THE INTERNATIONAL WHO'S WHO
1976-77

THE
INTERNATIONAL
WHO'S WHO

FORTIETH EDITION

1976-77

EUROPA PUBLICATIONS LIMITED
18 BEDFORD SQUARE LONDON WC1B 3JN

© EUROPA PUBLICATIONS LIMITED 1976

All rights reserved

ISBN 0 900 36293 6

Library of Congress Catalog Card Number 35-10257

AUSTRALIA AND NEW ZEALAND
James Bennett (Collaroy) Pty. Ltd., Collaroy, N.S.W., Australia

INDIA
UBS Publishers' Distributors Pvt. Ltd., P.O.B. 1882, 5 Ansari Road, Daryaganj, Delhi 6

JAPAN
Maruzen Co. Ltd., 6 Tori-Nichome, Nihonbashi, Tokyo 103

Printed and bound in England by
STAPLES PRINTERS LIMITED
at The Stanhope Press, Rochester, Kent.

FOREWORD TO THE 40th EDITION

EACH new edition of THE INTERNATIONAL WHO'S WHO is the result of a thorough revision of its predecessor. Daily records of changes to existing entries are maintained and the editors are constantly engaged in research directed towards the selection of new names. The book contains biographies of people from almost every country in the world and in almost every sphere of human activity.

Five hundred new biographies have been added to this latest edition and many of the existing entries have been expanded. In the case of a small number of entrants who have retired and whose biographies remain unchanged, we have referred readers to THE INTERNATIONAL WHO'S WHO 1975-76. In this way we have been able to accommodate new entries without increasing the size of the book beyond its present manageable proportions. An obituary list of persons whose deaths have been noted since the preparation of the previous edition appears at the front of the book, immediately after the section on Reigning Royal Families.

We would once again like to express our thanks to all those who, by completing questionnaires or by correcting proofs sent to them, have enabled us to bring our information up-to-date. We would particularly like to emphasize the necessity for proofs of entries to be returned to us without delay, since only in this way can we be certain that every entry is as accurate and as up-to-date as possible.

April 1976.

ABBREVIATIONS

A.A.A.	..	Agricultural Adjustment Administration
A.A.A.S.	..	American Association for the Advancement of Science
A.A.F.	..	Army Air Force
A.A.S.A.	..	Associate of the Australian Society of Accountants
A.B.	..	Bachelor of Arts
AB	..	Aktiebolag
A.C.A.	..	Associate of the Institute of Chartered Accountants
Acad.	..	Academy
Accad.	..	Accademia
Accred.	..	Accredited
A.C.I.S.	..	Associate of the Chartered Institute of Secretaries
A.C.S.	..	American Chemical Society
Act.	..	Acting
A.C.T.	..	Australian Capital Territory
ADC	..	Aide-de-camp
Adm.	..	Admiral
Admin.	..	Administrative, Administration, Administrator
A.E.R.E.	..	Atomic Energy Research Establishment
A.F.	..	Air Force
A.F.C.	..	Air Force Cross
affil.	..	affiliated
AFL	..	American Federation of Labor
A.F.M.	..	Air Force Medal
AG	..	Aktiengesellschaft (Joint Stock Company)
Agric.	..	Agriculture
a.i.	..	ad interim
A.I.A.	..	Associate of Institute of Actuaries; American Institute of Architects
A.I.A.A.	..	American Institute of Aeronautics and Astronautics
A.I.B.	..	Associate of the Institute of Bankers
AICC	..	All-India Congress Committee
A.I.C.E.	..	Associate of the Institution of Civil Engineers
A.I.Ch.E.	..	American Institute of Chemical Engineers
A.I.E.E.	..	American Institute of Electrical Engineers
A.I.M.E.	..	American Institute of Mining Engineers; Associate of the Institution of Mining Engineers
A.I.Mech.E.		Associate of the Institution of Mechanical Engineers
A.I.R.	..	All-India Radio
Akad.	..	Akademie
Ala.	..	Alabama
A.L.S.	..	Associate of the Linnaean Society
Alt.	..	Alternate
A.M.	..	Master of Arts; Alpes Maritimes; Albert Medal
Amb.	..	Ambassador
Amer.	..	American
A.M.I.C.E.	..	Associate Member of the Institution of Civil Engineers
A.M.I.E.E.		Associate Member of the Institution of Electrical Engineers
A.M.I.Mech.E.		Associate Member of the Institution of Mechanical Engineers
A.P.	..	Andhra Pradesh
approx.	..	approximately
Apptd.	..	Appointed
A.R.A.	..	Associate of the Royal Academy
A.R.A.M.	..	Associate of the Royal Academy of Music
A.R.C.A.	..	Associate of the Royal College of Art
A.R.C.M.	..	Associate of the Royal College of Music
A.R.C.S.	..	Associate of the Royal College of Science

A.R.I.B.A.	...	Associate of the Royal Institute of British Architects
Ariz.	..	Arizona
Ark.	..	Arkansas
A.R.S.A.	..	Associate of the Royal Scottish Academy; Associate of the Royal Society of Arts
A.S.L.I.B.	...	Association of Special Libraries and Information Bureaux.
A.S.M.E.	..	American Society of Mechanical Engineers
Asoc.	..	Asociación
Ass.	..	Assembly
Asscn.	..	Association
Assoc.	..	Associate
A.S.S.R.	..	Autonomous Soviet Socialist Republic
Asst.	..	Assistant
Aug.	..	August
b.	..	born
B.A.	..	Bachelor of Arts; British Airways
B.A.A.S.	..	British Association for the Advancement of Science
B.Agr.	..	Bachelor of Agriculture
B.A.O.	..	Bachelor of Obstetrics
B.Arch.	..	Bachelor of Architecture
Bart.	..	Baronet
B.A.S.	..	Bachelor in Agricultural Science
BBC	..	British Broadcasting Corporation
B.C.	..	British Columbia
B.Ch., B.Chir.		Bachelor of Surgery
B.C.L.	..	Bachelor of Civil Law; Bachelor of Canon Law
B.Com(m).	..	Bachelor of Commerce
B.C.S.	..	Bachelor of Commercial Sciences
B.D.	..	Bachelor of Divinity
Bd.	..	Board
B.D.S.	..	Bachelor of Dental Surgery
B.E.	..	Bachelor of Engineering; Bachelor of Education
BEA	..	British European Airways
B.E.E.	..	Bachelor of Electrical Engineering
B.Ed.	..	Bachelor of Education
Beds.	..	Bedfordshire
B.E.M.	..	British Empire Medal
B.Eng.	..	Bachelor of Engineering
Berks.	..	Berkshire
B.F.A.	..	Bachelor of Fine Arts
BIS	..	Bank for International Settlements
B.L.	..	Bachelor of Laws
Bldg.	..	Building
B.Lit(t).	..	Bachelor of Letters
B.LL.	..	Bachelor of Laws
B.L.S.	..	Bachelor in Library Science
B.M.	..	Bachelor of Medicine
B.M.A.	..	British Medical Association
B.Mus.	..	Bachelor of Music
Bn.	..	Battalion
BNOC	..	British National Oil Corporation
BOAC	..	British Overseas Airways Corporation
Brig.	..	Brigadier
B.S.	..	Bachelor of Science; Bachelor of Surgery
B.S.A.	..	Bachelor of Scientific Agriculture
B.Sc.	..	Bachelor of Science
Bt.	..	Baronet
Bucks.	..	Buckinghamshire
c.	..	child, children
C.A.	..	Chartered Accountant
Calif.	..	California
Cambs.	..	Cambridgeshire
Cand.	..	Candidate, Candidature
Cantab.	..	Of Cambridge University
Capt.	..	Captain

ABBREVIATIONS

Cards.	..	Cardiganshire
C.B.	..	Companion of the (Order of the) Bath
CBC	..	Canadian Broadcasting Corporation
C.B.E.	..	Commander of (the Order of) the British Empire
CBI	..	Confederation of British Industry
CBS	..	Columbia Broadcasting System
C.C.	..	Companion of Order of Canada
CCP	..	Chinese Communist Party
C.D.	..	Canadian Forces Decoration
CDU	..	Christlich-Demokratische Union
C.E.	..	Civil Engineer
CEAO	..	Communauté Economique de l'Afrique de l'Ouest
Cen.	..	Central
C.Eng.	..	Chartered Engineer
CENTO	..	Central Treaty Organization
C.E.O.	..	Chief Executive Officer
CERN	..	Conseil (now Organisation) Européen (ne) pour la Recherche Nucléaire
C.G.M.	..	Conspicuous Gallantry Medal
CGT	..	Confédération Générale du Travail
C.H.	..	Companion of Honour
Chair.	..	Chairman
Ch.B.	..	Bachelor of Surgery
C.Chem.	..	Chartered Chemist
Chem.	..	Chemistry
Ch.M.	..	Master of Surgery
C.I.	..	Channel Islands
CIA	..	Central Intelligence Agency
Cía.	..	Compañía (Company)
Cia.	..	Compagnia (Company)
CID	..	Criminal Investigation Department
C.I.E.	..	Companion of (the Order of) the Indian Empire
Cie.	..	Compagnie (Company)
C.I.E.E.	..	Companion of the Institution of Electrical Engineers
C.-in-C.	..	Commander-in-Chief
CIO	..	Congress of Industrial Organizations
C.L.D.	..	Doctor of Civil Law (U.S.A.)
C.Lit.	..	Companion of Literature
C.M.	..	Canada Medal; Master in Surgery
CMEA	..	Council for Mutual Economic Assistance
C.M.G.	..	Companion of (the Order of) St. Michael and St. George
C.N.R.S.	..	Centre National de la Recherche Scientifique
Co.	..	Company; County
C.O.	..	Commanding Officer
COI	..	Central Office of Information
Col.	..	Colonel
Coll.	..	College
Colo.	..	Colorado
COMECON		Council for Mutual Economic Assistance
Comm.	..	Commission
Commdg.	..	Commanding
Commdr.	..	Commander, Commandeur
Commdt.	..	Commandant
Commr.	..	Commissioner
Conf.	..	Conference
Confed.	..	Confederation
Conn.	..	Connecticut
Contrib.	..	Contributor; contribution
C.P.A.	..	Certified Public Accountant
Corp.	..	Corporate
Corpn.	..	Corporation
Corresp.	..	Correspondent; Corresponding
C.P.	..	Communist Party
C.P.P.	..	Convention People's Party (Ghana)
C.P.P.C.C.	..	Chinese People's Political Consultative Conference
C.P.S.U.	..	Communist Party of the Soviet Union
cr.	..	created
C.S.I.	..	Companion of (the Order of) the Star of India
CSIRO	..	Commonwealth Scientific and Industrial Research Organization
C.St.J.	..	Commander of (the Order of) St. John of Jerusalem
Cttee.	..	Committee
C.V.	..	Commanditaire Vennootschap
C.V.O.	..	Commander of the Royal Victorian Order
d.	..	daughter(s)
D.Arch.	..	Doctor of Architecture
D.B.	..	Bachelor of Divinity
D.B.A.	..	Doctor of Business Administration
D.B.E.	..	Dame Commander of (the Order of) the British Empire
D.C.	..	District of Columbia
D.C.L.	..	Doctor of Civil Law
D.C.M.	..	Distinguished Conduct Medal
D.C.M.G.	..	Dame Commander of (the Order of) St. Michael and St. George
D.Cn.L.	..	Doctor of Canon Law
D.Comm.	..	Doctor of Commerce
D.C.S.	..	Doctor of Commercial Sciences
D.C.T.	..	Doctor of Christian Theology
D.C.V.O.	..	Dame Commander of the Royal Victorian Order
D.D.	..	Doctor of Divinity
D.D.R.	..	Deutsche Demokratische Republik (German Democratic Republic)
D.D.S.	..	Doctor of Dental Surgery
Dec.	..	December
D.Econ.	..	Doctor of Economics
Denbighs.	..	Denbighshire
D. en D.	..	Docteur en Droit
D. en Med.	...	Docteur en Medicine
D.Eng.	..	Doctor of Engineering
Del.	..	Delegate, delegation, Delaware
Dem.	..	Democratic
Dep.	..	Deputy
Dept.	..	Department
D. ès L.	..	Docteur ès Lettres
D. ès Sc.	..	Docteur ès Sciences
Devt.	..	Development
D.F.	..	Distrito Federal
D.F.A.	..	Doctor of Fine Arts
D.F.C.	..	Distinguished Flying Cross
D.F.M.	..	Distinguished Flying Medal
D.H.	..	Doctor of Humanities
D.H.L.	..	Doctor of Hebrew Literature
D.Hum.Litt.	..	Doctor of Humane Letters
D.K.	..	Most Esteemed Family (Malaysia)
Dip.Agr.	..	Diploma in Agriculture
Dip.Ed.	..	Diploma in Education
Dip(l).Eng.	..	Diploma in Engineering
Dir.	..	Director
Dist.	..	District
D.Iur.	..	Doctor of Law
D. Iur. Utr.	..	Doctor of both Civil and Canon Law
Div.	..	Division; Divisional
D.Jur.	..	Doctor of Law
D.L.	..	Deputy Lieutenant
D.Lit(t).	..	Doctor of Letters; Doctor of Literature
D.L.S.	..	Doctor of Library Science
D.M.	..	Doctor of Medicine (Oxford)
D.M.D.	..	Doctor of Dental Medicine
D.Mus.	..	Doctor of Music
D.M.V.	..	Doctor of Veterinary Medicine
D.O.	..	Doctor of Ophthalmology
D.P.H.	..	Diploma in Public Health
D.P.M.	..	Diploma in Psychological Medicine
D.Phil.	..	Doctor of Philosophy
Dr. Agr.	..	Doctor of Agriculture
Dr.Ing.	..	Doctor of Engineering
Dr.Iur.	..	Doctor of Laws
D(r).Med.	..	Doctor of Medicine
Dr.Oec.(Publ.)		Doctor of (Public) Economy
Dr.Rer.Nat.		Doctor of Natural Sciences

Dr.rer.Pol.	..	Doctor of Political Science
D.S.	..	Doctor of Science
D.S.C.	..	Distinguished Service Cross
D.Sc.	..	Doctor of Science
D.Sc.S.	..	Doctor of Social Science
D.S.M.	..	Distinguished Service Medal
D.S.O.	..	Companion of the Distinguished Service Order
D.S.T.	..	Doctor of Sacred Theology
D.Theol.	..	Doctor of Theology
D.T.M.(& H.)		Diploma in Tropical Medicine (and Hygiene)
D.U.P.	..	Diploma of the University of Paris
E.	..	East
ECA	..	Economic Co-operation Administration; Economic Commission for Africa
ECAFE	..	Economic Commission for Asia and the Far East
ECE	..	Economic Commission for Europe
ECLA	..	Economic Commission for Latin America
Econ(s).	..	Economic(s)
ECOSOC	..	Economic and Social Council
ECSC	..	European Coal and Steel Community
ECWA	..	Economic Commission for Western Asia
ed.	..	educated
Ed.D.	..	Doctor of Education
Ed.M.	..	Master of Education
E.D.	..	Efficiency Decoration; Doctor of Engineering (U.S.A.)
Ed.	..	Editor
Edin.	..	Edinburgh
Edn.	..	Edition
Educ.	..	Education
EEC	..	European Economic Community
EFTA	..	European Free Trade Association
e.h.	..	Ehrenhalben (Honorary)
EIB	..	European Investment Bank
E.M.	..	Edward Medal; Master of Engineering (U.S.A.)
Emer.	..	Emeritus
Eng.	..	Engineering
Eng.D.	..	Doctor of Engineering
ESCAP	..	Economic and Social Commission for Asia and the Pacific
est.	..	established
ETH	..	Eidgenössische Technische Hochschule (Swiss Federal Institute of Technology)
Ets.	..	Establissements
EURATOM		European Atomic Energy Community
Exec.	..	Executive
Exhbn.	..	Exhibition
Ext.	..	Extension
f.	..	founded
F.A.A.	..	Fellow of Australian Academy of Science
F.A.C.C.	..	Fellow of the American College of Cardiology
F.A.C.C.A.		Fellow of the Association of Certified and Corporate Accountants
F.A.C.E.	..	Fellow of the Australian College of Education
F.A.C.P.	..	Fellow of American College of Physicians
F.A.C.S.	..	Fellow of the American College of Surgeons
F.A.I.A.	..	Fellow of the American Institute of Architects
F.A.I.A.S.		Fellow of the Australian Institute of Agricultural Science
F.A.I.M.	..	Fellow of the Australian Institute of Management
F.I.A.M.S.	..	Fellow of the Indian Academy of Medical Sciences
FAO	..	Food and Agriculture Organization
F.A.S.E.	..	Fellow of Antiquarian Society, Edinburgh
F.B.A.	..	Fellow of the British Academy
FBI	..	Federal Bureau of Investigation
F.B.I.M.	..	Fellow of the British Institute of Management
F.C.A.	..	Fellow of the Institute of Chartered Accountants
F.C.G.I.	..	Fellow of the City and Guilds of London Institute
F.C.I.C.	..	Fellow of the Chemical Institute of Canada
F.C.I.S.	..	Fellow of the Chartered Institute of Secretaries
FCO	..	Foreign and Commonwealth Office
F.C.T.	..	Federal Capital Territory
F.C.W.A.	..	Fellow of the Institute of Cost and Works Accountants
FDGB	..	Freier Deutscher Gewerkschaftsbund
Feb.	..	February
Fed.	..	Federation; Federal
F.G.S.	..	Fellow of the Geological Society
F.G.S.M.	..	Fellow of the Guildhall School of Music
F.I.A.	..	Fellow of the Institute of Actuaries
F.I.Arb.	..	Fellow of the Institute of Arbitrators
F.I.B.	..	Fellow of the Institute of Bankers
F.I.B.A.	..	Fellow of the Institute of Banking Associations
F.I.C.E.	..	Fellow of the Institution of Civil Engineers
F.I.D.	..	Fellow of the Institute of Directors
F.I.E.E.	..	Fellow of the Institution of Electrical Engineers
F.I.E.E.E.	..	Fellow of the Institute of Electrical and Electronics Engineers
Fil.Lic.	..	Licentiate in Philosophy
F.I.M.	..	Fellow of the Institute of Metallurgists
F.I.Mech.E.		Fellow of the Institute of Mechanical Engineers
F.Inst.F.	..	Fellow of the Institute of Fuel
F.Inst.P.	..	Fellow of the Institute of Physics
F.Inst.Pet.	..	Fellow of the Institute of Petroleum
F.I.P.M.	..	Fellow of the Institute of Personnel Management
F.I.R.E.	..	Fellow of the Institution of Radio Engineers
F.J.I.	..	Fellow of the Institute of Journalists
Fla.	..	Florida
F.L.A.	..	Fellow of the Library Association
Flints.	..	Flintshire
FLN	..	Front de Libération Nationale
F.L.S.	..	Fellow of the Linnaean Society
fmr.	..	former
fmrly.	..	formerly
F.N.I.	..	Fellow of the National Institute of Sciences of India
F.N.Z.I.A.	..	Fellow of the New Zealand Institute of Architects
F.R.A.C.P.	...	Fellow of the Royal Australasian College of Physicians
F.R.A.C.S.	...	Fellow of the Royal Australasian College of Surgeons
F.R.A.I.	..	Fellow of the Royal Anthropological Institute
F.R.A.I.A.	...	Fellow of the Royal Australian Institute of Architects
F.R.A.I.C.	..	Fellow of the Royal Architectural Institute of Canada
F.R.A.M.	..	Fellow of the Royal Academy of Music
F.R.A.S.	..	Fellow of the Royal Astronomical Society; Fellow of the Royal Asiatic Society
F.R.Ae.S.	..	Fellow of the Royal Aeronautical Society
F.R.B.S.	..	Fellow of the Royal Society of British Sculptors
F.R.C.M.	..	Fellow of the Royal College of Music
F.R.C.O.	..	Fellow of the Royal College of Organists
F.R.C.O.G.		Fellow of the Royal College of Obstetricians and Gynaecologists
F.R.C.P.(E.)		Fellow of the Royal College of Physicians (Edinburgh)

F.R.C.S.(E.)	..	Fellow of the Royal College of Surgeons (Edinburgh)
F.R.Econ.S.		Fellow of the Royal Economic Society
F.R.E.S.	..	Fellow of the Royal Entomological Society
F.R.F.P.S.	..	Fellow of the Royal Faculty of Physicians and Surgeons
F.R.G.S.	..	Fellow of the Royal Geographical Society
F.R.Hist.S.		Fellow of the Royal Historical Society
F.R.Hort.S.		Fellow of the Royal Horticultural Society
F.R.I.B.A.	..	Fellow of the Royal Institute of British Architects
F.R.I.C.	..	Fellow of the Royal Institute of Chemistry
F.R.I.C.S.	..	Fellow of the Royal Institute of Chartered Surveyors
F.R.Met.Soc.		Fellow of the Royal Meteorological Society
F.R.P.S.	..	Fellow of the Royal Photographic Society
F.R.S.	..	Fellow of the Royal Society
F.R.S.A.	..	Fellow of the Royal Society of Arts
F.R.S.A.M.D.		Fellow of the Royal Scottish Academy of Music and Drama
F.R.S.C.	..	Fellow of the Royal Society of Canada
F.R.S.E.	..	Fellow of the Royal Society of Edinburgh
F.R.S.L.	..	Fellow of the Royal Society of Literature
F.R.S.M.	..	Fellow of the Royal Society of Medicine
F.R.S.S.	..	Fellow of the Royal Statistical Society
F.S.A.	..	Fellow of the Society of Antiquaries
F.S.I.A.	..	Fellow of the Society of Industrial Artists
F.T.I.	..	Fellow of the Textile Institute
F.T.S.	..	Fellow of Technological Sciences
F.Z.S.	..	Fellow of the Zoological Society
Ga.	..	Georgia
GATT	..	General Agreement on Tariffs and Trade
G.B.	..	Great Britain
G.B.E.	..	Knight (or Dame) Grand Cross of (the Order of) the British Empire
G.C.	..	George Cross
G.C.B.	..	Knight Grand Cross of (the Order of) the Bath
G.C.I.E.	..	Knight Grand Commander of (the Order of) the Indian Empire
G.C.M.G.	..	Knight (or Dame) Grand Cross of (the Order of) St. Michael and St. George
G.C.S.I.	..	Knight Grand Commander of (the Order of) the Star of India
G.C.V.O.	..	Knight (or Dame) Grand Cross of the Royal Victorian Order
G.D.R.	..	German Democratic Republic
Gen.	..	General
GHQ	..	General Headquarters
Glam.	..	Glamorganshire
GLC	..	Greater London Council
Glos.	..	Gloucestershire
G.M.	..	George Medal
GmbH	..	Gesellschaft mit beschränkter Haftung (Limited Liability Company)
GOC (in C)	..	General Officer Commanding (in Chief)
Gov.	..	Governor
Govt.	..	Government
GPO	..	General Post Office
G.S.O.	..	General Staff Officer
Hants	..	Hampshire
h.c.	..	honoris causa
H.E.	..	His Eminence; His Excellency
Herefords.	..	Herefordshire
Herts.	..	Hertfordshire
H.H.	..	His (or Her) Highness
H.L.D.	..	Doctor of Humane Letters
H.M.	..	His (or Her) Majesty
H.M.S.	..	His (or Her) Majesty's Ship
Hon.	..	Honourable; Honorary
Hons.	..	Honours
Hosp.	..	Hospital
HQ	..	Headquarters
H.R.H.	..	His (or Her) Royal Highness
HSWP		Hungarian Socialist Workers' Party
Hunts.	..	Huntingdonshire
Ia.	..	Iowa
IAEA	..	International Atomic Energy Agency
IATA	..	International Air Transport Association
IBA	..	Independent Broadcasting Authority
IBRD	..	International Bank for Reconstruction and Development (World Bank)
ICAO	..	International Civil Aviation Organization
ICC	..	International Chamber of Commerce
ICE	..	Institution of Civil Engineers
ICEM	..	Intergovernmental Committee for European Migration
ICFTU	..	International Confederation of Free Trade Unions
ICI	..	Imperial Chemical Industries
ICOM	..	International Council of Museums
ICS	..	Indian Civil Service
ICSID	..	International Centre for Settlement of Investment Disputes
Ida.	..	Idaho
IDA	..	International Development Association
IDB	..	Inter-American Development Bank
I.E.E.	..	Institution of Electrical Engineers
IFC	..	International Finance Corporation
Ill.	..	Illinois
ILO	..	International Labour Organisation
IMCO	..	Inter-Governmental Maritime Consultative Organization
I.Mech.E.	..	Institution of Mechanical Engineers
IMF	..	International Monetary Fund
Inc.	..	Incorporated
Ind.	..	Indiana; Independent
Insp.	..	Inspector
Inst.	..	Institute; Institution
Int.	..	International
INTUC	..	Indian National Trades Union Congress
I.S.O.	..	Companion of the Imperial Service Order
ITA	..	Independent Television Authority
ITU	..	International Telecommunications Union
ITV	..	Independent Television
IUPAC	..	International Union of Pure and Applied Chemistry
IUPAP	..	International Union of Pure and Applied Physics
Jan.	..	January
J.C.B.	..	Bachelor of Canon Law
J.C.D.	..	Doctor of Canon Law
J.D.	..	Doctor of Jurisprudence
J.P.	..	Justice of the Peace
Jr.	..	Junior
Jt.	..	Joint
J.U.D.	..	Juris utriusque Doctor (Doctor of both Civil and Canon Law)
Ju.D.	..	Doctor of Law
Kan.	..	Kansas
K.B.E.	..	Knight Commander of (the Order of) the British Empire
K.C.	..	King's Counsel
K.C.B.	..	Knight Commander of (the Order of) the Bath
K.C.I.E.	..	Knight Commander of (the Order of) the Indian Empire
K.C.M.G.	..	Knight Commander of (the Order of) St. Michael and St. George
K.C.S.I.	..	Knight Commander of (the Order of) the Star of India
K.C.V.O.	..	Knight Commander of the Royal Victorian Order
K.G.	..	Knight of (the Order of) the Garter
KLM	..	Koninklijke Luchtvaart Maatschappij (Royal Dutch Airlines)
K.P.	..	Knight of (the Order of) St. Patrick
K.St.J.	..	Knight of (the Order of) St. John Jerusalem
K.T.	..	Knight of (the Order of) the Thistle

Kt.	..	Knight
Ky.	..	Kentucky
La.	..	Louisiana
L.A.	..	Los Angeles
Lab.	..	Laboratory
Lancs.	..	Lancashire
L.D.S.	..	Licentiate in Dental Surgery
Legis.	..	Legislative
Leics.	..	Leicestershire
L. en D.	..	Licencié en Droit
L. ès L.	..	Licencié ès Lettres
L.H.D.	..	Doctor of Humane Letters
L.I.	..	Long Island
Lic. en Der.	..	Licenciado en Derecho
Lic. en Fil.	..	Licenciado en Filosofía
Lic.Med.	..	Licentiate in Medicine
Lieut.	..	Lieutenant
Lincs.	..	Lincolnshire
Litt.D.	..	Doctor of Letters
LL.B.	..	Bachelor of Laws
LL.D.	..	Doctor of Laws
LL.L.	..	Licentiate of Laws
LL.M.	..	Master of Laws
L.M.	..	Licentiate of Medicine; or Midwifery
L.N.	..	League of Nations
L.R.A.M.	..	Licentiate of the Royal Academy of Music
L.R.C.P.	..	Licentiate of the Royal College of Physicians
Ltd(a).	..	Limited; Limitada
m.	..	married; marriage
M.A.	..	Master of Arts
M.Agr.	..	Master of Agriculture (U.S.A.)
Maj.	..	Major
Man.	..	Manager, Managing; Manitoba
M.Arch.	..	Master of Architecture
Mass.	..	Massachusetts
Math.	..	Mathematics, Mathematical
M.B.	..	Bachelor of Medicine
M.B.A.	..	Master of Business Administration
M.B.E.	..	Member of (the Order of) the British Empire
M.C.	..	Military Cross
MCC	..	Marylebone Cricket Club
M.Ch.	..	Master of Surgery
M.Ch.D.	..	Master of Dental Surgery
M.C.L.	..	Master of Civil Law
M.Com(m).	..	Master of Commerce
Md.	..	Maryland
M.D.	..	Doctor of Medicine
M.Div.	..	Master of Divinity
M.D.S.	..	Master of Dental Surgery
Me.	..	Maine
mem.	..	member
M.Eng.	..	Master of Engineering (Dublin)
M.F.A.	..	Master of Fine Arts
Mfg.	..	Manufacturing
Mfrs.	..	Manufacturers
Mgr.	..	Monseigneur; Monsignor
M.I.	..	Marshall Islands
M.I.A.	..	Master of International Affairs
M.I.C.E.	..	Member of the Institution of Civil Engineers
M.I.Chem.E.	..	Member of the Institution of Chemical Engineers
Mich.	..	Michigan
Middx.	..	Middlesex
M.I.E.E.	..	Member of the Institution of Electrical Engineers
Mil.	..	Military
M.I.Mar.E.	..	Member of the Institute of Marine Engineers
M.I.Mech.E.	..	Member of the Institution of Mechanical Engineers
M.I.Min.E.	..	Member of the Institution of Mining Engineers
Min.	..	Minister; Ministry
Minn.	..	Minnesota
M.Inst.T.	..	Member of the Institute of Transport
Miss.	..	Mississippi
M.I.Struct.E.	..	Member of the Institution of Structural Engineers
M.I.T.	..	Massachusetts Institute of Technology
M.J.	..	Master of Jurisprudence
M.L.A.	..	Member of the Legislative Assembly
M.L.C.	..	Member of the Legislative Council
M.M.	..	Military Medal
Mo.	..	Missouri
M.O.H.	..	Medical Officer of Health
Mon.	..	Monmouthshire
Mont.	..	Montana
M.P.	..	Member of Parliament; Madhya Pradesh (India)
M.P.A.	..	Master of Public Administration (Harvard)
M.Ph.	..	Master of Philosophy (U.S.A.)
M.P.P.	..	Member of Provincial Parliament (Canada)
M.R.A.S.	..	Member of the Royal Asiatic Society
MRC		Medical Research Council
M.R.C.P.(E.)		Member of the Royal College of Physicians (Edinburgh)
M.R.C.S.(E.)		Member of the Royal College of Surgeons (Edinburgh)
M.R.C.V.S.	..	Member of the Royal College of Veterinary Surgeons
M.R.I.	..	Member of the Royal Institution
M.R.I.A.	..	Member of the Royal Irish Academy
M.R.I.C.	..	Member of the Royal Institute of Chemistry
MRP	..	Mouvement Républicain Populaire
M.S.	..	Master of Science; Master of Surgery
M.Sc.	..	Master of Science
Mus.Bac. or B.		Bachelor of Music
Mus.Doc. or D.		Doctor of Music
Mus.M.	..	Master of Music (Cambridge)
M.V.D.	..	Master of Veterinary Medicine
M.V.O.	..	Member of the Royal Victorian Order
N.	..	North
N.A.S.	..	National Academy of Sciences (U.S.A.)
NASA		National Aeronautics and Space Administration
Nat.	..	National
NATO	..	North Atlantic Treaty Organization
Naz.	..	Nazionale
N.B.	..	New Brunswick
NBC	..	National Broadcasting Corporation
N.C.	..	North Carolina
N.D.	..	North Dakota
N.E.	..	North East, Near East
Neb.	..	Nebraska
NEDC	..	National Economic Development Council
Nev.	..	Nevada
N.H.	..	New Hampshire
N.J.	..	New Jersey
N.M.	..	New Mexico
Northants.	..	Northamptonshire
Notts.	..	Nottinghamshire
Nov.	..	November
NPC		National People's Congress
nr.	..	near
NRC	..	Nuclear Research Council
N.S.W.	..	New South Wales
NV	..	Naamloze Vennootschap
N.W.	..	North West
N.W.T.	..	North West Territories
N.Y.	..	New York
N.Y.C.	..	New York City
N.Z.	..	New Zealand
O.	..	Ohio
OAS		Organization of American States
OAU		Organization of African Unity
O.B.E.	..	Officer of (the Order of) the British Empire
O.C.	..	Officer of the Order of Canada
Oct.	..	October

OECD	..	Organization for Economic Co-operation and Development
OEEC	..	Organization for European Economic Co-operation
O.F.S.	..	Orange Free State
Okla.	..	Oklahoma
O.M.	..	Member of the Order of Merit
Ont.	..	Ontario
O.P.	..	Ordo Praedicatorum (Dominicans)
OPEC	..	Organization of the Petroleum Exporting Countries
O.P.M.	..	Office of Production Management
Ore.	..	Oregon
Org.	..	Organization
O.S.B.	..	Order of St. Benedict
Oxon.	..	Of Oxford University; Oxfordshire
Pa.	..	Pennsylvania
Parl.	..	Parliament; Parliamentary
P.C.	..	Privy Councillor
PCC	..	Provincial Congress Committee
Pd.B.	..	Bachelor of Pedagogy
Pd.D.	..	Doctor of Pedagogy
Pd.M.	..	Master of Pedagogy
P.E.I.	..	Prince Edward Island
Pembs.	..	Pembrokeshire
PEN	..	Poets, Playwrights, Essayists, Editors and Novelists (Club)
Perm.	..	Permanent
Ph.B.	..	Bachelor of Philosophy
Ph.D.	..	Doctor of Philosophy
Pharm.D.	..	Docteur en Pharmacie
Phil.	..	Philosophy
Phila.	..	Philadelphia
PLA	..	Port of London Authority
P.O.(B.)	..	Post Office (Box)
P.O.W.	..	Prisoner of War
P.P.R.A.	..	Past President of the Royal Academy
P.Q.	..	Province of Quebec
P.R.A.	..	President of the Royal Academy
Pref.	..	Prefecture
Prep.	..	Preparatory
Pres.	..	President
P.R.I.	..	President of the Royal Institute (of Painters in Water Colours)
P.R.I.B.A.	..	President of the Royal Institute of British Architects
Prin.	..	Principal
Priv.Doz.	..	Privat Dozent (recognized teacher not on the regular staff)
P.R.O.	..	Public Relations Officer
Proc.	..	Proceedings
Prof.	..	Professor
Propr.	..	Proprietor
Prov.	..	Province, Provincial
P.R.S.	..	President of the Royal Society
P.R.S.A.	..	President of the Royal Scottish Academy
Pty.	..	Proprietary
Publ(s).	..	Publication(s)
Publr.	..	Publisher
PUWP	..	Polish United Workers' Party
Pvt.	..	Private
PWP	..	Polish Workers' Party
Q.C.	..	Queen's Counsel
R.A.	..	Royal Academy; Royal Academician
R.A.A.F.	..	Royal Australian Air Force
R.A.C.	..	Royal Armoured Corps
R.A.C.P.	..	Royal Australasian College of Physicians
R.A.F.	..	Royal Air Force
R.A.F.V.R.	..	Royal Air Force Volunteer Reserve
R.A.M.	..	Royal Academy of Music
R.A.M.C.	..	Royal Army Medical Corps
R.C.	..	Roman Catholic
R.C.A.	..	Royal College of Art; Royal Canadian Academy; Radio Corporation of America
Regt.	..	Regiment

Rep.	..	Representative; Represented
Repub.	..	Republic
resgnd.	..	resigned
retd.	..	retired
Rev.	..	Reverend
R.I.	..	Rhode Island
R.I.B.A.	..	Royal Institute of British Architects
R.N.	..	Royal Navy
R.N.V.R.	..	Royal Naval Volunteer Reserve
R.N.Z.A.F.	..	Royal New Zealand Air Force
R.P.	..	Member Royal Society of Portrait Painters
R.S.A.	..	Royal Scottish Academy; Royal Society of Arts
R.S.C.	..	Royal Shakespeare Company
R.S.F.S.R.	..	Russian Soviet Federative Socialist Republic
Rt. Hon.	..	Right Honourable
Rt. Rev.	..	Right Reverend
R.V.O.	..	Royal Victorian Order
R.W.S.	..	Royal Society of Painters in Water Colours
s.	..	son(s)
S.	..	South
S.A.	..	South Africa; Société Anonyme, Sociedad Anónima
S.A.E.	..	Society of Aeronautical Engineers
Salop.	..	Shropshire
Sask.	..	Saskatchewan
S.B.	..	Bachelor of Science (U.S.A.)
S.C.	..	South Carolina
SCAP	..	Supreme Command Allied Powers
Sc.B.	..	Bachelor of Science
Sc.D.	..	Doctor of Science
S.Dak.	..	South Dakota
S.E.	..	South East
SEATO	..	South East Asia Treaty Organization
Sec.	..	Secretary
SEC.	..	Securities and Exchange Commission
Secr.	..	Secretariat
SED	..	Sozialistische Einheitspartei Deutschlands (Socialist Unity Party of the German Democratic Republic)
Sept.	..	September
S.-et-O.	..	Seine-et-Oise
SHAEF	..	Supreme Headquarters Allied Expeditionary Force
SHAPE	..	Supreme Headquarters Allied Powers in Europe
S.J.	..	Society of Jesus (Jesuits)
S.J.D.	..	Doctor of Juristic Science
S.M.	..	Master of Science
S.O.A.S.	..	School of Oriental and African Studies
Soc.	..	Society
S.p.A.	..	Società per Azioni
SPD	..	Sozialdemokratische Partei Deutschlands
Sr.	..	Senior
S.S.R.	..	Soviet Socialist Republic
Staffs.	..	Staffordshire
S.T.B.	..	Bachelor of Sacred Theology
S.T.D.	..	Doctor of Sacred Theology
S.T.L.	..	Licentiate of Sacred Theology
S.T.M.	..	Master of Sacred Theology
Supt.	..	Superintendent
S.W.	..	South West
T.A.	..	Territorial Army
T.D.	..	Territorial Decoration; Tealta Dáil (Mem. of the Dáil)
Tech.	..	Technical, Technology
Temp.	..	Temporary
Tenn.	..	Tennessee
Tex.	..	Texas
Th.B.	..	Bachelor of Theology
Th.D.	..	Doctor of Theology
Th.M.	..	Master of Theology
Trans.	..	Translation; translator
Treas.	..	Treasurer

ABBREVIATIONS

TU(C)	..	Trades Union (Congress)
U.A.E.	..	United Arab Emirates
U.A.R.	..	United Arab Republic
UDEAC	..	L'Union Douanière et Economique de l'Afrique Centrale.
UDR	..	Union des Démocrates pour la République
U.K.	..	United Kingdom (of Great Britain and Northern Ireland)
UMIST	..	University of Manchester Institute of Science and Technology
UN(O)	..	United Nations (Organization)
UNA	..	United Nations Association
UNCTAD	..	United Nations Conference on Trade and Development
UNDP	..	United Nations Development Programme
UNDRO	..	United Nations Disaster Relief Office
UNEF	..	United Nations Emergency Force
UNEP	..	United Nations Environment Programme
UNESCO	..	United Nations Educational, Scientific and Cultural Organisation
UNHCR	..	United Nations High Commission for Refugees
UNICEF	..	United Nations International Children's Emergency Fund
UNIDO	..	United Nations Industrial Development Organization
UNITAR	..	United Nations Institute for Training and Research
Univ.	..	University
UNKRA	..	United Nations Korean Relief Administration
UNRRA	..	United Nations Relief and Rehabilitation Administration
UNRWA	..	United Nations Relief and Works Agency
U.P.	..	United Provinces, Uttar Pradesh (India)
UPU	..	Universal Postal Union
U.S.A.	..	United States of America
U.S.A.F.	..	United States Air Force
U.S.N.	..	United States Navy
U.S.S.	..	United States Ship
U.S.S.R.	..	Union of Soviet Socialist Republics
Va.	..	Virginia
V.C.	..	Victoria Cross
Vol(s).	..	Volume(s)
Vt.	..	Vermont
W.	..	West
W.A.	..	Western Australia
Warwicks.	..	Warwickshire
Wash.	..	Washington
WEU	..	Western European Union
WFTU	..	World Federation of Trade Unions
WHO	..	World Health Organization
Wilts.	..	Wiltshire
WIPO	..	World Intellectual Property Organization
Wis.	..	Wisconsin
WMO	..	World Meteorological Organization
Worcs.	..	Worcestershire
W.R.A.C.	..	Women's Royal Army Corps
W.R.N.S.	..	Women's Royal Naval Service
W.Va.	..	West Virginia
Wyo.	..	Wyoming
YMCA	..	Young Men's Christian Association
Yorks.	..	Yorkshire
YWCA	..	Young Women's Christian Association

REIGNING ROYAL FAMILIES

*Biographical entries of most of the reigning monarchs and of
certain other members of the reigning royal families will be
found in their appropriate alphabetical order in the biographical section of this book.*

BELGIUM
Reigning King

KING BAUDOUIN ALBERT CHARLES LÉOPOLD AXEL
MARIE GUSTAVE; b. September 7, 1930; succeeded to
the throne July 17, 1951, after abdication of his father,
King Léopold III; married December 15, 1960, Doña
Fabiola de Mora y Aragón (b. June 11, 1928).

Father of the King

King Léopold III; b. November 3, 1901; married (1)
November 4, 1926, Princess Astrid of Sweden (b.
November 17, 1905, died August 29, 1935); (2) September 11, 1941, Mlle. Mary Liliane Baels (three
children).

Brother of the King

Prince Albert, Prince of Liège; b. June 6, 1934; married
July 2, 1959, Donna Paola Ruffo di Calabria (two
sons, one daughter).

Sister of the King

Joséphine Charlotte, Princess of Belgium; b. October 11,
1927; married April 9, 1953, Prince Jean of Luxembourg (b. January 5, 1921) (five children).

BHUTAN
Reigning King

THE DRUK GYALPO JIGME SINGHYE WANGCHUK, King
of Bhutan; b. November 11, 1955; succeeded to the
throne July 24, 1972, on the death of his father, the
Druk Gyalpo Jigme Dorji Wangchuk; crowned
June 2, 1974.

Parents of the King

The Druk Gyalpo Jigme Dorji Wangchuk; b. 1928;
married 1953, Queen Ashi Kesang Wangchuk;
succeeded to the throne October 28, 1952; died
July 21, 1972.

DENMARK
Reigning Queen

QUEEN MARGRETHE II; b. April 16, 1940; succeeded to
the throne January 14, 1972, on the death of her
father, King Frederik IX; married June 10, 1967,
Count Henri de Laborde de Monpezat (Prince
Henrik) (b. June 11, 1934).

Children of the Queen

Prince Frederik André Henrik Christian (heir-apparent);
b. May 26, 1968.
Prince Joachim Holger Waldemar Christian; b. June 7,
1969.

Parents of the Queen

King Frederik IX; b. March 11, 1899; son of King
Christian X and Queen Alexandrine; married May 24,
1935, Princess Ingrid of Sweden (b. March 28, 1910);
died January 14, 1972.

Sisters of the Queen

Princess Benedikte; b. April 29, 1944; married
February 3, 1968, Prince Richard zu Sayn-Wittgen-
stein-Berleburg; son Prince Gustav, b. January 12,

1969; daughter Princess Alexander, b. November 20,
1970; daughter Princess Nathalie, b. May 2, 1975.
Queen Anne-Marie of the Hellenes; b. August 30, 1946;
married September 18, 1964, King Constantine II of
the Hellenes; sons Prince Paul, b. May 20, 1967,
Prince Nicholas, b. October 1, 1969; daughter
Princess Alexia, b. July 10, 1965.

Uncle of the Queen

Prince Knud; b. July 27, 1900; married September 8
1933, Princess Caroline-Mathilde of Denmark, b.
April 27, 1912; sons H.E. Ingolf, Count of Rosenborg,
b. February 17, 1940, H.E. Christian, Count of
Rosenborg, b. October 22, 1942; daughter Princess
Elisabeth, b. May 8, 1935.

IRAN
Reigning Shah

MOHAMMAD REZA PAHLAVI ARYAMEHR, Shahanshah of
Iran; b. October 26, 1919; succeeded to the throne
September 16, 1941, on the abdication of his father,
Reza Shah the Great; married (1) March 15, 1939,
PRINCESS FAWZIA, daughter of King Fouad I of
Egypt (divorced November 19, 1948); (2) February
12, 1951, SORAYA ESFANDIARI-BAKHTIARI (divorced
March, 1958); (3) December 21, 1959, FARAH DIBA.

Children of the Shah

Princess Shahnaz; b. October 27, 1940.
Prince Reza; b. October 31, 1960 (Crown Prince).
Princess Maasoumeh Farahnaz; b. March 12, 1963.
Prince Ali Reza; b. April 28, 1966.
Princess Leila; b. March 27, 1970.

Father of the Shah

Reza Shah; b. March 15, 1878; elected Shah of Persia
December 13, 1925, abdicated September 16, 1941;
died July 26, 1944.

Brothers and Sisters of the Shah

Princess Shams.	Prince Ahmad Reza.
Princess Ashraf.	Prince Mahmood Reza.
Prince Gholam Reza.	Princess Fatemeh.
Prince Abdul Reza.	Prince Hamid Reza.

JAPAN
Reigning Emperor

EMPEROR HIROHITO; b. April 29, 1901; succeeded his
father December 25, 1926; married January 26, 1924,
PRINCESS NAGAKO KUNI (b. March 6, 1903), daughter
of Prince Kuni.

Children of the Emperor

Princess Shigeko (Terunomiya); b. December 6, 1925
(married); died July 1961.*
Princess Kazuko (Takanomiya); b. September 30, 1929
(married).*
Princess Atsuko (Yorinomiya); b. March 7, 1931
(married).*

Prince Akihito (Tsugunomiya); b. December 23, 1933; married April 10, 1959, Michiko Shoda; sons, Prince Naruhito Hironomiya; b. February 23, 1960; Prince Fumihito (Ayanomiya); b. November 30, 1965; daughter, Princess Nori; b. April 18, 1969.

Prince Masahito (Hitachinomiya); b. November 28, 1935; married September 1964, Hanako Tsugaru.

Princess Takako (Suganomiya); b. March 2, 1939; married March 10, 1960, Hisanaga Shimazu.*

* Denotes that under the postwar new law, married daughters of the Emperor are commoners. They are no longer listed as members of the Imperial Family in most reference books.

Parents of the Emperor

Emperor Yoshihito; b. August 21, 1879; married May 10, 1900, died 1926; Princess Sadako (b. June 25, 1884, died May 1951), daughter of Prince Kujo.

Surviving Brothers of the Emperor

Prince Nobuhito (Takamatsunomiya); b. January 3, 1905.

Prince Takahito (Mikasanomiya); b. December 2, 1915.

JORDAN
Reigning King

KING HUSSEIN; b. November 14, 1935; succeeded to the throne on the abdication of his father, August, 1952; ascended the throne May 2, 1953; married April 19, 1955, PRINCESS DINA, daughter of Abd-el-Hamid Aoun of Saudi Arabia (now divorced); married May 25, 1961, Miss Antoinette Gardner, PRINCESS MUNA AL-HUSSEIN (divorced 1972); married December 24, 1972, ALIA BAHA EDDIN TOUKAN (Queen Alia Al-Hussein).

Children of the King

Princess Alya; b. February 13, 1956.
Prince Abdullah; b. January 30, 1962.
Prince Feisal; b. October 11, 1963.
Princess Zein; b. April 26, 1968.
Princess Ayeshia; b. April 26, 1968.
Princess Haya; b. May 3, 1974.

Parents of the King

King Talal; b. February 26, 1907; married November 27, 1933, Queen Zein Al Sharaf; died July 8, 1972.

Brothers and Sister of the King

H.R.H. Prince Mohammed; married January 9, 1964, Princess Firyal; sons Prince Talal, b. July 26, 1965 and Prince Ghazi, b. October 15, 1966.

H.R.H. Prince Hassan (named as Crown Prince, April 1, 1965); married Princess Tharwat; daughters Princess Rahma, Princess Sunayya, Princess Badia.

H.R.H. Princess Basmah; married April 2, 1970, Lt. Timor al-Daghistani; daughter, Princess Farah, b. March 25, 1971; son, Prince Ghazi, b. October 15, 1974.

KUWAIT
Reigning Amir

SHEIKH SABAH AL-SALIM AL-SABAH; b. 1913; succeeded his brother Sheikh Abdullah al-Salim al-Sabah as Head of State, November 24, 1965.

Crown Prince

Sheikh Jaber al-Ahmad al-Jaber al-Sabah; b. 1928; proclaimed Crown Prince May 31, 1966.

LESOTHO
Reigning King

KING MOSHOESHOE II; b. May 2, 1938; married August 23, 1962, PRINCESS TABITHA 'MASENTLE; became King when Lesotho gained independence, 1966.

Children of the King

Prince Letsie David; b. July 17, 1963.
Prince Seeiso Simeone; b. April 16, 1966.
Princess Constance Christina Sebueng; b. December 24, 1969.

Parents of the King

Seeiso Griffith, late Paramount Chief of Basutoland (b. 1905) and 'Ma-Bereng.

LIECHTENSTEIN
Reigning Prince

FRANZ JOSEF II; b. August 16, 1906; succeeded his great-uncle, July 25, 1938; married March 7, 1943, COUNTESS GINA VON WILCZEK (PRINCESS GEORGINE) (b. October 24, 1921).

Children of the Prince

Prince Hans Adam; b. February 14, 1945; married July 30, 1967, Countess Maria Kinsky; sons, Prince Alois, b. June 10, 1968; Prince Maximilian, b. May 16, 1969; Prince Constantin, b. March 15, 1972; daughter Princess Tatjana, b. April 10, 1973.

Prince Philipp; b. August 19, 1946; married September 11, 1971, Mademoiselle Isabelle de l'Arbre de Malander; sons, Prince Alexander, b. May 19, 1972; Prince Wenzel, b. May 12, 1974.

Prince Nicolaus; b. October 24, 1947.
Prince Nora; b. October 31, 1950.
Prince Franz Josef Wenzel Georg Maria; b. November 19, 1962.

Brothers and Sisters of the Prince

Princess Maria Theresia (Countess Strachwitz); b. January 14, 1908; died September 30, 1973.
Prince Karl Alfred; b. August 16, 1910.
Prince Georg; b. November 11, 1911.
Prince Ulrich; b. August 29, 1913.
Princess Henriette; b. November 11, 1914.
Prince Alois; b. December 12, 1917; died February 14, 1967.
Prince Heinrich; b. October 21, 1920.

LUXEMBOURG
Reigning Monarch

GRAND DUKE JEAN; b. January 5, 1921; succeeded November 12, 1964, on the abdication of his mother, Grand Duchess Charlotte; married April 9, 1953, JOSEPHINE CHARLOTTE, PRINCESS OF BELGIUM (b. October 11, 1927).

Children of the Grand Duke

Princess Marie-Astrid; b. February 17, 1954.
Prince Henri; b. April 16, 1955.
Prince Jean; b. May 15, 1957.
Princess Margaretha; b. May 15, 1957.
Prince Guillaume; b. May 1, 1963.

Parents of the Grand Duke

Grand Duchess Charlotte, Duchess of Nassau; b. January 23, 1896; succeeded January 15, 1919; abdicated in favour of her son, Grand Duke Jean,

November 12, 1964; married November 6, 1919, Prince Félix of Bourbon Parma (b. September 28, 1893, died April 8, 1970).

Brother and Sisters of the Grand Duke

Princess Elisabeth; b. December 22, 1922; married May 9, 1956, Prince François Ferdinand of Hohenberg (b. September 13, 1927); two d.

Princess Marie-Adelaid; b. May 21, 1924; married April 10, 1958, Count Charles Joseph Henckel de Donnersmarck (b. November 7, 1928); three s. one d.

Princess Marie-Gabrielle; b. August 10, 1925; married November 6, 1951, Count Knud de Holstein-Ledreborg (b. October 2, 1919); seven d.

Prince Charles; b. August 7, 1927; married March 1, 1967, Joan Douglas Dillon; one s. one d.

Princess Alix; b. August 24, 1929; married August 17, 1950, H.H. Prince Antoine de Ligne (b. March 8, 1925); three s. three d.

MALAYSIA

Supreme Head of State (Yang di-Pertuan Agung)*

TUANKU YAHYA PETRA IBNI AL MARHUM SULTAN IBRAHIM, Sultan of Kelantan; b. December 10, 1917; elected sixth Yang di-Pertuan Agung June 19, 1975; installed September 21, 1975; married June 1939, Tengku Zainab binte Tengku Mohamed Petra; one son, four daughters.

* Reign ends in September 1980; to be succeeded by Sultan of Pahang (see p. 1298)

MONACO

PRINCE RAINIER III; b. May 31, 1923; succeeded his grandfather, Prince Louis II, May 9, 1949; married April 18, 1956, Miss GRACE PATRICIA KELLY, daughter of the late Mr. John Brendan Kelly and Mrs. Margaret Kelly, of Philadelphia, U.S.A.

Children of the Prince

Princess Caroline Louise Marguerite; b. January 23, 1957.

Prince Albert Alexandre Louis Pierre; b. March 14, 1958.

Princess Stéphanie Marie Elisabeth; b. February 1, 1965.

Parents of the Prince

Princess Charlotte, Duchess of Valentinois (b. September 30, 1898); married March 19, 1920, Comte Pierre de Polignac, who assumed the style and title of Prince Pierre of Monaco; died November 10, 1964.

MOROCCO
Reigning King

KING HASSAN II (formerly Crown Prince Moulay Hassan); b. July 9, 1929; son of King Mohammed V (died February 26, 1961); became King and Prime Minister of Morocco when he succeeded his father, February 1961.

Children of the King

Princess Myriam; b. August 26, 1962.

Prince Mohamed; b. August 21, 1963.

Princess Asma; b. 1965.

Princess Hasna; b. 1967.

Prince Rachid; b. July 1970.

Brother and Sisters of the King

Prince Moulay Abdullah; married Lamia Solh.

Princess Lalla Aicha.

Princess Lalla Malika.

Princess Lalla Nezha.

Princess Lalla Amina.

Princess Lalla Fatima Zohra.

NEPAL
Reigning King

KING BIRENDRA BIR BIKRAM SHAH DEV; b. December 28, 1945; succeeded to the throne, January 31, 1972, on the death of his father King Mahendra; crowned February 24, 1975; married 1970, PRINCESS AISHWARYA RAJYA LAXMI DEVI RANA.

Heir-Apparent

Crown Prince Deependra Bir Bikram Shah Dev; b. June 27, 1971.

NETHERLANDS
Reigning Queen

QUEEN JULIANA LOUISE EMMA MARIE WILHELMINA, Princess of Orange Nassau, Duchess of Mecklenburg; Princess of Lippe-Biesterfeld, etc.; b. April 30, 1909; succeeded to the throne on the abdication of her mother, September 4, 1948; inaugurated September 6, 1948; married January 7, 1937, PRINCE BERNHARD LEOPOLD FREDERIK EVERHARD JULIUS COERT KAREL GODFRIED PIETER OF LIPPE-BIESTERFELD (b. June 29, 1911).

Children of the Queen

Princess Beatrix Wilhelmina Armgard; b. January 31, 1938; married March 10, 1966, Claus George Willem Otto Frederik Geert van Amsberg; sons Prince Willem-Alexander Claus George Ferdinand, b. April 27, 1967, Prince Johan Friso Bernhard Christiaan David, b. September 25, 1968, Prince Constantijn Christof Frederik Aschwin, b. October 11, 1969.

Princess Irene Emma Elisabeth; b. August 5, 1939; married April 29, 1964, Prince Carlos Hugo of Bourbon Parma; sons Prince Carlos Javier Bernardo, b. January 27, 1970, Prince Jaime Bernardo, b. October 13, 1972; daughters Princess Marguerita Maria Beatrice, b. October 13, 1972, Princess Maria Carolina Christina, b. June 23, 1974.

Princess Margriet Francisca; b. January 19, 1943; married January 10, 1967, Pieter van Vollenhoven; sons, Prince Maurits Willem Pieter Hendrik van Orange Nassau van Vollenhoven, b. April 17, 1968, Prince Bernhard Lucas Emmanuel, b. December 25, 1969, Prince Pieter-Christiaan Michiel, b. March 22, 1972, Prince Floris Frederik Martyn, b. April 10, 1975.

Princess Maria Christina; b. February 18, 1947; married June 28, 1975, Jorge Guillermo.

Parents of the Queen

Princess Wilhelmina Helena Pauline Maria; b. August 31, 1880; daughter of King Willem III and his second wife, Princess Adelheid Emma Wilhelmina Theresia of Waldeck and Pyrmont; succeeded to the throne November 23, 1890; married February 7, 1901, Prince Hendrik Wladimir Albrecht Ernst of Mecklenburg-Schwerin (b. April 19, 1876, died July 3, 1934); abdicated September 4, 1948; died November 28, 1962.

NORWAY
Reigning King

KING OLAV V; b. July 2, 1903; succeeded to the throne on the death of his father, King Haakon VII, September 21, 1957; married March 21, 1929, Princess Märtha of Sweden (b. March 28, 1901, died April 5, 1954), daughter of Prince Carl (third son of King Oscar II of Norway and Sweden).

Children of the King

Crown Prince Harald; b. February 21, 1937; married August 29, 1968, Miss Sonja Haraldsen (now Crown Princess Sonja); daughter Princess Märtha Louise, b. September 22, 1971; son Prince Haakon Magnus, b. July 20, 1973.

Princess Ragnhild Alexandra; b. June 9, 1930; married May 15, 1953, H. Erling Lorentzen; three c.

Princess Astrid Maud Ingeborg; b. February 12, 1932; married January 12, 1961, Hr. Johan Martin Ferner; five children.

Parents of the King

King Haakon VII of Norway; b. August 3, 1872, died September 21, 1957; elected King of Norway by the Storting, November 18, 1905; married July 22, 1896, Princess Maud (b. November 27, 1869, died November 20, 1938), third daughter of King Edward VII of Great Britain.

OMAN
Reigning Sultan

SULTAN QABOOS BIN SAID; b. November 18, 1940; succeeded to the throne on the abdication of his father, Sultan Said bin Taimur (1910-72), July 23, 1970.

SAUDI ARABIA
Reigning King

KING KHALID IBN ABDUL AZIZ, Imam of the Moslems, Head of the Council of Ministers; b. 1909; acceded March 26, 1975.

Brothers of the King include

King Saud ibn Abdul Aziz; b. January 15, 1901; acceded November 9, 1953, relinquished throne November 2, 1964; died February 23, 1969.

King Faisal ibn Abdul Aziz; b. 1905; acceded November 2, 1964; died March 25, 1975.

Prince Fahd ibn Abdul Aziz; b. 1922; proclaimed Crown Prince March 1975.

Amir Mohammed; b. 1910.

Amir Sultan; b. 1924.

Amir Talal; b. 1930.

SPAIN
Reigning King

KING JUAN CARLOS I; b. January 5, 1938; succeeded to the throne November 22, 1975; married May 14, 1962, Princess Sophia of Greece (b. November 2, 1938), daughter of the late King Paul of the Hellenes and of Queen Frederica.

Children of the King

Princess Elena; b. December 20, 1963.

Princess Cristina; b. June 13, 1965.

Prince Felipe; b. January 30, 1968.

Parents of the King

Don Juan de Borbón y Battenberg, Count of Barcelona; b. June 20, 1913; married 1935, Doña María de las Mercedes de Borbón y Orleans.

SWAZILAND
Reigning King

KING SOBHUZA II; b. July 22, 1899; installed as constitutional ruler 1921.

Father of the King

Ngwane V.

SWEDEN
Reigning King

KING CARL XVI GUSTAF; b. April 30, 1946; succeeded to the throne September 15, 1973, on the death of his grandfather King Gustaf VI Adolf.

Parents of the King

Prince Gustaf Adolf, Duke of Västerbotten; b. April 22, 1906, died January 26, 1947; married October 20, 1932, Sibylla, Princess of Saxe-Coburg and Gotha (b. January 18, 1908, died November 28, 1972).

Sisters of the King

Princess Margaretha; b. October 31, 1934; married June 30, 1964, Mr. John Ambler; daughter, Sybilla Louise, b. April 14, 1965; sons, Charles Edward, b. July 14, 1966; James, b. June 10, 1969.

Princess Birgitta; b. January 19, 1937; married May 25, 1961, Prince of Hohenzollern Johann Georg; sons, Carl Christian, b. April 5, 1962; Hubertus, b. June 10, 1966; daughter, Desirée, b. November 27, 1963.

Princess Désirée; b. June 2, 1938; married June 5, 1964, Baron Niclas Silfverschiöld; son, Carl Otto Edmund, b. March 22, 1965; daughters, Christina Louise Madeleine, b. 1966, Hélène, b. September 20, 1968.

Princess Christina; b. August 3, 1943; married August 15, 1974, Tord Magnusson; son Gustaf, b. August 8, 1975.

THAILAND
Reigning King

KING BHUMIBOL ADULYADEJ; b. December 5, 1927 succeeded to the throne on the death of his brother, King Ananda Mahidol, June 9, 1946; married April 28, 1950, MOM RAJAWONG SIRIKIT KITIYAKARA (b. August 12, 1932), daughter of H.H. Prince Nakkhatra Mongkol Kitiyakara, Krommuen Chandaburi Suranat.

Children of the King

Princess Ubol Ratana; b. April 5, 1951; married August 1972, Peter Ladd Jensen (relinquished Royal claims).

Prince Vajiralongkorn; b. July 28, 1952.

Princess Sirindhorn; b. April 2, 1955.

Princess Chulabhorn; b. July 4, 1957.

Parents of the King

Prince Mahidol of Songkhla and Princess Sri Sangwalya.

Sister of the King

Princess Kalyani Vadhana.

TONGA
Reigning King

KING TAUFA'AHAU TUPOU IV; b. July 4, 1918; succeeded to the throne December 15, 1965, on death of his mother Queen Salote Tupou III; married 1947, Princess Halaevalu Mata'aho (b. 1926).

Mother of the King

Queen Salote Pilolevu Tupou III; b. March 13, 1900; married 1917, Prince Viliami Tungi (Prince Consort), died December 15, 1965.

Children of the King

Prince Tupouto'a (Crown Prince); b. May 4, 1948.

Princess Salote Mafile'o Pilolevu Tuku'aho; b. November 17, 1951.

Prince Fatafehi Alaivahamama'o Tuku'aho; b. December 17, 1954.

Prince Aho'eitu Unuakiotonga Tuku'aho; b. July 12, 1959.

UNITED ARAB EMIRATES
Reigning Rulers

Ruler of Sharjah: Sheikh SULTAN BIN MUHAMMAD AL-QASIMI; succeeded to the throne 1972.

Ruler of Ras al Khaimah: Sheikh SAQR BIN MUHAMMAD AL-QASIMI; succeeded to the throne 1948.

Ruler of Umm al Quwain: Sheikh AHMAD BIN RASHID AL-MU'ALLA, M.B.E.; succeeded to the throne 1929.

Ruler of Ajman: Sheikh RASHID BIN HUMAID AL-NU'AIMI; succeeded to the throne 1928.

Ruler of Dubai: Sheikh RASHID BIN SAID AL-MAKTUM; succeeded to the throne 1958.

Ruler of Abu Dhabi: Sheikh ZAYED BIN SULTAN AL-NHAYYAN; succeeded to throne 1966.

Ruler of Fujairah: Sheikh HAMAD BIN MUHAMMAD AL-SHARQI; succeeded to the throne 1974.

UNITED KINGDOM
Reigning Queen

QUEEN ELIZABETH II; b. April 21, 1926; succeeded to the throne February 6, 1952, on the death of her father, King George VI; crowned June 2, 1953; married November 20, 1947, H.R.H. The Prince Philip, DUKE OF EDINBURGH, K.G. (b. June 10, 1921), son of Prince Andrew of Greece and Princess Alice of Battenberg (Mountbatten).

Children of the Queen

Prince Charles Philip Arthur George, Prince of Wales, Duke of Cornwall and Rothesay, Earl of Chester and Carrick, Baron of Renfrew, Lord of the Isles and Great Steward of Scotland, K.G. (heir-apparent); b. November 14, 1948.

Princess Anne Elizabeth Alice Louise; b. August 15, 1950; married November 14, 1973, Captain Mark Phillips.

Prince Andrew Albert Christian Edward; b. February 19, 1960.

Prince Edward Antony Richard Louis; b. March 10, 1964.

Parents of the Queen

King George VI; b. December 14, 1895; son of King George V and Queen Mary; married April 26, 1923, Lady Elizabeth Angela Marguerite Bowes-Lyon (b. August 4, 1900); succeeded to the throne December 11, 1936; died February 6, 1952.

Sister of the Queen

Princess Margaret Rose; b. August 21, 1930; married May 6, 1960, the Earl of Snowdon, G.C.V.O.; son, Viscount Linley, b. November 3, 1961; daughter, Lady Sarah Frances Elizabeth Armstrong-Jones, b. May 1, 1964.

The full titles of Queen Elizabeth II are as follows:

United Kingdom
"Elizabeth the Second, by the Grace of God, of the United Kingdom of Great Britain and Northern Ireland and of her other Realms and Territories, Queen, Head of the Commonwealth, Defender of the Faith."

Canada
"Elizabeth the Second, by the Grace of God, of the United Kingdom, Canada, and her other Realms and Territories, Queen, Head of the Commonwealth, Defender of the Faith."

Australia
"Elizabeth the Second, by the Grace of God, Queen of Australia and of her other Realms and Territories, Head of the Commonwealth."

New Zealand
"Elizabeth the Second, by the Grace of God, of the United Kingdom, New Zealand, and her other Realms and Territories, Queen, Head of the Commonwealth, Defender of the Faith."

Jamaica
"Elizabeth the Second, by the Grace of God, of Jamaica and of her other Realms and Territories, Queen, Head of the Commonwealth."

Trinidad and Tobago
"Elizabeth the Second, by the Grace of God, Queen of Trinidad and Tobago and of her other Realms and Territories, Head of the Commonwealth."

Barbados
"Elizabeth the Second, by the Grace of God, Queen of Barbados and of her other Realms and Territories, Head of the Commonwealth."

Mauritius
"Elizabeth the Second, Queen of Mauritius and of her other Realms and Territories, Head of the Commonwealth."

Fiji
"Elizabeth the Second, by the Grace of God, Queen of Fiji and of her other Realms and Territories, Head of the Commonwealth."

The Bahamas
"Elizabeth the Second, by the Grace of God, Queen of The Bahamas and of her other Realms and Territories, Head of the Commonwealth."

Grenada
"Elizabeth the Second, by the Grace of God, Queen of Grenada and of her other Realms and Territories, Head of the Commonwealth."

Papua New Guinea
"Elizabeth the Second, Queen of Papua New Guinea and of her other Realms and Territories, Head of the Commonwealth."

The Republics of India, Ghana, Cyprus, Tanzania, Uganda, Kenya, Zambia, Malawi, Nigeria. Singapore, Botswana, Guyana, Nauru, Sierra Leone, The Gambia, Bangladesh, Sri Lanka and Malta, together with the Federation of Malaysia, the Kingdom of Lesotho, the Kingdom of Swaziland, the Kingdom of Tonga and the State of Western Samoa, recognize the Queen as "Head of the Commonwealth".

OBITUARY

Abdul Razak bin Hussein, Tun Haji	14 Jan. 1976
Acker, Achille H. Van	10 July 1975
Ahanda, Vincent de Paul	1975
*Ahmed, Tajuddin	Nov. 1975
*Albers, Josef	24 March 1976
Anderson, Clinton Presba	11 Nov. 1975
Anderson, Sir Donald George	30 Nov. 1975
Arendt, Hannah	4 Dec. 1975
Armstrong, Anthony	10 Feb. 1976
Asafu-Adjaye, Sir Edward Okyere	Feb. 1976
Auboin, Roger	16 Oct. 1974
Ayrton, Michael	17 Nov. 1975
Babotchkin, Boris Andreevich	July 1975
Bakhiet, Gaafar Mohed Ali	March 1976
Barnes, Nathan	16 July 1975
Barratt, Sir Sydney	28 Aug. 1975
Bastid, Paul Raymond Marie	30 Oct. 1974
Bek, Alexandr Alfredovich	Deceased
Benesz, Andrzej	Feb. 1976
Benoit, Jean-Paul	Deceased
Berggolts, Olga Fedorovna	14 Nov. 1975
*Berkeley, Busby	14 March 1976
Bernard, Sir Dallas Gerald Mercer	26 Nov. 1975
*Bernet Kempers, Karel Phillipus	30 Sept. 1974
*Beyen, Johan Willem	1976
Bianchi-Bandinelli, Ranuccio	Jan. 1975
Bodnaras, Gen. Emil	24 Jan. 1976
Bost, Pierre	Dec. 1975
*Braibant, Charles	23 April 1976
Branigan, Roger Douglas	19 Nov. 1975
Brennan, Joseph	3 March 1976
Briggs, Ellis Ormsbee	Feb. 1976
Bronk, Detlev Wulf	12 Nov. 1975
Brown, W(illiam) Norman	22 April 1975
Buchan, Alastair Francis	3 Feb. 1976
Calo, Giovanni	Deceased
Carrington, Most Rev. Philip	3 Oct. 1975
Cassin, René	20 Feb. 1976
Castro, Joao Augusto de Araujo	9 Dec. 1975
Cepek, Ladislav	15 Oct. 1974
Charon, Jacques	Oct. 1975
Chou En-lai	8 Jan. 1976
Chou Hsing	3 Oct. 1975
Christie, Dame Agatha	12 Jan. 1976
Cicogna, Furio	Dec. 1975
Cleland, Brig. Sir Donald Mackinnon	27 Aug. 1975
Clemence, Gerald Maurice	Deceased
*Cloete, (Edward Fairley) Stuart (Graham)	20 March 1976
Concha, H.E. Cardinal Luis	Sept. 1975
Constable, W. G.	3 Feb. 1976
Cook, Sir James Wilfred	21 Oct. 1975
Cordier, Andrew Wellington	11 July 1975
Corrigan, Leo F(rancis)	12 June 1975
Costello, John Aloysius	5 Jan. 1976
Crawford and Balcarres, Earl of; Lord David Lindsay Balniel	13 Dec. 1975
*Dam, (Carl Peter) Henrik	24 April 1976
Daubeny, Sir Peter Lauderdale	6 Aug. 1975
Davis, Joseph Stancliffe	23 July 1975
Delavignette, Robert	4 Feb. 1976
De La Warr, Earl; Herbrand Edward Dundonald Brassey Sackville	28 Jan. 1976
Denjoy, Arnaud	21 Jan. 1974
*Dennison, David Mathias	April 1976
De Valéra, Eamon	29 Aug. 1975
Dobzhansky, Theodosius	18 Dec. 1975

Dowty, Sir George	7 Dec. 1975
Dragstedt, Lester R.	14 Aug. 1975
Duncan, Sir Val (John Norman Valette)	19 Dec. 1975
Dunning, John Ray	25 Aug. 1975
Dvornik, Francis	4 Nov. 1975
Dyhrenfurth, Günter Oskar	14 Sept. 1975
Edwards, Prof. Sir Ronald Stanley	20 Jan. 1976
*Elazar, Lieut.-Gen. David	14 April 1976
Elling, Christian	Deceased
*Ernst, Max	1 April 1976
Esplá Triay, Oscar	6 Jan. 1976
Fajans, Kasimir	18 May 1975
Felsenstein, Walter	8 Oct. 1975
Feltin, H.E. Cardinal Maurice	27 Sept. 1975
*Fernando, Hugh Norman Gregory	March 1976
Fierlinger, Zdeněk	2 May 1976
Fock, Vladimir Alexandrovitch	27 Dec. 1974
Forssmann, Werner	Deceased
Foster, John Frederick	24 Sept. 1975
Franchon, Benoit	4 Aug. 1975
Franco Bahamonde, Generalísimo Francisco	20 Nov. 1975
Frauwallner, Erich	Deceased
Frewen, Admiral Sir John Byng	30 Aug. 1975
Friedrich, Otto Andreas	8 Dec. 1975
Gallimard, Gaston	25 Dec. 1975
Garner, Robert Livingston	Dec. 1975
*Georgiev, Alexandr Vasilievich	12 April 1976
*Gibbs, Hon. Sir Geoffrey Cokayne	6 July 1975
Gilliland, Edwin R.	12 March 1973
*Godber, Baron; Frederick Godber	10 April 1976
Gorham, Maurice Anthony Coneys	9 Aug. 1975
Grano, H.E. Cardinal Carlo	April 1976
Gray, Sir James	11 Dec. 1975
*Grechko, Marshal Andrei Antonovich	26 April 1976
Griffiths, Rt. Hon. James	7 Aug. 1975
Gui, Vittorio	16 Oct. 1975
György, Paul	1 March 1976
Haddow, Sir Alexander	22 Jan. 1979
Hahnloser, Hans Rob	Deceased
Haile Sellassie I, His Imperial Majesty	27 Aug. 1975
Hansen, Alvin Harvey	6 June 1975
Harrisson, Tom	Jan. 1976
Hayward, Sir Isaac James	3 Jan. 1976
Heald, Henry Townley	23 Nov. 1975
Heenan, H.E. Cardinal John Carmel	7 Nov. 1975
Heisenberg, Werner	1 Feb. 1976
Hertz, Gustav	30 Oct. 1975
Hessellund-Jensen, Aage	24 April 1974
Heyne, Hans	24 Dec. 1973
Hill, William Charles Osman	25 Jan. 1975
Hirst, Sir Edmund Langley	29 Oct. 1975
Hodge, Sir William Vallance Douglas	7 July 1975
Hogben, Lancelot	22 Aug. 1975
Holford, Baron; William Graham Holford	17 Oct. 1975
Holtedahl, Olaf	26 Aug. 1975
Hoover, Calvin Bryce	23 June 1974
Horák, Jiři	14 Sept. 1975
Huber, Paul	Deceased
*Hughes, Howard Robard	5 April 1976
Humphrey, George Duke	Deceased
Hurcomb, Baron; Cyril William Hurcomb	7 Aug. 1975
Husain, Mahmud	10 April 1975

In Tam	1975
Iturmendi Bañales, Antonio	4 March 1975
Ivanov, Semyon Pavlovich	Deceased
Job, Jakob	30 April 1973
Johnson, Howard Albert	Deceased
Jouve, Pierre Jean	8 Jan. 1976
Kaitila, Esa Heikki	18 June 1975
Kamaraj, K.	2 Oct. 1975
Kamaruzzaman, Abdul Hassanat Mohammed	Nov. 1975
K'ang Sheng	21 Dec. 1975
Kellner, Béla	27 July 1975
Kienle, Johann (Hans) Georg	Deceased
Kirchwey, Freda	3 Jan. 1976
Kirchbaum, Emil	Deceased
Kisfaludi-Strobl, Zsigmond	14 Aug. 1975
Klokoč, Andrej	26 March 1975
Knipper, Lev Konstantinovich	Deceased
Küchemann, Dietrich	23 Feb. 1976
Kulczyński, Stanisław	12 July 1975
Labbé, Roland Georges Joseph Marie	1973
Lavon, Pinhas	24 Jan. 1976
Lawther, Sir William	1 Feb. 1976
Lazarev, Viktor Nikitch	31 Jan. 1975
Leckwijck, William Peter Edward Joseph van	19 June 1975
Leger, Alexis Saint-Léger	20 Sept. 1975
Lemberger, Dr. Ernst	3 Dec. 1974
Lilar, Albert	16 March 1976
*Lin Yutang	March 1976
Linnett, John Wilfrid	7 Nov. 1975
Liu Hsing-yuan	Deceased
Lowry, Laurence Stephen	23 Feb. 1976
Lowson, Sir Denys Colquhoun Flowerdew	10 Sept. 1975
Loyen, André	1974
Lugeon, Jean	23 Feb. 1976
Luttig, Hendrik Gerhardus	12 July 1975
Maheu, Rene	19 Dec. 1975
Maisky, Ivan Mikhailovich	3 Sept. 1975
Manuwa, Chief the Hon. Sir Samuel Layinka Ayodeji	16 Sept. 1975
Marriott, Richard Michael Harris	12 Dec. 1975
Marsh, Ernest Sterling	Deceased
Martin, H.E. Cardinal Joseph Marie Eugene	23 Jan. 1976
Martinon, Jean	1 March 1976
Matter, Jean	May 1975
Meynell, Sir Francis	9 July 1975
Middleton, William Shainline	9 Sept. 1975
Mielziner, Jo	March 1976
Migot, Georges	1976
*Miller, William E.	13 April 1976
Mitrany, David	25 July 1975
Mollet, Guy	3 Oct. 1975
Monnington, Sir Walter Thomas	7 Jan. 1976
Montgomery of Alamein, Viscount; Field-Marshal Bernard Law Montgomery	24 March 1976
Murdock, Kenneth Ballard	15 Nov. 1975
Neale, Sir John Ernest	2 Sept. 1975
Neihardt, John Gneisenau	Deceased
Netchkina, Militsa Vasilyevna	Deceased
*Nicoll, (John Ramsay) Allardyce	17 April 1976
Nimmanheminda, Sukich	Feb. 1976
Noriega-Morales, Manuel	6 April 1975
Oleffe, André	18 Aug. 1975
Pachachi, Nadim	March 1976
Pasolini, Pier Paolo	2 Nov. 1975

*Penfield, Wilder Graves	5 April 1976
Phillips, Wendell	4 Dec. 1975
Plaude, Karl Karlovich	1 Jan. 1976
Polanyi, Michael	23 Feb. 1975
Rahman, Sheikh Mujibur	15 Aug. 1975
Rakotomalala, H.E. Cardinal Jérôme	1 Nov. 1975
*Reed, Sir Carol	26 April 1976
*Restivo, Franco	17 April 1976
Ritchie of Dundee, Baron; John Kenneth Ritchie	20 Oct. 1975
Robeson, Paul	23 Jan. 1976
Roullier, Jean Georges	Sept. 1974
Sachs, Hans-Georg	10 July 1975
Sallborg, John A.	July 1975
Salvatorelli, Luigi	3 Nov. 1974
Sapir, Pinhas	12 Aug. 1975
Schleinzer, Dr. Karl	19 July 1975
Selwyn-Clarke, Sir Selwyn	13 March 1976
Servais, Jean-Aimé	21 Feb. 1976
Shafik, Doria (Ahmed)	22 Sept. 1975
Shaw, Sir Patrick	27 Jan. 1976
Shchetinin, Semyon Nikolayevich	Dec. 1975
Sherriff, Robert Cedric	13 Nov. 1975
Shostakovich, Dmitry Dmitryevich	9 Aug. 1975
*Shtemenko, Gen. Sergei Matveyevich	23 April 1976
Sisowath Sirik Matak, (H.H. Prince) Lieut.-Gen.	April 1975
*Sivara, Gen. Kris	23 April 1976
Smart, William Marshall	17 Sept. 1975
*Solberg, Halvor Skappel	Deceased
*Soldevilla Zubiburu, Ferran	Deceased
Spence, Robert	10 March 1976
Staf, Cornelius	1973
Starovsky, Vladimir Nikonovich	20 Oct. 1975
Steen, Marguerite	4 Aug. 1975
Stein, Clarence S.	7 Feb. 1975
Steward, Julian H.	Deceased
Sudrabkains, Ianis (Arvid) Karlovich	4 Sept. 1975
Summers, Sir Spencer	19 Jan. 1976
Swartz, Thomas Robert	Sept. 1975
Tatum, Edward L(awrie)	5 Nov. 1975
Thompson, Sir George Paget	10 Sept. 1975
Tidblad, Inga Sophia	12 Sept. 1975
*Tobey, Mark	24 April 1976
Toynbee, Arnold Joseph	22 Oct. 1975
Trilling, Lionel	5 Nov. 1975
Unterman, Rabbi Iser Jehudah	24 Jan. 1976
Verissimo, Erico Lopes	28 Nov. 1975
Virsky, Pavel Pavlovich	July 1975
Visconti, Luchino	17 March 1976
Vishnevsky, Alexander Alexandrovich	21 Nov. 1975
Vorobyov, Vitaly Andreevich	Deceased
Waddington, Conrad Hal	26 Sept. 1975
Walker, Eric Anderson	Feb. 1976
Wallis, Mieczysław	25 Oct. 1975
Walters, Basil L.	29 Aug. 1975
Ward, John Harris	28 July 1974
Weatherhead, Rev. Leslie Dixon	3 Jan. 1976
Wheeler, Sir Charles Reginald	25 Nov. 1975
Wheeler, Gen. Earle Gilmore	18 Dec. 1975
Wheeler-Bennett, Sir John Wheeler	9 Dec. 1975
Wilder, Thornton Niven	8 Dec. 1975
Wiles, Reid	23 June 1975
Wotruba, Fritz	28 Aug. 1975
Wurster, Carl	14 Dec. 1975
Yazici, Bülent	4 Feb. 1976
Zhukov, (Yuri) Georgi Alexandrovich	18 June 1974

THE INTERNATIONAL WHO'S WHO

1976-77

A

Aalberse, Petrus Josephus Mattheus; Netherlands lawyer and politician; b. 1910, Leiden; *m.* Augusta I. Housz 1939; three *s.* three *d.*; ed. Gymnasium St. Aloysius and Univ. of Leiden.
Secretary Building Industry Asscn. 42–47; Adviser, social orgs. 47–62; mem. Wassenaar Town Council 45-54; Sec. and later Pres. Landelijk Comité Rechtszekerheid 47-52; Sec. Catholic Social Advice and "Raad van Overleg" 55-62; Pres. Catholic People's Party 62-68; mem. Second Chamber of States Gen. 63-69; mem. State Council 69-; Commdr. Order of Gregory the Great.
Leisure interests: books, television, golf.
Ruychrocklaan 370, The Hague, Netherlands.
Telephone: 070-248677.

Aalto, (Hugo) Alvar Henrik; Finnish architect; b. 3 Feb. 1898, Kuortane; *m.* 1st Aino Marsio (died 1949), one *s.* one *d.*; *m.* 2nd Elissa Mäkiniemi 1952; ed. Jyväskylän Lyseo and Univ. of Technology, Helsinki.
Graduated as architect 21, owner of architectural practice 23-; Prof. at Massachusetts Inst. of Technology 46-48; mem. Acad. of Finland 55-; Hon. mem. Royal Coll. of Arts, London, Assoc. per l'Architettura Organica, Rome, Instituto de Arquiteto do Brasil, Södra Sveriges Byggnadstekniska Samfund 57-, Accad. di Belle Arti, Venice, American Acad. of Arts and Sciences 57-, Asscn. of Finnish Architects 58-, Norske Arkitekters Lansforbund, Norway 59-, Colegio de Arquitectos del Perú 65-, V-Dala Nation, Uppsala 65-; mem. or corresp. mem. numerous other acads.; mem. Orden pour le Mérite für Wissenschaft und Künste 69; Chevalier, Légion d'Honneur, Akademisk Arkitekt-førenings Aeresmedaille, Denmark, Prins Eugen Medal, Sweden, Royal Gold Medal of Architecture (U.K.) 57, Commdr. Order of Dannebrog (Denmark), Gold Medal, American Inst. of Architects 63, Gold Cube, Svensk Arkitekters Riksförbund 63, Cordón del Calli de Oro, Soc. de Arquitectos Mexicanos 63, Bronzeplakette, Freie Akad. der Künste in Hamburg 65, Suomen Leijonan ritarikunta suurristi 65, Diplôme des Palmes d'Or du Mérite de l'Europe 66, Thomas Jefferson Medal, Univ. of Virginia 67; numerous hon. degrees.
Principal works: Finnish Pavilions at Paris Int. Exhbn. 37, New York World Fair 39, Paimio Sanatorium, Helsinki and Jyväskylä Univ. buildings, Viipuri Library, flats in Berlin, Dormitory Block for Mass. Inst. of Technology, Wolfsburg City Centre, government and office buildings, Helsinki.
Tiilímaki 20, 00330 Helsinki 33, Finland.

Aamiry, Muhammad Adeeb Al-, B.A.; Jordanian politician, educationist and author; b. 1907, Jaffa, Palestine; *s.* of Mahmoud Al-Aamiry and Zakia Al-Deeb; *m.* Siham Jabri Al-Aamiry 1942; one *s.* three *d.*; ed. American Univ. of Beirut and Palestine Law Inst.
Teacher 30; Headmaster 34; Ministry of Educ. Insp. 43; Deputy Dir. of Broadcasting Station, Jerusalem 44; Gen. Sec., Ministry of Foreign Affairs 50; Dir. Imports and Exports Dept. 51; Head, Civil Service Dept. 55-58; Under-Sec., Ministry of Educ. 52, Ministry of Reconstruction and Devt. 53; Minister of Foreign Affairs Aug.-Oct. 67, of Educ. Oct. 67-April 68; Amb. to U.A.R. May 68; Minister of Culture, Information, Tourism and Antiquities 68-69; mem. Jordan Writers Union, Soc. of Friends of Archaeology, Soc. of Scientific Establishment of Jerusalem; Al Kawkab Medal 1st Grade.
Publs. *How to Keep Your Health* (2 vols.), *Ray of Light* (short stories), *General Science, Plant Families, Life and Youth* (trans. from English) 67, *Jerusalem: The Arab Heritage* 70, *Palestine: The Arab Heritage* 72.
Leisure interests: extra-political activities, reading, writing.
P.O. Box 1514, Amman, Jordan.
Telephone: 44447.

Aars, Knut; Norwegian diplomatist; b. 14 July 1918, Oslo; *s.* of Jacob and Anna (née Broedsgaard) Aars; *m.* Gerd Sandvik 1943; one *s.* one *d.*; ed. Oslo Univ.
Lawyer, then deputy judge 41-44; Sec. Norwegian Legation, Stockholm 44-45, Lisbon 48-50; Sec. Ministry of Foreign Affairs 45-48; First Sec., Washington 50-52; Chief, Div. for NATO Affairs, Ministry of Foreign Affairs 52-55; Deputy Perm. Rep. to North Atlantic Council 55-58; Counsellor, London 58-62; Amb. to Iran and Pakistan 62-65, also accred. to Afghanistan 64-66; Special Adviser to Ministry of Foreign Affairs 66-70; Perm. Rep. of Norway to North Atlantic Council June 70-72; mem. Norwegian Inst. of Int. Affairs 72-73; Ministry of Foreign Affairs 73-; Amb. to Argentina, Paraguay and Uruguay 74-.
Leisure interest: mountaineering.
Norwegian Embassy, Buenos Aires, Argentina.

Aarvik, Egil; Norwegian politician; b. 12 Dec. 1912, Borsa, Central Norway; *s.* of Julius and Louise (née Lie) Aarvik; *m.* Anna C. Grove-Nielsen 1938; three *s.* one *d.*
Secretary, Norwegian Lutheran Inner Mission 34-37, Danish Inner Mission 37, Stavanger Inner Mission 40-46; journalist on daily newspaper *Dagsavisa*, Trondheim 47-50, Editor 50-55; Editor *Folkets Framtid* (organ of Christian People's Party) 48-65; mem. Nat. Board of Norwegian Blue Cross 58-, Chair. 60-; mem. Strinda Municipal Council 52-56; mem. Storting for Oslo 61-65, 69-, Chair. Social Affairs Cttee. 61-65; Minister of Social Affairs 65-70; Pres. Lagting 74-; Christian People's Party.
Tollef Gravs v. 127, 1342 Jar, Norway.
Telephone: 248325 (Home).

Abakanowicz, Magdalena; Polish artist and weaver; b. 20 June 1930, Falenty nr. Warsaw; ed. Warsaw Acad. of Fine Arts.
Member of ZAIKS asscn. of authors; work includes tapestry, screen structures, space forms of knotted, plaited and woven fibres; paintings with collage and gouache; teacher, Higher School of Fine Arts, Poznań 65-; State Prize, 3rd Class 65; Gold Medal, VIII Int.

Biennale of Arts, São Paulo; Gold Medal, FSP 67 and others; Silver Cross of Merit.
Works: Structural Gobelin for North Brabant Provincial Office, Netherlands; Gobelin for Public Library, Stuttgart, Fed. Repub. of Germany; Sculpture-Space Form, Elbląg, Poland. One-man exhbns.: Gallery Dautzenberg, Paris 62, Zachęta Museum, Warsaw 65, Public Museum, Oslo 67, Museum of Arts, Zürich 68, Frans Hals Museum, Haarlem 69, Public Museum, Rotterdam. Collections: Museum of Modern Art, N.Y.; Stedelijk Museum, Amsterdam; Museu de Arte Contemporanea, São Paulo; Frans Hals Museum, Haarlem; Musée des Beaux-Arts, Chaux-de-Fonds, Switzerland; museums in Oslo, Zürich and Poznań.
Al. Stanów Zjednoczonych 16 m. 53, 54-403 Warsaw, Poland.

Abbadi, Bashir Ahmed, D.SC.; Sudanese politician; b. 1936, Omdurman; s. of Ahmed B. El Abbadi and Fatima A. Beshir; m. Huda M. Logan 1963; four c.; ed. Univ. of Khartoum and Northwestern Univ., U.S.A.
Lecturer, Faculty of Eng., Univ. of Khartoum, Head, Dept. of Mechanical Eng. 70-71; mem. Board of Dirs. Sudan Railways 68-69, Chair. Board of Dirs. Sudan Airways 69-70; Minister of Communications 71-, and of Transport 73-.
Ministry of Communications, Khartoum, Sudan.

Abbado, Claudio; Italian conductor; b. 1933; ed. Conservatorio Giuseppe Verdi, Milan, and Musical Acad. in Vienna.
Guest conductor of principal orchestras in Europe and America; conductor at principal festivals and opera houses since 61; Perm. Conductor 68, and Musical Dir. 71, Scala Orchestra, Milan; Principal Conductor Vienna Philharmonic Orchestra 71; Principal Guest Conductor London Symphony Orchestra 74; Sergei Kussewitzky Prize, Tanglewood 58, Dmitri Mitropoulos Prize, New York 63, Mozart-Medaille of the Mozart Gemeinde, Vienna 73; since 65 yearly recipient of int. prizes for recordings (Diapason, Deutscher Schallplattenpreis, Grand Prix du Disque, etc.).
Via Nirone 2/A, 20123, Milan, Italy.

Abbas, Ferhat; Algerian politician; b. 1890; ed. Algiers Univ.
Formerly a chemist at Sétif; took part in organization of the Algerian People's Union 38; published "Manifesto of the Algerian People" 43; founded Amis du Manifeste et de la Liberté (A.M.L.) 44 and took part in the formation of the Union Démocratique du Manifeste Algérien (U.D.M.A.) 46; elected representative to French Constitutional Assembly 46, later member of French Union Assembly; elected to Algerian Assembly 48 and 54; Leader of U.D.M.A. 46-56; joined Nat. Liberation Front (F.L.N.) 55; mem. F.L.N. delegation to 11th Gen. Assembly of UN 57; leader del. to North African Conf., Tangier 58; Prime Minister of "Provisional Government of the Algerian Republic" (in Tunisia) 58-61; Pres. of the Chamber of the independent state of Algeria 62-63; under detention July 64-June 65.
Publs. Le jeune algérien 31, La Nuit coloniale 63.
Konba, Algiers, Algeria.

Abbott, Hon. Douglas Charles, P.C., Q.C., B.C.L., LL.D.; Canadian lawyer; b. 29 May 1899, Lennoxville, Quebec; s. of Lewis Duff Abbott and Mary J. Pearce; m. Mary W. Chisholm 1925; two s. one d.; ed. Bishop's Coll., Lennoxville, McGill Univ., and Dijon Univ. (France).
Member of Parl. 40-54; Parl. Asst. to the Minister of Finance 43-45, to Minister of Nat. Defence 45; Minister of Nat. Defence for Naval Services, later Minister of Nat. Defence 45; Minister of Finance 46-54; Puisne Justice, Supreme Court of Canada 54-; Chancellor, Bishop's Univ. 58-68.
Leisure interests: fishing and curling.
124 Springfield Road, Ottawa, Ontario 2, Canada.
Telephone: 745-6250.

Abbott, Very Rev. Eric Symes, K.C.V.O., M.A.; British ecclesiastic; b. 26 May 1906; ed. Nottingham High School and Jesus Coll., Cambridge.
Curate, St. John's, Smith Square, London, S.W.1 30-32; Chaplain, King's Coll., London 32-36, Lincoln's Inn 34-36; Warpen, Lincoln Theological Coll. 36-45; Dean, King's Coll., London 45-55; Warden, Keble Coll., Oxford 55-60; Dean of Westminster 59-74; Chaplain to H.M. The King 48-52, to H.M. The Queen 52-60, Extra Chaplain to H.M. The Queen 74-; Hon. Fellow Keble Coll., Oxford, and Jesus Coll., Cambridge; Hon. D.D. (London, Lambeth); Freeman of Westminster 73.
17 Vincent Square, London, S.W.1, England.

Abboud, A. Robert, M.B.A., LL.B.; American banker; b. 29 May 1929, Boston, Mass.; s. of Alfred and Jane Abboud; m. Joan Grover Abboud 1955; one s. two d.; ed. Harvard Coll., Harvard Law School, Harvard Business School.
Assistant Cashier, Int. Dept., First Nat. Bank of Chicago 60, Asst. Vice-Pres. Int. 62, Vice-Pres. 64, Senior Vice-Pres. 69, Exec. Vice-Pres. 72, Vice-Chair. 73, Deputy Chair. of Board 74-75, Chair. of Board Dec. 75-.
Publs. Introduction of U.S. Commercial Paper in Foreign Markets—Premature and Perilous? 70, A Proposed Course for U.S. Trade and Investment Policies 71, A Proposal to Help Reverse the Narrowing Balance in the U.S. Balance of Trade 71, The Outlook for a New Monetary System 71, Opportunities for Foreign Banks in Singapore 71, The International Competitiveness of U.S. Banks and the U.S. Economy 72.
First National Bank of Chicago, One First National Plaza, Chicago, Ill. 60670; Home: High Point Farm, Route 1, Box 209, Algonquin, Ill. 60102, U.S.A.
Telephone: (312) 732-8043 (Office); (312) 658-4808.

Abboud, Gen. Ibrahim; Sudanese army officer and politician; b. 26 Oct. 1900; ed. Gordon Coll., Khartoum, and Military Coll., Khartoum.
Commissioned 17, joined Sudan Defence Force 25, served Eritrea, Ethiopia and North Africa in Second World War; Deputy C.-in-C. Sudanese Army 54-56, C.-in-C. 56-64; Pres. Supreme Council of the Armed Forces, Prime Minister and Minister of Defence 58-64.
Suakin, Sudan.

Abdel Meguid, Ahmed Esmat, PH.D.; Egyptian diplomatist; b. 22 March 1923, Alexandria; m. Eglal Abou-Hamda 1950; three s.; ed. Faculty of Law, Alexandria Univ. and Univ. of Paris.
Attaché and Sec., Egyptian Embassy, London 50-54; Ministry of Foreign Affairs, Head British Desk 54-56, Asst. Dir. Legal Dept. 61-63, Head Cultural and Technical Assistance Dept. 67-68; Counsellor, Perm. Mission to European Office of UN, Geneva 57-61; Minister Counsellor, Egyptian Embassy, Paris 63-67; Official Spokesman of Govt. and Head Information Dept. 68-69; Amb. to France 69-70; Minister of State for Cabinet Affairs 70-72; Perm. Rep. to UN 72-; mem. Int. Law Asscn., took part in UN confs. on the Law of the Sea 59, on Consular Relations 63 and on the Law of Treaties 69; Ordre National du Mérite, Govt. of France 67; Grand Croix 71; 1st Class Decoration, Arab Repub. of Egypt 70.
Publs. several articles in Revue Egyptienne de Droit International.
Permanent Mission of Egypt to United Nations, 36 East 67th Street, New York, N.Y. 10021, U.S.A.
Telephone: 879-6300.

Abdel-Rahman, Aisha, PH.D. (pen name **Bint el-Shati**); Egyptian writer and university professor; ed. Cairo Univ.
Assistant Lecturer, Cairo Univ. 39-; Literary Critic Al Ahram 42-; Inspectress in Arabic Languages and Literature, Ministry of Educ. 42; Lecturer in Arabic, Ain Shams Univ. 50-57; Asst. Prof. 57-62; Prof. of

Arabic Literature and Chair. Univ. Coll. for Women 62-; mem. Higher Council of Arts and Letters 60-; State Prize 36; Acad. of Arabic Language Award for Textual Studies 50, for Short Story 54.
Publs. *Rissalet el Ghofram by Abul Ala'a* 50, *New Values in Arabic Literature* 61, *The Koran: Literary Interpretation* 62, *Ibn Seeda's Arabic Dictionary* 62, *Contemporary Arab Women Poets* 63; six books on illustrious women of Islam; two novels; four vols. of short stories.
13 Agam Street, Heliopolis, Cairo, Egypt.

Abdel-Rahman, Ibrahim Helmi, PH.D.; Egyptian United Nations official; b. 5 Jan. 1919; ed. Univs. of Cairo, London, Edinburgh, Cambridge and Leiden.
Lecturer in Astronomy and Astrophysics, later Asst. Prof., Cairo Univ. 42-54; Sec.-Gen. Council of Ministers; 54-58; Dir. Egyptian Atomic Energy Comm. 54-59; mem. and Sec.-Gen. Nat. Science Council 56-58; mem. Nat. Planning Comm. 57-60; Dir. Inst. of Nat. Planning 60-63; UN Commr. for Industrial Devt. 63-66; Exec. Dir. UN Industrial Devt. Org. (UNIDO) 67-74; Senior Adviser to Prime Minister 75; Minister of Nat. Planning and Admin. Reform April 75-; mem. Egyptian Del. UNESCO Gen. Conf. 48, 52, 54.
Council of Ministers, Cairo, Egypt.

Abdessalam, Belaid; Algerian politician; b. July 1928, Dehemcha.
Former Hon. Pres. Union Générale des Etudiants Musulmans Algériens (UGEMA); Instructor Front de Libération Nationale (FLN) School, Oujda; Political Adviser in Cabinet of M. Ben Khedda 61; in charge of Econ. Affairs, FLN Provisional Exec. 62; Pres., Dir.-Gen. Soc. Nat. pour la Recherche, la Production, le Transport, la Transformation et la Commercialisation des Hydrocarbures (SONATRACH) 64-66; Minister of Industry and Energy 65-.
Ministère de l'Industrie et de l'Energie, Algiers, Algeria.

Abdoh, Djalal, LL.D.; Iranian diplomatist; b. 1909, Teheran; s. of Mohamad and Batool Abdoh; m. Sedighe Etemad 1938; three d.; ed. Teheran and Paris Univs.
Assistant Dir. Ministry of Justice 37-39; Public Prosecutor, Court of Govt. Employees, Teheran 41-43; Dir.-Gen. Ministry of Justice 43-44; mem. Parl. 44-49; mem. Iranian Del. to UN 46-53, 54-59; Dep. Perm. Rep. Iranian Mission to UN 49-53; Dir.-Gen. of Political Affairs, Ministry of Foreign Affairs 54-55; Ambassador and Perm. Rep. to UN 55-59; Minister of Foreign Affairs 59; UN Plebiscite Commr. British Cameroons 59-61; Roving Ambassador of Iran 61-62; Prof. Int. Law and Pol. Science, Teheran Univ. 61; Admin.UN Temporary Exec. Authority (UNTEA. West New Guinea) Oct. 62-May 63; Amb. to India 65-68, to Italy 68-72; Man. Dir. Iranian Bankers' Asscn. 72-; mem. Currency and Credit Council 72-, Perm. Court of Arbitration 46-; Pres. Iranian Asscn. for the UN 72, Int. Law Asscn. Iranian Branch 73-.
Publs. *Civil Procedure of Iran, Comparative Law, International Private Law, Eléments psychologiques dans les Contrats, Le Ministère public, Le Régime pénitentiaire en Iran, The Political Situation in the Middle East* (Persian), *The Political Situation in Africa* (Persian).
41 Daraay-e-Noor Street, Takht-e-Javoos Avenue, Teheran, Iran.
Telephone: 622020.

Abdul Jamil bin Abdul Rais, Tan Sri, P.M.N., P.J.K.; Malaysian diplomatist; b. 14 Jan. 1912; ed. Clifford School and Oxford Univ., England.
Joined Admin. Service 32; State Sec. Perlis 51-52; State Financial Officer, Selangor 54-55, State Sec. 56; Chief Minister, State of Selangor 57-59; Deputy Sec. to the Treasury 59-61; Sec. to the Treasury (Federal) 61-64; Chief Sec. to Malaysian Govt., Head of Home and Foreign Service, Sec. to the Cabinet 64-67; High Commr. for Malaysia in U.K. Nov. 67-July 71, con-

currently Amb. to Ireland; Chair. Penang Port Comm.; fmr. Vice-Chair. Malaysian Red Cross; fmr. Chair. Malaysian Boy Scout Asscn.; fmr. Pres. Malaysian Lawn Tennis Asscn.
Jamnor, 32 Jalan Kia Beng, Kuala Lumpur, Malaysia.

Abdul Rahman Putra, Tunku (Prince), C.H.; Malaysian politician; b. 1903; m. 3rd Puan Sharifah Rodziah binti Syed Alwi Barakbah 1939; one s. one d. (both by 1st wife); one s. three d. (all adopted); ed. Alor Star, Bangkok, Penang, St. Catharine's Coll., Cambridge, and Inner Temple, London.
Joined Kedah State Civil Service 31, District Officer; appointed to Exec. and Legislative Councils, Malaya, as unofficial mem. 52; Leader Fed. Legislative Council; Chief Minister and Minister for Home Affairs 55; first Prime Minister and Minister of External Affairs, Malaya 57-63, Malaysia Sept. 63-Sept. 70, also Minister of Culture, Youth and Sports at various times; leader successively of United Malay Nat. Org. and Alliance Party; Chancellor, Univ. of Malaya 62; Sec.-Gen. Islamic Conf. 69-72; several hon. degrees and foreign decorations.
Leisure interests: golf, football, walking, swimming, racing, motor-boating, photography, collecting ancient weapons, particularly the Malay Kris.
Publs. *Mahsuri* (play about Malaya) 41, (film) 58; *Raja Bersiong* (a story of his ancestors) (filmed 66).
61 Ayer Road, Penang, Malaysia.
Telephone: 65970 (Home).

Abdulgani, Roeslan; Indonesian diplomatist, civil servant and politician; b. 1914, Surabaya, East Java; s. of Mr. Abdulgani and Siti Murad; m. Sihwati Nawangwulan 1938; two s. three d.; ed. Teacher Training Coll., Surabaya.
Active in Nat. Youth Movement seeking independence from Dutch; active in anti-Japanese underground during Japanese occupation; Editor *Bakti* (in East Java) 45; Sec.-Gen. Ministry of Information 47-53; Sec.-Gen. Ministry of Foreign Affairs 53-56; Del. to UN 51, 56, 66; Sec.-Gen. Afro-Asian Conf., Bandung 55; headed Del. to Suez Conf. 56; Minister of Foreign Affairs 56-57; mem. Constituent Assembly 57-; Vice-Chair. Nat. Council 57-59; Vice-Chair. Supreme Advisory Council 59-62; Co-ordinating Minister and Minister of Information 63-65; Deputy Prime Minister for Political Institutions 66; Perm. Rep. to UN 67-71; retd.; Lecturer Monash Univ. and other Australian univs. 72; Research Fellow Prince Bernhard Fund, Netherlands, U.K. 73; Vice-Pres. 24th UN Gen. Assembly 69; Consultant, Nat. Defence and Security Council of Indonesia; Indonesian medals; several hon. degrees; mem. P.N.I. (Indonesian Nat. Party).
Leisure interests: walking, reading, classical music.
Publs. *In Search of Indonesian Identity, The Bandung Spirit, Indonesian and Asian-African Nationalism, Pantjasila: The Prime Mover of the Indonesian Revolution, Hero's Day: In Memory of the Fighting in Surabaya on 10 November 1945, Impact of Utopian-Scientific and Religious Socialism on Indonesian Socialism, 25 Years: Indonesia in the UN, Personal Experiences During the Japanese Occupation,* etc.
11 Jalan Diponegro, Jakarta, Indonesia.

Abdulghani, Abdul Aziz, M.A.(ECON.); Yemeni economist; b. 4 July 1939, Haifan, Yemen Arab Repub.; s. of Abdulghani Saleh and Tohfa Moqbel; m. Aceya Hamza 1966; four s. one d.; ed. Colorado Coll. and Colorado Univ.
Minister of Health 67-68, of Economy 68-69, 70-71; Chair. Technical Office, Board of Planning 69-70; Gov. Central Bank of Yemen 71-75; Prime Minister Jan. 75-.
Leisure interests: swimming, hiking.
P.O. Box 38, Sana'a, Yemen Arab Republic.
Telephone: 2116.

Abdulla, Rahmatalla; Sudanese businessman and fmr. diplomatist; b. 1922; *m.*; four *c.*; ed. Trinity Coll., Cambridge.
Head of History Faculty, Sudan Inst. of Educ.; Exec. Sec. for Social Devt. and later Asst. Gen. Man. Sudan Gezira Board; Amb. to India and Japan 56-60, Nigeria 60-61, France, Netherlands, Belgium, Switzerland and Spain 60-64; Minister of Nat. Educ. 64-65, Deputy Under-Sec. for Foreign Affairs 65-67; Amb. to France, Netherlands, Switzerland and Spain (2nd term) 68-70, Zaire 70-72; Perm. Rep. to UN and Security Council 72-74; farming and business since Feb. 1974 with Rahmatalla Abdulla Business Bureau, Khartoum.
Rahmatalla Abdulla Business Bureau, P.O. Box 446, Khartoum, Sudan.
Telephone: 79378.

Abdulla Osman Daar, Aden; Somali businessman and politician; b. 1908, Beledwin; ed. Govt. School, Somalia.
Served in Italian Admin. 29-41; joined Somali Youth League 44, Leader 53, Pres. 54-56, 58-59; Pres. Nat. Assembly 56-60, Constituent Assembly 60; Pres. Somali Repub. 61-67; Deputy to Nat. Assembly 67-69; detained following coup 69, released 73.
c/o Government Offices, Mogadishu, Somalia.

Abdullah, Sheikh Mohammad; Indian politician; b. 1905, Soura, Srinagar, Kashmir; *s.* of Sheikh Mohammed Ibrahim; *m.* 1933; three *s.* two *d.*; ed. Kashmir, Lahore and Aligarh (U.P.).
Founder of Kashmir Muslim Conf., later Kashmir Nat. Conf., for representative govt. in Kashmir 38; Pres. All-India States People's Conf. 46; sentenced to 9 years' imprisonment for leading peoples of Jammu and Kashmir State in struggle against Maharajah of Kashmir for constitutional govt. and civil liberties Aug. 46 (sentence not carried out in full); Head of Interim Govt. Nov. 47; mem. Indian Del. to UN Jan. 48; Prime Minister of Jammu and Kashmir 48-53; mem. Indian Constituent Assembly 49; in detention 53-58, 58-64, 65-68; in exile 71-72; Chief Minister of Kashmir Feb. 75-.
Leisure interest: gardening.
Soura, Srinagar, Kashmir.
Telephone: 3809.

Abdullah bin Ali, Datuk; Malaysian diplomatist; b. 31 Aug. 1922, Johore; *m.* Datin Badariah binti Haji Abdul Aziz; two *s.* two *d.*; ed. Raffles Coll., Singapore.
Johore civil service; joined foreign service 57; served in India, Ethiopia, Morocco; between overseas appointments served as Chief of Protocol and Deputy Sec.-Gen. (Admin. and Gen. Affairs) in Foreign Ministry; High Commr. to Singapore 71-75; Amb. to Fed. Repub. of Germany 75; High Commr. to United Kingdom Sept. 75-; Dato Paduka Mahkota Johore (Order of Crown of Johore); Kesatria Mangku Negara (Malaysian order).
Leisure interests: tennis, golf, swimming, ornithology.
High Commission of Malaysia, 45 Belgrave Square, London, SW1X 8QT, England.
Telephone: 01-245 9221.

Abdurazakov, Malik Abdurazakovich; Soviet politician; b. 1919; ed. Namangan Teachers' Training Coll. and Higher Party School of C.P.S.U. Central Cttee.
Young Pioneer leader, teacher, school director, Insp. for Namangan Dept. of Educ. 33-40; mem. C.P.S.U. 40-; Young Communist League and C.P. work in Uzbekistan 40-; First Sec. Tashkent Regional Cttee. of C.P. of Uzbekistan 61-71; Minister of Agricultural Procurements, Uzbek S.S.R., 71-; mem. Central Cttee. of C.P. of Uzbekistan; Alt. mem. Central Cttee. of C.P.S.U. 61-; Alt. mem. Bureau of Central Cttee. of C.P. of Uzbekistan; Deputy to U.S.S.R. Supreme Soviet 62-70.
Uzbek S.S.R. Ministry of Agricultural Procurements, Tashkent, U.S.S.R.

Abe, Kobo; Japanese novelist and playwright; b. 7 March 1924, Tokyo; *m.* 1947; one *d.*; ed. Tokyo Univ. 25th Akutagawa Prize 51, Post-War Literature Prize 50, Yomiuri Literary Prize 62, Kishida Prize for Drama 58. Publs. *Owarishi Michino Shirubeni* (The Road Sign at the End of the Road), *Akai Mayu* (Red Cocoon) 49, *Kabe-S. Karumashi No Hanzai* (The Crimes of S. Karma, Esq.) 51, *Kiga Domei* (Hunger Union) 54, *Seifuku and other plays* (The Uniform) 55, *Doreigari* (Hunt for a Slave) 55, *Kemonotachi wa Kokyo o Mezasu* (Animals are Forwarding to Their Natives) 57, *Dai Yon Kanpyoki* (The Fourth Unglacial Period) 59, *Yurei wa Kokoniiru* (Here is a Ghost) 59, *Ishi no Me* (Eyes of Stone) 60, *Suna no Onna* (The Woman in the Dunes) 62, *Tanin no Kao* (The Face of Another) 64, *Omaenimo Tsumi Ga Aru* (You are Guilty, Too) 65, *Enomoto Buyo* (Buyo Enomoto) 65, *Moetsukita Chizu* (The Ruined Map) 69, *Bo ni natta otoko* (The Man Who Became a Stick) 69, *Inter Ice Age 4* 70, *Mihitsu no Koi* (Premeditated Act of Uncertain Consequences) 71, *Gaido Book* (Guide Book) 71, *Hoko otoko* (The Box Man) 73, *Ai no Megane wa iromegane* (Love's Spectacles Are Coloured Glass) 73, *Midoriiro no stocking* (Green Stocking) 74, *Ue* (Wee) 75, *Warau Thuki* (Smiling Moon) 75.
1-22-10, Wakaba Cho, Chofu City, Tokyo, Japan.
Telephone: 03-300-3833.

Abe, Shintaro; Japanese journalist and politician.
Member House of Reps. 58-; Private Sec. to Prime Minister Nobusuke Kishi; fmr. Deputy Sec.-Gen. Liberal Democratic Party, fmr. Vice-Pres. LDP Diet Policy Cttee.; Minister of Agriculture and Forestry Dec. 74-.
Ministry of Agriculture and Forestry, Tokyo, Japan.

Abel Smith, Sir Alexander, Kt., T.D., J.P.; British merchant banker and business exec. (retd.); b. 18 Sept. 1904, London; *s.* of Lt.-Col. Francis Abel-Smith, D.L. and Madeline St. Maur Seymour; *m.* 1st Elizabeth Morgan 1936 (died 1948), 2nd Lady (Henriette) Palmer, née Cadogan (Lady-in-Waiting to H.M. Queen Elizabeth II) 1953; two *s.* two *d.*; ed. Eton and Magdalen Coll., Oxford.
Military Service 39-45, retd. with rank of Brig.; Dir. J. Henry Schroeder Wagg & Co. Ltd. 47-67; Chair. Provident Mutual Life Assurance Asscn. 67-74; Dir. other companies; Deputy Chair. Export Council for Europe 64-69; Deputy Chair. Duke of Edinburgh's Award Scheme 67-; Legion of Merit (U.S.A.) 45; Knight Order of Dannebrog (Denmark) 64.
Leisure interests: shooting and fishing.
Old Rectory, Quenington, Cirencester, Gloucestershire, England.
Telephone: Coln St. Aldwyns 231.

Abelson, Philip Hauge, B.S., M.S., PH.D.; American physicist and editor; b. 27 April 1913, Tacoma, Wash.; *s.* of Ole Andrew and Ellen Hauge Abelson; *m.* Neva Martin 1936; one *d.*; ed. Washington State Coll. and Univ. of California at Berkeley.
Assistant Physicist, Dept. of Terrestrial Magnetism, Carnegie Inst. of Washington 39-41, Staff mem. (of Dept.) 46-53, Dir. Geophysical Laboratory 53-71; Pres. Carnegie Inst. of Washington 71-; Principal Physicist and Civilian-in-Charge, Naval Research Laboratory Branch, Navy Yard, Philadelphia 41-46; Co-Editor *Journal of Geophysical Research* 59-65; Editor *Science* 62-; mem. Nat. Insts. of Health Biophysics and Biophysical Chemistry Study Section 56-59, Gen. Advisory Cttee. to Atomic Energy Comm. 60-63, Cttee. on Science and Public Policy of Nat. Acad. of Sciences 62-63; Consultant to Nat. Aeronautics and Space Admin. 60-63; mem. Nat. Acad. of Sciences, American Acad. of Arts and Sciences, American Philosophical Soc. and many other learned socs.; Pres. American Geophysical Union 72-74, Int.

Union of Geological Sciences 72-; U.S. Navy Distinguished Civilian Service Medal 45, Physical Sciences Award, Washington Acad. of Sciences 50, Distinguished Alumnus Award, Washington State Univ. 62, Hillebrand Award, Chemical Soc. of Washington 62, *Modern Medicine* Award 67, Joseph Priestly Award 73, Kalinga Prize for Popularization of Science 73, American Medical Asscn. Scientific Achievement Award 74; Hon. D.Sc. (Yale Univ.) 64, (Southern Methodist Univ.) 69; D.H.L. (Univ. of Puget Sound) 68; work includes identification of uranium fission products 39-40, co-discovery of Neptunium 40, separation of uranium isotopes 43, bio-synthesis in microorganisms 53, amino acids in fossils 55, fatty acids in rocks 56.
Publs. (edited) *Researches in Geochemistry* vols. 1 and 2 59, 67, *Energy for Tomorrow* 75.
Carnegie Institution of Washington, 1530 P Street, N.W., Washington, D.C. 20005, U.S.A.
Telephone: 202-387-6400.

Aberconway, 3rd Baron, of Bodnant; **Charles Melville McLaren;** British business executive; b. 16 April 1913; ed. Eton Coll., and New Coll., Oxford.
Barrister, Middle Temple 37; **Army service 39-45;** Chair. John Brown & Co. Ltd., Sheepbridge Engineering Ltd., English China Clays Ltd.; Dir. Westland Aircraft Ltd.; Vice-Chair. Sun Alliance and London Insurance Co.; Dir. Nat. Westminster Bank Ltd.; Pres. Royal Horticultural Soc. 61-.
25 Egerton Terrace, London, S.W.3, England; and Bodnant, Tal-y-cafn, North Wales.

Abercrombie, Michael, M.A., B.SC., F.R.S.; British biologist; b. 14 Aug. 1912, Ryton (U.K.); s. of Lascelles and Catherine Abercrombie; m. Minnie Louie Johnson 1939; one s.; ed. Leeds Grammar School and Queen's Coll., Oxford.
Junior Research Fellow, Queen's Coll., Oxford 37-40; Beit Memorial Fellow for Medical Research 40-43; Lecturer in Zoology, Birmingham Univ. 45-46; Reader in Embryology, Univ. Coll. London 50-59, Prof. of Embryology 59-62; Jodrell Prof. of Zoology, Univ. Coll. London 62-70; Dir. Strangeways Research Lab., Cambridge 70-; Fellow, Clare Hall, Cambridge.
Publs. *Dictionary of Biology* (with C. J. Hickman and M. L. Johnson) 51; papers on embryology, tissue culture, cancer and wound healing.
Strangeways Research Laboratory, Wort's Causeway, Cambridge; Home: East Lodge, Little Shelford, Cambridge, England.
Telephone: 0223-43231 (Strangeways); 022-04-3366 (Home).

Abercrombie, Nigel James, M.A., D.PHIL.; British free-lance writer; b. 5 Aug. 1908, Satara, India; s. of late Lieut.-Col. A. W. Abercrombie and Ethel Emma Abercrombie (née Gordon); m. Dorothy Maud Elisabeth Brownlees 1931; one s. one d.; ed. Haileybury and Oriel Coll., Oxford.
Lecturer in French, Magdalen Coll., Oxford 31-36; Prof of French and Head of Modern Languages Dept., Univ. Coll., Exeter 36-40; Secretary's Dept., Admiralty 40-62; Cabinet Office 62-63; Sec.-Gen. Arts Council of Great Britain 63-68, Chief Regional Adviser, Arts Council of G.B. 68-73; Paget-Toynbee Prize 34.
Leisure interests: European literature and travel.
Publs. *The Origins of Jansenism* 36, *Saint Augustine and French Classical Thought* 38, *Life and Work of Edmund Bishop* 59, *Artists and Their Public* 75, contributor *Times Anthology of Detective Stories* 73, *The Arts in South-East England* 74, *Arts Council Anthology of Short Stories* 76.
32 Springett Avenue, Ringmer, Lewes, Sussex, England.
Telephone: Ringmer 813029.

Abernathy, Rev. Ralph David; American clergyman and civil rights leader; b. 11 March 1926, Linden, Ala.; m. Juanita Odessa Jones 1952; four c.; ed. Alabama State Coll. and Atlanta Univ.
Army service during Second World War; Pastor, First Baptist Church of Montgomery 51-61; organized Montgomery Improvement Asscn. 55; joined Southern Christian Leadership Conf., Atlanta 57, became Sec.-Treas., Vice-Pres. 65-68, Pres. 68-; Pastor, West Hunter Street Baptist Church, Atlanta 61-; mem. Nat. Asscn. for Advancement of Colored People (N.A.A.C.P.); has been jailed numerous times with late Dr. Martin Luther King; Hon. LL.D., Allen Univ. 60, Long Island Univ. 69, Alabama State Univ. 74; Hon. D.D., Morehouse Coll. 71; Peace Medallion (German Democratic Repub.) 71.
334 Auburn Avenue, N.E., Atlanta, Ga. 30303, U.S.A.

Abetti, Giorgio, C.B.E. (Hon.), D.SC.; Italian astronomer; b. 5 Oct. 1882, Florence; s. of Antonio Abetti and Giovanna Colbachini; m. Anna Maffei Garino 1920; one s.
Director Arcetri Observatory 21-52; Astronomer Roman Coll., Rome 10-19; mem. De Filippi Asiatic expedition 13-14; Prof. of Astronomy Florence Univ. 21-, Rector 36; mem. Accad. Naz. dei Lincei; fmr. Vice-Pres. Int. Astronomical Union; mem. Royal Astronomical Soc.; Chief Italian Acad. expeditions to Kazakhstan and Sudan for Solar eclipses 36, 52; fmr. Pres. Int. Cttee. for Study of Solar and Terrestrial Relationships; Pres. Italian Astronomical Soc. 53-64; awarded Silver Medal of Royal Italian Geographical Soc., Lincei Prize 25, Janssen Medal 37, Gold Medal of Ministry of Public Instruction 57, Gold Medal Italian Astronomical Soc. 64, Gold Medal City of Florence 72; mem. Royal Astronomical Soc. and Royal Soc. of Edinburgh; Pres. Nat. Inst. of Optics 52-70, Italian Fulbright Asscn. 59.
Leisure interest: divulgation of astronomy.
Publs. *Il Sole* 63 (English trans. 63), *Stelle e Pianeti* 56 (English trans. 66), *Amici e nemici di Galileo* 45, *Scienza d'oggi* 46, *Storia dell' Astronomia* 48, 63 (English trans. 52) 64, *Kepler* 51, *Esplorazione dell'Universo* 59, 65 (English trans. 68), *Le Nebulose e gli Universi-isole* (with M. Hack) 59 (English trans. 65), *Solar Research* 62, *Unità del Cosmo* 64; Editor *Osserv. e Mem. Oss. Arcetri* (22-53).
Istituto Nazionale di Ottica, Largo Enrico Fermi 7 50125 Florence, Italy.
Telephone: 221180; 221179.

Ablon, Ralph E.; American business executive; b. 1916, Tupelo, Mississippi; m.; four c.; ed. Ohio State Univ.
Teacher, Ohio State Univ. 38-39; worked for Luria Brothers and Co. 39-62; served in U.S. Navy during Second World War; Exec. Vice-Pres. Luria Brothers 48-55, Pres. 55-62; Chair. and Chief Exec. Officer, Ogden Corpn. 62-, Pres. 72-.
Ogden Corporation, 161 East 42nd Street, New York, N.Y. 10017, U.S.A.

Abouhamad, Khalil, L. EN D.; Lebanese Minister of Foreign Affairs 70-74; see *The International Who's Who 1975-76*.

Abourezk, James G.; American lawyer and politician; b. 24 Feb. 1931, Wood, S. Dak.; m. Mary Ann Houlton 1952; two s. one d.; ed. South Dakota School of Mines, Univ. of South Dakota School of Law.
Served U.S. Navy 48-52; fmr. partner, law firm of LaFleur and Abourezk; Congressional rep. for S. Dak. 71-73; Senator, S. Dak. 73-; Democrat.
Senate Office Building, Washington, D.C. 20510, U.S.A.

Abragam, Anatole, D.PHIL.; French physicist; b. 15 Dec. 1914, Griva-Semgallen, Russia; s. of Simon Abragam and Anna Maimin; m. Suzanne Lequesme 1944; ed. Lycée Jeanson, Sorbonne, Oxford Univ.

Research Assoc. Centre Nat. de la Recherche Scientifique 46; joined French Atomic Energy Comm. 47, Physicist, later Senior Physicist 47-55, Head of Magnetic Resonance Laboratory 55-58, Head of Solid State Physics and Nuclear Physics Dept. 59-65, Dir. of Physics 65-70, Dir. of Research 71-; Prof. of Nuclear Magnetism, Coll. de France 60-; Pres. French Physical Soc. 67; mem. Acad. of Sciences 73-; Hon. Fellow, U.S. Acad. of Arts and Sciences; Commdr. Ordre Nat. du Mérite; Officier Légion d'Honneur; Dr. h.c. (Univ. of Kent) 68; Holweck Prize, London Physical Soc. 58, Grand Prix Cognac-Jay, Acad. of Sciences 70, and others.
Leisure interest: English and Russian literature.
Publs. *Discovery of Anomalous Hyperfine Structure in Solids* 50, *Dynamic Polarization in Solids* 57, *The Principles of Nuclear Magnetism* 61, *Nuclear Antiferromagnetism* 69, *Electron Paramagnetic Resonance of Transition Elements* (with B. Bleaney) 70, *Nuclear Pseudomagnetism* 71, *Nuclear Ferromagnetism* 73.
Commissariat à l'Energie Atomique, Centre d'Etudes Nucléaires de Saclay, P.O. Box 2, 91190 Gif-sur-Yvette; Home: 33 rue Croulebarbe, 75013 Paris, France.

Abraham, Edward Penley, C.B.E., M.A., D.PHIL., F.R.S.; British biochemist; b. 10 June 1913, Southampton; *s.* of Albert Penley Abraham and Mary Hearn; *m.* Asbjörg Harung 1939; one *s.*; ed. Queen's Coll., Oxford. Fellow of Lincoln Coll., Oxford 48-; Reader in Chemical Pathology, Oxford Univ. 60-64, Prof. of Chemical Pathology 64-; Rockefeller Foundation Travelling Fellow at Univ. of Stockholm 39, Univ. of Calif. 48; CIBA Lecturer at Rutgers Univ., N.J. 57; Guest Lecturer, Univ. of Sydney 60; Rennebohm Lecturer, Univ. of Wisconsin 67; Hon. mem. American Acad. of Pharmaceutical Sciences 67; Squibb Lecturer, Rutgers Univ., N.J. 72; Royal Soc. Medal 73, Scheele Medal (Sweden) 75; Hon. Fellow Queen's Coll., Oxford 73.
Leisure interests: walking, skiing.
Publs. *Biochemistry of Some Peptide and Steroid Antibiotics*; part-author: *Antibiotics, The Chemistry of Penicillin, General Pathology, Biosynthesis and Enzymic Hydrolysis of Penicillins and Cephalosporins*; scientific papers on the penicillins and cephalosporins and other antibiotics.
Sir William Dunn School of Pathology, Oxford; Home: Badgers Wood, Bedwell Heath, Boars Hill, Oxford, England.
Telephone: 57321 (School of Pathology); 735395 (Home).

Abramov, Grigorii Grigorievich; Soviet politician; b. 10 Jan. 1908, Karandeevka, Ryazan; ed. Bauman Technical Inst., Moscow.
Engineer 41-47; party work 47-49; Second Sec. Mytishchi Town Cttee., Communist Party, First Sec. Shchelkovsk Town Cttee. 49-55; Section Leader, Moscow City Party Cttee. 55-59, Second Sec. 59-60, First Sec. 60-63; First Dep. Chair. Econ. Council 63-65; Dep. Minister Chemical and Oil Machine Building 65-; mem. Central Cttee. C.P.S.U. 61-66; Dep. to U.S.S.R. Supreme Soviet 62-66; mem. Presidium of Supreme Soviet 62-66; Order of Red Banner of Labour (four times).
Ministry of Chemical and Oil Machine Building, 25 Bezbozhny pereulok, Moscow, U.S.S.R.

Abramovitz, Max, B.S., M.S.; American architect; b. 23 May 1908, Chicago; *s.* of Benjamin Abramovitz and Sophia Maimon; *m.* 1st Anne Marie Causey 1937 (divorced), 2nd Anita Brooks 1964; one *s.* one *d.*; ed. Illinois and Columbia Univs., Ecole des Beaux Arts, Paris.
Member of Harrison, Fouilhoux & Abramovitz 41-45, Harrison & Abramovitz 45-; U.S. Army (Corps of Engineers) 42-45; Deputy Dir. of Planning, U.N., New York City 47-52; U.S. Air Force (Colonel) 50-52; Fellow,

American Inst. of Architects; mem. Architectural League of New York, American Soc. of Civil Engineers, Century Asscn.; Dir. Regional Plan Asscn. Inc.; Trustee, Mount Sinai Hospital; Legion of Merit 45; Dr. of Fine Arts, Univs. of Pittsburgh and Illinois; Award of Achievement, Univ. of Illinois Alumni Asscn. 63; Fellow, Brandeis Univ. 63.
Works include: Corning Glass Center (Corning, N.Y.) 51, Mellon Nat. Bank, U.S. Steel Building, Alcoa Building (Pittsburgh), U.S. Embassy (Rio de Janeiro) 52, U.S. Embassy (Havana) 53, Three Chapels at Brandeis Univ. 55, Commercial Investment Trust Building (New York City) 57, Wachovia Bank and Trust Co. Building (Charlotte, N.C.) 58, Corning Glass Building (New York City) 59, Gateway No. 4 (Pittsburgh) 60, Philharmonic Hall, Lincoln Center for the Performing Arts (New York City), Columbia Univ. Law School and Library (New York City) 62, Univ. of Illinois Assembly Hall (Champaign, Ill.) 63, Phoenix Mutual Life Insurance Bldg. (Hartford, Conn.) 64, Hilles Library, Radcliffe Coll., Cambridge, Mass. 66, Beth Zion Temple, Buffalo, N.Y. 67, Krannert Center for the Performing Arts, Urbana, Ill.
418 East 50th Street, New York, N.Y. 10022, U.S.A.

Abramowski, Helmut, DR.JUR.; German lawyer; b. 20 May 1923, Hanover; *s.* of Georg Abramowski and Else Krause; *m.* Helga Wemmie 1953; one *s.* one *d.*; ed. Viktoria Gymnasium, Potsdam, Christian-Albrecht-Univ., Kiel.
Referendar 49; Assessor 53; Dir. Monetary Affairs, Fed. Ministry of Econs. 53-63, Dir. Banking 65-66, Dir. Int. Financial Operations 69-73; Chair. Cttee. on Financial Aid to Developing Countries, Cttee. on Investment Guarantees; Alt. Exec. Dir. IBRD 63-65; mem. Board Asian Devt. Bank 67-69; Asst. Sec.-Gen. OECD 73-75.
Organisation for Economic Co-operation and Development, 2 rue André-Pascal, 75775 Paris 16; 24 bis 26 rue St.-James, 92200 Neuilly, France; and Auf dem Rosenberg 22, 5307 Wachtberg-Villiprot, Federal Republic of Germany.
Telephone: 747-59-17 (France); 36-64-02 (Fed. Germany).

Abrassimov, Pyotr Andreevich; Soviet diplomatist; b. 16 May 1912, Bogushevskoe, Byelorussia; ed. Byelorussian State Univ.
Electrician 28-31; Soviet Army 41-42; Party work 42-46, 50-52, 55-56; Perm. Rep. Byelorussian S.S.R. Council of Ministers at U.S.S.R. Council of Ministers 46-48; First Vice-Chair. Byelorussian S.S.R. Council of Ministers 48-50, 52-55; Minister-Counsellor, Soviet Embassy, Peking 56-57; Ambassador to Poland 57-61; First Sec. Smolensk Regional Cttee. of C.P.S.U. 61-62; Amb. to the German Democratic Republic 62-71, 75-; Amb. to France 71-73; mem. Cen. Cttee. C.P.S.U.; Deputy Supreme Soviet of U.S.S.R.; Order of Lenin (twice), Red Banner, Red Banner of Labour, October Revolution.
U.S.S.R. Embassy, Unter den Linden 63-65, 108 Berlin, German Democratic Republic.

Abrikosov, Alexei Alexeyevich; Soviet physicist; b. 25 June 1928, Moscow; *s.* of Alexei Ivanovich Abrikosov and Fanny Davidovna Vulf; *m.* 1st Tatiana Nikolayevna Lashko 1949, 2nd Annie Françoise Dao 1970; two *s.*; ed. Moscow Univ.
Postgraduate Research Assoc., Research Worker, Inst. of Physical Problems, U.S.S.R. Acad. of Sciences 48-65; Head of Dept., Inst. of Theoretical Physics, U.S.S.R. Acad. of Sciences 65-; Research Assoc., Asst. Prof., Prof. Moscow Univ. 65-; Corresp. mem. U.S.S.R. Acad. of Sciences 64-; Lenin Prize 66; Fritz London Award 72; D.S. h.c. (Lausanne Univ.) 75.
Leisure interests: skiing, mountaineering.
Publs. *Quantum Field Theory Methods in Statistical Physics* 62, *Introduction to the Theory of Normal Metals*

72, and works on plasma physics, quantum electro-dynamics, theory of superconductors, magnetism, astro-physics, quantum liquids and semimetals.
Landau Institute for Theoretical Physics, Vorobiev-skoye Chaussée 2 Moscow 117334, U.S.S.R.

Abs, Hermann J.; German banker; b. 15 Oct. 1901; ed. part-time studies, Univs. of Bonn and Cologne.
Joined staff of Delbrück Schickler & Co., bankers, Berlin 29, Partner 35-37; mem. Management Board, Deutsche Bank, Berlin 37; mem. Management Board, Reconstruction Loan Corpn., Frankfurt 48-59, Chair. 59-; Head, German Del. on German External Debts 51-53; mem. Management Board Süddeutsche Bank A.G. 52-67, now Deutsche Bank A.G., Frankfurt, mem. Supervisory Board 67, now Chair.; mem. Advisory Board Int. Finance Corpn. 62-; Chair. Supervisory Board Dahlbusch Verwaltungs-AG, Gelsenkirchen, Deutsche Bank AG, Frankfurt (Main), ESTEL N.V. Hoesch-Hoogovens, Arnhem, Hoesch Aktiengesellschaft, Dort-mund, Phoenix Gummiwerke AG, Hamburg-Harburg, Rheinisch-Westfälisches Elektrizitätswerk AG, Essen; Chair. Admin. Board Kreditanstalt für Wiederaufbau, Frankfurt (Main); Deputy Chair. Supervisory Board Siemens Aktiengesellschaft, Munich; mem. Supervisory Board BRASCAN Ltd., Toronto; mem. and Hon. Chair. Supervisory Board Deutsche Lufthansa AG, Cologne; Hon. Chair. Supervisory Board Daimler-Benz AG, Stuttgart-Untertürkheim, Flachglas AG DELOG-DETAG, Gelsenkirchen/Fürth, Deutsche Solvay-Werke G.m.b.H., Solingen-Ohligs, Deutsche Ueberseeische Bank AG, Hamburg, Enka Glanzstoff AG, Frankfurt (Main), Pittler Maschinenfabrik AG, Langen (Hessen), Papierwerke Waldhof-Aschaffenburg AG, Raubling (Obb), Salamander AG, Kornwestheim, Stumm Aktien-gesellschaft, Essen-Bredeney, Süddeutsche Zucker-AG, Mannheim; Dr. h.c. (Univ. of Göttingen, Wirt-schaftshochschule, Mannheim, etc.).
Junghofstrasse 5-11, Frankfurt/Main, Federal Republic of Germany.

Abushady, Mohamed Mahmoud, B.COM., PH.D., A.C.I.P.; Egyptian banker; b. 15 Aug. 1913, Fayoum; s. of Mahmoud and Seddika (Hashad) Abu Shadi; m. Colleen Althea Bennet 1947; two s. two d.; ed. Cairo Univ., Chartered Inst. of Patent Agents, and American Univ., Washington.
Controller-General, Insurance Dept., Ministry of Fin-ance 49-52; Dir.-Gen. Govt. Insurance and Provident Funds 53; Chair. and Man. Dir. Development and Popu-lar Housing Co. 54-55; Sub-Gov. Nat. Bank of Egypt 55-60, Man. Dir. 61-67, Chair. and Man. Dir. 67-70; Chair. Union de Banques Arabes et Françaises (UBAF), Paris 70-, UBAF Ltd., London 72-; Chair. Social Insurance Org. 56-57; Chair. and Man. Dir. Cairo Insurance Co. 56-57; Man. Dir. Cairo Bank 56-57; Order of the Repub., 2nd Class; Order of Merit, 1st Class.
Leisure interests: swiming, tennis.
Publs. *The Art of Central Banking and its Application in Egypt* 62, *Central Banking in Egypt* 52, *Will New York Attract Arab Capital?*, *The Experience of the Arab-French Banks.*
Union de Banques Arabes et Françaises, 4 rue Ancelle, 92 Neuilly sur Seine; Home: 52 avenue Foch, Paris 16e, France.
Telephone: 747-72-42.

Aceves Parra, Dr. Salvador; Mexican doctor and politician; b. 4 April 1904, Michoacán; s. of José M. Aceves and María Parra de Aceves; m. Carmen G. C. de Aceves 1934; two s. two d.; ed. Nat. Preparatory School, Mexico City, and Faculty of Medicine, Nat. Autonomous Univ., Mexico.
Assistant at Propadeutic Medical Clinic, Faculty of Medicine, Nat. Autonomous Univ. 33, Prof. of Medical Pathology 36-44, Prof. of Medical Clinic 44-; Prof. of Graduate Course in Cardiology 35-, Asst. Prof., later

Prof., at Graduate School; Intern Doctor, Gen. Hospital 33-36, attached to Intern Medical Service 36-38, Head of Medical Service, Gen. Hospital 38-44; Head, Nat. Inst. of Cardiology Service 44-61; Dir. Nat. Inst. of Cardiology 61-65; Under-Sec., Secr. of Public Health and Welfare 65-68, Sec. 68-70; Hon. mem. Council of Seminaries of Mexican Culture 60-; mem. Nat. Acad. of Medicine, Pres. 51, 52; Pres. Mexican Cardiology Soc. 47-49, 56-58; mem. Gov. Council, Nat. Univ. of Mexico; mem. numerous American and Latin American medical socs.; Commdr. Order of Merit (Italy) 64; Decoration for Medical Merit (Brazil) 67.
Leisure interests: reading, horse-riding.
B. Traven No. 166, México 13, D.F., Mexico.
Telephone: 524-16-84.

Acharya, Bejoy Krishna; Indian civil servant and diplomatist; b. 1 May 1912, Calcutta; s. of Dr. P. K. Acharya; m. Nilima Mukherji 1938; two s.; ed. Calcutta Univ. and Univ. Coll., London.
Joined I.C.S. 36; Chief Minister, Tripura State 48-49; Deputy Sec. in Ministries of Industry, External Affairs 49-51; Deputy High Commr. for India in East Pakistan 51-54; Minister and Political Rep. to Cambodia 55-56, Foreign Service Inspector, External Affairs 56, Joint Sec. External Affairs 57-59; Ambassador to Czecho-slovakia and Rumania 59-62, to Morocco and Tunisia 62-64, High Commr. in Canada 64-66; Amb. to Brazil, Bolivia and Venezuela 66-68; High Commr. in Pakistan 69-71; Vigilance Commr. West Bengal 71-72; Cen. Govt. Vigilance Commr. 72-.
Leisure interests: reading, photography, driving.
Central Vigilance Commission, 3 Dr. Rajendra Prasad Road, New Delhi, India.
Telephone: 383679 (Office); 375718 (Home).

Acheampong, Gen. Ignatius Kutu; Ghanaian army officer; b. 23 Sept. 1931, Kumasi; m.; seven c.; ed. St. Peter's Catholic School, Kumasi, R.C. School, Ejisu, Cen. Coll. of Commerce, Agona Swedru, Mons Officer Cadet School, U.K. and Gen. Staff Coll., Fort Leaven-worth, U.S.A.
Former labourer, school teacher and secretary; Prin-cipal, Western Commercial Inst., Achiase 49-50; Vice-Principal, Cen. Coll. of Commerce 50-51; Instructor, Kumasi Commercial Inst. 51-52; enlisted Ghana Army 53, commissioned 59; served in UN Congo Operations 62-63, mentioned in dispatches; Chair. W. Region Cttee. of Admin. in earlier military régime; Brigade Commdr. 1st Infantry Brigade Group, Accra 72; Head of State, Chair. Nat. Redemption Council, Commr. for Finance and Defence Jan. 72-, for Public Relations 72-73; C.-in-C. of Ghana Armed Forces 72-; Chair. of Supreme Mil. Council Oct. 75-; promoted Gen. 76.
Supreme Military Council, Accra, Ghana.

Achebe, Chinua, B.A.; Nigerian writer; b. 16 Nov. 1930, Ogidi, E.C.S.; s. of late Isaiah O. and Janet N. Achebe; m. Christie C. Okoli 1961; two s. two d.; ed. Government Coll., Umuahia, and Univ. Coll., Ibadan.
Producer, Nigerian Broadcasting Corpn., Lagos 54-58, Regional Controller, Enugu 58-61, Dir. Voice of Nigeria, Lagos 61-66; Dir. Heinemann Educational Books (Nigeria) Ltd.; Dir. Nwamife (Publishers), Enugu; Senior Research Fellow, Univ. of Nigeria, Nsukka 67-; Rockefeller Fellowship 60-61; UNESCO Fellowship 63; Foundation mem. Soc. of Nigerian Authors; mem. Gov. Council, Lagos Univ. 66; mem. E. Central State Library Board 71-; Founding Editor, *Okike* 71-; Prof. of English, Univ. of Massachusetts 72-75, Univ. of Connecticut 75-; Editorial Adviser, African Writers' Series (Heinemann) 62-72; Nigerian Nat. Trophy 60; Margaret Wrong Memorial Prize 59; Jock Campbell *New Statesman* Award 65; Commonwealth Poetry Prize 72; Hon. Fellow, Modern Language Asscn. of America 74; Neil Gunn Int. Fellow 75; Fellow, Ghana Asscn. of Writers 75; Hon. D.Univ.; Hon. D.Litt.

Leisure interest: music.
Publs. *Things Fall Apart* 58, *No Longer at Ease* 60, *Arrow of God* 64, *A Man of the People* 66, *Chike and the River* 66, *Poems* 71, *Girls at War* 72, *Beware Soul Brother* 72, *How the Leopard Got His Claws* 73, *Morning Yet on Creation Day* 75.
Department of English, University of Connecticut, Storrs, Conn. 06268, U.S.A.

Achille, Jean-Claude; French public administrator; b. 6 June 1926, Agen; *m.* Lise-Rose Rame 1961; one *s.*; ed. École Polytechnique and Ecole des Mines, Paris.
Engineer, Coal mines Bassin de Blanzy 50-51; Engineer of Mines, Valenciennes, then Asst. to Chief Engineer, Douai Mines 51-56; Technical Councillor and Dir. of Offices at Ministry of Industry and Commerce 56-59; Asst. Dir.-Gen. Gaz de France 59-63; Dir.-Gen. Charbonnages de France 63-68; Dir. Houillères du bassin du Nord et du Pas-de-Calais, Houillères du bassin de Lorraine 63-68; mem. Econ. and Social Cttee. European Community 63-68; mem. Board of Dirs. and Dir.-Gen. Rhône-Poulenc, S.A. 68-; mem. Advisory Council Banque de France 75-; Chair. Board Société des Usines Chimiques, Rhône-Poulenc 74-75; Dir. numerous other companies.
Rhône-Poulenc, S.A., 22 avenue Montaigne, F 75360 Paris Cédex 08, France.
Telephone: 256-40-00.

Acker, Sven Hermann; Danish public servant; b. 27 Feb. 1911, Copenhagen; *s.* of Fr. Acker and Karen Frisenette; *m.* Drude Kvalsund 1940; ed. Ordrup Gymnasium and Københavns Universitet.
Secretary to Minister of Public Works 46-48; Del. UN Transport Cttee., Geneva 47-50, 52-56; Chair. UN Cttee. on Road Transport, Geneva 54-56; Dir.-Gen. Nat. Travel Asscn. of Denmark 57-67, Danish Tourist Board 67-; Chair. Regional Comm. for Europe, Int. Union of Official Travel Orgs. 64-67; Chair. European Travel Comm. 71-73; mem. Exec. Cttee. for Preservation of Natural Amenities in Denmark 57-59; mem. Exec. Cttee. Europa Nostra; Vice-Chair. Cttee. Royal Danish Music and Ballet Festival 57-68; Knight 1st Class Order of Dannebrog; Commdr. Icelandic Order of the Falcon; Danish Tourist Board Medal.
Leisure interest: Danish history.
Danish Tourist Board, Vesterbrogade 6D, DK-1620 Copenhagen V; Hostrups Have 1, 1954 Copenhagen V; Summer: Nordre Strandvej 408, 3100 Hornbaek, Denmark.

Ackley, (Hugh) Gardner, PH.D.; American educationist, economist and diplomatist; b. 30 June 1915, Indianapolis, Ind.; *s.* of Hugh M. and Margaret (McKenzie) Ackley; *m.* Bonnie A. Lowry 1937; two *s.*; ed. Western State Teachers Coll. and Univ. of Michigan.
Instructor, Ohio State Univ. 39-40, Univ. of Michigan 40-41; Office of Price Administration, Washington 41-43, 44-46; Office of Strategic Services 43-44; Asst. Prof. Univ. of Michigan 46-47, Assoc. Prof. 47-52, Prof. 52-68; Econ. Adviser and Asst. Dir. Office of Price Stabilization 51-52; mem. Board of Editors, *American Economic Review* 53-56; Dir. Social Science Research Council 59-62; Vice-Pres. American Econ. Asscn. 63; 10em. Council of Econ. Advisers, Exec. Office of the Pres. of U.S. 62-68, Chair. 64-68; Amb. to Italy 68-69; Henry Carter Adams Univ. Prof. of Political Economy, Univ. of Mich. 69-; Consultant Baker, Weeks & Co. 70-74; Dir. Nat. Bureau of Econ. Research 71-, Banco di Roma (Chicago) 73-; Trustee Joint Council on Econ. Educ. 71-; Fellow, American Acad. of Arts and Sciences; mem. American Philosophical Society; Hon. LL.D. (Western Michigan Univ.) 64, (Kalamazoo Coll.) 67; Cavaliere del Gran Croce, Ordine al Merito della Repubblica d'Italia.
Publs. *Macroeconomic Theory* 61, *Un Modello Econometrico dello Sviluppo Italiano nel Dopoguerra* 63, *Stem-*

ming World Inflation 71; numerous articles, reviews, contributions to symposia, etc.
Department of Economics, University of Michigan, Ann Arbor, Mich. 48104; Home: 907 Berkshire Road, Ann Arbor, Mich. 48104, U.S.A.
Telephone: 313-764-2374 (Office); 313-665-8770 (Home).

Actis, Brig.-Gen. Omar Carlos; Argentine soldier and administrator; b. 25 April 1920, Oliva, Córdoba; *s.* of Domingo and Adela Ferrero; *m.* Delia Santanni 1946; one *s.* one *d.*; ed. Colegio Nacional Bernadino Rivadavia, Nat. Mil. Coll., Higher Technical School, Ecole des Ponts et Chaussées (France), Centro de Altos Estudios del Ejército.
Officer at Nat. Mil. Coll. 46-50, teacher 55; teacher at Army School of Mechanics 55; engineer at Mil. Steel Factory 55; Commdr. 5th Battalion Sappers 56; mil. engineer Army Gen. Supply office 57; Commdr. Bridge Construction Battalion 62; Army High Command, logistics section 63; Commdr. Construction Engineers 65-67; 2nd in command, Army Engineers 68; Pres. Inst. of Army Social Works 69-71; Gen. Admin. Yacimientos Petrolíferos Fiscales 71; Abdón Calderón Award 1st Class (Ecuador); Grand Officer, Orden al Mérito Nacional (Ecuador).
Avenida Presidente Roque Sáenz Peña 777, Buenos Aires, Argentina.
Telephone: 46-1580.

Acutt, Sir Keith (Courtney), K.B.E.; British mining executive; b. 6 Oct. 1909, South Africa; *s.* of late Guy Courtney Acutt.
War service 39-45; Joint Deputy Chair. Anglo-American Corpn. of South Africa Ltd.; Chair. Rand Selection Corpn. Ltd. until 74, Wankie Colliery Co.; Dir. De Beers Consolidated Mines Ltd.; Dir. numerous finance and mining companies.
Leisure interests: horse breeding and racing.
44 Main Street, Johannesburg, South Africa.

Aczél, György; Hungarian politician; b. 1917, Budapest.
Joined Workers' Movement 35; Party Sec., Borsod and Baranya after 45; First Deputy Minister of Educ. 58-67; mem. Central Cttee. Hungarian Socialist Workers' Party 56-, Chair. Propaganda Dept., Sec. Central Cttee. 67-74, mem. Politburo 70-; Deputy Prime Minister 74-; mem. Central Cttee. Agitation and Propaganda Board, with Hungarian Socialist Workers' Party 75-; Chair. Awarding Cttee. for State Prize and Kossuth Prize; Gold Medal, Labour Order of Merit.
Publs. *Eszménk erejével* (By Strength of our Idea) 70, *Szocialista kultúra-közösségi ember* (Socialist Culture-Community Man) 75.
Parliament Building, 1357 Budapest, Hungary.

Adade, Nicholas Yaw Boafo, B.SC. (ECON), B.COM., LL.B., B.L.; Ghanaian barrister-at-law; b. 1927, Wenchi; *s.* of T. E. Adade and late Afua Pokua; *m.* Agnes Wiafe; two *s.*; ed. Accra Acad., Univ. Coll. of the Gold Coast, and Lincoln's Inn, London.
Enrolled at Ghana Bar 57; private practice, Kumasi 57-64; Editor, *Ghana Law Reports* 64-67; Part-time Lecturer, Faculty of Law, Univ. of Ghana 65-67; mem. Nat. Liberation Council Legal Cttee. 66-67; Chair. Nat. Liberation Council Cttee. on Management Agreements 66-68; Sec. Ghana Bar Asscn. 66-69; mem. Gen. Legal Council 66-69; Dir. Ghana News Agency 67-68; Dir. Ghana Commercial Bank 68-69; mem. Parl. 69-72; Attorney-Gen. and Minister of Justice 69-71; Minister for Local Admin. and Interior 71-72; private law practice 73-.
P.O. Box 197, Accra, Ghana.
Telephone: 65216.

Adair, Frank Earl, LL.D., M.D., L.H.D.; American surgeon; b. 9 April 1887, Beverly, Ohio; *s.* of Samuel Graham and Ella (née Patterson); *m.* Marion Hopkinson

1935; two s.; ed. Marietta Coll. and Johns Hopkins Univ.

House Surgeon, New York Hosp. 14-15; Asst. Surgeon Hosp. for Special Surgery, New York, N.Y. 19-30; Asst. Surgeon Memorial Hosp. 20-26, Assoc. Surgeon 26-28, Attending Surgeon 29-52, Emer. 52-; Emer. Attending Surgeon Memorial Sloan-Kettering Cancer Center; Attending Surgeon Doctor's Hosp., Ewing Hosp. 50-, St. Clair's Hosp.; Assoc. Prof. Cornell Univ. Medical School; mem. Comm. to help settle cases in suits which involve Supreme Court Justices; Pres. Adair Fund for Cancer Research, Jackson Lab. for Cancer Research; Trustee Marietta Coll., Royal Society of Medicine Foundation; Hon. Fellow, Royal Soc. of Medicine; Fellow, American Coll. of Surgeons; Nat. Award, American Coll. of Surgeons 69; Nat. Cancer Award for Distinguished Service, American Board of Radiology; mem. American Medical Asscn., American Radium Soc., American Asscn. for Cancer Research and many other socs.

Publs. many articles in medical journals.

75 East 71st Street, New York, N.Y. 10021; Home: 1 East 66th Street, New York, N.Y. 10021, U.S.A.

Adam, James, M.SC., C.ENG., A.F.C., F.R.AE.S.; South African aviation executive; b. 19 Nov. 1913, Scotland; ed. Pretoria Univ.

Joined Fuel Research Inst. 35, Senior Technical Officer 40; Pilot S.A. Air Force 40-46; Graduate Empire Test Pilot School 44; Technical Adviser, S.A. Airways 46-57, Operations Man. 57-63, Deputy Chief Exec. 63-72, Chief Exec. 72-.

South African Airways, P.O. Box 7778, Johannesburg; Home: 115 Tenth Avenue, Highlands North, Johannesburg, South Africa.

Adam, Kenneth, C.B.E., M.A., F.R.S.A.; British television official; b. 1 March 1908; ed. Nottingham High School and St. John's Coll., Cambridge.

Manchester Guardian 30-34; Home News Editor, B.B.C. 34-36; Chief Correspondent, *The Star* 36-40; Press Officer, British Airways 40-41; Dir. Publicity, B.B.C. 41-49, Controller, Light Programme 49-55; Joint Gen. Man. Hulton Press 55-57; Controller, Television Programmes, B.B.C. 57-61, Dir. Television June 61-68; Visiting Prof. of Communications, Temple Univ., Philadelphia 69-.

Tomlinson Hall, Temple University, Philadelphia, Pa. 19122, U.S.A.; 19 Old Court House, London, W.8, England.

Adam, Robert (Robin) Wilson: British petroleum executive; b. 21 May 1923, Aberdeen; s. of Robert Ross Adam and Agnes Wilson Adam; m. Marion Nancy 1957; ed. Fettes Coll., Edinburgh.

War service in India and Burma; joined Anglo-Iranian Oil Co. (later The British Petroleum Co.) as an accountant 50, Asst. Chief Accountant 59-64, with Cen. Planning Dept. 64-67, Gen. Man. 66-67; Gen. Man. Finance and Planning Dept. of BP Chemicals 67-69; Pres. BP North America Inc. 69-73; Dir. BP Trading Ltd. 73-75, Man. Dir. The British Petroleum Co. Ltd. 75-.

Leisure interest: golf.

The British Petroleum Company Ltd., Britannic House, Moor Lane, London, E.C.2; Home: Squirrel Wood, Seven Hills Road, Cobham, Surrey, England.

Telephone: 01-920-8000 (Office); Cobham 2888 (Home).

Adam, Gen. Sir Ronald Forbes, G.C.B., D.S.O., O.B.E.; British army officer; b. 30 Oct. 1885; ed. Eton and Royal Military Acad., Woolwich.

Served Great War 14-18; Gen. Staff Officer Staff Coll. Camberley 32-35, Commandant 37; Gen. Staff Officer War Office 35-36; British Del. Gen. Staff conversations between Great Britain, France and Belgium 35; Commander 1st Div. Royal Artillery 36-37; Deputy Chief Imperial Gen. Staff 37-40; Gen. Officer Command-

ing Northern Command 40-41; Adjutant Gen. to Forces 41-46; mem. Army Council 42-46; Chair. British Council 46-55, Pres. 55-69; Pres. Nat. Inst. Adult Educ.; mem. Miners' Welfare Comm. 46-54; mem. Exec. Board UNESCO 50-52, Chair. 52-54; Principal, Working Men's Coll. 56-61; Chair. Council of Inst. of Education, London Univ.; Gov. Birkbeck Coll.; Trustee, Nat. Central Library; Pres. United Nations Asscn.; Hon. LL.D. (Aberdeen); Hon. Fellow, Worcester Coll., Oxford.

Carylls Lea, Faygate, Sussex, England.

Adama-Tamboux, Michel; Central African Republic Permanent Representative to UN 70-74; see *International Who's Who 1975-76.*

Adams, Arthur Stanton, M.A., SC.D.; American educationist; b. 1 July 1896, Winchester, Mass.; s. of Charles S. and Grace E. (Newhall) Adams; m. 1st Dorothy Anderson 1918 (died 1954), 2nd Irene H. Smith 1956 (died 1963); one s. (died 1974); ed. U.S. Naval Acad. and Submarine School, Univ. of Calif., and Colorado School of Mines.

Served in U.S. Navy 18-21; Teacher, Mathematics and Science, public and private schools, Denver 21-25; Asst. Prof. of Metallurgy and Mathematics, Assoc. Prof. of Mechanics, and Prof. Colorado School of Mines 27-40, Asst. to Pres. 38-40; Asst. Dean of Engineering and Dir. Engineering, Science and Management, War Training Programme, Cornell Univ. 40-42; Bureau of Naval Personnel 41-45; Provost of Cornell Univ. 46-48; Pres. Univ. of New Hampshire 48-51; Pres. American Council on Educ. 51-61; Pres. Salzburg Seminar in American Studies 61-65; Consultant, New England Center for Continuing Educ. 69-; Regents Lecturer, Univ. of California 61; Pres. Asscn. of Land-Grant Colls. and Univs. 49-50; Visiting Prof. of Higher Education, Univ. of Colorado 62; mem. American Asscn. for the Advancement of Science, etc.; Legion of Merit; 36 hon. degrees.

Leisure interests: sailing, gardening.

Publs. *The Development of Physical Thought* (with Leonard B. Loeb) 33, *Fundamentals of Thermodynamics* (with George D. Hilding) 45.

Cedar Point Road, Durham, N.H. 03824, U.S.A.

Telephone: 603-742-3050.

Adams, Charles Francis, A.B.; American industrialist; b. 2 May 1910; m. 1st Margaret Stockton, one s. two d.; m. 2nd Beatrice D. Penati 1973; ed. St. Mark's School and Harvard Univ.

Joined Paine, Webber, Jackson & Curtis (Investment Banking) 34, Partner 38; served with U.S. Navy (Commdr.) 40-46; with Paine, Webber, Jackson & Curtis 46-47; Exec. Vice-Pres. Raytheon Manufacturing Co. (now Raytheon Co.) 47, Pres. 48-60, 62, Chair. 64-; Dir. Liberty Mutual Insurance Co. 53-, Liberty Mutual Fire Insurance Co. 68-, Pan American World Airways Inc. 67-; First Nat. Bank of Boston 59-, The Gillette Co. 60-, A. C. Cossor Ltd. 61-67; hon. degrees, Bates Coll., Northeastern and Suffolk Univs.

Raytheon Company, 141 Spring Street, Lexington, Mass. 02173, U.S.A.

Telephone: 617-862-6600.

Adams, John Bertram, C.M.G., F.R.S., M.A., C.ENG., F.I.E.E., F.INST.P.; British scientist; b. 24 May 1920, Kingston, Surrey; s. of John A. Adams and Emily Searles; m. Renie Warburton 1943; one s. two d.; ed. Eltham Coll.

Worked at Radar Research Establishment, Malvern 40-45; Atomic Energy Research Establishment, Harwell 45-53; European Org. for Nuclear Research (CERN) 53-61, Dir. Proton Synchrotron Div. 54-60, Dir.-Gen. 60-61; Dir. Culham Laboratory, U.K. Atomic Energy Authority 60-67; Controller, Ministry of Technology 65-66; Board mem. for Research, U.K. Atomic Energy Authority 66-69; Dir.-Gen. Laboratory II, European Org. for Nuclear Research (CERN) 69-75, Exec. Dir.-Gen. 76-; Röntgen Prize (Univ. of Giessen)

60; Duddell Medal, Physical Soc. 61; Leverhulme Medal, Royal Soc. 72; Hon. D.Sc. (Geneva) 60, (Birmingham) 61, (Surrey) 66.

c/o European Organization for Nuclear Research, 1211 Geneva 23; Champ Rosset, 1297 Founex (Vaud), Switzerland.

Telephone: 41-98-11 (Office); 76-31-19 (Home).

Adams, Leonie, B.A., D.LITT.; American poet and teacher; b. 9 Dec. 1899, Brooklyn, New York; d. of Charles Frederick Adams and Henrietta Rozier (Adams); m. William Troy 1933 (died 1961); ed. Barnard Coll.

Editorial work Wilson Publishing Co., Metropolitan Museum of Art and others 22-28; Guggenheim Fellowship for Creative Writing 28-30; Instructor in Literature, New York Univ. 30-32, Sarah Lawrence Coll. 33-34, in Literature and Writing, Bennington Coll. 35-37, 41-44, in Writing, New Jersey Coll. for Women 46-48, Columbia Univ. 47-68; Visiting Prof. Univ. of Wash. 60, 68-69, Purdue Univ. 71-72; Consultant in Poetry, Library of Congress 48-49; Fellow in American Letters, Library of Congress 48-55; mem. Nat. Inst. of Arts and Letters (Sec. 59-61); D.Litt. (New Jersey Coll. for Women) 50; Harriet Monroe Award 54; Shelley Memorial Award 54; Bollingen Prize in Poetry 55 (jointly); Acad. of American Poets Award 59; Fulbright Lecturer in American Studies, France 55-56; Sabbatical Grant, Nat. Council on the Arts 66-67; Brandeis Univ. Poetry Medal and Award 69; Mark Rothke Foundation Award 73; Distinguished Alumna Medal, Barnard Coll. 74; Fellowship Acad. American Poets 74.

Leisure interest: gardening.

Publs. *Those Not Elect* (and other poems) 25, *High Falcon* 29, *Lyrics of François Villon* (edited, with translation) 33, *Poems, A Selection* 54.

Candlewood Mountain Road, R.D.2, New Milford, Conn. 06776, U.S.A.

Telephone: 201-354-9550.

Adams, Sir Philip George Doyne, K.C.M.G.; British diplomatist; b. 17 Dec. 1915, Wellington, New Zealand; ed. Lancing and Christ Church, Oxford.

Vice-Consul, Beirut 39-41; war service 41; Third Sec., Cairo 41-45; Second Sec., Jeddah 45-47; Foreign Office, London 47-51; First Sec., Vienna 51-54; Trade Commr., Khartoum 54-56; Regional Information Officer, Beirut 56-59; Foreign Office, London 59-63; Consul-Gen., Chicago 63-66; Amb. to Jordan 66-70; Asst. Under-Sec. Foreign and Commonwealth Office 70; Deputy Sec. Cabinet Office 71-72; Amb. to Egypt 73-75.

c/o Foreign and Commonwealth Office, King Charles Street, London, S.W.1, England.

Adams, Robert; British sculptor; b. 5 Oct. 1917, Northampton; s. of Arthur Adams and Ada Elizabeth Adams; m. Patricia Devine 1952; one d.; ed. Northampton School of Art.

Works in wood, stone, bronze, steel and concrete; Instructor Central School of Art, London 49-59; one-man exhibitions at Gimpel Fils, London, between 47 and 69, in Paris 49, New York 50, 63, Dublin 55, New Jersey 55, Wuppertal 57, Düsseldorf 57, Bonn 57, Dortmund 57; represented at Biennali: São Paulo 50-57, Antwerp 51, 53, 59, Venice 52-62; other group exhibitions: Holland Park, London 54-57 and Documenta III Kassel 65; works in various permanent collections including Arts Council, British Council, Museum of Modern Art, New York, Museum of Modern Art, Turin, São Paulo Museum, Univ. of Michigan, Tate Gallery, London.

Major works include sculptures: Kings Well, Hampstead, London; Fire Services Training Establishment, Moreton-in-the-Marsh; Kings Heath School, Northampton; Municipal Theatre, Gelsenkirchen; B.P. Building London, P. & O Liner *Canberra*, Union Castle Liner *Transvaal Castle*; Heathrow Airport, London; Sekers Showrooms, London; Queen Mary Coll., London.

Rangers Hall, Great Maplestead, Halstead, Essex, England.

Telephone: Hedingham 60142.

Adams, Robert McCormick, Jr., PH.D.; American archaeologist; b. 23 July 1926, Chicago, Ill.; s. of Robert McCormick Adams and Janet Lawrence Adams; m. Ruth S. Skinner 1953; one d.; ed. Univ. of Chicago.

Instructor, Univ. of Chicago 55-57, Asst. Prof. 57-61, Assoc. Prof. 61-62, Prof. 62-, Dir. Oriental Inst. 62-68, Dean of Social Sciences 70-74; Chair. Assembly of Behavioral and Social Sciences, Nat. Research Council; Visiting Prof., Harvard 62; Univ. of Calif. (Berkeley) 63; Annual Prof., Baghdad School, American Schools of Oriental Research 66-67; field research in Iraq, Iran, Mexico, Saudi Arabia and Syria; Lewis Henry Morgan Prof., Univ. of Rochester 65; mem. Nat. Acad. of Sciences, American Acad. of Arts and Sciences, American Philosophical Soc., German Archaeological Inst.

Leisure interests: skiing, mountaineering.

Publs. *Land behind Baghdad: a history of settlement on the Diyala plains* 65, *The evolution of urban society: early Mesopotamia and prehispanic Mexico* 66, (with H. J. Nissen) *The Uruk Countryside* 72.

5201 South Kimbark Avenue, Chicago, Ill. 60615; P.O.B. 101A, Basalt, Colo. 81621, U.S.A.

Telephone: 753-2477; MU4-8358; 927-3380.

Adams, Sherman; American politician and public servant; b. 8 Jan. 1899, East Dover, Vt.; s. of Clyde H. and Winnie Sherman; m. Rachel L. White 1923; one s. three d.; ed. Dartmouth Coll.

Treasurer Black River Lumber Co. 21-22; Manager timber and lumber operations, Parker-Young Co., Lincoln, New Hampshire (N.H.) 28-45; mem. N.H. House of Reps. 41-44; Chair. Comm. of Labor 41-42, Speaker 43-44; mem. 79th Congress, Second N.H. District 45-47; Gov. of New Hampshire 49-53; Chief of White House Staff and Asst. to the President 53-58; Lecturer in Govt. Dartmouth Coll., Wooster Coll., Princeton Univ. and other American institutions; Pres. Loon Mountain Recreation Corpn. 66-; Chair. Mt. Washington Commission 69-; Pres. White Mountain Music Festival 74-; served with U.S. Marine Corps 18; Hon. LL.D. (Dartmouth Coll., Univ. of N.H., Center Coll., Univ. of St. Lawrence, Univ. of Maine, Middlebury Coll., Bates Coll., Bryant Coll.), C.L.D. (New England Coll.); Republican.

Leisure interests: skiing, fishing.

Publs. *First Hand Report* 61; contributions to *American Forests, Appalachia,* etc.

Pollard Road, Lincoln, N.H., U.S.A.

Adams-Schneider, Hon. Lance Raymond, M.P.; New Zealand politician; b. 1919, Wellington, N.Z.; s. of A. A. Adams; two s. one d.; ed. Mt. Albert Grammar School.

Manager, Taumarunui dept. store; served in Second World War, N.Z. Medical Corps; Vice-Chair. Nat. Party in Waitomo electorate; mem. South Auckland Div. Exec.; M.P. for Hamilton 59-69, for Waikato 69-; Minister of Broadcasting, Minister Asst. to Minister of Customs 69; Minister of Customs, Asst. Minister of Industries and Commerce Dec. 69-Feb. 72; Minister of Health, Social Security and Social Welfare Feb.-Nov. 72; Opposition Spokesman on Health and Social Welfare 72-75, on Industry, Commerce and Customs 74-75; Minister of Trade and Industry Dec. 75-.

Parliament House, Wellington, New Zealand.

Adamson, Sir (William Owen) Campbell, Kt.; British economist and business executive; b. 26 June 1922, Glasgow, Scotland; s. of John and Elsie (née Glendinning) Adamson; m. Gilvray Allan 1945; two s. two d.; ed. Rugby School and Corpus Christi Coll., Cambridge.

Joined Baldwins Ltd. 45; various posts in Steel Co. of Wales and Richard Thomas & Baldwins after mergers 51-69, Dir. 65; mem. Iron and Steel Fed. team visiting U.S.S.R. 56; Industrial Adviser, Dept. of Econ. Affairs 67, Senior Industrial Adviser 67, Deputy Under-Sec. of State 68; Dir.-Gen. Confed. of British Industry 69-76; founder mem. Social Science Research Council; mem. B.B.C. Gen. Advisory Cttee.; mem. Council of Iron and Steel Inst. 60-72; mem. Council and Exec. Cttee., Industrial Soc.; Vice-Chair. Nat. Savings Cttee. for England and Wales; Visiting Fellow Lancaster Univ. 70, Nuffield Coll., Oxford 71.
Leisure interests: music, swimming, tennis, brass-rubbing.
Birchamp House, Newland, Glos.; and 31 Chesham Street, London, S.W.1, England.
Telephone: Coleford 3143 and 01-235-8623.

Adarkar, Bhaskar Namdeo, M.B.E., M.A.; Indian economist; b. 18 May 1910, Vengurla, Maharashtra State; s. of Tarabai and Namdeo Vishnu Adarkar; m. Sarla Wagle 1935; two s. one d.; ed. Wilson Coll., Bombay and Gonville and Caius Coll., Cambridge.
Agent, Bank of India Ltd., Bombay 38; Research Officer to the Economic Adviser to the Govt. of India 38-40; Chief Research Officer 40-41; Under-Sec. to the Govt. Commerce Dept. 41-43; Asst. Economic Adviser to the Govt. 43-45, Deputy Economic Adviser 45-49; mem. Indian Tariff Board 49 and 50-52; Sec. Reconstruction Cttees. 41-43, mem. Tariff Comm. 52-57; Exec. Dir. Int. Monetary Fund 57-61; Jt. Sec. Ministry of Commerce and Industry 61-63; Additional Sec. Ministry of Economic and Defence Co-ordination Feb.-Aug. 63, Additional Sec. Ministry of Finance Sept. 63-65; Deputy Gov. Reserve Bank of India 65-70, Gov. 70-; Custodian, Cen. Bank of India 71-72, Chair., Man. Dir. 72-74; Chair. Maharashtra State Road Transport Corpn. 74-.
Publs. include Indian Tariff Policy, Devaluation of the Rupee, The Gold Problem, History of the Indian Tariff.
Gulestan, Cuffe Parade, Colaba, Bombay 5, India.
Telephone: 21-18-67.

Addams, Charles Samuel; American cartoonist; b. 7 Jan. 1912; ed. Colgate Univ., Univ. of Pennsylvania, and Grand Central School of Art.
Artist for The New Yorker 33-.
Publs. Drawn and Quartered 42, Addams and Evil 48, Monster Rally 51, Home Bodies 54, Night Crawlers 57, Dear Dead Days 59, Black Maria 60, The Groaning Board 64, The Charles Addams Mother Goose 67, My Crowd 70.
25 West 43rd Street, New York, N.Y. 10036, U.S.A.

Addis, Sir John Mansfield, K.C.M.G.; British diplomatist; b. 11 June 1914; ed. Rugby and Christ Church, Oxford.
Third Sec. Foreign Office 38; with Allied Force H.Q. (Mediterranean) 42-44; Junior Private Sec. to Prime Minister 45-47; First Sec., Nanking 47-50, Peking 50; Counsellor, Peking 54-57; Counsellor, Foreign Office 57-60; Ambassador to Laos 60-62; Fellow Harvard Center for Int. Affairs 62-63; Ambassador to Philippines 63-70; Senior Civilian Instructor, Royal Coll. of Defence Studies 70-72; Chargé d'Affaires, Peking 72; Amb. to People's Repub. of China 72-74; Senior Research Fellow, Wolfson Coll., Oxford 75-.
Woodside, Frant, Sussex, England.

Adeane, Sir Robert, Kt., O.B.E.; British company director and farmer; b. 1905; ed. Eton and Trinity Coll., Cambridge.
Chairman Colonial Securities Trust Co. Ltd. -75, Dir. 76-; Dir. Drayton Consolidated Trust Ltd., Drayton Commercial Investment Co. Ltd., British Electric Traction Co. Ltd., The Ruberoid Co. Ltd., Decca Ltd., Drayton Group Ltd.; Man. Dir. and Dir. of other companies; Trustee, Tate Gallery 55-62.
Loudham Hall, Wickham Market, Suffolk, England.

Adebo, Simeon Olaosebikan, C.M.G., the Okanlomo of Itoko,; Nigerian lawyer and diplomatist; b. 5 Oct. 1913, Abeokuta, Nigeria; s. of Chief Adebo, the Okanlomo of Itoko, and Fowotade; m. Regina Abimbola Majekodunmi 1941; three s. one d.; ed. King's Coll., Lagos, London Univ. and Gray's Inn, London.
Permanent Sec. to Ministry of Finance, W. Nigeria 57-59, to Treasury 59-60; Head of Civil Service and Chief Sec. to Govt. of W. Nigeria 61-62; Perm. Rep. of Nigeria to the United Nations 62-67; UN Under-Sec.-Gen. and Exec. Dir. of UN Inst. for Training and Research 68-72; Pres. Soc. for Int. Devt. 66-67, 67-68; Vice-Pres. World Asscn. of World Federalists; Chair. Nat. Univs. Comm. of Nigeria; eleven hon. degrees.
Leisure interests: tennis and reading.
Fowotade House, P.O. Box 139, Abeokuta, Nigeria.
Telephone: AB 341.

Adedeji, Adebayo, B.SC.(ECON.), M.P.A., PH.D.; Nigerian economist; b. 21 Dec. 1930, Ijebu-Ode; s. of Mr. and Mrs. L. S. Adedeji; m. Susan Aderinola Ogun 1957; four s. two d.; ed. Ijebu-Ode Grammar School, Univ. Coll., Ibadan, Univ. Coll., Leicester and Harvard Univ.
Assistant Sec., Ministry of Econ. Planning, W. Nigeria 58-61, Principal Asst. Sec. (Finance) 62-63; Deputy Dir. Inst. of Admin., Univ. of Ife 63-66, Dir. 67- (on leave of absence 71-); Prof. of Public Admin., Univ. of Ife 68- (leave of absence 71-); Nat. Manpower Board 67-71; Fed. Commr. for Econ. Devt. and Reconstruction 71-75; Exec. Sec. UN Econ. Comm. for Africa June 75-; founder and editor Quarterly Journal of Administration 67-75; Fellow, Nigerian Inst. of Management; Pres. Nigerian Econ. Soc. 71-72; Pres. African Asscn. for Public Admin. and Management 74-; Vice-Chair. Asscn. of Schools and Inst. of Admin. of Int. Inst. of Admin. Sciences 70-.
Leisure interests: photography, lawn tennis, walking.
Publs. A Survey of Highway Development in Western Nigeria 60, Nigerian Administration and its Political Setting (Ed.) 69, Nigerian Federal Finance: Its Development, Problems and Prospects 69, Local Government Finance in Nigeria: Problems and Prospects (Co-ed.) 72, Management Problems of Rapid Urbanisation in Nigeria (Co-ed.) 73, The Tanzania Civil Service, a Decade after Independence 74.
United Nations Economic Commission for Africa, P.O. Box 3001, Addis Ababa, Ethiopia; and Adeola Lodge, 122 Apebi Street, Ijebu-Ode, Nigeria.
Telephone: Ijebu-Ode 256 (Home).

Ademola, Rt. Hon. Sir Adetokunbo Adegboyega, P.C., K.B.E., C.F.R.; Nigerian lawyer; b. 1 Feb. 1906, Abeokuta; s. of late Sir Ladapo Ademola, Paramount Ruler of Egbaland; m. Kofo Moore 1939; three s. two d.; ed. St. Gregory's Grammar School, Lagos, King's Coll., Lagos, Cambridge Univ. and Middle Temple, London.
In Crown Law Office, Lagos 34-35; Admin. officer, Enugu 35; in private practice as barrister and solicitor, Lagos 36-39; Magistrate in Nigeria 39-49; Puisne Judge, Nigeria 49-55; Chief Justice, Western Region 55-58; Chief Justice, Supreme Court 58-72; Chair. Census Board 72-; mem. Int. Comm. of Jurists; mem. Int. Olympic Cttee.; mem. Comm. of experts advising Int. Labour Org. on Convention; Hon. Bencher, Middle Temple 59; Grand Commdr. Order of Niger 72; Hon. LL.D., Hon. D.Sc.
Leisure interest: golf.
National Census Office, Lagos; and 1 The Close, Adetokunbo Ademola Street, Victoria Island, Lagos, Nigeria.
Telephone: 52219 and 50096.

Aderemi, Sir Adesoji, K.C.M.G., the Oni of Ife; Nigerian administrator; b. 1889; ed. St. Philip's School, Ife.
Served with Nigeria Railway Dept. 09-21; Oni of Ife 30-; mem. Nigerian Legislative Council 47; Del. African Conf., London 48; Pres. Western Region House

of Chiefs 51-63; mem. Nigerian House of Reps. 51-54; Central Minister without Portfolio 51-55; Del. to Nigerian Constitution Conf. 57 and 58; Gov. Western Region of Nigeria 60-62; mem. Nigerian Cocoa Marketing Board 47-51; Dir. Nigerian Produce Marketing Co Ltd. 47-51.

The Afin, Ife, Western Region, Nigeria.

Aders, Robert O., LL.B.; American lawyer and retail executive; ed. Miami Univ., Oxford, Ohio and Indiana Univ.

Formerly served in U.S. Dept. of Justice; joined The Kroger Co. 57, Gen. Attorney and Head, Legal Dept. 62, Vice-Pres. and Gen. Counsel 64, Sec. 66, Vice-Pres. and Sec. 67, Vice-Chair. 70, Chair. of Board 70-74; mem. Nat. Business Council for Consumer Affairs 72-; Vice-Pres. and Dir. Super Market Inst.; Dir. Ranco Inc.; mem. Board of Trustees, Ohio Wesleyan Univ.; mem. various civic orgs., etc.

The Kroger Company, 1014 Vine Street, Cincinnati, Ohio 45201, U.S.A.

Adiseshiah, Malcolm Sathianathan, M.A., PH.D.; Indian educationist; b. 18 April 1910, Madras; s. of Shri Veranaci P. Adiseshiah and Nessammah Adiseshiah; m. Elizabeth Adiseshiah 1952; ed. Madras, London and Cambridge Univs.

Professor of Econs., Calcutta, and Madras Univs. 30-46; Assoc. Gen. Sec. Int. Student Service 46-48; Dep. Dir. Exchange of Persons Service, UNESCO 48-50; Dir. Dept. of Tech. Assistance, UNESCO 50-54; Asst. Dir.-Gen. UNESCO 55-63; Deputy Dir.-Gen. 63-70; Dir. Madras Inst. of Devt. Studies 71-, Vice-Chancellor, Madras Univ. 75.

Publs. *Demand for Money* 38, *Agricultural Economic Development* 41, *Handicraft Industries* 42, *Rural Credit* 43, *Planning Industrial Development* 44, *Restless Nations* 62, *War on Poverty* 63, *Non-political UN* 64, *Welfare and Wisdom* 65, *Economics of Indian Natural Resources* 66, *Education and National Development* 67, *Adult Education* 68, *Some Thoughts on Unesco in the Second Development Decade* 69, *Brain Drain from the Arab World* 69, *Let My Country Awake* 70, *Madras Development Seminar Series* 71, *It is Time to Begin* 72, *Techniques of Perspective Planning* 73, *Plan Implementation: Problems and Prospects for the Fifth Plan* 74, *Towards University Excellence* 74, *Literacy Discussion* 76, *Towards a Functional Learning Society* 76.

74 Second Main Road, Gandhinagar, Madras 600 020, India.

Adjibade, Tiamiou; Benin diplomatist; b. 15 July 1937, Porto Novo; ed. Univ. of Dakar.

Entered Diplomatic Service 61; Dir. Int. Orgs. and Technical Assistance 61-70; Sec.-Gen. Ministry of Foreign Affairs 70-73; Perm. Rep. to UN 73-, concurrently Amb. to U.S.A. 73-75; rep. in several African and int. orgs.

Permanent Mission of Benin to United Nations, 4 East 73rd Street, New York, N.Y. 10021, U.S.A.

Adler, John Hans, PH.D., D.IUR., M.A.; American economist; b. 16 Nov. 1912, Tachov, Czechoslovakia; s. of August and Lilly (Beck) Adler; m. Vilma J. Rabl 1939; two d.; ed. German Univ., Prague, Czechoslovakia, and Yale Univ.

Research Asst., Yale Inst. of Int. Studies 41-42; Instructor in Economics, Oberlin Coll. 42-44; Economist, Federal Reserve Board 44-45; Deputy Chief, Finance Div., U.S. War Dept., Vienna 45-47; Economist, Fed. Reserve Bank, N.Y.C. 47-50; Economist Int. Bank for Reconstruction and Devt. 50-57, Econ. Adviser 57-61, Dir. Econ. Devt. Inst.; Int. Bank for Reconstruction and Devt. 62-67; Senior Adviser Int. Bank for Reconstruction and Devt. 67-68, now Dir. Programming and Budgeting Dept. and mem. President's Council; Chief, or Chief Economist, several World Bank Missions, Latin America, Africa, Far East.

Publs. *Public Finance in a Developing Country—El Salvador: A Case Study* (with H. C. Wallich) 49, *Public Finance and Economic Development in Guatemala* (with E. R. Schlesinger and E. C. Olsen) 52, *The Pattern of U.S. Import Trade since 1923* (with E. R. Schlesinger and E. Van Westerborg) 52, *Recursos Financieros y Reales para el Desarrollo* 61, 65.

International Bank for Reconstruction and Development, Programming and Budgeting Department, 1818 H Street, N.W., Washington, D.C. 20433; and 5620 Western Avenue, Chevy Chase, Md. 20015, U.S.A. Telephone: 654-2804 (Home).

Adler, Kurt Herbert; American conductor and opera director; b. 2 April 1905, Vienna, Austria; s. of Ernst and Ida (Bauer) Adler; m. Nancy Goodhue Miller 1965; two d.; ed. Acad. of Music, Vienna, Conservatory and Music-Historical Inst. of Univ. of Vienna.

Conducted in Max Reinhardt Theatres, Vienna 25-28, in Germany, Italy and Czechoslovakia 28-37; Asst. Conductor to Toscanini and Instructor at Mozarteum, Salzburg Festivals 36 and 37; went to U.S.A. 38; Conductor Chicago Opera Company 38-42, Conductor New York Opera Company 45; joined San Francisco Opera Company 43, Artistic Dir. 53-56, Gen. Dir. 56-; Producer, Spring Opera, San Francisco; Founder Western Opera Theater; Head, Merola Opera Program; Artistic Adviser, San Francisco Conservatory of Music 49-51; Guest Conductor with various operas and symphonies in U.S.A., and in Italy 38-58; Trustee, Nat. Opera Inst. 69-; Board mem. O.P.E.R.A.; Hon. Mus.D. (Coll. of Pacific) 56; various decorations from Austria, Germany, Italy and U.S.S.R.

The San Francisco Opera Association, War Memorial Opera House, San Francisco, Calif. 94102, U.S.A. Telephone: 415-861-4008.

Ado, Andrei Dmitrievich; Soviet physiologist; b. 12 Jan. 1909, Kazan; ed. Kazan Medical Inst.

Member C.P.S.U. 43-; Assoc., Prof., Head of Chair, Kazan Medical Inst. 31-52, Head of Chair, Second Moscow Medical Inst. 52-; Corresp. mem. U.S.S.R. Acad. of Medical Sciences 45-65, mem. 65-; Dir. Research Allergological Laboratory, U.S.S.R. Acad. of Medical Sciences 61-; Vice-Chair. Board U.S.S.R. and Moscow Socs. of Patologicophysiologists; Asst. Editor *Patologicheskaya fiziologiya*; Chair. Problem Comm. on Allergy; Order of Lenin, Badge of Honour, etc.

Publs. Over 200 works on inflammation, allergy and immunity.

Allergological Laboratory, U.S.S.R. Academy of Medical Sciences, 10 Leninsky Prospekt, Moscow, U.S.S.R.

Adomakoh, Albert, M.A.; Ghanaian banker, economist and lawyer; b. 8 April 1924; ed. Downing Coll., Cambridge.

Barrister-at-Law; Sec. Bank of Ghana 57-62; Postgraduate, London School of Econ. 61-62; Man. Dir. and Chair. Nat. Investment Bank 62-65; Gov. Bank of Ghana 65-68; Commr. (Minister) for Agriculture 68-69; Asst. Dir.-Gen. FAO 69-70; Dir. Investments, Africa and Middle East, IFC 70-72; Devt. and Finance Consultant 72-; Chair. Ghana Consolidated Diamonds Ltd. 73-; Dir. C.F.A.O. (Ghana) Ltd. 75-.

Publ. *The History of Currency and Banking in West African Countries* 62.

P.O. Box 4104, Accra, Ghana.

Adrian, 1st Baron, cr. 55, of Cambridge; **Edgar Douglas Adrian,** O.M., M.A., M.D., F.R.S., F.R.C.P.; British physiologist; b. 30 Nov. 1889, London; s. of Alfred Douglas Adrian, C.B., K.C.; m. Hester Agnes Pinsent 1923; one s. two d.; ed. Westminster and Trinity Coll., Cambridge.

Became Fellow of Trinity Coll., Cambridge 13; Foulerton Research Prof., Royal Society 29-37; Prof. of Physiology, Cambridge Univ. 37-51; Master of Trinity Coll.,

Cambridge 51-65; Vice-Chancellor Cambridge Univ. 57-59 and Chancellor 67-; Chancellor Leicester Univ. 58-71; Pres. Royal Soc. 50-55, Brit. Asscn. for the Advancement of Science 54, Royal Soc. of Medicine 60-62; mem. Acad. des Sciences and Acad. de Médecine, Paris, Accad. dei Lincei, Rome, Royal Acads. of Science, Netherlands, Denmark and Sweden, Royal Flemish Acad. of Medicine, American Philosophical Society, Nat. Acad. of Sciences, etc.; Hon. F.R.S.M., F.R.S.E., etc.; awarded Baly Medal 29; Nobel Prize for Medicine 32; Royal Medal of Royal Society 34; Copley Medal 47; Hon. D.Sc. (Pa., Oxford, Harvard, Lyons, London, Manchester, Durham, Belfast, Johns Hopkins, New York, Sheffield and Hull, Brazil, Bologna, Freiburg, Paris, etc.), Hon. LL.D. (McGill, St. Andrews, Glasgow, Wales, Liverpool, Dalhousie), Hon. M.D. (Brussels, Louvain, Montreal).
Publs. *The Basis of Sensation* 28, *The Mechanism of Nervous Action* 32, *The Physical Background of Perception* 47.
Trinity College, Cambridge, England.
Telephone: Cambridge 58201.

Adu, Amishadai Larson, C.M.G., O.B.E., M.A., G.M.; Ghanaian public servant; b. 1914, Anum, Ghana; s. of Eliezer M. Adu and Agnes Otubea Larson; m. Elizabeth Obeng 1944; three s. one d.; ed. Achimota School, Ghana, Queens' Coll., Cambridge and Imperial Defence Coll., London.
Science Master, Achimota School 39-42; joined Colonial Admin. Service, Gold Coast 42, Joint Sec. Cttee. on Constitutional Reform (Coussey Cttee.) 49; Commr. for Africanization, Gold Coast Civil Service 50-52, Dir. of Recruitment and Training 52-55; Sec. for External Affairs Gold Coast 55-57, Perm. Sec. Ministry of External Affairs, Ghana 57-59; Sec. to Cabinet, Ghana 59-61; Sec. Nat. Council for Higher Education and Research, Ghana 61-62; Sec.-Gen. East African Common Services Organization 62-63; Regional Rep. UN Technical Assistance Board and Dir. Special Fund Programmes in E. Africa 64-65; Deputy Sec.-Gen. Commonwealth Secretariat, London 66-Oct. 70; Dir. Consolidated African Selection Trust Oct. 70-; Man. Dir. Ghana Consolidated Diamonds Ltd. 73-.
Leisure interests: reading, photography, golf.
Publ. *The Civil Service in Commonwealth Africa* 69.
Ghana Consolidated Diamonds Ltd., Accra; Home: P.O. Box 20, Aburi, Ghana.

Aduko, Louis Antoine, B.A., M.A.; Ivory Coast diplomatist; b. 31 Dec. 1917, Bonoua; ed. Coll. of W. Africa, Liberia, Lycée Pugert, Algiers, Univs. of Chicago and London.
Director, Personnel Bureau, Ministry of Education 58-59, Scholarships Bureau 60-61; Deputy Dir. of Political Affairs, Ministry of Foreign Affairs 61-68, Dir. 68-73; Amb. to U.K. Nov. 73-.
Embassy of the Ivory Coast, 2 Upper Belgrave Street, London, S.W.1, England; and B.P. 1553, Ministère des Affaires Etrangères, Abidjan, Ivory Coast.

Afanasenko, Yevgeni Ivanovich; Soviet politician; b. 17 April 1914, Budishche Village, Byelorussia; ed. Herzen Pedagogical Inst., Leningrad.
Secondary school teacher 38-41; Soviet Army 41-46; mem. C.P.S.U. 43-; Head of Education Dept., Frunze Reg., Moscow 48-50; party work 50-56; Head of Org. Dept., Moscow City Cttee., C.P.S.U. 54-55, Sec. City Cttee. 55-56; Minister of Education for the R.S.F.S.R. 56-66; Amb. to Rwanda 66-71, Congo (Brazzaville) 71-73; Candidate mem. Central Cttee. of C.P.S.U. 61-60; Deputy to U.S.S.R. Supreme Soviet to 66; Order of Lenin, Order of Red Banner of Labour, Order of Red Star.
c/o Ministry of Foreign Affairs, Moscow, U.S.S.R.

Afanasiev, Georgii Dimitriyevich; Soviet geologist; b. 1906; ed. Leningrad State Univ.
Research work, Inst. of Petrology 30; mem. C.P.S.U.

48-; Head of Dept. of Gen. Petrography, U.S.S.R. Acad. of Sciences Inst. of Geology of Ore Deposits, Petrography, Mineralogy and Geochemistry 50-; Learned Sec., Dept. of Geological and Geographical Sciences, U.S.S.R. Acad. of Sciences 48-53; Corr. mem. U.S.S.R. Acad. of Sciences 53-; Deputy Chief Learned Sec., U.S.S.R. Acad. of Sciences 58-; Asst. to Chief Ed. of *Proceedings of the U.S.S.R. Acad. of Sciences, Geological Series* 54-59, Chief Editor 59-76; Editor *Pravda* 76-; Vice-Pres. Comm. for Absolute Dating of Geological Formations 62-63, Pres. 63-; Pres. of the Petrographic Cttee. 62-; Order of Lenin, Order of Red Banner of Labour, Badge of Honour, Order of Patriotic War.
U.S.S.R. Academy of Sciences, 14 Leninsky Prospekt, Moscow, U.S.S.R.

Afanasiev, Sergei Alexandrovich; Soviet politician; b. 17 March 1918, Novorossiysk, Krasnodar Territory; ed. Bauman Technical Inst., Moscow.
Engineer, Ministry of Armaments 41-46; Dep. Head, Dept. Ministry of Armaments of U.S.S.R. 46-53; Head of Technological Board, U.S.S.R. Ministry of Defence Industries 53-57; Deputy Chair. Leningrad Council of Nat. Economy 58-61; Chair. R.S.F.S.R. Council of Nat. Economy, Deputy Chair. Council of Ministers R.S.F.S.R. 61-65; U.S.S.R. Minister of General Machine Building 65-; mem. Central Cttee. C.P.S.U. 61-; Deputy to U.S.S.R. Supreme Soviet 62-; U.S.S.R. State Prize.
Ministry of General Machine Building, Moscow, U.S.S.R.

Aferi, Maj.-Gen. Nathan A., D.S.O.; Ghanaian army officer and diplomatist; b. 21 Sept. 1922, Mampong-Akwapim; m.; five c.; ed. Achimota Coll. and Akropong Seminary.
Education instructor, Gold Coast Regt., rising to Warrant Officer 47; Army Chief Educ. Instructor 47; trained at Officer Cadet Training School, Eaton Hall, Chester, England 49; Lieut. British Army 50, seconded to W. African Frontier Force; after further Army training in U.K., obtained PSC at Staff Coll., Camberley and JSSC at Staff Coll. Latimer, being first Ghanaian army officer to obtain these; rose to Co. Commdr., Ghana Army 53-55, 2nd in Command, Rifle Co. 57-58, Deputy Adjutant-Gen., Command HQ 58-60, Lieut.-Col. in Command of 2nd Battalion of Infantry 60; served Congo 60-61; rose to Brig. and Commdr. 2nd Infantry Brigade 61-65; Chief of Staff, Ministry of Defence 62; Commdr. Northern Command 62-65; Maj.-Gen., Chief of Defence Staff, Ghana Armed Forces, July 65; retd. from army June 66; Amb. to Mexico and Venezuela and High Commr. in Jamaica and Trinidad 66-70; High Commr., Nigeria 70; Commr. for Foreign Affairs Jan.-Nov. 72, for Local Govt. Nov. 72-75; served numerous dels. to Moscow, Canada, OAU Cttees., etc.; Honour of Merit, Egypt; Gold Aztec Eagle of Mexico (First Class).
Leisure interests: music, poetry reading, lawn tennis, driving, farming and gardening.
Publ. *Careers in the Army* 68.
c/o Ministry of Local Government, Accra, Ghana.

Affleck, Raymond Tait, B. ARCH.; Canadian architect; b. 20 Nov. 1922, Penticton, B.C.; s. of Dr. John Earnest Affleck and Barbara (Tait) Affleck; m. Betty Ann Henley 1951; four s. one d.; ed. McGill Univ.
Practising architect, Montreal 55-, Partner Arcop Assocs., Montreal and Toronto; Visiting Prof. McGill Univ. 65-; mem. Royal Canadian Acad.; Massey Medals in Architecture.
Leisure interests: gardening, skiing, travel.
Publs. *Exhibitions and International Fairs as a Means of Mass Communications* 68, and several articles.
1440 St. Catherine Street W., Montreal, P.Q.; Home: 16 St. George's Place, Montreal, P.Q., Canada.
Telephone: 878-3941; 488-1461.

Affra, João Rodrigues Simões; Portuguese diplomatist; b. 30 Sept. 1908, Lisbon; s. of José Simões de Brito and Carlota Rodrigues Affra; m. Maria Antonia C. da C. e Silva Affra 1945; two d.; ed. Lisbon Univ.
Entered diplomatic service 31, held posts in League of Nations, Washington, Mexico and China 37-51; Counsellor, Head of Admin. Dept., Ministry of Foreign Affairs 51; Consul-Gen., London 52; Counsellor, subsequently Minister-Counsellor, Washington 54-56; Minister-Plenipotentiary to Cuba 56-61, also accred. to Colombia and Ecuador; Amb. to Chile 61-65, to Sweden 65-71, also accred. to Finland; Perm. Del. of Portugal at OECD 71-75.
Leisure interest: numismatics.
c/o Ministry of Foreign Affairs, Lisbon, Portugal.

Afrifa, Lieut.-Gen. Okatakyie Akwasi Amankwaa, C.V., D.S.O.; Ghanaian army officer and politician; b. 24 April 1936, Mampong, Ashanti; s. of John Kwaku Amankwaa Afrifa and Sophia Amma Seiwaa Amaniampong; m. Christine Susanna Addaquay 1968; two s. two d.; ed. Adisadel Coll., Cape Coast and Royal Military Acad., Sandhurst, England.
Second Lieut. 60; in command of rifle platoon, Congo 60; Lieut. 61, Platoon Commdr. 5th Infantry Battalion, Tamale, Ghana 61; infantry courses in U.K. 61, later served again in Congo; 1st Brigade H.Q., Ghana 62, then 2nd Brigade, Kumasi; Maj. 65; mem. Nat. Liberation Council in charge of Finance 66-69; Chair. Nat. Liberation Council April-Sept. 69; Chair. Presidential Comm. 69-70; retd. from army 70; mem. Council of State 71-72; arrested Jan. 72, released from political detention Dec. 73.
Leisure interests: horse-riding, reading military history, participation in self-help projects.
Publ. *The Ghana Coup.*
P.O. Box 18, Mampong, Ashanti, Ghana.

Afshar, Amir Aslan; Iranian diplomatist; b. 21 Nov. 1922, Teheran; m. Camilla Saed; one s. one d.; ed. Hindenburg High School, Berlin and Univs. of Berlin, Greifswald, Vienna and Geneva.
Joined Ministry of Foreign Affairs 48; Attaché, Iranian Embassy, Netherlands 50-54; toured U.S.A. under Eisenhower Exchange Fellowship Program 55-56; Rep. to Nat. Assembly 56-61; Civil Adjutant to H.I.M. Shahanshah of Iran 57; Pres. Iranian Shipping Lines 60-63; Amb. to Austria 67-69; Pres. Board of Govs., Int. Atomic Energy Agency, Vienna 68-69; Amb. to U.S.A. 69-73, also accred. to Mexico 70-73; Amb. to Fed. Repub. of Germany 73-; del. to UN Gen. Assembly 57, 58, 59, 60 and to several other int. confs.; Order of Homayoun and numerous other nat. and foreign decorations.
Publs. in Persian: *Ways and Means of Iran's Participation in International Organizations, God created the World, The Dutch built Holland;* in German: *Study of the Constitution of the German Third Reich, Study of the Administrative Law of the German Reich, The Possibilities of the Expansion of the Iranian Economy;* in English: *Report on America.*
Imperial Iranian Embassy, Bonn-Godesberg, Kölnerstrasse 133-137, Federal Republic of Germany; Home: Hafez Avenue 283, Teheran, Iran.

Afshar, Amir Khosrow, K.C.M.G., L. EN D.; Iranian diplomatist; b. 1918, Teheran; s. of Seif Saltaneh Afshar and Sedigeh; m.; one s. two d.; ed. American Coll., Teheran, Univs. of Paris and Geneva.
Joined Ministry of Foreign Affairs 41; First Sec., Washington 46; First Sec., Perm. Del. to UN 47; Dir. UN Dept., Ministry of Foreign Affairs 49, Dir. Third Political Dept. 51, Fourth Political Dept. 53; Chargé d'Affaires, London 53, Minister Plenipotentiary 54; Dir.-Gen. for Political Affairs, Ministry of Foreign Affairs 58; Parl. and Political Under-Sec. 59; Amb. to Fed. Repub. of Germany 61, to France 63; Deputy and

Acting Minister for Foreign Affairs 67; Amb. to U.K. 69-74; Order of Homayoun; Order of the Crown; Grand Officier, Légion d'Honneur; Commdr. Cross of the Order of Merit (Fed. Germany).
Leisure interests: horse breeding, riding.
c/o Ministry of Foreign Affairs, Teheran, Iran.

Aga Khan IV, H.H. Prince Karim; spiritual leader and Imam of Ismaili Muslims; b. 13 Dec. 1936, Geneva; s. of late Prince Aly Salomon Khan and of Princess Joan Aly Khan; m. Sarah Frances Crichton-Stuart 1969; two s. one d.; ed. Le Rosey, Switzerland, Harvard Univ., U.S.A.
Became Aga Khan on the death of his grandfather Sir Sultan Mohamed Shah, Aga Khan III, G.C.S.I., G.C.I.E., G.C.V.O., 57; granted title of His Highness by Queen Elizabeth II 57, of His Royal Highness by the Shah of Iran 59; Commdr. Ordre du Mérite Mauritanien 60; Grand Croix, Ordre Nat. de la Côte d'Ivoire 65, Ordre Nat. de la Haute-Volta 65; Ordre Nat. Malgache 66, Ordre du Croissant Vert des Comores 66; Grand Cordon Ordre du Tadj de l'Empire d'Iran 67; Nishan-I-Imtiaz, Pakistan 70; Hon. LL.D. Peshawar Univ. 67, Univ. of Sind 70.
1 rue des Ursins, 75004 Paris, France.
Telephone: 633-85-47.

Aga Khan, Prince Sadruddin; Iranian UN official; b. 1933; ed. Harvard Univ. and Harvard Univ. Graduate School for Arts and Sciences.
UNESCO Consultant for Afro-Asian Projects 58; Head of Mission and Adviser to UN High Commr. for Refugees 59-60; UNESCO Special Consultant to Dir.-Gen. 61; Exec. Sec. Int. Action Cttee. for Preservation of Nubian Monuments 61; UN Dep. High Commr. for Refugees 62-65, High Commr. 65-; Publ. *The Paris Review;* Founder and Sec. Harvard Islamic Asscn.; Pres. Council on Islamic Affairs, New York City; mem. Inst. of Differing Civilizations, Brussels.
Office of UN High Commissioner for Refugees, Palais des Nations, 1211 Geneva 10, Switzerland.

Agaltsov, Marshal Filipp Alexandrovich; Soviet air force officer; b. 21 Jan. 1900, Soldatskoe Village, Tula Region; ed. Military-Political Acad.
Soviet Forces 19-; Spanish Civil War 37-38; successively Commdr. Air Regiment, Air Division, Air Corps, Second World War; later Deputy C.-in-C. Soviet Air Forces; Commdr. Soviet Long Range Air Force 62-69; mem. C.P.S.U. 42-; Order of Lenin (three times), Order of Suvorov (twice), Order of Red Banner (four times), Order of Red Star, Order of Patriotic War, etc.
Ministry of Defence, 34 Naberezhnaya M. Thoreza, Moscow, U.S.S.R.

Agam, Yaacoy; Israeli artist; b. 1928, Rishon Letzon; m. Clila Agam 1954; two s. one d.; ed. Bezalel School of Art, Jerusalem, Atelier d'art abstrait, Paris.
One-man exhbns. in Galerie Craven, Paris 53, Galerie Denise René, Paris 56, 58, Palais des Beaux-Arts, Brussels 58, Tel-Aviv Museum 58, Suzanne Bollag Gallery, Zurich 59, 62, Drian Gallery, London 59, Marlborough Gerson Gallery, New York 66, Galerie Denise René, New York 71; travelling retrospective exhbn. Paris, Amsterdam, Düsseldorf, Tel-Aviv 72-73; numerous group exhbns. 54-.
Works include: *Transformes Musicales* 61, *Double Metamorphosis,* Shalom Liner 64, *Sculptures in the City,* Reims 70, sculpture and mural, President's mansion, Israel 71, *Water-Fire* fountain, St. Louis 71, environment, Elysée Palace, Paris 72, mobile wall, School of Science, Montpellier 72, design and realization of a square in defence quarter, Paris, incl. water fountain and monumental sculpture 73; films produced incl. *Recherches et Inventions* 56, *Le Désert chante, Microsalon* (with I. Mambush) 57.
26 rue Boulard, Paris, France.

Ageev, Nikolai Vladimirovich, D.SC.; Soviet physical chemist; b. 30 June 1903, Tbilisi; ed. Leningrad Polytechnical Inst., Kaiser Wilhelm-Inst. für Metallforschung (Berlin-Dahlem).

Docent, Leningrad Polytechnical Inst. 29-38; Head of Lab. Inst. of Gen. and Inorganic Chem., U.S.S.R. Acad. of Sciences 38-51; Prof. Gen. Chem. 40-; mem. C.P.S.U. 44-; Deputy Dir. Baikov Inst. of Metallurgy, U.S.S.R. Acad. of Sciences 51-71, Dir. 71-75; Head of Lab., Baikov Inst. of Metallurgy 75-; Corresp. mem. U.S.S.R. Acad. of Sciences 46-68, Academician 68-; mem. Inst. of Metals (London) 29-48, Canadian Inst. Mining and Metallurgy 73-; Editor-in-Chief, *Problems of Contemporaneous Metallurgy* 51-62, *Metallurgical Abstract* 53-, *Phase Diagrams of Metallic Systems* 59-, U.S.S.R. Acad. of Sciences, *Bulletin-Metals* 65-; Order of Lenin (twice), Order of October Revolution, Order of Labour Red Banner (three times).

Publs. *X-Ray Metallography* 32, *Thermal Analysis of Metals and Alloys* 36, *The Chemistry of Metallic Alloys* 41, *The Nature of Chemical Bond in Metallic Alloys* 47, and works on metals and alloys.

A. A. Baikov Institute of Metallurgy, U.S.S.R. Academy of Sciences, Leninski Prospekt 49, Moscow 117334, U.S.S.R.

Telephone: 135-65-72.

Agnelli, Giovanni; Italian industrialist; b. 12 March 1921, Turin; s. of Edoardo Agnelli and Princess Virginia Bourbon del Monte; brother of Umberto Agnelli (q.v.); m. Princess Marella Caracciolo di Castagneto 1953; one s. one d.

Grandson of Giovanni Agnelli, founder of F.I.A.T. (manufacturers of land, sea and air engines and vehicles); Vice-Chair. Fiat 49-66, Chair. 66-; Chair. Fiat-Allis Inc. 73-; Chair. of R.I.V. (Factory at Villar Perosa), Istituto Finanziario Industriale (IFI), Casa Editrice *La Stampa*, Fondazione Giovanni Agnelli, Italian Mfrs. Asscn.; mem. Board Mediobanca, Torino Industrial Asscn., Italian Stock Companies Asscn., SKF of Sweden; mem. Int. Advisory Cttee. Chase Manhattan Bank, Int. Industrial Conf. of San Francisco, Atlantic Inst. for Int. Affairs; Mayor, Villar Perosa 45; Cross for Military Valour.

Fiat S.p.A., 10 Corso Marconi, Turin; Home: Villa Frescot, Strada di San Vito, 256-Turin, Italy.

Telephone: 65651.

Agnelli, Umberto, DR.JUR.; Italian motor executive; b. 1 Nov. 1934, Lausanne, Switzerland; s. of Edoardo Agnelli and Princess Virginia Bourbon del Monte; brother of Giovanni Agnelli (q.v.); one s.; ed. Univ. Turin.

President, Federazione Nazionale Calcio 59; Pres. and Dir. Società Assicuratrice Industriale (SAI) 60-71; Pres., Chair. Fiat-France 65-; Pres. Piaggio & Co. 65-; Dir. IFI 59-, RIV-SKF 62-; Man. Dir. Fiat S.p.A. 72-; Pres. IVECO; mem. Confederazione Generale dell'Industria Italiana, Board Fondazione Agnelli, Board Chambre Syndicale des Constructeurs d'Automobiles; Grand Officer Order of Merit (Italy).

Publs. numerous articles in journals and econ. reviews. Fiat S.p.a., Corso Marconi 10, Turin, Italy.

Agnew, Spiro Theodore, LL.B.; American lawyer and politician; b. 9 Nov. 1918, Baltimore, Md.; s. of Theodore Spiro Agnew and Margaret Akers Agnew (family name was Anagnostopoulos); m. Elinor Isabel Judefind 1942; one s. three d.; ed. Baltimore public schools, Johns Hopkins Univ. and Univ. of Baltimore.

Army officer, served France and Germany, Second World War; legal studies 47; Mil. service, Korean War; joined private law firm 52, later established own law office in Baltimore; Chief Exec., Baltimore County 62-66; Gov. of Maryland 67-69; Vice-Pres. of the United States 69-73, resigned; Republican.

Leisure interests: tennis, golf, reading, music.
Kenwood, Chevy Chase, Md. 20015, U.S.A.

Ago, Roberto, C.B.E., LL.D., P.S.D.; Italian university professor; b. 26 May 1907, Vigevano, Pavia; s. of late Gen. Pietro Ago and Maria Marini; m. Luciana Cova 1936; three s. two d.; ed. Univ. of Naples.

Lecturer in Int. Law, Univ. of Cagliari 30-33, Univ. of Messina 33-34; Prof. of Int. Law, Univ. of Catania 34, Univ. of Genoa 35, Milan Univ. 38, Rome Univ. 56-; Pres. Italian Society for Int. Organization; Italian Del. to ILO Conf. 45-, to UNESCO 49-50, Law of Sea Conf. 58-60, Vienna Conf. on Diplomatic Relations 61; Pres. Vienna Conf. Law of Treaties 68-69; mem. Comm. for drafting European Constitution 52; Chair. Gov. Board ILO 54-55, 67-68; mem. and fmr. Pres. Int. Law Comm. of UN 57-; mem. Perm. Court of Arbitration 57-; Hon. Pres. World Fed. of UN Asscns.; Judge *ad hoc,* Int. Court of Justice 59-60; Pres. Arbitration Tribunal France-Germany, France-U.S.A.; mem. and Pres. numerous other int. tribunals and conciliation comms.; mem. and Vice-Pres. Inst. de Droit Int.; mem. Curatorium Hague Acad. of Int. Law, American Acad. of Political and Social Sciences, Inst. Hellénique Droit Int., Accademia dei Lincei, Société Royale de Belgique; Hon. mem. Indian Soc. Int. Law, American Soc. Int. Law; Grand Croix, Order of Merit (Italy), Order of Merit (Fed. Germany); Officer Légion d'Honneur, Hon. C.B.E., Dr. h.c. (Nancy, Nice, Paris).

Leisure interests: collecting modern paintings, gardening.
Publs. *Teoria del diritto internazionale privato* 34, *Il requisito dell'effettività dell'occupazione in diritto internazionale* 34, *Règles générales des conflits de lois* 36, *La responsabilità indiretta in diritto internazionale* 36, *Lezioni di diritto internazionale privato* 39, *Le délit international* 39, *Lezioni di diritto internazionale* 43, *Scienza giuridica e diritto internazionale* 50, *Diritto positivo e diritto internazionale* 56, *International Organisations and their Functions in the Field of Internal Activities of States* 57, *Positive Law and International Law* 57, *Il Trattato istitutivo dell' Euratom* 61, *The State and International Organisation* 63, *La responsabilité internationale des Etats* 63, *La qualité de l'Etat pour agir en matière de protection diplomatique des sociétés* 64, *Le Nazioni Unite per il diritto internazionale* 65, *La coopération internationale dans le domaine du droit international public* 66, *La codification du droit international et les problèmes de sa réalisation* 68, *La fase conclusiva dell'opera di codificazione del diritto internazionale* 69, *Premier, deuxième, troisième et quatrième rapport à la C.D.I. sur la responsabilité des Etats* 69-73, *Nazioni Unite: venticinque anni dopo* 70, *Droit des traités à la lumière de la Convention de Vienne* 71, *Cours général de droit international public* 73.

143 Via della Mendola, Rome, Italy.
Telephone: 32-42-31.

Agoshkov, Mikhail Ivanovich; Soviet mining specialist; b. 12 Nov. 1905, Petrovsk-Zabaikalsky, Chita Region; ed. Far East Polytechnic Inst., Vladivostock.

Lecturer, Far East Polytechnic Inst. 31-33; Dean, North Caucasian Inst. of Mines and Metallurgy 33-41; Asst. Dir. Inst. of Mines, U.S.S.R. Acad. of Sciences 41-58; mem. C.P.S.U. 43-; Head, Laboratory of Mining Inst., U.S.S.R. Acad. of Sciences 54-; Prof. Inst. of Nonferrous Metals 51-; Deputy Chief Learned Sec., U.S.S.R. Acad. of Sciences 57; Corresp. mem. U.S.S.R. Acad. of Sciences 53; State prizewinner 51; four Orders.

Publs. *Mining of Ore Deposits* 45, *Methods of Estimating Output of Metal Mines* 49, *Research of Technological Processes of Underground Mining* 59, *Mining Methods of Vein Type Deposits* 60, *Mining of Ore and Placer Deposits* 62.

U.S.S.R. Academy of Sciences, 14 Leninsky Prospekt, Moscow, U.S.S.R.

Agranat, Simon, LL.D.; Israeli judge; b. 1906, U.S.A.; ed. Chicago Univ.

Settled in Palestine 30; law practice 31-40; Magistrate

40-48; Pres. District Court, Haifa 48-50; Judge Supreme
Court 50-, Deputy Pres. 61-66, Pres. 66-; mem. Perm.
Court of Arbitration (The Hague) 62-68; Chair. Inquiry
Commission, Yom Kippur War 74.
The Supreme Court, Jerusalem; 62 Nayot Street,
Rehavia, Jerusalem, Israel.

Agrawala, Vasudeva Sharan, M.A., PH.D., D.LITT.;
Indian university professor and writer; b. Aug. 1904; ed.
Banaras Hindu Univ. and Lucknow Univ.
Curator, Mathura Museum 31-39, Lucknow Museum
40-45; Supt. Nat. Museum and Nat. Museum Branch
of Archaeological Survey of India, New Delhi 46-51;
Prof. and Head of Dept. of Art and Architecture, Coll.
of Indology, Banaras Hindu Univ. 51-; Pres. Museums
Asscn. of India and other historical asscns.; Pres. All-
India Prakrit Text Soc. 64-.
Publs. *A Revised Catalogue of Mathura Museum* 50,
India as Known to Panini 53, *Paninikalina Bhara-
tavarsha* 55, *Jayasi's Padamavata* 55, *Kadambari: A
Cultural Study* 58, *Prithiviputra, or Essays on Indian
Culture* 60, *Sparks from the Vedic Fire* 62, *The Thousand-
Syllabled Speech of Vedic Symbolism, Vol. I* 63, *Vidya-
pati's Kirtilata* 62, *Matsya Purana: A Study* 63, *Devi
Mahatmya: Glorification of the Great Goddess* 63, *Solar
Symbolism of the Boar* 63, *Vedic Lectures* 63, *Harsha-
charita: A Cultural Commentary* 64, *Vamana Purana:
A Study* 64, *Bharata Savitri, Vol. I* 57, *Vol. II* 64,
Chakradhvaja: The Wheel Flag of India 64, *Ancient
Indian Folk-Cults* 64, *Divyavadana* 65, *Indian Art* 65,
Heritage of Indian Art 71.
Department of Art and Architecture, College of
Indology, Banaras Hindu University, Varanasi 5,
India.

Agt, Andries A.M. van; Netherlands politician; b.
2 Feb. 1931, Geldrop; s. of Frans van Agt and Anna
Frencken; m. Eugenie Krekelberg 1958; one s. two d.;
ed. Catholic Univ., Nijmegen.
Worked at Ministry of Agriculture and Fisheries, then
Ministry of Justice 58-68; Prof. of Penal Law, Univ. of
Nijmegen 68-; Minister of Justice 71-; Deputy Prime
Minister 73-; Catholic People's Party.
Leisure interest: tennis.
Ministry of Justice, The Hague; Joanneslaan 10,
Nijmegen, Netherlands.

Aguilar Mawdsley, Andres; Venezuelan diplomatist
and lawyer; b. 10 July 1924, Caracas; ed. Universidad
Central de Venezuela, Caracas and McGill Univ.,
Montreal.
Teacher of Civil Law, Univ. Central de Venezuela 48,
Prof. of Law 58-; Teacher of Civil Law, Univ. Católica
Andrés Bello, Caracas 54, Prof. 58, Vice-Rector 62-63;
legal adviser to Venezuela Chamber of Building 57-58;
mem. Gov. Board, Industrial Bank of Venezuela 58-59;
Minister of Justice until 63; Perm. Rep. to European
Office of the UN, Geneva 63-65; mem. several ILO
cttees. and Pres. ILO Conf. 64; Pres. of Council of
ICEM 64-65; Head of Venezuelan Del. to Int. Conf. on
Human Rights, Teheran 68; Pres. Nat. Gov. Board of
Caritas 66-69; mem. Gov. Board Inst. of Higher
Studies in Admin. 66; Chair. Nat. Council of Int.
Council on Social Welfare 68; Pres. Venezuelan Asscn.
for UN 67-68; has held posts in several orgs. concerned
with social welfare and educ.; Perm. Rep. to UN 69-72;
Amb. to U.S.A. 72-74; mem. Inter-American Comm. on
Human Rights 72-, Chair. 76; mem. Panel of Legal
Experts of INTELSAT 74.
Publs. *Possession in the Civil Law of the Province of
Quebec* (in French), *La responsabilidad contractual del
arquitecto y del empresario por vicios y defectos de la
obra* (The contractual responsibility of architects and
contractors for building faults and defects), *Protección
familiar* (Family protection), *La delincuencia en
Venezuela: Su prevención* (Delinquency in Venezuela:
its prevention), *La obligación de alimentos en derecho*

venezolano (The obligation of alimony in Venezuelan
law); articles on legal subjects published in specialized
journals.
c/o Ministry of Foreign Affairs, Caracas, Venezuela.

Aguirre Obarrio, Eduardo Enrique, DR. EN DERECHO;
Argentine lawyer and politician; b. 14 May 1923, Ber-
lin, Germany; s. of Luis M. Aguirre and Analía María
Obarrio de Aguirre; m. Diana María Braceras Santa-
marína; two s. two d.; ed. Univ. of Buenos Aires.
Adviser/Consultant, Ministry of Interior 55, Gen.
Assessor 55-57 and Deputy Departmental Dir. 57;
Deputy Sec. of Nat. Defence 62; majority leader in the
Senate 63-65; Private Sec. to Minister of Justice 67-70;
Under-Sec. of Justice 70-71; Pres. of Caja Fed. de
Ahorro y Préstamo para la Vivienda (Fed. Savings and
Lending Bank) 72; Minister of Defence 72-73; Prof. of
Criminal Law, Univ. of Buenos Aires 56-; Grand Cross
of Condor of the Andes (Bolivia).
Leisure interests: tennis, chess, bridge, piano.
Publs. various legal publications.
Sanchez de Bustamante 2657/59, primer piso "D",
Buenos Aires, Argentina.
Telephone: 83-4858.

Ágústsson, Einar; Icelandic politician; b. 23 Sept.
1922, Rangárvallasýsla; m. Thórunn Sigurdardóttir;
one s. two d.; ed. Univ. of Iceland.
Officer, Financial Council 47-54, Finance Ministry
54-57; Gen. Man. Co-operative Savings Bank 57-63;
Dir. Co-operative Bank of Iceland 63-71; mem. Cen.
Cttee. Progressive Party 58-, Vice-Pres. 68-; mem.
Reykjavík City Council 62-71; mem. Althing 63-;
Minister of Foreign Affairs July 71-; Commdr. with
Star of the Order of the Falcon (Iceland), Grand Cross
White Rose (Finland), Grand Cross Dannebrog (Den-
mark), Grand Cross St. Olav (Norway), Grand Cross
Polar Star (Sweden).
Ministry of Foreign Affairs, Reykjavík; Home: Hlyn-
gerdi 9, Reykjavík, Iceland.
Telephone: 3-04-36.

Ahidjo, Ahmadou; Cameroonian politician; b. 24 Aug.
1924, Garoua; ed. Ecole Supérieure d'Administration,
Yaoundé.
Began his career in radio administration; elected as
Rep. to Representative Assembly of Cameroon 47;
fmr. Sec. of Assembly, Pres. Admin. Affairs Comm.,
Vice-Pres.; Counsellor Assembly of the French Union
55-58, fmr. Sec.; Pres. Territorial Assembly of Cameroon
56-57; Minister of the Interior 57-59; Deputy Prime
Minister 57-58; Prime Minister 58-59; Prime Minister
and Minister of the Interior, independent state of
Cameroon Jan.-May 60; Pres. Repub. of Cameroon
May 60-61, of the Fed. Repub. of Cameroon 61-72,
United Repub. of Cameroon 72-; Pres. Union Nationale
Camerounaise (UNC); Titulaire Etoile Noire du Bénin.
Présidence de la République, Yaoundé, Cameroon.

Ahlers, Conrad; German journalist and government
official; b. 8 Nov. 1922, Hamburg; s. of Adolf and
Gertrud (née Krancke) Ahlers; m. Heilwig von der
Mehden 1949; one s. two d.; ed. Gymnasium and Univ.
of Hamburg.
Editor, German service of B.B.C., London 48-49;
Editor, *Sonntagsblatt* 49-51; Duty Information Officer,
Press and Information Office of Fed. Govt., sub-
sequently Press Adviser, Blank Office (now Ministry of
Defence) 51-53; Foreign Policy Editor, *Die Welt* 53-56;
Head, Bonn Office, *Der Spiegel* 56-59; Home Policy
Editor, *Frankfurter Rundschau* 59-62; Deputy Editor-
in-Chief, *Der Spiegel* 62-66; Deputy Head, Press and
Information Office of Fed. Govt. 66-69, State Sec.,
Govt. Spokesman and Head 69-72; mem. Bundestag
72-; Head of Publs., Friedrich-Krupp Stiftung 73-.
53 Bonn-Ippendorf, Ippendorfer Allee 8, Federal
Republic of Germany.

Ahlfors, Lars Valerian, PH.D.; American professor of mathematics; b. 18 April 1907, Helsinki, Finland; *m.* Erna Lehnert 1933; three *d.*; ed. Univ. of Helsinki.
Lecturer, Harvard Univ. 35-38; Prof., Univ. of Helsinki 39-44, Univ. of Zürich 45-46; Prof. of Mathematics, Harvard Univ. 46-, W. C. Graustein Prof. 64-; mem. Nat. Acad. of Sciences; Fields Medal for Mathematics, Vihuri Int. Prize.
Publs. *Complex Analysis* 53, *Riemann Surfaces* (with L. Sario) 60, *Quasiconformal Mappings* 66, and many articles in mathematical analysis.
Department of Mathematics, Harvard University, Cambridge, Mass. 02138, U.S.A.

Ahlmann, Hans Jakob Konrad Wilhelmsson, PH.D.; Swedish geographer and diplomatist; b. 14 Nov. 1889, Karlsborg; *s.* of the late Wilhelm Ahlman; *m.* Erica Harloff 1920; no *c.*
Assistant Prof. of Geography, Uppsala Univ. 21; Prof. of Geography, Stockholm Univ. 29-50; Swedish Amb. in Oslo 50-56; leader of Swedish-Norwegian expedition to the North-Eastland 31, to Spitzbergen 34; leader Swedish-Icelandic investigations of Vatnajökull 36-38; leader Swedish-Norwegian expedition to N.E. Greenland 39-40; Swedish leader of Norwegian-British-Swedish Antarctic Expedition 49-52; Pres. Int. Geographical Union 56-60.
Leisure interests: art and literature.
Publs. *Sommar vid Polhavet* (with S. Malmberg), *Nutida Sverige, Land of Ice and Fire, Norge, natur och näringsliv, Glaciological Research on the North Atlantic Coasts, Glacier Variations and Climatic Fluctuations* 53.
Fregattvägan 6, 11748 Stockholm, Sweden.
Telephone: 08-197401.

Ahmad, Mirza Muzaffar; Pakistani civil servant; b. 28 Feb. 1913, Qadian, Punjab; *s.* of Mirza Bashir Ahmad and Sarwar Sultan Begum; *m.* Amtul Qayyum Begum 1939; one *s.*; ed. Govt. Coll., Lahore, London and Oxford Univs.
Entered Indian Civil Service 37; Colonization Officer, Dam Irrigation Scheme 44, Irrigation and Land Settlement Scheme 46; Deputy Commr., Mianwali and Colonization Officer, Thal Irrigation Scheme 49-50; Finance Sec. Punjab Prov. 52-55, W. Pakistan Prov. 55-59, Additional Chief Sec. W. Pakistan Prov. 59-62; Sec. of Commerce, Govt. of Pakistan 62, Sec. of Finance 63-66; Deputy Chair. Planning Comm. 66-70; Econ. and Finance Adviser to Pres. of Pakistan 70-72; Exec. Dir. IBRD, IFC and IDA 72-74; Deputy Exec. Sec. IBRD/IMF Devt. Cttee. Nov. 74-; rep., head of del. to numerous int. confs., conducted negotiations with IBRD on Indus Basin Devt. Fund.
Leisure interests: photography, hunting, reading.
International Bank for Reconstruction and Development, 1818 H Street, N.W., Washington, D.C.; Home: 7524 Hackamore Drive, Potomac, Md. 20854, U.S.A.
Telephone: (202) 477-6435 (Office); (301) 299-3836 (Home).

Ahmad, Maj.-Gen. Mohammed al-Baqir; Sudanese army officer and politician; b. 1927, El Sofi; *m.*; four *s.* one *d.*; ed. Commercial Secondary School, Khartoum, Military Coll. and Cairo Univ.
Commissioned 50; Chief of Staff, Southern Command 58; Mil. Gov. Upper Nile Province 59; Mil. Attaché, London 60-67; Dir. of Training and Chief of Staff, Southern Command 68; Commdr. Mil. Coll. 68-69; Under-Sec. Ministry of Defence June-Dec. 69; First Deputy Chief of Staff of Armed Forces 69-70, Chief of Staff 70-71; Minister of the Interior 71-73, Jan.-Aug. 75; First Vice-Pres. of Sudan May 72-; mem. Council, Univ. of Khartoum; del. to several int. confs.; several decorations.
Office of the Vice-President, Khartoum, Sudan.

Ahmadi, Sadegh; Iranian lawyer; b. March 1920, Kermanshah; ed. Darol-Fonoon High School, Teheran, Univ. of Teheran.
Appointed Judge 46; Asst. Inspectorate Org. of the Prime Minister's Office, later Dir.-Gen.; Public Prosecutor of Teheran; First Asst., State Gen. Inspectorate; mem. Parl.; Under-Sec. in charge of Planning and Studies, Ministry of Justice, Parl. Under-Sec.; Minister of Justice Sept. 71-; mem. Parl. del. to U.S.S.R.; has studied judicial systems in European countries.
Ministry of Justice, Teheran, Iran.

Ahmadu-Suka, Osman; Nigerian diplomatist; b. 22 Sept. 1926, Wara, Sokoto; ed. Achimota Coll., Ghana, Loughborough Training Coll., England, Univs. of London and Columbia.
Education Service, Sokoto Native Authority and Govt. of Northern Nigeria 46-59; Premier's Office, Kaduna 60-62; First Sec. (Educ.), High Comm., U.K. 62-64; Counsellor and Head of Chancery, Embassy, U.S.A. 64-66; Consul-Gen. in New York 66-68; Amb. to Egypt 68-73, to Netherlands 73-75; High Commr. to U.K. 75-; Rep., Commonwealth Liaison Cttee. 62-64; Alt. Perm. Rep. to UNESCO 62-64.
Nigerian High Commission, Nigeria House, 9 Northumberland Avenue, London, W.C.2, England.
Telephone: 01-839-1244.

Ahmed, Aziz, O.B.E.; Pakistani civil servant and diplomatist; b. 1906; ed. Cambridge Univ.
Sub-Divisional Officer, Bengal 34-37; Dir. Debt Conciliation Bengal 37-39; District Magistrate, Raj Shahi District 39-41; Registrar Co-op Socs., Bengal 41-43; Dir. Procurement, Dept. of Civil Supplies, Bengal 43-44, Joint-Sec. (Planning) 44-46; Deputy Sec. Indian Dept. of Agriculture 46-47; Chief Sec. to Govt. of E. Pakistan 47-52; Sec. to Cabinet, Central Govt., Pakistan 52-56; Sec. to various Ministries, then Sec.-Gen. to Govt. of Pakistan 56-59; Amb. to U.S.A. 59-63; Sec. to Govt. of Pakistan Ministry of Foreign Affairs 63-66; Chair. Press Trust of Pakistan; Minister of State for Foreign Affairs and Defence 73-; Hilal-i-Pakistan, Hilal-i-Azam, Sitara-i-Pakistan.
Ministry of Foreign Affairs, Islamabad; Home: 55 Clifton, Karachi-6, Pakistan.

Ahmed, Fakhruddin Ali, B.A.; Indian barrister and politician; b. 13 May 1905, New Delhi; *s.* of Col. Z. A. Ahmed and Begum Roquiai Sultan; *m.* Begum Abida Hyder 1945; two *s.* one *d.*; ed. St. Stephen's Coll., Delhi, St. Catharine's Coll., Cambridge, and Inner Temple, London.
Called to Bar, Inner Temple 28; Advocate Punjab High Court, Assam High Court 28 and later Senior Advocate Supreme Court; joined Indian Nat. Congress 31; mem. Assam Pradesh Congress Cttee. 36, All-India Congress Cttee. 36; Minister of Finance and Revenue, Assam 38-39; detained 40-45; Advocate-Gen. of Assam 46-52; mem. Working Cttee. All India Congress Cttee. 46-47, of Working and Parl. Cttee. 66-74; mem. Rajya Sabha 52-53; Minister of Local Self-Government 57-62, of Finance, Law, Community Devt., and Panchayat 58-66; Union Minister for Irrigation and Power 66, of Educ. 66-67, of Industrial Devt. and Co. Affairs 67-69, of Industry, Internal Trade and Company Affairs 69-70, of Food, Agriculture, Community Devt. and Co-operation 70-72, of Agriculture 72-74; Pres. of India Aug. 74-; Hon. LL.D. Guru Nanak Univ., Amritsar 74, Gauhati Univ. 75; Tamra Patra Award 74.
Leisure interests: sport, reading, listening to good music.
Rashtrapati Bhavan, New Delhi, India.
Telephone: 375321.

Ahmed, Khandakar Moshtaque; Bangladesh lawyer and politician; b. 1918.
Was active in Indian independence movt.; helped found Awami league; Minister of Foreign Affairs, Law and Parliamentary Affairs, Govt. of Bangladesh (in

exile in India) April-Dec. 71, of Law, Parliamentary Affairs and Land Revenue 71-72, of Power, Irrigation and Flood Control 72-74, of Trade and Commerce July 74-75, Pres., Minister of Defence and Home Affairs Aug.-Nov. 75.

Ahmed, S. Habib, B.A.; Pakistani United Nations official; b. 1 April 1915, Delhi, India; s. of late Abdus Salam and Munawar Jahan; m. Amtul Hafeez 1941; two s. one d.; ed. Univ. of Delhi.
Administrator, Cen. Govt., India 35-41; Finance and Budget Officer, Tata Iron & Steel Co., India 41-47; Budget Officer, UN 49-50; Public Admin. Adviser UN Commr., Libya 51; Chief Africa and Middle East Unit, Public Admin. Div., Technical Assistance Admin. UN H.Q. 51-54; UN Taxation Adviser to Libya, Consultant in Public Admin. Training to Ethiopia, Iraq 54; Chief, Office for Asia and Far East, UN Technical Assistance Admin. 55-58; Chief Admin. Officer, UN Observation Group, Lebanon 58-59; Deputy Dir. Bureau of Tech. Assist. Operations UN H.Q. 59-60; UN Admin., Congo 60-61, Chief Admin. Officer, UN Mission in the Congo 61-62; Chief, Civilian Operations UN Operations in the Congo, Resident Rep. of Tech. Assist. Board, and Dir. of Special Fund Programme, Congo 62-63, Resident Rep. of UN Devt. Programme, Somalia and Fed. of South Arabia 64-67, Libya 67-71, Syria 71-75; Dir. Mahara Devt. Bureau, Winnipeg 76-. Leisure interests: gardening, bridge.
49 D'Arcy Drive, Winnipeg, Man. R3T 2K5, Canada. Telephone: (204) 269-9556.

Ahmed, Tajuddin; Bangladesh lawyer and politician; b. 1922.
Active in Awami League 49-75; Prime Minister of Bangladesh Dec. 71-Jan. 72; Minister of Finance, Planning and Revenue 72-73, of Finance and Revenue 73-74, of Finance, Forestry, Fisheries and Livestock July-Oct. 74; arrested Aug. 75.
[*Died 3 Nov. 1975.*]

Aho, Lauri Emil, M.A.; Finnish politician and journalist; b. 18 July 1901, Pyhäjärvi; s. of Dir. Johan Emil Aho and Hilda Sofia Åkman; m. Sisko Aira Kyllikki Heikkilä 1931 (died 1967); three s.; ed. Helsinki Univ.
Literary Dir., K. J. Gummerus Publishing Co. 31-34; Asst. Editor-in-Chief *Uusi Suomi* 34-37; Official, Employers' Asscn. 37-40; Editor-in-Chief *Uusi Suomi* 40-56; Chair. Helsinki City Council 53-56; Mayor of Helsinki 56-68; Pres. Asscn. of Finnish Cities 58-67; mem. Int. Press Inst.; Hon. Ph.D. (Helsinki Univ.) 73; numerous Finnish and foreign decorations.
Kaartintorpantie 6A, Helsinki, Finland. Telephone: 485085.

Ahomadegbé, Justin Tometin; Benin politician; b. 1917; ed. William Ponty School, Dakar, and School of Medicine, Dakar.
Medical work, Cotonou, Porto-Novo 44-47; mem. Gen. Council, Dahomey 47, Sec.-Gen. Bloc Populaire Africain; Sec.-Gen. Union Démocratique Dahoméenne (U.D.D.) 56; mem. Grand Council, A.O.F. 57; mem. Dahomey Legislative Assembly 59, Pres. 59-60; medical work 60-61; imprisoned 61-62; Minister of Health, Public Works and Nat. Education 63; Vice-Pres. of Dahomey, Pres. of Council of Ministers and Minister in Charge of Interior, Defence, Security and Information 64-65, also in charge of the Plan 65; mem. Presidential Council May 70-Oct. 72; Head of State May-Oct. 72.
c/o Ministry of Justice, Cotonou, Benin.

Ahuja, Vishnu K.; Indian diplomatist; b. 5 Sept. 1923; ed. Bombay and Oxford Univs.
Attaché, Third and Second Sec., Moscow 49-52; Under-Sec. Ministry of External Affairs 52-54; Second Sec., Paris 54-55, First Sec. 55-56; First Sec., Moscow 56-59,

Bangkok 59-62; Acting High Commr. in New Zealand 62-63, High Commr. 63-65; Joint Sec. Ministry of Commerce 66-68; Consul-Gen., New York 68-71, 72, also Amb. to Costa Rica; Amb. to Romania 72-75; Additional Sec., Ministry of Foreign Affairs, New Delhi 75-.
Ministry of Foreign Affairs, New Delhi 110011, India.

Aichinger, Ilse; German and Austrian writer; b. 1 Nov. 1921, Vienna; m. Günter Eich (died 1972); ed. high school and Universität Wien.
Formerly worked with Inge Scholl at Hochschule für Gestaltung, Ulm; later worked as a reader for S. Fischer (publishers), Frankfurt and Vienna; Förderungspreis des Österreichischen Staatspreises 52, Preis der *Gruppe 47* 52, Literaturpreis der Freien und Hansestadt Bremen 54, Immermannpreis der Stadt Düsseldorf 55, Literaturpreis der Bayerischen Akademie 61, Ny-ell Sachs-Preis, Dortmund 71.
Publs. *Die Grössere Hoffnung* (novel) 48, *Knöpfe* (radio play) 52, *Der Gefesselte* (short stories) 53, *Zu keiner Stunde* (dialogues) 57, *Besuch im Pfarrhaus* (radio play) 61, *Wo ich wohne* (stories, dialogues, poems) 63, *Eliza, Eliza* (stories) 65, *Nachricht von Tag* (stories) 70.
8232 Bayerisch Gmain, Postfach 27, Federal Republic of Germany.

Aiken, Frank; Irish politician; b. 13 Feb. 1898, Camlough, Co. Armagh; s. of James Aiken and Mary McGeeney; m. Maud David 1934; two s. one d.; ed. Christian Brothers' School, Newry.
Active in Volunteers and Gaelic League 13-; Commander Northern Div. I.R.A. 21; participated in negotiations resulting in Collins-de Valera pact; Chief of Staff I.R.A. 23-25; mem. Dáil for Co. Louth 23-73; Minister for Defence 32-39; Minister for Co-ordination of Defence 39-45; Minister for Finance 45-48; Minister for External Affairs 51-54 and 57-69; Tánaiste (Deputy Prime Minister) 65-69; fmr. Vice-Pres. Assembly Council of Europe; Grand Cross of Pian Order, Grand Cross Order of Merit (Fed. Germany), Grand Officer Order of St. Charles; Hon. LL.D. (Nat. Univ. of Ireland); Fianna Fáil.
"Dúngaoithe", Sandyford, Co. Dublin, Ireland.

Aikyo, Mitsuo; Japanese mining executive; b. 3 Jan. 1908; ed. Hitotsubashi Univ.
Former Pres. Mitsubishi Metal Corpn., Chair. 71-. Mitsubishi Metal Corpn., 6, 1-chome, Ohtemachi, Chiyoda-ku, Tokyo; Home: 137 Shinmeicho, Toshi-maku, Tokyo, Japan. Telephone: 391-9401.

Ailes, Stephen; American lawyer; b. 25 March 1912, Romney, W. Va.; s. of Eugene E. Ailes and Sallie Cornwell Ailes; m. Helen Wales 1939; three s. one d.; ed. Episcopal High School, Alexandria, Virginia, Princeton Univ., and West Virginia Univ. Law School.
Asst. Prof. of Law, West Virginia Univ. 37-40; private legal practice 40-42; Legal Staff, Office of Price Admin. 42-46; law firm Steptoe & Johnson, Washington, D.C. 46-47, 48-61, 65-70; Counsel, American Econ. Mission to Greece 47; Under-Sec. of Army 61-64; Sec. of the Army 64-65; Pres. and Chief Exec. Officer Asscn. of American Railroads 71-.
Office: Association of American Railroads, American Railroads Building, 1920 L Street, N.W., Washington, D.C. 20036; Home: 4521 Wetherill Road, Washington, D.C. 20016, U.S.A.

Ailleret, Pierre Marie Jean; French engineer; b. 10 March 1900, Vienne en Arthies (S. & O.); m. Denise Node Langlois 1935; three s. three d.; ed. Ecole Poly-technique.
Director of Studies and Research, Electricité de France 46-57, Asst. Gen. Man. 58-66; Prof., Ecole Nat. des Ponts et Chaussées 38-70; mem. Atomic Energy Cttee. 50-67, Admin. Council, Conservatoire Nat. des Arts et

Métiers 58-; Vice-Pres. Hispano-Francesca de Energía Nuclear; Pres. Union Technique d'Electricité 58-; Man. *La Revue générale de l'Electricité* 72-; Commdr. Légion d'Honneur.
34 rue des Vignes, 75016 Paris, France.

Aini, Mohsen Ahmed al-; Yemeni politician and diplomatist; b. 1932, N. Yemen; ed. Faculty of Law, Cairo Univ. and the Sorbonne, Paris.
School-teacher, Aden 58-60; Int. Confederation of Arab Trade Unions 60-62; Minister of Foreign Affairs, Yemeni Repub. Sept.-Dec. 62; Perm. Rep. to UN 62-65, 65-66, 67-69; Minister of Foreign Affairs May-July 65; Prime Minister Nov.-Dec. 67; Amb. to U.S.S.R. 68-70; Prime Minister, Minister of Foreign Affairs Feb. 70-Feb. 71, Sept. 71-Dec. 72, June 74-Jan. 75; Amb. to France Aug.-Sept. 71, 75-, to U.K. 73-74.
Embassy of the Yemen Arab Republic, avenue Paul Doumer 25, Paris 11e, France.

Airlie, 13th Earl of, **David George Coke Patrick Ogilvy;** British merchant banker; b. 17 May 1926, London; s. of 12th Earl of Airlie, K.T., G.C.V.O., M.C., and Lady Alexandra Marie Bridget Coke; m. Virginia Fortune Ryan 1952; three s., three d.; ed. Eton Coll.
Chairman, Westpool Investment Trust Ltd. 64-, Ashdown Investment Trust Ltd. 68-, J. Henry Schroder Wagg and Co. Ltd. 73-; Deputy Chair. Gen. Accident Fire and Life Assurance Corpn. Ltd. 75-; Dir. Scottish and Newcastle Breweries Ltd. 69-, Schroders Ltd. 70-, Schroder Int. Ltd. 73-, Leadenhall Securities Corpn. Ltd. 74-; D.L. (Angus) 64.
13 St. Leonards Terrace, Chelsea, London, S.W.3; Cortachy Castle, by Kirriemuir, Angus, Scotland.
Telephone: 01-730-8741 (London); Cortachy 231.

Aitken, Sir (John William) Max, Bart., D.S.O., D.F.C.; British newspaper executive; b. 15 Feb. 1910, Montreal, P.Q., Canada; one s. three d.; ed. Westminster School and Pembroke Coll., Cambridge.
Royal Air Force 39-45; Conservative M.P. 45-50; Chair. Beaverbrook Newspapers Ltd.; Dir. The Price Co. Ltd., Assoc. Television Ltd.; renounced peerage but succeeded to the Baronetcy of Sir Max Aitken (later Lord Beaverbrook) June 64.
The Garden House, Cherkley, Leatherhead, Surrey, England.
Telephone: 01-353-8000.

Aitken, Sir Robert Stevenson, M.D., D.PHIL., F.R.C.P., F.R.C.P.E., F.R.A.C.P.; British physician; b. 16 April 1901, Wyndham, New Zealand; m. Margaret G. Kane 1929; one s. two d.; ed. New Zealand Schools, Univs. of Otago and Oxford.
London Hospital 26-34; Reader in Medicine, British Postgraduate Medical School, Univ. of London 35-38; Regius Prof. of Medicine Univ. of Aberdeen 39-48; Vice-Chancellor, Univ. of Otago, N.Z. 48-53; Vice-Chancellor Univ. of Birmingham 53-Sept. 68; Deputy Chair. Univ. Grants Cttee. 68-73; Chair. Birmingham Repertory Theatre 61-74; Hon. LL.D. (Dalhousie, Melbourne, Panjab, McGill, Pennsylvania, Aberdeen, Newfoundland, Leicester, Birmingham, Otago), Hon. D.C.L. (Oxon.), Hon. D.Sc. (Sydney, Liverpool).
6 Hintlesham Avenue, Birmingham B15 2PH, England.

Aitmatov, Chingiz; Soviet writer; b. 12 Dec. 1928, Sheker Village, Kirghizia; ed. Kirghiz Agricultural Inst.
Writer 52-; mem. C.P.S.U. 59-; First Sec. of Cinema Union of Kirghiz S.S.R. 64-69, Chair. 69-; Candidate mem. Central Cttee. of C.P. of Kirghiz S.S.R.; People's Writer of Kirghiz S.S.R. 68; Vice-Chair. Cttee. of Solidarity with Peoples of Asian and African Countries; Deputy to U.S.S.R. Supreme Soviet; Order of Red Banner of Labour (twice); Lenin Prize for *Tales of the Hills and the Steppes* 63; State prizewinner 68.
Publs. include: stories: *Face to Face, Short Stories,*

Melody 61, *Tales of the Hills and the Steppes* 63; novels: *Djamilya* 59, *My Poplar in a Red Kerchief* 60, *Camel's Eye, The First Teacher, Farewell Gulsary.*
Kirghiz Branch of Union of Writers of U.S.S.R., Ulitsa Pushkina 52, Frunze, U.S.S.R.

Aitmuratov, Erezhep; Soviet politician; b. 1929; ed. Central Asia Polytechnical Inst.
Electrical engineer, Chief Power Engineer of Takhia-Tash Power Undertaking of Kara-Kalpak A.S.S.R. 52-57; mem. C.P.S.U. 55-; party official, Vice-Chair. Council of Ministers of Kara-Kalpak A.S S.R., Chair. Uzbek Farming Equipment Asscn., Sec. Khodzheili Industrial Production Party Cttee. 57-63; Chair. Council of Ministers of Kara-Kalpak A.S.S.R. 63-; mem. Central Cttee. Communist Party of Uzbekistan; Deputy to U.S.S.R. Supreme Soviet 66-; Sec. Comm. on Transport and Communications, Soviet of the Union, 70-.
Council of Ministers of Kara-Kalpak A.S.S.R., Nukus, U.S.S.R.

Aizawa, Hideyuki, LL.B.; Japanese finance official; b. 4 July 1919, Usa, Oh-ita; s. of Jiro Aizawa and Kume Ninomiya; m. Yoko Shoji 1969; three s.; ed. Tokyo Imperial Univ.
With Ministry of Finance 42-; Chief Shimogyo Taxation Office 49-50; Asst. Budget Examiner, Ministry of Finance 51-54, Budget Examiner in charge of Educ., Local Finance, Agric. and Forestry 54-63; Dir. Legal Div., Budget Bureau 63-64, Dir. Co-ordination Div. 64-65; Dir.-Gen. Kinki Local Finance Bureau 65-66; Deputy Dir.-Gen. Budget Bureau 66-69; Deputy Vice-Minister of Econ. Planning Agency 69-70; Dir.-Gen. Financial Bureau, Ministry of Finance 70-71, Dir.-Gen. Budget Bureau 71-73; Vice-Minister of Finance 73-74.
Leisure interests: golf, baseball.
Publ. *Expenditure for Education* 60.
Aizawa-Hideyuki Office, 17 Mori Bldg. 2, Sakuraga-cho, Shiba-Nishikubo, Minato-ku, Tokyo; Home: 7-10-3 Seijo Setagaya-ku, Tokyo 157, Japan.
Telephone: 03-508-7771 (Office); 03-484-0122 (Home).

Ajtai, Miklos; Hungarian government official; b. 19 May 1914, Rákosliget; s. of Dezsö Ajtai and Margit Gere; m. Magda Jóboru 1968; one s. one d.; ed. Budapest Univ. of Sciences.
Chemist, Chinoin factory; in resistance movement during Second World War; entered State service 45, successively Chief Departmental Leader, Ministry of Welfare, Section Head, Ministry of Industry, First Deputy Minister of Light Industry; Deputy Pres., State Planning Office 56-61, Pres. 61-67; Deputy Prime Minister 67-74; mem. Central Cttee. Hungarian Socialist Workers' Party 61-; alt. mem. Political Cttee. of Hungarian Socialist Workers' Party 62-70; Pres. State Office of Tech. Devt. 71; Pres. Fed. of Tech. and Scientific Socs. 74-; Vice-Pres. for the State Prize and Kossuth Prize Cttee. 74-; Red Banner Order of Merit.
1052 Budapest, Martinelli tér 8, Hungary.

Akama, Yoshihiro; Japanese banker; b. 2 Dec. 1916, Tokyo; s. of Nobuyoshi and Midori (Nannichi) Akama. m. Hiroko Nitta 1945; one s. three d.; ed. Tokyo Univ.
Managing Dir. Mitsubishi Trust & Banking Corpn; 65-69, Senior Man. Dir. 69-70, Deputy Pres. 70-71, Pres. 71-.
Leisure interests: Igo, fishing.
Mitsubishi Trust & Banking Corporation, 4-5, 1-chome Marunouchi, Chiyoda-ku, Tokyo 100; Home: 4-15-22 Komagome Toshimaku, Tokyo, Japan.
Telephone: 03-917-5755.

Akatani, Genichi; Japanese United Nations official; b. 29 Sept. 1918, Taipei; ed. Univ. of Oxford and Sophia Univ., Tokyo.
Joined Japanese Foreign Service 45; Second Sec., Paris 54, First Sec. 55; Head, East-West Trade Div.,

Econ. Affairs Bureau, Ministry of Foreign Affairs 58; Counsellor, Washington, D.C. 61-66; Counsellor, Public Information Bureau, Ministry of Foreign Affairs 66-72; Asst. Sec.-Gen. for Public Information, UN June 72-; del. to several sessions of UN Gen. Assembly.
United Nations Secretariat, First Avenue, New York, N.Y. 10017, U.S.A.

Akçal, Erol Yilmaz; Turkish lawyer and politician; b. 5 May 1931, Diyarbakir; s. of İzzet Akçal and Zemzem Akçal; ed. Faculty of Law, Ankara, New York Univ. and City Coll., New York.
Legal Adviser, Istanbul 59-61; mem. Parl. 61-63; mem. Council of Europe 64-66, 67-68, Vice-Pres. 69-70; Minister of Tourism and Information 72-73; Pres., Chair. of Bd. Transtürk Trade Inc., Istanbul 73-.
Leisure interests: reading, swimming, photography.
Publs. *Economy Aspects of NATO, Turkey and the Legal Status of the Straits.*
Halaskârgazi Caddesi 198, Osmanbey, Istanbul, Turkey. Telephone: 48-44-77.

Ake, Siméon; Ivory Coast lawyer and diplomatist; b. 4 Jan. 1932; ed. Univs. of Dakar and Grenoble.
Chef de Cabinet to Minister of Public Service, Ivory Coast 59-61; First Counsellor, Ivory Coast Mission to UN 61-63; Dir. of Protocol, Ministry of Foreign Affairs 63-64; Amb. to U.K., Sweden, Denmark and Norway 64-66; Perm. Rep. of Ivory Coast to UN Sept. 66-; Officer of Nat. Order of Republic of Ivory Coast.
Permanent Mission of Ivory Coast to United Nations, 46 East 74th Street, New York, N.Y. 10021, U.S.A.

Akenzua II, Oba Omonoba Ukuakpolokpolo, C.M.G.; traditional monarch (Oba) of Benin, Nigeria; b. 1899, Benin City, Mid-Western State; s. of Oba Eweka II; ed. Benin Govt. School, King's Coll., Lagos.
Transport clerk, Benin Native Authority, 21-24; confidential clerk to his father 24; ascended throne April 33; nominated mem. Western House of Assembly 47, later mem. Nigerian Legislative Council; mem. Western Nigeria House of Chiefs 51-; Cabinet Minister without portfolio 55-62; Pres. Mid-Western House of Chiefs 63-Jan. 66; Chancellor, Ahmadu Bello Univ., Zaria 66-72.
Residence of the Oba, Benin City, Western Nigeria.

Åkerman, Johan, M.B.A.; Swedish business executive; b. 19 Sept. 1925, Lund; s. of Prof. Gustaf Åkerman and Anna-Lisa Ekelund; m. Gunilla Bergenstråhle 1953 (divorced 1975); one s. two d.; ed. Stockholm Univ. and Univ. of Calif.
With Stockholms Enskilda Bank, Stockholm 47, World Bank (IBRD), Washington 53, Electro-Invest 55; Joined the Grängesberg Co. (now Gränges A.B.) 60, Pres. 71-.
Leisure interests: skiing, skating, sailing, golf.
Gränges AB, Fack, 103 26 Stockholm 16, Sweden.
Telephone: 08-223500.

Akhmadulina, Bella Akhatovna; Soviet poet; b. 10 April 1937, Moscow; ed. Gorky Inst. of Literature.
Poems include: *The String* 62, *The Rain* 63, *My Ancestry* 64, *Summer Leaves* 68, *The Lessons of Music.*
U.S.S.R. Union of Writers, Ulitsa Vorovskogo 52, Moscow, U.S.S.R.

Akhund, Iqbal Ahmad; Pakistani diplomatist; b. 1924, Hyderabad, Sind; s. of Abdullah Shaffimohammed and Maryam Shaikh; m. Yolanda née Gombert 1956; three s. one d.; ed. Bombay Univ.
Served in diplomatic missions in Canada, Spain, Netherlands, Saudi Arabia, Malaysia and the Perm. Mission to the UN in New York 49-56; Personal Sec. to the Foreign Minister 56-58; Dir. Foreign Office 64-66, Dir.-Gen. 66-68; Amb. to the U.A.R. 68-71; Amb. to Yugoslavia 71-72; Perm. Rep. to the UN 72-; mem. Pakistan del. to the Security Council meetings on the

Kashmir question; served as Rep. of Pakistan on the Sec.-Gen.'s Advisory Cttee. on the Congo and on the working group on the Admin. and Financial Procedures of the UN, Vice-Pres. UN Econ. and Social Council 74.
Leisure interests: reading, music, golf.
Pakistan House, 8 East 65th Street, New York, N.Y. 10021, U.S.A.
Telephone: 879-8600.

Akilandam, Perungalur Vaithialingam (*pseudonym* Akilon); Indian Tamil writer; b. 27 June 1922, Perungaur; s. of M. Vaithialingam and V. Amirdhammal; ed. Maharaja's Coll., Pudukkottai.
Writer 40-; in Indian Post & Telegraph Dept. 45-58; freelance writer 58-; Sec. Tamil Writers' Asscn. Tiruchy 53-57; Sec. Gen. Fed. of All-India Tamil Writers 62-; Dir. Tamil Writers' Co-op. Soc. 63-; mem. Tamil Advisory Board, Sahitya Akademi 64-; Producer, Spoken Word in Tamil, All-India Radio, Madras 65-; Pres. Tamil Writers' Asscn. 67; Kalai Magai Prize for *Penn* 46, Tamil Akademi Award for *Nenjin Alaigai* 53, Sahitya Akademi Award for *Vengaiyin Maindan* 63, Tamilnadu Govt. Award for *Kayalvizhi* 68, for *Erimalai* 73.
Leisure interests: reading and short travels.
Publs. include: novels: *Penn* 46, *Snehithi* 50, *Nenjin Alaigai* 50, *Pavai Vilakku* 58, *Vengaiyin Maindan* 61, *Ponmalar* 64, *Kayalvizhi* 64, *Chittirap Paavai* 67; short stories: *Sakthivel* 47, *Nilavinilay* 50, *Vazhi Pirandhadu* 52, *Sahodarar Andro?* 63, *Nellore Arisi* 67, *Erimalai* 71.
171 Lloyds Road, Madras 14, India.
Telephone: 81968.

Akins, James E.; American diplomatist; b. 15 Oct. 1926, Akron, Ohio; s. of Bernice Bikler and Quay Akins; m. Marjorie Abbott 1954; one s. one d.; ed. Akron Univ.
U.S. Navy 45-46; undertook relief work with non-profit org. 48-50; taught in Lebanon 51-52; asst. editor with research org. 53-54; entered Foreign Service 54; held numerous diplomatic posts in Paris 54-55, Strasbourg 55-56, Damascus 56-57, Kuwait 58-60, Baghdad 61-64; with Secr., Wash., D.C. 65-67, Acting Deputy Asst. Sec. Int. Resource Food Policy 69-70, Dir. Fuels and Energy Office 70-72; Amb. to Saudi Arabia 73-75.
Leisure interests: opera, archaeology.
Publs. articles on oil affairs.
Department of State, Washington, D.C. 20521, U.S.A.

Aknazarov, Zekeriya Sharafutdinovich; Soviet politician; b. 1924; ed. Sverdlovsk Inter-Regional Party School and Bashkirian Pedagogical Inst.
Soviet Army 42-45; mem. C.P.S.U. 45-; Second Sec. Baimak District Cttee. of Lenin Young Communist League; Young Communist League official 48-51; First Sec. Bashkir Regional Cttee. of Young Communist League 51-54; official of Bashkir Regional Cttee. of C.P.S.U. 54-60; Research student at Acad. of Social Sciences of C.P.S.U. Central Cttee. 60-62; Chair. Council of Ministers of Bashkir Autonomous S.S.R. 62-; mem. Central Auditing Comm. of C.P.S.U.; Deputy to U.S.S.R. Supreme Soviet 62-; Sec. Comm. on Transport and Communications, Soviet of Nationalities.
Council of Ministers of Bashkir A.S.S.R., Ufa, U.S.S.R.

Ako, Ernest; Ghanaian police official.
Joined Ghana Police Force 41, Insp. 54, Asst. Commr. 67, Commr. 70, Insp.-Gen. 74; Commr. for Internal Affairs, Nat. Redemption Council 74-; mem. Supreme Mil. Council Oct. 75-.
c/o Police Headquarters, Accra, Ghana.

Aksenov, Vassily Pavlovich; Soviet writer; b. 20 Aug. 1932, Kazan; s. of Pavel V. Aksenov and Eugenia Ginzburg; m. Kira L. Mendeleva 1957; one s.; ed. Leningrad Medical Inst.
Physician 56-60; professional writer 60-; mem. Union

of Soviet Writers; mem. Editorial Board *Yunost* (magazine).
Leisure interests: music, travelling, running.
Publs. Novels: *Colleagues* 60, *Starry Ticket* 61, *Oranges from Morocco* 63, *Time, My Friend, Time* 64, *The Empty Barrels* 68, *Love to Electricity* 71, *My Granpa is a Monument* 72, *The Box Inside Which Something Knocks* (children's book) 76; collected stories: *Catapult* 64, *Half Way to the Moon* 66; screenplay for films: *Colleague, My Young Friend, When They Raise the Bridges, Travelling* 67, *The Murmar House* 72; play: *Always Sell* 65; travel: *Twenty-Four Hours Non-Stop* 76.
Krasnoarmejskaja st. 21 apt. 20, 125319 Moscow, U.S.S.R.
Telephone: 151-8615.

Aksyonov, Alexander Nikiforovich; Soviet politician; b. 1924; ed. Higher Party School of C.P.S.U. Central Committee.
Collective farmer 41-42; Soviet Army 42-43; Young Communist League official 43-57; Minister of Public Order of Byelorussian S.S.R. 60-65; First Sec. Vitebsk Regional Cttee. of C.P. of Byelorussia 65-; mem. Central Cttee. C.P. of Byelorussia; Deputy to U.S.S.R. Supreme Soviet 66-; Chair. Comm. on Problems of Youth, Soviet of Nationalities.
Vitebsk Regional Committee of Communist Party of Byelorussia, Vitebsk, U.S.S.R.

Akufo-Addo, Edward, M.O.V., M.A.; Ghanaian lawyer; b. 1906; ed. Presbyterian Church Seminary, Akropong, Achimota School, St. Peter's Coll., Oxford, and Middle Temple, London.
Member Legis. Council, Ghana 49-50; mem. Coussey Constitutional Comm., Ghana 49; Judge of Ghana Supreme Court 62-64; Chair. Political Cttee. of Nat. Liberation Council 66; Chair. Board of Dirs. Ghana Commercial Bank 66; Chair. Constitutional Comm., Ghana 66; Chief Justice of Ghana 66-70; Chair. Gen. Legal Council, Ghana 66-70; Pres. of Ghana Aug. 70-Jan. 72; Chair. Council of Univ. of Ghana 66; mem. London Inst. of World Affairs; Hon. Fellow St. Peter's Coll., Oxford.
Home: Yeboaa Buw, 46/5 Nima Road, Ringway Central, Accra, Ghana.
Telephone: 63534.

Akurgal, Ekrem, PH.D.; Turkish archaeologist; b. 30 March 1911, Istanbul; ed. Germany.
Lecturer, Univ. of Ankara 41-49, Prof. of Archaeology 49; has conducted excavations at Smyrna, Sinope, Phokaia, Daskyleion, Pitane and Erythrai 53-, at Izmir 67-; Visiting Prof., Princeton Univ. 61-62; mem. Turkish Historical Soc. (Sec.-Gen. 51-61), Turkish High Comm. for Ancient Monuments; mem. Austrian and German Archaeol. Insts., British, Austrian and Swedish Acads.; Hon. mem. Soc. for Promotion of Hellenic Studies, London, American Inst. of Archaeol.; Dr. h.c. (Bordeaux) 61.
Publs. *Griechische Reliefs aus Lykien* 42, *Remarques Stylistiques sur les reliefs de Malatya* 46, *Späthethitische Bildkunst* 49, *Phrygische Kunst* 55, *Die Kunst Anatoliens von Homer bis Alexander* 61, *Die Kunst der Hethiter* 61, *Orient und Okzident* 66, *Treasures of Turkey* (with Mango and Ettinghausen) 66, *Urartäische und Altiranische Kunstzentren* 68, *Ancient Civilizations and Ruins of Turkey* (3rd edn.) 73.
University of Ankara, Dil ve Tarih-Coğrafya Fakültesi, Ankara; Home: Vali Dr. Reşit cad. 90/5 çankaya, Ankara, Turkey.

Akwaa', Brig. Mohamed Ali al-; Yemeni army officer; b. 1933, Sana'a; *m.*; five *c.*; ed. secondary school, Mil. Coll., Sana'a.
Participated in the movts. against last three Imams of Yemen, Free Yemenis Revolution 48, attempted coup 55, Revolution of 26 Sept. 62; leading figure in movt.

which ousted Pres. al-Sallal 67; has held several posts in mil. and civil service including Asst. Mil. Commdr. Taiz District, Head Criminal Investigation Dept., Head Nat. Security (Intelligence) Dept.; Chief of Staff, Army Operations, Head S. Yemen Relief Office attached to Presidency; Minister of the Interior 73-74.
Bir Al-Azab, Sana'a, Yemen Arab Republic.

Akwei, Richard Maximilian; Ghanaian diplomatist; b. 27 Nov. 1923, Accra; *s.* of Richard Mabuo Akwei and Martha Akwei; *m.* Josephine Akosua Afram 1956; two *s.* one *d.*; ed. Achimota Coll., Accra, London Univ. and Christ Church, Oxford.
Administration Officer, Ghana Civil Service 50-56; Ghana Diplomatic Service 56-; attached to U.K. High Comm., Ottawa 56-57; First Sec., Washington 57-60; Dir. W. European and E. European Depts. Ministry of Foreign Affairs, Accra 60-64; Amb. to Mexico 64-65; Perm. Rep. to UN, Geneva, and Amb. to Switzerland 65-67; Perm. Rep. to UN, New York 67-72; Amb. to People's Repub. of China 72-.
Leisure interests: tennis, music, photography, reading.
Ghanaian Embassy, 8 San Li Tung, Peking, People's Republic of China.
Telephone: 522296.

Alam, Assadollah; Iranian agriculturist and politician; b. 1919; ed. Karaj Agricultural Coll., Univ. of Teheran.
Gov.-Gen. of Baluchistan 45-48; Minister of the Interior 48, of Agriculture 49, of Labour 50; Superintendent of the Pahlavi Estates and mem. of the High Council for their disposal 51; fmr. Dir. Pahlavi Foundation; Minister of the Interior 55-57; Leader People's Party 56-; Prime Minister July 62-March 64; Chancellor Pahlavi Univ.; Minister of the Imperial Court 66-.
Ministry of the Imperial Court, Teheran, Iran.

Alamuddin, Najib Salim, B.A.; Lebanese airline executive; b. 9 March 1909, Baakline; *s.* of Wadad and Salim Alamuddin; *m.* Dr. Ida Kunzler Alamuddin 1940; two *s.* one *d.*; ed. American Univ. of Beirut and Coll. of South West, Exeter, England.
Teacher of Engineering and Mathematics, American Univ. of Beirut 30-33; Insp. of Mathematics, Education Dept., Govt. of Trans-Jordan 33-36; Insp.-Gen. of Customs, Trade and Industry, Trans-Jordan 39-40; Chief Sec. Govt. of Trans-Jordan 40-42; founded Near East Resources Co. 42; Gen. Man. Middle East Airlines 52-56, Chair. and Pres. 56-; Minister of Tourism and Information 65, of Public Works and Transport 66, 73; mem. Exec. Cttee. of Int. Air Transport Asscn.; Hon. mem. Board of Trustees, American Univ. of Beirut; Dir. Inst. du Transport Aérien, and several Lebanese cos.; several foreign decorations.
Leisure interest: farming.
Middle East Airlines Airliban, MEA Buildings, Airport Boulevard, P. O. Box 206, Beirut, Lebanon.
Telephone: 272220 or 274440.

Alarcón de Quesada, Ricardo; Cuban diplomatist; b. 21 May 1937; ed. Univ. de Habana.
Head of Student Section, Provincial Office of 26 July Revolutionary Movement 57-59; Pres. Univ. Students' Fed., Sec. Union of Young Communists; Dir. for Regional Policies (Latin America), Ministry of Foreign Affairs 62-66; mem. Governing Council of Inst. for Int. Politics, Ministry of Foreign Affairs; Perm. Rep. of Cuba to the UN 66-.
Permanent Mission of Cuba to the United Nations, 6 East 67th Street, New York, N.Y. 10021, U.S.A.

Alba, Jaime Delibes, LL.L.; Spanish diplomatist; b. 30 Nov. 1908, Madrid; *s.* of Santiago de Alba and Enriqueta D.; *m.* Ana María Fuster 1937; ed. Univs. of Valladolid and Madrid, Free Univ. of Brussels and New Coll., Oxford Univ.

Served in the Ministries of Foreign Affairs and Commerce, specializing in int. econ. affairs 33-52; Under-Sec. Foreign Econ. Relations and Trade 51; Econ. Counsellor, Embassy in Rome 52-57; Minister Counsellor, Spanish Embassy, Washington 57-62; Amb. to the Philippines 62, Brazil 63, Luxembourg and Belgium 67-72; Perm. Rep. to the UN 72-73; Amb. to U.S.A. 74-; mem. Spanish del. to FAO 53-57; Chair. Int. Oil Agreement Cttee. and mem. Spanish del. to twelfth session of UN Gen. Assembly 57; as Plenipotentiary signed Spain's accession to the Int. Bank for Reconstruction and Devt. and the Int. Monetary Fund; Pres. del. of Spanish observers to the Second Extraordinary Inter-American Conf., Rio de Janeiro; several Spanish and foreign decorations.
Leisure interests: travelling, golf.
Embassy of Spain, 2700 15th Street, N.W., Washington, D.C. 20009, U.S.A.

Alban-Hansen, Erik; Danish civil servant; b. 29 July 1920, Copenhagen; s. of Ejler Vilhelm Hansen and Vilhelmine Hansen (née Lorentzen); m. Vibeke Alban-Hansen (née Poulson) 1943; one s. two d.; ed. Univ. of Copenhagen.
Principal, Prices amd Monopoly Control 43; Principal, Dept. of Customs and Excise 44-47, Head of Section 47-62, Asst. Sec. 62-65, Deputy Sec. 65-73; Fed. of Danish Industries 46-59; Dir.-Gen. of Financial Institutions and Fiscal Matters, Comm. of European Communities 73-.
Leisure interest: music.
Commission of the European Communities, rue de la Loi 200, Brussels; 35 Square Marie-Louise, 1040 Brussels, Belgium; and Ildkulevej 27, Yderby Lyng, 4583 Sjaell. Odde, Denmark.
Telephone: 217-88-23 (Home); 0342-62-26 (Denmark).

Albee, Edward Franklin; American playwright; b. 12 March 1928; ed. Lawrenceville and Choate Schools, Washington, and Columbia Univ.
Has written a number of plays, including: *The Death of Bessie Smith, The American Dream, The Sand Box* 61, *The Zoo Story* 61, *Who's Afraid of Virginia Woolf* 62, stage adaptation of *The Ballad of the Sad Café* (Carson McCullers) 63, *Tiny Alice* 64, *Malcolm* (from novel by James Purdy) 66, *A Delicate Balance* (Pulitzer Prize 67) 66, *Everything in the Garden* (after a play by Giles Cooper) 67, *All Over* 71, *Seascape* (Pulitzer Prize 75) 75; two one-act plays: *Box, Quotations from Chairman Mao Tse-tung* 68.
c/o The William Morris Agency, 1350 Avenue of the Americas, New York, N.Y. 10019, U.S.A.

Albers, Josef; American (b. German) painter and art teacher; b. 19 March 1888, Bottrop, Westphalia; ed. Teachers' Seminary, Royal Art School, Berlin, Art Acad., Munich, Bauhaus, Weimar.
Teacher in public schools 08-13, 15-19; Prof. at Bauhaus, Weimar, Dessau, Berlin 23-33; Prof. of Art, Black Mountain Coll., N.C., U.S.A. 33-49; Prof. of Art and Chair. Yale Univ. School of Art 50-58, Prof. Emer. 58,- Visiting Critic 58-60; lecture tours in N. and S. America, Europe; over 200 one-man shows, represented internationally in more than 100 museums; mem. Nat. Inst. of Arts and Letters 68-; Benjamin Franklin Fellow, Royal Soc. of Arts, London 70; Extraordinary mem. Berlin Art Acad. 74; Ada S. Garret Prize 54; William Clark Prize 57; Award for Painting, Pittsburgh Int. Exhbn. 67; D.F.A. h.c. Univ. of Hartford, Conn. 57, Yale Univ. 62, Calif. Coll. of Arts and Crafts 64, Univ. of Chapel Hill 67, Univ. of Illinois 69, Minneapolis Art School 69, Kenyon Coll. 69, Washington Univ., St. Louis 71, Pratt Inst., Brooklyn, N.Y. 75; Hon. LL.D. (Univ. of Bridgeport) 66, York Univ., Toronto 73; Hon. Dr. Phil. (Ruhr Univ., Bochum) 67; Ford Foundation Grant 59, 1964 Gold Medal; American Inst. of Graphic Arts, Grosses Verdienstkreuz des Verdienstordens der Bundesrepublik Deutschland 68, etc.
Publs. numerous articles and books on art and art education, c. 500 graphic prints.
808 Birchwood Drive, Orange, Conn. 06477, U.S.A.
[*Died* 24 *March* 1976.]

Albert, Calvin; American sculptor; b. 19 Nov. 1918, Grand Rapids, Mich.; s. of Philip and Ethel Albert; m. Martha Neff 1941; one d.; ed. Inst. of Design, Chicago, Art Inst. of Chicago and Archipenko School of Sculpture.
Teacher, New York Univ. 49-52, Brooklyn Coll. 47-49, Inst. of Design 42-46; Prof. of Art Pratt Inst. 49-, Head of Graduate Sculpture Program 65-; 22 one-man exhbns. including Landmark, Stable and Borgenicht Galleries, N.Y.C., Palace of Legion of Honor, San Francisco, Art Inst. of Chicago; other exhbns. in the U.S. and Galleria George Lester, Rome; sculpture and drawings in collections of Whitney Museum, Metropolitan Museum, Jewish Museum, Art Inst. of Chicago, Detroit Inst. of Arts, Univ. of Nebraska, Chrysler Museum of Art and William Rockhill Nelson Gallery of Art; Fulbright Advanced Research Grant to Italy 61; Tiffany Grants 63, 65; Guggenheim Fellowship 66; Nat. Inst. of Arts and Letters Award 75.
Leisure interest: boating.
Publ. *Figure Drawing Comes to Life* (with Dorothy Seckler).
325 West 16th Street, New York, N.Y. 10011, U.S.A.

Albert, Carl Bert, A.B., B.A., B.C.L., LL.D.; American lawyer and politician; b. 10 May 1908; ed. Univ. of Oklahoma and Oxford Univ.
Admitted to Oklahoma Bar 36; Legal Clerk, Federal Housing Admin. 35-37; practised law, Oklahoma City 37; attorney and accountant Sayre Oil Co. 37-38; law practice, Mattoon, Ill. 38-39; legal dept., Ohio Oil Co. 39-40; served army 41-46; practised law McAlester, Oklahoma 46-47; mem. House of Reps. 47-, Democratic Whip 55; Majority Leader 62-71; Speaker of House of Reps. Jan. 71-; Bronze Star.
House of Representatives, Washington, D.C. 20515, U.S.A.

Alberty, Robert Arnold, B.S., M.S., PH.D.; American professor of chemistry; b. 21 June 1921, Winfield, Kan.; s. of Luman H. Alberty and Mattie Arnold Alberty; m. Lillian Jane Wind 1944; one s. two d.; ed. Lincoln High School, Lincoln, Neb., Univ. of Nebraska and Univ. of Wisconsin.
Instructor, Chemistry Dept., Univ. of Wisconsin 47-48, Asst. Prof. 48-50, Assoc. Prof. 50-56, Prof. 56-57, Assoc. Dean of Letters and Science Jan. 62-June 63, Dean of Graduate School 63-67; Prof. of Chemistry and Dean, School of Science, Mass. Inst. of Technology 67-; mem. Nat. Acad. of Sciences 65-, American Acad. of Arts and Sciences 68-; Chair. Comm. on Human Resources, Nat. Research Council; Eli Lilly Award for research in enzyme kinetics 56; Hon. Dr. Univ. of Nebraska 67, Lawrence Univ. 67.
Leisure interest: designing and building a summer cabin.
Publs. *Physical Chemistry* (co-author) 4th edn. 75, *Experimental Physical Chemistry* (with others) 62.
School of Science, Massachusetts Institute of Technology, Cambridge, Mass. 02139; Home: 7 Old Dee Road, Cambridge, Mass. 02138, U.S.A.
Telephone: 253-2456 (Office); 491-3689 (Home).

Albertz, Heinrich; German politician and ecclesiastic; b. 22 Jan. 1915; ed. theological studies in Berlin, Halle and Breslau.
Curate in Berlin 37, arrested during Second World War as active member of Protestant Church; Head of Refugee Office, City of Celle 46; mem. Social Democrat Party (S.P.D.) 46-; Rep. for Refugees, Lower Saxony Landtag 47; mem. Refugee Council, Exec. Cttee. of

S.P.D. 47; Dir. of Senate Cttee. for People's Welfare, West Berlin 55-59; Head of Senate Chancellery, West Berlin 61-63; Senator for Internal Affairs, West Berlin 61-63; Deputy Mayor and Senator for Internal Affairs 65-66; Mayor of West Berlin Dec. 66-67; Protestant Priest in West Berlin 68-; Niedersächsische Landesmedaille, Grosses Verdienstkreuz mit Stern und Schulterband.
1 Berlin 38, Rolandstrasse 6b, Germany.

Albuquerque, José Osório da Gama e Castro Saraiva de, LIC. EM DIR.; Portuguese judge; b. 3 Aug. 1910, Fornos de Algodres; s. of Conselheiro Luís Osório and Margarida de Albuquerque Osório; m. Zilia de Serpa Brandão 1934; six s. five d.; ed. Universidade de Coimbra.
Assistant to Procurator of Repub. 34-42; Judge 42-57; Procurator, Appeal Court, Oporto district 42-44; Deputy Procurator-Gen. of Repub. 46-54; Procurator-Gen. of the Repub. 54-57; Appeal Court Judge 57-61; Supreme Court Judge 61-; Pres. of the Supreme Court of Justice 66, Gran Cruz de Ordem de Cristo.
Leisure interest: gardening.
Rua do Francisco de Almeida 63, Lisbon 3, Portugal.
Telephone: 61 07 74.

Alcobre Ares, Manuel; Argentine writer; b. 7 June 1900; ed. Commercial Secondary School.
Editor daily *Crítica* 30-38, review *Estampa* 38-41; Sec.-Gen. Asscn. Argentine Writers 49-51; Prof. of Castilian Language and Literature in Technical Schools; Municipal Poetry Prize, Buenos Aires; Nat. Poetry Prize of Nat. Cultural Comm.
Publs. Poetry: *Paisajes Civiles* 28, *Poemas de Media Estación* 31, *Espuma en la Arena* 37, *Hogar y Paisajes Nuevos* 40, *Acento Forestal* 43, *El Arbol Solariego* 46, *Canción en Sol de Despedida* 49, *Silvas de la Tierra que Fue Mar* 55, *Estación Terminal* 57, *Epístola al Cielo* 60, *Patria! Argentina!* 60; prose: *Luces a la Distancia* 34, *Bajo el Paraguay* 35.
Calle Joaquín V. Gonzales 4292, Buenos Aires, Argentina.

Alcorn, (Hugh) Meade, Jr., A.B., LL.B.; American politician; b. 20 Oct. 1907, Suffield, Conn.; s. of late Hugh M. and Cora W. Alcorn; m. twice; one s. (deceased) one d.; ed. Dartmouth Coll. and Yale Univ.
Admitted to Connecticut Bar 33; Asst. State's Attorney, Hartford County, 35-42, State's Attorney 42-48; mem. Connecticut House of Reps. 37, 39 and 41, Majority Leader 39, Speaker 41; Republican Chair. Suffield, Conn. 38-53; del. Republican Nat. Convention 40, 48, 52, 56 (Chair.); alt. del. 44; Seventh District Committeeman; Nat. Committeeman from Conn. 53-61; Vice-Chair. Cttee. on Arrangements for 1956 Republican Nat. Convention 56; Chair. Republican Nat. Cttee. 57-59; mem. Hartford County, Conn. State (Pres. 50-51) and American Bar Asscns., American Judicature Soc.; Fellow, American Coll. of Trial Lawyers; Vice-Pres. and Dir. First Nat. Bank of Suffield; Dir. United Bank & Trust Co., Hartford, Conn.; Hon. LL.D. (Univ. of Hartford) 74.
Leisure interests: fishing, hunting.
49 Russell Avenue, Suffield, Conn., U.S.A.
Telephone: 668-7306.

Alder, Berni Julian, PH.D.; American theoretical physicist; b. 9 Sept. 1925, Duisburg, Germany; s. of Ludwig Alder and Ottilie Gottschalk; m. Esther Romella Berger 1956; two s. one d.; ed. Univ. of Calif. (Berkeley), and Calif. Inst. of Technology.
Instructor, Univ. of Calif. (Berkeley) 51-54; Theoretical Physicist, Univ. of Calif. Lawrence Radiation Lab. 55-; Nat. Science Foundation Senior Post Doctoral Fellow, Weizman Inst. (Israel) and Univ. of Rome 63-64; Van der Waals Prof., Univ. of Amsterdam 71; Guggenheim

Fellow, Cambridge (U.K.) and Leiden (Netherlands) 54-55; mem. Nat. Acad. of Sciences.
Leisure interests: hiking, skiing.
Publs. many chapters in books and articles in journals.
Lawrence Radiation Laboratory, P.O. Box 808, Livermore, Calif. 94550, U.S.A.

Aldewereld, Siem; Netherlands banker; b. 1909, Amsterdam; s. of Gerrit Aldewereld and Marianna Stodel; m. Kitty M. Erwteman 1939; no c.; ed. Amsterdam Univ.
Entered service of Rotterdam Bank, Amsterdam 30; Govt. Dir. of Foreign Exchange Control, Curaçao 40; during the war, Supervisor of Netherlands East Indies assets in Western Hemisphere, New York 42; Financial Adviser for Netherlands Indies affairs, Netherlands Embassy, Washington; Asst. to Treas. Int. Bank for Reconstruction and Development 46-52, Asst. Dir. 52-55, Dir. of Department of Technical Operations 55-65; Vice-Pres. for Finance, Int. Bank for Reconstruction and Devt. 56-74; Partner Lazard Frères & Co., N.Y. 74-.
2801 New Mexico Avenue, N.W., Apartment 1407, Washington, D.C. 20007, U.S.A.

Aldington, 1st Baron (cr. 62); Toby (Austin Richard William) Low, P.C., K.C.M.G., C.B.E., D.S.O., T.D.; British banker and industrialist; b. 25 May 1914, London; s. of Col. Stuart Low, D.S.O. and Hon. Lucy Gwen, d. of Lord Atkin; m. Araminta, d. of Sir Harold MacMichael, G.C.M.G., D.S.O., 1947; one s. two d.
Called to Bar 39; Army Service 39-45; Conservative M.P. 45-62; Parl. Sec. to Ministry of Supply 51-54; Minister of State, Board of Trade 54-57; Deputy Chair. Conservative Party Org. 59-63; Chair. Grindlays Bank Ltd. (fmrly. Nat. and Grindlays), Sun Alliance & London Insurance Group; Deputy Chair. Gen. Electric Co. Ltd.; Chair. Port of London Authority 71-, Nat. Nuclear Corpn. Ltd., Dir. Lloyds Bank Ltd., First Nat. City Corpn., Banque Grindlay Ottomane; Fellow, Royal Soc. of Arts 70.
Leisure interests: golf, gardening, stalking.
Knoll Farm, Aldington, nr. Ashford, Kent; and 21D Cadogan Gardens, London, S.W.3, England.

Aldiss, Brian Wilson; British writer; b. 18 Aug. 1925, Norfolk; m. 2nd Margaret Manson 1965; two s. two d.; ed. Framlingham Coll. and West Buckland School.
Formerly soldier, draughtsman, bookseller and film critic; Literary Editor *Oxford Mail* 57-69; Pres. British Science Fiction Asscn. 60-65; Hugo Award for *Hothouse* 62, Nebula Award for *The Saliva Tree* 65, Ditmar Award for World's Best Contemporary Science Fiction Writer 69, BSFA Award for *The Moment of Eclipse* 72.
Leisure interests: walking, meditating, travel, collecting water-colours, painting.
Publs. *The Brightfount Diaries* 55, *Space, Time & Nathaniel* 57, *Non-Stop* 58, *The Male Response* 59, *Hothouse* 62, *The Airs of Earth* 63, *The Dark Light Years* 64, *Greybeard* 64, *Earthworks* 65, *Best Science Fiction Stories of Brian W. Aldiss* 65, *Cities and Stones: A Traveller's Jugoslavia* 66, *Report on Probability A* 68, *Barefoot in the Head* 69, *Intangibles Inc.,* 69, *A Brian Aldiss Omnibus* 69, *The Hand-Reared Boy* 70, *The Shape of Further Things* 70, *A Soldier Erect* 71, *The Moment of Eclipse* 71, *Brian Aldiss Omnibus 2* 71, *Penguin Science Fiction Omnibus* (Ed.) 73, *Comic Inferno* 73, *Billion Year Spree* 73, *Frankenstein Unbound* 73, *The Eighty-Minute Hour* 74, *Hell's Cartographers* (Ed.) 75, *Space Odyssey's Evil Earths* 75.
Heath House, Southmoor, Abingdon, Oxfordshire, England.
Telephone: Longworth 820215.

Aldrich, Hulbert Stratton, PH.B.; American banker; b. 3 April 1907, Fall River, Mass.; s. of Stanley Alden Aldritch and Jane Stratton (Pratt) Aldrich; m. Amy

Durfee 1934; two *d.*; ed. Phillips Acad. and Yale Univ. Joined New York Trust Co. 30, Asst. Treas. 39-43, Vice-Pres. 43-52, Pres. 52-59 (co. merged with Chemical Corn Exchange Bank to form Chemical Bank New York Trust Co.); Vice-Chair. Chemical Bank 59-72; Chair. Hill Samuel Inc. 72-; Dir. numerous other companies.
Leisure interest: tennis.
375 Park Avenue, New York, N.Y. 10022, U.S.A.

Aldrich, Robert; American film director; b. 1918.
Films include: *Big Leaguer, World for Ransom, Apache* 54, *The Big Knife* 55, *Attack* 57, *Whatever Happened to Baby Jane* 62, *Hush, Hush, Sweet Charlotte* 64, *Flight of the Phoenix* 65, *The Dirty Dozen* 66, *The Killing of Sister George* 68, *The Grissom Gang* 71, *Ulzana's Raid* 72, *Emperor of the North* 72, *The Longest Yard* 74, *The Mean Machine* 75, *Hustle* 76.
Aldrich Studios, 201 N Occidental Boulevard, Los Angeles, California 90026, U.S.A.

Aldrin, Edwin Eugene, Jr.; American astronaut; b. 20 Jan. 1930, Montclair, N.J.; *s.* of Col. Edwin E. Aldrin and late Marion M. Aldrin; *m.* Joan A. Archer; two *s.* one *d.*; ed. U.S. Military Acad. and Massachusetts Inst. of Technology.
Member U.S. Air Force; completed pilot training 52; flew combat missions during Korean War; later became aerial gunnery instructor, Nellis Air Force Base, Nev.; attended Squadron Officers' School at Air Univ., Maxwell Air Force Base, Ala.; later Flight Commdr. 36th Tactical Fighter Wing, Bitburg, Germany; completed astronautics studies at Mass. Inst. of Technology 63; selected by NASA as astronaut 63; Gemini Target Office, Air Force Space Systems Div., Los Angeles, Calif. 63; later assigned to Manned Spacecraft Center, Houston, Tex.; pilot of backup crew for *Gemini IX* mission 66; pilot for *Gemini XII* 66; backup command module pilot for *Apollo VIII*; lunar module pilot for *Apollo XI*, landed on the moon 20 July 69; Commdt. Aerospace Research Pilot School 71-72; Fellow, American Inst. of Aeronautics and Astronautics; Hon. mem. Royal Aeronautical Soc.; several honorary degrees and numerous decorations and awards; retd. from U.S.A.F. 72.
Publs. *First on the Moon: A Voyage with Neil Armstrong* (with Michael Collins) 70, *Return to Earth* 73.
Aerospace Research Pilots School, Edward AFB, Calif. 93523, U.S.A.

Aleixandre, Vicente; Spanish writer; b. 1898, Seville; *s.* of Cirilo and Elvira Aleixandre; ed. Univ. of Madrid; Member Spanish Acad., Hispanic Soc. of America, Monde Latin Paris Acad.; Hon. Fellow, Professors of Spanish, U.S.A. Asscn.; corresp. mem. Sciences and Arts, Puerto Rico Acad. Arts, Malaga Acad., Hispanoamerican Bogotá Acad.; Nat. Prize of Literature.
Publs. *Ambito* 28, *Espadas como Labios* 32, *Pasión de la Tierra* 35, *La Destrucción o el Amor* 35, *Sombra del Paraíso* 44, *Mundo a Solas* 50, *Vida del Poeta: El amor y la poesía* 50, *Poemas Paradisíacos* 52, *Nacimiento Ultimo* 53, *Historia del Corazón* 54, *Algunos Carácteres de la Nueva Poesía Española* 55, *Ocho Poemas de Aleixandre* 55, *Mis Poemas Mejores* 57, *Los Encuentros* 58, *Poemas Amorosos* 60, *Poesías Completas* 60, *Picasso* 61, *Antigua Casa Madrileña* 61, *En Un Vasto Dominio* 62, *María la Gorda* 63, *Retratos con Nombre* 65, *Presencias* 65, *Dos Vidas* 67, *Obras Completas* 68, *Poemas de la Consumación* 68, *Antología del Mar y la Noche* 71, *Poesía Superrealista* 71, *Sonido de la Guerra* 71, *Diálogos del Conocimiento* 74.
Velintonia 3, Parque Metropolitano, Madrid 3, Spain.
Telephone: 233-47-94.

Alekperov, Aziz Aga-Aga-baba; Soviet foreign trade official; b. 1 Jan. 1916; ed. Inst. of Foreign Trade Moscow.
Has worked in foreign trade 38-; various posts in All-

Union *Vostokintorg* (Eastern Foreign Trade) Asscn., Chair. 65-.
All-Union *Vostokintorg* Association, 32-34 Smolenskaya-Sennaya Ploshchad, Moscow, U.S.S.R.

Alekseev, Mikhail Pavlovich; Soviet professor of literature; b. 5 June 1896, Kiev; *s.* of Pavel Petrovich Alekseev and Antonina Vassilievna Alekseeva; *m.* Nina Vladimirovna Alekseeva; two *d.*; ed. Univ. of Kiev.
Lecturer, Kiev Univ. 19-20, Odessa Univ. 21-27; Prof. Leningrad Univ. 32-60, Head of Dept. of Philology 45-47, 50-53; corresp. mem. U.S.S.R. Acad. of Sciences, 46-58, mem. 58-; mem. Inst. of Russian Literature of Acad. of Sciences, Leningrad; Head Sector of Interrelations of Russian and foreign literatures; Chair. Pushkin Comm., U.S.S.R. Acad. of Sciences; mem. Serbian Acad. of Science and Art; corresp. mem. British Acad.; Hon. mem. Modern Languages Asscn. of America; Hon. Ph.D. (Univ. of Rostock); Hon. D.Litt. (Univ. of Oxford); Hon. D. ès L. (Bordeaux and Paris); Hon. D.Phil. (Univ. of Budapest and Poznań); Order of Lenin, etc.
Publs. *Siberia in the References of European Travellers and Writers*, 2 vols. 32, 36, 2nd edn. 46, *History of English Literature* 43, 60, *The Russian Language in England* 44, *The English Language in Russia* 46, *Pushkin and the Science of his Time* 56, *Hogarth and his Analysis of Beauty* 58, *Byron MSS. in the U.S.S.R.* 58, *Letters of Turgenev* 61, *Hispano-Russian Literary Relations* 64, *Shakespeare and Russian Culture* 65, *Pushkin's "Monument"* 67, *Pushkin, Comparative Studies* 72, *Zur Geschichte Russisch-Europäische Literaturtraditionen* 75.
7 Linia 2, log. 3, Leningrad 199034, U.S.S.R.

Alekseevsky, Evgeny Evgenyevich; Soviet politician; b. 1906.
Deputy People's Commissar for Agric., Tajikistan 31; Commissar Cavalry Div., Second World War; in charge of agric. in various regions of Ukraine 46; Deputy Minister of Agriculture, Ukraine in 'fifties; Chair. U.S.S.R. State Cttee. for Irrigated Farming 63; Minister of Reclamation and Water Management 65-; Deputy to U.S.S.R. Supreme Soviet 66-; mem. Central Cttee., C.P.S.U. 72-.
Ministry of Reclamation and Water Management, Orlicov per. 1/11, 107139 Moscow, U.S.S.R.

Alemán, Miguel; Mexican government official; b. 1905; ed. Universidad Nacional Autónoma de Mexico.
Private law practice, later Magistrate, High Court of Justice 28-35; Senator 35-36; Gov. of Veracruz 36-40; Sec. for Govt. under Pres. Camacho 40-45; Pres. of Mexico 46-52; later Pres. Nat. Tourism Council.
Departamento de Turismo, Mariano Escobado 726, Mexico 5, D.F., Mexico.

Aler, Lieut.-Gen. Izaak Alphonse; Netherlands company director and Air Force officer; b. 3 May 1896, Amsterdam; *s.* of I. A. Aler and Th. M. M. Giroldi; *m.* Nessine A. van der Stok 1922; one *s.* two *d.*; ed. Royal Military Acad., Breda.
Air Force Pilot 18-25; KLM Pilot 26-39; recalled to Air Force as Staff Captain 39-40; prisoner of war in Stanislau and Neu Brandenburg 42-45; returned to active service 45-53; mem. Board of Royal Netherlands Aircraft Factories "Fokker" 53-67; Pres. KLM (Royal Dutch Airlines) 54-61; mem. of Air Advisory Cttee. of European Defence Community 48; Chief of Air Staff 50; Knight in the Order of the Netherlands Lion 51; Commander in the Legion of Merit 51-68; Knight in the Order of Orange-Nassau 48; Grand Officer in the Order of Orange-Nassau and awarded "General Snijders" Gold Medal 53.
Leisure interests: outdoor life and bridge.
Waardeel 17, Rolde, Netherlands.
Telephone: 05924-1984.

Alessandri Rodríguez, Jorge; Chilean businessman and politician; b. 1896; ed. Nat. Univ. of Chile.
Deputy from Santiago 25; fmr. Prof. School of Engineering, Santiago; fmr. mem. Public Works Comm.; Dir. of a number of paper factories and sugar refineries; Vice-Pres. Bank of South America; Minister of Finance 48-50; Senator 57; Pres. of Chile 58-64; candidate for Pres. election 70.
Santiago, Chile.

Alessandro, Victor Nicholas; American conductor; b. 27 Nov. 1915; ed. Eastman School of Music (Univ. of Rochester), N.Y., Mozarteum Acad., Salzburg, and Accad. Santa Cecilia, Rome.
Musical Dir. Oklahoma Symphony 38-51, San Antonio Symphony Orchestra and San Antonio Grand Opera Festival 51-; Alice M. Ditson Award, Columbia 56; Nat. Music Council Award 64.
San Antonio Symphony Society, 109 Lexington Avenue, Suite 207, San Antonio, Tex. 78205, U.S.A.

Alewyn, Richard, PH.D.; German professor of German literature; b. 24 Feb. 1902; ed. Lessing-Gymnasium, Frankfurt, and Univs. of Frankfurt, Marburg, Munich and Heidelberg.
Privatdozent, Univ. of Berlin 31; Assoc. Prof. Univ. of Heidelberg 32-33; Visiting Prof. Sorbonne, Paris 33-35; Assoc. Prof. Queens Coll., New York 39-48, Prof. 48-49; Prof. Univ. of Cologne 49-55, Free Univ. of Berlin 55-59; Prof. of German Literature, Univ. of Bonn 59-67, Emeritus 67; Guest Lecturer at several univs. in U.S.A. 52-; Editor *Euphorion* 56-62; Hon. mem. Modern Language Asscn. of America; mem. Akad. der Wissenschaften zu Göttingen, Rheinisch-Westfälische Akad. der Wissenschaften, PEN Club, Deutsche Akad. für Sprache und Dichtung.
Publs. *Vorbarocker Klassizismus* 26, 2nd edn. 62, *Johann Beer* 32, *Über Hugo von Hofmannsthal* 58, 4th edn. 67, *Das Grosse Welttheater* 59, French trans. *L'Univers du Baroque* 64, *Probleme und Gestalten* 74.
8131 Perchting bei Starnberg, Federal Republic of Germany.
Telephone: 08161/7308.

Alexander, Sir Alex (Sandor), Kt.; British business executive; b. 21 Nov. 1916; *m.* 1946; two *s.* two *d.*
Founder, Westwick Frosted Products (merged with Ross Group Ltd. 54); Dir. Ross Group 54, Chair. Ross Frozen Food Div. 54-61, Poultry Div. 61-68; Man. Dir. and Chief Exec. Ross Group Ltd. 67-69, Chair. 69-; Dir. Imperial Tobacco Group Ltd. 69-; Chair. Imperial Foods Ltd. 71-; Pres. Nat. Asscn. of Frozen Food Producers 57, 71; Chair. Pea Growers' Research Org. 59-61, Nat. Asscn. of Poultry Packers 65, Fed. of British Poultry Industries 66-68; Dir. British United Trawlers Ltd. 69, Deputy Chair. 73-; Dir. Nat. Westminster Bank Ltd., Eastern Region 73; Dir. Ransomes, Sims, Jefferies Ltd. 74; Gov. British Nutrition Foundation 75; mem. Court, Univ. of East Anglia 61, Agriculture Econ. Devt. Cttee. 74; Trustee Glyndebourne Arts Trust 75; Chair. Norwich Theatre Trust; Pres. British Food Export Council; Fellow, Royal Soc. of Arts, Inst. of Management, Inst. of Grocery Distribution 75.
Leisure interests: shooting, tennis, painting, theatre.
Westwick Hall, Norwich, Norfolk; 1 Lygon Place, Ebury Street, London, SW1W 0JR; Imperial House, Grosvenor Place, London, S.W.1, England.
Telephone: Swanton Abbott 664; 01-730-0288 (London).

Alexander, Sir Darnley Arthur Raymond, Kt., C.B.E., LL.B.; Nigerian chief justice (British nationality); b. 28 Jan. 1920, Castries, St. Lucia, West Indies; *s.* of Pamphile Joseph Alexander and the late Lucy Alexander; *m.* Mildred Margaret Alexander (née King) 1943; one *s.* one *d.*; ed. St. Mary's Coll., St. Lucia, Univ. Coll., London.
Middle Temple 38, called to bar 42; legal service in Jamaica and Turks and Caicos Islands 44-57, Western

Nigeria 57-63, Solicitor-Gen. 60, Q.C. 61; Judge, High Court of Lagos (later Lagos State) 64-69; Chief Justice of South-Eastern State 69-75, of Fed. Republic of Nigeria 75-; mem. Nigerian Soc of Int. Law 68-, Int. Advisory Board African Law Reports 73-; Chair. Nigerian Advisory Judicial Cttee. 75-.
Leisure interests: cricket, football, swimming, table tennis, reading.
Supreme Court, Lagos; Home: 15 Ikoyi Crescent, Ikoyi, Lagos, Nigeria.
Telephone: 21307 (Office); 23260 (Home).

Alexander, William Gemmell, M.B.E., M.A.; British administrative official; b. 19 Aug. 1918, Hooton, Ches.; *s.* of Harold Gemmell and Winifred A. (née Stott) Alexander; *m.* Janet Elias 1945; four *s.* one *d.*; ed. Sedbergh School and Brasenose Coll., Oxford.
Army Service 39-45; Co-operative Societies Officer. Gilbert and Ellice Islands 46-51; Registrar of Co-operative Societies, Mauritius 51-55; Co-operative posts, Cyprus 55-60; Manager, Agricultural Dept., Co-operative Wholesale Society 60-63; Dir. Int. Co-operative Alliance 63-68; Dir.-Gen. Royal Soc. for the Prevention of Accidents 68-74; County Road Safety Officer, West Yorkshire Metropolitan County Council 74-.
Leisure interests: sport and walking.
8 Woolgreaves Close, Sandal, Wakefield, West Yorkshire, England.
Telephone: Wakefield 55214.

Alexandrenne, Louis, DIPL. ING.; Senegalese engineer and politician; b. 28 Dec. 1933, Dakar; ed. Lycée de Dakar, Faculté des Sciences, Toulouse.
Former Engineer and Head of Geology and Mining Prospecting, Mining Board; Dir. of Mines and Geology, concurrently Dir. of Industry 65-69; Pres., Dir.-Gen. Société Nationale d'Etudes et de Promotion Industrielle Jan 69-; Minister of Industrial Devt. July 72-; Municipal Councillor, Dakar; fmr. Pres. Admin. Board, Institut de Technologie Alimentaire, Office Sénégalais de l'Artisanat.
Ministère du Développement Industriel, Dakar, Senegal.

Alexandrov, Alexandr Danilovich; Soviet mathematician; b. 4 March 1912, Volyn, Ryazan Region; ed. Leningrad Univ.
Lecturer Leningrad Univ. -52, Rector 52-64; mem. C.P.S.U. 51-; specialized in subject of convex bodies and general surfaces in geometry; corr. mem. Acad. of Sciences of U.S.S.R. 46-65, mem. 65-; Head of Dept., Inst. of Mathematics, Siberian Br. U.S.S.R. Acad. of Sciences 64-; State prizewinner; Order of Lenin.
Akademgorodok, Institute of Mathematics, Novosibirsk U.S.S.R.

Alexandrov, Anatoly Nikolaevich, D.SC.; Soviet composer; b. 25 May 1888, Moscow; ed. Moscow Conservatoire.
Professor of Composition at Moscow Conservatoire 26-; Order of Red Banner of Labour 43, State Prize 51, Order of Lenin 53; Merited Arts Worker R.S.F.S.R. 46; People's Artist of the R.S.F.S.R. 64-71, of the U.S.S.R. 71-.
Works include *Bela* (opera in 4 acts), *Wild Bara* (opera in 3 acts); Symphony in C Major (4 movements); 13 piano sonatas, and numerous other works for piano; 4 string quartets; over 100 songs and many other compositions; film music.
Moscow State Conservatoire, 13 Ulitsa Herzena, Moscow, U.S.S.R.

Alexandrov, Anatoly Petrovich; Soviet physicist; b. 13 Feb. 1903, Tarashcha, Kiev Region, Ukraine; ed. Kiev Univ.
Work devoted to physics of dielectrics, mechanical and electrical properties of high polymeric compounds; developed widely-used static theory of strength of

solids; invented relaxation theory of elasticity in polymers, etc.; Corresp. mem. U.S.S.R. Acad. of Sciences 43-53, mem. 53-; Dir. Inst. of Physical Problems, U.S.S.R. Acad. of Sciences 46-55, Dir. Inst. of Atomic Energy 60-, Pres. 75-; mem. C.P.S.U. 62-; Deputy to U.S.S.R. Supreme Soviet 62-70; mem. Central Cttee. C.P.S.U. 66-; Order of Lenin (six times); numerous medals and prizes.
I. V. Kurchatov Atomic Energy Institute, 46 Kurchatova, Moscow; U.S.S.R. Academy of Sciences, Leninsky Prospekt 14, Moscow, U.S.S.R.

Alexandrov, Col. Boris Alexandrovich; Soviet composer and conductor; b. 1905; ed. Moscow State Conservatoire.
Conductor, Central Theatre of Soviet Army 29-37; Deputy Chief, Soviet Army Song and Dance Co. 37-46; Chief 46-; Asst. Prof., Moscow Conservatoire 33-; People's Artist of R.S.F.S.R. 48, of U.S.S.R. 58; Order of Lenin 49, 67, Order of Red Banner of Labour 64.
Principal works: *Marriage in Malinovka* (operetta) 37, *A Year Later* (operetta) 40, *A Girl of Barcelona* (operetta) 42, *My Guzel* (orchestral) 46, *Left-hander* (ballet) 55, *October Soldier Defending Peace* (oratorio) 66; also songs and choral works.
Soviet Army House, Ploshchad Kommuny, Moscow, U.S.S.R.

Alexandrov, Grigory Vasilievich; Soviet film director; b. 23 Jan. 1903, Sverdlovsk.
Began career as actor in the Central Workers' Studio of Proletkult 21; began film work 24; worked with S. Eisenstein as director of *Strike*, as actor and assistant in *Battleship Potemkin*, and co-director of *October* 27, *Old and New* 28-29, *Mexico* 31; worked in Paris 29, Hollywood and Mexico 29-30; mem. C.P.S.U. 54-; People's Artist of the U.S.S.R.; mem. Lenin Int. Peace Prize Cttee.; State prizes 41, 50; Order Lenin (twice), Order of Red Banner of Labour and other decorations.
Made films: *Jolly Fellows* 34, *Circus* 36, *Volga-Volga* 38, *Bright Path* 39, *Spring* 47, *Meeting on the Elbe* 49, *Composer Glinka* 52, *Russian Souvenir* 60; produced *Dear Liar* (Kilthy) in Mossoviet Theatre.
Mosfilm Studio, Moscow. U.S.S.R.

Alexandrov, Pavel Sergeevich; Soviet mathematician; b. 7 May 1896, Noginsk, Moscow Region; ed. Moscow Univ.
Prof. of Mathematics at Moscow Univ. 29-; founded Soviet Topological School; Pres. Moscow Mathematical School; Academician, U.S.S.R. Acad. of Sciences 53-; foreign assoc. U.S. Nat. Acad. of Sciences 47; mem. American Philos. Soc., Polish Acad. of Sciences, corresp. mem. Acad. of Sciences, Berlin, Göttingen, Halle; Hero of Socialist Labour 69.
Publs. *Combinatorial Topology* 47, *Untersuchungen über Gestalt und Lage abgeschlossener Mengen beliebiger Dimension* (Annals of Mathematics, Princeton, N.Y., 29, vol. 30), *Topologische Dualitätssätze I, II* (59, 62), *Einführung in die Gruppentheorie von P.S.* 60, *Nichtabgeschlossene Mengen* 62.
Moscow State University, Leninskiye Gory, Moscow, U.S.S.R.

Alexeyev, Alexander Ivanovich; Soviet diplomatist and journalist; b. 3 Aug. 1913, Moscow; ed. Moscow Univ.
Diplomatic Service 41-; First Sec. Buenos Aires 54-58; Head of Dept. for Latin American Countries, State Cttee. of U.S.S.R. Council of Ministers for Cultural Relations with Foreign Countries 59-60; Counsellor, Havana 60-62, Amb. to Cuba 62-67; at staff of Ministry of Foreign Affairs 67-68; Vice-Chair. Board of Novosti Press Agency 69-; Order of Red Banner of Labour (thrice), Badge of Honour.
Novosti Press Agency, Ploshchad Pushkina, Moscow, U.S.S.R.

Alexeyev, Pyotr Fyodorovich; Soviet journalist; b. 8 July 1913, Sergeevka, Kustanai Region, Kazakh S.S.R.; ed. Tashkent Pedagogical Inst. and Higher Party School of the C.P.S.U.
Young Communist League Official, Uzbek S.S.R. 31-32; journalistic work 32-62; Editor-in-Chief *Selskaya Zhizn* (Country Life) 62-71; Editor-in-Chief *Sovietskaya Rossia* (Soviet Russia) 71-75; Amb. to Madagascar 75-; mem. Central Auditing Comm. of the C.P.S.U. 66; mem. C.P.S.U. 40-.
U.S.S.R. Embassy, 179 rue Rasamoely Maurice, Tananarive, Madagascar.

Alexiadis, George; Greek lawyer and public official; b. 18 Dec. 1911, Tropea, Arcadia; s. of Dr. Stavros Alexiadis and Panagiota Giannakopoylos; m. Katherine Tsarpalis 1967; ed. Athens Univ.
Practising lawyer 33-; Legal Adviser to Nat. Bank of Greece 40; head of a resistance organization and publisher of an underground newspaper 41-45; Counsellor to Athens Municipality 50; publ. *Perspective* 60-; fmr. Dir.-Gen. Hellenic Nat. Broadcasting Inst.; Minister of Employment Oct.-Nov. 73; Medal of Nat. Resistance; Progressive Party.
Leisure interests: stamps, gardening.
Publs. include: *Legal and Social Aspect of the Idea of the State* 39, *Introduction to Land Allotment* 41, *Geo-Economy and Geo-Policy of Greek Countries* 45 and 46, *The Reform of Criminal Law in Soviet Russia* 57, *Political History of Modern Greece* 60-63, *The First Balkan Alliance of 1867-1868* 71, *The Origins of the Greek-Italian War* 73, *A Strange Theory About the French Revolution* 75.
National Bank of Greece, 86 Aeolou Street, Athens; Home: 129 Kiphissias Avenue, Athens 606, Greece.
Telephone: 3218-930 (Office); 6922-192 (Home).

Alfaro Polanco, José María; Spanish writer and diplomatist; b. 1906.
Director of magazines *Vértice*, *Escorial*, *Fe*, and fmr. dir. *Arriba*; Vice-Pres. of Cortes; Amb to Argentina 59-72.
Publs. *Versos de un invierno, Leoncio Pancorbo, La última falsa, El molinero y el diablo, Fue en una venta*.
Eduardo Dato 20, Madrid, Spain.

Alföldi, András; Hungarian archaeologist and historian; b. 27 Aug. 1895; ed. Budapest Univ.
Former Prof. of Roman History, Inst. for Advanced Study, Princeton; mem. Institut de France, British, Royal Swedish, Lincei, Göttingen, Mainz, Bavarian, Danish, Hungarian, Austrian, Bulgarian and other Acads.; Hon. Fellow Soc. of Antiquaries, London and Scotland, Soc. for Promotion of Roman Studies, Royal Numismatic, Pontif. Accad. di Archeologia, Spanish, Turkish, and Finnish archaeological and historical socs., French, Swiss, Austrian and Bavarian numismatic socs.; Hon. Ph.D. (Utrecht, Bonn, Paris, Ghent Univs.); Gold Medal, City of Rome, Order "Pour le Mérite" (Germany), Les Palmes Académiques (France), Golden Cross of King George II (Greece), etc.
Publs. *Der Untergang der Römerherrschaft in Pannonien* 24-26, *Studies on the World Crisis of the Third Century A.D., The Huns, Studies on the Monarchical Representation in Rome* 34-35; contrib. to *Cambridge Ancient History* 35-38, *Festivals of Isis in Rome in the IVth Century* 37, *Studies on the Social Morphology, Art and Archaeology of the Nomads of Eurasia* 36-37, *Die Kontorniaten* 41-43, *Daci e Romani in Transilvania* 40, *A History of Aquincum* 42, *Zu den Schicksalen Siebenbürgens* 44, *The Conversion of Constantine and Pagan Rome* 48, *Valentinian I and the Senate* 50, *Studies on Zoomorphic Headgear* 50, *The Origins of the Roman Patriciate* 51, *The Birth of Imperial Symbolism* 52-53, *Caesar's Monarchy* 53, *The Tragic Costume* 54, *The Trojan Legend in Rome* 57, *The Roman Surname* 66, *The Domination of Cavalry in Greece and Rome after the*

Kings 66, *Early Rome and the Latins* 65, *Imperial vows and Alexandrine Gods* 66, *The Role of the Cavalry in Greece and Rome* 67, *Caesar in 44 B.C.* 71, *The Oldest Structural Patterns of the Roman State and Society* 72, *The Nummi Quadrigati* 72, *The Two Laurel Trees of Augustus* 73, *Early Roman History* (research report and new contrib.) 74, *Tempestas Mariana* 74, *Octavian's Rise to Power* 75.
Spiez, Switzerland.
Telephone: 541766.

Alfozan, Yusuf; Saudi Arabian diplomatist; b. 1913; ed. Arabia and Bombay, India.
Editor *Shubban's Voice* 36-38; Personal Agent in Bombay to H.M. King Abdulaziz Ibn Saud 38; Consul-Gen. Palestine 39-41, Bombay 49-55; Minister to India 55-57, Amb. 57-65, to Iran 66-68, to Spain 68-74, to India 74-.
Embassy of Saudi Arabia, 1 Eastern Avenue, Maharani Bagh, New Delhi, India.

Alfvén, Hannes Olof Gösta, PH.D.; Swedish professor of plasma physics; b. 30 May 1908; ed. Universitet i Uppsala.
Professor of Theory of Electricity, Royal Inst. of Technology, Stockholm 40-45, of Electronics 45-63, of Plasma Physics 63; mem. Swedish Science Advisory Council; mem. Swedish Acad. of Sciences, Swedish Acad. of Eng. Sciences; Foreign Assoc. U.S. Acad. of Sciences; mem. other foreign Acads.; Gold Medal, Royal Astronomical Soc. (U.K.) 67; Nobel Prize for Physics 70; Lomonosov Gold Medal, U.S.S.R. Acad. of Sciences 71.
Publs. papers in physics and astrophysics and: *Cosmical Electrodynamics* 50, *On the Origin of the Solar System* 54, *Cosmical Electrodynamics: Fundamental Principles* (with C.-G. Fälthammar) 63, *Worlds-Antiworlds* 66.
Division of Plasma Physics, Royal Institute of Technology, Stockholm 70, Sweden.

Ålgård, Ole, CAND.JUR.; Norwegian diplomatist; b. 9 Sept. 1921; s. of Gabriel and Bertha Ålgård; m. Rigmor née Braathe, one s. one d.; ed. Univ. of Oslo.
Joined Ministry of Foreign Affairs 46; Sec., Moscow 47-50; Chargé d'Affaires, Vienna 51-56; Ministry of Foreign Affairs, Chief of Section 56-71; Deputy Perm. Rep. to UN 61-64; Counsellor, Norwegian Embassy, Brussels and Perm. Rep. to Council of Europe 64-66; Amb. to People's Repub. of China 66-71; Perm. Rep. to UN Jan. 72-; del. to UN Gen. Assembly 70, 71.
Leisure interests: history, fishing.
Permanent Mission of Norway to United Nations, 825 Third Avenue, 18th Floor, New York, N.Y. 10017; Home: 10 Gracie Square, New York, N.Y. 10028, U.S.A.
Telephone: 212-879 8670.

Ali, (Chaudhri) Mohamad, M.SC.; Pakistani politician; b. 15 July 1905, Jullundhar, India; s. of Chaudri Khair-ud-din and Ayesha; m. Razia Sultana 1931; four s. one d.; ed. Lahore and Univ. of Punjab.
Lecturer in chemistry, Islamia Coll., Lahore 27-28; joined Indian Accounts and Audit Service 28; Accountant-Gen., Bahawalpur 32-36; entered Govt. of India service 36; Under-Sec. Finance Dept. 38-39; Deputy Financial Adviser 39-43; Joint Financial Adviser, Ministry of Supply 43-45; Financial Adviser War and Supply 45-47; mem. Steering Cttee. of Partition Council 47; Sec.-Gen. to Govt. of Pakistan 47-51; Minister of Finance 51; Minister of Finance and Econ Affairs 54-55; Prime Minister and other portfolios 55-56; Leader Nizam-E-Islam Party; retired from active politics Oct. 69.
Publ. *The Emergence of Pakistan* 67.
86-D/1, Gulberg III, Lahore, Pakistan.
Telephone: 81434.

Ali, H. A. Mukti; Indonesian comparative religion specialist; b. 1923, Central Java; m.; two s. one d.; ed. Indonesia, Pakistan, Canada.
Vice-Chancellor, IAIN "Sunan Kalijaga", Yogjakarta; Minister of Religious Affairs Sept. 71-.
Publs. *Modernization of Islamic Schools, Comparative Religion, its Method and System*, etc.
Leisure interest: table tennis.
Ministry of Religious Affairs, Jl. M. Husni Thamrin 6, Jakarta; Home: Perumahan Dinas Pejabat Tinggi 1, Jakarta, Indonesia.

Ali, Muhammad; American boxer; b. (as Cassius Marcellus Clay) 17 Jan. 1942, Louisville, Ky.; s. of Cassius Marcellus Clay Sr. and Odetta Lee Grady; m. 1st Sonje Roi (dissolved); 2nd Belinda Boyd 1967, four c.; ed. Louisville.
Amateur boxer 54-60, Olympic Games light-heavyweight champion 60; professional boxer 60-, won world heavyweight title Feb. 64, defeating Sonny Liston; adopted name Muhammad Ali 64; stripped of title after refusing to be drafted in U.S. Army 67, won case in U.S. Supreme Court and returned to professional boxing 70; regained world heavyweight title Oct. 74, defeating George Foreman in Zaire; 49 victories in 51 fights up to end of 75; mem. of U.S. Black Muslim movement.
Publ. *The Greatest: My Own Story* (autobiography) 75.
c/o Deer Lake Training Camp, Pennsylvania, U.S.A.

Ali, S. Osman; Pakistani international finance official; b. 1 July 1912; m.; three c.; ed. Univs. of Madras and Oxford.
Entered Indian Civil Service 35; various posts 35-47; exec. posts with Govt. of Pakistan 49-58, Commerce Sec. 59-62, Sec. Econ. Affairs Div. 62-66; Amb. to Belgium, Luxembourg and the EEC 66; Perm. Rep. to European Office of UN and Specialized Agencies in Geneva 66; Exec. Dir. IBRD, IFC and IDA 68; Man. Dir. Pakistan Industrial Credit and Investment Corpn. Ltd.; Sitara-i-Quaid-i-Azam 58; Sitara-i-Pakistan 64.
Jubilee Insurance House, McLeod Road, P.O. Box 5680, Karachi 2, Pakistan.

Ali, Sadiq, B.A.; Indian politician; b. 1910, Udaipur, Rajasthan; ed. Allahabad Univ.
General Sec. Indian Nat. Congress, New Delhi, Perm. Sec. All-India Congress Cttee. 38-48; mem. Lok Sabha 50-52, Rajya Sabha 58-; Gen. Sec. Indian Nat. Congress 58-64, 66-; Pres. Opposition Congress Party 71; Chief Editor *AICC Economic Review*; associated with Indian freedom movement 30.
Publs. *Know Your Country, Congress Ideology and Programme, Culture in India, General Elections 1957, Towards Socialist Thinking in Congress.*
27 Shri K.M. Munshi Marg, New Delhi 11, India.

Ali, Salem Rubia (see Rubbayi, Salem Ali).

Ali Khan, Begum Liaquat (widow of late Liaquat Ali Khan, fmr. Prime Minister of Pakistan), M.A., B.T.; Pakistani diplomatist; ed. Univs. of Lucknow and Calcutta.
Founder Pres. All-Pakistan Women's Asscn., Nat. Guard, Naval Reserve and Cottage Industry Projects; chair. various educational, hospital and social work groups; del. to U.N. General Assembly 52; mem. I.L.O. Expert Cttee. on Recommendations 55; Ambassador to the Netherlands 54-61, to Italy 61-66, to Tunisia 61-64; Gov. Sind Prov. 73-76.
Government House, Karachi, Pakistan.

Ali Samater, Gen. Mohammed; Somali army officer and politician.
Vice-Pres. Somali Repub. 71-, also Chief of the Armed Forces, Minister of Defence.
Army Headquarters, Mogadishu, Somalia.

Alier, Abel, LL.B., LL.M.; Sudanese politician; b. 1933, Bor District, Upper Nile Province; s. of Kwai and Anaai Alier; m. Siama Fatma Bilal 1970; one s. two d.; ed. Univs. of Khartoum and Yale.
Former advocate; District Judge in El Obeid, Wad Medani and Khartoum until 65; participant in Round Table Conf. and mem. Twelve Man Cttee. to Study the Southern problem 65; mem. Constitution Comms. 66-67, 68; fmr. mem. Law Reform Comm. and Southern Front; Minister of Supply and Internal Trade Oct. 69-June 70; Minister of Works June 70-July 71; Minister of Southern Affairs 71-72; Vice-Pres. Oct. 71-; Pres. Supreme Exec. Council for the South April 72-; mem. Board of Dirs., Industrial Planning Corpn.; mem. Nat. Scholarship Board.
Leisure interests: tennis, athletics, reading history and literature.
People's Palace, Khartoum, Sudan.

Aliev, Geidar Ali Rza Ogly; Soviet politician; b. 1923, Baku, Azerbaizhan; ed. Azerbaizhan State Univ.
Joined Azerbaizhan S.S.R. Ministry of Interior and State Security 45; Deputy Chair. Cttee. of State Security, Azerbaizhan S.S.R. Council of Ministers 65-67, Chair. 67-69; First Sec. Cen. Cttee. Azerbaizhan C.P. 69-; Deputy to U.S.S.R. Supreme Soviet 70-74; Vice-Chair. Soviet of the Union 74.
Central Committee of the Communist Party of the Azerbaizhan S.S.R., Baku, U.S.S.R.

Aliger, Margarita Iosifovna; Soviet poetess; b. 7 Oct. 1915, Odessa; ed. Gorky Literary Inst.
Member C.P.S.U. 42-; State prizewinner 43; Order of Red Banner of Labour 65; Badge of Honour.
Publs. *Year of Birth* 38, *The Railway* 39, *Stones and Grasses* 40, *To the Memory of the Brave* 42, *Zoya* 42, *Lyrics* 43, *Your Victory* 46, *Selected Poems* 47, *A Tale of Truth* 47, *First Thunder* 47, *First Signs* 48, *The Lenin Hills* 53, *The Beautiful Metcha-River* 53, *Man on His Way* 54, *Lyrics* 55, *From a Notebook* 57, *Lyrics and Poems* 59, *A Few Steps* 64, *Russia: My Native Country* 67, *Stronger than Death* 68; Essays: *Chilean Summer* 65, *Return to Chile* 66; trans. poems of Aragon, Pablo Neruda, Bagriana, etc.
U.S.S.R. Union of Writers, 52 Ulitsa Vorovskogo, Moscow, U.S.S.R.

Alikhani, Ali Naghi; Iranian economist and politician; b. 1929; m. Suzanne Demeuzes 1954; three s. one d.; ed. Alborz Coll., Teheran, Univ. of Teheran and Univ. of Paris.
Former Econ. Adviser to Nat. Iranian Oil Co. and other orgs.; Minister of Economy 63-69; Chancellor, Univ. of Teheran 69-71; Chair. Int. Bank of Iran, Iran Refractories Co., Alupan Aluminium Co. 71-; Chair. Council of Materials and Energy Research Center, Arya Mehr Univ. of Tech.; mem. High Council of Environmental Conservation, governing bds. of Inst. for Int. Political and Econ. Studies and Reza Shah Kabir Univ., bd. of trustees Abu-Ali Sina Univ., Iran Center for Man. Studies.
Leisure interest: hunting.
264 28th Street, Park Avenue (Abbassabad), Teheran, Iran.
Telephone: 686896.

Alikhanov, Enver Nazarovich; Soviet politician; b. 1917; ed. Azerbaijan Industrial Inst.
Soviet Army 41-42; Industrial Geologist 42-45; mem. C.P.S.U. 43-; Apparatus of Central Cttee. of Azerbaijan C.P. 45-51; Azerbaijan oil industry 51-59; Minister of Oil Industry, Azerbaijan 58-59; Sec. Central Cttee. of Azerbaijan C.P. 59-62; Chair. Council of Ministers of Azerbaijan 62-71; Alt. mem. Central Cttee. of C.P.S.U.; mem. Central Cttee. C.P. of Azerbaijan; Deputy to U.S.S.R Supreme Soviet; Lenin Prize 61.
c/o Council of Ministers of Azerbaijan S.S.R., Baku, U.S.S.R.

Alikhanyan, Artem Isaakovich; Soviet physicist; b. 24 June 1908, Tbilisi; ed. Leningrad Univ.
Began research work 31; discovered with his brother (Alikhanov, A. I.) and Kozodaev emission of "couples" (positron and electron) by agitated nuclei 34; discovered with brother and Nikitin varitrons 41; founder and Dir. of Yerevan Physics Inst. 43-; founder Aragats cosmic scientific station 45; Corresp. mem. U.S.S.R. Acad. of Sciences 45; mem. Armenian S.S.R. Acad. of Sciences 43; State Prize 41, 48; Order of Red Banner of Labour (twice).
Institute of Physics of the U.S.S.R. Academy of Sciences, 14 Leninsky Prospekt, Moscow, U.S.S.R.

Alimarin, Ivan Pavlovich; Soviet chemist; b. 11 Sept. 1903, Moscow; s. of Pavel and Maria Alimarin; m. Zoya Alimarina 1936; one s. one d.; ed. Moscow Univ.
At All-Union Research Inst. of Mineral Raw Materials 25-53; Prof. Moscow Inst. of Fine Chemical Technology 50-53, Moscow Univ. 53-; at Inst. of Geochemistry and Analytical Chem., U.S.S.R. Acad. of Sciences 49-; Corresp. mem. U.S.S.R. Acad. of Sciences 53-66, mem. 66; Hon. mem. Analytical Chem. Soc., England 68-, Acad. of Science, Finland 74-, Chemical Soc. of the German Democratic Repub.; Hon. D.Phil (Polytechnical Univ., Budapest) 71, (Univ. of Gothenburg) 73; State Prize; Order of Lenin (three times).
Leisure interests: photography, fishing.
V. I. Vernadsky Institute of Geochemistry and Analytical Chemistry, 47A Vorobyevskoe Shosse, 117334 Moscow, U.S.S.R.

Alioto, Joseph Lawrence; American lawyer and politician; b. 1916, San Francisco, Calif.; s. of Giuseppe and Domenica (Lazio) Alioto; m. Angelina Genaro 1941; five s. one d.; ed. Roman Catholic coll.
Former govt. lawyer, Washington, specializing in anti-trust cases; returned to private practice in Calif.; Sec. Rice Growers' Asscn. of Calif., Mayor of San Francisco; Jan. 68-76; Democrat.
Leisure interests: music, reading, golf.
City Hall, San Francisco, Calif. 94102, U.S.A.

Aliyeva, Sakina; Soviet (Azerbaijan) philologist and politician; b. 1925; ed. Azerbaijan State Univ. and Higher Party School.
Minister of Education, Nakhichevan Republic 60-61; Sec. Nakhichevan Regional Cttee., C.P. of Armenia 62-63; Pres. of Presidium of Supreme Soviet of Nakhichevan A.S.S.R. 63.
Presidium of Supreme Soviet of Nakhichevan A.S.S.R., Nakhichevani, Armenian Republic, U.S.S.R.

Alkhimov, Vladimir Sergeyevich; Soviet foreign trade official; b. 25 Oct. 1919; ed. Leningrad Financial and Economic Inst., and Acad. of Foreign Trade.
Member C.P.S.U. 42-; Chief of Dept., later Deputy Dir., Research Inst. of Commercial Exchange 50-57; Commercial Counsellor, U.S.A. 57-60; Deputy Chief, later Chief of Dept., Ministry of Foreign Trade 61-67; Deputy Minister of Foreign Trade 67-; Hero of Soviet Union; and other decorations.
U.S.S.R. Ministry of Foreign Trade, 32/34 Smolenskaya-Sennaya ploshchad, Moscow, U.S.S.R.

Alladaye, Maj. Michel; Benin army officer; b. 1940, Abomey; m.; five c.; ed. Lycée Victor Ballot, Ecole Mil. de Saint-Cyr, Ecole Supérieure Technique du Génie, Versailles.
Commander 1st Engineers Corps, Dahomey Armed Forces, Kandi 63-67; promoted to rank of Capt. 67; worked successively in Eng. Unit, Army Gen. Staff Command, Services Battalion Command; Commdr., Dir. Mil. Engs.; Minister of Foreign Affairs 72-; Chevalier Légion d'Honneur.
Ministère des Affaires Etrangères, Cotonou, Benin.

Allais, Maurice; French economist and engineer; b. 31 May 1911, Paris; s. of Maurice and Louise (Caubet) Allais; m. Jacqueline Bouteloup 1960; one d.; ed. Ecole Polytechnique and Ecole Nationale Supérieure des Mines de Paris.

Department of Mines and Quarries 37-43; Dir. Bureau de Documentation Minière 43-48; econ. research 48-; Prof. of Economic Analysis, Ecole Nationale Supérieure des Mines de Paris 44-; Prof. of Econ. Theory, Inst. of Statistics, Univ. of Paris 47-68; Dir. of Research, Centre Nat. de la Recherche Scientifique 54-; Dir. Centre for Econ. Analysis 44-; Prof. Graduate Inst. of Int. Studies, Geneva 67-70; Dir. Séminaire Clément Juglar d'Analyse Monétaire, Univ. of Paris X 70-; Chevalier Légion d'Honneur; Officier Palmes Académiques; Lanchester Prize, American Soc. for Operation Research and other awards; Dr. h.c. (Groningen); Ingénieur Général au Corps des Mines.

Publs. *Abondance ou Misère* 46, *Economie et Intérêt* 47, *Traité d'Economie Pure* 52, *La gestion des houillères nationalisées et la théorie économique* 53, *Les fondements comptables de la macroéconomique* 54, *Le pendule paraconique* 57-59, *Manifeste pour une Société Libre* 58, *L'Europe Unie, route de la prospérité* 60, *Le Tiers-Monde au Carrefour—Centralisation autoritaire ou planification concurrentielle* 62, *L'Algérie d'Evian* 62, *The Role of Capital in Economic Development* 63, *Reformulation de la théorie quantitative de la monnaie* 65, *L'Impôt sur le Capital* 66, *The Conditions of the Efficiency in the Economy* 67, *Growth without Inflation* 68, *Growth and Inflation* 69, *La Libéralisation des Relations Economiques Internationales* 70, *Les Théories de l'Equilibre Economique Général et de l'Efficacité Maximale* 71, *Forgetfulness and Interest* 72, *The General Theory of Surplus and Pareto's Fundamental Contribution* 73, *Inequality and Civilization* 73, *La Création de Monnaie et de Pouvoir d'Achat par le Mécanisme du Crédit* 74, *The Psychological Rate of Interest* 74, *L'Inflation Française et la Croissance* 74, *Classes Sociales et Civilisations* 74.
15 rue des Gâte-Ceps, 92210 Saint Cloud, France.
Telephone: 602-53-35.

Allan, Colin Hamilton, C.M.G., O.B.E., M.A.; British overseas administrator; b. 23 Oct. 1921, Wellington, New Zealand; ed. Hamilton High School, Canterbury Univ., Magdalene Coll., Cambridge Univ.
Cadet, Admin. Service, British Solomon Islands 45; District Commr., Western Solomons 46-49, Malaita 49-53; Special Lands Commr. 53-57; Senior Asst. Sec. Western Pacific High Comm. 57-59; Asst. Resident Commr. New Hebrides 59-66, Resident Commr. 66-73; Gov. and C.-in-C. Seychelles, Commr. British Indian Ocean Territory 73-; Commdr. Ordre Nat. du Mérite 66. Publs. *Customary Land Tenure in the British Solomon Islands Protectorate* 58; articles on overseas admin., anthropology, etc.
Government House, Seychelles; Home: 23 Alpha Street, Cambridge, New Zealand.

Allard, Sven; Swedish diplomatist; b. 6 July 1896, Tjällmo; m. Baroness Margaretha Silfverschiöld 1933; two s.
Attaché Foreign Office 21; Warsaw Legation 22; Riga, Reval, Kovno 23; Second Sec. Brussels and The Hague 25; First Vice-consul London 30; First Sec. Warsaw 32, Rome 33, Paris 34; Commercial Counsellor 34; Counsellor of Legation and Chargé d'Affaires Athens 38, Ankara 39-40, Sofia 41; Rep. Gov. for relief in Greece 42-43; Minister to China 43-47; Del. for Commercial Negotiations, Foreign Office 47-49; Minister to Romania (also accredited to Hungary and Bulgaria) 49-51; Minister to Czechoslovakia (also accredited to Hungary) 51-54, to Austria 54-56; Ambassador to Austria 56-64; Rep. to FAO, Rome 64-69.
Publs. *Diplomat in Vienna* (in Swedish, Finnish and German) 65, *Russia and the Austrian State Treaty: A Case Study of Soviet Foreign Policy in Europe* 70, *Stalin and Hitler: A Study in Soviet Foreign Policy in Europe 1933-41* 70.
c/o Ministry of Foreign Affairs, Stockholm, Sweden.

Allardt, Helmut, DR. JUR.; German Ambassador to U.S.S.R. 68-72; see *The International Who's Who 1975-76*

Allegro, John Marco; British philologist, archaeologist, author and playwright; b. 17 Feb. 1923, London; s. of John Marco Allegro and Mabel Jessie Perry; m. Joan Ruby née Lawrence 1948; one s. one d.; ed. Wallington County Grammar School and Univ. of Manchester.
Royal Navy 41-46; Manchester Univ. 47-52; research in Hebrew dialects, Magdalen Coll., Oxford 52-53; British rep. on Int. Editing Team for Dead Sea Scrolls, Jerusalem 53-; Lecturer in Comparative Semitic Philology and Hebrew, Univ. of Manchester 54-62, in Old Testament and Intertestamental Studies 62-70; Adviser to Jordanian Govt. on Dead Sea Scrolls 61-; Trustee and Hon. Sec. Dead Sea Scrolls Fund 62-70.
Leisure interests: sketching, photography.
Publs. *The Dead Sea Scrolls* 56, 64, *The People of the Dead Sea Scrolls* 58, *The Treasure of the Copper Scroll* 60, 64, *Search in the Desert* 64, *The Shapira Affair* 65, *Discoveries in the Judaean Desert of Jordan V* 68, *The Sacred Mushroom and the Cross* 70, *The End of a Road* 70, *The Chosen People* 71, *Lost Languages* 76.
Craigmore, Ballasalla, Isle of Man, United Kingdom.
Telephone: Castletown 2345.

Allen, Charles, Jr.; American investment banker; b. 1 Jan. 1903; ed. New York Public Schools and Commerce High School.
Founder, Allen & Co. (investment bankers) 22; Chair. of Board Allen Ranches, Pres. Bayou Interests Inc.; Dir. Evergreen Pk. Shopping Plaza, North Kansas City Devt. Co., Ogden Corpn.; official of numerous other companies.
Allen and Company, 30 Broad Street, New York, N.Y. 10004, U.S.A.

Allen, Sir Douglas Albert Vivian, G.C.B.; British civil servant; b. 15 Dec. 1917, Surrey; s. of Albert Allen and Elsie Maria (née Davies); m. Sybil Eileen Allegro 1941; two s. one d.; ed. Wallington County Grammar School and London School of Economics.
Assistant Principal, Board of Trade 39; served Royal Artillery 40-45; Principal, Board of Trade 45, Cabinet Office 47, Treasury 48; Asst. Sec., Treasury 49-58; Under-Sec., Ministry of Health 58-60, Treasury 60-62; Third Sec., Treasury 62-64; Deputy Under-Sec. of State, Dept. of Econ. Affairs 64-66, Second Perm. Under-Sec. of State 66; Perm. Under-Sec. of State, Dept. of Econ. Affairs 66-68; Perm. Sec., Treasury 68-74; Head Home Civil Service, Perm. Sec. Civil Service Dept. 74-; Chair. Econ. Policy Cttee., Org. for Econ. Co-operation and Devt. 72-.
Leisure interests: tennis, woodwork.
9 Manor Way, South Croydon, Surrey, England.
Telephone: 01-688-0496 (Home).

Allen, George Cyril, C.B.E., M.COM., PH.D., F.B.A.; British university professor Emeritus; b. 28 June 1900, Kenilworth, Warwicks.; s. of George Henry and Elizabeth Allen; m. Eleanora Cameron McKinlay Shanks 1929 (died 1972); ed. King Henry VIII School, Coventry, and Univ. of Birmingham.
Lecturer Nagoya Commercial Coll. Japan 22-25; Research Fellow and Lecturer, Univ. of Birmingham 25-29; Prof. of Economics and Commerce, Univ. Coll., Hull 29-33; Prof. of Economic Science, Univ. of Liverpool 33-47; Prof. of Political Economy, Univ. Coll., London Univ. 47-67; Temp. Asst. Sec. Board of Trade 40-44, Temp. Counsellor, Foreign Office Sept. 45-April 46; mem. various Govt. Cttees. 44- (mem. Monopolies

and Restrictive Practices Comm. 50-62); Pres. Economic Section, British Asscn. 50; Dir. Anglo-Nippon Trust 64-68; mem. Acad. Planning Board, new Univ. of Ulster 65-70; Order of the Rising Sun 3rd Class (Japan); Fellow British Acad.; Vice-Pres. Royal Econ. Soc., Econ. Research Council; Hon. Fellow, School of Oriental and African Studies, Univ. of London; Trustee, Inst. of Econ. Affairs.
Leisure interests: water-colour painting, literature.
Publs. *Modern Japan and its Problems* 28, *The Industrial Development of Birmingham and the Black Country* 29, *British Industries and their Organisation* 33, (6th revision 70), *Japan*, *The Hungary Guest* 38, *A Short Economic History of Japan* 46 (revised 72), *Japan's Economic Recovery* 58, part-author of *The Industrialisation of Japan and Manchukuo* 40, *Western Enterprise in Far Eastern Economic Development* 54, and of *Western Enterprise in Indonesia and Malaya* 57, *The Structure of Industry in Britain* 61 (revised 70), *Japan's Economic Expansion* 65, *Japan as a Market and Source of Supply* 67, *Japan's Place in Trade Strategy* 68, *Monopoly and Restrictive Practices* 68.
Flat 15, Sunnymeade House, 380 Banbury Road, Oxford, England.

Allen, Joseph P., IV; American astronaut; b. 27 June 1937, Crawfordsville, Ind.; *m.* Bonnie Jo Darling; ed. DePauw Univ. and Yale Univ.
Former Research Assoc., Univ. of Washington, Seattle; selected by NASA as scientist-astronaut 67-; mem. staff President's Council for Int. Econ. Policy 73.
NASA Spacecraft Center, Houston, Tex. 77058, U.S.A.

Allen, Percy B., M.P.; New Zealand politician; b. 1913, Auckland, New Zealand; one *s.* one *d.*; ed. Te Aroha and Rotorua.
Served in Second World War, demobilized 45, Major; Deputy Chair. Rotorua Branch of Nat. Party; M.P. Bay of Plenty 57-; Minister of Works and Minister in Charge of Police 63-69; Minister of Works and of Electricity 69-72, of Works and Police 72; Chair. Nat. Roads Board, Nat. Water Authority, New Zealand Gas Council.
Ministry of Works, Wellington, New Zealand.

Allen, Sir Peter Christopher, Kt., M.A., B.SC.; British industrial chemist and business executive; b. 8 Sept. 1905, Ashtead, Surrey; *s.* of the late Sir Ernest King Allen and Florence Mary (née Gellatly); *m.* 1st Violet Sylvester Wingate-Saul 1931 (died 1951), two *d.*; *m.* 2nd Consuelo Maria Linares Rivas; ed. Harrow School and Trinity Coll., Oxford.
Joined Brunner, Mond and Co. (now Mond Div. of I.C.I.) 28; Man. Dir. Plastics Div., Imperial Chemical Industries (I.C.I.) 42-48, Chair. Plastics Div. 48-51, Dir. of I.C.I. 51-71, Dep. Chair. 63-68, Chair. 68-71; Pres. Canadian Industries Ltd. 59-62, Chair. 62-68; Pres. and Chair. I.C.I. of Canada Ltd. 61-68; Dir. Royal Trust Co., Canada 61-64; mem. Export Council for Europe 62-65; Vice-Chair. of Asscn. of British Chemical Manufacturers 63-65; Pres. British Plastics Federation 63-65; mem. Iron & Steel Holding and Realisation Agency 63-67; mem. British National Export Council (Chair. 70-73), Chair. Cttee. for Exports to Canada 64-67; mem. National Econ. Devt. Cttee. for Chemical Industry 64-67; Commonwealth Export Council 64-67; Pres. Chemical Industries Asscn. Ltd. 65-67; mem. Council of Confederation of British Industry 65-67; Deputy Chair. African Explosives & Chemical Industries Ltd. 68-71; Dir. ICIANZ 68-71, Bank of Montreal 68-75, British Insulated Callender's Cables 71-; Pres. Univ. of Manchester Inst. of Science and Technology 68-71; mem. Industrial Policy Group 69-72; mem. British Overseas Trade Board 72-75; Advisory Dir. New Perspective Fund 73-; Fellow, British Inst. of Management, Inst. of Dirs.; Hon. D.Tech. (Lough-

borough); Hon. Fellow, Trinity Coll., Oxford; Gov. Harrow School.
Leisure interests: foreign travel, railways, golf, writing, philately.
Publs. *The Railways of the Isle of Wight* 28, *Locomotives of Many Lands* 54, *On the Old Lines* 57, *Narrow Gauge Railways of Europe* (with P. B. Whitehouse) 59, *Steam on the Sierra* (with R. A. Wheeler) 60, *Round the World on the Narrow Gauge* (with P. B. Whitehouse) 66, *The Curve of Earth's Shoulder* (with Consuelo Allen) 66, *Rails in the Isle of Wight* (with A. B. MacLeod) 67, *Famous Fairways* 68, *Play the Best Courses* 72.
Telham Hill House, Battle, Sussex, England.

Allen, Raymond Bernard, M.D., PH.D.; American educationist; b. 7 Aug. 1902, Cathay, N.D.; *s.* of Anthony James Allen and Ellen Faulkner; ed. Univ. of Minnesota and the Mayo Foundation.
Assoc. Dean in charge of Graduate Studies, Coll. of Physicians and Surgeons, Columbia Univ. 34-36; Assoc. Dir. N.Y. Post-Graduate Medical School and Hospital, Columbia Univ. 33-36; Dean, Wayne Univ. Coll. of Medicine 36-39; Exec. Dean, Chicago Colls. of Univ. of Illinois 39-46, Dean, Coll. of Medicine 43-46; Pres. Univ. of Washington, Seattle 46-52; Dir. Psychological Strategy Board 52; Chancellor, Univ. of California, Los Angeles 52-59; Dir. U.S. Operations Mission to Indonesia 59-61; Chief, Office of Research Co-ordination, Pan American Health Org., Washington 62-65, Office of Health and Population Dynamics 65-67; Consultant, Health-Educ., Population Dynamics 67-; Consultant on Research, Office of Population, U.S. AID 69-71; Consultant to Asia Foundation 71-.
Publs. include *Medical Education and the Changing Order*.
14136 Wadsworth Court, Annandale, Va. 22003, U.S.A.

Aller, Lawrence Hugh, M.A., PH.D.; American astronomer; b. 24 Sept. 1913, Tacoma, Wash.; *s.* of late Leslie E. Aller and late Lena B. Aller; *m.* Rosalind Duncan Hall 1941; two *s.* one *d.*; ed. Univ. of Calif., Berkeley, and Harvard Univs.
Society of Fellows, Harvard Univ. 39-42; Asst. Prof. Indiana Univ. 45-48; Assoc. Prof. Univ. of Michigan 48-54, Prof. 54-62; Prof. of Astronomy, Univ. of Calif., Los Angeles 62-; Visiting Prof. Australian Nat. Univ. 60-61, Univ. of Toronto 61-62, Univ. of Sydney 68, Univ. of Tasmania 69; Guest Investigator, Mount Wilson Observatory 46-; mem. Nat. Acad. of Sciences; Fellow, American Acad. of Arts and Sciences.
Leisure interests: photography, travel.
Publs. *Atoms, Stars and Nebulae* (with Leo Goldberg) 42 (revised edn. 71), *Atmospheres of Sun and Stars* 53, 63, *Nuclear Transformations, Stellar Interiors and Nebulae* 54, *Gaseous Nebulae* 56, *Abundance of Elements* 61.
Astronomy Department, University of California, Los Angeles, Calif. 90024, U.S.A.
Telephone: (213) 825 3515.

Allerslev Jensen, Erik; Danish library director; b. 22 May 1911; ed. Danish Library School.
Assistant Librarian, Frederiksberg Public Library 33-37; Head of Dept. of Printed Catalogue Cards, State Inspectorate for Public Libraries 37-42; Dir. Danish Library Bureau 42-46; Dep. Dir. State Inspection of Public Libraries 46-59, Dir. 60-; Dir. Danish Library School 46-56; Dir. School of Advanced Library Studies, Gothenburg 58-68.
Publs. *Dansk Bogfortegnelse* (The Danish National Bibliography) 35-60, *Decimal-Klassedeling* (Decimal Classification), 4th Edition, 54, *Lærebog i Biblioteksteknik* (Manual of Library Economy), 4th Edition, 59, *Dansk bibliotekslitteratur* (Danish Library Literature: A Bibliography) 50, *Biblioteker og Læsning* (Libraries and Reading) 6 vols. 56-64, *Skrifter udsendt af den Nordiske Fortsættelsesskole for Bibliotekarer* (Publs. from the

Scandinavian Library School in Gothenburg) 4 vols.
60-62, *Biblioteksstudier* (Library Studies) 7 vols. 63-70;
Editor *Reol* (Scandinavian Library Journal) 62-67;
Editor *Scandinavian* (Public Library Quarterly) 68-73.
State Inspection of Public Libraries, Niels Juels Gade 5,
DK 1059 Copenhagen K, Denmark.
Telephone: (01) 13 46 33.

Ailey, Col. Alphonse; Benin army officer and poli-
tician; b. 9 April 1930, Bassila; *s.* of Amadou Alley
and Amina Akim; *m.*; six *c.*; ed. primary schools at
Lomé, Togo, secondary school in Senegal, and military
colls. in France and Ivory Coast.
Joined 5th Senegalese Rifle Regt., Dakar; served in
Indo-China 50-53, Morocco 55-56, Algeria 59-61;
returned to Dahomey 61; Second-Lieut. Dahomeyan
Army 61, Capt. 62, Major 64, Lieut.-Col. 67, Chief of
Staff 67; Pres. of Dahomey Dec. 67-68; Sec.-Gen. for
Nat. Defence 70-72; arrested Feb. 73, sentenced to
twenty years' detention.
Leisure interests: all forms of sport.
Carré 181-182, B.P. No. 48, Cotonou, Benin.

Alliali, Camille; Ivory Coast lawyer and diplomatist;
b. 23 Nov. 1926; *m.*; five *c.*; ed. Dakar Lycée and Lycée
Champollion, Grenoble.
Former Advocate, Court of Appeal, Abidjan; Press Sec.
Parti Démocratique de la Côte d'Ivoire 59-, Deputy
58-60; Vice-Pres. Nat. Assembly, Ivory Coast 57-60;
Senator of French Community 59-61; Amb. to France
61-63; Perm. Del. UNESCO 61-63; Minister of Foreign
Affairs 63-66; Minister of Justice 66-; Commdr. Légion
d'Honneur and many other decorations.
Ministry of Justice, Abidjan, Ivory Coast.

Allibone, Thomas Edward, C.B.E., PH.D., D.SC., D.ENG.,
F.I.E.E., F.A.M.I.E.E., F.R.S.; British scientist; b. 11 Nov.
1903, Sheffield; *s.* of Henry James and Eliza Allibone;
m. Dorothy Margery Boulden, L.R.A.M., A.R.C.M. 1931;
two *d.*; ed. Sheffield and Cambridge Univs.
High Voltage Laboratory, Metropolitan Vickers Co.
30-44; Univ. of California (British team, Atomic
Bomb) 44-45; Dir. Research Laboratory, Associated
Electrical Industries, Aldermaston 46-63; Scientific
Adviser to A.E.I. Ltd. 63; Dir. Assoc. Elec. Industries
(Woolwich) Ltd. 50-63; Chief Scientist, Central Elec-
tricity Generating Board 63-70; External Prof. of Elec-
trical Engineering, Leeds Univ. 67-; Visiting Prof. of
Physics, City Univ. 71-; Vice-Pres. Inst. Physics 48-52;
Chair. Research Cttee., Electrical Research Asscn.
55-62; Vice-Pres. Royal Inst. 55-57, 69-; mem. Council,
Physical Soc. 53-57, Council of Inst. of Electrical
Engineers 37-53, Advisory Council, Royal Mil. Coll.,
Shrivenham; Pres. Section A British Asscn. 58, Inst. of
Information Scientists 67-69; Trustee, British Museum
68-.
Leisure interests: history, archaeology, gardening,
handicrafts.
Publs. *High Voltage Electrical Phenomena and Thermo-
nuclear Reactions, Release and Use of Atomic Energy,
Rutherford, the Father of Nuclear Energy, The Royal
Society and its Dining Clubs.*
York Cottage, Lovel Road, Winkfield, Windsor,
England.
Telephone: Winkfield Row 4501.

Allis, William Phelps; American physicist; b. 15 Nov.
1901, Menton, France; *s.* of Edward Phelps Allis, Jr.
and Amédine (Sgrena) Allis; *m.* Nancy Olive Morison
1935; two *s.* one *d.*; ed. Massachusetts Inst. of Technology, Univ. of Nancy (France), Princeton Univ. and
Univ. of Munich.
Member of Physics Faculty, Massachusetts Inst. of Technology 25-, Prof. of Physics 50-67, Prof. Emer. 67-; on
staff, Radiation Laboratory, Office of Scientific Research and Devt. 40-42; Consultant, Los Alamos
Scientific Laboratory 52-; Asst. Sec.-Gen. for Scientific
Affairs, NATO 62-64; Vice-Pres. American Acad. of

Arts and Sciences 60-62; U.S. Army 42-45; Visiting
Prof., Harvard Univ. 60; Visiting Fellow, Oxford Univ.
68; Exchange Prof., Univ. de Paris-Sud 69, 72, 74;
Visiting Prof., Middle East Technical Univ. 70, Univ.
of South Florida 71, Instituto Tecnico de Electrónica,
Lisbon, Univ. of Western Ontario 73; Fulbright Senior
Lecturer Univ. of Innsbruck, Austria 74-75; Fellow,
American Physical Soc., American Asscn. for the Ad-
vancement of Science, American Acad. of Arts and
Sciences, Inst. of Physics (London), Royal Soc. of Arts;
Legion of Merit (U.S.A.) 45; Légion d'Honneur (France)
69.
Leisure interests: climbing, skiing, canoeing, opera.
Publs. *Thermodynamics and Statistical Mechanics* 52,
Nuclear Fusion 60, *Waves in Anisotropic Plasmas* 63,
Electrons, Ions and Waves 67.
Massachusetts Institute of Technology, Cambridge,
Mass. 02139; Home: 33 Reservoir Street, Cambridge,
Mass. 02138, U.S.A.
Telephone: 617-876-7535.

Allison, Rt. Rev. Sherard Falkner, D.D., LL.D.; British
ecclesiastic; b. 19 Jan. 1907; *s.* of Rev. W. S. Allison; *m.*
Ruth Hills 1936; one *s.* (and one *s.* deceased) two *d.*; ed.
Jesus Coll. and Ridley Hall, Cambridge.
Curate, St. James's, Tunbridge Wells 31-34; Chaplain,
Ridley Hall, Cambridge 34-36; Vicar, Rodbourne
Cheney, Swindon 36-40, Erith 40-45; Principal, Ridley
Hall 45-50; Bishop of Chelmsford 51-61, of Winchester
and Prelate of the Order of the Garter 61-74.
Leisure interests: sailing, water-colour sketching, bird-
watching.
Winton Lodge, Aldeburgh, Suffolk, England.
Telephone: Aldeburgh 2485.

Allmand, Warren, B.A., B.C.L.; Canadian politician;
b. 19 Sept. 1932, Montreal; *m.* Patricia Burns 1966;
two *s.* one *d.*; Loyola Coll., St. Francis Xavier, McGill
and Paris Univs.
Admitted to Quebec Bar 58; practised law 58-66; part-
time Lecturer in Political Science and Commercial Law
62-65; mem. Parl. for Notre-Dame-de Grâce 65-; mem.
several Parl. Standing Cttees.; Solicitor-Gen. 72-75;
Liberal.
3522 Connaught Avenue, Montreal, Quebec, Canada.

Allon, Brig.-Gen. Yigal; Israeli soldier, agriculturalist
and politician; b. 10 Oct. 1918, Kfar Tabor, Lower
Galilee; *m.* one *s.* one *d.*; ed. Kaduri Agricultural Coll.,
Univs. of Jerusalem and Oxford.
Joined Hagana 31, Commdr. of Palmach Company 41,
in Syria and Lebanon with Allies, Dep. Commdr.,
Palmach 43, Commdr.-in-Chief, Palmach 45-48; charged
with Hagana operations in Palestine 45-47, in command,
Upper Galilee, Central Israel, Jerusalem Corridor, the
Negev and N. Sinai 47-48; Maj.-Gen. (Reserves) Zahal
(Israel Defence Forces); Mem. and Co-Founder Kib-
butz Genossar 37-; Minister of Labour 61-67; Deputy
Prime Minister 67-, Minister for Immigrant Absorption
67-69, of Educ. and Culture 69-74, of Foreign Affairs
June 74-; mem. Exec. Cttee. Hakibbutz Hameuchad;
fmr. Sec.-Gen. Achduth Ha-avodah Socialist Party;
mem. Labour Party and Labour-Mapam Alignment;
mem. 3rd, 4th, 6th and 7th Knessets.
Publs. *The Story of Palmach* 51, *Curtain of Sand* 60, *The
Making of Israel's Army* 70, *The Shield of David* 70,
Three Wars and One Peace.
Jewish Quarter, Old City, Jerusalem; Home: Kibbutz
Genossar, Israel.

Allott, Gordon Llewellyn, B.A., LL.B.; American
lawyer and politician; b. 2 Jan. 1907, Pueblo, Colo.; *s.*
of late Leonard J. Allott and Bertha Louise Allott; *m.*
Welda O. Hall 1934; two *s.*; ed. Univ. of Colorado.
Admitted to Colorado Bar; practised law in Lamar,
Colorado; District Attorney, Prowers County 46-48;
active in Young Republican League of Colorado 35-40;
Gen. Counsel, Young Republican Nat. Fed. 38-41,

Chair. 41-46, mem. Exec. Cttee. 46-49; served army 42-46; Lieut.-Gov. of Colorado 50-54; U.S. Senator from Colorado 55-73; Senate Chair., Republican Party Cttee. 69-73; U.S. del. to the UN 61; mem. Inter-Parl. Union 56-73, Vice-Chair. 58-66; mem. Gen. Advisory Comm. to the U.S. Arms Control and Disarmament Agency 74-.
Leisure interests: fishing, swimming, reading, music.
560 Capitol Life Center, Denver, Colorado 80203; Home: 3427 South Race Street, Englewood, Colorado 80110, U.S.A.
Telephone: 534-7414 (Office); 761-1777 (Home).

Almeida, Dr. Bernardo V.M. de, Count of Caria, c.b.e., dr.iur.; Portuguese business executive; b. 1912; ed. Pedro Nuñes High School and Univ. of Lisbon.
Vice-President, C. Santos S.A.R.L. 34-, Vidago, Melgaço & Pedras Salgadas S.A.R.L.36-; Man. Dir. Supersumos Lda. 59; mem. Board Siderurgia Nacional S.A.R.L. 60, Banco Pinto & Sotto Mayor 60; mem. Fiscal Board Companhia de Papel do Prado 60; mem. Board Associação Industrial Portuguesa 58; Pres. Associação Commercial de Lisboa 59-64; mem. Tribunal Tecnico 2da Instancia Aduaneiro.
Rua Rosa Araújo 8-2°, Lisbon, Portugal.

Almeida, Gen. Pedro Geraldo de; Brazilian army officer and administrator; b. 1901, Rio de Janeiro; s. of Marieta de Azevedo Almeida; m. Isabel Setembrino de Carvalho Almeida 1927; one s. one d.; ed. Military School, Realengo.
Assistant Instructor Realengo Military School 32-36. Head of Artillery Section 37-38; Brazilian Military Attaché Uruguay 38-41; Asst. to Dep. Chief of Army Staff 41-44; Cavalry Commdr. and mem. War Ministry Cabinet 44-50; Head of Military Comm. to U.S. 51-53; Commdr. Artillery School Regiment 53-55; Head of Chief Army Staff Cabinet 55-59; Commdr. Artillery Div. 59-60; Head Rio de Janeiro Military Coll. 60-61; Head Military Cabinet of the Presidency and Commdr. Military Region 61; Head Agulhas Negras Military Acad. 62; Exec. Dir. Brazilian Section of Interamerican Council for Commerce and Production (CICYP) 63-.
Office: Avenue Rio Branco, 50-5°, Rio de Janeiro; Home: Rua Gustavo Sampaio, 390/804, Rio de Janeiro, Brazil.
Telephone: 23-50-55 (Office); 237-96-16 (Home).

Almeida Costa, Mário Julio de, ll.d.; Portuguese lawyer; b. 20 Oct., Vagos-Aveiro; s. of Silvério dos Santos Costa and Maria Júlia de Almeida Costa; m. Maria da Soledade 1953; two s. one d.
Professor of Law Coimbra Univ. 52-67; Prof., Econs. Coll., Oporto 62-67; Prof. Int. Faculty for Teaching of Comparative Law, Strasbourg 67; Minister of Justice 67-73; Pres. Corporative Chamber 73; Deputy Gov. Bank of Portugal; Grand Cross Order of Christ (Portugal), Order of Cruzeiro do Sul (Brazil).
Leisure interests: reading, sports, music.
Avenida Infante Santo 15-7°, E-Lisbon 3, Portugal.
Telephone: 679135.

Almeyda Medina, Clodomiro; Chilean professor and politician; b. 1923, Santiago; m. Irma Cáceres; three c.; ed. Alemán High School and Faculty of Law, Univ. of Chile.
Joined Socialist Party 41; held various posts rising to Under Sec.-Gen.; Prof. of Philosophy, Teacher Training Inst., Univ. of Chile 52; Prof. of Philosophy, Popular Univ. "Valentín Latelier"; Prof. of Rural Econ., Univ. of Chile; Dir. School of Sociology, Univ. of Chile 66; Prof. of Political Sciences, Schools of Law and Political and Admin. Studies; Prof. of Dialectical Materialism, School of Sociology; mem. Central Cttee. Socialist Party; Minister of Labour 52-53, of Mines 53-61; Deputy 61-65; mem. Chilean del. to UN Gen. Assembly

70; Minister of Foreign Affairs 70-73, of Defence 73; imprisoned Sept. 73, released Jan. 75, granted political asylum in Romania.

Almogi, Yosef; Israeli politician; b. 4 May 1910, Poland; s. of Zevi and Hanna Almogi; m. Shifra Weinblatt 1934; two s.
Settled in Israel 30; mem. Kibbutz Hakovesh 30; mem. Hagana Command 33-39; with British Army 39-40; in German captivity 41-45; Gen. Sec. Haifa Labour Council, mem. Exec. Cttee. Histadrut 47-59; elected to Parl. 55; Gen. Sec. Mapai 59-61; Minister without Portfolio 61-62; Minister of Devt. and Housing 62-64; Minister of Labour 68-73; Mayor of Haifa 73-.
120 Arlozorov Street, Haifa, Israel.
Telephone: 04-640775.

Almond, Gabriel Abraham; American educator; b. 12 Jan. 1911, Rock Island, Ill.; s. of the late David and Lisa Almond; m. Dorothea Kaufmann 1937; three c.; ed. Univ. of Chicago.
Fellow, Social Science Research Council 35-36, 46; Instructor, Political Science, Brooklyn Coll. 39-42; Office of War Information, Washington 42-45, War Dept., European Theatre of Operations 45; Research Assoc., Inst. of Int. Studies, Yale Univ. 47-49, Assoc. Prof. of Political Science 49-51; Assoc. Prof. of Int. Affairs, Princeton Univ. 51-54, Prof. 54-57, Prof. of Politics 57-59; Prof. of Political Science, Yale 59-63; Prof. of Political Science, Stanford Univ. 63-, Exec. Head, Dept. of Political Science, Stanford Univ. 64-69; Consultant, Air Univ. 48, Dept. of State 50, Office of Naval Research 51, Science Advisory Board, U.S. Air Force 60-61; Fellow, American Acad. of Arts and Sciences; Pres. American Political Science Asscn. 65-66; mem. Social Science Research Council 56-, American Philosophical Soc.; Fellow, Nat. Endowment for Humanities; Overseas Fellowship, Churchill Coll., Cambridge 72-73.
Leisure interests: carpentry, swimming, bird-watching.
Publs. *The American People and Foreign Policy* 50, *The Appeals of Communism* 54; editor *The Struggle for Democracy in Germany* 49, *The Politics of the Developing Areas* 60; co-author *The Civic Culture* 63; *Comparative Politics: A Developmental Approach* 66, *Political Development* 70, *Crisis, Choice and Change* 73, *Comparative Politics Today* 74.
Stanford University, Stanford, Calif. 94305; Home: 4135 Old Trace Road, Palo Alto, Calif., U.S.A.
Telephone: 941-2302.

Almond, James Lindsay, Jr., ll.b.; American politician and lawyer; b. 15 June 1898, Charlottesville, Va.; s. of James Lindsay and Edmonia Burgess Almond; m. Josephine Minter 1925; ed. Univ. of Virginia.
Assistant Commonwealth's Attorney, Roanoake, Va. 30-33; Judge, Roanoake Hustings Court 33-46; mem. U.S. House of Representatives (Dem.) 46-48; Attorney-Gen. of Virginia 48-57; Gov. of Virginia 58-62; Judge, U.S. Court of Customs and Patent Appeals 63-73, Senior Judge 73-.
208 Wexleigh Drive, Richmond, Va. 23229, U.S.A.

Aloni, Shulamit; Israeli politician; ed. Teachers' Seminar, Hebrew Univ.
Columnist *Davar* (daily); mem. Knesset (for Labour Party until 69); formed Civil Rights List 73, Pres. 73-; Minister without Portfolio 74-75; Chair. Israel Consumers' Council.
The Knesset, Jerusalem, Israel.

Alonso, Dámaso, ph.d.; Spanish university professor and writer; b. 1898, Madrid; m. Eulalia Galvarriato (novelist) 1929; ed. Univ. of Madrid.
Former Lecturer in Spanish at Univs of Berlin, Cambridge, Stanford, California; Hunter College, N.Y.; Inst. of Int. Education, N.Y.; Columbia Univ. New York; Visiting Prof. at Yale, Johns Hopkins Univ.,

Harvard; Prof. at Centre of Historical Studies, Madrid 23-36; Prof. of Spanish Language and Literature, Valencia Univ. 33-39; Prof. of Romance Philology, Madrid Univ. 39-68; mem. Royal Spanish Acad. (Dir.), Royal Acad. of History, Madrid, Modern Humanities Research Asscn. (Pres. 60); foreign mem. Arcadia and Lincei (Rome), Crusca (Florence), American Philosophical Soc.; Corresp. mem. British Acad.; Pres. Int. Asscn. of Hispanists 62-65; Dr. h.c. (Univs. of Lima, Bordeaux, Rome, Hamburg, Oxford, Freiburg, Massachusetts, Leeds, Costa Rica and Lisbon).
Publs. Criticism: *Temas gongorinos* 27, *La Lengau poética de Góngora* 35, 50, 61, *La Poesía de San Juan de la Cruz* 46, 58, 67 (Italian trans.), *Ensayos sobre Poesía española* 44, *Vida y obra de Medrano* 48, Pt. II (with S. Reckert) 58, *Poesía Española* 50, 53, 57, 62, 68 (Portuguese, German and Italian trans.), *Seis calas en la expresión literaria española* (co-author) 51, 56, 63, *Poetas españoles contemporáneos* 52, 58, *La Primitiva Epica francesa a la luz de una "Nota Emilianense"* 45, *Estudios y Ensayos gongorinos* 55, 60, *Menéndez Pelayo, Crítico literario, De los siglos oscuros al de oro* 58, 64, *Primavera temprana de la literatura europea* 61, *Góngora y el Polifemo* 60, 61, 67, *Dos españoles del Siglo de Oro* 60, *Cuatro poetas españoles* 62, *Del Siglo de Oro a sete Siglo de siglas* 62, 68, *En Torno a Lope* 72; Poetry: *Poemas Puros* 21, *Oscura Noticia* 44, 59, *Hijos de la Ira* 44, 46, 58, 69, 73 (German and Italian trans.), *Hombre y Dios* 55, 59 (Italian trans.), *Poemas escogidos* 69; *Obras Completas I-III* 71-74; trans. of James Joyce, G. M. Hopkins and von Wartburg into Spanish.
Avenida A. Alcocer 23, Madrid 16, Spain.

Alonso-Fueyo, Sabino; Spanish university professor and newspaper editor; b. 1909.
Journalist 30-; fmr. Editor *Levante*, Valencia; fmr. Prof of Philosophy and Political Doctrine, Valencia Univ.; Editor *Arriba* 62; mem. Falange.
c/o Arriba, Avda. del Generalísimo 142, Madrid, Spain.

Alpatov, Mikhail Vladimirovitch, D.HIST. ART.; Soviet art historian; b. 10 Dec. 1902, Moscow; ed. St. Michael Secondary School, Moscow and Moscow Univ.
Lecturer, Moscow Inst. of Fine Arts and Moscow Univ. 25-, Prof. 43; mem. Acad. of Fine Arts 54; Merited Artist of R.S.F.S.R.
Publs. *Denkmäler der Ikonenmalerei* (with Oskar Wulff) 25, *Geschichte der altrussischen Kunst* (with N. Brunov) (two vols.) 32 (both in German), *Italian Art at the Time of Dante and Giotto* 39, *Essays on the History of Western Art* 64, *History of Art* (three vols.) 48-55 (all in Russian), *Russian Impact on Art* 50 (in English), *Alexander Ivanov, his Life and Work* (two vols.) 56 (in Russian), *Geschichte der Kunst* Vol. I 60, II 64 (in German), *Andrej Rublev* 62, *Il Maestro del Cremlino* 63 (both in Italian), *Die Dresdner Galerie* 66 (in German).
Surikov Institute of Fine Arts, Moscow, U.S.S.R.

Alphand, Hervé; French economist and diplomatist; b. 31 May 1907; ed. Lycée Janson de Sailly and Ecole des Sciences Politiques.
Insp. of Finances and Dir. Trade Agreements Div., Min. of Commerce 37-38; Sec.-Gen. Ministerial Cttee. of Nat. Economy 38; Financial Counsellor to Embassy Washington 40-41; Dir. of Economic Affairs French Nat. Cttee. 41-44; Dir.-Gen. French Foreign Office 45; French Amb. to OEEC; Deputy to Atlantic Council 50; mem. NATO Perm. Council 52-54; Amb. to UN 55, to U.S.A. 56-65; Sec.-Gen. French Foreign Office 65-72; retd.; Grand Officier Légion d'Honneur, Ordre Nat. du Mérite.
122 rue de Grenelle, 75007 Paris, France.
Telephone: 551-44-59.

Alport, 1st Baron, cr. 61, of Colchester; **Cuthbert James McCall Alport,** P.C., T.D., D.L.; British politician; b. 22 March 1912, Johannesburg, South Africa; s. of Prof. A. C. Alport, F.R.C.P. and Janet McCall; m. Rachel

Cecilia Bingham 1945; one s. two d.; ed. Haileybury, Cambridge Univ.
President, Cambridge Union Soc. 35; Tutor Ashridge Coll. 35-37; called to Bar; War Service 39-45; Dir. Conservative Political Centre 45-50; Conservative M.P. for Colchester 50-61; Chair. Joint East and Central African Board 53-55; Asst. Postmaster-Gen. 55-57; Parl. Under-Sec. of State, Commonwealth Relations Office 57-59, Minister of State 59-61; High Commr. to Fed. of Rhodesia and Nyasaland 61-June 63; U.K. Del. to Council of Europe, Strasbourg 64-65; Prime Minister's Special Envoy to Rhodesia 67; Fellow British Inst. of Management 67; Deputy Speaker, House of Lords 71-; Pro-Chancellor, City Univ. 72-; Deputy Lieut. of County of Essex 74.
Leisure interests: preservation and development of Colchester; family and home.
Publs. *Kingdom in Partnership* 37, *Hope in Africa* 52, *The Sudden Assignment* 65.
The Cross House, Layer de la Haye, Colchester, Essex, England.
Telephone: Layer de la Haye 217.

Alsen, Hans O.; Swedish commissioner; b. 16 Aug. 1926, Enköping.
Commissioner Uppsala 66; Under-Sec. of State, Cabinet Office 69-70; Mem. of Board Uplandsbanken 71; Pres. Kooperativa förbundet (Swedish Co-operative Union and Wholesale Soc.) 72-.
Kooperativa förbundet, Fack 104, 65 Stockholm 15, Stadsgarden 6, Sweden.

Alsop, Joseph Wright, B.A.; American journalist and author; b. 11 Oct. 1910, Avon, Conn.; s. of Joseph W. and Corinne D. (Robinson) Alsop; m. Mrs. Susan M. D. Patten 1961; ed. Groton School and Harvard Univ.
Member *New York Herald Tribune* staff, New York 32-35, Washington 36-37; author (with Robert Kintner) of syndicated column *The Capital Parade* (North American Newspaper Alliance) 37-40; Lieut.-Commdr. U.S. Navy 40, later joined Volunteer Air Force as aide to Gen. Chennault; captured by Japanese at Hong Kong, exchanged and returned to U.S.; Dir. Lend-Lease Mission to China, Chungking 42; author (with brother Stewart Alsop) of column *Matter of Fact* (New York Herald Tribune Syndicate) 46-58, sole author (*Los Angeles Times* Syndicate) 64-; Legion of Merit, Order of Cloud Banner (China).
Publs. *The 168 Days* (with Turner Catledge), *Men Around the President* (with Robert Kintner) 38, *The American White Paper* (with Robert Kintner) 40, *We Accuse* (with Stewart Alsop) 55, *The Reporter's Trade* (with Stewart Alsop) 58, *From the Silent Earth* 64.
2720 Dumbarton Avenue, N.W., Washington, D.C. 20007, U.S.A.
Telephone: 202-965-1770.

Alter, Gerald M., PH.D.; American banking official; b. 15 Dec. 1919, Mason City, Iowa; s. of William and Rebecca Alter; m. Charlotte Mae Kivo 1943; two s. one d.; ed. Harvard Univ. and Harvard Univ. Graduate School.
Former economist, U.S. Treasury, U.S. Bureau of the Budget, Commerce Dept., and Federal Reserve Board; Int. Bank for Reconstruction and Development 51-, Asst. to Economic Dir. and Chief of General Studies Div. 51-58, Economic Adviser, Dept. of Operations, W. Hemisphere 58-64, Dir. W. Hemisphere Dept. 64-69, Dir. S. America Dept. 70-72, Regional Vice-Pres. Latin America and the Caribbean 72-75, Senior Advisor to Senior Vice-Pres., Operations 75-.
Leisure interests: boating, tennis.
International Bank for Reconstruction and Development, Washington, D.C. 20433; Home: 5124 Linnean Terrace, N.W., Washington, D.C. 20008, U.S.A.
Telephone: EM2-8606.

Alvarado Puerto, Andrés; Honduran politician; b. 21 Jan. 1919, Olanchito; s. of Andrés Alvarado Meléndez and Alejandrina Puerto del Arca; m. Hazel Berther Downing Saler; five s. one d.; ed. St. Catherine's Acad., British Honduras, Instituto Saleciano San Miguel, Tegucigalpa and Universidad Autónoma de la República de México.
Under-Secretary of State, Dept. of Natural Resources 55, Sec. of State 56; Sec. of State, Dept. of Foreign Affairs 57; Pres. Exec. Council, Liberal Party of Honduras 62; Deputy to Nat. Congress 65; Man. Honduras Cotton Co-operative; Minister of Foreign Affairs 71-72; del. to various int. confs.; decorations from Honduras, Argentina, Brazil, Chile, Ecuador Egypt, Guatemala, Mexico, Netherlands, Panama, Peru, Taiwan, Vatican and Venezuela.
Publ. *Corte Centroamericana de Justicia.*
c/o Secretaria de Relaciones Exteriores, Tegucigalpa, D.C., Honduras.

Alvarez, Luis Walter, S.B., S.M., PH.D., SC.D.; American physicist; b. 13 June 1911; ed. Univ. of Chicago.
Research Associate, Instructor, Asst. Prof., and Assoc. Prof., Univ. of California 36-45, Prof. of Physics 45-; Assoc. Dir. Lawrence Radiation Laboratory 54-59; Pres. American Physical Soc. 69; Collier Trophy 46, Medal for Merit 47, John Scott Medal and Prize 53, Einstein Medal 61, Pioneer Award of American Inst. of Electrical Engineers 63, Nat. Medal of Science 64, Michelson Award 65, Nobel Prize in Physics 68.
Lawrence Berkeley Laboratory, University of California, Berkeley, Calif. 94720, U.S.A.
Telephone: 415-843-2740.

Alvarez Tabio, Fernando; Cuban judge and diplomatist; b. 15 July 1907, Havana; ed. University of Havana.
Municipal Judge, Cuba 33-47; Court Magistrate, Province of Las Villas 47-50; Magistrate, Court of Justice, Havana 50-57, Magistrate Pres. 57-58, dismissed for political reasons 58; Justice of Supreme Court 59, and Head of Court of Constitutional and Social Guarantees 59-; Dir. Inst. for Int. Affairs and Prof. of Constitutional Law and Comparative Govt., School of Political Sciences, Univ. of Havana 62-; Perm. Rep. of Cuba to UN 64; del. to U.N. Gen. Assembly 67, 68, 69, 70.
Supreme Court of Justice, Havana, Cuba.

Alverny, Marie-Thérèse d', DR.PHIL.; French palaeographical archivist; b. 25 Jan. 1903, Boën sur Lignon, Loire; d. of André d'Alverny and Magdeleine des Colombiers de Boismarmin; ed. Univ. de Strasbourg and Univ. de Paris à la Sorbonne, Ecole nat. des Chartes and Ecole pratique des Hautes Etudes, Paris.
Librarian Bibliothèque nationale 28, Asst. Keeper of MSS. 47-62; Prof. Centre of Higher Studies of Mediaeval Civilization, Univ. of Poitiers 57-; Maître de Recherche, Centre national de la Recherche scientifique (CNRS) 63-66, Dir. of Research 67-; Gen. Sec. Bibliographical Comm., Int. Union of the History of Sciences; Co.-Dir. *Archives d'Histoire doctrinale et littéraire du Moyen-Age* 54; mem. Editorial Cttee. *Scriptorium* 66-, *Manuscripta* 68-, *Vivazium* 74; mem. Soc. of Ecole Nat. des Chartes (Pres. 65-66), Soc. of Latin Studies and Int. Cttee. of Palaeography; Corresp. mem. Mediaeval Acad. of America, American Philosophical Soc., Acad. of Humanities of Barcelona and British Acad.; Chevalier Légion d'Honneur; Red Cross War Medal; Dr. h.c. (Oxford).
Leisure interest: gardening.
Publs. *La Sagesse et ses sept filles: Recherches sur les Allégories de la Philosphie et des Arts libéraux IXe-XIIe siècle* 46, *Catalogue général des manuscrits latins de la Bibliothèque nationale,* vols. III 52, IV 58, V 68, *Catalogues des Manuscrits Datés en Ecriture Latine,* vols. II 62 and III 74, *Deux traductions latines du Coran au Moyen Age* 48, *Marc de Tolède, Traducteur d'Ibn Tumart* 50-51, *Avicenna latinus* in vols. 62-, *Alain de Lille, Textes inédits, avec une introduction sur sa vie et ses oeuvres* 65, *Al-Kindi, De Radiis* 75.
Centre National de la Recherche Scientifique, 40 avenue d'Iéna, Paris 75116; Homes: 58 rue de Vaugirard, Paris 6e; and Clérac, par Meyrannes (Gard), France.
Telephone: 548-09-03 (Paris home).

Alzamera, Carlos; Peruvian diplomatist; b. 1926; m. Joined Ministry of Foreign Affairs 43, Foreign Service 49; served in missions to Bolivia, Brazil, Ecuador, Italy, OAS, Paraguay, U.S.A.; Under-Sec. for Econ. and Integration Affairs, Ministry of Foreign Affairs 69-71; Amb. and Perm. Rep. to UN Office in Geneva 72-75, to UN, New York Nov. 75-; mem. dels. to several sessions of Gen. Assembly incl. sixth and seventh special sessions, to ECOSOC, Conf. of Cttee. on Disarmament, UNCTAD III; head of dels. to various int. confs. on devt., of Group of 77, and on non-alignment.
Permanent Mission of Peru to the United Nations, 301 East 47th Street, Room 16A, New York, N.Y. 10017, U.S.A.

Amado, Jorge; Brazilian novelist; b. 10 Aug. 1912, Itabuna, Bahia; s. of João Amado de Faria and Eulalia Leal Amado; m. Zelia Gattai 1945; one s. one d.
Calouste Gulbenkian Prize, Acad. du Monde Latin 71.
Publs. include: *Mar Morto, Jubiabá, The Violent Land, São Jorge dos Ilheus, Cacau, Suor, Capitães da Areia, ABC de Castro Alves, Bahia de Todos os Santos, O Amor do Soldado, Seara Vermelha, O Cavaleiro da Esperança, O Mundo da Paz, Os subterrâneos da Liberdade, Gabriela Cravo e Canela, Os velhos marinheiros, Os pastores da noite, Dona Flor e seus dois maridos! Tenda dos Milagres, Tereza Batista Cansada de Guerra.*
Leisure interests: reading, gardening, cats, poker.
Rua Alagoinhas 33, Rio Vermelho-Salvador, Bahía, Brazil.
Telephone: 80362.

Amaldi, Edoardo, PH.D.; Italian physicist; b. 5 Sept. 1908; ed. Rome Univ.
Professor, Gen. Physics Rome Univ.; Vice-Pres. Istituto Nazionale di Fisica Nucleare; mem. Accademia Naz. dei Lincei, Royal Soc. of Sciences of Uppsala, U.S.S.R. Acad. of Sciences; Hon. mem. Royal Inst. of Great Britain, Nat. Acad. of Sciences of U.S.A., Royal Soc. (U.K.); Hon. D.Sc. (Oxford Univ.) 74, etc.
Publs. various papers on atomic and nuclear problems.
University of Rome, Piazzale delle Scienze 5, Rome, Italy.

Amatayakul, Manu, DR. PHIL., DR. RER. POL., DIPL. JUR.; Thai diplomatist and barrister-at-law; b. 1912, Bangkok; s. of H.E. Phya Amatayabongse and Khunying Tanom; m. Tuangratana Amatayakul 1947; two s.; ed. Bar Law School, Thailand, Chulalongkorn Univ., Univ. of Berlin and Univ. of Berne.
Lecturer in Public Finance, Econs., Journalism, Chulalongkorn Univ., lecturer in Int. Law, Thammasat Univ. 42-47; Sec.-Gen. and Alt. Rep. Thai Perm. Del. to UN 49-50; Dir.-Gen. of UN Dept., Ministry of Foreign Affairs 53-59; Prof. of Int. Relations, Chulalongkorn Univ. 55-58; mem. Thai Del. to UN Gen. Assembly 53, 58, 61; mem. Civil Aviation Board of Thailand 53-59; Amb. to U.S.S.R. 59-63, to Spain 63-65; Dir.-Gen. of Treaty and Legal Dept., Ministry of Foreign Affairs 65-70; Legal Adviser to Prime Minister 69-70; Amb. to Brazil and Peru 70-71, to Italy 75-; Special Grand Cordon of Most Noble Order of Crown of Thailand 65, and other decorations.
Leisure interest: photography.
Publs. *Umwandlung der Währungspolitik Europas von 1918-1939, Kreditpolitik Europas, United Nations,* and other works.
69 Prongchai Road, Mahamek, Bangkok, Thailand.
Telephone: 862427.

Amaury, Emilien; French editor and advertising manager; b. 5 March 1909, Etampes; *m.* Geneviève Aubin; ed. Univ. de Paris.
Founder, Office de Publicité Générale; creator of resistance movement called Groupe de la Rue de Lille during occupation; Perm. mem. Féd. de la Presse Clandestine during occupation; Dir. Agence Havas after liberation; Founder and Man. *Carrefour*; Pres. and Founder *Parisien Libéré* 66-, and several provincial journals; Pres. Syndicat de la Presse Hebdomadaire Parisienne, Comité National Intersyndical de la Presse Périodique Française; Grand Officer de la Légion d'Honneur, Croix de Guerre, Rosette de la Résistance.
114 avenue des Champs Elysées, 75008 Paris, France.

Ambartsumyan, Victor Amazaspovich; Soviet astrophysicist; b. 18 Sept. 1908, Tbilisi; ed. Leningrad Univ. and Pulkovo Observatory.
Lecturer and research worker Leningrad Univ. 31-43; Prof. Astrophysics Erevan Univ. 47-; Corresp. mem. U.S.S.R. Acad. of Sciences 39-53, mem. 53-; mem. C.P.S.U. 40-; founder and Dir. Byurakan Astrophysics Observatory 45-; Pres. Armenian Acad. of Sciences 47-; Vice-Pres. Int. Astronomical Union 48-55, Pres. 61-64; Past Pres. Int. Council of Scientific Unions (ICSU) 69; Deputy Supreme Soviet U.S.S.R. 50-; mem. Foreign Affairs Comm., Soviet of Union; mem. Central Cttee. Communist Party of Armenia; specialist on problems of stellar cosmogony; corresp. mem. French Acad. of Sciences; German Acad. of Sciences (Berlin); Hon. mem. American Acad. of Arts and Sciences; foreign assoc. U.S. Nat. Acad. of Sciences 59; Foreign mem. Royal Soc. 69; State Prize 46, 50; Hero of Socialist Labour, Hammer and Sickle Gold Medal, four Orders of Lenin, two Orders of Red Banner of Labour.
Publs. *Teoroticheskaya astrofizika* 39, *Evolyutsiya zvezd i astrofizika* 47, *Novyi sposob rascheta rassejania sveta v mutnoi srede* 42, *O rasseyaniis sveta atmosferami planet* 42, *K voprosu o diffusnom otrazhenii sveta mutnoi sredoi* 43, *Nauchnye Trudy* (2 vols.) 60.
Academy of Sciences of Armenian S.S.R., 24 Ulitsa Barekamutyan, Erevan, U.S.S.R.

Ambrière, Francis; French writer and journalist; b. 27 Sept. 1907; ed. Univs. of Dijon and Paris.
Before Second World War was Ed. *Nouvelles Littéraires* and dramatic critic *Mercure de France*; served in French Army in Second World War; prisoner in Germany and Poland; Dir. of *Guides Bleus* 45-72; Prés.-Dir. Gén. of *L'Université des Annales* 47-72; dramatic critic of monthly *Les Annales*; Vice-Pres. of Jury, Prix Albert-Londres 72-; Officer Légion d'Honneur, Commdr. des Arts et Lettres, Officer Order of Cedar (Lebanon), Order Polonia Restituta.
Publs. *La Vie Secrète des Grands Magasins* 32 (revised 38), *Le Favori de François Ier* 36, *Les Grandes Vacances* (Prix Goncourt 46), *Le Solitaire de La Cervara* 47, *La Galerie Dramatique* 49, *Le Maroc* 52.
15 rue Sainte Geneviève Bonvillers, 60 Cauvigny, France.

Ameling, Elly; Netherlands opera singer; b. Rotterdam.
Studied singing with Jo Bollekamp, with Jacoba and Sam Dresden, and with Bodi Rapp; studied French art song with Pierre Bernac; has given recitals in Europe, South Africa, Japan; debut in U.S.A. 68, annual tours of U.S.A. and Canada 68-; has sung with Concertgebouw, New Philharmonic Orchestra, BBC Symphony Orchestra, Berlin Philharmonic, Cincinnati Symphony, San Francisco Symphony, Toronto Symphony, Chicago Symphony; has appeared in Mozart Festival, Washington, D.C. 74, Caramoor Festival 74, 1974 Art Song Festival, Princeton, N.J. 74; major recordings, *Mozart Concert, Handel Concert, Cantatas* (Bach), *Mörike Lieder* (Wolf), *Aimez-vous Handel?, Aimez-vous Mozart?, Christmas Oratorio* (Bach), *Symphony No. 2* (Mahler),

Te Deum (Bruckner), *Italienisches Liederbuch* (Wolf); First Prize, Concours Int. de Musique, Geneva; Grand Prix du Disque, Edison Prize, Preis der Deutschen Schallplattenkritik, Stereo Review Record of the Year Award; Knight Order of Orange-Nassau.
c/o Mr. Silvio Samomar, Concert Directie Dr. G. de Koos & Co., Houtweg 11, Laren N.H., Netherlands.

Amelko, Admiral Nikolai Nikolayevich; Soviet naval officer; b. 22 Nov. 1914, Leningrad; ed. Frunze Higher Naval School and Acad. of General Staff.
Naval service 33-; Commdr. of ships, Baltic Fleet 37-41; Commdr. of ship formation 41-46; Chief of Staff, Pacific Fleet 56-62; Commdr. Pacific Fleet 62-69; Deputy C.-in-C. of U.S.S.R. Navy 69-; Alt. mem. Central Cttee. of C.P.S.U.; Deputy to U.S.S.R. Supreme Soviet 66-.
U.S.S.R. Ministry of Defence, 34 Naberezhnaya M. Thoreza, Moscow, U.S.S.R.

Amer, Subhi Ameen, M.D.; Jordanian politician; b. 1912, Hebron; *m.*; ed. American Univ. of Beirut.
Physician, Transjordan 38-46, Palestine Govt. 47-48; Dir. Govt. Hospital, Nablus 48-53; Chief Physician, Nablus District 53-57; Asst. Under-Sec. to Minister of Health 57-62; Minister of Health five times 62-67; Minister of Health, Reconstruction and Devt. Oct.-Dec. 62, 68-69; Minister of Reconstruction and Devt. 70.
Ministry of Reconstruction and Development, Amman, Jordan.

Amerasinghe, Hamilton Shirley; Ceylonese diplomatist; b. 18 March 1913, Colombo; ed. Royal Coll., Colombo and Ceylon Univ. Coll.
Ceylon Civil Service 37; Sec. to Minister of Health, Ceylon 41-46; Resident Manager, Gal Oya Development Board 50-52; Counsellor, Washington 53-55; Controller of Establishments, General Treasury, Ceylon 55-57; Alt. Del. Ceylon Del. to UN 57; Controller of Supply, Cadre and Finance, General Treasury, Ceylon 58; Perm. Sec. to Ministry of Nationalised Services and Chair. Port (Cargo) Corpn., Colombo 58; Sec. to Treasury and Perm. Sec. Ministry of Finance 61-63; Dir. Bank of Ceylon 62-63; High Commr. of Ceylon in India 63-67; Perm. Rep. to UN 67-; Chair. UN Cttee. on Peaceful Uses of Sea Bed and Ocean Floor Beyond Limits of Nat. Jurisdiction, Special Cttee to. Investigate Israeli Practices affecting the Human Rights of the Population of the Occupied Territories. UN *ad hoc* Cttee. on the Indian Ocean, Pres. Third UN Law of the Sea Conf. 73-74.
Leisure interests: classical music, photography, tennis and riding.
Permanent Mission of Sri Lanka to the United Nations, 630 Third Avenue, New York, N.Y. 10017; Home: Apartment 155W, 5 S.W. Park Avenue, New York, N.Y. 10028, U.S.A.
Telephone: 427-9303 (Home).

Amery, Rt. Hon. Julian, M.P.; British politician; b. 27 March 1919; *s.* of the late Rt. Hon. Leopold Amery; *m.* Catherine, *d.* of Rt. Hon. Harold Macmillan (*q.v.*), 1950; one *s.* three *d.*; ed. Eton and Oxford Univ.
War Correspondent, Spanish Civil War 38-39; Attaché H.M. Legation, Belgrade, and on special missions 39-40; Sergeant R.A.F. 40-41; commissioned and transferred to Army; active service, Egypt, Palestine, Adriatic 41-42; liaison officer to Albanian Resistance 44; on the staff of Mr. Churchill's personal mission to Generalissimo Chiang Kai-Shek 45; M.P. 50-66, 69-; Under-Sec. of State for War 57-58, for Colonies 58-60; Sec. of State for Air 60-62; Minister for Aviation 62-64; Minister of Public Building and Works June-Oct. 70; Minister for Housing and Construction 70-72; Minister of State, Foreign and Commonwealth Office 72-74; Conservative.
Leisure interests: skiing, travel.
Publs. *Sons of the Eagle, The Life of Joseph Chamberlain,*

Joseph Chamberlain and the Tariff Reform Campaign 69, *Autobiography* 70, *Approach March* 73.
112 Eaton Square, London, S.W.1, England.
Telephone: 01-235-1543.

Ames, Bruce N., PH.D.; American professor of biochemistry; b. 16 Dec. 1928, New York; s. of Dr. M. U. and Dorothy Andres Ames; m. Dr. Giovanna Ferro-Luzzi 1960; two c.; ed. Cornell Univ. and Calif. Inst. of Technology.
Postdoctoral Fellow, Nat. Insts. of Health 53-54, Biochemist 54-60; Nat. Science Foundation Fellow, Labs. of F. C. Crick, Cambridge and F. Jacob, Paris 61; Chief Section of Microbial Genetics, Lab. of Molecular Biology, Nat. Insts. of Health 62-67; Prof. of Biochemistry, Univ. of Calif., Berkeley 68-; mem. Nat. Acad. of Sciences, American Acad. of Arts and Sciences; Eli Lilly Award, American Chem. Soc. 64; Arthur Flemming Award 66, Rosenstiel Award 76.
Publs. scientific papers in areas of operons, biochemical genetics, histidine biosynthesis, mutagenesis, detection of environmental carcinogens and mutagens.
University of California, Department of Biochemistry, Berkeley, Calif. 94720; Home: 1324 Spruce Street, Berkeley, Calif. 94709, U.S.A.
Telephone: (415) 642-5165 (Office).

Amiama Tió, Fernando Arturo; Dominican politician, lawyer and university professor; b. 1 May 1913, San Pedro de Macoris; s. of late Luis Amiama and of Carmen Tió Amiama; m. Lucila Troncoso de Amiama; three d.; ed. elementary and secondary school.
Ambassador in charge of Cultural Dept.; Prof. of American Int. Law, Univ. of Santo Domingo 60; Acting Sec. of State 62; Amb. in charge of Admin., Dept. of Foreign Affairs, in charge of Legal Dept. 62; Prof. Univ. Pedro Henríquez Ureña 66; Amb. in charge of UN, OAS, Int. Confs. Dept., Ministry of Foreign Affairs 66; Sec. of State for Foreign Affairs 67-70; Perm. Rep. to UN 70-72; Sec. of State without Portfolio 72; Sec. of State for the Interior and Police 74-75, for Labour 75-; decorations from Dominican Repub., Lebanon, China, Nicaragua (two), El Salvador, Chile, Mexico, Venezuela and Spain.
Publs. *Las Funciones Consulares* (2 vols.) 57, *El Centrismo Político* (essay) 64, *Acuerdos Administrativos O Ejecutivos* (series of articles).
Secretaría de Estado de Trabajo, Santo Domingo; and Avenue Francia No. 127, Santo Domingo, Dominican Republic.
Telephone: 9-0837.

Amiel, Denys; French dramatist; b. 5 Oct. 1884, Villegailhenc, Aude; nephew of Paul Lafreyre (Catholic writer); m. Cécile Postel 1909; one d.
Former Vice-Pres. Société des Auteurs et Compositeurs Dramatiques; Hon. Sec. Int. Confed. of Authors and Composers; Officier, Légion d'Honneur; Commdr. Ordre de la Couronne d'Italie; Grand Prix du Théâtre.
Leisure interests: music, theatre.
Publs. *La Souriante Madame Beudet* 21, *Le Couple* 23, *Café-Tabac* 23, *Le Voyageur* 23, *La Carcasse* 26, *M. et Mme. Un Tel* 25, *L'Image* 27, *L'Age de Fer* 30, *Décalage* 31, *Trois et une* 31, *L'Homme* 34, *La femme en fleur* 35, *Ma liberté* 37, *Famille* 38, *La Maison Monestier* 39, *Mon Ami* 43, *"1939"* 40, *Le nouvel amour* 46, *Le Manoir de Gers* 49, *La Dormeuse éveillée* 50, *Pardonnez-leur* 51, *Vivre Ensemble* 51, *Le paysan du Danube* 51, *Les Naufragées* 52, *L'Age du Feu* 53, *Nature* 54, *Le Portrait* 55, *Vedettes* 57, *Terre, Confession, Confidences* 58, *Elle et Elle* 59, *Duplicata* 60.
Domaine de la Condamine, La Gaude, Alpes Maritimes, France.
Telephone: 32-40-09.

Amies, (Edwin) Hardy; British couturier; b. 17 July 1909; ed. Brentwood School.

Trainee, W. & T. Avery, Birmingham 30-34; Man. Designer Lachasse, Farm Street, London, W.1 34-39; Intelligence Corps 39-45; Man. Dir. Hardy Amies Ltd. 46-; opened Hardy Amies Boutique Ltd. 50; Dressmaker to the Queen 55-; Design Consultant to Alexandra Overalls Ltd., Brian Manufacturing Co. Ltd., D. Byford & Co. Ltd., Cambridge Clothing Co. Ltd. (New Zealand), Clarks Ltd., Coppley Noyes & Randall Ltd. (Canada), Crockett & Jones Ltd., Daito Woollen Spinning & Weaving Co. Ltd. (Japan), Hepworths Ltd., Hooper & Harrison (Australia) Pty. Ltd., Lichfield N.Z. Ltd. (New Zealand), T. Lipson & Son Ltd. (Canada), Michelsons Ltd., The Park Lane Neckwear Co. (Canada), B. Smuts Kennedy Ltd. (New Zealand), H. J. Stotter Inc. (U.S.A.), Susan Small Ltd., Veka Inc. Ltd. (S. Africa), Clubman Shirts Ltd., Bear Brand Ltd., Star Hat Co. Ltd. (New Zealand), Phoenix Clothes (U.S.A.), Jarman Shoe Co. (U.S.A.), Enro Shirt Co. (U.S.A.), Esquire Sportswear Mfg. Corp. Ltd. (U.S.A.); Chair. Inc. Soc. of London Fashion Designers 59-60; Officier de l'Ordre de la Couronne (Belgium) 46; Royal Designer for Industry 64; numerous design awards.
Publs. *Just So Far* 54, *ABC of Men's Fashions* 64.
Hardy Amies Ltd., 14 Savile Row, London, W.1, England.
Telephone: 01-734-2436.

Amin, Mohamed El Amir; Sudanese airline official; b. 1 June 1919; ed. Gordon Memorial Coll., Khartoum. Attached to Office of Civil Sec. (now Ministry of Interior) 38-48; Chief of Booking and Freight Office, Sudan Airways 48-54, Sales Supt. Sudan Airways 54-56; Gen. Man. Sudan Airways 66-68, 72-; Adviser-Gen. 68-.
Sudan Airways, P.O. Box 253, Khartoum, Sudan.
Telephone: 77637.

Amin, Mostafa, M.A.; Egyptian journalist; b. 21 Feb. 1914, Cairo; s. of Mohamed Amin Youssef and Ratibah Zagloul; ed. American Univ. of Cairo and Georgetown Univ., U.S.A.
Began his career publishing or writing for magazines, incl. *El Raghaeb, Rose el Youssef* 28; Deputy Chief Ed. *Akher Saa* weekly magazine 34, Ed.-in-Chief 38; City Ed. *Al Ahram* daily 39-44, Diplomatic Ed. 40; Ed.-in-Chief *Al Isnain* weekly 41-44; founder *Akhbar el Yom* weekly newspaper and publishing house, jointly with his brother Ali Amin 44; mem. House of Reps. 44; purchased *Akher Saa* weekly magazine 46; founded *Akher Lahza, El Guil* 51, weekly magazines; arrested 26 times for editorial policies during 51; founded *Al-Akhbar* daily 52; published *Al Mokhtar* for Reader's Digest 56-67; Vice-Chair. Press Board 60, dismissed by Pres. Gamal Abdul Nasser 60; Chair. of Board, Dar al Hilal Publishers 61; Chair. of Board, Akhbar el Yom Publishers 62-64, Editorial Man. 64-65; arrested 65, sentenced to life imprisonment 66, reprieved by Pres. Anwar Sadat 74; Ed.-in-Chief *Akhbar el Yom* May 74-.
Publs. *Laughing America* 43, *First Year in Prison*.
Dar Akhbar el Yom, 6 Sharia al-Safaha, Cairo, Egypt.

Amin, Samir, D.ECON.; Egyptian economist; b. 4 Sept. 1931, Cairo; s. of Farid and Odette Amin; m. Isabelle Eynard 1957; no c.; ed. Univ. of Paris.
Senior Economist, Econ. Devt. Org., Cairo 57-60; Technical Adviser for Planning to Govt. of Mali 60-63; Prof. of Econs., Univs. of Poitiers, Paris and Dakar; Dir. UN African Inst. for Econ. Devt. and Planning 70-.
Leisure interest: history.
Publs. *Trois Expériences Africaines de Développement, Mali, Guinée, Ghana* 65, *L'Economie du Maghreb* (2 vols.) 67, *Le développement du capitalisme en Côte d'Ivoire* 68, *Le monde des affaires Sénégalaises* 68, *Maghreb in the Modern World,* 70, *L'Accumulation à l'échelle mondiale* 70, *L'Afrique de l'Ouest bloquée* 71, *Le développement inégal* 73.

African Institute for Economic Development and Planning, B.P. 3186, Dakar, Senegal.
Telephone: 225-77.

Amin Dada, Field-Marshal Idi; Ugandan army officer and Head of State; b. 1925, West Nile; s. of late Amin Dada.
Joined King's African Rifles 46; rank of Corporal 49, Major 63, Col. 64; Deputy Commdr. of the Army 64; Commdr. of the Army and Air Force 66-70; rank of Brig-Gen. 67, Maj.-Gen. 68, promoted Field-Marshal July 75; leader of mil. *coup d'état* which deposed Milton Obote Jan. 71; Pres. and Chief of Armed Forces Feb. 71-; Minister of Defence 71-75; Chair. Defence Council 72-; Minister of Internal Affairs 73, of Information and Broadcasting 73; Chief of Staff of the Army 74-; Chair. of the OAU June 75-, presided over Kampala Summit 75, Addis Ababa Summit 76; Heavyweight Boxing Champion of Uganda 51-60; awarded eight highest mil. decorations of Uganda; Hon. LL.D. (Kampala) 76.
Office of the Head of State, Kampala, Uganda.

Amini, Ali, D.ECON. ET IUR; Iranian politician; b. 1905, Teheran; s. of Mohsen and Achraf Amini; m. Baloul Voosough 1932; one s.; ed. Ecole de Droit, Grenoble, and Faculté de Droit, Paris, France.
Alternate Judge, Court of First Instance, and Penal Branch, Court of Appeal, Teheran 31; Dir.-Gen. Dept. of Customs and Monopolies 33, Economic Section, Ministry of Finance 39; Asst. Prime Minister 40; Dir. Foreign Exchange Comm.; Deputy, 15th Legislative Session of the Majlis; Head of Narcotics Del. to Geneva and U.S.A.; Minister of Nat. Economy; Head of Iranian Trade Del. to Germany and France; Minister of Economy 52; Minister of Finance 53, of Justice 55; Ambassador to U.S.A. 56-58; Leader of Independents in general election 60; Prime Minister 61-July 62.
Publ. *L'institution du monopole de commerce extérieur en Perse.*
Park Aminodoleh, Avenue Ebnecina, Teheran, Iran.
Telephone: 39-32-32.

Amirmachmoed, Lieut.-Gen.; Indonesian army officer and politician; b. 21 Feb. 1923, Cimahi, West Java; ed. Technical School, Army Staff Coll. (SSKAD).
Several army posts 43-65, including Deputy Chief of Staff Dwikora Command I 61, Commdr. Mil. Territory X, Lambung Mangkurat, S. Kalimantan 62-65, Commdr. Mil. Territory V/Djaja 65; promoted to rank of Lieut.-Col. 57, Col. 61, Brig.-Gen. 64, Maj.-Gen. 66, Lieut.-Gen. 70; Minister of Home Affairs, Pembangunan (Devt.) Cabinet 69; Chair. of govt. body for the implementation of Act of Free Choice in W. Irian (now Irian Jaya) according to New York Agreement on Irian Jaya 69; implemented gen. elections 71; Minister of Home Affairs, 2nd Pembangunan Cabinet 73-.
Department of Home Affairs, Jalan Veteran, Jakarta, Indonesia.

Amis, Kingsley, M.A.; British author; b. 16 April 1922, London; s. of William Robert and Rosa Annie (née Lucas) Amis; m. 1st Hilary A. Bardwell 1948, two s. one d.; m. 2nd Elizabeth Jane Howard 1965; ed. City of London School and St. John's Coll., Oxford.
Lecturer in English, Univ. Coll. of Swansea 49-61; Fellow of Peterhouse, Cambridge 61-63; Visiting Fellow in Creative Writing, Princeton Univ. 58-59; Visiting Prof. of English, Vanderbilt Univ. 67-68; Somerset Maugham Award.
Leisure interests: classical music, thrillers, television.
Publs. *A Frame of Mind* 53, *Lucky Jim* 54, *That Uncertain Feeling* 55, *A Case of Samples* 56, *I Like it Here* 58, *New Maps of Hell* 60, *Take a Girl Like You* 60, *My Enemy's Enemy* 62, *One Fat Englishman* 63, *The James Bond Dossier* 65, *The Egyptologists* (with Robert Conquest) 65, *The Anti-Death League* 66, *A Look Around the Estate* (poems 1957-1967) 67, *Colonel Sun* 68 (as Robert Markham), *I Want it Now* 68, *The Green Man* 69, *What Became of Jane Austen?* 70, *Girl, 20* 71, *On Drink* 72, *The Riverside Villas Murder* 73, *Ending Up* 74, *Kipling and His World* 75.
c/o A. D. Peters, 10 Buckingham Street, London, W.C.2, England.

Amissah, John Kodwo, J.C.D., D.D., LL.D.; Ghanaian Roman Catholic ecclesiastic; b. 27 Nov. 1922, Elmina; ed. St. Peter's School, Kumasi, St. Teresa's Seminary at Amisano, St. Augustine's Coll., Pontifical Urban Univ., Rome.
Ordained as priest Dec. 49; taught at St. Teresa's Minor and Major Seminary 50-51 and 54-57; consecrated Auxiliary Bishop June 57; Archbishop of Cape Coast and Metropolitan of Ghana Dec. 59-70; Chair. first Pan-African Symposium of Catholic Episcopal Confs. Kampala 69; Chair. Gen. Assemblies 1st, 2nd and 3rd Symposiums of Episcopal Confs. of Africa and Madagascar (SECAM) 69-72; Chair. Univ. Coll. of Cape Coast 69; mem. Council of State 69-; awarded Grand Medal.
c/o Archbishop's House, P.O. Box 112, Cape Coast, Ghana.
Telephone: 042-2593.

Amit, Maj.-Gen. Meir, M.B.A.; Israeli business executive; b. 17 March 1921, Tiberias; s. of Simon and Chaya Slutsky; m. Yona Kelman 1941; three d.; ed. Columbia Univ., New York.
Member, Kibbutz Alonim 39; served in Israeli Defence Forces 48-68, sometime Head of Mil. Intelligence and Head of Israeli Security Service; Pres. Koor Industries 68-.
Leisure interests: photography, collecting toys and educational games.
Koor Building, Shderot Shaul 8, Tel-Aviv (P.O. Box 33333), Israel.
Telephone: 262392.

Ammash, Maj.-Gen. Saleh Mahdi; Iraqi soldier and politician; ed. Military Coll.
Minister of Defence Feb.-Nov. 63; C.-in-C. Supreme Defence Council of Iraq and Syria Oct.-Nov. 63; Minister of Foreign Affairs Nov. 63; mem. Revolutionary Command Council, Deputy Prime Minister and Minister of the Interior 68-70; Vice-Pres. 70-71; Amb. to U.S.S.R. 71-74, to France 74.
c/o Ministry of Foreign Affairs, Baghdad, Iraq.

Ammoun, Fouad; Lebanese politician; b. 26 Nov. 1899; ed. Beirut School of Law and Univ. de Paris à la Sorbonne.
President, Court of Appeal and of Cassation, Lebanon 35-42, Attorney-Gen. 42-43; Commr. of Govt. attached to Council of State 43-44; Joined Ministry of Foreign Affairs 44, Legal Expert 44-45 Gen. Sec. 45-56, 60-63; mem. Cttee. drafting Covenant of League of Arab States and numerous int. treaties 44-; Minister for Planning and Nat. Economy Feb.-March 64; Minister for Foreign Affairs 64-65; Judge Int. Court of Justice 65-; Vice-Pres. Int. Court of Justice 70; Chair. Lebanese Nat. Comm. UNESCO 45-55, 60-63, and Cttee. Int. Econ. Relations 60-63; mem. del. to UN seven sessions between 48-63; Cordon of the Phoenix (Greece).
Publs. several juridical articles, notably a commentary on the *Code Correctionnel Libanais* (with Ph. N. Boulos and W. El Kassar).
c/o International Court of Justice, The Hague, Netherlands.

Amory, 1st Viscount, cr. 60, of Tiverton in the County of Devon; **Derick Heathcoat Amory,** K.G., P.C., G.C.M.G.; British politician and public official; b. 26 Dec. 1899; ed. Eton Coll. and Christ Church, Oxford.
Served 39-45 war; Conservative M.P. for Tiverton Div. Devon 45-60; Minister of Pensions 51-53; Minister of State, Board of Trade 53-54; Minister of Agriculture and Fisheries July 54; Minister of Agriculture, Fisheries

and Food Oct. 54-Jan. 58; Chancellor of the Exchequer 58-60; Chair. Medical Research Council 60-61, 65-69; High Commr. for U.K. in Canada 61-63; Chair. Royal Comm. on Penal Reform 64-; Dir. Lloyds Bank 60-70, ICI Ltd. 60-61, 63-70; Deputy Gov. Hudson's Bay Co. 64-65, Gov. 65-70, Dir. 64-71; Chair. John Heathcoat and Co. 66-72; Chancellor, Exeter Univ. 72-; Hon. LL.D. (Exeter, McGill, Mount Allison and Bishop's), Hon. D.C.L. (Oxford Univ.) 74.
150 Marsham Court, Marsham Street, London, S.W.1, England.

Amouzegar, Jamshid, B.C.E., M.S., PH.D.; Iranian politician; b. 25 June 1923; ed. Univs. of Teheran, Cornell, Washington.
United Nations Expert, Mission to Iran 51; Chief, Engineering Dept. 52-55; Deputy Minister of Health 55-58; Minister of Labour 58-59, of Agriculture 59-60; Consulting Engineer 60-64; Minister of Health 64-65, of Finance 65-74, of Interior and Employment 74-; Chair. Int. Civil Service Advisory Board of UN.
Tajrish, Teheran, Iran.

Amritanand, Rt. Rev. Joseph; Indian ecclesiastic; b. 17 Feb. 1917; ed. Forman Christian Coll., Lahore and Bishop's Coll.
Ordained Deacon 41, Priest 43; Bishop of Assam 49-62; Bishop of Lucknow 62-70; Bishop of Calcutta 70-, also of Durgapur 72-74.
Bishop's House, 51 Chowringhee Road, Calcutta 700071, India.

Amsterdam, Gustave G.; American financier; b. 18 Aug. 1908; ed. Univ. of Pennsylvania.
Vice-Pres. Albert M. Greenfield & Co. 38-56; Vice-Pres. Bankers' Securities Corpn. 46-51, Exec. Vice-Pres. 51-55, Pres. 55-70, Chair. 59-; Chair. City Stores Co., Diversified Stores Co. Inc.; Pres. Benjamin Franklin Hotel Corpn., Albert M. Greenfield Foundation; Vice-Pres. Bankers' Realty Corpn., Lit Bros. Foundation. 1401 Walnut Street, Philadelphia, Pa. 19102; Home: 5209 Woodbine Avenue, Philadelphia, Pa. 19131, U.S.A.

Amuzegar, Jahangir, PH.D.; Iranian economist and politician; b. 13 Jan. 1920, Teheran; s. of Habibollah Amuzegar and Turan Azemudeh; m. Eleanor R. Horn 1958; ed. Univs. of Teheran, Washington and California.
Teaching Asst., Univ. of Calif., Los Angeles 51-53; Lecturer, Whittier Coll. 53, Univ. of Mich. 53-55; Asst. Prof. Pomona Coll., Claremont, Calif. 55-56; Asst. Prof. Mich. State Univ., E. Lansing, Mich. 56-58; Assoc. Prof. Occidental Coll. and Univ. of Calif., Los Angeles 58-60; Brookings Research Prof. 60-61; Lecturer, Univ. of Maryland 63-73; Adjunct Prof., American Univ. 75-; Econ. Adviser, Plan Org., Govt. of Iran 56-57; Minister of Commerce, Iran 61-62; mem. Council of Money and Credit 61-62, High Econ. Council 61-62; mem. Board of Dirs. Bank Melli Iran 61-62; Chair. Board, Foreign Trade Co. (Iranian Govt. Org.) 61-62; Minister of Finance 62; Chair. High Council of Nat. Iranian Oil Co. 62; Amb.-at-Large, Chief of Iranian Econ. Mission, Washington, D.C. 63-; Exec. Dir. Int. Monetary Fund 73-.
Publs. *Technical Assistance in Theory and Practice: The Case of Iran* 66, *Iran: Economic Development under Dualistic Conditions* 71, *Energy Policies of the World: Iran* 75; numerous articles in professional journals in U.S., Europe and Asia.
Iranian Economic Mission, 5530 Wisconsin Avenue, Washington, D.C. 20015; and International Monetary Fund, Washington, D.C. 20431, U.S.A.
Telephone: 654-7930; 477-5967.

Amuzegar, Kuros, M.SC., PH.D.; Iranian politician; b. 15 June 1927, Teheran; ed. Univ. of Teheran and in U.S.A.

Engineering Consultant to Karaj Dam; Technical Consultant to Planning Org.; official, Ministry of Devt. and Housing, subsequently Ministry of Labour; mem. Board of Dirs. and Man. Dir. Org. of Social Insurance; Minister of Devt. and Housing 71-74.
Ministry of Development and Housing, Teheran, Iran.

An P'ing-sheng; Chinese politician.
Provincial Cadre in Kwangtung 55, Vice-Gov. Kwangtung 56-61; Sec. Kwangsi CCP Cttee. 61-67, 71-75, First Sec. 75-; Vice-Chair. Kwangsi Revolutionary Cttee. 68-.
People's Republic of China.

Anand, Bal Krishan, M.B., B.S., M.D.; Indian physiologist; b. 19 Sept. 1917, Lahore; s. of V. D. Anand and Saraswati Anand; m. Kamla Puri 1942; one s. two d.; ed. Government Coll. and K.E. Medical Coll., Lahore.
Prof. of Physiology, Lady Hardinge Medical Coll., New Delhi 49-57, All India Inst. of Medical Sciences, New Delhi 57-; Pres. XXVI Int. Congress of Physiological Sciences, New Delhi 74; Rockefeller Foundation Fellow at Yale Univ. School of Medicine 50-51; Fellow, Indian Acad. of Medical Sciences, Nat. Inst. of Sciences (F.N.I.); Indian Council of Medical Research Senior Research Award 62; Watumull Foundation Award in Medicine 61; Sir Shanti Swaroof Bhatnagar Memorial Award for Scientific Research in Medicine 63; Padma Shri 69; Medical Council of India Silver Jubilee Research Award 69.
Leisure interests: literature, photography, tennis, hiking.
All India Institute of Medical Sciences, Ansari Nagar, New Delhi 16, India.
Telephone: 626792 (Office); 621720 (Home).

Anand, Mulk Raj, PH.D.; Indian author and critic; b. 12 Dec. 1905, Peshawar; s. of Lalchand Anand and Ishwar Kaur; m. 1st Kathleen van Gelder 1939 (divorced 1948), 2nd Shirin Vajifdar 1950; one d.; ed. Punjab and London Univs.
Active in Nationalist and Gandhi movements; lecturer, London County Council; B.B.C. broadcaster; film script writer, British Ministry of Information; edited (56) various magazines, Leverhulme Fellow for Research in Hindustani literature; Editor *Marg* magazine, India; mem. India Nat. Acad. of Letters; fmr. Tagore Prof. of Art and Literature, Punjab Univ., Chandigarh; fmr. Chair. Nat. Acad. of Art, New Delhi; Padma Bhushan 67.
Leisure interests: gardening, walking, travel.
Publs. Novels: *Morning Face, Private Life of an Indian Prince, The Big Heart, The Sword and the Sickle, Across the Black Waters, Untouchable, Coolie, The Barbers' Trade Union, Seven Summers,* etc.; Essays: *Apology for Heroism, Lines Written to an Indian Air,* etc.
Jassim House, 25 Cuffe Parade, Bombay 400005; c/o Marg Publications, Army Navy Building, Mahatma Gandhi Road, Bombay 1; Lokayata, Hauz Khas Village, New Delhi 16, India.
Telephone: Bombay 211371 (Jassim House); Bombay 252576 (Marg Publs.).

Ananian, Vakhtang Stepanovich; Soviet writer; b. 1905, Armenia.
Correspondent and later Editor *Matchkal*; full-time writing 30-; mem. C.P.S.U. 28-; Orders of Red Banner of Labour, Badge of Honour.
Publs. include: *A Chrestomathy of Hunters Stories* (7 vols.) 48-71, *At the Shore of Lake Sevan* 50 (translated into eighteen languages), *Steep Paths* 55 (translated into eight languages), *The Childhood in Mountains* 54, *The Prisoners of Leopard's Valley* 56 (translated into eleven languages), *Animal World of Armenia* Vol. I 61, II 62, III 65, IV 67, *Fatherland Mountains* 63, *Complete Works* (6 vols.) 68-71.
Erevan 15, Paronian Street 1, Floor 12, Armenian S.S.R., U.S.S.R.

Anatoli, A. (*formerly known as* Anatoli Kuznetsov); author; b. 18 Aug. 1929, Kiev, Ukraine; s. of Vasily Kuznetsov and Maria Kuznetsova; m. Irena Marchenko 1955; one s.; ed. Gorki Inst. of Literature, Moscow.
Commenced literary career at age 14 following Nazi occupation of Kiev; worked with Dnieper Hydro-Electric Scheme while also reporting and writing for a local newspaper; mem. Communist Party 55-69; mem. U.S.S.R. Union of Writers 59-69; winner of three literary competitions in Ukraine and Moscow; settled in United Kingdom 69.
Leisure interests: hiking, rowing, swimming, football, music, sightseeing; animal lover (mem. French section, Asscn. of Cat Lovers and Defenders resulting from description of cat in *Babi Yar*).
Publs. novels: *Sequel of a Legend* 57, *At Home* 64, *Babi Yar* (novel/documentary) 66, *Fire* 69; film scenarios: *We, Two Men, Encounter at Dawn*; four vols. of short stories.
c/o David Floyd, Esq., *The Daily Telegraph*, 135 Fleet Street, London, E.C.4, England.

Anclam, Kurt; German politician; b. 7 May 1918, Kowanz; m.; one c.; ed. secondary school.
Baker's apprentice, rising to master baker 32-51; Chair. People's Democratic Party Krembz group, Kr. Gadebusch 48; councillor, Krembz 48-50; mem. Freier Deutscher Gewerkschaftsbund 52; mem. and Deputy Chair. Schwerin-Land Council 52-54; mem. Schwerin Liberal Democratic Party Council 49-54; deputy to Schwerin-Land Council 50-54; deputy to Schwerin District Council 52-54; Deputy Chair. Schwerin District Liberal Democr atic Party Asscn. 51-57 mem. central cttee. 67-, mem. political sub-cttee. of central cttee. 67-; correspondence course at DASR "Walter Ulbricht" Potsdam-Babelsberg—qualified as lawyer 53-59; asst. to central cttee. of Liberal Democratic Party 54-57; Personal Adviser to Deputy Chair. of Council of Ministers 57-66; Chair. Halle District Asscn. of Liberal Democratic Party 66-; deputy to Halle District Council 67-71; mem. Halle sub-cttee. of Nat. Front 66-; Deputy to People's Chamber 54-63; Deputy Chair. sub-cttee. supervising elections 67-71; mem. Council of State; Silver and Bronze Fatherland Order of Merit, D.D.R. Medal of Merit.
Staatsrat, 102 Berlin den Marx-Engels-Platz, German Democratic Republic.

Anda, Geza; Swiss (b. Hungarian) pianist; b. 19 Nov. 1921, Budapest; s. of Géza G. and Mathilda (née von Tömösváry) Anda; m. Hortense Bührle 1964; one s.; ed. Budapest Acad. of Music.
Debut with Mengelberg 39; since then has appeared with Berlin Philharmonic, Vienna Philharmonic, New York Philharmonic, Amsterdam Concertgebouw, Philharmonia (London), Paris Conservatoire, Santa Cecilia (Rome), Philadelphia, Chicago, San Francisco Symphony Orchestras and many others; frequent soloist at Salzburg, Lucerne, Edinburgh, Vienna, Montreux and Besançon Festivals; annual appearances Royal Festival Hall, London; numerous recordings; Chevalier Ordre des Arts et des Lettres; Franz Liszt Prize 40; Grand Prix des Disques 61, 62, 63; Grand Prix des Discophiles 66; Preis der Deutschen Schallplattenkritik 66; Schallplattenpreis "Wiener Flötenuhr", Mozartgemeinde 69, 70; Hon. mem. Royal Acad. of Music 69; Ordre des Arts et des Lettres (France).
Publ. *13 Cadenzas for Piano Concertos by Mozart* 72.
Leisure interests: skiing, bookbinding.
Zollikerstrasse 178, 8008 Zürich, Switzerland.
Telephone: 55-33-35.

Anderheggen, Erwin, DR. ING. E.H.; German business executive; b. 23 Jan. 1909, Cologne; s. of Ernst and Eugenie (née Eschen) Anderheggen; m. Gerda Klinger 1962; ed. Univ. of Freiburg and Technische Hochschule, Berlin.

Engaged in copper and nickel mining in Iran 37; joined Steinkohlenbergwerk Friedrich Heinrich AG, Kamp-Lintfort 41, mem. Man. Board 51, Chair. Man. Board 56; mem. Man. Board and Planning Dir. Bergbau AG, Niederrhein (Ruhrkohle AG) 69; Chair. Man. Board, Saarbergwerke AG 72.
Publs. articles in journals.
Leisure interests: research and development, music.
6600 Saarbrücken, Trierer Strasse 1, Postfach 1030, Federal Republic of Germany.
Telephone: 405-3200.

Anders, William Alison, M.SC.; American astronaut; b. 17 Oct. 1933, Hong Kong; s. of Commdr. and Mrs. Arthur F. Anders; m. Valerie Hoard; four s. one d.; ed. U.S. Naval Acad. and Air Force Inst. of Technology, Wright-Patterson Air Force Base, Ohio.
Commissioned in the Air Force and received flight training; fighter pilot, Air Defense Command; nuclear engineer and instructor pilot, Air Force Weapons Laboratory, Kirtland Air Force Base, New Mexico; selected as astronaut by NASA 63; backup pilot for *Gemini XI* mission 66; lunar module pilot for the maiden voyage to the moon in *Apollo VIII* Dec. 68; backup command module pilot on *Apollo XI* mission 69; Exec. Sec. Nat. Aeronautics and Space Council 69-73; Commr. Atomic Energy Comm. 73-74; Chair. Nuclear Regulatory Comm. 74-.
Federal Energy Administration, Washington, D.C., U.S.A.

Andersch, Alfred; German writer; b. 4 Feb. 1914; m. Gisela Dichgans 1950; two s. one d.; ed. Wittelsbacher Gymnasium, Munich.
Spent six months in Dachau Concentration Camp as Communist Youth Leader 33; fmr. industrial worker; Editor of newspapers after Second World War (*Der Ruf, Texte und Zeichen, Studio Frankfurt*); now broadcaster and freelance writer; mem. Group 47; Deutscher Kritiker-Preis 58; Nelly Sachs-Preis 68; Prix Charles Veillon 68.
Publs. *Deutsche Literatur in der Entscheidung* (essays) 48, *Europäische Avantgarde* (anthology) 48, *Die Kirschen der Freiheit* (autobiog.) 52, *Sansibar oder der letzte Grund* (novel) 57, *San Gaetano* (narrative) 57, *Geister und Leute* (stories) 58, *Die Rote* (novel) 60, *Wanderungen im Norden* 62, *Ein Liebhaber des Halbschattens* (stories) 63, *Aus einem römischen Winter* 66, *Efraim* (novel) 67, *Hohe Breitengrade* 69, *Mein Verschwinden in Providence* (stories) 71, *Norden Süden rechts und links* (essays) 72, *Winterspelt* (novel) 74. For radio: *Strahlende Melancholie* 53, *Die Bürde des weissen Mannes, Brennpunkt Indochina* 53, *Die Feuerinsel oder Die Heimkehr des Kapitän Tizzoni* 55, *Fahrerflucht* 58, *Synnöves Halsband* 58, *Aktion ohne Fahnen* (adapted from *Sansibar oder der letzte Grund*) 58, *Der Tod des James Dean* 60, *Der Albino* 60, *Von Ratten und Evangelisten* 60, *In der Nacht der Giraffe* 60, *Biologie und Tennis* (with H. Krapp) 58, *Russisches Roulette* 61.
Berzona (Valle Onsernone), Ticino, Switzerland.
Telephone: Locarno (Switzerland) 85 12 33.

Andersen, Einar Anton, D.SC., M.SC.; Danish geodesist, mathematician and astronomer (retd.); see *The International Who's Who 1975-76*.

Andersen, Hans George, LL.B., LL.M.; Icelandic diplomatist; b. 1919, Winnipeg, Canada; s. of F. A. Andersen, C.P.A. and Thora Andersen; m. Astridur Helgadóttir 1945; one s. one d.; ed. Univ. of Iceland and Harvard Univ.
Legal Adviser, Ministry of Foreign Affairs, Lecturer, Univ. of Iceland 48-54; Ambassador to NATO 54-62, to OEEC 56-62, to France 61-62, to Sweden 62-63, to Norway 63-69; Legal Adviser, Ministry for Foreign Affairs 69-; Chair. Icelandic del. to Third UN Conf. on the Law of the Sea; Commdr. of the Order of the

Falcon (with Star); Grand Cross St. Olav (Norway), Grand Cross, Order of Merit (Italy).
Leisure interests: reading, swimming.
Ministry of Foreign Affairs, Reykjavík; Home: 5 Kvisthagi, Reykjavík, Iceland.
Telephone: 25185.

Andersen, Knud Børge, M.ECON.; Danish politician; b. 1 Dec. 1914, Copenhagen; s. of A. Chr. Andersen, cabinet-maker, and Karen Andersen; m. Grethe Trock 1943; four s.
Danmarks Radio 40-50; Teacher, Krogerup Folk High School 46-50; Headmaster, Workers' Folk High School, Roskilde 50-57; Scandinavian Folk High School, Geneva 53, 58; Adviser, Prison Education Dept. 57-64; mem. Danish Nat. Comm. for UNESCO 49-70; mem. Econ. Comm. of Labour Movement 52-; mem. Folketing 57-70, 73-; Minister of Educ. 64-68; mem. Nordic Council 62-64, 68-70, 73-75; Gen. Sec. Social Democratic Party of Denmark 70-71; Minister of Foreign Affairs 71-73, 75-; mem. Rask Ørsted Foundation 57-64; co-Editor *Verdens Gang* 53-58; Social Democrat.
Leisure interests: reading, theatre.
Publ. *Kamp og Fornyelse* (with J. O. Krag, q.v.).
Urbansgade 2, 2100 Copenhagen Ø, Denmark.
Telephone: TRIA 3301.

Andersen, Magnus Kristoffer; Norwegian politician and former fisherman; b. 20 March 1916, Andenes, Vesterålen.
Fisherman 31-55; mem. Nat. Board. Asscn. of Norwegian Fishermen 51-63, Chair. 55-63; mem. Norwegian Export Council 59-, Free Trade Comm. 61-; Chair. Lofoten Fisheries Comm. 61-; Chair. of Board, State Bank for Fishermen 69-; mem. Norwegian Agency for Int. Devt. (NORAD) 69-; mem. Parl. 65-; Minister of Fisheries Jan.-Oct. 72; Labour Party.
Youngstorget 2, Oslo, Norway.

Andersen, Mogens; Danish painter; b. 8 Aug. 1916, Copenhagen; s. of late Einar F. T. Andersen and late Erna Ingeborg, née Andersen; m. Inger Therkildsen 1947; one s. one d.; ed. in Copenhagen under art master P. Rostrup Boyesen.
Art teacher Copenhagen 52-59, Académie de la Grande Chaumière, Paris 63; mem. cttee. Danish Art Exhbn. Arrangement 56-58; mem. Royal Acad. of Fine Arts ;56 Eckersberg Medal 49, and other awards.
Exhibitions: Copenhagen 35-40, 42-50, 53-66, 67; Paris 50-74; Private Exhbns.: Copenhagen 53, 63, 66, 68, 69, Ålborg (Denmark) 54, 72, Lund (Sweden) 59, Paris 54, 59, 63, 66, 67, 73, 75, Warsaw 73, Belgrade 73, Zagreb; group exhbns. in Europe and the U.S.A.; Venice Biennale 68; paintings hung in Modern Museum, Skopje 65, and many other museums in Denmark, Sweden, Norway, Poland and U.S.A.
Major works: Composition in Niels Bohr Inst., Copenhagen 55, Mural, Central Library, Copenhagen 58-59, Composition in Central Library, Århus 63, *October*, State Art Museum 64, Mural, Gentofte Town Hall 71, Restaurante Copenhagen, Paris 73, Handelsbanken, Copenhagen 75.
Publs. *Moderne fransk malerkunst* 48, *Omkring Kilderne* 67, *Erindringer* 76.
Strandagervej 28, 2900 Hellerup, Copenhagen, Denmark.
Telephone: Hellerup 266.

Andersen, Svend, M.POL.ECON.; Danish banker; b. 26 Sept. 1915, Copenhagen; s. of Christen Andersen and Paula Ingrid, née Nielsen; m. Alice Elkiaer Hansen 1942; three s.; ed. Københavns Universitet.
Economist, Nat. Bank of Denmark 40, Chief of Secr. 50-61, Man. 61-62, Deputy Gov. 62-63, mem. Board of Govs. 63-; Economist, Int. Bank for Reconstruction and Devt. (World Bank) 46-50; mem. Boards, Deputy Chair. The Ship Credit Fund of Denmark 63-, War Risk Insurance of Danish Ships of Copenhagen and Danish War Risk Cargo Insurance of Copenhagen 63-,

Nat. Econ. Soc. 66-72; mem. Nordic Cttee. for Financial Matters 66, Chair. 66-74; Chair. Lauritz Andersens Fund 70, Monetary Cttee. of EEC 73; Knight Commdr. Order of Dannebrog.
Leisure interest: modern history.
Danmarks Nationalbank, Holmens Kanal 17, DK 1093 Copenhagen K; Home: Viggo Rothes Vej 31, DK 2920 Charlottenlund, Denmark.
Telephone: HE 2007.

Anderson, Carl David, B.S., PH.D., SC.D., LL.D.; American physicist; b. 3 Sept. 1905; ed. California Inst. of Technology.
Teaching Fellow in Physics 27-30, Research Fellow 30-33, Asst. Prof. of Physics 33-37, Assoc. Prof. California Inst. of Technology 37-39, Prof. 39-; Chair. Div. of Physics, Mathematics and Astronomy 62-; awarded gold medal of American Inst. 35, Nobel Prize for Physics 36, Elliott Cresson Medal of Franklin Inst. 37, John Ericsson Medal of American Soc. of Swedish Engineers 60; engaged in research on gamma rays and cosmic rays 30-; mem. Nat. Acad. of Sciences, American Acad. of Arts and Sciences and Amer. Philosophical Soc.
California Institute of Technology, Pasadena, Calif. 91109, U.S.A.
Telephone: 213-795-6841.

Anderson, Charles Alfred, PH.D., D.SC.; American research geologist; b. 6 June 1902, Bloomington, Calif.; s. of Amel A. Anderson and Mary Lyman; m. Helen Argall 1927; one s.; ed. Pomona Coll. and Univ. of Calif. (Berkeley).
Instructor, Univ. of Calif. 28-30, Asst. Prof. 30-38, Assoc. Prof. 38-42; U.S. Geological Survey, Washington, D.C. 42-72, Chief of Mineral Deposits Branch 53-58, Chief Geologist 59-64, Research Geologist 64-72, retd.; Pres. Soc. Econ. Geologists 68; mem. Nat. Acad. of Sciences, American Acad. of Arts and Sciences; Fellow, Geological Soc. of America, Mineral Soc. of America, American Geophysical Union; Distinguished Service Award 60, Penrose Medal, Soc. of Econ. Geologists 74.
Leisure interests: bird watching, photography.
Publs. *Tuscan Formation of Northern California* 33, *Volcanoes of Medicine Lake Highland, California* 41, *Reconnaissance survey of Roberts Mountains, Nevada* 42, *Geology of islands and neighbouring land areas, Gulf of California* 50, *Geology and ore deposits of Jerome area, Arizona* 58, *Massive sulfide deposits and volcanism* 69.
209 Northrop Place, Santa Cruz, Calif. 95060, U.S.A.
Telephone: 408-427-1554.

Anderson, Colin Bruce, M.A., B.ENG.; South African mining engineer and executive; b. 23 Oct. 1909, Benoni, Transvaal; s. of P. M. Anderson and Anne L. Hamilton; m. Eleanor Green 1941; two s. two d.; ed. King Edward VII School, Johannesburg, Caius Coll., Cambridge and McGill Univ., Montreal, Canada.
Worked as mining eng. in Canada and S. Africa 33-46; served S. African Engineering Corps, Middle East, World War II; Man. Union Corpn. Ltd. 46-68, Man. Dir. 68-72, Chair. 72-74; Hon. Life Pres., S.A. Nat. Council for the Blind; Hon. Freeman, Johannesburg 75; Chair., Soc. to Help Civilian Blind, Johannesburg; Hon. Life Pres. and mem. Witwatersrand Agricultural Soc.; Fellow, S.A. Inst. of Mining and Metallurgy; Life mem. Canadian Inst. of Mining and Metallurgy.
Leisure interests: gardening, farming, rowing, charitable work.
57 Harrow Road, Sandhurst, Sandton 2001, South Africa.
Telephone: 784-4012.

Anderson, Sir Colin (Skelton), K.B.E., Kt.; British shipowner; b. 15 July 1904, London; s. of Sir Alan Anderson, G.B.E.; m. Morna Campbell MacCormick 1932; two d.; ed. Eton and Trinity Coll., Oxford.
Former Dir. P. & O. Steam Navigation Co., Australia & N.Z. Bank; Chair. Anderson Green & Co. Ltd. 63-70;

Dir. Midland Bank Ltd. 50-74, Marine Insurance Co. Ltd. 50-70, Orient S.N. Co. Ltd. 50-70; Dir. Royal Opera House, Covent Garden Ltd. 61-73, City Arts Trust Ltd. 62-70; Chair. Nat. Asscn. of Port Employers 47-48, 50-54, I.C.C. Comm. on Sea Transport 65-71, Int. Chamber of Shipping 49-63, Hon. Pres. 63-; Chair. London Shipowners' Dock Labour Cttee. 44-45, London Port Employers (and mem. London Board of Nat. Dock Labour Board) 45-47; Pres. British Employers' Confed. 56-58 (Vice-Pres. 52-56), Chamber of Shipping of U.K. 49; mem. Royal Fine Art Comm. 59-, Chair. 68-; Chair. Trustees of Tate Gallery 60-67 (Vice-Chair. 53-59); Trustee Nat. Gallery 63-67; Chair. Contemporary Art Soc. 56-60; Provost, Royal Coll. of Art 67- (Chair. 52-56); mem. British Transport Comm. Design Panel 62-; Corresp. mem. Bavarian Acad. of Fine Arts 70-; Officer Order of Orange Nassau (Neths.); Hon. Designer of Royal Coll. of Art, Hon. Assoc. of Royal Inst. of British Architects; Hon. LL.D., Aberdeen; Hon. Fellow, Trinity Coll., Oxford.

Leisure interests: the home, the arts, the garden.

Admiral's House, Hampstead Grove, London, N.W.3, England.

Telephone: 01-435-0597.

Anderson, Eugenie Moore; American diplomatist; b. 26 May 1909, Adair, Iowa; d. of E. A. Moore and Flora McMillen Moore; m. John Pierce Anderson 1930; one s. one d.; ed. Stephens Coll., Simpson Coll., Carleton Coll., Inst. of Musical Art, New York City.

Ambassador to Denmark 49-53; Chair. Minnesota State Comm. for Fair Employment Practices 55-60; mem. Board, U.S. Cttee. for Refugees 59-60; mem. Democratic Nat. Advisory Cttee. on Foreign Policy 57-60; mem. Board of Dirs. American Asscn. for the UN 59-61; Vice-Chair. Citizens' Cttee. for Int. Devt. 61-62; Trustee, American Freedom from Hunger Foundation 62; Minister to Bulgaria 62-65; U.S. Rep. to UN Trusteeship Council and mem. U.S. Del. to UN as Amb. 65-68, Chair. Trusteeship Council 68-; Special Asst. to Sec. of State until 68.

Leisure interests: music, reading, art, travel, cooking.

Tower View, Red Wing, Minn. 55066, U.S.A.

Telephone: 612-388-6553.

Anderson, Herbert, A.B., B.S.E.E., PH.D.; American professor of physics; b. 24 May 1914, New York; s. of Joseph Anderson and Sima Goldberg Anderson; m. Jean Betty Clough 1947; three s. one d.; ed. Columbia Univ. University Fellow, Columbia Univ. 39-40, Research Asst. 40-42; Physicist and Group Leader, Metallurgical Lab., Univ. of Chicago 42-44; Physicist and Group Leader, Los Alamos Scientific Lab., N. Mexico 44-46; Asst. Prof. of Physics, Univ. of Chicago 46-47, Assoc. Prof. 47-50, Prof. 50-, Dir. Enrico Fermi Inst. 58-62; Guggenheim Fellow 56-57; Fulbright Lecturer, Italy 56-57; Fellow, Los Alamos Scientific Lab. 71-; mem. Nat. Acad. of Sciences, American Physical Soc., Italian Physical Soc., American Asscn. for Advancement of Science; current researches include high energy physics, pion and muon physics, mesic atoms.

Enrico Fermi Institute, University of Chicago, 5630 South Ellis, Chicago, Ill. 60637; Home: 4923 South Kimbark Avenue, Chicago, Ill. 60615, U.S.A.

Anderson, John Stuart, M.SC., PH.D., F.R.S., F.A.A.; British chemist; b. 9 Jan. 1908, London; s. of John Anderson and Emma Sarah Pitt; m. Joan Habershon Taylor 1935; one s. three d.; ed. Imperial Coll. of Science and Technology and Heidelberg Univ.

Assistant Lecturer, Imperial Coll. of Science 32-38; Senior Lecturer, Univ. of Melbourne 38-47, Prof. and Head of Chem. Dept. 54-59; Deputy Chief Scientific Officer, Atomic Energy Research Establishment, Harwell 47-53; Dir. Nat. Chemical Laboratory (U.K.) 59-63; Prof. of Inorganic Chem., Oxford Univ. 63-75; Hon. Professorial Fellow, Univ. Coll. of Wales, Aberyst-

wyth 75-; Treas. Australian Acad. of Science 56-59; Davy Medal (Royal Soc.) 73, Longstaff Medal (Chemical Soc.) 75.

Leisure interests: reading, painting, photography.

Publs. numerous papers in scientific journals.

Edward Davies Chemical Laboratory, University of Wales, Aberystwyth; Home: The Cottage, Abermagwr, Cardiganshire, Wales.

Telephone: (0970) 7645 (Office).

Anderson, Dame Judith, D.B.E.; Australian actress; b. 10 Feb. 1898, Adelaide; ed. Norwood High School.

Stage debut in *A Royal Divorce*, Theatre Royal, Sydney 15; went to New York 18; stage appearances have included: *The Dove, Behold the Bridegroom, Strange Interlude, Morning becomes Electra, Come of Age, The Old Maid, Hamlet, Macbeth, Family Portrait, Tower Beyond, Three Sisters, Medea*; films: *Rebecca, Edge of Darkness, Laura, King's Row, Spectre of the Rose, The Red House, Pursued, Tycoon, Cat on a Hot Tin Roof, Macbeth, Don't Bother to Knock, The Chinese Prime Minister* (TV) 74.

c/o Actors' Equity of New York, 165 West 4th Street, New York, N.Y., U.S.A.; 808 San Ysidro Lane, Santa Barbara, Calif. 93103, U.S.A.

Anderson, Hon. Sir Kenneth McColl, K.B.E.; Australian politician; b. 11 Oct. 1909, at sea off Adelaide; s. of D. M. Anderson; m. Madge Merrion; one d.

Served with Signals Corps of 8th Div. of Australian Imperial Force 41-45; prisoner-of-war for 3½ years; Mayor of Ryde 49-51; elected to Legislative Assembly of New South Wales 50-53; mem. Senate 53-; temporary Chair. of Cttees. of the Senate 56-64; Minister for Customs and Excise 64-68; Minister for Supply 68-71; Minister of Health Aug. 71-Dec. 72; Leader of the Govt. in the Senate 68-Dec. 72.

Leisure interest: bowls.

Australian Parliament Offices, Australian Government Centre, Chifley Square, Sydney, N.S.W. 2000, Australia

Anderson, Lindsay Gordon, M.A.; British film and theatre director; b. 17 April 1923, Bangalore, S. India; s. of Maj.-Gen. A. V. Anderson and Mrs. Estelle Bell Sleigh; ed. St. Ronan's School, Cheltenham Coll., and Wadham Coll., Oxford.

Co-Founder and Editor Film Review *Sequence* 47-52; Co-Founder Free Cinema Group, Nat. Film Theatre 56-59; Pres. Jury, Canadian Nat. Film Festival 63; Jury mem. Int. Festivals Delhi 65, Venice 66; Assoc. Dir. Royal Court Theatre 69-75.

Films directed: *Wakefield Express* 53, *Thursday's Children* (with Guy Brenton) 54, *O Dreamland* 54, *Every Day Except Christmas* 57, *This Sporting Life* 63, *The White Bus* 65/66, *Raz, Dwa, Trzy* (The Singing Lesson) for Documentary Studio, Warsaw 67, *If . . .* 68, *O Lucky Man!* 73, *In Celebration* 74.

Stage productions: *The Long and the Short and the Tall* 59, *Serjeant Musgrave's Dance* 59, *The Lily White Boys* 60, *Billy Liar* 60, *The Fire Raisers* 61, *The Diary of a Madman* 63, *Andorra* 64, *Julius Caesar* 64, *The Cherry Orchard* 66; directed Polish production of *Inadmissible Evidence* (Nig Do Obrony), Teatr Wspolczesny, Warsaw 66; *In Celebration* 69, *The Contractor* 69, *Home* (London and Broadway) 70, *The Changing Room* 71, *The Farm* 73, *Life Class* 74, *What the Butler Saw* 75, *The Sea Gull* 75, *The Bed Before Yesterday* 75.

Leisure interests: photography, resting.

Publ. *Making a Film* 62.

57 Greencroft Gardens, London, N.W.6, England.

Telephone: 01-624-3143.

Anderson, Marian; American singer; b. 17 Feb. 1902; ed. Philadelphia public school.

Studied with Agnes Reifsnider, Giuseppe Boghetti and Frank La Forge; concerts in U.S.A., Europe, Africa, S. America, Japan and W. Indies 26-53; operatic début 55, operatic tours 55-; U.S. Del. to UN 58; U.S.

Presidential Medal of Freedom Award 62, and numerous overseas awards.
Publ. *My Lord, What a Morning!* (autobiography) 56. Danbury, Conn. 06810, U.S.A.

Anderson, O. Kelley, B.A., M.B.A.; American investment executive; b. 1907, Lamoni, Iowa; s. of Oscar Anderson and Ella Belle Kelley; m. Alma U. Weichel 1935; one s.; ed. Univ. of Iowa and Harvard Graduate School of Business Administration.
Director and officer of financial and industrial companies 31-; Pres. Consolidated Investment Trust 39-50; Dir. New England Mutual Life Insurance Co. 47-71, Pres. 51-66, Chair. 66-71; Dir. Boston Edison Co., Gillette Co., Diversification Fund Inc., Exchange Fund of Boston Inc., Depositors Fund of Boston Inc., Fiduciary Exchange Fund Inc., Ritz-Carlton Hotel Co., Leverage Fund of Boston Inc., Second Fiduciary Exchange Fund Inc.; Chair. Exec. Cttee. and Trustee, Real Estate Investment Trust of America, Chair. Board of Trustees of Provident Inst. for Savings Boston; Trustee, Century Shares Trust, Consolidated Investment Trust; Hon. Trustee, Cttee. for Econ. Devt.; Dir. Vance Sanders Income Fund, Inc.; Fellow, American Acad. of Arts and Sciences.
Leisure interests: travel, golf, bridge.
294 Washington Street, Boston, Mass. 02108, U.S.A.

Anderson, Philip W., M.A., PH.D.; American physicist; b. 13 Dec. 1923, Indianapolis, Ind.; s. of Prof. H. W. Anderson and Elsie Osborne Anderson; m. Joyce Gothwaite 1947; one d.; ed. Univ. High School, Urbana, Ill., and Harvard Univ.
Naval Research Laboratory 43-45; mem. Technical Staff Bell Telephone Laboratories 49-74, Chair Theoretical Physics Dept. 59-61, Asst. Dir. Physical Research Laboratory 74; Visiting Lecturer, Univ. of Tokyo 53-54; Overseas Fellow, Churchill Coll., Cambridge 61-62; Editor *Physics* 64-68; Visiting Prof. of Theoretical Physics, Cambridge Univ. 67-75; Prof. Princeton Univ. 75-; mem. Nat. Acad. of Sciences 67-, American Acad. of Arts and Sciences 66-; mem. Japanese Physical Soc.; Fellow, American Physical Soc.; mem. Inst. of Physics and Physical Soc.; O. E. Buckley Prize, American Physical Soc., Dannie Heineman Prize, Acad. of Sciences, Gottingen; Fellow, Jesus Coll., Cambridge.
Leisure interests: hiking, Japanese game of Go (rank sho-dan), gardening and ecology, studying social and biological sciences, Romanesque architecture.
Publs. *Concepts in Solids* 63; review articles and book chapters on exchange in insulators, Josephson effect and quantum coherence, hard superconductors, localized moments, resonances in transition metals, etc.; approx. 150 research papers on spectral line broadening, magnetism, superconductivity, many-body theory, quantum chemistry, nuclear physics, etc.
Room 1D-268, Bell Laboratories Inc., Murray Hill, N.J. 07974; Princeton University, Princeton, N.J. 08540, U.S.A.

Anderson, Robert, M.A.E.; American business executive; b. 2 Nov. 1920, Columbus, Neb.; s. of late Robert Anderson and of Lillian Anderson Bays; m. 1st Constance Anderson (divorced 1972); one s. one d. 2nd Diane Clark Lowe 1973; ed. Fairfax High School, Los Angeles, Colorado State Univ. and Chrysler Inst. of Engineering.
With Chrysler Corpn. 46-68, Vice-Pres. and Gen. Man. Chrysler-Plymouth Div. 65, subsequently Vice-Pres. Products Planning and Devt.; Dir. and Pres. Commercial Products Group, North American Rockwell Corpn. 68; Exec. Vice-Pres. N. American Rockwell Corpn. 69-70, Pres. and Chief Operating Officer (now Rockwell Int. Corpn.) 70-74, Pres., Chief Exec. Officer 74-; Dir. Hospital Corpn. of America; Dir. Security Pacific Nat. Bank; mem. Board of Trustees, Calif.

Inst. of Tech. 75-; Hon. Alumnus Award and Hon. LL.D. (Colorado State Univ.).
Leisure interests: golf, tennis, flying.
Rockwell International Corporation, 600 Grant Street, Pittsburgh, Pa. 15219, U.S.A.

Anderson, Robert Bernerd; American lawyer and public servant; b. 4 June 1910, Burleson, Texas; s. of Robert Lee and Elizabeth (Haskew) Anderson; m. Ollie Mae Rawlings Anderson 1935; two s.; ed. Godley High School, Weatherford Coll. and Univ. of Texas.
Taught in Burleson High School 27-30; studied Univ. of Texas Law School 30-32, was meanwhile elected to the Texas legislature; practised law 32; Asst. Attorney-Gen. of Texas and Prof. of Law at Univ. of Texas 33; State Tax Commissioner 34-37, and Chair. and Exec. Dir. Texas Unemployment Comm. 36; Gen. Counsel for the Waggoner Estate (oil and ranching empire) 37-, Gen. Man. 41-53; U.S. Sec. of Navy 53-54; Deputy Sec. of Defense 54-55; Sec. of Treasury 57-61; Special Envoy of Pres. of U.S. to U.A.R. Oct. 67; Served as Pres. of Texas Board of Educ., Dir. of the Reserve Bank of Texas and on many other public bodies; fmr. Pres. Ventures Ltd., Chair. Robert B. Anderson and Co. Ltd., Dir. C.I.T. Financial Corpn., Copy Technology, Goodyear Tire and Rubber Co., Intercontinental Trailsea Corpn., Pan American World Airways Inc., Chair. ITC Commercial Credit Card Inc.
Robert B. Anderson and Co. Ltd., 1 Rockefeller Plaza, New York, N.Y. 10020; Home: 2 East 67th Street, New York, N.Y., U.S.A.

Anderson, Robert Orville, B.A.; American cattle rancher and business exec.; b. 1917, Chicago, Ill.; s. of Hugo A. and Hilda Nelson Anderson; m. Barbara Herrick Phelps 1939; two s. five d.; ed. Univ. of Chicago.
Founder and Pres. Hondo Oil and Gas Co. (fmrly. Malco Refineries Inc.) 41-63; Founder and Owner, Lincoln County Livestock Co., Texas and New Mexico; Chair. Federal Reserve Bank of Dallas 59-65; Dir. Northern Natural Gas Co. 60-63; Chair. of Exec. Cttee. and Dir. The Atlantic Refining Co. 63-65 (now Atlantic Richfield Co.), Chair. of Board 65-; mem. Nat. Petroleum Council 54-; Chair. Aspen Inst. for Humanistic Studies 59-, The Aspen Co.; Chair. Lovelace Foundation 62-; Chair. of Board Eisenhower Exchange Fellowships; Trustee, Univ. of Chicago 63-, Calif. Inst. of Technology; mem. Washington Inst. for Foreign Affairs 63-; official of numerous civic and business orgs.
Leisure interests: hunting and fishing.
Atlantic Richfield Co., Los Angeles, Calif., U.S.A.

Anderson, Roger E., B.S.; American banker; b. 29 July 1921, Chicago, Ill.; s. of Elmer and June Anderson; m. Marilyn Spence 1949; two s.; ed. Northwestern Univ.
Joined Continental Illinois Nat. Bank 46, Commercial Dept. 47-48, Asst. Cashier 49, successively Second Vice-Pres., Vice-Pres., Senior Vice-Pres. of Int. Banking 49-68, Exec. Vice-Pres., Dir. 68, Vice-Chair. 71; Chair. of Board of Dirs. of Continental Illinois Corpn. and Continental Illinois Nat. Bank March 73-.
Leisure interests: fishing, tennis.
Continental Illinois National Bank, 231 South LaSalle Street, Chicago, Ill. 60693; Home: 2423 Bennett Avenue, Evanston, Ill. 60201, U.S.A.
Telephone: (312) 828-7703 (Office).

Anderson, Thomas Foxen, B.S., PH.D.; American biologist; b. 7 Feb. 1911, Manitowoc, Wis.; s. of late Anton Anderson and late Mabel Foxen; m. Wilma Fay Ecton 1937; one s. one d.; ed. Calif. Inst. of Technology and Univ. of Munich.
Instructor in Chemistry, Univ. of Chicago 36-37; Investigator in Botany, Univ. of Wis. 37-39, Instructor in Physical Chemistry 39-40; R.C.A. Fellow of Nat. Research Council 40-42; Assoc. Johnson Foundation, Univ. of Pennsylvania 42-46, mem. of Faculty 46-,

Prof. of Biophysics 58-; Snr. mem. Inst. for Cancer Research 58-; Fulbright and Guggenheim Fellow, Inst. Pasteur, Paris 55-57; mem. Nat. Acad. of Sciences, Electron Microscope Soc. of America (Pres. 55), Int. Fed. of Electron Microscope Socs. (Pres. 60-64), Biophysical Soc. (Pres. 65), American Soc. of Naturalists, A.A.A.S., American Soc. of Microbiol., Deutsche Gesellschaft für Elektronenmikroscopie, Soc. Française de Microscopie Electronique (hon. mem.); mem. Int. Cttee. on Nomenclature of Viruses 68-; Silver Medal of Inst. Pasteur 57.
Leisure interests: golf, travel.
Publs. *The Reactions of bacterial viruses with their host cells* (Botanical Review 15) 49, *Bacteriophages* (Annual Review of Microbiology 4) 50, *Recombination and segregation in Escherichia coli* (Cold Spring Harbor Symposium on Quantitative Biology 23) 58, *The Molecular organization of virus particles* (Molecular Organization and Biological Function editor John M. Allen) 67, *Some Personal Memories of Research* (Annual Review of Microbiology) 75.
The Institute for Cancer Research, 7701 Burholme Avenue, Philadelphia, Pa. 19111, U.S.A.
Telephone: (215) FI2-1000.

Anderson, Wendell Richard, B.A., LL.B.; American state governor; b. 1 Feb. 1933, St. Paul, Minn.; s. of Theodore M. Anderson and Gladys Nord; m. Mary C. McKee 1963; one s. two d.; ed. Univ. of Minn.
Member Minnesota House of Reps. 58-62; elected to Minn. Senate 62, re-elected 66; Gov. of Minnesota Jan. 71-; Democrat.
Leisure interests: hockey, golf.
Office of the Governor, State Capitol, St. Paul, Minn. 55155, U.S.A.
Telephone: 612-296-3391.

Anderson, Capt. William R., U.S.N. (retd.); American naval officer; b. 17 June 1921, Bakerville, Tenn.; s. of Mr. and Mrs. D. H. Anderson; m. Yvonne Etzel 1943; two s.; ed. Columbia Military Acad. and U.S. Naval Acad.
Commissioned 42; service in submarines 42-59; Idaho Univ. Inst. of Naval Tactics 51; Naval Reactors Branch, Atomic Energy Comm. 56-57, 59; Commdr. *Nautilus*, the world's first atomic submarine 57-59 (in which he achieved the first totally submerged transit of the North Pole and N.W. Passage 58); Freedoms Foundation 62-64; mem. U.S. House of Reps. 64-72; Bronze Star Combat "V", various war and campaign medals; Legion of Merit 58, Christopher Columbus Int. Medal (Italy) 58, Patron's Medal, Royal Geographical Soc. 59, Freedom Leadership Award 60; Democrat.
Publs. *Nautilus 90 North* 59, *First under the North Pole* 59, *The Useful Atom* 66.
2700 Virginia Avenue, N.W., Washington, D.C. 20037, U.S.A.
Telephone: 202-333-3938.

Anderson, William Summers, A.A.S.A.; British business executive; b. 29 March 1919, Hankow, China; s. of William G. and Mabel Anderson; m. Janice Elizabeth Robb 1947; three d.; ed. Public and Thomas Hanbury School, Shanghai.
Internal Auditor Hong Kong and Shanghai Hotels Ltd. 38-39; Auditor Linstead and Davis 40-41; war service 41-45; Nat. Cash Register Corpn. (NCR) 45, Man. NCR Hong Kong 50-59, Vice-Pres. Far East and China NCR Japan 59-72, Corporate Pres. and Dir. 72, Pres. and Chief Exec. Officer 73-, Chair. 74-.
Leisure interests: sailing, golf.
NCR Corporation, Main and K Streets, Dayton, Ohio 45479, U.S.A.
Telephone: 513-449-2250.

Anderson-Imbert, Enrique, PH.D.; Argentine university professor; b. 12 Feb. 1910, Argentina; s. of José Enrique Anderson and Honorina Imbert; m. Margot

Di Clerico 1934; one s. one d.; ed. Universidad Nacional de Buenos Aires.
Professor, Univ. of Cuyo, Argentina 40-41, Univ. of Tucumán, Argentina 41-46, Univ. of Michigan 47-65; First Victor S. Thomas Prof. of Hispanic American Literature, Harvard Univ. 65-; mem. American Acad. of Arts and Sciences 67; Prize from Buenos Aires City for novel *Vigilia* 34.
Publs. *El arte de la prosa en Juan Montalvo* 48, *Historia de la literatura hispanoamericana* 54, *¿Qué és la prosa?* 58, *El grimorio* 61, *Vigilia-Fuga* 63, *El gato de Cheshire* 65, *Genio y figura de Sarmiento* 67, *La originalidad de Rubén Darío* 67, *La sandía y otros cuentos* 69, *Una aventura de Sarmiento en Chicago* 69, *Métodos de Crítica literaria* 69, *La locura juega al ajedrez* 71, *La flecha en el aire* 72, *Los domingos del profesor* 72, *Estudios sobre letras hispánicas* 74, *La Botella de Klein* 75.
Department of Romance Languages, 201 Boylston Hall, Harvard University, Cambridge, Massachusetts 02138, U.S.A.

Andersson, Bibi; Swedish actress; b. 11 Nov. 1935, ed. Terserus Drama School and Royal Dramatic Theatre School, Stockholm.
Malmö Theatre 56-59, Royal Dramatic Theatre, Stockholm 59-; appearances at Uppsala Theatre 62-.
Plays acted in include: *Erik XIV* 56, *Tre systrar* 61, *King John* 61, *Le Balcon* 61, *La Grotte* 62, *Uncle Vanya* 62, *Who's Afraid of Virginia Woolf* 63, *As You Like It* 64, *After the Fall* 64-65, *The Full Circle* 73, *Twelfth Night* 75.
Films acted in include: *Sjunde inseglet* (Seventh Seal) 56, *Smultronstället* (Wild Strawberries) 57, *Nära livet* (The Brink of Life) 58, *Sommarnöje Sökes* (Summer House Wanted) 58, *Djävulens öga* (Eye of the Devil) 61, *Älskarinnen* (The Mistress) 62, *För att inte tala om alla dessa kvinnor* (All those Women) 64, *Juninatt* (June Night) 65, *Ön* (The Island) 65, *Syskonbädd* (My Sister, My Love) 66, *Persona* 66, *Duel at Diablo* 66, *The Girls* 69, *The Kremlin Letter* 70, *A Passion, The Touch* 71, *Scenes from a Marriage* 74.
c/o Svenska Filminstitutet, Kungsgatan 48, Stockholm C; Home: Tykö Vägen 28, Lidingo, Sweden.
Telephone: 7663801.

Andersson, Harriet; Swedish actress; b. 1932, Stockholm.
Theatre career commenced in chorus at Oscars Theatre; subsequently appeared in reviews and then started serious dramatic career at Malmö City Theater 53; now appears regularly at Kunigliga Dramatiska Teatern, Stockholm; best-known stage appearances include performances of Anne Frank in *The Diary of Anne Frank*, Ophelia in *Hamlet*, in *The Beggar's Opera* and in plays by Chekhov; numerous film appearances including several by Ingmar Bergman (q.v.): *Summer with Monica* 53, *Sawdust and Tinsel* 53, *Women's Dreams* 55, *Dreams of a Summer Night* 55, *Through a Glass Darkly* 61, *All Those Women* 64, *Cries and Whispers* 73; films directed by Jörn Donner (q.v.): *One Sunday in September* 63, *To Love* 64, *Adventure starts here* 65, *Stimulantia* 65-66, *Rooftree* 66, *Anna* 70; other recent films include: *Siska* 62, *Dream of Happiness* 63, *Loving Couples* 64, *For the Sake of Friendship* 65, *Vine Bridge* 65, *The Serpent* 66, *The Deadly Affair* 67, *The Girls* 68, *The Stake*; German Film Critics' Grand Prize for *Through a Glass Darkly*; Swedish Film Asscn. plaque; Best Actress Award, Venice Film Festival 64 (for *To Love*).
c/o Sandrew Film & Theater AB, Box 5612, 114 86 Stockholm, Sweden.

Andersson, Sven Olof Morgan; Swedish politician; b. 5 April 1910, Gothenburg; ed. People's High School, Geneva.
President, Gothenburg District, Social-Democratic Youth Union 29-32; Instructor in W.E.A., Gothenburg

32-35; mem. Nat. Cttee. Social Democratic Youth Union 34-40; Sec. Gothenburg District, Social-Democratic Party 35-45; Town Councillor, Gothenburg 38-40; mem. Second Chamber of Parl. 40-44; Gen. Sec. Social-Democratic Party 45-48; mem. First Chamber of Parl. 48-; Minister without Portfolio 48-51; Minister of Communications 51-57, of Defence 57-73, of Foreign Affairs Nov. 73-.
Ministry of Foreign Affairs, Stockholm, Sweden.

Andics, Mrs. Erzsébet, PH.D.; Hungarian historian and university professor; b. 1902.
Professor of Modern Hungarian History, Eötvös Loránd Univ., Budapest; Deputy Minister for Education 53-56; mem. Hungarian Acad. of Sciences; awarded Kossuth Prize; Red Banner Labour Order of Merit 72.
Publs. include *Kossuth Lajos harca az árulók és megalkuvók ellen a reformkorban és a forradalom idején* (Lajos Kossuth's Struggle Against the Traitors and Opportunists during the Reform Era and the Time of the Revolution), *A magyarországi munkásmozgalom az 1848-49-es forradalomtol és Szabadságharctól az 1917-es Nagy Októberi Szocialista Forradalomig* (The Hungarian Working Class Movement from the 1848-49 Revolution and The War of Independence up to the 1917 Great October Revolution) 55, *A nagybirtokos arisztokrácia ellenforradalmi szerepe 1848-49-ben.* II-III 53-65. *Das Bündnis Habsburg-Romanow* 63, *1848-49 Tanulmányok* 68 *Metternich und die Frage Ungarns* 73, *Széchenyi and Metternich* 75, *Metternich and Hungary* 75.
Eötvös Loránd Tudományegyetem, Budapest V, Pesti Barnabás u. I; and H-1026 Budapest II, Orsó-utca 19, Hungary.
Telephone: 364-106.

Andras, Hon. Robert Knight; Canadian politician; b. 1921, Lachine, P.Q.; s. of John D. Andras and Angela E. Knight; m. Frances Hunt 1945; one s. one d.; ed. Wesley Coll., Winnipeg, Man.
Served with Queen's Own Cameron Highlanders 42-46; successive exec. positions, Ford Motor Co. 46-58; Pres. of several companies 58-65; elected Liberal mem. Fed. Parl. 65, re-elected 68, 72, 74; Minister without Portfolio responsible for Housing 68-71; Minister of State for Urban Affairs 71; Minister of Consumer and Corporate Affairs Jan.-Nov. 72; Minister of Manpower and Immigration Nov. 72-.
Room 425S, House of Commons, Ottawa, Ont., K1A 0A6; Home: Thunder Bay, Ontario and Ottawa, Ont., Canada.
Telephone: (613) 996-6861 (Office).

Andreadis, Stratis G., LL.D.; Greek banker; b. Vrontados, Island of Chios; ed. Univs. of Athens and Paris.
Called to the Bar, Athens 27; Prof. Admin. Law, Univ. of Salonica 39; Athens Graduate School of Econs. and Business Sciences, Prof. of Admin. Law 39-69, Prof. Emer. 69, Rector 43-44, 56-57, 60-61, 64-66, 67-68; Pres. and Chair. Commercial Bank of Greece, Ionian and Popular Bank of Greece and Bank of Piraeus; Chair. Investment Bank, Bank of Attica and Commercial Bank of the Near East Ltd. (London); Chair. and Financial-Admin. Man. Hellenic Electric Railways; Chair. The Phoenix Insurance Co., Ioniki Insurance Co., Gen. Insurance of Greece Co., Andreadis (U.K.) Ltd./ Shipping/London, Phosphoric Fertilizers Industry S.A., Eleusis Shipyard Co. Ltd., Greek Juice Processing and Canning Industry S.A., Ioniki Hotel Enterprises Ltd., Greek Gen. Enterprises Ltd., Greek Industry for Sacks and Plastic Products Co. Ltd., Hellenic Mutual Fund Management Co. S.A.; official of numerous nat. and int. business orgs.; Corresp. mem. Acad. of Moral and Political Sciences, France 72; Fellow, Historical and Ethnological Soc. of Greece; Knight Commdr. and Commdr. Royal Order of George I; Knight Commdr. Royal Order of the Phoenix; Grande Ufficiale dell' Ordine Al Merito della Repubblica Italiana; Officier

Légion d'Honneur; Officier Ordre de Léopold (Belgium); Archon Megas Ritor (Dignitary of the Ecumenical Patriarchate); Cross of Saint Mark Class A, Greek Orthodox Patriarchate of Alexandria; Grand Commander, Greek Orthodox Patriarchate of Jerusalem; Golden Cross Millenary of Mount Athos; Gold Medal Ministry of Merchant Marine; Gold Medal Société des Arts Sciences et Lettres, Paris; Grand Cross of Merit with Star of the Federal Republic of Germany.
Publs. *Le Contentieux Administratif des Etats Modernes* 34, *The Invalidating Jurisdiction of the Council of State* (two vols.) 36, 43, *Elements of Administrative Law* 56, *Elements of Constitutional Law* 53, *Lectures in Administrative Justice* 64, *Administrative Law* 68; *Essays* (three vols.) 61-62; numerous studies and articles on gen. econ., banking and shipping matters; many contributions to the Greek and int. press.
11 Sofocleous and 80 Aeolou Streets, Athens 122; 11 King George II Street, Athens 138, Greece.

Andreazza, Mario David; Brazilian army officer and politician; b. 20 Aug. 1918; ed. Escola Militar.
Second Lieut. 41, Lieut. 43, Capt. 45, Maj. 53, Lieut.-Col. 60, Col. 65; Brazilian Mil. Mission in Paraguay 52; fmr. Sec. of Council of Nat. Security, later at Fed. Dept. of Information, later with Dept. of Armed Forces; on staff of Minister of War 64; Minister of Transport 67-74; numerous decorations.
Praça XV de novembro, 2° andar, Rio de Janeiro, Brazil.

Andreev, Alexander Nikitovich; Soviet politician; b. 1917; ed. Uman Inst. of Agriculture and Higher Party School of Central Committee of C.P. of Ukraine.
Education service 33-42; Soviet Army 42-45; mem. C.P.S.U. 44-; party official 45-54; Sec., Second Sec. Cherkassy Regional Cttee. of C.P. of Ukraine 54-65, First Sec. 65-; mem. Central Cttee. C.P. of Ukraine; Deputy to U.S.S.R. Supreme Soviet; mem. Comm. on Legislation, Soviet of the Union.
Cherkassy Regional Committee, Communist Party of the Ukraine, Cherkassy, U.S.S.R.

Andreev, Vyacheslav Stepanovich; Soviet trade unionist; b. 31 March 1926, Stepurino Village, Smolensk Region; ed. Moscow Power Engineering Secondary School and All-Union Power Engineering Correspondence Inst.
Turner 42-46; technician, later Senior Laboratory Worker, Lebedev Physics Inst., U.S.S.R. Acad. of Sciences 47-51; Engineering Plant 51-62; Chair. Central Cttee. of Electrical and Power Workers' Trade Union 62-; mem. All-Union Central Council of Trade Unions 68-; mem. C.P.S.U. 54-; two medals.
Central Committee of the Electrical and Power Workers' Trade Union, 42 Leninsky Prospekt, Moscow, U.S.S.R.

Andreotti, Giulio; Italian journalist and politician; b. 14 Jan. 1919, Rome; m. Livia Danese 1945; four c.; ed. Univ. of Rome.
President, Fed. of Catholic Univs. in Italy 42-45; Deputy to the Constituent Assembly 45 and to Parl. 47-; Under-Sec. in the Govts. of De Gasperi and Pella 47-53; Minister for the Interior in Fanfani Govt. 54; Minister of Finance 55-58, of Treasury 58-59, of Defence 59-60, 60-66, of Industry and Commerce 66-68; Chair. Christian Democratic Parl. Party in Chamber of Deputies 68-72; Prime Minister 72-73; Chair. Foreign Affairs Cttee., Chamber of Deputies; Minister of Defence March-Oct. 74, for the Budget, and Econ. Planning and in charge of Southern Devt. Fund Nov. 74-.
Piazza Montecitorio 115, Rome, Italy.

Andrewes, Sir Christopher Howard, M.D., LL.D., F.R.S., F.R.C.P.; British physician; b. 7 June 1896, London; s. of Sir Frederick Andrewes, F.R.S. and Phyllis Mary Hamer; m. Kathleen Helen Lamb 1927; three c.; ed. Highgate School and St. Bartholomew's Hospital, London.

Surgeon Sub-Lieut. Royal Naval Volunteer Reserve 18-19; House Physician and Chief Asst. to Medical Professorial Unit, St. Bartholomew's Hospital 21-23, 25-26; Asst. Resident Physician, Hospital of Rockefeller Inst., New York City 23-25; William Julius Mickle Fellow, Univ. of London 31; Oliver-Sharpey Lecturer Royal Coll. of Physicians 34; mem. Nat. Inst. for Medical Research 27-61, Deputy Dir. 52-61; in charge of WHO World Influenza Centre, Mill Hill, London 48-61.
Leisure interests: natural history, especially entomology.
Publs. *Viruses of Vertebrates* 64, *The Common Cold* 65, *The Natural History of Viruses* 67, *The Lives of Wasps and Bees* 69.
Overchalke, Coombe Bissett, Salisbury, Wilts., England.
Telephone: Coombe Bissett 201.

Andrewes, Edward David Eden; British Managing Director, Tube Investments 72-75; see *The International Who's Who 1975-76.*

Andrews, Eamonn; Irish radio and television commentator and official; b. 19 Dec. 1922, Dublin; s. of William and Margaret Andrews; m. Grainne Bourke 1951; one s. two d.; ed. Synge School, Dublin.
Insurance Clerk, Dublin; boxing commentaries, Radio Eireann 40; *Irish Independent* 45; studied acting under Abbey Theatre actress Ria Mooney, wrote play *The Moon is Black*; came to England 50; radio and television appearances include Sports Programmes, Children's Programmes, *What's My Line, This is Your Life* and *Today*; Chair. Irish Television Authority (Radio Eireann) 60-66, joined ABC Television 64, presented *The Eamonn Andrews Show* and *World of Sport*; joined Thames Television on its formation 68; Chair. Eamonn Andrews Studios Ltd. and Gaiety Theatre, Dublin; Knight Order of St. Gregory the Great; Hon. C.B.E. 70.
Leisure interests: writing, reading, listening, golf.
Publ. *This is My Life* 63.
Windsor House, Heathfield Gardens, London, W4 4ND, England.

Andrews, Julie; British actress and singer; b. 1 Oct. 1935, Walton-on-Thames, Surrey; m. 1st Tony Walton 1959 (dissolved 1968), one d.; m. 2nd Blake Edwards 1969.
First stage appearance at the age of twelve as singer, London Hippodrome; played in revues and concert tours; appeared in pantomime *Cinderella*, London Palladium; played leading parts in *The Boy Friend* N.Y. 54, *My Fair Lady* 59-60, *Camelot* N.Y. 60-62; television play *High Tor*; several television shows including *The Julie Andrews Hour* 72-73; Academy Award (Oscar) Best Actress 64; three Golden Globe Awards.
Films: *Mary Poppins* 63, *The Americanization of Emily* 64, *The Sound of Music* 64, *Hawaii* 65, *Torn Curtain* 66, *Thoroughly Modern Millie* 66, *Star!* 67, *Darling Lili* 70, *The Tamarind Seed* 73.
Publs. *Mandy, The Last of the Great Wangdoogles* 74.
Chasin-Park-Citron Agency, 9255 Sunset Boulevard, Los Angeles, Calif. 90024, U.S.A.

Andriamahazo, Brig.-Gen. Gilles; Malagasy army officer; b. 1919, Fort-Dauphin, Tuléar Prov.; ed. Ecole Supérieure de Guerre, Paris.
Promoted to rank of Col.; then Inspector of Infantry and Artillery, Gen. Staff Headquarters at the Presidency; Brig.-Gen., Inspector-Gen. of the Armed Forces 70; Mil. Gov. of Tananarive 72; Minister of Territorial Admin. 72-75; Chair. Mil. Directorate Feb.-June 75; Head of Mil. Cttee. for Devt. June 75-.
Military Committee for Development, Tananarive, Madagascar.

Andrianov, Konstantin Alexandrovich; Soviet sports administrator; b. 16 Feb. 1910, Moscow; ed. High Party School of Central Cttee. of C.P.S.U.

Worked in Moscow factories 24-36; activities in Young Communist League 36-38; Chair. Moscow City Cttee. for Physical Culture and Sport 38-41; Deputy Chair. All-Union Cttee. for Physical Culture and Sport, U.S.S.R. Council of Ministers 41-47, 50-58; Chief of Dept. of Main Board of Labour Resources, U.S.S.R. Council of Ministers 58-59; Deputy Chief, Dept. of State Cttee. for Labour and Wages 59-64; mem. of U.S.S.R. People's Control Cttee. 64-; Chair. U.S.S.R. Olympic Cttee.; fmr. mem. Exec. Cttee. of Int. Olympic Cttee., Vice-Pres. 66; Order of Red Banner of Labour.
c/o U.S.S.R. Olympic Committee, Skatertny pereulok 4, Moscow, U.S.S.R.

Andrianov, Kuzma Andrianovich; Soviet chemist; b. 28 Dec. 1904, Kondrakovo Village, Kalinin Region; ed. Moscow Univ.
All-Union Electro-Technical Inst. 30; Instructor, Moscow Chemico-Technological Inst. 30-41, Moscow Power Eng. Inst. 41-46; Prof. Moscow Power Eng. Inst. 46-; mem. C.P.S.U. 49-; Assoc. Inst. of Elemental Organic Compounds, U.S.S.R. Acad. of Sciences 54-; Corresp. mem. U.S.S.R. Acad. of Sciences 53-64, mem. 64-; four State Prizes; Lenin Prize; Hero of Socialist Labour; Order of Lenin (three times); "Hammer and Sickle" Gold Medal; other decorations.
Institute of Elemental Organic Compounds, 28 Ulitsa Vavilova, Moscow, U.S.S.R.

Andriashev, Anatole Petrovich; Soviet zoologist; b. 19 Aug. 1910, Montpellier, France; s. of P. E. Waitashevsky and N. Y. Andriasheva; m. Nina M. Savelyeva 1934; two d.; ed. Leningrad Univ.
Postgraduate, Research Assoc., Asst. Prof. Leningrad Univ. 33-39; Sebastopol Biological Scientific Station 39-44; Chief, Antarctic Research Div., Inst. of Zoology, U.S.S.R. Acad. of Sciences 44-; Antarctic expeditions 55-58, 71-72; Corresp. mem. U.S.S.R. Acad. of Sciences 66-; Hon. foreign mem. of American Soc. of Ichthyological Herpetology; State prizewinner 71.
Leisure interests: skiing, photography, the French Impressionists.
Publs. works on ichthyology, zoogeography and Antarctic biology.
Zoological Institute, Academy of Sciences, Leningrad 164, U.S.S.R.

Andriessen, Jacobus Eye, PH.D.; Netherlands economist and business executive; b. 25 July 1928, Rotterdam; m. Josephina Hoogcwey 1952; ed. Erasmus Univ., Rotterdam and Amsterdam Free Univ.
Director Dept. of Gen. Econ. Policy, Ministry of Econ. Affairs 55-59; Prof., Legal Faculty, Univ. of Amsterdam 59; Adviser to Ministry of Econ. Affairs 59-63; mem. Econ. and Social Cttee. of European Econ. Community (EEC) 62-63; Minister of Econ. Affairs 63-65; mem. Management Council Royal Packaging Industries Van Leer; Dir. Ballast-Nedam, Chair. Board of Dirs. Elsevier Publishing Co., United Dutch Film Inst., Africa Inst.
Leisure interests: modern literature, painting and films, skiing, golf.
Publs. *Development of Modern Price Theory* 55, *Anticycle Policy in a Western European Context* 59, *Theory and Practice of Economics* 64 (5th edn. 76), *The Field of Force between Economics and Politics* 64.
Waldeck Pyrmontlaan 16, Wassenaar, Netherlands.
Telephone: 01751-79019.

Andrieu, René Gabriel, B.P., L.-ès-L.; French journalist; b. 24 March 1920, Beauregard (Lot); s. of Alphonse Andrieu and Esther Vernhet; m. Jeanine Vigie 1947; one d.; ed. Toulouse Univ.
Diplomatic Editor *Ce Soir* 46-58; Chief Editor *L'Humanité* 58-; Croix de Guerre, Médaille de la Résistance; mem. Central Cttee. French Communist Party 61-.
Publs. *Les communistes et la Révolution* 68, *Histoire de*

France du Front populaire à nos jours (with Jean Effel) 69.

3 allée Henri Wallon, 92 Nanterre, France.

Andropov, Yuri Vladimirovich; Soviet politician; b. 1914; ed. Inland Water Ways Transport Coll., Petrozavodsk State Univ. and Higher Party School.

Young Communist League, Yaroslavl Region and Karelo-Finnish Republic 36-44; mem. C.P.S.U. 39-; Counsellor, later Ambassador to Hungary 53-57; official responsible for party relations with other Communist countries 57-62; mem. Central Cttee. C.P.S.U. 61-; Deputy to U.S.S.R. Supreme Soviet 50-54, 62-; mem. Secretariat, Central Cttee. of C.P.S.U. 62; Candidate mem. Politburo, Central Cttee. of C.P.S.U. June 67-73, mem. Politburo 73-; Chair. State Security Cttee. of U.S.S.R. Council of Ministers 67-.

State Security Committee of U.S.S.R. Council of Ministers, Moscow, U.S.S.R.

Androsch, Dr. Hannes; Austrian politician; b. 18 April 1938, Vienna; *m.*; two *c.*; ed. Hochschule für Welthandel, Vienna.

Assistant auditor, Fed. Ministry of Finance 56-66; Sec. Econ. Affairs Section, Socialist Parl. Party 63-66; mem. Nationalrat 67-; Minister of Finance April 70-.

Federal Ministry of Finance, Vienna, Austria.

Androutsopoulos, Adamantios, LL.B., LL.M.; Greek politician; b. 1919, Psari, Greece; ed. Athens Univ., John Marshall Law School, Chicago, U.S.A., Chicago Univ.

Lawyer 47; Prof. of Law, Chicago Industrial School; Scientific collaborator at Roosevelt Univ., Mundelein Coll., John Marshall Law School, Fengen Coll.; returned to Greece 67; Minister of Finance 67-71, of Interior 71-73; Prime Minister 73-74; mem. Athens Lawyers' Union, American Judicature Soc., American Business Law Asscn.

Publs. *State distributions and national economy, The Problem of Causation in Maritime Law, Legal Terminology of the Greek-American Dictionary.*

c/o Office of the Prime Minister, Athens, Greece.

Andrus, Cecil D.; American state governor; b. 25 August 1931, Hood River, Ore.; *s.* of Hal S. and Dorothy (Johnson) Andrus; *m.* Carol M. May 1949; three *d.*; ed. Oregon State Univ.

Served, U.S. Navy 51-55; mem. Idaho Senate 61-66, 69-70; State Gen. Man. Paul Revere Life Insurance Co. 69-70; Gov. of Idaho 71-; Hon. LL.D. Gonzaga Univ., Spokane, Washington 75; Democrat.

Office of the Governor, State Capitol, Boise, Idaho 83707; Home: 1805 North 21st Street, Boise, Idaho 83702, U.S.A.

Andrzejewski, Jerzy; Polish writer; b. 19 Aug. 1909, Warsaw; *s.* of late Jan Andrzejewski and Eugenia Glinojecka; *m.* Maria Abgarowicz 1942; one *s.* one *d.*; ed. Warsaw Univ.

Literary debut 32; underground activity during German occupation; Editor-in-Chief *Przegląd Kulturalny* (Cultural Review) 52-54; Deputy to Seym 52-57; mem. Polish Writers' Asscn. 36-; Order of Banner of Labour (1st Class) 49.

Leisure interests: music, bridge.

Publs. Novels: *Ład serca* (Harmony of the Heart) (Young Writers' Prize, Polish Acad. of Literature) 39, *Popiół i diament* (Ashes and Diamonds) (Odrodzenie Award) 48 (Złoty Kłos Award 65), *Ciemności kryją ziemię* (Darkness Covers the Earth) 57, *Bramy Raju* (The Gates of Paradise) 61, *Idzie skacząc po gorach* (He Cometh Leaping Upon the Mountains) 63, *Apelacja* (The Appeal) 67, *Miazga* (Mash) 72; stories: *Drogi nieuniknione* (The Inevitable Ways) 37, *Noc* (Night) 45, *Złoty Lis* (The Golden Fox) 55, *Niby Gaj* (As If the Grove) 61, *Three Tales* 73, *Książka dla Marcina* (A Book for Martin—reminiscences) 54, *Święto Winkelrieda*

(Winkelried's Day—play with J. Zagorski) 45, *Prometheus* (play) 72.

Swierczewskiego 53/4, 03-402 Warsaw, Poland.

Telephone: 19-82-61.

Anfinsen, Christian Boehmer, PH.D.; American biochemist; b. 26 March 1916, Monessen, Pa.; *s.* of Christian Boehmer Anfinsen (deceased) and Sophie née Rasmussen; *m.* Florence Bernice Kenenger 1941; one *s.* two *d.*; ed. Swarthmore Coll., Univ. of Pennsylvania, Harvard Medical School.

Assistant instructor in organic chem. Univ. of Pennsylvania 38-39; Fellow American Scandinavian Foundation, visiting investigator Carlsberg laboratory Copenhagen, Denmark 39-40; Fellow, Harvard Univ. 41-43, Instructor in Biological Chem., Harvard Medical School 43-45; Civilian with Office of Scientific Research and Devt. CMR 44-46; Assoc. in Biological Chem., Harvard Medical School 45-48; Senior Fellow, American Cancer Soc., Visiting Investigator, Medical Noble Inst. with Prof. Hugo Theorell 47-48; Markle Scholar and Asst. Prof. Biological Chem., Harvard Medical School, also consultant in research anaesthesia, Massachusetts Gen. Hosp. 48-50; Chief, Laboratory of Cellular Physiology, Nat. Heart Inst. 50-52; Chief, Laboratory of Cellular Physiology and Metabolism, Nat. Heart Inst. 52-62; Prof. Dept. of Biological Chem., Harvard Medical School 62-63; Chief, Laboratory of Chemical Biology Nat. Inst. of Arthritis, Metabolism and Digestive Diseases 63-; mem. Board of Gov., Weizmann Inst. of Science, Rehovot, Israel; mem. American Soc. of Biological Chemists (Pres. 71-72), Nat. Acad. of Sciences, Royal Danish Acad.; Rockefeller Foundation Public Service Award 54; Hon. D.Sc. (Swarthmore Coll.) 65; Harvey Lecturer 66; Hon. D.Sc. (Georgetown Univ.) 67; Hon. D.Sc. (New York Medical Coll.) 69; Hon. Fellow, Weizmann Inst. of Science 69; EMBO Lecturer for Sweden 70; Visiting Fellow, All Souls Coll. Oxford 70; Jubilee Lecturer 72; Nobel Prize for Chem. 72.

Leisure interests: sailing, music.

Publs. *The Molecular Basis of Evolution* 59, numerous articles in learned journals on protein labelling, enzyme functions and properties, and allied subjects.

National Institute for Arthritis and Metabolic Diseases, Bethesda, Md. 20014; and 8 West Drive, Bethesda, Md. 20014, U.S.A.

Telephone: 301-496-5408 (Work); 301-657-2597.

Angelini, Arnaldo M.; Italian electrical engineer and nuclear energy administrator; b. 2 Feb. 1909, Force, Ascoli Piceno Prov.; *s.* of Licinio and Anita Lucangeli; *m.* Livia Rossi 1937; two *s.* one *d.*

Managing Dir., Gen. Man. Terni Co.; Gen. Man. ENEL 63-73, Chair. 73-; Prof. Electrical Eng., Univ. of Rome, Dir. Electric Eng. Inst.; fmrly. Vice-Pres. Comitato Nazionale per le Ricerche Nucleari; mem. Council Italian Forum for Nuclear Energy (FIEN), Pres. 59-60; mem. Steering Cttee. Comitato Nazionale per l'Energia Nucleare 60-73; mem. Scientific and Technical Cttee. EURATOM, Pres. 61, Vice-Pres. 64; mem. del. to Conf. on Peaceful Uses of Nuclear Energy, Geneva 55, 58, 64, 71; Pres. Associazione Elettrotecnica ed Elettronica Italiana (AEI) 59-61; Corresp. mem. Accad. Nazionale dei Lincei; Fellow, Inst. of Electrical and Electronic Eng., American Nuclear Soc.; mem. Soc. Française des Electriciens, and other socs.; Pugno Vanoni, Jona and Castellani Prizes, AEI.

ENEL, 3 Via G. B. Martini, 00198 Rome; Home: 5 Via Francesco Coletti, 00191 Rome, Italy.

Telephone: 8509 (Office).

Angelis, Gen. Odysseus; Greek army officer; b. 3 Feb. 1912, Chalkis; *s.* of Miltiadis Angelis; unmarried; ed. Army Cadets Coll., Higher War Coll. and Nat. Defence Coll.

Commissioned 34; served during World War II in

Albanian Campaign 40-41, Middle East Campaign 43-45, anti-communist campaign in Greece 46-49; Chief of Army Gen. Staff 67-68; C.-in-C. Hellenic Armed Forces 69-73; Vice-Pres. of Greece Aug.-Nov. 73; remanded in custody Feb. 75, sentenced to 20 years' imprisonment for high treason and insurrection Aug. 75; Golden Medal of Gallantry and several other orders and awards.

Ångström, Anders K., M.SC., PH.D.; Swedish meteorologist; b. 28 Feb. 1888, Stockholm; s. of Knut Ångström and Hélène Pilo; m. Anna-Greta Montelius 1923; three s. two d.; ed. Univs. of Uppsala, Cornell and Jena.
Fellow of Physics, Cornell Univ., N.Y. 12-13; Chair. Met. Section Swedish National Comm. for Geodesy and Geophysics 34-56; Asst. Prof. Meteorology Uppsala Univ. 16-18; First State Meteorologist 34; Chief Swedish Weather Bureau 40; Dir.-in-Chief Swedish Meteorological and Hydrological Inst. 49-54; mem. Smithsonian Inst. expedition to Algeria 12; leader expedition to Mount Whitney, California 13, to Switzerland 29; Pres. Int. Radiation Comm. 36-45; Pres. Swedish Society for Anthropology and Geography 39-40 and 50-52; mem. Royal Swedish Acad. of Agriculture 43, Royal Swedish Acad. of Military Sciences 46, Royal Swedish Acad. of Sciences 48, Int. Meteorological Cttee. 49-51, Permanent Rep. of Sweden at World Meteorological Organisation 51-54, Council Int. Union for Geodesy and Geophysics 49-60, Meteorological Expert of U.N. to Iceland Govt. 56, Vice-Pres. Int. Climatological Comm. of U.N. 53-57; Consultant Eppley Foundation for Research 58-74; Int. Meteorological Org. Prize 62; Rossby Prize, Swedish Geophysical Soc. 68.
Leisure interests: winter sports, sailing, tennis.
Publs. *A Study of the Radiation of the Atmosphere* 15, *Determinations of the Atmospheric Turbidity* 70, *The Climate of Sweden* (3rd edn.) 73, and other works on meteorology, and solar and terrestrial radiation.
Stavgårdsgatan 57, Stockholm-Bromma, Sweden.
Telephone: 08-250773.

Anguiano, Raúl; Mexican painter; b. 26 Feb. 1915, Guadalajara, Jalisco; s. of José Anguiano and Abigail V. de Anguiano; one s. one d.; studied under José Vizcarra and Ixca Farias.
Concerned in Modern Art movement, Mexico 34; founder mem. Taller de Gráfica Popular; studied at Art Students' League, New York 41; one-man exhbns. in Mexico, Paris 52, 65, 67, San Francisco 53-65, Havana 56, Chile 60, Moscow 62, Rome 65-67, Miami 65, San Antonio (Texas) 66, Quito 71, Mexico City 72, Palm Springs, Calif. 74; has exhibited in collective exhbns. in London, Warsaw, Tokyo, Berlin, Prague, Peking, Lille, Los Angeles, Lugano, etc.; works include murals for the Hormona Laboratories, Onyx-Mex Industries and the Nat. Museum of Anthropology, Mexico City; has completed series of works about *lacandones* of Lacandona Jungle; retrospective exhbn. Salón de la Plástica Mexicana, Mexico 69; guest teacher, lecturer and invited to exhibit works at Univ. of W. Indies, Kingston, Jamaica 70; painted mural at Olympia Hotel, Kingston; numerous prizes.
Leisure interests: music, reading, writing.
Anaxágoras 1326, Colonia Narvarte, México 13, D.F. México.
Telephone: 575-07-56, 575-14-54.

Angulo-Iñíguez, Diego; Spanish art historian; b. 18 July 1901, Valverde, Huelva; s. of Diego and Angela Angulo-Iñíguez; m. Pilar Romero 1965; ed. Univs. of Seville, Madrid, Berlin.
Professor of History of Art, Granada Univ. 25-26, Univ. of Seville 27-40, Madrid Univ. 40- (Emer. 71-); Emer. Dir. Instituto de Arte Diego Velázquez, Museo del Prado; mem. Real Academia de la Historia, Real Academia de Bellas Artes de San Fernando.

Publs. *La Arquitectura Mudéjar Sevillana* 35, *La Escultura en Andalucía* (3 vols.) 27-39, *Planos de Monumentos de América* (7 vols.) 33-39, *Historia del Arte Hispano Americano* (3 vols.) 45, *Velázquez* 47, *Historia del Arte* (2 vols.) 53, *Pintura del Renacimiento* 54, *Pintura Madrileña Siglo XVII* 68, *Pintura del Siglo XVII* 71, *Corpus of Spanish Drawings* 75.
Leisure interests: travel, country life.
Instituto Diego Velázquez, Medinaceli 4, Madrid 14, Spain.

Anichkov, Sergei Victorovich; Soviet pharmacologist and physiologist; b. 20 Sept. 1892, St. Petersburg (Leningrad); s. of Victor Anichkov and Marie Tillot; m. Maria Petrovna Urasova 1930; four d.; ed. First Leningrad Medical Inst.
Junior Assoc., Asst. Prof. First Leningrad Medical Inst. 22-24; Head of Chair, Leningrad Mil. Medical Acad. 24-37; Prof. Kirov Mil. Medical Acad. 37-44; Head of Chair, Second Leningrad Medical Inst. 45-62; Head of Dept. of Inst. of Experimental Medicine, U.S.S.R. Acad. of Medical Sciences 48; Corresp. mem. U.S.S.R. Acad. of Medical Sciences 47-50, mem. 50; mem. C.P.S.U. 62-; mem. Cen. Council U.S.S.R. Physiol. Soc.; Hon. Pres. All-Union Pharmacological Soc.; Hon. mem. Rome Medical Acad.; mem. Int. Brain Research Org.; Hon. Pres. Union of Pharmacologists 66-; Hero of Socialist Labour, Orders of Lenin (two), State Prize, etc.; Dr. h.c. Charles Univ., Prague, Helsinki Univ., Rostock Univ.
Leisure interest: fishing.
Publs. Over 120 on pharmacology of endocrine glands, physiology and pharmacology of carotid haemoreceptors, reflectory dystrophy and its pharmacotherapy, pharmacology of nervous systems and new original neurotropic preparations (antiphiens), etc.
Institute of Experimental Medicine, 69/71 Kirovsky prospekt, Leningrad, U.S.S.R.
Telephone: 34-27-42 (Home); 34-54-47.

Anin, Patrick Dankwa, M.A., LL.B.; Ghanaian judge; b. 27 July 1928, Bekwai, Ashanti; m.; two s. two d.; ed. Achimota Coll., Selwyn Coll., Cambridge, and London School of Economics.
Called to Bar, Middle Temple 56, Called to Gold Coast Bar 56; fmr. Dir. Bank of Ghana; mem. Electoral Comm. 66-67; Commr. for Communications 67-68, Commr. for External Affairs 68-69; Justice of Appeal 69-; Chair. Bribery and Corruption Comm. 71-.
Leisure interests: reading, tennis.
Judge's Chambers, Supreme Court, P.O. Box 119, Accra, Ghana.

Anisimov, Anatoly Vasilyevich; Soviet diplomatist; b. 17 March 1919, Stepanovo Village, Vologda Region; ed. Pokrovsky Pedagogical Inst. of Leningrad.
Attaché, Soviet Embassy, Iran 43-54; First Sec., Dept. for Near East and Middle East Countries, Ministry of Foreign Affairs 54-56; Counsellor, Deputy Head of Dept. for Middle East Countries, Ministry of Foreign Affairs, 56-68, 72-; Amb. to Jordan 68-72; Badge of Honour.
Ministry of Foreign Affairs, Moscow, U.S.S.R.

Ankrah, Gen. Joseph Arthur; Ghanaian army officer; b. 18 Aug. 1915, Accra; s. of Samuel P. K. Ankrah and Beatrice A. Quaynor; m. 1st Elizabeth Oyoe 1939, 2nd Felicia Kailey 1953, 3rd Mildred C. Akosua 1962; seven s. eleven d.; ed. Wesley Methodist School, Accra, and Accra Acad.
Comes from Ga tribe, S. Ghana; Warrant Officer II, Infantry and Staff, Second World War; commissioned 47; Battalion Commdr., later Brigadier, Kasai Province, Congo 60-61, awarded Ghana Mil. Cross; Deputy Chief of Defence Staff, Ghana 61-July 65; Chief of Defence Staff and Chair. Nat. Liberation Council, Ghana, Feb. 66-April 69; Officer Order of the Volta, Grand Cordon

Most Venerable Order of Knighthood of the Pioneers (Liberia).
Leisure interests: sport, horse racing, gardening, reading.
c/o House D594/3 Asylum Down, Accra, Ghana.
Telephone: Accra 24583.

Annan, Baron (Life Peer) cr. 65, of Royal Burgh of Annan; **Noel Gilroy Annan,** O.B.E., M.A.; British university official; b. 25 Dec. 1916, London; s. of late James Gilroy Annan and Fannie Quinn; m. Gabriele Ullstein 1950; two d.; ed. Stowe School, King's Coll., Cambridge.
Served in War Office, War Cabinet Offices and Military Intelligence 40-44, France and Germany 44-46; Gen. Staff Officer, Political Division, British Control Comm. 45-46; Fellow, King's Coll., Cambridge 44-56, 66, Asst. Tutor 47, Lecturer in Politics 48-66, Provost 56-66; Provost of Univ. Coll., London 66-; Gov. of Stowe School 45-66, Queen Mary Coll. 56-60; Senior Fellow, Eton Coll. 56-66; mem. Gulbenkian Cttee. for Art in U.K. 57-64, Chair. Educ. Cttee. 71-; mem. Academic Planning Board, Univ. of East Anglia 60; Chair. Academic Planning Board, Univ. of Essex 62; mem. Academic Advisory Board Brunel Univ. 64; mem. Public Schools Comm. 66-70; Chair. Cttee. of Enquiry into Broadcasting 74-; Trustee, British Museum 63-; Dir. Royal Opera House, Covent Garden 75-; F.R.Hist.S.; Fellow, Berkeley Coll., Yale 63; Hon. Fellow, Univ. Coll., London 68; Hon. D.Litt. York, (England), Ontario; D. Univ. Essex; Foreign Hon. mem. American Acad. of Arts and Sciences; Le Bas Prize 48, James Tait Black Memorial Prize 51.
Leisure interest: Mediterranean travel.
Publs. *Leslie Stephen: His Thought and Character in Relation to his Time* 51, *The Intellectual Aristocracy* (in *Studies in Social History*, edited by J. H. Plumb) 56, *The Curious Strength of Positivism in English Political Thought* 59, *Kipling's Place in the History of Ideas* (in *Kipling's Mind and Art*) 64, *Roxburgh of Stowe* 65 and articles in *Victorian Studies* and other periodicals.
University College, Gower Street, London, WC1E 6BT, England.
Telephone: 387-7050.

Anne, H.R.H. The Princess, Mrs. Mark Phillips, G.C.V.O. (Anne Elizabeth Alice Louise); b. 15 Aug. 1950; d. of Queen Elizabeth II and Prince Philip, Duke of Edinburgh; m. Capt. Mark Anthony Peter Phillips 1973; ed. Benenden School, Kent.
President of Save the Children Fund; Patron of the Riding for the Disabled Asscn.; Commdt.-in-Chief of the Nursing and Ambulance Cadets of the St. John Ambulance Brigade; Chief Commdt. The Women's Royal Naval Service; Col.-in-Chief of 14th/20th King's Hussars, Worcestershire and Sherwood Foresters Regt., 8th Canadian Hussars (Princess Louise's); Freeman of City of London, of Fishmongers' Co., Farriers' Co.; Yeoman of Saddlers' Co.; Hon. Freeman of Lorimers' Co.; official visits abroad to the 14th/20th King's Hussars in Fed. Repub. of Germany 69, to see the work of the Save the Children Fund in Kenya 71, to the 2,500th anniversary celebrations of the Iranian monarchy 71, to 14th/20th King's Hussars and to see the work of the Save the Children Fund, Hong Kong 71, to S.E. Asia 72, Munich 72, Yugoslavia 72, Ethiopia and the Sudan 73, to visit Worcestershire and Sherwood Foresters Regt. in Berlin 73, in Hereford, Fed. Repub. of Germany 74, to Canada 74, Australia 75; has accompanied the Queen and the Duke of Edinburgh on several State Visits; has taken part in numerous equestrian competitions including Horse of the Year Show, Wembley and Badminton Horse Trials; winner of Raleigh Trophy 71 and Silver Medal 75 in Individual European Three Day Event; Sportswoman of the Year,

Sports Writers' Asscn., *Daily Express, World of Sport,* BBC Sports Personality 71.
Oak Grove, Sandhurst, Camberley, Surrey, England.

Annenberg, Walter H.; American publisher and diplomatist; b. 13 March 1908, Milwaukee, Wis.; s. of M. L. Annenberg; m. 2nd Leonore Cohn 1951; one d.; ed. Peddie School, Univ. of Pennsylvania.
President Triangle Publications Inc., Pa.; publishes *TV Guide;* Amb. to U.K. 69-75; Officier Légion d'Honneur; Commdr., Orders of Lion of Finland, Crown of Italy; Commdr. Order of Merit (Italy).
Llanfair Road, Wynnewood, Pa. 19096, U.S.A.

Annenkov, Nikolai Alexandrovich; Soviet theatre and film actor; b. 21 Oct. 1899; ed. Higher Theatre School of Maly Theatre, Moscow.
Actor of Maly Theatre 24-; mem. C.P.S.U. 42-; People's Artist of U.S.S.R. 60; State Prize (thrice); Order of Lenin; other decorations.
Main roles include: Mitya (*Poverty is no Vice* by A. N. Ostrovsky), Cherkun (*Barbarians* by Maxim Gorky), Sintsov (*Enemies* by Gorky), Nil (*Lower Middle Classes* by Gorky), Plakun (*The Eternal Source* by Zorin), Ognev (*Front* by A. Korneichuk), Motylev (*Glozy* by V. Gusev).
Maly Theatre, 1/6 Ploshchad Sverdlova, Moscow, U.S.S.R.

Annigoni, Pietro; Italian painter; b. 7 June 1910, Milan; m. 1st Anna Maggini 1937 (died 1968); 2nd Rosella Segreto 1976; one s. one d.; ed. Accademia di Belle Arti, Florence.
First exhibition held in Florence 32; exhibition, Milan 36; helped found group of modern realistic painting, which exhibited in Milan 47, and subsequently in Rome and Florence; exhbns. Wildenstein's (London 50, New York 57), Paris, London 54; retrospective exhbn. Brooklyn Museum, N.Y. 69, Calif. Palace of Legion of Honor, San Francisco 69, Galleria Levi, Milan 71; mem. Accademia di S. Luca, Rome, Arti del Disegno, Florence.
Leisure interest: sailing.
Works include portraits of The Duchess of Devonshire, Miss Margaret Rawlings, Lord and Lady Howard de Walden, Dame Margot Fonteyn; *Deposition of Christ with Dominican Saints* 36-40, *Say You This is Man?* 53, *Way to the Sermon on the Mount* 54, Portrait of H.M. Queen Elizabeth II 55, Portrait of H.R.H. the Prince Philip, Duke of Edinburgh 57, Portrait of H.R.H. Princess Margaret 58, *Life* 61, Portrait of President Kennedy 61; fresco *Crucifix* in S. Martino Castagno, Florence; Portrait of Pope John XXIII; altarpiece, Church of Claretian Fathers, Hayes, Middlesex, *The Immaculate Heart of Mary* 62; Portrait of H.M. Queen Elizabeth, the Queen Mother 63; *St. Joseph,* altarpiece Church of S. Lorenzo, Florence 64; *Resurrection* fresco in Church of S. Michele, Ponte Buggianese (Montecatini) 67, *Apocalypse* fresco 73, *The Last Supper* 75, *St. Benedict,* Church of Montecassino altarpiece 75; Portraits of Shah of Iran and Queen Farah Diba 68; second portrait of H.M. Queen Elizabeth II for Nat. Portrait Gallery, London 70; *Il Misericordioso* for Venerabile Arciconfraternità della Misericordia, Florence 70; portrait of H.R.H. the Duchess of Kent for Univ. of Leeds 71; *The Golden Age* (Frescos), Sala Pontormo, at Wethersfield House, Amenia, New York 72-73.
Borgo degli Albizzi 8, Florence, Italy.
Telephone: 212438.

Annorkwei II, Nene, Q.M.C.; Ghanaian chief; b. 1900; ed. Wesleyan School, Accra.
Entered Nigerian civil service as Treasury Clerk 19; transferred to Gold Coast 30; promoted to Accountant 44; elected Manche of Prampram 48; appointed Treas. of Provincial Council, Eastern Province, and mem.

Council's Standing Cttee. 48; later Pres. Joint Provincial Council of Chiefs (representing Eastern and Western Regions); Chair. Ghana Museum and Monuments Board 57-; Queen's Medal for Chiefs 56.
Manche of Prampram, Prampram, Ghana.

Anouilh, Jean Marie Lucien Pierre; French playwright; b. 23 June 1910; ed. Collège Chaptal and Univ. of Paris.
Cino-del-Duca Prize 70.
Plays include: *L'Ermine* (The Ermine) 34, *Y'avait un prisonnier* 35, *Le Voyageur sans bagages* 37, *Le Bal des Voleurs* (Thieves' Carnival) 38, *La Sauvage* (Restless Heart) 38, *Cavalcade d'Amour* 41, *Le Rendez-vous de Senlis* 42, *Léocadia* (Time Remembered) 42, *Euridice* (Point of Departure) 42, *Oreste* 45, *Antigone* 46, *Roméo et Juliette* (Fading Mansion) 46, *Medée* 46, *L'invitation au château* (Ring Round the Moon) 48, *Ardèle ou la Marguerite* 49, *La Répétition, ou l'amour puni* 50, *Colombe* 50, *La Valse des toréadors* (Waltz of the Toreadors) 52, *L'Alouette* (The Lark) 53, *Ornifle* 55, *Pauvre Bitos* (Poor Bitos) 56, *L'Hurluberlu* 58, *Beckett ou l'amour de Dieu* (Becket) 59, *Foire d'Empoigne* 60, *La Grotte* 61, *L'Orchestre* 62, *Monsieur Barnett* (TV play), *Le Boulanger, la Boulangère et le Petit Mitron* 68, *Cher Antoine* 69, *Ne Réveillez Pas Madame* 70, *You Were So Sweet When You Were Little* 74, *Mr. Barnett* 75, *L'Arrestation* 75.
Films include: *Monsieur Vincent, Pattes Blanches, Caprice de Caroline, Becket.*
3 rue de Furstenberg, Paris 6e, France.

Ansari, Homayoun J., M.S.; Iranian civil servant; b. 20 Dec. 1929, Esfahan; m. Leily Sheibani 1962; one s. one d.; ed. in Iran and U.S.A.
Senior Exploration Geologist, Nat. Iranian Oil Co. 56-59, Head of Studies and Co-ordination, Exploration and Production Dept. 59-62; Dir.-Gen. Petroleum Affairs, Ministry of Finance 62-64; Chair. and Man. Dir. Telephone Co. of Iran 64-71; Chair. and Man. Dir. Telecommunication Co. of Iran 71-74; Minister of Housing and Urban Devt. April 74-.
Publs. several scientific papers on petroleum exploration.
122 Sheibani Street, Darrus, Teheran, Iran.
Telephone: 2371017.

Ansari, Dr. Hooshang, M.A.; Iranian politician and economist; b. 1928; ed. in U.K., U.S.A. and Japan.
Former Press, Commercial and Econ. Attaché, Japan; Chief, Supervisory Comm., Public Supplies; mem. High Council, Iranian Aviation; Technical Under-Sec., Ministry of Commerce; Special Amb., African Countries; Amb. to Pakistan and Ceylon; Minister of Information; Amb. to U.S.A.; Minister of Economy 69-, and of Finance 74-.
Ministry of the Economy, Teheran, Iran.

Anseele, Edouard; Belgian engineer and politician; b. 1902, Ghent; ed. Univ. of Ghent.
Echevin (elected magistrate) in Ghent 33-34, 39-41 and 52-, Burgomaster 44-46; Pres. Comm. for the Electrification of the Railways 45; mem. Chamber of Representatives 36-; Minister of Communications 54-58; Minister of Posts, Telegraphs and Communications 62-66, 68-73; fmr. Vice-Pres. Belgian Socialist Party.
76 rue du Perroquet, Ghent, Belgium.

Ansell, Graham Keith, B.A.; New Zealand diplomatist; b. 2 March 1931, Lower Hutt, New Zealand; ed. Horowhenua Coll., Palmerston North Boys' School and Victoria Univ., Wellington.
Department of Industries and Commerce 48-51, of External Affairs 51-56; Second Sec., High Comm. to Ottawa 56-59; Asst., then Acting Head, Econ. and Social Affairs Div., Dept. of External Affairs 59-62; Deputy High Commr., Canberra 64-68; Head, Econ.

Div., Ministry of Foreign Affairs 68-71; Minister, N.Z. Embassy, Tokyo 71-73; High Commr. Fiji 73-, Nauru 74-.
New Zealand High Commission, Suva; Home: 1 Marou Road, Suva, Fiji.

Ansett, Sir Reginald Myles, K.B.E.; Australian aviation, road transport and television company administrator; b. 13 Feb. 1909, Inglewood, Victoria; s. of C. J. Ansett; m. Joan McAuliffe Adams 1944; three d.
Chair. and Man. Dir. Ansett Transport Industries Ltd. and subsidiaries, Ansett Transport Industries (Operations) Pty. Ltd. (Trading as Ansett Airlines of Australia, Ansett Airlines of New South Wales, Ansett Airlines of S. Australia, Ansett Freight Express, Ansett Pioneer, Ansett Pioneer Ltd. (N.Z.), Aviation Engineering Supplies, Ansett Television Films, Barrier Reef Islands, MacRobertson Miller Airline Services, Provincial Motors, Ansett Motors, N.I.C. Instrument Co., Ansett General Aviation, Ansair, Mildura Bus Lines), Ansett Niugini Enterprises Ltd., Ansett Hotels Pty. Ltd., Ansett Hotels (P. and N.G.) Pty. Ltd., Austarama Television Pty. Ltd., Universal Telecasters Queensland Ltd., Wridgways Holdings Ltd., Ansett Industries Australia Ltd. (U.S.A.), Ansett Industries (Hong Kong) Ltd., Albury Border Transport Pty. Ltd., J. Sist and Co. Pty. Ltd., Transport Industries and Insurance Co. Ltd., Ansett Brewarrana Holdings Pty. Ltd., Van Dusen Aircraft Supplies Australia Ltd., Diners Clubs Ltd.
Leisure interests: horse racing, game shooting.
489 Swanston Street, Melbourne, Victoria, Australia.
Telephone: 3453144.

Ansiaux, Hubert-Jacques-Nicolas; Belgian banker; b. 24 Nov. 1908, Ixelles; s. of Jacques N. C. Ansiaux and Eva H. M. Olislager; m. Geneviève Mayer-Astruc; one s. one d.; ed. Univ. Libre de Bruxelles.
Director, Nat. Bank of Belgium 41-54, Deputy Gov. 54-57, Gov. 57-71; Chair. Inst. Belgo-Luxembourgeois du Change 57-; Dir. Bank for Int. Settlements 57-; Gov. for Belgium, Int. Monetary Fund 57-; Chair. Conseil des Institutions publiques de Crédit 57-; mem. Conseil général de la Caisse Générale d'Epargne et de Retraite 57-; Chair. Conseil d'Admin. de l'Office Central de la Petite Epargne 57-; mem. Man. Board and Chair. Standing Finance Cttee. of Carnegie Hero Fund 57-; mem. Conseil d'Administration de l'Université Libre de Bruxelles 59-; First Vice-Chair. Nat. Council on Scientific Policy 59-; Alt. Gov. for Belgium of Int. Bank for Reconstruction and Devt., Int. Finance Corpn. 60-; mem. Man. Board Fondation Nationale pour le Financement de la Recherche Scientifique 60-; Chair. Comité Consultatif des Finances de la Fondation Universitaire et du Fonds Nat. de la Recherche Scientifique; Chair. Cttee. of Govs. of Central Banks of European Econ. Community; Officer Order of Leopold and Grand Officer Order of Crown (Belgium) and decorations from Netherlands, Luxembourg, Syria, Italy, Greece, France, Thailand, Great Britain and U.S.A.
Home: Le Bois Sauvage, 158 avenue Circulaire, B-1180 Brussels, Belgium.
Telephone: 02/74-58-93.

Ansquer, Vincent, LIC. EN DROIT; French politician; b. 11 Jan. 1925, Vendée; s. of Vincent Ansquer and Berthe Ripoche; m. Monique Chaudière 1954; two d.; ed. Coll. St.-Stanislas, Nantes, Ecole Nat. de la France d'Outre-mer.
With Overseas Admin. 47; commercial activity in Guinea 48-52, in France 52-62; mem. Jeune Chambre Economique, la Roche sur Yon, Consular del., Chamber of Commerce 52-62; mem. Parl. 62-; Vice-Pres. Parl. Finance Comm. 63-; Rapporteur du Budget, Commissariat au Plan, Dél. a l'Aménagement du Territoire et à l'Action Régionale 63-; Mayor of La Bruffière 65-;

mem. Govt. Group on Property Laws 73; Pres. Regional Council for the Loire 74-; Minister of Commerce May 74-; Pres. Parl. Asscn. of Small and Medium Enterprises 72-73; Pres. UDR for Vendée 64-, Deputy Vice-Pres. UDR Group, mem. Exec. Bureau; Dir. *La Vendée Libre, Espaces.*
Ministère du Commerce, 19 rue de Constantine, 75007 Paris; Home: 85530 La Bruffière, Vendée, France.

Antes, Horst; German painter and sculptor; b. 28 Oct. 1936, Heppenheim a.d.B.; s. of Valentin Antes and Erika Antes; m. Dorothea Grossmann 1961; one s. one d.; ed. State Acad. of Fine Arts, Karlsruhe.
Worked in Florence, then Rome; Prof. at State Acad. of Fine Arts, Karlsruhe 65-71; now living in Karlsruhe and Tuscany, Italy; Villa Romana Prize, Florence 62; Villa Massimo Prize, Rome 63; mem. Acad. der Künste, Berlin.
One-man shows: Troisième Biennale de Paris, Museum Ulm, Städtische Galerie Munich 64; Gallery Stangl Munich 65, 68, 72; Gimpel and Hanover Gallery, Zürich and London 67, 70, 73; Lefèbre Gallery, New York 67, 69, 72, 74; 23rd Biennale Venice 66; 10th Biennale São Paulo 69; Staatliche Kunsthalle Baden-Baden, Kunsthalle Bern, Kunsthalle Bremen, Frankfurter Kunstverein 71-72. Group exhibitions: Pittsburgh International Exhibition 61, 64, 70; *Dokumenta*, Kassel 64, 68. Catalogues: *Catalog of Etchings* 62-66 (G. Gercken) 68, *Catalog of Books* (W. Euler) 68.
Hohenbergstrasse 11, 7500 Karlsruhe-41 (Wolfartsweier), Federal Republic of Germany.
Telephone: (0271) 491621.

Anthony, Rt. Hon. (John) Douglas, P.C.; Australian farmer and politician; b. 31 Dec. 1929, Murwillumbah; s. of Hubert Lawrence Anthony and Jessie, née Stirling; m. Margot Macdonald Budd 1957; two s. one d.; ed. Murwillumbah High School, The King's School, Paramatta, and Queensland Agricultural Coll.
Member House of Reps. 57-, Exec. Council 63-73, Minister for the Interior 64-67, of Primary Industry 67-71, for Trade and Industry 71-72, for Overseas Trade Nov. 75-, for Minerals and Energy Nov.-Dec. 75, for Natural Resources Dec. 75-; Deputy Prime Minister Feb. 71-Dec. 72, Nov. 75-; Deputy Leader Nat. Country Party of Australia 66-71, Leader 71-.
Leisure interests: golf, squash, tennis, swimming.
Parliament House, Canberra, A.C.T., Australia.
Telephone: Canberra 731026.

Antokolsky, Pavel Grigorievich; Soviet poet; b. 1 July 1896; Leningrad; ed. Moscow Univ. Law Faculty.
State prizewinner for *My Son* 43; Order of Red Banner of Labour (twice) and other decorations.
Publs. *Robespierre and Gorgon* 28, *1871 Commune* 31, *François Villon* 34, *Great Distances* 35, *Pushkin's Year* 38, *Half a Year* 42, *Iron and Fire* 42, *The Third Book of the War* 43, *My Son* 43, *A Lane in Arbat* 54, *Ocean* 55, *The Studio* 58, *The Strength of Vietnam* 60, *Pushkin* 60, *High Tension* 62, *Picasso* 63, *Adopted Brothers* 63, *Selected Poems* (2 vols.) 64, *Fourth Dimension* 64, *Les voies des poètes* 65, *Poèmes* (2 vols.) 66; trans. of French poets.
U.S.S.R. Union of Writers, Vorovskogo Ulitsa 52, Moscow, U.S.S.R.

Antonio (Antonio Ruiz Soler); Spanish dancer; b. 4 Nov. 1921, Seville; s. of Francisco and María Dolores.
Danced with Rosario under name *Los Chavalillos Sevillanos*, later *Rosario and Antonio* until 52; with own company, *Antonio, Ballet Español* 52- and *Antonio y sus Ballets de Madrid* 64; Cross of Isabel la Católica; Gold Medal of Swedish Dance Acad.; Medal of Ministry of Information 63; Cross of Commdr. of Civil Merit; Gold Plate of Spanish Artists Syndicate; Silver Plate of Min-

istry of Information to First Dancer of Spain; Medal of Work and numerous other medals and decorations.
Coslada 7, Madrid, Spain.
Telephone: Madrid 256-24-01.

Antonioni, Michelangelo, L. ECON. and COMM.; Italian film director; b. 29 Sept. 1912; ed. Univ. of Bologna.
Film critic *Corriere Padano* and *L'Italia Libera*; City of Munich Prize 68.
Films: *Gente del Po* 43-47, *Amorosa Menzogna* 49, *N.U.* 48, *Sette Canne un Vestito, La Villa dei Mostri, Superstizione* 49 (documentaries); *Cronaca di un Amore* 50, *La Signora Senza Camelie* 52-53, *I Vinti* 52, *Amore in Città* 53, *Le Amiche* 55, *Il Grido* 57, *L'Avventura* 59, *La Notte* 61 (Silver Bear, Berlin Film Festival 61), *L'Eclisse* 62, *Il Deserto Rosso* 64 (Golden Lion, XXV Venice Film Festival 64), *Blow Up* 66 (Golden Palm, Cannes Film Festival 67), *Zabriskie Point* 70, *Chung Kuo-China* 72, *The Passenger* 74.
Via Vincenzo Tiberio 18, Rome, Italy.

Antoniu, Costache; Romanian actor; b. 26 Feb. 1900, Țigănești, Jași; ed. Jași Coll. of Dramatic Arts.
Actor in provincial theatres until 35; mem. Romanian Nat. Theatre Co., Bucharest 35-; Rector and Prof. Theatre Inst. "I. L. Caragiale" 54-70; Deputy to Grand Nat. Assembly; mem. Nat. Peace Cttee.; Pres. Artistes' Asscn.; notable roles include Scapin, title role in *Les Fourberies de Scapin* (Molière), Nenea Iancu in *Acolo departe* (*There Far Away*, Ștefănescu) and, in recent years, Prof. Andronic in *Ultima oră* (*Stop Press*, Sebastian), Spiridon Hampu in *Ziua cea mare* (*The Great Day*, Banuș), Profirel in *Hagi Tudose* (Delavrrancea), Udrea in *Steaua fără nume* (*The Nameless Star*, Sebastian), title role in Chekov's *Uncle Vanya*, Prozorov in Chekhov's *Three Sisters*, Muromschi in *Nunta lui Crecinschi* (*Crecinshi's Wedding*, Suhovo-Cobylin), Micola in *Fericirea furată* (*Stolen Happiness*, Franco), Dr. Prell in *Institutorii* (Ernst), Cernogubov in *Personal Matter* (Stein), Pristanda, the Candidate in *D'Ale Carnavalului* (*Carnival Scenes*) and the tipsy citizen in *O Scrisoare Pierdută* (*A Lost Letter*, Caragiale), title role in *Conu Leonida* (Caragiale), Spirache in *Titanic Vals* (Mușatescu), etc.; Film roles include: Gounod in *Darclée*, Priest in *Pădurea Spînzuraților* (*The Forest of the Hanged*), *Vacanță la Mare* (*Holiday at the Seaside*), *Streinul* (*The Stranger*); Artist of the People, three State Prizes, Order of Labour Second Class, Star of Romanian People's Repub.
Publ. *From the Past of the Romanian Theatre* (memoirs) 53.
B-dul Schitu Măgureanu 1, Bucharest, Romania.
Telephone: 15-33-95.

Antonov, Alexei Konstantinovich; Soviet politician; b. 12; ed. Leningrad Polytechnic Inst.
Engineer, later Chief Factory Engineer 35-57; econ. work, Leningrad Regional Econ. Cttee. 57-59, Dep. Chair. Leningrad Regional Econ. Cttee. 59-61, Chair. 61-65; Candidate mem. Central Cttee. of C.P.S.U. 61-72, mem. 72-; Minister of Electro-Technical Industry (U.S.S.R.) 65-; Deputy to U.S.S.R. Supreme Soviet 62-.
Ministry of Electro-Technical Industry, 12 Bolshaya Gruzinskaya ulitsa, Moscow, U.S.S.R.

Antonov, Nikolai Afanasyevich; Soviet politician; b. 1921; ed. Leningrad Industrial Inst.
Member C.P.S.U. 44-; Soviet Army 41-45; Dir. Borovichi Mechanical Plant 45-55; Chair. Exec. Cttee. of Borovichi City Soviet of Workers' Deputies 55-56; Chief of Section, Novgorod Regional Cttee. of C.P. 56-60; Sec. Novgorod Regional Cttee. of C.P. 60-66; Chair. Exec. Cttee. Novgorod Regional Soviet of Workers' Deputies 66-72; First Sec. Novgorod Regional Cttee. of C.P.S.U. 72-; Deputy to U.S.S.R. Supreme Soviet 74-.
Regional Committee of the C.P.S.U., Novgorod. U.S.S.R.

Antonov, Oleg Konstantinovich; Soviet aircraft designer; b. 7 Feb. 1906, Leningrad; ed. Leningrad Polytechnical Inst.
Member C.P.S.U. 45-; Head Experimental Design Dept. 46-; Designer-Gen. for Aircraft Industry 62-; gliders and aeroplanes designed under his direction include: AN-2, AN-10, AN-12, AN-14, AN-22 (ANTEI); Corresp. mem. Ukrainian Acad. of Sciences 55-67, Academician 67-; Deputy to Supreme Soviet of U.S.S.R.; mem. comm. for Transport, Soviet of the Union; State Prize 52; Lenin Prize 62; Hero of Socialist Labour 66; Order of Lenin (twice); "Hammer and Sickle" Gold Medal; other decorations.
Ministry of Aircraft Industry, Moscow, U.S.S.R.

Antonov, Sergei Fyodorovich; Soviet engineer, diplomatist and politician; b. 1911; ed. Leningrad Inst. of Engineers for Dairy Products Industry.
Worked formerly in agencies and ministries of meat and milk industry; Minister of Milk and Dairy Products Industry 54-57; Envoy-Counsellor, Embassy to People's Repub. of China 58-60; Amb. to Afghanistan 60-65; Minister of Meat and Milk Industry 65-; Deputy U.S.S.R. Supreme Soviet 66-; mem. Central Auditory Comm. C.P.S.U. 66-.
Ministry of Meat and Milk Industry, Moscow, U.S.S.R.

Antonova, Irina Alexandrovna; Soviet art historian; b. 20 March 1922, Moscow; ed. Moscow Lomonosov Univ.
Scientist and Post-Graduate Student, State A.S. Pushkin Museum 46-49, Senior Scientific Worker 49-61; Dir. 61-; specialist in Italian art; contributor on ancient and modern Western art in journals *Iskusstvo* (Art), *Tvorchestvo* (Creative Work) and *Khudozhnik* (Artist); Dir. Soviet Art Exhbn. in Czechoslovakia 57, Austria 59; Head Soviet Pavilion, Venice 60; mem. C.P.S.U. 54-. Publs. *Venetian Painting of the 16th Century* 56, *Veronese* 63; script for film *Pictures in the Dresden Gallery*.
State A.S. Pushkin Museum of Fine Arts, Volkhonka 12, Moscow, U.S.S.R.

Antunovic, Rista; Yugoslav politician; b. 25 June 1917; ed. Belgrade Univ.
Former Sec. District Cttee. Yugoslav Communist Youth Fed.; fmr. mem. C.P. District Cttee. for Leskovac; mem. Communist Party 40-; a leader of liberation movement in S. Serbia, Second World War; later Sec. C.P. District Cttees. for Vranje and Leskovac; Commdr. First Div. Nat. Liberation Army, S. Serbia; mem. Central Cttee. C.P. of Serbia 45-; Central Cttee. of Yugoslav C.P. 52-; mem. Exec. Cttee. Central Cttee. of Serbian C.P. 48-; later Sec. Serbian C.P. City Cttee. for Belgrade, later Org. Sec. Central Cttee. Serbian C.P.; also Minister of Trade and Minister of Agriculture for Serbia, and mem. Exec. Council for Serbia; mem. Fed. Assembly 45-; later mem. Fed. Exec. Council, mem. Fed. Chamber of Fed. Assembly; decorations include Order of People's Hero, Order of Nat. Liberation, Order of Repub. with Gold Wreath, Partisan Memorial Order.
c/o Federal Executive Council, Belgrade, Yugoslavia.

Anwar Sani, Chaidir; Indonesian diplomatist; b. 19 Feb. 1918, Padang; m.; six c.; ed. Univ. of Leyden, Netherlands.
First Sec., Indonesian Embassy, Paris 50-52; Ministry of Foreign Affairs, Djakarta, Chief Asian Div. 52-55, Deputy Head Asian and Pacific Directorate 57-60, Head Directorate of Int. Orgs. 65-66, Chef de Cabinet 66 and Dir.-Gen. of Political Affairs 66-67; Counsellor, Embassy, Cairo 55 and Peking 55-57; Minister Counsellor, Embassy, New Delhi 60-64; Amb. to Belgium and Luxembourg and Head Indonesian Mission to the EEC 70-72; Perm. Rep. to UN 72-.
Permanent Mission of Indonesia to United Nations, 733 Third Avenue, 11th Floor, New York, N.Y. 10017, U.S.A.

Aoussou, Koffi; Ivory Coast public official; b. 1924, Yamoussokro; ed. Ecole Spéciale des Travaux Publics, Paris.
Formerly attached to Office of Public Works, Abidjan; subsequently Chef de Cabinet to the Minister of Public Works, then Sec. of State for Industry and the Plan; fmr. Amb. to Italy, to Belgium, Netherlands, Luxembourg and EEC; Pres., Autorité pour l'Aménagement de la Vallée du Bandama 69; Pres. Air Afrique 73-; mem. Exec. Cttee. IATA 73.
Air Afrique, Avenue L. Barthe, B.P. 21017, Adjbian, Ivory Coast.

Apel, Hans Eberhard, DR.RER.POL.; German economist and politician; b. 25 Feb. 1932, Hamburg; m. Ingrid Schwingel 1956; two d.; ed. Hamburg Univ.
Apprentice, Hamburg export and import business 51-54; Sec. Socialist Group in European Parl. 58-61, Head, Econ., Finance and Transport Dept. 62-65; mem. Bundestag 65-, Chair. Transport Cttee. 69-72; Deputy Chair. Social Democratic Group in Bundestag 69-72; mem. Nat. Exec. Social-Democratic Party (SPD) 70-; Parl. Sec. of State, Fed. Ministry of Foreign Affairs 72-73; Fed. Minister of Finance May 74-; mem. of Board, Howaldt-Deutsche Werft AG 70-74.
Leisure interest: football.
Publs. *Edwin Cannan und seine Schüler* 61, *Raumordnung in der Bundesrepublik* (in *Deutschland* 1975) 64, *Europas Neue Grenzen* 64, *Der Deutsche Parlamentarismus* 68, *Bonn, den..., Tagebuch eines Abgeordneten* 72.
53 Bonn, Rheindorfer Strasse 108, Federal Republic of Germany.

Apel, Willi, DR.PHIL.; American (b. German) musicologist; b. 1893, Konitz, W. Prussia (now Chojnice, Poland); s. of Max and Ida Apel (née Schoenlank); m. Ursula Siemering 1928; ed. Univs. of Bonn, Munich, Berlin.
Piano studies with Leonid Kreutzer, Edwin Fischer; lecturer on music 26-36; went to U.S.A. 36; taught at Longy School of Music 36-43, Harvard Univ. and Radcliffe Coll. 38-42, Boston Center for Adult Education 37-50; Prof. of Music, Indiana Univ. 50-63, Emeritus Prof. 64-; Fellow, Medieval Acad. of America; Gold Medal, Monteverdi Festival, Venice 68.
Publs. *The Notation of Polyphonic Music 800–1600* 42, *Harvard Dictionary of Music* 44 (rev. 69), *Historical Anthology of Music* (with A. T. Davison, 2 vols.) 46, 50, *Masters of the Keyboard* 47, *French Secular Music of the Late 14th Century* 50, *Gregorian Chant* 58, *Harvard Brief Dictionary of Music* 60, *Geschichte der Orgel- und Klaviermusik bis 1700* 67 (English trans. 72), *French Secular Compositions of the 14th Century*, 3 vols. 69-72.
1018 East Second Street, Bloomington, Ind., U.S.A.
Telephone: 33-2-1655.

Apithy, Sourou Migan; Benin politician; b. 8 April 1913; ed. Ecole Libre des Sciences Politiques, Ecole Nat. d'Organisation Economique et Sociale.
Deputy of Dahomey to French Constituent Assemblies 45-46; mem. Nat. Assembly 46-58; del. to seventh and eighth sessions UN 53; mem. Grand Council French West Africa 47-57; Pres. Gen. Council Dahomey 55-57; Prime Minister Provisional Govt. 58-59; Minister without Portfolio 60; Vice-Pres. and Minister of the Plan and Development 60; Ambassador of Dahomey to France, U.K., and Switzerland to 63; Minister of Finance, Economy and the Plan 63-64; Pres. of the Repub. of Dahomey 64-Nov. 65; mem. Pres. Council 70-72; detained following coup 72; Commdr. de la Grande-Comore.
Publ. *Au Service de mon Pays.*
c/o Ministry of Justice, Cotonou, Benin.

Apodaca, Jerry; American politician; b. 3 Oct. 1934, Las Cruces, New Mexico; s. of Raymond and Alisa Apodaca; m. Clara Melendres 1956; two s. three d.; ed. Univ. of New Mexico.

History teacher and football and track coach, Valley High School, Albuquerque, N.M. 57-60; Owner, Jerry Apodaca Insurance Agency, Jerry Apodaca Realty; Pres. Family Shoe Center; State Senator, Dona Ana County 66-74; Governor, State of New Mexico Jan. 75-. Leisure interest: sports.
Governor's Office, Executive-Legislative Building, Santa Fe, New Mexico 87503; Governor's Residence, Mansion Drive, Santa Fe, New Mexico 87501, U.S.A.

Aponte Martinez, H.E. Cardinal Luis; American (Puerto Rican) ecclesiastic; b. 4 Aug. 1922, Lajas; s. of Santiago Evangelista Aponte and Rosa Martínez; ed. St. Ildefonso Seminary, San Juan and St. John's Seminary, Boston, Mass., U.S.A.
Ordained priest 50; Curate, Patillas, then Pastor of Santa Isabel; Sec. to Bishop McManus, Vice-Chancellor of Diocese of Ponce 55-57; Pastor of Aibonito 57-60; Chaplain to Nat. Guard 57-60; Auxiliary Bishop of Ponce and Titular Bishop of Lares 60-63; Bishop of Ponce 63-64; Archbishop of San Juan 64-; created Cardinal by Pope Paul VI 73; Dir. of Devt. for Catholic Univ. of Puerto Rico 60-63; Pres. Puerto Rican Episcopal Conf. 66-; Hon. LL.D. (Fordham Univ.) 66; Hon. S.T.D. (Inter American Univ. of Puerto Rico) 69.
Arzobispado, Calle San Jorge 201, Santurce, Puerto Rico 00912.

Appel, André, D.D., L.H.D., D.S.T.; French ecclesiastic; b. 20 Dec. 1921, Strasbourg; three s. one d.
Former Chaplain Univ. of Paris; Sec.-Gen. French Protestant Fed. 56-64; Pastor Temple Neuf, Strasbourg 64-65; Sec.-Gen. Lutheran World Fed. 66-74; Pres. Lutheran Church in Alsace and Lorraine 74-.
1A quai St. Thomas, F67081 Strasbourg-Cédex, France. Telephone: 88-324586.

Appel, Karel Christian; Netherlands painter; b. 25 April 1921, Amsterdam; ed. Rijksakademie van Beeldende Kunsten, Amsterdam.
Began career as artist 38; exhibitions in Europe, America and Japan 50-; has executed murals in Amsterdam, The Hague, Rotterdam, Brussels and Paris; UNESCO Prize, Venice Biennale 53; Lissone Prize, Italy 58; Acquisition Prize, São Paulo Bienal 59; Graphique Int. Prize, Ljubljana, Yugoslavia 59; Guggenheim Nat. Prize, Netherlands 51; Guggenheim Int. Prize 61.
Office: c/o Galerie Statler, 51 rue de Seine, Paris; Home: 7 rue Brézin, Paris 14e, France.

Appiah, Joe; Ghanaian lawyer and politician; b. 16 Nov. 1918, Kumasi; m. Peggy Cripps 1953; ed. Mfantsipim Secondary School, Cape Coast.
Worked as lawyer, later politician; mem. Convention People's Party; formed Opposition Nat. Liberation Movement Feb. 55; imprisoned 60-62; mem. Political Cttee. July 66-69; goodwill Amb. to U.S.A. and U.K. Sept. 66; Leader, Nationalist Party with M.K. Apaloo May 69, merged to form United Nat. Party (UNP) July 69; defeated in elections Aug. 69; Pres. Ghana Bar Asscn.; Chair. opposition Justice Party Oct. 70-72; Roving Amb. for Nat. Redemption Council July 72-.
Office of the National Redemption Council, P.O. Box 1627, Accra, Ghana.

Appleton, Rt. Rev. George, C.M.G., M.A., M.B.E.; British ecclesiastic; b. 20 Feb. 1902, Windsor; s. of Thomas George and Lily Appleton; m. Marjorie A. Barrett 1929; one s. two d.; ed. County Boys' School, Maidenhead, Selwyn Coll., Cambridge and St. Augustine's Coll., Canterbury.
Ordained deacon 25, priest 26; Curate, Stepney Parish Church 25-27; Missionary in charge S.P.G. Mission, Irrawaddy Delta 27-33; Warden, Coll. of Holy Cross, Rangoon 33-41; Archdeacon of Rangoon 43-46; Dir. of Public Relations, Govt. of Burma 45-46; Vicar of Headstone 47-50; Sec. Conf. of British Missionary Socs.

50-57; Rector, St. Botolph, Aldgate, London 57-62; Archdeacon of London and Canon of St. Paul's Cathedral 62-63; Archbishop of Perth (Australia) 63-69; Anglican Archbishop in Jerusalem 69-74; retd. 74.
Publs. *John's Witness to Jesus* 55, *In His Name* 56, *Glad Encounter* 59, *On the Eightfold Path* 61, *Daily Prayer and Praise* 62, *Acts of Devotion* 63, *One Man's Prayers* 67, *Jerusalem Prayers for the World Today* 73, *Journey for a Soul* 74.
7/8 Ginge, Wantage, Oxon., OX12 8QR, England. Telephone: East Hendred 583.

Appleyard, Raymond K., M.A., PH.D.; British scientist; b. 5 Oct. 1922, Birkley; m.; one s. two d.; ed. Rugby School, Trinity Coll., Cambridge.
Instructor in Physics and Biophysics, Yale Univ. 49-51; Fellow in Natural Sciences, Rockefeller Foundation 51-53; Assoc. Research Officer, Atomic Energy of Canada Ltd. 53-56; Sec. UN Scientific Cttee. on the Effects of Atomic Radiation 57-61; Dir. Biology Services, European Atomic Energy Community (EURATOM) 61-73; Exec. Sec. European Molecular Biology Org. 65-73; Sec. European Molecular Biology Conf. 69-73; Dir.-Gen. Scientific and Technical Information, Information Management, Comm. of European Communities 73-.
Directorate-General for Scientific and Technical Information and Information Management, 29 rue Aldringen, Luxembourg.

Apró, Antal; Hungarian politician; b. 1913.
Joined Communist Party 31; Pres. of Building Workers' Asscn. 45; Gen. Sec. Trade Union Council 48-51; Minister of Building Materials Industry 52-53; Deputy Prime Minister 53-56, 61-71; Minister of Industry 56-57; First Deputy Prime Minister 58-61; Perm. Rep. to Council for Mutual Econ. Aid 62-71; Pres. Nat. Council, Patriotic People's Front 56-57; First Speaker of Parl. 71-; mem. Politburo, Socialist Workers' Party.
Houses of Parliament, H-1357 Kossuth L. tér, Budapest, Hungary.

Aquarone, Stanislas Raoul Adrien, B.A., A.M., PH.D.; Australian international civil servant; b. 13 Nov. 1915, Melbourne; m. 1941; two s. two d.; ed. Univ. of Toronto Schools, Univ. of Toronto, and Columbia Univ., N.Y.
Former teacher of French language and literature, Hamilton Coll. and in Columbia, Panama and Toronto Univs.; Sec. Int. Court of Justice 48-51, First Sec. 51-60, Deputy Registrar 60-66, Registrar 66-.
Publ. *The Life and Works of Emile Littré (1801–1881)* 58.
International Court of Justice, Peace Palace, The Hague; Home: Benoordenhoutsweg 93, The Hague, Netherlands.

Aquino, Francisco, M.P.A.; Salvadorian agricultural engineer and economist; b. 12 Sept. 1919; s. of Francisco Aquino and Lucila Herrera; m. María Dalila Negro 1946; three s. one d.; ed. Coll. for Agronomic Studies, San Salvador and Harvard Univ., U.S.A.
Land Appraiser, Mortgage Bank, San Salvador 42, Analyst, Nat. Planning Asscn., Washington, D.C. 43; Man. Fed. of Rural Credit Co-operatives, San Salvador 44; Adviser to Minister of Economy, Guatemala 46-47; Dir. Econs. Research Dept., Ministry of Agriculture, San Salvador 47-48; Economist, Econ. Comm. for Latin America (ECLA) 48-56; Chief, Cereals Section, Food and Agricultural Org. (FAO), Rome 56-59; Dir. ECLA-FAO Econs. Div., Santiago de Chile 59-61; Minister of Agriculture, El Salvador April-June 61; Pres. Cen. Reserve Bank of El Salvador, and concurrently, Gov. for El Salvador, in Int. Monetary Fund (IMF), in Int. Bank for Reconstruction and Devt. (IBRD—World Bank) and Affiliate in Cen. American Bank for Econ. Integration, also mem. Nat. Planning Council and Pres. Cen. American Monetary Council 61-66; Technical Man. Inter-American Devt. Bank, Washington, D.C. 67-68; Exec. Dir. UN-FAO World

Food Programme 68-; Chair. Joint Board of Govs. IMF-IBRD 64; Order of Christopher Columbus. Leisure interests: music and wild-life.
Via delle Terme di Caracalla, Rome; Home: via Degli Orti Flaviani 4, Rome, Italy.
Telephone: 5797 (Office); 5138018 (Home).

Arafat, Yasser (*pseudonym* of Mohammed Abed Ar'ouf Arafat); Palestinian resistance leader; b. 1929, Jerusalem; ed. Cairo Univ.
Joined League of Palestinian Students 44, mem. Exec. Cttee. 50, Pres. 52-56; formed, with others, Al Fatah movt. 56; engineer in Egypt 56, Kuwait 57-65; Pres. Exec. Cttee. of Palestine Liberation (Al Fatah) June 68-, Pres. Cen. Cttee., Head, Pol. Dept. 73-; Gen. Commdr. Palestinian Revolutionary Forces.
Palestine Liberation Organization, Colombani Street, Off Sadat Street, Dr. Raji Nasr Building, Ras Beirut, Lebanon.

Aragon, Louis; French novelist, poet and essayist; b. 3 Oct. 1897, Paris; ed. Univ. of Paris.
One of founders and fmr. leader Surrealist Movement, now leader Socialist Realism Movement; Sec. French section of Int. Asscn. of Writers for Defence of Culture; mem. Cttee. of Dirs. *Europe review*; Dir. fmr. Paris daily *Ce Soir*; Dir. *Les Lettres Françaises* (weekly) 53-72; mem. Communist Party; mem. Lenin Int. Peace Prize Cttee.; mem. Acad. Goncourt 67-68; served with Tank Div. 39-40, prisoner of war, escaped to unoccupied France, worked in Resistance movt.; Hon. mem. American Acad. of Arts and Letters 72.
Publs. Novels: *Anicet, Le Libertinage, Le Paysan de Paris, Les cloches de Bâle, Les Beaux Quartiers* (awarded Prix Renaudot), *Les voyageurs de l'Impériale, Aurélien, La Semaine Sainte, La mise à mort, Blanche ou l'Oubli*; essays: *Traité du Style, Les aventures de Télémaque, Pour un réalisme socialiste*; poems: *Feu de joie, Le Mouvement perpétuel, La grande Gaité, Persécuté persécuteur, Hourra l'Oural, Le Crève-Coeur, Les Yeux d'Elsa, La Diane française, Les Yeux et la Mémoire, Elsa, Le Fou d'Elsa, Les Chambres, Poème du temps qui ne passe pas*; history: *Histoire de l'U.R.S.S. de 1917-1960*.
56 rue de Varenne, Paris 7e, France.

Aram, Abbas; Iranian diplomatist; b. 1906.
Entered diplomatic service 31; Asst. Chief, Third Political Div., Foreign Ministry 43; First Sec. Berne 45; First Sec., Counsellor, and Chargé d'Affaires, Washington 46, 49 and 50; Dir. Fourth Political Div., Foreign Ministry 51; Counsellor, Embassy, Baghdad 53; Chargé d'Affaires and Minister, Washington 53 and 54-56; Dir.-Gen. Political Affairs, Foreign Ministry 58; Amb. to Japan 58, concurrently to Republic of China; Minister of Foreign Affairs 59-60; Amb. to Iraq 60-62; Minister of Foreign Affairs 62-67; Amb. to U.K. 67-69, to People's Repub. of China 72-75, also accred. to Dem. Repub. of Viet-Nam and to Dem. People's Repub. of Korea.
Foreign Ministry, Teheran, Iran.

Araña Osorio, Gen. Carlos Manuel; Guatemalan army officer and politician; b. 17 July 1918.
Former Commdr. Zacapa Brigade, Guatemala Army; fmr. Amb. to Nicaragua; mem. Nat. Liberation Movement; Pres. of Guatemala 70-74.
Office of the President, Guatemala City, Guatemala.

Arapov, Boris Alexandrovich; Soviet composer; b. 12 Sept. 1905, Leningrad; s. of Alexander Boris Arapov and Elizabeth Arapova; m. Tatjana Todorova 1933; two d.
Professor Leningrad Conservatoire 40-; Exec. mem. Leningrad Composers' Section, Soviet Composers' Union; Honoured Worker of Arts of Uzbek S.S.R. 44, of R.S.F.S.R. 57; Order of Red Banner of Labour 53, and other awards.
Compositions include: *Tadzhik Suite* 38, *Negro Protest*

Songs for Voice and Jazz Orchestra 40, *Hodja Nasreddin* (Uzbek opera) 43, *Four Songs for Voice and Piano* 49, *Russian Suite for Symphony Orchestra* 50, symphony-poem *Free China* 59, *The Frigate "Victory"* (opera) 58, *Third Symphony* 63, *Concerto for Violin and Orchestra* 64, *Rain* (chamber opera) 65, *Concerto for Big Symphony Orchestra* 69, *Soliloquy for Baritone* 69, *Sonata for Piano* 70, *Dorian Gray* (ballet) 73, *Concerto for Violin, Piano, Percussion and Chamber Orchestra* 73, *Fourth Symphony for Baritone, Mezzo-Soprano, Speaker, Two Choirs and Big Symphony Orchestra* 75, *Four Sonnets by Petrarch for Mezzo-Soprano and Piano* 75.
Leisure interests: travel, western European painting, oriental decorative art.
Prospekt Y. Gagarina 35 kw 65, Leningrad 196142, U.S.S.R.
Telephone: 93-82-63.

Araripe Macedo, Lieut.-Gen. Joelmir Campos de; Brazilian air force officer; b. 16 Feb. 1909, Rio de Janeiro; s. of José Araripe Macedo and Zulmira Campos de Araripe Macedo; m. Maria de Lourdes Vianna 1934; one s. one d.; ed. Colegio Militar, Escola Militar and Escola Técnica do Exército.
Former Instructor, Escola Técnica do Exército; Pres. Fabrica Nacional de Motores, Co-ordinating Cttee. of Int. Airport Project; Dir. Engenharia da Aeronáutica, Material Aeronáutica, Rotas Aéreas; mem. Industrial Devt. Comm., Nat. Petroleum Council; Insp.-Gen. of Aviation; Minister of Aeronautics 72-; decorations from Brazil, Italy, France, Portugal, Ecuador, Bolivia, Korea, China, Paraguay, Colombia and Venezuela.
Leisure interest: reading practical works on aviation.
Publs. various articles on aeronautical subjects.
Ministério da Aeronáutica, Esplanada dos Ministérios, Brasília, D.F., Brazil.
Telephone: 23-0409, 23-1409, 23-2409.

Araújo, José Emilio Gonçalves, DR.AGRON.; Brazilian soil scientist; b. 8 Sept. 1922, Rio de Janeiro; s. of Antonio Araújo Fernández and Emerenciana Goncalves; m. Laurinda Lopez 1946; one s. two d.; ed. Universidade Rural do Brasil, Rio de Janeiro and Universidade Federal Rural do Sul, Pelotas.
Acting Prof., Coll. of Agriculture, Universidade Federal de Pelotas 46-48, Prof. 48-65; Prof. Escola Agrotecnica Visconde da Graça, Pelotas 52-60; Natural Resources Expert, Inter-American Inst. of Agricultural Science,. OAS 65; Dir. Inter-American Center for Rural Devst and Agrarian Reform 65-70; Dir. Instituto Inter-americano de Ciencias Agricolas, OAS 70-; Chief Soils Section, Instituto Agronomico do Sul 47-50, Dir. 52-53, mem. Perm. Technical Council on Soils 58-61; mem. Brazilian Soc. for Soil Science, Brazilian Geological Soc., Brazilian Soc. for the Advancement of Science, American Soc. of Agronomy, Latin-American Soc. of Soil Science, Int. Soil Science Asscn., etc.; Officer, Orden del Mérito Agrícola (Colombia) 70, Commdr. Orden Mérito Agrícola (Peru) 73, and other awards.
Publs. more than 35 formal papers and two books on agricultural soil research, agrarian reform and other related subjects.
Instituto Interamericano de Ciencias Agrícolas de la OEA, P.O. Box 10281, San José, Costa Rica.
Telephone: 22-20-22.

Araújo Sales, H.E. Cardinal Eugenio de; Brazilian ecclesiastic; b. 8 Nov. 1920, Acari.
Ordained 43; Bishop 54; Apostolic Administrator, See of São Salvador de Bahia until 68; Archbishop of São Salvador da Bahia 68-71; cr. Cardinal 69.
Palácio Arquiepiscopal do Campo Grande, Av. 7 de Setembro 309, Salvador, Est. da Bahia, Brazil.

Arboussier, Gabriel Marie D'; Senegalese politician; b. 14 Jan. 1908, Djenne, Mali; s. of Henri Arboussier and Aminata Ali Koita; m. 1946; one s. three d.; ed. Collège des Dominicains, Sorèze, Lycée de Toulouse and Faculty of Law, Univ. of Paris.

Governor's Office, Dakar 37-41, Head of Office, Yako 41-43; Head of Political Office for Ivory Coast 43-44; Dep. for French Equatorial Africa to French Constituent Assembly 45-47; organizer of Conf. at Bamako, which formed R.D.A. (Rassemblement Démocratique Africain) 46, Gen. Sec. 49-50; Rep. for Ivory Coast in Assembly of French Union 47-53, Vice-Pres. 47-50; Rep. of Niger at Grand Council of French West Africa 56-60, Vice-Pres., later Pres.; Minister of Justice and Keeper of The Seals, Senegal 60-62; Ambassador to France 63-64, concurrently Perm. Del. to UNESCO, Exec. Dir. UN Inst. for Training and Research 65-68; Amb. to Fed. Repub. of Germany 68-72; Consultant to Pontifical Comm. for Studies on Justice and Peace 67; Pres. Int. Inst. on Immunology and Blood Transfusion (INNIT); Grand Croix de l'Ordre National du Sénégal, Commdr. Légion d'Honneur and other decorations; Hammarskjöld Prize 67.

Leisure interests: literature, riding, tennis, swimming.

14 rue Calvin, 1204 Geneva; and 9c Plateau de Trontenex, 1208 Geneva, Switzerland.

Telephone: 28-60-82 (Office); 35-38-03 (Home).

Arbuzov, Alexei Nikolaevich; Soviet playwright; b. 1908, Moscow; ed. Leningrad Theatrical School.

Actor in theatres in Leningrad and Moscow 23-30; mem. Union of U.S.S.R. Writers; Literary work 30-; Order of Red Banner of Labour 58, 68.

Publs. plays: *Six Favourites* 35, *The Long Road* 35, *Tanya* 39, *The Year of the Tsar* 41, *Little House on the Outskirts* 43, *The Wandering Years* 54, *They are Waiting for us Somewhere* 53, *Irkutsk Story* 59, *The Twelfth Hour* 59, *The Prodigal Son* 61, *My Poor Marat* 64, *The Promise* 66, *Confessions at Night* 67, *Lucky Days of an Unlucky Man* 68.

Union of U.S.S.R. Writers, 52 Ulitsa Vorovskogo, Moscow, U.S.S.R.

Arbuzov, Boris Alexandrovich; Soviet chemist; b. 4 Nov. 1903, Novaya Alexandriya; ed. Inst. of Agriculture and Forestry, Kazan, and Univ. of Kazan.

Docent Prof , Inst. of Chemical Technology, Kazan 30-38; Prof. of Organic Chemistry, Univ. of Kazan 38-, Dean of Chemistry Div. 40-50; Dir. Inst. of Organic Chemistry in Kazan, U.S.S.R. Acad. of Sciences 58-65; Dir. Arbuzov Inst. of Organic and Physical Chemistry 65-; mem. U.S.S.R. Acad. of Sciences 53-; Deputy to U.S.S.R. Supreme Soviet 66-; mem. Foreign Affairs Comm., Soviet of Union; State prizewinner; Hero of Socialist Labour, three Orders of Lenin, Order of Red Banner of Labour (twice); Hammer and Sickle Gold Medal; other decorations.

Publs. *Investigations in the Field of Isomeric Rearrangements of Bicyclic Terpens and their Epoxydes* 36, *The Arbuzov Transformation*, etc.

Arbuzov Institute of Organic and Physical Chemistry, Kazan, U.S.S.R.

Archambault, Pierre; French journalist; b. 24 June 1912.

Préfet (Acting) Indre-et-Loire 44; Dir.-Gen. *La Nouvelle République du Centre-Ouest* 44-72, Vice-Pres. du Directoire 72-; Pres. Syndicat Nat. de la Presse Quotidienne Régionale 52-71, later Man.; Pres. Confédération de la Presse Française 70-, mem. Council Agence France-Presse 57-69, 71-; mem. Man. Council ORTF 64-72.

4-18 rue de la Préfecture, Tours, Indre-et-Loire, France.

Arciniegas, Germán, D.L.; Colombian writer and diplomatist; b. 6 Dec. 1900, Bogotá; s. of Rafael Arciniegas and Aurora Angueyra; m. Gabriela Vieira 1929; two d.; ed. Univ. Nacional, Bogotá.

Vice-Consul, London 29; Chargé d'Affaires, Buenos Aires 40; Minister of Education, Republic of Colombia

42-46; Visiting Prof. Univ. of Chicago 44, Univ. of Calif. 45, Columbia Univ. 47; Prof. Columbia Univ. 54-59; Amb. to Italy 59-62; Editor *Cuadernos*, Paris 62; Colombian Amb. to Venezuela 67-70; Editor *Amérique Latine*, a monthly section of *Revue des deux Mondes* 74-; mem. Acad. of History and Letters of Colombia; corresp. mem. acads. in Spain, Argentina, Mexico, Cuba, etc.; Hammarsjköld Prize 67.

Publs. *El Estudiante de la Mesa Redonda* 32, *América Tierra Firme* 37, *Los Comuneros* 38, *The Knight of El Dorado* 42, *Germans in the Conquest of America* 43, *The Green Continent* 44, *Este Pueblo de América* 45, *Caribbean, Sea of the New World* 46, *The State of Latin America* 52, *Amerigo and the New World* 55, *Italia*, *Guía para Vagabundos* 59, *América Mágica* 59, *América Mágica II* 61, *Cosas del Pueblo* 62, *El Mundo de la Bella Simoneta* 62, *Entre el Mar Rojo y el Mar Muerto* 64, *Latin America: A Cultural History* 66, *Genio y Figura de Jorge Isaacs* 67, *Medio Mundo Entre un Zapato* 69, *Nuevo Diario de Noé* 69, *Colombia Itinerario y Espíritu de la Independencia* 69, *Roma Secretísima* 72, *America en Europa* 75.

c/o Consulat de Colombia, 22 rue de l'Elysée, Paris 75008, France.

Arcy, Jean Baron D'; French television administrator; b. 10 June 1913, Versailles; s. of Richard, Baron d'Arcy and Lucie Huyot; m. 1st Marie M. Duval 1946 (deceased), one s.; m. 2nd Countess Manuela Serra 1970; ed. Ecole des Hautes Etudes Commerciales, Paris, Faculté de Droit, Paris, and Ecole d'Application d'Artillerie, Fontainebleau.

Artillery officer 34-45; asst. dir. in Ministry of Deported Prisoners and Refugees 44-45; private sec. to Minister of Armies 45-46; Dir. of office of Minister of Youth, Arts and Letters 47; technical adviser to Minister of Information 48-49; seconded for special duties with Radiodiffusion-Télévision Française 50-52, Television Programme Dir. 52-59, Dir. of Int. Relations of R.T.F. 59-61; Dir. Radio and Visual Services Div., UN 61-72; Pres. Video-Cites S.A. 73-; Chair. Int. Broadcast. Inst.; Chevalier Légion d'Honneur; Croix de Guerre; Resistance Medal.

8 Rue Leroux, 75116 Paris, France.

Telephone: 704 4735

Arden, John; British playwright; b. 26 Oct. 1930; ed. Sedbergh School, King's Coll., Cambridge, and Edinburgh Coll. of Art.

Fellow in Playwriting, Bristol Univ. 59-60; Visiting Lecturer (Politics and Drama), New York Univ. 67.

Plays: *All Fall Down* 55, *The Life of Man* 56, *The Waters of Babylon* 57, *Live Like Pigs* 58, *Sergeant Musgrave's Dance* 59, *Soldier, Soldier* 60, *The Business of Good Government* 60, *Wet Fish* 62, *The Workhouse Donkey* 63, *Ironhand* 63, *Ars Longa Vita Brevis* (with Margaretta D'Arcy) 64, *Armstrong's Last Goodnight* 64, *Left Handed Liberty* 65, *Friday's Hiding* (with Margaretta D'Arcy) 66, *The Royal Pardon* (with Margaretta D'Arcy) 66, *The Hero Rises Up* (musical with Margaretta D'Arcy) 68, two autobiographical plays *The Ballygombeem Bequest* 72, *The Island of the Mighty* 72.

c/o Margaret Ramsay Ltd., 14A Goodwin's Court, London, W.C.2, England.

Ardizzone, Edward, C.B.E., R.A., R.D.I.; British artist; b. 16 Oct. 1900, Haiphong; s. of French and Italian father and Scots mother; m. Catherine J. Anderson 1928; two s. one d.; ed. Clayesmore School, Westminster School of Art.

Clerk in London 18-26; freelance artist 26-; served in Royal Artillery 39-40; full-time official War Artist 40-45; Tutor, Royal Coll. of Art, London; has illustrated more than 150 books for British and American publishers; works purchased by the Tate Gallery, the Arts Council of Great Britain and various provincial art galleries; Kate Greenaway Medal; Hon. A.R.C.A.

Publs. A series of children's books, with original illustrations, including *Little Tim and the Brave Sea Captain*, *Tim All Alone*, *Diana and Her Rhinoceros*, *The Young Ardizzone: An Autobiographical Fragment*, *Diary of a War Artist* 74, etc., and numerous book illustrations.
No. 5, Vine Cottages, Rodmersham Green, Sittingbourne, Kent, England.

Ardon, Mordechai; Israeli (b. Polish) artist; b. 13 July 1896; ed. Bauhaus, Weimar and Munich Acad. of Fine Arts.
After working in Berlin and teaching in the Itten School of Art, emigrated to Israel 33; Adviser on Art to Ministry of Educ. and Culture, Jerusalem.
c/o Cité International des Arts, 18 rue de Hôtel de Ville, Paris, France.

Ardwick, Baron (Life Peer), cr. 70, of Barnes in the London Borough of Richmond-upon-Thames; **John Beavan;** British journalist; b. 1910; ed. Manchester Grammar School.
With *Evening Chronicle*, Manchester 28-30, *Manchester Evening News*; Diarist, Leader Writer *Evening Standard* 40-42; News Editor and Chief Sub-Editor, *The Observer* 42-43; Editor, *Manchester Evening News*; Dir. Manchester Guardian and Evening News Ltd. 43-46; London Editor, *Manchester Guardian* 46-55; Asst. Dir. Nuffield Foundation 55-60; Editor, *Daily Herald* Oct. 60-62; Political Adviser, *Daily Mirror* Group 62-.
House of Lords, London, S.W.1, England.

Aref, Maj.-Gen. Abdul Rahman Mohammed (brother of late President Abdul Salam Aref); Iraqi army officer and politician; b. 1916; ed. Baghdad Military Acad.
Head of Armoured Corps until 62; Commdr. 5th Div. Feb. 63-Nov. 63; assisted in overthrow of Gen. Kassem 63; mem. Regency Council 65; Asst. Chief of Staff Iraqi Armed Forces Dec. 63-64; Acting Chief of Staff 64, Chief of Staff 64-68; Pres. of Iraq April 66-July 68, also Prime Minister May 67. Living outside Iraq.

Areilza, José María de, Count of Motrico; Spanish diplomatist and politician; b. 3 Aug. 1909, Bilbao; s. of Enrique de Areilza and Countess de Rodas; m. Mercedes de Churruca, Countess Motrico 1932; three s. two d.; ed. Bilbao Univ. and Univ. of Salamanca.
Mayor of Bilbao 37; Dir.-Gen. of Industry, Franco Cabinet 38-40; mem. Cortes 43-47; Amb. to Argentina 47-50; industrial and banking activities 50-54; Amb. to U.S.A. 54-60, to France 60-64; Sec.-Gen. Monarchist Party 66-69; Nat. Econ. Counsellor; mem. Nat. Council and Political Junta of Falange; mem. Federación de Estudios Independientes (Fedisa); Minister of Foreign Affairs Dec. 75-; Grand Cross of Carlos III, of Isabel la Católica, Merito Civil; Légion d'Honneur; Orden del Libertador (Argentina).
Leisure interests: books, travel, engravings.
Publs. *Reivindicaciones de España* 41, *Embajadores sobre Espana* 46, *Escritos Políticos* 68, *Cien Articulos* 71, *Figuras y Pareceres* 73, *Asi los he visto* 74.
Fuente del Rey, 11 Aravaca, Spain.
Telephone: 207 02 59.

Arenales Catalán, Lic. Jorge; Guatemalan lawyer and politician; b. 19 April 1914, Guatemala City; m. Dora Forno de Arenales; ed. Univ. Nacional de Guatemala.
Under-Secretary of Agriculture and Mining 44; Consul, New York 45; Minister of Economy and Labour 54-56: other administrative posts; Minister of the Interior 70-72, of Foreign Affairs 72-74.
c/o Ministerio de Asuntos Exteriores, Guatemala City, Guatemala.

Arendt, Walter; German politician; b. 17 Jan. 1925, Heessen; m. Erna Arendt 1948; one s.; ed. Akad. der Arbeit, Frankfurt and Akad. für Gemeinschaft, Hamburg.

Miner in Heessen 39-47; Editor IG Bergbau und Energie, Bochum 48, mem. Man. Board 55, Chair. 64-69; mem. Bundestag (S.P.D.) 61-, mem. European Parl. 61-69; Pres. Int. Union of Miners 67-69; Minister for Labour and Social Welfare Oct. 69-.
Office: Bundesministerium für Arbeit und Sozialordnung, 53 Bonn-Duisdorf, Bonner Strasse 85, Federal Republic of Germany.
Telephone: 74-2192 (Office).

Arespacochaga y Felipe, Juan de; Spanish civil engineer and economist; b. 1920, Madrid; s. of Nicolás de Arespacochaga; m. Marta Llopiz 1949; one s. eight d.; ed. Univ. of Madrid.
Former Dir.-Gen. for Tourist Promotion; Chair. Academie Internationale de Tourisme, Empresa Nacional de Turismo, Nat. Asscn. of Spanish Roads; chair. Civil Engineering Asscn., mem. Nat. Coll. of Economists, Nat. Coll. of Civil Engineers, etc.; Grand Cross of Civil Merit and Orders from Italy, Tunisia and Lebanon.
Leisure interests: yacht, golf, winter sports.
Publs. *Las Obras Hidráulicas y la decadencia económica de España* 48, *El aceite de Oliva, moneda mediterránea* 49, *El multiplicador económico en las obras de riego* 56, *Los transportes españoles y la integración europea* 59, *Las inversiones de O.P. en la Plan Nacional.*
Alberto Alcocer 13, Madrid 16, Spain.
Telephone: 250-31-16.

Argod, Hubert Aymard, DIP. SC. POL.; French diplomatist; b. 28 Aug. 1914, Bourg-de-Peage (Drôme); m. Andrée Lognos 1969; ed. Ecole des Roches, Ecole Libre des Sciences Politiques, Paris.
Diplomatic Service 41-; French Provisional Govt., Algiers; First Sec. French Del. to UN, New York 46; First Sec., Beirut 47-50, High Comm. in Germany 51; European Affairs Dept., Ministry of Foreign Affairs 52, Tunisian and Moroccan Affairs Dept. 56-58, Head, Levant Desk 58-61; First Counsellor, Tunis 61; Ambassador to Chad 61-62; Minister-Counsellor, Algiers 62; Deputy High Rep. Algiers 63; Ambassador to Cambodia 64-68, to Senegal and Gambia 69-73; Dir. de Cabinet of Sec. of State to Minister of Foreign Affairs April-May 74; with Cen. Admin. 74-, Officier, Légion d'Honneur, Croix de Guerre (39-45).
c/o Ministère des Affaires Etrangères, 37 quai d'Orsay, Paris 7e; and 2 boulevard des Sablons, 92 Neuilly-Sur-Seine, France.

Arian, Abdullah al-, LL.B., PH.D.; Egyptian diplomatist and lawyer; b. 21 March 1920, Damanhur; ed. Cairo, Harvard and Columbia (N.Y.) Univs.
Assistant District Attorney, Boheirah Province 42-43; Lecturer in Law, Cairo Univ. 43-45, Asst. Prof. of Int. Law and Int. Org., Inst. of Public Admin., Cairo 59-61; Prof. of Int. Law, Div. of Legal Studies, Inst. of Arab Higher Studies, Cairo 59-; Counsellor, Office of Pres. of Egypt 55-56; Counsellor and Legal Adviser, Perm. Mission at UN 57-59; Dir. Dept. of Legal Affairs and Treaties, Ministry of Foreign Affairs 59-68; Amb. and Deputy Perm. Rep. to UN 68-71; Amb. to France 71-74; Perm. Rep. to UN Office, Geneva 74-; mem. Int. Law Comm. 57-58, 61-65, 66-; del. to numerous UN and OAU confs. and several sessions of UN Gen. Assembly.
Publs. several books and articles on questions of international law and the UN.
Mission Permanente d'Egypte auprès les Nations Unies, 72 rue de Lausanne, Geneva, Switzerland.

Arias, Arnulfo; Panamanian politician; b. 15 Aug. 1901, Penonomé; ed. Univ. of Chicago and Harvard Univ. School of Dental Medicine.
Founded True Nat. Revolutionary Party in 1920s (renamed Panameñista Party 63); Pres. of Panama 40-41; banished and in exile 41-45; Pres. of Panama 49-51;

deposed and deprived of citizenship 51; Pres. of Panama Oct. 68 (deposed after ten days).
c/o Partido Panameñista, Panama City, Panama.

Arias, Dame Margot Fonteyn de, D.B.E. (wife of Roberto Arias, *q.v.*); British ballerina; b. 18 May 1919; ed. U.S.A. and China.
As prima ballerina of the Royal Ballet Company, London, has danced all principal classical roles as well as leading roles in many modern ballets, and has appeared in many countries all over the world; films include *I am a Dancer* 72; Pres. Royal Acad. of Dancing 54-; Order of Finnish Lion; Benjamin Franklin Medal 73; several hon. degrees.
Publ. *Margot Fonteyn* (autobiog.) 75.
c/o Royal Opera House, Covent Garden, London, W.C.2, England.

Arias, Roberto Emilio, B.A. (husband of Dame Margot Fonteyn de Arias, *q.v.*); Panamanian lawyer, editor and diplomatist; b. 1918; ed. Peddie School, New Jersey, and St. John's Coll. Cambridge.
Called to Panamanian Bar 39; Editor *El Panamá-América* 42-46; Publisher *La Hora* 48-; Del. to UN Assembly 53; Amb. to U.K. 55-58, 60-62; Deputy to Nat. Assembly of Panama 64-68.
Apartado 6307, Panama City, Panama.

Arias E., Ricardo M.; Panamanian diplomatist, politician and businessman; b. 1912, in Embassy of Panama, Washington, D.C., U.S.A.; s. of Francisco Arias Paredes and Carmen Espinosa de Arias; m. Olga Arias; two s. two d.; ed. Colegio La Salle, Panama, Shenandoah Valley Acad., Virginia, Georgetown Univ., Washington, U.S.A. and Univ. Católica, Santiago, Chile.
Mem. Nat. Electoral Jury 44-48; Minister of Agriculture, Commerce and Industries 49-51, of Labour, Health and Social Welfare 52-55; Second Vice-Pres. of the Republic 52-55, Acting Pres. Sept. 54; Minister of Foreign Affairs Jan. 55; Pres. of the Republic 55-56; fmr. Ambassador to U.S. and to Organization of American States; Rep. to Int. Bank for Reconstruction and Development 56; defeated candidate, Presidential election May 60; Amb. to U.S. 64-68; Exec. Vice-Pres. DISA, S.A. 68-; Leader, Coalición Patriótica Nacional; Pres. Sociedad Ganadera (Cattle Asscn.), Compañía Panameña de Aviación; Hon. LL.D. (Rockhurst Coll.); numerous Panamanian and foreign orders.
Leisure interest: golf.
Apartado 4549, Panama City, Panama.

Arias Navarro, Carlos; Spanish lawyer and politician; b. 11 Dec. 1908.
Legal Asst., Ministry of Justice; Public Prosecutions Dept., Supreme Court; Civil Gov. León Prov. 44-49, Navarre 49; Dir.-Gen. of Security 57; Mayor of Madrid 65-73; Minister of Interior June-Dec. 73; Prime Minister Jan. 74-.
Oficina del Presidente del Gobierno, Madrid, Spain.

Arifov, Ubai Arifovich, PH.D.; Soviet solid state and nuclear physicist; b. 15 June 1909, Kokand; m. Abdurasuleva Amina 1932; two s. one d.; ed. Samarkand Pedagogical Inst.
Dir. Physico-Technical Inst., Uzbek Acad. of Sciences 45-56; mem. Acad. of Sciences of Uzbekistan 56-, Pres. 62-66; Dir. Inst. of Nuclear Physics of Uzbek Acad. of Sciences and Head Nuclear Electronics Dept. 56-62, Dir. Inst. of Electronics and Head Secondary Process Lab. 66-; Chief Editor *Doklady Acad. Nauk Uzbeksky S.S.R.* 62-66, mem. editorial board 66-; Chief Ed. helio-tech. journal 65-; mem. editorial board *Izvestia Acad. Nauk Uzbesky S.S.R.* 66-.
Leisure interest: tennis.
Academy of Sciences of Uzbekistan, Tashkent, Observatorskaya 85, U.S.S.R.
Telephone: 33-95-64.

Arikpo, Okoi, PH.D.; Nigerian politician; b. 1916; Ugep, E. Nigeria; ed. Nigeria, and Univ. of London.
Teacher, Univ. of London 49-51; mem. E. Nigeria House of Assembly 52, later mem. Fed. House of Reps. until 54; later Minister of Lands and Mines; scientist and teacher 61-67; Fed. Commr. for Trade June 67-Sept. 68; Fed. Commr. for External Affairs Sept. 68-75; Sec. Nigerian Univ. Comm.
c/o Federal Ministry for External Affairs, Lagos, Nigeria.

Ariyoshi, George Ryoichi, JU.D.; American politician; b. 12 March 1925, Honolulu, Hawaii; s. of Ryozo Ariyoshi and Mitsue (Yoshikawa) Ariyoshi; two s. one d.; ed. McKinley High School, Honolulu, Michigan State Univ. and Univ. of Michigan Law School.
Private law practice, Honolulu 53-70; mem. Territorial House of Reps. 54-58, of Territorial Senate 59, of State Senate 60-70; Lieut. Gov. 70-74, Gov. of State of Hawaii 74-; Distinguished Alumni Awards, Univ. of Hawaii and Michigan State Univ.; Hon. LL.D. (Univ. of the Philippines).
Leisure interest: sports.
Executive Chambers, State Capitol, Honolulu, Hawaii 96813, U.S.A.
Telephone: (808) 548-5420.

Arkadyev, Georgy Petrovich; Soviet diplomatist; b. 5 Feb. 1905, Pokhvistnevo Village, Orenburg Region; ed. Economic Inst.
Publishing and pedagogical activities 19-36; joined Russian diplomatic service 36; People's Commissariat for Foreign Affairs 37-44; Ministry of Foreign Affairs 44-47; Soviet Mil. Administration, Germany 47-49; Counsellor, U.S.S.R. Diplomatic Mission to D.D.R. 49-51; Foreign Ministry U.S.S.R. 51-52, Chief U.S.A. Dept. 52-53; Ambassador to Norway 54-56; Dep. Perm. U.S.S.R. Rep. to UN 56-60; Under-Sec. UN, Head Dept. of Political and Security Council Affairs 60, Adviser to Sec.-Gen. 62; resigned 62; Head, Dept. of Int. Econ. Orgs. of Ministry of Foreign Affairs 62-66; Perm. Rep. of U.S.S.R. to IAEA, Vienna 66; Perm. U.S.S.R. Rep. at Int. Orgs. in Vienna 68-.
International Atomic Energy Agency, Vienna 1, Kärntnerring, Austria.

Arkell, John Heward, C.B.E., M.A., F.B.I.M.; British business executive; b. 20 May 1909, Tytherington, Glos.; s of Rev. H. H. Arkell, M.A. and Gertrude M. (née Heward) Arkell; m. 1st Helen B. Huitfeldt 1940, 2nd Meta B. Grundtvig; three s. one d.; ed. Dragon School, Oxford, Radley Coll. and Christ Church, Oxford.
Secretary, Sir Max Michaelis (Investment) Trust 31-37; Asst. Sec. Council for the Protection of Rural England 37-39; army service 39-45; Personnel Man., J. Lyons & Co. Ltd. 45-49; Controller of Staff Admin., BBC 49-58, Dir. 58-60; Dir. of Admin. BBC 60-70; Chair. Air Transport and Travel Industry Training Board 70-; Lay mem. Nat. Industrial Relations Court 72-; Dir. Boots Co. Ltd. 70-, The Coates Group of Companies 70-, U.K. Provident Institution 71-; Chair. British Inst. of Management 72-74; mem. Council of CBI 72; Fellow, Royal Coll. of Arts 73; Vice-Pres. Council for Preservation of Rural England 73.
Leisure interests: walking, sailing, swimming, riding, music.
Pinnocks, Fawley, Henley-on-Thames, Oxon, England.
Telephone: Henley 3017.

Arland, Marcel; French novelist and essayist; b. 5 July 1899.
Winner Goncourt Prize 29, Grand Prix de Littérature de l'Académie Française 52, Grand Prix Nat. des Lettres 60; Dir. of *La Nouvelle Revue Française*; mem. Acad. Française.

Publs. Novels: *Terres étrangères* 24, *Etienne* 25, *Monique* 26, *Les Ames en peine* 27, *L'Ordre* 29 (Goncourt Prize), *Antarès* 32, *Les Vivants* 33, *La Vigie* 35, *Les plus beaux de nos jours* 38, *Terre Natale* 38, *La Grace* 39, *Zélie dans le désert* 44, *Il faut de tout pour faire un monde* 47, *La Consolation du Voyageur* 52, *L'Eau et le Feu* 56, *A perdre Haleine* 60, *Le Grand Pardon* 65; Essays: *Etapes, Edith, La Route obscure* 25, *Où le cœur se partage* 27, *Essais critiques* 31, *Le promeneur* 44, *Les échanges* 45, *Pascal* 47, *Marivaux* 49, *Anthologie de la Poésie française* 41, *La Prose française: Anthologie, histoire et critique d'un art* 51, *Je vous écris . . .* 60, *La Nuit et les Sources* 62, *Carnets de Gilbert* 67, *La Musique des Anges* 67, *Attendez l'aube* 70, *Proche du Silence* 73.
5 rue Sébastien-Bottin, Paris 7e, France.

Arletty (*pseudonym* of Léonie Bathiat); French actress; b. 15 May 1898.
On stage has played in *Le Bonheur Mesdames, Fric-Frac* and *Un Tramway nommé Désir, La descente d'Orphée* (Tennessee Williams) 59, *Un Otage* at Théâtre de France 62, *L'Etouffé chrétien* 62, *Les monstres sacrés* 66; played title role in *Phèdre* on radio; has made a number of films including *Hôtel du Nord* 38, *Le Jour se Lève* 39, *Fric-Frac* 39, *Circonstances Atténuantes* 39, *Madame Sans-Gêne* 41, *Les Visiteurs du Soir* 42, *Les Enfants du Paradis* 44, *Maxime* 59, *Huis Clos* 59, *La Gamberge* 61, *Le Jour le Plus Long* 61, *Tempo di Roma* 62, *Le Voyage à Biarritz* 62, *Gibier de potence.* Publ. *La Défense* 71.
14 rue de Rémusat, Paris, France.
Telephone: 288-91-63.

Arley, Niels Henrik, DR. PHIL.; Danish physicist and mathematician; b. 7 Feb. 1911, Copenhagen; s. of Hjalmar and Ragnhild Petersen; m. Ellen Bruun 1935; one d.; ed. Københavns Universitet.
Mathematics teacher, Royal Danish Naval Acad. 35-55; Research Fellow, Inst. for Theoretical Physics, Univ. of Copenhagen 36-40, private scientific sec. to Prof. Niels Bohr 37-39, Asst. Prof. 40-54, Assoc. Prof. 54-; Dir. Geophysics Research Inst., Univ. of Copenhagen 47-53; mem. cttee. Danish Deep-sea Expedition 50-52; Assoc. Editor *Journal for Geophysical Research* 52-58; External Examiner Technical Univ. of Denmark 54-; Visiting Scientist, Norsk Hydro's Inst. Cancer Research, Oslo 54-; Visiting Prof. to numerous Univs.; Pres. Danish Soc. Protection Scientific Work 51-52; Knight Order of Dannebrog; Galathea Medal.
Leisure interests: music, history.
Publs. *Introduction to the Theory of Probability and Statistics* (with K. R. Buch) 40, *Theory of Stochastic Processes and their Application to the Theory of Cosmic Radiation* 43, *Cosmic Ray Physics* (with others) 49, *Lectures on Radiobiology* 54, *Atomic Power: An Introduction to the Technical, Military, Medical and Biological Problems of the Atomic Age* (with H. Skov) 59.
Norsk Hydros Institute for Cancer Research, Montebello, Oslo 3, Norway; The Niels Bohr Institute, University of Copenhagen; Blegdamsvej 17, 2100 Copenhagen Ø, Denmark.
Telephone: Oslo 554080.

Arlfink, H.E. Cardinal Bernardus Johannes; Netherlands ecclesiastic; b. 5 July 1900; ed. Aartsbisschoppelijk Seminarie, Culemborg, Groot-Seminarie, Rijsenburg, Pauselijk Bijbel-Instituut, Rome, and Jerusalem.
Professor of Holy Scripture, Aartsbisschoppelijk Groot-Seminarie, Rijsenburg 33-45; Prof. for Old Testament and Hebrew Language, Univ. of Nijmegen 45-51; tit. Archbishop of Tyana and Coadjutor of the Archdiocese of Utrecht 55-; Archbishop of Utrecht 55-; created Cardinal by Pope John XXIII 60.
Publs. *Het Boek Prediker, Het Boek Ecclesiasticus, Epistels en Evangelien volgens het Romeins Missaal, Het Passieverhaal der vier Evangelisten, Het Boek Josue.*
40 Maliebaan, Utrecht, Netherlands.

Armagh, Roman Catholic Archbishop of, and Primate of all Ireland (*see* Conway, H.E. Cardinal William).

Armand Ugon, Enrique C., D.IUR.; Uruguayan lawyer; b. 10 Aug. 1893, Valdense, Colonia; s. of Daniel Armand Ugon and Alice Rivoir; ed. Univ. of Montevideo.
Provincial Attorney 18; Judge, Court of First Instance 20, Court of Appeal 38; Pres. High Court 49; del. to 12th Session of League of Nations, Geneva 31, to 2nd Inter-American Conf. of Lawyers, Rio de Janeiro 43; Pres. del. to 3rd Session of U.N. Gen. Assembly, Paris 48, to 5th Session 50; del. of Uruguay and Costa Rica to Inter-American Council of Jurists 50; Judge, Int. Court of Justice 52-61; mem. Comm. of Inquiry (Ghana, Portugal) 61; Pres. Comm. of Inquiry (Portugal, Liberia) 62; Judge *ad hoc* Int. Court of Justice 63-70; Judge, Perm. Court of Arbitration, The Hague 71.
Publs. *Las Leyes Inconstitucionales* 16, *El Derecho de Resistencia* 50; (co-author) *Compilación de Leyes y Decretos del Uruguay* 30.
Plaza Cagancha 1344, Montevideo, Uruguay.
Telephone: 915063; 86482.

Armendáriz, Antonio; Mexican lawyer and diplomatist; b. 29 Sept. 1905, Coahuila; m. Ana María Etchegaray de Armendáriz 1936; three s. three d.; ed. National Univ. of Mexico.
Former Prof. of Sociology and Economy, Nat Univ. of Mexico; Dir.-Gen. of Secondary Education 41-43; private law practice 43-53; Pres. Nat. Comm. on Securities 49-52; Under-Sec. of Finance and Public Credit 53-59; Ambassador to United Kingdom 60-64; Pres. Nat. Bank for Foreign Trade 65-70; Pres. Nat. Warehouses 70-; mem. and fmr. Pres. Anglo-Mexican Cultural Inst.; Hon. K.B.E.
Leisure interests: music, hunting.
National Warehouses, Plaza de la Constitución No. 7, Mexico 1, D.F.; Home: Calle del Arbol 21, San Angel, Mexico 20, D.F., Mexico.
Telephone: 5-48-25-28 (Home); 5-10-11-68, 5-21-10-91 (Office).

Armitage, Sir Arthur, Kt., M.A., LL.D.; British professor and university administrator; b. 1 Aug. 1916, Marsden, Yorks,; s. of Kenyon Armitage; m. Joan Kenyon Marcroft 1940; two d.; ed. Oldham Hulme Grammar School and Queens' Coll., Cambridge.
Fellow of Queens' Coll., Cambridge 45-58, Lecturer in Law 47-70, Vice-Chancellor Univ. of Cambridge 65-67; Vice-Chancellor Univ. of Manchester 70-, Prof. of Common Law 70-; Commonwealth Fund Fellow at Yale Univ. 37-39.
Publs. *Case Book on Criminal Law* (with J. W. C. Turner), *Clerk & Lindsell on Torts* (Joint Editor).
Office of the Vice-Chancellor, University of Manchester, Oxford Road, Manchester, M13 9PL; Home: The Firs, Fallowfield, Manchester, M14 6HE, England.
Telephone: 061-273-3333 (Home).

Armitage, Kenneth, C.B.E.; British sculptor; b. 18 July 1916; ed. Leeds Coll. of Art and Slade School, London.
Teacher of Sculpture, Bath Acad. of Art 47-56; Gregory Fellowship, Leeds Univ. 53; British Council Visitor in Sculpture to Venezuela 63-64; One-man exhibitions London 52, 57, 62, 65, New York 54, 56, 58, 62, Retrospective exhibition Whitechapel Art Gallery, London 59, represented at Venice Biennale 58; Guest Artist, City of Berlin 67-69; Hakone Open-Air Sculpture, Japan 69; many group exhbns. in America and Europe; works in public collections in Belgium, France, Germany, Italy, Netherlands, Switzerland, U.K., U.S.A., Venezuela; David Bright Prize Venice Biennale 58.
22A Avonmore Road, London, W.14, England.

Armstrong, Mrs. Anne Legendre, B.A.; American company director and diplomat; b. 27 Dec. 1927, New Orleans, La.; d. of Armant and Olive Legendre; m. Tobin Armstrong 1950; three s. two d.; ed. Foxcroft School, Middleburg, Va., and Vassar Coll.

Chairman Kenedy (Tex.) Co. Republican Party 58-61; Deputy Vice-Chair. Texas Republican Party 65-66, State Vice-Chair. 66-68; Del. Nat. Convention 64, 68, 72; mem. Republican Nat. Cttee. 68-73, Co-Chair. 71-73, mem. Exec. Cttee. 71-73, Co-Chair. Exec. Cttee. 71-72; Counsellor to Pres. Nixon with cabinet rank 72-74; Chair. Fed. Property Council 72-74; resigned from govt. service 74; Dir. American Express Co., American Express Int. Banking Corpn. Jan. 75-; Ambassador to U.K. 76-; Trustee, Kenedy Co. School Board; Dir. Stratford Hall, Coastal Board Tuberculosis and Respiratory Disease Asscn.; mem. Advisory Cttee. Eagleton Centre for American Women and Politics, Rutgers Univ.
American Embassy, Grosvenor Square, London W1A 1AE, England; Armstrong Ranch, Armstrong, Tex. 78338, U.S.A.

Armstrong, Hon. John Ignatius; Australian politician; b. 6 July 1908, Sydney; s. of W. Armstrong (deceased); m. Joan C. Curran 1945; one s. four d.; ed. Marist Brothers High School, Darlinghurst.
Member, Sydney City Council 34, Chair. 63-65; Senator for N.S.W. 38-62; Govt. Rep., Nat. Film Board 45-49; Minister for Supply and Devt. 46-49, and mem. Commonwealth Rationing Comm.; Minister in Charge, Royal Visit March 48; Deputy Opposition Leader, Senate 51-56; Lord Mayor of Sydney 65-67; High Commissioner for Australia in the U.K. 72-75.
Leisure interests: golf, swimming, bowling.
47 Beach Road, Collaroy, N.S.W., Australia.
Telephone: 988-511.

Armstrong, Neil A.; American astronaut and professor of engineering; b. 5 Aug. 1930, Wapakoneta, Ohio; m. Janet Shearon; two s.; ed. Purdue Univ. and Univ. of Southern California.
Naval aviator 49-52, flew combat missions during Korean War; joined NASA Lewis Flight Propulsion Laboratory 55, later transferred to NASA High Speed Flight Station, Edwards, Calif.; as aeronautical research pilot, was X-15 project pilot flying to over 200,000 ft. and at approx. 4,000 m.p.h.; other flight test work included X-1 rocket research plane, F-100, F-101, F-104, F5D, B-47 and the paraglider; selected as astronaut by NASA Sept. 62; command pilot for *Gemini VIII* 66; backup pilot for *Gemini V* 65, *Gemini XI* 66; flew to the moon in *Apollo XI* July 69, first man to set foot on the moon 20 July 69; Chair. Peace Corps Nat. Advisory Council 69; Deputy Assoc. Admin for Aeronautics, NASA, Washington 70-71; Prof. of Engineering, Univ. of Cincinnati 71-; Fellow, Soc. of Experimental Test Pilots, American Inst. of Aeronautics and Astronautics; hon. mem. Int. Acad. of Astronautics, Int. Astron. Fed.; numerous decorations and awards from 17 countries including Presidential Medal of Freedom, NASA Exceptional Service Award, Royal Geographical Soc. Gold Medal and Harmon Int. Aviation Trophy 70.
Department of Engineering, University of Cincinnati, Cincinnati, Ohio 45221, U.S.A.

Armstrong, Sir Thomas Henry Wait, M.A., D.MUS., F.R.C.M.; British musician; b. 15 June 1898; ed. Keble Coll., Oxford and Royal Coll. of Music.
Organist Thorney Abbey 14; Sub-Organist, Peterborough Cathedral 15; served R.G.A. 17-19; Sub-Organist, Manchester Cathedral 22; Organist, St. Peter's, Eaton Square 23; Organist, Exeter Cathedral 28; Cramb Lecturer in Music, Univ. of Glasgow 49; Student of Christ Church, Oxford 39-55; Student Emeritus 55-; Choragus of the Univ. and Lecturer in Music 37-54; Conductor of Oxford Bach Choir and Oxford Orchestral Soc.; Organist, Christ Church, Oxford 53-55; Principal, Royal Acad. of Music 55-68; Hon. F.R.C.O., F.R.A.M.
The Old Rectory, Newton Blossomville, nr. Turvey, Beds., England.

Armstrong of Sanderstead, Baron (Life Peer), cr. 75, of the City of Westminster; **William Armstrong,** P.C., G.C.B., M.V.O.; British fmr. civil servant; b. 3 March 1915, London; s. of William and Priscilla (née Hopkins) Armstrong; m. Gwendoline Enid Bennett 1942; one s. one d.; ed. Bec School, London and Exeter Coll., Oxford.
Assistant Principal, Board of Educ. 38; Asst. Private Sec. to Pres. of Board of Educ. 40; Private Sec. to Sec. of War Cabinet 43-46; Principal Private Sec. to successive Chancellors of Exchequer 49-53; Under-Sec. Overseas Finance Div., H.M. Treasury 53-57, Home Finance Div. 57-58, Third Sec. and Treasury Officer of Accounts 58-62, Joint Perm. Sec. 62-68; Head of Home Civil Service and Perm. Sec. to Civil Service Dept. 68-74; Deputy Chair. Midland Bank 74-75, Chair. April 75-; Vice-Pres. of Council, Inst. of Bankers 75-; mem. Council Manchester Business School 70-74; Hon. Fellow, Exeter Coll., Oxford 63; Visiting Fellow, Nuffield Coll., Oxford 64-72; Hon. D.Cn.L. (Oxford) 71, Dr. h.c. (Open Univ.) 74, Hon. D.Litt. (City Univ.) 74, Hon. Degrees Cranfield Inst. Technology, Herriot-Watt Univ., Sheffield Univ. 75.
Leisure interests: talking, walking, reading.
143 Whitehall Court, London, SW1A 2EP, England.

Arnail, Ellis Gibbs; American politician and lawyer; b. 20 March 1907; ed. Univ. of the South, Sewanee and Georgia Univ.
Mem. Georgia legislature; Asst. Attorney-Gen. 37-39. Attorney-Gen. 39-43; Gov. of Georgia 43-47; Pres Soc. of Ind. Motion Picture Producers; Senior mem. Law Firm Arnall, Golden and Gregory; mem. U.S. Del. to 4th annual conf. UNESCO, Paris 49; U.S. Del. Anglo-American Film Conf., London 50; Trustee Univ. of the South, Mercer Univ.; Dir. U.S. Office of Price Stabilization 52; Pres. Ind. Film Producers' Export Asscn. 56-; Chair. Board of Dirs. Nat. Asscn. of Life Insurance Companies; Chair. Board of Dir. Coastal States Life Insurance; Dir. Manufacturers Nat. Bank; Dir. of numerous other companies; mem. U.S. Nat. Comm. for UNESCO 63-.
Publs. *The Shore Dimly Seen* 46, *What the People Want* 47.
Residence: 213 Jackson Street, Newnan, Ga. 30263; Office: Arnall, Golden & Gregory, 10th Floor, Fulton Federal Building, Atlanta, Ga. 30303, U.S.A.
Telephone: 404-577-5100 (Office).

Arnaud, Claude; French diplomatist; b. 9 Nov. 1919, Voiteur (Jura); s. of Dr. Paul Arnaud, M.D.; m. Sonia Larrain Beutner 1962; ed. Univs. de Dijon, Lyon et Paris à la Sorbonne.
Attaché, Washington 45-46; Office of Resident-Gen. in Morocco 46-51; First Sec. Bonn 52-55; Econ. Dept., Foreign Office, Paris 55-59; Counsellor, Chargé d'Affaires, Belgrade 59-62; Minister-Counsellor, Perm. Mission to UN 62-65; Amb. to Laos Jan. 66-68, to Kenya 68-69; Dir. European Dept., Ministry of Foreign Affairs 69-72, Asst. Dir. for Political Affairs 72-75; Amb. to People's Repub. of China 75-; Chevalier Légion d'Honneur, Croix de Guerre 39-45.
French Embassy, Peking, People's Repub. of China; and 6 rue du Général-Lambert, Paris, France.

Arndt, Otto; German building mechanic, railway engineer and politician; b. 1920.
General Man. Deutsche Reichsbahn (G.D.R. Railways); cand. mem. Cen. Cttee. Sozialistische Einheitspartei Deutschlands (SED); now Minister of Transport.
Ministerium für Verkehr, Berlin, German Democratic Republic.

Arnold, James R., M.A., PH.D.; American professor of chemistry; b. 5 May 1923, Metuchen, N.J.; s. of Abraham S. and Julia J. Arnold; m. Louise C. Arnold 1952; three s.; ed. Princeton Univ.
Assistant, Princeton 43, Manhattan Project 43-46;

Fellow, Inst. of Nuclear Studies, Univ. of Chicago 46; Nat. Research Fellow, Harvard 55-57; Assoc. Prof., Dept. of Chem., Univ. of Calif., San Diego 58-60, Prof. 60-; recipient of lunar samples from missions of *Apollo XI, XII, XIV, XV*; member of Nat. Acad. of Sciences, American Asscn. for Advancement of Science, American Chem. Soc., American Acad. of Arts and Sciences; Nat. Council of World Federalists 70-; Guggenheim Fellow, India 72-73; specializes in field of cosmic-ray produced nuclides, meteorites, lunar samples and cosmochemistry.

Publs. over fifty articles in scientific reviews and journals.

Department of Chemistry, University of California, San Diego, La Jolla, Calif. 92037, U.S.A.

Telephone: 713-453-2000, Ext. 1453.

Arnold, Malcolm, C.B.E.; British composer; b. 21 Oct. 1921, Northampton; *s.* of William and Annie Arnold; two *s.* one *d.*; ed. Royal Coll. of Music, London.

Principal Trumpet, London Philharmonic Orchestra 42-44 and 46-48; served army 44-46; full-time composer and conductor 48-; awarded Cobbett Prize 41, Mendelssohn Scholarship 48; Hon. D.Mus. (Exeter), Bard of the Cornish Gorsedd.

Leisure interests: reading and conversation.

Works include *Beckus the Dandipratt* (overture) 43, and 8 other overtures; 1st Symphony 49, 2nd Symphony 53, 3rd Symphony 57, 4th Symphony 60, 5th Symphony 61, 6th Symphony 67, 7th Symphony 73; 15 concertos; *Homage to the Queen*, Coronation Ballet performed at Covent Garden 53, and 4 other ballets; chamber music, vocal music, brass band music; film music *Bridge on the River Kwai* 58 (Hollywood Oscar), *Inn of the Sixth Happiness* (Ivor Novello Award) 59.

Meadowcroft, The Hill, Monkstown, Co. Dublin, Ireland.

Arnon, Daniel I(srael), B.S., PH.D.; American biochemist; b. 14 Nov. 1910, Poland; *s.* of Leon and Rachel (Chodes) Arnon; *m.* Lucile Jane Soule 1940; two *s.* three *d.*; ed. Univ. of California, Berkeley.

Instructor to Asst. Prof., Univ. of Calif., Berkeley 36-43; Lieut. to Major U.S. Army and Air Force 43-46; Assoc. Prof., Berkeley 46-50; Guggenheim Fellow, Cambridge Univ. 47-48; Prof. of Plant Physiology, Univ. of Calif., Berkeley 50-60, Prof. of Cell Physiology 61-, Chair. Dept. of Cell Physiology 61-, Biochemist in Calif. Agric. Experimental Station 58-; Fulbright Guest Investigator, Max-Planck Inst. für Zellphysiologie, Berlin-Dahlem 55-56; Guggenheim Fellow 62-63; mem. Nat. Acad. of Sciences; Fellow American Acad. of Arts and Sciences, American Asscn. for Advancement of Science, American Inst. of Chem.; mem. American Chem. Soc., American Soc. Photobiology, American Soc. Biological Chem., Biochem. Soc. (London), American Soc. Plant Physiology (Pres. 52-53); Scandinavian Soc. Plant Physiology; Foreign mem. Royal Swedish Acad. of Sciences, Acad. d'Agriculture de France; Charles F. Kettering Award in Photosynthesis; Co-recipient Newcomb Cleveland Prize; Gold Medal, Univ. of Pisa; Stephen Hales Award, American Soc. of Plant Physiologists; Nat. Medal of Science (U.S.A.) 73; Dr.h.c. Univ. of Bordeaux 75; mem. Deutsche Akademie der Naturforscher Leopoldina.

Leisure interests: swimming, mountaineering.

Department of Cell Physiology, 251 Hilgard Hall, University of California, Berkeley, Calif. 94720; Home: 28 Norwood Avenue, Berkeley, Calif. 94707, U.S.A.

Telephone: 415-642-3684 (Univ.); 415-526-5575 (Home).

Arnoul, Françoise (Françoise Gautsch); French actress; b. 9 June 1931; ed. Lycée de Rabat, Lycée Molière (Paris) and Paris Conservatoire.

Films include *Nous irons à Paris, La Maison Bonnadieu, Le Désir et l'Amour, La Plus Belle Fille du Monde,* *Les Compagnons de la Nuit, Les Amants du Tage, French-Cancan, Des Gens sans Importance, Thérèse Etienne, La Chatte, Asphalte, La Bête à l'Affût, Le Bal des Espions, La Chatte sort ses Griffes, La Morte-Saison des Amours, Le Testament d'Orphée, Les Parisiennes, Vacances portugaises, A Couteaux tirés, Lucky Joe, Le Dimanche de la Vie, Le Congrès s'amuse*; theatre debut in *Les Justes* (Camus) Versailles 66.

32 rue Monsieur-le-Prince, Paris 6e, France.

Arnould, Reynold; French artist; b. 7 Dec. 1919, Le Havre (Seine Maritime); *m.* Marthe Bourhis 1945; ed. Lycée Corneille, Rouen, Ecole des Beaux-arts, Rouen and Ecole nationale supérieure des Beaux-arts.

Information mission in U.S.A. 45-46; Dir. School of Art, Baylor Univ., Texas 49-52, Baylor Univ. Summer Arts School, Paris 52; Dir. Museum Maison de la Culture, Le Havre 52-65; Curator of Grand Palais 65-; numerous exhbns. in Paris; exhbn. by Musée des arts décoratifs at Louvre called *Reynold Arnould, forces et rythmes de l'industrie*; exhbn. at Galerie de France, Paris, called *Reynold Arnould, 40 ans de portraits* 69; works in Musée nationale d'art moderne, Paris, and museums and art galleries in U.S.A., Britain, Belgium, Switzerland, Italy and Norway; Chevalier Légion d'Honneur, Chevalier Ordre Nat. du Mérite, Officier Ordre des Arts et Lettres.

Leisure interests: sport, swimming.

Grand Palais, Porte A, avenue de Selves, Paris 8e, France.

Telephone: 231-81-24.

Arns, H.E. Cardinal Paulo Evaristo; Brazilian ecclesiastic; b. 14 Sept. 1921, Forquilhinha, Criciuma; *s.* of Gabriel and Helena Arns; ed. Univ. of Paris and Ecole des Hautes Etudes, Paris.

Taught theology and French Univ. Católica de Petrópolis; pastoral work in Petrópolis; Aux. Bishop of São Paulo 66; Archbishop of São Paulo; Metropolitan Bishop of São Paulo 70; Pres. Bishop's Conf. of São Paulo State; Grand Chancellor of Pontificia Univ. Católica de São Paulo; mem. Secr. for Non-Believers (Vatican); cr. Cardinal by Pope Paul VI 73.

Publs. numerous works and translations on religious and racial topics, including *A Quem iremos, Senhor?* 68, *Comunidade: União e Ação* 72.

Rua Mococa 71, Sumaré, 01255 São Paulo, S.P., Brazil.

Aron, Raymond Claude Ferdinand, LITT.D.; French journalist and university professor; b. 14 March 1905, Paris; *m.* Suzanne Gauchon 1933; two *d.*; ed. Univ. of Paris.

Lecturer, Univ. of Cologne 30-31; on staff, French Inst., Berlin 31-33; Prof. Lycée du Havre 33-34; Sec. Centre of Social Information, Ecole Normale Supérieure 34-39; Prof. Univ. of Toulouse 39; Editor *La France Libre,* London 40-44; on staff *Combat* 46, and *Figaro* 47-; Prof. Inst. d'Etudes politiques and Sorbonne; Prof. Collège de France 70; Prof.-at-Large, Cornell Univ.; mem. Académie des Sciences morales et politiques 63-; Foreign Hon. mem. American Acad. Arts and Sciences 61-; mem. American Philosophical Soc., British Acad.; Officier, Légion d'Honneur; Prix des Ambassadeurs 62; Prix Montaigne 68; Hon. Ph.D. (Harvard, Basle, Brussels, Columbia, Southampton, Oxford, Jerusalem and Louvain Univs.).

Publs. *Introduction à la Philosophie de l'Histoire* 38, *La Sociologie allemande contemporaine* 35, *Le grand schisme* 48, *Les guerres en chaîne* 51, *L'Opium des intellectuels* 55, *La Tragédie algérienne* 57, *Paix et guerre entre les nations* 62, *Dix-Huit Leçons sur la Société Industrielle* 63, *La lutte des classes* 64, *Démocratie et totalitarisme* 65, *Trois Essais sur l'Age industriel* 66, *Les Etapes de la pensée sociologique* 67, *Les Désillusions du Progrès* 69, *République Impériale* 73, *Histoire et*

Dialectique de la Violence 73, *Penser la Guerre, Clause-witz* 76.
Office: 6 rue de Tournon, Paris 6e; Home: 87 boulevard Saint Michel, Paris 5e, France.
Telephone: MED. 3900.

Arosemena Gómez, Otto, LL.D.; Ecuadorean lawyer and politician; b. 1922.
Former lawyer in Guayaquil; Leader of Coalición Institucionalista Democrática; Provisional Pres. of Ecuador 66-68.
c/o Ministerio de Asuntos Exteriores, Quito, Ecuador.

Arosemena Monroy, Carlos Julio, D.IUR.; Ecuadorean politician; b. 1920.
Counsellor, Ecuadorean Embassy, Washington 46-52; Chair. Chamber of Deputies 52; Minister of Defence 52-53; Vice-Pres. 60-61; Pres. of Ecuador 61-63.

Arpino, Giovanni; Italian writer; b. 27 Jan. 1927; ed. Univ. degli Studi, Turin.
Has worked as Editor for Einaudi and Editoriale Zanichelli; has contributed to *Il Giorno, Paese sera, Paese, Stasera* (dailies), *Il Mondo, Vie nuove, Mondo Nuovo, Le Ore, Tempo, Illustrazione italiana* (periodicals), *Botteghe Oscure, Il contemporaneo, Il Ponte, Paragone, Tempo presente, Nuova corrente, Europa letteraria, Itinerari, Cinema nuovo, Questo e altro* (cultural magazines); Strega Prize 64.
Publs. *Sei stato felice* (novel) 52, *Barbaresco* (poems) 54, *Il prezzo dell'oro* (poems) 55, *Gli anni del giudizio* (novel) 58, *La suora giovane* (novel) 59, *Rafé e Micropiede* (for children—Bancarellino Prize) 60, *Mille e una Italia* (for children) 61, *Una nuvola d'ira* (novel) 62, *L'ombra delle colline* (novel—Strega Prize) 64, *Un'anima persa* (novel) 66.
Via Leopardi 15, Milan, Italy.

Arrabal, Fernando; Spanish writer; b. 11 Aug. 1932, Melilla; *m.* Luce Moreau; one *s.* one *d.*
Political prisoner in Spain 67; now lives in Paris; founder "Panique" movt. with Topor, Jodorowsky, etc.; Grand Prix du Théâtre 67, Grand Prix Humour Noir 68.
Leisure interest: chess.
Publs. novels: *Baal Babylone* 59, *The Burial of Sardine* 62, *Fêtes et Rites de la Confusion* 65; poetry: *Pierre de la Folie* 63, *100 Sonnets* 66; plays: *The Architect and the Emperor of Assyria, And They Put Handcuffs on the Flowers, Garden of Delights, The Automobile Graveyard, Guernica, The Grand Ceremonial,* and 45 other plays published and performed in Paris, Berlin, New York and London; essays: *The Panic, The New York of Arrabal, Letter to General Franco, Fischer* 73; wrote and directed films, *Viva la Muerte, J'irai comme un cheval fou, L'arbre de Guernica.*
2 rue de Vienne, Paris 75008, France.
Telephone: 5226894.

Arrau, Claudio; concert pianist; b. 6 Feb. 1903, Chillán, Chile; *s.* of Carlos and Lucretia Arrau; *m.* Ruth Schneider 1938; two *s.* one *d.*; ed. privately.
Gave first concert at age of five in Santiago; Buenos Aires debut at age of seven; studied in Berlin with Martin Krause (pupil of Liszt) 10-15; first American concerts 23 returned 41 and annual tours since; world tours include Russia 29, 30, 68, Australia 47, 52, 58, 68, 74, South Africa 49, 52, 56, South America, Mexico and Israel 51, 53, 62, 70, India, Sri Lanka and Singapore 55, 56, Japan 65, 70, 72; bi-annual European tours; awarded Liszt and Ibach prizes 12, 16 and 17; First Prize Concours International des Pianistes de Genève 27.
Leisure interests: books, gardening, art, antiques.
Publs. *Beethoven Piano Sonatas* Vol. I 74, Vol. II 75.
c/o Hurok Concerts, 1370 Avenue of the Americas, New York, N.Y., U.S.A.

Arriaga, General Kaúlza de; Portuguese army officer; b. 18 Jan. 1915, Oporto; ed. Univ. of Oporto, Portuguese Mil. Acad. and Portuguese Inst. for Higher Mil. Studies.
Instructor, Field School for Mil. Engineers 39-45; attended Gen. Staff Course 45-49; Lisbon Mil. H.Q. and Army Gen. Staff 49-50; at Ministry for Nat. Defence and Rep. of Minister of Defence in Tech. Comm. for External Econ. Co-operation 50-53; Head of Office of Minister of Nat. Defence and Min. of Defence Rep. at Tech. Comm. for External Co-operation and Atomic Energy Board 54-55; Under-Sec. of State for Aeronautics, later Sec. 55-62; High Command Course 63-64; Brig. 64; Prof. of Strategy and Tactics, Inst. for High Mil. Studies 64-66; Chair. Atomic Energy Board 67; Gen. 68; Commdr. all Portuguese Ground Forces in Mozambique 69-70; C.-in-C. Portuguese Forces in Mozambique 70-73; retired May 74; arrested Sept. 74, released Jan. 76; mem. Overseas Council 65-69; Chair. Exec. Cttee. Soc. Portuguesa de Exploração de Petróleos (ANGOL) 66-69; Pres. Equestrian Fed. 68; several Portuguese and foreign decorations.
Publs. include works on engineering, atomic energy and military affairs.
c/o Junta de Energia Nuclear, Rua de S. Pedro de Alcântara 79, Lisbon, Portugal.

Arrow, Kenneth J., PH.D.; American professor of economics; b. 23 Aug. 1921, New York; *s.* of Harry I. and Lillian Arrow; *m.* Selma Schweitzer 1947; two *s.*; ed. The City College, Columbia Univ.
Captain, U.S. Army Air Forces 42-46; Research Assoc. Cowles Comm. for Research in Econ., Univ. of Chicago 47-49; Asst. Assoc. and Prof. of Econs., Statistics and Operations Research, Stanford Univ., 49-68; Prof. of Econs., Harvard Univ., 68-; Hon. LL.D. (City Univ., Univ. of Chicago); Hon. Dr. of Social and Econ. Sciences (Univ. of Vienna); Hon. Sc.D. (Columbia Univ.) 73; D.Sc.S. (Yale Univ.) 74; Hon. D. (Univ. René Descartes) 74; Hon. D. (Hebrew Univ. Jerusalem) 75; mem. Nat. Acad. of Sciences, American Acad. of Arts and Sciences, American Phil. Soc., Finnish Acad. of Sciences; Nobel Memorial Prize in Econ. Science 72.
Leisure interests: walking, square dancing.
Publs. *Social Choice and Individual Values* 51, 63, *Studies in the Mathematical Theory of Inventory and Production* (with S. Karlin and H. Scarf) 58, *Studies in Linear and Nonlinear Programming* (with L. Hurwicz and H. Uzawa) 58, *A Time Series Analysis of Inter-industry Demands* (with M. Hoffenberg) 59, *Public Investment, The Rate of Return and Optimal Fiscal Policy* (with M. Kurz) 70, *Essays in the Theory of Risk-Bearing* 71, *General Competitive Analysis* (with F. H. Hahn) 71, *The Limits of Organization* 73; about 100 articles in learned journals.
1737 Cambridge Street, Cambridge, Mass., 02138; Home: 6 Walnut Avenue, Cambridge, Mass., 02140, U.S.A.
Telephone: 617-495-4587 (Office); 617-868-8994 (Home).

Arrupe, Father Pedro, S.J.; Spanish ecclesiastic; b. 14 Nov. 1907, Bilbao; *s.* of Marcelino and María Gondra Arrupe; ed. with Fathers of Escuelas Pías, Bilbao, Univ. of Madrid (Medicine), and Jesuit studies in Spain, Belgium, Netherlands and U.S.A.
Entered Society of Jesus 27; in Japan 38-65, engaged in parish ministries, training of Novices, Provincial Superior 54-65; was in Hiroshima when first atomic bomb exploded; Superior-Gen. of Soc. of Jesus 65-.
Publs. eight spiritual books (Japanese); *Este Japón increíble—Memorias del P. Arrupe, Escala en España, Nuestra vida consagrada, Ante un mundo en cambio* (Spanish); *Witnessing to Justice, Men for Others* (English, French, Spanish).
Superiore Generale della Compagnia di Gesù, Borgo Santo Spirito 5, Rome, Italy.

Arteh Ghalib, Omar; Somali politician; b. 1930, Hargeisa; *m.*; seven *c.*; ed. St. Paul's Coll., Cheltenham, U.K. and Univ. of Bristol.
Teacher 46-49; Headmaster, various elementary schools 49-54; Vice-Principal, Intermediate School, Sheikh, Somalia 54-56; Principal, Intermediate School, Gabileh 58; Officer in charge of Adult Educ. 59; District Commr. in Public Admin. 60-61; First Sec. Somali Embassy, Moscow 61-62; Rapporteur, Special Cttee. on South-West Africa, UN 62-63; Counsellor, Perm. Mission of Somalia at UN 64; Amb. to Ethiopia 65-68; mem. Somali Nat. Assembly; Sec. of State for Foreign Affairs 69-.
Publs. include: *Back from the Lion of Judah.*
Ministry of Foreign Affairs, Mogadishu, Somalia.

Arthur, Sir Geoffrey (George), K.C.M.G., M.A.; British diplomatist; b. 19 March 1920, U.K.; *s.* of late G. J. Arthur; *m.* Margaret Woodcock 1946; ed. Ashby de la Zouch Grammar School and Christ Church, Oxford.
Army service 40-45; joined diplomatic service 47; posted to Baghdad 48-50, Ankara 50-53, Bonn 56-58, Cairo 59-63; Foreign Office 53-55, 63-66; Amb. to Kuwait 67-68; Asst. Under-Sec. Foreign and Commonwealth Office 69-70; Political Resident in the Persian Gulf 70-72; Visiting Fellow, St. Antony's Coll., Oxford 72-73; Deputy Under-Sec., Foreign and Commonwealth Office 73-75; Master Pembroke Coll., Oxford Aug. 75-; Dir. British Bank of the Middle East 75-.
c/o Pembroke College, Oxford, England.
Telephone: Oxford 42271.

Arthur, James Stanley, B.SC.; British diplomatist; b. 3 Feb. 1923; ed. Anderson Educ. Inst., Shetland Isles, Trinity Acad., Edinburgh and Liverpool Univs.
Ministry of Education (later Dept. of Educ. and Science) 47-66, Private Sec. to Parl. Sec. 49-51, Principal Private Sec. to Minister 60-63; Foreign Office 66-67; Counsellor, High Comm., Nairobi 67-70; Deputy High Commr., Malta 70-73; High Commr., Fiji 74-.
British High Commission, Suva, Fiji; and c/o Foreign and Commonwealth Office (Fiji), King Charles Street, London, S.W.1, England.

Artobolevsky, Ivan Ivanovich; Soviet scientist; b. 9 Oct. 1905, Moscow; *s.* of Ivan Artobolevsky and Zinaida Nikolina; *m.* Olga Kalachnikova 1936 (died 1975); ed. Moscow Timiriazev Acad. and Moscow Univ.
Worked in field of machines, mechanisms and automatics; invented classification of dimensional mechanisms; Lecturer 27-32; Prof. Moscow Univ. 32-49; Prof. of Applied Mechanics, Inst. of Machine Research, Moscow 37-; Deputy and mem. of Presidium of U.S.S.R. Supreme Soviet; mem. Acad. of Sciences of U.S.S.R.; Vice-Pres. Exec. Cttee. World Fed. of Scientists; Pres. of Union of Socs. of Friendship and Cultural Relations with Foreign Countries, U.S.S.R. Soc. *Znaniye* (Knowledge) 66-, Int. Fed. for the Theory of Machines and Mechanisms; foreign mem. of Serbian and Czechoslovakian Acads. of Science; hon. mem. Int. Acad. of History of Science; Hero of Socialist Labour, Order of Lenin (four times); Hammer and Sickle Gold Medal; Honoured Scientific and Technical Worker of R.S.F.S.R.; James Watt Medal; Acad. Tchebichev Prize; Acad. Goryatchkin Gold Medal.
Publs. *Theory of Dimensional Mechanisms* 37, *Theory of Mechanisms and Machines* 53, *Theory of Mechanisms for the Generation of Plan Curves* 59, *Synthesis of Plane Mechanisms* 59, *Theory of Mechanisms* 65, *Theory of Mechanisms and Machines* 75.
Institute of Machine Research, Ulitsa Griboyedova 4, Moscow, U.S.S.R.
Telephone: 223-02-34.

Artsikhovsky, Artemy Vladimirovich; Soviet archaeologist; b. 26 Dec. 1902, Leningrad; ed. Moscow Univ.
Professor of Archaeology at Moscow Univ. 37-, Head of Dept. of Archaeology 39-; carried on excavations at Novgorod for forty years; mem. C.P.S.U. 52-; Corresp. mem. U.S.S.R. Acad. of Sciences 60-.
Publs. *Ancient Russian Miniatures as Historical Source* 44, *Introduction to Archæology* 47, *Foundations of Archæology* 54, *Birch Bark Rolls of Novgorod* 54-63, etc.
Moscow State University, Leninskie Gory, Moscow, U.S.S.R.

Arup, Sir Ove Nyquist, Kt., C.B.E., M.ING.F., F.I.C.E., F.I.STRUCT.E., M.I.C.E.I., M.S.A.I.C.E.; British and Danish consulting engineer; b. 16 April 1895, Newcastle upon Tyne, England; *s.* of Jens Simon Johannes Arup and Mathilde Bolette Nyquist; *m.* Ruth Samuel Sørensen 1925; one *s.* two *d.*; ed. Preparatory School, Hamburg, Germany, Public School, Søro, Denmark, and Univ. of Copenhagen.
Designer, Christiani & Nielsen G.m.b.H., Hamburg 22; Chief Designer, Christiani & Nielsen Ltd., London 25-34 (Designer 23-25); Dir. and Chief Designer, J. L. Kier & Co. Ltd., London 34-38; Dir. Arup Designs Ltd., Arup & Arup Ltd., Pipes Ltd. 38-45; Senior Partner, Ove Arup and Partners, London, Dublin, W. Africa, S. Africa and Australia 49-; Senior Partner, Arup Associates 63-; Consulting Engineer for schools, flats, Irraid. shelters, industrial projects, marine work (Air Ministry), hospitals, universities, cathedrals, bridges; Chair, Soc. of Danish Civil Engineers in Great Britain and Ireland 55-59; Visiting Lecturer, Harvard Univ. 55; Commdr. First Class, Order of Dannebrog (Denmark) 75; Royal Gold Medal, Royal Inst. of British Architects 66; Hon. D.Sc. (Durham Univ., Univ of E. Anglia); Gold Medal, Inst. of Structural Engineers 73.
Leisure interests: most things.
Publs. *Design, Cost, Construction and Relative Safety of Trench, Surface, Bombproof and other Air Raid Shelters* 39, *Safe Housing in Wartime* 41.
Office: 13 Fitzroy Street, London W.1; Home: 6 Fitzroy Park, Highgate, London, N.6, England.
Telephone: 01-636-1531 (Office); 01-340-3388 (Home).

Arutyunov, Alexandr Ivanovich; Soviet neurosurgeon; b. 3 Jan. 1904, Yerevan; ed. North Caucasian Univ.
Head Doctor of Hospital, Mari Autonomous Republic 29-30; Intern at clinic 30-32; Postgraduate, Senior Assoc. Central Neurosurgical Inst. 32-41; Army Surgeon 41-45; Head of clinic, Kiev Psychoneurological Inst. 45-50; Dir. Ukrainian Inst. 50-64; Corresp. mem. U.S.S.R. Acad. of Medical Sciences 61-67, mem. 67-; Dir. Burdenko Inst. of Neurosurgery; Head of Chair, Central Medical Refresher Inst. 64-; mem. C.P.S.U. 40-; Deputy Academic Sec., Dept. of Clinical Medicine, U.S.S.R. Acad. of Medical Sciences; Chair. U.S.S.R. Soc. of Neurosurgeons 66; First Vice-Pres. Int. Fed. of Neurosurgical Socs.; Vice-Pres. Int. Neurosurgical Asscn. 65-; Order of Lenin, Red Banner of Labour, Red Star, Red Banner (twice).
Publs. About 120 works on traumas of central nervous system, treatment of consequences of cerebral and spinal inflammation, perfection of neurosurgical technique.
Burdenko Institute of Neurosurgery, 13/5 Pervy Tverskoy-Yamskoy Pereulok, Moscow, U.S.S.R.

Arutyunyan, Alexandr Grigoryevich; Soviet composer; b. 23 Sept. 1920, Yerevan; *s.* of Grigory and Eleonora Arutyunyan; *m.* Irina Arutyunyan 1950; one *s.* one *d.*; ed. Yerevan Conservatoire.
Executive mem. Armenian S.S.R. Composers' Union; mem. C.P.S.U. 52-; State Prize 49; Honoured Worker of Arts for Armenian S.S.R. 56; Red Banner of Labour 56; People's Artist of Armenia 62; People's Artist of the U.S.S.R. 70; State Prize of Armenia 71.
Leisure interests: literature, art.
Compositions include: Concerto for piano and orchestra 41, Overture No. 1 *Our Just Cause* 42, Overture No. 2 *Concert Overture* 44, Polyphonic partita for piano 45,

Motherland Cantata 47, Symphonic poem *In Memory of Collective Farmer Zakiyan* (with E. Mirzoyan) 48, Overture No. 3 *Festive Overture* 49, *Lenin Cantata* (with E. Mirzoyan) 50, Concerto for voice and orchestra, Concerto for trumpet and orchestra 50, Concertino for piano and orchestra 51, Dance suite for symphony orchestra 53, Symphony 58, *Lay of the Armenian People* (vocal symphonic poem) 61, *Sayat-Nova* (opera) 65-68, Symphonietta for string orchestra 66, *Lenin Oda* (cantata) 68, *With my Motherland* for choir and orchestra 69, *In Memory of Mother* vocal cycle 70, *Theme and Variations* for trumpet and orchestra 72, Rhapsody for piano and string orchestra 75.
Armenian Composer's Union, 25 Ulitsa Demirchyana, Yerevan, U.S.S.R.
Telephone: 524785 (Home).

Arutyunyan, Nagush Khachaturovich; Soviet mechanical engineer and politician; b. 1912; ed. Yrevan Polytechnic Inst., Moscow Military Engineering Acad. Former Hydrological Engineer; Researcher, Armenian S.S.R. Acad. of Sciences 45-50; Prof. Yerevan Univ. 50-, Rector 61-63; mem. Armenian Acad. of Sciences 50-, Vice-Pres. 60-61; mem. Communist Party 42-; Chair. of Presidium of Supreme Soviet of Armenian S.S.R. 63-; Deputy Chair. Supreme Soviet of U.S.S.R. 63-; mem. Central Auditing Cttee. of C.P.S.U. 66-; mem. Central Cttee. of Armenian C.P.
Presidium of Supreme Soviet of Armenian S.S.R., Yerevan, U.S.S.R.

Asada, Shizuo; Japanese aviation official; b. 13 Oct. 1911; ed. Law Dept., Tokyo Imperial Univ. (now Tokyo Univ.).
Dir. Bureau of Shipping, Ministry of Transport 58-61; Admin. Vice-Minister of Transport 61-63; Senior Vice-Pres. Japan Air Lines 63-69, Exec. Vice-Pres. 69-71, Pres. 71-.
Japan Air Lines, 7-3, Marunouchi 2-chome, Chiyoda-ku, Tokyo 100; Home: 30-19, Seijo 6-chome, Setagaya-ku, Tokyo 157, Japan.

Asai, Koji; Japanese banker; b. 3 Aug. 1902, Ishikawa Pref.; s. of Tasaburo and Sue Asai; m. Miyoko Mizutani 1927; two s. two d.; ed. Kobe Higher Commercial School.
Joined Sumitomo Bank Ltd. 25, Man. Tokyo Branch 47, Dir. 49, Man. Head Office 50, Senior Man. Dir. 58, Dir. and Deputy Pres. 63, Dir. and Pres. 71-73.
Leisure interests: reading, golf, appreciation of music.
12-5 Hamacho, Ashiya City, Hyogo Prefecture, Japan.

Asamov, Salakhitdin; Soviet politician; b. 1930; ed. Moscow Veterinary Acad.
Member C.P.S.U. 56-; zoo-technician, Dir. Nishan State Stud Farm, Karshi District, Surkhandarya Region 55-61; party official and Minister of Agriculture of Uzbek S.S.R. 61-64, also Chair. Samarkand Regional Soviet of Working People's Deputies; First Sec. Kashkadarya Regional Cttee. of C.P. of Uzbekistan 64-71; Chair. Exec. Cttee. Tashkent Regional Soviet of Working People's Deputies 71-; mem. Central Cttee. C.P. of Uzbekistan; Deputy to U.S.S.R. Supreme Soviet 66-70.
Tashkent Regional Soviet of Working People's Deputies, Tashkent, U.S.S.R.

Asbeck, Werner, DR. ING.; German business executive; b. 3 Jan. 1908; ed. Technische Hochschule, Aachen.
Superintendent, Leipziger Leichtmetallwerk Bernhard Berghaus, Rackwitz 39-43; Asst. to Pres. Vereinigte Stahlwerke, Düsseldorf 43-50; Dir. Investment Dept., Stahl-Treuhänder-Vereinigung, Düsseldorf 50-53; Asst. to Technical Board of Dirs., Dortmund-Hörder-Hüttenunion A.G., Dortmund 53-54; fmr. Chair. Management

Board, Klöckner-Werke A.G.; mem. numerous supervisory boards etc.
4 Düsseldorf, Eitelstrasse 40, Federal Republic of Germany.

Åsbrink, Per Valfrid; Swedish banker; b. 1912; ed. Univ. of Stockholm.
Co-operative Union 34-38; Editor *Social Yearbook*, Asscn. for Social Work 38-42; Sec. Stockholm Town Council 43-45; Sec. on 1946 Comm. on Education 46-47; Ministry of Communications 48-55, Under Sec. 51-55; Governor, Sveriges Riksbank (Bank of Sweden) 55-73; Chair. Board of Luossavaara-Kiirunavaara A.B. (iron mining) 57-74, A.B. Aerotransport 62-74, A.B. Tumbra bruk (papermaking) 63-73; mem. Board Scandinavian Airlines System 52-74, Bank for Int. Settlements, Basle 55-73, Exec. Dir. IMF 73-.
1600 South Eads Street, Arlington, Va. 22202, U.S.A.

Aschenborn, Hans Jürgen, M.A.BIBL., D.PHIL., F.S.A.L.A.; South African librarian; b. 19 Aug. 1920, Windhoek, S.W. Africa; s. of Hans A. Aschenborn and Emmy Bredow; m. Helga C. Hermenau; one s. three d.; ed. Univ. of S. Africa and Univ. of Pretoria.
Merensky Library, Univ. of Pretoria 49-51; head of various depts., Transvaal Provincial Library Services 51-53; Lecturer in Library Science, Univ. of Pretoria 53-59; joined The State Library, Pretoria 59, Dir. 64-; Fellow, Int. Micrographic Congress; John Harvey Medal 64.
Leisure interests: farming, Arab horse breeding, riding.
Publs. *Stimmen deutscher Dtchter* 49, *Titelbeskrywing* 56, *Sachkatalogisierung seit Trebst* 57, *Staatsbiblioteek der Z.A.R.* 70.
State Library, Box 397, Pretoria; Box 15294, Lynn, East Pretoria, South Africa.
Telephone: 483920 (State Library); 821460 (Home).

Asensio-Wunderlich, Julio; Guatemalan diplomatist; b. 5 Nov. 1911, Guatemala City; s. of Dr. José Luis Asensio and Mrs. Beatriz Wunderlich de Asensio; m. Elena Aguirre-Wyld 1938; four s. one d.; ed. Universidad de San Carlos, Guatemala and Loyola Coll., Montreal.
Deputy Minister of Foreign Relations, Guatemala 54-; Minister-Counsellor, Embassy of Guatemala, Washington, D.C. 55-58; Legal Counsellor, Foreign Office, Guatemala 58-64; Amb. to U.S.A. 70-; mem. Del. to UN Gen. Assembly 54-55; Orden del Mérito Civil (Spain), Caballero de San Silvestre (Vatican).
Leisure interests: reading, coffee growing.
Embassy of Guatemala, 2220 R Street, N.W., Washington, D.C. 20008; Home: 2839 Woodland Drive, N.W., Washington, D.C. 20008, U.S.A.
Telephone: 202-332-2865 (Embassy); 202-332-4117 (Home).

Asfia, Safi; Iranian engineer and politician; b. 1916, Teheran; m. Behjat Ziai 1941; three d.; ed. Ecole Polytechnique and Ecole des Mines, Paris.
Professor of Economic Geology Teheran Univ. 39-62; Dep. Dir. Plan Organization 54-61, Man. Dir. 61-68; Dep. Prime Minister and Minister of State for Econ. and Devt. Affairs 68-74; Minister of State 74-.
Office of Minister of State, Teheran, Iran.
Telephone: 68801.

Ash, Roy Lawrence, M.B.A.; American industrialist; b. 20 Oct. 1918, Los Angeles, Calif.; m. Lila M. Hornbek 1943; three s. two d.; ed. Harvard Univ.
Bank of America 36-42, 47-49; Chief Financial Officer, Hughes Aircraft Co. 49-53; Co-Founder, Dir. Litton Industries Inc. 53-72, Exec. Vice-Pres. 58-61, Pres. 61-72; mem. Board of Dirs., Bankamerica Corpn., Global Marine Inc., Pacific Mutual Life Insurance Co.; Dir. Los Angeles World Affairs Council; Trustee, Cttee. for Economic Development; Co-Chair. Japan-California

Asscn.; mem. Board of Trustees, Calif. Inst. of Technology; official of educational orgs.; Chair. President's Advisory Council on Exec. Org. 69-71; Trustee, The Urban Inst.; Dir. Office of Management and Budget 72-75.

655 Funchal Road, Los Angeles, Calif. 90024, U.S.A.

Ashby, Baron (Life Peer), cr. 73, of Brandon, Suffolk; **Eric Ashby,** Kt., F.R.S., D.SC., M.A., D.I.C.; British botanist and university administrator; b. 24 Aug. 1904, London; s. of Herbert C. Ashby and Helena M. Chater; m. Elizabeth H. Farries; two s.; ed. City of London School, Imperial Coll. of Science, London, and Univ. of Chicago.

Commonwealth Fund Fellow, U.S.A. 29-31; lecturer in Botany, Imperial Coll. 31-35; Reader in Botany, Univ. of Bristol 35-37; Prof. of Botany, Univ. of Sydney, Australia 38-46; Harrison Prof. of Botany, Manchester Univ. 46-50; Pres. and Vice-Chancellor, The Queen's Univ. Belfast 50-59; Counsellor and Chargé d'Affaires Australian Legation, Moscow 45; mem. Exec. Council Scientific and Industrial Research 56-60; Master of Clare Coll., Cambridge 58-75; Chair. Int. Comm. on Higher Education in Nigeria 59-61; Vice-Chair. Asscn. of Univs. of British Commonwealth 59-61; Vice-Chair. Commonwealth Scholarships Comm. 59-62; mem. Univ. Grants Cttee. 60-67; Chair. Cttee. of Award, Commonwealth Fund of N.Y. 63-69; Hon. Adviser, Nigerian Nat. Univ. Comm. 62-; Pres. British Asscn. for Advancement of Science 63; Council Royal Soc. 64-65; Trustee Ciba Foundation 66-; mem. Central Advisory Council for Science and Technology 67-69; Vice-Chancellor, Univ. of Cambridge 67-69; Chair. Royal Comm. on Pollution 70-73; Chancellor, Queen's Univ., Belfast 70-; Trustee, British Museum 69-; Fellow, Advisory Council, Science Policy Foundation 75-; Order of Andrés Bello 1st Class (Venezuela) 74.

Leisure interests: chamber music, mountain walking.

Publs. *Environment and Plant Development* 31, *English-German Botanical Terminology* 38, *Challenge to Education* 46, *Scientist in Russia* 47, *Science and the People* 53, *Technology and the Academics* 58, *Community of Universities* 63, *African Universities and Western Tradition* 64, *Universities, British, Indian, African* 66, *The Rise of the Student Estate in Britain* 70, *Masters and Scholars* 70, *Any Person, Any Study* 71, *Portrait of Haldane* 74.

Norman Cottage, Manor Road, Brandon, Suffolk; Clare College, Cambridge, England.

Ashcroft, Dame Peggy (Dame Edith Margaret Emily Hutchinson), D.B.E.; British actress; b. 22 Dec. 1907; ed. Croydon and Central School of Speech Training, Albert Hall, London.

First appeared at Birmingham Repertory Theatre 26; roles include: Constance Neville (*She Stoops to Conquer*), Naomi (*Jew Süss*) 29, Desdemona (with Paul Robeson) 30, Irina (*The Three Sisters*) 37-38, Cecily Cardew (*The Importance of Being Ernest*) 39-40, 42, Catherine (*The Dark River*) 43, Haymarket Repertory Season 44-45, Evelyn Holt (*Edward My Son*) 47, Catherine Sloper (*The Heiress*) 49, Hester Collyer (*The Deep Blue Sea*) 52, Hedda Gabler 54, Miss Madrigal (*The Chalk Garden*), Shen Te (*The Good Woman of Setzuan*) 56, Rebecca West (*Rosmersholm*) 59, title role *Duchess of Malfi* 61, Madame Ranevsky (*The Cherry Orchard*) 62, and numerous Shakespearian performances at The Old Vic, London, and as mem. Royal Shakespeare Company, Stratford and London 60-64; has appeared in London in *The Seagull* 64, *Days in the Trees* 66, *Ghosts* 67, *Delicate Balance* 68, *Landscape* 69, Katherine of Aragon in *Henry VIII* (Stratford-on-Avon), *The Plebeians* 70, *Lloyd George Knew my Father* 72, *Old Times* 72, *John Gabriel Borkman* 75, *Happy Days* 75. Films inc. *The Wandering Jew, Thirty Nine Steps, The Nun's Story, Sunday Bloody Sunday, Three into Two Won't Go;* King's Gold Medal (Norway); Hon. D.Litt.

(Oxon.) 61, Leicester 64; Hon. D.Lit., London 65, Cambridge 72.

Manor Lodge, Frognal Lane, London, N.W.3, England.

Ashe, Derick Rosslyn, C.M.G., M.A. (OXON.); British diplomatist; b. 20 Jan. 1919, Guildford, Surrey; s. of Frederick Allen and Rosalind Ashe (née Mitchell); m. Rissa Guinness (née Parker) 1957; one s. one d.; ed. Bradfield Coll., Trinity Coll., Oxford.

Served in H.M. Forces 40-46, mentioned in despatches 45; Second Sec. Control Comm. for Germany 47-49; Private Sec. to Perm. Under-Sec. of State for German Section, Foreign Office 50-53; First Sec. La Paz 53-55; Foreign Office 55-57; First Sec. Information, Madrid 57-61; Foreign Office 61-62; Counsellor, Head of Chancery, Addis Ababa 62-64, Havana 64-66; Head of Security Dept., Foreign and Commonwealth Office 66-69; Minister, Tokyo 69-71; Amb. to Romania 72-75, to Argentina 75 (withdrawn Jan. 76); Knight Order of Orange-Nassau.

Leisure interests: riding, antiques.

British Embassy, Buenos Aires, Argentina; and 30 Gloucester Square, London, W.2, England.

Ashenheim, Sir Neville Noel, Kt., C.B.E.; Jamaican lawyer, business executive and diplomatist; b. 18 Dec. 1900, Kingston; s. of late Lewis Ashenheim and Estelle L. DeCordova; m. Leonie V. Delevante 1926; three s.; ed. Jamaica Coll. and Wadham Coll., Oxford. Chairman, Jamaican Board Standard Life Assurance 58-61, 67-71, House of Myers Ltd. 44-61, Fred. L. Myers & Son (Produce) Ltd. 44-61, Gleaner Co. Ltd. 44-67, Consolidated Int. Corpn. Ltd. (now Wray & Nephew Group Ltd.) 58-, Blinds and Furnishings Ltd. 49-, Jamaica Industrial Devt. Corpn. 52-57, Caribbean Cement Co. 66; official of other companies; mem. Legislative Council 59-62; Minister without Portfolio and Leader of Govt. Business in Legislative Council, Jamaica 62; Amb. to U.S.A. 62-67; Minister without Portfolio, Leader of Govt. Business in Senate 67-72.

Leisure interests: reading, swimming, horse-racing, bridge, billiards, tennis.

3rd Floor, The British American Building, Knutsford Boulevard, Kingston 5, Jamaica.

Telephone: 936-8584.

Ashford, George Francis, O.B.E.; British oil executive; b. 1911, King's Norton, nr. Birmingham; ed. Malvern Coll. and Trinity Hall, Cambridge.

Admitted as solicitor 37, joined Legal Dept. of Distillers Co. Ltd.; rose to Lieut.-Col., Second World War; rejoined Legal Dept. of Distillers Co. Ltd. (D.C.L.) 45, Company Sec. of British Hydrocarbon Chemicals 47-51; Dir. of D.C.L. 56-57, British Hydrocarbon Chemicals Ltd. 58-67; Deputy Chair. D.C.L. Chemical Group 60-61, Chair. 61-62, Chair. Chemicals and Plastics Group 62-67; mem. Management Cttee. of D.C.L. 63-67; D.C.L. chemical and plastics interests acquired by British Petroleum 67; Dir. British Petroleum Co. Ltd. July 67-68, a Man. Dir. Jan. 69-72; Man. Dir. BP Chemicals Ltd. Aug. 67-70; Dir. Albright and Wilson Ltd. 73-; mem. Monopolies Comm. 73-; Vice-Pres. Chemical Industries Asscn. 67-70; Pres. British Plastics Fed. 68; mem. Econ. Devt. Cttee. for the Chemical Industry.

Meadow House, Kingston Hill, Surrey, England.

Ashihara, Yoshinobu, B.A., M.ARCH., D.ENG.; Japanese architect; b. 7 July 1918, Tokyo; s. of Dr. Nobuyuki Ashihara and Kikuko Fujita; m. Hatsuko Takahashi 1944; one s. one d.; ed. Univ. of Tokyo and Harvard Univ. Graduate School.

Worked in architectural firms, Tokyo 46-52; in Marcel Breuer's firm, New York 53; visited Europe on Rockefeller Travel Grant 54; Head, Yoshinobu Ashihara and Assocs. 55-; Lecturer in Architecture, Hosei Univ., Tokyo 55-59, Prof. of Architecture 59-65; Prof. of Architecture, Musashino Art Univ., Tokyo 64-70; Visiting Prof., School of Architecture and Building,

Univ. of New South Wales, Australia 66, Dept. of Architecture, Univ. of Hawaii 69; Prof. of Architecture, Univ. of Tokyo 70-; Award of Architectural Inst. of Japan for Chuo-Koron Building 60; Special Award of Architectural Inst. of Japan for Komazawa Olympic Gymnasium 65; Ministry of Educ. Award for Japan Pavilion, *Expo 67*, Montreal; NSID Golden Triangle Award (U.S.A.) 70, Order of Commendatore (Italy) 70.
Works include: Chuo-Koron Building, Sony Building, Komazawa Olympic Gymnasium 65, Japanese Pavilion, *Expo 67*, Montreal, Fuji Film Bldg. 69.
Leisure interests: sauna, travelling.
Publ. *Exterior Design in Architecture* 69.
Y. Ashihara, Architect and Associates, 7th Floor, Sumitomo-seimei Building, 31-15 Sakuragaoka-cho, Shibuya-ku, Tokyo 150; Home: 47 Nishihara-3, Shibuya-ku, Tokyo, Japan.
Telephone: 463-7461 (Office).

Ashimov, Baiken; Soviet politician; b. 1917; ed. Leningrad Zoological Inst. and C.P.S.U. Higher Party School.
Member, C.P.S.U. 40-; army service 38-45; party and local work, Kokchetav Region, Kazakh S.S.R. 45-60; Chair. Karaganda Regional Exec. Cttee. 61-63, 64-68; First Sec. Karaganda Agricultural C.P. Regional Cttee. 63-64; First Sec. Taldy-Kurgan C.P. Regional Cttee. 68-70; Chair. Kazakh S.S.R. Council of Ministers 70-; Deputy to U.S.S.R. Supreme Soviet 70-; mem. Cen. Cttee. C.P.S.U. 71-; mem. Cen. Cttee. Kazakhstan C.P.
Council of Ministers of the Kazakh S.S.R., Alma-Ata, U.S.S.R.

Ashiotis, Costas; Cypriot diplomatist; b. 1908; ed. Pancyprian Gymnasium, Nicosia, and London School of Economics.
Former journalist and editor; Govt. Service 42-; Asst. Commr. of Labour 48; Dir.-Gen. Ministry of Foreign Affairs 60; mem. Cypriot Dels. to UN and Int. Confs.; High Commr. in U.K. 66-; Hon. M.B.E.
Publ. *Labour Conditions in Cyprus During the War Years 1939–45.*
Cyprus High Commission, 93 Park Street, London, W1Y 4ET, England.

Ashkenazy, Vladimir; Russian-born concert pianist; b. 6 July 1937, Gorky, U.S.S.R.; s. of David Ashkenazy and Evstolia (née Plotnova); m. Thorunn Sofia Johanns-dottir 1961; two s. two d.; ed. Central Music School, Moscow, and Moscow Conservatoire.
Second Prize, Int. Chopin Competition, Warsaw 55; Gold Medal, Queen Elizabeth Int. Piano Competition, Brussels 56; Joint winner (with John Ogdon) Tchaikov-sky Piano Competition, Moscow 62; concerts in many countries.
Leisure interest: soccer.
Brekkugerdi 8, Reykjavík, Iceland.
Telephone: Reykjavik 36588.

Ashmole, Bernard, C.B.E., M.C., M.A., B.LITT., F.B.A.; British archaeologist; b. 22 June 1894, Ilford, Essex; s. of William Ashmole and Caroline Wharton Tiver; m. Dorothy De Peyer 1920; one s. two d.; ed. Hertford Coll., Oxford.
Craven Fellow, Athens and Rome British Schools 20-22; Asst. Curator of Coins, Ashmolean Museum, Oxford 23-25; Dir. British School at Rome 25-28; Yates Prof. Archaeology, London Univ. 29-48; Keeper, **Greek and Roman Antiquities,** British Museum 39-56; Lincoln Prof. of Classical Archaeology and Art, Oxford Univ. 56-61; Geddes-Harrower Prof. of Greek Archaeology and Art, Aberdeen Univ. 61-62; Hon. LL.D.; Fellow, Lincoln Coll., Oxford; Hon. Fellow, Hertford Coll., Oxford, University Coll., London.
Publs. *Catalogue of Ancient Marbles at Ince Blundell Hall, Greek Sculpture and Painting* (with Sir J. D. Beazley), *Olympia: The Sculptures of the Temple of*

Zeus (with N. Yalouris and A. Frantz), *Art of the Ancient World I* (with H. A. Groenewegen), *Architect and Sculptor in Classical Greece.*
5 Tweed Green, Peebles, Scotland.

Ashmore, Adm. Edward (Beckwith), G.C.B., D.S.C., A.D.C.; British naval officer; b. 11 Dec. 1919, Queens-town, Eire; s. of Vice-Adm. L. H. Ashmore, C.B., D.S.O., and T. V. Shutt; m. Elizabeth Mary Doveton Sturdee 1942; one s. one d.; ed. Royal Naval Coll., Dartmouth.
Served *H.M.S. Birmingham, Jupiter, Middleton* 38-42; Staff, C.-in-C. Home Fleet 44-45; mentioned in des-patches 46; Asst. Naval Attaché, British Embassy, Moscow 46-47; Squadron Communications Officer 3rd Aircraft Carrier Squadron 50; Commdr. 50; *H.M.S. Alert* 52-53; Capt. 55; Capt. (F) 6th Frigate Squadron, Commdg. Officer *H.M.S. Blackpool* 58; Dir. of Plans, Admiralty and Ministry of Defence 60-62; Commdr. British Forces Caribbean Area 63-64; Rear-Adm. 65; Asst. Chief of Defence Staff, Signals 65-67; Flag Officer, Second-in-Command, Far East Fleet 67-68; Vice-Adm. 68; Vice-Chief Naval Staff 69-71; Adm. 70; C.-in-C. Western Fleet Sept.-Oct. 71; C.-in-C. Fleet 71-73; Chief of Naval Staff and First Sea Lord March 74-; Principal A.D.C. to Her Majesty the Queen 74-.
Mall House Flat, Admiralty Arch, Whitehall, London S.W.1, England.
Telephone: 01-930 4146.

Ashtal, Abdalla Saleh; Yemeni diplomatist; b. 5 Oct. 1940; ed. Menelik II Secondary School, Addis Ababa, Ethiopia, American Univ. of Beirut, Lebanon.
Assistant Dir. of Sana'a Branch, Yemeni Bank for Reconstruction and Devt. 66-67; Editor *Ash-ara* (weekly) 67-68; mem. Exec. Cttee. of Gen. Command, Nat. Liberation Front 68-72; Political Adviser, Perm. Mission to UN 70, Senior Counsellor 72-73, Perm. Rep. May 73-, concurrently Amb. to Canada 74-.
Permanent Mission of People's Democratic Republic of Yemen, 211 East 43rd Street, Room 605, New York, N.Y. 10017, U.S.A.

Ashton, Sir Frederick, C.H., Kt., C.B.E.; British choreo-grapher and dancer; b. 17 Sept. 1906, Guayaquil, Ecuador; s. of George Ashton and Georgina Fulcher; ed. Dover Coll. and Dominican Fathers, Lima, Peru.
Principal choreographer Royal Ballet 35-70, Dir. 63-70; Flight-Lieut., R.A.F., during Second World War; Queen Elizabeth II Coronation Award; Legion of Honour (France); Commdr. of the Order of the Danne-brog; Hon. D.Litt. (Durham and E. Anglia), Hon. D.Mus. (London) 70.
Leisure interests: gardening, swimming, contemplating.
Choreography for *Symphonic Variations, Cinderella, Les Patineurs, Rendezvous, Façade, Scènes de Ballet, Wedding Bouquet, Capriol Suite, Sylvia, Romeo and Juliet, Ondine, La Fille Mal Gardée, Jazz Calendar, Enigma Variations, Lament of the Waves, The Tales of Beatrice Potter* (film) 71, *The Dream,* etc.
Royal Opera House, Covent Garden, London, W.C.2, England.

Asimov, Isaac, B.S., M.A., PH.D.; American bio-chemist and science fiction writer; b. Petrovichi, U.S.S.R.; s. of Judah Asimov and Anna Rachel (Berman) Asimov; m. 1st Gertrude Blugerman 1942, one s. one d.; m. 2nd Janet O. Jeppson 1973; ed. Columbia Univ.
Instructor in Biochemistry, Boston Univ. School of Medicine 49-51, Asst. Prof. 51-55, Assoc. Prof. 55-; professional writer 38-; numerous awards.
Leisure interests: no leisure.
Publs. 143 books including *The Human Body* 63, *The Human Brain* 64, *New Intelligent Man's Guide to Science* 65, *Asimov's Biographical Encyclopedia of Science and Technology* 64, *Understanding Physics* 66, *The Universe* 66, *Is Anyone There?* 67, *Asimov's Guide*

to the Bible 68, *Photosynthesis* 69, *Shaping of England* 69, *Opus 100* 69, *Solar System and Back* 70, *The Gods Themselves*, Editor *Nebula Award Stories* 73, *The Tragedy of the Moon* (essays) 74, *Words of Science* 74.
12 West 72nd Street, New York, N.Y. 10023, U.S.A.

Asimov, Mukhamed Saifitdinovich; Soviet physicist and politician; b. 25 Aug. 1920, Leninabad; *m.* Monand Asimova 1923; two *s.* three *d.*; ed. Uzbek State Univ., Samarkand, and Acad. of Social Sciences.
Army Service 41-46; mem. C.P.S.U. 45-; Senior Lecturer, Leninabad Pedagogical Inst. 46-54; Postgraduate student, Acad. of Social Sciences 54-55; Rector, Dushanbe Polytechnic Inst. 56-62; Minister of Educ. of Tajik S.S.R. 62; mem. Central Cttee. Tajik C.P. 62-; mem. Presidium, Sec. Central Cttee. of Tajik C.P., Chair. Party and State Control Cttee., Tajik S.S.R., Deputy Chair. Council of Ministers of Tajik S.S.R. 63-65; Pres. Acad. of Sciences of Tajik S.S.R. 65-; Deputy to U.S.S.R. Supreme Soviet 66-; mem. Central Cttee. C.P. of Tajikistan; Corresp. mem. U.S.S.R. Acad. of Sciences.
Leisure interest: chess.
Dushanbe 25, Academy of Sciences, Lenin Street 33, Tajikistan, U.S.S.R.
Telephone: 2-20-72.

Âşiroğlu, Vahap, L. EN D.; Turkish diplomatist; b. 14 Aug. 1916, Karamursel; *s.* of Tahsin and Safiye Âşiroğlu; *m.* Sevim Zeren 1946; one *s.*; ed. Galatasaray Lycée, Istanbul and Faculty of Law, Univ. of Istanbul.
Entered diplomatic service 43; served in Czechoslovakia, Turkish Ministry of Foreign Affairs and Perm. Mission of Turkey at UN 46-62; Minister and Deputy Perm. Rep. to UN 62-65; Amb. to Denmark 65-68, to Indonesia 68-71; Sec.-Gen. Regional Co-operation for Devt. (RCD) May 71-74; mem. UN Comm. on Human Rights 53-56; Leader, Turkish del. to ICAO Assembly 56; Chair. del., GATT Ministerial meeting, Tokyo 59; Chair. UN Conciliation Comm. for Palestine 62-65.
Leisure interests: riding, tennis, sailing, swimming, photography, antiques, sea shell collection.
c/o Ministry of Foreign Affairs, Ankara, Turkey.

Askarov, Asanbai; Soviet politician; b. 1922; ed. Frunze Teachers' Training Coll. and Higher Party School of C.P.S.U. Central Cttee.
In Educational Service 39-42; Soviet Army 42-46; Party Official 46-51, 54-58; Chair. Djambul Regional Soviet of Working People's Deputies 58-59; First Sec., Djambul Regional Cttee., Communist Party of Kazakhstan 59-65; First Sec. Alma Ata Regional Cttee., C.P. of Kazakhstan; mem. Central Cttee. of C.P.S.U. and of Central Cttee. of Kazakhstan C.P. 65-; Alt. mem. Bureau of Central Cttee., C.P. of Kazakhstan; Deputy to U.S.S.R. Supreme Soviet 66-; mem. Mandate Cttee., Soviet of Nationalities of U.S.S.R. Supreme Soviet; Chair. Youth Affairs Comm. 74-; mem. C.P.S.U. 44-.
Alma Ata Regional Committee, Communist Party of Kazakh S.S.R., Alma Ata, U.S.S.R.

Askenase, Stefan; Belgian (b. Polish) concert pianist; b. 10 July 1896; *m.* Ingrid Buchwald 1972; ed. Coll. in Lemberg and Acad. of Music, Vienna.
War service, Austrian officer 15-18; Teacher, Cairo Conservatoire 22-25; Prof. Royal Conservatoire of Music, Brussels 57-61; concert tours all over Europe and overseas; records for Deutsche Grammophon Gesellschaft.
Rodderbergstrasse 72, 53 Bonn-Bad Godesberg, Federal Republic of Germany; and c/o New Era International Concerts Ltd., 16 Lauriston Road, London, S.W.19, England.
Telephone: Bonn 341422.

Askew, Reubin O'Donovan, LL.B.; American state governor; b. 11 Sept. 1928, Muskogee, Okla.; *s.* of Leo Goldberg Askew and Alberta Nora O'Donovan; *m.*

Donna L. Harper 1956; one *s.* one *d.*; ed. Escambia County Public School System, Florida State Univ., Univ. of Florida Coll. of Law and Denver Univ.
Partner in law firm, Pensacola, Florida 56-70; Asst. County Solicitor, Escambia Co., Florida 56-58; mem. State of Florida House of Reps. 58, 60-62; State Senate 62-70; Gov. of Florida 70-; Chair. Education Commission of U.S.A. 73; Vice-Chair. Southern Govs. Conf., Chair. 74-; Hon. degrees Univ. of Notre Dame, Stetson Univ., Rollins Coll., Eckerd Coll., Florida Southern Coll.; John F. Kennedy Award, Nat. Council of Jewish Women 73; Democrat.
Office of the Governor, State Capitol, Tallahassee, Fla. 32304; Home: 700 N. Adams Street, Tallahassee, Fla. 32303, U.S.A.

Askin, Hon. Sir Robert William, G.C.M.G.; Australian politician; b. 4 April 1909, Sydney; *m.* Mollie Underhill 1937; ed. Sydney Technical High School, New South Wales.
Former bank official; with Australian Imperial Forces, Second World War; mem. New South Wales Parl. 50-75; Deputy Leader of Liberal Party 54-59, Leader 59-75; Premier and Treas. of New South Wales 65-75.
Leisure interests: surfing, gardening, racing.
86 Bower Street, Manly, Sydney, New South Wales, Australia.

Asmodi, Herbert Christian Ernst; German playwright; b. 30 March 1923; ed. Ruprecht-Karl Universität, Heidelberg.
War service 42-45; studies at Heidelberg 47-52; freelance writer, Munich 52-; mem. PEN; Gerhart Hauptmann-Preis der Freien Volksbühne Berlin 54, Tukan Prize, Munich 71.
Publs. comedies: *Pardon wird nicht gegeben, Nachsaison, Die Menschenfresser, Mohrenwäsche, Dichtung und Wahrheit oder der Pestalozzi-Preis, Stirb & Werde* (two episodes from the German recovery), *Nasarin oder Die Kunst zu Träumen, Marie von Brinvilliers, Geld.*
Munich 23, Occamstrasse 3, Federal Republic of Germany.
Telephone: 348436.

Asnag, Abdallah al-Majid al-; Yemeni trade union official and politician; b. 1933.
Senior Reservation Officer, Aden Airways 51-62; leader, People's Socialist Party; Gen. Sec. Aden Trade Union Congress until Dec. 62, 63-65; imprisoned Dec. 62-Dec. 63; Head of Political Bureau, Front for Liberation of Occupied S. Yemen (FLOSY); Minister of Foreign Affairs, Yemen Arab Repub. Aug.-Sept. 71, March-June 74, of Econ. 71-74; Deputy Premier for Communications June 74-Jan. 75; Minister of Foreign Affairs Jan. 75-.
Ministry of Foreign Affairs, Sana'a, Yemen Arab Republic.

Asp, Eero Rafael; Finnish monetary official; b. 24 Feb. 1922, Helsinki; *s.* of Einar Walfrid Asp and Eva Elisabet Tynell; *m.* Sisko Oili Karstila 1953; one *d.*; ed. Helsinki Univ.
Bank of Finland, Helsinki 48, Sec. Bank of Finland 55-58, 60-62; Alt. mem. Board of Govs. IMF 57-58, 61-62, mem. Board of Dirs. 58-60, 68-70; Man. Dir. Export Guarantee Board (export credit insurance agency), Helsinki 62-71, Finnish Export Credit Ltd., Helsinki 63-; Alt. mem. Board of Govs., Asian Devt. Bank 66-.
Leisure interest: golf.
Finnish Export Credit Ltd., Unioninkatu 7, 00130 Helsinki 13, Finland.
Telephone: 630-696.

Aspling, Sven; Swedish politician; b. 28 Aug. 1912.
Journalist 37-42; Constituency Organizer, Social Democrat Party 42-46, Asst. Sec.-Gen. 46-48, Sec.-Gen. 48-62; mem. Parl. 56-; Minister of Social Affairs 62-.
Ministry of Social Affairs, Stockholm 16, Sweden.

Asplund, Karl, B.A., PH.D.; Swedish professor, poet and art historian; b. 27 April 1890, Jader, Södermanland; s. of Conrad A. and Vendela Sahlin; m. 1st Astrid Fredriksson (died 1922), 2nd Elvira Sjödin 1950; one d.; ed. Uppsala Univ.
Secretary, Art History Soc. 15-16; Corresp. *Dagens Nyheter* 14-21 and *Svenska Dagbladet* 22-34; Man. Dir. Bukowski Co. 29-53; Pres. Bellman Soc. 43-64; mem. Vitterhetsakademi (Acad. of Letters), Stockholm.
Leisure interests: chess, collecting old drawings.
Publs. *Egron Lundgren* 14-15, *Katalog öv. utst. av äldre svenska Porträttminiatyrer i Stockholm* 15, *Den svenska porträttminiatyrens hist.* 16, *Vers från väster, Anders Zorn, his Life and Work* 21, *Zorn's Engraved Work* 20, *Ivar Arosenius* 28, *Borta bra* 32, *Orient* 37, *Axel Fridell* 37, *Selected Poems* 38, *Carl Eldh* 43, *Livets Smultronställen* 45, *Att överleva* 48, *Augusti* 52, *En Stenhammarkrönika* 54, *Septemberskyar* 57, *De Ljusa timmarna* 59, *Konst, Kännare, Köpmän* 62, Ed. *P. A. Hall, Sa correspondance de famille* 55, *Nils Dardel* 57, etc.
Rådmansg. 17, Stockholm, Sweden.

Asratyan, Ezras Asratov; Soviet physiologist; b. 31 May 1903, Metsik, Turkey; m. Janna Sayants 1937; three s.; ed. Yerevan State Univ.
Assistant Yerevan State Univ. 25-30; mem. C.P.S.U. 29-; scientific worker in Physiological Inst. U.S.S.R. Acad. of Sciences 30-41; Head of Neuro-Physiological Laboratory, Leningrad Brain Research Inst. 35-41; Head of Physiological Dept. Pedagogical Inst. Leningrad 36-41; Prof. of Physiology, Tashkent Medical Inst. 41-43; Professor, Medical Inst. Moscow 43-50; Head of Physiological Laboratory, U.S.S.R. Acad. of Sciences 44-50; Head of Physiological Dept. Moscow Second State Medical Inst. 50-60; Head, Inst. of Higher Nervous Activity and Neurophysiology 60-; mem. Armenian Acad. of Sciences 47-, mem. Czechoslovak Medical Soc. J. E. Purkyne, Pavlovian Soc. of America, Neurological and Neurochemical Soc. of Montevideo, Medicalbiological Soc. of Netherlands; corresp. mem. U.S.S.R. Acad. of Sciences 39-; Pavlov Prize 50, Gold Medal 61; Order of Lenin (twice), Order of Red Banner of Labour (twice), Order of Red Star, etc.
Leisure interests: gardening, swimming.
Publs. *Essays on Etiology, Functional Pathology and Therapy of the Traumatic Shock* 45, *Physiology of the Central Nervous System* 53, *Lectures on Some Problems of Neurophysiology* 58, *Reliability of Brain* 63, *Compensatory Adaptations, Reflex Activity and the Brain* 65, *Essays on Physiology of Conditioned Reflexes* 70, *I. P. Pavlov* 74.
Ulitsa Butlerova 5A, Moscow; and Ulitsa Petrovskogo 3, Apt. 20, 117419 Moscow, U.S.S.R.
Telephone: 334-70-00 (Office); 232-08-65 (Home).

Asri bin Haji Muda, Datuk Haji Mohamed, S.P.M.K.; Malaysian politician; b. 10 Oct. 1923.
Former teacher; Acting Sec.-Gen. Pan-Malayan Islamic Party 49-54, Commr., Kelantan 54-61, Vice-Pres. 61-64, Pres. 64-; mem. Kelantan State Assembly 59-68, Speaker 64-68; mem. Parl. 59-68; mem. Nat. Unity Council 69-; Minister of Lands, Mines and Special Functions 72-; Deputy Chair. Nat. Council for Islamic Affairs 73-.
Ministry of Lands, Mines and Special Functions, Kuala Lumpur, Malaysia.

Assad, Lt.-Gen. Hafiz al-; Syrian army officer and politician; b. 1928.
Minister of Defence and Commdr. of Air Force Feb. 66-Nov. 70; Prime Minister and Sec. Baath Party Nov. 70-April 71; Regional Sec.-Gen. Baath Party May 71-; Pres. of Syria March 71-; mem. Pres. Council, Fed. of Arab Repubs. 71-; Pres. Syrian Nat. Progressive Front 72-; Commdr. in Chief of Armed Forces 73-.
Office of the President, Damascus, Syria.

Assar, Nassir; Iranian diplomatist; b. 1926; s. of Mohammad Kazem Assar; ed. Teheran Univ.
Joined Ministry of Foreign Affairs 45; Vice-Consul, Stuttgart 49; Second Sec., Stuttgart 51; Vice-Consul, Hamburg 53; Deputy Dir. Dept. of Int. Orgs., Ministry of Foreign Affairs 54-56; First Sec., Ankara 56; First Sec., Iranian Mission to UN 58, Counsellor 59; Counsellor, Deputy Chief of Mission, Ankara 61; Deputy Prime Minister and Head, Org. for Public Trust and Endowment 64; Sec.-Gen. CENTO 72-75.
c/o Central Treaty Organisation, Old Grand National Assembly Building, Ankara, Turkey.

Assmann, Arno; German theatre producer and manager; b. 30 July 1908; ed. Gymnasium und Realschule zum heiligen Geist, Breslau, and Musikhochschule, Breslau.
At Schauspielhaus, Hamburg 46-47, Thalia-Theater, Hamburg 47-52, Schauspielhaus, Frankfurt/Main 52-55, Kammerspiele, Munich 55-58; Dir. Theater am Gärtnerplatz, Munich 59-63; Dir. Bühnen der Stadt Köln (Cologne City Theatres) Jan. 64-Sept. 64, Gen. Dir. Sept. 64-68.
Productions include: *Der Schulfreund* (Kammerspiele, Munich) 59, *Fiesko* (Residenztheater, Munich) 59, *Hoffmanns Erzählungen* (Staatsoper, Munich) 60, *Julius Caesar* (Bühnen der Stadt Köln) 64, *Don Carlos* (Opera, Cologne) 64, *Dantons Tod* (Cologne) 65, *Billy Budd* (Opera, Cologne) 65.
Agentur Kohler, 8000 Munich 23, Rümannstrasse 51, Federal Republic of Germany.

Astaikin, Ivan Pavlovich; Soviet politician; b. 1917; ed. Higher Party School of C.P.S.U. Central Cttee.
Teacher and Dir. of secondary school 34-39; Official, Young Communist League 39-48; Sec., Second Sec., Mordovian Regional Cttee. of C.P.S.U. 48-54; Chair. Council of Ministers of Mordovian S.S.R. 54-; Deputy to U.S.S.R. Supreme Soviet 58-; mem. C.P.S.U. 39-.
Council of Ministers, Mordovian Autonomous S.S.R., Saransk, U.S.S.R.

Astaire, Fred; American actor and dancer; b. 10 May 1899.
Co-starred with his sister as Fred and Adele Astaire 16-32; has appeared in numerous musical comedies and films, television dramas and Fred Astaire Specials (musical), including: *Lady Be Good, The Bandwaggon, Gay Divorce, Top Hat, Holiday Inn, The Sky's the Limit, The Ziegfield Follies, The Belle of New York, Daddy Long Legs, Silk Stockings, On the Beach, Pleasure of his Company, Finian's Rainbow, The Midas Run, The Towering Inferno.*
Publ. *Steps in Time* (autobiography) 60.
c/o Lambs Club, New York, N.Y., U.S.A.

Astapenko, Pavel Evmenovich; Soviet international official; b. 13 Dec. 1918, Mogilev Region, Byelorussia; m. Margarita Astapenko 1945; two d.; ed. Byelorussian State Univ., Minsk and Higher Diplomatic School.
Began career at Ministry of Foreign Affairs of the U.S.S.R.; Dep. Chief 49, subsequently Chief of Political Dept. of Ministry of Foreign Affairs of the Byelorussian S.S.R.; Dep. Minister of Foreign Affairs of Byelorussian S.S.R. 54-61; Chief Govt. Del. to Int. Labour Conf. 56-61; Perm. Rep. of Byelorussian S.S.R. to UN 61-64; Asst. Dir. Gen. Int. Labour Office (ILO) 70-; Order of Red Star; other decorations.
International Labour Office, 154 rue de Lausanne, 1211 Geneva 22; Home: 24 Chemin François Lehmann, 1218 Geneva, Switzerland.

Astigueta, José Manuel; Argentine diplomatist and lawyer; b. 24 Dec. 1918, Buenos Aires; s. of Jose M. Astigueta and Maria Luisa Caceres; m. Maria Ayerza 1945; one s.; ed. Faculty of Law and Social Sciences, Nat. Univ., Buenos Aires and Nat. Military School.

Joined diplomatic service 45; posts at Ministry of Foreign Affairs and at embassies in U.S.A., Mexico, Peru, Brazil and Portugal 45-58; Deputy Dir. Nat. Mil. School 59-62; Minister of Nat. Defence 62-63; Counsellor, Spain 63-66; Head, Dept. of N. American Affairs, Ministry of Foreign Affairs 67-69; Amb. to U.S.S.R. 69; Hon. Prof. Nat. War Coll., Inst. of High Studies of the Army, School of Command and Gen. Staff Aeronautics; del. to numerous int. confs.
Leisure interest: golf.
Martin Coronado 957, Acassusso, Province of Buenos Aires, Argentina.
Telephone: 743-3738.

Astin, Allen V(arley), M.S., PH.D.; American physicist; b. 12 June 1904, Salt Lake City, Utah; s. of John Andrew Astin and Catherine Varley; m. Margaret Linnie Mackenzie 1927; two s.; ed. Univ. of Utah and New York Univ.
National Research Council Fellow, Johns Hopkins Univ. 28-30; Research Assoc., Utilities Research Cttee., Nat. Bureau of Standards 30-32, Physicist 32, Asst. Chief Ordnance Devt. Div. 44-48, Chief Electronics and Ordnance Div. 48-50, Assoc. Dir. 51-52, Dir. 52-69, Dir. Emer. 69-; Chair. Consultative Cttee. on Standards for Measuring Ionizing Radiations of Int. Cttee. of Weights and Measures 54-65; Chair. Cttee. on Fed. Labs. of Fed. Council for Science and Technology 62-69; mem. Nat. Motor Vehicle Safety Advisory Council 68-72; U.S. Co-ordinator U.S.-French Scientific and Technological Co-operation Program 69-; Home Sec. Nat. Acad. of Sciences 71-75; Fellow, American Physical Soc., Inst. of Electrical and Electronic Engineers; mem. Nat. Acad. of Sciences, American Philosophical Soc., Int. Cttee. of Weights and Measures, American Ordnance Asscn., etc.; Presidential Certificate of Merit and numerous other awards.
5008 Battery Lane, Bethesda, Md. 20014, U.S.A.
Telephone: 301-652-8573.

Aston, James William, B.S.; American banker; b. 6 Oct. 1911, Farmersville, Tex.; s. of Joseph A. and Jimmie G. J. Aston; m. Sarah C. Orth 1935; one s.; ed. Texas A. & M. Coll.
Served U.S.A.A.F. 41-45; Vice-Pres. Repub. Nat. Bank of Dallas 45-55, Exec. Vice-Pres. 55-57, Pres. 57-61, Pres. and Chief Exec. Officer 61-65, Chair. and Chief Exec. Officer 65-; official of numerous civic and philanthropic orgs.
Leisure interests: golf, hunting.
Republic National Bank of Dallas, P.O. Box 5961, Dallas, Tex. 75222; 5000 Royal Lane, Dallas, Tex. 75229, U.S.A.

Astor, Hon. Francis David Langhorne; British journalist; b. 5 March 1912, London; s. of 2nd Viscount Astor; m. 1st Melanie Hauser 1945, one d.; m. 2nd Bridget Aphra Wreford 1952, two s. three d.; ed. Eton and Balliol Coll., Oxford.
Staff, *Yorkshire Post* 36; served Second World War 39-45; Foreign Editor *The Observer* 46-48, Editor 48-75; Croix de Guerre.
9 Cavendish Road, St. John's Wood, London, N.W.8; and Manor House, Sutton Courtenay, Berks., England.

Astor of Hever, 2nd Baron, cr. 56, of Hever Castle in the County of Kent; **Gavin Astor**; British company director; b. 1 June 1918; s. of late Lord Astor of Hever; m. Irene, d. of late Field-Marshal Earl Haig, 1945; two s. three d.; ed. Eton and New Coll., Oxford.
Served in Army in Second World War 39-45; Dir. Times Publishing Co. Ltd. 52-66, Chair. 59-66; Pres. Times Newspapers Ltd. 67-; Chair. Commonwealth Press Union 59-72, Pres. 72-; Dir. Alliance Assurance Co. Ltd. 54-; Lord Lieut. of Kent 72-.
Hever Castle, Edenbridge, Kent, England.
Telephone: Edenbridge 2204.

Astrom, C. Sverker; Swedish diplomatist; b. 1915, Uppsala; ed. Univ. of Uppsala.
Foreign Service 39-, Moscow 40-43, Ministry of Foreign Affairs 43-46, Washington 46-48, Ministry of Foreign Affairs 48-53, London 53-56; Head of Political Dept., Min. of Foreign Affairs 56-63; Perm. Rep. to UN 64-70; Deputy Perm. Sec.-Gen., Ministry of Foreign Affairs 70-72, Sec.-Gen. 72-.
c/o Ministry of Foreign Affairs, Stockholm, Sweden.

Astsatryan, Egish Tevosovich; Soviet politician; b. 1914; ed. Tbilisi Industrial Inst.
Member C.P.S.U. 44-; Deputy Chief Engineer of mine, Chief Engineer, Mining Trust 38-50; Sec. Yerevan Territorial Cttee. of C.P. of Armenia, and Chief of Section, Central Cttee. of Armenian C.P. 50-60; Chair. Econ. Council of Armenian S.S.R. 60-65; Chair. Cttee. of People's Control of Armenian S.S.R. 66-; mem. Central Cttee. of Armenian C.P.
Council of Ministers of Armenians S.S.R., Yerevan, U.S.S.R.

Astwood, Edwin Bennett, B.SC., M.D.CM., PH.D., SC.D.; American (naturalized 1943) physician and endocrinologist; b. 29 Dec. 1909, Bermuda; s. of Ernest Millard Astwood and Imogene Doe; m. Sara Ruth Merritt 1937; one s. one d.; ed. McGill Univ. Medical School and Harvard Univ.
Medical House Officer, Royal Victoria Hospital, Montreal 34-35; Assoc. in Obstetrics, Johns Hopkins Univ., and Asst. Obstetrician, Johns Hopkins Hospital 39-40; Asst. Prof. of Pharmacotherapy, Harvard Medical School 40-45; Assoc. in Medicine, Peter Bent Brigham Hospital 40-45; Research Prof. of Medicine, Tufts Medical School 45-52, Prof. of Medicine 52-73, Emer. 73-; endocrinologist, J. H. Pratt Diagnostic Hospital 45-48; Senior Physician, New England Medical Center Hospitals 45-73, Consulting Physician 73-; Consulting Physician, King Edward VII Memorial Hosp. 73-; mem. Nat. Acad. of Sciences, American Physiology Soc., American Acad. Arts and Sciences, etc.; Pres. Endocrine Soc. 61-62; Regent American Coll. of Clinical Pharmacology and Chemotherapy 64-67; numerous awards.
Leisure interests: woodwork, amateur electronics, tennis.
Publs. About 200 papers in scientific and medical journals on sex hormones, reproductive physiology, thyroid gland, antithyroid drugs, pituitary hormones and endocrine disorders.
Outerbridge Building, Pitt's Bay Road, Pembroke 5-33; Home: Covesidd, Shaw Wood, Pembroke 5-51, Bermuda.
Telephone: 2-4240 (Office); 2-4781 (Home).

Atalla, Anton Abdun-Nur; Jordanian lawyer, banker and politician; b. 18 Oct. 1897, Jerusalem; s. of Abdul-Nur Atalla and Maria Zacharia; m. Farida Issa Zacharia 1928; two s. one d.; ed. American Univ., Beirut, and Law Faculty, Jerusalem.
Crown Counsel 24-27, Magistrate 28-31, Senior Magistrate 32-37, Judge District Court, Palestine 37-43; Senior Partner A. & H. Atalla, law firm 43-48; Gen. Man. Arab Land Bank, Jordan 48-73, Consultant 74-; mem. and Chair. Finance Cttee., Jordan House of Reps. 54-56; Jordan Minister for Foreign Affairs 63-64, June-Sept. 70; mem. Jordan Senate, Legal Cttee., Foreign Relations Cttee. 63-74; mem. Bureau of Interpretation of Constitution 73-74; Pres. Arab Orthodox Exec. 52-; Pres. Nat. YMCA 59-; Past Gov. of Rotary District; Jordan Order of Star, Belgian Grand Order of Cross, Knight Grand Cross Order of St. Gregory (Vatican), Paraguayan Order of Grand Cross.
Leisure interests: walking, travelling.
Arab Land Bank, P.O. Box 6425, Jabal Amman, Amman, Jordan.
Telephone: 41308.

Atassi, Nureddin, M.D.; Syrian politician; b. 1929; ed. Damascus Univ.
Minister of the Interior Aug. 63; Deputy Prime Minister Oct. 64; mem. Syrian Presidential Council May 64-Dec. 65; Chief of the Syrian State Feb. 66-Oct. 70; also Prime Minister Oct. 68-Oct. 70; Sec.-Gen. Syrian Baath Party 66-70; in exile in Libya.

Ateeqy, Abdulreham Salim al-; Kuwaiti diplomatist and politician; b. 5 April 1928; ed. High School, Kuwait.
Secretary-General, Police Dept., Kuwait 49-59; Dir.-Gen. Health Dept. 59-61; Del. to UN 60-61, to WHO, Geneva 61, to UN Gen. Assembly 61; Amb. to U.S.A. 62-63; Under-Sec. Ministry of Foreign Affairs 63-67; Minister of Finance 67-, and Oil Affairs 67-75; Chair. Kuwait Fund for Arab Econ. Devt.
Ministry of Finance, P.O. Box Safat 9, Kuwait.

Athanasiadis-Novas, Georgios; Greek politician; b. 1893; s. of Themistoklis and Evdokia Athanasiadis-Novas; m. Maria S. Bulgari 1935; no c.; ed. Athens Univ.
Former journalist and lawyer; mem. Parl. 26-39, 51, 56, 58, 61, 63, 64; Minister of Interior 45, of Education 45, 50-51; Minister of Industry 51-52; Minister in charge of Prime Minister's Office 51-52, 63; Pres. of Chamber of Deputies 64-65; Prime Minister July-Aug. 65; Deputy Prime Minister 65-66; mem. Athens Acad. 55-; Centre Union.
Publs. (under pseudonym George Athanas) *Proino Xekinima* (Morning Start), *Agapi ston Epakto* (Love in Epaktos), *Prasino Kapello* (Green Hat), *Deka Erotes* (Ten Love Stories), *Aploikes Psiches* (Simple Souls), *Drosseri Kaimi* (Happy Trouble), *Tragoudia ton Vounon* (Mountain Songs), *Evdokia* (Good Will), *Vathies Rizes* (Deep Roots), *Timia Dora* (Honest Gifts), *Astegnoto Dakri* (Tears that do not dry), *Enos ke Thrinos* (Praise and Lament).
Akademia Athinon, Odos Panepistimiou, Athens, Greece.

Athanassiades, George; Greek newspaper proprietor; b. 13 Aug. 1912, Constantinople; s. of Athos and Helen Amira; m. Helen Abatzi 1939; three c.; ed. Saint Paul School, Piraeus.
General Man. *Vradyni*, daily, *Naftemboriki*, daily journal of finance, commerce, shipping and industry; mem. Union of Publrs. of Athenian Newspapers, Int. Press Inst., Int. Fed. of Journalists, Int. Fed. of Newspaper Publrs.; Silver Medal of Valour, Gold Medal of Oecumenical Patriarchate.
Leisure interest: sports.
c/o Vradyni, 9-11 Piraeus Street, Athens 112, Greece.

Athanassiades, Panos; Greek newspaper proprietor; b. 17 March 1899, Kydonias; ed. Commercial School of Chalke, Athens Univ.
Proprietor Delpa, maritime agency 20-; Publr. of *Bulletin Maritime de Constantinople*, daily 22-24, *Index Maritime de Constantinople* 23-24, *Naftemboriki*, daily journal of finance, commerce, shipping and industry 24-; Lecturer, School of Industry, Piraeus 59-62; Publr. *Vradyni*, daily 62-; Pres. Org. of Port of Piraeus 60-64, Int. Union of Transport 55-; mem. Council Nat. Org. of Tourism 56-59; Knight of Dannebrog (Denmark).
Publs. numerous articles.
132 Patission Street, Athens 802, Greece.

Athfield, Ian Charles, DIP.ARCH.; New Zealand architect; b. 15 July 1940, Christchurch; m. Nancy Clare Cookson 1962; two s.; ed. Christchurch Boys High School, Auckland Univ. School of Architecture.
A Principal of Structon Group Architects, Wellington 65-68; own practice 68-; N.Z.I.A. Silver Medal 70, AA Award 68, 72.
Leisure interests: building, gardening, drinking, laughing.

105 Amritsar Street, Khandallah, Wellington, New Zealand.
Telephone: 795-134, 793-758 (Office); 793-832 (Home).

Atiki, Abdul Rahman al- (*see* Ateeqy, Abdulreham Salim al-).

Atiya, Aziz Suryal, M.A., PH.D., LITT.D.; Egyptian historian and writer; b. 1898; ed. Univs. of Liverpool and London.
Charles Beard Fellow and Univ. Fellow, Univ. of Liverpool 30-32; History Tutor, School of Oriental Studies, Univ. of London 33-34; Prof. of Medieval and Oriental History, Univ. of Bonn 35-38; Prof. Medieval History, Cairo 38-42, Alexandria 42-54; consultant to Library of Congress, Washington, D.C. 50-51; visiting lecturer U.S. univs., Univ. of Zürich and Swiss Inst. of Int. Affairs 50-51; Pres. Inst. of Coptic Studies, Cairo 54-56; Medieval Acad. Visiting Prof. of Islamic Studies, Univ. of Michigan, Ann Arbor 55-56; Luce Prof. of World Christianity, Union Theological Seminary, and Visiting Prof. of History, Columbia Univ., New York 56-57; Visiting Prof. of Arabic and Islamic History, Princeton Univ. 57-58; mem. Inst. for Advanced Study, Princeton 58-59; Dir., Middle East Center, Utah Univ. 59-67; Distinguished Prof. of History, Utah 67-; corresp. mem. UNESCO Int. Comm. for the Scientific and Cultural History of Mankind; corresp. mem. Coptic Archaeological Soc.; mem. Medieval Acad. of America, Mediterranean Acad., Rome; Hon. D.H.L.
Publs. *The Crusade of Nicopolis* 34, *The Crusade in the Later Middle Ages* 38, *Egypt and Aragon—Embassies and Diplomatic Correspondence between 1300 and 1330* 38, *Kitab Qawanin al-Dawawin by Saladin's Wazir ibn Mammati* 43, *History of the Patriarchs of the Egyptian Church* (2 vols.) 48-59, *Monastery of St. Catherine in Mt. Sinai* 49, *The Mt. Sinai Arabic Microfilms* 54, *Coptic Music* 60, *Crusade, Commerce and Culture* 62, *The Crusades—Historiography and Bibliography* 62, *History of Eastern Christianity* 68, etc. (all books in either English or Arabic).
1335 Perry Avenue, Salt Lake City, Utah, U.S.A.
Telephone: Salt Lake City 328-1086.

Atiyah, Michael Francis, M.A., PH.D., F.R.S.; British mathematician; b. 22 April 1929, London; s. of Edward Selim Atiyah and Jean (Levens) Atiyah; m. Lily Brown 1955; three s.; ed. Victoria Coll., Egypt, Manchester Grammar School and Trinity Coll., Cambridge.
Research Fellow, Trinity Coll., Cambridge 54-58; Fellow, Pembroke Coll., Cambridge 58-61, Univ. Lecturer 57-61; Reader, Oxford Univ., and Fellow, St. Catherine's Coll., Oxford 61-63; Savilian Prof. of Geometry, Oxford Univ., and Fellow of New Coll., Oxford 63-69; Prof. of Mathematics, Inst. for Advanced Study, Princeton, N.J. 69-72; Royal Soc. Research Prof., Oxford Univ.; Fellow, St. Catherine's Coll. 73-; Pres. London Mathematical Soc. 74-; Fields Medal, Int. Congress of mathematicians, Moscow 66; Royal Medal of Royal Soc. (U.K.) 68; Hon. D.Sc. (Bonn, Warwick); Foreign mem. American Acad. of Arts and Sciences, Swedish Acad. of Sciences.
Leisure interests: gardening, music.
Publs. *K-Theory* 66, *Commutative Algebra* 69.
Mathematical Institute, 24 St. Giles, Oxford; Home: Shotover Mound, Headington, Oxford, England.
Telephone: Oxford 62359.

Atkins, Orin Ellsworth, LL.B.; American oil executive; b. 6 June 1924, Pittsburgh, Pa.; s. of Orin E. Atkins and Dorothy Whittaker Atkins; m. Kathryn Agee Atkins 1950; two s.; ed. Marshall Coll., Huntington, W. Va., Univs. of Pennsylvania and Virginia.
Admitted to W. Va. Bar 50, Kentucky Bar 52; with Ashland Oil Inc. (Ky.) 50-, Exec. Asst. 56-59, Admin. Vice-Pres. 59-65, Dir. 62-, Pres. and Chief Exec. Officer

65-72, Chair. of Board and Chief Exec. Officer 72-; Chair. Marshall Univ. Advisory Board.
Office: 1409 Winchester Avenue, Ashland, Ky. 41101
Home: 602 Amanda Drive, Ashland, Ky. 41101, U.S.A
Telephone: 606-329-3333 (Office); 606-324-2763 (Home)

Atkinson, Frederick John, C.B., M.A.; British civil servant; b. 7 Dec. 1919, London; s. of George E. Atkinson and Elizabeth S. Cooper; m. Margaret Grace Gibson 1947; two d.; ed. Jesus Coll., Oxford Univ.
Lecturer, Jesus and Trinity Colls., Oxford 47-49; Econ. Adviser, Cabinet Office 49-51, at Embassy, Washington 51-54 and at Treasury 55-69; Chief Econ. Adviser, Dept. of Trade and Industry 70-73; Asst. Sec.-Gen. OECD 73-75; Deputy Sec. Chief Econ. Adviser, Dept. of Energy 75-.
Leisure interest: reading.
26 Lee Terrace, London, S.E.3; Tickner Cottage, Church Lane, Aldington, Kent, England; 31 boulevard Raspail, 75007 Paris, France.
Telephone: 01-852-1040 (Office); Aldington 514 (Home).

Atkinson, Justin Brooks, A.B., L.H.D. (HON.); American writer; b. 28 Nov. 1894; ed. Harvard Univ.
Literary Editor *New York Times* 22-25, Dramatic Critic 25-42; War Correspondent in China 43-44; Correspondent in Russia 45-46; dramatic critic 46-60; columnist 60-64; Pulitzer Prize 47; Fellow, American Acad. of Arts and Sciences.
Publs. *Henry Thoreau, the Cosmic Yankee* 27, *East of the Hudson* 31, *Cingalese Prince* 35, *Once Around the Sun* 51, *Tuesdays and Fridays* 63, *Brief Chronicles* 66, *Broadway* 70, *This Bright Land* 72.
Durham, N.Y. 12422, U.S.A.

Attar, Mohamed Said al-; Yemeni economist; b. 26 Nov. 1927; m.; two c.; ed. Ecole Pratique des Hautes Etudes à la Sorbonne, Inst. d'Etude du Développement Econ. et Social (I.E.D.E.S.), Univ. de Paris.
Research I.E.D.E.S. 60-62; Dir.-Gen. Yemen Bank for Reconstruction and Devt. 62-65; Minister of Econ. March-Aug. 65; Pres. Econ. Comm. Oct. 65-Feb. 66; Pres. Board Yemen Bank and Pres. of Econ. High Comm. March 66-68; Perm. Rep. to UN 68-71, 73-74; Deputy Premier for Financial Affairs and Minister of Economy Aug.-Sept. 71, Exec. Sec. Econ. Comm. for W. Asia 74-.
Publs. *L'Industrie du gant en France* 61, *L'épicerie à Paris* 61, *Etude sur la croissance économique de l'Afrique Occidentale* 62, *Le marché industriel et les projets de l'Arabie Séoudite* 62, *Le sous-développement économique et social du Yémen* (*Perspectives de la Révolution Yémenite*) 64, Arabic edition 65.
Economic Commission for West Asia, UN Building, P.O. Box 4656, Bir Hassan, Beirut, Lebanon.

Attassi, Lt.-Gen. Louai; Syrian army officer and politician; b. 1926; ed. Syrian Military Acad., and Staff Officers' Coll., Homs.
Took part in Palestinian war 48; opposed Syrian break with Egypt 61; Garrison Commdr., Aleppo April 62; Military Attaché, Syrian Embassy, Washington 62-63; C.-in-C. of Syrian Armed Forces and Pres. of Revolutionary Council March-July 63.
Damascus, Syrian Arab Republic.

Attenborough, David Frederick, C.B.E., M.A.; British broadcaster and writer; b. 8 May 1926, London; s. of Frederick and Mary Attenborough; brother of Sir Richard Attenborough (q.v.); m. Jane Elizabeth Elsworth Oriel 1950; one s. one d.; ed. Wyggeston Grammar School, Leicester, and Clare Coll., Cambridge.
Royal Navy 47-49; Editorial Asst. in publishing house 49-52; with BBC Television 52-73, Trainee Producer BBC TV 52-54, Producer of zoological, archaeological, travel, political and other programmes 54-64, Controller BBC 2 64-68, Dir. of Programmes, TV 69-73;

mem. Man. Board, BBC 69-73; freelance broadcaster and writer 73-; Hon. D.Litt. (Leicester and City Univs.), Hon. D.Sc. (Liverpool Univ.); Special Award, Guild of TV Producers 61, Silver Medal, Royal TV Soc. 66, Silver Medal, Zoological Soc. of London 66, Desmond Davis Award, Soc. of Film and TV Arts 70, Cherry Kearton Award, Royal Geographical Soc. 72.
Leisure interests: music, tribal art, natural history.
5 Park Road, Richmond, Surrey, England.

Attenborough, Sir Richard Samuel, Kt., C.B.E.; British actor, producer and director; b. 29 Aug. 1923; s. of Frederick Attenborough; brother of David Attenborough (q.v.); m. Sheila Sim; one s. two d.; ed. Wyggeston Grammar School, Leics., and Royal Acad. of Dramatic Art, London.
First stage appearance in *Ah! Wilderness*, Palmers Green 41; West End debut in *Awake and Sing* 42; first film appearance *In Which we Serve* 42; R.A.F. 43, seconded to R.A.F. Film Unit 44-46; returned to stage 49; formed Beaver Films with Bryan Forbes (q.v.), appearing in and co-producing *The Angry Silence* 59; formed Allied Film Makers 60; produced *Whistle Down the Wind* 61, *The L-Shaped Room* 62, *Seance on a Wet Afternoon* 63; directed *Oh! What a Lovely War* 68; *Young Winston* 71; Chair. Royal Acad. of Dramatic Art (RADA); Pro-Chancellor, Sussex Univ.; Gov. Nat. Film School; Chair. Capital Radio 73-; mem. Cinematograph Films Council 67-73, Arts Council of Great Britain 70-73; Best Actor Award, San Sebastian 64, British Film Acad. 64; Hollywood Golden Globe Awards 66, 67, 69; First of Cinematograph Exhibitors Asscn. annual awards for Distinguished Service to British Cinema 67; Hon. D.Litt. (Leicester); Hon. D.C.L. (Newcastle); Trustee, Tate Gallery.
Leisure interests: collecting 20th-century painting and Picasso ceramics, gramophone records, Chelsea Football Club.
Stage appearances include *The Little Foxes* 42, *Brighton Rock* 43, *The Way Back* 49, *To Dorothy a Son* 50-51, *Sweet Madness* 52, *The Mousetrap* 52-54, *Double Image* 56-57, *The Rape of the Belt* 57-58.
Film appearances include *School for Secrets*, *The Man Within*, *Dancing with Crime*, *Brighton Rock*, *London Belongs to Me*, *The Guinea Pig*, *Morning Departure*, *Hell is Sold Out*, *The Magic Box*, *Gift Horse*, *Eight O'Clock Walk*, *The Ship that Died of Shame*, *Private's Progress*, *The Baby and the Battleship*, *Brothers in Law*, *Dunkirk*, *The Man Upstairs*, *Sea of Sand*, *Danger Within*, *I'm All Right Jack*, *Jet Storm*, *S.O.S. Pacific*, *The Angry Silence*, *The League of Gentlemen*, *Only Two Can Play*, *All Night Long*, *The Dock Brief*, *The Great Escape*, *Seance on a Wet Afternoon*, *The Third Secret*, *The Guns of Batasi*, *The Flight of the Phoenix*, *The Sand Pebbles*, *Dr. Dolittle*, *The Bliss of Mrs. Blossom*, *The Last Grenade*, *A Severed Head*, *David Copperfield*, *Loot*, *10 Rillington Place*, *Ten Little Indians*, *Brannigan*, *Rosebud*, *Death in Persepolis*, *Conduct Unbecoming*.
Old Friars, Richmond Green, Surrey, England.

Attiga, Ali Ahmad, PH.D.; Libyan economist; b. Oct. 1931, Misratah; one s. four d.; ed. Univs. of Wisconsin and Calif.
Assistant Econ. Adviser, Nat. Bank of Libya 59-60, Head, Econ. Research Dept. and Chief Ed. *Economic Bulletin* 60-64, 66-68; Under-Sec. Ministry of Planning and Devt. 64-66; Chair. Energy Cttee., Nat. Planning Council 65-66; Minister of Planning and Devt. 68-69, of Econ. 69; Gen. Man. Libya Insurance Co. 70-73, Chair. 73; Chair. and Founder, Nat. Investment Co. 71-73; Chair. Libyan Hotels and Tourist Co. 71-73; Dir. Arab Re-insurance Co., Beirut 71-73; Sec.-Gen. Org. of Arab Petroleum Exporting Countries 73-; mem. Joint Planning Cttee., Nat. Planning Council 63-68, Supreme Petroleum Council 64-66; mem. Board of Dirs., Coll. of Advanced Technology 64-66.

Publ. *Effect of Petroleum on the Libyan Economy 1956-1960* 74.
Organization of Arab Petroleum Exporting Countries, P.O. Box 20501, Al-Sour Street, Kuwait.
Telephone: 420061 (Office); 517963 (Home).

Attiyia, Mahmoud Ibrahim, B.SC.; Egyptian geologist; b. 1900; ed. Cairo and Imperial Coll. of Science and Technology, London.
Asst. Lecturer, School of Engineering, Giza 23-25; Geologist, Geological Survey of Egypt 29, Asst. Dir. 39, Dir. 49; Dir.-Gen. Mines and Quarries Dept. 54-56; Tech. Dir. Mineral Wealth Co. and Sinai Manganese Co., Cairo 56-62; Chair. and Man. Dir. Associated Mines Co. 62-65; delegated Prof. of Geology, Cairo Univ.; A.R.C.S. London 29; F.G.S. London 30; mem. Inst. d'Egypte 46; mem. Board of the Desert Inst. of Egypt 50; mem. Egyptian Acad. of Sciences 50; mem. Conseil d'Egypte 46-; mem. Board of the Desert Inst. of Egypt 51; State Prize in Geological and Chemical Sciences 50; Order of the Republic (Egypt) 54; Pres. Egyptian Acad. of Sciences 68.
Publs. *Notes on the Underground Water in Egypt* 42, *The Barramiya Mining District* 48, *New Mode of Occurrence of Iron-Ore Deposits* 49, *Iron-Ore Deposits of Egypt* 50, *Ground-Water in Egypt* 53, *Deposits in the Nile Valley and the Delta* 54, *Iron-Ore Deposits of the District East of Aswan* 55, *Manganese Deposits of Egypt* 56.
10 Diwan Street, Garden City, Cairo, Egypt.

Attwood, William, B.A.; American journalist and diplomatist; b. 14 July 1919, Paris, France; s. of Frederic Attwood and Gladys Hollingsworth; m. Simone Cadgene 1950; one s. two d.; ed. Choate School, Princeton Univ.
United States Army 41-45; Corresp. *New York Herald Tribune* 46-48, *Collier's Magazine* 49-51; European Editor *Look Magazine* 51-55, Nat. Editor 55-57, Foreign Editor 57-61; Amb. to Guinea 61-63; Special Adviser to U.S. UN Del. 63-64; Amb. to Kenya 64-66; Editor-in-Chief Cowles Communications Inc. 66-70; Pres. and Publisher *Newsday* 70-; Dir. Overseas Devt. Council, the Advertising Council; Trustee Kress Foundation; Democrat.
Publs. *The Man Who Could Grow Hair* 49, *Still the Most Exciting Country* 55, *The Reds and the Blacks* 67, *The Fairly Scary Adventure Book* 69.
Leisure interests: golf, reading, tennis, bridge.
423 Carter Street, New Canaan, Conn. 06840, U.S.A.
Telephone: 203-966-5831; 516-294-3488 (Office).

Atwood, John Leland, A.B., B.S.; American engineer; b. 26 Oct. 1904; ed. Hardin Simmons Univ. and Univ. Texas.
Junior Engineer, Army Air Corps, Wright Field, Ohio 28; Design Engineer, Douglas Aircraft Co. 30-34; Vice-Pres. and Chief Engineer, North American Aviation Inc. (became North American Rockwell, now Rockwell Int. Corpn.) 34, Pres. 48-70, Chief. Exec. Officer 60, Chair. of the Board 62, Senior Consultant and Dir. 70-; Hon. Fellow, American Inst. of Aeronautics and Astronautics, Pres. 54-; mem. Soc. Automotive Engineers.
Rockwell International Corporation, 2230 East Imperial Highway, El Segundo, Calif. 90245, U.S.A.

Atzmon, Moshe; Israeli conductor; b. 30 July 1931, Budapest, Hungary; m. 1954; two d.; ed. Tel-Aviv Acad. of Music, Guildhall School of Music, London.
Left Hungary for Israel 44; played the horn professionally in various orchestras for several years; second prize Dimitri Mitropoulos Competition for Conductors, N.Y. 63; Leonard Bernstein Prize 63; First Prize, Int. Conductors Competition, Liverpool, England 64; has conducted in Israel, England, Australia, Germany, Sweden, Norway, Switzerland, Spain, Finland, Italy, Austria, Turkey and U.S.A.; Chief Conductor, Sydney Symphony Orchestra 69-71; Chief Conductor, North German Symphony Orchestra 72; Musical Dir. Basle Symphony Orchestra 72.
Leisure interests: reading, travelling.
16 Canfield Gardens, London, N.W.6, England.
Telephone: 01-624-6322.

Aubert, Jacques, D. en D.; French administrator and politician; b. 6 Aug. 1913, Cherbourg; m. Nicole de la Hautière 1944; one s. three d.; ed. Lycée de Brest, Faculté de droit de Paris and Ecole libre des Sciences Politiques.
Legal Adviser Ministry of Foreign Affairs 39-40; Asst. to Sec.-Gen. of Comm. on Cotton Imports 41-42; Chef du Cabinet of Prefect 42; Asst. Prefect, Dir. of Security for French Occupation Zone in Austria 47, Sec.-Gen., Vienna 51; Asst. Prefect, Dreux 53; Asst. Dir. Private Office of Pierre Voizard, Resident Gen. of France at Tunis 54, Sec.-Gen. Martinique, Constantine 55; Dir. Private Office of Abdelkadar Barakrok, Sec. of State for Algeria, and Private Offices of Bourgès-Manoury and Félix Gaillard 57-58; Prefect and Technical Adviser, Private Office of Prefect of Police 58; Dir. Sûreté Nationale in Algeria 60-61; Prefect of Loir-et-Cher 61; Dir.-Gen. Sûreté Nationale 62; Dir. Private Office of R. Frey, Minister of the Interior 63-66; Sec.-Gen. of the Police 67-69; Counsellor of State 69-; Officier Légion d'Honneur, Croix de la Valeur Militaire, Commandeur du Mérite (Ordre National du Mérite).
33 rue Poussin, Paris 16e, France.

Aubinière, Gen. Robert Joseph; French air force officer and astronautical specialist; b. 24 Sept. 1912, Paris; m. Geneviève Beauville 1936; six d.; ed. Ecole Polytechnique, and air force training.
War service, North Africa 42, Chief of Operations, N. Region of France 43, then sent to a concentration camp; Vice-Commdt., Ecole de l'Air de Salon-de-Provence 45-48, Commdt. 60; Air Force Staff Colleges 49; Deputy Chief-of-Staff 5th Airborne Region 50-53; Commdt., Ground Staff Training School Rochefort 54-57, Centre Interarmées d'Essais d'Engins Spéciaux, Colomb-Béchar 57-58; promoted Gén. de Brigade Aérienne 58; Technical and Industrial dir. of Aeronautics 60; promoted Gén. de Division Aérienne 61; Dir.-Gen. Centre National d'Etudes Spatiales 62-71; Pres. of Council of Admin. of ELDO 68-70, Sec.-Gen. 72-74; Grand Officier Légion d'Honneur, Croix de Guerre, Médaille de l'Aéronautique.
1 rue Anatole-France, 92290 Châtenay-Malabry, France.

Aubréville, André Marie Alphonse; French forest and botanical specialist; b. 30 Nov. 1897, Pont St. Vincent; m. Marguerite Bertrand 1927; one d.; ed. Ecole Polytechnique and Ecole Nationale des Eaux et Forêts.
Career in Waters and Forests Service, Overseas France 25-55; Insp.-Gen. of Forest Services, Overseas France 39-55; numerous missions in tropical countries, mainly in Africa; Prof. in Muséum National d'Histoire Naturelle, holding titular chair of Phanerogamy, Dir. Lab. of Phanerogamy 58-68; Hon. Emer. Prof. at Muséum Nat. d'Histoire Naturelle 68-; mem. Acad. des Sciences and Acad. d'Agric. de France; mem. Acad. des Sciences and Acad. des Sciences d'Outre Mer; Officier, Légion d'Honneur; Médaille Militaire; Croix de Guerre (14-18).
Leisure interests: world-wide travel, gardening.
Publs. *Flore forestière de la Côte d'Ivoire* 36, *Climats, Forêts et Désertification de l'Afrique tropicale* 49, *Flore forestière soudano-guinéenne* 50, *Etude écologique des principales formations végétales du Brésil* 61, *Direction des Flores du Gabon, du Cameroun, de Madagascar et des Comores, du Cambodge-Laos-Vietnam, de la Nouvelle Calédonie*, etc.
Museum: 16 rue Buffon, Paris 5e; Home: 118 boulevard Raspail, Paris 6e, France.
Telephone: 331-30-35 (Office); 548-82-68 (Home).

Aubrun, Charles Vincent; French university professor; b. 4 April 1906, Clichy-Paris; s. of Charles F. and Suzanne (née Miraucourt) Aubrun; m. Hilda G. Donnelly 1929; ed. Univ. of Paris.
Professor, Univ. of Poitiers 39-45, Univ. of Bordeaux 45-51, Univ. of Paris 51-72, Dir. Centre of Hispanic Studies 53-72, Univ. of Nice 72-; Guest Prof. Univ. of Texas, Austin, Columbia Univ., U.C. Santa Barbara, Cornell, Stanford, Bloomington, San José de Costa Rica; Chevalier de la Légion d'Honneur.
Leisure interests: drawing, mathematics.
Publs. *Bolívar: choix de lettres, discours, proclamation* 34, *Lope de Vega*, *Peribáñez* 43, *Le Chansonnier espagnol d'Herberay des Essarts*, 15e siècle 51, *L'Amérique Centrale* 52-74, *Histoire des Lettres hispano-américaines* 54, *Calderón*, *La estatua de Prometeo* 61, *Calderón*, *Eco y Narciso* 61, *Bolívar*, *Cuatro cartas y una memoria* 61, *Lope de Vega*, *La Circe* 62. *Histoire du théâtre espagnol* 65, 68, *La comédie espagnole (1600-1680)* 66, *L'espagnol à l'Université* (2 vols.) 67, 70, *L'Espagne au Siècle d'or* 71.
23 boulevard de Cambrai, Nice, France.
Telephone: 86-52-43.

Auchincloss, Louis Stanton, LL.B., D.LITT.; American lawyer and author; b. 27 Sept. 1917; ed. Groton School, Yale Univ. and Univ. of Virginia.
Admitted to New York Bar 41, Assoc. Sullivan and Cromwell 41-51, Hawkins, Delafield and Wood, New York City 54-58, partner 58-; Lieut. U.S. Navy 41-45; Pres. Museum of the City of New York; mem. Nat. Inst. of Arts and Letters.
Publs. *The Indifferent Children* 47, *The Injustice Collectors* 50, *Sybil* 52, *A Law for the Lion* 53, *The Romantic Egoists* 54, *The Great World and Timothy Colt* 56, *Venus in Sparta* 58, *Pursuit of the Prodigal* 59, *House of Five Talents* 60, *Reflections of a Jacobite* 61, *Portrait in Brownstone* 62, *Powers of Attorney* 63, *The Rector of Justin* 64, *Pioneers and Caretakers* 65, *The Embezzler* 66, *Tales of Manhattan* 67, *A World of Profit* 69, *Motiveless Malignity* 69, *Edith Wharton: A Woman in Her Time* 71, *I Come as a Thief* 72, *Richelieu* 72, *The Partners* 74, *A Winter's Capital* 74, *Reading Henry James* 75.
1111 Park Avenue, New York City 28, N.Y. 10028, U.S.A.

Auchinleck, Field-Marshal Sir Claude John Etre, G.C.B., G.C.I.E., C.S.I, D.S.O., O.B.E.; British army officer; b. 21 June 1884, Aldershot; s. of Col. J. C. A. Auchinleck R.H.A. and Mary E. Eyre; ed. Wellington Coll. and Royal Mil. Coll., Sandhurst.
Commissioned Indian Army 03; joined 62nd Punjabis 04; served Egypt 14-15, Aden 15, Mesopotamia 16-19; Imperial Defence Coll. 27; commanded 1st Battalion 1st Punjab Regt. 29-30; Instructor Staff Coll. Quetta 30-33; Commander Peshawar Brigade 33-36; Deputy Chief of Gen. Staff Army Headquarters India 36-38, Commander Meerut District 38; mem. Expert Cttee. on Indian Defence 38; Commdr. Allied Land Forces in Northern Norway 40; G.O.C.-in-C. Southern Command 40; Commdr.-in-Chief India 41, Middle East 41-42, India 43-47; Chair. Dowsett Holdings Ltd. 54; Chair. Murrayfield Real Estate Co. Ltd. 58; Hon. LL.D. (Aberdeen, St. Andrews, Manchester); Virtuti Militari (Poland) 42; War Cross (Czechoslovakia) 44; Order of Chief Commdr., Legion of Merit (U.S.A.) 45; Order of Star of Nepal (1st Class) 45; Grand Cross, Order of St. Olaf (Norway) 47; Order of Cloud and Banner (China) 47; Grand Officier, Légion d'Honneur 49.
Leisure interests: travel, sketching, fishing, walking.
Villa Rikichou, rue Hafid Ibrahim, Marrakesh. Morocco; c/o National & Grindlays Bank, 13 St. James's Square, London, S.W.1, England.
Telephone: 300-13.

Audenhove, Omer Van; Belgian politician; b. 3 Dec, 1913.
Member Resistance, Second World War; mem. Municipal Council, Diest 46-, Mayor 47-58; mem. Belgian Senate 54-; Minister of Public Works and Reconstruction 55-58, 58-61; Président Parti Libéral de Belgique May-Oct. 61, Président-fondateur, Parti de la Liberté et du Progrès 61-; Officier de l'Ordre de la Couronne; Officier Ordre de Léopold II avec Palmes; Chevalier de l'Ordre de Léopold; Croix de Guerre avec Palmes; Grand Croix de l'Ordre Orange-Nassau (Netherlands).
Publ. *Deux lois indispensables.*
Villa Gilden Boom, Schaffen (lez Diest), Belgium.

Audry, Colette; French writer; b. 6 July 1906; ed. Ecole Normale Supérieure, Sèvres.
Professor of Literature, Lycée Molière, Paris 45-65; Literary Critic *Les Temps Modernes* 45-55; on staff Editions, Denoël 63-; film-set designer and script-writer; Prix Medicis for *Derrière la Baignoire* 62.
Publs. novels: *On joue perdant*, *Aux yeux du souvenir*, *Léon Blum ou la politique du Juste*, *Connaissance de Sartre*, *Sartre ou la Réalité humaine* 66, *L'Autre planète* 72; screen-plays: *Les malheurs de Sophie*, *La Bataille du rail*, *Olivia*, *Absence*, *Liberté surveillée*, *Derrière la Baignoire*, *Fruits amers*; play: *Soledad*.
Résidence du Val (3b), 91-Palaiseau, France.

Auer, Väinö, PH.D., F.I.A.L.; Finnish geologist and geographer; b. 7 Jan. 1895; ed. Helsinki Univ.
Member Forest Research Inst. 18-29; Geologist, Geological Survey of Canada 26; Lecturer in Geography, Helsinki Univ. 22-29, Prof. 29-53, Prof. in Geology 57-63; Rockefeller scholarship 26; leader geographical expedition, Patagonia and Tierra del Fuego 28-29; Pres. Finnish Geographical Society and Finnish Forestry Asscn. 35-36; leader geographical expeditions to Patagonia 37-38, 47-53 and 57; Hon. Dir. Forestry Research of Argentina 47; President Finnish Acad. of Science 59; mem. Finnish Scientific Acad., etc.; highest award of honour of Finnish Culture Foundation, Finnish Acad. of Sciences, Kordelin Foundation; Fennia Gold Medal 50; Kairamo Silver Medal 50; Cajander Medal 55; Martin Behaim Silver Medal 59; Rueppell Silver Medal 61; Helsinki Univ. Medal; Eskola Gold Medal 75; war medals; Commdr. (First Class) Order of Lion, Finland; Commdr. of White Rose, Finland; mem. numerous foreign socs.; Dr. h.c. (Bonn, Turku).
Publs. *Verschiebungen der Wald- und Steppengebiete Feuerlands in post-glazialer Zeit*, *Las Capas Volcánicas como Base de la Cronología Postglacial de Fuegopatagonia*, *Peat bogs in Southeastern Canada*, *Nuevos Aspectos de la Sequía en la Patagonia*, *The Pleistocene of Fuego-Patagonia: I The Ice and Inter-Glacial Ages*, *II History of the Flora and Vegetation*, *III Shoreline Displacements*, *IV Bog Profiles*, *V Quarternary Problems of Southern South America*, etc.
Rakuunantie 4, B, 14, Helsinki 33, Finland.
Telephone: Helsinki 486433.

Auerbach, Charlotte, D.SC., PH.D., F.R.S., F.R.S.E.; British geneticist; b. 14 May 1899, Crefeld, Germany; ed. Univs. of Würzburg, Freiburg, Berlin and Edinburgh.
Left Germany 33; Asst., Inst. of Animal Genetics, Univ. of Edinburgh, Lecturer 46, Reader 57, Prof. 67, Prof. Emer. 69-; Visiting Prof. Oak Ridge Nat. Laboratory, U.S.A. 58; mem. Japan Genetics Soc., Danish Acad. of Sciences; Foreign Assoc. Nat. Acad. of Sciences, U.S.A. 70.
Leisure interests: literature, music, hiking, gardening.
Publs. include: *Adventures with Rosalind* (children's book) 45; *Genetics in the Atomic Age* 56, 65, *The Science of Genetics* 62, 69, *Mutation* 62, *Heredity* 65, *Mutation Research* 76.
Institute of Animal Genetics, The University, West Mains Road, Edinburgh 9, Scotland.

Auerbach, Frank; German artist; b. 29 April 1931, Berlin; ed. St. Martin's School of Art, London (under David Bomberg), Royal Coll. of Art.

One-man exhbns. at Beaux-Arts Gallery, London 56, 59, 61, 62, 63, Marlborough Fine Art, London 65, 67, 71, 74, Marlborough Gallery Inc., New York 69, Villiers Art Gallery, Sydney 72, Univ. of Essex, Colchester 73, Galleria Bergamini, Milan 73; group exhbns. at Tooths Gallery, London 58, 71, N.Y. Foundation, Rome 58, Carnegie Int. Exhbn., Pittsburg 58, 61, Dum Int. Exhbn., London 63, Gulbenkian Exhbn., London 64, Marlborough Graphics, London 66-71, Peter Stuyvesant Foundation Collection, London 67, Graphics Triennial, Bienne 70, Palazzo dell' Acad. and Palazzo Reale, Genoa 72, Marlborough-Godard, Toronto 73; Los Angeles County Museum 75; works in public collections in U.K., Australia, Brazil, U.S.A.; Silver Medal for painting, Royal Coll. of Art.

c/o Marlborough Fine Art Gallery, 6 Albemarle Street, London, W1X 3HF, England.

Auerbach, Stanley Irving, M.S., PH.D.; American ecologist; b. 21 May 1921, Chicago, Ill.; s. of Abraham and Carrie Friedman Auerbach; m. Dawn Patricia Davey 1954; two s. two d.; ed. Univ. of Illinois and Northwestern Univ.

Second Lieut. U.S. Army 42-44; instructor, then Asst. Prof., Roosevelt Univ., Chicago 50-54; Assoc. scientist, then scientist, Health Physics Div., Oak Ridge Nat. Laboratory 54-59, Senior Scientist, Section Leader 59-70, Dir. Ecological Sciences Div. 70-72, Environmental Sciences Div. 72-; mem. U.S. Cttee. Int. Biological Program; Dir. Deciduous Forest Biome Project 69-; mem. Special Comm. on Biological Water Quality of Ohio River Valley Sanitation Comm. 71-, Board of Trustees, Inst. of Ecology 71-74, N.A.S.—NRC Bd. on Energy Studies, Board of Govs. American Inst. of Biological Sciences; Chair. Nominating Cttee. Ecological Soc. of America 72-; Pres. Oak Ridge Branch, Scientific Research Soc. of America 72-, Cttee. on Energy and the Environment (N.A.S.—NRC), Div. of Ecology American Soc. of Zoologists, British Ecological Soc., Nature Conservancy, Entomological Soc. of America, Nature Conservancy, Health Physics Soc., Wilderness Soc., Soc. of Systematic Zoology; Assoc. Ed. *Radiation Biology, Radiation Research* (A.A.A.S.).

Publs. miscellaneous publs. in ecology and radioecology.
Environmental Sciences Division, Oak Ridge National Laboratory, Oak Ridge, Tenn. 37830, U.S.A.
Telephone: 615-483-8611 Ext. 3-1935.

Auger, Pierre Victor, D. ès S.; French physicist and university professor; b. 14 May 1899; ed. Ecole Normale Supérieure, and Univ. of Paris.

Assistant, Faculty of Sciences, Univ. of Paris 27, Dir. of Studies 32, Prof. 37-; Research Assoc. Univ. of Chicago 41-44; Dir. of Higher Educ., Ministry of Educ., Paris 45-48; Dir. Dept. of Natural Sciences UNESCO 48-59; Chair. French Cttee. for Space Research 59-62; mem. Anglo-Canadian team on Atomic Energy, Canada 42-44; French del. to UN Atomic Energy Comm. 46-48; Dir.-Gen. European Space Research Org. 62-67; Grand Officier, Légion d'Honneur, Commandeur des Palmes Académiques; Int. Feltrinelli Prize 61, Kalinga Prize 72.
Publs. *Les rayons cosmiques* 41, *What are Cosmic Rays?* 44, *L'Homme Microscopique* 52, *Main Trends in Scientific Research* 61.
12 rue Emile Faguet, Paris 14e; and 21 *bis* rue Lapérouse, Paris 16e, France.
Telephone: 225-21-18 (Office); 331-96-34 (Home).

Augstein, Rudolf; German magazine publisher; b. 5 Nov. 1923; ed. High School.

Lieutenant, Second World War; Publisher *Der Spiegel* (weekly) 46-; under arrest (for alleged political offence) Oct. 62-Feb. 63, elected Bundestag Nov. 72, resigned Jan. 73.

Publs. *Spiegelungen* 64, *Konrad Adenauer* 64, *Preussens Friedrich und die Deutschen* 68, *Jesus Menschensohn* 72.
Der Spiegel, Ost-West-Strasse, Hamburg 11, Federal Republic of Germany.
Telephone: 040-3-00-71.

Augustincic, Antun; Yugoslav sculptor; b. 1900.
Joined Partisan movement 43; Vice-Pres. Anti-Fascist Council for Nat. Liberation of Yugoslavia.
Works include memorial in front of U.N. H.Q., New York, busts of Pres. Tito, Memorial to Red Army at Batina Skela on the Danube and Memorial to Pilsudski; Memorial to Miner, Geneva Memorial to Victims of Fascism, Addis Ababa Memorial to Ras Makonen; mem. Yugoslav Acad. Sciences and Arts.
Yugoslav Academy of Sciences and Arts, Braće, Kavurćia 1, Zagreb, Yugoslavia.

Aujaleu, Eugène Jean Yves; French physician; b. 29 Oct. 1903, Negrepelisse, Tarn et Garonne; s. of Eugène Henri Aujaleu (Dr. Med.) and Claire Pailler; m. Blanche Dumas 1937; two d. (one deceased); ed. Toulouse Faculty of Medicine.

Inspector-Gen. of Health 41; Dir. Health Service, Free French Govt. Algiers 42-44; Dir. of Social Hygiene, Ministry of Health 45; Dir.-Gen. of Public Health 56-64; Dir.-Gen. Nat. Inst. of Health and Medical Research 64-69, Hon. Dir.-Gen.; Councillor of State 66-70; Chair. WHO Exec. Board 59-60, Pres. 21st World Health Assembly 68, Int. Centre for Cancer Research, Lyon 65-71, Mental Health Asscn. 67-; mem. Conseil supérieur d'hygiène publique 72-.
Leisure interests: music, gardening.
144 boulevard du Montparnasse, Paris 14e, France.
Telephone: 326-59-18.

Aune, Leif Jørgen; Norwegian politician; b. 7 June 1925, Bodø.
Consultant, Industrial Devt. Asscn. for N. Norway 51; Sec. Office for Regional Planning, Nordland 53; Consultant, Devt. Fund for N. Norway 54; Deputy Dir.-Gen. Regional Devt. Fund 61; Exec. Dir. of Finance, Tromso 70-73; Under-Sec. of State, Ministry of Local Govt. and Labour 71-72; Minister of Local Govt. and Labour 73-; Labour.
Ministry of Local Government and Labour, Oslo Dep., Norway.

Aura, Teuvo Ensio, LL.M.; Finnish politician; b. 28 Dec. 1912, Ruskeala; s. of Jalo Aura and Aino Sofia Kolehmainen; m. Kaino Kielo Kivekäs 1939 (died 1970); two s. one d.; ed. Univ. of Helsinki.

Worked for Board of Supply 40-41, Chair. 42; Dir. Post Office Savings Bank 42-43, Dir. Gen. 43-68; Chair. Econ. Council 46-47, 51-56; mem. Joint Del. of Credit Inst. 49-68; Minister of Commerce and Industry 50-51, 53-54, 57; Minister of Justice 51; Chair. Admin. Board of Industrialization Fund 54-60; mem. Finance Board 53-; mem. Board, Mutual Life Insurance Co., Salama 50-71, Insurance Co. Pohjola 55-, Helsinki Chamber of Commerce 58-; mem. of Admin. Board, Rauma Repola and Kemira Oy 61-72; Chair. Admin. Board, Aluma Oy, IBM in Finland, Finnish Fair Co-operation, L.M. Ericsson in Finland Oy and Mankala Oy; mem. Bourse of Helsinki, Union of the Finnish Lawyer; Mayor of Helsinki 68-; Prime Minister 70, 71-72; Commdr., First Class, Order of the White Rose, Order of the Cross of Liberty, Commdr. Order of the Lion of Finland and many other honours.
Leisure interests: literature and art.
Publs. *Talous ja yhteiskunta* (Economy and Society): several articles on political economy and communal politics in various publications.
Helsinki City Hall, Pohjoisesplanadi, 11-13 Helsinki 17; Aleksanterinkatu 14, Helsinki 17, Finland.
Telephone: 169-2200 (Office); 625-506 (Home).

Auric, Georges; French composer; b. 15 Feb. 1899; ed. Paris Conservatoire and Schola Cantorum, Paris.
Member "Les Six" movement in France; Music Critic, *Marianne* 36, and later *Paris-Soir*; Dir. of Réunion des théâtres lyriques nationaux 62-68; Pres. Int. Confederation of Socs. of Authors and Composers 68-70; mem. Acad. des Beaux-Arts; Commandeur Légion d'Honneur, and other decorations.
Compositions include songs and piano music; film music, e.g. for René Clair's *A Nous la Liberté* 32 and Jean Cocteau's *L'Aigle à deux Têtes* 48; ballet music includes *Le Peintre et son Modèle* 49, *Phèdre* 50, *Chemin de Lumière* 52, *Coup de Feu* 52; *Le Masque* (opera); sonata for piano for unaccompanied four-part chorus) 50.
36 avenue Matignon, Paris 8e, France.

Austin, (John) Paul; American business executive; b. 14 Feb. 1915, Lagrange, Ga.; s. of late Samuel Yates Austin and Mrs. S. Y. Austin; m. Jeane Weed; two s.; ed. Harvard Univ., Harvard Law School and Culver Military Acad.
Legal practice, New York 40-41, 45-49; U.S. Navy 42-45; Legal Dept., The Coca-Cola Co. 49-50, Asst. to Pres. The Coca-Cola Export Corpn. 51-52, Vice-Pres. 52-58; Pres. and Dir. The Coca-Cola Export Corpn. 59-62, Exec. Vice-Pres. The Coca-Cola Co. 61-62, Pres. 62-71, Chief Exec. Officer 66-, Chair. of Board 70-; Dir. Morgan Guaranty Trust Co. of New York, Gen. Electric Co., Trust Co. of Georgia, and Continental Oil Co., Southern Mills Inc., Adela Investment Co., S.A., Grocery Mfrs. of America; Trustee, U.S. Council of Int. Chamber of Commerce; Chair. Bd. of Trustees, Rand Corpn.; mem. Bd. of Regents, Smithsonian Inst.; Legion of Merit.
P.O.B. 1734, Atlanta, Ga. 30301, U.S.A.

Austregésilo de Athayde, Belarmino Maria; Brazilian journalist; b. 25 Sept. 1898, Caruarú, Pernambuco; s. of José Feliciano Augusto de Athayde and Constância Adelaide Austregésilo de Athayde; m. Maria José de Queiroz; two s. one d.; ed. Seminário de Prainha, Fortaleza, Liceu do Ceará and Univ. of Rio de Janeiro.
Teacher 17-18; Dir. Sec. *A Tribuna* 18-21; on staff of *Correio da Manhã* 21; Dir. *O Jornal* (with Diários Asociados) 24-32; exiled for political reasons 32; Dir. *Diário da Noite*; Editor-in-Chief *O Jornal*; mem. Brazilian Del. UN Gen. Assembly, Paris 48; mem. Brazilian Acad. of Letters 31-, Pres. 59-; Ordem do Mérito Naval Aeronáutico 57, Militar 63, Jornalístico 65; numerous foreign decorations.
Publs. *Histórias Amargas* 21, *Quando as Hortencias Florescem* 21, *A Influência Espiritual Americana* 38, *Fora da Imprensa* 48, *Mestre de Liberismo* 52, *Na Academia* 53, *Discurso de recepção a José Lins do Rego* 56, *Vanaverba* 66, *Epístóla aos Contemporâneos* 67, *Conversas na Barbearia Sol* 71.
Academia Brasileira de Lettras, Avenida Presidente Wilson 203, Rio de Janeiro; Rua Cosme Velho 599, Rio de Janeiro, Brazil.
Telephone: 225-4368 (Home).

Austrheim, John; Norwegian politician and farmer; b. 10 Oct. 1912, Gloppen, Sogn og Fjordane.
Member Gloppen Municipal Council 45-52, Mayor 56-62; Deputy, Storting (Parl.) 58-61; Senterpartiet (Centre Party) M.P. for Sogn and Fjordane 61-67, Chair. Senterpartiet faction in the Storting 69-71; Minister of Communications 72-73; Vice-Chair. Central Board, Husbanken 66-; mem. Nature Conservancy Council 67-.
c/o Royal Ministry of Communications, Oslo, Norway.

Autant-Lara, Claude; French film director and author; b. 5 Aug. 1901; ed. Lycée Janson de Sailly, Mill Hill School, London, Ecole des Arts Décoratifs, and Ecole des Beaux-Arts.
Entered French film industry 20; directed first short

picture *Faits-Divers* 23; Hon. Pres. Syndicat des Techniciens du Cinéma Français; Pres. Fédération Nationale du Spectacle.
Principal films: *Le Diable au Corps*, *Douce*, *The Red Inn*, *Game of Love*, *Le Rouge et le Noir*, *Seven Sins*, *Marguerite de la Nuit*, *La Traversée de Paris*, *En cas de malheur*, *La Jument verte*, *Le Bois des Amants*, *Tu ne tueras point*, *Vive Henri-IV*, *Vive l'amour*, *Le Comte de Monte-Cristo*, *Le Meurtrier*, *Le Magot de Joséfa*, *Le Journal d'une femme en blanc*, *Le Nouveau Journal d'une femme en blanc*, *Le Plus Vieux Métier du Monde* 67, *Le Franciscain de Bourges* 68.
6 rue Ballu, Paris 9e, France.

Avedon, Richard; American photographer; b. 15 May 1923, New York; s. of Jack Avedon and Anna Polonsky; m. 1st Dorcas Nowell 1944, 2nd Evelyn Franklin 1951; one s.; ed. Columbia.
Staff photographer *Harper's Bazaar* 46-65, *Vogue* magazines 66-; contributing photographer *Life*, *Look*, *Graphics* magazines; U.S. Camera Annual; exhbns. at Museum of Modern Art, Philadelphia Museum of Modern Art; one man retrospective show Mpls. Inst. of Arts 70; one man show, perm. collection, Smithsonian Inst.; one man show Museum of Modern Art 74; retrospective exhbn., Marlborough Gallery, New York and Int. Tour 75; Highest Achievement Medal Awards, Art Dirs. Show 50-.
Leisure interest: photography.
Publs. *Observations* 59, *Nothing Personal* 64, Editor *Diary of a Century* (photographs by Jacques Henri Lartigue, q.v.) 70, *Alice in Wonderland* 73.
407 East 75th Street, New York, N.Y. 10021, U.S.A.

Aveline, Claude; French writer and painter; b. 19 July 1901, Paris; only s. of Georges Avtsine and Cecile Tchernomordik; m. Jeanne Barusseaud 1964; one adopted s.
Honorary Pres. Soc. Anatole France; Pres. of Jury for Prix Jean-Vigo (Cinema) 50-75; exhbns. of paintings in Paris 72, 74, Ljubljana 73, Brussels 75, Zagreb 76; Officier de la Légion d'Honneur; Médaille de la Résistance (with rosette), Commdr. des Arts et Lettres, etc.; Grand Prix Société des Gens de Lettres 52, Prix Italia 55.
Leisure interest: fibre-tip colour painting.
Publs. Novels: *Le Point du Jour* 28, *La vie de Philippe Denis* (*Madame Maillart* 30, *Les amours et les haines* 52, *Philippe* 55), *Le prisonnier* 36, *Le temps mort* 44, *Suite policière* (*La double mort de Frédéric Belot* 32, *Voiture 7 place 15* 37, *L'Abonné de la ligne U* 47, *Le jet d'eau* 47 *L'oeil-de-chat* 70), *Pour l'amour de la nuit* 56, *Le poids du feu* 59, *Le bestiaire inattendu* 59, *C'est vrai mais il ne faut pas le croire* 60; Essays and Travel Books: *La merveilleuse Légende du Bouddha* 28, *Routes de la Catalogne ou Le livre de l'amitié* 32, *La promenade égyptienne* 34, *Les devoirs de l'esprit* 45, *Anatole France* 49, *Et tout le reste n'est rien* (*La Religieuse Portugaise*) 51, *Les Mots de la fin* 57, *Le Code des jeux* 61, *Avec toi-même et coetera* 63, *Les réflexions de Monsieur F.A.T.* 63, *Célébration du lit* 67; *Le haut mal des créateurs* 73; Play: *L'as de coeur* (ballet, music by Henri Sauguet) 61, *Brouart et le désordre* 64, *La parade de la rengaine* 67; Poetry: *Io Hymen suivi de Chants funèbres* 25, *Portrait de l'Oiseau-Qui-N'Existe-Pas* 65, *De* 68, *Monologue pour un disparu* 74.
19 rue Servandoni, 75006 Paris; Ty Guennic, 56780 Ile-aux-Moines, France.

Averoff-Tossizza, Evangelos, LL.D., PH.D.; Greek economist, journalist and politician; b. 1910; ed. Univ. of Lausanne.
Began career as journalist, worked in Switzerland and Greece; active in resistance movement during 41-44 war, imprisoned in Northern Italy, later escaped and continued resistance work until end of war; mem. of

Parl. 46-; Gov. of Corfu 41; fmr. Minister of Supply, National Economy and Commerce, and Under-Sec. for Foreign Affairs; Minister of Agriculture Feb.-May 56, of Foreign Affairs May 56-63, joined National Radical Union 56; sentenced to five years imprisonment Aug. 67, later pardoned; imprisoned July 73 for leading the Mutiny of the Navy; Minister of Nat. Defence July 74-.
Publs. seven novels, a play, *History of the Decade 40-50*.
33 Pentelis Street, Kifissia, Athens; (Home): Ministry of National Defence, Athens, Greece.

Avidom (Mahler-Kalkstein), Menahem, B.A.; Israeli composer; b. 6 Jan. 1908, Stanislau (fmrly. Austria, now U.S.S.R.); *s.* of Isaac Kalkstein and Helena Mahler; *m.* Suzanne Soumis-Lyonnais 1935; two *d.*; ed. American Univ., Beirut, and in Paris.
Lecturer on theory of music, Hebrew Conservatoire of Music, Tel-Aviv 36-, and Music Teachers' Training Coll. Tel-Aviv 45-; Sec.-Gen. Israel Philharmonic Orchestra 45-; Vice-Pres. Board of Dirs. Acum Ltd. (Composers and Authors Asscn.), Dir.-Gen. 56-; Dir. Arts Dept. Jerusalem Convention Centre 52; Art Adviser, Govt. Tourist Centre, Ministry of Commerce and Industry 54-; Pres. League of Composers 58; mem. Nat. Arts Council 62; Israel State Prize 61, Tel Aviv Municipality Prize 48, 56; Israel Philharmonic Prize 53; Authors' and Composers' Asscn. Prize 62.
Leisure interests: painting, chess, music reviews.
Compositions include *A Folk Symphony 47, Symphony No. 2 David 48, Sinfonietta 51*, 2 Piano Sonatinas 49, *Concertino* for violinist Jascha Heifetz, *Concertino* for cellist Gregor Piatigorsky 51, *Alexandra Hashmonaith* (opera in 3 acts) 52, *Jubilee Suite, Triptyque Symphonique*, concerto for strings and flute, music for strings, symphonies 3, 4, 5 and 6, psalms and cantatas, *12 Preludes Variés* for piano, *Metamorphoses* for string quartet 60, *Symphony No. 7* (25th anniversary of Israel Philharmonic Orchestra), *Enigma*, septet for 5 **wood instruments, piano and percussion, Quartet for brass**, *Reflexions* for 2 flutes, Triptyque for Solo violin, **"B-A-C-H" Suite for Chamber Orchestra**, *Festival Sinfonietta* **(Symphony No. 8) 66**, *The Crook* **(comic opera) 66/67**, *Symphonie Variée* **(Symphony No. 9) for Chamber Orchestra 68**, Concertino for Violin and Chamber Orchestra 68, *The Farewell* (Chamber Opera in one act) 70, *Spring*, Overture for Symphony Orchestra 72, *6 Inventions for Piano in Homage and on the Name of Arthur Rubinstein 73, Passacaglia* for Piano 73, *Piece on the Name of SCHoEnBerG for Piano 74, The Emperor's New Clothes* (comic opera in one act) for Israel Festival 76.
Office: ACUM House, Rothschild Boulevard 118, Tel-Aviv; Home: Samadar Street, Ramat-Gan, Israel.
Telephone: 240105 (Office); 795512 (Home).

Avila, Rev. Fernando Bastos de; Brazilian ecclesiastic and sociologist; b. 17 March 1918; ed. Univs. of Nova Friburgo (Brazil), Louvain and Gregorian Univ., Rome.
Professor of Sociology, Catholic Pontifical Univ. of Rio de Janeiro 57-; Social Dir. Nat. Catholic Immigration Comm. 54-; mem. Council, Nat. Fed. of Trade 60-; Dir. Instituto Brasileiro de Desenvolvimento (IBRADES).
Publs. *Economic Impacts of Immigration 56, L'Immigration au Brésil 57, Introdução a Sociologia 62, Solidarismo 65, Pequena Enciclopédia de Moral Ecivismo 67.*
115 rua Bambina-Botatogo, Rio de Janeiro, Brazil.

Avon, Earl of, cr. 61 and **Eden,** 1st Viscount, cr. 61, of Royal Leamington Spa in the County of Warwick; **(Robert) Anthony Eden,** K.G., P.C., M.C.; British politician; b. 12 June 1897; 2nd surviving *s.* of Sir William Eden, 7th and 5th Bt.; *m.* 1st Beatrice Helen Beckett **(marriage dissolved 1950), 2nd Clarissa Anne Spencer Churchill 1952; one *s.* (and elder *s.* killed in R.A.F. 1945); ed. Eton and Christ Church, Oxford.**

Conservative M.P. for Warwick and Leamington 23-57; Parliamentary Private Sec. to Sir Austen Chamberlain 26-29; Under-Sec. of State for Foreign Affairs in Nat. Govt. Sept. 31-33; Lord Privy Seal without seat in Cabinet, assigned to special work at Foreign Office 34-35; Sec. for LN Affairs June-Dec. 35; Sec. of State for Foreign Affairs Dec. 35-Feb. 38, resgnd.; conducted diplomatic missions to Moscow, Warsaw and Prague 35; Sec. of State for the Dominions with special access to the War Cabinet Sept. 39-April 40; Sec. of State for War 40, for Foreign Affairs Dec. 40-July 45; Leader House of Commons 42-45; Chair. Conservative Foreign Affairs Cttee. 45-73, Army Cttee. 45; Chancellor Birmingham Univ. 45-73; Dir. Westminster Bank Ltd. 46-51; Chair. OEEC 52-54; Deputy Prime Minister and Sec. of State for Foreign Affairs 51-55; Prime Minister 55-Jan. 57; Hon. Master of the Bench, Middle Temple; Trustee, Nat. Gallery 35-49; Pres. Royal Shakespeare Theatre, Stratford on Avon 58-66, now Gov.; a Trustee of Shakespeare's Birthplace; Hon. Life Patron Young Conservative Org.; Pres.Anglo-Ethiopian Soc. 66-; Patron Hereford Herd Book Soc. 68-; Hon. D.C.L. (Oxford, Durham), Hon. LL.D. (Cambridge, Leeds, Sheffield, Belfast, Toronto, California, Birmingham, Bristol).
Publs. *Places in the Sun 26, Foreign Affairs 39, Freedom and Order* (Selected Speeches) 47, *Days for Decision 49, Full Circle* (memoirs) 60, *Facing the Dictators* (memoirs) 62, *The Reckoning* (memoirs) 65, *Towards Peace in Indo-China 66.*
Manor House, Alvediston, Salisbury, Wilts., England.

Avramenko, Stepan Stepanovich; Soviet politician; b. 1918; ed. Belotserkov Inst. of Agriculture.
Veterinary surgeon 41-49; Local Govt. and Party work 49-55; First Sec., Barabinsk Town Cttee. of C.P.S.U. (Novosibirsk Region) 55-59; Chair. Novosibirsk Regional Soviet 59-64; First Sec. Amur Regional Cttee. of C.P.S.U. 64-; Alt. mem. C.P.S.U. Central Cttee. 66-71, mem. 71-; mem. Comm. for Transport and Communications, Soviet of Union 74-; Deputy to U.S.S.R. Supreme Soviet 62-; mem. Mandate Comm., Soviet of Union, U.S.S.R. Supreme Soviet; mem. C.P.S.U. 50-.
Amur Regional Committee, Communist Party of Soviet Union, Blagoveshchensk, U.S.S.R.

Avriel, Ehud; Israeli diplomatist; b. 19 Oct. 1917, Vienna, Austria; *s.* of Isidor and Helena Avriel; *m.* Hannah Marie (née Eliasberg) 1940; four *d.*; ed. High School, Vienna.
Israeli Minister to Czechoslovakia 48, concurrently to Hungary 49; Minister to Rumania 50; Dir.-Gen. Prime Minister's Office, Jerusalem 51-57; Ambassador to Ghana and Liberia 57-61, to Congo (Léopoldville) 60-61; Deputy Dir. Gen. Ministry of Foreign Affairs 61-66; Amb. to Italy and Malta 66-69; Chair. World Zionist Action Cttee., Jerusalem 69-; Diplomatic Adviser and Amb. Extraordinary, Ministry of Foreign Affairs 72; Consul-Gen. to the Midwest 75-.
Leisure interest: photography.
Publ. *Open The Gates 75.*
Apartment 1308, 111 East Wacker Drive, Chicago, Ill. 60601, U.S.A.

Avtsin, Alexander Pavlovich; Soviet pathologist; b. 18 Sept. 1908, Moscow; ed. First Moscow Medical Inst.
Associate, Inst. of Neuropsychiatric Prophylaxis 33-38; Asst. Prof. Third Moscow Medical Inst. 37-41; Asst. Prof. First Moscow Medical Inst. 42-43; Army Surgeon 43-46; Head of Dept., Inst. of Normal and Pathological Morphology, U.S.S.R. Acad. of Medical Sciences 45-61; Corresp. mem. U.S.S.R. Acad. of Medical Sciences 61-65, mem. U.S.S.R. Acad. of Medical Sciences 65-; Dir. Inst. of Human Morphology, U.S.S.R. Acad. of Medical Sciences 61-; Vice-Chair. Moscow Soc. of Pathologicoanatomists, Vice-Chair. U.S.S.R. Soc. of

Pathalogicoanatomists; mem. Editorial Board *Arkhiv patologii*, Co-Editor Big Medical Encyclopaedia; Order of Lenin, Order of Red Banner of Labour and Bulgarian Red Banner of Labour.
Publs. Over 100 works on pathological anatomy of cerebral tumours, hormonotherapy of cerebral neoplasms, infectious diseases and military pathology.
Institute of Morphology, U.S.S.R. Academy of Medical Sciences, Block 18, 61/2 Ulitsa Shchepkina, Moscow, U.S.S.R.

Awad, Muhammad Hadi; Yemeni diplomatist; b. 5 May 1934; *m.* Adelah Moh'd Hadi Awad 1956; one *s.* three *d.*; ed. Murray House Coll. of Educ.
Teacher 53-59; Educ. Officer 60-62; Chief Insp. of Schools 63-65; Vice-Principal As-Shaab Coll. 65-67; Perm. Rep. to Arab League 68-70, concurrently Amb. to U.A.R., also accred. to Sudan, Lebanon, Libya and Iraq; Perm. Sec. Ministry of Foreign Affairs 70-73; Amb. to U.K. 73-, concurrently to Spain and Sweden 74-, to Denmark, Portugal, the Netherlands 75-.
Leisure interest: photography.
Embassy of the People's Democratic Republic of Yemen, 57 Cromwell Road, London, S.W.7, England.
Telephone: 584-6607.

Awadallah, Babikir; Sudanese jurist and politician; b. 1917; ed. School of Law, Gordon Coll., Khartoum.
District Judge, El Obeid; resigned to become Speaker of Sudanese House of Representatives 54-57; Judge of the Supreme Court 57-, Chief Justice Oct. 64-May 69; Prime Minister and Minister of Foreign Affairs May-Oct. 69; Deputy Chair. Revolutionary Council, Minister of Foreign Affairs Oct. 69-July 70, and Minister of Justice 69-71; First Vice-Pres. of Sudan Oct. 71-May 72.
Office of the First Vice-President, Khartoum, Sudan.

Awolowo, Chief Obafemi, B.COM. (HONS.), LL.B. (Lond.), B.L., LL.D., D.SC., D.LITT. (Ashiwaju of Ijebu Remo, Losi of Ikenne, Lisa of Ijeun, Apesin of Oshogbo, Odole of Ife, Ajagunla of Ado Ekiti, Odofin of Owo and Obong Ikpan Isong of Ibibioland); Nigerian politician; b. 6 March 1909, Ikenne; *s.* of David Sopolu and Mary Efunyela Awolowo; *m.* Hannah Idowu Dideolu 1937; two *s.* three *d.*; ed. London Univ.
Teacher 28-29; Stenographer 30-34; Newspaper Reporter 34-35; engaged in motor transport and produce buying 36-44; Solicitor and Advocate, Supreme Court of Nigeria 47-51; Minister of Local Govt. and Leader of Govt. Business Western Region 52-54; co-founder and first Gen. Sec. of Egbe Omo Oduduwa, a Yoruba cultural movement; founder and Fed. Pres. of Action Group of Nigeria; Premier, Govt. of the W. Region of Nigeria 54-59; Leader of the Opposition in Federal Parliament 60-May 62, detained May 62-Nov. 62, on trial for treasonable felony and conspiracy Nov. 62-Sept. 63; sentenced to 10 years imprisonment Sept. 63; given free pardon and released Aug. 66; elected Leader of Yorubas Aug. 66; Chancellor of Univ. of Ife, Nigeria 67-; Vice-Chair. Federal Exec. Council and in charge of Ministry of Finance June 67-June 71; private practice 71-.
Publs. *Path to Nigerian Freedom, Awo* (autobiography), *Thoughts on Nigerian Constitution, My Early Life, The People's Republic, The Strategy and Tactics of the People's Republic of Nigeria*; various pamphlets.
c/o P.O. Box 136, Ibadan, Nigeria.
Telephone: Ibadan 20087.

Awoonor, Kofi Nyidevu, M.A., PH.D.; Ghanaian professor of comparative literature; b. 13 March 1935; ed. Univ. of Ghana, Univ. Coll., London, and State Univ. of N.Y.
Research Fellow, Inst. of African Studies; Man. Dir. Film Corpn., Accra; Longmans Fellow, Univ. of London; Asst. Prof. and later Chair. Comparative Literature Program, State Univ. of N.Y., Stony Brook; Visiting Prof., Univ. of Texas, Austin and New School of Social Research, N.Y.; currently Prof. of Comparative Literature, State Univ. of N.Y., Stony Brook; Contributing Editor, *Transition* and *Alcheringa*; Gurrey Prize for Poetry; Longmans and Fairfield fellowships.
Publs. poetry: *Rediscovery* 64, *Messages* 70, *Night of My Blood* 71; prose: *This Earth My Brother* 71, *Guardians of the Sacred Word* 73, *Ride Me Memory* 73, *Breast of the Earth* 74 (history of African literature); novel: *Alien Corn* 74, *Where is the Mississippi Panorama* 74.
English Department, State University of New York, Stony Brook, N.Y. 11790, U.S.A.

Axelrod, Julius, PH.D.; American biochemical pharmacologist; b. 30 May 1912, New York City; *s.* of Isadore and Molly (Leichtling) Axelrod; *m.* Sally Taub Axelrod 1938; two *s.*; ed. Coll. of the City of New York, N.Y. Univ. and George Washington Univ.
Laboratory Asst., Dept. of Bacteriology, N.Y. Univ. Medical School 33-35; Chemist, Laboratory of Industrial Hygiene 35-46; Research Assoc., Third N.Y. Univ. Research Div., Goldwater Memorial Hosp. 46-49; Assoc. Chemist, Nat. Heart Inst., Nat. Inst. of Health 49-50; Chemist 50-53, Senior Chemist 53-55; Chief Section on Pharmacology, Lab. of Chemical Science, Nat. Inst. of Mental Health, Health Services and Mental Health Admin., Dept. of Health, Educ. and Welfare 55-; mem. Scientific Advisory Board, Nat. Foundation, Brookhaven Nat. Laboratory, Center for Biomedical Educ., and many others; mem. Int. Brain Research Organization; Fellow, American Coll. of Neuropsychopharmacology (mem. Council 66-69); mem. American Chem. Soc., American Soc. of Pharmacology and Experimental Therapeutics, American Soc. of Biological Chemists, American Asscn. for the Advancement of Science; Fellow, American Acad. of Arts and Sciences, Nat. Acad. of Sciences; corresp. mem. German Pharmacological Soc.; Gairdner Foundation Award 67; Distinguished Achievement Award, George Washington Univ. 68, Dept. of Health, Educ. and Welfare 70, Modern Medicine Magazine 70; Claude Bernard Medal, Univ. of Montreal 69, Nobel Prize for Medicine or Physiology 70, Albert Einstein Achievement Award, Yeshiva Univ. 71, etc.; several research awards, memorial lectureships etc.; Hon. Sc.D. (Univ. of Chicago, Medical Coll. of Wisconsin, New York Univ.); Hon. LL.D. (George Washington Univ.); Dr. h.c. (Univ. of Panama); Hon. LL.D. (Coll. City of New York), etc.
Leisure interests: music, reading.
Publs. Over 300 articles in professional journals, also abstracts and press articles.
Section on Pharmacology, Laboratory of Clinical Science, National Institute of Mental Health, Building 10, Room 2D-47, 9000 Rockville Pike Bethesda, Md. 20014; Home: 10401 Grosvenor Place, Rockville, Md. 20852, U.S.A.

Axen, Hermann; German journalist; b. 6 March 1916.
Mem. Communist Youth League 32; emigrated to France; imprisoned in concentration camps 40-45; mem. Central Cttee. Socialist Unity Party (S.E.D.) 50; Chief Editor *Neues Deutschland* 56-67; Candidate mem. of Politburo of Central Cttee. of Socialist Unity Party 67-71, mem. 71-; mem. Volkskammer; Silver Medal Vaterländische Verdienstorden.
Sozialistische Einheitspartei Deutschlands, 102 Berlin, Am Marx-Engels-Platz 2, German Democratic Republic.

Axer, Erwin; Polish theatre producer and director; b. 1 Jan. 1917, Vienna, Austria; *s.* of Maurycy Axer and Fryderyka Schuster; *m.* Bronisława Kreczmar 1945 (died 1973); two *s.*; ed. Lwów, and Nat. Acad. of Theatrical Art, Warsaw.
Assistant Producer, Nat. Theatre, Warsaw 38-39; Actor-Producer, Polish Drama Theatre, U.S.S.R. 39-41;

Artistic Dir., Teatr Kameralny, Łódź 46-49; Dir. and producer Teatr Współczesny (Contemporary Theatre) Warsaw 49-; Dir. and Chief Producer, Nat. Theatre, Warsaw 55-57; Ordinary Prof. Producers Dept. State Higher Theatrical School, Warsaw 57-66, Prof. Ordinary 66-; State Prizes for Artistic Achievement 51, 53, 55, 62, Nagroda Krytyki im Boya-Zelenskiego (Critics Award) 60; Commdr. Cross of Polonia Restituta; Order of Banner of Labour (2nd Class).
Productions include: *Major Barbara* (Shaw) 47, *Niemcy* (Kruczkowski) 55, *Kordian* (Slowacki) 56, *Pierwszy dzień wolności* 59, *Iphigenia in Tauris* 61, *Kariera Arturo Ui* (Brecht) Warsaw 62, Leningrad 63, *Three Sisters* (Chekhov) 63, Düsseldorf 67, *Androcles and the Lion* (Shaw) Warsaw 64, *Tango* (Mrożek) Warsaw 65, Düsseldorf 66, *Die Ermittlung* (Weiss) Warsaw 66, *Le Piéton de l'Air* (Ionesco) Warsaw 67, *Maria Stuart* (Schiller) Warsaw 69, *Dwa Teatry* (Szaniawski) Leningrad 69, *Matka* (Witkiewicz) Warsaw 70, *Porträt eines Planeten* Düsseldorf 70, *Old Times* and *Macbeth* Warsaw 72, *Uncle Vanya* Munich 72, *Ein Fest für Boris* Vienna 73, *Lear* Warsaw 74, *Endgame* Vienna 76.
Publs. include: *Listy ze sceny I* (Letters from the Stage) 55, *Listy ze sceny II* 57, *Sprawy Teatralne* (Things Theatrical) 66.
Ul. Odyńca 27 m. 11, 02-606 Warsaw, Poland.
Telephone: 44-01-16.

Ayari, Chedli, L. en D., D. ès Sc.(Econ.); Tunisian economist, diplomatist and politician; b. 24 Aug. 1933, Tunis; s. of Sadok and Fatouma Chedly; m. Elaine Vatteau 1959; one s. one d.; ed. Collège Sadiki and Inst. de Hautes Etudes.
With Société Tunisienne de Banque 58; Asst. Faculté de Droit et des Sciences Economiques et Politiques, Tunis 59; Econ. Counsellor, Perm. Mission of Tunis at UN 60-64; Exec. Dir. IBRD 64-65; Dean, Faculté de Droit, Tunis 65-67; Dir. C.E.R.E.S. 67-69; Sec. of State in charge of Plan 69-70; Minister of Nat. Educ., Youth and Sport 70-71; Amb. to Belgium Feb.-March 72; Minister of Nat. Economy 72-74, of Planning 74; Prof. of Economics, Agrégé de Sciences Economiques, Tunis; mem. UN Cttee. of Planning for Devt.; Grand Cordon, Ordre de la République.
Publs. numerous books and articles on economic and monetary problems.
Jardins de Gammarth, Tunis, Tunisia.
Telephone: 270-038.

Ayckbourn, Alan; British playwright and theatre director; b. 12 April 1939, London; s. of Horace Ayckbourn and Irene Maud (née Worley); m. Christine Helen (née Roland) 1959; two s.; ed. Haileybury.
Went straight into the theatre on leaving school as stage manager and actor with various repertory cos. in England; Founder Mem. Victoria Theatre Co., Stoke-on-Trent 62-64; Drama Producer, BBC Radio 64-69; Dir. of Productions, Library Theatre, Scarborough 70-; Evening Standard Award for Best New Comedy for *Absurd Person Singular* 73, for Best New Play for *The Norman Conquests* 74; Plays and Players Award for Best New Play for *The Norman Conquests* 74; Variety Club of Great Britain Playwright of the Year 74.
Leisure interests: music, cricket, astronomy.
Plays: *Relatively Speaking* 67, *How the Other Half Loves* 70, *Time and Time Again* 72, *Absurd Person Singular* 73 (N.Y. 74), *The Norman Conquests* 74 (N.Y. 75), *Absent Friends* 75, *Just Between Ourselves* 76.
c/o Margaret Ramsay Ltd., 14A Goodwin's Court, St. Martin's Lane, London WC2N 4LL, England.
Telephone: 01-240 0691.

Aydalot, Maurice, D. en D.; French judge; b. 22 June 1905; s. of Joseph Aydalot; ed. Faculté de Droit de Paris.

Magistrate, Ministry of Justice 30; Deputy Public Prosecutor, Paris 37, Public Prosecutor 51, Prosecutor-Gen., Court of Appeal, Paris 57-62; Prosecutor-Gen., Court of Cassation 62-67; First Pres. Court of Cassation 67-; Commandeur de la Légion d'Honneur.
Publs. *Les atteintes au crédit de l'Etat, L'expertise comptable judiciaire, Droit Pénal des Affaires.*
Palais de Justice, boulevard du Palais, Paris 1er; Home: 165 avenue de Wagram, 75017, Paris 16e, France.

Ayé, Hippolyte, D. en MED.; Ivory Coast politician; b. 1932, Anoumako, Abidjan; ed. Faculty of Medicine, Toulouse, Ecole Nat. de Santé Publique, Rennes and Paris, France.
Member, later Vice-Pres., Econ. and Social Council 63-66; Asst. lecturer in hygiene and public health, Ecole des Sages Femmes d'Abidjan 63-66; Asst. Head of clinical dept., Faculty of Medicine, Abidjan 66-69; Asst. Head of clinical dept., Centre hospitalier et universitaire, Pathology Service Oct. 66-; Pres. WHO Gen. Assembly May 70; Minister of Health and Population Jan. 70-; mem. French and Ivory Coast Comm. on Higher Educ. 64-.
Ministry of Health and Population, Abidjan, Ivory Coast.

Ayer, Sir Alfred Jules, Kt., M.A., F.B.A.; British university professor; b. 29 Oct. 1910, London; s. of late Jules L. C. and Reine (née Citroen) Ayer; m. 1st Grace I. R. Lees 1932, one s. one d.; m. 2nd Alberta C. Chapman 1960, one s.; ed. Eton Coll. and Christ Church, Oxford.
Lecturer in Philosophy, Christ Church, Oxford 32-35, Research Student of Christ Church 35-44; Fellow of Wadham Coll. Oxford 44-46, Dean of Wadham 45-46; Grote Prof. of the Philosophy of Mind and Logic, Univ. of London 46-Oct. 59; Wykeham Prof. of Logic, Oxford Oct. 59-; served in Welsh Guards and on Intelligence Duties during Second World War; Attaché British Embassy, Paris 45; Fellow of New Coll., Oxford; Hon. Fellow of Wadham Coll., Oxford 57-; Hon. mem American Acad. of Arts and Sciences 63; Dr. h.c. (Univ. of Brussels) 62, Hon. D.Litt. (Univ. of East Anglia).
Publs. *Language, Truth and Logic* 36, *The Foundations of Empirical Knowledge* 40, *Thinking and Meaning* 47, *British Empirical Philosophers* (editor, with Raymond Winch) 52, *Philosophical Essays* 54, *The Problem of Knowledge* 56, *Privacy* 60, *Philosophy and Language* 60, Editor *Logical Positivism* 60, *Concept of a Person and Other Essays* 63, *The Origins of Pragmatism* 68, *Metaphysics and Common Sense* 69, *Russell and Moore: The Analytical Heritage* 71, *Probability and Evidence* 72, *Russell* 72, *Bertrand Russell as a Philosopher* 72, *The Central Questions of Philosophy* 73.
New College, Oxford, OX1 3BN; Home: 10 Regents Park Terrace, London, NW1E 7EE, England.
Telephone: Oxford 48451; 01-485-4855 (London).

Ayers, Thomas G.; American business executive; b. 16 Feb. 1915, Detroit, Mich.; m. Mary Ayers; four s. one d.; ed. Univ. of Mich.
Joined Public Service Co. of Northern Illinois (formerly a div. of Commonwealth Edison) 38, Man. of Industrial Relations 48; Asst. Vice-Pres. of Industrial Relations, Commonwealth Edison Co. 52, Vice-Pres. 53, Exec. Vice-Pres. 62-64, Pres. 64-73, Dir. 65-, Chair., Chief Exec. Officer 73-; Dir. First Nat. Bank of Chicago, G. D. Searle and Co., Sears, Roebuck and Co., Zenith Radio Corpn.; Dir. and fmr. Pres. Chicago Asscn. of Commerce and Industry; Chair. Breeder Reactor Corpn.; Exec. Nat. Electric Reliability Council; Dir. Edison Electric Inst.; Trustee, North-western Univ.; Hon. LL.D. (Elmhurst Coll.)
Commonwealth Edison Company, P.O. Box 767, Chicago, Ill. 60690, U.S.A.

Aykroyd, Wallace Ruddell, C.B.E., M.D., SC.D.; British nutritionist; b. 30 July 1899, Dublin, Ireland; s. of Alfred Constantine Aykroyd and Wilhelmina Mary Ruddell; m. Freda Kathleen Buttery 1930; one s. two d.; ed. The Leys School, Cambridge, and Univ. of Dublin.

Beit Memorial Research Fellow 28-30; mem. Health Section, League of Nations 30-35; Dir. Nutrition Research Laboratories, Coonoor, India 35-45; mem. Indian Famine Inquiry 44-45; Dir. Nutrition Div. F.A.O. 46-60; Senior Lecturer, Dept. of Human Nutrition, London School of Hygiene and Tropical Medicine 61-66; Hon. Fellow American Public Health Asscn., American Inst. of Nutrition.

Leisure interests: reading and gardening.

Publs. *Vitamins and Other Dietary Essentials* 32, *Three Philosophers* 35, *Human Nutrition and Diet* 38, *Sweet Malefactor—Sugar, Slavery and Human Society* 67, *The Conquest of Famine* 74, articles on nutrition.

Queen Anne House, Charlbury, Oxford, England.
Telephone: Charlbury 441.

Aylestone, Baron (Life Peer), cr. 67, of Aylestone in the City of Leicester; **Herbert William Bowden,** P.C., .C.B.E., C.H.; British politician and television executive; b. 20 Jan. 1905; m. Louisa G. Brown 1928; one d.

President Leicester Labour Party 38; M.P. 45-67; Parl. Private Sec. to Postmaster-Gen. 47-49; Asst. Govt. Whip 49-50, Deputy Opposition Whip 51-55, Chief Opposition Whip 55-64; Lord Pres. of the Council 64-66; Leader House of Commons 64-66; Sec. of State for Commonwealth Affairs 66-67; Chair. Independent Broadcasting Authority (I.B.A.) 67-75.

House of Lords, London, SWIA oAA, England.

Aylmer, Sir Felix, Kt. (*pseudonym of* Sir Felix Aylmer Jones), O.B.E., B.A.; British actor; b. 21 Feb. 1889, Corsham, Wilts.; s. of Lieut.-Col. Edward Aylmer Jones, R.E.; m. Cecily Byrne 1915 (died 1975); two s. (deceased) one d.; ed. Magdalen Coll. School and Exeter Coll., Oxford.

First stage appearance at the Coliseum with Seymour Hicks 11; Birmingham Repertory Theatre 13; served in R.N.V.R. First World War 14-18; Pres. British Actors' Equity Asscn. 49-69; principal stage appearances in London: *R. E. Lee* 23, *The Terror* 27, *The Nelson Touch* 31, *The Voysey Inheritance, St. Joan, Bird in Hand* 34, *Heroes Don't Care, Waste* 36, *Yes and No* 37, *The Flashing Stream* 38, *Scandal at Barchester* 44, *Daphne Laureola* 49, *First Person Singular* 52, *Spider's Web* 54-56, *The Chalk Garden* 56; appeared on N.Y. stage, 22, 25, 39 and 53-54; principal films: *Tudor Rose, Victoria the Great, The Demi-Paradise, Henry V, Mr. Emmanuel, The Ghosts of Berkeley Square, Hamlet, Prince of Foxes, Quo Vadis, Ivanhoe, Knights of the Round Table, St. Joan, Captain Dreyfus, Separate Tables, The Doctor's Dilemma, Never Take Sweets from a Stranger, From the Terrace, Exodus, The Boys, Becket, The Chalk Garden.*

Publs. *Dickens Incognito* 59, *The Drood Case* 64.
6 Painshill House, Cobham, Surrey, England.
Telephone: Cobham (Surrey) 2463.

Aymond, Alphonse Henry, A.B., J.D.; American lawyer and public utilities official; b. 27 Sept. 1914, St. Louis, Mo.; s. of Alphonse H. Aymond and Anne Putz Aymond; m. Elizabeth Shierson 1939; three s.; ed. Northwestern Univ. and Univ. of Michigan.

Admitted to Illinois Bar 39, Michigan Bar 47; with Miller, Gorham, Wescott and Adams, Chicago 39-44; Commonwealth and Southern Corpn., New York City 46-47; Attorney, Consumers Power Co., Jackson, Mich. 46-51, Gen. Attorney 51-55, Vice-Pres. and Gen. Counsel 55-57, Exec. Vice-Pres. and Dir. 57-60, Chair. of Board and Dir. 60-, Pres. 72-75; Pres. and Dir. Michigan Gas Storage Co. 60-; Dir. City Bank and Trust Co.,

Nat. Bank of Detroit, American Seating Co., Kellogg Co., Nat. Detroit Corpn., S. S. Kresge Co.; Trustee, W. K. Kellogg Foundation, Northwestern Mutual Life Insurance Co., Northwestern Mutual Life Mortgage and Realty Investors.

Leisure interests: golf, gardening, bridge.
Consumers Power Co., 212 W. Michigan Avenue, Jackson, Mich., U.S.A.
Telephone: 517-788-0600.

Ayouné, Jean-Rémy; Gabonese administrator and politician; b. 5 June 1914, Assewé, Fernan-Vaz; ed. Catholic mission and seminaries in Libreville.

Worked in French Equatorial African Admin., Libreville 34-37; head of Audit Bureau, Dept. of Finance, Cabinet of the Gov.-Gen., Brazzaville 37-46; Editor, Press and Information Service, Cabinet of the Gov.-Gen. 46-52; Sec. of Inspection Dept., Acad. of Libreville 53-56; mem. Del. of A.E.F. to Paris 56-57; head, Press and Information Bureau, Cabinet of High Commr. to Congo (Brazzaville) 57-59; trainee, Quai d'Orsay and E.N.A. Jan.-April 60; Second Counsellor, French Embassy in German Fed. Repub. 60-61; first Amb. of Gabon to German Fed. Repub. March 61-March 63; Sec.-Gen. of Govt. March 64-Dec. 66; Minister of Civil Service and Technical Admin. Co-operation Dec. 66-July 68; Minister of Foreign Affairs July 68-April 70; Minister of Foreign Affairs and Co-operation April 70-June 71; Minister of Justice and Keeper of the Seals 71-72; First Pres. Gabonese Chamber of Commerce 72-.

Chambre de Commerce, d'Agriculture et d'Industrie et des Mines du Gabon, B.P. 110, Libreville, Gabon.

Ayyoubi, Mahmoud Ben Saleh al-; Syrian politician; b. 1932.

Former Dir.-Gen. for Admin. Affairs, Euphrates Dept.; Minister of Educ. 69-71; Deputy Premier Nov. 70-April 71; Vice-Pres. 71-75; Prime Minister Dec. 72-.
Office of the Prime Minister, Damascus, Syria.

Azad, Bhagwat Jha, M.A.; Indian politician; b. 28 Nov. 1922, Kasba Village, Bihar; s. of Jarab Lall Jha and Mrs. Yogmaya; m. Indira Jha Azad 1947; three s.; ed. TNB Collegiate School, TNB Coll., Patna Coll. and Patna Univ.

Joined Quit India Movement 42, sentenced to four years' imprisonment; Pres. Bihar State Students Congress 50; Sec. to Students and Econs. Depts. of Bihar State Congress 50-51; mem. All-India Congress Cttee. 52-; mem. Parl. 52-57, 62-67, 67-71, 71-; Minister of State, Ministry of Educ. 67-69, Ministry of Labour and Rehabilitation 69-71; mem. Public Account Cttee.

Leisure interests: composing poems, tunes and singing them; sport.
7 Ashoka Road, New Delhi, India.
Telephone: 387725.

Azeredo da Silveira, Antonio Francisco; Brazilian diplomatist; b. 22 Sept. 1917, Rio de Janeiro; s. of Flavio and Lea Maria Azeredo da Silveira, m. May Paranhos Azeredo da Silveira 1943; four s.; ed. Instituto Rio-Branco.

Joined foreign service 45, served in Havana, Buenos Aires, Florence, Madrid and Rome, Consul-Gen. Paris 61-63; Perm. Rep. to Office of UN at Geneva 66-68; Amb. to Argentina 68-74; Minister of Foreign Relations March 74-; del. to several confs. of OAS, GATT and UNCTAD, etc.; decorations from Fed. Germany, Italy, Ecuador, Peru, Chile, Netherlands, Austria, Spain and Malta.

Ministério Relações Exteriores, Brasília; Home: Avenida Vieira Souto, 408-apto, 401, Rio de Janeiro, B.B., Brazil.

Azevedo, Carlos de, M.A.; Portuguese museum administrator; b. 1918, Lisbon; s. of António Martins de Azevedo and Delfina M. de Azevedo; m. Maria Teresa Falcão 1940; three s.; ed. Lisbon Univ.

Lecturer in Portuguese, Oxford Univ. 45-47; at Lisbon Museum of Ancient Art 48-50; carried out official survey of Portuguese monuments in India 51; Curator, Lisbon Museum of Contemporary Art 55-60; Exec. Sec. Fulbright Comm. in Portugal 60-73; Head Div. of Foreign Cultural Relations, Ministry of Educ. 73-74, Dir. Internal Cultural Relations 74-; rep. of *The Connoisseur* in Portugal 54-; Sec. Portuguese Cttee. Int. Council of Museums (ICOM) 67-74; Fellow, Royal Soc. of Arts (London); Corresp. mem. Lisbon Nat. Acad. of Fine Arts.
Leisure interests: old organs, playing the harpsichord.
Publs. *Portuguese Country Houses*, two books on Portuguese colonial architecture, one on old Portuguese organ-cases, various studies and articles.
Rua Custódio Vieira, 2-3°-Dt°., Lisbon, Portugal.
Telephone: 68-34-25.

Azgur, Zair Isaakovich; Soviet monumental and portrait sculptor; b. 2 Jan. 1908, Molchany Village, Vitebsk Region, Byelorussia; ed. Leningrad Acad. of Arts and Kiev Arts Inst.
Known for his busts of revolutionary figures (*F. Dzerzhinsky, Gracchus Baboeuf*) 31-33, of figures of the Second World War and leading Soviet statesmen, workers, artists and scientists; mem. C.P.S.U. 43-; mem. Acad. of Arts of the U.S.S.R.; State prizewinner; People's Artist of the Byelorussian S.S.R.; Gold Medal, Exhibition to celebrate 40th anniversary of the Soviet Revolution; Brussels Int. Exhbn. 58; Order of Lenin, Red Banner of Labour (two), Red Star; People's Artist of the U.S.S.R.; Order of the October Revolution.
Byelorussian S.S.R. Union of Artists, Minsk, U.S.S.R.

Azikiwe, Rt. Hon. Nnamdi, P.C., M.A., M.SC., LL.D., D.LITT.; Nigerian politician; b. 16 Nov. 1904, Zungeru; s. of Obed Edom Chukwuemeka and Rachel Ogbenyeanu Azikiwe; three s. one d.; ed. Lincoln and Pennsylvania Univs.
Former Instructor in History and Political Science Lincoln Univ., Pa.; fmr. Gov. Dir. African Continental Bank Ltd.; Chair. Associated Newspapers of Nigeria Ltd., African Book Co. Ltd.; Pres. Nat. Council of Nigeria and the Cameroons; Vice-Pres. Nigerian Nat. Democratic Party; elected mem. of Legislative Council of Nigeria 47-51; mem. Brooke Arbitration Tribunal 44, Nigerianisation Comm. 48, MacDonald Arbitration Tribunal 48; mem. Western House of Assembly 52-53, Eastern House 54-59; former Minister of Local Govt., Eastern Region, and Minister of Internal Affairs 55-57; Premier, Eastern Nigeria 54-59; Pres. Fed. Senate 60; Gov.-Gen. and C.-in-C. Fed. of Nigeria 60-63, President of Nigeria 63-66; Fellow, Inst. of Journalists 61-; Chancellor and Chair. Council of the Univ. of Nigeria 61-66; Joint Pres. Anti-Slavery Soc. for Human Rights 70-; Chancellor, Univ. of Lagos Jan. 72-.
Leisure interests: walking, swimming, research in my private library.
Publs. *Liberia in World Politics* 34, *Renascent Africa* 37, *The African in Ancient and Medieval History* 38, *Land Tenure in Northern Nigeria* 42, *Political Blueprint of Nigeria* 43, *Economic Reconstruction of Nigeria* 43, *Economic Rehabilitation of Eastern Nigeria* 55, *Zik: a Selection of Speeches* 61, *Military Revolution in Nigeria* 72, *Meditations: A Collection of Poems* 65, *Dialogue on a New Capital for Nigeria* 74.
Onuiyi Haven, P.O. Box 7, Nsukka, Nigeria.

Azimi, Gen. Reza; Iranian army officer and politician; b. 1913; ed. Mil. Acad., Teheran.
Joined Imperial Army 29; Commdr. Armoured Corps, Chief of Army Staff Dept., Commdr. Central Army No. 1, Deputy Commdr. Ground Forces, Commdr. Western Army, Officer Commdg. Ground Forces 60-66,

Adjutant-Gen. to Shahanshah; Minister of Defence 71-; various army decorations.
Ministry of Defence, Teheran, Iran.

Azimov, Pigam Azimovich; Soviet specialist in Turkmenian language and literature; b. 1915; ed. Ashkhabad Pedagogic Inst.
Member C.P.S.U. 39-; at Ashkhabad Pedagogic Inst. 48-50; at Turkmenian State Univ. 50-63; mem. Turkmenian Acad. of Sciences 51-, Pres. 66-; Merited Scientific Worker of Turkmenian S.S.R. 61; several U.S.S.R. decorations.
Turkmenian S.S.R. Academy of Sciences, 15 Ulitsa Gogolya, Ashkhabad, U.S.S.R.

Azimov, Sarvar Alimadjanovich, DR. PHIL. SC.; Soviet philologist and diplomatist; b. 20 May 1923, Djizak Village, Uzbekistan; ed. Middle Asian State Univ.
First Sec. Board of Uzbek Writers' Union 56-57; Minister of Culture, Uzbek S.S.R. 57-59; Deputy Chair. Council of Ministers, and Minister of Foreign Affairs, Uzbek S.S.R. 59-69; Amb. to Lebanon 69-.
Publs. Many works on Middle Asian and Near Eastern Literature problems.
Soviet Embassy, Beirut, Lebanon.

Aziz, Ungku Abdul; Malaysian professor and university administrator; b. 28 Jan. 1922, London, U.K.; m. Sharifah Azah Aziz; one d.; ed. Raffles Coll. and Univ. of Malaya in Singapore, Waseda Univ., Tokyo, Univ. of Pittsburgh.
Johore State Civil Service; Lecturer in Econs., Univ. of Malaya in Singapore till 52; Head, Dept. of Econs., Univ. of Malaya, Kuala Lumpur 52-61, Dean of Faculty 61-65, Vice-Chancellor 68-; Pres. Nat. Co-operative Org. (ANGKASA) March 71, Asscn. of S.E. Asian Institutions of Higher Learning 73-75; Chair. Asscn. of Commonwealth Univs. 74-; mem. of Council, Soc. for Int. Devt. 71-74; Trustee, Asian Inst. of Technology 72-77; Corresp. mem. of Advisory Board, *Modern Asian Studies* 73-75; mem. Econ. Asscn. of Malaysia, Scientific Comm. of Int. Council of Research in Co-operative Devt., Int. Asscn. of Agricultural Economists, Joint Advisory Cttee. of FAO, UNESCO and ILO; mem. Nat. Consultative Council and Nat. Unity Advisory Council, Govt. of Malaysia; Fellow, World Acad. of Arts and Sciences 65-; Ordre des Arts et des Lettres (France) 65.
Office of the Vice Chancellor, University of Malaya, Kuala Lumpur 22-11 Malaysia.
Telephone: Kuala Lumpur 54400.

Aziz bin Yeop, Tan Sri Abdul, P.S.M., G.C.V.O.; Malaysian High Commissioner to United Kingdom 71-73; see *The International Who's Who 1975-76.*

Azkoul, Karim, PH.D.; Lebanese diplomatist and writer; b. 15 July 1915, Rachaya; s. of Najeeb Azkoul and Latifah Assaly; m. Eva Corey 1947; one s. one d.; ed. Jesuit Univ. of St. Joseph, Beirut, and Univs. of Paris, Berlin, Bonn and Munich.
Professor of History, Arab and French Literature, and Philosophy in various colls. in Lebanon 39-46; Dir. of an Arabic publishing house and monthly Arabic review *The Arab World*, Beirut 43-45; mem. Lebanese Del. to UN 47-50, Acting Perm. Del. to UN 50-53; Head of UN Affairs Dept., Ministry of Foreign Affairs 53-57; Head, Perm. Del. to UN 57-59; Consul-Gen. in Australia and New Zealand 59-61; Amb. to Ghana, Guinea and Mali 61-64, to Iran and Afghanistan 64-66; Journalist 66-68; Prof. of Philosophy, Beirut Coll. for Women 68-72, Lebanese Univ. 70-72; mem. PEN, Emergency World Council, Hague 71-; mem. Board of Trustees, Board of Management of Theological School of Balamand, Lebanon; Order of Cedar (Lebanon), Order of Holy

Sepulchre (Jerusalem), Order of St. Marc (Alexandria), Order of the Brilliant Star (Republic of China), Order of Southern Star (Brazil), Order of St. Peter and Paul (Damascus).

Leisure interests: reading and writing.

Publs. *Reason and Faith in Islam* (in German) 38, *Reason in Islam* (in Arabic) 46, *Freedom* (co-author) 56, *Freedom of Association* (UN) 68; trans. into Arabic *Consciencism* (Nkrumah) 64; *Arab Thought in the Liberal Age* (Albert Hourani) 69.

Union Building, Spaers Street, Alsanayeh, Beirut, Lebanon.

Telephone: 233390 (Office); 233250 (Home).

Aznavour, Charles (*pseudonym* for Varenagh Aznavourian); French singer and film star; b. 22 May 1924; ed. Ecole centrale de T.S.F., Centre de spectacle, Paris. With Jean Dasté Company 41; with Pierre Roche in *Les Fâcheux* and *Arlequin* 44; numerous song recitals in France, Europe and U.S.A.; actor in numerous films including: *La tête contre les murs* 59, *Tirez sur le pianiste* 60, *Un taxi pour Tobrouk*, *Le testament d'Orphée*, *Le diable et les dix commandements*, *Haute-Infidélité* 64, *La Métamorphose des cloportes* 65, *Paris au mois d'août* 66, *Le facteur s'en va-t-en guerre* 66, *Le diable par le queue* 68, *Candy* 69, *Les Intrus* 73.

Film music includes: *Soupe au lait*, *L'île du bout du monde*, *Ces dames préfèrent le mambo*, *Le cercle vicieux*, *De quoi tu te mêles Daniela*, *Douce Violence*, *Les Parisiennes*; also author and singer of numerous songs; composer of operetta *Monsieur Carnaval* 65.

4 avenue du Lieutel, 78 Galluis, France.

B

Ba, Babacar; Senegalese politician; b. 14 June 1930; ed. Univ. of Dakar.

Governor Oriental Province 60-61; Principal Private Sec. to the Presidency 61-62, 68-70; District Commr. 63-66; Principal Private Sec. to Minister of Foreign Affairs 68; Sec.-Gen. at the Presidency 70; Minister of Finance and Econ. Affairs April 71-; fmr. Pres. Banque Centrale des Etats de l'Afrique de l'Ouest.

Ministère des Finances et des Affaires Economiques, Dakar, Senegal.

Baah, Maj. Kwame R. M.; Ghanaian army officer; b. 21 May 1938, Dormaa Ahenkro, Brong-Ahafo Region; ed. Royal Officers' Specialist Training School, Accra, Mil. Acad., Dehra Dun, India.

Commissioned Regular Infantry Officer, Ghana Army 62; held various posts including Instructor, Ghana Mil. Acad. and Training School, Acting Commdg. Officer, 5th Infantry Battalion, Staff Officer to Defence Adviser, Ghana High Comm., London, Asst. Defence, Armed Forces Attaché, Ghana Embassy to U.S.A.; Commr. for Lands, Mineral Resources Jan.-Nov. 72, for Foreign Affairs 72-75, of Econ. Planning Oct. 75 (resigned); mem. Nat. Redemption Council 72-75.

Office of the National Redemption Council, P.O. Box 1627, Accra, Ghana.

Baba, Corneliu; Romanian artist; b. 18 Nov. 1906, Craiova; ed. Bucharest Univ. and Inst. of Fine Arts, Taşi.

Teacher Inst. of Fine Arts, Taşi, and N. Grigorescu Inst. of Fine Arts, Bucharest; First official exhbn. 34; numerous official exhbns. in Romania, Moscow, Venice, Vienna, Prague, Warsaw, Rome, Sofia, etc. 44-; one-man exhbns. Brussels 64, Berlin 64, New York 70; Hon. mem. U.S.S.R. Acad. of Art 58-; Corresp. mem. Acad. Socialist Republic of Romania 63-; mem. Acad. of Arts, Berlin 64-; People's Artist 62, State Prizewinner 53, 54. Major works: *Odihna la Cîmp* (Homecoming from the Fields) 54, *Intoarcerea de la Sapă* (Coming Back from Maize Hoeing) 42, *Tăranu* (Peasants) 58, *Oţelari* (Steelworkers) 60, portraits of M. Sadoveanu, Lucia Sturdza Bulandra, Tudor Arghezi and his wife, and book illustrations.

Uniunea Artiştilor Plastici, Bucureşti, Calea Victoriei 155, Bucharest, Romania.

Babaevsky, Semyon Petrovich; Soviet writer; b. 29 May 1909, Kunye village, Kharkov Region, Ukraine; *m.* 1929; two *s.*; ed. Moscow Literary Inst.

Member Communist Party of Soviet Union 39-, war corresp. 41-45; Deputy to Supreme Soviet of U.S.S.R. 50-58; mem. Board U.S.S.R. Union of Writers; State Prizewinner 48, 49, 50; Order of Red Banner of Labour 59, 69.

Publs. Novels: *Cavalier of the Golden Star, Geese Island* 47, *Light over the Earth* 49, *Well-Spring Grove* 56, *White Mosque, Sukhaya Buivola* 58, *Along Paths and Roads* 59, *Son's Mutiny* 61, *Native Land* 65, *The Whole World* 69, *Contemporaries* 72.

27 Ulitsa Krasnoarmeiskaya kv. 87, Moscow 125319, U.S.S.R.

Babajanyan, Arno Arutyunovich; Soviet composer; b. 22 Jan. 1921, Erevan; *s.* of Arutyun and Arszwick Babajanyan; *m.* Tereza Babajanyan 1939; one *s.*; ed. Erevan and Moscow Conservatoires.

Member C.P.S.U. 56; Asst. Prof. at Erevan Conservatoire 56; Merited Artist of Armenian S.S.R. 56, People's Artist of Armenian S.S.R. 56, of U.S.S.R. 71; State Prize 66.

Leisure interests: chess, hockey, football, cars, collecting paintings.

Principal works: Variations for Piano 37, Prelude 39, First Piano Concerto 42, Sonata for Piano 43, *Dance Vagarshapat* 44, Concerto for Violin and Orchestra 49, Heroic Ballade for Piano and Orchestra 51, Rhapsody for Two Pianos 54, Sonata for Violin and Piano 59 Holiday Suite for Two Pianos and Percussion 61, *My Heart is in the Mountains* (operetta) 62, Six Pieces for Piano 64, *Andante and Humoresk* 70, Meditation for Piano 71, Ballet Suite 72, *The Tram is Going to the Park* 73, Trio for Violin, Cello and Piano; variety, jazz, film and theatre music.

Ogareva str. 13, ap. 21, 103009 Moscow, U.S.S.R. Telephone: 229-82-29.

Babanova, Mariya Ivanovna; Soviet actress; b. 11 Nov. 1900, Moscow.

Started work at V.E. Meyerhold Theatre 20; later moved to Mayakovsky Theatre 20; People's Artist of the Soviet Union; State prize; most important parts Polina (*Profitable Post*—A. N. Ostrovsky), Goga (*A Man with a Portmanteau*—A. M. Faiko), Juliet (*Romeo and Juliet*), Countess Diana (*A Dog on the Loft*—Lopé de Vega), Tanya (*Tanya*—A. N. Arbuzov), Sofia (*Zykovy*—M. Gorky), Ranevskaya (*The Cherry Orchard*—Chekhov), Maggy (*What Every Woman Knows*—Barrie), Kay (*A Woman's Life*—K. Morimoto), Mary (*Mary October*—Duvilie), Ophelia (*Hamlet*), Elizabeth (*Circle*—Maugham), Mariya Alexandrovna (*Uncle's Dream*—Dostoevsky), Lidya (*Old Fashioned Comedy*—A. N. Arbuzov).

Moscow Mayakovsky Theatre, 19 Ulitsa Herzena, Moscow, U.S.S.R.

Babayev, Sabir; Soviet composer; b. 30 Dec. 1920, Tashkent, Uzbekistan; ed. Tashkent Conservatoire.

Executive mem. Uzbek S.S.R. Union of Composers; Sec. Soviet Union of Composers; Merited Worker of Arts of the Uzbek S.S.R.

Principal works: Two Suites for Symphony Orch. 46-48, Two Poems and *Festival Overture* for folk instrument orch. 50-52; Concerto for chang (Uzbek folk instrument) and orch. of folk instruments 52; Cantata, *Cotton Farmers of Uzbekistan* 55, *Segokh* (symphonic poem on folk themes) 56; *Love of Motherland* (musical drama) 57, *During the Festival* (symphonic poem) 58, *Khamza* (opera) 61, *Uzbek Poetic Songs* 66.

Uzbek S.S.R. Union of Composers, Tashkent, U.S.S.R.

Babbidge, Homer Daniels, Jr., M.A., PH.D.; American university president; b. 18 May 1925, West Newton, Mass.; *s.* of Homer Daniels Babbidge and Allalie Lavinia Adams; *m.* Marcia J. Adkisson 1956; one *s.* two *d.*; ed. Yale Univ.

Co-founder, American studies for foreign students, Yale Univ. 48; Exec. Fellow Pierson Coll. 49-57; Dir. of financial aids, lecturer in Educ., mem. Board of Admissions, Yale Univ. 54-57; Special Asst. to U.S. Commr. for Educ. 55-56; Asst. to Sec. Dept. of Health, Educ. and Welfare 57-58; Dir. Program of Financial Assistance to Higher Educ. 58-59; Asst. Commr., Dir. Div. of Higher Educ. 59-61; Pres. Univ. of Connecticut 62-72; Master Timothy Dwight Coll., Yale, Fellow Inst. for Social and Policy Studies 72-; Chair. U.S. Advisory Comm. on Int. Educ. and Cultural Affairs; Vice-Chair. Nat. Science Foundation Advisory Cttee. on Institutional Relations; mem. U.S. Public Health Service's Advisory Council on Health Research Facilities; Chair. Conn. Educ. Council and mem. numerous other cttees., etc.; Hon. L.H.D. (Hartford, Fairfield), Hon. D.Litt. (Rosary Hill Coll., Buffalo), Hon. LL.D. (Ithaca Coll., Yale Univ.); named as one of outstanding young men, U.S. Junior Chamber of Commerce 59; Distinguished

Service Medal, U.S. Dept. of Health, Educ. and Welfare 61.

Leisure interests: stone wall building, ice skating, reading.

Publs. *Student Financial Aid* 60, *A Federal Education Agency for the Future* 61, *The Federal Interest in Higher Education* (co-author) 62, *Noah Webster: On Being American* 67.

63 Wall Street, New Haven, Conn. 06510, U.S.A.

Babcock, Horace W., PH.D.; American astronomer; b. 13 Sept. 1912, Pasadena, Calif.; *s.* of Harold D. Babcock and Mary G. (Henderson); *m.* 1st M. B. Anderson 1940; one *s.* one *d.*; 2nd Elizabeth M. Aubrey 1958; one *s.*; ed. California Inst. of Technology and Univ. of California.

Instructor, Yerkes and McDonald Observatories 39-41; Staff mem. Radiation Laboratory, Mass. Inst of Technology 41-42; Staff mem. Office of Scientific Research and Devt. Project, Calif. Inst. of Technology 42-45; Staff mem. Mount Wilson and Palomar Observatories (now Hale Observatories) 46-, Asst. Dir. 57-64, Dir. 64-; mem. Nat. Acad. of Sciences (Draper Medal 57), Council mem. 73-76; American Philosophical Soc., American Acad. of Arts and Sciences; Assoc. Royal Astronomical Soc., Eddington Medal 57, Gold Medal 70; Bruce Medal, Astronomical Soc. of Pacific; Hon. Sc.D.

Leisure interest: sailing.

Publs. Articles in scientific and technical journals, mainly on magnetic fields of the sun and stars, theory of the sun's magnetic field, rotation of the spiral galaxy in Andromeda, ruling of diffraction gratings, astronomical instrumentation.

The Hale Observatories, 813 Santa Barbara Street, Pasadena, Calif. 91101, U.S.A.

Telephone: 213-577-1122.

Babics, Antal, DR. MED.; Hungarian surgeon and urologist; b. 4 Aug. 1902, Lovászpatona; *s.* of Endre Babics and Róza Moór; *m.* Ilona Esterházy 1940.

Lecturer, Urological Clinic, Budapest Medical Univ. 40, Prof. and Dir. of Clinic 45-74; Corresp. mem. Hungarian Acad. of Sciences 49-50, full mem. 50-, Sec. Medical Dept., Hungarian Acad. of Sciences; mem. Presidium Int. Urological Soc.; Hon. mem. Soviet Soc. of Surgeons, Urological Soc. of Italy, Germany, Austria and Romania, Purkinje Soc. of Czechoslovakia, Soviet Medical Acad.; Kossuth Prize 51; Labour Order of Merit, golden degree 70, Banner Order of Hungarian Repub.

Leisure interests: angling, walking, dogs, natural science books.

Publs. include: *Urology* 52, *The Theory and Clinical Aspects of Kidney Necrosis* 52.

Medical University, Budapest; and Budapest II, Pór Bertalan utca 5, Hungary.

Telephone: 343-727 (Office); 355-109 (Home).

Babiiha, John Kabwimukya, DIP. VET. SC.; Ugandan politician; b. 17 April 1913, Toro; *s.* of late Zachary Kubangisa and of Elizabeth Tibananuka; *m.* Elizabeth Kabahuma 1940; five *s.* nine *d.*; ed. St. Joseph's Coll., Mbarara, St. Mary's Coll., Kisubi, Makerere Univ. Coll. and Pretoria Univ.

Assistant Veterinary Officer 39-45; Asst. Treas. Toro District Admin. 46-53; Uganda Legislative Council 54-60; mem. Parl. 61-71; Minister of Animal Industry, Game and Fisheries 62-71; Vice-Pres. of Uganda 66-71; Chair. Council of Veterinary Educ. of E. Africa 63-71; Special Pres. Adviser on Animal Resources 73-; mem. Makerere Univ. Council 74; Knight Commdr. Order of Stars of Queen of Sheba (Ethiopia), Chevalier, Grand Cordon Order of the Leopard (Zaire), Knight Order of Grand Cross of Pope Pius IX (Vatican), Gold Medal and Distinguished Diploma (Vatican) 65, Independence Medal 62, Medal for Distinguished Service (Uganda) 73,

Medalha Pro Mundi Beneficio (Brazil) 75, and other awards.

Leisure interests: walking, reading, debates, social anthropology.

Publ. *The Bayaya Clan in the Western Region* 57.

P.O. Box 7168, Kampala; Home: P.O. Box 13, Fort Portal, Uganda.

Babikian, Khatchik Diran; Lebanese lawyer and politician; b. 1924, Cyprus; *m.* 1956; five *d.*; ed. Collège Italien Beirut, Faculté Française de Droit Beirut, Faculté de Paris, Univ. of London.

Barrister; Deputy for Beirut 57, 60, 64, 68, 72; mem. Parl. Comm. on Justice; Pres. Traffic Comm., Parl. Comm. on Planning, Lebanese Management Asscn. 72; Minister for Admin. Reform 60-61; Minister of Public Health 68-69; Minister of Tourism 69-70, of Information 72-73, of Planning 73; Pres. Armenian Nat. Assembly 72.

Place de l'Etoile, Beirut; Home: Rue Abrine, Achrafié, Beirut, Lebanon.

Telephone: 242033 (Office); 322013 (Home).

Babin, Jean; French professor; b. 26 Feb. 1905; ed. Univ. de Nancy.

High School teacher 27-29, Lycée Asst. 29-33, Prof. 33-41; School Inspector 41-47; Dir. of Education in the Saar 47-48; Prof. Faculty of Letters, Lille Univ. 48-55; Rector, Acad. de Strasbourg 55-58, Acad. de Bordeaux 60-72; Dir. du Centre Nat. des Œuvres Univs. 58-60; Gen. Del. of Minister of Educ. for Int. Univ. Affairs 72; Officier de la Légion d'Honneur, Commdr. Ordre des Palmes Acad.

Publs. (with A. Babin) *Du Français au latin et aux langues vivantes par l'analyse* 36, *Les lieux-dits de la Commune de Boureuilles* (*Meuse*) 52, *Le toponymiste dans la mine* 53, *Les lieux-dits de la mer* 54, *Les parlers de l'Argonne* 55.

173 boulevard Saint Germain, Paris 6e, France.

Babington Smith, Michael James, C.B.E.; British banking executive; b. 20 March 1901; ed. Eton and Trinity Coll., Cambridge.

Consultant, Williams & Glyns Bank (fmr. Deputy Chair.), Bank of England (until March 69), Bank for Int. Settlements, Cie. Financière de Suez until 74, Suez Int., Nat. and Grindlays Bank Ltd., and other companies; Chair. Cttee. in London, Ottoman Bank 75-; Sheriff of London 53 and 62.

Flat 6, 20 Embankment Gardens, London, S.W.3, England.

Telephone: 01-352-2854.

Babiuch, Edward, M.ECON.; Polish politician; b. 28 Dec. 1927, Bedzin District, Katowice Voivodship; ed. Silesian Technical Scientific Establishment and Gen. School of Planning and Statistics.

Member, Polish United Workers' Party (PZPR) 48; functions in Voivodship Board, Katowice 49 and subsequently in Cen. Board of Polish Youth Union; worked at Cen. Cttee. of PZPR 55-59; Sec. PZPR Warsaw Voivodship Cttee. 59-63; Deputy Head, Organization Dept., Cen. Cttee. 63-65, Head 65-70; Editor-in-Chief, *Zycie Partii* 63-65; Deputy to Seym 69-; mem. Cen. Cttee. PZPR 64-, mem. Politburo and Sec. Cen. Cttee. Dec. 70-; Chair. Seym Comm. of Nat. Defence 71-72; mem. Presidium, All-Polish Cttee. of Nat. Unity Front 71-; mem. State Council March 72-; Order of Banner of Labour (1st and 2nd Class), Officer's and Knight's Cross of Order of Polonia Restituta, Order of Yugoslav Star with Ribbon 73, Medal of 30th Anniversary of People's Poland.

Polska Zjednoczona Partia Robotnicza, Nowy Świat 6, 00-497 Warsaw, Poland.

Bacall, Lauren; American actress; b. 16 Sept. 1924; *m.* 1st Humphrey Bogart 1945 (died 1957), 2nd Jason Robards 1961; two *s.* one *d.*

Films since 45 include *To Have and Have Not, The Big Sleep, Confidential Agent, Dark Passage, Key Largo, Young Man with a Horn, Bright Leaf, How to Marry a Millionaire, Woman's World, The Cobweb, Blood Alley, Written on the Wind, Designing Woman, The Gift of Love, Flame over India, Sex and the Single Girl, Harper, Murder on the Orient Express* 74; plays: *Goodbye Charlie* 60, *Cactus Flower* 66, *Applause* 70 (London 72).
c/o Julius Lefkowitz & Company, 1350 Avenue of the Americas, New York, N.Y. 10019, U.S.A.

Bacchelli, Riccardo; Italian writer; b. 19 April 1891, Bologna; s. of Giuseppe and Anna Bumiller; m. Ada Fochesfati 1966.
Member Accad. Naz. dei Lincei, Accademia della Crusca, Florence, Accademia delle Scienze, Bologna, Accademia delle Scienze, Ferrara, Istituto Lombardo di Scienze e lettere; Grand Officer of Italian Republic 53, Dott. h.c. Univs. of Bologna and Milan.
Publs *Poemi lirici* 14, *Lo sa il tonno* 24, *Il diavolo al Pontelungo* 27, *Amore di poesia* 30, *La Congiura di Don Giulio d'Este* 31, *Oggi, domani e mai* 32, *Mal d'Africa* 34, *Iride* 37, *Il Mulion del Po* 38-40, *Gioacchino Rossini* 41, *Il Fiore della Mirabilis* 42, *Il Pianto del Figlio di Lais* 45, *Lo Sguardo di Gesù* 48, *L'Alba dell'Ultima Sera* 49, *La Cometa* 51, *Italia per terra e per mare* 52, *L'incendio di Milano* 52, *Memorie del Tempo Presente* 53, *Il Figlio di Stalin* 53, *Tre giorni di passione* 55, *Nel fiume della Storia* 55, *Amleto* 56, *I tre schiavi di Giulio Cesare* 57, *Viaggio in Grecia* 59, *Non ti chiamerò più padre* 59, *Leopardi e Manzoni* 60, *Viaggi all'estero e vagabondaggi di fantasia* 66, *Giorno per giorno 1912-1922* 66, *America in confidenza* 66, *Rapporto segreto* 67, *Giorno per Giorno 1932-1966* 68, *L'Afrodite* 69, *Africa tra Storia e Fantasia* 69, *La Stella del Mattino* 71, *Bellezza e Umanita* 72, *Giorni di Vita e Temo di Poesia* 73.
Borgonuovo 20, 20121 Milan, Italy.

Bach, Wilhelm Franz-Josef, DR. ING.; German engineer and diplomatist; b. 4 Feb. 1917, Neuss; s. of Gustav and Christine (née Kaiser) Bach; m. 1942; two d.; ed. Technical Univs. of Aachen, Berlin and Brunswick.
Assistant Prof. of Aerodynamics, Technical Univ., Aachen 42-45; Deputy Chief Editor *Aachener Volkszeitung* 47-50; Diplomatic Service 51-, Canberra, Washington 52-57; Personal Asst. to German Chancellor (Dr. Adenauer) 57-61; Consul-Gen., Hong Kong 61-64; Amb. to Iran 64-59; mem. Bundestag 69-72; Industrial Consultant 72-; numerous decorations.
Publ. *Pressure distribution on objects flying with supersonic velocity.*
Leisure interests: collector of coins and bronzes, golf.
Aachen, Preussweg 121, Federal Republic of Germany.
Telephone: 0241-72007.

Bachauer, Gina; British pianist; b. 21 May 1913, Athens, Greece; d. of John and Ersilia Bachauer; m. 1st John Christodoulou 1937, 2nd Alec Sherman 1951; ed. Athens Coll., Athens Conservatoire of Music, and Ecole Normale, Paris under Cortot and Rachmaninov.
Debut Athens Symphony Orchestra, conductor Mitropoulos 35; more than 600 concerts for Allied Forces 40-46; Debut in London 47 and in New York 50; Austria, Belgium, Canada, Cuba, Cyprus, Czechoslovakia, Finland, France, Federal Republic of Germany, Greece, Hong Kong, Honolulu, Ireland, Israel, Italy, Netherlands, New Zealand, Norway, Poland, Portugal, Romania, South Africa, Spain, Sweden, Switzerland, U.K., Venezuela and Yugoslavia; Order of Golden Phoenix and Commdr. Order of Welfare (Greece); Prize, Vienna Int. Piano Competition 33; Founding Artist, Kennedy Center for the Performing Arts, Washington 71; Hon. D. Hum., Univ. of Utah 71.
Leisure interests: swimming, cooking, reading.
6 Cumberland Terrace, Regent's Park, London, N.W.1, England.
Telephone: 01-935-0182.

Bacher, Robert Fox, B.S., PH.D.; American physicist; b. 31 Aug. 1905, Londonville, Ohio; s. of Harry and Bryl Fox Bacher; m. Jean Dow 1930; one s. one d.; ed. Univ. of Michigan.
Nat. Research Fellow Physics, Calif. Inst. of Technology 30-31; Mass. Inst. of Technology 31-32; Alfred Lloyd Fellow Univ. of Michigan 32-33; Instr. Columbia Univ. 34-35; Instructor to Prof., Cornell Univ. 35-49; Radiation Laboratory, Mass. Inst. of Technology 40-45 (on leave 43-45); Los Alamos Laboratory, Atomic Bomb Project 43-Jan. 46; Dir. of Laboratory of Nuclear Studies, Cornell Univ. 46; mem. U.S. Atomic Energy Comm. 46-49; Prof. of Physics, Calif. Inst. of Technology 49-, Chair. Div. of Physics, Mathematics and Astronomy 49-62, Provost 62-70; mem. President's Science Advisory Cttee. 57-60; Trustee, Carnegie Corpn. 59-75; Claremont Graduate School 71-, Universities Research Asscn. 65- (Chair. 69-73, Pres. 73-74), Rand Corpn. 50-60; Dir. Detroit Edison Co., Bell & Howell Co., TRW Inc.; Pres. Int. Union of Pure and Applied Physics 69-72; mem. Nat. Acad. of Sciences, American Philosophical Soc., American Acad. of Arts and Sciences, American Physical Soc. (Pres. 64), American Asscn. for Advancement of Science; awarded Medal for Merit by Pres. Truman Jan. 46.
Publ. *Atomic Energy States* (with S. Goudsmit) 32.
California Institute of Technology, Pasadena, Calif. 91125; and 345 South Michigan Avenue, Pasadena, Calif. 91106, U.S.A.

Bachmann, Kurt; German journalist and politician; b. 1909.
Former leatherworker; joined C.P. of Germany 32, worked underground in Cologne; fled to France 38, joined Resistance Movement 40; arrested in S. France 42, imprisoned in seven concentration camps; helped found Asscn. of Victims of Nazi Persecution 45, and helped publish *Volksstimme* (Communist newspaper), Cologne; mem. Exec. C.P. of Germany 50-56 (party banned 56); later became Bonn corresp. for *Die Tat* (weekly of Asscn. of Victims of Nazi Persecution); mem. Fed. Organizing Cttee., German C.P. 68; Chair. of German C.P. 69-73.
German Communist Party, Düsseldorf, Federal Republic of Germany.

Bächtold, Kurt, D.PHIL.; Swiss librarian; b. 13 Nov. 1918, Schaffhausen; m. Rös Egloff 1950; three s. one d.; ed. Gymnasium, Schaffhausen, Univs. of Lausanne, Zürich and Paris.
Editor *Schaffhausen Nachrichten* 47-68; mem. Schaffhausen City Council 48-52, Schaffhausen School Council 59-61; mem. Nat. Council, Fed. Assembly 61-, Pres. until 74; mem. European Parl. 72-; Dir. Schaffhausen City Library.
Leisure interests: walking, mountain climbing.
Publs. *Weltgeschichte im 20. Jahrhundert* 59, *Schaffhauser Biographien* 61, *Wasser im Gefahr* 71, *Protest und Dialog: Das Jugendproblem heute* 72, *Die Evolution der Demokratie* 73.
Vögelingässchen 34, 8200 Schaffhausen, Switzerland.
Telephone: 5 12 04 (Office); 5 65 20 (Home).

Backus, George Edward, S.M., PH.D.; American theoretical geophysicist; b. 24 May 1930, Chicago, Ill.; s. of late Milo Morlan Backus and of Dora Dare Backus; m. Elizabeth E. Allen 1961; two s. one d.; ed. Thornton Township High School, Harvey, Ill. and Univ. of Chicago.
Assistant Examiner, Univ. of Chicago 49-50; Junior Mathematician, Inst. for Air Weapons Research, Univ. of Chicago 50-54; Physicist, Project Matterhorn, Princeton Univ. 57-58; Asst. Prof. of Mathematics, Mass. Inst. of Technology 58-60; Assoc. Prof. of Geophysics, Univ. of Calif. (La Jolla) 60-62, Prof. 62;

Guggenheim Fellowship 63; Fellow American Geophysical Union, American Acad. of Arts and Sciences; mem. Nat. Acad. of Sciences.

Leisure interests: hiking, swimming, history, reading disciplined fiction, flying, skiing.

Publs. *Self-sustaining Dissipative Kinematic Fluid Dynamo* 58, *Rotational Splitting of the Free Oscillations of the Earth* 61, *Propagation of Short Waves on a Slowly Rotating Earth* 62, *Magnetic Anomalies over Oceanic Ridges* 64, *Possible Forms of Seismic Anistropy* 62, 65, 70, *Potentials for Tangent Tensor Fields on Spheroids* 66, *Inversion of Seismic Normal Mode Data* (with F Gilbert) 66-, *Geomagnetic Data and Core Motions* 67, *Reduction Languages and Variable-Free Programming* 72, *Inversion of Earth Normal Mode Data* (with F. Gilbert) 68, 69, 70, *Inference from Inaccurate and Inadequate Data* 71, 72.

Institute of Geophysics and Planetary Physics, University of California, San Diego, P.O.B. 109, La Jolla, Calif. 92037; Home: 7687 Hillside Drive, La Jolla, Calif. 92037, U.S.A.

Telephone: 714-453-2000 (Office); 714-454-5868 (Home).

Backus, John Warner, A.M.; American computer programmer and mathematician; b. 3 Dec. 1924, Phila.; s. of Cecil Franklin Backus and Elizabeth Edsall; m. 2nd Una Stannard 1968; two d.; ed. Columbia Univ. Research Staff mem., Thomas J. Watson Research Center 59-63; IBM Fellow, San José, Calif. 63-; Adjunct Prof. of Information Sciences, Univ. of Calif., Santa Cruz 74-; mem. Asscn. for Computing Machinery, American Mathematical Soc., NAS; W. W. McDowell Award, Inst. of Electrical and Electronics Engineers 67.

Leisure interests: music, sailing.

Publs. *Systems Design of the IBM 704 Computer* (with G. M Amdahl) 54, *The Fortran Automatic Coding System* (with others) 57, *The Syntax and Semantics of the Proposed International Algebraic Language of the Zürich ACM-GAMM Conference* 59, *Report on the Algorithmic Language ALGOL 60* (with others) 60, *Programming Language Semantics and Closed Applicative Languages* (conference record of ACM Symposium) 73.

91 St. Germain Avenue, San Francisco, Calif. 94114, U.S.A.

Telephone: 415-731-8155.

Bacon, Edmund Norwood, B.ARCH.; American architect and planner; b. 2 May 1910, Philadelphia; s. of Ellis W. and Helen Comly Bacon; m. Ruth Holmes 1938; two s. four d.; ed. Cornell Univ. and Cranbrook Acad.

Architectural Designer, Shanghai, China 34; housing projects for W. Pope Barney, Architect, Philadelphia 35; Supervisor of City Planning, Flint (Michigan) Inst. of Research and Planning; Man. Dir. Philadelphia Housing Asscn. 40-43; Co-Designer Better Philadelphia Exhibition and Senior Land Planner, Philadelphia City Planning Comm.; Exec. Dir. Philadelphia City Planning Comm. 49-70; Professional Adviser, Franklin Delano Roosevelt Memorial Competition 59; mem. President's Citizens' Advisory Cttee. on Environmental Quality 70; Vice-Pres. Design and Devt., Mondev International Ltd.; numerous awards.

Publ. *Design of Cities* 67 (revised edn. 74).

Home: 2117 Locust Street, Philadelphia, Pa. 19103, U.S.A.

Telephone: Locust 7-0693.

Bacon, Francis; Irish painter; b. 1910, Dublin.

Began to teach himself to paint 30; first One-Man Shows London 49, New York 53; exhibited at Venice Biennale 54; rep. at Brussels Int. Exhbn. 58; important works include triptychs: *Three Studies for Figures at the Base of a Crucifixion* 44, *Crucifixion* 62, *Sweeney Agonistes* 67, *Triptych* 1972, *Triptych* 1973, *Triptych* 1974; single oils: *Man with Dog* 53, *Study After Velazquez's*

Portrait of Pope Innocent X 53, *Two Figures* 53, *Study for a Portrait of Van Gogh* 57, *Portrait of Isabel Rawsthorne standing in a Street in Soho* 67; Retrospective Exhbn. Tate Gallery, London 62, Paris 71; exhbn. New London Gallery 63, Solomon Guggenheim Museum, N.Y. 63, Galerie Maeght, Paris 66, Marlborough New London Gallery 67, Marlborough-Gerson Gail, New York 68, Grand Palais, Paris 71, Kunsthalle, Düsseldorf 72, Metropolitan Museum, New York 75, Fundación Juan March, Madrid 76, Musée Cantini, Marseilles 76; travelling exhbns. Mannheim, Turin, Zürich, Amsterdam 62, Hamburg, Stockholm, Dublin 65; Rubens Prize, City of Siegen 66.

c/o Marlborough Fine Art Ltd., 6 Albemarle Street, London, W1X 3HF, England.

Bacon, Francis Thomas, O.B.E., F.R.S., M.A., M.I.MECH.E.; British mechanical engineer; b. 21 Dec. 1904, Billericay; s. of Mr. and Mrs. T. W. Bacon; m. Barbara Winifred Papillon 1934; one s. one d.; ed. Eton and Trinity Coll., Cambridge.

With C. A. Parsons & Co., Newcastle on Tyne 25-40; anti-submarine work for Admiralty in Second World War, research on Hydrox Fuel Cell, Cambridge Univ. 46-56; consultant to Nat. Research Development Corpn. on development of Hydrox Fuel Cells, Cambridge 57-62; consultant to Energy Conversion Ltd. 62-71, to Fuel Cells Ltd. 72-73; S. G. Brown Award (Royal Soc.) 65; British Silver Medal (Royal Aeronautical Soc.) 69; Churchill Gold Medal Award (Soc. of Engineers) 72, Melchett Medal (Inst. of Fuel) 72.

Leisure interests: walking in the hills, fishing.

Westfield, Little Shelford, Cambridge, CB2 5ES, England.

Telephone: Shelford 2244.

Bacon, Paul; French politician; b. 1 Nov. 1907, Paris; s. of Laurent Bacon and Maria Baradat; m. Marthe Rajaud 1933; two s.; ed. Ecole Professionnelle de Pau. Began career as furniture designer 23-27; mem. Gen. Secrétariat Jeunesse Ouvrière Chrétienne 27-37; Chief Editor of *Monde Ouvrier* 37-39; served French Army 39-40; mem. Assemblée Nationale Consultative 44-45 (Groupe Resistance Metropolitaine); Dir. of *Syndicalisme* (organ of Confédération Française des Travailleurs Chrétiens) 45; Deputy (M.R.P.), Vice-Pres. Ass. Nat. Constituante 46-; Sec. to Presidency of Council 49-50; Minister of Labour and Social Security, Bidault, Queuille, Pleven, Faure Cabinets 50-52, Mayer Cabinet 53, Laniel Cabinet 53-54, Faure Cabinet 55-56, Gaillard Cabinet 57-58; Minister without Portfolio, subsequently Minister of Labour, de Gaulle Cabinet 58; Minister of Labour, Debré Cabinet 59-May 62, Pompidou Cabinet 62; mem. Conseil Economique et Social 63; Dir. Turin Int. Centre for Advanced Technical and Vocational Training, Int. Labour Org. (I.L.O.) 64-67; Chair. Centre d'Etude des Revenus et des Couts (Commissariat-Gén. du Plan) 67-; mem. Conseil National de la Statistique 73-; Chevalier, Légion d'Honneur; Commdr. Mérite Social, Santé Publique.

Leisure interest: painting.

Publs. *La Naissance de la Classe Ouvrière*, *Vers la Réforme de l'Entreprise Capitaliste*, *La Démocratie Economique et Sociale*.

23 avenue Balzac, La Varenne-St.-Hilaire (Val de Marne); and C.E.R.C., 30 rue Las Cases, Paris 7e, France.

Telephone: 883-15-58; 551-75-70.

Bacquier, Gabriel; French (baritone) opera singer; b. 17 May 1924, Béziers; s. of Augustin Bacquier and Fernande Sévera; m. 1st Simone Teisseire 1943, and Mauricette Bénard 1958; two s.; ed. Paris Conservatoire.

Debut at Théâtre Royal de la Monnaie, Brussels 53; joined Opéra de Paris 56; debut at Carnegie Hall 60, Metropolitan Opera, New York 61; now appears

regularly at the Vienna State Opera, Covent Garden, La Scala, Opéra de Paris and most leading opera houses. repertoire includes *Otello, Don Giovanni, Pelléas et Mélisande, Damnation de Faust, Tosca, Falstaff*; several recordings; Prix National du disque français 64, and other prizes.
Leisure interests: painting, drawing.
141 rue de Rome, Paris 17e, France.
Telephone: 227-33-84.

Badarou, Dr. Daouda; Benin surgeon and politician; b. 7 Jan. 1929, Porto-Novo; ed. Dakar and Univ. of Paris.
Qualified as surgeon 61; fmr. mem. Exec. Council, W.H.O.; Minister of Public Health and Social Affairs Dec. 65-Dec. 67; mem. Bureau Nat. de l'Union pour le Renouveau du Dahomey (U.R.D.); Minister of Foreign Affairs 68-69, 70-71; Amb. to France, also accred. to U.K., Italy and Spain 71-73.
c/o Ministry of Foreign Affairs, Cotonou, Benin.

Baddiley, James, M.SC., PH.D., D.SC., F.R.S.E., F.R.S.; British professor of chemistry; b. 15 May 1918, Manchester; s. of the late James Baddiley; m. Hazel M. Townsend 1944; one s.; ed. Manchester Grammar School and Univ. of Manchester.
ICI Fellow, Univ. of Cambridge 44-49; Fellow, Swedish Medical Research Council, Stockholm 47-49; mem. of staff Dept. of Biochemistry, Lister Inst., London 49-54; Prof. of Organic Chem., Univ. of Durham (Newcastle Div.) 55; Head of the School of Chem. and Hon. Dir. Microbiological Chemistry Research Lab., Univ. of Newcastle upon Tyne 68-; Hon. mem. American Soc. of Biological Chemists; Rockefeller Fellow 54; Tilden Lecturer, Chemical Soc. 59, Karl Folkers Lecturer, Univ. of Illinois 62, Leeuwenhoek Lecturer, Royal Soc. 67; Meldola Medal, Royal Inst. of Chem. 47, Corday-Morgan Medal and Prize, Chem. Soc. 52, Davy Medal, Royal Soc. 74.
Leisure interests: music, photography.
Publs. Numerous publications in bio-chem. and microbiological chem.
Microbiological Chemistry Research Laboratory, University of Newcastle upon Tyne, Newcastle upon Tyne, NE1 7RU; Home: 26 Woolsington Park South, Woolsington, Newcastle upon Tyne, NE13 8BJ, England. Telephone: Newcastle 28511, Ext. 3071 (Office); Newcastle 860229 (Home).

Baden-Powell, Olave, Lady (Olave St. Clair), G.B.E.; British Chief Guide; b. 22 Feb. 1889; ed. privately.
Chief Guide of the British Commonwealth 17, World Chief Guide 30-; widow of Lord Baden-Powell, the founder of the Boy Scout and Girl Guide Movements; Grand Cross of the British Empire, Order of the Phoenix of Greece, Order of White Rose of Finland, decorations from Haiti, Peru and Panama, Order of the Sacred Treasure of Japan, Order of the Cedars of Lebanon, Order of the Oak of Luxembourg.
Publs. *Baden-Powell* 64, *Window on my Heart* (autobiog., with Mary Drewery) 73.
c/o The General Secretary, The Girl Guide Association, 17-19 Buckingham Palace Road, London, SW1W 0PT, England.

Badger, Richard McLean, PH.D.; American emeritus professor of chemistry; b. 4 May 1896, Elgin, Ill.; s. of Joseph Stillman Badger and Carrie Mable Hewitt; m Virginia Alice Sherman; one s. one d.; ed. Northwestern University and Calif. Inst. of Technology.
Assistant Prof., Calif. Inst. of Technology 29-38, Assoc. Prof. 38-45, Prof. 45-66, Prof. Emeritus 66-; Lecturer, Univ. of Calif. (Berkeley) 31; mem. Nat. Acad. of Sciences; Rockefeller Int. Research Fellow 28, 29; Guggenheim Fellow 60-61; Fellow, American Acad. of Arts and Sciences; Award for Excellence in Coll. Chem. Teaching, Manufacturing Chemists' Asscn. 61.

Leisure interests: gardening, making of jewellery.
Publs. 85 articles, mainly on spectra of molecules, in scientific journals.
1963 New York Drive, Attadena, Calif. 91001, U.S.A. Telephone: 213-797-4945 (Home).

Badillo, Herman, LL.B., C.P.A.; American politician, lawyer and accountant; b. 21 Aug. 1929, Caguas, Puerto Rico; s. of Francisco and Carmen (Rivera) Badillo; m. 2nd Irma (Deutsch) Liebling 1961; three c.; ed. Haaren High School, New York, City Coll., New York and Brooklyn Law School.
Accountant, Ferro, Berdon & Co. (certified public accountants) 51-55; admitted to New York Bar 55; practised law as partner in firm Permut & Badillo, New York 55-62; Commr. Dept. of Relocation, New York City 62-65; Pres. Borough of Bronx 65-70; partner, Stroock & Stroock & Lavan (Wall Street law firm) 70; mem. U.S. House of Reps. 72-; mem. Cttee. on Educ. and Labour; Adjunct Prof. Graduate School of Urban Educ., Fordham University; Hon. LL.D. (City College, New York); Democrat.
Publ. *A Bill of No Rights: Attica and the American Prison System.*
Longworth House Office Building, Washington, D.C. 20515; Home: 405 West 259th Street, Bronx, N.Y. 10471, U.S.A.

Badings, Henk, DR.ENG.; Netherlands composer; b. 17 Jan. 1907, Bandoeng, Indonesia (fmrly. Dutch East Indies); m. Jeannette Tukke 1946; one d.; ed. Tech. Univ., Delft.
Asst. in Palaeontology, Tech. Univ., Delft 31; first symphony performed in Amsterdam 30; Prof. of Composition, Rotterdam Conservatoire 34-37; Co.-Dir. Musical Lyceum, Amsterdam 37-41; Dir. State Conservatoire, The Hague 41-45; musical composition 45-; Dir. Electronic Music Studio, Univ. of Utrecht 61-64, Prof. of acoustics and information 64-; Prof. of Musical Composition, Musikhochschule, Stuttgart 62-72; Paganini Prize 53, Italia Prize 54, Marzotto Prize 64, Rai-Italia Prize 71, Sweelink Prize 72; mem. Royal Flemish Acad. of Art; Hon. Citizen of New Martinsville, W. Virginia, U.S.A.
Leisure interests: geology, plastic arts, literature, travelling, philately.
Compositions: sixteen symphonies, chamber music, choral works, operas, etc., as well as electronic music. Huize Hugten, Maarheeze, Netherlands. Telephone: 04957-327.

Badura-Skoda, Paul; Austrian pianist; b. 6 Oct. 1927; m. Eva Badura-Skoda; ed. Realgymnasium courses in conducting and piano, Konservatorium der Stadt Wien, and Edwin Fischer's Master Class in Lucerne.
Regular concerts since 48; tours all over the world as soloist and with leading orchestras; conductor of chamber orchestra 60-; yearly master classes fmrly. in Edinburgh, Salzburg and Vienna Festival 58-63; artist in residence, Univ. of Wisconsin, master classes in Madison, Wisconsin 66-71; First Prize Austrian Music Competition 47; recorded over 100 L.P. records including complete Beethoven and Schubert sonatas.
Compositions: *A Mass in D, Cadenzas to Piano and Violin Concertos by Mozart and Haydn.*
Publ. Co-author *Interpreting Mozart on the Keyboard* (with Eva Badura-Skoda), *Die Klaviersonaten von Beethoven* (with Jörg Demus) 70; Editions of Schubert, Mozart, Chopin; numerous articles.
Zuckerkandlgasse 14, Vienna 1190, Austria.

Baerdemaeker, Adolphe de, D. EN D.; Belgian Foreign Office official; b. 28 Oct. 1920, Brussels; m. Anne d'Udekem D'Acoz 1954; one s. one d.; ed. Univ. Catholique de Louvain.
Economic Surveys Branch, Ministry of Econ. Affairs 43; Attaché, Econ. and Financial Affairs, Belgian Embassy, London 45; Deputy Sec.-Gen. Brussels

Treaty Org., London 50; Deputy Sec. NATO Council, London, and Sec. of Econ. and Financial Bureau, Paris 51-52; Counsellor, Private Office of Minister of Econ. Affairs 52-54; Counsellor, Econ. Questions, Vice-Chair. OEEC Econ. Cttee., Belgian Dels. to NATO and OEEC, Paris 54-58; Dir., Gen. Directorate of External Relations, EEC 58; Perm. EEC Del. to OECD 66-.
Leisure interest: golf.
Office: 61 rue des Belles Feuilles, Paris 16e; Home: 129 avenue Malakoff, Paris 16e, France.
Telephone: 553-5326 (Office).

Baev, Alexandr Alexandrovich, D.SC.; Soviet biologist; b. 10 Jan. 1904, Chita; ed. Kazan State Univ.
Physician 27-30; Lecturer, Kazan Medical Inst. 30-35; Senior Research Worker, Bakh Inst. of Biochem., U.S.S.R. Acad. of Sciences 35-59; Head of Laboratory, Inst. of Molecular Biology 59-; C.P.S.U. 64-; corresp. mem. U.S.S.R. Acad. of Sciences 68-70, mem. 70-.
Publs. works on primary structure of nucleic acids and molecular genetics.
Institute of Molecular Biology, 32 Ulitsa Vavilova, Moscow, U.S.S.R.

Baez, Joan; American folk singer; b. 1941, Staten Island, N.Y.; d. of Albert V. and Joan (Bridge) Baez; m. David Harris 1968 (divorced 1973); one s.; ed. School of Fine and Applied Arts, Boston Univ.
Began career as singer in coffee houses, appeared at Ballad Room, Club 47 58-68, Gate of Horn, Chicago 58, Newport, R.I., Folk Festival 59-69, Town Hall and Carnegie Hall, New York 62, 67, 68; gave concerts in black colls. in southern U.S.A. 63-; toured Europe 70, 71, 72, U.S.A. 70, 71, 72, 73, Democratic Repub. of Viet-Nam 72; recordings with Vanguard Records 60-72, A & M Record Co. 72-; many TV appearances; began refusing payment of war taxes 64; detained for civil disobedience opposing conscription 67; speaking tour of U.S.A. and Canada for draft resistance 67-68; Founder, Vice-Pres. Inst. for Study of Non-Violence 65.
Publs. *Daybreak* 68, *Coming Out* (with David Harris) 71.
Chandos Productions, P.O. Box 1026, Menlo Park, Calif. 94025; Home: Los Altos, Calif. 94022, U.S.A.
Telephone: (415) 328-0266 (Office).

Báez-Camargo, Gonzalo; Mexican teacher; b. 13 Nov. 1899, Oaxaca; s. of Guillermo Camargo and Rosenda González Angulo; m. Urania Báez Rascón 1925; four s. one d.; ed. Methodist Mexican Inst., Union Evangelical Seminary, Mexico, and Nat. Univ., Mexico.
Vice-President Methodist Mexican Inst., Puebla 27; Exec. Sec. and Gen. Sec. on Christian Education, Evangelical Council of Mexico 29-41; Manager Union Publishing House 31-46; Prof. Christian Literature and Journalism 41-61, Old Testament 62, Hebrew 63-71, Union Evangelical Seminary; Sec. Cttee. on Literature, Cttee. on Co-operation in Latin America 46-60; Prof. Modern Ideologies, Presbyterian Seminary 63; Prof. Spanish, Iberoamerican Univ. 64-68; Prof. Old Testament, Baptist Seminary 64; Prof. Old Testament, Lutheran Seminary 66; Prof. of Hebrew, Theological Community 68-71; Prof. of Journalism, Carlos Septien School of Journalism 71; mem. Editorial Cttee., New Spanish Version of the Bible 60-73; Exegetical Adviser, Popular Version of the Bible 73-.
Leisure interests: music, photography.
Publs. *Hacia la Renovación Religiosa en Hispano-américa* 30, *Principios y Método de la Educación Cristiana* 32, *Religion in the Republic of Mexico* (co-author) 35, *Baltasar Gracián y Morales* 44, *El Artista y Otros Poemas* 46, *Biografía de un templo* 53, 74, *Tres poemas* 51, *La Nota Evangélica en la Poesía Hispanoamericana* 60, *Protestantes enjuiciados por la Inquisición en Iberoamérica* 60, *El Comunismo, el cristianismo, y los cristianos* 60, *Genio y espíritu del metodismo wesleyano* 62, *El "don de lenguas" en el Nuevo Testamento* 72, *La*

Cruz, símbolo cristiano universal 73, *Breve historia del texto bíblico* 75; under pseudonym of "Pedro Gringoire": *La Superstición de la Sangre "Aria"* 42, *Martin Niemoeller* 38, *Un Prefacio a la Educación para la Libertad* 46, *Las manos de Cristo* 50, *Los manuscritos de Qumrán* 57, *El materialismo zoológico* 63, *El doctor Mora, impulsor de la causa bíblica en México* 63, *Galería de retratos literarios* 67, *Pérate que trille y otros poemas populares* 70, *Oda clásica a la primavera* 71, *Una exhibición de ignorancia y male fe* 71, *U.R.S.S.: cárcel del pensamiento* 71, *Para que el mundo crea* 71, *Voces perdurables de nuestro tiempo* 71.
Ave. Nevado 133, México 13, D.F., Mexico.
Telephone: 539-54-40.

Baffi, Paolo; Italian banker; b. 5 Aug. 1911, Broni, Pavia; s. of Giovanni and Giuseppina Lolla; ed. Bocconi Univ. of Milan.
Joined Banca d'Italia 36, Research Dept. 36-56, Econ. Adviser 56-60, Gen. Man. 60-75, Gov. 75-; Econ. Adviser, BIS 56-60, mem. Board of Dirs. 75-; Visiting Prof. Cornell Univ. 59-60; Prof. Monetary History and Policy, Rome Univ.; Chair. Ufficio Italiano dei Cambi 75-; Gov. for Italy, IBRD (World Bank) 75-; mem. Cttee. of Central Bank Govs., EEC 75-; mem. Board of Dirs. Consiglio Nazionale delle Ricerche 75-; Cavaliere di Gran Croce; mem. Accad. Naz. dei Lincei; Chevalier, Légion d'Honneur (France).
Publs. *The Dollar and Gold* 53, *Monetary Developments in Italy from the War Economy to Limited Convertibility 1935-1958* 58, *Problems of European Economic Integration* 60, *Monetary Stability and Economic Development in Italy 1946-1960* 61, *Studi sulla Moneta* 65, *The Inflation Problem in Europe* 66, *Western European Inflation and the Reserve Currencies* 68, *Les mouvements des salaires et de la balance des paiments dans les récentes expériences italienne et internationale* 69, *Nuovi studi sulla Moneta* 73, *Saving in Italy today* 74, *Italy's Narrow Path* 75.
Banca d'Italia, Via Nazionale 91, 00184 Rome, Italy.
Telephone: 4672.

Bafia, Jerzy; Polish judge; b. 5 May 1926, Płociczno, Suwalki District; s. of Franciszek and Maria Bafia; m. Stanisława Bafia 1950; one s.; ed. Jagellonian Univ., Cracow.
Judge, District Court of Justice, then Voivodship Court of Justice 50-53; with Supreme Court of Justice 53-54; with Ministry of Justice 54-58, Dir. Dept. of Codification 58-69; Doctor of Legal Sciences, Warsaw Univ. 61-64, Asst. Prof. 64-70, Prof. Extraordinary 70-; Asst. Prof. Silesian Univ. 68-69; Head Chancellery, Seym (Parl.) 69-72; First Chief Justice of Supreme Court Jan. 72-; Deputy to Seym 72-; Sec.-Gen. Polish Lawyers' Asscn. 63-72, mem. Codifying Cttee., Sec. of Cttee. Presidium 64-; Vice-Pres. Int. Union of Lawyers (Democrats) 70-; mem. Polish United Workers' Party; Central Comm. of Party Control Dec. 75-; Minister of Justice 76-; Knight Cross Order of Polonia Restituta, and other decorations.
Ulica Sułkowicka 6 m. 3, 00-396 Warsaw, Poland.
Telephone: 41-15-82.

Bafile, Monsignor Corrado; Vatican diplomatist; b. 1903; ed. State Univ., Rome, and Lateran Univ., Rome.
Ordained priest 36; Vatican Secretariat of State 39-; Privy Chamberlain to Pope John XXIII 58-60; Papal Nuncio to Germany 60-; Titula Archbishop of Antiochia in Pisidia 60-.
Papal Nunciature, 53 Bonn-Bad Godesberg, Turmstrasse 29, Federal Republic of Germany.
Telephone: 02221/376901.

Baggio, H.E. Cardinal Sebastiano; Vatican ecclesiastic; b. 16 May 1913, Rosà, Italy; s. of Giovanni Battista and Pierina Baggio; ed. Seminario Vescovile di Vicenza, Pontificia Università Gregoriana, Pontificia Accademia

Ecclesiastica and Scuola di Paleografia e Biblioteconomia at the Vatican library.
Ordained priest 35; Sec. Nunciatures in El Salvador, Bolivia, Venezuela 38-46; with Secr. of State 46-48; Chargé d'Affaires, Colombia 48-50; Sacra Congregazione Concistoriale 50-53; Titular Archbishop of Ephesus 53-; Apostolic Nuncio, Chile 53-59; Apostolic Del., Canada 59-64; Apostolic Nuncio, Brazil 64-69; cr. Cardinal April 69; Archbishop of Cagliari 69-73; Prefect, Sacred Congregation for the Bishops 73-; orders from Bolivia, Brazil, Chile, Colombia, Ecuador, Malta and Venezuela.
Piazza Pio XII, 10 Rome, Italy.
Telephone: 6984217.

Bagramian, Marshal Ivan Kristoforovich; Soviet army officer and politician; b. 2 Dec. 1897, Kirovoabad, Armenia; ed. Frunze Military Acad., and General Staff Acad., Soviet Army.
Member, C.P.S.U. 41-; South West and Western Fronts 41-43; Commdr. First Baltic Front 43-45; Military Commdr. Baltic Military Area 45-54; Chief Insp. U.S.S.R. Ministry of Defence 55-56; Marshal of Soviet Union 55-; Chief, Rear Admin. and Supply Services of Soviet Army; Deputy Minister of Defence of U.S.S.R. 58-68; Inspector-Gen. Ministry of Defence 68-; Head of Gen. Staff, Mil. Acad. 56-58; Alternate mem. Central Cttee. of C.P.S.U. 52-61, mem. 61-; mem. Youth Affairs Comm., Soviet of Nationalities 74-; Deputy to U.S.S.R. Supreme Soviet 46-; Hero of Soviet Union; Order of Lenin (five times), Order of Suvorov (twice), Order of Kutuzov, Order of Red Banner (three times), Order of October Revolution, etc.
Publs. include: *Fighting Traditions of the Soviet Armed Forces, Warrior City on the Dnieper* 65.
Ministry of Defence, Naberezhnaya M. Thoreza 34, Moscow, U.S.S.R.

Bagrit, Sir Leon, Kt., C.I.E.E., F.R.S.A.; British business executive; b. 13 March 1902; m. Stella Feldman 1926; two d.; ed. St. Olave's School, London, and London Univ.
Deputy Chair. Elliot-Automation Ltd. 57-62, Chair. 63-; fmr. Deputy Chair. The English Electric Co. Ltd.; mem. Council of Dept. for Scientific and Industrial Research 63-65, Minister's Advisory Council on Technology (Ministry of Technology); Dir. Electronic Trust Ltd. 63-, Technology Investments Ltd. 63-, Royal Opera House, Covent Garden 62-70; Founder and Chair. Friends of Covent Garden 62-69; mem. of Council, Royal Coll. of Art 60-63; mem. Advisory Council, Science Museum, Victoria and Albert Museum; mem. Royal Inst.; B.B.C. Reith Lecturer 64; Gold Medal, Royal Soc. of Arts 65; Ambassador Award 65; Hon. D.Sc. (Reading), Hon. Dr. (Surrey).
Publ. *The Age of Automation.*
Upper Terrace House, Hampstead, London, N.W.3, England.

Baguidy, Fern D.; Haitian lawyer and diplomatist; b. 17 June 1920, Port-au-Prince; s. of Charles Damien Baguidy and Theolene Lherisson; m. Lucille Edith Young 1959; two s. two d.; ed. Lycée Nord Alexis, Jérémie, and Lycée Alexandre Pétion, Law School, and Inst. of Ethnology, Port-au-Prince.
Assistant Chief of Immigration and Emigration Service 47-51; Pan-American World Airways 51-57; First Sec. Haitian Del. to Organization of American States (OAS) 57-58, Minister-Counsellor 58-59; Minister-Counsellor, Embassy of Haiti in United States 60, 61-62; Chargé d'Affaires of Haiti to OAS 61, Amb. to OAS 62-, Pres. Perm. Council, OAS; mem. Int. Platform Asscn.; del. of Haiti to numerous int. confs.; Grand Cross Nat. Order of Honour and Merit of Haiti; Inter-American Defense Coll. Award 73.
Leisure interests: writing, football, basket ball.

Representation of Haiti at Organization of American States, 4400 Seventeenth Street, N.W., Washington, D.C., U.S.A.

Bahadur K. C., Kaisher; Nepalese educationist and diplomatist; b. 28 Jan. 1907, Kathmandu; s. of Maj. Dan Bahadur and Kumari Khattri Chettri; m. Home Kumari 1923; one s. one d.; ed. St. Paul's Mission School, St. Xavier's Coll., Calcutta, and Univ. Coll., Calcutta.
Translator and Lecturer, Tri-Chandra Coll. 30-32; research in MS., inscriptions and sculpture, Nepal 32-45; Nepalese Resident in Tibet 46-50; Sec. Ministry of Educ., Health and Local Self Govt. 56-61; Del. to UN 56-57, UNESCO 60; Amb. to People's Repub. of China, concurrently to Mongolian People's Repub. and Burma 61-65, also to Repub. of Indonesia and Kingdom of Laos 62-65; Chair. Nepal Public Service Comm. 66-70; Chief Editor, Civil Service Journal of Nepal; awarded Italian Order of Merit 53; Order of the Gurkhas (1st Class) of King Mahendra 61.
Publs. *Countries of the World* 35, *Ancient and Modern Nepal* 53, *Materials for the Study of Nepalese History and Culture* 58, *Judicial Customs of Nepal, Part I* 58 (revised versions of Parts I and II 65), *Eroticism in Nepalese Art* 60, *Introduction to Kathmandu and Patan* 61, *Universal Value of Nepalese Aesthetics, Parts I and II* 61-62, transl. of *Kirataruniye, Nepal and her Neighbours* 74.
636 Kamal Pokhari, Katmandu, Nepal.
Telephone: 11696.

Bahadur, Raj, B.SC., M.A., LL.B.; Indian lawyer and politician; b. 21 Aug. 1912; s. of Sunder Lal; m. Vidyawati Srivastava 1936; four s. one d.; ed. Maharaja's Coll., Jaipur, Agra Coll. and St. John's Coll., Agra.
Member Cen. Advisory Cttee. Bharatpur State 39-42, Municipal Comm. 41-42; resigned from these posts in connection with "Quit India" Movement; mem. Rep. Assembly 43; imprisoned for participation in freedom struggle 45 and 47; Sec. Assembly Praja Parishad Party 43-48, Gen. Sec. Matsya Union Congress Cttee. 48-49; Pres. Bharatpur Bar Asscn. 48-51; elected to Constituent Assembly of India 48-50; mem. Union Parl. 50-67, 71-; Sec. Congress Party in Parl. 50-52; Dept. Minister, later Minister of State for Communications 51-56; led Indian Del. to 10th Session of Int. Civil Aviation Org., Caracas; Minister of Communications Dec. 56-April 57; Minister of State for Transport and Communications 57-62; Minister of State for Transport 62-63, Minister of Transport 63-65, and of Civil Aviation 65; Minister of Information and Broadcasting 66-67; Advocate, Supreme Court of India 67-Dec. 67; Amb. to Nepal 68-71; Minister of Parl. Affairs, Shipping and Transport 71-73, of Communications 73-Jan. 74, of Tourism and Civil Aviation 73-; mem. Rajasthan P.C.C. and All-India Congress Cttee.; Congress Party.
Leisure interest: collecting books.
Ministry of Tourism and Civil Aviation, New Delhi; Home: Basan Gate, Bharatpur, Rajasthan, India.

Bahnini, Hadj M'Hammed, L. EN D., L. ÈS L.; Moroccan politician; b. 1914, Fez; ed. Lycée Gouraud (now "Lycée Hassan II"), Rabat.
Secretary, Royal Palace; Magistrate, Haut Tribunal Chérifien; Instructor, Collège Impérial and Private Tutor to H.R.H. Crown Prince Moulay El Hassan, Prince Moulay Abdallah, Princess Lalla Aïcha and Princess Lalla Malika; Dir. of the Imperial Cabinet 50-51; Del. Judge, Meknès 51; exiled Dec. 52-July 54; Sec.-Gen. of the Cabinet 55-72; Minister of Justice 58-60; Minister of Admin. Affairs 65-70; Minister of Nat. Defence 70-71; Minister of Justice, Sec.-Gen. of Govt. 71-72, also Deputy Prime Minister April-Nov. 72; Minister of State for Culture Nov. 72-.
Ministry of Culture, Rabat, Morocco.

Bahr, Egon; German government official; b. 18 March 1922, Treffurt; *m.* Dorothea Bahr 1945; one *s.* one *d.* Journalist 45-; Chief Commentator RIAS (Rundfunk im amerikanischen Sektor Berlins) 50-60; Dir. Press and Information Office of Berlin 60-66; promoted to rank of Amb. in diplomatic service 67; took part in negotiations for establishment of trade representation in Prague 67; Dir. of Planning Staff, Diplomatic Service 67-68; Ministerial Dir. 68-69; State Sec., Bundeskanzleramt and Plenipotentiary of the Federal Govt. in Berlin Oct. 69-72; Fed. Minister without Portfolio attached to the Fed. Chancellor's Office 72-74, for Overseas Devt. Aid (Economic Co-operation) July 74-. Friedrich-Ebert-Allee 114, 53 Bonn 1, Federal Republic of Germany.

Bahramy, Bahram, PH.D.; Iranian diplomatist; b. 1924, Tehran; *s.* of Fazlullah Bahramy; *m.* Solange Bahramy 1961; one *d.*; ed. Iran and Switzerland. Ministry of Econ. 47; Foreign Service 54-; Dir. of Cultural Admin., then of Second Political Admin.; Dir.-Gen. of Secretariat-Gen. of Ministry of Foreign Affairs, later of Protocol Admin.; Counsellor, Embassy in London; Minister Counsellor, Berne; mem. Perm. Mission to UN, Econ. Congress of Muslim States; Under-Sec. Ministry of Foreign Affairs; Amb. to Egypt 76-. Leisure interests: sports, reading. 11 Okbah Street, Dokki, Cairo, Egypt. Telephone: 987288.

Bahyl, Pavol, ING.; Czechoslovak politician; b. 12 April 1928, Badín, Banská Bystrica; ed. Technical Coll., Brno. Designer, Považské Eng. Works 48-49; Technologist, Turčianské Eng. Works 50-59, Deputy Gen. Man. 60-63; Gen. Man. Podpolianské Eng. Works 63-69; Deputy Minister-Chair. Fed. Cttee. for Industry 69, Vice-Chair. 71; First Deputy Minister for Metallurgy and Eng. of C.S.S.R. 71-73; Minister Vice-Chair. Fed. State Planning Comm. 73; Fed. Minister of Gen. Engineering Dec. 73-; Vice-Chair. Czechoslovak del., Intergovt. Czechoslovak-Soviet Comm. for Econ. and Scientific-Technical Co-operation; Distinction for Outstanding Labour 66. Ministry of General Engineering, Prague, Czechoslovakia.

Baibakov, Nikolai Konstantinovich; Soviet politician; b. 1911; ed. Azerbaijan Industrial Inst. Oil-mining engineer in Azerbaijan oil field 32-37; Chief Engineer and Manager of Leninneft Oil Trust in Baku 37; Dir. Vostokneft in Soviet East 38-39; Dir. Central Management Board for oil extraction in Eastern districts of the People's Commissariat of Oil Industry 39-40; Deputy People's Commissar of the Oil Industry of U.S.S.R. 40-44; Minister of Oil Industry of U.S.S.R. 44-45; Deputy to U.S.S.R. Supreme Soviet 46-50, 54-62, 66-; Chair. of U.S.S.R. State Planning Cttee. 55-57, 65-; first Deputy Chair. of Council of Ministers of R.S.F.S.R. and Chair. of State Planning Comm. of R.S.F.S.R. 57; Vice-Chair. U.S.S.R. Council of Ministers 66-; Chair. State Cttee. of the Chemical and Oil Industry 63-64; Chair. State Cttee. of Oil Production Industry 64-65; mem. Central Cttee. of C.P.S.U. 52-61, 66-; awarded four Orders of Lenin, two Orders of Red Banner of Labour, Lenin Prize, and medals. State Planning Committee, 4 1st Dyakovsky pereulok, Moscow, U.S.S.R.

Bailar, Benjamin Franklin, B.A., M.B.A.; American government official; b. 21 April 1934, Champaign, Ill.; *s.* of Dr. John C. Bailar, Jr.; *m.* Anne Tveit 1958; one *s.* one *d.*; ed. Univ. of Colorado and Harvard Graduate School of Business Admin. Continental Oil Co. 59-62; American Can Co. 62-72, Vice-Pres. 67-72; Senior Asst. Postmaster-Gen. U.S. Postal Service 72-74, Deputy Postmaster-Gen. 74-75, Postmaster-Gen. Feb. 75-. U.S. Postal Service, 475 L'Enfant Plaza West, S.W., Washington, D.C. 20260; Home: 6311 Friendship Court, Bethesda, Md. 20034, U.S.A. Telephone: (202) 245-5225 (Office).

Bailey, Sir Harold Walter, Kt., D.PHIL., M.A., F.B.A.; British oriental scholar; b. 16 Dec. 1899, Devizes, Wilts.; *s.* of Frederick C. Bailey and Emma J. Reichart; ed. Univ. of West Australia and Oxford Univ. Lecturer in Iranian Studies, School of Oriental Studies, London Univ. 29-36; Prof. of Sanskrit, Cambridge Univ. 36-67, Emeritus Prof. 67-; Corresp. mem. Danish Acad. 46, Norwegian Acad. 47, Acad. of History and Antiquities, Sweden; mem. Inst. de France (Acad. des Inscriptions et Belles-lettres) 68; Hon. Fellow, School of Oriental and African Studies, London 63; Fellow, Australian Acad. of the Humanities 70; Hon. D.Litt. (Univ. of W. Australia, Australian Nat. Univ.). Publs. *Zoroastrian Problems in the Ninth Century Books* 43, *Khotanese Texts I-VI* 45-68, *Khotanese Buddhist Texts* 51, *Saka Documents I-IV* 60-67, *Saka Documents Text Volume* 68; many articles in learned periodicals. Queens' College, Cambridge, England.

Bailly, Gen. Paul; French air force officer; b. 2 Sept. 1903; ed. Ecole Spéciale de St. Cyr. Commissioned 24, pilot 26, posted to the Levant; test pilot 29-31; staff course 35-37; commanded a reconnaissance group 40; joined French forces in U.K. 42; commanded a bomber group attached to the R.A.F. 43-45; A.O.C. French Air Forces in Morocco and Air Training in North Africa 45-47; Deputy Chief of Staff 47-49; in command of Air Defence 49-53; Chief of Staff to C.-in-C. Central Europe 53-55, of the French Air Force 55-58, Inspector-Gen. 58-59; mem. management Soc. Lorraine-Escaut 61-66; Grand Officier Légion d'Honneur, Croix de Guerre and other French and foreign decorations. 25 rue Le Primatrice, 77 Fontainebleau, France.

Bainbridge, Kenneth Tompkins, S.M., M.A., PH.D.; American physicist; b. 27 July 1904, Coopers-town, N.Y.; *s.* of William Warin and Mae Tompkins Bainbridge; *m.* 1st Margaret Pitkin 1931 (died 1967), one *s.* two *d.*; *m.* 2nd Helen Brinkley King 1969; ed. Mass. Inst. of Technology and Princeton Univ. Nat. Research Council Fellow 29-31; Bartol Research Foundation Fellow 31-33, Guggenheim Memorial Foundation Fellow 33-34; Asst. Prof. Harvard Univ. 34-38, Assoc. Prof. 38-46, Prof. of Physics 46, Chair. Dept. of Physics 53-56; George Vasmer Leverett Prof. of Physics, Harvard 61-74, Emer. Prof. 75; Div. Leader, Nat. Defense Research Cttee., Radiation Laboratory 40-43; Group and Division Leader, Los Alamos Laboratory 43-46; awarded Levy Medal, Franklin Inst. 33; elected American Acad. Arts and Sciences 38, Nat. Acad. Sciences 46; dir. first atomic bomb "Trinity" test Feb.-Sept. 45; awarded Presidential Certificate of Merit for war research work on radar 48; Trustee Assoc. Univs. Inc. 58-59. Leisure interests: painting, photography, travel. Lyman Laboratory, Harvard University, Cambridge, Mass. 02138, U.S.A. Telephone: 617-495-2868.

Bainton, Roland Herbert; American educationist; b. 1894, England; *s.* of James Bainton and Charlotte Blackham; *m.* Ruth Woodruff 1921; two *s.* three *d.*; ed. Whitman Coll. and Yale Univ. Emigrated to U.S.A. 02; Instructor in Church History, Yale Univ. 20-23, Asst. Prof. 23-32, Assoc. Prof. 32-36, Titus Street Prof. of Ecclesiastical History 36-62, Emer. 62-. Leisure interest: watercolour painting. Publs. include *Here I Stand* (A Life of Martin Luther)

50, *The Travail of Religious Liberty* 51, *The Reformation of the Sixteenth Century* 52, *Hunted Heretic: A Study of Michael Servetus* 53, *The Age of the Reformation* 56, *What Christianity Says about Sex, Love and Marriage* 57, *Yale and The Ministry* 57, *Pilgrim Parson, The Life of James Herbert Bainton* 58, *Christian Attitudes to War and Peace* 60, *Collected Papers* (3 vols.) 62, 63, 64, *Horizon History of Christianity* 64, *Erasmus of Christendom* 68, *Women of the Reformation* 2 vols., 71, 73, *Behold the Christ* (art) 74, and numerous paperbacks.
363 St. Ronan Street, New Haven, Conn. 06511, U.S.A.
Telephone: 203-624-7568, 203-426-9587.

Baird, Joseph Edward; American banker and company executive; b. 18 March 1934, Columbus, Ohio; *s.* of Judge Edward Graham Baird and Alice Hoover Baird; *m.* Anne Marie Baird 1958; one *s.* two *d.*; ed. Yale Univ.
Chase Manhattan Bank 59-66; Smith, Barney & Co. Inc. 66-67; Man. Dir., Chief Exec. Western American Bank (Europe) Ltd., London 68-73; Pres., Chief Operating Officer Occidental Petroleum Corpn. 73-.
Leisure interest: sailing.
Occidental Petroleum Corporation, 10889 Wilshire Boulevard, Suite 1500, Los Angeles, Calif. 90024, U.S.A.
Telephone: (213) 879-1700.

Baird, Tadeusz; Polish composer; b. 26 July 1928, Grodzisk, Mazuria; *s.* of Edward and Maria Baird.
Studied in State High School of Music, Warsaw; awarded State Prize for First Symphony 51, Olympics Prize for Second Piano Sonatina 52, City of Cologne Music Prize 63, State Prize 64, 70, Prize of the Union of Polish Composers 65, three First Prizes, Tribune Int. des Compositeurs, UNESCO, Paris, for *Four Essays, Variations without Theme,* and *Four Dialogues* 59, 63, 66, Sergius Koussevitzky Prize, U.S.A. 68, City of Warsaw Music Prize 70, Alfred Jurzykowski Foundation Award, New York 71, Arthur Honegger Music Award 74; numerous decorations.
Compositions include: Sinfonietta 49, Symphonies 50, 52, Piano Concerto 49, *Colas Breugnon* (suite for string orchestra and flute) 51, Concerto for orchestra 53, *Lyric Suite* (text by J. Tuwim) 53, Cassazione for orchestra 56, *Four Love Sonnets to Words by William Shakespeare* for baritone and chamber orchestra, *Four Essays for Orchestra* 57, *Divertimento* (for four wind instruments) 57, String Quartet 58 *Espressioni Varianti* (for violin and orchestra) 59, *Egzorta* (for speaker, choir and orchestra) 60, *Erotiques* (for soprano and orchestra) 61, *Study* (for vocal orchestra, percussion and piano) 61, *Variations without theme* (for orchestra) 62, *Epiphany Music* (for orchestra) 63, *Four Dialogues for Oboe and Chamber Orchestra* 64, *Tomorrow* (one-act opera after Conrad), *Four Songs* (for mezzosoprano and chamber orchestra) 66, *Four Novelletes* (for chamber orchestra) 67, *Five Songs* (for mezzosoprano and 16 players) 68, *Simfonia breve* 68, Third Symphony 69, *Goethe-Briefe* (cantata for baritone, mixed choir and orchestra) 70, *Play* (for string quartet) 71, *Psychodrama* (for orchestra) 72, Concerto for Oboe and Orchestra 73, *Elegeia* (for orchestra) 73, *Concerto for Viola and Orchestra* 75; chamber pieces, works for flute, oboe, piano, clarinet and bassoon, choral and solo songs, incidental music for stage and films.
Leisure interests: theatre, cars.
03-904 Warsaw, Lipska 11m.4; and c/o Union of Polish Composers, Rynek Starego Miasta 27, Warsaw, Poland.
Telephone: 17-43-12.

Bakala, Adrien; Congolese (Brazzaville) diplomatist; b. 1935, Mouyondzi; *s.* of Douma and Zoumba Bakala; *m.* 1962; one *d.* one *s.*; ed. Univ. de Caen and Inst. des Hautes Etudes d'Outre-Mer, Paris.
Director of Admin., Social and Cultural Affairs, Ministry of Foreign Affairs of Congo 65, Sec.-Gen., Ministry of Foreign Affairs 65-68, Dir. Dept. of Studies

and Documentation 70-71; Deputy Head of Congolese Del. to UN Gen. Assembly 66, Head 67-68; Perm. Rep. to UN 69-70; Prof., Ecole Nationale d'Administration 70; Amb. to Egypt 71-73, to Italy 73-75.
c/o Ministry of Foreign Affairs, Brazzaville, People's Republic of the Congo.

Bakarić, Vladimir, LL.D.; Yugoslav politician; b. 8 March 1912, Zagreb; *s.* of Stjepan and Zora Bakarić; *m.* Marija Bakarić; one *s.* two *d.*
Helped organize uprising in Croatia 41; mem. of Presidium of Anti-Fascist Council for Yugoslav Nat. Liberation; Sec. of the Central Cttee. of the League of Communists of Croatia 44-66, Pres. Cen. Cttee. 66-69; Pres. Govt. of the Nat. Repub. of Croatia, later Pres. of the Exec. Council 45-53; Pres. Assembly of the Nat. Repub. of Croatia 53; mem. of Presidency of the Socialist Fed. Repub. of Yugoslavia 74; Vice-Pres. of Yugoslavia 75-76; mem. Fed. Exec. Council; mem. Exec. Bureau, Presidium of League of Communists of Yugoslavia; mem. Yugoslav Acad. of Sciences and Arts; Orders of Nat. Hero, Partisan Star (1st Class), Brotherhood and Unity (1st Class), Bravery Partisan Commemoration Medal 41.
Zagreb, Šetalište Karla Marxa 2, Yugoslavia.
Telephone: 512-719.

Bakema, Jacob B.; Netherlands architect; b. 8 March 1914, Groningen; *s.* of Kiert Bakema and Tietsia Dijkhuis; *m.* S. Th. Van Borssum Waalkes 1939; two *s.* one *d.*; ed. Technical High School, Groningen, Acad. of Architecture, Amsterdam, and Technical Univ., Delft.
Worked in architectural and planning offices of van Eesteren 37, van Tijen 40-43, Rotterdam Municipal Housing Dept. 45-48, van de Broek en Bakema 48-; German concentration camp 43-44; Co-Ed. *Forum* (architectural magazine) 59-64; Prof. of Architectural Design, Technical Univ. Delft 63-; Prof. Town Planning Acad. of Hamburg 65-; Hon. Fellow A.I.A. and Asscn. of Scottish Architects; Hon. mem. Zentrale Vereinigung Architekten Österreichs and Bund Deutscher Architekten; mem. Int. Congress for Modern Architecture 47-, Council mem. 53-59; mem. Team-X 53-; Board mem. "Architectura et Amicitia" 55-67; Leader, Architectural Class, Salzburg Int. Summer Acad. 65-69, 73-75; Extraordinary mem. Akad. der Künste, Berlin; Hon. mem. Asscn. of Finnish Architects; Officer, Order of Orange-Nassau, Order of Crown of Belgium; Knight, Order of Netherlands Lion.
Major works: Social Centre, Cinema 't Venster, Shopping Centre Lijnbaan, Rotterdam; Montessori School, Rotterdam; church in Nagele; Town Hall, Marl (Fed. Germany); housing block, Hansaviertel, Berlin; Regional Plan, North-Kennemerland (North Holland); town planning for cities of Leeuwarden, Hengelo, Eindhoven and Amsterdam; Netherlands Pavilion, Brussels Int. Exhbn. (with other); World Broadcasting Building, Hilversum; "Pampus" plan for extension of Amsterdam; building and laboratories for Technical Univ., Delft; Netherlands Pavilion, Osaka Exposition (with other) 70; Het Dorp, Arnhem (village for handicapped people); AMRO Computer Centre, Amstelveen; Town Hall, Terneuzen.
Leisure interest: films.
Publs. *Naar een samenlevings-architectuur* (Towards an Architecture for Society) 63, *Architektur und Städtebau* (Architecture and Town Planning) 63, *Van Stoel tot Stad* (From Doorstep to Town) 64, *L. C. van der Vlugt* (Art and Architecture in the Netherlands Series) 68, *Team X-primer* (ed. Alison Smithson) 68, *The Possible City* 68, *Citizen and City in the Year* 2000 71, and numerous articles.
Van den Broek en Bakema, Posthoornstraat 12b, Rotterdam 1, Netherlands.
Telephone: 134780.

Baker, Carlos; American educator and writer; b. 5 May 1909; s. of Arthur E. and Edna H. Baker; m. Dorothy Scott 1932; one s. two d.; ed. Dartmouth Coll., Harvard Univ. and Princeton Univ.

Teacher of English, Thornton Acad. 33-34, Nichols School, Buffalo 34-36; Princeton Univ. 38-, Prof. of English 51-54, Woodrow Wilson Prof. of Literature 54-, Dept. Chair. 52-58; Guggenheim Fellowship 65-66.

Publs. inc. *Shelley's Major Poetry* 48, *Hemingway: The Writer as Artist* 52 (4th edn. 74), *A Friend in Power* (novel) 58, *The Land of Rumbelow* (novel) 63, *A Year and a Day* (poems) 63, *Ernest Hemingway: A Life Story* (biog.) 69; *The Gay Head Conspiracy* (novel) 73.

34 Allison Road, Princeton, New Jersey, U.S.A.
Telephone: 609-924-4435.

Baker, Crowdus; American merchandising executive; b. 27 Feb. 1906; ed. Terrill Prep. School, Staunton Military Acad. and Austin Coll., Texas.

Sears, Roebuck & Co. 29, Operating Supt. Mail Order Plant, Seattle 35-39, Boston 39-42, Philadelphia 42-45, Gen. Man. New England Operations 45-51, Treas. 51-54, Dir. 52-, Vice-Pres. and Comptroller 54-63, Pres. 60-67, Vice-Chair. Board 68-72; Dir. Allstate Insurance Co., Sears Bank and Trust Co., Calcasieu Chemical Co., Bethlehem Steel Corpn., official of several business and civic orgs.; Hon. D.Iur. Austin Coll. and Villanova Univ.

2298 Drury Lane, Northfield, Ill. 60094, U.S.A.

Baker, Field-Marshal Sir Geoffrey Harding, G.C.B., C.M.G., C.B.E., M.C.; British army officer; b. 20 June 1912, Murree, Pakistan; s. of the late Col. C. N. and Ella M. Baker; m. Valerie Lockhart 1946; two s. one d.; ed. Wellington Coll., Royal Military Acad., Woolwich.

Commissioned into Royal Artillery 32; India, with 11th Field Brigade 35; "F" (Sphinx) Battery, R.H.A. 37, Egypt 39; Middle East Staff Coll. 40; Brigade Maj. R.A. 4th Indian Div., Western Desert and Eritrea 40, 41; Instructor M.E. Staff Coll. 42; G.S.O. 1, H.Q. Eighth Army 42-43; C.O. 127th Field Regt., R.A., Sicily 43; B.G.S., H.Q. 21st Army Group, North-West Europe 44; Deputy Dir. War Office 47; C.O. 3rd Regt., R.H.A. 50-52; Dir. War Office 52-54; Dir. of Operations and Chief of Staff to Gov. of Cyprus Nov. 55-Feb. 57; C.R.A., 7th Armoured and 5 Divs. B.A.O.R. 57-59; Asst. Chief of Staff, H.Q. Northern Army Group, Germany 59; Chief of Staff, H.Q. Southern Command 60-61; Chief of Staff Contingencies Planning, Supreme H.Q. Allied Powers Europe 61-63; Vice-Chief of Gen. Staff 63-66; G.O.C.-in-C. H.Q. Southern Command 66-68; Chief of Gen. Staff 68-April 71; ADC to H.M. the Queen 68-71; Dir. Grindlays Bank, Central London Region of Lloyd's Bank; Gov. Wellington Coll. and Radley Coll.; Master Gunner, St. James's Park and Col. Commdt. Royal Horse Artillery; Constable, H.M. Tower of London; Pres. Army Benevolent Fund; U.S. Legion of Merit (Cmdr.) 46; Freeman of the City of London; Hon. Liveryman, Haberdashers Co.

c/o Lloyds Bank Ltd., 6 Pall Mall, London, S.W.1, England.

Baker, Rt. Hon. Sir George Gillespie, Kt., P.C., O.B.E.; British judge; b. 25 April 1910, Stirling, Scotland; s. of late Capt. John Kilgour Baker and Jane Gillespie; m. Jessie R. M. Findlay 1935; three s.; ed. Strathallan School, Perthshire and Brasenose Coll., Oxford.

Called to the Bar, Middle Temple 32; Bencher 61, Reader 75, Treas. 76; Q.C. 52; Recorder of Bridgenorth 46-51, of Smethwick 51-52, of Wolverhampton 52-61; Judge of the High Court 61-, Presiding Judge, Wales and Chester Circuit 70-71; Pres. Probate, Divorce and Admiralty Div. (now Family Div.) of the High Court of Justice April 71-; First Chair. Gen. Optical Council 59-61; Chair. Cttee. on Mechanical Recording of Court Proceedings 64-70; Hon. Fellow of Brasenose Coll., Oxford 67; Hon. mem. Canadian Bar Asscn. 72.

Leisure interests: golf, fishing, philately.
Camrie, Overstream, Loudwater, Rickmansworth, Herts., England.
Telephone: Rickmansworth 77296.

Baker, George Pierce, A.M., PH.D.; American educationist; b. 1 Nov. 1903, Cambridge, Mass.; s. of Geo. P. and Christina H. Baker; m. Ruth Bremer 1926; one s. three d.; ed. Harvard Univ.

Instructor in Economics and Tutor in Div. of Economics, History and Govt., Harvard Coll. 28-36; Asst. Prof. of Transportation, Harvard Business School 36-39; Associate Prof. of Transportation 39-46; mem. Civil Aeronautics Board 40-42, Vice-Chair. 42; Lieut.-Col. Quartermaster Corps 42, Col.-Gen. Staff Corps 43-45; Dir. Office of Transport and Communications Policy, State Dept. 45-46; Prof. of Int. Transport and Communications, Fletcher School of Law and Diplomacy 46-47; James J. Hill Prof. of Transportation, Harvard Univ. 46-63, Emeritus Prof. 70; George Fisher Baker Prof. of Admin. 63-70; U.S. mem. UN Transport and Communications Comm. 45-46; Pres. Transport Asscn. of America 54-62, Chair. of Board 62-68; Dean of Faculty, Harvard Business School 62-69; Trustee Penn Central Transportation Co. 70-74; Fellow, American Acad. of Arts and Sciences; Legion of Merit; several hon. degrees.

Publs. *The Formation of the New England Railroad Systems* 37, *Case Problems in Transportation Management* (with G. E. Germane) 57.

3 Center Plaza, Boston, Mass. 02108, U.S.A.
Telephone: 617-742-8076.

Baker, Howard Henry, Jr., LL.B.; American politician and attorney; b. 15 Nov. 1925, Huntsville, Tenn.; s. of Howard H. Baker and Dora Ladd; m. Joy Dirksen 1951; one s. one d.; ed. The McCallie School, Chattanooga, Univ. of the South, Sewanee, Tennessee, Tulane Univ. of New Orleans, and Univ. of Tennessee Coll. of Law.

U.S. Naval Reserve 43-46; fmr. partner in Baker, Worthington, Barnett & Crossley, Knoxville, Tenn.; fmr. Chair. Board First Nat. Bank, Oneida, Tenn.; Senator from Tennessee Jan. 67-; Republican.

Leisure interests: tennis, photography.
U.S. Senate, Washington, D.C.; Home: Huntsville, Tenn., U.S.A.

Baker, Dame Janet, D.B.E.; British mezzo-soprano; b. 21 Aug. 1933, Hatfield, Yorks.; m. James Keith Shelley 1957; ed. York Coll. for Girls, Wintringham, Grimsby.

Kathleen Ferrier Memorial Prize 56; Queen's Prize 59; Shakespeare Prize, F.v.S. Foundation of Hamburg; Hon. D.Mus. Birmingham, Hull, Leicester, London and Oxford; Hon. Fellow, St. Anne's Coll., Oxford 75.

Leisure interest: reading.
Bamford Cottage, South Hill Avenue, Harrow-on-the-Hill, Middlesex, England.

Baker, Sir John (Fleetwood), Kt., O.B.E., F.R.S., M.A., SC.D., D.SC., D.ENG., LL.D., F.INST.C.E., F.I.STRUCT.E.; British engineer; b. 19 March 1901, Wallasey, Cheshire; s. of J. W. Baker and Emily Fleetwood; m. Fiona Mary MacAlister Walker 1928; two d.; ed. Rossall School and Clare Coll., Cambridge.

Technical Asst. Royal Airship Works 25; Asst. Lecturer Univ. Coll. Cardiff 26; Scientific Asst. Building Research Station Dept. of Scientific and Industrial Research 28; Technical Officer to Steel Structures Research Cttee. 31-36; Prof. of Civil Engineering Bristol Univ. 33-43; mem. Civil Defence Research Cttee. 39-48; Scientific Adviser and Head of Design Section, A.R.P. Dept., Ministry of Home Security 39-43; Fellow Clare Coll. 43; Prof. of Mechanical Sciences and Head of Dept. of Engineering, Cambridge Univ. 43-68, Chair. Council,

School of Physical Sciences 45-71; mem. Council, Inst. of Civil Engineers 47-56, 58-66, Vice-Pres. 68-70; mem. of Council British Welding Research Asscn. 46-68, Univ. Grants Cttee. 54-64; Pres. Welding Inst. 70-71; Pres. British Asscn. for the Advancement of Science 75-76; Dir. John Brown & Co. Ltd. 63-71; Dir. Technical Devt. Capital Ltd. 63-74, I.D.C. Group Ltd., I.D.C. Project Management Consultants Ltd., Deputy Chair. I.D.C. Consultants Ltd.; Hon. F.I.Mech.E.; Hon. A.R.I.B.A.; Hon. F. Welding Inst.

Publs. *Differential Equations of Engineering Science* 29, *Analysis of Engineering Structures* 36, *The Steel Skeleton*, Vol. I 54, Vol. II 56, *Plastic Design of Frames* 69.
100 Long Road, Cambridge, England.
Telephone: Trumpington 2152.

Baker, Richard Edward St. Barbe; British silviculturist; b. 9 Oct. 1889, Southampton; s. of John St. Barbe Baker and Charlotte Purrot; m. 1st Doreen Long 1946, 2nd Catriona Burnett 1959; one s. one d.; ed. Dean Close School, Cheltenham, Saskatchewan Univ., Gonville and Caius Coll., Cambridge, and Imperial Forestry Inst., Oxford Univ.

Student, farmer and lumber camp employee, Canada 09-13; Army Service 14-17; Asst. Conservator of Forests, Kenya 20-23, Nigeria 24-29; founded Men of the Trees, Kenya 22, Great Britain 24, Palestine 29, as a world-wide society 32, Junior Men of the Trees 56, settled in New Zealand and established Commonwealth and Overseas Headquarters of Men of the Trees 59; lectured and conducted forestry planning in U.S.A., Canada, South America; Convenor, World Forestry Charter Gatherings 45-56; founded Friends of Sahara (U.S.A. and U.K.); prepared report and launched Sahara Reclamation Programme 63-64; Rep. Saharan countries to World Forestry Congress, Madrid 66 and Buenos Aires 72; Founder and Editor *Trees and Life* (Journal of Men of the Trees) 34-59; Hon. LL.D. (Univ. of Saskatchewan).

Leisure interests: tree photography, horses and riding.

Publs. *Tree Lovers' Calendar* 29-75, *Trees—Book of the Seasons* 40, *Africa Drums* 42, *The Redwoods* 43, 59, *I Planted Trees* 44, *Green Glory—Forests of the World* 47, *New Earth Charter* 49, *Famous Trees* 53, *Sahara Challenge* 54, *Kabongo* 55, *Land of Tane* 56, *British Isles Section of World Geography of Forest Resources* 56, *Dance of the Trees* 57, *Kamiti—A Forester's Dream* 58, *Horse Sense* 61, *Trees of New Zealand* 65, *True Book of Trees* 65, *Sahara Conquest* 66, *My Life—My Trees* 70, *Famous Trees of Bible Lands* 74.
Mount Cook, New Zealand.

Baker, William Oliver, B.S., PH.D.; American research chemist; b. 15 July 1915, Chestertown, Md.; s. of Harold M. and Helen (Stokes) Baker; m. Frances Burrill 1941; one s.; ed. Washington Coll., Maryland, and Princeton Univ.

With Bell Telephone Labs. 39-, in charge of polymer research and devt. 48-51, Asst. Dir. of Chemical and Metallurgical Research 51-54, Dir. of Research, Physical Sciences 54-55, Vice-Pres. Research 55-73, Pres. 73-; mem. Nat. Acad. of Sciences, Nat. Acad. of Engineering, Inst. of Medicine, American Philosophical Soc., American Acad. of Arts and Sciences; Harvard Fellow 37-38; Proctor Fellow 38-39; named one of top ten scientists in U.S. Industry 54; Nat. Insts. of Health, Lectureship 58; AIC Honor Scroll 62; Perkin Medal 63; Priestley Medal 66; Edgar Marburg Award 67; Arthur J. Schmitt Lecturer, Notre Dame 68; A.S.T.M. Award to Executives 67, Industrial Research Institute Medal 70; Harrelson Lecturer, North Carolina State Univ. 71; Frederik Philips Award (Inst. of Elec. and Electronics Engineers) 72; *Industrial Research* Man of the Year Award 73; Procter Prize 73; Herbert Spencer Lecturer,

Univ. of Pennsylvania 74; James Madison Medal, Princeton Univ. 75; Gold Medal, American Inst. of Chemists 75; Mellon Inst. Award 75; and many hon. degrees.

Publs. *Rheology*, Vol. III 60, *Listen to Leaders in Engineering* 65, *Science and Society: A Symposium* (Xerox Corpn.) 65, *Perspectives in Polymer Science* 66, *Research in the Service of National Purpose* 67, *Research in the Service of Man: Biomedical Knowledge, Development and Use* 67, *Washington Colloquium on Science and Society, Second Series* 67, *Science: The Achievement and the Promise* 68, *1942–1967, Twenty-five Years at RCA Laboratories*; *Materials Science and Engineering in the United States* 70, *A Look At Business In 1990 . . . A Summary of The White House Conference on the Industrial World Ahead* 72; about 75 research papers in *J. Am. Chem. Soc.*, *J. Chem. Phys.*, *Phys. Rev.*, *Ind. Eng. Chem.*, *J. Appl. Phys.*, etc. and holder of 13 patents.
Bell Telephone Laboratories, Murray Hill, N.J. 07974, U.S.A.
Telephone: 201-582-3423.

Bakhirev, Vyacheslav Vasilievich; Soviet engineer and politician; b. 17 Sept. 1916, Dudorovo village, Ivanovo Region; ed. Moscow State Univ.

Engineer, head of dept., chief design engineer, chief engineer then dir., mechanical and machine building factory 41-65; First Deputy Minister of Defence Industry 65-68; Minister of Machine Building 68-; mem. C.P.S.U. 51-, Central Cttee. 71-; Deputy, U.S.S.R. Supreme Soviet 62-; Lenin Prize; Order of Lenin, Badge of Honour, etc.
Ministry of Machine-Building, Moscow, U.S.S.R.

Bakhrakh, Lev Davidovich; Soviet physicist; b. 22 July 1921, Rostov-on-the-Don; ed. Zhukovsky Air Force Engineering Acad.

Research Assoc. Inst. of Instrumentmaking, Radio-engineering Inst. 47-; mem. C.P.S.U. 47-; Corresp. mem. U.S.S.R. Acad. of Sciences 66-; State Prize 51; Lenin Prize 61.
Publs. Works on radiophysics and radio engineering.
U.S.S.R. Academy of Sciences, 14 Leninsky Prospekt, Moscow, U.S.S.R.

Bakke, Hallvard, B.COMM.; Norwegian journalist and politician; b. 4 Feb. 1943, Flesberg; s. of Bjarne K. Bakke and Anne Ranvik Bakke; m. Inger Karine Skaanes 1969; one s. one d.

Member of Bergen Municipal Council 67-; Norwegian School of Econs. and Business Admin. 68; Alt. Rep. to Parl. 69-; Admin. Man. *Den Nationale Scene*, Bergen 69-76; Chair. Hordaland County Org., Labour Party 74-; Minister of Commerce and Shipping Jan. 76-.
Ministry of Commerce and Shipping, Fr. Nansenspl. 4, Oslo 1; Home: Kolstirusten 4, 5030 Landås, Bergen, Norway.
Telephone: 20-51-10 (Office); 05/28-37-71 (Home).

Bakkenkist, Siebrand Cornelis; Netherlands business executive; b. 23 Sept. 1914, Amsterdam; m. Elisabeth Wegenaar; two s.; ed. Univ. of Amsterdam.

Founder and Man. Bakkenkist, Spits & Co. (consultancy firm) 42-64; mem. Board of Dirs. Zwanenberg-Organon (now part of AKZO N.V.) 64; mem. Board of Dirs., AKZO N.V. 67; Deputy Pres. Man. Board, AKZO N.V. 69-; Pres. Verband von Nederlandsche Ondernemingen (Fed. of Netherlands Industry); Officer, Order of Orange-Nassau.
Herenweg 117, Breukeleveen, Netherlands.
Telephone: 02158-1072.

Bakr, Field Marshal Ahmed Hassan al-; Iraqi army officer and politician; b. 1914, Tikrit; ed. teacher training coll. and Military Acad.
Forced to retire from Iraq Army 58 following participation in revolutionary activities; participated in Revolution of 14th Ramadhan and appointed Prime Minister

and mem. of Council of Revolutionary Command 63; Vice-Pres. of Iraq Nov.-Dec. 63; participated in Revolution of July 68; elected Pres. of Iraq and Chair. of Council of Revolutionary Command 68-, Prime Minister 68-, Minister of Defence 73-; promoted to rank of Field Marshal 69.

Office of the President, Baghdad, Iraq.

Balafrej, Ahmed; Moroccan politician; b. 1908; ed. Univs. of Paris and Cairo.

Sec.-Gen. in Istiqlal (Independence) Party 44-; later exiled by French, returned to Morocco 55; Minister of Foreign Affairs 55-58; Prime Minister May-Dec. 58; Ambassador-at-Large 60-61; Dep. Prime Minister June 61; Minister of Foreign Affairs 61-Nov. 63; Personal Rep. of King with rank of Minister 63-72.

c/o The Royal Palace, Rabat, Morocco.

Balaguer, Joaquín; Dominican diplomatist and politician; b. 1 Sept. 1907, Villa Bisonó; s. of Joaquín Balaguer Lespier and Carmen Celia Ricardo Vda. Balaguer; ed. Univ. de Santo Domingo and Univ. de Paris à la Sorbonne.

Served Madrid 32-35; Under-Sec. of Foreign Affairs 36-40; Minister to Colombia 40-46; Alt. Rep. to UN 47; Minister of Foreign Affairs 54-55, of Educ. and Arts 55-57; Vice-Pres. of Dominican Repub. 57-60, Pres. 60, 66- (re-elected 70, 74); voluntary exile in U.S. 62-65; Founder-Leader Reformist Party 62-.

Office of the President, Santo Domingo, Dominican Republic.

Balanchine, George; American choreographer; b. 9 Jan. 1904, St. Petersburg (now Leningrad), Russia; ed. Imperial Ballet School and Conservatoire, St. Petersburg.

With Ballets Russes (Diaghilev) 24; Dir. Copenhagen Royal Theatre 29; founder mem. Ballets Russes de Monte Carlo 32; at Metropolitan Opera, New York 34-37; co-founder School of American Ballet 34; Artistic Dir., New York City Ballet Co. 48-; ballets include *Pastorale, Triumph of Neptune, Apollon, Bal, Cotillon, Mozartfina, Song of Norway, Agon, Monumentum pro Gesualdo, Movements, Jewels, Prodigal Son, Concerto Barocco Orpheus, Episodes, Coppelia, The Steadfast Tin Soldier;* choreography for films and plays include *On Your Toes, Goldwyn Follies, The Boys from Syracuse, Cabin in the Sky, I Married an Angel, House of Flowers.*

Publ. *Balanchine's Complete Stories of the Great Ballets* 54.

c/o School of American Ballet Inc., 155 West 65th Street, New York, N.Y. 10023, U.S.A.

Balanchivadze, Andrei Melitonovich; Soviet composer; b. 1 July 1906, Leningrad; ed. Tiflis and Leningrad Conservatories.

Wrote music to ballet *Heart of the Mountains* 38, and to twenty films, including *Georgy Saakadze, David Guramishvili, Lost Paradise, They Descended from the Mountains, Mameluk,* etc.; State prizewinner for symphony 44, and second concerto for piano and orchestra 46; People's Artist of Georgian S.S.R. and the U.S.S.R.; Order of Lenin and other decorations; Compositions include *Mzia* (opera) 49, third concerto for piano and string orchestra 53, concerto for bassoon and orchestra 54, *Ruby Stars* (ballet) 51; orchestral works: *Lake Ritza, The Sea, The Dnieper, Solemn Overture, On the Tbilisi Sea, Rhapsody, Ballade;* second symphony (with piano) 59, *Stranitsy Zhizni* (Pages of Life) (ballet) 61, Fourth Concerto for Piano and Orchestra 62, *Vecher* (Evening), Miniature for string quartet 64, *Fantasia* for piano 64, *Muvri* (ballet) 65.

Georgian S.S.R. Union of Composers, 22 Prospekt Rustaveli, Tbilisi, U.S.S.R.

Balancy, Pierre Guy Girald, C.B.E.; Mauritian journalist and diplomatist; b. 8 April 1924, Mauritius; s. of René Balancy and Alix Herse; m. Marie-Thérèse Louis 1947; two s. three d.; ed. Royal Coll., Port Louis, and Bhujoharry Coll.

Member Mauritius Legis. Assembly 63-68; Municipal Counsellor 63-64; Parl. Sec., Ministry of Educ. and Cultural Affairs 64-65; Minister of Information, Posts and Telegraphs 65-67, of Works 67-68; Founder and Editor-in-Chief *L'Express* (daily newspaper) 63-64; Sec. Cercle Littéraire de Port Louis 62; mem. Action Sociale 59-60; mem. Directing Cttee. French Cultural Centre 57-62; Editor *Escales* (quarterly literary review) 54-60; Perm. Rep. of Mauritius to UN April 68-June 69; Amb. of Mauritius to U.S.A. July 68-, concurrently High Commr. to Canada Jan. 70-.

Leisure interests: reading, writing.

4600 Cathedral Avenue, N.W., Washington, D.C. 20016, U.S.A.

Telephone: 362-5885.

Balandin, Anatoli Nikiforovich; Soviet politician; b. 1927; ed. Orenburg Inst. of Agriculture.

Agronomist, and Dir. of machine and tractor station 52-57; Official, Agricultural Dept. of Orenburg Regional Cttee. of C.P.S.U., and First Sec. Chkalovsk District Cttee. of C.P.S.U. 57-62; Head Sorochinsk Collective State Farm Production Dept., Head of Agricultural Dept. of Orenburg Regional Cttee. of C.P.S.U., then Sec. 62-66; Chair. Orenburg Regional Soviet, and Deputy to U.S.S.R. Supreme Soviet 66-; mem. C.P.S.U. 54-; mem. Planning and Budget Comm., Soviet of Union.

Orenburg Regional Soviet of Working People's Deputies, Orenburg, U.S.S.R.

Balasanyan, Sergei Artemyevich; Soviet composer; b. 26 Aug. 1902, Ashkhabad, Turkmen S.S.R.; ed. Moscow Conservatoire.

Secretary R.S.F.S.R. Composers' Union; Exec. mem. U.S.S.R. Composers' Union; Asst. Prof. 61-65, Prof. 65-; Honoured Worker of Arts of Tadjik S.S.R. 39, State Prize 49, People's Artist of Tadjik S.S.R. 57, Honoured Worker of Arts of R.S.F.S.R. 64; orders and medals of Soviet Union.

Principal works: *The Vose Uprising* (opera) 39, *Kova the Blacksmith* (opera) 41, *Leili and Medjnun* (ballet) 47, Two Sonatinas for Piano 48, Tadjik Suite (for symphony orchestra) 48, *Bakhtior and Nisso* (opera) 54, *Seven Armenian Songs* (symphonic suite) 55, *Afghan Suite* 56, Nine Songs by Komitas for Voice and Symphony Orchestra 57, Three Songs by Sayat-Nova for Voice and Symphony Orchestra 57, *Islands of Indonesia* (six symphonic pictures for orchestra) 59, 61, Rhapsody on a Theme of Rabindranath Tagore, Four Songs of Africa, Two Songs of Latin America, *Shakuntala* (ballet) 61.

Moscow Section of R.S.F.S.R. Composers' Union, 4-6 Tretya Miusskaya ulitsa, Moscow, U.S.S.R.

Balbín, Ricardo; Argentine politician; b. 29 July 1904; ed. Universidad de la Plata.

Deputy 31-52; imprisoned by Perón; anti-Perónist candidate for Presidency 51; founder and Pres. Unión Cívica Radical del Pueblo (U.C.R.P.); U.C.R.P. candidate for Presidency 58-62, March 73, Sept. 73.

544 calle 49, La Plata, Argentina.

Balcon, Sir Michael, Kt.; British film producer; b. 19 May 1896, Birmingham; s. of Louis and Laura Balcon; m. Aileen Leatherman, M.B.E., 1924; one s. one d.

Founder and Dir. Gainsborough Pictures Ltd. 28; Dir. of Production, Gaumont-British Picture Corpn. Ltd. 31; Dir. and Producer Ealing Films Ltd. 38-59; Chair. British Lion Films (Holdings) Ltd. until 65; Consultant, Border Television Ltd.; Senior Fellow, Royal Coll. of Art; Hon. Fellow, British Kinematograph Soc.; Knight (1st Class) Order of St. Olav (Norway); Hon. D.Litt. (Birmingham, Sussex).

Productions include: *The Good Companions, Evergreen, I Was a Spy, Man of Aran, A Yank at Oxford, The Foreman Went to France, Next of Kin, Dead of Night,*

The Captive Heart, The Overlanders, Hue and Cry, Scott of the Antarctic, Whisky Galore, Kind Hearts and Coronets, The Blue Lamp, The Lavender Hill Mob, The Man in the White Suit, Where No Vultures Fly, Mandy, The Cruel Sea, The Divided Heart, The Night My Number Came Up, Touch and Go, The Ladykillers, The Long Arm, The Shiralee, Dunkirk, The Scape-goat, The Siege of Pinchgut, The Long and the Short and the Tall, Sammy Going South.
Publ. *Michael Balcon Presents . . . A Lifetime of Films* 69.
Upper Parrock, Hartfield, Sussex, England.
Telephone: Forest Row 2370.

Balderston, C. Canby, B.S., A.M., PH.D.; American banker; b. 1 Feb. 1897; ed. Westtown School, Pennsylvania and Univ. of Pennsylvania.
Assistant Prof. of Industry, Univ. of Pennsylvania 25-31, Prof. 31-54; Dean, Wharton School of Finance and Commerce, Univ. of Pennsylvania 41-54; mem. Board of Dirs. Federal Reserve Bank of Philadelphia 43-53, Deputy Chair. 49-53; Chief, War Dept., Wage Administration Agency and Wage Administration Section, H.Q. Army Service Forces 42-45; mem. Board of Governors Fed. Reserve System 54-65, Vice-Chair. 55-65; Pres. Leeds and Lippincott 50-66, Chair. 75-; Adjunct Prof. of Finance, American Univ. 66-; official of several business and educational orgs.
Publs. *Managerial Profit-Sharing* 28, *Profit-Sharing for Wage-Earners* 37, *Group Incentives* 30, *Executive Guidance of Industrial Relations* 35, *Wage Setting* 40.
Penncrest, 749 W. Rose Tree Road, Media, Pa. 19063, U.S.A.

Baldwin, Charles F., B.S.; American diplomatist; b. 21 Jan. 1902, Zanesville, Ohio; s. of Charles Scott and Harriet Baldwin; one s. and one d. (deceased); ed. Georgetown Univ.
U.S. Foreign Commerce Service 27, Sydney 27-30, Oslo 46-48; U.S. Political Adviser, Trieste 48-49; Counsellor (Econ. Affairs), London 50-51; Consul-Gen. Singapore 52-53; Deputy Asst. Sec. of State for Far East Econ. Affairs 54-55; Ambassador to Fed. of Malaya 61-63, to Malaysia 63-64; Diplomat in Residence, Univ. of Virginia 64-69.
113 Falcon Drive, Colthurst, Charlotteville, Va., U.S.A.
Telephone: 296-4928.

Baldwin, James A.; American writer; b. 2 Aug. 1924; ed. DeWitt Clinton High School.
First professional publication *Nation* book review 46; articles and stories in *Nation, Reporter, Harper's Bazaar, Partisan Review, Commentary, Mademoiselle, The New Leader, Esquire, The New Yorker* 46; stories included in Martha Foley's *Best Short Stories* 58, 61, and O. Henry's *Best Short Stories of 1959*; play *Amen Corner* produced at Howard Univ. 55; mem. Dramatists' Guild, New Dramatists' Cttee., Actors' Studio; Eugene F. Saxton Fellowship 45, Rosenwald Fellowship 48, Guggenheim Fellowship 54, Partisan Review Fellowship and Nat. Inst. of Arts and Letters Award 56, Ford Foundation Grant 59.
Publs. *Go Tell It On The Mountain* (novel; published in U.S.A., Great Britain, Italy, France, Germany, Japan, Denmark and Sweden) 53, *Notes of a Native Son* (essays; U.S.A. and Sweden) 55, *Giovanni's Room* (novel; U.S.A., Great Britain, France, Germany, Sweden and Denmark) 56, *Nobody knows my Name* (essays; U.S.A. and Sweden) 61, *Another Country* (novel; U.S.A. and Great Britain) 62, *The Fire Next Time* (essays) 63, *Blues for Mr. Charlie* (play) 63, (with Richard Avedon) *Nothing Personal* 64, *Going to Meet the Man* 65, *Tell Me How Long the Train's Been Gone* (novel) 67, *A Rap on Race* (with Margaret Mead, q.v.) 71, *No Name in the Street* 72, *If Beale Street Could Talk* (novel) 74, *Little Man, Little Man* 75.
137 West 71st Street, New York, N.Y., U.S.A.

Baldwin, John Russel, B.A., M.A., B.LITT., D.C.L.; Canadian air executive; b. 7 Aug. 1912, Toronto, Ont.; s. of Rev. J. R. Baldwin and Florence Byers; m. Dorothy M. Pearson 1944; three s.; ed. public and secondary schools, Mount Brydges and Uxbridge, Ontario, McMaster Univ., Univ. of Ontario, Univ. of Toronto and Christ Church, Oxford.
Member Faculty of History, McMaster Univ. 37-38; Nat. Sec. of Canadian Inst. of Int. Affairs 38-41; joined Dept. of External Affairs 41, transfer to Cabinet Secr., Privy Council Office 42; Asst. Sec. to Cabinet War Cttee., later Asst. Sec. to Cabinet 43-48; Chair. of Air Transport Board 49; Deputy Minister of Transport 54; Pres. of Air Canada 68-73.
Leisure interests: skiing, boating, oenology.
1382 McGregor Avenue, Montreal 109, P.Q., Canada.

Balevsky, Angel Tonchev, D.SC.; Bulgarian engineer; b. 15 April 1910, Troyan; s. of Toncho Angelov Balesky and Penka Kalcheva Balevska; m. Laura Todorova Kemedulska 1938; one s. one d.; ed. Brno, Czechoslovakia.
Professor of Metals and Technology of Metals, Higher Inst. of Electrical and Mechanical Engineering 45-66, Rector 66-68; Vice-Pres. State Cttee. for Science and Technological Progress 60-61; Dir. Inst. of Metals and Technology of Metals 66-; mem. State Council 71-; Corresp. mem. Bulgarian Acad. of Sciences 52-66, mem. 67, Pres. 68; Hon. mem. Acad. of Science of Hungary 70, U.S.S.R. 71, Poland 71, Czechoslovakia 73, German Democratic Repub. 74, Mongolian People's Repub. 74; Hon. mem. Polish Soc. of Theoretical and Applied Mechanics; mem. Standing Cttee. of Pugwash Movt. 71-; Hon. D. Eng., Higher Technological School, Ilmenau (G.D.R.) 73; Dimitrov Prize Laureate 51, 60; Merited Scientist 66; People's Scientist 71; Order of Red Banner of Labour; Order of Georgi Dimitrov 70; Order of Cyril and Methodius (1st and 2nd Class); Gold Medal, French Soc. for the Promotion of Scientific Research and Invention Activities 70; Special Nicholas Copernicus Medal of Poland 73; M. V. Lomonosov Gold Medal, U.S.S.R. Acad. of Sciences 75.
Leisure interests: history and literature.
Publs. several articles in learned journals.
31 Asparouh Street, Sofia, Bulgaria.
Telephone: 87-82-94.

Balke, Siegfried, DR.ING.; German chemist and politician; b. 1 June 1902, Bochum; m. Anne Wagner 1927; ed. Technical Univ. of Munich.
Industrial chemist 25-53, 63-; Fed. Minister for Posts and Telecommunications 53-56; mem. Bundestag 57-69; Fed. Minister for Nuclear Energy 56-62; Chair. German Fed. Technical Asscn.; Hon. Prof. Munich Univ.; Dr.rer.nat. h.c., Technical Univ. of Clausthal.
8 Munich 22, Lerchenfeldstrasse 9, Federal Republic of Germany.
Telephone: 221174.

Ball, Alan Hugh; British business executive; b. 8 June 1924, England; s. of Sir Joseph Ball, K.B.E. and Lady Ball; m. Eleanor K. Turner 1948; two s. one d.; ed. Eton Coll.
Joined Lonrho Ltd. 47, Chair. and Joint Man. Dir. 61-72, Exec. Deputy Chair. 72-.
Leisure interests: shooting, fishing.
Lonrho Ltd., Cheapside House, Cheapside, London, E.C.2; Home: The Old Mill, Ramsbury, Wilts., England.
Telephone: 01-606-8131 (Office).

Ball, Eric Glendinning, B.S., M.A., PH.D.; American university professor; b. 12 July 1904, Coventry, England; s. of C. Sturges Ball and Nellie Glendinning; m. Grace L. Snavely 1927; ed. Haverford Coll. and Univ. of Pennsylvania.
Asst., School of Medicine, Univ. of Pa. 26-28; Nat. Research Fellow, Johns Hopkins Medical School 29-30, Instructor in Physiological Chemistry 30-33, Associate

in Physiological Chemistry 33-40; Int. Physiological Congress Fellow, Rome 32; Guggenheim Memorial Foundation Fellow, Berlin-Dahlem 37-38; Asst. Prof. of Biological Chemistry, Harvard Medical School 40-41, Assoc. Prof. 41-46, Prof. 46-72, Chair. Div. of Medical Sciences 52-68; Acting Head, Dept. of Biological Chemistry 43-46, 58-59, Edward S. Wood Prof. of Biological Chemistry 62-72, Prof. Emer. 72-; Independent Investigator, Marine Biological Laboratory, Woods Hole, Mass. 71-; Guggenheim Memorial Foundation Fellow and Visiting Investigator, Scripps Clinic and Research Foundation, La Jolla, Calif. 63-; Eli Lilly Prize in Biochemistry 40; Fellow American Asscn. for Advancement of Science; mem. of Nat. Acad. U.S.A., Society of Biological Chemists, American Chemical Society, American Acad. of Arts and Sciences, Biochemical Society of Great Britain, etc.; Hon. M.A. (Harvard Univ.) 42; Hon. D.Sc. (Haverford Coll.) 49; holder of Southern Cross, Brazil 45, Certificate of Merit, U.S.A. 48; mem. Editorial Board *Journal of Biological Chemistry* 50-60 and *Biochemical Preparations* 48-56 (Editor-in-Chief Vol. 2), *Biochemistry* 60-70.
Leisure interests: gardening, outdoor sports.
Marine Biological Laboratory, Woods Hole, Mass. 02543; P.O. Box 406, Falmouth, Mass. 02541, U.S.A. Telephone: 548-3705 (Office); 548-0556 (Home).

Ball, George Wildman; American lawyer and government official; b. 21 Dec. 1909; ed. Northwestern Univ. Admitted to Illinois Bar 34, D.C. Bar 46; law practice Chicago 35-42, Washington 46-61; Assoc. Gen. Counsel Lend-Lease Admin. 42-43, Foreign Econs. Admin. 43-44; Dir. U.S. Strategic Bombing Survey, London 44-45; Political Adviser to Adlai Stevenson; Under-Sec. of State for Econ. Affairs Feb.-Dec. 61; Under-Sec. of State Dec. 61-Sept. 66; Pres. of Board of Dirs. of Lehmann Brothers Int. Ltd. Oct. 66-May 68; Perm. Rep. to UN June-Sept. 68; Senior Partner, Lehman Brothers Int. Jan.-May 68, 69-; Hon. LL.D. (Northwestern Univ.); Democrat.
Publ. *The Discipline of Power* 68.
Office: 1 William Street, New York, N.Y. 10004; Home: 860 United Nations Plaza, New York, N.Y. 10017, U.S.A.

Ball, Lucille; American actress; b. 6 Aug. 1911, Jamestown, N.Y.; *m.* 1st Desi Arnaz 1940 (divorced 1960); one *s.* one *d.*; *m.* 2nd Gary Morton 1961.
Film actress 34-; TV actress; Pres. Desilu Productions Inc. 62-67; Lucille Ball Productions 67-.
Films include: *Roberta, Chatterbox, Follow the Fleet, Stage Door, Having a Wonderful Time, Affairs of Annabell, Room Service, Valley of the Sun, Seven Days Leave, DuBarry was a Lady, Best Foot Forward, Meet the People, Thousands Cheer, Without Love, Love from a Stranger, Her Husband's Affairs, Forever Darling, Facts of Life, Mame* 74; TV Shows: *I Love Lucy* 51-60, *The Lucy Show* 62-68, *Here's Lucy* 68-74.
Roxbury Drive/Lexington Road, Beverly Hills, California, U.S.A.

Ball, William, A.B., M.A.; American actor and theatrical director; b. 1931, Evanston, Ill.; *s.* of Catherine and Russell Ball; ed. Fordham Univ. and Carnegie Inst. of Technology.
Oregon Shakespearian Festival 50-53; Antioch Shakespeare Festival 54; Group 20 Players 55; San Diego Shakespeare Festival 56; Arena Stage, Washington D.C. 57-58; *Back to Methuselah*, Broadway, New York and tour 58; *Six Characters in Search of an Author, Così Fan Tutte* 59, *The Inspector General* 60, *Porgy and Bess* 61, *Midsummer Night's Dream* 63, New York City Center Opera Co. off-Broadway: *The Misanthrope, The Lady's Not for Burning, The Country Wife, Ivanov, A Month In The Country* 56-58, *Under Milk Wood* 56-61, *Six Characters In Search of an Author* 63, *The Tempest*, Stratford, Conn., Shakespeare Festival; *Yeoman of the*

Guard (Stratford, Canada) 64; Librettist and Dir. *Natalia Petrovna* (New York City Center Opera Co.) 64; *Tartuffe* (Lincoln Center Repertory Co.) 65; Founder and Gen. Dir. American Conservatory Theatre (A.C.T.) initiated at Pittsburgh Playhouse in 65 with a 16-play double repertory theatre; resident in San Francisco 67-; Fulbright Scholarship to Great Britain, NBC/RCA Fellowship to Carnegie Inst. of Technology, Ford Foundation Director's Grant 59, Ford Foundation Comm. for opera libretto *Natalia Petrovna*.
Leisure interests: meditation, photography, films, travel.
450 Geary Street, San Francisco, Calif., U.S.A.

Balladore Pallieri, Giorgio, LL.D.; Italian lawyer; b. 1905; ed. Univ. of Turin.
Lecturer, Univ. of Messina 30, Prof. 32; Prof., Univ. of Modena 33, Genoa 34, Univ. of Sacred Heart, Milan 35; Prof., Hague Acad. of Int. Law 35-49; Prof., Escuela de Funcionarios Internacionales, Madrid 55; now Prof. of Int. Law, Univ. of Sacred Heart, Milan; mem. Legal Advisory Council, Ministry of Foreign Affairs; Judge, European Court of Human Rights 60-, Vice-Pres. 71-74, Pres. 74-.
University of the Sacred Heart, Faculty of Law, 4 Via Stefano Jacini, Milan, Italy.

Ballantine, Duncan Smith, A.B., PH.D.; American college president; b. 5 Nov. 1912, Garden City, N.Y.; *s.* of Raymond and Amy Smith Ballantine; *m.* 1st Margarette Torbert 1941, 2nd Saffeti Acele 1962; one *s.* two *d.*; ed. Amherst Coll. (Mass.), and Harvard Univ.
Held various teaching appointments 36-42; served with U.S.N.R. 42-46; Assoc. Prof. History, Mass. Inst. Technology 47-52; Pres. Reed Coll. 52-55; Pres. Robert Coll. 55-61; Research Assoc. Harvard Univ. Center for Int. Affairs 62; now Dir. Educ. Dept., Int. Bank for Reconstruction and Devt. (World Bank); mem. Soc. for Int. Devt., Middle East Inst.; Trustee, Robert Coll., Istanbul; Trustee, Int. Inst. of Educ. Planning; Hon. LL.D.
Leisure interests: tennis, gardening, fishing, art.
Publ. *U.S. Naval Logistics in the Second World War* 47.
Home: 5306 Blackistone Road, Washington, D.C. 20016; Office: International Bank for Reconstruction & Development (World Bank), 1818 H Street, N.W., Washington, D.C., U.S.A.
Telephone: 229-7596 (Home).

Ballantrae, Baron (Life Peer), cr. 72, of Auchairne and The Bay of Islands; **Bernard Edward Fergusson,** K.T., G.C.M.G., G.C.V.O., D.S.O., O.B.E.; formerly Governor-General of New Zealand, British army officer and author; b. 6 May 1911, London; *s.* of Gen. Sir Charles Fergusson, Bart. and Lady Alice Boyle; *m.* Laura Margaret Grenfell 1950; one *s.*; ed. Eton Coll., Royal Military Coll. Sandhurst.
Joined the Black Watch 31; served in Palestine 37-38, in Middle East and Burma Second World War, including Wingate Expeditions into Burma 43-44; Palestine Police 46-47; Commanded the Black Watch 48-51; Col. Intelligence SHAPE 51-53; Commdr. 29 Infantry Brigade 57-58; retd. from army 58; Gov.-Gen. of New Zealand 62-67; Col. the Black Watch 69-; Chair. British Council 72-; Chancellor St. Andrews Univ. 73-; Lord High Commr. to Gen. Assembly of Church of Scotland 73-74; Hon. degrees from Canterbury, Waikato, Strathclyde, Dundee and St. Andrews.
Publs. *Eton Portrait* 37, *Beyond the Chindwin* 45, *Lowland Soldier* (verse) 45, *The Wild Green Earth* 46, *The Black Watch and the King's Enemies* 50, *Rupert of the Rhine* 52, *The Rare Adventure* 54, *The Watery Maze* 61, *Wavell: Portrait of a Soldier* 61, *Return to Burma* 63, *The Trumpet in the Hall* 71, *Captain John Niven* 72.
Auchairne, Ballantrae, Ayrshire, Scotland.
Telephone: Ballantrae 344.

Ballinger, Violet Margaret Livingstone, B.A., M.A.; South African politician; b. 1894, Scotland; *m.* William G. Ballinger (*q.v.*); ed. Holy Rosary Convent (Port Elizabeth), Huguenot Coll. (Wellington), Rhodes Univ. (Grahamstown) and Somerville Coll., Oxford.
Settled in South Africa 04; elected to Union Parl. 37, returned unopposed 42, re-elected 48, returned unopposed 54 as Native Rep. for Cape Eastern; parliamentary seat abolished by Bantu Self-Government Act 59; mem. South African Liberal Party 53- (1st Pres.); Dyason Memorial Lecturer, Inst. Int. Affairs, Australia 60; Assoc. Fellow, Nuffield Coll., Oxford 61; fmr. Senior Lecturer in History, Witwatersrand Univ.; Hon. LL.D. (Univ. of Cape Town, Rhodes Univ.).
Publs. *Influence of Holland on Africa, Britain in South Africa, Bechuanaland and Basutoland* (with W. G. Ballinger), *From Union to Apartheid—A Trek to Isolation* 70 and articles on race and economic problems.
8 Firdale Road, Newlands, Cape Province, South Africa.

Ballinger, William George; South African (b. British) politician; b. 1894; *m.* Violet Margaret L. Ballinger (*q.v.*); ed. Glasgow Univ. and Elsinore Coll., Denmark.
Town and Parish Councillor, Motherwell (Scotland) 22-28; Adviser on African Trade Union, Industrial and Co-operative Organizations; Adviser British Workers' Del. I.L.O. Confs. Geneva 35 and 36; Senator (Rep. of Transvaal and Orange Free State Africans) 48-60; seat abolished by Bantu Self-Government Act 60; Research student, Queen Elizabeth House, Oxford 61; Hon. Sec. Non-European Progress Trust, Cape Town.
Publs. *Race and Economic Contacts, Britain in South Africa, Bechuanaland and Basutoland* (with Margaret Ballinger).
8 Firdale Road, Newlands, Cape Province, South Africa.

Ballmer, Ray Wayne, M.SC.; American mining executive; b. 1926, New Mexico; *m.*; two *c.*; ed. N.M. School of Mines, Mass. Inst. of Technology.
Held senior posts with Kennecott Copper Corpn., U.S.A., with responsibilities in Ariz. and Bingham Canyon, Utah operations; now Man. Dir. Bougainville Copper Ltd., responsible for design, construction and commissioning of Bougainville copper operation.
Leisure interests: boating, golf, skiing.
Bougainville Copper Limited, 95 Collins Street, Melbourne, Australia.

Balluseck, Daniel J. von; Netherlands journalist and diplomatist; b. 8 March 1895, Utrecht; *s.* of F. A. von Balluseck and J. W. Soeterik; *m.* E. A. Eringaard 1932; one *s.*; ed. School of Economics, Rotterdam, and Univs. of Geneva and Amsterdam.
Correspondent of *Algemeen Handelsblad* in London, Paris, Geneva, Indonesia, Mexico, U.S.A. and Amsterdam 18-28, chief editor 28-41 and 45-49; civilian prisoner during occupation; Perm. Rep. to UN (with rank of Amb.) 50-55; Amb. to U.S.S.R. 55-57, to Canada 58-60; del. of Ministry of Foreign Affairs in Defence Coll., The Hague 61-69; Knight Order of Netherlands Lion; Officer Order of Orange-Nassau.
Leisure interests: music, theatre, travel.
Publs. *Holland's House: A Nation Building a Home*, by Peter Bricklayer (pen-name) 39; *Wij deelgenooten* (story of the Netherlands-Indonesian relationship) by Pieter Schakel (pen-name) 45.
96B Koninginnegracht, The Hague, Netherlands.
Telephone: The Hague 553774.

Balmain, Pierre Alexandre; French couturier; b. 18 May 1914, Saint-Jean de Maurienne; ed. Lycée de Chambéry and Ecole des Beaux Arts.
Designed for Molyneux 34-39, Lucien Lelong 41-45; began own business 46; wide activity in high fashion for women, and ready-to-wear for men and women; Chevalier de la Légion d'Honneur, etc.
Publ. *My Years and Seasons* (memoirs) 64.
44 rue François Ier, Paris 8e, France.
Telephone: BAL 6804.

Balogh, Baron (Life Peer), cr. 68, of Hampstead; **Thomas Balogh,** M.A., DR.RER.POL.; British political economist; b. 2 Nov. 1905, Budapest; *s.* of Emil Balogh; *m.* 1st Penelope Tower (widow of Oliver Gatty) 1945 (dissolved 1970), 2nd Dr. C. Storr; two *s.* one *d.*; four step *d.*; ed. Gymnasium, Univs. of Budapest, Berlin and Harvard.
Fellow, Hungarian Coll., Berlin 27-28; Rockefeller Fellow 28-30; banking 31-39; Lecturer, Balliol Coll., Oxford 39-45, Fellow 45-, Leverhulme Emeritus Fellow 73-; Reader in Econs., Oxford Univ. 60-73; Senior Research Associate, Queen Elizabeth House, Oxford 73-; mem. Econ. and Financial Sub-cttee. of Labour Party Exec. Cttee. 50-64, 70-; Vice-Chair. Fabian Soc. 69, Chair. 70; Consultant or Adviser to Reserve Bank of Australia, Govts. of Malta, India, Jamaica, British Guiana, Mauritius and Algeria, FAO and UN Econ. Comms. for Latin America and Africa; Visiting Prof., Minneapolis, Madison, Harvard, Delhi and New York; Econ. Adviser to British Cabinet 64-68 (on part-time basis Oct. 67-68); Minister of State for Energy 74-75; Deputy Chair. (part-time) British Nat. Oil Corpn.; Leverhulme Fellow 73; Fellow, Woodrow Wilson Center, Washington.
Leisure interests: planting trees, conversation.
Publs. *Studies in Financial Organisation* 47, *The Dollar Crisis* 49, *Fabian Essays* (Int. and Colonial), co-author *The Establishment, Economic Future of Malta* (with Seers) 55, *Planning and Monetary Organisation in Jamaica* 56, *The Economic Development of the Mediterranean* (with Ergas) 57, *Development Plans in Africa* (with Ergas) 59, *Economic Policy in Underdeveloped Areas and the Price Mechanism* 62, *Aspects of Development* 63, *Unequal Partners* 63, *Planning for Prosperity* 63, *The Economics of Poverty* 66, *The Limits of Economics* 69, *Labour and Inflation* 70, *Facts and Fancy in International Economic Relations* 73.
Old Bank House, 14 High Street, Hampstead, London, NW3 1PX, England.
Telephone: 01-435-9275.

Balogun, Kolawole, Chief **Balogun of Otan,** LL.B.; Nigerian lawyer, politician and diplomatist; b. 1926; ed. Govt. Coll., Ibadan.
On staff of *Nigerian Advocate*, later radio announcer, then Asst. Editor *West African Pilot*; legal studies in London 48-51, called to the Bar 51; Sec. London branch National Council of Nigeria and the Cameroons (NCNC) 51; Nat. Sec. NCNC 51-57; mem. of Fed. Parl. 54; Fed. Minister without Portfolio, later Fed. Minister of Information; resigned from govt. 58; Nigerian Commr. in Ghana 59-60, High Commr. 60-61; mem. of Ministry of Foreign Affairs 61-; Chair. Nigerian Nat. Shipping Line 62-65; Commr. for Econ. Planning and Social Devt., Mil. Govt. of W. Nigeria 67; Commr. for Education 68-70; Chair. Sketch Group of Newspapers, Ibadan 71.
c/o Ministry of Foreign Affairs, Lagos, Nigeria.

Balsis, Edwardas Kosto; Soviet composer; b. 20 Dec. 1919, Nikolaev, Ukraine; ed. Kaunas Conservatoire.
Chairman Lithuanian Composers' Union; Sec., Exec. mem. U.S.S.R. Composers' Union; Asst. Prof. 60-; Honoured Worker of the Arts of Lithuanian S.S.R. 59; People's Artist of Lithuanian S.S.R. 65; Order of Banner of Labour, Badge of Honour.
Principal works: Piano Sonata 49, *Vilnius* (poem for symphony orchestra) 50, *Heroic Poem* (for symphony orchestra) 52, String Quartet in G-minor 53, First Concerto for Violin and Orchestra 54, *Dance Suite of*

Lithuanian folk dances for symphony orchestra 57, Second Concerto for Violin and Orchestra 58, *Egle*, *Queen of the Snakes* (ballet) 60, Cantata for Choir and Symphony Orchestra 61; Film music: *The Bridge*, *Blue Roads* 57, *Adonas Wants to Become a Man* 59, *Living Heroes* 60, *The Cannonade* 61, *Old Sailor's Song*, *Going on a Long Sea Voyage* 64.
Lithuanian Composers' Union, 6 Ulitsa Reshitoyu, Vilnius, Lithuanian S.S.R., U.S.S.R.

Baltensweiler, Armin, M.A.; Swiss airline executive; b. 20 April 1920, Mollis, Canton Glarus; *m.*; two *s.* one *d.*; ed. Eidgenössische Technische Hochschule (ETH), Zürich.
Joined staff of ETH Inst. for Aeronautical Engineering 46; subsequently became research engineer, Fed. Swiss aircraft factory, Emmen; joined Swissair 48, mem. Man. Board and Head, Planning Service 56, Exec. Vice-Pres. 60, Pres. Jan. 72-.
Leisure interests: mountain climbing, skiing, hunting.
Publs. numerous specialized articles.
Swissair, 8058 Zürich-Flughafen, Switzerland.
Telephone: 01/812.12.12.

Balthus (Comte Balthasar Klossowski de Rola); French artist; b. 29 Feb. 1908.
Exhibited Galerie Pierre, Paris 34, Pierre Matisse Gallery, New York City 38, 39, 49, 56, Moos Gallery, Geneva 43, Wildenstein Galleries, Paris 46, 56, Dunn Int. Exhbn., London 63; Retrospective Exhbn. at Tate Gallery, London 68; Dir. Villa Medici, Rome 61-.
Works include: Frescoes, Church of Beatenberg, Switzerland 28, Costumes and Sets for Artaud's *The Cenci* 35, for *Cosi Fan Tutte*, Aix-en-Provence 50, numerous paintings.
Accademia di Francia, Villa Medici, Viale Trinità dei Monti 1, Rome 00187, Italy.

Baltimore, David, PH.D.; American biologist; b. 7 March 1938, New York, N.Y.; *s.* of Mr. and Mrs. Richard Baltimore; *m.* Alice Huang 1968; one *d.*; ed. Swarthmore Coll. and Rockefeller Univ.
Postdoctoral Fellow, Mass. Inst. of Technology (M.I.T.) 63-64; Albert Einstein Coll. of Medicine, N.Y. 64-65; Research Assoc., Salk Inst., La Jolla, Calif. 65-68; Assoc. Prof., M.I.T. 68-72, Prof. of Biology 72-; American Cancer Soc. Prof. of Microbiology 73-; Eli Lily Award in Microbiology and Immunology 71; U.S. Steel Foundation Award in Molecular Biology 74; Nobel Prize 75.
Center for Cancer Research, Massachusetts Institute of Technology, Cambridge, Mass. 02139, U.S.A.

Baltra, Alberto; Chilean lawyer and economist; b. 1912, Traiguén, Malleco; *s.* of Luis Baltra and Luisa Cortés; *m.* Adriana Olguin 1940; one *s.*
Professor of Political Economy and Director of School of Economics 35; Vice-Pres. Int. Exchange Comm. 39; Dir.-Gen. of Trade at Ministry of National Economy 42; Under-Sec. of State, Ministry of Nat. Economy 46; accompanied Pres. on trade missions to Brazil and the Argentine 47; Minister of Nat. Economy and Trade 47; mem. of Import Licensing Comm. 47; Pres. Radical Party 58; Prof. of Economic Theory and Dir. of Dept. of Social Sciences, Univ. of Chile, Santiago; Consultant to UN Econ. Comm. for Latin America (ECLA); Leader of Radical Party; Pres. of XII Nat. Convention of Radical Party; Senator 67-73; mem. Econ. and Govt. Comm. of Senate; Presidential candidate.
Leisure interest: music.
Publs. *Economía dirigida*, *El principio orgánico biológico en la economía*, *Organización económica de la U.R.S.S.*, *Crecimiento económico de América Latina* (trans. Polish and Russian), *La desnacionalización del petróleo chileno*, *Tres países del mundo socialista*, *Pedro Aguirre Cerda*, *Teoría económica*, *Nuestra América y sus problemas*, *Problemas del subdesarrollo latinoamericano*, *Otro camino para Chile*, *Socialismo y democracia*.
Avenida Antonio Varas 475, Santiago, Chile.

Bam, Arvind Shankar, B.SC.; Indian civil servant and United Nations official; b. 12 March 1918; *m.* Mrinal Coomarie 1945; one *s.* two *d.*; ed. Fergusson Coll., Poona, and King's Coll., London.
Entered Civil Service 41, Asst. Collector, Dharwar 42-44; Special Officer, Civil Supplies, Darjeeling 44-45; District Controller of Civil Supplies, Jalpaiguri 45-46; Asst. Collector, Broach 46-47; Under-Sec., Home Dept., Govt. of Bombay April-Aug. 47, Deputy Sec. 47-49; First Collector and District Magistrate, Kolhapur 49-52; Dep. Sec. Ministry of Rehabilitation, Calcutta 52-57; Controller for Iron and Steel 57-61; Chair. Tea Board, Govt. of India 61-65; Gen. Man. Indian Airlines Corpn. Dec. 65-Nov. 66, Chair. and Gen. Man. Dec. 66-June 67; Resident Rep. of UN Devt. Programme in Yugoslavia 67-74, in Liberia 74-; Leader, Indian Steel Del. to ECAFE 60; Leader, Indian Tea Del. to U.S., Canada, Australia, New Zealand and Singapore 62.
Leisure interests: golf, bridge.
Resident Representative of United Nations Development Programme, Latco Building, Broad Street, P.O. Box 274, Monrovia, Liberia.
Telephone: 21384, 22767 (Office); 26551 (Home).

Bamba, Nanlo, L. en D.; Ivory Coast magistrate and politician; b. 15 Nov. 1916, Bouaké; ed. Ecole Normale William-Ponty.
Served in the French Colonial Admin., Paris 47-51, Ivory Coast 52-54; substituted as Public Prosecutor in Cotonou 54-55; Justice of the Peace in Bondoukou 55-56; trainee of ENFOM 56-58; Deputy Public Prosecutor, then examining magistrate in Abidjan 58; Chef de Cabinet 59-61; Dir. Nat. Police Force Feb. 60-Jan. 61; Assoc. Dir. Cabinet of Félix Houphouet-Boigny, Pres. of the Repub. Aug. 61-Feb. 63; Keeper of the Seals and Minister of Justice Feb. 63-Jan. 66; Minister of the Interior 66-74, of Waters and Forests July 74-.
Ministry of Waters and Forests, Abidjan, Ivory Coast.

Banbury, (Frederick Harold) Frith; British theatrical director, actor and manager; b. 4 May 1912, Plymouth; *s.* of Rear Admiral Frederick Arthur Frith Banbury and Winifred Fink; ed. Stowe School, Oxford Univ. and Royal Acad. Dramatic Art.
Made first stage appearance 33 and appeared on the London stage, in plays and on television until 47; has since concentrated on direction; plays directed include: *Dark Summer* 47, *The Holly and the Ivy* 50, *Waters of the Moon* 51, *The Deep Blue Sea* 51, *Morosco* N.Y. 52, *A Question Of Fact* 53, *Marching Song* 54, *Love's Labours Lost* Old Vic. 54, *The Diary of Anne Frank* 56, *A Dead Secret* 57, *Flowering Cherry* 57, *A Touch of the Sun* 58, *The Ring of Truth* 59, *The Tiger and the Horse* 60, *The Wings of the Dove* 63, *The Right Honourable Gentleman* N.Y. 65, *Howards End* 67, *Dear Octopus* 67, *Enter a Free Man* 68, *My Darling Daisy* 70, *The Winslow Boy* 70, *Captain Brassbound's Conversion* 71, *Reunion in Vienna* 72, *The Day After the Fair* 72, in U.S.A. 73, *Glasstown* 73, and others in New York, Tel Aviv and Paris.
Leisure interest: playing the piano.
4 St. James Terrace, Prince Albert Road, London, N.W.8, England.
Telephone: 01-722 8481.

Bancroft, Anne; American actress; b. 17 Sept. 1931; *m.* 2nd Mel Brooks 1964; ed. Christopher Columbus High School, New York City.
Theatre: Broadway debut in *Two for the Seesaw* 58; played Anne Sullivan in *The Miracle Worker* 59-60, *The Devils* 65, *The Little Foxes* 67, *A Cry of Players* 68. Films: *The Miracle Worker*, *Don't Bother to Knock*,

Tonight we Sing, Demetrius and the Gladiators. The Pumpkin Eater, Seven Women, The Graduate 68, *Young Winston* 71, *The Prisoner of Second Avenue* 74, *The Hindenberg* 75.

Numerous TV appearances including *Mother Courage and her Children, Annie, the Woman in a Life of a Man*; Academy Award for film *The Miracle Worker* 62; Golden Globe Award 68.

c/o David J. Cogan, 350 Fifth Avenue, New York, N.Y., U.S.A.

Bancroft, Harding Foster; American newspaper executive; b. 29 Dec. 1910, New York; *s.* of Francis Sydney Bancroft and Beatrice F. Jordan; *m.* Jane Northrop 1936; two *s.* two *d.*; ed. Williams Coll. and Harvard Law School.

Lawyer 36-41; Office of Price Admin., Washington 41-43; Lend-Lease Admin. 43; U.S. Navy 43-45; Chief Div. UN Political Affairs, Dept. of State 45; U.S. Dep. Rep., UN Collective Measures Comm. 50-53; Legal Adviser, Int. Labour Org. (ILO), Geneva 53-56; Sec. *The New York Times* 57-63, Dir. 61-, Exec. Vice-Pres. 63-; mem. U.S. Del. UN Gen. Assembly 66; Dir. Gaspesia Pulp & Paper Co., Foreign Policy Asscn.; Trustee, Clark Art Inst., Williams Coll., Carnegie Corpn. of N.Y., Carnegie Endowment for Int. Peace; mem. Int. Council Museum of Modern Art, Council on Foreign Relations, Century Asscn.; mem. Board of Dirs. UN Asscn. of the U.S.A., Greer Children's Community.

The New York Times, 229 West 43rd Street, N.Y. 10036; and 180 East 9th Street, New York, N.Y. 10021, U.S.A.

Telephone: 212R-H4-3485.

Banda, Aleke Kadonaphani; Malawi journalist and politician; b. 19 Sept. 1939, Livingstone, Zambia; *s.* of Eliazar G. Banda and Lilian Phiri; *m.* Mbumba M. Kahumbe 1961; two *s.* one *d.*; ed. United Missionary School, Que Que and Inyati School, Bulawayo.

Secretary Nyasaland African Congress (N.A.C.), Que Que Branch 54; Gen. Sec. S. Rhodesia African Students Asscn. 57-59; arrested and detained in Rhodesia 59, deported to Nyasaland; Founder-mem. Malawi Congress Party (MCP), Sec.-Gen. 59-73, mem. 74-; Editor Nyasaland TUC newspaper *Ntendere Pa Nchito* and mem. TUC Council 59-60; Personal Political Sec. to Dr. Hastings Banda 60-73; Sec. MCP Del. to Lancaster House Conf. resulting in self-govt. for Malawi 60; Sec. to subsequent confs. 60, 62; Man. Editor *Malawi News* 59-66; Dir. Malawi Press Ltd. 60; Dir.-Gen. Malawi Broadcasting Corpn. 64-66; Nat. Chair. League of Malawi Youth and Commdr. Malawi Young Pioneers 63-73; Dir. Reserve Bank of Malawi 65-66; Minister of Devt. and Planning 66-67, of Econ. Affairs (incorporating Natural Resources, Trade and Industry, and Devt. and Planning), and Minister of Works and Supplies 67-68, of Trade and Industry (incorporating Tourism, Information and Broadcasting) 68-69, of Finance and of Information and Tourism 69-72, of Trade, Industry and Tourism 72-73; dismissed from Cabinet posts and party 73; reinstated as mem. party 74.

Leisure interest: tennis.

Malawi Congress Party, P.O. Box 5250, Limbe, Malawi.

Banda, Hastings Kamuzu, PH.B., B.SC., M.B., CH.B., M.D., L.R.C.S.; Malawi doctor and politician; b. 1906; ed. mission school, Edinburgh Univ. and in U.S.A. Worked in gold mine; spent twelve years in U.S. in study and medical practice; medical practice in Willesden, England, until 54, in Kumasi, Ghana 54-58; returned to Nyasaland to take up leadership of Malawi Congress Party 58-; detained during declared state of emergency March 59-April 60; Minister of Natural Resources, Survey and Local Govt. 61-63, Prime Minister of Nyasaland 63-July 64, of Malawi July 64-, also Minister of Agriculture, Natural Resources, External Affairs, Defence, Works and Supply, Youth;

Pres. of Repub. of Malawi July 66- (named Pres. for Life 71); Chancellor, Univ. of Malawi 65-.

Office of the President, Zomba, Malawi.

Banda, Rupiah Bwezani, B.A.; Zambian diplomatist; b. 19 Feb. 1937, Gwanda, S. Rhodesia; *m.*; four *c.*; ed. Secondary School, Munali, Zambia, Univ. of Ethiopia, Lund Univ., Sweden.

Representative of United Nat. Independence Party (UNIP) in N. Europe 60-64; First Sec. for Int. Affairs Nat. Union of N. Rhodesia Students; Amb. to United Arab Repub. 65-67, to U.S.A. 67-69; Exec. Chair. Rural Devt. Corpn. 70-71; Gen. Man. Nat. Marketing Board of Zambia 71-74; Perm. Rep. to UN 74-75, Minister of Foreign Affairs May 75-; Pres. UN Council for Namibia 74-75.

Ministry of Foreign Affairs, Lusaka, Zambia.

Bandaranaike, Sirimavo Ratwatte Dias; Ceylonese politician; b. 17 April 1916; ed. St. Bridget's Convent, Colombo.

Widow of the late S. W. R. D. Bandaranaike (Prime Minister of Ceylon 56-59); Pres. of Sri Lanka Freedom Party 60-; Prime Minister, Minister of Defence and External Affairs July 60-65; mem. Senate until 65; Leader of Opposition 65-70; Prime Minister, Minister of Defence and Foreign Affairs, Planning, Econ. Affairs and Plan Implementation May 70-.

Horagolla, Nittambuwa, Sri Lanka.

Bandeen, Robert Angus, PH.D.; Canadian railway administrator; b. 29 Oct. 1930, Rodney, Ont.; *s.* of John Robert and Jessie Marie (Thomson) Bandeen; *m.* Mona Helen Blair 1958; four *s.*; ed. Univ. of Western Ont. and Duke Univ., U.S.A.

Joined Canadian Nat. Railways 55, Research and Devt. Dept. 55-66, Dir. of Corporate Planning 66-68, Vice-Pres. Corporate Planning and Finance 68-71, Vice-Pres. Great Lakes Region, Toronto 71-72, Exec. Vice-Pres. Finance and Admin. 72-74, Pres. and Chief Exec. Officer 74-.

Leisure interests: squash, tennis, skiing.

935 Lagauchetiere Street, W., Montreal, Quebec, H3G 3N4; Home: 3289 Cedar Avenue, Montreal, Quebec, H3Y 1Z6, Canada.

Telephone: (514) 877-3648 (Office); (514) 937-3641 (Home).

Bandeira de Mello, Lydio Machado, DR.JUR.; Brazilian university professor emeritus; b. 19 July 1901, Abaete, Minas Gerais; *s.* of Dr. Lydio Alerano and Adélia Machado Bandeira de Mello; *m.* Amália Introcaso Bandeira de Mello 1928; two *s.* two *d.*; ed. Univ. of Brazil.

Professor of Criminal Law, Univ. of Minas Gerais 52-71, Comparative Criminal Law 59-71, Prof. Emer. 72-.

Leisure interests: walking, cinema-going, philately.

Publs. *O Problema do Mal* 35, *A Procura de Deus* 38, *Responsabilidade Penal* 41, *Prova Matemática da Existência de Deus* 42, *Teoria do Destino* 44, *A Predestinação Para O Bem* 48, *Metafísica do Número* 46, *Tabu, Pecado e Crime* 49, *O Real e o Possível* 53, *Manual de Direito Penal* Vols. 1-4, 53-58, *A Origem dos Sexos* 55, *Filosofia do Direito* 57, *Ontologia e Lógica da Contradição* 59, *Metafísica do Tempo* 61, *O Direito Penal Hispano-Luso Medievo* 2 vols. 61, *Tratado de Direito Penal, Crime e Exclusão de Criminalidade* 62, *Da Responsabilidade Penal e Da Isenção de Pena* 62, *Da Capitulação dos Crimes e da Fixação das Penas* 63, *Metafísica da Gravitação* 63, *Memória, Espaço e Tempo* 2 vols. 63, *Cosmologia do Movimento* 65, *Teologia Matemática* 65, *Metafísica do Espaço* 66, *A Pluralidade de Consciências* 67, *Crítica Cosmológica da Física Quântica* 68, *Fórmulas Gerais da Distribuição de Probabilidades* 68, *Evangelho para Bacharéis* 69, *O Criminoso, O Crime e a Pena* 70, *Trabalhos de Algoritmia (Aritmética e Algebra) Superior* 71, *A Existência e a Imortalidade da Alma* 72, *As Credenciais da Razão* 73,

Teoria Algébrica das Permutações Condicionadas 72, *Crítica do Princípio de Razão Suficiente* 74, *A Falibilidade da Indução* 74, *A Conquista do Reino de Deus* (2 vols.) 75, *O Possível Puro* 75.
Rua Rodrigues Caldas, 703 Belo Horizonte, Minas Gerais, Brazil.
Telephone: 370198.

Bandio, Jean-Arthur: Central African Republic diplomatist; b. 6 June 1928, Brazzaville, Congo People's Repub.; *m.*; thirteen *c.*; ed. Ecole Normale, Mouyondzi, Congo People's Repub., Ecole Normale, St. Cloud, France, and Ecole de la France d'Outre-Mer.
Headmaster Brazzaville School; District Chief and Sub-Commr. in Cen. African Repub., Dir. of Cabinet, Office of the Pres. of C.A.R.; Minister of the Interior, then of Foreign Affairs; Amb. to Italy, subsequently to Egypt; Perm. Rep. to UN Sept. 74-.
Permanent Mission of the Central African Republic to United Nations, 386 Park Avenue South, Room 1614, New York, N.Y. 10016, U.S.A.

Bandzar, Jambalyn; Mongolian diplomatist; b. 10 July 1922; ed. Mongolian State Univ., Ulan Bator.
Secondary school teacher 46-48; local govt. posts 48-50; First Sec., Moscow 50-54; Head of Dept., Ministry of Foreign Affairs 54-56; First Sec., Prague 56-58; Head of Dept., Ministry of Foreign Affairs, and Deputy Foreign Minister 58-60; Amb. to Hungary 60-64; Permanent Rep. of Mongolian People's Repub. to UN 66-68; Amb. to France 69-72, to Poland 72-.
Embassy of the Mongolian People's Republic, Ul. Ujazdowskie 12, Warsaw, Poland.

Banerji, Asoka Nath; Indian steel executive; b. 19 Dec. 1917, Banares, U.P.; *s.* of late Sikhar Nath Banerji and Anurupa Debi; *m.* Subrata Matilal 1948; two *s.* one *d.*; ed. Muzaffarpar, Patna, Calcutta and Massachusetts Inst. of Technology, U.S.A.
Army service 41-47; joined Indian Admin. Service 47; District Magistrate, W. Bengal, and Deputy Sec. to Govt. of W. Bengal; Chief Passport and Visa Officer for India, Dacca 52; Deputy Gen. Man. Durgapur Steel Project, Ministry of Iron and Steel 56-60; Sec. Hindustan Steel Ltd. 60-61; Iron and Steel Controller, Govt. of India 61-64; Gen. Man. Rourkela Steel Plant 64-67; Gen. Man. Rourkela Steel Plant and Dir. in charge, Durgapur Steel Plant Aug.-Dec. 67; Deputy Chair. Hindustan Steel Ltd. 67-69; Dir.-Gen. Bureau of Public Enterprises, Govt. of India 69-73; Special Sec. for Industrial Devt. 73-.
Leisure interests: reading, classical music.
Ministry of Industrial Development, Udyog Bhavan, New Delhi 11; Home: 77 Lodi Estate, New Delhi 3, India.
Telephone: 375446 (Office); 617773 (Home).

Banerji, Shishir Kumar, B.A.; Indian diplomatist; b. 21 Oct. 1913, Uttarpara; *s.* of Mr. and Mrs. A. D. Banerji; *m.* Gauri Chatterjee 1939; two *s.* two *d.*; ed. Univ. of Allahabad and New Coll., Oxford.
Joined ICS 37; Deputy Commr. Central Provinces 37-46; Sec. Civil Supplies, Cen. Provs. Govt. 46-47; First Sec., Chargé d'Affaires, Tehran 47-49; Deputy Sec. Ministry of External Affairs 49-51; Deputy High Commr., Lahore 51-54; Consul-Gen. San Francisco 54-56; Chair. UN Visiting Mission to British and French Togolands 55; Envoy to Syria 56, Ambassador 57-58; High Commissioner to Malaya 58-59; Joint Sec., Ministry of External Affairs 60-61; Chief of Protocol 61-64; Chief Inspector of Indian Missions abroad 64; Amb. to German Fed. Repub. 64-67, to Japan 67-70; Sec. Ministry of Foreign Affairs 70-72; Lieut. Gov. Goa 72-.
Leisure interests: photography, collection of old Indian sculpture, paintings and modern art.
Cabo Raj Niwas, Goa, India.

Bangerter, Hans Ernst; Swiss sports official; b. 10 June 1924, Studen, Bienne; *m.* Hedy Tanner 1948; one *s.* two *d.*; ed. Technical Coll., Bienne.
Assistant Sec. Int. Fed. of Association Football (FIFA), Zürich 53-59; Sec.-Gen. European Union of Association Football (UEFA), Berne 60-.
Leisure interests: gardening, golf, skiing, walking, mountaineering.
Office: UEFA, P.O. Box 16, Berne 15, Switzerland; Home: Hubelgasse 25, 3065 Bolligen, BE, Switzerland.
Telephone: 031 43 17 35.

Bangura, Samuel Lansana, B.SC.ECONS.; Sierra Leonean banker; b. 7 June 1930, Yele Northern Prov.; ed. Bo Govt. Secondary School, Hull Univ. and Queen's Coll., Oxford, England.
Worked as Asst., later District Commr., Bonthe District 59-62; Senior Asst. Sec., Deputy Financial Sec. Ministry of Devt. 62-64, Perm. Sec. 64-66; Asst. to Gov., Bank of Sierra Leone 66, Deputy Gov. 66-70, Gov. 70-; Chair. Board of Govs. for Int. School 69-, Board of Dirs., Nat. Devt. Bank 70-; Dir. Sierra Leone Produce Marketing Board 70-; Fellow, Int. Bankers' Asscn.
Bank of Sierra Leone, P.O.B. 30, Freetown; and Leone Lodge, Spur View, Wilberforce, Sierra Leone.

Bank-Anthony, Sir Mobolaji, K.B.E.; Nigerian business executive; b. 11 June 1907; ed. Methodist Boys High School, Lagos, Church Missionary Society Grammar School, Lagos, Ibeju-Ode Grammar School.
Postal Clerk, Nigerian Post and Telegraph Dept. 24; later built up palm oil business and after Second World War built up construction, haulage and cinema companies; Chair., Nigerian Stock Exchange; Fellow Inst. of Directors, London.
Executive House, 2A Oil Mill Street, P.O.B. 75, Lagos, Nigeria.

Bankole-Jones, Sir Samuel; Sierra Leonean judge; b. 23 Aug. 1911; ed. Methodist Boys' High School, Freetown, Fourah Bay Coll. and Middle Temple, London.
Teacher, Methodist Boys' High School, Freetown 32-34; called to the Bar 38; part-time lecturer in law and public admin., Fourah Bay Coll. 38-49; police magistrate 49-59; Puisne Judge 59-63; Chief Justice of Sierra Leone 63; Pres. of Sierra Leone Court of Appeal 65; Chancellor Univ. of Sierra Leone 69; Judge, Supreme Court 71-72; Legal Consultant 72-; Chair. of Fourah Bay Coll. Council.
c/o Supreme Court, Freetown, Sierra Leone.

Bannerman, David Armitage, O.B.E., M.B.E., LL.D., SC.D., F.R.S.E.; Scottish ornithologist and author; b. 27 Nov. 1886, Pendleton, Lancs.; *s.* of David Alexander Bannerman and Edith Bannerman (née Armitage); *m.* 1st Muriel G. Morgan 1911 (died 1945), one *s.* (deceased) two *d.*; 2nd Jane Priestley (née Holland) 1952; ed. Wellington Coll. and Pembroke Coll., Cambridge.
Zoological Dept. British Museum 10-52; served in France, First World War Staff Officer, B.R.C.S. H.Q.; Second World War Asst. Censor; Hon. Fellow, American, Cyprian, Gambian, Spanish and French Ornithologists' Unions; Hon. Pres. Scottish Ornithologists; Vice-Pres. Royal Soc. for the Protection of Birds; Scientific Fellow, Zoological Soc. of London; Hon. Curator, Royal Scottish Museum, Edinburgh; Order of St. John; Hon. Assoc., British Museum; Gold Medallist, British Ornithological Union.
Leisure interests: writing bird books, travel, fishing, bird-watching.
Publs. *The Canary Islands: Their History, Natural History and Scenery* 22, *The Birds of Tropical West Africa* (8 vols.) 30-51, *The Birds of West and Equatorial Africa* (2 vols.) 53, *The Birds of the British Isles* (12 vols.) 53-64, *The Birds of Cyprus* (with Jane Bannerman) 59, *The Birds of the Atlantic Islands:* vol. 1 (*Canary Islands*) 62, vol. 2 (*Madeira*) 65, vol. 3 (*Azores*)

with Jane Bannerman 66, vol. 4 (Cape Verde Islands) with Jane Bannerman, *Handbook of the Birds of Cyprus and Migrants of the Middle East* 71, *Birds of the Maltese Archipelago* (with J. A. Vella-Gaffiero) 76, and many scientific publications.
Bailiff's House, Slindon, Arundel, Sussex, England.
Telephone: Slindon 212.

Bannikov, Nikolai Vasilyevich; Soviet politician; b. 1914; ed. Kuibyshev Industrial Inst.
Shop Mechanic, then Man., later Chief Mechanic, then Dep. Dir. of factory, and Party Organizer of C.P.S.U. Central Cttee. at a Kuibyshev factory 37-45; Party Official 45-59; Second Sec., Karaganda Regional Cttee. of Communist Party of Kazakhstan 59-62, First Sec. 63-68; also mem. Central Cttee. of C.P. of Kazakhstan, Alt. mem. of C.P.S.U. Central Cttee., and Deputy to U.S.S.R. Supreme Soviet 66-, mem. Comm. on Construction and Industry of Bldg. Materials, Soviet of Union; mem. C.P.S.U. 40-, First Sec. Irkutsk Regional Cttee. 68-.
Irkutsk Regional Committee, Irkutsk, U.S.S.R.

Bansal, Ghamandi Lal, M.A., LL.B.; Indian commercial executive; b. 3 Dec. 1914, Ranikhet, U.P.; s. of Musaddi Lal; m. Mrs. Shanti Bansal 1941; three s. two d.; ed. A.V. Mission School, Ranikhet, Government Intermediate Coll., Almora, and Lucknow Univ.
Former Dir. State Bank of India; mem. Indian Parl. 52-57; Sec.-Gen. Fed. of Indian Chambers of Commerce and Industry, All-India Organization of Industrial Employers, Indian Nat. Cttee. of Int. Chamber of Commerce 54-75; Chair. Governing Body of Shri Ram Coll. of Commerce; Treas. Helen Keller Trust for the Blind, Deaf and Dumb; Hon. Treas. Indian Council of World Affairs; Chair. Nat. Cttee. for the Devt. of Backward Areas.
Leisure interests: reading, golf.
Publ. *India and Pakistan—An Analysis of Economic, Agricultural and Mineral Resources.*
28 Ferozeshah Road, New Delhi 1, India.
Telephone: 381528 (Office); 388120 (Home).

Bante, Brig-Gen. Teferi; Ethiopian army officer and politician.
Chairman of Provisional Mil. Council Nov. 74-.
c/o Provisional Military Council, Addis Ababa, Ethiopia.

Banzer Suárez, Gen. Hugo; Bolivian army officer and politician; b. 10 May 1926, Santa Cruz; s. of César Banzer and Luisa Suárez; m. Yolanda G. Prada 1926; two s. three d.; ed. Mil. Coll., La Paz.
Commander Bolivian 4th Cavalry Regiment; Minister of Educ. and Culture 64-66; Mil. Attaché Washington, D.C. 67-69; Dir. Mil. Coll. 69-71; in exile Jan.-Aug. 71; Pres. of Bolivia Aug. 71-; Order of Mil. Merit (U.S.A.), and other national and foreign decorations.
Palacio del Gobierno, La Paz, Bolivia.

Baram, Moshe: Israeli politician; b. 1911, Zdolvinov, Ukraine.
Member of Youth and Hechalutz movts. and Hachshara group in Ukraine; emigrated to Israel 31; worked as a bldg. labourer, active in Hagana, mem. Socialist Youth movt.; Sec. Israel Workers' Party, Jerusalem 42; mem. Yishuv (Reps. Assembly of Jewish Community) 44; del. to World Zionist Congresses 46-; mem. Israel Labour Party 46-, Cen. Exec. Bodies 46-; Sec.-Gen. Histadrut (Jerusalem Workers' Council) 48; mem. Hagana HQ in Jerusalem, Emergency Comm. 48, Jerusalem Municipal Council, Chair. Coalition Exec. 55-59; mem. Fourth and subsequent Knessets 59-, Chair. Labour Comm., mem. Finance Comm.; Coalition Whip in Sixth Knesset 65; Chair. Unemployment Insurance Comm., mem. Cen. Body of Histadrut Council's Fed. of Labour; Minister of Labour 74-.
Ministry of Labour, Jerusalem, Israel.

Baranov, Vasily Gavrilovich; Soviet endocrinologist; b. 25 Dec. 1899, Gatchina, Leningrad Region; s. of Gavril Petrovich Baranov and Julia Ivanovna Baranova; m. Maria Michailovna Tushinskaja 1952; ed. Leningrad Military Medical Acad.
Army therapeutist; Intern 25-29; Senior Assoc. Inst. of Experimental Medicine 32-40; Head of Dept., First Leningrad Medical Inst. 38-41, 45-46; Senior Research Assoc. 46-54; Head of Laboratory, Inst. of Physiology 54-, Prof. 54; Corresp. mem. U.S.S.R. Acad. of Medical Sciences 52-60, mem. 60-; mem. Board U.S.S.R. Soc. of Therapeutists; Chair. All-Union Soc. of Endocrinologists, Leningrad Soc. of Endocrinologists; Orders of Lenin, Red Banner of Labour and Red Star and other decorations.
Leisure interests: holidays at country house and travelling, boating, walking; thinking over scientific problems.
Publs. Over 135 works on endocrinology, including pathogenesis and treatment of toxic goitre, diabetes mellitus, physiology and pathology of ageing and climax.
Pavlov Institute of Physiology, U.S.S.R. Academy of Sciences, 6 Naberezhnaya Makarova, Leningrad, U.S.S.R.

Barata, Julio de Carvalho; Brazilian politician; b. 1905, Manaus; ed. Colégio Estanislau Kestka (São Paulo), Colégio Máximo Anchieta (Nova Friburgo), Universidade Federal do Estado do Rio de Janeiro, and Universidade do Estado da Guanabara.
Director-General, Dept. of Information; Dir. *Jornal do Comercio* (Santos) and *A Batalha* (Rio de Janeiro); Vice-Pres. Tribunal Superior do Trabalho; Minister of Labour 69-74.
c/o Ministério de Trabalho, Brasília, D.F., Brazil.

Barber, Baron (Life Peer), cr. 74, of Wentbridge in West Yorkshire; **Anthony Perrinot Lysberg Barber,** P.C., T.D.; British fmr. politician; b. 4 July 1920, Hull; s. of John Barber, C.B.E., and Katy Lysberg; m. Jean Patricia Asquith 1950; two d.; ed. Retford School and Oriel Coll., Oxford.
Army Service 39-40, Royal Air Force 40-45; mem. Parl. 51-64, 65-74; Parl. Private Sec., Air Ministry 52-54; Govt. Whip 55-57; Lord Commissioner of the Treasury 57-58; Parl. Private Sec. to Prime Minister 58-59; Econ. Sec. to the Treasury 59-62, Financial Sec. to the Treasury 62-63; Minister of Health 63-64; Chair. Conservative Party 67-70, Redfearn Nat. Glass 67; Dir. British Ropes (now Bridon) 64-70, 74-, Chartered Bank 66-70; Chancellor of Duchy of Lancaster June-July 70; Chancellor of Exchequer 70-74; Chair. Standard and Chartered Banking Group Sept. 74-; Conservative.
15 Montpelier Square, London, S.W.7, England.

Barber, John Norman Romney; British business executive; b. 22 April 1919, Leigh-on-Sea, Essex; m.; one s.
Principal in charge of Cen. Finance Dept., Ministry of Supply 46-55; with Ford Motor Co. Ltd. 55-65, Dir. of Finance 62, Founder, Chair. Ford Motor Credit Co. 63; Dir. of Finance, AEI Ltd. 65; Finance Dir. Leyland Motor Corpn. 68, Dir. of Finance and Planning, British Leyland Motor Corpn. 68, Deputy Man. Dir. 71, Deputy Chair. 73; Fellow, British Inst. of Management; Past Chair. Board of Trade Investments Grants Advisory Cttee.; fmr. mem. Royal Comm. on Medical Educ.
Leisure interests: motor sport, photography, reading.
Copthall Green House, Upshire, Essex, England.
Telephone: 23241.

Barber, Samuel, DR. MUS.; American composer; b. 9 March 1910; ed. Curtis Inst. of Music, Philadelphia.
Works include: String Quartet 36, Symphony 36, Adagio for Strings 36, Essay for Orchestra 37, Concerto

for Violin and Orchestra 40, Second Essay 42, Second Symphony 44, *Capricorn Concerto* 44, 'Cello Concerto 46, Ballet Suite, *Medea* 46, *Knoxville: Summer of 1915* (voice and orchestra) 47, *Piano Sonata* 49, *Souvenir* 53, *Prayers of Kierkegaard* (for chorus, soprano and orchestra) 54, *Vanessa* 58, *Die Natale* 60, *Piano Concerto* 62, *Andromache's Farewell* 63, *Antony and Cleopatra* (opera) 66, *Despite and Still* (song cycle) 68, cappella choruses, *Twelfth Night, To Be Sung on the Water* 69; Hon. D.Mus. (Harvard); mem. Nat. Inst. of Arts and Letters, U.S.A.; American Soc. of Composers, Authors and Publishers; Pulitzer Prize 58, 63.
c/o G. Schirmer Inc., 609 Fifth Avenue, New York, N.Y. 10017; Capricorn, Mount Kisco, N.Y. 10549, U.S.A.

Barbieri, H.E. Cardinal Antonio María; Uruguayan ecclesiastic; b. 12 Oct. 1892, Montevideo.
Joined the Capuchin Order; ordained priest 21; Titular Bishop of Macra 36; Archbishop of Montevideo 40-; created Cardinal by Pope John XXIII Dec. 58.
Arzobispado, Calle Trienta y Tres 1368, Montevideo, Uruguay.

Barbieri, Fedora; Italian singer; b. 4 June 1919; ed. Trieste High School and Conservatoire.
Scholarship to Teatro Lirico, Florence 40; début as Fidalma in Cimarosa's *The Secret Marriage*, Teatro Comunale, Florence 40; has appeared in leading roles at La Scala, Milan 42-, Teatro Colon, Buenos Aires 47-, Metropolitan Opera House, New York and Royal Opera House, Covent Garden, London 50-; has also appeared at numerous important festivals and opera seasons in Italy, Germany, U.S.A., France, Spain, Portugal, Brazil, Austria, etc.; has sung leading roles in recordings of *Aida, Il Trovatore, Requiem, Falstaff, Un Ballo in Maschera* (Verdi), *La Gioconda* (Ponchielli), *La Favorita* and *Linda di Chamonix* (Donizetti), *Suor Angelica* (Puccini).
Viale Belfiore 9, Florence, Italy.

Barbieri, Lázaro; Argentine politician; b. 1911; ed. Univ. Nacional de Tucumán.
Former Prof. of Sociology, Univ. Nacional de Tucumán; Prof. of Argentine History and Social Thought, Univ. Nacional de Tucumán; Governor of Tucumán Province.
Publs. *La Integración de Latinoamerica—Su Problemática Sociológica, La Reforma Religiosa y la Formación de la Conciencia Moderna, Sociología de la Educación y la Problemática del Sistema Educativo.*
Universidad Nacional de Tucumán, San Miguel de Tucumán, Argentina.

Barbosa, Raúl; Brazilian international finance official; b. 19 Aug. 1911, Fortaleza, Ceará; ed. School of Law, Fed. Univ. of Ceará.
Director-General, Justice Dept., State of Ceará 43-46; mem. Brazilian Chamber of Deputies 46-50; Gov. of State of Ceará 51-54; Legal Counsel, Banco do Nordeste 54-56, Pres. 56-68; Prof., School of Business Admin., Univ. of Tucumán; Exec. Dir. for Brazil and Ecuador, Inter-American Devt. Bank (IDB) 68-75.
Publs. several works on economics and related subjects.
c/o Ministério des Assuntos Exteriores, Brasília, Brazil.

Barboza, Mário Gibson; Brazilian diplomatist; b. 1918, Olinda, Pernambuco; ed. Faculdade de Direito de Recife.
Joined diplomatic service 40; Vice-Consul, Houston; Sec., Washington, Brussels; Minister-Counsellor, Buenos Aires; Deputy Perm. Rep. to UN 58-62; Amb. to Austria 62, to U.S.A. until 69; Minister of Foreign Affairs 69-74; Amb. to Greece 74-.
Embassy of Brazil, 14 Platia Philikis Eterias, Athens, Greece.

Barbour, Walworth; American Ambassador to Israel 61-73; see *The International Who's Who 1975-76*.

Barčák, Andrej, ING.; Czechoslovak economist and politician; b. 19 Jan. 1920, Mlynky, Slovakia; ed. mining colls. in Sopron, Hungary, and Ostrava.
Worked in various mines and enterprises in Hungary 42-47; returned to Slovakia 47; various leading posts in industry until 55; Ministry of Metallurgical Industry 55-57; Deputy Minister of Metallurgical Industry and Ore Mines 57-63; Dir. Slovak Magnesite Works, Košice 63-69; mem. Econ. Comm. of Central Cttee. C.P. of Slovakia 63-66; State Sec. Ministry of Foreign Trade Sept. 69-Jan. 70; Minister of Foreign Trade 70-; mem. Legislative Council 70-; Head of Del. to CMEA Perm. Comm. for Foreign Trade 70-; Deputy to House of the People, Fed. Assembly 71-; Order of Labour.
Ministry of Foreign Trade, Prague 1, tř. Politických vězňů 20, Czechoslovakia.

Barcikowski, Kazimierz, D.ECON.; Polish politician; b. 22 March 1927, Zglechowo, Mińsk Mazowiecki; ed. Higher School of Social Sciences, Warsaw.
During Second World War combatant in Home Army; active mem. Rural Youth Union ("Wici") 46-48; posts in Polish Youth Union, Łódź 48-49, mem. Gen. Board 50-56, Sec. 56; Vice-Chair. Rural Youth Union 57, subsequently Chair.; Sub-Editor, State Publishing House "Iskry" 54-56; mem. Polish United Workers' Party (PZPR) 53-; Deputy Head, Organizational Dept. Cen. Cttee. PZPR 65-Nov. 68; Editor-in-Chief *Życie Partii* (Party Life) 65-Nov. 68; Deputy mem. Cen. Cttee. PZPR 64-68, mem. Nov. 68-, Sec. 70-74, alt. mem. Politburo Dec. 71-; First Sec. Voivodship Cttee. PZPR, Poznań Nov. 68-Dec. 70; Deputy to Seym 65-; Minister of Agriculture 74-; mem. Presidium of Govt. 74-; Order of Banner of Labour 1st and 2nd Class.
Ministerstwo Rolnictwa, ul. Wspólna 30, 00-519 Warsaw, Poland.

Barclay, Sir Roderick Edward, G.C.V.O., K.C.M.G.; British retired diplomatist; b. 22 Feb. 1909, Kobe, Japan; s. of J. G. and Mrs. Barclay; m. Jean Gladstone 1934; one s. three d.; ed. Harrow School and Trinity Coll., Cambridge.
Entered Foreign Service 32; served Brussels, Paris and Washington; Principal Private Sec. to Sec. of State for Foreign Affairs 49-51; Asst. Under-Sec. of State 51, Deputy Under-Sec. of State 53; Amb. to Denmark 56-60; Deputy Under-Sec. of State for Foreign Affairs 60-63; Amb. to Belgium 63-69; Dir. Barclays Bank S.A. 69-, Chair. 70-74; Dir. Slough Estates Ltd. 69-, Barclays Bank Int. Ltd. 71, Banque de Bruxelles S.A. 71.
Leisure interests: shooting, fishing, travel.
Publ. *Ernest Bevin and the Foreign Office 1963-69* 75.
Great White End, Latimer, Bucks., England.
Telephone: Little Chalfont 2050.

Barco, Virgilio, S.B., A.M., PH.D.; Colombian international finance official; b. 17 Sept. 1921, Cúcuta; m.; one s. three d.; ed. M.I.T. and Boston Univ.
Secretary of Public Works and Finance, Norte de Santander 43-45; Sec.-Gen. and Acting Minister of Communications 45-46; mem. House of Reps. 49-51, Senator 58-66; Minister of Public Works 58-61; Pres. Eighth Pan-American Highway Congress 60; Amb. to U.K. 61-62; Minister of Agriculture and Acting Minister of Finance 63-64; Mayor of Bogotá 66-69; Exec. Dir. IBRD, IFC and IDA 69.
c/o Ministerio de Asuntos Exteriores, Bogotá, Colombia.

Barcroft, Henry, M.A., M.D., F.R.C.P., F.R.S.; British physiologist; b. 18 Oct. 1904, Cambridge; s. of Sir Joseph Barcroft and Mary A. Ball; m. Bridget M. Ramsey 1933; three s. one d.; ed. Marlborough Coll., King's Coll., Cambridge and St. Mary's Hospital. London.
Lecturer in Physiology, University Coll., London 32-35; Dunville Prof. of Physiology, Queen's Univ., Belfast 35-48; Prof. of Physiology, St. Thomas's Hospital Medical School, Univ. of London 48-71, Emer. 71-;

Sir Henry Wellcome Trustee 66-74; Chair. Research Defence Soc. 69-72, Sec. 72-; Hon. D.Sc. (W. Australia, Queen's Univ., Belfast); Hon. M.D. (Innsbruck); Hon. mem. Soc. Française d'Angiologie.
Leisure interests: sailing, golf.
Publs. *Sympathetic control of human blood vessels* (with H. J. C. Swan) 52; papers in *Journal of Physiology* and other scientific journals.
44 Wood Lane, Highgate, London, N6 5UB, England. Telephone: 01-340-2338.

Barcs, Sándor; Hungarian journalist; b. 10 Nov. 1912; s. of Sándor Barcs Sr. and M. Wack; m. 1st Maria Molnár 1945, 2nd Marta Kenéz 1962, 3rd Magdolna Szabó 1970; two s. one d.
Editor, Hungarian Telegraphic Agency 45-50, Gen. Man. 50-; mem. Council Patriotic People's Front, Parl. and Presidential Council; Chair. Hungarian Football Association 49-63; Vice-Pres. European Football Union (UEFA) 62-, Acting Chair. 72-; mem. Council Inter-parliamentary Union 63-; Chair. Nat. Fed. of Hungarian Journalists 65-74; Labour Order of Merit, golden degree 70; Order of the Red Banner 72.
Leisure interests: angling, soccer.
Hungarian Telegraphic Agency, Fém utca 5/7, H-1426 Budapest 1, Hungary.
Telephone: 159-490.

Barcsay, Jenö; Hungarian artist; b. 14 Jan. 1900, Katona; s. of Boldizsár Barcsay and Irén Kabdebó; ed. Acad. of Fine Arts, Budapest.
Studied on state scholarship in Paris 26-27, 29-30, and in Italy; mem. artists' colony at Szentendre 29-; Prof. of Anatomy and Perspective, Acad. of Fine Arts, Budapest 45-; principal works include paintings, drawings and mosaics; numerous exhbns. in Hungary and abroad; exhibited at Venice Biennale 64; Kossuth Prize 53; Honoured Artist Award 64; Gold Medal Pro Arte 67; Eminent Artist award 69; Prix National, Deuxième Festival International de Peinture, Cagnes-sur-Mer, France 70; Banner Order of Hungarian People's Repub., 2nd degree 75.
Publs. *Anatomy for the Artist* 53, *Man and Drapery* 58, *Form und Raum* 66.
H-1062 Budapest VI, Népköztásaság u. 87-89, Hungary. Telephone: 229-480.

Bard, Philip, A.B., A.M., PH.D.; American physiologist; b. 25 Oct. 1898, Hueneme, Calif.; s. of Hon. Thomas R. Bard and Mary Gerbeding Bard; m. 1st Harriet Hunt 1922 (died 1964), 2nd Janet Mackenzie Rioch 1965 (died 1974); two d.; ed. Thacher School, Ojai, Calif., Princeton and Harvard Univs.
Teaching Fellow in Physiology, Harvard 25-26, Instructor 26-28, Asst Prof. Biology, Princeton Univ. 28-31; Asst. Prof. Physiology and Tutor Normal Medical Sciences, Harvard Medical School 31-33; Prof. Physiology and Dir. Physiology Dept., Johns Hopkins Univ. 33-64, Prof. Emeritus 64-; Dean of Medical Faculty 53-57; mem. and fmr. Pres. American Physiological Soc., mem. Nat. Acad. Sciences, American Acad. Arts and Sciences, Asscn. of American Physicians, American Philosophical Soc., American Neurological Asscn., Soc. for Experimental Biology and Medicine (Pres. 59-61), Asscn. Research in Nervous and Mental Diseases (Pres. 50); served as mem. of Cttee. on Aviation Medicine; Chair. Sub-Cttee. on Motion Sickness; mem. Cttee. on Shock and Transfusions, Div. Medical Sciences, Nat. Research Council, Washington, D.C., during Second World War; Trustee, Rockefeller Univ. 57-; Pres. The International Foundation 69-; Lashley Award for Work in Neurobiology, American Philosophical Soc. 62; American Coll. of Physicians Award for Achievement in Science of Medicine 68; Hon. Sc.D. (Princeton 47, Washington and Lee Univ. 49), Dr. h.c. (Univ. Católica de Chile, Univ. Nacional Mayor de San Marcos de Lima); Hon. LL.D. (Johns Hopkins).

Office: Johns Hopkins Medical School, Baltimore, Md. 21205; Home: 6 Meadow Road, Baltimore, Md. 21212, U.S.A.
Telephone: 301-955-3881.

Bardeen, John, PH.D., D.SC.; American physicist; b. 23 May 1908, Wisconsin; s. of Charles Bardeen and Althea Harmer; m. Jane Maxwell 1938; two s. one d.; ed. Univs. of Wisconsin and Princeton.
Geophysicist with Gulf Research and Development Corpn. 30-33; Junior Fellow, Harvard Univ. 35-38; Asst. Prof. of Physics, Univ. of Minnesota 38-41; Physicist at U.S. Naval Ordnance Laboratory 41-45; Research Physicist, Bell Telephone Laboratory 45-51; Prof. of Electrical Engineering and Physics, Univ. of Illinois 51-; Fellow, American Physical Society, mem. Nat. Acad. of Sciences; Nobel Prize for Physics (with W. Shockley and W. H. Brattain) 56 for research leading to the invention of the transistor, Nobel Prize for Physics (with L. N. Cooper, q.v. and J. R. Schrieffer, q.v.) 72, U.S. Nat. Medal of Science 65.
55 Greencroft, Champaign, Ill. 61820, U.S.A.
Telephone: 217-352-6497.

Bardini, Adolfo, DR.ING.; Italian automobile executive; b. 9 April 1915, Genoa; s. of the late Emilio and Eugenia Baltuzzi; m. 1st Ernestina Zampaglione 1939; two d.; 2nd Mirella Noli Parmeggiani 1972; ed. Naples Univ.
General Man. Fabbrica Macchine Industriali, Naples 52-55; Dir. and Gen. Man. Nuova San Giorgio, Genoa 55-62; Dir. and Gen. Man. Alfa Romeo S.p.A. 62-74; Chair. Autodelta S.p.A. 62-74, ANFIA (Italian Asscn. of Motor Vehicle Mfrs.) 75-, Turin Int. Motor Show 75.
Leisure interest: skiing.
ANFIA, Corso Galileo Ferraris 61, 10128 Turin, Italy. Telephone: Turin 57-61.

Bardini, Aleksander; Polish theatre and opera director, actor and professor; b. 17 Nov. 1913, Łódź; m.; one d.; ed. State Inst. of Theatrical Arts, Warsaw.
Teacher, Warsaw State Coll. of Theatrical Arts 66-; developed contemporary style of musical interpretation; State Prize 53, Collective State Prize 55; Commdr.'s Cross, Order of Polonia Restituta; Ministry of Culture and Arts Prize, 1st Class.
Leisure interest: music.
Productions: operas: *Jutro* (Baird), *Electra* 71, *Boris Godunov, Otello, Cosi fan tutte*; plays: *Dziady* (Mickiewicz), *Midsummer Night's Dream, Henry IV, Measure for Measure, A Streetcar Named Desire, The Night of the Iguana, Tango* (Mrożek), *John Gabriel Borkman.*
Ul. Mokotowska 17 m. 21, 00-640 Warsaw, Poland. Telephone: 25-21-22.

Bardot, Brigitte; French actress; b. 28 Sept. 1934; m. 1st Roger Vadim (q.v.), 2nd Jacques Charrier, 3rd Gunther Sachs 1966 (dissolved 1969); ed. Paris Conservatoire.
Stage and film career 52-; films include *Manina: la Fille sans Voile, Le Fils de Caroline Chérie, Futures Vedettes, Les Grandes Manoeuvres, La Lumière d'en Face, Cette Sacrée Gamine, La Mariée est trop belle, Et Dieu Créa la Femme, En Effeuillant la Marguerite, Une Parisienne, Les Bijoutiers du Clair de Lune, En Cas de Malheur, La Femme et le Pantin, Babette s'en va-t-en Guerre, Voulez-vous Danser avec Moi?, La Vérité, Please not now?, Le Mépris, Le Repos du Guerrier, Une Ravissante Idiote, Viva Maria, A Coeur Joie 67, Two Weeks in September 67, Shalako 68, Les Femmes 69, Les Novices 70, Boulevard du Rhum 71, Les Pétroleuses 71, Don Juan 73, L'Histoire très bonne et très joyeuse de Colinot trousse-chemise 73.*
65 boulevard Lannes, 75116 Paris; and La Madrague, Saint-Tropez (Var.), France.

Barenboim, Daniel; Israeli concert pianist and conductor; b. 15 Nov. 1942, Buenos Aires, Argentina; s. of Prof. Enrique Barenboim; m. Jacqueline du Pré (q.v.)

1967; studied piano with his father and other musical subjects with Nadia Boulanger, Edwin Fischer and Igor Markevitch.

Debut in Buenos Aires at age of seven; played Bach D Minor Concerto with orchestra at Salzburg Mozarteum at age of nine; has played in Europe regularly 54-; yearly tours of U.S.A. 57-; has toured Japan, Australia and S. America; has played with or conducted New Philharmonia Orchestra, London Symphony Orchestra, New York Philharmonic, Philadelphia Orchestra, Israel Philharmonic, Vienna Philharmonic, Berlin Philharmonic, etc.; frequently tours with English Chamber Orchestra and with them records for E.M.I. (projects include complete Mozart Piano Concertos and late Symphonies); other recording projects include complete Beethoven Sonatas and Beethoven Concertos (with New Philharmonia Orchestra conducted by Klemperer); has appeared in series of Master-classes on B.B.C. television; presented Festival of Summer Music on South Bank, London, 68, 69; leading role in Brighton Festival 67-; appears regularly at Edinburgh Festival; conductor, Edinburgh Festival Opera 73; Musical Dir. Orchestre de Paris 75-.

c/o Harold Holt Ltd., 122 Wigmore Street, London, W.1, England.

Telephone: 01-935 2331.

Bargellini, Piero; Italian writer; b. 5 Aug. 1897.
Founder *Calendario dei pensieri e delle pratiche solari* 23, *Frontespizio* 29; Mayor of Florence 66-67; articles for numerous newspapers and magazines including the *Corriere della Sera*; Christian Democrat.
Publs. include: *Scritti a maggio* 31, *Fra Diavolo* 32, *San Bernardino da Siena* 33, *G. Carducci* 34, *Architettura con fregio polemico* 35, *David* 36, *Città di pittori* 39, *Via Larga* 41, *S. Francesco* 41, *Volti di pietra* 43, *Caffè Michelangiolo* 44, *Il Ghirlandaio del bel mondo fiorentino* 45, *La fiaba pittorica di Benozzo Gozzoli* 46, *Amor profano* 46, *Il sogno nostalgico di Sandro Botticelli* 46, *La pittura ascetica del Beato Angelico* 48, *La dolce mestizia del Perugino* 50, *Vedere e capire Firenze* 50, *Lui* 50, *Lei* 50, *Pian dei Giullari* (12 vols.) 50, *Nostalgico di Sandro Botticelli* 51, *Chiodi solari* 52, *Santa Chiara* 52, *Canto alle rondini* 53, *Sant'Antonino da Firenze* 54, *Tivurzi* 55, *Ghirlanda por Firenze* 56, *In Lizza per l'arte* 57, *Santi come uomini* 57, *Belvedere: arte Greca, arte etrusca* (2 vols.) 57-59, *I santi del giorno* 58, *Il Natale nella storia, nella leggenda e nell'arte* 59, *Assisi città santa* 60.
Via della Pinzochere 3, Florence, Italy.

Barger, Thomas C.; American oil executive (retd.); b. 30 Aug. 1909, Minneapolis, Minn.; s. of Michael T. Barger and Mary M. Donahue; m. 1st Kathleen Ray 1937 (died 1971); six c.; 2nd Kathleen Vachreau Loeb 1972; ed. Univ. of North Dakota, U.S.A.
Joined Arabian American Oil Co. (Aramco) as geologist 37; Dir. Local Govt. Relations; Rep. to Saudi Arabian Govt.; Vice-Pres. Aramco 58, Pres. 59, Chief Exec. Officer 61-69, Chair. of Board 68-69, Corporate Dir. and Petroleum Consultant 69-; Dir. Offshore Technology Inc., Calif. First Bank, Kratos Corpn., Northrop Corpn.; Trustee, Univ. of San Diego, Alumni Board, Univ. of North Dakota, Board of Overseers, Univ. of Calif. at San Diego.
Leisure interests: archaeology, photography, water skiing, tinkering, handball, golf.
Publ. *Energy Policies of Arab States of Persian Gulf* 75.
2685 Calle del Oro, La Jolla, Calif. 92037, U.S.A.
Telephone: 714-459-8680.

Barghoorn, Frederick Charles, PH.D.; American university professor; b. 4 July 1911; ed. Amherst Coll. and Harvard Univ.
Press Attaché, American Embassy, Moscow 43-47; Department of Political Science, Yale Univ. 47-, Prof. of Political Science 56-.

Publs. *The Soviet Image of the United States* 50, *Soviet Russian Nationalism* 56, *The Soviet Cultural Offensive* 60, *Soviet Foreign Propaganda* 64, *Politics in the U.S.S.R.* 66.
Department of Political Science, Yale University, New Haven, Connecticut, U.S.A.

Bargmann, Wolfgang L., DR. MED.; German anatomist; b. 27 Jan. 1906, Nuremberg; m. Charlotte Hauptfleisch 1935; two d.; ed. Frankfurt, Munich, Vienna and Berlin Univs.
Privat Dozent, Zürich Univ. 35-38; Prosector, Leipzig Univ. 38-42; Prof. Extraordinary, Königsberg Univ. 42-45, Göttingen 45; Prof. Ordinary, Kiel Univ. 46-74; Dir. Anatomical Inst. Kiel Univ. 45-; Rector, Kiel Univ. 50-51, 65-66; Vice-Pres. German Research Asscn. 55-61, mem. Wissenschaftsrat 58-64; Pres. Anatomical Soc. 58-61, 75-76; mem. Royal Swedish Acad. 53, Deutsche Akad. Naturforscher Leopoldina 58, Norwegian Acad. 61, Yugoslav Acad. 74; Corresp. mem. Mainz Acad. 63, Finnish Acad. 65; Hon. mem. Japanese Anatomical Soc. 59, Hungarian Anatomical Soc. 68, Anatomical Soc. of Great Britain and Ireland 71, Yugoslav Anatomical Soc. 75; Senator Max-Planck Gesellschaft 66; Hon. Senator Kiel Univ.; Schleiden Medal (Leopoldina) 67; Dr. med. vet. h.c. (Giessen) 67; Dr. med. h.c. (Ghent) 73; Grand Cross, Order of Merit (Fed. Repub. of Germany).
Publs. *Histologie und Mikroskopische Anatomie des Menschen* (6th edn.) 67, *Das Zwischenhirn-Hypophysensystem* 54, Editor, *Handbuch der Mikroskopischen Anatomie des Menschen*.
Niemannsweg 81, Kiel, Federal Republic of Germany.
Telephone: Kiel 85239.

Barich, Karl; German steel executive; b. 20 Oct. 1901; ed. Wirtschaftshochschule Mannheim.
Head Management Clerk, Geisweider Eisenwerke A.G. 41-45, mem. Management Board 45-47; mem. Management Board Hüttenwerk Geisweid A.G. (formed by merger) 47-51; mem. Management Board Stahlwerke Südwestfalen A.G. 51-54, Chair. 54-70, Chair. Advisory Board 71-75; Chair. Wirtschaftsvereinigung Eisen-und Stahlindustrie 48-49, and later until 54, now mem. Management Cttee.; mem. Boards of scientific, cultural and other insts.; Dr.rer.pol. h.c. (Wirtschaftshochschule, Mannheim) 57.
Stahlwerke Südwestfalen A.G., 5903 Hüttental-Geisweid, Postfach 6, Federal Republic of Germany.

Baring, Hon. John Francis Harcourt, M.A.; British merchant banker; b. 2 Nov. 1928, London; s. of 6th Baron Ashburton and Hon. Doris Mary Therese Harcourt; m. Susan Mary Renwick 1955; two s. two d.; ed. Eton Coll., Trinity Coll., Oxford.
Director Baring Bros. & Co. Ltd. 55-, Chair. 74-; Dir. Royal Insurance Co. Ltd. 64-, Trafford Park Estates Ltd. 64-, Outwich Investment Trust Ltd. (now Chair.) 65-, Pye Holdings Ltd. 67-, Outwich Ltd. (Johannesburg) 67-; mem. British Transport Docks Board 66-72; Rhodes Trustee 70-; mem. Council Baring Foundation 71-; Receiver-Gen. Duchy of Cornwall 74-.
Baring Bros. & Co. Ltd., 88 Leadenhall Street, London, EC3A 3DT, England.
Telephone: 01-588 2830.

Barke, (James) Allen; British motor executive; b. 16 April 1903; ed. technical school.
General engineering 22-32; Ford Motor Co. 32-; Chaser, Purchase Dept. 33-38; Buyer, Purchase Dept. 39-47; Chief Buyer (Tractors) 47-48; Man. Leamington Foundry 48-53; Exec. Dir. and Gen. Man. Briggs Motor Bodies Ltd. 53-59; Dir. Product Divs. Ford Motor Co. 59-61; Asst. Man. Dir. 61-62, Man. Dir. 62-63, Chief Exec. Officer and Man. Dir. 63-65, Vice-Chair. 65-68; Dir. De La Rue Co. 70-73, Falcon Engineering Co. 73-.
Thurlestone, Mill Green, Ingatestone, Essex, England.
Telephone: Ingatestone 2949.

Barker, Sir (Charles Frederic) James, Kt., M.B.E.; British business executive; b. 17 Feb. 1914, Walton-on-the-Naze; s. of Charles F.J. and Ethel (née Brook) Barker; m. Thora Daphne Perry 1940; two s.; ed. Colchester Royal Grammar School.
With L. Rose and Co. Ltd. 34-39; army service 39-45; rejoined L. Rose and Co. Ltd. 48, Man. Dir. 57; with Schweppes Ltd. 58-69, Dir. 62, Man. Dir. 69; Dir. Cadbury Schweppes Ltd. 70-71; Chair. and Chief Exec. Unigate Ltd. 70-72, Chair. and Joint Chief Exec. 72-74, Chair. 74-; Pres. Food Mfrs'. Fed. 67-70, Dairy Trade Fed. 73-75; Deputy Chair. CBI Overseas Cttee. 75-; Fellow, Inst. of Management; Croix de Guerre.
Leisure interests: sailing, reading, my family.
3 Lombardy Place, London, W.2; New Hall, Thorpe-le-Soken, Essex, England.
Telephone: 01-229-1536; Thorpe-le-Soken 507.

Barker, Denis William Knighton; British oil executive; b. 1908, Barnsley, Yorks.; m. Esmee D. Marsh; two d.; ed. Holgate Grammar School, Barnsley, and Sheffield Univ.
Joined the British Petroleum Co. Ltd. (then Anglo-Persian Oil Co.) 29, with assoc. companies in France 29-40; refinery engineer, Haifa 40-46; in U.K. 46-52; Man. Australian Div. Refineries Dept. BP 52-56; took over co-ordination of Continental and Commonwealth refineries, London 56-58; BP Rep. in New York 58, Pres. BP (N. America) 59-60; Asst. Gen. Man. Refineries Dept. 60-66, Gen. Man. 66-67, Dir. BP Trading Ltd. 67-72; a Man. Dir. The British Petroleum Co. Ltd. 67-72.
Leisure interests: golf, gardening.
Stable Cottage, Upper House Lane, Shamley Green, Surrey, England.
Telephone: Cranleigh 2726.

Barker, E. W., M.A., LL.B.; Singapore politician; b. 1921; ed. Raffles Coll., Singapore, St. Catharine's Coll., Cambridge and Inner Temple, London.
Practised law in Singapore 52-64; Assemblyman in constituency of Tanglin 63-; Speaker of Singapore Legislative Assembly 63-64; Minister for Law 64-65, for Law and Nat. Devt. 65-75, for Law and Environment June 75-.
Ministry of Law, Government Offices, St. Andrew's Road, Singapore 6.

Barker, George Granville; British writer; b. 26 Feb 1913, Loughton, Essex; s. of George Barker and Marion Frances Taaffe; m. Elspeth Cameron Langlands; two s. two d.; ed. Marlborough Road School, Chelsea, London.
Professor of English Literature, Imperial Tohoku Univ., Japan 39-41; lived in America 41-43; returned to England 44; in Italy 60-65; Visiting Prof. N.Y. State Univ. 65; Visiting Prof. of Literature, Univ. of Wis. 71-72, Florida Int. Univ. 74; Arts Fellow, York Univ. 66.
Leisure interests: painting, admiring architecture.
Publs. *Poems* 33, *Alanna Autumnal* 33, *Calamiterror*, *Janus* 35, *Lament and Triumph* 40, *News of the World*, *The True Confession of George Barker* 50, *Collected Poems* 57, *Two Plays*, *The View from a Blind I* 62, *The New Confession* 63, *Dreams of a Summer Night* 65, *The Golden Chains* 68, *Essays* 68, *Essays* 69, *Poems for Children* 69, *To Aylsham Fair* 70, *At Thurgarton Church* 70, *Poems of Places and People* 71, *The Alphabetical Zoo* 72, *In Memory of David Archer* 73.
c/o Faber and Faber, 3 Queen Square, London, W.C.1 and Bintry House, Itteringham, Aylesham, Norfolk, England.
Telephone: Saxthorpe 240.

Barker, Horace Albert, PH.D., D.SC.; American professor of biochemistry; b. 29 Nov. 1907, Oakland, Calif.; s. of A. C. Barker and Nettie H. Barker; m. Margaret D. McDowell 1933; one s. two d.; ed. Stanford Univ.
National Research Council Fellow in Biological Sciences, Hopkins Marine Station 33-35; Gen. Educ. Board Fellow, Technical Univ., Delft, Holland 35-36; Instructor in Soil Microbiology, Div. of Plant Nutrition, and Junior Soil Microbiologist in Agric. Experiment Station, Univ. of Calif. 36-40, Asst. Prof. and Asst. Soil Microbiologist 40-45, Assoc. Prof. and Assoc. Soil Microbiologist 45-46, Prof. and Soil Microbiologist 46-50, Prof. of Plant Biochemistry and Microbiologist 50-57, Prof. of Microbial Biochemistry and Microbiologist 57-59, Prof. of Biochemistry and Microbiologist 59-, Emer. Prof. 75; Chair. Dept. of Plant Nutrition 49-50, Dept. of Plant Biochemistry 50-53, Vice-Chair. Dept. of Agric. Biochemistry 58-59, Chair. Dept. of Biochemistry 62-64; on editorial boards of various scientific journals; mem. Nat. Acad. of Sciences, American Acad. of Arts and Sciences and other socs.; numerous awards including Gowland Hopkins Medal, Biochemistry Soc., London 67, Nat. Medal of Science 68.
Leisure interests: fishing and mountaineering.
Publs. *Bacterial Fermentations* 56; over 200 papers; research into various aspects of bacterial metabolism, including the synthesis and oxidation of fatty acids, fermentation of amino acids and purines, carbohydrate transformation and methane formation; isolation, structure and function of cobamide coenzymes; bacterial enzymes.
Department of Biochemistry, Biochemistry Building, University of California, Berkeley, Calif. 94720, U.S.A.
Telephone: 415-642-5688.

Barker, Robinson Franklin, A.B.; American glass executive; b. 20 Dec. 1913, Boston, Mass.; s. of Williston Wright Barker, M.D. and Gertrude Sherman Barker; m. Mary Lucinda Haskins 1938; one s. one d.; ed. Harvard Univ.
Served U.S. Naval Reserve 42-45; with PPG Industries Inc. 35-; various managerial positions, then Asst. to Pres., and Gen. Man. (Planning) Glass Div. 55-57, Vice-Pres., Gen. Man. Glass Div. 57-62, Vice-Pres. Glass and Fiber Glass Group 62-66, Pres. 66-67, Chair. of Board and Chief Exec. Officer 67-. also Dir. of Co.; Dir. PPG Industries Foundation, PPG Industries Canada Ltd. Carrier Corpn., Mellon Bank N.A., Mellon Nat. Corpn., Duplate Canada Ltd. and other companies.
Leisure interests: fishing, music.
Office: 1 Gateway Center, Pittsburgh, Pa. 15222; Home: 8 Woodland Road, Sewickley, Pa. 15143, U.S.A.
Telephone: 412-434-3311 (Office); 412-741-7384 (Home).

Barker, Sir William, K.C.M.G., O.B.E.; British diplomatist; b. 19 July 1909; ed. Univs. of Liverpool and Prague.
Foreign Office 43; First Sec., Prague 45-47, transferred Moscow 47; Counsellor and Chargé d'Affaires, Oslo 51-54; Consul-General, Boston, Mass. 54; Counsellor, Washington 55-60; Minister, Moscow 60-63; Fellow, Center for Int. Affairs, Harvard Univ. 63-64; Asst. Under-Sec. of State, Foreign Office 65-66; Amb. to Czechoslovakia 66-68; Prof. of Russian, Liverpool Univ. 69-.
Russian Department, The University, Liverpool 3; and 53 Eshe Road North, Liverpool L23 8UE, England.

Bar-Lev, Lieut.-Gen. Haim; Israeli soldier; b. 1924, Austria; m.; one s. one d.; ed. Mikhev Israel Agricultural School, Columbia Univ. School of Econs. and Admin., U.S.A.
Joined Palmach Units 42; Platoon Commdr., Beith-Ha'Arava 44; Commdr. D Co., Yesreel 45-46; Commdr. Palmach non-commdg. officer's course and C.O. Eight Regt., Negev Brigade 47, Operations Officer 48; Commdr. Armoured Units 48; Instructor and later Commdr., Bn. Commdrs. course 49-52; Chief of Staff, Northern Command 52-53; C.O., Givati Brigade 54-55;

Dir. G.H.Q. Training Div. 56; Commdr. Armoured Brigade during Sinai campaign; Commdr. Armoured Corps 57-61; made study tour of armoured corps of Western European countries and U.S.A. 61; after obtaining M.A., Columbia Univ., visited U.S. army installations and the armies of the Philippines, Japan, Thailand and S. Viet-Nam; Dir. Gen. Staff (Operations) Branch 64-66; Deputy Chief of Staff Israel Defence Forces 67, Chief of Staff 68-72; Minister of Commerce and Industry 72-.
Ministry of Commerce and Industry, Tel-Aviv, Israel.

Barlog, Boleslaw; German theatre director and producer; b. 28 March 1906, Breslau (now Wrocław); *m.* Herta Barlog 1939; ed. Oberrealschule, Berlin.
Assistant Producer, Volksbühne, Berlin 30-33; Asst. Dir. UFA and TERRA films 35-39, Dir. 39-45; Dir.-Gen. Berlin Municipal Theatres 45-72 (Schlosspark Theatre 45-72, Schiller Theatre 51-72, Schiller-Theatre Workshop 59-72); Dir.-Gen. Carl-Zuckmayer Gesellschaft 72-; mem. Acad. of Arts, Berlin; Grand Order of Merit (Fed. Germany) 50; Ordre National de l'Art et des Lettres and other decorations and awards.
Leisure interests: philately, travel, music.
Spindelmuehler Weg 7, 1 Berlin 45, Federal Republic of Germany.

Barlow, Charles Sydney; South African business executive; b. 1905, Durban; ed. Clifton Coll., Bristol, Caius Coll., Cambridge.
Entered Barlow Rand Ltd. 27, Branch Man. Johannesburg 29-41; Intelligence Officer with rank of Maj., 2nd Div., S.A. Army 41-44; Chair. War Stores Disposal Board 45-46; Chair. of the Board and Man. Dir. Barlow Rand Ltd. 48-; Dir. of all major cos. in the Barlow Rand Group; Dir. S.A. Breweries Ltd., Phalaborwa Mining Co., American S.A. Investment Co. Ltd. and many other cos.; Exec. Vice-Pres. and Trustee, S.A. Foundation; Hon. Fellow, Coll. of Medicine; Fellow Royal Soc. for the Encouragement of Arts, Manufactures and Commerce; mem. of various sporting bodies; Business Statesman Award, Harvard Business School Club 71.
Leisure interests: golf, fishing, farming, ornithology.
Barlow Rand Ltd., P.O. Box 4862, Johannesburg, South Africa.

Barlow, Harold Everard Monteagle, B.SC., PH.D., F.R.S.; British electrical engineer; b. 15 Nov. 1899, London; *s.* of Leonard Barlow, M.I.E.E. and Katherine Barlow (née Monteagle); *m.* Janet Hastings Eastwood 1931; three *s.* one *d.*; ed. City and Guilds Engineering Coll., London, and Univ. Coll., London.
Sub-Lieut. R.N.V.R. 17-18; East Surrey Ironworks Ltd. 23; Barlow & Young Ltd. 23-24; Supt. Radio Dept., Royal Aircraft Establishment, Farnborough 39-45; Academic Staff, Univ. Coll. London 24-67; Emer. Prof. of Electrical Engineering, Univ. of London 67-; War service 39-45; Dir. Marconi Instrument Co. Ltd. 67-; Chair. British Nat. Cttee. of Int. Radio Union 67-; Chair. High Frequency Measurements Cttee. and mem. Council, British Calibration Service, Ministry of Technology (now Dept. of Trade and Industry), London 67-; Hon. Research Fellow, Univ. Coll. London 67-; mem. Athlone Fellowships Cttee., Board of Trade, London 54-; mem. Royal Soc./Nuffield Foundation Fellowships Cttee. 68-, Nat. Electronics Council 70-; Foreign mem. Polish Acad. of Sciences; Fellow, Inst. of Electrical Engineers, London, and Faraday Medallist 67; Dellinger Gold Medal, Int. Union of Radio Science 69; Fellow, Inst. of Mechanical Engineers, City and Guilds Inst., London; Fellow, Inst. of Electronic and Electrical Engineers (U.S.A.) 56-; Hon. mem. Inst. of Electronic and Communications Engineers, Japan 74; Mervin J. Kelly Award 75; Hon. D.Sc., D.Eng.
Leisure interests: travel, walking, sailing.
Publs. *Microwaves and Waveguides* 50, *Microwave*

Measurements (with A. L. Cullen) 52, *Radio Surface Waves* (with J. Brown) 61, about 50 scientific papers.
13 Hookfield, Epsom, Surrey, England.
Telephone: Epsom 21586 (Home).

Barlow, Horace B., M.A., M.B., B.CH., SC.D., M.D., F.R.S.; British physiologist; b. 8 Dec. 1921, Chesham Bois; *s.* of James A. Barlow and Emma N. Darwin; *m.* Ruth Salaman 1954 (divorced 1970); four *d.*; ed. Trinity Coll., Cambridge, Harvard Medical School and Univ. Coll. Hospital.
Fellow, Trinity Coll., Cambridge 50-53, 73-; Fellow and Lecturer, King's Coll., and Demonstrator, Physiological Lab. 53-64; Prof. of Physiological Optics and Physiology, Univ. of Calif., Berkeley 64-73; Royal Soc. Research Prof., Physiological Laboratory, Cambridge 73-.
Leisure interests: walking, music, skiing, gliding.
Publs. papers on the neurophysiology of vision in *The Journal of Physiology*.
Physiological Laboratory, Cambridge, CB2 3EG; Home: 10 Green Street, Cambridge, CB2 3JU, England.

Barmin, Vladimir Pavlovich; Soviet engineer; b. 17 March 1909, Moscow; *s.* of Pavel Ivanovich Barmin and Maria Isayevna (Antonenkova) Barmina; *m.* Lydia Ivanovna Postnikova 1933; two *s.*; ed. Moscow Higher Technical School.
At compressor plant, U.S.S.R. Acad. of Sciences 30-, Chief Designer 41-; Instructor, Moscow Higher Technical School 31-, Prof. Mech. Eng. 60-; mem. C.P.S.U. 44-; Corresp. mem. U.S.S.R. Acad. of Sciences 58-66, mem. 66-; State Prize 43, 67; Lenin Prize 57; Hero of Socialist Labour 56; Order of Lenin (five times); Order of October Revolution; various medals.
Publs. on compressor engineering, refrigeration techniques, etc.
U.S.S.R. Academy of Sciences, 14 Leninsky Prospekt, Moscow, U.S.S.R.

Barnaby, Charles Frank, M.SC., PH.D.; British physicist; b. 27 Sept. 1927, Andover, Hants.; *s.* of Charles H. Barnaby and Lilian Sainsbury; *m.* Wendy Elizabeth Field 1972; one *d.*; ed. Andover Grammar School and Univ. of London.
Physicist, U.K. Atomic Energy Authority 50-57; mem. Senior Scientific Staff, Medical Research Council, Univ. Coll. Medical School 57-68; Exec. Sec. Pugwash Confs. on Science and World Affairs 68-70; Dir. Stockholm Int. Peace Research Inst. (SIPRI) Oct. 71-.
Leisure interest: natural history.
Publs. *Radionucleoles in Medicine* 70, *Man and the Atom* 71, Editor *Preventing the Spread of Nuclear Weapons* 71, Co-editor *Anti-ballistic Missile Systems* 71, *Disarmament and Arms Control* 73; articles in scientific journals.
Stocksundstorpsvägen 1, 17173 Solna, Sweden; San Kuai, Chilbolton, Stockbridge, Hants., England.
Telephone: 08/15 09 40 (Sweden); Chilbolton 423 (England).

Barnard, Christiaan Neethling, M.MED., M.D., M.S., PH.D., F.A.C.S., F.A.C.C.; South African heart surgeon; b. 1922, Beaufort West, Cape Province; *s.* of Adam Hendrik Barnard and Maria Elisabeth de Swart; *m.* 1st Aletta Gertruida Louw 1948 (divorced 1970); one *s.* one *d.*; *m.* 2nd Barbara M. Zoellner 1970; two *s.*; ed. Univ. of Cape Town.
Graduated as doctor 46; intern, Groote Schuur Hospital, Cape Town 47; then spent two years in general practice in Ceres; then Senior Resident Medical Officer, City Fever Hospital, Cape Town; returned to Groote Schuur Hospital; then Charles Adams Memorial Scholar, Univ. of Minnesota, concentrating on cardio-thoracic surgery; on return to Groote Schuur Hospital concentrated on open-heart operations and cardiac research; Head of Cardiac Research and Surgery, Univ. of Cape Town; developed the Barnard Valve, for use in

open-heart surgery; performed first successful open-heart operation in South Africa; performed first successful heart transplant operation in world 67, first successful double heart transplant operation 74; Hon. D.Sc. Univ. of Cape Town.
Leisure interests: power-boats, water skiing, fishing, flying.
Publs. *One Life* (autobiography, with C. B. Pepper) 70, *Heart Attack: All you have to know about it* 71, *The Unwanted* (with S. Stander) 74.
Department of Cardiac Surgery, Medical School, Observatory, Cape Town, South Africa.
Telephone: 55-1359.

Barnard, Lance Herbert; Australian politician; b. 1 May 1919; *m.* Jill Barnard; one *s.* three *d.*; ed. Launceston Technical Coll.
Military service in Second World War 40-45, Australian Cadet Corps, with rank of Captain 45-54; mem. Parliament 54-75; State Pres. Tasmanian Branch, Australian Labor Party 63-66, 70-72; Deputy Leader, Parl. Labor Party 67-75; Deputy Prime Minister 72-74; Minister for Defence 72-75; Amb. to Sweden, Finland and Norway Sept. 75-; mem. Joint Public Accounts Cttee. 56-58, Fed. Parl. Labor Party Exec. 58-61; fmr. mem. Joint Select Cttee. on Defence Forces Retirement Benefits Legislation.
Australian Embassy, Sergels Torg 12, Box 40 046, 103 42 Stockholm, Sweden; Home: 8 Lantana Avenue, Launceston, Tasmania, Australia.
Telephone: (08) 244660 (Residence); 442296 (Home).

Barnes, Clive; British journalist, dance and theatre critic; b. 13 May 1927, London; *m.*; two *c.*; ed. King's Coll., London and Oxford Univ.
Administrative officer, Town Planning Dept., London County Council 52-61; also active as freelance journalist contributing articles, reviews and criticisms on music, dance, theatre, films and television to *The New Statesman, The Spectator, The Daily Express, The New York Times*, etc.; Chief dance critic, *The Times*, London 61-65; Exec. Editor, *Dance and Dancers, Music and Musicians, Plays and Players* 61-65; Dance Critic, *The New York Times* 65-, also Drama Critic (weekdays only) 67-.
Publs. *Ballet in Britain Since the War, Frederick Ashton and His Ballet, Ballet Here and Now, Dance As It Happened, Dance in the Twentieth Century, Dance Scene: U.S.A.*
c/o The New York Times, 229 West 43rd Street, New York, N.Y. 10036, U.S.A.

Barnes, Edward Larrabee, B.A., M.A.; American architect; b. 22 April 1915, Chicago, Ill.; *s.* of Cecil and Margaret H. (Ayer) Barnes; *m.* Mary E. Coss 1944; one *s.*; ed. Milton Acad., Harvard Univ. and Graduate School of Design.
Sheldon Travelling Fellowship 42; architectural practice in New York City 49-; Critic of Architectural Design, Pratt Inst., Brooklyn 53-54, Yale School of Architecture 56-; work exhibited at Museum of Modern Art (New York), Carnegie Inst. (Pittsburgh, Pa.) and published in architectural magazines; Dir. Municipal Art Soc. of New York 60; Fellow, American Inst. of Architects; Trustee, American Acad. in Rome 63, Vice-Pres. 72, Museum of Modern Art, New York 75; Assoc. Nat. Acad. of Design 69, Academician 74; Yale Award for Distinction in the Arts, Arnold Brunner Prize, Nat. Inst. of, Arts and Letters 59, Silver Medal, Architectural League, N.Y. 60, Progressive Architecture Design Award 63, F.H.A. First Honor Award 63; A.I.A., Medal of Hon. (N.Y. chapter) 71, Collaborative Achievement in Architecture 72, Hon. Award 72; Harleston Parker Award, Boston Soc. of Architects 72.
Works include: Prefabricated aluminium house for Consolidated Vultee Aircraft Corpn.; private houses; Fresh Air Fund Camps; urban renewal housing projects

in Sacramento and San Juan; corporate identification programme for Pan American Airways; U.S. Consulate, Tabriz, Iran; Haystack Mountain School of Arts and Crafts, Maine; master plans for State Univ. of New York campuses at Purchase and Potsdam; office buildings for New England Merchants National Bank, Boston, and IBM, N.Y.; Walker Art Gallery, Minneapolis, Minn., etc.
Leisure interests: music, piano, sailing, climbing.
Office: 410 East 62nd Street, New York, N.Y. 10021; Home: Wood Road, Mount Kisco, N.Y., U.S.A.
Telephone: 212-838-8500.

Barnes, Harry George, Jr., M.A.; American diplomatist; b. 5 June 1926, St. Paul, Minn.; *s.* of Harry George and Bertha Pauline (Blaul) Barnes; *m.* Elizabeth Ann Sibley 1948; one *s.* three *d.*; ed. Amherst Coll. and Columbia Univ.
Served with A.U.S. 44-46; Vice-Consul, Bombay 51-53; Consular Officer, Prague 53-55; Russian Area and Language Trainee, Oberammergau, Germany 55-56; Second Sec., Consul, Moscow 56-69; Office of Soviet Union Affairs, Dept. of State 59-62; Nat. War Coll. 62-63; Deputy Chief of Mission, American Embassy, Nepal 63-67, Romania 68-71; Office of Personnel, Dept. of State 71-72; Deputy Exec. Sec., Dept. of State 72-74; Amb. to Romania March 74-.
Leisure interest: trekking.
American Embassy, Bucharest, Romania; and 7019 Armat Drive, Bethesda, Md. 20034, U.S.A.
Telephone: 12-40-40 (Bucharest).

Barnes, Sir John, K.C.M.G.; British diplomatist; b. 22 June 1917, London; *s.* of Rt. Rev. E. W. Barnes and Adelaide Ward; *m.* Cynthia M. R. Stewart 1948; two *s.* three *d.*; ed. Winchester Coll. and Trinity Coll., Cambridge.
Served in Royal Artillery 39-46; joined diplomatic service 46; postings to Washington, Beirut and Bonn; Amb. to Israel 69-72, to the Netherlands 72-.
British Embassy, Lange Voorhout 10, The Hague, Netherlands; Home: Hampton Lodge, Hurstpierpoint, Sussex, England.

Barnes, Robert Henry, B.S., M.D.; American psychiatrist; b. 4 Nov. 1921, Worcester, Mass.; *s.* of Harry Elmer Barnes and Grace Stone Barnes; *m.* Beverly R. Feingold 1967; one *s.* one *d.* and one stepson; ed. Union Coll., Schenectady, New York, Duke Univ. and Univ. of Colorado.
Instructor, Psychosomatic Medicine, Univ. of Colorado 52-53, Asst. Prof. of Psychiatry, Duke Univ. 53-56; Assoc. Prof., Prof. and Chair., Dept. of Psychiatry, Univ. of Missouri in Kansas City 56-68; Exec. Dir. Greater Kansas City Mental Health Foundation 56-68; Acting Dir. Epidemiological Field Station, Kansas City, Missouri 67-68; Prof. of Psychiatry, Univ. of Texas School of Medicine, San Antonio 68-72; Prof. and Chair. Dept. of Chemistry, Texas Technical Univ. School of Medicine 72-; Fellow, American Psychiatric Asscn.; Consultant Nat. Inst. of Mental Health in Community Mental Health Programs and Epidemiology 62-.
Leisure interests: private flying, hunting, fishing, cooking.
Publs. *A Community Concern* (with Epps and McPartland) 65; and 30 articles on geriatrics, psychosomatic medicine, electroencephalography, cerebral circulation, psychiatric education, and group therapy.
Texas Technical University School of Medicine, Tubbock, Tex. 79409, U.S.A.
Telephone: 806-742-5273.

Barnetson, Baron (Life Peer), cr. 75, of Crowborough in the County of Sussex; **William Denholm Barnetson,** Kt., M.A., British journalist; b. 21 March 1917; *s.* of William Denholm Barnetson and Ella Grigor Moir;

m. Joan F. Davidson 1940; one *s.* three *d.*; ed. Royal High School, Edinburgh and Edinburgh Univ.
Successively Leader Writer, Editor and Gen. Man., Edinburgh Evening News 48-61; Joint Man. Dir. United Newspapers Ltd. 61, Chair. 66-; Chair. Reuters Ltd. 68-; Chair. Bradbury Agnew 69-, Farming Press 74-, Sheffield Newspapers 63-, Council Commonwealth Press Union 72-; Pres. Press Club 73, Periodical Publrs'. Asscn. 74-, Newsvendors Benevolent Inst. 75-; Chair. Scottish Int. Information Cttee. 70-, Marketing Advisory Cttee., Open Univ. 73-, Appeal Newspaper Press Fund 74-; Dir. Argus Press Ltd., Drayton Consolidated Trust Ltd., Yorkshire Post Newspapers Ltd., British Electric Traction Co. Ltd., Olympia & Earls Court Ltd. and other companies.
Leisure interest: books.
United Newspapers Ltd., 23-27 Tudor Street, London, EC4Y 0HR; 1 Andrewes House, Fore Street, Barbican, London, E.C.2; Home: "Broom", Chillies Lane, Crowborough, Sussex, England.
Telephone: 01-583-9199; 01-628-6897; 089-26-5748.

Baron, Jean-Jacques; French engineer; b. 11 May 1909, Angerville L'Orcher, Seine Maritime; three *s.*; ed. Ecole Centrale des Arts et Manufactures, Paris.
Engineer, later Technical Dir. L'Aluminium Français 33-57; Dir. Compagnie Péchiney-Kuhlmann (fmrly. Péchiney) 58-71; Dir., Adviser Soc. Péchiney Ugine Kuhlmann 71-; Dir. Ecole Centrale des Arts et Manufactures, Paris; Officier Légion d'Honneur, Ordre des Palmes Académiques.
Office: 23 rue Balzac, Paris 8e; Home: Grande Voie des Vignes, 92 Chatenay-Malabry, France.
Telephone: 227-54-72 (Office); 660-36-10 (Home).

Barooah, Dev Kanta, LL.B.; Indian politician; b. 22 Feb. 1914, Dibrugarh (Assam); *s.* of late Nilkanta Barooah; *m.* Priyalata Barooah; one *s.*; ed. Nowgong Govt. School and Banaras Hindu Univ.
Secretary, Assam P.C.C. 38-45; Editor *Dainik, Assamiya* and *Natun Asamiya* (daily newspapers); mem. Constituent Assembly 49-51, Lok Sabha 52-57; mem. Legislative Assembly of Assam 57-60, Speaker 60; Chair. Oil Refinery 60; mem. Assam Legislative Assembly 62-66, 67; Minister of Educ. and Co-operation 62; Chair. Oil India 68; Gov. of Bihar 71-73; Minister of Petroleum and Chemicals 73-74; Pres. Indian Nat. Congress Party 74-.
Leisure interests: gardening, reading.
5 Dr. Rajendra Prasad Road, New Delhi; and 23 Tughlak Road, New Delhi, India.
Telephone: 615117, 72120.

Baroody, Jamil Murad; Saudi Arabian diplomatist; b. 8 Aug. 1905, Souk el Gharb, Lebanon; *s.* of Murad H. and Edma H. (Daoun) Baroody; *m.* Loraine Fischer; two *s.* two *d.*; ed. American Univ., Beirut.
Arab political and econ. observer, London 29, 35-39; Sec.-Gen., acting Commr.-Gen. for Lebanon, New York World's Fair 39-40; lecturer, Princeton Univ. 43; adviser to Arabic Edn., *Reader's Digest*; also freelance writer on Middle East 44-47; with Royal Del. of Saudi Arabia to UN, San Francisco 45, mem. Third Cttee. of Gen. Assembly 47-, alt. Perm. Rep. to UN (now Amb., Deputy Perm. Rep.) 47-; Hon. Citizen of New York City 39; Gold Medal, Order of Merit (Lebanon).
Publs. *Poems* 36; articles in periodicals.
Permanent Mission of Saudi Arabia to the United Nations, 6 East 43rd Street, New York, N.Y. 10017, U.S.A.

Baroyan, Oganes Vagarshakovich; Soviet health official; b. 24 Dec. 1906, Erevan; ed. First Medical Inst. of Moscow.
Professor of Epidemiology and Microbiology; Dir., Dept. of Epidemiology, Ivanovski Virology Inst. of Acad. of Medical Sciences; Dir. Gamaleya Inst. of Epidemiology and Microbiology, Acad. of Medical

Sciences 64-; Asst. Dir.-Gen. World Health Organization, Geneva 61-64; Prof. and Academician Acad. of Medical Sciences of U.S.S.R. 65-; mem. Int. Epidemiological Asscn.; Hon. mem. Soc. of Czechoslovak Epidemiologists and Microbiologists of Purkyně Medical Soc. of Czechoslovakia; State Prize; Order of Red Star (twice); Order of Red Banner of Labour; Badge of Honour; Iranian orders.
Publs. About 200 on epidemiology of virus infections.
N. F. Gamaleya Institute of Epidemiology and Microbiology, 2 Ulitsa Gamalei, Moscow, U.S.S.R.

Barr, Alfred Hamilton, Jr., PH.D.; American museum official and art historian; b. 28 Jan. 1902, Detroit, Mich.; *s.* of Alfred H. Barr and Annie Wilson; *m.* Margaret Scolari-Fitzmaurice 1930; one *d.*; ed. Boys' Latin School, Baltimore, Md., and Princeton and Harvard Univs.
Instructor, History of Art, Vassar Coll. 23-24, Princeton Univ. 25-26; Assoc. Prof. of Art, Wellesley Coll. 26-29; Dir., Museum of Modern Art, New York 29-43, Trustee 39-, Dir. of Museum Collections 47-67, Counsellor to the Trustees 67-; Hon. Litt.D. (Princeton), Hon. Ph.D. (Bonn), Hon. D.F.A. (Buffalo, Yale, Columbia); Nat. Inst. of Arts and Letters Award for Distinguished Service to the Arts 68, New York State Award 68; several foreign decorations.
Leisure interest: bird watching.
Publs. *Cubism and Abstract Art* 36, *What is Modern Painting?* 43, *Picasso: Fifty Years of his Art* 46, *20th Century Italian Art* (with J. T. Soby) 49, *Matisse: His Art and His Public* 51, *Masters of Modern Art* (ed.) 54; editor of several periodicals on art.
Home: 49 East 96th Street, New York, N.Y., U.S.A.

Barr, John Andrew, LL.B.; American lawyer, business executive and educator; b. 10 Sept. 1908, Akron, Ind.; *s.* of Earl and Bertha Barr; *m.* Louise Stentz 1933; three *s.* one *d.*; ed. DePauw and Indiana Univs.
With law firm of Wildermuth and Force (Gary, Ind.) 30-33; Attorney Montgomery Ward & Co. 33-35; Partner Wildermuth, Force and Barr 35-38; rejoined Montgomery Ward legal staff 38, Asst. Sec. 40-49, Vice-Pres. and Sec. 49-55, Dir. 50-65, Chair. 55-65; Dean, Graduate School of Management, Northwestern Univ. 65-75; Dir. Northern Trust Co., Commonwealth Edison Co., S.C. Johnson and Son Inc., Stewart-Warner Corpn., Marsh and McLennan Cos., Nortrust Corpn., Goldblatt Bros. Inc., Evanston Hospital Asscn., Mid-West Stock Exchange.
Leisure interests: golf, hunting, fishing, gardening.
Graduate School of Management, Northwestern Univ., 2001 Sheridan Road, Evanston, Ill. 60201; 670 Midfield Lane, Northbrook, Ill. 60062, U.S.A.

Barr, Joseph Walker; American businessman; b. 17 Jan. 1918, Vincennes, Ind.; *s.* of Oscar Lynn Barr and Stella F. Walker; *m.* Beth A. Williston 1939; one *s.* four *d.*; ed. DePauw Univ. and Harvard Univ.
Former Exec. Vice-Pres. Merz Engineering, Indianapolis; fmr. Sec.-Treas. Barr Devt. Corpn., Indianapolis; fmr. Treas. O. L. Barr Grain Co., Indianapolis; fmr. mem. U.S. House of Reps., mem. Banking and Currency Comm.; Asst. to Sec. (Congressional Relations), Dept. of Treasury 61-64; Chair. Board Fed. Deposit Insurance Corpn. 64-65; Under-Sec. of Treasury 65-68, Sec. 68-69; Pres. American Security and Trust Co. 69-72, Chair. of the Board 73-74; Chair. Barr Devt. Corpn.; U.S. Navy 42-45; Dir. 3M Co., Burlington Industries, Commercial Credit Co., Student Loan Marketing Asscn., Washington Gas Light Co.; mem. Advisory Cttee, Export-Import Bank of United States; mem. Board of Regents, Georgetown Univ.; Hon. LL.D. Vincennes Univ. 66, DePauw Univ. 67.
Suite 907, 730 15th Street, N.W., Washington, D.C. 20005; Home: Houyhnhnm Farm, Hume, Virginia 22639, U.S.A.

Barr, Morris Alfred, A.C.M.M., LL.D.; Australian international administrator and business executive; b. 23 Dec. 1922, Melbourne; s. of Benjamin Alfred Barr and Margaret Bell; m. Shirley Frances Deacon 1957; ed. Scotch Coll., Melbourne Univ. and Melbourne Conservatorium of Music.
Member editorial staff Melbourne *Argus*; served with Australian Imperial Forces and Far Eastern Liaison Office; Head, Melbourne Conservatorium of Music 48; with English-Speaking Union 51-, Dir. of Programmes 59-64, Dir.-Gen. 64-69; Part-time lecturer in int. affairs to British Armed Services 53-64; Partner and Dir. Int. Operations, Winner Marketing Communications 69-; Int. Co-ordinator Winston Churchill Memorial Trust 60-65; Chair. and Man. Dir. Associated Consultants (Construction) Ltd. 69-; Trustee, Univ. of Louisville (Humphrey Centenary Scholarship Trust); Chair. Australian Musical Asscn. 74-.
Leisure interests: music, swimming, golf.
106 Gloucester Place, London, W1H 3DB; Home: 16 Park Place Villas, London, W.2, England.
Telephone: 01-935-4253.

Barrachin, Edmond; French journalist and politician; b. 12 Jan. 1900.
Deputy 34-36, 46, 51, 56-58; Senator 59-; volunteer 39, prisoner 40, escaped and joined Free French; founder *Action* group; Minister-in-charge of Constitutional Reform 53-56; mem. Constitutional Consultative Cttee. 58; fmr. Pres. of Independent group in Senate; Médaille Militaire, Croix de Guerre.
15 rue du Cirque, Paris 8e, France.

Barran, Sir David Haven, Kt.; British oil executive; b. 23 May 1912, London; s. of John N. Barran, Bt., and Alice M. Parks; m. Jane Lechmere Macaskie 1944; four s. three d.; ed. Winchester Coll. and Trinity Coll., Cambridge.
Asiatic Petroleum Co. 34-61, served Egypt, Sudan, Red Sea, India, London 34-58, Pres. Asiatic Petroleum Corpn., New York 58-61; Managing Dir. The Shell Petroleum Co., Shell Int. Petroleum Co. 61-; Principal Dir. Bataafse Petroleum Mij. N.V. 61-; Dir. Shell Transport and Trading Co. Ltd. 61-64, Deputy Chair. 64-67, Man. Dir. 67-72, Chair. 67-72; Dir. Shell Oil Co. 64-, Chair. 70-72; Dir. Shell Caribbean Co. 64-68; Dir. City Investment Co. of N.Y. and Zurich 72-, Glaxo 72-, Midland Bank 72-, Gen. Accident Insurance 72-, Canadian Imperial Bank 72-.
Leisure interests: gardening, shooting, golf, embroidery.
Brent Eleigh Hall, Sudbury, Suffolk; and 36 Kensington Square, London, W.8, England.
Telephone: 01-937-5664 (London).

Barrault, Jean-Louis; French actor and producer; b. 8 Sept. 1910; m. Madeleine Renaud (q.v.); ed. Collège Chaptal.
Master at Collège Chaptal 31; began stage career in rôle of servant in *Volpone* 31; produced and acted in a number of plays, including: *Autour d'une Mère* 35, *Hamlet, Tandis que j'agonise, Numance* 37, *La Faim*; with the Comédie-Française, 40-47: *Antoine et Cléopâtre, Le Soulier de Satin*; founded Compagnie M. Renaud-J.-L. Barrault 47: *Les Nuits de la Colère, les Fausses Confidences, Amphitryon, Baptiste, Occupe-toi d'Amélie, Le Procès, Partage de Midi, Le Bossu, Christophe Colomb, Pour Lucrèce, La Cerisaie* 54, *Le Songe des Prisonniers* 55, (Théâtre Marigny) *Le Personnage Combattant, Madame Sans-Gêne, La Vie Parisienne* 58, *Rabelais* 69, *Jarry sur la Butte* 70, *Harold et Maude* 73, *Zarathustra* (dir., actor) 74; Dir. Théâtre de France (fmr. Odéon) 59-68, Théâtre des Nations 65-67, 71-; Officier, Légion d'Honneur; has made films, *Les Beaux Jours, Hélène* 36, *Mademoiselle Docteur, Drôle de Drame, Un Grand Amour de Beethoven, Le Puritain* 37, *L'Or dans la Montagne* 39, *La Symphonie Fantastique* 42, *Les*

Enfants du Paradis 44, *Le Cocu magnifique* 46, *La Ronde* 50, *Versailles* 55.
Publs. *Réflexions sur le Théâtre* 49, *Nouvelles Réflexions sur le Théâtre* 59, *Journal de bord* 61, *Mémoires de Demain* (autobiog.) 74; Editor: *Cahiers de la Compagnie M. Renaud-J.-L. Barrault*.
18 avenue du Président Wilson, Paris 16e, France.

Barre, Raymond; French international civil servant; b. 12 April 1924, Saint-Denis, Réunion; ed. Faculté de Droit, Paris, and Inst. d'Etudes politiques, Paris.
Professor at Inst. des Hautes Etudes, Tunis 51-54; Prof. at Faculté de Droit et de Sciences économiques, Caen 54-63; Prof. Inst. d'Etudes politiques, Paris 61-, Faculté de Droit et Sciences économiques, Paris 62-; Dir. du Cabinet to Minister of Industry 59-62; mem. Cttee. of Experts (Comité Lorain) studying financing of investments in France 63-64; mem. Comm. of Gen. Econ. and Financing of Fifth Plan and other govt. cttees.; Vice-Pres. of Comm. of European Communities, responsible for Econ. and Financial Affairs 67-72; mem. Gen. Council, Banque de France 73-.
Home: 6 rue de Bagatelle, 92 Neuilly-sur-Seine, France.

Barreiros Rodríguez, Eduardo; Spanish business executive; b. 1919.
Chairman of Board of Dirs. Barreiros Diesel S.A., Rheinstahl Hanomag Barreiros S.A., David Brown Engranajes S.A., Barreiros A.E.C. S.A., Barreiros Empresa Constructora S.A., Financiera Barreiros S.A., Comercial Internacional Barreiros S.A., Cía. Portuguesa de Motores y Camiones S.A.
Princesa 1, Madrid, Spain.

Barrenechea, Norberto M., PH.D.; Argentine business executive and diplomatist; b. 20 Aug. 1924, Buenos Aires; s. of Juan Carlos and Maria Elena Torres; m. Elisabeth M. Duhalde 1949; two s. two d.; ed. Universidad de Buenos Aires.
President of Board of Dirs. and Gen. Attorney Pedro D. Duhalde y Cía. S.A. (agricultural firm) 58-75; Vice-Pres. Board of Dirs. El Brasero, S.A., Indal S.A., Iquiyù S.A., El Boyero S.A.; Gen. Attorney El Grillo S.A., Don Pedro Dionisio S.A., El Caballito S.A., Maldonado S.A., Inaga S.A., El Candil S.C.A.; mem. Council Banco Frances e Italiano para la America del Sud; Amb. of Argentina in U.S.A. 64-66; Technical mem. Comm. for Promotion of Econ. Devt. in Argentina; mem. American-Argentine Univ. Asscn., Corporación Argentina de Aberdeen Angus, Jockey Club.
Leisure interest: collecting bulls.
Publs. *Treatise on Auditing, Treatise on Financial Mathematics.*
Sarmiento 329, Buenos Aires, Argentina.
Telephone: 783-3900; 31-6030.

Barrera de Irimo, Antonio; Spanish economist and politician; b. 1929, Ribadeo; m.; six c.; ed. Univ. of Deusto.
Entered Tax Inspectorate 54; Prof. of Finance, Univ. of Madrid and Deusto; Deputy Sec.-Gen. Ministry of Finance 58, Sec.-Gen. 62; Dir. Inst. of Fiscal Studies 61; Chair. Financial Comm. Devt. Plan 62; Chair. Compañía Telefónica Nacional de España 65-73; Minister of Finance and Second Vice-Pres. of the Govt. 73-74; mem. Board Compañía Telefónica Nacional, Banco Hispano Americano.
Leisure interest: music.
c/o 70 Paseo de la Castellana, Madrid, Spain.

Barrett, Charles S., M.A., PH.D.; American physicist, crystallographer and metallurgist; b. 28 Sept. 1902, Vermillion, S. Dakota; s. of Charles H. and Laura D. Barrett; m. Dorothy Adams 1928; one d.; ed. Univs. of S. Dakota and Chicago.
Division of Physical Metallurgy, Naval Research Laboratory, Anacostia, D.C. 28-32; Metals Research

Laboratory and Dept. of Metallurgy, Carnegie Inst. of Technology, Pittsburgh 32-46; Prof., James Franck Inst., Univ. of Chicago 46-70; now Senior Research Engineer of Denver Research Inst., Univ. of Denver; Eastman Visiting Prof., Oxford Univ. 65-66; Editor Metals and Alloys Section of *Structure Reports* for Int. Union of Crystallography 49-51; Pres. American Society for X-ray and Electron Diffraction 47; mem. Exec. Cttee. American Inst. for Mining and Metallurgical Engineers 54-57 (Mathewson Medal 34, 44, 50, Hume-Rothery Award 76), Fellow 65-; mem. Nat. Acad. of Sciences 67-; Hon. mem. American Soc. of Metals (Howe Medal 39); mem. Ship Steel Cttee. of Nat. Research Council 48-62, Advisory Cttee., Office of Ordnance Research 56-59; Fellow, American Physical Soc., American Crystallographic Asscn., Inst. of Metals, U.S.A. Nat. Cttee. of Int. Union of Crystallography 50-55; Clamer Medal of Franklin Inst. 50; Heyn Medal of Deutsche Gesellschaft für Metallkunde.
Leisure interests: travel, painting watercolours, tennis, scientific writing.
Publs. *Structure of Metals* 43, 53, 66; over 180 papers on research in metallurgy, crystallography and physics.
University of Denver, Denver, Colo. 80210, U.S.A.

Barrett, David, B.A., M.S.W.; Canadian politician; b. 2 Oct. 1930, Vancouver, B.C.; s. of Samuel Barrett and Rose Hyatt; m. Shirley Hackman 1953; two s. one d.; ed. Seattle and St. Louis Univs.
Social Worker, Probation Officer, St. Louis Co. Juvenile Court, St. Louis, Mo.; Supervisor of Social Training, Haney Correctional Inst.; Personnel and Staff Training Officer; Supervisor of Counselling Services, John Howard Soc. of B.C., Vancouver; first elected to B.C. Legislative Assembly 60; re-elected 63, 66, 69, 72; apptd. Leader of the Opposition 69; Premier of B.C., Minister of Finance 72-75; New Democratic Party.
c/o Legislative Assembly, Victoria, B.C., Canada.

Barrett, Edward Ware, A.B.; American journalist; b. 3 July 1910, Birmingham, Ala.; s. of Edward Ware and Lewis R. (Butt) Barrett; m. Mason Daniel 1939; two d.; ed. Princeton Univ. and Univ. of Dijon.
On staff of *Birmingham* (Ala.) *News* 30-31; with Columbia Broadcasting System 32-33; with *Newsweek* 33-50, Washington Corresp. 35-36, National Affairs Editor 36-37, assoc. Editor 37-42, Editorial Dir. 46-50; with Office of War Information 42-43, with Psychological Warfare Branch of Allied Force H.Q. 43-44; Exec. Dir. of O.W.I. overseas operations, then Dir. of overseas branch 44-45; U.S. Asst. Sec. of State for Public Affairs 50-52; Editor, Consultant, N.Y. 52-54; Pres. Edward W. Barrett and Associates 52-56; Exec. Vice-Pres. Hill and Knowlton 55-56; Dean, Graduate School of Journalism, Columbia Univ. 56-Aug. 68; Dir. Communications Inst., Acad. for Educational Devt. 69-; Trustee Inst. of Int. Educ. 52-60, Atlantic Council of the U.S. 62-; Dir. UN Asscn. 64-69; Pres. Asscn. for Educ. in Journalism 65; Dir. Race Relations Information Center 69-74, Chair. 73-74; Dir. Foreign Policy Asscn. 74-.
Publs. *Truth is Our Weapon* 53, *Educational T.V.— Who Should Pay?* 68; Editor: *This is Our Challenge* 58, *Journalists in Action* 63.
Home: Hawkwood Lane, Greenwich, Conn. 06830; Office: 680 Fifth Avenue, New York, N.Y. 10019, U.S.A.

Barrie, Sir Walter; British business executive; b. 31 May 1901, Coleraine, Co. Londonderry; s. of Rt. Hon. Hugh T. Barrie, M.P., and Katie Barrie; m. Noele Margaret Furness 1927 (died 1968); two s.; ed. Merchiston Castle, Edinburgh, and Gonville and Caius Coll., Cambridge.
Entered Lloyd's 26; mem. Cttee. of Lloyd's 46; Deputy Chair. of Lloyd's 51-52; Chair. of Lloyd's 53, 54, 57, 58; fmr. Dir. Lloyd's Life Assurance Ltd.; Pres. Insurance Inst. of London 55-56, Pres. Chartered Insurance Inst.

62-63; Dir. John Ferguson & Sons (Glasgow) Ltd., Joseph W. Hobbs & Co. Ltd., Westminster Bank 58-69, Ulster Bank 64-72; retd. 74.
Leisure interest: golf.
Compton Elms, Pinkneys Green, Maidenhead, SL6 6NR, Berkshire, England.
Telephone: Maidenhead 27151.

Barrington, Ernest James William, M.A., D.SC., F.R.S.; British professor of zoology; b. 17 Feb. 1909, London; only s. of William B. and Harriet Barrington; m. Muriel Catherine Anne Clinton 1943; one s. one d.; ed. Christ's Hospital and Oriel Coll., Oxford.
Lecturer in Zoology, Univ. Coll., Nottingham 32; Rockefeller Fellow in Comparative Physiology, McGill Univ. 39, Harvard Univ. 40; Prof. of Zoology, Nottingham Univ. 49-74, Public Orator 64-70; Buell Gallagher Visiting Prof., City Coll., New York 66; Visiting Prof., Univ. of São Paulo 72; Fellow, Royal Soc. 47-71; Vice-Pres. Zoological Soc. of London 67, mem. Council, Chair. Publs. Cttee.; mem. Council European Soc. of Comparative Endocrinology; European Editor *General and Comparative Endocrinology* 60-73; Royal Soc. Leverhulme Visiting Prof., Univ. of Buenos Aires 70; Hon. mem. European Soc. of Comparative Endocrinologists; mem. Société Royale Zoologique de Belgique.
Leisure interests: walking, music.
Publs. *Introduction to General and Comparative Endocrinology* 63, *Hormones and Evolution* 64, *The Biology of Hemichordata and Protochordata* 65, *Invertebrate Structure and Function* 67, *The Chemical Basis of Physiological Regulation* 68, *Perspectives in Endocrinology* (joint Editor) 69, *Hormones in Development* (joint Editor) 71; scientific papers on digestive structure and physiology, and comparative endocrinology.
Cornerways, 2 St. Margaret's Drive, Alderton, Tewkesbury, Gloucester, GL20 8NY, England.
Telephone: Alderton 375.

Barrios, Dr. Gonzalo; Venezuelan lawyer, historian and politician; b. 1903.
Former lawyer; fmr. Chair. Acción Democrática Party; Minister of Interior March 64-Nov. 66; unsuccessful Presidential candidate 68.
Acción Democrática, Calle Los Cedros, Edif. No. 4, La Florida, Caracas, Venezuela.

Barrow, Rt. Hon. Errol Walton, P.C., B.SC. (Econ.); Barbadian barrister and politician; b. 21 Jan. 1920, Barbados; s. of Reginald Grant Barrow and Ruth O'Neal; m. Carolyn Plaskett 1945; one s. one d.; ed. Combermere School, Harrison Coll., Lincoln's Inn London, and London Univ.
Flying duties, Royal Air Force 40-47; Founder-mem. Dem. Labour Party 55, Chair. 58-; Prime Minister of Barbados 61-, Prime Minister of independent Barbados Nov. 66-, also Minister of External Affairs 66-72, of Finance and Planning; Hon. LL.D.
Leisure interests: driving, flying, sailing.
Culloden Farm, St. Michael, Barbados.
Telephone: 63179.

Barry, Peter; Irish politician; b. 1928, Cork.
Managing Dir. of a tea firm; mem. of the Dáil 69-; fmr. Chair. Oireachtas Cttee., Fine Gael Party; fmr. Lord Mayor of Cork and Chair. Cork and Kerry Regional Devt. Board; Fine Gael Spokesman on Labour 69-73; Minister for Transport and Power March 73-.
Ministry for Transport and Power, Government Buildings, Dublin 2, Ireland.

Barschall, Henry Herman, PH.D.; American physicist; b. 29 April 1915, Berlin, Germany; m. Eleanor Folsom 1955; one s. one d.; ed. Princeton Univ.
Assistant Prof. Univ. of Wis. 46-47, Assoc. Prof. 47-50, Prof. 50; Chair. Dept. of Physics 51-54, 56-57, 63-64;

Visiting Prof. Univ. of Calif. 71-73; Assoc. Div. Leader Lawrence Livermore Lab., Univ. of Calif. 71-73; Bascom Prof. of Nuclear Engineering and Physics, Univ. of Wis.; Editor *Physical Review C* 72-; Bonner Prize American Physical Soc.; mem. Nat. Acad. of Sciences.
Engineering Research Bldg., Madison, Wis. 53706; Home: 1110 Tumalo Trail, Madison, Wis. 53711, U.S.A.
Telephone: 608-263-1647 (Office); 608-233-6920 (Home).

Barshai, Rudolf Borisovich; Soviet conductor; b. 1 Oct. 1924, Labinskaya, Krasnodar Territory; ed. Moscow Conservatoire.
Performed in chamber ensembles with Shostakovich, Richter, Oistrakh, Rostropovich; founded Moscow Chamber Orchestra 55; numerous tours abroad; composer of orchestrations and arrangements for chamber orchestra of old and contemporary music.
State Philharmonic Society, 31 Ulitsa Gorkogo, Moscow, U.S.S.R.

Barszczewska, Elżbieta; Polish actress; b. 29 Nov. 1913; d. of Witold Barszczewski and Maria Szumska; m. Marian Wyrzykowski; one s.; ed. Theatrical School, Warsaw.
Début, Teatr Nowy 34; mem. Teatr Polski Co. 45-; major roles include Ophelia (*Hamlet*), Infanta (*Le Cid*), Lilla Weneda (*Lilla Weneda*), Nora (*The Doll's House*), Helena (*A Midsummer Night's Dream*), Tessa (*Tessa* by Giraudoux), Maya (*The Simpleton of the Unexpected Isles*), Mimi (*La Bohème*), Camille (*Bataille de Dames*), Angelica (*Port Royal* by Montherlant), Hannah (*The Night of the Iguana*), Lubov (*The Cherry Orchard*), Helen (*Innocent Culprits* by Ostrovski), Helene Alving (*Ghosts*); guest appearances in U.S.S.R., Czechoslovakia, U.S.A.; many film appearances; many prizes and decorations including State Artistic Prize 72.
Leisure interests: collecting theatrical items.
Al. I Armii W.P. 11/20, 00-580 Warsaw, Poland.
Telephone: 28-9102.

Bart, Lionel; British composer and lyricist; b. 1 Aug. 1930.
Ivor Novello Awards as song writer 57 (three), 59 (four), 60 (two); Variety Club Silver Heart as Show Business Personality of the Year, Broadway, U.S.A. 60; Antoinette Perry Award (Tony) for *Oliver!* 62; Gold disc for soundtrack of *Oliver!* 69.
Principal works: Lyrics for *Lock Up Your Daughters* 59, music and lyrics for *Fings Ain't Wot They Used T'be* 59, music, lyrics and book for *Oliver!* 60 (film 68), music, lyrics and direction of *Blitz!* 62, music and lyrics of *Maggie May* 64; film scores include: *Serious Charge, In the Nick, Heart of a Man, Let's Get Married, Light Up the Sky, The Tommy Steele Story, The Duke Wore Jeans, Tommy the Toreador, Sparrers Can't Sing, From Russia with Love, Man in the Middle*; many individual hit songs.
Leslie Perrin Associates, Dumbarton House, 68 Oxford Street, London W.1, England.

Bartels, Eyvind, M. POL. SC.; Danish diplomatist; b. 13 Jan. 1916, Copenhagen; s. of Knud and Gudrun Sinding Bartels; m. Jytte Breum Bartels.
Entered Danish Foreign Service 42; Head. Econ. Dept., Ministry of Foreign Affairs 48; Perm. Del. to OEEC and Econ. Adviser, Danish Embassy, Paris 50; Rep. at European Coal and Steel Community (ECSC) 53-54; Consul-Gen., New York 55-56; Amb. and Head, Perm. Del. to OEEC 57-60; Head, Del. to ECSC 57-59; Amb. to France 60-65; Amb. to India (also accred. to Ceylon) 65-67; Amb. to Egypt (also accred. to Ethiopia and Sudan) 67-71; Amb. to U.S.A. Sept. 71-.
Danish Embassy, 3200 Whitehaven Street, N.W., Washington, D.C. 20008, U.S.A.
Telephone: 202-AD4-4300.

Bartelski, Leslaw, LL.M.; Polish writer; b. 8 Sept. 1920, Warsaw; s. of Zygmunt and Zofia Ulanowska; m. Maria Zembrzuska 1947; one s. one d.; ed. Univ. of Warsaw.

Member of resistance movement 39-44; mem. *Sztuka i Naród* (Art and Nation) 42-44; Co-Editor *Nowiny Literackie* 47-48, *Nowa Kultura* 53-63, *Kultura* 63-72; mem. Presidium of Gen. Council, Soc. of Fighters For Freedom and Democracy 69-; mem. PEN; Chair. Warsaw Branch, Polish Writers Asscn. 72-; Visiting Prof., Univ. of Warsaw 70-71; Vice-Pres. Warsaw City Council 73-; State Prize 51, Prize of Minister of Defence 69, Pietrzak Prize 69, Warsaw Prize 69.
Leisure interests: history of Second World War, sport.
Publs. novels include: *Ludzie zza rzeki* 51, *Pejzaż dwukrotny* 58, *Wodorosty* 65, *Mickiewicz na wschodzie* 65, *Dialog z cieniem* 68, *Niedziela bez dzwonów* 73, *Krwawe skizydta* 75; essays: *Genealogia ocalonych* 63, *Jeździec z Madary* 63, *Powstanie Warszawskie* 65, *Walcząca Warszawa* 68, *Mokotów 1944* 71, *Z głową na karabinie* 74.
Ul. Joliot Curie 17/1, Warsaw, Poland.
Telephone: 44-31-10.

Barth, John, M.A.; American novelist and professor of English; b. 27 May 1930, Cambridge, Md.; s. of John J. Barth and Georgia Simmons; m. Shelly Rosenberg; ed. Johns Hopkins Univ.
Instructor Pennsylvania State Univ. 53, Assoc. Prof. until 65; Prof. State Univ. of N.Y. at Buffalo 65-73, Johns Hopkins Univ. 73-; Nat. Acad. of Arts and Letters Award; Nat. Book Award; Rockefeller Foundation Grant; Brandeis Univ. Citation in Literature; Hon. Litt.D. (Univ. of Maryland).
Publs. Novels: *The Floating Opera* 56, *The End of the Road* 58, *The Sot-Weed Factor* 60, *Giles Goat-Boy* 66; *Lost in the Funhouse* (stories) 68, *Chimera* 72.
Johns Hopkins University, Baltimore, Md. 21218, U.S.A.

Bartha, Dénes (Dennis R.), DR. PHIL. HABIL.; Hungarian musicologist; b. 2 Oct. 1908, Budapest; s. of Richard Bartha and Paula Imling; m. Susan Bartha 1939; two s. one d.; ed. High School of Music, Budapest, and Berlin Univ.
Librarian, Music Dept. Nat. Library 30; joined staff Budapest High School of Music 35-42, Prof. of Musicology 42 (Deputy Chair. 51-); Music Critic *Pester Lloyd* 39-44; Editor monthly journal *Magyar Zenei Szemle* 41-44; Music Adviser to Budapest Municipal Orchestra 47-48; Editor *Zenei Szemle* 47-48, *Zenetudományi Tanulmányok* (with B. Szabolcsi) (Vols. I-10) 53-62; *Studia Musicologica* (with B. Szabolcsi) 61-; mem. Directorium Int. Soc. of Musicology, American Musical Soc.; Neilson Prof. Smith Coll., Northampton, Mass. 64; Visiting Prof. Harvard Univ. 64-65, Cornell Univ. 65-66, Univ. of Illinois 66, Univ. Coll. Santa Barbara 71, 73; A. Mellon Prof. Univ. of Pittsburgh 66-67, 69-; Dent Medal 63, Erkel Prize 69.
Leisure interests: Alpinism, chess.
Publs. include *Egyetemes Zenetörténet* (General History of Music) (2 vols.) 35, *Musik, Musikgeschichte, Musikleben in Ungarn* 40, *Die ungarische Musik* (with Zoltán Kodály) 43, *A Zenetörténet Antológidja* 48, 70, *Ötödfélszáz Énekek* 53, *The Nine Symphonies of Beethoven* 56, 58, 70, *J. S. Bach* 56, 60, *Haydn als Opernkapellmeister* 60, *J. Haydn, Ges. Briefe und Dokumente Krit. Ausgabe* 65, *Zenei Lexikon* (3 vols.) 65; Editor of *La Canterina* 59, *L'Infedeltà delusa* 64, *Le Pescatrici* 72 (Haydn operas).
University of Pittsburgh, Department of Music, Pittsburgh, Pa. 15260, U.S.A.
Telephone: 412-624-4185 (Office); 441-2295 (Home).

Barthel, Max; German writer; b. 17 Nov. 1893, Dresden; s. of Gustaf and Clara Barthel; m. Luise B. Moebius; two s. one d.
Publs. Verse: *Verse aus den Argonnen, Freiheit, Die Faust, Arbeiterseele, Sonne, Mond und Sterne, Botschaft und Befehl, Hutzlibum, Danksagung, Die Lachparade, Lobgesang, Roter Mohn, Das Lied vom Walde, Spielzeuglieder, Von Ostern bis Pfingsten, Lasset uns die Welt*

*gewinnen, Überfluss des Herzens, An den Mond, Morgen-
blau und Nachtmusik, Sachen zum Lachen (Kinderlieder),
Wir spielen Zirkus (Kindersingspiel), Die Sonne krönt
das Jahr* (cantata), *Das lachende Paradies, Tänzerische
Lieder, Frühling am Bodensee* (song cycles), *Das Lied
vom Leben* (cantata), *Es kommt der Star in jedem Jahr*
(children's poems); novels: *Das Spiel mit der Puppe,
Das Land auf den Bergen, Die Strasse der ewigen Sehn-
sucht, Das Haus an der Landstrasse, Kein Bedarf an
Weltgeschichte* (autobiography); short stories: *Der Bund
der Drei, Das vergitterte Land 13 Indianer*; reports:
Deutschland, Erde unter den Füssen.
Leisure interests: walking, reading.
5207 Litterscheid 29, Federal Republic of Germany.
Telephone: 02247-1456.

Barthelmeh, Hans Adolf; German business executive;
b. 19 Sept. 1923, Cologne; *s.* of Johann and Gertrud
(née Weiler) Barthelmeh; *m.* Helene Fries 1950; one *s.*
President and Chair. Man. Board, Ford-Werke AG,
Cologne; Chair. Board of Dirs. Ford-Credit AG,
Cologne; mem. Man. Board, Verband der Deutschen
Automobilindustrie e.V., Frankfurt; mem. Board of
Dirs. American Chamber of Commerce, Fed. Germany;
mem. Industry Cttee. Chamber of Industry and
Commerce, Cologne until 73; mem. Regional Council
Deutsche Bank AG; mem. Board of Dirs., Deutsche
Automobil-Treuhand GmbH.
Leisure interests: swimming, walking, books on
philosophy, psychology and history, playing the piano.
5 Cologne 80, Herrenstrunder Strasse 2a, Federal
Republic of Germany.
Telephone: 0221 682729.

Bartholomew, Frank H., LL.D.; American journalist;
b. 5 Oct. 1898, San Francisco, Calif.; *s.* of John W.
Bartholomew and Kate Leigh Schuck; *m.* Antonia L.
Patzelt 1922; ed. Oregon State Univ.
Joined United Press 21, Pacific Div. Man. 24-30, Vice-
Pres. (Pacific Area) 30; Pres. and Gen. Man. United
Press Int. 58-62, Chair. of the Board 62-71, Dir. and
Hon. Chair. 72-; Dir. United Feature Syndicate,
United Press Asscns. Co., Security Pacific Nat. Bank,
Los Angeles, San Francisco Fed. Savings and Loan
Asscn., Balboa Club de Mazatlan, Mexico, Scripps-
Howard Foundation, Cincinnati; Pres. Buena Vista
Vinicultural Soc., Sonoma, Calif.; war corresp. in
Pacific 42-45, China 49, Korea 50, Indo-China 54.
220 East 42nd Street, New York, N.Y. 10017; Home:
Glenbrook, Nevada 89413, U.S.A.
Telephone: 514-626-6300.

Bartlett, (Charles) Vernon (Oldfeld), C.B.E.; British
author, politician and publicist; b. 30 April 1894,
Westbury, Wilts.; *s.* of Thomas Oldfeld Bartlett and
Beatrice Jecks; *m.* 1st Marguerite van den Bemden
1917 (died 1966), 2nd Eleanor Menzel (née Ritchie)
1969; one *s.*
Formerly Reuter's correspondent at Peace Conf.; sub-
sequently *The Times* corresp. in Switzerland and Rome;
London Dir. L.N. Secretariat 22-32; speaker on inter-
national affairs for B.B.C. 28-34; Diplomatic Com-
mentator *News Chronicle* 34-54; Editor *World Review*
34-40; Independent M.P. for Bridgwater 38-50; Political
Commentator *Straits Times*, Singapore 55-61.
Leisure interests: exploring Italy, meeting people,
swimming.
Publs. *Journey's End* (with R. C. Sherriff), *Calf Love,
This is my Life, East of the Iron Curtain, Struggle for
Africa, And now To-morrow, Tuscan Retreat, A Book
About Elba, Introduction to Italy, The Past of Pastimes,
The Colour of Their Skin, Tuscan Harvest, Central
Italy, Northern Italy, I Know What I Liked,* etc.
603 Via di Tiglio, Centoni, 55062 Colle di Compito,
Lucca, Italy.
Telephone: Capannori 39241.

Bartlett, Dewey Follett, B.S.; American geologist and
politician; b. 28 March 1919, Marietta, Ohio; *s.* of David
A. and Jessie (Follett) Bartlett; *m.* Ann. C. Smith 1945;
two *s.* one *d.*; ed. Lawrenceville School, N.J., and
Princeton Univ.
Served as a pilot in Second World War; partner, Keener
Oil Co. 51-71; Pres. Dewey Supply Co., Tulsa 53-56;
mem. from Tulsa, Oklahoma Senate 62-66; Gov. of
Oklahoma 67-71; Senator from Oklahoma 73-; owner-
operator ranch in Del. County 68-; mem. Board of
Dirs. Ind. Petroleum Asscn. of America, Oklahoma Ind.
Producers Asscn.; Co-Chair. Ozark Regional Comm.;
Chair. Interstate Oil Compact Comms.; mem. Republi-
can Govs. Exec. Cttee.; Air Medal.
Leisure interests: jogging, tennis, ranching.
140 Old Senate Office Building, Washington, D.C.
20510; Home: 823 N.E. 23rd Street, Oklahoma City,
Okla. 73105, U.S.A.

Bartlett, Paul Doughty; American professor of
chemistry; b. 14 Aug. 1907, Ann Arbor, Mich.; *s.* of
George Miller and Mary L. (Doughty) Bartlett; *m.* Mary
Lula Court 1931; one *s.* two *d.*; ed. Amherst Coll. and
Harvard Univ.
National Research Fellow, Rockefeller Inst. 31-32;
Instructor Univ. of Minnesota 32-34, Harvard Univ.
34-37; Asst. Prof. Harvard Univ. 37-40, Assoc. Prof.
40-46, Prof. 46-48, Erving Prof. of Chem. 48-75; Robert
A. Welch Research Prof., Texas Christian Univ. 74-;
guest lecturer at many American and European Univs.;
exchange visitor Univ. of Leningrad 61; Centenary
Lecturer, Chemical Soc. London 69; Chair. Organic
Division American Chemical Society 48, Chair. North-
eastern Section 53-54; Pres. Organic Division Int.
Union of Pure and Applied Chemistry 67-69; Chair.
U.S. Nat. Cttee. for Int. Union of Pure and Applied
Chem. 69; Program Chair. 23rd Int. Congress of Pure
and Applied Chem. 71; fmr. mem. editorial boards of
*The Journal of the American Chemical Society, Journal
of Organic Chemistry, Journal of Polymer Science* and
mem. editorial advisory board of *Tetrahedron*; Guggen-
heim and Fulbright Fellow 57; mem. Nat. Acad. of
Sciences, American Acad. of Arts and Sciences, Deutsche
Akademie der Naturforscher Leopoldina; Hon. Fellow,
Chemical Soc. (London); Hon. mem. Swiss Chemical
Soc. 72-; Hon. Sc.D. (Amherst Coll. and Univ. of
Chicago), Dr. h.c. (Paris and Montpellier); many awards
including American Chem. Soc. Award in Pure Chem.
38, August Wilhelm von Hofmann Medal of Gesell-
schaft Deutscher Chemiker 62, Willard Gibbs Medal
(American Chem. Soc.) 63, Roger Adams Award
(A.C.S.) 63, President's Nat. Medal of Science 68, James
Flack Norris Award in Physical Organic Chem. (Ameri-
can Chem. Soc.) 69, John Price Wetherill Medal
(Franklin Inst.) 70, Linus Pauling Medal 76, Nichols
Medal 76, Alexander v. Humboldt Senior Scientist
Award (Freiburg Univ.) 76; Guggenheim Fellowship
71-72.
Leisure interests: skiing, skating, photography.
Publs. *Nonclassical Ions* and about 200 research papers
on reaction mechanisms in chemical journals.
Texas Christian University, Fort Worth, Tex. 76129,
U.S.A.

Bartlett, Vernon (see Bartlett (C.) V. (O.)).

Barton, Sir Derek Harold Richard, Kt., F.R.S.,
F.R.S.E.; British organic chemist; b. 8 Sept. 1918; ed.
Tonbridge School and Imperial Coll., Univ. of London.
Lecturer, Imperial Coll. 45-59; Visiting Prof., Harvard
Univ. 49-50; Reader in Organic Chemistry, Birkbeck
Coll., Univ. of London 50-53, Prof. 53-55; Regius Prof.
of Chemistry, Glasgow Univ. 55-57; Prof. of Organic
Chemistry, Imperial Coll. of Science and Technology,
Univ. of London 57-; Pedler Lecturer, Chem. Soc. 67;
Hon. Fellow Deutsche Akad. der Naturforscher Leo-
poldina 67; Hon. D.Sc. Univ. of Montpellier 62, Univ.

of Dublin 64, City Univ. 74; Nobel Prize for Chem. 69; Foreign Assoc. U.S. Nat. Sciences 70-; Royal Medal, Royal Soc. 72; Chevalier Légion d'Honneur; numerous other medals.
Department of Chemistry, Imperial College of Science and Technology, Prince Consort Road, London, SW7 2AY, England.
Telephone: 01-589-5111.

Barton, William Hickson; Canadian diplomatist; b. 10 Dec. 1917, Winnipeg, Man.; s. of Ernest J. and Norah M. (née Hickson) Barton; m. Jeanie Robinson 1947; one s.; ed. Univ. of British Columbia.
Canadian Army 40-46; Sec. Defence Research Board of Canada 46-52; joined Dept. of External Affairs, Ottawa 52; Counsellor, Canadian Embassy, Vienna 56; Minister, Canadian Mission at UN, New York 61; Dir.-Gen. UN Bureau, Dept. of External Affairs 64; Asst. Under-Sec. of State for External Affairs 70; Amb. and Perm. Rep. to Office of UN, Geneva 72-.
Permanent Mission of Canada, United Nations, 10A Avenue de Budé, 1202 Geneva; Home: 15 route de Collex, Bellevue, Geneva, Switzerland.
Telephone: 34-19-50 (Office); 74-12-43 (Home).

Barwick, Rt. Hon. Sir Garfield Edward John, P.C., G.C.M.G., B.A., LL.B.; Australian lawyer and politician; b. 22 June, 1903, Sydney; s. of Jabez Edward Barwick and Lily Grace Barwick (née Ellicot); m. Norma Mountier 1929; one s. one d.; ed. Fort St. Boys' High School Sydney, Sydney Univ.
Admitted to N.S.W. Bar 27, Victoria Bar 45, Queensland Bar 58; Pres. N.S.W. Bar Asscn. 50-52, 55-56, Law Council of Australia 52-54; mem. Fed. House of Reps. for Parramatta 58-64; Attorney-Gen. 58-64; Acting Minister for External Affairs Mar.-Apr., Aug.-Nov. 59, April-June 60, Minister for External Affairs Dec. 61-64; Chief Justice of Australia 64-; Chancellor Macquarie Univ., Sydney, March 67-; Pres. Australian Inst. of Int. Affairs 72-; Judge ad hoc, Int. Court of Justice 73-74; Leader, Australian Del. SEATO Council, Bangkok 61, Paris 63; UN Del. 60, 62-64; Australian Del. to ECAFE, Manila 63; Australian Del. ANZUS, Canberra 62, Wellington 63; Hon. LL.D. (Sydney).
Leisure interests: gardening, fishing, yachting.
Chambers of the Chief Justice, High Court of Australia, Sydney; and Mundroola, George Street, Careel Bay, Sydney, Australia.

Barzel, Rainer, DR. IUR.; German lawyer, civil servant and politician; b. 20 June 1924, Braunsberg, East Prussia; s. of Dr. Candidus Barzel and Maria Barzel; m. Kriemhild Schumacher 1948; one d.; ed. Gymnasium, Braunsberg (East Prussia), Berlin, and Univ. of Cologne.
Air Force, Second World War; Civil Service, North Rhine-Westphalia, Ministry for Fed. Affairs 49-56, resigned 56; mem. Bundestag 57-; Fed. Minister for All-German Affairs 62-63; Exec. mem. Christian Democrat Party (CDU), First Deputy Chair. CDU and Chair. CDU/CSU in Bundestag 64-73; Chair. CDU 71-73.
Publs. Die geistigen Grundlagen der politischen Parteien 47, Souveränität und Freiheit 50, Die deutschen Parteien 51, Gesichtspunkte eines Deutschen 68.
Leisure interests: skating, curling, archaeology.
Ferdinandstrasse 4, 479 Paderborn/W., Federal Republic of Germany.
Telephone: 02221-16-2565.

Barzini, Luigi, B.LITT.; Italian journalist and writer; b. 21 Dec. 1908, Milan; s. of Luigi and Mantica (née Pesavento) Barzini; m. 1st Giannalisa Gianzana 1940; m. 2nd Paola Gadola 1949; five c.; ed. School of Journalism, Columbia Univ., New York.
Special Correspondent Corriere della Sera 30-40; Editor and Publisher Il Globo, Rome 44-47; contributor to Italian and other magazines; mem. Italian Chamber of Deputies 58-72; Liberal.
Publs. Americans are Alone in the World 53, I Disarmati 57, Mosca Mosca 61, The Italians 64, L'Europa Domani Mattina 64.
Leisure interest: riding.
1055 Via Cassia, Tomba di Nerone, Rome, Italy.
Telephone: 366-1925.

Barzun, Jacques, PH.D.; American university professor and writer; b. 30 Nov. 1907, Créteil, France; two s. one d.; ed. Lycée Janson de Sailly and Columbia Univ.
Instructor in History, Columbia Univ. 29, Asst. Prof. 38, Assoc. Prof. 42, Prof. 45-, Dean of Graduate Faculties 55-58, Dean of Faculties and Provost 58-67, Univ. Prof. 67-75, Seth Low Prof. 60; Literary Adviser, Scribner's 75-; mem. Acad. Delphinale (Grenoble), American Nat. Inst. of Arts and Letters (Pres. 72-75), American Historical Asscn., Royal Soc. of Arts, American Arbitration Asscn.; Dir. Council for Basic Educ., New York Soc. Library, Open Court Publications Inc., Peabody Inst.; mem. Advisory Council, Univ. Coll. at Buckingham; Chevalier de la Légion d'Honneur; Extraordinary Fellow, Churchill Coll., Cambridge 61.
Publs. The French Race 32, Race: A Study in Modern Superstition 37, Of Human Freedom 39, Darwin, Marx, Wagner 41, Teacher in America 45, Berlioz and the Romantic Century 50, God's Country and Mine 54, The Energies of Art 56, Music in American Life 56, The Modern Researcher 57 (with H. Graff), The House of Intellect 59, Classic, Romantic and Modern 61, Science, the Glorious Entertainment 64, The American University 68, A Catalogue of Crime (with W. Taylor) 71, On Writing, Editing and Publishing 71, The Use and Abuse of Art 74, Clio and the Doctors 74; Editor Pleasures of Music 51, The Selected Letters of Lord Byron 53, New Letters of Berlioz (and trans.) 54, The Selected Writings of John Jay Chapman 57, Modern American Usage (with others); Trans.: Diderot: Rameau's Nephew 52, Flaubert's Dictionary of Accepted Ideas 54, Evenings with the Orchestra 56, Courteline: A Rule is a Rule 60, Beaumarchais: The Marriage of Figaro 61.
597 Fifth Avenue, New York, N.Y. 10017, U.S.A.

Basaldella, Afro; Italian painter; b. 1912; ed. Acad. of Fine Arts, Venice.
Works under the name of Afro; represented in the most important museums of U.S.A. and Europe; executed design for Ritratto di Don Chisciotte Rome 57; first prize Venice Biennale 56, second prize Pittsburgh Int. 59, UNESCO Award, Paris.
Via Nicolo Tartaglia 3, Rome, Italy.

Basford, Hon. (Stanley) Ronald, P.C., M.P., B.A., LL.B., Q.C.; Canadian politician; b. 22 April 1932, Winnipeg, Man.; s. of Douglas and Elizabeth Basford; m. Madeleine Nelson Kirk 1967; one s. one d.; ed. Univ. of British Columbia.
Practised in Vancouver law firm; mem of Parl. for Vancouver 63-; observer to many int. confs.; Co-Chair. Joint Commons-Senate Cttee. on Consumer Credit and Cost of Living 67; Minister of Consumer and Corporate Affairs 68, of Urban Affairs 72, of Nat. Revenue 74, of Justice and Attorney-General 75-; Liberal.
Leisure interest: fishing.
House of Commons, Ottawa, Ont.; Home: 31 Holborn, Ottawa, Ont., Canada.

Basie, (William) Count; American jazz and blues musician; b. 21 Aug. 1904, Red Bank, N.J.
Plays piano and occasionally organ; started playing in Harlem clubs; played with Walter Page Blue Devils, Kansas City; joined Bennie Moten Orchestra, Leader of renamed Count Basie Orchestra 36-; debut in New York 38; first appearance at Carnegie Hall 39; first European tour 54, first S. American tour 69, has also toured

Canada and Japan; played Inaugural Ball for Pres. Kennedy 61; Royal Command Performance, U.K. 66; has performed with Frank Sinatra, Tony Bennett, Ella Fitzgerald, Sammy Davis, Jr., etc., numerous concert, night club and television appearances, has played at all the major jazz festivals, including the Newport Jazz Festival, Int. Jazz Festival, France; Band awards include *Esquire* Silver Award, *Downbeat* Readers' Poll 55, *Metronome* Poll, *Downbeat* Int. Critics' Poll 56, and many others.

Film appearances in *Reveille with Beverly* 42, *Stage Door Canteen, Mr. Big, Crazy House, Cinderfella* 60, *Blazing Saddles* 74.

Compositions include: *One O'Clock Jump, The Mad Boogie*.

c/o Willard Alexander Inc., 660 Madison Avenue, New York, N.Y. 10021, U.S.A.

Telephone: (212) 751-7070.

Baskakov, Sergei Alexeyevich; Soviet politician; b. 1911; ed. Industrial Inst. of the Urals.

Member C.P.S.U. 31-; technologist, later Senior Engineer, U.S.S.R. Ministry of Armament 35-43; party and trade union work 43-51; Deputy Minister of Medium Machine Building, U.S.S.R. 53-54; on staff, Central Cttee. of C.P.S.U. 54-, Dept. Chief 56-, mem. Central Auditing Comm. 61-71.

Central Auditing Commission of the Communist Party of the Soviet Union, Moscow, U.S.S.R.

Basmaci, Ferid; Turkish banker; b. 13 Feb. 1911, Istanbul; *m.* Faize Basmaci 1938; two *d.*; ed. Faculty of Econs. and Commerce, Istanbul.

Treasurer, Türkiye İş Bankası 53-58, Vice-Pres. 58-60, Man. Galata Branch 60-66, Senior Vice-Pres. 66-67, Pres. 67-; Chair. Sınaî Yatırım ve Kredi Bankası 67-, Minin Bank 69-, Industrial Devt. Bank of Turkey 69-. Türkiye İş Bankası A.Ş., Ulus, Ankara; Home: Vali Dr. Reşit Caddesi 73, Çankaya, Ankara, Turkey.

Telephone: 124383 (Home).

Basnayake, Hema Henry, Q.C.; Ceylonese judge; b. 3 Aug. 1902, *s.* of Simon Samaringh Basnayake and Charlotte Siriwardene; *m.* Lilivati Gomes 1932; two *s.*; ed. St. Aloysius Coll., Galle, and St. Joseph's Coll., Colombo.

Admitted to the Bar 27; Crown Counsel 32; Commr. for preparing new revised edition of Legislative Enactments of Ceylon 37-38; Asst. Legal Draughtsman 39; Senior Crown Counsel 44; Acting Solicitor-Gen. 45, Jan. 46; Acting Attorney-Gen. 46, 47; mem. Local Govt. Service Comm. 45-47; Solicitor-Gen. 46; Puisne Justice 47-51; Attorney-Gen. 51-55; Acting Chief Justice 55; Chief Justice 56-64; Chair. Comm. of Inquiry on Police Force 65; Chair. Board of Trustees, Ceylon Univ. Sangharama and Vihara Trust, Musaeus Girls Coll., Kalutara Bodhi Trust; Pres. Child Protection Soc., Crippled Children's Aid Asscn., Sri Lanka Human Ecology Asscn.; Vice-Pres. St. John Ambulance Asscn.; Pres. Ceylon Farmers' Asscn. Maha Bodei Soc. of Sri Lanka, Int. Comm. of Jurists (Sri Lanka Section); Chair. Water Resources Board, Sri Lanka.

Leisure interests: encouraging farming and the production of food necessary for the land, care of the disabled and the needy, rural welfare.

Publ. *Legislative Enactments of Ceylon* 38, 56.

Elibank House, 39 Elibank Road, Havelock Town, Colombo 5, Sri Lanka.

Telephone: 85857, 81392.

Basov, Alexandr Vasilievich, M.SC.; Soviet politician and diplomatist; b. 20 March 1912, Stanitsa Baklanovskaya, Tsimlaynsk district, Rostov region; ed. Vologda Agricultural Inst.

Veterinary Inst. 30-42; teacher 42-54; Sec. Rostov Regional Cttee., C.P.S.U. 54-55; Chair. Rostov District Exec. Cttee. 55-60; First Sec. Rostov District Cttee., C.P.S.U. 60-62; mem. Central Cttee. C.P.S.U. 61-;

Counsellor, Cuba 62-65; Minister of Agriculture of R.S.F.S.R. 65; Ambassador to Romania 65-71, to Chile 71-73.

Ministry of Foreign Affairs, Moscow, U.S.S.R.

Basov, Nikolai Gennadievich; Soviet physicist; b. 14 Dec. 1922, Voronezh; *s.* of Prof. Gennadii Fedorovich Basov and Zinaida Andreevna Molchanova; *m.* Kseniya Tikhonovna Nazarova 1950; two *s.*; ed. Moscow Inst. of Physical Engineers.

P. N. Lebedev Physical Inst. 50-, Vice-Dir. 58-72, Dir. 73-; founded Laboratory of Quantum Radio-physics 63-; Prof. Moscow Inst. of Physical Engs. 63-; Deputy to U.S.S.R. Supreme Soviet 74-; Corresp. mem. U.S.S.R. Acad. of Sciences 62-66, Academician 66-, mem. Presidium 67-; mem. Optical Soc. of America, Deutsche Akad. der Wissenschaften, Berlin, Deutsche Akad. der Naturforscher Leopoldina, Bulgarian Acad. of Sciences, Polish Military-Technical Acad., Royal Swedish Acad. of Eng. Sciences, Prague Polytechnic Inst., Jena Univ.; Editor *Priroda* (Nature) popular science magazine, *Soviet Journal of Quantum Electronics*; Lenin Prize 59, Nobel Prize for Physics 64; Order of Lenin 67, 72, 75, Hero of Socialist Labour 69.

Leisure interests: photography, skiing.

P. N. Lebedev Physical Institute of the Academy of Sciences, 53 Leninsky Prospect, Moscow, U.S.S.R.

Bass, Lawrence Wade, PH.D.; American chemical engineer; b. 18 June 1898, Streator, Ill.; *s.* of the late John H. and Sara L. Bass; *m.* Edna M. Becker 1935; no *c.*; ed. Tulane, Yale, Lille and Paris Univs. and Inst. Pasteur, Paris.

Rockefeller Inst. 25-29; Exec. Staff Mellon Inst. 29-31; Dir. of Research Borden Co., New York 31-36; Asst. Dir. Mellon Inst. 37-42; Dir. New England Ind. Research Foundation 42-44; Dir. Chemical Research Air Reduction Co. Inc. 44-48; Research and Development U.S. Indus. Chemicals Inc. 44-48, Vice-Pres. 48-52; Exec. Arthur D. Little Inc. 52-54, Vice-Pres. 54-64; Consultant 64-; Pres. American Inst. Chemical Engs. 45.

Leisure interests: photography, travel.

Publs. *Chemistry of the Inorganic Complex Compounds* 23, *Nucleic Acids* 31, *Management of Technical Programs* 65, *Formulation of Research Policies* 67.

Office: 1735 Eye Street, N.W., Washington, D.C. 20006; Home: 2000 N. Street, N.W., Washington, D.C. 20036, U.S.A.

Bassani, Giorgio; Italian writer; b. 1916; ed. Univ. of Bologna.

Chief Editor *Botteghe Oscure* 48-60, Dir. of Literary Series with Feltrinelli including *Il Gattopardo*, G. di Lampedusa 57-63; Teacher History of Theatre, Acad. d'Arte Drammatica 57-68; Vice-Pres. Radio Televisione Italiana 64-65; Strega Prize 56, Viareggio Prize 62, Campiello Prize 69, Nelly Sachs Prize 69.

Publs. *Cinque storie ferraresi* 56, *Gli occhiali d'oro* (novel) 58, *Il giardino dei Finzi-Contini* (novel) 62, *L'alba ai vetri* (poems) 63, *Dietro la porta* (novel) 64, *Le parole preparate* (essays) 66, *L'airone* (novel) 68, *Heron* 70, *Epitaffio* (poems) 74.

Via G. B. De Rossi 33, Rome, Italy.

Basson, Jacob Daniel du Plessis ("Japie"); South African politician; b. 1918, Paarl, Cape Province; *s.* of late Senator and of Mrs. Danie J. Basson; *m.* Clarence Strauss 1947; two *d.*; ed. Stellenbosch Univ.

Political sec. and journalist in Repub. and S.W. Africa 39-50; mem. S. African Parl. for Namib, S.W. Africa 50-59 (Nat. Party of S.W.A.); expelled from Nat. Party Caucus over differences concerning Govt.'s race policies 59; Independent M.P., leading extra-Parl. Political Group (The Nat. Union) 59-61; merger of Nat. Union with United Party (official opposition party) 61; M.P. (United Party) for Bezuidenhout,

Johannesburg 61-; Leader United Party in the Transvaal 75; Shadow Minister of Foreign Affairs.
Leisure interests: reading, gardening, swimming.
House of Assembly, Cape Town; and 123 Kitchener Avenue, Bezuidenhout Valley, Johannesburg, South Africa.
Telephone: 24-5040 (Johannesburg).

Bastian, Paul Henri, LIC EN DROIT; Luxembourg government official; b. 9 Sept. 1896, Luxembourg; *m.* Edith Cazal 1922; two *d.*; ed. Luxembourg Athénée, Munich and Montpellier Univs.
Sec. Gen. Luxembourg Branch Soc. Gén. Alsacienne de Banque 22-29; Dir. Agence Economique et Financière, Luxembourg 29-39; Pres. Asscn. des Journalistes Luxembourgeois 36-38; Dir. Luxembourg City Food Services 40-41; Dir. Gewerbebank, Deputy Dir. Banque Gén. de Luxembourg 41-44; Hon. Commissaire du Gouvernement, Ministry of Finance 44-; mem. Council, Inst. Belgo-Luxembourgeois du Change 45-72; mem. Monetary Cttee. EEC 58-69; Benelux Cttee. Econ. Policy 60-; mem. Luxembourg Del. to OECD; Dir. of several companies; Commdr. Ordre Adolphe de Nassau, Commdr. Ordre de la Couronne de Chêne, Commdr. Ordre de Léopold, Commdr. Ordre de St. Grégoire le Grand, Officier Légion d'Honneur, Commdr. Order of Merit (Germany and Italy).
Leisure interests: reading, painting, swimming, walking.
Publs. *La Fortune Nationale du Grand-Duché de Luxembourg 34, Le Système Monétaire du Grand-Duché de Luxembourg 36, Le Commerce Extérieur du Grand-Duché de Luxembourg 39.*
20a boulevard Em Servais, Luxembourg.

Bastid, Suzanne; French lawyer; b. 15 Aug. 1906 Rennes; *d.* of Jules Basdevant and Renée Mallarmé; *m.* 1937; three *d.*; ed. Lycée de Grenoble, Lycée de Fénelon, Paris, and Univ. de Paris à la Sorbonne.
Professor, Faculty of Law, Lyon 33-46, Paris 46-; Prof. Inst. d'études politiques, Univ. de Paris 46-; Pres. Admin. Tribunal, UN 52-68, Vice-Pres. 69-; Sec.-Gen. Inst. of Law 63-69, First Vice-Pres. 69-71; Pres. Soc. française pour le droit international; mem. French Del. to UN Gen. Assembly (4th to 13th Sessions); mem. Acad. des Sciences Morales et Politiques; Officier Légion d'Honneur, Commdr. Royal Order of Sahametri (Cambodia).
Publs. include: *Les fonctionnaires internationaux, Jurisprudence de la Cour internationale de Justice, Les Tribunaux administratifs internationaux et leur jurisprudence, Les questions territoriales devant la C.I.J.*
88 rue de Grenelle, Paris 7e, France.
Telephone: 548 63 34.

Bastyan, Lieut.-Gen. Sir Edric (Montague), K.C.M.G., K.C.V.O., K.B.E., C.B.; British army officer and Australian governor; b. 5 April 1903; ed. Royal Military Coll., Sandhurst.
Army career began as Second Lieut. Sherwood Foresters 23, rising to Chief Admin. Officer, Eighth Army 43; Maj.-Gen. in charge Admin., Allied Land Forces, S.E. Asia 44-45; Imperial Defence Coll. 46; Maj.-Gen. in charge Admin., British Army of the Rhine 46-48; employed on special duties, War Office 49; Chief of Staff, Eastern Command 49-50; Dir. of Staff Duties, W.O. 50-52; Commdr. 53rd (Welsh) Infantry Div. (T.A.) and Mid-West District 52-55; Vice-Adjutant-Gen. War Office 55-57; Lieut.-Gen. 57; Commdr., British Forces, Hong Kong 57-60; retd. 60; Gov. of South Australia 61-Oct. 68; Gov. Tasmania 68-73; Hon. Col. Royal Tasmania Regiment 69; Hon. Air Commodore No. 24 Squadron, R.A.A.F.; K.St.J. 61.
c/o Government House, Hobart, Tasmania, Australia.

Bata, Thomas John, C.C.; Canadian shoe executive; b. 17 Sept. 1914 Prague, Czechoslovakia; *s.* of the late Thomas Bata and Marie Bata; *m.* Sonja Ingrid Wett-stein; one *s.* three *d.*; ed. privately and Acad. of Commerce Uherske Hradiste.
President Bata Ltd.; Chair. of Bata Shoe Co. of Canada Ltd. 39-, British Bata Shoe Co. Ltd. 46-, Bata Industries Ltd., Dir. and officer of several companies connected with Bata Group; Dir. IBM Canada Ltd., Toronto and Canadian Pacific Airlines; Dir. American Management Asscn. 58-61, Canadian Council Int. Chamber of Commerce, Canadian Exec. Service Overseas; Chair. Standing Group on Devt. Aid and Private Investment for the Business and Industry Advisory Cttee., OECD; mem. Board of Govs. Canadian Asscn. for Latin America, Canadian Export Asscn., Toronto Arts Foundation, Stratford Shakespearean Festival Foundation; Founding mem. and mem. Planning Council, The President's Professional Asscn. (U.S.A.) 61; Founder and fmr. Dir. Young President's Asscn.; mem. Chief Execs. Forum, Canadian Inst. of Int. Affairs, Canadian Econ. Policy Cttee., Board of Dirs. Nat. Ballet Guild of Canada; Vice-Chair. Board of Govs., Trent Univ., Peterborough, Ont.
Batawa, Ontario; 44 Park Lane Circle, Don Mills, Ontario, Canada.

Bataillon, Marcel Edouard, D. ÈS L.; French university professor; b. 20 May 1895, Dijon; *s.* of Eugène Bataillon and Marie-Henriette Wahl; *m.* Lucy Hovelacque 1922; three *s.* one *d.*; ed. Lycée Carnot, Dijon, Lycée Louis-le-Grand, Paris, Ecole Normale Supérieure, Paris, and Ecole des Hautes Etudes Hispaniques, Madrid.
Artillery Officer, First World War 14-18, Prof. Univ. of Lisbon 22-26, Lycée de Bordeaux 26-29, Univ. of Algiers 29-37, Univ. of Paris 37-45, Collège de France 45-65, Hon. Prof. Collège de France 65-; Dir. Collège de France 55-65; mem. Acad. des Inscriptions et Belles Lettres 52-; Hon. Pres. Féd. Int. des Langues et Littératures Modernes; mem. Royal Acads. of Belgium, Netherlands and Sweden, Accad. dei Lincei, Rome, Bavarian Acad. of Sciences, British Acad.; Corresp. mem. Spanish Acad., and Acad. of History, Madrid; Commdr. Légion d'Honneur; Commdr. des Palmes Académiques; Croix de Guerre; Dr. h.c. (Louvain, Exeter, Leiden, Turin and Montevideo).
Publs. *Erasme et l'Espagne 37, Etudes sur le Portugal au temps de l'humanisme 52, Le Docteur Laguna auteur du "Voyage en Turquie" 58, La Célestine selon F. de Rojas 61, Varia lección de clásicos españoles 64, Etudes sur Bartolomé de Casas 65.*
Leisure interests: walking, travelling.
14 rue de l'Abbé de l'Epée, Paris 5e, France.
Telephone: ODE-94-24.

Bateman, Leslie Clifford, C.M.G., D.SC., PH.D., F.R.S.; British scientist; b. 21 March 1915, Yiewsley; *s.* of Charles Samuel Bateman and Florence Skinner; *m.* 1st Marie Pakes 1945 (died 1967); two *s.*; *m.* 2nd Eileen Jones 1973; ed. Univ. Coll., London, and Oriel Coll., Oxford.
Chemist, Natural Rubber Producers' Research Asscn., England 41-53, Dir. of Research 53-62; Controller of Rubber Research, Malaysia 62-74, Special Adviser, Malaysian Rubber Research and Devt. Board 74-; Colwyn Medal 62, Jubilee Foundation Lecturer 71, Inst. of the Rubber Industry; Hon. D.Sc. (Malaya) 68, (Aston) 72; Fellow, Univ. Coll., London 74; Panglima Setia Makhota, Malaysia 74.
Leisure interests: outdoor activities, particularly cricket and golf.
Publs. Editor and contributor to *The Chemistry and Physics of Rubber-like Substances* 63; numerous publications in *Journal of Chemical Society*, etc. and on the techno-economic position of the natural rubber industry.
3 Palmerston Close, Welwyn Garden City, Herts., AL8 7DL, England.
Telephone: Welwyn Garden 22391.

Bateman, Sir Ralph (Melton), K.B.E., M.A., F.C.I.S.; British business executive; b. 15 May 1910, Rochdale, Lancs.; s. of the late Dr. and Mrs. W. H. Bateman; m. Barbara Yvonne Litton 1935; two s. two d.; ed. Epsom Coll. and Univ. Coll., Oxford.
Turner and Newall Ltd. 31-, Dir. 57-, Deputy Chair. and Joint Man. Dir. 59-67, Chair. 67-76; Dir. Certain-teed Products Corpn. of Philadelphia, U.S.A., Cassiar Asbestos Corpn. Ltd. of Toronto, Canada; Pres. of Confed. of British Industry 74-May 76; mem. Nat. Econ. Devt. Council; Gov. Nat. Inst. of Econ. and Social Research; Fellow British Inst. of Management, Chartered Inst. of Secs., Royal Soc. of Arts; mem. Council of Manchester Business School, mem. Court Manchester Univ., Univ. of Salford; Chair. Board of Govs., Ashridge Coll. of Management; Hon. D.Sc. Univ. of Salford.
Turner and Newall Ltd., 77-79 Fountain Street, Manchester, M2 2EA; Home: Highfield, Withinlee Road, Prestbury, Cheshire, England.
Telephone: 061-236-9381.

Batenburg, Andries, DR. ECON.; Netherlands banker; b. 11 Oct. 1922, Rotterdam; s. of A. Batenburg and C. C. Keller; m. Margaretha Hartman 1949; two d.; ed. Netherlands Econ. Univ.
Joined Nederlandsche Handel-Maatschappij N.V. 48; Man. Dir. Algemene Bank Nederland N.V. 66, mem. Presidium 70, Chair. Managing Board Sept. 74-.
Publ. Enkele Hoofdlijnen van de Monetaire Politiek (Some Principal Aspects of Monetary Policy).
Algemene Bank Nederland N.V., Vijzelstraat 32, Amsterdam, Netherlands.

Bates, Alan; British actor; b. 17 Feb. 1934, Allestree, Derbys.; s. of Harold A. Bates and Florence M. Wheatcroft; m. Victoria Ward 1970; twin s.; ed. Belper Grammar School and Royal Acad. of Dramatic Art (RADA).
Spent one year with Midland Repertory Co., Coventry; subsequent stage appearances in London include roles in The Mulberry Bush, Look Back in Anger (also in Moscow and New York), The Country Wife, In Celebration, Long Day's Journey into Night (also at Edinburgh Festival), The Caretaker (also in New York), The Four Seasons, Hamlet (also in Nottingham), Butley (also in New York, Los Angeles and San Francisco), Life Class, Otherwise Engaged 75; has also appeared at Canadian Shakespeare Festival, Stratford, Ont. in title role of Richard III and as Ford in The Merry Wives of Windsor; also in Poor Richard (New York), Venice Preserved (Bristol), The Taming of the Shrew (Stratford-upon-Avon); received Tony Award for Butley, Broadway, New York 73.
Films: The Entertainer 60, Whistle Down the Wind 61, A Kind of Loving 62, The Running Man 62, The Caretaker 63, Nothing but the Best 64, Zorba the Greek 65, Georgy Girl 65, King of Hearts 66, Far from the Madding Crowd 66, The Fixer 67, Women in Love 68, The Three Sisters 69, The Go-Between 71, A Day in the Death of Joe Egg 72, Butley 73, The Impossible Object 73, In Celebration 74, Royal Flash 74.
Leisure interests: squash, swimming, tennis, driving, travelling, reading.
c/o Michael Linnit, Chatto & Linnit Ltd., 13 Wardour Street, London, W.1, England.

Batitsky, Marshal Pavel Fyodorovich; Soviet army officer and politician; b. 27 July 1910, Kharkov, Ukraine; ed. Frunze Military Acad., and Acad. of General Staff.
Soviet Army 24-; mem. C.P.S.U. 38-; Chief of Div. Staff, then Div. and Corps Commdr. 41-45; Area Mil. Commdr. 48-50; Chief of Gen. Staff, Soviet Army Air Force 50-53; First Deputy Commdr. Area Anti-Aircraft Defence 53-54, Commdr. 54-65; First Deputy Chief Gen. Staff Soviet Armed Forces 65-66; C.-in-C.

U.S.S.R. Anti-Aircraft Defence, Deputy Minister of Defence 66-; Cand. mem. Central Cttee. of C.P.S.U. 61-66, mem. 66-; Deputy to U.S.S.R. Supreme Soviet; Hero of the Soviet Union; Order of Lenin (four times), Order of Kutuzov (twice), Order of Suvorov, Order of Red Banner (four times), Order of the October Revolution.
Ministry of Defence, 34 Naberezhnaya M. Thoreza, Moscow, U.S.S.R.

Batliner, Gerard, D.IUR.; Liechtenstein lawyer; b. 9 Dec. 1928, Eschen; s. of Andreas and Karolina Batliner; m. Christina Negele 1965; two s.; ed. Grammar School, Schwyz, Switzerland, and Univs. of Zürich, Fribourg, Paris, and Freiburg im Breisgau.
Practice at County Court of Principality of Liechtenstein 54-55; lawyer, Vaduz 56-62; Vice-Pres. Progressive Burgher Party 58; Vice-Mayor of Eschen 60; Pres. Liechtenstein Parl. 74-; Head of Govt. of Principality of Liechtenstein 62-70; Editor-in-Chief Liechtenstein Politische Schriften (Liechtenstein Political Publications); Fürstlicher Justizrat 70; Grand Cross of the Liechtenstein Order of Merit.
Am Schrägen Weg 2, FL-9490 Vaduz, Liechtenstein.
Telephone: 2-24-24.

Batov, Gen. Pavel Ivanovich; Soviet army officer; b. 1 June 1897, Filisovo Village, Yaroslav Region.
Tsarist Army 15-17, Red Army 18-; mem. Communist Party 29-; served in Spanish Civil War 36-37, gravely wounded; Corps Commdr. 37; served as Div. Commdr. in Finland War 39-40; Deputy Commdr. Bryansk front 42; made Commdr. 65th Army 42; served in Stalingrad, Byelorussia, Poland, Berlin 42-45; Commdr. Soviet forces in Germany 45-49; Commdr. Kaliningrad Mil. District 49-55, Carpathian Mil. District 55-58, Baltic Mil. District 58-60, U.S.S.R. Southern Army Group (Hungary) 60-62; Chief of Staff, Joint Armed Forces of Warsaw Pact Org. 62-65; First Deputy Chief of Staff Soviet Armed Forces 62-66; Insp.-Gen. Ministry of Defence 66-70; Chair. Soviet Cttee. of Veterans 70-; Deputy to Supreme Soviet of U.S.S.R. until 70; Order of Lenin (five times); Hero of the Soviet Union (twice); Order of Suvorov (three times); Order of Kutuzov; Order of Red Banner (three times); Order of the October Revolution, etc.
Publs. include: In Battles and On the March 62, The Oder Operation 65, Trusty Shield 65.
Soviet Committee of Veterans, Gogol Boulevard 4, Moscow, U.S.S.R.

Batten, Jean Gardner, C.B.E.; New Zealand aviator; b. 1909; ed. Cleveland House Coll., Auckland.
Obtained flying licence 30, commercial pilot's licence 32; London Aeroplane Club; made solo flights England-India 33, England-Australia (woman's record) 34, Australia-England (first woman to complete return flight) 35, England-Brazil (world record 61¼ hours; fastest crossing of S. Atlantic 13¼ hours; first England-S. America and solo S. Atlantic flight by woman) 36, England-New Zealand (first direct flight 11 days, establishing record England-Australia solo 5 days 21 hours, fastest Sydney-Auckland flight (10½ hours)) 37, Australia-England (solo record 5 days 18 hours 15 minutes) 37; many trophies and medals, including those of Fédération Aéronautique Internationale 38, and City of Paris 71; Chevalier Légion d'Honneur; Officer Order of Southern Cross of Brazil; Jean Batten Archive, Royal Air Force Museum, Hendon, London.
Leisure interests: travelling, music, swimming.
Publ. My Life 38.
c/o Barclays Bank Ltd., 25 Charing Cross Road, London, WC2H 0HZ, England.

Batten, William Milfred, B.S.; American business executive; b. 4 June 1909, Reedy, W. Va.; s. of Lewis A. Batten and Gurry Goff; m. Kathryn Pherabe Clark

1935; one *s*. one *d*.; ed. Parkersburg High School, W. Va. and Ohio State Univ.

Salesman, Section Man., Asst. Man., J. C. Penney Co. store, Lansing, Mich. 35-40; Training Dir. Personnel Dept. J. C. Penney Co., New York 40-42; consultant in Organization Planning & Control Div. Office of Q.M.G., Washington 42; military service, Office of Q.M.G., U.S. Army as Lieut.-Col. 42-45; Zone Personnel Rep. (Eastern Zone), J. C. Penney Co., New York 45-51, Asst. to Pres. 51-58, Vice-Pres. 53-58, Pres. 58-64, Chair. of Board 64-74; Dir. N.Y. Stock Exchange 72-74; Trustee Woodrow Wilson Int. Center for Scholars; Dir. American Telephone and Telegraph Co., Boeing Co., First Nat. City Bank, First Nat. City Corpn.; Chair. Business Council 71-72; Hon. LL.D. (Alderson-Broaddus Coll., Morris Harvey Coll. and West Virginia Univ.); Hon. L.H.D. (Marietta Coll.).

Mill Neck, Long Island, N.Y. 11765, U.S.A.

Battle, Lucius Durham, A.B., LL.B.; American educationist; b. 1 June 1918, Dawson, Ga.; *s*. of Warren L. Battle and Jewel B. Durham; *m*. Betty Davis 1949; two *s*. two *d*.; ed. Univ. of Florida.

Manager of student staff, Univ. of Florida Library 40-42; Assoc. Admin. Analyst, War Dept. 42-43; U.S. Naval Reserve 43-46; Foreign Affairs Specialist, Dept. of State, Washington 46-49; Special Asst. to Sec. of State 49-53, 61-64, also Exec. Sec. Dept. of State 61-62; First Sec., Copenhagen 53-55; Deputy Exec. Sec. NATO, Paris 55-56; Asst. Sec. of State for Educational and Cultural Affairs 62-64; Amb. to United Arab Repub. 64-67; Asst. Sec. of State for Near Eastern and S. Asian Affairs, Washington 67-68; Vice-Pres. for Corporate Affairs, Communications Satellite Corpn., Washington, D.C. 68-73, Senior Vice-Pres. for Corporate Affairs 74-; Pres. Middle East Inst., Washington, D.C., 73-74; Chair. UNESCO Gen. Conf., Paris 62; Vice-Pres. Colonial Williamsburg Inc., Williamsburg Restoration Inc. 56-61; Trustee Meridian House Int., American Univ. Cairo; mem. American Foreign Service Asscn. (Pres. 62-63); Chair., Visiting Comm. for Centre for Middle Eastern Studies of Harvard Coll.; Chair. of Board, St. Alban's School.

Home: 3200 Garfield Street, N.W., Washington, D.C., U.S.A.

Batty, Sir William (Bradshaw), Kt.; British motor executive; b. 15 May 1913, Manchester; *s*. of Rowland and Nellie Batty; *m*. Jean Ella Brice 1946; one *s*. one *d*.; ed. Hulme Grammar School, Manchester.

Apprentice toolmaker, Ford Motor Co. Ltd. 30, company trainee 33; Man. Tractor Div. 55; Gen. Man. Tractor Group 61; Dir. of Car and Truck Group 64; Exec. Dir. Ford Motor Co. Ltd. 63, Man. Dir. 67-73, Chair. 72-; Chair. Ford Motor Credit Co. Ltd. 68-; Automotive Finance Ltd. 70-; Dir. Henry Ford and Son Ltd., Cork 65-, Ford Lusitana SARL, Portugal 73-; Pres. Soc. of Motor Mfrs. and Traders 75-76.

Leisure interests: golf, sailing, gardening.

Ford Motor Co. Ltd., 4 Grafton Street, London, W1X 4RD; Home: Blackmore House, Hook End, Brentwood, Essex, England.

Telephone: 01-491-7878 (Office); Blackmore 821-352 (Home).

Baturone Colombo, Admiral Adolfo; Spanish naval officer and politician; b. 24 Feb. 1904, San Fernando; *s*. of Eugenio and María del Carmen Baturone; *m*. Josefina Santiago Sánchez 1928 (died 1966); six *s*. four *d*.; ed. Escuela Naval Militar.

Various war commands 36-39; Commdr. destroyer *Gravina* 43-45, cruiser *Galicia* 54-57; Dir. Escuela de Suboficiales 58; Commdr. Marina de Cádiz 58-62, promoted to Rear-Admiral and commanded Agrupación Naval del Estrecho 62; Chief Naval Div. of Catalonia 62-64; Admiral Personnel Service 65-66; 2nd Chief-of-Staff of Armada 66-67; Admiral Chief-of-Staff 67-69;

Minister of the Navy 69-73; Grandes Cruces del Mérito Naval, Mérito Aeronáutico y Mérito Militar and awards from Portugal, Peru and Chile.

Leisure interest: family life.

Paseo del Prado, 3-2°, Madrid, Spain.

Telephone: 222-65-10.

Baudet, Philippe; French diplomatist; b. 29 Aug. 1901, Argenteuil; *m*. Jacqueline Breguet (deceased); one *s*. one *d*.; ed. Lycée Condorcet, Faculty of Law and Ecole des Sciences Politiques, Paris.

Entered diplomatic service 28, occupied posts in Constantinople, Washington, Peking, Paris, Mexico and Chungking; Free French Forces in London 42; Washington 42-45; Dir. Asian Affairs, Ministry of Foreign Affairs 45-47; Minister-Counsellor, London 47-50; Ambassador to Yugoslavia 50-54, to Argentina 55-57, to Turkey 56-57; Diplomatic Counsellor to French Govt. 57-62; Civil Asst. to Sec. of State for Defence 59-62; Ambassador to Switzerland 62-64, to U.S.S.R. 64-66; Ambassadeur de France (Hon.) 65; Commdr. de la Légion d'Honneur, Hon. K.C.V.O. (U.K.), Grand Officer Order of Orange Nassau (Neths.), etc.

31 *bis* boulevard Suchet, Paris 16e, France.

Telephone: 288-65-62.

Baudouin I; King of the Belgians; Baudouin Albert Charles Léopold Axel Marie Gustave; b. 7 Sept. 1930; *s*. of King Léopold III and Queen Astrid; *m*. Doña Fabiola Mora y Aragón (b. 11 June 1928) 1960; no *c*.; ed. privately.

Prince Royal 50; succeeded his father on his abdication 17 July 51.

The Royal Palace, Brussels, Belgium.

Bauer, Ludwig; Austrian business executive; b. 23 Sept. 1908, Hadersdorf-Weidlingau; *s*. of Ludwig and Margarethe (née Marno) Bauer; *m*. Marta Karlin 1941 (died 1975); ed. Realschule and Handelsakademie.

With Vacuum Oil Co. 28-38, AG der Kohlenwertstoffverbände, Gruppe Benzin-Benzol 38-; "Martha" Erdöl G.m.b.H. 46, Man. 55, Gen. Dir. 60; Chair. Man. Board Österreichische Mineralölverwaltung AG 66-; Hon. Senator Montanistischen Hochschule, Leoben; Grosses Ehrenzeichen für Verdienste um die Republik Österreich; Silbernes Komturkreuz des Ehrenzeichens für Verdienste um das Bundesland Niederösterreich; Ordine al Merito (Italy).

Leisure interests: literature, music, art.

1091 Vienna, Otto-Wagner-Platz 5, Austria.

Telephone: 42-36-21.

Bauer, Peter Thomas, M.A., F.B.A.; British economist; b. 6 Nov. 1915, Budapest, Hungary; ed. Scholae Piae (Budapest) and Gonville and Caius Coll., Cambridge.

Fellow Gonville and Caius Coll. Cambridge 46-60, 68-; Reader, Agricultural Economics, Univ. of London 47-48; Univ. Lecturer in Economics, Cambridge Univ. 48-56, Smuts Reader in Commonwealth Studies 56-60; Prof. of Economics (with special reference to economic development and underdeveloped countries), Univ. of London 60-.

Publs. *The Rubber Industry* 48, *West African Trade* 54, *The Economics of Under-developed Countries* (with B. S. Yamey) 57, *Economic Analysis and Policy in Under-developed Countries* 58, *Indian Economic Policy and Development* 61, *Markets, Market Control and Marketing Reform* (Selected Papers, with B. S. Yamey) 69, *Dissent on Development: Studies and Debates in Development Economics* 72; numerous articles on economic subjects.

London School of Economics and Political Science, Houghton Street, London W.C.2, England.

Baum, Warren C., PH.D.; American international finance official; b. 2 Sept. 1922, New York; *s*. of William and Elsie Baum; *m*. Jessie Scullen 1946; two *d*.; ed. Columbia Coll. and Harvard Univ.

With Office of Strategic Services 42-46; Economic Co-operation Admin. 49-51; Mutual Security Agency 52-53; Economist, RAND Corpn. 53-56; Chief, Office of Network Study, Fed. Communications Comm. 56-59; Economist, European Dept., World Bank 59-62; Div. Chief, European Dept. 62-64; Asst. Dir. in charge of Transportation, Projects Dept. 64-68; Deputy Dir., Projects Dept. July 68; Assoc. Dir., Projects Nov. 68-72; Vice-Pres. Projects Staff 72-.
Publs. *The Marshall Plan and French Foreign Trade* 51, *The French Economy and the State* 56.
International Bank for Reconstruction and Development, 1818 H Street, N.W., Washington, D.C. 20433, U.S.A.

Baum, Most Rev. William Wakefield, S.T.D., S.T.L.; American ecclesiastic; b. 21 Nov. 1926, Dallas, Tex.; s. of Harold E. and Mary Leona (Hayes) White, step-father Jerome C. Baum; ed. Kenrick Seminary, St. Louis and Univ. of St. Thomas Aquinas, Rome.
Ordained to priesthood 51; Assoc. Pastor, St. Aloysius, St. Therese's and St. Peter's parishes, Kan. City, Mo. 51-56; Instructor and Prof., Avila Coll., Kan. City 54-56, 58-63; Admin. St. Cyril's Parish, Sugar Creek, Mo. 60-61; Hon. Chaplain of His Holiness the Pope 61; Peritus (Expert Adviser), Second Vatican Council 62-65; First Exec. Dir. Bishops' Comm. for Ecumenical and Interreligious Affairs, Wash. 64-67, Chair. 72; mem. Joint Working Group of reps. of Catholic Church and World Council of Churches 65-69; mem. Mixed Comm. of reps. of Catholic Church and Lutheran World Fed. 65-66; Chancellor, Diocese of Kan. City, St. Joseph 67-70; Hon. Prelate of His Holiness the Pope 68; Pastor, St. James Parish, Kan. City 68-70; Bishop, Diocese of Springfield-Cape Girardeau 70; mem. Synod of Bishops 71; Archbishop of Wash. and Chancellor of the Catholic Univ. 73-; Hon. D.D., Muhlenberg Coll., Allentown, Pa. 67, Georgetown Univ., Wash., St. John's Univ., Brooklyn, N.Y.
Leisure interests: reading, music.
Publs. *The Teaching of Cardinal Cajetan on the Sacrifice of the Mass* 58, *Considerations Toward the Theology on the Presbyterate* 61.
1721 Rhode Island Avenue, N.W., Washington, D.C. 20036, U.S.A.
Telephone: 202-783-1465.

Baumgartner, Wilfred Siegfried, D. EN D.; French financial administrator; b. 21 May 1902, Paris; s. of Dr. Amédée Baumgartner; m. Christiane Mercier 1930; one s. two d., ed. Ecole des Sciences Politiques and Univ. of Paris.
Inspector of Finance 25-30; Chef du Cabinet of Min. of Finance 30; Deputy Dir. of Treasury at Min. of Finance 30-34, Asst. Dir. 34-35, Dir. 35-37; Dir.-Gen. and Pres. of Conseil d'Administration du Crédit National 37-49; mem. Gen. Council of Banque de France 37-49; Gov. of Bank 49-60; Minister of Finance 60-62; Pres.-Dir.-Gen. Rhône-Poulenc S.A. 63-73, Hon. Pres.-Dir.-Gen. 73-75, Hon. Pres. 75-; Pres. Alliance Française 62-; Pres. Financial Comm. Int. Chamber of Commerce 65-; mem. Acad. des Sciences morales et politiques 65-, Econ. and Social Council 69-; Hon. LL.D. Law School of Paris; Hon. Gov. Banque de France; Grande Croix, Légion d'Honneur.
Leisure interests: tennis, mountaineering.
98 rue de Grenelle, Paris 7e, France; 22 avenue Montaigne, Paris 8e, France.

Baumont, Maurice Edmond Marie, D. ès L.; French historian; b. 26 Feb. 1892, Lunéville; widower; one d.; ed. Ecole Normale Supérieure, Univ. of Paris.
With Reparations Comm. in Berlin 20-27, with L.N. 27-39; Hon. Prof. Inst. Universitaire des Hautes Etudes Internationales (Geneva); Historical Adviser, Ministry of Foreign Affairs; Editor (France) Wilhelmstrasse documents (publ. in 10 vols. since 50); Hon. Prof. Univ.

of Paris; Curator Musée de Chantilly; mem. Acad. des sciences morales et politiques.
Publs. include *L'Allemagne, Lendemain de Guerre et de Révolution* 22, *Quinze Ans d'Histoire Universelle 1914-1929*, *L'Abdication de Guillaume II* 30, *L'Affaire Eulenburg* 33, *L'Essor Industriel et l'Impérialisme Colonial (1878-1904)* 49, *La Faillite de la Paix (1918-1939)* 51, *Histoire de la France pour tous les Français: Vol. II, 1878 à nos Jours* 50, *Gloires et Tragédies de la IIIe République* 56, *Aux sources de l'Affaire Dreyfus* 59, *La Grande Conjuration Contre Hitler* 63, *L'Europe de 1900 à 1914* 67, *La Troisième République* 68, *Les origines de la Deuxième Guerre Mondiale* 69, *L'Echiquier de Metz* 71, *Bazaine et ses secrets* 75.
10 avenue Emile Acollas, Paris 7e, France.
Telephone: 783-90-26.

Baunsgaard, Hilmar Tormod Ingolf; Danish businessman and politician; b. 26 Feb. 1920, Slagelse; m. Egone Baunsgaard; one d.; ed. commercial schools.
Deputy Man. grocery firm 44-47; Business Man. Købmaendenes Indkøbscentral A/S HOKI, Odense 47-61; Marketing Man. at WA Reklame-Marketing S/I 64-68; Pres. Social-Liberal Party Youth 48-50; mem. Exec. Social-Liberal Party 48-57 (Vice-Pres. 54-57); mem. of Parl. 57-; Minister of Commerce 61-64; Prime Minister Feb. 68-71; mem. Board Nat. Bank of Denmark 60-61, 66-68, 71; mem. Board Politiken 75.
Leisure interests: gardening, painting.
Blidahpark 34, 2900 Hellerup, Denmark.

Bavin, Rt. Rev. Timothy John, M.A.; South African bishop; b. 17 Sept. 1935, Northwood, England; ed. St. George School, Windsor, Brighton Coll., Worcester and Cuddesdon Colls., Oxford Univ.
Assistant Priest, St. Alban's Cathedral, Pretoria 61-64; Chaplain, St. Alban's Coll., Pretoria 64-69; Asst. Priest, Uckfield, Sussex, England 69-71; Vicar, Church of the Good Shepherd, Brighton 71-73; Dean of Johannesburg 73-74, Bishop Nov. 74-.
Bishop's House, 4 Crescent Drive, Westcliff, Johannesburg 2193; and P.O. Box 1131, Johannesburg 2000, South Africa.

Bawden, Edward, C.B.E., R.A., R.D.I.; British artist; b. 1903; ed. Cambridge School of Art and Royal Coll. of Art.
Tutor, Royal Coll. of Art 32-; Official War Artist, Middle East 40-45; work represented in Tate Gallery, London, and in other London, provincial and Commonwealth galleries; Trustee, Tate Gallery 51-58.
2 Park Lane, Saffron Waldon, Essex, England.

Bawoyeu Alingue; Chad finance official; b. 18 Aug. 1937, N'Djamena; m.; seven c.; ed. Nat. School for Treasury Services, Paris, Inst. of the IMF.
Principal Treasury Inspector; Accountant to Nat. Assembly; Cen. Treasurer of Chad, Dir. of Treasury and Public Accounts; Dir. of the Cabinet of Minister of Public Health and Social Affairs and the Minister of Foreign Affairs; Alt. Exec. Dir. IMF; Alt. Admin. Chad Devt. Bank; Perm. Rep. to UN April 74-75.
c/o Ministry of Foreign Affairs, N'Djamena, Chad.

Baxendell, Peter Brian, C.B.E., B.SC., A.R.S.M.; British petroleum engineer; b. 28 Feb. 1925, Runcorn; s. of Lesley Wilfred Baxendell and Evelyn Gaskin; m. Rosemary Lacey 1949; two s. two d.; ed. St. Francis Xaviers Coll., Liverpool, Royal School of Mines, Imperial Coll., London.
With Royal Dutch/Shell Group 46-; Anglo-Egyptian Oilfields 47-50; Compania Shell de Venezuela 50-63; Technical Dir. Shell-BP Nigeria 63-66, Man. Dir. 69-72; Shell Int. London, Eastern Region 66-69; Chair. Shell U.K. 73; Man. Dir. Royal Dutch/Shell Group 73-.
Leisure interests: squash, tennis.
Royal Dutch/Shell Group, Shell Centre, London, S.E.1, England.

Baxter, Sir John Philip, K.B.E., C.M.G., B.SC., PH.D., M.I.CHEM.E., F.R.A.C.I., M.I.E. (Aust.), F.A.A.; Australian chemical engineer and educationist; b. 7 May 1905; ed. Hereford, and Birmingham Univ.
Research Dir.-Gen. Chemicals Division I.C.I. and Dir. Thorium Ltd. -49; Prof. of Chemical Engineering N.S.W. Univ. of Technology 49-53. Dir. 53-54, Vice-Chancellor (now Univ. of New South Wales) 55-69; Chair. Atomic Energy Comm. 57-72; Chair. Sydney Opera House Trust 69-.
1 Kelso Street, Enfield, N.S.W., Australia.
Telephone: 7474261.

Bayar, Celâl; Turkish politician; b. 1883.
Minister of Nat. Economy 21; Minister of Reconstruction and Settlement (when Turkish and Greek populations were exchanged in accordance with Treaty of Lausanne) 23; founded Ish Bank 24; Minister of Nat. Economy 32; Prime Minister 37-39; Vice-Pres. Republican People's Party during Presidency of Kemal Atatürk; undertook leadership of new Democratic Party founded 46; Pres. of the Republic May 50-60; detained on Yassiada Island 60-61; sentenced to life imprisonment Sept. 61, released on grounds of health 63; imprisoned again 63-64; released again on health grounds Nov. 64; granted full pardon July 66.
Ankara, Turkey.

Bayer, Otto, DR. PHIL. NAT.; German chemical executive; b. 4 Nov. 1902, Frankfurt/Main; m. Eleonore Stellisch 1928; ed. Klinger-Oberrealschule, Frankfurt, and Univ. Frankfurt.
Private Asst. to Julius von Braun 24-27; entered Research Labs. of I.G. Farbenindustrie A.G., Mainkur Works 27, Dir. I.G. Farbenindustrie 39; Prof. ord. hon. Univ. of Cologne 44; mem. Management Board and Head of Research, Farbenfabriken Bayer A.G. 51-63; Deputy Chair. Supervisory Board of Farbenfabriken Bayer A.G. 63-64, Chair. 64-74; mem. German Research Council 50-56; official of numerous other firms and business orgs.; author of many publs. and holder of 400 German patents; inventor of Diisocyanat-Polyadditions-Process 37; corresp. mem. Acad. for Science and Literature, Mainz and Düsseldorf; A. v. Baeyer Medal, Gauss-Weber-Medal, Duisberg Medal, Soc. of German Chemists, and other medals; six hon. doctorates.
5673 Burscheid, Haus am Eifgen, Federal Republic of Germany.
Telephone: 02174-8555.

Bayero, Alhaji Ado; Nigerian administrator; b. 1930, Kano; s. of Alhaji Abdullahi Bayer, Emir of Kano; ed. Kano Middle School.
Clerk, Bank of W. Africa; M.P., N. House of Assembly 55-57; Chief of Kano Native Authority Police 57-62; Amb. to Senegal 62-63; Emir of Kano 63-; Chancellor, Univ. of Nigeria, Nsukka, E. Nigeria April 66-.
Leisure interests: photography, riding, reading.
University of Nigeria, Nsukka, E. Nigeria.

Bayh, Birch Evans, Jr.; American lawyer, farmer and politician; b. 22 Jan. 1928; ed. Purdue Univ. and Indiana Univ.
Former farmer, later in legal practice, Terre Haute; mem. Indiana House of Reps. 55-62, Minority Leader 57-58, 61-62, Speaker 59-60; U.S. Senator from Indiana 63-; Democrat.
Senate Office Building, Washington, D.C. 20510, U.S.A.

Bayne, Right Rev. Stephen Fielding, Jr., S.T.D.; American bishop; b. 21 May 1908, New York; s. of Stephen Fielding Bayne and Edna Ashley Bayne; m. Lucie Culver Gould 1934; four s. one d.; ed. Trinity School, New York, Amherst Coll. and General Theological Seminary.
Fellow and Tutor, New York Gen. Theological Seminary 32-34; ordained 33; Rector, Trinity Church, St.

Louis, Mo. 34-39, St. John's, Northampton, Mass. 39-42; Chaplain, Columbia Univ. 42-47, U.S.S. *Salerno Bay* 44-46; Bishop of Olympia, Wash. 47-59; Exec. Officer, Anglican Communion 60-64; Director of Overseas Dept., Episcopal Church of U.S. 64-68; First Vice-Pres. Exec. Council Episcopal Church in U.S.A. 68-70; Prof. of Ascetical Theology, Gen. Theological Seminary 70-, Dean 72-73, Dean Emeritus 73-; numerous hon. degrees.
Leisure interests: sailing, writing, railway history.
Publs. *The Optional God* 53, *Christian Living* 57, *In the Sight of the Lord* 58, *Enter with Joy* 61, *Mindful of the Love* 62, *An Anglican Turning Point* 64.
Chelsea Square 1, New York, N.Y. 10011, U.S.A.
Telephone: 212-CH3-5150.

Bayramoğlu, Fuat; Turkish diplomatist; b. 1912, Ankara; s. of Mehmet Tayyip and Hüsniye Bayramoğlu; m. Nesteren Bayramoğlu; ed. School of Political and Administrative Sciences, Istanbul, and Univ. of Liège.
Entered Diplomatic Service 39; mem. Gen. Directorate of Press and Publication Cttee. 43; Head of Secretariat Prime Minister's Office 44-46; Chair. Press Dept. Cttee. 46; Dir. in Foreign Ministry 48; Consul, Cyprus 49; Consul Gen., Jerusalem 51-53; Dir.-Gen. Consular and Claims Dept., Ministry of Foreign Affairs, Ankara 53-57; Ambassador to Norway 57-59, to Iraq 59-60, to Iran 60-62, to Italy 62-63; Sec.-Gen. Ministry of Foreign Affairs 63-65, Chair. Inspection Corps 71-; Amb. to Belgium 65-67, to Italy 67-69, to U.S.S.R. 69-71; Sec.-Gen. of the Presidency 72-; Homayoun Order of Iran 62; Grand Croix de Mérite Civil Espagnol 63; Grande Croce all'Ordine del Merito della Republica italiana 69; Presidential Distinguished Service Award 73; Foreign Ministry Distinguished Service Award 73.
Leisure interests: philately, clock and watch collection.
Publs. Turkish version of *The Rubaiyat* of H. G. Nakhai 67, 74, *Rubailer* (Book of quatrains with trans. into Persian)74, *Türk Cam Sanati ve Beyok Işleri* 74, and several legal and sociological articles.
Cumhurbaşkanlığı Köşkü, Ankara, Turkey.

Bayülken, Ümit Halûk; Turkish diplomatist; b. 7 July 1921, Istanbul; s. of Staff Officer H. Hüsnü Bayülken and Mrs. Melek Bayülken; m. Mrs. Valihe Salci 1952; one s. one d.; ed. Lycée of Haydarpasa, Istanbul, and Univ. of Ankara (Political Sciences).
Ministry of Foreign Affairs 44-; Reserve Officer in Army 45-47; Vice-Consul, Frankfurt (Main) 47-49; First Sec., Bonn 50-51; Ministry of Foreign Affairs 51-53; First Sec. Turkish Perm. Mission to UN 53-57, Counsellor 57-59; Turkish Rep. to London Joint Cttee. on Cyprus 59-60; Dir.-Gen., Policy Planning Group, Ankara 60-63, Deputy Sec.-Gen. for Political Affairs 63-64, Sec.-Gen. 64-66; Amb. to U.K. 66-69, concurrently accred. to Malta May 68-July 69; Perm. Rep. of Turkey to UN 69-71; Minister of Foreign Affairs 71-74; Sec.-Gen. Cen. Treaty Org. 75-; Hon. G.C.V.O. (U.K.); Order of Isabel la Católica (Spain); Grosses Bundesverdienstkreuz (Fed. Repub. of Germany).
Leisure interests: music, painting, reading.
Publs. lectures, articles, studies and essays on minorities, Cyprus, principles of foreign policy, int. relations and disputes.
Eski Büyük Millet Meclisi, Ulus, Ankara, Turkey.

Bazaine, Jean, L. ès L.; French painter; b. 21 Dec. 1904.
Executed stained glass windows for church at Assy 46, at Saint Severin, Paris 66, ceramic mural and windows at Audincourt 51-54, ceramic mural at UNESCO 60, and Maison de la Radio, Paris 63; exhibited Galerie Carré, Galerie Maeght, Paris; Retrospective Exhbns. Berne 58, Eindhoven 59, Hanover 63, Zürich 63, Oslo 63, Paris 65; Rep. at Biennali of Venice, São Paulo and

Carnegie; Grand Prix Nat. des Arts 64; paintings in most of the leading museums in U.S.A. and Europe.
Publs. *Notes sur la peinture d'aujourd'hui* 48, *Exercice de la peinture* 73.
36 rue Pierre Brossolette, 92140 Clamart, France.

Bazán Dávila, Raúl; Chilean lawyer and diplomatist; b. 1 July 1913, Santiago; ed. Sacred Heart Coll. and Catholic Univ., Santiago.
Professor of Int. Public Law, Catholic Univ. 41-45; practised law 41-52; Principal Lawyer Caja Nacional de Ahorros 52, Banco del Estado de Chile 53; Amb. to Brazil 54-62; Legal Adviser Ministry of Foreign Affairs 63, Political Adviser 64; held various diplomatic posts in Buenos Aires, Rio de Janeiro, Madrid, Jerusalem, at UN 64-72; Legal Adviser Ministry of Foreign Affairs 71-72, Perm. Mission of Chile to UN 73; Perm. Rep. to UN 73-74.
c/o Ministerio de Relaciones Exteriores, Santiago, Chile.

Bazelon, David Lionel; American judge; b. 3 Sept. 1909, Superior, Wis.; *m.* Miriam Kellner 1936; two *s.*; ed. Univ. of Ill. and Northwestern Univ.
Private practice, Illinois 32-35; Asst. U.S. Attorney, Northern District of Illinois 35-40; senior mem. Gottlieb and Schwartz 40-46; Asst. Attorney-Gen. U.S. Lands Div. 46-47, Office of Alien Property 47-49; Judge, U.S. Court of Appeals, District of Columbia circuit 49-, Chief Judge 62-; Lecturer, Law and Psychiatry, Univ. of Pennsylvania Law School 57-58, 58-59; Sloan Visiting Prof., Menninger Clinic, Topeka, Kansas 60-61, Regent's Lecturer, Univ. of Calif. at Los Angeles 64; Lecturer in Psychiatry, The Johns Hopkins Univ. School of Medicine 64-; Clinical Prof. of Psychiatry (Socio-legal aspects), George Washington Univ. 66-; Chair. Task Force on Law, President's Panel on Mental Retardation 61-62; mem. Board of Dirs. American Orthopsychiatric Asscn. 65-, Pres. 69-70; mem. Board of Dirs. Joint Comm. on Mental Health of Children Inc. 65-70; mem. Harvard Univ. Program on Technology and Soc. Advisory Cttee. 66-71, Nat. Advisory Mental Health Council, Public Health Service 67-71; mem. Board of Trustees, Salk Inst. for Biological Studies 61-; mem. U.S. Mission on Mental Health to U.S.S.R. 67; mem. Cttee. on Ethics, American Heart Asscn. 68-, John F. Kennedy Center for Research on Education and Human Development Nat. Advisory Cttee. 68-, Battelle-Northwest Behavioral and Social Science Consulting Panel 70-72; Chair. Advisory Board, Boston Univ. Center for Law and Life Sciences 70-; Fellow, American Acad. of Arts and Sciences, Boston, Mass. 70-; Isaac Ray Award, American Psychiatric Asscn. 60-61, Hon. Fellow 62, Distinguished Service Award 75; Hon. Fellow, American Coll. of Legal Medicine 75; Hon. LL.D. (Colby Coll.) 66, Boston Univ. Law School 69.
Home: 2700 Virginia Avenue, N.W., Apartment 1207, Washington, D.C. 20037, U.S.A.
Telephone: 426-7118.

Bazhan, Mikola (Nikolai Platonovich); Soviet poet; b. 9 Oct. 1904, Kamenets-Podolsk, Ukraine; ed. Inst. of Foreign Relations, Kiev.
Editor-in-Chief, Ukrainian Soviet Encyclopedia 59; mem. C.P.S.U. 40-; mem. Acad. of Sciences of Ukrainian S.S.R. 51-; mem. Board and Sec. of U.S.S.R. Union of Writers, Vice-Pres. European Community of Writers; State prizewinner; Hero of Socialist Labour, Order of Lenin (four times); Order of Red Banner; Order of Red Banner of Labour; Merited Worker of Arts and of Science of Georgian S.S.R.; translator of Russian and Georgian poets into Ukrainian.
Publs. *17th Patrol* 26, *Immortality* 37, *Fathers and Sons* 38, *Mother* 39, *Tambi* 40, *Daniil Galitsky* 42, *The Stalingrad Notebook* 43, *Impressions of England* 48, *Mickiewicz in Odessa* 56, *By the Saviour's Tower* 52,

Italian Meetings 61, *A Flight through the Storm* 63, *Immortality of the Stone* 67, *The Recollections of Uman* 72.
Ukrainian Branch, U.S.S.R. Union of Writers, Kiev, U.S.S.R.

Bazin, Germain (René Michel), D. ès L., L. en D.; French museum curator and university professor; b. Paris; *s.* of Ch. Bazin and J. Laurence Mounier-Pouthôt; *m.* Countess Heller Bielotzerkowka; ed. Coll. Ste. Croix, Neuilly, Ste. Croix, Orléans, Coll. de Pont Levoy and Univ. de Paris.
Professor, Brussels Free Univ. 34; began Museum career in Dept. of Drawings, Ecole des Beaux Arts; Keeper of Paintings, Louvre 37, Dir. of Paintings and Drawings 51-65 (Museum of Louvre), Dir. of Restoration, Paintings of French Museums 65; Prof. of Museum Studies at Ecole Louvre 41-70; now Hon. Curator Museum of Louvre and Research Prof. York Univ., Toronto; Infantry Capt. 39-45; active work in protection of French art treasures 40-45; organized over 40 exhbns. in France and abroad; has frequently lectured in Europe, U.S.A., S. America; has made film on *Impressionism*, Art Adviser for film *The Louvre* (N.B.C., New York); Del. to numerous UNESCO Cttees.; mem. Inst. de France (Acad. des Beaux-Arts); mem. Central Inst. of Conservation, Rome; mem. numerous acads.; Officier Légion d'Honneur; Commdr. Arts et Lettres; Grand Officer de l'Ordre de Léopold (Belgium); Commdr. de la Couronne (Belgium); Commdr. Ordre République Italienne and Orders from Italy, Portugal, Sweden and Brazil; Dr. h.c. Univ. do Brasil and D.H., Villanova Univ., Pennsylvania; books translated into twenty languages.
Publs. *Le Mont St. Michel* 32, *Le Louvre* 33, *Les Trésors de la Peinture française* 41, *Fra Angelico* 43, *Corot* 43, *L'époque impréssionniste* 44, *Le Crépuscule des Images* 46, *Les grands Maîtres hollandais* 49, *Histoire générale de l'art (de la Préhistoire à nos jours)* 53, *L'Art religieux baroque au Brésil* 56, *Les Trésors de la Peinture au Louvre* 58, *Les Maîtres des Ecoles étrangères au Musée de l'Ermitage* 60, *Gallery of Flowers* 60, *Les Trésors du Musée du Jeu de Paume* 61, *L'Aleijadinho* 63, *Le Message de l'Absolu* 64, *Baroque et Rococo* 65, *Le Temps des Musées* 67, *Trésors de la peinture au Musée Louvre, Avante-garde de la Peinture, Sculpture Mondiale, Destins du Baroque* 70, *Manet* 72.
4 avenue Raymond Poincaré, Paris 16e, France.

Bazin, Hervé (*see* Hervé-Bazin, Jean-Pierre Marie).

Beach, Frank Ambrose; American professor of psychology; b. 13 April 1911, Emporia, Kan.; *s.* of Frank A. and Bertha Robinson Beach; *m.* 1st Anna Beth Odenweller 1935 (died 1971); one *s.* one *d.*; *m.* 2nd Noel Gaustad 1972; ed. Kansas State Teachers' Coll. and Univ. of Chicago.
Fellow in Clinical Psychology, Kansas State Teachers' Coll. 32-33; High School Instructor, Yates Center, Kan. 34-35; Research Asst. in Neurophysiology, Harvard Univ. 35-36; Asst. Curator, Dept. Experimental Biology, American Museum of Natural History 36-42, Curator and Chair. Dept. of Animal Behavior 42-46; Prof. of Psychology, Yale Univ. 46-52, Sterling Prof. 52-58; Prof. of Psychology, Univ. of Calif., Berkeley 58-; Hon. D.Sc. McGill Univ. and Williams Coll.; many awards and prizes; mem. numerous scientific asscns.
Publs. *Hormones and Behavior* 48, *Patterns of Sexual Behavior* (co-author with C. S. Ford) 52, *Sex and Behavior* (Editor) 65; over 120 articles in scientific journals, many reviews and non-technical publs.
Department of Psychology, University of California, Berkeley, Calif. 94720, U.S.A.
Telephone: 415-642-6000.

Beach, Morrison H.; American insurance executive; b. 10 Jan. 1917, Winsted, Conn.; *s.* of Howard Edmund and Edith (Morrison) Beach; *m.* Evelyn R. Harris 1942;

one *s.* two *d.*; ed. Williams Coll., Massachusetts Inst. of Technology, Connecticut Univ. Law School.
Assistant Actuary Travelers Insurance Co. 50, Assoc. Actuary 54, Actuary 57, Second Vice-Pres. and Actuary 59, Second Vice-Pres. Exec. Dept. 62, Vice-Pres. 64, Senior Vice-Pres. 65, Exec. Vice-Pres. 70, Pres. 71-, Chair. and Chief Exec. Officer 73-; Dir. Travelers Corpn. and its principal U.S. and Canadian Insurance Subsidiaries, Hartford Nat. Bank and Trust Co., Hartford Nat. Corpn., Hartford Process, Health Insurance Assoc. of America, Chair. of numerous business and philanthropic concerns; Fellow, Soc. of Actuaries; mem. Amer. Acad. of Actuaries.
c/o The Travelers Insurance Companies, One Tower Square, Hartford, Conn. 06115, U.S.A.

Beadengar, Dessande; Chad diplomatist; b. 28 March 1936, Fort Sibut, Oubangui-Chari, French Equatorial Africa (F.E.A.); *m.*; ten *c.*; ed. in F.E.A. and Teachers' Coll. of Ecole Normale d'Auteuil, Paris.
Director of Schools, Fort Crampel, Oubangui-Chari (later Central African Repub.) 56-61; studied in Paris 61-63; teacher of English, Fort Sibut 64-65, Bambari 65-66 (both in Cen. African Repub.); joined public service of Chad 66; teacher of English, Ahmed Mangue School, Sarh; Dir. Koumra secondary school, Moyen-Chari 67; joined Chad Ministry of Information and Tourism 68; Minister of Tourism and Handicrafts 71-73, for Water, Forests, Fisheries, Hunting, National Parks and Animal Reserves 73-75; Perm. Rep. to UN Aug. 75-; Administrator for Chad on Governing Council, Soc. for the Devt. of Tourism in W. Africa (Hotafric) 71-73.
Permanent Mission of Chad to the United Nations, 221 East 43rd Street, Suite 1703, New York, N.Y. 10017, U.S.A.

Beadle, George Wells, M.SC., PH.D.; American biologist; b. 22 Oct. 1903, Nebraska; *s.* of Chauncey and Hattie Beadle; *m.* 1st Marion D. Hill 1928 (divorced 1953), 2nd Muriel M. Barnett 1953; two *s.*; ed. Univ. of Nebraska and Cornell Univ.
National Research Council, Calif. Inst. of Technology 31-33, Research Fellow and Instructor 33-36; Asst. Prof. of Genetics, Harvard Univ. 36-37; Prof. of Biology, Stanford Univ. 37-46; Prof. of Biology and Chair. Division of Biology, Calif. Inst. of Technology 46-61; Pres. American Asscn. for the Advancement of Science 56-57; Eastman Visiting Prof., Oxford 58-59; Pres. Chicago Univ. 61-69; Dir. American Medical Asscn. and Inst. for Biomedical Research 68-70; Prof. of Biology Univ. of Chicago 61-68, Prof. Emeritus, William E. Wrather Distinguished Service Prof., Hon. Trustee 69-; mem. National Acad. of Sciences, Amer. Acad. of Arts and Sciences, Royal Soc., Danish Royal Soc., National Science Acad. India, Inst. Lombardi de Lettre, Milan, Japan Acad., Indian Nat. Science Acad.; Lasker Award 50, Dyer Award 51, Emil C. Hansen Prize 53, Nobel Prize for Medicine (with Lederberg and Tatum) 58; Albert Einstein Award 58; Nat. Award, American Cancer Soc. 59, Kimber Genetics Award, Nat. Acad. of Sciences 60; D.Sc. (Hon.) Yale, Nebraska, North-western, Rutgers, Kenyon, Wesleyan, Oxford, Birmingham, and others.
Leisure interests: photography, mountaineering.
Publs. *An Introduction to Genetics* (jointly) 39, *Genetics and Modern Biology* 63, *The Language of Life* (with Muriel Beadle) 66.
Department of Biology, University of Chicago, Chicago, Ill. 60637; 5533 Dorchester Avenue, Chicago, Ill. 60637, U.S.A.
Telephone: (312) 493-2169.

Beadle, Rt. Hon. Sir (Thomas) Hugh (William), P.C., Kt., C.M.G., O.B.E.; Rhodesian politician and judge; b. 6 Feb. 1905; ed. Univ. of Capetown and Queen's Coll., Oxford.

Advocate, Bulawayo 30-39; Royal West African Frontier Force, Gold Coast 39-40; Deputy Judge Advocate-Gen. S. Rhodesian Forces, and Parl. Sec. to Prime Minister 40-46; M.P. 39-50; Minister of Justice, Internal Affairs, Health, Education, S. Rhodesia 46-50; Judge of High Court, S. Rhodesia 50-61, Chief Justice 61-; Hon. Fellow Queens Coll., Oxford 66.
Chief Justice's Chambers, High Court, Bulawayo, Rhodesia.

Beale, Hon. Sir Howard, K.B.E., Q.C.; Australian lawyer, diplomatist and company director; b. 1898, Tamworth; *s.* of Rev. Joseph and Clara Elizabeth (Vickery) Beale; *m.* Margery E. Wood 1927; one *s.*; ed. Univ. of Sydney.
Called to the Bar 25; apptd. King's Counsel 50; Lecturer, Army Educational Dept. 40; R.A.N. 42-45; Liberal mem. for Parramatta, House of Reps. 46-58; mem. Commonwealth Parl. Public Works Cttee. 47-49; Minister for Information and Transport 49-50, for Supply 50-58, and for Defence Production 56-58 and Minister-in-charge of Atomic Energy Comm. and Aluminium Production Comm. 50-58; Acting Minister for Immigration 51-52, 53, 54; Minister for Nat. Development 52-53, for Air 52, for Defence 57; mem. Australian Defence Council, Cabinet Defence Preparations Cttee., Cabinet Cttee. on Uranium and Atomic Energy 50-58; Ambassador to U.S.A. 58-64; Alternate Gov. Int. Monetary Fund 60, 62 and 64; Pres. Arts Council of Australia 64-68; Woodward Lecturer, Yale Univ. 60; Regents' Visiting Prof., Univ. of California 66, Marquette Univ. Wis. 67-69; now Dir. and Adviser to various Australian, British and U.S. industrial and financial corpns.; Hon. LL.D., Kent Univ., Ohio, Marquette Univ., Wis. 69; Hon. D.H. Lit., Nebraska 62.
Leisure interests: yachting, reading, music.
1/4 Marathon Road, Darling Point, 2027, Australia.

Beall, J. Glenn, Jr.; American senator; b. 19 June 1927, Cumberland, Md.; *s.* of late Senator J. Glenn Beall, Sr.; *m.* Nancy Lee Smith; one *d.*; ed. public schools in Frostburg, Md., Phillips Exeter Acad. and Yale Univ.
Associated with Beall, Garner and Geare Inc. (insurance co.) since graduation; mem. Maryland House of Delegates 62-68; mem. U.S. House of Reps. 68-70; Senator from Maryland 71-; Republican.
Old Senate Office Building, Washington, D.C. 20510, U.S.A.

Beals, Carleton, M.A.; American writer; b. 13 Nov. 1893, Medicine Lodge, Kan.; *s.* of Leon Eli Beals and Elvina Sybila Blickensderfer Beals; *m.* 1st Lillian Rine 1919, 2nd Elizabeth Daniel 1930, 3rd Blanca Rose Arquedes 1934, 4th Carolyn Kennedy 1956; ed. Calif., Columbia, Madrid, Rome and Mexico Univs.
Principal American High School Mexico City 19-20; Editor Latin-American Press Syndicate 34-36; Pres. Editorial Board *Latin-American Digest* 33-34; special corresp. Europe, Mexico, Central America, Spain, N. Africa, Italy, Turkey, U.S.S.R. and Germany 20-23, 29, 34, 37, 46, 57, 61; mem. expeditions to Indian Regions Mexico 30-31, Peru, Bolivia, Ecuador, Amazon, Patagonia 46, 61; Bryce Historical Prize 17, Bonnheim Essay Prize 15, 16, Guggenheim Foundation Award 31, Barnes Foundation Award 53-54, Best Essay Prize, *Arizona Quarterly* 61; Nat. Acad. of Recording Arts Award 65.
Leisure interests: chess, horse-back riding, swimming.
Publs. *Rome or Death—the Story of Fascism* 23, *Mexico—an Interpretation* 23, *Brimstone and Chili* 27, *Con Sandino en Nicaragua* 28, *Destroying Victor* 29, *Mexican Maze* 31, *Banana Gold* 32, *Porfirio Diaz, Dictator of Mexico* 33, *The Crime of Cuba, Fire on the Andes* 34, *Black River* 35, *The Story of Huey P. Long* 35, *The Stones Awake* 36, *America South* 37, *The Coming Struggle for Latin America, Glass Houses* 38, *American Earth* 39, *The Great*

Circle 41, *Pan America, A Program for the Western Hemisphere* 41, *Dawn Over the Amazon* 43, *Rio Grande to Cape Horn* 43, *Lands of the Dawning Morrow* 48, *The Long Land: Chile* 48, *Our Yankee Heritage: The Making of New Haven* 51, *Stephen Austin: Father of Texas* 53, *Our Yankee Heritage: The Making of Bristol* 54, *Our Yankee Heritage: New England's Contributions to American Civilisation* 55, *Adventure of the Western Sea: The Story of Robert Gray* 56, *Taste of Glory* 56, *John Elliot: The Man who loved the Indians* 58, *House in Mexico* 58, *Brass-Knuckle Crusade, The Great Knownothing Conspiracy* 60, *Nomads and Empire Builders* 61, *Cyclone Carry: The Story of Carry Nation* 62, *Latin America: World in Revolution* 63, *Eagles of the Andes* 63, *Under the Fifth Sun, Mexico Old and New* 64, *Arévalo, Anti-communism in Latin America* 64, *War within a War* 65, *Land of the Mayas, Past and Present* 67, *The Great Revolt and its Leaders* 68, *Stories Told by the Aztecs Before the Spaniards Came* 69, *Colonial Rhode Island* 70, *Great Guerilla Warriors* 70, *The Nature of Revolution* 70, *The Incredible Incas: Past and Present* 73; jointly: *The Mexican Genius* 31, *Recovery through Revolution, Contemporary Opinion* 33, *Rifle Rule in Cuba* (with Clifford Odets) 35, *Mississippi River Folklore, The Writer in a Changing World* 37, *We Testify* 41, *New Invitation to Learning* 44, *What South Americans Think of Us* 45, *The Price of Liberty* 47, *Exploring Life through Literature* 51, 57, *Politics, Bits of Silver* 61.
RFD2 Box 25, Killingworth, Conn. 06417, U.S.A.
Telephone: (203) 663-1696.

Beam, Jacob D., B.A.; American diplomatist; b. 24 March 1908; ed. Princeton and Cambridge Univs. Vice-Consul, Geneva 31-34; Third Sec., Berlin 34-40; Second Sec., London 41-45; Asst. Political Adviser, U.S. Forces, Germany 45-47; Chief, Central European Div., Dept. of State 47-49; Consul-Gen., Djakarta 49-51; Acting U.S. Rep., U.N. Comm. for Indonesia 51; Counsellor, Belgrade 51-52; Minister-Counsellor, Moscow 53; Deputy Asst. Sec. of State 53-57; Ambassador to Poland 57-61; in charge of political and negotiating affairs, Arms Control and Disarmament Agency 61-66; Amb. to Czechoslovakia 66-68, to U.S.S.R. 69-73; Head U.S. Del. to Int. Communications Union Conf., Malaga 73; Chair. Radio Free Europe 74.
3129 O Street, N.W., Washington, D.C., U.S.A.

Beament, Brigadier-Gen. George Edwin, O.B.E., K.ST.J., E.D., Q.C., B.A.SC. (retd.); Canadian officer and lawyer; b. 12 April 1908, Ottawa, Ont.; s. of Thomas Arthur Beament, Q.C. and Edith Louise Beament (née Belford); m. Brenda Yvonne Mary Thoms 1941; one s. one d.; ed. Royal Military Coll., Kingston, Toronto Univ., Osgoode Hall Law School, Staff Coll., Camberley.
Called to Ontario Bar 34; Partner Beament and Beament, Ottawa 37; mobilised 2nd Field Battery R.C.A., Major 39; proceeded to England in command 2/14 Field Battery R.C.A. 40; Brigade Major 1st Canadian Armoured Brigade 41; C.O. 6 Canadian Field Regiment R.C.A., Lieut.-Col. 42; Col., Gen. Staff First Canadian Army 43; Brig.-Gen. Staff First Canadian Army 45; mentioned in despatches; awarded Croix de Guerre avec Palme, Order of the White Lion, 3rd Class, Czechoslovak Military Cross; Pres. Khaki Univ. of Canada in the U.K. 45-46; now Counsel Beament, Fyfe, York, Barristers and Solicitors; Pres. Royal Mil. Coll. Club of Canada 53-54; Pres. Ottawa Community Chests 53-55; Pres. United Services Inst. 55-56; Pres. Ottawa Y.M.C.A. 58-60; Gov. Carleton Univ. 56-73; mem. Nat. Capital Comm. 60-66; Bencher Law Soc. Upper Canada 64-75; Chancellor, Ven. Order of St. John (Canada); Knight of Grace Ven. Order of St. John 64; Knight of Justice Ven. Order of St. John 75; Hon. Col. 30th Field Regiment R.C.A. 68-; Hon. Pres. Ottawa YM-YWCA

69-72; Gov. Corps of Commissionaires (Ottawa); Dir. Community Foundation of Ottawa and District.
Leisure interests: travel, historical research, reading.
Office: 1005 La Promenade, 151 Sparks Street, Ottawa 4, Ontario K1P 5E3; Home: Snowberry, Notch Road, Old Chelsea, P.Q. J0X 2H0, Canada.
Telephone: 235-6736 (Office); 827-2150 (Home).

Beams, Jesse Wakefield, A.B., M.A., PH.D.; American physicist; b. 25 Dec. 1898, Sumner County, Kan.; s. of J. W. Beams and Kathryn Wylie Beams; m. Maxine Sutherland; ed. Fairmount Coll., Kan., Wisconsin Univ., Virginia Univ.
Instructor of Physics and Mathematics, Alabama Polytechnic Inst. 22-23; Nat. Research Fellow in Physics, Virginia and Yale Univs. 25-27; Instructor in Physics Yale Univ. 27-28; Assoc. Prof. Physics, Virginia Univ. 28-30, Prof. 30-69, Chair. Dept. of Physics 48-62, Emer. Prof. 69-; mem. Gen. Advisory Cttee. Atomic Energy Comm. 54-60, Nat. Acad. Sciences, American Phil. Soc., Optical Soc. of America, American Asscn. Univ. Profs., American Physics Teachers' Asscn.; awarded Potts Medal of Franklin Inst.; Fellow American Physical Soc., American Acad. of Arts and Sciences; A.A.A.S. Chair., Section B 42; Pres. Virginia Acad. of Science 47; Francis H. Smith Prof. of Physics 53, Emer. 69; Naval Ordinance Development Award 46; Jefferson Award 55; Scott Award 56; Pres. American Physical Society 58-59; Lewis Prize 58; Alumni Award Wichita Univ. 59; Nat. Medal of Science 67; Atomic Energy Comm. Citation 73.
Publs. Numerous researches in field of electrical discharge in gases; electro-optical Kerr effect; studies of phenomena which occur in short intervals of time; studies of phenomena which occur in high centrifugal fields; the development of high speed centrifuges; the acceleration of ions to high energies; measurement of particle and molecular weights; magnetic balances, partial specific volumes viscosities; low temperature physics; strength of materials; isotope separation, gravitation.
Department of Physics, University of Virginia, Charlottesville, Va. 22903; Home: 1705 Kenwood Lane, Charlottesville, Va. 22903, U.S.A.
Telephone: (804) 924-3781 (Office); (804) 295-2048 (Home).

Bean, Alan L.; American astronaut; b. 15 March 1932, Wheeler, Texas; m. Sue Ragsdale; one s. one d.; ed. Univ. of Texas.
Commissioned in U.S. Navy; received pilot training and assigned to Attack Squadron; then attended Navy Test Pilot School, Patuxent, Md.; selected by NASA 63; command pilot for backup crew of *Gemini X* Mission 66; landed on the moon in *Apollo XII* Nov. 69; Commdr. *Skylab* 3 Mission 73; backup Commdr. U.S. flight crew, Apollo-Soyuz Test Project 75; holder of 10 world records in astronautics and space flights.
NASA Johnson Space Center, Houston, Texas 77058, U.S.A.

Bean, William Bennett, M.D.; American physician; b. 8 Nov. 1909, Manila, Philippines; s. of Robert Bennett and Adelaide Leiper (Martin) Bennett; two s. one d.; ed. Univ. of Virginia.
Intern, Johns Hopkins Univ. Hosp. 35-36; Asst. Resident Physician, Boston City Hosp. 36-37; Senior Medical Resident, Cincinnati Gen. Hosp. 37-38; Asst. Attending Physician 41-46, Clinician, Out-Patient Dept. 46-48, Attending Physician 46-48; Asst. Prof. Univ. of Cincinnati Medical Coll. 40-47, Assoc. Prof. 47-48; Prof., Head Dept. of Internal Medicine, Univ. of Iowa Medical Coll. 48-70, Physician-in-Chief Univ. Hosps. 48-70; Sir William Osler Prof., Kempner Prof. and Dir. Inst. for Medical Humanities, Univ. of Texas Medical Branch 70-; John Horsley Memorial Prize,

Univ. of Virginia 44; Groedel Medal 61; Fellow, American Acad. of Arts and Sciences and other orgs.; mem. New York Acad. of Sciences, World Medical Asscn., Royal Soc. of Medicine, Pan American Medical Asscn. and many other socs.

Publs. *Sir William Osler; from his Bedside Teachings and Writings* (3rd edn.) 68, *Vascular Spiders and Related Lesions of the Skin* 58, *Aphorisms from Latham* 62, *Rare Diseases and Lesions; their Contribution to Clinical Medicine* 67.
Editor *Monographs in Medicine* 51-52; Book Review Editor *Archives of Internal Medicine* 55-61, Editor-in-Chief 62-66; Editorial Consultant *Modern Medicine* 64-67, *Stedman's Medical Dictionary, Family Medical Quotations*; Editor *Current Medical Dialog* 67-.
2814 Dominique, Galveston, Tex. 77550, U.S.A.

Bearsted, 3rd Viscount, cr. 25, of Maidstone; Marcus Richard, T.D., D.L.; British banker; b. 1 June 1909, London; *s.* of 2nd Viscount and Dorothea Montefiore Micholls; *m.* 1st Elizabeth Heather Firmston-Williams 1947 (dissolved 1966), 2nd Jean Agnew Somerville 1968; one *d.*; ed. Eton and New Coll., Oxford.
Army service with Warwickshire Yeomanry (Major) 39-45; Chair. 1928 Investment Trust Ltd., Samuel Properties Ltd., Hill Samuel & Co. (Jersey) Ltd., Tanker Finance Ltd., Negit S.A. Luxembourg; fmr. Chair., now Dir. Hill Samuel Group Ltd.; Dir. Sun Alliance and London Insurance Group, Lloyd's Bank Ltd. and others; Deputy Lieut. of Warwickshire 50-; mem. Board of Kensington and Chelsea and Westminster Area Health Authority and official of several hospitals; fmr. Chair. Bearsted Memorial Hospital; Pres. St. Mary's Hospital Medical School.
Leisure interests: hunting, shooting, fishing, tapestry.
100 Wood Street, London, EC2P 2AJ; Home: 1 Eaton Close, London, SW1W 8JX; Upton House, Nr. Banbury, OX15 6HT, Oxon., England.
Telephone: 01-628-8011 (Office); 01-730-4040 (Home); 029-587-242 (Country).

Beaton, Sir Cecil Walter Hardy, Kt., C.B.E.; British photographer and designer; b. 14 Jan. 1904; ed. Harrow and Cambridge.
Photographer, stage and film designer; settings and costumes for *Black Vanities, Kipps, Pitt the Younger, Anna Karenina, An Ideal Husband, Gigi, The Doctor's Dilemma*; stage productions: *Lady Windermere's Fan* (London and New York), *The Second Mrs. Tanqueray, Quadrille* (London and New York), *Portrait of a Lady* (New York), *The Chalk Garden, My Fair Lady* (New York and London), *Vanessa* (New York), *Turandot, Coco*; exhbns. of paintings and stage designs Redfern Gallery, London 36, 58, 65, Sagitarrius Gallery, N.Y. 56, Lefevre Gallery, London 66; retrospective exhbn. of photographs at Nat. Portrait Gallery, London 68-69.
Publs. *The Book of Beauty* 30, *Cecil Beaton's Scrapbook* 37, *Cecil Beaton's New York* 39, *My Royal Past* 39, *History Under Fire* (with James Pope Hennessey) 41, *Time Exposure* (with Peter Quennell) 41, *Winged Squadrons* 42, *Near East* 43, *British Photographers* 44, *Far East* 45, *Chinese Album* 46, *Ashcombe* 49, *Photobiography* 51, *Ballet* 51, *Persona Grata* (with Kenneth Tynan) 53, *The Glass of Fashion* 54, *It Gives me Great Pleasure* 55, *The Face of the World* 57, *Japanese* 59, *Diaries 1922-1939: The Wandering Years* 61, *Quail in Aspic* 62, *My Fair Lady* 64, *Diaries: The Years Between* 65, *The Best of Beaton* 68, *My Bolivian Aunt* 71, *Diaries: The Happy Years* 72, *Diaries: The Strenuous Years* 73, *The Magic Image* 75.
Reddish House, Broadchalke, nr. Salisbury, Wilts., England.

Beattie, (John) Robert, B.A.; Canadian economist and banker; b. 30 May 1910, Greenwood, B.C.; *s.* of John Thomas Beattie and Mary Maude Minkler; *m.* 1st

Katharine McIntyre 1937 (deceased), 2nd Mary Angus Rogers 1964; four *d.*; ed. Univ. of Manitoba and Oxford Univ.
With Manufacturers' Life Insurance Co., Toronto 33-35; entered Bank of Canada, Ottawa 35, Deputy Chief of Research Dept. 40, Chief of Research Dept. 44, Exec. Asst. to Govs. 50, Deputy Gov. 55-72; Econ. Consultant to Canadian Arctic Gas Study Ltd. 72-.
Leisure interest: golf.
South Dene Farm, R.R.2 Mountain, Ont., Canada.
Telephone: 238-4634 (Office); 989-5202 (Home).

Beaudoin, Hon. Louis René, P.C., Q.C.; Canadian barrister and solicitor; b. 1912; ed. Montreal Coll., Coll. Ste-Marie, Seminary of Ste-Thérèse, Coll. S.-Laurent, Univ. of Montreal.
Member Board of Dirs. Global Life Insurance Co., Global Gen. Insurance Co., Global Reinsurance Co., Laurentide Acceptance Corpn., Paquette & Paquette Inc., etc.; mem. Canadian House of Commons 45-58; Deputy Chair. of Cttees. 49-52; Deputy Speaker 52-53; Speaker 53-57; Vice-Pres. Nat. Liberal Federation 49-51; Canadian Del. to Second Session of UN Gen. Assembly in New York 49; Del. Commonwealth Parl. Conf., Wellington (N.Z.) and Canberra 50; Pres. Exec. Cttee. Canadian Branch, Commonwealth Parl. Asscn. 47-54, Hon. Pres. 53-57; mem. Gen. Council C.P.A. 51-54; Q.C. 52; mem. Bar of Montreal and P.Q.
Suite 910, Aldred Building, 507 Place d'Armes, Montreal, Canada.

Beaulieu, Paul André; Canadian diplomatist; b. 1 April 1913; ed. Univ. of Montreal.
Joined diplomatic service 40; posts in Ottawa, Washington, Boston and London 40-58; Amb. to Lebanon 58-61, to Iraq 61-63, to Brazil 63-67, to UN 67-68, to France 68-70, to Portugal 70-72.
c/o Ministry of Foreign Affairs, Ottawa, Canada.

Beaulne, Joseph-Charles-Leonard Yvon; Canadian diplomatist; b. 22 Feb. 1919, Ottawa; *m.;* five *c.;* ed. Univ. of Ottawa.
Served with Canadian Army in U.K., N. Africa, Italy and N.W. Europe; joined Canadian Dept. of External Affairs 48, served Rome, Buenos Aires and Havana 48-61; Amb. to Venezuela 61-64; Minister in Washington 64-67; Amb. to Brazil 67-69; Perm. Rep. to UN 69-72; Asst. Sec. of State 72-74; Dir.-Gen. Bureau of African and Middle Eastern Affairs, Dept. of External Affairs 74-.
Department of External Affairs, Bureau of African and Middle Eastern Affairs, Lester B. Pearson Building A-5, Ottawa, Canada.
Telephone: 992-7133.

Beaumarchais, Jacques Delarue Caron de, L. EN D.; French diplomatist; b. 16 April 1913, Bayonne; ed. Ecole des Roches, Verneuil-sur-Avre, Faculté de Droit, Paris, and Ecole libre des sciences politiques. Entered French diplomatic service 42; has served in Rome, London, Moscow and held various posts in Ministry of Foreign Affairs; Dir. of Cabinet of Minister of Foreign Affairs 64; Dir. of Political Dept., Ministry of Foreign Affairs 65-72; Amb. to U.K. 72-; Hon. Fellow, St. Antony's Coll., Oxford 72; Officier, Légion d'Honneur, Commdr. Ordre Nat. du Mérite.
French Embassy, 58 Knightsbridge, London, S.W.1, England.

Beaumont, Sir Richard Ashton, K.C.M.G., O.B.E.; retired British diplomatist; b. 29 Dec. 1912; ed. Repton and Oriel Coll., Oxford.
Entered Consular Service 36, served Beirut 36, Damascus 38; war service 41-44; joined Foreign Office 45, served Mosul 46-47; Chargé d'Affaires, Damascus 47; Consul, Jerusalem 48-49, Caracas 49-53, Baghdad 53-57; Imperial Defence Coll. 58; Head of Arabian Dept. Foreign Office 59-61; Amb. to Morocco 61-65, to

Iraq 65-67; at Foreign Office 67-69; Amb. to Egypt 69-72; Dir.-Gen. Middle East Asscn. 73-.
14 Cadogan Square, London, S.W.1, England.

Beaupre, Robert Showers; American banker; b. 14 Feb. 1911, Anaconda, Mont.; *m.* Dorothy Fiala Beaupre 1940; one *s.* one *d.*; ed. Lewis and Clark High School, Spokane, Washington.
Seattle First Nat. Bank 29-, Pres., Dir. 61-; Chair. of Board, Junior Achievement of Seattle; mem. Board of Trustees, Pacific N.W. Research Foundation, N.W. Kidney Center, N.W. Council for Econ. Educ., Washington Bankers' Asscn., Legislative Comm.; mem. Business and Industry Advisory Board, Seattle Opportunities Industrialization Center Inc.
Seattle First National Bank, P.O. Box 3586, Seattle, Washington 98124, U.S.A.

Beaupre, Thomas Norbert, B.SC., M.SC.; Canadian business executive; b. 17 Aug. 1917; *m.* Hazel Genereux 1945; one *s.* one *d.*; ed. McGill Univ.
Served in Second World War with Royal Canadian Army Service Corps; in Trade and Commerce Dept., Govt. of Canada, Ottawa; later in Defence Production as Asst. Deputy Minister and Dir. of Aircraft Production; Vice-Pres. and Sec. Canadian Chemical and Cellulose Co. Ltd. 53-57; Exec. Vice-Pres. Columbia Cellulose Co. Ltd. and Celgar Ltd., Vancouver 57-58, Pres. 58-61; Pres. Brit. Columbia Forest Products Ltd. 61-64, Chair. of Board 64-; Chair. of Board and Pres. Domtar Ltd. 66-74; Dir. Argus Corpn., Royal Bank of Canada, Hudson's Bay Co., Hudson's Bay Oil and Gas Co. Ltd., Standard Broadcasting Corpn. Ltd., Standard Broadcast Sales Co. Ltd., CJAD Ltd., United Corpns. Ltd.; Gov. Canadian Export Asscn.
3207 The Boulevard, Westmount, Quebec, Canada.

Beauvoir, Simone Lucie Ernestine Marie Bertrand de; French writer; b. 9 Jan. 1908; ed. Paris Univ.
Taught in various lycées 31-43; awarded Prix Goncourt for *Les Mandarins* 45; Jerusalem Prize 75; Hon. LL.D. (Cantab.).
Publs. Novels: *L'Invitée* 43 (English edn. *She Came to Stay* 49, American edn. 54), *Le Sang des Autres* 45, (English and American edns. *The Blood of Others* 48), *Les Mandarins* 45 (American edn. *The Mandarins* 56, English edn. 57), *Tous les Hommes sont Mortels* 47 (American edn. *All Men are Mortal* 55); Play: *Les Bouches Inutiles* 54; non-fiction: *Pyrrus et Cinéas* 44, *Pour une Morale de l'Ambiguity* (American edn. *The Ethics of Ambiguity*) 48, *L'Amérique du Jour au Jour* 48 (English edn. *America Day by Day* 52, American edn. 53), *Le Deuxième Sexe* 49 (American edn. *The Second Sex* 52, English edn.), *Faut-il Brûler Sade?* 51 (English and American edns. *Must We Burn Sade?* 53), *Privilèges* 57, *La Longue Marche* 57 (American and English edns. *The Long March* 58), *Mémoires d'une Jeune Fille Rangée* 58, *Brigitte Bardot* 60, *La Force de l'Age*, *La Force des Choses* 63, *Une Mort très Douce* 64, *Les Belles Images* 66, *La Vieillesse* 70, *Tout compte fait* 72.
11 *bis* rue Schoelcher, Paris 14e, France.

Beaven, Peter Jamieson, DIP.ARCH., A.R.I.B.A., F.N.Z.I.A.; New Zealand architect; b. 13 Aug. 1925, Christchurch; *s.* of Eric Tamate Beaven and Maria Joan Jamieson; *m.* Anne Mary Beaglehole 1952; one *s.* two *d.*; ed. Christ's Coll., Christchurch, Univ. Coll., Auckland.
Sub Lieut. Royal Naval Volunteer Reserve, Far East; practised in Christchurch for twenty years; founded first New Zealand Civic Trust; Chair. Environment Advisory Cttee., Christchurch City Council; Principal, Beaven Hunt Assocs.; Gold Medal, N.Z. Inst. of Architects 66, various merit awards in N.Z. architecture.
Leisure interests: yachting, sketching, painting, walking, reading.
Publs. *Urban Renewal Report* (N.Z. Govt.), co-author *New Zealand Architecture 1840-1970* 73.

Beaven Hunt Associates, P.O. Box 1766, Christchurch; Home: 46 Esplanade, Sumner, Christchurch 8, New Zealand.

Beavogui, Louis Lansana; Guinean politician; b. 1923, Macenta; ed. West African Medical School, Dakar.
Former Asst. Medical Officer, Gueckedou, S. Guinea; later Medical Officer, Kissidougou, later becoming Mayor; Minister of Trade, Industry and Mining, Guinea 57-58, of Econs. 58-61, of Foreign Affairs 61-69, of Econ. Affairs 69-72; Prime Minister 72-, also responsible for the Army, Foreign Affairs, Planning, Financial Control and Information.
Office of the Premier, Conakry, Guinea.

Beazley, Kim Edward, M.A.; Australian politician; b. 30 Sept. 1917, Northam, W. Australia; ed. Perth Modern School, Claremont Teachers' Coll., Univ. of W. Australia, Australia Nat. Univ.
Worked as schoolteacher and tutor until 45; mem. Parl. for Fremantle, W. Australia 45-; mem., Vice-Chair. Joint Parl. Cttee. on Foreign Affairs 67-70; Minister of Educ. 72-75; mem. of Council, Australian Nat. Univ. 51-, Australian Inst. of Aboriginal Studies 64-, Advisory Council, Australian Commonwealth Scientific and Industrial Research Org. (CSIRO); fmr. Vice-Pres. Teachers' Union, Councillor Australian Teachers' Fed.; del. to Commonwealth Parl. Asscn. Conf., Nigeria 62; Labor Party.
Parliament House, Canberra, A.C.T., Australia.

Beb a Don, Philémon Louis Benjamin, D. EN D., DR.POL.SC.; Cameroonian diplomatist; b. 15 Aug. 1925; ed. Lycée d'Aix en Provence, Univs. of Aix en Provence and Toulouse.
With local, civil and financial admin. 45-48; studied law and political science 48-57; Principal Civil Administrator, Acad. of Int. Law, The Hague 57; Dir. Cabinet of Ministry of Econ. Affairs 57-58; Head, Dept. of Legal Affairs, Ministry of Interior 58-60; Deputy Head of Dept., Ministry of Foreign Affairs 60-61; Diplomatic Adviser to Pres. of the Repub. July 60-; Counsellor, Cameroon Embassy, France 61-62; Amb. to France, Italy, Spain 62-67, to Fed. Repub. of Germany 67-72, to Switzerland, Yugoslavia 68-72; Dir. of Cabinet 72-; Cameroonian mem. of dels. to many int. confs.; several national and foreign decorations.
Publs. numerous articles in law journals.
Office of the President, Yaoundé, Cameroon.

Becerra de la Flor, Dr. Daniel; Peruvian surgeon and politician; b. 23 Jan. 1906, Moquegua; *s.* of Dr. Daniel Becerra and Isabel de la Flor; *m.* Yolanda Tabini 1934; one *s.* one *d.*
Associate Prof. of Surgery, San Marcos Univ. 54-61; Principal Prof. and Head of Dept. of Surgery Cayetano Heredia School of medicine; Senator 63-68; Prime Minister and Minister of Public Health 65-67; Pres. Peruvian Acad. of Surgery 67-69; Founder-Pres. Peruvian Soc. of Gastroenterology 54; Consultant Surgeon Navy Medical Centre 53-; Grand Cross Orden del Sol 66; Grand Cross Hipólito Unanue 65; Grand Cross Daniel A. Carrion 65; many hon. degrees.
Leisure interests: painting, fishing, golf.
Av. Angamos 1192 (Miraflores), Lima, Peru.

Becher, Ulrich; Austrian-Swiss writer; b. 2 Jan. 1910, Berlin, Germany; *s.* of Richard Becher and Elisa Ulrich von Rickenbach; *m.* Dana Roda 1934; one *s.*; ed. Werner-Siemens-Gymnasium, Berlin, Freie Schulgemeinde Wickersdorf, and Univs. of Geneva, Berlin and Leipzig.
Former mem. George Grosz circle, Berlin; went to Vienna 33; newspaper corresp. Paris and Switzerland; escaped to Zürich 38; in Rio de Janeiro 41-43, Brazilian interior 44, New York City 45-48, Basle 49-; Drama Prize, German Stage Club, Cologne 55.
Leisure interests: politics, drawing, jazz-piano.

Publs. *Männer machen Fehler* (short stories) 32, *Die Eroberer* (short stories) 36, *Nachtigall will zum Vater fliegen* (novel) 50, *Kurz nach 4* (novel) 57, *Männer machen Fehler, Geschichten der Windrose* (collected short stories) 58, *Das Herz des Hais* (novel) 60, *Brasilianischer Romanzero* 62, plays: *Niemand* 34, *Der Bockerer* (with Peter Preses) 48, *Samba* 51, *Feuerwasser* 52, *Mademoiselle Löwenzorn* 54, *Die Kleinen und die Grossen* 57, *Der Herr kommt aus Bahia* 58, *Makumba* 65, *Biene gib mir Honig* 72; *Murmeljagd* (novel in five vols.): *Tote Zeit, Licht im See, Geisterbahn I, Geisterbahn II, Die Strasse über San Gian* 69, *Der schwarze Hut* 72, *Das Profil* (novel) 73, *William's Ex-Casino* (novel) 74.
Spalenring 95, Basle, Switzerland.
Telephone: 22-51-70.

Bechtel, Stephen Davison; American engineer-constructor; b. 24 Sept. 1900, Aurora, Ind.; *s.* of Warren A. and Clara (West) Bechtel; *m.* Laura Adaline Peart 1923; one *s.* one *d.*; ed. Univ. of Calif.
Joined W. A. Bechtel Co., Vice-Pres. 25-36, Pres. 36-46; First Vice-Pres. Six Companies Inc. (constructors of Hoover Dam) 31-35; Dir. Bechtel-McCone Corpn. 37-46; during Second World War Chair. Calif. Shipbuilding Corpn.; now Senior Dir. Bechtel Corpn.; Dir. various Bechtel engineering and construction corporations and international affiliates; Dir. Stanford Research Inst. 49-; Pres. Lakeside Corpn.; Dir. Industrial Indemnity Co. and Southern Pacific Co.; Trustee Ford Foundation 60-; mem. Business Advisory Council U.S. Dept. of Commerce 50-61 (Chair. 58-59), The Business Council 61-; Hon. LL.D., D.Eng.; John Fritz Medal 61; Nat. Defense Transportation Award 60; Order of Cedar (Lebanon), Knight Order of St. Sylvester (Holy See), Kt. Commdr. Court of Honour.
Home: 244 Lakeside Drive, Oakland, California 94612; Office: 155 Sansome Street, San Francisco, California 94104, U.S.A.

Beck, Béatrix Marie; Swiss writer; b. 30 July 1914; ed. Lycée de St. Germain-en-Laye and Université de Grenoble.
Former Sec. to André Gide; journalist; mem. Jury, Prix Fémina; Prix Goncourt for *Léon Morin, prêtre*; Prix Félix Fénéon.
Publs. *Barny, Une Mort irrégulière, Léon Morin, prêtre, Des accommodements avec le ciel, Le Premier Mai, Abram Krol, Le Muet, Cou coupé court toujours.*
c/o MM. Cailler (Editeurs), Geneva, Switzerland.

Beck, Conrad; Swiss composer; b. 16 June 1901, Lohn, Schaffhausen; *m.* Friedel Ehrsam 1941; two *s.*; ed. Konservatorium, Zürich.
Further musical studies in Paris with Ibert, Honegger and Roussel 23-32; Ludwig Spohr Prize, City of Brunswick; Composers Prize of Asscn. of Swiss composers; Kunstpreis, City of Basle; Commdr. Order of Cultural Merit, Monaco 73.
Leisure interest: mountaineering.
Principal works: Seven symphonies, many other symphonic works, concertos, two oratorios, cantatas, chamber music, etc., including *Der Tod zu Basel* (Miserère), *Die Sonnenfinsternis, Elegie.*
St. Johann Vorstadt 82, Basle, Switzerland.
Telephone: 250451.

Beck, Most Rev. George Andrew; British (Roman Catholic) ecclesiastic; b. 28 May 1904; ed. Clapham Coll., London, and St. Michael's Coll., Hitchin.
Priest 27; Staff St. Michael's Coll., Hitchin until 41, Headmaster 41-44; Headmaster, The Becket School, Nottingham 44-48; Titular Bishop of Tigia and Coadjutor Bishop of Brentwood 48-51, Bishop of Brentwood 51-55; Bishop of Salford 55-64; Archbishop of Liverpool 64-75; Chair. Catholic Educ. Council 48-70.
Publs. *Assumptionist Spirituality* 36, *The Family and the Future* 48.

c/o Archbishop's House, 87 Green Lane, Mossley Hill, Liverpool L18 2EP, England.
Telephone: 051-722-2379.

Becker, Aharon; Israeli labour official; b. 1906, Brest-Litovsk, Russia; *m.* Cyla Selzer 1930; one *s.* two *d.*
Went from Russia to Israel 24; mem. Kibbutz 25; building worker 25-28; Sec. Ramat Gan Labour Council 29-32; Sec. Union of Textile Workers 33-34; mem. Exec. of Labour Council in Tel-Aviv 34-43; Man. Dir. Industrial Dept., Co-operative Wholesale Soc. 43-47; Head of Supply Mission, Ministry of Defence 47-48; Head of Trade Union Dept. and mem. Exec. Bureau, Histadrut 49-60, Sec.-Gen. 61-69; Deputy mem. Governing Body of ILO 56-70; mem. Knesset; mem. Secr. of Israel Labour Party; mem. Council of Dirs., Bank of Israel.
Publs. Numerous articles in Hebrew and British press; various booklets and publications on economic and labour problems.
66 Keren Kayemet Boulevard, Tel-Aviv, Israel.

Becker, Carl Johan; Danish archaeologist; b. 3 Sept. 1915, Copenhagen; *s.* of Carl Becker and Henny Becker (née Döcker); *m.* Birgit Hilbert 1949; three *d.*; ed. Metropolitanskolen, Københavns Universitet.
Assistant, National Museum 34-41, Asst.-Keeper 41-52; Prof. of Prehistoric Archaeology, Univ. of Copenhagen 52-, Dean Faculty of Arts 63-64, mem. Konsistorium 64-70; Chief Editor *Acta Archaeologica* 48-; mem. Royal Danish Acad. of Sciences and Letters, Danish Research Council for the Humanities 68-75; Corresp. Fellow, British Acad.; mem. Cttee. of Thai-Danish Archaeological Expedition and numerous European Prehistoric and Archaeological societies; Knight First Class Order of Danebrog.
Leisure interest: numismatics.
Publs. *Enkeltgravkulturen på de danske Øer* 36, *Mosefundne Lerkar fra Yngre Stenalder* 48, *Die Mittel-Neolithischen Kulturen in Südskandinavien* 55, 71, *Förromersk Jernalder i Syd-og Midtjylland* 61.
23 Egernvej, DK-2000-Copenhagen F., Denmark.
Telephone: FA. 5711.

Becker, Hans Detlev; German publisher and journalist; b. 11 June 1921, Freiburg, Elbe; *s.* of Albert Becker and Hildegard Becker; *m.* Elisabeth Burkhard 1953; ed. Univ. of Münster.
Managing Editor *Der Spiegel* 50-58, Chief Editor 59-61, Publisher 62-; Publisher, Gen. Man. *Manager Magazine* 71; mem. German Press Council 75-.
Leisure interest: golf (captain of Reinbek-Wohltorfer Golf-club).
c/o Spiegel-Verlag, 2 Hamburg 11, Brandstwiete 19; Home: 2057 Wentorf, Bez. Hamburg, Am Golfplatz 3, Federal Republic of Germany.
Telephone: 040-3007246 (Office).

Becker, Jürgen; German writer; b. 10 July 1932, Cologne; *s.* of Robert Becker and Else Becker, née Schuchardt; *m.* 1st Marie Becker 1954 (dissolved 1965), one *s.*; *m.* 2nd Rango Bohne 1965, one step *s.* one step *d.*; ed. Univ. of Cologne.
Various jobs until 59; freelance writer and contributor to W. German Radio 59-64; Reader at Rowohlt Verlag 64-65; freelance writer 65-, living in Cologne, Berlin, Hamburg and Rome; Förderpreis des Landes Niedersachsen 64; Stipendium Deutsche Akad. Villa Massimo, Rome 65, 66; Group 47 Prize 67; Literaturpreis der Stadt Köln 68.
Publs. *Phasen* (Text and Typogramme with Wolf Vostell) 60, *Felder* (Prose) 64, *Ränder* (Prose) 68, *Bilder, Häuser* (Radio Play) 69; Editor *Happenings* (documentary with Wolf Vostell) 65.
c/o Suhrkamp-Verlag, 6 Frankfurt/M; 5 Köln-Bruck, Am Klausenberg 84, Federal Republic of Germany.
Telephone: 8401-53.

Beckett, Samuel, M.A.; Irish author; b. 13 April 1906; ed. Portora Royal School and Trinity Coll., Dublin. Lecturer Ecole Normale Supérieure, Paris, 28-30, Trinity Coll., Dublin 30-32; now lives in Paris; Foreign Hon. mem. American Acad. of Arts and Sciences 68; Prix Formentor 61; Nobel Prize for Literature 69.
Publs. Verse: *Whoroscope* 30, *Echo's Bones* 35; Novels: *Murphy* 38, *Watt* 44, *Mercier et Camier* 46 (English edn.) 74, *Molloy* 51 (English edn. 56), *Malone meurt* 52 (English edn. 56), *L'Innommable* 53 (English edn. 57), *Comment C'est* (English edn. 63), *Imagination Dead Imagine* 66; Short Stories: *More Pricks than Kicks* 34, *Nouvelles et textes pour rien* 55; Stage Plays: *En attendant Godot* 52 (English version *Waiting for Godot*), *Fin de Partie* 57 (English version *End Game*), *Krapp's Last Tape* 59, *Happy Days* 60, *Play* 63, *Not I* 73; Radio Plays: *All that Fall* 57, *Embers* 59, *Words and Music* 61, *Cascando* 64; Essay: *Proust* 65; *No's Knife: Collected Shorter Prose 1945-66* 67.
c/o Faber and Faber Ltd., 3 Queen Square, London, W.C.1, England; and c/o Editions de Minuit, 7 rue Bernard Palissy, Paris 6e, France.

Bedell, Ralph Clairon, A.M., PH.D.; American university professor and public servant; b. 4 June 1904, Hale, Mo.; *s.* of Charles Edward Bedell and Jennie Eaton Bedell; *m.* 1st Stella Virginia Bales 1929 (deceased), 2nd Ann Barclay Sorency 1968 (deceased); ed. Univ. of Missouri and Columbia Univ.
Professor of Educational Psychology, Northeast Missouri State Teachers Univ. 33-37; Dean of Faculty, Central Missouri State Univ. 37; Prof. of Educational Psychology and Measurements, Univ. of Nebraska 38-50; served Navy 43-46; Prof. of Psychology and Educ., The American Univ., Washington, D.C. 50-52; with U.S. Office of Educ., Dept. of Health, Educ. and Welfare 52-66; on leave 55-58; Sec.-Gen. South Pacific Comm. Nouméa, New Caledonia 55-58; Prof. of Educ., Univ. of Missouri-Columbia 67-74, Emer. Prof. and Research Assoc. 74-.
Publs. *General Science for To-day* (co-author) 36, *Pre-Flight Aeronautics* (co-author) 42, *Basic Guidance for Nebraska Schools* (Editor) 48.
300 Brandon Road East, Columbia, Mo. 65201, U.S.A. Telephone: 314-443-3006.

Bédié, Henri Konan, L. EN D., D. ÈS SC.; Ivory Coast economist and politician; b. 1934, Dadiékro; *m.* Henriette Koizan 1958; two *s.* two *d.*; ed. Poitiers Univ., France.
Worked as civil servant in France 59; Counsellor at the French Embassy, Washington March 60-Aug. 60; founded Ivory Coast mission to the UN 60; Chargé d'affaires for Ivory Coast to U.S.A. Aug. 60-Dec. 60, Amb. Dec. 60-Jan. 66; Minister Del. for Econ. and Financial Affairs Jan. 66-Sept. 68, Minister Sept. 68-; mem. Bureau Politique, Parti Démocratique de la Côte d'Ivoire (PDCI); Pres. OAMPI (Office africain et malgache de la propriété industrielle).
Ministry of Economic and Financial Affairs, Abidjan, Ivory Coast.

Bedjaoui, Mohammed; Algerian politician; b. 21 Sept. 1929; ed. Univ. of Grenoble and Institut d'Etudes Politiques, Grenoble.
Lawyer, Court of Appeal, Grenoble 51; research worker at Centre National de la Recherche Scientifique (CNRS) Paris 55; Legal Counsellor of the Arab League in Geneva 59-62; Legal Counsellor Provisional Republican Govt. of Algeria in Exile 58-61; Dir. Office of the Pres. of Nat. Constituent Assembly 62; mem. Del. to UN 62; Sec.-Gen. Council of Ministers, Algiers 62-63; Pres. Soc. Nat. des chemins de fer algériens (SNCFA) 64; Dean of the Faculty of Law, Algiers Univ. 64-; Minister of Justice and Keeper of the Seals 64-70; mem., special reporter, Comm. on Int. Law, UN 65-; Amb. to France 70-; Perm. Rep. to UNESCO 71-; Carnegie Endowment for Int. Peace 56; Ordre du Mérite Alaouite, Morocco; Order of the Repub., Egypt.
Publs. *International Civil Service* 56, *Fonction publique internationale et influences nationales* 58, *La révolution algérienne et le droit* 61, *Succession d'états* 70.
Embassy of Algeria, rue Hamelin 18, Paris 16e, France; and 39 rue des Pins, Hydra, Algiers, Algeria.

Beeby, Clarence Edward, C.M.G., M.A., PH.D.; New Zealand educationist and administrator; b. 16 June 1902, Leeds, England; *s.* of Anthony Beeby and Alice Beeby (née Rhodes); *m.* Beatrice Eleanor Newnham 1926; one *s.* one *d.*; ed. Christchurch Boys' High School, Canterbury Coll., Univ. of New Zealand, Univ. Coll., London, and Univ. of Manchester.
Lecturer in Philosophy and Education, Canterbury Univ. Coll., Univ. of N.Z. 23-34; Dir. N.Z. Council for Educational Research 34-38; Asst. Dir. of Education, Education Dept., N.Z. 38-40, Dir. of Education 40-60 (on leave of absence 48-49); Asst. Dir.-Gen. of UNESCO 48-49; Ambassador to France 60-63; leader N.Z. Dels. to Gen. Confs. of UNESCO 46, 47, 50, 53, 54, 56, 58, 60, 63; Hon. Counsellor of UNESCO 50; mem. of UNESCO Exec. Board 60-63, Chair. 63; Research Fellow, Harvard Univ. 63-67; Chair. UNESCO Evaluation Panel for World Functional Literacy Projects 67-70; Commonwealth Visiting Prof., Univ. of London 67-68; Consultant to Australian Govt. on educ. in Papua and New Guinea 69; Consultant to Ford Foundation in Indonesia 70-75; mem. Council of Consultant Fellows, Int. Inst. for Educ. Planning 72-78; Order of St. Gregory (first class); Hon. LL.D. (Otago), Hon. Lit.D. (Wellington); Mackie Medal (ANZAAS) 71.
Leisure interests: cabinet making, trout fishing, gardening.
Publs. *The Intermediate Schools of New Zealand* 38, *Entrance to University* (with W. Thomas and M. H. Oram) 39, *The Quality of Education in Developing Countries* 66, *Qualitative Aspects of Educational Planning* (editor) 69.
New Zealand Council for Educational Research, P.O. Box 3237, Wellington; Home: 73 Barnard Street, Wellington, New Zealand.
Telephone: 557-939 (Office); 725-088 (Home).

Beecher, Henry K., M.D.; American physician and professor; b. 4 Feb. 1904, Wichita, Kan.; ed. Univ. of Kansas and Harvard Univ.
Surgical Resident, Massachusetts Gen. Hosp. 32-35, Anesthetist-in-Chief 36-70; research under Prof. A. Krogh, Copenhagen 35; Instructor in Anesthesia, Harvard Medical School 36-39, Assoc. in Anesthesia 39-41, Henry Isiah Dorr Prof. of Research in Anesthesia 41-70, Emer. 70-; mil. service in U.S. Army 43-45, Lieut.-Col., five battle stars; mem. Editorial Board *Journal of Pharmacology and Experimental Therapeutics,* *International Journal of Neuropharmacology, Medical Documentation, Pharmakotherapia, Excerpta Medica* (Anesthesiology), *Methods of Information in Medicine;* Corresp. Editor *Der Anaesthetist;* Visiting Prof. Emory, Texas, North Carolina and New York Univs.; Senior mem. American Medical Asscn., American Asscn. for Thoracic Surgery; Fellow, A.A.A.S.; Senior Fellow, American Surgical Asscn.; mem. many socs.; 41 hon. lectureships; League of Merit, U.S. Army 45; Chevalier, Légion d'Honneur (France) 51; Citation for Distinguished Service to Humanity, Univ. of Kansas 58; Hon. M.D. (Univ. of Lund, Sweden) 61; Dr. h.c. (Univ. of Thessaloniki, Greece) 69; Hon. Citizen of Riga, U.S.S.R. 70; many other awards.
Publs. *Physiology of Anesthesia* 38, *Resuscitation and Anesthesia for Men Wounded in Battle* 49, *Measurement of Pain* 57, *Measurement of Subjective Responses: Quantitative Effects of Drugs* 59, *Research and the Individual* 70; Editor *Physiologic Effects of Wounds* 54,

Disease and the Advancement of Basic Science 60; 4 booklets; 261 articles.
Countway Library of Medicine, 10 Shattuck Street, Boston, Mass. 02115; Home: 101 Chestnut Street, Boston, Mass. 02108, U.S.A.

Beeching, Baron (Life Peer), cr. 65; **Richard Beeching,** A.R.C.S., B.SC., D.I.C., PH.D., C.I.MECH.E., F.B.I.M., F.INST.P., F.C.I.T.; British business executive; b. 21 April 1913, Sheerness, Kent; s. of Hubert Josiah Beeching and Annie Beeching (née Twigg); m. Ella Margaret Tiley 1938; ed. Maidstone Grammar School and Imperial Coll. of Science and Technology, London.
Fuel Research Station, Greenwich 36-37; Mond Nickel Co. 37-43; Armaments Design Dept., Fort Halstead 43-48; joined ICI 48, "Terylene" Council 51-53, Vice-Pres. ICI (Canada) Ltd. 53, Chair. Metals Div. 55, Dir. ICI 57-61; Dir. British Nylon Spinners Ltd. 59; Dir. ICI (Australia and New Zealand) Ltd. 60; Chair. British Transport Comm. 61-63, Chair. British Railways Board 63-65; rejoined ICI 65, Deputy Chair. 66-March 68; Chair. Royal Comm. on Assizes and Quarter Sessions 66-69; Chair. Redland Ltd. 70-, Furness Withy & Co. Ltd. 73-75, Econ. Insurance Co. Ltd. 73-75; Dir. Lloyds Bank Ltd. 65-; First Pres. Inst. of Work Study Practitioners 67-72, Royal Soc. for the Prevention of Accidents (RoSPA) 68-73; mem. Nat. Econ. Devt. Council (NEDC) 62-64, Top Salaries Review Body 71-75; Fellow of Imperial Coll.; Hon. LL.D. (London Univ.), Hon. D.Sc. (Nat. Univ. of Ireland).
Leisure interest: golf.
Little Manor, Lewes Road, East Grinstead, Sussex, England.
Telephone: East Grinstead 25477.

Beehgly, Charles Milton, A.B.; American steel executive; b. 6 Oct. 1908; ed. Ohio Wesleyan Univ.
Metal Carbides Co., Newark 31; Goff-Kirby Co., Cleveland 32-33; Buffalo Slag Co. 34; Cold Metal Products Co., Youngstown 35-38, Production Man. 39-42, Sales Man. 39-50, Vice-Pres. and Dir. 46-57, Gen. Man. 52-57; Pres. Jones & Laughlin Steel Corpn. (strip steel division) 57-71, Exec. Vice-Pres. Corpn. 58-60, Pres. 60-63, Chair. and Chief Exec. Officer 63-69, Chair. Exec. Cttee. 69-71; Vice-Pres., Gov. T. Mellon & Sons 69-; mem. Exec. Cttee. American Iron and Steel Inst.
Jones & Laughlin Steel Corporation, 3 Gateway Center, Pittsburgh 30, Pa., U.S.A.

Beeley, Sir Harold, K.C.M.G., C.B.E., M.A.; British diplomatist; b. 15 Feb. 1909, London; s. of Frank Arthur Beeley; m. Karen Brett-Smith (née Shields) 1958; one step s. three d., two step d.; ed. Highgate School and Queen's Coll., Oxford.
Lecturer at Univs. of Sheffield, London, Oxford and Leicester 30-39; entered Foreign Service 46; Counsellor, Copenhagen 49-50, Baghdad 50-53, Washington 53-55; Ambassador to Saudi Arabia 55; Asst. Under-Sec. Foreign Office 56-58; Deputy Perm. Rep. to UN 58-61; Amb. to United Arab Republic 61-64, 67-69; Perm. Rep. of U.K. to Disarmament Conf., Geneva 64-67; retired from Diplomatic Service 69; Lecturer, Queen Mary Coll., London 69-75; Chair. Unigulf Investments Ltd. 70-.
Publ. *Disraeli* 36.
2 Ormond Road, Richmond, Surrey, England.
Telephone: 01-940-1193.

Beer, (Georges) Henrik (Teodor W:son), M.A.; Swedish International Red Cross official; b. 22 Nov. 1915, Stockholm; s. of Waldemar Beer and Valborg Beer (née Granath); m. Barbro Selldén 1949; three s.; ed. Univ. of Stockholm.
Sec. Nat. Defence League 42-44; Dir. Swedish Govt. Comm. for Int. Relief 44-47; Sec.-Gen. Swedish Red Cross 47-60; Sec.-Gen. League of Red Cross Societies 60-; Sec.-Gen. XVII Int. Red Cross Conf. 48; Exec. Dir. Folke Bernadotte Memorial Foundation 51-62; Pres. Henry Dunant Inst. 70-72.
Leisure interests: ornithology, music.
League of Red Cross Societies, 17 Chemin des Crets, Petit-Saconnex, 1211 Geneva 19, Switzerland.
Telephone: 34-55-80.

Beer, Otto F., DR. PHIL.; Austrian writer, journalist and professor; b. 8 Sept. 1910, Vienna; s. of Leopold J. Beer and Emma Beer (née Pabst); m. Gerty Mothwurf 1949; ed. Univ. of Vienna.
Editor *Neues Wiener Journal* and *Neues Wiener Tagblatt* until 39; Chief Editor *Salzburger Nachrichten* 45; Drama Critic, *Welt am Abend* 46-48, *Der Standpunkt,* Merano 48-52, *Neues Österreich,* Vienna 52-67, Österreichischer Rundfunk 67-, *Süddeutsche Zeitung* 67-.
Leisure interest: music.
Publs. *Zehnte Symphonie* 52, *Wiedersehen in Meran* 52, *Ich-Rodolfo-Magier* 65, *Christin-Theres* 67; comedies: *Man ist nur zweimal jung* 55, *Operette* 60, *Die Eintagsfliege* 61, *Bummel durch Wien* 71, *Der Fenstergucker* 74.
Lederergasse 27, Vienna VIII, Austria.
Telephone: 42-04-84.

Beer, Samuel Hutchison, PH.D.; American university professor; b. 28 June 1911; ed. Staunton Military Acad., Univ. of Michigan, and Oxford and Harvard Univs.
Writer, Resettlement Admin. and Democratic Nat. Cttee. 35-36; Reporter *New York Post* 36-37; *Fortune* magazine 37-38; Instructor in Government, Harvard Univ. 38-42, Asst. Prof. 46-48, Assoc. Prof. 48-53, Prof. of Govt. 53-, Chair. Dept. of Govt. 54-58, Eaton Prof. of Science of Govt. 71-; Nat. Chair. Americans for Democratic Action 59-62; U.S. Army 42-45.
Publs. *The City of Reason* 49, *Treasury Control: The Coordination of Financial and Economic Policy in Great Britain* 56, *Patterns of Government: Major Political Systems of Europe* (co-author) 58 (3rd edn. 73), *Modern British Politics* 65, *The State and the Poor* 70.
87 Lakeview Avenue, Cambridge, Mass., U.S.A.

Beers, William O.; American food company executive; b. 26 May 1914; s. of Ernest and Rose (Binz) Beers; m. 1st Mary E. Holmes (deceased), 2nd Frances L. Miller 1954; two s. three d.; ed. Univ. of Wis.
Joined Kraftso Corpn. 37, Dir. 65-, Pres. 68-73, Chair. 72-; Pres. Kraft Foods Div. 65-68; Dir. Manufacturers Hanover Trust Co., Manufacturers Hanover Corpn., A. O. Smith Corpn., Allis-Chalmers, American Airlines, Sears, Roebuck, U.S. Steel Corpn.; Trustee, U.S. Council of Int. Chamber of Commerce, Consumer Research Inst.; Chair. Exec. Cttee. Food and Drug Law Inst.; mem. Agribusiness Industry Advisory Cttee.; Chair. GMA-FDA Council (Grocery Mfrs. of America Inc.-Food and Drug Admin.); mem. Business Council, Alumni Foundation, Wisconsin Univ.; Hon. LL.D. (Univ. of Wis.).
Kraftco Corporation, Kraftco Court, Glenview, Ill. 60025, U.S.A.

Beevers, Harry, PH.D.; American biologist; b. 10 Jan. 1924, Shildon, England; s. of Norman and Olive Beevers; m. Jean Sykes 1949; one s.; ed. Univ. of Durham.
Post-doctoral research, Univ. of Oxford 46-50; Asst. Prof. of Biology, Purdue Univ. 50-53, Assoc. Prof. 53-58, Prof. 58-69; Prof. of Biology, Univ. of Calif., Santa Cruz 69-; Pres. American Soc. of Plant Physiologists 61; mem. Nat. Acad. of Sciences; Sigma Xi Research Award, Purdue Univ. 58; McCoy Research Award 68, Stephen Hales Award, American Society of Plant Physiologists 70; Hon. D.Sc. Purdue Univ. 71, Univ. of Newcastle upon Tyne 74; Fellow American Acad. of Arts and Sciences 73.
Leisure interests: squash, gardening.

Publs. *Respiratory Metabolism in Plants* 61; 120 articles on plant metabolism in scientific journals.
Division of Natural Sciences, University of California, Santa Cruz, Calif. 95060; Home: 46 South Circle Drive, Santa Cruz, Calif. 95060, U.S.A.
Telephone: 408-429-2046 (Office); 408-423-7350 (Home).

Beevor, John Grosvenor, O.B.E.; British lawyer and financial administrator; b. 1 March 1905, Newark; s. of Henry and Mary Beevor; m. Mary Grepe 1957; three s.; ed. Winchester Coll. and Oxford Univ.
Adviser, British Del. Marshal Plan Conf., Paris 47; Man.-Dir. Commonwealth Development Finance Co. Ltd. 54-56; Vice-Pres. Int. Finance Corpn. 56-64; fmr. partner Slaughter and May, Solicitors (London); Chair. Doulton & Co., Lafarge Org., Tilbury Contracting; financial adviser and Dir. of several British companies.
Leisure interests: golf, history, literature.
51 Eaton Square, London, SW1W 9BE, England.
Telephone: 01-235 7987.

Begg, Admiral of the Fleet Sir Varyl, G.C.B., D.S.O., D.S.C., K.ST.J., P.M.N. (Malaysia); British naval officer; b. 1 Oct. 1908, London; s. of F. C. Begg and M. C. Robinson; m. Rosemary Cowan 1943; two s.; ed. St. Andrews School, Eastbourne, Malvern Coll., Naval Staff Coll. and Imperial Defence Coll.
Royal Navy 26-, Gunnery Officer 33, H.M.S. *Glasgow* 39-40, H.M.S. *Warspite* 40-43; commanded H.M. Gunnery School, Chatham 48-50, 8th Destroyer Flotilla 50-52, H.M.S. *Excellent* 52-54, H.M.S. *Triumph* 55-56, Chief of Staff to C.-in-C. Portsmouth 57-58; Flag Officer Commanding Fifth Cruiser Squadron and Flag Officer, Second-in-Command, Far East Station 58-60; a Lord Commr. of Admiralty and Vice-Chief of Naval Staff 61-63; C.-in-C. British Forces in Far East and U.K. Mil. Adviser to SEATO 63-65; C.-in-C. Portsmouth and Allied C.-in-C. Channel Aug. 65-Feb. 66; Chief of Naval Staff and First Sea Lord Feb. 66-68; Gov. and Commdr.-in-Chief Gibraltar 69-73.
Leisure interests: tennis, fishing, gardening.
Copyhold Cottage, Chilbolton, Stockbridge, Hants., England.
Telephone: Chilbolton 320.

Begin, Menachem, M.J.; Israeli lawyer and politician; b. 16 Aug. 1913, Brest-Litovsk, Russia; s. of Zeev-Dov and Hassia Begin; m. Aliza Arnold; one s. two d.; ed. Mizrachi Hebrew School, Univ. of Warsaw.
Head of Betar Zionist Youth Movement in Poland 39; arrested and held in concentration camp in Siberia 40-41; C.-in-C. of Irgun Zvai Leumi in Israel 42; founded (now Chair.) Herut (Freedom) Movement in Israel 48-; mem. Knesset (Parl.); Minister without Portfolio 67-70; Joint Chair. Likud (Unity) Party 73-.
Publs. *The Revolt: personal memoirs of the Commander of Irgun Zvai Leumi* 49, *The White Nights.*
1 Rosenbaum Street, Tel-Aviv, Israel.

Begmatova, Sakin Begmatovna; Soviet politician; b. 1921; ed. All-Union Financial and Economic Inst.
Teacher 39-41; Deputy People's Commissar for Food Industry of Kirghiz S.S.R. 41-49; Chief of Section, Frunze City Cttee. of Communist Party, Kirghizia 49-52; Deputy Minister of Finance, Kirghiz S.S.R. 52-61; Vice-Chair. Council of Ministers and Minister of Foreign Affairs, Kirghiz S.S.R. 61-; mem. C.P.S.U. 43-; mem. Central Cttee. of C.P., Kirghiz S.S.R.
Council of Ministers of Kirghiz S.S.R., Frunze, U.S.S.R.

Begougne de Juniac, Gontran; French diplomatist; b. 28 July 1908, Limoges; s. of Octave Begoügne de Juniac and Madeleine Desgranges; m. Myriam des Moutis 1959; one s.; ed. Ecole Montalambert, Limoges, Ecole libre des Sciences politiques, Paris, and Univ. de Paris à la Sorbonne.
Deputy Consul 35; Sec. of Embassy, Berlin 36-37, Moscow 37-41; Ministry of Foreign Affairs 41; Sec. of

Embassy, Dublin 45-47; Div. of Cultural Relations, Ministry of Foreign Affairs 47-49, Sec.-Gen. of Four Powers Conf. 49; Counsellor, Washington 49-55; Minister and Minister-Counsellor, London 55-60; Amb. to Ethiopia 60-65, to Turkey 65-70, to Belgium 70-73; Commdr. Légion d'Honneur, etc.
Publs. articles in *Revue des Deux Mondes.*
11 boulevard du Général Koenig, Neuilly/Seine, France.
Telephone: 624-07-06 (Home).

Begtrup, Mrs. Bodil Gertrud; Danish diplomatist; b. 12 Nov. 1903, Nyborg; d. of Judge C. A. and Carla Andreasen; m. 1st Dr. Begtrup 1929, 2nd L. B. Bolt-Jørgensen 1948 (died 1967); one d. (deceased); ed. Københavns Universitet.
Member of Danish delegation to League of Nations 38, and to U.N. 46-52; Film Censor 39-48; Minister to Iceland 49-55, Ambassador 55; Ministry of Foreign Affairs 56; Perm. Rep. Council of Europe 56-59; Ambassador to Switzerland 59-68, and accredited Minister to Austria 59-60; Amb. to Portugal 68-73; mem. board Danish Nat. Council of Women 29, Vice-Pres. 31, Pres. 46-49; Pres. UN Comm. on the Status of Women 46-47, mem. 48-49; Pres. Danish Soc. for the UN 56-59; Dr. Iur. h.c. Smith Coll. Massachusetts.
Leisure interests: politics, literature, flowers.
Strandvejen 16B¹, Copenhagen, Denmark.
Telephone: 01-202480.

Béguin, Bernard, L. ès L.; Swiss journalist; b. 14 Feb. 1923, Sion, Valais; s. of Bernard Béguin and Clemence Welten; m. Antoinette Waelbroeck 1948; two s. two d.; ed. Geneva High School, Geneva Univ. and Graduate Inst. of Int. Studies.
Swiss Sec. World Student Relief 45-46; corresp. at U.N. European Headquarters; *Journal de Genève* 46-70, Foreign Editor 47, Editor-in-Chief 59-70; Diplomatic Commentator, Swiss Broadcasting System 54-59, Swiss T.V. 59-; Head of Programmes, Swiss French-speaking T.V. 70-73, Deputy Dir. 73-; Central Pres. Swiss Press Asscn. 58-60; mem. Federal Comm. on Cartels 64-; mem. Board, Swiss Telegraphic Agency 68-71.
Leisure interests: sailing, camping.
6 avenue de la Gare, 1001 Lausanne; 41 avenue de Budé, 1202 Geneva 1, Switzerland.
Telephone: Lausanne 20 59 11 (Office); 33-75-30 (Home).

Beheiry, Mamoun Ahmed, B.A.; Sudanese banker; b. 3 Oct. 1925, Um Ruaba; s. of Ahmed Abdel Wahab el Beheiry and Um Bashayer Ali Dinar; m. Mamoun Soad 1957; two s. three d.; ed. Victoria Coll., Alexandria and Brasenose Coll., Oxford.
Inspector of Finance 50-52, Senior Insp. 52-54; Joint Sec. Ministry of Finance and Econs. 54-56; Deputy Under-Sec. for External Finance and Devt. 56-58; Dir. representing Minister of Finance and Econs. on the board of several companies 53-59; Chair. Sudan Currency Board 56-58, Nat. Technical Planning Comm. 61-63; Alt. Gov. IMF 57-62, Gov. 62-64; Gov. Central Bank of Sudan 58-63; Minister of Finance and Econs. 63-64; Gov. IBRD, IMF and IFC 63-64; Pres. African Devt. Bank 64-70; Pres. Board of Trustees, Special Fund for Southern Region 72-; mem. Municipal Council of Khartoum 57-62, Council of Univ. of Khartoum 52-63, UN Civil Service Advisory Board 60-62; UN Expert Group on Econ. and Social Consequences of Disarmament 61-62; Chair. Cttee. of Nine, African Devt. Bank; led many delegations abroad.
Leisure interest: lawn tennis.
c/o Special Fund for Southern Region, P.O. Box 778, Khartoum, Sudan.
Telephone: 79410.

Behnia, Abolhassan; Iranian banker; b. 5 Jan. 1910; ed. Univ. of Paris.
Professor, Technical Faculty, Teheran Univ. 42-67; Dir.-Gen. Ministry of Roads and Communications 46-47;

Chair. and Man. Dir. Irrigation Org. 50-55; Minister of Roads and Communications 60; Dir. of Technical Bureau, Plan Org. 61-64; Chair. and Man. Dir. Bank Rahni Iran (Mortgage Bank of Iran) 65-.
Bank Rahni Iran, Ferdowsi Street, Teheran; 41 avenue Heravi, Saltanatabad, Teheran, Iran.
Telephone: 310171-80, 311351-58 (Bank).

Behrens, Sir Leonard Frederick, Kt., C.B.E., J.P., M.COM.; British retired businessman; b. 15 Oct. 1890, Manchester; s. of Gustav Behrens and Fanny Warburg; m. Beatrice Mary Farrow (née Symes) 1920; two d.; ed. Manchester Grammar School, Rugby School and Manchester Univ.
Entered family firm of Sir Jacob Behrens & Sons, Bradford and Manchester 11, Partner 20, Dir. 48, retd. 54; Acting Pres. Liberal Party Sept. 55-Sept. 56, Pres. Sept. 56-57, Chair. Exec. 59-61; Hon. Pres. World Fed. of UN Asscns. (Acting Pres., Stockholm 51, New York 63); Chair. Hallé Concerts Soc. 52-59; Hon. mem. and Deputy Chair. Royal Manchester Coll. of Music; Dir. Emer. Manchester Chamber of Commerce; served with Serbian Relief Fund 15-18; Chair. Manchester Information Cttee. and Lecturer to H.M. Forces 40-45; Royal Observer Corps 41-52; Yugoslav Order of St. Sava, Chinese Order of Brilliant Star.
Leisure interests: music, university, Liberal party, United Nations.
Netherby, 119 Barlow Moor Road, Didsbury, Manchester M20 8TS, England.
Telephone: 061-445-3600.

Beier, Max Walter Peter, DR. PHIL.; Austrian museum curator and professor; b. 6 April 1903, Spittal-Drau, Kärnten; s. of Julius Beier and Marie Beier (née Mitis); m. Irmgard Zeitheim 1931; two s. one d.; ed. Univ. of Vienna.
Natural History Museum, Vienna 27-; Dir. Emer. Zoological Dept.; corresp. mem. Argentine Entomological Soc., Finland Entomological Soc.; Hon. mem. Netherlands Entomological Soc.; Fabricius Medal 66; Dr. h.c. (Innsbruck) 70.
Publs. Over 370 scientific publications.
Naturhistorisches Museum, Zoologische Abteilung, A-1014 Vienna 1, Burgring 7; Home: Proschkogasse 1/10, 1060 Vienna, Austria.
Telephone: 93-27-12, Ext. 267.

Beinecke, William Sperry; American lawyer and business executive; b. 22 May 1914; ed. Phillips Acad., Andover, Westminster School, Connecticut, Yale Univ. and Columbia Univ., New York.
Admitted to New York Bar 41; Assoc. Chadbourne, Wallace, Parke and Whiteside 40-41, 46-48; U.S. Navy 41-45; Partner, Casey, Beinecke and Chase 48-51; Gen. Counsel, The Sperry and Hutchinson Co. 52-54, Gen. Counsel and Vice-Pres. 54-60, Pres. 60-67, now Chair. and Chief Exec. Officer; Dir. of other companies.
Sperry and Hutchinson Building, 330 Madison Avenue, New York, N.Y. 10017, U.S.A.

Beise, S. Clark, B.S.; American banker; b. 13 Oct. 1898, Windom, Minn.; s. of Dr. Henry C. and Blanche (Johnson) Beise; m. Virginia Carter 1934; one s. one d.; ed. Univ. of Minnesota School of Business.
Regimental supply sergeant in First World War; worked with Minneapolis Trust Co. 22-24, with Nat. Bank Examiners Minneapolis Office (covering Ninth Fed. Reserve District) 24-27; with People's Nat. Bank Jackson (Mich.) rising to Vice-Pres. 27-33; Nat. Bank Examiner, Twelfth Fed. Reserve District 33-36; Vice-Pres. Bank of America 36-45, Exec. Vice-Pres. 45-51, Senior Vice-Pres. 51-54, Pres. 54-63, Chair. Exec. Cttee. 63-69, Hon. Dir. 69-; mem. Cttee. for Econ. Devt., Conf. Board; fmr. Dir. Stanford Research Inst., Walt Disney Productions; fmr. Chair. San Francisco Foundation; mem. Business Council, Board Fruehauf Corpn.; Hon. Chair. Golden Gate Chapter, American Red Cross;

mem. Advisory Council, San Francisco Planning and Urban Renewal Asscn.; Hon. LL.D. St. Mary's Coll. of Calif. 60; O.M. Italian Repub. 57.
Office: Bank of America Center, San Francisco, Calif. 94137; Home: 420 El Cerrito Avenue, Hillsborough, Calif. 94010, U.S.A.

Beith, Sir John Greville Stanley, K.C.M.G.; British diplomatist; b. 4 April 1914, London; s. of William Beith and Margaret Stanley; m. Diana Gregory-Hood (née Gilmour); one s. one d.; one step s. one step d.; ed. Eton and King's Coll., Cambridge.
Diplomatic Service 37-, Athens, Buenos Aires, Foreign Office 40-49; Head of U.K. Del. to UN, Geneva 49-53; First Sec. and Head of Chancery, Prague 53-54; Counsellor and Head of Chancery, Paris 54-59; Head of Levant Dept. Foreign Office 59-61, North and East African Dept. 61-63; Amb. to Israel 63-66; Asst. Sec.-Gen. NATO 66-67; Under-Sec. Foreign and Commonwealth Office 67-69; Amb. to Belgium 69-74.
Leisure interests: music, racing, tennis.
Dean Farm House, Sparsholt, Winchester, Hants., England.
Telephone: Sparsholt 326.

Beitz, Berthold; German industrialist; b. 26 Sept. 1913; ed. secondary school.
Bank apprentice; employment in Shell, Hamburg; in charge of the Galician oilfields, Poland 39-44; Deputy Chair. British Zonal Insurance Control Dept. 46; Dir.-Gen. Iduna Germania Insurance Co. 49-53; General-bevollmächtigter Dr. Alfred Krupp von Bohlen und Halbach 53-67; Chair. Board of Curators, Alfried Krupp von Bohlen und Halbach-Stiftung; Chair. Supervisory Board, Fried. Krupp G.m.b.H., Essen; mem. Int. Olympic Cttee. 72; Fed. Cross with Star; Commandorium with Star of Order of Merit (Poland).
Hügel 14, 43 Essen-Bredeney, Federal Republic of Germany.
Telephone: 188-4810.

Béjart, Maurice Jean, (b. Maurice Berger); French dancer, choreographer and stage director; b. 1 Jan. 1927, Marseilles; s. of Gaston Berger; ed. Lycée in Marseilles.
With Marseilles Opera and Royal Opera, Stockholm, before founding Ballet de l'Etoile, Paris 54, Dir. 54-57; Dir., Ballet Théâtre de Paris 57-59; Dir. Ballet du XXe. Siècle, Brussels 59-, Brussels Opera, Théâtre Royal de la Monnaie; Grand Prix de la Musique 70; Chevalier of the Order of Arts and Letters.
Productions include: *Orphée, Le Voyage, Le Sacré du Printemps, Les Noces, Don Juan, Boléro, Symphonie pour un Homme seul, Nijinsky, Clown of God* (ballets); *The Merry Widow, Tales of Hoffmann, Ode à la Joie* (IXe symphonie), *La damnation de Faust, Messe pour le temps présent, Romeo et Juliette, Prospective, Baudelaire, Ni fleurs—ni couronnes, La Tentation de St-Antoine, A la recherche de . . ., Le Marteau sans Maître, La Traviata, Per la Dolce Memoria di quel Giorno* 74, *Ce que L'Amour Me Dit* 74, *Chants d'Amour et de Guerre* 75, *Notre Faust* 75.
Publs. *Mathilde ou le temps perdu* (novel), *La Reine verte* (play).
Théatre royal de la Monnaie, Brussels, Belgium.

Bejm, Tadeusz; Polish politician; b. 27 April 1929, Kuźnica Stara nr. Klobuck; ed. Higher Econ. School, Sopot.
Member of Meat Industry Cen. Board, Katowice; army and navy service 50-53; Polish Ocean Lines, Gdynia 53-58; First Sec. Gdańsk-Portowa District Cttee. Polish United Workers' Party (PZPR) 58-59, Propaganda Sec. Gdańsk Town Cttee. 59-63; Chair. Presidium of Gdańsk Town Nat. Council 63-69; First Sec. Gdańsk Voivod Cttee., PZPR 71-75; Minister of Admin., Local Economy and Environmental Protection 75-76, of Transport March 76-; mem. Cen. Cttee., PZPR 71-;

Knight's Cross, Order of Polonia Restituta 69, Order of Banner of Labour, 2nd Class 74.
Polska Zjednoczona Partia Robotnicza, ul. Nowy Świat 6, 00-497 Warsaw, Poland.

Bel Abbes, Youssef, M.D.; Moroccan physician and politician; b. 15 Aug. 1921; ed. Marrakesh, Medical Coll. of Algiers and Paris.
Joined Public Health Service 49, Dir. several hospitals, then Insp.-Gen. of Health; Minister of Health 58-61, of Health and Educ. 61-62, of Educ. 62-65; Mayor of Marrakesh and Pres. Provincial Council; Amb. to U.A.R. 65-66, to Italy 67-69, to Algeria 69-70; Minister of Foreign Affairs Oct. 70-Aug. 71; Amb. to Spain May-Sept. 72, to France Oct. 72-.
Embassy of Morocco, rue le Tasse 3, Paris 16e, France.

Belafonte, Harry; American singer; b. 1 March 1927, New York; s. of Harold George Belafonte Sr. and Malvene Love Wright; m. 2nd Julie Robinson 1957; one s. three d.; ed. George Washington High School, New York.
In Jamaica 35-39; service with U.S. Navy 43-45; American Negro Theater; student at Manhattan New School for Social Research Dramatic Workshop 46-48; first engagement at the Vanguard, Greenwich Village; European tour 58; Pres. Belafonte Enterprises Inc.; Broadway appearances in *Three For Tonight, Almanac, Belafonte At The Palace,* and in films *Bright Road, Carmen Jones* 52, *Island in the Sun* 57, *The World, the Flesh and the Devil* 58, *Odds Against Tomorrow* 59, *The Angel Levine* (also producer) 69, *Buck and the Preacher* 71; Emmy Television Award for *Tonight with Belafonte* 60; Producer *Strolling —'s* 65, *A Time for Laughter* 67, *Harry and Lena* 70; Hon. D.Hum. (Park Coll., Mo.) 68, Hon. D.Arts, New School of Social Research, N.Y. 68; numerous recordings.
Leisure interests: photography, water skiing, recording.
c/o Mike Merrick Enterprises Inc., 9000 Sunset Boulevard, Los Angeles, Calif. 90069, U.S.A.

Belaúnde Terry, Fernando; Peruvian architect and politician; b. 7 Oct. 1913; ed. France and U.S.A.
Member Chamber of Deputies 45-48; Dean in School of Architecture, Lima 48-56; Leader Popular Action Party (Partido Acción Popular) 56-; Presidential Candidate 56, 62; Pres. of Peru 63-Oct. 68; fled to New York Oct. 68-; lecturing at Harvard Univ. Nov. 68-; returned to Peru briefly Dec. 70, deported at end of month, returned Jan. 76.
Publ. *Peru's Own Conquest* (autobiography).

Belcher, Taylor Garrison; American diplomatist; b. 1 July 1920; ed. Brown Univ., Providence, R.I.
U.S. Navy 42-45; U.S. Foreign Service 45-, Mexico City 45-49, Consul, Glasgow 50-54; International Affairs Officer, Dept. of State 54-57; Consul and Consul-Gen. Nicosia, Cyprus 57-60; Canadian National Defense Coll. 60-61; Dir. Office of West Coast Affairs, Bureau of Inter-American Affairs, Dept. of State 61-64; Amb. to Cyprus 64-69, to Peru 69-74.
Department of State, Washington, D.C. 20520, U.S.A.

Belfrage, Leif Axel Lorentz, LL.D.; Swedish diplomatist; b. 1 Feb. 1910; m. Greta Jering 1937; one s. three d.; ed. Stockholm Univ.
Practised law at Stockholm Magistrates Court 33, subsequently joined Ministry of Commerce; Dir. Swedish Clearing Office 40; Dir. Swedish Trade Comm. 43-45; entered Foreign Office 45, Head of Section in Commercial Dept. 45-46; Commercial Counsellor, Washington 57-60; Head of Commercial Dept., Foreign Office, Stockholm 49-53; Asst. Under-Sec. of State at Foreign Office 53-56, Perm. Under-Sec. of State 56-67; Amb. to U.K. Dec. 67-72; Amb. and Rep. to OECD and UNESCO 72-; Hon. G.B.E. (U.K.).
Délégation de Suède, 19 rue de Franqueville, 75016 Paris, France.
Telephone: 524-9860.

Belgium, King Baudouin I of (*see* Baudouin).

Belgium, Archbishop Primate of (*see* Suenens, Cardinal Joseph).

Belgodère, Paul Louis; French mathematician; b. 25 Feb. 1921, Saint-Denis; m. Madeleine Odette Sarros 1945; two d.; ed. Ecole Normale Supérieure.
Secretary-Gen. Intermédiaire des Recherches Mathématiques 43-49; Technical Assoc. Centre Nat. de la Recherche Scientifique 44-; Sec. Mathematical Soc. of France 46-; Mathematical Librarian, Ecole Normale Supérieure 50-54; Gen. Sec. Inst. Henri Poincaré 54-.
Institut Henri Poincaré, 11 rue Pierre et Marie Curie, F-75231 Paris Cedex 05, France.
Telephone: (1) 033-42-10.

Belichenko, Albert Nikolaevich; Soviet economist and banker; b. 2 July 1931, Dnepropetrovsk; ed. Moscow Financial Institute.
Deputy Man. Dir. Econ. and Foreign Exchange Dept., State Bank of the U.S.S.R. 64-66; Chair. of Board, Wozchod Handelsbank A.G., Zürich 66-72; First Deputy Chair. Bank for Foreign Trade of the U.S.S.R. 72-75; Chair. of Board, Int. Investment Bank, Moscow July 75-.
International Investment Bank, 17 Presnensky Val, Moscow, D-22, U.S.S.R.
Telephone: 252-30-22.

Belin, Roger, D.IUR.; French civil servant; b. 21 March 1916; m. Christiane Bressac 1961; ed. Univ. of Paris Law Faculty, Paris School of Political Sciences.
Auditeur Conseil d'Etat 43; Chargé de Mission, Présidence du Conseil 44; Maître des Requêtes, Conseil d'Etat 49; mem. Atomic Energy Cttee. 51; Dir. Présidence du Conseil 55; Sec.-Gen. of the Government 58-; Pres. Régie autonome des transports parisiens 64-; Conseiller d'Etat 65-; Pres. Union Int. des Transports Publics 73; Officier Légion d'Honneur.
9 boulevard Flandrin, Paris 16e, France.

Beliy, Victor Arkadyevich; Soviet composer; b. 14 Jan. 1904, Berdichev, Ukraine; ed. Moscow Conservatoire.
Member Board of U.S.S.R. Composers' Union; State Prize 52, Honoured Artist of Byelorussian S.S.R. 55, Honoured Worker of the Arts of R.S.F.S.R. 56; Order of Red Banner of Labour 47; Badge of Honour 64.
Principal compositions: Instrumental works: Lyric Sonatina 29, Sonata for Piano 41, Sonata for Piano No. 4 46, Sixteen Preludes on Folk Themes of the U.S.S.R. 47, Two Pieces for Piano on Byelorussian Themes 50, Sonata for Violin and Piano 53; Works for Voice and Piano: *26 Works* 26, *War Cycle* (words by E. Toller) 29, *Ten Chuvash Songs* 33, *Leavetaking* 35, *Song of the Partisan Girl* 35, *The Little Airman* 35, *Winter Road* 36, *Sea Songs* 39, *Ballade of Captain Gastello* 41, *Lenin's Birthday* 49; Choral works: *Hunger March* 30, Suite on Chuvash Themes 36, Two Fragments from the poem *V. I. Lenin* 38, *Three Roads* 39, *Slav Suite* 42, Two Choral Works on Russian Folk Themes 45; Songs: *Workers of All Lands Unite* 30, *Song of the 30th Division* 33, *Eaglet* 36, *Song of the Brave* 41, *Boldly, Red Navymen* 41, *October Song* 49, *In Defence of Peace* 49.
Composers' Union of the U.S.S.R., 8-10 Ulitsa Nezhdanovoi, Moscow, U.S.S.R.

Bell, Bernard R.; American international finance official; ed. Univs. of Pennsylvania and Paris.
Vice-President, later Chair. of Board, Surveys Research Inc. (consulting firm) 59-65; Transportation Adviser, World Bank Mission in Colombia 62; Dir. economic work, Indian Coal Transport Study 63-64; Chief, Mission to India 64; joined World Bank 65, later Asst. Dir. Economics, Projects Dept.; Deputy Dir., Projects Dept., IBRD 67; Dir. Resident Staff, Indonesia 68; Regional Vice-Pres. Eastern Africa 72; Regional Vice-Pres. East Asia and the Pacific 74.

c/o International Bank for Reconstruction and Development, Washington, D.C. 20433, U.S.A.

Bell, David Elliott; American economist; b. 20 Jan. 1919; ed. Pomona Coll., and Harvard Univ.
Joined Budget Bureau 39; served U.S. Marine Corps, Second World War; Budget Bureau 45-47; Asst. in White House 47-51; Admin. Asst. to Pres. Truman 51; Head, Stevenson's Research Staff, Pres. Election Campaign 52; Head, Littauer Center Economic Mission to Pakistan 54-57; Lecturer in Economics, Littauer Center (Harvard Graduate School of Public Admin.) 57, Sec. (Chief Admin. Officer) 59-61; Dir. U.S. Budget Bureau 61-62; Administrator, Agency for Int. Devt. 62-66; Vice-Pres. (Int. Activities), Ford Foundation 66-69, Exec. Vice-Pres. 69-.
Publ. *Allocating Development Resources: Some Observations Based on Pakistan Experience* 59.
Ford Foundation, 320 East 43rd Street, New York, N.Y. 10017, U.S.A.

Bell, Elliott Vallance, A.B.; American publisher; b. 25 Sept. 1902; ed. Columbia University.
Financial writer *N.Y. Herald-Tribune* 29, *New York Times* 29-39; First Pres. N.Y. Financial Writers' Asscn. 38-39; economic adviser to Thomas E. Dewey 39-40; research consultant to Wendell Wilkie 40; mem. Editorial Board *New York Times* 41-42; Supt. of Banks New York State 43-49; Chair. Exec. Cttee. McGraw-Hill Inc. 50-67; Editor and Publr. *Business Week* 51-64; Dir. Carrier Corpn., etc.; Trustee Emer., Council on Foreign Relations; Trustee, R. W. Strauss Memorial Foundation; Hon. LL.D. Bard Coll., St. Lawrence Univ., Hon. D.C.S. Pace Coll.
Publ. *We Saw It Happen* (with other correspondents *New York Times*) 38.
Office: 200 E. 66th Street, New York, N.Y. 10021; Home: Quaker Hill, Pawling, N.Y. 12564, U.S.A.

Bell, Sir Gawain (Westray), K.C.M.G., C.B.E., M.B.E. (MIL.); British administrator; b. 21 Jan. 1909, Cape Town, South Africa; s. of William W. Bell and Emily H. Bell; m. Silvia Cornwell-Clyne 1945; three d.; ed. Winchester Coll. and Hertford Coll., Oxford.
Sudan Political Service 31; seconded to Govt. of Palestine 38; Military Service, Middle East 41-45, Lt.-Col. Arab Legion 42-45; District Commr., Kordofan 45-49; Deputy Sudan Agent, Cairo 49-51; Deputy Civil Sec. Sudan Govt. 53-54; Perm. Under-Sec. Ministry of Interior 54-55; H.M. Political Agent, Kuwait 55-57; Gov., Northern Region of Nigeria 57-62; Sec.-Gen. Council for Middle East Trade 63-64; Joint Constitutional Adviser to Govt. of Fed. of South Arabia 65-66; Sec.-Gen. South Pacific Comm. 66-69; Chair. British Leprosy Relief Asscn. 71; mem. Gov. Body, School of Oriental and African Studies, Univ. of London 70-75; mem. Civil Service Selection Board 72-; K.St.J. 58; Order of Independence 3rd Class (Trans Jordan); mem. Chapter Gen. St. John of Jerusalem.
Leisure interests: walking, riding, rifle-shooting, skiing, military history.
Hidcote Bartrim Manor, Chipping Campden, Glos., England.
Telephone: Mickleton 305.

Bell, George Douglas Hutton, C.B.E., PH.D., F.R.S.; British agricultural scientist; b. 18 Oct. 1905, Swansea; s. of George H. Bell and Lilian M. Hutton; m. Eileen G. Wright 1934; two d.; ed. Bishop Gore's School, Swansea, Univ. Coll. of N. Wales, and Univ. of Cambridge.
Research Officer, Plant Breeding Inst. 31, Univ. Demonstrator, Cambridge 33, Lecturer 44; Fellow, Selwyn Coll., Cambridge 44-54, Hon. Fellow 65; Dir. Plant Breeding Inst., Cambridge 47-71; Research Medal, Royal Agric. Soc. of England 56; Mullard Medal, Royal Soc. 67; Hon. D.Sc. (Univs. of Reading, Wales and Liverpool); Massey Ferguson Nat. Award 73.

Leisure interests: music, theatre, natural history, sport, gardening.
Publs. *Cultivated Plants of the Farm* 48, *The Breeding of Barley Varieties in Barley and Malt* 62, *Cereal Breeding* in *Vistas in Botany* Vol. II 63, *Phylogeny of Temperate Cereals in Crop Plant Evolution* 65; papers on barley and breeding in *Journal of Agricultural Science*, etc.
6 Worts Causeway, Cambridge, England.
Telephone: 0223-47449.

Bell, Sir (George) Raymond, K.C.M.G., C.B.; British financial official; b. 13 March 1916; m. Joan Elizabeth Coltham 1944; four c.; ed. Bradford Grammar School, St. John's Coll., Cambridge.
Entered Civil Service, Asst. Principal 38; Ministry of Health 38; H.M. Treasury 39; war service Royal Navy, Lieut. R.N.V.R. 41-44; Principal, Civil Service 45, Sec. (Finance), Office of High Commr. in Canada 45-48; Asst. Sec. 51; Counsellor, U.K. Perm. Del. to OEEC/NATO, Paris 53-56; Principal Private Sec. to Chancellor of Exchequer 58-60; Under-Sec. 60; mem. U.K. Del. to Brussels Conf. 61-62, 70-72, Deputy Sec. 66; Deputy Sec. H.M. Treasury 66-72; Vice-Chair. European Investment Bank 73-.
Leisure interests: music, reading, travel.
European Investment Bank, 2 place de Metz, Luxembourg; Home: 24 rue de Bragance, Luxembourg; and Laburnum Cottage, Acton, Sudbury, Suffolk, England.
Telephone: 43-50-11 (Office); 23-515 (Luxembourg); Sudbury 77147 (Home).

Bell, James Dunbar, PH.D.; American fmr. diplomatist; b. 1 July 1911, Lebanon, New Hampshire; s. of Frank U. Bell and Louise Dunbar; m. Stephanie Ann Mathews 1961; three s. two d.; ed. Univs. of Chicago and New Mexico.
Reporter *Albuquerque Journal*, New Mexico 33-34; Chief Statistician, New Mexico Dept. of Public Welfare 36-37; Instructor Gary Coll. 39-41; Analyst, Office of Co-ordinator, Inter-American Affairs 41-42; Special Asst., Dept. of Justice 43-44; Prof. Hamilton Coll. 46-47; Dept. of State 44-70, Bogotá, Santiago, Manila 44-52; Officer-in-Charge, Philippine Affairs, Washington 53-54; Deputy Dir. Philippine and Southeast Asian Affairs 54-55; Dir. Office of Southwest Pacific Affairs 56-57, 60-64; Deputy Chief of Mission and Counsellor, Jakarta 57-59; Amb. to Malaysia 64-69; Lecturer Merrill Coll., Univ. of Calif., Santa Cruz 70-71; Acting Dir. Center for South Pacific Studies, Univ. of Calif., Santa Cruz 73-74; Fellow of Merrill Coll. 69-.
Leisure interests: golf, politics.
9 South Circle Drive, Santa Cruz, Calif. 95060, U.S.A.
Telephone: 408-423-5812.

Bell, John Alexander Gordon; Canadian business executive; b. 16 Aug. 1929, Rivers, Manitoba; s. of John Edwin Bell, D.D. and Mary MacDonald (McIlraith) Bell; m. Charlene Elizabeth McCabe 1959; one s. one d.; ed. primary and secondary schools in Man. and Ont.
With The Bank of Nova Scotia 48-; at Queen and Church Branch, Toronto 48; at Gen. Office on Inspection Staff 53; Special Rep., London 55; Man., West End, London 57, Asst. Man. Toronto Branch 59, Man., Halifax 62, Ottawa 64, Kingston, Jamaica 65, Asst. Gen. Man. Kingston 66, Man. Dir. 67, Gen. Man. Metropolitan Toronto Region 68, Deputy Chief Gen. Man. 69, Exec. Vice-Pres. and Chief Gen. Man. 72-.
The Bank of Nova Scotia, 44 King Street W., Toronto, Ontario, Canada.
Telephone: 866-6125.

Bell, Marie (*pseudonym of* Marie Bellon); French actress; b. 23 Dec. 1905; ed. Lycée de Bordeaux, Bordeaux and Paris Conservatoires.
Pensionnaire and later Sociétaire, Comédie Française 21-53; founded own company La Compagnie Marie Bell 53; Dir. Théâtre du Gymnase 59-; principal theatre

roles in *Phèdre, Le Misanthrope, Cyrano de Bergerac, Ruy Blas,* etc.; produced and acted in *Madame Princesse* 65-66; films include *Carnet de Bal* and *Le colonel Chabert*; Officier Légion d'Honneur.
32 avenue des Champs-Elysées, Paris 8e, France.

Bell, Robert Edward, C.C., M.A., PH.D., F.R.S., F.R.S.C.; Canadian professor of physics; b. 29 Nov. 1918, England; *s.* of Edward R. Bell and Edith E. Rich; *m.* Jeanne Atkinson 1947; one *d.*; ed. elementary and high school, Ladner, B.C., Univ. of British Columbia and McGill Univ.
Physicist, Nat. Research Council of Canada, Ottawa 41-45; Physicist, Chalk River Nuclear Labs. 46-56, on loan to McGill Univ. 52-56; Assoc. Prof. of Physics, McGill Univ. 56-60, Rutherford Prof. and Dir. Foster Radiation Lab. 60-69, Dean of Graduate Studies and Research 69-70; Principal and Vice-Chancellor, McGill Univ. 70-; Canadian Centennial Medal 67, Medal for Achievement in Physics, Canadian Asscn. of Physicists 68; Companion of the Order, Canada 71.
Leisure interests: reading, amateur carpentry.
Publs. over 50 articles in scientific journals and contributions to books.
McGill University, P.O. Box 6070, Station A, Montreal, Quebec H3C 3G1; Home: 363 Olivier Avenue, Montreal, Quebec H3Z 2C8, Canada.
Telephone: 514-392-5347; 514-935-3769.

Bell, Ronald Percy, M.A., LL.D., D.SC., D.TECH., F.R.S., F.R.S.E., F.R.I.C.; British professor of chemistry; b. 24 Nov. 1907, Maidenhead, Berks.; *s.* of Edwin Alfred Bell and Beatrice Annie Ash; *m.* Margery Mary West 1931; one *s.*; ed. Maidenhead County Boys' School and Balliol Coll., Oxford.
Fellow, Balliol Coll., Oxford 33-67, Vice-Master 65-66, Hon. Fellow 67; Univ. Reader in Physical Chemistry, Oxford 55-66; Prof. of Chemistry, Univ. of Stirling, Scotland 67-; Chemical Soc. Liversidge Lecturer 73-74; Spiers Memorial Lecturer 75; Foreign mem. Royal Danish Acad. of Arts and Sciences 62; Foreign Assoc. U.S. Nat. Acad. of Sciences 72-; Hon. LL.D., Ill. Inst. of Technology 64, Hon. D.Tech., Technical Univ. of Denmark 69; Hon. D.Sc., Univ. of Kent; Meldola Medal 36.
Leisure interests: music, hill-walking.
Publs. *Acid-Base Catalysis* 41, *Acids and Bases* 52 (2nd edn. 69), *The Proton in Chemistry* 59 (2nd edn. 73).
Chemistry Department, University of Stirling, Stirling; Home: 6 Victoria Square, Stirling, Scotland.
Telephone: Stirling 3171 (Office); Stirling 3502 (Home).

Bellanger, Claude; French journalists; b. 2 April 1910. Secretary-General, Ligue Française de l'Enseignement 36-39; Dir. Centre d'Entraide aux Etudiants Prisonniers 40-44; active with resistance and clandestine press 40-44; now Dir.-Gen. of *Le Parisien libéré*; Hon. Pres. Syndicat de la Presse Parisienne; Vice-Pres. Féd. Nationale de la Presse Française; Pres. Féd. Int. des Editeurs de Journaux; Vice-Pres. l'Institut Français de Presse, Conseil d'Administration de L'Agence France-Presse; mem. Admin. Council *Courrier de L'Ouest* (Angers), *Maine Libre* (Le Mans); Commdr. de la Légion d'Honneur, Médaille de la Résistance, Croix de Guerre, etc.
Publs. *Vers la Guerre ou Vers La Paix* 36, *Nouvelles Chroniques Interdites, Les Bannis* 44, *Poètes Prisonniers* 44, *La Presse des Barbelés* 51, *Presse Clandestine 1940-1944* 61, *Les débuts d'Emile Zola dans la presse* 64, co-direction *Histoire Générale de la Presse Française* (5 vols.) 69-76.
25 avenue Michelet, 93400 Saint Ouen, France.

Bellmon, Henry, B.S.; American farmer and politician; b. 3 Sept. 1921; ed. Oklahoma State Univ.
U.S. Marine Corps 42-46; mem. Oklahoma Legislature 46-48; Farmer 45-; State Chair. Republican Party

60-62; Gov. of Oklahoma 63-67; Chair. Nixon for President Cttee. 68; Senator from Okla. 69-.
125 Russell Building, Washington, D.C. 20510; and Route One, Red Rock, Oklahoma, U.S.A.

Bellow, Saul, B.S.; American writer; b. 10 June 1915, Montreal, Canada; ed. Northwestern Univ.
Professor, Univ. of Minn. 46-48; Prof. Princeton Univ. 52-53; Prof. Univ. of Chicago 64-; Nat. Book Award, Inst. of Arts and Letters 53, Ford Foundation Grant 59, Prix Int. de Littérature 65, U.S. Nat. Book Award for *Mr. Sammler's Planet* 71; Fellow American Acad. of Arts and Sciences.
Publs. include contributions to numerous magazines and journals; also *Dangling Man* 44, *The Victim* 47, *The Adventures of Augie March* 53, *Seize the Day* 56, *Henderson the Rain King* 59, *Great Jewish Short Stories* 63, *Herzog* 64, *The Last Analysis* 64, *Mosby's Memoirs and Other Stories* 68, *Mr. Sammler's Planet* 69, *Humboldt's Gift* 75.
University of Chicago, 1126 East 59th Street, Chicago, Ill. 60637, U.S.A.

Belluschi, Pietro, DOTT.ING.; American architect; b. 18 Aug. 1899, Ancona, Italy; *s.* of Guido Belluschi and Camilla Dogliani; *m.* 1st Helen Hemila 1934 (deceased), 2nd Marjorie Bruckner 1965; two *s.*; ed. Univ. of Rome and Cornell Univ.
Draftsman for A. E. Doyle, Architect, Portland, Ore. 25-28; chief designer A. E. Doyle & Assoc. 28-33, partner 33-43; own architectural practice 43-; Dean, School of Architecture and Planning, Mass. Inst. of Technology 51-65; Fellow, American Acad. of Arts and Sciences, Royal Acad. of Fine Arts, Copenhagen; mem. Nat. Acad. of Design; life mem. Nat. Inst. of Arts and Letters; Gold Medal, Italian Charitable Soc.; Commendatore della Repubblica Italiana; Gold Medal, American Inst. of Architects 72; numerous honorary degrees and other distinctions.
Principal works: Portland Art Museum, Equitable Building, Oregonian Publishing Plant (all Portland, Ore.); Library for Bennington Coll., Vt. 59; Juilliard School, Lincoln Center for the Performing Arts, N.Y. City 69; Bank of America World Headquarters Building (San Francisco); many churches and temples in U.S.A.
700 N.W. Rapidan Terrace, Portland, Ore. 97210, U.S.A.

Belmondo, Jean-Paul; French actor; b. 9 April 1933, Paris; *s.* of Paul Belmondo (*q.v.*); *m.* 1952, divorced 1967; one *s.* two *d.*; ed. Ecole Alsacienne, Paris, Cours Pascal and Conservatoire national d'art dramatique.
Started career on the stage; mainly film actor since 57; Pres. French Union of Actors 63-66.
Plays acted in include: *L'Hôtel du Libre-Echange, Oscar, Trésor-Party, Médée, La mégère apprivoisée*; Films acted in include: *Sois belle et tais-toi, A pied, à cheval et en voiture, Les Tricheurs, Charlotte et son Jules, Drôle de dimanche* 58, *Les Copains du dimanche, Mademoiselle Ange, A double tour, Classe tous risques, Au bout de souffle, L'Amour, La Novice, La Ciociara, Moderato Cantabile, Léon Morin Prêtre, Le Doulos* 62, *Dragées au poivre, L'Aîné des Ferchaux, Peau de banane, 100,000 dollars au soleil* 63, *Two Women, The Man From Rio, Echappement libre* 64, *Les tribulations d'un Chinois en Chine, Pierrot le Fou* 65, *Paris, brûlet-il?* 66, *Le Voleur* 66, *Casino Royale* 67, *The Brain* 69, *La Sirène du Mississippi* 69, *Un Homme qui me plaît* 70, *Borsalino* 70, *The Burglars* 72, *La Scoumoune* 72, *L'Héritier* 72, *Le Magnifique* 73, *Stavisky* 74, *Peur sue la Ville* 75.
Publ. *30 Ans et 25 Films* (autobiog.) 63.
Art Media, 37 rue Marbeuf, Paris 8e, France.

Belmondo, Paul; French sculptor; b. 8 Aug. 1898, Algiers; *s.* of Paul Belmondo and Rose Cerrito; *m.* Sarah M. Rainaud 1931; two *s.* (Jean-Paul Belmondo, *q.v.*) one *d.*; ed. Algeria and Ecole des Beaux-Arts.

Teacher, Ecole Nationale Supérieure des Beaux-Arts, Paris 53-; Pres. Inst. de France 70-71, Acad. des Beaux-Arts 70; Officier de la Légion d'Honneur; Commdr. des Arts et Lettres; Officier de l'Ordre de Léopold; Prix de l'Afrique du Nord; Prix Blumenthal 25; Prix des Beaux Arts, Paris 56; Médaille de Vermeil, Paris.
Works include: busts of Vlaminck, Clostermann, Maurice Genevoix and the Shah of Persia; reliefs, statues and works in the Musée National d'Art Moderne and Musée National d'Alger.
77 avenue Denfert Rochereau, Paris 75014, France.

Beloff, Max, M.A., D.LITT., F.R.HIST.S., F.B.A., F.R.S.A.; British historian; b. 2 July 1913, London; s. of S. and M. Beloff; m. Helen Dobrin 1938; two s.; ed. St. Paul's School and Corpus Christi Coll. and Magdalen Coll., Oxford.
Asst. Lecturer in History, Manchester Univ. 39-46; Nuffield Reader in Comparative Study of Institutions, Oxford Univ. 46-56; Fellow of Nuffield Coll. 47-57; Gladstone Prof. of Govt. and Public Admin. Univ. of Oxford and Fellow of All Souls Coll. 57-74; Principal, Univ. Coll. at Buckingham 74-; Fellow of St. Anthony's Coll., Oxford; Hon. D.C.L. (Bishop's Univ.); Hon. LL.D. (Univ. of Pittsburgh).
Publs. *Public Order and Popular Disturbances 1660-1714* 38, *The Foreign Policy of Soviet Russia 47-49, Thomas Jefferson and American Democracy 48, Soviet Policy in the Far East 1944-51 53, The Age of Absolutism 1660-1815 54, Foreign Policy and the Democratic Process 55, Europe and the Europeans 57, The Great Powers 59, The American Federal Government 59, New Dimensions in Foreign Policy 61, The United States and the Unity of Europe 63, Europe du XIX et XX Siècle 60-66 (Joint Editor), The Balance of Power 68, The Future of British Foreign Policy 69, Imperial Sunset, Vol. I 69, The Intellectual in Politics 70.*
Leisure interests: cricket, opera.
University College at Buckingham, Buckingham, England.
Telephone: Buckingham 4161.

Belokurov, Vladimir Vyacheslavovich; Soviet actor; b. 8 July 1904; ed. A. M. Gorky Higher Inst. of Public Education, Kazan.
Pevsov Company, Kazan 18-19; Kazan Theatre 19-23; Moscow Theatre of Revolution 24-36; Moscow Art Theatre Company 36-; has starred in films 32-; mem. All-Russian Theatrical Soc.; People's Artist of U.S.S.R.; State Prize; Order of Red Banner of Labour and medals.
Principal Roles: Kostylev (*Lower Depths,* Gorky), Yasha (*Cherry Orchard,* Chekhov), Kudryash (*The Storm,* Ostrovsky), Belogubov (*A Lucrative Post,* Ostrovsky), Mercutio (*Romeo and Juliet,* Shakespeare), Chichikov (*Dead Souls,* Gogol), Molchalin (*Woe from Wit,* Gribyedov), Grigory (*Fruits of Enlightenment,* Tolstoy), Alesha (*Land,* Virta), Veretennikov (*Officer of the Fleet,* Kron), Gvozdilin (*Third Pathétique,* Pogodin), Gavriil Nechai (*Over the Dnieper,* Kornei-chuk).
Moscow Art Theatre, 3 Proyezd Khudozhestvennogo Teatra, Moscow, U.S.S.R.

Belous, Nikolai Andreevich; Soviet diplomatist; b. 27 Oct. 1913, Dubovye Makharintsy Village, Vinnitsa Region; ed. Moscow Machine Building Inst.
Joined Diplomatic Service 45; Second, then First Sec. Soviet Embassy, Argentina 49-54; First Sec., Dept. of American Countries, Ministry of Foreign Affairs 55-57; Counsellor, Soviet Embassy, Argentina 57-59; Counsellor, Ministry of Foreign Affairs 59-61; Counsellor-envoy, Soviet Embassy, Cuba 61-65; Deputy Head, Latin American Countries Dept., Ministry of Foreign Affairs 65-68; Amb. to Colombia 68-71; staff, Ministry of Foreign Affairs 71-; Badge of Honour.
Ministry of Foreign Affairs, 32-34 Smolenskaya-Sennaya Ploshchad, Moscow, U.S.S.R.

Belousov, Vladimir Vladimirovich, D.SC.; Soviet geologist; b. 30 Oct. 1907, Moscow; s. of Vladimir and Xenia Belousov; m. Natalia Gourvitch 1931; one s.; ed. Moscow Univ.
Consultant, Council for Research of Productive Resources under U.S.S.R. Acad. of Sciences 31-32; geologist, Central Research Inst. of Prospecting 32-38; Senior Scientific Assoc., U.S.S.R. Acad. of Sciences 38-44; Head of Dept., Moscow Inst. for Prospecting 42-49; Prof. 40; Head of Geology Dept., Inst. of Physics of the Earth of U.S.S.R. Acad. of Sciences 44-; Vice-Chair. Technical Council, U.S.S.R. Ministry of Geology 47-56; Prof., Moscow Univ. 53-; Corresp. mem. U.S.S.R. Acad. of Sciences 53-; Vice-Chair. Int. Geophysics Cttee. 60-64; Pres. Int. Cttee. for Upper Mantle of the Earth Projects 64-70; mem. Swedish and N.Y. Acads. of Sciences; Hon. mem. Geological Socs. of U.S.A., France and U.K.
Leisure interests: skiing, tourism.
Publs. *Basic Problems in Geotectonics 62, Crust and Upper Mantle of Continents 66, Crust and Upper Mantle of Oceans 68, Principles of Geotectonics 75,* and several articles in professional journals; principal work in problems of structure and development of the Earth's crust, relationship between deep and geological processes, tectonophysics.
Soviet Geophysical Committee, Molodejnaia 3, Moscow 296, U.S.S.R.

Belov, Nicolai Vassilevich; Soviet crystallographer; b. 14 Dec. 1891, Yanov, Poland; s. of Vassili Vassilevich and Olga Andreevna; m. Alexandra Grigorevna (Ivanova); two d.; ed. St. Petersburg Polytechnic Inst.
Head, X-ray Dept., Inst. of Crystallography of U.S.S.R. Acad. of Sciences 38-; Prof. of Crystallography, Gorky Univ. 46-, Moscow Univ. 53-; Vice-Pres. Int. Union of Crystallography 57-63, Pres. 66-69; Pres. Nat. Comm. of Soviet Crystallographers; Corresp. mem. U.S.S.R. Acad. of Sciences 46-53, mem. 53-; Hon. mem. of Mineral Socs. of U.S.S.R., U.S.A., France, U.K.; Fedorov Prize 47, State Prize 52, Order of Red Banner, of Labour 53, Order of Lenin (three times), Lomonosov Medal 66, Hero of Socialist Labour 69, Lenin Prize 74.
Leisure interest: swimming.
Publs. *Structure of Ionic Crystals 47, Structural Crystallography 51, A Classroom Method of Deriving 230 Space Groups of Symmetry 51, 1651 Schubnikov Groups 56, Crystal Chemistry of Silicates with Large Cations 61, Mineralogy—Periodic System 75, Essays in Structural Mineralogy 1949-1975* (176 pieces), *Systematic Analysis of Patterson Function Starting from Crystal Symmetry* 74.
Institute of Crystallography, Academy of Sciences of U.S.S.R., 59 Leninsky Prospekt, Moscow, U.S.S.R.

Belsky, Igor Dmitrievich; Soviet choreographer; b. 28 March 1925; ed. Leningrad Ballet School.
Dancer with Leningrad Kirov Theatre of Opera and Ballet 43-62; Teacher of folk character dance at Leningrad Choreography School 46-; Producer and Choreographer, Leningrad Kirov Theatre of Opera and Ballet 59-62, Chief Choreographer 62-; People's Artist of the R.S.F.S.R.
Principal roles: Rotbart (*Swan Lake*), Nurali (*Fountain of Bakhchiserai*), Tybalt (*Romeo and Juliet*), Shurale (Yarushllin's *Shurale*), Severyan (Prokofiev's *Stone Flower*), Mako (Karayev's *Thunder Road*).
Chief productions: *Shores of Hope* (Petrov) 59, *Leningrad Symphony* (Shostakovich) 61, *Humpbacked Horse* (Shchedrin) 63.
Leningrad Kirov Theatre of Opera and Ballet, Ploshchad Iskusstv 1, Leningrad, U.S.S.R.

Beltrán, Pedro Gerardo; Peruvian newspaper publisher; b. 1897, Lima; m. Miriam Kropp 1950.
Former Pres. Nat. Agricultural Soc.; fmr. Chair. of Board, Central Reserve Bank of Peru; Peruvian Amb.

to Washington 44-45; mem. Advisory Board of Int. Bank for Reconstruction and Devt. 48-50; Peruvian del. to Econ., Financial and other Int. Confs. (Bretton Woods 44, Inter-American, Mexico 45, UN, San Francisco 45, etc.); Prime Minister and Minister of Finance 59-61; headed the political Alianza Nacional in Peru; Publisher of morning daily *La Prensa*, Lima 50-72; Hon. LL.D. Yale, Harvard and California Univs.; Grand Officier de la Légion d'Honneur; Hon. Fellow, London School of Economics and Political Science 60-.
Apartado 485, Lima, Peru.
Telephone: 28-3140.

Beltrán, Washington; Uruguayan newspaper executive and politician; b. 1914; ed. Universidad de la República, Montevideo.
Joined *El País* 39, Sub-Dir. 49-61, Co-Dir. 61-; mem. House of Representatives 46; founded Reconstrucción Blanca group 54, and Unión Blanca Democrática group within National Party 50; Senator 50-; Nat. Counsellor of Govt. 62-65; Pres. of National Council of Govt. 65-66.
c/o Ministerio de Asuntos Exteriores, Montevideo, Uruguay.

Beltrão, Alexandre Fontana; Brazilian coffee executive; b. 28 April 1924, Curitiba, Paraná; s. of Alexandre Beltrão and late Zilda Fontana Beltrão; m. Anna Emilia Beltrão 1964; two c.; ed. Instituto Santa Maria, Curitiba, Univ. of São Paulo, Escola Nacional de Engenharia, Rio de Janeiro.
Assistant engineer 44; army officer 45-46; asst. engineer, Dept. of Soil Mechanics, Inst. de Pesquisas Tecnologicas, São Paulo 48; trained in regional planning at Inst. Nat. d'Aerophotogrametrie, Ministère de la Reconstruction, Paris and at Ministry of Works, London 50-51; founder and Dir. of SPL (Planning Services Ltd.) 54-; observer, Govt. of State of Paraná to UN Int. Coffee Conf. 62; special adviser to Pres. Brazilian Coffee Inst. 64; Chief Brazilian Coffee Inst. Bureau, N.Y. 65-67; Pres. World Coffee Promotion Cttee. of Int. Coffee Org. 65-67; Exec. Dir. Int. Coffee Org. May 68-; Commdr. Order of Rio Branco.
Publs. *Paraná and the Coffee Economy* 63, essay on Economy of States of Paraná, Pará and Ceará (Brazil) 58.
International Coffee Organization, 22 Berners Street, London, W.1, England.
Telephone: 01-580-8595 (London); 267-2895 (Rio).

Beltrão, Hélio Marcos Penna; Brazilian lawyer and economist; b. 15 Oct. 1916, Rio de Janeiro; s. of Heitor and Christina Penna Beltrão; m. Maria Coutinho Beltrão 1966; one s. two d.; ed. Faculdade Nacional de Direito and New York Univ.
Director and Pres. of Social Security Agency (IPASE-IAPI) 41-46; Pres. Brazilian Petroleum Inst. 54-56; Dir. of Petrobrás S.A. (Govt. Oil Co.) 54-56; Sec. of Planning, State of Guanabara 60-61; mem. Board Nat. Bank for Econ. Devt. 61-62, 72, Nat. Housing Bank 65-, Itaipu Binacional 74-; mem. Cttee. on Fed. Admin. Reorganization 64-67; Minister of Planning and Gen. Co-ordination March 67-Oct. 69; Dir. and Vice-Pres. Mesbla S.A. (chain of dept. stores), Rio de Janeiro 62-71; Pres. Ultra Group of Companies 69-; Dir. and Vice-Pres. Paraiso Cement Co. 70-73; Pres. Brazilian Acad. of Science and Admin. 75-; Fellow, Int. Acad. of Management 71-.
Leisure interest: popular music.
Office: Avenida Graça Aranha, 206-12° andar, Rio de Janeiro; Home; Rua Prudente de Moraes, 1179 Penthouse Ipanema, Rio de Janeiro, Brazil.

Belukha, Nikolai Andreyevich; Soviet politician; b. 16 Oct. 1920, Poltava, Ukraine; ed. Moscow Bauman Higher Technical School.
Design Engineer, Chelyabinsk factory and research inst. in Leningrad 45-48; Party Official 48-63; Second

Sec., Central Cttee., Communist Party of Latvia 63-; mem. Bureau, Central Cttee., C.P. of Latvia; mem. Central Auditing Comm. of C.P.S.U. 66-71, Alternate mem. Central Cttee. 71-; Deputy Supreme Soviet of U.S.S.R. 62-; mem. Comm. for Problems of Youth, Soviet of Nationalities; mem. C.P.S.U. 48-.
Central Committee, Communist Party of Latvia, Riga, U.S.S.R.

Belyaev, Spartak Timofeevich, DR.SC.; Soviet physicist; b. 27 Oct. 1923, Moscow; ed. Moscow State Univ. Junior research worker, senior research worker, Head of Laboratory, I. Kurchatov Inst. of Nuclear Physics; Siberian Dept., Acad. of Sciences 62-; Prof., Rector, Novosibirsk State Univ. 65-; Corresp. mem. U.S.S.R. Acad of Sciences 64-68, Academician 68-; mem. C.P.S.U. 43-; Order of Lenin, Red Star, Order of October Revolution and medals.
Publs. Scientific works in field of theory of atomic nucleus, particle movement in cyclotron, physics of relativistic plasma, statistic physics of quantum, many body systems.
Akademgorodok, Novosibirsk, U.S.S.R.

Ben-Aharon, Yitzhak; Israeli administrator; b. 1906, Bukovina, Austria; ed. Berlin High School for Political Science and Econs.
Went to Palestine 28; founder of Kibbutz Givat Hayim; Sec. Tel-Aviv Labour Council 38-39; Lieut., British Army, Second World War; prisoner-of-war 41-45; mem. Knesset 49-62; Minister of Transport 59-62; mem. Knesset 69-; Sec.-Gen. Histradut 69-73.
Publs. *Listen Gentile, Michtavim Leuni, Bepheta Temura*.
Kibbutz Givat Hayim (Meyuhad), Doar Hedera, Israel.

Ben Baruch (Schwartz), Shalom; Israeli journalist; b. 29 Nov. 1886; ed. Odessa Univ., Russia.
Dir. Palestine Telegraphic Agency until 35; fmr. Dir. *Palestine Bulletin* and Jerusalem branch of daily *Haboker* 22-36; Founder *Echo of Jerusalem*.
Publs. *The Arab Question, The Poetry of Saul Tchernichovsky, The Jewish Question at the Peace Conference, The Shekel, The Zionist Organisation, Herzl in His Diaries, Herzl in His Letters* 40, *Jabotinsky the Nation's Fighter* 42, 43, *Max Nordau in His Letters* 44, *Diaspora and Palestine* 45, *Ussishkin in His Letters* 49, *Jerusalem in the New Hebrew Poetry* 54; edited *The United Nations Organisation* (essays) 52.
18 Histadruth Street, Jerusalem, Israel.

Ben Bella, Mohammed; Algerian politician; b. 1916.
Warrant Officer in Moroccan regiment during Second World War (decorated); Chief O.A.S. rebel military group in Algeria 47; imprisoned 49-52 (escaped); directed Algerian national movement from exile in Libya 52-56; arrested Oct. 56; held in France 59-62; Vice-Premier, Algerian Nationalist Provisional Govt., Tunis 62, Leader, Algerian Political Bureau, Algeria 62, Premier of Algeria Sept. 62-65, Pres. of Algeria Sept. 63-65; Lenin Peace Prize 64.
Algiers, Algeria.

Ben Haim, Paul; Israeli composer; b. 5 July 1897, Munich, Germany; s. of Dr. Heinrich Frankenburger and Anna Schulmann; m. Helena Acham 1934; one s.; ed. State Acad. of Music and Univ. of Munich.
Active as conductor, composer and pianist in Germany until 33; settled in Tel-Aviv permanently 33; composer and teacher since 33; Hon. Pres. League of Composers in Israel; Israel State Prize 57; Cross of Merit, First Class (Fed. Rep. of Germany) 68.
Leisure interest: books.
Compositions: 5 *Pieces for Piano* 48, *Sonatina for Piano* 49, *Sonata for Violin Solo* 51, *Melody and Variations* 53, *Sonata for Piano* 54, *Three Songs without Words* 54, *Concerto for Strings* 57, *The Sweet Psalmist of Israel* 59, *Concerto for Violin and Orchestra* 60, *Capriccio for Piano*

and Orchestra 61, *Concerto for Cello and Orchestra* 63, two symphonies and many other works.
11 Aharonovitz Street, Tel-Aviv, Israel.

Ben-Natan, Asher; Israeli diplomatist; b. 15 Feb. 1921, Vienna; m. Erika Frudt 1940; one s. one d.; ed. Z. P. Hayut Hebrew Coll., Vienna and Institut des Hautes Etudes Internationales, Geneva.
Co-founder and mem. Kibbutz Mederot-Zeraim 38-44, latterly Sec. and Treas.; Political Dept., Jewish Agency 44-45; on mission to Europe to organize rescue of Jews and illegal immigration to Palestine; attached to office of Head of Jewish Agency 47-48; Ministry of Foreign Affairs 48-51; studies in Geneva 51-53; Govt. Rep. on Board of Red Sea Inkodeh Co. 53-56, Gen. Man. 55-56; Rep. of Ministry of Defence in Europe 56-58; Dir.-Gen. Ministry of Defence 59-65; Ambassador to German Fed. Repub. 65-70, to France 70-75; Officier Légion d'Honneur; Commandeur de l'Ordre National (Ivory Coast); Commandeur de l'Ordre de l'Etoile Equatoriale (Gabon).
89 University Street, Tel-Aviv, Israel.
Telephone: 924-39-54 and 924-29-17.

Bénard, André Pierre Jacques; French oil executive; b. 19 Aug. 1922; ed. Lycée Janson de Sailly, Lycée Georges Clemenceau, Nantes, Lycée Thiers, Marseilles, Ecole Polytechnique, Paris.
Joined Royal Dutch/Shell Group 46; mem. Société Anonyme des Pétroles Jupiter 46-49; Shell Petroleum Co. Ltd., London 49-50; Head of Bitumen services, Société des Pétroles Shell Berre 50-58, Head Nat. Activities Dept. 58-59, Pres. 67-; Asst. Dir.-Gen. Société pour l'Utilisation Rationnelle des Gaz 60-61, Pres., Dir.-Gen. 62-64; Marketing Man. Shell Française 64-67, Pres., Man. Dir. 67-70; Man. Dir. Royal Dutch, Shell Petroleum Co. Ltd. 71-; Co-ordinator, Europe, Oil and Gas 70; Dir. Shell Petroleum N.V. 70, Principal Dir. 71; Dir. The Shell Petroleum Co. Ltd. 70; Médaille des Evadés; Médaille de la Résistance; Chevalier de l'Ordre National du Mérite, Chevalier Légion d'Honneur.
Royal Dutch Petroleum Company, Carel van Bylandtlaan 30, The Hague, Netherlands.
Telephone: 70-77-66-55.

Bénard, Jean Pierre, L. ès L.; French diplomatist; b. 29 Feb. 1908; s. of Georges Bénard and Reine Say; m. Yvonne Mamet 1928; ed. Lycée Janson de Sailly and Univ. de Paris à la Sorbonne.
Journalist, Agence Havas, Washington 34-36, Chief, News Service, Middle East and Cairo 36-39; Diplomatic Service 45-, Counsellor, U.S.A. 45-54; Dep. Dir. NATO Information Div. 55-57; Minister, Tunisia 57-60; Ambassador, Fed. Republic of Cameroon 60-65, Ethiopia 65-71; Dir. Cabinet of the Sec. of State for Foreign Affairs 71-72; Pres. GERDAT (Study and Research Group for Devt. of Tropical Agronomy); Officier, Légion d'Honneur.
42 rue Schaeffer, Paris 16e, France.

Benawa, Abdul Raouf; Afghan writer and administrator; b. 1913; ed. Ganj Public School, Kandahar.
Mem. Language Dept. Afghan Acad. 39; mem. Words Dept. Afghan Acad. and Asst. Information Dept. 40; Dir. Publication Dept. Afghan Acad. 41; Gen. Dir. *Pusthu Tolana*; Sec. Afghan Acad. and Dir. *Kabul* magazine; proprietor of weekly magazine *Hewad*; mem. History Dept. 50, Dir. Internal Publ Dept. 51, Gen. Dir. 52; Press Attaché India 53-56; Pres. Radio Kabul 56-63; Press and Cultural Counsellor, Cairo 63-.
Publs. *Women in Afghanistan, Mir Wiess Neeka, Literary Sciences, Pusthu Songs, De Ghanamo Wazhai, Pushtoonistan, A Survey of Pushtoonistan, Rahman Baba, Pir mohammad-Kakar, Khosh-hal Khan se Wai, Pushtoo Killi,* Vol. 4, *Kazim Khan-e-Shaida;* translations: *Mosa-fir Iqbal, Geetan-Jali Tagoor, Da Darmistatar Pusthoo Seerane, Leaders of Pashtoonistan. History*

of *Hootaki, Preshana afkar* (poem), *Da zra khwala, Pashto writers today* (2 vols.), *Pashto reader for schools, Pachakhan* (A leader of Pashtoni), *Landei* (public poems); plays: *I-Zoor gonahgar* (Old criminal), *Ishtebah* (confusion), *Kari bar asal, Aashyanae aqab, Zarang, Chaoki der khater, Hakoomat baidar.*
Afghan Embassy, Cairo, Egypt; and Ministry of Information and Culture, Kabul, Afghanistan.

Benda, Ernst; German lawyer and politician; b. 15 Jan. 1925, Berlin; m. Waltraut Vorbau 1956; one s. one d.; ed. Kant-Gymnasium, Berlin-Spandau, Humboldt Univ., Freie Univ. Berlin, Univ. of Wisconsin.
War service; prisoner-of-war; Humboldt Univ. 46-48; Freie Univ., Berlin 48-51; Univ. of Wisconsin 49-55; District appointment, Spandau 51-54; mem. Berlin House of Reps. 55-57, Bundestag 57-71; in practice as lawyer 56-71; Chair. Berlin Christian Democratic Union Youth Dept. 52-54; mem. Fed. Govt. 66; Under-Sec. in Interior Ministry; Minister of the Interior 68-69, Pres. Fed. Constitutional Court 71-; Hon. D.Jur. (Würzburg Univ.).
Leisure interests: fishing, garden, sailing.
Publs. *Notstandsverfassung und Arbeitskampf* 63, *Rechtsstaat und Verjährung* 65, *Industrielle Herrschaft und sozialer Staat* 66, *Die Notstandsverfassung* 66, *Der Rechtsstaat in der Krise* 71.
75 Karlsruhe 41, Käthe-Kollwitz-Strasse 46, Federal Republic of Germany.

Bender, Arnold Eric, PH.D.; British nutrition scientist; b. 24 July 1918, Liverpool; m.; two s.; ed. Liverpool Institute, Univs. of Liverpool and Sheffield.
Research Chemist, British Drug Houses 40-45; Nuffield Research Fellow, Univ. of Sheffield 45-47, Asst. Lecturer 47-49; Head of Nutrition Team, Crookes Laboratories 49-54; Head of Research, Bovril Ltd. 54-61; Head of Research and Devt., Farley's Infant Foods Ltd. 61-64; Senior Lecturer (later Reader) Queen Elizabeth Coll., Univ. of London 65-71, Prof. 71-.
Leisure interests: gardening, filming, lecturing.
Publs. *Dictionary of Nutrition and Food Technology* 60, *Nutrition and Dietetic Foods* 67, *Value of Food* 70, *Facts of Food* 76; research papers and review articles in scientific journals.
59 Perryn Road, London, W3 7LS, England.

Bender, Myron L(ee), B.S., PH.D.; American chemist and educator; b. 20 May 1924, St. Louis; s. of Averam Burton Bender and Fannie Leventhal Bender; m. Muriel Blossom Schulman 1952; three s.; ed. Purdue Univ.
Chemist, Eastman Kodak Co. 44-45; Postdoctoral student, Harvard 48-49; AEC Fellow, Univ. of Chicago 49-50; Instructor, Univ. of Connecticut 50-51; Instructor to Assoc. Prof. Illinois Inst. of Technology 51-60; mem. Faculty Northwestern Univ. 60-, Prof. of Chemistry 62-; Consultant to Govt. and industry 59-; Sloan Fellow 59-63; mem. Nat. Acad. of Sciences, Amer. Chem. Soc. and other socs.; Midwest Award of the ACS; D.Sc., Purdue Univ.
Leisure interests: gardening, sculpture.
Publs. 177 papers, ten monographs, and three books (one Russian, two English).
Northwestern University, Evanston, Ill. 60201; Home: 2514 Sheridan Road, Evanston, Ill. 60201, U.S.A
Telephone: 492-7675 (Univ.); 869-6307 (Home).

Bendetsen, Karl Robin, A.B., LL.B., O.B.E.; American lawyer and business executive; b. 11 Oct. 1907, Aberdeen, Wash.; s. of Albert M. and Anna (Bentson) Bendetsen; m. 1st Billie McIntosh, 2nd Maxine Bosworth 1947, 3rd Gladys Ponton de Arce 1972; one s. one d.; ed. Leland Stanford Univ.
Law practice 34-40; U.S. Army 40-46; Management Counsel 46-47; Special Counsel to Sec. of Defense 48; Asst. Sec. of Army 50-52; Under-Sec. of Army 52; Chair.

Board Panama Canal Co. 50; Dir.-Gen. U.S. Railroads 50-52; Champion Paper and Fiber Co. (now Champion Papers Inc.) 52-, Pres. and Chief Exec. Officer 60-, Chair. 65-67; Chair. of Board, Dir., Chief Exec. Officer U.S. Plywood-Champion Papers Inc. (now Champion Int. Corpn.) 67-72, Chair. Exec. Cttee. 73-75; Dir. Champion Int., Westinghouse, N.Y. Stock Exchange; Special Asst. to Sec. of Defense for German Affairs, also for Philippines 56; Chair. Advisory Council on Non-Mil. Instruction, Office of Sec. of Defense 62; Vice-Chair. Defense Manpower Comm. 74; Officier, Légion d'Honneur; Croix de Guerre; Medal of Freedom.
Leisure interest: Episcopal Church activities.
2918 Garfield Terrace, N.W., Washington, D.C. 20008, U.S.A.
Telephone: (202) 462-4091.

Benedetti, Mario; Uruguayan writer; b. 14 Sept. 1920, Paso de los Toros, Tacuarembo; s. of Brenno Benedetti and Matilde Farrugia; m. Luz López; ed. Colegio Alemán.
Journalist on *Marcha* (weekly) and Literary, Film and Theatre Critic on *El Diario*, *Tribuna Popular* and *La Mañana*; visited Europe 57, 66-67.
Publs. Fiction: *Esta mañana* 49, *El último viaje y otros cuentos* 51, *Quién de nosotros* 53, *Montevideanos* 59, *La Tregua* 63, *Gracias por el Fuego* 65, *La muerte y otras sorpresas* 68; plays: *Ustedes por ejemplo* 53, *El Reportaje* 58, *Ida y Vuelta* 58; poetry: *La víspera indeleble* 45, *Sólo mientras tanto* 50, *Poemas de la Oficina* 56, *Poemas del Hoyporhoy* 65, *Inventario* 65, *Contra los puentes levadizos* 66, *A ras de sueño* 67; essays: *Peripecia y novela* 48, *Marcel Proust y otros ensayos* 51, *Literatura uruguaya siglo XX* 63, *Letras del continente mestizo* 67, *Sobre artes y oficios* 68.
Velsen 4543, Montevideo, Uruguay.
Telephone: 591229.

Benedict, Manson, B.CHEM., M.S., PH.D.; American engineer; b 9 Oct. 1907, Lake Linden, Mich.; s. of C. Harry Benedict and Lena Manson Benedict; m. Marjorie Oliver Allen 1935; two d.; ed Cornell Univ. and Mass. Inst. of Technology.
National Research Fellow, Harvard Univ. 35-36, Research Assoc. in Geophysics 36-37; Research Chemist, M. W. Kellogg Co. 38-43; in charge of Process Design Uranium-235 Gaseous Diffusion Plant, Kellex Corpn. 43-46; Dir. Process Devt., Hydrocarbon Research Inc. 46-51; Prof. of Nuclear Eng., Mass. Inst. of Technology 51-73, Head of Nuclear Eng. Dept. 58-71, Inst. Prof. 69-73, Inst. Prof. Emer. 73-; Scientific Adviser, Nat. Research Corpn. 51-57, Dir. 60-66; mem. Gen. Advisory Cttee. U.S. Atomic Energy Comm. 58-68, Chair. 62-64; Dir. Atomic Industrial Forum 67-72; mem. Nat. Acad. of Sciences, Nat. Acad. of Eng.; Perkin Medal of Soc. of Chemical Industry, American Section; American Inst. of Chemical Engineers (three Awards), U.S. Atomic Energy Comm. Citation, Industrial and Eng. Chemistry Award of Amer. Chemical Soc.; Arthur H. Compton Award of American Nuclear Soc.; Enrico Fermi Award, U.S. Atomic Energy Comm.
Leisure interest: golf.
Publs. *Engineering Development in the Gaseous Diffusion Process* (Co-Editor), *Nuclear Chemical Engineering* (Co-Author) 57.
Room 24-109, Massachusetts Institute of Technology, Cambridge, Mass.; Home: 25 Byron Road, Weston, Mass., U.S.A.

Benedicto, Roberto S., A.A., LL.M.; Philippine lawyer and banker; b. 17 April 1917; ed. Univ. of the Philippines, George Washington Univ.
Major in the Philippines Armed Forces 41-45; Acting Provincial Fiscal, Negros Occidental 45; Prof. Commercial Law, Far Eastern Univ. 48-55; Gov. Devt. Bank of the Philippines 57-59; Exec. Vice-Pres., Treas. Philippines Commercial and Industrial Bank

62-65; Pres., Vice-Chair. Philippine Nat. Bank 66-70; Amb. to Japan 72-; mem. Monetary Board, Central Bank of the Philippines; Alt. Gov. IMF, IBRD; Legion of Merit, Rep. Community Chest of Greater Manila.
Embassy of the Philippines, 6-15, Roppongi 5-chome, Minato-ku, Tokyo, Japan; Home: 1420 San Marcelino, Malate, Manila, Philippines.

Benedictos (Vassilios Papadopoulos); Greek orthodox ecclesiastic; b. 1892; ed. Greek Orthodox Hieratic School, Jerusalem, and Athens Univ.
Clerk, Patriarchal Offices, Jerusalem 14; ordained deacon 14; accompanied the then Patriarch to Damascus during World War I; studies in Law and Theological Schools, Athens Univ. 21-25; Rep. of Patriarch of Jerusalem at World Christian Conf. of Faith and Order, Geneva 27; Exarch of the Holy Sepulchre in Athens 29-46; ordained priest and Archimandrite 46; mem. Holy Synod, Jerusalem Patriarchate 46-; Legal Adviser and Chair. Pending Property Cttee. 47; Chair. Financial Cttee. 50; rep. of Patriarch, Internationalisation of Jerusalem Trusteeship Conf. 50; Archbishop of Tiberias 51; Greek Orthodox Patriarch of Jerusalem 57-; Grand Cross of King George of Greece, Grand Cross and Cordon of Patriarchate of Antioch, Jordanian and Lebanese orders.
Greek Orthodox Patriarchate, P.O. Box 4074, Jerusalem, Israel.

Benediktsson, Einar, M.A.; Icelandic diplomatist; b. 30 April 1931, Reykjavík; s. of Stefan M. Benediktsson and Sigridur Oddsdóttir; m. Elsa Petursdóttir 1956; three s. two d.; ed. Colgate Univ., N.Y., Fletcher School of Law and Diplomacy, Mass., London School of Econs., Inst. des Etudes Européennes, Turin, Italy.
With Org. for European Econ. Co-operation, Paris 56-60; Head of Section, Ministries of Econ. Affairs and Commerce 60-64, Ministry of Foreign Affairs 64, 68-70; Counsellor, Icelandic Embassy, Paris 64-68; Perm. Rep. to Int. Orgs., Geneva 70-; Vice-Chair. EFTA Jan.-June 75; Commdr. Order of Falcon (Iceland), Ordre du Merite Nat. (France).
Délégation d'Islande, 9-11 rue de Varembé, 1211 Geneva 20; Home: 149E route de Ferney, 1218 Grand-Saconnex, Geneva, Switzerland.
Telephone: 34 02 28 (Office); 34 92 28 (Home).

Benediktsson, Jakob, M.A., PH.D.; Icelandic philologist; b. 20 July 1907, Fjall; s. of Benedikt Sigurdsson and Sigurlaug Sigurdardóttir; m. Grethe Kyhl 1936; ed. Univ. of Copenhagen.
Assistant Editor *Old-Icelandic Dictionary* (Copenhagen) 39-46; Librarian Univ. of Copenhagen 43-46; Editor-in-Chief *Icelandic Dictionary* Univ. of Iceland 48-; mem. Societas Scientiarum Islandica, Royal Danish Acad. of Sciences and Letters, Norwegian Acad. of Sciences and Letters, Swedish Acad.
Publs. *Gisli Magnússon* 39, *Chronologie de deux listes des prêtres kamiréens* 40, *Jardabók Árna Magnussonar og Páls Vídalíns* (vols. VII, X, XI) 40-43, *Skardsbók* (Corpus codicum Islandicorum XVI) 43, *Two Treatises on Iceland* 43, *Veraldar saga* 44, *Ferdabók Tómasar Sæmundssonar* 47, *Ole Worm's Correspondence with Icelanders* 48, *G. Andrésson Deilurit* 48, *Persius rimur* 49, *Arngrimi Jonae Opera I-IV* 50-57, *Arngrímur Jónsson and his Works* 57, *Skardsdrbók* 58, *Sturlunga Saga* (Early Icelandic Manuscript I) 58, *Islenzk-dönsk ordabók*, *Vidbaetir* 63, *Islemdingabók*, *Landnámabók* 68, *Landnámabók* 74.
2 Stigahlíd, Reykiavik, Iceland.
Telephone: 30987

Bénézit, Jacques Charles Victor; French oil executive; b. 7 Oct. 1913; ed. Ecole Polytechnique, Ecole des Mines.
Mining Engineer, Nancy, Paris; Dir. Exploration/Production Dept. 55; Dir. Compagnie Française des Pétroles; Pres. and Dir.-Gen. Compagnie Française des

Pétroles (Algeria); Vice-Pres. Compagnie Générale de Géophysique; Dir. French Petroleum Co. of Canada Ltd., Compagnie des Pétroles Total Libye, Société d'étude des marchés européens du gaz d'Hassi R'Mel transporté par canalisations (Somarel) and several other companies; Chevalier, Légion d'Honneur.
Compagnie Française des Pétroles, 5 rue Michel-Ange, Paris 16e; and 89 avenue de Villiers, Paris 17e, France.

Bengelloun, Ahmed Majid, L. EN D.; Moroccan lawyer and politician; b. 27 Dec. 1927, Fez; ed. Inst. of Political Science, Paris.
Public Prosecutor, Marrakesh 56, later Public Prosecutor of Mil. Tribunal, Meknés, Gen. Counsel, Supreme Court; Public Prosecutor Court of Appeal 60-64; Minister of Information 65-67, 72-74; Sec.-Gen. Ministry of Justice 67; Minister at the Royal Cabinet 67-71, of Civil Service 71-72; fmr. Prof. Inst. des Hautes Etudes Juridiques; Prof. Law Faculty, Univ. of Rabat, Ecole Morocaine d'Admin.; mem. Comm. for the Drafting of the Penal Code and Penal Procedure Code; has attended numerous int. judicial confs.; Order of the Throne, and several foreign decorations.
c/o Ministère de l'Information, Rabat, Morocco.

Bengsch, H.E. Cardinal Alfred, DR.THEOL.; German ecclesiastic; b. 10 Sept. 1921; ed. grammar school, Berlin, Philosophical-Theological Coll., Fulda, Ludwig Maximilians Universität, Munich.
Ordained 50; Chaplain in Berlin; further study and Asst. at Theological Coll., Erfurt 54-56; Lecturer in Dogma and Rhetoric at Theological and Sacerdotal Coll., Neuzelle 56-59; Titular Bishop of Tubia and Asst. Bishop of Berlin 59; Bishop of Berlin and Pres. of Berlin Bishops' Conference 61; Archbishop 62-; cr. Cardinal 67; mem. Sacred Congregation for Religious Orders and Secular Institutes; mem. Secr. for Promoting Christian Unity, Rome; mem. Pontifical Comm. for Revision of Canon Law.
Publs. *Heilsgeschichte und Heilswissen* 57, *Unterwegs zum Herrn* 59, *Heiligung, Umkehr, Vollendung* 59, *Berufung und Bewährung* 60, *Der Glaube an die Auferstehung* 62, *Den Glauben leben* Vol. I 65, *Konzil für Dich* 66, *In Erwartung der Wiederkunft* 66, *Den Glauben leben* Vol. II 67, *Glaube und Kritik* 68, *Würde des Dienstes* 69, *Kirche ohne Kreuz* 69, *Weder Gegenwärtiges noch Zukünftiges . . .* 74, *Wo steht die Predigt heute?* 74, *Zehn Gebote* 75.
108 Berlin Französische Strasse 34 (East Berlin); 1 Berlin 19, Wundtstrasse 48/50 (West Berlin), Germany. Telephone: 200 02 81 (East Berlin); 306-20-61 (West Berlin).

Bengtsson, Ingemund; Swedish politician; b. 1919, Veddinge, Halland; ed. County Coll.
Formerly Man. Halland County Labour Exchange; mem. of Parl. 51-; consultant to Ministry for Health and Welfare 54-65; mem. of Board, Social Democrat Party, fmrly. Vice-Pres. Social Democrat Party Member's Council; mem. Swedish del. to UN Gen. Assembly; Minister of Agriculture 69-73, of Labour 73-.
Ministry of Labour, Stockholm, Sweden.

Bengzon, Cesar, B.A., LL.B.; Philippine judge; b. 29 May 1896; ed. Ateneo de Manila and Univ. of the Philippines.
Law Clerk, Bureau of Justice 19, Special Attorney, then Asst. Attorney 20, Solicitor-Gen. 31; Dean and Prof. of Law, Univ. of Manila 28-32; Under-Sec. of Justice and Chair. Board of Pardons 33; Assoc. Justice, Court of Appeals 36; Assoc. Justice, Supreme Court 45; Prof. of Law, Univ. of Santo Tomas and Philippine Law School 48-54; Chair. Senate Electoral Tribunal 50-57; Chief Justice Supreme Court 61; Judge, Int. Court of Justice, The Hague 66-76; mem. Philippine Acad. of Sciences and Humanities 64-; Pres. Philippine Section, Int. Comm. of Jurists 64, 66; mem. Nat. Research Council

64-, American Judicature Soc. 65, Philippine Soc. of Int. Law 65-; LL.D. h.c. Univ. of Manila 57, Ateneo de Manila Univ. 64, Univ. of the Philippines 64.
c/o International Court of Justice, The Hague, Netherlands.

Benhima, Ahmed Taiba (brother of Dr. Mohamed Benhima, *q.v.*); Moroccan diplomatist; b. 13 Nov. 1927; s. of Tayeb Benhima and Ben Hida; ed. Univs. of Nancy and Paris.
Chargé d'Affaires, Paris 56-57, Ambassador to Italy 57-59; Sec.-Gen. of Ministry of Foreign Affairs 59-61; Perm. Rep. to UN 61-64; Minister of Foreign Affairs 64-66, 72-74; Dir. Cabinet of King 66-67; Perm. Rep. to UN 67-71; Minister of State for Information 74-.
Ministry of Information, Rabat, Morocco.

Benhima, Mohamed, M.D. (brother of Ahmed Benhima, *q.v.*); Moroccan physician and politician; b. 25 June 1924, Safi; s. of Tayeb Benhima and Ben Hida; four c.; ed. Faculté de Médecine de Nancy, France.
Chief Medical Officer, Had Court District 54-56; Chief of Central Service for Urban and Rural Hygiene 56-57; Head of Personal Office of Minister of Public Health 57-60; Sec.-Gen. Ministry of Public Health Jan.-June 60; Gov. of Provinces of Agadir and Tarfaya 60-61; Minister of Public Works 61-62, 63-65, 67-72, of Commerce, Industry, Mines, Handicrafts and Merchant Marine 62-63, of Nat. Educ. 65-67; Prime Minister 67-69; Minister of State for Agriculture and Agrarian Reform 69-70; Minister of Health 69-72, of Internal Affairs 72-73; Minister of State for Co-operation and Training 73-; Grand Cordon de Mérite, Côte D'Ivoire; decorations from Govts. of Belgium, Morocco, Sweden, Ethiopia, Tunisia, Liberia and United Arab Republic.
Km. 5.5, Route des Zaërs, Rabat, Morocco.

Benites Vinueza, Leopoldo, DR. RER. POL.; Ecuadorean diplomatist; b. 17 Oct. 1905; ed. Univ. of Guayaquil.
Minister to Uruguay 47-52; Alt. Rep. of Ecuador to UN 53-54; Amb. to Bolivia 54-56, to Argentina 56, to Uruguay 56-60; Perm. Rep. to UN 60-75; Pres. 28th UN Gen. Assembly 73.
c/o Ministry of Foreign Affairs, Quito, Ecuador.

Benítez, Jaime, LL.M., LL.D.; Puerto Rican educator and government official; b. 29 Oct. 1908, Vieques; s. of Don Luis Benítez and Doña Cándida Rexach Benítez; m. Luz A. Martínez 1941; one s. two d.; ed. Georgetown Univ. and Univ. of Chicago.
Instructor in Political Science, Univ. of Puerto Rico 31-41, Assoc. Prof. 41-42, Chancellor of Univ. 42-66, Pres. 66-71; Res. Commr. from Puerto Rico in the U.S. 72-; mem. House of Representatives Cttee. on Education and Labour 72-; Head Hearings Officer, Nat. War Labor Board, Washington; Del. to UNESCO Conf., Paris 51; mem. U.S. Nat. Comm. UNESCO 51-55; Pres. Cttee. of Bill of Rights, Puerto Rico Constitutional Convention 51; mem. Housing Cttee., U.S. Federal Housing Agency 57; U.S. Del., Conf. of Univs., Utrecht, Holland 48; Fellow American Acad. of Arts and Sciences, American Acad. of Political and Social Sciences, Federal Bar Asscn., Nat. Asscn. of State Univs. (Pres. 58), Colegio de Abogados de Puerto Rico; Hon. LL.D. (Inter-American, San German, New York, Fairleigh Dickinson Univs. and Catholic Univ. of Puerto Rico).
Leisure interest: flying kites.
Publs. *The Concept of the Family in Roman and Common Law Jurisprudence* 31, *Political and Philosophical Theories of José Ortega y Gasset* 39, *Reflexiones Sobre el Presente* 50, *La Iniciación Universitaria y las Ciencias Sociales* 52, *The United States, Cuba, and Latin America* 61, *Junto a la Torre* 63, *Discurso en Salamanca* 65, *Sobre el Futuro Cultural y Político de Puerto Rico* 65.
House of Representatives, Washington, D.C., U.S.A. Telephone: 225-2615 (Office); 7240-171 (San Juan).

Beniuc, Mihai, D.PHIL.; Romanian writer and scientist; b. 20 Nov. 1907, Sebis-Arad; s. of Atanasie and Veselina Beniuc; m. Emma-Sylvia Friedmann 1945; ed. Arad High Schools, Cluj Univ. and in Germany.

Professor, Cluj Univ. 30; now Prof. of Psychology, Chair. Univ. of Bucharest; revolutionary poet 26-; mem. Grand Nat. Assembly 57-65; Chair. Writers' Union of the Romanian People's Republic until 65; mem. Romanian Acad. 55-, State Prizes 51 and 54; Hero of Socialist Labour 71.

Publs. Verse: *Songs of Desolation* 38, *New Songs* 40, *Poems* 43, *The Lost City* 43, *A Man is Waiting for the Sunrise* 46, *Selected Poems* 49, *Banners* 52, *The Apple Tree near the Road* 54, *Durability* 55, *The Heart of the Old Vesuvius, Journeys Through Constellations* 57, *An Hour before Sunset* 59, *Songs of the Heart* 61, *The Matter and the Dreams* 61, *Colours of the Autumn* 62, *Strings of Time* 63, *Headlights* 64, *Rock Flowers* 65, *Day by Day* 65, *Other Ways* 67 (many translated); Prose: *Learning and Intelligence in Animals* 34, *The Roundabout Path of the Fighting Fish* 38, *Territoriality* 39, *Personal Hate, On the Edge of the Knife* 59, *An Ordinary Man has Disappeared* 64, *The Reciprocal Influence of Behaviour Patterns Learnt by Betta Splendens Regan, Animal Psychology* 70; Plays: *In the Cucu Valley* 59, *The Return* 60; Criticism: *Our Poetry* 56, *Mason Manole* 57. Leisure interests: philosophy, linguistics, biology, poetry.

Str. Grădina Bordei 51, 7000 Bucharest, Romania.
Telephone: 33-12-33.

Benjamin, Curtis G.; American publisher; b. 13 July 1901, Province, Ky.; m. Norma Olson 1931; one s. one d.; ed. Univ. of Kentucky, Univ. of Chicago and Univ. of Arizona.

McGraw-Hill Book Co. 26-, Manager, College Dept. 32-42, Vice-Pres. 42-46, Pres. 46-60, Chair. Board of Dirs. 61-65, Management Board 65-66; Dir. McGraw-Hill Inc. 47-72, McGraw-Hill Co. of Canada Ltd. 47-72, McGraw-Hill Publishing Co. Ltd. (London) 47-72; Exec. Consultant McGraw-Hill Inc. 67-; Pres. American Book Publishers Council 58-59; Chair. Govt. Advisory Cttee. on Int. Book Programs 62-64, Del. to U.S.S.R for State Dept. 62; mem. State Dept. Advisory Panel on Int. Copyright 70-; mem. Science Information Council, Nat. Science Foundation 59-60, 64-67, Advisory Council on College Library Resources 66-68, Board of Trustees, Norwalk Hospital, Conn. 70-; Dir. Save the Children Fed. and Community Development Foundation 68-73; Hon. LL.D. (Kentucky), Hon. Litt. D. (Arizona).

McGraw-Hill Inc., 1221 Avenue of the Americas, New York, N.Y. 10020; Home: Kellogg Hill Road, Weston, Conn. 06880, U.S.A.

Benjamin, Hilde; German lawyer and politician; b. 5 Feb. 1902; studied law.

Practising lawyer until 33; joined Communist Party 27; commercial employment during Nazi regime; State lawyer in Berlin 45; joined Sozialistische Einheitspartei Deutschlands (S.E.D.) 46; Vice-Pres. Supreme Court 49; Minister of Justice 53-67; Prof. of History of Admin. of Justice, Deutsche Akad. für Staats- und Rechtswissenschaft "Walter Ulbricht" 67-; mem. Central Cttee. S.E.D. 53; mem. Volkskammer; Clara-Zetkin Medal, two Distinguished Service Orders, Order of the Banner of Labour, medal for Fighters against Fascism, Order of Merit (Gold); Dr. h.c.

Deutsche Akademie für Staats-und Rechtswissenschaft "Walter Ulbricht", Potsdam-Babelsberg, German Democratic Republic.

Benjenk, Munir P.; Turkish international finance official; b. 12 June 1924, Istanbul; s. of Pertev Benjenk and Stella Habib; ed. Robert Coll., Istanbul and London School of Econs.

With B.B.C. 49-51; with Org. for Econ. Co-operation and Devt. (OECD) Paris 53-63, Dir. Technical Assistance Programme, OECD; joined IBRD 63, Chief of North Africa Div. 65-67, Deputy Dir. Middle East and North Africa Dept. 67-68, Europe, Middle East and North Africa Dept. 68-70, Dir. 70-72, Vice-Pres. for Europe, Middle East and North Africa 72-75, Regional Vice-Pres. 75-; Order of Merit of the Italian Repub. 60; Order of Cedars of Lebanon.

Leisure interests: classical music, history.

International Bank for Reconstruction and Development, 1818 H Street, N.W., Washington, D.C. 20433, U.S.A.

Benke, Mrs. Valéria; Hungarian politician; b. 26 June 1920, Gyönk; m. 1947; one s. two d.; ed. teacher training.

Joined Communist Party 41; Trade Union Sec., Szeged 44; Teacher, Party Acad. 45-46; performed party work, Budapest 46-48; Budapest Sec., Women's Fed. 48-50; Sec. Nat. Peace Council 50-54; Pres. Hungarian Radio and Television 54-58; Minister of Public Educ. 58-61; mem. of Parl. 49-71; mem. Cen. Cttee. of Hungarian Socialist Workers' Party 57-, Presidential Council 67-71, mem. Political Cttee. Hungarian Socialist Workers' Party 70-; Editor-in-Chief, *Társadalmi Szemle*.

Leisure interest: reading.

Hungarian Socialist Workers' Party, Budapest V, Széchenyi rakpart 19, Hungary.
Telephone: 111-400.

Benkei, András; Hungarian politician; b. 11 Sept. 1923, Nyiregyháza; s. of István Benkei; m. Erzsébet Habony 1949; two d.

Former mechanic; Sec. Szabolcs-Szatmár County Cttee. of Food Industry Trade Union 49; Head, Industrial Dept., Szabolcs-Szatmár County Party Cttee. 51-54; First Sec. Nyiregyháza Municipal Cttee., Hungarian Socialist Workers Party 54-56; First Sec. Szabolcs-Szatmár County Party Cttee. 56-63; Minister of Internal Affairs 63-; mem. Central Cttee. Hungarian Socialist Workers Party; mem. National Assembly.

Leisure interests: literature, sport.

Ministry of Internal Affairs, József Attila-u. 2-4, H-1903 Budapest V, Hungary.
Telephone: 313-700.

Benn, Rt. Hon. Anthony (Neil) Wedgwood, P.C., M.A., M.P.; British politician; b. 3 April 1925, London; s. of William Wedgwood Benn (1st Viscount Stansgate), P.C. and Margaret Eadie (Holmes); m. Caroline de Camp 1949; three s. one d.; ed. Westminster School and New Coll., Oxford.

R.A.F. Pilot 43-45; Oxford Univ. 46-49; Producer, BBC 49-50; Labour mem. Parl. for Bristol S.E. 50-60, compelled to leave House of Commons on inheriting peerage 60, re-elected and unseated 61, renounced peerage and re-elected 63; Nat. Exec. Labour Party 59-; Chair. Fabian Soc. 64; Postmaster-Gen. 64-66; Minister of Technology 66-70, of Power 69-70; Shadow Minister of Trade and Industry 70-74; Sec. of State for Industry and Minister of Posts and Telecommunications 74-75; Sec. of State for Energy 75-; Vice-Chair. Labour Party 71-72, Chair. 71-72; Hon. LL.D. (Strathclyde Univ.); Hon. D.Tech. (Bradford); Hon. D.Sc. (Aston).

Publs. *The Privy Council as a Second Chamber* 57, *The Regeneration of Britain* 64, *The New Politics* 70, *Speeches by Tony Benn* 74.

Department of Energy, Thames House South, Millbank, London, S.W.1, England.
Telephone: 01-211-3000.

Bennacerraf, Baruj, M.D.; American pathologist; b. 29 Oct. 1920, Caracas, Venezuela; s. of Abraham and Henriette Benacerraf; m. Annette Dreyfus 1943; one d.; ed. Lycée Janson, Paris, Columbia Univ., New York and Medical Coll. of Virginia.

Intern, Queens General Hosp., New York 45-46; U.S. Army 46-48; Research Fellow, Dept. of Microbiology,

Coll. of Physicians and Surgeons, Columbia Univ., New York 48-50; Chargé de Recherches, CNRS, Hôpital Broussais, Paris 50-56; Asst. Prof. of Pathology, New York Univ. School of Medicine 56-58, Assoc. Prof. of Pathology 58-60, Prof. 60-68; Chief, Lab. of Immunology, Nat. Inst. of Allergy and Infectious Diseases, Nat. Insts. of Health, Bethesda, Md. 68-70; Fabyan Prof. of Comparative Pathology and Chair. Dept. of Pathology, Harvard Medical School 70-; Past. Pres., mem. American Asscn. of Immunologists; Past Pres. Fed. of American Socs. for Experimental Biology; mem. American Acad. of Arts and Sciences, Nat. Acad. of Sciences, British Asscn. for Immunology, French Soc. for Biological Chem., etc.; Scientific Adviser for Immunology, WHO; trustee and mem. Scientific Advisory Board, Trudeau Foundation; mem. Scientific Advisory Board, Mass. Gen. Hosp.; mem. Board of Govs. Weizman Inst. of Sciences.
Leisure interests: music, art collecting.
Publs. *Immunological Tolerance* (with Katz), *Immunogenetics and Immunodeficiency*, *The Role of Products of the Histocompatibility Gene Complex in Immune Responses* (with Katz), and articles in professional journals.
Department of Pathology, Harvard Medical School, 25 Shattuck Street, Boston, Mass. 02115; Home: 111 Perkins Street, Boston, Mass. 02130, U.S.A.
Telephone: 617-734-3300 (Office); 617-522-6514 (Home).

Bennecke, Gen. Jürgen; German Commander-in-Chief Allied Forces, Central Europe 68-73; see *The International Who's Who 1975-76*.

Bennedsen, Mrs. Dorte; Danish politician; b. 2 July 1938, Copenhagen; d. of late Prof. Hal and Bodil Koch; m. Jørgen Bennedsen 1961; two s. one d.; ed. Copenhagen Univ.
Curate, Holmens Church 65-68; Sec.-Gen. Danish Youth Council 68-71; Chair. "The Little School", Copenhagen 68-70; Minister for Ecclesiastical Affairs 71-73; Chair. Consumers' Org. in Denmark 74-; mem. Board of Dirs. Danish Asscn. for Int. Co-operation 69; mem. Nat. UNESCO Comm. 70; mem. Frederiksberg Town Council 70; mem. Parl. 75.
Leisure interests: skiing, ice-skating.
Tesdorpfsvej 55, 2000F, Denmark.

Bennett, Lt.-Col. Sir Charles Moihi To Arawaka, Kt., D.S.O., M.A., DIP.ED., DIP.SOC.SC.; New Zealand diplomatist; b. 1913; ed. Univ. of N.Z. and Exeter Coll., Oxford.
Schoolmaster 37; Staff mem. New Zealand Broadcasting Service 38-39; service with New Zealand Army in U.K., Greece, Crete, North Africa, commanding Maori Battalion from Alamein to Tunis 39-46; Staff mem. War Histories Section, Internal Affairs Dept., mem. Ngarimu Scholarship Fund Board 47-50; Asst. Controller Maori Welfare Div., Maori Affairs Dept. 51-57, Dir. 57-58; mem. State Literary Advisory Cttee., New Zealand Parole Board 51; New Zealand High Commr. to Malaya (the first Maori to lead an overseas Mission) 59-63; Asst. Sec. Dept. of Maori Affairs, Wellington 63-69; Vice-Pres. New Zealand Labour Party 70-72, Pres. 73-; Hon. LL.D. (Univ. Canterbury, N.Z.).
33A High Street, Rotorua, New Zealand.

Bennett, Emmett Leslie, M.A., PH.D.; American classical scholar; b. 12 July 1918, Minneapolis, Minn.; s. of Emmett L. Bennett and Mary C. Buzzelle; m. Marja Adams 1942; five c.; ed. Univ. of Cincinnati.
Research analyst, U.S. War Dept. 42-45; taught in Dept. of Classics, Yale Univ. 47-58; Fulbright Research Scholar, Athens 53-54; Cambridge 65; mem. Inst. for Advanced Study, Guggenheim Fellow, Visiting Lecturer in Greek, Bryn Mawr Coll. 55-56; Dept. of Classical Languages, Univ. of Texas 58-59; Univ. of Wisconsin Inst. for Research Humanities 59-, Acting Dir. 68-69,

72-75, Dept. of Classics 60-; Visiting Prof. Univ. of Colorado 67, of Cincinnati 72; corresp. mem. German Archaeological Inst., Archaeological Soc. of Athens; mem. Comité Int. Permanent des Etudes Mycéniennes, Archaeological Inst. of America, American Philological Asscn., Linguistic Soc. of America.
Publs. *The Pylos Tablets* 51 and 56, *The Mycenae Tablets* 53 and 58, *Mycenaean Studies* 64, Editor, *Nestor* 57-, etc.
University of Wisconsin, Madison, Wis. 53706, U.S.A.
Telephone: 608-257-3162.

Bennett, Frederick Onslow Alexander Godwyn, B.A.(CANTAB.), T.D.; British business executive; b. 21 Dec. 1913, Shenley; s. of Alfred Bennett and Marjorie Muir Bremner; m. Rosemary Perks 1942; one s. four d.; ed. Winchester Coll., Trinity Coll., Cambridge.
Joined Whitbread & Co. as pupil brewer 35; military service, mentioned in despatches 39-45; Man. Dir. Whitbread & Co. Ltd. 49, Deputy Chair. 59, Chief Exec. 68-74, Chair. 72-; Master of Brewers' Co. 63-64; Chair. Brewers' Soc. 72-74; U.S. Bronze Star.
Leisure interests: shooting, racing.
Whitbread & Co. Ltd., Brewery, Chiswell Street, London, EC1Y 4SD; Home: Grove House, Selling, Faversham, Kent, ME13 9RW, England.
Telephone: 01-606-4455 (Office); Selling 250.

Bennett, Jack Franklin, M.A., PH.D.; American economist; b. 17 Jan. 1924, Macon, Ga.; s. of Andrew Jackson Bennett and Eloise Franklin Bennett; m. Shirley Elizabeth Goodwin 1949; three s. one d.; ed. Woodrow Wilson High School, Washington, D.C., Yale and Harvard Univs.
Communications Officer, U.S. Navy 44-46; Joint U.S./U.K. Export-Import Agency, Berlin 46; Econ. Co-operation Admin. 50; Special Asst. to Administrator, Technical Co-operation Admin. 51-53; Senior Economist, Presidential Comm. on Foreign Econ. Policy 53-54; Foreign Exchange Analyst, Standard Oil Co. (N.J.) 55; Presidential Citizens' Cttee. on Mutual Security 56-57; European Financial Rep., Standard (Oil N.J.) 58-60, Asst. Treas., Exec. Asst. to Chair. 61-64, Chief Economist, Man. Co-ordination and Planning 65-66, Gen. Man. Supply Dept. Humble Oil 67-69, Dir. and Vice-Pres. Esso Int. 69-71; Deputy Under-Sec. for Monetary Affairs U.S. Treasury Dept. 71-74, Under-Sec. March-July 74, Under-Sec. for Monetary Affairs 74-75; Alexander Hamilton Award 74.
Leisure interests: swimming, tennis, inventing.
Publs. articles in *Foreign Affairs, Journal of Finance, Economia Internazionale.*
Home: 4000 Massachusetts Avenue, N.W., Washington, D.C. 20016; and 141 Taconic Road, Greenwich, Conn. 06830, U.S.A.
Telephone: (202) 686-0117, (203) 869-8931 (Home).

Bennett, John Coleman, M.A., D.D., S.T.D.; American theologian; b. 22 July 1902; ed. Phillips Exeter Acad., Williams Coll., Oxford Univ. and Union Theological Seminary.
Mem. of Faculty, Auburn Theological Seminary 30-38; Prof. of Theology, Pacific School of Religion 38-43; Prof. of Christian Theology and Ethics, Union Theological Seminary 43-57, Dean of Faculty 55-63, William E. Dodge Jr. Prof. of Applied Christianity 57-61, Reinhold Niebuhr Prof. of Social Ethics 61-70, Pres. 63-70; Visiting Prof. Christian Ethics, Pacific School of Religion 70-; Pres. American Theological Soc. 54, American Soc. for Christian Social Ethics 61; Co-Editor *Christianity and Crisis*; several honorary degrees.
Publs. *Social Salvation* 35, *Christian Realism* 41, *Christian Ethics and Social Policy* 46, *Christianity and Communism* 48 (new ed. *Christianity and Communism Today* 60), *Christians and the State* 58, Ed. *Nuclear*

Weapons and the Conflict of Conscience 62, *Foreign Policy in Christian Perspective* 66.
2340 Virginia Street, Berkeley, Calif. 94709, U.S.A.

Bennett, Richard Rodney, A.R.A.M., F.R.A.M.; British composer; b. 29 March 1936, Broadstairs, Kent; s. of H. Rodney Bennett and Joan Esther Bennett; ed. Leighton Park School, Reading, Royal Acad. of Music, London and under Pierre Boulez, Paris.
Commissioned to write two operas by Sadler's Wells 62; Prof. of Composition, Royal Acad. of Music 63-65; Arnold Bax Soc. Prize for Commonwealth Composers 64; Anthony Asquith Memorial Award for *Murder on the Orient Express* film music, Soc. of Film and TV Awards 74.
Leisure interests: cinema, modern jazz.
Compositions: *The Approaches of Sleep* 59, *Journal, Calendar, Winter Music* 60, *The Ledge, Suite Française, Oboe Sonata* 61, *Nocturnes, London Pastoral, Fantasy* 62, *Aubade, Jazz Calendar, String Quartet No. Four, Five Studies* 64, *Symphony No. 1* 65, *Epithalamion* 66, *Symphony No. 2* 67, *Wind Quintet, Piano Concerto* 68, *Jazz Pastoral* 69, *Oboe Concerto* 70, *Guitar Concerto* 71, *Viola Concerto* 73, *Commedia I-IV* 72-73; Opera: *The Mines of Sulphur* 64, *A Penny for a Song* 66, *Victory* 69; Film Music: *Indiscreet, Devil's Disciple, Blind Date, The Mark, Only Two Can Play, Wrong Arm of the Law, Heavens Above, Billy Liar, One Way Pendulum, The Nanny, The Witches, Far from the Madding Crowd, Billion Dollar Brain, The Buttercup Chain, Secret Ceremony, Figures in a Landscape, Nicholas and Alexandra, Lady Caroline Lamb, Voices, Murder on the Orient Express.*
c/o London Management, Regent House, 235-241 Regent Street, London, W.1, England.

Bennett, Roy Frederick, C.A.; Canadian business executive; b. 18 March 1928, Winnipeg, Man.; s. of Charles William Bennett (deceased) and Gladys Mabel Matthews; m. Laurel Susan McDermott 1955; one s. two d.; ed. Collegiate Inst., N. Toronto and Inst. of Chartered Accountants.
Lever Hoskin & Co., Toronto 47-54; Kelvinator of Canada Ltd., Weston 54-56; Ford Motor Co. of Canada Ltd., Supervisor Financial Planning 56-57, Man. Financial Analysis 57-60, Asst. Controller 60-62, Dir. Vehicle Marketing 62-63, Dir. Corporate Planning 63-64, Gen. Marketing Man. 64-65, Vice-Pres. Finance 65-70, Dir. 66-, Pres. 70-, Chief Exec. Officer 72-; Chair. Advisory Council Better Business Bureau of Canada, Motor Vehicle Mfrs. Asscn.; mem. Premier's Advisory Cttee. on Econ. Policy, Ontario, Minister's Advisory Cttee., Dept. of Industry, Trade and Commerce, Ottawa, Canadian-American Cttee., C. D. Howe Research Inst., Exec. Council, Canadian Mfrs. Asscn., Board of Dirs. Mississauga Hospital.
Leisure interests: golf, squash, tennis, skiing.
Ford Motor Company of Canada Limited, The Canadian Road, Oakville, Ontario, Canada.

Bennett, Wallace Foster; American politician; b. 13 Nov. 1898; ed. Univ. of Utah.
President Bennett's (Paint and Glass) Co. and Bennett's Motor Co., Salt Lake City till 50, now Chair. of both; Pres. Nat. Glass Distributors Asscn. 37, Salt Lake Rotary Club 40, Salt Lake Community Chest 44-45; Nat. Asscn. of Manufacturers 49; mem. LDS (Mormon) Church; Republican Senator from Utah 50-74; mem. **Senate Banking and Currency Cttee. and Senate Finance Cttee., Joint Cttee. on Atomic Energy, Joint Cttee. on Defence Production.**
Publs. *Faith and Freedom* 50, *Why I am a Mormon* 58.
P.O. Box 1320, Salt Lake City, Utah, U.S.A.

Bennett, Hon. William Andrew Cecil, P.C., LL.D.; Canadian businessman and politician; b. 6 Sept. 1900, Hastings, New Brunswick; s. of Andrew Havelock Bennett and Emma Burns Bennett; m. A. E. May

Richards 1927; two s. one d.; ed. in New Brunswick and Alberta.
President Bennett's Stores Ltd. (est. 1930) operating chain of five stores (hardware, electrical appliances,etc.) in the Okanagan valley; B.C. Legislature 41-, Premier of British Columbia 52-72, and also Pres. of Exec. Council and Minister of Finance 55-72; leader of the Social Credit movement in B.C. 52-73; Freeman of the City of Kelowna.
Leisure interests: fishing, reading, bridge.
Seaview Apartments, 2768 Satellite Street, Victoria, B.C.; 1979 Ethel Street, Kelowna, B.C., Canada.

Bennett, William John, O.B.E., LL.D., B.A.; Canadian business executive; b. 3 Nov. 1911; ed. Fort William Collegiate Coll. and Univ. of Toronto.
Private Sec. to Minister of Transport 35-39; Chief Exec. Asst. to Minister of Munitions and Supply 39-46; Pres. and Man. Dir. Eldorado Mining and Refining Ltd. (the Govt. agency responsible for uranium procurement) 47-58; Pres. Northern Transportation Co. Ltd. 47-58; Eldorado Aviation Ltd. 53-58, Pres. Atomic Energy of Canada Ltd. 53-58; Dir. Canadian British Aluminium Co. Ltd., Pres. 58-60; Vice-Pres. and Dir. Iron Ore Co. of Canada 60-65, Pres. 65-; dir. of numerous other companies.
Iron Ore Company of Canada, 1245 Sherbrooke Street W., Montreal, P.Q.; Home: 4304 Montrose Avenue, Westmount, Quebec, Canada.

Bennett, William Tapley, Jr., A.B., LL.B., D.C.L.; American diplomatist; b. 1 April 1917, Griffin, Ga.; s. of William Tapley Bennett and Annie Mem Little Bennett; m. Margaret Rutherfurd White 1945; two s. three d.; ed. Univ. of Georgia, Univ. of Freiburg, Germany, and George Washington Univ.
Instructor in Political Science, Univ. of Georgia 37; with Nat. Inst. of Public Affairs 39-40; Dept. of Agriculture 40; Asst. to Co-ordinator, Office of Defense Housing 40-41; with State Dept. 41-, served in U.S. Army 44-46; Officer in charge Central American and Panama Affairs 49-51, Caribbean Affairs 51, Deputy Dir. South American Affairs 51-54; Nat. War Coll. 54-55; Special Asst. to Deputy Under-Sec. of State 55-57; Counsellor, Vienna 57-61, Rome 61; Counsellor (with rank of Minister), Athens 61-64; Amb. to Dominican Repub. 64-66, to Portugal 66-69; State Dept. Rep. to Air Force Univ. 69-71; Deputy U.S. Rep. and Amb. UN Security Council 71-; Alternate U.S. Rep. to 26th and 27th UN Gen. Assemblies 71, 72; Pres. UN Trusteeship Council 72-73.
Leisure interests: sailing, skiing, photography, travel, golf.
U.S. Mission to the United Nations, 799 UN Plaza, New York, N.Y. 10017, U.S.A.

Bennigsen-Foerder, Rudolf von; German business executive; b. 2 July 1926, Berlin; s. of Rudolf and Margarethe (née Welt) von Bennigsen-Foerder; m. Johanna Wirmer 1955; no c.; ed. Univs. of Erlangen, Bonn and Geneva.
With Ministry of Finance 57-59; joined VEBA AG 59, Chair. Man. Board 71-; Chair. Supervisory Board Chemische Werke Hüls AG 74-, Gelsenberg AG, Nordwestdeutsche Kraftwerke AG, Preussische Elektrizitäts-AG, Hugo Stinnes AG, VEBA-CHEMIE AG.
4 Düsseldorf 30, Karl-Arnold-Platz 3, Federal Republic of Germany.
Telephone: (0211) 45791.

Benning, Bernhard, DR.OEC.(PUBL.); German banker; b. 17 Sept. 1902, Munich; s. of Karl and Margaret Benning; m. Ilse Güssow 1939; two d.; ed. Maximiliansgymnasium and Universität München.
Bayerische Hypotheken- und Wechsel-Bank, Munich 23-28; Dept. for Issue and Investment of Capital, Statistisches Reichsamt 28-33; Dir. of Econ. Dept.,

Reichs-Kredit-Gesellschaft 33-45; prisoner-of-war 45-50; mem. Board of Mans., Bank Deutscher Länder 50-57; mem. Board of Mans. and of Zentralbankrat Deutsche Bundesbank 57-72; Deputy Chair. Board of Dirs. Deutsche Verkehrs-Kreditbank AG, Lastenausgleichsbank and Deutsche Gesellschaft für öffentliche Arbeiten; Grosses Verdienstkreuz mit Stern.
Leisure interests: books, coins, walking, gardening.
Publs. include *Der Schwarze Freitag: Eine Untersuchung des Börsenzusammenbruchs 27, Kapitalbildung und Investition in der Deutschen Volkswirtschaft 31*.
6 Frankfurt/M, Lindenring 41, Federal Republic of Germany.

Benslimane, Abdelkader; Moroccan politician; b. 1932; ed. Toulouse Univ., France.
Joined Ministry of Finance 57; Amb. to France 61-63; attached to Maghreb Consultative Comm., Ministry of Finance; Amb. to Belgium 72; Minister of Trade, Industry, Mines and Merchant Marine 72-74, of Finance April 74-.
Ministry of Finance, Rabat, Morocco.

Benson, Rt. Hon. Edgar John, P.C., M.P.; Canadian chartered accountant and politician; b. 1923; ed. Queen's Univ., Kingston, Ontario.
Joined firm England, Leonard and Macpherson (chartered accountants), Kingston, Ontario 52; Asst. Prof. of Commerce, Queen's Univ., Kingston 52-62; M.P. 62-72; Parl. Sec. to Minister of Finance 63-64; Minister of National Revenue 64-68; Pres. of Treasury Board 65-68; Minister of Finance 68-72, also Receiver-Gen. 68-72; Head of Central Mortgage and Housing Corpn. 68-72; Minister of Nat. Defence Jan.-Oct. 72; Pres. Canadian Transport Comm. 72-; Liberal.
275 Slater Street, Ottawa, Ont.; Home: 44 Strathcona Crescent, Kingston, Ont., Canada.

Benson, Ezra Taft, M.S.; American agriculturist and religious leader; b. 4 Aug. 1899; ed. Brigham Young Univ., Iowa State Coll., and Univ. of Calif.
Missionary of Church of Jesus Christ of Latter-day Saints in U.K. 21-23; County Agricultural Agent, Univ. of Idaho Extension Service 29, Extension Economist and Marketing Specialist 30-39, Head Dept. of Agricultural Economics and Marketing 31; Sec. Idaho Co-operative Council 33-38; Exec. Sec. Nat. Council of Farmer Co-operatives 39-43; served on several advisory cttees. and nat. boards in field of agriculture 39-; mem. Exec. Cttee. American Inst. of Co-operation 42-52, Chair. Board of Trustees 52; mem. Farm Foundation 46, 50; mem. Nat. Agricultural Advisory Cttee. during Second World War, mem. Nat. Farm Credit Cttee. 40-43; U.S. del. Int. Conf. of Farm Organisations, London 46; U.S. Sec. of Agriculture Jan. 53-61; Dir. Corn Products Inc. 61-; mem. Council of Twelve, Church of Jesus Christ of Latter-day Saints 43-, Pres. Mormon Church European Mission 63; Republican.
1907 Quincy Street, N.W., Washington, D.C. 20018; and c/o Church of Jesus Christ of Latter-Day Saints, 47 East Temple Street, Salt Lake City, Utah 84111, U.S.A.

Benson, Sir Henry, G.B.E., F.C.A.; British chartered accountant; b. 2 Aug. 1909, Johannesburg; s. of Alexander S. and Florence (née Cooper) Benson; m. Virginia Macleod 1939; two s. one d.; ed. South Africa.
Commissioned Grenadier Guards 40-45; Dir. Royal Ordnance Factories 43-44; Controller of Building Materials Ministry of Works 45; Adviser on housing production, Ministry of Health 45; Dir. Hudson's Bay Co. 53-62, Deputy Gov. 55-62; Dir. Finance Corpn. for Industry 53-; mem. Council, Inst. of Chartered Accountants 56-75, Pres. 66; Investigator Ulster Transport Authority 61, shipping services in N.Z. trade 62, turnover tax cttee. 63; Joint Commr. on formation of Confed. of British Ind. 63; Joint Insp. Rolls Razor Affair 64; Chair. Iron and Steel Fed. Devt. Cttee. 66; Trustee, Times Trust 67-; mem. Perm. Joint Hops

Cttee. 67-; Chair. Nat. Trust Inquiry Cttee., Racing Industry Inquiry Cttee. 67; Vice-Pres. UEC 69-70; mem. Ministry of Defence Admin. Cttee. 69-71, Dockyard Policy Board 70-75; Senior Partner, Coopers and Lybrand 47-75; mem. CBI Co. Affairs Cttee. 72-73; Chair. Int. Accounting Standards Cttee. 73-; Dir. Finance for Industry Ltd. 74-, Industrial and Commercial Finance Corpn. 74-; Exec. Dir. Hawker Siddeley 75-; mem. Govs.' City Liaison Cttee. 74-75; Treas. Open Univ. 75-; Adviser to Bank of England 75-.
Leisure interests: shooting, sailing, golf.
Bank of England, London, E.C.2; 9 Durward House, 31 Kensington Court, London, W.8, England.
Telephone: 01-937-4850.

Benthall, Sir Arthur Paul, K.B.E.; British business executive; b. 25 Jan. 1902, Wimbledon, Surrey; s. of Rev. C. F. Benthall and Annie Theodosia (née Wilson); m. Mary Lucy Pringle 1932; four s.; ed. Eton Coll. and Christ Church, Oxford.
Joined Bird and Co. and F. W. Heilgers and Co., Calcutta 24, partner in both firms 34; Vice-Pres. Bengal Chamber of Commerce 47, Pres. 48, 50; Pres. Asscn. of Chambers of Commerce of India 48, 50; mem. Calcutta Local Board, Imperial Bank of India 46-48, 50-53, Central Board 48, 50-53; Chair. All India Board of Technical Studies in Commerce and Business Admin. 50-53; Pres. Royal Agri-Horticultural Soc. of India 45-47; Vice-Pres. U.K. Citizens' Asscn. 51, Pres. 52; Chair. Amalgamated Metal Corpn. Ltd. 59-72; Chair. Bird and Co. (London) 53-72; Dir. The Chartered Bank 53-72, Royal Insurance Co. Ltd. and assoc. companies 53-72.
Leisure interests: botany, gardening, sailing.
Publ. *The Trees of Calcutta* 47.
Benthall Hall, Broseley, Salop, England.
Telephone: Telford 882254.

Bentley, Helen Delich; American government official, journalist and television and film producer; b. Ruth, Nev.; d. of Michael and Mary (Kovich) Delich; m. William Roy Bentley 1959; ed. Univ. of Nev., George Washington Univ. and Univ. of Mo.
Reporter, Ely Record, Nev. 40-42; Political Campaign Man. for Senator James G. Scrugham, White Pine Co., Nev. 42; Bureau Man., United Press, Fort Wayne, Ind. 44-45; Reporter Baltimore Sun 45-53, Maritime Editor 53-69; Television Producer, world trade and maritime shows 50-64; Public Relations Adviser, American Asscn. Port Authorities 58-62, 64-67; Chair. Fed. Maritime Comm. 69-; Chair. Amer. Bi-centennial Fleet Inc. 73-; Editor, Seaport Histories, Ports of Americas; Republican.
Federal Maritime Commission, 1405 I Street, N.W., Washington, D.C. 20573; 408 Chapelwood Lane, Lutherville, Md. 21093, U.S.A.

Bentley, Nicolas Clerihew, F.S.I.A.; British artist and author; b. 14 June 1907, Highgate, London; s. of E. C. and Violet (née Boileau) Bentley; m. Barbara Hastings 1934; one d.; ed. Univ. Coll. School, Heatherley School of Art.
Dir. André Deutsch Ltd.
Leisure interests: music, looking at paintings, travel.
Publs. *The Tongue-Tied Canary 48, The Floating Dutchman 50, Ballet-Hoo 52, Third Party Risk 53, A Choice of Ornaments 59, A Version of the Truth 60, The Victorian Scene 68, Golden Sovereigns 70, Tales from Shakespeare 72, The Events of That Week 72, Inside Information 74, An Edwardian Album 74*, etc.
The Old School, Downhead, Shepton Mallet, Somerset, England.
Telephone: 074-988-410.

Bentley, Phyllis Eleanor, O.B.E., B.A., D.LITT.; British novelist; b. 19 Nov. 1894, Halifax, Yorks.; d. of Joseph Edwin Bentley and Eleanor (née Kettlewell); ed. Halifax, Cheltenham Ladies' Coll.

Fellow Royal Soc. of Literature; Vice-Pres. English centre, P.E.N.; Vice-Pres. of Royal Literary Fund.
Leisure interests: amateur theatre, walking.
Publs. *The World's Bane* 18, *Environment* 22, *Cat-in-the-Manger* 23, *The Spinner of the Years* 28, *The Partnership* 28, *Carr* 29, *Trio* 30, *Inheritance* 32, *A Modern Tragedy* 34, *The Whole of the Story* 35, *Freedom, Farewell* 36, *Sleep in Peace* 38, *Take Courage* 39, *Manhold* 40, *Here is America* 42, *Regional Novel* 42, *The Rise of Henry Morcar* 46, *Some Observations on the Art of Narrative* 46, *The Brontës* 47, *Colne Valley Cloth* 47, *Life Story* 48, *Quorum* 50, *Panorama* 52, *The House of Moreys* 53, *Noble in Reason* 55, *Love and Money* 57, *Crescendo* 58, *Kith and Kin* 60, *The Young Brontës* 60, *Committees* 62, *O Dreams, O Destinations* 62, *Public Speaking* 64, *Enjoy Books* 64, *The Adventures of Tom Leigh* 64, *Tales of the West Riding* 65, *A Man of his Time* 66, *Ned Carver in Danger* 67, *Gold Pieces* 68, *Ring in the New* 69, *The Brontës and their World* 69, *Sheep May Safely Graze* 72, *The New Venturers* 73, *More Tales of the West Riding* 74.
The Grange, Warley, Halifax, Yorks., England.
Telephone: Halifax 31624.

Bentov, Mordechai; Israeli journalist and politician; b. 28 March 1900, Warsaw, Poland; s. of Joseph and Helen Bentov; m. Zipora Redlich 1926; two d.; ed. Inst. of Technology, Warsaw Univ. and Jerusalem Law Classes.
Settled in Palestine 20; Founder and Chief Editor *Al Hamishmar* 43-48 and 49-55; signed Declaration of Independence of Israel 48; mem. Knesset 49-; Minister of Labour and Reconstruction, Provisional Govt. 48-49; Minister of Development 55-61; mem. Jewish Agency Del. to U.N., Lake Success 47; Del. to Zionist Congresses, Round Table Conf. London 39, World Jewish Congress, U.S.A. 44, Geneva 53; mem. Secretariat, United Workers Party (MAPAM); Chair. Economic Affairs Cttee. of the Knesset 51-55; Minister of Housing 66-70; mem. World Exec. Hashomer Hatzair, Exec. Histadrut and Zionist Action Cttee.; mem. Exec. World Jewish Congress.
Leisure interests: photography, filming.
Publs. *The Case for Bi-National Palestine* 46, *Israel's Economy at the Crossroads* 65, *Israel, the Palestinians and the Left* 71.
Kibbutz Mishmar Haemek, Israel.

Bentsen, Lloyd Millard, Jr., LL.B.; American politician; b. 11 Feb. 1921, Mission, Tex.; s. of Lloyd M. Bentsen and Edna Ruth (Colbath) Bentsen; m. Beryl A. Longino 1943; two s. one d.; ed. Univ. of Texas, Austin.
Served U.S. Army 42-45; County Judge, Hidalgo County, Tex. 46-48; mem. House of Reps. 48-54; Dir. Lockheed Aircraft, Continental Oil, Bank of Southwest in Houston until 70; U.S. Senator from Tex. 71-; Chair. Armed Services Sub-Cttee. on Volunteer Forces and Selective Service 72; mem. Senate Finance Cttee.; Distinguished Flying Cross; Air Medal with Three Oak Leaf Clusters; Democrat.
115 Senate Office Building, Washington, D.C. 20510, U.S.A.

Bentz van den Berg, Pieter Rudolph; Netherlands iron and steel executive; b. 21 Feb. 1901; ed. Nederlandsche Economische Hoogeschool, Rotterdam.
Koninklijke Nederlandsche Hoogovens en Staalfabrieken N.V. (Royal Netherlands Blast Furnaces and Steelworks), Ijmuiden 24-67, Gen. Proxy 31-46, Man. Dir. 46-65, Senior Man. Dir. 65-, mem. Board 67-71; Vice-Pres. Economic League for European Co-operation, Pres. Dutch Section; fmr. Pres. Central Org. for Econ. Relations with Foreign Countries; Dir. various other companies; Commdr. Order of Vasa (Sweden), Knight of the Order Nederlandsche Leeuw.
Van Lennepweg 5, Oosterbeek, Netherlands.

Bentzon, Niels Viggo; Danish composer; b. 24 Aug. 1919; ed. Danish Royal Conservatory.
Musical works: Twelve symphonies, seven piano concertos, opera *Faust*, choral works, five ballets, pieces for chamber orchestra, string quartet and piano.
Solsortvej 33, Copenhagen, Denmark.
Telephone: Fasan 24.

Benya, Anton; Austrian trade union official; b. 1912; ed. occupational school.
Electromechanic, shop steward; mem. Exec. Cttee. Metal Workers and Miners Union 48, Chair. 62-; Sec. Austrian Trade Union Fed. 48, Vice-Pres. 59, Pres. 63-; mem. Parl. 56; mem. Exec. Cttee. Socialist Party; Pres. Nationalrat 71-.
1130 Vienna XIII, Elisabethallee 83; 1011 Vienna, Hohenstaufengasse 10-12, Austria.
Telephone: Vienna 63-37-11 (Office).

Benz, Ernst Wilhelm, DR. PHIL., LIC. THEOL., D.D. (Marburg); German university professor; b. 17 Nov. 1907, Friedrichshafen am Bodensee; s. of Ernst Benz and Line Benz (née Bofinger); m. Brigitte von Boxberger 1960; six s. one d.; ed. Univs. of Tübingen, Berlin and Rome.
Docent Univ. of Halle-Wittenberg 32-35; Extraordinary Prof. of Church History Univ. of Marburg 35-37; Ordinary Prof. 37-; mem. Acad. of Sciences, Mainz 49. Acad. Septentrionale, Paris 58, American Acad. of Arts and Sciences, Boston 65, Katholische Akademie, Vienna 69.
Leisure interests: hiking, cycling, accordion playing.
Publs. *Das Todesproblem in der Stoa* 29, *Marius Victorinus und die Entwicklung der abendländischen Willensmetaphysik* 32, *Ecclesia Spiritualis, Die Geschichtsanschauung und Kirchenidee der franziskanischen Reformation* 34, *Der vollkommene Mensch, nach Jakob Boehme* 37, *Nietzsches Ideen zur Geschichte des Christentums* 38, *Emanuel Swedenborg* 48, *Swedenborg in Deutschland* 48, *Leibniz und Peter der Grosse* 48, *Wittenberg und Byzanz* 48, *Die Ost-Kirche und die russische Christenheit* 49, *Die abendländische Sendung der östlich-orthodoxen Kirche* 50, *Indische Einflüsse auf die frühchristliche Theologie* 51, *Paulus als Visionär* 52, *Russische Heiligenlegenden* 53, *Bischofsamt und apostolische Sukzession* 53, *Die Ostkirche* 53, *Augustins Lehre von der Kirche* 54, *Schelling, Werden und Wirken seines Denkens* 55, *Schellings Theologische Geistesahnen* 55, *Adam, Der Mythus von Urmenschen* 56, *Geist und Leben der Ostkirche* 57, *Die christliche Kabbala* 58, *Der Prophet Jakob Boehme* 59, *Die Bedeutung der griechisch-orthodoxen Kirche für das Abendland* 59, *Ideen zu einer Theologie der Religionsgeschichte* 60, *Das Christentum und die nichtchristlichen Hochreligionen, Eine internationale Bibliographie* 60, *Kirchengeschichte in ökumenischer Sicht* 61, *Der Übermensch, Eine Diskussion* 61. *Zen in europäischer Sicht* 62, *Asiatische Begegnungen* 63, *Buddhas Wiederkehr und die Zukunft Asiens* 63, *The Eastern Orthodox Church: Its Thought and Life* 63, *Die protestantische Thebais* 63, *Patriarchen und Einsiedler: der tausendjährige Athos und die Zukunft der Ostkirche* 64, *Schöpfungsglaube und Endzeiterwartung* 65, *Buddhism or Communism, Which holds the Future of Asia?* 65, *Russische Kirche und abendländisches Christentum* 66, *Evolution and Christian Hope* 66, *Les Sources Mystiques de la Philosophie Romantique Allemande* 68, *Die Vision: Erfahrungsformen und Bilderwelt* 69, *Der Heilige Geist in Amerika* 70, *Theologie der Elektrizität* 71, *Der Philosoph von Sans-Souci im Urteil der Theologie und Philosophie seiner Zeit* 71, *Neue Religionen* 71; Edited *Sonderhefte Z.R.G.G.*, *Reinkarnation, Moderne Aktivität der nichtchristlichen Hochreligionen, Christliche Brüderschaften, Messianische Kirchen, Sekten und Bewegungen im heutigen Afrika, Geist und Landschaft* 72, *Endzeiterwartung zwischen Ost und West* 73, *Das Recht auf Faulheit (Lafargue-Studien)*

74, *Urbild und Abbild* (*Der Mensch und die mystische Welt*) 74.
Lutherstrasse 7a, 355 Marburg (Lahn), Hessen, Federal Republic of Germany.
Telephone: 06421-25209.

Benzer, Seymour, B.A., M.S., PH.D.; American biologist; b. 15 Oct. 1921, N.Y.C.; s. of Mayer Benzer and Eva Naidorf; m. Dorothy Vlosky 1942; two c.; ed. Brooklyn Coll. and Purdue Univ.
Assistant Prof. of Physics Purdue Univ. 47-53, Assoc. Prof. of Biophysics 53-58, Prof. 58-61, Stuart Distinguished Prof. 61-67; Biophysicist Oak Ridge Nat. Laboratory 48-49; Research Fellow California Inst. of Technology 49-51, Visiting Assoc. 65-67, Prof. of Biology 67-75, Boswell Prof. of Neuroscience 75-; Fulbright Research Scholar, Pasteur Inst., Paris 51-52; Senior Nat. Science Foundation Research Fellow Cambridge 57-58; Fellow, American Asscn. for the Advancement of Science; mem. Nat. Acad. of Sciences, Harvey Soc., Biophysical Soc., American Acad. of Arts and Sciences, American Philosophical Soc.; awards include Sigma Xi Research Award 57 and McCoy Award 65, Purdue Univ. and Gairdner Award of Merit (Canada) 64, Ricketts Award, Univ. of Chicago, Lasker Award 71, Prix Charles-Leopold Mayer, French Acad. of Sciences 75, T. Duckett Jones Award, Helen Hay Whitney Foundation 75; Hon. D.Sc., Purdue Univ. 68, Columbia Univ. 74.
Publs. *The Elementary Units of Heredity* 57, *Induction of Specific Mutations with 5-bromouracil* 58, *Topology of the Genetic Fine Structure* 59, *Topography of the Genetic Fine Structure* 61, *A Change from Nonsense to Sense in the Genetic Code* 62, *On the Role of Soluble Ribonucleic Acid in Coding for Amino Acids* 62, *A Physical Basis for Degeneracy in the Genetic Code* 62, *Adventures in the rII Region* 66, *Isolation of Behavioral Mutants of Drosophila by countercurrent Distribution* 67, *Genetic Dissection of the Drosophila Nervous System by means of Mosaics* 70, *Mapping of Behavior in Drosophila Mosaics* 72, *Genetic Dissection of Behavior* 73.
Division of Biology, California Institute of Technology, Pasadena, Calif. 91125, U.S.A.
Telephone: 795-7697.

Bérard, Armand; French diplomatist; b. 2 May 1904; s. of Victor Bérard and Alice Colin; m. Isabelle de Savignac 1945; two d.; ed. Ecole Normale Supérieure, Paris, Heidelberg Univ., and French School for Advanced Spanish Studies, Madrid.
Served Berlin 31, Office of Under-Sec., Foreign Affairs 36, Office of Foreign Minister 36-37, Washington 38, Rome (Quirinal) 39; mem. French Del. to Armistice Comm. Wiesbaden 40-42; mem. Underground Foreign Affairs Study Bureau 42; escaped to Algiers 44; Minister-Counsellor in Washington 45; Deputy High Commr. in Germany 49; Diplomatic Adviser to Prime Minister 55; Ambassador to Japan 56-59; Perm. Rep. to UN 59-62; Amb. to Italy 62-67; Perm. Rep. to UN 67-70; Gov. Fondation européenne de la Culture; Grand Officier Légion d'Honneur.
25 rue du Bois de Boulogne, 92 Neuilly, France.
Telephone: 624-35-44.

Berard, Maurice Robert Georges; French banker; b. 17 March 1891, Paris; s. of Philippe Berard; m. Yolande de Loys-Chandieu 1918 (deceased); two s. (deceased), one d.; ed. Paris Univ.
Hon. Pres. Bank of Syria and Lebanon; Hon. Pres. Friends of Nat. Museum of Modern Art; Vice-Pres. Friends of the Louvre; Hon. Pres. Asscn. Léonard de Vinci; Gold Medal Aero Club of America and Aero Club of France; Officer Legion of Honour; Croix de Guerre 14-18; D.C.M.; Mérite Agricole.
Leisure interests: art, archaeology, agriculture.

Publs. *Renoir à Wargemont, Une Famille du Dauphiné.*
7 rue Alfred Dehodencq, Paris 16e, France.
Telephone: TRO 16-94.

Bercot, Pierre, D. en D.; French businessman; b. 12 July 1903, Paris; m. Vivaldine Pinchon 1938; three c.; ed. Lycée Henri IV, Faculté de Droit, Paris, Ecole Nationale des Langues Orientales.
President and Gen. Man. Soc. Anonyme André Citroën (Citroën, S.A. since 68) 58-70, Hon. Pres. Jan. 71-; Pres. Comobil, S.A., Geneva 66-; Admin. Comotor, S.A., Luxembourg 67-.
Leisure interests: music, yachting.
Home: 24 *bis* Parc de Montretout, 92 Saint-Cloud; Office: 117 Quai André Citroën, Paris 15e, France.

Bere, James F., M.B.A.; American business executive; b. 25 July 1922, Chicago, Ill.; m.; three s. two d.; ed. Northwestern Univ., Ill.
Draughtsman for Clearing Machine Div., U.S. Industries, Inc., rising to Gen. Man. of the Div., Hamilton, Ohio, Pres. and Gen. Man. of Axelson Mfg. Div., Los Angeles 56-61; Pres. and Gen. Man. of Borg and Beck Div., Borg-Warner Corpn. 61-64, Group Vice-Pres. Borg-Warner Corpn. Jan. 64-66, Exec. Vice-Pres. 66-68, Pres. 68-75, Chief Exec. Officer 72-; Chair. June 75-, served with U.S.A.A.F. in Second World War; Dir. Continental Ill. Nat. Bank and Trust Co. of Chicago; mem. Young Presidents' Org., Soc. of Automotive Engineers, Board of Trustees of Ill. Inst. of Technology; mem. U.S. Council of the Int. Chamber of Commerce and Japan-U.S. Econ. Council and of various socs.
Borg-Warner Corporation, 200 S. Michigan Avenue, Chicago, Ill. 60604; 641 South Elm Street, Hinsdale, Ill., U.S.A.
Telephone: (312) 663-2060.

Beregovoy, Major-Gen. Georgi Timofeevich; Soviet cosmonaut; b. 15 April 1921, Fyodorovka, Poltava Region; m. Lydia Matveyevna; one s. one d.; ed. Zhukovsky Air Force Engineering Acad.
Entered Lugansk Training School for Pilots 38; in Soviet Air Force 38-; assault pilot in Second World War; after war attended Senior Officer's School and later took a test-pilot course; graduated from Air Force Acad. 56; joined cosmonaut detachment 64; mem. C.P.S.U. 43-; made flight in *Soyuz 3* (with space-docking experiments) Oct. 68; paid official visit to U.S.A. 69; Deputy, U.S.S.R. Supreme Soviet 70; mem. Comm. for Foreign Affairs, Soviet of Union; Merited test-pilot of U.S.S.R.; Hero of Soviet Union, Gold Star (twice), Order of Lenin (twice), Red Banner.
Zvezdny Gorodok, Moscow, U.S.S.R.

Berenblum, Isaac, M.D., M.SC.; Israeli pathologist and experimental biologist; b. 26 Aug. 1903, Białystok, Poland; s. of Paul and Michle Berenblum; m. Doris L. Bernstein 1928; two d.; ed. Bristol Grammar School and Leeds Univ.
Riley-Smith Research Fellow, Dept. Experimental Pathology and Cancer Research, Leeds Univ. Medical School 27-36; Beit Memorial Research Fellow, Dunn School of Pathology, Oxford Univ. 36-40; Departmental and Univ. Demonstrator in Pathology, Oxford Univ. 40-48; in charge of Oxford Univ. Research Centre of British Empire Cancer Campaign 40-48; Special Research Fellow, Nat. Cancer Inst., Bethesda, Md., U.S.A. 48-50; Visiting Prof. of Oncology, Hebrew Univ., Jerusalem 51-57; Jack Cotton Prof. of Cancer Research, Head of Dept. of Experimental Biology, The Weizmann Inst. of Science, Rehovot, Israel 50-71; Emeritus Prof. 71-; Scholar-in-Residence, Fogarty Int. Center, Nat. Insts. of Health, Bethesda, Md. 71; Hon. Life mem. New York Acad. of Sciences 58, mem. Israel Nat. Acad. Sciences and Humanities, World Acad. Arts and Sciences.

Leisure interests: chess, writing, listening to music.
Publs. *Science versus Cancer* 46, *Man against Cancer* 52,
Cancer Research Today 67, *Carcinogenesis as a Biological
Problem* 74.
Weizmann Institute of Science, Rehovot, Israel.
Telephone: 951721.

Beretta, David; American chemical engineer; b. 16
July 1928, Cranston, R.I.; *m.* Serena Shuebruk; two *s.*
one *d.*; ed. Univ. of Rhode Island, Rhode Island Coll.
and Univ. of Connecticut.
With Fram Corpn. of East Providence 49-51; service
with U.S. Army Chemical Corps, Korean War; joined
Chemical Div., Uniroyal Inc. 53, Factory Man.
Naugatuck Plant 65, Vice-Pres. Chemical Operations,
Uniroyal Ltd., Canada 66, Vice-Pres. Marketing 68-70,
Pres. Uniroyal Chemical 70, Group Vice-Pres. 72-73,
Dir., Pres., Chief Operating Officer Jan.-Dec. 74, Chair.,
Pres., Chief Exec. Jan. 75-; Dir. Rubicon Chemicals
Inc., Monochem Inc., Geismar Industries Inc.; Chair.
Research Inst., Univ. of Waterloo; mem. Advisory
Council, Coll. of Eng., Notre Dame Univ., Naugatuck
Chamber of Commerce, Conn. Public Expenditures
Council; mem. Amer. Chemical Soc., Amer. Inst. of
Chemical Engineers, Rhode Island Professional Engs.
Uniroyal Inc., Oxford Management and Research Cen-
ter, Middlebury, Conn. 06749, U.S.A.

Berg, Axel Ivanovich; Soviet scientist; b. 10 Nov.
1893, Orenburg; ed. Military Naval Acad.
Specialist in field of radio engineering; Instructor and
later Prof., Naval Engineering School 25-, Leningrad
Electrical Engineering Inst. 26-, Mil. Naval Acad.,
Leningrad 27-; Chair., All Union A. S. Popov Soc. of
Radio Engineering and Electrical Communications and
All Union Scientific Council for Radio-physics and
Radio Engineering, U.S.S.R. Acad. of Sciences, Corresp.
mem. 43-46, Academician 46-; Chair. Scientific Council
for Complex Problem of Cybernetics, U.S.S.R. Acad. of
Sciences 59-; Editor-in-Chief Encyclopedia *Automation
in Production and Industrial Electronics*; mem. C.P.S.U.
44-; Hero of Socialist Labour, Order of Lenin (three
times), Hammer and Sickle Gold Medal, etc.
Publs. include: *Theory of Vacuum Alternating-Current
Generators* 25, *Theory of Calculation of Thermionic
Generators* 32, *Selected Works* 64.
U.S.S.R. Academy of Sciences, 14 Leninsky Prospekt,
Moscow, U.S.S.R.

Berg, Fritz; German manufacturer; b. 27 Aug. 1901;
ed. Univ. of Cologne.
Pres. Bundesverband der Deutschen Industrie, Cologne,
Union des Industries de la Communauté Européenne
(UNICE), Brussels, Wirtschaftsverband Eisen-, Blech-
und Metallwaren, Düsseldorf, South Westphalian
Chamber of Commerce.
599 Attena/W., Lüdenscheiderstrasse 16, Federal
Republic of Germany.

Berg, Paul, B.S., PH.D.; American biochemist; b. 30
June 1926, New York; *s.* of Harry Berg and Sarah
Brodsky; *m.* Mildred Levy 1947; one *s.*; ed. Pa. State
Univ. and Western Reserve Univ.
Post-doctoral Fellow, Copenhagen Univ., Denmark
52-53; Postdoctoral Fellow, Washington Univ., St
Louis, Mo. 53-54, Scholar in Cancer Research 54-57
Asst. to Assoc. Prof. of Microbiology 55-59; Prof of
Biochemistry, Stanford Univ. School of Medicine,
Stanford, Calif. 59-, Chair. Dept. of Biochemistry
69-74; Senior Post-Doctoral Fellow of Material Science
Foundation 61-68; Pres. American Soc. of Biological
Chemists 75-76; mem. Nat. Acad. of Sciences 66-; Eli
Lilly Prize in Biochemistry 59, Calif. Scientist of the
Year 63, V. D. Mattia Award 72.
Leisure interests: travel, art, and sports.
Publs. 70 publs. in fields of biochemistry and micro
biology.

Stanford University Medical Center, Stanford, Calif.
94305, U.S.A.
Telephone: 415/497-6170.

Berganza, Teresa; Spanish mezzo-soprano singer; b.
16 March 1935.
Debut in Aix-en-Provence 57, in England, Glyndebourne 58; has sung at La Scala, Milan, Opera Roma,
Metropolitan, New York, Chicago Opera House, San
Francisco Opera, Covent Garden, etc.; has appeared at
festivals in Edinburgh, Holland, Glyndebourne; con-
certs in France, Belgium, Holland, Italy, Germany,
Spain, Austria, Portugal, Scandinavia, Israel, Mexico,
Buenos Aires, U.S.A., Canada, etc.; appeared as Rosina
in *Il Barbiere di Siviglia*, Covent Garden 67; Premio
Lucrezia Arana; Premio extraordinario del Conserva-
torio de Madrid; Grande Cruz, Isabel la Católica.
Joaquín María López 29, Madrid 15, Spain.
Telephone: 2336359.

Bergen, William Benjamin, B.S., AERO.E.; American
aerospace engineer and business executive; b. 29 March
1915; *s.* of Oldfield and Hazel Bergen; *m.* 1st Gertrude
Catherine Coxon 1943, 2nd Eleanor Mae Page 1968;
one *s.* one *d.*; ed. Mass. Inst. of Technology.
Glenn L. Martin Co., Baltimore, Md. (now Martin Co.)
37-, Chief Engineer 49-51, Vice-Pres. Engineering 51-
53, Exec. Vice-Pres. 53-55, Pres. 59; Rockwell Int.
(fmrly. North Amer. Rockwell) Pres. Space Div. 67-70,
Pres. Aerospace Operations 71, Corporate Vice-Pres.
Aerospace 74-; Dir. Calif. State Chamber of Commerce;
mem. S.A.E., Holland Soc.; Fellow A.I.A.A.; Lawrence
Sperry Award 43.
Leisure interests: flying, golf, hunting, tennis.
c/o Rockwell International, 1700 East Imperial Highway, El Segundo, Calif. 90245, U.S.A.
Telephone: 213/647-5552.

Bergenström, Stig Gullmar, LL.D.; Swedish administrator; b. 3 Dec. 1909, Cannes, France; *m.* Hélène
Renfer 1958; one *s.* one *d.* and six *c.* from previous
marriages; ed. Univ. of Uppsala.
Judiciary service at Court of Justice 34-37; Sec.-Gen.
Group of the Swedish Employers' Confed. 37, Asst.
Dir. 41, Vice-Dir. 44, Dir. 49-; mem. Employers' Group
of Governing Body of ILO 50-; Vice-Pres. Exec. Cttee.
of Int. Org. of Employers 52-62, Pres. Exec. Cttee.
63-; Chair. Int. Council of Danish, Finnish, Norwegian
and Swedish Employers' Confederations; Vice-Chair.
Governing Body ILO 69-.
Leisure interests: sailing, philately.
Swedish Employers' Confederation, S. Blasieholmshamn
4A, Stockholm; Box 16 120, 103/23 Stockholm, Sweden.
Telephone: Stockholm 14-05-00.

Berger, Hans, DR. JUR.; German lawyer and diplo-
matist; b. 29 Oct. 1909, Cologne; ed. Cologne Univ.
Assistant judge, Cologne 37-39; Adviser to Commr. for
Price-Control, Berlin 39-44; Judge, Cologne 45-47,
Supreme Court of British Zone of Germany, Cologne
48-49; Pres. Court, Düsseldorf 49-53; Ministerial Dir.,
Ministry of the Interior, Bonn 53-54; Head, Legal Dept.,
Foreign Office, Bonn 54-59; Amb. to Denmark 59-63,
to Netherlands 63-65; Sec. of State to the Pres. of the
German Fed. Repub. 65-69; Amb. to Holy See 69-71.
534 Bad Honnef, Schaaffhausenstrasse 1, Federal
Republic of Germany.
Telephone: 02224 3432.

Berger, Samuel D., PH.B.; American diplomatist; b.
6 Dec. 1911, Gloversville, N.Y.; *s.* of Harry I. Berger
and Bess Cohen; *m.* Elizabeth Lee Bonner 1969; ed.
Univ. of Wisconsin and London School of Economics.
Served U.K. 42-50; Special Asst. to Dir. for Mutual
Security 51-53; Counsellor Tokyo, Wellington (N.Z.),
Athens 53-61; Amb. to Repub. of Korea 61-64; Deputy
Commdt. Foreign Affairs, Nat. War Coll., Washington,
D.C. 64-65; Deputy Asst. Sec. of State for Far Eastern

Affairs 65-68; Deputy Amb. to Repub. of Viet-Nam 68-72; Co-ordinator, Senior Seminar, Foreign Service Inst., Dept. of State, Wash. 72-74; retd. 75.
Leisure interests: tennis, gardening.
2911 33rd Place, N.W., Washington, D.C. 20008, U.S.A.

Berger, Wilhelm Georg; Romanian composer and musicologist; b. 4 Dec. 1929, Rupea, Braşov Cty.; studied violin at Bucharest Conservatoire.
Member of Bucharest Filarmonica Orchestra 48-57; mem. Composers' Union Quartet 53-57; Sec. Romanian Composers' Union; "Prince Rainier III of Monaco" Prize, Monte Carlo, 64; Concours international de composition d'oeuvres pour quatuor à cordes Prize, Liège, 65; "Reine Elisabeth de Belgique" Int. Musical Contest Prize 66; "George Enescu" Prize of Romanian Acad. 66; Composers' Union Prize 69.
Compositions: Eight symphonies, chamber music (12 string quartets, sonatas, etc.).
Publs. Studies: *Moduri si proportii*; *Structuri sonore si aspectele lor armonice* (Modes and proportions; Sonorous structures and their harmonic aspects), articles and lectures; *Ghid pentru muzica instrumentala de camera* (Guidebook for instrumental chamber music) 65; *Muzica simfonica* (*Baroque-Classical* 67, *Romantic* 72, *Modern* 74); *Quartetul de coarde de la Haydn la Debussy* (The string quartet from Haydn to Debussy) 70.
Uniunea Compozitorilor din Republica Socialista Romănia, 141 Calea Victoriei, Bucharest, Romania.

Bergeron, André Louis; French printer and trade unionist; b. 1 Jan. 1922.
Secretary-Gen. of Typographical Union, Belfort 46-47; Force-Ouvrière 47-48, Perm. Sec. Belfort Area 48; Sec.-Gen. Fédération Force Ouvrière du Livre 48-50; Regional Del. Force Ouvrière and mem. Exec. Cttee. 50-56, mem. Bureau de la Confédération 56-63, Sec.-Gen. Force Ouvrière 63-.
Force Ouvrière, 198 avenue du Maine, Paris 14e, France.
Telephone: 539-22-03.

Bergeron, Tor Harold Percival, D.SC.; Swedish meteorologist; b. 15 Aug. 1891, Godstone, Surrey, England; s. of Armand Bergeron and Hilda Stawe; m. Vera I. Romanovsky 1932; one s.; ed. Univ. of Stockholm and at Bergen and Leipzig.
Junior meteorologist, Stockholm 20-22, Bergen 22-23; Senior meteorologist, Bergen 25-28, Oslo 29-35; Consultant and Visiting Lecturer, Malta 28, 29, Moscow 30, 32; Senior meteorologist, Swedish Meteorological and Hydrological Inst. 35-41, Chief of Synoptic Section 41-47; Asst. Prof. of Meteorology, Stockholm Univ. 41-47; Prof. of Meteorology Uppsala Univ. 47-60, Emeritus 60-; Leader Project Pluvius, Uppsala Univ. 61-; Consultant/Visiting Prof. Univ. of Calif. (Los Angeles) 47, 57, 59, 61, 63; mem. Royal Swedish Acad. of Sciences, Royal Scientific Soc., Uppsala, Norwegian Acad. of Sciences; Hon. mem. American Meteorological Soc., Royal Meteorological Soc. (London), Swedish Geophysical Soc.; Dr. h.c. (Uppsala); several decorations including Int. Meteorological Org. Prize 66.
Leisure interests: music, colour photography.
Publs. *Wellen und Wirbel an einer quasistationären Grenzfläche über Europa* (with G. Swoboda) 24, *Über die dreidimensional verknüpfende Wetteranalyse (I & II)* 28, 34, *Richtlinien einer dynamischen Klimatologie* 30, *Physikalische Hydrodynamik* (with others) 33, *Lectures on clouds and practical synoptic analysis* (in Russian) 34, *On the Physics of Clouds and Precipitation* 35, *On the Physics of Fronts* 37, *Sechssprachiges Meteorologisches Wörterbuch* 39, *General Effects of Ice-Nuclei in Clouds* 49, *The Coastal Orographic Maxima of Precipitation in Autumn and Winter* 49, *Über den Mechanismus ausgiebiger Niederschläge* 50, *A General Survey in the Field of Cloud Physics* 53, *The Problem of Tropical Hurricanes* 54, *Dynamic Meteorology and Weather Forecasting* (with others) 57, *Methods in Scientific Weather Analysis and Forecasting* 59, *Problems and Methods of Rainfall Investigation* 60, *Preliminary Results of Project Pluvius* 61, *The possible role of snow-drift in building up high inland ice-sheets* 65, *On the low-level redistribution of atmospheric water caused by orography* 65, *Mesometeorological Studies of Precipitation* (I-III) 67-68, *Cloud Physics research and the future freshwater supply of the World* 68.
Bredgränd 3, 753 20 Uppsala, Sweden.
Telephone: 018-1439-90.

Bergersen, Birger Martin, DR.PHIL.; Norwegian teacher and public servant; b. 25 July 1891, Kvefiord; s. of H. C. Bergersen and Kristine Bergersen; m. Benedicte Nicolaysen 1930; one s. one d.; ed. Oslo Univ.
Curator Paleontological Museum 21; Asst. at Zoological Laboratory 22; lecturer Norwegian Coll. of Dentistry 25, Dir. of Anatomy Department 29, Prof. of Anatomy 32, Vice-Rector 33-37, Rector 39-42 and 45; on staff of Ministry of Supply and Reconstruction in London 42-45; Minister to Sweden 46, Ambassador 47; Minister of Ecclesiastical Affairs and Educ. 53-60; mem. Oslo City Council 35-45; Chair. Whaling Council 36-54; Pres. Int. Whaling Comm., Chair. Joint Cttee. Norwegian Research Councils 49-54, 60-65; mem. Board of Dirs. Maritime Museum 28-67, Vice-Chair. Oslo Municipal Art Collection 45-64, etc.; mem. Norwegian Acad. of Science in Oslo, Tromso and Trondheim; Dr. (h.c.) Stockholm Univ.; mem. N.Y. Acad. of Science; Hon. mem. Dental Orgs. of Norway, Sweden and Finland.
Publs. Many books and papers on zoology, comparative anatomy, dental anatomy, pedagogy and history of science.
Geologisk Museum Toyen, Sars gt. 1, Oslo 4; Home: Anton Schjöth's gt. 13, Oslo 4, Norway.
Telephone: Oslo 460373.

Bergesen, d.y., Sigval; Norwegian shipowner; b. 27 April 1893; ed. Oslo Commercial Coll.
Joined firm Sigval Bergesen, Stavanger 16; partner and Head, Shipowning Dept. 18-35; established Sig. Bergesen d.y. & Co., Oslo and Stavanger (of which he is now Senior Partner) 35; co-Dir. A. P. Møller, Copenhagen and Odense Staalskibsvaerft, Odense 34-39; returned to Norway 39; Chair. and Dir. Skibsaktieselskapet Snefonn, Skipsaksjeselskapet Bergehus; Chair. of Board, Teknisk Bureau A/S, A/S Sigmalm, A/S Siganka; Commdr. Order of St. Olav, Commdr. Order of Dannebrog, Légion d'Honneur, Médaille de l'Alliance Française, Les Palmes d'Officier de L'Instr. Publique (France), Knight's Cross of the Order of the Redeemer (Greece), Royal Order of George I.
Home: Huk Avenue 15, Bygdøy Oslo; Office: Bergehus, Drammensveien 106, Oslo, Norway.

Berggren, Thommy; Swedish actor; b. 1937; ed. The Pickwick Club (private dramatic school), Atelierteatern, Stockholm, and Gothenburg Theatre.
Gothenburg Theatre 59-63; Royal Dramatic Theatre, Stockholm 63-.
Plays acted in include: *Gengangaren* (Ibsen) 62, *Romeo and Juliet* 62, *Chembalo* 62, *Who's Afraid of Virginia Woolf* 64.
Films acted in include: *Pärlemor* 61, *Barnvagnen* (The Pram) 62, *Kvarteret Korpen* (Ravens End) 63, *En söndag i september* (A Sunday in September) 63, *Karlek 65* (Love 65) 65, *Elvira Madigan* 67, *The Black Palm Trees* 69, *The Ballad of Joe Hill* 71.
c/o Svenska Filminstitutet, Kungsgatan 48, Stockholm C., Sweden.

Berghaus, Ruth; German theatre director; b. 2 July 1927, Dresden; m. Paul Dessau (q.v.); ed. Palluccaschule.
Formerly production asst. and choreographer at several Berlin theatres; joined Berliner Ensemble 64, Deputy Dir. 70-71, Dir. 71-; productions at Berliner Ensemble include *Viet Nam Diskurs* (Peter Weiss), Brecht's *Im Dickicht der Städte* 71, *Die Gewehre der Frau*

Carrar 71, *Omphale* (Peter Hacks) 72, *Zement* (Heiner Müller) 73, *Die Mutter* 74; also responsible for several productions at the State Opera, Berlin, including works by R. Strauss, Rossini, Weber and Dessau; extraordinary mem. Deutsche Akad. der Künste.
Berliner Ensemble, 104 Berlin, Am Bertolt-Brecht-Platz 1, German Democratic Republic.

Berghianu, Maxim; Romanian economist and politician; b. 19 Aug. 1925, Sighişoara; *m.* Silvia Popovici (actress); two *d.*; ed. Economic Sciences and Planning Inst., Bucharest.
First Sec. of Communist Party Cttee. of Braşov Region 55-59, Cluj Region 63-65; Chair. of State Planning Cttee. 65-72; Minister for Technical and Material Supply and for Fixed Assets Management Control 72-; alt. mem. Central Cttee. of R.C.P. 55, mem. 60; alt. mem. of Exec. Cttee. of Central Cttee. of R.C.P. 65, mem. 66-; Deputy to Grand Nat. Assembly 57-; mem. Defence Council of Romania 69-; Hero of Socialist Labour 71.
Central Committee of the Romanian Communist Party, Bucharest, Romania.

Bergman, Ingmar; Swedish film director and theatre producer; b. 14 July 1918, Uppsala; ed. Stockholm Univ.
Producer Royal Theatre, Stockholm 40-42; scriptwriter and producer Svensk Filmindustri 40-44; theatre-dir. Helsingborg 44-46, Gothenburg 46-49, Malmo 54-63; leading Dir. Royal Dramatic Theatre, Stockholm 63-66; has written the scripts of most of his films; Erasmus Prize 65; Award for Best Dir. Nat. Soc. of Film Critics 70; Order of the Yugoslav Flag 71; Luigi Pirandello Int. Theatre Prize 71; author of plays *A Painting on Wood, The City, The Rite* (TV play), *The Lie* (TV play), *Scenes from a Marriage* (TV play); Dir. *To Damascus* 74, *The Merry Widow, Twelfth Night* 75.
Films include: *Crisis* 45, *It Rains on our Love* 46, *A Ship Bound for India* 47, *Music in Darkness* 47, *Port of Call* 48, *Prison* 48, *Thirst* 49, *To Joy* 49, *Summer Interlude* 50, *This Can't Happen Here* 50, *Waiting Women* 52, *Summer with Monika* 52, *Sawdust and Tinsel* 53, *A Lesson in Love* 54, *Journey into Autumn* 55, *Smiles of a Summer Night* 55, *The Seventh Seal* 56, *Wild Strawberries* 57, *So Close to Life* 57, *The Face* 58, *The Virgin Spring* 59, *The Devil's Eye* 60, *Through a Glass Darkly* 61, *Winter Light* 62, *The Silence* 62, *Now About these Women* 63, episode in *Stimulantia* 65, *Persona* 66, *The Hour of the Wolf* 67, *Shame* 68, *The Rite* 70, *A Passion* 70, *The Touch* 71, *Cries and Whispers* 72, *Scenes from a Marriage* 74, *The Magic Flute* (film and TV) 75, *Face to Face* (TV) 75.
c/o Svensk Filmindustri, Kungsgatan 36, Stockholm, Sweden.

Bergman, Ingrid; Swedish actress and film star; b. 29 Aug. 1915; ed. Stockholm.
Starred in Swedish, German, American, Italian, British and French films, including *Intermezzo, Casablanca, Gaslight, Bells of St. Mary's, For Whom the Bell Tolls, Stromboli, Anastasia, Notorious, Spellbound, Indiscreet, Inn of the Sixth Happiness, Goodbye Again, The Visit, Yellow Rolls-Royce, Cactus Flower, Walk in the Spring Rain, Mixed Up Files of Mrs. Frankweiler, Murder on the Orient Express* 74; has also appeared on the stage in New York, Rome, Paris and London in *Joan of Lorraine* (U.S.A.) 46, *Tea and Sympathy* (Paris) 56, *A Month in the Country* (London) 65, *More Stately Mansions* (Los Angeles, New York) 67-68, *Captain Brassbound's Conversion* (London) 71, *The Constant Wife* (London, U.S.A.) 73-74, etc.; Pres. of Jury, Cannes Film Festival 73; Order of Vasa; Acad. Awards 44, 56; Best Supporting Actress Award, Soc. of Film and TV Awards 74; Acad. Award for Best Supporting Actress 74.
c/o International Famous Agency, 11-12 Hanover Street, London, W.1, England.

Bergonzi, Carlo; Italian tenor opera singer; b. 13 July 1924, Busseto, Parma; ed. Parma Conservatory.
Debut (baritone) as Figaro (*Il Barbiere di Siviglia*) at Lecce 48; debut as tenor in title role of *Andrea Chénier*, Teatro Petruzzelli, Bari 51; subsequently appeared at various Italian opera houses including La Scala, Milan; U.S. debut in *Il Tabarro* and *Cavalleria Rusticana*, Lyric Opera, Chicago 55; appeared at Metropolitan Opera, New York in *Aida* (as Radames) and *Il Trovatore* (as Manrico) 55-56; now appears at all the major opera houses in Europe, and also in U.S.A. and South America; repertoire includes many Verdi roles.
c/o Signor A. Ziliani, A.L.C.I., Via Paolo da Cannobio 2, Milan, Italy; c/o John Coast, 1 Park Close, London, S.W.1, England.

Bergquist, Kenneth Paul, B.S.; American aviation management consultant; b. 21 Nov. 1912, Crookston, Minn.; *s.* of late Carl W. Bergquist and Anna O. Bergquist; *m.* Alice Stark Porterfield 1937; one *s.* one *d.*; ed. U.S. Military Acad. and National War Coll.
Air Attaché, Athens 47-49; Dir. of Operations, Air Defence Command, Colorado 50-55; Dir. of Operations, Air Force H.Q., Washington D.C. 55-58; Commdr. Electronic Systems Div., Hanscom Field, Mass. 58-62; Commdr. Air Force Communications Service 62-65; retd. as Maj.-Gen. June 65; Admin. Asst. for Aviation and Communications, Bethlehem Steel Corpn. 66-72; mem. Board of Govs., Flight Safety Foundation 69-72; D.S.M., four Legion of Merit Awards. Bronze Star Medal, Air Medal. Greek Order of the Phoenix, Greek D.S.M.
Leisure interests: ski-ing, water ski-ing, swimming, boating, golf.
34 Aldebaran Avenue, Vandenberg Village, Lompoc, Calif. 93436, U.S.A.
Telephone: 805-733-2165.

Berinson, Zvi, SC.DIP., B.A.; Israeli judge; b. 1907, Safad; *s.* of Haim and Haya Berinson; *m.* Hana Wolf 1931; one *s.* one *d.*; ed. Scots Coll., Safad, Israel, Jesus Coll., Cambridge, and Gray's Inn, London.
Lecturer, Scots Coll. 29-31; Legal Adviser and Dir. Municipal Dept. Gen. Fed. of Jewish Labour, Palestine 36-49; Dir.-Gen. Ministry of Labour, Israel Govt. 49-53; Judge, Supreme Court 54-; Lecturer on Labour Law and Social Insurance, Hebrew Univ. 53-72; Chair. League of Socs. for the Rehabilitation of Offenders; Israel Nat. Opera; Pres. Public Council for the Prevention of Noise and Air Pollution in Israel; mem. of the Board Int. Prisoners' Aid Asscn.; head of Israel Del. to ILO 49-53, 58-59.
Leisure interests: gardening, hiking, public service.
The Supreme Court of Israel, Jerusalem; 18 Marcus Street, Jerusalem, Israel.
Telephone: 32483 (Home); 231924.

Berio, Luciano; Italian composer; b. 24 Oct. 1925; ed. Liceo Classico and Conservatorio G. Verdi, Milan.
Founder of Studio de Fonologia Musicale, Italian Radio; Teacher of Composition and Lecturer at Mills Coll. (Calif.), Darmstadt, and Harvard Univ.; now Prof. of Composition, Juilliard School of Music, N.Y.
Compositions include: *5 Variazioni* 51, *Nones for Orchestra* 54, *Alleluyah I and II* 55-57, *Thema (Omaggio a Joyce)* 58, *Circles* 60, *Visage* 61, *Epifanie* 63, *Passaggio* 62, *Laborintus* 65, *O King* 68, *Sinfonia* 69, *This Means That . . .* 70, *Opera* 70, *Laborintus 2.*
53 Potter Place, Weehawken, N.J. 07087, U.S.A.
Telephone: 201-863-8283.

Beriosova, Svetlana; British ballerina; b. 24 Sept. 1932, Lithuania.
With Metropolitan Ballet 46-49, Sadler's Wells Theatre Ballet 49-52, Sadler's Wells Ballet (now Royal Ballet) 52-; leading roles in *Swan Lake, The Sleeping Beauty,*

Giselle, Coppélia, Trumpet Concerto, The Shadow, Rinaldo and Armida, The Prince of the Pagodas, Antigone, Baiser de la Fée, Perséphone, Les Sylphides, The Lady and the Fool, Ondine, Sylvia, Apollo, Lilac Garden, Cinderella, Les Biches, Les Noces, Enigma Variations 68, *Jazz Calendar* 69, *La Bayadère, Checkpoint* 70, etc.
Royal Opera House, Covent Garden, London, W.C.2; 3 Hans Crescent, London, S.W.1, England.

Berkeley, Busby; American director; b. 29 Nov. 1895. Stage career with Warner Bros., then with MGM 39-. Directed musicals, *Whoopee* 31, *Palmy* 32, *Roman Scandals* 33, *42nd Street* 33, *Footlight Parade* 33, *Dames* 34, *Fashions* 34, *Wonder Bar* 34, *Gold Digger* series 33-37, and supervised revival of *No, No Nanette*, N.Y. 71. Directed films, *Go Into Your Dance* 36, *Stage Struck* 36, *Hollywood Hotel* 37, *Men Are Such Fools* 38, *They Made Me a Criminal* 39, *Babes in Arms* 39, *Babes on Broadway* 40, *Strike Up the Bank* 40, *Ziegfeld Girl, For Me and My Gal* 42, *The Gang's All Here* 44, *Cinderella Jones* 45, *Take Me Out to the Ball Game* 48, *Two Weeks with Love, Call Me Mister, Two Tickets to Broadway, Million Dollar Mermaid, Small Town Girl, Easy to Love, Rose Marie* 54, *Jumbo* 62.
[*Died* 14 *March* 1975].

Berkeley, Sir Lennox Randal, Kt., B.A.; British composer; b. 12 May 1903, Boars Hill, Oxford; s. of Hastings Fitzhardinge Berkeley and Aline Carla (née Harris); m. Elizabeth Freda Bernstein; three s.; ed. Gresham's School, Holt, and Merton Coll., Oxford.
Studied music in Paris with Mlle. Nadia Boulanger 27-31; mem. B.B.C. Music Dept. staff 42-45; awarded Collard Fellowship in Music 46; Composition Prof Royal Acad. of Music, London 46-68, Pres. Performing Right Soc. 75-.
Principal works incl.: Orchestra: three Symphonies, *Divertimento, Nocturne*, Concerto for piano and orchestra, Concerto for two pianos and orchestra, Concerto for violin and chamber orchestra, Five Pieces for violin and orchestra, *The Winter's Tale* (suite), *Voices of the Night*, Guitar Concerto, Sinfonia Concertante for Oboe and Orchestra; Chamber Music: Three string quartets, string trio, Sonata for viola and piano, Trio for violin, horn and piano, Sextet for clarinet, horn and string quartet, Duo for cello and piano; Piano: Sonata, six Preludes, four Concert studies; Vocal: *Four Poems of St Teresa* for contralto and strings, *Stabat Mater* for six soloists and twelve instruments, *Five Poems of W. H. Auden, Autumn Legacy*, Song Cycle for voice and piano, *Mass* for five voices, *Songs of the Half-Light* for high voice and guitar, *Magnificat* (City Festival, London) 68, *Guitar Concertino* 74, Five Chinese Songs; Opera: *Nelson, A Dinner Engagement, Ruth, Castaway*.
8 Warwick Avenue, London, W.2, England.

Berkhouwer, Cornelis, LL.D.; Netherlands barrister and politician; b. 19 March 1919, Alkmaar; s. of Cornelis Berkhouwer and Neeltje Vroegop; m. Michelle Martel 1966; two s.; ed. Univ. of Amsterdam.
Barrister 42-; M.P. 56-; European Parl., mem. 63-68, Pres. Liberal Group 68-72, Pres. European Parl. 73-75; Commdr. Order of the Netherlands Lion; Grand Officer, Order of Merit (Italy).
Leisure interests: tennis, swimming, cycling, athletics literature, music.
Publs. various articles in the field of law.
56 Stationsweg, Heiloo, Netherlands.

Berkin, John Phillip, C.B.E., M.A.; British oil execu tive; b. 23 Oct. 1905, Hankow, China; s. of John Berkin and Leila Louise Berkin (née Doolittle); m. 1st Elizabeth Mary Joseph Arnold 1934 (deceased 1967), one s.; 2nd Lilian Ivy Beatrice Chisholm 1968; ed. Taunton School and Sidney Sussex Coll., Cambridge.
Joined Royal Dutch/Shell Group 27 and served in

Far East, London and U.S.A.; Vice-Pres. Asiatic Petroleum Corpn. New York 42-46; Dir. Shell Petroleum Co. Ltd. 53-, Man. Dir. Royal Dutch/Shell Group 57-66; Dir. Bataafse Petroleum Maatschappij N.V. 57-68; Dir. "Shell" Transport and Trading Co. Ltd. 57-; Dir. Industrial Reorganisation Corpn. 66-68, National & Grindlays Bank Ltd. 66-, The Nuclear Power Group Ltd. 69-71.
Oriel, Fairfield Road, Southdown, Shawford, Winchester, Hants, England.

Berkol, Faruk N., LL.D.; Turkish diplomatist; b. 9 Sept. 1917, Istanbul; s. of Nurettin Ali Berkol and Pakize Berkol; ed. Univs. of Istanbul and Paris and School of Political Science, Paris.
Joined Ministry of Foreign Affairs 41; First Sec., Washington 45-50; Counsellor, later Chargé d'Affaires, London 52-56; Chief of Cabinet to Pres. of Turkey 56-60; Amb. to Tunisia 62-67, to Belgium 67-72; UN Under-Sec.-Gen., UN Disaster Relief Co-ordinator 72-.
Leisure interests: fishing, gardening.
Publs. works in Turkish and French on the Balkan *entente*, Turkish economic expansion and the legal status of eastern Mediterranean waterways.
United Nations Office of the Disaster Relief Coordinator (UNDRO), Palais des Nations, 1211 Geneva 10, Switzerland.
Telephone: 34 60 11.

Berliet, Paul; French industrialist; b. 5 Oct. 1918; ed. Lycée Ampère, Lyon.
Deputy Dir.-Gen. Société Automobiles M. Berliet 54-58, Admin. Dir.-Gen. 58-62, Pres., Dir.-Gen. 62-74, Vice-Pres. and Dir.-Gen. 75-; Pres. Société Africaine des Automobiles M. Berliet 68-; Admin. Citröen S.A. 68-; Chevalier Légion d'Honneur.
La Cerisaie, rue Carnot, 69 Saint-Cyr-au-Mont-d'Or, France.

Berlin, Irving, D.MUS.; American composer and song writer; b. 11 May 1888 in Russia; s. of Moses and Leah L. Baline; m. Ellin Mackay 1926; three d.; ed. public schools in New York City.
Went to U.S.A. 93; Pres. Irving Berlin Music Corpn.; Medal of Merit for *This is the Army*, special gold medal for *God Bless America*.
Songs include: *Alexander's Ragtime Band, Oh, How I Hate to get up in the morning, Always, Reaching for the Moon, White Christmas, God Bless America, Blue Skies, What'll I do, All Alone, Remember, Everybody's Doing It, There's No Business Like Show Business, How Deep is the Ocean*, among hundreds of others; musicals: *This is the Army* (comedy), *Easter Parade* (film), *Annie Get Your Gun, Miss Liberty, Mr. President* and *Call Me Madam* (stage musicals), *Top Hat, Follow the Fleet, Alexander's Ragtime Band, Holiday Inn* (films).
Irving Berlin Music Corporation, 1290 Avenue of the Americas, New York, N.Y., U.S.A.

Berlin, Sir Isaiah, O.M., Kt., C.B.E., M.A., F.B.A.; British university teacher; b. 6 June 1909; s. of Mendel and Marie Berlin; m. Aline de Gunzbourg 1956; ed. St. Paul's School and Corpus Christi Coll., Oxford.
Lecturer in Philosophy, New Coll., Oxford 32; Fellow of All Souls Coll., Oxford 32-38; Fellow and Tutor New Coll. 38-50; attached to British Information Service N.Y. 41; First Sec., British Embassy, Washington 42-46, Moscow 45; Lecturer, Oxford Univ. 47-; Sub-Warden New Coll. 49-50; Research Fellow, All Souls Coll. 50-57; Chichele Prof. of Social and Political Theory, Oxford Univ. 57-67; Visiting Lecturer, Harvard 49, 51, 53, Ford Research Prof. 62, Mellon Lecturer, Washington, D.C. 65; Visiting Prof., Princeton Univ. 66; Mary Flexner Lecturer, Bryn Mawr Coll. 52-53; Auguste Comte Memorial Lecturer, London School of Economics 53; Northcliffe Lecturer, University Coll., London; Alexander White Prof., Chicago Univ. 55; Romanes

Lecturer, Oxford Univ. 71; Gov. Univ. of Jerusalem; Trustee, Nat. Gallery 75-; Dir. Royal Opera House, Covent Garden 54-66, 74-; Prof. of Humanities, City Univ. of N.Y. 66-72; Pres. Wolfson Coll., Oxford 66-75; Fellow, All Souls Coll. 75-; Pres. British Acad. 74-; Hon. mem. Amer. Acads. of Arts and Sciences, Arts and Letters; Hon. Dr., Hull, Cambridge, Glasgow, East Anglia, Columbia, Brandeis, London, Liverpool, Jerusalem and Tel-Aviv Univs.; Hon. Fellow, Corpus Christi Coll., Oxford.

Publs. *Karl Marx* 39, *The Hedgehog and the Fox, Historical Inevitability* 54, *The Age of Enlightenment* 56, *Two Concepts of Liberty* 58, *The Life and Opinions of Moses Hess* 59, *Four Essays on Liberty* 69, *Fathers and Children* 72, *Vico and Herder* 76.

All Souls College, Oxford, England.

Berliner, Robert W., B.S., M.D.; American physician; b. 10 March 1915, New York; s. of William M. Berliner and Anna Weiner; m. Lea Silver 1941; two s. two d.; ed. Yale Univ. and Columbia Univ.

Intern, Presbyterian Hospital, N.Y. 39-41; Resident Physician, Goldwater Hospital, N.Y. 42-43; Research Fellow, Goldwater Memorial Hospital, and Asst. in Medicine, New York Univ. Coll. of Medicine 43-44; Research Asst., Goldwater Memorial Hospital, and Instructor in Medicine, N.Y. Univ. Coll. of Medicine 44-47; Asst. Prof. of Medicine, Columbia Univ. 47-50; Research Assoc., Dept. of Hospitals, City of N.Y. 47-50; Chief, Lab. of Kidney and Electrolyte Metabolism, Nat. Insts. of Health, Bethesda, Md. 50-62; Special Lecturer, George Washington School of Medicine, Washington, D.C. 51-; Dir. of Intramural Research, Nat. Heart Inst., Nat. Insts. of Health 54-68; Dir. of Labs. and Clinics, Nat. Insts. of Health 68-69; Deputy Dir. for Science 69-73; Prof. Lecturer, Georgetown Univ. Schools of Medicine and Dentistry 64-73; Prof. of Physiology and Medicine, Dean, Yale Univ. School of Medicine 73-; mem. Nat. Acad. of Sciences, Amer. Acad. of Arts and Sciences, Amer. Heart Asscn.; Pres. Amer. Soc. of Nephrology 68; mem. numerous other medical socs.; Distinguished Service Award, Dept. of Health, Educ. and Welfare 62; Homer W. Smith Award in Renal Physiology 65; Alumni Award for Distinguished Achievement, Coll. of Physicians and Surgeons, Columbia Univ. 66; Bicentennial Medal, Coll. of Physicians and Surgeons, Columbia Univ. 67; Distinguished Achievement Award by *Modern Medicine* 69; Amer. Heart Asscn. Research Achievement Award 70.

Leisure interests: hiking, birdwatching, music.

Publs. Approx. 100 publs. in medical literature.

Yale University School of Medicine, C203 Sterling Hall of Medicine, 333 Cedar Street, New Haven, Conn. 06510; Home: 36 Edgehill Terrace, New Haven, Conn. 06511, U.S.A.

Telephone: 203-432-4586 (Office); 203-777-1379 (Home).

Berlinguer, Enrico; Italian politician; b. 25 May 1922, Sasari, Sardinia; m.; four c.

Joined Italian Communist Party 44; active in communist youth movt. in Milan and Rome; mem. Cen. Cttee. Italian C.P. 45-, Deputy Sec. 68-72, Sec. 72-; Sec.-Gen. Youth Movt. 49-56; Chair. World Fed. of Democratic Youth 50-53; Regional Sec. Italian C.P., Sardinia 57-58; Chief, Organizational Dept., Cen. Cttee., Italian C.P. 58; mem. Chamber of Deputies 68-.

Partito Comunista Italiano, Via delle Botteghe Oscure 4, Rome, Italy.

Bernabei, Ettore; Italian journalist and broadcasting executive; b. 1921; ed. Univ. of Florence.

Director *Il Giornale del Mattino* (Florence) 51-56, *Il Popolo* (Rome) 56-60; Editor *La Nazione del Popolo* (Florence); Dir.-Gen. Radiotelevisione Italiana 61-74; Pres. Italstat 74-.

Italstat S.p.A., 9 Avenue Arno, Rome, Italy.

Telephone: 844-8141.

Bernabò-Brea, Luigi; Italian archaeologist; b. 27 Sept. 1910; ed. Univs. of Genoa and Rome and Italian School of Archaeology, Athens.

Inspector, Archaeological Museum, Taranto 38; Supt. of Antiquities for Liguria 39-41, for Eastern Sicily 41-; Dir. Archaeological Museum, Syracuse 41-; founder and Dir. Aeolian museum, Lipari; Dir. Italian archaeological mission to Poliochni, Lemnos; Dr. h.c. Clermont-Ferrand.

Publs. *Corpus vasorum Antiquorum, Museo Civico Genova-Pegli* 42, *Gli scavi nella Caverna delle Arene Candide di Finale Ligure,* Vol. I 46, Vol. II 56, *La scultura funeraria tarantina* 52, *L'Athenaion di Gela e le sue terrecotte architettoniche* 52, *Akrai* 56, *Sicily before the Greeks* 58, *Poliochni, città preistorica nell' Isola di Lemnos,* Vol. I 64, and other books in collaboration with M. Cavalier.

Museo Archeologico Nazionale, Piazza del Duomo 14, Syracuse, Sicily, Italy.

Bernadotte, Count Sigvard Oscar Fredrik, B.A.; Swedish industrial designer; b. 7 June 1907; s. of late King Gustav VI of Sweden; m. Marianne Lindberg 1961; ed. Uppsala Univ., Royal Acad. of Arts, Stockholm and Munich.

Designed silverware, textiles, bookbindings, glass, porcelain 29-; Partner, Bernadotte & Bjørn (Industrial Design) 49, own firm Bernadotte Design AB 64-; Pres. Int. Council of Socs. of Industrial Design (ICSID) 61-63; awarded Gold Medal, Silver Medal and Diploma at the Milan Triennale.

Villagatan 10, Stockholm, Sweden.

Telephone: 10-20-20.

Bernal y Garcia Pimentel, Ignacio, PH.D.; Mexican anthropologist; b. 13 Feb. 1910, Paris, France; s. of Rafael Bernal and Rafaela García Pimentel (de Bernal); m. Sofía Verea 1944; two s. two d.; ed. Loyola Coll., Montreal, Canada, National Univ. and National School of Anthropology, Mexico.

Director, Dept. of Anthropology, Mexico City Coll. 48-59; Prof., National Univ. of Mexico 49-; Sec. Soc. Mexicana de Antropología 54-62; Perm. Del. to UNESCO, Mexico 55-56; Dir., Nat. Museum of Anthropology, Mexico 62-68, Nat. Inst. of Anthropology and History, Mexico 68-70, Teotihuacan Project 62-64; Dir. Nat. Museum of Anthropology 71-; Regular mem. El Colegio Nacional de Mexico, British Acad., Academia Mexicana de la Historia; Foreign Fellow, American Acad. of Arts and Science; mem. other Mexican and foreign anthropological orgs.; decorations from Netherlands, France, Italy, Belgium, Denmark and German Fed. Repub.

Publs. *Introduction to Archaeology* 52, *Mesoamérica* 53, *Huitzilopochtli Vivo* 57, *Pintura Precolombina* 58, *Tenochtitlan en una Isla* 59, *Correspondencia de Bandelier* 60, *Toynbee y Mesoamérica* 60, *Bibliografía y Etnografía* 62, *Mexico before Cortez* 63, *Teotihuacan* 63, *Mexican Wall Paintings* 63, *Mexican Art* 63; various sections *Handbook of Middle American Indians* 65, *El Museo de Antropología* 67, *La Cerámica de Monte Albán* 67, *El Mundo Olmeca* 68, *Ancient Mexico in Colour* 68, *The Mexican National Museum of Anthropology* 68, *The Olmec World* 69.

Tres Picos 65, Mexico City 5, D.F., Mexico.

Bernar Castellanos, Ignacio; Spanish economist; b. 11 Nov. 1929; s. of Manuel Bernar and Rosario Castellanos; m. Virginia Elorza Losada 1955; one s. five d.; ed. Commercial Univ. of Deusto and Central Univ. of Madrid.

Director, Macmor, S.A. until 60; Dir.-Gen., Foreign Trade, Ministry of Trade 62-68; Councillor, Instituto Español de Moneda Extranjera (IEME), Empresa Nacional Bazán, Almadén, Credito y Caución, S.A. 62-68; Dir.-Gen. Supreme Council of the Chamber of

Commerce, Industry and Navigation 68-; Gran Cruz del Mérito Civil; Cruz de San Carlos, Colombia.
Leisure interests: hockey, golf, tennis, trout fishing, hunting.
Consejo Superior de la Cámaras Oficiales de Comercio, Industria y Navigación de España, Calle Claudio Coello 19, 1°, Madrid, Spain.

Bernard, Henry; French architect; b. 1912, Savoy; ed. Ecole Nationale des Beaux-Arts and in Rome.
Served during Second World War 39-45; architect to Palace of Versailles 45; Deputy Chief Architect to City of Caen 45, Architect-in-Chief 53, Inspector-Gen. of Civil Buildings and Nat. Palaces 63; work includes St. Julien Church, several lycées and buildings of Univ. of Caen; other projects include univ. hospital centres at Caen, Grenoble, Tours, town planning project at Grenoble, and schemes for Paris, etc.
Publs. articles in literary and specialized journals.
2 place Rodin, Paris 16e, France.

Bernard, Lucien, M.D.; French public health official; b. 30 Nov. 1913, Paris; s. of Noel Bernard and Paule Delage; m. Marguerite Hamelin 1939; one s. two d.; ed. Faculté de Paris and Inst. Pasteur, Paris.
Director of Health Services and Prof. of Microbiology, School of Medicine, Rheims 41-44; Chief of Communicable Diseases branch and Int. Health at Ministry of Public Health 46-56; Asst. to Dir.-Gen. of Public Health 56-58; Dir. of Health Services, Regional Office for South East Asia, World Health Org. (WHO) 58-63, Dir. in the office of the Dir.-Gen., Geneva, and Personal Rep. of the Dir.-Gen. at Regional Office for Africa 63-64; Asst. Dir.-Gen. WHO Feb. 64-; Corresp. Nat. Acad. of Medicine, Paris.
Leisure interests: music, oriental art.
Publs. on microbiology, epidemiology and public health administration.
World Health Organization, avenue Appia, 1211 Geneva; 29 Malagnou, 1208 Geneva, Switzerland.
Telephone: 34-60-61.

Bernardini, Gilberto, DR. PHYS.; Italian physicist; b. 20 Aug. 1906, Florence; s. of Alfredo Bernardini and Elvira Nannucci; m. Nella Magherini 1928; one s. one d.; ed. Univs. of Pisa and Florence and Kaiser Wilhelm Inst., Berlin-Dahlem.
Prof. of Physics, Univ. of Bologna 39, Univ. of Rome 45; Research Prof. of Physics, Univ. of Ill., U.S.A. 50; Visiting Prof., Columbia Univ. 48-49 and 49-50; Dir. of Research in S.C. Div. European Org. for Nuclear Research (CERN), Geneva 57; Dir. of S.C. Div. CERN, Geneva 58-59; Dir. of Research CERN 60-62, Univ. of Rome 63-64; Dir. Scuola Normale Superiore, Pisa 64-; Vice-Pres. Italian Inst. for Nuclear Studies; Pres. Italian Physical Soc. 60-67; Nat. mem. Accad. Nazionale dei XL, Accad. Pugliese delle Scienze 67, Accad. Nazionale dei Lincei; Fellow American Physical Soc.; Hon. Fellow, Inst. of Physics 71; Pres. European Physical Soc. 68; Vice-Pres. European Physical Soc. 70-; mem. Accad. Bologna, Modena and Bari; awarded Int. Medal Augusto Righi, Somaini Prize 55, Presidential Gold Medal (Italy), Italian Physical Soc. Gold Medal 69; hon. degree, Univ. of Rochester; J. T. Tate Gold Medal (U.S.A.) 71.
Leisure interests: music, poetry.
Scuola Normale Superiore, Piazza dei Cavalieri 7, 56100 Pisa, Italy.
Telephone: 43554.

Bernaris, Antonios; Greek economist; b. Kydoniais, Asia Minor; unmarried; ed. in France and U.K.
Government adviser and Sec.-Gen. of various ministries 42-49; Deputy Gov. Agricultural Bank of Greece 55-58; Minister of Agriculture 63; Chair. Farmers' Provident Fund; mem. Roual Soc. of Econs. (U.K.), Asscn. of American Agricultural Economy and other profes-

sional bodies; del. to various int. confs.; Minister of Social Services Aug. 71-72.
Publs. many specialized works on economics.
c/o Ministry of Social Services, Athens, Greece.

Bernasko, Col. Frank George, B.SC., LL.B.; Ghanaian army officer; b. 7 Dec. 1930, Cape Coast; s. of Frank George and Sophia Rosetta Bernasko; m. Esther Nyahan Aasku 1960; three s. (one deceased) one d. (deceased); ed. Cape Coast Govt. Boy's School, Adisadel Coll. and Univ. of Ghana, Legon.
Instructor Ghana Mil. Acad. 60-62; Deputy Adjutant-Gen. Ghana Armed Forces 62-65; Dir. of Studies Ghana Mil. Acad. 65-66; Chair. Scholarship Review Board 66-67; Dir. of Educ. Ghana Armed Forces 66-72; Pres. Military Court-Martial, Port-of-Spain, Trinidad 70-71; Regional Commr. Cen. Region 72-73; Commr. for Agriculture 73-75; Commr. for Cocoa Affairs Feb.-Sept. 75; now in private legal practice.
Leisure interests: music, athletics, voluntary work.
P.O. Box 9271, Airport Branch Post Office, Accra, Ghana.
Telephone: 22539 (Office); 29288 (Home).

Bernáth, Aurél; Hungarian painter and writer on art; b. 13 Nov. 1895, Marcali, Somogy; s. of Dr. Béla Bernáth and Attala Roboz; m. Alice Pártos 1927; one d.; ed. grammar school, Budapest, Nagybánya Art School, Vienna, Berlin, Italy, France, U.K., etc.
Professor, Coll. of Fine Arts 45-69; works in many public and private collections in Hungary and abroad; Kossuth Prize 48, 70; Eminent Artist of Hungarian People's People. 64; Banner Order of the Hungarian People's Republic 75. Most prominent works: *Riviera, Morning, Mother and Child, Violin, The Luncheon, The Kovács Family, On the Balcony, Portrait of Lőrinc Szabó, The History, State of the Worker, Tragedy of Man, Midsummer Night's Dream.*
Leisure interests: music, literature.
Publs. *Irások a müvészetről, A Múzsa Körül* (essays on art), *Igy Éltünk Pannoniában* (novel), *Utak Pannoniából* (novel) 60, *A Muzsa Udvarában* (essays on art) 66, *Gólyáról, Helgáról halálról* (novel), *Kisebb világok* (essays) 74, *Feljegyzések éjfél kőrül* (essays) 76.
Stollár Béla u. 4, 1055 Budapest V, Hungary.
Telephone: 125-524.

Berner, Endre Qvie, DR. TECHN.; Norwegian chemist; b. 24 Sept. 1893, Stavanger; s. of Endre Berner and Anna Marie Giemre; m. 1st Nathalia Adelaide Weidemann 1922 (deceased); two s. one d.; 2nd Erna Gay 1935; one d.; ed. State Univ. of Technology at Trondheim.
Lecturer in Organic Chemistry, Trondheim 22-33; Prof. of Chemistry, Univ. of Oslo 34-61; mem. Norwegian Chemical Society (Chair. Trondheim Div. 31-33, Chair Oslo Div. 39-40, Pres. 46-50, Hon. mem. 66), Royal Norwegian Society of Sciences, Norwegian Acad. of Science, Royal Swedish Acad. of Eng. Sciences, Chemical Soc. London, Royal Soc. of Arts; hon. foreign mem. Soc. of Chemical Industry; Vice-Pres. Int. Union of Chem. 51-55; Order of St. Olav (1st Class) 69.
Leisure interests: angling, stamps.
Publs. *Textbook of Organic Chemistry* (in Norwegian) 6th edn. 64, and many scientific papers.
Gyldenlovesgate 13, Oslo 2, Norway.

Bernet Kempers, Karel Phillipus, DR.PHIL.; Netherlands musicologist; b. 20 Sept. 1897, Nijkerk; s. of Karel J. W. Bernet Kempers; m. Gertrude Dorothea Boursse 1934; two d.; ed. Univ. of Munich.
Professor History of Music, Royal Conservatory, The Hague 29-49; Prof. Amsterdam Conservatory 34-53; Private teacher, Univ. of Amsterdam 29-37; Lecturer in Musicology, Univ. of Amsterdam 37-46, Prof. 46-68; Sec. Royal Dutch Society of Musicians 34-41, Chair. 45-65, Hon. Pres. 65-; Vice-Pres. Netherlands Council of Musicians 50-65; mem. Council of Concertgebouw

Orchestra 56-68; Editor *Preludium-Concertgebouwnieuws* 45-71; Pres. Consulting Cttee. Int. Musicological Soc.; Vice-Pres. Dutch Soc. of Musical History 71; Officer, Order of Orange-Nassau; Knight, Order of the Dutch Lion.

Publs. *Jacobus Clemens von Papa und seine Motetten* 28, *De Italiaanse Opera van Peri tot Puccini* 29, *Muziek-geschiedenis* 32 (6th edition 65), *Muziek in den Ban der letteren* 35, *Beknopte Geschiedenis van het Kerklied* (with Prof. Dr. G. v. d. Leeuw) 48, *Meesters der Muziek* (5th edition) 55, *Panorama der Muziek* 48, *Complete Works of Clemens von Papa* (21 vols.—72) (Editor), *The Leyden Codices* (with Dr. Chr. Maas).
[*Died 30 September* 1974].

Bernhard Leopold Frederik Everhard Julius Coert Karel Godfried Pieter, H.R.H. Prince (*see* under Netherlands).

Bernhard, Wilhelm; French scientist; b. 8 Nov. 1920, Worb, Berne, Switzerland; ed. Grammar School, Berne, Univs. of Berne and Geneva.
Assistant to Prof. C. Oberling 48-60; worked with Profs. Leroux and Pasteur Vallery-Radot, Dir. of Research, Centre Nat. de la Recherche Scientifique 61-; Head of Electron Microscopy, Lab. Inst. de Recherches sur le Cancer, Villejuif 48-; research on the fine structure of normal and cancer cells, and studies on oncogenic viruses; mem. Conseil Nat. de la Recherche Scientifique 60-66, 71-; Gen. Sec. Int. Fed. of Electron Microscopy Socs. 71-; Grand prix scientifique de la ville de Paris 64; Ehrlich Prize (with R. Dulbecco) 67, Howard Taylor Ricketts Award, Univ. of Chicago 72: Dr. h.c. Univs. of Brussels, Basle 69.
Leisure interests: music, literature.
Institut de Recherche sur le Cancer, Villejuif (Val-de Marne), France.
Telephone: 726-4658.

Bernstein, Baron (Life Peer), cr. 69, of Leigh; **Sidney Lewis Bernstein,** LL.D.; British business executive; b. 30 Jan. 1899.
A founder, Film Soc. 24; mem. Middx. County Council 25-31; Films Adviser, Ministry of Information 40-45; Liaison, British Embassy, Washington 42; Chief, Film Section, Allied Forces Headquarters, N. Africa 42-43; Chief, Film Section, SHAEF 43-45; Chair. Granada Group Ltd. 34-; Gov. Sevenoaks School 64-74; lectured on Film and Int. Affairs, New York and Yale Univs.; mem. Nuffield Foundation Resources for Learning Consultative Cttee. 65-72.
36 Golden Square, London, W1R 4AH; Coppings Farm, Leigh, Tonbridge, Kent, TN11 8PN, England.

Bernstein, Leonard; American conductor, composer and pianist; b. 25 Aug. 1918, Lawrence, Mass.; s. of Samuel J. and Jennie (Resnick) Bernstein; m. Felicia M. Cohn 1951; one s. two d.; ed. Boston Latin School Harvard and Curtis Inst. of Music.
Assistant at Berkshire Music Center 42, mem. of Faculty 48-55, Head, Conducting Dept. 51-55; Asst. Conductor N.Y. Philharmonic Orchestra 43-44; Dir. N.Y. City Symphony 45-48; Musical Adviser Israel Philharmonic Orchestra 48-49; Prof. of Music, Brandeis Univ. 51-56; Co-conductor N.Y. Philharmonic 57-58. Musical Dir. 58-69, Laureate Conductor for Life; conducted with leading orchestras of America and in the capitals of Europe; music lectures on "Omnibus" television programme 54-62; Dir. N.Y. Phil. Young People's Concerts on nationwide television 58-71; tours in S. America, Europe, Near East and U.S.S.R.; Pres. English Bach Festival 72-; Charles Eliot Norton Prof. of Poetry, Harvard Univ. 72-73.
Compositions: *Clarinet Sonata* 42, *Jeremiah* (symphony) 42, *On the Town* 45, *Symphony No. 2—The Age of Anxiety* 49, *Trouble in Tahiti* (one-act opera) 52, *Wonderful Town* 53, *On the Waterfront* 54, *Serenade for Violin, Strings and Percussion* 54, *Candide* 56, *West Side*

Story 57, *Symphony No. 3—Kaddish* 63, *Chichester Psalms* for chorus and orchestra 65, *Mass: A Theatre Piece for Singers, Players and Dancers* 71, and other scores for stage and songs.
Publs. *The Joy of Music* 59, *Leonard Bernstein's Young People's Concerts* 62, *The Infinite Variety of Music* 68. 205 West 57th Street, New York, N.Y. 10019, U.S.A.

Bernstein, Richard Barry, PH.D.; American professor of physical chemistry; b. 31 Oct. 1923, New York; s. of Simon and Stella Grossman Bernstein; m. Norma B. Olivier 1948; one s. three d.; ed. Columbia Coll. (N.Y.) and Columbia Univ. (N.Y.).
Assistant Prof. Illinois Inst. of Technology (Chicago) 48, Asst. Prof., Assoc. Prof., Prof. Univ. of Michigan 53-63; Prof. Univ. of Wisconsin 63-, W. W. Daniells Prof. 66-73; W. T. Doherty Prof. of Chemistry and Prof. of Physics, Univ. of Texas 73-; Chair. Office of Chem. and Chem. Tech., Nat. Research Council of Nat. Acad. of Sciences 74-; mem. Nat. Acad. of Sciences; mem. Basic Research Program Cttee., A. P. Sloan Foundation; Fellow, American Acad. of Arts and Sciences; A. P. Sloan Fellowship 56; awarded Nat. Science Foundation Senior Post-doctoral Fellowship 60.
Leisure interest: music.
Publs. *Molecular Reaction Dynamics* (with R. D. Levine) 74, and numerous scientific articles (particularly on molecular collisions) 47-.
Department of Chemistry, University of Texas, Austin, Texas 78712, U.S.A.

Bernstein, Robert Louis; American publisher; b. 5 Jan. 1923, New York City; s. of Alfred and Sylvia Bernstein; m. Helen Walter 1950; three s.; ed. Harvard Univ.
U.S. Army Air Force 43-46; with Simon & Schuster (book publishers) 46-57, Gen. Sales Man. 50-57; Random House Inc. 58-, Vice-Pres. (Sales) 61-63, First Vice-Pres. 63-65, Pres. and Chief Exec. Officer 66, Chair. 75; Vice-Chair. Asscn. of American Publrs. 70-72, Chair. 72-73; Chair. Assen. of American Publrs'. Cttee. on Soviet-American Publishing Relations 73-74; on Int. Freedom to Publish 75; mem. Council on Foreign Relations; mem. Board, Blythedale Children's Hospital and Tougaloo Coll., Jackson; mem. Board of Visitors, City Coll., City Univ., New York.
Leisure interests: skiing, tennis, swimming.
Office: Random House, Inc., 201 East 50th Street, New York, N.Y. 10022; Home: 20 Murray Hill Road, Scarsdale, N.Y., U.S.A.
Telephone: 212-PLI-2600.

Berrada, Abdeslam, DIP.SC.AGR.; Moroccan agronomist; b. 3 Oct. 1931, Fez; ed. secondary schools, Fez, Ecole Nat. d'Agriculture de Grignon, Ecole Nat. des Eaux et Forêts, Nancy, France.
Several posts in Waters and Forests Admin., subsequently Dir. 65; Sec.-Gen. Ministry of Agriculture and Agrarian Reform 71-72, Minister 72-74; Exec. Vice-Pres. Soc. Cellulose du Maroc 72-; rep. to numerous regional and int. confs.
c/o Ministère de l'Agriculture et de la Réforme Agraire, Rabat, Morocco.

Berrill, Sir Kenneth, K.C.B., B.SC.(ECON.), M.A.; British economist; b. 28 Aug. 1920, London; s. of Stanley Berrill and Lilian Blakeley; m. June Phillips 1950; one s. one d.; ed. London School of Econs. and Trinity Coll., Cambridge Univ.
H.M. Treasury (Cen. Econ. Planning Staff) 47-49; Lecturer in Econs., Cambridge Univ. 49-69; Special Adviser, H.M. Treasury 67-69; Brit. Nat. Comm. for UNESCO 67-70; mem. Council for Scientific Policy 69-72; Chair. Univ. Grants Cttee. of G.B. 69-73; mem. Advisory Board for Research Councils 72-73; apptd. Head of Govt. Econ. Service and Chief Econ. Adviser to H.M. Treasury 73-74; Dir. Cen. Policy Review Staff, Cabinet Office 74-; sometime Econ. Adviser to OECD,

IBRD, Guyana, Cameroon, Turkey; City Councillor, Cambridge 64-69; Hon. Fellow (London School of Econs., King's Coll. and St. Catherine's Coll., Oxford, Chelsea Coll., London); Hon. LL.D. (Bath, Cambridge, East Anglia, Leicester); Hon. D.Univ. (Open Univ.); Hon. D.Tech. (Loughborough); Hon. Sc.D. (Aston).
Leisure interests: skiing, hill walking, theatre.
11 Chester Place, Regents Park, London, N.W.1, England.

Berrill, Norman John, F.R.S., F.R.S.C., PH.D., D.SC.; Canadian zoologist; b. 28 April 1903; ed. Bristol and London Univs.
Lecturer in Zoology, Univ. of London 25-27; Lecturer in Physiology, Univ. of Leeds 27-28; Asst. Prof. in Zoology, McGill Univ. Montreal 28-31, Assoc. Prof. 31-46, Chair. Dept. of Zoology 37-47, Strathcona Prof. of Zoology 47-65, Research Assoc. 65; Lecturer in Biology, Swarthmore Coll., Pennsylvania 69.
Publs. *The Tunicata* 51, *The Living Tide* 51, *Journey into Wonder* 52, *Sex and the Nature of Things* 53, *Man's Emerging Mind* 55, *The Origin of Vertebrates* 55, *You and the Universe* 57, *Growth, Development and Pattern* 61, *Worlds Apart* 65, *Biology in Action* 66, *Inherit the Earth* 66, *Life of the Ocean* 66, *The Person in the Womb* 68, *Life of the Sea Islands* 69, *Developmental Biology* 71, *Animals in Action* 72.
Swarthmore College, Swarthmore, Pa.; Home: 410 N. Swarthmore Avenue, Swarthmore, Pa. 19081, U.S.A. Telephone: 215-544-1762.

Berry, Charles A., M.D.; American physician; b. 17 Sept. 1923, Rogers, Arkansas; s. of George Valentine Berry and Vera Helen Whitmore; m. Addella (Dell) Nance Berry 1944; one s. two d.; ed. Univ. of Calif. and Harvard School of Public Health.
Air Force positions, including Aviation Medicine Residency Training Program, and Chief of Dept. of Aviation Medicine at School of Aviation Medicine, Randolph Air Force Base, Texas 51-59; Chief, Flight Medicine Branch, U.S.A.F. Office of Surgeon-Gen. 59-62; Chief, Center Medical Operations Office, NASA Manned Spacecraft Center 62-66; Dir. of Medical Research and Operations. NASA Manned Spacecraft Center May 66-; Dir. for Life Sciences, NASA 71-74; Prof., Chair. Dept. of Aerospace Medicine, Univ. of Tex. Medical Branch, Galveston, Clinical Prof. of Aerospace Medicine, Univ. of Tex. School of Public Health, Houston; Pres. Univ. of Tex. Health Science Center 74-; Pres. Aerospace Medical Asscn. 69-70, mem. many medical and other socs.; Hon. Fellow, Amer. Heart Asscn. 74; Arnold D. Tuttle Award, Aerospace Medical Asscn.; Gold Medal, Amer. Coll. of Chest Physicians; Gold Medal, Czechoslovak Acad. of Medicine; Daniel and Florence Guggenheim Int. Astronautics Award 69; Amer. Coll. of Surgeons Annual Award 70; NASA Distinguished Service Award 73; Hermann Oberth Award 74; Cedars of Lebanon Award 74, and many others.
Leisure interests: fishing, tennis, violin.
University of Texas Health Science Center at Houston, P.O. Box 20036, Houston, Tex. 77025; Home: 10814 River View Drive, Houston, Tex. 77042, U.S.A. Telephone: (713) 792-4975 (Office).

Berry, Walter; Austrian baritone singer; b. 8 April 1929, Vienna; s. of Franz Berry and Hilde Jelinek; m. 1st Christa Ludwig (*q.v.*) 1957 (divorced 1970); one s.; m. 2nd Brigitte Hohenecker 1973; ed. Vienna School of Engineering and Vienna Music Acad.
Student mem. Vienna State Opera 50-53, ordinary mem. 53-; awarded title *Kammersaenger* by Austrian Govt. 63; Guest singer at openings of opera houses in Vienna, Munich, Berlin, Tokyo, New York (Metropolitan Opera), at festivals in Salzburg, Munich, Aix-en-Provence, Lucerne, Netherlands, Stockholm. Saratoga; appearances in New York, Chicago, Buenos Aires,

Tokyo, Paris, Berlin, Munich, etc.; Prizes from Music Concourses in Vienna, Verviers and Geneva.
Roles include: Wozzeck, Ochs von Lerchenau, Barak, Olivier, Escamillo, Pizarro, Telramund, Klingsor, Wotan, Amonasro, Scarpia, Figaro, Guglielmo, Leporello.
Leisure interests: listening to and taping music, yachting, swimming, archaeology, photography.
Office: c/o Music and Arts SA, Tobelhofstrasse 2, CH-8044 Zürich; Home: 6008 Lucerne, Seefeldstrasse 11, Switzerland.
Telephone: 47-19-88 (Office); 23-40-79 (Home).

Bers, Lipman, DR.RER.NAT.; American (naturalized 1949) mathematician; b. 22 May 1914, Riga, Latvia; s. of I. A. and Bertha (née Weinberg) Bers; m. Mary Kagan 1938; one s. one d.; ed. Univs. of Zurich, Latvia and Prague.
Research instructor, Brown Univ. 42-45; Asst. Prof., later Assoc. Prof. Syracuse Univ. 45-50; mem. Inst. for Advanced Study 48-50; Prof. New York Univ. 50-64, Chair. Dept. Mathematics 59-64; Prof. Columbia Univ., New York 64-, Davies Prof. of Maths., 75-; Pres. American Mathematical Soc.; mem. Nat. Acad. of Sciences, American Acad. of Arts and Sciences.
Publs. *Mathematical Aspects of Gas Dynamics* 58, co-author (with F. John and M. Schechter) *Partial Differential Equations* 67, *Calculus* 69, numerous research papers.
Department of Mathematics, Columbia University, New York, N.Y. 10027, U.S.A. •

Berson, Jerome Abraham, M.A., PH.D.; American professor of chemistry; b. 10 May 1924, Sanford, Fla.; s. of Joseph and Rebecca Bernicker Berson; m. Bella Zevitovsky 1946; two s. one d.; ed. City Coll. of New York, Columbia and Harvard Univs.
Assistant Prof., Univ. of Southern Calif. 50-53, Assoc. Prof. 53-58, Prof. 58-63; Prof., Univ. of Wisconsin 63-69, Yale Univ. 69-; Chair. Dept. of Chemistry, Yale Univ. 71-74; Fellow, American Acad. of Arts and Sciences; Nat. Research Council Post-doctoral Fellow, American Chem. Soc. (Calif. Section) Award; mem. Nat Acad. of Sciences.
Leisure interests: hiking, squash.
Publs. scientific papers on organic chemistry published mostly in *Journal of the American Chemical Society*.
Department of Chemistry, Yale University, New Haven, Conn. 06520, U.S.A.
Telephone: 203-432-4525.

Bertaux, Pierre, DR. ès L.; French civil servant; b. 8 Oct. 1907, Lyon; s. of Felix Bertaux; m. Denise Supervielle 1935; three s.; ed. Ecole Normale Supérieure. Paris and Berlin Univs.
Dir. of Spoken Word, Radiodiffusion d'Etat 34-36. Personal Sec. at Ministries of Foreign Affairs and Education 36-37; Prof. Faculty of Arts, Rennes; Prof. Faculty of Arts, Toulouse 38-39; served French Army 39-40; active in Resistance Movement; Commr. of the Republic, Toulouse 44-46; Dir. of Secretariat of Minister of Transport and Public Works 46-47; Prefect of Rhone 47-48; Inspector-Gen. of Administration 48-49; Dir.-Gen. of Sûreté Nationale 49-51; Senator of French Sudan 53-55; Pres. and Dir.-Gen. Acrow-France 55-58; Prof. Univ. Lille 58-64, Prof. Sorbonne, Paris 64-; Dir. Inst. d'Allemagne, Asnières; Expert, OECD-UNESCO; mem. Akademie der Künste, West Berlin; Corresp. mem. Akademie der Künste der D.D.R.; Officier de la Légion d'Honneur, Compagnon de la Libération, Grand Officier Orange-Nassau, Commdr. Nordstjarnoorden, Commdr. Order of Dannebrog, Heinrich Heine-Preis der Stadt (Düsseldorf) 75.
Publs. *Hoelderlin* 36, *Allemagne de Guillaume II* 62, *Geschichte Afrikas* 62, *Mutation der Menschheit* 63, Bertaux-Lepointe Dictionaries 67-68, *Hölderlin und die*

französische Revolution 69, *Civilisation Urbaine* 71, *Libération de Toulouse* 73.
Leisure interest: futurology.
106 rue Brancas, 92 Sèvres, France.
Telephone: Paris 027-0023.

Berthoin, Georges Paul, L. EN D., L. ÈS SC.; French civil servant; b. 17 May 1925, Nérac; *s.* of Jean Berthoin and Germaine Mourgnot; *m.* 1st Anne W. Whittlesey, 2nd Pamela Jenkins; two *s.* four *d.*; ed. Univ. of Grenoble, Ecole des Sciences Politiques, Paris and Harvard and McGill Univs.
Private Sec. to Minister of Finance 48-50; Head of Staff, Prefecture of Alsace-Lorraine-Champagne 50-52; Principal Private Sec. M. Jean Monnet, Pres. of ECSC 52-55; Counsellor for Information, ECSC 55-56; Deputy Chief Rep. of ECSC in U.K. 56; Acting Chief Rep. of Comm. of EEC 67-68, Deputy Chief Rep. 68-71, Chief Rep. 71-73; Exec. mem. Trilateral Comm. 73-75, European Chair. 76-; Médaille Militaire, Croix de Guerre, Médaille de la Résistance.
Leisure interests: art, theatre, walking, collecting objects.
96 *bis* rue de Longchamp, 92200 Neuilly; Château de Guran, Haute-Garonne, France.
Telephone: 7221054.

Berthoin, Jean; French politician; b. 12 Jan. 1895; *m.* Germaine Mourgnot 1924; one *s.* two *d.*
Served 14-18 war; entered civil service 19, served in Tunisia, Algeria and in various districts in France; Dir. to Cabinet (Colonies, Marine, Interior), Sarraut Govt. 32-36, Inspector-Gen. 36-38; Sec.-Gen. Ministry of the Interior 38-40; Treas., Dept. de l'Isère (and active in Resistance during 39-45 war) 40-47, Dept. de la Seine 47-48; mem. Parti Radical Socialiste; Senator for Isère 48-74; Minister of the Interior, Queuille Govt. 50, of Educ., Mendès-France Govt. 54-55, Faure Govt. 55-56, de Gaulle Govt. 58-59; Minister of Interior Jan. 59; mem. European Parl. 59-74; Hon. mem. Parl.; Pres. 10th UNESCO Gen. Conf. 58; mem. Acad. des Sciences d'Outre-mer 61; Grand Croix Légion d'Honneur, Croix de Guerre and nine citations.
67 avenue Niel, Paris 17e, France.

Berti, Luciano; Italian art historian; b. 28 Jan. 1922, Florence; *s.* of Ferdinando and Ines Berti; *m.* Anna Maria Tinacci 1959; no *c.*; ed. Univ. of Florence.
Attached to Superintendancy of Florence 49; arranged new museums of Casa Vasari, Arezzo 50, Palazzo Davanzati 55, Il Museo di Arezzo 58, Il Museo di S. Giovanni Valdarno 59, Museum of Verna 61, Museum of S. Croce, Florence 62; Dir. Museums of Arezzo, San Marco and Academy, Florence; Dir. Museo Nazionale del Bargello; Dir. Uffizi Gallery, Florence 69-; Dir. Monuments, Pisa Gallery 73-; Dir. of Galleries, Florence 74; Silver Medal, Ministry of Public Educ.; Dott. Laurea in Lettere.
Leisure interests: history of art, museology.
Publs. *Filippino Lippi* 57, *Masaccio* 64 (English trans. 67), *Pontormo* 64, *Pontormo disegni* 65, *Il Principe dello Studiolo* 67, *Il Museo tra Thanatos ed Eros* 73-74, various articles and catalogues.
Galleria degli Uffizi, Piazzale degli Uffizi, Florence; Home: Via Giusti 6, Florence, Italy.
Telephone: 57-73-29 (Home).

Bertoldi, Luigi; Italian politician; b. 31 Jan. 1920, San Candido, Bolzano.
Member Cen. Cttee. Partito Socialista Italiano (Italian Socialist Party) 51; Vice-Sec. PSI; mem. Chamber of Deputies 58-; Provincial Sec. Partito Socialista Unificato (Socialist Fed.), Verona; Pres. Socialist Parl. Group 70; Minister of Labour and Social Security 73-Oct. 74; Socialist.
c/o Ministry of Labour and Social Security, Rome, Italy.

Bertola, Giuseppe M., D.ENG.; Swiss electrical engineering executive; b. 7 May 1910, Vacallo; *s.* of Giovanni Bertola and Aida Agustoni; *m.* Maria Giussani 1935; four *d.*; ed. Milan School of Eng.
Engineering Dept., Brown Boveri Baden, Switzerland 33, Sales Dept. 44-45, Sales Man. 52-62, Man. Dir. 62-76; with various electro-mechanical firms in Germany, Italy and U.S.A. 34-43; worked for Brown Boveri in Latin America 45-58, Man. Dir. Brown Boveri Compañia Sudamericana de Electricidad, Buenos Aires 52-58; mem. Man. Cttee. Brown Boveri Group 70-76; Head of Brown Boveri Int. 70-76; Chair. Board Brown Boveri-Sulzer Turbomachines, TIBB (Milan), SACE (Bergamo); mem. Board CEM (Paris), Brown Boveri-Oerlikon (Barcelona), Brown Boveri Corpn. (New Jersey) and other cos. of Group; mem. Board Union Bank of Switzerland, SAE (Milan); Chair. Board Chambre de Commerce Latino-Américaine, Soc. Suisse pour l'Industrie Horlogère 75-.
Leisure interests: books, golf.
BBC Brown, Boveri & Company Ltd., CH-5401 Baden; Home: Schlössliweg 10, CH-8044 Zürich, Switzerland.
Telephone: 056-752002 (Office); 01-328883 (Home).

Bertoli, H.E. Cardinal Paolo; Vatican diplomatist; b. 1 Feb. 1908, Poggio Garf (Lucca); *s.* of Carlo and Aride Poli.
Ordained priest 30; Sec. Apostolic Nunciature, Belgrade 33-38, France 38-42; Chargé d'Affaires a.i., Antilles Apostolic Nunciature, Port-au-Prince, Haiti 42-46; Counsellor, Apostolic Nunciature, Berne 46-52; Head of Mission for Emigration to South America; Titular Archbishop of Nicomedia 52; Apostolic Del. in Turkey 52-53, Apostolic Nuncio in Colombia 53-59, in Lebanon 59-60; France 60-69; Prefect of Congregation for the Causes of Saints 69-73; cr. Cardinal 69.
Piazza della Città Leonina 1, 00193 Rome, Italy.
Telephone: 657312.

Bertolucci, Bernardo; Italian film director; b. 16 March 1940, Parma; *s.* of Attilio Bertolucci.
Worked with Pier Paolo Pasolini on *Accattone;* directed: *La Commare Secca* 62, *Prima della Rivoluzione* 64, *Il Fico Infruttuoso* in *Vangelo 70* 68, *Partner* 70, *La Strategia del Ragno* 70, *Il Conformista* 70, *Last Tango in Paris* 72, *1900* 75.
Publs. *In cerca del mistero* (poems) 62 (Viareggio Prize 62).
Via del Babuino 51, Rome, Italy.

Berutowicz, Włodzimierz; Polish lawyer and politician; b. 3 Oct. 1914, Przedmość, Wieluń district; ed. Wrocław Univ.
Former Chief Justice, Voivodship Court of Justice, Poznań and Wrocław; Chair. Dept. of Civil Law, Wrocław Univ., Rector, Wrocław Univ. 68-; mem. Central Comm. of Party Control, Polish United Workers' Party; Minister of Justice Oct. 71-; mem. Polish Lawyers' Asscn.; Order of Banner of Labour, Order of Polonia Restituta and other decorations.
Ministerstwo Sprawiedliwości, Aleje Ujazdowskie 11, 00-567 Warsaw, Poland.

Berzegov, Nukh Aslancherievich; Soviet politician; b. 1925; ed. Krasnodar Pedagogic Inst.
Member Communist Party of Soviet Union 44-; various posts in education in Adyge Autonomous Region 48-52; Head, Adyge Regional Dept. of Education 52-57; Vice-Chair. Adyge Regional Soviet 57-58; Sec. Adyge Regional Cttee. of C.P.S.U. 58-60, First Sec. 60-; Deputy to U.S.S.R. Supreme Soviet 62-; mem. Comm. for Legislation, Soviet of Nationalities.
Adyge Regional Committee, Communist Party of the Soviet Union, Maikop, U.S.S.R.

Beschev, Boris Pavlovich; Soviet politician; b. July 1903; ed. Leningrad Inst. of Railway Engineers.
Engineer on October Line 35-36; Dir. Orjonikidze Line (Northern Caucasus) 37-40; Dir. October Line (Leningrad) 40; Dir. Dept. of N.W. Lines and Dir. Kuibyshev Line 41-44; Deputy People's Commissar and subsequently Deputy Minister of Railways 44-48; Minister of Railways of U.S.S.R. 48-; Deputy, U.S.S.R. Supreme Soviet 54-; mem. Central Cttee. of C.P.S.U. 52-; awarded Order of Lenin (six times), Order of the Red Banner of Labour, Hero of Socialist Labour, Hammer and Sickle Gold Medal and other decorations.
Ministry of Railway Transport, 2 Novo-Basmannaya ulitsa, Moscow, U.S.S.R.

Bessemoulin, Jean; French meteorologist; b. 18 March 1913, Garches (Hauts-de-Seine); *m.* Jeanne Lapeyre 1941; one *d.* two *s.*; ed. Univ. de Paris à la Sorbonne and Univ. de Nancy.
National Meteorological Office 35-; Head successively of Banne d'Ordanche, Nancy and Clermont-Ferrand Meteorological Stations; Head South East Meteorological Region 42-45; Head, Forecast Division, Service Météorologique Métropolitain 45-58, Asst. Dir. 58-61; Asst. to Dir. of National Meteorology 61-64, Dir. of National Meteorology 64-; Principal Del. of France to the Fourth, Fifth and Sixth Congresses of the World Meteorological Org.; mem. Exec. Cttee., WMO 64-71, Second Vice-Pres. 71-75; mem. numerous WMO Cttees. and Meteorological Societies; Officier, Légion d' Honneur, Croix de Guerre avec palme, and other decorations.
Météorologie Nationale, 73 rue de Sèvres, 92100 Boulogne, France.
Telephone: 604-91-51.

Bessis, Marcel Claude; French research haematologist; b. 15 Nov. 1917, Tunis; *m.* Claude Perrot; three *d.*; ed. Lycée Janson de Sailly and Univ. de Paris (School of Medicine).
Director of Research Lab. of Nat. Centre for Blood Transfusion 47-65; Prof. Faculty of Medicine, Paris 63; Dir. Inst. of Cell Pathology, Bicêtre Hospital 65-; mem. Nat. Cttee. for Scientific Research 64-; Laureate Acad. des Sciences et de Médecine; Editor *Nouvelle Revue française d'Hématologie* 46-; Hon. mem. Harvey Soc. 63, Hon. Fellow American Coll. of Physicians; Chevalier Légion d'Honneur.
Publs. *Cytology of Blood and Blood-forming Organs* 56, *Living Blood Cells and their Ultra-structure* 73.
Institut de Pathologie Cellulaire, Hôpital Bicêtre, 94 Kremlin-Bicêtre, Paris; Home: 2 rue Saint Simon, Paris 7e, France.
Telephone: 548 48-74 (Home); 588-6195 (Office).

Bessmertnova, Natalya Igorevna; Soviet ballet dancer; b. 19 July 1941; ed. Bolshoi Theatre Ballet School.
Artiste of Bolshoi Theatre Ballet 61-; Award of Merit R.S.F.S.R.
Important roles include: Mazurka and 7th Valse (*Chopiniana*), Pas de trois (*Swan Lake*), variations (*Baiadere*), Giselle (*Giselle*), The Muse (*Paganini*, music by Rachmaninov), Florin (*Sleeping Beauty*), Leila (*Leila and Medjnun*, by Balasanyan), Shirin (*Legend of Love*), Odette-Odile (*Swan Lake*), Girl (*Le Spectre de la Rose*), Maria (*The Fountain of Bakhtchisaray*), Frigina (*Spartacus*).
State Academic Bolshoi Theatre of U.S.S.R., 1 Ploshchad Sverdlova, Moscow, U.S.S.R.

Best, Charles Herbert, C.H., C.C., C.B.E., M.A., M.D., D.SC., F.R.C.P., F.R.C.P.(C)., F.R.C.P.(E.), F.R.S.C., F.R.S.; Canadian physiologist; b. 27 Feb. 1899, West Pembroke, Maine, U.S.A.; *s.* of Herbert Huestis Best, M.D., and Luella Fisher Best; *m.* Margaret Hooper Mahon 1924; two *s.*; ed. Toronto and London Univs.
Fellow, Physiology Dept. Toronto Univ. 20-21; Research

mem. Connaught Labs. 22-32; Asst. Prof. of Physiological Hygiene 26-29, Acting Dir. of Dept. 29-41; Prof. of Physiology and Dir. of Dept. 29-65, Dir. Emer., Prof., Graduate Lecturer 65-; Assoc. Dir. Connaught Labs. 32-41; Consultant 41-; Research Assoc. 23-41, Dir., Prof. Banting-Best Dept. of Medical Research 41-67, Dir. Emer. 67-; Special Consultant 73-; Scientific Dir. Int. Health Div. of Rockefeller Foundation 41-43, 46-48; Surgeon Capt. R.C.N.V.R., Dir. R.C.N. Medical Research Unit; co-discoverer of Insulin with Dr. Banting; Vice-Pres. British Diabetic Asscn. 34-; First Hon. Pres. Canadian Diabetic Asscn. 52; Hon. mem. American Diabetes Asscn. 40-, Pres. 48-49, mem. of Council, Hon. Pres. 60-; mem. American Philosophical Soc.; Dir. Roscoe B. Jackson Laboratory 55-; Pres. Int. Union of Physiological Sciences 53-, Asscn. of American Physicians 54, Pontifical Acad. of Sciences 55; Foreign Assoc. Nat. Acad. of Sciences; Foreign mem. The Royal Swedish Acad. of Science 61; mem. Advisory Cttee. on Medical Research of WHO; hon. mem. European Asscn. for the Study of Diabetes; Baly Medal, Royal Coll. of Physicians 39; Banting Medal, American Diabetes Asscn. 49; Flavelle Medal, Royal Soc. of Canada 50; Dale Medal of Soc. for Endocrinology 59; Joslin Medal, New England Diabetes Asscn. 65; Hon. D.Sc. (Chicago, Oxford, Laval Maine, Northwestern), Hon. D.Sc. (Cambridge), Dr. h.c. (Paris), Hon. M.D. (Amsterdam, Louvain, Liège, Caracas, Thessaloniki, Freie Univ. of Berlin, Ottawa,) Hon. LL.D. (Dalhousie, Queen's, Melbourne, Toronto and Edinburgh); Hon. mem. Acad. of Medicine of Toronto 66; Legion of Merit (U.S.), Brazil Scientific Biennial Award 71; Hon. PH.D., Hebrew Univ. of Jerusalem 71, and many other awards.
Leisure interests: riding, golf, painting.
Publs. *The Internal Secretion of the Pancreas* (with F. G. Banting) 22, *The Human Body* (with N. B. Taylor) 32, *The Physiological Basis of Medical Practice* (with N. B Taylor) 37 (9th edn. 73), *Selected Papers of Charles H. Best* 63.
Charles H. Best Institute, 112 College Street, Toronto, Ont. M5G 1L6; and 105 Woodlawn Avenue W., Toronto, Ont. M4V 1G6, Canada.
Telephone: 928-2586 (Office); 922-4929 (Home).

Besterman, Theodore Deodatus Nathaniel, D.LITT., LL.D., D.ès L.; British scholar; b. 18 Sept. 1904; ed. Lycée de Londres, and Oxford Univ. (extra-mural).
Investigation Officer and Editor, Society for Psychical Research 27-35; special lecturer, London School of Librarianship 31-38; Joint Editor, Oxford Books on Bibliography, Gen. Editor Asscn. of Special Libraries 42-46; founder and editor *Journal of Documentation* 44-47; Editor and Exec. Officer *British Union Catalogue of Periodicals* 44-46; Editor *Studies on Voltaire and the Eighteenth Century* 55; successively Counsellor, World Bibliographical and Library Centre, and Head, Dept. for the Exchange of Information, UNESCO 46-49; Hon. Treas. Folk Lore Society 28-29; mem. of Council 26-37; Dir. Inst. et Musée Voltaire, Les Délices, Geneva 52-; Pres. Int. Congress on the Enlightenment 63-71, Int. Soc. for Eighteenth-century Studies 67-71; Editor of the Complete Works of Voltaire 68-; Chevalier Légion d'Honneur.
Publs. *The Beginnings of Systematic Bibliography* 35 (3rd edn. 52), *A World Bibliography of Bibliographies* (2 vols.) 39-40, 4th edn. (5 vols.) 65, *Early Printed Books to the End of the Sixteenth Century: a Bibliography of Bibliographies* 40, 2nd edn. 61, *British Sources of Reference and Information* 47, *Index Bibliographicus* (2 vols.) 51, 52, *Voltaire's Notebooks* (2 vols.) 52, *Voltaire's Correspondence* (107 vols.) 52-65, definitive edn. 68, *St. Jean de Brébeuf, les Relations de ce qui s'est passé au pays des Hurons* 57, *Lettres de la Marquise du Châtelet* (2 vols.) 57, *Lettres d'amour de Voltaire à sa nièce* 57,

Voltaire on Shakespeare 67, *Voltaire's Household Accounts* 68, *Voltaire* 69, *The Besterman Bibliographies* (25 vols.) 71, *Voltaire's Philosophical Dictionary* 71, editor *The Printed Sources of Western Art* (29 vols.) 72, *Voltaire Editions Unknown to Bengeres* 73, *Voltaire on the Arts* 73, and many other works.

Thorpe Manderville House, Banbury, Oxon., England.

Bestor, Arthur Eugene, M.A., PH.D., LL.D.; American historian; b. 20 Sept. 1908, Chautauqua, N.Y.; *s.* of Arthur Eugene Bestor and Jeanette Louise (Lemon) Bestor; *m.* 1st Dorothea Nolte 1931 (divorced), 2nd Anne Carr 1939 (deceased), 3rd Dorothy Alden Koch 1949; three *s.*; ed. Yale Univ.

Instructor, Yale 30-31, 34-36; Asst. Prof. Columbia Univ. 37-42; Asst. Prof. Humanities, Stanford Univ. 42-45, Assoc. Prof. History 45-46; Assoc. Prof. of History, Univ. of Illinois 47-51, Prof. 51-62; Guggenheim Fellow 53-54, 61-62; Harmsworth Prof. of American History, Oxford Univ. 56-57; Prof. of History, Univ. of Washington 62-; Visiting Lecturer, Univ. of Wis. 47; Fulbright Visiting Prof., Univ. of Tokyo 67; mem. American Historical Asscn. (Pres. Pacific Coast Br. 75-76), Org. of American Historians, Ill. State Historical Soc. (Pres. 54-55), Council for Basic Educ. (Pres. 56-57), American Studies Asscn., Univ. Centers for Rational Alternatives; Beveridge Prize of American Historical Asscn. 46.

Leisure interests: walking, photography.

Publs. *Education and Reform at New Harmony* 48, *Backwoods Utopias* 50 (revised edn. 70), *Problems of American History* (jointly) 52 (4th edn. 72), *Educational Wastelands* 53, *The Restoration of Learning* 55, *Three Presidents and Their Books* 55 (jointly), *State Sovereignty and Slavery* 61, *The American Civil War as a Constitutional Crisis* 64, *The American Territorial System* 73 (jointly), *Separation of Powers in the Domain of Foreign Affairs* 74.

Department of History, University of Washington, Seattle; and 4553 55th Avenue, N.E., Seattle, Wash. 98105, U.S.A.

Telephone: 206-LA4-4202.

Beswick, Baron (Life Peer), cr. 64; **Frank Beswick,** P.C., J.P.; British politician and aerospace expert; b. 1912; *m.*; one *s.* one *d.*

Member of Parl. for Uxbridge div. of Middx. 45-59; Chair. Parl. Labour Party Civil Aviation Sub-Cttee. 51-59; Parl. Under-Sec. Ministry of Civil Aviation 50-51; Dir. Derby Aviation Ltd. 52-60; Lord-in-Waiting 64-65; Parl. Under-Sec. of State, Commonwealth Relations Office 65-67; Capt. Hon. Corps of Gentlemen at Arms and Govt. Chief Whip, House of Lords 67-70; Special Adviser, British Aircraft Corpn. 70-74; Minister of State Dept. of Industry 74-75; Chair. (desig.) British Aerospace Board 76-.

House of Lords, London, S.W.1; British Aerospace Board, Metropole Buildings, Northumberland Avenue, London, S.W.1, England.

Betancourt, Rómulo; Venezuelan politician; b. 22 Feb. 1908; ed. Caracas Univ.

Imprisoned while still a student by the Vicente Gómez régime; exiled to Colombia; returned to Venezuela to lead anti-Communist underground left-wing movement 36; again in exile 39-41; organized Acción Democrática 41-; Pres. Revolutionary Governing Junta on overthrow of Medina Angarita 45; forced again into exile by Pérez Jiménez régime 48-58; Pres. of Venezuela 59-64.

Betancur-Mejía, Dr. Gabriel: Colombian international civil servant; b. 26 April 1918, Bogotá; *m.* Yolanda Pulecio 1959; two *d.*; ed. Javeriana Univ., Bogotá, Syracuse Univ., U.S.A., and School of Advanced International Studies, Washington.

Former Sec. of Technical and Econ. Affairs to Pres. of Colombia; fmr. Founder and Dir. Colombia Inst. for Advanced Training Abroad (ICETEX); Prof. of Finance and Int. Trade; fmr. Chair. Special Comm. for Programming and Devt. of Education, Science and Culture in Latin America, Org. of American States; fmr. Dir. Gen. Colombian Asscn. of Univs.; Asst. Dir.-Gen. of UNESCO (in charge of educational activities) 63-66; Minister of Educ., Colombia 55-56, 66-68; mem. Exec. Board UNESCO 70-75, Vice-Chair. 72-74; Pres. Int. Conf. Educ., Geneva 70.

Leisure interest: golf.

40 avenue Foch, Paris 16e, France; Apartado Aéreo 6113, Bogotá, Colombia.

Telephone: KLE 35-94.

Betham, Hon. Gustav Frederick Dertag, O.B.E.; Western Samoan politician and businessman; b. 11 April 1915; ed. Newton West School and Seddon Memorial Technical Coll., Auckland, N.Z.

Western Samoan public Service 32-39; O. F. Nelson & Co. Ltd. (Gen. merchants) 39-47; Man. Samoa Printing & Publishing Co. 47-49; Man. Dir. Greenline Service Ltd. 49-52; merchant 53-; mem. Legislative Council of Western Samoa 48-71; Minister of Finance 61-70, also of Econ. Devt., Inland Revenue and Customs; mem. Exec. Council 61-70; Gov. W. Samoa in Asian Devt. Bank (ADB) 66-70; Sec.-Gen. South Pacific Comm. 71-75; del. to numerous int. corps.

Nouméa Ceolex, New Caledonia, South Pacific.

Telephone: 620-00.

Bethe, Hans Albrecht, PH.D.; Alsatian-born American physicist; b. 2 July 1906; *m.* Rose Ewald 1939; one *s.* one *d.*; ed. Goethe Gymnasium (Frankfurt/Main), and Frankfurt/Main and Munich Univs.

Lecturer German Univs. 28-33, Manchester and Bristol Univs. (England) 33-35; Asst. Professor Cornell Univ. 35-37, Prof. 37-; Dir. Theoretical Physics Div. Los Alamos Scientific Laboratory 43-46; mem. President's Science Advisory Cttee. 56-59; mem. American Philosophical Soc., Nat. Acad. of Sciences, American Physical Soc. (Pres. 54), American Astronomical Soc.; foreign mem. Royal Soc. (London); Presidential Medal of Merit 46, Max Planck Medal 55, Enrico Fermi Award 61; Nobel Prize for Physics 67.

Publs. *Elementary Nuclear Theory* 47, *Mesons and Fields* 55, *Intermediate Quantum Mechanics* 64, 68; contributions to *Handbuch der Physik* 33, 57, *Review of Modern Physics* 36-37, etc., and to scientific journals.

Laboratory of Nuclear Studies, Cornell University, Ithaca, N.Y., U.S.A.

Betjeman, Sir John, Kt., C.B.E.; English poet and author; b. 1906; ed. Marlborough and Magdalen Coll., Oxford.

Heinemann Award; Duff Cooper Award; William Foyle Poetry Prize (twice); Queen's Medal for Poetry 60; C.Lit; Poet Laureate 72; Hon. Fellow Keble Coll., Oxford 72; Albert Medal, Royal Soc. of Arts 73; Hon. D.Lit. 74.

Publs. *Mount Zion, Ghastly Good Taste, Continual Dew, An Oxford University Chest, Antiquarian Prejudice, Old Lights for New Chancels, Selected Poems, First and Last Loves, A Few Late Chrysanthemums, The English Town in the Last Hundred Years, Collected Poems, Summoned by Bells* (autobiog. in verse), *English Churches* (with Rev. Basil Clarke), *High and Low, Victorian and Edwardian London* (photographs) 69, *A Pictorial History of English Architecture, London's Historic Railway Stations* 72, *Victorian and Edwardian Brighton from Old Photographs* (with J. S. Gray) 72, *West Country Churches* 73, *A Nip in the Air* 74; *Guides* to Cornwall, Devon and (with John Piper) Shropshire, Buckinghamshire and Berkshire.

c/o John Murray Ltd., 50 Albemarle Street, London, W1X 4BD; The Mead, Wantage, Berkshire, England.

Bettelheim, Bruno, PH.D.; American child-psychoanalyst; b. 25 Aug. 1903, Vienna, Austria; *m.*; one *s.* two *d.*; ed. Univ. of Vienna.

Took up residence in U.S. 39; currently Stella Rowley Prof. of Educ., Prof. of Psychology and Psychiatry at Univ. of Chicago and Dir. Univ. of Chicago Sonia Shankman Orthogenic School 44-73, the university's residential treatment centre for severely emotionally disturbed children; has written many books on severely disturbed children, social psychology and related issues; founder mem. Nat. Acad. of Educ.; Fellow, American Psychological Asscn., Orthopsychiatric Asscn.; mem. Chicago Psychoanalytic Soc., Chicago Council for Child Psychiatry.

Publs. include: *Love is Not Enough* 50, *Symbolic Wounds* 54, *Truants from Life* 55, *The Informed Heart* 60, *Dialogues with Mothers* 62, *The Empty Fortress* 67, *The Children of The Dream* 69, *Obsolete Youth* 70, *A Home for the Heart* 74, and numerous magazine articles.

5725 Kenwood, Chicago, Ill. 60637, U.S.A.

Telephone: FA-4-2688 (Home).

Bettelheim, Charles, D. en D., L. ès L.; French economist; b. 20 Nov. 1913, Paris; s. of Henri Bettelheim and Lucienne Jacquemin; m. Lucette Beauvallet; five c.; ed. Paris Univ.

Director Centre for Social Studies and Int. Relations Ministry of Labour, Paris 44-48; French rep. Conf. on Trade and Employment 47; Prof. of Political Economy at Ecole Pratique des Hautes Etudes 48-; Head of UN Mission for Technical Assistance to Indian Govt. 55-56; Prof. at Ecole Nationale d'Administration; Prof. at Inst. d'Etudes du Développement Economique et Social 58-; mem. French Sociological Inst.; Dir. of the review *Problèmes de Planification* and Centre d'Etudes de Planification Socialiste.

Publs. *La Planification Soviétique* 39, *Les Problèmes théoriques et pratiques de la Planification* 46, *L'Economie Allemande sous le Nazisme* 46, *Bilan de l'Economie Française de 1918 a 1946* 47, *Esquisse d'un Tableau Economique de l'Europe* 48, *Initiations aux recherches sur les idéologies économiques et les réalités sociales* 48, *Emploi et Chômage devant la Théorie Economique* 49, *L'Economie Soviétique* 50, *Auxerre en* 1950 50, *Théories contemporaines de l'emploi* 51, *Nouveaux aspects de la théorie de l'emploi* 52, *Long-Term Planning Problems* 56, *Foreign Trade and Planning for Economic Development* 56, *Studies in the Theory of Planning*, Bombay 59, *Some Basic Planning Problems* 60, *Teoría de la Planificación* 61, *Problemas Teóricos y Prácticos de la Planificación* 62, *L'Inde Indépendante* 62, *Planification et Croissance accélérée* 64, *La construction du socialisme en Chine* 65, *Los Marcos Socioeconómicos y la organización de la planificación Social* 66, *Problèmes Théoriques et Pratiques de la Planification* 66, *La Transition vers l'Economie Socialiste* 68, *India Independent* 68, *Calcul économique et formes de propriété* 70, *Révolution culturelle et organisation industrielle en Chine* 73, *Les luttes de classes en U.R.S.S.—1917-1923* 74.

17 rue des Feuillantines, Paris 5e, France.

Telephone: 633-36-38.

Bettencourt, André; French politician; b. 21 April 1919.

General Counsellor for Lillebonne 46-; mem. Chamber of Deputies 51-; Vice-Pres. Foreign Affairs Comm. Nat. Assembly; Sec. of State to Presidency of the Council 54-55; Sec. of State for Transport 66-67; Sec. of State, Ministry of Foreign Affairs 67-May 68; Minister of Posts and Telecommunications May 68-July 68, of Industry July 68-June 69, of State Plan June 69-July 72, Minister attached to Foreign Office July 72-; also Minister of Cultural Affairs *ad interim* Nov. 70-Jan. 71; Chevalier, Légion d'Honneur, Croix de Guerre.

18 rue Delabordère, 92 Neuilly-sur-Seine, France.

Beugel, Ernst Hans van der; Netherlands professor of international relations and business executive; b. 2 Feb. 1918; ed. Univ. of Amsterdam.

Government service 45-60; Sec., Econ. Cttee. of the Cabinet, Ministry of Econ. Affairs; Dir. Bureau of the Marshall Plan, Ministry for Foreign Affairs 47, Dir. Gen. Econ. and Mil. Aid Programme 52; Sec. of State (Ministry of Foreign Affairs) for Foreign Affairs 57-58; Ambassador and Special Consultant to the Minister for Foreign Affairs 59; Deputy Pres. KLM Royal Dutch Airlines 60-61, Pres. 61-63; now Dir. of several companies in Netherlands, U.K. and U.S.; Prof. of Int. Relations, Leiden Univ. 66-; Vice-Chair., Netherlands Inst. for Int. Affairs; Chair. Netherlands Cancer Inst.; Grand Cross of the Oak Crown (Luxembourg), Grand Cross of the Order of Leopold II (Belgium), Knight Commdr. of the Order of St. Michael and St. George (U.K.), Grand Officer of Dannebrog (Denmark), Commdr. Légion d'Honneur (France), Knight Netherlands Lion, Officer Order of Orange-Nassau.

Office: Smidswater 1, The Hague; Home: Van Ouwenlaan 50, The Hague, Netherlands.

Telephone: 653850 (Office); 241848 (Home).

Beuve-Méry, Hubert, L. ès L., D. en D.; French journalist; b. 5 Jan. 1902; m. Geneviève Deloye 1928; four s.; ed. Paris Univ.

Director, Legal and Econ. Section, Institut Français de Prague 28-39; diplomatic corresp. of *Temps*, Prague 34-38; with Inst. Français, Lisbon 40-42, Dir. Nat. School, Uriage; Founder *Le Monde* 44, Dir. 44-69; writes under pseudonym "Sirius"; Gold Medal, Inst. of Journalists 70; Golden Pen of Freedom, Int. Fed. of Newspaper Editors 72.

Publs. *La Théorie des Pouvoirs Publics d'après François de Vittoria et ses rapports avec le droit public contemporain* 28, *Vers la plus grande Allemagne* 39, *Réflexions politiques* 51, *Suicide de la IVe République* 58, *Onze ans de règne, 1958-1969, vus par Sirius* 74.

107 boulevard Raspail, 75006 Paris, France.

Telephone: 548-5478.

Beuys, Joseph; Austrian artist and sculptor; b. 12 May 1921, Kleve; s. of Joseph Beuys and Johanna Hülsermann; m. Eva Wurmbach; two c.

Professor Staatliche Kunstakademie, Düsseldorf 61-; one-man exhbns. in galleries throughout Europe including in Kranenburg 53, 63, Düsseldorf 65-66, 69, Vienna 66-71, Antwerp, Eindhoven 68, Basle 69, 70, Lucerne, Innsbruck, Stockholm 71.

Drakeplatz 4, 4 Düsseldorf-Oberkassel, Federal Republic of Germany.

Bevan, Timothy Hugh; British banker; b. 24 May 1927, London; s. of Hugh Bevan and Pleasance Scrutton; m. Pamela Murray (née Smith) 1952; two s. two d.; ed. Eton.

Called to the Bar, Middle Temple 50; Dir. Barclays Bank Ltd. 66, Vice-Chair. 68, Deputy Chair. 73-; Dir. Barclays Bank (France) Ltd., later Barclays Bank S.A. 65, Barclays Bank of Calif. 68, Barclays Bank Int. Ltd. 71; Chair. Barclays Bank U.K. Management Ltd. 72; London Dir. Bank of N.S.W. 66; Dir. Soc. Financière Européenne 67, Commercial Union Assurance Co. Ltd. 74-.

Barclays Bank Ltd., 54 Lombard Street, London, E.C.3; Home: Tyes Place, Staplefield, Near Haywards Heath, Sussex, England.

Telephone: Handcross 367 (Home).

Beverloo, Cornelis Van; Netherlands painter; b. 1922; ed. Amsterdam Acad. of Fine Arts.

Co-founder, with Appel and Constant, of the experimental "Reflex" group; co-founder of "Cobra" group 48; rep. at numerous exhibitions, including Brussels Int. Exhibition 58, Dunn Int. Exhibition, London 63; works under the name of "Corneille".

c/o Société des Artistes Indépendants, Grand Palais des Champs-Elysées, Cours la Reine, Paris 8e, France.

Bewoor, Gen. Gopal Gurunath; Indian army officer; b. 11 Aug. 1916; s. of Sir Gurunath Venkatesh and Lady Rukmini Bewoor; m. Radhika Bewoor; two s. one d.; ed. Dehra Dun Mil. Coll., Staff Coll., Quetta. Commissioned 37; Instructor, Staff Coll., Quetta 47; served 2nd Dogra Regiment 47-48; Commdr. Infantry Brigade 52; Dir. Personnel Services, Army H.Q. 53; Del. to UN Gen. Assembly 56; Commdr. Infantry Brigade 57; promoted Maj.-Gen., Chief of Staff Western Command 59; G.O.C. Infantry Div. 61; Dir. Mil. Training, H.Q. 63; promoted Lieut.-Gen., Corps Commdr. Eastern Theatre 64; Deputy Chief of Army Staff 67; G.O.C.-in-C. Southern Command 69-73; Chief of Army Staff 73-75; Col. 11 Gurkha Rifles 60-75; Amb. to Denmark 76-; Param Vishisht Seva Medal 69; Padma Bhushan 72.
Indian Embassy, Amagertorv 8, 1160 Copenhagen K, Denmark.

Bexelius, Tor Alfred, JUR.DR.; Swedish lawyer; b. 25 Sept. 1903, Stockholm; s. of Anton Bexelius and Gerda Tollstén; m. Gun Koch 1935; two s. one d.; ed. Stockholm Univ.
Appeal Court Judge 37-48, Presiding Judge 48-54; Chair. or mem. numerous Legislative Cttees. 42-; Chair. Näringsfrihetsråd (Nat. Anti-Cartel Board) 54-56; Chair. Nat. Employees' Inventions Board 55-75; Justitieombudsman (Parliamentary Commr for Justice) 56-72.
Leisure interest: history.
Publs. numerous treatises on law and legislation.
Alevägen 4, 182 63 Djursholm, Sweden.
Telephone: Stockholm 755-60-56.

Bezençon, Marcel, L. ès L.; Swiss broadcasting official; b. 1 May 1907, Orbe; s. of Ernest and Marie Bezençon-Bezuchet; m. Marthe Droguet; one s. one d.; ed. Lausanne and Vienna Univs.
Journalist; Dir. Société Romande de Radiodiffusion, Radio-Lausanne 39-50; Dir.-Gen. Société Suisse de Radiodiffusion et Télévision (Swiss Broadcasting Corpn.) 50-72; Pres. EBU Television Programme Cttee. 54-69; Pres. EBU 71-; Pres. S.A. pour la publicité à la télévision 71-; Pres. Théâtre de Lausanne; Founder Eurovision.
Leisure interests: fine arts, literature.
16 chemin de Renens, Château de Valency, 1000 Lausanne, Switzerland.
Telephone: 021-24-66-66.

Bezombes, Roger; French painter; b. 17 Jan. 1913. Has exhibited in Paris since 37 and taken part in most overseas exhibitions of French art; work shown in Musée d'Art Moderne and Musée des Beaux Arts (Paris) and in museums in Paris, Menton, Algiers, Oran, Rabat, Athens, Jerusalem, etc.; Prix Nat. de Peinture. Works include paintings, illustrations for *Le grain de Sable* 55, lithographs; mural decorations for the steamer *Ile de France* and for the liner *France*; apartments at the official residence of the Pres. of the Republic, etc.; tapestries executed at Aubusson, including the collection for the Maison d'Afrique, Univ. of Paris; Brussels Exhibition 58; Metropolitan Opera N.Y. 58; Nouvelle Maison de la Radio de Paris; Chevalier de la Légion d'Honneur; Prof. Académie Julian.
Publ. *L'Exotisme dans l'Art et la Pensée* 54.
3 quai Saint-Michel, 75005 Paris, France.

Bhabha, Cooverji Hormusji, M.A., B.COM., J.P.; Indian businessman; b. 22 July 1910, Bombay; s. of Hormusji Cursetjee Bhabha and Ratanbai Panday; m. Dr. Amy C. H. Bhabha 1955; one s. one d.; ed. St. Xavier's Coll. and Sydenham Coll. of Commerce, Bombay.
Fellow St. Xavier's Coll. 32-34; Fellow and Lecturer in Banking Law and Practice, Sydenham Coll. of Commerce 32-33; J.P. 38-; Commerce mem. Govt. of India Sept. 46; mem. Works, Mines and Power Nov. 46; Minister of Commerce, Govt. of India, Aug. 47-April

48; Leader Indian del. to World Trade Conf. Havana 47 (elected Vice-Pres. of Conf.); Chair. Indian Banks Asscn. 55-61; Dir. Investment Corpn. of India, Tata Power Supply Co. Ltd., Swadeshi Co. Ltd., Tata Iron & Steel Co. Ltd., Spencer & Co. Ltd., Icelvinator of India Ltd., United Carbon India Ltd.; Trustee, Commerce (1935) Ltd., etc.
Commerce (1935) Ltd., Manek Mahal, 90 Veer Nariman Road, Bombay 20; 49 Cuffe Parade, Colaba, Bombay, 5 India.
Telephone: 253505 (Office).

Bhagat, Bali Ram; Indian politician; b. 1922; ed. Patna Coll.
Secretary Bihar Provincial Congress Cttee. 49; mem. Provisional Parl. 50-52, Lok Sabha 52-, Speaker Jan. 76-; Parl. Sec. Ministry of Finance 52-55; Deputy Minister for Finance 55-63; Minister of State for Planning 63-67, for Defence March-Nov. 67, for External Affairs 67-69; Minister in charge of Foreign Trade and Supply 69-70; Minister for Steel and Heavy Industry 70-71.
Office of the Speaker, Lok Sabha, New Delhi, India.

Bhagat, Dhanraj; Indian sculptor; b. 20 Dec. 1917, Lahore, Pakistan; s. of B. Hargobind and Lakshmi Done; m. Kamla Devi 1943; two s. two d.; ed. Khalsa High School and Mayo School of Arts, Lahore.
Teacher, Mayo School of Arts 39 and 44; Lecturer in Sculpture, Delhi Polytechnic Art Dept. 46-60, Senior Lecturer 60-62, Asst. Prof. 62-68, Prof. 68-73; numerous commissions throughout India; works in stone, wood, plaster, cement and metal-sheet; ten one-man sculpture shows in India 50-72; exhibitions abroad in London and Paris 48, East European countries 55 and 58, U.S.A. 54, German Federal Republic 58, São Paulo 62, South Africa 65; mem. Lalit Kala Acad. Punjab; mem. Nat. Cttee. of Int. Asscn. of Plastic Arts, Paris; invited to participate in first and second triennial exhbn. of World Art, New Delhi; works in Govt. Museum, Punjab, National Gallery of Modern Art, New Delhi, Lalit Kala Acad., Baroda Museum and Punjab Univ. Museum; Nat. Award of Lalit Kala Acad. 61; State Award 69.
Leisure interest: reading art and philosophy books.
College of Art, 22 Harding Avenue, New Delhi; and H 20, New Delhi South Extension Part 1, New Delhi, India.

Bhagavantam, Suri, M.SC.; Indian scientist and university professor; b. 1909, Gudivada, A.P.; s. of S. V. S. Sastry and S. Sitamma; m. Sitamahalakshmi 1924; four s. one d.; ed. Nizam Coll., Hyderabad and Madras Univ.
Professor of Physics and Principal, Andhra Univ. until 48; Scientific Liaison Officer, B.C.S.O. and Scientific Adviser to Indian High Commr. in U.K., London 48-49, Prof. of Physics, Osmania Univ. 49-52, Vice-Chancellor and Dir. Physical Labs. 52-57; Dir. Indian Inst. of Science, Bangalore 57-62; Scientific Adviser to Minister of Defence 61-69; Chair. Bharat Electronics Ltd., Cttee. on Org. of Scientific Research; Vice-Pres. Int. Union of Pure and Applied Physics; Dir. Hindustan Aeronautics Ltd.; Hon. D.Sc., F.N.I. and F.A.Sc.
Leisure interests: light reading, writing.
Publs. *Scattering of Light and Raman Effect* 40, *Theory of Groups and Its Application to Physical Problems* 52, *Crystal Symmetry and Physical Properties* 66.
Indian Institute of Science, Bangalore 560012, India.
Telephone: 81698.

Bhandari, Sunder Singh, M.A., LL.B.; Indian politician; b. 12 April 1921, Udaipur, Rajasthan; s. of Dr. Sujan Singh Bhandari and Phool Bai; unmarried; ed. Sirohi, Udaipur and Kanpur.
Advocate, Mewar High Court, Udaipur 42-43; Headmaster, Shiksha Bhawan, Udaipur 43-46; Divisional Pracharak, Rashtriya Swayamsewak Sangh, Jodhpur 46-51; Provincial Sec. Bharatiya Jana Sangh (People's

Party), Rajasthan 51-57; All India Sec. Bharatiya Jana Sangh 61-65, 66-67, All India Organizing Sec. 65-66; mem. Rajya Sabha 66-72; Leader, Janasangh Group in Rajya Sabha 67-68; Gen. Sec. Bharatiya Jana Sangh 67-.
Leisure interest: reading.
Bharatiya Jana Sangh Office, Vithal Bhai Patel, Bhawan Rafi Marg, New Delhi; Panchayati Nohara, Udaipur, Rajasthan, India.
Telephone: 383349 (New Delhi); 495 (Udaipur).

Bhargava, Vashishtha, M.SC.; Indian judge; b. 5 Feb. 1906; *m.* Vishnu Kumari Bhargava 1925; three *s.*; ed. Univ. of Allahabad.
Joint Magistrate 30-35; Civil and Sessions Judge 36-37; District and Sessions Judge 37-47; Additional Commr. for Food and Supplies, Govt. of Uttar Pradesh 47-48; Legal Remembrancer and Judicial Sec. 48-49; Puisne Judge, High Court, Allahabad 49-66, Chief Justice Feb-July 66; Judge Supreme Court of India 66-71; Chair. Sugar Industry Inquiry Comm. 71-74.
A 16/3 Vasant Vihar, New Delhi 110057, India.

Bhatia, Prem Narain; Indian journalist and diploma-tist; b. 1911, Lahore; *s.* of late H. N. D. Bhatia and late Puran Devi Bhatia; *m.* Shakuntala Ram 1942; two *s.* one *d.*; ed. Government Coll., Lahore, and Punjab Univ.
Army Service, Second World War; Dir. of Public Information, Bengal Government 45-46; Political Correspondent *The Statesman* (Calcutta and New Delhi) 46-58; Public Relations Adviser, Indian Embassy, Moscow 48; Editor *The Tribune*, Ambala 59; Resident Editor *The Times of India*, Delhi 60-62; Delhi Editor *The Indian Express* 63-65; Indian corresp. *The Guardian* (Manchester and London); High Commr. in Kenya 65-68, in Singapore 69-72; Editor-in-Chief, Dir. India News and Features Alliance 73-.
Leisure interests: reading, golf.
Publs. *All My Yesterdays, Indian Ordeal in Africa.*
Jeevan Deep Building, Parliament Street, New Delhi, India.

Bhatt, Ravishanker, M.A.; Indian merchant banker; b. 13 Dec. 1909; *s.* of Santoshram Bhatt; *m.* Pushpa N. Pathak; two *s.* two *d.*; ed. Samaldas Coll., Bhavnagar, Bombay School of Econs. and Sociology and London School of Econs.
Secretary, Industrial Investment Trust Ltd. 36-40; Sec. Diwan's Office, Bhavnagar State, subsequently Nayab Diwan (finance and railway) 40-47; Finance Officer, Oriental Govt. Security Life Assurance Co. Ltd. 48-53; Man. Dir. Bombay State Finance Corpn. 53-57; mem. Govt. of India Tariff Comm. 57-60; Exec. Dir. Indian Investment Centre 60-64, Chair. 72-; Chair. Unit Trust of India 64-72, Govt. of India Advisory Cttee. on Control of Capital Issues 73-, Ahmedabad Electricity Co. Ltd.; Dir. Premier Automobiles Ltd., Atul Products Ltd., Industrial Investment Trust Ltd., Steel Authority of India, State Bank of India; Hon. Fellow, London School of Econs.
Leisure interests: reading plays and poetry, long walks.
Publs. *Capital for Medium and Small-Scale Industries*; various articles on economic and financial subjects.
Ewart House, Homi Mody Street, Bombay-1, India.
Telephone: 253756.

Bhattacharya, Bhabani, PH.D.; Indian author and journalist; b. 10 Nov. 1906, Bhagalpur; *s.* of late P. N. Bhattacharya and Mrs. K. Bhattacharya; *m.* Salila Mukerji 1935; one *s.* two *d.*; ed. Patna and London.
Press Attaché at Indian Embassy in Washington 49-50; Asst. Editor *The Illustrated Weekly of India*, Bombay 50-52; Sec. Tagore Commemorative Volume Soc. 59-60; invitations from Harvard Univ., America-Japan Soc., Tokyo, Govts. of Australia and of West Germany, British Council; Ford Foundation research grant and round-the-world travel award; Senior Specialist, Inst.

of Advanced Projects, Honolulu 69-70; Visiting Prof. Univ. of Hawaii 71-72; Walker-Ames Prof. Univ. of Wash. 73; mem. Nat. Acad. of Literature; Univ. of N.Z. Prestige Award 63; Indian Nat. Acad. of Letters Award 67; "Bhabani Bhattacharya Collection" established in Boston Univ. archives.
Leisure interests: travel in India and abroad.
Publs. *Some Memorable Yesterdays, Indian Cavalcade, The Golden Boat*, and the novels *So Many Hungers, Music for Mohini, He Who Rides a Tiger, A Goddess Named Gold, Shadow from Ladakh* (novels translated into 16 European languages), *Towards Universal Man, Gandhi, the writer: the image as it grew* 69, etc.
3 Otley Court, Glan Tai, Manchester, Mo. 63011, U.S.A.
Telephone: (314) 351-7961.

Bhattacharyya, Birendra Kumar, B.SC., M.A.; Indian journalist and writer; b. 16 March 1924, Suffry Sibsagar, Assam; *s.* of Sashidhar Bhattacharyya; *m.* Binita Bhattacharyya 1958; two *s.* one *d.*; ed. Jorhat Government High School, Cotton Coll., Gauhati, Calcutta Univ. and Gauhati Univ.
Former Science Teacher, Ukrul High School, Manipur; Editor *Ramdhenu* 51-61, *Sadiniya Navayung* 63-67; Exec. mem. Sanjukta Socialist Party, Assam; Sec. Archaeological Soc. of Assam; Sahitya Akademi Award for Assamese Literature 61.
Publs. novels: *Iyaruingam* (won Akademi Award), *Rajpathe Ringiai* (Call of the Main Street), *Mother, Sataghai* (Killer), *Mrityunjay, Pratipad*; collections of short stories: *Kolongajioboi* (Still Flows the Kolong), *Satsari* (Necklace).
Kharghuli Development Area, Gauhati 1, Assam, India.
Telephone: 5019.

Bhave, Acharya Vinoba; Indian philosopher and savant; b. 11 Sept. 1895, Gagode, Maharashtra; *s.* of Narhav Shambhurao Bhave.
Co-worker and disciple of late Mahatma Gandhi; Founder and Leader of *Bhoodan* (Land Gift) Movement, the purpose of which is to bring about fundamental social and economic change in society by peaceful means. The movement began by way of a collection of gifts of land from landowners to be distributed among the landless, later developing into voluntary renunciation of ownership of land in favour of village communities, or *Gramdan*; more than four million acres of land were collected by *Bhoodan* and about 97,000 villages have declared *Gramdan* or common ownership (March 1969). Leader of *Shanti Sena* (Peace Volunteers) a movement for conflict resolution and socio-economic reform.
Leisure interest: comparative study of all religions.
Publs. *Talks on the Gita* 60, *The Essence of the Quran* 62, *Democratic Values* 63, *Steadfast Wisdom* 66, *The Essence of Christian Teachings* 66, and many others.
Sarva Seva Sangh, Rajghat, Varanasi, Uttar Pradesh, India.
Telephone: 4391.

Bhaya, Hiten, M.A.; Indian business executive; b. 29 Feb. 1920, Muzaffarpur, Bihar; *s.* of U. N. Bhaya; *m.* Angela Bhaya; three *c.*; ed. Patna Univ.
Joined govt. service 44, with Ministry of Defence (Navy), trained in Royal Naval Establishment, Ceylon and U.K., Dir. of Naval Armament Supply 55-59, Industrial Management Pool 59; joined Bhilai Steel Plant, Hindustan Steel Ltd. as Dir. of Purchase and Stores 59-61; Sec. Hindustan Steel 61-67, Gen. Man. Alloy Steels Plant, Durgapur 67-70, Commercial Dir. Hindustan Steel 70-72, Chair. Hindustan Steel Ltd. 72-; Dir. Bokaro Steel Ltd., Heavy Engineering Corpn. Ltd., Indian Iron and Steel Co. Ltd.; mem. Exec. Cttee., Int. Iron and Steel Inst., mem. Council, Indian

Statistical Inst., Nat. Council of Applied Econ. Research.
Hindustan Steel Ltd., P.O. Hinoo, Ranchi-2; Home: 16 New Road, Calcutta 27, India.

Bhumibol Adulyadej; King of Thailand; b. 5 Dec. 1927; ed. Bangkok and Lausanne, Switzerland.
Youngest son of Their Royal Highnesses Prince and Princess Mahidol of Songkhla; succeeded his brother, the late King Ananda Mahidol, June 46; married Her Majesty the present Queen Sirikit, daughter of H.H. the late Prince Chandapuri Suranath, 28th April 50; formal Coronation 5th May 50; three daughters, H.R.H. Princess Ubol Ratana, b. 51, H.R.H. Princess Sirindhorn, b. 55, H.R.H. Princess Chulabhorn, b. 57; one son, H.R.H. Crown Prince Vajiralongkorn, b. 52.
Chitralada Villa, Bangkok, Thailand.

Bhutto, Mumtaz Ali, M.A. (OXON.); Pakistani politician; b. 13 March 1933, Pir Buksh Bhutto; s. of Nawab Nabi Buksh Bhutto; m. 1950; one s. two d.; ed. Christ Church, Oxford.
Called to Bar, Lincoln's Inn; practised law, High Court, Karachi Bench 59-61; mem. Nat. Assembly from Larkana 65-; mem. Movt. against Pres. Ayub Khan 66-69; founder mem. Pakistan People's Party 67; imprisoned by Ayub Khan 68; Gov. of Sind 71-72, Chief Minister 72-73; Minister of Communication, Govt. of Pakistan Oct. 74-.
Leisure interests: hunting, shooting, riding, reading.
Village Pir Buksh Bhutto, Taluka Ratodero District, Larkana, Pakistan.

Bhutto, Zulfikqar Ali; Pakistani lawyer and politician b. Jan. 1928, Larkana; s. of the late Sir Shahnawaz Khan Bhutto; ed. Univ. of California (Berkeley), Christ Church, Oxford, and Lincoln's Inn, London.
Lecturer in Int. Law, Univ. of Southampton 52-53; Teacher of Constitutional Law, Sind Muslim Law Coll., and private legal practice 53-58; Minister for Commerce 58-60, of Minority Affairs, Nat. Reconstruction and Information Jan. 60-62, of Fuel, Power and Natural Resources, and Kashmir Affairs April 60-62, of Industries and Natural Resources 62-65, of Foreign Affairs 63-June 66; formed People's Party Dec. 67; arrested Nov. 68, released Feb. 69; President of Pakistan 71-73; Minister of Foreign Affairs, of Defence 71-, of Atomic Energy 72-; Prime Minister 73-; mem. and leader Pakistan Dels. to UN Gen. Assembly; several decorations.
Publs. *The Myth of Independence* 69, *The Great Tragedy*. 71.
Office of the Prime Minister, Rawalpindi, Pakistan.

Biaggi, Francantonio; Italian consulting engineer. b. 1899; ed. Politecnico, Milan, and Pavia Univ.
Operation engineer, Società Orobia, Milan 24-46, Engineering Man. 46, later Deputy Gen. Man.; Gen. Man., later Man. Dir. Società Elettrica Bresciana Brescia 48-; Man. Dir. Società Energia Elettrica (SENEL), Rome, Società Elettrica Valle Camonica; Vice-Pres. Società Lago d'Idro, Brescia; Dir. Rezzato-Vobarno Railway, Brescia; Appointee for Foreign Relations, Società Edison, Milan; expert OEEC Cttee. for Tariffs; Councillor, Federazione Nazionale Imprese Elettriche (FENIEL), Associazione Imprese Elettriche Lombarde Trentine Emiliane (AIELTE); fmr. mem. Italo-Austrian Cttee. for East Tyrol Hydro-Electric Plants; Italian Govt. del. to European Technical Comm. of ECA for study of interconnection problems in U.S.A.49; Councillor Associazione Nazionale Imprese Produttrici e Distributrici di Energia Elettrica (ANIDEL); Dir. Società Italiana Autotrasporti (SIA).
Publs. *L'elettricità in Diritto* 46, *Ordnungsprobleme der elektrischen Energiewirtschaft im Rahmen der Erfahrungen in Italien* 51, *Report on the Tecaid Mission in the United States* (with Marin) 49. *Wechselwirkungen*

zwischen Tarifpolitik und Ausbauplanung der Energieerzeugung (with Boselli) 52.
Piazza Vittoria 7, Brescia, Italy.

Biaggini, Benjamin Franklin; American business executive; b. 15 April 1916, New Orleans, La.; s. of Benjamin F. Biaggini, Sr. and Maggie (Switzer) Biaggini; m. Anne Payton 1937; two d.; ed. St. Mary's Univ. of Texas and Harvard Business School.
President and Chief Exec. Officer, Southern Pacific Co. and Southern Pacific Transportation Co., San Francisco; Chair., Dir. St. Louis Southwestern Railway Co., St. Louis; mem. Business Council; Trustee, Conf. Board, Calif. Inst. of Technology, Nat. Safety Council; Dir. Tenneco Inc., Asscn. of Amer. Railroads, California State Chamber of Commerce, Stanford Research Inst.; mem. Nat. Pay Board 71-72; Hon. LL.D. (St. Mary's Univ. of Texas) 65.
Leisure interests: golf, photography.
Southern Pacific Company, 1 Market Street, San Francisco, Calif. 94105; Home: 1170 Sacramento Street, San Francisco. Calif. 94108, U.S.A.

Biancini, Angelo; Italian sculptor; b. 1911; ed. Accademia di Santa Luca.
Professor and Artistic Dir. Istituto d'Arte, Faenza; Regular Exhibitor Venice Biennali and Rome Quadriennali 34-58; international exhibitor throughout the world; Prize, Milan Triennale 40, Venice Biennale 58.
Major Works: three statues, Galleria d'Arte Moderna, Rome, Canadian Temple, Rome, Mosaic Marist Fathers' International Coll. etc.
Istituto d'Arte di Ceramica, Faenza, Italy.

Biayenda, H.E. Cardinal Emile; Congolese ecclesiastic; b. 1927, Mpangala, Vinza.
Ordained 58; consecrated titular Archbishop of Garba 70; Archbishop of Brazzaville 71-; created Cardinal by Pope Paul VI 73.
Archevêché, B.P. 2301, Brazzaville, People's Republic of the Congo.

Bibby, Sir (Arthur) Harold, Bt., D.S.O., D.L.; British shipowner; b. 18 Feb. 1889, Oxton, Cheshire; s. of Arthur Wilson Bibby and Beatrice Bibby (née Heald); m. Marjorie Guthrie Williamson 1920; one s. three d.; ed. Rugby.
Joined Bibby Bros. & Co. 07; served in First World War, France and Flanders 15-18; Chair. Liverpool Steam Ship Owners' Asscn. 27, 58 (centenary year); High Sheriff of Cheshire 34-35, apptd. Deputy Lieut. 35; Chair. Liverpool Sailors' Home 21-51, Pres. 51-; Chair. Indefatigable and Nat. Sea Training School for Boys 31-59, Pres. 59-72; Chair. Bibby Line Ltd. 35-69, Pres. 69-; Dir. Martins Bank 29-67, Chair. 47-62; Dir. The Sea Insurance Co. Ltd. 22-68, Chair. 30-56; Gov. Rugby School 32-67; Hon. LL.D. (Liverpool Univ.); Hon. Freeman, City of Liverpool 70.
Leisure interests: shooting, gardening.
Tilstone Lodge, Tarporley, Cheshire; and Martins Building, Water Street, Liverpool, England.

Bibó, István, DR. POL. and JUR.; Hungarian scholar and politician; b. 7 Aug. 1911, Budapest; s. of István Bibó and Irene Graul; m. Boriska Ravasz 1940; one s. one d.; ed. Grammar schools at Budapest and Szeged. Piarist Coll., Szeged Univ., Vienna, Geneva.
Called to the Bar 40; Lecturer Szeged Univ. 40; in Ministry of Justice 41-45; Counsellor, later departmental chief, Ministry of Interior 45-46; Prof. of Political Sciences Szeged Univ. 46-50; Deputy Pres. of East European Research Inst. Budapest 47-49; Librarian, Univ. of Budapest 51-56; Minister of State Nov. 56; imprisoned 56-63; Librarian, Central Statistical Office 63-71.
Leisure interests: cartography, historical and political atlases.
Publs. *A szankciók kérdése a nemzetközi jogban, Kényszer,*

jog, szabadság, Jogszerü közigazgatás, eredményes köz-igazgatás, erös végrehajtóhatalom, A magyar demokrdcia válsága, A keleteurópai kisnépek nyomorusága, Zsidó kérdés Magyarországon 1944 után. The Case of Hungary and the World Situation, The Paralysis of the International Community and its Remedies.
Berkenye-u. 4, 1025 Budapest II, Hungary.

Bickmore, Lee Smith; American food executive; b. 5 June 1908, Paradise, Utah; *s.* of Danford M. and Sarah Jane (Smith) Bickmore; *m.* Ellen McMinn 1939; two *d.*; ed. Utah State Univ. and Harvard School of Business Admin.
Joined Nat. Biscuit Co. (Nabisco) 33, District Sales Man., Newark (N.J.) 46-49, Admin. Asst. to Vice-Pres (Sales), General Office 49-50, Vice-Pres (Sales, Advertising and Marketing) 50-57, Senior Vice-Pres. and mem Exec. Dept. 57, Exec. Vice-Pres. and mem. Board of Dirs. 59, Pres. 60-66, Chief Exec. Officer 61-73, Chair. Board 68-73, Chair. Exec. Cttee. 73-; official of Nabisco subsidiaries and other companies.
c/o National Biscuit Company, 425 Park Avenue, New York, N.Y. 10022; Home: 15 Randall Drive, Short Hills, N.J. 07078, U.S.A.

Bidault, Georges; French politician; b. 5 Oct. 1899' Moulins (Allier); *s.* of Georges Bidault and Augustine Traverse; *m.* Suzanne Borel 1945; ed. Coll. des Jésuites de Turin, Univ. of Paris.
Served First World War 17-18, subsequently Prof at Valenciennes, Rheims and Paris Univs.; adviser and leader writer for *L'Aube* until 39; mobilised 39, prisoner 40, released, apptd. Prof. Univ. of Lyons; resistance leader; Minister of Foreign Affairs under de Gaulle 44. Geputy (Loire) 45-62; Prime Minister of Provisional Dovt. 46; Minister of Foreign Affairs 47; Pres M.R.P 49; Prime Minister 49-50, Deputy Prime Ministei (Queuille Govt.) 51, Minister of Nat. Defence (Pleven Govt.) 51-52; Minister of Foreign Affairs (Mayer and Laniel Govts.) 53-54; Pres. of temporary Council April 58; exile in Brazil 63-67, Belgium 67-68; returned to France June 68; Lecturer, Univ. of Guanabara 65; Grand Cross Légion d'Honneur etc.
Publs. *D'une Résistance à l'autre* (autobiographical) 65, *Le Point* 68.
21 rue du Colonel-Moll, Paris 17e, France.

Biddle, Eric H.; American administrator; b. 27 April 1898, Philadelphia, Pa.; *s.* of Fred Davis Biddle and Estelle Harbeson; *m.* 2nd Janet Mayo 1957; three *s.* one *d.*; ed. Univ. of Pennsylvania and Oxford Univ.
Industrial Management and Finance 22-32; Relief Administrator of Pennsylvania 32-35; Exec. Dir. Community Fund of Philadelphia 35-40; Exec. Vice-Pres. U.S. Cttee. for Care of European Children from the war zones 40-41; mission to U.K. 41, Head Special Mission to U.K. and missions to European, Middle East and Occupied Territories 42-46 for various U.S. Govt. Depts.; Adviser U.S. Del. UNRRA 45, UNESCO 46, UN 45-46; Chair. Advisory Group of Experts on Admin., Personnel and Budgetary questions to UN Gen. Assembly 45-47; Special Asst. to Sec.-Gen. UN 46; Special Asst. to Dir. of OIC, Consultant to Asst. Sec. of State for Public Affairs and special missions to Europe 47; Special Asst. for Overseas Admin. ECA, Acting Chief ECA Mission to Korea and Asst. to U.S. Ambassador to Korea 48; Consultant, ECA Mission to Italy and Special Asst. to Dir. of German and Austrian Affairs, Dept. of State 49; Consultant to Chair., Nat. Sec. Resources Board, Exec. Office of the Pres. 49-51. and to various ECA and MSA officials 51-52; Special Consultant to Exec. Chair. Tech. Assistance Board (UN); Management Consultant 53-57, Vice-Pres. and Dir. Porter Int. Co. 57-65; Vice-Pres. United States Leasing Corpn. 58-61; Pres. Biddle Associates 61-.
Suite 801, 815 Connecticut Avenue N.W., Washington,

D.C. 20006; 1200 N. Nash Street, Arlington, Va. 22209, U.S.A.
Telephone: (703) 243-4766.

Bide, Austin Ernest, B.SC., F.R.I.C., F.B.I.M.; British business executive; b. 1915; *m.*; three *d.*; ed. Univ. of London.
Member of staff, Dept. of Govt. Chemist until 40; Research Dept. Glaxo Laboratories Ltd., Deputy Sec. 54, Sec. 59; Dir. Glaxo Group Ltd. 63; Deputy Chair. Glaxo Holdings Ltd. 71-73, Chair. and Chief Exec. 73-. Glaxo Holdings Ltd., Clarges House, 6-12 Clarges Street, London, W.1, England.

Biden, Joseph Robinette, Jr., J.D.; American politician; b. 20 Nov. 1942, Scranton, Pa.; *s.* of Joseph R. Biden and Jean F. Biden; *m.* Neilia Hunter (deceased); two *s.* one *d.* (deceased); ed. Univ. of Del., Newark and Syracuse Univ. Coll. of Law, N.Y.
Trial Attorney in the Public Defender's Office, Del. 68; Founder of Biden & Walsh Law Firm, Wilmington; mem. New Castle Co., Del. and Amer. Bar Asscns.; Amer. Trial Lawyers' Asscn.; admitted to practise before the Del. Supreme Court; mem. New Castle Co. Council 70-72; Senator from Del. 72-, serving as a mem. of the Cttee. on Public Works and the Cttee. on Banking, Housing and Urban Devt; named to the Democratic Steering Cttee.
Leisure interests: sports, history, public speaking, American architecture.
228 North Star Road, North Star, Wilmington, Del., U.S.A.
Telephone: 239-4626.

Bieber, Margarete, PH.D.; American (naturalized 1940) classical archaeologist; b. 31 July 1879, Schoenau, West Prussia (now Pryscowo, Poland); *d.* of Jacob Heinrich Bieber and Vally Bukofzer; one adopted *d.*
Professor of Archaeology Giessen Univ. and Dir. of the Archaeological Inst. of the Univ. until 33; Hon. Fellow, Somerville Coll. Oxford 33-34; Lecturer, Barnard Coll. 34-36; Associate Prof. of Fine Arts and Archaeology Columbia Univ., New York 36-38 (retd. 48); Special Lecturer Barnard Coll. 48-50, Princeton Univ. 48-50, Inst. of Gen. Studies, Columbia Univ. 48-54; mem. German Archaeological Inst., Berlin, Council for Art and Archaeology, Boston; Gold Medal for Achievement in Archaeology, Amer. Inst. of Archaeology 74; Hon. D.Litt., Columbia Univ. 54; Hon. Senator, Giessen Univ. 59.
Leisure interests: collecting coins, listening to music.
Publs. *Katalog der Skulpturen in Kassel* 16, *Die Denkmäler zum Theaterwesen im Altertum* 20, *Griechische Kleidung* 28, *Entwicklungsgeschichte der griechischen Tracht* 34, 67, *The History of the Greek and Roman Theatre* 39, 61, *Laocoon: the Influence of the Group since its Re-discovery* 42, 67, *German Readings in the History and Theory of Fine Arts* 46, *German Readings I: A Short Survey of Greek and Roman Art* 58, 68, *The Sculpture of the Hellenistic Age* 55, 61, *A Bronze Statuette in Cincinnati* 57, *Romani Palliati* 59, *The Copies of the Herculaneum Women* 62, *Alexander the Great in Greek and Roman Art* 64, *New Trends in the New Books on Ancient Art* 65, *The Statue of Cybele in the J. Paul Getty Museum* 68, *Roman Copies as Roman Art* 70, *A Critical Review of Schuchhardt, Antike Plastik* 70, *Die Wichtigkeit der Römischen Spätrepublikanischen Münzen für dir Geschichte der Kunst* 71, *Copies: A Contribution to Greek and Roman Art* 75.
605 W. 113th Street, Apt. 33, New York, N.Y. 10025, U.S.A.
Telephone: 212-MO3-4454.

Bieberbach, Ludwig, PH.D.; German mathematician; b. 4 Dec. 1886, Goddelau; *s.* of Dr. Erhard Bieberbach and Lina Ludwig; four *s.*; ed. Heidelberg and Göttingen Univs.

Lecturer Königsberg Univ. 10; Prof. Basle 13, Frankfurt 15, and Berlin 21-45; mem. Prussian Acad. of Science 24-45, Deutsche Akademie der Naturforscher Leopoldina, Halle 24-.
Publs. *Differential-und Integralrechnung, Lehrbuch der Funktionentheorie, Theorie der Differentialgleichungen, Algebra, Analytische Geometrie, Projektive Geometrie, Differentialgeometrie, Höhere Geometrie, Konforme Abbildung, Theorie der geometrischen Konstruktionen, C. F Gauss, Galilei und die Inquisition, Analytische Fortsetzung, Theorie der gewöhnlichen Differentialgleichungen auf funktionentheoretischer Grundlage, Theorie der gewöhnlichen Differentialgleichungen im reellen Gebiet.*
Bahnhofstrasse 5, 8203 Oberaudorf, Federal Republic of Germany.
Telephone: 08033-331.

Bień, Witold, D.ECON.SC.; Polish economist and politician; b. 15 June 1927, Przysieka, Miechów District; s. of Antoni and Magdalena Bień; m. 1950; one s. two d.; ed. Main School of Planning and Statistics, Warsaw.
Worked in Accounting Organization Office 50-52; Ministry of Finance 52-63, Counsellor to Minister 64-68, Dir. Dept. of Industry 68-71; Under-Sec. of State, Ministry of Finance May 71-; Pres. Nat. Bank of Poland April 73-.
Narodwy Bank Polski, ul. Swiętokrzyska 11/21, 00-950 Warsaw, Poland.
Telephone: 26-99-55.

Biermann, Adm. Hugo Hendrik, S.S.A., O.B.E.; South African naval officer; b. 6 Aug. 1916, Johannesburg; s. of Hugo Hendrik Biermann; m. Margaret Elaine Cruwys 1940; one s. one d.; ed. Braamfontein Afrikaans Medium School, Volkskool Heidelberg, Transvaal, Jan van Riebeeck High School, Cape Town and training ship *General Botha.*
Served in Merchant Navy 34-39; transferred to S.A. Navy 40, with rank of Sub-Lieut.; served in Mediterranean and S.A. waters; Chief of S.A. Navy 52, with rank of Commodore; promoted to rank of Rear-Adm. 57, Vice-Adm. 67, Adm. 72; Chief of S.A. Defence Forces 72-.
Leisure interest: sports.
Defence Headquarters, Pretoria; Home: 41 Edward Street, Waterkloof, Pretoria; and Private Bag X414, Pretoria, South Africa.

Biermann, Ludwig Franz Benedikt, DR. PHIL.; German astrophysicist; b. 13 March 1907, Hamm, Westphalia; m. Ilse Biermann (née Wandel); one s. two d.; ed. Univs. of Hanover, Munich, Freiburg and Göttingen.
Assistant Univ. of Göttingen 33; Scholarship, Univ. of Edinburgh 34; at Univ. of Jena 34-36; Lecturer (Dozent) Univ. of Berlin 38, Univ. of Hamburg 45-47 Assoc. Prof. 47-48; Assoc. Prof. Univ. of Göttingen 48; Head of Astrophysics Dept., Max-Planck-Inst. for Physics 47-58; Dir. of Inst. for Astrophysics 58-75, Acting Dir. Max-Planck-Inst. for Physics and Astrophysics 71-75, Scientific mem. (emeritus) 75-; Prof. of Astronomy Univ. of Munich 59-; Chair. Scientific Policy Cttee., European Southern Observatory (ESO) 74, Kepler Comm., Bavarian Acad. of Sciences 74; Visiting Prof. Calif. Inst. of Technology, Haverford Coll., Princeton Univ. 55, Univ. of Calif. (Berkeley) 59-60, Univs. of Sydney and Canberra 60, Inst. for Advanced Studies, Princeton 61; Visiting Fellow, Univ. of Colorado, Boulder 67, Special Visiting Prof. 68-; mem. Bayerische Akad. der Wissenschaften; Corresp. mem. Soc. Royale des Sciences, Liège; Assoc. Royal Astronomical Soc., London, Int. Acad. of Astronautics, Deutsche Akademie der Naturforscher Leopoldina; Copernicus Prize 43; Bruce Gold Medal of Astronomical Soc. of the Pacific 67; Hon. D.Sc. (Univ. of Colorado) 69; Emil-Wiechert-Medal, German Geophysical Soc. 73; Gold Medal, Royal Astronomical Soc. 74.

Major work includes: Investigation on stellar evolution and stellar structure 31-39, theoretical work on the solar atmosphere and corona 33-, problems of cosmic radiation and interstellar magnetic fields 50-, physics of comets and problems related to interplanetary matter and the solar wind 51-, plasma physics and its relation to astrophysics 56-, problems of space research 63-.
Office: Max-Planck-Institut für Physik und Astrophysik, 8000 Munich 40, Föhringer Ring 6; Home: 8000 Munich 40, Rheinlandstr. 10B, Federal Republic of Germany.
Telephone: 327001 (Office); 325144 (Home).

Bierwirth, John E.; American business executive; b. 21 April 1895; ed. Yale Univ.
Vice-President and Dir. Thompson-Starrett Co. Inc. 19-29; Vice-Pres. New York Trust Co. 29-41, Pres. and Trustee 41-; Pres. Nat. Distillers and Chemical Corpn. 49-58, Chair. and Chief Exec. Officer 58-70, Chair. 70-.
National Distillers and Chemical Corporation, 99 Park Avenue, New York City, N.Y. 10016; Home: Briarwood Crossing, Lawrence, N.Y. 10016, U.S.A.

Biesheuvel, Barend William; Netherlands agriculturist and politician; b. 5 April 1920, Haarlemmerliede; m. Wilhelmina Meuring 1945; one s. two d.; ed. Free Univ. of Amsterdam.
Ministry of Agriculture 45-47; Sec. for Foreign Relations, Fed. of Agriculture 47-52; Gen. Sec. Nat. Protestant Farmers' Union 52-59, Pres. 59-63; mem. Parl. 57-63, 63-; mem. European Parl.; Deputy Prime Minister, Minister of Agriculture and Fisheries 63-67; mem. Second Chamber Parl.; leader of Anti-Revolutionary Party; Pres. Shipbuilding Advisory Board; Prime Minister July 71-73; mem. Advisory Board Unilever N.V. 73-; Pres. Supervisory Board Nat. Investment Bank 73-; mem. Supervisory Board Ogem.
Enschedeweg 7, Aerdenhout, Netherlands.

Bigeleisen, Jacob, A.B., M.S., PH.D.; American chemist; b. 2 May 1919, Paterson, N.J.; s. of Harry and Ida (Slomowitz) Bigeleisen; m. Grace Alice Simon 1945; three s.; ed. New York Univ., Washington State Univ. and Univ. of Calif. (Berkeley).
S.A.M. Labs., Columbia Univ. (Manhattan District) 43-45; Ohio State Univ. 45-46; Univ. of Chicago 46-48; Assoc. to Senior Chemist, Brookhaven Nat. Laboratory 48-68; Prof. of Chemistry, Univ. of Rochester 68-, Chair. Dept. of Chemistry 70-75, Tracy H. Harris Prof., Coll. of Arts and Sciences 73-; Visiting Prof. Cornell Univ. 53; Hon. Visiting Prof., Eidgenössische Technische Hochschule, Zürich 62-63; Senior Postdoctoral Fellow, Nat. Science Foundation 62-63; Visiting Distinguished Prof., State Univ. of N.Y. (Buffalo) 66; Guggenheim Fellow 74-75; mem. Nat. Acad. of Sciences; Fellow, American Acad. of Arts and Sciences; American Chem. Soc. Nuclear Applications to Chemistry Award 58; Gilbert N. Lewis Lecturer, Univ. of Calif. 63; E. O. Lawrence Memorial Award and Presidential Citation 64.
Leisure interests: sailing, architecture.
Publs. *Calculation of equilibrium Constants of Isotopic Exchange Reactions* 47, *Relative Reaction Velocities of Isotopic Molecules* 49, *The Significance of the Product and Sum Rules to Isotope Fractionation Studies* 57, *Statistical Mechanics of Isotope Effects in Condensed Systems* 61, and numerous publications on ionization of strong electrolytes, organic photochemistry, semiquinones, acids and bases and particularly theoretical and experimental studies on the chemistry of isotopes.
The University of Rochester, Department of Chemistry, River Campus, Rochester, N.Y. 14627, U.S.A.
Telephone: 716-275-4227.

Biggs, Edward George Power; American (b. British) organist; b. 29 March 1906; ed. Hurstpierpoint Coll., and Royal Acad. of Music, London.
Organist and Soloist Sir Henry Wood's Festival Orchestra at Queen's Hall; freelance concert organist in

America; many organ recital recordings on historic organs, and recordings first for R.C.A. Victor then Columbia Recording Companies; Fellow American Acad. of Arts and Sciences; D.Mus. (Hon.), Acadia Univ. Nova Scotia and New England Conservatory, Boston; Hon. Dr. Fine Arts Coe Co., Iowa; Hon. Fellow, Royal Acad. of Music, London, Hon. Fellow Royal Coll. of Organists, London.
53 Highland Street, Cambridge, Mass. 02138, U.S.A.

Biggs, Norman Parris; British banker; b. 23 Dec. 1907, Newry, Co. Down; s. of John G. Biggs and Mary Sharpe Dickson; m. Peggy Helena Stammwitz 1936; two s. one d.; ed. John Watson's School, Edinburgh.
Bank of England 27-46; Dir. Kleinwort, Sons & Co. Ltd. 46-52; Dir. Esso Petroleum Co. 52-57, Man. Dir. 57-64, Vice-Chair. 64-66; Vice-Pres. (Finance) Esso Europe Inc. 66-67; Chair. Esso Petroleum Co. Ltd. 68-71; Chair. United Int. Bank Ltd. 70-, Williams and Glyn's Bank Ltd. 72-; Deputy Chair. Nat. and Commercial Banking Group Ltd.; Dir. Gillett Bros. Discount Co. Ltd.
Leisure interests: sailing, travel.
8 Sussex Square, London, W.2. England.

Bihalji-Merin, Oto; Yugoslav critic, essayist and novelist; b. 3 Jan. 1904, Belgrade-Žemun; s. of David Bihalji and Klara (Schoemann) Bihalji; m. Lisa Bihalji 1938; one d.; ed. Belgrade and Berlin Acads. of Fine Art.
Began his career as a painter; now works as an author, editor and art critic; also writes under the pseudonyms Peter Merin and Peter Thoene; Editor-in-Chief *Jugoslavia* 49-58; mem. Selection Cttee., Art Exhibition, Brussels Int. Exhbn. 58; Order of People's Merit, 1st Class, Chevalier, Ordre de Léopold (Belgium), Herder Prize 64, Grand Cross of Distinguished Service of Federal Republic of Germany.
Leisure interests: talking with young people, travelling by aeroplane, listening to very old and very new music.
Publs. *Conquest of the Skies* 37 (English, French, German, Dutch and Swedish translations), *Spain Between Death and Birth* 38 (English and German translations), *Modern German Art* (English edn. 38, Serbo-Croat edn. 55), *Au Revoir in October* (novel) 47, *Thoughts and Colours* (essays), *The Foundry* (play) 50, *Yugoslavia, a Small Country between the Worlds* 54 (German edn. 55, Dutch edn. 56), *Yugoslav Sculpture of the XX Century* 55 (English, French and German translations), *Peter Lubarda and the Painting "The Battle of Kossovo", The Invisible Door* (play) 56, *Rencontres in Our Days* (essays) 57, *Icons and Frescoes in Serbia and Macedonia* (French, English and German translations) 58, *Primitive Arts of the XX Century in Europe and America* 59; chapter on Yugoslav and Polish art in *Neue Kunst nach 1945* 58, *The Adventure of Modern Art,* 62, 64, 68, *Bogosav Zivkovic, World of a Primitive Sculptor* 62, 63, *Bogomil Sculpture* 62, 64 (*The Bogomils* in English 63), *Architects of Modern Thought* 65, *Primitive Artists of Yugoslavia* 65, *Die Welt von oben* 66, *Thousands of Years of Art in Yugoslavia* (Editor and preface) 69, *Masks of the World* 70 (German), *The End of Art in the Age of Science?* (French and German) 69, *The Douanier Rousseau* (with Lisa Bihalji-Merin) 70, *Time-Light-Movement* (essay) 70, *Modern Primitives* (English) 71, *Masters of Naive Art* (English, German, French, Italian, Serbo-Croat) 71, 72, *Bridges of the World* (Editor and preface) 72, *Image and Imagination* 74, *Unity of the World in the Vision of Art* 74, monographs on painters: *Krsto Hegedusic* 65, *Gabrijel Stupica* 68, *Marij Pregelj* 71, *Naive Arts* (TV series) 74.
Nemanjina ul. 3, Belgrade, Yugoslavia.
Telephone: 641-571.

Bijedić, Džemal; Yugoslav politician; b. 1917, Mostar, Herzegovina; m.; three c.; ed. Faculty of Law, Belgrade.

Joined communist movt. as a student; organized partisans in Bosnia-Herzegovina during World War II; became successively Asst. Minister of Interior, Sec.-Gen. of Govt. and Minister responsible for Legal Problems, Govt. of Bosnia-Herzegovina; Pres. Assembly of Bosnia-Herzegovina 67-71; Prime Minister of Yugoslavia July 71-.
Office of the Prime Minister, Belgrade, Yugoslavia.

Bilac Pinto, Olavo; Brazilian lawyer and politician; b. 8 Feb. 1908, Minas Gerais; s. of João Pereira Pinto and Laura Domingues Pereira; m. Maria do Carmo Moreira 1933; one s. two d.; ed. Instituto Moderno de Educação, Minas Gerais, and Universidade de Minas Gerais.
Criminal lawyer, Belo Horizonte 31-33; Police Instructor, Minas Gerais 33-34; Deputy of Constituent and Legislative Assemblies, Minas Gerais 34; Dir. *Revista Forense* 35; Prof. Faculty of Law, Univ. of Minas Gerais 39-41; fmr. Prof. of Administrative Law, Univ. of Brazil; Fed. Deputy 50-; Financial Sec. State of Minas Gerais 61; Leader of União Democrática Nacional (U.D.N.) in Chamber of Deputies 62-63; Pres. of Nat. Cttee. U.D.N. 63; Del. to UN 64; Pres. Brazilian Chamber of Deputies 65-66; Amb. to France 66-70; Minister, Supreme Fed. Tribunal 70-72.
Publs. *Contribuição de Melhoria* 37, *Ministério Público* 37, *Regulamentação Efetiva dos Serviços de Utilidade Pública* 41, *Estudos de Direito Público* 53, *Le Financement de l'Hotellerie Touristique* 64, *Guerra Revolucionaria* 64.
Av. Vieira Souto 550, Rio de Janeiro, GB, Brazil.

Bil'ak, Vasil, D.SC.S.; Czechoslovak politician; b. 11 Aug. 1917, Krajná Bystrá; ed. School of Political Studies at Central Committee of Communist Party of Czechoslovakia, Prague.
Took part in Slovak Nat. Rising 44; full-time party official, Regional Cttee., C.P. of Slovakia, Bratislava 50-51; Dept. Head, Central Cttee., C.P. of Slovakia 53; Sec. and Chief Sec. Regional Cttee., C.P. of Slovakia, Prešov 54-58; Minister-Commr., Comm. for Educ. and Culture of Slovak Nat. Council 59-62, Minister 60-62; Deputy Chair. Slovak Nat. Council 60-63; Sec. Central Cttee. C.P. of Slovakia 62-68, First Sec. 68; mem. Central Cttee. C.P. of Czechoslovakia 54-, mem. Secr. 68-; mem. Presidium Central Cttee. C.P. of Czechoslovakia 68-, Chair. Ideological Cttee. 70-; Deputy to Slovak Nat. Council 54-64; mem. Central Cttee. of C.P. of Slovakia 55-71; Deputy to Nat. Assembly 60-69; mem. Presidium, Central Cttee. of C.P. of Slovakia 62-68; mem. Presidium Nat. Assembly 63-68; Deputy to House of The People, Fed. Assembly 69-; mem. Presidium of Fed. Assembly 69-71; mem. Presidium Nat. Assembly 75-; Order of Labour 67, Georgi Dimitrov Order 68, Soviet Order of the Red Banner 70, Soviet Memorial Medal 70, Order of Repub. 72, Order of Victorious February 73.
Central Committee of Communist Party of Czechoslovakia, nábř. Kyjevské brigády 12, Prague 1, Czechoslovakia.

Bilge, Ali Suat, LL.T.; Turkish professor of international law and politician; b. 1921, Istanbul; s. of Sulhiye and Sezai Bilge; m. Olcay Bilge 1965; one s.; ed. Univs. of Ankara and Geneva.
Assistant, Faculty of Political Science, Univ. of Ankara 50, Assoc. Prof. 52, Prof. 60-; Hon. Legal Adviser, Ministry of Foreign Affairs 60, First Hon. Legal Adviser 65; Judge, European Court of Human Rights 66; mem. Perm. Court of Arbitration, The Hague 66; mem. UN Cttee. of Human Rights 70; mem. Int. Law Comm. 71-; Minister of Justice 71-72; Amb. to Switzerland 72-.
Leisure interest: fishing.
Publs. *Diplomatic Protection of Compatriots* 53, *International Politics* 66.

Embassy of Turkey, Lombachweg 33, Berne, Switzerland; Home: Bahçelievler 58 nci Sokak No. 2, Ankara Turkey.
Telephone: 12-25-17.

Bilheimer, Rev. Robert Sperry, B.A., B.D., D.D.; American ecclesiastic; b. 28 Sept. 1917, Denver, Colo.; s. of George Steven and Katherine Elizabeth Bilheimer; m. Dorothy Dodge 1942; three s.; ed. Phillips Exeter Acad., Yale Univ., Yale Divinity School.
Minister, Westminster Presbyterian Church 46-48; Sec., The Inter-Seminary Movement 45-48; Programme Sec., World Council of Churches, New York 48-54, Assoc. Gen. Sec., Dir. of the Division of Studies, Geneva 54-63; Senior Minister, Central Presbyterian Church, Rochester, N.Y. 63-66; Dir. Int. Affairs Programs, The Nat. Council of Churches of Christ in the U.S.A. 66-.
Leisure interests: trout fishing, photography.
Publs. *What Must the Church Do?* 47, *The Quest for Christian Unity* 52.
Office: Room 566, 475 Riverside Drive, New York, N.Y. 10027; Home: 60 Pinewood Gardens, Hartsdale, N.Y. 10530, U.S.A.

Bilibin, Alexander Fedorovich; Soviet infectionist; b. 28 March 1897, Surazh, Bryansk Region; ed. Kiev Univ.
Physician, Head of Section in hospital 22-24; Head of Chair, Third Moscow Medical Inst. 44-50, Second Moscow Medical Inst. 50-; Corresp. mem. U.S.S.R. Acad. of Medical Sciences 50-60, mem. 60-; Hon. mem. Czechoslovak Purkinye Scientific Soc.; Order of Lenin, Red Banner of Labour; Merited Scientist of U.S.S.R.
Publs. About 150 works on acute infectious diseases (dysentery, salmonellosis, Botkin disease).
Second Medical Institute, 1 Malaya Pirogovskaya ulitsa, Moscow, U.S.S.R.

Bill, Max; Swiss architect, sculptor, painter, politician and writer; b. 22 Dec. 1908, Winterthur; s. of Erwin Bill and Marie Geiger; m. Binia Spoerri 1931; ed. Zürich School of Art and Craft and Dessau Bauhaus.
Professor at Zürich 44-45; Dir. Inst. for Design, Ulm, Germany 51-56; Prof. of Environmental Design, Inst. for Fine Arts, Hamburg 67-74; Grand Prix Triennale Milan 36 and 51, Biennale São Paulo 51 (1st Int. Sculpture prize) and 67; mem. Fed. of Swiss Architects; mem. Zürich City Council 61-68, Swiss Fed. Council 67-71; Hon. Fellow, American Inst. of Architects 64; mem. Acad. of Arts, Berlin, Royal Flemish Acad. of Science, Letters and Art; New York Guggenheim Int. Award 64; Art Prize, City of Zürich 68.
Home: Rebhusstrasse 50, 8126 Zumikon; Office: Albulastrasse 39, 8048 Zürich, Switzerland.
Telephone: (051)-52-60-60 (Office).

Billanovich, Giuseppe; Italian philologist; b. 6 Aug. 1913; ed. Univ. degli Studi, Padua.
Senior Research Fellow, Warburg Inst., London 48-50; Prof. Italian Literature Fribourg Univ., Switzerland 50-60; Prof. Mediaeval and Humanistic Philology, Catholic Univ. of Milan; Antonio Feltrinelli Prize for Philology 65; Co-Dir. *Thesaurus Mundi* and annual *Italia Medioevale e Umanistica.*
Publ. *I primi umanisti e le tradizioni dei classici latini* 53.
Corso Magenta 48, Milan, Italy.

Billera, I. John; American business executive; b. 20 July 1912, New York City; m.; ed. Coll. of the City of N.Y.
Former financial officer, Noma Electric Corpn., Edward Ermold Co., Sperry Gyroscope Co.; Treas. U.S. Industries Inc. 53, subsequently financial Vice-Pres., then Senior Vice-Pres. in charge of all overseas operations, Exec. Vice-Pres. 60, Dir. 63-, Pres. 65-70, Chief Exec. Officer 65-, Chair. of Board 66-.
U.S. Industries Inc., 250 Park Avenue, New York, N.Y. 10017, U.S.A.

Billeskov-Jansen, Frederik Julius, DR.PHIL.; Danish professor; b. 30 Sept. 1907, Hvidbjerg; s. of Hans Billeskov-Jansen and Bothilde Schack-Schou; m. Vibeke Collet Henrichsen 1938; one s. two d.; ed. Københavns Universitet.
Assistant Lecturer in Danish, Univ. of Copenhagen 35-38, Prof. 41-; Lecturer, Univ. de Paris à la Sorbonne 38-41; Editor *Orbis Litterarum* 43-50; mem. Royal Danish Acad. of Sciences and Letters, mem. Int. Asscns. of Comparative Literature and of German Language and Literature, mem. Danish Acad.; Pres. Søren Kierkegaard Soc., Alliance Française, Copenhagen; Kommandor af Dannebrog; Officier, Légion d'Honneur.
Publs. *Danmarks Digtekunst I-III* 44-58, 2nd edition 64, *Holberg som Epigrammatiker og Essayist* 39. Editions of Holberg: *Moralske Tanker* 43, *Epistler* 54, *Memoirer* 63, *Vaerker i tolv Bind* 69-71, *Ludvig Holberg* 74; *Søren Kierkegaards Litterære Kunst* 51, *Søren Kierkegaards: Vaerker i Udvalg* 50, *Poetik* (Vols. I and II) 41-48, *Den Danske Lyrik* 61-66, *Esthétique de l'œuvre d'art littéraire* 48, *L'Age d'or* 53, *Anthology of Danish Literature* (French edn. 64, English edn. 71, Italian edn. 73, Dutch edn. 73).
Frydendalsvej 20, 1809 Copenhagen V, Denmark.
Telephone: 01-316369.

Billetdoux, François-Paul; French writer, actor, director and producer; b. 7 Sept. 1927; ed. Ecole d'Art Dramatique Charles Dullin and Institut des Hautes Etudes Cinématographiques.
Producer and Dir. Radiodiffusion Française 46-, in Caribbean 49-50, Gen. Overseas Service 57-58; journalist 51; cabaret actor and disc jockey 51-53; work for theatre, radio, television and films 59-; numerous prizes.
Publs. *L'Animal* (novel) 55, *Une rose pour Charles Cros* 57, *Royal Garden Blues* 57, *Brouillon d'un bourgeois* 61; Plays: *Treize pièces à louer* 51, *A la nuit* 55, *Tchin-Tchin* 59, *Le comportement des époux Bredbury* 60, *Va donc chez Törpe* 61, *Pour Finalie* 62, *Comment va le monde, Môssieu?, Il tourne, Môssieu!* 64, *Il faut passer par les nuages* 64, *Silence! l'arbre remue encore!* 67, *Je n'étais pas chez moi* 68, *Quelqu'un devrait faire quelque chose* 69, *7 + Quoi?* 69, *Femmes parallèles* 70, *Rintru pa trou tar hin!* 71, *Ne m'attendez pas ce soir* 71, *Les veuves* 72, *La Nostalgie, Camarade* 74; Television: *Pitchi Poï ou la parole donnée* 67, *Musique pour une ville* 69, *Famine chez les rats* 70, *Cantique des créatures* 70, *L'Apocalypse des Animaux* 73; Radio: *Ai-je dit que je suis bossu?* 71.
31 square de Montsouris, Paris 14e, France.

Billingham, Rupert Everett, M.A., D.PHIL., D.SC., F.R.S.; British zoologist; b. 15 Oct. 1921, Warminster, Wilts.; s. of Albert Everett Billingham and Helen Louise Green; m. Jean Mary Morpeth 1951; two s. one d.; ed. Oxford Univ.
Lecturer, Dept. of Zoology, Birmingham Univ. 47-51; Research Fellow of British Empire Cancer Campaign, and Hon. Research Assoc., Dept. of Zoology, Univ. Coll. London 51-57; mem. Wistar Inst. of Anatomy and Biology, Phila., U.S.A. 57-65; Prof. of Zoology, Univ. of Pa. 58-71; Prof. and Chair. Dept. of Medical Genetics, and Dir. Phipps Inst. of Medical Genetics, Univ. of Pa., School of Medicine 65-71; Prof. and Chair. Dept. of Cell Biology, Univ. of Texas Southwestern Medical School at Dallas, Tex. 71-; Pres. Transplantation Soc. 74-76; Fellow, N.Y. Acad. of Sciences, Amer. Acad. Arts and Sciences; Fellow Royal Soc. 61-; Alvarenga Prize, Coll. of Physicians of Phila.; Hon. Award Medal, Amer. Asscn. of Plastic Surgeons; Hon. D.Sc., Trinity Coll. (Conn.), F. L. Adair Award, Amer. Gynaecological Soc. 71.
Leisure interest: gardening.
Publs. *Transplantation of Tissues and Cells* (ed. with

W. K. Silvers) 61, *Wound Healing* (ed. with W. Montagna) 64, *Epithelial-Mesenchymal Interactions* (ed. with R. Fleischmajer) 68, *Immunology and the Skin* (ed. with W. Montagna) 71, *The Immunobiology of Transplantation* (with W. K. Silvers) 71, *The Immunobiology of Mammalian Reproduction* (with A. E. Beer) 76, numerous scientific publications on tissue transplantation immunology, immunological tolerance, and the biology of skin, in Royal Soc. and other journals.
Office: Department of Cell Biology, University of Texas Southwestern Medical School, 5323 Harry Hines Boulevard, Dallas, Texas 75235; Home: 5211 Meaders Lane, Dallas, Texas 75229, U.S.A.
Telephone: 214-688-2224 (Office); 214-691-4435 (Home).

Billings, Marland Pratt, PH.D., D.SC.; American geologist; b. 11 March 1902, Boston; s. of George Bartlett and Helen Agnes (McDonough); m. Katharine Stevens Fowler 1938; one s. one d.; ed. Harvard Univ. Teaching Fellow and Instructor, Harvard Univ. 22-28, 30-, Asst. Prof. 30-39, Assoc. Prof. 39-46, Prof. 46-72, Prof. Emer. 72-, Chair. Div. of Geological Sciences 46-51; mem. Faculty, Bryn Mawr Coll. 28-30; mem. Staff U.S. Geological Survey, Part-time 29-44, Geologist 43-44; Civilian Technical Observer, U.S. Army 44; mem. American Asscn. for the Advancement of Science (Vice-Pres. 49), Nat. Acad. of Sciences, Geological Soc. of America (Pres. 59); Hon. D.Sc. (New Hampshire and Washington Univs.).
Publs. *Structural Geology* 42 (3rd edn. 72), *Bedrock Geology of New Hampshire* 56, *Chemical Analyses of Rocks and Rock-Minerals from New Hampshire* 64.
Harvard University, Dept. of Geological Sciences, 24 Oxford Street, Cambridge, Mass. 02138; Westside Road RFD, North Conway, New Hampshire 03860, U.S.A. Telephone: 617-495-2351 (Office); 603-383-6664.

Billotte, Gen. Pierre; French army officer and politician; b. 8 March 1906, Paris; s. of Gen. Gaston Billotte and Catherine Lathony; m. 1951: two d.; ed. Ecole Militaire de Saint-Cyr, Ecole Supérieure de Guerre.
Military Rep. of Free French in Moscow 41-42; Chief of Staff to Gen. de Gaulle in London 42-44, Sec. of Cttee. for Nat. Defence; Commdr. Brigade under Gen. Leclerc 44; Commdr. 10th Infantry Division 44; Asst. Gen. Chief of Staff Nat. Defence 45-46; French Mil. Rep. to UN 46-50; retired from army 50; mem. Chamber of Deputies 51-56, 62-66, 68-71, 71-; Minister of Nat. Defence and of the Armed Forces 55; Rep. of France on various UN Cttees. 55-62; Vice-Pres. U.N.R. Group in Nat. Assembly 62-66; Minister of State Overseas Depts. and Territories 66-68; Mayor of Créteil 65; Pres. Mouvement pour le socialisme par la participation; Commdr. Légion d'Honneur; Compagnon de la Libération.
Publs. *Fatalité de la defaite allemande* 41, *Le Temps du choix* 50, *L'Europe est Née* 55, *Considération sur la Stratégie Mondiale* 57, *Du Pain sur la Planche* 65, *Le Temps des Armes* 73.
39 Boulevard du Commandant Charcot, Neuilly-sur-Seine, France.

Billoux, François; French politician; b. 21 May 1903, St. Romain la Motte (Loire); s. of Michel Billoux and Marie Chavroche; m. Josette Rampini 1928; one d.; ed. Ecole pratique de Commerce et d'Industrie de Roanne (Loire).
Communist Dep., Marseille 36-; fmr. Town Councillor, Marseilles; Sec. Fed. of Young Communists 23-27, Sec.-Gen. 28-31; mem. Central Cttee. of French Communist Party 26-; Commr. of State French Cttee. Nat. Liberation 44; Minister for Public Health 44-45; Minister for Nat. Economy 45-46; Minister for Reconstruction 46; Minister for Nat. Defence Jan.-May 47; mem. Politbureau of French Communist Party 36-72; political dir. *France Nouvelle*; mem. Parl. Comm. on Foreign Affairs.

2 place du Colonel-Fabien, 75010 Paris; 25 rue St. Bazile, 13001 Marseilles, France.
Telephone: PRO-42-22.

Binaghi, Walter; Argentine civil engineer and international official; b. 13 July 1919, Buenos Aires; s. of Ambrosio Binaghi and Isolina Bertani; m. María Rosalía Unia 1945 (deceased); ed. Colegio Nacional de Buenos Aires and Buenos Aires Univ.
Assistant at Buenos Aires Univ. 43; Aerodrome designer, Directorate of Infrastructure 43, Dir. Runways Section 45, Aerodrome Planning 46; rep. ICAO Air Navigation Cttee. 47-49, Chair. Air Navigation Comm. 49-57; Pres. 8th and 21st Assembly, ICAO 54, 74, Pres. of Council of ICAO 57-; Hon. Dr. Eng. School of Mines and Engineering, South Dakota 59.
International Aviation Square, 1000 Sherbrooke St. West, Montreal, Quebec H3A 2R2, Canada.

Binder, Paul, DR.SC.POL.; German economist; b. 29 July 1902, Stuttgart; s. of Paul Martin Binder and Frieda Barth; m. Gisela Soll 1947; two d.; ed. Technical High School, Stuttgart, and Univs. of Tübingen, Rostock, Dijon.
Deputy Dir. of Dresdner Bank, Berlin 37-40; Provincial Dir., later State Sec. and Dir. of the Finance Ministry and Deputy Prime Minister of Württemberg-Hohenzollern; mem. of Parl. Council, Bonn 49; mem. Council of Economic Advisers for the Appraisal of General Econ. Devt. 64-68; mem. Board European Cttee. for Econ. and Social Progress (CEPES), and Dir. its German Board; mem. Board of Dirs. Econ. Cttee. of C.D.U.; Hon. Senator Tübingen Univ., Prof.; Grosses Verdienstkreuz mit Stern.
Leisure interest: history.
Publs. *Schalthebel der Konjunktur* 39, *Die Stabilisierung der Wirtschaftskonjunktur* 56, *U.S.A. und Wir* 56, *Kaufkraft, Produktivität, freie Kapitalbildung* 56, *Die Bundesbahn und ihre Konkurrenten* 61, *Dir Wirtschaft, die Materielle Grundlage unserer Existenz* 72, *Kritik der traditionellen Wirtschaftstheorie und der herkömmlichen Wirtschaftspolitik.*
Hermann-Kurz-Strasse 24, Stuttgart-N; Office: Königstrasse 48, Stuttgart-N, Federal Republic of Germany. Telephone: 292383 (Office); 295891 (Home).

Binder, Theodor, M.D.; Peruvian physician; b. 1919; ed. Hebel-Gymnasium Lörrach, Univs. of Freiburg, Strasbourg, and Basle, and Swiss Tropical Inst., Basle.
Clinic Chief, Swiss Tropical Inst. 47-48; Public Health Officer, Oxapampa, Peru 48-50; Staff, Medical School, Univ. of San Marcos, Lima 51-56; Founder of Clinic for the Poor, and constructor of Hospital, Pucallpa 56-60, Inauguration Hospital Amazónico Albert Schweitzer, Yarinacocha, Pucallpa 60, Director 60-; Founder and Dir. Instituto Tropical Amazónico 63-; Exec. Dir. Amazonian Indian Int. Devt., Toronto and N.Y. 71-.
Publs. Philosophy: *Friedrich Nietzsche* 50, *Goethe's Iphigenia and the Ethics* 51, *A. Schweitzer as a Philosopher* 54, *Heroism as an Attitude towards Life* 56, *Personal Ethics in a Depersonalizing Age* 63, *Tristes Tropiques or Land of Hope* 68, *The Right to an Independent Development in the Third World* 70, *Sense and Nonsense of the Christian Mission Among Jungle Indians* 70, *Problems of Intercultural Relations* 71; Medicine: *Congenital Malaria* 50, *Treatment of Hypertension* 52, *Latin-America: Nonanalytical Psychotherapy* 58, *Histoplasmosis in Eastern Peru* 64, *Dermatomycosis and Deep Mycosis in Eastern Peru* 65, etc.
Taos Canyon, Taos, N.M. 87571, U.S.A.

Bing, Sir Rudolf, K.B.E.; British impresario; b. 9 Jan. 1902, Vienna, Austria; s. of Ernst and Stefanie Hoenigsvald Bing; m. Nina Schelesmskaya-Schelesnaya 1929. Hessian State Theatre, Darmstadt 28-30; Civic Opera, Berlin-Charlottenburg 30-33; Gen. Man. Glyndebourne

Opera, England 35-49; Artistic Dir. Edinburgh Int. Festival 47-49; Gen. Man. Metropolitan Opera N.Y., 50-72; Distinguished Visiting Prof. of Music, Brooklyn Coll. 72-75; Consultant, Columbia Artists Management Inc. 74-; Adjunct Prof. of Theatre Management, N.Y. Univ. 72; Hon. D.Mus. (Lafayette Coll., Pa.), Hon. D.Litt. (Dickinson Coll., Pa.), Hon. D. Hum. Litt. (N.Y., Temple Univs., and Wagner Coll.), Hon. LL.D. (Jacksonville Univ., Fla.); Chevalier Légion d'Honneur, Grand Officer Order of Merit of Repub. of Italy, Grand Silver Medal of Honour of Repub. of Austria, Commander's Cross of Order of Merit of Fed. Repub. of Germany
Publ. *5000 Nights at the Opera* 72.
Essex House, 160 Central Park South, New York, N.Y. 10019, U.S.A.

Bing, R. H., B.SC., M.ED., PH.D.; American mathematician; b. 20 Oct. 1914, Oakwood, Tex.; s. of Rupert Henry Bing and Lula May Thompson Bing; m. Mary Blanche Hobbs 1938; one s. three d.; ed. Southwest Texas State Univ. and Univ. of Texas.
Assistant Prof., Univ. of Wisconsin, Assoc. Prof., Prof., Research Prof. 69-73; Prof. Univ. of Texas 73-; Chair. Conf. of Board of Mathematical Sciences 65-66, Chair. Div. of Mathematical Science of Nat. Research Council 67-69; Vice-Pres. and Chair. of Section A., American Asscn. for the Advancement of Science 59; Pres. Mathematical Asscn. of America 63-64; mem. Nat. Science Board 68-75, Nat. Acad. of Sciences; Vice-Pres. American Mathematical Soc. 67-69, Pres. 76.
Publs. Research articles on topology in mathematical journals.
Department of Mathematics, R. L. Moore Hall, University of Texas, Austin, Texas, U.S.A.
Telephone: 512-471-4257 (Office); 512-453-5317 (Home).

Binger, James Henry, A.B., LL.B.; American lawyer and business executive; b. 16 May 1916, Minneapolis, Minn.; s. of Dr. Henry E. and Vida Binger (née DeBar); m. Virginia E. McKnight 1939; one s. two d.; ed. Yale Univ. and Univ. of Minnesota.
Associate, Fletcher, Dorsey, Barker, Colman and Barber 41-43; Minneapolis-Honeywell Regulator Co. (Honeywell Inc. 64) 43-, Asst. Sec. 45-46, Asst. Vice-Pres. 46-50, Vice-Pres. and Gen. Man. Valve Div., Philadelphia 49, Vice-Pres. 52-61, Dir. 59-, Pres. 61-65, Chief Exec. Officer 64-74, Chair. 65-74, now Chair. Exec. Cttee.; Dir. North-western Bell Telephone Co., Northwest Airlines, Northwest Bancorporation, 3M Co., Chase Manhattan Bank; Vice-Pres. Univ. of Minnesota Foundation; Vice-Chair. Business Council.
Honeywell Inc., 2701 Fourth Avenue South, Minneapolis, Minnesota, U.S.A.

Bingham, Colin William Hugh; Australian journalist and author; b. 10 July 1898, Richmond, Queensland; s. of H. Bingham; m. Alexa Strachan 1923; one s. two d.; ed. Townsville Grammar School and Queensland Univ.
Literary staff *The Telegraph*, Brisbane 22-39; London staff Australian Assoc. Press 40-42; Foreign Corresp. *Sydney Morning Herald* 43-48, Assoc. Editor 57-61, Acting Editor 57-58, Editor 61-65; mem. N.S.W. State Advisory Cttee. of Australian Broadcasting Comm. 68-72; mem. Metropolitan Council Workers' Educational Asscn. (N.S.W.) 70-74; elected life mem. Queensland Univ. Union; Ford Memorial Prize for Verse, Queensland Univ. 20, 23, 24; Wilkie-Deamer Newspaper Address 65; Jubilee Lecturer, Queensland English Asscn. 73.
Leisure interests: decorative bark designs, birdwatching, gardening.
Publs. *Men and Affairs* 67, *The Affairs of Women* 69, *Poems* 70.
30 Arnold Street, Killara, N.S.W. 2071, Australia.
Telephone: 4982970 (Sydney).

Bingham, Jonathan Brewster; American politician; b. 24 April 1914, New Haven, Conn.; s. of Hiram and Alfreda (Mitchell) Bingham; m. June Rossbach 1939; one s. three d.; ed. Yale Univ.
Member, New York Bar; U.S. Army 43-45; private legal practice 39-41, 46-51, 53-54, 59-61; Office of Price Admin. 41-42; Dept. of State 45-46; Asst. Dir. Office of Int. Security Affairs, Dept. of State 51; Dep. Administrator, Tech. Co-op. Admin. 51-53; Sec. to State Gov. 55-58; U.S. Rep. UN Trusteeship Council 61-63, Pres. 62-63; U.S. Rep. UN Econ. and Social Council 63-64; mem. U.S. House of Reps. 65-.
Leisure interests: chamber music (violin, viola), tennis, golf.
House of Representatives, Washington, D.C. 20515; 5000 Independence Avenue, Bronx, N.Y. 10471, U.S.A. Telephone: 202-225-4411 (Washington), 212-933-2310 (New York).

Binkowski, Johannes Aloysius Joseph, D.PHIL.; German newspaper publisher; b. 27 Nov. 1908, Neisse; s. of Emil and Anna Binkowski; m. Helene Scholz 1937; ed. Univs. of Breslau and Cologne.
Co-Founder and head of adult educ. programme, Aalen 51; Co-Founder Südwestdeutscher Zeitungsverband 54; Chair. Cttee. for Political Journalism and Studies, Asscn. of Newspaper Publrs. 62, Pres. of Asscn. 70-; mem. German Press Council 66-70; Chair. Verein Südwestdeutscher Zeitungsverleger 67, Vice-Chair. 70-; mem. Television Council, Zweites Deutsches Fernsehn, Chair. Policy and Co-ordination Cttee. 62-; mem. Board of Govs. Stiftervereinigung der Presse 66-; Vice-Pres. Int. Fed. of Newspaper Publrs. 73-; Pres. Ritterorden vom Heiligen Grabe zu Jerusalem; Grosses Verdienstkreuz 69.
Publs. *Wertlehre des Duns Scotus* 35, *Religiöse Erwachsenenbildung* 36, *Christlicher Alltag* 37, *Der Mensch am Scheideweg* 47, *Die sozialen Enzykliken* 63, *Mit den Massenmedien leben* 70.
7 Stuttgart 1, Villastrasse 11; Home: 7 Stuttgart 75 (Sillenbuch), Oberwiesenstrasse 47, Federal Republic of Germany.
Telephone: 432981 (Office); 473804 (Home).

Biobaku, Saburi Oladeni, C.M.G., B.A., M.A., PH.D.; Nigerian historian and university official; b. 16 June 1918; m. Muhabat Folasade Agusto 1949; one s.; ed. Government Coll., Ibadan, Higher Coll., Yaba, Univ. Coll. Exeter, Trinity Coll. Cambridge and Inst. of Historical Research, London.
Master, Govt. Coll., Ibadan 41-44; Educ. Officer 47-50; Asst. Liaison Officer for Nigerian Students in U.K., Colonial Office, London 51-53; Registrar, Univ. Coll., Ibadan 53-57; Sec. to Premier and Exec. Council, W. Nigeria 57-61; Pro-Vice-Chancellor, Univ. of Ife and Dir. Institutes of African Studies and of Public Admin. 61-65; Vice-Chancellor Designate, Univ. of Zambia Feb.-March 65; Vice-Chancellor Univ. of Lagos 65-72, Prof. and Dir. of African Studies 65-; Dir. Yoruba Historical Research Scheme 56-; Chair. Management Consultant Services Ltd. 72-; Chair. Cttee. of Vice-Chancellors, Nigeria 67-70; Vice-Chair. Standing Cttee., *Encyclopaedia Africana* 67-; mem. Exec. Board Asscn. of African Univs. 67-; Pres. Historical Soc. of Nigeria 68-; created Are of Iddo, Abeokuta 58; Hon. Fellow, W. African Asscn. of Surgeons 68.
Publs. *The Origin of the Yoruba* 55, *The Egba and their Neighbours* 57, *African Studies in an African University* 63.
P.O. Box 7741, Lagos, Nigeria.
Telephone: 31430.

Birch, (Albert) Francis, B.S.E.E., M.A., PH.D., F.R.A.S.; American professor of geophysics; b. 22 Aug. 1903, Washington, D.C.; s. of George Albert Birch and Mary C. Hemmick; m. Barbara Channing 1933; one s. two d.; ed. Harvard Univ. and Univ. of Strasbourg.

Research Assoc. in Geophysics, Harvard Univ. 32-37, Asst. Prof. 37-43, Assoc. Prof. 43-46, Prof. 46-49, Sturgis Hooper Prof. of Geology 49-47, Emer. Prof. 74-; Sherman Fairchild Visiting Scholar, Calif. Inst. of Tech. 75; mem. Nat. Acad. of Sciences, American Acad. of Arts and Sciences, American Philosophical Soc., Geological Soc. of America (Pres. 64), American Geophysical Union, American Physical Soc., Seismological Soc. of America, Geological Soc. of London; Legion of Merit 45; Day Medal, Geological Soc. of America 50; Bowie Medal, American Geophysical Union 60; Nat. Medal of Science 68; Vetlesen Prize 68; Penrose Medal, Geological Soc. of America 69; Hon. D.Sc. (Univ. of Chicago); Gold Medal, Royal Astronomical Soc. 73.

Publs. Papers on geophysical topics: elasticity, composition of the Earth's interior, heat flow and geothermal problems, measurements of physical properties of rocks at high pressures and temperatures.
Hoffman Laboratory, Harvard University, Cambridge, Mass. 02138, U.S.A.

Birendra Bir Bikram Shah Dev, King of Nepal; b. 28 Dec. 1945, Kathmandu; s. of late King Mahendra and Princess Indra; m. Queen Aishwarya Rajya Laxmi Devi Rana 1970; one s.; ed. St. Joseph's Coll., Darjeeling, Eton Coll., England, Univ. of Tokyo and Harvard Univ.
Has travelled extensively throughout Europe, North and South America, U.S.S.R., Iran, Japan, China and several African countries; Grand Master and Col.-in-Chief, Royal Nepalese Army 64; Supreme Commdr.-in-Chief 72; Chief Scout, Nepal Boy and Girl Scouts; Chair. Nepal Asscn. of Fine Arts; Chancellor Tribhuvan Univ.; numerous decorations; came to the throne 31 Jan. 72, crowned 24 Feb. 75.
Leisure interests: painting, swimming, riding, playing games, parachuting.
Narayanhity Royal Palace, Kathmandu, Nepal.

Birgi, Muharrem Nuri; Turkish Permanent Representative to NATO 60-72; see *The International Who's Who 1975-76.*

Birkelund, Palle; Danish librarian; b. 29 Jan. 1912; ed. Københavns Universitet and Aarhus Universitet.
Library Asst., State Library, Aarhus and Univ. Library, Copenhagen, Asst. Librarian 44; UNESCO Fellowship, U.S.A. 49; Nat. Librarian 52-; UNESCO consultant, Burma 68; Vice-Chair. Danish Library Asscn.; Chair. Danish Asscn. of Research Libraries, Gen. Advisory Council for Research Libraries; mem. Exec. Council of League of European Research Libraries (LIBER), State Council for Information and Documentation, etc.
Publs. Co-editor: *Nordisk leksikon for bogvaesen* 47-62, *Libri, International Library Review,* library and bibliographical reviews, etc.
The Royal Library, Copenhagen; and 6 Strandgade, 1401 Copenhagen, Denmark.
Telephone: SU 189.

Birla, B. M.; Indian industrialist; b. 1904.
One of the founders of the Indian Chamber of Commerce and Pres. in 36 and 44; founder and Pres. Indian Sugar Mills Asscn. and Indian Paper Mills Asscn.; mem. Fiscal Comm., Govt. of India; Pres. Fed. of Indian Chambers of Commerce and Industry 54; fmr. Dir. Central Board Reserve Bank of India and Chair. of Local Board, Eastern Area; Chair. Hindustan Motors Ltd.; Man. Dir. Birla Bros. Private Ltd.; Dir. Ranchi Enterprises and Properties Ltd.
Office: Birla Bldg., 9/1 R.N. Mukherjee Road, Calcutta 1; Home: Birla House, 8/9 Alipore Road, Calcutta 27, India.

Birlădeanu, Alexandru; Romanian economist and politician; b. 25 Jan. 1911, Comrat, U.S.S.R.; widower; one s. one d.; ed. Univ. of Taşi.
Professor, Head of Dept. of Political Economy, Inst. of Econ. Sciences, Bucharest 46-51; mem. Romanian Communist Party 36-, mem. Cen. Cttee. 55-, alt. mem. Political Bureau 62-65, mem. 65-68; mem. Exec.Cttee. and Perm. Presidium 65-68, Cen. Cttee. of R.C.P.; Sec.-Gen. the Deputy Minister, Ministry of Nat. Economy 46-48; Minister of Foreign Trade 48-54; First Deputy Chair., then Chair., State Planning Cttee. 55; Deputy Chair. Council of Ministers 55-65, 67-68, First Deputy Chair. 65-67; Deputy to Grand Nat. Assembly; Chair. Nat. Council of Scientific Research 67; mem. Acad. of the Socialist Repub. of Romania 55-; Pres. Dept. of Econ. Sciences, Acad. of Social and Political Sciences 70-; Hero of Socialist Labour 64.
Leisure interest: reading.
Str. Arh. Cerchez No. 8, Bucharest, Romania.

Birley, Sir Robert, K.C.M.G., M.A.; British professor of rhetoric; b. 14 July 1903, Midnapore, Bengal, India; s. of Leonard Birley and Grace Maxwell-Smith; m. Elinor Margaret Frere 1930; two d.; ed. Rugby and Balliol Coll., Oxford.
Asst. master, Eton Coll. 26-35; Headmaster of Charterhouse 35-47; Educational Adviser, British Zone of Germany 47-49; Headmaster of Eton Coll. 49-63; Visiting Prof. of Educ., Univ. of Witwatersrand 64-66; mem. Fleming Cttee. 44; Burge Memorial Lecturer 47, Reith Lecturer 49; Gresham Prof. of Rhetoric; Prof. and Head Dept. of Social Science, Univ. of London 67-70; Chair. Gen. Council of the Selly Oak Colleges 69-; Grosses Bundesverdienstkreuz 57; Hon. Dr. Ing. Berlin Technical Univ., Hon. LL.D. Edinburgh, Witwatersrand, Leeds and Liverpool Univs., Hon. D.Phil. Frankfurt/Main Univ., Hon. D.C.L. Oxford Univ., Hon. D.Sc. Aston Univ.
Leisure interests: old books, travelling in France.
Publs. *Speeches and Documents in American History* (4 vols.), *The English Jacobins, Sunk Without Trace* 62.
Lomans, West End, Somerton, Somerset, England.
Telephone: Somerton 72640.

Birnbaum, Hans; German business executive; b. 14 Feb. 1912, Schwetz, Weichsel; s. of Dr. med. Hugo Birnbaum and Erika Birnbaum, née Boege; m. Ingeborg von Lettow 1951; three s. one d.; ed. Univs. of Freiburg, Leipzig and Königsberg.
Ministry of Econ. Affairs, Berlin 39-45; Ministry of Finance, Lower Saxony 49-50; Fed. Ministry of Finance, Bonn 50-57; Under-Sec. in Fed. Treasury, Bonn 57-61; mem. Management Board, Salzgitter AG (iron and steel, machinery) 61-, Chair. of Management Board 68-; Chair. Supervisory Board Volkswagenwerk AG 74-.
Salzgitter AG, 332 Salzgitter-Drütte 41, Federal Republic of Germany.
Telephone: 05341-212399/212499.

Birney, Earle, M.A., PH.D., LL.D., O.C., F.R.S.C.; Canadian author; b. 13 May 1904, Calgary, Alta.; s. of William G. Birney and Martha Robertson; m. Esther Bull 1940; one s.; ed. Univs. of British Columbia, Toronto, Calif. and London.
Lecturer during summer sessions, Univ. British Columbia 27-34, 36-37; Instructor in English Univ. of Utah 30-34; Lecturer, Asst. Prof. of English, Univ. of Toronto 36-42; Personnel Selection Officer, Canadian Army, retd. with rank of Maj. 42-45; Supervisor of European Foreign Language Broadcasts, Radio Canada 45-46; Prof. of English Univ. of British Columbia 46-62, Prof. of Creative Writing, Head of Dept. 63-65; Writer in Residence Univ. of Toronto 65-67, Univ. of Waterloo 67-68; Regents Prof. of Creative Writing Univ. of Calif. 68-; Royal Soc. of Canada Scholarship 34-36, Gov.-Gen.'s Medal for Poetry 42, 45, Leacock Medal for

Humour 49, Canadian Govt. Overseas Fellowship 53, L. Pierce Medal for Literature 54, Nuffield Fellowship 58, Canada Council Travelling Fellowships to Latin America 62, Australia, N.Z. 68, Africa, S. Asia 72, 74-75, U.K. 71, 73, Canada Council Medal 68.
Leisure interests: swimming, travelling.
Publs. poetry: *David* 42, *Now is Time* 45, *Strait of Anian* 48, *Twentieth Century Canadian Poetry* (anthology) 53, Editor *Selected Poetry of Malcolm Lowry* 62, *Ice, Cod, Bell or Stone* 62, *Near False Creek Mouth* 64, *Selected Poems* 66, *Pnomes, Jukollages and Other Stunzas* 67, *Memory No Servant* 68, *Poems of Earle Birney* 69, *Rag and Bone Shop* 71, *What's So Big About Green?* 73, *The Bear on the Delhi Road* 73, *Collected Poems* 74, *Damnation of Vancouver* 76; novels: *Turvey* 49 (revised edn. 76), *Down the Long Table* 55 (revised edn. 75); verse play: *Trial of a City* 52; criticism: *The Creative Writer* 66, *The Cow Jumped over the Moon* 72.
Apartment 2201, 200 Balliol Street, Toronto, Canada.
Telephone: (416) 489-8368.

Biró, József; Hungarian politician; b. 13 Feb. 1921; ed. Economic and Technical Academies, Univ. of Law. Former instrument maker, fitter and welder; fmr. Head of Wages Dept., Technical Dept., Imports Dept., Ministry of Foreign Trade; Managing Dir. foreign trade enterprise 55-57; Head Commercial Dept., Hungarian Legation, London 57-60; Sec., Party Cttee. of Ministry of Foreign Trade 60-62, Dep. Minister of Foreign Trade 62-63, Minister of Foreign Trade 63-; mem. State Planning Comm. 73-; mem. Central Cttee. Hungarian Socialist Workers' Party 66-.
Ministry of Foreign Trade, 1054 Honvéd-utca 13-15, Budapest, Hungary.
Telephone: 126-710.

Birrenbach, Kurt, D.IUR.; German business executive; b. 2 July 1907; ed. Paulinum Grammar School, Münster, and Univs. of Geneva, Paris, Munich, Berlin and Münster.
Adviser for financial affairs and foreign exchange transactions 35-39; importer and exporter of steel and steel products, S. America and Germany 39-54; Chair. Thyssen Vermögensverwaltung GmbH, Düsseldorf 55-; Vice-Chair. of Supervisory Board, August Thyssen-Hütte A.G., Duisburg-Hamborn 62-; Vice-Chair. Handelsunion A.G., Düsseldorf; Chair. Fritz Thyssen Stiftung, Cologne; mem. of the Bundestag; Vice-Pres. Atlantic Inst., Paris; official of other firms and int. orgs.; Christian Democrat.
Publ. *The Future of the Atlantic Community* 63.
Düsseldorf, Berliner Allee 33, Federal Republic of Germany.
Telephone: 81176.

Birtwistle, Harrison; British composer; b. 1934, Accrington, Lancs.; *m.* Sheila Birtwistle; three *s.*; ed. Royal Manchester Coll. of Music and Royal Acad. of Music, London.
Director of Music, Cranborne Chase School 62-65; Visiting Fellow Princeton Univ. (Harkness Int. Fellowship) 66; Cornell visiting Prof. of Music, Swarthmore Coll., Pa. 73-74; Slee Visiting Prof., New York State Univ., Buffalo, N.Y. 75; works have been widely performed at the major festivals in Europe including the Venice Biennale, the Int. Soc. of Contemporary Music Festivals in Vienna and Copenhagen, the Warsaw Autumn Festival and at Aldeburgh, Cheltenham and Edinburgh; formed, with Peter Maxwell Davies (*q.v.*), The Pierrot Players.
Works: operatic and dramatic: *The Mark of the Goat* (cantata) 65-66, *The Visions of Francesco Petrarca* (sonnets for baritone and orchestra) 66, *Punch and Judy* (one-act opera) 66-67; orchestral works: *Chorales for Orchestra* 62-63, *Three Movements with Fanfares* 64, *Nomos* 68, *The Triumph of Time* 70; for instrumental ensemble: *Refrains and Choruses* 57, *Monody for Corpus*

Christi 59, *The World is Discovered* 60, *Entr'actes and Sappho Fragments* 64, *Ring a Dumb Carillon* 65, *Tragoedia* 65, *Three Lessons in a Frame* 67, *Verses for Ensembles* 69, *Grimethorpe Aria* 73; choral works: *Narration: Description of the Passing of a Year* 64, *Carmen Paschale* 65; also several pieces of instrumental music.
22 Trafalgar Road, Twickenham, Middx.; c/o Alfred A. Kalmus Ltd., Universal Edition (London) Ltd., 2/3 Fareham Street, London, W1V 4DU, England.
Telephone: 01-437-5203/4/5 (Publisher).

Bisaglia, Antonio, D.JUR.; Italian politician; b. 31 March 1929, Rovigo.
Began career in journalism and insurance; Deputy Political Sec. Christian Democratic Party 70-73; Minister of Agriculture 74, of State Participation 75-.
Ministry of State Participation, via Sallustiana 53, 00187 Rome, Italy.

Bischoff, Bernhard, DR. PHIL.; German philologist; b. 20 Dec. 1906, Altendorf, Thuringia; *s.* of Emil Bischoff and Charlotte (née v. Gersdorff); *m.* Hanne Oehlerking 1935; two *s.* two *d.*; ed. Humanistisches Gymnasium Züllichau (Mark) and Univ. München.
Assistant to Prof. E. A. Lowe, Munich 33-39; Dozent, Munich Univ. 47, Full Prof. of Medieval Latin Philology 53-; mem. Bayerische Akad. der Wissenschaft, Royal Irish Acad., Medieval Acad. of America, British Acad., Royal Historical Soc., Österreichische Akad. der Wissenschaft, Koninklijke Vlaamse Acad., American Acad. of Arts and Sciences, Royal Danish Acad., Acad. des Inscriptions et Belles-Lettres; D.Litt. h.c. (Dublin and Oxford).
Leisure interest: music.
Publs. *Die Südostdeutschen Schreibschulen und Bibliotheken in der Karolingerzeit I* 40, *Libri Sancti Kyliani* 52, *Mittelalterliche Studien I/II* 66, 67, *Carmina Burana* (*facsimile edn.*) 68, *Carmina Burana* (*critical edn.*) *I, III* (with O. Schumann) 70, *Lorsch im Spiegel seiner Handschriften* 74.
8033 Planegg bei München, Ruffini-Allee 27, Federal Republic of Germany.
Telephone: (Munich) 8596631.

Bishara, Abdulla Yacoub; Kuwaiti diplomatist; *m.* Miriam Bishara; one *s.* one *d.*; ed. Cairo Univ. and Balliol Coll., Oxford.
Second Sec., Kuwait Embassy, Tunisia 63-64; Dir. Office of Ministry of Foreign Affairs, Kuwait 64-71; Perm. Rep. to UN Sept. 71-; Amb. (non-resident) to Brazil and Argentina 74-; del. to numerous int. confs.
Leisure interest: reading.
Permanent Mission of Kuwait to the United Nations, 235 East 42nd Street, 27th Floor, New York, N.Y. 10017, U.S.A.
Telephone: 212-687-8284.

Bishop, Elizabeth, B.A., LL.D.; American poet; b. 8 Feb. 1911; ed. Walnut Hill School, New England, and Vassar Coll., Poughkeepsie, New York.
Consultant in Poetry, Library of Congress, Washington D.C. 49-50; lecturer in English Harvard Univ. 70-; Houghton Mifflin Literary Fellowship, Guggenheim Fellowship, Shelley Memorial Award, Amy Lowell Fellowship, Partisan Review Fellowship, etc.; mem. American Inst. of Arts and Letters; Dr. h.c. (Smith Coll., Rutgers, Brown Univs.); Pulitzer Prize for Poetry 56; Nat. Book Award 69; Order of Rio Branco (Brazil) 70.
Publs. *North and South* (poems), *A Cold Spring* 55. *Poems* 55, *The Diary of Helena Morley* (trans. from Portuguese) 57, *Questions of Travel* 65, *Complete Poems* 69, *Anthology of 20th Century Brazilian Poetry* 72.
c/o Farrar, Straus & Giroux, New York, N.Y., U.S.A.

Bismarck, Klaus von; German radio executive; b. 6 March 1912; ed. High School, Doberan, agricultural education (training).

Army training 34-38; continued agricultural studies 38-39; Second World War service rising to Lieut.-Col. and commdr. of infantry regt. 39-45, prisoner-of-war 45; Dir. Juvenile Welfare Office, Herford 45-46, Jugendhof (Youth Leader Training Centre) Vlotho a.d. Weser 46-49; Dir.-Gen. Westdeutscher Rundfunk 61-74; mem. Board of Trustees Int. Broadcasting Inst.; Hon. D.Theol. (Münster Univ.); mem. Senate, Max Planck-Gesellschaft; Freiherr v. Stein Prize for social work. Publs. Papers on sociology and theology.
Marienburg, Eugen-Langen-Strasse 28, Federal Republic of Germany.

Bisplinghoff, Raymond Lewis; American aeronautical engineer; b. 7 Feb. 1917, Hamilton, Ohio; s. of Roscoe Earl Bisplinghoff and Isabelle Lewis Bisplinghoff; m. Ruth Doherty 1943; two s.; ed. Eidgenössische Technische Hochschule, Zürich, and Univ. of Cincinnati.
Engineer, Aeronca Aircraft Corpn. 37-40, Wright Field 40-41; Instructor, Univ. of Cincinnati 41-43; Engineer, Bureau of Aeronautics, Navy Dept., Washington 43-46; Asst. Prof. Massachusetts Inst. of Technology 46-48, Assoc. Prof. 48-53, Prof. 53; mem. Scientific Advisory Board, United States Air Force; mem. Cttee. of NASA (Nat. Aeronautics and Space Admin.), Dir. Office of Advanced Research and Technology, NASA until Nov. 63, Assoc. Administrator for Advanced Research and Technology Nov. 63-, Special Asst. to Administrator 65-; mem. Nat. Acad. of Engineering 65; Consultant to Admin., Fed. Aviation Agency 65-; Prof. and Head, Dept. of Aeronautics and Astronautics, Massachusetts Inst. of Technology 66-68; Dean, School of Engineering, M.I.T. 68-70; Chancellor, Univ. of Missouri at Rolla; Deputy Dir. Nat. Science Foundation 70-; Pres. American Inst. of Aeronautics and Astronautics 66; Chair. NASA Research and Technology Advisory Council; Chair. Aeronautics and Space Engineering Board; Vice-Chair. Sonic Boom Cttee., Nat. Acad. of Sciences; mem. Nat. Acad. of Sciences; Fellow American Acad. Art and Sciences, Royal Aeronautical Soc.; Dir. Allied Research Assocs., Allied Systems Ltd., General Aircraft Corpn., Engineering Council for Professional Devt.; Vice-Pres. Int. Astronautical Fed.; Fellow, American Astronautical Soc.; mem. Science Advisory Council, United Aircraft Corpn., Int. Acad. of Astronautics, Nat. Acad. of Sciences, Space Medicine Cttee.; U.S. mem. Int. Council of Aeronautical Sciences; mem. Defense Science Board; mem. of Council, Nat. Acad. of Engineering; Hon. Fellow, American Inst. of Aeronautics and Astronautics; various hon. degrees; NASA Distinguished Service Medal 67, Federal Aviation Agency Extraordinary Service Medal 68, NASA Apollo Achievement Award 69.
Leisure interests: sailing, flying (private pilot).
Publs. Three books and many papers in the field of aeronautics and astronautics.
Office of the Chancellor, University of Missouri, Rolla Mo. 65401, U.S.A.

Bissell, Claude T(homas), C.C., M.A., PH.D.; Canadian university administrator; b. 10 Feb. 1916, Meaford, Ont.; s. of George Thomas Bissell and Maggie Editha (Bowen) Bissell; m. Christina Flora Gray 1945; one d.; ed. Runnymede Collegiate Inst., Toronto, Cornell and Toronto Univs.
Reuben Wells Leonard Fellowship 36, Cornell Fellowship 37; Instructor in English, Cornell Univ. 38-41; Lecturer in English, Toronto Univ. 41-42; served in Canadian Army in Europe 42-45; on staff of Khaki Coll. England 45-46; Asst. Prof. of English, Dean in Residence, Univ. Coll. Toronto Univ. 47; Asst. to Pres. Toronto Univ. 48, Assoc. Prof. 51, Vice-Pres. of Univ. 52-56; Pres. Carleton Univ. Ottawa 56-58; Pres. Univ. of Toronto 58-71, Univ. Prof. 71-; Chair. Canada Council 60-62; Pres. Nat. Conf. Canadian Univs. and

Colls. 62-63; Chair. Canadian Univs. Foundation 62-63; Pres. World Univ. Service of Canada 62-63; Visiting Prof. of Canadian Studies on William Lyon Mackenzie King Endowment, Harvard Univ. 67-68; Chair. Carnegie Foundation for Advancement of Teaching; Hon. mem. American Acad. of Arts and Sciences 68; Hon. D.Litt. (Manitoba, Laval, Western Ont., Lethbridge, Leeds), Hon. LL.D. (McGill, Queen's, New Brunswick, Carleton, Montreal, St. Lawrence, British Columbia, Michigan, York, Windsor and Columbia Univs.); Companion of the Order of Canada 69.
Leisure interests: swimming, photography.
Publs. *Great Canadian Writing* 66, *The Strength of the University* 68, *Halfway Up Parnassus, A Personal Account of the University of Toronto, 1932-1971*, Editor and Contrib. to *University College: A Portrait 1853-1953, Canada's Crisis in Higher Education, Our Living Tradition*; many articles.
Simcoe Hall, University of Toronto, Toronto 5; Home: 229 Erskine Avenue, Toronto, Ont. M4P 1Z5, Canada. Telephone: 928-6446 (Office); 483-9616 (Home).

Bissinger, Frederick Lewis, M.E., M.S., J.D.; American chemical executive; b. 11 Jan. 1911, New York; s. of Jacob Frederick Bissinger and Rosel (Ensslin) Bissinger; m. Julia E. Stork 1935; one s. one d.; ed. Stevens Inst. of Technology and Fordham Univ.
Chemistry Instructor, Stevens Inst. of Technology 33-36; Lawyer, Pennie, Davis, Marvin & Edmonds 36-42; various exec. positions, including Pres., Industrial Rayon Corpn. 42-61; Group Vice-Pres. Midland-Ross Corpn. 61-62; Vice-Pres. and Dir. Stauffer Chem. Corpn. 62-65; Vice-Pres. Allied Chemical Corpn. 65-66, Dir. 66-, Exec. Vice-Pres. 66-69, Pres. 69-74, Vice-Chair. 74-76.
P.O. Box 3000-R, Columbia Road and Park Avenue, Morristown, N.J. 07960, U.S.A.
Telephone: 201-455-5125.

Bista, Kirti Nidhi, M.A.; Nepalese politician; b. 1927; ed. Tri-Chandra Coll., Katmandu and Lucknow Univ.
Assistant Minister for Education 61-62, Minister for Educ. 62-64, for Foreign Affairs 64; Vice-Chair. Council of Ministers and Minister for Foreign Affairs and Educ. 64-66; Vice-Chair. Council of Ministers and Minister for Foreign Affairs and Econ. Planning 66-67; Deputy Prime Minister and Minister for Foreign Affairs and Educ. Jan. 67-68; Perm. Rep. to UN 68-69; Prime Minister, Minister of Finance, Gen. Admin. and Palace Affairs 69-73; mem. Royal Advisory Cttee. 69-70; Leader Nepalese Dels. to UN Gen. Assemblies 64, 65, 66, and to UNESCO Gen. Confs. 62, 64, 66, and to various other confs.; accompanied H.M. the King on many State Visits; Order of the Right Hand of Gurkhas (First Class), Fed. German Order of Merit, French Legion of Honour.
Kshetra Pati, Kathmandu, Nepal.

Biszku, Béla; Hungarian politician; b. 13 Sept. 1921. Communist Party official 44; Staff mem., later Head of Dept. of Cadres, Budapest Party Cttee. 46-51; Sec. Budapest Party Cttee. 51-53; Minister of Home Affairs 57-61; Deputy Prime Minister 61-62; mem. Political Cttee., Hungarian Socialist Workers' Party 57-, Sec. Central Cttee. 62-.
Publs. *Topical Points of the proletarian dictatorship in Hungary* 57, *The 21st Congress of the Soviet Communist Party and its effects on the international workers movement* 59, *What are the Party's tasks in carrying the resolutions of the 8th Congress into effect?* 63, *The Party and the State in the Service of the People* 72.
Hungarian Socialist Workers' Party, Széchenyi Rakpart, 19, Budapest, Hungary.

Bitar, Salah ad-Din al-; Syrian politician; b. 1912; ed. Damascus and Univ. of Paris.
Secondary school teacher in Damascus 34-42; entered politics 42; co-founder, with Michel Aflaq, of Arab

Resurrection Party and Editor of party organ; left Syria after Shishekly coup 52; later returned and took part in merging of Renaissance and Socialist parties to form Baath Party; elected to Parliament after overthrow of Shishekly 54; Minister of Foreign Affairs 56; head of Syrian Del. to UN Gen. Assembly 57; Minister of Culture and Nat. Guidance, U.A.R. 58-59; Prime Minister of Syrian Arab Republic March-11 May 63, 13 May-Nov. 63, May-Oct. 64, Jan.-Feb. 66; concurrently Minister of Foreign Affairs May-Nov. 63; Vice-Pres. Council of Revolutionary Command Nov. 63-May 64; expelled from Baath Party Oct. 66.
c/o Pacific Hotel, Beirut, Lebanon.

Bitsios, Dimitri S.; Greek diplomatist and politician; b. 1915; *m.*; one *s.* one *d.*; ed. Univ. of Athens.
Entered Diplomatic Service 39, served Cairo, London and New York; Head, Economic Section, Ministry of Foreign Affairs; Head, 4th Political Dept., Ministry of Foreign Affairs; Del. to UN 56-61, Perm. Rep. 61-65, 67-72; Head, 1st Political Dept., Ministry of Foreign Affairs 65; Private Sec. to King of the Hellenes 66; resigned from Diplomatic Service 72; Under-Sec. of State July-Oct. 74; Minister of Foreign Affairs Oct. 74-; Order of George I and of the Phoenix; Distinguished Service Medal.
Leisure interests: collecting stamps and medals.
Publs. *Egypt and the Middle East, Greek Diplomatic History, Cyprus in Critical Hours* 74.
10 Herodoton Street, Athens, Greece.
Telephone: 712-487.

Bittner, Horst; German diplomatist.
Leader of German Trade Mission, Moscow 57-65, Amb. to U.S.S.R. 65; Vaterländischer Orden in Bronze 65.
c/o Ministry of Foreign Affairs, Berlin, German Democratic Republic.

Biya, Paul, L. EN D.; Cameroon politician; b. 13 Feb. 1933, Mvomeko; *m.* Jeanne (née Atacham); ed. Ndem Mission School, Edea and Akono Seminaries, Lycée Le Clerk, Yaoundé, Univ. of Paris.
Head of Dept. of Foreign Devt. Aid 62-63; Dir. of Cabinet in Ministry of Nat. Educ. 64-65; on goodwill mission to Ghana and Nigeria 65; Sec.-Gen. in Ministry of Educ., Youth and Culture 65-67; Dir. of Civil Cabinet of Head of State 67-68; Sec.-Gen. to Pres. Jan.-Aug. 68; Minister of State, Sec.-Gen. to Pres. 68-75; Prime Minister June 75-; Chevalier de l'Ordre de la Valeur Camerounaise, Commdr. of Nat. Order of Fed. Repub. of Germany and of Tunisia; mem. Union Nationale Camerounaise (UNC).
Office of the Prime Minister, Yaoundé, Cameroon.

Bizot, Henry; French banker; b. 27 Aug. 1901; ed. Inst. Sainte-Croix, Neuilly-sur-Seine.
Inspector of Finances 25; Asst. Sec.-Gen. Comptoir national d'escompte de Paris 30-59, Dir.-Gen. 59-62, Admin. Dir.-Gen. 62-63, Vice-Pres. Dir.-Gen. 63-64, Pres. 64-; Pres. Banque nationale de Paris 66-71; Chair. Unival; Dir. numerous companies including Banque industrielle de l'Afrique du Nord, Didot-Botton, Idéal-Standard; Commdr. Légion d' Honneur.
76 avenue Raymond-Poincaré, Paris 16e, France.

Bjarnason, Ásgeir; Icelandic farmer and politician; b. 6 Sept. 1914, Ásgarður; *s.* of Bjarni Jensson and Salbörg Ásgeirsdóttir; *m.* 1st Emma Benediktsdóttir 1945 (deceased), 2nd Ingibjörg Sigurðardóttir 1954; two *s.*
Farmer Ásgardur, Dalasýsla 43-; Parish Sec. 56-; mem. Althing 56-; Speaker, Upper House 71-73, United Althing 74-; mem. Board, Icelandic Agricultural Soc. 67-, Chair. 72-; mem. Nat. Research Council 65-, State Social Security Council 68-, Icelandic Del. to Nordic Council 64-66, 74-; Grand Cross, Order of the Knight.

Althing, Reykjavík; Home: Ásgarður, Dalasýsla, Sólheimar 42, Reykjavík, Iceland.
Telephone 11560 (Althing); 37997 (Home).

Bjarnason, Matthias; Icelandic businessman and politician; b. 15 Aug. 1921, Isafjordur; *s.* of Bjarni Bjarnason and Audur Johannesdóttir; *m.* Kristin Ingimundardóttir 1944; one *d.* one *s.*; ed. Commercial Coll. of Iceland.
Manager of ferry co., Isafjordur 42-68, Isafjordur Fishing Vessels' Mutual Insurance Soc. 60-74; Man. Kögur Fishing Co. 59-66; mem. Board Isfirdingur Fishing Co. 47-59, Chair. 50-59; mem. Isafjordur Town Council 46-70, Chair. 50-52; Chair. Board Isafjordur Electric Power Works 46-51; mem. Board Union of Icelandic Fishing Vessel Owners 62-74, also other owners' socs.; mem. Cttee. State Shipping Authority 66-; Chair. Icelandic Fishing Vessels Joint Insurance Inst. 67-74; mem. Board Icelandic Fish Industries Fund 69-74, Employment Equalization Fund 70-71, Econ. Devt. Inst. 72-; Chair. Exec. Cttee. Fish Industry Board 68-74; mem. Independence Party, on Cen. Cttee. 70-; Editor *Vesturland* 53-59; Supplementary mem. Althing 63-67, mem. for West Fjords 67-; Minister of Fisheries, Health and Social Security Aug. 74-.
Leisure interests: reading, travelling.
Hafnarstraeti 14, Isafjordur, Iceland.
Telephone: 25000.

Bjelke-Petersen, Hon. Johannes; Australian politician; b. 13 Jan. 1911, Dannevirke, New Zealand; *s.* of Carl G. and Maren (née Poulsen) Bjelke-Petersen; *m.* Florence Gilmour 1952; one *s.* three *d.*; ed. Taabinga Village Primary School, correspondence courses and private studies.
Farmer; mem. Queensland Parl. 47-; Minister for Works and Housing 63-68, later of Aboriginal and Island Affairs, and Police; Leader of Country (now National) Party of Queensland 68-; Premier of Queensland 68-.
Leisure interests: flying, reading, bush-walking.
Office of the Premier, Executive Building, Brisbane, Queensland 4000, Australia.

Bjerknes, Jakob Aall Bonnevie; Norwegian meteorologist; b. 2 Nov. 1897, Stockholm; *s.* of Prof. Vilhelm K.F. Bjerknes; *m.* Hedvig Borthen 1928; one *s.* one *d.*; ed. Oslo and Leipzig Univs.
Meteorologist, Bergen Observatory 18; Dir. Weather Service for Western Norway 20; Prof. Geophysical Inst. Bergen 31-40; Prof. Univ. of Calif., Los Angeles 40; hon. mem. Royal Meteorological Soc., London, awarded its Symons Gold Medal 40; Bowie Medal, American Geophysical Union 42, Royal Order of St. Olav 46, Vega Medal of Swedish Asscn. of Geography 58; elected to Nat. Acad. Washington, D.C. 47; mem. Royal Swedish Acad. of Sciences; foreign mem. Royal Norwegian Acad. of Sciences, Hon. Fellow Indian Acad. of Sciences; Hon. mem. American Meteorological Soc. 58; Pres. Meteorological Asscn. of the Int. Union of Geodesy and Geophysics 48-51, Vice-Pres. I.U.G.G. 51-54; Int. Meteorological Org. Prize 59; Rossby Award from American Meteorological Soc. 60; Nat. Medal of Science from Pres. of U.S. 66; mem. American Acad. of Arts and Sciences 60, American Acad. of Achievement 67; Hon. LL.D. Univ. of California (U.S.A.).
Leisure interest: travel.
Department of Meteorology, University of California, Los Angeles, Calif. 90024; 201 Ocean Avenue, Apartment 609 P, Santa Monica, Calif. 90402, U.S.A.
Telephone: 213-825-1852.

Bjerve, Petter Jakob, CAND. ECON. D.PHIL.; Norwegian economist and politician; b. 27 Sept. 1913, Stjördal; *s.* of Petter Jakob Bjerve and Kristine

Arnstad; *m.* Rannveig Bremer 1942; three *s.*; ed. Univ. of Oslo.
Research Asst. Economics Inst., Oslo Univ. 39-40; **Research Fellow,** Oslo Univ. 45-49; Chief of Div. Ministry of Finance 45-49; Dir.-Gen. Central Bureau of Statistics of Norway 49-60, 63-; Minister of Finance 60-63; mem. advisory missions to Zambia 64, Sri Lanka 71; Adviser to the Govt. of Pakistan 68-69, Bangladesh 73; mem. Labour Party.
Publs. *Hva krigen kostet Norge* (What the War Cost Norway) 45, *Government Economic Planning and Control* 50, *Planning in Norway 1974-56* 59, *Trends in Norwegian Planning 1945-1975* 76.
Central Bureau of Statistics, Oslo; Breidablikkvn 10b, Oslo 11, Norway.
Telephone: 283759.

Björk, Anita; Swedish actress; b. 25 April 1923, Tällberg Dalecarlia; *m.* Stig Dagerman (deceased); one *s.* two *d.*; ed. Royal Dramatic Theatre School, Stockholm.
Numerous stage appearances at Royal Dramatic Theatre, Stockholm, including *Miss Julie* 48, Agnes (*Brand*, Ibsen), Celia (*The Cocktail Party*, Eliot), Rosalind (*As You Like It*, Shakespeare), Juliet (*Romeo and Juliet*, Shakespeare), Eliza (*Pygmalion*, Shaw), Solange (*Les Bonnes*, Genet), The girl (*Look Back in Anger*, Osborne), Johanna (*Les séquestrés d'Altona*, Sartre).
Films acted in include: *Himlaspelet* 42, *Räkna de lyckliga stunderna blott* (Count Your Blessings) 44, *Hundra dragspel och en flicka* (One Hundred Concertinas and a Girl) 46, *Ingen väg tillbaka* (No Return) 47, *Kvinna utan ansikte* 47, *Det kom en gäst* (There Came a Guest) 47, *På dessa skuldror* (On these Shoulders) 48, *Människors rike* (The Realm of Men and Women) 49, *Kvartetten som sprängdes* (The Quartet that was Broken) 50, *Fröken Julie* 50-51, *Han glömde henne aldrig* 52, *Night People* 53, *Die Hexe* 54, *Giftas* 55, *Der Cornet* 55, *Moln över Hellesta* (Dark Clouds over Hellesta) 56, *Sången om den eldröda blommen* 56, *Gäst i eget hus* (Guest in One's Own House) 57, *Mannekäng i rött* 58, *Tärningen är kastad* 60, *Goda vänner trogna grannar* 60, *Vita frun* 62, *Älskande par* 64.
Jägarestigen 7, Saltsjo-Duvnäs, Stockholm, Sweden.

Björnsson, Henrik Sv., LL.B.; Icelandic diplomatist; b. 2 Sept. 1914, Reykjavík; *s.* of Sveinn Björnsson and Georgia Björnsson (née Hoff-Hansen); *m.* Groa Torfhildur Jonsdóttir 1941; one *s.* two *d.*; ed. Univ. of Iceland.
Graduated in law and joined Foreign Service 39, served Copenhagen, Reykjavík, Washington 39-44; Head of Dept. Ministry of Foreign Affairs, Reykjavík 44-47; Sec. Oslo 47-49; Counsellor, Paris 50-52; Sec. to Pres. of Iceland 52-56; Sec.-Gen. Ministry of Foreign Affairs 56-61; Amb. to Great Britain and Netherlands and Minister to Spain and Portugal 61-65; Amb. to Belgium and Perm. Rep. to NATO 65-67, Council of Europe 68-70; Amb. to France 65-, and concurrently to Luxembourg, Yugoslavia, Egypt and Ethiopia, and Perm. Rep. to OECD and UNESCO; Kt. Commdr. Order of Icelandic Falcon, Grand Cross, Orders of Lion (Finland), Mérito Civil (Spain), Couronne (Belgium), Hon. K.B.E. and other foreign decorations.
Ambassade d'Islande, 124 boulevard Haussmann, Paris 8e, France.
Telephone: 522-8154.

Björnstrand, Knut Gunnar; Swedish actor; b. 13 Nov. 1909, Stockholm; *s.* of Oscar Johansson and Ellen Maueleon; *m.* Lillie Lundahl 1935; three *d.*; ed. Royal Dramatic School, Stockholm.
First stage appearance at Swedish theatre, Vasa, Finland 36; worked at several theatres in Stockholm; began film career in *A Night in the Harbour* 41; Guest artist, Royal Dramatic Theatre 48; first worked with

Ingmar Bergman (*q.v.*) 51, playing leading parts in many of his films; appeared at Vasa Theatre, Stockholm in *Plaza Suite* 69; Swedish Film Soc. Gösta Ekman Prize 63; *Chaplin Magazine* "Oscar" for *The Seventh Seal* and others.
Leisure interests: fishing, sailing, art-collecting, music, literature.
Films include: *A Lesson in Love* 54, *Smile of a Summer Night* 55, *The Seventh Seal* 56, *Through a Glass Darkly* 61, *Winter Light* 62, *Shame* 68, *The Girls*, *The Rite* (TV), *Isola*, *Persona*, *Wild Strawberries*.
Odengatan 44, 11351 Stockholm, Sweden.
Telephone: 08-371840.

Bjørnvig, Thorkild Strange, DR. PHIL.; Danish poet and writer; b. 2 Feb. 1918; *s.* of Adda and Theodor Bjørnvig; *m.* 1st Grete Damgaard Pedersen 1946, 2nd Birgit Hornum 1970; two *d.*; ed. Cathedral School, Aarhus, and Univ. of Aarhus.
Member Danish Acad. 60; several prizes.
Publs. poetry: *Stjaernen bag gavlen* 47, *Anubis* 55, *Figur og Ild* 59, *Vibrationer* 66, *Ravnen* 68, *Udvalgte digte* 70; essays: *Rilke og tysk Tradition* 59, *Begyndelsen* 60, *Kains Alter* 64, *Oprør mod neonguden* 70, *Virkeligheden er til* 73, *Pagten, mit venskab med Karen Blixen* 74, *Delfinen* 75, *Stoffets Krystalhav* 75, *Det religiøse menneskes ansigter* 75.
Issehoved, 8795 Nordby, Denmark.
Telephone: 06596259.

Black, Baron (Life Peer), cr. 68, of Barrow-in-Furness; **William Rushton Black,** Kt.; British business executive; b. 12 Jan. 1893, Barrow-in-Furness; *m.* Patricia Margaret Dallas 1917; one *s.* (deceased) one *d.*; ed. Barrow Secondary School, Barrow Technical Coll.
With Vickers Ltd. 08-28; Man. Weymanns Motor Bodies 28; Gen. Man. Park Royal Vehicles Ltd. 34-39, Man. Dir. 39; Dir. Associated Commercial Vehicles Ltd. 49, Man. Dir. 57, now Chair.; Chair. A.E.C. Ltd. 58, Leyland Motor Corpn. 63-67, Park Royal Vehicles Ltd.
Leisure interests: golf, gardening.
Birchwood Grange, Ruxley Crescent, Claygate, Surrey, England.

Black, Sir Douglas Andrew Kilgour, M.D., F.R.C.P.; British physician; b. 29 May 1913, Delting, Shetland; *s.* of Rev. Walter Kilgour Black and Mary Jane Crichton; *m.* Mollie Thorn 1948; one *s.* two d.; ed. St. Andrews Univ.
Lecturer, Reader and Prof., Dept. of Medicine, Manchester Univ. 46-, Sir Arthur Sims Commonwealth Travelling Prof. 71; on secondment as Chief Scientist, Dept. of Health and Social Security 72-; Lectureships (Royal Coll. of Physicians, London): Goulstonian 53, Bradshaw 65, Lumleian 70.
Leisure interests: reading and writing.
Publs. *The Logic of Medicine* 68, *Essentials of Fluid Balance* (4th edn.) 67; Editor *Renal Disease* 72.
17 Woodsyre, Sydenham Hill, London, SE26 6SS, England.
Telephone: (01) 670-2965.

Black, Eugene R., B.A.; American banker; b. 1 May 1898; ed. Univ. of Georgia.
Served First World War; later associated with Harris, Forbes & Co. N.Y. investment bankers; Man. Atlanta Office Chase-Harris, Forbes Corpn. 31, Asst. Vice-Pres. 33; Second Vice-Pres. Chase Nat. Bank N.Y. 33, Vice-Pres. 37-47, Dir. and consultant The Chase Manhattan Bank 63-June 70; Exec. Dir. for U.S. Int. Bank for Reconstruction and Development 47-49; Senior Vice-Pres. Chase Nat. Bank N.Y. March-June 49; Pres. and Chair. Int. Bank for Reconstruction and Development July 49-63, Int. Finance Corpn. Oct. 61-63; Special Financial Consultant to Sec.-Gen. of UN 63-; Consultant American Express Co. June 70-; Dir. numerous companies 63-; many nat. and int. awards.

Publs. *The Diplomacy of Economic Development, Alternative in Southeast Asia* 69.
Office: 65 Broadway, New York 1006, N.Y.; Home: 178 Columbia Heights, Brooklyn 11421, N.Y., U.S.A.

Black, Sir Misha, Kt., O.B.E., R.D.I., F.S.I.A.; British architect and industrial designer; b. 16 Oct. 1910, Baku, Russia; *m.* 1st Helen Lillian Evans 1935 (dissolved), 2nd Edna Joan Fairbrother 1955; two *s.* one *d.*
Partner in Industrial Design Partnership 32-39; Principal Exhibition Architect to Ministry of Information 40-45; Exhibition Consultant to UNESCO 47 and 54; Co-ordinating Architect, Festival of Britain 1951; Consultant to Ceylon Govt., Colombo Exhibition 52 and 56; Industrial Design Consultant to B.O.A.C. 51-56; Senior Partner, Design Research Unit 46-; mem. MARS Group 38-57; mem. Council of Soc. of Industrial Artists 38-58, Pres. 54-56; Advisory Council, Inst. of Contemporary Art 51-67; mem. Council of Industrial Design 55-64; Design Consultant to British Transport Comm. 56-66; Royal Designer to Industry 58; Joint Interior Architect to Orient Line 57-60; Prof. of Industrial Design Royal Coll. of Art 59-75, Prof. Emer. 75-; Architect to Zoological Soc. of London for Small Mammal House 62-67; Architect and Industrial Designer to Hong Kong Rapid Transit Railway 69-; Pres. Int. Council of Socs. of Industrial Design 59-62; Design Consultant to London Transport Exec. 64-, to Vickers Ltd. 68-71; Vice-Pres. Modular Soc. 66-; Gold Medal, Soc. of Industrial Artists 65; mem. Advisory Council, Science Museum 66-; Trustee, British Museum 68-; Hon. Vice-Pres. Nat. Union of Students 65-; Companion, Inst. of Mechanical Engineers 69.
Designs for Spanish-American Exhibition, Seville 28, Int. Exhibition Paris 37, Empire Exhibition Glasgow 38, N.Y. World's Fair 39, Brussels International Exhbn. 58, Montreal Int. Exhbn. 67; and for public and private companies.
Publs. Article in *The Practice of Design* 45, *Exhibition of Design* (Editor) 50, *Public Interiors* 70.
32 Aybrook Street, London, W1M 4BB, England.
Telephone: 01-486-1681.

Black, Shirley Temple; American actress and diplomat; b. 23 April 1928, Santa Monica, Calif.; *d.* of George F. and Gertrude Temple; *m.* 1st John Agar, Jr. 1945 (dissolved 1949), one *d.*; *m.* 2nd Charles A. Black 1950, two *c.*; ed. privately and Westlake School for Girls.
Career as film actress commenced at $3\frac{1}{2}$ years; first full-length film was *Stand Up and Cheer*; narrator/actress in TV series *Shirley Temple Storybook* 57-; hostess/actress *Shirley Temple Show* 60; Del. to UN, New York 69-; Amb. to Ghana 74-; Dir. Nat. Multiple Sclerosis Soc.; Dame, Order of Knights of Malta (Paris) 68; numerous state decorations.
Films include: *Little Miss Marker, Baby Take a Bow, Bright Eyes, Our Little Girl, The Little Colonel, Curly Top, The Littlest Rebel, Captain January, Poor Little Rich Girl, Dimples, Stowaway, Wee Willie Winkie, Heidi, Rebecca of Sunnybrook Farm, Little Miss Broadway, Just Around the Corner, The Little Princess, Susannah of the Mounties, The Blue Bird, Kathleen, Miss Annie Rooney, Since You Went Away, Kiss and Tell, That Hagen Girl, War Party, The Bachelor and the Bobby-Soxer* and *Honeymoon.*
American Embassy, Accra, Ghana; and Woodside, California, U.S.A.

Blackie, William; American business executive; b. 1 May 1906, Glasgow, Scotland; *s.* of William and Catherine Hyne Blackie; *m.* Florence M. Hewens 1934; one *s.*; ed. Scotland.
Apprenticed to chartered accountant, Glasgow, Scotland 24-29; Price, Waterhouse & Co., Chicago 30-39; Controller, Caterpillar Tractor Co., Peoria, Illinois 39-44, Vice-Pres. 44-54, Exec. Vice-Pres. 54-62, Dir. 58-, Pres. 62-66, Chair. and Chief Exec. Officer 66-72; Dir.

Ampex Corpn., Shell Oil Co.; Senior partner and dir. Lehman Bros.; Chair. Marconaflo Inc. 74-.
2305 Skyfarm Drive, Hillsborough, Calif. 94010, U.S.A.

Blackman, Geoffrey Emett, M.A., F.R.S.; British agricultural scientist; b. 17 April 1903, London; *s.* of Prof. V. H. Blackman and Edith Delta Emett; *m.* Audrey Babette 1931; ed. King's Coll. School and St. John's Coll., Cambridge.
Head of Botany Section, Jealott's Hill Agricultural Research Station, Warfield, Berks. 27-35; Lecturer in Ecology, Imperial Coll. of Science and Technology 35-45; Sibthorpian Prof. of Rural Econ. and Head of Dept. of Agricultural Science, Oxford Univ. 45-70, now Prof. Emer.; Hon. Dir. Agricultural Research Council Unit of experimental agronomy concerned with introduction of new crops, principles of selective toxicity and devt. of selective herbicides 41-70; Sec. of Biology War Cttee. 42-46; Del. of Clarendon Press 50-70; Chair. Advisory Cttee. enquiring into Production Devt. and Consumption Research in Natural Rubber Industry 56; mem. Biological Sciences Sub-Cttee. of Univ. Grants Cttee. 68-70; Fellow of Royal Soc. 59, Vice-Pres. 66-68; U.S. Nat. Acad. of Sciences Cttee. on the effects of herbicides in Vietnam.
Leisure interests: skiing, gardening with the Ericaceae, collecting water-colours.
Publs. Papers in scientific journals on agricultural ecological, physiological and statistical investigations.
Woodcroft, Foxcombe Lane, Boars Hill, Oxford, England.

Blackmun, Harry A.; American judge; b. 12 Nov. 1908, Nashville, Ill.; *s.* of Corwin Manning and Theo Huegely (Reuter) Blackmun; *m.* Dorothy E. Clark 1941; three *d.*; ed. Harvard Univ. and Harvard Law School.
Admitted to Minnesota Bar 32; private legal practice until 50; Instructor, William Mitchell Coll. of Law 35-41, Univ. of Minnesota Law School 45-47; Judge, U.S. Court of Appeals Eighth Circuit 59-70; Assoc. Justice U.S. Supreme Court 70-; mem. American Bar Asscn., Minnesota State, Third Judicial District (Minn.) and Olmsted County (Minn.) Bar Asscns., American Judicature Soc.; Hon. LL.D. (DePauw, Drake, Hamline and Ohio Wesleyan Univs., Morningside Coll., Wilson Coll., Dickinson School of Law, Ohio Northern Univ.).
United States Supreme Court, Washington, D.C. 20543, U.S.A.

Blackwell, Sir Basil Henry, Kt., M.A., J.P.; British bookseller and publisher; b. 29 May 1889, Oxford; *s.* of Benjamin Henry Blackwell and Lydia (née Taylor); *m.* Marion Christine Soans 1914; two *s.* three *d.*; ed. Magdalen Coll. School and Merton Coll., Oxford.
Chairman, Basil Blackwell and Mott Ltd. 22-69, B. H. Blackwell Ltd. 24-69, Pres. 69-, and Blackwell Scientific Publications Ltd. 39-72; Pres. Antiquarian Booksellers Asscn. 25 and 26, Pres. Associated Booksellers of Great Britain and Ireland 34 and 35, Pres. The Classical Asscn. 65, The English Asscn. 70; Officier d'Académie; Hon. Fellow, Merton Coll., Oxford; Hon. LL.D. (Manchester Univ.) 65; Hon. Freeman of Oxford City 70; Hon. mem. Stationers' Co. 72.
Leisure interest: reading.
Osse Field, Appleton, Abingdon, Oxon., England.

Blackwood, Sir Robert (Rutherford), Kt., M.C.E., B.E.E., F.I.E.A.; Australian business executive; b. 3 June 1906, Melbourne; *s.* of late Robert Leslie Blackwood and Muriel Pearl Blackwood (née Henry); *m.* Hazel Lavinia McLeod 1932; one *s.* one *d.*; ed. Melbourne Church of England Grammar School, Melbourne Univ.
Testing Officer, Engineering School, Univ. of Melbourne 28-30, Lecturer Agricultural Engineering 31-33, Prof. of Mechanical Engineering 47; Research Engineer

Dunlop Australia Ltd. 33-36, Technical Man. 37-46, Gen. Man. 48-66, Chair. Board of Dirs. 72-; Chair. Interim Council, Monash Univ. 59-61, First Chancellor 61-68; Dir. Humes Ltd. 66-; Chair. Board of Dirs., Steel Mains Pty. Ltd. 70-; Pres. Nat. Museum of Victoria Council 70-, Royal Soc. of Victoria 73-75; Trustee, Asian Inst. of Technology, Bangkok 67-; Hon. LL.D. (Monash Univ.); Peter Nicol Russell Memorial Medal 66.
Leisure interests: archaeology, painting.
Publs. *Monash University: The First Ten Years* 68, *Beautiful Bali* 70, and scientific papers.
8 Huntingfield Road, Middle Brighton, Victoria 3186, Australia.
Telephone: 92-5925.

Blair, William McCormick, Jr., A.B., LL.B.; American lawyer and diplomatist; b. 24 Oct. 1916; ed. Stanford Univ. and Univ. of Virginia.
United States Air Force (Capt.) 42-46; admitted to Illinois Bar 48; with Wilson & McIlvaine, Chicago 47-50; Admin. Asst. to Adlai E. Stevenson 50-56; Partner Stevenson, Rifkind and Wirtz, Chicago 57-61, Paul, Weiss, Rifkind, Wharton and Garrison, N.Y. 57-61; Amb. to Denmark 61-64, to Philippines 64-68; Gen. Dir. John F. Kennedy Center 68-72; law practice; Bronze Star; Officer of Order of the Crown (Belgium); Order of Sikatuna (Philippines).
2510 Foxhall Road, Washington, D.C. 20007, U.S.A.

Blais, Marie-Claire, C.C.; Canadian writer; b. 5 Oct. 1939, Quebec City; ed. Quebec, Paris and United States. Guggenheim Foundation Fellowship, New York 63; Prix de la langue française 61, Prix France-Quebec 64, Prix Médicis 66.
Leisure interests: painting, handwriting analysis.
Publs. *La Belle Bête* 59, *Tête blanche* 60, *Le jour est noir* 62, *Une saison dans la vie d'Emmanuel* 65, *L'Insoumise* 66, *Les voyageurs sacrés* 69, *Manuscrits de Pauline Archange* 70 (novels); *Pays Voiles, Existences* (poems) 64.
c/o Les Editions du Jour, 1651 St. Denis, Montreal, P.Q., Canada.

Blaizot, Jean P. M. L. F., D. ès SC.; French university official; b. 14 Jan. 1915, Mauvezin; s. of Prof. Louis Blaizot and Madeleine Palanque; m. Simone Guénot 1946; three s. one d.; ed. Lycée de Versailles, Sorbonne, Paris.
Teacher, Evreux 40-44, Paris 44-45; worked for Nat. Centre of Scientific Research 45-48, Tutor, then Prof. Toulouse Univ. 48-60, Dean 65-69; Prof. Bordeaux Univ. 69-; Rector, Poitiers Univ. 61-64; fmr. Dir. Inst. of Physiology, Toulouse; mem. Asscn. of French Speaking Physiologists, Soc. of Biological Chem.; Commdr. Palmes Académiques 61; Chevalier Légion d'Honneur 62.
Publs. *Les Relations physiologiques entre la glande thyroide et la vitamine B1, Journal de Physiologie, Annales de la Nutrition.*
Office: Institut de Biologie Animale, Avenue des Facultés, 33405 Talence, France.
Telephone: (56) 80-68-00.

Blajovici, Petre; Romanian politician; b. 26 Aug. 1922, Inand, Bihor County; s. of Petru and Maria Blajovici; two d.; ed. Acad. of Social and Political Studies, Bucharest.
Member of Communist Party 47; First Sec. Cîmpeni District Party Cttee. 50-52; Sec. of Cluj Region Party Cttee. 52-54; alt. mem. Central Cttee. of the R.C.P. 60-65, mem. 65-; First Sec. Banat Region Cttee. of C.P. 60-64; Vice-Chair. Council of Ministers 64-67; Minister of Labour 67-69; Chair. of the State Cttee. for Local Economy and Admin. 69-73; Vice-Chair. Nat. Council for Physical Educ. and Sport 73-; First Sec. Bihar County Cttee. of R.C.P. 73-; alt. mem. of Exec. Cttee., Cen. Cttee. of R.C.P. 65-; Deputy to Grand Nat.

Assembly 61-; Star of the Repub., Order of 23rd August; Order of Labour 62.
Leisure interests: hunting, literature, reading.
Central Committee of the Romanian Communist Party, Bucharest, Romania.

Blake, Rev. Eugene Carson, A.B., TH.B.; American church official; b. 7 Nov. 1906, St. Louis, Mo.; m. Valina Gillespie 1929; ed. Princeton Univ., Edinburgh Univ., and Princeton Theological Seminary.
Teacher, Forman Christian Coll., Lahore, India 28-29; Asst. Pastor, Collegiate Church of St. Nicholas, New York 32-35; Pastor, First Presbyterian Church, Albany, N.Y. 35-40, Pasadena (Calif.) Presbyterian Church 40-51; Stated Clerk, The United Presbyterian Church in the U.S.A. 51-66 (The Presbyterian Church in the U.S.A. until 58); Gen. Sec. World Council of Churches 66-72; Pres. Nat. Council of Churches (U.S.A.) 54-57; Trustee, Princeton Univ. 57-61; Chair. Div. of Inter-Church Aid, Refugee and World Service, World Council of Churches 62-66; Chair. American Advisory Cttee. Programme to combat racism; World Council of Churches 73; Chair. American Friends Ethiopian Orthodox Church 73, Bread for the World, U.S.A. 74; 21 hon. degrees.
Leisure interests: golf, bridge.
Publ. *He is Lord of All, The Church in the Next Decade.*
204 Davenport Drive, Stamford, Conn. 06902, U.S.A.

Blakemore, Colin Brian, M.A., PH.D.; British neurophysiologist and lecturer in physiology; b. 1 June 1944, Stratford-on-Avon; s. of Cedric Norman and Beryl Ann Blakemore; m. Andrée Elizabeth Washbourne 1965; one d.; ed. King Henry VIII School, Coventry, Corpus Christi Coll., Cambridge, Univ. of Calif., Berkeley.
Harkness Fellowship, Univ. of Calif. 65-67; Univ. Demonstrator, Physiological Laboratory, Cambridge 68-72; Lecturer in Physiology, Cambridge 72-; Fellow and Dir. of Medical Studies, Downing Coll. 71-; Dir. of Medical Research Council Programme Grant 72-; Visiting Prof. New York Univ. 70, M.I.T. 71; mem. Editorial Board *Perception* 71-; mem. Nat. Cttee. Brain Research Asscn. 73-, Cen. Council of Int. Brain Research Org. 73-, Cttee. European Brain and Behaviour Soc. 74-, Council, Cambridge Philosophical Soc. 75-, BBC Science Consultative Group 75-, Physiological Soc., Experimental Psychology Soc. and others; Leverhulme Fellowship 74-75; BBC Reith Lecturer 76; Robert Bing Prize, Swiss Acad. of Medical Sciences 75.
Publs. Editor *Handbook of Psychobiology* 75; contributions to *Constraints on Learning* 73, *Illusion in Art and Nature* 73, *The Neurosciences Third Program* 74, and to professional journals.
The Physiological Laboratory, Cambridge, CB2 3EG; Downing College, Cambridge, CB2 1DQ, England.
Telephone: 0223-64131 (Laboratory); 0223-59491 (Downing Coll.).

Blakeney, Allan Emrys, M.L.A., L.L.B., M.A.; Canadian politician; b. 7 Sept. 1925, Bridgewater, Nova Scotia; s. of John Cline Blakeney and Bertha May Davies; m. 1st. Mary Elizabeth Schwartz 1950 (died 1957), one s. one d.; 2nd Anne Gorham, one s. one d.; ed. Dalhousie and Oxford Univs.
Secretary and legal adviser to Crown Corpn., Govt. of Saskatchewan 50-55; Chair. Sask. Securities Comm. 55-58; partner law firm of Davidson, Davidson & Blakeney 58-60; Govt. of Sask. Minister of Educ. 60-61; Provincial Treas. 61-62; Minister of Health 62-64; partner law firm of Griffin, Blakeney, Beke 64-70; Govt. of Sask. Leader of the Opposition 70-71; Premier 71-; mem. Rhodes Scholarship Selection Cttee. of Sask.; mem. Senate, Univ. of Sask. 60-62; Chair. of Wascana Centre Authority 62-64; Pres. New Democratic Party of Canada 69-71.
Publs. Articles on Sask. Crown Corpns. in *Proc. of the Inst. of Public Admin. of Canada* and *The Public*

Corporation edited by W. Freedman, *Press Coverage of Saskatchewan Medicare Dispute*, Queens' Quarterly, Autumn, 63.
Office of the Premier, Regina, Saskatchewan, Canada.

Blakenham, 1st Viscount (cr. 63) of Little Blakenham, in the County of Suffolk; **John Hugh Hare**, P.C., O.B.E., D.L., V.M.H.; British politician; b. 22 Jan. 1911; s. of Earl and Countess of Listowel; m. Hon. Beryl Nancy Pearson 1934; one s. two d.; ed. Eton Coll.
Lieutenant-Colonel, Suffolk Yeomanry 39-45; Alderman London County Council 37-52; M.P. 45-63; Vice-Chair. Conservative Party Org. 51-55, Chair. 63-65; Minister of State for Colonial Affairs 55-56; Sec. of State for War 56-58; Minister of Agriculture 58-59, of Labour 60-63; Chancellor of Duchy of Lancaster and Dep. Leader, House of Lords 63-64; Chair. Toynbee Hall 66-, Gov. Body, Peabody Trust 67-; Treasurer Royal Horticultural Soc. 70-; Deputy Lieut. for Suffolk 68.
Leisure interest: gardening.
10 Holland Park, London, W.11; Cottage Farm, Little Blakenham, Ipswich, Suffolk, England.
Telephone: 01-727-5885 (London); 0473 830344 (Suffolk).

Blamont, Philippe Lucien, DIPL.SC.POL.; French international official; b. 17 Nov. 1927, Paris; s. of Emile Armand Blamont and Perle Odette Amélie Cohen; m. Evelyne Bernheim 1950; two d.; ed. Faculté de Droit de Paris, Inst. d'Etudes politiques de Paris, Cambridge Univ. and Georg-August-Universität zu Göttingen.
Secretary of conf. of Advocates at Council of State and Court of Cassation 51; mem. office of Dir.-Gen., Int. Labour Office (ILO), Geneva 52-53, Int. Organizations Div. 53-57, Liaison Office with UN, New York 57-59, Exec. Asst. to Dir.-Gen., Geneva 60-64, Dir. Liaison Office with UN 64-66; Dir., Int. Centre for Advanced Technical and Vocational Training, Turin 66-74; Pres. Nat. Comm. on Future Training 74-75; Pres., Dir.-Gen. Bossard Inst. 75-.
Bossard Institut, 12 rue Jean-Jaurès, Hauts de Seine, 92807 Puteaux; 92 rue du Bac, Paris 7e, France.
Telephone: 776-42-01 (Office); 222-00-19 (Home).

Blancard, Jean Raymond Edouard; French engineering administrator; b. 18 Aug. 1914; ed. Ecole Polytechnique.
Engineer, then Chief Engineer of Mines; Dir. of Fuels Central Admin. of Industry and Commerce until 60; mem. Admin. Council Gaz de France 59-; Ministerial Del. for Air Force 59-61; Pres. Bureau de recherches de pétrole (B.R.P.) 59-65; Vice-Pres. Entreprise de recherches et d'activités pétrolières (ERAP) 65-68; Pres. Dir.-Gen. Soc. auxiliare de l'Erap (AUXERAP) 65, Soc. francaise de recherches et d'exploitation petrolières (SOFREP) 66-68; Pres. Industrial Equipment Cttee., Atomic Energy Comm. 61-; Vice-Pres. Régie nat. des Usines Renault 61-65; Pres., Dir.-Gen. SNECMA 64-68; Perm. Under Sec. for Armaments 68-; Dir. Turboméca, Nord-Aviation, Sud-Aviation; Vice-Pres. Union Syndicale des industries aéronautiques et spatiales 65-; Officier Légion d'Honneur.
19 boulevard Flandrin, Paris 16e, France.

Blanch, Most Rev. and Rt. Hon. Stuart Yarworth, P.C., M.A. (OXON.); British ecclesiastic; b. 2 Feb. 1918, Blakeney, Glos.; s. of the late William Edwin and Elizabeth Blanch; m. Brenda Coyte 1943; one s. four d.; ed. Alleyn's School, Dulwich, St. Catherine's Soc. and Wycliffe Hall, Oxford.
Law Fire Insurance Soc. Ltd. 36-40; Navigator, R.A.F. 40-46; Curate, Highfield, Oxford 49-52; Vicar of Eynsham, Oxford 52-57; Tutor and Vice-Principal, Wycliffe Hall 57-60, Chair. 67-; Oriel Canon of Rochester and Warden of Rochester Theological Coll. 60-66; Bishop of Liverpool 66-75; Archbishop of York 75-; LL.D. h.c. (Liverpool Univ.) 75.
Leisure interests: music, walking.

Publs. *The World Our Orphanage 72, For all Mankind 76.*
Bishopthorpe, York, YO2 1QE, England.

Blanchard, Francis; French international civil servant; b. 21 July 1916, Paris; m. Marie Claire Boué 1940; two s.; ed. Univ. of Paris.
French Home Office; Int. Org. for Refugees, Geneva 47-51; Int. Labour Office, Geneva 51-, Asst. Dir.-Gen. 56-, Deputy Dir.-Gen. 68-74, Dir.-Gen. 74-.
Leisure interests: skiing, hunting, horse-riding.
International Labour Office, 4 chemin des Morillons, Geneva, Switzerland; Home: Prébailly, Gex (Ain), France.
Telephone: 985211 (Office); 41-51-70 Gex (Home).

Blanc-Lapierre, André Joseph Lucien, D. ÈS SC.; French scientist; b. 7 July 1915, Lavaur; s. of Victor Blanc-Lapierre and Jeanne Garrigues; m. Jacqueline Masson 1940; two s. six d.; ed. Ecole Normale Supérieure de Paris.
Member of Staff, Ecole Normale Supérieure 40-44; Head of electronic dept., Centre National d'Etudes des Télécommunications 44-48; Prof. Univ. of Algiers and Dir. Inst. d'Etudes Nucléaires 48-61; Dir. Laboratoire de l'Accélérateur Linéaire, Paris 61-69; Prof. Univ. of Paris XI 61-, Dir. Ecole Supérieure d'Electricité 69-; Pres. Consultative Cttee. for Scientific and Technical Research 63-65; Pres. Comm. for Scientific Research of Plan 64-66; Free mem. Acad. des Sciences 71-; Commdr. Légion d'Honneur, Ordre Nat. du Mérite; several prizes.
Leisure interests: bridge, travel.
Publs. numerous books and articles in professional journals.
Plateau du Moulon, 91190 Gif-sur-Yvette, France.
Telephone: 941-80-40 (Office).

Blanco-Cervantes, Dr. Raúl; Costa Rican chest specialist and politician; b. 1903, San José; s. of Macedonio Blanco Alvarez and Dolores Cervantes Castro; m. Dora Martín Chavarría 1939; one s. four d.; ed. Liceo de Costa Rica and Luis Maximilian Univ., Munich.
Medical Dir., Sanatorio Carlos Durán 33-67; Dir. of Anti-Tuberculosis Dept., Ministry of Public Health 37-67; Minister of Public Health 48-49; Pres. College of Physicians and Surgeons of Costa Rica 46, 47; Dir.-Gen. of Assistance, Ministry of Public Health 50, 51; First Vice-Pres. of Costa Rica 53-58, 62-66; Acting Pres. of Costa Rica 55; Dir. Hospital Nacional para Tuberculosis 58-; Pres. Colegio de Médicos y Cirujanos de Costa Rica 46-47; Hon. mem. Sociedad Mexicana de Tisiología; mem. of WHO Expert Advisory Panel on tuberculosis 54-71; Gov. American Thoracic Soc., American Coll. of Chest Physicians until 66; First Pres. and Founder Sociedad Centroamericana de Tisiología; several decorations.
Leisure interests: reading, gardening.
P.O. Box 918, San José, Costa Rica.
Telephone: 21-20-82.

Blanco Estrade, Dr. Juan Carlos; Uruguayan politician; b. 9 June 1934, Montevideo; ed. Univ. of Montevideo.
Worked in Banco Hipotecario, Uruguay; Central Govt. office, later Presidents' office, until 65; Gen. offices of Org. of American States, and simultaneously alternate Rep. of Latin-American Asscn. of Free Trade (Lafta) 65-68; Dir. Lafta 68-71; Under-Sec. for Foreign Affairs April 71-Nov. 72; Minister for Foreign Affairs Nov. 72-.
Ministerio de Relaciones Exteriores, 18 de Julio 1205, Montevideo, Uruguay.

Blanco Villalta, Jorge Gastón; Argentine diplomatist and writer; b. 1909.
Vice-Consul, Istanbul 34-35; First Sec. Ministry of Foreign Affairs 46; Head of UN Div., Political Dept.,

Ministry of Foreign Affairs 46; in charge of liaison with Nat. Congress 47; Sec.-Gen. Argentine del. UN Assemblies 47, 48; Counsellor 48; Dir. Intellectual Co-operation and Counsellor attached to Presidency 48-53; Sec.-Gen. and Del. Inter-American Conf. 54; Dir. Middle East and East Europe Dept. Ministry of Foreign Affairs 54- (Minister 54, Amb. 55-); Royal Order of Phoenix (Greece), Order of the Cedar (Lebanon).
Publs. *El Pueblo Turco* 36, *Cuadros de la Estambul Actual* 37, *Literatura turca* 39, *Kemal Ataturk* 39, *Literatura turca contemporánea* 40, *El Milagro Turco* 40, *Conquista del Río de la Plata* 43, *Historia de la Conquista del Río de la Plata* 46, *Antropofagía ritual americana* 48, *Montoya, apóstol de los guaraníes* 55, *Organización de los Estados Americanos* 57, *La Organización de la Comunidad Internacional* 60.
Las Heras 4095, Buenos Aires, Argentina.

Blancpain, Marc; French writer; b. 29 Sept. 1909; ed. Collèges d'Hirson et de Laon, Université de Nancy, Univ. de Paris à la Sorbonne and Ecole Normale Supérieure, Saint-Cloud.
Teacher, Ecole Internationale de Genève 31-35, Lycée Français, Cairo 35-39; Sec.-Gen. of Alliance Française 45-; mem. PEN Club, Soc. des Gens de Lettres, Acad. Stanislas, Acad. des Sciences d'Outre-Mer; Commdr. Légion d'Honneur, Croix de Guerre 39-45, Commandeur des Palmes Académiques, Commandeur Ordre National du Mérite, Commdr. Ordre des Arts et Lettres, and orders from Peru, Chile, Senegal, Brazil and Belgium; Grand Prix du Roman, Acad. Française 45, Prix Courteline 46, Prix Scarron 55, Prix Engelmann (Belgium) 56, Grand Prix du Rayonnement Français (Acad. Française) 61.
Publs. include: *Le Solitaire* (novel) 45, *Les Contes de la Lampe à Graisse* (novel) 46, *Le Carrefour de la Désolation* (novel) 51, *Voyages et Verres d'Eau* (essay) 52, *La Femme d'Arnaud vient de mourir* (novel) 58, *Contes de Vermeil* (for children) 58, *Les Peupliers de la Prétentaine* 61, *Vincennes Neuilly* (short stories) 61, *Grandes Heures d'un Village de la Frontière* 64, *Les Truffes du Voyage* 65, *Aujourd'hui, l'Amérique latine* 66, *Ulla des Antipodes* (novel) 67, *Les Lumières de la France* (essay) 67, *La Saga des Amants Séparés*, Vol. I 69, Vol. II 70, Vol. III 72-, *Le plus long amour* 71, *En français malgré tout* 73, *Nous l'appelions Bismarck* 74.
Office: 101 boulevard Raspail, Paris 6e; Home: 12 boulevard Jean Mermoz, 92 Neuilly-sur-Seine, France. Telephone: 747-92-10 (Home).

Blanding, Sarah Gibson, LL.D.; American educationist; b. 22 Nov. 1898, Fayette County, Ky.; s. of William de Saussure Blanding and Sarah Gibson Anderson; ed. New Haven Normal School of Gymnastics; Kentucky and Columbia Univs., and London School of Economics.
Instructor in physical education, Kentucky Univ. 19-22; Acting Dean of Women 23-24; Dean of Women and Asst. Prof. 26-36; Dean of Women and Associate Prof. 37-41; Dir. New York State Coll. of Home Economics, Cornell Univ. 41-42; Dean 42-46; Pres. Vassar Coll. 46-64, Pres. Emer. 64-; mem. Governor's Cttee. on Educ. and Employment of Women; Board of Trustees, The Edward W. Hazen Foundation, Wykeham Rise School, Chatham Coll.; Cttee. for Econ. Devt., mem. Acad. Freedom Cttee., American Civil Liberties Union; mem. Comm. on Independent Colls. and Univs. of the Asscn. of Colls. and Univs. of N.Y. State; mem. Nat. Advisory Council, American Asscn. for UN.
Leisure interests: walking, bird-watching, swimming, reading.
Lakeville, Conn. 06039, U.S.A.
Telephone: 203-435-2181.

Blankenhorn, Herbert; German diplomatist; b. 15 Dec. 1904, Mülhausen-Alscace; m. Gisela Krug 1944; two s. two d.; ed. Gymnasiums in Strasbourg, Berlin and Karlsruhe, and Univs. of Munich, London, Heidelberg and Paris.
Entered Foreign Service 29; served Athens 32-35, Washington 35-39, Helsinki 40, Berne 40-43; Foreign Office, Berlin (Protocol Section) 43-45; Deputy Sec.-Gen. Zonal Advisory Council, Hamburg 46-48; Sec.-Gen. Christian Democratic Party (British Zone) 48; Private Sec. to Pres. of the Parl. Council, Bonn (Dr. Adenauer) 48-49; Chief of Liaison Office with Allied High Commission 49; Political Dir. Foreign Office 50-55; Amb. to NATO 55-58; Amb. to France 58-63, to Italy 64-65, to U.K. 65-70; mem. UNESCO Exec. Council 70-, Vice-Pres. Exec. Board.
7847 Badenweiler (Baden), 2 Hintere Avenue, Federal Republic of Germany.
Telephone: 7632-354.

Blanton, Leonard Ray, B.S.; American businessman and politician; b. 10 April 1930, Hardin Co., Tenn.; s. of Leonard Alonzá Blanton and Ova A. Delaney Blanton; m. Betty Littlefield 1949; two s. one d.; ed. Old Shiloh High School and Univ. of Tenn.
Member Tennessee House of Reps. 64-66; mem. for Tenn., U.S. House of Reps. 66-72; Gov. of Tenn. 75-; mem. Exec. Cttee. Nat. Governor's Conf.; Chair. Tennessee-Tombigbee Waterway Devt. Authority; Democrat.
Leisure interests: hunting, fishing, golf.
Tennessee State Capitol, Nashville, Tenn. 37; Governor's Residence, Curtiswood Lane, Nashville, Tenn. 37204, U.S.A.
Telephone: (615) 741-2001 (Office); (615) 383-5401 (Home).

Blanzat, Jean; French writer; b. 1905; ed. Collège de Bellac and Ecole normale d'instituteurs de Versailles.
Literary Dir. Editions Grasset 45-53; mem. Publisher's Readers' Cttee. Editions Gallimard 53-; Grand Prix du roman de l'Académie française 42; Prix Fémina 65.
Publs. novels: *Enfance* 30, *A moi-même ennemi* 33, *Septembre* 36, *L'Orage du matin* 42, *La Gartempe* 57, *Le Faussaire* 65, *L'Iguane* 66.
7 rue de Navarre, Paris 5e, France.

Blaškovič, Dionýz, M.D., D.SC.; Czechoslovak virologist; b. 2 Aug. 1913, Jablonica; s. of Koloman Blaškovič and Gabriela Blaškovič (née Blaškovičova); m. 1st Milada Janatová 1941; m. 2nd Vlasta Černá 1972; one s. two d.; ed. Charles Univ., Prague.
Research work, Inst. of Bacteriology and Immunology, Charles Univ.; bacteriological research 34-46; Rockefeller Foundation Fellow, United States 46-47; Head, Dept. of Epidemiology and Microbiology, State Health Inst., Bratislava 45-52; Prof. Med. Faculty, Comenius Univ., Bratislava 54-, Prof. Nat. Science Faculty 69-; Dir. Inst. of Virology, Slovak Acad. of Sciences, Bratislava 53-; Sec.-Gen. Int. Council of Scientific Unions (ICSU) 63-66; Pres. Slovak Acad. of Sciences 61-65; mem. Presidium Czechoslovak Acad. of Sciences 65-70; Editor-in-Chief *Acta Virologica*; Hon. mem. All-Union Soc. of Hygienists, Epidemiologists, Microbiologists and Infectionists of U.S.S.R. 56; WHO expert; Fellow, New York Acad. of Sciences 60; Hon. mem. Polish Microbiological Soc. 63, Austrian Microbiological Soc. 63; Foreign mem. U.S.S.R. Acad. of Sciences 66; mem. Int. Org. for Cell Research, Brussels; mem. Soc. Gen. Microbiology, London; mem. Deutsche Akad. Naturforscher Halle/Saale 67; State Prize for Science 51; Purkyně Medal in Medical Sciences 56; Order of Labour 63; Max Planck Gold Medal 65; J. E. Purkyně Gold Plaque 68.
Virological Institute, Bratislava, Mlynská dolina 1; Novosvetská 18, Bratislava, Czechoslovakia.
Telephone: 483-37 (Office), 314-88 (Home).

Blatchford, Joseph Hoffer, LL.B.; American government official; b. 7 June 1934, Milwaukee, Wis.; s. of Mr. and Mrs. George Blatchford; m. Winifred Marich 1967; one s. one d.; ed. Beverly Hills High School,

Univ. of Calif. at Los Angeles and Univ. of Calif. Berkeley Law School.
Organizer of community devt. programme, Accion; Calif. Candidate for Congress 68; Dir. Peace Corps 69-71; Dir. ACTION 71-72; law practice 72-73; Prof. of Political Science, Whittier Coll. 73-.
545 South Norton Avenue, Los Angeles, Calif. 90020, U.S.A.
Telephone: (213) 380-4522.

Blattný, Ctibor, DR.ING., DR.SC.; Czechoslovak botanist; b. 8 Sept. 1897, Česká Skalice; ed. Coll. of Agricultural Engineering, Prague.
Director Inst. for Experimental Botany, Czechoslovak Acad. of Sciences 60-68; Prof. Agric. Coll., Prague 67-; mem. Czechoslovak Acad. of Sciences 60, Academician 60-; State Prize 58; Silver Plaque of Czechoslovak Acad. of Sciences 67; Dr. h.c., Schiller Univ., Jena.
Publs. Scientific papers on plant viruses, especially agricultural plant viruses.
Říčanova 29, Prague 6-Břevnov, Czechoslovakia.

Blauvelt, Howard W., C.P.A.; American petroleum executive; b. 11 Feb. 1917, New York; s. of the late Harry O. W. Blauvelt and Lillian M. Woelfert Blauvelt; m. 1st Margaret D. Hahn 1939 (deceased 1970), 2nd Mary E. Cassity 1970; one s. one d.; ed. Yale Univ. and Columbia Graduate School of Business Admin., N.Y.
Treasurer, Meyer and Medelsohn, Inc. 49-51; Asst. Controller, Continental Oil Company, Oklahoma 52-57, Controller, Texas 62-65, Vice-Pres. Co-ordinating and Planning, New York 65-66, Exec. Vice-Pres. New York 66-69, Pres. Conoco Chemicals Div. 69-72, Exec. Vice-Pres., Stamford, Conn. 72-74, Pres. March-May 74, Chair. and Chief Exec. Officer May 74-; Senior Vice-Pres. Hudson's Bay Oil & Gas Co. Ltd., Canada 57-62; Dir. Continental Oil Co. 66-, Bankers Trust, New York 75-, General Telephone & Electronics 75-, American Petroleum Inst. 74-.
Leisure interest: golf.
Continental Oil Company, High Ridge Park, Stamford, Conn. 06904, U.S.A.
Telephone: (203) 359-3500.

Blazevic, Juraj Jakov; Croatian politician; b. 24 March 1912, Bužim near Gospić; ed. Zagreb Univ.
Joined Communist Party of Yugoslavia 28; imprisoned for six months for communist activities 31; Sec. District Cttee. of Croatia in Lika 40; del. First Nat. Conference of C.P. of Croatia; mem. Central Cttee. C.P. of Croatia; at Fifth Party Conference elected mem. Central Cttee. C.P. of Yugoslavia; organized Croatian uprising First Partisan Detachment Velebit in Lika district; sentenced to death by Italian Mil. Court 43; mem. 1st, 2nd and 3rd Zavnoh Convention; Public Prosecutor of Croatia 45-48; Minister of Commerce and Supply 48-50; Vice-Pres. Govt. and Pres. Econ. Council of Croatia 50-53; Pres. of Croatia 53-62; Pres. Fed. Chamber of Commerce, mem. Fed. Exec. Council 62-65; Vice-Pres. 65-67; Pres. of Assembly of Croatia 67-; fmr. mem. Presidency of Yugoslavia; Medal of Nat. Hero; Partisan Memorial Medal 41; numerous other decorations.
The Croatian Assembly, Zagreb, Yugoslavia.

Bleaney, Brebis, C.B.E., F.R.S., M.A., D.PHIL.; British physicist and university professor; b. 6 June 1915, London; s. of Frederick Bleaney and Eva Johanne Petersen; m. Betty Isabelle Plumpton 1949; one s. one d.; ed. St. John's Coll., Oxford.
University Lecturer in Physics, Oxford 45-57; Fellow of St. John's Coll., Oxford 47-57, Hon. Fellow 68-; Dr. Lee's Prof. of Experimental Philosophy, Oxford 57-; Fellow of Wadham Coll. 57-; Corresp. mem. Acad. des Sciences de l'Institut de France 74-; Hughes Medal, Royal Soc. 62; C. V. Boys Prize, Physical Soc. of London.
Leisure interests: music, tennis, travel.
Publs. *Electricity and Magnetism* (with B. I. Bleaney) 57,

Electron Paramagnetic Resonance (with A. Abragam) 70.
Clarendon Laboratory, Oxford; Home: Garford House, Garford Road, Oxford, England.
Telephone: 59291 (Laboratory); 59589 (Home).

Blech, Harry, O.B.E.; British conductor; b. 2 March 1910, London; s. of Polish parents; m. 2nd Marion Manley 1957; one s. three d. (and one s. two d. by 1st marriage); ed. Central London Foundation, Trinity Coll. of Music and Manchester Coll. of Music.
Violin soloist 28-30; with B.B.C. Symphony Orchestra 30-36; Founder-mem. Blech Quartet 33-50, London Wind Players 42, London Mozart Players 49, Haydn-Mozart Soc. 49, London Mozart Choir 52; Hon. mem. Royal Acad. of Music; Fellow, Royal Manchester Coll. of Music, Trinity Coll. of Music.
Leisure interest: reading.
The Owls, 70 Leopold Road, London, S.W.19, England.
Telephone: 01-946-8135.

Bleuler, Manfred Eugen, M.D.; Swiss physician; b. 4 Jan. 1903, Zurich; s. of Prof. Eugen Bleuler and Hedwig Waser; m. Monica Bisaz; one d.; ed. Univs. of Geneva and Zürich.
Various hospital posts in Switzerland and U.S.A. 27-32; Senior Medical Officer, St. Pirminsberg Hospital, Pfäfers 33-36; Senior Medical Officer, Univ. Psychiatric Clinic, Friedmatt, Basle 37-42; Prof. of Psychiatry and Dir. Psychiatric Clinic, Univ. of Zürich 42-69, now Hon. Prof.; Hon. mem. Vienna Soc. of Doctors.
Publs. *Krankheitsverlauf, Persönlichkeit und Verwandt-schaft Schizophrener* 41, *Endokrinologische Psychiatrie* 54, *Begleiterscheinungen körperlicher Krankheiten* 66, *Neuauflage Lehrbuch Psychiatrie* 69, *Die schizophrenen Geisteskrankheiten im Lichte langer Kranken & Familien-Geschichten* 70, and other works.
CH 8702 Zollikon, Bahnhofstrasse 49, Switzerland.

Bleustein-Blanchet, Marcel; French advertising executive; b. 21 Aug. 1906.
Founder and Pres. Publicis 27-; founded Radio Cité 35; founder and Dir.-Gen. Régie Presse 38-; founder and Pres. Fondation de la Vocation 60-; Founding Co-Pres. Confédération de la Publicité Française 66-67; founder Les Drugstores Publicis 58; Commdr. Légion d'Honneur, Croix de Guerre, Médaille de la Résistance, etc.
Publs. *Sur mon Antenne* 48, *La rage de convaincre* 70.
Office: 133 avenue des Champs-Elysées, Paris 8e; Home: 23 rue Albéric-Magnard, Paris 16e, France.

Blind, Adolf, DR.RER.POL.; German university professor and business executive; b. 16 Oct. 1906; ed. Univ. of Frankfurt.
Privat Dozent, Univ. of Frankfurt 34-36; Head of Statistical Office, Saarland, and City of Saarbrücken 36-42; Extra-Mural Prof., Univ. of Heidelberg 42-49; Prof., Univ. of Saarbrücken 49; Minister of Finance, Saarland 55-57; Prof. of Statistics, Univ. of Frankfurt 57; fmr. Chair. of Advisory Board Saarbergwerke; mem. Int. Statistical Inst.; Dep. Chair. German Statistical Asscn.; Grosses Verdienstkreuz.
Publs. *Die Heimarbeit in der Schweiz* 29, *Beiträge zur deutschen Statistik* 36, *Wesen und Eigentümlichkeit sozialstatistischer Erkenntnis* 53, *Das derzeitige Verhältnis zwischen Statistik und Nationalökonomie* 63, *Wirt-schaftsstatistik in Forschung und Lehre* 66.
Passavantstrasse 10, 6000 Frankfurt am Main, Federal Republic of Germany.
Telephone: 61-89-67.

Bliss, Anthony Addison, B.A., LL.B.; American lawyer; b. 19 April 1913, New York; s. of Cornelius Newton Bliss and Zaidee Cobb Bliss; m. 1st Barbara Field 1937 (divorced 1941); 2nd Jo Ann Sayers 1942 (divorced 1967); 3rd Sally Brayley 1967; four s. two d.; ed. Groton Harvard Coll. and Univ. of Virginia Law School.
Associate, Milbank, Tweed, Hope & Hadley 40-41,

45-51, Partner 52-61, Partner Milbank, Tweed, Hadley & McCloy 61-74, Consulting Partner 74-; Dir. Metropolitan Opera Asscn. Inc. 49-, Pres. 56-67, Exec. Dir., Chair. Admin. Cttee. 74-; Chair. Foundation for American Dance, Inc., City Center Joffrey Ballet 70; Co-Chair., Dir. Nat. Corporate Fund for Dance, Inc. 72-; Trustee, U.S. Trust Co. of New York 59-; Dir. Lincoln Center for the Performing Arts, Inc. 61-67, Great Atlantic and Pacific Tea Co., Inc. 63-70; mem. Nat. Council on the Arts 65-68, Advisory Panel on Dance, Nat. Endowment for the Arts 68-71, Music Panel 68-69; Trustee, Nat. Opera Inst. 69-74; Dir. New York Foundation for the Arts, Inc. 71-; Trustee, Portledge School 73-, Foundation Center 74-75; mem. American Bar Asscn., N.Y. State Bar Asscn., Asscn. of the Bar of the City of New York, Nassau County Bar Asscn.
Leisure interests: breeding Chesapeake Bay Retrievers, tennis, swimming.
Metropolitan Opera Association, Inc., Lincoln Center Plaza, New York, N.Y. 10023; Milbank, Tweed, Hadley & McCloy, 1211 Avenue of the Americas, New York, N.Y. 10036; Home: 144 Centre Island Road, Centre Island, Oyster Bay, N.Y. 11771, U.S.A.
Telephone: (212) 799-3100, (212) 422-2660 (Office); (516) 922-4843 (Home).

Bliss, Ray Charles, A.B.; American insurance executive and politician; b. 16 Dec. 1907, Akron, Ohio; s. of Emil and Emilie (Wieland) Bliss; m. Ellen Palmer 1959; ed. Univ. of Akron, Ohio.
Secretary, Treas. Wells & Bliss Inc. 33-37; Pres. Tower Agencies Inc. (general insurance) 47-; mem. Summit County Board of Elections 36-, Chair. 45-46, 49-50; Chair. Summit County Repub. Central Cttee. 42-64; Chair. Ohio Repub. State Central and Exec. Cttee. 49-65; Presiding Officer Repub. Joint Leadership of Congress, and Nat. Repub. Co-ordinating Cttee. 65-69; mem. Repub. Nat. Cttee. 52-, mem. Exec. Cttee. 52-, Vice-Chair. Repub. Nat. Cttee. 60-65, 70-, Chair. 65-69; mem. Univ. of Akron, Board of Trustees 70-74, 75-; Univ. of Akron Alumni Hon. Award 65; Hon. H.L.D. (Akron Univ.) 68.
Leisure interest: rose-growing.
Home: 2535 Addyston Road, Akron, Ohio 44313; Office: 425 First National Tower, Akron, Ohio 44308, U.S.A.
Telephone: 762-8903 (Office); 864-4563 (Home).

Blitz, Gérard; Belgian business executive; b. 28 Feb. 1912; ed. Collège d'Anvers.
Diamond cutter 32-50; Founder, Vice-Chair., Club Méditerranée (holiday org.) 50-; Pres. S.P.V.Y. 66-; Croix de Guerre.
Office: 8 rue de la Bourse, Paris 2e; Home: 6 rue du Printemps, Paris 17e, France.

Bliven, Bruce, A.B.; American journalist; b. 27 July 1889, Emmetsburg, Ia.; s. of Charles Franklin Bliven and Lilla (Ormsby) Bliven; m. Rose Emery 1913; one s.; ed. Stanford Univ.
Director, Dept. of Journalism Southern Calif. Univ. 14-16; mem. editorial staff Printers' Ink 16-18; mem. Editorial Board, N.Y. Globe 19-23, The New Republic 23-54; New York corresp. The Manchester Guardian 27-47; mem. Nat. Asscn. of Science Writers 40-; Lecturer in Communication and Journalism, Stanford Univ. 57-; Trustee, Twentieth Century Fund (emeritus).
Leisure interests: reading, music, theatre, walking.
Publs. The Men Who Make the Future 42, What the Informed Citizen Needs to Know (co-editor) 45, Twentieth Century Unlimited (Editor) 50, Preview for Tomorrow: The Unfinished Business of Science 53, The World Changers 65, Five Million Words Later (autobiography) 70, A Mirror for Greatness 75.
Kingscote Gardens, Stanford, Calif. 94305, U.S.A.
Telephone: 415-328-0497.

Bloch, Ernst, DR. PHIL.; German professor of philosophy; b. 8 July 1885, Ludwigshafen am Rhein; m. Karola Piotrkowska 1934; one s. one d.; ed. Munich and Würzburg Univs.
In Switzerland, France, Czechoslovakia and U.S.A. 38-49; Prof. of Philosophy Leipzig Univ. 49-57, Visiting Prof. Tübingen Univ. 61-; Peace Prize of German Booksellers 67, Sigmund Freud Prize, Akademie für Sprache und Dichtung, Darmstadt 75; Dr. h.c.(Zagreb, Sorbonne, Tübingen).
Publs. Geist der Utopie 18, 23, 64, 71, Thomas Münzer als Theologe der Revolution 21, 62, 69, Spuren 30, 59, 69, Erbschaft dieser Zeit 35, 62, Subjekt-Objekt, Erläuterungen zu Hegel 51, 62, Avicenna und die Aristotelische Linke 52, Das Prinzip Hoffnung 54, 59, Zur Ontologie des Noch-Nicht-Seins 61, Naturrecht und menschliche Würde 61, Verfremdungen I and II 62, 64, Tübinger Einleitung in die Philosophie 1 and 2, 63, 64, 69, Literarische Aufsätze 65, Über Karl Marx 68, Widerstand und Friede 68, Atheismus im Christentum 68, Philosophische Aufsätze 69, Über Methode und System bei Hegel 70, Politische Messungen, Pestzeit Vormärz 70, Vom Hasard zur Katastrophe 72, Vorlesungen zur Philosophie der Renaissance 72, Das Materialismusproblem, seine Geschichte und Substanz 72, Experimentum Mundi 74, Gespräche mit Ernst Bloch 75
Im Schwanzer 35, 74 Tübingen, Federal Republic of Germany.
Telephone: 5959.

Bloch, Felix, PH.D.; American university professor; b. 23 Oct. 1905; s. of Gustav and Agnes Bloch; m. Lore Misch 1940; three s. one d.; ed. Fed. Inst. of Technology, Zürich, and Univ. of Leipzig.
Lecturer, Univ. of Leipzig 32-33; Acting Assoc. Prof. Stanford Univ. 34-36, Prof. of Physics 36-71, Prof. Emer. 71-; Dir.-Gen. European Council for Nuclear Research, Geneva 54-55; mem. Nat. Acad. of Sciences; Pres. American Physical Soc. 65-66; Fellow, Churchill Coll., Cambridge 67; Nobel Prize for Physics 52.
Leisure interest: piano.
1551 Emerson Street, Palo Alto, Calif. 94301, U.S.A.
Telephone: 415-327-8156.

Bloch, Konrad, PH.D.; American (b. German) biochemist; b. 21 Jan. 1912; ed. Technische Hochschule, Munich, and Columbia Univ.
Emigrated to U.S.A. 36, naturalized 44; Instructor and Research Assoc., Columbia Univ. 39-46, Asst. Prof. of Biochemistry, Univ. of Chicago 46-50, Prof. 50-54; Higgins Prof. of Biochemistry, Harvard Univ. 54-; Fellow American Acad. of Sciences; mem. Nat. Acad. of Sciences; Fritzsche Award, American Chemical Soc. 64; Nobel Prize for Medicine with Prof. Theodor Lynen for discoveries concerning the mechanism and regulation of cholesterol and fatty acid metabolism 64.
Publ. Lipide Metabolism 61.
38 Oxford Street, Cambridge, Mass. 02138, U.S.A.

Bloch-Lainé, François, D. en D.; French banker; b. 25 March 1912, Paris; s. of Jean-Frédéric Bloch-Lainé and Georgette Lainé; m. Anne-Marie d'Abbadie d'Arrast 1935; four s.; ed. Univ. of Paris.
Entered Inspection des Finances 36; directed finances of Resistance; Deputy Dir. of Treasury 44; financial adviser in China and Chief, French Financial Mission to Far East 45-46; Dir. of Schuman Cabinet 46; Dir. of Treasury 47-53; Dir.-Gen. Caisse des Dépôts 53-67; Insp.-Gen. of Finances 63-; Pres. Crédit Lyonnais 67-74; posts in Soc. Nat. des Pétroles d'Aquitaine, Banque de Bruxelles, la Cie. Bancaire, Crédit Nat., Crédit Foncier Franco-Canadien, Crédit Foncier de France; Vice-Pres. Asscn. professionelles des Banques; Grand Officier Légion d'Honneur; Croix de Guerre; Médaille de la Résistance; Commdr. des Palmes Académiques.
Publs. L'Emploi des Loisirs Ouvriers et l'Education

Populaire 35, *La Zone Franc* 53, *Le Trésor Public* 60, *La Réforme de l'Entreprise* 63.
11 rue de l'Hôtel-Colbert, 75005 Paris, France.

Block, Joseph Leopold; retired American steel company executive; b. 6 Oct. 1902, Chicago, Ill.; *s.* of Leopold and Cora (Bloom) Block; *m.* Lucille Eichengreen 1924; one *s.* (deceased) one *d.*; ed. Harvard School (Chicago) and Cornell Univ.
Joined Inland Steel Co. 22, sales dept. 23-27, Asst. Vice-Pres. 27-36, Vice-Pres., Sales 36-51, Vice-Chair. 49-52, Exec. Vice-Pres. and Chair. Finance Cttee. 52-53, Pres. 53-56, Pres. and Chief Exec. Officer 56-59, Chair. and Chief Exec. Officer 59-67, Chair. Exec. Cttee. 67-71, Dir. 30-75, Hon. Dir. 75-; on leave of absence with Steel Div. War Production Board, Wash. 41-44; Chair. Steel Production Cttee., War Production Board 41-43, Asst. Dir. 43-44, Deputy Dir. 44; Pres. Chicago Asscn. of Commerce and Industry 57-59; Dir. Nat. Merit Scholarship Corpn. 63-, Chair. 71-75, Community Fund of Chicago, Vice-Pres. 50-61, Pres. 61-63; Dir. Jewish Fed. of Chicago 31-52, Pres. 47-50; Trustee Cttee. for Econ. Devt., Ill. Inst. of Technology; Hon. Dir. Museum of Science and Industry, Chicago; Vice-Chair. of Ill. Board of Higher Educ.; mem. Welfare Service Cttee., Cook Co. Dept. of Public Aid; Hon. LL.D. St. Joseph's Coll. (Collegeville), Ind., Bradley Univ., Roosevelt Univ., Ill. Inst. of Technology, Northwestern Univ.; Hon. D.Eng. Rose Polytechnic Inst.
Leisure interests: golf, collecting Lincolnia.
Office: 30 West Monroe Street, Chicago, Ill.; Home: 1325 Astor Street, Chicago, Ill., U.S.A.

Block, Leo de, LL.D.; b. 14 Aug. 1904, The Hague; *s.* of H. C. A. de Block and M. C. D. Bonnike; *m.* D. E. C. van Lede 1944; three *d.*; ed. Rijksuniversiteit te Leiden.
Various posts in Dutch and foreign banks 23-47; Ministry of Finance 47-59; Ministry of Econ. Affairs 59-60; Exec. Vice-Pres. K.L.M. (Royal Dutch Airlines) 60-63; State Sec. Foreign Affairs 63-67 and State Sec. for Transport and Waterways 66-67; Minister of Econ. Affairs 67-70; Commdr. Order of Netherlands Lion, Royal Wedding Medal 66, Grand Cross Orders of Merit (Austria, Luxembourg), St. Olav (Norway), Leopold II (Belgium), Oak Wreath of Luxembourg.
5 St. Hubertusweg, The Hague, Netherlands.

Bloembergen, Nicolaas, DR. PHIL.; American (naturalized 1958) professor of applied physics; b. 11 March 1920, Dordrecht, Netherlands; *s.* of Auke Bloembergen and Sophia M. Quint; *m.* Huberta D. Brink 1950; one *s.* two *d.*; ed. Univs. of Utrecht and Leiden.
Research Fellow, Leiden Univ. 47-49; Soc. of Fellows, Harvard Univ. 49-51, Gordon McKay Assoc. Prof. 51-57, Prof. of Applied Physics 57-; Rumford Prof. of Physics 74-; Lorentz Guest Prof., Leiden 73; Guggenheim Fellow 57; mem. Nat. Acad. of Sciences (U.S.A.); Corresp. mem. Royal Dutch Acad. of Sciences; Buckley Prize, Amer. Physical Soc.; Liebmann Prize, Inst. of Radio Engineers; Ballantine Medal, Franklin Inst., Dutch Royal Acad. of Arts and Sciences; Half Moon Trophy, Netherland Club of New York; Nat. Medal of Science 74.
Leisure interests: travel, skiing, tennis.
Publs. *Nuclear Magnetic Relaxation* 61, *Nonlinear Optics* 65, over 150 papers in professional journals.
Pierce Hall, Harvard University, Cambridge, Mass., U.S.A.
Telephone: 617-495-3336.

Blokhin, Nikolai Konstantinovich; Soviet politician; b. 1915; ed. Astrakhan River School, Leningrad Inst. of Water Transport Engineers, and Higher Party School.
Teacher 35-40; Chief Mechanic, Astrakhan Ship Repair Plant 40-41; Soviet Army 41-44; Chief of Section, Volgotanker Shipping Co. 44-45; Deputy First Sec. Astrakhan Regional Cttee. of C.P. 53-59; First Deputy

Chair. Astrakhan Econ. Council 59-61; First Sec. Astrakhan City Cttee., of C.P. 61-63; Chair. Exec. Cttee., Astrakhan Regional Soviet of Workers' Deputies 63-70; Head, Volga Oil-Tanker Steamship Co. 70-; mem. C.P.S.U. 42-; Deputy to R.S.F.S.R. Supreme Soviet.
Volga Oil-Tanker Steamship Company, Astrakhan, U.S.S.R.

Blokhin, Nikolai Nikolayevich, M.D.; Soviet surgeon and cancer specialist; b. 4 May 1912, Gorky; *s.* of Nikolai I. Blokhin and Evdokiya I. Blokhina; *m.* Nadezhda G. Blokhina 1956; one *d.*; ed. Gorky State Medical Inst.
Intern at Gorky Medical Inst. 34-37, Asst. Prof. in Surgical Clinic 37-47, Prof. and Chief of Surgical Clinic 47-52, Dir. of Inst. 51-52; Dir. Inst. of Experimental and Clinical Oncology of U.S.S.R. Acad. Medical Sciences 52-; Pres. U.S.S.R. Acad. Medical Sciences 60-68, mem. 60-; Deputy to U.S.S.R. Supreme Soviet; mem. C.P.S.U. 48-; Pres. Comm. awarding Int. Lenin prizes 74-; Pres. Inst. of Soviet-American Relations; Pres. Int. Union against Cancer 66-70; Foreign mem. Polish Acad. Sciences; Hon. mem. Purkyné Czech Med. Soc.; Life mem. N.Y. Acad. of Sciences; Hero of Socialist Labour; Order of Lenin (three times), Order of Labour Red Banner, Order of Red Star; Hammer and Sickle Gold Medal.
Publs. *Skinplastic* 56, *Problems of Chemiotherapy of Malignant Tumours* (Editor) 60, *Modern Diagnostic Methods in Malignant Tumours* (Editor) 67, *Manual on clinical oncology* 72, and numerous other publications on surgery and cancer research.
Institute of Experimental and Clinical Oncology, U.S.S.R. Academy of Medical Sciences, Kashirscoye shousse 6, Moscow 115478, U.S.S.R.
Telephone: 111-83-71.

Blokhintsev, Dmitri Ivanovich; Soviet physicist; b. 11 Jan. 1908, Moscow; ed. Moscow Univ.
Instructor, Moscow Univ. 30-, Prof. 36-; Scientific Worker, P. M. Lebedev Physical Inst., U.S.S.R. Acad. of Sciences 35-56; Dir. Joint Inst. for Nuclear Research 56-64, Dir. Laboratory of Theoretical Physics 65-; Corresp. mem. U.S.S.R. Acad. of Sciences 58-, Ukrainian S.S.R. Acad. of Sciences 39-; mem. Hungarian Acad. of Sciences, German Leopoldina Acad.; Pres. Int. Union of Pure and Applied Physics 69; mem. C.P.S.U. 43-; State and Lenin prizewinner; Order of Lenin (four); Hammer and Sickle Gold Medal; Hero of Socialist Labour, etc.
Publs. *On the Theory of Phosphorescence* 34, *On the theory of Solid Rectifiers* 38, *Spectra fluorescences and absorptions of various molecules* 39, *Bases of Quantum Mechanics* 49, 63, *Elementary Particles and Field* 50, *Reactor of Atomic Power Station* (with others) 58, *Collection of Scientific Works and Articles* 58, 60, *Diffusion of the Signal inside a Telemetric Particle* 62.
Joint Institute for Nuclear Research, Dubna, Moscow Region, U.S.S.R.

Blondin, Antoine, L. ès L.; French writer; b. 11 April 1922, Paris; *m.* 1st Sylviane Dollfus, one *s.* one *d.*; *m.* 2nd Françoise Barrère; ed. Lycée Louis-le-Grand and Univ. de Paris.
Contributor to *Paris-Presse, Arts, La Parisienne,* etc.; wrote scenarios for the films *La Route Napoléon, Obsession, La Foire aux Femmes*; Prix des Deux-Magots 49, Prix Interallié for *Un Singe en Hiver* 59.
Leisure interests: sport, gastronomy.
Publs. *L'Europe Buissonnière, Les Enfants du Bon Dieu, L'Humeur Vagabonde, Un Singe en Hiver, Un Garçon d'honneur.*
72 rue Mazarine, Paris 7e, France.

Bloom, Claire; British actress; b. 15 Feb. 1931, London; *d.* of Edward Bloom and Elizabeth Grew; *m.* 1st Rod Steiger (*q.v.*) 1959 (divorced), 2nd Hillard

Elkins 1969; one *d*.; ed. London, Bristol and New York. Oxford Repertory Theatre 46, Stratford-on-Avon 48; first major stage appearances in *The Lady's Not For Burning* 49, *Ring Around the Moon* 50; at Old Vic 51-53, *Duel of Angels* 56; other stage performances include, Andromache in *The Trojan Women* 64, Sascha in *Ivanov*, London 66, Nora in *A Doll's House*, New York 71, London 73, Hedda Gabler in *Hedda Gabler*, N.Y. 71, Mary, Queen of Scots in *Vivat, Vivat Regina!*, N.Y. 72, *A Streetcar Named Desire*, London (Evening Standard Drama Award for Best Actress) 74; Fellow Guildhall School of Music and Drama 75.
Films include, *Limelight*, *Man Between*, *Richard III*, *Alexander the Great*, *Brothers Karamazov*, *Buccaneer*, *Look Back in Anger*, *Three Steps to Freedom* 60, *The Brothers Grimm*, *The Chapman Report* 62, *The Haunting* 63, *80,000 Suspects* 63, *Alta Infedeltà* 63, *Il Maestro di Vigevano* 63, *The Outrage* 64, *Spy Who Came in from the Cold* 65, *Three into Two Won't Go* 67, *Illustrated Man* 68, *Red Sky at Morning* 70, *A Doll's House* 73, *A Legacy* (TV) 75, *Islands in the Stream* 75.
Leisure interests: walking, music.
c/o Larry Dalzell, 3 Godwins Court, St. Martins Lane, London, W.C.2, England.
Telephone: 01-499 3811.

Blough, Roger M(iles), A.B., LL.B.; American lawyer and industrialist; b. 19 Jan. 1904, Riverside, near Johnstown, Pa.; *s.* of Christian E. Blough and Viola Hoffman; *m.* Helen Decker 1928; twin *d*.; ed. Susquehanna Univ. Pa. and Yale Law School.
Taught in Pa. High School 25-28; studied law 28-31; with law firm. of White & Case, N.Y. 31-42; Gen. Solicitor for U.S. Steel Corpn. of Delaware 42-51; Exec. Vice-Pres. (Law) U.S. Steel Co. (in 53 merged into U.S. Steel Corpn.) 51, Vice-Chair. Board of Dirs. 52, Dir. 52-, Gen. Counsel 53, Chair. and Chief Exec. Officer 55-69; partner, White & Case 69-; Dir. and founding mem. Business Cttee. for the Arts; Dir. The Commonwealth Fund; Hon. mem. Japan Iron and Steel Fed.; Hon. Vice-Pres. American Iron and Steel Inst.; mem. Center for Inter-American Relations, Council on Foreign Relations, New York State Bar Asscn.; mem. and Fellow American Bar Asscn.; Life mem. Acad. of Political Science; numerous other civic affiliations; eighteen hon. degrees.
Leisure interests: fishing, golfing.
Office: 14 Wall Street, New York, N.Y. 10005; Home: Blooming Grove, Hawley, Pa. 18428, U.S.A.

Blount, Winton M.; American business executive; b. 1 Feb. 1921, Union Springs, Ala.; *s.* of Winton M. Blount and Clara Belle Chalker Blount; *m.* Mary Katherine Archibald 1942; four *s.* one *d*.; ed. Public School, Union Springs, Staunton Military Acad., Univ. of Alabama.
Bomber pilot—World War II; founded Blount Brothers Corpn. 46, Pres. and Chair.; Pres. Chamber of Commerce of U.S. April-Dec. 68; Postmaster-Gen. of U.S. 69-71; Chair. Exec. Cttee. Blount Inc. 73, Chair. of Board, Pres. 74; Republican; Hon. doctorates at Judson Coll., Huntingdon Coll., Birmingham-Southern, Southwestern Univ., Seattle Pacific Coll., Univ. of Alabama, Samford Univ.; Citation for Distinguished Service to City of Montgomery and other awards.
Leisure interests: skiing, tennis, hunting.
Route 10, Box 43, Vaughn Road, Montgomery, Ala. 36111, U.S.A.

Blout, Elkan R(ogers), A.B., PH.D.; American biochemist; b. 2 July 1919, New York, N.Y.; *s.* of Eugene and Lillian Blout; *m.* Joan Dreyfus Blout 1939; two *s.* one *d*.; ed. Phillips Exeter Acad. and Princeton and Columbia Univs.
Associate Dir. of Research, Polaroid Corpn. 48-58, Vice-Pres. and Gen. Man. of Research 58-62; Lecturer in Biophysics, Harvard Medical School 60-62, Prof. of

Biological Chem. 62-, Edward S. Harkness Prof. of Biological Chem. 64-, Chair. Dept. of Biological Chem. 65-69; Nat. Research Fellow, Harvard Univ.; Fellow, American Acad. of Arts and Sciences, A.A.A.S., Optical Soc. of America, New York Acad. of Sciences, mem. Nat. Acad. of Sciences; Hon. A.M.
Leisure interests: boating, deep-sea fishing.
Publs. Various articles in specialized journals, including *Journal of American Chemical Society*, etc.
Department of Biological Chemistry, Harvard Medical School, 25 Shattuck Street, Boston, Mass. 02115; Home: 1010 Memorial Drive, Cambridge, Mass. 02138, U.S.A.
Telephone: 617-734-3300, Ext. 721 (Office); 617-876-3227 (Home).

Bluhdorn, Charles G.; American business executive; b. 20 Sept. 1926, Vienna, Austria; *m.* Yvette LeMarrec 1953; one *s.* one *d*.; ed. City Coll. of N.Y. and Columbia Univ.
Formed own company, Intramex Devt. Co. (import-export co.) 49; acquired Michigan Bumper Co. 56, from which Gulf and Western Corpn. (name changed to Gulf and Western Industries Inc. 60) was formed 58; Chair. and Chief Exec. Gulf and Western Industries Inc. 58-; Chair. Paramount Pictures Corpn., Famous Players' Canadian Corpn.; Exec. Vice-Pres. Southwest Holdings, Inc.; Partner Intramex Devt. Co.; Pres. Fortune Coffee Corpn.
Gulf and Western Industries Inc., 1 Gulf and Western Plaza, New York, N.Y. 10023, U.S.A.

Blume, Peter; American painter; b. 27 Oct. 1906, Smorgon, Russia; *s.* of Harry and Rose Blume; *m.* Grace Douglas Gibbs Craton 1931; ed. New York Educational Alliance Art School.
Exhibited Daniel Gallery New York 26-31, Julien Levy Gallery 37, Durlacher Bros. 47, Kennedy Gallery 68, Danenberg Gallery N.Y. 70, Koe Kerr Gallery 74; Retrospective Exhbn., Paintings and Drawings 26-65, Manchester N.H., and Hartford, Conn. 64, Paintings, Drawings and Sculpture, Museum of Contemporary Art, Chicago 76, and museums throughout U.S.; works in Museum of Modern Art, Whitney, Metropolitan, Newark, Boston, Columbus, Cleveland, Philadelphia and Fogg Museums, Wadsworth Atheneum, Williams, Randolf-Macon Colls., Art Inst. Chicago; prizeman Carnegie Int. Exhbn., Pittsburgh 34, and Artists for Victory Exhbn. 42; Guggenheim Fellowship 32, renewal 36; awarded grant of American Acad. of Arts and Letters and Inst. of Arts and Letters 47; elected Assoc. Nat. Acad. of Design 48; mem. Nat. Inst. of Arts and Letters 50, American Acad. of Arts and Letters 60.
Leisure interest: gardening.
Works: *South of Scranton*, *Parade*, *Light of the World*, *The Eternal City*, *The Rock*, *Passage to Etna*, *Tasso's Oak*, *Winter*, *Summer*, *Recollection of the Flood*, etc.
Sherman Church Road, Sherman, Conn. 06784, U.S.A.
Telephone: 203-354-7429.

Blumenthal W(erner) Michael, PH.D.; American business executive; b. 3 Jan. 1926, Germany; *s.* of Ewald Blumenthal and Rose Valerie (Markt) Blumenthal; *m.* Margaret Eileen Polley 1951; three *d*.; ed. Univ. of California at Berkeley and Princeton Univ.
Went to U.S. 47, naturalized 52; Research Assoc., Princeton Univ. 54-57; Labor Arbitrator, State of New Jersey 55-57; Vice-Pres., Dir. Crown Cork Int. Corpn. 57-61; Deputy Asst. Sec. of State for Econ. Affairs, Dept. of State 61-63; also served as U.S.A. Rep. to UN Comm. on Int. Commodity Trade; mem. U.S.A. Del. to 1961 Punta del Este Conf. which initiated The Alliance for Progress; President's Deputy Special Rep. for Trade Negotiations (with rank of Amb.) 63-67; Chair. U.S. Del. to Kennedy Round tariff talks in Geneva; Pres. Bendix Int. Aug. 67-70; Dir. Bendix Corpn. Nov. 67-, Vice-Chair. June 70-Dec. 70, Pres.

and Chief Operating Officer Jan. 71-March 72, Chair., Chief Exec. Officer and Pres. April 72-; Trustee, The Rockefeller Foundation and Princeton Univ.; Dir. The Equitable Life Assurance Soc. of U.S.A., Atlantic Council of U.S.A., Council on Foreign Relations, Nat. Council for U.S.A.-China Trade; Chair. Board Nat. Cttee. on U.S.A.-China Relations Inc.; mem. Advisory Council on Japan-U.S.A. Econ. Relations and Emergency Cttee. for American Trade (ECAT).
Leisure interests: tennis, skiing.
Office: The Bendix Corporation Executive Offices, Bendix Center, Southfield, Mich. 48076; Home: 505 Barton North Drive, Ann Arbor, Mich. 48105, U.S.A. Telephone: 313-352-5110 (Office).

Blundell, Sir (Edward) Denis, G.C.M.G., G.C.V.O., K.B.E., O.B.E. (Mil.); New Zealand lawyer and diplomatist; b. 29 May 1907, Wellington; s. of Henry Percy Fabian Blundell; m. June Halligan 1945; one s. one d.; ed. Waitaki High School and Trinity Hall, Cambridge. Called to the Bar 29; Barrister and Solicitor, Wellington 30-68; Senior Partner, Bell, Gully and Co.; Served with N.Z.E.F. 39-44; High Commr. for New Zealand in United Kingdom 68-72; Amb. to Ireland 68-72; Chair. Royal Comms. on Parl. Salaries 61, 64, 67-68; Chair. Air Services Licensing Authority 52-62; Pres. N.Z. Cricket Council 57-60, of "Birthright" 61-68, of N.Z. Law Soc. 62-68; fmr. Dir. N.Z. Shipping Co. Ltd., N.Z. Breweries Ltd. and others; Gov.-Gen. of New Zealand 72-.
Leisure interests: cricket, golf, swimming, tennis, walking, squash.
Government House, Wellington, New Zealand.

Blundell, Sir Michael, K.B.E.; British farmer and politician; b. 7 April 1907, London; s. of Alfred Herbert Blundell and Amelia Woodward Richardson; m. Geraldine Lötte Robarts 1946; one d.; ed. Wellington Coll.
Emigrated to Kenya 25; served in Royal Engineers (Col.) 39-45; Comm. for European Settlement 46-47; Chair. Pyrethrum Board of Kenya 49-54, Allsopps African Investments 49-54; mem. Kenya Legislative Council for Rift Valley Constituency 48-58, 61-62; specially selected mem. under Lennox-Boyd Constitution for Kenya, April 58-61; Acting Leader, European Elected mems. 51, Leader 52; Minister on Emergency War Council 54; Minister of Agriculture 55-59, 61-62; Leader New Kenya Party 59-63; Chair. E. A. Breweries Ltd. 64-, Uganda Breweries Ltd. 65-; Dir. Barclays Bank D.C.O. (Kenya) 69; Chair. Egerton Agricultural College 62-72.
Leisure interests: gardening, music, porcelain, wild-life.
Publ. *So Rough a Wind* 64.
P.O. Box 30181, Nairobi, Kenya.
Telephone: Nairobi 63278 and 802701.

Blunden, George, M.A.; British central banker; b. 31 Dec. 1922, Sutton, Surrey; s. of George Blunden and Florence Holder; m. Anne Bulford 1949; two s. one d.; ed. City of London School, Univ. Coll., Oxford.
War service, Royal Sussex Regt. 41-45; Bank of England 47-55; Economist, Balance of Payments Div., Int. Monetary Fund 55-58; various posts, Bank of England 58-65, Deputy Principal, Discount Office 65-67, seconded to Monopolies Comm. 68, Deputy Chief Cashier 68-73, Chief of Man. Services 73-74, responsible for banking supervision with rank of head of dept. 74-76, Exec. Dir. 76-; Chair. Group of Ten Cttee. on banking supervision 75-.
Bank of England, Threadneedle Street, London, EC2R 8AH; Home: Fir Trees, Heath Drive, Walton-on-the-Hill, Tadworth, Surrey, KT20 7QQ, England.

Blunt, Sir Anthony (Frederick), K.C.V.O., M.A., PH.D., F.B.A., F.S.A.; British art historian; b. 26 Sept. 1907, Bournemouth, Dorset; s. of late Rev. A. S. V. Blunt

and Hilda Violet Master; ed. Marlborough and Trinity Coll., Cambridge.
Fellow of Trinity Coll., Cambridge 32-36; on staff of Warburg Inst., London 37-39; Reader in History of Art London Univ. and Deputy Dir. Courtauld Inst. of Art 39; war service, France 39-40, War Office 40-45; Surveyor of the Pictures of King George VI 45-52, of the Queen's Pictures 52-; Prof. of History of Art London Univ. and Dir. Courtauld Inst. of Art 47-74; Slade Prof. of Fine Art, Univ. of Oxford 62-63, Univ. of Cambridge 65-66; Commdr. of Order of Orange-Nassau 48, of Legion of Honour 58; Hon. D.Litt. (Bristol) 61, (Durham) 63, (Oxford) 71; Hon. D. ès L. (Paris) 66; Hon. Fellow, Trinity Coll., Cambridge 67; Fellow Royal Coll. of Art; Hon. F.R.I.B.A.
Publs. *Artistic Theory in Italy* 40, *François Mansart* 41, *French Drawings at Windsor Castle* 45, *Rouault's Miserere* 51, *The Drawings of Nicolas Poussin* (with Walter Friedlaender) 39-75, *Art and Architecture in France 1500-1700* 53, *The Drawings of G. B. Castiglione and Stefano Della Bella at Windsor Castle* 54, *Venetian Drawings at Windsor Castle* 57, *Philibert de l'Orme* 58, *The Art of William Blake* 59, *Roman Drawings at Windsor Castle* (with H. L. Cooke) 60, *Picasso, the Formative Years* (with Phoebe Pool) 62, *Seurat* (introduction and notes) 65, *The Paintings of Nicolas Poussin* 66, *Nicolas Poussin* (2 vols.) 67, *Picasso's Guernica* 67, *Sicilian Baroque* 68, *Supplements to the catalogues of the Italian and French Drawings at Windsor Castle* 71, *Baroque and Rococo Architecture in Naples* 75.
45 Portsea Hall, Portsea Place, London, W.2, England.

Bluyssen, Most Rev. Johannes Wilhelmus Maria; Netherlands ecclesiastic; b. 10 April 1926, Nijmegen; ed. St. Michielsgestel and Haaren Episcopal Seminaries.
Curate Veghel 50-52; Vice-Prefect Seminary St. Michielsgestel 52-54; studied in Rome 54-57; Spiritual Dir. Seminary St. Michielsgestel 57-61; Joint Bishop of 's-Hertogenbosch 61-66, Bishop 66-.
Parade 10, 's-Hertogenbosch, Netherlands.
Telephone: 073-133551.

Blyden, Edward Wilmot, PH.D.; Sierra Leone diplomatist; b. 19 May 1918, Freetown; m.; eight c.; ed. in Sierra Leone and Harvard Univ.
Ozias Goodwin Scholar in Political Science and UNESCO Fellow in Int. Relations, Harvard 51-52; Prof. of Political Science, Fourah Bay Coll., Freetown 51-71; Prof. and Dir. Inst. of African Studies, Nigeria 60-67, Inst. of African Studies, Sierra Leone 67; Amb. to U.S.S.R., also accred. to Bulgaria, Czechoslovakia, Hungary, Poland, Romania, Yugoslavia 71-74, to UN Dec. 74-; visiting prof. and guest lecturer at many colls. and univs. in U.S.A.; has lectured at colls. and univs. in Europe, Africa, Middle East, S.E. Asia, Latin America; rep. at many int. confs.
Publs. articles and publs. on African and int. legal and political questions.
Permanent Mission of Sierra Leone to the United Nations, 919 Third Avenue, 22nd Floor, New York, N.Y. 10017, U.S.A.

Boaten, Frank Edmund; Ghanaian diplomatist; b. 17 Dec. 1923; s. of late Hanson Edmund Acheampong and of Madam Christiana Tumtuo; m. Christina Esther (Amoo-Gottfried) 1955; ed. Univ. Coll. of the Gold Coast and Univ. of London..
First Sec., Ghana High Comm., New Delhi 57-59; Counsellor, Ghanaian Embassy, Moscow 60; Dir. Eastern European Div. and later Dir. of Admin., Accra 60-66; Sec.-Gen. Accra Assembly 62-66; del. numerous confs. Australia, Finland, Sweden, Switzerland, U.S.S.R., U.K. and U.S.A.; Principal Sec. Ministry of Foreign Affairs 66-71; mem. Ghana Constitutional Assembly 69; Visiting Fellow, Queen Elizabeth House and Senior Assoc. mem. St. Antony's Coll., Oxford 71-72; Perm. Rep. to UN. 72-, concurrently Amb. to

Cuba 74-; fmrly. Assoc. mem. Royal Inst. of Int. Affairs, Inst. of Commonwealth Studies.
Leisure interests: coin collecting, tennis.
Permanent Mission of Ghana to United Nations, 150 East 58th Street, 27th Floor, New York, N.Y. 10022, U.S.A.
Telephone: 832-1300.

Bobba, Franco, DR. JUR., DR. RER. POL.; Italian diplomatist; b. 2 Oct. 1913, San Giorgio Lomellina, Pavia; ed. Univ. of Pavia, Acad. of Int. Law, The Hague, Univs. of Berlin and Poitiers.
Entered Ministry of Foreign Affairs 38; Sec. Bône and Berlin 39-43; Ministry of Foreign Affairs 50, concerned with matters relating to European integration and economic co-operation; mem. Italian Del. to Brussels Conf. for negotiation of Rome Treaties and to Interim Cttee. of Rome Treaties; Dir.-Gen. Econ. and Financial Affairs Section, Comm. of EEC; Dir. European Investment Bank until 70; Ministerial rank 62-68; mem. Board of Dirs. and Gen. Man. Istituto Finanzario Industriale (IFI); Vice-Chair. and Man. Dir. Società Assicuratrice Industriale (SAI); Chair. SAIFI S.p.A., SAIFI Management S.p.A.
Corso Galileo Galilei, 12 Turin, Italy.
Telephone: 6562.

Bobbio, Norberto, DR. JUR. ET PHIL.; Italian professor; b. 18 Oct. 1909, Turin; s. of Luigi and Rosa Caviglia; m. Valeria Cova 1943; three c.; ed. Univ. of Turin.
Professor of Legal Philosophy, Univs. of Camerino 35-38, Siena 38-40, Padua 40-48 and Turin 48-; Ordinary Fellow, Accad. dei Lincei.
Publs. *L'analogia nella logica del diritto* 38, *La consuetudine come fatto normativo* 42, *La filosofia del decadentismo* 44, *Studi di teoria generale del diritto* 55, *Politica e cultura* 55, *Italia civile* 64, *Da Hobbes a Marx* 65, *Giusnaturalismo e positivismo giuridico* 65, *Saggi sulla scienza politica in Italia* 69, *Una filosofia militante* 71.
Via Sacchi 66, Turin, Italy.
Telephone: 59-70-56.

Bobleter, Carl H.; Austrian diplomatist; b. 5 July 1912; ed. Innsbrück, Vienna and Paris.
Consul in Hamburg and Düsseldorf 48-50; Attaché, Ministry of Foreign Affairs, Directorate for Political Economy 50-53; Rep. of Austria to High Authority of European Iron and Steel Community 53-58; Rep. of Austria on Council of OEEC, later OECD May 58-60; Austrian Rep. to Council of EFTA in Geneva 60-64; Sec. of State, Ministry for Foreign Affairs, Vienna 64-68; Head, Perm. Austrian Del. to OECD 68-.
Organisation for Economic Co-operation and Development (OECD), Château de la Muette, 2 rue André-Pascal, Paris 16e, France.

Bobrowski, Czeslaw, LL.M.; Polish economist and politician; b. 1 May 1904, Sarny; ed. Warsaw Univ. and Ecole des Sciences Politiques, Paris.
Director, Dept. of Economics, Ministry of Agriculture and Agrarian Reform 45; Pres. Cen. Planning Bureau, Vice-Chair. Economic Cttee., Council of Ministers 45-47; Deputy Chair. Economic Council, Council of Ministers 57-62; Prof. of Econ. Planning, Warsaw Univ. 59-73; Prof. of Econs. Univ. of Paris 69-71, Algiers 71-74.
Ul. Smiala 36 m.2, Warsaw, Poland.

Bochenski, Joseph, O.P., D.D., PH.D.; Swiss (b. Polish) philosopher; b. 30 Aug. 1902, Czuszów, Poland; s. of Adolph and Maria G. Dunin-Borkowska; ed. Univs. of Lwów and Poznań.
Lecturer, Angelicum, Rome 34-36; Prof. 37-40; Docent Univ. of Cracow 38; served Polish Army Great Britain 40-44; Italy 44-45; Extr. Prof. Univ. of Fribourg 45-48, Prof. 48-72; Dean. Faculty of Arts 50-52; Visiting Prof. Univ. of Notre Dame. Ind. 55-56, Univ. of Pittsburgh

58, Univ. of Calif. 58-59; Univ. of Kansas 60; Dir. East-European Study Centre, Fribourg 58, Ost-Kolleg, Cologne 62; Rector, Univ. of Fribourg 64-66, Vice-Rector 66-68; LL.D. h.c.
Leisure interest: flying.
Publs. *De cognitione Exist. Dei* 36, *Elementa logicae Graecae* 37, *Nove Lezioni di Logica Simbolica* 38, *S. Thomae Aq. De modalibus* 40, *La Logique de Théophraste* 47, *Petri Hispani Summulae Logicales* 47, *Europäische Philosophie der Gegenwart* 47, *On Analogy* 48, *Précis de logique mathématique* 49, *Diamat* 50, *Ancient Formal Logic* 51, *Die zeitgenössischen Denkmethoden* 54, *Formale Logik* 56, *Handbuch des Weltkommunismus* (ed.) 58, *Wege zum philosophischen Denken* 60, *Die dogmatischen Grundlagen der sowjetischen Philosophie* 60, *Logic of Religion* 65, Editor *Studies in Soviet Thought* and *Sovietica*.
1 Place Georges Python, CH-1700 Fribourg, Switzerland.
Telephone: 037-22-28-02.

Bochner, Salomon, DR. PHIL.; American mathematician; b. 20 Aug. 1899, Cracow, Poland; s. of Joseph and Rude Bochner; m. Naomi Weinberg 1937 (deceased 1971); one d.; ed. Berlin Univ. and Univs. of Copenhagen, Oxford and Cambridge.
International Educ. Board Fellow 25-27; Lecturer Univ. of Munich 27-33; Faculty mem., Princeton Univ. 33-68, Henry Burchard Fine Prof. 59-68, Prof. Emer. 68-; Edgar Lovett Prof. of Mathematics, Rice Univ. 68-; Assoc. Editor *McGraw Hill Encyclopedia of Science and Technology* 60-; mem. Editorial Board, *Dictionary of the History of Ideas* 67-.
Publs. include *The Role of Mathematics in the Rise of Science* 66, *Eclosion and Synthesis, Perspectives on the History of Knowledge* 69, articles in the *Dictionary of the History of Ideas* 73.
Fine Hall, Princeton University, Princeton, N.J. 08540; and Department of Mathematics, Rice University, Houston, Tex. 77001, U.S.A.
Telephone: (609) 452-4200 (Princeton); (713) 527-4829, Ext. 237 (Houston).

Bochvar, Andrey Anatolevich; Soviet metallographer; b. 8 Aug. 1902, Moscow; ed. Moscow Higher Technical School.
Instructor, Moscow Higher Technical School 23-30; Instructor, Moscow Inst. of Non-Ferrous Metals and Gold 30-34, Prof. 34-60; Prof. Moscow Inst. of Steel 61-; mem. U.S.S.R. Acad. of Sciences 46-; Bureau mem. Physical Chemistry and Technology of Inorganic Materials, U.S.S.R. Acad. of Sciences 63-; State Prize (four), Lenin Prize 61, Hero of Socialist Labour, Hammer and Sickle Gold Medal, Order of Lenin (four), and other awards.
Publs. *Study of Mechanism and Kinetics of Alloy Crystallisation of Eutectic Types* 35, *Principles of Hot Working of Alloys* 40, *On Different Mechanisms of Plasticity in Metallic Alloys* 48, *Metallography* 56, *On the Development of Doubles by Deforming Metals* 64.
Academy of Sciences of U.S.S.R., Leninsky Prospekt 14, Moscow, U.S.S.R.

Bock, Edward John, B.S., M.S.; American chemicals executive; b. 1 Sept. 1916, Fort Dodge, Ia.; s. of Edward J. and Maude (Juday) Bock; m. Ruth Kunerth 1941; two s. two d.; ed. Iowa State Univ.
Joined Monsanto Co. as an engineer 41; Plant Man. Columbia, Tenn. 48; Assoc. Dir. of Marketing, Inorganic Chemicals Div. 56; Dir. of Marketing 57; Asst. Gen. Man. 58, Vice-Pres. 60, Gen. Man. Inorganic Chemicals Div. 60; Vice-Pres. (Admin.), mem. Board of Dirs. and mem. Exec. Cttee. 65; mem. Corporate Devt. Cttee. 67; Pres. of Monsanto Co., Chair. Corporate Devt. Cttee. and Exec. Cttee. 68-72; Dir. Northern Natural Gas Co. of Omaha, Tri-Continental Leasing Co., Curlee Clothing Co.; Pres. and Chief Exec. Officer

Cupples Co., St. Louis 76-; mem. Board of Govs., Iowa State Univ. Foundation.
Leisure interests: amateur radio, golf, hunting, boating.
7 Huntleigh Woods, St. Louis, Mo. 63131, U.S.A.

Bock, Fritz, LL.D.; Austrian politician; b. 1911; ed. Univ. of Vienna.
Joined Austrian People's Party 45; Head of section of Social Policy, Austrian People's Party 47; Gen. Counsellor Austrian Nat. Bank 47-51; M.P. 49-62; Sec. of State, Fed. Ministry of Commerce and Reconstruction 52-55, Fed. Ministry of Finance 55-56; Fed. Minister of Commerce and Reconstruction 56-66; Vice-Chancellor and Minister of Commerce, Trade and Industry 66-68; Vice-Pres. Austrian Econ. Fed.; Chair. Board of Dirs. Creditanstalt Bankverein; Pres. Org. for Int. Econ. Relations; numerous decorations.
Braungasse 47, Vienna XVII, Austria.

Bock, Jerry (Jerrold Lewis); American composer; b. 23 Nov. 1928; ed. Univ. of Wisconsin.
Wrote scores for high school and coll. musicals; author of sketches for television 51-54; composed songs for film *Wonders of Manhattan* 56; composed music for show *Mr. Wonderful* 56, and with Sheldon Harnick (*q.v.*) *The Body Beautiful* 58, *Fiorello* 59 (Pulitzer Prize, Antoinette Perry (Tony) Awards), *Tenderloin* 60, *She Loves Me* 63, *Fiddler on the Roof* 64, *The Apple Tree* 66, *The Rothschilds* 70.
145 Wellington Avenue, New Rochelle, N.Y., U.S.A.

Bod'a, Koloman, D.SC.; Czechoslovak doctor of veterinary medicine and politician; b. 4 April 1927, Horná Strehová; ed. Coll. of Veterinary Medicine, Brno.
Assistant, Faculty of Veterinary Medicine, Agricultural Coll., Košice 51-63; Postgraduate studies, Moscow Veterinary Acad. 55-58; Asst. Prof. Agricultural Coll., Košice 59-62, Prof. 62, Vice-Dean 58-60, Pro-Rector 60-63; Commr. of Slovak Nat. Council for Agriculture and Food 63-68; Minister, Chair. of Fed. Cttee. for Agriculture and Food 69-70; Alt. mem. Central Cttee. of C.P. of Slovakia 58-62, 66-69, mem. 69-71; Alt. mem. Central Cttee. C.P. of Czechoslovakia 62-66, mem. 66-71; mem. Presidium Slovak Nat. Council 63-68, Deputy 66-71; Alt. mem. Presidium of Cen. Cttee. C.P. of Slovakia 66-68, mem. 68-69; Deputy to House of Nations, Fed. Assembly 68-71; mem. Econ. Council of Fed. Govt. 69-70; Corresp. mem. Czechoslovak Acad. of Sciences 65-, Slovak Acad. of Sciences 66-; Chair. Czechoslovak Agricultural Acad. 69-74; Dir. of Research Inst. of the Physiology of Farm Animals, Slovak Acad. of Sciences 72-; Distinction for Merit in Construction 62; Klement Gottwald State Prize 67.
Czechoslovak Academy of Agriculture, Gorkého 32, Prague, Czechoslovakia.

Bode, Hendrik Wade, A.M., PH.D.; American research engineer; b. 24 Dec. 1905, Madison, Wis.; s. of Boyd Henry Bode and Bernice Ballard; m. Barbara L. Poore 1933; two d.; ed. Ohio State Univ. and Columbia Univ.
Assistant, Mathematics Dept., Ohio State Univ. 25-26; mem. Technical Staff, Bell Telephone Lab. 26-67, Research Mathematician 44-52, Dir. Mathematical Research 52-55, Dir. of Research (Physical Sciences) 55-58, Vice-Pres. 58-67; Gordon McKay Prof. of Systems Engineering, Harvard Univ. 67-74, Emer. Prof. 74-; Visiting Fellow, Princeton Univ. 48-49; mem. Nat. Acad. of Sciences (Councillor 67-70); mem. Nat. Acad. of Engineering, Physical Soc., Inst. of Electrical and Electronic Engineers, Amer. Inst. of Aeronautics and Astronautics, Mathematical Soc., Amer. Acad. of Arts and Sciences, etc.; Presidential Certificate of Merit 48; Edison Medal of Inst. of Electrical and Electronic Engineers 69; Oldenburger Medal, A.S.M.E. 75; Hon. Sc.D. (Ohio State Univ.) 70.
Leisure interests: gardening, boating.

Publs. *Network Analysis and Feedback Amplifier Design* 45; patents and papers mostly on electric circuit theory published especially in *Bell System Technical Journal*.
321 Pierce Hall, 29 Oxford Street, Harvard University, Cambridge, Mass. 02138, U.S.A.
Telephone: 617-495-2850.

Boden, Dr. Hans August Constantin; German industrialist; b. 28 July 1893, Brunswick; m. Ellinor Gutheiz 1932; one s. three d.; ed. Univs. of Würzburg and Oxford.
Served with Ministry of Reconstruction and at Finance Ministry; German rep. Reparations Comm. Paris 25-29; Gen. Sec. German Del. to Young Plan Conf. Paris and The Hague 29; Man. Finance Dept. Allgemeine Elektricitäts-Gesellschaft Berlin 29; mem. German Negotiating Cttee. to Schuman Plan Conf. Paris June 50; fmr. Chair. Allgemeine Elektricitäts-Gesellschaft AEG-Telefunken; Hon. Pres. I.C.C., Paris 61.
Kurhessenstrasse 44, 6 Frankfurt/Main, Federal Republic of Germany.
Telephone: 0611-600-3598.

Bodenstein, Dietrich H. F. A., PH.D.; American professor of biology; b. 1 Feb. 1908, Corwingen, E. Prussia; s. of Hans and Charlotte (Lilienthal) Bodenstein; m. Jean Coon 1947; one d.; ed. Univ. of Freiburg, Germany.
Research Asst., Kaiser Wilhelm Inst. of Biology, Berlin 28-33; Research Assoc., German-Italian Inst. of Marine Biology, Rovigno d'Istria, Italy 33-34, Stanford School of Biology, Calif. 34-41; John Simon Guggenheim Memorial Fellow, Dept. of Zoology, Columbia Univ. 41-43; Asst. Entomologist, Conn. Agricultural Experimental Station, New Haven, Conn. 44; Insect Physiologist, Medical Div. Army Chemical Center, Md. 45-57; Embryologist, Nat. Heart Inst., Gerontology Branch, Baltimore City Hospitals 58-60; Lewis and Clark Prof. of Biology, Univ. of Virginia 60-, Chair. of Dept. 60-73; mem. Nat. Acad. of Sciences, American Acad. of Arts and Sciences; Hon. mem. Biological Soc. of Brazil.
Leisure interests: gardening, reading.
Publs. Some 80 publs. in learned scientific journals.
Department of Biology, Gilmer Hall, University of Virginia, Charlottesville, Va. 22903; 536 Valley Road, Charlottesville, Va. 22903, U.S.A.
Telephone: 293-9270 (Home).

Bodian, David, S.B., PH.D., M.D.; American medical scientist and professor of anatomy; b. 15 May 1910, St. Louis, Mo.; s. of Harry Bodian and Tillie Franzel; m. Elinor Widmont 1944; two s. three d.; ed. Univs. of Chicago, Michigan and Johns Hopkins Univ.
Assistant in Anatomy, Univ. of Chicago 35-38; Research Fellow, Univ. of Mich. 38, Johns Hopkins Univ. 39-40; Asst. Prof. of Anatomy, Western Reserve Univ. 41-42; Asst. Prof. of Epidemiology, Johns Hopkins Univ. 42-46, Assoc. Prof. 46-57, Prof. of Anatomy and Dir. Dept. of Anatomy 57-; mem. Nat. Acad. of Sciences, American Acad. of Arts and Sciences, American Asscn. of Anatomists, American Physiological Asscn., American Soc. of Cell Biology, American Philosophical Soc., Soc. for Neuroscience; Hon. mem. Soc. Française de Neurologie, Paris; E. Mead Johnson Award 41, Distinguished Service Award, Univ. of Chicago Alumni 55, U.S. Public Health Service Award 56, Poliomyelitis Hall of Fame, Georgia Warm Springs 57.
Leisure interests: gardening, reading, music, tennis, chess.
Publs. *Neural Mechanisms in Poliomyelitis* (with H. A. Howe) 42; numerous articles on neurobiology, poliomyelitis and experimental neurology in scientific journals 36-71.
School of Medicine, Johns Hopkins University, 725 North Wolfe Street, Baltimore, Md. 21205, U.S.A.
Telephone: 301-825-4608.

Bodson, Victor Hubert Joseph, LL.D.; Luxembourg barrister; b. 24 March 1902, Luxembourg; *m.* Aline Krancher 1952; two *s.* three *d.*; ed. Athénée de Luxembourg and Univs. of Strasbourg, Algiers and Montpellier.
Member Luxembourg Socialist Labour Party 30; mem. Chamber of Deputies 34-61, Communal Council 34-40; Minister of Justice, of Transport and of Public Works 40-47, 51-59; Vice-Pres. Chamber of Deputies 37-40, 48-51, 59-61, Pres. 64-67, Hon. Pres. 67-; Councillor of State 61-64, Hon. Councillor of State 64-; Pres. Int. Asscn. of French-language Parliamentarians 67-72; mem. Comm. of European Communities 67-70; mem. for Luxembourg (Socialist) of Action Cttee. for United States of Europe 59-67; numerous foreign decorations.
Leisure interests: hunting, travel, archaeology, history.
Office: 7 rue Nicolas Welter, Luxembourg; Home: Villa Malpaartes, Mondorf-les-Bains, Grand Duchy of Luxembourg.
Telephone: 42155 (Office); 68915 (Home).

Bodyul, Ivan Ivanovich; Soviet politician; b. 1918; ed. Moscow Military Veterinary Acad. and Higher Party School, Central Committee of C.P.S.U.,
Veterinary Surgeon, Soviet Army 42-46; Asst. Chief. Agricultural Group, Moldavian Council of Ministers 46-48; Govt. Controller of State Farms, Moldavian S.S.R. 48-51; econ. work 52-54; party work 51-52, 54-56; Apparatus of Central Cttee. of C.P.S.U. 58-59; Second Sec. Communist Party of Moldavian S.S.R. 59-61, First Sec. 61-; mem. Central Cttee. of C.P.S.U. 61-; Deputy to Supreme Soviets of U.S.S.R. 65-, and Moldavian S.S.R.
Central Committee of the Communist Party of Moldavia, Kishinev, U.S.S.R.

Boekelheide, Virgil Carl, PH.D.; American professor of chemistry; b. 28 July 1919, S. Dakota; *s.* of Charles F. Boekelheide and Eleanor Toennies; *m.* Caroline A. Barrett 1945; two *s.* one *d.*; ed. Univ. of Minnesota.
Instructor, Univ. of Illinois 43-46; Asst. Prof. to Prof., Univ. of Rochester 46-60; Prof. of Chem., Univ. of Oregon 60-; mem. Nat. Acad. of Sciences 62-; Guggenheim Fellow 53-54; Swiss American Foundation Fellow 60; Roche Anniversary Fellow 63-64; Welch Lecturer 68; Fulbright Distinguished Prof., Yugoslavia 72; mem. Board of Editors *Organic Reactions* 56-, *Organic Syntheses* 56-64, *Journal of American Chemical Society* 64-74; mem. Council for Int. Exchange of Scholars (Sr. Fulbright-Hayes Awards).
Leisure interests: tennis and music.
Publs. 175 original research papers.
2017 Elk Drive, Eugene, Oregon 97403, U.S.A.

Boenisch, Peter H.; German journalist; b. 4 May 1927, Berlin; *s.* of Konstantin Boenisch and Eva Boenisch (née Premysler); *m.* Victoria von Schack 1959; ed. Dr. Hugo Eckner Coll., Berlin Univ.
Political Editor *Die Neue Zeitung* 45-49; Editor *Tagespost* 49-52; Special Asst. to Pres. Nordwest-Deutsche-Rundfunk 52-55; Editor Kindler Publishing Co. 55-59, Springer Publishing Corpn. 59-, *Berliner Illustrierte*; Editor *Bild-Zeitung, Bild am Sonntag*; Vice-Chair. Axel Springer Group, responsible for planning & development; Order of Merit (Fed. Repub. of Germany).
Leisure interests: golf, antiques.
Verlag Axel Springer, Kochstr. 50, 1 Berlin 61, Federal Republic of Germany.
Telephone: Berlin 25 91 449.

Boerma, Addeke Hendrik; Netherlands agricultural engineer; b. 3 April 1912; ed. Agricultural Univ., Wageningen.
Netherlands Farmers' Organisation 34-38; Adviser to Food Office, Ministry of Agriculture 38-41; Dir. Crop Marketing Board 41-44; Govt. Commr. for Food and Agriculture, liberated parts of Netherlands 44; Acting Dir.-Gen. of Food 45; Govt. Commr. for Foreign Agricultural Relations 46; Regional Rep. for Europe, Food and Agriculture Organization of the United Nations (FAO) 48-51, Dir. Econs. Div. FAO 51-58, Head of Program and Budgetary Service, FAO 58-62, Asst. Dir.-Gen. FAO 60-67, Exec. Dir., World Food Program, FAO 62-67, Dir.-Gen. FAO 68-75; Knight, Order of Lion (Netherlands), etc.
c/o Ministry of Foreign Affairs, The Hague, Netherlands.

Boersma, Jacob; Netherlands politician; b. 2 Dec. 1929, Leeuwarden; *m.*; ed. Econ. Inst., Rotterdam and Free (Calvinist) Univ., Amsterdam.
Formerly held various exec. positions in planning, social, advisory and consumer orgs.; mem. Second Chamber of Parl.; mem. European Parl., Strasbourg; Minister of Social Affairs 71-; Calvinist Protestant.
Ministry of Social Affairs, 73 Zeestraat, The Hague, Netherlands.
Telephone: 070-469-470.

Boesch, Hans H., PH.D.; Swiss university professor; b. 24 March 1911; ed. Universität Zürich and Clark Univ., U.S.A.
Professor of Geography, Zürich Univ. 41-, Dir. Geography Inst., Zürich Univ. 42-; Vice-Pres. Int. Geographical Union 49-56, Sec.-Gen. 56-68; Vice-Pres. Int. Council of Scientific Unions 65-68; Hon. D.Sc. (Clark).
Publs. scientific works in field of physical, regional and economic geography.
Geographisches Institut, Universität Zürich, 10 Blümlisalpstrasse, 8006 Zürich, Switzerland.
Telephone: 01-28-96-32.

Boeschenstein, William Wade; American glass executive; b. 7 Sept. 1925, Chicago, Ill.; *s.* of Harold and Elizabeth (Wade) Boeschenstein; *m.* Josephine Moll 1953; four *s.*; ed. Phillips Acad. and Yale Univ.
Owens-Corning Fiberglas Corpn., Detroit 50-, Branch Man. 55-59, Vice-Pres. (Central Region) 59-61, Vice-Pres. (Sales Branch Operations) 61-63, Vice-Pres. (Marketing) 63-67, Exec. Vice-Pres. 67-71, Pres. Aug. 71-, Chief Exec. Officer 73-.
Leisure interests: golf, skiing, tennis.
Owens-Corning Fiberglas Corporation, Fiberglas Tower, Toledo, Ohio 43659, U.S.A.
Telephone: 419-259-3100.

Boeynants, Paul Van Den; Belgian politician; b. 22 May 1919; ed. Collège Saint-Michel.
Former butcher; mem. Chamber of Reps. 49-; Minister of Middle Classes 58; Dir. 1958 Exhbn., Brussels; Chair. Social Christian Party 61-68; Prime Minister 66-68; Minister of Defence 72-, and of Brussels Affairs 74-.
c/o Ministry of Defence, Brussels, Belgium.

Bogaers, Petrus Clemens Wilhelmus Maria, DRS.ECON.; Netherlands trade unionist and politician; b. 2 July 1924, Cuyk a/d Maas; *s.* of Petrus P. M. J. Bogaers and Henrica Maria Hermans; *m.* Femmigje Visscher 1950; four *s.* three *d.*; ed. Episcopal Coll. Grammar School, Roermond, and Tilburg School of Economics.
Assistant to Prof. v.d. Brink 47; Econ. Adviser to Roman Catholic Worker's Union 48, Head, Scientific Advisory Section, Roman Catholic Workers' Union 57-63; Dep. mem. Socio-Economic Council 54; mem. Econ. and Social Cttee. European Economic Communities 58; mem. Second Chamber, Netherlands Parl. 59; Minister of Housing and Building 63-65; Minister of Housing and Physical Planning 65-66; Pres. Gooiland Region 68-74; Commdr., Order of Orange-Nassau.
Leisure interests: reading, tennis, open-air life.
Lingenskamp 25, Laren, North Holland, Netherlands.
Telephone: 83148 (02153).

Bogarde, Dirk (Van den Bogaerde, Derek Niven); British actor; b. 28 March 1920; ed. Allan Glen's School, Glasgow, Univ. Coll. School, London, and Chelsea Polytechnic.

Army Service 40-46.

Roles in plays include Cliff in *Power without Glory* 47, Orpheus in *Point of Departure* 50, Nicky in *The Vortex* 53, Alberto in *Summertime* 55-56, *Jezebel* 58.

Films include *Hunted, Appointment in London, They Who Dare, The Sleeping Tiger, Doctor in the House, Doctor at Sea, Doctor at Large, The Spanish Gardener, Cast a Dark Shadow, Ill Met by Moonlight, A Tale of Two Cities, The Wind Cannot Read, The Doctor's Dilemma, Libel, Song Without End, The Angel Wore Red, The Singer Not the Song, Victim, H.M.S. Defiant, Password is Courage, The Mind Benders, I Could Go On Singing, The Servant, Doctor in Distress, Hot Enough for June, High Bright Sun, King and Country, Darling . . . , Modesty Blaise, Accident, Our Mother's House, Sebastian, Justine, The Fixer, Upon This Rock, The Damned, Death in Venice, The Serpent, The Night Porter, Permission to Kill.*

c/o Harbottle and Lewis, 34 South Molton Street, London, W.1, England.

Bogdan, Corneliu; Romanian diplomatist; b. 5 Nov. 1921, Bucharest; s. of Horia and Silvia Bogdan; m. Emilia Milco 1949; three d.; ed. Inst. for Economic Studies, Int. Relations Dept., Bucharest.

Joined Ministry of Foreign Affairs 48; Counsellor, Wash. 51-53; Deputy Dir. Western Dept., Ministry of Foreign Affairs 53-55, Dir. of Press 55-61, Dir. for Western Europe 61-67; Amb. to U.S.A. 67-; various orders.

Embassy of the Socialist Republic of Romania, 1607 23rd Street, N.W., Washington, D.C. 20008; Home: 2236 Massachusetts Avenue, N.W., Washington, D.C. 20008, U.S.A.

Telephone: (202) 232-4747 (Office).

Bogdanovich, Peter; American film director; b. 30 July 1939, Kingston, N.Y.; s. of Borislav and Herma (Robinson) Bogdanovich; m. Polly Platt 1962 (divorced 1973); two d.

Actor, American Shakespeare Festival, Stratford, Conn. 56, N.Y. Shakespeare Festival 58; Dir. Producer off-Broadway plays, *The Big Knife* 59, *Once in a Lifetime* 64; film critic, writer for *Esquire, New York Times, Village Voice* 59-; Owner Saticoy Productions Inc., Los Angeles 68-; Co-Founder Directors Co. 72; mem. Dirs. Guild of America, Writers' Guild of America, Acad. of Motion Picture Arts and Sciences; N.Y. Film Critics' Award for Best Screenplay (*The Last Picture Show*) 71, Soc. of Film and TV Arts Award 72, Writers' Guild of America Award for Best Screenplay (*What's Up, Doc?*) 72.

Films include: *Targets* (directed, wrote, produced, acted in) 68, *The Last Picture Show* (dir., wrote) 71, *Directed by John Ford* (dir., wrote) 71, *What's Up, Doc?* (dir., wrote, prod.) 72, *Paper Moon* (dir., prod.) 73, *Daisy Miller* (dir., prod.) 74, *At Long Last Love* (dir., wrote, prod.) 75.

Publs. *John Ford* 68, *Fritz Lang in America* 69, *Allan Dwan, the Last Pioneer* 71, *Pieces of Time: Peter Bogdanovich on the Movies* 73, *Picture Shows* 75.

Columbia Pictures, 300 Colgems Square, Burbank, California 91505, U.S.A.

Bogers, Willem Adrianus Johannes; Netherlands business executive; b. 18 June 1922, Venlo; s. of Petrus A. Bogers and Wilhelmina A. C. van Rijt; m. Willy J.Th.M. Coehorst 1951; one s. two d.; ed. Univ. of Econ. Science, Tilburg.

With Univ. of Econ. Science; joined DSM 50, Man.-Dir. 66-73, Chair. 73-; Knight, Order of Netherlands Lion.

Leisure interests: reading, walking, swimming.

DSM, 2 Van der Maesenstraat, Heerlen; Home: Zandweg 22, Heerlen, Netherlands.

Telephone: 045-782520.

Boggs, James Caleb, B.A., LL.B.; American lawyer and politician; b. 15 May 1909, Cheswolc, Del.; s. of Edgar J. and Lettie (Vaughan) Boggs; m. Elizabeth Muir 1931; one s. one d.; ed. Dover High School, Del., Univ. of Delaware and Georgetown Univ. Law School.

Army Command and Gen. Staff Coll., Fort Leavenworth, Kentucky 42; admitted to Bar, Del. Supreme Court 38, U.S. Supreme Court 46; Judge Family Court, New Castle County, Del. 46; mem. U.S. House of Reps. 46-52; U.S. Rep. in Congress 47-53; mem. House Cttees. on Exec. Expenditures, Admin., and Judiciary; Gov. of Delaware 61-73; U.S. Senator for Delaware 61-73; of counsel law firm Bayard, Brill and Handelsman, Wilmington, Del. 73-; Dir. Rollins Int. Inc.; Chair. Nat. Govs'. Conf. 59; Pres. Council State Govts. 60; mem. U.S. Nat. Comm. for UNESCO 64-66, White House Conf. on Int. Co-operation 65, Joint Comm. on Org. Congress 65-66, Nat. Comm. Fire Prevention and Control 71-72, Board Dirs. Blood Bank of Del. Inc., apptd. mem. Joint Cttee. on Econ. Report, 82nd Congress; served to rank of Col. in U.S. army 41-46; mem. American Bar Asscn., Delaware Bar Asscn. American Judicature Soc., American Legion; Croix de Guerre avec Palmes, Legion of Merit, Bronze Star with Cluster, European Theatre Operations ribbon with 5 campaign stars; Republican.

1203 Grinnell Road, Wilmington, Delaware 19806; and 901 Market Street, Wilmington, Delaware 19801, U.S.A.

Boggs, Jean Sutherland, O.C., M.A., PH.D.; Canadian art gallery director; b. 11 June 1922, Negritos, Peru; d. of Oliver Desmond and Humia Marguerite (Sutherland) Boggs; ed. Trinity Coll., Univ. of Toronto, and Radcliffe Coll., Harvard Univ.

Assistant Prof. of Art, Skidmore Coll. 48-49, Mount Holyoke Coll. 49-52; Assoc. Prof. of Art, Univ. of Calif. at Riverside 54-62; Curator, The Art Gallery of Toronto 62-64; Steinberg Prof. of History of Art, Washington Univ. 64-66; Dir. Nat. Gallery of Canada 66-; mem. Canadian Art Museum Dirs. Org., Asscn. of Art Museum Dirs.; Fellow, Royal Soc. of Canada; Trustee American Assoc. of Museums, American Fed. of the Arts; Hon. LL.D. (Univ. of Toronto) 67, (Laurentian Univ., Sudbury) 67, (McMaster Univ., Ont.), Hon. D.U.C. (Univ. of Calgary) 67, Hon. LL.D. (Dalhousie Univ.) 71, Hon. D.Litt. (Mount Holyoke, Mass.) 71, LL.D. (Univ. of Victoria B.C.) 72, (Smith Coll., Mass.) 75.

Publs. *Portraits by Degas* 62; Exhbn. Catalogues: *Picasso the Man* (The Art Gallery of Toronto) 64, *Drawings by Degas* (City Art Museum of St. Louis) 67, *The National Gallery of Canada* 71, *Picasso 1881-1973* 73.

The National Gallery of Canada, Ottawa K1A OM8; Home: 85 Range Road, Ottawa K1N 8J7, Canada.

Telephone: 992-3110 (Office).

Bogianckino, Massimo, PH.D.; Italian opera director; b. 10 Nov. 1922, Rome; s. of Edoardo T. Bogianckino and Fiorangela Liberi; m. Judith Matthias 1950; ed. Conservatory of Music and Acad. Santa Cecilia, Rome and Univ. of Rome.

Former musicologist and concert pianist; Dir. Enciclopedia dello Spettacolo 57-62; Dir. Accademia Filarmonica, Rome 60-63; Dir. Teatro dell' Opera, Rome 63-68; Artistic Dir. Festival of Two Worlds, Spoleto 68-71; Dir. of Concert Programs, Accad. Santa Cecilia, Rome 70-71; Artistic Dir. La Scala, Milan 71-74; Gen. Artistic Consultant Teatro Comunale, Florence 74-; Grosses Bundesverdienstkreuz (Fed. Germany).

Publs. *L'arte clavicembalistica di D. Scarlatti* 56

(English version 68), *Aspetti del Teatro musicale in Italia e in Francia nell' età Barocca* 68.
Teatro Comunale, Florence, Italy.
Telephone: 262842.

Bognár, József; Hungarian politician and scholar; b. 5 Feb. 1917, Szombathely; m. Ida Kutzián 1946; ed. in Budapest.
Studied literature and philosophy; taught in a grammar school; joined the "March Front" Resistance Movement during 39-45 war; joined Smallholders Party; mem. of Parl. 45 and organizer and secretary of the Smallholders Party; Minister of Information 46; Mayor of Budapest 47-48; Vice-Pres. Smallholders Party 48-49; Minister of Internal Trade 48-53, of Internal and Foreign Trade 53-54, of External Trade 54-56; Prof. of Trade Econs., Karl Marx Univ. of Econ. Science, Budapest 57-; Pres. Inst. for Cultural Relations 61-69; mem. Presidium Hungarian-Soviet Friendship Soc. 59-63; mem. Hungarian Acad. of Sciences 65-; Econ. Adviser to Ghanaian Govt. 62; Dir. Inst. for World Econs., Hungarian Acad. of Sciences 66-; Chair. Scientific Council for World Economy 69-; Vice-Pres. Hungarian Econ. Soc.; mem. Board of Dirs., Int. Council of Social Sciences; mem. Scientific Cttee. Istituto di Studi e Documentazione Sull'Est Europeo, Trieste; Editor-in-Chief *Studies on Developing Countries, Acta Oeconomica, Trends in World Economy*, mem. Editorial Board *The New Hungarian Quarterly, Mondes en Développement,* Paris, Hon. Editorial Advisory Board *World Development,* Oxford; Deputy, Hungarian Parl. 45-; Chair. Cttee for Planning and Budget; Vice-Pres. Presidium Patriotic People's Front 65-; Chair. Hungarian World Alliance 59-; Hungarian State Prize 70.
Leisure interests: reading memoirs and historical novels.
Publs. include: *Planned Economy in Hungary: Achievements and Problems* 59, *Kereslet és Kereslethutatás a Szocializmusban* (Demand and Demand Analysis in Socialism) 61, *Economic Growth in the Developing Countries* 66, *Economic Policy and Planning in Developing Countries* 68, *Les nouveaux Mécanismes de l'économie socialiste en Hongrie* 69, and numerous articles.
Scientific Council for World Economy, Budapest XII, Kálló esperes u. 15; Budapest II, Érmelléki-utca 1, Hungary.
Telephone: 664-572; 155-206.

Bogolyubov, Mikhail Nikolayevich; Soviet philologist; b. 24 Jan. 1918, Kiev; ed. Leningrad Univ.
Service in the Army 41-45; Lecturer and Researcher Leningrad Univ. 44-60, Prof. 59-; Dean Oriental Dept. 60-; Corresp. mem. U.S.S.R. Acad. of Sciences 66-.
Leningrad University, Oriental Faculty, 11 Universitetskaya Naberezhnaya, Leningrad, U.S.S.R.

Bogolyubov, Nikolai Nikolayevich; Soviet mathematician; b. 21 Aug. 1909, Gorky.
Professor, Kiev and Moscow Univs. 36-; mem. U.S.S.R. Acad. of Sciences 53-, Academician-Sec. Dept. of Mathematics 63-; mem. Presidium U.S.S.R. Acad. of Sciences; mem. Ukrainian S.S.R. Acad. of Sciences 48-; Foreign mem. Bulgarian and Polish Acads. of Sciences; Foreign mem. German Acad. of Science, Berlin 66, American Acad. of Sciences and Arts, Boston; Dir. Joint Inst. for Nuclear Research, Dubna 65-; Foreign Assoc., Nat. Acad. of Sciences of U.S.A. 69-; Deputy to U.S.S.R. Supreme Soviet 66-; State Prize 47, 53; Lenin Prize; Hero of Socialist Labour; Order of Lenin (five); Hammer and Sickle Gold Medal; Max Planck Medal 73; Franklin Medal 74.
Publs. *New Methods in Calculus of Variations* 32, *Introduction into Non-Linear Mechanics* 37, *Basic Theory of Measuring in Non-Linear Mechanics* 37, *On Some Statistical Methods in Mathematical Physics* 45, *Problems of Dynamic Theory in Statistical Physics* 46,
New Method in Theory of Superconductivity 58, *On the Problem of Hydrodynamics of Superfluid Liquids* 63, *Quasimeans in Problems of Statistical Mechanics* 63, *Asymptomatic Methods in the Theory of Non-Linear Oscillations* 63.
Joint Institute for Nuclear Research, Dubna, Moscow Region, U.S.S.R.

Bogomolov, Alexei Fedorovich; Soviet physicist; b. 2 June 1913, Sitskoe Village, Smolensk Region; ed. Moscow Power Inst.
Postgraduate, Research Assoc. Moscow Power Inst. 37-41; Army Service 41-45; mem. C.P.S.U. 44; Asst. Prof., Head of Chair, Moscow Power Inst. 45-; Doctor of Tech. Sciences, Prof. 58-; Merited Scientist of R.S.F.S.R.; Corresp. mem. U.S.S.R. Acad. of Sciences 66-; Hero of Socialist Labour 57; Order of Lenin (three times); Hammer and Sickle Gold Medal.
Publs. Works on radiophysics and radio engineering.
Moscow Power Institute, 14 Krasnokazarmennaya ulitsa, Moscow, U.S.S.R.

Bogorad, Lawrence, PH.D.; American biologist; b. 29 Aug. 1921, Tashkent, U.S.S.R.; s. of Boris and Florence (Bernard) Bogorad; m. Rosalyn G. Sagen 1943; one s. one d.; ed. Univ. of Chicago.
Instructor, Dept. of Botany, Univ. of Chicago 48-51; Visiting Investigator, Rockefeller Inst. 51-53; Asst. Prof., Dept. of Botany, Univ. of Chicago 53-57, Assoc. Prof. 57-61, Prof. 61-67; Prof. Dept. of Biology, Harvard Univ. 67-, Chair. 74-; mem. Nat. Acad. of Sciences, Chair. Botany Section 74-; Fellow, Amer. Acad. of Arts and Sciences; Pres. Amer. Soc. of Plant Physiologists 68; Fulbright Fellowship 60 and other academic awards.
Publs. various papers in scientific journals.
Harvard University, The Biological Laboratories, 16 Divinity Avenue, Cambridge, Mass. 02138, U.S.A.
Telephone: 617-495-4292.

Bogush, Lev Konstantinovich; Soviet surgeon; b 3 March 1905, Moscow; s. of Konstantin Fedorovich and Antonina Stepanovna Bogush; m. Tamara Vasiljevna Bogush; two s. one d.; ed. Nizhni Novgorod Univ.
Head of Dept. at hospital, Gorky Region 29-40; Master of Medicine 37, Doctor 43; Army Surgeon 40-46; Senior Research Assoc., Inst. of Tuberculosis 46-51; Head of Dept., Central Inst. of Tuberculosis 56-; Prof. Central Advanced Training Inst. 51-; Corresp. mem. U.S.S.R. Acad. of Medical Sciences 57, mem. 63-; mem. Board U.S.S.R. and Moscow Soc. of Phthisiatrists; Order of Red Banner of Labour, Red Star, Patriotic War; Lenin Prize 61; State Prize 74.
Leisure interest: hunting.
Publs. Over 250 works on surgery of pulmonary tuberculosis.
Central Institute of Tuberculosis, Yauza Railway Station, Moscow, U.S.S.R.

Bohan, Marc; French couturier; b. 22 Aug. 1926; s. of Alfred Bohan; ed. Lycée Lakanal, Sceaux.
Assistant with Piguet 45, later with Molyneux and Patou; Dior organization, London 58, later Paris; Artistic Dir. Soc. Christian Dior 60-.
Office: 30 avenue Montaigne, Paris 8e; Home: 18 rue Jean-Goujon, 75008 Paris, France.

Boheman, Erik; Swedish diplomatist, politician and business executive; b. 19 Jan. 1895, Stockholm; s. of Carl and Ellen (née Abramson) Boheman; m. Margaret Mattsson 1932; two s. two d.; ed. Stockholm High School and Univ. of Stockholm.
Army Service 15-18, Foreign Service 18-60, served Paris, London, Foreign Office, Turkey, Bulgaria, Greece, Poland and Romania 18-37; Sec.-Gen., Foreign Office 38-45; Amb. to France 45-47, to U.K. 47-48, to U.S.A. 48-58; Senator for City of Gothenburg 59-70, Vice-Chair. Parl. Foreign Relations Cttee. and Chief

Rep. Opposition 59-, Speaker of First Chamber of Parl. 65-70; Chair. Board AB Svenska Järnvägsverkstäderna, Robert Bosch AB, Svenska Tändsticks AB 73-; Vice-Chair. Board L. M. Ericsson Telephone Co., SAAB-Scania AB, AB Papyrus, Nymoilla Paper Mill Co.; mem. Board Holmens Bruks and Fabrics AB, Scandinavian Airlines System (SAS), Stockholms Enskilda Bank 58-70; the Order of the Seraphim; Grand Cross Order of Vasa; Grand Cross Order of Dannebrog; Grand Cross Finnish White Rose; Grand Officier Légion d'Honneur; Hon. K.B.E. (U.K.) and numerous other foreign decorations; Hon. LL.D. (Tufts Coll., Augustana Coll., Gustav Adolphus Coll., Upsala Coll.).
Publ. *Pd Vakt* (memoirs—2 vols.) 63, 64.
Leisure interests: travelling, golf and farming.
Svenska Tändsticks Aktiebolaget, v. Trädgardsgatan 15, Box 16100, 103 22 Stockholm 16; Home: Anneberg, Graenna, Sweden.

Böhm, Karl, D.IUR.; Austrian musician; b. 28 Aug. 1894; ed. Graz Classical Secondary School, Karl-Franzens Univ., Graz, and under Eusebius Mandyczewski, Vienna.
Conductor, Graz City Theatre 17-21; at Munich State Opera 21-27; Gen. Music Dir., Darmstadt 27-31; at Hamburg 31-33; Dir. Dresden State Opera 34-42; Dir. Vienna State Opera 43-45, 54-56; Conductor, Vienna Philharmonic Orchestra 33-, Berlin Philharmonic Orchestra, New York Philharmonic Orchestra etc.; Guest Conductor Teatro San-Carlo, Naples, Teatro alla Scala, Milan, Teatro Colón, Buenos Aires, Metropolitan Opera, New York, etc.; Conductor at Salzburg Festival, Bayreuth Festival, etc.; Hon. mem. Mozarteum, Salzburg, Music Acad., Graz, Music Soc. of Steiermark, Soc. for Music Theatre, Vienna, Concerthouse Soc., Vienna, Cultural Circle, Vienna, German Opera, Berlin, Vienna Philharmonic Orchestra; Hon. Senator Karl-Franzens Univ., Graz; Hon. Ring of Vienna, Graz, Bayreuth, Steiermark, Vienna Philharmonic Orchestra; Bruckner-Ring of Vienna Symphonic Orchestra; Schalk Medal, Vienna Philharmonic Orchestra; Schmidt Medal, Soc. of Friends of Music, Vienna; Mozart Medal, Mozarteum, Salzburg and Mozart Soc., Prague; Brahms Medal, Hamburg; Great Badge of Honour in Silver; Great Distinguished Service Cross in Gold with Star, etc.; Hon. Citizen of Salzburg, Hon. Prof., Gen. Music Dir. of Austria, Hon. Conductor of Vienna Philharmonic Orchestra; Music Prize of Steiermark, Prize of Art, Berlin, and other awards.
1190 Vienna, Himmelstrasse 41, Austria.

Böhm, Siegfried; German economist and politician; b. 1928.
Member Cen. Cttee. Sozialistische Einheitspartei Deutschlands (SED); Minister of Finance 69-.
Ministerrat, Berlin, German Democratic Republic.

Böhme, Hans-Joachim; German politician and history teacher; b. 1931.
Candidate mem. Cen. Cttee., Sozialistische Einheitspartei Deutschlands (SED); Minister of Higher and Technical Educ.
Ministerrat, Berlin, German Democratic Republic.

Bohr, Aage Niels, DR.PHIL., D.SC.; Danish physicist; b. 19 June 1922, Copenhagen; s. of Prof. Niels Bohr and Margrethe Nørlund; m. Marietta Bettina (née Soffer); two s. one d.; ed. Univ. of Copenhagen.
Associate D.S.I.R., London 43-45; research asst., Inst. of Theoretical Physics, Copenhagen 46; Prof. of Physics, Univ. of Copenhagen 56-; Dir. Niels Bohr Inst. 62-70, Nordita 75-; Hon. Ph.D. (Oslo, Heidelberg, Trondheim, Manchester, Uppsala); mem. Danish, Norwegian, Swedish Acads. of Science, Nat. Acad. of Sciences, U.S.A., American Acad. of Arts and Sciences, American Philosophical Soc.; Dannie Heineman Prize 60, Pius XI Medal 63, Atoms for Peace Award 69, Ørsted Medal 70,

Rutherford Medal 72, John Price Wetherill Medal 74; Nobel Prize for Physics 75.
Publs. *Rotational States of Atomic Nuclei* 54, *Nuclear Structure* Vol. I 69, Vol. II 75 (with Ben R. Mottelson).
Granhøjen 10, Hellerup, Copenhagen, Denmark.
Telephone: GE 346.

Boichenko, Viktor Kuzmich; Soviet government official; b. 21 July 1925; ed. Foreign Trade Inst.
Red Army 42-46; Soviet Trade Mission, Peking 54-55; Dep. Consul, U.S.S.R. Gen. Consulate, Shanghai 55-57, First Sec. Soviet Embassy, Peking 57-59; Dep. Chair. *Intourist* 59-62, First Deputy Chair. 62-64, Chair. 64-69; Dir. Main Board of Foreign Tourism under Council of Ministers 70-; Vice-Pres. Int. Fed. of Nat. Tourist Asscns. 64-66; mem. Joint Temporary Man. Cttee., Universal Fed. of Travel Agents' Asscns. (UFTAA) 66-67; Hero of Soviet Union, Order of Lenin, Order of Red Banner of Labour, Order of Red Star, Gold Star Medal, etc.
Intourist, 16 Prospekt Marxa, Moscow, U.S.S.R.

Boikova, Anna Petrovna; Soviet politician; b. 28 Nov. 1918; ed. Pskov Pedagogical Inst.
Member C.P.S.U. 40-; Teacher, later Headmistress and Education Officer 40-43; party work 43-54; First Sec. Kuibyshev District Cttee. of C.P.S.U. (Leningrad) 54-56; Second Sec. Leningrad City Cttee. C.P.S.U. 56-63; Deputy Chair. Leningrad City Council of Workers' Deputies 63-64, First Deputy Chair. 64-; mem. Central Auditing Comm. C.P.S.U. 56-61; mem. Presidium R.S.F.S.R. Supreme Soviet.
Leningrad City Council of Workers' Deputies, Leningrad, U.S.S.R.

Boisdeffre (Néraud le Mouton de), Pierre Jules Marie Raoul; French writer, diplomatist and broadcasting official; b. 11 July 1926, Paris; s. of Gen. de Boisdeffre; m.; three s.; ed. Lycée Condorcet, Collège Stanislas, Ecole Libre des Sciences Politiques, Ecole Nationale d'Administration and Harvard Univ.
Civil Servant, Ministry of Nat. Educ. 50-55; Deputy Dir. of Press Affairs, Ministry of Foreign Affairs 58-63; Dir. of Sound Broadcasting, Office de Radiodiffusion et Télévision Française (O.R.T.F.) 63-68; Cultural Counsellor, French Embassy, London 68-71, Brussels 71-; Chevalier de l'Ordre National du Mérite, Officier des Arts et Lettres, Chevalier des Palmes Académiques, Officier de l'Etoile Polaire, Chevalier de l'Ordre de la Couronne, Commdr. de l'Ordre Nat. du Cèdre, Commdr. de l'Ordre du Christ; Grand Prix de la Critique (for *Métamorphose de la Littérature*) 50.
Publs. *Métamorphose de la Littérature* (Vol. I *de Barrès à Malraux*, Vol. II *de Proust à Sartre*) 50, *Où va le Roman?* 62, *Les Ecrivains français d'aujourd'hui* 63, *Une histoire vivante de la littérature d'aujourd'hui (1939-64)* 64, *Une anthologie vivante de la littérature d'aujourd'hui* I 65, II 66, *La Cafetière est sur la table* 67, *Lettre ouverte aux hommes de gauche* 69; critical portraits: *Barrès parmi nous* 52, *André Malraux* 52, *Kafka* (with R. M. Albérès) 60, *Barrès* 62, *Giono* 65, *Vie d'André Gide* (Vol. I: *Gide avant la fondation de la N.R.F.*) 70, *Les Ecrivains de la Nuit, Les Poètes Français d'aujourd' hui* 73.
1 Square Marguerite, 1040 Brussels, Belgium.

Boissard, Adéodat Louis; French banker; b. 21 Nov. 1901; ed. Ecole Saint-François-de-Sales, Dijon, Lycée de Dijon, and Univ. de Paris à la Sorbonne.
Inspector of Finances 27; Dir.-Gen. of Estates, Ministry of Finance 40; Gov. Crédit Foncier de France 55-67; Pres. Service d'exploitation industrielle des tabacs et des allumettes (S.E.I.T.A.) 67-71; Pres. Compagnie Française d'Epargne et de Crédit 67-71; Grand Officier Légion d'Honneur.
1 boulevard Beauséjour, Paris 16e, France.

**Boissieu Dean de Luigné, Gen. Alain Henri Paul
Marie-Joseph de;** French army officer; b. 5 July 1914,
Chartres; s. of Henri de Boissieu Dean de Luigné and
Marguérite Froger de Mauny; m. Elizabeth de Gaulle,
d. of Gen. Charles de Gaulle, 1946; one d.; ed. Saint-Cyr
Mil. Acad.
Cavalry Second Lieut. 38, First Lieut. 40; prisoner of
war, escaped, later detained in U.S.S.R.; joined Free
French Forces 41; Capt. 42; Staff, High Commr. in
Indian Ocean 44-45; Maj. 45, Lieut.-Col. 53; Commdg.
Officer 4th Regiment of Chasseurs, Algeria 56-58; Col.
58; Chief Mil. Staff, High Commr. in Algeria 58; Chief of
Staff Armour Directorate 59; Commdg. Officer 2nd
Armoured Brigade 62; Brig.-Gen. 64; Commdg. Gen.
Saint-Cyr Mil. Acad. and Ecole Mil. Inter-Armes de
Coëtquidan 64-67; Commdg. Gen. 7th Div. 67; Maj.-
Gen. 68; Inspector of Armour 69; Lieut.-Gen. 70; mem.
Army Council 71; Gen., Chief of Staff of French Army
75-; Grand Chancellor, Order of the Legion of Honour
Feb. 75-; Grand Croix Légion d'Honneur; Compagnon
de la Libération; Croix de Guerre; Croix de la Valeur
Mil.; Knight of Malta; Hon. K.B.E., and other decora-
tions.
Leisure interests: riding, hunting.
Grande Chancellerie, 1 rue de Solférino, 75007 Paris,
France.

Boitsov, Vassily Vassilevich; Soviet technologist and
politician; b. 1908; ed. Moscow Higher Technical School.
Engineering posts 37-46; Dir. of Scientific Research of
technological institute 47-63; Chair. State Cttee. of
Standards, Measures and Measuring Instruments 63-70,
State Cttee. of Standards, U.S.S.R. Council of Ministers
70-; mem. Communist Party of Soviet Union; Deputy
to Supreme Soviet of R.S.F.S.R.
State Committee of Standards, 9 Leninsky Prospekt,
Moscow, U.S.S.R.

Bojart Ortega, Rafael; Argentine university professor;
b. 12 April 1920, Buenos Aires; s. of Rafael Bojart
Ceballos and Hemilce Ortega; m. Haydée Albistur
Pando 1944; two s.; ed. Univs. of Buenos Aires, El
Salvador, Barcelona and Columbia Univ., New York.
Founder Academia de Estudios Históricos Bartolomé
Mitre 58, Univ. of Morón 60, Instituto Enrique Larreta
64, Academia Internacional de Historia 65, Instituto
Americano de Futurología 75; Pres. Academia de
Estudios Históricos Bartolomé Mitre, Academia Inter-
nacional de la Historia, Rector, Univ. of Morón; mem.
Real Academia Hispano-americana de Cádiz, Academia
Argentina de Diplomacia, Academia de Estudios Par-
lamentarios y Legislativos Internacionales, Instituto
de Cultura Americana de Madrid, Instituto Argentino
Hispánico, Asociación Internacional de Derecho;
Médaille Etoile Civique, Paris.
Publs. *Introducción a la filosofía, Filosofía de la Historia,
La Poesía Epica Medieval, La Estética Contemporánea,
La Esencia de la Poesía, El Motivo de la Angustia en el
Existencialismo, La Poesía de Carlos Obligado, La
Inteligencia en el Gobierno de los Pueblos, Ricardo Rojas
y el Futuro de América, El Hispanismo en Larreta,
La Poesía de Cesar Rosales, Como Hacer un Best Seller,
Qué es la Futurología, Borges Escritor, La Fuerza del
Occidente;* novels *La Música de la Montaña, El Hombre
Nuevo, Una Aventura en el Año 2000;* plays: *Polichinela,
Los Hijos que no Nacieron.*
San Martín 933, piso 7°, Depto. 51, Buenos Aires,
Argentina.
Telephone: TE-31-2052.

Bok, Bart Jan, PH.D.; American (naturalized 1938)
emeritus professor of astronomy; b. 28 April 1906,
Hoorn, Holland; s. of Jan Bok and Gesina Annetta Van
Der Lee; m. Priscilla Fairfield 1929; two c.; ed. Univs.
of Leiden and Groningen.
R. W. Willson Fellow in Astronomy, Harvard Univ.
29-33, Asst. Prof. in Astronomy 33-39, Assoc. Prof. of
Astronomy 39-46, Assoc. Dir. Harvard Observatory
46-52, Robert Wheeler Willson Prof. of Astronomy,
Harvard Univ. 47-57; Prof. of Astronomy, Australian
Nat. Univ. 57-66; Dir. Mount Stromlo Observatory,
Canberra, Australia 57-66; Prof. of Astronomy, Univ.
of Arizona 66-74; Head, Dept. of Astronomy, and Dir.
Steward Observatory 66-70; Vice-Pres. Int. Astrono-
mical Union 70-76, Nat. Acad. of Sciences; mem.
American Astronomical Soc. (Pres. 72-74), American
Asscn. for Advancement of Science, American
Acad. of Arts and Sciences; Fellow, Royal Astronomical
Soc., London, Inst. of Physics, Australia; Hon. mem.
Royal Astronomical Soc. of Canada, Royal Astrono-
nomical Soc. of N.Z., Astronomical Soc. of Australia;
Corresp. mem. Royal Netherlands Acad. of Arts and
Sciences; mem. Royal Soc. of Sciences, Uppsala;
Orange-Nassau Medal, Netherlands.
Publs. *The Distribution of Stars in Space* 37, *The Milky
Way* (with Mrs. Bok) 41 (fourth revised edn. 74), *Basic
Marine Navigation* (with F. W. Wright) 44, *The
Astronomer's Universe* 58; 200 articles; principal field is
Milky Way research, with long-standing emphasis on
S. Milky Way; also cosmic evolution, star clouds of
Magellan, radio astronomy.
Steward Observatory, University of Arizona, Tucson,
Ariz. 85721; Home: 200 Sierra Vista Drive, Tucson,
Ariz. 85719, U.S.A.
Telephone: 602-795-0061, 604-884-2589.

Bok, Derek Curtis, M.A., LL.B.; American university
administrator; b. 22 March 1930, Bryn Mawr, Pa.; s. of
late Curtis Bok and Margaret Plummer (now Mrs. W. S.
Kiskadden); m. Sissela Ann Myrdal (d. of Karl Gunnar
and Alva Myrdal q.v.) 1955; one s. two d.; ed. Stanford
Univ., Harvard Univ., Inst. of Political Science, Paris
Univ. and George Washington Univ.
Served U.S. Army 56-58; Asst. Prof. of Law, Harvard
Univ. 58, Prof. 61-; Dean, Harvard Law School 68-71;
Pres. Harvard Univ. July 71-.
Leisure interests: gardening, tennis, swimming.
Publs. include: *The First Three Years of the Schuman
Plan, Cases and Materials on Labor Law* (with Archi-
bald Cox), *Labor in the American Community* (with
John Dunlop).
Office of President, Harvard University, Cambridge,
Mass. 02138, U.S.A.
Telephone: 617-495-1502.

Bokassa, Marshal Jean Bédel; Central African Repub-
lic army officer and politician; b. 22 Feb. 1921, Boban-
gui, Lobay; s. of the late Mindogon Mgboundoulou and
Marie Yokowo; m. Catherine Dengueade; ed. Ecole
Sainte Jeanne-d'Arc, M'Baiki, Ecole Missionnaire,
Bangui, and Ecole Missionnaire, Brazzaville.
Joined French Army 39, rose to Captain 61; organized
Central African Repub. (CAR) Army, C.-in-C. 63-; took
power in military coup Dec. 65; Pres. of CAR Jan. 66-,
Prime Minister 66-75; Minister of Defence 66-, of Jus-
tice 66-70, of Information 70-74, of Agriculture and
Stockbreeding 70-74, of Public Health and Population
Jan. 71-, also Minister of Civil and Mil. Aviation and of
Civil Service 73-, of Land, River and Air Transport
Oct. 73-, of Trade and Industry 73-74, of Mines 73-;
Leader Mouvement d'évolution sociale de l'Afrique
noire (MESAN); Pres. Union douanière et économique
de l'Afrique centrale (UDEAC); Légion d'Honneur,
Croix de Guerre; Marshal of CAR 74.
Office of the President, Bangui, Central African
Republic.

Bokhorst, Matthys, LITT.D., D.PHIL.; South African
art historian; b. 28 Aug. 1900, Rotterdam, Netherlands;
s. of P. F. Bokhorst and J. C. de Kok; m. P. W. M.
Groenhart 1946; three s.; ed. Rotterdam, Leyden Univ.
and Switzerland.
Professor of Netherlands Cultural History and Dir.
Neths. Inst. Pretoria Univ. 29-51; Editor *Nederlandse*

Post 51-; Prof. of Cultural History of Western Europe, Univ. of Cape Town 73-; Pres. South African Asscn. of Arts 51-58; Chair. Govt. Art Advisory Comm. 52-68; Dir. Michaelis Art Gallery 56-64; Dir. South African National Gallery 62-73; mem. Exec. Council of South African Museums Asscn. 58-, Pres. 71-73; mem. Nat. Arts Comm. 68-; Medal of Honour, S.A. Akademie vir Wetenskap en Kuns 70; Officer Order of Orange-Nassau 73.
Leisure interest: fine arts.
Publs. *Nederlands-Zwitserse Betrekkingen voor en na 1700* 30, *Kultuur van een Waterland* 37, *Handvest der Vryheid* 44, *Die Kuns van'n Kwarteeu* 54, *Art at the Cape* 64, *The S.A. National Gallery* 65, *François Levaillant* (co-author) 73.
"Het Trappenhuis", Talma Road, Muizenberg, Cape Town, South Africa.
Telephone: 85345.

Boland, Frederick Henry, B.A., LL.B.; Irish former diplomatist and businessman; b. 1904, Dublin; *s.* of Henry Patrick Boland and Charlotte (née Nolan); *m.* Frances Josephine Kelly; one *s.* four *d.*; ed. Clongowes Wood Coll., Trinity Coll., Dublin, King's Inn, Dublin, Harvard and Chicago Univs.
Third Sec. Irish Foreign Service 29; First Sec. Paris 32; Head of L.N. Section, Dublin 34; Head of Div., Dept. of Industry and Commerce 36; Asst. Sec. Dept. of External Affairs 38, Perm. Sec. 46; Amb. to Great Britain 50-56; Rep. to UN 56-64; Chancellor, Dublin Univ. 64-; Chair. IBM Ireland Ltd.; Dir. Investment Bank of Ireland 64-, Arthur Guinness Son & Co. 64-, Irish Distillers Ltd., Insurance Corpn. of Ireland Ltd., Fitzwilton Ltd., Cement Ltd., Gresham Hotels Ltd.; Pres. 15th Session, UN Gen. Assembly; mem. Royal Irish Acad.; Knight Commdr. Order of St. Gregory (Holy See), Grand Cross, Order of North Star (Sweden); Hon. LL.D.
Leisure interests: reading, fly fishing, piano.
60 Ailesbury Road, Dublin, Ireland.
Telephone: 693599.

Boland, Kevin; Irish politician; b. 15 Oct. 1917, Dublin; *s.* of Gerald Boland and Annie Keating; *m.* Cecilia Finneran 1951; two *d.*; ed. St. Joseph's Christian Brothers' Schools, Marino, Dublin, O'Connell Schools, Dublin, and Univ. Coll., Dublin.
Member Dublin Corpn., Grangegoram Mental Hospital Board and Dublin Fever Hospital Board 55-57; mem Parl. Dublin 57-June 70; Minister for Defence 57-61, for Social Welfare 61-66, for Local Govt. 66-70, and for Social Welfare 69-70; Leader, Republican Unity Party (Aontacht Éireann) 71-.
Red Gap, Rathcoole, Co. Dublin, Ireland

Boldizsár, Iván; Hungarian writer and journalist; b. 30 Oct. 1912, Budapest; *m.* Josette Dubruel 1941; two *s.* one *d.*; ed. Budapest Univ.
An early member of the progressive village research movement in Hungary; Editor-in-Chief of Information, Peace Conf. Del. 46; Del. for UNESCO 46; Sec. of State in Hungarian Ministry of Foreign Affairs 47-51; Editor *Magyar Nemzet* 51-55, *Hetfoi Hirlap* 56, *Tukor (Mirror)* 57-58, *The New Hungarian Quarterly* 60-; Pres. Hungarian PEN Club 64-; Dr. h.c. (Union Coll., Schenectady, N.Y.) 71; Labour Order of Merit Golden Degree; State Prize, 1st Degree 75.
Leisure interest: grandchildren.
Publs. *A nyugati kapu Tiborc, A gazdag parasztok orszaga, Fortocska Téli parbaj, Magyarorszagi Napló, A toll fegyverével, A reménység üzenete, Reggeltől reggelig, Tiborc uj arca, Balatoni Kaland, Magyarorszag Utikönyu, Születésnap, Az éjszaka végén, Rokonok és indegenek, Zsiráffal Angliában* (Doing England with a Giraffe 69), *Királyalma, Tulélök* (play), *Az angyal lába,*

New York Percrol percre, A filozófus oroszlán, Halálaim, A Szárnyas ló.
Balogh Adám-utca 29, 1026 Budapest II, Hungary.
Telephone: Budapest 136-857.

Bolduman, Mikhail Panteleimonovich; Soviet actor; b. 12 July 1898.
Zhmerinka Drama Group, Ukraine 23; Kiev Russian Drama Theatre 24-31; Moscow Korsh Theatre 31-33; Moscow Art Theatre 33-; also films; State Prize of the U.S.S.R. (twice), People's Actor of R.S.F.S.R. and other awards.
Moscow Art Theatre, 3 Proyezd Khudozhestvennogo Teatra, Moscow, U.S.S.R.

Bolin, (Axel) Bertil; Swedish lawyer and international official; b. 8 Nov. 1923, Törnevalla; *s.* of A. G. and Gotty Bolin; *m.* Thea Burland 1971; one *s.* one *d.* (by previous marriage); ed. Univ. of Uppsala.
Legal Adviser to Swedish Confederation of Trade Unions 56-62, Dir. for Int. Affairs 62; mem. Swedish Del. to UN Gen. Assembly, mem. Industrial Devt. Board 62-69; mem. ILO Gov. Body 65-68, Asst. Dir.-Gen. 68-74, Deputy Dir.-Gen. 74-; mem. Int. Comm. of Jurists, Int. Asscn. for Industrial Relations, Swedish Labour Law Asscn., several Swedish Royal Comms.
Leisure interests: skiing, tennis, gardening.
Publs. *Swedish Labour Law, Holidays with Pay* (in Swedish), *Labour Market and Trade Unions in Developing Countries* (in Swedish), *Consumer Rights.*
International Labour Organisation, route de Morillon, 1218 Geneva; Home: 14 chemin de la Tourelle, 1209 Geneva, Switzerland.
Telephone: 98-10-88 (Geneva).

Boling, Edward J., M.S., ED.D.; American university president; b. 19 Feb. 1922, Sevier County, Tenn.; *s.* of Sam R. and Nerissa (Clark) Boling; *m.* Carolyn Pierce 1950; three *s.*; ed. Univ. of Tenn. and George Peabody Coll.
With Union Carbide Corpn. of Oak Ridge, Tenn. 51-54; State Budget Director 54-58; Commr. of Finance and Admin. 58-61; Vice-Pres. for Devt. and Admin., Univ. of Tenn. 61-70; Pres. Univ. of Tenn. 70-.
Leisure interests: boating, golf.
Suite 800, Andy Holt Tower, Tennessee University, Knoxville, Tennessee 37916, U.S.A.
Telephone: 615-974-2241 (Office); 615-588-1924 (Home).

Bolkiah Mu'izuddin Waddaulah, H.H. Sultan Hassanal, D.K., P.S.P.N.B., P.S.N.B., P.S.L.J., S.P.M.B., P.A.N.B.; Sultan of Brunei; b. 15 July 1946; *s.* of former Sultan Sir Muda Omar Ali Saifuddin, K.C.M.G. (q.v.); ed. privately, and Victoria Inst., Kuala Lumpur, Malaysia, and Royal Military Acad., Sandhurst.
Appointed Crown Prince and Heir Apparent 61; Ruler of State of Brunei Oct. 67-; Hon. Capt. Coldstream Guards 68; Sovereign and Chief of Royal Orders instituted by Sultans of Brunei.
Istana Darul Hana, Brunei.

Bölkow, Ludwig, DIP.ENG.; German aviation executive; b. 30 June 1912, Schwerin; ed. Technische Hochschule, Berlin.
Engineer, Messerschmitt AG 39-45; Founder Bölkow (IBB) engineering co., Stuttgart 48; Founder Bölkow-Entwicklungen KG (later Bölkow G.m.b.H.) 56; Shareholder and Pres. Messerschmitt-Bölkow-Blohm G.m.b.H., Ottobrunn; Deputy Chair. of Supervisory Board, Deutsche Airbus G.m.b.H., Munich; Chair. Board of Dirs. Panavia Aircraft G.m.b.H., Munich; mem. Admin. Board, Airbus-Industrie, Paris; mem. Board of Dirs., Deutsche Gesellschaft für Luft- und Raumfahrt e.V., Berlin; mem. of Senate, Deutsche Forschungs- und Versuchsanstalt für Luft- und Raumfahrt e.V., Porz-Wahn; Bavarian Order of Merit; Ring of Honour Soc. of German Engineers; Gold Diesel medal; Ludwig-Prandtl Ring, Deutsche Gesellschaft

für Luft- und Raumfahrt; Pionierkette der Windrose; Distinguished Service Cross, Fed. Repub. of Germany Order of Merit; Werner-von-Siemens Ring of Honour; Dr. Ing. h.c. Technische Universität, Stuttgart.
Messerschmitt-Bölkow-Blohm G.m.b.H., 8012 Ottobrunn, Federal Republic of Germany.

Böll, Heinrich Theodor; German writer; b. 21 Dec. 1917; *m.*; three *s.*
President, Int. PEN until 74; Nobel Prize for Literature 72.
Publs. *Der Zug war pünktlich* 49, *Wanderer, kommst du nach Spa?* 50, *Die schwarzen Schafe* 51, *Wo warst du, Adam?* 51, *Und sagte kein einziges Wort* 52, *Nicht nur zur Weihnachtszeit* 52, *Haus ohne Hüter* 54, *Das Brot der frühen Jahre* 55, *So ward Abend und Morgen* 54, *Unberechenbare Gäste* 56, *Im Tal der donnernden Hufe* 57, *Irisches Tagebuch* 57, *Die Spurlosen* 57, *Dr. Murkes Gesammeltes Schweigen* 58, *Billard um Halbzehn* 59, *Erzählungen, Hörspiele, Aufsätze* 61, *Ein Schluck Erde* 62, *Ansichten eines Clowns* 63, *Entfernung von der Truppe* 64, *Als der Krieg ausbrach* (stories) 65, *Frankfurter Vorlesungen* 66, *Ende einer Dienstfahrt* 66, *Aufsätze, Kritiken, Reden* 67, *Hausfriedensbruch* 70, *Aussatz* 70, *Gruppenbild mit Dame* 71, *Gedichte* 73, *Die verlorene Ehre von Katharina Blum* 74.
Belvederestrasse 35, Cologne-Müngersdorf, Federal Republic of Germany.

Bolle, Eivind; Norwegian fisherman and politician; b. 13 Oct. 1923.
Member Vestvågøy Municipal Council 63-, Chair. 72-; mem. Board Nordland County Fishermen's Asscn. 65-71, Nat. Exec. Norwegian Fishermen's Asscn. 65-73; mem. Board Norwegian Raw Fish Dealers' Asscn. 70-, Deputy Chair. 72-; mem. Cen. Board, State Bank for Fisheries; mem. Storting (Parl.) for Nordland 73-; Minister of Fisheries 73-; Labour.
Ministry of Fisheries, Oslo Dep., Norway.

Bollnow, Otto Friedrich, DR. PHIL.; German philosopher; b. 14 March 1903, Stettin; *s.* of Otto and Frida Bollnow; *m.* Dr. Ortrud Bürger 1938; one *s.* two *d.*; ed. Univs. of Berlin, Greifswald and Göttingen.
Teacher of Philosophy and Education, Göttingen 31-39; Prof. of Psychology and Education, Giessen 39-46; Prof. of Philosophy and Education, Mainz 46-53, Univ. of Tübingen 53-, Prof. Emer. 70.
Publs. *Dilthey* 36, *Das Wesen der Stimmungen* 41, *Existenzphilosophie* 43, *Einfache Sittlichkeit* 47, *Rilke* 51, *Die Pädagogik der deutschen Romantik* 52, *Neue Geborgenheit: Das Problem einer Überwindung des Existenzialismus* 55, *Die Lebensphilosophie* 58, *Wesen und Wandel der Tugenden* 58, *Existenzphilosophie und Pädagogik* 59, *Mass und Vermessenheit des Menschen* 62, *Mensch und Raum* 63, *Die Pädagogische Atmosphäre* 64, *Französischer Existentialismus* 65, *Krise und neuer Anfang* 66, *Sprache und Erziehung* 66, *Philosophie der Erkenntnis* Vol. I 70, Vol. II 75, *Das Verhältnis zur Zeit* 72.
Waldeckstrasse 27, 74 Tübingen, Federal Germany.
Telephone: 07071-4076.

Bolshukhin, Vasily Ivanovich; Soviet politician; b. 1924; ed. special secondary school.
Army service 42-47; Foreman, copper works plant 41, 47-; Deputy to U.S.S.R. Supreme Soviet 66-, also mem. Presidium; Hero of Socialist Labour, Order of Lenin, Hammer and Sickle Gold Medal, etc.
Presidium of U.S.S.R. Supreme Soviet, Kremlin, Moscow, U.S.S.R.

Bolt, Robert Oxton, C.B.E.; British playwright; b. 15 Aug. 1924; *s.* of Ralph and Leah Bolt (née Binnion); *m.* 1st Celia Roberts 1950, 2nd Sarah Miles 1967 (divorced); two *s.* two *d.*; ed. Manchester Grammar School and Manchester Univ.
Office Boy, Insurance Office, Manchester 41-42;

Manchester Univ. 43; R.A.F. and W. African Frontier Force 43-46; Teacher, Bishopsteignton Village School 50-51, Millfield School, Somerset 51-58; freelance writer 58-; Oscar for *A Man for All Seasons* (film) 67.
Plays: *Flowering Cherry* 57, *The Tiger and the Horse* 59, *A Man for all Seasons* 61 (film 67), *Gentle Jack* 63, *The Thwarting of Baron Bolligrew* (for children) 66, *Brother and Sister* 67, *Vivat! Vivat! Regina* 70; Filmscripts: *Lawrence of Arabia* 62, *Dr. Zhivago* 64, *Ryan's Daughter* 70, (also Dir.) *Lady Caroline Lamb* 72.
c/o Margaret Ramsay Ltd., 14A Goodwin's Court, St. Martin's Lane, London, W.C.2, England.

Bolte, Hon. Sir Henry Edward, G.C.M.G., M.P.; Australian farmer and politician; b. 20 May 1908, Ballarat, Victoria; *s.* of late J. H. Bolte and Mrs. A. J. Bolte; *m.* Edith L. Elder 1934; ed. Ballarat Church of England Grammar School.
Served Second World War in Australian Imperial Forces; mem. Victoria Legislative Assembly for Hampden 47-; Minister of Water Supply, Mines and Conservation 48-50; Premier, Treasurer 55-72, and Minister for Conservation (Victoria) 55-61; Leader, Liberal Party of Victoria 53-72; Hon. LL.D. Melbourne Univ. 65, Monash Univ. 67.
Leisure interests: horse racing, cricket, shooting, golf.
"Kialla", Meredith 3333, Victoria, Australia.

Bolton, Sir George Lewis French, K.C.M.G.; British banker; b. 16 Oct. 1900, London; *s.* of William Lewis George and Beatrice Louise Bolton; *m.* May Howcroft 1928; one *s.* two *d.*
Société Générale de Paris 17; Helbert, Wagg & Co. Ltd. 20; Bank of England to assist in management of Exchange Equalisation Fund 33; Tripartite Monetary Agreement 36; Adviser to Bank of England 41-48; Exec. Dir. of Bank of England 48-57, Dir. 57-68; Dir. Bank for Int. Settlements 49-57; Exec. Dir. Int. Monetary Fund 46-52, Alt. Gov. 52-57; Chair. Bank of London and South America 57-70; Chair. Commonwealth Devt. Finance Co. Ltd. 68-, Australian Urban Investments Ltd., Int. Banking Services 68-, London United Investments Ltd. 71-, Premier Consolidated Oilfields Ltd. 74; Deputy Chair. Lonrho 73-; fmr. Chair. Bank of London and Montreal Ltd.; Dir. Canadian Pacific Steamships Ltd., Canadian Pacific Oil & Gas of Canada Ltd., Lloyds Bank Int. Ltd., Sun Life Assurance Co. of Canada (U.K.) Ltd., Canadian Enterprise Devt. Corpn. Ltd.
Lloyds Bank International Ltd., 100 Pall Mall, London, S.W.1; Pollards Cross, Hempstead, Essex, England.
Telephone: 01-930-2313.

Bolz, Lothar, DR. JUR.; German lawyer and politician; b. 3 Sept. 1903; ed. Univs. of Munich, Kiel and Breslau.
Held various legal positions 26-30; law practice 30-33; in exile in Poland and U.S.S.R. 33-47; Minister for Construction, German Democratic Repub. 49-53; Chair. Council of Ministers 50-67, Minister of Foreign Affairs 53-65; Chair. Nat. Democratic Party of Germany 48-69; Vaterländischer Verdienstorden in Gold, Orden Banner der Arbeit and other awards.
Friedrichstrasse 65, Berlin, German Democratic Republic.

Bomani Paul Lazaro; Tanzanian politician; b. 1 Jan. 1925, Musoma; *s.* of Rev. Lazaro Bomani; ed. Ikizu Secondary School.
Employee, Williamson Diamonds Ltd. 45-47; Asst. Sec., later Sec. Mwanza African Traders' Co-operative Soc.; Organizer, Lake Province Growers' Asscn. 52; studied Co-operative Development at Loughborough Coll. 53-54; mem. Legislative Council 55; Manager Victoria Fed. of Co-operative Unions Ltd. 55; Minister of Agriculture, Tanganyika 60-62, of Finance 62-64, Minister of Finance of Tanzania 64-65, for Econ. Affairs and Devt. Planning 65-67, of Commerce 67-72,

and of Industries 70-72; Gov. of IBRD (World Bank) for Tanzania 67-70; Amb. to U.S.A. 72-.
Leisure interests: soccer, swimming, fishing, music, reading.
Embassy of Tanzania, 2010 Massachusetts Avenue, N.W., Washington, D.C., U.S.A.

Bombassei Frascani de Vettor, Giorgio; Italian diplomatist; b. 29 June 1910, Florence; *s.* of Alfredo Bombassei Frascani de Vettor and Margherita Tidone Peri; *m.* Eli Tramontani 1940; one *s.*; ed. Università degli Studi, Florence and Inst. of Political and Social Sciences "Cesare Alfieri", Florence.
Italian Diplomatic Service 33-, served Egypt, U.S.A., France, Ceylon, U.S.S.R., Switzerland, Brazil 33-52; Deputy Dir. of Int. Co-operation, Ministry of Foreign Affairs 52-56, Deputy Dir.-Gen. of Political Affairs 56-57; Perm. Rep. of Italy to Council of Europe 57-61; Ambassador to Luxembourg 61-67; Perm. mem. Italian Del. to Special Council of Ministers of European Coal and Steel Community (ECSC) 61-67; Amb. to the Netherlands 65-67; Perm. Rep. of Italy to the European Communities 67-; Grand Cross Officer Order of Merit (Italy), Medal of Freedom (U.S.A.) and other decorations.
Leisure interests: golf, bridge.
Italian Permanent Delegation to the European Communities, 74 rue de la Loi, Brussels, Belgium.
Telephone: 513-45-90.

Bompiani, Conte Valentino; Italian publisher; b. 27 Sept. 1898, Ascoli Piceno; *s.* of Gen. Giorgio Bompiani and Anna Chiari; *m.* Lucia Bregoli 1932; two *d.*; graduated in law.
Founded own publishing house, Milan 29; Bompiani have published *Dizionario Letterario delle Opere e dei Personaggi, Dizionario Biografico degli Autori* (under auspices of UNESCO); has written nine plays which have been produced; Pres. Soc. Italiana degli Autori ed Editori, Rome; Libro d'Oro from Presidency of Council of Ministers; Medaglia d'Oro from City of Milan; Medaglia d'Argento al Valor Civile; Silver Medal, Carnegie Foundation; other decorations.
Office: Via Carlo Pisacane 26, 20129 Milan; Home: Via San Primo 6, 20121 Milan, Italy.
Telephone: 27-16-241 (Office); 700-103 (Home).

Bonami, Charles Victor; French broadcasting official; b. 16 May 1908, Ceilhes; *s.* of Charles Bonami and Maria Galabrun; *m.* Fernande Alvernhe 1932; one *s.* one *d.*
Posts, Telegraphs and Telecommunications Services 26-34; Radiodiffusion Télévision Française 35-, successively Asst. Head of Section, Head of Section, Asst. Dir., Head of Service, Head of Dept., Head of Dept. of Gen. Affairs and Public Relations, now retd.; founder *RTF Information-Documentation* 47-64; Founder-mem. European Broadcasting Union (EBU) 50-, Admin. 50-64; mem. Admin. Council, Office de Coopération Radiophonique (O.C.O.R.A.) 62-64, retd. 68; Officier, Légion d'Honneur, Chevalier du Mérite postal.
Leisure interest: research into local history.
2 rue Henri Duchène, Paris 15e, France.
Telephone: 579-6806.

Bond, Christopher Samuel; American state governor; b. 6 March 1939, St. Louis; *s.* of Arthur Doerr and Elizabeth Green Bond; *m.* Carolyn Reid 1967; ed. Deerfield Acad., Mass., Woodrow Wilson School of Public and Int. Affairs, Princeton Univ., Univ. of Virginia.
Clerk, Fifth Circuit, U.S. Court of Appeals 63-64; with law firm, Covington and Burling, Washington, D.C. 64-67; private practice; Asst. Attorney-Gen., Chief Counsel of Consumer Protection Div. 69-70; State Auditor, Missouri 70-72; Gov. of Missouri 73-; Chair. Republican Govs'. Asscn. 74-75; Exec. Cttee. Nat. Govs'. Conf. 74-75; U.S. Jaycees Ten Outstanding

Young Men Award 74; Hon. LL.D. (Westminster and William Jewell Colls., Mo.) 73; Republican.
Office of the Governor, State Capitol, Jefferson City, Missouri; Home: 14 S. Jefferson Road, Mexico, Missouri 65265, U.S.A.

Bond, Richard C., M.B.A.; American business executive; ed. Swarthmore Coll. and Harvard Business School.
President, Board of Trustees, John Wanamaker Philadelphia Inc.; Trustee, Penn Central Transportation Co. 70; Dir. Philadelphia Saving Fund Soc., Insurance Co. of N. America, Kraftco Corpn., Rorer-Amchem Inc., Bell Telephone Co. of Pennsylvania, Lenox Inc., etc.; Dir. and Trustee of many civic and educational boards; numerous citations and awards; Hon. LL.D. (St. Joseph's Coll., Swarthmore Coll.).
412 Caversham Road, Bryn Mawr, Pa., U.S.A.

Bondarchuk, Sergei Fedorovich; Soviet film actor and director; b. 25 Sept. 1920, Byelozerka, Odessa Region; ed. All Union State Inst. of Cinematography.
Principal roles: Othello, Shevchenko (*Taras Shevchenko*), Valko (*The Young Guard*), Dymov (*The Grasshopper*) Yershov (*An Unfinished Tale*), Ivan Franko (*Ivan Franko*), Matvei Krylov (*The Soldiers Go On*), Sokolov (*Destiny of a Man*), Kozostylov (*Seryozha*), Pierre Bezukhov (*War and Peace*), The Doctor (*Uncle Vanya*); Dir., acted in film *Destiny of a Man*; directed *War and Peace* 62-67, *Waterloo* 70; acted in film *Uncle Vanya* 74; Order of Lenin; People's Artist of U.S.S.R.; Lenin and State Prizes.
"Mosfilm" Studio, 1 Mosfilmovskaya ulitsa, Moscow, U.S.S.R.

Bondarenko, Ivan Afansyevich; Soviet politician; b. 1926; ed. Azov Agricultural Inst.
Checker with collective farm field crop team 42-43; Soviet Army service 43-45; Sectional Agronomist for Machine and Tractor Station, then Chief Agronomist for Forest-Shelterbelt Station 45-56; Dir. Educational-Experimental Farm and Lecturer at Azov Black Sea Inst. of Agriculture 56-59; Party Official, and Sec. of Rostov Regional Cttee. of C.P.S.U. 59-64; Chair. Rostov Regional Soviet 64-66; First Sec., Rostov Regional Cttee. of C.P.S.U. and Deputy to U.S.S.R. Supreme Soviet 66-; mem. C.P.S.U. 50-, Central Cttee. 71-; mem. Comm. for Agriculture, Soviet of Union.
Rostov Regional Committee of Communist Party of the Soviet Union, Rostov-on-Don, U.S.S.R.

Bonde, Gen. Count Thord; Swedish army officer; b. 17 March 1900.
Entered army 20, Capt. 33, Major 41, Lieut.-Col. 43, Col. 46, Major-Gen. 55, Lieut.-Gen. 57, Gen. 63; Mil. Attaché to Washington 43-45; Chief of National Defence Coll. 53-55; C.-in-C. Swedish Army 57-63; Chief of Staff to H.M. the King of Sweden 63-.
Skärkiksvägen 22, Djursholm, Sweden.

Bonde, Peder, B.L.; Swedish business executive; b. 2 Sept. 1923, Stockholm; *s.* of Count Carl Bonde and Countess Ebba Bonde (née Wallenberg); *m.* Jacqueline Madeleine Fernande Rouchier 1957; two *s.* one *d.*
Assistant Vice-Pres. Stockholms Enskilda Bank 57, Vice-Pres. 61, Exec. Vice-Pres. 69; Man. Dir. and Deputy Chief Exec. Skandinavska Enskilda Banken 72-73; Exec. Vice-Pres. Saléninvest AB 73-.
Saléninvest, S-10440 Stockholm; Home: Strandvägen 49, S-115 23 Stockholm, Sweden.
Telephone: 635560 (Office); 67-71-73 (Home).

Bondevik, Kjell, M.A.; Norwegian politician; b. 11 March 1901, Leikanger; *s.* of Ola and Severina Bondevik; *m.* 1st Agnes Sundal 1928, 2nd Torhild Bjørnstad 1957; three *s.* one *d.*; ed. Universitetet i Oslo.
Schoolteacher 27-37; Headmaster Sauda High School 37-64; Senior Lecturer in Social History, Univ. of

Bergen 65-70; Chair. Christian People's Party in Roga-
land 39-50; mem. Nat. Board of Party 49-61; mem.
Storting 50-65, Chair. of its Social Affairs Cttee. 54-61;
Parl. Leader Christian People's Party 61-65; Minister of
Social Affairs Aug.-Sept. 63, Ecclesiastical Affairs and
Educ. 65-71.
Publs. works on Norwegian folklore and traditions:
Kristent innslag i norsk politikk 1800-1930 (Christian
feature in Norwegian policy) 75.
Oberst Rodes v. 90, Oslo II, Norway.
Telephone: (02) 29-44-28.

Bondeville, Emmanuel; French composer; b. 29 Oct.
1898, Rouen; *m.* 1st Jacqueline Petitalot 1955 (died
1970); *m.* 2nd Viorica Cortez 1974; two *s.*
Dir. des Emissions artistiques, Radiodiffusion Française
35-45; Dir. Opéra de Monte-Carlo 45-49; Dir. Théâtre
National de l'Opéra-Comique 49-52; Dir. du Théâtre
National de l'Opéra 52-70, Hon. Dir.; mem. Académie
des Beaux Arts 59-64, Perm. Sec. 64-. Pres. then Hon.
Pres. (64-) Comité nat. de la musique; Grand Prix de
la musique, Soc. des auteurs 66.
Works: *Illuminations* (Marine, Ophélie, Baldes Pendus)
30-33, *L'Ecole des Maris 35, Sonate pour Piano, La
Cloche Felée, Trois Pochades, La Rhapsodie Foraine, Le
Pardon de Saint-Anne, Illustrations pour Faust 42,
Madame Bovary 51, Gaultier-Garguille 53, Symphonie
Lyrique 57, Symphonie Choréographique 65, Antoine et
Cléopâtre 74.*
Palais Mazarin, 25 Quai de Conti, Paris 6e, France.

Bondi, Sir Hermann, K.C.B., M.A., F.R.S.; British
mathematician; b. 1 Nov. 1919, Vienna; *s.* of late
Samuel and Helene Bondi; *m.* Christine M. Stockman
1947; two *s.* three *d.*; ed. Real Gymnasium, Vienna and
Trinity Coll., Cambridge.
Fellow, Trinity Coll. Cambridge 43-49, 52-54; Lecturer
in Mathematics, Cambridge Univ. 48-54; Prof. of
Applied Mathematics, Univ. of London (King's Coll.)
54-, on leave of absence 67-; Dir.-Gen. European Space
Research Org. (ESRO), Paris 67-March 71; Chief
Scientific Adviser to Ministry of Defence 71-, Research
Assoc. Cornell Univ. 51, Harvard Coll. Observatory 53;
Visiting Prof. Cornell Univ. 60; Fellow, Royal Society
59, Royal Astronomical Soc. (Sec. 56-64), Cambridge
Philosophical Soc.; Chair. Nat. Cttee. for Astronomy
64-67; Pres., Inst. of Math. and its applications 74;
K.C.B. 73.
Publs. *Cosmology* 52, (2nd edn. 60), *The Universe at
Large* 61, *Relativity and Common Sense* 64, *Assumption
and Myth in Physical Theory* 67, numerous papers.
Ministry of Defence, Main Building, Whitehall, London,
S.W.1; East House, Buckland Corner, Reigate Heath,
Reigate, Surrey, England.

Bondor, József; Hungarian building engineer and
politician; b. 19 Jan. 1917, Elesd; *s.* of Ferenc Bondor
and Teréz Pap; *m.* Sarolta Csonka 1943; one *d.*
Former mason's apprentice; joined workers movement
40, Communist Party 45; directed reconstruction of
Lenin Foundry Works in County Borsod; one of
founders and builders of town of Dunaujváros; Chief
Engineer, later Vice-Pres. of Budapest Metropolitan
Council 61-65; Deputy Minister of Building Construc-
tion and City Planning 65-68, Minister 68-; Chair. Nat.
Council for Environmental Protection 74-; Labour
Order of Merit, Golden degree 70.
Ministry of Building and City Planning, Budapest V,
Beloiannisz-utca 2-4, Hungary.
Telephone: 112-200.

Bongo, Albert-Bernard; Gabonese politician; b. 30
Dec. 1935, Lewai, Franceville; *m.*; two *c.*; ed. primary
school at Bacongo (Congo—Brazzaville) and technical
coll., Brazzaville.
Civil servant; served Air Force 58-60; entered Ministry
of Foreign Affairs 60; Dir. of Private Office of Pres.
Léon Mba 62, in charge of Information 63-64, Nat.

Defence 64-65; Minister-Del. to Presidency in charge
of Nat. Defence and Co-ordination, Information and
Tourism 65-66; Vice-Pres. of Govt., in charge of Co-
ordination, Nat. Defence Planning, Information and
Tourism 66-67; Vice-Pres. of Gabon March-Nov. 67,
Pres., Minister of Defence, of Information, of Planning
Dec. 67-, Prime Minister 67-75, Minister of the Interior
67-70, of Devt. 70-, of Mines 70-71, of Foreign Affairs
73-74; Founder and Sec.-Gen. Parti Démocratique
Gabonais 68; High Chancellor, Ordre Nat. de l'Etoile
Equatoriale; decorations from the Ivory Coast, Niger,
Chad, Cameroon, Central African Republic, Mauritius,
Togo, Taiwan, Zaire, France, U.K. and Guinea.
Boîte Postale 546, Libreville, Gabon.
Telephone: 26-90.

Bonhomme, Albert; French public servant; b. 7 July
1913, Polminhac Cantal; *m.* Gilberte Sebaut 1953;
three *c.*; ed. Faculty of Law, Paris and Toulouse.
Army service 39-45; Dep. Prefect of Tiaret 45-47, of
Oran 47-49; Sec.-Gen. of Guadeloupe 49-51; Dep.
Prefect of Tlemcen 51-56; Prefect of Medea 56-58, of
Aveyron 58-60, of Guadeloupe 60-65; Prefect without
Portfolio 65-; Adviser to Govt. of Panama 67; Public
Security 68; Prefect without Portfolio 70; Mayor of
Castagniers 71-; Officier, Légion d'Honneur; Commdr.
Ordre National du Mérite.
Leisure interest: aviation.
Publs. *Monsieur Aimé Lafleur 57, Adieu Foulards,
Adieu Madras 61.*
06670 Castagniers, France.
Telephone: 08-05-22.

Bonilla, Lempira E; Honduran international finance
official; b. 16 Sept. 1920, Marcala; ed. George Washington Univ.
Economic Counsellor, Embassy of Honduras, Washington, D.C. 57-63; Alt. Exec. Dir. IBRD 60-63; Alt. Exec.
Dir. IMF 63; held senior post in Div. for Admin. of
Loans, Inter-American Devt. Bank (IDB); Exec. Dir.
for Costa Rica, El Salvador, Guatemala, Haiti, Honduras and Nicaragua, at IDB 69-.
Inter-American Development Bank, 808 17th Street,
N.W., Washington, D.C. 20577, U.S.A.

Bonjour, Edgar Conrad, DR. PHIL.; Swiss university
professor; b. 21 Aug. 1898, Berne; *m.* Dora Kocher
1941; two *s.* two *d.*; ed. Univs. of Berne, Geneva, Paris
and Berlin.
High school teacher 21-32; Deputy Director of Federal
Archives 32; Priv. Doz. Univ. of Berne 33-35; Prof. of
History, Univ. of Basle 35-, Dean of the Faculty of
Philosophy 40, Rector and Pres. of Assembly of Swiss
univ. rectors 46; Pres. of Basle Historic Society 46-49;
mem. of Polish Acad., Bavarian Acad.; Dr. h.c. Univ.
of Neuchâtel 59.
Leisure interest: music.
Publs. *Geschichte der Schweiz 38, Schillers Historische
Schriften 44, Geschichte der schweizerischen Neutralität
46, Das Schicksal des Sonderbundes in zeitgenössischer
Darstellung 47, Die Gründung des schweizerischen
Bundesstaates 48, Theodor Kocher 50, Basel im Schweizer-
bund 51, Johannes von Müller 52, Der Neuenburger
Konflikt 56, Studien zu Johannes von Müller 57, Die
Universität Basel 60, Die Geschichtsschreibung der
Schweiz (2 vols.) 62 (in collaboration with R. Feller),
Geschichte der schweizerischen Neutralität* (revised,
enlarged edn., 8 vols., publ. in French 70-71) 67-74,
Discordia Concors (2 vols.) 68, *Die Schweiz und Europa*
(4 vols.) 75.
Benkenstrasse 56, Basle, Switzerland.
Telephone: 061-382610.

Bonnefous, Edouard; French politician; b. 24 Aug.
1907; ed. Ecole des Sciences Politiques and Inst. des
Hautes Etudes Internationales.
Former Pres. Comm. on Foreign Affairs, Nat. Assembly;
Minister of Commerce, Faure Cabinet 52; Minister of

State, Mayer Cabinet Jan. 53; Minister of Posts and Telegraphs until 56; Minister of Transport and Public Works 57-58; Deputy from Seine-et-Oise 46-58, Senator 59-; Chair. Comm. on Finance, Senate 72-; mem. Consultative Assembly, Council of Europe; del. to UN 48-52, Pres. French Cttee., Ligue Européenne de Coopération Economique; Prof. Inst. des Hautes Etudes Internationales; Pres. Soc. of Political Economy, Asscn. Nat. de Protection des Eaux, Asscn. professionnelle de la Presse Républicaine; Vice-Pres. Inst. Océanographique, Institut des Hautes Etudes de l'Amérique; mem. de l'Institut de France; Pres. Asscn. and Féd. Française pour la Défence de l'Environnement contre les Pollutions et les Nuisances; Pres. Conservatoire Nat. des Arts et Métiers 75; Grand Prix Gobert of Académie Française 68.

Publs. *Le Corporatisme, Devant et derrière le Rideau de Fer, A travers l'Europe Mutilée, L'Idée Européenne et sa Réalisation, L'Europe en face de son destin, Encyclopédie de l'Amérique Latine, La réforme administrative, Les grands Travaux, Histoire Politique de la IIIe République* (7 vols.), *La Terre et la Faim des Hommes, L'Année Politique* (26 vols.), *Les milliards qui s'envolent, Le monde est-il surpeuplé? L'Homme ou la Nature.*

6 rue de l'Elysée, Paris, France.

Bonnefoy, Yves Jean, L. ès L.; French writer; b. 24 June 1923, Tours; s. of Elie Bonnefoy and Hélène Maury; m. Lucille Vine; one d.; ed. Lycée Descartes, Tours, Faculté des Sciences, Poitiers, and Faculté des Lettres, Paris.

Lived in Paris 43-; contributor to *Mercure de France, Critique, Encounter, L'Ephémère*, etc.; has travelled in Europe, Asia and N. America; lectures or seminars at Brandeis, Johns Hopkins, Princeton, Geneva, Nice and other Univs.; Co-Editor *L'Ephémère*.

Publs. *Du Mouvement et de l'Immobilité de Douve* (poems) 53 (On the Motion and Immobility of Douve 68), *Hier régnant Desert* 58, *L'Improbable* (essays) 59, *Pierre écrite* (poems) 64, *Arthur Rimbaud* (essay) 61, *Un rêve fait à Mantoue* (essays) 67, *Selected Poems* 68, *Dans le leurre du Seuil* (poems) 75; Art: *Peintures murales de la France Gothique* 54, *Miró* 63, *Rome 1630* 69, *L'Arrière-Pays* (essays) 72; translations of Shakespeare.

63 rue Lepic, Paris 18e, France.
Telephone: 606-88-12.

Bonner, James, PH.D.; American professor of biology; b. 1 Sept. 1910, Ansley, Neb.; s. of Walter D. and Grace Gaylord Bonner; m. Ingelore Silberbach 1967; one s. three d.; ed. Univ. of Utah, Calif. Inst. of Technology and Oxford Univ.

National Research Council Fellow, Utrecht, Zürich and Leiden 34-35; Instructor, Calif. Inst. of Technology 36-38, Asst. Prof. 38-43, Assoc. Prof. 43-46, Prof. 46-; mem. Nat. Acad. of Sciences.

Leisure interests: skiing, mountain climbing, travel.

Publs. *Plant Biochemistry* 50, *Principles of Plant Physiology* 52, *The Next 100 Years* 57, *The Nucleohistones* 64, *The Molecular Biology of Development* 65, *The Next 90 Years* 67, and c. 400 scientific publs.

California Institute of Technology, Pasadena, Calif. 91109; Home: 3119 Mesaloa Lane, Pasadena, Calif. 91107, U.S.A.
Telephone: 213-695-6841, Ext. 1928 (Office); 213-797-7194 (Home).

Bonner, Robert William; Canadian politician and business executive; b. 10 Sept. 1920, Vancouver; m. Barbara Newman 1942; one s. two d.; ed. Univ. of British Columbia.

Army service in U.K., N. Africa, Sicily, Italy 42-45; mem. Legis. Assembly, B.C. 52-68; Attorney-Gen., B.C. 52-68, at various times concurrently Minister of Educ., of Industrial Devt., of Trade and Commerce, of Commercial Transport; Senior Vice-Pres. Admin.,

MacMillan Bloedel Ltd. 68-71, Dir. 68-, mem. Exec. Cttee. 69, Vice-Chair. 71-72, Pres., Chief Exec. Officer 72-73, Chair. 73-74, retd. 74; Chair. B. C. Hydro & Power Authority 76-; mem. Board, Int. Nickel Co. of Canada Ltd., Canadian Cable Systems Ltd., J. Henry Shroder & Co. Ltd.; mem. Canadian Bar Asscn., Vancouver Bar Asscn., Law Soc. of B.C.

Leisure interests: photography, boating.

British Columbia Hydro & Power Authority, 970 Burrard Street, Vancouver, B.C. V6Z 1Y3, Canada.

Bonnet, Christian, D. EN D.; French industrialist and politician; b. 14 June 1921, Paris; s. of Pierre Bonnet and Suzanne Delebecque; m. Christiane Mertian 1943; five c.; ed. Univ. of Paris and Ecole des sciences politiques.

President of Les Grandes Marques de la conserve 52-61, Del. Conseil supérieure de la conserve; M.R.P. Deputy for Morbihan 56-58; Deputy for the second constituency of Morbihan 58-; Gen. Councillor, Belle-Ile 63-; Mayor of Carnac 64-; Sec.-Gen. Républicains Indépendants; Chair. Cttee. on the Merchant Marine budget; Pres. Supervisory Council, Caisse des dépôts et consignations; Sec. of State for Supply, Housing and Territorial Devt. 72-74; Minister of Agriculture May 74-.

Ministère d'Agriculture, 78 rue de Varenne, Paris 7e, France.

Bonnet, Henri; French scholar and diplomatist; b. 26 May 1888, Châteauponsac, Haute-Vienne; s. of Jules Théobald Bonnet and Marie-Thérèse Lascoux; m. Hellé Zervoudakl 1932 (deceased 1962); ed. Ecole Normale Supérieure and Paris Univ.

Member LN Secretariat 20-31; Dir. Inst. of Intellectual Co-operation 31-40; Prof. Political Science Free School of Social Research, N.Y. 41-43; Commr. and Minister for Information Provisional Govt. of the French Renublic 43-44; Amb. to U.S.A. 44-55; Vice-Pres. Franco-American Cttee.; mem. Board Dirs. Centre of Studies of Foreign Policy; Pres. Franco-American Cttee. for Industrial Co-operation; Grand Officier de la Légion d'Honneur, Croix de Guerre (14-18), Médaille de Résistance.

23 rue Verneuil, Paris 7e, France.
Telephone: 261-15-40.

Bono, Gaudenzio, DR. ENG.; Italian industrialist; b. 17 May 1901, Turin; s. of Stefano Bono and Giuseppina Caire; m. Giuseppina Bono; three s.; ed. Politecnico of Turin.

Sole Man. Dir. and Gen. Man. FIAT, Turin until Feb. 69, Man. Dir. Feb. 69-Jan. 72 and Vice-Chair. 72-75; Chair. "Galileo Ferraris" Nat. Electrical Eng. Inst.; Dir several Italian companies; Cavaliere del Lavoro; Knight Grand Cross of the Italian Republic.

10, Corso Marconi, Turin, Italy.

Bonow, (Karl Daniel) Mauritz, LIC. PHIL.; Swedish co-operative official; b. 5 Sept. 1904, Luleå; s. of Walfrid Mauritz Bonow and Andréa Jonsson; m. Anna Margareta Edlund 1931; one s. three d.; ed. Uppsala Univ. and London School of Economics.

Assistant Chief of Secr., Kooperativa förbundet 31-39; Chief of Research Bureau, State Food Comm. 40-41; Gen. Sec. and Dir. Kooperativa förbundet 41-69; Vice-Pres. Int. Co-operative Alliance 55-60, Pres. 60-75.

Leisure interest: gardening.

Publs. *Staten och jordbrukskrisen* (The State and the Agricultural Crisis) 35, *Staten och näringslivet* (The State and Economic Life) 43, *Kooperationen och folkförsörjningen* (Co-operation and the Structure of Society) 36, *Producer and Consumer* 54, *Co-operation in a Changing World* 60, *Demokratisk ekonomi* 69, *Co-operative Consumer Policy* 72, *International Co-operation for Self-Reliance* 75.

Björns Trädgårdsgränd 3, Stockholm, Sweden.
Telephone: 40-97-83.

Bonvin, Roger; Swiss public servant; b. 12 Sept. 1907; ed. Sion and Einsiedeln Colls.

Constructed tunnels for Dixence S.A. 32-34; Fed. Topography Service 34-35; Local Govt. Depts. 36-49; Collaborator in Elektrowatt S.A. 49-55, Mayor of Sion 55-62; Nat. Councillor 55-62; mem. Swiss Fed. Council 62-73, Vice-Pres. Jan.-Dec. 66, Jan.-Dec. 72, Pres. Jan.-Dec. 67, Jan.-Dec. 73; Head of Finance Dept. 62-68, of Transport Dept. 68-73; Christian Dem.

Grand Pont 29, Sion, Switzerland.

Bonvoisin, Baron Pierre de, D. en D., M.A.; Belgian banker; b. 1903, Verviers; *m.* Elisabeth Galopin 1933; two *s.* two *d.*; ed. Liège and Princeton Univs.

Honorary Chair. of Board, Société Générale de Banque, Brussels; Extraordinary Prof. Emer. of Money and Banking, Univ. of Louvain; Hon. Chair. Belgian Amer. Banking Corpn., N.Y., Belgian Amer. Bank & Trust Co., N.Y., Crédit Foncier International, Banque Belge Ltd. (London); Dir. Compagnie Financière et de Réassurance du Groupe A.G., Brussels, Agence Maritime Internationale, Antwerp.

Home: 30 Boulevard Saint Michel, 1040 Brussels; Office: 3 Montagne du Parc, 1000 Brussels, Belgium.

Telephone: (02) 513-66-00 (Office); (02) 733-72-35 (Home).

Bonynge, Richard; Australian conductor; b. 1930, Sydney; *m.* Joan Sutherland (*q.v.*) 1954.

Trained as a pianist; debut as conductor with Santa Cecilia Orchestra, Rome 62; conducted first opera *Faust*, Vancouver 63; has conducted in most of leading opera houses; Artistic Dir., Principal Conductor Sutherland/Williamson Int. Grand Opera Co., Australia 65; Artistic Dir. Vancouver Opera Asscn. 74-; Musical Dir. Australian Opera 75-.

Has conducted *La Sonnambula, La Traviata, Faust, Eugene Onegin, L'Elisir d'Amore, Orfeo* 67, *Semiramide*, Florence 68, *Giulio Cesare, Lucia*, Hamburg, New York 69-71, *Norma* and *Orfeo*, N.Y. 70, *The Tales of Hoffmann*, N.Y. 73, Sydney Opera House 74.

Major recordings include: *Alcina, La Sonnambula, Norma, Beatrice di Tenda, I Puritani, Faust, Semiramide, Lakmé, La Fille du Régiment, The Messiah, Don Giovanni, Les Huguenots, L'Elisir d'Amore, Lucia, Rigoletto, The Tales of Hoffmann, Thérèse* (Massenet), numerous orchestral works, ballet including *Giselle, Coppelia, Sylvia, Nutcracker.*

c/o Ingpen and Williams, 14 Kensington Court, London, W.8, England.

Booher, Edward E.; American publisher; b. 29 June 1911, Dayton, Ohio; *s.* of Wilfred Elsworth Booher and Cora Bell Middlestetter Booher; *m.* 1st Selena Read Knight 1939, 2nd Agnes Martin Whitaker 1961; two *s.* one *d.*; two stepsons, one stepdaughter; ed. Antioch Coll.

McGraw-Hill Book Co., Vice-Pres. 44-54, Exec. Vice-Pres. 54-60, Pres. 60-68, Chair. 68-70; Pres. Books and Educ. Services Group, McGraw-Hill Inc. 70-; Trustee, Asia Soc., Univ. of the Negev; mem. Board of Higher Educ. of New Jersey, Visiting Cttee. of Harvard Graduate School of Educ., U.S. State Dept. U.S.-India Joint Sub-Comm. for Educ. and Culture; Dir. Fidelity Union Trust; mem. Advisory Board, *The Partisan Review*; Gov. Yale Univ. Press; Woodrow Wilson Fellow.

Leisure interest: education.

McGraw-Hill Inc., 1221 Avenue of the Americas, New York, N.Y. 10020, U.S.A.

Telephone: 212-997-2033.

Böök, Klas Erik, FIL. LIC.; Swedish banker and diplomatist; b. 10 March 1909, Lund; *m.* Aina Hakon-Pettersson 1933; three *s.* two *d.*

Sec. Bank of Sweden 37; Head of Research Dept., Bank of Sweden 40; Deputy Man. Foreign Exchange Control Office 40; Man. Bank of Sweden 43; Deputy Gov. 44; mem. Foreign Trade Comm. Board 44; Envoy Extraordinary and Min. Plen.; Head of Commercial Dept.

Foreign Office 47; Deputy Chair. Export Credit Guarantee Board; Chair. Foreign Exchange Control Board, mem. Foreign Funds Control Board; Gov. Bank of Sweden 48-51; Swedish Minister in Canada 51-55; Ambassador to China and Thailand 55-61, to India, Ceylon and Nepal 61-65, to Switzerland 65-72, Special Commr. in Foreign Office 72-.

Lya, 260 97, O. Karup, Sweden.

Telephone: 0431-71-601.

Booker, Henry George, PH.D.; American professor of applied physics; b. 14 Dec. 1910, Barking, Essex, U.K.; *s.* of Charles Henry Booker and Gertrude Mary Booker; *m.* Adelaide Mary McNish 1938; two *s.* two *d.*; ed. Cambridge Univ.

Research Fellow, Christ's Coll., Cambridge 35-40; Scientific Officer in British Radar Research Establishment 40-45; Univ. Lecturer in Mathematics, Cambridge Univ. 45-48; Prof. of Electrical Engineering, Cornell Univ. 48-65; Prof. of Engineering Physics, Cornell Univ. 49-65; IBM Prof. of Engineering and Applied Mathematics, Cornell Univ. 62-65; Dir. School of Electrical Engineering, Cornell Univ. 59-63; Prof. of Applied Physics, Univ. of Calif., San Diego 65-; Research Assoc. Carnegie Inst. of Washington 37-39; Guggenheim Fellow, Cambridge Univ. 54-55; Staff Scientist, Stanford Research Inst. 62-63; mem. Nat. Acad. of Sciences and numerous other socs.; numerous prizes.

Leisure interest: swimming.

Publs. Over fifty scientific works.

Department of Applied Physics and Information Science, University of California, San Diego, La Jolla, Calif. 92037, U.S.A.

Boomstra, Sjoerd, D.JUR.; Netherlands financial executive; b. 12 Sept. 1913, Rotterdam; *m.* Henny Brons 1954; two *c.*; ed. secondary school, Bandung, Indonesia, Univ. of Leiden.

Netherlands Clearing Inst. and Deviezen Inst. 38; joined Ministry of Finance 45, Deputy Dir., then Dir. External Finance 53; Vice-Chair. European Investment Bank 70-.

European Investment Bank, 2 place de Metz, Luxembourg; Home: Ridderlaan 25, The Hague, Netherlands.

Telephone: 43-50-11 (Office); 24-41-67 (Home).

Boon, Henrik Nicolaas, LL.D.; Netherlands diplomatist; b. 23 Aug. 1911, Rotterdam; *s.* of Jan Boon and Elizabeth Johanna Mees; *m.* Charlotte Talitha Mees 1936; four *d.*; ed. Univs. of London, Paris and Leyden and Geneva School of Int. Studies.

Served Ministry of Foreign Affairs 36-39; served in Madrid, Brussels, Washington, Tsjoengking, Batavia and Nanking 39-47; Deputy and later Chief of Diplomatic Affairs Division, Ministry of Foreign Affairs 47-49; Sec.-Gen. Ministry of Foreign Affairs 49-52, Minister later Amb. to Italy 52-58, Amb. to Venezuela 58-61; Amb. on Special Mission; Perm. Rep. to NATO 61-70; Amb. to Italy, also accred. to Malta 71-; Knight Order of Netherlands Lion, Commdr. Order of Orange-Nassau, Grand Cross Order of Adolf van Nassau of Luxembourg, Grand Officer Order of the Crown of Belgium, Commdr. Légion d'Honneur, Grand Cross Ordine al Merito, Italy.

Leisure interests: archaeology, classical music, skiing, horse-riding.

Publs. *Rêve et réalité dans l'oeuvre économique et social de Napoléon III, Bagatellen.*

Royal Netherlands Embassy, Via Michele Mercati 8, 00197 Rome, Italy.

Boorstin, Daniel J., M.A., LL.D.; American educator, author and librarian; b. 1 Oct. 1914, Atlanta, Ga.; *s.* of late Samuel Boorstin and Dora Olsan; *m.* Ruth Carolyn Frankel 1941; three *s.*; ed. Harvard Coll., Balliol Coll., Oxford, Cambridge and Yale Univs.

Harvard Coll. and Harvard Law School 38-42; Office of Lend-Lease Admin., Washington 42; Asst. Prof., Swarthmore Coll. 42-44; Prof. of American History and Preston and Stirling Morton Distinguished Service Prof. of History, Univ. of Chicago 44-69; Prof. Amer. History, Univ. of Paris 61-62; Pitt Prof. Amer. History and Institutions and Fellow, Trinity Coll. Cambridge 64-65, Shelby and Kathryn Cullom Davis Lecturer, Graduate Inst. of Int. Studies, Geneva 73-74; Senior Historian Smithsonian Inst., Washington, D.C. 73-75; The Librarian of Congress 75-; Dir. Nat. Museum of History and Technology 69-73; mem. Board Trustees Colonial Williamsburg, Board Dirs. Thomas Gilcrease Museum, Comm. on Critical Choices for Americans; Trustee American Film Inst.; Pulitzer Prize for History 74, and several other prizes.
Leisure interests: gardening, bird watching, cross-country skiing.
Publs. *The Mysterious Science of the Law* 41, *Delaware Cases 1792-1830* (3 vols.) 43, *The Lost World of Thomas Jefferson* 48, *The Genius of American Politics* 53, *The Americans: The Colonial Experience* 58, *America and the Image of Europe* 60, *The Image or What Happened to the American Dream* 62, *The Americans: The National Experience* 65, *The Landmark History of the American People* (2 vols.) 68, 70, *The Decline of Radicalism* 69, *The Sociology of the Absurd* 70, *The Americans: The Democratic Experience* 73, *Democracy and its Discontent* 74; Editor: *An American Primer* 66, *American Civilization* 72.
The Library of Congress, Washington, D.C. 20540; Home: 3541 Ordway Street, N.W., Washington, D.C. 20016, U.S.A.
Telephone: (202) 426-5205 (Office).

Booth, Rt. Hon. Albert Edward, P.C., M.P.; British politician; b. 28 May 1928; s. of Albert Henry Booth and Janet Mathieson; m. Joan Amis 1957; three s.; ed. South Shields Marine School, Rutherford Coll. of Technology.
Worked as a shipbuilding draughtsman; elected to Tynemouth Borough Council 62; Tynemouth Election Agent 51, 55; M.P. for Barrow-in-Furness 66-; Minister of State, Dept. of Employment 74-76; Sec. of State for Employment April 76-; Labour.
House of Commons, Westminster, London, S.W.1, England.

Boothby, Baron (Life Peer), of Buchan and Rattray Head; **Robert J. G. Boothby,** K.B.E., LL.D.; British politician; b. 1900, Edinburgh; s. of Sir R. T. Boothby, K.B.E.; m. Wanda Sanna 1967; ed. Eton and Magdalen Coll., Oxford.
Unionist M.P. for East Aberdeenshire 24-58; Parl Private Sec. to Mr. Winston Churchill (Chancellor of the Exchequer) 26-29; Parl. Sec. to Ministry of Food 40-41; British del. to Consultative Assembly of Council of Europe 49-57, Vice-Chair. Cttee. on Economic Affairs 52-56; Rector of St. Andrews Univ. 58-61; Pres. Anglo-Israel Asscn.; Officier de la Légion d'Honneur 50.
Publs. *The New Economy* 43, *I Fight to Live* 47, *My Yesterday, Your Tomorrow* 62.
1 Eaton Square, London, S.W.1; House of Lords, London, S.W.1, England.

Boothe, Clare (*see* Luce, Mrs. Clare).

Borbándi, János; Hungarian politician; b. 1923; ed. Univ. of Political Econ., Party Acad.
Joined Communist Party 45; machine fitter Csepel Iron Works until 49; political posts in factory and party headquarters 49-53; Sec. Factory Party Cttee., Lenin Foundry Works, Diósgyór 53-55; First Sec. Party Cttee., Budapest District II 58-61; Deputy Minister of Defence 61-66; Leader Admin. Dept., Cen. Cttee., Hungarian Socialist Workers' Party 66, mem. Cen.

Supervisory Dept. 62-66, Cen. Cttee. 70-; mem. Parl 62-66; Deputy Prime Minister 74-.
Office of the Prime Minister, Kossuth Lajos tér, 1357 Budapest, Hungary.
Telephone: 123-500.

Borch, Fred J.; American business executive; b. 28 April 1910, Brooklyn, New York; m. 1st Martha Kananen (died 1969), one s. one d.; m. 2nd Lucia M. Lowles 1970; ed. Western Reserve Univ.
General Electric Co. 31-, Vice-Pres. (Marketing) 54-59; Vice-Pres. and Group Exec. (Consumer Products) 59-61, Exec. Vice-Pres. (Operations) 61-63, Pres. and Chief Exec. Officer 63-68, Chair. and Chief Exec. Officer 68-72.
Leisure interest: golf.
570 Lexington Avenue, New York, N.Y. 10022, U.S.A.
Telephone: 212-750-2511.

Bord, André; French politician; b. 30 Nov. 1922, Strasbourg; s. of Alphonse Bord and Marie-Anne Sigrist; m. Germaine Fend; two s.
Member Chamber of Deputies for Bas-Rhin 58-; mem. Municipal Council, Strasbourg 59-, Deputy Mayor 59-; mem. Conseil Général, Strasbourg 61-, Pres. 67-; Pres. Groupe des Non-Inscrits pour Union Nat. des Anciens Combattants, European Parl. 61-66; Sec. of State for Interior 66-72, for Ex-Servicemen and War Victims 72-; Sec.-Gen. U.D.R. June 75-; Founder, Pres. Asscn. for Industrial Devt., Alsace 67; Pres. Regional Council of Alsace 73-, Asscn. Départementale du Tourisme; Médaille Mil., Médaille de la France Libre, Médaille de la Résistance; Croix de Guerre avec palme; Grand Officer, Order of Orange-Nassau (Netherlands), Order of Polonia Restituta (Poland), and others; U.D.R.
37 rue de Bellechasse, 75007 Paris, France.
Telephone: 551-41-29.

Borda, Guillermo Antonio; Argentine lawyer and politician; b. 22 Sept. 1914; ed. Univ. de Buenos Aires.
Professor of Argentine History, School of Commerce No. 6 41-46; Prof. in Faculty of Law and Social Sciences, Univ. of Buenos Aires 47-56; Prof. of Civil Law, Univ. of Salvador 57-, Catholic Univ. of Buenos Aires 58-; Minister of Finance, Public Works and Agriculture, Province of San Luis 45; Sec. of Public and Urban Works, City of Buenos Aires 58; mem. Court of Civil Appeals 59-62, Vice-Pres. 62-63, Pres. 63-66; Minister of Interior 66-69.
Publs. *Error de hecho y de derecho* 46, *Historia Argentina* 46, *Retroactividad de la ley y derechos adquiridos* 51, *Tratado de Derecho Civil Argentino, Parte General* 53, *Familia* 55.
Montevideo 471, Buenos Aires, Argentina.

Bordaberry Arocena, Juan María; Uruguayan politician; b. 1928, Montevideo; s. of Domingo Bordaberry and Elisa Arocena de Bordaberry; m. Josefina Herrán Puig; seven s. one d.; ed. Univ. of Montevideo.
Chairman, Nat. Meat Board 59; mem. Hon. Comm. for Agricultural Devt. Plan 60; mem. Nat. Wool Board 60-62; Chair. Comm. Against Foot and Mouth Disease 62; mem. Senate 62-64; Chair. Liga Federal de Acción Ruralista 64; Minister of Agriculture 69-72; Pres. of Uruguay March 72-.
Joaquín Suárez 2868, Montevideo, Uruguay.
Telephone: 20-14-12.

Bordaz, Robert, D. en D., L. ès L.; French government official; b. 6 July 1908, Argenton Chateau, Deux Sèvres; s. of Louis Bordaz and Marguerite Michel; m. 1947, two s. one d.
Communications and Merchant Marine Office, Algiers 43; Ministry of Public Works, Paris; Master of Petitions, Council of State 44; Ministry of Nat. Economy 45; Govt. Commr., Banque de Paris et des Pays Bas 46-48; Head of Private Office of Minister of Construction

48-51; Dir. Bank Inst. of Cambodia, Laos and Viet-Nam 51-54; Deputy Commr. Indo-China 54-56; Commercial Counsellor and Head of Dept. of Econ. Expansion, Moscow 56-58; Counsellor of State 58-; Pres. Inst. d'Aménagement et d'Urbanisme de la Ville de Paris 60-62; Dir.-Gen. Radiodiffusion-Télévision Française 62-64; mem. Board of Agence France-Presse; Commr.-Gen. French section Expo 67, Montreal 64-67; Pres. Etablissement Public du Centre Georges Pompidou 70-; Commr. Légion d'Honneur; Médaille de la Résistance; Commdr. des Arts et Lettres.
Leisure interest: cinema.
Publs. La nouvelle Economie Soviétique 1935-1960 60, monthly column in La Nouvelle Revue des Deux Mondes since 70.
15 rue Gay-Lussac, Paris 5e, France.
Telephone: 033-10-31.

Border, Lewis Harold, M.V.O.; Australian diplomatist; b. 16 April 1920, Bundarra, N.S.W.; s. of late Arch-deacon Harold Border and Nellie Lillyman; m. Margaret Fae Gerrand 1956; one s. three d.; ed. The Armidale School, Armidale, and Univ. of Sydney.
Australian Army 41-45; entered Australian Diplomatic Service 45, served Japan, Switzerland, India and Washington, D.C. 47-59; Amb. to Burma 63-65, to Republic of Viet-Nam 66-68; Australian High Commr. in Pakistan and Amb. to Afghanistan 68-70; Deputy Sec. Dept. of Foreign Affairs 71-75; Amb. to Fed. Repub. of Germany 75-.
Leisure interests: reading, golf.
Australian Embassy, Bonn, Federal Republic of Germany.

Bordier, Paul; French Inspector of Finances; b. 16 Jan. 1921; ed. Rochefort-sur-Mer and Bordeaux Lycées, Ecole Nat. de la France d'Outre-Mer.
Service in Morocco, French colonies and in Ministry of Overseas France; Dir.-Gen. of Economic Affairs, French Equatorial Africa until 56; Gov. Niger 56-58; High Commr. Central African Republic 58-60; Technical Adviser, Ministry of Co-operation 61; Inspector of Finances 62-; Pres. Groupe Foncier du Plan 65-66; Pres. Chambre Syndicale Commerce et Industrie des Eaux Minérales 68-.
1 rue de Sfax, Paris 16e; and 10 rue Clément Marot, Paris 8e, France.
Telephone: PAS 65-91; BAL 5422.

Bordier, Roger; French writer; b. 5 March 1923; s. of Robert Bordier and Valentine Jeufraux; m. Jacqueline Bouchaud; ed. secondary school.
Journalist in the provinces, later in Paris; Contributor to Nouvelles Littéraires and Aujourd'hui; radio and television writer; Prix Renaudot 61.
Publs. poems: Les Epicentres 51; novels: La Cinquième Saison 59, Les Blés 61, Le Mime 63, L'Entracte 65, Un âge d'or 67, Le Tour de Ville 69, Les Eventails 71, L'océan 74; Play: Les Somnambules 63, Les Visiteurs 72; Essays: L'Object contre l'art 72, Le Progrès: Pour qui? 73.
8 rue Geoffrey St. Hilaire, Paris 5e, France.
Telephone: 535-22-56.

Borel, Jacques; French writer, teacher and critic; b. 17 Dec. 1925, Paris; s. of Pierre Borel and Lucie Dubée; m. Christiane Idrac 1948; one s. four d.; ed. Lycée Henri IV, Paris and Univ. de Paris.
Teacher, Lycée de Clermont-Ferrand 52-56, Lycée Rodin, Paris 56-67; Visiting Prof. Middlebury Coll. 66, Portland State Coll. 67, Univ. of Hawaii 68, Univ. of Calif. (Irvine) 69; contributes poems and essays to Nouvelle Revue française, Critique, Cahiers du Chemin, Mercure de France, Botteghe Oscure, Cahiers du Sud, Figaro, etc.; Prix Goncourt 65, Chevalier Arts et Lettres 71.
Publs. Editor Verlaine's Complete Works 59-60, Poetical Works 62, Complete Works in Prose 72; L'Adoration

(novel) 65, Tata ou de l'Education (play) 67, Le Retour (novel) 70, Marcel Proust (essay) 72, La Dépossession (diary) 73, Commentaires (essays) 74, Un Voyage Ordinaire (diary) 75; Trans. James Joyce's The Cat and the Devil 66, Collected Poems 67, Prefaces to Romanciers au Travail 67, Du Bellay's Poetical Works 67, Guillevic's Terraqué 68, Fargue's Vulturne and Epaisseurs 71, Francis Jammes' De l'Angélus de l'Aube a l'Angélus du Soir 71, Verlaine's Poèmes Saturniens, Fêtes Galantes, Romances sans Paroles 73.
22 rue Charles de Gaulle, 91440 Bures-sur-Yvette, Essonne, France.
Telephone: 907-57-29.

Borel, Jacques Paul; French restaurant executive; b. 9 April 1927, Courbevoie; s. of William and Marie (née Le Monnier) Borel; m. Christiane Roubit 1949; two s. one d.; ed. Lycées Condorcet and Carnot, Paris, Ecole des Hautes Etudes Commerciales.
Member Sales Force IBM France 50-57, Manager Saigon (Viet-Nam) Branch Office IBM; Pres. Soc. française de distribution de produits alimentaires (Sofradipa) 57-, Dir. 60-; Pres. Jacques-Borel Restaurants Co. 60- (now Jacques Borel International); Pres. Cie. des Hôtels Jacques Borel; Hon. Pres. du Syndicat National des Chaînes d'Hôtels et de Restaurants de Tourisme et d'Entreprise, Soc. Hoteles Jacques Borel (Spain), Geschäftsführer Jacques Borel Gastronomie und Hotel G.m.b.H. (Germany); Pres. Groupe H.E.C. Tourisme-Hôtellerie; Pres. Consejo General de Restaurantes, Madrid; Dir. Gestione Mense Aziendali Cusin Alimentari (Italy), Soc. de Promotion Touristique des Autoroutes, Soc. du Ticket Restaurant, Soc. Générale Belge de Restauration, Cie. Méditerranéennc de Restauration et d'Hôtellerie, Montparnasse 56, Aéro-Tourisme-Côte d'Azur; Dir.-Gen. Soc. de Promotion des Auto-routes de Provence Cote d'Azur, Soc. d'Etude d'Organisation et de Réalisation des Infrastructures Modernes (SEORIM), Soc. de Promotion des Auto-routes de Bourgogne, Restaurants (Belgium), Restaurants (Spain); Censeur Soc. des Autoroutes Rhône Alpes (AREA).
Leisure interests: skiing, swimming.
Tour Maine Montparnasse 33, avenue du Maine, 75755 Paris-Cédex 15; Home: Les Villepreux, 47 avenue de Villepreux, 92 Vaucresson, Hauts de Seine, France.
Telephone: 260-35-25 (Office); 970-65-84 (Home).

Boren, David L., M.A., J.D.; American lawyer and state governor; b. 21 April 1941, Washington, D.C.; s. of Lyle H. and Christine (McKown) Boren; m. Janna Lou Little 1967 (divorced 1975); one s. one d.; ed. Yale, Oxford and Oklahoma Univs.
Rhodes Scholar 65; Asst. to Dir. of Liaison, Office of Civil and Defense Mobilization 60-62; Propaganda Analyst, Soviet Affairs, U.S. Information Agency 62-63; Speakers Bureau, U.S. Embassy, London 63-65; mem. residential counselling staff, Univ. of Okla. 65-66; mem. Okla. House of Reps. 66-74; Chair. Govt. Dept., Okla. Baptist Univ. 69-74; Gov. of Okla. Jan. 75-.
Leisure interests: family, reading, rowing, tennis.
State Capitol Building, Oklahoma City, Okla. 73105, U.S.A.
Telephone: 521-2821.

Boreskov, Georgy Konstantinovich; Soviet chemist; b. 20 April 1907, Omsk; ed. Odessa Chemical Inst.
At Ukrainian Chemico-Radiological Inst., Odessa 28-37; Instructor, Odessa Inst. of Chemical Technology 30-37, Odessa Univ. 34-37; Dir. Catalysis Lab., Moscow Fertilizer, Insecticide and Fungicide Research Inst. 37-49; Assoc. Karpov Physico-Chemical Inst. 46-; Prof. Moscow Inst. of Chemical Technology 49-; Corresp. mem. U.S.S.R. Acad. of Sciences 58-66, mem. 66-; Dir. Inst. of Catalysis, Siberian Dept., U.S.S.R. Acad. of Sciences 61-; State Prize 42; Hero of Socialist Labour 67;

Order of Lenin (twice); Hammer and Sickle Gold Medal. Publs. on investigations of catalytic processes.
Institute of Catalysis, Siberian Department of U.S.S.R. Academy of Sciences, Akademgorodok, Novosibirsk, U.S.S.R.

Borg, Kim, M.SC.; Finnish singer; b. 1919, Helsinki; s. of Kaarlo Borg and Hilkka Stenius; m. Ebon Ringblom 1950; one s. one d.; ed. Helsinki Inst. of Technology and Sibelius-Acad., Helsinki.
Début, Helsinki 47; Royal Theatre, Copenhagen 52-70; Finnish National Opera 52-70; Munich State Opera 56-57; Glyndebourne Opera Co. 56, 59 and 68; Metropolitan Opera Co., New York 59-62; Royal Theatre, Stockholm 63-75; Hamburg State Opera 64-69; Prof. Royal Conservatory, Copenhagen 72-; guest appearances at State Opera, Vienna and Bolshoi Theatre, Moscow; tours in Europe, N. and S. America, Asia, Australia and Africa; numerous recordings; composed chamber music and orchestrated songs; Chair. Det danske Sangselskab; mem. Board Dirs. Danish-Finnish Soc.; Cross of Liberty (Finland); Kt. of White Rose (Finland); Pro-Finlandia Medal; Hon. Cross for Arts and Sciences (Austria).
Leisure interests: painting, fishing.
Publ. *Suomalainen laulajanaapinen* (ABC for the Finnish singer) 72.
Office: Det Kgl. danske Musikkonservatorium, Copenhagen; Home: Österbrogade 158, DK 2100 Copenhagen, Denmark.
Telephone: 290731 and 03-190027.

Borg, Lars Göran, M.SC., LIC.SC., DR.SC.; Swedish mathematician; b. 19 Nov. 1913, Kumla; s. of Eric J. Borg and Elna Peterson; m. Gunborg Sjölinder, M.D., 1939; two s. one d.; ed. Univ. of Uppsala.
Research Professor Univ. of Uppsala 45-52; Prof. of Math. Royal Inst. of Technology, Stockholm 53-, Rector 68-; Pres. Board for Educ. Org. for Teachers in Technology 64-67, Board Microwave Inst. Stockholm 68-; Deputy Board of L. M. Ericsson Telephone Co. 72-; mem. Nat. Science Council 61-67, Advisory Council of Board of Univ. Chancellor 64-70, Swedish Board for Technical Development 71-, Royal Acad. of Eng. Sciences (Vice-Pres. 72-74), Advisory Council to Wallenberg Foundation 72-74, Swedish Math. Soc. (Pres. 57-60), Swedish Operational Analysis Soc. (Pres. 63), Swedish Soc. of Future Studies (Pres. 71), Amer. Math. Soc., Amer. Assoc. for the Advancement of Science, Board of SEFI, Brussels, several govt. cttees. on education, research, radio and television, etc.; Hon. LL.D. (Dundee); Commdr. Order of Polar Star.
Leisure interests: technical constructions, building.
Publs. *Uber die Stabilität gewisser Klassen von linearen Differentialgleichungen* 44, *Eine Umkehrung der Sturm-Liouvilleschen Eigenwertaufgabe* 45, *Inverse problems in the theory of characteristic values* 47, *Bounded Solution of a System of Differential Equations* 48, *On a Liapounoff Criterion* 49, *On the completeness of some sets of functions* 49, etc.
Royal Institute of Technology, S-100 44 Stockholm 70; Home: 118 Alviksvagen, S-161 38 Stockholm-Bromma, Sweden.
Telephone: 23-65-20 (Office); 25-21-40 (Home).

Borg Olivier, Dr. George, LL.D.; Maltese politician; b. 5 July 1911, Valletta; ed. Lyceum and Royal Univ. of Malta.
Elected to Council of Govt. 39, to Legislative Assembly 47; Minister of Works and Reconstruction and Minister of Education 50; Prime Minister and Minister of Works and Reconstruction 50-55; Leader of Opposition 55-58; Prime Minister and Minister of Economic Planning and Finance 62-71, also Minister of Commonwealth and Foreign Affairs 65-72; Hon. D.Litt.; Knight Grand Cross Order of St. Sylvester and Order of Pius IX (Vatican); Leader Nationalist Party.
House of Representatives, Valletta, Malta.

Borge, Victor; American entertainer; b. 3 Jan. 1909, Denmark; m.; two s. three d.; ed. Borgerdydskolen and Copenhagen Conservatoire, and in Berlin and Vienna under Frederic Lamond and Egon Petri.
Concert pianist 22-34; revue, theatre and film career as composer, actor and musical comedian 34-; settled in U.S.A. 40, U.S. citizen 48; Order of Dannebrog, Order of Vasa (Sweden) 72, Order of St. Olav (Norway) 73.
Leisure interest: boating.
Publ. *My Favourite Intervals* 74.
Field Point Park, Greenwich, Conn., U.S.A.

Borgeaud, Maurice Camille; French metals executive; b. 5 Oct. 1909; ed. Ecole Polytechnique.
Former Vice-Pres. of USINOR (Union sidérurgique du Nord et de l'Est de la France), Pres., Dir.-Gen., Chair., Hon. Chair. 73-; Vice-Pres. Denain Nord-Est Longwy, Pres., Dir.-Gen. 73-; Officier Légion d'Honneur.

Borges, Jacobo; Venezuelan painter; b. 28 Nov. 1931; ed. Escuela de Artes Plásticas Cristóbal Rojas, Caracas and Ecole des Beaux Arts, Paris.
Member of Young Painters' Group and Illustrator of magazines and record covers while in Paris 51-56, also exhibited in French Nat. Exhbns.; Prof. of Scenography and Plastic Analysis, Escuela de Artes Plásticas Cristóbal Rojas, Caracas 58-65; Prof. of Scenography, Theatre School of Valencia and Dir. Experimental Art Centre, Univ. of Venezuela 66-; one-man exhbns. in Caracas at Galería Lauro 56, Museo de Bellas Artes 56, Galería G 63 and Galería Techo 65; represented in numerous group exhbns. including São Paulo Bienal 57, 63, 65, Venice Biennale 58, Brussels World Fair 58, and Int. Exhbns. at Guggenheim Museum, New York 64, 65; Nat. Painting Prize 63, Armando Reverón Bienal Prize 65.
Major works: *La Lámpara y la Silla* 51, *La Pesca* 57, *Sala de Espera* 60, *Todos a la Fiesta* 62, *Ha Comenzado el Espectáculo* 64, *Altas Finanzas* 65; series of *Las Jugadoras* and *Las Comedoras de Helados* 65-66.
c/o Museo de Bellas Artes, Avenida los Caobos, Caracas, Venezuela.

Borges, Jorge Luis; Argentine author and university professor; b. 24 Aug. 1899; ed. in Switzerland, Cambridge and Buenos Aires Univs.
Municipal Librarian of Buenos Aires 39-43; Dir. Nat. Library of Buenos Aires 55-73; fmr. Prof. of English and North American Literature, Buenos Aires Univ.; mem. Acad. Argentina de Letras; Hon. K.B.E.; Premio de Honor, Prix Formentor 61 (with Samuel Beckett), Fondo de las Artes 63; Inter-American Literary Prize 70; Hon. D.Litt. (Oxford) 70; Hon. doctorate (Jerusalem) 71; Alfonso Reyes Prize 73.
Publs. many short stories, poems and essays, including *Luna de Enfrente, Cuaderno San Martín, Historia de la Eternidad, Antología Clásica de la Literatura Argentina, El Martín Fierro* (with Margarita Guerrero), *La Poesía Gauchesca, El Aleph, El Jardin de Senderos que se bifurcan, Inquisiciones, Otras Inquisiciones, Historia Universal de la Infamia, Fervor de Buenos Aires, Ficciones, Labyrinths, Libro de Cielo y del Infierno* (poems) 60, *El Hacedor* 60, *Antología personal* 61, *Elogia de la Sombra* (poems) 69, *El Informe de Brodie* (stories) 71.
México 564, Buenos Aires, Argentina.

Borgnine, Ernest; American actor; b. 24 Jan. 1917; ed. New Haven public schools.
Films include *From Here to Eternity, Bad Day at Black Rock, Marty, Violent Saturday, Square Jungle, Three Brave Men, Hell Below, The Rabbit Trap, Man on String, Barabbas, Flight of the Phoenix* 66, *The Oscar* 66,

The Split, Ice Station Zebra, The Dirty Dozen 68, *Willard* 71, *The Poseidon Adventure* 72, *Emperor of the North* 72, *Sunday in the Country* 74, *Law and Disorder* 75; Acad. Award for Best Performance 56.
CMA, 8899 Beverly Boulevard, Los Angeles, Calif. 90048, U.S.A.

Borgonovo Pohl, Ing. Mauricio Alfredo; Salvadorian engineer and politician; b. 20 Dec. 1939, San Salvador; *s.* of Mauricio Borgonovo and Sara Pohl de Borgonovo; *m.* Patricia Baldocchi Dueñas de Borgonovo 1964; one *s.* one *d.*; ed. San José Univ. and Massachusetts Inst. of Technology.
Director Salvadorian Asscn. of Industries (ASI) 66-72; Pres. Comisión Ejecutiva Portuaria Autónoma (CEPA) 71-72; Pres. Organization Cttee. of Central American Inst.; Dir.-Gen. Foreign Policy, Ministry of Foreign Affairs 72; Minister of Foreign Affairs 72-; Nat. Order of Merit, Grand Cross Extraordinary of Paraguay.
Leisure interests: tennis, swimming, flying.
Ministerio de Relaciones Exteriores, Calle Santa Tecla, Km. 6, San Salvador; Home: 72-73 Avenida Norte, San Salvador, El Salvador.

Borin, Vadim Ivanovich; Soviet trade corporation official; b. 14 Jan. 1926; ed. Steel Inst., Moscow, and All-Union Acad. for Foreign Trade, Moscow.
Senior Engineer, Chief of Dept., U.S.S.R. Trade Del. in U.K. 55-60; Dir. *Promsyrioimport* 60-62; Deputy Trade Rep. of U.S.S.R. in Finland 62-66; Pres. *Soyuzchimexport* (export and import of chemical products) 66-69; Commercial Rep. in Japan 69-.
U.S.S.R. Trade Representation, Tokyo, Japan.

Borisenko, Nikolai Mikhailovich; Soviet politician; b. 1918; ed. Kharkov Veterinary Inst.
Veterinary technician 39-41; Soviet Army 41-45; mem. C.P.S.U. 43-; State farm dir. and Man. of Ukrainian agricultural trust 45-55; Chair. of local Soviet, Chair. Chernigov Regional Soviet of Working People's Deputies 55-63; First Sec. Chernigov Regional Cttee. of C.P. of Ukraine 63-70; mem. Central Cttee. C.P. of Ukraine, Sec. 70; Alternate mem. Political Bureau 70-; Alternate mem. C.P.S.U. Central Cttee. 71-; Deputy to U.S.S.R. Supreme Soviet 66-; Chair. Comm. for Agriculture, Soviet of Nationalities.
Central Committee, Communist Party of Ukraine, Kiev, U.S.S.R.

Borisov, Alexandr Vasilyevich; Soviet politician; b. 1913; ed. Gorky Inst. of Agriculture.
Agronomist 36, 38-41; Soviet Army 36-38, 41-46; Chief Agronomist, Krasnoufimsk District Dept. of Agriculture 46-59, later Head Sverdlovsk Regional Dept. of Agriculture; Vice-Chair. Sverdlovsk Regional Soviet 59-64, Chair. 64-; mem. C.P.S.U. 45-; Deputy to U.S.S.R. Supreme Soviet 66-; mem. Comm. for Public Health and Social Welfare, Soviet of Union.
Sverdlovsk Regional Soviet of Working People's Deputies, Sverdlovsk, U.S.S.R.

Bork, Robert Heron, J.D.; American government official and lawyer; b. 1 March 1927, Pittsburgh; *s.* of Harry Philip Bork and Elizabeth Kunkle; *m.* Claire Davidson 1952; two *s.* one *d.*; ed. Univ. of Chicago.
Admitted to Illinois Bar 53; Assoc., mem. Kirkland, Ellis, Houston, Chaffetz & Masters 55-62; Assoc. Prof. Yale Law School 62-65, Prof. of Law 65-73; Solicitor-Gen. 73-; Acting Attorney-Gen. 73.
Solicitor-General, Department of Justice, Washington, D.C. 20530; Home: 1007 Turkey Run Road, McLean, Virginia 22101, U.S.A.

Borkh, Inge; Swiss soprano opera singer; b. 26 May 1921; ed. Drama School, Vienna, and Vienna Acad.
Theatre performances (dancing, piano) in Vienna and Milan, then in Switzerland in German version of *Konsul* (Menotti); int. career 51-, Bayreuth, Paris, Vienna, Edinburgh Festival; first visit to U.S.A. 53; World

Première of *Irische Legende* (Egk) 55; appeared as Salome and Elektra, Carnegie Hall, New York 58; Metropolitan Opera, N.Y. 58; Bavarian Court Singer 63; appeared at opening of Nationaltheater, Munich, in *Die Frau ohne Schatten* Nov. 63; Grand Prix du Disque for *Elektra, Antigone* (Orff), and Schönberg's *Gurrelieder*; Reinhard Ring Award 73.
Haus Weitblick, CH 9405 Wienacht, Switzerland.
Telephone: Heiden 912091.

Borlaug, Norman Ernest, PH.D.; American agricultural scientist; b. 25 March 1914, Cresco, Ia.; *s.* of Henry O. and Clara (Vaala) Borlaug; *m.* Margaret G. Gibson 1937; one *s.* one *d.*; ed. Univ. of Minnesota.
With U.S. Forest Service 38-39; Instructor, Univ. of Minn. 41; Microbiologist, E. I. DuPont de Nemours Foundation 42-44; Research Scientist, Wheat Rockefeller Foundation, Mexico 44-60, Centro Internacional de Mejoramiento de Maíz y Trigo (Int. Maize and Wheat Improvement Center), Mexico 64-; Leonard L. Klinck Lecturer, Agricultural Inst. of Canada 66; mem. Citizen's Comm. on Science, Law and Food Supply 73-, Comm. on Critical Choices for America 73-, Nat. Acad. of Sciences; Hon. Fellow Indian Soc. of Genetics and Plant Breeding 68; Hon. Foreign mem. Acad. Nacional de Agronomía y Veterinaria de Argentina, N. I. Vavilovi Acad. (U.S.S.R.); Foreign mem. Royal Swedish Acad. of Agriculture and Forestry 71, Indian Nat. Science Acad. 73; numerous Mexican awards; Nobel Peace Prize 70; Hon. D.Sc. Punjab Agricultural Univ. 69, Royal Norwegian Agricultural Coll. 70, Michigan State Univ. 71, Universidad de la Plata, Argentina 71, Univ. of Florida 73, and others.
Leisure interests: hunting, fishing, baseball, wrestling, football, golf.
International Maize and Wheat Improvement Center, Londres 40, Mexico City 6; Home: Sierra Gorda 69, Lomas de Chapultepec, Mexico City, Mexico.

Borman, Frank; American astronaut; b. 14 March 1928, Gary, Ind.; *m.* Susan Bugbee; two *s.*; ed. U.S. Military Acad.
Pilot training, Williams Air Force Base, Arizona; assigned to various fighter squadrons in U.S. and Philippines; Instructor in Thermodynamics and Fluid Mechanics, U.S. Mil. Acad. 57; Master's degree from Calif. Inst. of Technology 57; graduated from U.S. Air Force Aerospace Research Pilots School 60; Instructor 60-62; selected by NASA as astronaut Sept. 62; Command Pilot *Gemini VII* 65; Commdr. *Apollo VIII* spacecraft which made flight round the moon Dec. 68; Deputy Dir. for Flight Operations, NASA, until May 69; Field Dir. of a NASA Space Station Task Group 69-70; Vice-Pres. Electronic Data Systems July 70-; Vice-Pres. Eastern Airlines Inc. 70-74, Vice-Pres. for Eastern Operations July 74-; NASA Exceptional Service Medal; Harmon Int. Aviation Trophy 66; Gold Space Medal, Int. Aeronautics Feb. 69.
Eastern Airlines Inc., Eastern Airlines Building, 10 Rockefeller Plaza, New York 20, N.Y., U.S.A.

Born, Jorge; Argentine industrial, commercial and financial company director; b. 24 July 1900; ed. Athenée Royal, Antwerp, Belgium, and Univ. de Bruxelles, Belgium.
Director, Bunge y Born S.A. 26-, Pres. and Chair. 56-; Vice-Pres. Molinos Río de la Plata S.A. 51-, Bunge y Born Foundation 64-; breeder of pedigree cattle (Hereford) and controls ownership of ranches in several Argentine provinces; Knight Order of Leopold, Officer Order of Crown (Belgium).
25 de Mayo 501, Buenos Aires, Argentina.

Borodin, Andrei Mikhailovich; Soviet veterinary surgeon and politician; b. 1912; ed. Alma Ata Zoo-Veterinary Inst.
Acting Veterinary Surgeon on state farm, and Veterinary Surgeon for an agricultural combine in Kazakhstan

32-39; exec. post, Agricultural Dept., Kustanai Region, Kazakh S.S.R. 39-42; exec. Party and local govt. posts 42-45; Asst. Head of Dept., Central Cttee., C.P. of Kazakhstan, then First Deputy Minister of Agriculture and Procurements, Kazakhstan S.S.R. 45-53; Rep. of U.S.S.R. Ministry of Procurements for Kazakh S.S.R. 53-56; First Sec., Akmolinsk Regional Cttee., C.P. of Kazakhstan 56-57; Minister of Agriculture, then Vice-Chair., State Planning Cttee., Kazakh Council of Ministers 57-58; at H.Q. of Central Cttee., C.P. of Kazakhstan 58-59; First Sec., Kustanai Regional Cttee., C.P. of Kazakhstan; mem. Central Cttee. of C.P.S.U. 66-, of C.P. of Kazakhstan 59-; Deputy to U.S.S.R. Supreme Soviet 62-, mem. Comm. for Agriculture, Soviet of Union; mem. C.P.S.U. 41; Hero of Socialist Labour, Order of Lenin, Hammer and Sickle Gold Medal, etc.
Kustanai Regional Committee, Communist Party of Kazakhstan, Kustanai, U.S.S.R.

Borodin, Victor Petrovich; Soviet politician; b. 1924; ed. Volgograd Inst. of Agriculture.
Soviet Army 42-52; Official, Volgograd Regional Cttee., C.P.S.U., Head of Dept. of Agriculture, then Second Sec., Volgograd Regional Cttee. of C.P.S.U. 52-65; Chair. Volgograd Regional Soviet 65-; mem. C.P.S.U. 46-; Deputy to Supreme Soviet 66-; mem. Planning and Budget Cttee., Soviet of Union, Cttee. of U.S.S.R. Parl. Group.
Volgograd Regional Soviet of Working People's Deputies, Volgograd, U.S.S.R.

Borotra, Jean (Robert); French civil engineer, company director and fmr. tennis player; b. 13 Aug. 1898, Biarritz; s. of Henry Borotra and Marguerite Revet; m. Mabel de Forest 1938 (divorced 1947); one s.; ed. Lycées Saint Louis and Michelet, Paris, Univ. de Paris and Ecole Polytechnique.
Civil Engineer 22; Commercial Man. Satam 24-30, Dir. 30-; Commissar-Gen. Gen. Educ. and Sport in Marshal Pétain's Govt. 40-42, deported by Gestapo 42-45; Vice-Pres. French Lawn Tennis Asscn. 30-68, Hon. Pres.; Pres. Comm. *Doctrine of Sport*, High Cttee. of Sport, Paris 62-68; Pres. Int. Lawn Tennis Fed. 60-61, Vice-Pres. 61-69, Hon. Vice-Pres. 69-; Vice-Pres. Int. Council for Sport and Physical Educ. (ICSPE) 60-68, Deputy Pres. 68-; Pres. Int. Cttee. for Fair Play; Pres. and Dir. several French and foreign cos.; Commdr. Légion d'Honneur, Croix de Guerre (14-18, 39-45); Hon. C.B.E. and several other foreign decorations; winner of numerous lawn tennis prizes, including six Wimbledon Championships (two for singles, three for doubles, and one for mixed doubles), and mem. French Davis Cup Team 22-47.
Office: 18 rue de Varize, Paris 16e; Home: 35 avenue Foch, Paris 16e, France.
Telephone: 224-44-02 (Office); 727-61-31 (Home).

Borov, Todor; Bulgarian bibliographer and librarian; b. 1901, Lom; m. Haritina Ivanowa Peeva 1930; two s.; ed. Sofia and Berlin Univs.
Professor in Library Science, Univ. of Sofia; Editor *Bălgarska kniga* (The Bulgarian Book) 30, *Yearbook of Bulgarian Bibliographical Inst.* 45-63.
Publs. *Knigi, biblioteki, bibliografija* (Books, Libraries, Bibliography) 41, *Pătija kăm knigite* (The Road to Books) 42, *Cehov i Bălgarija* 55, *Bulgarische Biblio-graphie* 60, *Die Bibliographie als Universitätslehrfach* 63, *Ausbildung von Bibliothekaren* 64.
Zar Krŭm 15, Sofia, Bulgaria.
Telephone: 87-52-40.

Borovik-Romanov, Andrei Stanislavovich; Soviet physicist; b. 18 March 1920, Leningrad; m. Belikova Tatjana Petrovna 1947; one s.; ed. Moscow Univ.
Research Assoc. Inst. of Physical Problems U.S.S.R. Acad. of Sciences 47-48; Research Assoc. Moscow Inst. of Measures and Measuring Instruments 48-55; Inst. of

Physico-Technical and Radio Measurements, U.S.S.R. Cttee. of Standards, Measures and Measuring Instruments 55-56; Assoc. and Deputy Dir. Inst. of Physical Problems U.S.S.R. Acad. of Sciences 56-; Prof. Moscow Physico-Technical Inst. 67-; Editor *JETP Letters* 68-; Corresp. mem. U.S.S.R. Acad of Sciences 66-, Acade-mician 72-.
Publs. Works on experimental and theoretical physics.
S. I. Vavilov Institute of Physical Problems, 2 Voro-byevskoe Shosse, Moscow, U.S.S.R.

Borovkov, Alexander Alexeyevich; Soviet mathe-matician; b. 6 March 1931, Moscow; ed. Moscow Univ. Postgraduate, Research Assoc. Moscow Univ. 54-60; Assoc. Head of Dept. Inst. of Mathematics, Siberian Branch U.S.S.R. Acad. of Sciences 60-; Lecturer, Head of Chair Novosibirsk Univ. 61-, Prof. 65-; Corresp. mem. U.S.S.R. Acad. of Sciences 66.
Publs. Works on contiguous problems of theory probabilities.
Institute of Mathematics, Akademgorodok, Novosi-birsk, U.S.S.R.

Borrelli, Rev. Mario, L.S.T.; Italian ecclesiastic; b. 1922, Naples; s. of Gennaro Borrelli and Lucia Morvillo; ed. Major Archdiocesan Seminary, Naples.
One of the founders of O.N.A.R.M.O., Naples 46; founder of first J.O.C. in Naples 47, of I.R.P., Naples 48, of "Casa dello Scugnizzo", Naples 50; Founder-Dir. *Lo Scugnizzo* (monthly magazine) 50-.
Publ. *La Concezione Copernico Galileiana e la Filosofia di Tomaso D'Aquino* 61, *La Relazione tra il Conservatorio dei Poveri di Gesù Cristo e l'Oratorio di Napoli* 61, *Il Largo dei Girolamini* 62, *A Streetlamp and the Stars* 63, *Memorie Baroniane dell'Oratorio di Napoli* 63, *Opere e Documenti sul Baronio presso la British Museum Library* 64, *I Documenti dell'Oratorio Napoletano* 64, *Le Testimonianze Baroniane dell'Oratorio di Napoli, Documenti sul Baronio presso la Bodleian Library, L'Epistolario del Giusto Calvino nei suoi Rapporti col Baronio* 65, *L'Architetto Nencioni Dionisio Di Bar-tolomeo* 67, *Le Costituzioni dell' Oratorio Napoletano* 68, *Diario delle Baracche* 69.
Largo San Gennaro a Materdei, Naples; Oratory of St. Philip, Via Duomo 142, Naples, Italy.
Telephone: 449139.

Borrie, Wilfred David, O.B.E., M.A.; British demo-grapher; b. 2 Sept. 1913, Waimate, New Zealand; s. of Peter and Isobella Borrie; m. Alice H. Miller 1941; one d.; ed. Waitaki Boys High School, Oamaru, New Zealand, Univ. of Otago, N.Z. and Cambridge Univ.
Lecturer, Social History and Econs., Sydney Univ. 44-46, Senior Lecturer 46-47; Research Fellow, Research School of Social Sciences, Australian Nat. Univ. 49-52, Reader 52-57, Prof. and Head of Dept. of Demography 57-68; Dir. Research School of Social Sciences 68-73, Prof. of Demography 73-; Vice-Pres. Int. Union for Scientific Study of Population 61-63; Pres. Social Science Research Council of Australia 62-64, Australian Council of Social Services 63-64; Chair. Population Comm., UN 65-69; mem. Immigration Planning Council of Australia 65-.
Leisure interests: surfing, tennis.
Publs. *Population Trends and Policies* 47, *Immigration* 48, *Italians and Germans in Australia* 54, *The Cultural Integration of Immigrants* (Part I and General Editor) 59, *Australia's Population Structure and Growth* (with G. Spencer) 65, *The Growth and Control of World Population* 70, *Population Environment and Society* 73.
Research School of Social Sciences, Australian National University, P.O. Box 4, Canberra, A.C.T.; Home: 29 Norman Street, Deakin, A.C.T., Australia 2600.
Telephone: 814114.

Borschette, Albert, D. ès L.; Luxembourg diplomatist; b. 14 June 1920; ed. Univs. of Aix-en-Provence, Inns-bruck, Munich, Erlangen and Paris.

Press Attaché, Ministry of State, Luxembourg 45-47; Head of Luxembourg Mission to French Zone of Germany 47-49; mem. Luxembourg Mission to Allied Control Comm., Berlin 49-50; Sec. Luxembourg Legation, Bonn 50-53, Sec., later Counsellor, Brussels 53-56; Deputy Head of Del. to Intergovernmental Cttee. for the Common Market and Euratom 56-57, to Interim Cttee. 57-58; Luxembourg Rep. to Euratom 58-59, Amb., Perm. Rep. to European Communities 58-70; mem. Comm. of European Communities July 70-; numerous decorations.
Publs. *Journal Russe* 46, *Literatur und Politik* 51, *Itinéraries I* 52, *Itinéraries Soviétiques* 71; novel: *Continuez à mourir* 57.
Commission of the European Communities, 200 rue de la Loi, Brussels, Belgium.

Borsos, Miklós; Hungarian sculptor and graphic artist; b. 13 Aug. 1906, Nagyszeben; s. of Lajos Miklós Borsos and Erzsébet Mosolygó; m. Ilona Gabriella Kéry 1933; no c.; ed. Budapest Coll. of Fine Arts and self-taught in Italy and France.
Started as painter, switched to stone-modelling and copper engraving 33; mem. Arts Council 45; Prof. Budapest Coll. of Applied Arts 46-60; Exhbns. Budapest 57, Tihany 65; exhibited at Venice Biennale 66, Zürich and Rome 67; First Prize Carrara sculpture exhbn. 59; Munkácsy Prize 54, Kossuth Prize 57, Merited Artist 67; Labour Order of Merit, Golden Degree 71; Eminent Artist 72.
Leisure interest: playing violin.
Romer Flóris-utca 53, Budapest II, Hungary.
Telephone: 357-958.

Borsuk, Karol, PH.D.; Polish mathematician; b. 8 May 1905, Warsaw; ed. Warsaw Univ.
Assistant lecturer, Warsaw Univ. 29-35, Docent 34-38, Assoc. Prof. 38-46; Head of Topology Group in Mathematical Inst. of Polish Acad. of Sciences 49-; Corresp. mem. Polish Acad. of Sciences 52-56, mem. 56-; Ed. *Rozprawy Matematyczne* 52-70; Deputy Editor *Fundamenta Mathematicae* 52-70; mem. Editorial Staff *Mathematical Monographs* 46-70; initiated and developed the theory of retracts; elaborated the theory of shape; Officer's Cross, Order of Polonia Restituta 54, Commdr.'s Cross 58; State Prize (1st Class) 55, 72.
Publs. *Geometria analityczna wielowymiarowa* (Multidimensional Analytical Geometry) 69; *Podstawy geometrii* (co-author); about 100 publs. on topology.
Ul. Filtrowa 63 m. 18, 02-056 Warsaw, Poland.

Borten, Per; Norwegian agronomist and politician; b. 3 April 1913, Flå Gauldal; s. of Lars and Karen Borten; m. Magnhild Rathe 1948; three c.; ed. Norwegian Agricultural Univ., Ås.
Head, Technical Section, Provincial Agricultural Admin., Sör-Tröndelag 46-65; Chair. Flå Municipal Council 45; Provincial Council, Sör-Tröndelag 48; fmr. Head of Youth Movement of Agrarian Movement, Sör-Tröndelag; mem. Storting 50-, Pres. Odelsting 61-65; Chair. Senterpartiet 55-67, Parl. Leader 57; Prime Minister 65-March 71; Deputy Chair. Housing Bank 55-; mem. Council of Farmers' Bank 65-; Chair. Council of United Life Insurance Cos. in Norway 59-.
Storting, Oslo, Norway.
Telephone: Oslo 442424.

Bortoluzzi, Paolo; Italian ballet dancer; b. 17 May 1938, Genoa; m. Jaleh Kerendi 1970; one s. one d.
Studied ballet under Ugo Dell'Ara, Genoa 54; joined Del Balletto Italiano, Milan 57; Leone Massine's Festival de Nervi 60; with Maurice Béjart's Ballet of the Twentieth Century 60-72; Perm. Guest Artist, American Ballet Theater 72, La Scala, Milan, Düsseldorf Opera; repertoire includes *Romeo and Juliet, Les Sylphides, Giselle, The Sleeping Beauty, Orpheo, The Nutcracker, Cinderella, Lac des Cygnes, Firebird, Nomos Alpha, La Sylphide* as well as many avant-garde works,

notably Béjart's *Nijinsky: Clown of God, IXe Symphonie, Messe Baudelaire.*
16 avenue des Merles, 1150 Brussels, Belgium; 11 Nuovo Corso Torino, 10098 Rivoli, Italy.
Telephone: Brussels 6732958; 39-11-9530733 (Italy).

Bosch, Baron Jean van den, G.C.V.O., LL.D.; Belgian diplomatist and banker; b. 27 Jan. 1910, Ghent; s. of Firmin and Anna de Volder; m. Helène Cloquet 1944; two d.; ed. Université Catholique de Louvain.
Diplomatic Service 34-; Sec., Peking 37-40, Ottawa 40; Chargé d'Affaires to Luxembourg Govt. in London 42-44; Counsellor 44, attached to Household of Prince Charles, Regent of Belgium, later served Cairo, Paris; Minister 53; Consul-Gen., Hong Kong, Singapore and Saigon 54; Amb. to Egypt and Minister to Libya 55; Perm. Under-Sec. of State, Ministry of Foreign Affairs and Foreign Trade 59, 60-65; Amb. to Congo (Léopoldville) 60; Amb. to U.K. 65-72; Perm. Rep. to Council of WEU 66-72; Dir. Lloyds Bank Int. 72-; Chair. LBI (Belgium) S.A. 73-; numerous decorations.
Lloyds Bank International (Belgium) S.A., 2-6 rue Royale, 1000 Brussels; 1 avenue de l'Hippodrome, 1050 Brussels, Belgium.
Telephone: 512-67-90 (Office); 648-79-03 (Home).

Bosch, Juan; Dominican writer and politician; b. 1909; ed. La Vega and Santo Domingo.
Founded literary group *Las Cuevas* (The Caves); exile in Puerto Rico and Cuba, travelled extensively in Latin America 37-61; founded Dominican Revolutionary Party 39, Pres. until Oct. 66; fmr. Prof. of Inst. of Political Science of Costa Rica; Pres. of Dominican Repub. 63; unsuccessful candidate for Presidency 66.
Publs. *Camino Real* (Royal Path—short stories), *Indios* (Indians), *La Mañosa* (The Shrew—novel), *Mujeres en la Vida de Hostos* (Women in the life of Hostos), *Hostos —El Sembrador* (Hostos, the Sower), *Dos Pesos de Agua* (Two Pesos worth of Water), *Ocho Cuentos* (Eight Tales), *La Muchacha de la Guaira* (The Girl from La Guaira), *Cuba, la Isla Fascinante* (Cuba, the Fascinating Island), *Cuentos de Navidad* (Christmas Stories), *Life of Bolívar, Cuentos escritos en el Exilio* (Tales written in Exile), *Trujillo: Causas de una tiranía sin Ejemplo* (Trujillo: Causes of a Tyranny without Equal), *The Unfinished Experiment: Democracy in the Dominican Republic* 65, *David* 66, *Pentagonism* 69.

Bosch-Gimpera, Pere, PH.D.; Mexican historian and archaeologist; b. 22 March 1891, Barcelona, Spain; s. of Pedro Bosch-Padró and Dolores Gimpera-Juncá; m. Josefina García-Díaz 1917; two s. one d.; ed. Barcelona, Madrid and Berlin Univs.
Director Catalan Archaeological Service 15-, and of Archaeological Museum 21-; Prof. of Prehistory and Ancient History Barcelona Univ. 16-39, Dean Philosophical Faculty 31-33, Rector of the Univ. 33-39; Pres. conf. for foundation of Congress of Prehistorical and Protohistorical Science, Berne 31; Minister of Justice, Catalan Autonomous Govt. 37-39; Prof. Oxford Univ. 39-40; Prof. School of Anthropology, Univ. of Mexico 41-48, Univ. of Guatemala 45-46; Chief of the Div. of Philosophy and Humanities, UNESCO 48-52; Sec.-Gen. Int. Union for Anthropological and Ethnological Sciences 53-66; Prof. Univ. of Mexico and School of Anthropology, Mexico 53-; Dr. h.c. (Heidelberg); Hon. mem. Royal Anthropological Inst., Soc. Antiquaries London; Ordinary mem. Deutsches Archaeologisches Inst., Inst. d'Estudis Catalans, Hispanic Soc. (Wash.); Corresp. mem. Académie des Inscriptions et Belles Lettres, Paris, Pontificia Academia Romana di Archeologia, etc.; Foreign Fellow, American Anthropological Asscn.; Prix Raoul Dusseigneur, Price Sahagun; Commdr. Ordre Palmes Académiques.
Leisure interests: literature, classical music, drawing.
Publs. *Prehistoria catalana* 19, *Études sur le néolithique et l'énéolithique de France* (with J. Serra-Ràfols) 27,

Etnología de la Península Ibérica 32, *La conquista romana de España* (with P. Aguado) 35, *España* 37, *L'art grec à Catalunya* 37, *Two Celtic Waves in Spain* 42, *España un mundo en formación* 43, *El poblamiento y la formación de los pueblos de España* 45, *Historia de Catalunya* (with F. Soldevila) 45, *Historia de Oriente* 47-51, *Los Iberos* 48, *Phéniciens et Grecs dans l'extrême Occident* 51, *Mouvements Celtiques* 50-55, *Ibères, Basques, Celtes* 56-57, *Todavía el problema de la cerámica ibérica* 58, *Asia y América en el paleolítico inferior, Supervivencias* 58, *L'Amérique: Paléolithique et Mésolithique, Néolithique et Pré-Colombien* 59, *El Problema Indo-europeo* 60, *Les Indoeuropéens* 61, *Civilisation mégalithique portugaise et civilisations espagnoles* (*L'Anthropologie*) 67, *L'Amérique avant Christophe Colomb* 67, *Las Relaciones Prehistóricas mediterráneas* 67, *Europe, Asie, Amérique au paléolithique supérieur* 67, *Paralelos transpacíficos de las altas culturas americanas y su cronología* 70 (trans. in German 71), *Historia de Oriente I* 70, *L'América pre-colombiana* 70.
Leisure interests: literature, classical music, drawing.
Office: Instituto de Investigaciones Anthropológicas, Torre de Humanidades 1, Ciudad Universitaria, México 20, D.F.; Home: Callejón de Olivo 84-4, Colonia Agrícola, México 20, D.F., Mexico.
Telephone: 5-24-29-37.

Bosco, Giacinto; Italian lawyer and politician; b. 25 Jan. 1905.
Professor of Int. Law, Rome Univ.; fmr. Editor *Rivista di Studi Politici Internazionali*, Florence; Editor *Rivista di Studi Europei*, Rome; fmr. Legal Adviser, Ministry of Foreign Affairs; mem. Senate 48-, Vice-Pres. 58-60; Under-Sec. of State for Defence 53-58, Minister for Educ. 60-62, of Justice 62-63, of Labour and Social Security Dec. 63-July 64; Chief, Italian Del. at UN 65; Minister of Labour and Social Security Feb. 66-Dec. 68, for Special Political Affairs, and Chief of Italian Del. at UN Dec. 68-69; Minister without Portfolio March-July 70; Minister of Posts and Telecommunications Aug. 70-Feb. 72; Christian Democrat.
Il Senato, Rome, Italy.

Bose, Vivian, B.A., LL.B.; Indian jurist; b. Ahmedabad; s. of Lalit Mohan Bose; m. Irene Mott 1930; one s. one d.; ed. Dulwich Coll., England, and Pembroke Coll., Cambridge.
Called to Bar, Middle Temple, London 13; practised at Nagpur Bar, India 13-36; Principal, Univ. Coll. of Law 24-30; Govt. Advocate and Standing Counsel to Govt. of Central Provinces and Berar 30-36; Additional Judicial Commr., Nagpur 31-36; Puisne Judge, Nagpur High Court 36-49, Chief Justice, Nagpur High Court 49-51; Puisne Judge, Supreme Court of India 51-56, retd. 56, ad. hoc. Judge 58-59; mem. Int. Comm. of Jurists 58-, Pres. 59-66, Hon. Pres. 66-; Chief Commr. for India, Boy Scouts Asscn. 48-49, Nat. Commr. 59-62.
Leisure interests: photography, motoring.
Henessy Road, Nagpur 1, Maharashtra, India.

Boskovsky, Willi; Austrian conductor; b. 16 June 1909; ed. Akad. für Musik, Vienna.
Conductor of New Year Concerts of Vienna Philharmonic Orchestra 54-; Founder of Vienna Octet; Leader of Philharmonic Orchestra of Vienna State Opera; soloist in chamber music; numerous decorations including Mozart Medal, Salzburg and Vienna; Österreichisches Ehrenkreuz; Kreisler Prize.
1030 Vienna 3, Jacquingasse 51, Austria.
Telephone: 72-6459.

Bosquet, Alain, M.A. (*pseudonym* of Anatole Bisk); French writer and critic; b. 28 March 1919, Odessa, Russia; s. of Alexander Bisk and Berthe Bisk (née Turiansky); m. Norma E. Caplan 1954; ed. Athénée d'Uccle, Univ. Libre de Bruxelles and Univ. de Paris à la Sorbonne.
Served with Belgian, French and U.S. Armies 40-45;

Editorial Sec. *la Voix de France*, New York 42-43; served with Allied Control Council, Berlin, then with Dept. of State 45-51; Prof. of French Literature, Brandeis Univ., U.S.A. 58-59; Prof. of American Literature, Univ. of Lyons 59-60; Columnist, *Combat* 53-; critic, French Nat. Broadcasting System 56-; columnist, *Le Monde* 61-; Prix Guillaume Apollinaire for *Langue Morte* 52; Prix Sainte-Beuve for *Premier Testament* 57; Prix Max Jacob for *Deuxième Testament* 59; Prix Fémina-Vacaresco for *Verbe et Vertige* 62; Prix Interallié for *La Confession Mexicaine* 65; Grand Prix de Poésie de l'Académie Française for *Quatre Testaments et Autres Poèmes* 67.
Leisure interests: Pre-Columbian art, postage stamps.
Publs. poems: *La vie est clandestine* 45, *A la mémoire de ma planète* 48, *Langue morte* 51, *Quel royaume oublié* 55, *Premier Testament* 57, *Deuxième Testament* 59, *Maître Objet* 62, Selected Poems, translated by Samuel Beckett, Charles Guenther, and Edouard Roditi 63, *100 Notes Pour Une Solitude* 70, *Penser contre soi* 73, *Notes pour un pluriel* 74; essays: *Saint-John Perse, Pierre Emmanuel, Emily Dickinson, Walt Whitman, Anthologie de la poésie américaine* 56, *35 jeunes poètes américaines* 61, *Verbe et Vertige* (on contemporary poetry) 61, *Entretiens avec Salvador Dali* 67, *Dorothea Tanning, Le Middle West* 67, *Les Américains sont-ils Adultes?* 69, *Roger Caillois* 71, *En Compagnie de Marcel Arland* 73, *Pas d'accord* 74, *Soljenitsyne* 74; novels: *La Grande Eclipse* 52, *Ni Singe, ni Dieu* 53, *Le Mécréant* 60, *Un besoin de malheur* 63, *Les Petites Eternités* 64, *La Confession mexicaine* 65, *Les Tigres de papier* 68, *Les poèmes de l'année 1970* (with P. Seghers) 70, *L'Amour à deux têtes* 70, *Chicago oignon sauvage* 71, *Notes Pour Un Amour* 72, *Monsieur Vaudeville* 73, *L'Amour bourgeois* 74.
32 rue de Laborde, Paris 8e, France.
Telephone: 387-96-76.

Bot, Theodorus H.; Netherlands politician and diplomatist; b. 1911, Dordrecht; m. Elisabeth W. van Hal 1936; seven c.; ed. State Univ., Utrecht.
Former civil servant 36-59; East Asiatic Affairs Bureau Indonesia 36-42; Japanese P.O.W. Burma-Thailand 42-45; General Political Adviser The Hague and Djakarta 46-54; Dir. Western Co-operation Foreign Affairs The Hague 54-59; State Sec. for Interior (Netherlands New Guinea Affairs) 59-63; Minister of Education, Arts and Sciences 63-65; Minister without Portfolio for the Under-Developed Countries 65-67; Amb. to Canada 68-73, to Austria 73-; Knight Commdr. Order Netherlands Lion, Knight Grand Cross St. Olav of Norway; Catholic People's Party.
Leisure interests: music, skiing, mountaineering, riding, literature.
Publs. articles in various magazines.
Royal Netherlands Embassy, Vienna; and Jacquingasse 8-10, 1030 Vienna III, Austria.

Botelho, Carlos; Portuguese painter; b. 18 Sept. 1899, Lisbon; s. of Carlos and Josefina Botelho; m. Beatriz Dos Santos 1922; one s. one d.; ed. Lisbon and Paris Acads. of Fine Arts.
Decorated Portuguese pavilion, Colonial Exhibition, Paris 31, Universal Exhibition, Paris 37; rep. XXV Venice Biennale 50, São Paulo Biennale 51-53, 55, 57, Brussels Int. Exhibition 58; Grand Prix, Paris Int. Exhibition; Sousa Cardoso Prize 39, Columbano Prize 40, S. Paulo Biennale; Prix d'Acquisition 51, Mention d'Honneur 53; Hallmark Award Prix, New York 52; Silver Medal Brussels Exhibition 58; Exhibited at 50 Years of Modern Art Exhibition Brussels and Art and Work Exhibition Charleroi 58; organized in conjunction with British Council Henry Moore Exhibition in Lisbon 59; retrospective exhibition Lisbon 59; "Promotion of Architecture" Exhibition, Barcelona 60; Rep., XXX Biennale, Venice 60; Exhibition, Madrid 61; one-man

Exhbn., New York 63, Lisbon 64, New York 65; Exhbns. São Paulo, London, Rio de Janeiro 65, Madrid 66; Gulbenkian Exhbn., Brussels, Paris, Madrid 67; itinerant exhbn. in major cities of Brazil 70; Bertrand Russell Centenary Exhbn., London 72; Gulbenkian Prize, Lisbon 61.
Leisure interest: playing the violin.
Atelier Buzano, Parede, Portugal.
Telephone: 2471667.

Botero; Colombian artist; b. 19 April 1932, Medellín; s. of David and Flora Botero; m. Cecilia Botero 1964; four c.
First group exhbn., Medellín 48; first one-man exhbn., Galeria Leo Matiz, Bogotá 51; studied at Acad. San Fernando and Prado Museum, Madrid 52; visited Paris and Italy and studied art history with Roberto Longhi, Univ. of Florence 53-54; lived in Mexico 56; one-man exhbn. Pan American Union, Washington, D.C. 57; Colombia 58-59; lived in New York 60-; first one-man exhbn. in Europe, Baden-Baden, Munich 66; visited Italy and Germany 67, studied work of Dürer; travelling retrospective exhbn. of 80 paintings in five German museums 70; one-man exhbn. Hanover Gallery, London 70; paintings in public collections in U.S.A., Germany, Spain and S. America; Guggenheim Nat. Prize for Colombia 60.
5 blvd. du Palais, Paris 4e, France.
Telephone: 0330674.

Botha, Johan Samuel Frederik, B.ECON.; South African diplomatist; b. 18 Feb. 1919, South Africa; s. of Philip J. Botha and Johanna P. du Plessis; m. Teresa M. Robbins 1949; three s. one d.; ed. Univ. of Stellenbosch and Univ. of South Africa.
Served, S. African Army 40-45; Second Sec., S. African Embassy, Washington 49-54, Ottawa 54-57; Perm. Rep. to UN 57-59; Asst. Sec. Dept. of Foreign Affairs, Pretoria 59-62; Consul-Gen., Tokyo 62-64; Minister, S. African Embassy, Washington 64-67; Deputy Sec. for Foreign Affairs 67-71; Amb. to U.S.A. 71-75; Under Sec., Dept. of Foreign Affairs.
Leisure interests: Africana, genealogy, cabinet making.
c/o Dept. of Foreign Affairs, Pretoria, South Africa.

Botha, Matthys Izak, B.A., LL.B.; South African diplomatist; b. 1913, Bloemfontein; s. of Johannes H. J. Botha and Anna M. J. Botha (née Joubert); m. Hester le Roux (née Bosman) 1940; two s.; ed. Selborne Coll., East London and Univ. of Pretoria.
Department of Finance 31-44; Dept. of Foreign Affairs 44-, Washington 44-51, New York 51-54; Head of Political Div., Dept. of Foreign Affairs, Pretoria 55-58; Minister to Switzerland 59-60; Minister, London 60-62; Perm. Rep. to UN 62-70; Amb. to Canada 70-73, to Italy and Panama 73-, also accred. to Costa Rica and El Salvador 73-74.
Leisure interests: boating, skiing, golfing.
South African Embassy, Fourth Floor, Philips Building, Piazza Monte Grappa 4, Rome 00195, Italy.

Botha, Michiel Coenraad; South African politician; b. 14 Dec. 1912, Lindley, O.F.S.; m. Lorraine Gouws 1940; five s. two d.; ed. Univ. of Stellenbosch, Pretoria Univ. and Univ. of Cape Town.
Teacher, Transvaal schools 35-36; Lecturer, Pretoria Technical Coll. 37-43; Sec. Afrikaanse Taal-en Kultuurvereniging 43-53; mem. Parl. 53-; later Deputy Minister of Bantu Admin. and Devt.; Minister of Bantu Admin. and Devt., and Minister of Bantu Educ. 66-; Nat. Party.
Ministry of Bantu Administration and Development and of Bantu Education, Pretoria, South Africa.

Botha, Pieter Willem, M.P.; South African politician; b. 12 Jan. 1916, Paul Roux district, O.F.S.; m. Elize Rossouw 1943; five c.; ed. Univ. of Orange Free State.

Member of Parl.; Chief Sec. Cape Nat. Party 48-58; Deputy Minister of the Interior 58-61; Minister of Community Devt., Public Works and Coloured Affairs 61-66, of Defence 65-; Leader Nat. Party in Cape Province Nov. 66-.
Leisure interests: shooting, hunting game.
Ministry of Defence, Pretoria, South Africa.

Botha, Roelof Frederik, B.A., LL.B.; South African diplomatist; b. 27 April 1932; ed. Volkskool, Potchefstroom, Univ. of Pretoria.
Joined Dept. of Foreign Affairs 53; served with diplomatic missions in Europe 56-62; mem. S. African legal team in S.W. Africa case, Int. Court of Justice, The Hague 63-66, 70-71; Agent of S. African Govt., Int. Court of Justice 65-66; Legal Adviser Dept. of Foreign Affairs 66-68, Under-Sec. and Head S.W. Africa and UN sections 68-70; mem. Parl. for Wonderboom 70-, served on various select Parl. cttees. 70-74; Sec. Foreign Affairs Study Group of Nat. Party's mems. of Parl. 74; Amb. and Perm. Rep. to UN 74; Amb. to U.S.A. 75-; mem. S. African Del. to UN Gen. Assembly 67-69, 71, 73-74; National Party.
Embassy of South Africa, 3051 Massachusetts Avenue, N.W., Washington, D.C. 20008, U.S.A.

Botha, Hon. Stephanus Petrus, B.COM.; South African politician; b. 5 May 1922, Lusaka, N. Rhodesia; s. of D. P. Botha; m. Martina Roos; two s. three d.; ed. Paarl Boys High School.
Joined Dr. Anton Rupert's Technical Industrial Investment Organization, became financial organizer; estab. Soutpansberg Regional Devt. Soc. 57, Chair. and Hon. Pres.; M.P. for Soutpansberg; Chair. Nat. Party's Land Group; Sec. Water Affairs Group; Deputy Sec. Study Group on Bantu Affairs; mem. Bantu Affairs Comm. 66-; mem. Exec. Cttee. of Nat. Party in Transvaal; Deputy Minister of Water Affairs 66-68; Minister of Water Affairs and of Forestry 68-76, of Labour and Mines 76-; Dir. Volkskas Ltd., Rondalia Ltd., Alt. Trustee Dagbreek Trust.
Ministry of Labour and Mines, Pretoria, South Africa.

Bothereau, Robert; French trade unionist; b. 22 Feb. 1901.
Metal worker; Sec. State Workers' Trade Union, Orleans 26-28; Sec.-Gen. Loiret Département Union 28-33; Sec.-Gen. Confederation of Labour (C.G.T.) 33-48; Sec.-Gen. Gen. Confederation of Labour—Force Ouvrière (C.G.T.F.O.) 47-64; mem. French Econ. and Social Council 48-63; mem. Gen. Council Banque de France 63-72, Counsellor of State 64-67.
21 rue du Puits de Roussy, 45-Beaugency, France.
Telephone: (38) 44-52-55.

Bott, Raoul, D.SC.; American (naturalized) mathematician; b. 24 Sept. 1923, Budapest, Hungary; s. of Rudolph and Margit (Kovacs) Bott; m. Phyllis H. Aikman 1947; one s. three d.; ed. McGill Univ. and Carnegie Inst. of Technology.
Member Inst. for Advanced Study, Princeton 49-51, 55-57; Instructor in Mathematics, Univ. of Mich. 51-52, Asst. Prof. 52-55, Prof. 57-59; Prof. of Maths. Harvard Univ. 59-; Higgins Prof. of Maths. 68-; Editor *Topology*, *Annals of Mathematics* 58-59, *American Journal of Mathematics* 69-; mem. Nat. Acad. of Sciences, American Mathematical Soc., American Acad. of Arts and Sciences; Veblen Prize, American Math. Soc. 64 (Vice-Pres. 73-75); Fellow, Quincy House 69-.
Leisure interests: music, swimming, skiing.
Office: Mathematics Department, Harvard University, Science Center, 1 Oxford Street, Cambridge, Mass. 02138; Home: 77 Kirkstall Road, Newtonville, Mass. 02160, U.S.A.
Telephone: B14-7960 (Home).

Bottomley, Sir James Reginald Alfred, K.C.M.G., M.A.; British diplomatist; b. 12 Jan. 1920, London; s. of Sir Cecil Bottomley and Alice T. Bottomley (née Robinson);

m. Barbara E. Vardon 1941; two *s.* (and one deceased) two *d.*; ed. King's Coll. School, Wimbledon and Trinity Coll., Cambridge.

Served in British Army 40-46; joined Dominions Office 46 (now Foreign and Commonwealth Office); served in South Africa 48-50, Pakistan 53-55, U.S.A. 55-59, Malaysia 63-67; mem. British Nat. Export Council 70-71, British Overseas Trade Board 72, Cttee. on invisible exports 70-72; Amb. to South Africa 73-76; Perm. Rep. to UN Office and other orgs. in Geneva May 76-.
Leisure interests: gardening, reading, golf.
United Nations Geneva Office, Palais des Nations, Geneva, Switzerland.

Bottrall, Francis James Ronald, O.B.E., K.ST.J., F.R.S.L.; British poet and literary historian; b. 2 Sept. 1906, Camborne, Cornwall; *s.* of Francis John Bottrall and Clara Jane Rowe; *m.* 1st Margaret F. Saumarez-Smith 1934, 2nd Margot Pamela Samuel 1954; one *s.*; ed. Redruth County School and Pembroke Coll., Cambridge.
Lecturer in English Helsinki Univ. 29-31; Commonwealth Fund Fellowship Princeton Univ. U.S.A. 31-33; Johore Prof. of English Language and Literature Raffles Coll. Singapore 33-37; Asst. Dir. and Prof. of English Literature British Inst. Florence 37-38; Sec. London Univ. School of Oriental and African Studies 39-45; seconded to Air Min., Priority Officer 40; British Council Rep. Sweden 41-44, Italy 45-50; Controller Education Div. British Council 50-54; Rep. Brazil 54-56, Greece 57-59, Japan 59-61; Chief, Fellowships and Training Branch, Food and Agriculture Org. (FAO) of UN 63-65; Syracuse Int. Poetry Prize 54; Grand Officer of Order of Merit of Republic of Italy 73.
Leisure interests: music, travel, watching sport.
Publs. *The Loosening and Other Poems* 31, *Festivals of Fire* 34, *The Turning Path* 39, *T. S. Eliot: Dikter i Urval* 42, *Farewell and Welcome* 45, *Zephyr Book of English Verse* 45, *Selected Poems* 46, *The Palisades of Fear* 49, *Adam Unparadised* 54, *Collected Poems* 61, *Rome* (Art Centres of the World) 68, *Day and Night* 74, *Poems 1955-1973* 74.
Via IV Fontane 16, Int. 6, 00184 Rome, Italy.

Botvinnik, Mikhail Moiseevich, D.SC.; Soviet chess player; b. 17 Aug. 1911, Repino (near Leningrad); *s.* of Moisey and Serafina Botvinnik; *m.* Gajane Ananova 1935; one *d.*; ed. Leningrad M. I. Kalinin Polytechnic Inst.
Chess Champion of U.S.S.R. 31, 33, 39, 41, 44, 45, 52; World Champion 48-57, 58-60, 61-63; Chess Grandmaster of U.S.S.R.; Senior Scientific Assoc. All-Union Scientific Research Inst. of Electrical Energy 55-; mem. C.P.S.U. 40-; Int. Grand Master; Order of Lenin; Order of Red Banner of Labour, Order of Honour (twice).
Flat 154, 3 ja Frunzenskaja W. 7, Moscow G-270, U.S.S.R.
Telephone: 2421586.

Bouchard, Marcel Félix; French university professor; b. 30 June 1898, Vosne Romanée, Côte d'Or; *m.* Marguerite Helminger 1926; five *c.*; ed. Ecole Normale Supérieure.
Professor, Lycée de Vesoul 20, Belfort 22, Dijon 25; Lecturer in French Classical Literature, Faculty of Letters Nancy 33, Prof. 37, Dean of Faculty 45-46; Rector of Académie de Dijon and Pres. of the Univ. Council 46-; served in both World Wars; fmr. Pres. Académie des Sciences, Arts et Belles-Lettres de Dijon 62; fmr. Pres. Perm. Conf. of Rectors and Vice-Chancellors of European Univs.; fmr. Vice-Pres. of Asscn. of French Speaking Univs.; fmr. Vice-Pres. Int. Asscn. of Univs.; Officier Légion d'Honneur; Officier Mérite Agricole; Commdr. Ordre des Palmes Académiques; Grand Cross, Order of

Merit of Germany; Dr. h.c. Univ. of Montreal, Univ. of Manchester; hon. mem. Univ. of Göttingen.
Leisure interests: hunting, yachting.
Publs. *De l'Humanisme a l'Encyclopédie* 30, *Les caractères véritables de Pierre Legouz* 30, *Lamartine ou le sens de l'amour* 40, *L'histoire des oracles de Fontenelle* 46, *L'Académie de Dijon et le premier Discours de Rousseau* 50, *Pour la Bourgogne son Université* 73.
Gilly-Les-Citeaux, 21 Vougeot, France.
Telephone: 80-06-86-49.

Bouey, Gerald Keith, B.A.; Canadian banker; b. 2 April 1920, Axford, Sask.; *s.* of J. A. Bouey; *m.* 1945; one *s.* one *d.*; ed. Queen's Univ., Kingston, Ont.
Joined Research Dept., Bank of Canada 48, Asst. Chief 53-56, Deputy Chief 56-62, Chief 62-65, Adviser to the Govs. 65-69, Deputy Gov. 69-71; Senior Deputy Gov. Jan. 72-Jan. 73; Gov. Bank of Canada Feb. 73-.
Leisure interests: reading, golf, curling.
Office: 234 Wellington Street, Ottawa; Home: 79 Kamloops Avenue, Ottawa, Canada.
Telephone: 563-8330 (Office); 733-5710 (Home).

Bouladoux, Maurice; French trade unionist; b. 16 July 1907.
Accountant, textile factory 22-23; Founder, Constitution of Young Christian Trade Unionists, Pres. of Paris Region 29; Sec.-Gen. French Confederation of Christian Workers 37; Head Buyer, Chemical Industry 40-45; Sec.-Gen. French Confederation of Christian Workers 48-53, Pres. 53-61; Pres. Int. Federation of Christian Trade Unions 61-73 (now called World Confederation of Labour—WCL); mem. Admin. Council, Int. Labour Org. (ILO) 60-63; Vice-Pres. Econ. and Social Cttee. of European Econ. Community and Euratom 58-73; Counsellor of State 64-68.
98 rue de St. Prix, 95320 St. Leu la Forêt, France.
Telephone: 960-02-72.

Boulanger, Nadia (Juliette); French composer, conductor and music teacher; b. 16 Sept. 1887; ed. Paris Conservatoire.
Honorary Prof. Paris Conservatoire, Dir. and Prof. American Conservatory of Music, Fontainebleau 49-; Maître de Chapelle of H.H. the Prince of Monaco; compositions include orchestral and instrumental pieces and songs; mem. American Acad. of Arts and Sciences; Commdr. Légion d'Honneur, Commdr. Arts et Lettres; Commdr. St. Charles; Commdr. Polonia Restituta; Dr. h.c. (Univs. of Oxford, and Newcastle, and Harvard Univ.)
1 place Lili-Boulanger, 75009 Paris, France.
Telephone: 874-57-91.

Boulanger, Yuri Dmitriyevich; Soviet geophysicist; b. 10 Aug. 1911, Moscow; *s.* of Dimitry and Vera Boulanger; *m.* Kira Koziakkova 1958; two *s.*; ed. Moscow Geodesy Inst.
Research Assoc. Schmidt Inst. of Physics of Earth, U.S.S.R. Acad of Sciences 34-; Corresp. mem. U.S.S.R. Acad. of Sciences 66-; Pres. Int. Geodesy Asscn. 71-75; Hon. D.Eng. (Tech. Univ. Dresden).
Publs. Works on experimental studies in gravimetry and experimental studies of recent crustal movements (geokinematics).
O. Schmidt Institute of Earth Physics, 10 Ulitsa Bolshaya Gruzinskaya, Moscow; Apart. 64, Block 2, D. Ulianov Str., Moscow W-333, U.S.S.R.

Boulding, Kenneth Ewart, M.A.; American university professor; b. 18 Jan. 1910, Liverpool, England; *s.* of William C. Boulding and Elizabeth Ann Boulding (née Rowe); *m.* Elise Biorn-Hansen 1941; four *s.* one *d.*; ed. Liverpool Collegiate School, New Coll., Oxford, and Univ. of Chicago.
Commonwealth Fellow 32-34; Asst. Edinburgh Univ.

34-37; Instructor, Colgate Univ., U.S.A. 37-41; Economist, L.N. 41-42; Prof. Fisk Univ. 42-43; Assoc. Prof. Iowa State Coll. 43-46; Angus Prof. of Political Economy and Chair. of Dept., McGill Univ. 46-47; Prof. Iowa State Coll. 47-49; Prof. of Economics, Univ. of Michigan 49-68; Prof. of Econs. and a Programme Dir. Inst. of Behavioral Science, Univ. of Colorado 68-; Pres. American Econ. Asscn. 68, Distinguished Fellow 69; Fellow, Center for Advanced Study of Behavioral Science, Stanford, Calif. 54-55; Fellow, American Acad. Arts and Sciences, American Philosophical Soc.; mem. Nat. Acad. of Sciences; John Bates Clark Medal, American Econ. Asscn. 49, Prize for Distinguished Scholarship in the Humanities 62; many hon. degrees. Leisure interests: poetry, sketching, water-colours.
Publs. *Economic Analysis* 41 (fourth edn. 66), *The Economics of Peace* 45, *The Naylor Sonnets* 45, *A Reconstruction of Economics* 50, *The Organizational Revolution* 53, *The Image* 56, *Principles of Economic Policy* 58, *The Skills of the Economist* 58, *Conflict and Defense* 62, *The Meaning of the Twentieth Century* 64, *The Impact of the Social Sciences* 66, *Beyond Economics* 68, *Economics as a Science* 70, *A Primer on Social Dynamics* 70, *The Prospering of Truth* (1970 Swarthmore Lecture) 70, *Peace and the War Industry* (ed.) 70, *Readings in Price Theory* (ed. with W. G. Stigler) 52, *Linear Programming and the Theory of the Firm* (ed. with W. A. Spivey) 60, *Disarmament and the Economy* (ed. with Emile Benoit) 63, *Economic Imperialism* (ed. with T. Mukerjee) 72, *Redistribution to the Rich and the Poor* (ed. with Marin Pfaff) 72, *The Appraisal of Change* (in Japanese) 72, *Kenneth E. Boulding/Collected Papers* Vols. I and II (ed. Fred Glahe) 71, Vols. III and V (ed. Larry Singell) 73-75, *Transfers in an Urbanized Economy* (ed. with Martin and Anita Pfaff) 73, *The Economy of Love and Fear: a Preface to Grants Economics* 73, *Sonnets from the Interior Life and Other Autobiographical Verse* 75.
Institute of Behavioral Science, University of Colorado, Boulder, Colo. 80309, U.S.A.
Telephone: (303) 492-7526.

Boulez, Pierre; French composer; b. 26 March 1925; ed. Paris Conservatoire.
Studied with Messiaen, Vaurabourg-Honegger and Leibowitz; Dir. of Music to Jean-Louis Barrault theatre company 48; aided by Barrault and Madeleine Renaud Barrault he founded the *Concert Marigny* which later became the *Domaine Musicale*, Paris; Principal Guest Conductor Cleveland Symphony Orchestra 68; Musical Dir. New York Philharmonic 71-(77); Principal Conductor BBC Symphony Orchestra 71-75; Dir. Inst. de Recherches et de Coordination Acoustique/Musique Sept. 75-; has conducted concerts at Amsterdam, the Donaueschingen Festival and elsewhere.
Works: First Piano Sonata 46, Sonata for Two Pianos 46, Sonatina for Flute and Piano 46, *Le Visage Nuptial* (5 poems of René Char for 2 solo voices, female choir and orch.) 46-50, Second Piano Sonata 48, *Le Soleil des Eaux* (2 poems of René Char for voice and orch.) 48, *Livre pour Quattuor* (string quartet) 49, *Symphonie Concertante* (piano and orch.) 50, *Le Marteau sans Maître* (cantata for voice and instruments to texts by René Char, also ballet 65) 55, *Structures* (2 pianos) 64, Third Piano Sonata 57-58, *Improvisations sur Mallarmé* (soprano and chamber ensemble) 58, *Doubles* (orch.) 58, *Poésie pour Pouvoir* (orch. and eight-track tape-recorder) 58, *Tombeau* (soprano and orch.) 59, *Pli selon Pli* 58-62, *Figures—doubles—prismes* 64/74, *Eclats* and *Eclats Multiples* 65, *Domaines* 68-69, *Cummings ist der Dichter* 70, *Explosante Fixe* 73, *Memoriales* 74.
Publs. *Penser la musique aujourd'hui* 66, *Relevés d'apprenti* (essays) 67.
c/o Ingpen and Williams Ltd., Concert Agents, 14 Kensington Court, London, W.8, England.

Boulin, Robert; French lawyer and politician; b. 20 July 1920; s. of Daniel Boulin and Marcelle Martineau; m. Colette Lalande 1947; one s. one d.
Lawyer 46-; U.N.R. (Union pour la Nouvelle République) Dep. 58-61, 62-; mem. Central Cttee. U.N.R.; Sec. of State for Repatriation Jan.-Sept. 62; Sec. of State for the Budget Sept. 62-May 68; Minister of Civil Service May-June 68, of Agriculture 68-69, of Public Health June 69-72, for Parl. July 72-April 73; Mayor of Libourne 59.
14 rue de Géraud, 33500 Libourne; 32 boulevard Maillot, 92200 Neuilly-sur-Seine, France.
Telephone: Libourne 51-08-89.

Boulloche, André François Roger Jacques, L. ès D.; French politician; b. 7 Sept. 1915, Paris; m. 1st 1949, 2nd Odile Pathé 1959; two s. one d.; ed. Ecole Polytechnique, Paris.
Director du Cabinet of Paul Ramadier 47-49; Dir. Service de l'Infrastructure, Sec. of State for Air 53-55; Dir. of Public Works and Urbanization, Morocco 55; Minister without Portfolio, de Gaulle Cabinet July 58-Jan. 59; Minister of Educ. Debré Cabinet Jan.-Dec. 59; Counsellor of State 60-63; Mayor of Montbéliard 65-; Deputy from Doubs 67-; Commdr. Légion d'Honneur, Compagnon de la Libération, Médaille de la Résistance, Croix de Guerre.
87 avenue Paul Doumer, Paris 16e, France.
Telephone: JAS 44-25.

Boult, Sir Adrian C., C.H., Kt., M.A., D.MUS., F.R.C.M.; British musician; b. 8 April 1889; ed. Westminster School, Christ Church, Oxford, and Leipzig Conservatorium.
Former Conductor British Symphony Orchestra; has conducted in London, Vienna, Munich, Prague, Barcelona, Boston, Brussels, Zürich, Paris and New York; Dir. Birmingham City Orchestra 24-30; Dir. of Music BBC 30-42; Conductor BBC Symphony Orchestra until 50; Chief Conductor London Phil. Orch. 50-57, Birmingham Symphony Orchestra 59-60; on staff of Royal Coll. of Music 19-30, 62-66; Vice-Pres. Council of Royal Coll. of Music 63-; Royal Phil. Soc. Gold Medallist 44, Hon. mem. Royal Acad. of Sweden; Hon. LL.D. (Birmingham, Liverpool), Hon. Mus. Doc. (Edinburgh and Cambridge), Hon. R.A.M., Hon. G.S.M.
Publs. *Thoughts on Conducting* 63, *My Own Trumpet* 73.
96 West Street, Farnham, Surrey, GU9 7EN, England.
Telephone: 025-73-26345.

Boulting, John Edward; British film director and writer; b. 21 Nov. 1913, Bray; s. of Arthur Boulting and Rose Bennet; twin brother of Roy Boulting, q.v.; ed. Reading School.
Started film making 37, Joint Man. Dir. Charter Film Productions Ltd. with Roy Boulting 73-; mem. Board, British Lion Films 58-73; Man. Dir. 66-73, resgnd.
Leisure interests: cricket, tennis, falling off horses, reading, talking, listening.
Films include, *Pastor Hall, Thunder Rock, Fame is the Spur, Brighton Rock, The Guinea Pig, Seven Days to Noon, The Magic Box, Private's Progress, Brothers in Law, I'm all Right Jack, Heaven's Above, The Family Way, There's a Girl in My Soup, Soft Beds, Hard Battles.*
Charter Film Productions, 95 Wigmore Street, London, W.1; Home: Warfield Dale House, Warfield Dale, Nr. Bracknell, Berkshire, RG12 6HR, England.
Telephone: 01-352-8822 (Office); 03447-3404 (Home).

Boulting, Roy; British film producer and director; b. 21 Nov. 1913; s. of Arthur Boulting and Rose Bennet; twin brother of John Boulting, q.v.; ed. Reading School.
Formed independent film production co. with John Boulting 37; war service, RAC, finishing as Capt.; Dir.

British Lion Films Ltd. 58-72; Joint Man. Dir. Charter Film Productions Ltd. 73-.

Films produced include, *Brighton Rock* 47, *Seven Days to Noon* 50, *Private's Progress* 55, *Lucky Jim* 57, *I'm All Right Jack* 59, *Heavens Above!* 62.

Films directed include, *Pastor Hall* 39, *Thunder Rock* 42, *Fame is the Spur* 47, *The Guinea Pig* 48, *High Treason* 51, *Singlehanded* 52, *Seagulls over Sorrento*, *Crest of the Wave* 53, *Josephine and Men* 55, *Run for the Sun* 55, *Brothers in Law* 56, *Happy is the Bride* 58, *Carlton-Browne of the FO* 58-59, *I'm All Right Jack* 59, *The Risk* 60, *The French Mistress* 60, *Suspect* 60, *The Family Way* 66, *Twisted Nerve* 68, *There's a Girl in My Soup* 70, *Soft Beds, Hard Battles* 74.

Charter Film Productions Ltd., 95 Wigmore Street, London, W.1, England.

Boumah, Augustin; Gabonese politician; b. 7 Nov. 1927, Libreville; ed. French Inst. of Overseas Studies. Directeur de cabinet, Ministry of Labour 63; fmr. Dir. Gabonese School of Admin.; Minister of Youth, Sports and Cultural Affairs Jan.-April 67; Minister of Justice and Keeper of the Seals April-Sept. 67; mem. Exec. Cttee., Parti Démocratique Gabonais (PDG); Minister of the Interior 67-68, of Finance and the Budget 68-72; Minister of State at Presidency in charge of Planning and Devt. 72, 72-75; Pres. Supreme Court 75-.

Supreme Court, B.P. 1043, Libreville, Gabon.

Boumedienne, Houari (real name: **Mohammed Boukharouba**); Algerian army officer and politician; b. 1927; ed. Islamic Inst., Constantine, and Cairo.

Former teacher, Guelma; promoted rebel activities in Oran area, Algeria 55; Commdr. of Wilaya 55-57; Chief of Staff, F.L.N. 60-62; Minister of Defence 62-; First Deputy Premier 63-65; Pres. Revolutionary Council 65-; Pres. Council of Ministers 65-.

Council of Ministers, Algiers, Algeria.

Boun Oum Na Champassak, Prince; Laotian politician; b. 11 Dec. 1911, Champassak; ed. Lycée Chasseloup Laubat, Saigon.

Member resistance movement against Japanese 41-45; Pres. Del. of 1946 for Franco-Lao Co-operation; renounced right of succession to South Laotian throne in interests of Lao Unity; Prime Minister 49-50; Pres. Nat. Assembly which negotiated independence 49; Pres. Revolutionary Cttee., Anti-Communist League of Savannakhet after *coup d'état* of 1960; Prime Minister, Pres. Nat. Assembly 61-62; Perm. Del. of H.R.H. for Gen. Inspection of the Kingdom 62-; Minister of Religion 66-72.

c/o Ministry of Religion, Vientiane, Laos.

Bourassa, Robert, M.A.; Canadian politician and economist; b. 14 July 1933, St. Pierre Claver, Mercier; s. of Aubert Bourassa and Adrienne Courville; m. Andrée Simard 1958; one s. one d.; ed. Jean-de-Brébeuf Coll., Montreal, Montreal Univ., Univs. of Oxford and Harvard.

Admitted to Quebec Bar 57; Fiscal Adviser to Dept. of Nat. Revenue, Lecturer in Econs. and Public Finance, Ottawa Univ. 60-63; Sec., Dir. of Research, Bélanger Comm. on Public Finance 63-65; Special Adviser to Fed. Dept. of Finance; mem. Nat. Assembly for Mercier 66-; Pres. Liberal Party Political Comm., mem. Party's Strategy Cttee.; Prof. of Public Finances, Montreal and Laval Univs.; Leader Liberal Party of Quebec Jan. 70, Financial Critic; Prime Minister of Quebec May 70-, Minister of Finance 70, of Intergovt. Affairs 71-72.

Office of the Prime Minister of Quebec, Quebec City, P.Q., Canada.

Bourbon, H.R.H. Prince Alfonso de, Duke of Cadiz; Spanish diplomatist; b. 20 April 1936, Rome, Italy; s. of H.R.H. Jaime de Bourbon, Infante of Spain and H.R.H. Emanuela de Dampierre, Duke and Duchess of

Segovia and Anjou; m. María del Carmen Martinez-Bordiu 1972; two s.; ed. Switzerland, Italy, France, Univs. of Deusto, Valladolid and Madrid.

With Banco Exterior de España, Vice-Pres. Italian Chamber of Commerce 60-69; Amb. to Sweden 70-73; Pres. Inst. of Hispanic Culture 73-; Lieut. Spanish Air Force; Grand Cross Order of Isabel la Católica, G.C. Polar Star (Sweden), and other decorations.

Leisure interests: skiing, tennis, golf, flying, scuba diving.

San Francisco de Sales 33, Madrid, Spain.

Telephone: 253-93-63.

Bourdet, Claude; French journalist; b. 28 Oct. 1909, Paris; s. of Edouard Bourdet and Catherine Pozzi; m. Ida Adamoff 1935; two s. one d.; ed. Coll. de Normandie, Lycée Hoche (Versailles), Fed. Inst. of Technology (Zürich).

Attached to Cabinet of Minister of Nat. Economy 36-39; Man. La Manda (soap and oil firm) 40-41; mem. Dir. Cttee. "Combat" Movement and Man. of secret paper 42; mem. Conseil Nat. de la Résistance; arrested and imprisoned in Oranienburg and Buchenwald concentration camps 44; Vice-Pres. Consultative Assembly 45; Dir.-Gen. Radiodiffusion Française 45; Man. *Combat* 47-50; Founder and Editor *L'Observateur* (now *Le Nouvel Observateur*) 50-63; founder Centre d'Action des Gauches Indépendants 52; mem. Municipal Council of Paris 59-71, Nat. Cttee. Parti Socialiste Unifié 60-63; Pres. Mouvement pour le Désarmement, la Paix, la Liberté, Int. Confed. for Disarmament and Peace; Foreign Editor *Témoignage Chrétien* 67-; Compagnon de la Libération.

Publs. *Le Schisme Yougoslave* 50, *Les chemins de l'Unité* 64, *A qui appartient Paris* 72, *L'aventure incertaine* 75.

47 avenue d'Iéna, Paris 16e, France.

Telephone: 720-88-75.

Bourgeois, Paul, D.PHIL.; Belgian astronomer; b. 13 Feb. 1898, Brussels; m. Louise Dauby 1925; one s. one d.; ed. Univ. Libre, Brussels.

Assistant Belgian Royal Observatory 24, Assoc. Astronomer 36, Astronomer 38, Dir. 47, Hon. Dir. 63; Hon. Prof. Université Libre, Brussels 54; Hon. Past Pres. Abstracting Board, Int. Council of Scientific Unions; Vice-Pres. Centre Nat. de calcul mécanique; corresp. mem. Bureau des Longitudes; mem. Int. Astronomical Union; fmr. mem. Conseil Nat. de la Politique scientifique; Vice-Pres. Inst. pour la Recherche Scientifique en Afrique Centrale; Assoc. mem. Académie Royale des Sciences d'Outre-Mer; Quinquennial Prize for Statistics 29-33; Officier, Ordre de Léopold, Commdr. Ordre de la Couronne, Grand Officier Ordre de Léopold II.

Leisure interests: reading, travel.

Publs. Numerous scientific papers on meridian astronomy, astrometry, astrophysics and stellar statistics.

31 rue Paul Hankar, 1180 Brussels, Belgium.

Telephone: 02-743058.

Bourges, Yvon, L. en D.; French overseas administrator and politician; b. 29 June 1921, Pau; ed. Univ. de Rennes.

Chef de Cabinet to Prefect of the Somme 44-45, of Bas-Rhin 45-47; Sub-Prefect of Erstein 47-48; with Ministry of Overseas Territories 48; Dir. de Cabinet, High Comm. in French Equatorial Africa 48-51, in French West Africa 51-56; Gov. Upper Volta 56-58; High Commr. French Equatorial Africa 58-60, Brazzaville 60-61; Chef de Cabinet, Ministry of Interior 61-62; Deputy for Ille-et-Vilaine 62-75; Mayor of Dinard 62-67, 71-; Sec. of State for Scientific Research 65-66, for Information 66-67, for Co-operation 67-68, for Foreign Affairs 68-72; Minister of Commerce 72-73, of Defence 75-; mem. Comm. de développement écono-

mique régionale (CODER) 65-; Chevalier Légion d'Honneur.
21 rue Surcouf, 75007 Paris; 98 avenue Pasteur, 35400 Saint-Malo, France.

Bourgès-Maunoury, Maurice; French politician; b. 19 Aug. 1914.
Active with Resistance Movement 41-44; mem. Constituent Assembly 46; Radical Socialist Dep. for Haute Garonne 56-58; Sec. of State (Budget) in Schuman Cabinet Nov. 47-July 48; Sec. of State (Armed Forces) in Marie and Schuman Cabinets July-Sept. 48; returned to Govt. as Minister of Public Works July 50; Sec. of State, Présidence du Conseil July 50-July 51; Deputy Minister of Nat. Defence, Pleven Cabinet Aug. 51-Jan. 52; Minister of Armaments, Faure Cabinet Jan.-Feb. 52; French delegate to 7th Session of the U.N. 52; Minister of Finance, Mayer Cabinet Jan.-July 53; Minister of the Interior until 56, of Nat. Defence 56-57; Prime Minister 57; Minister of Interior 57-58; Pres. Société Industrielle et financière de l'Artois et des Mines de Kali; Chevalier Légion d'Honneur, etc.
94 boulevard Flandrin, 75116 Paris, France.

Bourget, Maurice; Canadian engineer and politician; b. 20 Oct. 1907, Lévis, P.Q.; *m.* Marguerite Cleary 1949; two *d.*
Member of Parl. 40-62; fmr. Parl. Asst. to Minister of Public Works; Speaker of Senate 63-66; mem. Privy Council Feb. 66-; Dir. Hall Corpn. of Canada; Liberal. Leisure interests: reading, golf, fishing.
3 Place Baribeau, Lévis, Province of Quebec, Canada. Telephone: 833-3642.

Bourguiba, Habib Ben Ali; Tunisian politician; b. 3 Aug. 1903, Monastir; *m.* 2nd Mrs. Wassila Ben Ammar 1962; ed. Univ. of Paris, Ecole Libre des Sciences Politiques.
Active in politics and journalism since 28; mem. Destour Party 21, broke away and formed Neo-Destour Party (outlawed by the French) 34; imprisoned by the French 34-36 and 38-43; escaped to Middle East 45, travelled to promote Tunisian independence 45-49, world tour during Tunisian negotiations with French Govt. 51; arrested 52, placed under surveillance at Tabarka (Jan.), imprisoned at Remada (March), in solitary confinement, Ile de la Galite (May) until 54; released 54, under surveillance in France 54-55, during negotiations; returned to Tunisia following Franco-Tunisian Agreements 55; Pres. Tunisian Nat. Assembly, Prime Minister, Pres. of the Council, Minister of Foreign Affairs, of Defence 56-57; Pres. of Tunisia, Head of Cabinet 57- (Pres. for Life 75); Pres. Neo-Destour Party (Pres. for Life 74); Ordre du Sang, Ordre de la confiance en diamants.
Publs. *Le Destour et la France* 37, *La Tunisie et la France* 55.
Office of the President, Tunis, Tunisia.

Bourguiba, Habib, Jr., L. ès D.; Tunisian diplomatist; b. 9 April 1927, Paris, France; *s.* of Pres. Habib Bourguiba (*q.v.*); *m.* Neila Zouiten 1954; two *s.* one *d.*; ed. Collège Sadiki, Law School, France.
Collaborated in national liberation movement, especially 51-54; lawyer in training, Tunis 54-56; Counsellor, Tunisian Embassy, Washington 56-57; Ambassador to Italy 57-58, to France 58-61, to U.S.A. 61-63, to Canada 61-62; Perm. Rep. to UN 61-62; Ambassador to Mexico 62-63; Sec.-Gen. to Presidency of Republic Dec. 63-64; in charge of Dept. of Youth and Sports, Dept. of Tourism, Nat. Office of Artisanship and Information Dept. Dec. 63-64; elected mem. Nat. Assembly Nov. 64; Sec. of State for Foreign Affairs 64-70.
Leisure interests: staying home with family, golf.
Villa Al Mahroussa, Avenue Salammbo, Tunis, Tunisia. Telephone: 281-727 (Home).

Bourliére, François (Marie Gabriel), M.D., L. ès S., SC.D.; French biologist and university professor; b. 21 Dec. 1913, Roanne, Loire; *s.* of Gabriel Bourlière and Marie

Deroche; *m.* Jacqueline Butez 1942; two *s.* one *d.*; ed. Univ. of Paris.
Research Asst., School of Medicine, Paris Univ. 42; Prof. of Physiology, School of Medicine, Rouen 46-49; Prof. of Gerontology, Univ. of Paris 59-; Editor of *La Terre et la Vie* and *Gerontologia;* Pres. Int. Union for Conservation of Nature and Natural Resources 63-66; Convener Int. Biological Programme (Terrestrial Ecology) 64-69; Dir. Nat. Foundation of Gerontology 68-; mem. Int. Ethological Cttee. 68-; Pres. special Cttee. for the Int. Biological Programme (ICSU) 69-74; Chair. Int. Co-ordination Cttee. Man and the Biosphere Program, UNESCO 71-75; Chevalier, Légion d'Honneur 70; Commdr. Order of Golden Ark (Netherlands) 74.
Publs. *Eléments d'un Guide Bibliographique du Naturaliste* (2 vols.) 40-41, *Formulaire technique du Zoologiste* 41, *Vie et Moeurs des Mammifères* 51, *Le Monde des Mammifères* 54, *The Natural History of Mammals* 54, *Sénescence et Sénilité* 58, *Introduction à l'écologie des Ongulés* 60, *The Land and Wildlife of Eurasia* 64; co-author: *Traité de Zoologie,* Vol. 15 *Oiseaux,* and Vol. 17 *Mammifères, Précis de Gérontologie* 56, *Problèmes de Production Biologique* 67, *Progrès en Gérontologie* 69, *Problèmes d'échantillonnage des peuplements animaux terrestres* 69, *Problèmes d'Echantillonage des Peuplements Animaux Aquatiques* 71, *Zoologie,* Vol. IV, *Pléiade* 74, *La démographie des populations sauvages de Vertébrés* 75.
Leisure interest: wildlife photography.
15 avenue de Tourville, 75007 Paris, France. Telephone: 551-44-83.

Bourne, Geoffrey Howard, D.SC., D.PHIL.; British professor and anatomist; b. 17 Nov. 1909, Perth, W. Australia; *s.* of Walter Howard Bourne and Mary Anne Bourne; *m.* Maria Nelly Golarz 1965; two *s.* by previous marriage; ed. Univs. of W. Australia and Melbourne.
Biologist, Australian Inst. of Anatomy 34-36; Biochemist, Commonwealth of Australia Advisory Council on Nutrition 36-38; Beit Memorial Fellow for Medical Research at Oxford 38-41; Mackenzie Mackinnon Research Fellow of the Royal Coll. of Surgeons and Royal Coll. of Physicians 41-43; Demonstrator in Physiology, Oxford 40-43 and 46-47; in charge of Research and Development, Rations and Biological Problems, Special Forces in S.E. Asia (Major) 44; Nutritional Adviser, British Mil. Admin. of Malaya (Lieut.-Col.) 45-46; Reader in Histology, Univ. of London, London Hospital 47-57; Prof. and Chair. Anatomy Dept., Emory Univ., Ga., U.S.A. 57-61; Dir. Yerkes Regional Primate Research Center, Emory Univ. 61-.
Leisure interests: water skiing, scuba diving, running.
Publs. include *Starvation in Europe* 43, *The Mammalian Adrenal Gland* 49, *An Introduction to Functional Histology* 55, 61, *Division of Labour in Cells* 61, *Structure and Function of Muscle* 63, *Muscular Dystrophy in Man and Animals* 63, *Atherosclerosis and its Origins* 63, *International Review of Dietetics* vols. 1-10 continuing, *Structure and Function of Nervous Tissue* Vols. 1-3, *The Chimpanzee* Vols. 1, 2, 3, 4 and 5, *The Ape People, Primate Odyssey* 74.
Yerkes Primate Center, Emory University, Atlanta, Ga. 30322, U.S.A.
Telephone: 378-0104.

Boustany, Foaud Ephrem, D. ès L.; Lebanese scholar; b. 15 Aug. 1906; ed. Deir-el-Kamar Coll. and Univ. St. Joseph, Beirut.
Teacher in Arab Literature, Islamic Insts. and History of Arab Civilization, Institut des Lettres Orientales 33-45; Dir. Ecole Normale 42-53; Prof. of Near Eastern History and Civilizations, Inst. des Sciences Politiques 45-55; Prof. of Arab Literature, Islamic Philosophy and Arab History, Acad. Libanaise des Beaux-Arts 47-53; Rector Univ. Libanaise 53-70; Sec.-Gen. Lebanese Nat.

Comm. for UNESCO 48-55; Sec.-Gen. Int. Comm. for
Translation of Classic Works 49-, Acad. Libanaise;
Dr. h.c. Univs. of Lyon 57, Austin, Texas 58, Georgetown, Washington, D.C. 58; Lebanese, French, Vatican
and other decorations.
Publs. *Au temps de l'Emir* 26, *Ar-Rawae* (critical
studies) 27, *Pourquoi* 30, *Histoire du Liban sous les
Chéhab* of Emir Haïdar Chéhab (with Dr. A. Rustem)
33-35, *Bagdad, capitale des lettres abbassides* 34, *Le rôle
des chrétiens dans l'établissement de la Omayyade* 38, *Le
style orale chez les Arabes préislamiques* 41, *Al-Magani
al Haditah* (5 vols.) 46-50, *Cinq jours à travers la Syrie* 50,
Les dits des mois 73, *Encyclopaedia Arabica* (10 vols.)
56-73.
Université Libanaise, Beirut, Lebanon.

Boustead, Col. Sir John Edmund Hugh, K.B.E., C.M.G.,
D.S.O., M.C. and bar; fmr. British political agent; b. 14
April 1895, Ceylon; s. of Lawrence Twentyman and
Ethel Margaret (née Alers-Hankey) Boustead; ed. Royal
Naval Colls., Osborne and Dartmouth, H.M.S. *Cornwall*
and Oxford Univ.
Midshipman and Acting Sub-Lieut. 13-15; Royal Navy,
German East and German South-West Africa and Cape
Station; S. African Brigade, Egypt, Western Desert and
France 15-19; Capt. S. African Brigade attached to Gen.
Denikin's Army in South Russia 19; apptd. Gordon
Highlanders, Malta, Constantinople, Chanak and East-
ern Thrace 21-24; led Kanchenjunga Expedition 26;
Sudan Camel Corps 24-29; Gen. Staff S.D.F. Khartoum
30; Commdr. Sudan Camel Corps 31; mem. Everest
Expedition 33; retd. from Army to Sudan Political
Service 34; District Commr. Western District, Darfur
35-40; recalled to service 40; raised and trained Sudan
Frontier Battn. S.D.F. and commanded it Jan.-July 41;
served in Central Abyssinia; S.D.F. Brigade in Eritrea
43; commd. 2nd S.D.F. Brigade 45; recalled to Political
Service Aug. 45; Resident Adviser to the Hadhramaut
States and British Agent Eastern Aden Protectorate
49-58; Devt. Sec., Muscat 58-61; Political Agent, Abu
Dhabi 61-65; several foreign orders; F.R.G.S.
Leisure interests: mountaineering, riding, sailing.
Publ. *The Wind of Morning* (autobiography) 71.
c/o Athenaeum Club, Pall Mall, London, S.W.1; and
Naval and Military Club, 94 Piccadilly, London, W.1,
England.

Boutaleb, Abdelhadi; Moroccan politician and
educationist; b. 23 Dec. 1923, Fez; m. Touria Chraibi
1946; two s. one d.; ed. Al Qarawiyin Univ.
Professor of Arabic History and Literature, and Tutor
to Prince Moulay Hassan and Prince Moulay Abdallah;
Founder-mem. Democratic Party of Independence
44-51; campaigned, through the Party, for Moroccan
independence, and for this purpose attended UN
Session, Paris 51, and Negotiating Conf. at Aix-les-
Bains 55; Minister of Labour and Social Affairs in
Bekkai Govt. 56; Chief Editor of journal *Al Rayal
Am* 56-61; Amb. to Syria Feb 62; Sec. of State, Ministry
of Information Nov. 62, Ministry of Information, Youth
and Sports Jan. 63; Minister of Information, Youth and
Sports June 63; Interim Minister in Charge of Mauri-
tania and Sahara Nov. 63; Minister of Justice 64-67,
of Nat. Educ. and Fine Arts 67; Minister of State 68;
Minister of Foreign Affairs 69-70; Pres. Chamber of
Reps. 70-71; Prof. of Constitutional Law and Political
Insts. 75-; Rabat Law Univ. 74; Amb. to U.S.A.,
Jan. 75-; Commdr. of the Throne of Morocco, Grand
Cordon of the Repub. of U.A.R., and other decorations.
Leisure interests: sports, music, reading.
Publs. Many cultural and literary works.
Moroccan Embassy, 1601 21st Street, N.W., Washing-
ton, D.C. 20009, U.S.A.

Bouteflika, Abdul Aziz; Algerian politician; b. 2
March 1937, Melilla; ed. Morocco.
Former Captain, Nat. Liberation Army; mem. Parl. for

Tlemcen 62-; Minister of Sports 62-63, of Foreign Affairs
Sept. 63-; mem. F.L.N. Political Bureau 64-; mem.
Revolutionary Council 65-; Pres. 29th UN Gen.
Assembly 74.
Ministry of Foreign Affairs, Algiers, Algeria.

Boutin, Bernard Louis, PH.B.; American college
president; b. 2 July 1923, Belmont, N.H.; s. of Joseph
L. Boutin and Annie E. (Laflam) Boutin; m. Alice M.
Boucher 1945; six s. five d.; ed. St. Michael's Coll.,
Winooski, Vermont, and Catholic Univ. of America,
Washington, D.C.
President and Treas., Boutin Insurance Agency Inc.,
Laconia, New Hampshire 48-63; Proprietor, Boutin
Real Estate Co., Laconia 55-63; Mayor of Laconia 55-
59; Deputy Admin., Gen. Services Admin., Washington
D.C. Feb.-Nov. 61; Admin. of Gen. Services 61-64;
Exec. Vice-Pres. Nat. Asscn. Home Builders 64-65;
Admin. of Small Business Admin. 66-67; Deputy Dir.
Office of Econ. Opportunity 65-66; Exec. Sanders
Assoc. Inc. 67-69; Chair. N.H. State Board of Educ.
68-69; mem. Nat. Highway Safety Comm. 69-70;
Democratic Candidate for Gov. of New Hampshire 58,
60; Pres. St. Michael's Coll. 69-; numerous awards;
Hon. LL.D., St. Michael's Coll.; Hon. Ph.D., Franklin
Pierce Coll.; Hon. L.H.D., Univ. of New Hampshire.
Leisure interests: golf, fishing.
503 Dalton Drive, Winooski, Vt. 05404, U.S.A.
Telephone: 802-655-2000.

Boutos, Ioannis; Greek politician; b. 1925, Athens;
m. Maria V. Sourrapa 1957; three s.; ed. Univ. of
Athens, London School of Econs.
Member Parl. 50, re-elected 56, 61, 63, 64; Under-Sec.
of Co-ordination 61-63, 67; Under-Sec. to Prime
Minister; Minister of Commerce 74-75, Alt. Minister for
Co-ordination 75-; mem. Interparl. European Comm.
for asscn. of Greece with EEC.
Ministry of Co-ordination, Athens, Greece.

Boutros, Fouad; Lebanese lawyer and politician; b.
1920, Beirut; m. Tania Shehade 1953; one s. two d.;
ed. Coll. des Frères, Beirut.
Judge, Civil and Mixed Commercial Court, Beirut 44-
47; Judge Mil. Tribunal and Court Lawyer 47-50; Govt.
Lawyer 51-57; Minister of Nat. Educ. and of the Plan
59-60; mem. Chamber of Deputies 60-; Deputy Speaker,
Chamber of Deputies 60-61; Minister of Justice 61-64;
Vice-Pres. of the Council, Minister of Educ. and Defence
66-67; Vice-Pres., Council of Ministers, Minister of
Foreign Affairs and of Tourism 68-69; numerous
decorations.
Damascus Street-Al Kamal Building, P.O.B. 5848;
Home: Sursock Street, Fouad Boutros Building, Beirut,
Lebanon.
Telephone: 230715, 239407, 297790 (Office); 334110
(Home).

Boutteville, Roger; French businessman; b. 25 Sept.
1892; ed. Ecole Polytechnique de Paris.
Pres. and Gen. Man. Soc. Alsacienne de Constructions
Mécaniques; Pres. Maisons Phénix; Vice-Pres. Soc.
Gén. de Constructions Electriques et Mécaniques
(Als-Thom); Dir. Soc. Lyonnaise des Eaux et de
l'Eclairage, Soc. de Force et Lumière Electrique,
Crédit Industriel et Commercial, Soc. Nat. d'Investisse-
ment, etc.; Commdr. Légion d'Honneur,Croix de Guerre.
Home: 47 rue de Bellechasse, Paris 7e, France.

Bouziri, Najib; Tunisian diplomatist; b. 1925; ed.
School of Law, Paris, and Inst. d'Etudes Politiques,
Paris.
Former advocate, Court of Appeals, Tunis; later
worked in Ministry of State and Ministry of Interior;
later Chef de Cabinet, Ministry of Foreign Affairs;
Chargé d'Affaires, Rome 57-58; Amb. to Italy 58-61, to
German Fed. Rep. 61-64; Sec. of State for Posts and
Telecommunications 64; Vice-Pres. Nat. Assembly

64-65; Amb. to U.S.S.R. 65-70, to Belgium and Luxembourg 70-72, to Morocco 72-73, to Algeria 73-74, to Spain 74-; Chair. Admin. and Budgetary Cttee. of UN Gen. Assembly 65.
Tunisian Embassy, Plaza Alonso Martínez 3, Madrid, Spain.

Bovet, Daniel, DR.SC.; Italian physiologist; b. 1907, Neuchâtel, Switzerland; s. of Pierre Bovet and Amy Babut; m. Filomena Nitti 1938; one s.; ed. Univ. of Geneva.
Assistant in Physiology, Univ. of Geneva 28-29; Asst. Inst. Pasteur, Paris 29-39, Dir. of Laboratory 39-47; Dir. of Laboratories of Therapeutical Chemistry, Istituto Superiore di Sanità, Rome 47-64; Prof. of Pharmacology, Univ. of Sassari 64-71; Prof. of Psychobiology, Univ. of Rome; Dir. Laboratory of Psychobiology and Psychopharmacology, Consiglio Naz. delle Ricerche 69-; Nobel Prize for Physiology and Medicine 57; mem. Accad. Naz. dei Lincei; Foreign mem. Royal Soc. (U.K.); Grand Officer of the Order of the Italian Repub.; Hon. Doctorates Palermo, Geneva, Rio de Janeiro, etc.
Publs. *Structure chimique et activité pharmacodynamique des médicaments du système nerveux végétatif* (with F. Bovet-Nitti) 48, *Curare and Curare-like Agents* (with F. Bovet-Nitti and G. B. Marini-Bettolò) 59, *Controlling Drugs* (with R. H. Blum and J. Moore), 74.
Laboratorio di Psicobiologia, Via Reno 1, 00198 Rome; Home: Piazza San Apollinare 33, 00186 Rome, Italy.
Telephone: (06) 864898 (Office); (06) 565297 (Home).

Bowden, Baron (Life Peer), cr. 63, of Chesterfield, **Bertram Vivian Bowden,** M.A., PH.D., M.SC.TECH., F.I.E.E.; British college principal and politician; b. 18 Jan. 1910, Chesterfield; s. of Bert C. Bowden; m. 1st Marjorie Browne 1939 (died 1957), 2nd Mary Maltby 1967 (died 1971), 3rd Phyllis James 1974; one s. two d.; ed. Chesterfield Grammar School, Emmanuel Coll., Cambridge, and Univ. of Amsterdam.
Schoolmaster, The Collegiate School, Liverpool 35-37; Chief Physics Master, Oundle School 37-40; Telecommunications Research Establishment, Swanage and Malvern 40-43; Naval Research Laboratory, Washington 43-45; Mass. Inst. of Technology (M.I.T.) 45-46; Atomic Energy Research Establishment, Harwell 46; Partner, Sir Robert Watson-Watt and Partners 46-50; Ferranti Ltd. (in charge of application of digital computers) 50-53; Principal, Manchester Municipal Coll. of Technology (now Univ. of Manchester Inst. of Science and Technology) 53-64, 65-76; Minister of State, Dept. of Educ. and Science 64-65.
Leisure interests: garden, music, reading.
Publs. *Faster than Thought—A Symposium on Digital Computers* 53, *The Proposals for the Development of the Manchester College of Science and Technology* 56, numerous papers and articles on education.
Pine Croft, Stanhope Road, Bowdon, Altrincham, Cheshire, England.
Telephone: 061-928-4005.

Bowen, Hon. Nigel Hubert, B.A., LL.B., Q.C.; Australian judge; b. 26 May 1911, Summerland, British Columbia, Canada; s. of Otway Percival Bowen and Dorothy Joan Bowen; m. Eileen Cecily Mullens 1947; three d.; ed. King's School, Parramatta, N.S.W. and St. Paul's Coll., Univ. of Sydney.
Admitted to N.S.W. Bar 36, Victoria Bar 54; Q.C. 53; Editor *Australian Law Journal* 46-58; Vice-Pres. Law Council of Australia 57-60; Lecturer in Company Law and Taxation, Univ. of Sydney 57-58; Pres. N.S.W. Bar Council 59-61; mem. of Parl. 64-73; Attorney-Gen. 66-69; Minister of Educ. and Science 69-71, Attorney-Gen. 71; Minister of Foreign Affairs 71-72; Judge, N.S.W. Supreme Court and Court of Appeal 73-; Chief Judge in Equity 74-; leader of Australian del., Vice-Pres. UN Int. Conf. on Human Rights 68, leader of del. UNESCO

Int. Conf. on Cultural Policies 70, UN Gen. Assembly 71, 72; Liberal.
Leisure interests: music, swimming.
43 Grosvenor Street, Wahroonga, N.S.W., Australia.

Bowen, Otis Ray, M.D.; American physician and politician; b. 26 Feb. 1918, Fulton Co., Ind.; s. of Vernie Bowen and Pearl Bowen; m. Elizabeth A. Steinmann 1939; three s. one d.; ed. Ind. Univ. and Ind. Univ. Medical School.
Physician 42-; served U.S. Army Medical Corps, commissioned First Lieut. later Capt. 42-45; fmr. Marshall County Coroner; mem. House of Reps. 58-72, Speaker 67-72, also fmr. House Minority Leader, mem. Legislative Advisory Cttee. and Vice-Chair., later Chair., Legislative Council; Gov. of Indiana Jan. 73-; fmr. mem. Intergovt. Relations Cttee. and Task Force on Urban Affairs, Nat. Legislative Conf.; Trustee, Ancilla Coll.; mem. Advisory Cttee. for curricula, Vincennes Univ.; mem. District, State and American Medical Asscns., Bremen Chamber of Commerce; mem. President's Comm. on Fed. Paperwork; Merit Award, Ind. Public Health Asscn. 71, Dr. Benjamin Rush Bicentennial Award, American Medical Asscn. 73, and other awards; Republican.
Leisure interests: collecting quotes, fishing, watching baseball, basketball, football and racing.
Office of the Governor, 206 State Capitol, Indianapolis, Ind. 46204; Home: Executive Residence, 4750 N. Meridian, Indianapolis, Ind., U.S.A.
Telephone: 317-633-4567 (Office).

Bowen, William Gordon, PH.D.; American university president; b. 6 Oct. 1933, Cincinnati, Ohio; s. of Albert A. Bowen and Bernice Pomert; m. Mary Ellen Maxwell 1956; one s. one d.; ed. Denison and Princeton Univs.
Assistant Prof. of Econs., Princeton Univ. 58-61, Assoc. Prof. 61-65, Prof. 65-; Dir. of Graduate Studies, Woodrow Wilson School of Public and Int. Affairs, Princeton Univ. 64-66; Provost, Princeton Univ. 67-72, Pres. 72-.
Leisure interests: sports in general, particularly swimming and tennis, reading.
Publs. *The Wage-Price Issue: A Theoretical Analysis* 60, *Performing Arts: The Economic Dilemma* (with W. J. Baumol) 66, *The Economics of Labor Force Participation* (with T. A. Finegan) 69.
Princeton University, 1 Nassau Hall, Princeton, N.J. 08540; Home: 83 Stockton Street, Princeton, N.J. 08540, U.S.A.

Bowie, Robert Richardson; American lawyer and university professor; b. 24 Aug. 1909; s. of Clarence K. and Helen R. Bowie; m. Theodosia Chapman 1944; two s.; ed. Gilman School, Baltimore, Maryland, Princeton Univ. and Harvard Law School.
Admitted to Maryland Bar 34, mem. firm Bowie and Burke, Baltimore 34-42; Reporter, Maryland Comm. on Civil Procedure 39-41; Asst. Dir. Maryland Legis. Council 40-41; Asst. Attorney-Gen., Maryland 41-42; U.S. Army 42-46; Special Asst. to Dep. Military Governor for Germany 45-46; Prof. of Law, Harvard Univ. 45-55; Gen. Counsel, Special Adviser U.S. High Commissioner for Germany 50-51; Dir. Policy Planning Staff, Dept. of State 53-55; Asst. Sec. of State for Policy Planning 55-57; Counsellor, Dept. of State 66-68; Prof. of Government, Harvard Univ. 57-; Dir. Center for Int. Affairs, Harvard Univ. 57-72; Legion of Merit with Oak Leaf Cluster.
Leisure interests: reading, sailing, golf, music.
Publs. various studies, and *Shaping the Future Foreign Policy in an Age of Transition* 64, *Suez 1956* 74.
6 Divinity Avenue, Cambridge, Mass. 02138; Home: 170 Coolidge Hill, Cambridge, Massachusetts 02138. U.S.A.
Telephone: 617-495-2124 (Office).

Bowles, Chester, B.S.; American diplomatist; b.
5 April 1901, Springfield, Mass.; s. of Charles Allen
Bowles and Nellie (Harris); m. Dorothy Stibbins 1934;
two s. three d.; ed. Yale Univ.
Business in N.Y., Chair. of Board, Benton and Bowles
Inc. 25-40; Dir. Price and Rationing Controls, State
of Conn. 41-43; Administrator of Wartime Price, Rent
and Rationing Controls for the U.S., mem. Production
Board 43-46; Dir. of Economic Stabilisation 46; U.S.
Del. UNESCO Conf. Paris 46; Consultant to Trygve
Lie, U.N., Int. Chair. U.N. Appeal for Children 47-48;
Gov. State of Conn. 49-51; U.S. Ambassador to India
and Nepal 51-53; U.S. Congressman 59-61; mem.
Foreign Affairs Cttee. and Foreign Policy Adviser to
the Pres. 59-60; Under-Sec. of State Jan.-Nov. 61;
Special Rep. and Adviser to the Pres. for African,
Asian and Latin American Affairs Dec. 61-63; Amb. to
India 63-69; numerous hon. degrees; Democrat.
Publs. *Tomorrow Without Fear* 46, *Ambassador's Report*
54, *The New Dimensions of Peace* 55, *Africa's Challenge
to America* 56, *American Politics in a Revolutionary
World* 56, *Ideas, People and Peace* 58, *The Coming
Political Breakthrough* 60, *Conscience of a Liberal* 62,
Makings of a Just Society 63, *A View from New Delhi*
69, *Promises to Keep* 71.
Hayden's Point, Essex, Conn., U.S.A.

Bowles, Paul; American composer and writer; b.
30 Dec. 1910, New York; s. of Dr. Claude Dietz and
Rena Winnewisser; m. Jane Auer 1938; ed. Univ. of
Va. and in Berlin and Paris.
Music Critic for *New York Herald Tribune* 42-45; re-
cipient of Guggenheim Fellowship and Rockefeller
Grant.
Compositions of music for films, for the theatre: *Doctor
Faustus, Twelfth Night, The Glass Menagerie, Cyrano de
Bergerac, Watch on the Rhine, Summer and Smoke,
Sweet Bird of Youth, The Milk Train Doesn't Stop Here
Any More*, etc.; scores for ballets: *Yankee Clipper,
Pastorela* (American Ballet Company), *Colloque Senti-
mental* (Marquis de Cuevas); operas: *Denmark Vesey,
The Wind Remains, Yerma*; and a number of sonatas,
concertos, etc.; also wrote novels, *The Sheltering Sky,
Let it come Down, The Spider's House, Up Above the
World*; short stories, collections, *A Little Stone, The
Hours after Noon, A Hundred Camels in the Courtyard,
Pages from Cold Point*; non-fiction, *Their Heads are
Green, Yallah! Without Stopping*; Poetry: *Scenes, The
Thicket of Spring*; trans. *A Life Full of Holes* (with
Driss ben Hamed Charhadi), *Love With a Few Hairs,
The Lemon* (with Mohammed Mrabet), *M'Hashish, The
Boy Who Set the Fire* (with Mohammed Mrabet), *For
Bread Alone* (with Mohamed Choukri), *The Oblivion
Seekers* (by Isabelle Eberhardt), *Look and Move On* (with
Mohammed Mrabet).
2117 Tanger Socco, Tangier, Morocco.

Boyd, Aquilino Edgardo; Panamanian lawyer and
diplomatist; b. 21; ed. La Salle, Panama City, Holy
Cross Coll., U.S.A., Univs. of Havana and Panama.
First Sec. Cuba 46-47, Washington 47-48; Congressman,
Panama Nat. Assembly 48-64; Pres. Nat. Assembly 49;
Min. Foreign Affairs 56-58; Perm. Rep. to UN 62-67,
68-.
Permanent Mission of Panama to the United Nations,
866 UN Plaza, Room 544-545, New York, N.Y. 10017,
U.S.A.
Telephone: 421-5420.

Boyd, Arthur Merric Bloomfield, O.B.E.; Australian
painter; b. 24 July 1920, Murrumbeena; s. of Merric
Boyd and Doris Gough; m. Yvonne Lennie 1945; one s.
two d.; ed. State School, Murrumbeena, Victoria.
Taught painting and sculpture by parents and grandfather; painted and exhibited in Australia 37-59, in
England 59-; designed for theatre, Melbourne 55-57,
ballet, Edinburgh Festival and Sadler's Wells 61,

Covent Garden 63; Retrospective Exhibition, Whitechapel Gallery, London 62, Adelaide 64; exhbns.
Adelaide, Sydney, Melbourne 68, Edinburgh 69, London
69, 73, Nat. Gallery of Victoria 70; Creative Arts Fellowship, Australian Nat. Univ., Canberra 71.
Leisure interest: music.
Publ. *Monograph* 67.
c/o Commercial Bank of Australia Ltd., 34 Piccadilly,
London, W.1, England.

Boyd, Howard Taney, J.D.; American business execu-
tive; b. 5 June 1909, Woodside, Maryland; s. of Howard
T. Boyd and Mary Violet (Stewart); m. Lucille Bel-
humeur 1935; one s. two d.; ed. Georgetown Univ.
Admitted D.C. Bar 34, Texas Bar; Sec. to Attorney-
Gen. of U.S. 34; Asst. U.S. Attorney, D.C. 35-39;
Partner, law firm Hogan and Hartson, Washington
39-52; Vice-Pres., Asst. Gen. Counsel, El Paso Natural
Gas Co. (renamed The El Paso Company, 74) 52-57,
Dir. 53-, Exec. Vice-Pres. 57-60, Pres. 60-65, Chair. 65-;
Dir. The Greyhound Corpn., Armour and Co., Texas
Commerce Bank N.A.
2727 Allen Parkway, Houston, Texas; and 6042 Crab
Orchard, Houston, Texas, U.S.A.

Boyd, Virgil Edward; American automobile executive
(retd.); b. 8 July 1912; ed. American Business Coll.,
Omaha, Neb.
Assistant to Pres., American Motors Corpn. 54-56,
Field Sales Man., then Dir. of Sales Operations, Auto-
motive Div. 56-61, Vice-Pres. Automotive Sales 61-62;
Vice-Pres. and Gen. Sales Man. Chrysler Corpn. 62-63,
Vice-Pres. and Group Exec., Automotive Sales 63-64,
Group Vice-Pres. Domestic Automotive 64-66, mem.
Board of Dirs. 64-, Pres. Jan. 67-Jan. 70, Vice-Chair.
70-72.
111 Bird Lane, Litchfield Park, Arizona 85340, U.S.A.

Boyd of Merton, 1st Viscount, cr. 60, of Merton-in-
Penninghame in the county of Wigtown; **Alan Tindal
Lennox-Boyd,** P.C., C.H.; British politician; b. 18 Nov.
1904, Bournemouth; s. of Alan Walter Lennox-Boyd
and Florence Begbie; m. Lady Patricia Florence Susan
Guinness 1938; three s.; ed. Sherborne and Christ
Church, Oxford.
President of the Union, Oxford 26; Conservative M.P.
for Mid-Beds. 31-60; Parl. Sec., Ministries of Labour
38, of Home Security 39, of Food 39-40, and of Aircraft
Production 43-45; served R.N.V.R. 40-43; Minister of
State for Colonial Affairs 51-52; Minister of Transport
and Civil Aviation 52-54; Sec. of State for Colonies
54-59; Exec. Dir. Arthur Guinness Son & Co. Ltd.
59-61, Man. Dir. 61-67, Joint Vice-Chair. 67-; Dir. Tate
and Lyle 66-74, Imperial Chemical Industries 67-;
Trustee, British Museum 62-, Natural History Museum
63-; D.L. Cornwall 65-.
Leisure interests: sailing, fishing, shooting.
6 Iveagh House, Ormond Yard, London, S.W.1; and
Ince Castle, Saltash, Cornwall, England.
Telephone: 01-839-3969.

Boyd-Carpenter, Baron (Life Peer), cr. 72, of Crux
Easton in the County Borough of Southampton; **Rt.
Hon. John Archibald Boyd-Carpenter,** P.C.; British
administrator; b. 2 June 1908; s. of late Sir Archibald,
M.P., and Lady Boyd-Carpenter; m. Margaret Mary
Hall 1937; one s. two d.; ed. Stowe School and Balliol
Coll., Oxford.
President Oxford Union Soc. 30; called to Bar 34;
practised S.E. Circuit; joined Scots Guards 39, served
until 45; M.P. 45-72; Financial Sec. to Treasury 51-54;
Privy Councillor 54; Minister of Transport and Civil
Aviation 54-55, of Pensions and Nat. Insurance 55-62,
Chief Sec. to Treasury and Paymaster-Gen. 62-64;
Opposition Front Bench Spokesman on Housing and
Land 64-66; Chair. Public Accounts Cttee. House of
Commons 64-70, Local Govt. Advisory Cttee. of Con-
servative Greater London Area Org. 68; Dir. Orion

Insurance Co. 67, 72, Chair. 69-72, C.L.R.P. Investment Trust 67, Chair. 70-72, City and Int. Investment Trust 66-, Life Asscn. of Scotland 70-72; mem. Council, Trust Houses-Forte Ltd. 70-72; Dir. Rugby Portland Cement Co. 71; Chair. U.K. Civil Aviation Authority 72-; Reith Lecturer (77); High Steward of Kingston-upon-Thames and Deputy Lieut. for Greater London 73-.
Leisure interests: swimming, tennis.
Aviation House, 129 Kingsway, London, WC2B 6NN, England.
Telephone: 01-405-6922.

Boye, Ibrahima; Senegalese judge; b. 29 March 1924, Saint Louis; s. of Amadou Abdoulaye Boye and Marème Sène; m. Marie Anne Cissé 1948; three s. four d.; ed. Univ. de Montpellier.
Attorney-at-Law, Court of Appeals, Nîmes, France; later mem. Public Prosecutor's Office at Court of Appeals of Montpellier; later French Judge, Guinea, Pres. of Colonial Court of Appeals, Dahomey; Examining Magistrate, Cotonou and Abidjan; Justice of the Peace, Agbonville, Ivory Coast; Technical Adviser in Ministry of Justice, Senegal 60, later Dir. of Cabinet and Justice of Supreme Court; Attorney-Gen., Senegal 61; Chair. UN Comm. on Human Rights 68; Amb. and Perm. Rep. of Senegal to UN until 71; Rep. of Senegal, UN Security Council 68, 69, Pres. 69; Vice-Pres. UN Gen. Assembly 70; Amb. to U.S.S.R., Poland, Hungary, Romania, Czechoslovakia 71-, to Bulgaria 73-.
Leisure interests: African-negro poetry.
Publs. Works on human rights, study of racial discrimination throughout the world.
ul. Donskaya 12, Moscow, U.S.S.R.
Telephone: 236-70-24, 236-85-28, 236-70-27.

Boyer, Paul Delos, PH.D.; American professor of chemistry; b. 31 July 1918, Provo, Utah; s. of Dell Delos Boyer and Grace Guymon; m. Lyda Whicker 1939; one s. two d.; ed. Brigham Young Univ. and Univ. of Wisconsin.
Research Asst., Univ. of Wis. 39-43; Instructor, Stanford Univ. 43-45; Assoc. Prof., Univ. of Minn. 47-53, Prof. 53-56, Hill Prof. of Biochem. 56-63; Prof. of Chem., Univ. of Calif. at Los Angeles 63-, Dir. Molecular Biology Inst. 65-; mem. Nat. Acad. of Sciences; Fellow, American Acad. of Arts and Sciences; Pres. American Soc. of Biol. Chemists 69-70; Guggenheim Fellowship 55; American Chem. Soc. Award 55; Dr. h.c., Univ. of Stockholm 74.
Publs. Author or co-author of over 150 scientific papers in biochem. and molecular biology.
University of California at Los Angeles, Molecular Biology Institute, 408 Hilgard Avenue, Los Angeles, Calif. 90024, U.S.A.
Telephone: 213-825-1018.

Boyesen, Jens Mogens; Norwegian diplomatist; b. 9 Oct. 1920, Oslo; s. of Einar Boyesen; m. Erle Bryn 1955; ed. Oslo Univ.
Active in Resistance 40-45; degree in law 47; Asst. Judge 48; entered Foreign Service 49; Under-Sec. Ministry of Foreign Affairs 51-54, Ministry of Defence 54-55; Amb. to NATO 55-63, to OEEC 55-61, to OECD 61-63; Under-Sec. of State for Foreign Affairs 64-65; Assoc., Norwegian Defence Research Establishment Jan. 67-; Amb. to Int. Orgs. in Geneva 68-73, Amb. to European Communities, and to Belgium and Luxembourg 73-.
Norwegian Embassy, 17 rue Archimède, Brussels 1040, Belgium.
Telephone: (Brussels) 36-20-45.

Boyland, Eric, D.SC., PH.D.; British university professor; b. 24 Feb. 1905, Manchester; s. of Alfred E. and Helen Boyland; m. Margaret Esther Maurice; two s. one d.; ed. Univs. of Manchester and London.
Lister Inst. for Preventive Medicine 28-30; Kaiser Wilhelm Inst. für Medizinische Forschung, Heidelberg

30-31; Physiological Chemist to Royal Cancer Hospital, London 31; Reader in Biochemistry, Univ. of London 35-47, Prof. of Biochemistry in Univ. of London, at the Chester Beatty Research Inst. of the Royal Cancer Hospital 48-70; Visiting Prof. in Toxicology, London School of Hygiene and Tropical Medicine 70-; Judd Award for Cancer Research, N.Y. 48; Medal of Société de Chimie biologique 56.
Leisure interests: walking, looking at paintings.
London School of Hygiene and Tropical Medicine, Keppel Street, London, WC1E 7HT; Home: 42 Bramerton Street, London, S.W.3, England.
Telephone: 01-352-2601 (Home); 01-636-8636 (Office).

Boyle, Marshal of the R.A.F. Sir Dermot Alexander, G.C.B., K.C.V.O., K.B.E., A.F.C.; British officer; b. 2 Oct. 1904, Durrow, Eire; s. of A. F. Boyle; m. Una Carey 1931; two s. one d.; ed. St. Columba's Coll., Ireland, and R.A.F. Coll., Cranwell.
Commissioned R.A.F. 24; Staff Officer, H.Q., R.A.F. India 33-35; Staff Coll., Andover 36; Chief Flying Instructor, Cranwell 37-39; 83 Squadron, Scampton 40-41; Asst. Sec. War Cabinet Office 41; Senior Air Staff Officer, H.Q. No. 83 Group 43-45; A.D.C. to the King 43; A.O.C. No. 11 Group 45; Imperial Defence Coll. 46; Dir.-Gen. of Manning 49-51; A.O.C. No. 1 Group, Bomber Command 51-53; C.-in-C. Fighter Command 53-55; Air Chief Marshal 56; Chief of Air Staff 56-59; Vice-Chair. British Aircraft Corpn. 62-71; Chair. of Trustees, R.A.F. Museum 65-74; Master of Guild of Air Pilots and Air Navigators 65-66; Chair. Court of Govs. Mill Hill School 69-.
Pauls Place, Sway, Lymington, Hants., England.

Boyle of Handsworth, Baron (Life Peer), cr. 70, of Salehurst in the County of Sussex; **Edward Charles Gurney Boyle,** Bt., P.C.; British politician; b. 31 Aug. 1923; ed. Eton Coll. and Christ Church, Oxford.
Member of Parl. 50-70; Parl. Private Sec. to Under-Sec. for Air 51-52, and to Parl. Sec. to Ministry of Defence 52-53; Parl. Sec. Ministry of Supply 54-55; Econ. Sec. to Treasury 55-56; Parl. Sec. Ministry of Education 57-59; Financial Sec. to Treasury 59-62; Minister of Education 62-64; Minister of State under Sec. of State for Educ. and Science April 64-Oct. 64; Conservative; Pro-Chancellor Sussex Univ. 65-70; Dir. Penguin Books Ltd. 65-; Chair. Top Salaries Review Body; Vice-Chancellor, Univ. of Leeds Sept. 70-; Trustee, British Museum 70-; mem. High Council, European Univ. Inst.; Hon. LL.D. (Leeds, Bath, Sussex and Southampton), Hon. D.Sc. (Univ. of Aston in Birmingham).
University of Leeds, Leeds 2, England.

Boyles, Thomas Albert; Canadian banker; b. 6 Jan. 1906, London, England; s. of Albert E. Boyles and Sarah M. Stringer; m. Cora E. McBride 1953; ed. public and high schools.
Joined the Bank of Nova Scotia 21, Chief Accountant 40, Exec. Asst. 46, Supervisor of branch office 48, Man. Ottawa branch 50, Toronto branch 52, Asst. Gen. Man. 56, Deputy Gen. Man. 58, Gen. Man. 63, Chief Gen. Man. 64, Exec. Vice-Pres. and Dir. 66, Deputy Chair. 69, Chair. of Board 72-74, Hon. Chair. of Board 74-; Chair. and Dir. of numerous foreign subsidiaries of Bank of Nova Scotia; Pres. and Dir. Empire Realty Co. Ltd.; Dir. MICC Investments Ltd., Mortgage Insurance Co. of Canada, Export Finance Corpn. of Canada Ltd.; mem. Toronto Redevelopment Advisory Council.
Leisure interests: golf, fishing, philately.
The Bank of Nova Scotia, 44 King Street, West Toronto M5H 1E2, Ont.; Home: 24 Edmund Avenue, Toronto M4V 1H3, Ontario, Canada.

Bozer, Prof. Dr. Ali Husrev, Turkish jurist; b. 28 July 1925, Ankara; s. of Mustafa Fevzi Bozer and Zehra Bozer; m.; three s.; ed. Ankara and Neuchâtel Univs. and Harvard Law School.

Assistant judge, Ankara 51; Asst., Faculty of Law, Ankara Univ. 52-60, Agrégé 55-60, Head of Dept. 61-, Prof. of Commercial Law 65-; lawyer at bar, Ankara 52-; Dir. Inst. de Recherche sur le Droit commercial et bancaire 60-; Judge, European Court of Human Rights 74-; mem. Admin. Council, Turkish Radio-TV Corpn. 68-71, Vice-Pres. 71-73.
Leisure interest: tennis.
Publs. *Les Droits d'Administration et de Jouissance des Père et Mère sur les Biens de l'Enfant, Nantissement Commercial, Aperçu général sur le Droit des Assurances Sociales en Droit turc, Droit commercial pour les Employés de Banques, Papiers valeurs pour les Employés de Banques*; monographs and articles in several reviews in Turkish and French.
Ahmet Rasim sok. 35/5, Gankaya, Ankara, Turkey.
Telephone: 271845, 191322.

Braams, Cornelis Marius, PH.D.; Netherlands physicist; b. 5 July 1925, Den Bosch; s. of R. Braams and B. J. Straver; m. A. G. Planting 1952; two s. two d.; ed. Univ. of Utrecht.
Experimental nuclear physics at M.I.T., Cambridge, U.S.A. 52-54; with Foundation for Fundamental Research on Matter (FOM) 55-, Research Assoc. 55-57, Scientific Head of Thermonuclear Group 57-58, Dir. Inst. for Plasma Physics 58-; part-time Prof. of Plasma Physics, Univ. of Utrecht 62-; Visiting Scientist, Boeing Scientific Research Laboratories, Seattle 63-65.
Leisure interests: sailing, field-hockey, gardening.
FOM-Institute for Plasma Physics, Rijnhuizen, P.O.B. 7, Nieuwegein, Jutphaas; Home: Joh. Wagenaarkade 33, Utrecht, Netherlands.
Telephone: 3402-1224 (Office); 30-931132 (Home).

Brabham, John Arthur (Jack Brabham), O.B.E.; Australian professional racing driver (retd.); b. 2 April 1926, Sydney, Australia; m. Betty Evelyn, 1951; three s.; ed. Hurstville Technical Coll., Sydney.
Served in R.A.A.F. 44-46; started own engineering business 46; Midget Speedway racing 46-52; numerous wins driving a Cooper-Bristol, Australia 53-54; came to Europe 55; Australian Grand Prix 55, 63; World Champion, Formula II 58; Formula II Champion of France 64; World Champion Driver 59-60, 60-61, 66; First in Monaco and U.K. Grandes Epreuves 59; won Grand Prix of Netherlands, Belgium, France, U.K., Portugal, Denmark 60, Belgium 61, France 66, 67, U.K. 66; began building own cars 61; Man. Dir. Jack Brabham (Motors) Ltd., Jack Brabham (Worcester Park) Ltd., Brabham Racing Org. Ltd., Engine Devts. Ltd.; Ferodo Trophy 64, 66; RAC Gold Medal 66, BARC Gold Medal 59, 66, 67; Formula I Mfrs. Championship 66, 67.
c/o 248 Hook Road, Chessington, Surrey, England.
Telephone: 01-397 4343.

Brace, William Francis, PH.D.; American professor of geology; b. 26 Aug. 1926, Littleton, N.H.; s. of Frank Charles Brace and Frances Badger Dodge Brace; m. Margaret T. Grant 1955; two s. one d.; ed. M.I.T., Cambridge, Mass.
Asst. Prof. of Geology M.I.T., 54-61, Assoc. Prof. of Geology 61-64, Prof. of Geology 64-; mem. Nat. Acad. of Sciences.
Leisure interests: music, rowing, running, climbing, skiing.
Publs. numerous technical articles.
Room 54-720, Department of Earth and Planetary Sciences, Massachusetts Institute of Technology, Cambridge, Mass. 02139, U.S.A.
Telephone: 617-253-3391.

Bracher, Karl Dietrich, DR. PHIL.; German political scientist and historian; b. 13 March 1922, Stuttgart; s. of Theodor and Gertrud Bracher; m. Dorothee Schleicher 1951; one s. one d.; ed. Gymnasium, Stuttgart, Univ. of Tübingen and Harvard Univ.

Research Asst. and Head of Dept., Inst. of Political Science, Berlin 50-58; Lecturer, German Hochschule für Politik, Berlin; Privatdozent and Prof. Free Univ., Berlin 55-58; Prof. of Political Science and Contemporary History, Univ. of Bonn 59-; Pres. Comm. for History of Parl. and Political Parties, Bonn 62-68; Fellow, Center for Advanced Study in the Behavioral Sciences, Stanford, U.S.A. 63-64; Pres. German Asscn. of Political Science 65-67; mem. Inst. for Advanced Study, Princeton, U.S.A. 67-68, 74-75; mem. Board, Institut für Zeitgeschichte, Munich, German Asscn. of Foreign Policy, Asscn. of German Scientists, German PEN Centre; Guest Prof. Oxford Univ. 71, Tel Aviv Univ. 74; Prof. European Univ. Inst. (Florence) 75; Hon. Mem. American Acad. of Arts and Sciences 73; hon. D. Hum. Litt.; mem. Editorial Board, *Politische Vierteljahresschrift, Vierteljahrshefte für Zeitgeschichte, Neue Politische Literatur, Bonner Historische Forschungen, Journal of Contemporary History, Government and Opposition, Societas* (Review of Social History), *History of the Twentieth Century, Bonner Schriften zur Politik und Zeitgeschichte, Modern Constitutionalism and Democracy* (joint editor) 2 vols. 66, *Nach 25 Jahren* (editor) 70, *Bibliographie zur Politik* (joint editor) 70, *Dokumente zur Deutschlandspolitik* 72-.
Leisure interest: piano music.
Publs. *Conscience in Revolt* (with others) 54, *Nationalsozialistische Machtergreifung und Reichskonkordat* 56, *Die Auflösung der Weimarer Republik* 55, *Staat und Politik* (with E. Fraenkel) 57, *Die Nationalsozialistische Machtergreifung* (with others) 60, *The Foreign Policy of the Federal Republic of Germany* 63, *Problems of Parliamentary Democracy in Europe* 64, *Adolf Hitler* 64, *Deutschland zwischen Demokratie und Diktatur* 64, *Internationale Beziehungen* (with E. Fraenkel) 69, *The German Dictatorship* 70, *Das deutsche Dilemma* 71, *Western Europe* (in *Times History of Our Times*) 71, *Democracy* (in *Europe Tomorrow*) 72.
Am Hofgarten 15, Bonn; Stationsweg 17, Bonn, Federal Republic of Germany.
Telephone: 655158.

Brachet, Jean Louis Auguste, M.D.; Belgian biologist; b. 19 March 1909, Eherbeek; s. of Albert Brachet and Marguerite Guchez; m. Françoise de Barsy 1934; two s. one d.; ed. Univ. Libre de Bruxelles.
Assistant in Anatomy, Faculty of Medicine, Univ. of Brussels 34-38, Dir. of Studies 38, Prof. 42-, Dir. Laboratory of Molecular Cytology and Embryology Sciences Faculty; also Foreign Consultant of Laboratory of Molecular Embryology, Naples; Rockefeller Fellow, Princeton 37; Visiting Prof. Inst. Pasteur, Paris 46, Univ. of Pa. 47, Indian Cancer Research Centre, Bombay 56, Rockefeller Inst. 58, Weizmann Inst., Israel 60, Univ. of Texas 65, Univ. of Jerusalem 66; Francqui Prof., Univs. of Liège, Ghent and Louvain; mem. Acad. royale des Sciences de Belgique, Acad. royale de Médecine de Belgique, Royal Danish Acad., Nat. Acad. of Sciences, Washington, American Acad. of Arts and Sciences, Royal Soc., London, Royal Soc., Edinburgh, Deutsche Akad. der Naturforscher Leopoldina, Halle, Yugoslav Acad. of Sciences, Istituto Lombardo, Milan, Soc. Française de Biologie, Inst. grand-ducal de Luxembourg; Dr. h.c. (Univs. of Strasbourg, Poitiers, Turin, Palermo, Edinburgh, Weizmann Inst., Israel, and Inst. agronomique de Gembloux.).
Leisure interests: archaeology, history, gardening.
Publs. *Embryologie chimique* 44, 45 (trans. English, Russian and Chinese), *Biochemical Cytology* 57 (trans. Russian and Polish), *The Biological Role of Ribonucleic Acids* 60, *Introduction to Molecular Embryology* 73, *Embriologia molecolare* 73; Co-editor *The Cell* (6 vols.); over 300 publications on the biochemical bases of embryonic development, the role of nucleic acids in the

synthesis of proteins, the role of the nucleus in the differentiation and synthesis of macromolecules.
Faculté des Sciences, Université Libre de Bruxelles, 67 rue des Chevaux Rhode-St.-Genese, Brussels, Belgium.

Brack, Robert William, B.A., F.A.I.M.; Australian business executive; b. 15 Nov. 1921, Hawthorn, Victoria; s. of James Brack and late Frances Lillian Brack (née Downey); m. Ethel J. Mackey 1952; one s. one d.; ed. Telopea Park High School, Canberra and Melbourne Univs.
With Dept. of Trade and Customs 38-41; served 8th Div. A.I.F. 41-45, P.O.W. Singapore and Thailand; Australian High Comm., London 49-51, 56-57; Australian Embassy, Washington, D.C. 52-53; Asst. Comptroller-Gen. of Customs, Canberra 59-63, Collector of Customs for N.S.W. 63-64; joined Australian Consolidated Industries Ltd., Commercial Man. 64-66, Asst. Gen. Man. 66-67, Gen. Man. 67-, Dir. 74-; Dir. Alex Harvey Industries Ltd., Malayan Containers Berhad; Chair. Pak Pacific Corpn. Pty. Ltd.; Dir. of other cos.
Australian Consolidated Industries Ltd., 550 Bourke Street, Melbourne, Victoria 3000; Home: 2 Evans Court, Toorak, Victoria 3142, Australia.
Telephone: 600441 (Office); 203757 (Home).

Bradbrook, Muriel Clara, M.A., PH.D., LITT.D.; British university professor; b. 27 April 1909; d. of Samuel Bradbrook; ed. Hutchesons' School, Glasgow, Oldershaw School, Wallasey, and Girton Coll., Cambridge.
Fellow of Girton Coll., Cambridge 32-35, 36-; Mistress of Girton Coll. 68-76; in residence Somerville Coll., Oxford 35-36; Board of Trade, Industries and Manufactures Depts. 2 and 3 41-45; Univ. Lecturer, Cambridge 45-62, Reader 62-65, Prof. of English 65-; in residence Folger Library, Washington, and Huntingdon Library, Calif. 58-59; tour of Far East for Shakespeare's Fourth Centenary 64; Trustee, Shakespeare's Birthplace 67; Visiting Prof. Santa Cruz, Calif. 66; Visiting Prof. Kuwait 69; Foreign mem. Norwegian Acad. of Arts and Sciences 66; Freedom of City of Hiroshima; F.R.S.L. 47; Hon. Litt.D. (Liverpool Univ.) 64, (Sussex Univ.) 72, (London Univ.) 73; Hon. LL.D. (Smith Coll., U.S.A.) 65; Hon. Ph.D. (Gothenburg) 75.
Leisure interests: travel, theatre.
Publs. *Elizabethan Stage Conditions* 32, *Themes and Conventions of Elizabethan Tragedy* 34, *The School of Night* 36, *Andrew Marvell* (with M. G. Lloyd Thomas) 40, *Joseph Conrad* 41, *Ibsen the Norwegian* 47, *T. S. Eliot* 50, *Shakespeare and Elizabethan Poetry* 51, *The Queen's Garland* 53, *The Growth and Structure of Elizabethan Comedy* 55, *Sir Thomas Malory* 57, *The Rise of the Common Player* 62, *English Dramatic Form* 65, *That Infidel Place: A History of Girton College* 69, *Shakespeare the Craftsman* 69, *Literature in Action* 72, *T. S. Eliot: the Making of "The Waste Land"* 72, *Malcolm Lowry: His Art and Early Life* 74.
91 Chesterton Road, Cambridge, CB4 3AP, England.
Telephone: 52765.

Bradbury, Norris Edwin, B.A., PH.D.; American physicist; b. 30 May 1909; ed. Pomona Coll., Calif., Univ. of Calif. and Mass. Inst. of Technology.
Assistant Prof. of Physics, Stanford Univ. 34-37, Assoc. Prof. 37-42, Prof. 42-51; Prof. of Physics, Univ. of Calif. 51-70; Dir. Los Alamos Scientific Laboratory, New Mexico 45-70; Capt. U.S. Naval Reserve 41-61; Fellow of the Nat. Acad. of Sciences and of the American Physical Soc.; Enrico Fermi Award 70.
Home: 1451 47th Street, Los Alamos, New Mexico 87544, U.S.A.

Bradfield, John Ross, LL.D.; Canadian business executive.
Hon. Chair. Noranda Mines Ltd.; Dir. Noranda Metal Industries Ltd., St. Lawrence Cement Co.; Pres. Ontario Geriatrics Research Soc.; Vice-Pres. Orthopaedic and Arthritic Hospital; Companion of Order of Canada.
Noranda Mines Ltd., Commerce Court West, Toronto 1; Home: 151 Dunvegan Road, Toronto, Ontario, Canada.
Telephone: 485-3446 (Home).

Bradley, Gen. Omar Nelson; American business executive and retd. army officer; b. 12 Feb. 1893, Clark, Missouri; s. of John S. Bradley and Elizabeth Hubbard; m. 1st Mary Quayle 1916 (died 1965), 2nd Kitty Buhler 1966; one d.; ed. U.S. Military Acad., West Point.
Second-Lieut. of infantry 15; advanced through grades to Gen. of the Army Sept. 50; Prof. of Mil. Science and Tactics, S. Dakota State Coll. Sept. 19-20; Instructor in Hawaii 25-28; graduated from Command and Gen. Staff School, Fort Leavenworth, Kan. July 29; Instructor at Infantry School, Fort Benning, Ga. 29-33; graduated from War Coll., Washington June 34; Instructor in Tactics, later Plans and Training Officer, West Point 34-38; Asst. Sec., Gen. Staff July 39-Feb. 41; Commandant of Infantry School, Fort Benning Feb. 41-Feb. 42; commanded 82nd Infantry Div. Feb. 42; commanded U.S. Second Corps in Tunisia and in invasion of Sicily 43; commanded First U.S. Army during invasion of Europe 44; later commanded 12th Army Group; Administrator of Veterans' Affairs 45-47; Chief of Staff U.S. Army 48-49; Chair. Joint Chiefs of Staff U.S. Dept. of Defense 49-53; U.S. Rep., NATO Military Cttee. (Chair. 49-50) and Standing Cttee. 49-53; Chair. Bulova Research Devt. Laboratories, N.Y. 53-; Bulova Watch Co. 58-; decorations incl. D.S.M. (3 Oak Leaf Clusters), D.S.M. of U.S. Navy, Legion of Merit with Oak Leaf Clusters, Silver Star, Bronze Star Medal, Hon. K.C.B. (Great Britain), Grand Cross of the Legion of Honour and Croix de Guerre with Palm (France), Order of Suvorov 1st degree and of Kutuzov 1st degree (U.S.S.R.), and many other awards.
Leisure interests: hunting, fishing, golf, writing.
Publ. *A Soldier's Story* 51.
630 Fifth Avenue, New York, N.Y. 10020, U.S.A.

Bradman, Sir Donald George, Kt.; Australian cricketer and company director; b. 27 Aug. 1908, Cootamundra, N.S.W.; s. of George and Emily Bradman; m. Jessie Menzies 1932; two s. (one deceased) one d.; ed. Bowral Intermediate High School.
Played cricket for N.S.W. 27-34, for S. Australia 35-49; played for Australia 28-48, Capt. 36-48; in test cricket made 6,996 runs (average 99.9), in all first-class cricket 28,067 runs (average 95); scored 117 centuries in first-class matches; mem. Australian Board of Control for Int. Cricket 45-, Chair. 60-63, 69-72; Vice-Pres. S. Australia Cricket Asscn. 51-65, Pres. 65-73, now Trustee and mem. Ground and Finance Cttee.; fmr. Australian Test Selector; fmr. mem. Stock Exchange of Adelaide; now Dir. many public cos.; Champion Mt. Osmond Country Club (Golf) 36, 49; fmr. S. Australia Amateur Squash Champion.
Leisure interests: cricket, tennis, golf, squash.
Publs. *Don Bradman's Book* 30, *How to Play Cricket* 35, *My Cricketing Life* 38, *Farewell to Cricket* 50, *The Art of Cricket* 58.
2 Holden Street, Kensington Park, S. Australia 5068, Australia.

Bradshaw, Thornton F.; American business executive; b. 4 Aug. 1917, Wash.; s. of Frederick and Julia See Bradshaw; m. 1st Sally Bradford Davis 1940, one s. two d.; m. 2nd Patricia S. West 1974; ed. Phillips Exeter Acad., Harvard Coll. and Harvard Graduate School of Business Admin.
Associate Prof., Harvard Business School 42-52; Partner, Cresap, McCormick and Paget, New York 52-56; Dir. The Atlantic Refining Co., Philadelphia (now Atlantic Richfield Co.) 56-, Vice-Pres. 56-62, Exec. Vice-Pres. 62-64, Pres. 64-, mem. Exec. Cttee. 66-; Dir. RCA Corpn., Champion Int., Diebold Venture Capital Corpn., American Petroleum Inst., The Conf. Board,

Foreign Policy Asscn., Aspen Inst. for Humanistic Studies; mem. Board Los Angeles World Affairs Council; mem. Board of Dirs. Security Pacific Nat. Bank, Security Pacific Corpn.; Board of Trustees and Chair. Board of Fellows, Claremont Univ. Center; Visiting Cttee. of U.C.L.A. Graduate School of Management; Visiting Cttee. for Div. of Chemistry and Chemical Engineering, Calif. Inst. of Technology; Chair. UNA Conventional Arms Control Policy Panel.
Leisure interests: boating, tennis, swimming.
Publs. *Controllership in Modern Management* 49, *Developing Men for Controllership* 50.
Atlantic Richfield Co., 515 South Flower Street, Los Angeles, Calif. 90071, U.S.A.
Telephone: (213) 486-1738.

Bradwell, Baron (Life Peer), cr. 75, of Bradwell juxta Mare in the County of Essex; **Thomas Edward Neil Driberg;** British journalist and politician; b. 22 May 1905, Crowborough, Sussex; *s.* of John J. S. Street Driberg and Amy M. Irving Bell; *m.* Mrs. Ena Mary Binfield 1951; ed. Lancing and Christ Church, Oxford.
Member Editorial Staff *Daily Express* 28-43; Ind. M.P. for Maldon Div. of Essex 42-45, Lab. 45-55; M.P. for Barking 59-74; mem. Nat. Exec. Cttee., Labour Party 49-72, Chair. 57-58; contributor *Sunday Citizen* (formerly *Reynolds News*) 43-66; television and radio critic for *New Statesman* 55-61; war corresp. 44-45 and in Korea 50; mem. Parl. Delegation, Buchenwald Camp 45; Chair. Commonwealth Group, Parl. Labour Party 64-68; Chair. Select Cttee. on Broadcasting etc. of Proceedings in Parl. 66-67; mem. Historic Buildings Council for England 66-.
Publs. *Colonnade* 49, *The Best of Both Worlds* 53, *Beaverbrook: a Study in Power and Frustration* 56, *Guy Burgess: A Portrait with Background* 56, *The Mystery of Moral Re-Armament: A Study of Frank Buchman and His Movement* 64, *Swaff* 74.
c/o Higham Associates Ltd., 5-8 Lower John Street, Golden Square, London, W1R 4HA, England.

Bræk, Ola Skjåk; Norwegian banker and politician; b. 4 Feb. 1912, Eidsvoll; *s.* of Gudbrand and Elisabeth (Fisher) Bræk; *m.* Ingeborg Wergeland 1938; two *s.* one *d.*
Lawyer, Ullensaker 36-38; Asst. judge, Eidsvoll 38-40, Insp. Norwegian Bank Inspection Board, Oslo 40-50; Chief Man. Dir. Sunmøre Kreditbank A/S Aalesund 50-; Chair. Board Statens Fryseri Aalesund 56-70; mem. Board, Norinvest A/S Oslo 62-65, A/S Forretningsbankenes Finansierings—og Eksportkredittinstitutt 62-, A/S Olivin, Aaheim, Statens Kornforretning 67-70, Fondet for nye industrielle tiltak, Oslo 69-; Chair. Council, Regional Banks in Norway 71-; Chair. Board of Reps. Sunmøre Fiskeindustri A/S, Aalesund 70-; mem. board of reps. of several other orgs.; First Deputy mem. Storting 65-68; Minister of Industry and Handicraft 72-73.
Leisure interest: angling.
Sunmøre Kreditbank A/S Korsegatan 8, Ålesund; 6001 Ålesund, Norway.

Braga, Ney; Brazilian politician; b. 25 July 1917; ed. in Curitiba and Escola Militar de Realengo.
Second Lieut. 38, rising to Reserve Brig.-Gen. in 63 on retirement from army; Chief of Police for Paraná 52-54, Prefect 54-58; Fed. Deputy 58; Gov. of Paraná 60-65; responsible for the creation of various companies during his governorship including Companhia de Desenvolvimento Econômico do Paraná (CODEPAR) and Companhia Paranaense de Energia Elétrica (COPEL); mem. Senate 65, 66-; Minister of Agriculture 65-66, of Educ. and Culture 74-; Pres. Council for the Extreme South (CODSEUL) 63; Christian Democrat (Nat. Pres.); Dr. h.c. Univ. of Paraná; numerous honours and awards.
Ministério da Educação e Cultura, Brasília, Brazil.

Braga, Ruben; Brazilian journalist and diplomatist; b. 12 Jan. 1913; ed. Univ. de Minas Gerais.
Professional journalist in Brazil 32-; roving correspondent for Brazilian newspapers in America and Europe; covered elections of Perón and Eisenhower; War Correspondent for *Diários Associados*, Brazilian Revolution 32, with Brazilian Expeditionary Force in Italy 44-45; Head of Commercial Writers in Brazil 35; Ambassador to Morocco 61-63.
Publs. *O Conde e o Passarinho* 36, *O Morro do Isolamento* 44, *Com a FEB na Itália* 45, *Um Pé de Milho* 48, *O Homem Rouco* 49, *50 Crônicas Escolhidas* 51, *Três Primitivos* 54, *A Borboleta Amarela* 55, *A Cidade e a Roça* 57, *100 Crônicas Escolhidas* 58, *Ai de ti, Copacabana* 60, *Chroniques de Copacabana de Paris et d'Ailleurs* 63.
c/o Ministério de Relaçoes Exteriores, Brasília, Brazil.

Braga da Cruz, Guilherme, DR. JUR.; Portuguese university professor; b. 11 June 1916, Braga, Portugal; *s.* of José Maria Braga da Cruz and Maria Isabel de Sousa Gomes; *m.* Ofélia de Azevedo Garcia; four *s.* five *d.*; ed. Lyceum of Braga, Univ. of Coimbra, Univ. of Paris.
Vice-Pres. Centro Académico de Democracia Cristã, Coimbra 36-37; Asst. Prof. Faculty of Law, Coimbra Univ. 42-47, Prof. 47-, Dean, Faculty of Law 58-61, Rector 61-62; mem. "Câmara Corporativa" 53-57, 57-61, Vice-Pres. 55-57; mem. Comm. New Civil Code 54-66; Portuguese mem. Int. Court of Justice, Right of Passage over Indian Territory case 57-59; Dir. Univ. Library 71-; Academician, Portuguese Acad. of History 51-, Acad. of Sciences 62-, Acad. Int. des Sciences Politiques 63-, Acad. de Législation, Toulouse 64-, Société Européenne de Culture 67-, and Int. Acad. of Portuguese Culture 67-; Dr. h.c. Faculty of Law, São Paulo Univ. 62, Navarra Univ. (Pamplona) 67; several national and foreign decorations.
Publs. *Algumas Considerações Sôbre a "Perfiliatio"* 38, *O Direito de Troncalidade*, 2 vols. 41, 47, *O Problema da Sucessão dos Ascendentes no Antigo Direito Grego* 47, *A Posse de Ano e Dia* 49, *O Direito de Superfície no Direito Romano* 49, *S. Martinho de Dume e a Legislação Visigótica* 50, *Direitos e Deveres do Estado na Educação* 52, *Origem e Evolução da Universidade* 53, *A Sucessão Legítima no Código Euricano* 53, *Formação Histórica do Moderno Direito Português e Brasileiro* 55, *O Problema do Regime de Bens Supletivo* 56, *Regimes de Bens do Casamento* 57, *Capacidade Patrimonial dos Cônjuges* 57, *O Problema da Universidade* 61, *Afinidade (Subsistência do vínculo após a dissolução do casamento)* 62, *Le Code Napoléon dans la formation du droit civil portugais moderne* 63, *Les pactes successoraux dans l'ancien droit portugais* 63, *Casamento: Contrato e Sacramento* 64, *Propriedade da Farmácia* 64, *O Movimento Abolicionista e a Abolição da Pena de Morte em Portugal (Resenha Histórica)* 67, *A Revista de Legislação e de Jurisprudência (Esboço da sua história)* 69, *El Derecho Subsidiario en la Historia del Derecho Português* 71, *Reforma do Ensino Superior* 73, *O Latim e o Direito* 73.
Avenida Dias da Silva, 6, Coimbra, Portugal.
Telephone: 2-32-45.

Brahimi, Lakhdar; Algerian diplomatist; b. 1934; ed. Medersa Algiers, Faculté de Droit et Institut des Sciences Politiques, Algiers, then Paris.
Student Leader 53-56; Algerian Front of Nat. Liberation (F.L.N.) to 56; Perm. Rep. of F.L.N. and later of Provisional Govt. of Algeria in South East Asia 56-61; Gen. Secretariat Ministry of External Affairs 61-63; Amb. to U.A.R. (Egypt) and Sudan 63-69; Perm. Rep. to Arab League 63-70; Amb. to U.K. 71-.
Algerian Embassy, 6 Hyde Park Gate, London, SW7 5EW, England.

Braibant, Charles, L. ÈS D., L. ÈS L.; French writer and archivist; b. 31 March 1889; ed. Lycées Janson-de-Sailly and Louis-le-Grand and Paris Univ.

Served French Army 14-18; Curator of Naval Archives 19-44; Insp.-Gen. of Archives of France 44-48; Dir.-Gen. of Archives of France 48-59, Hon. Dir.-Gen. 59-; Pres. Int. Archives Council 50-53, Hon. Pres. 53-; Nat. handwriting expert; Grand Officier, Légion d'Honneur, Commdr. des Palmes Académiques and other decorations; Prix Theophraste Renaudot 33.
Publs. *Le Roi Dort, Le Soleil de Mars, Le Rive des Dieux, Irène Soubeyran, Resplendine et autres Victimes, Lumière bleue, La Guerre à Paris, Le Métier d'Ecrivain, Mer franque, Le Secret d'Anatole France, Un Bourgeois sous trois Républiques, Félix Faure à l'Elysée, Histoire de la tour Eiffel.*
7 rue Louis-Boilly, Paris 16e, France.
Telephone: 870-3578.

Braidwood, Robert John: American archaeologist and anthropologist; b. 29 July 1907; m. Linda Schreiber 1937; one s. one d.; ed. Michigan, Berlin and Chicago Univs.
Field archaeology in Iraq, Illinois, Syria, New Mexico, Turkey and Iran; Prof. of Anthropology and Old World Prehistory, Univ. of Chicago 54-; Fellow, American Acad. of Arts and Sciences, Nat. Acad. of Sciences, American Philosophical Soc.; Corresp. mem. Deutsches Archäologisches Institut, Österreichische Akademie der Wissenschaft, etc., Dr.h.c. Sorbonne 75.
Publs. *Excavations in the plain of Antioch I* (with Linda Braidwood), *Prehistoric investigations in Iraqi Kurdistan* (with Bruce Howe, *et al.*).
c/o National Academy of Sciences, 2101 Constitution Avenue, Washington, D.C., 20418 U.S.A.

Brain, Sir Hugh Gerner, Kt., C.B.E., M.S.M., HON.M. AUST.I.M.M.; Australian retd. company secretary and director; b. 3 Dec. 1890, Toorak, Victoria; s. of W. J. and Florence Brain; m. Monica Eva Futcher 1920; one s. two d.; ed. State School, and Univ. High School, Melbourne.
Clerical employment in Victoria Public Service 07-13, Commonwealth Public Service 13-18; abroad with Australian Imp. Force 15-19; discharged as Capt. and D.A.A.G.; Dir. Australasian Temperance and Gen. Mutual Life Assurance Soc. Ltd. 40-72; Asst. Hon. Sec. Dept. of Defence Co-ordination 40; business mem. (hon.) Australian Naval Board 41-46; Chair. The Baillieu Educational Trusts 36-51.
Leisure interests: reading, music, Legacy Club (welfare of ex-servicemen's dependents).
415 Kooyong Road, Elsternwick, Victoria 3185, Australia.
Telephone: 53-5158 (Home).

Braine, John Gerard, A.L.A.; British author; b. 13 April 1922; s. of Fred and Katharine Braine; m. Helen Patricia Wood 1955; one s. three d.; ed. St. Bede's Grammar School, Bradford and Leeds School of Librarianship.
Assistant Librarian, Bingley Public Library 40-51; Branch Librarian, Northumberland County Library 54-56, Yorkshire West Riding County Library 56-57; mem. B.B.C. North Region Advisory Council 60-64.
Leisure interests: walking, talking, model-making, Victoriana, painting.
Publs. *Room at the Top* 57, *The Vodi* 59, *Life at the Top* 62, *The Jealous God* 64, *The Crying Game* 68, *Stay With Me Till Morning* 70, *The Queen of a Distant Country* 72, *Writing a Novel* 74, *The Pious Agent* 75, *The Stirrer* (play) 75, *Waiting for Sheila* 76.
Pentons, Onslow Crescent, Woking, Surrey, England.
Telephone: Woking 67014.

Braithwaite, Eustace Adolphe, M.SC.; Guyanese author and diplomatist; b. 27 June 1912; ed. New York Univ. and Cambridge Univ.
Royal Air Force, Second World War; schoolteacher, London 50-57; Welfare Officer, London County Council

58-60; Human Rights Officer, World Veterans Foundation, Paris 60-63; Lecturer and Educ. Consultant, UNESCO, Paris 63-66; Perm. Rep. of Guyana to UN 67-68; Amb. to Venezuela 68-69; Ainsfield Wolff Literary Award for *To Sir, With Love*.
Publs. *To Sir, With Love* 59 (film 67), *A Kind of Homecoming* 61, *Paid Servant* 62, *A Choice of Straws* 65, *Reluctant Neighbours* 72.
c/o Timber Trails Club, Sherman, Connecticut 06784, U.S.A.

Branca, Vittore (Felice Giovanni), D.LITT.; Italian educationist; b. 9 July 1913, Savona; m. Olga Montagner 1938; one s. three d.; ed. Univ. of Pisa.
Professor Accad. della Crusca, Florence 37-48; Prof. of Italian Literature, Maria Assunta Univ., Rome 48-50; Prof. of Italian Literature, Univ. of Catania 50-53, Univ. of Padua 53-; Rector Univ. of Bergamo 68-72; Head, Div. of Arts and Letters, UNESCO 50-53; Vice-Pres. Cultural Cttee. Nat. Italian Comm. of UNESCO; Chair. Cultural Cttee. RAI-TV; Chair. Int. Asscn. for Study of Italian Language and Literature; Vice-Pres. Fondazione Giorgio Cini; mem. Cttee. Int. Fed. of Modern Languages and Literatures; literary adviser to publishing houses; Editor *Lettere Italiane* and *Studi sul Boccaccio* (magazines) and of numerous series of classical texts and essays; mem. Accad. dei Lincei, Accad. Arcadia, Istituto Veneto Scienze Lettere e Arti, Accad. Polacca della Scienze, Acad. du Monde Latin (Inst. de France) Medieval Acad. of America, Hon. mem. Modern Language Asscn. of America, Nat. Comm. of UNESCO; Dr. h.c. (Univs. of Budapest, New York and Bergamo); Gold Medal of Italian Ministry of Educ.
Publs. Editions and critical studies of San Francesco, Petrarca, Boccaccio, Poliziano, Alfieri, Manzoni and other classical authors.
San Marco 2885, Venice, Italy.
Telephone: 89-819.

Branch, Harllee, Jr., B.A., LL.B.; American business executive (retd.); b. 21 June 1906, Atlanta, Ga.; s. of Harllee Branch and Bernice Simpson Branch; m. Katherine Hunter 1932; three s. one d.; ed. Boys High School, Atlanta, Davidson Coll., N. Carolina, and Lamar School of Law, Emory Univ., Atlanta.
Director, Fed. Reserve Bank of Atlanta 53-55; Pres. Southeastern Electric Exchange 54-55, Edison Electric Inst. 55-56; Pres. and Dir. The Southern Co. 57-69, Chair. of Board 69-71; Chair. of Board, Southern Services Inc. 61-71; Vice-Pres. and Dir. Alabama, Georgia, Gulf and Mississippi Power Companies 57-68; mem. U.S. Business Advisory Council 62-, Nat. Comm. on Productivity 70-71; Dir. Nat. Center for Voluntary Action 70-71; Senior Fellow Woodrow Wilson Nat. Fellowship Foundation 73-; Hon. LL.D., Hon. D.H.L.
Leisure interests: golf, fishing.
3106 Nancy Creek Road, N.W., Atlanta, Ga. 30327, U.S.A.
Telephone: 404-355-7906.

Brand, Hon. Sir David, K.C.M.G., M.L.A.; Australian politician; b. 1912, Dongara, Western Australia; s. of Albert John and Hilda (née Mitchell) Brand; m. Doris Elspeth McNeill; two s. one d.; ed. Government School, Mullewa, Western Australia.
Member Western Australian Legislative Assembly for Greenough 45-; Hon. Minister for Housing, Forests and Local Govt. 49; Minister for Works, Water Supply and Housing 50; Leader of the Opposition and Parliamentary Leader, Liberal and Country League 57-59; Premier, Treasurer and Minister for Tourists, Govt. of Western Australia 59-71; Leader of Opposition 71-73.
Leisure interests: golf, tennis.
Home: 24 Ednah Street, Como; and Parliament House, Perth, Western Australia.
Telephone: 21-8711.

Brand, Lindsay Brownfield, O.B.E., M.A., A.I.A.; Australian financial official; b. 29 Nov. 1916, Melbourne; s. of Walter Edgar and Mabel Eliza Brand; m. Betty Rosalind Delpratt 1947; two s.; ed. Univ. of Melbourne. With Bureau of Census and Statistics, Canberra 39-40, 46-54; Served, Royal Australian Navy 40-46; with Australian Treasury 54-70; Sec. Australian Loan Council 55-70; mem. Decimal Currency Board 63-68; Exec. Dir. IMF 70-75.
Leisure interests: tennis, golf.
Home: 4915 Van Ness Street, N.W., Washington, D.C. 20016, U.S.A.
Telephone: 966-4730.

Brand, Vance D.; American astronaut; b. 9 May 1931, Longmont, Colo.; s. of Dr. and Mrs. R. W. Brand; m. Joan Virginia Weninger; two s. two d.; ed. Univ. of Colorado and Univ. of California at Los Angeles.
Officer, U.S. Marine Corps 53-57; completed naval flight training 55, served as jet fighter pilot, Japan, for fifteen months; Flight Test Engineer, Lockheed Corpn., attended U.S. Naval Test Pilot School, Patuxent River, Md. under Lockheed sponsorship, later became an engineering test pilot for Lockheed; selected as astronaut by NASA April 66; backup command module pilot for Apollo XV; backup commdr. for Skylabs II and III; flew on Apollo-Soyuz joint docking mission July 75.
NASA Johnson Space Center, Houston, Tex. 77058, U.S.A.

Brandi, Cesare, PH.D.; Italian author and art critic; b. 8 April 1906; ed. Univs. of Siena, Pisa and Florence. Inspector for the Superintendence of the Monuments and Galleries of Siena 33-39; founder and Dir. Central Restoration Inst., Rome 39-; started publishing Immagine (a review) 48, and the Bollettino of the Inst. 50; Superintendent, Dept. of Antiquities and Fine Arts 53-; Commendatore dell'Ordine al Merito della Repubblica 54.
Publs. Rutilio Manetti 32, La R. Pinacoteca di Siena 33, Mostra della pittura riminese del '300 35, Giotto 38, Carmine o della pittura con due saggi su Duccio e Picasso 47, Morandi 42, Giovanni di Paolo 47, Quattrocentisti senesi 49, La fine dell'avanguardia 50, La fine dell'avanguardia e l'arte di oggi 52, Duccio 51, Celso o della poesia 57, Teoria generale della critica, etc.
Piazza S. Francesco di Paola 7, Rome, Italy.

Brando, Marlon; American actor; b. 3 April 1924; m. Anna Kashfi 1957 (divorced 1959); one s.; ed. Shattuck Military Acad.
Academy Award for the best actor of the year 54, Golden Globe Award for the most popular actor of 72; refused Oscar for The Godfather 73; has appeared in the plays I Remember Mama, Candida, A Flag is Born, The Eagle has Two Heads, A Streetcar Named Desire, etc., and the films The Men, A Streetcar Named Desire, Viva Zapata, Julius Caesar, The Wild Ones, Desirée, On the Waterfront, Guys and Dolls, Teahouse of the August Moon, Sayonara, The Young Lions, The Fugitive Kind, The Ugly American, Bedtime Story, Mutiny on the Bounty, The Chase, Appaloosa, A Countess from Hong Kong, Morituri, Southwest to Sonora 66, Reflections in a Golden Eye 67, Candy 68, The Night of the Following Day 69, The Nightcomers 71, The Godfather 72, Last Tango in Paris 72, The Missouri Breaks 75; Dir. The One-Eyed Jacks, etc.
P.O. Box 809, Beverley Hills, California, U.S.A.

Brandon, Henry; British journalist; b. 3 Sept. 1916, Liberec, Czechoslovakia; s. of Oscar and Ida Brandon; m. Mabel H. Brandon 1971; one d.; ed. Prague and Lausanne Univs.
With The Sunday Times, London 39-, War Corresp. in N. Africa and W. Europe 43-45, Paris Corresp. 45-46, Roving Diplomatic Corresp. 47-49, Washington Corresp. and Chief American Corresp. 50-; Foreign Corresp. Award, Univ. of Calif. 57, Lincoln Univ. Award, Mo. 62, Hannen Swaffer Award 64.
Leisure interests: skiing, tennis, swimming, photography.
Publs. As We Are 61, In the Red 66, Conversations with Henry Brandon 66, The Anatomy of Error 70, The Retreat of American Power 73.
814 National Press Building, Washington, D.C. 20045, U.S.A.
Telephone: (202) 628-4310.

Brandt, Cornelis J.; Netherlands executive and journalist; b. 14 Feb. 1913, Amsterdam; m. W. J. van den Bosch 1937; two s.; ed. Netherlands Inst. of Chartered Accountants.
Began career as accountant and Sec. to agricultural and banking organisations; Acting Editor-in-Chief Amsterdamsche Effectenblad and Het Financieele Dagblad 43-49; Financial Editor De Telegraaf 49-52, Editor-in-Chief 52-, Man. Dir. 64-.
Publ. Preference Shares 46.
Hartelstein 3, Amsterdam-Buitenveldert, Netherlands.
Telephone: 020-421023.

Brandt, Karl, DR. AGR.; American economic adviser and agriculturalist; b. Germany 9 Jan. 1899; ed. Berlin and Württemberg Univs.
Member Board of Dirs. German Farm Tenants Bank 25-27; Agricultural Adviser Central Co-operative Bank Berlin 28-29, mem. Board of Trustees 29-33; Prof., Coll. of Agriculture, Berlin Univ. 29-33; Prof., Graduate Faculty, New School for Social Research, New York 33-38; Visiting Research Prof., Louisiana State Univ. 37-38; Econ. Adviser to Sec. of Agriculture 42; Consultant to War Dept. 43, War Food Admin. 44, Farm Credit Admin. 44-45; Econ. Adviser on Food and Agriculture to U.S. Mil. Govt. in Germany 45-46; Guest Prof., Univ. Heidelberg and Goettingen 48-49; Prof. Agricultural Economy, Food Research Inst. Stanford Univ., Calif. 38-61, Assoc. Dir. 52-61, Dir. 61-64, Emer 64; mem. Joint Technical Mission to Uruguay of Int. Bank for Reconstruction and Devt. and FAO 50-51; Consultant to Ford Foundation 51-53; Adviser to Belgian Royal deputy on Kilombwe Valley (Congo) 54; Consultant to Stanford Research Inst. 44-62, Senior Econ. Consultant 63-; mem. Econ. Advisory Mission to Prime Minister of Malaya 63; Adviser to Pres., Di Tella Foundation, Buenos Aires 64; Consultant to Rockefeller and Ford Foundations in Colombia 65; mem. Board of Trustees, Foundation for Econ. Educ. 63-, American Enterprise Inst. for Governmental Research 58-; mem. Editorial Advisory Board The Intercollegiate Review 64-; Pres. Emer. Western Agricultural Econ. Asscn.; mem. Int. Conf. of Agricultural Economists, Philadelphia Soc., Mont Pelerin Soc.; Fellow, Royal Econ. Asscn., American Agricultural Econ. Asscn.; Hon. Dr. Phil (Heidelberg); Hon. mem. Soc. Royale d'Economie de Belgique; mem. Acad. d'Agriculture, Paris; Chevalier Ordre Nat. du Mérite (France) 67; Order of the Brilliant Star (Taiwan) 68; Justus-von-Liebig Prize 69; Distinguished Service Award, Wm. Volker Fund 70.
Publs. The Principles and Theory of Farm Tenancy 28, The German Fat Plan and its Economic Setting 38, Reconstruction of World Agriculture 45, Germany is our problem 46, The Management of Agriculture and Food in the German Occupied and other Areas of Fortress Europe 59, and others.
221 Kingsley Avenue, Palo Alto, Calif. 94301, U.S.A.

Brandt, Leo Wolfgang, DIPL.-ING.; German scientific civil servant; b. 17 Nov. 1908, Bernberg, Anhalt; s. of Berthold Brandt and Alwine née Kämper; m. Maria Emschermann 1930; three s. one d.; ed. Lessing-Oberrealschule, Düsseldorf and Technische Hochschule, Aachen and Berlin.
Head of Devt., Telefunken Gesellschaft für drahtlose

Telegraphie; Dir.-Gen., Rheinische Bahngesellschaft A.G., Düsseldorf; Sec. of State, Ministry for Economy and Transport, North-Rhine-Westfalia; Lecturer, Technische Hochschule, Aachen and Berlin; Sec. of State and Dir. Landesamt für Forschung 61-; Deputy Chair. Deutsche Atomkommission; several hon. degrees.
4006 Erkrath bei Düsseldorf, Sperberweg 2, Federal Republic of Germany.
Telephone: 64-26-26.

Brandt, Willy; German politician; b. 18 Dec. 1913, Lübeck; *m.* Rut Hansen; three *s.* one *d.*; ed. Lübeck and Oslo Univ.
Apprentice ship-broker 32; emigrated to Norway 33; journalist and Sec. of Norwegian charity 33-40; German and Norwegian resistance movements 40-45; journalist and Norwegian Press Attaché in Berlin 45-48; Chief Editor *Berliner Stadtblatt* 50-51; Sec. Exec. Cttee. of SPD in Berlin 48-49, mem. 50-63, Deputy Chair. 54-58, Chair. 58-63; Deputy Chair. SPD 62-64, Chair. 64-; mem. Berlin Chamber of Deputies 50-69, Pres. 55-57; Gov. Mayor of Berlin 57-66; mem. Federal Parl. (Bundestag) 49-57, 69-; Pres. Fed. Council (Bundesrat) 57-58; Pres. Deutscher Städtetag 58-63; Minister of Foreign Affairs and Vice-Chancellor Fed. Germany 66-69; Fed. Chancellor 69-74; Senator Max-Planck Asscn.; numerous hon. degrees and foreign decorations; Nobel Peace Prize 71; Reinhold Niebuhr Award 72; Aspen Inst. for Humanistic Studies Prize 73; Social Democrat (SPD).
Leisure interests: reading, fishing, swimming.
Publs. include *Krigen i Norge* 45, *Ernst Reuter* (with R. Lowenthal) 57, *Von Bonn nach Berlin* 57, *My Road to Berlin* 60, *The Ordeal of Co-existence* 63, *Begegnung mit Kennedy* 64, *Draussen* (with G. Struve) 66, *Schriften Während der Emigration* 66, *A Peace Policy for Europe* 68, *Der Wille zum Frieden* 71.
Sozialdemokratische Partei Deutschlands, Erich-Ollenhauer-Haus, 53 Bonn, Federal Republic of Germany.
Telephone: 221901.

Brandys, Kazimierz; Polish writer; b. 27 Oct. 1916, Łódź; *s.* of Henryk Brandys and Eugenia Landau; *m.* Maria Zenowicz 1944; ed. Univ. of Warsaw.
Co-Editor *Kuźnica Odrodzenie*, after war (weekly), Cracow 46-49 and of *Nowa Kultura* 56-58; mem. Exec. Cttee. Polish Writers' Union; State Literary Prize 50; Warsaw Literary Prize 48; State Prize 55; Premio Elba (Italy) 64; Officer's Cross, Order of Polonia Restituta 52; Order of Banner of Labour 2nd Class 54.
Publs. novels: *The Invincible City* 46, *The Wooden Horse* 46, *Between the Two Wars* (4 vols.) 48-51, *The Citizens* 54, *The Red Cap* 56, *Defence of Granada* (apology for writers and actors) 56, *Matka Królów* (Sons and Commanders, English edn.) 57, *Listy do pani Z.* (Letters to Mrs. Z.) 58-61, *Romantyczność* (Romanticism) 60, *Sposób bycia* (The Way to be) 64, *Dżoker* (Joker) 66, *Rynek* (The Market Place) 68, *Jak być kochaną* (How to be Loved) 70, *Mała księga* (A Little Book) 70, *Wariacje pocztowe* (Postal Variations) 72, *Pomysł* (The Concept) 74.
Nowomiejska 5m.5, Warsaw 00-271, Poland.
Telephone: 31-37-42.

Branscomb, B. Harvie, B.A., PH.D., D.LITT., LL.D., D.H.L.; American educationist; b. 25 Dec. 1894, Huntsville, Alabama; *s.* of Lewis C. Branscombe and Nancy McAdory; *m.* Margaret Vaughan 1921; three *s.*; ed. Birmingham-Southern Coll., Oxford and Columbia Univs.
Asst. Prof. Southern Methodist Univ. 19-25; Prof. Duke Univ. 25-46; Dir. Univ. Libraries, Duke Univ. 32-37; Dean Divinity School 44-46; Chancellor Vanderbilt Univ. 46-63; Consultant to World Bank on Educational Policy 62-63; Trustee Gen. Education Board 47; Chair. U.S. Educational Exchange Advisory Comm. 47-51;

Chair. Comm. on Education and Int. Affairs, American Council of Education 58; Chair. U.S. Nat. Comm. for UNESCO; Delegate General Conference, World Health Org. 65 and 66; Chair. U.S. Del., World Conf. on Illiteracy 65, Conf. of Ministers of Educ. of Latin American countries 66; mem. U.S. Nat. Advisory Health Council 63-67; Consultant, Acad. Educational Devt. 67-; Dir. Tennessee Fine Arts Center, Parthenon Fund; Trustee, several educational orgs.; Médaille du Roi Albert (Belgium); Médaille de la Reine (Belgium); Commdr. Order of the Southern Cross (Brazil).
Leisure interest: archaeological remains of the American Indians.
Publs. *The Message of Jesus* 25, *Jesus and the Law of Moses* 30, *The Teachings of Jesus* 31, *The Gospel according to Mark* 37, *Teaching with Books* 40.
1620 Chickering Road, Nashville 15, Tenn. 37215, U.S.A.
Telephone: 615-269-6821.

Branscomb, Lewis McAdory, M.S., PH.D.; American astrophysicist; b. 17 Aug. 1926, Asheville, N.C.; *s.* of Dr. and Mrs. Harvie Branscomb; *m.* Anne Wells 1951; one *s.* one *d.*; ed. Duke and Harvard Univs.
Instructor in Physics, Harvard Univ. 50; Lecturer in Physics, Univ. of Maryland 50-51; Chief, Atomic Physics Section, Nat. Bureau of Standards, Washington, D.C. 54-60, Chief Atomic Physics Div. 60-62; Chair. Joint Inst. for Laboratory Astrophysics 62-65, 68-70; Chief, Lab. Astrophysics Div., Nat. Bureau of Standards, Boulder, Colo. 62-69; Dir. Nat. Bureau of Standards Sept. 69-72; Chief Scientist, Vice-Pres. IBM Corpn. 72-; mem. Nat. Acad. of Sciences, Inst. of Medicine, Nat. Acad. of Eng.; Fellow, American Acad. of Arts and Sciences, American Philosophical Soc.; Trustee, Carnegie Inst. of Washington, Rand Corpn., Polytechnic Inst. of New York; several awards and hon. degrees.
Leisure interest: sailing.
Publs. numerous articles in professional journals.
IBM Corpn., Armonk, N.Y. 10504, U.S.A.
Telephone: 914-765-6467.

Brassens, Georges; French musician; b. 22 Oct. 1921; ed. Coll. de Sète, Lycée de Montpellier.
Composer and singer of songs in cabarets and music halls 52-; acted in and composed music and songs for the film *Porte des Lilas* 56; songs include *La Mauvaise Réputation*, *Le Gorille*, *Le Fossoyeur*, *Hécatombe*, etc., Grand prix du Disque 64; Prix de poésie, Acad. Française 67.
Publs. *La Tour des Miracles* (novel), *Poèmes et Chansons* (collection of poems and songs).
c/o Pierre Onténiente, 138 boulevard du Montparnasse, Paris 14e, France.

Brasseur, Maurice Paul; Belgian politician; b. 1909.
Teacher, Namur and Mons; served with Resistance 40-45; Burgomaster, Loverval 41-65; Minister of the Interior 50-52; mem. Chamber of Reps. 49-65, Vice-Pres. 58-61; Minister of Foreign Trade and Technical Assistance to under-developed countries 61; Gov. for Province of Luxembourg 65-; mem. of many Belgian missions abroad; numerous Belgian and foreign decorations, including Grand Croix de l'Ordre de Léopold II; Christian Socialist.
Palais Provincial, Arlon, Belgium.

Bratby, John, A.R.A., A.R.C.A., R.B.A., F.I.A.L.; British painter; b. 19 July 1928; ed. Tiffin Boys School, Kingston Art School, Royal Coll. of Art, London.
Works in Tate Gallery, London, Nat. Gallery of Canada, Nat. Gallery of New South Wales, New York Museum of Modern Art, Walker Art Gallery, Arts Council, Glasgow Museum of Art, etc.; rep. at Pittsburgh Int. Festival 55, 57, Venice Biennale 56; executed painting for the film *The Horse's Mouth* 58; Editorial Adviser *Art Quarterly*; Guggenheim Nat. Award 56 and 58.

Publs. *Breakdown* 60, *Breakfast and Elevenses* 61, *Brake-Pedal Down* 62, *Break 50 Kill* 63.
7 Hardy Road, Blackheath, London, S.E.3, England.
Telephone: 01-858-6288.

Bratchenko, Boris Fedorovich; Soviet mining engineer, economist and politician; b. 1912.
Has worked at coal mines in Rostov Region 35-49, at big combine in Karaganda, Kazakhstan 49-53; Govt. posts 53-; fmr. Vice-Chair. Council of Ministers of Kazakh Planning Cttee.; Minister of Coal Industry 65-; Candidate mem. Central Cttee. of C.P.S.U. 66-71, mem. 71-; Deputy to U.S.S.R. Supreme Soviet 62-; mem. C.P.S.U. 40-; U.S.S.R. State Prize.
Ministry of Coal Industry, 23 Building 2, Prospekt Kalinina, Moscow, U.S.S.R.

Bratsiotis, Panayotis, D.TH.; Greek university professor; b. 26 July 1889, Thebes; s. of John and Aphrodite Bratsiotis; m. Euphrosyne Trembelas 1927; three s. one d.; ed. Athens, Leipzig and Jena Univs.
Professor, Pedagogical Acad. of Piraeus 15-22; Prof. of Biblical Science, Athens Univ. 25-29, Prof. of Old Testament 29, Rector of Univ. 55-56; mem. Acad. of Athens 55, Pres. 60; foreign mem. Royal Flemish Acad. of Brussels; Hon. D.D. (Glasgow, Thessalonika Univs.).
Leisure interest: harmonium.
Publs. *St. John Baptist* 21, *Christianity and Culture* 40, *Humanism and Christianity, Social Thought of the Old Testament, Commentary to the Apocalypse of St. John* 50, *Commentary to the Ecclesiastes* 52, *Introduction to the Old Testament* 55, *Commentary to Isaiah, Chap. 1-12* 56-, *Meaning of Christian Agape* 56, *Die Orthodoxe Kirche in griechischer Sicht* 59-60, *Ein orthodoxes Bekenntnis* 66; collaborated on *Bible Oecuménique*, Paris 65.
Akadimia Athinon, Odos Panepistimiou, Athens; Apostel Paulus Street 5, Agia Paraskevi, Athens, Greece.
Telephone: 6592757.

Brattain, Walter H., B.S., M.A., D.PHIL.; American research physicist; b. 10 Feb. 1902, Amoy, China; s. of Ross and Ottilie Houser Brattain; m. 1st Keren Gilmore 1935 (deceased), 2nd Emma Jane (Kirsch) Miller 1958; one s.; ed. Whitman Coll., Oregon and Minnesota Univs.
Research physicist Radio Section, Bureau of Standards 28-29, Bell Telephone Laboratories Inc. 29-41, 44-67; Columbia Univ. War Research Div. 42-43; Visiting Lecturer, Harvard Univ. 52-53; Visiting Prof. of Physics, Whitman Coll., Walla Walla, Washington, Prof. Emer. 72-; mem. Nat. Acad. of Sciences; Stuart Ballantine Medal 52, John Scott Medal 55 (both with Dr. John Bardeen, q.v.), Nobel Prize in Physics 56 (with Dr. John Bardeen and Dr. William Shockley, q.v.); Fellow, American Physical Soc., American Acad. of Arts and Sciences, mem. Franklin Inst.; Hon. D.Sc. (Minnesota and Portland Univs., Whitman, Gustavus Adolphus and Union Colls.), Hon. D.Hum.Litt. (Hartwick Coll.).
Leisure interests: golf, fishing, reading.
Whitman College, Walla Walla, Washington 99362, U.S.A.
Telephone: 529-5100.

Bratteli, Trygve Martin; Norwegian journalist and politician; b. 11 Jan. 1910, Nøtterøy; s. of Terje Hansen Bratteli and Martha Barmen; m. Randi Helene Larssen 1946; one s. two d.; ed. public elementary school.
Editor Socialist newspaper *Folkets Frihet* 34; Editor fortnightly journal *Arbeider-Ungdommen*; Sec. Labour League of Youth 34-40, Chair. 45-46; Vice-Chair. Norwegian Labour Party 45-65, Chair. 65-75; Chair. Defence Cttee. 46, Finance Cttee. 50-51; M.P. 50-; Minister of Finance 51-55 and 56-60, of Communications 60-64; mem. Nordic Council 56-57, Electoral

Cttee. 64-71; Chair. Labour Party Parl. Group 64-71, 72-73; Prime Minister 71-72, Oct. 73-Jan. 76.
Leisure interest: open-air life.
Publs. *Aktuell ungdomspolitikk* 40, *Ungdommen og samfunnet* 46.
Home: Ullevålsvegen 58, Oslo 1, Norway.

Brauchitsch, Eberhard, von; German barrister and publisher; b. 28 Nov. 1926, Berlin; m. Dr. Helga Hempe; four c.; ed. legal studies, Berlin.
Admitted to the Bar 54; Man. Deutsche Flugdienst G.m.b.H., Frankfurt 57-65; Dir. and mem. of the Board, Friedrich Flick K.G., Düsseldorf, Man. Verwaltungsgesellschaft für industrielle Unternehmungen, Friedrich Flick G.m.b.H., Düsseldorf and Hessische Gesellschaft für industrielle Unternehmungen Friedrich Flick G.m.b.H., Wetzlar 65; Gen. Man. Axel Springer Publishing Co. until 72; Partner and Gen. Man. Friedrich Flick group 72-.
4021 Metzkausen bei Mettmann, Weiermannsbuschweg 21, Federal Republic of Germany.

Braudel, Fernand, D. ès L.; French historian; b. 24 Aug. 1902, Luméville (Meuse); m. Paule Pradel 1933; two d.; ed. Lycée Voltaire, Paris and the Sorbonne.
Professor, Algiers 23-32; Lycées Condorcet and Henri IV, Paris 32-35; Faculty of Arts, São Paulo 35-38; Ecole Pratique des Hautes Etudes 38-39, 45-; Prof. Coll. de France 49-72, Hon. Prof. 72-; Admin. Maison des Sciences de l'Homme 63-; Dr. h.c. (São Paulo, Madrid, Brussels, Geneva, Oxford, Cologne, Warsaw, Chicago, Cambridge, Florence, Padua, London, Hull).
Publs. *La Méditerranée et le Monde Méditerranéen à l'Epoque de Philippe II* 49 (2nd edn. 67), *Vol. II* 73, *Navires et marchandises à l'entrée du port de Livourne, 1547-1611* (with R. Romano) 51, *Le Monde actuel* 63, *Civilisation matérielle et capitalisme* Vol. I 68, *Ecrits sur l'histoire* 69.
59 rue Brillat-Savarin, Paris 13e, France.

Brauer, Erich; Austrian artist; b. 1929, Vienna; m.; ed. Wiener Kunstakademie.
Forced labour, Vienna 42-45; after studies in Vienna travelled in France, Spain, Africa, Greece and Israel 51-58, U.S.A. and Europe 58-70, Ethiopia 70, U.S.A., Japan 71-72; one-man exhbns. 56-, in Austria, Germany, Switzerland, France, Denmark, Liechtenstein, Italy, Israel and U.S.A.; group exhbns., incl. travelling exhbns. with Wiener Schule des Phantastischen Realismus 62-, in W. Europe, U.S.A., Israel, Iran, Turkey, Japan; two gold records for *Erik Brauer LP* (poetry, music and songs) 71.
c/o Eyn-Hod Israel, P.O. Box 989, 1011 Vienna, Austria.
Telephone: 344673.

Brauer, Jerald Carl, A.B., B.D., PH.D.; American church historian and educator; b. 16 Sept. 1921, Fond du Lac, Wisconsin; s. of Carl L. and Anna M. Brauer; m. Muriel I. Nelson 1945; two s. one d.; ed. Carthage Coll., Northwestern Lutheran Theological Seminary and Univ. of Chicago.
Instructor, Church History and History of Christian Thought, Union Theological Seminary, New York City 48-50; Asst. Prof. of Church History, Federated Theological Faculty, Univ. of Chicago 50-54, Assoc. Prof. 54-60, Dean, Federated Theological Faculty 55-60; Visiting Prof. Univ. of Frankfurt 61; Naomi Shenstone Donnelley Prof. History of Christianity 69-, Dean, Divinity School 60-70, mem. Center for Policy Studies; Visiting Lecturer Univ. of Tokyo and Kokugakin Univ. 66; mem. Board of Augustana Coll.; mem. Board of Theological Educ., Lutheran Church in America 61-69; Pres. 61-68; mem. Board of Govs., International House 70-73, Pres. 73-; Visiting Fellow, Center for the Study of Democratic Insts. 72, 74; Trustee Council on Religious and International Affairs; Del. of Lutheran Church in America to Lutheran World Fed. Assembly,

Helsinki 63; Observer to Vatican Council Sessions 64, 65; mem. American Soc. of Church History, Pres. 61; Hon. D.D. (Miami), Hon. L.L.D. (Carthage Coll.), Hon. S.T.D. (Ripon Coll.), Hon. L.H.D. (Gettysburg Coll.).
Leisure interests: painting, music, drama.
Publs. *Protestantism in America* 53, rev. edn. 66, *Luther and the Reformation* (with Jaroslav Pelikan) 53, *Basic Questions for the Christian Scholar* 54; Editor: *The Future of Religions* by Paul Tillich 66, *Essays in Divinity* (8 vols.) 67, *My Travel Diary* by Paul Tillich 70, *Westminster Dictionary of Church History* 71.
5620 South Blackstone Avenue, Chicago, Ill. 60637; Swift Hall 207, Univ. of Chicago, Chicago, Ill. 60637, U.S.A.
Telephone: 493-6886 (Home); 753-4061 (Office).

Brauer, Richard Dagobert, PH.D.; American mathematician; b. 10 Feb. 1901, Berlin, Germany; s. of Max Brauer and Caroline Jacob Brauer; m. Ilse Karger 1925; two c.; ed. Univ. of Berlin.
Privatdozent, Univ. of Königsberg 27-33; Visiting Prof., Univ. of Kentucky 33-34; Asst., Inst. for Advanced Study, Princeton 34-35; Asst. Prof., Assoc. Prof., Prof., Univ. of Toronto 35-48; Prof., Univ. of Michigan 48-52; Prof., Harvard Univ. 52-66, Perkins Prof. of Mathematics, Harvard Univ. 66-71, Emer. 71-; mem. Nat. Acad. of Sciences; Cole Prize, American Mathematical Soc. 49; Nat. Medal for Scientific Merit 71; Hon. Dr. of Math. (Univ. of Waterloo) 68, Hon. D.Sc. (Univ. of Chicago) 69.
Publs. About 100 mathematical papers in scientific journals 25-69.
c/o Department of Mathematics, Harvard University, Cambridge, Massachusetts 02138, U.S.A.

Brauksiepe, Änne; German politician; b. 23 Feb. 1912; m.; one s.
Spent several years in U.K. and Netherlands before 37; housewife and care of young cripples 37-45; mem. Bundestag 49-, later Deputy Chair. C.D.U. Parl. Party; Fed. Minister of Family and Youth Affairs 68-69; mem. Central Cttee. of German Catholics; Provincial Chair. European Women's Union.
474 Oelde/W., Hindenburgstrasse 13, Federal Republic of Germany.

Braun, Ferdinard; Luxembourg administrator; b. 14 March 1925, Esch-sur-Alzette.
Joined EEC 58, Chef de Cabinet to Head of Luxembourg del. to EEC Comm., then Chef de Div., Secr.; Dir. for Industry, Commerce and Crafts, Directorate-Gen. of Internal Market 61; mem. del. to negotiations of Kennedy Round; Chef de Cabinet to Luxembourg mem. of Comm. responsible for transport 67-68; Principal Adviser Directorate-Gen. of Industrial Affairs 68-69, Asst. Dir.-Gen. 69-73; Dir.-Gen. of Internal Market 73-.
Directorate General of Internal Market, Commission of the European Communities, 200 rue de la Loi, 1040 Brussels, Belgium.
Telephone: 35 00 40/35 80 40.

Braun, Baron Sigismund von; German diplomatist; b. 15 April 1911, Berlin; s. of the late Baron Magnus von Braun and Emmy von Braun (née von Quistorp); brother of Wernher von Braun (q.v.); m. Hildegard Margis 1940; one s. four d.; ed. Univs. of Hamburg, Berlin, and Cincinnati, Ohio.
Counsellor, German Embassy, London 53-58; Chief of Protocol, Foreign Office, Bonn 58-62; Observer (with rank of Amb.) of Fed. Repub. of Germany to the UN 62-68; Amb. to France 68-70, 72-; State Sec. Ministry of Foreign Affairs 70-72; Dr. h.c. and numerous decorations.
Leisure interests: shooting, water skiing.
13/15 avenue Franklin D. Roosevelt, 75008, Paris, France.
Telephone: 359-33-51.

Braun, Wernher von, B.S., PH.D.; American scientist (b. German, naturalized American 55); b. 23 March 1912, Wirsitz, Germany; s. of the late Baron Magnus von Braun and Emmy von Braun (née von Quistorp); brother of Baron Sigismund von Braun (q.v.); m. Maria von Quistorp, 1947; one s. two d.; ed. Federal Inst. Technology, Zürich, Inst. Technology, Berlin, and Univ. of Berlin.
Research on Rocket Motors since 30; research with German Ordnance Dept. on liquid fuel rocket development 32; tested successful launchings of two rudimentary liquid fuel rockets of the A-2 type which reached altitudes of 1.6 miles 34; Technical Dir. of Peenemuende Rocket and Devt. Centre 37; Project Dir. Research and Devt. Service, U.S. Army Ordnance Corps, Fort Bliss, Texas and Adviser for V-2 test firings at White Sands Proving Grounds, New Mexico 45; Tech. Dir. and later Chief Guided Missile Devt. Group, Redstone Arsenal, Ala. 50; Dir. Devt. Operations Div., Army Ballistic Missile Agency, Redstone Arsenal, Ala. 56 (responsible for Redstone, Jupiter and Pershing missiles and early Explorer satellites); Dir. George C. Marshall Space Flight Center, Nat. Aeronautics and Space Admin., Huntsville, Ala. 60- (responsible for devt. of Saturn launch vehicles for American Lunar Landing Program); Deputy Assoc. Admin. for Plans, NASA 70-72; Vice-Pres. Engineering and Devt., Fairchild Industries July 72-; Hon. Fellow, American Inst. of Aeronautics, American Astronautical Soc., Int. Acad. of Astronautics, Norwegian Interplanetary Soc., British Interplanetary Soc.; mem. Nat. Acad. of Engineering; Hon. mem. numerous foreign socs.; Space Flight Award, American Astronautical Soc. 57, Dr. Robert H. Goddard Memorial Trophy 58, Pres. Award for Distinguished Fed. Civilian Service 59, Smithsonian Inst. Langley Medal 67, U.S. Space Hall of Fame 69, and others; numerous hon. degrees.
Leisure interests: boating, scuba-diving, gliding, flying.
Publs. include *The Mars Project* 53, *Across the Space Frontier* 52, *Space Medicine* 52, co-author *Physics and Medicine of the Upper Atmosphere* 52, *Conquest of the Moon* 53, *Exploration of Mars* 56, *Project Satellite* 58, *First Men to the Moon* 60, *A Journey Through Space and the Atom* 62, (with Frederick I. Ordway) *History of Rocketry and Space Travel* 67 (third edn. 75), *Space Frontier* 67 (revised edn. 71), *The Rocket's Red Flare* (with F. I. Ordway) 76.
Fairchild Industries, Germantown, Md. 20767, U.S.A.
Telephone: 301-428-6137.

Braunshteyn, Alexander Yevseevich, M.D., D.BIOL.SC.; Soviet biochemist; 26 May 1902, Kharkov; ed. Kharkov Medical Inst.
Biochemical Inst., U.S.S.R. People's Commissariat of Health 28-36; All-Union Inst. of Experimental Medicine 36-45; Head of Laboratory, Inst. of Biological and Medical Chem., U.S.S.R. Acad. of Medical Sciences 45-60; Head of Laboratory, Inst. of Molecular Biology 60-; mem. U.S.S.R. Acad. of Medical Sciences; Corresp. mem. U.S.S.R. Acad. of Sciences 60-64, mem. 64-; State Prize; Hero of Socialist Labour; Order of Lenin; Hammer and Sickle Gold Medal; Foreign Assoc. mem. Nat. Acad. of Sciences, U.S.A.; Hon. mem. other acads. and learned socs. in Germany, France, U.S.A.; Dr. h.c.
Leisure interests: classic and modern literature, colour photography.
Publs. 190 experimental and theoretical papers on intermediary metabolism and enzymic catalysis.
Institute of Molecular Biology, 32 Ulitsa Vavilova, Moscow, U.S.S.R.

Brauw, Jonkheer M. L. de; Netherlands politician; b. 14 Sept. 1925, the Hague; m. Anna-Maria Röelly 1955; two s. three d.; ed. Leiden Univ.
Former Sec. to Man. Dirs., Unilever N.V., Rotterdam; Dir. Nationale Nederlanden Insurance Co. 60-; Minister

without Portfolio for Science Policy 71-72; mem. Second Chamber of Parl. 72-75; Pres. Board of Raadgevend Bureau Berenschot B.V. (Utrecht) 75; New Democratic Socialist.
Leisure interests: flying, horse riding, skiing.
Raadgevend Bureau Berenschot B.V., Churchill-laan 11, P.O. Box 8039, Utrecht, Netherlands.
Telephone: 030-916-916.

Bravo Ahuja, Victor; Mexican educationist and politician; b. 20 Feb. 1918, Tuxtepec, Oaxaca; *m.*; Instituto Politécnico Nacional, Escuela Militar de Aviación, Univ. Nacional Autónoma de Mexico, and Calif. Inst. of Tech. and Univ. of Mich., U.S.A.
Director, School of Engineering, Instituto Tecnológico y de Estudios Superiores de Monterey 46-49, Sec.-Gen. 49-51, Rector 51-59; Under-Sec. for Technical and Higher Educ., Sec. of Educ. 58-68; Gov. State of Oaxaca 68-70; Sec. for Educ. 70-; del. to numerous int. confs. and mem. many educational cttees., orgs. etc.; many honours and awards.
Publs. books on educational and political topics.
Secretaría de Educación Pública, Argentina 18, Mexico, D.F., Mexico.

Bray, Gen. Sir Robert Napier Hubert Campbell, G.B.E., K.C.B., D.S.O.; British army officer; b. 14 June 1908, Dacca, Pakistan; *s.* of Brig.-Gen. R. N. Bray, C.M.G., D.S.O.; *m.* Nora Gee 1936; three *s.*; ed. Gresham's School, Holt, and Royal Military Coll., Sandhurst.
Second Lieutenant, Duke of Wellington's Regt. 28; Norway, Middle East and North Western Europe 39-45; Brigadier, General Staff, British Army of the Rhine 50-52, Korea 54; Dir. of Land Air Warfare, and Dir. of NATO Standardisation, War Office 54-57; Major-Gen. 54; General Officer Commanding, 56th Infantry Div. (T.A.) 57-59; Commander, Land Forces, Arabian Peninsula 59-61; G.O.C. Middle East 60-66; G.O.C. in C. Southern Command 61-63; C.-in-C. Allied Forces, N. Europe 63-67; Deputy Supreme Allied Commdr. Europe, North Atlantic Treaty Org. (NATO) 67-70.
Leisure interests: sailing, shooting, fishing.
c/o Army and Navy Club, Pall Mall, London, S.W.1, England.

Brayer, Yves; French painter; b. 18 Nov. 1907, Versailles; *s.* of Gen. Victor Brayer; *m.* Hermione Falex 1945; one *s.*; ed. Ecole Nationale des Beaux-Arts, Paris.
Has exhibited in Paris, New York, London, Nice 59, 67, Geneva 61, Bordeaux 63, Madrid 63, Cologne, Berlin, Bourges; sets and costumes for ballet at the Paris Opéra, Royal Opera in Amsterdam and Festival of Cimiez; has painted murals for public buildings and illustrated numerous books; work represented in Musée National de l'Art Moderne, Paris and in numerous museums and private collections throughout the world; Pres. Acad. des Beaux-Arts 69-70; Officier Légion d'Honneur, Commdr. des Arts et des Lettres, Commdr. du Mérite de la République Italienne.
22 rue Monsieur le Prince, Paris 6e, France.
Telephone: 033-00-01.

Braynen, Alvin Rudolph, J.P.; Bahamian diplomatist; b. 6 Dec. 1904, Bahamas; *s.* of William Rudolph and Lulu Isabel Braynen; *m.* 2nd Ena Estelle 1969; one *s.* one *d.* (by previous marriage); ed. Public School, Current, Eleuthera, Bahamas.
Headmaster Govt. Public Schools 23-25; Rep. Sinclair Co. 30-65, Consultant 65-69; Consultant Shell Oil Co., Bahamas 69-; mem. House of Assembly 35-72, Deputy Speaker 49-53, 63-66, Speaker 67-72; mem. Exec. Council 53-58; del. to parl. confs., London 63, 68; Chair. Standing Cttee. of Conf. of Caribbean Parls. 70-72; Chair. Advisory Council for Public Records 71-73; High Commr. in U.K. July 73-.
Leisure interests: coin and stamp collecting.

High Commission for the Bahamas, 39 Pall Mall, London, SW1Y 5JG, England.
Telephone: 01-930-6967.

Bream, Julian, O.B.E.; British guitarist and lutanist; b. 15 July 1933; ed. Royal Coll. of Music.
Began professional career Cheltenham 47, London début 50; tours in Europe, America, Japan and Australia; appeared at festivals at Aldeburgh, Bath, Edinburgh, Three Choirs, King's Lynn, Holland, Ansbach, Berlin, and Stratford (Canada); research into Elizabethan Lute music which led to revival of interest in that instrument; has encouraged contemporary English compositions for the guitar.
c/o Harold Holt Ltd., 122 Wigmore Street, London, W.1, England.

Breder, Charles M.; American ichthyologist; b. 25 June 1897, Jersey City, N.J.; ed. High School, Newark.
Scientific Asst. and Fishery Expert with U.S. Bureau of Fisheries 18-21; aquarist N.Y. Aquarium 21-25, Research Assoc., Asst. Dir., Acting Dir., Dir. 25-43; Chair. and Curator Dept. of Fishes and Aquatic Biology, American Museum of Natural History, Ichthyology Dept. 44-65, Curator Emeritus 65-; Visiting Prof. New York Univ. 41-50; Dir. Lerner Marine Laboratory, Bimini, Bahamas 47-57; Advisory Board Cape Haze Marine Laboratory, Florida (now the Mote Marine Laboratory) 57-66, mem. Board of Dirs. 67-73, Senior Researcher 70-75; Research Assoc., Bingham Oceanographic Laboratory, Yale Univ. 33-60; Fellow, New York Zoological Soc.; Hon. D.Sc. (Newark Univ.).
Publs. *Field Book of the Marine Fishes of the Atlantic Coast from Labrador to Texas* 29, *Modes of Reproduction in Fishes* (with D. E. Rosen) 66, and technical papers.
Englewood, Florida, RFD 1, Box 452, U.S.A.
Telephone: 813-474-1810.

Breit, Gregory, A.M., PH.D.; American (naturalized 1918) physicist; b. 14 July 1899, Russia; *s.* of Alfred and Alexandra Smirnova Breit; *m.* Marjorie E. MacDill 1927; ed. Johns Hopkins Univ.
National Research Council Fellow, Univ. of Leyden 21-22, Harvard Univ. 22-23; Asst. Prof. of Physics, Minnesota Univ. 23-24; Mathematical Physicist, Dept. of Terrestrial Magnetism, Carnegie Inst. of Washington 24-29; Prof. of Physics, New York Univ. 29-34, Wisconsin Univ. 34-47, Yale Univ. 47-58, Donner Prof. of Physics 58-68; Distinguished Prof. of Physics, State Univ. of New York at Buffalo 68-74, Distinguished Service Prof. Emer. 74-; Research Assoc., Carnegie Inst. 29-44; Visiting mem. Inst. for Advanced Study, Princeton, New Jersey 35-36; on leave of absence as mem. of Uranium Cttee. (Section S), Office of Scientific Research and Development and other war work 40-45; mem. Nat. Acad. of Sciences; Fellow American Acad. of Arts and Sciences, American Physical Soc., Inst. of Electronic and Electrical Engineers, Geophysical Union; Assoc. Editor *Physical Review* 27-29, 39-41, 54-56, 61-63, Assoc. Editor, *Proceedings of National Academy of Sciences* 51-60, *Il Nuovo Cimento* 64-67; Councillor American Physical Soc. 35-38; mem. Div. of Physical Sciences, Nat. Research Council 32-33, 38-41; Franklin Medal 64; Nat. Medal of Science 67; Tom Bonner Prize, American Physical Soc. 69; Hon. D.Sc. (Univ. of Wisconsin).
Publs. *A Test of the Existence of the Conducting Layer* (with M. A. Tuve) 26, *The Effect of Retardation on the Interaction of Two Electrons* 29, *Quantum Theory of Dispersion*, Parts I-V 32, Parts VI and VII 33, *Capture of Slow Neutrons* (with E. Wigner) 36, *Theory of Scattering of Protons by Protons* 36, *Handbuch der Physik*, Vol. 42, part I, *Nuclear Reactions: II, Theory* (with others); **and other publications on kindred subjects.**
73 Allenhurst Road, Buffalo, N.Y. 14214, U.S.A.
Telephone: 716 836-7110.

Brekhov, Konstantin Ivanovich; Soviet engineer and politician; b. 1907; ed. Kharkov Machine Building Inst. Engineer, machine-building factories 31-42; mem. C.P.S.U. 31-; Dir. Irkutsk Heavy Machine-Building Works 44-54; Dep. Minister of Building and Road Machine Building, U.S.S.R. 54-57; econ. work, Moscow Region 57-59; Chair. Moscow Regional Econ. Cttee. 59-63; Chair. State Cttee. for Building of Machinery for Chemical and Oil Industries 64-65; Minister for Chemical and Oil Engineering 65-; Cand. mem. Central Cttee. of C.P.S.U. 61-71, mem. 71-; Deputy to Supreme Soviet of U.S.S.R. 62-.
Ministry for Chemical and Oil Engineering, 25 Bezbozhny Pereulok, Moscow, U.S.S.R.

Brekhovskikh, Leonid Maksimovich, D.SC.; Soviet physicist; b. 6 May 1917, Strunkino Village, Arkhangelsk Region; ed. Perm. State Univ.
Junior research worker, Senior research worker, Head of Dept., Inst. of Physics, U.S.S.R. Acad. of Sciences 39-54; Dir. Inst. of Acoustics 54-64, Head of Laboratory 64-; Sec.-Academician, Dept. of Oceanography, Physics of Earth Atmosphere and Geography, U.S.S.R. Acad. of Sciences 69-; mem. C.P.S.U. 59-; Prof. Moscow Univ. 53; Corresp. mem. U.S.S.R. Acad. of Sciences 53-68, Academician 68-; State Prize 50.
Publs. Numerous scientific works in fields of ocean acoustics, radiophysics and theoretical physics.
U.S.S.R. Academy of Sciences, 14 Leninski Prospekt, Moscow, U.S.S.R.

Bremer, Frédéric; Belgian physiologist; b. June 1892, Arlon; s. of Gaston Bremer and Amélie Leyder; m. Claire Baar 1921; one s. and one d.; ed. Univ. of Brussels.
Honorary Prof. and Dir. Laboratory of Physiopathology, Univ. of Brussels 32-; Pres. Nat. Centre for Neurophysiological and Muscular Research 54; mem. Belgian Acad. of Medicine and Sciences Div. Belgian Royal Acad.; Hon. mem. American Physiological Soc., Biology Soc., Paris, American Acad. of Arts and Sciences, Int. Brain Research Org.; mem. Physiological Soc. of Great Britain; Assoc. mem. Nat. Acad. Medicine of France, Accad. Nazionale dei Lincei (Rome); Corresp. mem. Inst. de France; Dr. h.c. (Univs. of Aix-Marseille, Montpellier, Strasbourg and Utrecht); Grand Officier de l'Ordre de Léopold; Croix de Guerre and Croix du Feu 14-18.
Leisure interests: gardening, travelling.
Publs. *L'activité électrique de l'écorce cérébrale* 38, *Some Problems in Neurophysiology* 53.
115 boulevard de Waterloo, Brussels, Belgium.
Telephone: 380844.

Brenchley, Thomas Frank, C.M.G., M.A.; British diplomatist; b. 9 April 1918, Stockton-on-Tees; s. of Robert B. and Alice (née Brough) Brenchley; m. Edith Helen Helfand 1946; three d.; ed. Merton Coll., Oxford.
Served in British Army 39-46; entered Civil Service 47, transferred to Foreign Office 49; served in Singapore, Cairo, Foreign Office and Middle East Centre for Arabic Studies 50-59; Khartoum, Jedda and Foreign Office 60-66; Asst. Under-Sec. for Middle East Affairs, Foreign and Commonwealth Office 67-68; Amb. to Norway 68-72, to Poland 72-74; Deputy Sec., Cabinet Office 75-.
Leisure interests: tennis, skiing, collecting books.
15 Cadogan Sq., London, S.W.1, England.
Telephone: 01-235 5976.

Brendel, Alfred; Austrian pianist; b. 5 Jan. 1931, Wiesenberg; s. of Ing. Albert and Ida (née Wieltschnig) Brendel; m. 1st Iris Heymann-Gonzala 1960 (divorced 1972), 2nd Irene Semler 1975; one d.
Studied piano under Sofija Deželić (Zagreb), Ludovika v. Kaan (Graz), Edwin Fischer (Lucerne), Paul Baumgartner (Basle), Edward Steuermann (Salzburg); studied composition under A. Michl (Graz) and har-

mony under Franjo Dugan (Zagreb); first piano recital 48; concert tours through Europe, Latin America, North America (63-), Australia (63, 66, 69); has appeared at many music festivals, including Salzburg 60-, Vienna, Edinburgh, Aldeburgh, Athens, Granada, Puerto Rico and has performed with most of the major orchestras of Europe and U.S.A. etc.; numerous recordings, including complete piano works of Beethoven, Schubert's piano works 1822-8; Premio Città de Bolzano, Concorso Busoni 49; Grand Prix du Disque 65, Edison Prize 74, Grand Prix des Disquaires de France 75.
Leisure interests: books, theatre, the visual arts, films, baroque and romanesque architecture, unintentional humour, kitsch.
Publs. Essays on music and musicians in *Phono, Fono Forum, Österreichische Musikzeitschrift, Music and Musicians, Hi-Fi Stereophonie, Musical Thoughts and Afterthoughts* 75, etc.
c/o Ingpen and Williams, 14 Kensington Court, London W.8, England.

Brennan, Peter J.; American politician; b. 1918, Manhattan.
Worked as painter, Macy's Dept. Store; served U.S. Navy 2nd World War; rose through Union ranks to Pres. Construction Trades Council 57; supported Pres. Nixon's election May 70; Sec. of Labour 73-75.
2100 Massachusetts Avenue, Washington, D.C. 20008, U.S.A.

Brennan, William Joseph, Jr., B.S., LL.B.; American judge; b. 25 April 1906; ed. Pa. and Harvard Univs.
Admitted to New Jersey Bar 31; practised in Newark, N.J. 31-49; Superior Court Judge 49-50, Appellate Division Judge 50-52; Justice, Supreme Court of New Jersey 52-56; Assoc. Justice, Supreme Court of the U.S. 56-; served as Colonel, General Staff Corps, U.S. Army in Second World War; Legion of Merit; Hon. D.C.L. (New York and Colgate Univs.), Hon. S.J.D. (Suffolk Univ.), Hon. LL.D. (Wesleyan, St. John's, Pennsylvania, Rutger's, George Washington, Harvard and Notre Dame Univs., Jewish Theological Seminary of America).
Supreme Court of the United States, Washington, D.C. 20543; and 3037 Dumbarton Avenue, N.W., Washington, D.C., U.S.A.

Brenner, Sydney, M.B., D.PHIL., F.R.S.; British scientist; b. 13 Jan. 1927; ed. Univ. of the Witwatersrand, Johannesburg, and Oxford Univ.
Lecturer in Physiology, Univ. of Witwatersrand 55-57; mem. Scientific Staff of Medical Research Council at M.R.C. Laboratory of Molecular Biology, Cambridge 57-; Fellow of King's Coll., Cambridge 59-; Foreign Hon. mem. American Acad. of Arts and Sciences; Hon. D.Sc. (Dublin); Warren Triennial Prize 68; William Bate Hardy Prize, Cambridge Philosophical Soc. 69; Gregor Mendel Medal of German Acad. of Science Leopoldina 70; Lasker Award 71; Hon. D.Sc. (Johannesburg) 72; Royal Medal of Royal Soc. 74; Prix Charles Leopold Mayer 75.
Medical Research Council Laboratory of Molecular Biology, Cambridge, CB2 2QH; Home: 26 Coton Road, Grantchester, Cambridge, England.

Breslow, Ronald, PH.D.; American professor of chemistry; b. 14 March 1931, Rahway, N.J.; s. of Alexander Breslow and Gladys Fellows; m. Esther Greenberg 1956; two d.; ed. Harvard Univ.
Instructor, Columbia Univ. 56-59, Assoc. Prof. 59-62, Prof. 62-67, Mitchill Prof. of Chem. 67-; Sloan Fellowship 61-63; mem. Nat. Acad. of Sciences, American Acad. of Arts and Sciences, Exec. Cttee. of Organic Div. of American Chemical Soc.; mem. Editorial Board *Organic Syntheses* 65-, Board of Editors Journal of Organic Chem. 68; Trustee, American-Swiss Foundation for Scientific Exchange Inc. 69-71; Chair. Div. of

Organic Chem., American Chemical Soc. 70-71; Chair. Div. of Chem., N.A.S. 74; American Chemical Soc. Award in Pure Chem. 66; Fresinius Award 66; Mark van Doren Award 69; Baekeland Medal 69; Centenary Lecturer, London Chemical Soc. 72; Harrison Howe Award 74.
Publs. *Organic Reaction Mechanisms* 65; over 100 scientific papers.
566 Chandler Laboratories, Department of Chemistry, Columbia University, New York, N.Y. 10027, U.S.A.
Telephone: 212-280-2170.

Bresson, Robert; French film producer; b. 25 Sept. 1901.
Started as painter; made first film 34; awarded many prizes for *Journal d'un Curé de Campagne*.
Films produced include: *Anges du Péché* 43, *Les Dames du Bois de Boulogne* 45, *Journal d'un Curé de Campagne* 51, *Un Condamné à Mort s'est échappé* 56, *Pickpocket* 59, *Le Procès de Jeanne d'Arc* 62, *Au Hasard, Balthasar* 66, *Mouchette* 66, *Une Femme Douce* 69, *Quatre nuits d'un rêveur* 71, *Lancelot du Lac* 74.
49 Quai Bourbon, Paris 4e, France.

Bressou, Clément Jean Pierre François Emmanuel, DR. VET.; French veterinary professor; b. 22 Feb. 1887, Montauban (Tarn et Garonne); s. of François Bressou and Marguerite Bourdelles; m. Madeleine Sizes 1913; one s. one d.; ed. Collège de Castelsarrasin and Ecole Nat. Vétérinaire, Toulouse.
Head of Anatomy Dept., Toulouse 12-17, Prof. of Anatomy 17-26; Prof. of Anatomy, Alfort (Paris) 26-57, Dir. of Veterinary School, Alfort 34-57; Insp. Veterinary School 41; Vice-Pres. Acad. de Sciences 56-, Acad. de Medicine 50-, Acad. D'Agric. 53-, Acad. Vet. 42-, Acad. de Pharm. 61-, Acad. Dentaire 66-, World Asscn. of Veterinary Anatomy 60; Commdr. Légion d'Honneur and several other French and foreign decorations; Dr. h.c. Univs. of Thessaloniki, Bern, Munich, Vienna, Madrid.
Leisure interests: conservation of nature, study of bulls, philately.
Publs. *Dissection des Animaux domicils* 35, *Traité d'Anatomie des Animaux domestiques: Equidés* 37, *Carnivores* 51, *Porcins* 61, *Ruminants* 69, *Ostéologie comparée, Animaux domestiques* 52, *Enseignement Vétérinaire en Europe* 42, *Problèmes de Protection de la Nature* 46, *Histoire de la Médecine Vétérinaire* 71.
Boulevard de Port-Royal 46, Paris 5e, France.
Telephone: 707-08-42.

Bretscher, Willy; Swiss journalist; b. 26 Oct. 1897, Winterthur; m. Hedwig Wohlwend 1924; ed. District School, Olten, Secondary School, Winterthur, Commercial School of Swiss Merchants' Asscn. and Univ. of Zürich.
Journalist *Neues Winterthurer Tagblatt* 14; Editor *Neue Zürcher Zeitung* 17, Berlin Corresp. 25-29 and Chief Editor 33-67; Vice-Pres. Exec. Cttee. Liberal Int. 48-70; mem. Nat. Council 51-67, Pres. of its Foreign Affairs Cttee. 54-55, 62-63; Pres. Swiss Winston Churchill Foundation 66-72; Pres. Swiss Asscn. on Foreign Policy 68-71; Hon. doctorate, Univ. of Zürich 68.
Leisure interest: fly fishing.
Publs. *Geschichte der Sozialistischen Bewegung in der Schweiz* 24, *Siebzig Leitartikel* 44, *Die politische Lage der Schweiz am Kriegsende* 45, *Schweizerische Aussenpolitik in der Nachkriegszeit* 51, *Russia by Twilight* 56, *The Defence of the West* 57, *Der Kampf um Berlin* 61, etc.
Freiestrasse 29, 8032 Zürich, Switzerland.
Telephone: 47-69-50.

Breuer, Marcel Lajos, M.A., F.A.I.A.; American architect; b. 22 May 1902, Pecs, Hungary; s. of Jacques and Franciska Kan Breuer; m. Constance Crocker

Leighton 1940; one s. one d.; ed. Hungarian Public School, and Bauhaus, Weimar.
Teacher Bauhaus, Dessau 24-28; architect Berlin 28-31; travels and architectural comms. Spain, Morocco, Switzerland, Germany, Hungary, Greece, England, Haiti, Pakistan, Japan, Mexico, Venezuela, Brazil, Argentina, Peru 31-35; architect London 35-37, Cambridge, Mass. 37-46; Assoc. Prof. Graduate School of Design, Harvard Univ. 37-46; with Marcel Breuer and Associates, Architects, New York 46-; mem. Nat. Inst. Arts and Letters; Fellow, American Acad. Arts and Sciences; Hon. mem. of Architectural Socs. in Columbia, Peru, Argentina; Hon. Dr. Fine Arts, Pratt Inst., Hon. Dr. Arts, Harvard Univ., Univ. Notre Dame, Hon. Dr. Govt. of Hungary; First Int. Prize, La Rinascente's "Compasso d'oro" 57; N.Y. State Council on Arts Award for Whitney Museum 67; America Hungarian Studies Foundation, George Washington Award 67; Fifth Ave. Asscn. Award for best institutional bldg. 66-67 for Whitney Museum; City Club of N.Y. Bard Award for Whitney Museum 68; Metropolitan Washington Board of Trade Award 69; Office of the Year Award 68; Concrete Industry Board Award 69 and 70; AIA Award for Excellence 70; Honor Award 70, 72, 73; AIA Medal of Honor 65; T. Jefferson Foundation Medal 68; AIA Gold Medal 68; several other awards and honours.
Leisure interest: photography.
Principal works include: UNESCO World Headquarters Bldgs., Paris (with others) 53-58; U.S. Embassy Bldg., The Hague 54-58; de Bijenkorf Dept. Store, Rotterdam 57-58; Van Leer World Headquarters Bldg., Amstelveen 57-58; IBM-France Research Centre, La Gaude 60-61; Whitney Museum of American Art, New York 63-66; Satellite Town, Bayonne (France) 63-69; Mary Coll., Bismarck, N.D. (four bldgs.) 68; Armstrong Rubber Co. Headquarters, New Haven, Conn. 65-70; Flaine (resort town in French Alps) 69-; Univ. of Massachusetts Campus Centre 70; IBM Bldgs., Boca Raton, Fa. 70-; The Cleveland Museum of Art 70; Cleveland Trust Co. Headquarters 71; Third Power Plant and Forebay Dam, Grand Coulee Dam (under construction).
Office: 635 Madison Avenue, New York, N.Y. 10022, U.S.A.; and 48 rue Chapon, Paris 3e, France; Home: 139 East 63 Street, New York, N.Y. 10022, U.S.A.
Telephone: 212-758-1766 (Office); 212-755-8882 (Home).

Brewer, Albert Preston, A.B., LL.B.; American lawyer and politician; b. 26 Oct. 1928; s. of Mr. and Mrs. Daniel Austin Brewer; m. Martha Farmer; two d.; ed. Decatur public schools and Univ. of Alabama.
Worked in Tuscaloosa Drug Store to earn law school tuition; began legal practice, Decatur 52; mem. Alabama House of Reps. 54-63, Speaker 63; Lieut.-Gov. of Alabama 66-68, Gov. 68-70; Vice-Chair. Southern Govs. Conf.; mem. Exec. Cttee., Nat. Govs. Conf.; Vice-Pres. and mem. Board of Dirs., Albama Tuberculosis Asscn.; mem. American, Alabama, and Morgan County Bar Asscns.; Dr. h.c. Jacksonville State Univ. and Samford Univ.; Democrat.
c/o State Capitol, Montgomery, Ala., U.S.A.

Brewer, Leo, PH.D.; American professor of chemistry; b. 13 June 1919, St. Louis, Mo.; s. of Abraham and Hannah (Resnik) Brewer; m. Rose Strugo 1945; one s. two d.; ed. Calif. Inst. of Technology and Univ. of California (Berkeley).
Research Assoc. Manhattan District Project, Univ. of Calif. (Berkeley); Research Assoc. Lawrence Berkeley Lab. (Univ. of Calif.) 43-61, Head Inorganic Materials Div. 61-; Assoc. Dir. Lawrence Berkeley Lab. 67-; Asst. Prof. Coll. of Chem., Univ. of Calif. 46-50, Assoc. Prof. 50-55, Prof. 55-; mem. Nat. Acad. of Sciences; Great Western Dow Fellow 42, Guggenheim Fellow 50, Leo H. Baekland Award 53, E. O. Lawrence Award 61; Palladium Medal and Award of Electrochemical Soc.

71; several hon. lectureships 63-67, 70-72, 74; Distinguished Alumni Award, Calif. Inst. of Technology 74.
Leisure interest: gardening.
Publs. Numerous articles in professional journals.
Department of Chemistry, University of California, Berkeley, Calif. 94720, U.S.A.
Telephone: 415-642-5176.

Brewster, Kingman, Jr.; American educator; b. 17 June 1919, Longmeadow, Mass.; s. of late Kingman Brewster and Florence Brewster; m. Mary Louise Phillips 1942; three s. two d.; ed. Yale Univ. and Harvard Univ.
Chairman *Yale Daily News* 40-41; Special Asst. Co-ordinator, Inter-American Affairs 41; Research Assoc.; Dept. of Economics, Mass. Inst. of Technology 49-50, Asst. Prof. of Law, Harvard Univ. 50-53, Prof. 53-60; Provost, Yale Univ. 60-63, Pres. 63-; U.S. Naval Reserve 42-46; Hon. LL.D. from numerous Univs.
Publs. *Antitrust and American Business Abroad* (with M. Katz) 59, *Law of International Transactions and Relations* 60.
105 Wall Street, New Haven, Conn., U.S.A.

Breycha-Vauthier, Arthur, D.IUR., DR.RER.POL.; Austrian librarian and diplomatist; b. 1 July 1903, Vienna; s. of Arthur and Maria Czyhlarz; m. Graziella Segantini 1943; ed. Theresianum, Vienna, and Univs. of Vienna, Louvain, London and Innsbruck.
Law Librarian, League of Nations Library 28, Asst. Librarian 34-37, Acting Librarian 37-45; Prof. Geneva Library School 39-64; Asst. Sec. Int. Fed. of Library Asscns. 29-, Treas. 58-; Chief Librarian, UN Library, Geneva 46-64, Librarian Emeritus 64-; Ambassador to Lebanon, concurrently to Syria, Jordan, Saudi Arabia, Iraq and Kuwait 64-68; Dir. Diplomatic Academy.
Leisure interests: gardening, Cistercians, collecting manuscripts on diplomatic history.
Publs. *Sources of Information—a Handbook of the Publications of the League of Nations* 39, *La Stirpe trentina di Giovanni Segantini* 59, *Le fonctionnaire international* 59, *Internationale Bibliotheksarbeit* 60, *Die Zeitschriften der Österreichischen Emigration* 60, *Tantur* 61, *Metternich-Maximen* 62, *Documentación internacional* 62, *Sie trugen Österreich mit sich in die Welt* 62; Editor *Actes du Conseil de la F.I.A.B.*, Vols. I-XXVII, *Vital Problems of International Libraries* 65, *Qusair' Amra* 67, *Deir Balamand* 69, *Österreich in der Levante* 72, *Tantur* 73.
Diplomatic Academy, Favoritenstrasse 15, Vienna IV, Austria.
Telephone: 657272.

Brezhnev, Leonid Ilyich; Soviet politician; b. 19 Dec. 1906; Dneprodzerzhinsk, Ukraine; ed. secondary school for Land Organization and Reclamation, Kursk, and Dneprodzerzhinsk Metallurgical Inst.
Chief of District Land Dept., Deputy Chair. of District Exec. Cttee., later Deputy Chief, Urals Regional Land Dept. 27-30; Engineer, Dneprodzerzhinsk Metallurgical Plant 31-35; Soviet Army 35-36; Deputy Chair. Exec. Cttee. Dneprodzerzhinsk City Council, Chief of Dept., Dnepropetrovsk Regional Party Cttee. 37-39, Sec. 39-41; Political Officer, Soviet Army 41-46; First Sec. Zaporozhye Regional Party Cttee., Ukraine C.P. 46-47, Dnepropetrovsk Regional Party Cttee. 47-50; First Sec. Central Cttee., C.P. of Moldavia 50-52; mem. Central Cttee. of C.P.S.U. 52-, Alt. mem. Presidium 52-53, Sec. Central Cttee. of C.P.S.U. 52-53; Deputy Chief Central Political Dept., Soviet Army and Navy 53-54; Second Sec. Central Cttee. of Kazakh C.P. 54, First Sec. 55-56; Alt. mem. Presidium Central Cttee. of C.P.S.U. 56-57, mem. 57-66, mem. Politburo 66-; Sec. Central Cttee. of C.P.S.U. 56-60; Chair. of Presidium of Supreme Soviet of U.S.S.R. 60-64, mem. Sept. 65-; Sec. Central Cttee. of C.P.S.U. 63, First Sec. 64-66, Gen. Sec. 66-; Hero of Socialist Labour 61, Hero of the

Soviet Union, Gold Star Medal, Hammer and Sickle Gold Medal, three Orders of Lenin, two Orders of Red Banner, Lenin Peace Prize 73, Hero of People's Repub. of Bulgaria 73, and other decorations.
Central Committee of the Communist Party of the Soviet Union, 4 Staraya ploshchad, Moscow, U.S.S.R.
Telephone: 206-25-11.

Bridgeman, Hon. Sir Maurice Richard, K.B.E., K.ST.J.; British businessman; b. 26 Jan. 1904; s. of Viscount Bridgeman; ed. Eton and Trinity Coll., Cambridge.
Joined Anglo-Persian Oil Co. 26; Adviser Ministry of Econ. Warfare 39; Joint Sec. Oil Control Board 40; Adviser Govt. of India 42; Principal Asst. Sec. (Petroleum Div.) Ministry of Fuel and Power 44-46; mem. Advisory Council on Middle East Trade 58-61; Chair. and Man. Dir. British Petroleum Co. 60-69; mem. Industrial Reorg. Corpn. 69-71; Knight Grand Cross of Order of Italian Repub., Grand Officer Order of Orange-Nassau.
10 Kylestrome House, Ebury Street, London, S.W.1; The Glebe House, Selham, Petworth, Sussex, England.
Telephone: Lodsworth 205.

Bridges, Harold; British oil executive; b. 14 March 1916, Derbys.; s. of George H. and Alice Allen Bridges; m. Shirley M. Cresswell 1943; one s. two d.; ed. Durham Univ.
Joined Royal Dutch Petroleum 37; Geophysicist in New Guinea, India, Australia, U.S.A., Indonesia, Ecuador, Colombia; Chief Geophysicist, Pakistan, Netherlands, Indonesia, U.S.A.; Gen. Man. Shell B.P. Petroleum Co. of Nigeria 56; Deputy Gen. Rep. of Shell in Indonesia 57; Deputy Group Personnel Co-ordinator, The Hague 59; Regional Co-ordinator (Oil), Caribbean, Central and South America 61; Dir. and Planning Co-ordinator, Shell Int. Petroleum Co., London 64; Dir. Shell Petroleum N.V., The Hague, and Shell Petroleum Co., London 67; Pres. and Dir. Shell Canada Ltd. 68-70; Exec. Vice-Pres. and Chief Operating Officer, Shell Oil Co., New York 70-71; Pres. and Chief Exec. Officer, Houston 71-May 76; Dir. American Petroleum Inst. 70-.
Leisure interest: golf.
Shell Oil Co., One Shell Plaza, P.O. Box 2463, Houston, Texas 77001; Home: 324 Buckingham Drive, Houston, Tex. 77024, U.S.A.
Telephone: 713-220-4016 (Office).

Bridges, Sir Phillip Rodney, Kt., C.M.G., Q.C.; British lawyer; b. 9 July 1922; ed. Bedford School, England.
Army service 41-47, Capt. Royal Artillery with Royal West African Frontier Force, W. Africa, India, Burma; Solicitor of Supreme Court, England 51; Barrister and Solicitor, The Gambia 54; Solicitor-Gen. 61; Attorney-Gen. 64; Queen's Counsel, The Gambia 64; Chief Justice of The Gambia 68-.
Chief Justice's Chambers, Supreme Court, Banjul, The Gambia; and Weavers, Coney Weston, Bury St. Edmunds, Suffolk, England.

Briggs, Sir (Alfred) George Ernest, Kt.; British businessman; b. 12 Feb. 1900; ed. Oundle School.
Deputy Controller Ministry of Supply 42-45, 51-52; Chair. John Scott & Partners, Unit Trusts Information and Broking Service, Bedward Windale Group; Dir. Hepworth Ceramic Holdings Ltd., Court Line Ltd., Gulf Devt. Co., Ltd.; mem. London Electricity Board.
Courtyard House, Lavershot Hall, London Road, Windlesham, Surrey, England.
Telephone: Ascot 20144.

Briggs, Asa, M.A., B.SC.; British historian; b. 7 May 1921, Keighley, Yorks.; s. of William Walker Briggs and Jane Briggs; m. Susan Anne Banwell 1955; two s. two d.; ed. Keighley Grammar School and Sidney Sussex Coll., Cambridge.
Fellow, Worcester Coll., Oxford 45-55, Reader in Recent

Social and Econ. History, Univ. of Oxford 50-55; Prof. of Modern History, Leeds Univ. 55-61; Prof. of History, Univ. of Sussex 61-, Dean of Social Studies 61-65, Pro-Vice-Chancellor 61-67, Vice-Chancellor 67-Sept. 76; apptd. Provost Worcester Coll., Oxford 75; Deputy Pres. Workers Educational Asscn. 54-58, Pres. 58-67; mem. Univ. Grants Cttee. 59-67; Trustee, Int. Broadcast Inst. 68-; Gov. British Film Inst. 70-; Chair. European Inst. of Education 74-; mem. Council of UN Univ. 74-; Hon. mem. American Acad. of Arts and Sciences 70-; Hon. LL.D., Hon. D.Litt., Hon. D.Sc.
Leisure interest: travel.
Publs. *Patterns of Peacemaking* (with D. Thomson and E. Meyer) 45, *History of Birmingham, 1865-1938* 52, *Victorian People* 54, *Friends of the People* 56, *The Age of Improvement* 59, Ed. *Chartist Studies* 59, *History of Broadcasting*, Vol. I 61, Vol. II 65, Vol. III 70, *Victorian Cities* 63, *The Nineteenth Century* (editor) 70, *Cap and Bell* (with Susan Briggs) 72, *Essays in the History of Publishing* (editor) 74.
Home: The Caprons, Keere Street, Lewes, Sussex, England.
Telephone: Lewes 4704 (Home).

Briggs, Robert William, PH.D.; American biologist; b. 10 Dec. 1911, Watertown, Mass.; s. of Robin Briggs and Bridget McGonigle; m. Janet Bloch 1940; two s. one d.; ed. Boston and Harvard Univs.
Research Fellow, McGill Univ., Montreal 38-42; Biologist, Lankenau Hospital Research Inst., Philadelphia 42-56; Prof., Indiana Univ. 56-62, Research Prof. 62-; mem. American Acad. of Arts and Sciences, Nat. Acad. of Sciences.
Leisure interest: contrabassoon.
Publs. *Transplantation of living nuclei in the frog* (with T. J. King) in *Proceedings* of Nat. Acad. of Sciences 52, *On the nature of the changes in nuclei during cell differentiation* (with T. J. King) in *Cold Spring Harbor Symposium* and *Journal of Experimental Biology* 56, 57, *Nucleocytoplasmic interactions in eggs and embryos* (with T. J. King) 59, *Nuclear transplantation studies in the axolotl* (with Signoret and Humphrey) 62, 64, *Accumulation in the oocyte nucleus of a gene product essential for embryonic development beyond gastrulation* (with G. Cassens and J. T. Justus) in *Proceedings* of Nat. Acad. of Sciences and *Journal of Experimental Zoology* 66, 68, 72, *Developmental Genetics of the Axolotl* (editor F. Ruddle) 73.
Department of Zoology, Indiana University, Bloomington, Ind. 47401, U.S.A.
Telephone: 812-337-3788.

Briggs, Wenike Opurum, LL.B.; Nigerian politician; b. 10 March 1918, Abonnema, Rivers State; m.; three c.; ed. Nyemoni School, Abonnema, King's Coll., Lagos, Regent St. Polytechnic, London, Univ. of Sheffield and Univ. of London (external student).
Postal Clerk, Dept. of Posts and Telegraphs; Customs Official, Dept. of Customs and Excise 42; Sub-editor *Daily Service* 45; founder and editor *The Nigerian Statesman* 47; studied in U.K., called to the Bar, Gray's Inn, London 55; mem. House of Reps. 59-66; Fed. Commr. for Educ. 67-71, for Trade 71-75.
Leisure interests: reading, gardening, swimming.
Ministry of Trade, Lagos, Nigeria.

Brignone, Carlos Santiago, M.P.A., C.P.A.; Argentine banker; b. 30 Oct. 1918, Oliva, Córdoba; s. of Carlos Brignone and Dolores Margarita Cuquejo; m. Nélida E. Castelli 1942; three s. one d.; ed. Univ. of Buenos Aires and Harvard Univ.
Worked at Banco Central de la República Argentina 36-47; Statistical Office 47-56; Adviser, to the Minister of the Economy 56-57; Exec. Dir. IBRD 58-64; First Vice-Pres. Banco Central de la República Argentina 67-68; Exec. Dir IDB 68-69; Pres. Banco Central da la República Argentina 71; Grand Officer of Merit

for distinguished service (Peru); Commendatore, Ordine al Merito (Italy).
Pueyrredón 2355-3° piso, 1119 Buenos Aires, Argentina.
Telephone: 80-2293.

Brilej, Joža, LL.D.; Yugoslav lawyer and diplomatist; b. 1910; ed. Univ. of Ljubljana.
Barrister in Ljubljana until 41; Organizer of Liberation Movement in Slovenia; Colonel, Nat. Liberation Army until 45; mem. Slovene Nat. Assembly; mem. Nat. Council of Slovenia 43; Head of Political Dept., Ministry of Foreign Affairs until 50, when apptd. Asst. Foreign Minster; Ambassador to Great Britain 50-53; Perm. Rep. to UN 54-58; fmr. Counsellor of State for Foreign Affairs; Amb. to United Arab Repub. 61-63; Pres. Cttee. for Econ. Relations with Foreign Countries and mem. Federal Exec. Council 63-67; Deputy to Federal Assembly; Vice-Pres. Nat. Assembly of Repub. of Slovenia; Pres. Constitutional Court, Slovenian Repub.; Yugoslav Orders for Bravery, of Brotherhood and Unity (1st Class), of Merit for the People (2nd Class), of Labour (1st Class), of Partisan Star (1st Class), etc.
Federal Executive Council, Belgrade, Yugoslavia.

Brimelow, Baron (Life Peer) cr. 76, of Tyldesley in the County of Lancashire; **Thomas Brimelow,** G.C.M.G., O.B.E.; British diplomatist; b. 25 Oct. 1915, Tyldesley, Lancs.; s. of William Brimelow and Hannah Smith; m. Jean E. Cull 1945; two d.; ed. New Mills Grammar School and Oriel Coll. Oxford.
Laming Travelling Fellow, Queen's Coll., Oxford 37; Probationer Vice-Consul, Danzig 38; Consulate, Riga 39, Acting Consul 40; served in Consulate-Gen., New York 40; in charge of Consular Section of Embassy, Moscow 42-45; Foreign Office 45; First Sec., Havana 48; in Moscow 51-54; Counsellor (Commercial) Ankara 54-56; Head of Northern Dept., Foreign Office 56-60; Counsellor, Washington 60-63; Minister, Moscow 63-66; Amb. to Poland 66-69; Deputy Under-Sec. Foreign and Commonwealth Office 69-73, Rep. on Council of WEU 69-73; Perm. Under-Sec., Head of Diplomatic Service 73-75; Hon. Fellow, Oriel Coll., Oxford 73, Queen's Coll., Oxford 74.
12 West Hill Court, Millfield Lane, London, N6 6JJ, England.
Telephone: 01-340-8722.

Brimmer, Andrew Felton, M.A., PH.D.; American economist and government official; b. 13 Sept. 1926, Newellton, La.; s. of Andrew Brimmer and Vellar Davis Brimmer; m. Doris Millicent Scott 1953; one d.; ed. Univ. of Washington, Univs. of Delhi and Bombay (India), and Harvard Univ.
Teaching Fellow, Harvard Univ. 54-55; Economist, Fed. Reserve Bank of New York 55-58; Asst. Prof. of Econs. Michigan State Univ. 58-61, Asst. Prof. of Finance, Wharton School, Univ. of Pa. 61-63; Deputy Asst. Sec. for Econ. Affairs, U.S. Dept. of Commerce 63-65, Asst. Sec. 65-66; mem. Board of Govs. Fed. Reserve System 66-74; Dir. Du Pont Co. 74-; Overseer Harvard Coll.; Trustee, Tustegee Inst., Negro Student Fund; Fellow, American Acad. of Arts and Sciences; mem. American Econ. Asscn., American Finance Asscn., Nat. Economists Club, Council on Foreign Relations; Pres. Asscn. for the Study of Negro Life and History; Govt. Man of Year, Nat. Business League 63; Arthur S. Flemming Award 66; Russworm Award 66; Golden Plate Award American Acad. of Achievement 67; Public Affairs Award of Capital Press Club; Hon. LL.D. (Marquette, Nebraska Wesleyan, Atlanta, Colgate and Tufts Univs., Univ. of Notre Dame and Middlebury and Bishop Colls.), other hon. degrees from Univ. of Miami, Boston and Oberlin Colls., Ohio and Long Island Univ.
Publs. *Life Insurance Companies in the Capital Market*

62, *Survey of Mutual Fund Investors* (with Arthur Freedman) 63.
Harvard University, Cambridge, Mass. 02138, U.S.A.

Brinckerhoff, Charles M.; American mining executive; b. 15 March 1901, Minneapolis; s. of William Brinckerhoff and Mary Belle Sharp; m. Florence Andreen 1926; one d.; ed. Columbia Coll. and Columbia School of Mines.
Phelps-Dodge Corpn., Arizona, Inspiration Consolidated Copper Co., Andes Copper Mining Co. 25-48; Gen. Man. Chile Exploration Co., Chile 48-56, Exec. Vice-Pres. 57-58; Pres. and Dir. Anaconda Co. 58-64, Vice-Chair. and Chief Exec. Officer 64-65, Chair. and Chief Exec. Officer 65-68, Consultant in Mining and Metallurgy 68-.
784 Park Avenue, New York, N.Y. 10021, U.S.A.
Telephone: 212-RE7-7208.

Brink, Frank, Jr., B.S., M.S., PH.D.; American biophysicist; b. 4 Nov. 1910, Easton, Pa.; s. of Frank Brink, Sr., and Lydia (Wilhelm) Brink; m. Marjory Gaylord 1939; one s. one d.; ed. Easton High School, Pennsylvania State Univ., Calif. Inst. of Technology and Univ. of Pennsylvania.
Research Assistant, Johnson Research Foundation, Univ. of Pennsylvania 37-38; Fellow 38-40; Instructor in Physiology, Cornell Medical Coll., New York City 40-41; Johnson Foundation Fellow and Lecturer in Biophysics, Univ. of Pennsylvania 41-47, Asst. Prof. 47-48; Assoc. Prof. Johns Hopkins Univ. 48-53; Prof. and mem. Rockefeller Inst. (now Univ.) 53-, Acting Dean of Graduate Studies 54-58, Dean of Graduate Studies 58-72, Detlev W. Bronk Prof. 74-; White Fellowship, Pennsylvania State Coll. (now Univ.); Lalor Fellowship, Univ. of Pennsylvania; mem. Nat. Acad. of Sciences, American Acad. of Arts and Sciences.
Leisure interest: reading.
Publs. Articles in scientific journals.
Rockefeller University, New York, N.Y. 10021; Home: R.D.1., Pleasant Valley Road, Titusville, N.J. 08560, U.S.A.
Telephone: 212-360-1431 (Office).

Brink, Johannes Roelof Maria van den, DR. ECON.; Netherlands banker and politician; b. 1915; ed. Catholic High School, Tilburg.
With Ministry of Commerce and Industry 40-42; Prof. Roman Catholic Univ., Nijmegen 45-48; mem. First Chamber, States-Gen. 45-48; Minister of Econ. Affairs 48-52; Gen. Adviser Amsterdam-Rotterdam Bank, N.V., and Incasso-Bank, N.V. 52-53, Gen. Man. 54, now Joint Man.; fmr. Chair. Supervisory Board, AKZO N.V.
Herengracht 595, Amsterdam, Netherlands.

Brink, R(oyal) Alexander, D.SC.; American geneticist; b. 16 Sept. 1897, Ont., Canada; s. of Royal Wilson Brink and Elizabeth Ann (Cuthbert) Brink; m. 1st Edith Margaret Whitelaw 1922 (deceased), 2nd Joyce Hickling 1963; one s. one d.; ed. Ont. Agricultural Coll., Univ. of Ill. and Harvard Univ.
Assistant Chemist, Western Canada Flour Mills 19-20; Asst. Prof. of Genetics, Univ. of Wis. 22-27, Assoc. Prof. 27-31, Prof. 31-68, Emer. Prof. 68-, Chair. Dept. of Genetics 39-51; Man. Editor *Genetics* 51-56; Pres. Genetics Soc. of America 57, American Soc. of Naturalists 63; mem. Nat. Acad. of Sciences, American Acad. of Arts and Sciences.
Leisure interest: colour photography.
Publs. Numerous research articles in scientific journals on pollen physiology, the role of endosperm in seed development, plant breeding, gene action and mutation in maize, and paramutation; editor *Heritage from Mendel*.
Laboratory of Genetics, University of Wisconsin, Madison, Wis. 53706; Home: 4237 Manitou Way, Madison, Wis. 53711, U.S.A.
Telephone: 608-262-3344 (Office); 608-274-1349 (Home).

Brinkhous, Kenneth Merle, M.D., D.SC.; American pathologist; b. 29 May 1908, Clayton County, Iowa; m. Frances Benton 1936; two s.; ed. Univs. of Iowa and Chicago.
Associate in Pathology, Univ. of Iowa 35-37, Asst. Prof. of Pathology 37-45, Assoc. Prof. of Pathology 45-46, Prof. 46-61; Chair. of Pathology, Univ. of N. Carolina 46-73, Alumni Distinguished Prof. of Pathology 61-; mem. Nat. Acad. of Sciences; several awards including J. F. Mitchell Int. Award for Heart and Vascular Research, N. Carolina Award in Sciences 69 and Murray Thelin Award, Nat. Hemophilia Foundation 41.
Publs. several publications on hemophilia, blood coagulation, thrombosis and related topics.
Department of Pathology, University of North Carolina, School of Medicine, Chapel Hill, N.C. 27514; Home: 524 Dogwood Drive, Chapel Hill, N.C. 27514, U.S.A.
Telephone: 919-966-1061 (Office); 919-942-4956 (Home).

Brion, Marcel; French writer; b. 21 Nov. 1895, Marseille; s. of Raoul Brion and Jeanne Berrin de Faultrier; m. Liliane Guerry 1940; one s. one d.; ed. Collège Champittet, Lausanne and Faculty of Law, Aix-en-Provence.
Lawyer 20-24; writer 25-; mem. Académie Française 64-; Grand Prix de Littérature, Académie Française 53, Prix des Ambassadeurs 55, Prix littéraire de Monaco 56; Officier, Légion d'Honneur, Officier, Crown of Italy, Officer of the Order of Merit of Italy, Commdr. of the Order of Merit of France, Order of Merit of the Repub. of Germany.
Leisure interests: geology, gardening.
Publs. include *Château d'Ombres* 43, *Goethe* 50, *Léonard de Vinci* 54, *Robert Schumann et l'âme romantique* 56, *Romantic Art* 58, *La chanson de l'oiseau étranger* 60, *La ville de sable* 62, *L'Art abstrait, L'Art fantastique, L'Allemagne romantique* (2 vols.) 63, *La Folie Céladon* 63, *La Rose de cire* 64, *L'enchanteur, Les escales de la haute nuit* 65, *De l'autre côté de la forêt* 66, *La Peinture romantique* 66, *Les Miroirs et les Gouffres* 67, *L'Ombre d'un arbre mort* 70, *Nous avons traversé la montagne* 72, *La Fête de la tour des âmes* 74.
32 rue de Bac, Paris 7e, France.
Telephone: 548-50-56.

Brisco, Milo Martin; American business executive; b. 1912, Maud, Okla.; m.; two d.; ed. Univ. of Oklahoma.
With Tropical Oil Co., Colombia, and other affiliates of Standard Oil Co. (New Jersey) 35-51; Asst. Gen. Man. Int. Petroleum, Colombia 51-53, Gen. Man., Peru 53, Colombia 54-56; Exec. Vice-Pres. Int. Petroleum 57-61, Pres. 61-66; mem. Board of Dirs. Jersey Standard 66-69; Vice-Pres. 67, Exec. Vice-Pres. and mem. Board Exec. Cttee. 68, Pres. Standard Oil Co. (New Jersey) 69-72; Dir. Int. Exec. Service Corps, Econ. Devt. Council N.Y.C., American Petroleum Inst., First Nat. City Bank, First Nat. Corpn., Council for Financial Aid to Educ. Inc.; Trustee, Univ. of Miami; mem. Board of Govs., United Way of America; mem. American Inst. of Mining, Metallurgical and Petroleum Engineers, N.Y. Urban Coalition Inc., Council on Foreign Relations Inc., Brookings Inst., Econ. Club. of New York.
c/o Exxon Corpn., 1251 Avenue of the Americas, New York, N.Y. 10020, U.S.A.

Brissaud, Raymond; French business executive; b. 3 June 1905, Paris; s. of Charles Brissaud and Marguerite Magnin; m. Yvonne Latou 1937; two s.; ed. Ecole St. Louis de Gonzague and Ecole Nationale Supérieure des Mines de Paris.
Administrator Dir.-Gen. Electrorail, Belgium 57-72, Hon. Admin. Dir.-Gen. 72-; Pres. Dir.-Gen. Soc. Française des Distilleries de l'Indochine 58-73, Admin. 73-; Admin. Dir.-Gen. Schneider S.A. 68-72, Hon. Admin. Dir.-Gen. 72-; Pres. Jeumont-Schneider 70-73, Admin. 73-; Admin. Creusot-Loire, Spie-Batignolles,

Banque de l'Union Européenne, Jeumont-Industrie, Lignes Télégraphiques et Téléphones (L.T.T.); Officier Légion d'Honneur, Chevalier, Ordre de la Couronne de Belgique.
Schneider S.A., 42 rue d'Anjou, Paris 8e; Home: 15 avenue de Madrid, 92 Neuilly-sur-Seine, France.

Brito de Almeida Costa, Mário Júlio, D.IUR.; Portuguese law professor and politician; b. 20 Oct. 1927, Boco, Vagos; ed. Univ. de Coimbra.
Extraordinary Prof. Faculty of Law, Univ. of Coimbra 60-62, Full Prof. 62; Minister of Justice 67-73; Fellow, Portuguese Acad. of History, Inst. of Coimbra; has taken part in law confs. in Portugal and abroad.
Publs. Numerous works on Portuguese law.
Av. Infante Santo 15 7°, Lisbon 3, Portugal.

Brittain, Alfred, III, B.A.; American business executive; b. 22 July 1922, Evanston, Ill.; m. Beatrice Memhard; one s. one d.; ed. Phillips Exeter Acad. and Yale Univ.
Served with Army Air Corps 42-46; with Bankers Trust Co. N.Y. 47-, Nat. Banking Dept. 51-64, Head of Dept. 64, later Vice-Pres. Special Industries Div., Asst. Treas. 51, Asst. Vice-Pres. 54, Vice-Pres. 57, First Vice-Pres. 62, Senior Vice-Pres. 64, Pres. 66-74, Chair. Jan. 75-; Chair. and Dir. Bankers Int. Corpn.; Dir. Bankers Trust N.Y. Corpn., Philip Morris Inc., Collings & Aikman Corpn., Bancom Devt. Corpn.; Trustee Carnegie Endowment for Int. Peace, Phillips Exeter Acad.
Bankers Trust N.Y. Corpn., P.O. Box 318, Church Street Station, New York, N.Y. 10015; and Cognewaugh Road, Cos Cob, Connecticut, U.S.A.

Britten, (Edward) Benjamin, O.M., C.H.; British composer; b. 22 Nov. 1913, Lowestoft, Suffolk; s. of Robert Victor and Edith Rhoda Britten; ed. Gresham's School, Holt, and Royal Coll. of Music, London.
Hon. D.Mus. (Belfast, Cambridge, Nottingham, Hull, Oxford, Manchester, London, Leicester, East Anglia, Wales, Warwick)); Hanseatic Goethe Prize 62, Aspen Award and Royal Philharmonic Soc. Gold Medal 64, Sibelius Prize 65, Sonning Prize 68, Ernst von Siemens Foundation Award 73, Maurice Ravel Prize 74.
Works include: *Simple Symphony* 23-26, *String Quartet* 31, *Sinfonietta* 32, *Phantasy* 32, *A Boy Was Born* 32-33, *Friday Afternoons* 34, *Suite for Violin and Piano* 34-35, *Our Hunting Fathers* 36, *Soirées Musicales I* 36, *Variations on a Theme of Frank Bridge* 37, *On This Island* 37, *Mont Juic* (with Lennox Berkeley) 37, *Piano Concerto No. 1 in D Major* 38, *Violin Concerto No. 1 in D Minor* 39, *Kermesse Canadienne* 39, *Ballad of Heroes* 39, *Les Illuminations* 39, *Diversions* 40, *Seven Sonnets of Michelangelo* 40, *Sinfonia da Requiem* 40, *Paul Bunyan* 41, *Matinées Musicales* 41, *String Quartet No. 1 in D Major* 41, *Scottish Ballad* 41, *Hymn to St. Cecilia* 42, *A Ceremony of Carols* 42, *Rejoice in the Lamb* 43, *Prelude and Fugue for String Orchestra* 43, *Serenade* 43, *Festival Te Deum* 45, *String Quartet No. 2 in C* 45, *Peter Grimes* 45, *Holy Sonnets of John Donne* 45, *Young Person's Guide to the Orchestra* 46, *The Rape of Lucretia* 46, *Albert Herring* 47, *Canticle I* (Francis Quarles) 47, *A Charm of Lullabies* 47, *Saint Nicolas* (cantata) 48, *The Beggar's Opera* (new version) 48, *The Little Sweep* 49, *Spring Symphony* 49, *Billy Budd* 51, *Canticle II* (Abraham and Isaac) 52, *Gloriana* 53, *Winter Words* (Hardy) 53, *The Turn of the Screw* 54, *Canticle III* (Sitwell) 54, *The Prince of the Pagodas* (ballet) 56, *Songs from the Chinese* 58, *Noye's Fludde* (opera) 58, *Nocturne* 58, *6 Hölderlin Fragments* 58, *Cantata Academica* 59, *Missa Brevis* 59, *A Midsummer Night's Dream* (opera) 60, *Sonata in C* (cello and piano) 61, *War Requiem* 62, *Psalm 150* 63, *Cantata Misericordium* 63, *Symphony for Cello and Orchestra* 63, *Nocturnal* (guitar) 63, *Curlew River* (church parable) 64, *First Suite for Cello* 64, *Songs*

and Proverbs of William Blake 65, *Voices for Today* 65, *The Poet's Echo* 65, *Gemini Variations* 65, *The Burning Fiery Furnace* (church parable) 66, *The Golden Vanity* (Vaudeville for boys' voices and piano) 66, *The Building of the House* (overture with chorus) 67, *Second Suite for Cello* 67, *The Prodigal Son* (church parable) 68, *Children's Crusade* 69, *Suite for Harp* 69, *Who are these Children?* (Soutar songs) 69, *Owen Wingrave* 70, *Canticle IV* (Eliot) 71, *Third Suite for Cello* 71, *Death in Venice* 73, *Canticle V* (Eliot) 74, *Suite on English Folk Tunes* 74, *Sacred and Profane: Eight Medieval Lyrics* 75, *A Birthday Hansel* (Burns) 75, *Phaedra* 75.
The Red House, Aldeburgh, Suffolk, IP15 5PZ, England.

Britton, Cedric John Charles, M.D., CH.B., D.P.H., F.R.C. PATH; British consulting physician; b. 1904, Wellington, New Zealand; m. Miryem Adèle Gédance 1935; two s. one d.; ed. Nelson Coll., N.Z., Univ. of Otago, and Middlesex Hospital, London.
Bacteriologist, Univ. of Otago 31; Asst. Pathologist, The Middlesex Hospital 32-33 and 37-46, Christchurch Hospital, N.Z. 34-36; fmr. Physician-in-charge Dept. Allergy and Hon. Haematologist, Prince of Wales's Hospital, London; Pathologist and Allergist, St. Andrew's Hospital, London; Hon. Pathologist, Finchley Memorial Hospital and Hendon District Hospital; fmr. Treas. British Allergy Soc.; fmr. Councillor, British Medical Asscn.; mem. Int. Soc. of Allergy, Int. Soc. of Haematology, British and European Socs. of Haematology, Pathology Soc. of Great Britain and Ireland, Asscn. Clinical Pathologists, American Acad. of Sciences; hon. mem. Argentine and French Allergy Societies.
Leisure interests: gardening, philately.
Publs. *Disorders of the Blood* (10th edn.) 69, *Bone Marrow Biopsy* 49, numerous articles on haematological and allergic subjects.
21 Wimpole Street, London, W1M 7AD, England.
Telephone: 01-636-1361.

Broadbent, Donald Eric, C.B.E., SC.D., F.R.S.; British psychologist; b. 6 May 1926, Birmingham; s. of Herbert Arthur Broadbent and Hannah Elizabeth Broadbent (née Williams); m. 1st Margaret Elizabeth Wright 1949, two d.; m. 2nd Margaret Hope Pattison Gregory 1972; ed. Pembroke Coll., Cambridge.
Staff mem. Applied Psychology Unit, Medical Research Council 49-58, Dir. 58-74, External Staff 74-; Pres. British Psychological Soc. 65, Psychological Section, British Asscn. for the Advancement of Science 67, Experimental Psychology Soc. 73; Fellow, British Psychological Soc., Acoustical Soc. of America, Human Factors Soc., Wolfson Coll., Oxford; Foreign Assoc. U.S. Nat. Acad. of Sciences; H. M. Vernon Prize; Kenneth Craik Award; Dist. Scientific Contribution Award of American Psychological Assoc.; Lister Lecturer, British Asscn. for the Advancement of Science; Gregynog Lecturer (Aberystwyth), Pillsbury Lecturer (Cornell), Fitts Lecturer (Michigan), William James Lecturer (Harvard); Fletcher-Stevens Lecturer (Utah); Hon. D.Sc. (Southampton).
Leisure interests: reading, camping, photography.
Publs. *Perception and Communication* 58, *Behaviour* 61, *Decision and Stress* 71, *In Defence of Empirical Psychology* 73.
Department of Psychology, 1 South Parks Road, Oxford, England.
Telephone: 0865-56789.

Broadbent, John Edward, M.A., PH.D.; Canadian professor and politician; b. 21 March 1936, Oshawa, Ont.; s. of Percy E. Broadbent and Mary A. Welsh; m. Lucille Munroe 1971; one s. one d.; ed. High School in Oshawa, Univ. of Ont., London School of Econs. and Political Science.

Professor of Political Science, York Univ., Ont. 65-68; mem. House of Commons 68-; Co-Chair. Policy Review Cttee. for New Democratic Party Fed. Convention 69; Chair. Fed. Caucus 72-74, Parl. Leader of Fed. Caucus 74-75; Nat. Leader of New Democratic Party July 75-. Leisure interests: reading contemporary fiction, listening to music, skiing.
Publ. *The Liberal Rip-Off* 70.
Room 629C, House of Commons, Ottawa, Ont.; Home: 803-373 Laurier Avenue East, Ottawa, Ont., Canada.
Telephone: 995-7224 (Office); 232-6941 (Home).

Broch, Henrik Andreas; Norwegian diplomatist; b. 20 Feb. 1909, Vang; *s.* of late Peter F. Broch and Elisabeth Rustad; *m.* Fanny Paus 1935; one *d.*; ed. Univ. of Caen and Norwegian Military Acad., Oslo.
Army Officer 30-39; Sec. Ministry of Foreign Affairs 31-33; Sec. of Legation, London 33-34; Ministry of Foreign Affairs 34-35, Chief of Div. 45-46; Counsellor, Stockholm 46-51; Minister Rio de Janeiro 51-55, Berne 55-57; Amb. to Switzerland 57-62, to Spain 62-66, to Sweden 66-73, to Czechoslovakia 76-; Commdr. Order of St. Olav (Norway), and orders from Denmark, Sweden, Spain, Brazil, Austria and Czechoslovakia.
Norwegian Embassy, Zitna 2, 125 41 Prague, Czechoslovakia.

Broches, Aron, LL.D.,; Netherlands lawyer; b. 22 March 1914, Amsterdam; *s.* of Abraham Broches and Chaja Broches (née Person); *m.* Catherina Johanna Pothast 1939; one *s.* one *d.*; ed. Univ. of Amsterdam and Fordham Univ. Law School.
Legal adviser, Netherlands Economic Mission and Netherlands Embassy, New York and Washington, D.C. 42-46; Sec. Neths. Del. to U.N. Monetary and Financial Conf., Bretton Woods 44; Sec. and Legal Adviser, Neths. Del. to Inaugural Meeting, Int. Monetary Fund and Int. Bank for Reconstruction and Development 46; Attorney in Legal Dept., I.B.R.D. 46-51, Asst. Gen. Counsel 51-56, Dir. Legal Dept. and Assoc. Gen. Counsel 56-59, Gen. Counsel 59-, mem. President's Council 65-, Vice-Pres. 72-; Sec.-Gen. Int. Centre for Settlement of Investment Disputes 67-; Chief IBRD Econ. Survey Mission to Nigeria 53-54; Trustee, Int. Legal Center 69-; mem. Exec. Council, American Soc. of Int. Law 69-73, Int. Council for Commercial Arbitration 72-.
Leisure interest: music.
Publs. numerous works on legal aspects of economic development including *International Legal Aspects of the Operations of the World Bank* 59, *The Convention on the Settlement of Investment Disputes between States and Nationals of Other States* 72.
World Bank, Washington D.C. 20433, U.S.A.
Telephone: 202-477-2087.

Brøchner-Mortensen, Knud, M.D.; Danish physician; b. 4 July 1906, Fredericia; *s.* of Vald Brøchner-Mortensen and Ingrid Schaffer; *m.* Else Stein 1932; two *s.* two *d.*; ed. Univ. of Copenhagen.
Professor of Medicine and Dir. of Medical Dept. A., Univ. Hospital of Copenhagen; Dean of Medical Faculty, Univ. of Copenhagen 56-57, mem. Konsistorium 63-74, Chair. Medical Educ. Cttee. 62-64; mem. Danish State Research Foundation 63-68; Chair. Medical Council, Univ. Hospital of Copenhagen 58-64; mem. Danish Forensic Council 64; Hon. mem. American Rheumatism Asscn., Sociedad Argentina de Reumatologia, Japanese Rheumatism Asscn., Swedish Rheumatism Asscn., Norwegian and Finnish Soc. of Internal Medicine; Heberden Oration Medal 57.
Leisure interest: history of medicine.
Publ. *Uric Acid in Blood and Urine* 37.
Fridtjof Nansens Plads 3, 2100 Copenhagen Ø, Denmark.
Telephone: (01) 391610.

Brock, Baron (Life Peer), cr. 65, of Wimbledon; **Russell Claude Brock,** Kt., M.D., M.S., F.R.C.S., F.R.A.C.S., F.A.C.S.; British surgeon; b. 24 Oct. 1903; ed. Christ's Hospital and Guy's Hospital (Univ. of London).
Surgeon to Guy's Hospital 36-68, to the Brompton Hospital 36-68; Hunterian Prof., Royal Coll. of Surgeons 38; Exchange Prof. of Surgery, Johns Hopkins Hospital 49; mem. Council Royal Coll. of Surgeons 49-, Vice-Pres. 57-58, Pres. 63-66; Dir. Dept. of Surgical Sciences, Royal Coll. of Surgeons 68-; numerous medals and prizes.
Publs. *Anatomy of the Bronchial Tree* 46, *Life and Work of Astley Cooper* 52, *Lung Abscess* 52, *Anatomy of Pulmonary Stenosis* 57.
2 Harley Street, London, W.1; The Old Rectory House, 84 Church Road, Wimbledon, London, S.W.19, England.
Telephone: 01-580-1441.

Brock, John Fleming, D.M., F.R.C.P.; South African professor of medicine; b. 27 March 1905; *s.* of Dr. John Brock and Mrs. E. E. Brock (née Fleming); *m.* Ruth M. Lomberg 1933; two *s.* two *d.*; ed. Grey School, Port Elizabeth, Univ. of Cape Town, Oxford Univ. and Harvard Medical School.
Taught at British Postgraduate Medical School, London 35; Asst. Dir. of Research in Medicine, Cambridge Univ. 36-38; Prof. of Medicine, Univ. of Cape Town 38-71, Emer. 71-; Pres. S.A. Coll. of Physicians, Surgeons and Gynaecologists 65-68; Nutrition Consultant, WHO 49-; mem. Council, Univ. of Cape Town 60-; Consulting Physician, Groote Schuur Hosp.; Hon. F.A.C.P. 66; Hon. F.C.P. (S.A.) 73; Hon. D.Sc. (Univ. of Natal) 71; Hon. LL.D. (Univ. of Witwatersrand) 75.
Leisure interests: tennis, bowls, medical history, philosophy.
Publs. *Recent Advances in Human Nutrition* 61; co-author *Human Nutrition and Dietetics* (6th Edn.) 75; papers, monographs and lectures on clinical medicine, metabolism and human nutrition.
University of Cape Town, Department of Medicine, Medical School, Observatory, Cape 7900; Home: Bendoran, Bishopscourt Drive, Claremont, Cape 7700, South Africa.
Telephone: 55-3921 (Office); 716082 (Home).

Brockway, Baron (Life Peer), cr. 64, of Eton and Slough; **(Archibald) Fenner Brockway;** British politician; b. 1 Nov. 1888; ed. School for Sons of Missionaries (now Eltham Coll.).
Leader War Resisters' Movement during First World War; journalist; Chair. No More War Movement and War Resisters' Int. 23-28; Gen. Sec. Independent Labour Party 23-26 and 33-39, Political Sec. 39-46, and Editor *New Leader* 26-29 and 31-46; Chair. Congress of Peoples against Imperialism 48-54; Chair. The Movement for Colonial Freedom 54-; Labour M.P. 29-31, 50-64.
Publs. *The Devil's Business* 15, *Socialism and Pacifism* 17, *The Government of India* 20, *English Prisons To-day* (with Stephen Hobhouse) 21, *A New Way with Crime* 28, *The Indian Crisis* 30, *Bloody Traffic* 33, *Hungry England* 32, *Will Roosevelt Succeed?* 34, *Purple Plague* (novel) 35, *Workers' Front* 38, *Inside the Left* 42, *Death Pays a Dividend* (with F. Mullally) 44, *German Diary* 46, *Socialism over Sixty Years: Life of Jowett of Bradford* 46, *Bermondsey Story: Life of Alfred Salter* 49, *Why Mau-Mau?* 53, *African Journeys* 55, *1960—Africa's Year of Destiny* 60, *Red Liner* 62, *Outside the Right* 62, *African Socialism* 63, *Immigration* (with Norman Pannell) 65, *This Shrinking Explosive World: A Study in Race Relations* 67, *The Next Step to Peace* 70, *The Colonial Revolution* 73.
House of Lords, London, S.W.1, and 67 Southway, London, N.20, England.
Telephone: 01-219-3193 (House of Lords); 01-445-3054 (Home).

Broda, Dr. Christian; Austrian lawyer and politician; b. 12 March 1916, Vienna; ed. Akademische Gymnasium, Vienna and Univ. of Vienna.
Political imprisonment 34; served in army 40-45; subsequently in private legal practice, Vienna; mem. Bundesrat 57-59, Nationalrat 59-; mem. Penal Law Comm. 57; Minister of Justice 60-66, April 70-; Socialist Party.
Federal Ministry of Justice, Vienna, Austria.

Brodal, Alf, M.D.; Norwegian neuroanatomist; b. 25 Jan. 1910, Oslo; s. of Peter Brodal and Helene Obenauer; m. Inger Hannestad 1935; one s. two d.; ed. Univ. of Oslo.
Assistant Dept. of Anatomy, Odontological High School of Norway, Oslo 37-43; Prosector of Anatomy, Univ. of Oslo 43-50, Prof. of Anatomy 50-, Dean Medical Faculty 64-66, Pro-Rector 67-69; Co-Editor *Ergebn. Anat. Entwickl. gesch.*; Rockefeller Fellowship, Dept. of Human Anatomy, Oxford Univ. 46-47; Fellow, Norwegian Acad. of Sciences 44; mem. Royal Soc. of Medicine, London 46; Assoc. mem. Nordic Neurosurgical Asscn. 47, Anatomical Soc. of Great Britain and Ireland 72; Hon. mem. American Neurological Asscn. 67, Norwegian Neurological Asscn. 73; mem. Deutsche Akad. Naturforscher Leopoldina 64-; Corresp. mem. Belgian Acad. of Medicine 69; Order of St. Olaf 69; Fridtjof Nansen Prize 52, Monrad-Krohn Prize 41 and 60; Barany Medal (Uppsala) 63-; Anders Jahre's Medical Prize 66; Dr. h.c. Univ. of Uppsala 66, Univ. of Paris 75.
Leisure interests: literature (fiction), carpentry, painting, out-door recreation.
Publs. (Monographs) *The Reticular Formation of the Brain Stem* 57 (Russian edn. 60), (with Jan Jansen) *Aspects of Cerebellar Anatomy* 54, (with Jan Jansen) *Das Kleinhirn* 58, (with Pompeiano and Walberg) *The Vestibular Nuclei and their Connections* 62 (Russian edn. 66); (Textbooks) *Neurological Anatomy in Relation to Clinical Medicine* 48, 69 (Japanese edn. 61), *The Cranial Nerves* 59, 65.
Anatomical Institute, University of Oslo, Karl Johans gt. 47, Oslo 1; Home: Preståsen 14, Blommenholm, Baerum, Norway.
Telephone: 33-00-70 (Office); 54-83-50 (Home).

Brodie, Bernard Beryl, PH.D.; American pharmacologist; b. 7 Aug. 1909, Liverpool, England; s. of Samuel Brodie and Esther Ginsburg; m. Anne L. Smith 1950; no c.; ed. McGill Univ., Montreal and New York Univ.
Research Asst. in Pharmacology, New York Univ. Medical School 35-38, Instructor in Pharmacology 38-41, Instructor, Dept. of Medicine (Biochem.) 41-43, Asst. Prof. of Pharmacology 43-47, Assoc. Prof. of Biochem. 47-50; Chief, Laboratory of Chemical Pharmacology, Nat. Heart and Lung Inst., Bethesda, Md. 50-70; Senior Consultant Hoffman-La Roche Inc. 71-; Founder *Life Sciences*; U.S. Editor and Co-Founder *Pharmacology*; Editor *Medicina et Pharmacologia Experimentalis*; Co-Founder and mem. Editorial Advisory Board *International Journal of Neuropharmacology*; mem. of Editorial and Advisory Boards of other medical journals; Claude Bernard Prof. Univ. of Montreal; Fellow N.Y. Acad. of Science; mem. Nat. Acad. of Sciences, Inst. of Medicine; Hon. mem. Soc. of Pharmaceutical Sciences, Italy; Paul Lamson Memorial Lecture, Vanderbilt Univ. 71; Rosemary Cass Memorial Lecture, Univ. of Dundee 71; T. Edward Hicks Memorial Lectureship in Pharmacy, Univ. of Iowa 71; Hon. D.Sc. (Univs. of Louvain, Paris and Barcelona. Philadelphia Coll. and New York Medical Coll); Hon. M.D. (Karolinska Institutet); Distinguished Service Award of Dept. of Health, Educ. and Welfare 58, Torald Sollmann Award in Pharmacology 63, Distinguished Achievement, Modern Medicine 64, Albert Lasker Award for Basic Medical Research 67, Nat. Medal of Science 68, Schmiedeberg-Plakette 69, Oscar B. Hunter Memorial Award, Golden Plate Award 70, Intra-Science Foundation Medallist 72.
Leisure interests: bridge, swimming, reading.
Publs. *Metabolic Factors Controlling Duration of Drug Action* 63, *Drug Enzyme Interactions* 64, *Handbuch der exp. Pharmakologie* 71, *Bioavailability of Drugs* 73.
Laboratory of Chemical Pharmacology, National Heart and Lung Institute, National Institutes of Health, Bethesda, Md. 20014; Eden Rock Gardens, 39406 Timrod Street, Apt. 272, Tucson, Ariz. 85711, U.S.A.
Telephone: 301-496-2593.

Brodie, Very Rev. Rabbi Sir Israel, K.B.E., B.A., B.LITT.; British Rabbi; b. 10 May 1895; ed. Jews' Coll., London, Univ. Coll., London and Balliol Coll., Oxford.
Jewish Chaplain to the Forces 17-19 and 40-48; Senior Jewish Chaplain 44-48; Minister, Melbourne Hebrew Congregation 22-37; Tutor and Lecturer in Homiletics, Jews' Coll. London 38-48; Chief Rabbi, United Hebrew Congregations of the British Commonwealth 48-65, Emer. Chief Rabbi; Fellow Univ. Coll., London; D.D. (Hon.); Hon. D.C.L. (Durham).
Flat R, 82 Portland Place, London, W1N 3DH, England.

Brodsky, Joseph Alexander: Russian-born poet (stateless); b. 27 May 1940, Leningrad; s. of Alexander Brodsky and Maria Volpert; one s.; ed. secondary school.
Employed as metalworker, deckhand, geologist, photographer, stoker, orderly, farmhand etc.; imprisoned three times; later worked as translator of poetry, drama; ordered to leave U.S.S.R. for Israel 72; poet-in-residence, Univ. of Michigan 72-; mem. Bavarian Acad. of Fine Arts.
Leisure interest: sleeping.
Publs. include *Colianes* (Selected poems in French) 66, *Stop in a Desert* (in Russian) 71, *Selected Poems* 73, others in Italian and German.
309 Wesley St., Ann Arbor, Mich. 48103, U.S.A.
Telephone: (313) 994-6697.

Brofoss, Erik, CAND. JUR., CAND. ECON.; Norwegian banker; b. 21 June 1908; ed. Oslo Univ.
Assistant Judge, West Telemark 33-35; employed by State Insurance Service 35-37, by Oslo Tax Assessment Office 37-41; escaped to Sweden Dec. 41, where employed by Norwegian Refugee Office; travelled to London April 42, mem. staff Norwegian Ministry of Finance until Oct. 42; Dir. Ministry of Supply (London); fmr. Vice-Chair. Econ. Co-ordinating Council; Minister of Finance Nov. 45-47; Minister of Trade Dec. 47-54; Gov. Bank of Norway (Central Bank) 54-70; Chair. Joint Consultation Council 54-65; Chair. Regional Devt. Fund 62-; mem. of Board, Alcan Aluminium Ltd. 71-; Lecturer, Univ. of Oslo 57-66; fmr. Gov. Int. Monetary Fund, Exec. Dir. 70-73; mem. Labour Party.
c/o Norges Bank, Bankpl. 2, Oslo 1, Norway.

Broglie, Prince Jean de, D. en D.; French politician; b. 21 June 1921; ed. Ecole des Sciences Politiques.
Auditor, Council of State 46; Conseiller-Gen., Rugles 51-58, 58-; Master of Petitions, Council of State 54-; Ind. Deputy for Eure 58-65, 67-; Mayor of Broglie; Sec. of State for the Sahara and Overseas Territories and Depts. 61-62, for Public Functions 62, for Algerian Affairs Dec. 62-65, for Foreign Affairs 66-67; Chevalier, Légion d'Honneur, Croix de Guerre, Médaille de la Résistance.
9 rue Adolphe-Yvon, Paris 16e, France.

Broglie, Prince Louis de, D.SC.; French scientist; b. 15 Aug. 1892; ed. Univ. of Paris.
Professor of Theoretical Physics Paris Univ. (Inst. Henri Poincaré) 28-; awarded Nobel Prize for Physics 29; mem. Inst. de France, Acad. des Sciences 33-; Life Sec. Acad. des Sciences 42-; mem. Acad. Française 43-; mem.

Scientific Cttee. Atomic Energy Comm. 46-; mem. Comité d'action scientifique de défense nationale 50-67; Foreign Assoc. U.S. Nat. Acad of Sciences 48; Foreign mem. Royal Soc. 53; Hon. mem. Romanian Acad. 65.
Publs. *La théorie de Quanta* 24, *Ondes et Mouvements* 30, *Introduction à l'étude de la mécanique ondulatoire* 26, *Conséquences de la rélativité dans le développement de la mécanique ondulatoire* 33, *Matière et Lumière, la Physique moderne et les quanta* 37, *Une nouvelle théorie de la lumière* 40, *Continue et Discontinue* 41, *Mécanique ondulatoire des corpuscules à spire* 42, *De la mécanique ondulatoire à la théorie du Noyau* 43, *Physique et Microphysique, Savants et Découvertes, Nouvelles perspectives en Microphysique, Sur les Sentiers de la Science*, etc.
94 rue Perronet, 92 Neuilly-sur-Seine, France.
Telephone: Maillot 76-09.

Broglio, Luigi; Italian aerospace engineer; b. 6 Nov. 1911, Venice.
Full Professor of Aeronautical Structures, Rome Univ. 44-, Head of School of Aerospace Eng. 52-; Chair. Italian Space Comm. of Nat. Research Council 59-68, Gen. Dir. San Marco Project (joint project with United States NASA); mem. NATO Advisory Group for Aeronautical Research; mem. Int. Acad. of Astronautics, American Soc. of Mech. Eng.
Publs. over 100 papers on theory of elasticity, aerodynamics, dynamics, heat conduction in solids, orbit analysis, astronautics.
Scuola Ingegneria Aerospaziale dell'Università degli Studi di Roma, Via Eudossiana 16, 00184 Rome, Italy.
Telephone: 461381, 4750887.

Bromberger, Merry Marie Louis (brother of Serge Paul Bromberger, *q.v.*); French journalist; b. 10 July 1906, Strasbourg; ed. Lycée d'Aix-en-Provence, Aix-en-Provence and Strasbourg Univs.
Founded *Le Courrier de Provence* (daily) 26; Editor *Petit Marseillais*; legal corresp. *Le Matin* 30; Chief Reporter *L'Intransigeant* 30-39, later with *Paris-Soir, Combat, Paris-Presse-L'Intransigeant*; with *Constellation* 49-; Chevalier Légion d'Honneur.
Publs. *Le Roman de l'Elysée, Comment ils ont fait Fortune, Le Comte de Paris et la Maison de France, Le Destin Secret de Georges Pompidou*; with Serge Paul Bromberger: *Les Secrets de l'expédition d'Egypte, Les 13 complots du 13 mai, Barricades et Colonels, Les Coulisses de l'Europe, Jean Monnet and the United States of Europe* 69.
96 boulevard Maurice Barrès, Neuilly-sur-Seine (Seine), France.
Telephone: MAI-26-23.

Bromberger, Serge Paul (brother of Merry Marie Louis Bromberger, *q.v.*); French journalist; b. 29 Aug. 1912; ed. Lycée Mignet (Aix-en-Provence).
Journalist 34-; Reporter on *Figaro* 45-; Dir. Service des Enquêtes et Reportage 72; mem. Asscn. des grands reporters français; Officier Légion d'Honneur, Croix du Combattant Volontaire.
Publs. *Retour de Corée* (co-author) 51, *Les Rebelles Algériens* 58, *En 1990* 64; with Merry Bromberger: *Les Secrets de l'expédition d'Egypte, Les 13 Complots du 13 mai* 59, *Barricades et Colonels* 60, *Les Coulisses de l'Europe* 68, *Jean Monnet and the United States of Europe* 69.
219 avenue de Versailles, Paris 16e, France.

Bromley, Yulian Vladimirovich; Soviet historian; b. 21 Feb. 1921, Moscow; ed. Moscow Univ.
Junior Research Assoc. Inst. of Slav Studies 50-51; Scientific Sec. Dept. of History, U.S.S.R. Acad. of Sciences 51-66; Dir. Inst. of Ethnography, U.S.S.R. Acad. of Sciences 66-; Corresp. mem. U.S.S.R. Acad. of Sciences 66-.
Publs. Works on general history and ethnology.
N. N. Miklukho-Maklai Institute of Ethnography, 19 Ulitsa Dmitriya Ulyanova, Moscow 117036, U.S.S.R.

Bronfman, Edgar M., B.A.; American business executive; b. 20 June 1929, Montreal, P.Q.; *s.* of late Samuel Bronfman and of Saidye (Rosner) Bronfman; *m.* Ann M Loeb; four *s.* one *d.*; ed. Trinity Coll. School, Port Hope, Ont., Williams Coll., Williamstown, Mass., and McGill Univ., Montreal.
Executive in charge of company's plants in Canada, Distillers Corpn.-Seagrams Ltd. 53-55; Chair. Admin. Cttee., Joseph E. Seagram & Sons Inc., New York 55. Pres. and Dir. 57-71; Pres. Distillers Corpn.-Seagrams (now The Seagrams Co. Ltd.) July 71-75, Chair. and Chief Exec. Officer May 75-; Dir. Adela Investment Co. S.A., Clevepak Corpn., Metropolitan Applied Research Center Inc., Int. Exec. Service Corps., American Technion Soc.; Founding mem. Rockefeller Univ. Council; Co-Chair. Devt. Fund for UN Int. School; Trustee Salk Inst. for Biological Studies, Nat. Urban League Inc., Mt. Sinai Hosp. and School of Medicine; mem. Board of Dirs. Interracial Council for Business Opportunity; mem. Foreign Policy Asscn., American Foreign Service Asscn., Center for Inter-American Relations Inc., Cttee. for Econ. Devt., etc.
Distillers Corporation—Seagrams Ltd., 1430 Peel Street, Montreal 110, P.Q., Canada; Home: 60 Lincoln Avenue, Purchase, N.Y., U.S.A.

Broniarek, Zygmunt; Polish journalist; b. 27 Aug. 1925, Warsaw; *s.* of Wacław Broniarek and Marianna Broniarek; *m.*; ed. Cen. School of Planning and Statistics, Warsaw.
Radiotelegraphic operator and stenographer, Czytelnik publishers, Warsaw 45-48; Corresp. *Trybuna Ludu* 49-; in U.S.A. 55, 58, Latin America 56, Paris 59-60, 69-73, Washington, 60-67; Chair. Polish Asscn. of Int. Journalists and Writers 74-; Gold Cross of Merit, Knight's Cross, Order of Polonia Restituta.
Publs. *Od Hustonu do Mississipi, Gorące dni Manhattanu, Szczeble do Białego Domu*.
Ul. Grójecka 81/87 m. 79, 02-094 Warsaw, Poland.

Bronston, Samuel; American film producer; ed. Université de Paris à la Sorbonne.
Former film distributor, Paris; fmr. unit production exec. with Columbia Studios Hollywood; founder Samuel Bronston Pictures Inc., now Pres.
Productions include: *King of Kings, El Cid* 60, *55 Days to Peking* 62, *Fall of the Roman Empire* 63, *The Magnificent Showman (Circus World,* U.K.) 64.

Brook, Alexander; American artist; b. 14 July 1898; ed. Art Students' League.
Logan Medal, Chicago Art Inst. 29, Beck Gold Medal, Pennsylvania Acad. 48; and several other awards.
Represented permanently in Metropolitan Museum New York City; Brooklyn (N.Y.) Museum; Art Inst. Chicago; Carnegie Inst. Pittsburgh; Nebraska Univ.; William Nelson Gallery, Kansas City, Mo.; Wadsworth Athenæum, Hartford, Conn.; Museum of Modern Art, New York City; Newark (N.J.) Museum; and many other U.S. museums, etc.
c/o Larcada Gallery, 23 East 67th Street, New York, N.Y. 10021; and Sag Harbor, Long Island, N.Y., U.S.A.

Brook, Peter, C.B.E.; British theatre and film director; b. 21 March 1925; *m.* Natasha Parry 1951; one *s.* one *d.*; ed. Westminster and Gresham's Schools, and Magdalen Coll., Oxford.
Joined Royal Shakespeare Co. 62; Producer, Co-Dir. Royal Shakespeare Theatre; founded Int. Theatre Research Centre, Paris 70, has toured with group in Iran, N. Africa; productions include *Dr. Faustus* 43, *Pygmalion, King John, Lady from the Sea* 45, *Romeo and Juliet* (at Stratford) 47, Dir. of Productions at Covent Garden Opera 49-50, *The Beggar's Opera* (film) 52, *Faust* (at Metropolitan Opera, N.Y.) 53, *The Dark is Light Enough* (in London) 54, *House of Flowers* (in N.Y.) 54, *Cat on a Hot Tin Roof* (in Paris) 56, *Eugene Onegin*

N.Y.) 58, *View from the Bridge* (Paris) 58, *The Fighting ock* (N.Y.) 59, *Moderato Cantabile* (film) 60, *Irma la Douce* 60, *Lord of the Flies* (film) 62, *King Lear* 63, *The Physicists* (N.Y.) 64, *The Marat/Sade* (N.Y.) 65 (film) 6, *US* 66, *Tell Me Lies* (film) 68, *Oedipus* (Seneca) 68, *Midsummer Night's Dream* 70, *King Lear* (film) 71, *The Conference of the Birds* 73, *Timon of Athens* (Paris) 4, *The Ik* (Paris) 75, (London) 76.
Publ. *The Empty Space* 68.
c/o C.I.R.T., 9 rue du Cirque, 75008 Paris, France.

Brook, Sir Robin (Ralph Ellis), Kt., C.M.G., O.B.E.; British business executive; b. 19 June 1908; s. of Francis Brook, F.R.C.S.; m. Helen Knewstub 1937; two .; ed. Eton and Kings Coll., Cambridge.
Military service 41-46, Brig. 45; Dir. Bank of England 6-49; Deputy Chair. British Tourist and Holidays Board 46-50, Colonial Devt. Corpn. 49-53; Chair. London Chamber of Commerce and Industry 66-68, Pres. 68-72; Pres. Asscn. of British Chambers of Commerce 72-74, Conf. of Chambers of Commerce of EEC; Dir. British Petroleum Co. 70-73; Chair. Ionian Bank, Jove Investment Trust, Danae Investment Trust, Leda Investment Trust Ltd., CARCLO Ltd.; Deputy Chair. United City Merchants; Dir. Dimplex Ltd.; mem. Cttee. on Invisible Exports 69-75, mem. ports Council 71-, Chair. 75-; Vice-Chair. City and East London AHA 74-; British Sabre Champion 36; Olympic Games 36, 48; Commdr. Legion of Merit; Legion of Honour; Croix de Guerre and Bar; Order of Leopold (Belgium); Belgian Croix de Guerre.
3 Bryanston Square, London, W.1, England.
Telephone: 01-262-1607.

Brooke, Edward William; American lawyer and politician; b. 26 Oct. 1919; ed. Howard Univ. and Boston Univ.
Admitted to Massachusetts Bar 48; Chair. Finance Comm., Boston 61-62; Attorney-Gen. of Massachusetts 3-67; Senator from Mass. 67-; Fellow, American Bar Asscn., American Acad. of Arts and Sciences; Republican.
Office: Senate Office Building, Washington, D.C.; Home: 535 Beacon Street, Newton Centre, Mass., U.S.A.

Brooke, John; British Chairman of Brooke Bond Liebig Ltd. 68-71; see *The International Who's Who* 975-76.

Brooke of Cumnor, Baron (Life Peer), cr. 66; **Rt. Hon. Henry Brooke,** P.C., C.H.; British politician; b. 9 April 1903, Oxford; s. of Leonard Leslie Brooke and Sybil Diana Brooke; m. Barbara Mathews (Baroness Brooke of Ystradfellte) 1933; two s. two d.; ed. Marlborough Coll. and Balliol Coll., Oxford.
Member of Parl. 38-45, 50-66; Deputy Chair. Southern Railway Co. 46-48; Financial Sec. to Treasury 54-57; Minister of Housing and Local Govt., Minister for Welsh Affairs 57-61, Chief Sec. to Treasury and Paymaster-Gen. 61-62; Home Sec. 62-64; mem. Cen. Housing Advisory Cttee. 44-54, London County Council 5-55, Hampstead Borough Council 36-57; Chair. Marlborough Coll. Council 71-; Chair. Asscn. of Independent Conservative Peers 74-; Conservative.
The Glebe House, Mildenhall, Marlborough, Wilts., England.
Telephone: Marlborough 2769.

Brooker, Robert Elton; American businessman; b. 8 July 1905, Cleveland; s. of Robert and Isadora (Roberts) Brooker; m. Sally Burton Smith 1933; two s.; ed. Univ. of Southern California.
With Southern California Edison Co. 28-34, Firestone Tire and Rubber Co. 34-44, Sears, Roebuck & Co. 4-58; Pres. Whirlpool Corpn. 58-61; Pres. Montgomery Ward & Co. 61-66, Chair. 66-70, Chair. Exec. Cttee. 0-; Chair. Marcor Inc. 68-70, Chair. Exec. Cttee. 70-75;

Dir. Marcor Inc., Montgomery Ward, C.N.A. Income Shares, and North Western Transportation Co.
One First National Plaza, Suite 2656, Chicago, Ill. 60603; Home: 1500 Sheridan Road, Wilmette, Ill. 60091, U.S.A.
Telephone: 312-467-3859 (Office).

Brookes, Rev. Edgar Harry, M.A., D.LITT., LL.D.; South African journalist, writer and ecclesiastic; b. 4 Feb. 1897, Smethwick, England; s. of Job H. Brookes and Emily E. Brookes (née Thomas); m. Heidi G. Bourquin 1925; three s. two d.
Professor of Public Admin. and Political Science Univ. of Pretoria 23-33; Principal, Adams Coll., Natal 34-45; Senator representing Africans of Natal and Zululand in Union Parl. 37-52; mem. Perm. Native Affairs Comm. 45-50; Pres. S.A. Inst. of Race Relations 32-33, 46-48, 59-60; S.A. Del. to L.N. 27, and to UNESCO 47; Prof. of History and Political Science, Univ. of Natal 59-62; Nat. Chair. Liberal Party of South Africa 63-68.
Publs. *History of Native Policy in South Africa* 24, *Native Education in South Africa* 29, *The Colour Problems of South Africa* 33, *The House of Bread* (poems) 44, *The Bantu in South African Life* 46, *South Africa in a Changing World* 53, *The Native Reserves of Natal* 56, *Civil Liberty in South Africa* 58, *The City of God* and *Politics of Crisis* 60, *Power, Law, Right and Love* 63, *A History of Natal* (with C. de B. Webb) 65, *A History of the University of Natal* 67, *Apartheid: A documentary Study of South African Politics* 68, *White Rule in South Africa 1830-1910* 74.
15 Elgarth, St. Patrick's Road, Pietermaritzburg 3201, Natal, South Africa.
Telephone: 22714.

Brookes, Baron (Life Peer) cr. 75 of West Bromwich, West Midlands; **Raymond Percival Brookes,** Kt.; British business executive; b. 10 April 1909, West Bromwich, Staffs.; s. of William Percival Brookes; m. Florence E. Sharman 1937; one s.; ed. West Bromwich School, Kenrick Technical Coll.
Apprenticed as engineer 23; joined GKN as joint Gen. Man. of Carringtons Ltd. 41, subsequently Man. Dir. and Chair.; Chair. GKN Forgings and Castings Ltd.; fmr. Chair. Joseph Sankey and Sons Ltd. (now GKN Sankey Ltd.); Dir. Guest Keen and Nettlefolds Ltd. 53, Deputy Group Man. Dir. 62, Group Man. Dir. 64, Group Chair. and Man. Dir. (subsequently relinquished Man. Directorship) 64, Group Chair. and Chief Exec. 66-75, Life Pres. 75-; part-time mem. British Steel Corpn. 67-68; First Pres. British Mechanical Eng. Confederation 68-70; Vice-Pres. Engineering Employers' Fed. 67-; mem. Council Soc. of Motor Manufacturers and Traders Ltd. 69-, mem. Exec. Cttee. 70-, Pres. 74-; mem. Council CBI 68-, BNEC 69-71, Wilberforce Court of Inquiry into electricity supply industry dispute Jan. 71, Industrial Development Advisory Board 72-75, Management Board UNI-Cardan Group Lohmar, Fed. Repub. of Germany 75-; Dir. BHP-GKN Holdings Ltd. (Australia), GKN Australia Ltd., ATV Network Ltd.; non-Exec. Dir. Plessey Co.; Court of Govs. Univ. of Birmingham 66-75, mem. Council 68-75; Hon. Fellow Inst. of Sales Engineers 73; Pres. Motor Ind. Research Asscn. 73-.
Leisure interests: fly-fishing, golf.
Guest, Keen and Nettlefolds Ltd., GKN House, 22 Kingsway, London, WC2B 6LG, England.
Telephone: 01-242-1616.

Brooks-Randolph, Angie Elizabeth, LL.D.; Liberian laywer and UN official; b. 24 Aug. 1928, Virginia, Montserrado County; m. Isaac Rudolph 1970; two s. (by previous marriage); ed. Shaw Univ., N.C., Howard Univ., Univs. of Wisconsin, London and Liberia.
Counsellor-at-law, Supreme Court of Liberia 53; Asst. Attorney-Gen. 53-58; Asst. Sec. of State 58-71; Prof. of Law, Liberia Univ. 54-58; Vice-Pres. Int. Fed. of

Women Lawyers 56-58, Pres. 64-67; Liberian Del., UN Gen. Assembly 54-; Vice-Chair. Fourth UN Cttee. 56; Vice-Pres. Cttee. on Information from Non-Self-Governing Territories 61; Chair. Fourth Cttee. 61; Chair. UN Comm. for Ruanda-Urundi 62; Chair. of UN Visiting Mission to Trust Territory of Pacific Islands 64; Vice-Pres. Trusteeship Council 65, Pres. 66; Pres. XXIVth Session UN Gen. Assembly 69; Pres. Congress on Adoption and Placement, Milan 71.
c/o United Nations, First Avenue, New York, N.Y., U.S.A.

Brooks, Cleanth, A.B., A.M., B.A., B.LITT., D.LITT., L.H.D.; American university professor; b. 16 Oct. 1906; ed. The McTyeire School, Vanderbilt Univ., Tulane Univ. and Oxford Univ.
Professor of English, Louisiana State Univ. 32-47, Yale Univ. (now Gray Prof. Emer. of Rhetoric) 47-; Man. Editor, later Editor (with Robert Penn Warren) *Southern Review*, Baton Rouge, Louisiana 35-42; Hon. Consultant, Library of Congress 52-62; Cultural Attaché American Embassy, London 64-66; mem. American Acad. of Arts and Sciences, Nat. Inst. of Arts and Letters, American Philosophical Soc.
Publs. *Modern Poetry and the Tradition* 39, *The Well-Wrought Urn* 47; with Robert Penn Warren: *Understanding Poetry* 38, *Understanding Fiction* 43, *Modern Rhetoric* 50; *Literary Criticism: A Short History* (with W. K. Wimsatt, Jr.) 57, *The Hidden God* 63, *William Faulkner: the Yoknapatawpha Country* 63, *A Shaping Joy* 71, *American Literature: the Makers and the Making* (with R. W. B. Lewis and R. P. Warren) 73; Gen. Editor (with David N. Smith) *The Percy Letters*, 10 vols. 42-; Editor: *The Correspondence of Thomas Percy and Richard Farmer* 46.
Forest Road, Northford, Conn., U.S.A.

Brooks, Gwendolyn; American writer; *m.* Henry Blakely; two *c.*; ed. Englewood High School and Wilson Junior Coll.,
Poet Laureate for State of Illinois 68-; Teacher of poetry at Northeastern Illinois State Coll., Columbia Coll., Chicago and Elmhurst Coll.; cited for creative writing by American Acad. of Arts and Letters 46; Guggenheim Fellow 46, 47; Pulitzer Prize for Poetry for *Annie Allen* 50.
Publs. *A Street in Bronzeville* 45, *Annie Allen* 49, *Maud Martha* 53, *Bronzeville Boys and Girls* 56, *The Bean Eaters* 60, *Selected Poems* 63, *In the Mecca* 68, *Riot* 69, *Family Pictures* 70, *Aloneness* 71, *Report From Part One* (autobiography) 72.
7428 South Evans Avenue, Chicago, Ill., U.S.A.

Brooks, Harvey, A.B., PH.D.; American physicist; b. 5 Aug. 1915, Cleveland, Ohio; *s.* of Chester Kingsley Brooks and Elizabeth Brown Brooks; *m.* Helen Gordon Lathrop 1945; one *s.* three *d.*; ed. Yale and Harvard Univs.
Society of Fellows, Harvard Univ. 40-41, Research Assoc. Harvard Underwater Sound Laboratory 42-45; Gordon McKay Prof. of Applied Physics 50-, Dean of Engineering and Applied Physics 57-; Asst. Dir. Ordnance Research Laboratory, Pennsylvania State Univ. 45-46; Assoc. Laboratory Head, Knolls Power Laboratory, Gen. Electric, Schenectady 46-50; Editor-in-Chief *Physics and Chemistry of Solids*; Dir. Raytheon Co.; Chair. Board of Trustees, German Marshall Fund; mem. Board of Trustees, Case Western Reserve Univ., Woods Hole Oceanographic Inst.; Pres. American Acad. of Arts and Sciences; mem. Council on Library Resources, Nat. Acad. of Engineering, Nat. Acad. of Sciences, American Philosophical Soc.; Hon. D.Sc.; Ernest Orlando Lawrence Award 60.
Publs. *The Government of Science* 68; numerous articles in *Physical Review, Nuclear Science and Engineering*, and other scientific journals.

217 Pierce Hall, Harvard University, Cambridge, Mass 02138; Home: 46 Brewster Street, Cambridge, Mass 02138, U.S.A.
Telephone: 868-7600, Ext. 2831 (Office); 354-717° (Home).

Brooks, James; American painter; b. 18 Oct. 1906 St. Louis, Mo.; *s.* of William R. Brooks and Abigai Williamson; *m.* 1st Mary Macdonald 1933, 2nd Char lotte Park 1947; ed. Southern Methodist Univ., Ar Students League, N.Y.C., and with Wallace Harrison Federal Arts Mural Projects 38-42; taught at Columbia and Yale Univs. and at Queens Coll. 47-67; severa one-man shows 49-72; represented in Museum of Moderr Art, Metropolitan Museum, Guggenheim, Whitney Brooklyn, New York; Tate Gallery, London, etc. several shows abroad; retrospective exhbn. Whitney Museum of American Art 63-64, Dallas Museum of Ar 72; Artist in Residence, American Acad. in Rome 63 Prof., Queen's Coll. 68; Guggenheim Fellowship 67-68 Visiting Critic, Univ. of Pennsylvania 71-72, 73 Carnegie Int. Prize 52; Art Inst. of Chicago Prize 57 61; Ford Foundation 62; mem. Nat. Inst. of Arts and Letters, Century Asscn. N.Y.C.
128 Neckpath, Springs, East Hampton, N.Y., U.S.A.

Brooks, John Wood, A.B.; American chemical execu tive; b. 9 Oct. 1917; ed. Groton School and Harvard.
Sales positions in textile industry 39-53; Vice-Pres. Gen. Sales Man., Textile Div., Spring Mills, Inc. 53-54 Gen. Merchandise Man., Textile Div., Celanese Corpn 55, Dir. Fibers Marketing 55-56, Vice-Pres., Gen. Man Fibers Div. 56-59, Exec. Vice-Pres. 60-65, Dir. 61, Pres 65-73, Chief Exec. Officer 68-, Chair. 71-; Dir. ACI Industries Inc., Bankers Trust Co., The Anaconda Co.
Office: 1211 Avenue of the Americas, New York City N.Y. 10036; Home: 363 Cantitoe Road, Bedford Hills N.Y. 10507, U.S.A.

Brooks, Richard; American film writer and director b. 18 May 1912; *m.* Jean Simmons; ed. Temple Univ. Formerly worked for NBC as writer and commentator now directs and writes screenplays for films.
Wrote and directed: *Deadline, U.S.A., Battle Circus Last Hunt, Something of Value, The Brothers Kara mazov, Cat on a Hot Tin Roof, Elmer Gantry* (Acad Award for Screenplay 61), *Sweet Bird of Youth, Lora Jim* (also producer), *In Cold Blood, The Professionals* Directed and collaborated on screenplays of *Last Time I Saw Paris, Blackboard Jungle*; Directed *Take the Higl Ground, Flame and the Flesh, Catered Affair, The Happy Ending, Dollars (The Heist*, U.K.), *Bite The Bullet* Wrote screenplay for *Swell Guy, White Savage, Brute Force, To the Victor, Crossfire*.
Publs. (novels) *Boiling Point, The Producer.*
c/o Metro-Goldwyn-Mayer, 10202 Washington Boule vard, Culver City, Calif. 90230, U.S.A.

Broomberg, Elias; Rhodesian politician; b. 23 Dec 1915, Johannesburg, S. Africa; *m.* Fay Golub 1939 three *s.*; ed. Forest High School, Johannesburg.
Came to Rhodesia 56; Dir. Sentax Weaving Mills (Pvt' Ltd., Trans-Ocean Import Corpn. (Pty.) Ltd., U.D.C (Rhodesia) Ltd. until 74; mem. of Parl. for Bulawayo East; Minister of Commerce and Industry 74-76, ot Information, Immigration and Tourism 76-; Pres. Cen African Textile Mfrs. Asscn. 58-60, 66-69; Nat. Chair Council for the Blind; Chair. Cotlands Babies Sanctuary Johannesburg 46-56, Southern Communal Centre Building Fund 48-56, Co-ordinating Council of Southern Suburbs Vigilance Asscns. 54-56, Queenshaven Corona tion Foundation 55-56; mem. Hosp. Board, S. Rand Hosp., Johannesburg 56; Chair. King George VI Rehabilitation Centre for Blind and Physically Handi capped Children; Vice-Pres. Rhodesia Soc. for the Blind

and Physically Handicapped; Pres. Lions Club of Bulawayo.
Ministry of Information, Immigration and Tourism, Salisbury; Home: 234 Selborne Avenue, Suburbs, Bulawayo, Rhodesia.

Broome, David, O.B.E.; British farmer and professional show jumper; b. 1 March 1940, Cardiff; *s.* of Fred and Amelia Broome; ed. Monmouth Grammar School for Boys.
European Show Jumping Champion, riding Sunsalve, Aachen 61, riding Mr. Softee, Rotterdam 67 and Hickstead 69; World Champion, riding Beethoven, La Baule (France) 70; Professional Champion of World, riding Sportsman and Philco, Cardiff 74; Master of Foxhounds.
Leisure interests: hunting, shooting, golf.
Publ. *Jump-Off* 70.
Mount Ballan Manor, Crick, Newport, Gwent, Wales, United Kingdom.
Telephone: Caldicot 420777.

Brophy, Brigid, F.R.S.L.; British novelist and critic; b. 12 June 1929, London; *d.* of late author John Brophy and Charis (Grundy); *m.* Michael Levey (*q.v.*) 1954; one *d.*; ed. St. Paul's Girls' School, London, and St. Hugh's Coll., Oxford.
Founder mem. Writers' Action Group 72; Exec. Councillor Writers' Guild of Great Britain 75.
Publs. *Hackenfeller's Ape* 53, *The King of a Rainy Country* 56, *Black Ship to Hell* (non-fiction) 62, *Flesh* 62, *The Finishing Touch* 63, *The Snow Ball* 64, *Mozart the Dramatist* (non-fiction) 64, *The Waste Disposal Unit* (play) 65, *Don't Never Forget* (non-fiction) 66, *The Burglar* (play) 67, published with preface 68, *Black and White, A Portrait of Aubrey Beardsley* (non-fiction) 68, *In Transit* 69, *Prancing Novelist* (non-fiction) 73, *The Adventures of God in His Search for the Black Girl* 73, *Pussy Owl* 76, *Beardsley and his World* (non-fiction) 76.
Flat 3, 185 Old Brompton Road, London, S.W.5, England.

Brophy, Theodore F., B.A., LL.B.; American business executive; b. 4 April 1923, New York; *m.* Sallie M. Showalter; two *c.*; ed. Yale Univ. and Harvard Univ. Law School.
Associate, law firm of Root, Ballantine, Harlan, Bushby & Palmer 50-55; Gen. Counsel, The Lummus Co. 55-58; Gen. Telephone and Electronics Corpn., Counsel 58-59, Vice-Pres. and Gen. Counsel 59-68, Exec. Vice-Pres. and Gen. Counsel 68-69, Dir. 69-72, Pres. 72-; mem. American Bar Asscn. and Past Chair. Public Utility Law Section; mem. Asscn. of the Bar N.Y.C., N.Y. State Bar Asscn. and Fed. Communications Bar Asscn.; Public mem. Admin. Conf. of the U.S. 70-.
One Stamford Forum, Stamford, Conn. 06940; and 730 Third Avenue, New York, N.Y. 10017, U.S.A.
Telephone: 212-551-1581, 551-1121.

Brosio, Manlio, LL.D.; Italian lawyer and diplomatist; b. 10 July 1897; *s.* of Edoardo and Fortunata Curadelli; *m.* Clotilde Brosio 1936; ed. Turin Univ.
Commenced practising law 20; joined political anti-Fascist movement "Rivoluzione Liberale"; collaborated in publications 19-26; political sec. of movement; mem. opposition cttee. against Fascism 24-26; mem. Cttee. of Nat. Liberation, Rome 43-44; Sec. Italian Liberal Party; Minister without Portfolio, Vice-Pres. of Council and Minister of War 45-46; Italian Amb. to U.S.S.R. 47-52, to Great Britain 52-54, to U.S.A. 55-61, to France 61-64; Sec.-Gen. North Atlantic Treaty Org. (NATO) 64-71; retd. 71; Senator of the Repub. for Turin (Liberal) 72-.
Office: Senate of the Republic, Palazzo Madama, Rome; Home: Corso Re Umberto 29 *bis*, 10128 Turin, Italy.
Telephone: 532441-548597.

Brost, Erich Eduard; German publisher and journalist; b. 29 Oct. 1903; ed. St. Peter and St. Paul's High School, Danzig.
Editor *Danziger Volksstimme* 24-36; journalist in Poland, Sweden, Finland and Great Britain 36-45, in Essen and Berlin 45-48; Publisher *Westdeutsche Allgemeine Zeitung*, Essen 48-.
36-38 Friedrichstr., 43 Essen, Federal Republic of Germany.
Telephone: Essen 20641.

Broström, Dan-Axel; Swedish shipowner; b. 17 May 1915.
Director Ångfartygs AB Tirfing, Ferm Steamship Co., Swedish American Line, Swedish East Asia Co. Ltd., Swedish Orient Line, Gothenburg Towing and Salvage Co., Neptun Salvage Co., Skandinaviska Enskilda Banken, Atlantica Insurance Co., Swedish Shipowners Insurance Asscn., Lloyd's Register of Shipping, Swedish Cttee.
Office: Broströmia, Box 2521, 403 17 Gothenburg 2; Home: Viktor Rydbergsgatan 16, 411 32 Gothenburg, Sweden.

Brouillet, René Alexis, K.C.V.O.; French diplomatist and civil servant; b. 9 May 1909, Cleppé; *s.* of Antonin Brouillet and Marie Legay; *m.* Noëlle Dibsky 1939; one *s.* four *d.*; ed. Lycée St. Etienne, Lycée Louis-le-Grand, Ecole Normale Supérieure, Ecole des Sciences Politiques.
Asst., Inst. Scientifique de Recherches Economiques et Sociales 35; Sec.-Gen. Centre Polytechnicien d'Etudes Economiques 36; Auditeur, Cour des Comptes 37; Chef Adjoint du Cabinet of Pres. of Senate 39-40; Dir. Juridical Service, Secretariat of State for Industrial Production 41-42; Conseiller Référendaire, Cour des Comptes 43; Dir. du Cabinet of Georges Bidault when Pres. Conseil Nat. de la Résistance 43-44; Dir. Adjoint du Cabinet, Gen. de Gaulle 44-46; mem. Council of Admin. Ecole Nat. d'Administration 45; Sec.-Gen. Tunisian Govt. 46-50; 1st Counsellor French Embassy Berne 50-53; Dir. Adjoint du Cabinet, Ministry of Foreign Affairs (Bidault) 53; 1st Counsellor French Embassy, Vatican 53-58; Sec.-Gen. to President of Council for Algerian Affairs June 58; Dir. du Cabinet, Gen. de Gaulle Jan 59-61; Ambassador to Austria 61-63, to Vatican 63-73; promoted to the rank of Ambassadeur de France 69; mem. Conseil Constitutionnel 74; Grand Officier de la Légion d'Honneur, Grand Cross of the Order of Pius IX, Grand Cross Order of Merit of the Austrian Repub.
Leisure interests: history, literature and public law.
77 rue Claude Bernard, Paris 5e; and Cleppé (Loire), France.

Brousse, Pierre; French politician; b. 1926, Limoges, Haute Vienne; *m.* Edmée Nouchy 1954; ed. Lycée de Tulle, Corrèze, Institut d'Etudes Politiques, Paris and Univ. of Paris.
President, Radical Students Group 49; Ministry of Industry 54-56; Pres., Young Radicals Group 56-58; Joint Sec.-Gen. Radical Party 58-61, Sec.-Gen. 61-69; mem. and Délégué général, Fédération de la gauche démocrate et socialiste 66-; Mayor of Béziers 67-; Gen. Counsellor of Hérault 67-; Senator for Hérault 68-; Vice-Pres. Radical Party 69-71.
6 rue Ernest Psichari, Paris 7e; 1 Impasse Baudin, Béziers, France.

Brouwenstyn, Gerarda; Netherlands opera singer.
Studied in Amsterdam; joined the Amsterdam opera and subsequently became First Soprano; has appeared in London, Berlin, Stuttgart, Brussels, Copenhagen, Paris, Vienna, Bayreuth, Barcelona, Buenos Aires, etc.; repertoire includes *Forza del Destino, Tosca, Aida, Othello, Un Ballo in Maschera, Tannhäuser, Walküre,*

Meistersinger, Le Nozze di Figaro, Jenufa, Troubadour, Cavalleria Rusticana, Don Carlos, etc.; Order of Orange-Nassau.
3 Bachplein, Amsterdam, Netherlands.

Brouwer, Luitzen Egbertus Jan; Netherlands oil executive; b. 1 July 1910, Amsterdam; *m.* Maria F. Rueb 1938; ed. Technische Hogeschool te Delft.
Royal Dutch/Shell Group 31-, assignments in Germany, Indonesia and Egypt; Mil. Service 40-46; assignments with Royal Dutch/Shell Group in U.S.A. and Netherlands; co-ordinator for exploration and production in Netherlands 51-; Gen. Man. Dir. Iranian Oil Exploration & Producing Co. and Iranian Oil Refining Co., Teheran 54; Man. Dir. Royal Dutch Petroleum Co. 56, Pres. 65-71, Dir. 71-; Principal Dir. Shell Petroleum N.V. 56-71, mem. Board of Dirs. 71-; Man. Dir. Shell Petroleum Co. Ltd. 56-71, Dir. 71-; Chair. Shell Canada; Dir. Shell Oil Co. 65-71; Dir. Algemene Bank Nederland N.V. (Amsterdam) 71-, Bos Kalis Westminster Dredging Group N.V. (Papendrecht) 72-, N.V. Petroleum Maatschappij Moeara Enim (Amsterdam) 72-, Naarden Int. N.V. 72-, N.V. Ned. Scheepvaart Unie (Rijswijk) 72-; Knight Order of Netherlands Lion; Officer and Commdr. Order of Orange-Nassau; Officer Légion d'Honneur 72.
N.V. Koninklijke Nederlandsche Petroleum Maatschappij, Carel van Bylandtlaan 30, The Hague, Netherlands.

Brouwers, Gerard; Netherlands civil servant; b. 2 Aug. 1908, Flushing; *m.* Johanna Montagne 1937; one *s.* two *d.*; ed. Rotterdam School of Economics.
Assistant Sec. to Econ. Council in Netherlands 33-37; Head, Planning Dept., Ministry of Econ. Affairs 37-39; Head, Price Policy Dept., Ministry of Econ. Affairs, later Head of Secretariat, Ministry of Econ. Affairs; Dir.-Gen. of Prices 45-49; Sec.-Gen. Ministry of Econ. Affairs 49-; Pres. of Chamber of Commerce and Industry of The Hague; mem. Board of Dirs. Royal Netherlands Blast Furnaces and Steelworks Ltd.; numerous decorations.
Leisure interests: literature, sailing.
70 Bloemcamplaan, Wassenaar, Netherlands.

Brovka, Pyotr Ustinovich; Soviet poet; b. 25 June 1905, Putilkovichi, Byelorussia; *s.* of Ustin Adamovich and Elena Stepanovna Brovka; *m.* Elena Michajlovna Brovka 1932; one *s.*; ed. Byelorussian State Univ.
Corresponding mem. Acad. of Sciences of Byelorussian S.S.R. 53-66, Academician 66-; mem. C.P.S.U. 40-; Deputy to Supreme Soviet of U.S.S.R., mem. U.S.S.R. Parl. Group Supreme Soviet; mem. Board and Sec. U.S.S.R. Union of Writers; Editor-in-Chief *Byelorussian Soviet Encyclopaedia* 67-; People's Writer of Byelorussian S.S.R. 62-; mem. Central Cttee. of C.P. of Byelorussia; State Prize (twice); Lenin Prize; Hero of Socialist Labour; Order of Lenin (four times); Hammer and Sickle Gold Medal; Badge of Honour; Red Star; Order of October Revolution; Order of Kiril and Mefodij (Bulgaria); Order of People's Friendship.
Leisure interests: floriculture, mushrooms.
Publs. *Hero's Arrival* 35, *Spring of the Homeland* 37, *Byelorus* 43, *Bread* 46, *Road of Life* 50, *The Days Go By* 62, *Collected Works* (4 Vols.) 67, *Among Red Mountain Ashes* 69, *Welcome* 72, *Both in the Day-Time and at Night* 74.
Karl Marx Street 30-4, Minsk 30, Byelorussia, U.S.S.R.
Telephone: 22-27-50.

Browaldh, Tore, B.A., LL.M., DR.ENG.; Swedish banker; b. 23 Aug. 1917, Vaesteraas; *s.* of Ernfrid and Ingrid (née Gezelius) Browaldh; *m.* Gunnel Ericson 1942; three *s.* one *d.*
Financial Attaché Swedish Legation, Washington, D.C. 43; Asst. Sec. The Swedish Royal Cttee. of Post-

War Econ. Planning 44-45; Admin. Sec. the Swedish Industrial Inst. for Econ. and Social Research; 44-45; Sec. to Board of Management, Svenska Handelsbanken 46-49, Chief Gen. Man. 55-66, Chair. March 66-; Dir. Econ., Social, Cultural and Refugee Dept., Sec.-Gen. Council of Europe 49-51; Exec. Vice-Pres. Confed. of Swedish Employers 51-54; mem. Board Swedish Bankers Asscn., Chair. 59-61; Chair. AB Industrivärden Svenska Cellulosa AB, Swedish Esso AB, Esso Chemical AB, Ahlén and Holm AB; Deputy Chair. Nobel Foundation, Swedish IBM; Dir. AB Volvo, AB Graenges Essem, Swedish Unilever AB, Skandia Insurance Co., etc.; mem. Board Dag Hammarskjöld Foundation 61-63, Swedish Govt. Research Advisory Board 66-70, Swedish Govt. Industrial Policy Comm. 68-70, Swedish Govt. Econ. Planning Comm. 62-; Special Adviser to Int. Fed. of Insts. for Advanced Studies; mem. UN Group to Study Multinational Corpns.; mem. Swedish Acad. of Engineering Sciences, Royal Acad. of Arts and Sciences, Uppsala; St. Erik Medal, Commdr. Order of Vasa.
Publ. *Management and Society* 61.
Svenska Handelsbanken, Arsenalsgatan 11, S-103 28 Stockholm; Home: Skeppargatan 66, 114 59 Stockholm, Sweden.
Telephone: 08-61 96 43.

Brower, Charles Hendrickson; American retd. advertising executive; b. 13 Nov. 1901; *s.* of Charles H. Brower and Mary Hendrickson Brower; *m.* Mary Elizabeth Nelson 1930; two *s.* one *d.*; ed. Rutgers Univ.
Teacher, Bound Brook High School, New Jersey 25-26; Writer, Batten, Barton, Durstine and Osborn, New York 28-40, Vice-Pres. and Dir. 40-46, Exec. Vice-Pres. (Creative Services) 46, mem. Exec. Cttee. 51-70, Gen. Man. and Vice-Chair. Exec. Cttee. 57, Pres. and Chair. Exec. Cttee. 57-64, Chair. of Board, Chief Exec. Officer 64-67, Chair. Exec. Cttee. 64-70; mem. Board of Trustees Rutgers Univ. 46-, Chair. Board of Govs. 62-71; Hon. L.H.D., Pace Coll. 52, Hon. LL.D., Monmouth Coll. 65, Rutgers Univ. 66.
914 Cole Drive, Brielle, N.J. 08730, U.S.A.
Telephone: (201) 528-5327.

Brown, Baron (Life Peer), cr. 64, of Machrihanish; **Wilfred Banks Duncan Brown,** P.C., M.B.E.; British business executive and politician; b. 29 Nov. 1908, Greenock, Scotland; *s.* of Peter Brown and Emily J. Brown; *m.* Marjorie Hershel Skinner 1939; three *s.*; ed. Rossall School.
With Glacier Metal Co. Ltd. 31-65, Man. Dir. and Chair. 39-65; Dir. Associated Engineering Ltd. 64-65; Chair. Docks Modernization Cttee. 65-68; Minister of State, Board of Trade 65-70; Fellow British Inst. of Management; mem. Int. Acad. of Management; mem. Industrial Devt. Advisory Board 75; Chair. Machine Tool Advisory Board; Pro-Chancellor Brunel Univ.; Hon. D.Tech. (Brunel Univ.), Hon. LL.D. (Univ. of Southern Illinois, U.S.A.), Hon. D.Sc. (Cranfield Inst. of Technology).
Leisure interests: golf, tennis, writing on organization.
Publs. *Managers, Men and Morale* (with Mrs. W. Raphael) 47, *Exploration in Management* 60, *Piecework Abandoned* 62, *Product Analysis Pricing* (with Dr. E. Jaques) 64, *Glacier Project Papers* (with Dr. E. Jaques) 65, *Organization* 71, *The Earnings Conflict* 73.
23 Prince Albert Road, London, NW1 7ST, England.
Telephone: 01-722-8040.

Brown, Sir Allen Stanley, Kt., C.B.E., M.A., LL.M.; Australian diplomatist; b. 3 July 1911; ed. Wesley Coll., Melbourne, and Queen's Coll., Univ. of Melbourne.
Director-General of Post-War Reconstruction 48; Sec. Prime Minister's Dept. and Sec. to Cabinet 49-58; Deputy High Commr. for Australia in U.K. 58-65; Amb. to Japan 65-70; Australian Commr. British Phosphate Commrs. and Christmas Island Phosphate

Comm. 70-; Vice-Pres. European Launcher Devt. Org. 64-65.
3 Devorgilla Avenue, Toorak 3142; 515 Collins Street, Melbourne 3000, Australia.

Brown, Sir David, Kt., M.I.A.E., M.I.MECH.E.; British engineer and business exec.; b. 1904; s. of Frank and Caroline Brown; m. 1st Daisie M. Firth 1926 (dissolved 1955), one s. one d.; m. 2nd Marjorie Deans 1955; ed. Rossall School, private tuition, and Huddersfield Technical Coll.
David Brown and Sons (Huddersfield) Ltd. 21, Dir. 29-32, Managing Dir. 32; founder David Brown Tractors Ltd. 35; Chair. David Brown Holdings 51-; Chair. Vosper Thorneycroft, David Brown-Vosper (Offshore) Ltd.; Dir. David Brown Gear Industries Ltd., Richardson, David Brown Ltd., Australia; underwriting mem. Lloyd's; past mem. Board of Govs. Huddersfield Royal Infirmary, Council of Huddersfield Chamber of Commerce.
Leisure interests: hunting, yachting, tennis.
32 Curzon Street, London, W1Y 8BH; Chequers Manor, Cadmore End, nr. High Wycombe, Bucks., England.
Telephone: 01-629-7373 (Office); High Wycombe 881282 (Home).

Brown, Edmund Gerald (Pat), LL.B.; American lawyer and politician; b. 21 April 1905; ed. Lowell High School, San Francisco, Univ. of California Extension Division, San Francisco Coll. of Law.
Admitted to bar 27; asst. and successor to Milton L. Schmitt; District Attorney, San Francisco 43; Attorney General, California 50, re-elected on nomination of both Democratic and Republican parties 54; Gov. of California 59-66; Chair. Nat. Comm. on Reform of Criminal Laws 67-; Vice-Pres. N.Y. Board of Trade; Democrat.
San Francisco, Calif., U.S.A.

Brown, Edmund G., Jr., A.B., J.D.; American lawyer and politician; b. 7 July 1938, San Francisco; s. of Edmund G. Brown (q.v.) and Bernice Brown; ed. Univ. of Calif. at Berkeley, Yale Law School.
Research Attorney, Calif. Supreme Court 64-65, Attorney, L.A. 66-69; Sec. of State, Calif. 71-74, Gov. 75-.
Governor's Office, State Capital, Sacramento, California 95814, U.S.A.

Brown, Ernest Henry Phelps, M.B.E., M.A., F.B.A.; British economist; b. 10 Feb. 1906, Calne, Wilts; s. of Edgar W. Brown and Ada L. Bibbing; m. Dorothy E. M. Bowlby 1932; two s. one d.; ed. Taunton School, Wadham Coll., Oxford.
Fellow of New Coll., Oxford 30-47; Rockefeller Travelling Fellow in U.S.A. 30-31; served with Royal Artillery 39-45; Prof. of Econs. of Labour, Univ. of London 47-68; mem. Council on Prices, Productivity and Incomes 59, Nat. Econ. Devt. Council 62-66, Royal Comm. on the Distribution of Income and Wealth 74-.
Leisure interests: walking, gardening.
Publs. *The Framework of the Pricing System* 36, *A Course in Applied Economics* 51, *The Balloon* (novel) 53, *The Growth of British Industrial Relations* 59, *The Economics of Labour* 62, *A Century of Pay* 68.
16 Bradmore Road, Oxford, OX2 6QP, England.
Telephone: Oxford 56320.

Brown, Sir (Frederick Herbert) Stanley, Kt., C.B.E., B.SC., C.ENG., F.I.MECH.E., F.I.E.E.; British electrical engineer; b. 9 Dec. 1910; ed. King Edward School and Birmingham Univ.
Birmingham Electric Supply Dept. 32-46; W. Midlands Jt. Electricity Authority 46-47; Liverpool Corpn. Electric Supply Dept. 47-48; British Electricity Authority 48-54; Generation Design Engineer, Central Electricity Authority 54-57, Chief Engineer 57; mem. for Engineering, Central Electricity Generating Board

57-59, Deputy Chair. 59-64, Chair. 65-72; Pres. Inst. of Electrical Engineers 67-68; Hon. D.Sc.
Cobbler's Hill, Compton Abdale, Cheltenham, Glos., GL54 4DR, England.

Brown, Gen. George Scratchley, B.S.; American air force officer; b. 17 Aug. 1918, Montclair, N.J.; s. of Thoburn Kay Brown and Frances Scratchley Brown; m. Alice Colhoun Brown 1942; two s. one d.; ed. U.S. Mil. Acad., West Point, Nat. War Coll., Washington, D.C.
Commissioned Second Lieut., U.S. Army Air Force 41, Col. 44, Brig.-Gen. 62, Maj.-Gen. 64, Lieut.-Gen. 66, Gen. 68; leader of Ploesti raid on oil fields in Romania 44; various troop carrier air defence and training command assignments 46-56; Exec. to Chief of Staff, U.S.A.F. 57-59; Mil. Asst. to Deputy Sec. and Sec. of Defense 59-63; Commdr. Eastern Transport Air Force 63-64; Commdr. Joint Task Force II, Sandia Base, N. Mexico 64-66; Asst. to Chair., Joint Chiefs of Staff 66-68; Commdr. 7th Air Force, Deputy Commdr. Air Operations, U.S. Forces in Viet-Nam 68-70; Commdr. Air Force Systems Command 70-73; Chief of Staff of U.S. Air Force 73-74; Chair. Joint Chiefs of Staff 74-; Distinguished Service Cross, Distinguished Service Medal with Three Oak Leaf Clusters, Silver Star, Legion of Merit with Two Oak Leaf Clusters, Distinguished Flying Cross with One Oak Leaf Cluster, Distinguished Flying Cross (U.K.), Croix de Guerre avec Palme (France), Order of Mil. Merit EULJI (Korea), Nat. Order of Viet-Nam, Third Class, Vietnamese Air Force Distinguished Service Order, First Class, and many others.
Leisure interests: tennis, fishing, woodwork.
Pentagon, Washington, D.C. 20301; Home: Quarters 6, Fort Myer, Va. 22211, U.S.A.
Telephone: (202) 697-9121 (Office); (703) 524-7361 (Home).

Brown, Harold, PH.D.; American physicist; b. 19 Sept. 1927; ed. New York City public schools and Columbia Univ.
Lecturer in Physics, Columbia Univ. 47-50, Stevens Inst. of Technology 49-50; Univ. of California Radiation Laboratory, Berkeley 50-52; Livermore Radiation Laboratory 52-61, Group Leader 53, Div. Leader 55, Assoc. Dir. 58, Deputy Dir. 59, Dir. 60-61; mem. Polaris Steering Cttee., Dept. of Defense 56-58; Consultant to Air Force Scientific Advisory Board 56-57; mem. Scientific Advisory Cttee. on Ballistic Missiles to Sec. of Defense 58-61; mem. President's Science Advisory Cttee. 61; Dir. of Air Force 65-69; Pres. California Inst. of Technology 69-; mem. U.S. Del. to Strategic Arms Limitation Talks 69-; Hon. D.Eng. (Stevens Inst. of Technology), Hon. LL.D. (Long Island Univ., Gettysburg Coll., Univ. of California).
415 South Hill Avenue, Pasadena, Calif. 91106, U.S.A.

Brown, Harrison (Scott), B.S., PH.D.; American professor of chemistry, educator and writer; b. 26 Sept. 1917, Sheridan, Wyo.; s. of late Harrison Harvey Brown and late Agatha Scott; m. Rudd Owen 1949; one s.; ed. Univ. of Calif., Berkeley, and Johns Hopkins Univ.
Instructor in Chem., Johns Hopkins Univ. 41-42; Research Assoc., Chem., Univ. of Chicago 42-43; Asst. Dir. Chem. Div., Clinton Labs., Oak Ridge 43-46; Asst. Prof. of Chem., Inst. for Nuclear Studies, Univ. of Chicago 46-48; Assoc. Prof. 48-51; Prof. of Geochem., Calif. Inst. of Technology 51-, and of Science and Govt. 67-; mem. Nat. Acad. of Sciences 55-, Foreign Sec. 62-; American Asscn. for Advancement of Science Award 47; American Chemical Soc. Award 52; Lasker Award 58. Carnegie-Mellon Award 71.
Leisure interest: music.
Publs. *Must Destruction Be Our Destiny?* 46, *The*

Challenge of Man's Future 54, *The Next Hundred Years* (with Bonner and Weir) 57, *The Next Ninety Years* (with Bonner and Weir) 67, *The Cassiopeia Affair* (with Zerwick) 68.
Office: Division of Humanities and Social Sciences, California Institute of Technology, Pasadena, Calif. 91109; Home: 623 East California Boulevard, Pasadena, Calif. 91106, U.S.A.
Telephone: 213-795-6841, Ext. 1074 (Office); 213-792-9474 (Home).

Brown, Herbert Charles, PH.D., D.SC.; American (naturalized 1935) professor of chemistry; b. 22 May 1912, London, England; s. of Charles Brown and Pearl Stine; m. Sarah Baylen 1937; one s.; ed. Wright Junior Coll., Chicago and Univ. of Chicago.
Eli Lilly Post-doctorate Fellow, Univ. of Chicago 38-39, Instructor 39-43; Asst. Prof. and Assoc. Prof. Wayne Univ. 43-47; Prof. Purdue Univ. 47-59, R. B. Wetherill Research Prof. 59-; mem. Board of Govs., Hebrew Univ., Jerusalem; Harrison Howe Lecturer 53; Centenary Lecturer, Chem. Soc. London 55; mem. Nat. Acad. of Sciences, American Acad. of Arts and Sciences; Nichols Medal 59, American Chem. Soc. Award 60, S.O.C.M.A. Medal 60, Linus Pauling Medal 68, Nat. Medal of Science 69, Roger Adams Medal 71, Chandler Medal 73; Madison Marshall Award 75; CCNY Scientific Achievement Award Medal 76; Hon. D.Sc. (Chicago).
Leisure interest: travel.
Publs. *Hydroboration* 62, *Boranes in Organic Chemistry* 72, *Organic Syntheses via Boranes* 75; many articles in professional journals.
Department of Chemistry, Purdue University, Lafayette, Ind. 47907; Home: 1840 Garden Street, West Lafayette, Ind. 47906, U.S.A.
Telephone: 317-494-8765 (Office); 317-463-5651 (Home).

Brown, Sir John Douglas Keith, Kt.; British chartered accountant and company director; b. 8 Sept. 1913, North Shields, Tynemouth; s. of Ralph D. Brown and Rhoda M. Keith; m. Margaret Eleanor Burnet 1940; two s.; ed. Glasgow Acad.
Joined Lovelock & Lewes, Chartered Accountants, Calcutta 37, Partner 46-49; Man. Dir. Jardine Henderson Ltd., Calcutta 49, Chair. 57-63; Pres. Bengal Chamber of Commerce and Industry and Associated Chambers of Commerce of India 58-60; Dir. Industrial Credit and Investment Corpn. of India Ltd. and Chair. Indian Oxygen Ltd. for six years; fmr. Chair. India Cable Co. Ltd.; mem. (Indian) Central Excise Reorganization Cttee. 60-63; Govt. of India Company Law Advisory Cttee. and Capital Issued Advisory Cttee. 58-63; Exec. Dir. McLeod Russel & Co. Ltd. 63, Chair. 72-; Chair. Samnuggur Jute Factory Co. Ltd. 68-, Robb Caledon Shipbuilders Ltd. 68-.
Leisure interests: gardening, golf, walking.
Windover, Whitmore Vale Road, Hindhead, Surrey, England.

Brown, Sir John Gilbert Newton, Kt., C.B.E.; British publisher; b. 7 July 1916, London; s. of John Brown and Molly Purchas; m. Virginia Braddell 1946; one s. two d.; ed. Lancing Coll., Hertford Coll., Oxford.
Manager O.U.P., Bombay 37-40, London 46-49; Sales Man. 49-55, Deputy Publr. 55, Publr. Gen. Div. 56-, Deputy Sec. 74-; served Royal Artillery 40-41, Japanese P.O.W. 42-45; Dir. Harlequin Enterprises Ltd., Toronto; mem. Publrs. Asscn., Pres. 63-65, mem. Board British Library; Prof. Fellow of Hertford Coll., Oxon.; Joint Treas. Royal Literary Fund.
Leisure interest: gardening.
Oxford University Press, 37 Dover Street, London, W1X 4AH; Home: 3 Alma Terrace, Allen Street, London, W8 6QY, England.
Telephone: 01-629-8494 (Office); 01-937-3779 (Home).

Brown, L. Dean; American diplomatist; b. 1920, U.S.A.; s. of Lewis P. Brown and Elizabeth Crossley; m. June Vereker Farquhar 1942; one s.; ed. Wesleyan Univ. and Imperial Defence Coll., London.
Served in U.S. Army 42-46; joined U.S. Foreign Service 46; postings to Congo, Canada, France, U.K., Morocco, Senegal; Amb. to Senegal and The Gambia 67-70, to Jordan 70-73; Deputy Under-Sec. of State for Management 73-.
c/o Department of State, Washington, D.C. 20520, U.S.A.

Brown, Mervyn, C.M.G., O.B.E., M.A.(OXON.); British diplomatist; b. 24 Sept. 1923, Durham; s. of William Brown and Edna Penman; m. Elizabeth Gittings 1949; ed. Ryhope Grammar School, Sunderland and St. John's Coll., Oxford.
Third Sec., Foreign Office 49-50; Buenos Aires 50-53; Second Sec., New York 53-56; First Sec., Foreign Office 56-59; Singapore 59-60; Vientiane 60-63; Foreign Office 63-67; Amb. to Madagascar 67-70; Diplomatic Service Inspector 70-72; Head of Communications Operations Dept., Foreign and Commonwealth Office 73-74, Dir. of Communications 74; High Commr. in Tanzania 75-, concurrently Amb. to Madagascar 76-.
Leisure interests: music, history, tennis.
British High Commission, P.O. Box 9200, Dar es Salaam, Tanzania.

Brown, Peter McKenzie; South African politician; b. 1924; ed. Michaelhouse, Cambridge Univ. and Univ. of Cape Town.
Natal Health Comm. 51; organized inter-racial discussion group which became South African Liberal Asscn.; mem. Liberal Party 53-64, Deputy Nat. Chair. 57-59, Nat. Chair. 59-64; detained under State of Emergency March-June 60; confined to Magisterial District of Pietermaritzburg since 64.
268 Longmarket Street, Pietermaritzburg, Natal, South Africa.

Brown, Roger William, M.A., PH.D.; American professor of social psychology; b. 14 April 1925; s. of Frank H. Brown and Muriel L. Brown; ed. Univ. of Mich.
Assistant Prof. Social Psychology, Harvard Univ. 52-57; Assoc. Prof. of Social Psychology, Mass. Inst. of Technology, Prof. of Social Psychology 60-62; Prof. of Social Psychology, Harvard Univ. 62-; mem. Nat. Acad. of Sciences; Hon. Doctorate York Univ., England.
Publs. *Words and Things*, 58 *The Acquisition of Language* 64, *Social Psychology* 65, *Psycholinguistics* 70, *A First Language* 73, *Psychology* (with R. Herristein) 75.
1270 William James Hall, Harvard University, Cambridge, Mass. 02138; Home: 100 Memorial Drive, Cambridge, Mass. 02142, U.S.A.

Brown, Sir Stephen, K.B.E.; British engineer; b. 15 Feb. 1906, Lincoln; s. of Arthur Mogg Brown and Ada Kelk (née Upton); m. Margaret Alexandra McArthur 1935; one s. one d.; ed. Taunton School and Bristol Univ.
Joined J. Stone & Co. Ltd. 32, Dir. 45-51; Man. Dir. J. Stone & Co. (Deptford) Ltd. 51, Chair. 56-59; Joint Man. Dir. J. Stone & Co. (Holdings) Ltd. 58, Chair. 59-66; Divisional Dir. Stone-Platt Industries Ltd. 58-59, Deputy Chair. 65, Chair. May 68-; Dir. Chloride Electrical Storage Co. Ltd. 55, Deputy Chair. 65; Chair. Molins Ltd. 71-; Dir. The Fairey Co. Ltd. 71-, Porvair Ltd. 71-; Pres. Engineering Employers Fed. 64-65; Deputy Pres. Confederation of British Industry Aug. 65, Pres. Sept. 66-May 68; Founder-mem. Export Council for Europe 60, Deputy Chair. Sept. 62-Dec. 63; Hon. D.Sc. (Univ. of Aston).
Leisure interests: shooting, fishing, golf.

Stone-Platt Industries Ltd., 25 St. James's Street, London, S.W.1; Coombe House, Bolney, Sussex, England.
Telephone: 01-930-9683 (Office); 0444-82-202 (Home).

Brown, Winthrop Gilman, B.A., LL.B.; American retd. government official and diplomatist; b. 12 July 1907; ed. St. Paul's School, Concord, Yale Univ. and Yale Law School.
Private law practice 32-41; Lend Lease Admin. 41; Exec. Officer Harriman Mission, U.S. Embassy, London 41-45; State Dept. Trade Policy posts 45-52; Economic Affairs U.S. Embassy, London 52-57; Minister-Counsellor, New Delhi 57-60; Amb. to Laos 60-62; Deputy Commdt. for Foreign Affairs, Nat. War Coll. 62-64; Amb. to Repub. of Korea 64-67; Special Asst. to Sec. of State for Liaison with Governors 67-72; Deputy Asst. Sec. of State, East Asian and Pacific Affairs 68-72; State Dept. Meritorious and Superior Service and Distinguished Honor Awards; President's Medal for Distinguished Federal Civilian Service.
Leisure interest: golf.
2435 Tracy Place, N.W., Washington, D.C., U.S.A.
Telephone: 483-2435.

Browne, Sir (Edward) Humphrey, Kt., C.B.E.; British business executive; b. 7 April 1911, Astley, Warwicks.; s. of James T. Browne and Ethel Mary (née Hills); m. Barbara Stone 1934; (died 1970) two s.; ed. Repton School, Magdalene Coll., Cambridge, and Birmingham Univ.
Former Manager, Chanters Colliery; Dir. and Chief Mining Engineer Manchester Collieries Ltd. 43-46; Production Dir. North Western Div. Coal Board 47-48; Dir.-Gen. of Production, National Coal Board 48-55; Chair. W. Midlands Div., Nat. Coal Board 55-60; Dep. Chair. Nat. Coal Board 60-67; Chair. John Thompson 67-70; Chair. Woodhall Duckham Ltd. 70-73; Chair. British Transport Docks Board 71-; Pres. British Coal Utilization Research Council 63-67; Chair. Bestobell Ltd. 73-; Dir. Haden Carrier Ltd. 73-; Pro-Chancellor Keele Univ. 71-75; mem. Commonwealth Devt. Corpn. 64-73.
Leisure interests: music, shooting.
Beckbury Hall, Shifnal, Shropshire; and 31 Dorset House, Gloucester Place, London, N.W.1, England.
Telephone: Ryton 207 and 01-935-8958.

Browne, Secor D.; American engineer, aviation specialist and government official; b. 22 July 1916, Chicago, Ill.; ed. Harvard Univ.
Former Dir. Colonial Equities Inc., Nat. Aviation Corpn.; fmr. Senior Vice-Pres. Nat. Aeronautic Asscn.; fmr. Chair. Board of Govs. Flight Safety Foundation; Pres. Browne and Shaw Co., Waltham, Mass. 55-69; Assoc. Prof. of Air Transport, Mass. Inst. of Technology 58-69; Vice-Pres. Int. Studies Div., Bolt, Beranek and Newman Inc., Cambridge, Mass. 68-69; Asst. Sec. for Research and Technology, U.S. Dept. of Transportation 69; Chair. U.S. Civil Aeronautics Board 69-73; Visiting Prof. and Consultant MIT 73-.
Secor D. Browne Assocs. Inc., Suite 409, 1730 R. I. Avenue, N.W., Washington, D.C. 20036, U.S.A.

Browne, Stanley George, O.B.E., M.D., F.R.C.P., F.R.C.S., D.T.M.; British consultant leprologist; b. 8 Dec. 1907, London; s. of Arthur Browne and Edith Lilly-white; m. Ethel Marion Williamson, 1940; three s.; ed. King's Coll. and King's Coll. Hosp., London, Inst. de Médecine Tropicale, Antwerp.
Medical Missionary, Yakusu, Belgian Congo 36-59; Prin. Ecole agréée d'Infirmiers; Dir. Yalisombo Leprosarium, Uzuakoli, Eastern Nigeria 59-65; Consultant Advisor in Leprosy 66-; Hon. Consultant, Univ. Coll., London 66-; medical consultant, The Leprosy Mission 66-; Medical Secretary LEPRA, Editor *Leprosy Review* 66-74; Sec.-Treas. Int. Leprosy Asscn. 66-;

Africa Medal, Stewart Prize and several foreign orders.
Leisure interests: photography, reading.
Publs. *Leprosy—New Hope and Continuing Challenge* 66, *Leprosy* (Acta Clinica No. 11) 68, and over 350 scientific articles on leprosy, tropical dermatology, filariasis, medical ethics, etc.
57A Wimpole Street, London, WIM 7DF; Home: 16 Bridgefield Road, Sutton, Surrey SM1 2DG.
Telephone: 01-642-1656.

Browne, William Herman; Canadian business executive; b. 25 March 1901; ed. Queen's Univ., Kingston, Ontario.
Cashier, British American Oil Co. Ltd. 23-25; Technical Service, Goodyear Tire and Rubber Co., Canada, Ltd. 25; Moore Corpn. Ltd., Toronto (business forms, etc.) 25-, Sec. 35-55, Exec. Vice-Pres. and Sec. 55-59, Exec. Vice-Pres. 59-62, Pres. 62-68, Chair. 68-75; Pres. and Dir. of subsidiary companies; mem. Canadian Council, Nat. Industrial Conf. Board.
c/o Moore Corporation Ltd., 330 University Avenue, Toronto, Ontario, Canada.

Brownell, Herbert, A.B., LL.B.; American lawyer; b. 20 Feb. 1904, Peru, Neb.; s. of Herbert Brownell and May Miller Brownell; brother of Samuel Miller Brownell (q.v.); m. Doris McC. Brownell 1934; two s. two d.; ed. Univ. of Nebraska and Yale Univ. School of Law.
Admitted to New York Bar 28; law practice, Root, Clark, Buckner, Howland and Ballantine 28-29; mem. New York State Assembly 32-37; practising attorney Lord, Day & Lord 29-53, 57-; Attorney-Gen. of United States 53-57; Pres. Asscn. of Bar of City of New York 62-64; Chubb Fellowship, Yale Univ. 59-; Assoc. Fellow Silliman Coll., Yale Univ. 55-; Chair. Comm. on Int. Rules of Judicial Procedure 58-59, American Bar Asscn. Cttee. on Constitutional Amendment relating to Presidential Disability; Pres. American Judicature Soc. 66-68; official of other legal orgs.; U.S. mem. Perm. Court of Arbitration, The Hague; Special Amb. to Mexico for Colorado River Dispute.
Lord, Day & Lord, 25 Broadway, New York, N.Y. 10004, U.S.A.
Telephone: 212-344-8480.

Brownell, Samuel Miller, A.B., M.A., PH.D.; American educationist; b. 3 April 1900, Peru, Neb.; s. of Herbert Brownell and May Miller Brownell; brother of Herbert Brownell (q.v.); m. Esther Delzell 1927; four c.; ed. Lincoln (Nebraska) High School, Univ. of Nebraska and Yale Univ.
Teacher, Demonstration High School, State Teachers Coll., Peru 21-23; Asst. Prof. of Educ., New York State Coll. for Teachers 26-27; Supt. of Schools, Grosse Pointe, Mich. 27-38; Prof. of Educational Admin., Yale Univ. 38-56; Pres. New Haven State Teachers' Coll. 47-53; U.S. Commr. of Educ. 53-56; Supt. of Schools, Detroit 56-66; Prof. Urban Educational Admin., Yale Univ. and Univ. of Conn. 66-70; Consultant Urban Educ. and Dir. Mid-Career Program, City School Admin. 70-73; Prof. Emeritus, Yale Univ.; many hon. degrees.
Leisure interests: spectator sports, travel.
Publs. *Progress in Educational Administration* 35, *Urban Education* 62; Editor *Issues in Urban Education* 71.
Apartment 1L, 70 Livingston Street, New Haven, Conn. 06511, U.S.A.

Broz, Josip (*see* Tito).

Brubeck, David Warren, B.A.; American musician; b. 6 Dec. 1920, Concord, Calif.; s. of Howard P. Brubeck and Elizabeth Ivey; m. Iola Whitlock 1942; five s. one d.; ed. Pacific and Mills Colls.
Formed his own trio 50, Dave Brubeck Quartet 51; numerous tours and recordings; many awards from trade magazines, *Metronome, Downbeat, Billboard,*

Melodymaker; Hon. Ph.D. (Univ. of Pacific, Fairfield Univ.); composer of 250 songs; *Points of Jazz* (ballet), *Elementals* (orchestral), *The Light in the Wilderness* (oratorio), *The Gates of Justice* (cantata), *Truth Is Fallen* (cantata).
Leisure interests: nature study, hiking, gardening, camping.
c/o Sutton Artists, 505 Park Avenue, New York, N.Y. 10022; and 221 Millstone Road, Wilton, Conn. 06897, U.S.A.

Brubeck, William H.; American government official; b. 19 Aug. 1920; ed. St. John's Coll., Maryland and Harvard Univ.
U.S. Army service 42-46; Teaching Fellow, St. John's Coll. 46-48, Harvard Univ. 50-52; Asst. Prof. Williams Coll. 52-56; Visiting Lecturer, Salzburg Seminary, Austria 55, Columbia Univ. 57; Legislative Asst. to mems. of Congress 56; Consultant, private firm 57-60, to Development Loan Fund 61; Special Asst. to Under-Sec. of State 61, Deputy Exec. Sec., Exec. Secr. 61-62, Special Asst. to Sec. of State, Exec. Sec. of Dept. of State 62-63; mem. Nat. Security Council, White House 63-65; Political Counsellor, London 65-69; Deputy Head of Mission, Jordan 70-73; Consul-Gen. Morocco 73-.
American Consulate-General, Casablanca, Morocco.
Telephone: 26-05-21.

Bruce, David K. E.; American diplomatist; b. 12 Feb. 1898, Baltimore, Maryland; s. of William Cabell Bruce and Louise E. F. Bruce; brother of James Bruce (*q.v.*); m. 1st Ailsa Mellon 1926, one d. (deceased); m. 2nd Evangeline Bell 1945, two s. one d. (deceased 76); ed. Princeton Univ. and Univs. of Virginia and Maryland.
Served First World War; practised law in Baltimore 21-25; mem. Md. House of Dels. 24-26, Va. House of Dels. 39-42; foreign service of U.S. State Dept. 26-28; engaged in various banking and business enterprises 28-39; chief rep. American Red Cross, Great Britain 40; with Office of Strategic Services 41-45, Col. in Army Air Forces 43-45; Asst. Sec. of Commerce 47; Chief French Mission for the E.C.A. 48; Amb. to France 49-52; Under-Sec. of State 52-53; Special U.S. Observer, Interim Cttee., European Defence Community 53; Special rep. to European High Authority for Coal and Steel 53-54; Amb. to Fed. Repub. of Germany 57-59, to U.K. 61-69; U.S. Rep. at Paris on Viet-Nam Peace Talks 70-71; Head, U.S. Liaison Office, Peking 73-74; Amb. to NATO 74-76; awarded mil. decorations by U.S., Great Britain, France, Norway, Poland, Denmark, Czechoslovakia.
Publs. *Revolution to Reconstruction* 38, *16 American Presidents* 63.
c/o Department of State, 2201 C Street, N.W., Washington, D.C. 20520, U.S.A.

Bruce, James, LITT.B., LL.B.; American executive; b. 23 Dec. 1892, Baltimore, Md.; s. of William C. Bruce and Louise Este Fisher Bruce; brother of David Bruce (*q.v.*); m. 1919; two d.; ed. Princeton Univ. and Univ. of Maryland.
Captain in U.S. Field Artillery, First World War; mil. aide to Pres. Wilson at Treaty of Versailles; Asst. Mil. Attaché, Italy, and Rep. of Versailles Peace Conf. in Montenegro and Albania 19; Vice-Pres. Atlantic Exchange Bank 21-26; Vice-Pres. Chase Nat. Bank 26-31; Pres. Baltimore Trust Co. 31-33; Financial Adviser Home Owners' Loan Corpn., Washington 33-34; Vice-Pres. and Dir. Nat. Dairy Products Corpn. 35-47; U.S. Amb. to Argentina 47-49; First Dir. Mutual Defence Assistance Programme 49-50; Dir. Avco Manufacturing Co., Loews Theatres Inc., Gen. American Investors, Ramco Enterprises, J. B. Stetson Co., Stanrock Uranium.
Publs. *Those Perplexing Argentines, College Journalism.*
825 Fifth Avenue, New York, N.Y. 10021, U.S.A.

Bruce, Noel Hugh Botha, G.L.M., I.D., F.I.B.R., F.I.B.S.A.; South African banker; b. 13 Nov. 1921. Fauresmith, O.F.S.; s. of late Lennox G. C. Bruce; m. Winifred M. Robertson 1946; two s. one d.; ed. Outeniqua High School, George Rondebosch High School, Cape Town and Univ. of S. Africa.
With S. Africa Reserve Bank 38-55; Chief Cashier, Bank of Rhodesia and Nyasaland 56-65; Gov. Reserve Bank of Rhodesia 64-; Pres. Inst. of Bankers in Rhodesia 73-74; Chair. Nat. Arts Foundation; Registrar of Banks and Financial Insts., Rhodesia 64-65; Trustee, Post Office Savings Bank and various pension funds; mem. Prime Minister's Econ. Council; Dir. Ipcorn Ltd.; has served on many govt. comms.; Independence Decoration 70, Grand Officer of the Legion of Merit 74.
Leisure interests: golf, fishing, photography.
Publs. articles in econ. and scientific journals.
Blue Gums, Radnor Road, Emerald Hill, Avondale, Salisbury (P.O. Box 1283, Salisbury), Rhodesia.
Telephone: 35807, 28791.

Bruch, Walter; German development engineer; b. 2 March 1908, Neustadt; m. Ruth Jeskulke 1938; one s.; ed. Technische Hochschule.
Development Engineer in Denes V. Mihaly Physical Technical Research Lab. 33-35; at Lab. for Physical Research, Telefunken AG until 45; now Dir. of Advanced Devt., AEG-Telefunken; Prof. of Govt. of Saarland; Chair. Fernsehtechnische Gesellschaft; Geoffrey Parr Award, Royal Television Soc.; Grosses Bundesverdienstkreuz mit Stern; Goldener Ehrenring der Deutschen Gesellschaft für Film-und Fernsehforschung; Medaille für Verdienste um die Hauptstadt Hannover; Dr. Ing. E.h. Technische Universität, Hanover.
Publs. 27 technical articles in field of colour television; *Kleine Geschichte des deutschen Fernsehens, Die Fernseh-Story*; contributor *Fernsehempfanger* in *Fernsehtechnik* 63.
AEG - Telefunken, 3 Hanover, Göttinger Chaussee 76; Home: 3 Hanover, Menschingstrasse 13, Federal Republic of Germany.
Telephone: 0511-630961 (Office); 0511-817222 (Home).

Bruchési, Jean, B.A., LL.L., D.POL.SC.; Canadian university professor and civil servant; b. 1901; ed. Univs. of Montreal and Paris, Ecole Libre des Sciences Politiques, Paris, and Ecole des Chartes, Paris.
Admitted to the Bar 24; Prof. of Gen. History, Univ. of Montreal 27-37, Prof. of Political Science and External Politics 29-58; Prof. of Canadian History, Marguerite-Bourgeoys Coll. Montreal 32-; Prof. of Economic History of Canada, Ecole Supérieure de Commerce, Laval Univ. 43-52; Under-Sec. of the Province of Quebec 37-; Editor of Foreign Politics, *Le Canada*, Montreal 28-31; Chief Editor *La Revue Moderne* 30-35, *L'Action Universitaire* 34-37; mem. (and founder) La Société des Ecrivains canadiens 37-, mem. Royal Society of Canada 40- (Pres. 53-54); Pres. Inst. Canadien de Québec 46-.
Publs. *Aux Marches de l'Europe* 31, *L'Epopée Canadienne* 34, *Histoire du Canada pour tous* 34-36, *Rappels* 41, *De Ville-Marie à Montréal* 42, *Le Chemin des Ecoliers* 44, *Evocations* 47, *Canada, réalités d'hier et d'aujourd'hui* 48, *Histoire du Canada* 51, *Le Canada* 52, *L'Université* 53, *Voyages . . . Mirages* 57.
185 avenue Laurier, Quebec, Canada.

Brück, Hermann Alexander, C.B.E., D.PHIL., PH.D., M.R.I.A., F.R.S.E.; British astronomer; b. 15 Aug. 1905, Berlin, Germany; s. of H. H. Brück and Margaret Brück; m. 1st Irma Waitzfelder 1936 (died 1950), 2nd Mary T. Conway 1951; two s. three d.; ed. Augusta Gymnasium, Berlin-Charlottenburg and Univs. of Bonn, Kiel, Munich and Cambridge.
Astronomer, Potsdam Astrophysical Observatory 28; Lecturer, Berlin Univ. 35; Research Assoc., Vatican Observatory 36; Asst. Observer, Solar Physics Observatory, Cambridge 37; John Couch Adams Astronomer,

Cambridge Univ. 43; Asst. Dir. Cambridge Observatory 46; Dir. Dunsink Observatory and Prof. of Astronomy, Dublin Inst. for Advanced Studies 47-57; Astronomer Royal for Scotland and Regius Prof. of Astronomy, Univ. of Edinburgh 57-75, Dean Faculty of Science 68-70; Vice-Pres. Royal Astronomical Soc. 59-61; mem. Pontifical Acad. of Sciences; Corresp. mem. Akad. der Wissenschaften, Mainz; Hon. D.Sc. (Nat. Univ. of Ireland, St. Andrew's Univ.).
Leisure interest: music.
Publs. Scientific papers in journals and observatory publications.
Craigower, Penicuik, EH26 9LA, Midlothian, Scotland. Telephone: Penicuik 75918.

Brück, Jean François Julien; Belgian trade union official; b. 4 July 1918, Verviers; m. Jeanne Cuypers 1947; two s. one d.; ed. state secondary school, Verviers. Permanent Sec. Young Christian Workers Regional Fed., Verviers 37-39; Nat. Treas. Belgian Young Christian Workers 39-47; Deputy Sec.-Gen. Office Employees' Nat. Union 47-51, Sec.-Gen. 51-57; Sec.-Gen. Confed. of Christian Trade Unions of the Congo 57-62; Dir. Int. Solidarity Fund, Int. Fed. of Christian Trade Unions (IFCTU) 62-68; Sec.-Gen. World Confed. of Labour 68-.
Leisure interests: physical education, swimming, mountaineering.
320 rue F. Gay, 1150 Brussels, Belgium. Telephone: 771-22-26.

Bruckner, Albert, PH.D.; Swiss historian; b. 13 July 1904, Basle; s. of Albert Bruckner and Anita Haas; m. Elizabeth Mitterer; two c.; ed. Lausanne, Basle, Berlin, Florence, Münster, Cologne.
Chief Asst. Int. Press Exhibition, Cologne 26-27; Pers. Asst. Prof. Kehr (Monumenta Germaniae) Berlin 29-30; 1st Asst. Basle Univ. Library 31-33; Chief Asst Archives, Basle 33-41, Privatdozent Basle Univ. 36-48; Extra. Prof. 48-66, Prof. 67-; State Archivist, Basle Town 61-66; mem. staff Schweiz. Herald. Gesellschaft 48-59; hon. mem. Öst. Inst. für Geschichtsforschung, Vienna; corresp. mem. Coimbra Acad.; corresp. Fellow Medieval Acad. of America, Cambridge, Mass.; corresp. Fellow, Monumenta Germaniae, Munich; D.Phil h.c. (Univ. Fribourg) 72; Editor-in-Chief Neue Schweizer Biographie; Co-Editor Umbrae Codicum Occidentalium 60-; Pres. Curatorium Helvetia Sacra; Ordre Palmes Académiques 68.
Publs. Scriptoria medii aevi helvetica I-XIII 35-73, Schweizer Fahnenbuch 41-42; Schweizer Stempelschneider und Schriftgiesser 43; Regesta Alsatiae Merovingici et Karolini Aevi 49; Basel und die Eidgenossen (with Bonjour) 51; Das Notariatsformularbuch des Ulrich Manot (Schweizer Rechtsquellen) 58; Das Herkommen der Schwyzer und Oberhasler 61; Chartae Latinae Antiquiores I-VII, 54-75, Diplomata Karolinorum 69-74, Die Bibel von Moutier-Grandval 72, Riehen 72, Liber Viventium Fabariensis 72, etc.
6292 Finkenberg 219, Austria.
Telephone: 05285-672 (Finkenberg).

Brueckner, Keith Allan, M.A., PH.D.; American professor of physics; b. 19 March 1924, Minneapolis, Minn.; s. of Leo John and Agnes Holland Brueckner; m. Elsa Dekking 1960; two s. one d.; ed. Univs. of Minnesota and California (Berkeley), Inst. for Advanced Study, Princeton.
Assistant Prof. Indiana Univ. 51-54, Assoc. Prof. 54-55; Physicist, Brookhaven Nat. Lab. (N.Y.) 55-56; Prof. of Physics, Univ. of Pennsylvania 56-59; Prof. of Physics, Univ. of Calif. (San Diego) 59-; Vice-Pres. and Dir. of Research, Inst. for Defense Analyses, Wash., D.C. 61-62; Technical Dir. KMS Technology Center, San Diego 68-71; Exec. Vice-Pres. and Technical Dir. KMS Fusion Inc., Ann Arbor, 71-74; mem. Nat. Acad. of Sciences, American Acad. of Arts and Sciences,

American Physical Soc.; Dannie Heinemann Prize for Mathematical Physics 63.
Leisure interests: mountain climbing, skiing, sailing, surfing.
Publs. Numerous articles in scientific journals.
Department of Physics, University of California at San Diego, La Jolla, Calif. 92093; Home: 7723 Ludington Place, La Jolla, Calif. 92037, U.S.A.
Telephone: 714-452-2892 (Office); 714-454-6834 (Home).

Brugger, Ernst; Swiss politician; b. 10 March 1914. Bellinzona; s. of Alois Brugger and Ida Müller; m. Eleonora Ringer 1937; five s.; ed. Univs. of Zürich, London, Paris.
Secondary school teacher, Gossau 36; Deputy to Kantonsrat 47-59; Mayor of Gossau 62; mem. Zürich Canton Govt. 59-70, Dir. of Interior and Justice Depts. 59-67, Dir. of Public Economy Dept. 67-69; mem. Fed. Council Jan. 70-, Vice-Pres. Jan.-Dec. 73, Pres. Jan.-Dec. 74; Head of Fed. Dept. of Public Economy Feb. 70-; Chair. EFTA Consultative Cttee., Finland-EFTA Joint Council; Ministerial Chair. EFTA Council; Radical Democrat.
Leisure interest: mountaineering.
Berne, Egelbergstrasse 17, Switzerland.

Brugmans, Hendrik, D. ès L.; Netherlands literary critic and historian; b. 13 Dec. 1906, Amsterdam; s. of Prof. Hajo Brugmans; m. Engelina Karolina Mary Kan 1934 (divorced); two s. (one deceased) two d.; ed. Lycée Fontanes, Paris, Amsterdam Univ. and the Sorbonne.
Teacher at Arnhem, Terneuzen and Amersfoort; Pres. Workers' Educational Inst.; Socialist mem. of Parliament 39-40; teacher at Amersfoort and Amsterdam 40-42; arrested and imprisoned as hostage in St. Michielsgestel camp 42-44; released and joined "Je Maintiendrai" resistance movement 44; sent to report to Netherlands Govt. in Exile in London 45; Dir. of Information and Political Sec. of Prime Minister in first post-war Govt.; mission in Siam and Indonesia 46; has devoted himself to the European Federalist Movement since 46; first Pres. Union Européenne des Fédéralistes 46; Rector, Coll. of Europe, Bruges 50-72; Gold Medal "Bene Meriti della Cultura" (Italy); Charlemagne Prize; Légion d'Honneur; Officer Order of Orange-Nassau; Commander, Order of Leopold II; Grosses Verdienstkreuz des Verdienstordens der Bundesrepublik Deutschland; Dr. h.c. (Catholic Univ. of Louvain); Netherlands Labour Party (Partij van de Arbeid).
Leisure interests: reading, mountain climbing, listening to people.
Publs. Denis de Rougemont et le Personalisme français, La Littérature française contemporaine, Les Trésors littéraires de la France, Jean-Jacques Rousseau, Histoire de la Littérature Française Moderne, Crise et Vocation de l'Occident, Introduction a une Histoire Européenne (Vol. I Les Origines de la Civilisation Européenne 58, Vol. II L'Europe prend le Large 71); also the federalist programme La Cité Européenne, Panorama de la Pensée fédéraliste, Le Fédéralisme contemporain (with P. Duclos), L'Idée européenne, 1920-1970, Visages de l'Europe, La pensée politique du Fédéralisme, L'Europe des Nations; together with numerous articles on European problems in periodicals.
Stalpertstraat 47, The Hague, Netherlands 240231; 85 Carmersstraat, 331012, 8000 Bruges, Belgium.

Bruhn, Erik Belton Evers; Danish ballet dancer; b. 3 Oct. 1928; ed. Royal Ballet School, Copenhagen.
Début with Danish ballet 46, Leading Dancer 49, 58-61; Guest Artiste, Metropolitan Ballet, London 47-49, American Nat. Ballet Theatre 49, 51, 53, Perm. mem. 53-58, New York City Ballet 59, American Ballet 60; appeared with Bolshoi Ballet 61, Danish Ballet 61, Royal Ballet (London) 62, Stockholm Opera Ballet 67-73; Resident Producer Nat. Ballet of Canada 73-.
57 King Street, East Toronto, Ont., Canada.

Bruller, Jean Marcel (see Vercors).

Brun, Edmond Antoine Sylvestre; French space scientist; b. 31 Dec. 1898, Saint Cannat; s. of Antoine Brun and Marie Villecrose; m. Suzanne Vincent 1923; ed. Lycée de Marseille and Univ. de Marseille.
Teacher, Nice 23-31, Paris 31-42; Hon. Prof., Faculty of Sciences, Paris 42-72; Hon. Dir. Laboratoire d'aéro-thermique, Centre nat. de la recherche scientifique 42-72; Pres. French Soc. of Astronautics 60-62, Int. Fed. of Astronautics 62-64; Vice-Pres. Int. Acad. of Astro-nautics 63-; Pres. Soc. française des thermiciens 64-66; Pres. Société des Ingénieurs Civils de France 69; Pres. of COVOS (Conséquences des vols stratosphériques) 73-; Officier Légion d'Honneur; mem. Nat. Acad. of Sciences (U.S.A.); Fellow Royal Aeronautical Soc., London; Hon. Fellow American Inst. of Aeronautics and Astro-nautics; Fellow American Astronautical Soc.; mem. Acad. des Sciences de l'Institut de France.
Leisure interest: agriculture.
Laboratoire d'aérothermique, 4 ter route des Gardes, Meudon (Hauts-de-Seine); 8 place du Commerce, 75 Paris 15e, France.
Telephone: 532-7729.

Brundage, Howard Denton, B.A.; American publisher and advertising executive; b. 9 Nov. 1923, Newark, N.J.; s. of Edgar Rae and Salome (Denton) Brundage; m. Nancy Williams 1945; one s. three d.; ed. Dart-mouth Coll. and Harvard Graduate School of Business Admin.
With Morgan, Stanley and Co., New York 45-50; Asst. Sec. The Hanover Bank, New York 50-52; with J. H. Whitney and Co., New York 52-58, Partner 58-61; Pres. New York Herald Tribune Inc. 58; Exec. Vice-Pres. (Finance) and Dir. J. Walter Thompson Co. 62-; Dir. Faber, Coe and Gregg Inc., Smith, Barney Equity Fund, and various insurance companies; Trustee, Mountainside Hospital, Montclair, N.J.
Leisure interests: golf, sailing, paddle tennis, bridge.
120 Lloyd Road, Montclair, N.J., U.S.A.
Telephone: 201-744-0650.

Brundage, Percival Flack; American consultant; b. 2 April 1892, Amsterdam, N.Y.; s. of Rev. William M. Brundage and Charlotte Hannah Flack; m. Amittai Ostrander 1918; one s. one d.; ed. Harvard and New York Univs.
Partner, Price, Waterhouse & Co. 30-54, Consultant 58-; Dep. Dir. Bureau of the Budget 54-56, Dir. 56-58; Dir. Montclair Community Chest 50-54; Dir. Nat. Bureau of Econ. Research 42-67, Pres. 54, Hon. Dir. 67-; mem. Int. Asscn. for Liberal Christianity and Religious Freedom, Pres. 52-55; Dir. Fed. Union Inc. (Chair. 51-54), American Asscn. for UN; Dir., Treas. Int. Movt. for Atlantic Union; Treas. Atlantic Council of the U.S. Inc.; Treas. People to People Health Foundation; mem. Unitarian Service Comm. (Dir. 49-54), American Unitarian Asscn. (Dir. 42-48), American Inst. of Accountants (Pres. 48-49), Council of Foreign Rela-tions, Foreign Policy Asscn.; Hon. D.C.S.
Leisure interests: golf, painting, travel.
Publ. The Bureau of the Budget 70.
2601 Woodley Place, N.W., Washington, D.C. 20008; Winter: 969 Hillsboro Mile, Pompano Beach, Fla. 33062, U.S.A.
Telephone: AD2-8894 (Summer); 941-0941 (Winter).

Brundtland, Gro Harlem, M.D., M.P.H.; Norwegian physician and politician; b. 20 April 1939, Oslo; s. of Gudmund and Inga Harlem; m. Arne Olav 1960; three s. one d.; ed. Oslo and Harvard Univs.
Consultant, Ministry of Health and Social Affairs 65-67; Medical Officer, Oslo City Health Dept. 68-69; Deputy Dir. School Health Services, Oslo 70-; Minister of Environment Sept. 74-; Vice-Chair. Labour Party 75-.
Leisure interest: cross-country skiing.

Publs. articles on preventive medicine, school health and growth studies.
Ministry of the Environment, Oslo Dept, Oslo; Home: Th. Lövstadsvei 19, Oslo 2, Norway.
Telephone: 119090 (Office); 559510 (Home).

Brunei, Sultan of (see Bolkiah).

Brunet, Jacques, L. ès D.; French banker; b. 10 May 1901, Paris; ed. Paris Univ.
Secretary to Raymond Poincaré 28; Deputy Dir., later Dir. Ministry of Finance 35-46; Gen. Man. Banque d'Algérie et de Tunisie 46-48; Pres. and Gen. Man. Crédit Nat. 49-60; Gov. Banque de France 60-69, Hon. Gov. 69-; Grand Croix de la Légion d'Honneur.
9 rue de Valois, Paris 1er, France.

Brunet, Jean-Pierre; French diplomatist; b. 20 Jan. 1920; m. Geneviève Didry 1970; ed. Lycée Saint-Louis, Paris and Ecole Navale, Brest.
Sub-Lieut., French Navy 40; joined Free French Naval Forces 40, served in submarines 40-45; Diplomatic Service 45-; French Embassy, London 46-47; Ministry of Foreign Affairs 48-61; Deputy Rep. of France to EEC 61-64; Head of Econ. Co-operation Section, Ministry of Foreign Affairs 65-66, Dir. of Econ. and Financial Affairs 66-75, Amb. to Japan 75-; mem. Gen. Council of Banque de France 66-73; Commander Légion d'Honneur.
Leisure interests: skiing, sailing.
French Embassy, 11-44, Minami-Azabu, 4-chome, Minato-ku, Tokyo, Japan; 4 rue Monsieur, 75007 Paris, France.
Telephone: 473-01-71 (Office); 783-81-61 (Home).

Bruneton, Pierre Adolphe Gaston; French business executive; b. 28 August 1901, Saint-Cloud; s. of Jean Bruneton and Cécile Morin; m. Yvonne Sautter 1925; one s. four d.; ed. Lycée Carnot, Paris, Ecole Centrale des Arts et Manufactures, Paris.
Engineer Sociedad Ibérica del Nitrógeno, Madrid 24-29; Deputy Dir. Foreign Dept., Société L'Air Liquide 32, Sec.-Gen. 42, Dir. 46, Deputy Dir.-Gen. 50, Deputy Admin. Dir.-Gen. 54, Admin. Dir.-Gen. 69-, Admin. 71-; Dir. of various subsidiary companies; Pres. Société Chimique de la Grande Paroisse; Officier, Légion d'Honneur; Croix de Guerre.
Société L'Air Liquide, 75 Quai d'Orsay, Paris 7e; Home: 5 Square Perronet, 92 Neuilly-sur-Seine, France.
Telephone: 555-44-30 (Office); 624-34-30 (Home).

Brunhes, Julien; French public servant; b. 25 Nov. 1900; ed. Lycée de Clermont-Ferrand, Lycée Saint-Louis, Paris, Ecole Navale, Ecole supérieure d'élec-tricité.
Assistant Sec.-Gen. Etablissements d'Aviation Louis Breguet 45-46, Sec.-Gen. Cttee. of liaison between Transport and Management 49-; Counsellor of the Republic, Senator 46-48, 52-60; mem. European Parl. 60-68, Vice-Pres. 64-66; Pres. Nat. Council of French Engineers; mem. numerous asscns; Chevalier Légion d'Honneur.
Office: 48 avenue de Villiers, Paris 17e; Home: 25 rue Galilée, Paris 16e, France.

Brunner, Guido, D.JUR.; German international civil servant; b. 27 May 1930, Madrid; ed. German School, Madrid and Univs. of Munich, Heidelberg and Madrid.
Diplomatic service 56-74; Foreign Minister's Office 56, Office of Sec. of State for Foreign Affairs 58-60, mem., later Head of Political Div., Del. to U.S.A. 60-68; Scientific and Technological Relations Div., Foreign Office 68-70, Spokesman 70-72, Head, Planning Dept. 72-74; Head, del. to Conf. on Security and Co-operation in Europe; Commr. for Research, Science, Educ. and the Statistical Office, European Communities Nov. 74-; Free Democratic Party (FDP).
Commission of the European Communities, 200 rue de la Loi, 1040 Brussels, Belgium.

Brustad, Tor; Norwegian biophysicist; b. 20 Dec. 1926; s. of Johan Ludwig and Aslaug Brustad; m. Berte-Marie Brustad 1953; one s. two d.; ed. Univs. of Oslo and California.

Research Fellow, Univ. of Oslo 53-54, Norwegian Cancer Soc. 54-57, U.S. Nat. Acad. of Sciences 57-59; Research Assoc. Univ. of California 59-60, Consultant in Biophysics 60-; Chair. Dept. of Biophysics, Norsk Hydro's Inst. for Cancer Research, Oslo 62-; Chair. Dept. of Medical Physics, The Norwegian Radium Hospital, Oslo 68-; Prof. of Radiation Biophysics, Univ. of Trondheim 70-.

Publs. on radiation effects on enzymes and micro-organisms.

Norsk Hydro's Institute for Cancer Research, Montebello, Oslo; and Nordvegen 30, 1342 Jar, Norway. Telephone: Oslo 24-29-05 (Home).

Brutelle, Georges; French politician; b. 20 Nov. 1922, Paris; m. Janette Brutelle-Duba 1957; one s. one d.; ed. Ecole Normale d'Instituteurs, Rouen, Ecole Supérieure de Commerce, Rouen and Univ. of Caen.

Resistance Movement 40-45; Chef du Cabinet, Ministry of Posts and Telecommunications 45-46; Sec.-Gen. Fédération des Déportés de la Résistance 46; mem. Policy Cttee. Parti Socialiste, Section Française de l'Internationale Ouvrière 46, Joint Sec.-Gen. 47-65, mem. Nat. Bureau 67-; Army Service in Algeria 56-57; Pres. des Colloques Socialistes 64; Sec. Fed. of Democratic Left and Socialists 65-67, Dir. de documentations, Soc. Générale de presse March 66-June 67; contributor to *Paris Normandie*, Man. 69-, and *L'Action de Tunis* 68-; Dir. Public Relations, Soc. d'études et constructions immobilières Oct. 68-, Asst. Dir.-Gen. 69, Dir.-Gen. 71-74; Dir. Gerpresse Jan. 74-; Officier de la Légion d'Honneur, Croix de Guerre, Rosette de la résistance.

Leisure interests: aquaria, hunting.

Publs. *La Pensée Socialiste Contemporaine* 65.

Gerpresse, 41 boulevard Barbès, Paris 18e; Home: 8 rue Léon Vaudoyer, Paris 7e, France.

Telephone: 076-59-39.

Brutus, Dennis, B.A.; South African educationist and poet; b. 28 Nov. 1924, Salisbury, S. Rhodesia; s. of Francis Henry Brutus and Margaret Winifred (née Bloemetjie); m. May Jaggers 1950; four s. four d.; ed. Paterson High School, Port Elizabeth, Fort Hare and Witwatersrand Univs.

Language teacher, Paterson High School, Cen. Indian High School; office boy and law student, Witwatersrand Univ.; Dir. World Campaign for Release of S. African Political Prisoners; worked for Int. Defence and Aid Fund, currently UN Rep.; Visiting Prof. Denver Univ.; Prof. of English, Northwestern Univ., Evanston, Ill.; Visiting Prof., English Dept., African and Afro-American Studies and Research Center, Univ. Tex., Austin, 74-75; Pres. S. African Non-Racial Olympic Cttee. (SAN-ROC); Chair. Int. Campaign Against Racism in Sport (ICARIS); Chair. Steering Cttee., African Literature Asscn.; Mbari Prize for Poetry in Africa, Chancellor's Prize for Bilingualism (Univ. of S. Africa); Freedom Writers' Award.

Leisure interests: sport, music, chess.

Publs. poetry: *Sirens, Knuckles, Boots* 63, *Letters to Martha* 68, *Poems from Algeria* 70, *Thoughts Abroad* (John Bruin) 71, *A Simple Lust* 73, *China Poems* 75, *Strains* 75, *The Stubborn Hope* 76.

English Department, Northwestern University, Evanston, Ill. 60201; 624 Clark Street, Evanston, Ill. 60201, U.S.A.; 18 Hilton Avenue, London, N.12, England.

Telephone: 312-328-9154 (Evanston); 01-445-6109 (London).

Brutyó, János; Hungarian trade union official; b. 20 Nov. 1911, Mako; s. of Pál Brutyó and Mária Tóth; m. Mária Takács 1937; one s. one d.

Former carpenter; Building Workers' Union 33, mem. Central Board 36, Sec.-Gen. 55; Deputy Minister of Building Industry 56; mem. Central Cttee. Hungarian Socialist Workers' Party 57-66, Substitute mem. Political Cttee. 62-66; mem. Nat. Council, Patriotic People's Front 56, Presidential Council 61; Gen. Sec. Hungarian Nat. Council of Trade Unions 59, Pres. 65-66; Pres. Supervisory Cttee., Hungarian Socialist Workers' Party 66-; Red Banner, Order of Labour.

Leisure interests: reading, angling.

c/o Hungarian Socialist Workers' Party, H-1387, Széchenyi rakpart 19, Budapest, Hungary.

Bruun, Egon, M.D.; Danish physician; b. 1 Feb. 1909, Copenhagen; m. Birte Dela 1936; two s. one d.; ed. Københavns Universitet.

Specialist in allergies; has trained at Univs. of Münster and Berlin 38, Forlanini Inst., Rome 40, Stockholm 43, Hôpital Broussais and Institut Pasteur, Paris 50, London and Oxford 52; Head Physician, Danish Red Cross Asthma Sanatorium in Norway 46-52; Lecturer on Clinical Allergy, Univ. of Copenhagen 50-; Head Physician of Allergy Clinic, Univ. Hospital, Copenhagen 55-; Pres. Danish Soc. of Allergology 50-54, 58-60; Treas. Int. Asscn. of Allergology 54-64; Fellow, American Acad. of Allergy 52; Pres.-elect, European Acad. of Allergology 58-62, Pres. 62-65; Pres. Northern Soc. of Allergology 62-65; official of other medical orgs.; Hon. mem. French, Argentine, Belgian, Finnish and Northern Allergy Soc., European Acad. of Allergology; Illum Prize of Honour and several awards.

Leisure interests: editing *Acta Allergologica*, gardening, historical literature.

8 Gersonsvej, Copenhagen-Hellerup, Denmark.

Telephone: HE 178.

Bruun-Rasmussen, Knud; Danish writer; b. 21 July 1898, Hilleröd; s. of Bishop Fr. Bruun-Rasmussen and Emilie Spies; m. 1st Dagny Hansen 1931 (died 1962), 2nd Britta Jansson 1969; two s. one d.

Novelist, poet and essayist.

Publs. *Digte* 20, *Kentaur* 26, *Novemberstorm* 27, *En Herre viser sig* 29, *Gaden og Mennesket* 30, *Dette ene Liv* 32, *Morgendrömme* 33, *Ansiglet i Spejlet* 47, *Hvordan skal jeg undervise?* 53, *Grundbog for talere* 54, *Bedömmelse af Mennesker* 54, *Kvinde og Mand i dagens lys* 55, *Talerkunst* 63, *Mundtlig Fremstilling* 69, *Mödeteknik* 70, *Indgang til Venezia* 72.

Strandallien 1C, 3000 Helsingør, Denmark.

Telephone: (03) 21-2308.

Lecturer, Zhukovsky Air Force Engineering Acad. 29-61; mem. U.S.S.R. Acad. of Sciences 42-; Assoc. Inst. of Machine Studies, U.S.S.R. Acad. of Sciences 51-; mem. Communist Party 21-; three Orders of Lenin; other decorations.

Publs. include: *Kinematics of very simple Spatial Mechanisms with Pairs of the Fifth Class* 37, *Kinestatics of Spatial Mechanisms* 37, *Foundations of the Theory of Calculation Systems* 64.

Institute of Machine Studies of Academy of Sciences of U.S.S.R., 4 ulitsa Griboedova, Moscow, U.S.S.R.

Bryan, Sir Arthur, Kt.; British company director; b. 4 March 1923, Stoke-on-Trent; s. of William Woodall Bryan and Isobel Alan (née Tweedie); m. Betty Ratford 1947; one s. one d.; ed. Longton High School.

Served with R.A.F.V.R. 41-45; joined Wedgwood Ltd. 47, sales rep. 49, Asst. London Man. 50-53, London Man. and Gen. Man. of Wedgwood Rooms 53-59, Gen. Sales Man. 59-60; Dir. and Pres. Josiah Wedgwood & Sons Inc. of America 60-62; Man. Dir. Wedgwood Ltd. 63-, Chair. 68-; Pres. British Ceramic Mfrs. Fed. 70-71; Fellow British Inst. of Management 68, Inst. of Marketing, Royal Soc. of Arts 64; Companion, Inst. of Ceramics; mem. Court, Univ. of Keele; K. St. J. 72; Lord Lt. of Staffordshire 68-.

Leisure interests: walking, tennis, reading.

Wedgwood Ltd., Barlaston, Stoke-on-Trent, Staffordshire; Parkfields Cottage, Tittensor, Stoke-on-Trent, Staffordshire, England.

Bryan, John H., Jr., B.A., M.B.A.; American business executive; b. West Point, Miss.; *m.*; four *c.*; ed. Southwestern Univ., Memphis, Univ. of Virginia School of Business.
Joined Bryan Packing Co. 60, Pres., Chief Exec. Officer 68-74; Exec. Vice-Pres., Dir. Consolidated Foods Corpn. March-Oct. 74, Pres., Chief Operating Officer Oct. 74-75, Pres., Chief Exec. Officer Feb. 75-; Trustee Southwestern Univ.
Consolidated Foods Corpn., 135 South LaSalle Street, Chicago, Ill. 60603, U.S.A.

Bryan, Wright, B.S.; American journalist; b. 6 Aug. 1905, Atlanta, Ga.; *s.* of Arthur Buist Bryan and Inez Sledge Bryan; *m.* Ellen Hillyer Newell 1932; one *s.* two *d.*; ed. Clemson Coll. and Univ. of Missouri School of Journalism.
With *Atlanta Journal* 27-53, Editor 45-53; Editor *Cleveland Plain Dealer* 54-63; Vice-Pres. Devt. Clemson Univ. 64-70; mem. American Soc. of Newspaper Editors, Pres. 52-53; U.S. Medal of Freedom; Hon. Litt.D. (Clemson); Hon. LL.D. (Coll. of Wooster).
100 Wyatt Avenue, Clemson, South Carolina, U.S.A.
Telephone: 803-654-3531.

Bryant, Sir Arthur, Kt., C.H., C.B.E., M.A., F.R.HIST.S., F.R.S.L.; British historian; b. 18 Feb. 1899, Dersingham, Norfolk; *m.* 1st Sylvia (née Shakerley) 1924, 2nd Anne (*d.* of Bertram Brooke, H.H. Tuan Muda of Sarawak) 1941 (divorced 1976); ed. Harrow and Queen's Coll., Oxford.
Principal Cambridge School of Arts, Crafts and Technology 23-25; Lecturer in History and English Literature Oxford Univ. Delegacy for Extra-Mural Studies 25-35; Producer Cambridge Pageant 24, Oxford Pageant 26, Fenland Pageant 31, Naval Pageant Greenwich 33; Editor *Ashridge Journal* 30-39; writer of "Our Note Book" in *Illustrated London News* 36-; a Gov. of Ashridge 36-49; Lecturer to H.M. Forces 40-46; Pres. English Assocn. 46; Chair. Soc. of Authors Management Cttee. 49-51; Chair. St. John and Red Cross Hospital Library 45-; Pres. Common Market Safeguards Campaign 69-, Friends of the Vale of Aylesbury 69-; Vice-Pres. Royal Literary Fund; Trustee, Historic Churches Preservation Council, English Folk Music Fund; Chesney Gold Medal 55; Hon. LL.D. (Edinburgh, St. Andrews, New Brunswick); Knight of Grace of St. John of Jerusalem.
Publs. *King Charles II* 31, *Macaulay* 32, *Samuel Pepys* 33, 35, 38, *The National Character* 33, *The England of Charles II* 34, *King George V* 36, *Letters and Speeches of Charles II* 36, *The American Ideal* 36, *Stanley Baldwin* 37, *Postman's Horn* 37, *Humanity in Politics* 38, *Unfinished Victory* 40, *English Saga 1840-1940*, 40, *The Years of Endurance* 42, *Dunkirk* 43, *Years of Victory* 44, *Historian's Holiday* 47, *The Age of Elegance* 50 (*Sunday Times* Gold Medal and £1,000 Award), *The Turn of the Tide* 57, *Triumph in the West* 59, *Restoration England* 61, *The Story of England: Makers of the Realm* 53, *The Age of Chivalry* 63, *The Fire and the Rose* 65, *The Medieval Foundation* 66, *Protestant Island* 67, *The Lion and the Unicorn* 69, *Nelson* 70, *The Great Duke* 71, *Jackets of Green* 72, *The Thousand Years of British Monarchy* 75.
Myles Place, The Close, Salisbury.

Bryant, Douglas Wallace, A.B., A.M.L.S.; American librarian; b. 20 June 1913, Visalia, Calif.; *s.* of Albert George and Ethel (Wallace) Bryant; *m.* Rene Kuhn 1953; one *d.*; ed. Univs. of Munich, Stanford, Michigan.
Translator, Stanford Univ. 34-35; Asst. Curator of Printed Books, Univ. of Michigan 36-38; Detroit Public Library 38-42; Lt.-Commdr., U.S. Naval Reserve 42-46; Asst. Librarian, Univ. of Calif. 46-49;

Dir. of Libraries, American Embassy, London 49-52; Admin. Asst. Librarian, Harvard Coll. Library 52-56, Assoc. Dir., Harvard Univ. Library and Assoc. Librarian, Harvard Coll. 56-64; Univ. Librarian, Harvard Univ. 64-72, Dir. of Library and Prof. of Bibliography 72-.
Widener Library, Harvard University, Cambridge, Mass., U.S.A.

Bryce, Robert; Canadian financial official; b. 27 Feb. 1910, Toronto, Ont.; *m.*; three *c.*; ed. Univs. of Toronto and Cambridge and Harvard Univ.
With Sun Life Insurance Co., Montreal 37; Dept. of Finance, Canada 38; Exec. Dir. IBRD 46; Asst. Deputy Minister of Finance and Sec. to Treasury Board 47; Sec. to Cabinet, Canada 54; Deputy Minister of Finance 63; Econ. Adviser to Prime Minister 70; Exec. Dir. IMF 71-74.
c/o Ministry of Finance, Ottawa, Ont., Canada.

Bryl, Ivan Antonovich; Soviet writer; b. 4 Aug. 1917, Odessa.
Began publishing 38; Sec. of Board, Union of Writers of Byelorussion S.S.R. 66-; State Prize 52, Order of Red Banner of Labour 67; other decorations.
Publs. *Dark-Browed Girl* 49, *Maria* 50, *The Righteous and the Wicked* 50, *Downing in Zabolotye* 50, *Galya* 53, *Inscription on a Wooden House* 56, *The Heart of a Communist* 57, *Confusion* 59, *My Native Land* 59, *Collected Works* (2 vols.) 60, *House of Orphans* 61, *Conversation is Continued* 62, *Green School* 63, *Lyrical Notes* 65, *Birds and Nests* 67, *Talks of Camp Fire* 66.
Union of Writers of Byelorussian S.S.R., Minsk, U.S.S.R.

Brymer, Jack, O.B.E.; British clarinettist; b. 27 Jan. 1915, South Shields, Co. Durham; *s.* of John Brymer and Mary Dixon; *m.* Joan Richardson 1939; one *s.*; ed. Goldsmith's Coll., London Univ.
Principal Clarinet, Royal Philharmonic Orchestra 47-63, BBC Symphony Orchestra 63-72, London Symphony Orchestra 72-; mem. Wigmore Ensemble, Prometheus Ensemble, London Baroque Ensemble, Delme Ensemble, Robles Ensemble and Dir./Founder London Wind Soloists; Prof. Royal Acad. of Music 50-56; Hon. RAM; world-wide soloist recitals and numerous recordings; lecturer on musical topics on radio and television; two demonstration films on history, development and use of the clarinet as a solo and orchestral instrument; Prof. of clarinet, Royal Mil. School of Music, Kneller Hall 70-73; Hon. M.A. (Univ. of Newcastle) 73.
Leisure interests: golf, tennis, swimming, gardening, carpentry, photography.
Underwood, Ballards Farm Road, South Croydon, Surrey, England.
Telephone: 01-657-1698.

Brynielsson, Harry Anders Bertil; Swedish executive; b. 20 March 1914, Stockholm; *s.* of Georg and Gurli Brynielsson; *m.* Wera Wahrenby 1940; two *s.* one *d.*; ed. Royal Inst. of Technology; Stockholm.
With Kema- Bolagen, Stockholm 36-43; Man. Dir. LKB-Produkter Fabriks Aktiebolag, Stockholm 43-51; Man. Dir. Aktiebolaget Atomenergi (Swedish Atomic Energy Co.) 51-69; Pres. European Atomic Energy Soc. 58-61; Chair. Swedish Corrosion Inst. 72-, Swedish Centre of Technical Terminology and Swedish Plant Inspection 75-; mem. Swedish Acad. of Engineering Sciences.
c/o Aktiebolaget Atomenergi, P.O. Box 43041, S-100 72 Stockholm 43; Ytterbyudd, S-185 00 Vaxholm, Sweden.
Telephone: Stockholm 18-80-20 (Office); 0764-373-65 (Home).

Brynner, Yul; film actor; b. 11 July 1920, Sakhalin, Japan (now U.S.S.R.); *m.* 1st Virginia Gilmore 1944, 2nd Jacqueline Brynner 1972; one *s.* three *d.*; ed. Sorbonne.

Connected with entertainment field from an early age; first appeared in circus and on stage in Paris; went to U.S.A. 40, appearing on stage in same year; radio announcer and commentator in French for Office of War Information 42-46; first appeared on Broadway 46; nightclub entertainer in Paris 47-48; TV actor and dir. for NBC 48, and subsequently for CBS; appeared on stage in *The King and I* 51-54, leading role 52-54; also play *Home Sweet Homer* 75 (N.Y.); acted in films 55-; film appearances include *The Ten Commandments* 55, *The King and I*, *Anastasia* 56, *The Brothers Karamazov* 58, *Journey*, *The Sound and the Fury*, *Solomon and Sheba* 59, *Once More with Feeling*, *The Magnificent Seven* 60, *Cast a Giant Shadow* 66, *Triple Cross*, *The Long Duel* 67, *The Double Man* 68, *The Madwoman of Chaillot* 69, *File of the Golden Goose* 69, *The Magic Christian* 70, *The Battle of Neretua* 71, *The Light at the Edge of the World* 71, *Romance of a Horse Thief* 71, *Catblow* 72, *Fuzz* 72, *The Happening* 72, TV Series *Anna and the King* 72, *The Serpent* 73, *Westworld* 73, *The Ultimate Warrior* 75, etc.; Donaldson Award 46; Antoinette Perry Award 51, Nat. Board Review Motion Pictures Award 56 for *The King and I*; Acad. Award in Motion Pictures 57.

Publ. *Bring Forth the Children* 60.

Office: c/o Diane Hoppenot, B.P. 275-16, 75766 Paris Cédex 16, France; 151 East 74th Street, New York, N.Y. 10021, U.S.A.

Brzezinski, Zbigniew K., B.A., PH.D.; American (naturalized 1949) professor of government; b. 28 March 1928, Warsaw, Poland; ed. McGill and Harvard Univs.

Settled in N. America 38; Instructor in Govt. and Research Fellow, Russian Research Center, Harvard Univ. 53-56; Asst. Prof. of Govt., Research Assoc. of Russian Research Center and of Center for Int. Affairs, Harvard Univ. 56-60; Assoc. Prof. of Public Law and Govt., Columbia Univ. 60-62, Prof. 62- (on leave 66-68) and Dir. Research Inst. on Communist Affairs 61- (on leave 66-68); mem. Policy Planning Council, Dept. of State 66-68; mem. Hon. Steering Cttee., Young Citizens for Johnson 64; Dir. Foreign Policy Task Force for Vice-Pres. Humphreys 68; Fellow, American Acad. of Arts and Sciences 69-; mem. Council on Foreign Relations, New York, Inst. for Strategic Studies (London), Nat. Assoc. for the Advancement of Colored People, Advisory Board of Int. Inst. for Peace and Conflict Research (Berlin), Research Inst. on Int. Change; Consultant to Dept. of State; Board of Trustees, Freedom House, Inst. of Defense Analysis (Washington, D.C.); Board of Dirs. Amnesty Int.; Foreign Affairs columnist *Newsweek*; Editorial Board *Foreign Policy*; Guggenheim Fellowship 60.

Publs. include: *Political Controls in the Soviet Army* 54, *The Permanent Purge—Politics in Soviet Totalitarianism* 56, *Totalitarian Dictatorship and Autocracy* (co-author) 57, *The Soviet Bloc—Unity and Conflict* 60, *Ideology and Power in Soviet Politics* 62, *Africa and the Communist World* (Editor and contrib.) 63, *Political Power: U.S.A./U.S.S.R.* (co-author) 64, *Alternative to Partition: For a Broader Conception of America's Role in Europe* 65, *Dilemmas of Change in Soviet Politics* (Editor and contrib.) 69, *Between Two Ages: America's Role in the Technetronic Era* 70, *The Fragile Blossom: Crisis and Change in Japan* 72.

Office: Columbia University, 420 West 118th Street, New York, N.Y. 10025; Home: 40 Brayton Street, Englewood, New Jersey, U.S.A.

Telephone: 212-280-4638 (Office); 201-567-7223 (Home).

Bubennov, Mikhail Semenovich; Soviet writer; b. 20 Nov. 1909, Polomoshnovo, Altai Territory.

Member Communist Party 51-; State Prize 47, Order of Red Banner of Labour 59, Order of Red Star.

Publs. Novels: *The Thundering Year* 32, *Immortality* 41,

The Silver Birch Tree 47, *Orlinaya Steppe* 59; Stories: *At Flood Time* 40, *Immortality* 69.

U.S.S.R. Union of Writers, 52 Ulitsa Vorovskogo, Moscow, U.S.S.R.

Bucalossi, Pietro; Italian cancer specialist; b. 9 Aug. 1905, San Miniato; s. of Alfredo and Cosetti Maria Bucalossi; m. Eugenia Goisis 1938; ed. Università degli Studi, Pisa.

Director-Gen. Nat. Cancer Inst., Milan; fmr. Pres. Fatebenefratelli Hospital, Milan; Mayor of Milan 64-; mem. Exec. Cttee. of the Int. Union Against Cancer (UICC), Italian League Against Cancer; Pres. Italian Cancer Soc., fmr. Pres. Work and Social Care Comm.; Dir. *Tumori*; mem. numerous medical socs.; Hon. Deputy Chamber of Deputies; fmr. Pres. Justice Comm ; Minister without Portfolio in charge of Scientific Research 73-March 74; Minister of Public Works Nov. 74-; numerous articles on cancer and malignant tumours.

Via Bigli 15, 20121 Milan, Italy.

Telephone: 700510.

Bucciarelli Ducci, Brunetto; Italian politician; b. 18 June 1914; ed. Collegio Nazionale, Arezzo and Univ. degli Studi, Florence.

Judge, Tribunale di Arezzo; joined Christian Democrat Party immediately after the war; Deputy; Vice-Pres. Chamber of Deputies 58-63, Pres. 63-68.

Publs. *Partiti, Gruppi e Parlamento, Introduzione allo Studio del Diritto Parlamentare, Cento Anni di Vita del Parlamento Italiano, Alcide de Gasperi e il suo Magistere Politico, La crisi dei partiti e la responsabilita dei cattolici, Siena e Dante, La figura e l'opera di Pio XI, Legislazione e Sport, Il Voto alle Donne, Il poeta Giosué Borsi a 50 anni dalla morte.*

Camera dei Deputati, Rome, Italy.

Buchanan, Sir Colin Douglas, Kt., C.B.E.; British town planner; b. 22 Aug. 1907, Simla, India; s. of William Ernest and Laura Kate Buchanan; m. Elsie Alice Mitchell 1933; two s. one d.; ed. Berkhamsted School and Imperial Coll. of Science and Technology, London.

With Public Works Dept., Sudan 30-32; Regional Planning Studies with F. Longstreth-Thompson, London 32-35; at Ministry of Transport 35-39; served with Royal Engineers 39-46; at Ministry of Town and Country Planning (later Ministry of Housing and Local Govt.) 46-61; Urban Planning Adviser, Ministry of Transport 61-63; Prof. of Transport, Imperial Coll., London 63-72; Dir. School of Advanced Urban Studies, Univ. of Bristol 73-75; Visiting Prof., Imperial Coll. 75-; Consultant to various public authorities; mem. Comm. on Third London Airport 68-70, Royal Fine Art Comm. 72-73; Gold Medal, Town Planning Inst. 68; Int. Road Fed. "Man of the Year" 71.

Leisure interests: woodworking, photography, caravanning.

Publs. *Mixed Blessing, the Motor in Britain* 58, *Traffic in Towns* 63, *Bath: A Study in Conservation* 69 and numerous papers on town planning and related subjects.

Tunnel House, Box, Minchinhampton, Glos., England.

Telephone: Nailsworth 2951.

Buchanan, J. Judd, M.B.A.; Canadian politician; b. 25 July 1929, Edmonton; s. of Nelles V. Buchanan and Helen de Silva; m. Kay Eleena Balfour 1952; three c.; ed. Univs. of Alberta and W. Ontario.

Member Board of Educ., London, Ont. 66-68; mem. Parl. for London West, Ont. 68-; Parl. Sec. to Minister of Indian Affairs and Northern Devt. 70-74, Minister Aug. 74-; Liberal.

House of Commons, Ottawa, Ont., Canada.

Buchanan, John Machlin, D.SC., PH.D.; American professor of biochemistry; b. 29 Sept. 1917, Winamac; s. of Harry J. and Eunice B. (Miller) Buchanan; m.

Elsa Nilsby 1948; two *s.* two *d.*; ed. De Pauw Univ., Univ. of Michigan and Harvard Univ.

Instructor, Dept. of Physiological Chem., School of Medicine, Univ. of Pa. 43-46, Asst. Prof. 46-49, Assoc. Prof. 49-50, Prof. 50-53; Nat. Research Council Fellow in Medicine, Nobel Inst., Stockholm, 46-48; Prof., Head, Div. of Biochem., Dept. of Biology, Mass. Inst. of Technology 53-67, Wilson Prof. of Biochem. 67-; mem. Medical Fellowship Board 54-; Fellow, Guggenheim Memorial Foundation; mem. Nat. Acad. of Sciences, American Soc. of Biological Chemists, American Chem. Soc., Int. Union of Biochemists, Amer. Acad. of Arts and Sciences; Eli Lilly Award in Biological Chem., A.C.S. 51.

Room 16-619, Department of Biology, Massachusetts Institute of Technology, Cambridge, Mass. 02139; Home: 56 Meriam St., Lexington, Mass. 02173, U.S.A.

Buchen, Philip William, A.B., J.D.; American lawyer and government official; b. 27 Feb. 1916, Sheboygan, Wis.; *s.* of Gustav W. and Elenor Buchen; *m.* Beatrice Loomis Gold 1947; one *s.* one *d.*; ed. Univ. of Mich. With Ford and Buchen 41-42; Butterfield, Keeney & Amberg 43-47; Amberg, Law & Buchen 48-55; Vice-Pres. Business Affairs, Grand Valley State Coll. 61-67; Law, Buchen, Weathers, Richardson & Dutcher 67-74; Counsel to Pres. of U.S.A. 74-; Hon. LL.D., Grand Valley State Coll.

Leisure interests: swimming, reading, the arts.

The White House, Washington, D.C. 20500; and 1200 16th Street, N.W., Washington, D.C. 20500, U.S.A. Telephone: 456-2632 (Office); DI 7-4704.

Bucher, Ewald, D.IUR.; German Minister of Justice 62-65; see *The International Who's Who 1975-76.*

Büchi, George H., D.SC.; American professor of chemistry; b. 1 Aug. 1921, Baden, Switzerland; *s.* of George and Martha Büchi; *m.* Anne Westfall Barkman 1955; ed. Fed. Inst. of Technology, Zürich.

Firestone Fellow, Univ. of Chicago 48-49; Instructor, Univ. of Chicago 49-51; Asst. Prof. of Chem., Mass. Inst. of Technology 51-56, Assoc. Prof. 56-58, Prof. 58-68, Dreyfus Prof. 68-; mem. Nat. Acad. of Sciences 65-; Ruzicka Award, Swiss Chemical Soc. 57, American Chemical Soc.; Fritzsche Award for outstanding contributions to field of structure determination of terpenes, American Chemical Soc. 58; Award for creative work in synthetic organic chem. 73.

Leisure interests: hunting, hiking and skiing.

Publs. *Photochemical Reactions XIII: A Total Synthesis of Thujopsene* 64, *Terpenes XIX: Synthesis of Patchouli Alcohol* 64, *The Structures of Aflatoxins B_1 and G_1* 65, *The Total Synthesis of Iboga Alkaloids* 66, *A Structurally Selective Method for the Preparation of Certain Diels-Alder Adducts* 67, *Biosynthesis of Aflatoxins* 68.

Massachusetts Institute of Technology, 77 Massachusetts Avenue, Boston, Mass. 02139, U.S.A. Telephone: 617-253-1838.

Buchler, Jean-Pierre; Luxembourg politician; b. 6 July 1908, Haller; ed. Inst. Agronomique de l'Etat, Gembloux, Belgium.

Instructor in Agriculture, Ecole d'Agriculture de l'Etat, Ettelbruck 31-34; Head of Dept. of Rural Economy, Ministry of Agriculture 34-45; Head of Luxembourg Office of Recovery 45-48; Head of Studies at Ministry of Econ. Affairs 45; Adviser to Ministry of Agriculture and Viticulture and Del. of Luxembourg for int. agricultural questions at FAO, GATT and OECD 48-64; several special missions 57-61; Sec. of State at Ministry of Agriculture and Viticulture 64-67; Ministry of Agriculture, Viticulture and Public Works 67; Minister of Family Affairs, Social Welfare and Housing until 74; Officier Ordre de la Couronne de Chêne (Luxembourg); Grand Croix Ordre de la Couronne (Belgium); Grand-Croix de l'Ordre d'Orange-Nassau (Netherlands).

Ministry of Family Affairs, Social Welfare and Housing, Luxembourg, Grand Duchy of Luxembourg.

Buchthal, Fritz, M.D.; Danish neurophysiologist; b. 19 Aug. 1907, Witten, Germany; *s.* of Sally Buchthal and Hedvig Weyl; *m.* Margaret A. Lennox, M.D.; ed. Albert-Ludwig-Universität, Freiburg im Breisgau, Germany, Stanford Univ., California, U.S.A., and Humboldt-Universität zu Berlin.

Assistant in Physiology, Univ. of Berlin 30-32; Inst. for Theory of Gymnastics, Copenhagen Univ. 33-43; Physiological Inst., Lund Univ. 43-45; Dir. Inst. of Neurophysiology, Copenhagen Univ. 46-, Prof. of Neurophysiology 55-; Chief, Dept. of Neurophysiology, Univ. Hospital 45-; Consultant, Nat. Inst. of Health, U.S.A. 59; Visiting Prof. Univ. of California 62, Academia Sinica 64, N.Y. Univ. 65; mem. Royal Danish Acad. Sciences 46, Danish Acad. of Technical Sciences, Royal Swedish Acad. of Sciences 68, Royal Soc. of Sciences (Sweden) 72; Hon. mem. French Neurological Soc., Polish Neurological Soc., German EEG Soc, English EEG Soc., Italian EEG and Clinical Neurophysiological Soc. and American Soc. for Electrodiagnosis and Electromyography; Corresp. mem. German Physiological and Neurological Socs., American Neurological Asscn., Italian Neurological Soc.; Hon. M.D. (Münster, Zürich); numerous awards.

Leisure interest: gardening.

Publs. *Mechanical Properties of Muscle Fibre* 42, *Rheology of Muscle* 51, *An Introduction to Electromyography* 57, *Electrophysiological Aspects of Myopathy* 63, *Evoked action potential and conduction velocity in human sensory nerve* 66, *Electrical and Mechanical Responses of Normal and Myasthenic Muscle* 68.

Jöbredden 24, Gentofte, Denmark 2820. Telephone: Gentofte 6629.

Buchwald, Art; American journalist, author and playwright; b. 20 Oct. 1925, New York; *s.* of Helen Kleinberger and Joseph Buchwald; *m.* Ann McGarry 1952; one *s.* two *d.*; ed. Univ. of Southern Calif., Los Angeles.

Columnist, *Herald Tribune,* Paris 48-62; syndicated columnist to 450 newspapers throughout the world 52-: Prix de la Bonne Humeur.

Publs. *Paris After Dark, Art Buchwald's Paris, I Chose Caviar, More Caviar, A Gift from the Boys, Don't Forget to Write, How much is that in Dollars?* 61, *Is It Safe to Drink the Water?* 62, *I Chose Capitol Punishment* 63, *And Then I told the President* 65, *Son of the Great Society* 67, *Have I ever Lied to you?* 68, *Oh, to be a Swinger* 70, *Getting High in Government Circles* 71, *I Never Danced at the White House* 73.

1750 Penn Avenue, N.W., Washington, D.C., U.S.A. Telephone: Washington 298-7990.

Buckle, (Christopher) Richard (Sandford); British writer, critic and exhibition designer; b. 6 Aug. 1916; ed. Marlborough Coll. and Balliol Coll., Oxford.

Founded *Ballet* 39; army service 40-46; Ballet Critic, *The Observer* 48-55, *Sunday Times* 59-; organizer The Diaghilev Exhibition, Edinburgh Festival and London 54, *The Observer* Film Exhibition, London 56, Telford Bicentenary Exhibition 57, Epstein Memorial Exhibition, Edinburgh, 61, The Shakespeare Exhibition (for Quatercentenary), Stratford-on-Avon and Edinburgh 64; designer, Exhibition Rooms, Harewood House, Yorks. and area in "Man in the Community" Pavilion, Expo 67 exhbn. Montreal, Gala of Ballet, London 71; Plays: *Gossip Column,* Q Theatre 53 and *Family Tree,* Worthing 56.

Publs. *John Innocent at Oxford* (novel) 39, *The Adventures of a Ballet Critic* 53, *In Search of Diaghilev* 55, *Modern Ballet Design* 55, *The Prettiest Girl in England* 58, *Harewood* (a guide book) 59, *Dancing for Diaghilev* (the Memoirs of Lydia Sokolova) 60, introductions to *Epstein Drawings* 62, and *Epstein: An Autobiography*

63, *Jacob Epstein: Sculptor* 63, *Monsters at Midnight* (limited edn.) 66, *The Message, a Gothick Tale of the A1* (limited edn.) 69, *Nijinsky* 71.
34 Henrietta Street, Covent Garden, London, W.C.2, England.
Telephone: 01-240-2111.

Buckley, James Lane, LL.B.; American politician; b. 9 March 1923, New York City; m. Anne F. Cooley 1953; six c.; ed. Yale Univ.
Served U.S. Navy 43-46; Senator from New York 71-; Republican.
2801 New Mexico Avenue, Washington, D.C. 20007, U.S.A.

Buckley, William Frank, Jr.; American editor and author; b. 24 Nov. 1925, New York; s. of William Frank and Aloise (Steiner) Buckley; m. Patricia Taylor 1950; one s.; ed. Univ. of Mexico and Yale Univ.
Formerly on staff *American Mercury*; Editor-in-Chief *National Review* 55-; syndicated columnist 62-; host of weekly television series *Firing Line* 66-; lecturer New School for Social Research 67; mem. U.S.I.A. Advisory Comm. 69-72; Chair. Starr Broadcasting Group; mem. U.S. del. to UN; contributor to *Harper's, Esquire, Saturday review, Atlantic,* etc.
Leisure interests: skiing, sailing, music.
Publs. *God and Man at Yale* 51, *Up from Liberalism* 59, *Rumbles Left and Right* 63, *The Unmaking of a Mayor* 66, *The Jeweler's Eye* 68, *The Governor Listeth* 70, *Crusing Speed* 71, *Inveighing We Will Go* 72, *Four Reforms* 73, *United Nations Journal* 74; co-author *McCarthy and His Enemies* 54; Editor *The Committee and Its Critics* 62, *Odyssey of a Friend* 70, *Did You Ever See A Dream Walking* 70.
National Review, 150 East 35th Street, New York, N.Y. 10016, U.S.A.
Telephone: OR 9-7330.

Buckwitz, Harry; German theatre director and producer; b. 31 March 1904, Munich, Bavaria; s. of Alfred and Helene Buckwitz; m. Nuri Buckwitz (née Wagner) 1959; two d.; ed. Realgymnasium and Univ. of Munich.
Hotel Man., Tanganyika 37-40; Dir. Münchner Kammerspiele 45-51; Gen. Man. Frankfurt/Main Municipal Theatres 51-; Dir. Schauspielhaus, Zurich 70-; producer of opera, plays, TV; first production several plays of Brecht, Thornton Wilder, Arthur Miller, Dürrenmatt, Max Frisch.
Leisure interest: mountaineering.
6242 Kronberg im Taunus, Königsteiner Strasse 2, Hellhof, Federal Republic of Germany; and 8044 Zürich, Krähbühlstrasse 6, Switzerland.
Telephone: 0-61-73/47-14 (Kronberg); 32-66-92 (Zürich).

Budashkin, Nikolai Pavlovich; Soviet composer; b. 6 August 1910, Mikhailovskaya Village, Kaluga Region; ed. Moscow Conservatoire.
Honoured R.S.F.S.R. Art Worker; Order of Red Star 43.
Compositions include 1st *Symphony* 37, *Sonatina for Piano* 37, *Holiday Overture* 37, *Russian Rhapsody, At the Fair*; State Prizes 47, 49, for *Russian Fantasia, Second Rhapsody* and *Thought*.
U.S.S.R. Union of Composers, 8-10 Nezhdanova ulitsa, Moscow, U.S.S.R.

Budd, John Marshall; American railway executive; see *The International Who's Who 1975-76*.

Buddington, Arthur F., PH.B., M.S., PH.D.; American geologist; b. 29 Nov. 1890, Wilmington, Del.; s. of Osmer G. Buddington and Mary S. Wheeler; m. Jene E. Muntz 1924; one d.; ed. Brown and Princeton Univs.
Instructor Brown Univ. 17; Petrologist Geophysical Laboratory Carnegie Inst. Washington 19-20; Asst. Prof. of Geology Princeton Univ. 20-26, Assoc. Prof. 26-32 and fmr. Prof., Chair. Geology Dept. 36-50;

Geologist U.S. Geological Survey, Summers 21-25, 30, 43-61; Geologist N.Y. State Museum, Summers 16-17, 26-29, 31-41; mem. Emer. Nat. Acad. of Sciences; mem., American Philosophical Soc., American Acad. of Arts and Sciences; Hon. mem. Mineralogical Soc., U.K.; Penrose Medal (American Geological Soc.) 54; Roebling Medal (American Mineralogical Soc.) 56; André Dumont Medal (Geological Soc., Belgium) 60; Hon. D.Sc. (Brown Univ.), Hon. LL.D. (Franklin and Marshall Coll.), Hon. Dr. of Applied Science (Liège Univ.).
Publs. *Geology of S.E. Alaska* 29, *Adirondack Igneous Rocks and their Metamorphism* 39, *Iron—Titanium Oxide Minerals* 64, *Origin of Anorthosite* 69.
Department of Geology, Princeton University, Princeton, N.J. 08540, U.S.A.

Budker, Gersh Itskovich; Soviet physicist; b. 1 May 1918, Muraffa Village, Ukraine; ed. Moscow Univ.
Associate Inst. of Atomic Energy, U.S.S.R. Acad. of Sciences 46-57; Prof., Moscow Eng. and Physics Inst. 56-57; Dir. Inst. of Nuclear Physics, Siberian Dept., U.S.S.R. Acad. of Sciences 57-; Presidium mem. Siberian Dept. U.S.S.R. Acad. of Sciences 58-; mem. U.S.S.R. Acad. of Sciences 64-; Lenin Prize 67; Order of Lenin; Order of Red Banner of Labour; various medals.
Institute of Nuclear Physics, Siberian Department, U.S.S.R. Academy of Sciences, Akademgorodok, Novosibirsk, U.S.S.R.

Budowski, Gerardo, PH.D.; Venezuelan agronomist and silviculturalist; b. 10 June 1925, Berlin, Germany; s. of Dr. Issar Budowski and Marguerite Wolffgang; m. Thelma T. Palma 1958; two d.; ed. Univ. Central, El Valle, Caracas, Inter-American Inst. of Agricultural Sciences, Turrialba, Costa Rica and Yale Univ. School of Forestry.
Director of Research, Ministry of Agriculture Forestry Service 47-49, Head 49-52; Forester, Inter-American Inst. of Agricultural Sciences, Havana 53-55, Turrialba 56-58, Head, Forestry Dept. 58-67; Visiting Prof. of Geography and Forestry, Univ. of Calif., Berkeley 67; Programme Specialist for Ecology and Conservation, UNESCO, Paris 67-70; Dir.-Gen. Int. Union for Conservation of Nature and Natural Resources.
Leisure interest: chess (several times champion of Venezuela and mem. of Olympic team).
Publs. over 100 publications.
International Union for Conservation of Nature and Natural Resources, 1110 Morges, Switzerland.
Telephone: (021) 71-44-01.

Bueche, Dr. Arthur Maynard, B.S., PH.D.; American chemist; b. 14 Nov. 1920, Flushing, Mich.; s. of late Bernard Paul and Margaret Rekert Bueche; one s. three d.; ed. Univ. of Michigan, Ohio State and Cornell Univs.
Research Assoc., Cornell Univ. 47-49; Gen. Electric Research Laboratory, Physical Chemist 50-53, Man. Polymer and Interface Studies 53-61, Man. Chem. Research 61-65, Vice-Pres. Research and Devt. and Dir. Research and Devt. Centre Schenectady, N.Y. 65-; mem. Nat. Acad. of Sciences 71-, Nat. Acad. of Eng. 74; Hon. Sc.D. (St. Lawrence Univ., Union Coll., D. Clarkson Coll. of Tech., Univ. of Akron), Hon. LL.D. (Knox Coll.), Eng. D. (Rensselaer Polytechnic Inst.).
Leisure interests: golf, skiing, photography.
Publs. more than thirty scientific papers; eleven patents.
P.O. Box 8, Schenectady, N.Y. 12301, U.S.A.
Telephone: 518-346-8771 Ext. 6331.

Bueno y Monreal, H.E. Cardinal José Maria, D.THEOL., D.PHIL., D.IUR.UTR.; Spanish ecclesiastic; b. 11 Sept. 1904; ed. Madrid Seminary, Gregorian Univ., Rome, and Madrid Univ.
Ordained priest 27; fmr. Prof. of Dogmatic Theology,

Canon Law and Moral Theology, Madrid Seminary; fmr. Prof. Inst. Cen. de Cultura Religiosa Superior; Fiscal, Archbishopric of Madrid 29-45, Doctoral Canon 45; Bishop of Jaca 45-50, of Vitoria 50-54; Titular Archbishop of Antioch in Pisidia and Coadjutor Archbishop of Seville 54-57; Archbishop of Seville 57-; created Cardinal by Pope John XXIII 58; mem. Sacred Congregations of Religious, of Rites and of Ceremonies; Gran Oficial, Orden del Sol (Peru), Cruz Meritísima de San Raimundo de Peñafort, Gran Cruz, Orden de Isabel la Católica; Dr. h.c., Zaragoza Univ.
Publs. *Las Relaciones entre la Iglesia y el Estado en los modernos Concordatos* 31, *Principios fundamentales de Derecho público eclesiástico* 45.
Palacio Arzobispal, Seville, Spain.
Telephone: 22-56-57.

Buerger, Martin Julian, S.M., PH.D.; American mineralogist and crystallographer; b. 8 April 1903, Detroit, Mich.; s. of Martin J. G. Buerger and Julie E. Buerger; m. Lila Mae MacAskill 1938; five d.; ed. Mass. Inst. of Technology.
Research Asst., Dept. of Geology, Mass. Inst. of Technology 25, Instructor 27, Asst. Prof. of Mineralogy 29, Assoc. Prof. 35, Prof. of Mineralogy and Crystallography 44-56, Faculty Chair. 54-56, Dir. School for Advanced Study 56-63, Inst. Prof. 56-68, Inst. Prof. Emer. 68-; Univ. Prof. Univ. of Conn. 68-73, Prof. Emer. 73-; Hon. Research Assoc., Harvard Univ. 73-; Visiting Prof. Univs. Rio de Janeiro 48, Santiago 62, Minneapolis 69, Va. Polytechnic Inst. 74; Pres. American Soc. of X-ray and Electron Diffraction 48, Crystallographic Soc. of America 39-46; Pres. Mineralogical Soc. of America 47; Co-Editor *International Tables for X-ray Crystallography* 46; Councillor American Acad. of Arts and Sciences 50-54; Vice-Pres. Geological Soc. of America 48; mem. Exec. Cttee. Int. Union of Crystallography 46; Ed. *Wiley Monographs on Crystallography* 65-; mem. Nat. Acad. of Sciences; foreign mem. Brazilian Acad. of Sciences and Turin Acad. of Sciences; Hon. mem. Real Sociedad Española de Historia Natural 64; Corresp. mem. Bavarian Acad. of Sciences 60-, Austrian Acad. of Sciences 62-; Hon. mem. German Mineralogical Soc. 57; Day Medallist, Geological Soc. of America 51; Roebling Medallist, Mineralogical Soc. of America 58; Isidor Fankuchen Memorial Award, Amer. Crystallographic Assoc. 71; Dr. h.c. Berne 58; Co-Editor *Zeitschrift für Kristallographie* 55-.
Publs. *Optical Crystallography* 35, *X-ray Crystallography* 42, *Elementary Crystallography* 56, *The Powder Method in X-ray Crystallography* (with L. V. Azaroff) 58, *Vector Space* 59, *Crystal-Structure Analysis* 60, *The Precession Method in X-ray Crystallography* 64, *Contemporary Crystallography* 70, *Introduction to Crystal Geometry* 71, *The LAUE Method* (with J. L. and M. C. Amoros) 75, about 200 scientific journal articles.
Department of Geological Sciences, Harvard University, 20 Oxford Street, Cambridge, Mass. 02138; and Weston Road, Lincoln, Mass., U.S.A.

Buero Vallejo, Antonio; Spanish playwright; b. 29 Sept. 1916, Guadalajara; s. of Teniente Coronel Francisco Buero and Cruz Vallejo; m. Victoria Rodríguez 1959; two s.; ed. Instituto de Segunda Enseñanza de Guadalajara and Escuela de Bellas Artes de Madrid.
Visiting Lecturer numerous Univs. in U.S.A. 66; Hon. Fellow, Círculo de Bellas Artes, American Asscn. of Teachers of Spanish and Portuguese; mem. Hispanic Soc. of America, Real Acad. Española, Int. Cttee. of the Theatre of the Nations; Premio Lope de Vega 49; Premio Nacional de Teatro 57, 58, 59; Premio Maria Rolland 56, 58, 60; Premio March de Teatro 59; Premio de la Crítica de Barcelona 60; Premio Larra 62; Medalla de Oro del Espectador y la Crítica 67, 70, 74; Premio Leopoldo Cano 68, 71, 72, Premio Mayte 74.

Leisure interest: painting.
Plays: *Historia de una Escalera* 49, *Las palabras en la arena* 49, *En la Ardiente Oscuridad* 50, *La Tejedora de Sueños* 52, *La señal que se espera* 52, *Casi un Cuento de Hadas* 53, *Madrugada* 53, *Irene, o el Tesoro* 54, *Hoy es Fiesta* 56, *Las Cartas boca Abajo* 57, *Un Soñador para un Pueblo* 58, *Las Meninas* 60, *El Concierto de San Ovidio* 62, *Aventura en lo Gris* 63, *El Tragaluz* 67, *La doble historia del Dr. Valmy* 67, *Mito* 68, *El Sueño de la razón* 70, *Llegada de los dioses* 71, *La Fundación* 74; essays: *Tres Maestros ante el público* 73.
Calle Hermanos Miralles 36, Madrid 1, Spain.
Telephone: 402-56-14.

Bueso, Guillermo; Honduran government official; b. 8 Dec. 1931; m.; seven c.; ed. Univ. of Honduras and Harvard Univ.
Banco Central de Honduras, Economist and Div. Chief, Research, Balance of Payments and Industrial Research depts. 51-62, Dir. Research Dept. 62-, Technical Adviser 71-; Rep. for Honduras in a number of int. bodies and at int. confs., including Inter-American Econ. and Social Council, and Alliance for Progress 62-68, UNCTAD 64, Central American Monetary Council and Central American Common Market 64-72, meetings of Govs. of the Latin American Central Banks 65-72; Prof. of Money and Banking, Faculty of Econ. Sciences, Nat. Autonomous Univ. of Honduras 63-64; Int. Monetary Fund, Alternate Gov. for Honduras 64-72, Exec. Dir. IMF 72-74.
Publs. articles on econs. and finance.
c/o Banco Central de Honduras, Tegucigalpa, Honduras.

Buffet, Bernard; French painter; b. 10 July 1928; ed. Lycée Carnot, Ecole Nat. Supérieure des Beaux-Arts.
Annual exhbns. 49-56 in Galerie Drouant-David, and in Galerie David & Garnier 57-; exhbns. in many foreign countries, including retrospective exhbns. Paris 58, Berlin 58, Belgium 59, Tokyo 63; illustrator of books, engraver, lithographer and stage designer; Grand Prix de la Critique 48.
Galerie Maurice Garnier, 6 avenue Matignon, Paris 8e, France.

Buffum, William Burnside, M.LITT.; American diplomatist; b. 10 Sept. 1921, Binghampton, N.Y.; m. Alma Bauman; three c.; ed. Oneonta State Teachers' Coll., Univ. of Pittsburgh, Oxford and Harvard Univs.
Served U.S. Army 43-46; entered Foreign Service 49; has served in Stuttgart 49, Bonn 53-58; Deputy Dir. UN Political Affairs, Dept. of State 63-65, Dir. 65-66; Deputy Asst. Sec. of State for Int. Org. Affairs 65-67; Deputy Perm. Rep. to UN 67-70; Amb. to Lebanon 70-73; Asst. Sec. of State for Int. Org. Affairs 74-75; UN Under Sec.-Gen. in Charge of Political and General Assembly Affairs Dec. 75-; rep. to several sessions of UN Gen. Assembly.
Department of State, Washington, D.C. 20520, U.S.A.

Bugayev, Lieut.-Gen. Boris Pavlovich; Soviet pilot and politician; b. 29 July 1923, Cherkassy Region, Ukraine; ed. School of Civil Aviation.
Entered Soviet Army 43, served World War II; Deputy Minister, then First Deputy Minister, U.S.S.R. Ministry of Civil Aviation 66-70; Minister of Civil Aviation May 70-; Deputy to U.S.S.R. Supreme Soviet 70-; Merited Pilot, Hero of Socialist Labour, Hammer and Sickle Gold Medal, Order of Lenin (twice), Red Banner (twice), Badge of Honour, U.S.S.R. State prizewinner, etc.
Ministry of Civil Aviation, 37 Leningradsky prospekt, Moscow, U.S.S.R.

Bugayev, Yevgeni Iosifovich; Soviet politician and journalist; b. 26 Nov. 1912, Krasovo Village, Byelorussia; ed. Chernyshevsky Inst. of History, Philosophy and Literature, Moscow, and Higher Party School Moscow.

Komsomol work 38-40; mem. C.P.S.U. 39-; party work 42-44; Sec. Gomel Regional Cttee., C.P. of Byelorussia 44-46; Sec. Central Cttee., C.P. of Byelorussia 46-47; Sec. Minsk Regional Cttee. of C.P.S.U. 48-49, Omsk 49-54; Chief Editor *Partiinaya Zhizn* (Party Life) 54-56, 61-66; Apparatus of Central Cttee. of C.P.S.U. 56-58; Editorial Dept. Head *Problemy Mira i Sotsialisma* (Problems of Peace and Socialism) 58-60; Chief Editor *Voprosy Istorii K.P.S.S.* (Questions of History of C.P.S.U.) 60-61; Editor-in-Chief *Party Life* 61-66; Deputy Editor-in-Chief and mem. Editorial Board *Kommunist* 66-; mem. Central Auditing Comm. of C.P.S.U. 61-66; Order of Lenin, Red Banner of Labour (2) and medals.
Kommunist, ul. Marx-Engels 5, Moscow, U.S.S.R.

Bugnard, Louis; French biophysicist; b. 7 July 1901, Foix, Ariège; *m.* Marguerite Blayac 1931; one *s.*; ed. Ecole Polytechnique and Univ. of Toulouse.
Professor, Faculty of Medicine, Paris 30-46, Hon. Prof. 46-71; Dir. Inst. Nat. d'Hygiène, Paris 46-64; Conseiller Scientifique, Commissariat of Atomic Energy 64-71; Commdr. Légion d'Honneur; mem. Acad. de Médecine; mem. Acad. de Chirurgie.
1 rue Las-Cases, Paris 75007, France.
Telephone: 551-1104.

Bühler, Hans, DR. RER. POL.; German business executive; b. 25 Nov. 1903, Freiburg i. Br.; ed. Univs. of Freiburg, Kiel und Tübingen.
Joined AEG 29, Gen. Man. 57; mem. Man. Board AEG-Telefunken 64, Chair. Man. Board 66-70, Chair. Supervisory Board 70-; hon. adviser to numerous econ. orgs. and insts.; Ehrensenator, Univ. of Erlangen 60; Bayerischer Verdienstorden 62; Grosses Bundesverdienstkreuz.
AEG-Telefunken, 6 Frankfurt 70, AEG Hochhaus, Federal Republic of Germany.
Telephone: (0611) 600-41-95.

Buiter, Harm Geert, D.ECON.; Netherlands trade unionist; b. 8 Jan. 1922, Tubbergen; *s.* of Klaas Buiter and J. Buiter-Van Dalen; *m.* Hendrien Van Schooten 1947; two *s.* one *d.*; ed. Univ. van Amsterdam.
Former mem. Socialist Youth Movement; Chair. Socialist Students Union of Amsterdam Univ.; active in Dutch resistance during Second World War; Research Officer Dutch Metalworkers Fed. 47; headed Joint Industrial Cttee. for metal industry in The Hague 48-51; Sec. to Workers' Group of Metal Trades Cttee. of Int. Labour Org.; Pres. European Coal and Steel Community study mission sent to U.S. 54; headed Gen. Secretariat of ECSC Trade Union Cttee. in Luxembourg 56; Gen. Sec. European Trade Union Secretariat, Brussels 58-67; Gen. Sec. Int. Confederation of Free Trade Unions (ICFTU) 67-71; Burgomaster of Groningen 71-.
Leisure interests: reading, theatre, stamp collecting.
Town Hall, Grote Markt. 1, Groningen; Kamplaan 10, Groningen, Netherlands.
Telephone: 179111 (Office).

Bulatović, Miodrag; Yugoslav writer; b. 20 Feb. 1930; ed. Univ. of Belgrade.
Wrote his early works in hospitals and Red Cross centres while leading a wandering life.
Publs. *Djavoli dolaze* (Devils Arrive) short stories 56, *Vuk i Zvono* (The Wolf and the Bell) novel-poem 58, *Crveni Petao leti prema nebu* (The Red Cockerel) novel 60, *Hero on a Donkey* novel 65, *Godot Game* play 66.
Ljubljana, Krekov 'rg 7, Yugoslavia.

Bulatović, Vukoje; Yugoslav journalist; b. 18 March 1927, Medevci, Medvedja; *s.* of Sava and Milosava Čalovec; *m.* Branka Gavrilović 1960; one *s.*; ed. Univ. of Belgrade.

Scientific Assoc., Inst. for Int. Labour Movt., Belgrade 57-60; Rome Corresp. for *Komunist* newspaper 64-69, Foreign Desk Editor 70; Sec. of Information, Socialist Repub. of Serbia 70-74; mem. Exec. Cttee. of the Presidency of the Cen. Cttee., League of Communists of Serbia 74-75; Dir. of *Politika* Publrs., Editor-in-Chief *Politika* daily Feb. 75-; Memorial Order 41; Order for Courage (twice); Order of Merit for the People; Grand Officer of Italian Repub.
Leisure interest: fishing.
Politika, Makedonska ulica 29, Belgrade, Yugoslavia.
Telephone: 329-367, 325-609.

Bulgakov, Alexandr Alexandrovich; Soviet politician; b. 1907; ed. Kharkov Electrotechnical Inst.
Member C.P.S.U. 37-; electrical engineer, factory party organizer, later Sec. Kharkov City Cttee., C.P. Ukraine 39-43; Chair. Exec. Cttee. Kharkov City Soviet of Workers' Deputies 53-54; Second Sec. Kharkov Regional Cttee. C.P. Ukraine 54-59; Sec. All-Union Central Council of Trade Unions 59-64; Chair. State Cttee. for Professional and Technical Education, U.S.S.R. Council of Ministers 64-; Cand. mem. Central Cttee. C.P.S.U. 61-71; Deputy to U.S.S.R. Supreme Soviet 62-.
State Committee for Professional and Technical Education in U.S.S.R. Council of Ministers, 16 Sadovo Sukharevskaya ul., Moscow, U.S.S.R.

Bulin, René Henri; French aeronautical engineer; b. 8 Aug. 1920; ed. Ecole Polytechnique Paris, Ecole Nationale Supérieure de l'Aéronautique.
Engineer responsible for setting up Centre d'Essais des Propulseurs 46-53; instructor, Ecole Nationale de l'Aviation Civile 53-63; Deputy Dir., then Dir. Air Navigation, Secrétariat Général de l'Aviation Civile, France 56-61; first Dir.-Gen. European Org. for the Safety of Air Navigation (EUROCONTROL) 61-, responsible for having set up the Air Traffic Services Agency, Brussels and the EUROCONTROL Experimental Centre, Bretigny-sur-Orge and for establishing the Upper Area Control Centres, Maastricht, Netherlands; Karlsruhe, Germany; Shannon, Ireland; and the EUROCONTROL Inst. of Air Navigation Services, Luxembourg; Officier de la Légion d'Honneur, Officier de l'Ordre de Léopold 1er, Officier du Lion de Juda, Médaille de l'Aéronautique, Chevalier des Palmes Académiques, Commdr. Ordre de Luxembourg.
Publ. *Technique du Transport Aérien* 58
EUROCONTROL, 72 rue de la Loi, 1040 Brussels, Belgium.
Telephone: 13-83-00.

Buliro, Joshua Davies; Kenyan civil servant; b. 1932, Ebwali, Bunyore; *s.* of Mr. and Mrs. Zakayo Kwenda; *m.* Wathoni Waiyaki 1963; one *s.* two *d.*; ed. Maseno School, Kakamega Govt. School, Maseno Secondary School, and Makerere Univ. Coll., Uganda.
Operations Asst., Sales-Rep. and Asst. Operations Man., Shell Oil Co. 56-63; Kenya Civil Service 63-64; Asst. Sec.-Gen. Organisation of African Unity (OAU) 64-75.
Leisure interests: hockey, cultural presentations/exhibitions.
c/o Ministry of Foreign Affairs, Nairobi, Kenya.

Bull, Lt.-Gen. Odd; Norwegian air force officer and United Nations official; b. 28 June 1907, Oslo; *s.* of Gjert Bull and Sigrid Bull (née Oddvin); *m.* Inga-Lisa Furugård 1953; one *s.*; ed. Vestheim School, Oslo Univ. and Norwegian Army Acad.
Norwegian Army 28-31, Air Force 31-; Norwegian Air Force in Norway, U.K. and Canada 40-45, Norway 45-48; Deputy Chief of Air Staff, Royal Norwegian Air Force 48-51; Deputy Chief of Staff Operations, Allied Air Forces, N. Europe 51-53; Air Commdr., N. Norway 53-56; Commdr. Tactical Air Forces, Norway 56-58; Exec. mem. UN Observation Group, Lebanon 58;

Special Rep. of UN Sec.-Gen. for British Air Evacuation and Flight Control from Jordan Oct. 58; Commdr. Tactical Air Forces, Norway 59-60, Chief of Air Staff, Royal Norwegian Air Force 60-63; Chief of Staff, UN Truce Supervision Org. Palestine June 63-70; co-operated with Israel and Jordanian authorities to secure Pope Paul's pilgrimage to the Holy Land, Jan. 64; mem. Int. Peace Acad.; Grand Cross Order of St. Olav and other Norwegian and foreign awards; UN Medal "In the Service of Peace" (twice); Hon. Citizen of Texas.

Leisure interests: skiing, swimming, reading (especially history).

Nedre Baastad Vei 48, 1370 Asker, Norway.

Telephone: 02-782274.

Bullard, Sir Edward C., Kt., sc.D., f.r.s.; British geophysicist; b. 21 Sept. 1907, Norwich; s. of Edward John Bullard and Eleanor Howes Crisp; m. 1st Margaret Ellen Thomas 1931 (divorced 1974), four d.; m. 2nd Ursula Margery Curnow 1975; ed. Repton and Clare Coll., Cambridge.

Demonstrator in Geodesy Cambridge 31-35; Smithson Research Fellow Royal Society 36-43; F.R.S. 41; research work for Admiralty 39-45; Fellow of Clare Coll., Cambridge 43-48 and 57-60, Churchill Coll., Cambridge 60-, Reader in Geophysics 45-48, 60-64; Head of Physics Dept., Univ. of Toronto 48-49; Dir. Nat. Physical Lab. 50-55; Fellow, Caius Coll., Cambridge 55-56, Prof. of Geophysics 64-74; Prof. Univ. of Calif. 63-; mem. Natural Environment Research Council 65-68, 70-72; foreign assoc. U.S. Nat. Acad. of Sciences; foreign hon. mem. American Acad. of Arts and Sciences; foreign corresp. Geological Soc. of America; foreign mem. American Philosophical Soc.; Hughes Medal of Royal Soc. 53, Chree Medal of Physical Soc. 57, Day Medal of Geological Soc. of America 59, Agassiz Medal of U.S. Nat. Acad. of Sciences 65, Gold Medal of Royal Astronomical Soc. 65, Wollaston Medal of Geological Soc. of London 67, Vetlesen Prize 68, Bowie Medal American Geophysical Union 75, Royal Medal of Royal Soc. 75.

IGPP A-025, University of California, La Jolla, Calif. 92093, U.S.A.

Telephone: (714) 452-2159.

Bullard, Sir Reader (William), k.c.b., k.c.m.g., c.i.e.; British diplomatist; b. 5 Dec. 1885.

Acting Vice-Consul Beirut 09-10, Vice-Consul Bitlis 10-11; Acting Consul Trebizond 12, Erzerum 13, Basra 14; Civil Adviser to Principal Military Gov. Basra 14; Political Officer Kifri 18; Deputy Revenue Sec. Mesopotamia 19; Military Gov. Baghdad 20; Middle East Dept. Colonial Office 21; British Agent and Consul Jeddah 23-25; Consul Athens 25-28, Addis Ababa 28; Consul Gen. Moscow 30, Leningrad 31-34; Minister to Arabia 36-39, to Iran 39-44, Ambassador 44-46, retd. 46; Dir. Inst. of Colonial Studies, Oxford 51-56; mem. Governing Board of School of Oriental and African Studies, Univ. of London 53-65; mem. Buraimi Oasis Arbitration Tribunal 54-55.

Publs. *Britain and the Middle East* 52, *The Camels Must Go* (autobiog.) 61.

46 Plantation Road, Oxford, England.

Telephone: Oxford 59259.

Bullen, Keith Edward, M.A., B.SC., PH.D., SC.D., F.R.S., F.A.A.; Australian university professor; b. 29 June 1906, Auckland; s. of George Sherrar Bullen and Maud Hannah Bullen (née Burfoot); m. Florence Mary Pressley 1935; one s. one d.; ed. Auckland Grammar School and Auckland Univ., New Zealand, and St. John's Coll., Cambridge.

Master, Auckland Grammar School, New Zealand 26-27; Lecturer in Mathematics, Auckland Univ. 27-31, 34-40; Special Lectureship, Hull Univ. 33; Senior

Lecturer in Mathematics, Melbourne Univ. 40-45; Prof. of Applied Mathematics, Univ. of Sydney 46-71, now Emeritus Prof.; Flinders Lecturer, Australian Acad. of Science 69; Pres. Int. Asscn. of Seismology and Physics of Earth's Interior 54-57; Vice-Pres. Int. Union of Geodesy and Geophysics 63-67, Int. Scientific Cttee. for Antarctic Research 58-62; Chair. Australian Nat. Cttee. for Int. Geophysical Year 55-60; Convener, Australian Nat. Cttee. for Antarctic Research 58-62; Chair. Int. Cttee. on Standard Earth Model 71-75; Visiting Prof. Univ. of British Columbia 72-73; Foreign Assoc. U.S. Nat. Acad. of Sciences; Foreign Hon. mem. American Acad. of Arts and Science; Hon. mem. Royal Soc. of New Zealand, Hon. Fellow Royal Soc. of N.S.W. 74; Pontifical Academician; Foreign and Commonwealth mem. Geological Soc. of London; Hon. D.Sc.; Gold Medal, Royal Astronomical Soc. 74 and numerous other medals.

Leisure interest: numismatics.

Publs. *Introduction to the Theory of Seismology* 47 (3rd edn. 63), *Introduction to the Theory of Mechanics* 49 (8th edn. 71), *Seismology* 54, *The Earth's Density* 75.

c/o Department of Applied Mathematics, University of Sydney, N.S.W. 2006; and 132 Fuller's Road, Chatswood, N.S.W. 2067, Australia.

Bullitt, John C.; American lawyer; b. 6 June 1925, Philadelphia, Pa.; s. of Orville H. Bullitt and Susan Ingersoll; m. Lelia M. Wardwell 1954; one s. one d.; ed. Harvard Coll. and Univ. of Pennsylvania Law School.

Lawyer, Shearman Sterling, New York 53-60; Deputy Asst. Sec. for Int. Affairs, U.S. Treasury 61-62, Asst. Sec. 62-64; Exec. Dir. Int. Bank for Reconstruction and Devt. 62-65; Dir. N.J. Office of Econ. Opportunity 65-67; Asst. Admin. for East Asia, AID, Dept. of State 67-69; Partner, Shearman Sterling; Trustee, Chair. Finance Cttee. The Population Council; Trustee Franklin Book Programs, W. Hem. Int. Planned Parenthood Fed.

53 Wall Street, New York, N.Y. 10005, U.S.A.

Telephone: (212) 483-1000.

Bullock, Baron (Life Peer) cr. 76, of Leafield in the County of Oxfordshire; **Alan Louis Charles Bullock,** Kt., F.B.A., M.A., D.LITT.; British author and university administrator; b. 13 Dec. 1914, Trowbridge; s. of Rev. Frank A. Bullock; m. Hilda Yates Handy 1940; three s. two d. (one deceased); ed. Bradford Grammar School, Wadham and Merton Colls., Oxford.

B.B.C. European Service diplomatic and political corresp. 40-45; Fellow, Dean and Tutor of New Coll., Oxford 45-52; Master of St. Catherine's Coll., Oxford 60-; Censor, St. Catherine's Soc., Oxford 52-60; mem. Arts Council 61-64, British Library Organizing Cttee. 72-73, Cttee. of Vice-Chancellors and Principals 69-73; Vice-Chancellor, Univ. of Oxford 69-73; Chair. Inquiry into Teaching of Reading and Other Uses of Language 72-74; Chair. Trustees of Tate Gallery 73-; Chair. Cttee. on Industrial Democracy 75-; Trustee Wolfson Foundation; Trustee and Fellow Aspen Inst.; Chair. Research Committee and mem. Council, Royal Institute of Int. Affairs (Chatham House); former Chair. Nat. Advisory Council on Training and Supply of Teachers; mem. Advisory Council on Public Records; fmr. Chair. The Schools Council, Board of Int. Asscn. for Cultural Freedom; Joint Editor *Oxford History of Modern Europe*, Int. Comm. of Historians for publication of documents on German Foreign Policy 1918-45; Hon. doctorates Aix-Marseilles, Bradford and Reading Univs.; Hon. Fellow, Merton, Wadham, Wolfson and Linacre Colls., Oxford; Chevalier Légion d'Honneur 70. Publs. *Hitler, a Study in Tyranny* 52, 62, *The Liberal Tradition* 56, *Schellenberg Memoirs* 56, *The Life and Times of Ernest Bevin*, Vol. I 60, Vol. II 67, *The Twentieth Century* (editor) 71.

The Master's Lodgings, St. Catherine's College, Oxford, England.
Telephone: Oxford 49541.

Bullock, Sir Ernest, Kt., C.V.O., D.MUS., LL.D. F.R.C.M., F.R.C.O., F.R.S.A.M.D., F.R.S.C.M.; British musician; b. 15 Sept. 1890, Wigan, Lancs.; s. of late Thomas Bullock; m. Margery Newborn 1919; two s. one d.; ed. Wigan Grammar School and privately; studied music under Sir Edward C. Bairstow.
Assistant Organist, Leeds Parish Church; Organist, Micklefield Church and Adel Church; Sub-Organist, Manchester Cathedral 12; with H.M. Forces 15-19; Organist, St. Michael's Coll., Tenbury 19, Exeter Cathedral 19-27; Organist and Master of the Choristers, Westminster Abbey 28-41, in charge of the music and conductor at the Coronation of King George VI 37; Gardiner Prof. of Music in the Univ. of Glasgow, and Principal of the Royal Scottish Acad. of Music and Drama 41-52; Dir. Royal Coll. of Music 53-60; held office as Pres. of Incorporated Soc. of Musicians, Royal Coll. of Organists, Incorporated Asscn. of Organists, etc.; Hon. RAM.
Leisure interests: pottering in the garden, playing patience, writing music for own amusement.
Works include songs, part-songs, organ music, church music, choral, etc.
Welby Cottage, Long Crendon, Aylesbury, Bucks., England.

Bullock, Theodore Holmes, PH.D.; American professor of neurosciences; b. 16 May 1915, Nanking, China; s. of A. Archibald and Ruth Beckwith Bullock; m. Martha Runquist 1937; one s. one d.; ed. Univ. of Calif., Berkeley.
Sterling Fellow, Yale Univ. 40-41; Rockefeller Fellow 41-42; Instructor in Neuroanatomy, Yale Univ. 42-44; Asst. Prof. of Anatomy, Univ. of Missouri 44-46; Instructor and sometime Head, Invertebrate Zoology, Marine Biol. Lab., Woods Hole, Mass.; Asst. Prof., Assoc. Prof., Prof. of Zoology, Univ. of Calif., Los Angeles 46-66; Prof. of Neurosciences, Univ. of Calif. San Diego School of Medicine 66-; Head of Neurobiology Unit, Scripps Inst. of Oceanography; mem. Brain Research Inst., Univ. of Calif. at Los Angeles; Assoc., Neuroscience Research Program, Brookline, Mass.; mem. Nat. Acad. of Sciences, Amer. Phil. Soc.; former Pres. Amer. Soc. of Zoology, Soc. for Neuroscience; Lashley Prize, American Philosophical Soc. 68.
Publs. *Structure and Function in the Nervous Systems of Invertebrates* (with G. A. Horridge) 65.
A-001 Department of Neurosciences, University of California, San Diego, La Jolla, Calif. 92093, U.S.A.
Telephone: 714-452-3636.

Bulmer-Thomas, Ivor (see Thomas, Ivor Bulmer-).

Bultmann, Rudolf Karl; German theologian; b. 20 Aug. 1884, Wiefelstede, Oldenburg; s. of Arthur and Helene Bultmann; m. Helene Feldmann 1917; three d.; ed. Univs. of Tübingen, Berlin and Marburg.
Privatdozent for New Testament Exegesis, Univ. of Marburg 12-16; Asst. Prof. Univ. of Breslau 16-20; Prof. in Giessen 20-21; Prof. Univ. of Marburg 21-51, Emeritus 51-; hon. mem. Soc. of Biblical Literature and Exegesis; D.Theol. (Marburg), D.D. (St. Andrews); D.S.Th. (Syracuse, N.Y.), Dr.Phil. h.c. (Marburg); mem. Accademia Nazionale dei Lincei, Rome; Orden pour le mérite für Wissenschaften und Künste.
Leisure interests: literature, history, evangelical theology.
Publs. *Die Geschichte der synoptischen Tradition* 8th edn. 70, *Ergänzungsheft* 4th edn. 71, *Jesus* 64, *Das Evangelium des Johannes* 9th edn. 68, *Das Urchristentum im Rahmen der antiken Religionen* 3rd edn. 63, *Theologie des neuen Testaments* 6th edn. 68, *Geschichte und Eschatologie* 2nd edn. 64, *Glauben und Verstehen* Vols. I-IV 33-65, *Die 3 Johannesbriefe* 2nd edn. 69,

Exegetica (ed. E. Dinkler) 67, *Jesus Christus und die Mythologie* 3rd edn. 67, *Die Erforschung der synoptischen Evangelien* 5th edn. 66, *Das Verhältnis der urchristlichen Christusbotschaft zum historischen Jesus* 4th edn. 65, *Briefwechsel 1922-1966* (with Karl Barth; ed. B. Jaspert) 71, *Der zweiter Brief an die Korinther* 75.
355 Marburg/Lahn, Calvinstrasse 14, Federal Republic of Germany.
Telephone: 25265.

Bultrikova, Mrs. Balzhan; Soviet politician; b. 1921; ed. Kazakh Pedagogical Inst.
Member C.P.S.U. 43-; Head of a secondary school 41-49; Chair. Central Cttee. Elementary and Secondary School Workers' Union, Kazakh Repub. 49-55; Minister of Social Maintenance, Kazakh S.S.R. 55-66; Vice-Chair. Kazakh Council of Ministers and Minister of Foreign Affairs, Kazakh S.S.R. 66-71, Minister of Public Educ. 71-; Deputy to Supreme Soviet of U.S.S.R. 66-70; Deputy to Supreme Soviet of Kazakh S.S.R. 47-; mem. Central Cttee. C.P. of Kazakhstan.
Kazakh S.S.R. Ministry of Public Education, Alma-Ata, U.S.S.R.

Bulundwe, Kitongo Pengemali, (formerly Edouard Bulundwe); Zairian politician; b. in Katanga (now Shaba).
Former Pres.-Gen. of AKAKAT, tribal asscn. of the Kaonde; CONAKAT (Confédération des asscns. tribales du Katanga) Deputy for Haut-Katanga 60; in charge of work camps for political delinquents 60-61; one of twenty Katangan deputies who petitioned Pres. Kasavubu to release fmr. Prime Minister Tshombe and recognize the independent state of Katanga 61; Gov. of Katanga Orientale; visited the U.S.A. as official rep. of the Democratic Republic of the Congo Dec. 65; Minister of Public Works 66; Admin. of Collieries, Luena 66-67; Dir. of Katangan Provincial Cttee., Mouvement populaire de la révolution (MPR) 67-69; Gov. of Equateur Prov. March-Aug. 69, of Orientale 69-70; Minister of the Interior 70-72; mem. Political Bureau, MPR 70-.
Bureau Politique du Mouvement populaire de la révolution, Kinshasa, Zaire.

Bumbry, Grace; American opera singer; b. 4 Jan. 1937, St. Louis, Mo.; d. of Benjamin and Melzia Bumbry; ed. Boston, Chicago and Northwestern Univs.
Debut, Paris Opera as Amneris, *Aida* March 60; Basle Opera 60-63; *Carmen* with Paris Opera, and toured Japan; Royal Opera, Brussels; *Die Schwarze Venus*, *Tannhäuser*, Bayreuth Festival 62; Vienna State Opera 63; Covent Garden 63, 68, 69; Salzburg Festival 64; Metropolitan Opera 65; La Scala 66; Richard Wagner Medal 63; Hon. D.H. (Univ. of St. Louis).
Leisure interests: interior decorating, designing clothes.
c/o Metropolitan Opera Association, Lincoln Center Plaza, New York, N.Y. 10023, U.S.A.

Bumpers, Dale, LL.D.; American politician; b. 12 Aug. 1925, Charleston, Ark.; m. Betty Flanagan 1949; two s. one d.; ed. Univ. of Arkansas and North-western Law School.
Proprietor Charleston Hardware and Furniture Co. 51-66, Angus Breeding Farm 66-70; Attorney, Charleston, Ark. 51-70; Gov. of Arkansas 71-74; U.S. Senator from Arkansas Jan. 75-; Democrat.
Leisure interests: reading, tennis, hunting.
U.S. Senate, Washington, D.C. 20510, U.S.A.
Telephone: 202-224-4843.

Bunaciu, Avram, D.IUR.; Romanian politician; b. 11 Nov. 1909, Gurba, Arad; s. of Ioan Bunaciu and Raveca Brădean; m. Noemi Nussbächer 1939; one s. two d.; ed. Law Faculty, Cluj Univ.
Joined the Communist Party 39; active in the resistance during the war; Sec.-Gen. Ministry of Internal Affairs 45-47; Deputy of Grand Nat. Assembly 48-; Minister of

Justice 48-49; Pres. State Control Comm. 49; Asst. Minister of Foreign Affairs 50-52; Sec. Presidium, Grand Nat. Assembly 54-57; Minister of Justice 57-58, of Foreign Affairs 58-61; Vice-Pres. of State Council 61-65; alt. mem. Central Cttee. Romanian C.P. 48-55, full mem. 55-69; Pres. Constitutional Cttee., Grand Nat. Assembly 65-; Rector, C.I. Parhon Univ. (now Bucharest Univ.) 52.
Leisure interests: hiking, gardening.
Marea Adunare Natională a R.S. Romania, Bucharest; 10 Herăstrău Street, Bucharest, Romania.
Telephone: 162150 (Office); 336529 (Home).

Bundvad, Kaj; Danish politician; b. 8 July 1904, Fredrikshavn; s. of Christian and Karen Bundvad; m. 1st Ingrid Winther Bundvad (née Sørensen) 1934; m. 2nd Marie Winther Bundvad (née Sørensen) 1951, one s.
Engineering Apprentice 19-24, Mechanic 24-35; High School Teacher 35-45; M.P. 43-71; Sec. to Information Centre of Labour Movement 45-56; Sec. to Social Democratic Federation 56-57; Minister of Labour and Housing 57-60, Labour 60-61, Labour and Social Affairs 61-63, Social Affairs 63-68; mem. Nordic Council 53-57, 68-71, Cttee. of Foreign Affairs 56-57; Chair. Danish Section Scandinavian Parl. Cttee. for Freer Communication 53-57; Chair. of Board Copenhagen Telephone Co. 69-75.
Gyvelvej 4A, 4000 Roskilde, Denmark.
Telephone: 03-35-28-26.

Bundy, McGeorge; American professor and foundation official; b. 30 March 1919, Boston, Mass.; s. of Harvey H. and Katharine L. (Putnam) Bundy; brother of William P. Bundy, q.v.; m. Mary B. Lothrop 1950; four s.; ed. Yale Univ.
Political Analyst, Council of Foreign Relations 48-49; Visiting Lecturer, Harvard Univ. 49-51, Assoc. Prof. of Govt. 51-54, Dean, Faculty of Arts and Sciences 53-61, Prof. 54-61; Special Asst. for Nat. Security Affairs, The White House 61-66; Pres. Ford Foundation 66-.
Publs. *On Active Service in Peace and War* (with H. L. Stimson) 48, *Pattern of Responsibility* (Editor) 52, *The Strength of Government* 68.
Ford Foundation, 320 East 43rd Street, New York, N.Y. 10017, U.S.A.
Telephone: 212-573-4700.

Bundy, William Putnam; American editor and former government official; b. 24 Sept. 1917, Washington, D.C.; s. of Harvey H. and Katharine L. (Putnam) Bundy; brother of McGeorge Bundy, q.v.; m. Mary Acheson 1943; two s. one d.; ed. Groton School, Yale Coll., Harvard Graduate School and Harvard Law School.
U.S. Army 41-46; Lawyer with Covington and Burling, Washington D.C. 47-51; Central Intelligence Agency 51-61; Dep. Asst. Sec. of Defense, International Security Affairs 61-63, Asst. Sec. of Defense, Int. Security Affairs Nov. 63-64; Asst. Sec. for Far Eastern Affairs, Dept. of State 64-69; Massachusetts Inst. of Technology May 69-71; Editor *Foreign Affairs* (quarterly) 72-; Legion of Merit, Hon. M.B.E.; Fellow, Yale Corpn. 61-; Trustee, American Assembly 63-; Board of Dirs., Council on Foreign Relations 64-.
Leisure interest: tennis.
58 East 68th Street, New York, N.Y. 10021, U.S.A.
Telephone: 212-535-3300.

Büngeler, Walter, DR.MED.; German pathologist; b. 30 Dec. 1900, Niedermendig; m. 1st Vilma Nachtrab 1926, 2nd Ingeborg Hofrichter 1971; ed. Rostock, Frankfurt-a.-M., and Bonn.
Lecturer in Pathology Frankfurt-a.-M. 29; Prof. of Pathology, Danzig 34-36; Prof. of Pathology and Dir. of Pathological Section State Leprosy Research Inst., São Paulo, Brazil 36-42; Prof. of Pathology and Dir. of

Pathological Inst. Kiel Univ. 42; Dean of Medical Faculty Kiel 46-47; Prof. of Pathology and Dir. of the Munich Inst. of Pathology 56-71; Dean of Medical Faculty, Munich 57-58, Emer. 69; Senator Emer. German-Latin, American Medical Acad.; Hon. mem. and Corresp. mem. of many medical socs.; Commdr. Ordem Cruzeiro do Sul (Brazil).
Publs. *Die Gasbehandlung bösartiger Geschwülste* (with Fischer-Wasels) 29, *Patología Morfológica de las Enfermedades Tropicales* 44, *Molestias osseas na lepra* 42, *Krankheiten des Blutes und der blutbildenden Organe, Lehrbuch der Speziellen Pathologie von Kaufmann, Bösartige Geschwülste* in handbook *Das ärztliche Gutachten im Versicherungswesen* 54, *Theorien der Geschulstenstehnung, Lepra, Lehrbuch Doerr, Allgemeine Pathologie.*
8 Munich 19, Schlagintweitstrasse 15, Federal Republic of Germany.
Telephone: 152535.

Bunker, Ellsworth, B.A.; American business executive and public servant; b. 11 May 1894, Yonkers, N.Y.; s. of George R. and Jean Polhemus (Cobb) Bunker; m. 1st Harriet Allen Butler (died 1964), 2nd Carol Laise 1967; two s. one d.; ed. Yale Univ.
Director Nat. Sugar Refining Co. 27-66, Pres. 40, Chair. of Board 48-51; Dir. Trustee Atlantic Mutual Insurance Co., Centennial Insurance Co. and other companies, Bureau of Social Science Research, Asia Foundation, Inst. for Int. Social Research, Hampton Inst.; Amb. to Argentina 51, to Italy 52-53, to India 56-61 and Nepal 56-59, to Org. of American States 64-66, Chair. 65; Amb.-at-Large 66-67, to Repub. of Viet-Nam 67-73; Amb.-at-Large 73-; negotiation of agreement between Netherlands and Indonesia on transfer of Netherlands New Guinea (West Irian) 62; Head U.S. del. to Panama Canal talks 73; Pres. American Nat. Red Cross 53-66; mem. Council on Foreign Relations, American Acad. of Arts and Sciences; Grand Cross Knight of the Repub. of Italy; Presidential Medal of Freedom with Special Distinction 63, 68.
Leisure interests: farming, sailing, golf, tennis.
Department of State, Washington, D.C. 20520, U.S.A.

Bunker, George M.; American business executive; b. 2 Jan. 1908; ed. Massachusetts Inst. of Technology. Campbell Soup Co. 31-34; Wilson & Co. 34-36; Partner A. T. Kearney & Co. (Management Engineers) 36-42; Vice-Pres. The Kroger Co. 42-49; Pres., Gen. Manager and Dir. Trailmobile Inc. 49-52; Pres., Gen. Manager and Dir. The Martin Co., Baltimore 52-59, Chair. Board 59-61; Pres. and Chief Exec. Officer Martin-Marietta Corpn., New York City 61-, Chair. of Board 67-.
Martin-Marietta Corporation, 277 Park Avenue, New York, N.Y. 10017; and 4940 Indian Lane, N.W., Washington, D.C., U.S.A.

Bünning, Erwin, DR. PHIL.; German botanist; b. 23 Jan. 1906, Hamburg; s. of Hinrich and Hermine Bünning; m. Eleonore Walter 1935; one s. two d.; ed. Univs. of Berlin and Göttingen.
Lecturer, Univ. of Jena 31-35, Univ. of Königsberg 35-42, Prof. 38; Prof., Univ. of Strasbourg 42-44, Univ. of Cologne 44-46; Prof. of Botany, Univ. of Tübingen 46-; mem. Leopoldina Acad., Halle, and Acads. of Berlin, Heidelberg, Göttingen, Munich, New York; Foreign Assoc., Nat. Acad. of Sciences, Washington; Hon. mem. Japanese Botanical Soc., Amer. Soc. Plant Physiology; Corresp. mem. Amer. Botanical Soc.; Hon. LL.D. (Glasgow).
Publs. *Entwicklungs-und Bewegungsphysiologie der Pflanze* (3rd edn.) 53, *Theoretische Grundfragen der Physiologie* (2nd edn.) 48, *In den Wäldern Nord-Sumatras* 48, *Der tropische Regenwald* 56, *Die physiologische Uhr* (2nd edn.) 63, (in Russian 58), *The Physiological Clock* (3rd edn.) 73, (in Chinese 65, Japanese 76)

Vilhelm Pfeffer 75; about 250 publs. in several fields of biology, especially plant physiology, movements, differentiation, photobiology.
Institut für Biologie 1, Auf der Morgenstelle 1, 74 Tübingen, Federal Republic of Germany.
Telephone: Tübingen 292605.

Bunshaft, Gordon, B.ARCH., M.ARCH.; American architect; b. 9 May 1909, Buffalo, N.Y.; *s.* of David and Yetta Bunshaft; *m.* Nina Elizabeth Wayler 1943; ed. Mass. Inst. of Technology.
Chief Designer, Skidmore, Owings and Merrill 37-42, Partner 49-; mem. Comm. of Fine Arts, Int. Council of Museum of Modern Art, American Inst. of Architects, Nat. Acad. of Design, Nat. Inst. of Arts and Letters; Fellow American Inst. of Architects; Hon. mem. Buffalo Fine Arts Acad.; American Inst. of Arts and Letters Architectural Award 55; Hon. Dir. Fine Arts Univ. of Buffalo; Chancellor's Medal, Univ. of Buffalo 69. Projects include Lever House (New York), Manufacturers Trust Co. (Fifth Avenue, New York), Conn. Gen. Life Insurance Co. building (Hartford, Conn.), Beinecke Rare Book and Manuscript Library (Yale Univ.), Banque Lambert (Brussels), Albright-Knox Art Gallery (Buffalo, N.Y.), Library-Museum of Performing Arts (Lincoln Center, N.Y.), H. J. Heinz Co. Ltd. (Middx., England), Joseph H. Hirshhorn Museum (Washington), Lyndon Baines Johnson Library and East Campus Library and Research Building (Austin, Tex.).
Leisure interest: collecting of art.
Skidmore, Owings and Merrill, 400 Park Avenue, New York, N.Y. 10022; Home: 200 East 66th Street, New York City, N.Y., U.S.A.
Telephone: 212 PLaza 9-2121 (Office).

Bunting, Sir (Edward) John, Kt., C.B.E., B.A.; Australian civil servant; b. 13 Aug. 1918, Ballarat, Vic.; *s.* of late G. B. Bunting and Ellen Withers; *m.* Peggy MacGruer 1942; three *s.*; ed. Trinity Grammar, Trinity Coll., Melbourne Univ.
Assistant Sec., Prime Minister's Dept. 49-53; Official Sec. Australian High Comm., London 53-55; Deputy Sec., Prime Minister's Dept. 55-58, Sec. and Sec. to Australian Cabinet 59-68; Sec. Dept. of Cabinet Office 68-71, Dept. of Prime Minister and Cabinet and Sec. to Cabinet 71-75; High Commr. in U.K. Feb. 75-.
Leisure interests: golf, music.
Australian High Commission, Australia House, Strand, London, W.C.2; Residence: 45 Hyde Park Gate, London, S.W.7, England; Home: 3 Wickham Crescent, Red Hill, A.C.T., Australia, 2603.

Bunting, John R.; American banker; b. 29 June 1925, Philadelphia, Pa.; *m.*; two *c.*; ed. The Hill School, Pottstown, Pa. and Temple Univ.
Federal Reserve Bank of Philadelphia 50-64, Vice-Pres. 62-64; Vice-Pres. and Economist, The First Pennsylvania Banking and Trust Co. 64, Exec. Vice-Pres. 65, Pres. and Chief Exec. Officer Sept. 68-, Chair. 72-; Lecturer in Econs., Temple Univ. 56-60; guest lecturer at many other univs. and colls.; Dir. City Stores Co., Fidelity Mutual Life Insurance Co., Greater Philadelphia Chamber of Commerce; Dir. or Trustee of many civic and educational orgs.; Hon. D.B.A. (St. Joseph's Coll., Philadelphia); Hon. LL.D. (Temple Univ.); Hon. Fellow, Hebrew Univ., Israel.
Publs. *The Hidden Face of Free Enterprise* 64, and numerous articles in business and financial publications.
First Pennsylvania Corporation and The First Pennsylvania Banking and Trust Co., 15th and Chestnut Streets, Philadelphia, Pa. 19101, U.S.A.

Buñuel, Luis; Mexican (b. Spanish) film director; b. 22 Feb. 1900.
Prize, Venice Film Festival 69; Order of the Yugoslav Flag 71.

Films include: *Un Chien Andalou* 29, *L'Age d'Or* 30, *Land without Bread* 36, *Los Olvidados* 50, *The Adventures of Robinson Crusoe* 53, *The Criminal Life of Archibald de la Cruz* 55, *La Mort en ce Jardin* (*Evil Eden*) 56, *Nazarin* 58, *La Fièvre monte à El Pao, The Young One* 60, *Viridiana* 61 (Prize, Cannes Festival), *El Angel Exterminador* 62, *Le Journal d'une femme de chambre* 64, *Simon of the Desert* 65 (Prize, Venice Festival), *Belle de Jour* 66 (Golden Lion of Saint Mark, Venice Film Festival 67), *La Voie Lactée* 69, *Tristana* 70, *The Discreet Charm of the Bourgeoisie* 72 (Oscar 73), *Le Fantôme de la Liberté* 74, *La Femme aux Bottes Rouges*.
c/o Directores Cinematográficos, Chihuahua 167, Mexico D.F.; Telimex, Division del Norte 2462, Mexico City, Mexico.

Bunwaree, Goorpersad; Mauritius banker; b. 12 May 1919, Mauritius; ed. Royal Coll., Mauritius, Oxford Univ. and Econ. Devt. Inst., Washington, D.C.
Assistant Sec., Cen. Admin. Secr. 56-57; Principal Asst. Sec., Ministry of Industry, Commerce and External Communications 57-63; Deputy Financial Sec. 63-66; Perm. Sec., Ministry of Works and Internal Communications 66-67; Financial Sec. 67-69; Man. Dir. Bank of Mauritius 70-72, Gov. Jan. 73-.
Bank of Mauritius, P.O. Box 29, Port Louis; Home: Sir Virgil Naz Avenue, Quatre Bornes, Mauritius.

Burakiewicz, Janusz; Polish politician; b. 20 Nov. 1916, Leningrad, U.S.S.R.; *s.* of Wincenty Burakiewicz and Janina Chelminska; *m.* Wanda Slusarczyk 1945; three *s.*; ed. Main School of Commerce, Warsaw.
Bank employee, Warsaw until 39; during Second World War took part in campaign of Sept. 39, in Auschwitz and Sachsenhausen Concentration Camps 41-45; at Cen. Board of Metallurgical Industry, Katowice 45-47; at various important posts at Ministry of Industry and Trade, Ministry of Foreign Trade and Office of Council of Ministers 45-56; Commercial Counsellor, Budapest 50-53; Commercial Counsellor, Berlin 56-58; Deputy Minister of Foreign Trade 58-64; Minister of Shipping 64-69; Minister of Foreign Trade 69-71; mem. Polish Workers' Party 45-48, Polish United Workers' Party 48-; Vice-Pres. Union of Fighters for Freedom and Democracy 69-72; Amb. to Yugoslavia 71-; Order of Banner of Labour 1st and 2nd Class, Order Polonia Restituta 3rd and 5th Class, Great Ribbon of the Homayoun Order of Iran, Gold Cross of Merit, Medal of 10th Anniversary of People's Poland.
Leisure interests: gardening, fishing.
Embassy of Poland, Belgrade, Yugoslavia.

Burbidge, (Eleanor) Margaret Peachey, PH.D., F.R.S.; British astronomer; *d.* of Stanley John and Marjorie (née Stott) Peachey; *m.* Geoffrey Burbidge (*q.v.*) 1948; one *d.*; ed. Frances Holland School, London and Univ. Coll., London.
Acting Dir. Univ. of London Observatory 50-51; Research Fellow, Yerkes Observatory, Univ. of Chicago 51-53, Calif. Inst. of Technology 55-57; Shirley Farr Fellow, later Assoc. Prof. Yerkes Observatory and mem. Fermi Inst., Univ. of Chicago 57-62; Assoc. Prof., later Prof. of Astronomy Univ. of Calif., San Diego 62-; Dir. Royal Greenwich Observatory 72-73; mem. Royal Astronomical Soc., Amer. Astronomical Soc., Int. Astronomical Union, Amer. Acad. of Arts and Science; Fellow, Univ. Coll., London; Helen B. Warner Prize (jointly with Geoffrey Burbidge) 59; Hon. D.Sc. (Smith Coll., Mass., and Univs. of Sussex, Leicester, Bristol and City Univ., London).
Publs. *Quasi-Stellar Objects* (with Geoffrey Burbidge) 67; numerous articles in scientific journals.
Department of Physics, University of California at San Diego, P.O. Box 109, La Jolla, Calif. 92037, U.S.A.

Burbidge, Frederick Stewart, B.A., LL.B.; Canadian transport executive; b. 30 Sept. 1918, Winnipeg; *s.* of

Frederick M. and Susan M. (Stewart) Burbidge; *m.* Cynthia A. Bennest 1942; two *s.*; ed. Ravenscourt School, Winnipeg, Univ. of Manitoba, Manitoba Law School.

Called to the Bar, Manitoba 46; joined Law Dept. of Canadian Pacific 47, Asst. Solicitor Winnipeg 47-50, Montreal 50-57, Winnipeg 57-60, Asst. Gen. Counsel 60, Asst. Vice-Pres. Traffic 62, Vice-Pres. Rail Admin. 66, Vice-Pres. and Exec. Asst. 67, Vice-Pres. Admin. 69, Marketing and Sales 69, Senior Exec. Officer Canadian Pacific Rail, Vice-Pres. 71, Pres. Canadian Pacific May 72-; Dir. Canadian Pacific Ltd., Canadian Pacific Steamships Ltd., Canadian Pacific (Bermuda) Ltd., Canadian Pacific Investments, Cominco Ltd., Bank of Montreal, Soo Line Railroad Co., Toronto, Hamilton and Buffalo Railroad Co., Marathon Realty Co. Ltd., Canadian Pacific Transport Co. Ltd., Canadian Industries Ltd.; mem. Board of Dirs. Bishop's Coll. School, Gen. Council of Industry (Quebec); Dir. Royal Victoria Hosp. Foundation; mem. Montreal Board of Trade, La Chambre de Commerce du district de Montréal, Law Soc. of Man., Fed. Advisory Council to the Minister of Industry, Trade and Commerce; Hon. Vice-Pres. Quebec Provincial Council, Boy Scouts of Canada.

Canadian Pacific, Windsor Station, Montreal H3C 3E4, Quebec, Canada.

Telephone: 861-6811.

Burbidge, Geoffrey (Ronald), PH.D., F.R.S.; British physicist; b. 24 Sept. 1925; *s.* of Leslie and Eveline Burbidge; *m.* Margaret Peachey 1948 (*q.v.* Eleanor Margaret Peachey Burbidge); one *d.*; ed. Bristol Univ. and Univ. Coll., London.

Assistant Lecturer, Univ. Coll. London 50-51; Agassiz Fellow, Harvard Univ. 51-52; Research Fellow, Cavendish Lab., Cambridge 53-55; Carnegie Fellow, Mount Wilson and Palomar Observatories 55-57; Asst. Prof. Dept. of Astronomy, Univ. of Chicago 57-58; Assoc. Prof. 58-62; Assoc. Prof. Univ. of Calif. (San Diego) 62-63, Prof. 63-; Phillips Visiting Prof., Harvard Univ. 68; Fellow, Univ. Coll., London.

Publs. *Quasi-Stellar Objects* (with Margaret Burbidge) 67, many scientific papers.

University of California, San Diego Campus, P.O. Box 109, La Jolla, California 92037, U.S.A.

Burbridge, Kenneth Joseph, M.A., B.C.L., PH.D.; Canadian diplomatist; b. 2 July 1911, Bathurst, N.B.; *s.* of Harry J. Burbridge and Elizabeth Foley; *m.* Marion C. Smith 1943; one *s.* one *d.*; ed. St. Thomas and St. Francis Xavier Univs., and Univs. of New Brunswick and Ottawa.

Private legal practice, St. John, New Brunswick 39-41; various public appointments incl. Legal Counsel, Dept. of Munitions and Supply, Ottawa 41-43; Chief Legal Adviser to Nat. Selective Service, Dept. of Labour, Ottawa 43-44; Legal Adviser to Unemployment Insurance Comm., Ottawa 45; Counsellor to Sec. of State and War Legal Adviser, Dept. of External Affairs and Claims Branch, Dept. of Sec. of State, Ottawa 45-47; Adviser and Del. to various int. bodies 47-53; Canadian Deputy Perm. Rep. to North Atlantic Council (NATO) and OEEC 54-57; Consul-Gen. of Canada, Seattle 57-63; Canadian del. to Colombo Plan Conf., Seattle 58; High Commr. to New Zealand 63-67; Dir. U.S.A. Div., Dept. of External Affairs 68-70; Canadian del. to IMCO and ECE Conf. on Int. Combined Transport, London 70, to IMCO/ECE Conf. on Int. Shipping Legislation, Geneva 70, to Int. Conf. on Unlawful Interference with Civil Aviation 71; Canadian Del. UN/IMCO Conf. on Int. Container Traffic 72; Exec. Dir. Int. Transport Policy Cttee., Canadian Transport Comm. 70-.

Leisure interests: oil painting, golf, skiing.

930 Sadler Crescent, Ottawa K2B 5H7, Ont., Canada.

Telephone: 729-2324.

Burbury, Hon. Sir Stanley Charles, K.B.E., K.ST.J.; Australian judge; b. 2 Dec. 1909; *s.* of Daniel Charle[s] Burbury; *m.* Pearl Christine Barren 1934; ed. Hutchin[s] School, Hobart, Univ. of Tasmania.

Admitted to Bar 34; Queen's Counsel 50; Solicitor-Gen[.] Tasmania 52; Chief Justice of Tasmania 56-73; Gov. o[f] Tasmania 73-; Nat. Pres. Heart Foundation of Aus[-] tralia 67-73; Dir. Winston Churchill Memorial Trust; Hon. LL.D., Tasmania 70; Hon. Col. Royal Tasmania[n] Regiment 74.

Leisure interests: music, bowls.

Government House, Hobart, Tasmania, Australia.

Burch, Dean, LL.B.; American attorney and government official; b. 20 Dec. 1927, Enid, Okla.; *s.* of Bert Alexander and Leola (Atkisson) Burch; *m.* Patricia Meeks 1961; one *s.* two *d.*; ed. Univ. of Arizona.

Assistant Attorney-Gen., Ariz. 53-54; Admin. Asst. to Senator Barry Goldwater 55-59; mem. firm Dunseath, Stubbs & Burch, Tucson 59-63; Deputy Dir. Goldwater for Pres. Cttee. 63-64; Chair. Republican Nat. Cttee. 64-65; Partner, Dunseath, Stubbs & Burch 65-69; Chair. Fed. Communications Comm. 69-74; Counsellor to Pres. Nixon March-Aug. 74, to Pres. Ford 74-Jan. 75; Partner, Pierson, Ball & Dowd, Washington, D.C.

Leisure interests: golf, tennis.

9311 Persimmon Tree Road, Potomac, Md. 20854, U.S.A.

Telephone: 301-983-1294.

Burcham, Lester Arthur; American retailing executive; b. 26 April 1913; ed. Public Schools, Lancaster.

F. W. Woolworth Co., New York City 31-, Trainee, Manager, Superintendent, Sales Manager, District Manager 31-58, Vice-Pres. 58-62, Exec. Vice-Pres. 62-64, Pres. 65-69, Chair. and Chief Exec. Officer 70-; Dir. F. W. Woolworth Ltd. (Canada), F. W. Woolworth Co. (Mexico), F. W. Woolworth Co. Ltd. (England), Woolworth Española, SA (Spain), Western Electric Co. Inc., Charter New York Corpn., Kinney Shoe Corpn., Richman Brothers Co.

F. W. Woolworth Co., 233 Broadway, New York City, N.Y., U.S.A.

Burden, William Armistead Moale, A.B.; American financier and diplomatist; b. 8 April 1906; ed. Harvard Univ.

Vice-Pres. Nat. Aviation Corpn. 39-41, Defence Supplies Corpn. 41-42; Asst. Sec. of Commerce for Air 43-47; Aviation Consultant Smith Barney & Co. Inc. 47-49; Partner William A. M. Burden & Co. 49-; Special Asst. for Research & Development to Sec. of Air Force 50-52; mem. Nat. Aeronautics and Space Council 58; Amb. to Belgium 59-61; Dir. Aerospace Corpn., American Metal Climax, Columbia Broadcasting Co.; Trustee (Past Pres.), Museum of Modern Art; Chair. Board of Trustees, Inst. of Defense Analyses; Pres. France America Soc.; Chair. Council of French-Amer. Socs. in N.Y.C.; mem. U.S. Citizens' Comm. for NATO 61-62; Grand Officier Légion d'Honneur, El Sol del Peru; Commdr. Cruzeiro do Sul (Brazil), Order of Merit (Italy); Assoc. Commdr. Order of St. John; Commdr.'s Cross, Order of Merit (Germany); Grand Cordon Ordre de Léopold II; Hon. D.Sc. (Clarkson Coll. of Technology), Hon. LL.D. (Fairleigh Dickinson and Johns Hopkins Univs.).

Publ. *The Struggle for Airways in Latin America* 43.

820 Fifth Avenue, New York City, N.Y. 10021, U.S.A.

Burdick, Quentin Northrop, B.A., LL.B.; American lawyer and politician; b. 19 June 1908, Munich, N.D.; *s.* of late Usher L. Burdick and Emma Robertson; *m.* 1st Marietta Janecky (died 1958), one *s.* three *d.*; *m.* 2nd Mrs. Jocelyn Burch Peterson, one *s.* two stepchildren; ed. Williston High School, Univ. of Minnesota.

Admitted to N. Dakota Bar 32, practised Fargo 32-58;

Candidate for Gov. 46, for U.S. Senator 56; elected to House of Reps. 58; Senator from N. Dakota 61-; Democrat.
U.S. Senate, Washington, D.C.; and 1110 South 9th Street, Fargo, North Dakota, U.S.A.

Burelli Rivas, Miguel Angel, LL.B., DR.POL.SC.; Venezuelan lawyer and diplomatist; b. 8 July 1922; ed. Univ. of Los Andes, Bogotá, Central Univs., Venezuela and Ecuador, Nat. Univ. of Bogotá, and Univs. of Madrid and Florence.
Pre-Seminary Prof. of Political Sociology and Chief Prof. of Mining and Agrarian Legislation, Faculty of Law, Univ. of Los Andes, Bogotá, Chief Prof. of Humanities I and II, Faculty of Civil Eng., Dir. of Univ. Culture, Founder of School of Humanities, Founder-Dir. of Univ. reviews, *Bibliotheca* and *Universitas Emeritensis*; Political Dir. Ministry of the Interior; Dir.-Gen. Ministry of Foreign Affairs (nine times Acting Minister); Interim Minister of Foreign Affairs; returned to legal profession 61; mem. Venezuelan Supreme-Electoral Council 61; Minister of Justice 64-65; Amb. to Colombia 65-67, U.K. 67-69; Presidential Candidate 68, 73; Amb. to U.S.A. 74-; Vice-Dir. Grand Colombian Merchant Fleet; Gen. Sec. Venezuelan Del. to Fourth Session UN Gen. Assembly; Asst. Sec.-Gen. Tenth Interamerican Conf.; Del. Perm. Coffee Comm. of Pan American Union; mem. Inquiry Comm. on British Guiana-Venezuela Boundary; mem. Editorial Cttee. *Meridanian Themes and Collection of Authors* 64-; Grand Cordon, Order of the Liberator, Grand Cross, Order of Merit (Fed. Repub. of Germany), Grand Cross of Merit (U.A.R.), Grand Officer, Order of Merit and Grand Cross, Order of St. Gregory the Great (Italy), Grand Cross, Order of Boyacá and Medal of Postal Merit, First Class (Colombia).
Embassy of Venezuela, 2445 Massachusetts Avenue, N.W., Washington, D.C. 20008, U.S.A.

Buresch, Eugen F., LL.D.; Austrian diplomatist; b. 9 Oct. 1915, Vienna; s. of Karl Buresch, LL.D., Federal Chancellor; m. Edda Grieshoffer 1961; two s. three d.; ed. High School Theresianum, Vienna, Univ. of Vienna and Ecole des Sciences Politiques, Paris.
Officer, Comité Int. du Bois, Brussels 38-39; First Sec., Rome 46-49; in Political Dept., Foreign Office, Vienna 49; First Sec., London 50-51; Dir. Austrian Information Service, New York 52-55; Chargé d'Affaires, Austrian Embassy, Iran 55, Minister 58, Amb. 60, concurrently to Afghanistan; Amb. to Canada 60-64; Head of Austrian negotiating del. with EEC, Brussels and Luxembourg 65-68; Amb. to UN at Geneva 68; now Amb. to Mexico; mem. Alumni Theresianische Akad.
Publs. Articles in newspapers.
Embassy of Austria, Campos Elíseos 305, Polanco, Mexico City, Mexico.

Burg, Josef, DR. PHIL.; Israeli politician; b. 31 Jan. 1909, Germany; m. Rivga Slonim 1943; one s. two d.; ed. Univs. of Berlin and Leipzig; Pedagogical Inst. Leipzig; Rabbinical Seminary Berlin; and Hebrew Univ. of Jerusalem.
Directorate, Palestine Office, Berlin 36; Nat. Exec. Mizrachi; Zionist Gen. Council 39-51; mem. Exec. Hapoel Hamizrachi 44-; Deputy Speaker First Knesset (Israeli Parl.) 49-51; Minister of Health, Govt. of Israel 51-52; Minister of Posts and Telegraphs Dec. 52-58; Minister of Social Welfare 59-70, Minister of the Interior 70-; Nat. Religious Party.
6 Ben Maymon Street, Jerusalem, Israel.

Burgan, Salih Khalil, M.D.; Jordanian physician, politician and international civil servant; b. 19 July 1918, Kerak; s. of Khalil Burgan and Labeebah (née Halasa); m. Blanche (née Khoury) 1949; three s. one d.; ed. American Univ. of Beirut.
Physician, Transjordan Frontier Forces (T.J.F.F.) 43-46, Dir. of Arab Physicians (T.J.F.F.) 46-48; private

physician at Zerka, Jordan 48-63; mem. Parl. 61-62, Senate 63-69; Minister of Health 63-64, of Social Affairs and Labour 66, of Public Health 66-67, of Social Affairs and Labour and Minister of Interior for Municipal and Rural Affairs 67-69; Dir. Int. Labour Office, Beirut 69-75, Asst. Dir.-Gen., Geneva June 75-; Al Kawkab Medal (1st Grade); Grand Kt. of the Holy Tomb.
Leisure interests: reading, classical music.
International Labour Office, Case Postale 500, CH-1211 Geneva 22; Residence: 11 Parc de Budé, 1202 Geneva, Switzerland.

Burgbacher, Fritz, DR.RER.POL.; German businessman and university professor; b. 1 Sept. 1900, Mainz; s. of Karl Burgbacher and Elisabeth Finkenäuer; m. Elisabeth Kinkel 1922; one s. three d.; ed. Frankfurt/Main Univ.
Syndikus, Dresdner Bank, Mainz 23-25; auditor 25-29; Dir. Rhenag Rheinische Energie A.G., Cologne 29-70; Dir. of various industrial and power-supplying companies; Hon. mem. Verband der Deutschen Gas- und Wasserwerke; Chair. Board and Power Cttee. Landesplanungsgemeinschaft Rheinland; mem. Bundestag; Vice-Pres. European Parliament, mem. Power and Econ. Cttee.; Christian Democrat.
Publs. *Wesen und Gestaltungsformen der Gasverbundwirtschaft* 50, *Die Bedeutung sozialer, politischer und psychologischer Faktoren in der Entwicklung der Energiewirtschaft, Das Problem der oberen Führungskräfte* 53, *Der Bildungsauftrag des christlichen Unternehmers* 54, *Gedanken zu unserer Zeit* 57, *Politik auf drei Ebenen* 61, *Politik, Idee und Wirklichkeit* 65, *Freiheit und Ordnung* 69, *Produktivkapital für jeden—die Pflicht zum Eigentum* 71.
Bayenthalgürtel 9, 5 Cologne-Marienburg, Federal Republic of Germany.
Telephone: 380281.

Burger, Warren E(arl); American judge; b. 17 Sept. 1907, St. Paul; ed. Univ. of Minnesota, St. Paul Coll. of Law.
Admitted to Minn. Bar 31; Partner, Faricy, Burger Moore & Costello 35-53; mem. Faculty, Mitchell Coll. of Law 31-48; Asst. Attorney-Gen. of U.S. 53-56; Judge, U.S. Court of Appeals, Washington, D.C. 56-69; Chief Justice of U.S. 69-76; Hon. Chair. Inst. of Judicial Admin.; Hon. Chair. Criminal Justice Project, American Bar Asscn.; Pres. Bentham Club, Univ. Coll. London 72-73; Chancellor, Board of Regents, Smithsonian Inst., Washington, D.C.; Chair. Board of Trustees, Nat. Gallery of Art, Washington, D.C.; Trustee Emer. Wm. Mitchell Coll. of Law, St. Paul, Minn., Mayo Foundation, Rochester, Minn., and Macalester Coll., St. Paul, Minn.; Hon. Master of the Bench, Middle Temple, London 69.
c/o Supreme Court Building, 1 First Street, N.E., Washington, D.C. 20543, U.S.A.

Burgers, Johannes Martinus, DR. PHIL.; Netherlands university professor; b. 13 Jan. 1895, Arnhem; s. of Johannes Martinus Burgers and Johanna Hendrika Romijn; m. 1st Jeannette Dolvina Roosenschoon (died 1939), one s. two d. (one deceased); 2nd Anna Margretha Verhoeven 1941; ed. Univ. of Leiden.
Professor Aero- and Hydro-dynamics Technical Univ. of Delft 18-55; Research Prof. Inst. for Fluid Dynamics and Applied Mathematics, Univ. of Maryland 55-; mem. Royal Neths. Acad. of Sciences 31-; Foreign mem. Accad. delle Scienze di Torino 64; Dr. h.c. Univ. Libre de Bruxelles 48, Univ. of Poitiers 50; mem. American Acad. of Arts and Sciences and of several societies; Knight Order of Netherlands Lion.
Leisure interests: many, of great diversity.
Publs. *Experience and Conceptual Activity* 65, *Flow Equations for Composite Gases* 69, *The Nonlinear Diffusion Equation* 75, and on hydro- and aerodynamics, etc., since 20.

Home: 4622 Knox Road, Apt. 7, College Park, Md. 20740; Office: Institute for Fluid Dynamics and Applied Mathematics, Univ. of Maryland, Md. 20742, U.S.A.
Telephone: 301-454-2705 (Office); 301-277-6939 (Home).

Burgess, Anthony, B.A., F.R.S.L.; British writer; b. 25 Feb. 1917, Manchester; s. of Joseph Wilson and Elizabeth Burgess; m. 1st Llewela Isherwood Jones 1942 (deceased), 2nd Liliana Macellari, Countess Pasi 1968; one s.; ed. Xaverian Coll., Manchester and Manchester Univ.
British Army 40-46; Chief Instructor, Western Command Coll. 46-48; Lecturer in Speech and Drama, Ministry of Educ. 48-50; Master Banbury Grammar School 50-54; Educ. Officer Malaya and Borneo 54-59; freelance writer 59-; reviewer for many British newspapers and journals including *Listener, Observer, Sunday Times, Spectator, Queen*; Visiting Prof. Univ. of N. Carolina 69-70, Princeton Univ. 70-71; Distinguished Prof., City Coll., N.Y. 72-73; Prof. Columbia Univ. 73-; Fellow, Royal Soc. of Literature; Literary Adviser, Guthrie Theater, Minn.; U.S. Nat. Arts Club Gold Medal; Knight of Mark Twain.
Leisure interests: travel, playing organ, piano, harpsichord, musical composition, philology, linguistics, cooking.
Publs. fiction: *Malayan Trilogy (The Long Day Wanes)* 56-59, *The Doctor is Sick* 60, *A Clockwork Orange* 62, *The Wanting Seed* 62, *Nothing Like the Sun* 64, *Tremor of Intent* 65, *Enderby* 68, *MF* 70, *Napoleon Symphony* 74, *The Clockwork Testament* 74; biography: *Shakespeare* 71; transls.: *Cyrano de Bergerac* 71, *Oedipus the King* 72; philology: *Language Made Plain* 65; television: *Lots of Fun at Finnegan's Wake* 73, *Moses* 73, *Michelangelo* 75.
2 Piazza Padella, Bracciano; and 16a Piazza Santa Cecilia, Rome, Italy; and 168 Triq Il-Kbira, Malta.

Burgess, Sir John Lawie, Kt., O.B.E. (Mil.), T.D., J.P.; British journalist; b. 17 Nov. 1912, Carlisle; s. of late R. N. Burgess; m. Alice Elizabeth Gillieron; two s. one d.; ed. Trinity Coll., Glenalmond, Scotland.
Secretary, Cumberland Newspapers Ltd. 34-45; war service abroad with Border Regt. 39-45; Chair. and Editor-in-Chief Cumberland Newspapers Ltd. 45-; Dir. Press Asscn. 50-57, Chair. 57; Dir. Reuters 55-68, Chair. 58-68; Chair. Border TV Ltd. 60-; Vice-Pres. Int. Publrs'. Asscn.; mem. of Council, Commonwealth Press Union; Hon. Col. 4th Battalion Border Regt. 56-68; D.L. Cumberland 56.
The Old Hall, Rockcliffe, Carlisle, Cumberland, England.

Burian, Jiří, ING.; Czechoslovak agriculturalist and politician; b. 3 Jan. 1921, Rosovice; ed. agricultural coll.
Apprenticed as bricklayer; agricultural work 42-48; Chair. Local Nat. Cttee., Dobříš, Bohemia 48-50; mem. Agricultural Dept., Regional Nat. Cttee., Prague 50-54; Head, Agricultural Dept., District Cttee. of Communist Party, Prague 54-58; Head of Div., Agricultural Dept., Central Cttee. of C.P. 62-63; Minister of Agriculture Sept. 63-67; mem. Agricultural Comm., Central Cttee. of C.P. of Czechoslovakia 63-69; mem. Nat. Assembly 64-69; Sec. Central Bohemian Regional Nat. Cttee.; Deputy to Czech Nat. Council 68-; Deputy to House of the People, Fed. Assembly 69-71; mem. Presidium; Chair. Comm. for Agriculture and Food, House of the People 69-71; Chair. Cen. Bohemian Regional Nat. Cttee. 71-; Order of Victorious February 73.
The Federal Assembly, Prague, Czechoslovakia.

Burin des Roziers, Etienne; French diplomatist; b. 11 Aug. 1913, Paris; s. of André Burin des Roziers and Madeleine Heurteau; m. Jane d'Oilliamson 1950; two s. one d.; ed. Ecole Libre des Sciences Politiques, Faculties of Law and Letters, Univ. of Paris, and Univ. of Oxford.
Head, French Del. to Int. Comm. of Enquiry on Former Italian Colonies 47-48; Sub-Dir. of the Saar,

Ministry of Foreign Affairs 48-50; Atlantic Pact Del. 50-52; Technical Adviser to Prime Minister 53; Chargé d'Affaires, Yugoslavia 54-55; Deputy to French Resident in Morocco 55-56; Consul-Gen., Milan 56-58; Amb. to Poland 58-62; Sec.-Gen. of the Presidency of the Repub. 62-67; Amb. to Italy 67-72; Perm. Rep. to Comm. of European Communities 72-75; Conseiller d'Etat 75-; Commdr. de la Légion d'Honneur, Croix de Guerre, Médaille de la Résistance, other decorations.
40 Quai des Libertins, Paris 4e, France.

Burkatskaya, Galina Evgenievna; Soviet agronomist and politician; b. 1916; ed. Kharkov Artem Communist Univ.
Chairman, Radyanska Ukraine Collective Farm 49-; Deputy of the Supreme Soviet of the U.S.S.R. until 66; mem. C.P.S.U. 46-; Hero of Socialist Labour (twice).
Radyanska Ukraine Collective Farm, Geronimovka Village, Cherkassy Region, Ukraine, U.S.S.R.

Burke, Admiral Arleigh A., American naval officer; b. 19 Oct. 1901, Boulder, Colo.; s. of Oscar A. Burke and Claire Mokler Burke; m. Roberta Gorsuch 1923; ed. U.S. Naval Acad. and Univ. of Michigan.
Commissioned 23, served all ranks to Rear-Admiral 50; served 1939-45 war; Head of Research and Development Div., Bureau of Ordnance, Washington 45; Chief of Staff to Commdr. Eighth Fleet in Atlantic 46, to C.-in-C Atlantic Fleet 45-47; Dep. Chief of Staff to Commdr. Naval Forces, Far East; Commdr. Cruiser Div. Five; mem. Mil. Armistice Comm. under Commdr. Naval Forces, Far East 51; Dir. Strategic Plans Div., Navy Dep. 52; Commdr. Cruiser Div. Six 54; Commdr. Destroyers Atlantic Fleet 55; Chief of Naval Operations (with rank of Admiral) 55-61, retd. 61; Counsellor to Center for Strategic and Int. Studies, Georgetown Univ.; Dir. of numerous companies; Hon. D.Sc., Hon. LL.D., Hon. D.Eng.; Navy Cross; Legion of Merit (two gold stars with oak leaf cluster); Purple Heart; and others.
Leisure interests: gardening, hunting, sailing.
Office: Suite 310, 1015 18th Street, N.W., Washington, D.C. 20036; Home: 8624 Fenway Drive, Bethesda, Md. 20034, U.S.A.
Telephone: 833-8764 (Office); 365-0906 (Home).

Burke, Bernard Flood, PH.D.; American physicist and astrophysicist; b. 7 June 1928, Boston, Mass.; s. of Vincent Paul Burke and Clare Aloyse Brine; m. Jane Chapin Pann 1953; three s. one d.; ed. Mass. Inst. of Technology.
Member of staff, Carnegie Inst. of Washington 53-65; Chair. Radio Astronomy Section, Carnegie Inst. of Washington, Dept. of Terrestrial Magnetism 62-65; Prof. of Physics, Mass. Inst. of Technology 65-; Visiting Prof., Leiden Univ. 71-72; Trustee Associated Univs. Inc. 72-; Trustee and Vice-Chair. N.E. Radio Observatory Corpn. 73-; mem. American Acad. of Arts and Sciences, Nat. Acad. of Sciences; Fellow, American Acad. for Advancement of Science; Helen B. Warner Prize, American Astron. Soc. 63; Rumford Prize, American Acad. of Arts and Sciences 71.
Leisure interests: skiing, sailing, hiking, chamber music.
Publs. *Microwave Spectroscopy* 53-54, *Radio Noise from Jupiter* 55-61, *Galactic Structure* 59, *Very Long Baseline Interferometry* 68-; miscellaneous publs. in radio astronomy 55-.
Room 26-335, Department of Physics, Massachusetts Institute of Technology, Cambridge, Mass. 02139; Home: 10 Bloomfield Street, Lexington, Mass., U.S.A.
Telephone: 617-253-2572 (Office); 617-862-8939 (Home).

Burke, Kenneth; American writer; b. 5 May 1897, Pittsburgh, Pa.; s. of James Leslie Burke and Lillyan May Duva; m. 1st Lily Mary Batterham 1919, 2nd Elizabeth Batterham 1933; two s. three d.; ed. Ohio State and Columbia Univs.

Research worker Laura Spelman Rockefeller Memorial 26-27; music critic *The Dial* 27-29; mem. staff Bureau of Social Hygiene 28-29; Music Critic *Nation* 34-36; Lecturer in Practice and Theory of Literary Criticism New School for Social Research 37, Univ. of Chicago 38, 49-50, Kenyon Coll. 50, Ind. Univ. 52, 58, Drew Univ. 62, 64, Bennington Coll. 43-61, Pennsylvania State Univ. 63; Regents Prof., Univ. of Calif. (Santa Barbara) 64-65, Central Washington State Coll. 66, Harvard 67-68, Washington Univ. 70-71, Wesleyan Univ. 72; Guggenheim Fellowship 35; mem. Nat. Inst. of Arts and Letters, American Acad. of Arts and Letters, American Acad. of Arts and Sciences; Fellow Center for Advanced Study in Behavioral Sciences 57-58; Hon. D.Litt., Bennington Coll., Rutgers Univ., Dartmouth Coll.; Hon. D.Hum.Litt. (Fairfield Univ., Northwestern Univ., Univ. of Rochester); Brandeis Univ. Creative Arts Awards Comm. Award for Notable Achievements in the Arts 67; award from Nat. Council on the Arts 69; Horace Gregory Award, New School for Social Research 70; Ingram Merrill Foundation Award in literature 70; mem. Century Asscn.
Leisure interests: trying to keep from becoming too unfit, punishing the piano, worrying about the military industrial complex.
Publs. *The White Oxen* 24, *Counter-Statement* 31, 53, 68, *Towards a Better Life* 32, 66, *Permanence and Change—Anatomy of Purpose* 35, 54, 65, *Attitudes Towards History*—Vol. I *Acceptance and Rejection, The Curve of History*, Vol. II *Analysis of Symbolic Structure* 37, 59, 61, *The Philosophy of Literary Form-Studies in Symbolic Action* 41, 57, revised edn. 67, *A Grammar of Motives* 45, 62, 69, *A Rhetoric of Motives* 50, 62, 69, *Book of Moments: Poems 15-54* 55, *The Rhetoric of Religion* 61, 70, *Perspectives by Incongruity* 65, *Terms for Order* 65, *Language as Symbolic Action, Essays on Life, Literature and Method* 66, *Collected Poems 15-67* 68, *Complete White Oxen* 68, *Dramatism and Development* 72; translator Thomas Mann's *Death in Venice* 25, Emil Ludwig's *Genius and Character* 27, and Emil Baumann's *Saint Paul* 29.
R.D.2, Andover, New Jersey 07821, U.S.A.
Telephone: 201-347-3249.

Burke, Richard, M.A.; Irish politician; b. 1929; ed. Christian Brothers, Tipperary and Univ. Coll., Dublin. Teacher in Blackrock until 69; mem. of the Dáil for Dublin South Co. 69-; fmr. Chief Whip of Fine Gael; Shadow Minister for Posts and Telegraphs 69-73; served on many Dáil cttees. including Public Accounts Cttee.; fmrly. County Councillor, Dublin Co. Council, Chair. 72-; Minister of Educ. 73-.
Ministry of Education, Government Buildings, Dublin 2, Ireland.

Burke, Samuel Martin, B.A. (HONS.), M.A., F.R.S.A.; Pakistani diplomatist; b. 3 July 1906, Martinpur; s. of K. D. Burke; m. Queenie Louise Burke; four d.; ed. Govt. Coll., Lahore, and School of Oriental Studies, London.
Indian Civil Service 31-47; District Officer and District and Sessions Judge; Pres. Election Tribunal, Punjab 46; Pakistani Foreign Office 48-49; served as Sec. to Pakistani Del. to Inter-Dominion Confs. with India 48 and 49; Counsellor to Pakistani High Comm. in London 49-52; Minister in Washington 52-53; led Special Missions to Dominican Republic and Mexico 52; Chargé d'Affaires, Rio de Janeiro 53; mem. UN Cttee. on Contributions 53-55; Deputy High Commr. for Pakistan in United Kingdom 53; Minister to Sweden (concurrently to Norway, Denmark and Finland) 53-56; Ambassador to Thailand and Minister to Cambodia and Laos 56-59; mem. Pakistani Del. to SEATO Council Meetings 57, 58, 59; High Commr. in Canada 59-61; led Special Mission to Argentina 60; Prof. and Consultant in South

Asian Studies, Dept. of Int. Relations, Univ. of Minnesota 61-; Sitara-i-Pakistan.
Leisure interests: cricket, riding, tennis.
Publs. *Zafrulla Khan: The Man and his Career, Pakistan's Foreign Policy: An Historical Analysis, Mainsprings of Indian and Pakistani Foreign Policies.*
Home: 810 Thornton Street S.E., Minneapolis, Minn. 55414; Office: 1246 Social Science Building, University of Minnesota, Minneapolis, Minn. 55455, U.S.A.
Telephone: 339-0480 (Home).

Burkill, John Charles, SC.D, F.R.S.; British mathematician; b. 1 Feb. 1900, Holt; s. of H. R. Burkill; m Margareta Braun 1928; one s. two d.; ed. St. Paul's School, and Trinity Coll., Cambridge.
Professor of Pure Maths., Univ. of Liverpool 24-29; Fellow, Lecturer and Tutor of Peterhouse, Cambridge 29-67, Master of Peterhouse 68-73; mem. Inst. of Advanced Study, Princeton 47, Visiting Prof. Rice Inst. 56, Tata Inst., Bombay 59; Adams Prize 49.
Publs. Mathematical books and papers.
2 Archway Court, Barton Road, Cambridge, CB3 9LW, England.

Burkitt, Denis Parsons, C.M.G., M.D., F.R.C.S., F.R.S.; British medical research scientist; b. 28 Feb. 1911, Enniskillen; s. of James P. and Gwendoline (née Hill) Burkitt; m. Olive M. Rogers 1943; three d.; ed. Dublin Univ.
Surgeon, R.A.M.C. 41-46; joined H.M. Colonial Service, Uganda 46, Govt. Surgeon and Lecturer in Surgery, Makerere Univ. Coll. Medical School 46-64; Senior Consultant Surgeon, Ministry of Health, Uganda 61-64; mem. Medical Research Council External Scientific Staff, Uganda 64-66, London 66-; Harrison Prize, Ear Nose and Throat Section, Royal Soc. of Medicine 66, Stuart Prize, British Medical Asscn. 66, Arnott Gold Medal, Irish Hospitals and Medical Schools Asscn. 68, K. B. Judd Award, Sloan Kettering Inst., N.Y. 69, Robert de Villiers Award, American Leukemia Soc. 70, Walker Prize, Royal Coll. of Surgeons 71, Paul Ehrlich-Ludwig Darmstaedter Prize (with Jan Waldenström, *q.v.*) 72; Hon. D.Sc. (Univ. of E. Africa) 70; shared Albert Lasker Medical Award in Clinical Cancer Chemotherapy 72, Gairdner Foundation Award 73; Hon. F.R.C.S. (Ireland) 73.
Leisure interests: photography, carpentry.
Publs. *Treatment of Burkitt's Lymphoma* (co-editor) 67, *Burkitt's Lymphoma* (co-editor) 70.
Medical Research Council, External Staff, 172 Tottenham Court Road, London, W.1; Home: The Knoll, Shiplake, Oxon., England.

Burkov, Boris Sergeevich; Soviet journalist, publisher and social worker; b. 11 May 1908, Kurkino Village, Tula Region; ed. agricultural technical school and Moscow Pedagogic Inst.
Journalist 38-; Chief Editor *Komsomolskaya pravda* (Komsomol Truth) 42-48; Deputy Chief Editor *Ogonyek* (Little Light) 51-54; Chief Editor *Trud* (Labour), Trade Union Newspaper 54-61; Chair. of Board of Novosti Press Agency 61-70; Sec. Union of Journalists of U.S.S.R. 57-70; now retd.; awarded orders: Lenin, Red Banner of Labour (2), Red Star and medals.
c/o Novosti Press Agency, M. Putinkovsky 2, Moscow, U.S.S.R.

Burn, Joshua Harold, M.D., F.R.S.; British pharmacologist; b. 6 March 1892, Barnard Castle, Co. Durham; m. 1st Margaret I. Parkinson 1920, 2nd Katherine F. Pemberton 1928, 3rd Elizabeth Haslam-Jones 1971; two s. four d.; ed. Barnard Castle School, Emmanuel Coll., Cambridge and Guy's Hospital.
Member staff Medical Research Council 20-25; fmr. Prof. of Pharmacology Univ. of London; Prof. of Pharmacology in Oxford Univ. 37-59; Visiting Prof. Washington Univ. St. Louis, Missouri 59-68; Emer.

Prof. of Pharmacology, Univ. of Oxford; Emer. Fellow, Balliol Coll., Oxford; Hon. Fellow, Nat. Inst. of Sciences of India; Hon. Pres. Int. Union of Pharmacology; Hon. mem. Pharmaceutical Soc.; Hon. mem. Soc. of Pharmacology and Therapeutics of Argentine Medical Asscn., British Pharmacological Society, Deutsche Pharmakologische Gesellschaft; mem. Deutsche Akademie der Naturforscher (Leopoldina); Hon. D.Sc. Yale Univ.; Hon. M.D. Johannes Gutenberg Univ. Mainz; Dr. h.c. Paris Univ.; Gairdner Int. Award 59; Hon. D.Sc. (Bradford Univ.).
Leisure interests: walking, writing history.
Publs. *Biological Standardisation* 37, *The Background of Therapeutics* 48, *Practical Pharmacology* 52, *Functions of Automatic Transmitters* 56, *Drugs, Medicines and Man, Automatic Nervous System* 64, *Our Most Interesting Diseases* 64.
3 Squitchey Lane, Oxford, England.
Telephone: Oxford 58209.

Burnet, Alastair (*see* Burnet, J. W. A.).

Burnet, Sir Frank Macfarlane, O.M., K.B.E., F.R.S., SC.D., F.R.C.P., F.R.A.C.P., F.A.C.P.; Australian scientist; b. 3 Sept. 1899, Traralgon, Victoria; s. of late Frank Burnet; m. 1st Linda Druce 1928 (died 1973), one s. two d.; m. 2nd Hazel Jenkin 1976; ed. Melbourne Univ.
Resident Pathologist, Melbourne Hospital 23-24; Beit Fellow for Medical Research at Lister Inst., London 26-27; Asst. Dir. Walter and Eliza Hall Inst. for Medical Research 28-31 and 34-44, Dir. 44-65; Dunham Lecturer, Harvard Medical School 44; Croonian Lecturer, Royal Society 50; Herter Lecturer, Johns Hopkins Univ. 50, Flexner Lecturer at Vanderbilt Univ. 58; Chair. Board of Trustees, Commonwealth Foundation 66-69; Foreign mem. Royal Swedish Acad. of Science 57; Foreign Assoc. Nat. Acad. of Sciences, U.S.A. 54, Copley Medal Royal Soc. 59, Nobel Prize for Medicine 60; Pres. Australian Acad. of Sciences 65-69, Hon. F.R.C.S.Eng.
Publs. *Biological Aspects of Infectious Disease* 40, *Production of Antibodies* 49, *Viruses and Man* 53, *Principles of Animal Virology* 55, *Enzyme, Antigen and Virus* 56, *Clonal Selection Theory of Immunity* 59, *Integrity of the Body* 62, *Auto-Immune Diseases* (with I. R. Mackay) 63, *Changing Patterns* (autobiography) 68, *Cellular Immunology* 69, *Immunological Surveillance* 70, *Dominant Mammal* 70, *Genes, Dreams and Realities* 71, *Walter and Eliza Hall Institute 1915-1965* 71, *Autoimmunity and Auto-immune Disease* 72, *Intrinsic Mutagenesis* 74.
48 Monomeath Avenue, Canterbury, Vic. 3126, Australia.
Telephone: 83 4526.

Burnet, James William Alexander (Alastair); British journalist; b. 12 July 1928, Sheffield, Yorks.; s. of late Alexander and Schonaid Burnet; m. Maureen Sinclair 1958; ed. The Leys School, Cambridge, and Worcester Coll., Oxford.
Sub-Editor and Leader Writer *Glasgow Herald* 51-58, Leader Writer *The Economist* 58-62; Political Editor, Independent Television News 63-64, rejoined ITN 76-; Editor *The Economist* 65-74; Editor *Daily Express* 74-76; Contributor to TV current affairs programmes, *This Week, Panorama, News at Ten*, etc.
43 Hornton Court, Campden Hill Road, London, W.8, England; and 33 Westbourne Gardens, Glasgow, W.2, Scotland.
Telephone: 01-937-7563 (London); 041-339-8073 (Glasgow).

Burnett, Most Rev. Bill Bendyshe, M.A., L.TH.; South African ecclesiastic; b. 31 May 1917, Koffiefontein; s. of Richard Evelyn Burnett and Louisa Martha Dobinsom; m. 1945; two s. one d.; ed. Diocesan Coll., Rondebosch, Michaelhouse School, Rhodes Univ. Coll. and St. Paul's Coll., Grahamstown and Queen's Coll., Birmingham, U.K.
Bishop of Bloemfontein 57-67; Gen. Sec. S. A. Council of Churches 67-69; Bishop of Grahamstown 69-74; Archbishop of Cape Town 74-.
Bishopscourt, Claremont, Cape Province, South Africa.
Telephone: 71-2531.

Burney, Leroy Edgar, M.D., M.P.H.; American physician; b. 31 Dec. 1906, Burney, Ind.; s. of Robert E. Burney and Mabel C. Howell; m. Mildred Hewins 1932; one s. one d.; ed. Indiana and Johns Hopkins Univs.
Joined U.S. Public Health Service 32, established first mobile venereal disease clinic in Brunswick, Georgia 37-39; Asst. Chief, Division of States Relations 43-44; detailed to U.S. Navy 44; Dir. U.S. Public Health Service, District IV, New Orleans 45; Sec. and State Health Commr., Indiana State Board of Health 45-54; Asst. Surgeon-Gen. and Deputy Chief, Bureau of State Service, U.S. Public Health Service 54-56; Surgeon-Gen. U.S. Public Health Service 56-61; Pres. World Health Assembly 58; Vice-Pres. Health Sciences, Temple Univ. 61-70; Pres. Milbank Memorial Fund Jan. 70-; Sedgwick Memorial Award, American Public Health Asscn. 75; Hon. D.Sc. (Jefferson, Woman's Medical Colls., Indiana Univ., De Pauw Univ.), Hon. LL.D. Seton Hall Univ.).
Leisure interests: golf and gardening.
Milbank Memorial Fund, 40 Wall Street, New York, N.Y. 10005, U.S.A.
Telephone: Whitehall 4-4989.

Burnham, Linden Forbes Sampson, B.A., LL.B., Q.C., O.E., S.C., M.P.; Guyanese lawyer and politician; b. 20 Feb. 1923, Kitty; s. of James Ethelbert Burnham and Rachel Abigail Burnham (née Sampson); m. 1st Sheila Bernice Lataste 1951, three d.; m. 2nd Viola Victorine Harper 1967, two d.; ed. Kitty Methodist School, Central High School and Queen's Coll., British Guiana, London Univ. and Gray's Inn.
Called to the Bar 48; Pres. Bar Asscn. 59; Queen's Counsel 60; Senior Counsel 66; Pres. W. Indian Students' Union, London 47-48; Del. of Union of the Int. Union of Students' Congress, Prague 47, Paris 48; Co-founder People's Progressive Party 49, Chair. 49-55; mem. Georgetown Town Council 52; Guyana Labour Union 52-56, 63-65, Pres. on leave 65-; Minister of Educ. 53; Founder and Leader People's Nat. Congress 57-; Leader of Parl. Opposition 57-64; Mayor of Georgetown 59, 64; Prime Minister British Guiana 64-66, Guyana 66-; Order of Excellence of Guyana.
Leisure interests: horse-riding, chess, swimming, fishing, hunting, farming.
Publ. *A Destiny to Mould* 70.
Office of the Prime Minister, Public Buildings, Georgetown; Home: The Residence, Vlissengen Road, Georgetown, Guyana.

Burns, Arthur Edward, PH.D.; American economist and former government official; b. 3 Sept. 1908, Oakland, Calif.; m. Marcella Eugenie Wyss 1933; ed. Univ. of Calif. and George Washington Univ.
Instructor, George Washington Univ. 34-35, Asst. Prof. 35-37, Assoc. Prof. 37-40, Adjunct Prof. 40-45, Prof. of Econs. 45-74, Emeritus 74-, Acting Dean, School of Govt. 46-49, Dean 49-57, Dean Graduate Council 57-67; Dean Graduate School of Arts and Sciences 67-74; Visiting Prof. Univ. of Calif. 49, Univ. of Brazil 52, Economist, Fed. Emergency Relief Admin. 34-35; Economist and Asst. Dir. of Research, Works Progress Admin. 35-40, Adviser 41-42; Special Consultant, Office of Price Admin. 42-43; Deputy Dir. Office of Materials and Facilities, War Food Admin. 43-45; Consultant to White House 57-60; Private Consultant 73-.
Publs. *Modern Economics* (with Neal and Watson) 48, 53, Arabic edn. 60, *Government Spending and Economic Expansion* (with D. S. Watson) 40, *Federal Work,*

Security and Relief Programs (with E. A. Williams) 41; numerous articles.
4000 Massachusetts Avenue, N.W., Washington, D.C. 20016, U.S.A.

Burns, Arthur F.; American government official and economist; b. 27 April 1904, Stanislau, Austria; *m.* Helen Bernstein 1930; two *s.*; ed. Columbia Univ. Instructor in Econs., Rutgers Univ. 27-30, Asst. Prof. 30-33, Assoc. Prof. 33-43, Prof. 43-44; Prof. of Econs. Columbia Univ. 44-58, John Bates Clark Prof. of Econs. 59-69; mem. Research Staff, Nat. Bureau of Econ. Research 33-69, Dir. of Research 45-53, Pres. 57-67, Hon. Chair. 68; Chair. President's Advisory Board on Econ. Growth and Stability 53-56, President's Council of Econ. Advisers 53-56, Cabinet Cttee. on Small Business 56; mem. Advisory Council on Social Security Financing 57-58; mem. President's Advisory Cttee. on Labor-Management Policy 61-66; Counsellor to Pres. of U.S.A. 69; Chair. Fed. Reserve Board 70-; U.S. Alt. Gov., IMF 73-; mem. American Econ. Assen. (Pres. 59), American Statistical Assen., American Acad. of Arts and Sciences, Acad. of Political Science (Pres. 62-68), American Philosophical Soc., etc.; several awards and numerous hon. degrees.
Publs. include: *Production Trends in the United States since 1870* 34, *Measuring Business Cycles* (with W. C. Mitchell) 46, *Economic Research and the Keynesian Thinking of our Times* 46, *Frontiers of Economic Knowledge* 54, *Prosperity Without Inflation* 57, *The Management of Prosperity* 66, *Full Employment, Guideposts and Economic Stability* (with P. A. Samuelson) 67, *The Defense Sector and the American Economy* (with others) 68, *The Business Cycle in the Changing World* 69.
Home: 2510 Virginia Avenue, N.W., Washington, D.C. 20037; Office: Board of Governors of the Federal Reserve System, Washington, D.C. 20551, U.S.A.

Burns, Norman, M.A.; American economist and educationist; b. 14 Nov. 1905, Versailles, O.; *s.* of Marley and Mabel B. Burns; *m.* Constance Albrech 1935; ed. Wittenberg Univ., Ohio, Yale Univ. and Univ. of Montpellier, France.
Assistant Prof. of Econs., American Univ. of Beirut 29-32; U.S. Govt. Service as Foreign Trade Economist, U.S. Tariff Comm., Dir. Foreign Service Inst. of State Dept., Deputy Dir. for Near East and South Asia, Int. Co-operation Admin., Econ. Adviser, UN Relief and Works Agency, Beirut, Dir. United States Operations Missions, Amman 34-61; Pres. American Univ. of Beirut 61-65; mem. Board of Govs., Middle East Inst., Washington 67-; Hon. LL.D. (Wittenberg Univ.).
Leisure interests: hiking and local history.
Publs. *Government Budgets of Middle East Countries* 56, *Planning Economic Development in the Arab World* 59, *Education in the Middle East* 65, *Management Factor in Economic Development* 70, *The Challenge of Education in the Developing Countries* 73, *The Energy Crisis and U.S. Middle East Policy* 73.
3813 North 37th Street, Arlington, Va. 22207, U.S.A. Telephone: 703-525-2724.

Burquan, Saleh Khalil, M.D.; Jordanian politician; b. 1917, Al Karak; *m.*; four *c.*; ed. American Univ. of Beirut.
Physician, Transjordan Frontier Forces 43-46, Dir. of Arab Physicians, T.F.F. 46-48; Private Physician, Zerka 48; M.P. 51-63; Minister of Health April 63-July 64, of Social Affairs and Labour Feb. 66, Oct. 67, 68-69, of Public Health Sept. 66-March 67, April-Aug. 67, of Public Health and Agriculture March-April 67, of Social, Home, Municipal and Rural Affairs April 68-Aug. 69; mem. of Senate 63, 67; Regional Dir. ILO, Beirut 69-; Al Kawkab Medal 1st Grade.
International Labour Organization, P.O.B. 4656, Beirut, Lebanon.

Burri, Alberto; Italian artist; b. 1915.
Qualified as surgeon; began painting while prisoner-of-war in U.S.A. 44; exhbns. throughout the world; winner of awards at Pittsburg, Venice, São Paulo; has pictures in many int. collections.
Via Nera 9, Rome, Italy.

Burris, Robert Harza, PH.D., D.SC.; American professor of biochemistry; b. 13 April 1914, Brookings, S. Dak.; *s.* of Edward Thomas Burris and Mable Harza Burris; *m.* Katherine Irene Brusse 1945; one *s.* two *d.*; ed. S. Dakota State Coll. and Univ. of Wisconsin.
Research Asst., Univ. of Wisconsin 36-40; Nat. Research Council Postdoctoral Fellow, Columbia Univ. 40-41; Instructor in Bacteriology, Univ. of Wisconsin 41-44, Asst. Prof. of Biochemistry 44-46, Assoc. Prof. 46-51, Prof. 51-, Chair. Dept. of Biochemistry 58-70; mem. Nat. Acad. of Sciences, American Acad. of Arts and Sciences; Guggenheim Fellow 54; Pres. American Soc. of Plant Physiologists 60; Merit Award of Botanical Soc. of America 66; Stephen Hales Award of American Soc. of Plant Physiologists 68; Hon. D.Sc. (S. Dakota State Univ.) 66.
Leisure interests: photography, canoeing.
Publs. *Manometric Techniques* 45; 195 scientific papers 36-75.
Department of Biochemistry, University of Wisconsin, Madison, Wis. 53706, U.S.A.
Telephone: 608-262-3042.

Burroughs, William S.; American writer; b. 1914, St. Louis; ed. Harvard Univ.
Publs. include: *Junkie: Confessions of an Unredeemed Drug Addict, The Naked Lunch, The Exterminator* (with Brion Gysin), *The Soft Machine, The Ticket that Exploded, The Yage Letters* (with Allen Ginsberg), *Nova Express, Dead Fingers Talk, The Wild Boys.*
c/o Grove Press, 80 University Place, New York, N.Y. 10003, U.S.A.

Burrows, Sir Bernard Alexander Brocas, G.C.M.G.; British fmr. diplomatist; b. 3 July 1910; *m.* Ines Walter 1944; one *d.* one *s.*; ed. Eton and Oxford Univ. Entered Foreign Service 34; served Cairo 38-45; Foreign Office 45-50; Counsellor, Washington 50-53; Political Resident in the Persian Gulf 53-58; Ambassador to Turkey 58-63; Deputy Under-Sec. at the Foreign Office 63-66; U.K. Perm. Rep., North Atlantic Council 66-70; Dir.-Gen. Fed. Trust for Educ. and Research.
Publ. *The Security of Western Europe* (with C. Irwin) 72.
Steep Farm, Petersfield, Hants., England.
Telephone: Petersfield 2287.

Burton, Richard, C.B.E.; British stage and film actor; b. 10 Nov. 1925, Pontrhyd-y-fen, Glam.; *m.* 1st Sybil Williams (divorced), two *d.*; *m.* 2nd Elizabeth Taylor (*q.v.*) 1964 (divorced 1974, remarried 1975); ed. Port Talbot Secondary School and Exeter Coll., Oxford Univ.
First appearance as Glan in *Druid's Rest*, Royal Court Theatre, Liverpool 43; St. Martin's Theatre, London 44; R.A.F. service 44-47; Hon. Fellow, St. Peter's Coll., Oxford 72.
Stage appearances include Richard in *The Lady's Not For Burning* 49, Cuthman in *The Boy With A Cart* 50, Hamlet, Sir Toby Belch, Henry V, Othello, Iago, Caliban with The Old Vic Company 53-54, 55-56; *Time Remembered* 57, *Camelot* 60, *Hamlet* 64; in *Doctor Faustus*, Oxford 66, *Equus* (N.Y.) 76.
Films include *The Last Days of Dolwyn, The Desert Rats, The Robe, Look Back In Anger, Ice Palace, Cleopatra, The V.I.P.s, Becket, The Night of the Iguana, The Sandpiper, The Spy who Came in from the Cold, Who's Afraid of Virginia Woolf, The Taming of the Shrew, Dr. Faustus, The Comedians, Boom, Candy,*

Where Eagles Dare, Staircase, Anne of the Thousand Days, Raid on Rommel, Villain, Under Milk Wood, Hammersmith is Out, The Assassination of Trotsky 71, *Bluebeard* 73, *Massacre in Rome* 74, *Brief Encounter* 74, *The Klansman* 74, *The Voyage* 74, *Walk with Destiny* (TV) 74.
c/o Major D. Neville-Willing, 85 Kinnerton Street, London, S.W.1, England; c/o Hugh French Agency Inc., 9348 Santa Monica Boulevard, Beverley Hills, Calif., U.S.A.
Telephone: 01-235-4640 (London).

Bury, Hon. Leslie Harry Ernest, M.A.; Australian politician; b. 25 Feb. 1913, London; m. Anne Helen Sise Weigall 1940; four s.; ed. Queen's Coll., Cambridge. Bank of New South Wales 35-45; Econ. Relations, Dept. of External Affairs 45-48; Commonwealth Treasury 48-51; Alt. Dir. Int. Bank for Reconstruction and Devt., Int. Monetary Fund 51-53, Exec. Dir. 53-56; mem. Parl. 56-74; Minister for Air 61-62, for Housing 63-66, for Labour and Nat. Service 66-69; Treas. 69-71; Minister of Foreign Affairs March-Aug. 71.
Leisure interests: carpentry, home maintenance and repairs, gardening.
Vaucluse Road, Vaucluse, N.S.W., Australia.
Telephone: Sydney 337-1431.

Busch, August A., Jr.; American brewing executive; b. 28 March 1899; ed. Smith Acad.
General Supt. Anheuser-Busch Inc. 24-26, Sixth Vice-Pres. and Gen. Man. 26-31, Second Vice-Pres. and Gen. Man. 31-34, First Vice-Pres. and Gen. Man. 34-41, Pres. 46-, Chair. 56-, Chief Exec. 71-; official of numerous other companies.
Anheuser-Busch Inc., 721 Pestalozzi Street, St. Louis, Mo. 63118, U.S.A.

Busch, Ernst; German actor; b. 22 Jan. 1900, Kiel; s. of Friedrich and Emma Busch; m. Irene Busch 1964; one s.
Acted in *Kaufmann von Berlin* (Piscator), *Die Mutter* (Brecht-Eisler), *Dreigroschenoper* (Brecht), *Galilei* (Brecht), and in films, including *Kühle Wampe*; emigrated 33; joined Int. Brigade in Spain; imprisoned by Nazis on return to Germany; resumed career as actor 45; joined Berliner Ensemble; Nat. Prize, 3rd Class 49, 2nd Class 56, 1st Class 66; Vaterländischer Verdienstorden in Silber 60, Gold 65; Johannes-R.-Becher-Medaille in Gold 65; Karl-Marx-Orden 70; Lenin Peace Prize 72.
Leonhard-Frank-Strasse 11, 111 Berlin, German Democratic Republic.

Busch, Rolf T.; Norwegian diplomatist; b. 15 Nov. 1920, Spydeberg; s. of Aksel Busch and Alette (née Tunby); m. Solveig Helle 1950; one s.; ed. Oslo Univ. and Nat. Defence Coll.
Deputy Judge 46-47; entered Norwegian Foreign Service 47; Ministry of Foreign Affairs 47-50; Sec., Cairo 50-52; Vice-Consul, New York 52-54; Ministry of Foreign Affairs 54-56; Nat. Defence Coll. 56-57; First Sec., Norwegian Del. to NATO, Paris 57-60; Ministry of Foreign Affairs 60-65; Counsellor and Deputy Perm. Rep. Norwegian Del. to NATO, Paris and Brussels 65-70; Dir.-Gen. Ministry of Foreign Affairs 70-; Perm. Rep. to North Atlantic Council 71-; Officer, Order of the Nile, Commdr. with Star, Icelandic Order of the Falcon.
20 avenue de Lothier, Woluwé-St.-Pierre, Brussels, Belgium; Hafrsfjordgt. 2, Oslo, Norway.
Telephone: 70-94-37 (Brussels); 56-54-39 (Oslo).

Bush, Alan, D.MUS. (LOND.); British composer, conductor and pianist; b. 22 Dec. 1900, London; s. of Alfred Walter Bush and Alice Maud Bush (née Brinsley); m. Nancy Rachel Head 1931; three d. (one

deceased); ed. Highgate School, Royal Acad. of Music and Humboldt Univ., Berlin.
Professor of Composition, Royal Acad. of Music 25-, Fellow 38-, Lecturer on History of Music 36-38; served army 41-45; Chair. Composers' Guild of G.B. 47-48; Pres. Workers' Music Asscn. 41-; has conducted leading orchestras in Europe and the U.S.S.R. and appeared frequently as pianist and lecturer; Carnegie Award for String Quartet 24; Arts Council Opera Prize 51; Corresp. mem. German Acad. of Arts 58; Handel Prize 62; D.Mus. h.c. (Dunelm) 71.
Leisure interests: walking, foreign travel.
Works include: Choral: *Winter Journey* 46, *Ballad of Freedom's Soldier* 53, *Alps and Andes of the Living World* 68; Orchestral: *Dance Overture* 35, *Piano Concerto* 37, *First Symphony* 40, *English Suite* 46, *Violin Concerto* 48, *Nottingham Symphony* 49, *Concert Suite for 'Cello* 52, *Dorian Passacaglia and Fugue* 59, *Byron Symphony* 60, *Variations, Nocturne and Finale for Piano and Orchestra* 62, *Partita Concertante* 64, *Scherzo* (for Wind Orchestra with Percussion) 69, *Africa* (for Piano and Orchestra) 71, *Concert-Overture for an Occasion* 71, *Liverpool Overture* 73; Chamber music: *Dialectic* (for String Quartet) 29, *Concert Piece* (for Cello and Piano) 36, *Lyric Interlude* (for Violin and Piano) 44, *Three Concert Studies* (for Piano Trio) 47, *Prelude, Air and Dance* (for Violin, String Quartet and Percussion) 63, *Suite* (for Two Pianos) 67, *Time Remembered* (for Chamber Orchestra) 69, *Serenade* (for String Quartet) 69, *Suite of Six* (for String Quartet); Piano solo: *Prelude and Fugue* 27, *Relinquishment* 28, *Le Quatorze Juillet* 43, *Nocturne* 57, *Sonata in A Flat* 70, *Letter Galliard*; Operatic: *Wat Tyler* 50, *Men of Blackmoor* 55, *The Sugar Reapers* 63, *Joe Hill: The Man Who Never Died* 67; Operas for Schools: *The Press Gang* 46, *The Spell Unbound* 53, *The Ferryman's Daughter* 61; Vocal solo: Song-Cycle *Voices of the Prophets* (for Tenor and Piano) 53, Song-Cycle *The Freight of Harvest* (for Tenor and Piano) 69, *Two Songs to Poems by Pablo Neruda* 73, Song Cycle *Life's Span* (for Mezzo-Soprano and Piano) 74.
Publ. *Strict Counterpoint in Palestrina Style*.
25 Christchurch Crescent, Radlett, Herts., England.
Telephone: Radlett 6422.

Bush, Dorothy Vredenburgh; American politician; b. 8 Dec. 1916, Baldwyn, Miss.; d. of Will Lee McElroy and Lany Holland McElroy; m. 1st Peter Vredenburgh, 1940 (deceased), one step s. (deceased); 2nd John W. Bush 1962; ed. George Washington Univ. and Miss. State Coll. for Women.
Secretary to Dir. of Tenn. Coal, Iron and Rail Road Co. 37-40; Asst. Sec. Young Democrats of America 41, Vice-Pres. 43-48, Acting Pres. 44; Sec. Democratic Nat. Cttee. 44-; Democratic Nat. Conventions 44, 48, 52, 56, 60, 64, 68, 72; Dir. Coastal Caribbean Oils & Minerals Ltd., Pancoastal Inc.; mem. Nat. Fed. of Business and Professional Women.
Democratic National Committee, 1625 Massachusetts Avenue, N.W., Washington, D.C. 20036; Home: The Cliffs, 1409 Lake Shore Drive, Columbus, Ohio 43204, U.S.A.

Bush, George; American diplomatist; b. 12 June 1924, Milton, Mass.; s. of Prescott S. and Dorothy Walker Bush; m. Barbara Pierce Bush 1945; four s. one d.; ed. Phillips Acad., Andover, Mass. and Yale Univ.
Naval Carrier Pilot 42-45; Co-founder Zapata Petroleum Corpn. 53; Co-founder-Pres. Zapata Off-Shore Co. 54-66; Rep. from 7th district, Texas, House of Reps. 66; Perm. Rep. to UN 70-73; Chair. Republican Nat. Cttee. 73-74; Head U.S. Liaison Office, Peking 74-75; Dir. of C.I.A. Nov. 75-.
Leisure interests: tennis, boating, golf.
Office of the Director, Central Intelligence Agency, Washington, D.C. 20505, U.S.A.

Bush, John Nash Douglas, M.A., PH.D.; American university professor; b. 21 March 1896, Morrisburg, Canada; s. of Dexter C. and Mary E. Bush; m. Hazel Cleaver 1927; one s.; ed. Toronto and Harvard Univs.

Sheldon Fellow, Harvard 23-24; Instructor, Harvard 24-27; Asst. Prof. of English, Univ. of Minn. 27-28, Assoc. Prof. 28-31, Prof. 31-36; Guggenheim Fellow 34-35; Assoc. Prof., Harvard 36-37, Prof. of English 37-57, Gurney Prof., Harvard 57-66; mem. American Philosophical Society; Pres. Modern Humanities Research Asscn. 55; corresp. Fellow, British Acad.; Hon. Litt.D. (Tufts, Oberlin, Merrimack, Swarthmore Colls., Harvard, Princeton, Mich. State, Toronto Univs., Boston Coll.); L.H.D. (Southern Illinois Univ. and Marlboro Coll.).

Publs. *Mythology and the Renaissance Tradition in English Poetry* 32, 63, *Mythology and the Romantic Tradition in English Poetry* 37, 69, *The Renaissance and English Humanism* 39, *Paradise Lost in Our Time* 45, *English Literature in the Earlier Seventeenth Century (Oxford History of English Literature)* 45, 62, *Science and English Poetry* 50, *Classical Influences in Renaissance Literature* 52, *English Poetry: the Main Currents from Chaucer to the Present* 52, *John Milton* 64, *Prefaces to Renaissance Literature* 65, *John Keats* 66, *Engaged and Disengaged* 66, *Pagan Myth and Christian Tradition in English Poetry* 68, *Matthew Arnold* 71, *Jane Austen* 75; Editor: *The Portable Milton* 49, *Tennyson: Selected Poetry* 51, *Keats: Selected Poems and Letters* 59, *Shakespeare's Sonnets* (with A. Harbage) 61, *Complete Poetical Works of Milton* 65, *Variorum Commentary on the Poems of John Milton* Vol. 1 70, Vol. 2 (with A. S. P. Woodhouse and E. Weismiller) 72.

3 Clement Circle, Cambridge, Mass. 02138; Summer: Norwich, Vt. 05055, U.S.A.
Telephone: 876-9548.

Busia, Kofi Abrefa, M.A., D.PHIL.; Ghanaian university teacher and politician; b. 11 July 1913; m.; four c.; ed. Mfantsipim (Cape Coast), Achimota Coll., London and Oxford Univs.

Awarded Carnegie Research Fellowship, Oxford Univ. 45; Admin. Officer, Gold Coast Govt. 47-49; fmr. Prof. Sociology, Univ. Coll. of Ghana; fmr. Leader of the Opposition, Ghana Parl.; fmr. Leader of United Party; Visiting Prof. Northwestern Univ. 54, Wageningen Univ. (Netherlands) 56-57, Visiting Fellow Nuffield Coll., Oxford 55; Prof. of Sociology, Inst. of Social Studies, The Hague 59-61; Prof. of Sociology and Culture of Africa, Univ. of Leiden 60-61; Visiting Prof. Colegio de Mexico, Mexico City 62; Exec. mem. Int. Sociological Asscn. 53-60; returned to Ghana 66; Chair. Nat. Liberation Advisory Council 66-69; founded Progress Party, Ghana 69; Leader of the Progress Party 69; Prime Minister Sept. 69-Jan. 72; mem. Int. Social Science Council, Int. African Inst., Asscn. of Social Anthropologists.

Publs. include *Position of the Chief in the Political System of Ashanti* 51, *Self-Government, Education for Citizenship, Industrialisation in West Africa* 55, *Challenge of Africa* 62, *Purposeful Education for Africa* 64, *Africa in Search of Democracy* 67.
St. Antony's College, Oxford, England.

Buslenko, Nikolai Panteleymonovich; Soviet mathematician; b. 15 Feb. 1922, Rzhishchev, Kiev Region, Ukraine; ed. Dzerzhinsky Military Engineering Acad.

Service in the army 41-; mem. C.P.S.U. 62-; Corresp. mem. U.S.S.R. Acad. of Sciences 66-; mem. Presidium Sciences Council of Cybernetics.

Publs. Works on machine mathematics and theory of large systems.
U.S.S.R. Academy of Sciences, 14 Leninsky Prospekt, Moscow, U.S.S.R.

Bustamante, Rt. Hon. Sir William Alexander, P.C., G.B.E.; Jamaican politician; b. 24 Feb. 1884.

Former soldier, policeman, and journalist; organized Bustamante Trade Union; Leader Jamaica Labour Party 43-; secured majority in Elections 44 and 49; mem. House of Representatives for Clarendon South; mem. Exec. Council as Minister for Communications 44-53; Chief Minister 53-55, Prime Minister 62-67; Commr. British Section Caribbean Comm. 50-55.
24 Tucker Avenue, Kingston 6, Jamaica.

Bustamante y Rivero, José Luis; Peruvian judge; b. 15 Jan. 1894; ed. Univs. of Arequipa and Cuzco.

Member Bars of Arequipa 18, Cuzco 18, Puno 26; Legal practice 18-34; Substitute Judge and Deputy Public Prosecutor, Superior Court of Arequipa 20-34; mem. Bar of Lima 56, Legal Practice 56-60, Dean of Lima Bar 60, now Hon. mem.; Teacher of American Archaeology, Univ. of Arequipa 21, Peruvian Social Geography 21, Modern Philosophy (Asst. Prof.) 21, Asst. Prof. in Legal Procedure 27, Prof. of Civil Law 30-34; mem. Arequipa City Council 21-24; Minister of Justice and Educ., Peru 30-31; Minister to Bolivia 34-38, to Uruguay 39-42; Amb. to Bolivia 42-45; Pres. of Peru 45-48; mem. Consultative Comm. of Ministry of Foreign Affairs 60; Judge, Int. Court of Justice, The Hague 61-70, Pres. Int. Court of Justice 67-70; mem. Peruvian Soc. of Int. Law, Nat. Acad. of Law and Political Sciences, Peruvian Acad. of Language, Lima, Affil. Royal Spanish Acad. of Language, Madrid; Hon. mem. Inter-American Bar Asscn., Washington; mem. Francisco de Vitoria Inst. of Int. Law and Hispano-Luso-Americano-Filipino Inst. of Int. Law, Madrid; Corresp. mem. Colombian and Uruguayan Acads. of Language.

Publs. include: *Organización y procedimientos de la Justicia Militar en el Perú* 18, *Proyecto de ley de Juzgados de Paz, con exposición de motivos* 19, *El laudo arbitral sobre Tacna y Arica* 29, *La Teoría del abuso del Derecho* 32, *Las Transformaciones del Contrato Civil* 35, *Una visión del Perú* 41, *Ensayo histórico sobre Arequipa* 41, *El Tratado de Derecho Civil Internacional de 1940 de Montevideo* 42, *La O.N.U. en el Palacio de Chaillot* 52, *Panamericanismo e Ibero-americanismo* 53, *La subestimación del Derecho en el mundo moderno* 54, *Las nuevas Concepciones Jurídicas sobre el alcance del mar territorial* 55, *Las clases sociales en el Perú* 59.
c/o Ministerio de Justicia, Lima, Peru.

Butcher, Willard Carlisle; American banker; b. 25 Nov. 1926, Bronxville, N.Y.; s. of Willard F. and Helen Calhoun Butcher; m. 1st Sarah C. Payne 1949 (died 1955), 2nd Elisabeth Allen 1956; one s. three d.; ed. Scarsdale High School, N.Y., Middlebury Coll., Vt. and Brown Univ., R.I.

Joined the Chase Manhattan Bank 47, Asst. Vice-Pres. 56, Vice-Pres. 58, Senior Vice-Pres. 60, assigned to Int. Dept. 68, Exec. Vice-Pres. in charge of Int. Dept. 69, Vice-Chair. Jan. 72, Pres. Oct. 72-.
Leisure interests, golf, sailing.
The Chase Manhattan Bank N.A., One Chase Manhattan Plaza, New York, N.Y. 10015; Home: 39 Trail's End Road, Wilton, Conn. 06897, U.S.A.
Telephone: 212-552-7251 (Office); 203-762-7959 (Home).

Butement, William Alan Stewart, C.B.E., B.SC., D.SC., F.I.E.E., F.INST.P., F.A.I.P., F.I.R.E.E., F.T.S.; Australian scientist; b. 18 Aug. 1904, Masterton, New Zealand; s. of Dr. William Butement; m. Ursula Florence Alberta Parish 1933; two d.; ed. Scots Coll., Sydney, Australia, Univ. Coll. School, Hampstead and Univ. Coll., London.

Scientific Officer, War Office 28-39; Asst. Dir. Scientific Research, Ministry of Supply 39-47; First Chief Supt., Research Establishment and Rocket Range, Woomera, Australia 47-49; Chief Scientist, Australian Dept. of Supply in charge Australian Defence Science 49-66; Dir. Plessey Pacific 67-.

Leisure interests: amateur radio transmission, fishing.
Publ. *Precision Radar* 45-46.
5A Barry Street, Kew, Victoria, Australia.
Telephone: 868375.

Butenandt, Adolf Friedrich Johann, D.PHIL.; German physiological chemist; b. 24 March 1903, Bremerhaven-Lehe; s. of Otto Butenandt and Wilhemine Butenandt (née Thomfohrde); m. Erika von Ziegner 1931; two s. five d.; ed. Oberrealschule Bremerhaven, Univs. of Marburg and Göttingen.
Scientific Asst. Chemical Inst., Göttingen Univ. 27-30, Dozent in organic and biological chemistry 31, leader organic and biological chemistry laboratories 31-33; Prof. of Chemistry, Dir. Organic Chemistry Inst., Danzig Inst. of Technology 33-36; Dir. Kaiser Wilhelm Inst. of Biochemistry, Berlin-Dahlem (later at Tübingen) (now Max Planck Inst. of Biochemistry, Munich) 36-72; Prof. of Physiological Chemistry, Munich Univ. 56-72, Prof. Emer. 72-; Pres. Max-Planck Soc. 60-72; Hon. Pres. Max-Planck Soc. 72; Foreign mem. Royal Soc. (U.K.) 68; Nobel Prize for Chem. 39; Orden Pour le Mérite (Arts and Sciences) 62, Österreichisches Ehrenzeichen für Wissenschaft und Kunst 64; Commdr. Légion d'Honneur 69; Commdr. dans l'Ordre des Palmes Académiques 72; Adolf-von-Harnack-Medaille, Max-Planck-Soc. 73; Foreign mem. Acad. of Sciences, Paris 74.
Publs. *Biochemie der Wirkstoffe (Sexualhormone, Genchemie, Insektenphysiologie)*; numerous articles in *Hoppe-Seyler's Zeitschrift für Physiologische Chemie, Chemische Berichte, Zeitschrift für Naturforschung*, etc.
Home: Marsopstrasse 5, 8 Munich 60, Federal Republic of Germany.
Telephone: 885490 (Home).

Buthelezi, Chief Gatsha; South African (Zulu) leader and politician; b. 27 Aug. 1928, Mahlabatini; s. of late Chief Mathole Buthelezi and Princess Magogo; m. Irene Audrey Thandekile Mzila 1952; three s. four d.; ed. Adams Coll., Fort-Hare Univ.
Installed as Chief of Buthelezi Tribe 53; assisted King Cyprian in admin. of Zulu people 53-68; elected leader of Zululand territorial authority 70; Prime Minister of KwaZulu 72-.
KwaPhindangene, P.O. Box 1, Mahlabatini, KwaZulu, South Africa.
Telephone: Ngilazi 2.

Butler, Clifford Charles, PH.D., F.R.S.; British physicist; b. 20 May 1922, Reading, Berks.; s. of Charles and Olive Butler; m. Kathleen Betty Collins 1947; two d.; ed. Reading Univ.
Assistant Lecturer in Physics, Manchester Univ. 45-47, Lecturer 47-53; Reader in Physics, Imperial Coll., London 53-57; Prof. 57-70, Head, Dept. of Physics 63-70; Dir. Nuffield Foundation 70-75; Vice-Chancellor, Loughborough Univ. of Technology 75-; Sec.-Gen. Int. Union of Pure and Applied Physics 63-72, First Vice-Pres. 72-75, Pres. 75-.
Publs. scientific papers on cosmic rays and high energy physics.
University of Technology, Loughborough, Leicestershire, LE11 3TU, England.
Telephone: 050-93-63171.

Butler, Frederick Guy, M.A., D.LITT.; South African university professor; b. 1918, Cradock, Cape Province; s. of E. C. Butler and Alice E. (née Stringer) Butler; m. Jean Murray Satchwell 1940; three s. one d.; ed. Rhodes Univ., Grahamstown, and Brasenose Coll., Oxford.
War service Egypt, Lebanon, Italy, U.K. 40-45; Oxford 45-47; lecturer in English, Univ. of Witwatersrand 48-50; Prof. of English, Rhodes Univ. 52-; Editor *New Coin* (poetry quarterly).
Leisure interests: producing plays, restoring old houses.
Publs. *Stranger to Europe* (poems) 52, 60, *The Dam*

(play) 53, *The Dove Returns* (play) 56, *A Book of South African Verse* 59, *South of the Zambesi* (poems) 66, *Cape Charade* (play) 68, *When Boys were Men* 69, *Take Root or Die* (play) 70, *The 1820 Settlers* (history) 74, *Selected Poems* 75.
c/o Rhodes University, Grahamstown, South Africa.
Telephone: 3823.

Butler, Hon. Michel; American financier; b. 26 Nov. 1926, Chicago; ed. Univ. of Colorado.
Chairman Natoma Productions Inc., Talisman Co., Michael Butler Associates; fmr. Vice-Pres. Butler Co.; Exec. Vice-Pres. and Dir. Butler Engineering & Construction, Butler Overseas; Dir. Butler Paper Corpn., Int. Sports Core, J. W. Butler Paper Co. of Chicago, Butler Paper Co., Basic Investment Corpn., Intrafi, Overseas Bank Ltd., Drake Oak Brook Hotel, Oak Brook Landscaping Co., Oak Brook Utility, Ondine Inc.; frmrly. Civic Chancellor, Lincoln Acad. of Illinois; Pres. Org. of Econ. Devt., Illinois Sports Council; Commr. Chicago Regional Port District; Special Adviser on India and Middle East Affairs to the late Senator John F. Kennedy; World Producer of *Hair*; Co-Producer of *Lenny*; mem. Chicago Historical Soc., English-speaking Union, Chicago Nat. History Museum, Oceanographic Inst.; Order of the Sword and Cutlass, Order of Lincoln, Order of Colonial Wars.
Natoma, Oak Brook, Ill., U.S.A.

Butler, Sir Milo Boughton, G.C.M.G., Kt.; Governor-General of the Bahamas; b. 11 Aug. 1906; ed. George Washington School, Fla., U.S.A., Rum Cay, Bahamas, and Central School, Nassau Court, Bahamas.
Independent mem. Legislative Council for Bains Town, New Providence, after other constituencies; Minister of Labour, Welfare, Agriculture and Fisheries 68-72, without Portfolio 72; Gov.-Gen. Aug. 73-; fmr. Pres. Milo B. Butler and Sons Ltd.; mem. Synod of Anglican Church.
Government House, Nassau, Bahamas.

Butler, Reg(inald Cotterell), A.R.I.B.A.; British sculptor; b. 1913; ed. Hertford Grammar School.
Lecturer, Architectural Asscn. School of Architecture, London 37-39; Technical Editor, Architectural Press 46-51; Gregory Fellow in Sculpture, Univ. of Leeds 51-53; First one-man show, London 49; Winner Int. Competition, The Unknown Political Prisoner 53; Retrospective exhbn. J. B. Speed Art Museum, Louisville, U.S. 63, Pierre Matisse Gallery, New York; Assoc., Acad. Royale des Sciences, des Lettres et des Beaux-Arts de Belgique.
Publ. *Creative Development* 62.
Studio: Ash, Berkhamsted Place, Berkhamsted, Hertfordshire, England.
Telephone: Berkhamsted 2933.

Butler, Thomas Clifton; American Chairman of Grand Union Company 68-74; see *The International Who's Who 1975-76*.

Butler of Saffron Walden, Baron (Life Peer), cr. 65, of Halstead; **Richard Austen Butler,** K.G., P.C., C.H., M.A.; British politician; b. 9 Dec. 1902, Attock Serai, India; s. of late Sir Montagu S. D. Butler, K.C.S.I.; m. 1st Sydney Courtauld 1926 (died 1954), three s. one d.; m. 2nd Mollie Courtauld (née Montgomerie) 1959; ed. Marlborough and Pembroke Coll., Cambridge.
Fellow Corpus Christi Coll., Cambridge 25-29; Conservative M.P. for Saffron Walden Div. of Essex 29-65; Parl. Private Sec. to the Sec. of State for India 31 and Under-Sec. of State for India 32-May 37; Parl. Sec. to Minister of Labour May 37-Feb. 38; Under-Sec. for Foreign Affairs Feb. 38-41, Pres. Board of Educ. 41-44, Minister of Educ. 44-45; Minister of Labour and Nat. Service May-July 45; Chancellor of the Exchequer 51-55; Lord Privy Seal and Leader of the House of Commons 55-57; Home Secretary, Lord Privy Seal and

eader of the House of Commons 57-59; Home Sec., eader of the House of Commons and Chair. of the onservative Party 59-61; Home Sec. 61-62; Cabinet inister charged with overseeing of Common Market egotiations 61, Minister responsible for Central frican Fed. 62-Oct. 63; Deputy Prime Minister and irst Sec. of State July 62-Oct. 63; Sec. of State for oreign Affairs Oct. 63-64; Master of Trinity Coll., ambridge 65-; fmr. Chair., Conservative Party esearch Dept.; Dir. Courtaulds Jan. 46-51, Dec. 65-69; hair. Home Office Cttee. on Mentally Abnormal ffenders 73-75; Pres. Royal Soc. of Literature; Rector lasgow Univ. 56-59; High Steward Cambridge Univ. 3-66; High Steward of City of Cambridge 63-; Chancel-r, Sheffield Univ. 60-, Univ. of Essex 62-; numerous on. degrees.

ubls. *The Responsibilities of Education* 69, *The Art of e Possible* (autobiography) 71.

ouse of Lords, London, S.W.1; and The Master's odge, Trinity College, Cambridge, England.

elephone: Cambridge 58201.

Butlin, Sir William Edmund, Kt., M.B.E.; retired British holiday camp proprietor; b. 29 Sept. 1899; ed. anada and England.

hairman and Man. Dir. Butlin's Ltd. 36-68; Pres. audeville Golfing Soc.; Companion Grand Order of Vater Rats; Elder Statesman, Variety Club of Great Iritain; Int. Vice-Pres. Variety Club; Statesman, ariety Club of Jersey.

utlin Building, 439 Oxford Street, London, W.1, ngland.

elephone: 01-629-6616.

Butoma, Boris Evstafievich; Soviet politician; b. 907; ed. Leningrad Shipbuilding Inst.

Vorked in various shipyards 37-48; Head of Board of Iinistry of Shipbuilding Industry 48-52; U.S.S.R.)eputy Minister of Shipbuilding 52-57; Chair. State ttee. for Shipbuilding 57-65; U.S.S.R. Minister of hipbuilding 65-; Deputy to U.S.S.R. Supreme Soviet 2-; State Prize 49; mem. Central Cttee. C.P.S.U. 66-; Iero of Socialist Labour 59; Order of Lenin; Hammer nd Sickle Gold Medal; other awards.

J.S.S.R. Ministry of Shipbuilding, 11/13 Sadovo-Kudrinskaya ulitsa, Moscow, U.S.S.R.

Butor, Michel; French lecturer and writer; b. 14 Sept. 926, Mons-en-Baroeul, Nord; s. of Emile Butor and nne Brajeux; m. Marie-Josephe Mas 1958; four d.; d. Univ. of Paris.

eacher at Sens (France) 50, Minieh (Egypt) 50-51, Ianchester (England) 51-53, Salonica (Greece) 54-55, ieneva (Switzerland) 56-57; Visiting Prof. Bryn Mawr nd Middlebury, U.S.A. 60, Buffalo, U.S.A. 62, Evans-on, U.S.A. 65, Vincennes (France) 69, Albuquerque, J.S.A. 69-70, Nice 70-73, Seattle, Albuquerque and Iiddlebury, U.S.A. 73-74, Nice and Geneva 74-75; rix Felix Féneon 57, Prix Renaudot 57, Grand prix de a critique littéraire 60.

eisure interest: teaching.

ubls. Novels: *Passage de Milan* 54, *L'Emploi du Temps* 56, *La Modification* 57, *Degrés* 60, *Intervalle* 73; Essays: *Le Génie du Lieu* 58, *Répertoire* 60, *Histoire Extraordinaire* 61, *Mobile* 62, *Réseau Aérien* 63, *Descrip-ion de San Marco* 63, *Les Oeuvres d'art imaginaires chez Proust* 64, *Répertoire II* 64, *Portrait de l'artiste en jeune inge* 67, *Répertoire III* 68, *Essais sur les Essais* 68, *Les Mots dans la Peinture* 69, *La Rose des Vents* 70, *Le iénie du Lieu II* 71, *Dialogue avec 33 Variations de L. Van Beethoven* 71, *Répertoire IV* 74, *Matière de Rêves* 5; Poetry: *Illustrations* 64, *6,801.000 litres d'eau par econde* 65, *Illustrations II* 69, *Travaux d'Approche* 72, *llustrations III* 73.

Aux Antipodes, Chemin de Terra Amata, 23 boulevard Carnot, 06300 Nice, France.

elephone: (93) 897118.

Butterfield, Alexander P., D.F.C., M.S.; American fmr. public official; b. 6 April 1926, Pensacola, Fla.; s. of Admiral Horace Butterfield; m. Charlotte Mary Maguire; three c.; ed. Univ. Coll. Los Angeles, Univ. of Maryland, George Washington Univ. and Nat. War Coll.

Served with U.S. Air Force 49-69; pilot; promoted to rank of Col.; Operations Officer McGhee-Tyson Base, Knoxville, Tenn.; Commdr. fighter squadron Kadena Base, Okinawa; Commdr. low and medium level air reconnaissance operations, S.E. Asia; F-111 Project Officer and Senior Defence Dept. Rep., Australia; staff positions include Academic Instructor, Air Force Acad., Senior Aide to C.-in-C. Pacific Air Forces, Policy Planner, Pentagon, Mil. Asst. to Special Asst. to Sec. of Defence; Deputy Asst. to Pres. Nixon 69-73; Admi-nistrator Fed. Aviation Admin. 73-March 75; mem. Sky Blazers aerobatic team; Legion of Merit and other awards.

Federal Aviation Administration, Washington, D.C. 20590, U.S.A.

Telephone: (202) 462-8521.

Butterfield, Sir Herbert, Kt., M.A., F.B.A.; British his-torian; b. 7 Oct. 1900, Oxenhope, Keighley, Yorks.; s. of Albert Butterfield and Ada Mary Buckland; m. Edith Joyce (Pamela) Crawshaw 1929; three s. (one deceased); ed. Trade and Grammar School, Keighley and Peterhouse, Cambridge.

Fellow of Peterhouse 23-55, Master 55-68, Hon. Fellow 68-; Visiting Fellow, Univ. of Princeton 24-25; Lecturer in History, Cambridge 30-44; Editor *Cambridge Histori-cal Journal* 38-52; Prof. of Modern History, Cambridge Univ. 44-63, Regius Prof. 63-68, Vice-Chancellor 59-Oct. 61; Foreign Hon. mem. American Acad. Arts and Sciences; Hon. mem. Royal Irish Acad.; Pres. His-torical Asscn. 55-58; mem. Admin Board Int. Asscn. of Univs. 60-65, Comm. on Higher Educ. in Ireland 60-68, Court of Govs., London School of Econs. 61-68, Advisory Council on Public Records 62-69, Cttee. Inst. of Historical Research 63-68; Gifford Lecturer, Glasgow Univ. 65-67; Hon. Vice-Pres. Royal Historical Soc. 67; Hon. LL.D. (Aberdeen) 52; Hon. D.Litt. (Dublin) 54, (Sheffield) 62, (Hull) 63, (Warwick) 67, (Bonn) 68; Hon. D.Lit. (Belfast) 55; Hon. Litt.D. (Harvard) 56, (Colum-bia) 56, (Hong Kong) 61, (Manchester) 66, (London) 68, (Bradford) 74.

Leisure interest: music.

Publs. *The Historical Novel* 24, *The Peace Tactics of Napoleon, 1806-8* 29, *The Whig Interpretation of History* 31, (ed.) *Select Documents of European History, Vol. III, 1715-1920* 31, *Napoleon* (*Great Lives*) 39, *The Statecraft of Machiavelli* 40, *The Englishman and His History* 44, *Inaugural Lecture on the Study of Modern History* 44, *The Origins of Modern Science 1300-1800* 49, *George III, Lord North, and The People 1779-1780* 49, *Christianity and History* 49, *History and Human Relations* 51, Riddell Memorial Lectures on *Christianity in European History* 51, *Liberty in the Modern World* 52, Beckly lecture *Christianity, Diplomacy and War* 53, *Man on His Past* 55, *George III and the Historians* 57, *International Conflict in the Twentieth Century* 60, *The Universities and Education Today* 62, (ed. with Martin Wright) *Diplomatic In-vestigations* 66, *Sincerity and Insincerity in Charles James Fox* 72, *The Discontinuities between the Generations in History* 72.

28 High Street, Sawston, Cambridge, CB2 4BG, England.

Telephone: Sawston 3322.

Butterworth, Sir (George) Neville, Kt.; British busi-ness executive; b. 27 Dec. 1911, Hastings; s. of Richard Butterworth and Hannah Wright; m. Barbara M. Briggs 1947; two s.; ed. Malvern Coll. and St. John's Coll., Cambridge.

Joined English Sewing Cotton Co. Ltd. 33, Commercial Dir. 48, Deputy Man. Dir. 61, Joint Man. Dir. 64, Man. Dir. 66, Deputy Chair. 67, Chair. Tootal Ltd. (fmrly. English Calico Ltd.) 68-74; High Sheriff of County of Greater Manchester 74, Deputy Lieut. 74-; Dir. Renold Ltd.; fmr. Chair. North West Regional Council, Confed. of British Industry (CBI); Trustee, Civic Trust for the North West; mem. North Regional Board, Nat. Westminster Bank Ltd., Court of Govs. and Council of Univ. of Manchester Inst. of Science and Technology, Textile Council; mem. Royal Comm. on the Distribution of Income and Wealth 74-; fmr. mem. Grand Council of CBI; Fellow, British Inst. of Management; Companion of the Textile Inst.
Leisure interest: farming.
Oak Farm, Ollerton, Knutsford, Cheshire, England.
Telephone: Knutsford 3150 (Home).

Buttigieg, Anton, LL.D.; Maltese lawyer and politician; b. 19 Feb. 1912, Gozo; s. of Saviour and Concetta (née Falzon) Buttigieg; m. Carmen Bezzina 1944; two s. one d.; ed. Royal Malta Univ.
Notary Public 39; Police Insp. during Second World War; Law reporter and leader writer *Times of Malta* 44-48; Acting Magistrate 55; Editor, *The Voice of Malta* 59-; mem. Parl. 56-; Pres. Malta Labour Party 59-61, Deputy Leader 62-; Del. to Malta Constitutional Confs., London 58-64; Rep. to Consultative Assembly, Council of Europe 67-, Vice-Pres. 67-68; Deputy Prime Minister 71-74, Minister of Justice and Parl. Affairs June 71-; mem. Acad. of the Maltese Language; mem. Gen. Council, Royal Malta Univ.; First Prize for Poetry, Govt. of Malta 71.
Leisure interests: football, horse racing, bathing.
Publs. Lyric poetry: *Mill-Gallerija ta' Zghoziti* (From the Balcony of my Youth) 45, *Fanali bil-Lejl* (Lamps in the Night) 49, *Qasba mar-Rih* (A Reed in the Wind) 68, *Fl-Arena* (In the Arena) 70; Humorous poetry: *Ejjew nidhku Ftit* (Let us Laugh a Bit) 63, *Ejjew nidhku ftit iehor* (Let us Laugh a Bit More) 66; Haikus and Tankas: *Il-Muza bil-Kimono* (The Muse in Kimono) (also in Japanese and English) 68.
653 St. Joseph High Road, Hamrun, Malta.
Telephone: 25558.

Butting, Max; German composer; b. 6 Oct. 1888, Berlin; m. Rita Zabekow 1912.
Studied with Walter Courvoisier; Prof. German Soc. of Composers; Chair. Dir. of A.W.A.; radio lecturer; mem. German Acad. of Arts; Nat. Prize; Dr. h.c. Compositions include 10 symphonies and other orchestral works, *Plautus im Nonnenkloster* (opera), 10 string quartets and other chamber music, piano concerto, flute concerto, piano music and children's pieces.
Waldstrasse 81, 111 Berlin, Germany.

Butz, Earl, PH.D.; American agriculturist; b. 3 July 1909, Noble County, Ind.; s. of Herman Lee Butz and Ada Tillie Lower; m. Mary Emma Powell 1937; two s.; ed. Purdue Univ.
Farmer, Noble County 32-33; Fellow in Agricultural Econs., Purdue Univ. 33-35; Research Fellow, Fed. Land Bank of Louisville 35-37; Instructor in Agricultural Econs., Purdue Univ. 37-38, Asst. Prof. 38-42, Assoc. Prof. 42-46, Prof. and Head of Agricultural Econs. 46-54; Asst. Sec. of Agriculture, Washington, D.C., and mem. Board of Dirs. Commodity Credit Corpn 54-57; Dean of Agriculture 57-67, Dean of Continuing Educ. and Vice-Pres. Purdue Research Foundation, Purdue Univ. 68-71; U.S. Sec. of Agriculture Dec. 71-, Counsellor to the Pres. for Natural Resources Jan.-May 73; Chair. U.S. Del. to FAO, Rome 55-56; mem. American Farm Econs. Asscn., Int. Conf. of Agricultural Economists, American Asscn. of Univ. Profs., etc.; numerous directorships, awards and hon. degrees.

Publs. *The Production Credit System for Farmers* 44, *Price Fixing for Foodstuffs* 52, various pamphlets, research bulletins and articles in journals and magazines.
U.S. Department of Agriculture, Room 200-A, Washington, D.C. 20250, U.S.A.
Telephone: 202-447-3631.

Buwono, Hamengku, IX (see Hamengkubuwono IX).

Buzaid, Alfredo; Brazilian lawyer and politician; b. 1914, Jaboticabal; ed. Faculdade do Largo de São Francisco.
Director, Faculdade do Largo de São Francisco 66-69, Vice-Rector Universidade de São Paulo 69; Minister of Justice 69-74.
Publs. *Da Ação Declaratória do Direito Brasileiro* 43, *Do Agrávo de Pétição* 56, *Da Ação Renovatória* 58, *Da Ação Direta de Declaração de Inconstitucionalidade* 58.
c/o Ministério de Justiça, Brasília, Brazil.

Buzick, William A., Jr., A.B., LL.B.; American business executive; b. 4 Nov. 1920, Sylvan Grove, Kansas; ed. Univ. of Kansas and Washburn Univ. in Topeka.
Served in U.S. Navy during Second World War; attorney in Kansas; Pres. Shasta Water Co. 59 (later acquired by Consolidated Foods Corpn.); Pres. Shasta Beverages Div. 60; Vice-Pres. and Dir. Consolidated Foods 64, Exec. Vice-Pres. Operations 66-68, Pres. and Chief Operating Officer June 68-69, Chair. of Board and Chief Exec. Officer 69-74.
50 Woodley Road, Winnetka, Ill. 60093, U.S.A.

Buzzati-Traverso, Adriano; Italian geneticist and international official; b. 6 April 1913, Milan; s. of Prof. Giulio Buzzati-Traverso and Alba Mantovani; ed. Univ. of Milan.
Director, Inst. of Genetics, Univ. of Pavia 48-62; Dir. Dept. of Marine Genetics 53-59; Research Assoc. Scripps Inst. of Oceanography, La Jolla, Calif.; human genetics expert to WHO 60-69; mem. Advisory Cttee. on Radiobiology, Int. Comm. of Radiological Protection; Pres. Italian group, Pugwash Conf. 66-69; fmr. mem. Exec. Cttee. Int. Cell Research Org., UNESCO and European Molecular Biology Org.; Asst. Dir.-Gen. for Science, UNESCO 69-73; Sr. Scientific Adviser, UN Environment Programme, Nairobi 73-.
Leisure interests: science, writing and abstract art.
Publs. Four books and numerous articles on population genetics and biophysics, *The Scientific Enterprise Today and Tomorrow* 76.
2 bis, Avenue de Ségur, Paris 75007, France; Lungotevere Mellini 34, Rome 00193, Italy.
Telephone: 7054087 (Paris); 3604964 (Rome).

Byam Shaw, Glen, C.B.E.; British theatrical director; b. 13 Dec. 1904, London; s. of Byam Shaw and Evelyn Pyke-Nott; m. Angela Baddeley, C.B.E. 1929 (died 1976); one s. one d.; ed. Westminster School, London.
First stage appearance, Pavilion Theatre, Torquay 23; mem. J. B. Fagan Co., Oxford Repertory Theatre; played Trophimof (*The Cherry Orchard*), New York, Konstantin Treplev (*The Seagull*), Baron Tusenbach (*The Three Sisters*), London; played in Max Reinhardt's production of *The Miracle*; repertory tour in South Africa with Angela Baddeley; played Darnley in *Queen of Scots* and Laertes in John Gielgud's production of *Hamlet*; mem. Gielgud Co., Queen's Theatre, London; produced plays in London, New York and Stratford-upon-Avon; Dir. Old Vic Theatre School 47-51; Co-Dir. Shakespeare Memorial Theatre 52-55, Dir. 56-59, Gov. 60; Dir. of Productions, Sadler's Wells Opera House 62-; mem. of Directorate of Sadler's Wells Opera 66-; mem. of Directorate of English Nat. Opera 74-; Army Service with Royal Scots 39-45; Hon. D.Litt. (Birmingham Univ.).
Leisure interest: friends and relations.

59 Ashley Gardens, London, S.W.1; Barnacre, oddon Drive, Berkshire, England. elephone: 01-828-9165 (London).

Bykhovsky, Bernard Emmanuilovich; Soviet philo- opher; b. 12 Sept. 1898; ed. Byelorussian Univ., Minsk. Member C.P.S.U. 20-; Prof. 29-; mem. U.S.S.R. Acad. f Sciences 66-; State Prize 44.
ubls. Numerous philosophical works.
U.S.S.R. Academy of Sciences, 14 Leninsky prospekt, Moscow, U.S.S.R.

Bykovsky, Col. Valery Fyodorovich; Soviet cosmo- aut; b. 2 Aug. 1934; ed. secondary school and Zhukov- ky Air Force Engng. Acad., Moscow.
Member C.P. 63-; Student Pilot, Moscow Aeroclub 52; oviet Army 52-, Katcha Air Force School of Pilots 54, et pilot 54-59, cosmonaut training 60-; Chief Asst. o Maj. Andrian Nikolayev in preparations for Niko- ayev's Space Flight Aug. 62; made 81 orbits of the arth (48 orbits with Valentina Tereshkova *q.v.*) une 14 to June 19, 1963; Order of Red Star, Order of enin, Hero of Soviet Union; Gold Star Medal; Pilot- osmonaut of U.S.S.R.
vezdny Gorodok, Moscow, U.S.S.R.

Bynum, William; American business executive; b. Sept. 1902, Oneonta, Ala.; s. of Dalton Perry and ena Hendricks Bynum; m. Margaret Garrett 1935; wo s.; ed. Univ. of Alabama and Auburn Univ.
thletic Dir., Troy Univ. 25-27; Carrier Corpn., yracuse 30-, Exec. Vice-Pres. 51-56, Dir. 52-, Pres. 6-, Pres. and Chief Exec. Officer 63-65, Chair. and hief Exec. Officer 65-69; Dir. Marine Midland Grace rust Co. of N.Y., Carrier Corpn., Otis Elevator Co., rouse-Hines Co., and other companies; mem. Nat. ndustrial Conf. Board; Hon. Sc.D. Univ. of Alabama, nd Hon. LL.D., Syracuse Univ.
eisure interests: community affairs, golf, fishing, ridge, reading.
Iunt Lane, Fayetteville, N.Y., U.S.A.

Byrd, David Harold; American business executive; . 24 April 1900, Detroit, Tex.; s. of Edward and Mollie yrd; m. Mattie Caruth; two s.; ed. Trinity Univ., Waxahachie and Univ. of Texas, Austin.
o-founder Civil Air Patrol and Chair. Emer. Nat. xec. Board; Co-founder and Dir. Emer. Ling-Temco- ought Inc.; Chair. of Board, Space Corpn.; Owner, D. H. Byrd Enterprises (cattle, oil, gas operations, rusts, foundations, financial, investment, industrial nd real estate companies); Charter mem. Chancellor's ouncil, Univ. of Texas; Distinguished Alumnus Award, Univ. of Texas 66.
eisure interests: hunting, golfing, painting.
Office: 1110 Tower Petroleum Building, Dallas, Tex.

75201; Home: 6909 Vassar Drive, Dallas, Tex. 75205, U.S.A.
Telephone: 214-741-5991.

Byrd, Harry Flood, Jr. (son of late Harry Flood Byrd); American newspaperman and politician; b. 20 Dec. 1914; ed. John Marshall High School, Richmond, Virginia Military Inst. and Univ. of Virginia.
Editorial writer Winchester *Evening Star* 33, Editor and Publisher 35-, Editor and Publisher Harrisonburg *Daily News-Record* 37-; also active in firm of H. F. Byrd, Inc., apple growers; mem. Virginia State Senate 47-65; mem. Democratic State Central Cttee. 40-70; served U.S. Naval Reserve 41-46; Dir. Associated Press 50-; U.S. Senator from Virginia (succeeding his father, Harry Flood Byrd) 65-; Independent.
U.S. Senate, Washington, D.C. 20510, U.S.A.

Byrd, Robert C., J.D.; American politician; b. 20 Nov 1917, North Wilkesboro, N.C.; s. of Cornelius Sale and Ada Kirby; m. Erma O. James 1936; two d.; ed. George Washington Univ. Law School and Washington Coll. of Law (American Univ.).
Member West Virginia House of Delegates 46-50, West Virginia Senate 50-52; mem. U.S. House of Repre- senatives rep. 6th District of West Virginia 52-58; Senator from West Virginia 58-; Asst. Democratic Leader in Senate Jan. 71-; mem. Senate Appropriations, Judiciary and Rules and Admin. Cttees.; Democrat.
105 Senate Office Building, Washington, D.C. 20510, U.S.A.

Byrom, Fletcher Lauman; American business execu- tive; b. 13 July 1918; m. Marie McIntyre 1945; one s. two d.; ed. Pennsylvania State Univ.
Sales Engineer, American Steel and Wire Co., Cleveland 40-42; Naval Ordnance Laboratory and Bureau of Ordnance and Research Planning Board, Navy Dept. 42-47; Asst. to Gen. Man. Tar Products Div., Koppers Co. Inc., Pittsburg 47-54; Asst. Vice-Pres. 54-55, Vice- Pres. 55-58, Vice-Pres. and Gen. Man. 58-60, Pres., Chief Admin. Officer and Dir. 60-67, Pres. and Chief Exec. Officer 67-70, Chair. of Board and Chief Exec. Officer 70-.
Leisure interests: sailing, shooting, reading.
Koppers Co. Inc., Koppers Building, Pittsburgh, Pa. 15219, U.S.A.

Byushgens, Georgy Sergeyevich; Soviet scientist (mechanics); b. 19 Sept. 1916, Moscow; ed. Moscow Aviation Inst.
Research Assoc. Central Airhydrodynamic Inst. 40; mem. C.P.S.U. 63-; Prof. 63; Corresp. mem. U.S.S.R. Acad. of Sciences 66-.
U.S.S.R. Academy of Sciences, 14 Leninsky Prospekt, Moscow, U.S.S.R.

C

Caballé, Montserrat; Spanish (soprano) opera singer; b. Barcelona; *m.* Bernabe Marti (tenor); one *s.*; ed. Conservatorio del Liceo.

Studied under Eugenia Kemeny, Conchita Badia and Maestro Annovazi; debut as Mimi (*La Bohème*), State Opera of Basle; N. American debut in *Manon*, Mexico City 64; U.S. debut in *Lucrezia Borgia*, Carnegie Hall 65; appeared at Glyndebourne Festival as Marschallin in *Der Rosenkavalier* and as the Countess in *The Marriage of Figaro* 65; debut at Metropolitan Opera as Marguerite (*Faust*) Dec. 65; now appears frequently at the Metropolitan Opera and numerous other opera houses throughout the U.S.A.; has performed in most of the leading opera houses of Europe including Gran Teatro del Liceo, Barcelona, La Scala, Milan, Vienna State Opera, Paris and Rome Operas, Bayerische Staatsoper (Munich), etc., and also at Teatro Colón, Buenos Aires; repertoire of over forty roles; recordings of *Lucrezia Borgia*, *La Traviata*, *Salome*; Most Excellent and Illustrious Doña and Cross of Isabella the Catholic.

c/o Columbia Artists Management Inc., 165 West 57th Street, New York, N.Y. 10019, U.S.A.

Caballero Calderón, Eduardo; Colombian diplomatist and writer; b. 6 March 1910; ed. Gimnasio Moderna de Bogotá and Universidad Externado de Colombia.

Secretary, Embassy, Lima 37-40; business official, Madrid 46-48; Rep. in Congress, Bogotá 58-61; Amb. to UN Educational, Scientific and Cultural Org. (UNESCO), Paris 62-66; Editor *El Tiempo* 66; mem. Colombian Acad. 66; Corresp. mem. Royal Spanish Acad.; Eugenio Nadal Prize for *El Buen Salvaje* 65.

Publs. *Tipacoque* (short stories) 39, *Suramérica, Tierra del Hombre* (essays) 41, *Brevario del Quijote* 47, *Ancha es Castilla* 47, *Siervo sin tierra* 48, *Diario de Tipacoque* 49, *Americanos y Europeos* 49, *Historia Privada de Los Colombianos* 49, *Cartas Colombianas* 51; novels: *El Cristo Espaldas* 50, *El Arte de Vivir sin soñar* 50, *La Penúltima Hora* 53, *Siervo sin Tierra* 54, *Memorias Infantiles* 64, *Manuel Pacho* 65, *El Buen Salvaje* 65, *Cain* 69.

Calle 37, No. 19-07, Bogotá, Colombia.

Caballero Tamayo, Xavier; Bolivian international official; b. 1918, La Paz; ed. Univ. of San Andrés, La Paz.

With Central Bank of Bolivia, Sec.-Gen., Chief of Personnel and Asst. Insp. Gen. 39-48; joined Int. Labour Office 48; various posts in Latin America and Geneva; Deputy Dir., field office for Near and Middle East 57, Dir. 63, Regional Co-ordinator 66, Regional Co-ordinator for the Americas 67, Asst. Dir.-Gen. Aug. 69-.

International Labour Organization, 154 rue de Lausanne, 1211 Geneva 22, Switzerland.

Cabanillas Gallas, Pío; Spanish lawyer and politician; b. 1923; *m.*; one *s.*; ed. Univ. of Granada.

Prof. of Commercial Law, Univ. of Madrid; founder *Revista de Derecho Notarial*; Under-Sec. Ministry of Information and Tourism 62-73; Minister of Information and Tourism 73-Oct. 74; Pres. Tabacalera, S.A.; Grand Cross of Civil Merit, Order of San Raimundo de Peñafort.

Publs. *La Ley de Venta a Plazos, Estatuo de la Publicidad, Modernas Orientaciones del Derecho Inmobilario, El Convenio de Exclusiva, Tópica y Dogmática Jurídica, El Poder en la Sociedad Anónima.*

Ministerio de Información y Turismo, Madrid, Spain.

Cabanis, José; French writer; b. 24 March 1922; ed. Univ. de Toulouse.

Chevalier des Arts et Lettres; Chevalier Légio d'Honneur.

Works include: novels: *l'Age ingrat* 52, *Juliette Bonviol* 54, *les Mariages de raison* 58, *le Bonheur du jour* (Pr des Critiques) 61, *les Cartes du temps* (Prix des Libraire 62, *les Jeux de la Nuit* 64, *la Bataille de Toulouse* (Pr Théophraste Renaudot) 66, *les Jardins de la Nuit* 7. criticism: *un essai sur Marcel Jounandeau* 60, *Plaisir lectures* 64, *Plaisir et Lectures II* 68, *Des Jardins e Espagne* 69, *Le Sacre de Napoléon* 70, *Charles X r ultra* (Prix des Ambassadeurs) 72.

5 rue Darquié, 31000 Toulouse, France.

Cabot, John Moors, B.LITT.; American diplomatis b. 11 Dec. 1901, Cambridge, Mass.; *s.* of Godfrey Lowe Cabot and Maria Buckminster Moors; *m.* Elizabet Lewis 1932; two *s.* two *d.*; ed. Harvard Univ. an Oxford Univ.

Entered U.S. Foreign Service 26; Vice-Consul Per 27-28; Third Sec. Dominican Republic 29-31, Mexic 31-32; Third Sec., later Second Sec., Brazil 32-3 Second Sec. Netherlands 36-38; Sec. Sweden 38-3 Guatemala 39-41; assigned Dept. of State; Asst. Chie Div. of American Republics 42; Chief, Div. of Carib bean and Central American Affairs 44; Counsellor Embassy, Argentina 45-46, Yugoslavia 47; Consul-Gen Shanghai 48-49; apptd. Career Minister 48; technic officer, U.S. dels., Dumbarton Oaks, Mexico City an San Francisco Confs.; Minister to Finland 50-52 Amb. to Pakistan 52-53; Asst. Sec. of State 53-54; De to Tenth Int. Conf. American States, Caracas 54 Amb. to Sweden 54-57, to Colombia 57-59, to Braz 59-61, to Poland 62-65; Deputy Commdt. Nat. Wa Coll. 65-66; retd. from foreign service Oct. 66; lecture Tufts Univ. 67-68; Grand Cross, Order of Souther Cross (Brazil) 68.

Publs. *The Racial Conflict in Transylvania* 26, *Toward our Common American Destiny* 55.

1610 28th Street, N.W., Washington, D.C. 20607 Summer: Watch House, Manchester, Mass. 01944 U.S.A.

Cabot, Paul Codman, A.B., M.B.A.; American banker b. 21 Oct. 1898, Brookline, Mass.; *s.* of Henry B. Cabo and Anne Codman; *m.* Virginia Converse 1924; five *c.* ed. Harvard Univ.

With First Nat. Bank 23-24; Treas. State Street Invest ment Corpn. 24-34, Pres. 34-58, Chair. of Board 58 partner State Street Research and Management Co 28-; Dir. Morgan Guaranty Trust Co. of New York mem. Business Council, Treas. Harvard Univ. 48-65 Chair. Fed. Street Fund, Inc.; Trustee Eastern Gas an Fuel Asscn.

Home: 653 Chestnut Street, Needham, Mass.; Office 225 Franklin Street, Boston, Mass. 02110, U.S.A.

Cabou, Daniel, L. en D.; Senegalese politician; b. 1 July, 1919, Ziguinchor; ed. France.

Responsible for liaisons with the Grand Council of the French African Community in the Cabinet of Xavier Torre, Sec-Gen. of the French African Community 54 58; Chef de Cabinet for Pierre Lami, Head of Senega lese Territory 58; Technical Councillor for Mamadou Dia; Pres. Council of Ministers 59; Dir.-Gen. Entente coopérative Sénégalaise (ENCOOP) 59; Gov. Fleuve region 60-61; Dir. de Cabinet for André Peytavin, Minister of Finances 61-62; Sec. of State for Public Works, responsible for Hydraulics, Housing and Urban Devt. Nov.-Dec. 62; Sec. of State for Finance and Econ. Affairs 62-63; Minister of Finance 63-64, of Commerce, Industry and Labour 64-68, for Secr. of the

Presidency 68-70, of Industrial Devt. 70-72; Deputy Gov. Central Bank of West African States 72-.
Banque Centrale des Etats de l'Afrique de l'Ouest, B.P. 3159, Dakar, Senegal.

Cabral, Luis de Almeida; Guinean politician; b. 1931, Bissau; brother of late Amílcar Cabral.
Founded Partido Africano da Independência da Guiné e Cabo Verde (PAIGC) with Amílcar Cabral 56; mem. Political Bureau and Cen. Cttee., PAIGC 56-70; fled to Senegal; Sec.-Gen. Nat. Union of Workers of Guinea-Bissau 61; mem. PAIGC Council of War 65-, Perm. Comm. of Exec. Cttee., in charge of Nat. Reconstruction of the liberated areas 70-72, Asst. Sec.-Gen. 72; Pres. Council of State of the self-proclaimed independent state of Guinea-Bissau 73-74, Pres. of Guinea-Bissau Sept. 74-.
Office of the President, Bissau, Guinea-Bissau.

Caccia, Baron (Life Peer), cr. 65, of Abernant; **Harold Anthony Caccia,** G.C.M.G., G.C.V.O.; British diplomatist; b. 21 Dec. 1905, Pachmarhi, India; s. of late Anthony Caccia, C.B., M.V.O. and Fanny Theodora Birch; m. Anne Catherine Barstow 1932; one s. two d.; ed. Eton, Trinity Coll., and Queen's Coll., Oxford.
Entered Foreign Service as Third Sec., Foreign Office 29, Legation, Peking 32; promoted to Second Sec. 34; transferred to Foreign Office 35; Asst. Private Sec. to Sec. of State 36; Legation, Athens 39; First Sec. 40; Foreign Office 41; seconded for service with Resident Minister North Africa 43; Vice-Pres. Political Section Allied Control Comm., Italy 44; Political Adviser G.O.C.-in-C. Land Forces, Greece 44; Minister, local rank, British Embassy Athens 45; Asst. Under-Sec. of State, Foreign Office 46, Deputy Under-Sec. of State 49; Minister, Vienna 49, Minister and High Commr. 50-51; Ambassador and High Commr. 51-54; Deputy Under-Sec., Foreign Office 54-56; Ambassador to the U.S.A. 56-61; Perm. Under-Sec. Foreign Office 61-64; Head of Diplomatic Service 64-65; Provost of Eton 65-; Chair. Standard Telephones and Cables Ltd. 68-; Dir. Nat. Westminster Bank, Int. Westminster Bank, Orion Bank, Prudential Assurance Co., Foreign and Colonial Investment Trust 65-; Lord Prior, Order of St. John 69; Hon. Fellow, Trinity Coll., Oxford 63, Queen's Coll., Oxford 74.
The Provost's Lodge, Eton College, Windsor, Berks., England.
Telephone: Windsor 66304.

Cáceres Monié, José Rafael; Argentine politician; b. 6 July 1918, Paraná, Entre Ríos; m. Maria Antoniaf Calabrese 1949; three s. two d.
University Dir., Centre of Law Studies, Faculty of Juridical and Social Sciences, Santa Fe 39-45; editor Ideas 41; mem. Directive Comm., Rural Soc. of Curuzú Cuatiá 45-55, Assessor and Attorney until 58; Deputy Chief of Police, Curuzú Cuatiá 46-47; Under-Sec., Ministry of Public Works and Services 58-59; Under-Sec. Nat. Defence 59-62; Sec.-Gen. to the Pres. 62; Amb. to Paraguay 67-69; Minister of Defence 69-72.
c/o Ministerio de Defensa de la Nación, Buenos Aires, Argentina.

Cacoyannis, Michael, Barrister-at-law (brother of Mrs. Stella Soulioti, q.v.); Greek film and stage director and actor; b. 11 June 1922, Limassol, Cyprus; s. of Sir Panayotis and Lady Cacoyannis; ed. Greek Gymnasium, and in London at Gray's Inn, Central School of Dramatic Art and Old Vic School.
Called to the Bar 43; Producer for Overseas Service of B.B.C. 41-50; screen and stage producer 50-; Order of the Phoenix (Greece) 65.
Appeared as Herod in Wilde's Salomé 47, in Camus's Caligula 49, in Two Dozen Red Roses 49, etc.; directed films Windfall in Athens 53, Stella 55, A Girl in Black 57, A Matter of Dignity 58, Our Last Spring 59, The

Wastrel 60, Electra 61, Zorba the Greek 64, The Day the Fish Came Out 67, The Trojan Women 71, The Story of Jacob and Joseph 74, Attila 74 75; also a number of stage productions in Athens, New York, etc., including The Trojan Women, Paris 65, The Devils, New York 66, Mourning Becomes Electra, Metropolitan Opera, New York 67, Romeo and Juliet, Paris 68, Iphigenia in Aulis, New York 68, La Bohème, New York 72, King Oedipus, Dublin 73.
15 Monson Street, Athens, Greece.

Cadbury, George Adrian Hayhurst, M.A.; British food manufacturer; b. 15 April 1929, Birmingham; s. of Laurence J. Cadbury (q.v.) and Joyce Cadbury; m. G. M. Skepper 1956; two s. one d.; ed. Eton and King's Coll., Cambridge.
Managing Dir. Cadbury Schweppes Ltd. 69-73, Deputy Chair. 74, Chair. 75-; Chair. West Midlands Econ. Planning Council 67-70; Dir. Daily News Ltd., Bank of England 70-, IBM U.K. Ltd., IBM U.K. Holdings Ltd. 75-; Hon. D.Sc.
Rising Sun House, Baker's Lane, Knowle, Solihull, West Midlands B93 8PT, England.
Telephone: Knowle 2931.

Cadbury, Laurence John, O.B.E., M.A. (father of George Adrian Cadbury, q.v.); British industrialist; b. 30 March 1889, Birmingham; s. of George Cadbury and Dame Elizabeth Cadbury; m. Joyce Matthews 1925; four s. (one deceased) two d. (one deceased); ed. Leighton Park School and Trinity Coll., Cambridge.
Managing Dir. British Cocoa & Chocolate Co. Ltd., Cadbury Bros. Ltd. and Associated Companies 20-59; Chair. E.M.B. Co. Ltd. 26-, Daily News Ltd. 30-; Dir. Tyne Tees Television 59-67; Chair. Bournville Village Trust 54-; Dir. Bank of England 36-61; Head Econ. Section, Mission to Moscow 41; High Sheriff, County of London 47-48, 60-61; Croix de Guerre, Mons Medal 1914 Bar; Hon. LL.D. (Birmingham Univ.).
Leisure interest: golf.
The Davids, Northfield, Birmingham, B31 2AN, England.
Telephone: 01-472-3654 (Office); 01-475-1441 (Home).

Cadbury, Paul Strangman, C.B.E.; British business executive; b. 3 Nov. 1895; ed. Leighton Park School, Reading.
Friends' Ambulance Unit 15-18, Chair. Friends' Ambulance Unit 39-48; Vice-Chair. Cadbury Bros. Ltd. 49-59, Chair. 59-65; mem. Bournville Village Trust; fmr. Chair. J. S. Fry & Sons Ltd., British Cocoa & Chocolate Co. Ltd.
Publ. Birmingham—Fifty Years On 52.
Low Wood, 32 St. Mary's Road, Harborne, Birmingham, B17 0HA, England.
Telephone: 021-427-1636.

Cadieux, Hon. Léo, P.C., O.C.; Canadian newspaperman and politician; b. 28 May 1908, St. Jerome, Quebec; s. of Joseph E. Cadieux and Rosa Paquette; m. Monique Plante 1962; one s.; ed. Commercial Coll. of St. Jerome and Seminary of Ste. Thérèse de Blainville, Quebec.
On editorial staff of La Presse, Montreal, Que. 30-41; Assoc. Dir. of Public Relations, Canadian Army 41-44; War Corresp. for La Presse, Montreal 44; Mayor of St. Antoine des Laurentides, Que. 48; mem. Canadian House of Commons 62-; Assoc. Minister of Nat. Defence 65-67, Minister of Nat. Defence 67-70; Amb. to France 70-75; Liberal.
20 Driveway, Appt. 1106, Ottawa, Canada.

Cadieux, Marcel, C.C., LL.D., Q.C., F.R.S.C.; Canadian diplomatist; b. 17 June 1915, Montreal; s. of Roméo Cadieux and Berthe Patenaude; m. Anita Comtois 1956; two s.; ed. André Grasset Coll., Montreal, Univ. of Montreal and McGill Univ.
Joined Dept. of External Affairs 41, served in London

and Brussels and as adviser to Canadian Del. to Paris Peace Conf.; Head, Personnel Div., Ottawa 48; attended NATO Defence Coll., Paris 51; Counsellor, Canadian Del. to N. Atlantic Council 52; Senior Political Adviser to Canadian Comm. on Int. Supervisory Comm.; Head, UN Div., Ottawa 55; Asst. Under Sec. of State for External Affairs and Legal Adviser 56, Deputy Under-Sec. 60; Under-Sec. Dept. of External Affairs 64; Amb. to U.S.A. 70-75, to France 75-; Vanier Gold Medal (Inst. of Public Admin. of Canada), Outstanding Achievement Award (Public Service of Canada).
Leisure interests: reading, films, travel.
Publs. *Le Ministère des Affaires extérieures* 49, *Embruns* 51, *Le Diplomate Canadien* 61 (English trans. 63); contributions to academic publs. and magazines.
Canadian Embassy, avenue Montaigne 35, Paris 8e, France.

Cadisch, Joos; Swiss geologist; b. 1 Sept. 1895; ed. Univ. of Berne.
Privat Dozent Fed. Inst. of Technology, Zürich 25; Prof. of Geology Basle Univ. 35; Prof. of Geology and Dir. Geological Inst. Berne Univ. 43-66, Prof. Emer. 66-, Rector of the Univ. 58; attached to Swiss Geological Comm. 20-30, mem. 45-; Hon. mem. Geologists' Asscn. (London); foreign mem. Geological Soc. of London and Accademia Nazionale dei Lincei.
Publs. *Der Bau der Schweizeralpen* 26, *Geologie der Insel Elba* 29, *Geologie der Schweizerischen Mineral- und Thermalquellen* 31, *Geologie der Schweizeralpen* (2nd edition) 53; co-editor Geological Map of Mittelbünden, Geological Map of Liechtenstein, Geological Atlas of Switzerland.
Gutenbergstrasse 26, Berne, Switzerland.

Cadwallader, Sir John, Kt.; Australian business executive; b. 25 Aug. 1902, Melbourne; *s.* of Daniel Cadwallader and Florinda Margaretta Cust; *m.* Helen S. Moxham 1935; two *s.* one *d.*; ed. Sydney Church of England Grammar School.
Managing Dir. Mungo Scott Pty. Ltd. until incorporation of Allied Mills Ltd. 19-49; Chair. and Man. Dir. Allied Mills Ltd. 49-; Dir. Bank of New South Wales 45, Pres. 59-; Chair. Bushells Investments Ltd. 63-; Dir. Queensland Insurance Co. Ltd. 46-74.
Leisure interests: golf, reading, rural interests.
27 Marian Street, Killara, N.S.W. 2071, Australia.
Telephone: 49-1974.

Caetano, Marcello José das Neves Alves, LL.D.; Portuguese lawyer and politician; b. 17 Aug. 1906, Lisbon; ed. Univ. of Lisbon.
Professor of Law of Lisbon Univ. 33-68; elected to Council of Colonial Empire 36; drafted Admin. Code promulgated in 36; Nat. Commr. for Youth 40; Special Envoy to Brazil 41; Minister for Colonies 44-47; Pres. of Corporative Chamber 49-55; Asst. Prime Minister 55-58; Prime Minister 68-74; Rector, Univ. of Lisbon 59-62; in exile following coup May 74; Head Inst. of Comparative Law, Rio de Janeiro 74-.
Publs. *A Depreciação da Moeda depois da Guerra* 31, *Manual de Direito Administrativo* 36, *Tratado Elementar de Direito Administrativo* 44, *Portugal e o direito Colonial Internacional* 48, *Ciência Política e Direito Constitucional* 55, etc.
Institute of Comparative Law, Gama Filho University, Rua Miguel Vitorino 623, Rio de Janeiro, RJ, Brazil.

Cage, John; American composer, author and artist; b. 5 Sept. 1912, Los Angeles, Calif.; *s.* of John Milton Cage and Lucretia Harvey; *m.* Xenia Andreyevna Kashevaroff 1935 (divorced 1945); ed. Pomona Coll.
Studied composition, harmony and counterpoint with Richard Buhlig, Adolph Weiss, Arnold Schoenberg and Henry Cowell; Teacher of Composition, New School for Social Research, N.Y.C. 55-60; Musical Dir. Merce Cunningham and Dance Co., N.Y.C. 44-68; Fellow,

Center for Advanced Studies, Wesleyan Univ. 60-61 Composer in Residence, Univ. of Cincinnati 67; Visiting Research Prof., School of Music, Univ. of Illinois 67-69 Artist in Residence, Univ. of Calif. (Davis) 69; Dir. concert percussion music sponsored by Museum of Modern Art and League of Composers 43; mem. Cunningham Dance Foundation; mem. of Board Foundation for Contemporary Performance Arts, mem. Nat. Inst. of Arts and Letters 69-; Guggenheim Fellow 49; Thorne Music Grant 68-69; award for extending boundaries of Musical Art, Nat. Acad. of Arts and Letters, and other awards; commissioned works include *The Seasons* (Ballet Soc.) 49, *34'46, 766* *for Two Pianists* (Donaueschinger Musiktage) 54, *Atlas Eclipticalis* (Montreal Festival) 61, *Cheap Imitation* (Koussevitzky Music Foundation).
Leisure interest: amateur mycology (founding mem. New York Mycological Soc.).
Publs. include *The Life and Works of Virgil Thomson* (with Kathleen O'Donnell Hoover) 58, *Silence* 61, *A Year from Monday* 67, *Notations* 69, *Not Wanting to Say Anything About Marcel*, M 73.
107 Bank Street, New York, N.Y. 10014, U.S.A.

Caggiano, H.E. Cardinal Antonio, Argentine ecclesiastic and fmr. Archbishop of Buenos Aires and fmr. Primate of Argentina; see *The International Who's Who* 1975-76.

Çağlayangil, İhsan Sabri; Turkish politician; b. 1907; ed. School of Law, Istanbul.
Formerly with Ministry of Interior; Gov. of Antalya 48-53, of Çannakale 53-54, of Sivas 54, of Bursa 54-60; Senator for Bursa 61-; Minister of Labour Feb.-Oct. 65. of Foreign Affairs 65-71; Pres. Senate Foreign Affairs Cttee. 72-; Minister of Foreign Affairs April 75-; Justice Party.
Ministry of Foreign Affairs, Ankara, Turkey.

Caglioti, Vincenzo; Italian chemist and university professor; b. 26 May 1902; ed. Università di Napoli.
Professor Univ. of Florence 36; Prof. Univ. of Rome 38-; Pres. Consiglio Nazionale delle Ricerche 65; mem. Accademia Nazionale dei Lincei; Nat. Prize for Chemistry Accademia Nazionale dei Lincei 57.
Consiglio Nazionale delle Ricerche, Piazzale delle Scienze 7, Rome; Istituto di Chimica Generale dell'Università di Roma, Piazzale delle Scienze 5, Rome, Italy.
Telephone: 4953635; 490324 (Univ.).

Cagney, James; American actor; b. 17 July 1899, New York.
Worked in films 31-; Pres. Cagney-Montgomery Productions; Vice-Pres. Cagney Productions 42; Pres. Screen Actors Guild 42-43; Acad. Award for *Yankee Doodle Dandy* 42.
Films include, *Public Enemy* 31, *The Crowd Roars* 32, *Footlight Parade* 33, *Jimmy the Gent* 34, *Here Comes the Navy* 34, *G-Men* 35, *A Midsummer Night's Dream* 35, *Angels with Dirty Faces* 38, *Each Dawn I Die* 39, *The Roaring Twenties* 39, *Strawberry Blonde* 41, *Yankee Doodle Dandy, What Price Glory?, Run for Cover, Love Me or Leave Me, Mr. Roberts, 1, 2, 3, Johnny Come Lately, 13 Rue Madeleine, Time of Your Life, Shake Hands with the Devil, The Gallant Heart.*
MGM Studios, Culver City, Calif. 90230, U.S.A.

Cahill, William Thomas; American politician; b. 25 June 1912; *s.* of the late William P. Cahill and of Rose J. Cahill; *m.* Elizabeth Myrtetus; two *s.* six *d.*; ed. St. Joseph's Coll. and Rutgers South Jersey Law School.
School teacher 33-37; special agent F.B.I. 37-38; practised law with Cahill and Wilinski; First Asst. County Prosecutor, Camden County 48-51; mem. New Jersey Assembly 51-53; admitted to practise before Supreme Court 59; mem. U.S. Congress 58-69; Gov. New Jersey 70-73; Republican.
Morven, Princeton, N.J. 08540, U.S.A.

Caicedo-Hyerbe, Aurelio; Colombian diplomatist; b. 4 March 1921, Popayan; ed. Univ. of Cauca.
Held several posts in Ministry of Foreign Affairs, including Diplomatic Under-Sec., Counsellor in Peru; Senator 51-56; mem. Advisory Cttee. to Ministry of Foreign Affairs; Minister of Labour 53-54, of Nat. Educ. 54-55; Amb. to Holy See 55-57; mem. Cttee. negotiating concordat between Colombia and Vatican 71, 72; Perm. Rep. to UN Sept. 73-75.
c/o Ministerio de Asuntos Exteriores, Bogotá, Colombia.

Caillois, Roger, AGRÉGÉ DE L'UNIV.; French writer; b. 3 March 1913, Rheims; s. of Gaston Caillois and Andrée Colmart; m. 2nd Alena Vichrova 1957; one d. (by 1st marriage); ed. Lycée de Reims, Sorbonne, and Ecole Normale Supérieure.
Founder French Inst., Buenos Aires; Editor-Dir. *Lettres françaises* 41-45; Chief Editor *France libre* 45-47; Dir. *La Croix du Sud* (collection of Ibero-American authors), Gallimard; Chief Editor *Diogène* (int. review of philosophy and human sciences); mem. Académie Française 71-; Officier Légion d'Honneur; Commdr. Ordre du Mérite 73.
Leisure interest: collection of minerals.
Publs. *Le Mythe et l'Homme* 38, *L'Homme et le Sacré* 39, *Puissance du Roman* 40, *Le Rocher de Sisyphe* 45, *Babel* 48, *Poétique de St. John Perse* 54, *L'Incertitude qui vient des Rêves* 56, *Les Jeux et les Hommes* 58, *Art poétique* 58, *Trésor de la Poésie universelle* (with Jean-Clarence Lambert) 58, *Méduse et Compagnie* 60, *Ponce-Pilate* 61, *Esthétique Généralisée* 62, *Bellone ou la Pente de la Guerre* 63, *Instincts et société* 64, *Au Coeur du Fantastique* 65, *Pierres* 66, *Images, images . . .* 66, *Obliques* 67, *L'Ecriture des Pierres* 70, *Cases d'un Echiquier* 70, *La Pieuvre* 73, *La Dissymétrie* 73, *Approches de l'Imaginaire* 74.
34 avenue Charles Floquet, 75007 Paris, France.
Telephone: 306-50-60.

Cain, Stanley Adair, PH.D.; American ecologist and professor of botany; b. 19 June 1902; s. of Oliver E. and Lillian F. Cain; m. Louise Gilbert Mavsten 1940; one s.; ed. Butler Univ. and Univ. of Chicago.
Engaged in research at Butler Univ. 24-30, Indiana Univ. 31-33, Cold Spring Harbor Biological Laboratory 35-39; Chief, Science Section, American Army Univ. 45-46; worked at Cranbrook Inst. of Science 46-50; UNESCO Expert in Ecology, Technical Mission to Brazil 55-56; Asst. Sec. for Fish, Wildlife, Parks and Marine Resources, Dept. of the Interior 65-68; Dir. Inst. for Environmental Quality, Prof. of Botany and Prof. of Conservation, Univ. of Michigan 68-71; Prof. of Environmental Studies, Univ. of California 71-; mem. World Acad. of Art and Science, Nat. Acad. of Sciences 70; fmr. mem. Task Force on Natural Resources 68; Benjamin Franklin Fellow, Royal Soc. of Arts; Pres. First Nat. Biological Congress, American Inst. of Biological Sciences 70; Hon. D.Sc. (Univ. of Montreal, Williams Coll., Butler Univ. and Drury Coll.); Conservation Award, U.S. Dept. of the Interior 64; Eminent Ecologist, Ecological Soc. of America 69; Distinguished Service Award, U.S. Dept. of the Interior 70.
Leisure interest: horticulture.
Department of Environmental Studies, University of California, Santa Cruz, Calif. 95060; 109 Oak Knoll Drive, Santa Cruz, Calif., U.S.A.
Telephone: 408-438-0677.

Caine, Sir Sydney, K.C.M.G.; British civil servant and university administrator; b. 27 June 1902, London; s. of Harry Edward Caine; m. 1st Muriel Anne Harris (died 1962), 2nd Doris Winifred Folkard 1965 (died 1973), 3rd Elizabeth Crane Bowyer 1975; one s.; ed. Harrow County School and London School of Economics.
Assistant Inspector of Taxes 23-26; Asst. Principal, Colonial Office 26-35, Principal 35-37; Financial Sec.,

Hong Kong 37-40; Asst. Sec., Colonial Office 40-44; Asst. Under-Sec. of State, Colonial Office 44-47, Deputy Under-Sec. of State 47-48; Third Sec., H.M. Treasury 48; Head of U.K. Treasury Delegation and British Supply Office, Washington, Jan. 49-51; Head of Int. Bank Mission to Ceylon 51-52; Vice-Chancellor Univ. of Malaya 52-56; Chair. Caribbean Fed. Fiscal Comm. June-Sept. 55; Dir. London School of Economics 57-67; Chair. Int. Inst. of Educational Planning (UNESCO) 63-70; Gov. Reserve Bank of Rhodesia Dec. 65-67; Head, Indonesian Sugar Study 71-72; Grand Officer Order of Orange-Nassau (Netherlands).
Publ. *British Universities: Purpose and Prospects* 69.
1 Buckland Court, 37 Belsize Park, London, NW3 4EB, England.
Telephone: 01-435-4703.

Cairncross, Sir Alexander Kirkland, K.C.M.G., M.A., PH.D., F.B.A.; British economist and civil servant; b. 11 Feb. 1911, Lesmahagow, Scotland; s. of Alexander Kirkland Cairncross and Elizabeth Andrew Wishart; m. Mary Frances Glynn 1943; three s. two d.; ed. Hamilton Acad., Univ. of Glasgow and Trinity Coll., Cambridge.
Lecturer, Univ. of Glasgow 35-39; held various Civil Service posts 40-46; on staff of *The Economist* 46; Economic Adviser, Board of Trade 46-49; Dir. Economic Div. O.E.E.C. 50; Prof. of Applied Economics, Univ. of Glasgow 51-61; Dir., Economic Development Inst., Wash. 55-56; Economic Adviser to British Govt. 61-64; Head of British Govt. Econ. Service 64-69; Master, St. Peter's Coll., Oxford 69-; Pres. Royal Econ. Soc. 68-70, Scottish Econ. Soc. 69-73; mem. Council of Man. Nat. Inst. of Social and Econ. Research, Advisory Cttee. Houblon-Norman Trustees, Council of Trade Policy Research Centre, Court of Governors London School of Econs.; numerous cttees. (including Working of the Monetary System 57-59); Editor *Scottish Journal of Political Economy* 53-61; Pres. Section F, British Asscn. for Advancement of Science 69; Pres. British Asscn. for Advancement of Science 70-71; Chancellor Univ. of Glasgow 72-; Dir. Ailsa and Alva Investment Trusts 59-61; Trustee, Urwick Orr and Partners 70; Pres. Girls' Public Day School Trust 72; Hon. LL.D. (Mount Allison Univ., Glasgow Univ., Reading, Exeter); Hon. D.Litt. (Heriot Watt Univ.); Hon. D.Sc. (Univ. of Wales, Queen's Univ., Belfast); Dr. h.c. (Univ. of Stirling); Foreign mem. American Acad. of Arts and Sciences.
Publs. *Introduction to Economics* 44, *Home and Foreign Investment 1870-1913* 53, *Monetary Policy in a Mixed Economy* 60, *Economic Development and the Atlantic Provinces* 61, *Factors in Economic Development* 62, *Essays in Economic Management* 71, *Control over Long-term International Capital Movements* 73, *Inflation Growth* 75, *International Finance* 75.
St. Peter's College, Oxford, England; University of Glasgow, Glasgow G12 8QCP, Scotland.
Telephone: 48436 (Oxford); 041-399 8855 (Glasgow).

Cairns, James Ford, PH.D.; Australian politician; b. 4 Oct. 1914, Carlton, Victoria; ed. state schools, Univ. of Melbourne.
Junior Clerk, Australian Estates Co. Ltd. 32-35; with Victoria Police Detective Force 35-44; Australian Infantry Forces 44-46; Senior Lecturer of Econ. History, Univ. of Melbourne 46-55; mem. House of Reps. for Yarra 55-69, for Lalor 69-; Minister for Overseas Trade 72-74, of Secondary Industry 72-73; Deputy Prime Minister 74-75, Fed. Treas. Dec. 74-June 75, Minister of Environment and Conservation June-July 75; mem. Fed. Parl. Labor Party Exec. 60-62, 64-.
Publs. *Australia* 52, *Living with Asia* 65, *The Eagle and the Lotus* 69, *Silence Kills* 70, *Tariffs and Planning* 71, *The Quiet Revolution* 72.
21 Wattle Road, Hawthorn 3122, Australia.

Cairns, Theodore L., PH.D.; American organic chemist; b. 20 July 1914, Edmonton, Alberta, Canada; s. of Albert W. Cairns and Theodora I. Cairns; m. Margaret Jean McDonald 1940; two s. two d.; ed. Univs. of Alberta and Illinois.
Instructor in Organic Chem., Univ. of Rochester 39-41; Research Chemist, Cen. Research and Devt. Dept., E. I. du Pont de Nemours & Co. 41-45, Research supervisor 45-51, Lab. Dir. 51-61, Dir. Basic Sciences 62-66, Dir. of Research 66-67, Asst. Dir. 67-71, Dir. 71-; mem. Nat. Acad. of Sciences, American Chem. Soc.; mem. Editorial Board *Organic Reactions*; mem. Soc. of Chem. Industry; mem. Governor's Council on Science and Technology 69; mem. President's Science Advisory Comm. 70-73; mem. of Pres. Cttee. on Nat. Medal of Science 74-75; Regents Prof. Univ. of Calif., Los Angeles 65-66; Fuson Lecture, Univ. of Nevada 68; Marvel Lecture, Univ. of Arizona 71; Perkin Medal, American Section of Soc. of Chemical Industry 73; Cresson Medal, Fránklin Inst. 74; Hon. Dr. of Laws (Univ. of Alberta).
Leisure interest: tennis.
Publs. Numerous patents and articles on chemistry.
Office: Central Research and Development Department, Room 6032, Du Pont Building, Wilmington, Del. 19898; Home: P.O. Box 3941, Greenville, Wilmington, Del. 19807, U.S.A.
Telephone: 774-2107 (Office); 658-4508 (Home).

Cakobau, Ratu Sir George Kadavulevu, G.C.M.G., O.B.E.; Fijian administrator and politician, b. 6 Nov. 1912, Suva; s. of Ratu Popi Epeli Seniloli Cakobau; m. 1st Adi Veniana Gavoka, one s. two d.; 2nd Adi Seruwaia Lealea Belekiwai, three s. one d.; ed. Levuka Public School, Queen Victoria School, Fiji, Newington Coll., N.S.W. and Wanganui Technical Coll., N.Z.
Fiji Civil Service 36-39; Roko and Fijian Magistrate 40-42, 46-56; Sub-Insp. of Police 44-46; mem. Legislative Council and Parl. 51-72; Econ. Devt. Officer and Roko 56-62; Native Lands Commr. 62-67; Asst. Minister for Fijian Affairs and Local Govt. 69, Minister 70-72; Minister without Portfolio May-Dec. 72; Gov.-Gen. of Fiji 73-.
Leisure interests: fishing, shooting, rugby, cricket, tennis and athletics.
Government House, Suva, Fiji.

Caldecote, 2nd Viscount, cr. 39, of Bristol; **Robert Andrew Inskip,** D.S.C., F.I.MECH.E., F.I.E.E., M.R.I.N.A.; British chartered engineer and business executive; b. 8 Oct. 1917, London; s. of Thomas Walker Hobart Inskip, 1st Viscount Caldecote, and Lady Augusta, widow of Charles Orr Ewing; m. Jean Hamilla Hamilton 1942; one s. two d.; ed. Eton and King's Coll., Cambridge.
R.N.V.R. 39-45; Royal Naval Coll., Greenwich 46-47; Asst. Man. Vickers-Armstrong Naval Yard, Walker-on-Tyne 47-48; Fellow, King's Coll., Cambridge, and Lecturer, Engineering Dept., Cambridge Univ. 48-55; Man. Dir. English Electric Aviation 60-63; Deputy Man. Dir. British Aircraft Corpn. 61-67; Dir. English Electric Co. 53-69, D. Napier and Son Ltd. 59-69, British Aircraft Corpn. (Holdings) 60-69, Marconi International Marine Co. Ltd. 60-71, Delta Metal Co. Ltd. 69-71 (Chair. 72-); Dir. Consolidated Gold Fields Ltd. 69-; Dir. Cincinnati Milacron Ltd. 69-75; Dir. Lloyds Bank Ltd. 75-; Chair. The Design Council 72-; Pres. Soc. of British Aerospace Companies 65-66, Parl. and Scientific Cttee. 66-69, Asscn. Int. des Constructeurs de Matériel Aerospatial (AICMA) 66-68; Chair. Econ. Devt. Cttee. for the Movement of Exports 65-72; mem. Review Board for Govt. Contracts 69-, Eng. Industries Council 75-; Chair. Export Council for Europe April 70-71; Pres. Dean School Close.
Leisure interests: sailing, shooting, golf.
c/o Delta Metal Co. Ltd., 1 Kingsway, London,

WC2B 6XF; Orchard Cottage, South Harting, Petersfield, Hants., England.
Telephone: 01-836-9303 (Office); Harting 264 (Home).

Calder, Alexander; American mechanical engineer and sculptor; b. 22 July 1898; ed. Stevens Inst. of Technology and Arts Student League, N.Y.
Worked as engineer until 23, when decided to take up painting as career; went to Paris 26; made wire sculptures 26-29, wood sculptures 28-30, "mobiles" first exhibited in Paris 32, "stabiles" 31, and also "constellations" and "towers"; designed Mercury Fountain, Spanish Pavilion, Paris 37; first prize for foreign sculptor, Biennale de Venezia 52; commissioned to do an outdoor "mobile" for UNESCO Building, Paris; 45-foot "mobile" at Idlewild Airport, New York; acoustic ceiling, Aréa Magna, Ciudad Universitaria, Caracas 53-54; large "mobile" in U.S. Pavilion, Brussels 58; first prize for sculpture Carnegie Int. 58; exhbn. at Tate Gallery, London 62; retrospective exhbn., Guggenheim Museum, New York, Nov. 64; exhbn. at Museum of Modern Art, Paris 65; "stabile" *Le Guichet* 65; 67-foot high stainless steel "stabile", *Expo 67*, Montreal 67; Commdr. Légion d'Honneur 74.
Publs. *Fables d'Aesop* 31, *Three Young Rats* 44, *Autobiography with Pictures* 67.
Painter Hill Road, R.F.D., Roxbury, Conn., U.S.A.

Caldera Rodriguez, Dr. Rafael; Venezuelan lawyer and politician; b. 24 Jan. 1916, San Felipe, Yaracuy; s. of Dr. Rafael and Rosa Sofia R. Caldera; m. Alicia P. Caldera 1941; three s. three d.
Secretary, Cen. Council of Soc. of Venezuelan Catholic Youth 32-34; founded U.N.E. (Nat. Union of Students) 36; graduated as lawyer 39; founded Acción Nacional 42; mem. Chamber of Deputies 42; unsuccessful Pres. Candidate for Cttee. of Ind. Political Electoral Org. (COPEI) 47; Fellow of Acad. of Political and Social Sciences 52; unsuccessful COPEI Pres. Candidate 58; Pres. of Chamber of Deputies 59-61; unsuccessful COPEI Pres. Candidate 63; Pres. of Dem. Christian Org. of America (ODCA) 64-69; Pres. (COPEI) of Venezuela 69-74; Senator-for-life 74; Prof. of Sociology and Labour Jurisprudence, Venezuelan Cen. Univ.; Fellow of Venezuelan Acad. of Languages; mem. many Venezuelan and Latin American Insts. of Political Science, Spanish Language and Sociology.
Publs. Essays on legal matters, sociology and politics.
COPEI, Edificio Celca, Esq. Dr. Díaz, Caracas, Venezuela.

Calderón, Alberto Pedro, PH.D.; American mathematician; b. 14 Sept. 1920, Mendoza, Argentina; s. of Dr. Pedro J. Calderón and Haydée Cores; m. Mabel Molinelli Wells 1950; one s. one d.; ed. Montana Inst., Zug, Switzerland, Colegio Nacional, Mendoza, Argentina, Univs. of Buenos Aires and Chicago.
Head of Practical Studies, Univ. of Buenos Aires 47-48; Rockefeller Fellow, Univ. of Chicago 49-50; Visiting Assoc. Prof., Ohio State Univ. 50-53; mem. Inst. of Advanced Study, Princeton 53-55; Assoc.Prof. of Mathematics, Mass. Inst. of Technology 55-59; fmr. Visiting Prof., Univs. of Buenos Aires, Cornell, Sorbonne, Stanford, Madrid, Bogotá (Colombia), Rome and Collège de France; Prof. of Mathematics, Univ. of Chicago 59-; Louis Block Prof. of Mathematics, Univ. of Chicago 68-; Chair. Dept. of Mathematics, Univ. of Chicago 70-72; fmr. Editor, *Transactions of the American Medical Soc.*, *Duke Mathematical Journal, Illinois Journal of Mathematics*; Assoc. Editor, *Journal of Functional Analysis, Journal of Differential Equations, Annals of Mathematics*; mem. American Acad. of Arts and Sciences, Nat. Acad. of Sciences of Buenos Aires, Nat. Acad. of Sciences, U.S.A., Royal Acad. of Sciences, Spain; Hon. Ph.D. (Buenos Aires 69).
Publs. numerous papers on mathematical topics.

Department of Mathematics, University of Chicago, Chicago, Ill., U.S.A.; also Departamento de Matemáticas, Facultad de Ciencas Exactas, Ciudad Universitaria, Buenos Aires, Argentina.

Calderón Aranguiz, Rolando; Chilean politician; b. 17 Sept. 1944, Paine; *m.* Ana María Leyton Urzúa; one *d.*; ed. State School, Paine.
Joined Socialist Party 58, became Party Leader, Province of O'Higgins, mem. Central Cttee. 67, Under-Sec. Masses Front 71; Founder and First Pres. Peasant and Indian Fed. of Chile 61; Founder and First Vice-Pres. Peasant Fed. Ranquil 68; contributed to the creation of several peasant unions throughout the country; Nat. Leader United Confed. of Workers of Chile (CUT), Sec.-Gen. 72-73; Minister of Labour 73; mem. Works Comms., Sixth Nat. Congress, CUT, participated in plenary meetings Dec. 71; Rep. of Socialist Party, 1st of May Festivities Cuba 66, first Latin American meeting of the youth workers Paraguay 68; participated in discussions with the Revolutionary Govt. of Cuba 71, with the Sec.-Gen. of the Workers' Party, Democratic People's Repub. of Korea and with the Sec. of the Central Cttee. of the U.S.S.R.

Caldeyro-Barcia, Roberto, M.D., F.A.C.S.; Uruguayan physiologist; b. 26 Sept. 1921, Montevideo; *s.* of Joaquín Caldeyro and Elvira Barcia; *m.* Ofelia Stajano 1946; four *s.* two *d.*; ed. Univ. of Uruguay.
Assistant Prof. of Physiology, Medical School Univ. of Uruguay 47-50, Prof. 50-, Prof. and Chair. Dept. of Physiopathology 65-; Chair. Service of Obstetrical Physiology 55-; Hon. mem. American Coll. of Surgeons, American Asscn. of Obstetricians and Gynaecologists; Dir. Latin American Center of Perinatology and Human Devt., Montevideo.
Publs. articles on obstetrics, *Oxytocin* (with H. Heller) 61.
Servicio de Fisiología Obstétrica, Hospital de Clínicas, piso 16, Avda. Italia, Montevideo, Uruguay.
Telephone: 401151, Extension 216.

Caldwell, Erskine; American writer; b. 17 Dec. 1903, Moreland, Georgia; *s.* of Ira S. Caldwell and Caroline Bell Caldwell; *m.* 1st Helen Lannington 1925, 2nd Margaret Bourke-White 1939, 3rd June Johnson 1942, 4th Virginia Moffett Fletcher 1957; three *s.* one *d.*; ed. Erskine Coll., Univ. of Virginia, Univ. of Pennsylvania.
Former newspaper writer, cotton picker, stage hand, professional footballer, book reviewer, lecturer, editor; Motion Picture Screen Writer in Hollywood 30-34, 42-43; awarded Yale Review award for fiction 33; mem. Authors' League of America, Nat. Inst. of Arts and Letters, P.E.N. Club; Newspaper Corresp. in Mexico, Spain, Czechoslovakia 38-39; Newspaper and Radio Corresp. Russia 41; Editor of *American Folkways* 40-55.
Publs. *The Bastard* 29, *Poor Fool* 30, *American Earth* 31, *Tobacco Road* 32, *God's Little Acre, We Are the Living* 33, *Journeyman, Kneel to the Rising Sun, Some American People* 35, *Southways* 39, *Trouble in July* 40, *Jackpot* 40, *All Out on the Road to Smolensk* 42, *Moscow under Fire* 42, *All Night Long* 42, *Georgia Boy* 43, *Stories* 44, *Tragic Ground* 44, *A House in the Uplands* 46, *The Sure Hand of God* 47, *This Very Earth* 48, *Place Called Estherville* 49, *Episode in Palmetto* 50, *Call it Experience* 51, *The Courting of Susie Brown* 52, *A Lamp for Nightfall* 52, *The Complete Stories of Erskine Caldwell* 53, *Love and Money* 54, *Gretta* 55, *Gulf Coast Stories* 56, *Certain Women* 57, *Molly Cottontail* (juvenile) 58, *Claudelle Inglish* 59, *When You Think of Me* 59, *Jenny by Nature* 61, *Close to Home* 62, *The Last Night of Summer* 63, *Around About America* 64, *In Search of Bisco* 65, *The Deer at Our House* (juvenile) 66, *In the Shadow of the Steeple* 66, *Miss Mamma Aimee* 67, *Writing in America* 67, *Deep South* 68, *Summertime Island* 68, *The Weather Shelter* 69, *The Earnshaw Neighborhood* 71, *Annette* 73; with

Margaret Bourke-White: *You Have Seen Their Faces* 37, *North of the Danube* 39, *Is This the U.S.A.?* 41.
c/o McIntosh and Otis Inc., 475 Fifth Avenue, New York, N.Y. 10017; and P.O.B. 820, Dunedin, Florida 33528, U.S.A.
Telephone: MU9-1050 (New York).

Califano, Joseph Anthony, Jr., A.B., LL.B.; American lawyer and government official; b. 15 May 1931, Brooklyn, New York; *s.* of Joseph A. and Katherine Gill Califano; *m.* Gertrude Zawacki 1955; two *s.* one *d.*; ed. Holy Cross Coll. and Harvard Univ.
Admitted to New York Bar 55; U.S. Naval Reserve 55-58; with firm Dewey Ballantine, Bushby, Palmer and Wood, New York City 58-61; Special Asst. to Gen. Counsel, Dept. of Defense 61-62; Special Asst. to Sec. of Army 62-63; Gen. Counsel, Dept. of Army 63-64; Special Asst. to Sec. and Deputy Sec. of Defense 64-65; Special Asst. to Pres. 65-69; admitted to U.S. District Court; U.S. Court of Appeals for 2nd Circuit; U.S. Supreme Court Bar 66; mem. Fed. Bar Asscn., Amer. Bar Asscn., Amer. Judicature Soc.; mem. firm Arnold & Porter 69-71; Williams, Connolly & Califano 71-; General Counsel, Democratic Nat. Cttee. 70-72; mem. Democratic Party's Nat. Charter Comm. 72-74; mem. Board Overseers Law School Visiting Cttee. Harvard Univ., Child Welfare League; mem. Annual Corp. Bd. of Children's Hospital, Washington; mem. Bd. of Dirs. Federal City Club and of Trustees of Mater Dei School, Washington; Distinguished Civilian Service Medal, Dept. of Army 64, Dept. of Defence 68; Man of Year Award, Justinian Soc. Lawyers 66.
Leisure interest: writing.
Publs. *The Student Revolution, A Global Confrontation* 69, *A Presidential Nation* 75; numerous articles for various newspapers and other publications.
Office: 1000 Hill Building, Washington, D.C. 20006; Home: 3551 Springland Lane, N.W., Washington, D.C. 20008, U.S.A.

Califice, Alfred; Belgian politician; b. 2 Oct. 1916, Melen; *m.* Marcelle David; four *d.*
Publicity section, Jeunesse Ouvrière Chrétienne 37-40; local govt. employee 40-42; Sec. Fédération des Syndicats Chrétiens, Charleroi district 44-65; mem. Parl. 65-, of European Parl. 68-72; Sec. of State for Housing and Planning 72-73; Minister of Public Works 73-74, of Employment and Labour, Walloon Affairs, Planning and Housing April 74-.
Ministry of Employment and Labour, Walloon Affairs, Planning and Housing, 53 rue Belliard, 1040 Brussels; Home: 13 rue du Transvaal, 6090 Couillet, Belgium.

Calkins, Robert D., B.S., M.A., LL.D., PH.D.; American economist; b. 19 Jan. 1903, Lebanon, Conn.; *s.* of Robert D. Calkins and Ethel Mae (Chambers); *m.* 1929; one *s.* one *d.*; ed. Coll. of William and Mary, and Stanford Univ.
Research Assoc., Food Research Inst., Stanford 25-27, 30-32; Teaching Asst. and Instructor, Stanford 29-31; Asst. Prof. of Econs., Univ. of Calif. 32-36, Assoc. Prof. 36-40, Prof. 40-41, Chair. of Dept. of Econs. 35-41, Dean, Coll. of Commerce 37-41; Prof. and Dean, School of Business, Columbia Univ. 41-46; Vice-Pres. and Dir. Gen. Educ. Board, N.Y.C. 47-52; Pres. The Brookings Inst., Washington, D.C. 52-67, Dir. 52-; Vice-Chancellor, Social Sciences and Prof. of Econs., Univ. of Calif.-Santa Cruz 67-70; Dir. N.Y. Fed. Reserve Bank 43-49; Mediator, War Labor Board 42-45; Consultant to Nat. Resources Planning Board 40-42, Office of Price Admin. 42, War Dept. 42, etc.
1775 Massachusetts Avenue, Washington, D.C. 20036; Home: 5415 Connecticut Avenue, Washington, D.C. 20015, U.S.A.

Callaghan, Sir Allan Robert, Kt., C.M.G., D.PHIL., B.SC., B.SC.AGR., F.A.I.A.S.; Australian agricultural official; b. 24 Nov. 1903, Perthville, N.S.W.; *s.* of late Phillip

George Callaghan and late Jane Peacock; *m.* 1st Zillah May Sampson (deceased); *m.* 2nd Doreen Winifred Draper; three *s.* (one deceased) one *d.*; ed. Univs. of Sydney and Oxford.

Agronomist (cereal breeding and genetics), N.S.W Dept. of Agriculture 28-32; Principal, Roseworthy Agricultural Coll., S. Australia 32-49; Asst. Dir. (Rural Industries), Australian Commonwealth Dept. of War Org. of Industry 42-43; Chair. Crown Lands Devt. Cttee. for S. Australia 42-46; Chair. Land Devt. Exec. (S. Australia) 46-50; Dir. of Agriculture in S. Australia 49-59; Commercial Counsellor, Australian Embassy, Washington, D.C. 59-65; Chair. Australian Wheat Board 65-72; Agricultural Consultant, Dept. Agriculture 72-75; Farrer Memorial Medal 54; Carnegie Foundation Grant to visit U.S.A. 56.

Leisure interests: music, gardening, swimming.

Publs. *The Wheat Industry in Australia* (with A. J. Millington) 56; Handbooks: *Crops and Pastures* (with E. J. Breakwell) 46, *Sheep Husbandry* (with D. S. Thompson) 46; articles on agronomy, animal husbandry and agricultural extension in scientific and extension journals.

2 Villanova, 45 Coolangatta Road, Kirra, Qd. 4225, Australia.

Telephone: Gold Coast 36-2668.

Callaghan, Rt. Hon. (Leonard) James, P.C., M.P.; British politician; b. 27 March 1912, Portsmouth; *m.* Audrey Elizabeth Moulton 1938; one *s.* two *d.*; ed. Portsmouth Northern Secondary School.

Tax Officer 29; Asst. Sec. Inland Revenue Staff Asscn. 36-47; service in Royal Navy 39-45; M.P. 45-; Parl. Sec. Ministry of Transport 47-50; Parl. and Financial Sec., Admiralty 50-51; Chancellor of the Exchequer 64-67; Home Secretary 67-70; Sec. of State for Foreign and Commonwealth Affairs 74-76; Leader of Parl. Labour Party April 76-; Prime Minister April 76-; mem. Consultative Ass., Council of Europe 48-50, 54; Chair. Co-ordinating Advisory Cttee. on Oil Pollution of the Sea 53-64; Consultant to Police Fed. 55-64; mem. Nat. Exec. Cttee. Labour Party; Treas. Labour Party 67-, Chair. 73-74; Hon. Life Fellow, Nuffield Coll., Oxford 67; Pres. U.K. Pilots' Asscn. 63-; Hon. Pres. Int. Maritime Pilots' Asscn. 71-; Freedom of City of Cardiff 75.

Publ. *A House Divided* 73.

10 Downing Street, London, S.W.1, England.

Callaghan, Morley (Edward); Canadian novelist; b. 1903; ed. St. Michael's Coll., Univ. of Toronto, and Osgoode Hall Law School.

Canada Council Medal Winner 66; Royal Bank of Canada Award 70.

Publs. *Strange Fugitive* 28, *Native Argosy* 29, *It's Never Over* 30, *No Man's Meat* 31, *Broken Journey* 32, *Such is My Beloved* 34, *They Shall Inherit The Earth* 35, *More Joy in Heaven* 36, *Now that April's Here* 37, *Jake Baldwin's Vow* (for children) 48, *The Varsity Story* 48, *The Loved and the Lost* 55, *The Man with the Coat* 55, *A Many Coloured Coat* 60, *A Passion in Rome* 61, *That Summer in Paris* 63, *Morley Callaghan* Vols. I and II 64.

20 Dale Avenue, Toronto, Ontario, Canada.

Callan, Harold Garnet, M.A., D.SC., F.R.S.; British professor of zoology; b. 5 March 1917, Maidenhead, Berks.; *s.* of Garnet George Callan and Winifred Edith (née Brazier); *m.* Amarillis M. S. Dohrn 1944; one *s.* two *d.*; ed. King's Coll. School, Wimbledon, and St. John's Coll., Oxford.

Served Second World War, Telecommunications Research Establishment 40-45; Senior Scientific Officer, Agricultural Research Council, Inst. of Animal Genetics, Edinburgh 46-50; Prof. of Natural History, St. Salvator's Coll., St. Andrews 50-; Master of United Coll. of St. Salvator's and St. Leonard's 67-68; mem. Advisory

Council on Scientific Policy 63-64; Trustee, British Museum (Natural History) 63-66; Visiting Prof., Univ. of Indiana 64-65; mem. Science Research Council 72-; mem. Council Royal Soc. 74-.

Leisure interests: shooting, carpentry.

Publs. Scientific papers, mostly on cytology and cell physiology.

Zoology Department, University, St. Andrews; Home. 2 St. Mary's Street, St. Andrews, Scotland.

Telephone: St. Andrews 2823 (Univ.); St. Andrews 2311 (Home).

Callard, Sir (Eric) John, Kt., M.A., C.ENG., F.I.MECH.E., F.R.S.A.; British business executive; b. 15 March 1913, Torquay, Devon; *s.* of late Frank and Ada Mary Callard; *m.* Pauline Mary Pengelly 1938; three *d.*; ed. Queen's Coll., Taunton, St. John's Coll., Cambridge.

Chairman Imperial Chemical Industries Ltd. (I.C.I.), Paints Div. 51-55, Man. Dir. 55-59, Chair. 59-64; Dir. I.C.I. Ltd. April 64-, Deputy Chair. 67-71, Chair. 71-April 75; Dir. Pension Funds Securities Ltd. 63-67, Imperial Metal Industries 64-67, Imperial Chemical Insurance 66-; Chair. I.C.I. (Europa) Ltd. 65-67; mem. Council Univ. of Manchester, Manchester Business School 64-71, Vice-Pres. 71-; mem. Council, British Inst. of Management 64-69, Fellow 66-; mem. Council, Export Council for Europe 66-71; Chair. Industrial Co-partnership Asscn. 67-71; Pres. Industrial Participation Asscn. 71-; mem. Council of Industry for Management Education 67-73; Co-opt. mem. Univ. of Cambridge Appointments Board 68-71; Vice-Pres. Combustion Engineering Asscn. 68-; Dir. Midland Bank Ltd. 71-, British Home Stores 75- (Chair. desig. 76-); Gov. London Graduate School of Business Studies 72-.

Leisure interests: games, gardening, fell walking.

Imperial Chemical Industries Ltd., Imperial Chemical House, Millbank, London S.W.1; Home: Farthings, Jordans, nr. Beaconsfield, Bucks., England.

Callas, Maria; Greek opera singer; b. 2 Dec. 1923, New York, U.S.A.; ed. Athens Conservatoire.

In Greece during 39-45 war; studied under Elvira de Hidalgo; sang with Athens Opera; sang in *Gioconda*, Verona 47; major rôles include, *Madame Butterfly*, *Aida*, *Norma*, *Rigoletto*, *Medea*, *Tosca*, etc.; has sung in Rome, Florence, Naples, Milan, New York, San Francisco, London, Mexico, Vienna, etc.; title role in film *Medea* 70; numerous recordings.

36 avenue George Mandel, Paris 16e, France; Monte Carlo, Monaco.

Calloway, Howard H.; American public official; b. 2 April 1927, LaGrange, Georgia; *m.* Elizabeth Walton; three *s.* two *d.*; ed. U.S. Military Acad.

Served in Infantry, participating in Korean War in Far Eastern Command, later becoming Instructor, Infantry School, Fort Benning, Ga. 49-52; mem. 89th Congress, rep. third district of Georgia 65-66; Republican candidate for Gov. of Georgia 66; Civilian Aide for Third Army Area 70-73; Sec. of the Army May 73-75; fmr. Campaign Man. for President Ford, 1976 Pres. Election; Pres. Interfinancial Inc. of Atlanta; fmr. mem. Board of Regents Univ. System of Georgia, Nat. 4-H Service Cttee., Board of Trustees, Nat. Recreation Asscn.

c/o Presidential Campaign Office, The White House, Washington, D.C. 20500, U.S.A.

Calmann-Lévy, Robert Paul Michel: French publisher; b. 20 Oct. 1899.

Director, Calmann-Lévy, publishers of French and foreign books.

3 rue Auber, 75009 Paris, France.

Calmes, Christian, D. EN D.; Luxembourg lawyer and civil servant; b. 11 July 1913, Oberursel, Germany; *s.* of Albert Calmes; *m.* Anne Raus 1939; three *s.* two *d.*;

ed. Echternach Gymnasium, Strasbourg and Paris Univs.
Called to the bar 38; successively Attaché, Sec., Counsellor and Minister Plenipotentiary, Ministry of Foreign Affairs; Sec.-Gen. Special Council of Ministers of ECSC 52-58, Council of Ministers of European Communities (ECSC, EEC, and EURATOM) 58-73, Hon. Sec.-Gen. 73-; mem. historic section of Institut Grand-Ducal de Luxembourg; Minister Plenipotentiary; Chamberlain to H.R.H. the Grand-Duke of Luxembourg.
Leisure interest: history.
Publs. *Geôles sanglantes* 48, *1867, L'Affaire du Luxembourg* 70, *Le Luxembourg dans la guerre de 1870* 70, *Au Fil de l'Histoire Tome 3*.
Ehnen, Luxembourg, Grand Duchy of Luxembourg. Telephone: 761 33.

Calmon de Sá, Ângelo; Brazilian banker; b. 1 Nov. 1935, Salvador; *s.* of Francisco de Sá and Maria dos Prazeres Calmon de Sá; *m.* Ana Maria Carvalho de Sá 1962; two *s.* two *d.*; ed. Fed. Univ. of Bahia.
Secretary of Industry and Commerce, Bahia State 67-70, Sec. of Finance 70-71; Pres. Econômico S.A. 71-74, Banco do Brasil S.A. March 74-; Pres. Bahia Asscn. of Banks 72-74; Vice-Pres. Bahia Asscn. of Commerce 72-74; Dir. Nat. Fed. of Banks 73-74; Chair. European Brazilian Bank 74-; Dir. Cie. Arabe et Internationale d'Investissement 74-, Euro-Latinamerican Bank Ltd. 74-; several Brazilian honours.
Leisure interests: riding, tennis, golf.
Publ. study on the Bank of Brazil as an agent of development and a factor of national integration.
Banco do Brasil S.A., Setor Bancário Sul Lote 23-20° andar, Caixa Postal 562, Brasília (DF) 40,000, Brazil. Telephone: 24-2553, 24-3553.

Calogero, Guido; Italian philosopher and university professor; b. 4 Dec. 1904.
Former Prof., Florence and Pisa Univs.; one of the leaders of Liberal-Socialist Movement, arrested 42 as anti-Fascist; Editor for the section of philosophy of Italian Encyclopaedia; Visiting Prof. of Philosophy, McGill Univ., Montreal 48-49; Dir. Italian Inst., London 50-55; Visiting Prof. of Philosophy, Univ. of Calif., Berkeley 56-57; mem. Inst. for Advanced Study, Princeton 62-63; Pres. Institut International de Philosophie 63-66; Prof. of Philosophy, Rome Univ.
Publs. *I fondamenti della logica aristotelica* 27, *Studi sull'Eleatismo* 32, *La scuola dell' uomo* 39, *Lezioni di Filosofia* 46-48, *Logo e Dialogo* 50, *Scuola sotto inchiesta* 57, *Filosofia del Dialogo* 62.
Via S. Alberto Magno 5, Rome, Italy.

Calvani, Aristides, D.IUR.; Venezuelan politician; b. 19 Jan. 1918, Port of Spain, Trinidad; *m.* Adelita Abbo de Calvani; seven *s.*; ed. Univ. of Louvain, Belgium and Central Univ. of Venezuela.
Teacher San Ignacio Coll., Caracas 41-46, 48-51; Prof. of Law and Philosophy of Law, Central Univ. of Venezuela 47-; Prof. of Law, Catholic Univ. "Andres Bello" 53-59; Founder, Dir. School of Social Sciences, Catholic Univ. "Andres Bello" 59-69; Pres. Inst. de Formación Demócrata Cristiana 62-69; Speaker, Court of Cassation, also Vice-Pres. 58, fmr. Pres. of Civil Hall; Deputy for Partido Social-Cristiano (COPEI) 59-62; Minister for Foreign Affairs 69-74; has represented Venezuela at numerous int. confs., including Thirteenth Consultative Conference of Foreign Ministers, Washington, D.C. 69, Gen. Ass. of UN 69, 70, 72, Gen. Ass. of OAS 70, 71, 73, Twelfth Conf. of Comisión Especial de Coordinación Latinoamericana 71, Third Conf. of UNCTAD 72; Legal Assessor Movimiento Sindical Cristiano 51-; Cofounder Inst. Nacional de Estudios Sindicales 61; organizer of Movimiento Familiar Cristiano in Venezuela, Pres. 59-61; numerous decorations from European and Latin American countries.
Universidad Central de Venezuela, Ciudad Universitaria, Caracas, Venezuela.

Calvet, Pierre Louis, LL.L.; French civil servant; b. 27 June 1910, Troyes; *m.* Luce Petitjean-Saglio 1933; one *s.* one *d.*; ed. Lycée Buffon, Law Faculty, Univ. of Paris, Ecole Libre des Sciences Politiques.
Financial Inspector 33; Financial Attaché, London 45; Gen. Dir. Office des Changes 47; Vice-Pres. European Payments Union 50; Deputy Gov. Bank of France 52; Vice-Pres. Banque Nationale de Paris 66-70, Admin. Jan. 71-; mem. Council Nat. Museums; Commdr. Légion d'Honneur, Order of Orange-Nassau; Officier Ordre de Léopold; Grand Officer, Order of Merit (Italian Repub.).
Leisure interests: reading, walking, music, painting.
Banque Nationale de Paris S.A., 16 Boulevard des Italiens, Paris 9e; Home: 33-35 rue de Valois, Paris 1er, France.
Telephone: 261-54-54 (Office); 261-49-14 (Home).

Calvet de Magalhães, José; Portuguese diplomatist; b. 2 Oct. 1915, Lisbon; *s.* of Manuel de Faria e Sousa Calvet de Magalhães and Judith de Sousa Cabral; *m.* Linda Calvet de Magalhães 1946; one *s.*; ed. Univ. of Lisbon.
Entered Foreign Service 41, served New York, Boston, Canton, Paris; mem. Del. to NATO 52-56; Minister and Head of Del. to OEEC 56-60, Amb. to OEEC 60-61, to OECD 61-64; Head, Del. to ECSC 59-64; Amb. to EEC and EURATOM 62-64; Dir.-Gen. Econ. Affairs 64-71, Sec.-Gen. 71-74; Amb. to Holy See 74-; Pres. Grêmio Literario of Lisbon 69-71; Grand Cross, Cross of the South and Grand Cross Order of Rio Branco (Brazil), Grand Cross, Order of Merit and Grand Cross Order of Isabel la Católica (Spain), Grand Officer, Order of Merit (Germany), Grand Cross, Order of the Falcon (Iceland), Grand Cross Pro Merito Melitensis Order of Malta, Grand Cross of Christ (Portuguese).
Publs. *The Criminal Responsibility of Doctors in Case of the Patients' Death* 44, *Anthero de Quental and Socialism* 45, *José Accursio das Neves* (anthology and introduction) 45, *Anthero de Quental* (anthology and introduction) 46, *History of Economic Thought in Portugal* 67.
Portuguese Embassy, Villa Lusa, Via S. Valentino 9, 00197 Rome, Vatican City, Italy.

Calvin, Melvin, B.S., PH.D.; American chemist; b. 8 April 1911, St. Paul, Minnesota; *s.* of Elias and Rose (Hervitz) Calvin; *m.* Marie Genevieve Jemtegaard 1942; one *s.* two *d.*; ed. Michigan Coll. of Mining and Technology and Univ. of Minnesota.
Instructor Dept. of Chemistry, Univ. of Calif., Berkeley 37-40, Asst. Prof. 41-45, Assoc. Prof. 45-47, Prof. 47-; Dir. Chem. Biodynamics Group, Lawrence Radiation Laboratory 46-; nat. defence work 41-45; Dir., Laboratory of Chem. Biodynamics, Univ. of Calif. Berkeley 60-; Assoc. Dir. Lawrence Radiation Laboratory, Berkeley 67-; selected to carry out research on lunar samples from *Apollo XI, XII*; mem. Nat. Acad. of Sciences; Foreign mem. The Royal Society; recipient of several scientific awards; Nobel Prize for Chemistry 61; Davy Medal, Royal Society 64.
Publs. *The Theory of Organic Chemistry* (with G.E.K. Branch) 41, *Isotopic Carbon* (with Heidelberger, Reid, Tolbert and Yankwich) 49, *The Chemistry of the Metal Chelate Compounds* (with Martell) 52, *The Path of Carbon in Photosynthesis* (with Bassham) 57, *Chemical Evolution* 61, 69, *Photosynthesis of Carbon Compounds* (with Bassham) 62.
Laboratory of Chemical Biodynamics, University of California, Berkeley, Calif. 94720; Home: 2683 Buena Vista Way, Berkeley, Calif., U.S.A.
Telephone: 642-0838 (Office); 848-4036 (Home).

Calvino, Italo; Italian writer; b. 15 Oct. 1923, San Remo; *m.* Chichita Singer 1964; one *d.*
Member of editorial staff Giulio Einaudi Editore.
Publs. *Il Sentiero dei Nidi Ragno* 47, *Ultimo viene il Corvo* 49, *Il Visconte dimezzato* 52, *L'Entrata in Guerra* 54, *Fiabe Italiane* 56, *Il Barone Rampante* 57, *I Racconti* 58, *Il Cavaliere Inesistente* 59, *La Giornata di uno Scrutatore* 63, *Marcovaldo* 63, *Le Cosmicomiche* 66, *Ti con zero* 67, *Le Citta Invisibili* 73, *Il Castello dei Destini Incrociati* 74.
c/o Giulio Einaudi Editore, Via Umberto Biancamano 1, Turin, Italy.

Calvo-Sotelo Bustelo, Leopoldo; Spanish engineer and politician; b. 14 April 1926, Madrid; *m.*; eight *c.*; ed. Escuela de Ingenieros de Caminos, Canales y Puertos, Madrid.
Pres. Spanish Railways 67-68; now Adviser, Unión Explosivos Rio Tinto; Procurador 71-; Minister of Commerce 75-.
Ministerio de Comercio, Madrid, Spain.

Calvocoressi, Peter; British writer and book publisher; b. 17 Nov. 1912, Karachi, India; *s.* of Pandia J. Calvocoressi and Irene (Ralli); *m.* Barbara Dorothy Eden 1938; two *s.*; ed. Eton Coll. and Balliol Coll., Oxford.
Called to Bar 35; R.A.F. Intelligence 40-45; assisted Trial of Major War Criminals, Nuremberg 45-46; on staff, Royal Inst. of Int. Affairs 49-54; partner Chatto & Windus, publishers 55-65; Reader in Int. Relations, Sussex Univ. 65-71; Editorial Dir. Penguin Books 72, Publisher and Chief Exec. 73-; mem. UN Sub-comm. on the Prevention of Discrimination 61-71; Chair. The London Library 70-73.
Leisure interests: music, tennis.
Publs. *Nuremberg: The Facts, the Law and the Consequences* 47, *Survey of International Affairs:* Vols. for 47-48, 49-50, 51, 52 and 53, *Middle East Crisis* (with Guy Wint) 57, *South Africa and World Opinion* 61, *World Order and New States* 62, *World Politics Since 1945* 68, *Total War* (with Guy Wint) 72.
Guise House, Aspley Guise, Milton Keynes, MK17 8HQ, England.

Camara, Assan Musa; Gambian politician; b. Andrew David Camara 1923, Mansajang.
Teacher in govt. and mission schools 48-58; entered politics 58; mem. House of Assembly (Independent) 60-; Minister of Educ. 63, of Foreign Affairs 67-74; Vice-Pres. of The Gambia 72-, also Minister of Local Govt. and Lands July 74-.
Office of the Vice-President, Banjul, The Gambia.

Câmara, Most Rev. Helder Pessoa; Brazilian (Roman Catholic) ecclesiastic; b. 7 Feb. 1909, Fortaleza.
Ordained priest 31; Consecrated Bishop 52; Titular Bishop of Salde 52; Titular Archbishop of Salde 55-64; Archbishop of Olinda and Recife 64-; organized Brazilian Conf. of Bishops and co-operated in organization of CELAM (the Latin-American Conf. of Bishops); an active campaigner for social reform in Latin-America; René Sande Award 62, Via Int. Peace Prize (Italy) 70, Martin Luther King Jr. Award 70, John XXII Memorial Award from Pax Christi, Spain 70; Dr. h.c. (Univs. of St. Louis, Louvain, Münster, Fribourg and Sorbonne); People's Peace Prize 74.
Rua do Giriquiti 48, Recife, Estado de Pernambuco, Brazil.

Camara, Ousmane; Senegalese politician; b. 1933, Kaolack; ed. Lycée Faidherbe, St. Louis, Dakar Univ., Centre Nat. d'Etudes Judiciaire, Paris.
Adviser to Supreme Court 61-64; Dir. Nat. Security 64-70; Minister of Labour and Civil Service March-Dec. 70, of Information in charge of Assembly Relations Dec. 70-73, of Higher Educ. 73-.
Ministry of Higher Education, Dakar, Senegal.

Camargo, Sérgio de; Brazilian sculptor; b. 1930; ed. Academia Altamira, Buenos Aires, and Univ. de Paris à la Sorbonne.
In France 48-50, 51-54, 61-; visited China 54; specializes in wood reliefs; Int. Sculpture Prize, Paris Biennale 63. Works are in permanent collections of Nat. Museum of Art, Rio de Janeiro, Museum of Art, São Paulo, Musée d'Art Moderne de la Ville de Paris, Tate Gallery, London, Galleria d'Arte Moderna, Rome, and in numerous private collections; represented in exhibitions in Paris and Brussels 63, Mannheim, Arras, London and Paris 64, 74, New York 65, and Latin-American exhibitions 54-.
27 rue Leplanquais, 92 Malakoff, France.

Cambanellis, Iakovos; Greek writer and film director; b. 1922.
Publications, plays include: *Dance on the Sheaves* 50, *The Seventh Day of Creation* 56, *The Courtyard of Miracles* 57, *Story Without a Title* 59, *Neighbourhood of Angels* 63; film scripts for *Stella, The River, Snowdrop;* dir. of films including documentary *The Root;* regular contributor to Greek Radio and *Eleftheria.*
Dervenion 19, Athens, Greece.

Cambournac, Francisco José Carrasqueiro, M.D.; Portuguese medical scientist; b. 26 Dec. 1903, Rio de Mouro (Sintra); *s.* of Pedro Roque Cambournac and Maria Carlota Carrasqueiro; *m.* Maria Estefânia Cambournac 1934; one *d.*; ed. Lisbon Univ., Lisbon, Paris, Hamburg and London Schools of Hygiene and Tropical Medicine, League of Nations Malaria Training Course, France, Yugoslavia and Italy.
Fellow and staff mem. Rockefeller Foundation, engaged mainly on malaria research and teaching 34-41; Assoc. Prof. of Hygiene, Public Health and Climatology, Lisbon Inst. of Tropical Medicine 42-44, Prof. 44-, Dir. 64-, also Dir. Portuguese Malaria Inst. 38-43; del. to Int. Health Conf., New York 46; mem. del. to World Health Ass. 47-53; mem. WHO Expert Panel on Malaria 48-53; Head del. WHO Cttee. for S.E. Asia 49, Africa 51-53; WHO Consultant for Africa 49 to prepare first African Malaria Conf. 50; Chief Epidemiological Services Mission of Angola, Co-ordinator yellow fever survey of Angola, Mozambique and São Tomé and Príncipe 50-54; mem. CCTA, African Scientific Council (CSA), Admin. Inst. des Parcs Nat. du Congo et du Rwanda 59-67; Dir. WHO Regional Office for Africa 54-64; mem. WHO Expert Panel Public Health Admin. 64-; Pres. of the Direction of Liga Portuguesa de Educação Sanitaria 64-67, Sociedade Portuguesa de Medicina Tropical (Secção de Medicina Tropical da Sociedade de Ciências Médicas) 64-67; Dir. and Prof. Public Health in Tropical Regions, Escola Nacional de Saúde Pública e de Medicina Tropical 67-72; Prof. Discipline of Public Health, Head Dept. of Public Health, and Dir., Instituto de Higiene e Medicina Tropical 72-73; Vice-Pres. Council of European Schools and Insts. of Tropical Medicine and Hygiene 71-72, Pres. Local Organizing Cttee. 72; mem. Int. Interim Cttee. of the Int. Congresses of Tropical Medicine and Malaria 73; mem. WHO Int. Ind. Comm. for Assessment of Smallpox Eradication in the Americas 73; Pres. of Tech. Board Escola de Ensino e Administração de Enfermagem; mem. Tech. Board Escola de Enfermagem de Saúde Pública; mem. Scientific Advisory Council, Int. Green Cross; Hon. Fellow American Public Health Asscn.; Hon. mem. Asscn. de Especialistas de Análises Clínicos (Spain); Hon. mem. Soc. Belge de Médecine Tropicale; Hon. mem. Société de Pathologie Exotique 67; mem. Hon. Cttee. Asscn. Provence-Portugal; mem. Comissão Regional da Especialidade de Doenças Tropicais (Ordems dos Médicos), American Soc. of Tropical Medicine, German Tropical Medicine Asscn., Amer. Mosquito Control Asscn., Int. Epidemiological Asscn., etc.; mem. Scientific Cttee., *Médecine d'Afrique*

Noire, O Médico, Rivista di Malariologia; Encomienda conplaca Orden Civil de Sanidad (Spain), Comendador Ordem Sant'Iago da Espada (Portugal) 73; Medal of Third Congresso Pan-Americano de Medicina do Trabalho-S. Paulo (Brazil).

Leisure interests: natural history, animal (especially bird) photography.

Publs. More than 150 papers, particularly on epidemiology, parasitology, entomology, public health, nutrition, health education, malaria, sleeping sickness and relapsing fever.

Instituto de Higiene e Medicina Tropical, Rua da Junqueira 96, Lisbon 3; Home: Rua de S. Francisco de Sales 17, 6 Esq. Lisbon 1, Portugal.

Telephone: 632141 (Office); 650575 (Home).

Cambronne, Luckner J.; Haitian politician; b. 24 Oct. 1930, Arcahaie, Port-au-Prince; s. of Pierre Cambronne and Romaine (née Bernadotte); m.; three s. two d.; ed. Lycée Pétion, Port-au-Prince.

Private Sec. to Pres. François Duvalier 57-60; Minister of Public Works 60-64; Deputy, Nat. Assistant April 61-Feb. 73; Minister of Interior and Defence April 71-Nov. 72; Amb.-at-large and Insp.-Gen. of Embassies and Consulates in the Americas March 73-.

Air Haiti, Miami International Airport, Miami, Florida, U.S.A.

Camden, John, B.SC.; British civil engineer; b. 18 Nov. 1925, Malvern, Worcs.; s. of late Joseph R. R. J. Camden and of Lilian Kate McCann; m. 1st Helen Demel 1951 (dissolved 1959), 2nd Irmgard Steinbrink 1959 (dissolved 1971), 3rd Diane Mae Yarbrough 1972; one s. four d.; ed. Worcester Royal Grammar School, Birmingham Univ.

Royal Tank Corps and Intelligence Corps 43-47; joined Ready Mixed Concrete Group 52, Dir. European Operations 62, Group Man. Dir. 66-, Chair. 74-.

Leisure interests: golf, gardening.

Ready Mixed Concrete Ltd., RMC House, 53-55 High Street, Feltham, Middx.; Home: Westbourn, Wentworth, Surrey, England.

Cameron, Clyde Robert; Australian politician; b. 11 Feb. 1914; ed. Gawler High School, South Australia.

Worked in shearing sheds 28-38; Organizer Adelaide Branch, Australian Workers' Union 38, Sec. 41-49; Fed. Vice-Pres. AWU 42-50; Industrial Officer 44-48; mem. House of Reps. for Hindmarsh 49-; mem. Fed. Parl. Labor Party Exec. 53-; Minister for Labour 72-75, and for Immigration 74-June 75, of Science and Consumer Affairs June-Nov. 75; mem. S.A. Broadcasting Advisory Cttee. 45-49, 64-; Pres. S.A. Branch, Australian Labor Party 46-48; Labor Party.

Parliament House, Canberra, A.C.T., Australia.

Cameron, Donald Alastair, O.B.E., M.B., B.S.; Australian physician and politician; b. 17 March 1900, Ipswich, Queensland; s. of Dr. J. A. Cameron; m. Rhoda McLean 1933; one s. one d.; ed. Sydney Univ.

Former Hon. Medical Officer, Ipswich Hospital; served Second World War; mem. Fed. Parl. for Oxley, Queensland 49-61; Minister for Health 56-61; Minister in Charge Commonwealth Scientific and Industrial Research Organization; High Commr. in New Zealand 62-65; Pres. Queensland Branch Australian Medical Asscn.; mem. Liberal Party of Australia.

Leisure interest: sailing.

43 Sefton Road, Clayfield, Brisbane, Queensland 4011, Australia.

Telephone: 621791.

Cameron, James; British author and journalist; b. 17 June 1911, London; s. of William Ernest Cameron and Margaret Douglas Robertson; m. 1st Elma Murray 1939 (deceased), 2nd Elizabeth O'Conor 1944 (divorced), 3rd Moneesha Sarkar 1971; one s. two step s. one d. one step d.; ed. in France and Scotland.

Started work on Dundee newspapers 27; in London associated with *News Chronicle* as Chief Foreign Corresp.; freelance work; opened BBC TV Series *One Pair of Eyes*, then films *Cameron Country*; currently working on books and on radio; Hon. D.Lit. (Lancaster Univ.); Granada Journalist of the Year 66, Granada Foreign Corresp. of the Decade 67, Prix Italia 74.

Publs. *Touch of the Sun* 50, *Mandarin Red* 55, *1914* 59, *The African Revolution* 61, *1916* 62, *Witness* 68, *Point of Departure* 69, *What a Way to Run a Tribe* 69, *An Indian Summer* 75.

16 Binden Road, London, W.12, England.

Telephone: 01-743-1623.

Cameron, Air Chief Marshal Sir Neil, K.C.B., C.B.E., D.S.O., D.F.C.; British air force officer; b. 8 July 1920, Perth, Australia; s. of Neil and Isabella Cameron; m. Patricia Louise Asprey 1947; one s. one d.; ed. Perth Acad.

Member Selection Bd., Combined Selection Centre 52-53; Dir. of Staff, R.A.F. Staff Coll., Bracknell 53-56; Officer Commdg. Univ. of London Air Squadron 56-58; Personal Staff Officer to Chief of Air Staff, Air Ministry 58-60; Officer Commdg. R.A.F. Abingdon 60-63; Principal Staff Officer to Deputy Supreme Allied Commdr. SHAPE 63-65; Asst. Commdt. (Cadets) R.A.F. Cranwell 65-66; mem. R.A.F. Ministry of Defence Programme Evaluation Group 66-68; Asst. Chief of Defence Staff, Ministry of Defence 68-70; Senior Air Staff Officer, HQ Air Support Command 70-72; Chief of Staff, HQ 46 Group 72; Deputy Commdr. HQ R.A.F. Germany 72-73; Air Officer Commdg. No. 46 Group 73-74; Air mem. for Personnel, Ministry of Defence 74-76; Chief of Air Staff (desig.) Aug. 76-.

Leisure interests: reading, rugby football, defence affairs.

c/o Ministry of Defence, Main Building, Whitehall, London SW1A 2HB.

Cameron, Roy James, M.ECON., PH.D.; Australian diplomatist; b. 11 March 1923, S. Australia; s. of Kenneth and Amy Jean Cameron (née Davidson); m. Dorothy Olive Lober 1951; two s. one d.; ed. Univs. of Adelaide and Harvard, U.S.A.

Lecturer in Econs., Canberra 49-51; Economist Int. Bank for Reconstruction and Devt. 55-56; with Australian Treasury 56-73, First Asst. Sec., Transport and Industry Div. 66-73; Amb., Del. to OECD Sept. 73-.

Australian Delegation to Organisation for Economic Co-operation and Development, 66 Avenue d'Iéna, Paris 16e, France.

Telephone: 723 54 23.

Cammann, Helmuth Carl, DR. RER. POL.; German economist; b. 8 Feb. 1927, Düsseldorf; s. of Carl Cammann and Maria Döpp; m. Helga Herweg 1957; one s. one d.; ed. Technological Univ., Karlsruhe and Cologne Univ.

Foreign Trade and Balance of Payments Section, Econ. Research Inst., Essen 50-53; Econ. Adviser, Perm. German Del. to OEEC 53-56; Head of Div., Econ. Directorate, ECSC, Luxembourg 56-57; Econ. Sec. Del. in U.K. of ECSC 57-61; Head of Perm. Del. of EEC Comm. to OECD, Paris 61-66; Sec.-Gen. Bundesverband deutscher Banken e.V., Cologne (Asscn. of German Banks) 66-.

Cologne, Mohrenstrasse 35, Federal Republic of Germany.

Telephone: 2063215.

Campaigne, Jameson Gilbert, B.A.; American editor and writer; b. 16 Jan. 1914, Brooklyn, N.Y.; s. of Curtis Campaigne and Edna Amory Foote; m. Edith Louise Baker 1938; three s. one d.; ed. Montclair Acad., Williams Coll.

Salesman, Yardley & Co. 36-40; writer with Compton Advertising 40-44; U.S. Marine Corps 44-46; Chief Editorial Writer, *Indianapolis Star* 46-51, Editor, Editorial Page 51-60, Editor 60-69, editorial writer and columnist 69-73; Editorial Writer, *New York News* 73-; mem. Mont Pelerin Soc.; Lincoln Nat. Life Foundation Award for best editorial on Lincoln; Freedoms Foundation Award for editorial writing 51, 52, 57; Indiana Univ. World Affairs Award 60.
Leisure interests: golf, squash, tennis.
Publs. *American Might and Soviet Myth* 60, *Check-off* 61.
220 East 42nd Street, New York, N.Y.; Home: 170 Highland Avenue, Montclair, N.J., U.S.A.
Telephone: 744-1721.

Campbell, Hon. Alexander Bradshaw, P.C., Q.C., B.A., LL.B., LL.D.; Canadian lawyer and politician; b. 1 Dec. 1933, Summerside, Prince Edward Island; s. of Thane A. Campbell (*q.v.*) and late Cecilia Bradshaw; m. Marilyn Gilmour 1961; two s. one d.
Practised law in Summerside, Prince Edward Island 59-66; mem. P.E.I. Legislature Feb. 65-, Leader of Liberal Party for P.E.I. Dec. 65-; Premier of P.E.I July 66-, Minister of Devt. 69-72, of Agriculture and Forestry 72-74, Pres. Exec. Council, Minister of Justice, Attorney and Advocate-Gen. 74-; mem. Privy Council for Canada Jan. 67-; mem. and fmr. Sec. Summerside Board of Trade; Past Pres. of Y's Men's Club; fmr. Vice-Pres. and Exec. mem. P.E.I. Young Liberal Asscn.; Elder, United Church, Summerside; Hon. LL.D. (McGill Univ.) 67.
Office: Provincial Administrative Buildings, Charlottetown, Prince Edward Island; Home: 330 Beaver Street, Summerside, Prince Edward Island, Canada.
Telephone: 892-3535 (Office).

Campbell, Allan McCulloch, M.S., PH.D.; American professor of biology; b. 27 April 1929, Berkeley, Calif.; s. of Lindsay and Virginia Campbell; m. Alice Del Campillo 1958; one s. one d.; ed. Univ. of Calif. (Berkeley) and Univ. of Illinois.
Instructor in Bacteriology, Univ. of Mich. Medical School, Ann Arbor 53-57; Research Assoc., Carnegie Inst. of Washington, Dept. of Genetics 57-58; Asst. Prof. to Prof. of Biology, Univ. of Rochester, 58-68; Prof. of Biological Sciences, Stanford Univ. 68-; Fellow, American Acad. of Arts and Sciences; mem. Nat. Acad. of Sciences.
Publ. *Episomes* 69.
Department of Biological Sciences, Stanford University, Stanford, Calif. 94305; Home: 947 Mears Court, Stanford, Calif. 94305, U.S.A.
Telephone: 497-1170 (Office); 493-6155 (Home).

Campbell, Sir Clifford Clarence, G.C.M.G., G.C.V.O.; Jamaican teacher and administrator; b. 28 June 1892, Petersfield, Westmoreland; m. Alice Estephene 1920; two s. two d.; ed. Petersfield Elementary School and Mico Training Coll.
Headmaster of various govt. schools 16-44; mem. House of Reps. (Jamaica Labour Party) 44-52, Chair. Cttee. for Educ. 45-49; Speaker, House of Reps. 50; Pres. of Senate 62; Gov.-Gen. of Jamaica 62-73.
Leisure interests: music, painting, reading, agriculture, community and professional service.
King's House, Kingston 10, Jamaica.

Campbell, Sir David, M.C., M.A., B.SC., M.D., LL.D., D.C.L., F.R.C.P., F.R.C.P.S., F.R.S.E.; British university professor; b. 6 May 1889, Patna, Ayrshire; m. Margaret Lyle 1921; ed. Univ. of Glasgow and Johns Hopkins Univ.
Pollok Lecturer in Pharmacology, Univ. of Glasgow 20-30; Asst. Physician, Western Infirmary, Glasgow 20-30; Rockefeller Medical Fellow 25-26; Regius Prof. of Materia Medica, Univ. of Aberdeen 30-59, Dean,

Faculty of Medicine 32-59; Physician, Aberdeen Royal Infirmary 30-59; mem. Gen. Medical Council 36-61, Pres. 49-61; Hon. LL.D. (Glasgow, Dublin, Liverpool and Aberdeen Univs.), Hon. D.C.L. (Durham).
Publ. *Handbook of Therapeutics* 30.
Carskeoch, Milltimber, Aberdeenshire, Scotland.
Telephone: Culter 733335.

Campbell, Douglas Lloyd; Canadian farmer and politician (retd.); b. 27 May 1895, Portage La Prairie, Manitoba; m. Margaret Gladys Crampton, 1920; three s. four d.; ed. Brandon Coll., Manitoba.
Member Manitoba Legislature 22-69; mem. Exec. Council 36-58; Ministry of Agriculture and Immigration 36-48; Prime Min. of Manitoba 48-58; Leader of the Opposition 58-62; Liberal-Progressive.
Leisure interests: golf, reading, travelling.
3 Ayr Blvd., Winnipeg 29, Manitoba, Canada.
Telephone: 888-2920.

Campbell, Evan Roy, C.B.E.; Rhodesian farmer and business executive; b. 2 Sept. 1908; ed. St. Andrews Coll., Grahamstown, Potchefstroom Agricultural Coll.
Farmer, Umvukwes, Southern Rhodesia 31-35, Inyazura 35-; Army service 40-45; mem. Rhodesia Tobacco Asscn. 46-50, Vice-Pres. 50-52, Pres. 52-58; Chair. Tobacco Export Promotion Council 58-63, Standard Bank Ltd., Commercial Union Assurance Co. of Rhodesia (Pvt.) Ltd., Rhodesia Tea Estates Ltd., Metal Box Co. of Central Africa Ltd., Fisons Pest Control (C.A.) (Pvt.) Ltd., Central African Branch of Inst. of Dirs. 65-, Manica Trading Co. of Rhodesia Ltd., Rhodesia Fertilizer Corpn. Ltd.; High Commr. of Southern Rhodesia in U.K. Dec. 63-June 65; Dir. Sable Chemical Industries Ltd., Discount Co. of Rhodesia Ltd. and other cos. 69-; Dir. Rhodesian Promotion Council 65-.
Courtney Rise, Addington Lane, Highlands, Salisbury, Rhodesia.
Telephone: Salisbury 882715.

Campbell, John Garfield, C.A.; Canadian business executive; b. 13 March 1916; ed. public and high schools, Regina, Saskatchewan.
Audit Clerk, Rooke Thomas & Co., Regina 35-41; Gen. Auditor, Defense Industries Ltd., Montreal 41-46; Comptroller, Victory Mills Ltd. 46-51; Comptroller Canadian Breweries Ltd. 51; Pres. Victory Mills Ltd. 52; Vice-Pres. Canadian Breweries Ltd. 54-59, Exec. Vice-Pres. 59-65, Pres. 65-.
Office: Canadian Breweries Ltd., 297 Victoria Street, Toronto 2, Ontario; Home: 18 Saintfield Avenue, Don Mills, Ontario, Canada.

Campbell, Joseph; American Comptroller-General 54-65; see *The International Who's Who 1975-76.*

Campbell, Nicholas Joseph, Jr., A.B., JUR.D., LL.D.; American lawyer and oil executive; b. 22 April 1915, Jersey City, N.J.; s. of Nicholas J. Campbell and Clara Campbell (née Zimmerman); m. Katherine M. Hickey 1944; one d.; ed. St. Vincent Coll., Latrobe, Pennsylvania, and Harvard Law Scool.
Practising Attorney, Satterlee Warfield & Stephens, New York 40-47; U.S. Air Force 42-46; Counsel, Creole Petroleum Corpn., New York 47-50; Man. Law Dept. Creole Petroleum Corpn., Caracas, Venezuela 51-56; Vice-Pres. and Dir. Creole Petroleum Corpn., New York 56; Assoc. Gen. Counsel Exxon Corpn., fmr. Standard Oil Co. (N.J.), New York 56-62; Dir. Esso Int. Inc., New York 57-62; Dir. Esso Standard Sekiyu K.K., Tokyo, Japan 62-64, Pres. 63-64; Dir. Toa Nenryo Kogyo K.K., Tokyo 63-64; Exec. Asst. to L. W. Elliott (Exec. Vice-Pres. Standard Oil Co. (N.J.), New York) 64-65; mem. Board of Dirs. Exxon Corpn., New York 65-66; Dir. and Pres. Esso Europe Inc., London 66-70; Dir. and Chair.

Esso Africa Inc. and affiliated cos., London 68-70; Dir. and Senior Vice-Pres. Exxon Corpn. 71-.
1251 Avenue of the Americas, New York, N.Y. 10020; Home: 359 Hollywood Avenue, Crestwood, N.Y. 10707. U.S.A.

Campbell, Ross, D.S.C.; Canadian diplomatist; b. 4 Nov. 1918, Toronto, Ont.; *s.* of late William M. Campbell and Helen I. Campbell; *m.* Penelope Grantham-Hill 1945; two *s.*; ed. Univ. of Toronto Schools and Univ. of Toronto.
Royal Canadian Navy 40-45; Third Sec., Oslo 46-47; Second Sec., Copenhagen 47-50; European Div., Dept. of External Affairs, Ottawa 50-52; First Sec., Ankara 52-56; Head of Middle East Div., Ottawa 57-59; Special Asst. to Sec. of State for External Affairs 59-62; Asst. Under-Sec. of State for External Affairs 62-64; Adviser to Canadian Dels. to UN Gen. Assemblies 58-63, Adviser to Canadian Dels. to North Atlantic Council 59-64; Amb. to Yugoslavia 64-67, concurrently accred. to Algeria 65-67; Perm. Rep. and Amb. to NATO, Paris May 67, Brussels Oct. 67-72; Amb. to Japan 73- (concurrently accred. to Repub. of Korea 73-74).
Leisure interests: tennis, gardening.
Canadian Embassy, 3-38, Akasaka 8-chome, Minato-ku, Toyko, Japan.

Campbell, Hon. Thane Alexander, M.A., LL.D.; Canadian judge; b. 7 July 1895, Summerside, P.E.I.; *s.* of Alexander and Clara Campbell; *m.* 1st Lillian Cecilia Bradshaw 1930 (died 1968), two *s.* two *d.*; *m.* 2nd Pauline A. L. Champ 1970; ed. Prince of Wales Coll., Charlottetown, Dalhousie and Oxford Univs.
Attorney-General of P.E.I. 30-31, 35-43; Chief Justice of P.E.I. 43-July 70; mem. P.E.I. Legislative Assembly 31-43; Premier of P.E.I. 36-43; mem. Bar of P.E.I. 27-43; Man. P.E.I. Mutual Fire Insurance Co. 30-43; mem. Historic Sites and Monuments Board of Canada 48-59, Board of Govs. of Dalhousie Univ. and Saint Dunstan's Univ.; (first) Chancellor of Univ. of P.E.I. 70-74; Chief War Claims Commr. for Canada 52-; Adviser on Claims by Canadians under Agreement with Bulgaria 67; Chief Commr. Foreign Claims Comm. 70-; mem. Nat. Library Advisory Council 48-59.
Leisure interest: curling.
Box 1358, Summerside, Prince Edward Island; Box 432, Ottawa, Ont., Canada.
Telephone: Ottawa 995-8702 (Office); 436-2556 (Home).

Campbell of Croy, Baron (Life Peer), cr. 74; **Gordon Thomas Calthrop Campbell,** M.C.; British politician; b. 8 June 1921, Quetta, Pakistan; *s.* of Maj.-Gen. and Mrs. J. A. Campbell; *m.* Nicola Madan 1949; two *s.* one *d.*; ed. Wellington Coll.
Served in regular army 39-46, wounded and disabled; diplomatic service 46-57, mem. U.K. mission to UN 49-52, Cabinet Office 54-56; mem. Parl. for Moray and Nairn 59-74; Lord Commr. of the Treasury 62; Parl. Under-Sec. of State for Scotland 63-64; Sec. of State for Scotland 70-74; Conservative.
Leisure interests: music, birds.
Holme Rose, Cawdor, Nairn, Scotland.
Telephone: Croy 223.

Campbell of Eskan, Baron (Life Peer) cr. 66, of Camis Eskan; **John (Jock) Middleton Campbell,** Kt.; British business executive; b. 8 Aug. 1912, London; *s.* of the late Colin Algernon Campbell and Mary C. G. Barrington; *m.* 1st Barbara N. Roffey 1938, two *s.* two *d.*; *m.* 2nd Phyllis J. Gilmour Taylor 1949; ed. Eton and Exeter Coll., Oxford.
Chairman, Booker McConnell Ltd. 52-67, Pres. 67-; Chair. Commonwealth Sugar Exporters 50-, Statesman and Nation Publishing Co. 63-, Milton Keynes Devt. Corpn. 67-; Pres. W. India Cttee., Dir. Commonwealth Devt. Corpn. 68-; mem. Community Relations Comm.

68-; Trustee Runnymede Trust, Chequers Trust.
Leisure interests: reading, hitting balls, painting.
Office and Homes: 15 Eaton Square, London, SW1W 9DD; and Crocker End House, Nettlebed, Oxford, England.
Telephone: 01-839-5133 (Office); Nettlebed 202 (Country).

Campen, Dr. Philippus Canisius Maria van; Netherlands business executive; b. 1 Jan. 1911, Nijmegen.
Manager, Co-operative Central Bank, Eindhoven 46, Gen. Man. 57-73; mem. Netherlands Senate and European Parl. until 67; mem. Supervisory Board, N.V. Philips Gloeilampenfabrieken 63-, Chair. 68, now Vice-Chair.; Pres. Asscn. Co-operative Credit Banks, EEC 71; mem. Supervisory Board, Friesch-Groningsche Hypotheek Bank, Ballast Nedam (Chair.), D.S.M., Kas-Associatie.
Fellenoord 15, Eindhoven, Netherlands.
Telephone: 040-433144.

Campenhausen, Hans Erich, Freiherr von, D.THEOL.; German university professor; b. 16 Dec. 1903, Rosenbeck, Livland; *s.* of Balthasar von Campenhausen and Lilli von Löwis of Menar; *m.* 1st Dorothee von Eichel 1931, 2nd Dorothee Anders 1966; three *s.* one *d.*; ed. Marburg, Heidelberg, Berlin and Rome.
Lecturer in ecclesiastical history Marburg 28-30, Göttingen 30-35; Lecturer in Giessen, Kiel, Greifswald, Heidelberg and Vienna 35-45; Prof. of Ecclesiastical History Heidelberg 45-; Rector Univ. of Heidelberg 46-47; mem. Heidelberg Akademie der Wissenschaften 46, Göttingen Akad. der Wissenschaften, Brit. Academy, American Acad. of Arts and Sciences; Hon. doctorates in Theology (St. Andrews, Göttingen, Oslo, Vienna and Uppsala Univs.).
Publs. *Ambrosius v. Mailand als Kirchenpolitiker* 29, *Die Passionssarkophage* 30, *Die Idee des Martyriums in der alten Kirche* 36, 2nd ed. 64, *Luther: Die Hauptschriften, Karl Müller: Kirchengeschichte I* 41, *Kirchliches Amt und Geistliche Vollmacht in den ersten drei Jahrhunderten* 53, 63 (English 69), *Die griechischen Kirchenväter* 55, *Lateinische Kirchenväter* 60, *Tradition und Leben* 60 (English 68), *Die Jungfrauengeburt in der alten Kirche* 62 (English 64), *Aus der Frühzeit des Christentums* 63, *Die Entstehung der Christlichen Bibel* 68 (English 72), *Theologenspiess und -Spass* 73, 74.
Ladenburger Strasse 69, Heidelberg, Baden-Württemberg, Federal Republic of Germany.

Campenhout, André Van; Belgian executive director, International Bank for Reconstruction and Development 60-73; see *The International Who's Who 1975-76.*

Campos Salos, Octaviano; Mexican economist and politician; b. 22 March 1916; ed. Escuela Nacional de Economía, Univ. Nacional Autónoma de Mexico, and Univ. of Chicago.
Former Man., Bank of Mexico; fmr. Exec. Sec. Mexican Cttee., Latin American Free Trade Area; fmr. Dir. School of Econs., Nat. Univ. of Mexico; fmr. Dir.-Gen., Inst. of Political, Econ. and Social Studies of Partido Revolucionario Institucional (PRI); fmr. Co-ordinator-Gen. of Planning, PRI; fmr. Dir.-Gen. of Commerce, Secr. of Industry and Commerce; later held posts with Secr. of Finance and Public Credit; fmr. Chief of Dept. of Econ. Studies, Bank of Mexico; fmr. Economist, UN Comm. for Latin America, Int. Monetary Fund; fmr. Visiting Prof., Univ. of Mexico; Sec.-Gen. of Teachers' Union of Mexico 38-40; Pres. Colegio de Economistas de México 56-58; mem. Exec. Council Int. Soc. of Econometrics 61-63; Sec. for Industry and Commerce 64-70.
Publs. numerous articles on foreign trade, int. econs., Latin American econ. integration, balance of payments, central banking, public finance and nat. economy.
c/o Secretaría de Industria y Comercio, Mexico, D.F., Mexico.

Campus, Ferdinand-Alexis-Auguste; Belgian university professor; b. 14 Feb. 1894, Brussels; s. of Alexis-Auguste Campus and Zelie Durand; m. Suzanne Dubois 1919; two s. two d.; ed. Inst. Rachez, Ghent, Athénée Royal, Brussels, Univs. of Brussels and Liège.
Served in army, both World Wars; Civil Engineer, Ministry of Public Works, Liège and Nieuport 19-20; Technical Dir. of Public Works, Railways, Post, Telegraph and Telephone of Saar Territory 20-26; Prof. Univ. of Liège 26-64, Prof. Emer. 64-, Rector 50-53; Technical Dir. construction of new Insts. of Univ. of Liège, Val-Benoît 29-37; founder 30 and Dir. Civil Eng. Laboratories of Univ. of Liège; Provincial Commr. for Reconstruction, Liège 40-44; mem. State Comm. for protection of Liège region against floods 27, Pres. 47-; Pres. Belgian Society for Testing Materials; Hon. mem. of Int. Asscn. for Bridge and Structural Engineering; Hon. mem. R.I.L.E.M.; mem. many Belgian, foreign and int. asscns. in civil engineering and testing of materials; mem. Royal Overseas Acad., mem. Royal Acad. Belgium; Corresp. mem. Royal Acad. Sciences Madrid; mem. Polish Acad. Sciences; hon. degrees Univs. of Cambridge and Brussels and Eidgenössische Technische Hochschule, Zürich; various medals and awards.
Publs. *Recherches, Etudes et Considérations sur les Constructions Soudées* 46; and many papers.
Leisure interests: travelling, classical music, drawings and etchings.
77 Avenue Armand Huysmans, Brussels 5, Belgium.
Telephone: 02-49-69-64.

Camu, Louis; Belgian bank official; b. 1905; ed. Univ. of Liège.
Former Lecturer, Univ. of Liège; Chef de Cabinet, Ministry of Public Information 34, Prime Minister's Office 38; Royal Comm. on Administrative Reform 35-39; Vice-Pres. Banque de Bruxelles 49, now Chair.; Pres. Council, EEC Banking Fed. 73-.
Banque de Bruxelles, S.A., 2 rue de la Régence, Brussels, Belgium.

Camu, Pierre, PH.D.; Canadian public official; b. 19 March 1923, Montreal; m. Marie-Marthe Trudeau; one s. two d.; ed. Univ. of Montreal and Johns Hopkins Univ., Baltimore.
Professor, Econ. Geography and Dir. Research Center, Faculty of Commerce, Laval Univ. 56-60; Consultant to shipping orgs. in Eastern Canada and U.S.A. 56-60; Vice-Pres. St. Lawrence Seaway Authority 60-65, Pres. 65-73; Administrator Canadian Marine Transportation Admin. 70-; Pres. Royal Canadian Geog. Soc. 67-.
Ministry of Transport, Hunter Building, Ottawa, K1A 0N7, Ont., Canada.
Telephone: 992-0531.

Candau, Marcolino Gomes, M.D., M.P.H.; Brazilian physician; b. 30 May 1911, Rio de Janeiro; s. of Julio Candau and Augusta Gomes; m. 1st Ena de Carvalho 1936, two s.; m. 2nd Sita Reelfs 1973; ed. Univ. of Brazil and Johns Hopkins Univ., U.S.A.
Held various positions in Health Service of State of Rio de Janeiro, Nat. Health Dept. and Ministry of Educ. and Public Health 34-50; Asst. Prof. of Hygiene, School of Medicine, Rio de Janeiro 38- (leave of absence 50-); Asst. Prof. of Epidemiology, Nat. Health Dept. 48-50; Dir. Div. of Org. of Public Health Services, WHO 50-51, Asst. Dir.-Gen. Dept. of Advisory Services 51-52; Asst. Dir. Pan-American Sanitary Bureau and Deputy Regional Dir. for the Americas, WHO 52-53; Dir.-Gen. WHO 53-73; Dir.-Gen. Emer. WHO 73-; mem. Brazilian Soc. of Hygiene, Rio de Janeiro State Soc. of Medicine and Surgery, Royal Soc. of Tropical Medicine and Hygiene, London; Hon. Fellow (Foreign) Argentine Medical Asscn., Nat. Acad. of Medicine, Peru, Royal Acad. of Medicine in Ireland, American Public Health Asscn., Royal Soc. for the Promotion

of Health (U.K.), Peruvian Public Health Asscn., Royal Soc. of Medicine London, American Coll. of Dentists; hon. mem. Nat. Acad. of Medicine, Brazil, American Venereal Disease Asscn., Canadian Public Health Asscn., Inter-American Asscn. of Sanitary Eng., American Hospital Asscn., Geneva Medical Soc. and other societies; Fellow Royal Coll. of Physicians, London; Mary Kingsley Medal of Liverpool School of Tropical Medicine 66, Royal Soc. of Health Gold Medal (London) 66; numerous hon. degrees; Moinho Santista Prize (São Paulo) 67; Univ. of Michigan Sesquicentennial Award 67; Foreign mem. U.S.S.R. Acad. of Medical Sciences 68; Commonwealth of Massachusetts Dept. of Health Centennial Award 69; Jo. Baptistae Morgagni Int. Prize of Associazione Artistico Letteraria Internazionale, Florence 73; Harben Gold Medal of Royal Inst. of Public Health and Hygiene, London 73; Geraldo Paula Souza Medal of Public Health Asscn., São Paulo 74; Léon Bernard Prize and Medal of World Health Asscn. 74; Life mem. of Johns Hopkins Soc. of Scholars 74.
Leisure interests: history, gardening.
"Le Mas", Route du Jura, 1296 Coppet, Switzerland.
Telephone: 022-76-16-49.

Candela (Outeriño), Félix; Mexican builder, engineer and architect; b. 27 Jan. 1910, Madrid, Spain; s. of Felix Candela Magro and Julia Outeriño Escheverria; m. 1st Eladia Martin 1940 (died 1963), 2nd Dorothy Davies 1967; ed. Instituto de Cardenal Cisneros, Madrid, and Escuela Superior de Arquitectura, Madrid.
Service in Spanish Civil War on Republican side 36-39; interned in France 39; emigrated to Mexico 39; supervision of architecture of La Colonia Santa Clara (Spanish Colony), Chihuahua 39-40; draftsman Mexico City 40; contractor Acapulco 41; assistant architect, Mexico City 42; partnership with his brother Antonio 45-; first Structure in thin-shell concrete 49; established Cubiertas Alá, S.A. with his brother 51; buildings include Cosmic Ray Pavilion, Mexico Univ. City 50, Mexico City Stock Exchange, Church of San Antonio de las Huertas, Church of La Virgen Milagrosa, Lederle Laboratories, and warehouses, Sports Palace for 1968 Olympic Games, Mexico City; major exhbn. of his work, Univ. of South Calif. 57; Prof., Escuela Nacional de Arquitectura, Mexico 53-; Jefferson Memorial Prof., Univ. of Virginia 66; Charles E. Norton Prof. of Poetry Harvard Univ. 61-62; Andrew White Prof.-at-Large, Cornell Univ. 71-; Prof. Dept. of Architecture, Univ. of Ill. at Chicago 71-; William Hoffman Wood Chair. of Architecture, Univ. of Leeds, England 74-75; Hon. mem. Sociedad de Arquitectos Colombianos, Sociedad Venezolana de Arquitectos and other societies; Gold Medal Inst. of Structural Engineers 61, Auguste Perret Prize of the Int. Union of Architects 61, Gold Medal, Soc. of Mexican Architects 63, and other awards; Hon. Fellow American Inst. of Architects 63, Hon. Corresp. mem. R.I.B.A. 63; Hon. D.F.A. (Univ. of New Mexico) 64.
University of Illinois At Chicago Circle Campus, Chicago, Ill. 60680; 1514 W. Jackson Boulevard, Chicago, Ill. 60607, U.S.A.
Telephone: (312) 829-6029.

Candilis, Georges; French architect; b. 1913, Russia; ed. Athens Polytechnical School.
Architectural practice, Athens until 40; fmr. Architect Greek Air Force, Asst. Prof. Athens Polytechnical School, Prof. Greek Nat. School of Building Technicians; Reserve Lieut. Greek Army 40-45 (Cross of St. George); went to France 45; Asst. to Le Corbusier, Paris and Architect of Le Corbusier's Housing Unit, Marseilles 45-51; Dir. Atbat-Afrique Co., Casablanca 51-54; Architectural practice, Paris 54-, specializing in tropical architecture; Prof. Ecole Nat. Supérieure des Beaux-Arts 63-; Pres. group of architects for the devt. of

Languedoc-Roussillon seashore; Chief Architect Barcarès Leucate Tourist Station, Languedoc-Roussillon; Pres. Syndicat des Architectes de la Seine; mem. French Order of Architects and other professional orgs.; Hon. Fellow AIA; Chevalier Légion d'Honneur; many prizes.

Major works include: new city of Bagnols sur Cèze; new city of Toulouse-Mirail; Free Univ. of Berlin; urban planning of Fort-Lamy (now N'Djamena) Chad, and numerous housing units, shopping centres, schools, hotels, etc. in France and abroad, incl. Algeria, Morocco, Iran, Tahiti and New Caledonia.

18 rue Dauphine, 75006 Paris, France.

Telephone: 633 61 70.

Canham, Erwin Dain, A.B., M.A., D.LITT., L.H.D., LL.D.; American newspaper editor; b. 13 Feb. 1904, Auburn, Maine; s. of Vincent Walter Canham and Elizabeth May Gowell; m. 1st Thelma Whitman Hart, 1930 (died 1967), 2nd Patience Mary Daltry 1968; two d.; ed. Bates Coll., and Oxford Univ.

With *The Christian Science Monitor* 25-, covered League of Nations Assembly 26-28, chief corresp. at London Naval Conf. 30, corresp. Geneva 30-32, head of Washington Bureau 32-39, Gen. News Editor 39-41, Man. Editor 41-44, Editor 45-64, Editor-in-Chief 64-74 Editor Emer. 74-; Radio commentator 38-39, 45-; Plebiscite Commissioner, North Mariana Islands 75; U.S. alternate Del. UN Gen. Ass. 49; mem. American Society of Newspaper Editors, Pres. 48-49; mem. U.S. Advisory Comm. on Information 48-51; mem. Corpn., Simmons College; Dir. Nat. Manpower Council; Trustee Bates and Wellesley Colls.; Trustee of Twentieth Century Fund; mem. U.S. Chamber of Commerce, Pres. 59-60, Chair. of Board 60-61, Chair. of Exec. Comm. 61-62; Chair. Foreign Policy Cttee.; Dir. John Hancock Mutual Life Insurance Co.; Chair. Dirs. Fed. Reserve Bank of Boston 62-67; Dir. Keystone Custodian Funds Inc. 70-; Dir. Nat. Bureau of Econ. Research, Resources for the Future Inc.; Dir. Electric Power Research Inst. 73-; Trustee Museum of Fine Arts, Boston; Board of Dirs. Datran; Fellow American Acad. of Arts and Sciences; Officer Southern Cross of Brazil; Commdr. Order of Orange-Nassau; Order of George I (Greece); Officier Légion d'Honneur; Grosses Bundesverdienstkreuz (German Fed. Republic); Hon. C.B.E.

Home: 242 Beacon Street, Boston, Mass. 02116; Office: 1 Norway Street, Boston, Mass., U.S.A.

Telephone: 247-2123 (Home).

Cannon, Howard Walter, B.S., LL.B.; American lawyer and politician; b. 1912; ed. Arizona State Teachers' Coll. and Arizona Univ.

Admitted to Arizona Bar 37, to Utah Bar 38, to Nevada Bar 46; fmr. Reference Attorney, Utah State Senate and County Attorney, Washington County, Utah; City Attorney, Las Vegas 49-59; Senator from Nevada 59-; service with Air Force in Second World War, rising to rank of Maj. Gen. U.S.A.F. Reserve; D.F.C., Air Medal with two Oak Leaf Clusters, American Defense Citation, Presidential Unit Citation, Croix de Guerre with silver star; Democrat.

Senate Office Building, Washington, D.C. 20510, U.S.A.

Canonge, Henri Albert; French trade union official; b. 13 May 1914, Barre-des-Cévennes; s. of Albert Canonge and Alix Lamarche; m. Germaine Puech 1939; two s.; ed. Lycée du Parc, Lyons, Nat. Agricultural Inst., Paris.

Assistant Insp. Agricultural Credit Bank 37-40; Dir. Dairy Industry Asscn. of Aveyron, Roquefort Interregional Cttee. 40, Gen. Confed. of Agriculture 45-63, Nat. Fed. of Farmers' Unions 45-47; Dir.-Gen. Nat. Agricultural Confed. for Mutual Assistance, Co-operation and Credit 52-74; mem. Econ. and Social Cttee., European Communities 58-, Vice-Pres. 72-74, Pres.

74-; mem. French Council of State 71-74; mem. Econ. and Social Council, France 45-52; Leader writer *Libération Paysanne* 45-52; mem. Nat. Cttee. on Prices 45-47, Agricultural Audit Comm. 60-73; Commdr. du Mérite Agricole, mem. Council, Ordre du Mérite Agricole; Commdr. des Palmes académiques.

Leisure interest: fly fishing.

Confédération nationale de la mutualité, de la coopération et du crédit agricoles, Maison de l'agriculture, 129 boulevard St.-Germain, 75006 Paris, France; and Economic and Social Committee of the European Communities, 2 rue Ravenstein, 1000 Brussels, Belgium.

Telephone: 033-93-31 (Paris); 513-95-95 (Brussels).

Canterbury, Archbishop of (*see* Coggan, Most Rev. Frederick Donald).

Cantini, José Luis; Argentine professor of law and politician; b. 6 March 1924, Rosario; s. of José Juan Cantini and Valentina María Josefa de Agostini; m. Gladys L. Serra 1950; three s. five d.; ed. Colegio San José (Rosario) and Universidad Nacional del Litoral.

Vice-Rector, Univ. Tecnológica Nacional 63-66; Dir. Colegio de Abogados de Rosario 64-66; Legal Assessor, Univ. Tecnológica Nacional 66-67; Rector, Univ. Nacional del Litoral 67-68, Univ. Nacional de Rosario 68-70; Vice-Pres. Council of Rectors of the National Univs. 68-69; Minister of Educ. and Culture 70-71.

Av. Pellegrini 438, Rosario, Argentina.

Canto, Jorge del; Chilean economist; b. 1916; ed. Univs. of Chile and Calif. (at Berkeley).

Officer, Chilean Foreign Office 37-38; Adviser, Central Bank of Chile 42-46; fmr. Prof. School of Econs. Univ. of Chile; Int. Monetary Fund 46-, Dir. Western Hemisphere Dept. 57-.

5412 Christy Drive, Washington 16, D.C., U.S.A.

Cao Van Bon; Vietnamese politician; b. 1908, Vinh Long Province; studied electronics in France.

Technical Director for several industrial firms in France; joined French resistance during World War II; politically active in overthrow of Diem Govt. 63; detained 65, 67-68 for joining opposition movements; joined NLF 68; Minister of Econ. and Finance, Provisional Revolutionary Govt. 69- (in Saigon 75-).

Ministry of Economy and Finance, Saigon, South Viet-Nam.

Caouette, Real; Canadian politician; b. 26 Sept. 1917, Amos, Abitibi, P.Q.; m. Suzanne Curé 1937; two s.; ed. Collège du Sacré-Coeur de Limbour, Collège de Victoriaville.

Former bank employee and commercial traveller; mem. of Parl. 46-49, 62, 63, 65, 68, 72; founded Le Ralliement des Créditistes (now Social Credit Party of Canada) 58, Leader in House of Commons 63; Deputy Nat. Leader, Social Credit Asscn. of Canada 61-62.

Leisure interests: boating, swimming in summer, snow mobile and reading in winter.

Parliamentary Building, Ottawa, Ontario, Canada.

Capanna, Alberto; Italian businessman; b. 8 July 1910; ed. Univ. Commerciale Luigi Bocconi, Milan.

Free-lance 34-36; staff of Ministry for Africa 36; Dir. Commissariat-Gen. for Food and Econ. Co-ordination in Libya 40-42, for Food in Sicily 42-43; Technical Sec. Ministry for Industry and Commerce 43-49; joined Istituto per la Ricostruzione Industriale (I.R.I.) 50, successively First Dir. Finsider, Central Dir., Exec. Vice-Pres., Chair. Finsider; June 75-, Dir. of numerous companies including Italsider, Dalmine, Sidercomit, Cementur, A.T.B.; founder mem. and Chair. Consultative Cttee. ECSC; Cavaliere del Lavoro e Cavaliere di Gran Croce al merito della Repubblica Italiana.

Publs. include *Gli scambi dell'Italia con l'estero dalla fondazione del Regno ad oggi* 40, and books on economic subjects.

Via Nomentana 373, Rome, Italy.

Capdevila, Arturo, DR. LAWS and SOC. SC.; Argentine lawyer and writer; b. 18 March 1889; ed. Univ. of Córdoba.
Judge and Prof. of Philosophy in Córdoba 19-22; Prof. of Literature, Univ. Nacional de la Plata 22; Spanish and Argentine awards.
Publs.Over 100 works including (poetry): *Melpómene, E Poema de Nenúfar, Córdoba Azul;* (plays): *La Sulamita, El Amor de Scharazada;* (history): *Las Vísperas de Caseros, Las Invasiones Inglesas;* (miscellaneous): *La dulce patria, Córdoba del Recuerdo, Babel y el Castellano, El gitano y su leyenda, Loores Platenses, Tierra Mía, Abraces, Maestro de amor, Advenimiento, El gran Reidor Segovia;* also treatises on medicine.
Juncal 3575, Buenos Aires, Argentina.

Capelle, Jean; French university professor and politician; b. 16 March 1909, Cales, Dordogne; s. of Henri Capelle and Berthe Vaysse; m. Marie de Chaignon 1933; one s.; ed. Ecole Nat. Supérieure des Mines de Paris and Ecole Normale Supérieure, Université de Paris.
Professor (Faculty of Science) at Nancy Univ. 43-46; Dir. Ecole Nat. Supérieure d'Electricité et de Mécanique 44-46; Dir.-Gen. of Educ. in French West Africa 47-49; Rector Nancy Univ. 49-54; Dir.-Gen. of Educ. in French West Africa and Rector, Dakar Univ. 54-57; Dir.-Gen. Inst. Nat. des Sciences Appliquées, Lyon 57-61, Pres. 73-; Dir.-Gen. Ministry of Educ. 61-64; Mayor of Saint-Avit Sénieur 65-; Deputy for the Dordogne 68-73; French Rep. to Council of Europe 68-73; Dir. Ecole Nat. Supérieure d'Electricité et de Mécanique de Nancy 73-.
Publs. *Génération des Engrenages par la Méthode des Roulettes* 38; *Théorie des Engrenages Hypoïdes* 48, *Cours de Résistance des Matériaux* 49; Editor *Bulletin de la Société d'Etudes de l'Industrie de l'Engrenage* 44, *En-cylopédie Française,* Vol. 13 61, *Tomorrow's Education* 67, *Pour ou Contre le Baccalauréat* 68, *Education et Politique* 75.
Home: 24440 St. Avit Sénieur, France.
Telephone: St. Avit Sénieur 61-31-99.

Caplin, Mortimer M., B.S., LL.B., J.S.D.; American lawyer, educator and government official; b. 11 July 1916, New York City; s. of Daniel Caplin and Lillian Epstein; m. Ruth Sacks 1942; three s. two d.; ed. Univ. of Virginia and New York Univ. Law School.
Law Clerk to U.S. Circuit Judge 40-41; legal practice with Paul, Weiss, Rifkind, Wharton & Garrison, New York City 41-50; U.S. Naval Reserve, Beachmaster in Normandy landings 42-45; Prof. of Law, Univ. of Virginia 50-61, Lecturer and Visiting Prof. 64-; Counsel to Perkins, Battle & Minor 52-61; U.S. Commr. of Internal Revenue 61-64; Partner, Caplin & Drysdale, Washington 64-; Chair. Finance Cttee. Prentice-Hall Inc.; Pres. Nat. Civil Service League; Vice-Pres. People-to-People Sports Cttee; Dir. Variable Annuity Life Insurance Co., Norton Simon Inc., Webb Resources Inc.; mem. Amer. Bar Assen., D.C., Va. and N.Y. State Bar Asscns., Nat. Tax Assen., Fed. Bar Assen., Amer. Law Inst.; Raven Award, Alexander Hamilton Award, and other awards; Editor-in-Chief *Virginia Law Review* 39-40; mem. Board of Trustees, George Washington Univ. and Coll. of the Virgin Islands; Hon. LL.D. (St. Michael Coll.) 64.
Leisure interests: swimming, horseback riding, gardening.
Publs. Numerous articles on tax and corporate matters.
Caplin & Drysdale, 1101 17th Street, N.W., Washington, D.C. 20036; Home: 4536 29th Street, N.W., Washington, D.C. 20008.
Telephone: 202-293-3900 (Office); 202-244-3040 (Home).

Capote, Truman; American author; b. 30 Sept. 1924, New Orleans; ed. Greenwich High School, New York.
Writer from early years; first published story *Miriam* 44; mem. Nat. Inst. Arts and Letters; O. Henry Memorial Award 46, 48, 51; creative writing award Nat. Inst. Arts and Letters 59.
Publs. *Other Voices, Other Rooms* (novel) 48, *Tree of Night* (short stories) 49, *Local Colour* (travel essays) 50, *The Grass Harp* (novel, later dramatized by the author) 51, *The House of Flowers* (musical) 54, *The Muses are Heard* (essay) 56, *Breakfast at Tiffany's* (short stories) 58, *Selected Writings* 63, *In Cold Blood* 64 (film 68), *A Christmas Memory* 66, *The Thanksgiving Visitor* 69, *Trilogy: An Experiment in Multimedia* 71, *The Dogs Bark* 74; short stories and articles in many nat. magazines.
c/o Random House Inc., 457 Madison Avenue, New York, N.Y. 10022, U.S.A.

Capp, Al(fred) Gerald; American author and artist; b. 28 Sept. 1909, New Haven; s. of Otto and Matilda (Davidson) Capp; m. Catherine Wingate Cameron; two d. one s.; ed. Philadelphia Acad. of Fine Arts, Boston Museum of Fine Arts.
Created comic strip " Li'l Abner" 34, appearing in over 1,000 newspapers throughout the world.
Publs. *Life and Times of the Shmoo, World of Li'l Abner,* and articles in *Atlantic Monthly, Life, Picture Post, Reader's Digest, Pageant.*
Capp Enterprises, 122 Beacon Street, Boston, Mass., U.S.A.

Cappelen, Andreas Zeier; Norwegian lawyer and politician; b. 31 Jan. 1915, Vang, Hedmark; s. of Hans Blom Cappelen and Erna Margrethe Zeier; m. Olene Liberg; three s.; ed. Univ. of Oslo.
Assistant, District Court 39-40, Barrister at Stavanger 41-45, District Attorney, County of Rogaland 45-47; Legal Lawyer and Asst. Chief of Wages to Municipal Authorities, Stavanger 47-57, Dep. Mayor of Stavanger 53, Sec. for Finance, Stavanger 57-58; Minister for Municipal and Labour Affairs 58-63, of Finance 63-65; Sec. for Finance, Stavanger 66-67; Judge, Stavanger 67-71, Chair. of Bench 69-71, Pres. of Town Court 69-71, 73-; Minister of Foreign Affairs 71-72.
Syftesakveien 15, 4042 Hafrsfjord, Norway.
Telephone: Stavanger 90-493 (Home).

Cappello, Carmelo; Italian sculptor; b. 21 May 1912; m. Selene Varale Cappello; one s. one d.; ed. Istituto Superiore d'Arte di Monza.
Sculptor 37-; regular exhibitor at Venice Biennali, Milan Triennali and Rome Quadriennali since 47; represented in major collections and int. exhibitions throughout the world; mem. Nat. Cttee. of UNESCO Div. of Plastic Arts; mem. Accad. Nazionale di San Luca; numerous awards.
Major Works: *Freddoloso* 38, *Uomo nello spazio* 55, *Tempesta* 56, *Cristo e i due ladroni* 55, *Volo Stratosferico* 58, *Il Folle* 48, *Il Filosofo* 49, *Tuffatori* 58, *Gli Acrobati* 55, *Eclisse* 59, *Fughe ritmiche* 61, *Involuzione del cerchio* 62, *Fontana per curve d'acqua* 58, *Ala* 60, *Ritmi Chiusi* 63, *Superficie-Spazio: Itinerario Circolare* 64, *Traiet toria Dal Piano Dello Spazio:* 65, *Occhio di Cielo* 66.
Via Melone 2, Milan, Italy.
Telephone: 898457 (Office); 8394658 (Home).

Cappuyns, Hendrik Frans Ferdinand, D. EN D.; Belgian business executive; b. 24 April 1913; s. of Hendrik and Maria Van Dingenen; m. Judith Smeets 1942; one s. one d.; ed. Univ. of Louvain.
Lawyer, Brussels bar 36-37; Sec.-Gen. S.N.C.B., Brussels 37-45, 45-52, Dir.-Gen. 52-64; Admin. Gevaert Photo Producten N.V.; Sec.-Gen. 56-; Chair. Agfa-Gevaert N.V., Mortsel 64-71; Chair. Agfa-Gevaert Group 71-75; Chair. and Man. Dir. Gevaert Photo-Producten N.V. 75-; Commdr. Ordre de la Couronne, Chevalier Ordre Léopold, Commdr. Ordre Léopold II, Officier Ordre Orange-Nassau.
Agfa-Gevaert N.V., B-2510 Mortsel; Home: Wilgendael, Horstebaan 109, B-2120 Schoten, Belgium.

Capra, Frank R.; American film director and pro-1ucer; b. 18 May 1897, Palermo, Italy; m. Lucille Warner 1933; two s. one d.; ed. Calif. Inst. of Tech. Came to U.S.A. 03; film dir. 21-; served U.S. Army both World Wars; fmr. Pres. Acad. of Motion Picture Arts and Sciences, Screen Directors' Guild; Dir. Calif. Inst. Tech.; three Acad. Awards for best direction of year; twice produced films which won Acad. Award as best picture of year.
Films produced, directed include: *Tramp, Tramp, Tramp* 26, *The Strong Man* 26, *Long Pants* 27, *For the Love of Mike* 27, *That Certain Thing* 28, *Submarine* 28, *Power of the Press* 28, *The Donovan Affair* 29, *Ladies of Leisure* 30, *Platinum Blonde* 31, *Forbidden* 32, *American Madness* 32, *Lady for a Day* 33, *It Happened One Night* (Acad. Awards for best picture and best dir.) 34, *Broadway Bill* 34, *Mr. Deeds Goes to Town* (Acad. Award for best dir.) 36, *Lost Horizon* 37, *You Can't Take it With You* (Acad. Awards for best picture and best dir.) 38, *Mr. Smith Goes to Washington* 39, *Meet John Doe* 41, *Why we Fight* (propaganda series) 41-45, *Arsenic and Old Lace* 44, *It's a Wonderful Life* 46, *State of the Union* 48, *Double Dynamite* 49, *Riding High* 50, *Here Comes the Groom* 51, *A Hole in the Head* 59, *Pocketful of Miracles* 61.
Publ. *The Name Above the Title* 71.
P.O. Box 98, La Quinta, Calif. 92253; and S.G. Colgems Square, Burbank, Calif. 91505, U.S.A.

Caprioglio, Vittorio; Italian chemist; b. 28 April 1929; ed. Univ. of Milan.
Worked in pharmaceutical field; worked in technological nuclear research, successively for Centro Informazioni e Studi Esperienze (CISE), AGIP Nucleare and EURATOM; Dir. Soc. Progettazioni Meccaniche Nucleari (IRI Group) 67-69; Dir. Ispra Establishment, EURATOM; Dir.-Gen. Joint Research Centre 71-74.
c/o Joint Research Centre, Commission of the European Communities, 200 rue de la Loi, Brussels, Belgium.

Caradon, Baron (Life Peer), cr. 64, of St. Cleer in the County of Cornwall; **Hugh Mackintosh Foot,** P.C., G.C.M.G., K.C.V.O., O.B.E. (brother of Sir Dingle Foot *q.v.,* Lord Foot of Buckland Monachorum and Michael Foot, *q.v.*); British overseas administrator; b. 8 Oct. 1907, Plymouth; s. of Rt. Hon. Isaac Foot, P.C.; m. Sylvia Tod 1936; three s. one d.; ed. Leighton Park School, Reading and St. Johns' Coll., Cambridge.
President Cambridge Union 29; Admin. Officer Palestine Govt. 29-37; attached to Colonial Office 38-39; Asst. British Resident, Transjordan 39-42; British Military Admin., Cyrenaica 43; Colonial Sec. Cyprus 43-45; Colonial Sec. Jamaica 45-47; Chief Sec. Nigeria 47-50; Capt.-Gen. and Gov.-in-Chief of Jamaica 51-57; Gov. and Commdr.-in-Chief of Cyprus 57-60; U.K. Perm. Rep. UN Trusteeship Council 61-62; Consultant to UN Special Fund 63; Minister of State for Foreign Affairs and Perm. Rep. to UN Oct. 64-70.
Publ. *A Start in Freedom* 64.
Home: Trematon Castle, Saltash, Cornwall, England.
Telephone: Saltash 3778.

Carafoli, Elie; Romanian professor of aerodynamics; b. 15 Sept. 1901, Veria-Salonica, Greece; s. of Nicolae and Emilia Ceara Carafoli; m. Monique Cosma; two d.; ed. Polytechnic Inst. of Bucharest and the Sorbonne, Paris.
Professor of Aerodynamics, Polytechnic Inst. of Bucharest 28-; Hon. Dir. Inst. of Fluid Mechanics and Aerospace 49-; mem. Romanian Acad. 48, Int. Acad. of Astronautics; Hon. Fellow of Royal Aeronautical Soc.; Corresp. mem. Acad. of Arts and Sciences of Toulouse; Pres. Int. Astronautical Fed. 68-70; Foreign mem. Braunschweigische Wissenschaftliche Gesellschaft; extraordinary mem. H. Oberth-Gesellschaft; State Prize, Order of Labour, Order of Scientific Merit; Honoured Scientist of Socialist Repub. of Romania,

Carl-Friedrich-Gauss Medal, Médaille Honneur Argent, Soc. Nat. de l'Encouragement au Progrès, and other awards.
Leisure interests: theatre, pictures, travel.
Publs. Nearly two hundred books, papers, monographs and articles.
Institute of Fluid Mechanics, str. Const. Mille 15, Bucharest; Home: Str. Vasile Conta 3, Bucharest, Romania.
Telephone: 145841 (Office); 162634 (Home).

Caragea, Boris; Romanian sculptor; b. 11 Jan. 1906, Balcic, Bulgaria; s. of Tudor and Raïna Caragea; divorced; one d.; ed. Bucharest School of Fine Arts.
Teacher of Sculpture, N. Grigorescu Fine Arts Inst., Bucharest; Chair. Plastic Artists Union 51-57; Chair. Plastic Arts Council of State Cttee. for Culture and Art 62-68; mem. Exec. Cttee. of Plastic Artists Union; Corresp. mem. Romanian Acad. 55-; One-man exhbn. Vienna 63; official exhbns. in Romania, Venice, Moscow, Belgrade, Prague, Berlin, Helsinki, Leningrad, Paris and Warsaw; represented at Venice Biennale 64; Merited Master of Arts 51, People's Artist 62, State prizewinner 51 and 53.
Major works: *The Meeting, The Mother, Liberation, V. I. Lenin, Fisher,* bas-relief on façade of Bucharest Opera, *Song, G. Enescu, The Victory.*
Uniunea Artistilor Plastici, Calea Victoriei 155, Bucharest; Home: 37 Davila Carol Street, Bucharest VI, Romania.
Telephone: 31-64-90.

Caram, Angel R., PH.D.; Argentine economist; b. 9 April 1921, Buenos Aires; s. of Assad Caram and Yamile Meouchi; m. Yolanda Elies 1956; no c.; ed. Univ. of Buenos Aires.
Economic Research Dept., Central Bank of Argentine Repub. 39-44; External Auditor, Ministry of Industry and Commerce 44-45; Financial Dept., Industrial Bank of the Argentine Repub. 45-48; Dir. of Commercial Studies, Ministry of Industry and Commerce 53-57; Nat. Deputy Dir. of Econ. and Financial Policy, Ministry of Economy 57, Dir. 63-65; Under Sec. of Economy 65; Financial Counsellor, Argentine Embassy, Washington, D.C. 65-68; Exec. Dir. Int. Bank for Reconstruction and Devt., Int. Finance Corpn. and Int. Devt. Asscn. Nov. 68-70; Finance Minister, Argentine Embassy, Washington 70-.
Argentine Embassy, 1600 New Hampshire Avenue, N.W., Washington, D.C.; Home: 1300 Army Navy Drive, Arlington, Va. 22202, U.S.A.

Caraway, Paul Wyatt; American retd. army officer and lawyer; b. 23 Dec. 1905; ed. U.S. Military Acad. and Georgetown Univ.
Commissioned 29, rose to Lieut.-Gen. 61; Senior Instructor (U.S.), Army Dept., NATO Defence Coll., Paris 51-53; Chief, Plans Div. Dept., Army Gen. Staff, Washington 53-55; Commanding Gen. 7th Infantry Div., Korea 55-56; Asst. Chief of Staff, H.Q. U.S. Forces, Japan 56-57, Chief of Staff 57-58, mem. Joint Strategic Survey Council, Office of Joint Chiefs of Staff, Washington 58-61; High Commr., Ryukyu Islands, Commdg. Gen. U.S. Army, Ryukyu Islands 61-65; mem. of firm, Reed and Caraway, Arkansas 65-68; Instructor Business Law, Benjamin Franklin Univ. 68-; numerous mil. decorations.
Benjamin Franklin University, 16th and L Streets, Washington, D.C. 20036; Home: 4450 South Park Avenue, Apartment 516, Chevy Chase, Md. 20015, U.S.A.

Carayannis, Denis; Greek diplomatist; b. 1918.
Joined Ministry of Foreign Affairs 47; Consul, Chicago 51-52, New York 52; Sec. Perm. Mission of Greece to UN 52-58; Ministry of Foreign Affairs 58-62; Consul-Gen. Paris 62-64; Dir. Dept. of Political Affairs of

Middle East and Africa 64-70; Minister Plenipotentiary 68; Amb. to Albania 71-73; Perm. Rep. to UN July 74-75; del. to several sessions of UN Gen. Assembly.
c/o Ministry of Foreign Affairs, Athens, Greece.

Carberry, H.E. Cardinal John J.; American ecclesiastic; b. 31 July 1904, Brooklyn.
Ordained 29; Titular Bishop of Elis 56; Bishop of Lafayette, Indiana 57-65, of Columbus, Ohio 65-68; Archbishop of St. Louis 68-; cr. Cardinal 69.
4445 Lindell Boulevard, Saint Louis 8, Missouri 63108, U.S.A.

Cardin, Hon. Lucien, P.C.; Canadian lawyer and politician; b. 1 March 1919; ed. Loyola Coll. and Montreal Univ.
Naval service 41-45; Barrister, Montreal; mem. House of Commons 52-, Assoc. Minister of Defence with seat in Cabinet 63-65; Minister of Public Works 65, of Justice July 65-67; mem. Immigration Appeal Board 70-72; Asst. Chair. Income Tax Revision Board 72-; Liberal.
House of Commons, Ottawa, Ontario; Home: 900 Abbott, Ville Saint-Laurent, Quebec, Canada.
Telephone: 323-2531.

Cardin, Pierre; French couturier; b. 7 July 1922, Italy.
Formerly worked with Christian Dior; founded own fashion house 49; f. Espace Pierre Cardin (theatre group); Chevalier Légion d'Honneur 74.
118 rue du Faubourg-Saint-Honoré, 75008 Paris, France.

Cardinale, Claudia; Italian film actress; b. 15 April 1938, Tunis; d. of Franco and Yolanda Cardinale; m. Franco Cristaldi 1966; one s.; ed. Lycée Carnot and Collège Paul Cambon, Tunis.
Made first film 58; awards include Nastro d'Argento, David di Donatello, Grolla d'Oro; has made 38 films, including 8½, *The Pink Panther, The Leopard, The Professionals, Once Upon a Time in the West, Fury, The Magnificent Showman, La Scoumoune.*
Vides Piazza, Pitagora 9, Rome, Italy.

Cardinale, Most Rev. Hyginus Eugene; Vatican ecclesiastic and diplomatist; b. 14 Oct. 1916; ed. St. Agnes Acad. (U.S.A.), Pontifical Roman Major Seminary, Pontifical Lateran Univ., Pontifical Gregorian Univ. and Pontifical Ecclesiastical Acad., Rome.
Attaché of Nunciature 45, Sec. of Nunciature 46; Papal Representations Egypt, Palestine, Arabia, Cyprus 46-52; Domestic Prelate 58; Counsellor of Nunciature 58; Chief of Protocol, Papal Secretariat 61; Under-Sec. of Tech. Org. Comm., Second Vatican Ecumenical Council 62; Apostolic Del. to Great Britain, Malta, Gibraltar and Bermuda and Titular Archbishop of Nepte 63-69; Apostolic Nuncio to Belgium and Luxembourg April 69-, and to the European Econ. Communities 70-; Holy See Special Envoy and Perm. Observer to Council of Europe (Strasbourg) 70-74; numerous decorations.
Publs. *La Représentation Pontificale* 48, *Church and State in the U.S.A.* 58, *Pontifical Diplomacy* 59, *Le Chiese Dissidenti d'Oriente dinanzi al Concilio* 61, *La Fedeltà del Patriarcato Greco-Melchita d'Antiochia alla Sede Apostolica* 61, *La Santa Sede e la Politica* 62, *Le Saint-Siège et la Diplomatie* 62, *Signs of the Times and Ecumenical Aspirations* 67, *The Unity of the Church* 68, *The Contribution of the Holy See to World Peace* 70, *The Holy See and the International Order* 75.
Apostolic Nunciature, Avenue de Tervueren 58, Brussels, Belgium.

Carey, Hugh L., J.D.; American state governor; b. 11 April 1919, Park Slope, Brooklyn; s. of Margaret Collins and Dennis J. Carey; m. Helen Owen Twohy 1945 (deceased); nine s. four d. one adopted d.; ed. St. Augustine's Acad., High School, Brooklyn, St. John's Univ.
Served with U.S. Army in Europe 39-46, rank of Lt.-

Col.; joined family petrochemical business 47; called to bar 51; mem. U.S. House of Reps. rep. 12th District of Brooklyn 60-74, apptd. Deputy Whip, mem. House Educ. and Labour Cttee., House Cttee. on Interior and Insular Affairs, Senate-House Joint Econ. Cttee., Sub-cttee. on National Parks; Chair. Sub-cttee. on Territorial and Insular Affairs; mem. House Ways and Means Cttee. 70; Gov., New York State Nov. 74-; much work for disabled and handicapped; Bronze Star, Croix de Guerre with Silver Star, Combat Infantryman's Badge; Democrat.
Governor's Residence, State Capitol, Albany, N.Y. 12224, U.S.A.

Cargill, Ian Peter M.; British international bank official; ed. Oxford Univ.
Indian Civil Service 38-47; British Treasury, London and Washington Office 48-52; World Bank, Desk Officer, Ethiopia, Sudan and Thailand 52-57; Asst. Dir., Dept. of Operations, Far East, World Bank 57-61, Dir. 61-66. Dir. Asia Dept. 66-68, Dir. S. Asia Dept. 68-72, Regional Vice-Pres. Asia 72-74, Vice-Pres. for Finance July 74-.
International Bank for Reconstruction and Development (World Bank), Washington, D.C. 20433, U.S.A.

Carl XVI Gustaf; King of Sweden; b. 30 April 1946; s. of Prince Gustaf Adolf and Sibylla, Princess of Saxe-Coburg-Gotha; ed. in Sigtuna and Univ. of Uppsala.
Created Duke of Jämtland; became Crown Prince 50; succeeded to the throne on death of his grandfather, King Gustaf VI Adolf 15 Sept. 73.
Royal Palace, Stockholm, Sweden.

Carli, Guido, D. IUR.; Italian economist and banker; b. 1914; ed. Padua Univ.
Director Ufficio Italiano dei Cambi 45; mem. Consulta Nazionale 45; mem. Man. Board Int. Monetary Fund 47; Gen. Adviser Ufficio Italiano dei Cambi 48; mem. European Payments Union Man. Board 50-58; Pres. 51-52; Pres. Mediocredito 52, Consorzio Credito Opere Pubbliche 59, Istituto Credito Imprese Pubblica Utilità 59; Vice-Pres. Istituto Mobiliare Italiano 59, Ufficio Italiano dei Cambi 59; Gen. Man. Banca d'Italia 59-61, Gov. 61; mem. Board Dirs. Bank of Int. Settlements 60-70; Board European Monetary Agreement 59-; mem. EEC Monetary Cttee. 59-; Gov. for Italy Int. Bank for Reconstruction and Devt. 62-; Minister of Foreign Trade 57-58; Einaudi Prize 64.
Publs. *Verso il multilateralismo degli scambi e la convertibilità delle monete, Evoluzione della legislazione italiana sul controllo degli scambi e dei cambi, Commercio Estero-Maggio 1957-Giugno 1958.*
Piazza Borghese 3, Rome, Italy.

Carlson, Edward Elmer; American airline executive, b. 4 June 1911, Tacoma, Wash.; s. of Elmer E. and Lula (Powers) Carlson; m. Nell Hinckley Cox; one s. one d.; ed. Univ. of Washington.
U.S. Navy 42-46; Asst. to Pres. Western International Hotels 46, Vice-Pres. 47, Exec. Vice-Pres. 53-61, Pres. 61-69, Chair. and Chief Exec. Officer 69-, Chair. Exec. Cttee. 71-; mem. Board of Dirs. UAL Inc. Aug. 70 (following merger of Western Int. Hotels and UAL, Inc.), Pres. and Chief Exec. Officer UAL Inc. and United Airlines 70-75, Chair. and Chief Exec. Officer Jan. 75-; Dir. Seattle First Nat. Bank, Safeco Insurance Corpn., Air Transport Assen. of America, First Chicago Corpn. (and its subsidiary First Nat. Bank of Chicago), etc.; Order of St. John of Jerusalem.
Leisure interests: golf, sailing.
UAL Inc., P.O. Box 66100, Chicago, Ill. 60666, U.S.A.

Carlsson, Ingvar Gösta, M.A.; Swedish politician; b. 9 Nov. 1934, Borås; m. Ingrid Melander 1957; two d.; ed. Lund Univ. and Northwestern Univ. U.S.A.
Secretary in Statsradsberedningen (Prime Minister's Office) 58-60; Pres. Social Democratic Youth League

61-67; Member of Parl. 64-; Under Sec. of State, Statsradsberedningen (Prime Minister's office) 67-69; Minister of Educ. 69-73, of Housing and Physical Planning 73-; mem. Exec. Cttee. Social Dem. Party. Ministry of Housing and Physical Planning, Kanslihuset, Stockholm, Sweden.

Carlu, Jacques; French architect; b. 7 April 1890. Premier Grand Prix of Rome; Prof. of Architecture. Massachusetts Inst. of Technology 24-23; architect of many famous buildings including Palais de Chaillot and NATO headquarters in Paris; elected mem. Académie des Beaux-Arts, Paris 57; Commandeur de la Légion d'Honneur.
7 rue Michel-Ange, 75016 Paris, France.
Telephone: 224-89-69; 224-88-93.

Carlucci, Frank Charles; American diplomatist; b. 18 Oct. 1930, Scranton, Pa.; s. of Frank and Ruth Carlucci; m. Jean Anthony 1954 (separated 1974); one s. one d.; ed. Princeton Univ. and Harvard Graduate School of Business Admin.
With Jantzen Co., Portland, Ore. 55-56; Foreign Service Officer, Dept. of State 56; Vice-Consul, Econ. Officer, Johannesburg 57-59; Second Sec. Political Officer, Kinshasa 60-62; Officer in charge of Congolese Political Affairs, Consul-Gen., Zanzibar 62-65; Counsellor for Political Affairs, Rio de Janeiro 65-69; Asst. Dir. for Operations, Office of Econ. Opportunity 69-70, Dir. OEO 71; Assoc. Dir. Office of Management and Budget 71-72, Deputy Dir. 72-73; Under-Sec. Dept. of Health, Educ. and Welfare 73-74; Amb. to Portugal Dec. 74-; Hon. D.Hum.Litt.; Superior Service Award and Superior Honour Award, Dept. of State.
Leisure interests: tennis, swimming, jogging, squash.
American Embassy, Avenue Duque de Loulé 39, Lisbon, Portugal.

Carlyle, Joan Hildred; British soprano; b. 6 April 1931; d. of late Edgar J. Carlyle and Margaret M. Carlyle; m. Robert Duray Aiyar; two d.; ed. Howell's School, Denbigh, N. Wales.
Principal Lyric Soprano, Covent Garden 55-; major roles sung in U.K. include: Oscar, *Ballo in Maschera* 57-58, Sophie, *Der Rosenkavalier* 58-, Nedda, *Pagliacci* (Zeffirelli production) 59, Mimi, *La Bohème* 60, Titania, *Midsummer Night's Dream*, Britten (Gielgud production) 60, Pamina, *Magic Flute* 62, 66, Countess, *Marriage of Figaro* 63, Zdenka, *Arabella* (Hartman Production) 64, *Suor Angelica* 65, Desdemona, *Othello* 65, *Arabella* 67, Marschallin, *Der Rosenkavalier* 68, Jenifer, *Midsummer Marriage* 69, *Donna Anna* 70, Reiza, *Oberon* 70, *Adrianna Lecouvreur* 70, *Russalka*, Elizabetta, *Don Carlos*; major roles sung abroad include Oscar, Nedda, Mimi, Pamina, Zdenka, Micaela, Donna Anna, Arabella, Elizabetta and Desdemona; debut at Salzburg, Metropolitan Opera, New York and Teatro Colón, Buenos Aires 68; several recordings including Von Karajan's production of *Pagliacci* as Nedda and *Midsummer Marriage* as Jenifer.
Leisure interests: gardening, travel, preservation of the countryside, interior design, cooking.
44 Abbey Road, St. John's Wood, London, N.W.8, England.

Carmichael, Harry J., C.M.G.; Canadian industrialist; b. 29 Sept. 1891; s. of late William A. Carmichael and Mary Ann Moran; m. Helen Marie Moran Woods 1942; ed. New Haven High School.
Joined McKinnon Industries, St. Catharines, Ont. 12, becoming Pres. and Gen. Man. on acquisition by Gen. Motors Corpn. 29; Vice-Pres. and Gen. Man. General Motors of Canada Ltd. 36-41; Joint Dir.-Gen. of Munitions Production, Dept. of Munitions and Supply 41-42; Co-ordinator of Production and Chair. War Production Board; Canadian Chair. Joint U.S.-Canada W.P.B. 42-45; Dir. Argus Corpn. Ltd., Foster Wheeler Ltd.,

Continental Can Co. of Canada Ltd., Hayes-Dana Ltd. 619 Avenue Road, Apartment 1601-2, Toronto M4V 2K6, Ont., Canada.

Carmoy, Guy de, L. EN D., L. ÈS L.; French administrator and professor; b. 20 Feb. 1907, Paris; s. of Pierre de Carmoy and Marguerite Perquer; m. Marie de Gourcuff 1934; one s. three d. (one d. deceased).
Inspector of Finances 30-60; Gen. Information Commissariat 39; Head of Film Dept., Ministry of Information 40-41; Budgetary Controller 41-43; deported to Germany 43-45; Alternate Exec. Director Int. Bank for Reconstruction and Development 46-48; mem. French del. for European Economic Co-operation 48; Dir. of Admin. and Confs. Organisation for European Economic Co-operation 48-52; Prof. Inst. d'Etudes Politiques 50-; Prof. Inst. Européen d'Administration des Affaires 61-; Officier Légion d'Honneur.
Leisure interest: interior decoration.
Publs. *Fortune de l'Europe* 53, *Les politiques étrangères de la France (1944-1966)* 67, *The Foreign Policies of France (1944-68)* 70, *Le Dossier Européen de l'Energie* 71.
22 avenue de Suffren, 75015 Paris, France.
Telephone: 56 7-12-73.

Carné, Marcel; French film director; b. 18 Aug. 1906; s. of Paul Carné and Marie Racouët.
Took course for film technicians; work interrupted by military service; on discharge entered insurance business, later returned to film work; assistant operator for *Les Nouveaux Messieurs* 28, asst. to Dir., Richard Oswald, for *Cagliostro* 29; won competition for film criticism organised by *Cinémagazine* and joined editorial staff of this publication, directed *Nogent*, *Eldorado du Dimanche* 29, assisted René Clair in direction of *Sous les Toits de Paris* 30; wrote criticisms for various journals; Asst. Dir. for *Le Grand Jeu, Pension Mimosa,* and *La Kermesse Héroïque;* scored first great success as dir. with *Jenny* 36; Knight Légion d'Honneur; Commdr. des Arts et des Lettres; Prix Int., Venice Biennale 38, 53, Grand Prix de Cinéma 58, Médaille de Vermeil 72.
Films include, *Drôle de Drame* 37, *Quai des Brumes* 38, *Le Jour se lève* 39, *Les Enfants du Paradis* 43, *Les Portes de la Nuit* 46, *La Marie du Port* 49, *Juliette ou la clé des songes* 50, *Thérèse Raquin* 53, *L'Air de Paris* 54, *Le Pays d'où je viens* 56, *Les Tricheurs* 58, *Terrain Vague* 60, *Du mouron pour les petits oiseaux* 63, *Trois chambres à Manhattan* 65, *Les Jeunes Loups* 68, *Les Assassins de l'Ordre* 70, *La Merveilleuse Visite* 74.
Publ. *La Vie à Belles Dents* (autobiography) 75.
10 rue Masseran, Paris 75007, France.
Telephone: 567-41-40.

Carnegie, Roderick Howard, B.SC., M.A. (OXON), M.B.A.; Australian mining executive; b. 27 Nov. 1932; s. of D. H. Carnegie; m. Carmen Clarke 1959; three s.; ed. Trinity Coll. Melbourne Univ., New Coll., Oxford, Harvard Business School, Boston, U.S.A.
Associate McKinsey and Co., Melbourne and New York 59-64, Principal Assoc. 64-68, Dir. 68-70; Dir. Conzinc Riotinto of Aust. Ltd. 70, Jt. Man. Dir. 71-72, Man. Dir. and Chief Exec. 72-74, Chair. and Chief Exec. 74-; Dir. Rio Tinto-Zinc Corpn. Ltd., Bougainville Copper Ltd., Hamersley Holdings Ltd., Australian Mining and Smelting Co. Ltd., Comalco Ltd., and several other cos. in the CRA group.
Conzinc Riotinto of Australia Ltd., 95 Collins Street, Melbourne 3000; Home: 15 St. Georges Road, Toorak, Victoria 3142, Australia.
Telephone: 63 0491.

Carneiro, Paulo de Berredo, D.SC.; Brazilian biochemist and diplomatist; b. 1901, Rio de Janeiro; s. of Mario Barboza Carneiro and Maria de Berredo; m. Corina de Lima e Silva 1927; one s. one d.; ed. Polytechnic School, Rio de Janeiro, and Université de Paris à la Sorbonne.

Professor Agregé, Polytechnic School, Rio de Janeiro 31-; Sec. of State for Agriculture, Industry and Commerce, State of Pernambuco 35; founded Pernambuco Agronomical Inst. 35; research at Institut Pasteur, Paris 36-41; Del. to numerous General Confs. of UNESCO 45-; mem. Exec. Board UNESCO 46-, Chair. 51-54; Head Brazilian Perm. Del. to UNESCO 47-58, Ambassador to UNESCO 58-; Pres. Int. Comm. for a *History of the Scientific and Cultural Development of Mankind* 51-; Pres. Int. Assen. *La Maison d'Auguste Comte* 58-; Vice-Pres. Int. Children's Centre; mem. Brazilian Acad. of Sciences 38, Acad. des Sciences Morales et Politiques (Inst. de France) 68, Brazilian Acad. of Letters 71; Pres. Acad. du monde Latin 69-; Prix Nativelle, Paris Acad. of Medicine 51.
Leisure interest: philosophy.
Publs. *Vers un nouvel humanisme* 70; numerous articles and essays on Comte and UNESCO.
UNESCO, Place de Fontenoy, Paris 7e; Home: 14 rue José Maria Heredia, Paris 7e, France.
Telephone: 273-15-35 (Home).

Carney, David, PH.D., M.A., M.SC., DIP. PUB. ADMIN.; Sierra Leonean economist, administrator, teacher; b. 27 May 1925, Freetown; s. of David Edward and Esther Victoria Carney; m. Helen Elizabeth Smith-Hall 1960; one s. one d.; ed. Fourah Bay Coll., Sierra Leone, Univ. of Pennsylvania and School of Advanced Int. Studies, Johns Hopkins Univ., U.S.A.
Lecturer, Fourah Bay Coll., Sierra Leone 45-47; Statistician, Dept. of Statistics, Govt. of Nigeria, Lagos, and Lecturer, Extra-Mural Dept., Univ. of Ibadan 48-52; Headmaster, Ghana Nat. Coll., Cape Coast, Ghana 52-53; Lecturer, Lincoln Univ., Franklin and Marshall Coll., Pa., Fairleigh Dickinson Univ., N.J. 53-58; Econ. Affairs Officer, Dept. of Econ. and Social Affairs, UN, New York 58-60; Asst. Prof. of Econs., Antioch Coll., Yellow Springs, Ohio 60-61; Econ. Adviser, Govt. of Sierra Leone 61-63; UN African Inst. for Econ. Devt. and Planning, Dakar, Senegal 63-70, Project Man. and Dir. April 67-Aug. 70; Chair. Comm. on Higher Educ. Sierra Leone 69, East African Community 70-72; Deputy Chief Economist 70-72; UN Econ. Devt. Planning Adviser, St. Lucia 73-75; mem. Governing Board UNESCO Int. Inst. for Educational Planning 70-73.
Leisure interests: writing poetry, stamp collecting.
Publs. *Government and Economy in British West Africa* 61, *A Ten-Year Plan of Economic and Social Development for Sierra Leone 1962/3-1971/2* 62, *Patterns and Mechanics of Economic Growth* 67; numerous papers in national and int. journals.
c/o Office of the Premier, Castries, St. Lucia, West Indies.
Telephone: St. Lucia 3142.

Carnot, Lazare; French businessman; b. 9 Nov. 1903, Paris; s. of Ernest Carnot; m. Marie Rose Françoy 1936; two s. two d.; ed. Ecole Nationale Supérieure des Mines de Paris.
Military service 26-27; mining engineer 27-28; Dir. Pricel; Dir. Rhône-Poulenc S.A., Rhône-Poulenc-Textile, La Cellophane, Compagnie Financière de Suez; Chevalier Légion d'Honneur, Croix de Guerre.
24 Boulevard Maillot, 92 Neuilly sur Seine, France.

Caro, Anthony, C.B.E., M.A.; British sculptor; b. 8 March 1924, London; s. of Alfred and Mary Caro; m. Sheila Girling 1949; two s.; ed. Charterhouse School, Christs' Coll., Cambridge, Regent St. Polytechnic and Royal Acad. Schools, London.
Assistant to Henry Moore 51-53; Part-time Lecturer St. Martin's School of Art, London 53-; taught at Bennington Coll. Vermont 63-65; one-man show in Milan 56, others subsequently in London, Washington,

Toronto, New York, Zürich and in Holland; retrospective show Arts Council (Hayward Gallery, London) 69; works in Tate Gallery, Arts Council, Museum of Modern Art (New York), Brandeis Univ. (Boston), Albright Knox Museum, Buffalo, N.Y., Cleveland Museum Ohio, Rijksmuseum Kroller-Muller (Otterlo, Netherlands); Sculpture Prize, Paris Biennale 59, David E. Bright Award, Venice Biennale 67, Prize for sculpture, São Paulo Biennale 69.
Leisure interest: travel.
111 Frognal, Hampstead, London N.W.3, England.

Carpeaux, Otto Maria, PH.D., LIT.D.; Brazilian journalist; b. 1900; ed. Vienna Univ.
Dir. Library, Nat. Faculty of Philosophy, Rio de Janeiro 41-45; Dir. Library, Getúlio Vargas Foundation, Rio de Janeiro 45-49; Editor *Correio da Manha*, Rio de Janeiro until 67, Co-editor Brazilian *Encyclopaedia Larousse* 67; Co-editor *Visão*, Rio de Janeiro 69; Co-editor *Encyclopaedia Mirador Internacional*, Rio de Janeiro 71; Italian Order of Merit.
Publs. 12 vols. of essays, *Short Critical Bibliography of Brazilian Literature* 51, *History of the Occidental Literatures* (9 vols.) 59-64, *A New History of Music* 58, *History of German Literature* 61, political essays 65, 66.
101 Rua República do Peru, Rio de Janeiro, Brazil.

Carpenter, Commdr. Malcolm Scott; American naval officer and astronaut; b. 1 May 1925, Boulder, Colorado; m. Louise Price; two s. two d.; ed. secondary school and Univ. of Colorado.
Aviation Cadet, U.S. Navy 43-45; Pilot, South Korea 49, later Navy Flight Officer, Electronics and Intelligence Officer; Project Mercury Astronaut 59-67, made triple orbit of the earth, May 24, 1962; spent 30 days beneath ocean in Sealab II, Aug.-Sept. 65; mem. U.S. Navy's Sealab Project 67; retd. from Navy to enter private business July 69.
9840 Airport, Los Angeles, Calif. 90045, U.S.A.

Carpentier y Valmont, Alejo; Cuban writer; b. 26 Dec. 1904; ed. Universidad de Habana.
Former journalist, radio station dir. and musicologist; travelled in Mexico, France, Spain, Belgium, Holland, Haiti, U.S.A. and upper reaches of Orinoco River; lectured in many countries including Eastern and Western Europe, China, Viet-Nam, U.S.S.R.; fmr. columnist *El Nacional*, Caracas, Venezuela; Cultural Attaché of Cuba in Paris 70-; Prix du Meilleur Livre Etranger for *The Lost Steps* 56, Cino del Duca Prize 75.
Publs. *Ecue-Yamba-O* (novel) 33, *A History of Cuban Music*, *El Reino de Este Mundo* (The Kingdom of this World) (novel) 49, *Los Pasos Perdidos* (The Lost Steps) (novel) 53, *El Acoso* (The Pursuit) (novel) 56, *Guerra de Tiempo* (The War of Time) (short stories) 58, *El Siglo de las Luces* (Explosion in a Cathedral) (novel) 63, *Reasons of State* 76.
Embassy of Cuba, 51 rue de la Faisanderie, Paris, 16e, France; Apartado 6153, Havana, Cuba.

Carpino, H.E. Cardinal Francesco; Italian ecclesiastic; b. 18 May 1905.
Ordained Priest 27; Titular Archbishop of Nicomedia 51; Titular Archbishop of Sardica 61; Archbishop of Palermo 67-70; Assessor, Sacred Congregation of Bishops 70-; created Cardinal by Pope Paul VI 67.
96010 Palazzolo Acreide, Syracuse, Italy.

Carr, Edward Hallett, C.B.E.; British diplomatist, political scientist and historian; b. 28 June 1892, London; ed. Merchant Taylors School and Cambridge Univ.
Entered Foreign Office 16; mem. British Del. to Peace Conf. 19; attached to Ambassadors' Conf. Paris 20-21; First Sec. Legation Riga 25-29; Asst. Adviser on L.N. Affairs, Foreign Office 30-33, First Sec. 33-36; Prof. of Int. Politics, Univ. Coll. Wales 36-46; Dir. Foreign Div.

Min. of Information 39-40; Asst. Editor *The Times* 41-45; Tutor in Politics, Balliol Coll. 53-55, Hon. Fellow Balliol Coll. 67-; Fellow Trinity Coll., Cambridge 55-.
Publs. *Dostoevsky: a new biography* 31, *The Romantic Exiles* 33, *Karl Marx* 34, *International Relations Since the Peace Treaties* 37, *Michael Bakunin* 37, *The Twenty Years' Crisis* 39, *Britain: A Study of Foreign Policy from Versailles to the Outbreak of War* 39, *Conditions of Peace* 42, *Nationalism and After* 45, *The Soviet Impact on the Western World* 46, *Studies in Revolution* 50, *The Bolshevik Revolution, 1917-1923*, Vol. I 50, Vol. II 52, Vol. III 53, *The New Society* 51, *German-Soviet Relations Between the Two World Wars* 51, *The Interregnum 1923-1924* (continuation of *The Bolshevik Revolution 1917-1923*) 54, *Socialism in One Country 1924-26* Vol. I 58, Vol. II 59, Vol. III 64, *What is History?* (The Trevelyan Lectures) 61, *1917: Before and After* 69, *Foundations of a Planned Economy*, Vol. I (with R. W. Davies) 69, Vol. II 71.
Trinity College, Cambridge, England.

Carr, Lt.-Col. Gerald Paul, M.SC.; American astronaut; b. 22 Aug. 1932, Denver, Colo.; *m.* JoAnn R. Petrie; three *s.* three *d.*; ed. Univ. of S. Calif., U.S. Naval Postgraduate School and Princeton Univ.
Entered U.S. Navy 49, commissioned 54; selected as NASA astronaut April 66; mem. astronaut support crew, *Apollo VIII* and *XII* flights; Nat. Defence Service Medal and other military decorations.
Leisure interests: sailing, golf, tennis, badminton, handball, woodworking and restoration of an old automobile.
NASA Johnson Space Center, Houston, Tex. 77058, U.S.A.

Carr of Hadley, Baron (Life Peer) cr. 75, of Monken Hadley in Greater London; **Robert Carr,** P.C., M.P.; British politician and business executive; b. 11 Nov. 1916, London; *s.* of Ralph Edward and Katie Elizabeth Carr; *m.* Joan Kathleen Twining 1943; one *s.* (deceased) two *d.*; ed. Westminster School and Gonville and Caius Coll., Cambridge.
Member of Parl. 50-75, Parl. Private Sec. to Sec. of State for Foreign Affairs 51-55, to Prime Minister April-Dec. 55, Parl. Sec. Ministry of Labour and Nat. Service 55-58, Sec. for Technical Co-operation May 63-Oct. 64; Sec. of State for Employment 70-72; Lord Pres. of Council and Leader of House of Commons April-Nov. 72; Sec. of State Home Dept. 72-74; joined John Dale Ltd. 38, Chief Metallurgist 45-48, Dir. of Research and Development 48-55, Chair. 59-63 and 65-70; Dir. Carr, Day & Martin Ltd. 47-55; Isotope Developments Ltd. 50-55; Deputy Chair. and Joint Man. Dir. Metal Closures Group Ltd. 60-63, Dir. 65-70; Dir. Scottish Union and Nat. Insurance Co. (London) 58-63; Dir. S. Hoffnung and Co. 63, 65-70, 74-, Securicor Ltd. 65-70, 74-; Norwich Union Insurance Group (London) 65-70, 74-; Dir. S.G.B. Group Ltd. 74-; Conservative.
Leisure interests: lawn tennis, gardening, music.
Publs. Co-author *One Nation, Change is our Ally* 54, *The Responsible Society* 58, *One Europe* 65.
House of Lords, Westminster, London, S.W.1; Home: Monkenholt, Hadley Green, Hertfordshire, England.

Carrelli, Antonio; Italian physicist; b. 1 July 1900, Naples; *s.* of Raffaele and Silvia (Scardaccione) Carrelli; *m.* 1st Nora Laliccia 1937, 2nd Lisetta Pellerano 1965; two *s.* one *d.*; ed. Università degli Studi, Naples.
Professor of Experimental Physics, Naples Univ. 32-; Vice-Pres. Italian Radio and Television (R.T.I.) 46-55, Pres. 55-59; Pres. Microlamba Co. 48-52 and Filotecnica Salmoiraghi Co. 48-52; Chair. Nat. Cttee. for Physics of Nat. Research Council, Scientific Cttee. of Italian Nat. Comm. of UNESCO; Vice-Pres. European Atomic Energy Comm. (EURATOM) 64-67; mem.

Accad. dei Lincei; several decorations; Pres. Board of Dirs. of Post and Telecommunications Ministry.
Via dei Mille, Naples, Italy.
Telephone: 417909.

Carrick, Hon. John Leslie; Australian politician; b. 4 Sept. 1918, Sydney; *m.*; three *d.*; ed. Sydney Technical High School, Univ. of Sydney.
Commissioned Univ. of Sydney Regt. 39, served in Australian Imperial Force, Sparrow Force; prisoner-of-war 42-45; mem. Citizen Mil. Force 48-51; Gen. Sec. N.S.W. Div. of Liberal Party of Australia 48-71; mem. Senate 71-; mem. Library Cttee. 71-73, Senate Standing Cttee. on Educ., Science and the Arts 71-75, Senate Standing Cttee. on Foreign Affairs and Defence 71-75, Joint Cttee. on Foreign Affairs 71-72, on Foreign Affairs and Defence 73-75; Opposition Spokesman for Federalism and Intergovernment Relations 75; Minister for Housing and Construction, for Urban and Regional Devt. Nov.-Dec. 75; Minister for Educ. and Minister assisting the Prime Minister in Fed. Affairs Dec. 75-.
Parliament Buildings, Canberra, A.C.T., Australia.

Carrier, George Francis, PH.D.; American professor of applied mathematics; b. 4 May 1918, Millinocket, Maine; *s.* of Charles Mosher Carrier and Mary Marcoux Carrier; *m.* Mary Casey Carrier; three *s.*; ed. Cornell Univ.
Research Engineer, Harvard Univ. 44-46; Asst. Prof. Brown Univ. 46-47, Assoc. Prof. 47-48, Prof. 48-52; Gordon McKay Prof. of Mech. Engineering, Harvard Univ. 52-72, Coolidge Prof. of Applied Maths. 72-; mem. Nat. Acad. of Sciences; Fellow, Amer. Acad. of Arts and Sciences, Nat. Acad. of Eng.; Assoc. Editor, *Journal of Fluid Mechanics*; mem. Editorial Board SIAM *Journal of Applied Mathematics*; mem. Corpn. of Woods Hole Oceanographic Inst.; mem. Board of Trustees, Rensellaer Poly. Inst.; Hon. mem. A.S.M.E.; Hon. Fellow, Inst. for Maths. and its Applications; Pi Tan Sigma Richards Memorial Award, A.S.M.E. 63.
Publs. *Functions of a Complex Variable: Theory and Technique* (with M. Krook and C. E. Pearson) 66, *Ordinary Differential Equations* (with C. E. Pearson) 68, *Partial Differential Equations* (with C.E. Pearson) 76; numerous articles.
Pierce Hall, Harvard University, Cambridge, Mass. 02138; Home: Rice Spring Lane, Wayland, Mass. 01778, U.S.A.

Carrière, Jean P.; French international civil servant; b. 7 Nov. 1925, Chalon/Saône; *s.* of Julien Carrière and Alice Daubard; *m.* Françoise Emery 1953; two *s.* one *d.*; ed. Dijon Law School and Ecole Nationale d'Admin.
Administrateur Civil, Ministry of Finance 57; Financial Attaché for Near and Middle East, Beirut 62; Dir. Office of Int. Orgs., Ministry of Finance 64, Deputy Dir. Information Dept. 67; Financial Attaché, French Embassy, Washington and Alt. Exec. Dir. IBRD 68-72; Dir. European Office of World Bank (IBRD) July 72-; Order of the Cedar of Lebanon.
Publ. *La Relève de l'Or* 66.
Office: 66 avenue d'Iéna, 75116 Paris; Home: 52 avenue Bosquet, 75007 Paris, France.
Telephone: 723-5421 (Office); 555-1686 (Home).

Carrillo Flores, Antonio; Mexican lawyer, banker and politician; b. 1909, Coyoacan, D.F.; *s.* of Julián Carrillo; *m.* Fanny Gamboa 1935; four *s.* two *d.*; ed. in New York and Nat. School of Jurisprudence, Mexico.
Prof. Faculty of Jurisprudence, Univ. of **Mexico** 32-; Joint Sec. Supreme Court of Justice 33; Head Law Dept. Attorney-Gen.'s Office 30-34 (except while with Supreme Court); Head, Law Dept., Ministry of Finance 35-36; mem. Admin. Council Bank of Mexico 38; Dir.-Gen. of Credit Ministry of Finance 41-45, of Nacional Financiera 45-52, Sec. of the Treasury 52-58; Amb. to U.S.A. 59-64; Minister of Foreign Affairs 64-70; Dir. Fondo de Cultura Económica 70-; Sec.-Gen. UN World Popula-

tion Conf. 72-74; decorations from Belgium, Fed. Repub. of Germany, Netherlands, France, Italy, Brazil, Paraguay, Argentina, Guatemala, El Salvador, Honduras, Nicaragua, Panama, Chile, etc.; Dr. h.c. (Lincoln Coll., Southern Methodist Univ. and Harvard Univ.).
Publs. *Administrative Justice in Mexico* 39, *The Mexican Financial System* 46, *The Economy and Human Rights in the Mexican Constitution* 59, *The Ideas and the Economic Development in the Process of the Mexican Revolution* 60, *The Supreme Court in the United States and in Mexico* 64, *Some Aspects of International Economic Co-operation* 67, *Homages and Testimonies* 67, *The Protection of the Civil Rights in Today's Mexico* 71.
Texas No. 26, Mexico 18, D.F., Mexico.

Carrington, 6th Baron; Peter Alexander Rupert Carington, P.C., K.C.M.G., M.C.; British politician; b. 6 June 1919, London; s. of 5th Baron Carrington and The Hon. Sybil Marion Colville; m. Iona McClean; one s. two d.; ed. Eton Coll. and Royal Military Coll., Sandhurst.
Grenadier Guards 39, and served N.W. Europe; Parl. Sec. Ministry of Agriculture 51-54, Ministry of Defence 54-56; High Commr. in Australia 56-59; First Lord of the Admiralty 59-63; Minister without Portfolio (at the Foreign Office), Leader of the House of Lords 63-64; Leader of the Opposition in the House of Lords 64-70; Sec. of State for Defence 70-74, also Minister of Aviation Supply 71-74; Sec. of State for Energy Jan.-March 74; Leader of the Opposition, House of Lords Oct. 74-; Chair. Conservative Party 72-74; Chair. Australia and New Zealand Bank Ltd. 67-70; Dir. Amalgamated Metal Corpn. Ltd. 65-70, Cadbury Schweppes Ltd. 68-70, 74-, Barclays Bank Ltd. 67-70, 74-, Hambros Bank Ltd. 67-70, Rio Tinto Zinc Corpn. Ltd. 74-.
House of Lords, London, S.W.1; Manor House, Bledlow, nr. Aylesbury, Buckinghamshire, England.
Telephone: 08444-3499.

Carro Martinez, Antonio; Spanish lawyer, economist and politician; b. 1923; m.; five c.
Member Parl.; Sec.-Gen. (technical) Ministry of the Presidency; Dir.-Gen. Inst. of Local Admin. Studies; Dir.-Gen. of Local Admin. June-Dec. 73; Minister of Presidential Affairs Dec. 73-75; Grand Cross of Civil Merit, Order of Cisneros.
Publs. *Derecho Político, Principios de Ciencia Política, La Constitución Española de 1869.*
c/o Ministerio de la Presidencia, Madrid, Spain.

Carroll, Donal Shemus Allingham, F.C.A.; Irish banker; b. 26 Dec. 1927, Ireland; s. of Col. J. D. Carroll and Sheila Maunsell (née Flynn); m. Monica D. M. Moran 1951; one s. one d.; ed. Glenstal Abbey School, Limerick and Trinity Coll., Dublin.
Joined P. J. Carroll & Co. Ltd. 52; Dir. 55, Chair. 60- and Man. Dir. 60-71; mem. court of Dirs., Bank of Ireland 56-, Deputy Gov. 62-64; Gov. and Chair. Irish Banks Standing Cttee. 64-70; Dir. Carreras Ltd. 62, Vice-Chair. 71-72; Dir. Rothmans Int. Ltd. 72-; Chair. Carreras Rothmans Ltd. 72-; Dir. Cen. Bank of Ireland 70-; Chair. Lloyds & BOLSA International Bank Ltd 71-73; mem. Public Services Advisory Council 73-; Dir. Dunlop Holdings Ltd.; Dir. Irish Times Holdings, Irish Times Trust; Hon. LL.D. (Dublin) 69.
Leisure interests: gardening, reading.
P. J. Carroll & Co. Ltd., Grand Parade, Dublin 6, Ireland.
Telephone: Dublin 767555.

Carruthers, Robert, B.SC. (ENG.), C.ENG., A.C.G.I, F.I.E.E.; British electrical engineer; b. 29 Jan. 1921, Leeds; s. of Mr. and Mrs. J. Carruthers; m. Phyllis Kathleen Deal 1945; two d.; ed. Harrow County School and London Univ., City and Guilds Coll.
Research at Telecommunications Research Establishment, Swanage and Great Malvern 41-46; Research

engineer with Messrs. Standard Telecommunication Laboratories Ltd. development of R.F. equipment for microwave radio links 46-47; research and development of synchrotrons, Atomic Energy Research Establishment 47-51; research work on gas discharge phenomena and its application to the field of controlled thermonuclear reactors; Senior Principal Scientist, Atomic Energy Research Establishment, Harwell; Head, Applied Physics and Technology Division, Culham Laboratory 61-.
Norman Cottage, 32 Norman Avenue, Abingdon, Berks., England.
Telephone: Abingdon 22386.

Carstairs, George Morrison, M.A., M.D., F.R.C.P.E., F.R.C.PSYCH.; British psychiatrist; b. 18 June 1916, Mussoorie, India; s. of Rev. George Carstairs, D.D., and Elizabeth H. Carstairs; m. Vera Hunt 1950; two s. one d.; ed. George Watson's Coll., Edinburgh and Edinburgh Univ.
Medical Officer, Fighter Command, R.A.F. 42-46; Commonwealth Fund Fellow, U.S.A. 48-49, Rockefeller Research Fellow, India 50-51, Henderson Research Scholar, India 51-52; Registrar, Maudsley Hospital, London 53; Scientific Staff, Medical Research Council Social Psychiatry Research Unit 54-60, Hon. Consultant, Maudsley Hospital 56-60; Dir. Medical Research Council Unit for Research on Epidemiology of Psychiatric Illness 60-71; Prof. of Psychiatry, Univ. of Edinburgh 61-73; Vice-Chancellor, Univ. of York 74-; B.B.C. Reith Lecturer 62; Pres. World Fed. for Mental Health 67-71.
Leisure interests: theatre, travel.
Publs. *The Twice Born* 57, *This Island Now* (the 1962 Reith Lectures) 63, *The Great Universe of Kota* 76.
Vice-Chancellor's House, University of York, York, England.
Telephone: 0904-59861.

Carstens, Karl, DR. IUR.; German lawyer and diplomatist; b. 14 Dec. 1914, Bremen; m. Veronica Prior 1944; ed. Univs. of Frankfurt, Dijon, Munich, Königsberg, Hamburg and Yale.
War service 39-45; lawyer, Bremen 45-49; Rep. of Free Hanseatic City of Bremen to Fed. Govt., Bonn 49-54; Fed. German Del. to Council of Europe, Strasbourg 54-55; Dep. Head. Political Div., Fed. Foreign Office, Bonn 55-58, Head, European Div. 58-60, State Sec. 60-, Deputy of Fed. Minister of Foreign Affairs 61-66; Deputy of Fed. Minister of Defence 66-67; Head of the Fed. Chancellor's Office 68-69; Prof. of Law, Univ. of Cologne 60-73; Dir. Research Inst., German Soc. for Foreign Affairs 70-73; mem. Bundestag 72-; Parl. Leader Christian Democrats 73-.
Publs. *Basic Ideas of the American Constitution and their Realisation* 54, *The Law of the Council of Europe* 56, *Politische Führung* 71.
Bundeshaus, 53 Bonn, Federal Republic of Germany.
Telephone: Bonn 161.

Cartan, Henri Paul, D. ès sc.; French mathematician; b. 8 July 1904, Nancy; s. of Elie Cartan; m. Nicole Weiss 1935; two s. three d.; ed. Lycée Buffon, Lycée Hoche, Versailles and Ecole Normale Supérieure.
Teacher, Lycée, Caen 28; Lecturer, Faculty of Science, Lille Univ. 29-31; Prof. Faculty of Science, Strasbourg Univ. 31-40, Univ. of Paris 40-69, Univ. de Paris-Sud (Orsay) 69-75; Pres. French Section, European Assen. of Teachers 57-75; Pres. Int. Mathematical Union 67-70; Pres. Mouvement Fédéraliste Européen (France) 74-; Corresp. Acad. des Sciences 65, mem. 74-; Foreign mem. Royal Soc. 71; Foreign Assoc. Nat. Acad. of Sciences, Wash. 72; Officier de la Légion d'Honneur.
Département de Mathématique, Université de Paris-Sud, 91405-Orsay; Home: 95 boulevard Jourdan, 75014 Paris, France.
Telephone: 540-51-78 (Home).

Carter, Benjamin Chadwick, A.B., C.P.A.; American business executive; b. 14 Jan. 1907, Rainier, Ore.; s. of Frank F. Carter and Mary R. Chadwick; m. Thelma R. Grothe 1934; one s. three d.; ed. Menlo School and Stanford Univ.
Accountant, Price, Waterhouse and Co. 29-34; Asst. to Controller FMC, San José 34, Asst. Controller 34-40, Controller 40-52, Vice-Pres. 46-52, Dir. 46-, Exec. Vice-Pres., Machinery Divs. 52-60, Exec. Vice-Pres., Finance, 60-66, Vice-Chair. Board of Dirs. 66-71, Chair. 71-73; Dir. Bank of Calif., Atari Inc.; mem. Board of Litronix Inc.
Leisure interests: golf, bridge, travel, gardening.
15600 Alum Rock Av., San José, Calif. 95127, U.S.A.
Telephone: 408-272-0397.

Carter, Hon. Douglas Julien; New Zealand farmer, politician and diplomatist; b. 5 Aug. 1908, Foxton; s. of Walter Stephen Carter and Agnes Isobel Nimmo; m. Mavis R. Miles 1936; ed. Palmerston North High School, Waitaki Boys' High School.
Member Parl. (Nat.) Raglan 57-75; Parl. Under-Sec. of Agriculture 67-70; Minister of Agriculture 70-72; High Commr. to U.K. (desig.) June 76-; Chair. N.Z. Pig Producers' Council 52-57, N.Z. Sharemilker Employers Asscn. 54-69.
Leisure interests: travel.
New Zealand House, Haymarket, London SW1Y 4TQ, England.

Carter, Edward Robert Erskine, B.C.L.; Canadian business executive; b. 20 Feb. 1923, Saint John, New Brunswick; s. of Arthur Norwood and Edith Isobel Ireland; m. Verna Leman Andrews 1947; two s. two d.; ed. Univ. of New Brunswick, Osgoode Hall, Toronto, and Oxford Univ. (Rhodes Scholar).
Military Service 42-45; read law with McMillan, Binch, Wilkinson, Berry & Wright, Toronto; called to Bar of New Brunswick 47, Bar of Ontario 51; Assoc. with A. N. Carter, Q.C., law practice, Saint John, N.B. 49-53; Legal Officer, Abitibi Power & Paper Co. Ltd., Toronto 53-54; joined Fennell, McLean, Seed & Carter 54, Partner, 55-58; Pres. and Chief Exec. Officer Hambro Canada Ltd.; Chair. and Dir. Consolidated Tin Smelters Ltd., British Amalgamated Metal Investments Ltd., Foodex Systems Ltd.; Chair. and Pres. Advocate Mines Ltd.; Deputy Chair. and Dir. Peel Village Developments Co. Ltd.; Vice-Chair., mem. Exec. Cttee. and Dir. Rio Tinto Patiño, S.A.; Dir. Bank of Montreal, Hambros Ltd., Westroc Industries Ltd., Bishopsgate Platinum Ltd., Sun Alliance Insurance Co. and numerous other companies; mem. Law Soc. of Upper Canada, New Brunswick Barristers Soc.
Hambro Canada Ltd., Suite 1104, Royal Trust Tower, Toronto-Dominion Center, Toronto M5K 1H6; Home: 21 Dale Avenue, Toronto M5K 1H6, Canada.
Telephone: 863-0014 (Toronto).

Carter, Edward W.; American businessman; b. 29 June 1911; ed. Univ. of California, Harvard Univ.
Chairman of Board Carter Hawley Hale Stores, Inc., Los Angeles; Dir. American Telephone and Telegraph Co., Del Monte Corpn., Pacific Mutual Life Insurance Co., Southern Calif. Edison Co., United Calif. Bank, Western Bancorporation; mem. Board of Regents, Univ. of Calif.; Trustee of Los Angeles County Museum of Art, Occidental Coll., The Brookings Inst., Washington, D.C., Cttee. for Econ. Devt.; Dir. Southern Calif. Symphony-Hollywood Bowl Asscn., San Francisco Opera Asscn., Stanford Research Inst., James Irvine Foundation, Santa Anita Foundation; mem. Business Council Business Cttee. for the Arts, Harvard Business School Overseas Visiting Cttee., UCLA Business School Visiting Cttee., The Conf. Board, Council on Foreign Relations.
550 South Flower Street, Los Angeles, Calif., U.S.A.
Telephone: 213-620-0150.

Carter, Elliott Cook, Jr., A.B., A.M.; American composer; b. 11 Dec. 1908; m. Helen Frost-Jones 1939; one s.; ed. Harvard Univ., Ecole Normale de Musique, Paris.
Musical Dir. Ballet Caravan 37-39; critic *Modern Music* 37-42; tutor St. John's Coll., Annapolis 39-41; teacher of composition Peabody Conservatory 46-48, Columbia Univ. 48-50, Queen's Coll. (N.Y.) 55-56; Prof. of Music, Yale Univ. 60; Andrew White Prof.-at-Large, Cornell Univ. 67-; mem. Board of Trustees, American Acad., Rome; American Composers' Alliance Prize for Quartet for Four Saxophones 43, First Prize Liège Int. Music Competition 53; mem. Int. Soc. for Contemporary Music, Dir. 46-52, Pres. American Section 52, Nat. Inst. of Arts and Letters, awarded two Guggenheim Fellowships, Pulitzer Prize (for 2nd String Quartet), Sibelius Medal 60, New York Critics Circle Award (for Double Concerto) 61, Hon. degrees Swarthmore Coll. and Princeton Univ. 69, Harvard Univ., Yale Univ., Boston Univ. 70; Gold Medal, Nat. Inst. of Arts and Letters 71; Pulitzer Prize (for 3rd String Quartet) 73.
Works include: Symphony, Double Concerto, Variations for Orchestra, Piano Concerto, Woodwind Quintet, Sonatas for piano and cello and for flute, oboe, cello, and harpsichord, two String Quartets, a duo for violin and piano, a brass quintet, the ballets *Pocahontas* and *The Minotaur*, a concerto for orchestra, choral and incidental music.
Mead Street, Waccabuc, N.Y. 10597, U.S.A.

Carter, Herbert Edmund, A.B., M.S., PH.D.; American professor of biochemistry and college administrator; b. 29 Sept. 1910, Mooresville, Ind.; s. of George B. Carter and Edna Pidgeon Carter; m. Elizabeth DeWees 1933; two d.; ed. DePauw Univ. and Univ. of Illinois.
Instructor in Biochemistry, Univ. of Ill., Urbana 32-35, Assoc. 35-37, Asst. Prof. of Biochem. 37-43, Assoc. Prof. 43-45, Prof. 45-, Head of Dept. of Chem. and Chem. Engineering 54-67, Acting Dean, Graduate Coll. 63-65, Vice-Chancellor for Academic Affairs 67-71; Co-ordinator Interdisciplinary Programmes, Univ. of Ariz. 71-; mem. Nat. Acad. of Sciences, Amer. Acad. of Arts and Sciences, Nat. Science Board 64, Chair. 70; Eli Lilly Award in Biochem. 43; Nichols Medal 65; Amer. Oil Chemists Soc. Award in Lipid Chem. 66; Kenneth A. Sencer Award 68, Alton E. Bailey Award 70.
Leisure interests: squash, golf.
Publs. Some 130 papers in various chemical and biochemical journals; Editor-in-Chief Vol. I of *Biochemical Preparations*.
University of Arizona, Tucson, Ariz.; Home: 2401 Cerrada de Promesa, Tucson, Ariz. 85718, U.S.A.

Carter, James Earl, Jr.; American politician and peanut farmer; b. 1 Oct. 1924, Plains, Georgia; s. of Earl and Lillian Carter; m. Rosalynn Smith; three s. one d.; ed. Georgia Tech. Coll. and U.S. Naval Acad.
U.S. Navy until 53; peanut farmer, warehouseman, Plains, Georgia; State Senator 62-66; Gov. of Georgia 70-74; Democrat.
1 Woodland Drive Plains, Ga. 31780, U.S.A.

Carter, Sir John, Kt., LL.B., Q.C.; Guyanese diplomatist; b. 27 Jan. 1919; ed. Queen's Coll., Georgetown, and London Univ.
Called to Bar, Middle Temple, London 42; Law practice British Guiana 45-66; mem. British Guiana Legislature 48-53, 61-64; Pro-Chancellor Univ. of Guyana 62-66; Perm. Rep. of Guyana to UN 66; Amb. to U.S.A. 66-70, to Yugoslavia 69-; High Commr. to U.K. 70-, concurrently Amb. to Fed Repub. of Germany, France, Netherlands and U.S.S.R. 70-.
Guyana High Commission, 3 Palace Court, Bayswater Road, London, W.2, England.

Carter, Lieut.-Gen. Marshall Sylvester, B.S., M.S.; American army officer and government official; b. 16 Sept. 1909, Fortress Monroe, Va.; s. of the late Brig.

Gen. Clifton Carroll Carter and Mai Coleman Carter; *m.* Préot Nichols 1934; one *s.* two *d.*; ed. U.S. Military Acad., Mass. Inst. of Technology, and Nat. War Coll. 2nd Lieut., U.S. Army 31; service with artillery, Honolulu, Panama; Staff Officer, Washington 42-45; China Theater 45-46; Special Asst. to Sec. of State 47-49; Minister, Amer. Embassy, London 49; Exec. to Sec. of Defense 50-52; Dep. Commdg. Gen., U.S. Army Alaska 52-55; Commdg. Gen. 5th Army Air Defence Region 55-56; Chief of Staff, North American Air Defense Command, Colorado Springs 57-59, Continental Air Defense Command 56-59; Chief of Staff, 8th Army, Korea 59-61; Commdg. Gen., Army Air Defense Center, Commdt. Army Air Defense School 61-62; Dep. Dir. Central Intelligence Agency 62-65; Dir. Nat. Security Agency 65-69; retd. from military service as Lieut.-Gen. 69; Pres. George C. Marshall Research Foundation 69-, Cheyenne Mountain Zoological Soc.; Distinguished Service Medal with two Oak Leaf Cluster, Legion of Merit with Oak Leaf Cluster, Bronze Star Medal, Distinguished Intelligence Medal, etc.
Leisure interests: hunting, fishing, ecology.
2685 Spring Grove Terrace, Colorado Springs, Colo. 80906, U.S.A.
Telephone: 303-576-8590.

Cartier-Bresson, Henri; French photographer; b. 22 Aug. 1908, Paris.
Studied painting in André Lhote's studio; took up photography 31; Asst. Dir. to Jean Renoir 36, 39; prisoner of war 40-43, escaped; founded Magnum-Photos with Capa, Chim, and Rodger 46; exhibitions Madrid, New York 33, New York Museum of Modern Art 46, The Louvre, Paris 54, (later tour in Germany, Switzerland, London, Milan, Tokyo, U.S.A.) 55, Phillips Collection, Washington 64, Tokyo 65, New York Museum of Modern Art 68, Victoria and Albert Museum, London 69; drawing exhibitions New York, Zurich 75; Overseas Press Club awards; D.Lit.h.c., Oxford Univ. 75.
Publs. *Images à la Sauvette* (U.S. edition *The Decisive Moment*), *The Europeans*, *From One China to the Other*, *The People of Moscow*, *Danses à Bali*, *The World of Henri Cartier-Bresson* 68, *L'Homme et la Machine* 68, *Vive la France* 70, *Cartier-Bresson's France* 71, *Faces of Asia* 72, *About Russia* 74.
c/o Magnum-Photos, 2 rue Christine, 75006, Paris, France; c/o Helen Wright, 135 East 74 Street, New York, N.Y., U.S.A.; c/o John Hillelson, 145 Fleet Street, London, England.

Cartwright, Rt. Hon. John Robert, P.C., C.C., M.C., Q.C., D.C.L., LL.D.; Canadian judge; b. 23 March 1895, Toronto; *s.* of James Strachan Cartwright, K.C., and Jane Elizabeth Young; *m.* 1st Jessie Carnegie Gibson 1915, one *d.*; *m.* 2nd Mrs. Mabel Ethelwyn Tremaine 1967; ed. Upper Canada Coll., Toronto, and Osgoode Hall, Toronto.
Served in First World War 14-19; awarded Military Cross 17; called to the Bar, Toronto 20; practised Toronto 20-49; K.C. 33; Judge Supreme Court of Canada 49-67, Chief Justice 67-70; Bencher of the Law Soc. of Upper Canada 46-; retd. 70; Order of Canada 70.
Apt. 707, 85 Range Road, Ottawa, K1N 8J6, Canada.
Telephone: 232-1990 (Home).

Cartwright, Dame Mary Lucy, D.B.E., M.A., D.PHIL., SC.D., F.R.S.; British mathematician; b. 17 Dec. 1900, Aynhoe, Northants.; *d.* of Rev. W. D. Cartwright and Lucy H. M. Cartwright, sister of William Frederick Cartwright, *q.v.*; ed. Godolphin School, Salisbury, and St. Hugh's Coll., Oxford.
Assistant Mistress, Alice Ottley School, Worcester 23-24, Wycombe Abbey School, Bucks. 24-27; Yarrow Research Fellow, Girton Coll. 30-34; Faculty Asst. Lecturer in Mathematics, Cambridge 33-35; Fellow and Lecturer, Girton Coll. 34-49; Mistress of Girton Coll. 49-

68, Life Fellow 68-, Univ. Lecturer in Mathematics Cambridge 36-59, Reader in the Theory of Functions 59-68, Emer. Reader 68-; Consultant on U.S. Navy Mathematical Research Projects at Stanford and Princeton Univs. 49; Fellow, Cambridge Philosophical Society; Vice-Pres. London Mathematical Society 36-38; Pres. Mathematical Association 51-52, London Mathematical Soc. 61-63; Visiting Prof. Brown Univ., Providence R.I. 68-69, Claremont Graduate School 69, Case Western Reserve Univ. 70, Poland 70, Univ. of Wales 71, Case Western Reserve Univ. 71, Cleveland Univ. 71; Commdr. of the Order of the Dannebrog; Sylvester Medal of Royal Soc.; De Morgan Medal of London Mathematical Soc.; Medal of Univ. of Jyväskylä, Finland; Hon. F.R.S. Edinburgh; Hon. LL.D. (Edinburgh Univ.), Hon. D.Sc. (Leeds Univ., Hull Univ., Univs. of Wales, Oxford and Brown).
38, Sherlock Close, Cambridge, CB3 0HP, England.
Telephone: 52574.

Cartwright, William Frederick, D.L., LL.D., M.I. MECH.E.; British engineer; b. 13 Nov. 1906, Aynhoe, Northants; *s.* of Rev. W. D. Cartwright and Lucy H. M. Cartwright, brother of M. L. Cartwright *q.v.*; *m.* Sally Chrystobel Ware 1937; two *s.* one *d.*; ed. Dragon School, Oxford, and Rugby.
Chief Mechanical Engineer's Dept., Great Western Railway 25-29; Guest, Keen and Nettlefolds Ltd., Dowlais 29-30; student, German and French steelworks 30-31; Asst. to Works Man. Guest, Keen, Baldwins Iron and Steel Co. Ltd., Port Talbot 31-35, Technical Asst. to Man. Dir. 35-40, Dir. and Chief Engineer, Guest, Keen, Baldwins Iron and Steel Co. Ltd. 40-43, Gen. Man. Margam and Port Talbot Works 43-47; Dir. Steel Co. of Wales 47-, Gen. Man. Steel Div. 47-62, Asst. Managing Dir. and Gen. Manager 54-62, Managing Dir. 62-67, Chair. Feb.-July 67; Man. Dir. S. Wales Group, British Steel Corpn. 67-70; Deputy Chair. British Steel Corpn. 70-73; Chair. S. Wales Regional Board; Dir. BSC (Int.) Ltd., Lloyds Bank; Bessemer Gold Medal, Iron and Steel Inst. 58.
Leisure interests: riding and yachting.
Castle-upon-Alun, St. Bride's Major, nr. Bridgend, Glamorgan, Wales.
Telephone: Southerndown 298.

Carvalho, José Candido de Melo, M.SC., PH.D.; Brazilian zoologist and entomologist; b. 11 June 1914, Carmo do Rio Claro, State of Minas Gerais; *s.* of João Candido de Melo Carvalho and Ana da Silva Vilela Carvalho; *m.* Milza Freire Carvalho 1939; one *d.*; ed. Escola Superior de Agricultura e Veterinária, Viçosa, Univ. of Nebraska, and Iowa Univ. of Science and Technology.
Professor of Biology and Zoology, Viçosa 42-46; Zoologist, Museu Nacional, Rio de Janeiro 46-, Dir. of Museu Nacional 55-61; Dir. Museu Goeldi, Belém 54-55; Vice-Pres. Nat. Research Council, Brazil 62-63; mem. Exec. Board Int. Union for Conservation of Nature 63-70; Pres. Asscn. for Tropical Biology 65-66; Prof. Nat. Coll. of Geology, Rio de Janeiro 60-; mem. Council, Univ. of Brazil 55-61, Nat. Council for Protection of Indians 55-58, Council for Nat. Culture 59-60; Pres. Perm. Cttee. Int. Congress on Entomology 52-, Latin American Congresses on Zoology 62-; mem. Brazilian Acad. of Sciences, Vice-Pres. 55-56; John Simon Guggenheim Fellow 54-55; British Council Fellow 51; Corresp. mem. Zoological Soc. of London; carried out twelve expeditions to Hyléa (Amazonas); Pres. Brazilian Foundation for Nature Conservation 66-69; Hon. mem. Mexican Inst. Nat. Research 67; Fellow Agra Zoological Soc. 64-; mem. Directorate of Nat. Indian Foundation 67-70; mem. Natural Resources Res. Comm. UNESCO 69-; Chief Assessor Pres. Brazilian Inst. Forestry Devt. 71-; Vice-Pres. Brazilian Soc. for Ecology 71-; Pres. Section Entomology, Int. Union of Biological Sciences 72-; mem. Council for Research and Post-Graduation, Fed.

Jniv. of Rio de Janeiro 73-; Consulting Editor *Biological Conservation* 68-; mem. Fed. Council of Culture 74-; Senior Scientific Fellow, N.S.F. 71-; Co-ditor *Amazoniana* 71-; mem. Brazilian Comm. on Man and the Biosphere 75; Co-ordinator on Tech. Comm. of Brazilian Foundation for Nature Con-ervation 75; Chair. Comm. on Zoology, Ecology, Botany, Brazilian Nat. Reserve Council 75; Prizes: Mello Leitão 51, Costa Lima of Brazilian Acad. of Sciences 66, Gold Medal World Wildlife Fund 73.
Leisure interests: field trips, miridae collection.
Publs. *Notas de Viagem ao Rio Negro* 52, *Notas de Viagem ao Javari-Itacoai-Jurua* 55, *Notas de Viagem ao Paru de Leste* 55, *Key to the Genera of Miridae of the World* 55, *Insects of Micronesia (Miridae)* 56, *Catalogue of the Miridae of the World* (5 vols.) 57-60, *The Miridae of Galapagos* 67, *Notas de viagem de um zoólogo à região das catingas e áreas limítrofes* 69, and numerous papers on zoology, entomology, etc.
Museu Nacional, Quinta da Boa Vista, Rio de Janeiro; Rua Campos Sales 143, Apt. 601, Rio de Janeiro, Brazil.
Telephone: 2287010 (Office); 2486794 (Home).

Carver, Field-Marshal Sir Richard Michael Power, G.C.B., C.B.E., D.S.O., M.C.; British army officer; b. 24 April 1915, Bletchingley, Surrey; s. of Harold Power Carver and Winifred A. G. née Wellesley; m. Edith Lowry-Corry 1947; two s. two d.; ed. Winchester Coll. and Royal Military Acad., Sandhurst.
With 7th Armoured Div. 42, 1st Royal Tank Regt. 43, 4th Armoured Brigade 44; Ministry of Supply 47; Allied Forces, Central Europe and SHAPE 51-54; Deputy Chief of Staff, East Africa Command 54-56; Dir. of Plans, War Office 58-59; Commdr. 6th Infantry Brigade 60-62; G.O.C. 3rd Div. (Maj.-Gen.) 62-64; Dir. Army Staff Duties 64-66; Commdr. Far East Land Forces (Lieut.-Gen.) 66-67; C.-in-C. Far East (Gen.) 67-69; G.O.C.-in-C. Southern Command 69-71; Chief of Gen. Staff 71-73; Chief of Defence Staff Oct. 73- Aug. 76.
Leisure interests: music, drama, art, history, writing, reading, gardening, bird-watching, tennis, sailing.
Publs. *Second to None* 50, *El Alamein* 62, *Tobruk* 64.
Shackleford Old Rectory, Eashing, Godalming, Surrey, England.
Telephone: Godalming 22483.

Cary, Frank T., M.B.A.; American business executive; b. Idaho; m.; four c.; ed. Univ. of Calif. (Los Angeles) and Stanford Univ.
Joined International Business Machine Corpn. 48; Asst. Dir. IBM Corporate Staff 61; Vice-Pres. Field Operations, Data Processing Div. 62, Vice-Pres. Management Controls, 64; Pres. Data Processing Div. 64-66; IBM Vice-Pres. and Group Exec. and Gen. Man. Data Processing Group 66; Senior Vice-Pres. 67; mem. Board of Dirs. IBM Corpn. 68, mem. Management Review Cttee. 69, Exec. Vice-Pres. and mem. Exec. Cttee. March 71; Pres. IBM Corpn. 71-74, Chair. of the Board and Chief Exec. 73-; Dir. J. P. Morgan & Co., Morgan Guaranty Trust Co., AMF Inc.; mem. Business Council, Board of Trustees, Amer. Museum of Natural History, the Conf. Board.
International Business Machines Corpn., Armonk, N.Y. 10504, U.S.A.
Telephone: 914-765-1900.

Cary, William Lucius, A.B., LL.B., LL.D., M.B.A.; American university professor, lawyer and government official; b. 27 Nov. 1910, Columbus, Ohio; s. of late William L. and Ellen K. Cary; m. Katherine L. Fenimore Cooper 1954; two d.; ed. Yale and Harvard Univs.
Admitted Ohio Bar 34, law practice 34-36; Securities & Exchange Comm. 38-40, Dept. of Justice 40-42, Office of Co-ordinator of Inter-American Affairs, Rio de Janeiro 42; Dir. Newark Telephone Co. 36-; Lecturer, Finance and Law, Harvard Graduate School of Business Admin. 46-47; Prof. Law Northwestern Univ. School

of Law 47-55, Columbia Univ. 55-61, Dwight Prof. of Law, Columbia Univ. 64-; Counsel, Patterson, Belknap and Webb, N.Y.; Chair. Securities and Exchange Comm. 61-64; Democrat.
Leisure interests: tennis, music.
Publs. *The Effect of Taxation on Corporate Mergers* 51, *Cases and Materials on Corporations* 59 and 69, *Politics and the Regulatory Agencies* 67, *The Law and the Lore of Endowment Funds* 69.
Columbia University School of Law, New York, N.Y. 10027, U.S.A.
Telephone: 280-2644.

Casa-Debeljevic, Lisa Della; Swiss singer; ed. Berne Conservatoire.
Début at Zürich Opera House 43; mem. Vienna State Opera Co. 47-, New York Metropolitan Opera Co. 53-; has appeared at Festivals at Salzburg 47, 48, 50, 53-58, Glyndebourne 51, Bayreuth, Edinburgh 52, Zürich, Lucerne, Munich 51-58; has also appeared in London, Berlin, Paris, Milan, San Francisco and in South America, etc.; apptd. Austrian State Kammersängerin.
Schloss Gottlieben, Thurgau, Switzerland.

Casardi, Alberico Aubrey; b. 3 Feb. 1903, Siena; s. of Ruggero Casardi and Margaret Haskard; m. Virginia Harris 1935.
Diplomatic Service 27-, New York, Lima, London, Berlin, Buenos Aires, UN; joined Ministry of Foreign Affairs in Brindisi-Salerno 43-44; Asst. to Sec.-Gen. 44-48, and mem. Italian Del. to peace negotiations, Council of Foreign Ministers, London 47, Peace Conf., Paris 47, Council of Foreign Ministers, New York 47; fmr. Dep. Sec.-Gen. of NATO, Paris; Ambassador to Belgium 63-65; Ambassador to Japan 65-68; Italian Comm.-Gen. to *Expo 70*, 68-70; special adviser to Banca Commerciale Italiana 70-.
Leisure interest: painting.
Villa il Frosino, via delle Fontanelle 22, San Domenico di Fiesole, Florence, Italy.
Telephone: (055) 59-111.

Casarès, Maria; French actress; b. 21 Nov. 1922, Spain; ed. Conservatoire nationale d'art dramatique.
Debut, Théâtre des Mathurins, Paris 42; mem. Comédie Française 52, Théâtre national populaire 55; appearances have included roles in *Six personnages en quête d'auteur, Le Triomphe de l'amour, Macbeth, La Ville, Phèdre, La Danse de mort*; film appearances include: *Les Enfants du Paradis, Les Dames du Bois de Boulogne, La Chartreuse de Parme, Orphée, Ombre et Lumière, Le Testament d'Orphée*; also appears on television; Officier des Arts et des Lettres.
8 rue Asseline, 75014 Paris, France.

Casariego, H.E. Cardinal Mario; Guatemalan ecclesiastic; b. 13 Feb. 1909, Figueras de Castropol, Spain.
Ordained 36; Titular Bishop of Pudenziana 58, of Perge 63; Archbishop of Guatemala 64-; cr. Cardinal 69.
Arzobispado, Apartado 723, Ciudad de Guatemala, Guatemala.

Case, Clifford Philip, A.B., LL.B., HON. LL.D.; American lawyer and politician; b. 16 April 1904, Franklin Park, N.J.; s. of Clifford P. and Jeannette (Benedict) Case; m. Ruth M. Smith 1928; one s. two d.; ed. Rutgers and Columbia Univs.
Associate Simpson Thacher and Bartlett, New York 28-39, mem. firm 39-53; mem. Rahway (N.J.) Common Council 38-42; mem. House of Assembly of N.J. 43 and 44; mem. 79th-83rd U.S. Congresses, resigned 53; Pres. and Dir. of the Fund for the Repub. 53-54; Republican Senator from N.J. 54-; mem. N.Y. Bar 28-; Liberty Magazine Award as outstanding mem. 82nd Congress; N.J. Society for Crippled Children and Adults (Board of Dirs.); mem. Advisory Board N.J. Chapter. Arthritis and Rheumatism Foundation, Rahway (N.J.) Red Cross (Trustee); mem. Council of Foreign Relations;

Hon. Trustee, Roper Public Opinion Research Center; mem. Advisory Council Woodrow Wilson School, Princeton Univ.; Dir. Columbia Univ. Law School Alumni Asscn.; mem. Bar Asscn., City of N.Y., N.Y. County, N.Y. State, and American Bar Asscns.; mem. American Judicature Soc.; mem. N.J. Historical Soc. (Hon. Trustee); Sponsor, Inst. for American Democracy; Hon. LL.D. from nine U.S. Colls. and Univs.

Leisure interests: music, reading, gardening, nature walks, travel.

315 Senate Office Building, Washington, D.C.; Home: 191 West Milton Avenue, Rahway, N.J., U.S.A.

Telephone: 202-224-3224 (Office).

Case, Everett Needham, B.A., M.A.; American educator and historian; b. 9 April 1901, Plainfield, N.J.; s. of James Herbert and Alice Needham Case; m. Josephine Young; three s. one d.; ed. Princeton Univ., Corpus Christi Coll., Cambridge, and Harvard Univ.

Assistant in History, Harvard Univ. 26-27; Asst. to Owen D. Young 27-33; Exec. Sec. Central Banking and Industrial Cttee., Washington D.C. 32-33; Asst. Dean, Harvard Graduate School of Business Admin. 39-42; Pres. Colgate Univ. 42-62, Emer. 62-; Consultant on Far Eastern Affairs to Sec. of State 49; Chair. American Council on Educ. 51-52; Pres. Alfred P. Sloan Foundation 62-68; Dir. Fed. Reserve Bank of New York 61-68, Chair. 66-68; Dir. Nat. Educational Television 54-61, 62- (Chair. 63-69); Trustee, Memorial Sloan-Kettering Cancer Center 63-68, Sloan-Kettering Inst. for Cancer Research 66-68, Millbrook School 44-69, (Chair. 60-68), Educational Broadcasting Corpn. 65-68; mem. Council on Foreign Relations, UNA-U.S.A. China Panel 66-68; Dir. Nat. Cttee. on U.S.-China Relations 66-; several hon. degrees.

Leisure interests: music, tennis.

Van Hornesville, Herkimer County, N.Y. 13475, U.S.A.

Telephone: 315-858-0036.

Casey, Baron (Life Peer) cr. 60, of Berwick (Victoria) and the City of Westminster; **Richard Gardiner Casey,** K.G., P.C., G.C.M.G., C.H., D.S.O., M.C., K.ST.J.; Australian politician and diplomatist; b. 29 Aug. 1890, Brisbane, Queensland; s. of R. G. Casey of Melbourne; m. Ethel Marian Sumner Ryan 1926; one s. one d.; ed. Melbourne and Cambridge Univs.

Political Liaison Officer between British and Australian Govts. in London 24-30; mem. Federal Parliament 31-40, 49-60; Asst. Treas. to Commonwealth Govt. 33-35; Treas. of the Commonwealth 35-39, and Min. of Development 37-39; Privy Councillor 39; Min. for Supply and Development 39-40; resgnd. from Parl. and Cabinet on appointment as first Minister to U.S.A. 40-42; British Minister of State Resident in Middle East 42-44; Gov. of Bengal 44-46; Federal Pres. Liberal Party of Australia 47-49; Minister of Supply 49; Minister in Charge of C.S.I.R.O. 49-60; Minister of Nat. Devt. 50; Minister for External Affairs 51-60; mem. Exec. C.S.I.R.O. 60-65; Gov.-Gen. Australia 65-69; Freeman, City of Melbourne 69.

Leisure interests: writing, flying.

Publs. *An Australian in India* 46, *Double or Quit* 49, *Friends and Neighbours* 54, *Australian Foreign Policy* 54, *Personal Experience 39-46* 62, *The Future of the Commonwealth* 63, *Australian Father and Son* 66, *Australian Foreign Minister—The Diaries of R. G. Casey 1951-60* 72.

Edrington, Berwick, Victoria 3806, Australia.

Casey, Albert V., M.B.A.; American airline executive; b. 28 Feb. 1920, Boston, Mass.; m. Eleanor Anne Welch; one s. one d.; ed. Harvard Univ. and Graduate School of Business Admin.

Assistant Vice-Pres. and Asst. Treas. Southern Pacific Co. 53-61; Vice-Pres. and Treas. REA Express 61-63;

Vice-Pres. Finance, Times Mirror Co. 63-64, Exec. Vice-Pres. and Dir. 64-66, Pres. and mem. Exec. Cttee. 66-74; Pres. and Chief Exec. Amer. Airlines Inc. Feb. 74-, Chair. April 74-; Dir. Pacific Amer. Income Shares Inc., Boys' Club of America; mem. Advisory Cttee. to Communications Policy Program of Rand Corpn. Board of Visitors of UCLA Graduate School of Management, Board of Councillors of Univ. of S. Calif. School of Business Admin., Board of Govs. of Performing Arts Council of Music Center of Los Angeles.

American Airlines, 633 Third Avenue, New York, N.Y. 10017, U.S.A.

Casey, William Joseph, B.S., LL.B.; American lawyer, author and government official; b. 13 March 1913, New York; s. of William J. and Blanche (La Vigne) Casey; m. Sophia Kurz 1941; one d.; ed. Fordham Univ. and St. John's Law School.

Chairman Board of Editors, Research Inst. of America 38-40, Inst. for Business Planning 54-70; partner, Hall, Casey, Dickler and Howley, N.Y. 57-71; mem. Gen. Advisory Cttee. on Arms Control and Disarmament 69-71; mem. Presidential Task Force on Int. Devt. 69-70; Pres. Chair. Long Island Asscn. of Commerce and Industry 68-71; Pres. Int. Rescue Cttee. 70-71; Chair. Securities and Exchange Comm. Washington, D.C. 71-72; Under-Sec. of State for Econ. Affairs 72-73; Pres. Export-Import Bank 73-; Trustee, Fordham Univ. 66-71; mem. Advisory Cttee. Notre Dame Law School; E.T.O. Bronze Star.

Leisure interests: sailing, skiing and reading.

Publs: *Tax Sheltered Investments* 52, *Lawyers Desk Book* 65, *Forms of Business Agreements* 66, *Accounting Desk Book* 67, and other works.

Home: Glenwood Road, Roslyn Harbour, Long Island, N.Y.; and 2501 Massachusetts Avenue, N.W., Washington, D.C. 20008, U.S.A.

Telephone: 202-755-1130 (Home).

Casimir, Hendrik Brugt Gerhard, PH.D.; Netherlands physicist; b. 15 July 1909, The Hague; s. of Rommert Casimir and Teunsina Dina Borgman; m. Josina Maria Jonker 1933; one s. four d.; ed. Univs. of Leyden, Copenhagen, and at Zürich.

Various research positions, Leyden 33-42; joined staff of Philips Research Laboratories, Eindhoven 42, Dir. of Laboratories 46, mem. Board of Management of Philips 57-72, supervising Philips research activities in various countries; Pres. European Physical Soc. 72-75; Pres. Royal Acad. of Netherlands 73; Foreign Hon. mem. American Acad. of Arts and Sciences; mem. Royal Flemish Acad. of Science, Letters and Arts; Corresp. mem. Heidelberg Acad. of Science, Austrian Acad. of Sciences, Vienna; Alfred Ewing Medal (London); Hon. D.Sc. Technical Univ. Copenhagen, Univ. of Louvain, Technical Univ. Aachen, Univ. of Edinburgh, Cranfield Inst. of Technology; Foreign mem. Royal Soc., London 70, Finnish Acad. of Technical Sciences, Helsinki, American Philosophical Soc., Philadelphia; Foreign Assoc. Nat. Acad. of Sciences, Washington; mem. Board of Trustees Rockefeller Univ., New York.

Publs. Many papers on theoretical physics, applied mathematics and low temperature physics.

Philips' Gloeilampen Fabrieken, Eindhoven; De Zegge 7, Heeze, Netherlands.

Telephone: 040-862233.

Caskey, John L., PH.D.; American classical archaeologist; b. 7 Dec. 1908, Boston, Mass.; s. of Lacey D. and Elsie (Stern) Caskey; m. Miriam Ervin 1967; ed. Yale Univ. and Univ. of Cincinnati.

Teaching fellow, acting instructor, and mem. of staff of Univ. of Cincinnati Excavations at Troy 32-38; Instructor, Asst. Prof. Univ. of Cincinnati 39-48; U.S. Army 42-46; Asst. Dir. American School of Classical Studies, Athens 48-49, Dir. 49-59, Vice-Chair. Man.

ttee. 65-75, Visiting Prof. 75-76; Prof. of Classical Archaeology, Univ. of Cincinnati 59-, and Head, Dept. f Classics, 59-72, Fellow of Graduate School; Field Dir. Excavations at Lerna 52-58, in Ceos 60-; mem. Inst. for Advanced Study 60, 65; mem. Archaeological Soc. of Athens 56-, German Archaeological Institute 56-; mem. American Philosophical Soc. 67-; Legion of Merit (U.S.A.); Commdr. Order of the Phoenix (Greece); Hon. Citizen of Athens.
Publs. *Troy* (co-editor and co-author) Vols. I-IV, *Preliminary Reports on Excavations at Lerna* 54-59, *The Early Helladic Period in the Argolid* 60, *Preliminary Reports on Excavations in Ceos* 60-75; contrib. to *Cambridge Ancient History* Vols. I, II, new edn. 64, 65.
Department of Classics, University of Cincinnati, Ohio 45221, U.S.A.
Telephone: Cincinnati 475-6097.

Caso y Andrade, Alfonso, PH.D.; Mexican archaeologist; b. 1 Feb. 1896, Mexico; *s.* of Antonio Caso and María Andrade; *m.* 1st María Lombardo 1922, 2nd Aida Lombardo 1966; two *s.* two *d.*; ed. Nat. Univ. of Mexico.
Professor Faculty of Letters 18-40, School of Law 19-29; Dir. Nat. Preparatory School 28; Head of Dept. of Archaeology Nat. Museum 30-33, Dir. Nat. Museum 33-34, Explorations, Monte Albán, Oax. 31-43; Dir. Gen. of Higher Education and Scientific Research Mar.-Aug. 44; Rector of Nat. Autonomous Univ. of Mexico Aug. 44-Mar. 45; Sec. of State in the Office of Nat. Estates and Admin. Inspection Dec. 46-; Dir. Nat. Inst. for Indian Affairs 49-; Hon. mem. New York Acad. of Sciences, American Acad. of Arts and Sciences, Deutsche Gesellschaft für Völkerkunde, Academia Mexicana de la Historia; corresp. Academician Nat. Acad. of Arts and Letters, Cuba, etc.; Officier de la Légion d'Honneur (France), Commdr. Order of North Star (Sweden), etc.; Hon. Ph.D. (Albuquerque, N. Mexico); Sciences and Arts Nat. Prize (Mexico 1960), Dr. h.c. Univ. of California; corresp. Fellow British Acad.
Publs. *El Teocali de la Guerra Sagrada* 27, *Las Estelas Zapotecas* 28, *Las exploraciones de Monte Albán, Oaxaca* 32-34, *Exploraciones en Mitla* 34, *Urnas de Oaxaca* 52, *The Aztecs: People of the Sun* 58, *Interpretación del Códice Bodley 2858* 60, *Interpretación del Códice Selden 3135 (A.2), Interpretación Códice Colombino, La Cerámica de Monte Albán, Los Calendarios Prehispánicos, El Tesoro de Monte Albán* 69.
Av. Central 234, Tlacopac, Villa Obregón, D.F., Zona 20, Mexico.

Cassavetes, John; American actor and film director; b. 9 Dec. 1929, New York; *m.* Gena Rowlands 1954; ed. Colgate Univ. and N.Y. Acad. of Dramatic Arts.
Assistant Man. Broadway play *Fifth Season*; television appearances include *Omnibus, Elgin Playhouse*; film appearances include *Taxi, Might Holds Terror, Crime in the Streets, Edge of the City, Fever, The Dirty Dozen, Rosemary's Baby, Husbands*; Dir. of *Shadows* 60, *Too Late Blues* 61, *A Child is Waiting* 62, *Faces* 68, *Husbands* 70, *Minnie and Moskowitz* 71, *A Woman Under the Influence* 74.
c/o Public Relations, United Artists, 729 Seventh Avenue, New York City, N.Y. 10017, U.S.A.

Cassels, Field Marshal Sir (Archibald) James (Halkett), G.C.B., K.B.E., D.S.O.; British army officer; b. 28 Feb. 1907, Quetta, then India; *s.* of late Gen. Sir Robert A. Cassels and the late Lady Florence E. Cassels; *m.* Joyce Kirk 1935; one *s.*; ed. Rugby School and Royal Military Coll., Sandhurst.
Commissioned 26; served Second World War, G.O.C. 51st Highland Div. 45, G.O.C. 6th Airborne 46; G.O.C. 1st British Commonwealth Div., Korea 51-52; Commr. 1st British Corps 53-54; Dir.-Gen. of Military Training, War Office 54-57; Dir. of Operations, Malaya 57-59; G.O.C.-in-C. Eastern Command 59; C.-in-C. British

Army of the Rhine and Commr. NATO Northern Army Group 60-63; Adjutant-General to the Forces 63-65; Chief of General Staff 65-68.
Leisure interests: shooting and fishing.
Pitearn, Alves, by Forres, Moray, Scotland.
Telephone: Alves 616.

Cassels, James Macdonald, M.A., PH.D., F.R.S.; British physicist; b. 9 Sept. 1924; *s.* of Alastair Macdonald Cassels and Ada White Scott; *m.* Jane Helen Thera Lawrence; one *s.* one *d.*; ed. Rochester House School, Edinburgh, St. Lawrence Coll., Ramsgate, and Cambridge Univ.
Harwell Fellow and Principal Scientific Officer, A.E.R.E., Harwell 49-53; Lecturer 53, Senior Lecturer, Univ. of Liverpool, Prof. of Experimental Physics, Univ. of Liverpool 56-59; Visiting Prof. Cornell Univ. 59-60; Lyon Jones Prof. of Physics, Univ. of Liverpool Oct. 60-; mem. Council Royal Soc. 68-69, Fellow; Rutherford Medal, Inst. of Physics 73.
Leisure interest: travelling hopefully, by air and otherwise.
Publs. *Basic Quantum Mechanics* 70, and articles in scientific journals on atomic, nuclear and elementary particle physics.
14 Dudlow Court, Dudlow Nook Road, Liverpool, L18 2EU, England.
Telephone: 051,722 2594.

Cassels, John William Scott, M.A., PH.D., F.R.S.; British mathematician; b. 11 July 1922, Durham City; *s.* of John William Cassels and Muriel Speakman Cassels, (née Lobjoit); *m.* Constance Mabel Senior 1949; one *s.* one *d.*; ed. Neville's Cross Council School, Durham, George Heriot's School, Edinburgh, and Edinburgh and Cambridge Univs.
Lecturer, Manchester Univ. 49-50, Cambridge Univ. 50-65; Reader in Arithmetic, Cambridge Univ. 65-67; Sadleirian Prof. of Pure Mathematics, Cambridge Univ. 67-; Fellow of Trinity Coll., Cambridge 49-.
Leisure interests: The Higher Arithmetic, gardening.
Publs. *An Introduction to Diophantine Approximations* 57, *An Introduction to the Geometry of Numbers* 59.
Department of Pure Mathematics and Mathematical Statistics, 16 Mill Lane, Cambridge CB2 1SB; Home: 3 Luard Close, Cambridge CB2 2PL, England.
Telephone: 65621 (Univ.); 41608 (Home).

Cassilly, Richard; American (tenor) opera singer; b. 14 Dec. 1927, Washington, D.C.; *s.* of Robert Rogers Cassily and Vera F. Swart; *m.* Helen Koliopulos 1951; four *s.* three *d.*; ed. Peabody Conservatory of Music, Baltimore, Md.
With New York City Opera 55-66, Chicago Lyric 59-, San Francisco Opera 66-; Deutsche Oper Berlin 65-, Hamburgische Staatsoper 66-, Covent Garden 68-, La Scala, Milan 70, Wiener Staatsoper 70, Staatsoper München 70, Paris Opera 72, Metropolitan Opera 73-; Kammersänger 73; television performances of *Otello, Peter Grimes, St. of Bleeker Street, Fidelio, Wozzeck* and *Die Meistersinger*; recordings for D.G., C.B.S., E.M.I.
Hamburgische Staatsoper, 2 Hamburg 36, Damtorstrasse, Federal Republic of Germany.

Cassirer, Henry R., B.A., PH.D.; American radio and television administrator; b. 2 Sept. 1911, Berlin; *s.* of Kurt and Eva (née Solmitz) Cassirer; divorced; one *d.*; ed. Odenwaldschule, Univs. of Frankfurt, Paris, Cologne, London School of Econs. and London Univ.
Announcer/translator, B.B.C. European Service 38-40; Foreign News Editor, Columbia Broadcasting System (C.B.S.), New York 40-44; Television News Editor, C.B.S. 44-49; freelance producer of TV documentary programmes 49-52; teacher of TV Production and Public Affairs Programming, New School for Social Research, New York Univ. School of Radio Techniques; with UNESCO 52-71, Dir. Use of Mass Media in Out-of-

School Educ.; Adviser on Educational Radio/TV to Govt. of India 57, Pakistan 60-, Israel 61-, Senegal 63-, Brazil 67-, Mali 68-, Algeria 69-, Singapore, United States (Alaska) 70, Morocco 74-, Ghana 75; Int. Consultant communication and educ. 71-; Visiting Prof. Ontario Inst. for Studies in Educ. 74.
Leisure interest: stereo photography.
Publs. *Television, a World Survey* 54, *Television Teaching Today* 60; films: *Man of our Age—The Sculpture of Jo Davidson* 48, *Buma-African Sculpture Speaks* 52, *Television Comes to the Land* 58, *Bildung und Kommunikation* 74.
Les Moulins, 74290 Menthon St. Bernard, France.
Telephone: (50) 44 88 53.

Cassola, Carlo; Italian writer; b. 17 March 1917. Strega Prize 60.
Publs. *La Visita* (short stories) 42, *Fausto e Anna* (novel) 52, *Il Taglio del Bosco* (short stories) 59, *La Ragazza di Bube* (novel) 60, *Un Cuore Arido* (novel) 61, *Il Cacciatore* (novel) 64, *Tempi Memorabili* (novel) 66, *Ferrovia Locale* (novel) 68, *Monte Mario, Giselle* 74.
Via Michelangelo 12, Grosseto, Italy.

Casson, Sir Hugh Maxwell, Kt., M.A., R.A., F.R.I.B.A., R.D.I., HON. DES. R.C.A.; British architect; b. 23 May 1910; ed. Eastbourne Coll., St. John.'s Coll., Cambridge, and Bartlett School of Architecture, Univ. Coll., London.
Private practice as architect 35-; Camouflage Officer in Air Ministry 40-44; Technical Officer Ministry of Town and Country Planning 44-46; Dir. of Architecture, Festival of Britain 51; mem. MARS Group 45-; Prof. of Environmental Design, Royal Coll. of Art 53-75; Pres. Royal Acad. of Arts 76-; mem. Royal Danish Acad. 54, Royal Fine Art Comm. 60.
Publs. *Bombed Churches as War Memorials* 44, *Houses: Permanence and Prefabrication* (with Anthony Chitty) 45, *Homes by the Million* 45, *An Introduction to Victorian Architecture* 48, *Inscape: the design of interiors* 68, *Nanny Says* (with Joyce Grenfell) 72.
35 Victoria Road, London, W8 5RH, England.
Telephone: 01-937 0842.

Cassou, Jean, L. ès L.; French writer; b. 9 July 1897; ed. Univ. de Paris à la Sorbonne.
Secretary, *Mercure de France* 20, later Editor at Ministry of Public Instruction; on personal staff of M. Jean Zay (Front Populaire) Minister of Nat. Educ. and Fine Arts 36; Asst. Keeper, Musée du Luxembourg 38; forced to retire and later imprisoned by Vichy régime 40, later fought in resistance and seriously wounded 44; Head Keeper, Musée Nat. d'Art Moderne 45-65; now Dir. of Studies, Ecole Pratique des Hautes Etudes; mem. Acad. Royale de langue et littérature françaises de Belgique; Compagnon de la Libération, Commdr. Légion d'Honneur, Croix de Guerre 39-45.
Publs. Novels include: *Les Harmonies Viennoises* 25, *Les Massacres de Paris* 36, *Le Voisinage des Cavernes* 71; Essays include: *Grandeur et Infamie de Tolstoi* 32, *Parti pris* 53; Poetry includes: *Trente-trois sonnets composés au secret* 44; Art criticism includes: *Picasso* 39, *Ingres* 47, *Situation de l'Art Moderne* 51, *La Création des Mondes* 71.
4 rue du Cardinal-Lemoine, Paris 5e, France.

Castaneda, Jorge; Mexican diplomatist; ed. Universidad Nacional Autónoma de México.
Joined Mexican Foreign Service 50; Legal Counsel, Ministry of Foreign Affairs 55-58, Dir. Gen. for Int. Orgs. 59-60; Alt. Rep. to UN 61-62; Amb. to Egypt 62-65; Principal Dir., Ministry of Foreign Affairs 65-; now Perm. Rep. to Int. Orgs. in Geneva; Prof. of Int. Public Law, Escuela Libre de Derecho 58; Prof. of Int. Public Law, Nat. Univ. of Mexico 59-60; mem. UN Int. Law Comm. 67-; del. to numerous int. confs. including many sessions of UN Gen. Assembly; Assoc.

mem. Inst. of Int. Law; mem. Int. Law Asscn., Hispano Luso-American Inst. of Int. Law.
Publs. *México y el Orden Internacional* 56, *Mexico an* *the United Nations* 58, *Valor Juridico de las Resolucione de las Naciones Unidas,* 67 (English version 69), *La N Proliferacion de las Armas Nucleares en el Orde Universal* 69, and articles in various legal journals.
Ministerio de Relaciones Exteriores, Mexico, D.F. Mexico.

Castañón de Mena, Juan, D.ARCH.; Spanish arm officer; ed. Escuela Técnica Superior de Arquitectura Madrid, and Acad. de Infantería and Escuela Superio de Guerra.
Captain, Gen. Staff 31; active service Corunna, 8th military div. and Gallegas Columns campaign 36, later C.-in-C. Gen. Staff 82nd Div. at Teruel, Alfambra Levante, Ebro, Cataluña and liberation of Madrid promoted Lt. Col.; Prof., Gen. Staff School; Brig.-Gen 59; Tactics Prof. Senior Army School 59; A.D.C. to Gen. Franco 51-75; Mil. Gov., Madrid 62; C.-in-C. 11th Mechanized Div. 64; Lt.-Gen. 65; Chief of Mil. House o Gen. Franco 65; Minister of the Army Oct.69-June 73 several decorations including Great Cross of Isabel la Católica, Great Cross of Carlos III, Commdr. Legion of Merit, U.S.A.
Lopez de Hoyez 15, Madrid 6; Home: Lagasca 77-6° Madrid 6, Spain.

Castberg, Frede, D.L.; Norwegian university professor; b. 4 July 1893, Vardal, Norway; s. of Johan Castberg (sometime Minister of Justice and Social Affairs) and Karen Anker; m. Ella Anker 1927; three d.; ed. Oslo Katedralskole and Oslo Univ.
Professor at Oslo Univ. 28-63; Rector 52-57; Legal Adviser to Ministry of Foreign Affairs; Pres. Curatorium of the Acad. of Int. Law, Hague; mem. of the Inst. of Int. Law; hon. mem. Finnish Asscn. Lawyers; mem. Institut de France and of several scientific socs.; hon. mem. of Finska Vetenskaps Societeten; LL.D. St. Olafs Coll., Colgate Univ., U.S.A.; Dr. h.c. Univs. of Uppsala, Paris and Helsinki.
Leisure interests: history, music, skiing.
Publs. *Norges Statsforfatning* 35, *Folkerett* 37, *Innledning til Forvaltningsretten* 38, *Problems of Legal Philosophy* 39, *Norge under Okkupasjonen* 45, *Fra Norsk og Fremmed Statsliv* 46, *Studier i Folkerett* 52, *Freedom of Speech in the West* 60, *Forelesninger over rettsfilosofi* 65, *La Philosophie du Droit* 70, *Minner om politikk og vitenskap fra drene 1900-1970* 71, *Den europeiske konvensjon om menneskerettighetene* 71 (English edn. 74), *Rett og revolusjon i Norge* 74.
Holmenkollveien 16, Smestad pr. Oslo, Norway.
Telephone: 144476.

Castillero Reyes, Ernesto de Jesus; Panamanian educationist and historian; b. 28 June 1889, Ocu, Herrera Province; s. of Mteo Castillero and Manuela Reyes de Castillero; m. Librada Pimentel de Castillero 1914; three s. three d.; ed. Nat. Inst. of Panama.
Primary School Teacher 13-17; Provincial Inspector of Public Instruction 17-22; Sec.-Gen. Inspectorate of Education 22-27; Sec. Nat. Inst. 27-33; Prof. of History Colegio de Artes y Oficios, Escuela Normal de Institutoras 36-40; Nat. Inst. 29-35; Insp.-Gen. of Education 36-40; Dir. Nat. Library of Panama 42-45; special Ambassador for Rep. of Honduras 57; Pres. Panama Acad. of History 58-61; Hon. Pres. Bolivarian Soc.; corresp. mem. Spanish and ten Latin American Acads. of History; mem. Ateneo Dominicano, U.S. Int. Acad. etc.; Dir. Panamanian Inst. of Hispanic Culture 53; Pres. Nat. Comm. on Historical Monuments 61-.
Publs. *Documentos históricos sobre la independencia del istmo de Panamá* 30, *La causa inmediata de la emancipación de Panamá, Historia de los orígenes, la formación y el rechazo por el Senado colombiano del Tratado Herrán Hay* 33, *Breve curso de Historia del Comercio* 35, *El*

Profeta de Panamá y su gran traición 36, *Panamá: Breve istoria de la República* 39, *Galería de Presidentes de Panamá* 36, 53, *Historia de la Comunicación Interceánica y de su influencia en el desarrollo de la entidad nacional panameña* 43, *La universidad interamericana: Historia de sus antecedentes y fundación* 43, *Historia de los Símbolos de la patria panameña* 47, *Leyendas e Historias de Panamá la Vieja* 50, *El General José Domingo Espinar* 51, *Historia de Panamá* 55, *Gonzalo Fernández de Oviedo* 57, *Episodios de la independencia de Panamá* 58, *Intimidades del Congreso de Panamá de 1826* 61, *La Isla que se transformó en Ciudad* 62, *El Canal de Panamá* 64, *Breve Historia de la Iglesia panameña* 65, *Lecciones de Historia Patria* 67, *Chiriquí: Ensayo de Monografía de la Provincia de Chiriquí* 68, *Historia de los Protocolos del Istmo de 1826* 70, *Ilmo.Sr.Dr. Rafael Lasso de la Vega, Diputado Istmeño a la Asemblea Constituyente de Cucuta en 1821* 71, *Historia de la Academia Panameña de la Historia* 71, *La Contribución de Panamá a la independencia del Perú* 74, *Panamá y Colombia: Historia de su reconciliación* 75.

Calle 31E, No. 4-23, P.O. Box 1563, Panama.
Telephone: 250668.

Castillo Morales, Carlos Manuel, PH.D., M.SC., D.ECON.; Costa Rican economist; b. 19 Dec. 1928; ed. Univ. de Costa Rica, and Univs. of Tennessee and Wisconsin. Head of Agricultural Section, UN Econ. Cttee. for Latin America (ECLA) 56-59, in Mexican Office of ECLA as Sec. of Central Isthmus Econ. Co-operation Cttee. 59-61, Asst. Dir. later Dir. of Office 61-63, 63-66; Sec.-Gen. Perm. Secretariat of Gen. Treaty for Central American Econ. Integration 66-70; Minister of Econs., Industry and Commerce 71-72; Vice-Pres., Minister of the Presidency May 74-.
Publs. *Análisis Exploratorio del Sistema de Tenencia de la Tierra en Costa Rica* 53, *La Reforma Agraria y sus Efectos sobre la Tasa de Acumulación de Capital en la Economía* 53, *El Régimen Agrario y el Funcionamiento de Mercado de los Factores* 55, *La Economía Agrícola en la Región del Bajío* 56, *Aspectos Políticos y Administrativos del Desarrollo Económico* 59, *Growth and Integration in Central America* 66.
c/o Office of the Vice-President, San José, Costa Rica.

Castillo-Valdes, Rafael Eduardo; Guatemalan civil engineer and diplomatist; b. 15 Jan. 1928, Cunen; s. of Manuel Trinidad Castillo and Carmen Imeldina Valdes; m. Janice Gordon 1958; four s. three d.; ed. Escuela Nacional de Comercio, Escuela Politécnica de Guatemala, Brigham Young Univ., Utah and Universidad de San Carlos de Guatemala.
Military service 48-53; civil engineer in charge of bridges and road construction for Govt. of Guatemala 57-59, in charge of construction of thermoelectric plants for private industry in Guatemala 59-61; designer for James Williamson and Partners, Scotland 61-62; with Instituto Nacional de Electrificación, Guatemala 63-66; mem. Nat. Congress of Guatemala 66-70, also Chair. Agricultural Cttee. and Dir. Org. of Partido Institucional Democratico (PID); Perm. Rep. of Guatemala to UN 70-74.
Leisure interests: reading (history, politics, geography, economics, engineering), languages (Spanish, English, French), music (piano), sports (golf, hiking).
c/o Ministerio de Relaciones Exteriores, Guatemala City, Guatemala.

Castillo Yurrita, Alberto del, DR.HIST.; Spanish university professor; b. 3 July 1899, Oñate (Guipúzcoa); s. of Gonzalo del Castillo and Jesusa de Yurrita; m. Marie Louise Jaquolot 1924; one s.; ed. Univs. of Barcelona, Paris, London, Berlin, Munich and Bologna.
Prof. Medieval History, Univ. of Barcelona 31-; Art Critic 39; Cultural Attaché, Spanish Embassy, Paris 44-45; Curator, Archaeological Museum, Barcelona

31-65; Dir. Spanish Inst. of Mediterranean Studies 42-; Dir. Romantic Provincial Museum 49; Vice-Editor *Diario de Barcelona* 53-; Vice-Pres. Spanish Asscn. of Art Critics 62; Spanish Delegate at European Council for Modern Art 67; Hon. Archaeological Inspector, Barcelona province.
Publs. include: *La Cultura del Vaso Campaniforme* 29, *Historia General* (3 vols.) 41, *Barcelona a través de los tiempos* 42, *De la Puerta del Angel a la Plaza de Lesseps* 43, *El Neolítico y el Eneolítico de la Península Ibérica* 43, *Cronología del Vaso Campaniforme en Europa* 44; *José María Sert: Su vida y su obra* 46, *Estética del Arte Paleolítico* 53, *La Maquinista Terrestre y Marítima, personaje histórico* 55, *La Barcelona de Menéndez y Pelayo (1871-1873)* 56, *Ramón Casas y su época* 58, *Lasar Segall* 58, (with M. Riu) *Historia del Transporte Colectivo en Barcelona (1872-1959)* 59, *Narciso Monturiol, inventor del Ictineo (1819-1885)* 63, *Historia de la Asociación de Ingenieros Industriales de Barcelona (1863-1963)* 63, *El manso medieval A de Vilosiu* 65, *Guía del Museo Romántico Provincial* 68, *Guía Abreviada del Museo Romántico Provincial* 68, *Excavaciones altomedievales en las provincias de Soria, Logroño y Burgos* 72.
Mallorca 305, Barcelona 9, Spain.

Castle, Rt. Hon. Barbara Anne, P.C., B.A., M.P., British politician; b, 6 Oct. 1911, Chesterfield; d. of F. Betts and Annie Rebecca Farraud; m. Edward Castle (now Lord Castle of Islington) 1944; ed. Bradford Girls' Grammar School, St. Hugh's Coll., Oxford Univ.
Admin. Officer, Ministry of Food 41-44; Corresp. for *Daily Mirror* 44-45; M.P. 45-; mem. St. Pancras Borough Council, London 37-45, Metropolitan Water Board 40-45, Nat. Exec. Cttee. of Labour Party 49-; Chair. of Labour Party 58-59; Minister of Overseas Development 64-65, Transport 65-68; First Sec. of State and Sec. of State for Employment and Productivity 68-70, for Social Services 74-76.
Leisure interests: walking, gardening, reading.
House of Commons, London, S.W.1, England.

Castle, William Bosworth, M.D., D.SC., M.S.; American physician and educator; b. 21 Oct. 1897, Cambridge, Mass.; s. of William Ernest and Clara (Sears) Bosworth Castle; m. Louise Müller 1933; one s. one d.; ed. Harvard.
Professor of Medicine, Harvard Univ. 37-57; George R. Minot Prof. of Medicine 57-63; Dir. Thorndike Laboratory, Boston City Hosp. 48-63, Hon. Dir. 63-68; Francis W. Peabody Faculty Prof. of Medicine, Harvard Univ. 63-68, Emeritus 68-; Distinguished Physician, U.S. Veterans Admin. 68-72; John Phillips Memorial Prize 32, Proctor Award, Philadelphia Coll. of Pharmacy and Science 35, Walter Reed Medal, American Soc. of Tropical Medicine 39, and Mead, Johnson and Co. Award 50, for discovery of gastric intrinsic factor and its relation to vitamin B12 deficiency in pernicious anaemia, etc.; Hon. D.Sc. (Harvard, Pa., Mount Sinai), Hon. LL.D. (Jefferson), Hon. S.M. (Yale), Hon. M.D. (Utrecht), Hon. S.D. (Chicago), Hon. L.H.D. (Boston Coll.), Hon. D.Sc. (Marquette), Kober Medal of the Asscn. of American Physicians 62, John M. Russell Award of the Markle Scholars 64; Oscar B. Hunter Memorial Award of the American Therapeutic Soc.; Joseph Goldberger Award for Clinical Nutrition.
Leisure interests: small boat sailing, home repairs.
22 Irving Street, Brookline, Mass. 02146, U.S.A.
Telephone: 617-566-2676.

Castries, René, Duc de; French historian and viticulturist; b. 6 Aug. 1908, La Bastide d'Engras; m. Mlle de Cassagne 1934; one s. two d.; ed. Collège Saint-Jean, Fribourg, Ecole Saint-Geneviève, Versailles and Ecole libre des Sciences politiques, Paris.
Mayor of Castries 41-51; Vice-Pres. Société des Gens de Lettres 64; Pres. Société d'Histoire diplomatique;

Chevalier des Arts et Lettres, Chevalier de Cincinnatus; numerous literary awards including Prix Balzac.
Publs. include: *Le testament de la Monarchie* (5 vols.) 58-70, *Mirabeau ou l'échec du destin* 60, *Maurice de Saxe* 63, *Henri IV, roi de coeur, roi de France* 70, *Histoire de France des origines à 1970, Figaro ou la vie de Beaumarchais* 72; articles in newspapers and journals, etc.
45 avenue Montaigne, 75008 Paris; Château de Castries, 34160, France.
Telephone: 225-77-41 (Paris); (67) 29-24-02 (Castries).

Castro, Federico de, D.LITT., D.PHIL., LL.D.; Spanish judge; b. 21 Oct. 1903, Seville; ed. Univs. of Seville, Madrid, Heidelberg and Berlin.
Assistant Prof. in Faculty of Law, Univ. of Seville 29, Prof. of Civil Law 33; Prof. of Civil Law, Univ. of La Laguna 30; Prof. of Civil Law, Univ. of Salamanca 31; Prof. of Private Int. Law, Univ. of Madrid 34, then Prof. of Civil Law; Adviser on Int. Legal Questions, Ministry of Foreign Affairs 57-68, Pres. Int. Law Section of Higher Council for Foreign Affairs at the Ministry 68; Editor *Anuario de Derecho Civil* and mem. Board of Editors *Revista Española de Derecho Internacional* 48-; Judge *ad hoc* Int. Court of Justice, The Hague (Barcelona Traction case) 59-61; Judge, European Court for Nuclear Energy 60; Pres. Int. Board of Arbitration of Int. Olive Oil Council 66; mem. Perm. Court of Arbitration 68; Judge, Int. Court of Justice 70-; mem. Higher Council for Scientific Research, Special Cttee. for drafting law on int. sale of goods, The Hague 51-57, Governing Council of Int. Inst. for Unification of Private Law 52-, and numerous other legal Cttees. and Insts.; Adviser to Spanish Del. to 22nd Session of UN Gen. Assembly; Leader of Del. to UN Conf. on the Law of Treaties, Vienna, and Vice-Pres. of Conf. 68-69.
International Court of Justice, Peace Palace, The Hague, Netherlands.

Castro, Raul H., A.B., LL.B.; American lawyer and state governor; b. 12 June 1916, Cananea, Sonora, Mexico; s. of Francisco D. Castro and Rosario Acosta de Castro; m. 1951; two d.; ed. Arizona State Coll., Flagstaff, and Univ. of Arizona, Tucson.
Former owner and operator Castro Pony Farm, Tucson, Arizona; in U.S. Foreign Service in Mexico 41-46; Spanish Instructor, Univ. of Arizona 46-49; Senior Partner law firm Castro and Wolfe 49-52; Deputy District Attorney, Pima County, Arizona 52-54, District Attorney 54-58; Judge of Superior Court, Arizona 59-61, Presiding Judge, Juvenile Court 63-64; Amb. to El Salvador 64-68, to Bolivia 68-70; private law practice, Tucson 69-75; Gov. of Arizona Jan. 75-; Hon. S.J.D., N. Arizona Univ.
Leisure interests: horseback-riding, hiking, reading.
State Capitol, Tucson, Ariz., U.S.A.

Castro Jijón, Rear-Admiral Ramón; Ecuadorean naval officer and politician; b. 1915.
Studied naval engineering in United States; fmr. Naval Attaché, London; C. in C. of Navy, Ecuador; Pres. Military Junta July 63-66; in exile 66-.
Rio de Janeiro, Brazil.

Castro Real, Juan Manuel; Spanish lawyer and diplomatist; b. 9 Feb. 1915, La Coruña, Cee; ed. Univs. of Madrid and Montreal.
Assistant Prof. of Public Int. Law, Univ. of Madrid 35, now Prof.; Prof. of Int. Law, Univs. of Valladolid and Salamanca; Sec. Int. Legal Affairs Office, Ministry of Foreign Affairs 46; Sec. Consulate-Gen., Montreal 48; Sec. for Cultural Affairs, Bonn 50; mem. Int. Legal Affairs Office 53; Asst. Dir. of UN Affairs 56, Dir. 58, 61; served in The Hague 60, Minister Plenipotentiary 62; Amb. to Denmark 71-; del. to various int. confs. and UN Gen. Assembly.

Publs. *La Represalias* 39, *La personalité international du Canada* 50, and various articles.
Spanish Embassy, Upsalagade 26, Copenhagen, Denmark.

Castro Ruz, Fidel, D.IUR.; Cuban politician; b. 13 Aug. 1927; ed. Jesuit schools at Santiago and Havana Havana Univ.
Law practice in Havana; began active opposition to Batista régime by attack on Moncada barracks at Santiago 26th July 53; sentenced to 15 years imprisonment 53; amnestied 56; went into exile in Mexico and began to organize armed rebellion; landed in Oriente Province with small force 2nd Dec. 56; carried on armed struggle against Batista régime until flight of Batista Jan. 59; Prime Minister of Cuba Feb. 59-; Chair. Agrarian Reform Inst. 65-; First Sec. Partido Unido de la Revolución Socialista (P.U.R.S.) 63-65, Partido Comunista 65-; Lenin Peace Prize 61; Hero of the Soviet Union 63; Order of Lenin 72.
Publs. *Ten Years of Revolution* 64, *History Will Absolve Me* 68.
Palacio del Gobierno, Havana, Cuba.

Castro Ruz, Maj. Raúl; Cuban politician; ed. Jesuit schools.
Younger brother of Fidel Castro (*q.v.*); sentenced with him to fifteen years imprisonment for insurrection 53; amnestied 54; assisted his brother's movement in Mexico, and in Cuba after Dec. 56; Chief of the Armed Forces Feb. 59; Deputy Prime Minister 60-72; Minister of the Armed Forces 60-; First Deputy Prime Minister Nov. 72-.
Office of the First Deputy Prime Minister, Havana, Cuba.

Catalano di Melilli, Felice; Italian diplomatist; b. 24 Jan. 1914; s. of Antonio and Verga Caterina Catalano di Melilli; m. Rosana Muscatello; two s.; ed. Univ. degli Studi, Florence.
Joined Diplomatic Service 38; Vice-Consul, Jerusalem 39, Leipzig 41-43; Sec., Washington 45-52; at Ministry of Foreign Affairs 52-55, 58-59, 61-65; Counsellor, Athens 55-58; Minister, Bonn 59-61; Acting Sec.-Gen. Ministry of Foreign Affairs 65-66; Amb. to the United Arab Repub. 66-69; Diplomatic Adviser to Prime Minister 69-70; Perm. Rep. to N. Atlantic Council 70-; numerous honours including Gran Croce Ordine al Merito della Repubblica Italiana, Grosses Deutsches Verdienstkreuz.
North Atlantic Council, NATO, Brussels 1110, Belgium.

Catargi, Henri; Romanian painter; b. 6 Dec. 1894, Bucharest; s. of Henri and Caterina Catargi; m. Aure Catargi 1970; ed. Académie Julian, Paris and Académie Ranson.
Chairman of the Plastic Fund 57-59; One-man exhbns. in Romania, Paris, Brussels, Dresden, Moscow, Tokyo; represented in Venice Biennale 58; Merited Master of Arts 62, State prizewinner 62, People's Artist 64.
Leisure interest: painting.
Major works include: *Landscape in Pasárea, The Brăila Shipbuilding Yards, Vase with Flowers, Gathering Apples, Relaxation, Landscape in Ciurel*.
Str. Drubeta 19, Bucharest 2, Romania.

Catcheside, David Guthrie, M.SC., M.A., F.R.S., F.A.A.; British professor of genetics; b. 31 May 1907, Bristol; s. of David Guthrie and Florence S. Catcheside; m. Kathleen M. Whiteman 1931; one s. one d.; ed. Strand School and King's Coll., Univ. of London.
Assistant to Prof. of Botany, Glasgow Univ. 28-30; Asst. Lecturer King's Coll., London 31-33, Lecturer 33-37; Rockefeller Int. Fellow, Calif. Inst. of Technology 36-37; Lecturer in Botany, Cambridge Univ. 37-50, Reader in Cytogenics 50-51; Fellow and Lecturer, Trinity Coll., Cambridge 44-51; Prof. of Genetics,

Adelaide Univ. 52-55; Prof. of Microbiology, Birmingham Univ. 56-64; Research Assoc. Carnegie Inst. of Washington 58; Visiting Prof. Calif. Inst. of Technology 61; Prof. of Genetics, John Curtin School of Medical Research, Australian Nat. Univ. 64-67; Dir. and Prof. of Genetics, Research School of Biological Sciences, ANU 67-73, Visiting Fellow 73-; Foreign Assoc. U.S. Nat. Acad. of Sciences 74.
Leisure interests: natural history, walking.
Publ. *The Genetics of Microrganisms* 51.
32 Moss Street, Cook, A.C.T., Australia.
Telephone: 512758.

Cater, Douglass; American writer, editor and government official; b. 24 Aug. 1923, Montgomery, Alabama; s. of Silas D. Cater, Sr. and Nancy Chesnutt Cater; m. Libby Anderson 1950; two s. two d.; ed. Harvard Univ.
Washington Editor *The Reporter* (magazine) 50-63, Nat. Affairs Editor 63-64; Special Asst. to Pres. of United States 64-68; writer and consultant 68-; Dir. Aspen Inst. Programme on Communications and Society 70-; Visiting Prof. Stanford Univ.; Special Asst. to Sec. of Army 51; Consultant to Dir. of Mutual Security Agency 52.
Publs. *Ethics in a Business Society* (with Marquis Childs) 53, *The Fourth Branch of Government* 59, *Power in Washington* 63, *Dana: The Irrelevant Man* 70.
928 Mears Court, Stanford, Calif. 94305, U.S.A.

Catherwood, Sir (Henry) Frederick Ross, Kt.; British industrialist and public official; b. 30 Jan. 1925, Co. Londonderry, N. Ireland; s. of Stuart and Jean Catherwood; m. Elizabeth Lloyd-Jones 1954; two s. one d.; ed. Shrewsbury and Clare Coll., Cambridge.
Chartered Accountant 51; Sec. Laws Stores Ltd., Gateshead 52-54; Sec. and Controller, Richard Costain Ltd. 54-55, Chief Exec. 55-60; Asst. Man. Dir. British Aluminium Co. Ltd. 60-62, Man. Dir. 62-64; Chief Industrial Adviser, Dept. of Econ. Affairs 64-66; mem. Nat. Econ. Devt. Council (N.E.D.C.) 64-71, Dir. Gen. 66-71; mem. British Nat. Export Council 65-70; Vice-Chair. British Inst. of Management 72-74, Chair. 74-76; Chair. British Overseas Trade Board, Dir. John Laing & Son, Group Man. Dir. and Chief Exec. 72-74; 75-; Chair. William Mallinson & Denny Mott Dec. 75-, Goodyear Tyre and Rubber Co. (GB) Ltd. 75-.
Publs. *The Christian in Industrial Society* 64, *Britain with the Brakes Off* 66, *The Christian Citizen* 69, *A Better Way* 75.
25 Woodville Gardens, London, W.5, England.
Telephone: 01-997 4117.

Catledge, Turner, B.S.; American newspaperman; b. 17 March 1901, Ackerman, Miss.; s. of Lee Johnson Catledge and Willie Anna (Turner) Catledge; m. 2nd Abby Ray Izard 1958; two d. (from 1st marriage); ed. Mississippi State Coll.
Employed *Neshoba* (Miss.) *Democrat* 21; Res. Editor *Tunica* (Miss.) *Times* 22-23; Man. Editor *Tupelo* (Miss.) *Journal* 23; reporter *Memphis* (Tenn.) *Commercial Appeal* 23-27, *Baltimore* (Md.) *Sun* 27-29; City Staff *New York Times* 29, corresp. Washington Bureau 30-36, Chief Washington News Corresp. 36-41; Chief Corresp. *New York Times* 43-44, Exec. Man. Editor 50-51, Managing Editor 51-64, Exec. Editor 64-68, Vice-Pres. 68-70, Dir. 68-73; Hon. D.Litt. (Washington and Lee Univ.), L.H.D. (South-Western Univ.); Hon. D.Iur. (Kentucky Univ.) 57, Hon. LL.D. (Tulane Univ.).
Publs. *The 168 Days* (with Joseph W. Alsop, Jnr.) 37, *My Life and the Times* 71.
229 West 43rd Street, New York, N.Y.; Home: 2316 Prytania Street, New Orleans, La., U.S.A.

Catlin, Sir George Edward Gordon, Kt., M.A., PH.D., F.R.S.L., F.R.S.A.; British university professor, philosopher and political scientist; b. 29 July 1896, Liverpool; s. of Rev. George E. Catlin and Edith Kate (née Orton);

m. 1st Vera Brittain 1925 (died 1970), 2nd Linda Gates (née Tassi) 1970; one s. one d. (q.v. Rt. Hon. Shirley Williams, M.P.); ed. New Coll., Oxford.
Professor of Politics, Cornell Univ. 24-35; candidate for Parl. 31 and 35; mem. of exec. of Fabian Society 35-37; mem. Int. Exec. Cttee., Int. Cttee. of Christian Socialist and Democratic Parties (Nouvelles Equipes Internationales) 48; Bronfman Prof. of Political Science and Chair. of Dept. of Econ. and Political Science, McGill Univ. 56-60; a pioneer of the idea of the Atlantic Community and draftsman of the Int. Declaration in support of Indian independence; Vice-Pres. World Acad. of Arts and Sciences; Vice-Pres. Anglo-German Asscn.; Provost, Mar Ivanios Coll., Travancore 53-54; Tagore Centenary Lecturer (Royal Soc. Arts and Royal Soc. Literature) 61; Goethe Centenary Lecturer, Heidelberg Univ.; Lecturer, Bologna, Yale and Peking Univs., etc.; Miembro de Honor, Instituto de Estudios Politicos, Spain 62; Grosses Verdienstkreuz, German Fed. Repub. 64; Médaille de Vermeil, Société à l'Encouragement au Progrès (France) 68; Vice-Pres. War on Want; Sponsor Martin Luther King Foundation; Winston Churchill Memorial Lecture "Atlanticism", Fulton, Mo., 69; Kierkegaard Lecture, Copenhagen; mem. Foreign Office Liaison Cttee., U.S.A. Bicentenary.
Publs. *Thomas Hobbes* 21, *The Science and Method of Politics* 26, 64, *Study of the Principles of Politics* 29, *Liquor Control* 31, *Preface to Action* 34, 67, *New Trends in Socialism* (editor) 35, *Studies in War and Democracy* (editor) 37, *Durkheim's Rules of Sociological Method* (editor) 37, *The Anglo-Saxon Tradition* 39, *Story of the Political Philosophers* 39, *One Anglo-American Nation*, *The Foundation of Anglo-Saxony* 41, *Anglo-American Union as Nucleus of World Federation* 42, *The Unity of Europe* 44, *Above All Nations* (in collaboration) 45, *In the Path of Mahatma Gandhi* 48, *Political Goals* 57, *The Atlantic Community* 59, *Systematic Politics* 62, *Political and Sociological Theory and its Applications* 64, *The Grandeur of England and the Atlantic Community* 64, *The Atlantic Commonwealth* 69, *For God's Sake, Go* (autobiography) 72, *Kissinger's Atlantic Charter* 74.

Caton-Thompson, Gertrude, F.B.A.; British archaeologist; b. 1888; ed. Miss Hawtrey's, Eastbourne, Paris and Newnham Coll. Cambridge (research).
Employed Ministry of Shipping 15-19; Paris Peace Conf. 19; Student British School of Archaeology in Egypt 21-26; excavated at Abydos and Oxyrhynchos 21-22, Malta 21, 24, Qau and Badari 23-25, Northern Faiyum 24-26, 27-28, Zimbabwe and other Rhodesian sites 28-29, Kharga Oasis 30-33, Hadhramaut (Southern Arabia) 37-38; Pres. Prehistoric Society 39-46; fmr. Vice-Pres. Royal Anthropological Inst., fmr. Gov. Bedford Coll., Univ. of London, and School of Oriental and African Studies; mem. Governing Council, British School of East Africa; Fellow Newnham Coll., Cambridge 34-51; Cuthbert Peake Award, Royal Geographical Soc. 32; Rivers Medal, Royal Anthropological Inst. 34, Huxley Medal 46, Burton Medal, Royal Asiatic Soc. 54; Hon. Litt.D. (Cambridge).
Publs. *The Badarian Civilisation* (with Guy Brunton) 28, *The Zimbabwe Culture* 31 (re-issued 69), *The Desert Fayum* 35, *The Tombs and Moon Temple of Hureidha* 44, *Kharga Oasis in Prehistory* 52.
Court Farm, Broadway, Worcs., England.

Catto, 2nd Baron, of Cairncatto; **Stephen Gordon Catto;** British company director; b. 14 Jan. 1923; s. of 1st Baron Catto and Gladys Forbes Gordon; m. 1st Josephine Innes Packer 1948, 2nd Margaret Forrest 1966; three s. three d.; ed. Eton Coll. and Cambridge Univ.
Air Force service 43-47; Chair. Morgan Grenfell & Co. Ltd., Australian Mutual Provident Soc. (U.K. Branch), Yule Catto & Co. Ltd., European Property Investment

Co. N.V.; Dir. Australian United Corpn. Ltd., The General Electric Co. Ltd., Hongkong & Shanghai Banking Corpn. Ltd. (London Cttee.) and other companies; mem. Advisory Council, Export Credits Guarantee Dept. 59-65; part-time mem. London Transport Board 62-68.
Leisure interests: gardening, music.
Morgan Grenfell and Co. Ltd., 23 Great Winchester Street, London, E.C.2, England.
Telephone: 01-588 4545.

Catton, Bruce; American writer and civil servant; b. 9 Oct. 1899, Petoskey, Mich.; s. of George R. and Adella M. Catton; m. Hazel Cherry 1924; one s.; ed. Oberlin Coll., Ohio.
Reporter, editorial writer and Washington correspondent 20-40; Dir. of Information, War Production Board 40-45; Dir. of Information, U.S. Dept. of Commerce, and Asst. Dir. of Information, U.S. Dept. of Interior; Senior Editor *American Heritage Magazine* 56-75; Nat. Book Award, non-fiction 53; Pulitzer Prize for History 54.
Leisure interests: general reading, study of American history, work with ship models.
Publs. *The War Lords of Washington* 48, *Mr. Lincoln's Army* 50, *Glory Road* 51, *A Stillness at Appomattox* 53, *U.S. Grant and the American Military Tradition* 54, *Banner at Shenandoah* 55, *This Hallowed Ground* 56, *America Goes to War* 58, *Grant Moves South* 60, *The Coming Fury* 61, *Terrible Swift Sword* 63, *Never Call Retreat* 65, *Grant Takes Command* 69, *Prefaces to History* 70, *Waiting for the Morning Train: a Michigan Boyhood* 72, *Gettysburg: The Final Fury* 74.
American Heritage, 1221 Avenue of the Americas, New York, N.Y 10020, U.S.A.

Cau, Jean, LIC. PHIL.; French writer and journalist; b. 8 July 1925; ed. Lycée Carcassonne, Lycée Louis-le-Grand, and Univ. of Paris.
Former Sec. to Jean-Paul Sartre; Ed. *Les Temps Modernes* 49-54; travelled extensively in U.S.A., Brazil, Greece, Italy, Spain, North Africa; journalist on *L'Express, le Figaro littéraire, Candide, France-Observateur* etc., Paris; Prix Goncourt 61.
Publs. novels: *Le coup de barre, Les Paroissiens, La Pitié de Dieu;* stories: *Mon village;* chronicle: *Les oreilles et la queue, L'Incendie de Rome* 64; plays: *Les Parachutistes, Le Maître du Monde, Dans un Nuage de Poussière* 67, *Les Yeux Crevés* 68; translation of *Who's Afraid of Virginia Woolf, Numance; Lettre ouverte aux têtes de chiens de l'Occident* 67, *L'Agonie de la Vieille* 69, *Tropicanas* 70, *Le Temps des esclaves, Les Entrailles du taureau* 71, *Pauvre France* (theatre) 72, *Traité de morale* I: *les Ecuries de l'occident* 73, II: *la Grande Prostituée* 74, *Toros* 73; scripts of films *La Curée* 66, *Don Juan 1973* 73.
13 rue de Seine, Paris 6e, France.

Causse, Jean-Pierre; French scientist; b. 4 Oct. 1926, Montpellier; m. Françoise Villard; three d.; ed. Lycée de Montpellier and Ecole Normale Supérieure.
Observatoire de Paris 52-55; Physicist, Schlumberger Ltd. 55-62; Dir. of Satellites Div., Centre Nat. d'Etudes Spatiales 62-66, Dir. of Programmes FR-1 and D-1 Dir. Brétigny Space Centre 66-69; Deputy Sec.-Gen., European Launcher Devt. Org. 69-73; Head Spacelab Programme, European Space Research Org. 73-74; Scientific Dir. Cie. de Saint-Gobain-Pont-à-Mousson 74-; Chevalier Légion d'Honneur; Prix Galabert 66.
54 Avenue Hoche, 75 Paris, France.
Telephone: 924 49 29.

Cauwenberg, Willy Van, DR. ECON.; Belgian diplomatist; b. 18 July 1914; m. Nini Wenger 1940; ed. Rijksuniversiteit te Gent.
Joined Diplomatic Service 38; Vice-Consul New York 45, Consul, New York 46-52; Consul-Gen. Kansas City

52-54, San Francisco 54-58; Econ. Minister, Washington 58-63; Amb. to Australia 63-66, to Netherlands 66-74, to U.S.A. 74-; Grand Officer Order of the Crown (Belgium), Grand Officer Order of Merit (Luxembourg), Commdr. Order of Leopold (Belgium), Grand Officer Order of Leopold II (Belgium), Order of Orange-Nassau, Grand Cross (Netherlands).
Royal Belgian Embassy, 3330 Garfield Street, N.W., Washington, D.C. 20008, U.S.A.
Telephone: (202) 333-6900.

Cavalcânti, José Costa; Brazilian army officer and politician; b. 6 Jan. 1918, Fortaleza, Ceará; m. Haideia Correia Cavalcânti; four s.; ed. Colégio dos Irmaõs Maristas and Escola Militar do Realengo.
Second Lieut. 38, rose to Col. 64; Instructor at Gen. Staff Coll. after Second World War; U.S. Infantry Training 52; Brazilian Mil. Attaché in U.S.A. 55-57; Sec. of Mixed Comm. on Brazilian-U.S. Defence 58; Sec. for Security, Pernambuco 59; mem. Fed. Chamber of Deputies 62-, Pres. Comm. on Nat. Security; Minister of Mines and Power 67-68; Minister of Interior and of Regional Orgs. 68-74.
Federal Chamber of Deputies, Brasília, Brazil.

Cavalierato, Phedon Annino; Greek diplomatist; b. 1912; ed. Univ. of Athens.
Foreign Service Egypt, Ankara, and Moscow 36-; Econ. Affairs Dept., Foreign Ministry, Athens 48; Greek Embassy, Washington 50; Head of Private Office of Ministry of Foreign Affairs 58; Dir. of Political Affairs for Western Europe at Foreign Ministry 59; Amb. to Australia and New Zealand 61; Dir.-Gen. Ministry of Foreign Affairs, Athens 63; Dir. of Econ. Affairs 64; Amb. to Bulgaria 64-66; Dir. of Political Affairs for Eastern Europe, Ministry of Foreign Affairs 66; Under-Sec. of State, Ministry of Foreign Affairs 67, later Greek Perm. Rep. to NATO 67; Grand Commdr. Order of Phoenix, Greece; Commdr. Order of George the First; numerous foreign decorations.
c/o Ministry of Foreign Affairs, Athens, Greece.

Cavalletti di Oliveto Sabino, Francesco; Italian diplomatist; b. 18 March 1907, Rome; s. of Giorgio Cavalletti di Oliveto Sabino and Giulia Pediconi; m. Maria Giulia Alvera 1942; two c.; ed. studied law.
Entered diplomatic service 32; Amb. to Luxembourg 53-56, to Yugoslavia 58-60; Head, Italian Del., Disarmament Conf. 60-67; Amb. to Spain 67; Head, Italian Del. to OECD; mem. Del. to UN Gen. Assembly 56, 57, 60-67. Publs. Contributions to many political reviews.
34 Via degli Orsini, Rome, Italy.
Telephone: 654-38-27.

Cavanagh, James Luke; Australian politician; b. 21 June 1913, S. Australia; s. of James Luke and Isobel Cavanagh; m. Elfreda Barbara Lamm 1941; two s. one d.; ed. Primary School.
Trades Union Sec. 46-62; Senator 62-; Minister of Works 72-73, of Aboriginal Affairs Oct. 73-June 75, of Policy and Customs June-Nov. 75.
Leisure interest: reading.
Parliament House, Canberra, A.C.T.; Home: 17 Hennessy Terrace, Rosewater, S. Australia 5013, Australia.
Telephone: 47-22-41 (Home).

Cavanaugh, Robert W., B.C.S.; American international banker; b. 27 Jan. 1914, Oil City, Pa.; s. of D. J. and Clara Straub Cavanaugh; m. Ruth Virginia Paul 1943; one s.; ed. Univ. of Notre Dame.
With Fed. Deposit Corpn. 36; U.S. Office of Alien Property Custodian 42; U.S. Foreign Economic Admin. 44; State Dept. 46; Treasury Dept. 47; Treas., Int. Bank, Int. Devt. Asscn. and Int. Finance Corpn. 47; Chair. and Chief Exec. Officer, Chase Manhattan Trust Corpn. Ltd. 69-; Officer, Order of Leopold II.
Chase Manhattan Trust Corpn. Ltd., P.O.B. 1543, Nassau, Bahamas.

Cavendish-Bentinck, Victor Frederick William, C.M.G.;
British company director; b. 18 June 1897, London;
s. of F. W. Cavendish Bentinck and Ruth Mary St.
Maur; m. Kathleen E. Barry 1948; one s. one d.; ed.
Wellington Coll., Berkshire.
Attaché, British Legation, Oslo 15; Army service 18;
Diplomatic service 19-47; served in Paris, The Hague,
Athens and Santiago, Asst. Under-Sec. of State 44,
Amb. to Poland 45-47; Chair. Bayer U.K. Ltd.; Pres.
British Nuclear Forum; Dir. NUKEM Nuklear-
Chemie und Metallurgie G.m.b.H. (Germany), S.A.
Métallurgie et Mécanique Nucléaires (Belgium), Franco-
Belge de Fabrications de Combustibles; Grosses
Verdienstkreuz.
21 Carlyle Square, Chelsea, London, S.W.3, England.
Telephone: 01-352 1258.

Cavert, Rev. Samuel McCrea, D.D., LL.D.; American
ecclesiastic; b. 9 Sept. 1888, Charlton, N.Y.; s. of
Walter I. Cavert and Elizabeth Brann; m. 1st Ruth
Miller 1918 (deceased); 2nd Twila Lytton 1927; one d.;
ed. Union Coll., Columbia Univ. and Union Theological
Seminary.
Ordained Presbyterian ministry 15; Fellow of Union
Theological Seminary 15-17; Chaplain U.S. Army 18-19;
Assoc. Sec. Federal Council of Churches of Christ in
America 20, Gen. Sec. 21-50; Gen. Sec. Nat. Council of
the Churches of Christ in the U.S.A. 51-54; American
Sec., World Council of Churches 54-57; Protestant
liaison official between U.S. Mil. Govt. and German
Churches, U.S. Zone 46; mem. Board of Dirs. Union
Theological Seminary; Dir. The Interchurch Center,
New York 63-64; Trustee, the Christian Century
Foundation; mem. Editorial Board *Religion in Life*
(quarterly); Senior Editor *The Pulpit Digest* 58-68;
Hon. Chancellor, Union Coll.; Hon. D.Theol. (Göttin-
gen), L.H.D., Litt.D.
Publs. *The Adventure of the Church, Christian Leaders
for Tomorrow, The Church Through Half a Century*
(with H. P. Van Dusen), *On the Road to Christian Unity,
The American Churches in the Ecumenical Movement,
Church Cooperation and Unity in America 1900-1970.*
161 Boulder Trail, Bronxville, N.Y., U.S.A.
Telephone: 914-DE7-4624.

Cayzer, Sir William Nicholas, Bt.; British shipowner;
b. 21 Jan. 1910, Scotland; s. of the late Sir Augustus
Cayzer, 1st Bt. and the late Ina Frances Stancomb;
m. Elizabeth Catherine Williams 1935; two d.; ed. Eton
and Corpus Christi Coll., Cambridge.
Joined Clan Line Steamers Ltd. 31; Chair. Liverpool
Steamship Owners Assen. 44-45; Chair. Gen. Council of
British Shipping 59; Pres. Chamber of Shipping of the
U.K. 59; Pres. Inst. of Marine Engineers 63; Prime
Warden of the Worshipful Co. of Shipwrights 69-70;
Chair. British and Commonwealth Shipping Co. Ltd.,
Union Castle Mail Steamship Co. Ltd., Clan Line
Steamers Ltd., Cayzer Irvine and Co. Ltd., Cayzer
Steel Bowater Holdings Ltd., Caledonia Investments
Ltd., Scottish Lion Insurance Co. Ltd., English and
Scottish Investors, Air Holdings Ltd.; Dir. Sun
Alliance and London Insurance Ltd., and various
other cos.
Leisure interests: gardening, golf.
Cayzer House, 2-4 St. Mary Axe, London, E.C.3; and
95J Eaton Square, London, S.W.1, England.

Cazzaniga, Vincenzo; Italian oil executive; b. 3 Nov.
1907; ed. Bocconi Univ., Milan.
Executive, Società Italiana Lubrificanti Bedford (affiliate of Standard Oil Co.) 32, Man. Dir. 38; Head, N. Italy
Mineral Oils Industrial Cttee. 45, N. Italy Mineral Oils
Dept. 45-48, Head N. Italy Lubricants Dept., Italian
Petroleum Cttee. 45-48; Pres. Esso Standard Italiana
51-74; mem. Exec. Cttee. Confindustria (Italian Manufacturers' Assen.) 57; Dir. Int. Chamber of Commerce
57; Pres. Unione Petrolifera 58-73, Sarpom 61, Esso

Chimica 66, Milan Experimental Fuel Station; Dir.
Rasiom 61, Stanic 63, Esso Europe Inc. 66-, Minnesota
Mining and Manufacturing Co. 70, Montedison 72-, In-
stituto Bancario Italiano S.p.A. 73, Fiduciaria Mobiliare
& Immobiliare S.p.A. 73; Vice-Pres. Bastogi Finanziaria
72; Chair. and Chief Exec. Bastogi Int. Ltd. 73-; Pres.
UCID (Christian Execs. Assen.) 72-; Cavaliere del
Lavoro, etc.; Ad honorem Degree 71.
Via Porta Latina 8, Rome, Italy.

Ceauşescu, Nicolae; Romanian politician; b. 26 Jan.
1918, Scorniceşti-Olt; m. Elena Ceauşescu; two s. one
d.; ed. Acad. of Economic Studies, Bucharest.
Member, Union of Communist Youth 33-, Communist
Party of Romania 33-; imprisoned for antifascist
activities 36-38, 40-44; Sec. Cen. Cttee., Union of Com-
munist Youth 39-40, 44-45; alternate mem. Cen. Cttee.
Romanian Workers' Party (now Communist Party)
45, mem. 52-; Deputy Minister of Agriculture 48-50;
Deputy in the Grand Nat. Assembly 48-; Deputy
Minister of Armed Forces 50-54; Alt. mem. of Political
Bureau 54, mem. 55-65; Sec. Cen. Cttee. of Romanian
Workers' Party (now Communist Party) 54-65, First
Sec. 65; mem. Exec. Cttee. 65-, Perm. Presidium 65-
74, Sec.-Gen. Cen. Cttee. 65-69; Pres. State Council
67-, Nat. Council of Socialist Unity Front 68-; Sec.-
Gen. Romanian Communist Party 69-; Pres. Defence
Council and Supreme Commdr. Armed Forces 69-; Hon.
Pres. Acad. of Social and Political Sciences 70-; Chair.
Supreme Council on Social and Econ. Devt.; Pres.
Socialist Repub. of Romania 74-; Dr. h.c. Univs. of
Bucharest 73, Bogotá 73, Beirut 74, Buenos Aires 74,
Bahia Blanca 74; Hero of Socialist Labour 64; Hero of
Socialist Repub. of Romania 71.
Publs. *Romania on the way to Completing Socialist
Construction* (3 vols.) 69-72, *For a Policy of Peace and
International Co-operation* 70, *Romania on the Way to
Building Up the Multilaterally Developed Socialist
Society* (Vols. IV-VIII) 70-73.
Central Committee of Romanian Communist Party,
Bucharest, Romania.

Cecil, Lord (Edward Christian) David (Gascoyne), C.H.;
British writer; b. 9 April 1902; ed. Eton, Christ Church,
Oxford.
Trustee Nat. Portrait Gallery 37-51; Goldsmiths' Prof.
of English Literature, Oxford Univ. 48-69, Fellow New
Coll., Oxford 39-69, now Hon. Fellow; C.Lit. 72.
Publs. *The Stricken Deer* 29, *Sir Walter Scott* 33, *Early
Victorian Novelists* 34, *Jane Austen* 35, *The Young
Melbourne* 39, *The Oxford Book of Christian Verse*
(Editor) 40, *Hardy, the Novelist* 43, *Two Quiet Lives* 48,
Poets and Story-Tellers 49, *Lord M* 54, *The Fine Art of
Reading* 57, *Max* 64, *Visionary and Dreamer* 69, Editor
The Bodley Head Max Beerbohm 70, *A Choice of
Tennyson's Verse* 71, *The Cecils of Hatfield House* 73.
Red Lion House, Cranborne, Wimborne, Dorset, England.

Cecil, Lester LeFevre; American judge; b. 21 Nov.
1893, Miami County, Ohio; s. of Harry E. and Edna
Furrow Cecil; m. Celia Carroll 1921 (died 1970), 2nd
Lucile Thomas 1972; two s. two d.; ed. Univ. of
Michigan.
Attorney, E. H. and W. B. Turner 17-21; City Prosecut-
ing Attorney, Dayton 22-25, Judge, Municipal Court
26-29; Judge, Common Pleas Court, Montgomery
County 29-53; Judge, U.S. District Court, Southern
District, Ohio 53-59, Judge, U.S. Court of Appeals,
Sixth Circuit 59, Chief Judge 62-63, Senior Circuit
Judge 65-; Hon. LL.D. (Ohio Northern Univ.).
P.O. Box 1053, Mid City Station, Dayton, Ohio 45402;
and 531 Belmont Park N., Dayton, Ohio 45405, U.S.A.
Telephone: 228-6062 (Office); 223-1168 (Home).

Cefis, Eugenio; Italian business executive; b. 21 July
1921, Cividale; m. 1943; ed. Univ. of Milan.
Commissioned in Sardinian Grenadiers; Vice-Pres. Ente

Nazionale Idrocarburi (ENI) until 67, Pres. 67-71; Pres. Montedison April 71-; Dir. Snia Viscosa 71-. Montedison, Foro Bonaparte 31, Milan, Italy.

Cejka, Karl, D.IUR.; Austrian civil servant; b. 1 Dec. 1917, Schrems Lawer, Austria; s. of Karl and Maria (née Tomek) Cejka; m. Editha Gersch; two s.; ed. Vienna Univ.
Began his career as journalist and lawyer; Asst. Man. Supervising Dept. Ministry of Food; Adviser to Ministry of Finance on financial management of Radio, Posts and Telegraph; mem. Radio Advisory Cttee.; Chair. Preparatory Cttee. for Radio Reorganization 56-57; Dir.-Gen. Austrian Radio 57-60; Counsellor, Ministry of Finance; Head, Dept. for Development Aid; Head, Dept. for Public Debt and Export Promotion, Dept. for Credit Policy, Debt Administration and Int. Orgs.; mem. Supervisory Boards of several companies.
Leisure interests: music, writing.
Montecuccoliplatz 12, 1130 Vienna, Austria.
Telephone: 82-41-44.

Cela, Camilo José; Spanish writer; b. 11 May 1916; ed. Univ. de Madrid.
Director and Publisher of journal *Papeles de Son Armadans*; mem. Real Acad. Española 57; Premio de la critica 55.
Publs. include: *La Familia de Pascual Duarte* (novel) 42, *Pabellón de reposo* 43-57, *Nuevas andanzas y desventuras de Lazarillo de Tormes* (short stories) 44-55, *Pisando la dudosa luz del día* (poems) 45, *Mesa revuelta* 45 and 57, *Viaje a la Alcarria* 48, *La colmena* 51, *Del Miño al Bidasoa* 52, *Mrs. Caldwell habla con su hijo* 53, *La Catira* 55, *Judíos, moros y cristianos* 56, *El molino de viento* (short stories) 56, *Nuevo retablo de don Cristobita* 57, *Viaje al Pirineo de Lerida* 65, *Diccionario Secreto I* 68, *II* 71, *San Camilo 1936* 69, *María Sabina* 70, *A vueltas con España* (essays) 73, *Oficio de tinieblas 5* 73.
La Bonanova, Palma de Mallorca, Spain.
Telephone: 233670.

Celebrezze, Anthony J., LL.B.; American politician and lawyer; b. 4 Sept. 1910, Anzi, Potenza, Italy; m. Anne Marco 1938; one s. two d.; ed. John Carroll and Ohio Northern Univs.
Admitted Ohio Bar 36; practised law in Cleveland; U.S. Navy Second World War; Senator, Ohio State 52-53; Mayor of Cleveland 53-62; U.S. Sec. of Health, Educ. and Welfare, July 62-65; Judge, U.S. Court of Appeals 65-; Order of Merit (Italy); Doctor of Humanity (Wilberforce Univ.) and many other hon. degrees; Democrat.
Leisure interests: reading, fishing, hunting.
312 Federal Building, Cleveland, Ohio 44114, U.S.A.
Telephone: 522-4270 (Home).

Celibidache, Sergiu; Romanian-born German conductor, composer and musicologist; b. 28 June 1912; ed. Jassy and Berlin.
Conductor and Artistic Dir. Berlin Philharmonic Orchestra 46-51; now guest conductor to leading European orchestras; German Critics' Prize 53, Berlin City Art Prize 55; Grosses Verdienstkreuz (Fed. Germany).
1955 Kunstpreis Stadt, Berlin, Federal Republic of Germany.

Célier, Pierre, B.A., LL.B.; French company executive; b. 25 Feb. 1917, Paris 7e; s. of Comte Alexandre Célier and Comtesse Elisabeth de Gastines; m. France-Victoire de Wendel 1942; one s. one d.; ed. Coll. Saint-Louis de Gonzague, Faculty of Arts and Faculty of Law (Paris).
Inspecteur des Finances 42-48; Asst. Dir. Gen. Wendel et Cie. 52-68; Dir. Gen. Wendel-Sidélot 68-73; Pres. of Directoire, Sacilor July 73-; Pres. Admin. Board Marine-Wendel July 75-; Officer Légion d'Honneur; Croix de Guerre 45.

3 rue Paul Baudry, 75008 Paris; Home: 37 rue de l'Université, 75067 Paris, France.
Telephone: 395 97 31 (Office); 228 81 36 (Home).

Celio, Nello, D.IUR.; Swiss lawyer and politician; b. 12 Feb. 1914; ed. Univs. of Basle and Berne.
Secretary Cantonal Interior Dept. 41-45; Public Procurator 45-46; State Councillor 46-49; Nat. Councillor 63-; Minister of Defence 66-67, of Finance 68-70; Pres. Swiss Fed. Council and Head, Finance Dept. 72-73; fmr. Pres. Radical Democrat Party.
c/o Radikal-Demokratische Partei, Berne, Switzerland.

Celler, Emanuel; American politician; b. 6 May 1888; ed. Columbia Univ.
Legal practice, New York City 12-; mem. U.S. House of Reps. 23-72, Chair. Judiciary Cttee. until 72; Author, Fed. Register Act, Foreign Trade Zone Act, Celler Anti-Merger Act, Celler Civil Rights Acts, 57-60; Dir. philanthropic and religious orgs.; Democrat.
Publ. *You Never Leave Brooklyn* (autobiog.).
425 Park Avenue, New York, N.Y. 10022; Home: 9 Prospect Park, West Brooklyn, N.Y. 11215, U.S.A.

Cépède, Michel; French agriculturalist; b. 20 Oct. 1908 Wimereux, Pas de Calais; s. of the late Casimir Cépède and Léonie Paccard; m. Yvonne Troude 1930; one s. three d.; ed. Lycées Louis-le-Grand and Saint Louis Institut National Agronomique and Univ. de Paris à la Sorbonne.
Assistant Prof. Rural Economy, Nat. Agronomic Inst. 31-47, Prof. 47-; with Ministry of Agriculture 44-59, Dir. of Studies and of the Plan 57-59; Pres. Agricultural Cttee. 59-62; mem. French Del. to FAO 45-69, Vice-Pres. 65; mem. Programme Cttee. 56-69, Pres. 63-69; Ind. Chair. of the Council 69-73; numerous other posts with FAO and UN; Sec.-Gen. Interministerial Cttee. for Food and Agriculture 46-57, Pres. 57; Pres. Interministerial Cttee. of World Campaign against Hunger 60-69; mem. Acad. d'Agriculture de France; Foreign mem. Acad. of Agrarian Econ., Florence; numerous decorations and honours.
Leisure interest: archaeology.
Publs. *Du Prix de Revient au Produit net en Agriculture* 46, *Economie alimentaire du Globe* 53, *Economía Mundial de la Alimentación* 55, *L'Economie des Besoins* 56, *La Vie Rurale dans l'Arc Alpin* 60, *Agriculture et Alimentation en France durant la II Guerre Mondiale* 61, *Nourrir les Hommes* 63, *Population and Food* 65, *L'Agriculture en l'Administration française* 65, *La Faim* 67, *La Science contre la Faim* 70, *La Solidarité* 73, and numerous articles on agricultural subjects.
135 rue Falguière, Paris 15e, France.
Telephone: 551-61-38 (Office); 783-28-08 (Home).

Cernan, Eugene A.; American astronaut; b. 14 March 1934, Chicago, Ill.; m. Barbara J. Atchley; one d.; ed. Purdue Univ.
Commissioned in U.S. Navy and entered flight training; assigned to Attack Squadrons 126 and 113, Miramar, Calif.; entered U.S. Naval Postgraduate School, Monterey, Calif. 61; selected as astronaut by NASA Oct. 63; pilot of *Gemini IX* mission 66, performed two-hour space walk; pilot of backup crew for *Gemini XII* 66; lunar module pilot in *Apollo X* mission May 69; Mission Commdr. *Apollo XVII* 72; NASA Exceptional Service Medal.
NASA Johnson Space Center, Houston, Tex. 77058, U.S.A.

Černík, Oldřich; Czechoslovak politician; b. 27 Oct. 1921, Ostrava; ed. Mining Coll., Ostrava.
Former machine fitter at Vítkovice Iron Works 37-49; Sec. District Cttee. of C.P. of Czechoslovakia, Opava 49-54, Chair. Regional Nat. Cttee., Ostrava 54-56; Sec. Central Cttee. of C.P. of Czechoslovakia 56-60; mem. Econ. Comm. Central Cttee. 63-70; Minister of Fuel and

Power 60-63, of Fuel 63; Deputy Prime Minister and Chair. State Planning Comm. 63-April 68; Prime Minister April 68-Dec. 68, Prime Minister Fed. Govt. of Czechoslovak Socialist Repub. 69-70; mem. Presidium Central Cttee. C.P. of Czechoslovakia 66-70; mem. of Central Cttee. Bureau for directing party work in Czech lands 69; Minister, Chair. of Cttee. for Technological and Investment Devt. 70; Dep. to Nat. Assembly 60-69; Dep. to House of the People, Fed. Assembly 69-70.
Committee for Technological and Investment Development, Prague 2, Slezská 7, Czechoslovakia.

Černík, Dr. Zdeněk; Czechoslovak diplomatist; b. 26 Feb. 1921, Ostrava; *m.*; two *c.*; ed. Inst. of Political and Social Sciences, Prague.
Joined Ministry of Foreign Affairs 50; Deputy Head of Dept. of Int. Orgs. 56-62, Head 62-68; Deputy Perm. Rep. to UN 59-62, Perm. Rep. 68-73; Head Czechoslovak Del. to Eighteen Nation Disarmament Conf., Geneva 65-67; Head Diplomatic Corps of Foreign Affairs 73-.
c/o Ministry of Foreign Affairs, Prague, Czechoslovakia.

Cerulli, Enrico, LL.D.; Italian diplomatist (retd.), anthropologist and linguist; b. 15 Feb. 1898, Naples; *m.* Lina Ciotola 1936; two *s.*; ed. Univ. of Naples.
Entered Civil Service 20; Sec. and later Dir. of Political Affairs, Italian Somaliland 20-25; First Sec. and later Counsellor, Italian Legation, Ethiopia 26-29; Italian rep. Anglo-Italian Boundary Comm., Somaliland 30-31; Head of Political Dept., later Sec.-Gen., Ministry for Italian Africa 32-35; mem. Italian del. to L.N. 35-37; Deputy Gov.-Gen. Italian East Africa 38-39; retd. 40-44; Counsellor of State and mem. of del. to Peace Conf. 44-47; Italian rep. Four-Power Confs., London, and later to UN on question of Italian African territories 47-49; Italian rep. UN Trusteeship Council 49-50; Ambassador to Iran 50-54; Counsellor of State 55-68; mem. Acad. dei Lincei (Pres. 68-), British Acad., Institut de France, Académie Royale de Belgique, Real Acad. Española, Acad. Portuguesa de Historia, Akad. der Wissenschaften, Göttingen, Pontifical Acad. of Archaeology, etc.; Hon. Litt.D. (Univs. of Brussels, Rome, Manchester); Corresp. Prof., School of Oriental Studies, Univ. of London; Hon. mem. Royal Asiatic Soc., London, Royal Anthropological Inst., London; fmr. Pres. Italian Anthropological Inst.
Publs. *The Folk Literature of the Galla in Southern Ethiopia* 22, *Etiopia Occidentale* (2 vols.) 30-33, *Studi Etiopici* (4 vols.) 36-51, *The Book of the Staircase and the Spanish-Arabic Sources of Dante* 49, *History of Ethiopic Literature* 56, *Somalia* (3 vols.) 58-59, *Islam of Yesterday and Today* 71, *New Researches on the Book of the Staircase* 72, *A Collection of Persian Tales translated in Venice in 1557* 75.
Accademia Nazionale dei Lincei, Palazzo Corsini, 00165 Rome; and 11 Via Lovanio, 00198 Rome, Italy.

Césaire, Aimé Fernand, L. ès L.; French (Martiniquais) poet, dramatist and politician; b. 25 June 1913, Basse-Pointe, Martinique; *s.* of Fernand and Marie (Hermine) Césaire; *m.* Suzanne Roussi 1937; six *c.*; ed. Fort-de-France (Martinique) and Lycée Louis-le-Grand (Paris), Ecole Normale Supérieure and the Sorbonne.
Teaching career until 45; mem. Constituent Assemblies 45 and 46; Dep. for Martinique 46-; Pres. Parti Progressiste Martiniquais; Mayor of Fort-de-France 45-.
Publs. Verse: *Cahier d'un Retour au Pays Natal, Les Armes Miraculeuses, Et les chiens se taisaient, Soleil cou coupé, Corps perdu, Cadastre, Ferrements*; Essays: *Discours sur le Colonialisme*; Theatre: *la Tragédie du roi Christophe, Une saison au Congo, Une tempête.*
Assemblée Nationale, Paris 7e, France; La Mairie, Fort-de-France, Martinique, West Indies.

Ceyrac, François; French trade union administrator; b. 12 Sept. 1912, Meyssac; ed. Lycée Louis-le-Grand and Univ. of Paris.
Metal Workers' and Miners' Union branch chief 36, Asst. Sec.-Gen. 45, Deputy Sec.-Gen. 52-68, Pres. 69-; social comm. of Patronat Français 46-, mem. of council 67-, Vice-Pres. 68-73, Pres. 73-; Dir. Wendel et Cie., Soc. Fonderie de Précision, Soc. Peugeot; founding mem. of Comité National pour le Développement des Grandes Ecoles.
Leisure interest: sailing.
31 avenue Pierre-Ier-de-Serbie, Paris 8e; Home: 16 avenue des Courlis, 78 Le Vésinet, France.

Chaban-Delmas, Jacques Michel Pierre; French politician; b. 7 March 1915; ed. Lycée Lakanal, Sceaux, Ecole Libre des Sciences Politiques, Paris.
Served army 39-40, Brig.-Gen. 40; nat. mil. del. responsible for co-ordination of mil. planning, Resistance 44; Inspector-Gen. of Army Nov. 44; Sec.-Gen. Ministry of Information 45; elected Radical deputy for Gironde 46; Mayor of Bordeaux 47-; leader of Gaullist group (Républicains Sociaux) in Nat. Assembly 53-56; mem. Consultative Assembly, Council of Europe; Inspecteur des Finances 56-57; Minister of Nat. Defence 57-58; Pres. of Nat. Assembly 58-69; Pres. of Comm. for Regional Econ. Devt. of Aquitaine 64-69; Pres. of European Ass. of Local Authorities; Prime Minister 69-72; Insp.-Gen. des Finances 73-; Pres. Regional Council, Aquitaine 74-; Candidate for Pres. of France May 74; Commdr. Légion d'Honneur; Croix de Guerre.
4 avenue Raymond-Poincaré, 75116 Paris, France.

Chabert, Jos, DR. EN DROIT; Belgian lawyer and politician; b. 16 March 1933, Etterbeek; ed. Univs. of Brussels and Louvain.
Advocate, Court of Appeal; Alderman, Meise; mem. Board of Admin. Intercommunale Haviland; mem. Chamber of Reps. 68-74, Senator 74-; Pres. of Christian Social Party Group in Parl. 72-73; mem. Finance and Steering Cttees., Cultural Council for the Dutch cultural community, Pres. of Christian Social Party Group 72-73; Minister of Dutch Culture and Flemish Affairs 73-74, of Communications 74-; Pres. Atelier protégé pour handicapés de Meise.
Ministry of Communications, rue de la Loi 65, 1040 Brussels, Belgium.

Chabrol, Claude; French film director and producer; b. 24 June 1930; ed. Paris Univ., Ecole Libre des Sciences Politiques.
Formerly film critic and Public Relations Officer in Paris for 20th-Century Fox; director and producer 58-.
Films directed include *Le Beau Serge* 57, *Les Cousins* 58, *A Double Tour* 59, *Les Bonnes Femmes* 59, *Les Godelureaux* 60, *Ophélia* 62, *l'Œil du Malin* 61, *Landru* 62, *les Plus Belles Escroqueries du Monde* 63, *Le tigre aime la chair fraîche* 64, *Le tigre se parfume à la dynamite* 65, *Marie-Chantal contre le Docteur Kha* 65, *Le Scandale* 67, *Les Biches* 68, *La Femme infidèle* 68, *Que la bête meure* 69, *Le Boucher* 70, *La Rupture* 70, *Juste Avant la Nuit* 71, *Doctor Popaul* 72, *La Décade Prodigieuse* 72, *Les Noces Rouges* 73, *Nada* 74, *Les Innocents aux Mains Sales* 75; Locarno Festival Grand Prix 58, Berlin Festival Golden Bear 59.
Publ. *Alfred Hitchcock* (with E. Rohmer).
49 boulevard de Château, 92 Neuilly-sur-Seine, France.
Telephone: Maillot 8849.

Chadenet, Bernard; French international civil servant; b. 16 Sept. 1915, Paris; *m.* Françoise Chêne-Carrère 1944; three *d.*; ed. Univ. de Paris à la Sorbonne and Ecole Supérieure d'Electricité, Paris, and Harvard Business School.
Engineer and Chief, Public Utilities Div., Projects Dept., Int. Bank for Reconstruction and Devt. (World

Bank) 54-58; Gen. Man. NEYRPIC, Grenoble 58-64; Assoc. Dir. Projects Dept., World Bank 64-67, Deputy Dir. 68-72, Vice-Pres. for Org., Planning and Personnel Management 72-; Chevalier Légion d'Honneur.
Leisure interest: skiing.
4759 Berkeley Terrace N.W., Washington, D.C. 20007, U.S.A.
Telephone: 333-1441.

Chadwick, John, M.A., LITT.D., F.B.A.; British classical scholar; b. 21 May 1920, East Sheen, Surrey; s. of Fred Chadwick and Margaret Bray; m. Joan Isobel Hill 1947; one s.; ed. St. Paul's School, London, Corpus Christi Coll., Cambridge Univ.
War service in Royal Navy 40-45; Editorial Asst. *Oxford Latin Dictionary* 46-52; Lecturer in Classics, Cambridge Univ. 52-66, Reader in Greek Language 66-69, Perceval Maitland Laurence Reader in Greek Language 69-; Collins Fellow, Downing Coll., Cambridge 60-; Sec. Gen. Perm. Int. Cttee. for Mycenaean Studies 75-; co-operated with Michael Ventris in the decipherment of the Minoan Linear B script; Corresp. mem. German Archaeological Inst. 57, Austrian Acad. of Sciences 74, Acad. des Inscriptions et Belles Lettres, Institut de France 75; Hon. Doctorate, Athens Univ. Philosophical School 58, Université Libre de Bruxelles 69; Hon. Litt.D. (Trinity Coll., Dublin) 71; Hon. Fellow, Athens Archaeological Soc. 74.
Leisure interest: travel.
Publs. *The Medical Works of Hippocrates* (with W. N. Mann) 50; *Documents in Mycenaean Greek* (with Michael Ventris) 56, 2nd edn. 73; *The Decipherment of Linear B* 58 (trans. into German and Italian 59, Swedish 60, Dutch 61, Danish, Spanish, Greek, Japanese 62, Polish 64, French 72); *The Pre-History of the Greek Language* (in Cambridge Ancient History, Vol. II) 63; *The Mycenaean World* 76; Editor *The Mycenae Tablets III* 63; Joint Editor *The Knossos Tablets IV* 71; various articles in learned journals.
Downing College, Cambridge CB2 1DQ, England.
Telephone: Cambridge 59491.

Chadwick, Lynn Russell, C.B.E.; British sculptor; b. 24 Nov. 1914; ed. Merchant Taylors School.
Works shown in London, New York, Paris, Brussels (Exposition 58) and Venice, where he won the International Sculpture Prize at the Biennale 56; 1st Prize Padua Int. Competition 59; Hors Concours, Bienal São Paulo 61.
Lypiatt Park, Stroud, Glos., England.

Chadwick, William Owen, F.B.A.; British historian; b. 20 May 1916, Bromley, Kent; s. of John and Edith (née Horrocks) Chadwick; m. Ruth Hallward 1949; two s. two d.; ed. St. John's Coll., Cambridge.
Fellow, Trinity Hall, Cambridge 47-56; Master of Selwyn Coll., Cambridge 56-; Dixie Prof. of Ecclesiastical History, Cambridge Univ. 58-68, Regius Prof. of Modern History 68-; Vice-Chancellor of Cambridge Univ. 69-71; Hon. D.D. (St. Andrews) 60, (Oxford) 73; Hon. D.Litt. (Kent) 70.
Leisure interests: music, sailing.
Publs. *From Bossuet to Newman* 57, *The Victorian Church* (2 vols.) 66-70, *The Mind of the Oxford Movement* (2nd edn.) 67, *John Cassian* (2nd edn.) 68, *The Reformation* (8th edn.) 75, *The Secularization of the European Mind* 76; numerous articles and reviews in learned journals.
The Master's Lodge, Selwyn College, Cambridge, England.

Chafee, John H., B.A., LL.B.; American lawyer and politician; b. 22 Oct. 1922, Providence, R.I.; s. of John Sharpe and Janet Hunter Chafee; m. Virginia Coates, 1950; four s. one d.; ed. Deerfield Acad., Yale Univ., and Harvard Law School.
U.S. Marine Corps 42-46, 51-52; admitted to Rhode

Island Bar 51; State Rep. Rhode Island House 56-62; Gov. of Rhode Island 63-69; Sec. of the Navy 69-72; Hon. LL.D. (Brown Univ., Providence Coll., Univ. of Rhode Island); Visiting Chubb Fellow, Yale Univ. 65; Chair. Compact for Educ. 65, Republican Govs'. Assen. 67-68; Trustee, Deerfield Acad. 70-, Yale Univ. 72-; Republican.
Leisure interests: squash, tennis, sailing, skiing.
Hospital Trust Tower, Providence, R.I.; Ives Road, East Greenwich, R.I., U.S.A.
Telephone: 401-274-9200 (Office).

Chagall, Marc; French (Russian-born) artist; b. 7 July 1887, Vitebsk.
Lived in France 10-14, Russia 14-22, France 22-41, U.S.A. 41-48, France 48-; works include paintings, engravings, murals, costumes and décor for ballet and theatre, and ceramics; stained glass windows for synagogue of Medical Centre near Jerusalem; ceiling for Paris Opera 64; murals for Metropolitan Opera House, Lincoln Center, New York 66; sets for *The Magic Flute* (Mozart), Metropolitan Opera 67; has exhibited in Tate Gallery, London, museums in Amsterdam, Paris, Chicago, New York, Venice, Jerusalem, Tel-Aviv, Berne, Zürich, Turin, Rome, Milan; exhbn. at Zürich Kunsthaus 67, at Tretyakov Art Gallery, Moscow 73; Int. Prize for Engraving, Venice Biennale 48, Erasmus Prize 60; Commdr. des Arts et des Lettres; Grand Officier, Légion d'Honneur; Grand Cross Nat. Order of Merit (France).
Publ. *Ma Vie* 31, English trans. 65.
Villa la Colline, Quartier les Gardettes, 06570 Saint-Paul, France.

Chagas, Carlos, M.D., SC.D.; Brazilian biophysicist; b. 1910; ed. Colégio Rezende, Univs. of Brazil and Paris.
Began career as Asst. at Inst. Oswaldo Cruz and Medical School, Univ. of Brazil; Prof. Univ. of Brazil Medical School 37, Dir. Inst. of Biophysics 46-64; mem. Brazilian Nat. Research Council 50-55, U.N. Scientific Cttee. 56-, WHO Scientific Advisory Cttee. 59-61, Pan American Health Org. Scientific Advisory Cttee. 62-; Chair. Exec. Cttee. Int. Brain Research Org.; Perm. Del. of Brazil to UNESCO; Adviser Puerto Rico Atomic Energy Comm.; mem. Brazilian Acads. of Science, Medicine and Pharmacy, Pontifical Acad. of Sciences, assoc. mem. Acad. de Médecine (Paris), Soc. de Biologie (Paris), London Physiological Soc.; Vice-Pres. ICSU; Dr. h.c. Paris, Coimbra, Mexico, Recife Univs.; Premio Moinho Santista 60; Commdr. Order of Christ (Portugal), of Merit (Italy); Officer Legion of Honour (France), Order of Polar Star (Sweden), of Public Health (France).
Publs. include *Homems e Cousas de Ciência* (essays) and a large number of medical and scientific papers 36-.
38 Francisco Otaviano, Rio de Janeiro, Brazil.

Chagla, Mahomedali Currim, B.A.; Indian barrister; b. 30 Sept. 1900; ed. St. Xavier's High School and Coll., Bombay, and Lincoln Coll., Oxford.
President Oxford Indian Majlis 22; called to Bar (Inner Temple) 22; Prof. of Constitutional Law, Govt. Law Coll., Bombay 27-30; Hon. Sec. Bar Council of High Court of Judicature, Bombay 33-41; Puisne Judge Bombay High Court 41-47; Chair. Legal Education Cttee. 48; Vice-Chancellor, Bombay Univ. 47; Chief Justice, High Court, Bombay 47-58; Del. to UN 46; Pres. Bombay Branch Royal Asiatic Soc. 47-58; Gov. of Bombay 56; Judge, Int. Court of Justice 57; mem. Law Commission 55-58; Ambassador to U.S., Mexico and Cuba 58-61; High Commissioner in the United Kingdom, Ambassador to Ireland 62-63; Minister of Educ., Govt. of India 63-66, of External Affairs 66-Sept. 67; numerous Indian dels., including UN Gen. Assembly 67; mem. Rajya Sabha; Chair. Life Insurance Corpn. Inquiry Comm. 58; mem. Sikh Grievances Enquiry Comm. 61; Hon. Fellow, Lincoln Coll., Oxford 61; Hon. LL.D. Hartford, Temple,

Boston, Leningrad and Punjab Univs., Dartmouth Coll., Benares Univ.

Publs. *The Indian Constitution* 29, *Law, Liberty and Life* 50, *The Individual and the State, An Ambassador Speaks* 62, *Education and the Nation, Unity and Language, Roses in December—an Autobiography.*

Pallonji Mansion, New Cuffe Parade, Bombay 5, India.

Chagula, Dr. Wilbert K., M.B., CH.B., M.A.; Tanzanian public servant and administrator; b. 1926; ed. Makerere Univ. Coll., Uganda, Cambridge Univ., Univ. of W. Indies, Jamaica, Yale Univ., U.S.A.

Assistant Medical Officer, Tanganyika 52; Asst. Lecturer, Lecturer in Anatomy, Makerere Univ. Coll. 55-61; Rockefeller Foundation Fellow in Histochemistry, Jamaica and Yale Univs. 61-62; Registrar and Vice-Principal, Univ. Coll., Dar es Salaam 63-65, Principal 65-70; Pres. E. African Acad. 63-, Fellow 71; mem. UNACAST 71-; Chair. Tanzania Nat. Scientific Research Council 72-; Minister for Water Devt. and Power 70-72, for Econ. Affairs and Dev . Planning 72-75, of Energy and Minerals Nov. 75-.

Ministry of Energy and Minerals Planning, Dar es Salaam, Tanzania.

Chaikovsky, Boris Alexandrovich; Soviet composer; b. 10 Sept. 1925, Moscow; ed. Moscow Conservatoire.

Major works include: Sonata for piano 44, suite for 'cello 46, First Symphony 47, Fantasia on Russian folk themes 50, *Slav Rhapsody* 51, Sonata for piano 52, *Symphonietta* for string orchestra 53, Trio for violin, 'cello and piano 53, *Cappriccio on English Themes* 54, First String Quartet 54, Trio for strings 55, Concerto for clarinet and orchestra 57, Sonata for cello and piano 57, Sonata for violin and piano 59, Second String Quartet 61, Piano Quintet 62, Concerto for cello and orchestra 64, Partita for cello and Chamber ensemble 66, Third String Quartet 67, Chamber Symphony 67, Second Symphony 67, Concerto for violin and orchestra 69, Concerto for piano and orchestra 71, Poushkin Lyrics for soprano and piano 72, Fourth String Quartet 72, Theme and Eight Variations for Orchestra 73, Sonata for Piano Duet 73, Fifth String Quartet 74, *Signs of the Zodiac* Cantata for Soprano and Orchestra 74; Exec. mem. Moscow Section, Composers' Union of R.S.F.S.R.; Honoured Worker Artist 69; State Prize 69.

Composers' Union of R.S.F.S.R., 8-10 Ulitsa Nezhdanovoy, Moscow, U.S.S.R.

Chailakhayan, Mikhail Khristoforovich, DR.SC.; Soviet plant physiologist; b. 21 March 1902; ed. Erevan State Univ.

Agronomist, Erevan 26-29; Lecturer, Faculty of Botany, Transcaucasian Zootechnical and Veterinary Inst. 28-31; Aspirant (postgraduate), Laboratory of Plant Physiology and Biochemistry, U.S.S.R. Acad. of Sciences, Leningrad 31-34; Head of Laboratory, K. A. Timiriazev Inst. of Plant Physiology, U.S.S.R. Acad. of Sciences, Moscow 35-; Chair. of Plant Anatomy and Physiology, Erevan State Univ. 41-46; Chair. of Plant Physiology and Microbiology, Erevan Agric. Inst., Prof. 43-; Corresp. mem. Armenian S.S.R. Acad. of Sciences, Erevan 45-70, mem. 70-, Hon. Scientist, Armenian S.S.R., Erevan 70-; mem. U.S.S.R. Acad. of Sciences, Moscow 68-, German Acad. Leopoldina, Halle 69-; Corresp. mem. Amer. Soc. of Plant Physiologists 63-, Amer. Botanical Soc. 69-; Foreign mem. Bulgarian Botanical Soc., Sofia 74-; Dr. h.c. (Rostock Univ., G.D.R.) 69-.

Publs. many scientific works in field of physiology of higher plant growth and development processes.

K. A. Timiriazev Institute of Plant Physiology, U.S.S.R. Academy of Sciences, Botanicheskaya 35, Moscow 127273, U.S.S.R.

Telephone: 482-53-12.

Chain, Sir Ernst Boris, Kt., F.R.S., M.A., PH.D.; British bio-chemist; b. 19 June 1906; s. of Dr. Michael Chain and Margarete Eisner; m. Anne Beloff 1948; two s. one d.; ed. Luisengymnasium and Friedrich-Wilhelm Univ., Berlin.

Research in Chemical Dept., Pathological Inst., Charité Hospital, Berlin 30-33; emigrated to England because of racial persecution 33; research in School of Biochemistry, Cambridge 33-35; Univ. Demonstrator and Lecturer in Chemical Pathology, Univ. of Oxford 35-49; Guest Prof. of Biochemistry, Istituto Superiore di Sanità, Rome 49; Prof. of Biochemistry and Scientific Dir. Int. Research Centre for Chemical Microbiology, Istituto Superiore di Sanità 50-61; Prof. of Biochemistry Imperial Coll. of Science and Technology, London 61-73, Emer. Prof., Senior Research Fellow 73-; awards include Nobel Prize for Physiology and Medicine 45, and Paul Ehrlich Prize 54; Commdr. Légion d'Honneur (France) 47; Grand Ufficiale al Merito della Repubblica Italiana; Grand Decoration in Gold for services to the Republic of Austria; many hon. degrees; hon. mem. many foreign acads. and learned societies.

Leisure interest: music.

Department of Biochemistry, Imperial College of Science, Imperial Institute Road, London, S.W.7; 7 Northview, Wimbledon Common, London, S.W.19, England.

Chakovsky, Alexander Borisovich; Soviet writer; b. 26 Aug. 1913, St. Petersburg (Leningrad); s. of Nina and Boris Chakovsky; m. Raisa Chakovskya 1945; one s. one d.; ed. Maxim Gorky Institute for Literature, Moscow.

Member C.P.S.U. 41-; Editor-in-Chief *Literaturnaya Gazeta* 62-; Sec. of Board, Union of Writers of U.S.S.R. 63-; Deputy U.S.S.R. Supreme Soviet 66-; Alternate mem. Central Cttee. C.P.S.U. 71-; U.S.S.R. State Prize 50; Hero of Socialist Labour 73; Orders of Lenin (twice), Order of October Revolution, Red Banner of Labour, Red Star, War Medals.

Leisure interest: tennis.

Publs. include: *It Was in Leningrad* (trilogy) 44, *Lyda* 45, *Peaceful Days* 47, *It's Already Morning with Us* 50, *Khvan Cher is on Guard* 52, *A Year of One Life* 56, *Roads We Take* 60, *Light of Distant Star* 62 (made into Film and play), *Fiancée* 66 (made into Film and play), *Blockade* (5 vols.) 68-73 (made into Film).

Literaturnaya Gazeta, 30 Tsvetnoi Bulvar, Moscow, U.S.S.R.

Telephone: 291-78-65.

Chakravarti, Subramaniam, M.A.; Indian state governor; b. 30 Aug. 1910, Madras; s. of T. K. Subramaniam and Bungaramma; m. Naina Rao 1940; two s.; ed. Hindu High School and Presidency Coll., Madras, London School of Econs. and Trinity Coll., Cambridge.

Joint Sec. Ministry of Transport 48-49; Chief, Industry Div., UN Econ. Mission for Asia and Far East 50-51; Devt. Commr. and Sec. Planning and Devt. Dept., Govt. of Andhra Pradesh 55; Admin., Nagarjunsagar Project 55-59; Principal, Nat. Inst. of Study and Research in Community Devt., Mussoorie 59-62; Sec. Ministry of Community Devt. and Co-operation 63-65, Ministry of Food, Agriculture, Community Devt. and Co-operation 66, Ministry of Transport 67-69, Ministry of Educ. and Youth Services 69-70; Gov. Himachal Pradesh 71-; fmr. del. to many int. confs. including ECAFE, UNICEF and UNESCO.

Leisure interests: gardening, treks, golf.

Raj Bharan, Simla 4, Himachal Pradesh, India.

Telephone: 3440 (Office); 3152 (Home).

Chakravarty, Birendra Narayan, B.SC.; Indian state governor; b. 20 Dec. 1904, Bogra (Bangladesh); m.

Indira Sanyal 1931; one *s.* one *d.*; ed. Presidency Coll., Calcutta Univ., Univ. Coll., London, School of Oriental Studies, London.
Joined Indian Civil Service 29; held various appointments in Bengal districts and Bengal Secretariat; Finance Sec., Bengal Govt. 44; Sec. to Gov., West Bengal 47; Chargé d'Affaires, Embassy of India, Nanking Feb.-June 48; Head of Indian Liaison Mission, Tokyo, with personal rank of Minister 48-49; Joint Sec., Ministry of External Affairs 49-51; Sec. (Commonwealth Relations) 51-52; Ambassador to Netherlands 52-54; Senior Alt. Chair. Neutral Nations Repatriation Comm., Korea 53; Acting High Commr. to Great Britain 54, High Commr. to Ceylon 55-56; Special Sec. Ministry of External Affairs 56-60; High Commr. to Canada 60-62; Perm. Rep. to UN 62-65; Gov. of Haryana 67-.
Leisure interests: gardening, photography.
Publ. *India Speaks to America.*
Haryana Raj Bhavan, Chandigarh, India.
Telephone: 26085.

Chalandon, Albin Paul Henri, L. ès L.; French businessman and politician; b. 11 June 1920, Reyrieux, Ain; *s.* of Pierre Chalandon and Claire Cambon; *m.* Princess Salomé Murat 1951; three *c.*
Inspecteur des Finances; Dir. Banque Nationale pour le Commerce et l'Industrie (Afrique) 49; Admin. and Dir-.Gen. Banque Commerciale de Paris until 64, Président-Directeur Général 64-68; Minister of Industry May 68, of Supply and Housing 68-72; Special Asst., Ministry of Foreign Affairs 74; mem. Central Cttee. Union pour la Nouvelle République (now Union des Démocrates pour la République) 58-, Sec.-Gen. 59, Deputy Sec.-Gen. UDR Dec. 74-; mem. Social and Econ. Council; Officier Légion d'Honneur, Croix de Guerre.
39 boulevard de Montmorency, Paris 16e, France.

Chałasiński, Józef, PH.D.; Polish sociologist; b. 17 Feb. 1904 Rudnik, Lublin; *m.* Krystyna Chałasińska; ed. Poznan Univ.
Post doctorate fellowship in U.S.A. and U.K. 31-33; Prof. Free Univ., Warsaw 36-39; Dir. State Inst. of Country Culture 36-39; Prof. and Rector Lódz Univ. 49-52; Prof. Warsaw Univ. 53-; collaborated in *Yearbook of Education* 50-53; mem. Exec. Cttee. Int. Seminar for Family Research; Editor-in-Chief *Nauka Polska* 53-57, *Przeglad Socjologiczny* 35-39, 57-, *Kultura i Spoteczeństwo* 57-, *Młode Pokolenie Wsi Polski Ludowej* 64-; mem. Polish Acad. of Sciences 52- (fmr. Deputy Scientific Sec.), mem. Presidium 68-71, Sec. Dept. Social Sciences 69-72; mem. Presidium Polish Cttee. for UNESCO Affairs; mem. Int. Social Science Council 59-; Visiting Prof. California Univ. 58; Chair. Study on Sociological and Cultural Problems of Contemporary Africa, Polish Acad. of Sciences; Gold Cross of Merit, Commdr. Cross, Order of Polonia Restituta 51, etc.; Wlodzimierz Pietrzak Scientific Prize 67; Medal of 30th Anniversary of People's Poland 74.
Publs. *Młode pokolenie chlopów* (The Young Generation of Peasants) 38, *Spoteczeństwo i wychowanie* (Society and Upbringing) 48, *Przeszłość i Przyszłość Inteligencji Polskiej* (Past and Future of the Polish Intelligentsia) 58, *Kultura Amerykańska* (American Civilization) 62, *Bliżej Afryki* (Closer to Africa) with Krystyna Chałasińska 65, *Kultura i Naród* (Culture and the Nations) 68, *Tradycje i perspektywy przyszłości kultury* (Traditions and Perspectives of Future of Culture) 70, *The Diaries of the Young Peasant Generation as a Manifestation of Contemporary Culture* 72, *Drogi awansu spotecznego robotnika* (Ways for the Social Rise of the Worker), *Szkota w spoteczeństwie amerykańskim* (The School in American Society), 30 *lat socjologii polskiej* (Thirty Years of Polish Sociology).
Mraszalkowska 16, m. 19, 00-590 Warsaw, Poland.

Chalfont, Baron (Life Peer), cr. 64; **(Arthur) Alun Gwynne-Jones,** P.C., O.B.E., M.C.; British politician; b. 5 Dec. 1919, Llantarnam, Wales; *s.* of Arthur Gwynne Jones; *m.* Mona Mitchell, M.D., CH.B., 1948; ed. West Monmouth School.
Commissioned into S. Wales Borderers (24th Foot) 40; Military Service Burma and India 40-44, Cyprus, Malaya and East Africa 44-61; Defence Corresp. *The Times*, London 61-64; Minister of State for Foreign Affairs 64-70, Minister for Disarmament 64-67, 69-70, in charge of day-to-day negotiations for Britain's entry into Common Market 67-69; resigned from Labour Party 74; Perm. Rep. to Western European Union 69; Dir. IBM (U.K.) Ltd. 73-.
Leisure interests: theatre, music.
Publ. *The Sword and the Spirit* 63, contribs. to journal of Royal United Services Inst. (*The Ulster Debate* 72).
65 Ashley Gardens, London, SW1P 1QG, England.

Chalid, Idham (*see* Idham Chalid, Dr. Kjai Hadji).

Chalmers, Floyd Sherman, O.C., LL.D., LITT.D., B.F.A.; Canadian publisher; b. 14 Sept. 1898, Chicago, Ill., U.S.A.; of Scottish parentage; *m.* Jean A. Boxall 1921; one *s.* one *d.*
With Bank of Nova Scotia 14; Reporter on *Toronto News* and *Toronto World*; joined *Financial Post* 19, Montreal Editor 23, Editor 25-42; Exec. Vice-Pres. Maclean-Hunter Publishing Co. 42-52, Pres. 52-64, Chair. 64-69; Chancellor, York Univ. 69-73; Chair. Floyd S. Chalmers Foundation; Officer, Order of Canada 67; Civic Award of Merit, Toronto 74; Diplôme d'hon., Canadian Conf. of the Arts 74; Canadian News Hall of Fame 75.
Leisure interests: golf, theatre.
Room 805, 481 University Avenue, Toronto M5W 1A7; Home: Apartment 4611, 44 Charles Street W., Toronto M4Y 1R8, Canada.
Telephone: 597-0319(Office); 964-7667 (Home).

Chalupa, Vlastimil, Ing.; Czechoslovak politician; b. 17 Oct. 1919, Ratenice; ed. Transport Inst., Žilina.
Held various economic and Communist Party posts 45-51; engaged in govt. admin. and postal services 52-69; Deputy Chair., Fed. Cttee. for Posts and Telecommunications 70; Minister of Posts and Telecommunications 71-; Head of Del. to CMEA Comm. for Posts and Telecommunications 71-; Distinctions for "Merit in Construction" 73.
Ministry of Posts and Telecommunications, Olšanská 5, Prague 3, Czechoslovakia.

Chamant, Jean, L. EN D.; French lawyer and politician; b. 23 Nov. 1913; *m.* Hélène Claret 1936; one *s.* three *d.*
Advocate, Court of Appeal, Paris; Deputy for l'Yonne 46-; Sec. of State, Ministry of Foreign Affairs 55-56; Vice-Pres. Nat. Assembly 59-67; Minister of Transport 67-June 69, Jan. 71-July 72; Republican-Independent.
6 rue Masseran, 75007 Paris, France.
Telephone: 567-29-05.

Chamberlain, Joseph Wyan, A.B., A.M., M.S., PH.D.; American astronomer and geophysicist; b. 24 Aug. 1928, Boonville, Mo.; *s.* of Gilbert Lee Chamberlain and Jessie Wyan Chamberlain; *m.* Marilyn Roesler Chamberlain 1949; two *s.* one *d.*; ed. Univs of Missouri and Michigan.
Project Scientist in Aurora and Airglow, U.S. Air Force, Cambridge Research Center 51-53; Research Assoc., Yerkes Observatory, Univ. of Chicago 53-55, Asst. Prof. of Astronomy 55-59, Assoc. Prof. 59-60, Assoc. Dir. Yerkes Observatory 60-62, Prof. of Astronomy Jan.-June 61, Prof. of Astronomy and Geophysical Sciences 61-62; Assoc. Dir. for Planetary Sciences Div. (fmrly. Space Div.), Kitt Peak Nat. Observatory, Tucson, Ariz. 62-70; Astronomer 70-71; Dir. Lunar Science

Inst., Houston, Texas 71-73; Prof. Space Physics and Astronomy Dept., Rice Univ., Houston 71-; Editor Reviews of Geophysics and Space Physics 74-; mem. Nat. Acad. of Sciences; mem. numerous int. comms. and recipient of numerous awards.

Leisure interests: golf, music, reading.

Publs. Over one hundred technical publs. on aurora, airglow and planetary astronomy.

Space Physics and Astronomy Department, Rice Univ., Houston, Texas 77001, U.S.A.

Telephone: (713) 527-8101.

Chamberlain, Owen, PH.D.; American physicist; b. 10 July 1920, San Francisco; s. of Edward and Genevieve Lucinda (Owen) Chamberlain; ed. Germantown Friends School, Dartmouth Coll., and Univ. of Chicago.

Research physicist Manhattan Project, Berkeley 42-43, Los Alamos 43-46; graduate student (under Enrico Fermi) Univ. of Chicago 46-48; Instructor in Physics Univ. of Calif., Berkeley 48-50, Asst. Prof. 50-54, Assoc. Prof. 54-58, Prof. 58-; on leave at Univ. of Rome as Guggenheim Fellow 57-58; Loeb Lecturer, Harvard Univ. 59; mem. Nat. Acad. of Sciences; Fellow, American Acad. of Arts and Sciences; has specialized in research in spontaneous fission, proton scattering, discovery of antiproton, properties of antinucleons, etc.; shared Nobel Prize for Physics with Emilio Segre 59.

Department of Physics, University of California, Berkeley 4, Calif., U.S.A.

Chambers, Sir (Stanley) Paul, K.B.E., C.B., C.I.E., B.COM., M.SC.(ECON.); British businessman; b. 2 April 1904, London; s. of the late Philip Joseph Chambers; m. Edith Pollack 1955; two d.; ed. City of London Coll., and London School of Economics.

Member Indian Income Tax Enquiry Cttee. 35-36; Income Tax Adviser to the Government of India 37-40; Dir. of Statistics, Sec. and Commissioner of Board of Inland Revenue 40-47; Chief of Finance Div. Control Comm. for Germany, British Element 45-47; Dir. ICI Ltd. 47, Financial Dir. 48-52, Deputy Chair. 52-60, Chair. 60-68; mem. Cttee. appointed to review the organization of Customs and Excise 51-53; mem. Cttee. on Departmental Records 52-54; Chair. Cttee. of Inquiry into London Transport 53-55; Dir. Nat. Provincial Bank Ltd. 51-69, Nat. Westminster Bank Ltd. 69-74, Royal Insurance Co. Ltd. 53-57 (Deputy Chair. 66-68, Chair. 68-74); Pres. Inst. of Dirs. 64-68; British Shippers' Council 63-68; Vice-Pres. The India, Pakistan, Burma Asscn. 55-71; Dir. Imperial Chemical Industries of Australia & New Zealand Ltd. 52-68; Deputy Chair. of African Explosives & Chemical Industries Ltd. 60-68; Pro-Chancellor Univ. of Kent 71-; Treas. The Open Univ. 69-75; several hon. degrees.

Home: 1A Frognal Gardens, Hampstead, London, N.W.3, England.

Telephone: 01-794-6906.

Chamoun, Camille, LL.D.; Lebanese lawyer and politician; b. 3 April 1900; ed. Coll. des Frères and Law School, Beirut.

Qualified as lawyer 24; mem. Parliament 34-; Minister of Finance 38; Minister of Interior 43-44; Minister to Allied Governments in London 44; Head of Del. to Int. Civil Aviation Conf., Chicago 44, UNESCO Conf. and UN Preparatory Comm. 45; Del. to UN Gen. Assembly, London and N.Y. 46; Lebanese rep. Interim Comm., UN 48; Pres. Lebanese Republic 52-58; Leader Liberal Nationalist Party 58-; Minister of Interior, Posts, Telephones, Telecommunications, Power and Electricity 75-.

Ministry of Interior, Beirut, Lebanon.

Champetier, Georges, D. es SC. PHY.; French scientist; b. 3 Feb. 1905, Paris; s. of Hippolyte Champetier and Berthe Constant; m. Eugénie Haussonville 1927; two s. two d.

Demonstrator, Ecole Pratique des Hautes Etudes, Paris 28-30; Asst. Inst. de Biologie Physico-chimique, Paris 30-37; Head of Laboratory, Faculty of Sciences, Univ. of Paris 37-39; in charge of Research, Nat. Centre of Scientific Research 39-45; Deputy Prof. Faculty of Sciences, Univ. of Paris 45-47, Asst. Prof. 47; Dir. Ecole Supérieure de Physique et de Chimie Industrielles Paris 69-; Prof. Faculty of Sciences Univ. of Paris 49-; Hon. Dir. Nat. Centre of Scientific Research 57; Pres. Société Chimique de France 62-64; Pres. Admin. Council, Institut Pasteur 66-70; Pres. French Nat. Cttee. of Chemistry 72; mem. Académie des Sciences 60-; Commdr. Légion d'Honneur; Grand Officier de l'Ordre National du Mérite.

Leisure interests: photography, amateur cinema.

Publs. *Traité de Chimie Générale, Notions et Principes fondamentaux* 39, *Les Eléments de la Chimie* 43, *La Chimie Générale* 45, *Dérivés cellulosiques* 47, *Les Molécules géantes* 48, *Chimie macromoléculaire* 72.

10 rue Vauquelin, Paris 5e, France.

Telephone: 337-77-00.

Champin, Pierre Marcel Henri; French businessman; b. 26 Aug. 1903; ed. Ecole des Sciences Politiques, Paris.

Former Pres. and Gen. Man. Vallourec, now Hon. Pres.; fmr. Pres. and Gen. Man. Denain-Nord-Est-Longwy, now Hon. Pres.; Admin. Usinor, Metal Deployé, Usines à Tubes de la Sarre, Brossette et Fils and of several other concerns; Officier Légion d'Honneur.

Home: 11 *bis* rue Jean Goujon, Paris 8e; Office: 7 place Chancelier Adenauer, 75-Paris 16e, France.

Chamson, André Louis Jules; French writer and museum curator; b. 6 June 1900, Nimes (Gard); s. of Jean Chamson and Madeleine Aldebert; m. Lucie Mazauric 1924; one d.; ed. Ecole des Chartes.

Curator Château de Versailles 33-39; Curator Petit Palais 45-59; mem. Acad. Française 56-; Int. Pres. PEN Club 56; Dir.-Gen. Archives de France 59-71; mem. Board of Dirs. ORTF 64-72; Pres. of Coll. of Curators of Museum of Chantilly 73-; Grand Croix de la Légion d'Honneur; Croix de Guerre; Médaille de la Résistance; many foreign honours; Hon. Dr. Laval Univ. (Quebec).

Leisure interests: hunting, riding.

Publs. *Roux le Bandit* 25, *Les Hommes de la route* 27, *Le Crime des Justes* 28, *Héritages* 30, *L'année des vaincus* 35, *Les quatre éléments* 36, *L'auberge de l'abîme* 36, *La Gèalre* 38, *Le Puits des Miracles* 45, *Le dernier village* 46, *L'homme qui marchait devant moi* 48, *La neige et la fleur* 51, *On ne voit pas le coeur* 52, *Le chiffre de nos jours* 54, *Languedoc* 56, *Adeline Venician* 56, *Nos ancêtres, les Gaulois* 58, *Devenir ce qu'on est* 60, *Le rendez-vous des espérances* 61, *Comme une pierre qui tombe* 64, *La Petite Odyssée* 65, *La Superbe* 67, *Suite cévenole* 68, *Suite pathétique* 69, *La Tour de Constance* 70, *Les Taillons ou la Terreur Blanche* 74, *La Reconquête* 74, *Suite Guerrière* 75.

35 rue Mirabeau, Paris 16e, France.

Chance, Britton, M.S., PH.D., D.SC.; American biophysicist; b. 24 July 1913, Wilkes Barre, Pa.; s. of Edwin M. and Eleanor (Kent) Chance; m. 1st Jane Earle 1938 (divorced), 2nd Lilian Streeter Lucas 1955; four s. four d., two step s. two step d.; ed. Univ. of Pennsylvania and Cambridge Univ., England.

Acting Dir. Johnson Foundation 40-41; Investigator Office of Scientific Research and Development 41; staff mem. Radiation Laboratory, M.I.T.; Asst. Prof. of Biophysics, Univ. of Pennsylvania 41-46, Prof. and Dir. Johnson Foundation 49-, E. R. Johnson Prof. of Biophysics 49-; Guggenheim Fellow, Nobel and Molteno Inst. 46-48; scientific consultant, research attaché, U.S. Navy, London 48; consultant, Nat. Science Foundation 51-56; President's Scientific Advisory Cttee. 59-60; NCI Working Group on Molecular Control

73-; NIAAA Council 71-75; Vice-Pres. Int. Union Pure and Applied Biophysics 72-75, Pres. 75-, mem. Nat. Acad. of Sciences, American Acad. of Arts and Sciences, American Philosophical Soc., Royal Acad. of Science, Uppsala, Biochemical Soc., Biophysical Soc., Int. Soc. for Cell Biology, Royal Soc. of Arts, Royal Swedish Acad., Acad. Leopoldina, etc.; Foreign mem. Max-Planck-Institut für Systemphysiologie und Ernährungs-physiologie, Dortmund; Fellow, Inst. of Radio Engineers; Presidential Certificate of Merit 50; Paul Lewis award in enzyme chemistry, American Chemical Soc. 50; William J. Morlock award in biochemical electronics, Inst. of Radio Engineers 61; Netherlands Biochemical Soc. Award 66; Keilin Medal 66; Franklin Medal 66; Heineken Prize 70; Gairdner Award 72; Festschrift Symposium, Stockholm 73; Semmelweis Medal 74; Nat. Medal of Science 74.
Leisure interests: yacht sailing and cruising, amateur radio.
Publs. *Waveforms* (with Williams, Hughes, McNichol, Sayre) 49, *Electronic Time Measurements* (with Hulsizer, McNichol, Williams) 49, *Enzyme-Substrate Compounds* 51, *Enzymes in Action in Living Cells* 55, *The Respiratory Chain and Oxidative Phosphorylation* 56, *Techniques for Assay of Respiratory Enzymes* 57, *Energy-Linked Functions of Mitochondria* 63, *Rapid Mixing and Sampling Techniques in Biochemistry* 64, *Control of Energy Metabolism* 65, *Hemes and Hemoproteins* 66, *Probes of Structure and Function of Macromolecules and Enzymes* 72.
Johnson Research Foundation, Richards Building D-501 G4, University of Pennsylvania, Philadelphia, Pa. 19174, U.S.A.
Telephone: 215-243-7159.

Chancellor, Sir Christopher (John), Kt., C.M.G., M.A.; British business executive; b. 29 March 1904, Cobham, Surrey; s. of Sir John and Lady Chancellor; m. Sylvia Mary Paget 1926; two s. two d.; ed. Eton Coll., and Trinity Coll., Cambridge.
Joined Reuters 30, Gen. Man. 44-59; Chair. Odhams Press Ltd. 60-61, Daily Herald (1929) Ltd. 60-61, The Bowater Paper Corpn. 62-69; Vice-Pres. Nat. Council of Social Service 59-71; Chair. Pilgrims Soc. 59-68; Dir. Madame Tussaud's Ltd. (fmr. Chair.), Bristol Evening Post Ltd.; mem. of Council, Univ. of Bath; Trustee, American Museum in Britain.
Hunstrete House, Pensford, Somerset, England.

Chancellor, John; American newspaperman and TV compère; b. 14 July 1927; ed. Univ. of Illinois.
Chicago *Sun-Times*; NBC news staff 50-, corresp. Chicago, Vienna, London, Moscow, Brussels, Berlin; compère NBC TV programme *To-day* 61-62; Producer of Special Programmes 62-63; Head of NBC Brussels Bureau to cover European Common Market July 63-64; White House Corresp. of NBC 64-65; Dir. Voice of America 65-67, with NBC 67-; Principal Reporter NBC Nightly News 71-.
c/o NBC News, 30 Rockefeller Plaza, New York, N.Y. 10020, U.S.A.

Chand, Khub, B.A.; Indian diplomatist and international development consultant; b. 16 Dec. 1911, Khurd (Jhelum); m. Nirmal Singh 1948; ed. Univ. of Delhi and Oriel Coll., Oxford.
Joined I.C.S. 35; Asst. and later Joint Magistrate, Shahjahanpur (U.P.) 35-37; Joint and later Additional District Magistrate, Kanpur (U.P.) 37-39; Under Sec. to Govt. of India, Dept. of Defence and Sec. Indian Soldiers' Board, later Asst. Financial Adviser, Mil. Finance 39-43; District Magistrate, Azamgarh (U.P.) 43-45; Regional Food Controller, U.P. 45-47; Deputy Sec. Ministry of Defence 47-48; Head Indian Mil. Mission in Germany, with rank of Major-Gen., Indian Army 48-50; Head of Indian Mission Allied High Comm. for Germany 49-50; Deputy High Commr. for

India in Pakistan 50-52, Acting High Commr. 50-51; Minister to Iraq April 52-55, concurrently Minister to Jordan 54-55; Joint Sec. to Govt. of India, Ministry of External Affairs 55-57; Amb. to Italy 57-60, concurrently Minister to Albania; High Commr. for India in Ghana and Sierra Leone, Commr. in Nigeria and Amb. to Liberia, Guinea and Mali 60-62; Amb. to Sweden and Finland 62-66; Leader of Indian delegation to 41st session of Economic and Social Council of UN 66; Indian rep. on Ad Hoc Cttee. of Narcotics Comm. of UN; Amb. to Lebanon, Jordan, Kuwait and High Commr. in Cyprus 66-67; Amb. to Fed. Repub. of Germany 67-70; mem. Exec. Board, Indian Council of World Affairs 72, Vice-Pres. 74; mem. for American and W. European Studies, Cttee. of Jawaharlal Nehru Univ. School of Int. Studies 74-.
Leisure interests: travel, bridge.
c/o 1/8A Shanti Niketan, New Delhi 21, India.
Telephone: 672473.

Chanda, Asok Kumar, B.SC., O.B.E.; Indian financier and economist; b. 25 Oct. 1902, Silchar, Assam; s. of late Kamini Kumar Chanda and late Chandraprabha Chanda; m. Monica Gupta 1928; two d.; ed. Calcutta Univ. and London School of Economics.
Joined Indian Audit and Accounts Service 26; mem. Lend-Lease Del. to U.S.A. 46; Adviser, Punjab Partition Council 47; Sec. of Defence 47-48; Deputy High Commr. to U.K. 48-49; Financial Commr. for Railways 49-52; Sec. Ministry of Production 52-54; Chair. Board of Dirs., Sindri Fertilizers & Chemicals Ltd., Hindustan Machine Tools Ltd. and Hindustan Steel Ltd. 52-54; Comptroller and Auditor-General 54-60; Chair. Third Finance Comm. 61, Union Excise Reorganization Cttee. 63, Cttee. on Broadcasting and Information Media 67; Chair. Jessop and Co. Ltd., Delhi 60-; Pres. Bengal Lawn Tennis Asscn.
Leisure interests: golf, swimming, photography.
Publs. *Indian Administration, Aspects of Audit Control, Federalism in India: A Study of Union-State Relations*.
54e Sujan Singh Park, New Delhi 3, India.
Telephone: 388081.

Chandavimol, Abhai, M.A. (CANTAB.); Thai educationist; b. 16 Feb. 1908, Carthaburi; s. of Meng Chandavimol and Wann Punyasthiti; m. Tongkorn Punyasthiti 1942; three s. one d.; ed. Suan Kularb School, Bangkok, Imperial Service Coll., Windsor, Gonville and Caius Coll., Cambridge, Inner Temple, London.
Teacher 25-28, 35-36; Sec. Dept. of Physical Educ. 36-43; Chief Private School Div. 43-47; Asst. Dir.-Gen. Dept. of Gen. Educ. 47-51; Dir.-Gen. Dept. of Physical Educ. 51-52, Dept. of Elementary and Adult Educ. 52-61; Under-Sec. of State for Educ. 61-68; Deputy Minister of Educ. 70-71, Minister 72-74; Senator 75-; mem. Exec. Cttee. Boy Scouts of Thailand 52-; elected Boy Scouts World Cttee. 65-71; elected Chair. Far East Scouts advisory Cttee. 66-68; Order of Crown of Thailand, Order of the White Elephant.
Leisure interests: scouting, gardening, orchid cultivation, golf.
85 Rajatapan Lane, Makkasan Bangkok 4, Thailand.
Telephone: 51-5058.

Chandler, George, M.A., PH.D., F.L.A., F.R.HIST.S.; British librarian; b. 2 July 1915, Birmingham; s. of late William Chandler and Mrs. F. W. Chandler; m. Dorothy Lowe 1937; one s.; ed. Central Grammar School, Birmingham, Birmingham and Midland Inst., Leeds Coll. of Commerce and Univ. of London.
With Birmingham Public Libraries 31-37, Leeds Public Libraries 37-46; Borough Librarian and Curator, Dudley 47-50; Deputy City Librarian, Liverpool 50-52; City Librarian 52-74; established Int. Library 57, American Library 59, Commonwealth Library 59; organizer of int. literary and historical exhibitions of books, manuscripts and prints; External Examiner, Sheffield

Univ.; Pres. Soc. of Municipal and County Chief Librarians 62-70; Chair. Exec. Cttee. of the Library Asscn. 65-70; mem. Library Advisory Council for England and Wales 65-72; Dir. Ladsirlac Technical Information Centre; Editor, Int. Series of Monographs on Libraries and Information Science, Editor Int. Bibliographical and Library Surveys 71; Pres. Int. Asscn. of Metropolitan City Libraries 67-71; mem. Organizing Cttee., British Library 71-73, British Library Board 73-74; Dir.-Gen. Nat. Library of Australia 74-; Hon. Editor *Int. Library Review* 69-; Pres. Library Asscn. 71.
Leisure interests: travel, walking, country cottage, dancing, foreign languages.
Publs. *Dudley* 49, *William Roscoe* 53, *Liverpool* 57, *Liverpool Shipping* 60, *Liverpool under James I* 60, *How to Find Out* 63, 67, 68, 73, *The Grasshopper and the Liver Bird* 64, *Liverpool under Charles I* 65, *Libraries in the Modern World* 65, *Four Centuries of Banking* 64, 68, *How to find out about Literature* 68-, *Libraries in the East* 71, *International Librarianship* 72, *Victorian and Edwardian Liverpool and the North West* 72, *Libraries, Bibliography and Documentation in the Soviet Union* 72, *Social History of Liverpool* 72, *Merchant Venturers* 73, *Victorian and Edwardian Manchester* 74.
c/o National Library of Australia, Canberra, A.C.T., Australia.

Chandler, Otis; American newspaper executive; b. 23 Nov. 1927, Los Angeles; s. of Norman Chandler and Dorothy Buffum Chandler; m. Marilyn Jane Brant 1951; three s. two d.; ed. Andover Acad., Mass., and Stanford Univ.
Trainee, Times Mirror Co. 53, Asst. to President (assigned to *Mirror-News*) 57, Marketing Manager, *Los Angeles Times* 58-60, Publisher, *Los Angeles Times* 60-, Vice-Pres. Times Mirror Co. 61-, Sr. Vice-Pres. 66-, Dir. 62; Vice-Chair. Board Times Mirror Co. 68.
Leisure interests: board surfing, hunting, fishing, photography, tennis, water skiing, track and field, sports cars.
Times Mirror Square, Los Angeles, Calif. 90053; 1048 Oak Grove Place, San Marino, Calif., U.S.A.

Chandra, Avinash; Indian artist; b. 28 Aug. 1931, Simla; ed. Delhi Polytechnic, Delhi.
On staff of Delhi Polytechnic, Delhi 53-56; in London 56-; executed glass mural for Pilkington Brothers' Head Office, St. Helens, Lancs. and fibreglass mural for Indian Tea Centre, London 64; Gold Medal, Prix Européen, Ostend 62; John D. Rockefeller Third Fund Fellowship 65.
Works in following collections: National Gallery of Modern Art, New Delhi, Tate Gallery, London, Victoria and Albert Museum, London, Arts Council of Great Britain, London, Ashmolean Museum, Oxford, Ulster Museum, Belfast, City Art Gallery, Birmingham, Gulbenkian Museum, Durham, Musée National d'Art Moderne, Paris, Whitworth Art Gallery, Manchester, Museum of Modern Art, Haifa, Punjab Museum, Chandigarh, etc.; one-man exhbns. in Srinagar, New Delhi, Belfast, London, Oxford, Paris, Bristol, Arnhem, Amsterdam, Zürich, Copenhagen, Stockholm, Chicago, Toronto, Geneva, etc.
24 Willoughby Road, Hampstead, London, N.W.3, England.

Chandra, Satish, M.A., B.SC.; Indian business exec. and politician; b. 17; ed. S.M. Coll., Chandausi, Govt. Agricultural Coll., Kanpur, and Bareilly Coll., Bareilly (Agra Univ.).
Indian Nat. Congress 36-; mem. Indian Constituent Ass. 48-50, Provisional Parl. 50-52, Lok Sabha 52-62; Parl. Sec. to Prime Minister 51-52; Union Dep. Minister for Defence 52-55, for Production 55-57, for Commerce and Industry 57-62; Chair. Indian Airlines Corpn. and Dir. Air-India 63, 64; Chair. British India Corpn. Ltd.,

The Elgin Mills Co. Ltd., Cawnpore Textiles Ltd., Cawnpore Sugar Works Ltd., Champarun Sugar Co. Ltd., Saran Engineering Co. Ltd. 62-; Dir. other cos.
Chitrakut, Parbati Bagla Road, Kanpur, U.P., India.

Chandrasekhar, Sripati, M.A., M.LITT., M.SC., PH.D., Indian economist and demographer; b. 22 Nov. 1918, Rajahmundry; s. of Prof. Sripati Sarangapanni and Mrs. Rajamma Sarangapanni; m. Dorothy Anne Downes 1947; three d.; ed. Univ. of Madras and Columbia, New York and Princeton Univs.
Visiting Lecturer, Univ. of Pa. and Asia Inst., New York 44-46; Prof. of Economics, Annamalai Univ. 47-50; Dir. Demographic Research, UNESCO, Paris 47-49; Prof. of Economics and Head of Dept., Baroda Univ. 50-53; Nuffield Fellow, London School of Economics 53-55; Dir. Indian Inst. for Population Studies 56-67; mem. Rajya Sabha 64-70; Minister of State for Health and Family Planning 67-Nov. 67; Minister of State in Ministry of Health, Family Planning and Urban Development 67-70; Research Prof. of Demography, Univ. of Calif.; Visiting Fellow Battelle Research Centre ("Think Tank") Seattle 71-72; Distinguished Visiting Prof. of Sociology, Calif. State Univ.; San Diego 72-74; Prof. of Demography and Public Health, Univ. of Calif., Los Angeles, 74-75; Vice Chancellor Annamalai Univ., Chidambaram, South India 75-; Editor *Population Review*; Hon. D.Litt. (Redlands Univ., Kurukshetra Univ.); Hon. M.D. (Budapest); Hon. D.Sc. (Univ. of Pacific).
Leisure interests: reading, especially detective stories, European classical music.
Publs. *India's Population* 46, *Census and Statistics in India* 47, *Indian Emigration* 48, *Hungry People and Empty Lands* 52, *Population and Planned Parenthood in India* 55, *Infant Mortality in India* 59, *China's Population* 59, *Communist China Today* 61, *Red China: An Asian View* 62, *A Decade of Mao's China* (Editor) 63, *American Aid and India's Economic Development* 65, *Asia's Population Problems* 67, *Problems of Economic Development* 67, *India's Population: Fact, Problem and Policy* 68, *Infant Mortality, Population Growth and Family Planning in India* 72, *Abortion in a Crowded World: the Problem of Abortion with Special Reference to India* 74.
Annamalai University, Chidambaram, South India; and 8976 Cliffridge Avenue, La Jolla, Calif., U.S.A.

Chandrasekhar, Subrahmanyan, B.A., PH.D., SC.D., F.R.S.; American (b. Indian) university professor; b. 19 Oct. 1910, Lahore; m. Lalitha Doraiswamy 1936; ed. Presidency Coll., Madras, and Cambridge Univ.
Fellow of Trinity Coll., Cambridge 33-37; Research Assoc. Univ. of Chicago 37-38, Asst. Prof. 38-41, Assoc. Prof. 42-43, Prof. 44-46; Distinguished Service Prof. of Theoretical Astrophysics 47-52, Morton D. Hull Distinguished Service Prof. of Theoretical Astrophysics 52-; Man. Editor *Astrophysical Journal* 52-71; mem. American Philosophical Society, American Academy of Arts and Sciences, U.S. Nat. Acad. of Sciences, Royal Soc. London; Bruce Gold Medal of Astronomical Soc. of the Pacific 52, Gold Medal, Royal Astronomical Soc. 53, Rumford Medal, American Acad. of Arts and Sciences 57, Royal Medal, Royal Soc., London 62, Nat. Medal of Science, U.S.A. 67, Nehru Memorial Lecture 68, Draper Medal, U.S. Nat. Acad. of Sciences 71, Heineman Prize, American Physical Soc. 74.
Publs. *Introduction to the Study of Stellar Structure* 39, *Principles of Stellar Dynamics* 42, *Radiative Transfer* 50, *Hydrodynamic and Hydromagnetic Stability* 61, *Ellipsoidal Figures of Equilibrium* 69.
Laboratory for Astrophysics and Space Research, 933 East 56th Street, Chicago, Illinois 60637, U.S.A.
Telephone: 312-753-8562.

Chandrasekharan, Komaravolu, M.A., M.SC., PH.D., Indian mathematician; b. 21 Nov. 1920, Masulipatam;

India; *m*. A. Sarada 1944; two *s*.; ed. Presidency Coll., Madras, and Inst. for Advanced Study, Princeton.
Prof. Eidgenössische Technische Hochschule, Zürich; Sec. Int. Mathematical Union 61-66, Pres. 71-74; Vice-Pres. Int Council of Scientific Unions 63-66, Sec.-Gen. 66-70; mem. Scientific Advisory Cttee. to Cabinet, Govt. of India 61-66; Fellow Nat. Inst. of Sciences of India, Indian Acad. of Sciences; Foreign mem. Finnish Acad. of Science and Letters 75; Padma Shri 59; Shanti Swarup Bhatnagar Memorial Award for Scientific Research 63; Ramanujan Medal 66.
Leisure interests: painting, book design.
Publs. *Fourier Transforms* (with S. Bochner) 49, *Typical Means* (with S. Minakshisundaram) 52, *Lectures on the Riemann Zeta-function* 53, *Analytic Number Theory* 69, *Arithmetical Functions* 70.
Eidgenössische Technische Hochschule, 8006 Zürich, Rämistrasse 101; Home: Hedwigstrasse 29, 8032 Zürich, Switzerland.
Telephone: 53-96-86.

Chandy, Kanianthra Thomas, M.A., LL.M.; Indian business executive; b. 13 Jan. 1913; *s*. of K. J.Thomas and Mrs. A. Thomas; *m*. 1938; three *s*. two *d*.; ed. London Univ.
In legal practice; later joined Hindustan Lever Ltd., Dir. 56-61; Dir. of Research Hyderabad Adm. Staff Coll. 56-61; Dir. Indian Inst. of Management, Calcutta 66-62; fmr. Chair. Food Corpn. of India; Chair. Hindustan Steel Ltd. 68-72; fmr. mem. Nat. Planning Council; fmr. mem. Nat. Credit Council; fmr. mem. Prime Minister's Review Cttee. reviewing the activities of the Council of Scientific and Industrial Research; Chair. Kerala State Industrial Devt. Corpn. 72-; Vice-Chair. Kerala State Planning Board; Chair. Board of Govs., Indian Inst. of Technology, Madras, Nat. Productivity Council of India, Steel Complex Ltd.; mem. Univ. Grants Comm., Govt. of India.
P.O. Box 105, Trivandrum 1, Kerala, India.

Chang Ch'ih-ming; Chinese army officer.
Political Commissar, 4th Field Army, People's Liberation Army 50; Political Commissar in Gen. Logistics Dept., Central-South Mil. District, PLA 54; re-assigned to Gen. Mil. Org. 54; Lieut.-Gen. PLA 55; Pres. Logistics Inst., PLA 60; Deputy Dir., Gen. Logistics Dept., PLA 65, Political Commissar 67-.
People's Republic of China.

Chang Ch'ing-fu; Chinese government official.
Vice-Minister of Forestry 56-58; Minister of Finance 75-.
People's Republic of China.

Chang Ching-yao; Chinese army officer.
Commander Kwangtung Mil. District, People's Liberation Army 73-.
People's Republic of China.

Chang Ch'un-chi'ao; Chinese party official; b. *circa* 1911.
Director East China Gen. Branch, New China News Agency 50; Dir. *Liberation Daily*, Shanghai 54; Alt. Sec. CCP Shanghai 64, Sec. 65; Chair. Shanghai Revolutionary Cttee. 67; Deputy Head Cen. Cultural Revolution Group 67; First Political Commissar Nanking Mil. Region, People's Liberation Army 67; mem. Politburo, 9th Cen. Cttee., CCP 69; First Sec. CCP Shanghai 71; mem. Standing Cttee., Politburo, 10th Cen. Cttee. of CCP 73; Vice-Premier State Council 75; Dir., Gen. Political Dept., PLA 75.
People's Republic of China.

Chang Chung; Chinese army officer.
Commander Kansu Mil. District, People's Liberation Army 67-; Vice-Chair. Kansu Revolutionary Cttee. 68; Sec. CCP Kansu 72.
People's Republic of China.

Chang Dai-Chien; Chinese painter; b. 1 April 1899; ed. Chui-ch'ing School, Chungking and under Li Ch'ing, Shanghai.
Member Cttee. first Nat. Exhbn. of Fine Arts 29; Prof. Central Univ. Nanking 36; moved to Argentina 52; first one-man exhbn. Peking 34, then Shanghai 36, Chungking 39, 40, Chengtu 43, Shanghai 46, 47, Hong Kong 48, 62, New Delhi and Hyderabad 50, Buenos Aires 52, Tokyo 55, 56, Museum of Modern Art, Paris 56, Salon Nationale, Paris 60, Brussels 60, Athens 60, Madrid 60, Geneva 61, São Paulo 61, Singapore 63, Kuala Lumpur 63, New York 63, Cologne 64, Grosvenor Gallery, London 65; represented at Paris Exhbn. of Chinese Painting 33, London 35, UNESCO Exhbn., Paris 46; Gold Medal, Int. Council of Fine Arts, N.Y. 58.
Major works: *The Lotuses*, Jeu-de-Paume Museum, Paris 33, copied two hundred frescoes, caves of Tun-huang 40, *Giant Lotus* 45, twelve major works, Perm. Exhbn. Contemporary Chinese Art, Cernuschi Museum 59, Lotus painting, Museum of Modern Art, N.Y. 61.
P.O. Box 249, Mogi das Cruzes, São Paulo, Brazil.

Chang Do Yung, General; Korean army officer; b. 1923; ed. Tongyang Univ., Japan.
Fought in Japanese army in Second World War; further education in U.S.A. 53; Dep. C.-in-C. of Gen. Staff, S. Korean Army 56, later Cmmdr. Second Army; C.-in-C. of General Staff; Minister of Defence May-June 61, Chair. Supreme Council of Nat.Reconstruction and Prime Minister May-June 61; under house arrest July 61; sentenced to death Jan. 62, sentence commuted, later released 62.
Seoul, Republic of Korea.

Chang Hai-t'ang; Chinese army officer.
Deputy Chief of Staff Liaoning Mil. District, People's Liberation Army 59, Deputy Commdr. 60, Commdr. 72-; Maj.-Gen. PLA 59; Vice-Chair. Liaoning Revolutionary Cttee. 72.
People's Republic of China.

Chang Hsien-yueh; Chinese army officer.
Lieutenant-General, People's Liberation Army 55; Deputy Dir., Gen. Logistics Dept., PLA 64-.
People's Republic of China.

Chang Lin-pin; Chinese army officer.
Deputy Dir., Gen. Logistics Dept., People's Liberation Army 50-; Lieut.-Gen. PLA 55; Alt. mem. 9th Cen. Cttee. of CCP 69, 10th Cen. Cttee. 73.
People's Republic of China.

Chang P'ing-hua; Chinese party official; b. 1903, Hunan.
Political Commissar in 120th Div. 47; Third Sec. CCP Wuhan 49-52; First Sec. CCP Hupeh 55-56, Second Sec. 56, Sec. 57-59; Alt. mem. 8th Cen. Cttee. of CCP 56; First Sec. CCP Hunan 59-67; First Political Commissar Hunan Mil. District, People's Liberation Army 60; Sec. Cen.-South Bureau, CCP 66-67; Deputy Dir. Propaganda Dept., CCP 66; criticized and removed from office during Cultural Revolution 67; Vice-Chair. Shansi Revolutionary Cttee. 71; Sec. CCP Shansi 71; Sec. CCP Hunan 73, Second Sec. 74-; mem. 10th Cen. Cttee. of CCP 73.
People's Republic of China.

Chang Shu-chih; Chinese army officer.
Commander Honan Mil. District, People's Liberation Army 64-; Deputy Commdr. Wuhan Mil. Region, PLA 70; Sec. CCP Honan 71; mem. 10th Cen. Cttee. of CCP 73.
People's Republic of China.

Chang Ts'ai-ch'ien; Chinese army officer.
Guerilla leader in Hupeh, Honan, Anhwei and Hunan 46; Chief of Staff Hupeh Mil. District, People's Liberation Army 50; Lieut.-Gen. PLA 58; Deputy Commdr.

Nanking Mil. Region, PLA 58-70; mem. 9th Cen. Cttee. of CCP 69, 10th Cen. Cttee. 73; Deputy Chief of Staff PLA 71-.
People's Republic of China.

Chang Tsung-hsun; Chinese military officer; b. 1898, Shensi; ed. Whampoa Mil. Acad.
Graduated 1925; Div. Commdr. Red Army 29; Chief of Staff, 4th Front Army on "Long March" 34; Brigade Commdr. 37; Alt. mem. 7th Central Cttee. 45; Deputy Commdr. First Field Army, People's Liberation Army 49-54, Deputy Chief of Gen. Staff 54-75; Alt. mem. 8th Cen. Cttee. CCP 56; visited Eastern Europe 59; Dir., Gen. Logistics Dept., PLA 75-.
People's Republic of China.

Chang Wei-hsun; Chinese civil servant and United Nations official.
Formerly in Foreign Relations Dept., Ministry of Health, Peking; Asst. Dir.-Gen. World Health Org. (WHO), in charge of family health and health services divs. 73-.
World Health Organization, Avenue Appia, 1121 Geneva, Switzerland.

Changufu, Lewis; Zambian politician; b. 1927, Kasama; ed. locally and by correspondence.
Entered politics 50; fmr. mem., African Nat. Congress 58; restricted 59; attended course in public relations and leadership, U.S.A.; Parl. Sec. to Prime Minister's Office 64-Jan. 65; Minister of Information and Postal Services Jan. 65-Dec. 66; Nat. Chief Trustee, United Nat. Independence Party (U.N.I.P.); Minister of Home Affairs Dec. 66-Sept. 67; Minister of Labour Sept. 67-Dec. 68; Minister of Labour and Social Services Dec. 68, later Minister of Transport; Minister of Home Affairs 70-73; Dir. of cos. 74-.
c/o Chibote House, Lusaka, Zambia.

Channing, Carol; American actress; b. 31 Jan. 1923.
Critics' Circle Award for *Lend an Ear*; Tony Award for *Hello Dolly* 63, Golden Globe Award for Best Supporting Actress, *Thoroughly Modern Millie* 67, Tony Award 68.
Stage productions include, *No for an Answer, Let's Face It, So Proudly We Hail, Lend an Ear, Gentlemen Prefer Blondes, Wonderful Town, The Vamp, Hello Dolly, Lorelei.*
Films include *The First Traveling Saleslady* 56, *Thoroughly Modern Millie* 67.
8749 Sunset Boulevard, Hollywood, Calif. 90046, U.S.A.

Chao Hsin-chu; Chinese party official.
Secretary, CCP Hupeh 57-65; Vice Gov. Hupeh 58-64; Vice-Minister of Culture 65; criticized and removed from office during Cultural Revolution 66; rehabilitated as a "leading cadre" in Inner Mongolia 72; Vice-Chair. Provincial Revolutionary Cttee. and Secretary CCP, Hupeh 73, Chair. Revolutionary Cttee. and First Sec., Hupeh 75.
Peoples' Republic of China.

Chao Tzu-yang; Chinese party official.
Secretary-General S. China Sub-bureau, CCP 50-54, Third Sec. 54-55; Third Deputy Sec. CCP Kwangtung 55, Sec. 62, First Sec. 65-67; Political Commissar Kwangtung Mil. District, People's Liberation Army 64; Sec. Cen.-South Bureau, CCP 65-67; criticized and removed from office during Cultural Revolution 67; Vice-Chair. Inner Mongolia Revolutionary Cttee. 71; Sec. CCP Inner Mongolia 71, CCP Kwangtung 72; Vice-Chair. Kwangtung Revolutionary Cttee. 72; mem. 10th Cen. Cttee. of CCP 73; First Sec. CCP Kwangtung 74; First Sec. Szechuan CCP Cttee. 75; Chair. Kwangtung Revolutionary Cttee. 74.
People's Republic of China.

Chapelain-Midy, Roger; French painter; b. 24 Aug. 1904, Paris; s. of Maurice and Hélène Chapelain-Midy; m. Ginette Pierre-Alype 1935; two s.; ed. Lycée Louis le Grand, Paris.

Pictures hung in Musée d'Art Moderne and Musée des Beaux Arts, Paris, in museums in Boulogne, La Rochelle, Lyon, Saint-Etienne, Cambrai, Bordeaux, Dijon, Algiers, Tunis, etc.; also in Venice, Amsterdam, Brussels, Buenos Aires, Cairo, São Paulo and London; awards include Carnegie Prize 38, Prix de l'Ile de France 52, Prix de la Biennale de Menton 53; Grand Prix de la Ville de Paris 55; Prix du Costume de Théâtre at Int. Biennale São Paulo 61; Officier de la Légion d'Honneur; Commdr. des Arts et Lettres; mem. Académie Royale de Belgique.
Leisure interests: everything related to gardens, plants, and nature in general.
Works include (in addition to pictures): murals in the theatre of the Palais de Chaillot, the Inst. Nat. Agronomique, and on the steamships *Provence, Bretagne, Jean Laborde, France*; and theatrical costumes and decors, in particular for *Les Indes Galantes* 52, *Die Zauberflöte* (Mozart) for the Théâtre National de l'Opéra 54, and *La Répétition* (ballet) for Cologne Opera 63, *Les Femmes Savantes* for the Comédie Française 72.
68 rue Lhomond, Paris 5e, France.
Telephone: 707-27-90.

Chapin, Roy Dikeman, Jr., A.B.; American automobile executive; b. 21 Sept. 1915; s. of Roy D. Chapin; m. Loise Chapin; ed. Yale Univ.
Held various positions with Hudson Motor Car Co. and Hudson Sales Corpn. 38-54; Asst. Sales Man. Hudson Div. American Motors Corpn. 52-54; Asst. Treas. and Dir. American Motors Corpn. 54-55, Treas. 55, Vice-Pres. 56-60, Exec. Vice-Pres., int. operations 60-66, Exec. Vice-Pres. and Gen. Man. 66-67, Chair. of Board and Chief Exec. Officer 67-; Chair. and Dir. American Motors (Can.) Ltd.; Dir. Rambler Motors Ltd., Amer. Natural Gas Co., Whirlpool Corpn. and other cos.; Vice-Pres. and Trustee, Roy D. Chapin Foundation 48-.
American Motors Corporation, 14250 Plymouth Road, Detroit, Mich. 48232, U.S.A.

Chapin, Schuyler Garrison; American musical impresario; b. 13 Feb. 1923, New York; s. of L. H. Paul Chapin and Leila H. Burden; m. Elizabeth Steinway 1947; four s.; ed. Longy School of Music and Harvard Coll.
Spot Sales, NBC Television, N.Y.C. 47-53; Gen. Man. Tex and Jinx McCrary Enterprises, N.Y.C. 53; Booking Dir. Judson O'Neill and Judd Div., Columbia Artists Management 53-59; Columbia Broadcasting System (CBS), Dir. Masterworks, Columbia Records Div. 59-62, Vice-Pres. Creative Services 62-63; Vice-Pres. Programming, Lincoln Center for the Performing Arts Inc. 64-69; Exec. Producer, Amberson Productions 69-72; Gen. Man. Metropolitan Opera Asscn. Inc. 72-75; Trustee, Naumburg Foundation 62-; Vice-Pres. Bagby Music Lovers Foundation 59-; Trustee, LeRoy Hospital; mem. Board of Dir., Amberson Enterprises Inc. 72-; mem. Coffee House, The Century Asscn.; Air Medal 45; N.Y. State Conspicuous Service Cross 51; Christopher Award 72; Hon. L.H.D. (New York Univ. and Hobart-William Smith Colls.).
Leisure interests: reading, tennis, bridge, swimming, gentle sailing.
901 Lexington Avenue, New York, N.Y. 10021, U.S.A.
Telephone: (212) RE 7-1761.

Chaplin, Arthur Hugh, C.B., B.A., F.L.A.; British librarian; b. 17 April 1905, Bexhill; s. of Rev. H. F Chaplin and Florence B. Lusher; m. Irene Marcousé 1938; ed. Univ. Coll., London.
Asst. Librarian, Reading Univ. 27-28, Queen's Univ. Belfast 28-29; Asst. Keeper, Dept. of Printed Books, British Museum 30-55, Deputy Keeper 55-59, Keeper 59-66, Principal Keeper 66-70; Exec. Sec. I.F.L.A. Working Group on Cataloguing Principles 54-59, Exec. Sec. Organizing Cttee. Int. Conf. on Cataloguing

Principles (1961) 59-66; mem. Council, Library Asscn. 64-70; Chair. I.F.L.A. Cttee. on Cataloguing 66-74; Pres. Microfilm Asscn. of Great Britain 67-71.
44 Russell Square, London, W.C.1, England. Telephone: 01-636-7217.

Chaplin, Sir Charles Spencer, Kt.; British film actor and producer; b. 16 April 1889, London; s. of Charles and Hannah Chaplin; m. 1st Mildred Harris 1918 (dissolved); m. 2nd Lita Grey 1924 (dissolved), two s. (one deceased); m. 3rd Paulette Goddard 1936 (dissolved); m. 4th Oona O'Neill, d. of late Eugene O'Neill, 1943, three s. five d.
Formed own producing organization and built Chaplin Studios, Hollywood 18; joint founder United Artists' Corpn. (with British affiliation Allied Artists); Officier de l'Instruction Publique (France); Commdr. Légion d'Honneur; Hon. D.Litt. (Oxford, Durham); Erasmus Prize 65; mem. American Acad. of Arts and Sciences 70; Life mem. Dirs. Guild of America 75; Order of the Yugoslav Flag with Sash 71; Acad. Award (Oscar) for services to cinema 72.
Films include: *Shoulder Arms* 18, *The Kid* 20, *The Gold Rush* 25, *The Circus* 28, *City Lights* 31, *Modern Times* 36, *The Great Dictator* 40, *Monsieur Verdoux* 47, *Limelight* 52, *A King in New York* 57, *La Revue de Charlot, The Countess from Hong Kong* 66.
Publs. *My Autobiography* 64, *My Life in Pictures* 74.
c/o United Artists Ltd., 142 Wardour Street, London, W.1., England; Vevey, Vaud, Switzerland.

Chapman, Albert Kinkade, A.B., A.M., PH.D.; American businessman; b. 31 May 1890, Marysville, Ohio; s. of Charles S. and Anna T. (Kinkade) Chapman; m. Ercil Howard 1916; two d.; ed. Ohio State and Princeton Univs.
Physiological optical research at Clark Univ. 16-17; served in U.S. Signal Corps and later in U.S. Air Corps (development of aerial photography) 17-19; with Eastman Kodak Co. 19-67, Asst. to Vice-Pres. (Manufacturing) 22-29, Production Man. 30-41, Asst. Vice-Pres. 36-41, Vice-Pres. and Asst. Gen. Man. 41-43, Dir. 43-66, Vice-Pres. and Gen. Man. 43-52, Pres. 52-60, Vice-Chair. of the Board 60-62, Chair. 62-66, Chair. of Exec. Cttee. 61-66; Dir. Canadian Kodak Co. Ltd. 31-66, Kodak Ltd. 59-66; mem. of Advisory Cttee. to the Board Lincoln First Bank of Rochester; Hon. Trustee Univ. of Rochester; Hon. Chair. Board of Trustees, Rochester Inst. of Technology; Trustee Int. Museum of Photography at George Eastman House (Exec. Cttee.); Chevalier Légion d'Honneur.
Eastman Kodak Co., 343 State Street, Rochester, N.Y. 14650, U.S.A.

Chapman-Andrews, Sir Edwin Arthur, K.C.M.G., O.B.E., B.A.; British diplomatist; b. 9 Sept. 1903, Exeter; s. of Arthur John and Ada Chapman-Andrews (née Allen); m. Sadie Barbara Nixon 1931; two s. two d.; ed. Univ. Coll., London, Sorbonne, Paris, and St. John's Coll., Cambridge.
Appointed to the Levant Consular Service 26; studied Oriental languages, Cambridge 26-28; consular appts. Port Said, Cairo, Suez, Addis Ababa, Kirkuk, Harar 28-36; Asst. Oriental Sec. British Embassy, Cairo 37; commissioned Royal Sussex Regt. and apptd. Major on staff of C.-in-C., Middle East; liaison officer with H.I.M. Emperor Haile Selassie and entered Abyssinia with H.I.M. 41. Foreign Office 42; Counsellor and Head, Personnel Dept. 44; one of H.M. Inspectors-Gen. of Overseas Establishments 46; Minister, British Embassy, Cairo 47; Minister to the Lebanon 51, Ambassador 52-56; Ambassador to the Sudan 56-61; London Rep. Massey-Ferguson (Export) Co. Ltd. 61-, Dir. Massey-Ferguson (Export) Co. Ltd. 64-, Mitchell Cotts (Exports) Ltd. 65-73; Fellow, Univ. Coll. London 52; K.St.J. 52; mem. of Council of Lord Kitchener Nat. Memorial Fund;

mem. Council for Middle East Trade 63-68, Chair. 65-68; mem. Nat. Export Council 65-68; mem. Council of Royal Albert Hall, mem. Council Anglo-Arab asscn. 71-; mem. Hon. Soc. of Gray's Inn; K.C.S.G. (Papal) 62.
2 The Leys, Brim Hill, London, N.2, England.

Chapman Nyaho, Daniel Ahmling, C.B.E., M.A., HON. LL.D.; Ghanaian teacher, public servant and business executive; b. 5 July 1909, Keta; s. of William and Jane (née Atriki) Chapman; m. Jane Abam Quashie 1941; two s. five d. (one deceased); ed. Bremen Mission School (Keta), Achimota Coll., Univ. of Oxford, Columbia Univ. and New York Univ.
Teacher Govt. Senior Boys' School, Accra 30, Achimota Coll. 30-33, 37-46; Gen. Sec. All-Ewe Conf. 44-46; Area Specialist, UN Secr. Dept. of Trusteeship and Information from Non-Self-Governing Territories 46-54; mem. Board of Management of UN Int. School, New York 50-54, 58-59; Sec. to Prime Minister and Cabinet, Gold Coast 54-57; Head of Ghana Civil Service 57; Amb. to U.S.A. and Perm. Rep. to UN 57-59; Chair. Mission of Ind. African States to Cuba, Dominican Repub., Haiti, Venezuela, Bolivia, Paraguay, Uruguay, Brazil, Argentina, Chile 58; mem. Board of Management of the UN Int. School, N.Y. 50-54, 58-59; Headmaster Achimota School 59-63; Vice-Chair. Comm. on Higher Educ. in Ghana 60-61, mem. Interim Nat. Council of Higher Educ. and Research, Ghana 61-62; Fellow, Ghana Acad. of Arts and Sciences; mem. UN Middle East/ North Africa Technical Assistance Mission on Narcotics Control 63; First Vice-Chair. Governing Council UN Special Fund 59; Dir. UN Div. of Narcotic Drugs 63-66; mem. Political Cttee. of Nat. Liberation Council 67; mem. Board of Trustees, Gen. Kotoka Trust Fund; Amb. Ministry of External Affairs 67; Exec. Dir. Pioneer Tobacco Co. Ltd. (British-American Tobacco Group) 67-70, Dir. 70-; Dir. Standard Bank Ghana Ltd. 70-; Chair. Arts Council of Ghana 68-69; Danforth Visiting Lecturer for Asscn. of American Colleges 69, 70; Chair. Council of Univ. of Science and Technology, Kumasi 72-; mem. Nat. Advisory Cttee. 72-; Hon. LL.D.
Leisure interests: music, walking, gardening, reading.
Publs. *Our Homeland* (Book I—*A Regional Geography of South-East Gold Coast*) 45, *The Human Geography of Eweland* 45.
Office: Tobacco House, Liberty Avenue, P.O.B. 5211, Accra; Home: 7 Ninth Avenue, Tesano, Accra, Ghana. Telephone: 21111 (Office); 27180 (Home).

Chapsal, Jacques (Jean René); French political scientist; b. 11 May 1909; ed. Ecole des Sciences Politiques and Faculty of Law, Paris (Docteur en Droit).
Librarian of the Senate 36; Sec.-Gen. Ecole des Sciences Politiques 39; Dir. of Institut d'Etudes Politiques, Univ. of Paris 47-; Administrator Fondation Nationale des Sciences Politiques 50.
27 rue Saint-Guillaume, Paris 7e, France.

Char, René; French poet; b. 14 June 1907; ed. Lycée d'Avignon and Univ. d'Aix en Provence.
Chevalier Légion d'Honneur; Croix de Guerre.
Publs. *Le Marteau sans Maître, Placard pour un chemin des écoliers, Dehors la nuit est gouvernée, Seuls demeurent, Feuillets d'Hypnos, Fureur et mystère, Les Matinaux, Le Soleil des eaux, A une Sérénité crispée, Poèmes et prose choisis, La Parole en archipel, Recherche de la base et du Sommet, Commune Présence, Poèmes des deux années, La Bibliothèque est en feu, L'âge cassant, Retour amont, Dans la Pluie Giboyeuse, Le Nu Perdu, Recherche de la base et du sommet* 71, *l'Effroi, la voie, Arrière-histoire du "poème pulvérisé"* 73, *Se rencontrer paysage avec Joseph Sima, Le Monde de l'art n'est pas le monde du pardon* 74.
c/o Editions Gallimard, 5 rue Sébastien-Bottin, Paris 7e; Home: Les Busclats, L'Isle-sur-Sorgue, Vaucluse, France.

Charbonnel, Jean; French politician; b. 22 April 1927; ed. Lycées Henri IV and Louis-le-Grand, Paris; Univ. de Paris à la Sorbonne, Ecole normale supérieure and Ecole nationale d'administration.

Research worker Centre National de Recherches Scientifiques; with Cour des Comptes 56; Asst. Prof. Inst. for Political Sciences, Sorbonne 57-59; Technical Counsellor Ministry of Public Health and later Ministry of Justice 59-62; Appeal Court Counsellor, Cour des Comptes 62; mem. Chamber of Deputies 62-; Gen. Counsellor Brive-Nord area 64-66; Mayor of Brive 66-; Sec. of State for Foreign Affairs (Co-operation) 66-69; Nat. Sec. Union des Démocrates pour la 5e République 67-68; Asst. Sec.-Gen. to the Union des Démocrates pour la République 68-71; Pres. Comm. des Finances, Assemblée nationale 71-72; Minister of Industrial and Scientific Devt. 72-74; with Cour des Comptes 74-.

Publ. *Louis Veuillot et la deuxième république.*

14 rue Dupont-des-Loges, Paris 7e, France.

Chargaff, Erwin, DR.PHIL.; American professor of biochemistry; b. 11 Aug. 1905, Austria; s. of Hermann and Rosa Chargaff; m. Vera Broido 1929; one s.; ed. Maximiliansgymnasium, Vienna, and Univ. of Vienna. Research Fellow, Yale Univ. 28-30; Asst., Univ. of Berlin 30-33; Research Assoc., Inst. Pasteur, Paris 33-34; Columbia Univ., N.Y. 35-, Asst. Prof. 38-46, Assoc. Prof. 46-52, Prof. of Biochemistry 52-74, Chair. Biochemistry Department 70-74, Prof. Emer. of Biochemistry 74; Visiting Prof., Sweden 49, Japan 58, Brazil 59; Einstein Chair., Collège de France, Paris 65, Cornell Univ. 67; mem. Nat. Acad. of Sciences, Wash.; Fellow American Acad. of Arts and Sciences, Boston; mem. Deutsche Akad. der Naturforscher Leopoldina; Foreign mem. Royal Swedish Physiographic Soc., Lund; Guggenheim Fellow 49, 58; Pasteur Medal, Paris 49; Neuberg Medal, N.Y. 59; Charles Leopold Mayer Prize, Acad. des Sciences, Paris 63; Dr. H. P. Heineken Prize, Royal Netherlands Acad. of Sciences, Amsterdam 64; Bertner Foundation Award, Houston 65; Gregor Mendel Medal, Halle 73; Nat. Medal of Science, Washington 75.

Publs. *Essays on Nucleic Acids* 63; Editor: *The Nucleic Acids* (3 vols.) 55, 60; numerous scientific articles and other literary work.

350 Central Park West, New York, N.Y. 10025, U.S.A. Telephone: 222-7994.

Charles, Ray (b. Ray Charles Robinson); American jazz musician; b. 23 Sept. 1930, Albany, Ga.; s. of late Bailey and Aretha Robinson; m. Della Charles; three s.; ed. St. Augustine's School, Orlando, Fla.

Taught himself to play and write for every bass and wind instrument in the orchestra, specializing in piano, organ and saxophone; composes and arranges; played at Rockin' Chair Club, Seattle Elks Club, Seattle; joined Lowell Fulsom's Blues Band, toured for a year; played at Apollo, Harlem; formed group to accompany singer Ruth Brown; Leader of Maxim Trio; with Atlantic Records 54-59, ABC Records 59-62, formed own co., Tangerine 62-; tours with Ray Charles Revue; major albums include *Ray Charles' Greatest Hits, Modern Sounds in Country and Western Music* (Vols. I and 2), *Message from the People, Volcanic Action of my Soul, Through the Eyes of Love.*

RPM International, 2107 West Washington Boulevard, Los Angeles, Calif. 90018, U.S.A.

Charles-Roux, Edmonde; French writer; b. 17 April 1920, Neuilly-sur-Seine; d. of François Charles-Roux and Sabine Gounelle; m. Gaston Deferre 1973; ed. Italy. Served as nurse, then in Resistance Movement, during Second World War, in which she was twice wounded; Reporter, magazine *Elle;* Features Editor, French edn. of *Vogue* 47-54, Editor-in-Chief 54-66; awarded Prix Goncourt 66.

Leisure interests: music, sea and sailing.

Publs. *Oublier Palerme* 66, *Elle Adrienne* 71, *L'Irregulière* 74.

Editions Grasset, 61 rue des Saints-Pères, Paris 6e, France.

Charlot, Gaston; French chemist; b. 11 June 1904, Paris; m. Dora Haimovici; one d.; ed. Ecole de Physique et de Chimie de Paris.

Professor, Faculté des Sciences, Ecole de Physique et de Chimie de Paris; also Prof., Inst. des Sciences et Techniques Nucléaires; mem. Acad. des Sciences (Inst. de France); Chevalier, Légion d'Honneur; Grand Prix Scientifique de la Ville de Paris.

Publs. numerous works on analytical chemistry.

18 rue Berthollet, Paris 5e, France.

Telephone: 587-0036.

Charlotte, H.R.H., Grand-Duchess of Luxembourg, Duchess of Nassau; b. 1896, Colmar Berg; m. Felix, Prince of Bourbon and Parma, Prince of Luxembourg 1919; two s. four d.

Ascended throne Jan. 19; abdicated Nov. 64 in favour of eldest son, now Grand-Duke Jean of Luxembourg.

Leisure interest: rose culture.

Grand-Ducal Palace, Luxembourg.

Charlton, Alfred Evan, C.B.E.; British journalist and writer; b. 9 June 1912, Brentford, Middx.; s. of Arthur Herbert Charlton and Margaret Icely Charlton; m. Joyce Edgeworth Johnstone; one s. one d.; ed. St. Paul's School.

Sub-Editor *The Statesman,* New Delhi and Calcutta 36, Editor 64-67; Indian Army 40-46; Deputy Corresp. in India for *The Times,* London 54-62, now with External Services of B.B.C.

Publs. *Go and Order the Drums* 64, *India* 71.

8 Elm Bank Gardens, Barnes, London, S.W.13, England. Telephone: 01-876 1754.

Charney, Jule Gregory, PH.D.; American professor of meteorology and oceanography; b. 1 Jan. 1917, San Francisco, Calif.; s. of Ely Charney and Stella Litman; ed. Univ. of Calif. at Los Angeles.

Research Assoc. Univ. of Chicago 46-47; Nat. Research Council Fellow, Univ. of Oslo 47-48; Staff mem., longterm mem., Dir. Theoretical Meteorology Group, Inst. for Advanced Study, Princeton, N.J. 48-56; Prof. of Meteorology, Mass. Inst. of Technology 56-64, Alfred P. Sloan Prof. of Meteorology 65-, Chair. Dept. of Meteorology 74-; Guggenheim Fellow, Cambridge Univ., Weizmann Inst. 72-73; Symons Lecturer, Royal Meteorological Soc. 74; von Neumann Lecturer, Soc. for Ind. and Applied Maths. 74; mem. Nat. Acad. of Sciences; Fellow American Acad. of Arts and Sciences, American Meteorological Soc., American Geophysical Union; Foreign mem. Royal Swedish Acad. of Sciences, Norwegian Acad. of Sciences; Meisinger Award, American Meteorological Soc. 49; Losey Award, Inst. of Aeronautical Sciences 57; Symons Memorial Gold Medal, Royal Meteorological Soc. 61; Rossby Research Medal, American Met. Soc. 64; Hodgkins Medal, Smithsonian Inst. 69; Int. Meteorological Org. Prize 71; Hon. D.Sc. (Univ. of Chicago) 70.

Leisure interests: music, reading, hiking.

Publs. Articles on stability of atmospheric motions, geostrophic scaling theory, extra-tropical and tropical cyclogenesis, maintenance of westerlies, numerical weather prediction, Gulf-Stream, Equatorial Undercurrent, mechanical coupling of troposphere and stratosphere, dynamics of deserts, general circulation of atmosphere.

Department of Meteorology, Massachusetts Institute of Technology, Cambridge, Mass. 02139, U.S.A. Telephone: 617-253-2451.

Charnock, Henry, M.SC.; British meteorologist and oceanographer; b. 25 Dec. 1920, Blackburn; s. of Henry Charnock and Mary Gray (McLeod); m. Eva M.

Dickinson 1946; one s. two d.; ed. Queen Elizabeth's Grammar School, Municipal Technical Coll., Blackburn and Imperial Coll., London.
RAFVR 43-46; Nat. Inst. of Oceanography 49-58, 60-66; Imperial Coll. 58-59; Prof. of Physical Oceanography, Univ. of Southampton 66-71, Visiting Prof. 71-; Dir. Nat. Inst. of Oceanography (now Inst. of Oceanographic Sciences) 71-; Pres. Int. Union of Geodesy and Geophysics 71-75.
Publs. papers in scientific journals.
Institute of Oceanographic Sciences, Wormley, Godalming, Surrey, England.
Telephone: Wormley 2122.

Charry, René; French orthopaedic surgeon; b. 28 March 1898; ed. Univ. of Toulouse.
Career dedicated to orthopaedic surgery and pathology of the hip in Toulouse, then grafting of bones and gerontology in Paris 55-; mem. Soc. of Surgeons, Paris, Int. Soc. of Orthopaedic Surgeons, Int. Coll. of Surgeons, Socs. of German, Belgian and Italian Orthopaedic Surgeons, French League against Rheumatism; Chevalier Légion d'Honneur, Commdr. Nichan Iftikhar.
Leisure interests: skiing, painting.
Surgical films: *La reconstruction articulaire du coude, de la hanche, du genou, reconstruction plastique de la hanche au nylon, l'ostéotomie sous-trochantérienne avec synthèse permettant la marche précoce, La résection-angulation, L'Opération mobilisatrice en chirurgie coxo-fémorale, Les meilleurs résultats de la Résection-Angulation, Aux deux pôles de la Résection-Angulation, Dynamic Reconstructive Osteotomy 71.*
Publs. *La Chirurgie moderne de la hanche 48, Dix consultations d'orthopédie, La résection-angulation de la hanche en deux temps 64.*
16 rue Alphonse de Neuville, Paris 17e; and 33 boulevard de la Saussaye, Neuilly, France.
Telephone: 227-35-31.

Charteris, Leslie, F.R.S.A.; American author; b. 12 May 1907, Singapore; m. 1st Pauline Schishkin 1931, one d.; m. 2nd Barbara Meyer 1939, 3rd Elizabeth Borst 1943, 4th Audrey Long 1952; ed. Rossall School and King's Coll., Cambridge.
Editor *The Saint Magazine* (now discontinued); producer of *The Saint* and other radio programmes; writer of the internationally syndicated *Saint* comic strip; originator of *The Saint* television programme; has written several film scripts; mem. Mensa; mem. Council of Int. Foundation for Gifted Children; Pres. Saint Club and Arbour Youth Centre; invented universal sign language *Paleneo* 69.
Leisure interests: reading, languages, horse racing, swimming, food and wine.
Publs. *Meet the Tiger* 29, *Enter the Saint* 31, *The Last Hero* 31, *The Avenging Saint* 31, *Wanted for Murder* 31, *Angels of Doom* 32, *The Saint v. Scotland Yard* 32, *Getaway* 33, *The Saint and Mr. Teal* 33, *The Brighter Buccaneer* 33, *The Misfortunes of Mr. Teal* 34, *The Saint Intervenes* 34, *The Saint Goes On* 35, *The Saint in New York* 35, *Saint Overboard* 36, *The Ace of Knaves* 37, *Thieves' Picnic* 37, *Juan Belmonte: Killer of Bulls* (translated from Spanish) 37, *Follow the Saint* 38, *Prelude for War* 38, *The First Saint Omnibus* 39, *The Saint in Miami* 40, *The Saint Goes West* 42, *The Saint Steps In* 43, *The Saint at Large* 43, *The Saint on Guard* 44, *The Saint Sees It Through* 46, *Call for the Saint* 48, *Saint Errant* 48, *The Second Saint Omnibus* 51, *The Saint in Europe* 53, *The Saint on the Spanish Main* 55, *The Saint Around the World* 56, *Thanks to the Saint* 57, *Señor Saint* 58, *The Saint to the Rescue* 59, *Trust the Saint* 62, *Saint in the Sun* 63, *Vendetta for the Saint* 64, *The Saint on TV* 68, *The Saint Returns* 68, *The Saint Abroad* 69, *The Saint and the Fiction Makers* 69, *The Saint in Pursuit* 70, *The Saint and the People Importers*

71, *Saints Alive* 74, *Catch the Saint* 75, *The Saint and the Hapsburg Necklace* 76.
8 Southampton Row, London, W.C.1, England.

Charue, André-Marie; Belgian ecclesiastic; b. 1 July 1898, Jemeppe-sur-Sambre; ed. Grand Séminaire de Namur, Catholic Univ. of Louvain.
Professor of Scriptures, Grand Séminaire de Namur 28-41; Bishop of Namur 41-; Vice-Pres. Theological Cttee. of Second Vatican Council; gave permission for the veneration of the shrine of Beaurang 43, declared that the authenticity of the apparitions should be admitted 49.
Publs. include *L'Incrédulité des Juifs dans le Nouveau Testament* 29, *L'Année sociale dans le diocèse de Namur* 50, *Les Epîtres Catholiques* (commentary on the collection *La Sainte Bible*) 51, *Le Clergé Diocésain tel qu'un Evêque le voit et le souhaite* 60.
Evêché de Namur, Rue de l'Eveché 1, B5000 Namur, Belgium.

Charusathira, General Prapas; Thai army officer and politician; b. 25 Nov. 1912, Udorn Prov.; m. Khunying Sawai; one s. four d.; ed. Chulachomklao Royal Military Acad. and National Defence Coll.
Army service 33, rose through infantry to Gen. 60; Minister of Interior 57-71; Deputy Prime Minister 63-71; Army Deputy Commdr. and Deputy Supreme Commdr. 63-64; Supreme Commdr. 64; mem. Nat. Exec. Council and Dir. of Security Council (Defence and Interior) 71-72; Deputy Prime Minister, Minister of Interior 72-73; Vice-Pres. and Rector, Chulalongkorn Univ. 61-69; numerous decorations.
Leisure interests: sport: boxing, soccer, golf, hunting, amateur ranching, arms collecting.
Publs. *The Role of the Ministry of Interior in the Development of National Security, The Role of the Ministry of Interior in Maintenance of National Peace and Order.*
Taiwan.

Charvát, Josef, M.D., D.SC.; Czechoslovak professor of medicine; b. 6 Aug. 1897, Prague; s. of late Václav and Anna Charvát; m. Božena 1920 (deceased); two d.; ed. Charles Univ., Prague.
Lecturer in Internal Medicine Univ. of Prague 28-33, Prof. 33-, Dir. Univ. Polyclinic 39-, Dir. 3rd Medical Dept., Faculty of Medicine 45-70; Dir. Laboratory for Endocrinology and Metabolism 56-; mem. Scientific Council, Ministry of Health 52-68; mem. Advisory Cttee. for Medical Research, W.H.O. 58-61, Pres. Endocrinological Soc. 37-74; mem. UN Advisory Cttee, for Applications of Science and Technology 64-71; mem. Czechoslovak Acad. of Sciences 54-; Foreign mem. Serbian Acad. of Sciences and Arts 65, Polish Acad. of Sciences 66; Dep. to Czech Nat. Council 68-71; Rector, Charles Univ., Prague 69; Pres. Inter. Congress Endocrinology, Washington 72; Hon. degree Cracow Univ. 64, Charles Univ., Prague 68, Comenius Univ., Bratislava 69; Order of Labour 57, State Prize 62, Hero of Socialist Labour and Holder of the Gold Star 67, Léon Barnard Prize 68, Purkyne Prize 72.
Publs. *Internal Secretions* 35, *Avitaminoses* 38, *Metabolism of Carbohydrates* 42, *Steroid Hormones* 52, *Manual for Practitioners* 52, 55, 67, *Parathyroid* 54, *Growth Hormones* 52, *Neurohypophysis* 56, *Life Adaptation and Stress* 69, 70, 73, *Man and his World* 74.
Ostrovní 5, 110 00 Prague 1, Czechoslovakia.
Telephone: 29-17-13.

Charyk, Joseph Vincent, PH.D., M.S., B.SC.; American scientist and administrator; b. 9 Sept. 1920, Canmore, Alberta, Canada; s. of John and Anna (Dorosh) Charyk; m. Edwina Rhodes Charyk; three s. one d.; ed. Univ. of Alberta, Calif. Inst. of Technology.
Instructor of Aeronautics, Calif. Inst. of Technology 45; Asst. (later Assoc.) Prof. of Aeronautics, Princeton Univ. 46; Dir. of Aerophysics and Chemistry Lab., Lockheed Aircraft Corpn. 55-; Dir. of Missile Tech-

nology Lab., Gen. Man. Space Technology Div. Aeronutronic Systems Inc. (Subsidiary of Ford Motor Co.) 56-59; Chief Scientist U.S. Air Force 59, Asst. Sec. of Air Force for Research and Development 59; Under-Sec. U.S. Air Force 60-63; Pres. and Dir. Communications Satellite Corpn. March 63-; mem. Board of Dirs., Abbott Laboratories, CML Satellite Corpn., Comsat Gen. Corpn.; mem. Int. Acad of Astronautics; Fellow in Amer. Inst. of Aeronautics and Astronautics; mem. Nat. Space Club, Armed Forces Communications and Electronics Asscn., Newcomen Soc., Nat. Inst. Social Sciences, and Conf. Board, Nat. Acad. of Eng.; Hon. LL.D., Hon. Dr.Ing.
Leisure interests: golf, tennis, photography.
5126 Tilden Street, N.W., Washington, D.C. 20016, U.S.A.
Telephone: (202) 244-3761.

Chase, Stuart, S.B.; American social scientist; b. 8 March 1888; ed. Mass. Inst. Technology and Harvard Univ.
Certified Public Accountant 16; Staff U.S. Federal Trade Comm. 17 and U.S. Food Administration 18-19; Consulting Economist for Nat. Resources Board, Resettlement Administration, and Securities Exchange Comm., Tennessee Valley Authority; mem. Nat. Inst. of Arts and Letters; Hon. Litt.D. (American Univ., Washington) 70, (Emerson Coll., Boston) 70.
Publs. *The Tragedy of Waste* 25, *Your Money's Worth* 27, *Men and Machines* 29, *Mexico: a Study of Two Americas* 31, *A New Deal* 32, *The Economy of Abundance* 34, *Government in Business* 35, *Rich Land, Poor Land* 36, *The Tyranny of Words* 38, *The New Western Front* 39, *Idle Money, Idle Men* 40, *A Primer of Economics* 41, *The Road We are Travelling* 42, *Goals for America* 42, *Where's the Money Coming From?* 43, *Democracy under Pressure* 45, *Men at Work* 45, *To-morrow's Trade* 46, *For This We Fought* 47, *The Proper Study of Mankind* 48, *Roads to Agreement* 51, *Power of Words* 54, *Guides to Straight Thinking* 56, *Some Things Worth Knowing* 58, *Live and Let Live* 60, *American Credos* 62, *Money into Grow On* 64, *The Most Probable World* 67, *Danger Man Talking* 69.
P.O. Box 422, Georgetown, Conn. 06829, U.S.A.

Chastel, André (Adrien), DR. ès LETTRES; French art historian; b. 15 Nov. 1912, Paris; s. of Adrien Chastel and Marie-Isabelle Morin; m. P.-M. Grand 1942; three s.; ed. Sorbonne, Paris.
Assistant in Art History, Sorbonne 45-48; Focillon Fellowship, Yale 49; Dir. of Studies for the History of the Renaissance, Ecole Pratique des Hautes Etudes 51-; Prof. History of Modern Art, Sorbonne 55-; Prof. Collège de France 70-; art critic, *Le Monde* 50-; Sec. Comité International d'Histoire de l'Art 61-, Vice-Pres. 69; Croix de Guerre 39-40; Officier Légion d'Honneur 74; Membre de l'Institut de France 75.
Leisure interest: member of R.C.F.
Publs. *Vuillard* 46, *L'art italien* (2 vols.) 57, *Botticelli* 58, *Art et Humanisme à Florence au temps de Laurent le Magnifique* 59, *L'Age de l'Humanisme* (with R. Klein) 63, *Italie 1460-1500* (2 vols.) 65, *Crise de la Renaissance* 68, *Mythe de la Renaissance* 69, edition of *Gauricus de Sculptura* (1504) 69.
30 rue de Lubeck, Paris 16e, France.

Chastenet de Castaing, Jacques, LL.D., C.B.E.; French journalist and historian; b. 20 April 1893, Paris; s. of Mr. and Mrs. G. Chastenet de Castaing; m. Germaine Saladin 1919; two s.
Former Editor *Le Temps*; mem. Acad. des Sciences Morales et Politiques 47-, and Académie Française 56-; Grand Officier, Légion d'Honneur.
Leisure interest: viticulture.
Publs. *William Pitt, Godoy Prince de la Paix, Wellington, Vingt ans d'histoire diplomatique, Le Parlement d'Angle-*

terre, *Le Siècle de Victoria, R. Poincaré, La France de M. Fallières, Histoire de la Troisième République* (7 vols.), *Winston Churchill et l'Angleterre du XX Siècle, La vie privée en Angleterre au début du Règne de Victoria, Jours Sanglants 1914-1918, L'Angleterre d'aujourd'hui, En avant vers l'Ouest, Cent ans de République* (9 vols.), *De Pétain à de Gaulle, Quatre Fois Vingt Ans.*
14 rue d'Aumale, Paris 9e, France.

Chataway, Rt. Hon. Christopher John, P.C.; British fmr. politician and fmr. athlete; b. 31 Jan. 1931; m. Carola Walker 1976; ed. Sherborne School and Magdalen Coll., Oxford.
Represented U.K. at Olympic Games 52, 56; holder of world 5,000 metres record 54; Junior Exec., Arthur Guinness, Son and Co. 53-55; Staff Reporter, Independent Television News 55-56; Current Affairs Commentator, B.B.C. Television 56-59; mem. London County Council 58-61; mem. Parl. for Lewisham North 59-66, for Chichester 69-74; Parl. Private Sec. to Minister of Power 61-62; Joint Parl. Under-Sec. of State, Dept. of Educ. and Science 62-64; Alderman, Greater London Council 67-70; Minister of Posts and Telecommunications 70-72, for Industrial Devt. 72-74; Man. Dir. Orion Bank; Dir. Fisons, B.E.T., Allied Investments; Conservative.
40 Addison Road, London, W.14, England.

Chatenet, Pierre, LIC. en DR.; French politician; b. 6 March 1917, Paris; s. of Henri Chatenet and Andrée Genès; m. Jacqueline Parodi 1947; one s.; ed. Lycée Buffon and Ecole des Sciences Politiques.
Auditor Conseil d'Etat 41; Chargé de Mission, Provisional Govt. 44, Labour Office 44-45; mem. French Del. UN Conf. San Francisco 45; Maître des Requêtes, Conseil d'Etat 46; Counsellor French Del. to UN 46-47; Political Dir. Residence Gen. Tunis 47-50; Counsellor French Perm. Del. to NATO 50-54; Dir. of Civil Service (Présidence du Conseil) 54; mem. UN Rights of Man Comm., Consultative Cttee. Fonction Publique Int.; Sec. of State (Prime Minister's Office) Jan.-May 59; Minister of the Interior May 59-61; Pres. of EURATOM 62-67; Conseiller d'Etat 63-; Pres. Comm. des Opérations de Bourse 67-72; mem. Conseil Constitutionnel 68; Pres. CREDITEL 73; Officier Légion d'Honneur; Grand Croix de l'Ordre de la Couronne de Belgique.
3 avenue Robert Schuman, Paris 7e, France.

Chatt, Joseph, M.A., PH.D., SC.D.; British chemist; b. 6 Nov. 1914, Horden; s. of Joseph Chatt and Elsie Chatt (née Parker); m. Ethel Williams 1947; one s. one d.; ed. Nelson School, Wigton, Cumberland and Cambridge Univ.
Deputy Chief Chemist, later Chief Chemist, Peter Spence & Son Ltd. 42-46; I.C.I. Research Fellow, Imperial Coll., London 46-47; Head of Inorganic Chemistry Dept., Butterwick, later Akers Research Labs., I.C.I. Ltd. 47-60; Akers Group Man. Research Dept. Heavy Organic Chemicals Div., I.C.I. 60-62; Group Head and Consultant, Petrochemical and Polymer Lab., I.C.I. 63; Dir. Unit of Nitrogen Fixation, Agricultural Research Council 63-; Prof. of Chemistry, Queen Mary Coll., London Univ. 63-64, Univ. of Sussex Jan. 65-; Fellow of Royal Soc.; mem. Chemical Soc., American Chemical Soc., Royal Inst. of Chemistry; Distinguished Visiting Prof. of Chemistry, Pennsylvania State Univ.; Visiting Prof. of Chemistry, Yale, Rajasthan and South Carolina Univs.; Debye Lecturer, Cornell Univ. 75; Gordon Wigan Prize for Research in Chemistry, Univ. of Cambridge 39; Tilden Lecturer of Chemical Soc. 62, Liversidge Lecturer 71-72; Pres. Dalton Div. Chemical Soc. 71-74; American Chemical Soc. Award for Distinguished Service in the Advancement of Inorganic Chemistry 71, Organometallic Award of Chemical Soc. 71; Hon. D.Sc. (East Anglia).
Leisure interest: numismatics.

Publs. Scientific papers on complex chemistry, A.R.C. Unit of Nitrogen Fixation, University of Sussex, Brighton BN1 9QJ; Home: 28 Tongdean Avenue, Hove, Sussex BN3 6TN, England.
Telephone: 66755 (Office); 54377 (Home).

Chatterjee, Dwarka Nath, B.A.; Indian diplomatist; b. 2 Nov. 1914, Calcutta; s. of P. N. Chatterjee; four d.; ed. Calcutta Univ., King's Coll., London, London School of Economics and School of Oriental Studies, London. Army Service 40-47; Indian Foreign Service 47-; First Sec., Paris 48-49, London 49-54; Deputy Sec., Ministry of External Affairs 54-55; Deputy High Commr. in Pakistan 56-58; Consul-Gen., Geneva 58-59; Minister, Washington 59-62; Ambassador to Congo (Léopoldville) 62-64; High Commr. in Australia 65-67; Deputy High Commr. in U.K. 67; Amb. to France 69-.
Indian Embassy, 15 rue Dehodencq, Paris 16e, France; and 9 Lovelock Place, Ballygune, Calcutta, India.

Chatterji, Suniti Kumar, M.A., D.LIT. (London); Indian educationist, philologist and writer; b. 26 Nov. 1890, Sibpur Howrah, Bengal; s. of late Haridas Chatterji and late Katyayani Devi; m. Kamala Devi Mukherji 1914 (died 1964); one s. five d.; ed. Calcutta, School of Oriental Studies, London, and Univ. of Paris. Khaira Prof. of Indian Linguistics and Phonetics, Calcutta Univ. 22-52, Emer. Prof. of Comparative Philology 52-; Visiting Prof., Univ. of Pa., U.S.A. 51-52; Chair., Upper House, West Bengal State Legislature 52-65; Nat. Prof. of India in Humanities 65-; Pres. Bangiya Sahitya Parishad, Linguistic Soc. of India; fmr. Pres. Asiatic Soc. of Bengal; hon. mem. Société Asiatique, Paris, American Oriental Soc., Norwegian Acad. of Sciences, Royal Siam Soc., Ecole Française de l'Extrême Orient, Linguistic Soc. of America, Soc. of Arts and Sciences, Utrecht; Fellow, Indian Council for Cultural Relations 61-; Pres. Sahitya Acad., New Delhi; Pres. Int. Phonetic Asscn., London 69-; awarded Padma-Vibhushana (Order of the Repub. of India); Hon. F.A.S., D.Litt. (Univs. of Rome, Delhi, Visva-Bharati Univ., Osmania, Rabindra-Bharati, Calcutta and Buddhist Univ., Nava-Nalanda). Leisure interests: collections of small art, listening to music, study of art, travel.
Publs. *Origin and Development of the Bengali Language* 26, *Dvipamaya Bharat* 40, 2nd edn. 64, *Indo-Aryan and Hindi* 42, 60, *Kirata-janakriti or the Indo-Mongoloids* 51, 74, *Africanism* 60, *Indianism and the Indian Synthesis* 62, *Languages and Literatures of Modern India* 64, *Dravidian* 66, *People, Language and Culture of Orissa* 66, *Balts and Aryans* 68, *India and Ethiopia* 69, *World Literature and Tagore* 71, *Iranianism* 72, *Jayadera* 74, and other works in English, Bengali and Hindi.
"Sudharma", 16 Hindusthan Park, Calcutta 29, India.
Telephone: 46-1121 (Home); 45-5319 (Office).

Chattopadhyaya, Harindranath; Indian poet, dramatist, musician and actor; b. 1898; ed. U.K., Germany, U.S.A. and U.S.S.R.
Studied theatrecraft under Stanislavsky and Meyerholdt; pioneer modern Indian Theatre; leader progessive movt. in literature; produced a film, *Azadi* (Freedom); has written screen script for *Legend of Gautam, Buddha,* 1942, and *Abul Hassan* (musical comedy); mem. of Lok Sabha (Parliament) 52.
Publs. *The Coffin, Feast of Youth, Ancient Wings, Grey Clouds and White Showers, Poems and Plays, Five Plays in Verse, Five Plays in Prose, Dark Well, The Divine Vagabond, Horizon—Ends, Edgeways and the Saint, Lyrics, Blood of Stones, Perfume of Earth, Magic Tree, Crossroads, Life and Myself* (Vol. I: Autobiography), *Hunter of Kalahasti* (play), *Treasury of Poems, Land of the New Man, The Toy-Maker of Kondapalli* (play), *Spring in Winter* (lyrics), etc.
3 Krishna Iyer Street, Nungumbakam, Madras, India.

Chatty, Habib; Tunisian diplomatist; b. 1916; ed. Sadiki Coll., Tunis.
Journalist 37-52, Editor *Ez-Zohra* 43-50, *Es-Sabah* 50-52; imprisoned 52, 53; Head, Press Cabinet of Pres. of Council 54-55, Head, Information Service 55; mem. Nat. Council, Neo-Destour Party 55; Dir. *Al Amal* 56; Vice-Pres. Constituent Nat. Assembly 56; Amb. to Lebanon and Iraq 57-59, to Turkey and Iran 59-62, to U.K. 62-64, to Morocco 64-70, to Algeria 70-72; Dir. of Presidential Cabinet 72-74; Minister of Foreign Affairs 74-; mem. of Political Bureau and Central Cttee. of Destour Socialist Party 74; Deputy to Nat. Assembly 74; several decorations.
Ministry of Foreign Affairs, Tunis, Tunisia.

Chatzidakis, Manos; Greek composer; b. 1925. Composer of ballet music, incidental music for theatre and films, piano and orchestral music, and popular songs; numerous national and int. awards, including Oscar 61; composed music for *Lysistrata, Birds, Plautos* (Aristophanes), and for films *Stella* 56, *Never on Sunday* 60, *Topkapi* 64, etc.

Chau, Dr. the Hon. Sir Sik-Nin, Kt., C.B.E., LL.D., M.B., B.S.; Hong Kong business executive; b. 1903, Hong Kong; s. of late Cheuk-Fan Chau; m. Ida Hing-Kwai Lau 1927 (died 1967); two s.; ed. St. Stephen's Coll., Hong Kong, Univs. of Hong Kong, London and Vienna.
Chairman, Hong Kong Trade Devt. Council 66-70, Hong Kong Model Housing Soc., The Hong Kong Chinese Bank Ltd., Kowloon Motor Bus Co., Pioneer Trade Devt. Co. Ltd., Repulse Bay Enterprises Ltd., Far East Insurance Co. Ltd., Nin Fung Hong Ltd., Oriental Express Ltd., Sik Yuen Co. Ltd., State Trading Corpn. Ltd.; Pres. Hong Kong Productivity Council 70-73; Pres. Designate World Council of Management; Hong Kong Cttee. for *Expo 70,* Osaka, Japan; Hon. Pres. Fed. of Hong Kong Industries; mem, Textiles Advisory Board, Legislative Council 46-60, Executive Council 47-62; Chair. Sub-Comm. on Trade, UN Econ. Comm. for Asia and Far East Conf. 55, Indo-Pacific Comm., Int. Council for Scientific Management 64-67; Pres. Japan Soc. of Hong Kong; Dir. official, educational and philanthropic orgs; Order of Sacred Treasure (Japan) 69.
Leisure interest: racing.
The Hong Kong Chinese Bank Ltd., 61-65 Des Voeux Road; 3547 Hatton Road, Hong Kong.
Telephone: 433695.

Chaudet, Paul; Swiss vine-grower and politician; b. 17 Nov. 1904, Rivaz; m. Madeleine Rogivue 1930; three s. one d.
Treas. Rivaz Commune; mem. Council of States; Nat. Councillor; Head, Dept. of Justice and Police 46-47, of Agriculture, Industry and Commerce 48-55; Federal Councillor 55-; Chief Defence Dept. 55-66; Vice-Pres. Fed. Council 58, 61, Pres. 59 and 62; Radical Liberal. Leisure interest: president of several humanitarian organizations.
Clos du Rocher, 1812 Rivaz/Vd., Switzerland.
Telephone: 021-56-13-77.

Chaudhuri, Gen. Joyanto Nath, O.B.E.; Indian army officer; b. 10 June 1908, Calcutta; s. of Amiya Nath Chaudhuri; m. 1st Aruna Chatterjee 1938 (died 1966), 2nd Helen Smith 1971; two s.; ed. Highgate School and Royal Military Coll., Sandhurst.
Served North Staffordshire Regt., Indian 7th Cavalry, Middle East and Burma 39-45; Military Gov. Hyderabad 48-49; fmr. G.O.C.-in-C. Indian Southern Command; Commdr. Goa Operation 62; Chief of Indian Army Staff Nov. 62-June 66; High Commr. in Canada 66-69; Visiting Prof. McGill Univ., Montreal 69-71; Int. Inst. for Strategic Studies, London 71-72; Chair. and Man.

Dir. Andrew Yule & Co., Calcutta 73-; awarded Padma-Vibhushan.
Leisure interests: music, photography, travel.
Publs. *Operation Polo, Arms, Aims and Aspects.*
Cavalry Club, 127 Piccadilly, London, England; c/o National and Grindlays Bank, 41 Chowringee, Calcutta, India.

Chaudhuri, Naranarain (Sankho), B.A.; Indian sculptor; b. 25 Feb. 1916; ed. Armanitoba High School, Dacca and Bishwa Bharti Santiniketan, West Bengal.
Freelance artist 47-; Chief, Dept. of Sculpture, Maharaja Sayajirao Univ. of Baroda 51-, Prof. 57-, Dean of Faculty 60-68; mem. Lalit Kala Akademi 56-; Pres. Indian Sculptors' Asscn. 64-65; mem. Indian Cttee. Int. Asscn. of Plastic Arts; Exhibited São Paulo Bienal 61, One-Man Exhibitions Bombay and Delhi; numerous Indian awards.
Major works: Sculptures, All India Radio, Delhi 55, Statue of Mahatma Gandhi, Rio de Janeiro, and works in collections in India, U.K. and U.S.A.
c/o Indian High Commission, Aldwych, W.C.2, England.

Chaudhuri, Nirad Chandra, B.A.; Indian writer; b. 23 Nov. 1897; ed. Calcutta Univ.
Former Asst. Editor *The Modern Review* (Calcutta); fmr. Sec. to Sarat Bose (Leader of Congress Party, Bengal); fmr. Commentator, All India Radio; has contributed to *The Times, Encounter, New English Review, The Atlantic Monthly, Pacific Affairs;* also contributed to Indian papers *The Statesman, The Illustrated Weekly, The Hindustan Standard, The Times of India;* Duff Cooper Memorial Prize for *The Continent of Circe* 67.
Publs. *The Autobiography of an Unknown Indian* 51 (published as *Jaico,* India 64), *A Passage to England* 59, *The Continent of Circe* 65, *Woman in Bengali Life* (in Bengali) 68, *Clive of India* 75.
P. and O. Buildings, Nicholson Road, Delhi-6, India

Chaudhury, Mahendra Mohan, B.A., B.L.; Indian politician; b. 12 April 1908, Nagaon, Assam; *m.* Sukhalata Chaudhury 1934; two *s.* four *d.;* ed. Cotton Coll., Gauhati, and Earle Law Coll., Gauhati.
Admitted to Barpeta Bar 36; joined freedom struggle under Mahatma Gandhi, imprisoned 32, 41 and 42; mem. Assam Legis. Assembly 46; Sec. Assam Congress Parl. Party; Parl. Sec. 47; Advocate of Assam High Court 49; Cabinet Minister, Assam 50-55; Pres. Assam Pradesh Congress Cttee. 55-56; Gen. Sec. All India Congress Cttee. 56-57; mem. Rajya Sabha 56, 72; Speaker Assam Legis. Assembly 58; Chief Minister of Assam 70-72; Gov. of Punjab May 73-.
Leisure interests: gardening, cattle rearing, wildlife, horticulture, agriculture.
Publs. *Life of Mahatma Gandhi, Life and Philosophy of Acharya Vinoba Bhave.*
Raj Bhavan, Punjab, Chandigarh, India.
Telephone: 24481, 24400.

Chaudhury, Moinul Haque; Indian politician; b. 13 May 1923, Sonabarighat, Assam; *s.* of M. A. Chaudhury and Safarunnessa Chaudhury; *m.* Rashida Mazumder 1948; one *s.* three *d.;* ed. Aligarh Univ.
Elected Congress, M.L.A., Assam 52, 57, 62, 67; mem. All-India Congress Cttee. 59-; Minister of Agriculture, Community Devt., Fisheries, Parl. Affairs, Irrigation, Govt. of Assam 57-67; represented India at UN 1961 and 1968 and in other Int. bodies, mem. Parl., Minister of Industrial Devt., Govt. of India 71-72; Senior Advocate, Supreme Court.
Leisure interests: reading, gardening.
4 Motilal Nehru Marg, New Delhi, India.
Telephone: 38-7217.

Chaufournier, Roger, D. en D.; French international bank official; b. 23 Jan. 1924, Lignières; *s.* of Louis Chaufournier and Josephine Rome; *m.* Edna Hylton

1951; two *s.* one *d.;* ed. Univ. de Paris (Sorbonne) and Ecole des Hautes Etudes Commerciales, Paris.
Post Doctoral Studies and Research, Univs. of Uppsala and Illinois; mem. Teaching and Research Staff, Dept. of Econs., Univ. of Illinois 49-52; Int. Bank for Reconstruction and Devt. (World Bank) 52-, economist 52-56, Bank Rep. in Peru and Adviser to Peruvian Govt. 56-60, Div. Chief, W. Hemisphere and European Depts. 60-64, Deputy Dir. W. Hemisphere Dept. 64-68, Dir. W. African Dept. Nov. 68-72, Regional Vice-Pres. for Africa Oct. 72-; Fellow, Swedish Inst. 48; Fulbright Fellow 49; Fellow, Inst. of Int. Educ.
Leisure interests: reading, bridge, tennis, swimming, sailing.
Office: 1818 H Street, N.W., Washington, D.C. 20433; Home: 5004 Nahant Street, Washington, D.C. 20016, U.S.A.
Telephone: 477-4504 (Office); 229-2967 (Home).

Chauvel, Jean Michel Henri, D. en D.; French diplomatist; b. 16 April 1897, Paris; *s.* of Fernand Chauvel and Marthe Derrien; *m.* Diane Le Maire de Warzée d'Hermalle 1926; two *s.* two *d.*
Secretary, French Embassy Peking 24; Sec.-Gen. of High Commissariat in Syria and the Lebanon; Consul-Gen. in Vienna 38; Sub-Dir. Asia-Oceania 38; Del. in France of the Commr. for Foreign Affairs of French Cttee. of Nat. Liberation 43; Sec.-Gen. Commissariat of Foreign Affairs 44; Amb. of France and Sec.-Gen. of Ministry of Foreign Affairs 44-49; Perm. Rep. on Security Council and Perm. Head of French del. to UN 49-52; Amb. to Switzerland 52-54; High Commr. and Amb. to Austria 54; Amb. to U.K. 55-62; Conseiller Diplomatique du Gouvernement 62-63; Grand Cross Legion of Honour; D.C.L. h.c. Oxon.; Hon. G.C.M.G., G.C.V.O.
Leisure interests: literature, music, painting.
Publs. *Préludes, Labyrinthe, D'une Eau Profonde, Infidèle, Imaginaires, Clepsydre, Sables, Commentaire I, II, III, L'Aventure Terrestre d'Arthur Rimbaud.*
123 rue de la Tour, Paris 16e; Le Ruluet, par Pont l'Abbé, 29-120, France.
Telephone: 504-29-38 (Paris); 91-04-88.

Chauviré, Yvette; French ballerina; b. 22 April 1917, Paris; ed. Paris Opera Ballet School.
Joined Paris Opera Ballet 30, Danseuse Etoile 42; with Monte Carlo Opera Ballet 46-47; Artistic and Technical Adviser to Admin. of Paris Opera 63-; Chevalier Légion d'Honneur; Officier des Arts et des Lettres; ballets in which she has performed leading roles include *Istar, Les Deux Pigeons, David Triomphant, Giselle, Les Créateurs de Prométhée, Roméo et Juliette, L'Ecuyère, Les Suites Romantiques, Lac des Cygnes, l'Oiseau de Feu, Petrouchka, Sylvia, La Belle Hélène, Casse-Noisette, Les Mirages, Le Cygne, La Dame aux Camélias.*
Leisure interests: drawings, watercolours, collecting swans.
Publ. *Je suis Ballerine.*
21 Place du Commerce, Paris 15e, France.
Telephone: 250-4242.

Chavan, Yeshwantrao Balwantrao, B.A., LL.B.; Indian politician; b. 12 March 1913, Sangli district of Maharashtra; *s.* of Shri Balwantrao Chavan; *m.* Smt. Venubai 1942; ed. Rajaram Coll., Kolhapur, and Law Coll., Poona.
Practised law at Karad; participated in Quit India Movt. 42; directed underground movement in Satara, District 42-43; arrested 43-44; Pres. District Congress Cttee., Satara 40; Sec. Maharashtra Provincial Congress Cttee. 48-50; mem. Bombay Legislative Assembly and Parl. Sec. 46; started a Marathi daily, *Prakash,* at Satara; Minister for Civil Supplies 52, later Minister of Local Self-Govt. and Forests; Chief Minister, Bombay State 56-60, Maharashtra State 60-62; Treas. Working Cttee. All-India Congress 58; Minister of Defence, India 62-66, of Home Affairs 66-70, Minister of Finance

70-74, of External Affairs Oct. 74-; Pres. Inst. for Defence Studies and Analysis; leader of Congress Party in Upper House 63, mem. Lower House 64.
Leisure interests: reading, fine arts and sports.
Ministry of External Affairs, Room 169, South Block, New Delhi 1; Home: 1 Race Course Road, New Delhi, India.

Chavanon, Christian, D. en D.; French lawyer and radio administrator; b. 12 March 1913.
Law practice in Bordeaux; Auditeur 41, later Maître des Requêtes, Conseil d'Etat 46, Conseiller d'Etat 63-; Dir. du Cabinet, Ministry of Reconstruction 51-53; Prof. Inst. d'Etudes Politiques; Prés.-Dir. Gén. Soc. Nat. des Entreprises de Presse 53-55, Hon. Prés. Dir.-Gén. 55-; Sec.-Gén. of Information June 58, Dir.-Gén. Radio-diffusion-Télévision Française July 58-60; Prés.-Dir. Gén. l'Agence Havas 60-73; Pres. Dir.-Gen. Havas Conseil 60-73; Pres. Nat. Confed. for French Publicity 67-69, Hon. Pres. 69; Admin. Cie. Luxembourgeoise Télédiffusion 60-75, Admin. Délegué Cie. Luxem-bourgeoise Télédiffusion 75-; Pres. Finance Section, Conseil d'Etat 73; Commdr. Légion d'Honneur.
18 Boulevard Maillot, 92 Neuilly-sur-Seine, France.

Chávez, Carlos; Mexican composer; b. 1899.
Studied the piano with Manuel Ponce 09-14, with Pedro Luis Ogazón 15-20, harmony with Juan B. Fuentes 17-18; first public concert of own compositions Mexico City 21; organized and conducted "Conciertos de Música Nueva" Mexico City 23-25; Founder Conductor Orquesta Sinfónica de México 28-48; Dir. Nat. Conservatoire 28-29, 34, founded Coro del Conservatorio 29; Chief Dept. of Fine Arts 33-34; Founder Dir. Nat. Inst. of Fine Arts 47-52; Founder Orquesta Sinfónica Nacional; con-ducted orchestras in North and South America 35-; Charles Eliot Norton Prof. Harvard 58-59; Head, Music Dept., Nat. Fine Arts Inst. 73-; numerous commissions including Guggenheim Memorial Founda-tion, Museum of Modern Art (New York), Library of Congress, Mexican Ministry of Education; Caro de Boesi Prize, Caracas 54; Officier de la Légion d'Honneur, Commdr. Order of the Crown of Belgium, Order of the Polar Star (Sweden), Cross of the Star of Italian Solidarity.
Publ. *Toward a New Music* 37.
Works include: Stage works: *El Fuego Nuevo* 21, *Los Cuatro Soles* 26, *Caballos de Vapor* 27, *La Hija de Cólquide* 44 (ballets), *Pánfilo and Lauretta* (opera) 56; Orchestral works: *Sinfonía de Antígona* 33, *Sinfonía India* 36, Concerto for Four Horns 38, Piano Concerto 40, Violin Concerto 48, Third Symphony 54, Fourth Symphony 53, Fifth Symphony (for strings), Sixth Symphony, Seventh Symphony; Chamber works: three String Quartets, Violin and Cello Sonatinas, Sonata for Four Horns, Toccata for Percussion; three Piano Sonatas, piano pieces, choral and vocal works.
Av. Pirincos 775, Lomas de Chapultepec, Mexico City, D.F., Mexico.

Chávez, Ignacio, M.D.; Mexican physician; b. 31 Jan. 1897, Zirándaro, Michoacán, Mexico; s. of Ignacio Chávez and Socorro Sánchez de Chávez; m. Celia Rivera de Chávez 1928 (died 1969); one s. one d.; ed. National Univ. of Mexico.
Clinical Prof. Nat. Univ. of Mexico 23-50, Dir. Nat. School of Medicine 33-34; Prof. of Cardiology, School of Graduates 46-61, Rector of Nat. Univ. 61-66; Founder and Dir. Nat. Inst. of Cardiology of Mexico 44-66, Hon. Dir. 66-; Founder Mexican Cardiological Soc. 35; founder-mem. Colegio Nacional 43; Hon. Rector Univ. of Michoacán; Hon. Prof. Univs. of Guadalajara, Guatemala, San Salvador, Rio de Janeiro, etc.; Hon. Pres. Interamerican Soc. of Cardiology; Pres. Int. Soc. of Cardiology 58-62, Hon. Pres. 62-; mem. Acads. of Medicine of Mexico, N.Y., Buenos Aires, etc.; Scientific

Prize of Mexico; hon. degrees from Univs. of Paris, Montpellier, Lyons, Mexico, São Paulo, Oxford, Bologna, Prague, Cracow, etc.; numerous Mexican and foreign decorations.
Leisure interests: reading, history and literature, travelling, photography.
Publs. *Enfermedades del Corazón, Cirugía y Embarazo* 45, *México en la Cultura Médica* 47, *La Digitalina a pequeñas dosis en el tratamiento de las Cardiopatías* 20, *Lecciones de Clínica Cardiológica* 31, *Exploración Fun-cional de los Riñones y Clasificación de la Nefropatías* 31, *Diego Rivera, Sus Frescos en el Instituto Nacional de Cardiología* 46, *México en la Cultura Médica* 47, *El Instituto Nacional de Cardiología a los diez años de su fundación* 54, . . . *a los veinte años de su fundación* 64.
Paseo de la Reforma 1310, Lomas, México 10, D.F., Mexico.
Telephone: 5-201176.

Chavunduka, Gordon Lloyd, M.A., PH.D.; Rhodesian educationalist; b. 16 Aug. 1931, Umtali; s. of Solomon and Lillian Chavunduka; m. Rachel Chavunduka 1959; two s. four d.; ed. Univ. of Calif. at Los Angeles, Univs. of Manchester and London.
Lecturer in Sociology, Univ. of Rhodesia, Salisbury 66-, Acting Head, Dept. of Sociology 74-75; Sec.-Gen. African Nat. Council 73-; mem. Univ. Senate 72-; Pres. Assen. of Univ. Teachers of Rhodesia 74-.
Leisure interests: gardening, boxing (spectator), football.
Publs. *Traditional Healers and the Shona Patient;* also papers in the field of sociology and contribs. to *INCIDI, The Rhodesian Journal of Economics, The Society of Malawi Journal,* etc.
University of Rhodesia, P.O. Box MP 167, Mount Pleasant, Salisbury; Home: 6163 Mangwende Drive East, P.O. Highfield, Salisbury, Rhodesia.

Chayefsky, Paddy; American writer; b. 29 Jan. 1923, Bronx, N.Y.; s. of Harry Chayefsky and Gussie Stuchevsky Chayefsky; m. Susan Sackler 1949; one s.; ed. New York.
Author of television plays 52-; Writer, Producer and Assoc. Producer of the films: *Marty* 55, *Bachelor Party* 57; Writer of films: *The Goddess* 58, *Middle of the Night* 59, *The Americanization of Emily* 64, *Paint Your Wagon* 68, *The Hospital* 71, *Network* 75; of Broadway plays incl. *Middle of the Night* 56, *The Tenth Man* 59, *Gideon* 62, *The Passion of Josef D.* 64, *The Latent Heterosexual* 68; Pres. Sudan Corpn. 56-, Carnegie Productions 57, S.P.D. Inc. 59, Sidney Productions Inc. 67, Simcha Productions Inc. 71; mem. Dramatists Guild, Screen-writers Guild, etc.
Leisure interest: photography.
Publs. *Television Plays* 55, *The Goddess* 58, *Middle of the Night* 59, *The Tenth Man* 60, *Gideon* 61, *The Passion of Joseph D.* 64, *The Latent Heterosexual* 68.
850 7th Avenue, New York, N.Y. 10019, U.S.A.

Chayes, Abram J., A.B., LL.B.; American professor of law; b. 18 July 1922, Chicago; m. Antonia Handler 1947; one s. four d.; ed. Harvard Univ.
U.S. Army service 43-46; Legal Adviser to Gov. of Connecticut 49-50; Assoc.-Gen. Counsel President's Materials Policy Comm. 51; Law Clerk to Justice Felix Frankfurter 51-52; private legal practice 52-55; Asst. Prof. of Law, Harvard Univ. 55-58, Prof. of Law 58-61, 65-; The Legal Adviser, Dept. of State 61-64; Fellow, American Acad. of Arts and Sciences; mem. Bars of Washington, D.C., Conn. and Mass., American Law Inst., American Soc. of Int. Law, Assen. of the Bar of City of New York.
Publs. *The International Legal Process,* (with T. Ehrlich and A. Lowenfeld) 68, 69, *ABM, An Evaluation of the Decision to Deploy an Anti-Ballistic Missile System* (with J. Wiesner) 69, *The Cuban Missile Crisis* 74.

c/o Harvard Law School, Cambridge, Mass. 02138; Home: 3 Hubbard Park, Cambridge, Mass. 02138, U.S.A.
Telephone: (617) 495-3122 (Office).

Chebotarev, Dmitry Fedorovich; Soviet gerontologist; b. 17 Sept. 1908, Kiev; ed. Kiev Medical Inst.
Intern Physiotherapeutical Inst., hospital, Chernigov 33-36; Postgraduate 2nd Kiev Medical Inst. 36-40; Army Surgeon 41-44; Postgraduate, Senior Research Assoc. 45-53; Deputy Dir. Inst. of Clinical Medicine, Kiev 53-54, Prof. 54; Chair. Learned Council of the U.S.S.R. Health Ministry 55-64; Head of Chair, Inst. of Postgraduate Medical Training, Kiev 53-61; Dir., Head of Dept., Inst. of Gerontology, U.S.S.R. Acad. of Medical Sciences 61-; Corresp. mem. U.S.S.R. Acad. of Medical Sciences 61, mem. 66-; Pres. Int. Asscn. of Gerontology 72-75; Chair. U.S.S.R. Soc. of Gerontologists and Geriatrists; Deputy Chair. U.S.S.R. and Ukrainian Socs. of Internists; mem. Presidium U.S.S.R. Soc. of Cardiologists; Chair. Gerontology and Geriatrics Comm., U.S.S.R. Ministry of Public Health; Order of Red Banner of Labour (three times); Merited Scientist Ukrainian S.S.R.
Publs. Over 150 works; monographs *Hypertensive Syndrome of Pregnancy, Internal Pathology in Clinic of Obstetrics and Gynecology, Cardio-vascular System of Ageing Organism, Care for Elderly and Old Patients, Geriatrics in the Clinic of Diseases of the Inner Organs.*
Institute of Gerontology A.M.S. U.S.S.R., Vyshgorodskaya 67, 252655 Kiev-114, U.S.S.R.
Telephone: 35-40-05 (Office).

Cheek, James Edward, PH.D.; American university president; b. 4 Dec. 1932, Roanoke Rapids, N.C.; s. of late King Virgil Cheek and Lee Ella (Williams) Cheek; m. Celestine J. Williams 1953; one s. one d.; ed. Shaw Univ., Raleigh, N.C., Colgate-Rochester Divinity School, Drew Univ., Madison, Trinity Coll., Washington D.C., and A and I State Univ.
Teaching Asst. in Theology, Drew Theological School, Madison, N.J. 59-60; Instructor in Western History, Union Junior Coll., Cranford, N.J. 59-61; Asst. Prof. of New Testament and Historical Theology, Virginia Union Univ. 61-63; Pres. Shaw Univ. 63-69; Pres. Howard Univ. July 69-; Dir. First Nat. Bank of Washington, Educational Policy Center Inc., Joint Center for Political Studies, Int. African Chamber of Commerce; Trustee, Colgate-Rochester Divinity School, Washington Center for Metropolitan Studies, American Asscn. of Higher Educ., Univ. of Miami etc.; professional memberships include American Soc. of Church History, American Asscn. of Univ. Profs., American Acad. of Religion; mem. numerous advisory boards and cttees.; various honorary degrees.
Howard University, Washington, D.C. 20001; 8035 16th Street, N.W., Washington, D.C. 20001, U.S.A.

Cheever, John; American writer; b. 27 May 1912, Quincy, Mass.
Regular contributor to *The New Yorker*; American Nat. Book Award for *The Wapshot Chronicle* (first novel) 57. Publs. include *The Wapshot Chronicle, The Wapshot Scandal, The Brigadier and the Golf Widow, Bullet Park, The World of Apples* 73, and four vols. of short stories.
Cedar Lane, Ossining, N.Y., U.S.A.

Chéhab, Emir Maurice; Lebanese archaeologist and historian; b. 1904; s. of Emir Hafez; m. Olga Choribane 1945; two s. three d.; ed. Univ. St. Joseph, Beirut, Ecole du Louvre, and Ecole des Hautes Etudes Historiques, Paris.
Conservator Lebanese Nat. Museum 28; Chief of Antiquities Service 37, Dir. 44; Prof. Lebanese History Ecole Normale and Gen. Diplomatic History Ecole des Sciences Politiques 45; Prof. of Oriental Archaeology Inst. of Oriental Literature 46; Prof., Ancient History,

Univ. of Lebanon; Dir. Tyre and Anjar Excavations 48-; Curator of Lebanese Antiquities 53-59, Gen. Dir. 59-.
Direction des Antiquités, rue de Damas, Beirut, Lebanon.

Chehou, Mehmet (*see* Shehu, Mehmet).

Chekmarev, Alexandr Petrovich, DR.TECH.SC.; Soviet metallurgist; b. 12 Sept. 1902, Iljinka Village, Ukraine; ed. Dnepropetrovsk Mining Inst.
Engineer, metallurgical plant 27-30; Docent, Chief of faculty, Prof., Dnepropetrovsk Metallurgical Inst. 31-41, 44-; Head of Dept., Inst. of Ferrous Metallurgy, Ukrainian S.S.R. Acad. of Sciences 48-; Deputy Chief Engineer, Stalingrad Metallurgical Plant 42; Prof. Magnitogorsk Mining Metallurgical Inst. 42-44; mem. C.P.S.U. 45-; Prof. 34; Academician, U.S.S.R. Acad. of Sciences 68-; State Prize 41, 49.
Institute of Ferrous Metallurgy, Dnepropetrovsk, U.S.S.R.

Chelli, Tijani; Tunisian politician; b. 23 March 1931, Nabeul; m.; three c.; ed. Collège Sadiki, Tunis and Ecole Polytechnique, Paris.
Engineer, Ministry of Public Works, Kef 59-60; Deputy Chief Engineer of Roads and Bridges 60; Dir. of Transport 61; Dir. of Sea and Air Transport 62; Pres. Dir.-Gen. Société Nationale des Chemins de Fer Tunisiens 65-67; Dir. of Industry, Dept. of Planning and Nat. Economy 67-69; Pres.-Dir. Gen. Industries Chimiques Maghrébines (I.C.M.) Jan.-Nov. 69; Minister of Public Works 69-70, of Economy 70-72; Pres., Dir.-Gen. Investment Promotion and Industrial Land Agency 73-.
Agence de Promotion des Investissements, 18 avenue Mohamed V, Tunis, Tunisia.

Chelomey, Vladimir Nikolayevich; Soviet applied mathematician; b. 30 June 1914, Sedlets, Ukraine; ed. Kiev Aviation Inst.
Instructor, Kiev Aviation Inst. 36-41; mem. C.P.S.U. 41-; research work, Central Inst. Aircraft Engines and other research orgs. 41-44; Prof. at Moscow Higher Technical School 52-; Corresp. mem. U.S.S.R. Acad. of Sciences 58-62, mem. 62-.
Publs. *Spring Theory* 38, *The Dynamic Stability of Aircraft Structural Elements* 39, *Pneumatic Servomechanisms* 54, *Stability Increasing Possibility of Elastic Systems by Vibrations* 56.
U.S.S.R. Academy of Sciences, 14 Leninsky Prospekt, Moscow, U.S.S.R.

Ch'en Chang-feng; Chinese army officer.
Deputy Commdr. Kiangsi Mil. District, People's Liberation Army 67, Commdr. 73-; Sec. CCP Kiangsi 73.
People's Republic of China.

Chen Chia-kang; Chinese diplomatist; ed. Wuhan Univ.
Active in int. youth activities; Asst. Head of Asian Dept. of Ministry of Foreign Affairs 49; Head of same Dept. 52; mem. of Council of Institute of Foreign Affairs 55; Ambassador to the United Arab Republic 56-66; Vice-Minister of Foreign Affairs 66-.
People's Republic of China.

Ch'en Hsi-lien; Chinese army officer; b. 1913, Hungan, Hupeh; ed. Red Army Acad.
Joined CCP 27; Battalion Commdr. 31-33; on Long March 34-35; Regimental Commdr. 37; Commdr. 3rd Army Corps, 2nd Field Army 49; Mayor of Chungking 49; Commdr. of Artillery Force, People's Liberation Army 51; Gen. 55; Alt. mem. 8th Cen. Cttee. of CCP 56; Commdr. Shenyang Mil. Region, PLA 59-73; Sec. N.E. Bureau, CCP 63-67; Chair. Liaoning Revolutionary Cttee. 68; mem. Politburo, 9th Cen. Cttee. of CCP 69, Politburo, 10th Cen. Cttee. 73; First Sec. CCP Liaoning

71-73; Commdr. Peking Mil. Region, PLA 74-; Vice-Premier State Council 75.
People's Republic of China.

Ch'en Ming-yi; Chinese army officer.
Deputy Commdr. Tibet Mil. Region, People's Liberation Army 55, Commdr. 71-; Maj.-Gen. PLA 57; Vice-Chair. Tibet Revolutionary Cttee. 68; Sec. CCP Tibet 71.
People's Republic of China.

Chen, Reignson C.; Chinese financial officer; b. 1896; ed. Tsinghua Coll., Peking, Colorado Coll. and New York Univ.
Manager, Wah Chang, Trading Corpn., Shanghai 23-26; Prof. Coll. of Commerce, Southeastern Univ., Shanghai 23-25, Peiyang Univ., Tientsin 26-27; Chief Rep., China Defence Supplies Inc. for China-Burma-India (U.S.A. Lend-Lease Supplies) 40-45; Sec.-Gen. Export-Import Board, Shanghai 46-48; Chair. Foreign Exchange Bankers Asscn., Shanghai 46-49; Man. Dir. and Gen. Man. Bank of China (Taipei), Gen. Man. China Insurance Co. (Taipei); Chair. China Products Trading Corpn. (Taipei) 52-60; Exec. Dir. for China (Taiwan), Int. Bank for Reconstruction and Development and Int. Devt. Asscn. 60-72; U.S. Medal of Freedom.
c/o International Bank for Reconstruction and Development, 1818 H Street, N.W., Washington, D.C., U.S.A.

Ch'en Shao-kun; Chinese politician.
Minister of Metallurgical Industry.
People's Republic of China.

Ch'en Tsai-tao; Chinese army officer; b. 1908, Macheng, Hupeh.
Guerilla leader 27; Commdr. 4th Army 34, 2nd Column, Cen. Plains Field Army 44; Commdr. Honan Mil. District, People's Liberation Army 49; Wuhan Mil. Region, PLA 54-67; Gen. 55; Leader of Wuhan Incident uprising (an anti-Maoist army revolt during Cultural Revolution, for which he was criticized and removed from office) 20th July 67; Deputy Commdr. Foochow Mil. Region, PLA 73-.
People's Republic of China.

Ch'en Yun; Chinese politician; b. 1905, Ching-pu, Kiangsu.
Joined CCP 25; Trade Union activist 25-27; mem. 6th Cen. Cttee. of CCP 31; on Long March 34-35; Deputy Dir. Org. Dept., CCP 37, Dir. 43; Dir. Peasants Dept., CCP 39; mem. 7th Cen. Cttee. of CCP 45; Vice-Premier, State Council 49-74; Minister of Heavy Industry 49-50; Sec., Secr. of Cen. Cttee., CCP 54; Vice-Chair. CCP 56-69; mem. Standing Cttee., Politburo of CCP 56-69; Minister of Commerce 56-58; Chair. State Capital Construction Comm. 58-61; mem. 9th Cen. Cttee. of CCP 69, 10th Cen. Cttee. 73.
People's Republic of China.

Ch'en Yung-kuei; Chinese party official; b. Shiyang, Shansi.
National Model Worker; Sec. CCP Tachai Production Brigade, Shansi 63-; Vice-Chair. Shansi Revolutionary Cttee. 67; mem. 9th Cen. Cttee. of CCP 69; Sec. CCP Shansi 71; mem. Politburo, Cen. Cttee. of CCP 73; Vice-Premier State Council 75.
People's Republic of China.

Chenery, Hollis Burnley, B.S., PH.D.; American economist; b. 6 Jan. 1918, Richmond, Virginia; s. of Christopher Chenery and Helen Bates; m. Louise Seamster 1942 (divorced); two d.; ed. Arizona, Oklahoma and Harvard Univs.
Officer, U.S. Army Air Corps 42-46; Economist, U.S. Econ. Co-operation Admin., Paris 49-50; Head, Programme Div., U.S. Mutual Security Agency, Rome 50-52; Econ. Consultant to Pakistan Govt. 55, Japanese Govt. 56, UN 57-61, Bank of Israel 59-61, Bank of Sicily 61, Govt. of South Korea 70; Prof. of Econs.,

Stanford Univ. 52-61; Asst. Admin. for Program, Agency for Int. Devt., Dept. of State 61-65; Prof. of Econs. and mem. Center for Int. Affairs, Harvard Univ. 65- (on sabbatical leave 70-); Econ. Adviser to Pres. Int. Bank for Reconstruction and Devt. 70-73, Vice-Pres., Devt. Policy 73-; Dir. Southern Natural Gas Co., Alabama; mem. Council of Econometric Soc., American Econ. Asscn., American Acad. of Arts and Sciences; Guggenheim Fellowship.
Leisure interests: tennis, hiking, skiing.
Publs. with others *Arabian Oil* 49, *Interindustry Economics* 59, *Studies in Development Planning* 70.
International Bank for Reconstruction and Development, 1818 H Street, N.W., Washington, D.C. 20433; 1010 Memorial Drive, Cambridge, Mass. 02138, U.S.A. Telephone: 617-864-4457.

Chenevière, Jacques, L. ès L.; Swiss writer; b. 17 April 1886; ed. Paris Univ.
Hon. Vice-Chair. Int. Red Cross Cttee.; Hon. D. ès L. (Geneva); Grand Prix de Littérature Française hors de France (Acad. Royale Belge) 66, Grand Prix du Rayonnement de la Langue Française 68.
Publs. *Les Beaux Jours* (crowned by French Acad.), *La Chambre et le Jardin* (poems), *l'Ile déserte, Jouvence ou la Chimère, Les Messagers inutiles, La Jeune fille de neige, Innocences, Les Aveux Complets, Connais ton Coeur, Valet, dames, roi, Les Captives, Le Bouquet de la Mariée,* (novels and short stories); *La Comtesse de Ségur, née Rostopchine* (a biography), *Campagne Genevoise, Retours et images.*
1293 Bellevue, near Geneva, Switzerland.
Telephone: 74-10-96.

Cheney, Richard B.; American political administrator; b. 30 Jan. 1941, Lincoln, Neb.; m. Lynne Vincent; two c.; ed. Univ. of Wyoming, Univ. of Wisconsin.
Engaged on staff of Gov. of Wis. and as a Congressional Fellow on staff of a mem. of House of Reps.; also worked for an investment advisory firm; Exec. Asst. to Donald Rumsfeld 69-71, Deputy 71-73; Deputy Asst. to the Pres. 74-75, Chief of White House Staff Nov. 75-.
The White House, Washington, D.C., U.S.A.

Ch'eng Chun; Chinese army officer.
Commander, 35th Army, 10th Army Corps, 3rd Field Army, People's Liberation Army 49; Deputy Commdr. Fukien Mil. District 50; Lieut.-Gen. PLA Air Force 55; Deputy Commdr. PLA Air Force 57-.
People's Republic of China.

Cheng Heng; Khmer politician; b. 1916, Takéo province; m.; seven c.; ed. Lycée Sisowath, Phnom Penh and Ecole d'Administration cambodgienne.
Former civil servant and Asst. Gov. of Province of Kandal; Deputy for Takhmau (Kandal) 58-68; Vice-Pres. Nat. Assembly 58; Sec. of State for Agriculture 60-61; Deputy for Phnom Penh and Pres. Nat. Assembly 68; Head of State 70-72; mem. Supreme State Council 73-74; has attended numerous int. confs. including Colombo Plan confs. and conf. of Union Parlementaire, Manila 69; founding mem. and fmr. Pres. Asscn. des planteurs des Cultures Tropicales du Cambodge.

Chenot, Bernard, L. en DR.; French politician; b. 20 May 1909, Paris; s. of André Chenot and Marcelle Pellerin; m. Clélie Schmit 1934; one s. two d.; ed. Lycée Montaigne, Lycée Louis-le-Grand, Ecole libre des Sciences Politiques, Faculté de Droit, Paris.
Chef de Cabinet in numerous Ministries 32-39, including Public Health 35, Public Works 38 and 39; Del.-Gen. of Tourism 38-42; Sec. Gen. Houillères Nat. du Nord et du Pas de Calais 44-46; Sec. Gen. Conseil Economique 51-58; Minister of Public Health and Population July 58-Jan. 59 (de Gaulle Cabinet), Jan. 59-Aug. 61 (Debré Cabinet), Minister of Justice Aug. 61-April 62 (Debré

Cabinet); mem. Conseil Constitutionnel 62; Président de la Cité internationale de l'Université de Paris; Pres. of Compagnies d'assurances générales 64, Groupe des Assurances Générales de France 68-70; Admin. Paribas Int. 68-70; Pres. Comité de liaison d'étude et d'action républicaines 68-71; Vice-Pres. Conseil d'Etat 71-; Pres. Institut français des sciences administratives 74; fmr. Prof. Ecole Libre des Sciences Politiques, Inst. d'Etudes Politiques; Pres. French Section, Centre Européen de l'Entreprise Publique; mem. Admin. Council, Fondation des Sciences Politiques; Commdr. Légion d'Honneur, Grand Cross, Sovereign Order of Malta, Gran Ufficiale, Ordine del Merito della Repubblica Italiana, Grand Croix Ordre de St.-Charles, Grand Croix Ordre du Cèdre (Lebanon); Médaille d'Or, Education Physique et des Sports.
Leisure interests: literature, sport.
Publs. *Organisation Economique de l'Etat* 51, *Les Entreprises Nationalisées* (Collection *Que sais-je?*) 56; various published lectures, including *Les Institutions administratives de la France* and *Histoire des Doctrines Politiques, Etre Ministre* 67.
16 avenue Pierre de Serbie, Paris 16e, France.
Telephone: 231-87-05.

Cherednichenko, Evgeny Trofimovich; Soviet trade union official; b. 12 Oct. 1912, Krasnodar; ed. Leningrad Inst. of Railway Transport Engineers and Higher Party School.
Departmental Head, Railway Line Section 38-40, 42-43; Party work 44-48; Asst. Head Div., Ministry of Railways 48-51; Chair. Central Cttee. Railwaymen's Trade Union 51-70; Sec. World Fed. Trade Unions 70; mem. Central Auditing Cttee. of C.P.S.U.; mem. Presidium of All-Union Central Cttee. of Trade Unions; Order of Red Banner of Labour (three times); Badge of Honour (twice), etc.
c/o World Federation of Trade Unions, Nám. Curieovych 1, Prague 1, Czechoslovakia.

Cherenkov, Pavel Alexeevich; Soviet physicist; b. 27 July 1904, Novaya Chigla, Voronezh; ed. Voronezh Univ.
Discoverer of the Cherenkov Effect; mem. Inst. of Physics, U.S.S.R. Acad. of Sciences; State Prize 46, Nobel Prize for Physics (with Tamm and Frank) 58; Corresp. mem. Acad. of Sciences 64-70, Academician 70-; Order of Red Banner of Labour (twice), Badge of Honour, etc.
Lebedev Physics Institute of U.S.S.R. Academy of Sciences, Leninsky Prospekt 53, Moscow, U.S.S.R.

Cherkassky, Shura; Russian-born American pianist; b. 7 Oct. 1911, Odessa; s. of Isaac Cherkassky and Lydia Schlemenson; m. Genia Ganz 1946 (divorced 1948); no c.; ed. Curtis Inst. of Music, Philadelphia.
Studied under his mother and then Josef Hofmann; emigrated to U.S.A. 22; debut Baltimore 23; first major European tour 46; numerous world tours and frequent tours of Germany and South Africa in particular; regular contributor to Salzburg Festival concerts; has recorded for Deutsche Grammophon, Philips, Decca.
Leisure interests: travelling, sight-seeing, air transport.
c/o Ibbs and Tillett, Ltd., 124 Wigmore Street, London, W.1, England.
Telephone: 01-486-4021.

Cherkes, Alexander Ilyich; Soviet pharmacologist; b. 3 May 1894, Kharkov; ed. Kharkov Univ.
Physician 17-21; Research Assoc., Asst. Prof. Kharkov Medical Inst. 21-29; Head of Laboratory, Ukrainian Inst. of Labour Hygiene 24-36; Head of Dept. Ukrainian Inst. of Experimental Medicine 33-41; Prof., Head of Chair, Kharkov Medical Inst. 29-44; Head of Chair, Kiev Medical Inst. 44-; Corresp. mem. U.S.S.R. Acad. of Medical Sciences 45; mem. U.S.S.R. Acad. of Medical Sciences 60-; mem. Board U.S.S.R. Soc. of

Pharmacologists 65-; Chair. Board Ukrainian Soc. of Pharmacologists 61-; Deputy Chair. Kiev Branch Soc. of Pharmacologists 64-; Order of Red Banner of Labour (twice), Badge of Honour, Merited Scientist of Ukrainian S.S.R.
Publs. Over 100 publs. on developing new medicines, investigating therapeutic effects of medicines and toxic substances.
Academy of Medical Sciences of the U.S.S.R., Ul. Solyanka 14, Moscow 109801, U.S.S.R.

Chern, Shiing-Shen, B.S., M.S., D.SC.; American (naturalized 1961) professor of mathematics; b. 26 Oct. 1911, Kashing, China; s. of Lien Chin Chern and Mei Han; m. Shih Ning Cheng 1939; one s. one d.; ed. Nankai Univ., Tientsin, Tsing Hua Univ., Peking, and Univ. of Hamburg, Germany.
Professor of Mathematics, Tsing Hua Univ., Peking 37-43; mem. Inst. for Advanced Study, Princeton, N.J., U.S.A. 43-45; Acting Dir. Inst. of Mathematics, Academia Sinica, Nanking, China 46-48; Prof. of Mathematics, Univ. of Chicago, U.S.A. 49-60, Univ. of Calif. at Berkeley 60-; mem. Academia Sinica, Nat. Acad. of Sciences (U.S.A.), American Acad. of Arts and Sciences; Hon. mem. Indian Mathematical Soc.; Corresp. mem. Brazilian Acad. of Sciences; Hon. LL.D. (Univ. of Hong Kong) 69; Hon. D.Sc. (Univ. of Chicago) 69, (Univ. of Hamburg, Germany) 71.
Publs. Scientific papers in various journals.
8336 Kent Court, El Cerrito, Calif., U.S.A.
Telephone: 415-232-4148.

Chernigovsky, Vladimir Nikolaievich; Soviet physiologist and neurophysiologist; b. 16 Feb. 1907, Ekaterinburg, now Sverdlovsk; s. of Nikolai E. and Natalia P. Chernigovsky; m. Natalia V. Chernigovsky; one s. one d.; ed. Perm State Univ.
Began physiological investigations of circulation, hæmatology and neurophysiology 33; Prof. of Physiology, Naval Medical Acad., Leningrad 43-52; Dir. of Inst. of Normal and Pathological Physiology, Moscow 52-59; Vice-Pres. Acad. of Medical Sciences 53-56; Head of Pavlov Inst. 59-; mem. U.S.S.R. Acad. of Medical Sciences, mem. and Vice-Sec. Dept. of Physiology, U.S.S.R. Acad. of Sciences; Corresp. mem. Romanian Acad. of Sciences; Hon. mem. J. Purkyňe Soc., Czechoslovakia 62; mem. Int. Acad. of Astonautics 65; Deputy to U.S.S.R. Supreme Soviet; Pavlov Prize 43, Pavlov Gold Medal 64 and I. M. Sechenov Prize 74, U.S.S.R. Acad. of Sciences; Order of Red Banner of Labour (twice), Order of Red Star.
Publs. include: *The Afferent Systems of the Internal Organs* 43, *Problems of the Nervous Regulation of Blood Compositions* 53, *Morpho-physiological Structure of Interoceptive Analyser and Some Details of its Function* 59, *The Interceptors* 60, *Participation of Some Structures of Limbic System in Conducting Visceral and Somatic Signals* 64, *Morpho-physiological Architecture of Subcortical and Cortical Projections of Afferent Fibres of Vagus* 64, *Cortical and Subcortical Representation of Visceral Systems* 73.
I. P. Pavlov Institute of Physiology, Nabereznaja Markarova 6, Leningrad 199164, U.S.S.R.

Chernyakov, Yury Nikolayevich; Soviet diplomatist; b. 1 Aug. 1918, Gorky; ed. Gorky Inst. of River Transport Engineers and Higher Diplomatic School.
Instructor, Gorky Inst. of River Transport Engineers 43-46; entered diplomatic service 48; Third Sec., Archives, Ministry of Foreign Affairs 48-50; Third, Second then First Sec., Soviet Embassy, Budapest 50-55; Counsellor, Ministry of Foreign Affairs 55-57, Soviet Embassy, Budapest 57-59; Deputy Head, Press Dept. 59-65; Counsellor, Minister-Counsellor, Soviet Embassy, Washington, D.C. 65-70; Head, Press Dept., Ministry of Foreign Affairs 70-73; Sec.-Gen., Ministry of Foreign Affairs 73-; Badge of Honour, Order of the

Patriotic War, Order of the Red Banner of Labour, etc.
Ministry of Foreign Affairs, 32-34 Smolenskaya-Sennaya Ploshchad, Moscow, U.S.S.R.

Chernyshev, Vyacheslav Ivanovich; Soviet journalist and politician; b. 14 Feb. 1914, Plyes, Ivanovo; ed. Communist Inst. of Journalism, Leningrad.
Compositor 30-33; Deputy Editor-in-Chief *Tikhookeansky Komsomolyets* (Pacific Komsomol Member), Khabarovsk 35-37; Corresp., later Head of Dept. *Komsomolskaya Pravda* (Komsomol Truth) 38-43; Press Attaché, Soviet Embassy, Mexico 43-46, Chile 46-47; Head of Dept. *Literaturnaya Gazeta* (Literary Paper) 47-48; Chief Editor Moscow Radio, later Deputy Head Supreme Broadcasting Board, U.S.S.R. Ministry of Culture 48-56; Head of Dept. *Sovietskaya Rossia* (Soviet Russia) 56-58; Deputy Head of Dept. of Int. Problems *Problemy mira i sotsialisma* (Problems of Peace and Socialism) 58-60; Head of U.S.S.R. Supreme Broadcasting Board and Deputy Chair. U.S.S.R. State Cttee. for Radio and Television 60-65; Sec.; Union of Journalists of U.S.S.R. 65-; mem. C.P.S.U. 37; Order of Red Banner of Labour.
Union of Journalists of U.S.S.R., Prospekt Mira 30, Moscow, U.S.S.R.

Chervonenko, Stepan Vasilievich, M.SC.; Soviet diplomatist; b. 16 Sept. 1915, Okop, Poltava; s. of Vassily Chervonenko and Agafia Kiritchenko; m. Loudmilla Chervonenko 1948; ed. Kiev State Univ.
Headmaster, secondary school 37-41; mem. C.P.S.U. 40-; Soviet Army service 41-44; teacher of Marxism-Leninism, Dep. Dir. Cherkass Pedagogical Inst. 44-48; on staff of Central Cttee. C.P. Ukraine 49-56; Sec. Central Cttee. C.P. Ukraine 56-59; Amb. to Chinese People's Repub. 59-65, to Czechoslovakia 65-73, to France 73-; mem. Central Cttee. C.P.S.U., parliamentary group of Supreme Soviet; Deputy to Supreme Soviet of U.S.S.R. and to Soviet Socialist Repub. of Ukraine; Order of Lenin, Order of Red Banner of Labour, Order of White Lion, etc.
Leisure interests: hunting, sport.
U.S.S.R. Embassy, 79 rue de Grenelle, Paris 7e, France.

Cheshire, Geoffrey Chevalier, D.C.L., F.B.A.; British barrister-at-law; b. 27 June 1886, Hartford, Cheshire; s. of Walter Christopher and Clara (Cook) Cheshire; m. 1st Primrose Barstow 1915 (died 1962), two s.; m. 2nd Mary Kathleen Lloyd, D.B.E., 1963 (died 1972); ed. Denston Coll., and Merton Coll., Oxford.
Lecturer Univ. Coll. of Wales, Aberystwyth 09-10; Fellow of Exeter Coll. Oxford 12-44; All Souls' Lecturer in Private Int. Law 22-33; All Souls' Reader in English Law 33-44; Vinerian Prof. of English Law, Univ. of Oxford 44-49, Fellow of All Souls 44-49; Reader in Private Int. Law to Council of Legal Education 45-60; Hon. Bencher Lincoln's Inn; fmr. mem. of Inst. of Int. Law 50-65; Fellow of British Acad., Hon. Fellow Merton and Exeter Colls., Oxford.
Publs. *Modern Real Property* 25, *Private International Law* 35; joint author of *Cheshire and Fifoot on Contract* 45, *International Contracts* 48, Gen. Editor *Stephen's Commentaries* 19th edn., *The Private International Law of Husband and Wife* 63.
Laundry Cottage, Empshott, Liss, Hants,. England.
Telephone: Blackmoor (Hampshire) 202.

Cheshire, Group Captain Geoffrey Leonard, V.C., D.S.O., D.F.C., B.A.; British air force officer (retd.); b. 7 Sept. 1917, Chester; s. of Prof. G. C. Cheshire, F.B.A., D.C.L. and Primrose (Burella) Cheshire; m. Margaret Susan Ryder, O.B.E.; one s. one d.; ed. Stowe School, Merton Coll., Oxford.
Commissioned 39; Flying Officer 40; Wing Commdr. commanding 76 Squadron 42, 617 Squadron 43; attached Eastern Air Command H.Q., South-East Asia 44, British Joint Staff Mission, Washington 45; observer at dropping of atomic bomb on Nagasaki 45; Founder

Cheshire Foundation Homes for the Disabled (operating 110 homes in 22 countries) and co-founder Ryder Cheshire Mission for the Relief of Suffering; Humanitarian Award, Variety Clubs Int. (with Susan Cheshire 74.
Publs. *Bomber Pilot* 43, *Pilgrimage to the Shroud* 56, *Face of Victory* 61; Films: *Dilip* 71, *To Be A Pilgrim* 72.
Leisure interests: tennis, photography.
Cavendish, Suffolk, England.
Telephone: 01-499-2267.

Chester, Sir (Daniel) Norman, Kt., C.B.E., M.A.; British political scientist; b. 27 Oct. 1907, Manchester; s. of Daniel and Edith Chester; m. Eva Jeavons 1936; ed. Manchester Univ.
Rockefeller Fellow 35-36; Lecturer in Public Admin., Manchester Univ. 36-45; mem. Economic Section, War Cabinet Secretariat 40-45; Official Fellow, Nuffield Coll., Oxford 45-54, Warden 54-; mem. Oxford City Council 52-74; fmr. Chair. and now Vice-Pres. Royal Inst. of Public Admin.; fmr. Pres. Int. Political Science Asscn.; Chair. Oxford Centre for Management Studies 65-75; fmr. mem. South-East Regional Economic Planning Council; Corresp. mem. Acad. des Sciences Morales et Politiques, Inst. de France; fmr. Editor *Public Administration*; Hon. D.Litt.
Publs. *Public Control of Road Passenger Transport* 36, *Central and Local Government, Financial and Administrative Relations* 51, *The Nationalised Industries* 51, *Lessons of the British War Economy* (Editor) 51, *Organisation of British Central Government 1914-1956* (Editor) 57, *Questions in Parliament* (with Mrs. Bowring) 62, *The Nationalization of British Industry, 1945-51* 75.
Leisure interests: football and bridge.
Nuffield College, Oxford; Home: 136 Woodstock Road, Oxford, England.
Telephone: Oxford 48014 (Office), Oxford 55323 (Home).

Chevalier, Louis; French university professor and political scientist; b. 29 May 1911; ed. Ecole Normale Supérieure.
Professor Coll. de France; Prof. Institut d'Etudes Politiques de Paris; mem. Conseil supérieur de la Recherche Scientifique; Pres. du Conseil Scientifique du Centre Int. d'Etude des Problèmes Humains de Monaco; mem. Conseil Economique et Social du District de Paris; Hon. degree Columbia Univ.
Publs. *Les Paysans, Le Problème démographique nord-africain, La Formation de la population parisienne, Madagascar, Démographie générale;* contributor to *Population, Le choléra de 1832, Classes laborieuses et classes dangereuses, Les Parisiens, Histoire Anachronique des Français.*
Collège de France, 11 place Marcelin-Berthelot, Paris 5e, France.

Chevalier, Roger; French aeronautical engineer; b. 3 May 1922, Marseilles; m. Monique Blin 1947; two s.; ed. Ecole Polytechnique and Ecole nationale supérieure de l'aéronautique.
Head of Dept., Aeronautical Arsenal 48-53; Chief Engineer, Nord-Aviation 54-60; Technical Dir. Soc. pour l'Etude et la Réalisation d'Engins Balistiques (SEREB) 60-, Dir.-Gen. 67; Gen. Man. Société Nationale de l'Industrie Aérospatiale (SNIAS), Vice-Pres. 74-; Pres. Asscn. Aéronautique et Astronautique de France; mem. Int. Acad. of Astronautics; Officier Légion d'Honneur; Médaille de l'Aéronautique; Prix Galabert 66; Commdr. Ordre du Mérite.
Leisure interests: tennis, hunting, reading.
4 rue Edouard Detaille, Paris 17e, France.
Telephone: CAR 59 28.

Chevallaz, Georges-André, D.LITT.; Swiss politician; b. 7 Feb. 1915, Lausanne; m. Madeleine Roch 1945; two s.; ed. Univ. of Lausanne.
Teacher, School of Commerce 42-55; Dir. Canton

Library, Reader in Diplomatic History, Univ. of Lausanne 55-58; Syndic de Lausanne 57-73; Nat. Councillor 59-73; mem. Fed. Council 73-, Head Finance Dept. 74-; Radical Democrat.

Publs. *Aspects de l'agriculture vaudoise à la fin de l'ancien régime* 49, *Histoire générale de 1789 à nos jours* 57, 67, 73, *Les grandes conférences diplomatiques* 64, *La Suisse ou le sommeil du juste* 67, etc.

Département des Finances et des Douanes, Bernerhof, Bundesgasse 3, Berne; Home: Elfenauweg 91, Berne, Switzerland.

Telephone: 61 60 01 (Office); 44 78 78 (Home).

Chevrier, Hon. Lionel, P.C., C.C., Q.C.; Canadian lawyer; b. Cornwall, Ont.; s. of Joseph E. Chevrier and Malvina de Repentigny; m. Lucienne Brulé 1932; three s. three d.; ed. Cornwall, Ont., High School, Cornwall Collegiate Inst., Univ. of Ottawa, Osgoode Hall (Law School) Toronto, Ont.

Called to Bar (Ont.) 28, 57 (P.Q.); apptd. K.C. 38; mem. of Dominion Parl. 35-54, 57-63; Deputy Chief Govt. Whip 40; Chair. Sub-Cttee. on Production and Munitions Contracts (Parl. War Expenditure Cttee.) 42; Parl. Asst. to Minister of Munitions and Supply 43; Minister of Transport April 45-54; Pres. The St. Lawrence Seaway Authority 54-57; Pres. of Privy Council 57; Minister of Justice 63-64; High Commr. for Canada in U.K. 64-67; Commr.-Gen. for Overseas Visits, *Expo 67*, Montreal; Head of Special Mission to Francophone Countries of Africa 68; Head of Mission to Canadian Consular Posts in U.S.A. 68; retd. from govt. service 69; retd. mem. of law firm Geoffrion, Prud'homme, Chevrier, Cardinal, Marchessault, Mercier and Greenstein; Pres. Québecair; Chair. UN Inst. for Training and Research Del. to Study Aspects of Waterways for Int. Navigation, Buenos Aires 70; Del. Bretton Woods Conf. 45; Chair. Canadian del. to UN Gen. Assembly, Paris 48; Freeman, City of London 65; Hon. LL.D. (Univ. of Ottawa, Queen's Univ., Laval Univ.); Hon. D.C.L. (Bishop's Univ.).

Leisure interests: walking, reading, travelling.

Publ. *The St. Lawrence Seaway* 59.

500 Place d'Armes, Montreal 126, P.Q., Canada.

Telephone: 288-9161.

Chew, Geoffrey Foucar, PH.D.; American professor of physics; b. 5 June 1924, Washington, D.C.; s. of Arthur Percy Chew and Pauline Lisette Foucar; m. 1st Ruth Elva Wright 1945 (died 1971), one s. one d.; m. 2nd Denyse Mettel 1972, two s.; ed. George Washington Univ. and Univ. of Chicago.

Research Physicist Los Alamos Scientific Lab. 44-46; Research Physicist, Lawrence Radiation Lab. 48-49, Head of Theoretical Group 67-; Asst. Prof. of Physics, Univ. of Calif. at Berkeley 49-50, Prof. of Physics 57-; Chair. Dept. of Physics 74-; Asst. Prof., the Assoc. Prof. of Physics, Univ. of Ill. 50-55, Prof. 55-56; Fellow Inst. for Advanced Study 56; Overseas Fellow Churchill Coll., Cambridge 62-63; mem. Nat. Acad. of Sciences, American Acad. of Arts and Sciences; Hughes Prize of American Physical Soc. 62, Lawrence Award of U.S. Atomic Energy Comm. 69.

Leisure interests: gardening, hiking.

Publs. *The S-Matrix Theory of Strong Interactions* 61, *The Analytic S Matrix* 66; over 100 scientific articles.

Department of Physics, University of California, Berkeley, Calif. 94720; and Lawrence Radiation Laboratory, Berkeley, Calif. 94720; Home: 10 Maybeck Twin Drive, Berkeley, Calif. 94708, U.S.A.

Telephone: 642-4505 (Dept. of Physics); 843-2740, Ext. 5851 (Lawrence Radiation Lab.); 848-1830 (Home).

Cheysson, Claude; French public servant; b. 13 April 1920; ed. Ecole Normale Supérieure, Ecole Polytechnique and Ecole d'Administration, Paris.

Escaped from occupied France to Spanish prison 43; Officer in the Free French Forces 43-45; entered French

Diplomatic Service 48; attached to U.N. Mission in Palestine 48; Head of French liaison office with Fed. German Govt., Bonn 49-52; adviser to Prime Minister of Vietnam, Saigon 52-54; Chef de Cabinet to French Prime Minister (Mendès-France) 54-55; technical adviser to Minister for Moroccan and Tunisian Affairs 55-56; Sec.-Gen. Comm. for Technical Co-operation in Africa (C.C.T.A.), Lagos 57-62; Dir.-Gen. Sahara Authority (Organisme Saharien), Algiers 62-65; Dir.-Gen. Organisme coopération industrielle, Algiers 66; Amb. to Indonesia 66-69; Pres. Entreprise minière et chimique and Pres. Dir.-Gen. Compagnie des potasses du Congo 70-73; Commr. for Devt. Aid, Comm. of European Communities 73-; Officier, Légion d'Honneur; Croix de Guerre (five citations).

Office: 11 avenue de Friedland, Paris 8e; Home: 9 quai Malaquais, Paris 6e, France.

Chi Peng-fei; Chinese politician; b. 1910, Yung-chi, Shensi; ed. Mil. Medical Coll.

Joined Communist Party 31; on Long March in Medical Dept., Red Army 35; Deputy Political Commissar, Army Corps, 3rd Field Army 50; Amb. to German Democratic Repub. 50-55; Vice-Minister of Foreign Affairs 55-72; Acting Minister of Foreign Affairs 68-72; Minister 72-74; mem. 10th Cen. Cttee., CCP 73.

People's Republic of China.

Chi Teng-k'uei; Chinese party official.

First Sec. CCP Loyang District, Honan 59; Alt. Sec. CCP Honan 66; Vice-Chair. Honan Revolutionary Cttee. 68; Alt. mem. Politburo, 9th Cen. Cttee. of CCP 69; mem. Politburo, 10th Cen. Cttee. of CCP 73; First Political Commissar, Peking Mil. Region, People's Liberation Army 74-; Vice-Premier State Council 75.

People's Republic of China.

Chia Chi-yun; Chinese party official.

Deputy Dir. State Statistical Bureau 54-58, Dir. 58-61; Sec. S.W. Bureau of Cen. Cttee. CCP 61-67; Sec. CCP Szechuan 63; First Sec. CCP Kweichow 65; criticized and removed from office during Cultural Revolution 67; Chair. Yunnan Revolutionary Cttee. 75-; First Sec. CCP Yunnan 75-.

People's Republic of China.

Chiang Ch'ing; Chinese party official; b. 1914, Chucheng, Shantung; m. Mao Tse-tung (q.v.) 1939; ed. Shantung Experimental Drama Acad., Tsinan.

Librarian, Tsingtao Univ. 33; Film Actress 34-38; joined CCP 37; Instructor Lu Hsun Art Acad., Yenan 39; Head of Cen. Film Admin. Bureau, Propaganda Dept., CCP 49; with Ministry of Culture 50-54; Organizer of Reforms in Peking Opera 63; First Deputy Head of Cen. Cultural Revolution Group 66; leading pro-Maoist activist in propaganda work during Cultural Revolution 65-69; mem. Politburo, 9th Cen. Cttee. of CCP 69, Politburo, 10th Cen. Cttee. 73.

People's Republic of China.

Chiang Ching-kuo; Chinese politician; b. 18 March 1910, Chekiang Prov.; s. of Chiang Kai-shek (died 1975); m. Chiang Fang-liang; three s. one d.; ed. Sun Yat-sen Univ., Moscow, and U.S.S.R. Military and Political Inst.

Eldest son of Generalissimo Chiang Kai-shek; Admin. Commdr. for South Kiangsi 39-45; Foreign Affairs Commdr. of Mil. and Political Admin. for N.E. China 45-47; Deputy Econ. Control Supervisor for Shanghai 48; Chair. Kuomintang Taiwan Province H.Q. 49-50; Dir., Gen. Political Dept., Ministry of Nat. Defence 50-54; mem. Central Revision Cttee. of Kuomintang 50-52; Minister without Portfolio 63; Deputy Minister of Nat. Defence 64-65; Minister of Nat. Defence 65-69; Vice-Premier 69-72, Premier May 72-; Dir.-Gen. of Kuomintang 75-; Deputy Sec.-Gen. Nat. Defence Council 54-67; Chair. Nat. Gen. Mobilization Cttee.

18 Chang An East Road, 1st Section, Taipei, Taiwan.

Chiang Hua; Chinese party official; b. Hupeh.
Guerrilla activist with new 4th Army, CCP 40; Mayor of
Hangchow 49-51; Deputy Sec. CCP Chekiang 52-55,
First Sec. 52-68; Alt. mem. 8th Cen. Cttee. of CCP 56;
First Political Commissar Chekiang Mil. District,
People's Liberation Army 56-68; Prof. of Political
Theories, Chekiang Univ. 58; Sec. E. China Bureau 65;
criticized and removed from office during Cultural
Revolution 68; Alt. mem. 10th Cen. Cttee. of CCP 73.
People's Republic of China.

Chiang Kai-shek, Madame (Soong, Mayling), LL.D.,
L.H.D.; Chinese sociologist; ed. Wellesley Coll., U.S.A.
Married (Pres.) Chiang Kai-shek 27; first Chinese woman
appointed mem. of Child Labour Comm.; inaugurated
Moral Endeavour Asscn.; established schools in Nanking for orphans of revolutionary soldiers; fmr. mem.
Legislative Yuan; served as Sec.-Gen. of Chinese Comm.
on Aeronautical Affairs; Dir.-Gen. New Life Movement;
founded and directed Nat. Chinese Women's Asscn. for
War Relief and Nat. Asscn. for Refugee Children;
accompanied husband on mil. campaigns; Hon. Chair.
American Bureau for Medical Aid to China and Cttee.
for the promotion of the Welfare of the Blind; Patroness
Int. Red. Cross Cttee.; Hon. Chair. British United Aid
to China Fund and United China Relief; First Hon.
Mem. Bill of Rights Commemorative Soc.; first
Chinese woman to be decorated by Nat. Govt. of China,
awards include Gold Medal of Nat. Inst. of Social
Sciences; L.H.D. John B. Stetson Univ., Bryant Coll.,
Hobart and William Smith Colls., Nebraska Wesleyan
Univ.; LL.D. Rutgers Univ., Goucher Coll., Wellesley
Coll., Loyola Univ., Russell Sage Coll., Hahnemann
Medical Coll., Univs. of Michigan and Hawaii, and
Wesleyan Coll., Macon; Hon. F.R.C.S. (Eng.); Hon.
mem. numerous socs.
Publs. *Sian: A Coup d'Etat* 37, *China in Peace and War*
39, *China Shall Rise Again* 39, *This is Our China* 40,
We Chinese Women 41, *American Tour Speeches* 42-43,
Little Sister Su 43, *The Sure Victory* 55, *Madame Chiang
Kai-shek: Selected Speeches* 58-59, *Album of Reproduc-
tions of Paintings* Vol. I 52, Vol. II 62, *Religious
Writings* 63, *Madame Chiang Kai-shek: Selected Speeches*
65-66, *Album of Chinese Orchid Paintings* 71, *Album of
Chinese Bamboo Paintings* 72, *Album of Chinese
Landscape Painting* 73, *Album of Chinese Floral
Paintings* 74.
c/o The President's Residence, Taipei, Taiwan.

Chiang Wei-ch'ing; Chinese party official; b. Kiangsu.
Deputy Political Commissar, People's Liberation Army,
Nanking 49; Second Sec. CCP Kiangsu 53-55, First Sec.
56-68; Alt. mem. 8th Cen. Cttee. of CCP 56; First
Political Commissar Kiangsu Mil. District, PLA 60-68;
Sec. E. China Bureau, CCP 66; criticized and removed
from office during Cultural Revolution 68; Alt. mem.
10th Cen. Cttee. of CCP 73; First Sec. CCP Kiangsi 75.
People's Republic of China.

Chiang Yee, B.SC., F.R.A.S., H.L.D., D.LITT., D.ARTS;
Chinese artist, calligrapher and author; b. 19 May 1903,
Kiukiang, China; s. of late Chiang Ho-an and Hsiang-
lin; m. Tseng-yun 1924 (separated); three c.; ed. Nat.
South Eastern Univ., Nanking.
Lecturer in Chemistry, Nat. Univ., Shanghai; District
Gov. of Kiukiang and Yushan (Kiangsi Prov.) Tangton
and Wuhu (Anhui Prov.); emigrated to London 33;
worked as writer and artist 33-; Lecturer in Chinese,
School of Oriental Studies, London Univ. 35-38; in
charge of Chinese Section, Wellcome Inst. of the
History of Medicine 38-40; executed series of portraits
of *Giant Panda* painted from life (first Giant Panda in
captivity, Regents Park Zoo) 38; other works of this
period include *Trafalgar Square in Fog* and numerous
Lake District landscapes; designed decor and costumes
for Sadlers' Wells performance of *The Birds* 42; after
World War II went to live in America; paintings at

this time include *The Tops of New York Skyscrapers
Appeared Above the Evening Clouds*; Curator of Chinese
Ethnology, Peabody Museum, Salem, Mass. 56-;
Ralph Waldo Emerson Fellow in Poetry, Harvard Univ.
58-59; Prof. of Chinese Studies, Columbia Univ. 60-;
mem. American Acad. of Arts and Sciences etc.; works
in numerous collections including Fogg Art Museum,
Cambridge, Mass., Utah State Univ. Museum, Logan;
recent exhibitions include City Hall, Hong Kong 72,
Australian Nat. Univ. 73.
Leisure interests: reading, walking, calligraphy.
Publs. *A book of poems in Chinese* 35, *The Chinese Eye*
35, *Chinese Calligraphy* 38, *A Chinese Childhood* 40,
Chinese Painting 53, *One Hundred quatrains of Chung-
ya* 55, *Chinese Ch'an Poetry* 66; the *Silent Traveller*
series: *The Silent Traveller in Lakeland* 37, *in London*
38, *in Wartime* 39, *in Yorkshire Dales* 41, *in Oxford* 44,
in Edinburgh 46, *in New York* 50, *in Dublin* 55, *in
Paris* 56, *in Boston* 59, *in Japan* 60, *in San Francisco*
64, *in Australia* 76; mainly for children: *Birds and
Beasts* 39, *Chinpo and The Giant Pandas* 39, *Chinpo at
The Zoo* 41, *Lo Cheng, the boy who wouldn't keep still* 41,
The Men of The Burma Road 42, *A Story of Ming* 43,
Dabbitse 44, *Yebbin* 47.
520 West 123 Street, New York, N.Y. 10027; c/o
W. W. Norton Co., 55 Fifth Avenue, New York, N.Y
10003, U.S.A.
Telephone: UN4-4321.

Chiang Yu-an; Chinese army officer.
Commander Ninghsia Mil. District, People's Liberation
Army 72-.
People's Republic of China.

Chiao Hung-kuang; Chinese army officer.
Commander Kwangsi Mil. District, People's Liberation
Army 67-; Political Commissar PLA Air Force, Kwangsi
67; Vice-Chair. Kwangsi Revolutionary Cttee. 68.
People's Republic of China.

Ch'iao Kuan-hua; Chinese politician; b. 1908, Yen-
cheng, Kiangsu; ed. Tsinghua Univ., Peking and in
Germany.
Director S. China Branch, New China News Agency
46-49; Deputy Dir., Gen. Office, Cen. People's Govt.
49-54; Asst. to Minister of Foreign Affairs 54-64; Vice-
Minister of Foreign Affairs 64-74, Minister 74-; Head of
Chinese del. to Sino-Soviet Border talks 69; Leader of
del. to UN Gen. Assembly 71; mem. 10th Cen. Cttee.
of CCP 73.
People's Republic of China.

Chiari, Roberto; Panamanian businessman and
politician; b. 2 March 1905.
Sugar manufacturer; President of Panama 60-64; Conservative.
Panama City, Panama.

Chiba, Saburo; Japanese industrialist and politician;
b. 1894; ed. Tokyo Imperial and Princeton Univs.
Entered Royal Oil Co., U.S.A. 21; Dir. Japanese
Business Joint Organisation 22; mem. House of Reps.
25-; Dir. South American Development Co. 28; Dir. and
Chief of Sales Dept., Jijishimpo Newspaper Co. Ltd. 32;
Man. Dir. Showa Petroleum Co. Ltd. 35; Pres. Japan
Petro-chemical Industry Co. Ltd. 38; Vice-Pres.
Technical Authority 45; Gov. Miyagi Prefecture 45;
Sec.-Gen. Democratic Party 49; Dir. Tokyo Agricul-
tural Univ. 51, Pres. and Chair. Board of Dirs. 55;
Chair. Finance Cttee. House of Reps. 53; mem. Gen.
Affairs Cttee. 63-; Minister of Labour 54-55; Chief Dir.
Soshinkai (LDP political group) 60-, mem. Board of
Counsellors LDP 69-; Pres. Japanese Nat. Group, Asian
Parliamentarians' Union 65-.
31 Maruyama-cho, Bunkyo-ku, Tokyo, Japan.

Chidzanja Nkhoma, R. Beston; Malawian (Chewa)
politician; b. 5 May 1921.
Joined Nyasaland African Congress 46 (now Malawi

ongress Party); Provincial Chair. Cen. Region 56-59, o-67; detained 59-60; mem. of Parl. for Lilongwe South I, Lilongwe Cen. 64; Parl. Sec. to Ministry of Trade nd Industry 63-64; Minister of Trade and Industry 64, f Home Affairs 64-65, of Local Govt. 65-67, of the en. Region 64-67; Amb.-at-large 67-68; Minister of Natural Resources 69, of Agriculture and Natural Resources 69-71, of Transport and Communications 72; Minister without Portfolio 72-74; Minister of OAU Affairs June 74-.
Ministry of OAU Affairs, Blantyre, Malawi.

Ch'ien Cheng-ying; Chinese government official; b. 1922; ed. Tatung Univ., Shanghai.
Vice-Minister of Water Conservancy 52-58, of Water Conservancy and Electrical Power 58; Minister of Water Conservancy and Electrical Power 75-.
People's Republic of China.

Ch'ien Chih-kuang; Chinese government official.
Vice-Minister of Textile Industry 49; Minister of Light Industry 75-.
People's Republic of China.

Chiepe, Miss Gaositwe Keagakwa Tibe, M.B.E., B.SC., M.A., LL.D. (HON.); Botswana diplomatist and politician; b. Serowe; d. of the late T. and S. T. Chiepe (née Sebina); un-married; ed. primary school in Serowe, secondary school in Tigerloof, S. Africa and Univs. of Fort Hare and Bristol.
Education Officer, Botswana 48, Senior Educ. Officer 62, Deputy Dir. of Educ. 65, Dir. of Educ. 68; High Commr. in U.K. and Nigeria 70-74, concurrently accredited to Sweden, Norway, Denmark, Fed. Germany, France, Belgium and the EEC; Minister of Commerce and Industry Nov. 74-.
Leisure interests: music, gardening.
Ministry of Commerce and Industry, Gaborone, Botswana.

Chikami, Teruomi; Japanese banker; b. 11 Aug. 1902, Tokyo, Japan; s. of Kiyoomi and Toku Chikami; m. Mari Katayama 1930; one s. three d.; ed. Tokyo Univ.
Managing Dir. The Mitsubishi Trust and Banking Corpn. 58, Senior Man. Dir. 62, Deputy Pres. 64, Pres. 65-71, Chair. 71-75, Counsellor 75-; Blue Ribbon Medal 68, Second Order of Merit, Order of the Sacred Treasure 74.
Leisure interests: music, pictures.
The Mitsubishi Trust and Banking Corpn., 4-5, 1-chome, Marunouchi, Chiyoda-ku, Tokyo; Home: No. 503 Town House Akasaka, 8-5-25 Akasaka, Minato-ku, Tokyo, Japan.
Telephone: 212-1211 (Office); 403-8410 (Home).

Chikovani, Mikhail Gerasimovich; Soviet politician; b. 1911; ed. Higher Party School.
Worker, then foreman 29-34; Sec. District Cttee. of C.P., Uzbekistan; later, Sec. Central Cttee. of Young Communist League of Uzbekistan; then Sec., Tashkent and Samarkand Regional Cttees. of C.P., Uzbekistan 34-41; Soviet Army 41-45; Sec. Tashkent City Cttee. of C.P., Uzbekistan 46-50; First Sec. Sukhumi City Cttee. of C.P., Georgia 54-58; Chair. Council of Ministers, Abkhazian A.S.S.R. 58-71; Chair. Georgian S.S.R. State Cttee. for Usage of Labour Resources 71-; mem. C.P.S.U. 32-, Central Cttee. of C.P., Georgia; Deputy to Supreme Soviet 58-70.
Georgian S.S.R. State Committee for Usage of Labour Resources, Tbilisi, U.S.S.R.

Childs, Marquis William, A.B., A.M.; American journalist; b. 17 March 1903; ed. Wisconsin and Iowa Univs.
With United Press 23 and 25-26; Corresp. *St. Louis Post Dispatch* 26-44, Special Corresp. 54-62, Washington Corresp. 62-68; United Feature Syndicate Columnist 44-54; Hon. LL.D. (Upsala Coll.).
Publs. *Sweden: The Middle Way, They Hate Roosevelt* 36, *Washington Calling* 37, *This is Democracy* 38, *This is*

Your War, I Write from Washington 42, *The Cabin* 44, *The Farmer Takes a Hand* 52, *Ethics in Business Society* (with D. Cater) 54, *The Ragged Edge* 55, *Eisenhower: Captive Hero* 59, *The Peacemakers* 61, *A Taint of Innocence* 67.
1701 Pennsylvania Avenue, N.W., Washington, D.C. 20036; Home: 2703 Dumbarton Avenue, N.W., Washington, D.C. 20007, U.S.A.

Chiles, Lawton Mainor; American politician; b. 3 April 1930, Lakeland, Fla.; s. of Lawton Chiles; ed. Univ. of Florida.
Served U.S. Army, Korea 53-54; law practice, Lakeland 55-; Senator from Florida 71-; mem. Democratic Steering Cttee. 71-; Govt. Award for Conservation 64; Wildlife Conservation Award of Nat. Wildlife Fed. 65; Democrat.
New Senate Office Building, Washington, D.C., U.S.A.

Chillida Juantegui, Eduardo; Spanish sculptor; b. 10 Jan. 1924; ed. Colegio Marianistas, San Sebastian, and Univ. de Madrid.
Started executing sculptures 47; first one-man exhbn., Madrid 54; one-man exhbns. at Duisburg and Houston, Texas 66, and at New York 67; has exhibited in numerous group exhbns. in America, France, Germany, Italy, Spain, Switzerland, and U.K. since 49 including Venice Biennali 58, 62; Premio del Comune di Venezia per la Scultura, Venice Biennale 58, Prix Kandinsky 60, Carnegie Prize, Pittsburgh Int. 64, North Rhine Westphalian Prize for Sculpture 65, Wilhelm Lehmbruck Prize, Duisburg.
Villa Paz, Alto de Maracruz, San Sebastian, Spain.

Ch'in Chi-wei; Chinese army officer; b. Hung-an, Hupeh.
Company Commdr. Red Army 31; Deputy Commdr. Yunnan Mil. District, People's Liberation Army 54; Deputy Commdr. Kunming Mil. Region, PLA 55, Commdr. 58; Lieut.-Gen. PLA 55; Sec. CCP Yunnan 66-68; Commdr. Chengtu Mil. Region, PLA 73-; mem. 10th Cen. Cttee. of CCP 73.
People's Republic of China.

Chipp, Hon. Donald Leslie, B.COM., A.A.S.A.; Australian politician; b. 21 Aug. 1925, Melbourne, Victoria; s. of L. T. Chipp; m. Monica T. Lalor 1951; two s. two d.; ed. Northcote High School.
Served in R.A.A.F. 43-45; Registrar, Commonwealth Inst. of Accountants and Australian Soc. of Accountants 50-55; Chief Exec. Officer Olympic Civic Cttee. 55-56; Councillor, City of Kew 55-61; mem. House of Reps. 60-; Minister for Navy and Minister in charge of Tourist Activities 66-68, Minister for Customs and Excise 69-72; Minister assisting Minister for Nat. Devt. 71-72; Minister for Social Security, Health, Repatriation and Compensation Nov.-Dec. 75; Liberal.
Parliament House, Canberra, A.C.T. 2600; Home: 60 Bluff Road, Black Rock, Victoria 3195, Australia.
Telephone: 62-2521 (Office).

Chipunza, Chad Magumise, B.A.; Rhodesian politician, farmer and businessman; b. 1925, Rusape; m. Constance Chieza 1951; four s. two d.; ed. teacher training college.
Headmaster, Highfield North School, Salisbury 51-54; Exec. Officer Capricorn Africa Soc. 55-57; Mem. of Parl. (United Federal Party) for Harare 58-63, Party Whip, subsequently Parliamentary Sec. to Minister of External Affairs until Dec. 63; Senior Lecturer, Domborhawa Training Centre 64-65; Mem. of Parl. for Bindura 65-; Leader of Official Opposition in Parl. (United People's Party) 66-69, re-elected Leader of Opposition (Nat. People's Union) 69-; Pres. African Progressive Party 74-; mem. Board of Govs. Bernard Mizeki Coll.
African Progressive Party, P.O. Box ST. 323, Southerton, Salisbury; and No. 34 Marimba Park, Salisbury, Rhodesia.
Telephone: 24530.

Chirac, Jacques; French politician; b. 29 Nov. 1932; ed. Lycée Carnot, Lycée Louis-le-Grand and Ecole Nationale d'Administration.
Military Service in Algeria; Auditor, Cour des Comptes 59-62; Head of Dept., Secr.-Gen. of Govt. 62; Head of Dept., Private Office of M. Pompidou 62-65; Counsellor, Cour des Comptes 65-67; State Sec. for Employment Problems 67-68; State Sec. for Economy and Finance 68-71; Minister for Parl. Relations 71-72, for Agriculture and Rural Devt. 72-74, of the Interior March-May 74; Prime Minister May 74-; Sec.-Gen. Union des Démocrates pour la République Jan.-June 75, Hon. Sec.-Gen. June 75-.
Hotel Matignon, Paris 7e; and 57 rue Boissière, Paris 16e, France.

Chirkov, Boris Petrovich; Soviet actor; b. 13 Aug. 1901; ed. Leningrad Inst. of State Art.
Acted at Leningrad Theatre of the Young Spectator 25-30 Leningrad Red Theatre 30-32, Leningrad New Theatre of the Young Spectator 36-38, Theatre Studio of the Film Actor, Moscow 45-50, Moscow Pushkin Drama Theatre 50-; People's Artist of the U.S.S.R. 50; State prizewinner 41, 47, 49, 52; awarded Order of Lenin; First prize in the All-Union Film Festival for the best male part (film *Kievlanka*) 60. Principal roles: Maxim (*Youth of Maxim* 35, *Return of Maxim* 37, *Vyborg Side* 39), Makhno (*Alexander Parkhomenko* 42), Udivitelno (*Front* 43), Dr. Chizhov (*True Friends* 54), Biryukov (*The Living and the Dead*) 63, The Little Man (*Extraordinary Mission* 65).
Publs. *Actor and his Role*, from *Thirty Years of the Soviet Cinematograph Industry* 50, 4 books of essays, *About Us, The Actors, On the Screen and Behind the Screen* 61, *Experience and Reflections* 64.
Moscow Pushkin Drama Theatre, 9 Tverskoi Boulevard, Moscow, U.S.S.R.

Chiryaev, Gavriil Iosifovich; Soviet politician; b. 1925; ed. Yakutsk Pedagogical Inst.
Teacher 42-43; Soviet Army 43-50; educational work 51-53; Instructor, Schools Sector, Yakutsk Regional Cttee. of C.P., later, Second Sec., Verkhny Vilyui District Cttee. of C.P. 53-58; Deputy Chief, later Chief, of Section, Yakutsk Regional Cttee. of C.P. 58-61; Sec. Yakutsk Regional Cttee. of C.P. 61-65, First Sec. 65-; Candidate mem. Central Cttee. C.P.S.U. 66-71, mem. 71-; mem. C.P.S.U. 44-; Deputy to U.S.S.R. Supreme Soviet 66-; mem. Comm. for Legislation, Soviet of Nationalities.
Yakutsk Regional Committee of Communist Party, Yakutsk, U.S.S.R.

Chissano, Joaquim; Mozambique politician; b. 1939.
Secretary and Minister of Defence, Frente de Libertação de Moçambique (FRELIMO) 64-74, also in charge of conduct and co-ordination of war against Portuguese army; mem. Cen. Cttee. FRELIMO; Prime Minister, Transitional Govt. of Mozambique 74-75, Minister of Foreign Affairs 75-.
Ministry of Foreign Affairs, Maputo (Lourenço Marques), Mozambique.

Chit Myaing, U; Burmese retd. army officer and diplomatist; b. Oct. 1922; ed. Univ. of Rangoon.
Joined Burma Independence Army under Gen. Aung San 42; Leader of Burmese Forces, Tharawaddy District during Liberation Movt. 45; Battalion Commdr. 48; Mil. Administrator 50, Brigade Commdr. 50; Insp.-Gen. Ministry of Immigration and Nat. Registration 58-60; Commdt. Army Staff Coll. 61; Minister of Trade and Industry 63-64; retd. from Army 67; Amb. to Yugoslavia 68-71, to U.K. 71-75; Sithu (Order of Burma).
c/o Ministry of Foreign Affairs, Rangoon, Burma.

Chňoupek, Bohuslav, Ing.; Czechoslovak politician; b. 10 Aug. 1925, Bratislava; ed. Coll. of Econ. Sciences, Bratislava.
Member of editorial staff, *Pravda* 58-60; Moscow corresp., *Pravda* 60-65; Chief Editor, *Predvoj* 65-67; Deputy Minister of Culture 67-69; Gen. Dir. Czechoslovak Radio 69-70; Amb. to U.S.S.R. Sept. 70-Dec. 71; Minister of Foreign Affairs Dec. 71-; alt. mem. Cen. Cttee. C.P. of Czechoslovakia 67-69, mem. 69-; Klement Gottwald State Prize 66; Order of Labour 70.
Publs. *Dunaj sa konči v Izmaile* 56, *Dobyvatel vesmiru* 61, *Generál s levom* (The General with the Lion).
Ministry of Foreign Affairs, Prague, Czechoslovakia.

Cho, Kiyoko Takeda, D.LITT.; Japanese university professor; b. 20 June 1917, Hyogoken; d. of Takehira and Hiroko Takeda; m. Yukio Cho 1953; one s.; ed. Kobe Coll., Olivet Coll., U.S.A., Union Theological Seminary, Columbia Univ., U.S.A., and Tokyo Univ.
Instructor in History of Thought, Int. Christian Univ. 53-55, Asst. Prof. 55-61, Prof. 61-; Lecturer, Tokyo Univ. 62-72; Dir. Cttee. on Asian Cultural Studies 58-71; Research Assoc. Princeton Univ. 65-66, on Asian Studies, Harvard Univ. 66-67; Dean Liberal Coll. of Arts, Int. Christian Univ. 67-69, Dean Graduate School 70-74; Dir. Inst. of Asian Cultural Studies 71-; mem. Pres. Cttee. World Council of Churches 71-75; Senior Assoc. Fellow, St. Antony's Coll., Oxford 75-76.
Leisure interests: folk art, floriculture.
Publs. *Man, Society and History* 53, *Conflict in Concept of Man in Modern Japan* 59, *The Emperor System and Education* 64, *Indigenization and Apostasy: Traditional Ethos and Protestants* 67, *The Genealogy of Apostates: The Japanese and Christianity* 73, *Between Orthodoxy and Heterodoxy* 76; Editor *Method and Objectives of History of Thoughts—Japan and the West* 61, *Educational Thoughts and Activities of Japanese Protestants* 63, *Christianity in Modern Japan* 64, *Theory of Comparative Modernization* 70, *Human Rights in Modern Japan* 70.
1-51-6 Nishigahara Kita-ku, Tokyo, Japan.
Telephone: 03-915-0886.

Chodorow, Marvin, PH.D.; American physicist; b. 16 July 1913, Buffalo, N.Y. s. of Isidor and Lena (Cohen) Chodorow; m. Leah Ruth Turitz 1937; two d.; ed. Univ. of Buffalo and Mass. Inst. of Technology.
Research Assoc., Pennsylvania State Coll. 40-41; Instructor in Physics, Coll. of City of N.Y. 41-43; Senior Project Engineer, Sperry Gyroscope Co. 43-47; Prof. Dept. of Physics and Electrical Engineering, Stanford Univ. 47-62, Dept. of Electrical Engineering and Applied Physics 62-, Dir. Microwave Lab. 59-, Chair. Dept. of Applied Physics 62-69; Lecturer, Ecole Normale Supérieure, Paris 55-56; Visiting Research Assoc., Univ. Coll., London 69-70; mem. Nat. Acad. of Sciences, Nat. Acad. of Engineering; Fellow, American Acad. of Arts and Sciences, American Physical Soc., Inst. of Electrical and Electronic Engineers; Fulbright Fellow, Cambridge Univ. (U.K.) 62; W.R.G. Baker Award 62; Hon. D. of Laws, Glasgow Univ. 72.
Leisure interests: travel, bridge, reading.
Publs. *Fundamentals of Microwave Electronics* (co-author).
Microwave Laboratory, Stanford University, Stanford, Calif. 94305; Home: 247 La Cuesta Drive, Menlo Park, Calif. 94025, U.S.A.
Telephone: 415-497-0201 (Office); 415-854-5747 (Home).

Choi Kyu Hah; Korean politician; b. 16 July 1919, Wonju City, Kangwon-do; m.; two s. one d.; ed. Kyungg High School, Seoul, Tokyo Coll. of Educ., Japan and Nat. Daedong Inst., Manchuria.
Professor, Coll. of Educ., Seoul Nat. Univ. 45-46; Dir. Econ. Affairs Bureau, Ministry of Foreign Affairs 51-52; Consul-Gen. Korean Mission, Japan 52-57, Minister 59; Vice-Minister of Foreign Affairs 59-60; Amb. to Malaysia 64-67; Minister of Foreign Affairs 67-71; Special Pres. Asst. for Foreign Affairs 71-75, Acting Prime Minister 75-; Chair. Korean del. to UN Gen.

Assembly, 67, 68, 69; del. to numerous int. confs. 55-; decorations from Ethiopia, Panama, El Salvador, Malaysia, Repub. of Viet-Nam, Tunisia and Belgium; Order of Diplomatic Service Merit; Hon. Litt. D. Hankook Univ. of Foreign Studies, Seoul).

-17, 1-ga, Myongnyun-dorig, Chongnogu, Seoul, Republic of Korea.

Choi, Kyung Nok; Korean army officer and diplomatist; b. 21 Sept. 1920, Eumsung-Gun, Choongbuk Province; *m.*; two *s.* two *d.*; ed. mil. colls. in Korea and U.S.A. and George Washington Univ., Washington, D.C. Served in Korean Army 46-61, rank of Commdg. Gen.; Supt. Mil. Mil. Acad. 52, Nat. Defence Coll. 59; Chief of Staff 61; Amb. to Mexico 67-71, also accred. to Costa Rica, Dominican Republic, El Salvador, Guatemala, Honduras, Nicaragua, Jamaica, Panama, Haiti; Amb. to U.K. 71-74, also accred. to The Gambia and Mauritius; Minister of Transport 74-.
Leisure interests: golf, tennis, swimming, skiing.
Ministry of Transport, Seoul, Republic of Korea.

Choi Siew Hong, B.A.; Malaysian banker; b. 16 July 1921, Pahang; *s.* of late Choi Soon and of Chan Yew; *m.* Maria Lim Kheng Chew 1943; three *s.* two *d.*; ed. Clifford School, Kuala Lipis, Raffles Coll., Singapore, Univ. of Malaya.
Teacher in Malaysian Educ. Service 46-55; joined Civil Service 55; Asst. Sec. Econ. Div., Treasury, Asst. Sec., then Acting Principal Asst. Sec., Econ. Sec., Prime Minister's Dept. 55-59; Sec. Bank Negara Malaysia (Cen. Bank of Malaysia) 59-60, Adviser 60-66, Deputy Gov. 66-72; Exec. Dir. IBRD 72-; Commdr. Order of Defender of the Realm (Johan Mangku Negara).
International Bank for Reconstruction and Development, 1818 H Street, N.W., Washington, D.C. 20433, U.S.A.
Telephone: (202) 477-2221.

Chomsky, (Avram) Noam; American theoretical linguist; b. 7 Dec. 1928, Pennsylvania; *s.* of William Chomsky and Elsie Simonofsky; *m.* Carol Schatz 1949; one *s.* two *d.*; ed. Univ. of Pennsylvania.
At Massachusetts Inst. of Technology (M.I.T.) 55-, Ferrari Ward Prof. of Linguistics 66-; Nat. Science Foundation Fellow, Princeton Inst. for Advanced Study; American Council of Learned Socs. Fellow, Center for Cognitive Studies, Harvard Univ.; mem. American Acad. of Arts and Sciences, Linguistics Soc. of America, American Philological Asscn., American Acad. of Political and Social Science, Nat. Acad. of Sciences, etc.; Hon. D.H.L., Univ. of Chicago 67, Loyola Univ., Swarthmore Coll. 70, Bard Coll. 71, Univ. of Mass. 73; Hon. D.Lit., London 67, Delhi 72.
Publs. include: *Syntactic Structures, Aspects of the Theory of Syntax, Cartesian Linguistics, Language and Mind, The Sound Pattern of English* (with Morris Hall), *American Power and the New Mandarins, At war with Asia* 70, *Problems of Knowledge and Freedom* 71, *Studies on Semantics in Generative Grammar* 72, *For Reasons of State* 73, *The Backroom Boys* 73, *Bains de Sang* (trans. of *Bloodbaths in Fact and Propaganda*) 74, *Peace in the Middle East?* 74, *Reflections on Language* 75, *The Logical Structure of Linguistic Theory* 76.
Department of Linguistics, Massachusetts Institute of Technology, Massachusetts Avenue, Cambridge, Mass. 02139.
Telephone: 617-864-7819 (Office).

Chona, Mathias Mainza, BAR.-AT-LAW; Zambian politician; b. 21 Jan. 1930, Nampeyo, Monze; *s.* of Chief Chona; *m.* Yolanta Mainza 1953; two *s.* five *d.*; ed. Chona School, Chikuni Catholic Mission, Munali Govt. School, Lusaka and Gray's Inn, London.
Interim Pres. UNIP (United National Independence

Party) 59-60, Vice-Pres. 60-61, Gen. Sec. 61-69, mem. Interim Exec. Cttee. 69-71, mem. Central Cttee. 71-; M.P. for Livingstone 64, for Mankoya 68; Minister of Justice 64; Minister of Home Affairs 64-66; Minister for Presidential Affairs 67; Minister without Portfolio 68; Minister for Central Province, Minister of Provincial and Local Govt. and Amb. to U.S.A. (also accred. to Chile) 69-70; Vice-Pres. of Zambia 70-73, also Minister of Nat. Guidance and Devt. 71-73, of Information 71-74; Prime Minister 73-75, also Minister of Nat. Guidance and Culture 73-75; Minister of Legal Affairs and Attorney Gen. May 75-; Sec.-Gen. 3rd Non-Aligned Conf. (Lusaka) 70; Pres. OAU Mediation Comm. 71-; del. to numerous int. congresses.
Leisure interests: reading, writing.
Publ. *Kabuca Uleta Tunji* (novel-Margaret Wrong Medal 56).
Ministry of Legal Affairs, Lusaka; and P.O. Box 208, Lusaka, Zambia.

Chopra, Mulk Raj, D.ENG.; Indian civil engineer and university vice-chancellor; b. 18 Aug. 1906, Lahore (now Pakistan); *s.* of Dina Nath Chopra and Mrs. Chopra; *m.* Subersh Chopra 1933; one *s.* two *d.*; ed. Govt. Coll., Lahore and Thomason Coll. (now Roorkee Univ.).
Joined Irrigation Branch, Punjab 30, rising to position of Under-Sec. to Govt., Punjab Irrigation Branch; promoted to Superintending Engineer 48; in charge of Harrike Barrage construction 49; Sec. Bhakra Control Board 50; Joint Dir., Directorate of Construction and Plant Design, Bhakra Dam and Power Plant 53, promoted to Chief Engineer, then Gen. Man. 53; in charge of Beas Project Admin. 60; Chair. Central Water and Power Comm., Govt. of India 62-66; Vice-Chancellor, Roorkee Univ. 66-71; Assessor Narmada Water Disputes Tribunal, New Delhi 72-; Padma Bhushan Award 67.
Narmada Water Disputes Tribunal, A-23-A, Kailash Colony, New Delhi 48; N-40 Panch Sheel Park, New Delhi, India.
Telephone: 631798 (Office); 78040 (Home).

Chorley, 1st Baron, cr. 45, of Kendal; **Robert Samuel Theodore Chorley,** M.A.; British jurist; b. 29 May 1895; Kendal, Westmorland; *s.* of Richard Fisher Chorley and Annie Elizabeth Frost; *m.* Katherine Campbell Hopkinson 1925; two *s.* one *d.*; ed. Kendal Grammar School and Queen's Coll., Oxford.
Formerly in Foreign Office and Ministry of Labour; Barrister 20; Pres. Hardwicke Soc. 21-22; Tutor Law Society's School of Law 20-24, Lecturer in Commercial Law 24-30; Sir Ernest Cassel Prof. of Commercial and Industrial Law, London Univ. 30-47; Hon. Sec. Council for Preservation of Rural England 38-67, Vice-Pres. 69-; Vice-Chair. Nat. Trust; mem. staff Ministry Home Security 41-42; Nat. Parks Cttee.; Deputy Regional Commr. for Civil Defence, N.W. Region 42-45; Chair. Westmorland Court of Quarter Sessions 45-68; mem. Parl. del. to India 46; Royal Comm. on Justices of the Peace 46; Chair. Cttee. on Civil Service Salaries 48; a Lord-in-Waiting to the King 46-49; mem. Mocatta Cttee. on Cheque Endorsements 55; Pres. Commons and Footpaths Preservation Soc. 61-; Gen. Editor *Modern Law Review* 37-71.
Publs. *Law of Banking, Leading Cases in Commercial Law* (in collaboration), *Shipping Law* (in collaboration), *Arnould's Law of Marine Insurance* (ed. 13th, 14th and 15th edns.), *Leading Cases in the Law of Banking* (in collaboration).
The Rookery, Stanmore, Middlesex, England.
Telephone: 01-954-1845.

Chorzempa, Daniel Walter, PH.D.; American pianist, organist, musicologist and composer; b. 7 Dec. 1944, Minneapolis; *s.* of Martin Chorzempa Sr. and Henrietta Reiswig; ed. Univ. of Minnesota.

Former church organist; Organ Instructor, Univ. of Minn. 62-65; Fulbright Scholar, Cologne 65-66; extensive piano and organ recitals in Germany, Denmark, Italy and U.K. etc. since 68; J. S. Bach Prize, Leipzig 68; records for Philips.
Leisure interests: mathematics, architecture, poetry, renaissance history and literature.
5000 Cologne 1, Grosse Budengasse 11, Federal Republic of Germany.
Telephone: 231271.

Chou Chien-jen; Chinese biologist; b. 1887, Shaohsing, Chekiang; brother of Lu Hsun (died 1936).
Founder mem. China Asscn. for Promoting Democracy 45; Vice-Gov. Chekiang 51-54, Gov. 58-68; Vice-Minister of Higher Educ. 54-58; Vice-Chair. Standing Cttee., Nat. People's Congress 65-; Vice-Chair. Chekiang Revolutionary Cttee. 68; mem. 9th Cen. Cttee. of CCP 69, 10th Cen. Cttee. 73.
People's Republic of China.

Chou Jung-hsin; Chinese government official.
Second Sec. N. China Bureau, CCP Cen. Cttee. 50-52; Vice-Minister of Building 52-58; Pres. Chekiang Univ. 58-60; Vice-Minister of Educ. 61-63; Acting Sec.-Gen. State Council 63-65; criticized and removed from office during Cultural Revolution 67; Minister of Educ. 75-.
People's Republic of China.

Chouard, Pierre; French botanist and plant physiologist; b. 29 Oct. 1903; s. of Louis-Jules Chouard and Marie Loudierre; m. Denise Petit-Dutaillis 1929; two s. one d.; ed. Ecole Saint-Aspais, Melun, Univ. de Paris, Inst. catholique, Paris, and Ecole normale supérieure.
At Ecole normale supérieure 28-32; Teacher, Ecole nationale d'horticulture 32-35; Editor-in-Chief *Revue Horticole* 32-50; Dir. of Studies in Botany, Univ. of Bordeaux 35-37; Prof. of Pure and Applied Botany, Univ. of Rennes 37-38; Prof. of Agriculture, Conservatoire nat. des arts et métiers 38-54; Prof. of Plant Physiology, Univ. of Paris 53-; Founder, Laboratory of the Phytotron 53, Dir. 57-; Sec.-Gen. 8th Int. Congress of Botany 54; Pres. Botany Section, Int. Union of Biological Sciences 53-; Vice-Pres. Int. Union of Biological Sciences 55-64; mem. Acad. d'Agriculture 53-; Pres. Botanical Soc. of France 49-50; Officier Légion d'Honneur; Commdr. des Palmes Académiques; Dr. h.c. (Montreal and Louvain).
Leisure interest: mountaineering.
11 rue du Val-de-Grâce, Paris 5e, France.

Chow Shu-kai; Chinese diplomatist; b. 21 Aug. 1913, Hupeh, China; ed. National Central Univ., Nanking and Univ. of London.
Chinese Consul, Manchester, England 44-45; Assoc. Prof. of Int. Relations, Univ. of Nanking 46-47; Deputy Dir. Information Dept., Ministry of Foreign Affairs 47-49; Minister, Chargé d'Affaires, Manila 53-55; Deputy Minister of Foreign Affairs 56-60; Cabinet Minister and Chair. overseas Chinese Affairs 60-62; Amb. to Spain 63-65, to U.S.A. 65-71; Minister of Foreign Affairs 71-72; Minister without Portfolio, Exec. Yuan (Cabinet) 72-.
Executive Yuan, Taipei, Taiwan.

Chrétien, Hon. Jean, P.C., B.A., LL.L.; Canadian lawyer and politician; b. 11 Jan. 1934, Shawinigan; s. of Wellie Chrétien and Marie Boisvert; m. Aline Chaîné 1957; two s. one d.; ed. Laval Univ., Quebec.
Director, Shawinigan Senior Chamber of Commerce 62; Liberal mem. House of Commons 63-; Parl. Sec. to Prime Minister, July 65, to Minister of Finance Jan. 66; Minister without Portfolio April 67-Jan. 68, of Nat. Revenue Jan.-July 68, of Indian Affairs and N. Devt. 68-74; Pres. Treas. Board 74-.
Leisure interests: skiing, fishing.
Office: House of Commons, Ottawa, Ont.; Home: P.O. Box 576, Shawinigan, Quebec, Canada.

Christensen, Henry; Danish newspaper editor an politician; b. 5 Jan. 1922, Copenhagen; s. of Ca Christensen and Anna née Hansen; m. Kirsten I Rasmussen.
Editor, *Dagbladet*, Roskilde 59-; mem. Folketing 53 Minister of Agriculture July 70-Oct. 71.
Solsortvej 11, 4000 Roskilde, Denmark.

Christensen, Kai; Danish architect; b. 28 Dec. 1916 Copenhagen; s. of late J. C. Christensen and Jenn Christensen; m. Kirsten Vitrup Andersen 1941; two d. ed. Royal Acad. of Fine Arts, Copenhagen.
Director, Technical Dept. of Fed. of Danish Architect 47-52; Man. Dir. Danish Bldg. Centre 52-61; Attache to Danish Ministry of Housing 61-; Chief, Scandinavia Design Cavalcade 62-68; mem. Danish Soc. of Arts an Crafts and Industrial Design, Swedish Soc. for Indus trial Design, Fed. of Danish Architects, The Architec tural Asscn., London; mem. Danish Cttee. for Bldg Documentation 50-; Sec. Scandinavian Bldg. Conf. 50 Pres. Int. Conf. of Building Centres 60; mem. Scan dinavian Liaison Cttee. concerning Govt. Bldg. 63-72 associated Editor *Building Research and Practice*/Bâti ment International (C.I.B. magazine); awards anc prizes in public competition.
Major works: designs for arts and crafts, exhibitions furniture for the Copenhagen Cabinet Makers' Exhibi tions, and articles and treatises in technical magazines
Leisure interests: chamber music, chess, fencing.
Office: Ministry of Housing, 12 Slotsholmsgade DK-1216 Copenhagen K; Home: 100 Vester Voldgade DK-1552 Copenhagen V, Denmark.
Telephone: 01-121337 (Home); 01-110201 (Office).

Christiansen, Ernst; Danish journalist and politician, b. 28 March 1891.
Chair. and Manager, Union of Social Democratic Youth 13-19; mem. Council and Exec. Cttee. Social Democratic Party 15-19; Chair. Left Socialist (later Communist) Party and Co-editor of its periodicals 19-27; on the staff of the Social Democratic daily newspaper, Copenhagen 31; mem. Exec. Cttee. Workers Radio Union 30-, Chair. 50-51 and 53-66; mem. Council, Danish Broadcasting Service 40-55 and 57-63; mem. *Landsting* 47-53, Danish Del. to UN 47, 53 and 54; Chair. for UN Delegation 55, 56, 57, 58, 59 and 60; Consultative Assembly of the Council of Europe 50-55, Danish Board of Foreign Policy 50-53; Minister without Portfolio 55-57; mem. Social Democratic Party.
Publs. *Statskapitalismen* 33, *Fra Lenin til Stalin* 36, *Amerika* 39, *Radioen under Krigen* (with P. Nørgaard) 45, *Danske Smede 1888-1948* 48, *Hvorfor er Social-demokratiet forsvarsvenligt?* 49, *Statsradiofonien 1925-50* (co-author) 50, *En Stjernevogn kørte ud* (with J. Christensen) 52, *Arbejderne og socialismen* 52, *En bygning vi rejser* (co-author) 54, *— men det gik anderledes* 60; *Smede för og nu* 63; translation of More's *Utopia*.
31 Tagensvej, Copenhagen, Denmark.
Telephone: 371-711.

Christiansen, Ragnar Karl Viktor; Norwegian politician; b. 28 Dec. 1922, Drammen; ed. secondary school and Railway School.
Norwegian State Railways, Drammen 40, telegraphist 42, Head Clerk 61; mem. Nedre Eiker Municipal Council 46-59, Chair. 56-57; mem. Supervisory Board for Armaments Factories 51-68; mem. Supervisory Board, Kongsberg Arms Factory and Raufoss Munitions Factory 69; mem. Consumers Council 53-60; fmr. Chair. Nedre Eiker Labour Party; mem. Labour Party Central Council 65-; Minister of Finance 71-72, of Transport Jan. 76-.
Arbeiderpartiet, Youngstorget 2, Oslo, Norway.

Christidis, Theodore; Greek economist; b. 24 Oct. 1900, Constantinople; m. Anny Papastavrianou 1940; one s. one d.; ed. English High School, Constantinople and Ecole Supérieure de Commerce de Marseille.

Director of Athens Chamber of Commerce and Industry 44-45; Gen. Sec. Ministry of Nat. Economy 46; Counsellor to Greek Perm. Del. to OEEC (now OECD) 48-50, Gen. Counsellor 50-53, Deputy Head of Delegation 53-55, Head 56-71; concurrently Amb. to European Econ. Community, Brussels 59-62; decorations include: Officier Légion d'Honneur, Grand Officer Order of Phoenix (Greece), Grand Officer Order of King George (Greece) and Grand Officer Order of Merit of Italian Republic, Grand Cross of Fed. Repub. of Germany. Publs. Author of many economic essays and articles. 3 rue Xenías, Athens, Greece.

Christie, John Traill; British educationist; b. 19 Oct. 1899; ed. Winchester and Trinity Coll., Oxford. Sixth Form Master Rugby 22-28; Fellow and Tutor of Magdalen Coll., Oxford 28-32; Head Master of Repton 32-37, of Westminster School 37-49; Principal of Jesus Coll., Oxford 50-67; Hon. Fellow, Jesus Coll., Oxford 67; Asst. Master, Westminster School 67-69. Great Henny, Sudbury, Suffolk, England.

Christie, Julie Frances; British actress; b. 14 April 1940, Assam, India; ed. Brighton Technical Coll., and Central School of Speech and Drama. Films: *Crooks Anonymous, The Fast Lady, Billy Liar, Young Cassidy, Darling,* (Acad. Award 66), *Doctor Zhivago, Fahrenheit 451, Petulia, Far From the Madding Crowd, In Search of Gregory, The Go-Between, McCabe & Mrs. Miller, Don't Look Now, Shampoo.* c/o International Creative Management, 22 Grafton St., London, W.1, England. Telephone: 01-629 8080.

Christie, Ronald Victor, M.D., D.SC., F.R.C.P., F.A.C.P.; British physician; b. 1902, Edinburgh; s. of Dr. Dugald Christie, C.M.G.; m. Joyce M. Ervine 1933; one s. one d.; ed. George Watson's Coll., Edinburgh and Edinburgh Univ. Assistant Rockefeller Inst. for Medical Research, New York City 26-28; Asst. Dept. of Pathology, Freiburg Univ. 29-30; Assoc. McGill Univ. Clinic, Royal Victoria Hospital, Montreal 30-35, Asst. Dir. and Asst. Physician Medical Unit, London Hospital 35-38; Dir. Medical Professorial Unit and Physician St. Bartholomew's Hospital 38-55; Prof. of Medicine, London Univ. 38-55, McGill Univ. 55-68; Physician-in-Chief, Royal Victoria Hospital, Montreal 55-64; Dean Faculty of Medicine, McGill Univ. 64-67; Hon. Sc.D. (Dublin), Hon. D.Sc. (Edinburgh) 70. Leisure interests: travel, fishing. c/o Faculty of Medicine, McGill University, Montreal, Quebec, Canada.

Christo (Christo Javacheff); American (naturalized) artist; b. 13 June 1935, Gabrovo, Bulgaria; m. Jeanne-Claude de Guillebon; one s.; ed. Fine Arts Acad., Sofia. Work involves wrapping up and packaging objects, buildings and landscape; went to Paris, first wrapped objects 58; first project for packaging of public building 61; "Iron Curtain" wall of oil drums blocking rue Visconti, Paris, "Wrapping a Girl", London 62; first Showcases 63; first Store Front 64; first Air Package and Wrapped Tree, Eindhoven, Netherlands 66; 42,390 cu. ft. Package, Walker Art Center, Minneapolis School of Art 66; first packaging of public building, Kunsthalle Bern 68; 5,600 cu. m. Package for Kassel Documenta 4 68; Packed Museum of Contemporary Art, Chicago 69; Wrapped Coast, Little Bay, Sydney, Australia, 1 m. sq. ft. of erosion control fabric, 36 miles of rope 69; Valley Curtain, Grand Hogback, Rifle, Colorado, suspended fabric curtain 70-72; project for Running Fence, Calif. 72-76; Wrapped Roman Wall 74; Ocean Front, Newport 74. 48 Howard Street, New York, N.Y. 10013, U.S.A. Telephone: (212) 966-4437.

Christofas, Kenneth Cavendish, C.M.G., M.B.E.; British diplomatist; b. 1917; m. Jessica Laura Sparshott 1948; two d.; ed. Univ. Coll., London. Served war 39-45; rose to hon. rank of Lieut.-Col.; Foreign Service 48-; Deputy Head of U.K. Del. to EEC 59-61; Counsellor British High Comm., Lagos 61-64; Head of Econs. Dept., Colonial Office 64-66; Counsellor, Foreign and Commonwealth Office 66-69; Minister and Deputy Head, U.K. del. to EEC 69-72; Dir.-Gen. for Econ., Financial and Parl. Affairs, Council of Ministers of European Communities 73-. Directorate General F, General Secretariat of the Council of Ministers of European Communities, 170 rue de la Loi, Brussels, Belgium. Telephone: 736-79-00.

Christoff, Boris, D.JUR.; Bulgarian singer; b. 18 May 1919, Plovdiv, Bulgaria; ed. Sofia Univ. and Italy. Began career as a lawyer; studied singing in Rome; interned in Austria in World War II; professional debut in Italy 45; has appeared at principal European opera houses, including La Scala, Milan, Rome, Naples, Venice, Palermo, Paris, London and Vienna and in America; major roles include Boris Godunov, King Philip, Don Quixote, Ivan the Terrible, Mephistopheles, Pizarro, and others; Dr. (h.c.) Paris Opera. Complete recordings of *Boris Godunov,* Gounod's *Faust, Don Carlos* and Mussorgsky's Songs. Via Bertolini 1, Rome, Italy.

Christopherson, Sir Derman Guy, Kt., O.B.E., S.M., D.PHIL., F.R.S.; British university vice-chancellor; b. 6 Sept. 1915, Plumstead, Kent; s. of Derman and Edith F. Christopherson; m. Frances Edith Tearle 1940; three s. one d.; ed. Sherborne School, Univ. Coll., Oxford and Harvard Univ. Scientific Officer, Research and Experiments Dept., Ministry of Home Security 41-45; Lecturer in Engineering, Cambridge Univ. and Fellow and Bursar of Magdalene Coll., Cambridge 45-49; Prof. of Mechanical Engineering, Univ. of Leeds 49-55; Prof. of Applied Science, Imperial Coll. of Science and Technology, London 55-60; Vice-Chancellor and Warden, Univ. of Durham 60-; Clayton Prize, Inst. of Mechanical Engineers 63; Fellow, Imperial Coll. of Science and Technology 66-; Hon. Fellow, Magdalene Coll., Cambridge 69-; several hon. degrees. Publs. *The Engineer in the University* 67, *The University at Work* 73, and various articles in learned journals. University of Durham, Old Shire Hall, Old Elvet, Durham, DH1 3HP, England. Telephone: Durham 64466 (Office).

Christophides, Ioannis; Cypriot barrister and politician; b. 21 Jan. 1924, Nicosia; s. of Cleanthis and Maris (née Ypsilantis) Christophides; m. Marvel Georgiadis 1953; two d. ed. Pancyprian Gymnasium. Called to the Bar, Gray's Inn, London 47; joined Comptoir d'Escompte de Nicosie (family banking firm) and Cleanthis Christophides Ltd. (family insurance firm) 48, Chief Exec. 54-57; founder mem. and Chair. (until 72), Merchant Credit Ltd., Universal Life Insurance Co. Ltd.; mem. Board, Cyprus Telecommunications Authority, Chair. 66-72; Vice-Chair. Commonwealth Telecommunications Council 70-72; Pres. Cyprus Red Cross 64-; Minister of Foreign Affairs 72-74, Jan. 75-. Leisure interest: reading. Ministry of Foreign Affairs, Nicosia; Home: 25 El. Venizelou Street, Nicosia T.T. 109, Cyprus. Telephone: 402101 (Office); 64653 (Home).

Christy, Robert Frederick, B.A., M.A., PH.D.; American physicist; b. 14 May 1916; ed. Univs. of British Columbia, and California (Berkeley). On U.S. Atomic Energy Project, Chicago and Los Alamos (Calif.) 42-46; Prof. of Physics, Calif. Inst. of

Technology, Pasadena 46-, Vice-Pres. and Provost 70-; mem. U.S. Nat. Acad. of Sciences 65; Eddington Medal, Royal Astronomical Soc. (U.K.) 67.

Publs. *Cosmic Ray Bursts* 41, *The μ Meson Spin* 41, *Determination of the Fine Structure Constant* 42, *Angular Distribution of γ Rays* 49, *The Coupling of Angular Momenta in Nuclear Reactions* 53, *Low Excited States of F¹⁹* 54, *Analysis of Nuclear Scattering Data* 56, *Corrections to Nuclear Q Values* 61, *Direct Capture Nuclear γ Rays* 61, *The Calculation of Stellar Pulsation* 64, *A Study of Pulsation in RR Lyrae Models* 66, *Review of Pulsation Theory* 66.

California Institute of Technology, Pasadena, Calif. 91109; Home: 1230 Arden Road, Pasadena, Calif. 91106, U.S.A.

Chrysler, Walter P., Jr.; American art collector; ed Dartmouth Coll.
Organizer, York Publishing House 26; Pres. and Chair. Cheshire House, Inc., Publications, N.Y.C. 30; Pres. Chrysler Building, N.Y.C. 37; Pres. Chrysler Art Museum, Provincetown, Mass.; collection of paintings and sculpture.
c/o Chrysler Art Museum at Norfolk, Norfolk, Va. 23510, U.S.A.

Chu Mu-chih; Chinese journalist.
Deputy Dir. New China News Agency 54-72, Dir. 72-; Vice-Chair. Nat. Journalists Asscn. 60; mem. 10th Cen. Cttee. of CCP 73.
People's Republic of China.

Chu, Peter, D. ès LETTRES; Chinese professor and businessman; b. 1902; ed. Univ. of Paris.
Man. Dir. The Agricultural & Industrial Bank of China 41-49; Publisher of *Life Today;* Prof. of Kwang Hsia Univ.; Dean of the Great China Univ.; Dir. South-Eastern Asia Development Corpn. Ltd.
Publs. *L'Emigration Japonaise depuis 1918, A Study of Scientific Management* 45.
26 Homantin Street, Hong Kong.

Chu Te; Chinese politician and fmr. army officer; b. 1886, Ma-an, Szechuan; ed. Chengtu Higher Normal School, Yunnan Mil. Acad. and in Paris, Berlin and Göttingen.
Detachment Commdr. 13; Brigade Commdr. 1916; participated in Nanchang Uprising 27; formed Red Army, with Mao Tse-tung (*q.v.*) as Political Commissar and himself as Commdr. at Chingkangshan 28; mem. Politburo, 6th Cen. Cttee. of CCP 34; on Long March as Commdr. of 1st Front Army 34-36; mem. Politburo, 7th Cen. Cttee. of CCP 45; Commdr.-in-Chief People's Liberation Army 46-54; Vice-Chair. People's Repub. of China 54-59; Marshall PLA 55; Vice-Chair. mem. Politburo, 8th Cen. Cttee. of CCP 56; Chair. Standing Cttee., Nat. People's Congress 59-; mem. Standing Cttee. of Politburo, 9th Cen. Cttee. of CCP 69, 10th Cen. Cttee. 73.
Publ. *The Battle Front of the Liberated Areas* 52.
People's Republic of China.

Chu Yao-hua; Chinese army officer.
Major-General Fukien Mil. District, People's Liberation Army 64, Commdr. 68-; Vice-Chair. Fukien Revolution-ary Cttee. 68.
People's Republic of China.

Chuang Tse-tung; Chinese government official.
Former World Table-Tennis Champion; Minister of Physical Culture and Sports 75-.
People's Republic of China.

Chudakov, Alexander Evgenievich; Soviet physicist; b. 16 Feb. 1921, Moscow; ed. Moscow Univ.
Research Assoc. Lebedev Inst. of Physics, U.S.S.R.

Acad. of Sciences 46-; Corresp. mem. U.S.S.R. Acad. of Sciences 66-.
Publs: Works on nuclear physics.
U.S.S.R. Academy of Sciences, 14 Leninsky Prospekt, Moscow, U.S.S.R.

Chudik, Michal; Czechoslovak politician and dip-lomatist; b. 29 Sept. 1914, Polomka.
Commissioner for Nutrition, Slovak Nat. Council 48-49; Chair. Regional Nat. Cttee., Košice 48-55; First Deputy Chair. Board of Commrs. and Comm. for Agriculture, Slovak Nat. Council 55; Chair. Slovak Nat. Council 63-68; Deputy Chair. Nat. Assembly 65-68; mem. Central Cttee. of C.P. of Czechoslovakia 50-68; mem. Agricultural Comm. of Central Cttee. of C.P. of Slovakia 63-66; mem. Presidium of Central Cttee. 64-68; Deputy to Nat. Assembly 64-Jan.69; Deputy to House of the People, Fed. Assembly Jan. 69-; Amb. to Bulgaria 71-; Order of 25th Feb. 48, 49; Order of the Republic 64.
Embassy of Czechoslovakia, Boulevard Vladimir Zaimov 9, Sofia, Bulgaria.

Chuikov, Marshal Vasili Ivanovich; Supreme Com-mander of Soviet Land Forces 60-64; see *The Inter-national Who's Who 1975-76*.

Chukhrai, Grigori Naumovich; Soviet film director; b. 23 May 1921, Melitopol, Zaporozhye Region; ed. All-Union State Inst. of Cinematography.
Soviet Army 39-45; mem. C.P.S.U. 44-; Dir. Mosfilm 55-64; Dir. Experimental Film Studio 65-; Honoured Art Worker of R.S.F.S.R., Lenin Prize 61, Order of Red Star, Order of Patriotic War, Order of Red Banner of Labour (three times), Labour Order of Hungary, Partisan Star of Czechoslovakia.
Films: *The 41st* 56, *Ballad of a Soldier* 59, *The Clear Sky* 61, *There Lived an Old Man and Old Woman* 64, *Memory* 67.
Mosfilm Studio, 1 Mosfilmovskaya ulitsa, Moscow, U.S.S.R.

Chulaki, Mikhail Ivanovich; Soviet composer; b. 19 Jan. 1908; Simferopol, Crimea; ed. Leningrad Con-servatoire.
Taught at the Leningrad Conservatoire 33, Moscow Conservatoire 48-; Sec. of the Union of Soviet Composers of the U.S.S.R. 48-57; Vice-Chair. of Cttee. for Arts Affairs under the U.S.S.R. Council of Ministers 51-53; Deputy Chief of Dept. for Arts Affairs of the U.S.S.R. Ministry of Culture 53-55; Dir. of the Bolshoi Theatre 55-59, 63-71; Sec. of Union of Composers of R.S.F.S.R. 59-; mem. Supreme Soviet R.S.F.S.R. 63-70; State prizewinner 47, 48, 50; awarded Badge of Honour and title of Honoured Art Worker of R.S.F.S.R.
Works: Three symphonies 34, 45, 59; ballets: *The Story of the Priest and his Servant Balda* 39, *The Imaginary Bridegroom* (based on the Goldoni comedy *Servant of Two Masters*) 46, *Youth* (based on the novel by N. Ostrovsky *How the Steel was Tempered*) 47, Cantata *On the Banks of the Volhov River* 43, *A Symphony Cycle of Songs and Dances of Old France* 59, nine choruses (a capella), *Lenin is with us* 60, *Russian Festival* (for violin ensemble), *Romances on Whitman's verses* 62.
c/o State Academic Bolshoi Theatre, 1 Ploshchad Sverdlova, Moscow, U.S.S.R.

Chullasapya, Air Chief Marshal Dawee; Thai air force officer and politician; b. 8 Aug. 1914; ed. Chula Chomklae Mil. Acad., Command and Gen. Staff Coll., Fort Leavenworth, U.S.A.
Air Attaché to India and Burma; Dir. of Intelligence; Dir. of Civil Aviation; Deputy Minister of Defence; Minister of Communications; Dir. of Nat. Devt., Agriculture and Communications; Chief of Staff, Supreme Command 61-; Minister of Agriculture and Co-operatives 72-73, of Defence 73-74; Medals of Courage 72, and numerous other awards.
c/o Ministry of Defence, Bangkok, Thailand.

Chumakov, Mikhail Petrovich; Soviet virologist; b. 4 Nov. 1909, Ivanovka, Tula; ed. First Moscow Medical Inst.
Physician, Postgraduate, Senior Research Associate, Institute of Microbiology, U.S.S.R. Acad. of Sciences 1-38; Senior Research Assoc., Head of Lab., U.S.S.R. Inst. of Experimental Medicine 38-44; Head of Dept. Inst. of Neurology, U.S.S.R. Acad. of Medical Sciences 4-50, Corresp. mem. 48, mem. 60, Dir., Head of Lab. Inst. of Virology 50-55, Organizer, Dir. Inst. of Poliomyelitis and Virus Encephalitis 55-; mem. C.P.S.U. 40; mem. Purkyně Medical Soc., Czechoslovakia; Order Badge of Honour, Red Banner of Labour, State Prize 41, Ivanovsky Prize, Lenin Prize 63.
Publs. Over 170 works on epidemiology of virus infections (tick encephalitis, trachoma, poliomyelitis, tick fever); monographs *Poliomyelitis—Epidemic Infantile Paralysis, Antibioticotherapy of Trachoma.*
Institute of Poliomyelitis and Virus Encephalitis, 27th Kilometre, Kievskoe Chaussée, Moscow Region, U.S.S.R.

Chung, Arthur; Guyanese judge; b. 10 Jan. 1918, Windsor Forest, West Coast, Demerara; s. of Joseph and Lucy Chung; m. Doreen Pamela Ng-See-Quan 1954; one s. one d.; ed. Modern High School, Georgetown and Middle Temple, London.
Land Surveyor 40; lived in England 46-48; Asst. Legal Examiner, U.K. Inland Revenue Dept. 47; returned to Guyana 48; Magistrate 54, Senior Magistrate 60; Registrar of Deeds of the Supreme Court 61; Judge of the Supreme Court 62-70; First Pres. of the Repub. of Guyana March 70-.
Office of the President, Georgetown, Guyana.

Chung Fu-hsiang; Chinese government official; b. Kwangsi.
Vice-Minister of Posts and Telecommunications 53-57, of Second Ministry of Machine Building 57-58, of First Ministry of Machine Building 58-61, of Posts and Telecommunications 62-67; criticized and removed from office during Cultural Revolution 67; Minister of Posts and Telecommunications 75-.
People's Republic of China.

Chung Il Kwon, Gen.; Korean army officer (retd.), diplomatist and politician; b. 1917; m. Kye Won Yoon 1946; three d.; ed. Military Acad. of Japan, U.S.A. Command and General Staff Coll., Harvard and Oxford Univs.
Former Army Chief of Staff, Chair. Joint Chiefs of Staff; Amb. to Turkey, France, U.S.A., concurrently to Brazil, Chile, Colombia, Argentina, Paraguay and Ecuador; Minister of Foreign Affairs 63; Prime Minister 64-70, concurrently Minister of Foreign Affairs 66-67; Chair. Korean-Japan Co-operation Council 71-; Chair. Democratic Republican Party 72-73; mem. Nat. Assembly 71-, Speaker 73-.
Leisure interests: horse-riding, skating.
91-19 Oksu-dong, Sungdong-ku, Seoul, Republic of Korea.

Chung, Kyung-Wha; Korean violinist; b. 26 March 1948, Seoul.
Studied under Ivan Galamian; started career in U.S.A.; winner of Leventritt Competition 67; European debut 70; has played under conductors such as Giulini, Haitink, Jochum, Maazel, Solti and Previn; has played with major orchestras including London Symphony Orchestra, New Philharmonia Orchestra, Pittsburgh Symphony Orchestra; has toured world; recordings for Decca; played at Salzburg Festival with London Symphony Orchestra 73.
Leisure interests: arts, antiques, French, farming.
c/o Harrison/Parrott Ltd., 22 Hillgate Street, London, W8 7SR, England.

Chung Yul Kim; Korean diplomatist and former air force officer; b. 1917; ed. Japanese Military Acad.

Commandant, Republic of Korea Air Acad. 49, Chief of Staff, Korea Air Force 49-52, 54-56; Chief, Korean Liaison Group to United Nations Command, Tokyo 52; Special Asst. to Minister of Nat. Defence 54-57, Minister of Nat. Defence 57-60; Ambassador to U.S.A. 63-68; mem. Nat. Assembly 67-71; Chief Commdr. Legion of Merit, Order of Mil. Merit Taeguk.
c/o Ministry of Foreign Affairs, Seoul, Republic of Korea.

Church, Alonzo, A.B., PH.D.; American professor of mathematics and philosophy; b. 14 June 1903, Washington, D.C.; s. of Samuel Robbins Church and Mildred H. L. Parker; m. Mary Julia Kuczinski 1925; one s. two d.; ed. Ridgefield School, Conn. and Princeton Univ.
National Research Fellow in Mathematics, Harvard, Göttingen and Amsterdam Univs. 27-29; Asst. Prof. of Maths. Princeton Univ. 29-39, Assoc. Prof. 39-47, Prof. 47-61, Prof. of Maths. and Philosophy 61-67; Editor *The Journal of Symbolic Logic* 36-; Prof. of Philosophy and Maths. Univ. of Calif. at Los Angeles 67-; mem. American Acad. of Arts and Sciences, Acad. Internationale de Philosophie des Sciences; Corresp. mem. British Acad.
Publs. *The Calculi of Lambda-Conversion* 41, *Introduction to Mathematical Logic* vol. I 56.
c/o Department of Philosophy, University of California at Los Angeles, Los Angeles, Calif. 90024, U.S.A.
Telephone: 213-825-4641.

Church, Frank, A.B., LL.B.; American politician; b. 25 July 1924; ed. Stanford and Harvard Univs.
Commissioned Infantry Officer 44; Military Intelligence in China, India and Burma; law practice in Boise, Idaho 50-56; Senator from Idaho 56-; del. O.A.S. Economic Conf., Buenos Aires 57; del. to Interparliamentary Union Conf., Warsaw 59; del. to Canadian-American Parliamentary Conferences, Ottawa, Montreal and Washington 59-60; Keynoter, Democratic Nat. Convention 60; Senatorial mem. U.S. Mission to the UN 66; Chair., Senate Foreign Relations Sub-cttee. on Western Hemisphere Affairs, Chair. Interior Sub-cttee. on Public Lands, Sub-cttee. on Consumer Interests of the Elderly, Chair. Special Cttee. on Ageing, Chair. U.S. Del. U.S.-Canada Interparliamentary Conf. 69-; Steering Cttee. of Finance Cttee. 73-, Chair. Select Cttee. on Amer. Intelligence Activities 75-; Democrat.
204 Old Senate Office Building, Washington, D.C., U.S.A.
Telephone: 225-6142.

Churchill, Odette Marie Céline (see Hallowes).

Chynoweth, Alan Gerald, B.SC., PH.D.; British physicist; b. 18 Nov. 1927, Harrow, Middx., England; s. of James Charles Chynoweth and Marjorie Fairhurst; m. Betty Freda Edith Boyce 1950; two s.; ed. King's College, Univ. of London.
Postdoctoral Fellow of Nat. Research Council of Canada, Chemistry Div., Ottawa 50-52; mem. Tech. Staff, Bell Telephone Labs. 53-60, Head, Crystal Electronics Dept. 60-65, Asst. Dir. Metallurgical Research Lab. 65-73, Dir., Materials Research Lab. 73-; Survey Dir. of Nat. Acad. of Sciences Cttee. on Survey of Materials Science and Eng. 71-75, Comm. on Mineral Resources and the Environment 73-75, mem. of Nat. Materials Advisory Board, Wash., Metallurgical Soc.; Senior mem. Inst. of Electrical and Electronic Engineers; Fellow American Physical Soc., Inst. of Physics, London; W. R. G. Baker Prize Award 67.
Leisure interests: travel, boating.
Publs. over 60 papers in professional journals on solid state physics, 12 patents on solid state devices, Nat. Acad. of Sciences reports: *Materials and Man's Needs, Materials Conservation Through Technology, Resource Recovery from Municipal Solid Wastes.*

Bell Telephone Laboratories, Murray Hill, New Jersey 07974; 6 Londonderry Way Summit, New Jersey 07901, U.S.A.
Telephone: 201-582-6810 (Office); 201-273-3956 (Home).

Chyorny, Alexei Klementyevich; Soviet politician; b. 1921; ed. Moscow Inst. of Chemical Engineering.
Shop Supt., then Deputy Dir. of plant in Komsomolsk-on-Amur 42-49; Chief of Section, later, Second Sec., Komsomolsk-on-Amur City Cttee. of C.P., then First Sec., District Cttee. of C.P. 49-56; Sec., later Second Sec., Regional Cttee. of C.P., Jewish Autonomous Region 56-62; Chair. Exec. Cttee., Khabarovsk Territorial Soviet of Working People's Deputies 62-70; First Sec., Khabarovsk Territorial Cttee. of C.P.S.U. 70-; mem. C.P.S.U. 46-; Deputy to U.S.S.R. Supreme Soviet 62-; mem. Comm. on Trade, Municipal Catering and Economy, Soviet of Nationalities; mem. Cttee. U.S.S.R. Parl. Group 70-; mem. C.P.S.U. Central Cttee. 71-.
Khabarovsk Territorial Committee of C.P.S.U., Khabarovsk, U.S.S.R.

Chyorny, Vassily Ilyich; Soviet politician; b. 1913; ed. Belgorod Agricultural School and Higher Party School.
Agronomist, Crimea 32-35, 39-41; in Soviet Army 35-37; Leader, Komsomol 37-39; Sec., District Cttee. of C.P. 39-41; Commissar, Bakhchisarai Partisan Regt. 41-42; in machine and tractor station, Kirghiz S.S.R. 42-43; Party and Soviet worker 44-50; Official, Central Cttee., C.P.S.U. 50-54, 60-61; First Vice-Chair. Council of Ministers, North Ossetian A.S.S.R. 54-55; Second Sec., North Ossetian Regional Cttee. of C.P. 55-60; First Sec. of Tambov Regional Cttee. of C.P. 66-; mem. Central Auditing Comm. of C.P.S.U. 66-71; Alternating mem. C.P.S.U. Central Cttee. 71-; mem. C.P.S.U. 39-; Deputy to U.S.S.R. Supreme Soviet 66-; mem. Comm. for Planning and Budget, Soviet of Union.
Tambov Regional Committee of Communist Party of U.S.S.R., Tambov, U.S.S.R.

Cieślewicz, Roman; Polish graphic artist; b. 13 Jan. 1930, Lwów; ed. Cracow Acad. of Fine Arts.
Member AGI 56-, ICTA 67-; work includes posters and book typography; worked for RSW Prasa, WAG, WAF and Czytelnik (publishers in Poland); Graphic Editor *Ty i Ja* (You and I) magazine 59-63; with *Elle* 63-65, Art Dir. 66-; with *Vogue* 66; works with C. Tchou, Juilliard, J. J. Pauvert, Adam (publishers in Paris); Grand Prix, Int. Exhbn. of Film Posters, Karlovy Vary 64; Bronze Medal, Toulouse-Lautrec Centenary Competition, Paris; Gold Medal, 1st Industricke Oblikowanie Biennale, Ljubljana; 1st Prize, All-Poland Biennale of Posters, Katowice 67.
Work includes panels in: Polish Industry Pavilion at Leipzig Int. Fair 57, Navigation Pavilion, Poznań, Int. Fair 59, Piombino Steelworks, Italy 63; illustrations for *Sklepy Cynamonowe* (novel by B. Schultz) 57; graphic layout for *Guide de la France Mystérieuse* 64; One-man exhbns.: BWA, Cracow 60; Moderna Galerija, Rijeka 61; Mandragore Bookshop, Paris 63; Synergie Club, Paris 64; Biebergalerie, Vienn 66; Kordegarda, Warsaw 67; Aurora Gallery, Geneva 68.
Collections: Museum of Modern Art, N.Y.; Stedelijk Museum, Amsterdam; Musée d'Art Décoratif, Paris; Library of Congress, Washington, D.C.; Museum of Modern Art, São Paulo; Fagersta Stadsbibliotek, Sweden.
"Elle", 100 rue Réaumur, Paris 2e, France.

Cikker, Ján; Czechoslovak (Slovak) composer; b. 29 July 1911, Banská Bystrica; m. Kitty Fiedler 1950; ed. Banská Bystrica, Conservatoire and Master School of Composition, Prague, and conducting under Felix Weingartner in Vienna.

Professor of Theory of Music Bratislava Conservatoir 39-51; Dramaturge, Opera House 45-48; Prof. o Composition, School of Musical Arts 51-; mem. Sloval Theatre Council 70-; Czechoslovak Peace Prize 51, Stat Prize 55, 63, 75, Nat. Artist 66, Herder Prize of Vienn Univ. 66, Madach Prize, Hungary 66, Order of Labou 71.
Works include *Sonatina for Piano* 33, *Symphoni Prologue* 34, Two string quartets 35, 37, *Capriccio* 36 *Cantus Filiorum* (cantata) 40, *About Life* (trilogy o: symphonic poems) 41, 43, 46, *Concertino for Piano and Orchestra* 42, *Bucolic Poem* (ballet music) 44, Scenic music for *Hamlet* 47, and *The Taming of the Shrew* 50, *The Tatra Streams* (three studies for piano) 54, *Wha* the Children Told Me 57; Meditation on the H. Schütz Theme *Glorified are the Dead* 64; Orchestral studies 65 *Hommage à Beethoven* 70, *Over the Old Trench* (symphony) 74, *Symphonia 1945* 75; and operas: *Jur Jánošik* 54, *Beg Bajazid* 57, *Resurrection* 62, *Mr. Scrooge* 63, *A play about Love and Death* (after Romain Rolland) 67, *Coriolanus* (after Shakespeare) 74.
Fialkové údolie č. 2, Bratislava, Czechoslovakia.
Telephone: 359-34.

Cilento, Sir Raphael West, Kt. M.D., B.S., D.T.M. & H.ENG.; Australian barrister; b. 2 Dec. 1893, Jamestown, S. Africa; ed. Prince Alfred Coll., Adelaide Univ. and School of Tropical Medicine, London.
Director Australian Inst. of Tropical Medicine; Dir. Public Health and Quarantine Mandated Territory of New Guinea for four years; Dir. Div. Tropical Hygiene and Chief Quarantine Officer N.E. Div. of Commonwealth 28-33; Senior Admin. Health officer Commonwealth Dept. of Health 34; Dir.-Gen. Health and Medical Services, Queensland 34-45; Hon. Prof. Social and Tropical Medicine Queensland Univ. 37-46; Pres. Medical Board Queensland 39-45; Barrister, Supreme Court, Queensland 39-; Assessor, Medical Assessment Tribunal Queensland 39-45; apptd. head of U.N.R.R.A. work in British zone of occupation in Germany 45-46; Dir. Div. of Refugees and Displaced Persons UN 46, Div. of Social Activities, Economic and Social Council UN 46-50; Pres. Royal Hist. Soc. of Queensland 34-35, 43-44, 53-68, Nat. Trust of Queensland 67-71.
Publs. *Malaria* 23, *Filariasis* 23, *Diagnosis of Bowel Diseases in North Australia* 24, *White Man in the Tropics* 25, *Health Conditions in the Pacific* 29, *Tropical Diseases in Australasia* 40, *Blue Print for the Health of a Nation* 44.
Altaville, 56 Glen Road, Toowong, Queensland 4066; and Supreme Court, Brisbane, Queensland, Australia.

Cintra do Prado, Luiz; Brazilian professor and physicist; ed. Escola Politécnica, Univ. de São Paulo, Univ. de Paris à la Sorbonne and Collège de France.
Laboratory Asst. Polytechnic Univ. of São Paulo 28-30, Asst. Lecturer Physics 29-33, Prof. 38-64, Prof. Emer. 64-; Lecturer Physics, Faculty of Medicine and Faculty of Sciences, Univ. of São Paulo 33-37; Dir. Escola Politécnica, Univ. of São Paulo 40-42, Vice-Rector 53-54; Prof. Pontificia Univ. Catolica, São Paulo 38-54; Chief, Nuclear Engineering Dept. Inst. of Atomic Energy 60-63, Dir. 61-63; Pres. Nat. Comm. for Nuclear Energy 64-66; mem. Del. to Int. Atomic Energy Agency (IAEA) 57-67; mem. Nat. Research Council 51-64; Vice-Pres. Brazilian Acad. of Sciences 59-64; mem. Scientific Advisory Cttee. of UN and of IAEA 60-; mem. Int. Cttee. on Weights and Measures 67-; over 120 publs.
Escola Politécnica, Universidade de São Paulo; Home: 840 rua Altino Arantes, Ribeirao Preto, Est São Paulo, Brazil.

Ciolkosz, Adam; Polish politician, writer and journalist; b. 1901, Cracow; s. of Kasper and Maria Ciolkosz; m. Lidia Ciolkosz 1925; ed. Cracow Univ. and Cracow School of Political Science.

Served and wounded Polish Wars 18-20; participated in Silesian Uprising 21; Socialist mem. Diet 28 and 30 and Sec. Polish Parl. Socialist Party; imprisoned in fortress of Brest Litovsk as one of opposition leaders 30 and 33-34; mem. Central Exec. Cttee., Polish Socialist Party 31-; mem. Nat. Council in Great Britain 40-45; fmr. Editor *Robotnik* London; mem. in charge external relations, Exec. of Polish Political Council 49-54; Vice-Chair. Polish Council of Nat. Unity Exec. Cttee. 54-56, Chair. 56-59 and 63-67; Chair. Polish Socialist Party in Great Britain 47-57; Chair. Central Council, Polish Socialist Party in Exile 57-59; Chair. Central Cttee., Polish Socialist Party in Exile 64-; Chair. London Del. Assembly of Captive European Nations 57-59, 64-65.
Leisure interest: collecting books.
Publs. *Trzy wspomnienia* 45, *The Curtain Falls* (with others) 51. *Rocznik spraw krajowych* (with others) 60, *Róza Luksemburg a rewolucja rosyjska* 61, *Od Marksa do Chruszczowa* 62, *Karol Marks a Powstanie Styczniowe* 63, *Koniec monolitu* 64, *Zarys dziejów socjalizmu polskiego* (with Dr. Lidia Ciolkosz) Vol. I 66, Vol. II 72, *Granice odwagi myslenia* 66, *Ludzie P.P.S.* 67, *Socjalizm na zachodzie Europy* 68, *Moskalofilskie pojmowanie dziejów* 69, *Polska wciaz na wulkanie* 71, *Sprawa najwazniejsza* 74, *Najwazniejszy sprzymierzeniec* 74, *Konferencja w Jałcie 1945 r.* 75.
9 Balmuir Gardens, London, SW15 6NG, England.
Telephone: 01-788-5231.

Cipa, Walter Johannes, DR. RER. NAT.; German business executive; b. 29 Nov. 1928, Gleiwitz/Oberschl.; *s.* of Ernst and Marie (née Kus) Cipa; *m.* Eva Mayer 1958; no *c.*; ed. Technische Hochschule, Aachen and Universität Freiburg.
Deutsche Erdöl AG, Hamburg 55; Gelsenkirchener Bergwerks AG 61- (name of firm changed to Gelsenberg AG 69), mem. Man. Board 65-75, Chair. of Man. Board 69-75; Chair. Supervisory Board Aral AG until 73, Deputy Chief Exec. AEG-Telefunken 75-76, Chair. Man. Board 76-.
AEG-Telefunken, Hohenzollerndamm 150, Berlin-Grunewald, Federal Republic of Germany.

Cirne Lima, Luis Fernando; Brazilian army officer and politician; b. 1930, Rio Grande do Sul; *s.* of Rui Cirne Lima and Maria Velho Cirne Lima; *m.* Miriam Obino Cirne Lima.
President Federação da Agricultura do Rio Grande do Sul; founder *Correio do Povo Rural*; Minister of Agriculture 69-73.
c/o Ministério de Agricultura, Brasília, D.f., Brazil.

Ciroma, Adamu, B.A.; Nigerian businessman and central banker; b. 1934, Potiskum; *s.* of Muhammadu and Aishatu Ciroma; *m.* 1970; one *d.*; ed. Barewa Coll. and Univ. Coll. Ibadan.
Administrative Officer, N. Nigeria Civil Service 61-65; Senior Asst. Sec., Fed. Civil Service 65-66; Editor *New Nigerian* 66-69, Man. Dir. New Nigerian Newspapers 69-74; business activities 74-75; Gov. Cen. Bank of Nigeria Sept. 75-.
Leisure interest: golf.
Central Bank of Nigeria, Tinubu Square, P.M.B. 12194, Lagos, Nigeria.
Telephone: 23306, 53700/100.

Ciry, Michel; French painter, etcher and graphic artist; b. 31 Aug. 1919; ed. Ecole des Arts Appliqués, Paris.
Religious and secular paintings and etchings; Prof. School of Fine Arts Fontainebleau 57-58, Académie Julian 60; fmr. mem. Conseil Supérieur de l'Enseignement des Beaux-Arts; Vice-Pres. Comité National de la Gravure; numerous exhbns. in Europe and America including Paris, London, New York, Boston, Amsterdam, Rome and Berlin; works in Museums of Europe and America; has illustrated numerous books including books by Montherlant, Green, Claudel and Mauriac; Prix National des Arts 45, Grande médaille de vermeil de la Ville de Paris 62, Prix de l'Ile de France 64, Prix Eugène Carrière 64, Laureate Acad. des Beaux-Arts 68; mem. Acad. des Beaux-Arts, Florence 64-; Prix Wildenstein 68.
Major works: *Chemin de Croix* 60-64, *Stabat Mater* 60, 61, 63, 65, *Fièvres* 65, *Christ's Passion* 55, 57, 60, 64, *Marie-Madeleine* 61, 63, 65, *Saint François* 50, 54, 59, 60, 64, 65.
La Bergerie, 76 Varengeville-sur-Mer, Seine-Maritime, France.

Cisař, Čestmír; Czechoslovak politician; b. 2 Jan. 1920, Hostomice; *m.* Irina Pěčková, 1943; one *s.* one *d.*; ed. Grammar School, Duchcov and Charles Univ., Prague.
Department of Propaganda and Agitation, Regional Cttee. of C.P., Prague, later Central Cttee. of C.P. 47-51; Head of Dept. for Propaganda and Agitation, Central Cttee. of C.P. 51-52; Sec. of C.P. Regional Cttee., Plzň 52-57, later Deputy Chief Editor *Rudé právo;* Chief Editor *Nová mysl* 61-63; Sec. Central Cttee. of C.P. April-Sept. 63; Minister of Education and Culture Sept. 63-65; Deputy to Nat. Assembly 64-66; Amb. to Romania 65-68; Sec. Central Cttee. of Czechoslovak C.P. March-Aug. 68; Pres. of Czech Nat. Council 68-69; mem. of Bureau of C.P. of Czechoslovakia Central Cttee. for directing Party Work in the Czech lands 68-69; Deputy to House of Nations, Fed. Assembly 69-70; mem. Fed. Assembly Presidium Jan. 69-70.
Obránců Míru 86, Prague 7, Czechoslovakia.
Telephone: 382528.

Cisler, Walker Lee; American engineer; b. 8 Oct. 1897, Marietta, Ohio; *s.* of Louis H. and Sara S. (Walker) Cisler; *m.* Gertrude Demuth Rippe 1939; two adopted *c.*; ed. Cornell Univ.
Joined Public Service Electric & Gas Co., Newark 22, rose to Asst. Chief Engineer Electric Dept. by 41; Chief, Equipment Production Branch, Office War Utilities, War Planning Board, Washington 41-43; Chief Engineer power plants, Detroit Edison Co. 45-47, Exec. Vice-Pres. 48-51, Pres. 51-64, Chair. 64-; Chair. Exec. Cttee. Fruehauf Corpn.; Pres. Overseas Advisory Assocs. Inc., Power Reactor Devt. Co; Dir. numerous other companies; Chair. Thomas Alva Edison Foundation; Official Adviser U.S. Del. Int. Conf. on Peaceful Uses Atomic Energy 55; official of numerous other scientific and educational institutions; Chief, Public Utilities Section, SHAEF, later Chief, Public Utilities Section, Office Mil. Govt. for Germany 43-45.
Home: 1071 Devonshire Road, Grosse Pointe Park, Mich. 48230; Office: 2000 2nd Avenue, Detroit 26, Mich., U.S.A.
Telephone: 313-963-6903.

Cissé, Jeanne Martin; Guinean diplomatist; b. April 1926, Kankan; *m.;* six *c.*
Teacher, Guinea 45-54; Dir. of school 54-58; mem. Teachers' Union 58-64; Parti Démocratique de Guinée, Kindia Office of the Fed. Bureau 59-68, Regional Women's Cttee. of Dalaba and Kindia and Nat. Women's Cttee.; Nat. Assembly, successively First Sec., Second Vice-Pres. and First Vice-Pres. until 72; Sec.-Gen. Conf. of African Women 62-72; Rep. UN Comm. on the Status of Women 63-69; Perm. Rep. to UN 72-; attended sessions of Gen. Assembly 61-63, 66-68, OAU 64, 65, 67-70, 72 and Afro-Asian Conf. 61; participated in UN Seminars on the Status of Women 64 and 71, and in world confs. of women, Moscow 63 and Helsinki 69; Lenin Peace Prize 75.
Permanent Mission of Guinea to United Nations, 295 Madison Avenue, 24th Floor, New York, N.Y. 10017, U.S.A.

Citrine, 1st Baron, cr. 46, of Wembley; **Walter McLennan Citrine,** P.C., G.B.E., COMP.I.E.E.; British trade unionist and administrator; b. 22 Aug. 1887, Liverpool; s. of Alfred Citrine and Isabella McLennan; m. Doris Helen Slade 1913; two s.
Mersey District Sec. Electrical Trades Union 14-20; Pres. 17-18 and Sec. 18-20 Mersey Fed. of Engineering and Shipbuilding Trades; Asst. Gen. Sec. Electrical Trades Union 20-23; Asst. Sec. Trades Union Congress 24-26 and Gen. Sec. 26-46; mem. Nat. Coal Board 46-47; Chair. Central Electricity Authority 47-57; part-time mem. Electricity Council, Atomic Energy Authority 58-62; Chair. Miners' Welfare Comm. 46-47; Pres. Int. Fed. of Trade Unions 28-45; Chair. World Fed. of Trades Unions 45-46; mem. H.M. Economic Advisory Council 30-33; Dir. Daily Herald Ltd. 29-46; mem. Gen. Advisory Council B.B.C. 34; Gov. London School of Economics 32-36; Trustee Imperial Relations Trust 37-49; mem. Cinematograph Council 38-48; mem. Royal Comm. on West Indies 38; mem. Consultative Council to Treasury 40-46; Chair. Production Cttee. on Regional Boards (Munitions) 42; Pres. British Electrical Approvals Board; Hon. LL.D. (Manchester).
Publs. *The British Trade Union Movement* 26, *Labour and the Community, I Search for Truth in Russia* 36, 38, *A B C of Chairmanship, My Finnish Diary* 40, *My American Diary* 41, *In Russia Now* 42, *Men and Work* (autobiography) 64, *Two Careers* 67.
Gorse Cottage, Berry Head, Brixham, South Devon, England.
Telephone: 08-045-51091.

Ciulei, Liviu; Romanian actor, director, scenographer and architect; b. 7 July 1923, Bucharest; ed. Bucharest Univ. and Bucharest Acad. of Dramatic Art.
Actor since 45; stage dir. and scenographer since 46; Dir. "Lucia Sturdza Bulandra" Theatre, Bucharest 63-72, First. Dir. 72-; mem. Union of Plastic Artists, Asscn. Artists of Theatrical and Musical Insts.; Pres. Romanian Centre of the O.I.S.T.T. (Int. Org. of Scenographers and Theatre Technicians); Artist Emer. 57; acted at Bulandra, Odeon and C. Nottara theatres in Bucharest, as Puck in *A Midsummer Night's Dream*, Oliver in *As You Like It*, Krogstadt in *Nora*, Piotr in *The Last Ones*, Protasov in *The Children Of The Sun*, Treplev in *The Seagull*, Dunois in *St. Joan*, Danton in *Danton's Death*; directed *Danton's Death*, Bucharest 66, and Schillertheater, West Berlin 67, *As You Like It* Bucharest 61, Deutsches Theater Göttingen 67, *Macbeth* Bucharest 68, *The Seagull* Schillertheater 68, *Richard II* Düsseldorfschauspielhaus 69, *Volpone* Freie Volksbühne, West Berlin 70, *Leonce and Lena* Bucharest 70, Washington 74, Vancouver 76, Ionesco's *Macbett* Munich 73, *The Threepenny Opera* Mannheim 73, Paul Foster's *Elizabeth the First*, Bucharest 74, Essen 74, West German television 75, *The Lower Depths*, Bucharest 75, *The Cherry Orchard*, Essen 75, *Long Day's Journey into Night*, Bucharest 75, numerous tours abroad with Romanian productions, including Budapest 60, Leningrad and Moscow 66, Florence 69, 70, Regensburg, Frankfurt/Main, Essen 70, Edinburgh Festival 71, The Hague, Amsterdam 72, etc.; State Prize 62 for films; Grand Prize at the Int. Festival of Karlovy Vary 60, for the film *Valurile Dunării* (The Waves of the Danube) as dir. and interpreter; prize for the best direction at the Int. Festival at Cannes 65, for the film *Padurea Spinzuratilor* (The Forest of the Hanged) as dir. and interpreter.
Teatrul "Lucia Sturdza Bulandra", Bd. Schitu Magureanu Nr. 1, Bucharest, Romania.

Civil, Alan; British horn player and composer; b. 13 June 1929; ed. studied under Aubrey Brain, London, and Willy von Stemm, Hamburg.
Principal Horn, Royal Philharmonic Orchestra 52-55; Co-Principal Horn with late Dennis Brain, Philharmonia Orchestra 55-57, Principal 57-66; Prof. of the Horn Royal College of Music; Solo Horn B.B.C. Symphony Orchestra 66-; Guest Principal Horn with Berlin Philharmonic Orchestra; mem. several Chamber Music Ensembles including London Wind Quintet, London Wind Soloists, Wigmore Ensemble, Prometheus Ensemble, Alan Civil Horn Trio, Music Group of London; has performed horn concertos as soloist in the U.S.A., South America, the Caribbean and Europe; records for Columbia.
Compositions: *Symphony* (for Brass and Percussion) 50, *Wind Octet* 51, *Wind Quintet* 51, *Horn Trio in E Flat* 52, *Divertimento for Trombone Quartet, Suite for Two Horns*; Songs, Music for Brass Ensemble, Horn Studies.
Downe Hall, Downe, Kent, England.

Claes, Willy; Belgian politician; b. 24 Nov. 1938, Hasselt; m. Suzanne Meynen 1965; one s. one d.; ed. Univ. Libre de Bruxelles.
Member Exec. Cttee., Belgian Socialist Party, Joint Pres. 75-; mem. Limbourg Council 64; mem. Chamber of Deputies 68-; Minister of Educ. (Flemish) Jan. 72-73, of Econ. Affairs 73-74.
Berkenlaan 23, B3500 Hasselt, Belgium.
Telephone: 011/22-01-08.

Clair, René; French film director and writer; b. 11 Nov. 1898.
Began life as a journalist and writer, then actor; later became film director; worked in France, England and America; mem. Acad. Française 60-; Légion d'Honneur and other nat. and foreign decorations; Dr. h.c. (Cambridge Univ., Royal Coll. of Art (U.K.)).
His films include *The Italian Straw Hat, Sous les Toits de Paris, Le Million, A nous la Liberté, 14 Juillet, The Ghost Goes West, I Married a Witch, It Happened Tomorrow, Le Silence est d'or, La Beauté du Diable, Les Belles-de-Nuit, Les Grandes Manoeuvres, Porte des Lilas, Tout l'or du Monde, Les Fêtes Galantes.*
Publs. *Reflections on the Cinema, Star Turn, La Princesse de Chine, Comédies et Commentaires, La Serrure* (play) 67, *Cinéma d'hier et d'aujourd'hui* 70, *L'Etrange ouvrage des cieux* 71, *Jeux du Hasard* (Short Stories) 76.
11 bis avenue de Madrid, 92200 Neuilly-sur-Seine, France.

Clapham, Sir Michael John Sinclair, K.B.E., M.A.; British printer and business executive; b. 17 Jan. 1912, Cambridge; s. of Sir John Clapham, C.B.E., and Lady Mary Margaret Clapham (née Green); m. Hon. Elisabeth Russell Rea (d. of 1st Baron Rea) 1935; three s. one d.; ed. King's Coll. Choir School, Cambridge, Marlborough Coll. and King's Coll., Cambridge.
Trained as printer 33-38; joined Imperial Chemical Industries Ltd. (ICI) as Man. of Kynoch Press 38; seconded to Tube Alloys Project (Atomic Energy) in Second World War; Dir. Metals Div., ICI (now Imperial Metal Industries Ltd.) 46-60, Chair. 60-61, 74-; Dir. Main Board of ICI 61-68, Deputy Chair. 68-74; Dir. ICI of Australia and New Zealand Ltd. (renamed ICI Australia Ltd. 71) 61-74, Imperial Metal Industries Ltd. 62-70, Chair. 74-; mem. Industrial Reorganization Corpn. April 69-71; Chair. Council for Nat. Academic Awards 71-; Deputy Pres. CBI 71-72, 74-, Pres. 72-74; Deputy Chair. Lloyds Bank 74-; Dir., Chair. BPM Holdings 74-.
Leisure interests: sailing, swimming, cooking.
Publs. *Printing* in *History of Technology*, Vol. III 57, *Multinational Enterprises and Nation States* 75.
Office: Lloyds Bank Ltd., 71 Lombard Street, London, E.C.3; Home: 26 Hill Street, London, W.1, England.
Telephone: 01-626-1500 (Office); 01-499-1240 (Home).

Clapp, Norton, B.A., PH.B., J.D.; American businessman; b. 15 April 1906, Pasadena, Calif.; four s.; ed. Occidental Coll., and Univ. of Chicago.
Admitted to Calif. and Wash. bars 29, private practice

29-42; U.S. Navy 42-46; Chair. Metropolitan Building Corpn., Seattle 54-; Pres. Pelican (Alaska) Cold Storage Co. 47-60; Boise (Ida.) Payette Lumber Co. 49-55, Laird, Norton Co. 50-60; mem. Board of Dirs. 46, Vice-Pres. Weyerhaeuser Timber Co. 55-57, Chair. 57-60, 66-, Pres. 60-66; dir. numerous other companies; Vice-Pres. Nat. Council Boy Scouts of America; Chair. Trustees Univ. of Puget Sound, Tacoma, The Menninger Foundation, Univ. of Chicago; Officer Order of Leopold II (Belgium).

Tacoma Building, Tacoma, 923 Evergreen Pt. Rd., Medina, Washington, U.S.A.

Clappier, Bernard; French economist; b. 9 Nov. 1913; ed. Ecole Polytechnique, Ecole Libre des Sciences Politiques.

Deputy Sec.-Gen. Office of Industrial Production 43; Dir. of the Cabinet of R. Schuman (Minister of Finance) 47, (Minister of Foreign Affairs) 48-50; Dir. External Econ. Relations, Ministry of Econ. Affairs 51-61; Chair. Conf. between Member States of the European Communities and other states which applied for membership of the Communities 62; Deputy Gov. Banque de France 63-70, mem. Gen. Council 73-, Gov. 74-; Insp.-Gen. of Finances 64; Vice-Pres. of Monetary Cttee. EEC; Alt. Dir. Bank for Int. Settlements until 73; Pres., Dir.-Gen. Crédit Nat. 73-74.

Banque de France, B.P. 140-01, 75049 Paris; 45 rue Saint-Dominique, Paris 7e, France.

Claret, Lucien Armand Joseph; French industrialist; b. 8 Jan. 1903, Barentin, Seine-Maritime; s. of Jean-Baptiste Claret and Jeanne Greux; m. Lydie Pujol; one s.; ed. Ecole Spéciale des Travaux Publics, Paris. Founded Etablissements A. L. Claret, Colombes 26, Société Industrielle de Travaux Electro-Mécaniques, Asnières 41, Société Industrielle de Découpage et d'Emboutissage, Paris 44, Société d'Exploitation des Procédés Leland & Claret 45, Fonderies de Carrières 47, Société Immobilière Claret, Colombes 48, Société Starlec, Paris 49, L'Unité Hermétique S.A., La Verpillière (Isère) 54, Société S.E.I.R.A.R., Paris 56, Claret-Normandie, St. Pierre-de-Varengeville (Seine-Maritime) 57, Claret-Ouest, Barentin (Seine-Maritime) 59, Unidad Hermetica (Spain) 62, C.M.E.P., Paris 62, Sociéte Lectra Paris 64, Motores Claret (Spain) 66; Pres./Dir.-Gen. Société d'Exploitation des Procédés Leland & Claret 55-68, Société L'Unité Hermétique S.A. 58-68, Man. Etablissements A. L. Claret 26-68, Fonderies de Carrières 53-68, Société de Distribution de Matériel 49-68, Claret-Normandie 57-68, Claret-Ouest 59-68; Pres./Dir.-Gen. Fabriques de Fraises Dentaires et Mécaniques 69; Vice-Pres. Unidad Hermetica, Sabadell (Spain) 62-72 and Motores Claret, Sabadell 66-72; Pres. Lectra 70; Pres. Dir.-Gen. Société Nouvelle des Ateliers de Constructions Electriques de Lagny 71; Vice-Pres., Dir.-Gen. Le Matériel Hydraulique S.A., Saint Denis 71; Dir. and Vice-Pres. Etablissements Willème; Man. Société d'Exploitation F.F.D.M.-Pneumat 72, Stedell 72-75, Ets. A. L. Claret 75; Adviser, French Foreign Trade; officer of several other companies; Officer Légion d'Honneur; Commdr. Mérite Commercial et Industriel.

Leisure interests: philately, music, binding, riding, mem. Yacht Club of France.

43 boulevard Malesherbes, Paris 8e; Home: 20 boulevard du Château, 92200 Neuilly-sur-Seine, France.

Clark, Baron (Life Peer), cr. 69, of Saltwood; **Kenneth Mackenzie Clark,** O.M., C.H., K.C.B.; British art historian; b. 13 July 1903, London; s. of Kenneth Mackenzie Clark and Margaret Alice McArthur; m. Elizabeth Martin 1927; two s. one d.; ed. Winchester and Trinity Coll., Oxford.

Worked with Bernard Berenson in Florence 26-28; mem. Cttee. Exhibition of Italian Art at Burlington House

30; Keeper Dept. of Fine Art, Ashmolean Museum, Oxford 31-33; Dir. Nat. Gallery, London 34-45; Surveyor of the King's Pictures 34-45; Ryerson Lecturer, Yale Univ. 36; Dir. Film Dept., Ministry of Information 39-41; Chair. War Artists Advisory Cttee. 39-45; Slade Prof. of Fine Art, Oxford Univ. 46-50 and 61-62; Chair. Arts Council of Great Britain 53-60; Chair. Independent Television Authority 54-57; Trustee British Museum; Conseil Artistique des Musées Nationaux; Chancellor, York Univ. 70-; Hon. mem. Royal Scottish Acad., Swedish Acad., Spanish Acad., American Acad. of Arts and Letters, French Acad.; Commendatore della Corona d'Italia and Commendatore al Ordine di Merito; Commdr. Légion d'Honneur, Knight of the Lion of Finland, Austrian Silver Medal of Honour; Fellow, British Acad. and Royal Coll. of Arts; U.S. Nat. Gallery of Art Award for distinguished services for *Civilisation* 70; Hon. D.Lit. (Columbia, New York), Hon. LL.D. (Glasgow, Liverpool), Hon. D.Lit. (Oxford, Cambridge, York, Warwick, London and Sheffield Univs.); C.Lit. 74.

Publs. *The Gothic Revival* 30, *Catalogue of Drawings by Leonardo da Vinci at Windsor* 35, *Leonardo da Vinci* 39, *One Hundred Details from the National Gallery* (two vols.), *Hay Wain* 44, *Landscape into Art* 49, *Piero della Francesca* 51, *Moments of Vision* 54, *The Nude* 55, *Looking at Pictures* 60, *Ruskin Today* 64, *Rembrandt and the Italian Renaissance* 66, *A Failure of Nerve* 67, *Civilisation* 69, *The Romantic Rebellion—Romantic versus Classic Art* 73, *The Drawings of Henry Moore* 74, *Another Part of the Wood* (autobiography) 74.

B.5 Albany, Piccadilly, London, W.1, England.

Clark, (Charles) Joseph, M.A.; Canadian politician; b. 5 June 1939, High River, Alberta; s. of Charles A. Clark and Grace R. Welch; m. Maureen Anne (née McTeer) 1973; ed. Univ. of Alberta, Dalhousie Univ. Began career as a journalist; Nat. Pres. Progressive Conservative Party of Canada (PCP) Student Fed. 63-65; First Vice-Pres. PCP Asscn. of Alberta 66-67; Lecturer, Univ. of Alberta 65-67; Special Asst. to Davie Fulton 67; Exec. Asst. to PCP Leader Robert Stanfield (q.v.) 67-70; mem. House of Commons 72-; Leader of PCP Feb. 76-; mem. Hillcrest Miners' Literary and Athletic Asscn.

House of Commons, Ottawa, Ontario; Home: Box 128, Edson, Alberta, Canada.

Clark, Col. Charles Willoughby, D.S.O., O.B.E., M.C.; British engineering executive; b. 6 April 1888; ed. Atherstone Grammar School.

Apprentice, Alfred Herbert Ltd., Coventry 04, Dir. 34-, Chair. and Joint Man. Dir. 58-66, Pres. 66-; Pres. of all subsidiaries; Army service 14-18; Pres. Coventry Chamber of Commerce 51-53; Chair., Mfrs. Section, Cttee. of Machine Tool Trades Asscn. 46-55; mem. Board of Trade Machine Tool Advisory Council 57-66; Deputy Lieut. of Warwickshire; Fellow, Royal Commonwealth Soc.

Flat 41, Regency House, Newbold Terrace, Leamington Spa, Warwickshire, England.

Clark, Colin Grant, M.A.; British economist; b. 2 Nov. 1905; ed. Dragon School, Oxford, Winchester Coll., and Brasenose Coll., Oxford.

Asst. Social Surveys of London 28-29, of Merseyside 29-30; Economic Advisory Council 30-31; Lecturer, Cambridge Univ. 31-37; Visiting Lecturer, Univs. of Sydney, Melbourne and Western Australia 37-38; Under-Sec. of State for Labour and Industry, Dir. Bureau of Industry, Financial Adviser to Treasury, Queensland 38-52; Dir. Inst. for Research in Agricultural Econs., Oxford 53-69; now Research Fellow, Monash Univ., Australia.

Publs. *The National Income, The Conditions of Economic Progress, The Economics of 1960, Welfare and Taxation, British Trade in the Common Market, Economics of*

Irrigation, Population Growth and Land Use, Starvation or Plenty?, The Value of Agricultural Land, etc.
Mannix College, Monash University, Clayton, Victoria 3168, Australia.

Clark, Dick, M.A.; American politician; b. 14 Sept. 1929, Paris, Ia.; s. of Clarence and Bernice Clark; m. Jean Gross 1954; one s. one d.; ed. Univ. of Md., Wiesbaden, Germany, Univ. of Frankfurt, Upper Ia. Univ. and Univ. of Ia.
U.S. Army, Germany, Private 50, Corporal 52; Teaching Asst., State Univ. of Ia. 56-59; Asst. Prof. of History and Political Science, Upper Ia. Univ. 59-64; Chair. Office of Emergency Planning in Ia., and Ia. Civil Defense Admin. 63-65; Admin. Asst. to Congressman John C. Culver 65-72; Senator from Ia. 72-; mem. American Historical Asscn., Conf. on European History, American Asscn. of Univ. Profs. and Conf. on Slavic and East European History, Members of Congress for Peace Through Law, Senate Agriculture and Foreign Relations Cttees., Special Cttee. on Aging, Rules Cttee., Democratic Steering Cttee.; Nat. Oratorical and Debate Champion 53.
Leisure interests: reading, debating, walking.
404 Russell Office Building, Washington, D.C. 20510, U.S.A.
Telephone: 202-224-3254.

Clark, Sir Fife, Kt., C.B.E.; British public servant; b. 29 May 1907; ed. Middlesbrough High School.
Political and diplomatic corresp. Westminster Press provincial newspapers 36-39; P.R.O. Ministry of Health 39-49; Controller, Central Office of Information (C.O.I.) 49-52; Adviser on Govt. Public Relations and to the Prime Minister 52-55; Dir.-Gen. C.O.I. 54-71; Consultant, Crown Agents for Overseas Govts. and Admins., London 71-75; First Pres. Int. Public Relations Assen. 55-57; Fellow and founder mem. of Council, British Inst. of Public Relations, Pres. 58-59; mem. Management Council, Brighton Int. Arts Festival 66-.
Publ. *The Central Office of Information* 71.
Wave Hill, Nevill Road, Rottingdean, Sussex, England.
Telephone: Brighton 33020.

Clark, Sir George Norman, M.A., D.LITT., F.B.A.; British historian; b. 27 Feb. 1890, Halifax; s. of J. W. Clark, C.B.E., J.P.; m. Barbara Keen 1919; one s. one d.; ed. Balliol Coll., Oxford.
Fellow of All Souls Coll., Oxford 12 and 61-75; served in Army 14-18; Fellow of Oriel Coll. 19-31; Editor *English Historical Review* 20-26, 38-39; Chichele Prof. of Econ. History, Oxford 31-43; Regius Prof. of Modern History, Cambridge 43-47; work for Govt. Depts. 39-45; Provost of Oriel Coll., Oxford 47-57; Pres. British Acad. 54-58; Foreign mem. Royal Danish Acad., Royal Netherlands Acad., Holl. Maatsch der Wetensch., Amer. Acad. of Arts and Sciences, Amer. Historical Soc.; Commdr. Order of Orange-Nassau (Neths.); Hon. LL.D. (Aberdeen); Hon. Litt.D. (Dublin, Cambridge); Hon. D.Litt. (Durham, Sheffield, Columbia, Hull); Hon. Fellow Balliol, Oriel and All Souls Colls. Oxford, Trinity Coll., Cambridge, Trinity Coll., Dublin, and Royal Coll. of Physicians; Dr. h.c. (Utrecht).
Publs. *The Dutch Alliance and the War against French Trade* 23, *The Seventeenth Century* 29, *The Later Stuarts* 34, *Science and Social Welfare in the Age of Newton* 37; edited *The Campden Wonder* 59, *History of the Royal College of Physicians*, 2 vols. 64-66, *English History, A Survey* 71.
7 Ethelred Court, Dunstan Road, Headington, Oxford, England.
Telephone: Oxford 61028.

Clark, Most Rev. Howard Hewlett, C.C., D.D., D.C.L.; Canadian ecclesiastic; b. 23 April 1903, Macleod, Alta.; s. of Douglass Clark and Florence L. Hewlett; m. Anna E. Wilson 1935; one s. three d.; ed. Thorold

High School, St. Catherine's Collegiate, Trinity Coll., Toronto, and Univ. of Toronto.
Asst. Curate St. John's Church, Norway, Toronto 30; Curate Christ Church Cathedral, Ottawa 32-39, Rector 39-41, Canon 41-45, Dean 45-54; Bishop of Edmonton 54-59; Archbishop of Edmonton and Primate of the Anglican Church of Canada 59-61; Archbishop and Metropolitan of Rupert's Land and Primate of the Anglican Church of Canada 61-70; Chancellor, Univ. of Trinity Coll. 72-; D.D. Trinity Coll. 45, D.C.L. Bishop's Univ. 60, LL.D. Univ. of Manitoba 66, etc. Publ. *The Christian Life, according to the Prayer Book* 57.
252 Glenrose Avenue, Toronto, Ont. M4T 1K9, Canada.
Telephone: 483-6497.

Clark, Howard Longstreth; American business executive; b. 14 March 1916, South Pasadena, Calif.; s. of Warren and Florence Clark; m. Jean Beaven 1961; nine c.; ed. Stanford Univ., Harvard Law School and Columbia Univ. Graduate Business School.
Price Waterhouse and Co. 37-39; admitted to New York Bar 42; War Service, Navy 42-45; American Express Co. 45-, Vice-Pres. 48, Senior Vice-Pres. 52-56, Exec. Vice-Pres. 56-60, Pres. and Chief Exec. Officer 60-68, Chair. and Chief Exec. Officer 68-, Pres. 74; Dir. of numerous companies.
65 Broadway, New York, N.Y. 10006; Home: 607 Riversville Road, Greenwich, Conn., U.S.A.

Clark, Sir John A., Kt.; British business executive; b. 1926; s. of Sir Allen Clark and Lady Jocelyn Clark; m. 1st Deidre Waterhouse 1952 (dissolved 1962), one s. one d.; m. 2nd Olivia Pratt 1970, two s. one d.; ed. Harrow and Cambridge.
Royal Naval Volunteer Reserve, Second World War; formerly with Metropolitan Vickers and Ford Motor Co.; studied American electronics industry in U.S.A.; Asst. to Gen. Man., Plessey Int. Ltd. 49; Dir. and Gen. Man. Plessey (Ireland) Ltd. and Wireless Telephone Co. Ltd. 50; mem. Board of Dirs. Plessey Co. Ltd. 53, Gen. Man. Components Group 57, Man. Dir. and Chief Exec. 62-70, Deputy Chair. 67-70, Chair. and Chief Exec. 70-; Dir. Int. Computers (Holdings) Ltd. 68-; Pres. Telecommunication Engineering and Mfg. Assen. 64-66, 72-74; Vice-Pres. Inst. of Works Mans.; Vice-Pres. Engineering Employers' Fed.
Leisure interests: golf, shooting, swimming, flying helicopters.
The Plessey Co. Ltd., Ilford, Essex, England.
Telephone: 01-478-3040.

Clark, J(ohn) Desmond, C.B.E., F.B.A., F.S.A., SC.D., PH.D.; British anthropologist; b. 10 April 1916, London; s. of Thomas J. C. Clark and Katherine Wynne; m. Betty Cable Baume 1938; one s. one d.; ed. Monkton Combe School and Christ's Coll., Cambridge.
Director Rhodes-Livingstone Museum, Livingstone, N. Rhodesia 38-61; Prof. of Anthropology, Univ. of Calif. (Berkeley) 61-; Mil. Service in E. Africa, Abyssinia, the Somalilands and Madagascar 41-46; Founder mem. and Sec. N. Rhodesia Nat. Monuments Comm. 48; Fellow, American Acad. of Arts and Sciences 65.
Leisure interests: walking, photography, wood-cutting.
Publs. *The Stone Age Cultures of Northern Rhodesia* 50, *The Prehistoric Cultures of the Horn of Africa* 54, *The Prehistory of Southern Africa* 59, *Prehistoric Cultures of Northeast Angola and their Significance in Tropical Africa* 63, *Atlas of African Prehistory* 67, *Kalambo Falls Prehistoric Site* Vol. I 69, Vol. II 74, *The Prehistory of Africa* 70.
Dept. of Anthropology, University of California, Berkeley, Calif. 94720; Home: 1941 Yosemite Road, Berkeley, Calif. 94707, U.S.A.
Telephone: 642-2533 (Office).

Clark, John Grahame Douglas, C.B.E., M.A., PH.D., SC.D., F.B.A.; British archaeologist; b. 28 July 1907, Shortlands, Kent; s. of Lt.-Col. Charles Douglas Clark and Maud Shaw; *m.* Gwladys Maud White 1936; two *s.* one *d.*; ed. Marlborough Coll., and Peterhouse, Cambridge.

Research student Peterhouse, Cambridge 30-32, By-Fellow 32-35; Faculty Asst. Lecturer in Archaeology, Cambridge 35-46; Squadron Leader, R.A.F.V.R. 41-45; Univ. Lecthrer in Archaeology, Cambridge 46-52, Disney Prof. 52-74; Head Dept. of Archaeology and Anthropology 56-61, 68, Master of Peterhouse 73-; Pres. Prehistoric Society 59-62, also its Editor 35-70; Vice-Pres. Soc. of Antiquaries of London 60-62; mem. Royal Comm. on Ancient Monuments 57-69; mem. Ancient Monuments Board; Hodgkins Medal Smithsonian Inst. 67; hon. mem. or Fellow of Danish, Dutch, Finnish, German, Italian, Swedish, Swiss and American Acads. and Socs.; Order of Dannebrog; Viking Medal, Wenner-Gren Foundation 72; Drexel Medal, Pennsylvania.
Leisure interests: gardening, sailing, contemporary art, oriental ceramics.
Publs. *The Mesolithic Settlement of Northern Europe* 36, *Archaeology and Society* 39, 58, *Prehistoric England* 40, *Prehistoric Europe: the Economic Basis* 52, *Excavations at Star Carr* 54, *World Prehistory—an Outline* 61, (with Stuart Piggott) *Prehistoric Societies* 65, 70, *The Stone Age Hunters* 67, *World Prehistory—a New Outline* 69, *Aspects of Prehistory* 70, *The Early Stone Age Settlement of Scandinavia* 75.
The Master's Lodge, Peterhouse, Cambridge, England. Telephone: Cambridge 50256.

Clark, Joseph Sill, LL.B.; American politician; b. 21 Oct. 1901; ed. Harvard Univ., and Univ. of Pa. Law School.
Practised law in Philadelphia 26-50; Col. U.S. Air Force in World War II; Mayor of Philadelphia 52-56; U.S. Senator from Pennsylvania 56-68; mem. Foreign Relations Cttee., Labor and Public Welfare Cttee.; World Federalists, U.S.A. 69-71; Chair. Coalition on Nat. Priorities and Mil. Policy 69-; mem. Amer., Pennsylvania and Philadelphia Bar Asscns.; Philadelphia (Bok) Award 56, Drexel Inst.; numerous hon. degrees; Democrat.
Publs. *The Senate Establishment* 63, *Congress, The Sapless Branch* 64.
440 Rex Avenue, Chestnut Hill, Philadelphia, Pa. 19118, U.S.A.

Clark, Ligia; Brazilian sculptress; b. 23 Oct. 1920; ed. Sacré Coeur de Marie, Belo Horizonte, Minas Gerais, and in Paris under Fernand Léger, Dobrinsky and Arpad Szénes.
Co-founder Brazilian Neo-concrete Group 59; first exhbn. of transformable sculptures *Bichos* 60; Exhibitions in Paris, Rio de Janeiro, New York, São Paulo, Stuttgart and London; Group exhbns. in France, Argentina, Germany, U.S.A., Italy, U.K., Israel, Czechoslovakia; numerous prizes and special exhbn., São Paulo Biennal 63.
Avenida Prado Junior 16, Apdo. 801, Copacabana, Rio de Janeiro, Brazil.

Clark, Gen. Mark W., D.S.C.; American army officer; b. 1 May 1896; ed. U.S. Military Acad.
2nd Lieut. 17, promoted through grades to Brig.-Gen. 41, Major-Gen. 42, Lieut.-Gen. 42, Gen. 45; served as an infantry officer in France in First World War; mem. Gen. Staff Corps 35-36, 37-40, March-June 42; apptd. Chief of Staff for Ground Forces in Europe July 42; led secret mission by submarine to obtain information in N. Africa preparatory to Allied invasion 42; Commanded Fifth Army in invasion of Italy 43, capture of Rome 44; Gen. in Command 15th Army Group Dec. 44, U.S. forces in Austria 45-47, 6th U.S. Army 47-49; Deputy U.S. Sec. of State 47; Chief of Army Field Forces, Fort Monroe, Va. 49-52; C.-in-C. UN Command and U.S. Far East Command 52-53;

Pres. The Citadel (Mil. Coll.) 54-65, Pres. Emeritus 65-; Chair. Govt. Cttee. to investigate Central Intelligence Agency 54; numerous hon. degrees; decorations include Hon. K.B.E. 44, Grand Officier Légion d'Honneur, Mil. Order of Suvorov 1st Degree (U.S.S.R.), D.S.M. with three oak leaf clusters (U.S. Army), D.S.C. (U.S.A.), K.C.B.
Publs. *Calculated Risk* 50, *From the Danube to the Yalu* 54.
The Citadel, Charleston, South Carolina 29409, U.S.A. Telephone: 577-5959.

Clark, Michael William, C.I.E.R.E., C.I.E.E.; British business executive; b. 7 May 1927, London; *s.* of late Sir Allen and Lady Clark (née Culverhouse); *m.* Shirley MacPhadyen 1955 (died 1974); two *s.* two *d.*; ed. Harrow School.
Assistant to Central Sales Man. The Plessey Co. Ltd. 50, Exec. Dir. 51, Dir. 53, Dir. Electronics and Equipment Group 58; Chair. and Man. Dir. Plessey U.K. Ltd. 62-65; Deputy Man. Dir. The Plessey Co. Ltd. 62, Dir. of Corporate Planning 65-67, Man. Dir. Telecommunications Group 67-68; Dir. Home-based operations, The Plessey Co. Ltd. 69; Man. Dir. The Plessey Co. Ltd. 70-75, Group Deputy Chair. and Deputy Chief Exec. 76-; mem. Council, Inst. of Dirs. Nat. Electronics Council; fmr. Vice-Pres. Soc. of British Aerospace Cttee.; mem. of the Court, Univ. of Essex; mem. of Council, British Inst. of Management.
Leisure interests: fishing, golf, forestry.
The Plessey Co. Ltd., Ilford, Essex, England.

Clark, Ramsey, B.A., A.M., J.D.; American lawyer and government official; b. 18 Dec. 1927, Dallas, Tex.; *s.* of Thomas Campbell Clark (*q.v.*); *m.* Georgia Welch 1949; one *s.* one *d.*; ed. Univs. of Texas and Chicago.
Marine Corps 45-46; admitted to Texas Bar 51, U.S. Supreme Court 56; Asst. Attorney-Gen., Dept. of Justice 61-65, Deputy Attorney-Gen. 65-67, Attorney-Gen. 67-69.
Publ. *Crime in America* 70.
37 West 12th Street, New York, N.Y. 10011, U.S.A. Telephone: 212-989-6613.

Clark, Sir Robert Anthony, Kt., D.S.C.; British merchant banker; b. 6 Jan. 1924, London; *s.* of John Anthony Clark and Gladys Clark (née Dyer); *m.* Marjorie Lewis 1949; two *s.* one *d.*; ed. Highgate School, King's Coll., Cambridge.
Served in Royal Navy 42-46; qualified as lawyer with Messrs. Slaughter and May, became partner 53; Dir. Philip Hill, Higginson, Erlangers Ltd., now Hill Samuel & Co. Ltd. 62-, Chair. and Chief Exec. 74-; Chair. Industrial Devt. Advisory Board 73-.
Leisure interests: music, reading.
100 Wood Street, London, EC2P 2AJ; Home: Munstead Wood, Godalming, Surrey, England.
Telephone: 01-628-8011 (Office); Godalming 7867 (Home).

Clark, Thomas (Tom) Campbell, A.B., LL.B. (father of Ramsey Clark, *q.v.*); American lawyer; b. 23 Sept. 1899; *s.* of William H. and Jennie Falls Clark; *m.* Mary Ramsey 1924; one *s.* one *d.*; ed. Virginia Military Inst. and Univ. of Texas.
Admitted to Texas Bar 22; practised in Dallas 22-37; civil district attorney for Dallas County, Texas 27-32; Partner in firm McCraw and Clark of Dallas 33-35; U.S. Dept. of Justice 37-43; Asst. Attorney-Gen. of U.S. 43-45; Attorney-Gen. of U.S. 45-49; Assoc. Justice Supreme Court of U.S. 49-67; Chair. Joint Cttee. for Effective Admin. of Justice 61-64, Chair. Board of Dirs. Nat. Coll. of State Trial Judges 63-71; Fellow, Inst. of Judicial Admin., Pres. 66-68; Chair. Board of Dirs. American Judicature Soc. 67-69; Chair. Advisory Board Nat. Comm. on Reform of Fed. Criminal Laws 67-; Dir. Fed. Judicial Center 68-69; mem. American, Texas,

Federal Bar Assens. and other socs.; holds hon. degrees from various American univs. and colleges.
Leisure interests: golf, hunting, fishing.
Supreme Court of United States, Washington, D.C. 20543; Home: 2101 Connecticut Avenue, N.W., Washington, D.C. 20008, U.S.A.

Clark, William Donaldson, M.A.; British author and civil servant; b. 28 July 1916, Haltwhistle, Northumberland; s. of John McClare Clark and Marion Jackson; ed. Oriel Coll., Oxford.
Commonwealth Fellowship, Univ. of Chicago 38; served Ministry of Information Services, Chicago, and British Embassy, Washington, D.C. 39-45; London Editor *Encyclopaedia Britannica* 46-49; Diplomatic Correspondent *The Observer* 49-55; Adviser on Public Relations to the Prime Minister 55-56; Corresp. of *The Observer* at New Delhi Mar.-Dec. 57; Ed. of *The Week* section of *The Observer* 58-60; Consultant on current affairs to Associated Television 58-66; Dir. of Overseas Development Inst. 60-68; Dir. of Information and Public Affairs, World Bank 68-72, Dir. External Relations 73-74, Vice-Pres. External Relations 74-.
Leisure interests: writing, talking and travel.
Publs. *Less than Kin* 57, *Number 10* (novel and play) 66, *Special Relationship* (novel).
3407 Rodman Street N.W., Washington, D.C. 20008; International Bank for Reconstruction and Development, 1818 H Street, N.W., Washington, D.C. 20433, U.S.A.
Telephone: 202-477-2466 (World Bank); 202-363-0499 (Washington).

Clarke, Arthur Charles, B.SC.; British science writer and underwater explorer; b. 16 Dec. 1917, Minehead, Somerset; s. of Charles W. Clarke and Mary N. Willis; m. Marilyn Mayfield 1953 (dissolved 1964); ed. Huish's Grammar School, Taunton, and King's Coll., London.
H.M. Exchequer and Audit Dept. 36-41; R.A.F. 41-46; Inst. of Electrical Engineers 49-50; Technical Officer on first G.C.A. radar 43; originated communications satellites 45; Chair. British Interplanetary Soc. 46-47, 50-53; Asst. Editor *Science Abstracts* 49-50; engaged on underwater exploration on Great Barrier Reef of Australia and coast of Ceylon 54-; extensive lecturing, radio and TV, U.K. and U.S.; UNESCO Kalinga Prize 61; Stuart Ballantine Medal, Franklin Inst. 63; AAAS—Westinghouse Science Writing Award 69; AIAA Aerospace Communications Award 74; John Campbell and Nebula Science Fiction Awards 74; Hugo Award 74.
Leisure interests: photography, table tennis, diving.
Publs. Non-fiction: *Interplanetary Flight* 50, *The Exploration of Space* 51, *The Young Traveller in Space* 54 (publ. in U.S.A. as *Going into Space*), *The Coast of Coral* 56, *The Making of a Moon* 57, *The Reefs of Taprobane* 57, *Voice across the Sea* 58, *The Challenge of the Spaceship* 60, *The Challenge of the Sea* 60, *Profiles of the Future* 62, *Voices from the Sky* 65, *The Promise of Space* 68; with Mike Wilson: *Boy Beneath the Sea* 58, *The First Five Fathoms* 60, *Indian Ocean Adventure* 61, *The Treasure of the Great Reef* 64, *Indian Ocean Treasure* 64; with R. A. Smith: *The Exploration of the Moon* 54; with Editors of *Life: Man and Space* 64; with the Apollo XI Astronauts: *First on the Moon* 70; *Report on Planet Three* 72; with Chesley Bonestell: *Beyond Jupiter* 72; Fiction: *Prelude to Space* 51, *The Sands of Mars* 51, *Islands in the Sky* 52, *Against the Fall of Night* 53, *Childhood's End* 53, *Expedition to Earth* 53, *Earthlight* 55, *Reach for Tomorrow* 56, *The City and the Stars* 56, *Tales from the White Hart* 57, *The Deep Range* 57, *The Other Side of the Sky* 58, *Across the Sea of Stars* 59, *A Fall of Moondust* 61, *Fron the Ocean, From the Stars* 62, *Tales of Ten Worlds* 62, *Dolphin Island* 63, *Glide Path* 63, *Prelude to Mars* 65; with Stanley

Kubrick: *2001: A Space Odyssey* (novel and screenplay) 68; *The Lost Worlds of 2001* 71, 72, *Of Time and Stars* 72, *The Wind from the Sun* 72, *Rendezvous with Rama* 73, *The Best of Arthur C. Clarke* 73, *Imperial Earth* 75.

Clarke, Sir Cyril Astley, K.B.E., M.D., P.R.C.P., F.R.C.O.G., F.R.S., F.F.C.M.; British professor of medicine; b. 22 Aug. 1907, Leicester; s. of Astley V. and Ethel Mary (née Gee) Clarke; m. Frieda M. M. (Féo) Hart 1935; three s.; ed. Oundle School, Caius Coll., Cambridge, and Guy's Hospital Medical School.
House physician, Guy's Hospital 32-34, Demonstrator, Dept. of Pathology and Physiology 34-35, Chief Clinical Asst., Dept. of Dermatology 35-36; Life Insurance Work 36-39; Medical Specialist, R.N. 39-45; Medical Registrar, Queen Elizabeth Hospital, Birmingham 46; Consultant Physician, United Liverpool Hospitals and Liverpool Regional Hospital Board 46-58; Reader in Medicine, Univ. of Liverpool 58, Dir. Nuffield Unit of Medical Genetics 63-72, Prof. of Medicine 65-72; Pres. Royal Coll. of Physicians; Nuffield Research Fellow, Dept. of Genetics, Univ. of Liverpool Oct. 72-; Hon. Consultant Physician, United Liverpool Hospitals and Liverpool Regional Hospital Board 58-; Hon. Fellow, Caius Coll., Cambridge; Fellow, Royal Australasian Coll. of Physicians 73, Royal Coll. of Physicians of Edinburgh 75; Chair. of Council, Bedford Coll., London Univ.; BMA Essay Prize 32; Soc. of Apothecaries of London Gold Medal for Therapeutics 70; James Spence Medal 73; Hon. D.Sc. (Edinburgh, Leicester, East Anglia, Birmingham. Liverpool, Sussex).
Leisure interests: small boat sailing, breeding butterflies.
Publs. *Genetics for the Clinician* 62 (2nd edn. 64), *Selected Topics in Medical Genetics* 69 (Editor), *Human Genetics and Medicine* 70, *Rhesus Haemolytic Disease, Selected papers and extracts* (Editor) 75, papers in professional journals.
Department of Medicine, Ashton Street, P.O. Box 147, Liverpool L69 3X; Home: High Close, Thorsway, Caldy, Cheshire, England.
Telephone: 051-709-6022 and 051-709-4852 (Liverpool); 051-625-8811 (Home).

Clarke, Denzil Robert Noble; British chartered accountant and business executive; b. 9 July 1908, Simla, India; s. of Robert T. Clarke, I.C.S.; m. Ismay Preston 1942; one s. two d.; ed. Stonyhurst Coll.
Joined British-American Tobacco Co. Ltd. (accounting), travelling in U.S.A., India, Burma, Ceylon, Europe and Caribbean 32; Army Service 42-45; Asst. to Finance Dir., British-American Tobacco Co. Ltd. 45, Finance Dir. 54-60, Deputy Chair. 60-62, Vice-Chair. 62-66, Chair. July 66-July 70; Dir. Sun Life Assurance Soc., Tobacco Securities Trust Co.
Leisure interests: gardening, tennis.
Puffins, South Drive, Wokingham, Berks., England.

Clarke, Sir Ellis Emmanuel Innocent, T.C., G.C.M.G., LL.B.; Trinidadian lawyer and diplomatist; b. 28 Dec. 1917, Port of Spain; s. of Cecil E. I. Clarke and Elma Pollard; m. Eyrmyntrude Hagley 1952; one s. one d.; ed. St. Mary's Coll., Port of Spain, Trinidad, London Univ. and Gray's Inn, London.
Private law practice, Trinidad 41-54; Solicitor-Gen. Trinidad and Tobago 54-56; Deputy Colonial Sec. 56-57; Attorney-Gen. 57-61; Constitutional Adviser to the Cabinet 61-62; Amb. to the United States 62-73, and to Mexico 66-73; Perm. Rep. to UN 62-66; Rep. on the Council of the Org. of American States 67-73; Chair. of Board, British West Indian Airways 68-73; Gov.-Gen. and C.-in-C. of Trinidad and Tobago 73-; Awarded first Trinity Cross (T.C.) 69.
Governor-General's House, St. Ann's, Trinidad and Tobago.
Telephone: 62-41261.

Clarke, Sir (Henry) Ashley, G.C.M.G., G.C.V.O.; British diplomatist; b. 26 June 1903, Stourbridge, Worcs.; s. of H. H. R. Clarke, M.D.; m. Frances Pickett Molyneux 1962; ed. Repton and Pembroke Coll., Cambridge.
Served with diplomatic missions in Hungary 25, Poland 27, Turkey 28-31; mem. British Del. to League of Nations and Disarmament Conf. 32-34; mission to Japan 34-38; at Foreign Office 39-44, latterly as Head, Far-Eastern Dept., Minister at Lisbon 44-46; Minister in Paris 46-69; Deputy Under-Sec. of State, Foreign Office 50-53; Ambassador to Italy 53-62; Gov. of B.B.C. 62-67, of Nat. Theatre 62-66, of British Inst. of Recorded Sound 64-67; Chair. Royal Acad. of Dancing 54-69; Chair. Italian Art and Archives Rescue Fund 66-70; mem. Cttee. of Man., Royal Acad. of Music 67-73; mem. Advisory Council Victoria and Albert Museum 69-73; Sec.-Gen. Europa Nostra 69-71; London Adviser Banca Commerciale Italiana 62-70, and mem. of Gen. Board Assicurazioni Generali, Trieste 64-75; Vice-Chair. Venice in Peril Fund 71-; Hon. Fellow, Pembroke Coll., Cambridge, Royal Acad. of Music; Hon. Dr.Pol.Sc. of Genoa Univ.; Grand Cross of the Order of Merit of the Italian Repub.; Torta Prize 74.
Leisure interests: music and the arts.
Dorsoduro, 1113 Venice, Italy.
Telephone: 706-530.

Clarke, Mrs. Irene Fortune Irwin, M.A.; Canadian publisher; b. 21 March 1903; d. of John and Martha (Fortune) Irwin; m. William Henry Clarke 1927 (deceased); two s. one d.; ed. Parkdale Collegiate Inst., Victoria Univ., and Univ. of Toronto.
Associated with her husband, the late William Henry Clarke, founder and Pres. of Clarke, Irwin & Co. Ltd., Book Publishers, until his death 55, Pres. and Chair. of Board 55-; official of several civic and educational orgs.
Office: Clarke, Irwin & Co. Ltd., 791 St. Clair Avenue West, Toronto 10, Ont., Canada.
Telephone: 416-654-3211.

Claude, Albert; American (born Belgian) cell biologist and cancer research worker; b. 23 Aug. 1899, Longlier; ed. Univ. of Liège.
Institut für Krebsforschung, Berlin Univ. and Kaiser Wilhelm Inst., Berlin-Dahlem 28-29; joined Rockefeller Inst. (now Univ.) 29, Adjunct Prof. 72-; Visiting Research Prof. Johnson Research Foundation 67-; Dir. Jules Bordet Inst., Brussels 49-71, Emer. 71-; Prof. Emer., Univ. of Brussels; Prof. Univ. Catholique de Louvain, Dir. Laboratoire de Biologie Cellulaire et Cancérologie 70-; Hon. mem. American Acad. of Arts and Sciences 71, Royal Belgian Acad. of Medicine 47, Int. Soc. for Cell Biology; Foreign Assoc. mem. Royal Belgian Acad. of Sciences, Letters and Arts; Membre d'Honneur, Soc. Française de Microscopie Electronique 65; mem. Acad. Libre de Belgique; Assoc. mem. Inst. de France; Prix du Fonds Nat. de la Recherche Scientifique and Prix Scientifique Baron Holvoet 65; Medal of Royal Belgian Acad. of Medicine 65; L. G. Horwitz Prize (jointly), Columbia Univ. 70; Paul Ehrlich and Ludwig Darmstaedter Prizes (jointly) 71; Nobel Prize for Medicine 74; Dr. h.c. (Modena) 63, (Univ. J. Purkinje, Brno) 70, (Rockefeller Univ.) 71; Commdr., Ordre des Palmes Académiques.
Laboratoire de Biologie Cellulaire, rue des Champs Elysées 62, 1050 Brussels, Belgium.

Claudius-Petit, Eugène Pierre; French politician and town planner; b. 22 May 1907; m. Marie-Louise Moire (died 1975); one s. two d.; ed. Ecole Nationale Supérieure des Arts Décoratifs.
Former cabinet maker and teacher; mem. Provisional Consultative Assembly of Algiers 43-44; Pres. Mouvement de Libération Nationale (Algeria) 45; mem. two Constitutent Assemblies 45-46; mem. Chamber of Deputies 46-55, 58-62, 67-; Minister of Reconstruction and Town Planning 48-53; Minister of Labour 54; Mayor of Firminy 53-71; Pres. Parl. group of Union Démocratique et Socialiste de la Résistance 58; Vice Pres. Nat. Assembly 59-62, 68-73; Pres. Entente Démocratique group, Nat. Assembly 62, Progrès et Démocratie Moderne 69-73; Vice-Pres. Centre Démocratie et Progrès; Officier de la Légion d'Honneur, Compagnon de la Libération, Rosette de la Résistance, Croix de Guerre avec Palme.
15 rue des Barres, 75004 Paris, France.

Clausen, Alden Winship (Tom); American banker; b. 17 Feb. 1923, Hamilton, Ill.; s. of Morton and Elsie (Kroll) Clausen; m. Mary Margaret Crassweller 1950; two s.; ed. Carthage Coll., and Univ. of Minnesota.
Joined Bank of America 49; assigned to Nat. Div., Southern Calif. 55; Asst. Vice-Pres. for financial relationships in electronics 61-65; Head Nat. Div., San Francisco World H.Q. 63; Senior Vice-Pres. 65-68; Exec. Vice-Pres. and mem. Man. Cttee. 68-69; Vice-Chair. Board of Directors 69; Pres. and Chief Exec. Officer, Bank of America Jan. 70-; Dir. Fed. Reserve Bank of San Francisco; Vice-Chair. Advisory Council on Japan-U.S. Econ. Relations; Dir. Assocs. of Harvard Business School; San Francisco Clearing House Asscn.; mem. Asscn. of Reserve City Bankers, Calif. Bar Asscn., Fed. Advisory Council (fmrly. Pres.) Govt. Borrowing Cttee. of American Bankers Asscn., Dir. United Way of America, mem. Business Council, mem. U.S. Treasury's Advisory Cttee. on Reform of the Int. Monetary System; Dir. U.S.-U.S.S.R. Trade and Econ. Council.
Bank of America, P.O. Box 37000, San Francisco, Calif. 94137, U.S.A.
Telephone: 415-622-2472 (Office).

Clausetti, Eugenio, D.IUR.; Italian music publisher; b. 7 Jan. 1905, Naples.
Managing Dir. G. Ricordi & Co., Milan 44, Vice-Pres.; Pres. Soc. of Italian Music Publishers; Vice-Pres. Dischi Ricordi S.p.A.; Vice-Pres. International Union of Publishers, Music Section; Pres. Italian Music Publishers' Asscn.
Via Cernaia 6, Milan, Italy.

Clausse, Gilbert-Roger; Belgian professor; b. 1 Dec. 1902, Saint-Mard, Luxembourg; m. Janine Huriau 1950; ed. Univ. of Liège.
Professor Athénée de St. Gilles 28-37; Dir. French broadcasts, Institut Nat. Belge de Radiodiffusion 37-46, Asst. Dir. of the Institut 47-53, Dir.-Gen. 53-57; Prof. Université Libre de Bruxelles 45-; Dir. of Centre d'Etude des Techniques de diffusion collective 58-.
Publs. Critique matérialiste de l'Education 34, L'Education de base pour un Humanisme social 35, Mesure des Humanités anciennes 37, La Radio, Huitième Art 45, La Radio scolaire 49, L'Information à la Recherche d'un Statut 51, L'Information d'Actualité: Critique de la Relation 53, Synopsis de l'information d'actualité 61, Les Nouvelles: Synthèse critique 63, Turquie: développement du Journalisme 64, Le Journal et l'Actualité 67, Belgique 1965—Presse, radio et télévision aux prises avec les élections 68, L'enseignement universitaire du journalisme et de la communication sociale 70.
87 avenue Carsoel, 1180 Brussels, Belgium.

Clavé, Antoni; Spanish painter; b. 5 April 1913, Barcelona; ed. evening classes at Escuela Superior de Bellas Artes de San Jorge, Barcelona.
Magazine and book illustrator 30-49; First Studio 45 rue Boissonade, Paris 41; influenced by Picasso's blue period 40, and by Vuillard and Bonnard 42; designed sets for theatre 46-55, starting with Los Caprichos, for Ballets des Champs-Elysées 46; full-time painter since 55; commenced carpet painting 57 and metal work 60; first one-man exhbn., Perpignan, France 39, later in

Paris, London, Oran, Gothenburg, Buenos Aires, Rome, Milan, Barcelona, Bilbao, Los Angeles, Geneva, Cologne and Tokyo; exhbn. "Thirty Years of Painting", Tokyo 72; Matarasso Prize, Bienal São Paulo 57.
Major works: Illustrations for *La Dame de Pique*, Pushkin 46, black lithographs *Candide*, Voltaire 48, *Gargantua*, Rabelais 53.
4 rue de Châtillon, Paris 14e, France.

Clavel, Bernard; French writer; b. 29 May 1923, Lons-le-Saunier; *s.* of Henri Clavel and Héloïse Dubois; *m.* Andrée David 1945; three *s.*; ed. primary school.
Left school aged 14 and apprenticed as pâtissier 37; subsequently held various jobs on the land and in offices; painter and writer since age 15; has written numerous plays for radio and television and contributes to reviews on the arts and pacifist journals; mem. Acad. Goncourt 71-; Prix Eugène Leroy, Prix populiste, Prix Jean Maci, Prix Goncourt (for *Les Fruits de l'Hiver*), Grand Prix littéraire de la Ville de Paris.
Leisure interests: sport, manual labour.
Publs. Major works include: *L'ouvrier de la nuit* 56, *Qui m'emporte* 58, *L'Espagnol* 59, *Malataverne* 60, *Le Voyage du père* 65, *L'Hercule sur la place* 66, *La Maison des Autres* 62, *Celui qui voulait voir la mer* 63, *Le coeur des vivants* 64, *Les Fruits de l'Hiver* 68, *Victoire au Mans* 68, *L'Espion aux yeux verts* 69, *Le Tambour du Bief* 70, *Le massacre des Innocents* 70, *Le Seigneur du Fleuve* 72, *Le Silence des Armes* 74, *Lettre à un Képi Blanc* 75, *La Boule de Neige* 75.
6 Villa Poirer, 75015 Paris; c/o Robert Laffont, 6 place Saint-Sulpice, Paris 6e, France.
Telephone: 273-35-02.

Clay, Gen. Lucius DuB., B.S.; American business executive and retired army officer; b. 23 April 1897, Marietta, Georgia; *s.* of Alexander and Frances Clay; *m.* Marjorie McKeown 1918; two *s.*; ed. U.S. Military Acad.
Commissioned as Second Lieut. 18; advanced through grades to General 47; instructor Officers' Training School (Engineers) 18; with Engineer troops 18-24. instructor in civil and military engineering, U.S. Military Acad. 24-28; river and harbour assignments; rep. U.S. at Permanent Int. Navigation Conf., Brussels 34; on Gen. MacArthur's staff in Philippines 37; in charge of construction of Red River Dam, Denison, Texas 38-40; in charge of defence airport programme, Civil Aeronautics Administration 40-41; Dir. of Material, U.S. Army 42-44; Deputy Dir. for War Mobilization and Reconversion 44-45; Deputy Mil. Gov. Germany (U.S.) 45-47; C.-in-C. European Command and Military Gov. of Germany (U.S.) Mar. 47-49; Pres. Kennedy's Personal Rep. in Berlin 61-62; Chair. of Board, Continental Can Co. 50-62, Dir. and mem. of Exec. Cttee. 70; Senior Partner, Lehman Brothers 63-73; mem. American Soc. of Civil Engineers, Soc. of American Mil. Engineers, Perm. Int. Navigation Congress, Amer. Red Cross, Amer. Acad. Arts and Sciences; Konrad Adenauer Prize 73.
Leisure interests: reading, golf.
Publs. *Decision in Germany* 50, *Germany and the Fight for Freedom*.
633 Third Avenue, New York, N.Y. 10017, U.S.A.
Telephone: (212) 551-7348.

Clayden, Rt. Hon. Sir (Henry) John, P.C.; lawyer; b. 26 April 1904, Transvaal; *s.* of Harold Clayden and Florence Richardson; *m.* Gwendolen Lawrance 1948; ed. Capetown, Charterhouse and Brasenose Coll., Oxford.
Barrister Inner Temple 26; Advocate Transvaal 27; war service 40-45, S.A. Engineer Corps, S.A. Staff Corps; K.C. 45; Judge of Supreme Court of S. Africa, Transvaal Provincial Division 46-55, 64-65; Judge of Federal Supreme Court, Federation of Rhodesia and Nyasaland 55-60; Chief Justice of Federal Supreme Court, Federation of Rhodesia and Nyasaland 60-64. Acting Gov.-

Gen. of Fed. May-June 61; Chair. Hammarskjöld Accident Comm. 62, Industrial Tribunals, London.
8 Walton Street, London, S.W.3, England.
Telephone: 01-589-1300.

Clayton, Jack; British film director; b. 1921.
Entered film industry 35; served in R.A.F. Film Unit 39-45; Production Man. for *An Ideal Husband*; Assoc. Producer *Queen of Spades, Flesh and Blood, Moulin Rouge, Beat the Devil, The Good Die Young, I am a Camera*; Producer and Dir. *The Bespoke Overcoat* 55; Dir. *Room at the Top* 58; Producer and Dir. *The Innocents* 61; Dir. *The Pumpkin Eater* 64; Producer and Dir. *Our Mother's House* 67; Dir. *The Great Gatsby* 74.
c/o Romulus Films Ltd., Brook House, Park Lane, London, W.1, England.

Clegg, Sir Cuthbert Barwick, Kt., T.D.; British banker b. 9 Aug. 1904, Lancashire; *s.* of Edmund Barwick Clegg, J.P., D.L.; *m.* Helen Margaret Jefferson 1930; one *s.*; ed. Charterhouse and Trinity Coll., Oxford.
Cotton Industry Working Party 46; Cotton Manufacturing Comm. 47-49; Anglo-American Council on Productivity 48-52; Pres. British Employers' Confederation 50-52; mem. Economic Planning Board 49-53, British Productivity Council 52-54; Pres. U.K. Textile Manufacturers Asscn. 61-69, Cotton, Silk and Man-made Fibres Research Asscn. 62-67, Inst. of Bankers 68-69; Chair. Martins Bank Ltd. 64-69; Local Advisory Dir., Preston District, Barclays Bank Ltd.; Dir. Halifax Building Soc.
Willow Cottage, Arkholme, Carnforth, Lancs., England.
Telephone: Hornby 21205.

Clemen, Wolfgang; German university professor; b. 29 March 1909, Bonn; *s.* of Prof. Paul Clemen; *m.* Ursula Gauhe 1943; two *s.* one *d.*; ed. Univs. of Heidelberg, Freiburg, Bonn, Berlin, Munich and Cambridge.
Lecturer, Cologne Univ. 38, Kiel Univ. 39; Prof. of English, Kiel Univ. 40-46, Munich Univ. 46-; mem. Bavarian Acad. of Sciences 48; Vice-Pres. German Shakespeare Soc. 49; Visiting Prof. Columbia Univ., New York 53; Pres. Modern Humanities Research Asscn. 64; Corresp. mem. British Acad. 64; Churchill Foundation Visiting Prof. Bristol 64; Hon. mem. American Modern Language Asscn. and Modern Humanities Research Asscn. 65; Hon. D.Litt. (Birmingham) 64; Hon. D.Phil. (Rouen) 67; Grosses Bundesverdienstkreuz 69; Hon. C.B.E. 72.
Leisure interest: chamber music.
Publs. *Shakespeares Bilder* 36, *Der junge Chaucer* 38, *Shelleys Geisterwelt* 48, *The Development of Shakespeare's Imagery* 51, 59, *English Tragedy before Shakespeare* 61, *Chaucer's Early Poetry* 63, *Kommentar zu Shakespeares Richard III* 57, *Shakespeare's Soliloquies* 64, *Spenser's Epithalamion* 64, *Shakespeare's Midsummer Night's Dream* (ed.) 63, *Past and Future in Shakespeare's Drama* 66, *A Commentary on Shakespeare's Richard III* 68, *Das Problem des Stilwandels in der engl. Dichtung* 68, *Was ist literarischer Einfluss?* 68, *Das Drama Shakespeares* 69, *Shakespeare's Dramatic Art* 72, *Shakespeare and Marlowe* 72, *G. M. Hopkins Gedichte* (English and German edn). 73, *The Pursuit of Influence* 74.
8207 Endorf, Upper Bavaria, Federal Republic of Germany.
Telephone: 326.

Clément, René; French film director; b. 18 March 1913; ed. School of Architecture, Paris.
Films include *Bataille du rail* 46, *Les Maudits* 47, *Walls of Malapaga* 48, *Château de verre* 50, *Jeux interdits* 52, *Lion d'or* 52, *Monsieur Ripois* 54, *Gervaise* 56, *Sea Wall* 58, *Demain est un autre jour* 62, *Quelle joie de vivre, Purple Noon* (*Plein Soleil*) 60, *The Love Cage* (*Les Félins*) 64, *Paris brûle-t-il?* 65, *A la Recherche du Temps Perdu* 66, *Le Passager de la Pluie* 70, *La Maison sous les arbres* 71, *La Course du lièvre à travers les champs* 71, *The Baby Sitter*.

Publs. *Bataille du rail* (with C. Audry) 47.
10 avenue Saint-Roman, Monte Carlo, Monaco; **and**
91 avenue Henri Martin, Paris 16e, France.

Clements, George L.; American businessman; b. 24
Feb. 1909, Chicago; *s.* of Fred Clements and Ina Small;
m. Ruth Howell 1933; one *s.* one *d.*; ed. Univ. of Illinois.
Joined Jewel Tea Co. Inc. (now Jewel Cos., Inc.)
Chicago 29, Dir. 48-51, Pres. 51-64, Chair. 65-70, Chair.
Exec. Cttee. 70-; Dir. G. B. Enterprises, Belgium,
Super Bazars, S.A., Belgium, Northern Illinois Gas Co.,
Universal Oil Products Co.; Dir. Chicago Asscn. of
Commerce; Dir. and mem. Exec. Cttee. Nat. Asscn. of
Food Chains; Chair. Board of Higher Educ., State of
Illinois 69-.
Leisure interests: hunting, golf, reading.
5725 East River Road, Chicago, Ill. 60631, U.S.A.

Clements, Sir John, Kt., C.B.E., F.R.S.A.; British actor,
manager and producer; b. 25 April 1910; *m.* Kay
Hammond 1946.
Made first stage appearance 30; played many Shakespearean parts with Ben Greet's Co.; founded Intimate
Theatre, Palmers Green, London, appearing in and
directing weekly repertory 35-40; produced *Yes and No*
at Ambassadors Theatre 37, *Private Lives* 44; played
Coriolanus, Petruchio with Old Vic. Co. 47-48; appeared
in *Edward My Son* 48; directed and appeared in *The
Beaux' Stratagem* 49-50; managed Saville Theatre 55-57,
presenting and appearing in *The Wild Duck, The
Rivals, The Seagull, The Doctor's Dilemma, The Way of
the World*; mem. Arts Council Drama Panel 53-58;
adviser on Drama to Associated Rediffusion Ltd. 55-56,
producing films for them; mem. Council Royal Acad.
Dramatic Art 57-; appeared in and directed *The Rape
of the Belt* 57-58; appeared in *Gilt and Gingerbread* 59,
The Marriage-go-round 59-60, *J.B.* 61, *The Affair* 61;
Old Vic American tour 62; played in *The Tulip Tree*
62, *The Masters* 63; directed and appeared in *Robert and
Elizabeth* 64; Dir. Chichester Festival Theatre 66-73; pro-
ductions include *The Clandestine Marriage, The Fighting
Cock, The Cherry Orchard, Macbeth* 66, *The Farmer's
Wife, Heartbreak House, The Beaux' Stratagem, An
Italian Straw Hat* 67, *The Unknown Soldier and his
Wife, The Cocktail Party, The Tempest, The Skin of our
Teeth* 68, *Antony and Cleopatra, The Magistrate, The
Caucasian Chalk Circle, The Country Wife* 69, *Peer
Gynt, Vivat, Vivat Regina!, The Proposal, Arms and the
Man, The Alchemist* 70, *The Rivals, Dear Antoine,
Caesar and Cleopatra, Reunion in Vienna* 71, *The
Beggar's Opera, The Dictor's Dilemma* 72, *The Director
of the Opera, Dandy Dick* 73, (directed and acted in)
The Fortune Hunters 75, (directed and acted in) *The
Case in Question* 75.
Films include: *Things to Come, Knight without Armour,
The Divine Spark, South Riding, Rembrandt, The Four
Feathers, Convoy, Ships with Wings, Undercover, They
Came to a City, The Silent Enemy, Train of Events, The
Mind Benders, Oh What a Lovely War!*
4 Rufford Court, 109 Marine Parade, Brighton, Sussex,
BN2 1AT, England.

Cleminson, James Arnold Stacey, M.C.; British com-
pany director; b. 31 Aug. 1921, Hull, Yorkshire; *s.* of
Arnold Russell and Florence Stacey Cleminson; *m.*
Helen Juliet Measor; one *s.* two *d.*; ed. Bramcote and
Rugby schools.
Served British Army, Parachute Regt. 40-46; joined
Reckitt and Colman Overseas 46; Dir. and later Vice-
Chair. J. J. Colman Norwich 60-69; Dir. Reckitt and
Colman Ltd. 69, Chair. Food Div. 70, Chief Exec. 73-;
Chair. Exec. Cttee., Endeavour Training; Trustee,
Airborne Forces Security Fund.
Leisure interests: riding, fishing, shooting, tennis, golf.
Reckitt and Colman Ltd., P.O. Box 26, Burlington Lane,
London W.4; Loddon Hall, Hales, Norfolk, England.

Clemmensen, Carl Johan; Danish economist; b.
26 Dec. 1916; *m.* Ingrid Clemmensen 1945; ed. Rungsted
Statsskole and Københavns Universitet.
Secretary, Danish Employers' Confederation 46-49,
Principal 49-55, Chief of Statistical-Econ. Dept. 55-60,
Vice-Dir. 60-62, Dir. and mem. Board of Dirs. 62-; **mem.**
numerous Govt. and other Cttees.; Editor *Statistiken*.
Office: Dansk Arbejdsgiverforening, Vester Voldgade
113, Copenhagen V; Home: Hummeltoften 13a, Virum,
Denmark.
Telephone: (02) 85-57-57 (Home).

Clemmesen, Johannes, D.M.SC.; Danish pathologist;
b. 14 Nov. 1908, Copenhagen; *s.* of Capt. Johan
Clemmesen and Marie Gran; ed. Metropolitan School
and Univ. of Copenhagen.
Pathologist, Old People's Town 50-55; Assoc. Prof. of
Pathology, Royal Dental Coll. 50-56; Chief Pathologist,
Finsen Inst., Copenhagen 55-; Dir. Danish Cancer
Registry 42-; mem. WHO Sub-cttee. on Cancer Regis-
tration and other cttees. on statistics and endemiology
of cancer 50-; mem. Exec. Cttee. Int. Union against
Cancer 54-62; mem. Secr., Cttee. on Geographical
Pathology of Cancer 50-62, Cttees. on Tumour Nomen-
clature 50-65; Chair. Co-ordinating Cttee. for Human
Tumour Investigations 73-75; Pres. Int. Asscn. for
Comparative Leukemia Research 75.
Publs. *X-radiation and Immunity to Heterotrans-
plantation* 38, *Statistical Studies in the Aetiology of
Malignant Neoplasms* 65, 69, 74.
Finsen Institute, Strandboulevard 49, Copenhagen
2100; Home: Stockholmsgade 43, Copenhagen 2100,
Denmark.
Telephone: 01-26-2696 (Office); 01-TR-8600 (Home).

Clercq, Willy De, LL.D.; Belgian barrister and politician; b. 8 July 1927, Ghent; *m.* Fernande Fazzi; two *s.*
one *d.*
Barrister, Court of Appeal, Ghent; with Gen. Secretariat
of UN, New York 52; mem. Chamber of Reps. for Ghent-
Eklo 58-; Deputy Prime Minister, in charge of Budget
66-68; Deputy Prime Minister 73-74, Minister of Finance
73-; Parti pour la liberté et le progrès (P.L.P.); Head
of P.L.P. Group; Chair. P.L.P. 71; mem. Inter-
parliamentary Union; part-time teacher Univ. of Ghent.
Leisure interests: sport, travel.
Ministère des Finances, Brussels, Belgium.

Clerdent, Baron Pierre Charles Jean Joseph, D. EN D.;
Belgian business executive; b. 29 April 1909, Liège;
s. of Frédéric Clerdent; *m.* Simone Lambeaux 1940; ed.
Univ. of Liège.
Advocate, Court of Appeal 45-53; Gov. Province of
Luxembourg, later Province of Liège until 71; Pres.
Admin. Board S. A. Cockerill; Pres. European Cttee.
for use of River Meuse; decorations from Belgium,
France, U.K., U.S.A., Germany, Italy, Netherlands,
Luxembourg, Greece, Austria, Poland, Sweden, Iran
and Senegal.
Leisure interest: golf.
Le Hinon, 1 rue de Tilff, B-4950 Beaufays, Belgium.

Clerides, Glavkos John, B.A., LL.B.; Cypriot lawyer
and politician; b. 24 April 1919, Nicosia; *s.* of John
Clerides, Q.C., C.B.E.; *m.*; one *c.*; ed. Pancyprian
Gymnasium, Nicosia, King's Coll., London Univ.,
Gray's Inn, London.
Served with R.A.F. 39-45; shot down and taken prisoner
42-45 (mentioned in despatches); practised law in
Cyprus 51-60; Head of Greek Cypriot Del., Constitu-
tional Comm. 59-60; Minister of Justice 59-60; mem.
House of Reps. 60-, Pres. of House 60-; Acting Pres. of
Cyprus July-Dec. 74; founder and leader of Unified
Party; Gold Medal, Order of the Holy Sepulchre.
56 Metochiou Street, Nicosia, Cyprus.

Clermont, Friedrich; German agriculturalist and
politician; b. 1934.
Chairman, Agricultural Production Co., Neubranden-

burg; mem. Volkskammer 63-; mem. Cttee. for Agriculture, Forestry and Food Supply, Volkskammer; mem. State Council 71-.
Staatsrat der Deutschen Demokratischen Republik, Marx-Engels-Platz, 102 Berlin, German Democratic Republic.

Cleve, Nils Joachim Otto, PH.D.; Finnish archaeologist; b. 1905, Helsinki; s. of Otto Cleve and Anna Stråhlman; m. Marianne Albrecht 1931; one s. one d.; ed. Univ. of Helsinki and Åbo Acad.
Director, Municipal Museum of Turku 34-45; Dir., Historical Dept., Nat. Museum (Kansallismuseo) 45-59; Lecturer Åbo Acad. 44-59, Univ. of Helsinki 48-63; State Archaeologist (Nat. Museum) 59-71.
Mäyrätie 6. B, Helsinki 80, Finland.
Telephone: 789918.

Cleveland, Harlan, A.B.; American administrator, educationist and government official; b. 19 Jan. 1918, New York City; s. of Stanley Matthews and Marian Phelps (van Buren); m. Lois W. Burton 1941; one s. two d.; ed. Princeton Univ. and Oxford Univ.
Served Allied Control Commission, Rome 44-45; served UNRRA, Rome and Shanghai 46-48; Economic Co-operation Admin., Washington 48-51; Asst. Dir. for Europe, Mutual Security Agency 52-53; Exec. Editor *The Reporter*, New York City 53-55, Publisher 55-56; Dean, Maxwell Graduate School of Citizenship and Public Affairs, Syracuse Univ. 56-61; Asst. Sec. for International Organization Affairs, State Dept. 61-65; Amb. to NATO 65-69; Pres. Univ. of Hawaii 69-74; Dir. Aspen Program in Int. Affairs Sept. 74-; Democrat.
Leisure interests: sailing, golf, writing.
Publs. *The Obligations of Power* 66, *NATO: The Transatlantic Bargain* 70, *The Future Executive* 72; Co-author: *The Overseas Americans* 60.
P.O. Box 2820, Princeton, N.J. 08540, U.S.A.
Telephone: (609) 921-1141.

Cliburn, Van (Harvey Lavan, Jr.); American pianist; b. 12 July 1934; studied with mother and at Juilliard School of Music.
Public appearances, Shreveport 40; début, Houston Symphony Orchestra 52, N.Y. Philharmonic Orchestra 54, 58; concert pianist on tour U.S. 55-, U.S.S.R. 58; appearances in Brussels, London, Amsterdam, Paris, etc.; Hon. H.H.D. (Baylor), numerous prizes.
c/o Hurok Attractions Inc., 1370 Avenue of the Americas, New York, N.Y. 10022, U.S.A.

Clifford, Clark McAdams; American lawyer and government official; b. 25 Dec. 1906, Fort Scott, Kan.; ed. Washington Univ.
Holland, Lashly and Donnell, St. Louis, Missouri 28-33, Holland, Lashly and Lashly 33-37, Partner, Lashly, Lashly, Miller and Clifford 38-68, Senior Partner, Clifford & Miller, Washington 50-68, 69-; Special Counsel, President of U.S.A. 46-50; Chair. Foreign Intelligence Advisory Board 63-68; Sec. for Defense 68-69; Dir. Nat. Bank of Washington, Washington-Sheraton Corpn.
815 Connecticut Avenue, Washington, D.C. 20006; Home: 9421 Rockville Pike, Bethesda, Maryland 20014, U.S.A.
Telephone: OLiver 2-2842 (Home).

Clifford, John McLean, LL.B., J.D.; American lawyer; b. 9 Dec. 1904; ed. Univ. of Utah, and Southwestern Univ.
Admitted to Californian Bar 30, D.C. Bar 39; Vice-Pres. Nat. Broadcasting Co. Inc. New York 53-54, Admin. Vice-Pres. 54-56, Exec. Vice-Pres. 56-61; Staff Vice-Pres. Radio Corpn. of America 61-62; Exec. Vice-Pres. and Dir. Curtis Publishing Co. Philadelphia 62-64, Pres. 64-68; Chair. Board, New York and Pennsylvania Co. Inc.; Dir. Curtis Circulation Co., Beehive Medical Electronics Inc.; Trustee, Sansum Clinic Research Inst.

965 Via Fruteria, Hope Ranch Park, Santa Barbara, California 93105, U.S.A.

Clinchy, Everett Ross, B.S., M.A., PH.D.; American educationalist; b. 16 Dec. 1896, N.Y.; s. of James Hugh Clinchy and Lydie Stagg; m. Winifred Mead 1918; one s. two d.; ed. Wesleyan Univ., Lafayette Coll., Columbia Univ., and Drew Univ.
Chaplain, Wesleyan Univ. 24-28; Pres. Nat. Conf. of Christians and Jews Inc. 28-58; Pres. The Council on World Tensions 50-65; fmr. Dir. Williamstown Inst. of Human Relations; Pres. Inst. on Man and Science 63-72, Chair. Exec. Cttee. 73-.
Publs. *All in the Name of God* 31, *Centers in Human Relations* 40, *Handbook on Human Relations* 50.
Rensselaerville, N.Y. 12147, U.S.A.
Telephone: 518-797-3477.

Clinton, Mark; Irish politician; m.; seven c.; ed. Warrenstown Coll. of Agriculture, Univ. Coll. Dublin.
Fine Gael M.P. for West County Dublin 61-; fmr. Chair. Dublin County Council, County Dublin Vocational Educ. Cttee., Eastern Health Board; fmr. Del. to Inter-Parl. Union; mem. Council of Europe; Minister for Agriculture and Fisheries March 73-.
Department of Agriculture and Fisheries, Agriculture House, Kildare Street, Dublin 2, Ireland.

Clitheroe, 1st Baron, cr. 55, of Downham; **Ralph Assheton,** Bt. ,P.C., D.L., M.A. F.S.A.; British businessman; b. 24 Feb. 1901, Worston; s. of Sir Ralph Assheton, 1st Bart.; m. Hon. Sylvia Hotham, F.L.A.S., F.R.I.C.S., 1924; two s. one d.; ed. Eton Coll., and Christ Church, Oxford.
Barrister, Inner Temple 25; mem. London Stock Exchange 27-39; Nat. Conservative M.P. Rushcliffe Div. of Notts. 34-45, City of London Nov. 45-50, Blackburn West 50-55; Parl. Sec. to Ministry of Labour and Nat. Service Sept. 39-Feb. 42, to Ministry of Supply 42-43; Financial Sec. to Treasury 43-44; Chair. Conservative Party 44-46; Chair. Public Accounts Cttee. 48-50, Select Cttee. on Nationalized Industries 51; Chair. Mercantile Investment Trust Co. Ltd. 58-71; Dir. Tanganyika Concessions Ltd.; fmrly. Dir. Tube Investments (Ltd.), Nat. Westminster Bank Ltd., Borax (Holdings) Ltd., Coutts and Co., Rio Tinto Zinc Ltd., and other companies; Lord Lieut. County of Lancs.; mem. Council Duchy of Lancaster; High Steward of Westminster.
Leisure interests: shooting, farming.
17 Chelsea Park Gardens, London, S.W.3; Downham Hall, Clitheroe, Lancs., England.
Telephone: 01-352-4020; Clitheroe 41210.

Cloete, (Edward Fairley) Stuart (Graham), F.I.A.L.; South African soldier, farmer and author; b. 23 July 1897, Paris; s. of Laurence Cloete and Edith Park; m. 1st Florence Horsman 1918 (dissolved), 2nd Mildred West 1941; ed. Lancing Coll., England.
Army officer 14-25, Coldstream Guards, retd.; farming and ranching in South Africa 23-35; Trustee, South African Foundation.
Leisure interests: painting, gardening, aviary.
Publs. *Turning Wheels* 37, *Watch for the Dawn* 39, *Yesterday is Dead* 39, *Hill of Doves* 41, *The Young Men and the Old* (poems) 42, *Congo Song* 43, *The Third Way* 45, *African Portraits, The Curve and the Tusk* 53, *The African Giant* 55, *Mamba* 56, *The Mask* 57, *Gazella* 58, *The Soldier's Peaches* (short stories) 59, *The Fiercest Heart* 60, *The Silver Trumpet* 60 and *The Looking Glass* 63 (short stories), *Rags of Glory* 63, *The Honey Bird* 64, *The 1001 Nights of Jean Macacque* 65, *The Abductors* 66, *The Writing on the Wall* (short stories) 69, *South Africa* 69, *How Young They Died* 70, *Three White Swans* 71, *A Victorian Son* 72, *The Gambler* 73, *The Company* 73, *A Heart of Gold* (short stories) 73, *More Nights of Jean Macacque* 75, *The Gladiator* (autobiog.) 76, *Canary Pie* (short stories) 76.
[*Died 20 March* 1976.]

Clore, Sir Charles, Kt.; British businessman; b. 26 Dec. 1904; *m.* 1943 (dissolved); one *s.* one *d.*; ed. in London.

Chairman, Sears Holdings Ltd., Sears Engineering Ltd., British Shoe Corpn., Scottish Motor Traction Ltd., Princes Investments Ltd., Taylor & Lodge Ltd., Garrard & Co. Ltd., Mappin & Webb Ltd., Selfridge's Ltd., Kaye & Stewart Ltd., Lewis's Investment Trust Ltd., Bentley Engineering Group Ltd., Lewis's Ltd.; Dir. Sears Industries Inc. (U.S.A.), Orange Free State Investment Trust Ltd., Ritz Hotel (London), and other companies.

Leisure interests: farming, shooting.

22 Park Street, London, W1Y 4AE, England.

Cloud, Preston, PH.D.; American research biogeologist; b. 26 Sept. 1912, Massachusetts; *s.* of Preston Cloud and Pauline Wiedemann; *m.* Janice Gibson 1972; one *s.* two *d.* (by previous marriage); ed. George Washington and Yale Univs.

Geologist, U.S. Geological Survey 42-61, 74, Chief Paleontology and Stratigraphy Branch 49-59, Rep. in Oceanography 59-61; taught at Harvard Univ. 46-48, Mo. School of Mines and Metallurgy 40-41, Univ. of Minn. 61-65, Univ. of Tex. 62, U.C.L.A. 65-68, Univ. of Calif. Santa Barbara 68-74, Salzburg Seminar Amer. Studies 73, A. L. du Toit Memorial Lecturer 75; has served on advisory panels to numerous orgs., including NASA, U.S. Dept. of Interior and Smithsonian Inst. and on Congressional panels; Assoc. Editor *American Journal of Science, Quarterly Review of Biology, Resources Policy* and *Precambrian Research*; mem. and Chair. various cttees. of Nat. Research Council, Nat. Acad. of Sciences and Geological Soc. of America; mem. Nat. Acad. of Sciences (Council 72-75, Exec. Cttee. 73-75), Nat. Research Council (Gov. Board 72-75), Amer. Philosophical Soc., Amer. Acad. of Arts and Sciences; Fellow, Amer. Soc. of Naturalists, Paleontological Soc. of America, Amer. Geophysical Union; Life Fellow, Geological Soc. of America (Council 72-75), Amer. Asscn. for Advancement of Science; hon. mem. Paleontological Soc. of India and several other nat. and int. socs.; A. Cressy Morrison Prize, N.Y. Acad. of Sciences 40, Rockefeller Public Service Award 56, Distinguished Service Award and Medal, U.S. Dept. of Interior 59, Medal, Paleontological Soc. of America 71, Lucius Wilbur Cross Medal, Yale Graduate School 73.

Leisure interests: skiing, back-packing, music.

Publs. include *Resources and Man, Adventures in Earth History* and various technical books; contributions to professional journals on the biological and sedimentological aspects of geology, both land and marine, on the origin and early evolution of life and on the interactions between biospheric, atmospheric and lithospheric evolution.

U.S. Geological Survey, Biogeology Clean Laboratory, University of California, Santa Barbara, Calif. 93106; 400 Mountain Drive, Santa Barbara, Calif. 93103, U.S.A.

Telephone: 805-961-3514 (Office).

Clouzot, Henri-Georges, L. EN D.; French film director; b. 20 Nov. 1907; ed. Lycée de Brest, Lycée Sainte-Barbe and Paris Univ.

Int. Prize Venice Film Festival 47 and 49, Cannes Grand Prix 53, Prix Louis-Delluc for *Les Diaboliques* 54, Cannes Special Prize for *Le Mystère Picasso* 56, Grand Prix du Cinéma français for *La Vérité* 60; Officier des Arts et des Lettres.

Films include *L'Assassin Habite au 21, Le Corbeau, Quai des Orfèvres, Manon, Le Salaire de la Peur, Les Diaboliques, Le Mystère Picasso, Les Espions, La Vérité, L'Enfer.*

"La Colombe d'Or", 06 Saint-Paul-de-Vence (Alpes-Maritimes), France.

Clurman, Harold Edgar; American theatrical director and critic; b. 18 Sept. 1901; *s.* of Samuel M. Clurman and Bertha Saphir; ed. New York public schools, Columbia Univ. and the Sorbonne, Paris.

Actor and stage manager 24-29; playreader for Theatre Guild, New York 29-31; co-founder Group Theatre, New York 31, Man. Dir. 37-41; Art Columnist *To-Morrow* magazine 46-53; Drama Critic *New Republic* 48-53, *The Nation* 53-; Exec. Consultant Repertory Theatre Lincoln Center 63-; Visiting Prof. Hunter Coll., New York 68-; productions directed include *Awake and Sing* 35, *Golden Boy* (Odets) 37, *Montserrat* (Robles) (Habimah Theatre, Tel Aviv) 41, *Member of the Wedding* (Carson McCullers) 49, *Desire Under the Elms* (O'Neill) 52, *The Autumn Garden* (Hellman) 53, *Tiger at the Gates* (Giraudoux) (London and N.Y.), in television 60, *Waltz of the Toreadors* (Anouilh) 56, *Orpheus Descending* (Tennessee Williams), *The Touch of the Poet* (O'Neill) 58, *Heartbreak House* (Shaw) 59, *A Shot in the Dark* (Achard-Kurnitz) 61, *Uncle Vanya*; Chevalier, Légion d'Honneur; Hon. D.Litt. (Bard Coll.); Hon. D. (Boston Univ., Ripon Coll., Carnegie Mellon Inst.).

Leisure interests: travel, music, art, dance, reading.

Publs. *The Fervent Years* 45, *Lies like Truth* 58, *The Naked Image* 69, *On Direction* 72, *The Divine Pastime* 74, *All People Are Famous* 74.

205 West 57th Street, New York, N.Y. 10019, U.S.A.

Clutton-Brock, (Arthur) Guy; British and Rhodesian (dual nationality) agriculturist and social worker; b. 5 April 1906, Northwood, Mddx.; *s.* of Henry and Rosa Clutton-Brock; *m.* Frances M. Allen 1934; one *d.*; ed. Rugby School and Magdalene Coll., Cambridge Univ.

Cambridge House University Settlement 27-29; Rugby House Settlement 29-33; Borstal Service 33-36; Principal Probation Officer, Metropolitan Area of London 36-40; Head Oxford House University Settlement 40-45; Youth and Religious Affairs Officer, British Military Govt., Berlin 45; with Christian Reconstruction in Europe 46; farm labourer in U.K. 47-48; Diocesan Agricultural Officer, Mashonaland (Southern Rhodesia) and Dir. of Farm Activities, St. Faith's Mission, Rusape (Southern Rhodesia) 49-59; briefly detained by Rhodesian Govt. on declaration of emergency March 59; Hon. Dir. Bamangwato Development Asscn., Bechuanaland Protectorate 61-62; Field Officer of the African Development Trust 62-65; retd. 66; Treas. non-racial Cold Comfort Farm Soc.; deported to Britain 71; Hon. Fellow Magdalene Coll., Univ. of Cambridge 73.

Leisure interest: sitting under a tree with others talking and smoking.

Publs. *Dawn in Nyasaland* 59, *Cold Comfort Confronted.*

Gelli Uchaf, Llandyrnog, Denbigh, L16 4HR, N. Wales.

Telephone: Llandyrnog 482.

Cluver, Eustace H., K.ST.J., E.D., M.A., M.D., B.CH., D.PH., F.R.S.H.; South African emeritus professor of preventive medicine; b. 28 Aug. 1894; *m.* Eileen Ledger 1929; three *d.*; ed. Victoria Coll., Stellenbosch, and Oxford Univ.

Rhodes Scholar to Oxford 13; fmr. Prof. of Physiology Witwatersrand Univ. Medical School, Sec. for Public Health and Dir. S. African Inst. for Medical Research Johannesburg; Prof. of Medical Education and Dean Faculty of Medicine, Univ. of Witwatersrand.

Leisure interest: afforestation.

Publs. *Medical and Health Legislation in the Union of South Africa* 49 (6th edn. 68), *Social Medicine* 51, *Recent Medical and Health Legislation* 55, *Public Health in South Africa* (6th edn.) 59.

Mornhill Farm, Walkerville, Transvaal, South Africa.

Telephone: Walkerville 1212.

Clyne, Hon. John Valentine, c.c.; Canadian business executive; b. 14 Feb. 1902, Vancouver; *s.* of Henry Clyne and Martha Clyne; *m.* Betty Ventris Ann

Somerset 1927; one *s.* one *d.*; ed. Florence Nightingale School and King Edward High School, Vancouver, Univ. of British Columbia, London School of Economics and King's Coll., London.

Various business firms 23-29; Partner, Macrae, Duncan and Clyne, Vancouver 29-46, Campney, Owen, Clyne and Murphy 47-50; Judge of Supreme Court of British Columbia 50-57; Chair. of Board MacMillan and Bloedel Ltd., Vancouver 58-59; Chair. of Board and Chief Exec. Officer, MacMillan, Bloedel and Powell River Ltd. (name changed to MacMillan Bloedel Ltd. April 66), Vancouver 60-72, Chair. of the Board 72-73; fmr. Chair. Canadian Maritime Comm.; Dir. MacMillan Bloedel Ltd., Canada Trust Co.

Leisure interests: sport, especially rugby football, theatre.

MacMillan Bloedel Ltd., 1075 W. Georgia Street, Vancouver V6E 3R9; Home: 3738 Angus Drive, Vancouver V6J 4H5, B.C., Canada.

Telephone: 683-6711 (Office); 733-6120 (Home).

Cobbina, John Henry; Ghanaian police officer; b. 29 Sept. 1919, Essikado, Sekondi; *m.*; one *s.* one *d.*; ed. Sekondi and Achimota Colls. and Metropolitan Police Training Centre, Hendon, England.

Teacher, Aggrey Coll., Sekondi 39-42; joined W. African Frontier Forces 42, Capt. and Co. Commdr. 49-50; joined Ghana Police Service 51, Asst. Supt. of Police 51-54; rose through ranks, becoming Chief Supt. 59; Asst. Commr. of Police and later Commr. of Police Admin. 60-72; Insp.-Gen. of Police 72-74, Commr. for Internal Affairs 72-75; Grand Medal 69.

Leisure interests: gardening, poultry keeping.

Ministry of Internal Affairs, Accra, Ghana.

Cobbold, 1st Baron, cr. 60, of Knebworth; **Cameron Fromanteel Cobbold,** K.G., P.C., G.C.V.O.; British banker and Palace official; b. 14 Sept. 1904, London; *s.* of Col. Clement Cobbold and Stella Cameron; *m.* Lady Hermione Lytton 1930; two *s.* one *d.*; ed. Eton and King's Coll., Cambridge.

Deputy Governor Bank of England until 49, Gov. 49-61; Lord Chamberlain 63-71; Perm. Lord-in-Waiting to H.M. The Queen 71; H.M. Lt. for City of London; High Sheriff County of London 46-47; mem. H.M. Privy Council 59; fmr. Dir. British Petroleum Co. Ltd., Guardian Royal Exchange Assurance Ltd.; Chair. Italian Int. Bank, London 72-74, now Dir.; Hon. LL.D. (McGill Univ.); Hon. D.Sc. (London Univ.).

Lake House, Knebworth, Herts., England.

Cochereau, Pierre; French organist; b. 9th July 1924, Saint-Mandé; *s.* of Georges Cochereau and Anne Gros; *m.* Nicole Lacroix 1948; one *s.* one *d.*; ed. Paris Acad. and Paris Conservatory of Music.

Director, Conservatory of Le Mans 51; Organist of Notre Dame, Paris 55-; Dir. Conservatory of Music, Dancing and Drama, Nice 60-; Concert tours throughout Europe, U.S.A., U.S.S.R., Australia, Japan and U.K.; Chevalier, Légion d'Honneur; 50 records; Chevalier des Arts et des Lettres.

Leisure interests: recording, organ building.

15 *bis* rue des Ursins, Paris 4e; 10 avenue Jean Lorrain, 06 Nice, France.

Telephone: MED-74-56 (Paris); 89-30-13 (Nice).

Cochran, Jacqueline; American airwoman and business executive; b. Muskogee, Florida; *m.* Floyd B. Odlum 1936.

Pilot since 32; winner Bendix Transcontinental Air Race 38; headed U.S. Women's Airforce Service Pilots in Second World War (Col. U.S.A.F.R.); holds numerous world air speed records; first woman to break sonic barrier 53; Dir. Northeast Airlines; Pres. Nat. Aeronautic Asscn. 60; Pres. Int. Aeronautic Fed. 58-; Consultant to Nat. Aeronautics and Space Admin.; Dir. Storer Broadcasting Co.; Dir. George Washington Univ.; Hon. Fellow, Soc. of Experimental Test Pilots; D.S.M.;

Hon. LL.D. (Elmira Coll., N.Y.), Hon. Sc.D. (Wisconsin Univ.), Sc.D. (Manchester Univ., N.H.); Légion d'Honneur; Gold Medal Int. Aeronautic Fed. 54; Distinguished Flying Cross 69, etc.

Leisure interests: flying, golf, reading, cooking.

Publ. *The Stars at Noon* 54.

Cochran Odlum Ranch, Indio, Calif., U.S.A.

Cochrane, Robert Greenhill, C.M.G., M.D., F.R.C.P., D.T.M.&H.; British consultant physician and leprologist; b. 11 Aug. 1899, Pei-Tai Ho, N. China; *s.* of Dr. Thomas Cochrane and Grace Hamilton Cochrane; *m.* 1st Ivy Gladys Nunn 1927, 2nd Martha Jeane Shaw 1968; two *s.* one *d.*; ed. Eltham Coll., Glasgow Univ. and St. Bartholomew's Hosp.

Secretary of Medical Work, Mission to Lepers (now Leprosy Mission), stationed at Purulia, Bihar, India 24-27; Medical Supt., Leprosy Mission Hosp., Bankura, Bengal 28-30; Medical Sec., British Empire Leprosy Relief Asscn. (now LEPRA) 30-35, 51-53; Chief Medical Officer, Lady Willingdon Leprosy Sanatorium, Chingleput 35-44, 48-51; Dir. of Leprosy Campaign, Dir. of Leprosy Research, Madras State 41-51; Dir. and Principal Prof. of Medicine and Dermatology and Dir. of Rural Medicine, Christian Medical Coll., Vellore, S. India 44-48; Adviser in Leprosy to Ministry of Health, London 51-65; Consultant and Lecturer in Leprosy, Hosp. for Tropical Diseases, St. Thomas's Hosp., St. John's Hosp. for Diseases of the Skin 51-65; Visiting Medical Officer, Homes of St. Giles, E. Hanningfield 51-65; Technical Medical Adviser, American Leprosy Missions, Inc. 53-65; Founder and Dir., Leprosy Study Centre, London 53-66; Medical Supt., Leprosy Home and Hosp., Vadothorasalur, Madras State, India 66-68; Medical Supt., Kola Noloto Leprosarium, Shinyanga, Tanzania (Africa Inland Mission) 68-72; Pres. Int. Leprosy Asscn. 63-68, Pres. Emer. 68-; Consultant to WHO; introduced use of D.D.S. for treatment of leprosy; integrated leprosy into gen. medicine; Kaiser-i-Hind gold medal 46; Coronation Medal, King George VI; Damien-Dutton Award 64.

Publ. *A Practical Textbook of Leprosy* 47, *Leprosy, Its Challenge and Hope* 49; Editor *Leprosy in Theory and Practice* 59, Co-editor 2nd edn. 64; *Biblical Leprosy, A Suggested Interpretation* 61.

606 Swede Street, Norristown, Pennsylvania 19401, U.S.A.

Telephone: (215) 272-0244.

Cockburn, Sir Robert, K.B.E., C.B., PH.D., M.SC., M.A. (CANTAB.); British civil servant; b. 31 March 1909, Portsmouth, Hants.; *s.* of Rev. R. T. Cockburn; *m.* Phyllis Hoyland 1935; two *d.*; ed. Municipal Coll., Portsmouth, and London Univ.

Taught science at West Ham Municipal Coll. 30-37; research in communications at Royal Aircraft Establishment, Farnborough 37-39; radar research at Telecommunications Research Establishment, Malvern 39-45; atomic energy research at A.E.R.E., Harwell 45-48; scientific adviser to Air Ministry 48-53; Principal Dir. of Scientific Research (Guided Weapons and Electronics), Ministry of Supply 54-55, Deputy Controller of Electronics 55-56, Controller of Guided Weapons and Electronics 56-59; Chief Scientist, Ministry of Aviation 59-64; Dir. Royal Aircraft Establishment, Farnborough 64-69; Chair. Council, Nat. Computing Centre 70-; Fellow, Churchill Coll., Cambridge 69-; Chair. TV Advisory Cttee. 71-; Chair. BBC Engineering Advisory Cttee. 73; Hon. Fellow, Royal Aeronautical Soc.; U.S. Congressional Medal for Merit.

Leisure interest: sailing.

21 Fitzroy Road, Fleet, Hampshire, England.

Telephone: 02514-5518.

Cockerell, Sir Christopher (Sydney), Kt., C.B.E., M.A., F.R.S.; British engineer; b. 4 June 1910, Cambridge; *s.* of Sir Sydney Cockerell and Florence Kingsford; *m.*

Margaret E. Belsham 1937; two *d.*; ed. Gresham's, Holt and Peterhouse, Cambridge.
Radio research Cambridge 33-35; joined Marconi's 35, in charge Airborne Div. and Navigational Research 46-48, research 48-50; started boat-building business later known as Ripplecraft Co. Ltd. 48-; inventor of Hovercraft 54, formed Hovercraft Ltd. 57; consultant to Ministry of Supply on Hovercraft Project 57-58; consultant Hovercraft Devt. Ltd. 58-70; Dir. 59-66; Chair. Ripplecraft Co. Ltd. 50-, Hovercraft Ltd.; mem. Ministry of Technology's Advisory Cttee. for Hovercraft 68-70; Pres. Int. Air Cushion Engineering Soc. 69-71; Pres. British Hovercraft Engineering Soc. 72-; Fellow, Royal Soc. of Arts 60-70; Hon. Fellow, Soc. of Engineers, Manchester Univ. of Science and Technology, Swedish Soc. of Aeronautics; hon. mem. Southampton Chamber of Commerce 63; Trustee, Nat. Portrait Gallery 67-; Hon. D.Sc. (Leicester and Heriot-Watt Univs.), Hon. D.Sc. (Royal Coll. of Art) 68; Hon. Fellow, Downing Coll., Cambridge 69, Fellow of the Royal Soc. 67; Hon. Fellow, Peterhouse, Cambridge 74; awarded numerous medals by various learned socs.
Leisure interests: fishing, gardening, antiquities.
16 Prospect Place, Hythe, Southampton, Hants. 804 6AU, England.
Telephone: Southampton 842931.

Cockfield, Sir (Francis) Arthur, Kt., LL.B., B.SC.(ECON.); British business executive; b. 28 Sept. 1916; ed. Dover County School, London School of Economics.
Called to Bar, Inner Temple 42; Inland Revenue Dept. of Civil Service 38; Asst. Sec. Bd. of Inland Revenue 45, Commr. 51-52, also Dir. of Statistics and Intelligence to Bd. of Inland Revenue 45-52; Finance Dir. Boots Pure Drug Co. Ltd. 53-61, Man. Dir. and Chair. Exec. Man. Cttee. 61-67; mem. Nat. Econ. Development Council (N.E.D.C.) 62-64; Special Adviser on Taxation to the Chancellor of the Exchequer 70-73; Chair. Price Comm. 73-; Hon. Fellow London School of Econs. 72.
Connaught House, Mount Row, Berkeley Square, London, W.1, England.

Cocks, Michael Francis Lovell, M.P.; British politician; b. 19 Aug. 1929; *m.* Janet Macfarlane 1954; two *s.* two *d.*; ed. Bristol Univ.
Former lecturer at Bristol Polytechnic; M.P. for Bristol South 70-; Asst. Govt. Whip 74-76, Govt. Chief Whip April 76-; Labour.
House of Commons, Westminster, London, S.W.1, England.

Cody, H.E. Cardinal John; American ecclesiastic; b. 24 Dec. 1907, St. Louis, Missouri; *s.* of Thomas and Mary (Begley) Cody; ed. N. American Coll., Rome.
Ordained 31; Auxiliary Bishop, Diocese of St. Louis 47-54; Coadjutor with right of succession to the Bishop of St. Joseph, Missouri 54, Apostolic Admin. 55; Coadjutor to Archbishop-Bishop of Kansas City, St. Joseph Aug. 56, Bishop 56-61; Coadjutor with right of succession to Archdiocese of New Orleans 61, Apostolic Admin. 62-64; Archbishop of New Orleans 64-65; Archbishop of Chicago 65-; cr. Cardinal 67; mem. Sacred Congregation for Catholic Educ., etc.; mem. Nat. Conf. of Bishops.
P.O. Box 1979, Chicago, Illinois 60690, U.S.A.
Telephone: 312-SU7-2315.

Coelho, Vincent H.; Indian diplomatist; b. 20 July 1917; ed. Madras Univ.
Indian Audit and Accounts Service 42, later Indian Foreign Service; Asst. Financial Adviser (Supply Dept.) 44; Under-Sec. Ministry of Finance 45-46; Under-Sec. Cabinet Secr. 46-47; Private Sec. to Prime Minister 47-48; Foreign Service 48-; First Sec. Berne 48-49; Trade Commr., Alexandria 49-50; Consul-Gen., Goa 51-54; Deputy Sec. Ministry of External Affairs 54-57; Chargé d'Affaires, Ankara 57-59; Joint Sec. Ministry of External Affairs 59-61; Ambassador to Brazil 63-65;

Indian Political Officer in Sikkim 66-68; Sec. II in Ministry of External Affairs 68; Amb. to Japan July 70-Nov. 72; High Commr. for India in Sri Lanka 72-.
Indian High Commission, India House, 86 Thurstan Road, Colombo, Sri Lanka.

Coetzee, Johannes Petrus, B.SC.; South African business executive; b. 25 April 1918, Magaliesburg, Transvaal; *s.* of J. C. Coetzee; *m.* Hester E. van Niekerk 1944; three *s.* one *d.*; ed. High School, Rustenburg and Univ. of the Witwatersrand.
Works Man. Amcor Works, Meyerton 57; Gen. Man. Feralloys Ltd., Cato Ridge, Natal 58-62; Gen. Man. Armament Board 63-65, Man. Dir. 65; Production Man. Amcor Group 65-66; Asst. Gen. Man. ISCOR 66-68, Gen. Man. 68-71, Dir. and Gen. Man. 71-72, Man. Dir. 72-.
Leisure interests: cattle farming, golf.
South African Iron and Steel Industrial Corporation (ISCOR) Ltd., P.O. Box 450, Pretoria; Home: 115 Drakensberg Drive, Waterkloof Park, Pretoria, South Africa.
Telephone: 3-9151, Ext. 2982 (Office); 78-9661 (Home).

Coetzer, William Bedford, B.COMM., C.A.(S.A.), F.C.I.S.; South African business executive; b. 13 Sept. 1909, Rouxville; *s.* of Hendrik Coetzer and Sylvia Elza Coetzer (née Blake); *m.* Margaret de Waal-Davies 1935; two *s.* three *d.*; ed. Grey Univ., Bloemfontein and Stellenbosch Univ.
Chairman, Federale Mynbou Bpk., Gen. Mining and Finance Corpn. Ltd., Hollardstraat-Ses Beleggings (Edms.) Bpk., Sentrust Ltd., Union Carriage and Wagon Co. Ltd.
6 Hollard Street, Johannesburg; 21 Tugela Road, Emmarentia, Johannesburg, South Africa.
Telephone: JHB. 836-1121 (Office).

Coffin, Frank Morey; American lawyer and government official; b. 11 July 1919, Lewiston, Maine; *s.* of Herbert and Ruth Coffin; *m.* Ruth Ulrich 1942; one *s.* three *d.*; ed. Bates Coll., and Harvard Univ.
Admitted to Maine Bar 47, legal practice 47-56; mem. U.S. House of Reps. 57-61; Man. Dir. Development Loan Fund, Dept. of State 61; Dep. Administrator, Agency for Int. Development 61-62, Dep. Administrator for Operations 62-64; U.S. Rep. to Development Assistance Cttee., Organisation for European Co-operation and Development (OECD), Paris 64-; U.S. Circuit Judge, Court of Appeals for First Circuit 65-, Chief. Judge; Dir. Overseas Devt. Council; mem. American Acad. of Arts and Sciences, Int. Legal Centre.
Leisure interests: sculpture, painting, boating.
1 Ocean Road, South Portland, Maine, U.S.A.

Coggan, Most Rev. (Frederick) Donald, D.D.; British ecclesiastic; b. 9 Oct. 1909, London; *s.* of Cornish and Fannie Coggan; *m.* Jean Strain 1935; two *d.*; ed. Merchant Taylors' School, St. John's Coll., Cambridge and Wycliffe Hall, Oxford.
Assistant Lecturer in Semitic Languages and Literature, Manchester Univ. 31-34; Curate, St. Mary, Islington 34-37; Prof. at Wycliffe Coll. Toronto 37-44; Principal, London Coll. of Divinity 44-56; Bishop of Bradford 56-61; Archbishop of York 61-74, of Canterbury Dec. 74-; Hon. Fellow, St. John's Coll., Cambridge 61; Prelate Order of St. John of Jerusalem 67-;
Leisure interests: gardening, motoring, music.
Publs. *A People's Heritage* 44, *The Ministry of the Word* 45, revised edn. 64, *The Glory of God* 50, *Stewards of Grace* 58, *Five Makers of the New Testament* 62, *Christian Priorities* 63, *The Prayers of the New Testament* 67, *Sinews of Faith* 69, *Word and World* 71, *Convictions* 75.
Lambeth Palace, London, S.E.1; Old Palace, Canterbury, Kent, England.

Coghill, Nevill Henry Kendal Aylmer, M.A.; British university teacher; b. 19 April 1899, Castle Townshend,

Co. Cork; *s.* of Sir Egerton Coghill, Bart., and Hilde-garde Coghill; *m.* Elspeth Nora Harley 1927 (dissolved 1933); one *d.*; ed. Haileybury Coll. and Oxford Univ.

Research Fellow, Exeter Coll., Oxford 24; Fellow and Tutor in English Literature 25; Fellow Royal Soc. of English Literature 54; Merton Prof. of English Literature, Oxford 57-66; produced *A Midsummer Night's Dream* (Haymarket Theatre, London) 45, *Pilgrim's Progress* (Covent Garden, London) 51; Gov. Shakespeare Memorial Theatre, Stratford 56; has broadcast on Shakespeare, Chaucer, Langland, etc.; F.R.S.L. 50; Pres. of the Poetry Soc. 64-68; Pres. of the English Assen. 70-71.

Leisure interests: pictures, music, writing.

Publs. *Visions from Piers Plowman, The Poet Chaucer* 49, *The Canterbury Tales* (in modern English) 51, *Geoffrey Chaucer* 56, *Shakespeare's Professional Skills* 64, Co-author (with Martin Starkie) *Canterbury Tales* (theatre) 68, *Troilus and Criseyde* (in modern English); Editor: T. S. Eliot's *Murder in the Cathedral* 65, *The Family Reunion* 69, *The Cocktail Party* 74.

Savran House, Aylburton, nr. Lydney, Glos., England. Telephone: Lydney 2240.

Cohen, Alexander H.; American theatre and television producer; b. 24 July 1920, New York; *s.* of Alexander H. and Laura (Tarantous) Cohen; *m.* 1st Jocelyn Newmark 1942 (divorced), 2nd Hildy Parks 1956; two *s.* one *d.*; ed. New York Univ.

Producer, Broadway 41-, London 63-; Producer, Antoinette Perry (Tony) Awards 67-; productions include *Ivanov, The School for Scandal, At the Drop of a Hat, The Homecoming, The Devils, Unknown Soldier and his Wife, Marlene Dietrich, Victor Borge, Beyond the Fringe, Good Evening, Ulysses in Nighttown, Black Comedy, Ages of Man, Home*; London Productions include *The Price, 1776, Harvey, The Comedians*.

225 West 44th Street, New York, N.Y. 10036; Home: 25 West 54th Street, New York, N.Y. 10019, U.S.A.; Queen's Theatre, 51 Shaftesbury Avenue, London, W1V 8BA; and 21 Parkside, Knightsbridge, London, SW1X 7JW, England.

Telephone: New York 757-1200 (Office); 01-734-6601 (London Office), 01-235-1725 (Home).

Cohen, Manuel Frederick; American fmr. government official; b. 9 Oct. 1912, New York City; *s.* of Edward and Lena Cohen; *m.* Pauline Grossman 1940; one *s.* one *d.*; ed. Brooklyn Coll. of City of New York, and Brooklyn Law School of St. Lawrence Univ.

Research Assoc., Twentieth Century Fund studies of securities markets 33-34; private corporate and real estate practice, New York 37-42; Securities and Exchange Comm. 42-69; Chief Counsel, Div. of Corpn. Finance 52-59, Adviser 59-60, Dir. Div. of Corpn. Finance 60-61, Commr. 61-64, Chair. Securities and Exchange Comm. 64-69; Professorial Lecturer in Law, George Washington Univ. 58-; Chair. Comm. on Auditors Responsibilities; Adviser, American Law Inst., Securities Codification Project; mem. Admin. Conf. of the United States.

Leisure interests: golf, music.

Office: Wilmer, Cutler & Pickering, 1666 K Street, N.W., Washington, D.C.; Home: 6403 Marjory Lane, Bethesda, Md. 20034, U.S.A.

Cohen, Morris, D.SC.; American metallurgist and materials scientist; b. 27 Nov. 1911, Chelsea, Mass.; *s.* of Julius H. and Alice Cohen; *m.* Ruth Krentzman 1937 (deceased); one *s.* one *d.*; ed. Massachusetts Inst. of Technology.

Instructor of Metallurgy M.I.T. 36, Asst. Prof. 37, Assoc. Prof. 41, Prof. of Physical Metallurgy 46, Ford Prof. of Materials Science and Eng. 62-, Institute Prof. 74-; fmr. consultant to U.S. Atomic Energy Comm. and mem. of several govt. panels and advisory cttees.; mem. Nat. Acad. of Sciences, Nat. Acad. of Eng.; Fellow,

American Acad. of Arts and Sciences, N.Y. Acad. of Sciences; Hon. mem. American Soc. for Metals (Pres. 69), Metallurgical Soc. of AIME, British Inst. of Metals, British Iron and Steel Inst., Japan Iron and Steel Inst., Japan Inst. of Metals, American Physical Soc., American Assen. for Advancement of Science, etc.; Hon. mem. Indian Inst. of Metals; has delivered numerous memorial lectures including several to American Soc. for Metals, and Coleman Lecture, Franklin Inst. 60; Kamani Medal, Indian Inst. of Metals 52, Mathewson Gold Medal, AIME 53; Clamer Medal, Franklin Inst. 59, Gold Medal, American Soc. for Metals 68, Gold Medal, Japan Inst. of Metals 70, Médaille Pierre Chevenard, Soc. Française de Métallurgie 71, Killian Faculty Achievement Award, M.I.T. 74.

Leisure interest: art collecting.

Room 13-5046, Department of Materials Science and Engineering, Massachusetts Institute of Technology, Cambridge, Mass. 02139; Home: 491 Puritan Road, Swampscott, Mass. 01907, U.S.A.

Telephone 617-595-1443 (Home); 617-253-3325 (Office).

Cohen, Philip Pacy, PH.D., M.D.; American professor of physiological chemistry; b. 26 Sept. 1908, Derry, N.H.; *s.* of David and Ada (Cottler) Cohen; *m.* Rubye H. Tepper 1935; three *s.* one *d.*; ed. Tufts Coll. and Univ. of Wisconsin.

Professor and Chair., Dept. of Physiological Chem., Univ. of Wisconsin 48-75, H. C. Bradley Prof. of Physiological Chem. 68-; Visiting Prof. Univ. of Calif. at Los Angeles 76; Chair. Cttee. on Growth, Nat. Research Council 54-56; mem. Board of Scientific Counsellors, Nat. Cancer Inst. 57-59, Chair. 59-61; mem. Nat. Advisory Cancer Council, Nat. Insts. of Health 63-67; Dir. Advisory Cttee. Nat. Insts. of Health 66-70; mem. Advisory Cttee. for Medical Research, Pan American Health Org. 67-; mem. Advisory Cttee. for Biology and Medicine, U.S. Atomic Energy Comm. 63-71, Chair. 69-70; mem. Nat. Advisory Arthritis and Metabolic Diseases Council, Nat. Insts. of Health 70-74; mem. Nat. Acad. of Sciences, American Chem. Soc., American Soc. of Biological Chemists, Biochemical Soc. (U.K.); hon. mem. Sociedad Argentina de Investigación Bioquímica, Nat. Acad. of Medicine, Mexico; Fellow, A.A.A.S.; hon. mem. Harvey Soc.

Publs. over 200 papers in fields of intermediary nitrogen metabolism, enzymology, differentiation and development, comparative biochemistry.

Department of Physiological Chemistry, 589 Medical Sciences Bldg., University of Wisconsin, Madison, Wis. 53706; Home: 1117 Oak Way, Madison, Wis. 53706, U.S.A.

Telephone: 608-262-1347 (Office); 608-233-1883 (Home).

Cohen, Ruth Louisa, C.B.E., M.A.; British university official; b. 10 Nov. 1906, Bushey Heath; *d.* of Walter Cohen and Lucy Cobb; ed. Newnham Coll., Cambridge. Commonwealth Fund Fellow, Stanford and Cornell Univs., U.S.A. 30-32; Research Officer, Agricultural Research Inst., Oxford 33-39; with Ministry of Food 39-42, Board of Trade 42-45; Fellow, Newnham Coll., Cambridge 39-54, Principal 54-72, Univ. Lecturer in Econs. 45-.

Publs. *History of Milk Prices* 36, *Economics of Agriculture* 39.

25 Gough Way, Cambridge, England. Telephone: Cambridge 62699.

Cohen, Seymour Stanley, B.S., PH.D.; American bio-chemist; b. 30 April 1917, New York City; *s.* of Herman Cohen and Lena Tanz; *m.* Elaine Pear 1940; one *s.* one *d.*; ed. Coll. of City of New York and Columbia Univ.

NRC Fellow 41-42 (to work with W. Stanley at Rockefeller Inst.), Research Assoc., Johnson Foundation, Univ. of Pa. 43-45; Instructor in Dept. of Pediatrics, Univ. of Pa. 45-50, Assoc. Prof. of Biochemistry and Pediatrics 50-54, Prof. 54-57, Charles Hayden American Cancer Soc. Prof. of Biochemistry 57, Hartzell Prof. and Chair. Dept. of Therapeutic Research, School of Medicine, Univ. of Pa. 63-71; American Cancer Soc. Prof. of Microbiology, Univ. of Colorado School of Medicine 71-; Fellow John Simon Guggenheim Foundation (to work with A. Lwoff and J. Monod at Pasteur Inst., Paris) 47-48; Lalor Fellow, Marine Biology Lab., Woods Hole, Mass. 51-52; Visiting Investigator, Virus Lab., Univ. of Calif. 55, Inst. de Radium, Paris 67; Instructor in Physiology, Marine Biology Lab. 68-; mem. Nat. Acad. of Sciences, Serbian Acad. of Science and Arts; mem. American Acad. of Arts and Sciences; Visiting Prof. Hebrew University (Jerusalem) 69, Collège de France 70-74; Consultant for Science, Amer. Cancer Soc. 73-; mem. Inst. of Medicine 73-; Fogarty Scholar, Nat. Insts. of Health 73-74; Visiting Smithsonian Scholar 73-; Dr. h.c. (Univ. of Louvain, Belgium) 72; Eli Lilly Award of Amer. Soc. of Bacteriology, 51, Mead Johnson Award, Amer. Acad. of Pediatrics 52, Newcomb Cleveland Award (AAAS) 55, Medal, Soc. Chimie Biologique 64, Borden Award, Asscn. Amer. Medical Colls., Passano Award 74.

Leisure interests: tennis, history.

Publs. *Virus-Induced Enzymes* (The Jesup Lectures) 68, *Introduction to the Polyamines* 71, about 200 papers.

635 Ash Street, Denver, Colo. 80220, U.S.A.

Telephone: 322-6783 (Home); 394-8049 (Office).

Cohen, Wilbur Joseph, PH.B., L.H.D.; American government official and educator; b. 10 June 1913, Milwaukee, Wis.; s. of Aaron Cohen and Bessie Rubenstein; m. Eloise Bittel 1938; three s.; ed. Univ. of Wisconsin.

With Cttee. Econ. Security 34-35; Social Security Admin. 36-56; Prof. Public Welfare Admin., Univ. of Michigan 56-; Asst. Sec. Dept. of Health, Educ. and Welfare 61-65, Under-Sec. 65-68, Sec. 68-69; Dean, School of Education, Univ. of Michigan 69-; Prof. of Educ., Univ. of Michigan 69-; mem. Board of Govs., Haifa Univ. 71-; Chair. President's Task Force on Health and Social Security 60; Pres. American Public Welfare Asscn. 75-76; mem. American Econ. Asscn., Industrial Relations Research Asscn., American Public Welfare Asscn., American Public Health Asscn. and numerous cttees.; Distinguished Service Award of Dept. of Health, Educ. and Welfare 56, Group Health Asscn. 56; Florina Lasker Award 61; Blanche Ittleson Award 62; Nat. Conf. Social Welfare, Distinguished Service Award 57, Bronfman Public Health Prize 57, Rockefeller Public Service Award 67, Arthur J. Altmeyer Award, Dept. of Health, Educ. and Welfare 72.

Leisure interests: philately, sawing wood.

Publs. *Retirement Policies in Social Security* 57, *Social Security: Programs, Problems and Policies* (with W. Haber) 60, Co-author *Income and Welfare in the United States* 62, numerous articles.

School of Education, University of Michigan, Ann Arbor, Mich.; Home: 620 Oxford Road, Ann Arbor, Mich. 48104; 9819 Capitol View Avenue, Silver Spring, Md. 29010, U.S.A.

Telephone: 313-764-9470 (Office); 313-663-6931, 301-565-0731 (Home).

Cohen of Birkenhead, 1st Baron, cr. 56; **Rt. Hon. Henry Cohen,** Kt., C.H., K.ST.J., M.D., F.R.C.P., F.S.A., F.R.S.A., J.P., D.L.; British physician; b. 1900, Birkenhead; s. of Isaac and Dora Cohen; ed. St. John's School, Birkenhead, Birkenhead Inst., Liverpool, London and Paris Univs.

Physician, Royal Infirmary, Liverpool 24-65; Prof. of Medicine, Liverpool Univ. 34-65; Bradshaw Lecturer, R.C.P. 40; Skinner Lecturer, Faculty of Radiologists 42; Lettsomian Lecturer, Medical Soc. of London 44; Moynihan Lecturer, Royal Coll. of Surgeons 48; Newsholme Lecturer, Univ. of London 50; Croonian Lecturer, Royal Coll. of Physicians 63, Harveian Orator 70, Woodhull Lecturer, Royal Inst. 73; Pres. Royal Soc. of Medicine, Royal Soc. of Health, Gen. Medical Council, Int. Acad. of History of Medicine, Asscn. for Study of Medical Educ., Nat. Children's Bureau, Children's Research Fund, Nat. Soc. of Clean Air, Asscn. of Physicians, Great Britain and Ireland; fmr. Chair. Cen. Health Services Council, Standing Medical Advisory Cttee., Ministry of Health; Governing Trustee, Nuffield Provincial Hospitals Trust; mem. Asscn. British Neurologists, Physiological Soc., Société Internationale de Gastro-entérologie; Crown rep. on Gen. Medical Council 45-72; Pres. B.M.A. 50; Chancellor Univ. of Hull 70-; Hon. Fellow, Jesus Coll., Cambridge Univ.; Hon. Master of the Bench, Inner Temple, London; medals include Gold Medal of B.M.A., Nuffield and Triennial Gold Medals of Royal Soc. of Medicine; Hon. F.A.C.P., F.R.C.P.Ed., F.R.C.P.I., F.R.C.P.S., F.R.I.C., F.C.S., F.R.C.R., F.F.A.R.C.S. Eng., F.D.S.R.C.S.Eng., F.R.C.S.Eng., F.R.S.M., F.A.P.H.A., F.R.S.H., F.R.C.O.G., F.R.C.G.P., F.B.Ps.S., F.P.S.; Hon. Freeman of Birkenhead 56, of Liverpool 70; Hon. Freeman of Soc. of Apothecaries 68; numerous hon. degrees including Oxford, Cambridge, London, Liverpool, Manchester, Hull, Dublin, New York.

Leisure interests: theatre, music, literature.

Publs. *New Pathways in Medicine* 35, *The Nature, Method and Purpose of Diagnosis* 43, *Sherrington* 58, articles in *Surgery of Modern Warfare* 41, contributed to *Lancet* volume on *Prognosis*, *Modern Methods of Treatment*, *Pye's Surgical Handicraft*, also *British Encyclopaedia of Medical Practice* (Editor).

31 Rodney Street, Liverpool 1, England.

Telephone: 051-709-2233.

Cohn, Haim; Israeli lawyer; b. 11 March 1911, Lübeck, Germany; s. of Zeev Cohn and Miriam Cohn (née Carlebach); m. 1st Else Benjamin 1933, 2nd Michal Smoira; one s. one d.; ed. Univs. of Munich, Hamburg and Frankfurt-on-Main, Germany, Hebrew Univ. of Jerusalem and Govt. Law School, Jerusalem.

Admitted to Bar of Palestine 37; Sec. Legal Council, Jewish Agency for Palestine, Jerusalem 47; State Attorney, Ministry of Justice, Hakirya 48, Dir.-Gen. 49; Attorney-Gen., Govt. of Israel 50; Minister of Justice and Acting Attorney-Gen. 52; Attorney-Gen., later Justice, Supreme Court of Israel 60-; mem. Perm. Court of Arbitration, The Hague 62-, UN Comm. on Human Rights 57-59, 65-67; Deputy Chair. Council of Higher Educ., Israel 58-71; mem. Board of Govs., Int. Inst. of Human Rights, Strasbourg; Chair. Exec. Council Hebrew Univ. of Jerusalem; Visiting Prof. of Law, Univ. of Tel-Aviv; Visiting Prof. of Jurisprudence, Hebrew University of Jerusalem; mem. Int. Comm. of Jurists, Pres. Int. Asscn. of Jewish Lawyers and Jurists.

Publ. *The Foreign Laws of Marriage and Divorce* (English) 37, *Glaube and Glaubensfreiheit* (German) 67, *The Trial and Death of Jesus* (Hebrew) 68, *The Trial and Death of Jesus* (English) 71, *Jewish Law in Ancient and Modern Israel* (English) 72.

36 Tchernihovsky Street, Jerusalem, Israel.

Telephone: (02) 3-9973.

Cohn, Mildred, M.A., PH.D.; American professor of biophysics; b. 12 July 1913, New York City; d. of Isidore M. Cohn and Bertha Klein; m. Henry Primakoff 1938; one s. two d.; ed. Hunter Coll. and Columbia Univ. Cornell Univ. Medical Coll., New York 38-46; Washington Univ. Medical School, St. Louis, Mo. 46-60; Prof. of Biophysics and Physical Biochem., Univ. of Pennsylvania School of Medicine 61-; mem. American Acad. of Arts and Sciences, Nat. Acad. of Sciences; Garvan Medal, American Chem. Soc.; Hon. Sc.D. (Women's Medical Coll. of Pennsylvania) 66.

Leisure interest: hiking.

Publs. articles in professional journals etc.

Johnson Research Foundation, University of Pennsylvania School of Medicine, A-611 Richards Bldg., Philadelphia, Pa. 19174; Home: Hampton House, 1600 Hagy's Ford Road, Narberth, Pa. 19072, U.S.A. Telephone: 215-594-8794 (Office); MO7-4674 (215) (Home).

Coïdan, Paul, LIC. EN DROIT; French civil servant; b. 3 Aug. 1911, Tripoli, Lebanon; s. of Michel and Marie Henriette Coïdan (née Pierson); m. Evelyn C. Sandison 1938; two s. one d.; ed. Univ. of Paris.
Joined Cen. Admin. of Finance 32, with Budget Office, then Senate Finance Comm.; Head, Office of Econ. Affairs 44; with UN 46-, Head Budget Div. 49, Head Financial Services, Geneva 55, Dir. Internal Audit 60, Dir. World Food Programme 63; Dir. External Relations, UNCTAD 65; Dir. Budget, UN 70; Asst. Dir.-Gen. UN, Geneva 73-.
United Nations Office, Palais des Nations, Geneva; Home: La Tuilière, 1249 Dardagny/Geneva, Switzerland.

Coing, Helmut, DR. JUR.; German jurist; b. 28 Feb. 1912; ed. Hanover, Lille, Kiel, Munich and Göttingen.
Professor of Jurisprudence, Goethe Univ. Frankfurt (Main) 40, Ord. Prof. 48, Faculty Dean 50-51, Univ. Rector 55-57; Pres. West German Conf. of Rectors 56-57, Wissenschaftsrat 58-61; Chair. Wissenschaftlicher Beirat, F. Thyssen-Stiftung 61-; Dir. Max Planck Inst. for History of European Law 64-; mem. Bayerische Akad. der Wissenschaften, Accademia delle Scienze dell'Istituto di Bologna 65; Commendatore Ordine al Merito (Italy); Grosses Verdienstkreuz des Verdienstordens der Bundesrepublik Deutschland, Officier de la Légion d'Honneur (France), Orden Pour le Mérite für Wissenschaft und Künste 73, etc.; Dr. Iur. h.c. Lyon, Montpellier, Vienna, Aberdeen and Brussels.
Publs. *Die Rezeption des Römischen Rechts in Frankfurt am Main* 39, *Die obersten Grundsätze des Rechts* 47, *Grundzüge der Rechtsphilosophie* 50, 69, *Lehrbuch des Erbrechts* 53, *Staudinger-Kommentar zum Allgemeinen Teil des BGB* 57, *Römisches Recht in Deutschland* (contribution to *Ius Romanum Medii Aevi*) 64, *Epochen d. Rechtsgeschichte in Deutschland* 67, 71, *Rechtsformen der privaten Vermögensverwaltung insbesondere durch Banken in U.S.A. und Deutschland* 67, *Die Treuhand kraft privaten Rechtsgeschäfts* 73; Editor; *Grundzüge der Rechtsphilosophie* 69, *Handbuch der Quellen und Literatur der neueren europäischen Privatrechtsgeschichte* 73, *Methoden der Rechts-Leitlichung* 74.
Holzhecke 14, 6 Frankfurt-am-Main, Federal Republic of Germany.

Cointat, Michel; French agronomist and politician; b. 13 April 1921; Paris, s. of Lucien Cointat and Marie-Louise Adam; m. Simone Dubois 1942; two s.; ed. Ecole Nat. des Eaux et Forêts.
Inspector of water and forests, Uzès, Gard 43-49; Inspector forests of Haute-Marne 50-58; Dir. Gen. Soc. for Devt. of waste ground and scrub lands of East Chaumont 58-61, Pres. 61-71; Dir. du Cabinet, Ministry of Agriculture 61-62, Dir. Gen. of Production and Supply 62-67; Pres. Special Agricultural Cttee. to EEC 65; Minister of Agriculture 71-72; Deputy Union Démocratique pour la République for Ille-et-Vilaine 67-; mem. European Parl. 68-71, 74-; Mayor of Fougères 71-; mem. Nat. Assembly; Pres. Financial Comm. in Regional Council of Brittany; Pres. Special Comm. to examine proposed land law; mem. various local socs.; Chev. de la Légion d'Honneur; Officier de l'Ordre Nat. du Mérite; Commandeur du Mérite Agricole; Officier des Palmes Académiques; Chevalier de L'Economie Nat.; Grand Officier du Mérite de l'Allemagne Fédérale; Grand Officier de l'Ordre de Victoria; Commandeur du Mérite Italien; Grand Officier de l'Ordre de la Haute-Volta.
Publs. About 400 articles on agriculture, forestry,

fishing and related subjects; collections of poems: *Souvenirs du Temps Perdu* 57, *Poèmes à Clio* 65, *Les Heures Orangées* 74.
Assemblée Nationale, Paris 7e; 89 Faubourg St. Denis, Paris 10e, France.
Telephone: 770-58-27.

Coke, Gerald Edward, C.B.E.; British merchant banker; b. 25 Oct. 1907, London; s. of Hon. Sir John Coke, K.C.V.O., and Hon. Mrs. Coke; m. Patricia Cadogan 1939; three s. (one s. deceased) one d.; ed. Eton and New Coll., Oxford.
Lieutenant-Colonel, Second World War; Chair. Rio Tinto Co. Ltd. 56-62; Dep. Chair. Rio Tinto-Zinc Corpn. 62-66, Dir. 47-75; Deputy Chair. Mercury Securities Ltd. 64-70; fmr. Dir. S. G. Warburg and Co. Ltd., United Kingdom Provident Inst. and other companies; Treas. Bridewell Royal Hospital (King Edward's School), Witley 46-72; Chair. Glyndebourne Arts Trust 55-; Gov. Royal Acad. of Music 57-73; Dir. Royal Opera House, Covent Garden 59-64; Gov. of BBC 61-66; Hon. F.R.A.M.; D.L. (Hants.) 74.
Jenkyn Place, Bentley, Hants., England.

Colbert, Edwin Harris, A.M., D.SC. PH.D.; American vertebrate palaeontologist; b. 25 Sept. 1905, Clarinda, Iowa; s. of George H. and Mary A. Colbert; m. Margaret Matthew 1933; five s.; ed. Univ. of Nebraska and Columbia Univ.
Student Asst. Univ. of Nebraska 26-29; Univ. Fellow Columbia Univ. 29-30; Research Asst. American Museum of Natural History 30-32, Asst. Curator 33-42, Curator and Chair. Dept. of Amphibians and Reptiles 44-45, Chair. Dept. of Geology and Palaeontology 58-60; Dept. of Vertebrate Palaeontology 60-66, Curator 66-70, Curator Emer. 70-; Prof. Vertebrate Palaeontology, Columbia Univ. 45-69, Prof. Emer. 69-; Assoc. Curator, Acad. of Natural Sciences of Philadelphia 37-48; Research Assoc., Museum of N. Arizona 54-68, Curator of Vertebrate Palaeontology 69-; mem. Nat. Acad. of Sciences; Pres. Society of Vertebrate Palaeontology 46-47, Society for Study of Evolution 58; Vice-Pres. Palaeontological Soc. 63-; Daniel Giraud Elliot Medal (N.A.S.); American Museum of Nat. History Medal 70.
Leisure interests: history, travel.
Publs. *The Dinosaur Book* 51, *Evolution of the Vertebrates* 55, 69, *Millions of Years Ago: Prehistoric Life in North America* 58, *Dinosaurs* 61, *Stratigraphy and Life History* (with Marshall Kay) 65, *The Age of Reptiles* 65, *Men and Dinosaurs* 68, *Wandering Lands and Animals* 73, and over 300 papers, etc.
The Museum of Northern Arizona, Flagstaff, Arizona 86001, U.S.A.
Telephone: 602-774-6265.

Colbert, Lester Lum, B.B.A., LL.B.; American automobile manufacturer; b. 13 June 1905; ed. Texas and Harvard Univs.
Cotton buyer, Texas 21-29; Law practice with Larkin, Rathbone and Perry (New York City) 29-33; joined Chrysler Corpn. 33; Resident Attorney 33-36; Vice-Pres. Dodge Div. 36-46; Gen. Man. Dodge Chicago plant (aircraft engines) 43-46; Pres. Dodge Div. 46-51; Vice-Pres. Chrysler Corpn. 49-50, Dir. 49-61, Pres. 50-61, Chair of Board 60-61; Trustee Hanover Bank and Automotive Safety Foundation 55-61; mem. Automobile Manufacturers' Asscn.; mem. American Bar Asscn.; mem. National Industrial Conf. Board; Hon. LL.D. Bethany Coll.; Chevalier de la Légion d'Honneur.
Office: Fisher Building, Detroit 31, Mich.; Home: 491 Martell Drive, Bloomfield Hills, Mich., U.S.A.

Colby, William Egan, B.A., LL.B.; American lawyer and government official; b. 4 Jan. 1920, St. Paul, Minn.; s. of Elbridge and Margaret Colby (née Egan); m.

Barbara Heinzen 1945; three *s.* one *d.*; ed. Princeton and Columbia Univs.

Served to rank of Maj., U.S. Army 41-45; admitted to N.Y. State Bar 47; Attorney Donovan, Leisure, Newton & Irvine 47-49; mem. Nat. Labor Relations Board 49-50; Attaché, American Embassy, Stockholm 51-53, Rome 53-58, First Sec., Saigon 59-62; Head, Far East Div., Cen. Intelligence Agency 62-67; Amb., Dir. Civil Operations and Rural Devt. Support, Saigon 68-71; Exec. Dir. CIA 72-73, Dir. Sept. 73-75; Silver Star, St. Olav Medal (Norway), Croix de Guerre (France), Dept. of State Distinguished Honor Award, Grand Officer, Nat. Order of Viet-Nam.

Central Intelligence Agency, Washington, D.C. 20505, U.S.A.

Coldstream, Sir William Menzies, Kt., C.B.E., D.LITT.; British painter and university professor; b. 28 Feb. 1908, Belford, Northumberland; *s.* of George Probyn Coldstream and Lillian Mercer Tod; *m.* 1st Nancy Culliford Sharp 1931 (dissolved 1942), two *d.*; *m.* 2nd Monica M. Hoyer 1961, one *s.* two *d.*; ed. privately and Slade School of Fine Art, Univ. Coll., London.

Slade Prof., Slade School of Fine Art, Univ. Coll. London 49-75; Trustee Nat. Gallery 48-55, 56-63, Tate Gallery 49-55, 56-63; Chair. Art Panel, Arts Council 53-62, Vice-Chair. Arts Council of Great Britain 62-69; Dir. Royal Opera House, Covent Garden 57-62; Chair. Nat. Advisory Council on Art Educ. 58-72, British Film Inst. 64-71; Hon. D.Litt. (Nottingham and Birmingham Univs.).

Slade School of Fine Art, University College London, Gower Street, London, W.C.1, England.

Telephone: 01-387-7050.

Cole, Baron (Life Peer) cr. 65, of Blackfriars; **George James Cole,** G.B.E.; British businessman; b. 3 Feb. 1906, Singapore; *s.* of James Cole and Alice Wheeler; *m.* Ruth Harpham 1940; one *s.* one *d.*; ed. Raffles Inst., Singapore.

Joined Niger Co. Ltd. (subsidiary of Lever Bros. Ltd. later merged into United Africa Co. Ltd.) 23; various posts in London and Africa, Controller for British West Africa 39; Dir. United Africa Co. Ltd. 45-63, Joint Man. Dir. 52-55; Dir. Taylor Woodrow (West Africa) Ltd. 47-55; Dir. Palm Line Ltd. 49-55, Chair. 52-55; Dir. Unilever Ltd. 48-, Vice-Chair. 56-60, Chair. 60-70; Chair. Rolls-Royce (1971) Ltd. 71-72; Dir. Unilever N.V. 48-, Vice-Chair. 60-70; Dir. Finance Corpn. for Industry Ltd. 57-73; Dir. Shell Transport and Trading Co. 71-; Chair. The Leverhulme Trust Fund, Trustee of the Civic Trust; Deputy Chair. Board of Govs., London Graduate School of Business Studies 63-70; Chair. Govt. Advisory Cttee. on the Appointment of Advertising Agents 60-70; Vice-Pres. Royal African Soc., The Luso-Brazilian Council, The Hispanic Council, The Inc. Liverpool School of Tropical Medicine; Gov. Nat. Inst. of Econ. and Social Research; mem. of Council of Royal Inst. of Int. Affairs.

50 Victoria Road, London, W.8, England.

Telephone: 01-937-9085.

Cole, Charles Woolsey, M.A., PH.D., L.H.D., LL.D., LITT.D., SC.D.; American ex-college president, diplomatist, consultant and author; b. 8 Feb. 1906, Montclair, N.J.; *s.* of Charles and Bertha Cole; *m.* 1st Katharine Salmon 1928 (deceased 1972), two *d.*; *m.* 2nd Marie G. Donahoe 1974; ed. Amherst Coll., and Columbia Univ.

Instructor in History, Columbia Univ. 29-35; Travelling Fellow, Social Science Research Council (Paris) 32-33; Assoc. Prof. Econs., Amherst Coll. 35-37, George D. Olds Prof. of Econs. 37-40; Prof. of History, Columbia Univ. 40-46; Pres. Amherst Coll. 46-60; Vice-Pres. Rockefeller Foundation 60-61; U.S. Ambassador to Chile 61-64; mem. Council on Foreign Relations. Leisure interests: fly-fishing, gardening.

Publs. *French Mercantilist Doctrines Before Colbert* 31, *Colbert and a Century of French Mercantilism* (2 vols.) 39, *Economic History of Europe* (with S. B. Clough) 41, *French Mercantilism 1638-1700* 43, *History of Europe* (with C. J. H. Hayes and M. Baldwin) 49, *History of Western Civilization* (with C. J. H. Hayes and M. Baldwin) 62, 67, *A Free People* (2 vols.) (with H. W. Bragdon and S. P. McCutchen) 70.

The Highlands, Seattle, Wash. 98177, U.S.A.

Telephone: 206-364-5747.

Cole, Sir David Lee, K.C.M.G., M.C.; British diplomatist; b. 31 Aug. 1920, Newmarket, Suffolk; *s.* of Brig. and Mrs. D. H. Cole; *m.* Dorothy Patton 1945; one *s.*; ed. Cheltenham Coll., and Sidney Sussex Coll., Cambridge.

Royal Inniskilling Fusiliers, Second World War; Dominions Office 47; U.K. Del. to United Nations, New York 48-51; First Sec., British High Comm., New Delhi 53-56; Private Sec. to Sec.of State for Commonwealth Relations 56-60; Head, Personnel Dept., Commonwealth Relations Office 61-63; Dep. High Commr. in Ghana 63-64, Acting High Commr. 63; High Commr. in Malawi 64-67; Minister (Political), High Comm., New Delhi, 67-70; Asst. Under-Sec. of State, Foreign and Commonwealth Office 70-73; Amb. to Thailand 73-.

Leisure interest: watercolour painting.

British Embassy, Ploenchit Road, Bangkok, Thailand; and c/o Foreign and Commonwealth Office, London, S.W.1, England.

Cole, Edward N.; American automobile executive; b. 17 Sept. 1909, Michigan; *s.* of Franklin B. Cole and Lucy C. Blasen; *m.* twice; five *c.*; ed. Grand Rapids Junior Coll., and General Motors Inst., Flint, Michigan.

Joined Gen. Motors Corpn. as Lab. Asst. 30; successively lab. technician, technician and designer, engineer, Chief Design Engineer, Asst. Chief Engineer, Chief Engineer, Works Man., Plant Man. Cadillac—Cleveland Tank Plant, Chief Engineer and Gen. Man. Chevrolet Motors Div. Detroit, Group Vice-Pres. of Car and Truck Divs. Gen. Motors; Exec. Vice-Pres. and Head of Operations Staff, Gen. Motors 65-67; Pres. Gen. Motors 67-74; Chair. of Exec. Cttee. Maritime Fruit Carriers 75-; designed new engine for G.M. Tank used in World War II, the *Corvair* rear-engine car; mem. Soc. Automotive Engineers, American Ordnance Asscn., Motor Vehicle Manufacturers Asscn. of U.S.; many hon. degrees.

Leisure interests: hunting, fishing, skiing, sailing, flying, gardening, working in home repair shop.

c/o General Motors Building, Detroit, Mich. 48202, U.S.A.

Cole, Kenneth S(tewart), A.B., PH.D., SC.D., M.D.; American biophysicist; b. 10 July 1900, Ithaca, N.Y.; *s.* of Charles Nelson Cole and Mabel Stewart Cole; *m.* Elizabeth Evans Roberts 1932 (deceased); one *s.* one *d.*; ed. Oberlin Coll. and Cornell Univ.

Assistant and Assoc. Prof. or Physiology, Coll. of Physicians and Surgeons, Columbia Univ. 29-46; Principal Biophysicist, Metallurgical Lab., Univ. of Chicago 42-46; Prof. of Biophysics and Physiology, Univ. of Chicago 46-49; Dir. Naval Medical Research Inst. 49-54; Chief, Laboratory of Biophysics, Nat. Inst. of Neurological Diseases and Blindness, Nat. Insts. of Health 54-66, Senior Research Biophysicist 66-; Prof. of Biophysics, Univ. of Calif., Berkeley 65-; mem. Nat. Acad. of Sciences; Foreign mem Royal Soc., London; Order of Southern Cross, Brazil 66; Nat. Medal of Science, U.S.A. 67.

Leisure interests: sailing, music.

Publ. *Membranes, Ions and Impulses* 68.

36-2A31 National Institutes of Health, Bethesda, Md. 20014, U.S.A.

Telephone: 301-496-3204.

Cole, Dame Margaret Isabel, D.B.E.; British historian and writer; b. 6 May 1893, Cambridge; *d.* of Prof. J. P. Postgate and Edith Allen; *m.* G. D. H. Cole 1918 (deceased); one *s.* two *d.*; ed. Roedean School and Girton Coll., Cambridge.
Classical Mistress St. Paul's Girls' School London 14-17; Asst. Sec. Labour Research Dept. 17-26; Tutorial Class Tutor Univ. of London 25-46; Hon. Sec. New Fabian Research Bureau 35-39; Hon. Sec. Fabian Society 39-53, Vice-Chair. 54-55, Chair. 55-56, Pres. 62-; Alderman, London County Council 52-65, Chair. Further Educ. Cttee. 50-59, 60-65, Vice-Chair. 59-60, 64-67; Chair. Battersea Coll. of Educ. 62-67; mem. Inner London Educ. Authority 64-67; Chair. Geffrye Museum 52-67; Chair. Sidney Webb Coll. 61-72, Vice-Chair. 72-75.
Publs. *The New Economic Revolution, Books and the People, Women of To-Day, Marriage, Past and Present, Education for Democracy, Evacuation Survey* (with R. Padley), *Beatrice Webb, Makers of the Labour Movement, Growing up into Revolution, Robert Owen, Servant of the County, Story of Fabian Socialism, Life of G. D. H. Cole* 71; Editor: *Democratic Sweden, Our Soviet Ally, Twelve Studies in Soviet Russia, The Road to Success, The Webbs and their Work, Our Partnership, Beatrice Webb's Diaries 1912-24* and *1924-32*; wrote many detective novels, books and pamphlets on social subjects jointly with the late G. D. H. Cole, contributor to periodicals and collective works.
Leisure interests: reading, art galleries.
4 Ashdown, Clivedon Court, Clevelands, London, W13 8DR, England.
Telephone: 01-997-8114.

Cole, Sterling, B.A., LL.B.; American lawyer and public servant; b. 18 April 1904, Painted Post, N.Y.; *s.* of Ernest and Minnie (Pierce) Cole; *m.* Mary Elizabeth Thomas 1929; three *s.*; ed. Colgate Univ. and Albany Law School, Union Univ.
Practised law in Bath, N.Y. 29-34; mem. U.S. House of Representatives 34-57, Chair. Joint Cttee. on Atomic Energy 53-54, and mem. of several other House Cttees.; Dir.-Gen. Int. Atomic Energy Agency, Vienna 57-61; mem. Washington Inst. of Foreign Affairs; Advisory Council for Center for Int. Studies, Graz, Austria; private legal practice, Washington 61-; Fed. Rep. to the Southern Inter-state Nuclear Board; mem. American, Fed., State of Va. and District of Columbia Bar Asscns.; Hon. LL.D. (Colgate Univ.), Hon. D.Sc. (Union Coll.), Hon. LL.D. (Elmira Coll.); Order of Merit (Italy); Great Golden Decoration of Honour for Merits (Austria); Republican.
Cole & Cole, 919 18th Street, N.W., Washington, D.C., U.S.A.
Telephone: 452-0166.

Coleman, James Samuel, PH.D.; American sociologist; b. 12 May 1926, Bedford, Ind.; *s.* of late James F. Coleman and of Maurine L. Coleman; *m.* 1st Lucille Richley 1949 (divorced 1973), 2nd Zdzislawa Walaszek 1973; three *s.*; ed. Purdue and Columbia Univs.
Research Assoc., Bureau of Applied Social Research, Columbia Univ. 53-55; Fellow, Center for Advanced Study in the Behavioural Sciences 55-56; Asst. Prof., Dept. of Sociology, Univ. of Chicago 56-59; Assoc. Prof., Dept. of Social Relations, Johns Hopkins Univ. 59, Prof. of Social Relations 61-73; Prof. of Sociology, Univ. of Chicago 73-; mem. President's Science Advisory Cttee. 70-73; mem. American Acad. of Arts and Sciences, Nat. Acad. of Science; Guggenheim Fellow 66; Hon. LL.D. (Purdue Univ.).
Publs. *Union Democracy* (co-author) 56, *The Adolescent Society* 61, *Introduction to Mathematical Sociology* 64, *Equality of Educational Opportunity* (co-author) 66, *Resources for Social Change: Race in the United States* 71, *The Mathematics of Collective Action* 73, *Power and the Structure of Society* 74.

Department of Sociology, University of Chicago, Chicago, Ill. 60637; Home: 5535 Blackstone Street, Chicago, Ill. 60637, U.S.A.
Telephone: 312-753-2363 (Office); 312-241-7461 (Home).

Coleman, S. Othello; Liberian international bank official; b. 12 Feb. 1928, Monrovia, Liberia; *m.*; four *c.*; ed. Liberia Coll., American Int. Coll., Springfield, Mass.
Self-employed 54-60; Asst. Research Officer, Bureau of Econ. Research, then Research Officer 60-61; Asst. Dir. of Econ. Research and Planning in charge of Bureau of Plans, Preparation and Co-ordination, Nat. Planning Agency 62-63; Dir. of Projects Preparation, Review, Evaluation and Aid Co-ordination, Nat. Planning Agency 64; Alternate Dir., Int. Bank for Reconstruction and Devt., Int. Finance Corpn., and Int. Devt. Asscn. 64-66, Exec. Dir. Nov. 66-70; Amb. to European Communities 74-.
1640 Rhode-St.-Genèse, 18 avenue des Touristes, Brussels, Belgium.

Coleman, William Thaddeus, Jr.; American lawyer and government official; b. 7 July 1920, Philadelphia; ed. Univ. of Pennsylvania, Harvard Law School.
Law Sec. to Judge Herbert Goodrich, U.S. Court of Appeals, Third Circuit 47; Law Clerk, U.S. Supreme Court 48; Assoc. Paul, Weiss, Rifkind, Wharton & Garrison, law firm 49-52; Assoc. Dilworth, Paxson, Kalish, Levy & Coleman 52, Partner 56-75; mem. President's Cttee. on Govt. Employment Policy 59-61; Consultant to U.S. Arms Control and Disarmament Agency 63-75; mem. Nat. Comm. on Productivity 71-72; U.S. Sec. for Transportation March 75-; Dir. Pan American Airways Inc., Penn Mutual Life Insurance Co., First Pa. Corpn.; mem. Board of Govs., American Stock Exchange; Trustee, Rand Corpn., Brookings Inst.
Department of Transportation, Washington, D.C. 20590, U.S.A.

Colin, André, D. EN D.; French politician; b. 19 Jan. 1910; ed. Collège de Brest and Paris Univ.
After military service, Sec. French Asscn. Catholic Youth; elected Pres. Gen. 36; Prof. of Faculty of Law, Lille; naval officer for Maritime Law in Levant 39; opposed Armistice and appealed to all Frenchmen to support De Gaulle; returned to France and active in Resistance; mem. Algiers Consultative Assembly 43; worked secretly to found Mouvement Républicain de Libération which became Mouvement Républicain Populaire (Christian Party) of which he was appointed Sec. Gen.; mem. Nat. Council of Resistance and Consultative Assembly Paris elected Sec. of its Youth Comm.; Deputy for Finistère 45-; Sec. of State in Prime Minister's Office 46-48; Minister for Merchant Navy 48-50; Sec. of State for Interior 50 and 51; Minister of the Interior 53; Minister, France d'Outre-Mer May 58; del. European Parl. 58; Senator 59; National Pres. Mouvement Républicain Populaire 59-63, Pres. M.R.P. in Senate 63-68, Groupe d'Union centriste des démocrates de progrès 68-71; mem. European Parl. 58, 66-; Pres. Conseil général du Finistère; Chevalier Légion d'Honneur, Croix de Guerre, Médaille de la Résistance.
Sénat, Palais du Luxembourg, Paris 6e, France.

Colina Riquelme, Rafael de la; Mexican diplomatist; b. 20 Sept. 1898, Tulancingo; *s.* of the late Prof. Manuel and Mrs. de la Colina; *m.* Amanda Steinmeyer 1944; three *c.*
Chancellor, Consular Service of Mexico, Philadelphia, Pa. 18-22; various diplomatic posts rising to Amb. to U S A. 49-53; Perm. Rep. to UN 53-59; Amb. to Canada 59-62, to Japan 62-64; Perm. Rep. to Org. of American State 65-; mem. INTELSAT Arbitration Panel 71; several foreign decorations.
Secretaría de Relaciones Exteriores, Mexico, D.F., Mexico.

Collado, Emilio Gabriel, S.B., A.M., PH.D.; American oil company executive; b. 20 Dec. 1910, Cranford, N.J.; s. of Emilio Gabriel Collado and Carrie (Hansee) Collado; m. 1st Janet Gilbert 1932, one s. one d.; m. 2nd Maria Elvira Tanco 1972; ed. Phillips Acad., Andover, Massachusetts Inst. of Technology and Harvard.
U.S. Treasury Dept. 34-36; Fed. Reserve Bank of N.Y. 36-38; U.S. State Dept. 38-46; Associate Economic Adviser, Special Asst. to Under-Sec., Dir. of Office of Financial and Development Policy, Deputy on Financial Affairs; Alternate, Inter-American Financial and Economic Advisory Cttee. 39-45; Alternate, Inter-American Economic and Social Council 45-46; mem. Inter-American Statistical Inst. 43-46; Chair. Inter-American Coffee Board 43-44; Trustee Export-Import Bank of Washington 44-45; U.S. Exec. Dir. Int. Bank of Reconstruction and Development 46-47; Standard Oil Co. (New Jersey) (now Exxon Corpn.) 47-, Treas. 54-60, Dir. 60, Vice-Pres. 62-66, Exec. Vice-Pres. 66-; Chair. U.S.A./B.I.A.C. for Organization for European Co-operation and Development (OECD), Discount Corpn. of New York; mem. Council on Foreign Relations; mem. and Dir. Nat. Bureau of Econ. Research; Chair. Cttee. for Econ. Devt. and Chair. of its Research and Policy Cttee.; Trustee American Econ. Assen., Hispanic Soc. of America; mem. American Acad. of Arts and Sciences, U.S. Council of Int. Chamber of Commerce.
Leisure interests: racquets, tennis.
Exxon Corporation, 1251 Avenue of the Americas, New York, N.Y. 10020; 435 East 52nd Street, New York, N.Y. 10022, U.S.A.

Colley, George Joseph; Irish solicitor and politician; b. 18 Oct. 1925, Dublin; s. of Henry E. Colley and Christina Nugent; m. Mary Doolan 1950; three s. four d.; ed. Scoil Mhuire, Marino, St. Joseph's Christian Brothers' School, Fairview, and Univ. Coll., Dublin.
Member of Dáil Éireann for Dublin N.E. 61-69, for Dublin N.C. 69-; mem. Legal Cttee. and Political Cttee., Council of Europe (Irish Parl. Del.) 62-64; Leader, Irish Del. to Council of Europe 64-65; Parl. Sec. to Minister for Lands and Fisheries 64-65; Minister for Educ. 65-66, for Industry and Commerce 66-69, for Industry, Commerce and the Gaeltacht 69-70, for Finance and the Gaeltacht 70-73; Chair. OECD Council 72; Fianna Fáil.
10 Palmerston Gardens, Rathmines, Dublin 6, Ireland.

Collier, Gershon Beresford Onesimus, M.A., B.C.L., B.L., LL.M., J.S.D.; Sierra Leonean professor and lawyer; b. 16 Feb. 1927; s. of Samuel Adolphus Collier and Maria Jeanette Collier; m. Fashn Dora 1954; one s.; ed. Fourah Bay Coll., Sierra Leone, Durham Univ., England, Middle Temple, London and N.Y. Univ.
Ambassador of Sierra Leone to UN 61-63, 64-67, to U.S.A. 63-67; Vice-Pres. UN Gen. Assembly (19th Session) 65-66; Chair. UN Cttee. on Colonialism; mem. UN Legal Cttee. on Peaceful Uses of Outer Space 64-67; Chief Justice of Sierra Leone Jan.-April 67; Senior Fellow, Centre for Int. Studies, N.Y. Univ. 67-69; mem. many Sierra Leonean and UN dels. to int. confs.; Prof. of Law and African Politics, State Univ. of N.Y. at Albany 72-; study leave and general legal practice, Sierra Leone 74-; Hon. LL.D. (Univ. of N.Y., Troy).
Leisure interests: tennis, swimming, fishing.
Publs. Sierra Leone: Experiment in Democracy in an African Nation 70; chapter in: Committee of 24 Review of United Nations Affairs 65 and Human Rights in Sierra Leone 65.
Department of Afro-American Studies, State University of New York at Albany, Albany, New York, U.S.A.; Home: 4 Percival Street, Freetown, Sierra Leone; c/o Principal's Residence, Methodist Girls' High School, Freetown, Sierra Leone.
Telephone: 24300 and 30139 (Home).

Collin, Fernand (Jozef Maria Fanny), LL.D.; Belgian company director and university professor; b. 18 Dec. 1897, Antwerp; s. of John F. Collin and Jeanne Verelst; m. Maria Bellekens 1968; two s. three d.; ed. Univ. of Louvain.
Lawyer, Antwerp 23-38; Lecturer, Univ. of Louvain 25, Prof. 27-68, Dean Faculty of Law and mem. Rectorial Council 45-48; Chair. Board of Dirs. Kredietbank 38-73 Chair. Imperial Products Co. 59-; Dir. Gevaert Photo-Products 52-; Chair. Banque Diamantaire Anversoise 64-68; mem. Higher Council for Physical Educ. and Sports 30-40; Royal Commissary to middle classes 37; Chair. Central Social Section, Belgian Banking Assen. 39-45; Chair. Supreme Family Council 52-59, Utrecht-Allerlei Risico's 59-71; mem. Man. Cttee. Inst. de Réescompte et de Garantie 40-63; Chair. Benelux Cttee. 59-66; Chair. Belgian Assoc. Investment Funds 58-62; Chair. Cardiology Foundation Princess Liliane 61-73; Chair. Continental Foods 68-; Pres. Int. Cardiology Fed. 70-72; Commdr. Order of the Crown and Commdr. Order of Léopold, Grand Officer Order Léopold II (Belgium); Commdr. Order of Orange-Nassau (Neths.), Commdr. Italian Order of Merit, Commdr. Order St. Gregory the Great, Grand Officer Order of the Crown (Belgium), Grand Officer Order of Merit (Luxembourg), and other decorations.
Leisure interests: music, horse-riding.
Publs. Enrico Ferri et l'Avant-Projet du Code pénal italien de 1921 25, Rapport sur les Classes Moyennes 37, Strafrecht 48, Code d'instruction criminelle et Lois complémentaires (with M. H. Bekaert) 49.
Mechelsesteenweg 196, Antwerp, Belgium.
Telephone: 03/37-86-39.

Collin, Jean, L. en D.; Senegalese politician; b. 19 Sept. 1924, Paris, France; s. of Lonis Collin and Madeleine Meunier; m. Marianne Turpin 1973; one s. one d.
Chief administrator, French Overseas Territories; Chief Information Service and Dir. Radio-Dakar 48; posted to Cameroon 51-56; Dir. of Cabinet of Mamadou Dia, Vice-Pres. then Pres. of the Council 57-58; Gov. of Cap-Vert March 60-Dec. 60; Sec.-Gen. of the Govt. Dec. 60-Aug. 64; Gen. Commr. of the Govt. to the Supreme Court 60; Perm. Sec. to the Higher Council for Defence June 61-May 63; Sec.-Gen. to the Presidency of the Repub. May 63-Feb. 64; Minister of Finance and Econ. Affairs 64-71; Minister of Interior April 71-.
Ministry of Interior, Dakar, Senegal.

Collingwood, Charles; American radio and television broadcaster; b. 4 June 1917; ed. Cornell Univ. and New Coll., Oxford.
Foreign Corresp. United Press, London 39, Amsterdam 40; Foreign Corresp. Columbia Broadcasting System, North Africa 42-43, France and Germany 44-45; CBS U.N. Corresp. 46-47; CBS White House Corresp. 48-51; Special Asst. Dir. for Mutual Security (U.S. Govt.) 51-52; Chief, London Bureau CBS 57-59; corresp. New York 59-64, Chief European Corresp. CBS News 64-67, Chief Foreign Corresp. 67-; Chevalier, Légion d'Honneur.
Publ. The Defector 70.
CBS News, 100 Brompton Road, London, S.W.3, England.

Collins, Vice-Admiral Sir John Augustine, K.B.E., C.B.; Australian retired naval officer and High Commissioner to New Zealand 56-62; see The International Who's Who 1975-76.

Collins, Gen. Joseph Lawton; American retd. army officer; b. 1 May 1896; ed. Louisiana State Univ., and U.S. Mil. Acad.
Graduated Mil. Acad. 17, instructor U.S. Mil. Acad. 21-25, Infantry School 27-31; student Command & Gen-Staff School 31-35, Army Industrial Coll. 36-37, Army War Coll. 37-38; advanced through grades to Brig.-Gen. 42, Major-Gen. 42, Lieut.-Gen. 45, Gen. 48; Instructor Army War Coll. 38-40; Asst. Sec. War Dept.

Gen. Staff 40-41; Chief of Staff, VII Army Corps 41, Hawaiian Dept. 41-42; Commdr. 25th Div. 42-44, VII Corps 44-45; Deputy Commdg.-Gen. and Chief of Staff Army Ground Forces 45; Chief of Public Information War Dept. 45-47; Deputy Chief of Staff, then Vice-Chief of Staff, U.S. Army 47-49, Chief of Staff Aug. 49-53; U.S. Representative to Military Cttee. and Standing Group, N.A.T.O. 53-56; spec. representative of U.S. in Viet-Nam with rank of Ambassador 54-55; retd. from active service 56; Dir. and Vice-Chair. of the President's Cttee. for Hungarian Refugee Relief 56-57; elected to Bd. of Dirs., Chas. Pfizer & Co. Inc., New York City; Vice-Chair. of the Bd., Pfizer International Inc., N.Y. City 57-69; Chair. Board of Dirs., Foreign Student Service Council of Greater Washington 57-58, Hon. Chair. 58-; Board of Trustees of Inst. of Int. Education Inc., New York 57-65; mem. USO Corpn. 59-60, USO Nat. Council 60-63; Chair. Greater Washington Council of Organizations Serving Int. Visitors 62-64.
1700 Pennsylvania Avenue, N.W., Washington 5, D.C., U.S.A.

Collins, Rev. Canon L(ewis) John, M.A.; British ecclesiastic; b. 23 March 1905, Hawkhurst, Kent; four s.; ed. Cranbrook School, Sidney Sussex Coll., Cambridge and Westcott House, Cambridge.
Chaplain, Sidney Sussex Coll., Cambridge 29-31; Minor Canon, St. Paul's Cathedral, London 31-34; Priest-in-Ordinary to H.M. King George V; Vice-Principal, Westcott House, Cambridge 34-37; Dean, Chaplain and Fellow, Oriel Coll., Oxford 38-48; R.A.F. Chaplain 40-45; Canon Residentiary, St. Paul's Cathedral 48-; Chair. Campaign for Nuclear Disarmament 58-64; Co-Pres. Western European Movt. against Nuclear Weapons 59-64; Pres. Int. Defence and Aid Fund 64-; Chair. Christian Action 47-72, Pres. 50-.
Leisure interests: walking, gardening.
Publs. The New Testament Problem 38, Theology of Christian Action 47, Faith under Fire 66 and contributions to various books and journals.
2 Amen Court, London, EC4M 7BX, England.

Collins, Michael; American astronaut; b. 31 Oct. 1930, Rome, Italy; m. Patricia M. Finnegan; one s. two d.; ed. U.S. Military Acad.
Commissioned by U.S. Air Force, served as experimental flight test officer, Air Force Flight Test Center, Edwards Air Force Base, Calif.; selected by NASA as astronaut Oct. 63; backup pilot for Gemini VII mission 65; pilot of Gemini X 66; command pilot, Apollo XI Mission for first moon landing July 69; Asst. Sec. for Public Affairs, Dept. of State 70-71; Dir. Nat. Air and Space Museum 71-; Fellow, Royal Aeronautical Soc.; NASA Exceptional Service Medal.
Publ. Carrying the Fire 74.
National Air and Space Museum, Smithsonian Institution, Washington, D.C., U.S.A.

Collins, Norman Richard; British writer; b. 3 Oct. 1907; ed. William Ellis School, Hampstead.
With Oxford Univ. Press 26-29; Asst. Literary Editor News Chronicle 29-33; Deputy Chair. Victor Gollancz 34-41; Empire Talks Man., BBC 41-44, Dir.-Gen. Overseas Service 44-46, Head of Light Programme 46-47, Controller of Television 47-50; Chair. Hyde Park Films and Watergate Productions Ltd.; Gov. British Film Inst. 49-51; Pres. Radio Industries Club 50; Deputy Chair. Assoc. Television Corpn. Ltd.; Dir. Orchestral Concerts Soc.; Councillor English State Co.; Gov. Sadler's Wells; Pres. Lifeline 62-70; Chair. Central School of Speech and Drama, Independent Broadcasting Services Ltd.; Dir. Independent Television News Ltd., UPITN Corpn.; Chair. Lord Mayor of London's 1976 National Appeal for the Aged.
Publs. The Facts of Fiction 32, Penang Appointment 34, The Three Friends 35, Trinity Town 36, Flames Coming Out of the Top 37, Love in Our Time 38, The

Captain's Lamp (play) 38, I Shall Not Want 40, Anna 42, London Belongs to Me 45, Black Ivory 48, Children of the Archbishop 51, The Bat that Flits 53, The Bond Street Story 59, The Governor's Lady 68.
1 Radlett Place, London, N.W.8, England.

Collins, Ralph Edgar, M.A.; Canadian diplomatist; b. 23 Nov. 1914, Yunnanfu, China; m. Jane Irwin; three c.; ed. Univ. of Alberta, Zimmern School of Int. Studies, Geneva, Univ. of Calif. and Harvard and Oxford Univs.
Joined Dept. of External Affairs 40, served in Washington, Ottawa, London and Moscow 40-56; Head, Far Eastern Div., Dept. of External Affairs 57; Fellow, Harvard Center for Int. Affairs 60-61; Head, African and Middle East Div., Dept. of External Affairs 61; Amb. to South Africa 64-65; Asst. Under-Sec. of State for External Affairs 65-71; Amb. to People's Repub. of China 71-72; Asst. Under-Sec. of State for External Affairs 72-.
c/o Department of External Affairs, Ottawa, Ont. K1A 0G2, Canada.

Collins, Samuel Cornette, M.S., PH.D., LL.D., D.SC., American professor of mechanical engineering; b. 1898, Kentucky; s. of John W. and Rachel (Caudill) Collins; m. Lena Masterson 1929; no c.; ed. Univs. of Tennessee and North Carolina.
Taught successively at Carson-Newman Coll., Univ. of Tenn., Tenn. State Teachers' Coll. and Univ. of N.C.; joined staff Mass. Inst. of Technology 30, Assoc. Prof. of Chem. 43, Prof. of Mechanical Engineering 49-64; previously engaged in further devt. and manufacture of cryogenic equipment and now Consultant, Naval Research Laboratory, Washington, D.C.; Vice-Pres. Cryogenic Technology Inc. 69; mem. Nat. Acad. of Sciences; Fellow, American Acad. of Arts and Sciences; John Price Wetherill Medal, Franklin Inst. 51, Kamerling Onnes Gold Medal 58; Rumford Premium, American Acad. of Arts and Sciences 65, Gold Medal, American Soc. of Mech. Engineers; Hon. D.Sc. (Univ. of N.C.), Hon. LL.D. (St. Andrews).
Publs. Expansion Machines (with R. L. Cannaday) 58; contributions to scientific journals, etc.
12322 Riverview Road, Oxon Hill, Md. 20022, U.S.A.
Telephone: 292-1367.

Coloma Gallegos, Francisco; Spanish army officer and politician; b. 1912; widower; six c.; ed. Acad. General Militar.
Army career 30-72, Col. 59; Military Attaché, Spanish Embassy, Washington 60; Brig.-Gen., Chief of Staff Eighth Mil. Region 65, transferred to Cen. Staff 67; Maj.-Gen. 69, Lt.-Gen. 72; Under-Sec. Ministry for the Army 69, Minister 73-.
Ministerio del Ejército, Madrid, Spain.

Colombani, Ignace Jean Aristide; French overseas administrator; b. 1908, Montreal, Canada; s. of Paul-Marie Colombani and Victorine Cormier; m. Marie-Laure Pellegrini 1943; one s.; ed. Ecole Pascal-Paoli; Morosaglia, Bastia Lycée and Ecole Nat. de la France d'Outre-Mer.
Administrator, French West Africa 33-49; Gov. Niger 49-50, Oubangui-Chari (now Cen. African Repub.) 50-51, Chad 51-56; Officier de la Légion d'Honneur, Commandeur de l'Etoile Noire, Chevalier du Mérite Agricole, Croix du Mérite de 1ère Classe de l'Ordre Souverain de Malte; Pres. "Lingua Corsa".
Leisure interest: Corsican dialect.
15 rue César Campinchi, Bastia, Corsica.
Telephone: Bastia 31-43-23.

Colombo, Duilio; Italian industrial executive; b. 31 Jan. 1913, Rome; m. Luciana Di Nola; four c.
Manager, Finsider S.p.A. 48-51, Dir.-Gen. 74-75, Vice-Chair. 75-; Commercial Dir. Cornigliano S.p.A. 51-58; Dir.-Gen. Siderexport S.p.A. 59-61, Pres. 70-; Vice-Dir.-

Gen. Italsider S.p.A. 61-64, Dir.-Gen. 66-74; Dir.-Gen. Deriver S.p.A. 64-66.
Via F. Denza, 21-Rome, Italy.
Telephone: 87.29.40.

Colombo, Emilio; Italian politician; b. 11 April 1920; ed. Rome Univ.
Took active part in Catholic youth organizations; fmr. Vice-Pres. Italian Catholic Youth Asscn.; Deputy, Constituent Assembly 46-48, Parl. 48-; Under-Sec. of Agriculture 48-51, of Public Works 53-55; Minister of Agriculture 55-58, of Foreign Trade 58-59, of Industry and Commerce 59-60, March-April 60, July 60-63, of the Treasury 63-70, Feb.-May 72; Prime Minister Aug. 70-Feb. 72; Minister without Portfolio in charge of Italian representation at UN 72-73; Minister of Finance 73-74, of the Treasury March 74-; Pres. Nat. Cttee. for Nuclear Research 61; mem. Cen. Cttee. Christian Dem. Party 52 and 53.
The Treasury, Rome; and Via Aurelia 239, Rome, Italy.

Colombo, H.E. Cardinal Giovanni; Italian ecclesiastic; b. 6 Dec. 1902.
Ordained priest 26; consecrated Titular Bishop of Philippopolis in Arabia 60; Archbishop of Milan 63-; mem. Cttee. of the Ecumenical Council on Catholic Seminaries and Educ.; created Cardinal 65.
Palazzo Arcivescovile, Piazza Fontana 2, Milan, Italy

Colombo, Vittorino; Italian politician; b. 3 April 1925, Albiate (Milan); ed. Università Cattolica, Milan.
Deputy for Milan-Pavia to Chamber of Deputies 58-; mem. Nat. Council, Italian Workers' Catholic Action; mem. Federchimici. Fed. of Independent Trade Unions; mem. Nat. Council, Christian Democratic Party; fmr. Under-Sec. of State to Ministry of Finance; Ministry of Foreign Trade 68-69; Minister of Health March-Oct. 74.
Ministry of Health, Rome, Italy.

Colonna di Paliano, Don Guido; Italian diplomatist; b. 16 April 1908; ed. Università degli Studi, Naples.
Foreign Service 33-, served New York, Toronto, Cairo, Stockholm, London, OEEC, Paris; Dep. Dir. of Political Affairs, Ministry of Foreign Affairs 56-58; Ambassador to Norway 58-62; Dep. Sec.-Gen. North Atlantic Treaty Org. (NATO) 62-64; mem. Comm. of European Economic Community, Brussels 64-67; mem. Combined Comm. of EEC, ECSC and Euratom 67-70; Pres. La Rinascente (Italian dept. store) 70-; mem. Board of Dirs. Exxon Corpn. 70-75.
La Rinascente, Piazza Carlo Erba 6, Milan, Italy.

Colotka, Peter, LL.D., C.SC.; Czechoslovak lawyer and politician; b. 10 Jan. 1925, Sedliacka Dubová; ed. Comenius Univ., Bratislava.
Assistant Lecturer, Faculty of Law, Comenius Univ., Bratislava 50-56, Asst. Prof. 56-64, Prof. 64-, Vice-Dean 56-57, Dean 57-58, Pro-Rector of Univ. 58-61; Commr. for Justice, Slovak Nat. Council 63-68; Deputy to Slovak Nat. Council 63-; mem. Presidium, Slovak Nat. Council 63-68; Deputy Premier 68; Deputy Premier, Fed. Govt. Sept. 69-; mem. Cen. Cttee. C.P. of Czechoslovakia and Cen. Cttee. of C.P. of Slovakia 66-; Deputy to House of Nations Fed. Assembly Dec. 68-, Pres. of Fed. Assembly Jan.-April 69; mem. Presidium of Fed. Assembly Jan.-April 69; Premier of Slovak Socialist Repub. May 69-; mem. Presidium of Central Cttee. C.P. of Slovakia May 69-; mem. Presidium of Central Cttee. C.P. of Czechoslovakia April 69-; mem. Int. Court of Arbitration, The Hague 62-70; Distinction for Merit in Construction 65, Order of Labour 69, Gold Medal of J. A. Comenius Univ. 69, Order of Victorious February 73, Order of the Repub. 75.
Publs. *Personal Property* 56, *Our Socialist Constitution* 61; scientific studies and articles in collaboration with Dr. Matoušek.
Government of S.S.R., Bratislava, Czechoslovakia.

Colquhoun, (Cecil) Brian (Hugh), B.SC.(ENG.), F.K.C., C.ENG., F.I.C.E., F.I.STRUCT.E., M.CONS.E., F.A.S.C.E., M.E.I.C., M.SOC.C.E. (France); British consulting engineer; b. 13 Nov. 1902, London; s. of the late Mr. and Mrs. Arthur H. Colquhoun; m. Beryl Cowan 1936; two s.; ed. King's Coll., London Univ.
Served with Dr. C. H. Lobban on design and construction of various buildings in London 25-26; with Eagle Oil Company Ltd. in Mexico 26-30; apptd. Resident Engineer on construction of Mersey Tunnel 30; later became Resident Engineer-in-Charge; Engineer-in-Chief Royal Ordnance Factories at Chorley, Risley and Kirkby 36-39, also Adviser on Maas (Rotterdam) Tunnel, Tamar (Plymouth) Tunnel, and Rossall sea wall 35-39; Rehabilitation of war-production factories in main industrial centres 40; with Ministry of Aircraft Production as Dir.-Gen. of Aircraft Production Factories 41-44; seconded as Engineering Adviser to Int. Bank for Reconstruction and Devt., Washington 54-56; Engineering Adviser to Parl. Channel Tunnel Cttee. 56-57; Senior Partner, Brian Colquhoun and Partners, Consulting Engineers.
3 Fountain House, Park Lane, London, W.1; also Mill Farm, Milland, West Sussex, England.

Comas Camps, Juan, D.SC.; Mexican anthropologist; b. 23 Jan. 1900, Alayor, Spain; s. of Gabriel Comas and Rita Camps; m. Camille Destillieres 1948; ed. Madrid and Univ. of Geneva.
Inspector of Primary Education Spain 21-39; Adviser, Council of Cultural Relations, Ministry of Foreign Affairs, Madrid 33-39; Sec.-Gen. Ministry of Public Instruction 38; Sec. *Revista de Pedagogía* Madrid 33-36; Anthropologist Nat. Anthropological Inst. of Mexico 40-43; Prof. Nat. School of Anthropology of Mexico 41-59; Sec. Inter-American Indian Inst. 42-55; Research Prof. Univ. of Mexico 55-74, Head Dept. of Anthropology 63-73, Prof. Emeritus 75-; Dir. *Boletín Bibliografico de Antropologia Americana* 45-52; Editor-in-Chief *America Indígena* and *Boletin Indigensita* 42-55; Editor *Anales de Antropologia* 63-.
Publs. *El sistema de Winnetka en la práctica* 30, *Las prácticas de las pruebas mentales y de instrucción* 34, *Aportaciones al estudio de la prehistoria de Menorca* 36, *Como se comprueba el trabajo escolar* 40, *Existe una raza judía?* 41, *Contribution à l'étude du Métopisme* 42, *La Antropología física en México y Centroamérica* 43, *La discriminación racial en América* 44, *Osteometria Olmeca* 44, *Bosquejo histórico de la Antropología en México* 50, *Les Mythes Raciaux* 51, *Cultural Anthropology and Fundamental Education in Latin America* 52, *Ensayos sobre Indigenismo* 53, *Bibliografía Selectiva de las Culturas Indígenas de América* 53, *Influencia indígena en la Medicina hipocrática en la Nueva España del siglo XVI* 54, *Ensayo sobre "raza" y Economía* 55, *Las lenguas vernáculas y el bilinguismo en Educación* 56, *Contribuciones indígenas Precolombinas a la Cultura Universal* 56, *Historia y Bibliografía de los Congresos Internacionales de Ciencias Antropológicas* 56, *Buffon, precursor de la Antropología* 58, *La educación ante la discriminación racial* 58, *La deformación cefálica intencional en la región del Ucayali, Perú* 58, *L'Anthropologie américaine et le diffusionisme de P. Laviosa Zambotti* 58, *Manual of Physical Anthropology* (Eng. ed.) 60, *Pigmeos en América* 60, *La heterogeneidad cultural y el planeamiento integral de la educación en América Latina* 60, *Datos para la historia de la deformación craneal en México* 60, *Las culturas agrícolas de América y sus relaciones con el Viejo Mundo* 61, *Race Relations—in Latin America* 61, *Scientific Racism Again?* 61, *El origen del hombre americano y la Antropología física* 61, *Primeras Instrucciones para la investigación antropológica: 1862* 62, *Combatir el racismo es defender la paz* 64. *Trayectoria de la Antropología social en México* 64, *El antigeno Diego entre los amerindios* 65, *Cranes mexicaines scaphocephals* 65, *Somato-*

metría de los indios Triques, México 65, *Manual de Antropología Física* 2nd edn. 66, *Características físicas de la familia lingüística Maya* 66, *Unidad y variedad de la especie humana* 67, *Medicina y antropología* 68, *Dos microcéfalos aztecas* 68, *La medicina aborigen mexicana en la obra de fray Augustín de Vetancourt* 68, *Anthropometric Studies in Latin America's Indian Populations* 71, *Cien años de Congresos Internacionales de Americanistas* 74, *Origen de la momificación prehistórica en América* 74, *Antropología de los pueblos iberoamericanos* 74, *Origen de las culturas precolombinas* 75, *Manuel Gamio en la antropología mexicana* 75.
Alberto Zamora 69, Coyoacán, 21 D.F., Mexico.
Telephone: 5-54-62-71.

Comay, Michael, B.A., LL.B.; Israeli diplomatist; b. 18 Oct. 1908; *m.*; two *c.*; ed. Cape Town Univ., South Africa.
Barrister, Supreme Court 31-40; Major, South African Army 40-45; Special Rep. South African Zionist Fed., attached to Political Dept. Jewish Agency, Jerusalem 46-48; mem. Israel del. to UN 47-48; Dir. British Commonwealth Div., Israel Foreign Ministry 48-51; Amb. to Canada 53-57; Asst. Dir.-Gen. Ministry for Foreign Affairs 57-59; Perm. Rep. to UN 60-67; Political Adviser to Foreign Minister and Amb.-at-Large 67-70; Amb. to U.K. 70-73; Fellow Jerusalem Inst. of Int. Affairs.
47 Harav Berlin Street, Jerusalem, Israel.

Comfort, Alexander, M.A., M.B., D.SC., M.R.C.S., L.R.C.P., D.C.H.; British medical biologist and writer; b. 10 Feb. 1920; ed. Highgate School, Trinity Coll., Cambridge, and The London Hospital.
Medical and hospital practice 44-48; Lecturer in Physiology The London Hospital 48-51; Nuffield Research Asst. Univ. Coll., London 51-54, Nuffield Research Fellow in Biology of Senescence 54-63; Dir. Medical Research Council Research Group in Ageing, Univ. Coll., London 63-70; Dir. of Research, Gerontology, Univ. Coll., London 70-73; Senior Fellow, Center for the Study of Democratic Insts. 74-75; Clinical Lectures, Dept. Psychiatry, Stanford Univ. 74-; Fellow Inst. of Higher Studies, Santa Barbara, Calif. 75-.
Publs. Novels: *No Such Liberty* 41, *The Almond Tree* 43, *The Powerhouse* 45, *On This Side of Nothing* 48, *A Giant's Strength* 52, *Come out to Play* 61; Verse: *A Wreath for the Living* 42, *Elegies* 44, *The Signal to Engage* 46, *And All but he Departed* 52, *Haste to the Wedding* 62; stories: *Letters from an Outpost* 47; Essays: *Art and Social Responsibility* 46, *The Novel and Our Time* 48, *The Pattern of the Future* 51, *Darwin and the Naked Lady* 61; Other: *Barbarism and Sexual Freedom* 48, *Sexual Behaviour in Society* 49, *First-Year Physiological Technique* 49, *Authority and Delinquency in the Modern State* 50, *The Biology of Senescence* 56, *Sex in Society* 63, *Ageing* 64, *The Koka Shastra* (trans.) 64, *The Process of Ageing* 64, *Nature and Human Nature* (essay) 66, *The Anxiety Makers* 67, *The Joy of Sex* 72, *More Joy* 74, *A Good Age* 76, *I and That: the Biology of Religion* 76.
2311 Garden Street, Santa Barbara, Calif. 93105; Home: 683 Oakgrove Drive, Santa Barbara, Calif. 93108, U.S.A.
Telephone: (805) 969-4330 (Home).

Comiti, Joseph; French surgeon and politician; b. 1920.
Secretary of State for Youth and Sports 68-69; Sec. of State in charge of Youth, Sports and Leisure 69-72; Minister for Youth and Sports 72-73; Minister in charge of Relations with Parl. April-Oct. 73; Sec. of State for Overseas Depts., and Territories March-May 74; mem. Bureau exécutif, Union des Démocrates pour la République; Pres. Haut Comité de la Jeunesse, des Sports et des Loisirs 70-.
14 rue de Lorraine, 13008 Marseilles; Home: 7 avenue Maréchal-Lyautey, Parc Talabot, 13067 Marseilles, France.

Commager, Henry Steele, PH.B., M.A., PH.D., M.A. (Cantab.), M.A. (Oxon.); American historian; b. 25 Oct. 1902; ed. Chicago and Copenhagen Univ.
Prof. New York Univ. 25-39, Columbia 39-56, Cambridge 42-43; Pitt Prof. American History, Cambridge Univ. 47-48; Harmsworth Prof. of American History, Oxford Univ. 52-53; Gottesman Prof. Uppsala 53; Prof. History, Amherst Coll. 56-, Simoson Lecturer 71-; Hon. Fellow, Peterhouse, Cambridge; Visiting Prof. Univ. of Copenhagen 56; Commonwealth Lecturer, Univ. of London 65; consultant U.S. War Dept. Historical Branch, U.S. Office War Information, State Dept., U.S. Army I. & E. Div.; Trustee American Scandinavian Foundation; mem. U.S. War Dept. Comm. on History of War, UNESCO Nat. Comm., Exec. Cttee., U.S. Del. to UNESCO, American Acad. of Arts and Letters; numerous hon. degrees; Gold Medal for History, American Acad. of Arts and Letters 72; Knight Order of Dannebrog.
Publs. *The American Republic* (2 vols., with S. E. Morison) 30, *Documents of American History* 34, *Theodore Parker* 36, *America: Story of a Free People* (with A. Nevins) 42, *Majority Rule and Minority Rights* 43, *History of the Second World War* 45, *The American Mind* 50, *The Great Declaration* 59, *The Great Proclamation* 60, *The Great Constitution* 61, *The Story of Human Rights* 61, *Living Ideas in America* 51, *America's Robert E. Lee* 51, *The Blue and the Gray* (2 vols.) 51, *Freedom, Loyalty and Dissent* 54, *Joseph Story* 54, *The Spirit of Seventy-Six* (with R. B. Morris), *Europe and America* (with G. Bruun), *Writings of Theodore Parker* 61, *The Era of Reform* 61, *Studies in Immigration* 61, *Crusaders for Freedom* 61, *History: Nature and Purpose* 65, *Freedom and Order* 66, *Search for a Usable Past* 67, *Was America a Mistake?* 68, *The Commonwealth of Learning* 68, *The American Character* 70, *The Use and Abuse of History* 72, *Britain Through American Eyes* 74, *The Defeat of America* 74, *Essays on the Enlightenment* 74; Editor Tocqueville's *Democracy in America* 47, *America in Perspective* 48, *St. Nicholas Anthology* 48, *The Rise of the American Nation* (50 vols. in progress), *Documents of American History* 50, *Chester Bowles: An American Purpose* 61, *Lester Ward and the Welfare State, Defeat of the Confederacy, The Nature and Study of History* 65, *The Struggle for Racial Equality* 67.
405 S. Pleasant Street, Amherst, Mass., U.S.A.; and Linton, Cambridgeshire, England.

Commins, Thomas Vincent; Irish diplomatist; b. 3 Oct. 1913, Ballymoreen, Co. Tipperary; *s.* of the late James and Mary Commins; ed. Rockwell Coll., and Univ. Coll., Dublin.
Irish Govt. Service 33-46; Diplomatic Service 46-; Commercial Sec., Washington, D.C. 46-48; Counsellor, Dept. of External Affairs 48-54; Counsellor, Paris 54-55; Chargé d'Affaires *en titre*, Lisbon 55-59; Minister to Argentina 59-60; Ambassador to Italy 60-62, to Holy See 62-66, to France 66-70; also Perm. Rep. of Ireland to OECD; Knight Grand Cross Order of Pius IX.
Leisure interests: music, theatre, golf.
Embassy of Ireland, Villa Spada, Via Giacomo Medici 1, Rome, Italy.
Telephone: 581 0134; 581 0777.

Commoner, Barry, A.B., M.A., PH.D.; American professor of plant physiology; b. 28 May 1917, New York City; *s.* of Isidore Commoner and Goldie Yarmolinsky; *m.* Gloria Gordon 1946; one *s.* one *d.*; ed. Columbia Coll. and Harvard Univ.
Assistant in Biology, Harvard Univ. 38-40; Instructor, Queens Coll. 40-42; U.S. Naval Reserve 42-46; Assoc. Editor *Science Illustrated* 46-47; Assoc. Prof. of Plant Physiology, Washington Univ., St. Louis 47-53; Prof. 53-; Chair. Dept. of Botany, Wash. Univ. 65-69, Dir. Center for the Biology of Natural Systems 65-; Newcomb Cleveland Prize, American Asscn. for Advance-

ment of Science 53; Hon. Life Vice-Pres. Soil Asscn. 68; Dir. A.A.S.S. 67-; Chair. A.A.A.S. Comm. on Environmental Alterations 69; Pres. St. Louis Comm. for Nuclear Information 65-66, for Environmental Information 66-; mem. Board of Dirs. Scientists' Inst. for Public Information 63-, Co-Chair. 67-69; Chair. 69-; mem. Gov. Board American Inst. of Biological Sciences 65-67; mem. of other consultatory boards; mem. Editorial Board *The World Book Encyclopedia* and *Environmental Pollution*; mem. Advisory Board *Science Year*; mem. Soc. of Biological Chemists, American Chem. Soc., Soc. Plant Physiologists, Soc. Gen. Physiologists, Nat. Parks Asscn., Ecological Soc., Fed. of American Science, Editorial Board *Nat. Wildlife*, *Journal of Human Ecology* and others; several honorary degrees; First Int. Humanist Award 70; Phi Beta Kappa Award for *The Closing Circle* 72, Int. Prize from the City of Cervia, for Safeguarding the Environment, Italy 73; D.Sc. (Williams Coll.) 70.
Leisure interest: walking.
Publs. *Science and Survival* 66, *The Closing Circle* 71; and over 200 articles, many of which are concerned with the origins and significance of alterations in the environment, especially in relation to modern technology.
Center for the Biology of Natural Systems, Box 1126, Washington University, St. Louis, Mo. 63130; 25 Crestwood Drive, Clayton, Mo. 63105, U.S.A.
Telephone: (314)-863-0100, Ext. 4485 or 4685 (Univ.).

Compton, Denis Charles Scott, C.B.E.; British cricketer (retd.), journalist and advertising executive; b. 23 May 1918, Hendon; s. of Harry Ernest Compton and Jessie Douthie; m. Christine Franklin Tobias 1975; three s. from previous marriages; ed. Bell Lane School, Hendon. First played for Middlesex County Cricket Club 36, for England v. New Zealand 37, v. Australia 38, v. West Indies 39, v. India 46, v. South Africa 47; played in 78 Test Matches; made 122 centuries in first class cricket; retd. 57; played Association Football, mem. Arsenal XI; England XI 43; Cricket Corresp., *Sunday Express* 51-; Commentator, BBC Television 58-; Exec. in Advertising Co. 58-; one of Wisden's Cricketers of the Year 39; Sportsman of the Year 47, 48; Hon. mem. MCC 57-; FA Cup Winners' Medal 49-50.
Leisure interests: golf, tennis, theatre.
Publs. *Testing Time for England* 48, *Playing for England* 48, *End of an Innings* 58.
15 Charterhouse Street, London, EC1N 6RH, England.
Telephone: 01-242 4388.

Compton, Sir Edmund Gerald, G.C.B., K.B.E., M.A.; British civil servant; b. 30 June 1906; m. Betty Tresyllian Williams 1934; one s. four d.; ed. Rugby School and New Coll., Oxford Univ.
Joined Civil Service 29; attached to Colonial Office 30; joined Treasury 31; Private Sec. to Financial Sec. to Treasury 34-36; Private Sec. to Minister of Aircraft Production 40; with Ministry of Supply 41; Asst. Sec., Treasury 42-47, Under Sec. 47-49, Third Sec. 49-58; Comptroller and Auditor Gen. 58-66; Parl. Commr. for Admin. (Ombudsman) 67-March 71, and in Northern Ireland 69-71; Chair. Local Govt. Boundary Comm. 71-, Royal Acad. of Music 75-.
53 Evelyn Gardens, London, S.W.7, England.
Telephone: 01-370-3220.

Comroe, Julius H., Jr., A.B., M.D.; American physiologist and medical educator; b. 13 March 1911, York, Pa.; s. of Julius Comroe and Mollie (Levy) Comroe; m. Jeanette Wolfson 1936; one d.; ed. Univ. of Pennsylvania.
Instructor, Univ. of Pennsylvania School of Medicine 36-40, Assoc. in Pharmacology 40-42, Asst. Prof. 42-46; Prof. and Chair., Dept. of Physiology and Pharmacology, Univ. of Pennsylvania Graduate School of Medicine 46-57; Dir. Cardiovascular Research Inst.

and Prof. of Physiology, Univ. of Calif. Medical Center, San Francisco 57-73, Prof. of Biology 74-; Editor *Circulation Research* (American Heart Asscn.) 66-71; mem. Nat. Acad. of Sciences; Fellow, Royal Coll. of Physicians (U.K.) 71; Research Achievement Award, American Heart Asscn. 68; Hon. medical degree, Karolinska Inst., Stockholm 68; Hon. D.Sc., Univ. of Chicago 68; Trudeau Medal, American Lung Asscn. 74.
Publs. *Physiological Basis for Oxygen Therapy* (with R. D. Dripps) 50, *Pulmonary Function Tests, Vol. II* (in English and Japanese) 50, *The Lung: Clinical Physiology and Pulmonary Function Tests* (with Foster, DuBois, Briscoe and Carlsen—in English, Spanish, Japanese, French, Russian, German, Italian and Turkish) 55, 62, *Physiology of Respiration* (in English, French, Italian, Spanish, German) 65, 74.
Cardiovascular Research Institute, University of California Medical Center, San Francisco, Calif. 94122; Home: 555 Laurent Road, Hillsborough, Calif. 94010, U.S.A.
Telephone: 415-666-1048 (Office); 415-342-2631 (Home).

Conant, James Bryant, A.B., PH.D., L.H.D., LITT.D., S.D., LL.D., D.C.L.; American educationist; b. 26 March 1893, Boston, Mass.; m. Grace Thayer Richards; two s.; ed. Harvard Univ.
Chemistry Dept. Harvard Univ. 16-33, Prof. of Organic Chemistry 29-33, Pres. Harvard Univ. 33-53, Emeritus Pres. 53-; U.S. High Commr. in Germany 53-55; Ambassador to Fed. Republic of Germany 55-57; Dir. Study of the American High School 57-61; Study of the Educ. of American Teachers 63-65, and of American Educ.; Lieut. Sanitary Corps, U.S. Army 17, Maj. Chemical Warfare Service 18; mem. Nat. Acad. of Sciences, Royal Socs. London and Edinburgh (foreign mem.), Royal Inst. of Chem. and Chemical Soc. of England, Educational Policies Comm. 41-46, 47-50, 57-63; Chair. National Defense Research Cttee. and Deputy Director of Office of Scientific Research and Development 41-46, Steering Cttee. for Manhattan District 42-45, Gen. Advisory Cttee. of Atomic Energy Commission 47-52; Commdr. Légion d'Honneur; C.B.E., Medal for Merit with Oak Leaf Clusters, Freedom House Award 53; Hon. Sc.D. (Cambridge, London, Lyon Univs. and Free University of Berlin and American universities); LL.D. (Princeton, Yale, California, Pennsylvania, Bristol, Queens, Toronto, Michigan, Yeshiva, Birmingham, Harvard, Edinburgh, Leeds Univs. and other American universities and colleges); L.H.D. (Boston); Litt.D. (Hamilton Coll.); Honoris causa (Melbourne, Canterbury, Univ. Coll. New Zealand); F.E.I.S. (Educ. Inst. Scotland); admitted to Univ. of Adelaide *ad eundem gradum*; Dr. (Univ. of Algiers); Atomic Pioneer's Award from Pres. Nixon 70.
Leisure interests: mountain climbing, trout fishing.
Publs. *Our Fighting Faith* 43, *On Understanding Science* 47, *Education in a Divided World* 48, *Science and Commonsense* 51, *Modern Science and Modern Man* 52, *Education and Liberty* 53, *The Citadel of Learning* 56, *Germany and Freedom* 58, *The American High School Today* 59, *The Child, The Parent, and the State* 59, *Education in the Junior High School Years* 60, *Slums and Suburbs* 61, *Thomas Jefferson and the Development of American Public Education* 62, *The Education of American Teachers* 63, *Two Modes of Thought* 64, *Shaping Educational Policy* 64, *The Comprehensive High School* 67, *My Several Lives: Memoirs of a Social Inventor* 70; Editor Vols. 2 and 9 *Harvard Case Histories in Experimental Science*; chemistry textbooks.
Manhattan House, 200 East 66th Street, New York, N.Y. 10021, U.S.A.

Conant, Kenneth John, A.B., M.ARCH., PH.D.; American archaeologist; b. 28 June 1894, Neenah, Wisconsin; s. of John F. Conant and Lucie E. Micklesen; m. 1st Marie

A. Schneider 1923, two *s.*; *m.* 2nd Isabel Pope 1956; ed. Harvard Univ.

Appointed to Harvard Univ. staff 20, Asst. Prof. 25, Prof. of Architecture 36-55, Prof. Emer. 56-; Harvard Exchange Prof., Sorbonne 35-36 and 50, Nat. Univ. of Mexico 42; Guggenheim Fellowships 27-29 (for expeditions to Cluny) and 55; excavations at Cluny 28-50; expeds. to cathedrals of Santiago de Compostela 20, 24 and 50, expeditions to Middle America 26, Kiev 35 and 36, to Abbey of Montecassino 35, Holy Sepulchre 38, 55, St. Sophia, Constantinople 35 and 38; hon. mem. Faculty of Architecture, Univ. of Buenos Aires, Acad. de Mâcon, France, American Inst. of Architects, Acad. d'Aix-en-Provence; Hon. F.S.A. London, Royal Soc. of Arts, Benjamin Franklin Fellow 60; corresp. Fellow of Société des Antiquaires de France; non-resident mem. Acad. de Dijon; Fellow American Philosophical Soc., Mediaeval Acad. of America; Hon. Pres. Archaeological Inst. of America, Soc. of Architectural Historians; Hon. Corresp. Compagnie des Architectes en Chef des Monuments Historiques; Medallist of the Soc. of Architectural Historians, of the Signet 60, of Mediaeval Acad. of America, and the Acad. d'Architecture, Paris, France 72; Officier de la Légion d'Honneur, and other decorations; Dr. (h.c.) Lawrence Univ., Univs. of Dijon (France) and Illinois; Hon. citizen Ville de Cluny, France.

Leisure interests: historical research, drawing, travel.
Publs. *The Early Architectural History of the Cathedral of Santiago de Compostela* 26, *Brief Commentary on Early Mediaeval Church Architecture* 42, *Benedictine Contributions to Church Architecture* 49, *Arquitectura Moderna en los Estados Unidos* 49, *Carolingian and Romanesque Architecture* 59, 66, 74, *Cluny-Les Eglises et la Maison du Chef d'Ordre* 68, etc.
274 Grove Street, Wellesley, Mass. 02181, U.S.A.
Telephone: 617-235-4502.

Concepción, Roberto, A.A., LL.B.; Philippine lawyer; b. 7 June 1903, Manila; *s.* of Isidro Bernardino Concepción and Catalina Cabral Reyes; *m.* Dolores Buenaventura Concepción 1926; two *s.* three *d.*; ed. San Beda Coll. and Univ. of Santo Tomás.

Private practice 29-29; Asst. Attorney, Office of the Attorney-Gen. 29-38; successively Asst. Solicitor-Gen., Judge of First Instance, Under-Sec. of Justice, Assoc. Justice of Court of Appeals; Assoc. Justice of Supreme Court 54, Chief Justice and Chair. Presidential Electoral Tribunal 66-73; Prof. of Law at several leading univs.; active in many local and int. orgs. engaged in the promotion of the rule of law; rep. of the Philippines at several int. confs.; Knight Grand Cross of Rizal; Hon. D.C.L. (Univs. of Santo Tomás and the Philippines and St. Louis Univ.).

Leisure interests: golf, yoga.
Publs. Various lectures and papers, etc.
Integrated Bar of the Philippines, 915 Quezon Boulevard Ext., Quezon City; Home: 18 Kitanlad, Quezon City, Philippines.
Telephone: 97-23-88 (Office); 62-32-73 (Home).

Conchon, Georges; French writer and journalist; b. 9 May 1925, Saint-Avit; *s.* of Gilbert Conchon and Marcelle Gancille; *m.* Yvonne Message 1946; one *d.*; ed. Lycée Henri IV, Paris, and Univ. de Paris à la Sorbonne.

Secretary of Debates, Assemblée de l'Union française 47-52, Divisional Head 52-58; Sec.-Gen. Parl. Central African Repub. 59; Sec. of Debates at the Senate 60-; Prix des Libraires de France 60, Prix Goncourt 64.
Publs. *Les Grandes Lessives* 53, *Les Honneurs de la Guerre* 55, *La Corrida de la Victoire* 59, *L'Etat Sauvage* 64, *Pourquoi pas Vamos* (play) 65, *L'Apprenti gaucher* 67, *Nous, la Gauche, devant Louis-Napoléon* 69, *L'Amour en Face* 72.
132 rue de Rennes, Paris 6e, France.
Telephone: 222-89-96.

Condliffe, John Bell, M.A., D.SC., LL.D., LITT.D.; American economist; b. 23 Dec. 1891, Melbourne, Australia; *s.* of Alfred Bell and Margaret (Marley) Condliffe; *m.* Olive Grace Mills 1916; two *s.* one *d.*; ed. Canterbury Coll. of New Zealand, Gonville and Caius Coll., Cambridge.

Professor of Econs. Canterbury Coll. 20-26; Research Sec. Inst. of Pacific Relations, Hawaii 27-31; Visiting Prof. of Economics Univ. of Michigan 30-31; mem. Economic Intelligence Service L.N. 31-37; Prof. of Commerce London Univ. 37-39; Prof. of Economics Univ. of California 40-58; Adviser Indian Nat. Council of Applied Economic Research 59-60; Sen. Economist Stanford Research Inst. 61-67; Erskine Fellow, Univ. of Canterbury 73; Assoc. Dir. Div. Econs. and History, Carnegie Endowment for Int. Peace 43-47; mem. Royal Econ. Soc., American Econ. Asscn., Econ. Soc. of Australia and N.Z.; Fellow A.A.A.S. 53; Howland Memorial Prize Yale Univ. 39; Wendell Wilkie Prize 50; Gold Cross, Royal Order of Phoenix (Greece).

Leisure interest: golf.
Publs. *New Zealand in the Making* 30 (revised 58), *Problems of the Pacific* 27, 29, *China Today—Economic* 32, *World Economic Survey* 31-37, *Reconstruction of World Trade* 40, *Agenda for a Post-War World* 42, *Commerce of Nations* 50, *The Welfare State in New Zealand* 59, *The Development of Australia* 63, *Foresight and Enterprise* 65, *The Economic Outlook for New Zealand* 69, *Te Rangi Hiroa: The Life of Sir Peter Buck* 72, *Defunct Economists* 74.
1641 Canyonwood Court No. 1, Walnut Creek, Calif. 94595, U.S.A.

Cone, Fairfax Mastick; American business executive; b. 21 Feb. 1903, San Francisco, Calif.; *s.* of William H. and Isabelle (Williams) Cone; *m.* Gertrude Kennedy 1929; one *d.*; ed. Univ. of California.

San Francisco Examiner 26-29; copywriter and account exec. Lord and Thomas advertising agency 29-38, Vice-Pres. and Man. 38-40, Vice-Pres. New York 41, Chicago 42; organizer of Foote, Cone & Belding 42, Chair., Exec. Cttee. 42-48, Chair. of Board 48-51, Pres. 51-57, Chair. Exec. Cttee. 57-67, Dir. 67-.
c/o Foote, Cone & Belding Inc., 200 Park Avenue, New York, N.Y. 10017, U.S.A.

Confalonieri, H.E. Cardinal Carlo; Vatican ecclesiastic; b. 25 July 1893, Seveso.

Ordained priest 16; fmr. Private Sec. to Pope Pius XI; Archbishop of Aquila 41-50; Titular Archbishop of Nicopolis al Nesto and Sec. Sacred Congregation of Seminaries and Universities 50-58; created Cardinal 58; Archpriest of Liberian Patriarchal Basilica; Prefect Sacred Consistorial Congregation 61-; mem. Sacred Congregations for the Doctrine of Faith, Oriental Churches, Clergy, De Propaganda Fide, Saints, Divine Cult, Catholic Educ., Council for Public Affairs.
Publs. *Pio XI visto da vicino* 57, *Decennio Aquilano esperienze pastorali* 67.
Via Rusticucci 13, Rome, Italy.

Conn, Jerome W., M.D.; American professor of medicine; b. 24 Sept. 1907, New York, N.Y.; *s.* of Joseph H. Conn and Dora Kobrin; *m.* Elizabeth Stern 1932; one *s.* one *d.*; ed. Rutgers Univ. and Univ. of Mich. Medical School.

Instructor of Internal Medicine, Univ. of Mich. Medical School 35-38, Asst. Prof. 38-44, Head of Div. of Endocrinology and Metabolism and Dir. of Metabolism Research Unit 43-, Assoc. Prof. 44-50, Prof. of Internal Medicine 50-68, Louis Harry Newburgh Distinguished Univ. Prof. of Internal Medicine 68-74; Prof. Emer. 74-; Veterans' Admin. Distinguished Physician 74-; F.A.C.P.; Hon. F.A.C.S., Hon. Sc.D. (Rutgers Univ.); mem. Nat. Acad. of Sciences, U.S.A., Inst. of Medicine, U.S.A., Nat. Acad. of Medicine, Argentina; numerous U.S. and foreign awards, including Modern Medicine

Award and Citation 57, Banting Medal of Amer. Diabetes Asscn. 58, Gordon Wilson Medal of Amer. Clinical and Climatological Asscn. 62, John Phillips Memorial Award of Amer. Coll. of Physicians 65, Gold Medal of Int. Soc. for Progress in Internal Medicine, Buenos Aires 69, Gairdner Int. Award 69, Stouffer Int. Award 71.

Leisure interests: tennis, squash, fishing, writing.

Publs. 428, and contribs. to 17 books, on metabolism, endocrinology and hypertension.

Veterans' Administration Hospital, 2215 Fuller Road, Ann Arbor, Mich. 48105; Home: 200 Orchard Hill Drive, Ann Arbor, Mich. 48104, U.S.A.

Telephone: 313-769-7100 (Office); 313-761-3966 (Home).

Connally, John Bowden, Jr., LL.B.; American lawyer and politician; b. 27 Feb. 1917, Floresville, Texas; s. of John B. Connally and Lela Wright Connally; m. Idanell Brill 1940; two s. one d.; ed. Univ. of Texas. Served in U.S. Navy 41-46; fmr. executive in oil, oilfield services, radio and television, carbon, ranches, insurance, New York Central Railroad; Sec. of the Navy Jan.-Nov. 61; Gov. of Texas 63-69; Dir. Texas Instruments 69-70, United States Trust Co., Halliburton Co.; Senior Partner, Vinson, Elkins, Searls, Connally & Smith, Houston (law firm) 69-70, Partner 72-; Sec. of the Treasury 71-72; Dir. Pan American World Airways 73-, Falconbridge Nickel Mines Ltd. 73-; mem. and trustee Andrew W. Mellon Foundation 73-; mem. Senior Execs. Council, Conf. Board 73-; Vice-Chair. Houston Chamber of Commerce 75-; Adviser to Pres. June-July 73; Democrat until 73, Republican 73-.

c/o Vinson, Elkins, Searls, Connally & Smith, First City National Bank Building, Houston, Tex., U.S.A.

Telephone: 713-236-2100 (Office).

Connelly, Brig.-Gen. Alan Burton, C.B.E., C.D., B.ENG.; Canadian army officer, engineer and international civil servant; b. 25 March 1908, Amble, Northumberland, England; s. of Thomas Connelly and Janet Burton; m. 1st Margaret Woodbury Forbes 1937, one s. one d.; m. 2nd Mary Evelyn Sharpe (née Brock) 1974; ed. Calgary Normal School, Royal Mil. Coll. of Canada, Nova Scotia Tech. Coll., McGill Univ. and School of Mil. Engineering, Chatham, England.

Canadian Army 31-53; Chief Engineer, 1 Canadian Corps 43-44; Commdr. "B" Group and Canadian Reinf. and Repat. Units 44-46; Commdr. Canadian Troops, N.W. Europe 46; Deputy Adjutant-Gen. 46-48; Commdr. Northwest Highway System 48-50; Commdr. Saskatchewan Area and G.O.C. Prairie Command 50-51; Commdr. Canadian Military Mission, Far East 51-52; Gen. Supt. Dufresne Engineering, Montreal 53-55; Vice-Pres. Mannix Construction and Empire Devt. 55-57; Chief, Engineering Div., Dept. of Northern Affairs and Nat. Resources 58-62; Dir. of Capital Assistance, External Aid Bureau, and Canadian Int. Devt. Agency 63-69; Dir. Colombo Plan Bureau 69-73; Adviser Ministry of Finance and Planning, Burma 74-75.

Leisure interests: drawing, swimming, golf, tennis, music, books, antiques.

360 Lake St. Louis Road, Ville de Lery, Quebec, Canada.

Telephone: 514-692-6563.

Connelly, Marc; American dramatist; b. 13 Dec. 1890; ed. Trinity Hall, Washington.

Fmr. Pres. Authors' League of America, Nat. Inst. of Arts and Letters; fmr. Prof. of Playwriting, Yale Univ.; Pulitzer Prize, O. Henry Award 30; Hon. Litt.D. Bowdoin.

Publs. *The Green Pastures, The Wisdom Tooth, A Souvenir from Qam* 65. *Voices Off Stage* 68; co-author *Beggar on Horseback, Dulcy, Merton of the Movies, To the Ladies, The Farmer Takes a Wife, Hunter's Moon* 58 (plays); *Helen of Troy N.Y.* (musical comedy).

25 Central Park West, New York City; and Players' Club, New York City, N.Y., U.S.A.

Connelly, Michael Aynsley, B.COM., F.C.A., C.M.A.; New Zealand politician; b. 21 Feb. 1916; ed. Univ. of Otago.

Served World War II; mem. Parl. for Riccarton 56-69, for Wigram 69-; served on numerous parl. cttees.; fmr. Christchurch City Councillor; fmr. Pres. Canterbury Savings Bank; Minister of Police 72-75, of Customs 72-74, Assoc. Minister of Finance 72-74; Minister of Statistics 74-75, of Works and Development 75; Chair. Nat. Roads Board 75, Nat. Water and Soil Conservation Authority 75; fmr. mem. Lincoln Coll. Council; Pres. Adult Cerebral Palsy Soc.; fmr. Chair. Exec. Cttee., Canterbury Provincial Bldgs. Board; Labour. Parliament Buildings, Wellington; Home: Corner of Yaldhurst and Pound Roads, Yaldhurst, Christchurch 5RD, New Zealand.

Connery, Sean; Scottish actor; b. 25 Aug. 1930; s. of Joseph and Euphamia Connery; m. 1st Diane Cilento 1962 (diss. 1974), 2nd Michelin Boglio Roquebrun 1975. Served in Royal Navy; Dir. Tantallon Films Ltd. 72-. Films include, *No Road Back* 55, *Time Lock* 56, *Action of the Tiger* 57, *Another Time, Another Place, Hell Drivers* 58, *Darby O'Gill and the Little People* 59, *Tarzan's Greatest Adventure* 59, *On the Fiddle* 61, *The Longest Day* 62, *The Frightened City* 62, *Woman of Straw* 64, *Marnie* 64, *The Hill* 65, *A Fine Madness* 66, *Shalako* 68, *The Molly Maguires* 68, *The Red Tent* 69, *The Anderson Tapes* 70, *The Offence* 73, *Zardoz* 74, *Murder on the Orient Express* 74, *Ransom* 74, *The Wind and the Lion* 75, *The Man Who Would Be King* 75; as James Bond in *Dr. No* 63, *From Russia with Love* 64, *Goldfinger* 65, *Thunderball* 65, *You Only Live Twice* 67, *Diamonds are Forever* 71.

c/o ICM, 22 Grafton Street, London, W.1, England.

Connick, Robert Elwell, B.S., PH.D.; American professor of chemistry; b. 29 July 1917, Eureka, Calif.; s. of Arthur E. Connick and Florence Robertson Connick; m. Frances Spieth 1951; two s. four d.; ed. Univ. of Calif.

Professor of Chemistry, Univ. of Calif., Berkeley 52-, Chair. Dept. of Chemistry, Univ. of Calif., Berkeley 58-60, Dean of Coll. of Chemistry 60-65, Vice-Chancellor for Academic Affairs 65-67, 69-71; mem. Nat. Acad. of Sciences.

Leisure interest: Indian petroglyphs.

Publs. Numerous articles in *Journal of American Chem. Soc., Journal of Chem. Physics, Inorganic Chem.,* etc.

Department of Chemistry, University of California, Berkeley, Calif. 94720; Home: 50 Marguerita Road, Berkeley, Calif. 94707, U.S.A.

Telephone: 524-4693 (Home).

Connolly, Hon. John Joseph, P.C., O.B.E., Q.C., PH.D., LL.D.; Canadian lawyer and politician; b. 1906; ed. Ottawa Separate Schools, Univ. of Ottawa, Queen's Univ., Kingston, Ontario, Univ. of Notre Dame, South Bend, Indiana, U.S.A., and Univ. of Montreal.

Member of Bar of Province of Ontario and Province of Quebec; Exec. Asst. to Minister of Nat. Defence for Naval Services 41-45; now Counsel to Honeywell Wotherspoon; Pres. Nat. Liberal Fed. 61-64; Senator from Ontario 53-; Minister without Portfolio and Leader of Govt. in Senate 64-68; Past Pres. Nat. Liberal Fed. of Canada; Pres. Gen. Council Commonwealth Parl. Assoc. 65-66, mem. of Working Party and Exec. Cttee. 66-70; Liberal.

The Senate, Ottawa, Ont., Canada.

Connor, John Thomas, J.D., A.B.; American business executive and government official; b. 3 Nov. 1914, Syracuse, N.Y.; s. of Michael J. and Mary Sullivan Connor; m. Mary O'Boyle 1940; two s. one d.; ed. Holy Rosary High School, Syracuse, N.Y., Holy

Rosary Grammar School, Harvard Law School and Syracuse Univ.

Formerly assoc. with law firm Cravath, de Gersdorff, Swaine and Wood; General Counsel, Office of Scientific Research and Development 42-44; U.S. Marine Corps 44-45; Counsel, Office of Naval Research, later Special Asst. to U.S. Sec. of Navy 45-47; General Attorney, Merck & Co. (pharmaceuticals) 47, Pres. 55-65; U.S. Sec. of Commerce 65-66; Pres. Allied Chemical Corpn. 67-69, Chair. of Board, Chief Exec. Officer and Dir. 69-; Dir., Gen. Motors Corpn., Chase Manhattan Bank, Chase Manhattan Corpn.; numerous hon. degrees.

P.O. Box 3000R, Morristown, N.J.; Home: Blue Mill Road, New Vernon, N.J., U.S.A.

Connor, Ralph, B.S., PH.D.; American chemist; b. 12 July 1907, Newton, Ill.; s. of Stephen A. and Minnie (Ross) Connor; m. Margaret Raef 1931; one s.; ed. Univs. of Illinois and Wisconsin.

Assistant Professor, Assoc. Professor and Prof. of Chemistry, Univ. of Pennsylvania 35-41; Technical Aide, Section Chief, and Chief of Div. 8, Nat. Defense Research Cttee. of Office of Scientific Research and Development 41-45; Assoc. Dir. of Research, Rohm & Haas Co. 45-48, Vice-Pres. and Dir. 48-73 (in charge of Research 48-70), Chair. of Board 60-70, Chair. of Exec. Cttee. 70-73; mem. Board of Dirs. American Chemical Soc. 54-65, Chair. 56-58; Hon. D.Sc. (Philadelphia Coll. of Pharmacy and Science, Univ. of Pennsylvania, Polytechnic Inst. of Brooklyn), Hon. LL.D. (Lehigh Univ.); several medals.

Home: 234 North Bent Road, Wyncote, Pa. 19095, U.S.A.

Conrad, Anthony Lee; American business executive; b. 3 May 1921, Norwood, Mass.; s. of Charles W. and Flora (Tandy) Conrad; m. 1st Katherine W. Wolfe 1943 (died 1968), two s. one d.; m. 2nd Nancy R. Morrison 1969; ed. Phillips Exeter Acad. and Lafayette Coll.

President, RCA Service Co. 60-68; Vice-Pres. Educ. Systems RCA Corpn. 68-69, Exec. Vice-Pres., Services 69-71, Pres. and Chief Operating Officer RCA Corpn. 71-, Chief Exec. Jan. 76-; Dir. Banquet Foods Corpn., Coronet Industries Inc., Cushman & Wakefield Inc., RCA Corpn., The Hertz Corpn., Random House Inc., RCA Global Communications Inc., ICI Americas, Chesebrough-Pond's Inc.; Vice-Chair. Lafayette Coll. Board of Trustees; Hon. D.Sc. (Florida Inst. of Technology) 70.

RCA Corporation, 30 Rockefeller Plaza, New York, N.Y. 10020, U.S.A.

Conrad, Charles, Jr.; American astronaut; b. 2 June 1930, Philadelphia, Pa.; m. Jane Du Bose; four s.; ed. Princeton Univ.

Entered U.S. Navy after graduation; attended Navy Test Pilot School, Patuxent River, Md., later project test pilot; also flight instructor and performance engineer, Patuxent; later Safety Officer, Fighter Squadron 96, Naval Air Station, Miramar, Calif.; selected as astronaut by NASA Sept. 62; pilot, *Gemini V* Mission 65; backup pilot *Gemini VIII* Mission 66; Command pilot *Gemini XI* 66; *Apollo XII* moon landing mission Nov. 69; Captain, *Skylab* 73; NASA Exceptional Service Medals; Yuri Gagarin Gold Space Medal 70.

NASA Johnson Space Center, Houston, Tex. 77058, U.S.A.

Conrad, Hermann, DR. JUR.; German university professor; b. 21 Oct. 1904, Cologne; s. of Paul and Julia (née Nacken) Conrad; ed. Univ. of Cologne.

Dozent Cologne Univ. 36; Lecturer Univs. of Lausanne and Geneva 38-40; Prof. of Law, Univ. of Marburg/Lahn 42-48, Univ. of Bonn 48-; mem. Rheinisch-Westfälische Akad. der Wissenschaften; Dr. h.c., Dr. rer. pol. h.c.

Publs. *Liegenschaftsübereignung und Grundbucheintragung in Köln während des Mittelalters* 35, *Die Amtleutebücher der Kölnischen Sondergemeinden* (with Dr. Thea Buyken) 36, *Dantes Staatslehre im Spiegel der scholastischen Philosophie seiner Zeit* 46, *Geschichte der deutschen Wehrverfassung* 39, *Deutsche Rechtsgeschichte Frühzeit und Mittelalter* 54, 2nd edn. 62, *Individuum und Gemeinschaft in der Privat-Rechtsordnung des 18. und beginnenden 19. Jahrhunderts* 56, *Das Gottesurteil in den Konstitutionen von Melfi, Friedrich II. von Hohenstaufen (1237)* (*Festschrift für Schmidt-Rimpler*) 57, *Freiherr von Stein als Staatsmann im Übergang vom Absolutismus zum Verfassungsstaat* 58, *Der Deutsche Juristentag 1860-1960, Festschr. z 100. Dt. Juristentag* 60; Ed. (with G. Kleinheyer) *C. G. Suarez, Vorträge über Recht und Staat* 60, *Rechtsstaatliche Bestrebungen im Absolutismus Preussens und Österreichs am Ende des 18. Jahrhdts.* 61, *Religionsbann, Toleranz und Parität am Ende des alten Reiches, Röm. Quartalschr.* 61, *Recht und Verfassung des Reiches in der Zeit Maria Theresia* (with Kleinheyer and others) 64, *Zu den geistigen Grundlagen der Strafrechtsreform Josephs II* (Festschrift für H. v. Weber) 64, *Das Allgemeine Landrecht von 1794 als Grundgesetz des friderizianischen Staates* 65, *Deutsche Rechtsgeschichte Neuzeit bis 1806* 66, *Rheinbund und Norddeutscher Reichsbund* (Gedächtnisschrift für Peters) 67, *Staatliche Theorie und kirchliche Dogmatik im Ringen um die Ehegesetzgebung Josephs II* (Festschrift für Schmaus) 67, *Staatsverfassung und Prinzenerziehung* (Festschrift für Brandt) 68, *Preussen und das Französische Recht in den Rheinländern* (Festschrift Oberlandesgericht Köln) 69, *Das Zivilrecht im Rechtsunterricht für den Erzherzog Joseph* (Festschrift für Hans Lentze) 69, *Der Reichsgedanke bei Dante und Nikolaus von Kues* 69, *Richter und Gesetz im Übergang vom Absolutismus zum Verfassungsstaat* 71, *Staatsgedanke und Staatspraxis des aufgeklärten Absolutismus* 71.

Oberaustr. 31, 53 Bonn-Bad Godesberg 1, Federal Republic of Germany.

Telephone: Bad Godesberg 12141.

Conrad, Wilhelm, DR. RER. POL.; German financier; b. 21 June 1911, Giessen; m.; two d.

Formerly Assistant, Inst. for Econ. Studies, Univ. of Giessen; Civic Treas., Giessen 46-49; Vice-Pres. Central Office for Emergency Aid, Bad Homburg 49-52, Fed. Compensation Office, Bad Homburg 53-56; Minister of Finance, Hesse 56-64; Pres. and Chair. Man. Board, Hessische Landesbank Girozentrale 64-67; Counsellor, Landeszentralbank, Hessen; mem. Board, Deutsche Unionbank, GmbH; Investitions- und Handelsbank A.G., Banque Worms & Cie., Paris and Casablanca; mem. Admin. Board, Deutsche Girozentrale-Deutsche Kommunalbank; mem. Man. Board, Deutscher Sparkassen- und Giroverband, Bonn, Hessischer Sparkassen- und Giroverband, Frankfurt/M; Grosses Bundesverdienstkreuz mit Stern und Schulterband.

Bad Homburg, Herderstrasse 20, Federal Republic ot Germany.

Telephone: 28641.

Conroy, Sir Diarmaid William, Kt., C.M.G., O.B.E., T.D., Q.C.; British jurist; b. 22 Dec. 1913, London; m. Elizabeth Craig 1939; one s. two d.; ed. Gray's Inn; London.

Practised at English Bar 35-39; served in army 39-46; Crown Counsel, N. Rhodesia 46-50, Legal Draftsman 50-52; Attorney-Gen., Gibraltar 52-55; Solicitor-Gen. and Deputy Speaker, Kenya 55-61; Chief Justice, N. Rhodesia 61-65; Pres. Industrial Tribunals (England and Wales) 65-74, Chair. Industrial Tribunals (Southampton) 74-.

Leisure interest: sailing.

26 Ward Avenue, Cowes, Isle of Wight, PO31 8AY, England.

Telephone: Cowes 5949.

Consagra, Pietro; Italian sculptor; b. 4 Oct. 1920, Mazara; two s. two d.; ed. Acad. of Fine Arts, Palermo. One-man shows: Rome 47, 49, 51, 59, 61; Milan 58, 61; Venice 48; Brussels 58; Paris 59; Zürich 61; São Paulo Bienal 55, 59; Venice Biennale 56, 60, New York 62, Buenos Aires 62, Boston 62; Works in following museums: Tate Gallery, London; Nat. Museum and Middleheim Park, Antwerp; Museums of Modern Art, São Paulo, Paris, Rome, New York, Buenos Aires, Caracas, Zagreb, Helsinki; Guggenheim Museum, New York; Art Inst., Chicago; Carnegie Inst., Pittsburgh; Inst. of Fine Arts, Minneapolis and Houston; Grand Prize for Sculpture, Venice Biennale 60.
c/o Galleria Nazionale d'Arte Moderna, viale delle Belle Arti 131, 00197, Rome; Via Cassia 1162, Rome, Italy.
Telephone: 6995119.

Consalvi, Simon Alberto; Venezuelan diplomatist; b. 7 July 1929; m.; two c.; ed. Cen. Univ. of Venezuela.
Member Nat. Congress 59-64, 74-; Amb. to Yugoslavia 61-64; Dir. Cen. Office of Information for the Presidency 64-67; Pres. Nat. Inst. of Culture and Art 67-69; Dir. Nat. Magazine of Culture; Int. Editor El Nacional newspaper 71-74; Minister of State for Information 74; Perm. Rep. to UN Oct. 74-; mem. Nat. Congress Foreign Relations Comm.
Permanent Mission of Venezuela to the United Nations, 231 East 46th Street, New York, N.Y. 10017, U.S.A.

Consigli, Carlos Alberto; Argentine doctor and politician; b. 20 Aug. 1918, Río Cuarto; ed. Faculty of Medicine, Nat. Univ., Córdoba, also Madrid, Barcelona and São Paulo.
Practised in Hospital Nacional de Clínicas, Patronato de Leprosos (Leprosy Foundation), Hospital Español (Skin Dept.); Ward doctor, subsequently Chief Clinician, Teaching Instructor, Dept. of Dermatology, Faculty of Medicine, Nat. Univ. of Córdoba; Chief of Dermatology Section, Ministry of Public Health and Social Assistance, Córdoba Province 55-67; Minister for Social Welfare 69-70; mem. numerous Argentinian and foreign medical socs., fmr. Vice-Pres. Sociedad Argentina de Leprología; fmr. Pres. Dermatological Union, Córdoba.
Publs. more than thirty scientific works.
c/o Ministerio de Bienestar Social de la Nación, Buenos Aires, Argentina.

Consolo, Federico; Italian international bank official; b. 18 March 1906, Palermo; m. Rysia Consolo-Toeplitz; ed. in Milan and London, and Univs. of Cambridge and Rome.
With Montecatini S.p.A. and Pirelli S.p.A. 28-43; liaison between Italian Govt. and Allied Comm. and subsequently UNRRA, Rome 45-47; with Int. Bank for Reconstruction and Devt., rising to Asst. Dir., W. Hemisphere Dept. 47-58; Dir.-Gen. Special Adviser to Comm., EURATOM, Brussels 58-64; Special Rep. for UN Orgs., Int. Bank for Reconstruction and Devt. 64-71.
c/o International Bank for Reconstruction and Development, 1818 H. Street, N.W., Washington, D.C. 20433, U.S.A.

Constantine XII; ex-King of the Hellenes; b. 2 June 1940; m. Princess Anne-Marie of Denmark 1964; two s. one d.; ed. Anavryta School and Law School, Athens Univ.
Military Training 56-58; visited United States 58, 59; succeeded to throne March 64; left Greece Dec. 67; deposed June 73; Monarchy abolished by Nat. Referendum Dec. 74; Gold Medal, Yachting, Olympic Games, Rome 60.
c/o Claridge's, Brook Street, London, W.1, England.

Conte, Arthur; French journalist, politician and broadcasting executive; b. 31 March 1920, Salses, Pyrénées-Orientales; s. of Pierre Conte and Marie-Thérèse Parazols; m. Colette Lacassagne 1951; one s. one d.; ed. Montpellier Univ.
Foreign leader writer, Indépendant de Perpignan 45; later worked for Paris Match; subsequently leader-writer for Les Informations and contributor to Le Figaro, Historia, Les Nouvelles Littéraires; Sec. Socialist Party Fed. for Pyrénées-Orientales; Deputy to Nat. Assembly 51-62; Sec. of State for Industry and Commerce 57; Deputy to Nat. Assembly (U.D.R.) 68-72; Mayor of Salses 47-; Del. to Assembly of Council of Europe 56-62; Pres. WEU Assembly 61-62; Chair. and Dir.-Gen. ORTF 72-73.
Leisure interest: golf.
Publs. La Légende de Pablo Casals, Les étonnements de Mister Newborn, Les Promenades de M. Tripoire, Les hommes ne sont pas des Héros, La Vigne sous le rempart, Yalta ou le partage du monde, Bandoung, tournant de l'histoire, Sans de Gaulle, Lénine et Staline, Les Frères Burns, Hommes Libres, l'Epopée mondiale d'un siècle (5 vols.).
94 avenue de Suffren, Paris 15e, France.

Conté, Sadiou, DR.MED.; Guinean surgeon and diplomatist; b. 1925; ed. Ecole William Ponty and Lycée, Dakar, Paris Univ. Medical Faculty.
Asst. Surgeon Dakar hospitals 57-58; Chief Surgeon, Ballay Hospital, Conakry 59; Ambassador to U.S.S.R. 59-61, to U.S.A. 61-63; Minister of Educ. 63, of Justice 67; now Prof. of Surgery and Chief Surgeon, Ignace Deen Hospital, Conakry.
Publs. Surgical papers in French and African journals; Le Noir et les Cultures indo-européennes 56, Réflexions sur la lymphadénie mésentérique 57, Notre expérience de l'abord direct du Mal de Pott 57, De la fausse rareté de la pathologie vésiculaire en Afrique 57, Un cas d'exulcé-ratio Simplex et Problèmes connexes 58, La spondylo-discite melitococcique 58, Au fil de la Liberté (collected poems) 66.
Hôpital Ignace Deen, Conakry, Guinea.

Conti, Luciano; Italian diplomatist; b. 29 Sept. 1917, Leghorn; m.; ed. Univ. of Siena.
Entered Diplomatic Service 40; held successive diplomatic posts in Stockholm, Vienna, Denver (U.S.A.) 43-50; Consul successively in Munich, Hamburg 51-54; Head of Section, Cultural Affairs Directorate, Ministry of Foreign Affairs; Deputy Dir.-Gen. of Personnel, Ministry of Foreign Affairs 58; Consul-Gen. Munich 59-62; Amb. to Lebanon, concurrently accred. to Kuwait 62-64, to Denmark 64-68; Amb.-at-Large, Econ. Affairs Gen. Directorate, Ministry of Foreign Affairs 68-73; Perm. Rep. to OECD 73-.
Italian Delegation to Organisation for Economic Co-operation and Development, 50 rue de Varenne, 75007 Paris, France.

Conway, H.E. Cardinal William John, D.D., D.C.L.; Irish ecclesiastic; b. 22 Jan. 1913; ed. Queen's Univ., Belfast, St. Patrick's Coll., Maynooth and Gregorian Univ., Rome.
Professor of Moral Theology and Canon Law, St. Patrick's Coll., Maynooth 42-57, Vice-Pres. 57-58; Titular Bishop of Neve, Auxiliary to His Eminence Cardinal D'Alton 58-63; Archbishop of Armagh and Primate of all Ireland Sept. 63-; created Cardinal 65.
Publs. The Church and State Control 52, Problems in Canon Law 55, The new law on the Eucharistic Fast 55, The Child and the Catechism 59, Youth Problems 60.
Ara Coeli, Armagh, Northern Ireland.
Telephone: Armagh 522045.

Conyers, John, Jr., J.D.; American politician; b. 16 May 1929, Detroit, Mich.; s. of John and Lucy Simpson Conyers; unmarried; ed. Detroit public schools and Wayne Univ.
Legislative Asst. to Congressman J. Dingell 58-61; Senior partner, Conyers, Bell & Townsend 59-61; Referee, Michigan workmens Compensation Dept.

61-63; fmr. Gen. Counsel, Detroit Trade Union Leadership Council; mem. Advisory Council, Mich. Civil Liberties Union; Rep. from Michigan, U.S. Congress 64-; Democrat; Hon. LL.D. (Wilberforce Univ.).
Leisure interests: tennis, jazz.
Publs. *Politics and the Black Revolution* 69, *To Change the Course of History* (in *Many Shades of Black*) 69.
222 Cannon House Office Building, Washington, D.C. 20515; 305 Federal Building, 231 W. Lafayette Boulevard, Detroit, Mich. 48226, U.S.A.
Telephone: 202-225-5126 (Washington); 313-226-7022 (Detroit).

Coobar, Abdulmegid; Libyan politician; b. 1909; ed. Arabic and Italian schools in Tripoli, and privately. With Birth Registration Section, Tripoli Municipal Council and later its Section Head, Adviser on Arab Affairs for the Council 43-44; resigned from Govt. Service 44; mem. Nat. Constitutional Assembly 50, and mem. its Cttee. to draft the Libyan Constitution; mem. of Parl. for Eastern Gharian 52-55, Pres. of Parl. Assembly 52-55; Deputy Prime Minister and Minister of Communications 55-56; again elected for Eastern Gharian to the new Chamber of Deputies 55-, Pres. 56; mem. of Council of Viceroy 56; Deputy Prime Minister and Minister of Foreign Affairs 57; Prime Minister 57-60; concurrently Minister for Foreign Affairs 58; Independence Award (First Class).
Asadu el-Furat Street 29, Garden City, Tripoli, Libya.

Cook, Chauncey William Wallace; American food company executive (retd.); b. 22 June 1909; ed. Univ. of Texas, Columbia Univ. Graduate School of Business Admin.
Proctor and Gamble Co. 31-42; Gen. Foods Corpn. 42-74, Chief Engineer 42-44, Div. Manager (Manufacturing and Engineering) 44-46, Production Manager Maxwell House Div. 46-51, Product Man., Instant Maxwell House Coffee 51-52, Sales and Advertising Man., Maxwell House Div. 53-55, Gen. Man., Maxwell House Div. and Vice-Pres. Gen. Foods 55-59, Exec. Vice-Pres. (Operations) 59-62, Pres. 62-65, Pres. and Chief Exec. Officer 65-66, Chair. and Chief Exec. 66-73, Chair. 73-74, Chair. Exec. Cttee. 74-; Dir., Gen. Foods Corpn. 60-, Whirlpool Corpn. 62-, Chase Manhattan Bank 63-74, AMF Inc. 72-, Shell Oil Co. 73-, Capital Nat. Bank (Austin, Texas) 73-; Trustee Conf. Board, Univ. of Texas Devt. Board; mem. Business Council; served on various national food advisory boards as chair.; several honorary degrees in Laws, Humane Letters and Engineering.
General Foods Corporation, 250 North Street, White Plains, N.Y. 10625, U.S.A.
Telephone: 914-253-4414.

Cook, Donald C., A.B., M.B.A., J.D., L.L.M.; American public utility executive; b. 14 April 1909, Escanaba, Mich.; s. of Nelson Cook, Jr. and Edith Bryant; m. Winifred V. Carlsen 1943; one s.; ed. Univ. of Michigan and George Washington Univ. Law School.
Securities and Exchange Commission 35-45; Exec. Asst. to Attorney-Gen. of U.S. 45-46; Dir. Office of Alien Property, U.S. Dept. of Justice 46-47; Partner, Cook & Berger (attorneys) 47-49; Commr., Securities and Exchange Comm. 49-50, Vice-Chair. 50-52, Chair. 52-53; Vice-Pres. American Electric Power Service Corpn. 53-54, Dir. 54-, Exec. Vice-Pres. 54-61, Pres. 61-72, Chief Exec. Officer 61-, Chair. of Board 72-; Pres. American Electric Power Co. 61-72, Dir. and Chief Exec. Officer 61-, Chair. of Board 71-, also Pres. and Chief Exec. Officer of subsidiaries.
Leisure interests: collector of Islamic Art, travel.
American Electric Power Co., 2 Broadway, New York, N.Y. 10004, U.S.A.
Telephone: 212-422-4800.

Cook, G(eorge) Bradford, J.D.; American lawyer; b. 10 May 1937, Lincoln, Neb.; s. of George B. Cook

and Margaret Colman; m. Laura Shedd Armour 1966; one s. three d.; ed. Stanford Univ. and Univ. of Neb. Law School.
Partner, Winston & Strawn, Chicago, Ill. 62-71; U.S. Securities and Exchange Comm. (SEC), Washington, D.C., Gen. Counsel 71-72, Dir. Div. of Market Regulation 72-73, Chair. March-May 73 (resigned).
Leisure interests: skiing, hunting, fishing.
4808 Rockwood Parkway, N.W., Washington, D.C. 20016; and Woman Lake, Longville, Minn. 56655, U.S.A.
Telephone: 202-244-1240 and 218-363-2078 (Homes).

Cook, Mercer, A.B., A.M., PH.D.; American university professor and diplomatist; b. 30 March 1903, Washington; s. of William Cook and Abbie Mitchell; m. Vashti Smith 1929 (died 1969); two s.; ed. Amherst Coll., Univ. of Paris and Brown Univ.
Assistant Professor of French, Howard Univ. 27-36; Prof. of French, Atlanta Univ. 36-43; Supervisor, English-Teaching, Haitian Schools 43-45; Prof. of French, Howard Univ. 45-58, 66-70; Foreign Rep. American Soc. of African Culture 58-60; Dir. African Programme, Congress for Cultural Freedom 60-61; Amb. to Repub. of Niger 61-64, to Senegal 64-66, concurrently to The Gambia 65-66; Visiting Prof. Harvard Univ. 70; Prof. Emer., Howard Univ. 70-.
Publs. *Le Noir* 34, *Five French Negro Authors* 44, *Education in Haiti* 49; trans. Senghor's *African Socialism* 59, Mamadou Dia's *African Nations and World Solidarity* 61; *The Militant Black Writer in Africa and the U.S.A.* 69.
4811 Blagden Avenue, N.W., Washington, D.C. 20011, U.S.A.
Telephone: 291-7388.

Cook, Sir William Richard Joseph, Kt., K.C.B., F.R.S., M.SC.; British physical research scientist; b. 10 April 1905; m. Gladys Allen 1939; one s. two d.; ed. Bristol Univ.
Various scientific posts in Research Establishments of War Office and Ministry of Supply 28-47; Dir. of Physical Research, Admiralty 47-50; Chief of the Royal Scientific Service 50-54; Deputy Dir. Atomic Weapons Research Establishment, Aldermaston 54-58; mem. for Engineering and Production of the U.K. Atomic Energy Authority 58-59, for Development and Engineering 59-61, for Reactors 61-64; Deputy Chief Scientific Adviser, Ministry of Defence 64-67; Chief Adviser (Projects and Research) to Minister of Defence (Equipment) 68-70; Chair. Buck and Hickman Ltd. 70-75, Dir. 70-; Dir. Rolls-Royce (1971) Ltd. 71-; Chair. Marconi Int. Marine Co. 71-75; Dir. GEC-Marconi Electronics 72-.
Adbury Springs, Newbury, Berks., England.
Telephone: Newbury 40409 (Home).

Cooke, (Alfred) Alistair; writer and broadcaster; b. 20 Nov. 1908, Manchester, England; s. of Samuel Cooke and Mary Elizabeth Byrne; m. 1st Ruth Emerson 1934, 2nd Jane White Hawkes; one s. one d.; ed. Jesus Coll., Cambridge, Yale and Harvard Univs.
Film Critic, B.B.C. 34-37; London Corresp. Nat. Broadcasting Co. 36-37; Special Corresp. on American Affairs, *The Times* 38-41; Special Corresp. BBC 38-, wrote and narrated *America: a personal history of the United States,* BBC TV 72-73; American feature writer, *Daily Herald* 41-44; UN Corresp. *The Manchester Guardian* 45-48 (now *The Guardian*), Chief Corresp. in U.S.A. 48-72; Peabody Award 52, 72, Writers' Guild Award for best documentary 72, Dimbleby Award 73, four Emmy Awards (Nat. Acad. of TV Arts and Sciences, U.S.A.) 73, Benjamin Franklin Award 73, Hon. K.B.E. 73; Hon. LL.D. (Edinburgh, Manchester); Hon. Litt.D. (St. Andrews Univ.) 75.
Leisure interests: golf, music, travel, photography.
Publs. *Garbo and the Night Watchmen* (edited) 37,

Douglas Fairbanks 40, *A Generation on Trial: U.S.A. v. Alger Hiss* 50, *One Man's America* (English title *Letters from America*) 52, *Christmas Eve* 52, *A Commencement Address* 54, *The Vintage Mencken* (edited) 55, *Around the World in Fifty Years* 66, *Talk About America* 68, *Alistair Cooke's America* 73.
1150 Fifth Avenue, New York; and Nassau Point, Cutchogue, Long Island, N.Y., U.S.A.

Cooke, James, B.S.; American retail executive; b. 13 Nov. 1909; ed. Wharton School, Univ. of Pennsylvania. Store Clerk, The Penn Fruit Co., Philadelphia 27, rose to Vice-Pres. and Gen. Man. 27-59, Pres. and Chief Exec. Officer 64-71, Chair. and Chief Exec. 71-; Pres. and Chief Exec. Officer Allied Supermarkets Inc. 59-65; Dir. and Sec.-Treas. of Topco Assocs. Inc.; Dir. Nat. Asscn. of Food Chains (Chair. 63-64), Dir. Supermarket Inst.; Chair. Rolling Hill Hospital.
Cedarbrook Hill Apartments, Wyncote, Pa. 19095, U.S.A.

Cooke, H. E. Cardinal Terence James, M.A.; American ecclesiastic; b. 1 March 1921, New York.
Ordained to the Priesthood 45; Sec. to Cardinal Spellman 57; Vicar-Gen. Archdiocese of New York 65; Archbishop of New York 68-; cr. Cardinal 69.
1011 First Avenue, New York, N.Y. 10022, U.S.A.

Cool, Pierre Auguste; Belgian trade unionist; b. 28 Aug. 1903, St. Niklaas-Waas; s. of Petrus Cool and Clémentine Heirman; m. Maria Wieers 1925; one s. five d.; ed. Technical High School St. Antonius, St. Niklaas-Waas, High School for Workers, Louvain.
Engineer, St. Niklaas-Waas 19-20, Eisden 20-21; studied High School for Workers, Louvain 21-24; Sec. Regional Union, Beringen 24-25, Free Miners Union for Limburg 25-28, for Flemish Region of Belgium 28-32; Sec.-Gen. Fed. of Christian Trade Unions of Belgium 32-46, Pres. 46-68; fmr. Vice-Pres. Int. Fed. of Christian Trade Unions, Hon. Regent Nat. Bank of Belgium; fmr. Pres. European Org. of ICFTU; Pres. Belgian Nat. Comm. for Peace and Justice; Vice-Pres. Belgian Campaign against Cancer; Minister of State; fmr. mem. Econ. and Social Cttee. of Common Market-Euratom; mem. Nat. Board for Scientific Policy; mem. of Board, Catholic Univ. of Louvain; Grand Officier, Order of Leopold II (Belgium); Commdr. Order, of St. Gregory the Great, Chevalier Légion d'Honneur (France); Grosses Verdienstkreuz (German Fed. Republic); Commdr. Order of Orange-Nassau (Netherlands).
Ter Beuken, Park Ten Doorn, 1852 Beigem, Belgium. Telephone: 02/269-46-63.

Cool, Rodney Lee, B.S., M.A., PH.D.; American professor of high energy physics; b. 8 March 1920, Platte, S. Dak.; s. of George E. and Muriel Post Cool; m. Margaret E. Macmillan 1949; one s. three d.; ed. Univ. of S. Dak., Harvard Univ.
Served Army Signal Corps (rose to Major) 42-46; Brookhaven Nat. Laboratory, Upton, research physicist 49-59, Deputy Chair. High Energy Physics 60-64, Asst. Dir. High Energy Physics 64-66, Assoc. Dir. High Energy Physics 66-70; Prof. Experimental High Energy Physics, Rockefeller Univ. 70-; mem. Stanford Linear Acceleration Center Policy Cttee. 62-67; Assoc. Univs. High Energy Panel, Assoc. Univs. Inc. 63-70; Walker Panel Cttee. on Science and Public Policy, Nat. Acad. of Science 64; mem. High Energy Physics Advisory Panel, Atomic Energy Comm. 67-70; Programme Consultant, Div. of Particles and Fields, American Physical Soc. 68-70; Chair. High Energy Advisory Cttee., Brookhaven Nat. Laboratory 67-70; mem. Nat. Science Foundation, Advisory Panel for Physics 70-73; Chair. Physics Advisory Cttee. Nat. Accelerator Laboratory 67-70; mem. Nat. Acad. of Sciences; Fellow, American Physical Soc.
Publs. *Advances in Particle Physics* (ed. with R. E. Marshak) 68, and many research papers.

Rockefeller University, New York, N.Y. 10021; Home: 450 East 63rd Street, New York, N.Y. 10021, U.S.A. Telephone: (212) 360-1750 (Office).

Cools, André; Belgian politician; b. 1 Aug. 1927, Flémalle-Grande, Liège; s. of Marcel Cools (died 1942); m. Thérèse Josis 1948; one s. one d.
Former Sec.-Receiver of Public Assistance Comm.; Socialist Deputy from Liège 58-; Mayor of Flémalle-Haute; Minister of the Budget 68-71, 72-73, of Econ. Affairs 71-72; Deputy Prime Minister 69-73; Co-Pres. Belgian Socialist Party 73-; Chevalier Ordre de Léopold; Grand Officer Order of Merit (Italy).
Home: 35 Rue Omer Maisin, Flémalle-Haute (Liège), Belgium.

Coombs, Herbert Cole, A.C.F.A.A., M.A., PH.D.; Australian former banker; b. 24 Feb. 1906, Kalamunda, W. Australia; s. of the late F. R. H. Coombs and Rebecca M. Coombs; m. Mary A. Ross 1931; three s. one d.; ed. Univ. of Western Australia and London School of Economics and Political Science.
Assistant Economist, Commonwealth Bank of Australia 35; Economist to Commonwealth Treasury 39; mem. Commonwealth Bank Board 42; Dir. of Rationing 42; Dir.-Gen. of Post-War Reconstruction 43; Gov. Commonwealth Bank of Australia 49-60; Chair. Commonwealth Bank Board 51-60; Gov. Reserve Bank of Australia 60-68, Chair. Reserve Bank Board 60-68; Chair. Australian Council for Aboriginal Affairs 68-; Chair. Australian Council for the Arts 68-74; Chancellor Australian Nat. Univ. 68-76; Consultant to the Prime Minister 72-75; Chair. Royal Comm. on Australian Govt. Admin. 74-76; Hon. LL.D. (Melbourne, Sydney and Australian Nat. Univs.), Hon. D.Litt. (Western Australia); Hon. Fellow, London School of Econs.
Leisure interests: golf, theatre, squash.
Publ. *Other People's Money* 71.
P.O. Box E223, Canberra, A.C.T. 2600; 119 Milson Road, Cremorne, N.S.W. 2090, Australia.
Telephone: 062-474544 (Office); 90-2866 (Home).

Coombs, Philip H.; American economist and educator; b. 15 Aug. 1915, Holyoke, Mass.; s. of Chas and Nellie Coombs; m. Helena Brooks 1941; one s. one d.; ed. Holyoke Public Schools, Amherst Coll., Univ. of Chicago and Brookings Inst.
Instructor in Economics, Williams Coll., Mass. 40-41; Economist, Office of Price Admin. 41-42; Econ. Adviser, Office of Strategic Services 42-45; Econ. Adviser to Dir. of Office of Econ. Stabilization 45-46; Dep. Dir. Veterans Emergency Housing Program 46-47; Prof. of Economics, Amherst Coll. 47-49; Exec. Dir. President's Materials Policy Comm. (Paley Comm.) 51-52; Sec. and Dir. of Research, Fund for Advancement of Education (Ford Foundation) 52-61, Program Dir., Education Div., Ford Foundation 57-61; Asst. Sec. of State for Educational and Cultural Affairs, Dept. of State 61-62; Fellow Council on Foreign Relations 62-63; Dir. Int. Inst. for Educational Planning (UNESCO), Paris 63-68; Dir. of Research 69-; Co-founder Center for Educational Enquiry 70; Vice-Chair. Int. Council for Educational Devt. 70-; Faculty mem. Inst. of Social and Policy Studies, Yale Univ.; official numerous educational orgs.; Hon. L.H.D. (Amherst Coll.), LL.D. (Brandeis Univ. and Monmouth Coll.).
Leisure interests: sailing, fishing, swimming, reading, touring, house repairs, community service.
Publs. *The Fourth Dimension of Foreign Policy* 64, *Education and Foreign Aid* 65, *The World Educational Crisis—A Systems Analysis* 68, *Managing Educational Costs* 72, *New Paths to Learning: for Rural Children and Youth* 73, *Attacking Rural Poverty: How Nonformal Education Can Help* 74, *Education for Rural Development: Case Studies for Planners* 75.
River Road, Essex, Conn., U.S.A.

Coon, Carleton Stevens, B.A., M.A., PH.D.; American anthropologist; b. 23 June 1904, Wakefield, Mass.; s. of John and Bessie Coon; m. 1st Mary Goodale 1927, 2nd Lisa Dougherty 1945; two s.; ed. Phillips Acad., Andover, Harvard Coll., and Harvard Univ.
Instructor and later Assoc. Prof. Harvard 34-41; Assoc. Prof. and later Prof. Harvard 45-48; Prof. and Curator Univ. of Pennsylvania 48-63, Research Curator 63-; Research Assoc., Peabody Museum, Harvard 68-, Lecturer Harvard 69-; expeditions to Morocco 24-28, 62, Albania 29-30, Ethiopia, Yemen and Aden Protectorate 33-34, Iraq 48-49, Iran 48-49, 51, Afghanistan 54, Syria 55, Japan and India 56-57, S. Chile (Alakaluf Indians) 59, Sierra Leone 65, Chad, Cameroon and Libya 66-67; mem. Nat. Acad. of Sciences 55; served in Second World War in diplomatic and mil. posts 42-45; Legion of Merit; hon. mem. Asscn. de la Libération Française; Wenner-Gren Foundation Medallist 51; Gold Medal of Philadelphia Athenaeum for book *The Origin of Races* 63; Gold Medal, Harvard Travellers' Club 72.
Leisure interests: forestry, boating.
Publs. include: *Measuring Ethiopia* 35, *The Races of Europe* 39, *Southern Arabia* 43, *Principles of Anthropology* (with E. D. Chapple) 42, *A Reader in General Anthropology* 48, *Races* (with S. M. Garn and J. B. Birdsell) 49, *The Mountains of Giants* 50, *Caravan* 51, 58, *Cave Explorations in Iran* 51, *The Story of Man* 54, 62, *The Seven Caves* 57, *The Origin of Races* 62, *The Living Races of Man* 65, *Yengema Cave Report* 68, *The Hunting Peoples* 71.
207 Concord Street, Gloucester, Mass. 01930, U.S.A.
Telephone: 617-283-1612.

Cooney, Patrick, LL.B.; Irish solicitor and politician; ed. Castleknock Coll., Univ. Coll., Dublin.
Fine Gael M.P. for Longford and Westmeath 70-; Minister of Justice March 73-.
Department of the Taoiseach, Government Buildings, Dublin 2, Ireland.

Coons, Albert Hewett, M.D., SC.D.; American immunologist; b. 28 June 1912, Gloversville, N.Y.; s. of Albert Selmser Coons and Marion Hewett (Coons); m. Phyllis Watts 1947; one s. four d.; ed. Williamstown Coll., Williamstown, Mass. and Harvard Medical School.
House Officer, Medical Service, Mass. Gen. Hosp. 37-39; Asst. Resident, Medicine, Boston City Hosp. 39-40; Resident Fellow, Harvard Medical School, 39-40, Res. Fellow, Bacteriology and Immunology 40-42; Instructor to Asst. Prof. of Bacteriology and Immunology, Harvard Medical School 47-53, Visiting Prof. 53-70, Prof. 70-; Career Investigator, American Heart Asscn. 53-; mem. Nat. Acad. of Sciences; Harvey Lecturer 57, Lasker Award 59, Paul Ehrlich Award 61, Passano Award 62, T. Duckett Jones Memorial Award 62, Gairdner Foundation Annual Award 62, Emil von Behring Prize 66, Albion O. Bernstein, M.D., Award, N.Y. State Medical Soc. 73; several hon. degrees.
Publs. papers in various scientific journals concerning immunofluorescence and antibody formation.
Department of Pathology, Harvard Medical School, 25 Shattuck Street, Boston, Mass. 02115; Home: 132 High Street, Brookline, Mass. 02146, U.S.A.
Telephone: 617-734-3300.

Cooper, Charles Arthur, PH.D.; American economist; b. 23 Dec. 1933, Chicago, Ill.; s. of Arthur Shires and Elizabeth Burton Greenebaum; m. Janis Starr 1966; two d. one s.; ed. Swarthmore Coll., Pa. Mass. Inst. of Technology, Russian Research Center of Harvard Univ.
Assistant to the Chair. and Economist, Rand Corpn. 61-63, Economist 63-66, 68-70; Econ. Adviser to Special Asst. to the Pres. 66-67; Assoc. Dir. and Econ. Counsellor, Agency for Int. Devt. (AID) Saigon 67-68; Minister-Counsellor for Econ. Affairs, U.S. Embassy, Saigon 70-73; Deputy Asst. to Pres. for Int. Econ.

Affairs, Nat. Security Council 73-74; Asst. Sec. of Treasury for Int. Affairs 74; Exec. Dir. for U.S.A., IBRD, IDA, IFC June 75-; AID Superior Honor Award 68; U.S. State Dept. Distinguished Honor Award 73.
Leisure interests: skiing, tennis.
Room E1112, World Bank, 1818 H Street, N.W., Washington, D.C. 20433; Home: 1061 Spring Hill Road, McLean, Va. 22101, U.S.A.
Telephone: (202) 477-2776 (Office); (703) 356-5402 (Home).

Cooper, James Lees; British journalist; b. 6 March 1907; ed. Darwen Grammar School, Lancs.
Articled journalist, *Darwen News*, later reporter Ashton-under-Lyne, Allied Newspapers, Manchester, *Daily Express*, London; War Correspondent 41-45; *Daily Express* Staff Correspondent, Canada 47-55, Head, New York Bureau 55-57; Organizer, Overseas Edition, *The Globe and Mail*, Toronto 58, Asst. to Editor and Publisher, Canada 59-63, Vice-Pres., Editor-in-Chief 63-74 Publr. 65-74; Dir. The Globe and Mail Ltd., Imperial Trust, Montreal; Chair. Canadian Section Commonwealth Press Union; Trustee, Toronto Gen. Hospital.
140 King Street West, Toronto 1, Ont., Canada.
Telephone: 368-7851.

Cooper, John Sherman, A.B., LL.D.; American lawyer and politician; b. 23 Aug. 1901, Somerset, Ky.; s. of John Sherman and Helen (Tartar) Cooper; m. Lorraine R. Shevlin 1955; ed. Yale and Harvard Univs. and Univ. of Kentucky.
Member Lower House Kentucky State Legislature 28-30; Judge Pulaski County, Ky. 30-38; served army 42-46; Circuit Judge 28th Judicial District, Kentucky 45-51; Senator from Kentucky 46-48, 52-54; with law firm, Gardner, Morrison & Rogers, Wash., D.C. 49-51; Amb. to India and Nepal 55-56; Republican Senator from Kentucky 56-73; Amb. to German Democratic Repub. 74-; Rapporteur for Mil. Cttee. of NATO Parliamentarians Conf. 66-67, 67-68; mem. Board of Trustees Univ. of Kentucky 35-46, Yale Univ. Council 60-65; mem. American Bar Asscn.; Bronze Star Medal for Services in Second World War; Hon. degrees from many American Univs.
American Embassy, Berlin, German Democratic Republic.

Cooper, Leon N., D.SC., PH.D.; American professor of physics; b. 28 Feb. 1930, New York City; s. of Irving Cooper and Anna Zola; m. Kay Anne Allard 1969; two d.; ed. Columbia Univ.
Member Inst. for Advanced Study 54-55; Research Assoc., Univ. of Ill. 55-57; Asst. Prof., Ohio State Univ. 57-58; Brown Univ., Assoc. Prof. 58-62, Prof. 74, Thomas J. Watson, Sr. Prof. of Science 74-; Dir. Center for Neural Studies; Visiting Lecturer, Varenna, Italy 55; Visiting Prof., Brandeis Summer Inst. 59, Bergen Int. School of Physics, Norway 61, Scuola Internazionale Di Fisica, Erice, Italy 65, L'Ecole Normale Supérieure, Centre Universitaire Int., Paris 66, Cargèse Summer School 66, Radiation Laboratory, Univ. of Calif., Berkeley 69, Faculty of Sciences, Quai St. Bernard, Paris 70, 71, Brookhaven Nat. Laboratory 72; Consultant for various industrial and educational orgs.; NSF Post-doctoral Fellow 54-55; Alfred P. Sloan Foundation Research Fellow 59-66; John Simon Guggenheim Memorial Foundation Fellow 65-66; Fellow, Amer. Physical Soc., Amer. Acad. of Arts and Sciences; Sponsor, Amer. Fed. of Scientists; mem. Nat. Acad. of Sciences, American Philosophical Soc.; Comstock Prize, Nat. Acad. of Sciences 68; Nobel Prize 72; Hon. D.Sc. (Columbia, Sussex) 73, (Illinois, Brown) 74.
Leisure interests: skiing, music, theatre.

Publs. *An Introduction to the Meaning and Structure of Physics* 68; numerous scientific papers.
Physics Department, Brown University, Providence, R.I. 02912; Home: 31 Summit Avenue, Providence, R.I. 02906, U.S.A.
Telephone: (401) 863-2172 (Office); (401) 421-1181 (Home).

Cooper, Martin Du Pré, C.B.E.; British music critic and writer; b. 17 Jan. 1910, Winchester; *s.* of Cecil H. H. Cooper and Cecil Hatherley Stephens; *m.* Mary Stewart, 1940; one *s.* three *d.*; ed. Winchester Coll., Hertford Coll.. St. Edmund Hall, Oxford.
Studied music in Vienna with Egon Wellesz 32-34; Hon. Fellow, Trinity Coll. Music, London; Asst. Editor *Royal Geographical Society Journal* 35-36; Music Critic, *London Mercury* 35-39, *Daily Herald* 46-50, *The Spectator* 46-54; joined music staff *Daily Telegraph* 50 and since 54 music editor; Editor *The Musical Times* 53-56; Pres. Critics' Circle 59-60; mem. Editorial Board *New Oxford History of Music* 61-, Editor Vol. X (1975).
Leisure interests: walking, languages.
Publs. *Gluck* 35, *Bizet* 38, *Opéra Comique* 49, *French Music from the Death of Berlioz to the Death of Fauré* 51, *Russian Opera* 51, *Les Musiciens anglais d'aujourd'hui* 52, *Ideas and Music* 66, *Beethoven—the last decade* 70.
34 Halford Road, Richmond, Surrey, TW10 6AP, England.

Cooray, H.E. Cardinal Thomas B.; Ceylonese ecclesiastic; b. 28 Dec. 1901.
Ordained priest 29; Titular Archbishop of Preslavo and Co-adjutor Archbishop of Colombo 45; Archbishop of Colombo 47-; created Cardinal 65; mem. Pontifical Comm. for Canon Law; Pres. Ceylon Bishops Conf.
Archbishop's House, Colombo 8, Sri Lanka.
Telephone: 95471.

Coore, David Hilton, B.A., B.C.L., Q.C., M.P.; Jamaican politician; b. 22 Aug. 1925, St. Andrew; *s.* of Clarence Reuben Coore and Ethlyn Maud Hilton; *m.* Rita Innis 1949; three *s.*; ed. Jamaica Coll., McGill Univ., Exeter Coll., Oxford.
Practised as barrister-at-law in Jamaica 50-72; mem. Legis. Council 60-62; Opposition Spokesman on Finance 67-72; Chair. People's Nat. Party 69-; mem. Parl. 72-; Deputy Prime Minister, Minister of Finance and of Public Service Feb. 72-; Chair. Board of Govs. Caribbean Devt. Bank 72-73, Inter-American Devt. Bank 73-74; Queen's Counsel 61.
Leisure interests: reading, swimming, golf.
Ministry of Finance, 30 National Heroes Circle, Kingston 4; Home: Vale Royal, 3 Montrose Road, Kingston 10, Jamaica.
Telephone: 929-5080 (Office); 927-6696 (Home).

Cooremans, Lucien, D. EN D.; Belgian administrator; b. 1899; ed. Univ. Libre de Bruxelles.
Secretary to Paul Hymans 28-34; Sec. of the Cabinet and Minister of Justice 40; fmr. mem. Chamber of Reps.; Pres. Brussels Exhibition 58; Pres. Brussels Int. Fair; fmr. Pres. Union of Int. Fairs; Mayor of Brussels 56-; Hon. Pres. and founder of the Union of Capitals of the European Community; many Belgian and foreign orders.
Hôtel de Ville, Brussels, Belgium.

Coote, Sir Colin Reith, Kt., D.S.O.; British journalist; b. 19 Oct. 1893; ed. Rugby School and Balliol Coll., Oxford.
Served Gloucestershire Regiment 14-18; M.P. for Isle of Ely 17-22; Rome corresp. of *The Times* 22-25, Parliamentary Sketch-writer 25-30, Leader writer 30-42; Deputy Editor *The Daily Telegraph* 42-50, Managing Editor 50-64; Légion d'Honneur.
Publs. include *In and About Rome* and *Italian Town and Country Life* 21, *Maxims and Reflections of Winston*

Churchill 50, *Sir Winston Churchill: a Self-Portrait* 54 (with P. D. Bunyan), *History of the Butterley Company* (with R. A. Mottram) 49, *Companion of Honour* 65, *Editorial* 65, *The Government We Deserve* 69, *The Other Club* 71.
16 Bigwood Road, London, N.W.11, England.

Cope, James Francis; Australian politician; b. 26 Nov. 1907, Sydney; *m.*; one *d.*
Active in Australian Labor Party, holding many exec. positions 30-; alderman Redfern Council 48-; Hon. Treas. and del. to Fed. Council of Australian Glassworkers' Union 53-55; M.P. for Cook 55, then Watson, then Sydney 69-; Parl. Public Accounts Cttee. 56-72; Temp. Chair. of Cttees. 67-72; Speaker, House of Reps. Australian Fed. Parl. 73-75.
The House of Representatives, Canberra, A.C.T., Australia.

Cope, S. Raymond, B.SC.(ECON.), PH.D.; British financial administrator (World Bank); b. 14 May 1907; *s.* of Sydney C. and Madeleine E. (née Pugh) Cope; ed. London School of Economics and Political Science.
Mem. of Guinness, Mahon and Co., merchant bankers 23-41, 46-47; Private Sec., Air Ministry Controller of Communications, Sec. Airborne Forces Cttee. 41-45; Finance Division, Control Comm. for Germany 45-46; Sec. and Treas. Esso Transportation Co. Ltd. 47; Int. Bank for Reconstruction and Devt. 47-, Loans Dept. 47-52, Asst. Dir., Dept. of Operations, Europe, Africa and Australasia 52-55, Dir. Dept. of Operations, Europe, Africa and Australasia 55-62, Dir. Dept. of Operations, Europe 62-65, Dir. Europe and Middle East Dept. 65-67, Dir. Europe Dept. 67-68, Office of Pres. 68-.
IBRD, Washington, D.C. 20433; Home: 3413 R Street, N.W., Washington, D.C. 20007, U.S.A.
Telephone: 338-1972 (Home).

Copeland, Lammot du Pont; American business executive; b. 19 May 1905, Christiana Hundred, Del.; *s.* of Charles and Louisa d'Andelot du Pont Copeland; *m.* Pamela Cunningham 1930; two *s.* one *d.*; ed. Harvard Univ.
E. I. du Pont de Nemours & Co. Inc. 29-, Dir. 42-, mem. Finance Cttee. 43-59, Sec. 47-54, Vice-Pres. 54-62, Pres. 62-67, Chair. of Board 67-71, mem. Exec. Cttee. 59-71; Dir. Chemical Bank of New York Trust Co.; Dir. and Trustee of numerous financial orgs.; Officer Legion of Honour (France), Officer Order of Leopold (Belgium), Commdr., Order of the Couronne de Chêne (Luxembourg); various honorary degrees in Laws, Science and Engineering.
Leisure interests: hunting, yachting.
Du Pont Building, Wilmington, Del. 19898, U.S.A.

Copic, Branko; Yugoslav writer; b. 1915; ed. Belgrade Univ.
Recipient of several Yugoslav literary awards; Order of Meritorious Service to the People, First and Second Class, Order of Brotherhood and Unity, First Class, 1941 Partisan Commemoration Medal.
Publs. include *A Warrior's Spring, Fighters and Fugitives, Dew on the Bayonets, Partisan Stories,* and volumes of verse.
c/o Yugoslav Academy of Sciences and Arts, Zrinski trg. 11, Zagreb 1, Yugoslavia.

Copland, Aaron; American composer; b. 14 Nov. 1900, Brooklyn, N.Y.; *s.* of Harris and Sarah (Mittenthal) Copland.
Enrolled Fontainebleau School of Music 21; studied with Nadia Boulanger in Paris 21-24; returned to U.S. 24; Guggenheim Fellowship 25-27; with Roger Sessions organised Copland-Sessions Concerts 28-31; Dir. American Festival of Contemporary Music, Yaddo; toured South America 41 and 47; Lecturer on Music, New School for Social Research N.Y. 27-37; has taught

composition at Harvard and Berkshire Music Center, Charles Eliot Norton Prof. 51-52; Dir. League of Composers, Edward MacDowell Asscn., Koussevitsky Music Foundation, Walter W. Naumberg Music Foundation and American Music Center; numerous awards.
Works include: *First Symphony* 25, *Concerto for Piano and Orchestra* 26, *Two Pieces for String Quartet* 28, *Lincoln Portrait* 42, *Billy the Kid* 38, *Violin Sonata* 43, *Appalachian Spring* 44, *Clarinet Concerto* 48, *Twelve Poems by Emily Dickinson* 50, *John Henry* (revised 57), *The Tender Land* 54, *Symphonic Ode* 55, *Piano Fantasy* 57, *Orchestral Variations* 58, *Nonet* 60, *Connotations for Orchestra* 62, *Music for a Great City* 63, *Emblems for Band* 64, *Inscape for Orchestra* 67, *Duo for Flute and Piano* 71, *Three Latin American Sketches* 71, *Night Thoughts for Piano* 71.
Publs. *What to Listen for in Music* 39, *Our New Music* 41, *Music and Imagination* 52, *Copland on Music* 60, *The New Music 1900-1960* 68.
c/o Boosey & Hawkes Inc., 30 West 57th Street, New York, N.Y. 10019, U.S.A.

Coppé, Albert; Belgian politician; b. 26 Nov. 1911, Bruges; s. of Albert Coppé and Helene Mahieu; m. M.-H. van Driessche 1940; four s. four d.; ed. Catholic Univ. of Louvain.
Member (Christian-Social Party) Chamber of Representatives 46-52; Minister of Public Works 50, of Economic Affairs and the Middle Classes 50-51, of Reconstruction 52; Vice-Pres. High Authority of the European Coal and Steel Community 52-67, Acting Pres. 67; mem. Combined Comm. of EEC, ECSC, and Euratom 67-73; mem. Board Philips Eindhoven, Generale Bank maatschappij; Chair. AKZO—Belgium; Prof. Extraordinary, Univ. of Louvain; Commdr. Ordre de Léopold, Grand Cordon, Ordre du Chêne (Luxembourg), Great Cross Leopold II, Great Cross Verdienstorden (Fed. Germany); Dr. h.c. (Univs. of Montreal and San Antonio, Texas).
Leisure interests: walking, philosophy, paleontology.
Publs. *De Europes e Uitdaging* 70, *De Multinationale Onderneming* 72, *Inflatie* 74.
Liskensstraat 2, Tervuren 1980, Belgium.

Coppieters, Emmanuel (Coppieters de ter Zaele, chevalier Emmanuel), DR. ECON., DR. IUR., M.SC. (ECON.); Belgian economist and jurist; b. 1925; three s. one d.; ed. Louvain and London Univs.
Professor Int. Econ. Orgs., Nat. Univ. Faculty of Econs., Antwerp (now Univ. of Antwerp) 54-, Royal Mil. Coll. 63-66; Dir.-Gen. Institut Royal des Relations Internationales, Brussels 54-; Editor *Chronique de Politique Etrangère*; Co-Editor *Internationale Spectator, Tijdschrift voor Internationale Politiek*; Consul-Gen. of Honduras 61-; Minister chargé d'affaires a.i. of Honduras to the European Communities 73-; Public Auditor of Banks 62-; Adviser for Foreign Trade to Govt. 64-; mem. Belg. Nat. Council of Statistics; Assoc. mem. Royal Acad. of Overseas Sciences; mem. Belgian Nat. Comm. UNESCO, Gov. Asscn. pour l'Etude des Problèmes de l'Europe, Paris; Gov. European Cultural Foundation 73-; Barrister; mem. American Political Science Asscn.; Reserve Lieut.-Col.; Officier Ordre de Léopold, Commdr. Order of the Holy Sepulchre, Résistance and Volontaire de Guerre Medals, Commdr. Order of Merit (Senegal), Orange-Nassau (Netherlands), Luxembourg, Morazan (Honduras), Tudor Vladimirescu (Romania); Officer Order of Rwanda, Order of Polonia Restituta; Knight of the Order of Malta; mem. Order of the Leopard (Zaire).
Publs. *English Bank Note Circulation 1694-1954, L'Accord Monétaire Européen et le Progrès de la Convertibilité des Monnaies, Internationale Organisaties en Belgische Economie, La integración monetaria y fiscal europea, culminación de la integración política*, etc.

88 avenue de la Couronne, Brussels; and Vijverskasteel, Loppem bij Brugge, Belgium.
Telephone: 648-20-00; and (050)-822-888.

Corbally, John Edward, M.A., PH.D.; American university administrator; b. 14 Oct. 1924, South Bend, Washington; s. of John E. and Grace Williams Corbally; m. Marguerite Walker 1946; one s. one d.; ed. Univs. of Washington and California (Berkeley).
High School Teacher and principal, State of Washington 47-53; College of Educ. Faculty, Ohio State Univ. 55-61, Dir. Personnel Budget 59-61, Exec. Asst. to Pres. 61-64, Vice-Pres. for Admin. 64-66, Vice-Pres. for Academic Affairs and Provost 66-69; Chancellor and Pres. Syracuse Univ. 69-71; Pres. Univ. of Illinois 71-; Chair. Nat. Council on Educational Research, Nat. Inst. of Educ. 73-76; Hon. LL.D. (Univ. of Md.) 71, (Blackburn Coll.) 72.
Leisure interests: golf, model railroading, travel.
Publs. co-author: *An Introduction to Educational Administration* 58 (4th edn. 71), *Educational Administration: The Secondary School* 61, *School Finance* 62.
Office: 364 Administration Building, Urbana, Ill. 61801; Home: 711 West Florida Avenue, Urbana, Ill. 61801, U.S.A.
Telephone: 217-333-3070 (Office); 217-344-2010 (Home).

Corbière, Jacques; French industrialist; b. 11 June 1906, Paris; s. of Paul Corbière and Marguerite Gervais; m. Odette Gravelin 1934; three s. one d.; ed. Ecole Fénelon and Lycée Condorcet, Paris.
President and Dir.-Gen. Fromageries Charles Gervais 60-67, Société Charles Gervais 62-67 and Compagnie Gervais Danone 67-; Vice-Pres. Conseil de Surveillance, Gervais Danone S.A. 67-73; Admin. Vice-Pres. BSN Gervais Danone 73-; Admin. Société Diététique Gallia and Société France-Glaces Findus; Pres. Syndicat professionnel des industriels laitiers de la Seine-Maritime 53-57, Hon. Pres. 57-; mem. Admin. Council, Fédération Nationale de l'Industrie Laitière 63-75; Pres. Centre d'études et de recherches technologiques des industries alimentaires 68-73; Admin. St. Hubert Club; mem. Cercle du Bois de Boulogne and Cercle du Golf de St.-Germain; Officier Légion d'Honneur; Croix de Guerre 39-45; Officier du Mérite Agricole; Chevalier Ordre de Léopold.
Leisure interests: ornithology, cattle breeding, hunting, fishing.
126 rue Jules Guesde, 92302 Levallois-Perret; 45 rue Emile-Ménier, 75116 Paris, France.
Telephone: 739 33 50.

Corbin, Edmond Emile; French engineer and international civil servant; b. 11 April 1908, Rennes; m. Geneviève Audet 1935; three s. one d.; ed. Ecole Polytechnique and Ecole Nationale des Ponts et Chaussées.
Bridges and Highways Engineer, Lorient 32-34, Cherbourg 34-41, Nancy 41-45; Chief Engineer of Bridges and Highways, Asst. to Dir.-Gen. of Railways and Transport, Ministry of Public Works and Transport, later Head of Dept. of Int. Affairs 45-61; Engineer-Gen. of Bridges and Highways in charge of Int. Relations 61-66; Sec.-Gen. of European Conf. of Ministers of Transport Jan. 66-; Officier Légion d'Honneur, Commdr. Ordre National du Mérite; Knight Order of Isabel the Catholic (Spain), Officer Order of Vasa (Sweden).
33 rue de Franqueville, Paris 16e; 18 avenue Charles Floquet, Paris 7e, France.
Telephone: 524-97-10; 783-72-18 (Home).

Cordeiro, H.E. Cardinal Joseph; Pakistani ecclesiastic; b. 19 Jan. 1918, Bombay.
Ordained 46; Archbishop of Karachi 58-; created Cardinal by Pope Paul VI 73.
St. Patrick's Cathedral, Karachi 3, Pakistan.
Telephone: 515-870.

Corea, Gamani, M.A., D.PHIL.; Ceylonese economist and civil servant; b. 4 Nov. 1925, Colombo; s. of Dr. :. V. S. and Freda (née Kotelawala) Corea; ed. Royal Coll., Colombo, Corpus Christi Coll., Cambridge, and Nuffield Coll., Oxford.
Director, Planning Secr. and Sec. Nat. Planning Council 56-60; Dir. of Econ. Research and Asst. to Gov. of Central Bank of Ceylon 60-65; Perm. Sec. to Ministry of Planning and Econ. Affairs and Econ. Sec. to Cabinet 65-70; Deputy Gov. Central Bank of Ceylon 70-; Consultant to Sec.-Gen., UN Conf. on Trade and Devt.; fmr. Chief, UN Econ. Mission to British Honduras; Chair. UN Cttee. on Devt. Planning; fmr. Pres. Section F, Ceylon Asscn. for Advancement of Science; mem. Consultative Cttee. Asian Agricultural Survey, Asian Devt. Bank; Chair. Expert Group on Int. Monetary Reform and Developing Countries (UNCTAD) 59 and Expert Group on Regional Performance Evaluation, ECAFE 72; Pres. Ceylon Asscn. for Advancement of Science 71; Chair. Expert Panel on Devt. and Environment 71; Senior Adviser to Sec.-Gen. UN Conf. on Human Environment (Stockholm) 71-72; Chair. UN Cttee. for Devt. Planning 72-74, UN Cocoa Conf. 72, ECAFE Group on Review and Appraisal of 2nd Devt. Decade 71, 72; Amb. to EEC and Benelux Countries 73-74; Research Fellow, Int. Devt. Research Centre, Canada 73, Visiting Fellow, Inst. of Devt. Studies, Univ. of Sussex 73, mem. Board of Govs. 74; Visiting Fellow, Nuffield College, Oxford 74; Sec.-Gen. UN Conf. on Trade and Devt. (UNCTAD) 74-.
Leisure interests: photography, golf.
United Nations Conference on Trade and Development, Palais des Nations, 1211 Geneva 10, Switzerland; and Horton Lodge, 21 Horton Place, Colombo 7, Sri Lanka. Telephone: 34 60 11 (Office).

Corelli, Franco; Italian tenor; b. Ancona; ed. Pesaro Conservatory, Maggio Musicale, Florence.
First appearance as Don Jose in *Carmen*, Spoleto; appeared in Spontoni's *La Vestale*, La Scala, Milan 54, Teatro San Carlo, Naples 55, *Cavaradossi*, Covent Garden, London 56, Rome 57, 58, Naples 58, La Scala (with Maria Callas *q.v.*) 60; Metropolitan Opera début as Manrico in *Il Trovatore* 61; has sung major parts in *Andrea Chénier, La Bohème, Turandot, Tosca, Ernani, Aida, Don Carlos, Forza del Destino, Cavalleria Rusticana, I Pagliacci,* etc.; performs regularly on American TV; completed recital tour with Renata Tebaldi; 1st Prize Spoleto Nat. Competition.
c/o S. A. Gorlinsky, 35 Dover Street, London, W.1, England.

Corey, Elias James, S.B., PH.D.; American professor of chemistry; b. 11 July 1928, Methuen, Mass.; s. of Elias J. Corey and Tina Hasham; m. Claire Higham 1961; two s. one d.; ed. Mass. Inst. of Technology.
Instructor in Chem., Univ. of Ill. 51-53, Asst. Prof. of Chem. 53-55, Prof. 56-59; Sheldon Emery Prof. of Chem., Harvard Univ. 59-, Chair. Dept. of Chem. 65-68; Alfred P. Sloan Foundation Fellow 55-57, Guggenheim Fellow 57, 68-69; mem. American Acad. of Arts and Sciences 60-68, Nat. Acad. of Sciences 66-; Hon. A.M., Hon. D.Sc.; Pure Chem. Award of American Chemical Soc. 60, Fritzsche Award of American Chemical Soc. 67, Intra-Science Foundation Award 67, Harrison Howe Award, Amer. Chemical Soc. 70, Award for Synthetic Organic Chem. 71, CIBA Foundation Award 72, Evans Award, Ohio State Univ. 72, Linus Pauling Award 73.
Leisure interests: outdoor activities and music.
Publs. approx. 300 chemical papers.
Department of Chemistry, Harvard University, 12 Oxford Street, Cambridge, Mass. 02138; Home: 20 Avon Hill Street, Cambridge, Mass. 02140, U.S.A. Telephone: 617-495-4033 (Office); 617-864-0627 (Home).

Corfield, Rt. Hon. Sir Frederick Vernon, Kt., P.C., Q.C.; British barrister-at-law and politician; b. 1 June 1915, London; s. of Brig. Frederick A. Corfield, D.S.O. and Mary Vernon; m. Elizabeth M. R. Taylor; ed. Cheltenham Coll. and Royal Military Acad., Woolwich.
Regular army 35-45; prisoner-of-war 40-45; called to Bar, Middle Temple 45; Judge Advocate Gen.'s Branch, War Office 45-46; farming 46-56; mem. Parl. for S. Gloucester 55-74; Joint Parl. Sec. Ministry of Housing and Local Govt. 62-64; Minister of State, Board of Trade June-Oct. 70; Minister of Aviation Supply 70-71, Minister for Aerospace, Dept. of Trade and Industry 71-72; mem. British Waterways Board 74-; Conservative.
Leisure interest: gardening.
Publ. *Corfield on Compensation* 59.
9 Randolph Mews, London, W.9; 2 Paper Buildings, Temple, London, E.C.4; Wording's Orchard, Sheepscombe, Stroud, Glos., GL6 7RE, England.

Cori, Carl Ferdinand, M.D.; American university professor; b. 5 Dec. 1896; ed. German Univ., Prague.
Assistant in Pharmacology Univ. of Graz 20-21; went to U.S.A. 22, naturalized U.S. citizen 28; Biochemist, State Inst. for Study of Malignant Disease, Buffalo, N.Y. 22-31; Prof. of Pharmacology and Biochemistry, Wash. Univ. School of Medicine, St. Louis, Mo. 31-67; Visiting Prof. of Biochemistry at Mass. Gen. Hospital, Harvard Medical School, Boston, Mass. 67-; mem. Nat. Acad. of Sciences, American Asscn. for Advancement of Science, American Philosophical Soc., American Chemical Soc.; American Soc. of Biological Chemists (Pres. 49-50), Pres. Fourth Int. Congress of Biochemistry, Vienna 58; foreign mem. Royal Soc.; Lasker Award 46, Mid-West Award (American Chemical Soc.) 46, Sugar Research Foundation Award 47, 50, Squibb Award 47; Nobel Prize in Medicine and Physiology 47; Willard Gibbs Medal (American Chemical Soc.) 48; numerous hon. degrees.
Enzyme Research Laboratory, Massachusetts General Hospital, Fruit Street, Boston, Mass. 02114, U.S.A. Telephone: 617-726-3737.

Corish, Brendan; Irish politician; b. 1918.
Mem. of Parl. 45-; Vice-Chair. Labour Party 46, Chair. 49-53, Parl. Leader 60-, mem. Council of State 64-; Parl. Party Whip 45-54; Parl. Sec. to Minister of Local Govt. and Minister of Defence 48; Minister of Social Welfare 54-57; Del. to Council of Europe 55-59; Del. to Int. Affairs Asscn. Conf. 49; Del. to Inter-Parl. Union Conf., Istanbul 51; assoc. mem. Del. to Commonwealth Relations Conf., Ottawa 52; Deputy Prime Minister and Minister for Health and Social Welfare 73-.
Belvedere Road, Wexford, Ireland.

Cormack, Sir Magnus Cameron, K.B.E.; Australian farmer and politician; b. 12 Feb. 1906, Caithness, Scotland; s. of William P. Cormack and Violet M. Cameron; m. Mary I. G. Macmeiken; one s. three d.; ed. St. Peter's School, Adelaide.
Member Senate 51-53, 61-, Pres. 71-74; del. to Commonwealth Parliamentary Asscn. Conf., Kuala Lumpur 63, UN Gen. Assembly 65; Liberal.
Leisure interests: sailing, deep sea cruising.
The Senate, Parliament House, Canberra, A.C.T.; Home: Lower Crawford, Via Heywood, Victoria, Australia.

Corneille (*see* Beverloo, Cornelis Van).

Cornelis, Henri Arthur Adolf Antoon Marie Christophe; Belgian administrator; b. 18 Sept. 1910; ed. Univ. of Ghent and Geneva School of International Studies.
Belgian Congo 34-60, Territorial Administrator 34-38, Head, Finance and Customs Office 38-42, Principal Territorial Administrator 42-46, Sub.-Dir. Econ. Affairs 46-48, Dir. Econ. Affairs 48-50, Dir.-Gen. Econ. Affairs 50-51, Commr. Ten Year Plan 51-53, Vice-Gov.-Gen.

of Belgian Congo 53-58, Gov.-Gen. 58-60; Adviser Banque de Paris et des Pays-Bas, Brussels 61-64; Dir., Adviser to the Chair. Cominière, Brussels 65-.
2 rue de la Sarte, Dion le Mont, Belgium.

Cornelius, Alvin Robert; Pakistani Chief Justice 60-67; see *The International Who's Who 1975-76.*

Corner, Edred John Henry, C.B.E., F.R.S., F.L.S.; British fmr. botanist; b. 12 Jan. 1906, London; s. of Edred Moss Corner and Henrietta (née Henderson) Corner; ed. Rugby School.
Assistant Dir. Gardens Dept., Straits Settlements 29-45; Principal Field Scientific Officer, Latin America, UNESCO 47-48; Lecturer in Botany, Cambridge Univ. 49-59, Reader in Plant Taxonomy 59-65, Prof. of Tropical Botany 66-73; Fellow, American Asscn. for Advancement of Science and mem. or corresp. mem. of many other foreign botanical and mycological socs.; Darwin Medal, Royal Soc. 60; Patron's Medal, Royal Geographical Soc. 66; Gold Medal, Linnean Soc. 70; Victoria Medal of Honour, Royal Horticultural Soc. 74.
Leisure interest: kindness.
Publs. *Wayside Trees of Malaya* 40, *Monograph of Clavaria* 50, *Life of Plants* 64, *Monograph of Cantharelliod Fungi* 66, *Natural History of Palms* 66, *Illustrated Guide to Tropical Plants* (with K. Watanabe) 69, *Boletus in Malaysia* 72, *Seeds of Dicotyledons* 76.
91 Hinton Way, Great Shelford, Cambridge, CB2 5AH, England.
Telephone: Shelford 2167.

Corner, Frank Henry, M.A.; New Zealand diplomatist; b. 17 May 1920, Napier; s. of C. W. Corner and S. O. Smith; m. Lynette Robinson 1943; two d.; ed. Victoria Univ. of Wellington.
First Sec. Washington 48-51; Senior Counsellor, London 52-58; Deputy Sec. of External Affairs 58-62; Perm. Rep. to UN 62-67; Amb. to U.S.A. 67-72; Sec. of Foreign Affairs 73-.
Leisure interests: gardening, walking, music.
26 Burnell Avenue, Wellington, New Zealand.
Telephone: 736-678 (Office); 737-022 (Home).

Corner, George Washington, A.B., M.A., M.D., SC.D., LITT.D., LL.D.; American physician and scientist; b. 12 Dec. 1889, Baltimore, Md.; s. of George W. Corner, Jr. and Florence E. Evans; m. Betsy Lyon Copping; one s. one d. (deceased); ed. Johns Hopkins Univ.
Assistant in Anatomy, Johns Hopkins Univ. 13-14, Resident House Officer, Johns Hopkins Hospital 14-15; Asst. Prof. Univ. of Calif. 15-19; Assoc. Prof. Johns Hopkins Univ. 19-23; Prof. Univ. of Rochester 23-40; Dir. Dept. of Embryology, Carnegie Inst. of Wash., Baltimore 40-55; Eastman Prof. Oxford 52-53; Historian, The Rockefeller Inst. N.Y. 56-60, Visiting Prof. 61-; mem. U.S. Acad. of Sciences (Vice-Pres. 53-57), Amer. Philosophical Soc. (Vice-Pres. 53-56, Exec. Officer 60-); Hon. Fellow, Zoological Society (London), Hon. F.R.C.O.G.; foreign mem. Royal Soc. of London; Fellow, Royal Soc. of Edinburgh.
Leisure interest: travel.
Publs. *Anatomical Texts of the Earlier Middle Ages* 27, *The Hormones in Human Reproduction* 42, *Ourselves Unborn* 45, *Anatomist at Large* 58, *George Hoyt Whipple and his Friends* 63, *Two Centuries of Medicine* 65, *History of the Rockefeller Institute* 65, *Doctor Kane of the Arctic Seas* 72.
American Philosophical Society, 104 S. 5th Street, Philadelphia, Pa. 19106, U.S.A.
Telephone: WALnut 5-3606 (Office).

Cornforth, John Warcup, C.B.E., M.SC., D.PHIL., F.R.S.; Australian research scientist; b. 7 Sept. 1917, Sydney; s. of J. W. Cornforth and the late Hilda Eipper; m. Rita H. Harradence; one s. two d.; ed. Univs. of Sydney and Oxford.
Scientific Staff, Medical Research Council 46-62; Dir.

Milstead Laboratory of Chemical Enzymology, Shel Research Ltd. 62-75; Assoc. Prof. Univ. of Warwicl 65-71; Visiting Prof. Univ. of Sussex 71-75; Royal Soc Prof. Univ. of Sussex 75-; Pedler Lecturer, Chem. Soc 68-69, Andrews' Lecturer, Univ. of N.S.W. 70, Max Tischler Lecturer, Harvard Univ. 70, Robert Robinson Lecturer, Chem. Soc. 72, Pacific Coast Lecturer 73 Foreign Hon. mem. Amer. Acad. 73; Corday-Morgan Medal, Chem. Soc. 53, Flintoft Medal, Chem. Soc. 66 Ciba Medal, Biochem. Soc. 66; Stouffer Prize 67; Davy Medal (Royal Soc.) 68; Ernest Guenther Award Amer. Chemical Soc. 69; Prix Roussel 72; Nobel Prize for Chemistry 75.
Leisure interests: tennis, gardening, chess.
Publs. *The Chemistry of Penicillin* (part author) 49, and numerous papers on chemical and biochemical topics.
University of Sussex, The School of Molecular Sciences, Falmer, Brighton, Sussex, BN1 9QJ, England.
Telephone: Brighton (0273) 66755.

Cornwell, David John Moore (*pseudonym* John Le Carré); British writer; b. 19 Oct. 1931; ed. St. Andrew's Preparatory School, Pangbourne, Sherborne School, Berne Univ., and Lincoln Coll., Oxford.
Teacher, Eton Coll. 56-58; in Foreign Service 60-64; Somerset Maugham Award 63.
Publs. *Call For the Dead* 61 (filmed as *The Deadly Affair* 67), *Murder of Quality* 62, *The Spy Who Came in From the Cold* 63, *The Looking Glass War* 65, *A Small Town in Germany* 68, *The Naive and Sentimental Lover* 71, *Tinker, Tailor, Soldier, Spy* 74.
c/o John Farquharson Ltd., 15 Red Lion Square, London, WC1R 4QW, England.

Corona Martín, Ramón; Mexican architect; b. 1906; ed. Xaverian Coll., Brighton, Oxford Univ., Escuela Nacional Preparatoria, Escuela Nacional de Arquitectos de México, and Universidad Nacional de México.
Architectural Practice 29-; Vice-Pres. Int. Union of Architects; mem. Board of Dirs. Universidad Autónoma de Guadalajara; mem. Board of Honour, Colégio de Arquitectos de México and Sociedad de Arquitectos de México; mem. numerous int. architectural societies.
Monte Libano 670, Mexico 10, D.F., Mexico.

Coronel de Palma, Luis, LL.B.; Spanish banker; b. 4 May 1925, Madrid; m. María del Rosario Martínez-Agulló Sanchis 1953; five c.; ed. Cen. Univ. of Madrid.
Called to the Bar 54; with Barcelona Treasury Office; Deputy Magistrate, High Court of Barcelona 56; Dir.-Gen. Savings and Investment, Gen. Banking and Exchange Office, Secr. of Board of Investments, Ministry of Finance 57; Dir.-Gen. Confed. of Savings Banks 59; Savings Banks Credit Inst. 62; Nat. Econ. Adviser 65; Gov. IBRD, IMF 70; Gov. Banco de España 70-; mem. Royal Acad. of Jurisprudence 55; Grand Cross, Civil Merit, Military Merit, and other decorations.
Leisure interests: music, reading.
Banco de España, Alcalá 50, Madrid, Spain.

Corre, Max, L. ès L.; French journalist; b. 25 Feb. 1912; ed. Paris Univ.
Former Editor-in-Chief *Samedi-Soir*; Dir. of *Paris-Match;* Dir.-Gen. of *Paris Presse, France-Dimanche;* Admin. *Télé-7-jours* 63; co-Dir. Aigle-Azur Presse 68-70; Adviser Hebdo Press Group 68-73; Dir. Soc. Animatique de presse 72; Editor *Paris-Paris* 73; Officier Légion d'Honneur, Croix de Guerre.
19 rue Octave-Feuillet, Paris 16e, France.

Correa, José Antonio, IUR.D.; Ecuadorean diplomatist and banker; b. 1915, Quito; s. of Alberto Correa and Maria Escobar; m. Elba Arteta 1940; two s. two d.; ed. Universidad Central de Quito.
Assistant Chief, Diplomatic Section, Ministry of Foreign

(49)

LOST/WITHDRAWN REPORT FORM
TO: PROCESSING DEPARTMENT

CALL NO. REF. CT 120 15 1976-1977

VOLUME/YEAR
ACCESSION or COPY NO. 3876125

AUTHOR ....

TITLE *International Who's Who*

BOOK LOST .... WITHDRAWN ✓

TO BE REPLACED: Yes* .... No.** ....

REPORTED BY ....

BRANCH .... DATE ....

* Please send order slips to the Acquisitions Dept.

** ☐ Withdraw catalog cards and/or COM records

☐ Retain COM records

Affairs 35-38, Chief 38-40; Second Sec., Ecuadorean Embassy, Washington 40-44, First Sec. 44; Dir. Diplomatic Dept., Ministry of Foreign Affairs 45; Sec.-Gen. Perm. Del. of Ecuador to UN 46-48, Alt. Rep. of Ecuador to UN. 48-50; Senior Officer, Exec. Office of Sec.-Gen. of UN 51-56; Dep. Dir., Div. of Trusteeship, Dept. of Trusteeship and Non-self-governing Territories of UN 56-57; Perm. Rep. of Ecuador to UN 58-60; Dir. Bureau of Relations with Member States, UNESCO 61-63; Ambassador of Ecuador to U.S.A. 63-64; Pres. José Antonio Correa y Compañía (law firm) 65-; Pres. Ecuatoriana de Desarrollo S.A. (COFIEC) (Devt. finance company) 66-.
Leisure interests: art collector, travel.
Office: Avenida 10 de Agosto 1564, P.O.B. 411, Quito, Ecuador.
Telephone: 239-129.

Corrêa da Costa, Sérgio; Brazilian diplomatist; b. 19 Feb. 1919, Rio de Janeiro; s. of Dr. I. Alfonso da Costa and Lavinia Corrêa da Costa; m. Zazi Aranha 1943; one s. two d.; ed. Univ. of Brazil and Univ. of Calif. (Los Angeles).
Secretary, Brazilian Embassy, Buenos Aires 44-46, Washington D.C. 46; Acting Rep. to Council of OAS and Inter-American ECOSOC 46-48; Deputy Head, Econ. Dept., Ministry of Foreign Relations 52; Head Div. of Int. Affairs, Brazilian War Coll. 52; Acting Pres. Brazilian Nat. Technical Assistance Comm. 55-58; Minister Counsellor, Rome 59-62; Amb. to Canada 62-65; Sec.-Gen. Ministry of Foreign Relations 67-68, Acting Minister 68; Amb. to U.K. 68-74; Perm. Rep. to UN 74-; Brazilian Rep., 18th and 21st Sessions, UN Gen. Assembly 63 and 66; numerous orders.
Leisure interests: swimming, yachting, reading.
Publs. *As Quatro Coróas de D. Pedro I* 41, *Pedro I e Metternich—Tracos de uma guerra diplomatica* 42, *A Diplomacia Brasileira na questão de Letícia* 42, *A Diplomacia do Marechal-Intervenção Estrangeira na Revolta da Armada* 45, *Every Inch a King—A Biography Of Dom Pedro I, First Emperor of Brazil* 50.
Permanent Mission of Brazil to United Nations, 747 Third Avenue, 9th Floor, New York, N.Y. 10017, U.S.A.

Corrêa do Lago, Antonio, M.A., LL.B.; Brazilian diplomatist; b. 28 Aug. 1918 ,Pau, France; s. of Gen. Manoel Corrêa do Lago and Maria Helena Guerra do Lago; m. Delminda Aranha Corrêa do Lago 1948; five s.; ed. Colégio Santo Ignácio, Rio de Janeiro, Univ. of Brazil, Rio de Janeiro, and Univ. of S. California, Los Angeles.
Foreign Service 39-, Buenos Aires 44, Montevideo 45-47; Consul, Los Angeles 51-53; Head, Econ. Div., Ministry of External Relations 54-58; Consul-Gen. Paris 59-61; Head of Brazilian Del. to Conf. of Latin American Free Trade Asscn. 61; Ambassador to Venezuela 61-64; Perm. Rep. to European Office of UN, Geneva, and Del. to Disarmament Cttee. 64-66; Dir. Instituto Rio Branco (Foreign Service Inst.) 66-69; Del. to XXII Session UN Gen. Assembly 67; Amb., Head Mission to European Communities, Brussels 70-74; Amb. to Uruguay 74-.
Brazilian Embassy, Bulevar Artigas 1410, Montevideo, Uruguay.
Telephone: 79-68-21.

Corrêa d'Oliveira (*see* da Cunha Sottomayor Corrêa d'Oliveira).

Correns, Erich, DR. h.c.; German chemist and politician; b. 12 May 1896; ed. Univs. of Berlin and Tübingen.
Chemist in rayon industry; works dir. cellulose and paper factory, Blankenstein, and rayon factory, Schwarza; Dir. Fibre Research Inst., German Acad. of Sciences, Berlin 51; mem. German Acad. of Sciences; mem. Volkskammer; Pres. of Nat. Council of Nat. Front of Demo-

cratic Germany 54-; mem. Council of State 61-; Vaterländischer Verdienstorden in Gold and other awards.
Staatsrat, Berlin, German Democratic Republic.

Corson, Dale R., PH.D.; American university president; b. 5 April 1914, Pittsburg, Kansas; s. of the late Harry R. Corson and of Alta Hill Corson; m. Nellie E. Griswold 1938; three s. one d.; ed. Coll. of Emporia, Univs. of Kansas and California.
With Los Alamos Scientific Lab. 45-46; Asst. Prof. of Physics, Cornell Univ. 46-47, Assoc. Prof. 47-52, Prof. 52-56, Chair., Dept. of Physics 56-59, Dean, Coll. of Eng. 59-63, Univ. Provost 63-69; Pres. Cornell Univ. 69-; Fellow, American Acad. of Arts and Sciences.
Leisure interests: hiking, mountain climbing, canoeing, photography, sailing.
Publs. *Introduction to Electromagnetic Fields and Waves* (with Lorrain), *Particle Accelerators* in *Encyclopedia Americana*.
300 Day Hall, Cornell University, Ithaca, N.Y. 14853; Home: 144 Northview Road, Ithaca, N.Y. 14850, U.S.A.
Telephone: (607) 256-5201; (607) 272-1815 (Home).

Corson, Bishop Fred Pierce, M.A., LL.D.; American ecclesiastic; b. 11 April 1896, Millville, N.J.; s. of Jeremiah and Mary Corson; m. Frances Blount Beaman 1922; one s.; ed. Dickinson Coll., and Drew Univ.
Ordained 20, successively Pastor, Jackson Heights (N.Y.), New Haven (Conn.), Pt. Washington (N.Y.), Simpson Church, Brooklyn (N.Y.) until 29; Superintendent, N.Y. East Methodist Conf. 30-34; Pres. Dickinson Coll. (Carlisle, Pa.) 34-44; Methodist Bishop of Philadelphia 44-68; Pres. Methodist Gen. Board of Educ. 48-60; Pres. Council of Methodist Bishops 52-53; Pres. World Methodist Council 61-66; Vice-Pres. Methodist Council on World Service and Finance 60-; Protestant Observer to the Vatican Council 62, 63, 64, 65; Trustee, numerous Colls.; Hon. Chancellor, Union Coll., Schenectady, N.Y.; mem. numerous socs.; Hon. D.D., L.H.D., Litt.D., S.T.D., Sc.D., J.U.D., D.C.L., D.S.L., Pd.D., D.R.E., Arts D., Ecu.D., E.J.D.; Order of St. Olav of Norway 64, Peace Medal Award of Third Order of St. Francis of Assisi 67, Rerum Novarum Medal from Pope Paul VI 67, John Wesley Ecumenical Medal 67.
Publs. include *Dickinson College, A Christian Philosophy of Education for the Postwar World, The Minister and Christian Higher Education, The Education we have and the Education we need, Free Masonry and the Framing of the Constitution, Your Church and You, American Methodism's Magna Charta, How Good is Communism? Pattern for Successful Living, The Christian Imprint*; co-author: *Steps to Christian Unity, Doctrines and Vatican Council II, Augustin Cardinal Bea*; editor: *Anniversary Edition of John Wesley's Translation of the New Testament*.
Cornwall Manor, Cornwall, Pa. 17016, U.S.A.
Telephone: 717-273-1077.

Cort, Stewart Shaw; American steel executive; b. 9 May 1911, Duquesne, Pa.; s. of Stewart J. and Carolyn (Schreiner) Cort; m. Elizabeth Bumiller 1961; ed. Yale Univ. and Harvard Business School.
Bethlehem Steel Corpn. 37-, Clerk, Commercial Research Div. 37-39, Sales Dept., Pacific Coast Div. 39, later Manager, Commercial Research and Sheet and Tinplate Sales; Asst. Gen. Manager, Sales, Pacific Coast Div. 50-52, Gen. Man. 52-54, Vice-Pres. Sales (Pacific Coast Div.) 54-60, Asst. Gen. Man. Sales 60-61, Vice-Pres. 61-63, Dir. 63-, Pres. 63-70, Chair. 70-74; Chair., Chief Exec. Officer and Dir., American Iron and Steel Inst.; Dir. Continental Ill. Nat. Bank and Trust Co. of Chicago; Dir. Met-Mex Penoles; Dir. Continental Illinois Corpn., Int. Iron and Steel Inst. and Highway Users Fed. for Safety and Mobility; Trustee, Blair Acad., Cttee. for Econ. Devt., Princeton Theological Seminary, Nat.

12

Safety Council, U.S. Council of the Int. Chamber of Commerce; mem. many insts. and cttees. inc. Exec. Cttee., Yale Devt. Board, Industries Advisory Cttee. of the Advertising Council, the Nat. Task Force on Econ. Growth and Opportunity, the Conf. Board Inc., the Business Council, Exec. Council of Harvard Business School Assoc., Steel Service Center Inst., Newcomen Soc., Int. Iron and Steel Inst., The Pa. Soc. (Pres. 71-72), Council of Int. Advisers, Swiss Bank Corpn., American Inst. of Steel Construction, Chair. Radio Free Europe 71-73; Grand Commdr. of the Order of African Redemption (Liberia).
Leisure interests: bridge, golf.
Bethlehem Steel Corporation, Bethlehem, Pennsylvania 18016, U.S.A.

Cortázar, Julio; Argentine writer; b. 1914.
Shorter works have appeared in *New World Writing* (New York), *La Table Ronde* (Paris), *Akzente* (Germany); on staff of UNESCO, Paris; mem. Jury, Casa de las Américas Award; Prix Médicis 74.
Publs. *Bestiario* (short stories) 51, *Final del juego* (short stories) 56, *Las armas secretas* (short stories) 59, *Rayuela* (novel) 63, *Los premios* (novel) 64, *Story of Cronopios and Famas* (stories), *All the Fires, Fire* (stories), *Devil's Drool* 62, *Modelo Para Armar* 68, *Relatos* (short stories) 70, *Libro de Manuel* (novel) 73.
Place Général Beuret, Paris 15e, France.

Cortina Mauri, Pedro; Spanish lawyer, diplomatist and politician; b. 1908; ed. Univ. of Madrid, Acad. of International Law, The Hague.
Legal Adviser on Int. Affairs, Ministry of Foreign Affairs 37-52; Consul-Gen. Tangiers 45-52; Dir. Int. Orgs., Ministry of Foreign Affairs 52-55; Consul-Gen. Paris, del. to int. orgs., Paris 55-58; mem. del. to UN Gen. Assembly 56; Under-Sec. Ministry of Foreign Affairs 58-66; Amb. to France 66-74; Minister of Foreign Affairs 74-75; mem. Inst. of Int. Law; Grand Cross Order of Isabel la Católica, Order of Civil Merit, Order of San Raimundo de Penafort, Légion d'Honneur.
Ministerio de Asuntos Exteriores, Madrid, Spain.

Cortlandt, Lyn, B.A., F.I.A.L., F.R.S.A.; American artist; b. New York; d. of Graf Karl Gustav von Lubieński and Elinor Ernestine (Thiel) Cortlandt; ed. Chouinard Art Inst., Jepson Art Inst. (Los Angeles), Art School of Pratt Inst., Columbia Univ. School of Painting and Sculpture, Hans Hofmann School of Fine Arts, China Inst. in America, Art Students' League of New York (all in New York City), and private instruction.
Advisory mem., Marquis Biographical Library Soc.; Comitato Internazionale, Centro Studi e Scambi Internazionali.
Works in Metropolitan Museum of Art, New York, Museum of Fine Arts, Boston, Fogg Museum of Art, Art Inst. of Chicago, Brooklyn Museum, Baltimore Museum of Art, Cincinnati Art Museum, Musée National d'Art Moderne, Paris, Stedelijk Museum, Amsterdam, Springfield Museum of Fine Arts, Mass., New York Public Library, Boston Public Library, etc.
Exhibitions in U.S.A., Belgium, Switzerland, Greece, Netherlands, Japan, Italy, Portugal, France, Brazil, Argentina, Curaçao, Puerto Rico, Jamaica, and Trinidad; mem. many socs. including Int. Platform Asscn., American Acad. of Political and Social Science, American Judicature Soc., Nat. Trust for Historic Preservation, Acad. of Political Science, UN/U.S.A., Nat. Soc. of Literature and the Arts, Allied Artists of America; Fellow, Royal Soc. of Arts (London), Int. Inst. of Arts and Letters (Germany); many awards for oils and water-colours.
Leisure interests: music, reading (non-fiction), tennis, foreign travel.
1070 Park Avenue, New York City, N.Y. 10028, U.S.A. Telephone: (212) 289-6370 and (212) 831-3536.

Corwin, Norman; American writer-producer-director of radio, television, stage and cinema; b. 3 May 1910, Boston, Mass.; s. of Samuel H. Corwin and Rose Ober; m. Katherine Locke 1947; one s. one d.
Newspaperman 29-38; writer, director, producer for Columbia Broadcasting System 38-48; Chief, Special Projects, UN Radio 49-53; mem. Faculty of Theatre Arts Univ. of Calif., Los Angeles; Regents Lecturer Univ. of Calif., Santa Barbara; mem. Telecommunications faculty, Univ. of Southern Calif.; writer in residence Univ. of N. Carolina; Chair. Documentary Awards Cttee. of Motion Picture Arts and Sciences; Co-Chair. Scholarship Cttee. of Acad. of Motion Picture Arts and Sciences; Chair. Documentary Awards Cttee. of Acad. of Motion Picture Arts and Sciences 64-; mem. Board of Dirs. Writers Guild of America; Trustee Filmex; writer, dir. and host TV series, *Norman Corwin Presents*, Westinghouse Broadcasting Co.; recipient of Peabody Medal, Edward Bok Medal; Award of American Acad. of Arts and Sciences 42; American Newspaper Guide Page One Award 44, 45; Wendell Wilkie One-World Award 46, entered in Radio Hall of Fame 62; Hon. D.Litt. (Columbia Coll. of Communications); other awards.
Leisure interests: mineralogy, music, painting, chess.
Publs. *They Fly through the Air* 39, *Thirteen by Corwin* 42, *More by Corwin* 44, *On a Note of Triumph* (both as a book and album of recordings) 45, *Untitled, and Other Dramas* 47, *Dog in the Sky* 52, *Overkill and Megalove* 62; Films: *The Blue Veil, The Grand Design, Lust for Life, The Story of Ruth, Prayer for the 70's* 69; Cantatas: *The Golden Door, Yes Speak Out Yes* (commissioned by UN 68); Stage plays: *The Rivalry, The World of Carl Sandburg, The Hyphen, Cervantes*.
Office: 10401 Wellworth Avenue, Los Angeles, Calif. 90024; Home: 4477 Colbath Avenue, Sherman Oaks, Calif. 91403, U.S.A.
Telephone: 213-27-48601 (Writers' Guild of America, West).

Cosgrave, Liam, LL.B.; Irish politician; b. 30 April 1920, Templeogue, Co. Dublin; s. of William T. Cosgrave and Louise Flanagan; m. Vera Osborne 1952; two s. one d.; ed. Christian Brothers' Schools, Dublin, St. Vincent's Coll., Castleknock, Co. Dublin and Kings Inns.
Called to the Bar 43; called to the Inner Bar 58; served in Army, first as Private and later in commissioned rank; T.D., Dublin Co. 43-48, Dún Laoghaire and Rathdown 48-; leader, *Fine Gael* Party 65-; Parl. Sec. to the Prime Minister and to Minister for Industry and Commerce 48-51; Minister for External Affairs 54-57; Prime Minister 73-; Chair. and Leader of first Irish Del. to UN Gen. Assembly 56; Knight Grand Cross of Pius IX; Hon. LL.D. (Duquesne Univ., Pittsburg, Pennsylvania, St. John's Univ., Brooklyn 56, DePaul Univ., Chicago 58, Nat. Univ. of Ireland and Dublin Univ. 74).
c/o Government Buildings, Dublin 2, Ireland.

Cosslett, Vernon Ellis, PH.D., SC.D., F.R.S.; British physicist; b. 16 June 1908, Cirencester; s. of Edgar Williams Cosslett and Annie Williams; m. 1st Rosemary Wilson 1936 (divorced 1940), 2nd Anna Joanna Wischin 1940 (deceased 1969); ed. Cirencester Grammar School, Bristol and London Univs., Kaiser Wilhelm Institut, Berlin-Dahlem.
Lecturer, Faraday House Electrical Eng. Coll., London, 35-39, Keddey-Fletcher Warr Research Student, London Univ. 39-41, Lecturer, Electrical Lab., Oxford 41-46, ICI Research Fellow, Cavendish Lab., Cambridge Univ. 46-49, Lecturer in Physics 49-65, Reader in Electronic Physics 65-75, Emer. 75-; Fellow, Corpus Christi Coll., Cambridge 63-; Pres. Royal Microscopical Soc., London 61-64, Int. Fed. of Socs. for Electron Microscopy 72-75; Hon. D.Sc. (Tübingen), Hon. D.Med.Sci. (Gothenburg), Duddell Medal of Inst. of Physics.

Leisure interests: gardening, listening to music, skiing, mountain walking.

Publs. *Introduction to Electron Optics* 46, 50, *The Electron Microscope* 47, *Bibliography of Electron Microscopy* 50, *Practical Electron Microscopy* 51, *X-Ray Microscopy* (with W. C. Nixon) 60, *Modern Microscopy* 66, *Advances in Optical and Electron Microscopy* (with R. Barer) 66, 68, 69, 71, 73, 75.

31 Comberton Road, Barton, Cambridge; Corpus Christi College, Cambridge University; Old Cavendish Laboratory, Free School Lane, Cambridge University, England.

Telephone: Comberton 2428; Cambridge 59418; Cambridge 58381.

Costa, Angelo; Italian industrialist; b. 18 April 1901; ed. Scuola Superiore di Commercio, Genoa.

President Confederazione Generale dell'Industria Italiana 45-55, Life mem. of Admin. and Exec. Cttee. 55-, Pres. 66; Vice-Pres. Pirelli 64; Pres. Asscn. of Shipowners of Tirreno 46-; Pres. Confed. of Independent Shipowners (now Nat. Confed. of Independent Shipowners) 46-, Nat. Asscn. for the Oil Industry.

Publs. numerous books and articles on economic and social subjects.

Centro Pirelli, Piazza Duca d'Aosta 3, Milan, Italy.

Costa, Lucio; Brazilian architect; b. 1902; ed. England, France and Escola Nacional de Belas Artes, Rio de Janeiro.

With Le Corbusier and others designed Brazilian Govt. buildings 36, with Niemeyer designed Brazilian Pavilion at New York World Fair 39, won int. competition for design of city of Brasília 57.

Brasília, Brazil.

Costanzo, Henry J., M.A.; American international finance official; b. 20 June 1925, Alabama; s. of Joseph and Mary Costanzo; m. Maxine Kruse 1955; two d.; ed. St. Mary's Univ. and Columbia Univ.

Economist, Econ. Co-operation Admin., Italy 49-52; Asst. U.S. Treasury Rep., Rome 52-53, Seoul 54-55; Financial Adviser and Chief of Programme Planning, Int. Co-operation Admin. 55; Adviser to IMF 57-61; Economist, Office of Asst. Sec. of Treasury for Int. Affairs 61; Dir. Office of Latin America, Treasury Dept. 62-67; Dir. Agency for Int. Devt., Seoul, 67-69; Exec. Dir. for U.S.A. Inter-American Devt. Bank (IDB) 69-71, Exec. Vice-Pres. 72-74; Exec. Sec. Joint Ministerial Devt. Cttee. IBRD/IMF 74-.

International Bank for Reconstruction and Development, 1818 H Street, N.W., Washington, D.C. 20433, U.S.A.

Telephone: 202-477-6424.

Costar, Sir Norman, K.C.M.G.; British diplomatist; b. 18 May 1909; ed. Battersea Grammar School and Jesus Coll., Cambridge.

Assistant Principal, Colonial Office 32-35; Private Sec. to Perm. Under-Sec., Dominions Office 35; U.K. High Commr.'s Office, Australia 37-39, New Zealand 45-47; Dep. High Commr. for U.K. in Ceylon 53-57; Asst. Under-Sec. Commonwealth Relations Office 58-60; Dep. High Commr. in Australia 60-62; British High Commr., Trinidad and Tobago 62-66, Cyprus 67-69; Immigration Appeals Adjudicator 70-.

c/o Foreign and Commonwealth Office, Downing Street, London, S.W.1, England.

Coste-Floret, Paul, D. EN D.; French lawyer and politician; b. 9 April 1911, Montpellier; s. of Jules Coste-Floret and Juliette Pierron; m. Andrée Railhac 1937; one s.; ed. Coll. Saint-François-Régis and Grand Lycée Montpellier, Univs. of Montpellier and Paris.

Assistant Prof. Faculty of Law, Paris 33-37; Prof. Faculty of Law, Algiers 38; Prof. of Law, Montpellier Univ. 47; after Armistice one of founders of Resistance Movement organ *Combat* and mem. of Liberation

Assen.; technical adviser to Comm. for Interior; Sec. to Minister of Justice in Provisional Govt. Algiers 43; Joint Sec. at Ministry of Justice 44-45; Sec.-Gen. of Comm. for Reform of Civil Code and then Joint Procurator-General for France at Trials of War Criminals, Nuremberg 45; Extraordinary Counsellor of State 45-46; Deputy for L'Hérault 45-67, Counsellor-Gen. 67-; Minister of War 47; Minister for Overseas Territories 47-50; Minister of Information Jan.-Feb. 52, of State Jan.-June 53, of Public Health and Population June 53-June 54; Mayor of Lamolon-les-Bains 53-59, 71-; mem. of Finance Comm. of Nat. Assembly 49; Pres. Comm. Universal Suffrage and Constitutional Laws 52; associated with newspaper *L'Aube* and several legal publications; Mayor of Lodève 59-67; mem. Conseil Constitutionnel 71-; Chevalier de la Légion d'Honneur, Médaille de la Résistance.

16 rue du Cardinal-de-Cabrières, 34 Montpellier, France.

Telephone: (Montpellier) 72-52-47.

Cot, Pierre-Donatien; French engineer and airline executive; b. 10 Sept. 1911, Paris; m. Claude Bouguen 1939; two s. two d.; ed. Lycée Louis-le-Grand, Paris, and Ecole Polytechnique, Paris.

Engineer, Paris 36; Chief Exec. of Port of Le Havre 45; Technical Man., Paris Airport Authority 51-55, Pres. 55-67; Man. Dir. of Air France 67-74; Pres., Dir.-Gen. Soc. Générale d'Entreprises 74-; Commdr. Légion d'Honneur, Croix de Guerre (39-45), Hon. M.V.O., Médaille de l'Aéronautique.

2 avenue Emile-Bergerat, Paris 16e, France.

Cottesloe, 4th Baron, cr. 1874, Baron of the Austrian Empire (Baron Fremantle); **Sir John Walgrave Halford Fremantle,** Bt., G.B.E., T.D., D.L., M.A.; British businessman; b. 2 March 1900; m. 1st Lady Elizabeth Harris 1926, one s. one d.; m. 2nd Gloria Dunn 1959, one s. two d.; ed. Eton and Trinity Coll., Cambridge.

Chairman, Thomas Tapling & Co., Yiewsley Engineering Co., Tate Gallery 59-60, Arts Council of Great Britain 60-65, Reviewing Cttee. on Export of Works of Art 54-72, South Bank Theatre Board, N. W. Metropolitan Regional Hosp. Board 53-60, Nat. Rifle Assen. 60-72, Hammersmith Hospital 67-73, British Postgraduate Medical Fed. 59-73; Gov. King Edward VII's Hospital Fund; Fellow Royal Postgraduate Medical School; Pres. Hosp. Saving Assen. 75; fmr. Vice-Chair. Port of London Authority; fmr. Pres. of Leander Club.

Leisure interests: rowing, shooting.

21 Lyndhurst Road, London, N.W.3, England.

Telephone: 01-435-6626.

Cottier, Jean; French civil servant; b. 2 Sept. 1912, Chalon sur Saône; s. of Pierre Cottier and Jeanne Jouard; m. Yvette Billod 1952; two d.; ed. Lycées Rollin and Henri IV, Sorbonne and Ecole Normale Supérieure, Paris.

Inspector of Finances 41-51; Financial Counsellor, Latin America 51-53; Deputy Dir. Foreign Finance Dept., Ministry of Finance 53-57; Financial Counsellor, French Embassy, Washington 57-61; Alt. Exec. Dir. Int. Bank for Reconstruction and Devt. 58-61; Deputy Sec.-Gen., Org. for European Econ. Co-operation (OEEC), Org. for Econ. Co-operation and Devt. (OECD) 61-69; Insp. Gen. of Finances 67-; Chair. Comm. Export Credit 70; Head, Service Inspection Générale des Finances 71; Minister (Financial), French Embassy, London 71-74; Chair. Banque Française du Commerce Extérieur 74-; Dir. United Int. Bank, Compagnie Française d'Assurance pour le Commerce Extérieur; Officier Légion d'Honneur, Commdr. Ordre du Mérite, Croix de Guerre.

21 boulevard Haussmann, 75427 Paris; 2 place de Bagatelle, 92 Neuilly-sur-Seine, France.

Telephone: 233-4445 (Paris).

Cotton, Frank Albert, PH.D.; American chemist; b. 9 April 1930, Philadelphia, Pa.; s. of Albert Cotton and Helen M. Taylor; m. Diane Dornacher 1959; two d.; ed.

Drexel Inst. of Technology, Temple and Harvard Univs.
Assistant Prof. Massachusetts Inst. of Technology (M.I.T.) 55-60, Assoc. Prof. 60-61, Prof. 61-71; Robert A. Welch Distinguished Prof., Texas A & G Univ. 72-; mem. Nat. Acad. of Sciences, American Acad. of Arts and Sciences, Royal Danish Acad. of Sciences and Letters; American Chem. Soc. Awards in Inorganic Chem. 62, 74, Baekeland Award (N.J. section) 63, Dwyer Medal (Univ. of N.S.W.) 66, Centenary Medal (Chemical Soc. London) 74, Nichols Medal (N.Y. section) 75, Harrison Howe Award (Rochester section) 75, Edgar Fahs Smith Award (Phila. section) 76.
Leisure interests: equitation, conservation.
Publs. *Advanced Inorganic Chemistry* (with G. Wilkinson, F.R.S.) 3rd edn. 72, *Chemical Applications of Group Theory* 2nd edn. 71, *Chemistry, An Investigative Approach* 2nd edn. 73, *Basic Inorganic Chemistry* (with G. Wilkinson) 75, approx. 450 research papers.
Department of Chemistry, Tex. A & G University, College Station, Tex. 77843; Home: Twafcliffe Ranch, Route 2, Box 230, Bryan, Tex. 77801, U.S.A.
Telephone: (713) 845-4432 (Office); (713) 589-2501 (Home).

Cotton, Norris; American lawyer and politician; b. 11 May 1900; ed. Wesleyan and George Washington Univs.
Member New Hampshire Legislature 23; Editor *Granite Monthly*, Concord 23-24; Sec. to Senator George H. Moses 24-28; admitted to N.H. Bar 28; with firm Demond, Woodworth, Sulloway and Rogers, Concord 28-33; with firm Cotton, Tesreau and Stebbins since 45; District Attorney Grafton County 33-39; Justice Municipal Court of Lebanon, N.H. 39-44; mem. N.H. House of Reps. 43, Speaker 45; mem. House of Reps. 47-54; Senator from New Hampshire 54-74; Republican.
15 Kimball Street, Lebanon, N.H., U.S.A.

Cotton, Hon. Robert Carrington, A.A.S.A.; Australian politician; b. 29 Nov. 1915, Broken Hill, N.S.W.; s. of H. L. Carrington and Laura Cotton; m. Eve MacDougall 1937; one s. two d.; ed. St. Peter's Coll., Adelaide.
Former Federal Vice-Pres. Liberal Party of Australia, State Pres. Liberal Party, N.S.W. 57-60, Acting Pres. 65; Senator for N.S.W. 65-; leader Del. of Federal Parl. to meetings of Inter-Parl. Union in Majorca and Geneva 67; Chair. Cottons' Pty. Ltd., Broken Hill; Minister of State for Civil Aviation 69-72, Minister of Manufacturing Industry, Science and Consumer Affairs Nov.-Dec. 75, of Industry and Commerce Dec. 75-.
Leisure interest: golf.
The Senate, Parliament House, Canberra, A.C.T.; Carrington Park, Oberon, N.S.W. 2787, Australia.

Cottrell, Sir Alan Howard, Kt., B.SC., PH.D., M.A., F.R.S.; British scientist; b. 17 July 1919, Birmingham; s. of Albert and Elizabeth Cottrell; m. Jean Elizabeth Harber 1944; one s.; ed. Moseley Grammar School and Univ. of Birmingham.
Lecturer in Metallurgy, Univ. of Birmingham 43-49, Prof. of Physical Metallurgy 49-55; Deputy Head, Metallurgy Div., Atomic Energy Research Establishment, Harwell 55-58; Goldsmith's Prof. of Metallurgy and Fellow of Christ's Coll., Cambridge 58-65; mem. Advisory Council on Scientific Policy 63-64; Deputy Chief Adviser (Studies), Ministry of Defence 65-67, Chief Adviser (Studies) 67; mem. Central Advisory Council for Science and Tech. 67-; Deputy Chief Scientific Adviser to Govt. 68-71, Chief Scientific Adviser 71-74; Master, Jesus Coll., Cambridge 74-; Fellow Royal Soc., Vice-Pres. 64; Fellow Royal Swedish Acad. of Sciences; Fellow Christ's College, Cambridge 58-70, Hon. Fellow 70; Foreign Hon. mem. American Acad. of Arts and Sciences 60; Foreign Assoc. U.S. Nat. Acad. of Sciences 72; Hon. mem. American Soc. for Metals 72, Fellow 74; Hon. D.Sc. (Columbia (N.Y.),

Newcastle, Liverpool, Manchester, Warwick, Sussex, Bath, Strathclyde and Aston Univs. and Cranfield Inst. of Tech.); numerous medals, including Rosenhain Medal of Inst. of Metals, Rumford and Hughes Medals, Royal Soc., Réaumur Medal of Soc. Française de Métallurgie; Harvey Science Prize, Technion-Israel Inst. of Tech. 74.
Leisure interest: music.
Publs. *Theoretical Structural Metallurgy* 48, *Dislocations and Plastic Flow in Crystals* 53, *The Mechanical Properties of Matter* 64, *Theory of Crystal Dislocations* 64, *An Introduction to Metallurgy* 67, *Portrait of Nature* 75, and various scientific papers.
The Master's Lodge, Jesus College, Cambridge, England. Telephone: Cambridge 53310.

Cottrell, Donald Peery, M.A., PH.D.; American university teacher and administrator; b. 17 Feb. 1902, Columbus, Ohio; s. of Dr. Harvey V. Cottrell and Della Stone Miller; m. Eleanor H. Westberg 1928; one s. one d.; ed. The Ohio State Univ. and Columbia Univ.
Public School Teaching and Admin. in Ohio 23-26; Tutor, Hunter Coll. of the City of New York 27-29; Asst. and Assoc. in Coll. Admin., Teachers' Coll., Columbia Univ. 27-29; Asst Prof. 29-31, Assoc. Prof. 31-41, Prof. 41-46 (Education); Asst. Dir., Div. of Instruction 41-44, Exec. Dir. Horace Mann-Lincoln School 43-46, Exec. Officer, Division of Instruction 46 (all at Teachers' Coll., Columbia Univ.); Dean, Coll. of Education, The Ohio State Univ. 46-67, Prof. of Educ. 67-72, Prof. Emer. 72-; Expert Consultant, U.S. War Dept. to advise Military Govt. (U.S.) in the field of University Education in Germany 47; Chair. of Comm. to survey the educational institutions of the Foreign Missions Conf. of N. America in the Philippines 48; Chief UN Educational Planning Mission to Korea 52-53; Pres. The American Asscn. of Colleges for Teacher Education 57; Chair. The Nat. Comm. on Teacher Education and Professional Standards of the Nat. Education Asscn.62; Exec. Consultant in Secondary and Teacher Education to Ministry of Education, Govt. of India, and U.S. A.I.D. Mission, India, 58, 61, 64; Chair. Comm. on Education for the Teaching Profession 66; mem. Board of Trustees, Talladega Coll., Alabama.
Leisure interest: painting (oils and acrylics).
Home: 6671 Olentangy River Road, Worthington, Ohio 43085, U.S.A.

Cotzias, George Constantin; American professor of neurology; b. 16 June 1918, Greece; s. of Constantin G. Cotzias and Katherine Strumpuli; m. Betty Ghinos 1951; one s.; ed. Nat. Univ. of Athens, Harvard Medical School.
Assistant Scientist and Asst. Physician Rockefeller Inst. N.Y. 46-52; Fellow Nat. Research Council 51-52; Exec. Officer Physiology Div. Medical Research Center, Brookhaven Nat. Lab. 53-55, Head Physiology Div. and Senior Scientist 55-; Prof. of Neurology, Mount Sinai School of Medicine 69-; Prof. of Medicine, State Univ. of New York (Stony Brook) 69-; Fellow, American Acad. of Arts and Sciences; mem. Nat. Acad. of Sciences 73; Hon. D.Sc. (Catholic Univ., Santiago, Chile) 69 (St. John's Univ., N.Y.) 71, Hon. Ph.D. (Women's Medical Coll., Pa.) 70; Grand Commdr. Greek Royal Order of the Phoenix; Albert Lasker Award in Clinical Medical Research 69, Borden Award, Asscn. American Medical Coll. 72, Harvey Lecturer, Rockefeller Univ., N.Y. 72, Oscar B. Hunter Award, American Soc. Clinical Pharmacology and Therapeutics, New Orleans 73, Archon Actuarius, Ecumenical Patriarchate, Istanbul 72 and other prizes.
Leisure interests: chess, gardening, boating.
Publs. *Metabolism of Amines and Relevant Enzymes, Metabolism of Trace Metals, Isotopes in Medicine, Neutron Activation Analysis, Treatment of Parkinson's Disease and of Chronic Manganese Poisoning.*
Memorial Sloan-Kettering Cancer Center, 1275 York

venue, New York, N.Y. 10021; Mount Sinai School of Medicine, 100th Street and 5th Avenue, New York, N.Y.; Home: 36 Brown's Lane, Bellport, N.Y. 11713, U.S.A.
Telephone: 212-TR6-1000; 516-286-1184 (Home).

Couch, John Nathaniel, A.M., PH.D.; American teacher and research worker; b. 12 Oct. 1896, Prince Edward, Va.; s. of John Henry Couch and Sallie Love Terry; m. Dorothy Else Ruprecht 1927; one s. one d.; ed. Univ. of North Carolina, Duke Univ., Univ. of Wisconsin, Univ. of Nancy, France.
Instructor in Botany 17-18 and 22-25, Asst. Prof. 25-28, Assoc. Prof. 28-32, Prof. 32-, all of North Carolina Univ.; Chair. Botanical Dept., Univ. of North Carolina 4-60, Kenan Prof. of Botany 45-; Visiting Assoc. Prof. Johns Hopkins Univ. 33 and Prof. 35; Hopkins Tropical Experimental Station, Jamaica 26; awarded Jefferson Medal, N. Carolina Acad. of Sciences 37; Walker Grand Prize in Nat. History 38; Certificate of Merit, Botany Soc. of America 56; Pres. of North Carolina Acad. of Sciences 46; mem. Nat. Acad. of Sciences 43, Nat. Acad. of Sciences of India; Pres. Mycological Soc. of America 43; Chair. South-Eastern Section Botanical Soc. of America; Hon. Vice-Pres. Int. Botany Congress, Seattle 69; Assoc. Editor *Mycologia* 37; Editor *Journal Elisha Mitchell Scientific Society* 46-60; Hon. Sc.D. (Catawba Coll., Duke Univ. and Univ. of N. Carolina); discovered sporangia and motile cells in actinomyce-ales 49.
Leisure interests: flower and vegetable gardening, foreign and domestic travelling.
Publs. *The Gasteromycetes of the Eastern United States and Canada* (W. C. Coker and J. N. Couch) 28, *The Genus Septobasidium* 38.
University of North Carolina, Chapel Hill, N.C.; Rocky Ridge Road, Chapel Hill, N.C. 27514, U.S.A.
Telephone: 919-933-6932 (Office); 919-942-3097 (Home).

Couder, André, DR. ès SCIENCES PHYSIQUES; French astronomer; b. 27 Nov. 1897, Alençon; m. Anne-Marie Pelletier 1925; one s.; ed. Univs. of Paris and Strasbourg.
Began astronomical career at Strasbourg Observatory; moved to Paris Observatory 25, Asst. Astronomer 30, Deputy 37, Astronomer 43, Dir. Optics Laboratory, Vice-Pres. Admin. Council 53-68; mem. Nat. Cttee. of Scientific Research 45-66; mem. and Pres. Bureau des Longitudes 51-53; mem. of the Inst. de France (Acad. des Sciences) 54-, Vice-Pres. 67, Pres. 68; Vice-Pres. Int. Astronomical Union 52-58; Pres. Société Astronomique de France 55-57; Pres. Comité de direction de l'Observatoire de Haute-Provence 64-73; Assoc. Royal Astronomical Soc. 46-, Royal Acad. of Belgium 61-; Grand-Prix Scientifique de la Ville de Paris 61; Dr. h.c. (Univ. de Liège) 73; Officier Légion d'Honneur, and other decorations.
Publs. *Lunettes et Téléscopes* (with A. Danjon) 35, and numerous papers.
11 rue Bobierre de Vallière, 92340 Bourg-la-Reine, France.
Telephone: 661-0981.

Couderc, Paul; French astronomer; b. 15 July 1899; ed. Faculté des Sciences, Paris, and Ecole Normale Supérieure.
Teacher of Mathematics, Lycée, Chartres 26-29, then at Lycées Montaigne, Charlemagne and Janson-de-Sailly, Paris 30-44; Astronomer, Paris Observatory 44-69, Hon. Astronomer 70-; fmr. Sec.-Gen. French Nat. Cttee. for Astronomy; fmr. Vice-Pres. Astronomical Soc. of France; Officier de la Légion d'Honneur; Officier des Palmes Académiques; UNESCO Kalinga Prize for 1966-67.
Publs. include: *L'Architecture de l'Univers* 30, *Parmi les étoiles* 38, *La Relativité* 42, *L'Expansion de l'Univers* 52.
61 avenue de l'Observatoire, Paris 14e, France.

Coulet, François, L. ès L., L. en D., HON. C.B.E.; French diplomatist; b. 16 Jan. 1906, Montpellier; m. Natalie Sullivan 1945; ed. Univs. of Montpellier and Paris.
Entered Diplomatic Service 35; Third Sec. Moscow 36-37, Second Sec. Helsinki 37-40; served Free French Forces 40-44; Private Sec. to Gen. de Gaulle 41-42; C.O. Free French Airborne Forces in U.K. 42-43; Sec.-Gen. of Corsica 43; Commr. of the Repub. for the Liberated Territories of the Normandy Beachhead 44; in charge of inter-allied relations 45; Dir. European Dept. (with rank of Minister) Ministry of Foreign Affairs 46-47; Minister to Finland 47-50; Amb. to Iran 50-55, to Yugoslavia 55-56; granted leave on personal request 56; volunteered for service in Algeria; Lieut.-Col. C.O. Parachute Regt., French Air Force 56-60; Minister and Dir. of Political Affairs to Del. Gen., Algiers 60; Pres. Société Financière de Radio-diffusion 62-65; Dir. C.G.C.T. 70; Dir. Pigier 70; Del.-Gen. Fédération Française des Clubs Automobiles 71-74; Commdr. de la Légion d'Honneur, Croix Val. Mil. with 3 palms and gold star, etc.
Publ. *Vertu des Temps Difficiles* 67.
81 boulevard de Port-Royal, 75013 Paris; and Juvanzé, 10140 Vendeuvre-sur-Barse, France.
Telephone: 336-45-90; 2 Juvanzé.

Coulibaly, Sori; Malian diplomatist; b. 1925, Sokolo; s. of Bakari Coulibaly and Binta Arma; m. Fanta Libidé 1949.
Served French Foreign Ministry, Paris; fmr. Sec.-Gen. Ministry of Foreign Affairs, Mali; Perm. Rep. to UN 62-66; Amb. to U.S.S.R. 67-68; Technical Adviser for Foreign Affairs to the Presidency 68-69, Minister of Foreign Affairs 69-70, of Labour and Public Works 70-75, of Rural Devt. 75-.
Ministry of Rural Development, Bamako, Mali.
Telephone: 24901.

Coulomb, Jean; French physicist; b. 7 Nov. 1904, Blida, Algeria; s. of Charles Coulomb and Blanche d'Izalguier; m. Alice Gaydier 1928; two s. two d.; ed. Ecole Normale Supérieure.
Director Institut de Physique du Globe Algiers 37-41; Dir. Institut de Physique du Globe Paris 41-56; Prof. at the Sorbonne 41-72; Visiting Prof. Istanbul Univ. 54-55; Pres. Int. Asscn. of Terrestrial Magnetism and Electricity 51-54; Dir.-Gen. Centre Nat. de la Recherche Scientifique 56-62; mem. of Cttee. for the Int. Geophysical Year 57-59; Pres. of the Centre National d'Études Spatiales 62-67; Pres. Int. Union of Geodesy and Geophysics 67-71; Pres. Bureau des Longitudes 66-69; Vice-Pres. Int. Council of Scientific Unions 68-72, Pres. 72-74; mem. Acad. of Sciences 60, Int. Acad. of Astronautics 66, Royal Danish Acad. 69, Acad. Royale de Belgique 71.
Publs. *La Physique des Nuages* (in collaboration) 40, *La Constitution Physique de la Terre* 52, *Physical Constitution of the Earth* (in collaboration) 63, *Expansion des Fonds Océaniques* 69, *Sea Floor Spreading and Continental Drift* 72, *Traité de Géophysique Interne*, Vol. I 73, Vol. II 75 (in collaboration).
4 rue Emile Dubois, 75014 Paris, France.
Telephone: 707-01-54.

Coulson, Sir John Eltringham, K.C.M.G.; British diplomatist; b. 13 Sept. 1909, Gosforth, Northumberland; s. of Henry Coulson and Florence Eltringham; m. Mavis Beazley 1944; two s.; ed. Cambridge Univ.
Entered Foreign Service 32; served Rumania 34-37, Foreign Office, Ministry of Economic Warfare and War Cabinet 37-46; Counsellor, Paris 46-48; Deputy U.K. Rep. OEEC, Paris 48-50; Deputy Permanent Rep. to UN 50-52; Asst. Under-Sec. of State, Foreign Office 52-55; Minister in Washington 55-57; Adviser to the Paymaster-Gen. 57-59; Ambassador to Sweden 60-63; Deputy Under-Sec. of State, Foreign Office 63-64; Chief

COU INTERNATIONAL WHO'S WHO CO

of Admin., Diplomatic Service 65; Sec.-Gen. European Free Trade Assen. (EFTA) 65-72.
Leisure interests: golf, tennis, fishing.
The Old Mill, Selborne, Hants., England.

Courcel, Geoffroy Chodron de, D. en DR., L. ès L., DIP. ECOLE DES SC. POL.; French diplomatist; b. 11 Sept. 1912, Tours; s. of Louis de Courcel and Alice Lambert-Champy; m. Martine Hallade 1954; two s.; ed. Coll. Stanislas and Paris Univ.
Attaché Warsaw 37; Sec. Athens 38-39; joined Free French forces June 40; Chef de Cabinet, Gen. de Gaulle 40-41; military service in Egypt, Libya and Tunisia 41-43; Dep. Dir. du Cabinet, Gen. de Gaulle 43-44; Regional Commr. for Liberated Territories 44; Deputy Dir. Cen. and Northern European Sections, Ministry of Foreign Affairs 45-47; First Counsellor Rome 47-50; Dir. Bilateral Trade Agreements' Section, Ministry of Foreign Affairs 50-53; Dir. African and Middle East Section, Ministry of Foreign Affairs 53-54; Dir.-Gen. Political and Economic Affairs, Ministry of Moroccan and Tunisian Affairs 54-55; Permanent Sec. of Nat. Defence 55-58; Permanent Rep. to N.A.T.O. 58-59; Sec. Gen. Présidence de la République 59-62; Ambassador to U.K. 62-72; Ambassadeur de France 65; Sec. Gen. French Ministry of Foreign Affairs 72-; Grand Officier Légion d'Honneur, Compagnon de la Libération, Croix de Guerre, Military Cross, Hon. G.C.V.O., etc.; Hon. D.C.L. (Oxford); Hon. LL.D. (Birmingham).
Leisure interests: shooting, swimming.
Publ. *L'influence de la Conférence de Berlin de 1885 sur le droit Colonial International* 36.
Ministère des Affaires Etrangères, quai d'Orsay, Paris 7e; 7 rue de Medicis, Paris 6e, France.

Cournand, André; American physician; b. 24 Sept. 1895, Paris; s. of Jules Cournand and Marguerite Weber; m. 1st Sybille Blumer (deceased 1959), 2nd Ruth Fabian 1963; one s. (deceased) three d.; ed. Sorbonne, Paris.
Resident U.S. since 30; held teaching appointments with Coll. of Physicians and Surgeons, Columbia Univ. 35-, Prof. of Medicine same Coll. 51-60, Emer. 64-; Chair. cardiovascular study section of Nat. Heart Inst. of Washington; mem. several medical and research societies, including American Physiological Society, Assen. of American Physicians, American Clinical and Climatological Assen., Nat. Acad. of Sciences; Foreign mem. Académie Nationale de Médecine, Académie des Sciences, Institut de France; hon. mem. British Cardiac Society, Royal Society of Medicine, Swedish Cardiac Society, Soc. Médicale des Hôpitaux de Paris, and Columbia Univ. Chapter of Alpha Omega Alpha; on editorial board of *Circulation* (journal of American Heart Assen.), *Journal de Physiologie* (Paris), *Revue Française d'Etudes Cliniques et Biologiques* (Paris), and *American Journal of Physiology*; Andreas Retzius Silver Medal of the Swedish Society of Internal Medicine 46; Lasker Award of U.S. Public Health Assen. 49; John Phillips Memorial Award of American Coll. of Physicians 52; Gold Medal of Royal Academy of Medicine, Brussels 56; Jiménez Díaz Prize, Madrid 70; Trudeau Medal, American Thoracic Soc. 71; served in French Army 15-18, awarded Croix de Guerre with three stars; joint winner Nobel Prize for Medicine 56; Hon. Dr. Univ. of Strasbourg; Hon. Dr. (Univ. of Lyon, Univ. of Brussels, and other univs.); Commandeur de la Légion d'Honneur.
Columbia University College of Physicians and Surgeons, 630 West 168th Street, New York, N.Y. 10032; 1361 Madison Avenue, New York, N.Y. 10028, U.S.A. Telephone: (212)-579-4031 (Office); (212)-289-4456 (Home).

Courrèges, André; French couturier; b. 9 March 1923, Pau (Pyrenees); s. of Lucien Courrèges and Céline Coupe; ed. Ecole Supérieure Technique.

Studied engineering, specialising in roads and bridge moved to Paris and spent year as fashion designer 4 went to Balenciaga's workrooms 48 and served 11 yea apprenticeship; launched own fashion house in Par August 61 and moved to larger premises 66; launche his "Couture-Future" 67; distribution extended t America, England and Belgium 68; opened secon *Boutique Courrèges* in Paris and shop in Tokyo 69.
Leisure interests: pelote basque, swimming, skiing.
Office: 40 rue François 1er, Paris 8e; Home: 27 ru Delabordère, 92 Neuilly-sur-Seine, France.

Courrier, Robert, D.SC., D.MÉD.; French professor; l 6 Oct. 1895, Saxon-Sion; m. Juliette Desmots 192 two d.; ed. Coll. de France, Paris.
Prof. of Experimental Morphology and Endocrinolog at Coll. de France; mem. Scientific Council, Atomi Energy Comm. 57-; mem. Inst. de France; mem Académie Nationale de Médicine 41-, Vice-Pres. 71 Pres. 72; Pres. of Council, Nat. Natural Histor Museum 64-71; foreign mem. Royal Soc. 53; Dr. h.c (Univs. of Brazil, Brussels, Istanbul, Louvain, Athens Quebec and Geneva); Perm. Sec., Acad. des Sciences Grand Officier Légion d'Honneur; Médaille d'Or d' Centre National de la Recherche Scientifique.
Publs. include *Endocrinologie de la Gestation*, and variou biographies.
Home: 3 rue Mazarine, Paris 6e, France.
Telephone: 326.66.21.

Courson de la Villeneuve, Tanguy de, L. EN D.; French diplomatist (retd.); b. 27 April 1911, Kharkhov; s. o Guy and Elisabeth de Courson de la Villeneuve; m Francine Bérard 1952; ed. Ecole Libre des Science Politiques, Paris Univ.
Posts at embassies in London 37, Brussels 44, Berlin 49; Counsellor, The Hague 52; Deputy Dir. in charge of Saarland Affairs, Direction d'Europe 53-56; Minister-Del. to Saarbrücken 57-59, Minister Plenipotentiary 60; Consul Gen. Düsseldorf Jan.-Aug. 60; Minister-Counsellor, French Embassy, Bonn 60; Head, Dept. o Bilateral Agreements, Ministry of Foreign Affairs 63-68; Amb. to Democratic Republic of Congo (Kinshasa) 68-70; Amb. to Norway 71-75; Officier, Légion d'Hon-neur, Ordre de Léopold, Ordre de la Couronne, etc.
Kalina, Place Maure, 06780 Saint-Cézaire, France.
Telephone: 60-20-59 (Home).

Court, Hon. Sir Charles Walter Michael, Kt., O.B.E. (MIL.), M.L.A., F.C.A., F.C.I.S.; Australian politician; b. 29 Sept. 1911, Crawley, Sussex; s. of late W. J. Court and Rose R. Court; m. Rita Steffanoni 1936; five s.; ed. Perth.
Founder Partner, Hendry, Rae & Court, chartered accountants 38; served Australian Imperial Forces 40-46, rising to rank of Lt.-Col.; mem. Legis. As-sembly for Nedlands 53-; Deputy Leader of Opposition W. Australian Parl. 57-59; Minister for Railways 59-67, for Industrial Devt. and the N.W. 59-71, for Transport 65-66; Deputy Leader of Opposition 71-72, Leader 72-73; Premier, State Treas., Minister Co-ordinating Econ. and Regional Devt., W. Australia April 74-; State Registrar (W. Australia) Inst. of Chartered Accountants in Australia 46-52; Senator Junior Chamber Int. 71; Hon. Col. W. Australia Univ. Regt. 69; Hon. LL.D. (W. Australia Univ.) 69; Aus-tralian Mfrs. Export Council Award 70, Inst. of Production Engs. Award 71; Liberal.
Leisure interest: music, occasional appearances as guest conductor.
Publs. many papers on industrial, economic and resource development matters.
Premier's Department, 32 St. George's Terrace, Perth, W. Australia 6000; Home: 46 Waratah Avenue, Dalkeith, W. Australia 6009, Australia.
Telephone: Perth 25-3749 (Office); 86-1257 (Home).

Courtemanche, Henri, P.C., B.A., LL.B.; Canadian politician and businessman; b. 1916; ed. Acad. de Mont Laurier, Séminaire St. Joseph, Mont Laurier, Coll. St. Laurent, Montreal, and Univ. of Montreal.
Hon. Vice-Pres. of the Rural Bar Assen. of the Province of Quebec; Dir. and Treas. Hôpital Jean Talon, Montreal; mem. House of Commons 49-53 and 57-60, Deputy Speaker 57; Sec. of State 58-60; Senator 60; mem. Knights of Columbus; Progressive Conservative.
44 Madona Street, P.O. Box 499, Mont-Laurier, Quebec, Canada.

Courtenay, Tom; British actor; b. 25 Feb. 1937; s. of Henry Courtenay and late Anne Eliza Quest; m. Cheryl Kennedy 1973; ed. Kingston High School, Hull, Univ. Coll., London, Royal Acad. of Dramatic Art.
Started acting professionally 60; stage performances in *Billy Liar* 61-62, *The Cherry Orchard* 66, *Macbeth* 66, *Hamlet* 68, *She Stoops to Conquer* 69, *Charley's Aunt* 71, *Time and Time Again* 72, *Table Manners* 74, *The Norman Conquests* 74-75, *The Fool* 75.
Films include, *The Loneliness of the Long Distance Runner* 62, *Private Potter* 62, *Billy Liar* 63, *King and Country* 64, *Operation Crossbow* 65, *King Rat* 65, *Doctor Zhivago* 65, *The Night of the Generals* 66, *The Day the Fish Came Out* 67, *A Dandy in Aspic* 68, *Otley* 69, *One Day in the Life of Ivan Denisovitch* 72, *Catch Me a Spy*.
c/o ICM, 22 Grafton Street, London, W.1, England.

Courthion, Pierre-Barthélemy; French art historian; b. 14 Jan. 1902, Geneva; s. of Louis Courthion and Elisa Bocquet; m. Pierrette Karcher 1927; one d.; ed. Univ. de Genève, Ecole des Beaux-Arts, Paris and Ecole du Louvre.
Former Asst. Dir. Arts section at Int. Inst. of Intellectual Co-operation of Soc. des Nations and Dir. Archaeological Museum, Valère; fmr. Dir. fondation Suisse dans la Cité universitaire de Paris; fmr. Vice-Pres. Union of French Artistic Press; Vice-Pres. Int. Assen. of Art Critics; mem. Jury of Int. Guggenheim Prize 60-; Cultural Mission to Brazil and Venezuela 63, to Amer. Univs. 65, 67, 74, to Canadian Univs. 69, to Japan and Republic of Korea 73; Silver Medal Reconnaissance française.
Publs. *Gabriele d'Annunzio* 25, *Panorama de la peinture contemporaine* 27, *Vie d'Eugène Delacroix* 27, *Nicolas Poussin* 29, *Claude Lorrain* 32, *Courbet* (2 vols.), *Henri Matisse* 34, *Genève ou le Portrait des Töpffer* 36, *Delacroix* 40, *Henri Rousseau le Douanier* 44, *Le Visage de Matisse* 45, *Bonnard, Peintre du merveilleux* 45, *Géricault* 47, *Utrillo* 48, *Peintres d'aujourd'hui, Raoul Dufy* 51, *La Montagne, L'Art indépendant, Montmartre* 55, *Paris d'autrefois* 57, *Paris des temps nouveaux* 57, *Le Romantisme* 61, *Manet* 62, *Georges Rouault* 62, *Autour de l'impressionnisme* 65, *Paris de sa naissance à nos jours* 66, *L'Ecole de Paris de Picasso à nos jours* 68, *Seurat* 68; Dir. of art films: *Ingres peintre du nu* 68, *Georges Rouault* 71, *Impressionism* 72, *Soutine* 73, *Pablo Gargallo* 73.
Leisure interests: mountaineering, mushroom picking and music.
11 rue des Marronniers, Paris 16e, France.
Telephone: 647-58-03.

Cousins, Rt. Hon. Frank, P.C.; British trade unionist; b. 8 Sept. 1904; ed. King Edward School, Doncaster.
Service with Transport and General Workers Union; appointed successively Organizer (38), Nat. Officer (44), Nat. Sec. (48) of Road Transport Section; Asst. Gen.-Sec. T. & G.W.U. 55, Gen. Sec. 56-64, 66-69; mem. British Transport Joint Consultative Council 55-63, Ministry of Labour Nat. Joint Advisory Council 56-, Exec. Council Int. Transport Workers Fed. 56-64, Pres. 58-60, 62-64, Vice-Pres. 68-; Chair. Central Training Council; Community Relations Comm. 68-70; elected mem. Gen. Council T.U.C. 56-64, 66-69; mem.

Dept. Scientific and Industrial Research 60-66, Export Credits Guarantee Dept., Advisory Cttee. 62, Nat. Econ. Devt. Council (N.E.D.C.) 62-69, British Nat. Export Council 67-69, Central Advisory Council for Science and Technology 67-, Nat. Freight Corpn.; Chair. Port of London Trade Devt. Cttee. 75-; Minister of Technology 64-66; M.P. 65-66; Labour.
Ramsfold Cottage, Roundhurst, Haslemere, Surrey, England.

Cousins, Norman, LITT.D., L.D.H., LL.D., D.E.; American editor and author; b. 24 June 1915; ed. Columbia Univ.
Education writer with *New York Evening Post* 35-36; Man. Editor *Current History* 36-40; Editor *Saturday Review* 40-72; Editor *Saturday Review/World* 73-; mem. Board Dirs. McCall Corpn. and Chair. Editorial Cttee. 61-70; Editor *U.S.A.* during Second World War; Chair. Connecticut Fact-Finding Comm. on Educ. 51-54; Pres. United World Federalists 54-56, Hon. Pres. 56-; U.S. Presidential Rep. at Inauguration of Pres. of Philippines 66; Pres. World Assen. of World Federalists 65-; mem. Board of Dirs. UN Assen. of U.S.A., Nat. Educational Television, The Charles F. Kettering Foundation, Samuel H. Kress Foundation; officer of many orgs.
Publs. *The Good Inheritance, A Treasury of Democracy* 41, *The Poetry of Freedom* (with William Rose Benet) 43, *Modern Man is Obsolete* 45, *Talks with Nehru* 51, *Who Speaks for Man* 53, *In God We Trust* 58, Ed. *March's Dictionary Thesaurus* 58, *Dr. Schweitzer of Lambaréné* 60, *In Place of Folly* 61, *Present Tense* 66, *The Improbable Triumvirate* 72, *The Celebration of Life* 74.
488 Madison Avenue, New York 22, N.Y., U.S.A.

Cousins, Ralph Wynne; American naval officer (retd); b. 24 July 1915, Eldorado, Okla.; s. of Richard Clyde Cousins and Louise Hennessey Cousins; m. Mary Gordon (McBride) Cousins June 1947; ed. L.L. Wright High School and Ironwood Junior Coll., Ironwood, Mich. and U.S. Naval Acad. Annapolis, Md.
Commissioned 37; Commdr. 45; Commanded Attack Carrier Air Group Eleven 45-47; Commdr. Naval Air Facility, Annapolis, Md. 52-54; Capt. 55; Deputy Chief of Staff, COMSIXTHFLT 58-59; Commdg. Officer, U.S.S. *Nantahala* 59-60; and U.S.S. *Midway* 60-61; Rear-Admiral 64; Mil. Asst. to Deputy Sec. of Defense 63-65; Commdr. Carrier Div. Nine 65-66; Asst. Chief of Staff (Plans), CINCPAC 66-67; Vice-Adm. 68; Attack Carrier Striking Forces Seventh Fleet (CTF 77) and Commdr. Carrier Div. Five 67-69; Deputy Chief of Naval Operations (Fleet Operations and Readiness) 69-70; Adm. 70; Vice-Chief of Naval Operations 70-72; Supreme Allied Commdr. Atlantic (NATO) 72-75; Asst. to Pres. Newport News Shipbuilding and Drydock Co. 75-; numerous medals incl. Navy Cross, Distinguished Service Medal with two gold stars, Legion of Merit with gold star, Air Medal with gold star, Presidential Unit Citation, Vietnamese decorations.
Leisure interests: fly fishing, tennis.
Newport News Shipbuilding and Drydock Co., Va. 23607, U.S.A.

Cousteau, Jacques-Yves: French marine explorer; b. 11 June 1910. St. André de Cubzac; s. of Daniel P. and Elizabeth (Duranthon) Cousteau; m. Simone Melchior 1937; two s.; ed. Acad. Stanislas Paris and Brest Naval Acad.
Lieutenant, French Navy, World War II; partly responsible for invention of the Aqualung 43; founder, Groupe d'études et de recherches sous-marines, Toulon 46; Founder and Pres. Campagnes Océanographiques Françaises, Marseilles 50; Founder and Pres. Centre d'Etudes Marines Avancées, Marseilles 52; Leader Calypso Oceanographic Expeditions; Dir. Oceanographic Museum, Monaco 57-; promoted Conshelf dive programme 62; Gen. Sec. ICSEM 66; Foreign Assoc.

U.S. Nat. Acad. of Sciences 68; Fellow, Soc. of Film and TV Arts 74; Corresp. mem. Hellenic Inst. of Marine Archaeology 75; author of documentary films incl. *Le Monde du Silence* (Acad. Award for Best Doc., Grand Prix. Palme d'or, Cannes) 56, *Le Monde sans Soleil* (Acad. Award for Best Doc.), *The Golden Fish* (Acad. Award for Best Short Film) 60; TV series: *The World of Jacques-Yves Cousteau* 66-68, *The Undersea World of Jacques-Yves Cousteau* 68-; TV series "South to Fire and Ice" etc. 73; Commdr. Légion d'Honneur; Croix de Guerre avec palmes; Mérite agricole, Mérite maritime; Officier Arts et Lettres; Potts Medal, Franklin Inst. 70; Hon. D.Sc. (Berkeley and Brandeis Univs.) 70; Gold Medal, Grand Prix d'océanographie Albert Ier 71; Gold Medal, Nat. Geographic Soc., Grande Médaille d'Or, Soc. d'encouragement au progrès 73; Award of New England Aquarium 73; Prix de la Couronne française 73, Grande médaille d'or "Sciences" 74, la Pollena della Bravura 74.

Publs. *Par 18 Métres de Fonds* 46, *La Plongée en Scaphandre* 50, *The Silent World* (Editor with James Duggan) 52, *Captain Cousteau's Underwater Treasury* (with James Duggan) 62, *The Living Sea* 62, *World Without Sun* (with P. Cousteau) 65, *The Shark: Splendid Savage of the Sea* (with Ph. Diolé) 70, *Life and Death in a Coral Sea* 71, *Diving for Sunken Treasure* 71, *The Whale: Mighty Monarch of the Sea* 72, *Octopus and Squid* 73, *Galapagos, Titicaca, the Blue Holes: Three Adventures* 73, *Compagnons de Plongeé* 74, *Encyclopedia: The Ocean World of J.-Y. Cousteau* 74, *Dolphins* 75.
Musée océanographique, Avenue Saint-Martin, Monaco-ville M.C., Monaco.

Coutinho, Vice-Admiral António Alba Rosa; Portuguese naval officer; b. 14 Feb. 1926, Lisbon; s. of António Rodrigues Coutinho and Ilda dos Prazeres Alva Rose Coutinho; m. Maria Candida Maldonado 1950; three s. one d.; ed. Portuguese Naval Acad., Lisbon Univ., Scripps Inst. of Oceanography, U.S.A. Commissioned in Portuguese Navy 47; served on board naval vessels and attended naval courses 48-54; Hydrographic Engineer, Chief of Hydrographic Mission, Angola 59-61; in prison in Zaire 61; several commissions and naval courses 62-64; Dir. of Dredging Services, Mozambique 64-72; Commdg. Officer of Frigate *Admiral P. Silva* 73-74; mem. Portuguese Armed Forces Movt. 74, mem. Mil. Junta 74-75, mem. Supreme Revolutionary Council March-Nov. 75; Pres. Angola Gov. Junta 74, High Commr. in Angola 74-Nov. 75; Distinguished Services Medal, Mil. Merit; Knight Aviz Order; Commdr. Order of Henry the Navigator; Vasco da Gama Naval Medal; Knight of Spanish Naval Merit.
Leisure interests: big game hunting, angling, sailing.
Rua Carlos Macheiro Dias 18, 3° esq., Lisbon, Portugal.
Telephone: 723638.

Coutsoheras, John; Greek lawyer, politician and poet; b. 1904, Ziria, Patras; ed. Univs. of Athens, Paris. Called to the Bar 27; mem. Social Democratic Party 32; Founder, Gen. Sec. Movt. for Democracy in Greece 35; Pres. Soc. for the Study of Greek Problems 56-; mem. Centre Union Party 61; mem. Parl. for Athens 64-67, 74-; under house arrest 68-70; founder mem. Socialist Party 74; mem. Council of Europe 75; Pres. Greek PEN 59-; Founder Universal Centre of the World Citizen—Cosmopolitis, Brussels 70; mem. many literary socs.; Medaglia d'oro di Poesia (Italy) 69, Grand Prix de la Poésie libre, Syndicat des Journalistes et Ecrivains 70, Grand Prix de la Poésie, Cercle Int. de la Pensée et des Arts Français 70, Grand Prix Int. du Disque d'Or, CIPAF 71, and many others.
Publs. poetry: *Thoughts and Echoes* 42, *Blue Breaths* 49, *Greek Nights* 54, *The Supper of Bethany* 59, *The March of the Lilies* 59, *Jordan, the Ever Running* 60, *Smoke Spiralling Up* 60, *Golgotha* 61, *Markos Evgenikos* 64, *The*

Man and the Sea 65, *Aphaia* 65, *The Charioteer* 66, *Men for Human Rights, Arise!* 69, *The Golden Fleece* 70 *With the Gull's Wing and Poseidon's Trident* 71; essays *Poetry and Language* 54, *Mon credo à l'homme libre* 70 and publications on law, economics and politics.
60a Skoufa Street, Athens 144, Greece.
Telephone: 61-35-16.

Couture, Jean Désiré; French mining and nuclear energy executive; b. 23 June 1913, Paris; s. of Julien Couture and Mathilde Bouneau; ed. Lycées Montaigne Saint-Louis and Louis-le-Grand, Ecole Polytechnique and Ecole Nationale Supérieure des Mines de Paris. Engineer 37-45, Chief Engineer 45-64 and Engineer-Gen. of Mines 64-; Dir. Cabinet of the Minister for Industrial Production 46; Dir. of Industrial Production and Mines of Morocco 47-48; Deputy Dir.-Gen. Charbonnages de France 48-49, 53-63; Deputy Dir.-Gen. Houillères de Bassin du Nord et du Pas-de-Calais 49-53; Pres. Admin. Council 57-63, Hon. Pres. 63; Vice-Pres. Comité consultatif de l'énergie 46-64; Pres. Institut français des combustibles et de l'énergie 65; Sec.-Gen. for Energy, Ministère de l'Industrie 63-73; Admin., Société Nationale des Chemins de fer Français 64-74; Pres. Commission consultative pour la production d'électricité d'origine nucleaire 63-73; Pres. French Nat. Cttee. of World Energy Conf. 75-; Senior Adv. to Chair. of Société Générale 74-; Commandeur Légion d'Honneur; Croix de Guerre 39-45.
29 bd. Haussmann, 75009 Paris; Home: 13 rue Monsieur, 75007 Paris, France.
Telephone: 266-54-00 (Office).

Couture, Pierre Julien; French mining executive; b. 25 Feb. 1909, Paris; s. of Julien Couture and Mathilde Bouneau; m. Yvonne Galot 1957; two s. three d.; ed. Lycée St. Louis, Ecole Polytechnique and Ecole Nationale Supérieure des Mines de Paris. Engineer, Chief Engineer and Engineer-Gen. of Mines 33-72; Asst. Dir.-Gen., Houillères de Lorraine 46-50; Dir.-Gen. Mines de la Sarre 50-57; Govt. Admin.-Gen., Commissariat of Atomic Energy 58-63; Adviser, Charbonnages de France 59-63; mem. Board of Admins., Electricité de France 59-63; mem. Council, Ecole Nat. des Mines de Paris 59-69; Pres. Council Ecole Nationale des Mines de St-Etienne 60-73; mem. Devt. Cttee., Ecole Polytechnique 58-63; Pres. of Board of Dirs., Les Mines Domaniales de Potasse d'Alsace 64-67; Pres. Supervisory Board Soc. Commerciale des Potasses d'Alsace 64-68; Pres. Soc. Potasses et Engrais Chimiques 64-67; Pres. S.A. Pec-Rhin 67-73, S.A. Tessenderloo-Chemie (Belgium) 67-; Pres. Board of Dirs. Entreprise minière et chimique 67-72, Mines de Potasses d'Alsace S.A. 68-72, SOFDI 72-, ENERCO 74-; Commdr. Légion d'Honneur; Officier du Mérite Saharien; Officier des Palmes Académiques; Commandeur Ordre Couronne (Belgium).
Leisure interests: Rotary Club of Paris, shooting, tennis, skiing.
22 rue Beaujon, 75008 Paris, France.
Telephone: 924-37-95.

Couve de Murville, (Jacques) Maurice; French politician; b. 24 Jan. 1907; ed. Paris Univ.
Principal Personal Sec. to Gen. Giraud, Algiers; mem. French Cttee. for Nat. Liberation June-Nov. 43; Commr. for Finance to 44; Italian Advisory Council 44; Ambassador to Italy 45; Dir.-Gen. Political Affairs, Foreign Office 45-50; Ambassador to Egypt 50-54, to U.S.A. 55-56, to Fed. Repub. of Germany 56-58; Minister of Foreign Affairs 58-68, of Finance May-July 68; Prime Minister July 68-June 69; Pres. North Atlantic Council 67-68; Inspector of Finance 69-73; Chair. Foreign Affairs Cttee. of the Assembly 73; mediator in Lebanon civil war 75.
Publ. *Une Politique étrangère 1958-69* 73.
Home: 44 rue du Bac, Paris 7e, France.

Cowdrey, (Michael) Colin, C.B.E.; British cricketer and businessman; b. 24 Dec. 1932, Bangalore, India; s. of Ernest Arthur Cowdrey and Kathleen Mary Cowdrey (née Taylor); m. Penelope Susan Chiesman 1956; ed. Homefield, Sutton, Tonbridge and Brasenose Coll., Oxford.

Captain of Cricket Team, Oxford 54, Kent 57-70, England 59- (25 times), MCC to West Indies 68, to Pakistan and Ceylon 69; Dir. Chiesmans 62-67, Whitbread Fremlins 74-; Exec. Dir. Barclays Int. 75-; mem. Council, Winston Churchill Memorial Trust 71-, Australia Soc. 75-.

Leisure interest: golf.

Publs. *Cricket Today* 57, *Tackle Cricket This Way* 60, *Time for Reflection* 63, *Incomparable Game* 69, *MCC Life of a Cricketer* 75.

Kentish Border, Limpsfield, Surrey, England.
Telephone: 283-8989 (Office); Limpsfield Chart 2377 (Home).

Cowles, Gardner, A.B.; American publisher; b. 31 Jan. 1903, Algona, Iowa; s. of Gardner Cowles and Florence Call; m. Jan Streate Cox 1956; one s. three d.; ed. Phillips Exeter Acad., and Harvard Univ.

City Editor *Des Moines Register* 25, News Editor 26-27; Assoc. Man. Editor *Des Moines Register and Tribune* 27, Man. Editor 27-31, Exec. Editor 31-39, Assoc. Publisher 39-43, Pres. 43-71, Chair. 71-73; Hon. Dir. United Air Lines, R. H. Macy & Co., Bankers Life Co., Kemperco Inc.; Hon. Chair. Cowles Communications Inc.; Vice-Chair. and Trustee, Museum of Modern Art, New York; fmr. mem. Board of Overseers of Harvard Univ.; Hon. LL.D. (Drake Univ.) 42, (Coe Coll.) 48, (Long Island Univ.) 55, (Grinnell Coll.) 57; Litt.D. (Iowa Wesleyan Coll.) 55, (Morningside Coll.) 58; L.H.D. (Bard Coll.) 50, (Cornell Coll.) 51; and other hon. degrees.

Leisure interests: reading, bridge, golf, travel.
Cowles Communications Inc., 488 Madison Avenue, N.Y. 10022, U.S.A.

Cowles, John, A.B.; American newspaperman; b. 14 Dec. 1898, Algona, Iowa; s. of Gardner and Florence (Call) Cowles; m. Elizabeth Bates 1923; two s. two d.; ed. Phillips Exeter Acad., and Harvard Univ.

Chairman, *Minneapolis Star and Tribune* 54-73; Chair. *Des Moines Register and Tribune* 45-70; Dir. Associated Press 34-43, First Nat. Bank of Mpls. 40-68; mem. Hoover Comm. Nat. Defense Establishment Cttee. 48; mem. Business Council; Consultant Nat. Security Council 53; mem. White House Educ. Conf. Cttee. 54-55; mem. Gen. Advisory Cttee. U.S. Arms Control and Disarmament Agency 62-69; Trustee Phillips Exeter Acad. 36-54, American Assembly, Ford Foundation 50-68; Carnegie Endowment for Int. Peace; mem. Board of Overseers, Harvard Univ. 44-50, 60-66, Pres. Alumni Asscn. 53-54; Presidential Certificate of Merit (Lease-Lend Admin.), Centennial Award Northwestern Univ., Award for Distinguished Service in Journalism Univ. of Minnesota; Hon. LL.D. (Harvard, Grinnell Coll., Boston Univ., Macalester Coll., Allegheny Coll., Rochester Univ., Carleton), Hon. L.H.D. (Simpson Coll., Drake Univ., Coe Coll.), Hon. Litt.D. (Jamestown Coll.).

Minneapolis Star and Tribune, 425 Portland Avenue, Minneapolis, Minnesota 55415, U.S.A.
Telephone: 612-372-4141.

Cowles, John, Jr.; American publisher; b. 27 May 1929, Des Moines, Iowa; s. of John and Elizabeth Bates Cowles; m. Jane Sage Fuller 1952; two s. two d.; ed. Phillips Exeter Acad. and Harvard Coll.

Joined Minneapolis Star and Tribune Co. 53, Vice-Pres. 57-68, Pres. 68-73, Editor 61-69, Editorial Chair. 69-73, Chair. 73-; Pres. Harper's Magazine Inc. 65-68, Chair. 68-; Dir. Harper and Row, Publishers Inc. 65-, Chair. 68-; Dir. Des Moines Register and Tribune Co., Associated Press, Guthrie Theatre Foundation, Minneapolis

American Newspaper Publishers Asscn. Foundation, etc.; fmr. Dir. Equitable Life Insurance Co. of Iowa, Phillips Exeter Acad., First Bank System, Inc. (Minneapolis), etc.; Campaign Chair. Minneapolis United Fund 67.

Office: 425 Portland Avenue, Minneapolis, Minn. 55413; Home: 1418 Curve Avenue, Minneapolis, Minn. 55403, U.S.A.

Cowley, Malcolm, A.B.; American writer; b. 24 Aug. 1898, Belsano, Pa.; s. of William and Josephine (Hutmacher) Cowley; m. 2nd Muriel Maurer 1932; one s.; ed. Harvard and Montpellier Univs.

Copy writer Sweet's Architectural Catalogue 20 and 23-25; free-lance writer 25-29; Literary Editor *The New Republic* 29-40; staff critic 40-53; literary adviser to the Viking Press 48-; mem. Harvard and Century Clubs, N.Y., American Acad. of Arts and Letters (Chancellor 67-), Nat. Inst. of Arts and Letters (Pres. 56-59, 62-65); Hon. D. Litt.

Leisure interest: gardening.

Publs. *Exile's Return* 34 (revised 51), *The Literary Situation* 54, *Black Cargoes* 62 (with Daniel P. Mannix), *The Faulkner-Cowley File* 66, *Think Back on Us* 67, *Blue Juniata: Collected Poems* 68, *A Many-Windowed House* 70, *A Second Flowering* 73; trans. Valéry's *Variety* 26, Princess Bibesco's *Catherine-Paris* 27, Gide's *Imaginary Interviews* 44, etc.; Editor: *Adventures of an African Slaver* 27, *After the Genteel Tradition* 37, *Books that Changed our Minds* 39, *The Portable Hemingway* 44, *The Portable Faulkner* 46, *The Portable Hawthorne* 48, *The Complete Whitman* 48, *The Stories of F. Scott Fitzgerald* 51, *Writers at Work* 58, etc.

Sherman, Conn. 06784, U.S.A.
Telephone: 203-354-6636.

Cox, Allan, M.A., PH.D.; American geophysicist; b. 17 Dec. 1926, Santa Ana, Calif.; s. of Vernon D. Cox and Hilda Cox; ed. Univ. of Calif. at Berkeley.

Geophysicist U.S. Geological Survey 59-67; Prof., Stanford Univ. 67-; mem. Nat. Acad. of Sciences, Amer. Acad. of Arts and Sciences; Vetlesen Prize; Fleming Award of American Geophysical Union; Day Medal, Geological Soc. of America.

Publs. *Rock Glaciers in the Alaska Range* (with C. Wahrhaftig) 59, *Long Period Variations of the Geomagnetic Field* (with R. R. Doell), 64, *Radiometric Time Scale for Geomagnetic Reversals* (with R. R. Doell and G. B. Dalrymple) 68, *The Lengths of Geomagnetic Polarity Intervals* 68, *Geomagnetic Reversals* 69, *Paleomagnetism of San Cristobal Island, Galapagos* 71, *Pacific Geomagnetic Secular Variation* (with R. R. Doell) 71, *Magnetism of Pillow Basalts and their Petrology* (with M. Marshall) 71, *Plate Tectonics and Geomagnetic Reversals* 73, *Frequency of Geomagnetic Reversals and the Symmetry of the Nondipole Field* 75.

Leisure interests: hiking, chopping firewood, theatre.
Department of Geophysics, Stanford University, Stanford, Calif. 94305, U.S.A.
Telephone: 415-327-3720.

Cox, Archibald, A.B., LL.B.; American lawyer; b. 17 May 1912, Plainfield, N.J.; s. of Archibald Cox and Frances Bruen; m. Phyllis Ames 1937; one s. two d.; ed. St. Paul's School, Concord, and Harvard Univ.

Admitted to Mass. Bar 37; in practice with Ropes, Gray, Best, Coolidge and Rugg, Boston 38-41; Attorney, Office of Solicitor-Gen., U.S. Dept. of Justice 41-43; Assoc. Solicitor, Dept. of Labor 43-45; Lecturer on Law, Harvard Univ. 45-46, Wilson Prof. of Law 46-; Chair. Wage Stabilization Board 52, Advisory Panel to Senate Cttee. on Educ. and Labour 58-59; Solicitor-Gen. of U.S. 61-65; Prosecutor, Watergate Investigation 73; Pitt Prof. of American History and Insts., Cambridge Univ. 74-75; mem. American Bar Asscn., American Acad. of Arts and Sciences, Board of Overseers, Harvard Univ. 62-65.

Publs. *Law and the National Labor Policy* 60, *Cases on Labor Law* (6th edn.) 65, *Civil Rights, the Constitution and the Courts* 67, *The Warren Court* 68, and articles in legal periodicals.
Glezen Lane, Wayland, Mass., U.S.A.

Cox, Sir (Ernest) Gordon, K.B.E., T.D., F.R.I.C., F.INST.P., LL.D., D.SC., F.R.S.; British scientist; b. 24 April 1906, Bath, Somerset; s. of Ernest and Rosina (née Ring) Cox; m. 1st Lucie Baker 1929 (died 1962), 2nd Mary Truter (née Jackman) 1968; one s. one d.; ed. City of Bath Boys' School and Univ. of Bristol.
Research Asst. Davy-Faraday Laboratory, Royal Inst. 27; Asst. Lecturer in Chemistry, Univ. of Birmingham 29, Lecturer 32, Senior Lecturer 39, Reader in Chemical Crystallography 40; Prof. of Inorganic and Structural Chemistry, Univ. of Leeds 45-60; mem. Agricultural Research Council 57-60, Sec. 60-71; Vice-Pres. Inst. of Physics 50-53; Treas. Royal Inst. of Great Britain 71-76; Hon. Sec. British Asscn. 71-75.
Leisure interests: gardening, natural history, music, books.
Publs. papers, chiefly on the crystal structures of chemical compounds.
117 Hampstead Way, London, NW11 7JN, England. Telephone: 01-455-2618.

Cox, Sir Trenchard, Kt., C.B.E., D.LITT., M.A., F.S.A., F.M.A.; British museum official; b. 31 July 1905; ed. Eton Coll., and King's Coll., Cambridge.
Asst. to Keeper, Wallace Collection 32-39; served 39-45 war in Home Office; Dir. City Museum and Art Gallery, Birmingham 44-55; Dir. and Sec. Victoria and Albert Museum 56-66; Chevalier Légion d'Honneur 67.
Publs. *Jehan Foucquet* 31, *David Cox* 47, *Peter Bruegel* 51, *Pictures: A Handbook for Collectors* 56.
33 Queen's Gate Gardens, London, S.W.7, England.

Coxeter, Harold Scott MacDonald, B.A., PH.D., LL.D., D.MATH., D.SC., F.R.S., F.R.S.C.; British mathematician; b. 9 Feb. 1907, London; s. of Harold Samuel Coxeter and Lucy (née Gee) Coxeter; m. Hendrina Johanna Brouwer 1936; one s. one d.; ed. King Alfred School, London, St. George's School, Harpenden, and Trinity Coll., Cambridge.
Rockefeller Foundation Fellow, Princeton 32-33; Procter Fellow, Princeton 34-35; Asst. Prof., Toronto 36-43, Assoc. Prof. 43-48, Prof. of Mathematics 48-; Visiting Prof., Notre Dame 47, Columbia Univ. 49, Dartmouth Coll. 64, Univ. of Amsterdam 66, Univ. of Edinburgh 67, Univ. of E. Anglia 68, Australian Nat. Univ. 70, Univ. of Sussex 72, Univ. of Warwick 76; mem. Koninklijke Nederlandse Akademie van Wetenschappen, Mathematische Gesellschaft in Hamburg, London Mathematical Soc., etc.
Leisure interests: music, travel.
Publs. *Non-Euclidean Geometry* 42, 65, *Regular Polytopes* 48, 73, *The Real Projective Plane* 49, 59, *Introduction to Geometry* 61, 69, *Projective Geometry* 46, *Twelve Geometric Essays* 68, *Regular Complex Polytopes* 74.
67 Roxborough Drive, Toronto M4W1X2, Ont., Canada.

Cozzens, James Gould; American writer; b. 19 Aug. 1903; ed. Harvard Univ.
Mem. Nat. Inst. Arts and Letters; Pulitzer Prize 49; Howells Medal, American Acad. of Arts and Letters 60.
Publs. *Confusion* 24, *Michael Scarlett* 25, *Cockpit* 28, *The Son of Perdition* 29, *S.S. San Pedro* 31, *The Last Adam* 33, *Castaway* 34, *Men and Brethren* 36, *Ask Me Tomorrow* 40, *The Just and the Unjust* 42, *Guard of Honor* 48, *By Love Possessed* 57, *Children and Others* 64, *Morning, Noon and Night* 68, *A Flower in her Hair* 74.
P.O. Box 2372, Stuart. Fla. 33494, U.S.A.

Crabbe, Hon. Samuel Azu, B.A., LL.B.; Ghanaian judge; b. 18 Nov. 1918; s. of Q. L. Crabbe; m. Dorice Martinson; three s. two d.; ed. Achimota Coll. and Univ. Coll., London.
Called to the Bar, Middle Temple 48; Barrister and Solicitor, Gold Coast Bar 48-52; mem. Accra Town Council 50-51; District Magistrate 53-57, Acting Senior Magistrate 57; Acting Chief Registrar, Supreme Court and Acting Registrar, Ghana Court of Appeal 57-58 Senior Crown Counsel, Attorney-Gen.'s Office 58 Acting Solicitor-Gen. 59; Judge, High Court of Justice 59-61, Supreme Court 61; mem. Gen. Legal Council of Ghana 61, Deputy Chair. 65-66; Chair. Concessions Tribunal 62; Justice of Appeal, Court of Appeal for Eastern Africa 63-65; Judge, Court of Appeal 66; Chair. Govt. Finance Board 67; Acting Chief Justice of Ghana 70, 72; Justice Supreme Court 71-; Chief Justice of Ghana 73-; Pro-Chancellor Univ. of Cape Coast, Chair. Univ. Council 72-; Justice of the First Demonstration Int. Court of Justice, Belgrade; Pres. Olympic and Commonwealth Games Asscn. of Ghana 68.
Leisure interests: football, cricket, reading, swimming golf.
Publ. *John Mensah Sarbah (1874-1910), His Life and Works.*
Office of the Chief Justice, P.O. Box 119, Accra, Ghana Telephone: 65292 (Office); 76223 (Residence).

Craig, Rev. Robert, M.A., B.D., S.T.M., PH.D., D.D. British ecclesiastic, university professor and administrator; b. 22 March 1917, Markinch, Fife, Scotland; s. of late John Craig and Anne Peggie Craig; m. Olga Wanda Strzelec 1950; one s. one d.; ed. St. Andrews Univ. and Union Theological Seminary, N.Y.
Assistant Minister, St. John's Kirk, Perth 41-42 British Army Infantry Chaplain 42-47; Prof. of Divinity, Natal Univ., S. Africa 50-57, Dean of Coll. 53-54; Prof. of Religion, Smith Coll., Northampton, Mass., U.S.A. 58-63; Prof. of Theology, Univ. Coll. of Rhodesia 63-69, Vice-Principal 66-69, Principal 69-70; Principal and Vice-Chancellor, Univ. of Rhodesia 70-; Hon. D.D. (St. Andrews Univ.) 67.
Leisure interests: cinema, theatre, recent and contemporary history, light classical music, listening and talking to people.
Publs. *The Reasonableness of True Religion* 54, *Social Concern in the Thought of William Temple* 63, *Religion: Its Reality and its Relevance* 65, *The Church: Unity in Integrity* 66, *Politics and Religion: A Christian View* 72, *On Belonging to a University* 74.
University of Rhodesia, P.O. Box 2702, Salisbury, Rhodesia.
Telephone: Salisbury 36635.

Craig, Thomas Rae, C.B.E., T.D., LL.D.; British steel executive; b. 11 July 1906, Motherwell; s. of Sir John Craig, C.B.E., D.L., and Lady Jessie Craig; m. Christina Moodie 1931; three s. one d.; ed. Glasgow Acad., and Lycée Malherbe, Caen.
Army Service 39-45; Entire career with Colvilles Ltd., Chair. 65-67; Man. Dir. Scottish and Northwest Group, British Steel Corpn. 67, mem. Board, British Steel Corpn. 67-72; Deputy Gov. Bank of Scotland 72-.
Leisure interest: farming.
Invergare, Rhu, Dunbartonshire, Scotland.
Telephone: Rhu 427.

Craig, Walter Early, A.B., LL.B.; American lawyer and judge; b. 26 May 1909; ed. Stanford Univ.
Law practice 34-; Assoc. Fennemore, Craig, Allen and Bledsoe 36-45, Partner 45-55; Partner Fennemore, Craig, Allen and McClennen 55-64; Pres. Maricopa County Bar Asscn. 41, Board of Govs. 49-53, Pres. 51-52; Vice-Pres. Western States Bar Council 55-56, Pres. 56-57; House of Delegates 47-, Board of Govs. 58-65, Pres. American Bar Asscn. 63-64; Council Inter-American Bar Asscn. 64-, and Int. Bar Asscn. 64-; U.S. District Judge Arizona 63-; Chair. Nat. Conf. of Fed. Trial Judges 72-73; mem. numerous judicial bodies, several hon. degrees, and numerous awards.
U.S. Court House, Phoenix, Ariz. 85025, U.S.A.
Telephone: 602-261-3547.

Craig, Rt. Hon. William; British politician; b. 2 Dec. 924; ed. Queen's Univ. Belfast.
Member (Ulster Unionist) Parl. of N. Ireland (Stormont) 60-72; mem. N. Ireland Assembly 73-74; Chief Whip 62-63; Minister of Home Affairs 63-64, 66-68; Minister of Health and Local Govt. 64; Minister of Devt. 65-66; Leader, Ulster Vanguard 72-, Vanguard Unionist Party 73; mem. Parl. (United Ulster Unionist Coalition) 74; mem. Northern Ireland Convention, East Belfast 75-76.
23 Annadale Avenue, Belfast 7, Northern Ireland.

Cram, Donald James, M.S., PH.D.; American professor of chemistry; b. 22 April 1919, Chester, Vt.; s. of Joanna Shelley and William Moffet Cram; m. Jane Maxwell 1969; no c.; ed. Rollins College, Fla., Univ. of Nebraska and Harvard Univ.
Researcher, Merck & Co., Rahway, N.J. 42-45; Instructor, American Chem. Soc. Fellowship, Univ. of Calif. L.A. (UCLA) 47-48, Asst. Prof. 48-51, Assoc. Prof. 51-56, Prof. 56-; Nat. Acad. of Sciences Award 61, A.C.S. Award 65, American Acad. of Arts and Sciences Award 67; Calif. Scientist of the Year 74, A.C.S. Cope Award in Organic Chem. 65, 75, McCoy Award for Contributions to Chem.
Leisure interests: tennis, surfing, skiing, guitar.
Publs. *Organic Chemistry* (with Prof. George Hammond and Prof. James Hendrickson), *Elements of Organic Chemistry* (with John Richards and Prof. George Hammond), monograph *Fundamentals of Organic Chemistry*, 270 papers in *Journal of American Chemical Society* and other chemical journals from 1943.
Department of Chemistry, University of California, 405 Hilgard Avenue, Los Angeles, Calif. 90069; 1250 Roscomare Road, Los Angeles, Calif. 90024, U.S.A.
Telephone: (213)-825-1562 (Office); (213)-472-8477 (Home).

Cramér, Harald, PH.D.; Swedish university professor; b. 25 Sept. 1893, Stockholm; s. of Carl Cramér and Emily Cramér; m. Marta Hansson 1918; two s. one d.; ed. Stockholm Univ.
Membership of Govt. Cttees. on Insurance Questions 17-; Prof. of Mathematical Statistics and Actuarial Mathematics, Univ. of Stockholm 29-58, Pres. 50-58; Chancellor of Univs. 58-61; Visiting Prof. Princeton, Yale and Berkeley Univs. 46-47, Columbia Univ. 63, Moscow and Leningrad 63, Berkeley 66; mem. Royal Swedish Acad. of Science, Norwegian, Danish and Finnish Acads. of Science, mem. American Acad. of Arts and Sciences; Hon. mem Int. Statistical Inst.; Hon. Pres. Swedish Soc. of Actuaries; Hon. D.Sc. (Princeton and Copenhagen Univs., Univs. of Helsinki and Edinburgh); Hon. LL.D. (Stockholm Univ.); Guy Gold Medal, Royal Statistical Soc., London 72.
Publs. *Random Variables and Probability Distributions* 37, *Mathematical Methods of Statistics* 45, *Elements of Probability Theory* 54, *Collective Risk Theory* 55, *Stationary and Related Stochastic Processes* (with M. R. Leadbetter) 67.
Sjötullsbacken 15, Blockhusudden, 115 25, Stockholm, Sweden.
Telephone: 08-62-37-19.

Cramer, Morgan J.; American business executive; b. 6 Oct. 1906, Monessen, Pa.; s. of Morgan J. and Cecilia (Michaels) Cramer; m. Miriam Fuchs 1933; one d.; ed. Lehigh Univ., Bethlehem, Pennsylvania.
Served in U.S. Army 43-46; P. Lorillard Company 31-66, Sales Dept. 31-60, Dir. 58-65, Vice-Pres. 60-61, Asst. to Pres. 61, Pres. 61-62, Pres. and Chief Exec. Officer 62-65; Pres. and Chief Exec. Officer Royal Crown Cola Int. Ltd. 66-68, Chair. of Board and Chief Exec. Officer 69-70; Dir. Greater New York Fund; Pres. and Dir. Morgan J. Cramer Associates Inc. 70-; Trustee, Polytechnic Hospital, Lehigh Univ. 73-.
530 East 72nd Street, New York City 10021, N.Y., U.S.A.

Crane, Horace Richard, PH.D.; American professor of physics; b. 4 Nov. 1907, Turlock, Calif.; s. of Horace Stephen Crane and Mary Alice Roselle; m. Florence Rohmer LeBaron 1934; one s. one d.; ed. Calif. Inst. of Technology.
Research Fellow Calif. Inst. of Technology 34-35; on Faculty of Univ. of Mich. 35-, Chair. of Dept. of Physics 65-72; Mass. Inst. of Technology Radiation Lab. 40; at Carnegie Inst. of Washington 41; Henry Russel Lecturer Univ. of Mich.; mem. Standing Cttee. on Controlled Thermonuclear Research, U.S. Atomic Energy Comm. 69-72; Chair. Board of Govs. Amer. Inst. of Physics 71-75; Fellow, American Acad. of Arts and Sciences; mem. Nat. Acad. of Sciences; Distinguished Service Award of Univ. of Mich. 57, and of Calif. Inst. of Technology 68; Davisson-Germer Prize of American Physical Soc. 68.
Leisure interests: ham radio, photography, horticulture.
Publs. over 150 scientific papers on nuclear physics, accelerators, electronics, biophysics and physics education, including *Principles and Problems of Biological Growth* (*Scientific Monthly* Vol. 70), *Precision Measurement of the g-factor of the Free Electron* (with D. Wilkinson, *The Physical Review* Vol. 121) 61.
Physics Department, University of Michigan, Ann Arbor, Mich. 48104, U.S.A.

Crane, Jacob Leslie; American engineer, administrator, town planning consultant; b. 14 Sept. 1892, Benzonia, Mich.; s. of Jacob L. and Sarah T. Maley Crane; m. 1st Ruth Fifield 1915; m. 2nd Jane Watson; two s. three d.; ed. Univs. of Harvard and Michigan.
Engineer on municipal works and housing 13-21; consulting engineer and city planner since 21; worked on development plans for 60 towns and cities in U.S., China, Russia and Latin America; U.S. Housing Authority 38-40; Asst. Co-ordinator Defense Housing 40-42; Dir. Div. of Urban Development Nat. Housing 42-45; Special Asst. to Administrator 45-48; Asst. to Administrator, Housing and Home Finance Agency 48-54, Consultant 54-; lecturer at several Univs.; consultation on housing and urban reconstruction in Britain, France, Italy 44-45, in South America 45-46; Consultant to UN 46-; Senior Consultant Doxiadis Associates 55-68; Chair. Special UN Housing Mission to S. Asia 50-51; Past Pres. American City Planning Inst.; mem. American Soc. of Civil Engineers and Int. Fed. for Housing and Planning.
Leisure interests: sailing, music.
Publ. *Urban Planning—Illusion and Reality* 73.
Cosmos Club, Washington, D.C.; and 4200 Cathedral Ave., N.W., Washington, D.C. 20016, U.S.A.

Cranston, Alan; American politician; b. 19 June 1914, Palo Alto, Calif.; m. Geneva McMath 1940; two s.; ed. Mount View High School, Los Altos, Pomona Coll., Pomona, Univ. of Mexico, and Stanford Univ.
International News Service, England, Germany, Italy, Ethiopia 37-38; Chief, Foreign Language Div., Office of War Information 40-44; U.S. Army 44-45; Nat. Pres. United World Federalists 49-52; Pres. Calif. Democratic Council 53-58; Controller of Calif. 58; re-elected 62; business career in land investment and home construction; U.S. Senator from Calif. 69-.
Leisure interests: painting in oils, running.
United States Senate, Washington, D.C. 20510, U.S.A.
Telephone: 202/224-3553.

Crawford, Bryce, Jr., A.B., A.M., PH.D.; American professor of chemistry; b. 27 Nov. 1914, New Orleans, La.; s. of Bryce Low Crawford and Clara Hall Crawford; m. Ruth Raney 1940; ed. Stanford Univ.
National Research Council Fellow, Harvard Univ. 37-39; Instructor, Yale Univ. 39-40; Asst. Prof., Univ. of Minn. 40-43, Assoc. Prof. 43-46, Prof. 46-, Chair. Dept. of Chem. 55-60, Dean, Graduate School 60-72; Fulbright Prof., Oxford Univ. 51, Tokyo Univ. 66;

Editor *Journal of Physical Chemistry* 70-; Chair. Council of Graduate Schools 62-63; Pres. Assen. of Graduate Schools 70, Graduate Record Examinations Board 68-72; mem. Nat. Acad. of Sciences, American Chem. Soc. (Board of Dirs. 69-), Coblenz Soc., American Philosophical Soc.; Fellow, American Physical Soc.; mem. Board of Dirs. American Chemical Soc. 69; Presidential Certificate of Merit 46; Guggenheim Fellowships 50, 72; Fulbright Professorship 51, 66; Minn. Award, American Chem. Soc. 69.
Publs. Articles in scientific journals.
Molecular Spectroscopy Laboratory, Dept. of Chemistry, University of Minnesota, Minneapolis, Minn. 55455; Home: 1545 Branston, St. Paul, Minn. 55108, U.S.A. Telephone: 612-373-9947.

Crawford, Sir Frederick, G.C.M.G., O.B.E.; British overseas administrator; b. 9 March 1906, Norham-on-Tweed, Northumberland; *m.* 1st Maimie Green 1936 (died 1959), two *s.*; *m.* 2nd Clio Georgiadis (née Colocotronis); ed. Hymers Coll., Hull, and Balliol Coll., Oxford.
Cadet, Tanganyika 29, Asst. District Officer 31, District Officer 41; seconded to East Africa Governors Conf. 42-43 and 45-46; Economic Sec. N. Rhodesia 47, Dir. of Development 48-50; Gov. and C.-in-C. Seychelles 51-53; Dep. Gov., Kenya 53-57; Gov. of Uganda 57-61; fmr. Dir. (Rhodesia) Anglo-American Corpn. of South Africa Ltd., Dir. Barclays Int. Bank, Rhodesia, Union Corpn. Investments Ltd. of Johannesburg, S. Africa and other companies.
Leisure interests: golf, fishing.
P.O.B. 1108, Salisbury, Rhodesia.
Telephone: 61431 and 33569.

Crawford, Joan; American film actress and business executive; b. 23 March 1908, San Antonio, Texas; ed. Stephens Coll., Columbia, Missouri.
Appeared in more than seventy films 25-; Dir. Pepsi Cola Co. 59-; in silent films 25-29.
Talking films include: *Hollywood Revue* 29, *Untamed* 29, *Montana Moon* 30, *Paid* 30, *Dance, Fools, Dance, Laughing Sinners* 31, *This Modern Age* 31, *Possessed* 32, *Letty Lynton* 32, *Grand Hotel* 32, *Rain* 32, *Today We Live* 33, *Dancing Lady* 33, *Sadie McKee* 34, *Chained* 34, *Forsaking All Others* 34, *No More Ladies* 35, *I Live My Life* 35, *The Gorgeous Hussy* 36, *Love on the Run* 36, *The Last of Mrs. Cheyney* 37, *The Bride Wore Red* 38, *Mannequin* 38, *The Shining Hour* 39, *The Ice Follies of 1939* 39, *The Women* 39, *Strange Cargo* 39, *The Gay Mrs. Trexel* 40, *A Woman's Face* 41, *When Ladies Meet* 42, *They All Kissed the Bride* 42, *Reunion in France* 43, *Above Suspicion* 43, *Mildred Pierce* 46, *Humoresque, Daisy Kenyon* 48, *Flamingo Road, The Damned Don't Cry* 50, *Harriet Craig* 50, *Goodbye My Fancy* 51, *This Woman is Dangerous* 52, *Sudden Fear* 52, *Torch Song* 53, *Johnny Guitar* 54, *Female on the Beach* 55, *Queen Bee* 56, *Autumn Leaves* 56, *Story of Esther Costello* 57, *The Best of Everything* 59, *The Caretakers* 62, *What Ever Happened to Baby Jane* 62, *Strait-Jacket* 63, *I Saw What You Did* 65, *Berserk* 68, *Trog* 71.
Publs. *A Portrait of Joan* (autobiog.), *My Way of Life* 72.
8008 W. Norton Avenue, Los Angeles, California 90046, U.S.A.

Crawford, Sir John Grenfell, Kt., C.B.E., M.EC.; Australian administrator; b. 4 April 1910, Sydney; *s.* of Harry Crawford and Harriet Wood; *m.* Jessie Morgan 1935; one *d.*; ed. Univ. of Sydney.
Lecturer in Rural Economics, Univ. of Sydney 34-41; Economic Adviser, Rural Bank of N.S.W. 35-43; Adviser, Dept. of War Organization of Industry 42-43; Dir. of Research, Commonwealth Ministry of Post-War Reconstruction 43-45; Dir. Commonwealth Bureau of Agricultural Economics 45-50; Commonwealth Wool Adviser 49-55; Sec. Dept. of Commerce and Agriculture, Canberra 50-56, Dept. of Trade 56-60; Senior Consultant

to Int. Bank for Reconstruction and Devt. 64-; Dir. School of Pacific Studies, and Prof. of Econs., Australia Nat. Univ. 60-67, Vice-Chancellor of Australian Nat Univ. 68-73; Chancellor, Univ. of Papua New Guinea 72-75; Vice-Chair. Commonwealth Econ. Enquir 62-64; Chair. Tech. Advisory Cttee., Int. Agricultura Research, FAO 71-; Special Commr. Australia Industries Assistance Comm. 74-; Chair. Australia Devt. Assistance Advisory Board 75-; Walter an Eliza Hall Fellow 33-35; Commonwealth Fund Fellow U.S.A. 38-40; Farrer Medallist (and Orator) 57; Fellow Australian Inst. of Agricultural Science 58; Hon D.Sc., Hon. D.Ec., Hon. LL.D., Hon. D.Sc.Ec.
Leisure interests: reading, tennis, fishing.
Publs. *Australian National Income* (with Colin Clark) 38; *War-Time Agriculture in Australia and New Zealand* (with C. M. Donald, D. B. Williams and A. A. Ross) 54; *Australian Trade Policy 1942-1966: A Documentary History* 68.
32 Melbourne Avenue, Deakin, A.C.T. 2600, Australia.

Crawford, Sir (Robert) Stewart, B.A., G.C.M.G., C.V.O.; retd. British diplomatist; b. 27 Aug. 1913, London; *s.* of the late Sir William Crawford, K.B.E.; *m.* Mary Corbett 1938; three *s.* one *d.*; ed. Gresham's School, Holt, and Oriel Coll., Oxford.
Air Ministry 36; Private Sec. to Chief of Air Staff 40-46; Asst. Sec. Control Office for Germany and Austria 46-47; Foreign Office 47-54; Counsellor, Oslo 54-56; Counsellor, later Minister, Baghdad 57-59; Deputy U.K. Del. to OEEC, Paris 59-60; Asst. Under-Sec., Foreign Office 61-65; Political Resident in Persian Gulf, Bahrain 66-70; Deputy Under-Sec. Foreign and Commonwealth Office 70-73.
Leisure interests: opera, travel, literature.
5 Manchester Street, London, W1M 5PH, England.
Telephone: 01-935-5347.

Crawford, William Avery; American diplomatist; b. 14 Jan. 1915, New York; *s.* of John Raymond Crawford and Pauline Avery Crawford; *m.* Barbara Gardner 1940; two *s.* three *d.*; ed. Haverford Coll., Haverford, Pa., Centro de Estudios Históricos, Madrid, Ecole Libre des Sciences Politiques, Paris, Harvard Coll., Columbia Univ. and Nat. War Coll., Washington, D.C.
Foreign Service 41-, Havana 41-44, Dept. of State 44-45, Moscow 45-47, Dept. of State 47-50, Paris 50-54, Dept. of State 54-57, Prague 57-59; Dir. Office of Research and Analysis for Sino-Soviet Bloc, Dept. of State 59-61; Minister to Romania 61-64, Ambassador 64-65; Special Asst. for Int. Affairs to Supreme Allied Commdr., Europe, NATO 65-67; Senior Foreign Service Inspector 67-70, Editorial Dir. Scholarly Resources Inc. 70-73; Dir. Foreign Relations Webster, Johnson & Stowell Inc. 73-.
4402 Boxwood Road, Washington, D.C. 20016, U.S.A.
Telephone: (301) 229-3880.

Crean, Frank, B.A., B.COM., A.A.S.A.; Australian accountant and politician; b. 28 Feb. 1916, Hamilton, Victoria; ed. state schools, Melbourne Univ.
Income Tax Assessor for ten years; mem. Victoria Legislative Assembly for Albert Park 45-47, for Prahan 49-51; mem. Parl. for Melbourne Ports 51-; mem. Fed. Parl. Labor Party Exec. 56-, Deputy Leader July 75-Jan. 76; mem. Privileges Cttee. 67-, Joint Cttee. on Defence Forces Retirement Benefits Legislation 70-72; Treas. 72-74; Minister for Overseas Trade 74-75; Deputy Prime Minister July-Nov. 75; mem. several Parl. dels. abroad; Labor Party.
Parliament House, Canberra, A.C.T.; and 106 Harold Street, Middle Park, Vic. 3206, Australia.

Crean, Gordon Gale, M.A., F.R.S.A.; Canadian barrister and diplomatist; b. 29 April 1914, Toronto; *s.* of Gordon Crean and Louisa Gale; *m.* Elizabeth Grant 1948; two *s.* two *d.*; ed. Upper Canada Coll., Toronto, Trinity Coll.,

Univ. of Toronto, New Coll., Oxford Univ., and Gray's Inn.
British Army 40-45; Second Sec., Dept. of External Affairs, Canada 45-, First Sec., Canadian Embassy, Belgrade, Counsellor, Office of High Commr., London 52; Head of Division, Dept. of External Affairs, Ottawa 53-58; Minister, Canadian Embassy, France 58-61; Amb. to Yugoslavia 61-64, to Italy 64-70, and High Commr. to Malta 65-70; Amb. to Fed. Germany 70-; assoc. mem. Inst. of Strategic Studies, Asscn. of Canadian Slavists.
Leisure interests: skiing, golf, tennis.
Canadian Embassy, 18 Friedrich-Wilhelm-Strasse, 53 Bonn, Federal Republic of Germany.

Creeley, Robert White, M.A.; American writer and professor of English; b. 21 May 1926, Arlington, Mass.; *s.* of Oscar Slade and Genevieve (Jules) Creeley; three *d.*; ed. Univ. of New Mexico and Harvard Univ.
Instructor Black Mountain Coll. 54-55; Visiting Lecturer Univ. of New Mexico, Albuquerque 61-62, Lecturer in English 63-66, Visiting Prof. 68-69; Lecturer Univ. of British Columbia, Vancouver 62-63; Prof. of English State Univ. of New York, Buffalo 67-; Visiting Prof., San Francisco State Coll. 70-71; Editor *Black Mountain Review* 54-57; American Field Service 44-45; D. H. Lawrence Fellow 60, Guggenheim Fellow 64, 71; Rockefeller Grantee 65; Levinson Prize of *Poetry Magazine* 60, Blumenthal-Leviton Award of *Poetry Magazine* 65.
Publs. *Le Fou* 52, *The Immoral Proposition* 53, *The Kind of Act of* 53, *The Gold Diggers* 54, revised edn. 65, *All That is Lovely in Men* 55, *If You* 56, *The Whip* 57, *A Form of Women* 59, *For Love, Poems 50-60,* 62, *The Island* 63, *Words* 67, *Numbers* 68, *Pieces* 69, *The Charm* 69, *A Quick Graph* 70, *The Finger* 70, *A Day Book* 72, *Listen* 72, *A Sense of Measure* 73, *His Idea* 73, *Contents of Poetry* 73; Edited: *New American Story* (with Donald M. Allen) 65, *The New Writings in the U.S.A.* (with Donald M. Allen) 67, *Selected Writings of Charles Olson* 67, *St. Martins* 71, *Whitman: Selected Poems* 72.
Annex B, State University of New York, Buffalo, N.Y. 14214; Home: Box 344, Bolinas, Calif. 94924, U.S.A.
Telephone: 415-868-0147 (Home).

Creighton, Donald Grant, C.C., B.A., M.A., D.LITT., LL.D.; Canadian univ. professor; b. 15 July 1902, Toronto; *s.* of William and Laura Creighton; *m.* Luella Bruce 1926; one *s.* one *d.*; ed. Victoria Coll., Univ. of Toronto and Balliol Coll., Oxford.
Lecturer in History, Univ. of Toronto 27-32, Asst. Prof. 32-39, Assoc. Prof. 39-45, Prof. 45-; Chair. Dept. of History 55-59; Research Asst. Royal Comm. on Dominion-Provincial Relations 38-39; John Simon Guggenheim Memorial Fellowship 40-41; Rockefeller Fellow 44-45; Nuffield Fellow 51-52; Pres. Canadian Historical Assoc. 56-57; mem. Historic Sites and Monuments Board of Canada; Chair. Canadian Board of Editors, *Encyclopaedia Americana;* Fellow, Royal Soc. of Canada, British Acad., Royal Historical Soc.; mem. Monckton Comm. 60, Ontario Advisory Cttee. on Confed. 65; Sir John A. Macdonald Prof. of History, Univ. of Toronto 55, Univ. Prof. 67-; Tyrell Medal for History 51, Gov.-General's Medal for Academic Non-Fiction 52 and 55, Univ. of British Columbia Medal for Popular Biography 55, Univ. of Alberta Nat. Award in Letters 57, Molson Prize of Canada Council 64; numerous hon. degrees.
Leisure interests: travel, music, water colours.
Publs. *The Commercial Empire of the St. Lawrence* 37, *Dominion of the North: a History of Canada* 44, *John A. Macdonald: The Young Politician* 52, *John A. Macdonald: The Old Chieftain* 55, *Harold Adams Innis: Portrait of a Scholar* 57, *The Story of Canada* 59, *The Road to Confederation: The Emergence of Canada 1863-1867* 64, *Canada's First Century* 70, *Towards the Discovery of Canada* 72, *Canada, the Heroic Beginnings* 74.
15 Princess Street, Brooklin, Ontario, Canada.
Telephone: 655-4402.

Cremer, Fritz; German sculptor; b. 22 Oct. 1906; ed. Hochschule für bildende Künste, Berlin-Charlottenburg. Studied in France, England and Italy; master's studio, Prussian Acad. of Arts, Berlin 38; Prof. of Sculpture, Akad. für angewandte Kunst, Vienna; mem. Deutsche Akad. der Künste, Berlin 50- (Vice-Pres. 75); Nat. Prize; Art Prize of Freier Deutscher Gewerkschaftsbund 61; Vaterländischer Verdienstorden in Gold 65.
Akademie der Künste der Deutschen Demokratischen Republik, 104 Berlin, Robert-Koch-Platz 7, German Democratic Republic.

Cremin, Cornelius Christopher, M.A., B.COMM.; Irish diplomatist; b. 6 Dec. 1908; ed. Nat. Univ. of Ireland, British Schools at Athens and Rome, Oxford Univ.
Served Paris 37-43, Berlin 43-45, Lisbon 45-46; Asst. Sec. Dept. of External Affairs 48-50; Irish Del. to O.E.E.C. Conf. 48; Ambassador to France and Head of Irish Del. to O.E.E.C. 50-54; Ambassador to Holy See 54-56, to the U.K. 56-58, 63-64; Perm. Rep. to UN 64-74; Sec. Dept. of External Affairs, Dublin 58-62; Chair. Irish Del. to UNCLOS III 73-; Grand Officier Légion d'Honneur; Knight Grand Cross Order of Pius, Grosses Bundesverdienstkreuz; Hon. LL.D. Nat. Univ. of Ireland 65.
c/o Ministry of Foreign Affairs, Dublin, Ireland.

Cremona, His Honour John Joseph, K.M., B.A., LL.D., D.LITT., PH.D., DR.JUR.; Maltese jurist, historian and writer; b. 6 Jan. 1918, Gozo; *s.* of Dr. Antonio Cremona and Anne Camilleri; *m.* Beatrice Barbaro 1949; one *s.* two *d.*; ed. Malta, Rome, London and Cambridge Univs.
Crown Counsel 47; Lecturer in Constitutional Law, Royal Univ. of Malta 47-65; Attorney Gen. 57-64; Prof. of Criminal Law, Royal Univ. of Malta 59-65; Pres. of Council 72-; Crown Advocate-Gen. 64-65; Vice-Pres. Constitutional Court and Court of Appeal 65-71; Judge, European Court of Human Rights 65; Pro-Chancellor, Royal Univ. of Malta 71-; Chief Justice of Malta, Pres. the Constitutional Court, the Court of Appeal and the Court of Criminal Appeal 71-; Fellow, Royal Historical Soc.; Hon. Fellow, London School of Econs.; Hon. mem. Real Academia de Jurisprudencia y Legislación (Madrid); Knight of Magisterial Grace, Sovereign Mil. Order of Malta; Commdr. Order of Merit (Italy); Knight Commdr. Constantine St. George; Knight Order of St. Gregory the Great.
Publs. include: *The Treatment of Young Offenders in Malta* 56, *The Malta Constitution of 1835* 59, *The Legal Consequences of a Conviction in the Criminal Law of Malta* 62, *The Constitutional Development of Malta* 63, *From the Declaration of Rights to Independence* 65, *Human Rights Documentation in Malta* 66; two volumes of poetry; articles in French, Italian and American Law Reviews.
Chambers of the Chief Justice of Malta, Valletta; 5 Victoria Gardens, Sliema, Malta, G.C.
Telephone: 33203.

Crépin, Général d'Armée Jean-Albert-Emile; French army officer; b. 1 Sept. 1908; ed. Ecole Polytechnique. Served China, Cameroun 33-39; with Free French Army 40-44, served Chad, Fezzan, Tunisia, France, Germany; served Indo-China 45; attached to 8th Infantry Div., Paris 51; Inspector-General of Works and Planning for the Armed Forces 54-60; Général de Corps d'Armée, Algeria 59; Commdr. Forces in Algeria 60-61; Général d'Armée, C-in-C. French Forces in Germany 61-63; C.-in-C. Allied Forces, Central Europe 63-66; Pres. Nord-Aviation 67-69; Vice-Pres. Société Nationale Industrielle Aérospatiale (SNIAS) 70-73, Counsellor for Military Affairs 74-; Grand Officier, Légion d'Honneur,

Compagnon de la Libération, Croix de Guerre (39-45), Croix de la Valeur Militaire.
51 rue de l'Assomption, Paris 16e, France.

Crespin, Régine; French soprano; b. 23 Feb. 1927, Marseilles; ed. Conservatoire National d'Art Dramatique.
Singer, Opéra, Paris 51-; has sung in principal concert houses, Europe and America; Chevalier de la Légion d'Honneur, Chevalier de l'Ordre National du Mérite, Commandeur des Arts et Lettres.
c/o Michel Glotz, 141 boulevard Saint-Michel, 75005 Paris, France.

Crewe, Albert Victor, PH.D.; American physicist and professor; b. 18 Feb. 1927, Bradford, England; *m.* Doreen Crewe; one *s.* three *d.*; ed. Liverpool Univ.
Assistant Lecturer, Liverpool Univ. 50-52, Lecturer 52-53; Research Assoc. Chicago Univ. 55-56, Asst. Prof. of Physics 56-59, Assoc. Prof. 59-63; Dir. Particle Accelerator Div. Argonne Nat. Laboratory 58-61, Dir. 61-67; Prof. Dept. of Physics and Biophysics Enrico Fermi Inst., Univ. of Chicago 63-, Dean, Physical Sciences Div. 71-76; constructed England's first diffusion cloud chamber with Dr. W. H. Evans at Liverpool Univ.; directed construction of large magnetic spectrometer for Chicago Univ.'s synchrocyclotron; consultant Sweden, Argentina; directed much of design and construction of Argonne's Zero Gradient Synchrotron; as Dir. Argonne Nat. Laboratory, developed relationships with U.S. Atomic Energy Comm., Argonne Univ. and Chicago Univ., expressed in Tripartite Agreement; Fellow, American Physical Soc., American Nuclear Soc.; mem. Nat. Acad. of Sciences, American Acad. of Arts and Sciences, Scientific Research Soc. for America, Electron Microscopy Soc. of America, Chicago Area Research and Devt. Council (Chair. 64), Governor's Science Advisory Cttee. for State of Ill.; Immigrant's Service League's Annual Award for Outstanding Achievement in the Field of Science 62; "Industrial Research Man of the Year 1970".
Leisure interests: archery, sculpture, photography, home design.
Department of Physics, University of Chicago, Chicago, Ill., U.S.A.

Crichton, Sir Andrew James Maitland-Makgill-, Kt.; British shipping executive; b. 28 Dec. 1910, Bryn Garth, Hereford; *s.* of Lieut. Col. D. M.-M.-Crichton and Phyllis née Cuthbert; *m.* Isabel McGill 1948; ed. Wellington College.
Managing Dir. P. & O. S. N. Co. 57-69, Dir. 70-; Dir. General Steam Navigation Co. Ltd. 58-68; Chair. Port Employers and Registered Dock Workers Pension Fund Trustees Ltd. 61-69, Nat. Asscn. of Port Employers and Joint Chair. Nat. Council for Port Transport Industry 58-65, E. Higgs (Air Agency) Ltd. 63-, investigation on the Post Office on behalf of N.E.D.C. 65; Vice-Chair. British Transport Docks Board 63-67, Port of London Authority (P.L.A.) 67-; Dir. British United Airways Ltd. 62-68, British India Steam Navigation Co. Ltd. 61-68; mem. Civil Service Arbitration Tribunal 63-69, Nat. Freight Corpn. 68-73, Council, Chamber of Shipping in U.K. 58-, Industrial Court 64; Chair. Overseas Containers Ltd. 65-73; Vice-Pres. Inst. of Transport; mem. Police Council for Great Britain 66-75, Arbitrator 75-; mem. Court of the Chartered Bank 70.
Leisure interests: golf, collecting paintings, music.
55 Hans Place, Knightsbridge, London, S.W.1; The Mill House, Earl Soham, Nr. Woodbridge, Suffolk, England.
Telephone: 01-584-1209 (London); 072-882-330 (Suffolk).

Crick, Francis Harry Compton, PH.D., F.R.S.; British biologist; b. 8 June 1916; ed. Univ. Coll., London, and Cambridge Univ.

Scientist, Admiralty, Second World War; Medical Research Council (M.R.C.) Student, Strangeways Laboratory, Cambridge 47-49; M.R.C. Laboratory of Molecular Biology, Cambridge 49-; Protein Structure Project, Brooklyn Polytechnic, New York 53-54; Fellow, Churchill Coll., Cambridge 60-61, Univ. Coll., London 62; Foreign Assoc. American Nat. Acad. of Sciences 69-; mem. German Acad. of Science 69; Nobel Prize for Medicine (with J. D. Watson and M. H. F. Wilkins) 62; Royal Medal, Royal Soc. 72; Copley Medal, Royal Soc. 75.
Publs. Over 70 papers on the structure of deoxyribonucleic acid (DNA) polynucleotides, polypeptides, proteins, viruses; *Of Molecules and Men* 67, etc.
Laboratory of Molecular Biology, Hills Road, Cambridge; and The Golden Helix, 19 Portugal Place, Cambridge, England.

Cristofini, Charles; French civil servant; b. 16 July 1913, Garlin; *m.* Solange Demerliac 1939; two *d.*
With Ministry of Finance 38-48, Air Ministry 48; Staff Dir. to M. Bourgès-Maunory 50-52; Dir. Financial Dept. and Programmes, Ministry of Nat. Defence and Armed Forces 52-55; Asst. Sec.-Gen. Western European Union 55-59; founded Soc. pour l'Etude et la Réalisation d'Engins Balistiques (SEREB) 59, Pres., Man. Dir. until 69; Special Adviser to Pres. Soc. Nat. Industrielle Aérospatiale 70, now Pres. of Directorate; Commdr. Légion d'Honneur.
Société Nationale Industrielle Aérospatiale, 37 Boulevard de Montmorency, 75016 Paris, France.
Telephone: 224-84-00.

Cristol, Stanley Jerome; American professor of chemistry; b. 14 June 1916, Chicago, Ill.; *s.* of Myer J. and Lillian (Young) Cristol; *m.* Barbara Wright Swingle 1957; one *s.* one *d.*; ed. Northwestern Univ. and Univ. of California, Los Angeles.
Assistant in Chem., Univ. of Calif. at Los Angeles (UCLA) 37-38, 41-42; Research Chemist, Standard Oil Co. of Calif. 38-41; Instructor, UCLA 42-43; Postdoctoral Fellow, Univ. of Ill. 43-44; Research Chemist, Bureau of Entomology and Plant Quarantine U.S. Dept. of Agriculture 44-46; Univ. of Colo., Asst. Prof. 46-49, Assoc. Prof. 49-55, Prof. 55-, Chair. Dept. of Chem. 60-62; mem. Nat. Acad. of Sciences; Guggenheim Fellow 55-56; Robert L. Stearns Award 71; James Flack Norris Award of the American Chemical Soc. 72.
Leisure interests: skiing and fishing.
Publs. *Organic Chemistry* 66 (with L. O. Smith, Jr.), numerous articles in scientific journals.
Department of Chemistry, University of Colorado, Boulder, Colo. 80302; Home: 2918 Third Street, Boulder, Colo. 80302, U.S.A.
Telephone: 303-492-6661 (Office); 303-443-1781 (Home).

Critchfield, Charles Louis, B.S., M.A., PH.D.; American physicist; b. 7 June 1910, Shreve, Ohio; *s.* of Roy and Clara (Prince) Critchfield; *m.* Jean La Zelle Anderson 1935; three *s.* one *d.*; ed. Eastern High School, George Washington Univ.
With Nat. Bureau of Standards 30-37; Instructor Univ. of Rochester 39-40; Nat. Research Fellow Princeton Univ. and Inst. for Advanced Study 40-41; Instructor Harvard Univ. 41-42; physicist, Geophysical Laboratory 42-43; group leader Los Alamos 43-46; Assoc. Prof. George Washington Univ. 46; physicist, Monsanto Chemical Co., Oak Ridge, Tenn. 46-47; Assoc. Prof. Univ. of Minnesota 47-49, Prof. of Physics 49-55; Dir. of Scientific Research, Convair Div. of Gen. Dynamics Corpn. 55-60; Vice-Pres. Research Telecomputing Corpn. 60-61; assoc. division leader Theoretical Physics Division, Los Alamos Scientific Laboratory 61-; mem. Editorial Board *Annual Review of Nuclear Science* 57-61; Assoc. Editor *Journal of the Franklin Inst.* 56-62; Assoc. Editor *Physical Review*

51-54; Fellow American Physical Soc.; Nat. Research Fellowship 40.
Leisure interests: chess, golf.
Publs. *Theory of Atomic Nucleus and Nuclear Energy Sources* (with G. Gamow) 49, and many papers.
Home: 391 El Conejo, Los Alamos, New Mexico 87544; Office: Theoretical Division, Los Alamos Scientific Laboratory, Los Alamos, N.M., U.S.A.
Telephone: 662-7336.

Critchley, Thomas Kingston, C.B.E., B.EC.; Australian diplomatist; b. 1916, Melbourne; *s.* of the late G. L. Critchley; *m.* Susan Cappel 1962; four *d.*; ed. North Sydney Boys' High School and Sydney Univ.
Assistant Econ. Adviser, Dept. of War Organization of Industry 43-44; Head, Research Section, Far Eastern Bureau, New Delhi, British Ministry of Information 44-46; Head, Economic Relations Section, Dept. of External Affairs, Canberra 46-47; Australian Rep. UN Cttee. of Good Offices on Indonesian Question 48-49; Rep. UN Comm. for Indonesia 49-50; Acting Australian Commr. Malaya 51-52; Rep. UN Comm. for Unification and Rehabilitation of Korea (UNCURK) 52-54; Head, Pacific and Americas Branch, Dept. of External Affairs, Canberra 54-55; Commr. Fed. of Malaya 55-57, High Commr. 57-63, High Commr. in Malaysia 63-65; Senior External Affairs Rep., Australian High Comm., London 66-69; Amb. to Thailand 69-75.
Leisure interests: golf, tennis.
c/o Ministry of Foreign Affairs, Canberra, Australia.

Crnobrnja, Bogdan; Yugoslav diplomatist; b. 16 Dec. 1916, Vrgin Most; *s.* of Mihailo Crnobrnja and Saveta Cumura; *m.* Angelina Grabric 1944; two *s.*; ed. Teacher's Coll.
Temporarily employed as teacher and studied philosophy; Col. in Nat. Liberation Struggle, Second World War; mem. Parl. 45-49, 49-53; Deputy Minister for Foreign Trade 46-51; Deputy Minister for Foreign Affairs 51-54, 58-61; Amb. to India 54-58; Sec.-Gen. to Pres. of Yugoslavia 61-67; Amb. to U.S.A. 67-71; Pres. Cttee. for Social Planning and Devt. Policy at Fed. Assembly; Pres. Machinery and Equipment Mfrs., Belgrade; Yugoslav and foreign decorations.
Leisure interests: fishing, hunting.
Nemanjina 4/x, 11000 Belgrade, Yugoslavia.

Crocker, Walter Russell, C.B.E.; Australian diplomatist; b. 25 March 1902, Broken Hill; *s.* of Robert Crocker and Alma Bray; *m.* Claire Ward 1950 (divorced 1968); two *s.*; ed. Balliol Coll., Oxford, Univ. of Adelaide, Australia, and Stanford Univ., California.
With British Colonial Service 30-34, L.N. and I.L.O. 34-40; served army 40-46; with U.N. 46-49; Prof. of Int. Relations, Australian Nat. Univ. 49-52, Acting Vice-Chancellor 51; High Commr. for Australia in India 52-55; Ambassador to Indonesia 55-57; High Commr. in Canada 57-59; High Commr. in India 59-62 and Ambassador to Nepal 60-62; Ambassador to the Netherlands and Belgium 62-65; Ambassador to Ethiopia and High Commr. to Kenya and to Uganda 65-67, to Italy 68-70; Lieut.-Gov. of S. Australia 73-; Croix de Guerre, Order of the Lion (Belgium), Knight Grand Cross of Italy, Grand Officier of the Order of Merit, Order of Malta.
Leisure interests: gardening, music.
Publs. *The Japanese Population Problem* 31, *Nigeria*: *Critique of Colonial Administration* 36, *On Governing Colonies* 46, *Self-Government for Colonies* 49, *Can the U.N. Succeed?* 51, *The Racial Factor in International Relations* 55, *Nehru* 66, *Australian Ambassador* 71.
Peak Farm, Tarlee and 8 Fowlers Road, Glen Osmond, South Australia 5064, Australia.

Croft-Cooke, Rupert, B.E.M. (Military); British writer and poet; b. 20 June 1903, Edenbridge, Kent; *s.* of Hubert Bruce Cooke and Lucy Taylor; ed. Tonbridge School and Wellington Coll., Shropshire.

Publs. *Some Poems* 29; novels: *Troubadour* 30, *Give Him the Earth* 30, *Night Out* 32, *Cosmopolis* 32, *Release the Lions* 33, *Picaro* 34, *Shoulder the Sky* 34, *Blind Gunner* 35, *Crusade* 36, *Kingdom Come* 37, *Rule, Britannia* 38, *Same Way Home* 39, *Glorious* 41, *Octopus* 46, *Ladies Gay* 46, *Wilkie* 48, *Brass Farthing* 50, *Three Names for Nicholas* 51, *Nine Days with Edward* 52, *Harvest Moon* 53, *Fall of Man* 55, *Seven Thunders* 56, *Barbary Night* 58, *Thief* 60, *Clash by Night* 61, *Paper Albatross* 65; general: *Madeira* 61; play: *Banquo's Chair*; autobiography: *The World is Young* 37, *The Man in Europe Street* 38, *The Circus Has No Home* 40, *The Moon in my Pocket* 48, *The Life for Me* 53, *The Blood Red Island* 53, *The Verdict of You All* 55, *The Tangerine House* 56, *The Gardens of Camelot* 58, *The Circus Book* (anthology) 47, *The Quest of Quixote* 59, *The Altar in the Loft* 60, *English Cooking* 60, *The Glittering Pastures* 62, *The Numbers Came* 63, *The Last of Spring* 64; *Bosie: The Life of Lord Alfred Douglas* 63 (biography), *The Wintry Sea* 64, *The Gorgeous East* 65, *The Purple Streak* 66, *The Wild Hills* 66, *The Happy Highways* 67, *Feasting with Panthers* 68, *The Sound of Revelry* 69, *Wolf from the Door* 69, *Exiles* 70, *Under the Rose Garden* 71, *The Licentious Soldiery* 71, *The Dogs of Peace* 73, *Nasty Piece of Work* 73, *The Caves of Hercules* 74.
c/o A. M. Heath and Co. Ltd., 40-42 William IV Street, London, WC2N 4DD, England; Glenageary, Dunlaoghaire, Co. Dublin, Ireland.
Telephone: Dublin 852095.

Cromer, 3rd Earl of; **George Rowland Stanley Baring,** G.C.M.G., M.B.E., P.C.; British merchant banker and financial administrator; b. 28 July 1918; ed. Eton Coll., and Trinity Coll., Cambridge.
Served with Grenadier Guards, rising to rank of Lt. Col. 39-46; Man. Dir. Baring Brothers and Co. Ltd. 47-58, 67-70, Adviser 74-; Economic Minister and Head of U.K. Treasury Del., Washington, U.K. Exec. Dir. Int. Monetary Fund, Int. Bank for Reconstruction and Development, Int. Finance Corpn. 59-61; Gov. Bank of England 61-66; U.K. Gov., Int. Bank for Reconstruction and Devt., Int. Finance Corpn., Int. Devt. Asscn. 63-66; Partner Baring Brothers and Co. Ltd.; Dir. Union Carbide Corpn. 67-71; Chair. IBM (U.K.) Ltd. 67-71, 74-; Amb. to U.S.A. 71-74; mem. Board Cie. Financière de Suez et de l'Union Parisienne, Paris; Dir. Shell Transport and Trading Co. 74-; mem. Board P. & O. Steam Navigation Co. 74-, Imperial Group Ltd., Daily Mail and General Trust Ltd.; Chair. London Multinational Bank 74-; Hon. LL.D. (N.Y. Univ.) 66.
Frenchstreet Farm, Westerham, Kent, England.
Telephone: 01-588-2830.

Cronin, Archibald Joseph, M.D., M.R.C.P., D.PH.; British physician and writer; b. 19 July 1896, Helensburgh, Dumbarton; *s.* of Patrick Cronin and Jessie Montgomerie; *m.* Agnes Gibson 1921; three *s.*; ed. Glasgow Univ.
Practised medicine until 30; Hon. D.Litt. Bowdoin Coll. and Lafayette Coll.
Leisure interests: golf, salmon-fishing, gardening.
Publs. *Hatter's Castle, Three Loves, Grand Canary, The Stars Look Down, The Citadel, Jupiter Laughs* (play), *The Keys of the Kingdom, The Green Years, Shannon's Way, The Spanish Gardener, Adventures in Two Worlds, Beyond this Place, Crusaders' Tomb, The Northern Light, The Judas Tree, A Song of Sixpence, A Pocketful of Rye, The Minstrel Boy* 75; creator *Dr. Finlay's Casebook*.
Champ-Riond, Baugy sur Clarens, VD, Switzerland.
Telephone: (021)-61-50-43.

Cronkite, Walter Leland, Jr.; American television correspondent; b. 4 Nov. 1916, St. Joseph, Missouri; *s.* of W. L. Cronkite (deceased) and Helene Fritsche; *m.* Mary Elizabeth Maxwell 1940; one *s.* two *d.*; ed. Univ. of Texas.

News writer and Editor, Scripps-Howard & United Press, Houston, Kansas City, Dallas, Austin, El Paso and New York City; United Press War Corresp. 42-45, later Foreign Corresp., Chief Corresp. Nuremberg War Crimes Trials, Bureau Manager, Moscow 46-48; Lecturer 48-49; Columbia Broadcasting System, television commentator 50-, News Analyst, CBS T.V. News 50-, Managing Editor CBS *Evening News with Walter Cronkite*; Narrator for *Twentieth Century*; Emmy Award, Acad. TV Arts and Sciences 70, George Polk Journalism Award 71, and other awards.
Leisure interest: yachting.
Columbia Broadcasting System Inc., 524 West 57th Street, New York City, New York, U.S.A.

Crosby, Bing (Harry Lillis); American actor and singer; b. 2 May 1904; ed. Gonzaga Univ., Spokane.
Singer with dance bands 25-30; has broadcast since 31; has appeared in numerous films, including *Pennies from Heaven, Holiday Inn, Going My Way, Blue Skies, Mr. Music, Little Boy Lost, White Christmas, Country Girl, Anything Goes, High Society, Say One For Me, The Jimmy Durante Story, The Bells of St. Mary's, Road to Hong Kong*; Bing Crosby Productions Ltd. 65-70; Acad. Award 44; Hon. Ph.D. Gonzaga Univ.
170 N. Robertson, Beverly Hills, Calif. 90211, U.S.A.

Crosby, John Campbell; American writer; b. 18 May 1912, Milwaukee, Wis.; *s.* of Frederick and Edna (née Campbell) Crosby; *m.* Katherine Blachford Wood 1964; two *s.* two *d.*; ed. Exeter, Yale Univ.
Reporter *Milwaukee Sentinel* 33, *New York Herald Tribune* 35-41, syndicated columnist 46-65; U.S. Army 41-46; columnist *Observer*, London 65-; John Crosby TV Programme (New York); Peabody Award, Newspaper Guild Award.
Leisure interests: travel, skiing, reading, theatre, movies, sailing, carpentry.
Publs. *Out of the Blue* 52, *With Love and Loathing* 63, *Sappho in Absence* 70, *The Literary Obsession* 73, *The White Telephone* 74, *An Affair of Strangers* 75.
c/o Elain Green Literary Agency, 31 Newington Green, London N.16, England.

Crosland, Rt. Hon. (Charles) Anthony Raven, P.C., M.A., M.P.; British politician; b. 29 Aug. 1918; ed. Highgate School and Trinity Coll., Oxford.
War service 40-45; Fellow and Lecturer in Economics Trinity Coll., Oxford 47-50; M.P. (Lab.) South Gloucestershire 50-55, Grimsby 59-; Sec. Independent Comm. of Enquiry into Co-operative Movement 56-58; Minister of State, Dept. of Econ. Affairs 64-65; Sec. of State for Educ. and Science 65-67; Pres. of the Board of Trade 67-69; Sec. of State for Local Govt. and Regional Planning 69-70, for the Environment 74-76, for Foreign and Commonwealth Affairs April 76-.
Publs. *New Fabian Essays* (contrib.) 52, *Britain's Economic Problem* 53, *The Future of Socialism* 56, *The Conservative Enemy* 62, *Socialism Now, and Other Essays* 74.
House of Commons, Westminster, London, S.W.1, and 37 Lansdowne Road, London, W.11, England.

Cross, Bert S.; American business executive; b. 16 Oct. 1905; *m.* Bernice Fischer 1927; one *s.* two *d.*; ed. Univ. of Minnesota.
Laboratory Technician, Minnesota Mining and Manufacturing Co. 26-29, Chief Chemist first 3M overseas lab., Factory Manager, Abrasives Div. 31-42, New Products Manager 42-45, Gen. Manager Scotchlite Div. 45-48, Vice-Pres. Scotchlite Div. 48-52, Vice-Pres. Graphic Products Group 52-57, Dir., mem. Management Cttee. 57-71, Pres., Chief Exec. Officer and mem. Finance Cttee. 63-66, Chair. and Chief Exec. Officer 66-70, Chair. Finance Cttee. 70-75; fmr. Dir. Dow-Jones; Dir. First Nat. Bank of St. Paul, Northwestern Bell Telephone Co., St. Paul Companies Inc., Exxon

Corpn.; mem. of numerous clubs and councils; Outstanding Achievement Award Univ. of Minnesota 67, Knight Commdr. of the Order of Merit of the Italian Repub. 68, U.S. Treasury Dept. Distinguished Service Award 68.
Office: E-1314 First National Bank Building, St. Paul, Minn. 55101; Home: 45 Evergreen Road, Pine Tree Hills, Dellwood, Min. 55110, U.S.A.

Cross, G(eorge) L(ynn), M.S., PH.D.; American university president and professor; b. 12 May 1905, Woonsocket, S. Dakota; *s.* of George Warren Cross and Jemima Jane Dawson; *m.* Cleo Sikkink 1926; two *s.* one *d.*; ed. South Dakota Coll., and Univ. of Chicago.
Instructor Bacteriology, South Dakota State Coll. 27-28; Head Botany Dept. Univ. of South Dakota 30-34; Prof. of Botany Univ. of Oklahoma 34-38, Head of Botany Dept. 38-42, Act. Dean Graduate Coll. 42-44, Act. Dir. Research Inst. 42-44, Pres. of the Univ. 44-68; Chair. Board American Exchange Bank, Norman, Okla. 64-; Pres. Oklahoma Health Sciences Foundation 68-; mem. of many learned socs.
Leisure interests: golf, art, music, writing.
812 Mockingbird Lane, Norman, Okla. 73069, U.S.A.
Telephone: 405-321-4527.

Cross, Ira B., A.M., PH.D.; American economist; b. 1 Dec. 1880; *s.* of Bradford Cross and Orietta Clemmons; *m.* Blanche Mobley 1911 (deceased); two *s.* (one deceased); ed. Univ. of Wisconsin and Stanford Univ.
Instructor and Asst. Prof. Stanford Univ. 09-14; Asst. and Associate Prof. Univ. of Calif. 14-19 and Prof. of Economics 19-51, Emeritus 51-; Vice-Pres. American Economic Asscn. 26; Pres. Pacific Coast Economic Asscn. 29; Assoc. Editor, Bulletin, Nat. Chrysanthemum Soc. 55; Hon. LL.D. (Univ. of Wisconsin) 51, (Univ. of California) 57; Fellow American Genealogical Soc.; Highest Award, Nat. Chrysanthemum Soc. 63.
Leisure interest: hybridizing chrysanthemums.
Publs. include: *Economics, Money and Banking, Domestic and Foreign Exchange, History of Banking in California, History of the Labour Movement in California, Frank Roney: Irish Rebel and California Labour Leader, Essentials of Socialism, Collective Bargaining in San Francisco*; numerous articles on economics and chrysanthemums.
16 Coleman Place, Menlo Park, Calif. 94025, U.S.A.

Cross, Richard Eugene; American lawyer and automobile executive; b. 20 Sept. 1910; ed. St. Thomas Military Acad., Assumption Coll., Univ. of Wisconsin and Univ. of Michigan.
Chairman, Board of Dirs. Amer. Motors Corpn. 62-66, now mem. Finance and Audit Cttees. and Dir.; Legal Counsel, Cross, Wrock, Miller & Vieson (lawyers); Dir. Hiram Walker-Gooderham & Worts Ltd., Mfrs. Life Insurance Co., Gen. Real Estate Shares Inc., Mountain States Pipe and Supply Co., The Packer Corpn.
4200 Penobscot Building, Detroit, Mich.; 20008 Lichfield Road, Detroit 21, Mich., U.S.A.

Cross of Chelsea, Baron (Life Peer), cr. 71; **Geoffrey Cross**, P.C.; British judge (retd.); b. 1 Dec. 1904, Chelsea, London; *s.* of Arthur G. Cross and Mary E. Dalton; *m.* Joan Eardley Wilmot 1952; one *d.*; ed. Westminster School and Trinity Coll., Cambridge.
Fellow, Trinity Coll., Cambridge 27; called to the Bar 30; K.C. 49; Judge, Chancery Div., The High Court 60-69; Lord Justice of Appeal 69-71; Lord of Appeal in Ordinary 71-75.
66 Oakwood Court, London, W.14, England.
Telephone: 01-602-2131.

Crossland, Sir Leonard, Kt.; British motor executive; b. 2 March 1914; *s.* of Joseph and Frances Crossland; *m.* 1st Rhona Griffin 1941, 2nd Joan Brewer 1963; two *d.*; ed. Penistone Grammar School.
Purchase Dept., Ford Motor Co. Ltd. 37-39; Royal

Army Service Corps 39-45; Purchase Dept., Ford Motor Co. Ltd. 45-54, Chief Buyer, Tractor and Implement Dept. 54-57, Chief Buyer, Car and Truck Dept. 57-59, Asst. Purchase Man. 59-60, Purchase Man. 60-62, Exec. Dir. 62-68, Supply and Services 62-66, Dir. Mfg. Staff and Services 66, Asst. Man. Dir. 66-67, Man. Dir. June-Dec. 67, Deputy Chair. Jan.-May 68, Chair. May 68-72; Deputy Chair. Lotus Cars; mem. Board Eaton Corpn. 74-; Chair. Eaton Ltd. U.K., Sedgeminster Technical Devts. Ltd.
Leisure interests: fishing, shooting, golf.
Abbotts Hall, Great Wigborough, Colchester, Essex, England.
Telephone: Peldon 456.

Crow, James F(ranklin), PH.D.; American geneticist; b. 18 Jan. 1916, Phoenixville, Pa.; s. of H. E. Crow and Lena Whitaker Crow; m. Ann Crockett 1941; one s. two d.; ed. Friends Univ. (Wichita, Kan.) and Univ. of Texas.
Instructor and Asst. Prof. Dartmouth Coll. 41-48; Asst. Prof., Assoc. Prof., now Prof. and Chair. Dept. of Genetics, Univ. of Wisconsin 48-; Acting Dean, Medical School, Univ. of Wis. 63-65; mem. Nat. Acad. of Sciences; Pres. Genetics Soc. of America 59, American Soc. of Human Genetics 67.
Leisure interest: orchestral and chamber music.
Publs. *Genetics Notes* (6th edn.) 66; various technical articles on genetics; *Introduction to Population Genetics Theory* 70.
Genetics Building, University of Wisconsin, Madison, Wis. 53706, U.S.A.
Telephone: 608-263-1993.

Crowe, Sir Colin Tradescant, G.C.M.G.; British diplomatist; b. 7 Sept. 1913, Yokohama, Japan; s. of Sir Edward Crowe, K.C.M.G.; m. Bettina Lum 1938; ed. Stowe School and Oriel Coll., Oxford.
Served Embassy Peking 36-38, 50-53, Shanghai 39-40, Washington 40-45; mem. U.K. Del. to OEEC Paris 48; served Tel-Aviv Legation 49, Imperial Defence Coll. 57; Chargé d'Affaires Cairo Dec. 59-61; Dep. Perm. Rep. to UN 61-63; Ambassador to Saudi Arabia 63-64; Chief of Admin., Diplomatic Service 65-68; High Commr. in Canada 68-70; Perm. Rep. to UN 70-73; Supernumerary Fellow, St. Antony's Coll., Oxford 64-65; Chair. Marshall Aid Commemoration Comm. 73-, Council Cheltenham Ladies Coll. 74-, Exec. Cttee. United World Colls.; Dir. Brandt's Ltd. 74.
Leisure interests: bird watching, gardening.
Pigeon House, Bibury, Glos., England.

Crowe, Hon. Philip Kingsland; American journalist and diplomatist; b. 7 Jan. 1908; m. Irene Pettus 1938; three d.; ed. Univ. of Virginia.
Reporter, and Asst. Financial Editor, *New York Evening Post* 30-34; explorer and big game hunter in French Indo-China 35-36; on advertising staff of *Life* and later *Fortune* 37-41, 45-48; Lieut.-Col. U.S. Army Air Force 41-45; Special Rep. of E.C.A. Mission to China 48-49; farmer and writer 49-53; Ambassador to Ceylon 53-57; U.S. Del. to ECAFE Conf. 54; Special Asst. to Sec. of State 57-58; Ambassador to the Union of South Africa 59-61, to the Repub. of South Africa 61; Amb. to Norway 69-73, to Denmark 73-; Dir. World Wildlife Fund, School of Advanced Int. Studies Johns Hopkins Univ., Foreign Service Educational Foundation, African Wildlife Leadership Foundation, Atlantic Salmon Asscn., American Cttee. for Int. Wildlife Protection; mem. of numerous clubs and socs.; Bronze Star Medal, Officier Légion d'Honneur, Cloud Banner of the Repub. of China, Military Order of Christ, Portugal; Grand Cross of the Order of St. Olav of Norway; Grand Cross of Order of Dannebrog of Denmark.
Leisure interests: shooting, fishing, hunting.
Publs. *Sport is Where You Find It* 54, *Diversions of a*

Diplomat 58, *Sporting Journeys* 66, *The Empty Ark* 67, *World Wildlife: The Last Stand* 70, *Out of the Mainstream* 70.
"Third Haven", Route 5, Easton, Md. 21601, U.S.A.
Telephone: 301-822-0249.

Crown, Henry; American business executive; b. 13 June 1896, Chicago; s. of Arie and Ida (Gordon) Crown; m. 1st Rebecca Kranz 1920 (died 1943), three s. (one s. died 1969); m. 2nd Gladys Kay 1946; ed. Chicago.
Clerk Chicago Firebrick Co. 10-12; Traffic Man. Union Drop Forge Co. 12-16; Partner S.R. Crown & Co. 16-19; Treasurer, Material Service Corpn. 19-21, Pres. 21-41, Chair. 41-59; Chair. Material Service Div. of General Dynamics Corpn., Chair. Exec. Cttee. and Dir. 59-66, 70-; Chair. Board, Henry Crown & Co. 67-; Dir. Waldorf Astoria Corpn.; Vice-Pres., Dir. 208 S. LaSalle St. Bldg. Corpn.; Dir., Chair. Finance Cttee., mem. Exec. Cttee., Chicago, Rock Island and Pacific Railway; mem. Chicago Civil Defence Corps; Trustee, Univ. of Chicago Cancer Research Foundation, De Paul Univ.; Fellow, St. Joseph's Coll., Rensselaer, Ind.; Assoc. Fellow, Brandeis Univ.; mem. of several orgs. and cttees.; Col. of Engineers in Second World War; Legion of Merit; Chevalier Légion d'Honneur, Gold Cross, Royal Order of the Phoenix (Greece), Order of Reuben Dario (Nicaragua); Horatio Alger Award (American Schools and Colls. Asscn.) 53, and several other awards; Hon. Dr.Eng. (Tri-State Coll., Angola, Ind.) 55, Hon. LL.D. (Barat Coll., Lake Forest, Ill.) 55, (Syracuse Univ.) 57, (De Pauw Univ.) 64.
Home: 900 Edgemere Court, Evanston, Ill. 60202; Office: 300 W. Washington, Chicago, Ill. 60606, U.S.A.

Crumb, George, B.M., M.M., D.M.A.; American composer; b. 24 Oct. 1929, Charleston, W. Va.; s. of George Henry and Vivian Reed; m. Elizabeth Brown 1949; two s. one d.; ed. Mason Coll. of Music, Univ. of Illinois, Univ. of Michigan, Hochschule für Musik (Berlin).
Professor, Univ. of Colorado 59-63; Creative Assoc., State Univ. of New York at Buffalo 63-64; Prof., Univ. of Pennsylvania 64-; Koussevitsky Int. Recording Award 71; Pulitzer Prize for Music 68.
Leisure interest: reading.
Publs. *Ancient Voices of Children, Black Angels, Eleven Echoes of Autumn,* 1965, *Songs, Drones and Refrains of Death, Makrokosmos* Vols. I-III, *Music for a Summer Evening.*
240 Kirk Lane, Media, Pa., U.S.A.
Telephone: (215) 565-2438.

Cruz, Ivo; Portuguese composer and conductor; b. 1901, Corumba, Brazil; s. of Manuel Pereira and Palmira Machado da Cruz; m. Maria Cardoso 1931; three s. one d.; ed. Univs. of Lisbon and Munich.
Has conducted in Austria, France, Germany, Switzerland, Spain, Holland, Belgium, Eire, Romania, Brazil and Portugal; his compositions have been played in Europe, North America, Brazil, New Zealand, North Africa and the Republic of South Africa; founder and Pres. Nat. Union of Musicians; Dir. Conservatoire National de Lisbonne; Head of the Lisbon Philharmonic Orchestra, of the Duarte Lobo Choral Soc., Pres. Pro Arte; Commdr. Order of St. Jacques; Knight Order of Alfonso el Sabio (Spain).
Compositions include two concertos for piano and orchestra, a violin sonata and many pieces for orchestra (e.g. *Sinfonia de Amadis, Sinfonia de Queluz* and *Pastoral* (ballet)), piano (e.g. *Aquarelas, Homenagens,* Suite and Caleidoscopio), and guitar: songs include *Triptico* (with Orchestra), *Les Amours du Poète, Ballades Lunatiques, Chansons Perdues, Chansons Profanes, Chansons Sentimentales.*
Leisure interest: antiques.
Rua do Salitre, 166, 2° E, Lisbon, Portugal.
Telephone: 680646.

Cruz-Diez, Carlos; Venezuelan painter; b. 17 Aug. 1923; ed. School of Plastic and Applied Arts, Caracas. Director of Art, Venezuelan subsidiary of McCann-Erickson Advertising Agency 46-51; Teacher, History of Applied Arts, School of Arts, Caracas 53-55; in Barcelona and Paris working on physical qualities of colour now named *Physichromies* 55-56; opened studio of visual arts and industrial design, Caracas 57; Prof. and Asst. Dir. School of Arts, Caracas 59-60; moved to Paris 60; First one-man exhbn., Caracas 47, later in Madrid, Genoa, Turin, London, Paris, Cologne, Oslo, Brussels, Ostwald Museum, Dortmund and Essen; Retrospective exhbns. at Signals, London and Galerie Kerchache, Paris 65; represented at numerous Group exhbns.; works in Museum of Fine Arts, Caracas, Victoria and Albert Museum, London, Casa de la Cultura, Havana, Städtisches Museum, Leverkusen, Germany, Museum of Modern Art, New York, Museum of Contemporary Art, Montreal, Museum des 20. Jahrhunderts, Vienna, Univ. of Dublin, Museo Civico di Torino, Wallraf-Richartz Museum, Cologne, Museum of Contemporary Art, Chicago, Musée de Grenoble; Grand Prix at 3rd Biennale, Cordoba, Argentina; Prix Int. de Peinture à la IX Biennale de São Paulo. 24 rue Pierre Semard, Paris 9e, France.

Cruz Uclés, Ramon Ernesto; Honduran international lawyer; b. 4 Jan. 1903. Former teacher; Magistrate, Supreme Court of Justice 49-54; Prof., Univ. Nacional Autónoma de Honduras 61-; Leader Partido Nacional; Pres. of Honduras 71-72. Universidad Nacional Autónoma de Honduras, 8A Avenida 804, Tegucigalpa, D.C., Honduras.

Crvenkovski, Krste; Yugoslav politician; b. 16 July 1921, Prilep, Macedonia; s. of Trajko and Balga Crvenkovski; m. Margarette Crvenkovski 1947; one s. one d.; ed. Higher Party School, Belgrade. Member, Communist Party of Yugoslavia 39-; active in People's Liberation Movt.; imprisoned 43-44; mem. Political Bureau, Cen. Cttee. League of Communists of Macedonia 48-51; Minister for Science and Culture, Govt. of Macedonia 49-51; Organizational Sec., Cen. Cttee., League of Communists of Macedonia 51-58, Political Sec. 63-66, Pres. Cen. Cttee. 66-69; mem. Fed. Exec. Council, Macedonia 54-63, Sec. for Educ. and Culture 58-63; mem. Exec. Bureau, Presidium of League of Communists of Yugoslavia (LCY) 69-71; mem. Council of Federation 69; First Vice-Pres. Presidency of Repub. of Yugoslavia June 71-72; Deputy to Assembly, Socialist Repub. of Macedonia; Deputy to Fed. Assembly; del. to IPU 65; leader or mem. del. to numerous congresses of Communist parties in other countries; numerous national decorations including Order of Nat. Hero, Order of Brotherhood and Unity, Order of Partisan Star, etc. Leisure interests: hunting, philately. Publs. *The Problems of Education, The Leading Role of the League of Communists of Yugoslavia, The League of Communists and the National Question, The League of Communists and Society.* Vodnjanska 78, Skoplje, Yugoslavia.

Cseterki, Lajos; Hungarian trade unionist and politician; b. 29 Oct. 1921; m. Piroska Martinovszki; two s. one d.; ed. teachers' training coll. and Soviet political school. Lecturer, Soviet anti-fascist school until 47; Lecturer, Trades Union Council, Budapest 47-50; Tutor, Party Acad. of Hungarian Working People's Party 50-51; Sec.-Gen. Teachers' Union 51-53; Sec. Trades Union Council 54-56; Liaison Duties, Revolutionary Worker-Peasant Govt., County Fejér 56-57, First Sec., County Fejér Cttee. 57-61; County Borsod Cttee. 61-62; mem. Cen. Cttee. Hungarian Socialist Workers' Party 59-, Substitute mem. Political Cttee. Nov. 62-66, Sec.

Central Cttee. 63-67; Sec. Presidential Council 67-. Presidential Council of the Hungarian People's Republic, Parliament Building, Budapest, Hungary.

Csikós-Nagy, Béla; Hungarian economist; b. 9 Sept. 1915, Szeged; s. of Dr. József Csikós-Nagy and Jolán Jedlicska; m. Dr. Livia Kneppó 1944; two d.; ed. Szeged Univ. and Univ. of Pécs. Joined Hungarian C.P. 45; Chair. Hungarian Board of Prices and Materials; Lecturer on Price Theory at Karl Marx Univ. of Econ. Sciences, Budapest 59-, title of univ. prof. 64, Dr. of Econ. Sc. 67; Under-Sec. of State 68-; Pres. Hungarian Econ. Asscn. 70-; Chair. Hungarian Soc. of Economists 75-; mem. Exec. Cttee. Int. Econ. Asscn.; Hungarian State Prize 70. Leisure interest: card patience. Publs. *Pricing in Hungary* (London) 68, *General and Socialist Price Theory* 68, *Hungarian Economic Policy* 71, *Socialist Economic Policy* (Budapest-London) 73, *Socialist Price Theory and Price Policy* 75; other studies on pricing theory and political economy. Office: Országos Anyag-és Arhivatal (National Board of Materials and Prices), Budapest V, Guszev-utca 23, Hungary. Telephone: 113-650.

Cuadra Medina, Lieut.-Gen. Mariano; Spanish air force officer; b. 12 May 1912, Madrid; m. Carmen Lores Gutiérrez 1944; three s. one d.; ed. Cavalry Acad. Spanish Army 30-36, Lieutenant, Cavalry Regiment 34-36; entered Air Force 36; Commdr. Air Base, Torrejon; Deputy Chief of Staff of Air Force; Dir. Higher Coll. for Nat. Defence Studies; Chief of Staff of Air Force; Minister for the Air Force 73-76; several decorations including Grand Cross of Mil. Merit, of Naval Merit, of San Hermenegildo. Ministerio del Aire, Plaza de la Moncloa, Madrid, Spain. Telephone: 2-44-04-19.

Cucino, Gen. Andrea; Italian army officer; b. 23 July 1914, Montecorvino Rovella; s. of Matteo and Giuseppina Lenza; m. Iolanda Saviani 1953; one s.; ed. Artillery and Engineering Acad., Scuola di Guerra, NATO Defence Coll. Promoted to the rank of Second Lt., Artillery 35, Lt. 37, Capt. 42, Maj. 46, Lt.-Col. 51, Col. 57, Brig.-Gen. 62, Div. Gen. 67, Gen. of Army Corps 70; Commdg. Officer 132 Regt. 59-60, 3rd Brigade of Ariete Corps 63-64; Div. Commdr. Ariete Corps 67-68; Insp. of Artillery 68-72; Sec.-Gen. Ministry of Defence 72-75; Chief of Gen. Staff Feb. 75-; Cavaliere di Gran Croce, Ordine al Merito della Repubblica Italiana; Grand Officer, Order of Merit, Fed. Repub. of Germany; Order of Tudor Vladimirescu, 2nd Class, Romania, and several mil. decorations. Leisure interests: sports, particularly tennis. Via XX Settembre 123A, Rome; Home: Via della Lungara 61, 00165 Rome, Italy. Telephone: 478248 (Office); 659343 (Home).

Cuckney, John Graham, M.A.; British civil servant; b. 12 July 1925, India; s. of late Air Vice-Marshal E. J. Cuckney; m. 2nd Muriel Boyd 1969; ed. Shrewsbury, Univ. of St. Andrews. Civil Assistant, Gen. Staff, War Office, 49-57; Dir. of various industrial and financial companies 57-72 incl. Lazard Bros. & Co. 64-70, J. Bibby & Sons 70-72; Chair. Standard Industrial Trust 66-70, Mersey Docks and Harbour Board 70-72, Building Econ. Devt. Council 76-; Ind. mem. Railway Policy Review Cttee. 66-67; Special mem. Hops Marketing Board 71-72; Chief Exec., Property Services Agency 72-74; Senior Crown Agent and Chair. of Crown Agents for Oversea Govts. and Administrations 74-. 4 Millbank, Westminster, London, S.W.1. Telephone: 222-7730.

Cudlipp, Baron (Life Peer), cr. 74, of Aldingbourne in the County of West Sussex; **Hugh Cudlipp,** Kt., O.B.E.; British journalist; b. 28 Aug. 1913; ed. in Wales. With various provincial newspapers in Cardiff and Manchester 27-32; Features Editor *Sunday Chronicle* 32-35, *Daily Mirror* 35-37; Editor *Sunday Pictorial* 37-40; served army 40-46; Editor *Sunday Pictorial* 46-49; Man. Editor *Sunday Express* 50-52, Editorial Dir. *Daily Mirror* and *Sunday Pictorial* (now *Sunday Mirror*) 52-63; Jt.-Man. Dir. Daily Mirror Newspapers Ltd., Sunday Pictorial Newspapers Ltd. 60-63; Chair. Daily Mirror Newspapers Ltd. 63-68; Chair. Odhams Press Ltd. 61-63, Daily Herald (1929) Ltd. 61-64; Dir. Associated Television Ltd. 56-73, Reuters Ltd.; Editorial Dir. Int. Publishing Corpn. 63-May 68, Deputy Chair. 64-May 68, Chair. 68-73; Deputy Chair. The Reed Group 70-73.
Publs. *Publish and be Damned!* 53, *At Your Peril* 62.
The Dene, Hook Lane, Aldingbourne, Sussex, England.

Cudmore, Derek George, C.B.E.; British overseas administrator; b. 9 Nov. 1923, Great Bentley, Essex; s. of H. T. and W. L. (née Burgess) Cudmore; m. Vera Beatrice Makin 1952; no c.; ed. Slough Grammar School and Regent Street Polytechnic.
Military Service 42-46; Admin. Officer, Colonial Service 47, served in Nigeria and Southern Cameroons 47-56, N. Rhodesia 56-57; Senior Asst. Sec. and Deputy Financial Sec., British Solomon Islands 57-67, Asst. Resident Commr., Gilbert and Ellice Islands 67-71; Gov. British Virgin Islands 71-74.
Leisure interests: golf, reading, sailing.
Perhams, Honiton, Devon, England.

Cuenca Díaz, Gen. Hermenegildo; Mexican army officer and politician; b. 13 April 1902, Mexico City; ed. Colegio Militar.
Chief of Staff, Secr. of Nat. Defence 51; Gen. of Div. 58; Senator for the State of Lower California 64-70; Sec. for Nat. Defence 70-.
Secretaría de la Defensa Nacional, Lomas de Sotelo, D.F., Mexico.

Cuevas, José Luis; Mexican painter; b. 26 Feb. 1934, Mexico City; s. of Alberto Cuevas and María Regla; m. Bertha Riestra 1961; two d.; ed. Univ. de Mexico, School of Painting and Sculpture "La Esmeralda", Mexico.
Over forty one-man exhbns. in New York, Paris, Milan, Mexico, Buenos Aires, Toronto, Los Angeles, Washington, etc.; Group Exhbns. all over N. and S. America, Europe, India and Japan; works are in Museum of Modern Art, Solomon R. Guggenheim Museum, Brooklyn Museum (New York), Art Inst. Chicago, Phillips Collection, Washington, D.C., Museums of Albi and Lyons, France, etc.; First Int. Award for Drawing, São Paulo Bienal 59; First Int. Award, Mostra Internazionale di Bianco e Nero de Lugano, Zürich 62; First Prize, Bienal de Grabado, Santiago, Chile 64; First Int. Prize for engraving, first Biennial of New Delhi, India 68; has illustrated following books: *The Worlds of Kafka and Cuevas* 59, *The Ends of Legends String, Recollections of Childhood* 62, *Cuevas por Cuevas* (autobiog.) 64, *Cuevas Charenton* 65, *Crime by Cuevas* 68, *Homage to Quevedo* 69, *El Mundo de José Luis Cuevas* 70.
Publs. *Cuevas by Cuevas* 64, *Cuevario* 73, *Confesiones de José Luis Cuevas* 75.
Galeana 109, San Angel Inn, México 20, D.F., Mexico; c/o Grace Borgenicht Gallery, 1018 Madison Avenue, New York City, U.S.A.
Telephone: 548-78-20; 548-80-54 (both Mexico D.F.)

Cukor, George; American film director; b. 7 July 1899.
Stage dir. New York until 28; started work in films 29; dir. of Metro-Goldwyn-Mayer 33-.
Films include: *A Bill of Divorcement* 32, *Little Women*

33, *David Copperfield* 34, *Romeo and Juliet* 36, *Camille* 36, *Holiday* 37, *The Women* 39, *The Philadelphia Story* 40, *Two Faced Woman* 41, *A Double Life* 47, *Adam's Rib* 49, *Born Yesterday* 50, *The Marrying Kind* 52, *Pat and Mike* 52, *A Star is Born* 54, *Wild is the Wind* 57, *Let's Make Love* 61, *My Fair Lady* 64, *Justine* 69, *Travels with my Aunt* 72, *Love Among the Ruins* 74, *The Bluebird* 75.
9166 Cordell Drive, Los Angeles, Calif. 90069, U.S.A.

Cullberg, Birgit Ragnhild; Swedish choreographer; b. 3 Aug. 1908, Nyköping; d. of Carl Cullberg and Elna Westerström; m. Anders Ek 1942 (divorced); two s. one d.; ed. Univ. of Stockholm, Jooss School of Dance, Lilian Karina Ballet School.
Choreographer, Swedish Opera Ballet 51-57; Guest Choreographer, Royal Danish Ballet 57-61, 75, American Ballet Theatre 58-64, New York City Ballet 58, Nat. Ballet of Santiago de Chile, City Ballets of Cologne, Munich, Düsseldorf, Zürich, Dortmund, Oslo, Helsinki, Antwerp and Geneva; Artistic Dir. Cullberg Ballet, The Swedish Nat. Theatre Centre 67-; choreography includes: *Miss Julie, Medea, Moon-reindeer, The Evil Queen* (Prix d'Italia 61), *Lady from the Sea, Adam and Eve, Eurydice is dead, Romeo and Juliet, Red Wine in Green Glasses* (Prix d'Italia 71), *Revolt, School for Wives, The Dreamer, Peer Gynt.*
Leisure interests: theatre, art, political and social problems, peace.
Publ. *Ballet and Us* 54.
Kommendörsgatan 8c, 114 48 Stockholm, Sweden.
Telephone: 615835.

Cullen, Hon. Jack Sydney George (Bud), P.C., M.P.; Canadian politician; b. 20 April 1927, Creighton Mine, Ont.; s. of Chaffey Roi Cullen and Margaret Evelyn Leck; m. Marion Ann Hawley 1956; one s. two d.; ed. Sudbury High School, Univ. of Toronto and Osgoode Hall.
Barrister-at-Law; mem. Parl. for Sarnia-Lambton 68-; Parl. Sec. to Minister of Nat. Defence, Minister of Energy, Mines and Resources and Minister of Finance; Minister of Nat. Revenue Sept. 75-; first Pres. Sarnia Educ. Authority; mem. Sarnia School Board, Sarnia and District Assen. for the Mentally Retarded; Liberal. House of Commons, Ottawa, Ont.; Home: 1844 Kilborn Avenue, Ottawa, Ont. K1H 6N4, Canada.
Telephone: 995-2960 (Office); 733-4996 (Home).

Culligan, John William; American business executive; b. 22 Nov. 1916, Newark, N.J.; m. Rita McBride 1944; two s. four d.; ed. Seton Hall, Utah, Chicago and Philippine Univs.
President Whitehall Laboratories (div. of Amer. Home Products Corpn.) 64-67; Vice-Pres. and mem. Operations and Finance Cttees., Amer. Home Products Corpn. 67-70, Exec. Vice-Pres. 70-73, Dir. 70-, Pres. and Chair. Operations Cttee. 73-; Vice-Pres. and Dir. The Proprietary Assen.; Dir. Prestige Group, London; Treas. Council on Family Health; Trustee, Valley Hosp., N.J.; Knight of Malta.
Leisure interest: golf.
American Home Products Corporation, 685 Third Avenue, New York, N.Y. 10017; Home: 119 Berkeley Place, Glen Rock, N.J. 07452, U.S.A.
Telephone: (201) 444-8407 (Home).

Cullman, Joseph Frederick, III, B.A.; American business executive; b. 9 April 1912, New York; s. of Joseph F. Cullman, Jr. and Frances Nathan (Wolff) Cullman; one d.; ed. Hotchkiss School, Yale Univ.
Sales Man. Eastern Area, Webster Tobacco Co. 36-41; served in U.S. Navy as Air Defence Officer and Commdr. 41-45; Vice-Pres. Benson & Hedges 46-53, Exec. Vice-Pres. 53-55, Pres. 55-61; Vice-Pres. Philip Morris Inc. 54, Exec. Vice-Pres. 55, Pres. and Chief Exec. Officer 57-66, Chair. and Chief Exec. Officer 66-; Dir. Philip Morris (Australia) Ltd., Benson and Hedges (Canada)

Ltd., Mission Viejo Co. (operating co. of Philip Morris), IBM World Trade Europe/Middle East/Africa Corpn., Bankers Trust Co., Ford Motor Co., Braniff Int. and Levi Strauss and Co.; mem. Exec. Cttee. of Tobacco Inst., Washington, D.C.; mem. Finance Cttee. of Cttee. for Econ. Devt.; mem. Nat. Board of Smithsonian Assocs.; Trustee, New York State Nature and Historical Preserve Trust, American Museum of Natural History, Colonial Williamsburg Foundation; mem. Yale Devt. Board, Advisory Council of Graduate School of Business, Stanford Univ., Conf. Board; Pres. Int. Atlantic Salmon Foundation; Dir. World Wildlife Fund—U.S. Appeal; Pres., Dir. Whitney M. Young, Jr. Memorial Foundation; New York City Chair. of United Negro Coll. Fund 1972 Campaign; Chair. U.S. Open Tennis Championships at Forest Hills 69-70, Hon. Chair. 71; Ordre du Mérite Commercial et Industriel (France) 63, Commdr. Order of Merit (Italy) 66; Hon. D.Iur (Bellarmine Coll., Louisville, Kentucky) 73; Hon. Dr. Commercial Science (Univ. of Richmond, Va.).
Leisure interests: tennis, golf, fishing, hunting.
100 Park Avenue, New York, N.Y. 10017, U.S.A.
Telephone: 212-679-1800.

Culmann, Herbert Ernst, DR.IUR.; German airline executive; b. 15 Feb. 1921, Neustadt; *m.* two *s.* one *d.*; ed. Gymnasium Neustadt and Ruprecht-Karl Universität, Heidelberg.
German Air Force 39-45; legal studies and legal practice 45-53; Deutsche Lufthansa A.G. 53-, Dir. of Central Admin. Div. (Int. relations, Org. Legal,, Planning, Financial divs.) 57-64, mem. Management Board 64-72, Chair. Exec. Board 72-; official of other companies; mem. Int. Law Asscn. 54-; Chair. Exec. Board Int. Air Transport Asscn. 72, mem. Exec. Cttee.; mem. Aviation Advisory Cttee., Fed. Transport Ministry.
Leisure interests: flying, music, sailing, skiing.
Deutsche Lufthansa AG, 5 Cologne 21 (Deutz), Von-Gablenz Strasse 2-6; Home: 506 Bensberg-Refrath, Neuertrassweg 30, Federal Republic of Germany.
Telephone: (0221) 8261 (Office).

Culver, John C., A.B., LL.B.; American politician; b. 8 Aug. 1932, Rochester, Minn.; *s.* of William Culver; *m.* Ann Cooper 1958; one *s.* three *d.*; ed. Franklin High School, Cedar Rapids, Harvard Coll., Emmanuel Coll., Cambridge, Harvard Univ.
Dean of Men, Harvard Univ. Summer School 60; Legis. Asst. to U.S. Senator Edward M. Kennedy 62-63; mem. Congress (Iowa) 65-75; U.S. Senator for Iowa Jan. 75-; Democrat.
Leisure interests: reading, sports, historical restoration.
United States Senate Office Building, Washington, D.C. 20510; Home: 6800 Connecticut Avenue, N.W., Chevy Chase, Md., U.S.A.
Telephone: 224-3121 (Office); 656-2691 (Home).

Cummings, Constance, C.B.E.; British actress; b. 15 May 1910, Seattle, U.S.A.; *m.* Benn W. Levy 1933; one *s.* one *d.*; ed. St. Nicholas School, Seattle.
First appeared on the stage in *Four Grapes*, since then in many stage, film and television roles; has performed *Peter and the Wolf* and played Joan in the Claudel-Honegger oratorio *St. Joan at the Stake* with the orchestra at the Albert Hall and Festival Hall; mem. Arts Council 65-70; Chair. of Arts Council Young People's Theatre Panel 65-74; mem. Royal Society of Arts 75.
Plays incl. *Emma Bovary, The Taming of the Shrew, Romeo and Juliet, St. Joan, Lysistrata, Coriolanus, Long Day's Journey into Night, The Cherry Orchard, The Bacchae.*
Leisure interests: needlework, gardening.
68 Old Church Street, London, S.W.3; Cote House, Aston, Oxfordshire.
Telephone: 352-0437.

Cummings, Nathan; American business executive. b. 14 Oct. 1896, St. John, N.B., Canada; *m.* Joanne Toor Cummings 1959; three *c.*; ed. Economist Training School, New York.
Retail shoe business 14-17; wholesale shoe business 17-24; shoe manufacturing 24-30; importing gen. merchandise 30-34; manufacturing biscuits and candy 34-38 (all in Canada); took up residence in U.S.A. 39; Pres. C. D. Kenny Co. (wholesale food), Baltimore 39-; acquired this and other firms to form Consolidated Foods Corpn., of which he is Hon. Chair., Chair. Exec. Cttee.; Chair. Board Associated Products Inc.; Dir. Soc. Nat. Bank Cleveland; Dir. Gen. Dynamics Corpn.; Patron and benefactor several art socs.; Chevalier Légion d'Honneur, Commendatore Al Merito della Repubblica Italiana and other awards, including hon. degrees from American and Canadian Univs.
Leisure interests: art collection and exhibition.
Home: Waldorf Astoria Towers, 100 East 50th Street, New York; Office: 375 Park Avenue, New York, U.S.A.
Telephone: Plaza 1-3330.

Cummings, Ralph W., PH.D.; American agriculturist; b. 13 Dec. 1911, Reidsville, N.C.; *m.* Mary Parrish Cummings; three *s.* one *d.*; ed. N. Carolina State Univ., Ohio State Univ.
Assistant and Assoc. Prof. Cornell Univ. 37-42; Prof. Head of Agronomy, N. Carolina State Univ. 42-47, Asst. Dir. of Agricultural Research 45-47, Dir. 48-54; Chief N. Carolina Agricultural Research, Mission in Peru 55-56; Field Dir., Chief Rep. in India, Rockefeller Foundation 57-66, Assoc. Dir. for Agricultural Sciences 63-68; Admin. Dean for Research N. Carolina State Univ. 68-71; Agriculture Programme Adviser in Asia and the Pacific, Ford Foundation 71-72; Dir. Int. Rice Research Inst., Philippines June-Nov. 72, Int. Crops Research Inst. for the Semi-Arid Tropics, Hyderabad 72-; Chair. Govt. of India Cttee. on Agricultural Univs. 60-64; Consultant Agricultural Research Org., Indonesia 70; Vice-Chair. Cttee. on Study of African Agricultural Research Capabilities, Nat. Acad. of Sciences, U.S.A. 70-73; many hon. degrees; Int. Agronomy Award, Soc. of Agronomy 70.
International Crops Research Institute for Semi-Arid Tropics, 1-11-256 Begumpet, Hyderabad, India.

Cummings, Tilden, B.S., M.B.A.; American banker; b. 18 Sept. 1907; ed. Princeton Univ. and Harvard Graduate School of Business Administration.
Dir. Continental Illinois Nat. Bank and Trust Co. of Chicago, Pres. 60-73; Dir. Northern Natural Gas Co., Omaha, American Brake Shoe Co., New York, Consolidated Foods Corpn., Chicago; Vice-Pres. Board of Trustees, Northwestern Univ.; Dir. Chicago, Milwaukee, St. Paul and Pacific Railroad Co. 70-, Canteen Corpn., Chicago, Northern Natural Gas Co., Omaha; official of many civic and philanthropic orgs.
Continental Illinois National Bank and Trust Co. of Chicago, 231 South La Salle Street, Chicago, Ill. 60690, U.S.A.

Cunhal, Alvaro; Portuguese politician; b. Coímbra; ed. Lisbon Univ.
Member of Portuguese Communist Party 31-; Sec.-Gen. Fed. of Communist Youth Movts. 35; mem. PCP Cen. Cttee. 36, Cen. Cttee. Secr. 42-49, 60-; active in party reorganization and devt. of links with int. communist movt. 42-49; imprisoned for political activities 37-38, 40, 49-60; Sec.-Gen. PCP 61-; Minister without Portfolio 74-75; mem. many PCP dels. abroad.
Leisure interests: drawing and painting.
Portuguese Communist Party, Avenue Antonio Serpa 26-2°, Lisbon, Portugal.

Cunningham, Alexander A.; American business executive; b. 7 Jan. 1926, Sofia, Bulgaria.
Navigator-electronics radar specialist, R.A.F., World

War II; joined Gen. Motors 48, Gen. Motors Overseas Operations Div. 53, Adam Opel A.G., Fed. Germany 53, Gen. Motors Ltd., London 56; Works Man. Gen. Motors do Brasil 58-62, Man. Dir. 63; Works Man. Gen. Motors Argentina S.A. 62-63; Man. Adam Opel, Bochum 64; Asst. Gen. Mfg. Man. Adam Opel A.G. 66-69, Ge . Mfg. Man. 69-70, Man. Dir. 70-74; Dir. European Operations, Gen. Motors Overseas Corpn. Feb. 74-.
General Motors Overseas Corporation, Stag Lane, Kingsbury, London, N.W.9, England.

Cunningham, Sir Graham, K.B.E., LL.B.; British company director; b. 19 May 1892, Walthamstow, Essex; s. of Daniel Cunningham; m. Edith Smith 1958; two s. one d.; ed. Bancroft's School.
Solicitor 14; served Royal Fusiliers 15-19; with Parson, Lee & Co., solicitors 19-33; Man. Dir. Tuck & Co. Ltd. 24-30; Man. Dir. Triplex Safety Glass Co. Ltd. 29-60; Chair. 35-61; Chair. Triplex Holdings Ltd., Stern & Bell Ltd., Weddall and Assembly Ltd. 61, Deputy Dir.-Gen. Children's Overseas Reception Board 40; Dir. of Claims, War Damage Comm. 41; Chief Exec. and Controller-Gen. of Munitions Production, Ministry of Supply 41-46; Gov. Bancroft's School; Gov. and Dep. Chair. and Hon. Fellow Imperial Coll. of Science and Technology; Chair. Shipbuilding Advisory Cttee. 46-60; Dir. Disabled Persons Employment Corpn. Ltd. 46-49; mem. Econ. Planning Board 47-61, Royal Comm. on Press 61-62; Chair. Dollar Exports Board 49; Fellow and Past Pres. Soc. of Glass Technology, Past Pres. Soc. of British Gas Industries; Past Master of Curriers Company and Glaziers Company.
Leisure interest: gardening.
Woolmers, Mannings Heath, near Horsham, Sussex, England.
Telephone: Horsham 3809.

Cunningham, Harry Blair; American retail executive; b. 23 July 1907; ed. Miami Univ., Oxford, Ohio.
Newspaper Reporter *Harrisburg Patriot* 27-28; S. S. Kresge Co., Lynchburg, Va. 28-29, Washington 30, Brooklyn 31-32, Detroit 33-35, Wheeling 36, Lafayette (Ind.) 36-38, Muncie (Ind.) 39-40, Grosse Pointe (Mich.) 40-41, Highland Park (Mich.) 42-46, Superintendent, Stores 47-50, Asst. Sales Dir. 51-52, Sales Dir. 53-57, Gen. Vice-Pres. 57-59, Pres. 59-70, Chair. of Board 67-72, Hon. Chair. 73-; official of other companies.
210 Lowell Court, Bloomfield Hills, Mich. 48013, U.S.A.

Cunningham, Merce; American dancer and choreographer; b. 16 April 1919, Centralia, Wash.; s. of Mr. and Mrs. C. D. Cunningham; ed. Cornish School, Seattle and Bennington Coll. School of Dance.
Soloist with Martha Graham Dance Co. 39-45; began solo concerts 42; on faculty of School of American Ballet, N.Y. 48-50; formed own company 53; has been in residence with his company at Black Mountain Coll., N.C., Connecticut Coll. School of Dance, Univ. of Calif. at Los Angeles, State Univ. of N.Y. at Buffalo, Univ. of Colo.; opened his own dance school in N.Y. 59; leads resident modern dance company at Brooklyn Acad. of Music, N.Y. 69-; mem. Mayor of New York's Cultural Cttee. 68; Guggenheim Fellowships 54, 59; Dance Magazine Award 60; Soc. for Advancement of The Dance in Sweden Gold Medal 64; Gold Star for Choreographic Invention Paris 66.
Leisure interests: reading, cooking, dominoes.
Works include: *The Seasons* 47, *16 Dances for Soloist and Company of Three* 51, *Septet* 53, *Minutiae* 54, *Spring-weather and People* 55, *Suite for Five* 56, *Nocturnes* 56, *Antic Meet* 58, *Summerspace* 58, *Rune* 59, *Crises* 60, *Aeon* 61, *Story* 63, *Winterbranch* 64, *Variations V* 65, *How to Pass, Kick, Fall and Run* 65, *Place* 66, *Scramble* 67, *Rain Forest* 68, *Walkaround Time* 68,

Canfield 69, *Second Hand* 70, *Tread* 70, *Signals* 70, *Objects* 70, *Un Jour ou Deux* 73.
Publ. *Notes on Choreography* 69.
463 West Street, New York, N.Y. 10014, U.S.A.

Cunningham, R. Walter; American astronaut; b. 16 March 1932, Creston, Iowa; m. Lo Ella Irby; one s. one d.; ed. Univ. of Calif. at Los Angeles.
Joined U.S. Navy 51, flight training 52; assigned to Marine Squadron 53; later, research scientist, Rand Corpn.; later at Univ. of Calif.; selected as astronaut Oct. 63; took part in *Apollo VII* Mission Oct. 68; Senior Vice-Pres. Century Devt. Corpn. 71-74; Pres. Hydrotech Devt. Co. 74-.
Leisure interest: sport.
Hydrotech Development Co., P.O. Box 55364, Houston, Tex. 77055, U.S.A.

Cupp, Paul J.; American businessman; b. 12 July 1902; ed. Wharton School of Commerce, Univ. of Pennsylvania.
Chairman Board, American Stores Co.; Chair. Univ. City Science Center; Pres. Presbyterian Univ. of Penna Medical Center; Dir. Philadelphia Nat. Bank, Provident Mutual Life Insurance Co.; John Wanamaker Phila., Chem. Leaman Tank Lines Inc., Greater Phila. Movement; Man. Western Savings Fund Soc.; Trustee, Univ. of Pennsylvania; mem. Philadelphia Chamber of Commerce; Hon. LL.D.
Home: 933 Muirfield Road, Bryn Mawr, Pa.; Office: 124 N. 15th Street, Philadelphia, Pa. 19102, U.S.A.

Curie, Eve Denise (*see* Labouisse, Eve Denise).

Curien, Hubert, D. ès sc.; French scientist; b. 30 Oct. 1924, Cornimont; s. of Robert Curien; m. Anne-Perrine Duménzil 1949; three s.; ed. Lycée d'Epinal, Coll. de Remiremont, Lycée Saint-Louis, Ecole Normale Supérieure and Faculté des Sciences, Paris.
Professor, Faculté des Sciences, Paris 56-; Scientific Dir. Centre Nat. de la Recherche Scientifique (CNRS) 66-69, Dir.-Gen. 69-73, Gen. Del. of Scientific and Technical Research 73-; fmr. Pres. Soc. Française de Minéralogie et Cristallographie; Chevalier, Légion d'Honneur; Military Medal; Prize, Acad. des Sciences.
Publs. scientific articles on solid state physics and mineralogy.
35 rue Saint-Dominique, Paris 7e; Home: 24 rue des Fossés Saint-Jacques, Paris 5e, France.
Telephone: 551-7430 (Office); 633-2636 (Home).

Curran, Sir Charles John, Kt.; British broadcasting executive; b. 13 Oct. 1921, Dublin; s. of Felix Curran and Alicia Isabella (née Bruce); m. Silvia Meyer 1949; one d.; ed. Wath-on-Dearne Grammar School, S. Yorkshire, and Magdalene Coll., Cambridge.
Indian Army 41-45; Producer, Home Talks, British Broadcasting Corpn. (BBC) 47-50; Asst. Editor *Fishing News* 50-51; BBC 51-, Canadian Rep. 56-59, Sec. 63-66, Dir. of External Broadcasting 67-68; Dir.-Gen. BBC April 69-; Pres. European Broadcasting Union 73-; mem. Exec. Cttee., British Council.
Leisure interest: opera.
British Broadcasting Corporation, Broadcasting House, London, W1A 1AA, England.
Telephone: 01-580-4468.

Curran, Sir Samuel Crowe, Kt., D.L., M.A., D.SC., PH.D., D.SC., LL.D., F.R.S.; British university principal and vice-chancellor; b. 23 May 1912, Ballymena, Ulster; s. of John Curran and Sarah Owen Crowe; m. Joan Elizabeth Strothers 1940; three s. one d.; ed. Glasgow Univ. and St. John's Coll., Cambridge.
Royal Aircraft Establishment 39-40; Ministry of Aircraft Production and Ministry of Supply 40-44; Manhattan Project (Ministry of Supply), Univ. of Calif. 44-45 (invention of scintillation counter 44); Natural

Philosophy Dept., Glasgow Univ. 45-55; U.K Atomic Energy Authority, Chief Scientist, Atomic Weapons Research Establishment, Aldermaston 55-59; Principal, Royal Coll. of Science and Technology, Glasgow 59-64; Principal and Vice-Chancellor, Univ. of Strathclyde, Glasgow 64-; mem. Council for Scientific and Industrial Research 62-65; Science Research Council 65-68, Advisory Council on Technology 64-70; Chair. Advisory Cttee. on Medical Research 62-75, Advisory Board on Relations with Univs. 66-70; Chief Scientific Adviser to Sec. of State for Scotland 67-; Dir. Scottish Television Ltd., Cetec. Systems Ltd., Hall-Thermotank Ltd.; Int. Research and Devt. Co. Ltd.; Fellow, Royal Soc. of Edinburgh; Hon. FRCPS (Glasgow); Commdr. of Order of St. Olav (Norway); Freeman of Burgh of Motherwell and Wishaw; Hon. Fellow, St. John's Coll., Cambridge; Officer's Cross, Order of Polonia Restituta.
Leisure interests: golf, skiing.
Publs. *Counting Tubes* 49, *Luminescence and the Scintillation Counter* 53, *Alpha, Beta and Gamma Ray Spectroscopy* 64, *Energy Resources and the Environment* (with others) 75; papers on nuclear research and educ.
University of Strathclyde, Royal College, 204 George Street, Glasgow, G1 1XW; Home: 5 Camstradden Drive East, Bearsden, Glasgow, G61 4AH, Scotland.
Telephone: 041-552-4400 (Office); 041-942-3936 (Home).

Currea Cubides, Maj.-Gen. Hernando; Colombian army officer and politician; b. 7 Dec. 1919, Bogotá; s. of Miguel Angel Currea and María Cubides de Currea; m. Stella Pombo de Currea Cubides 1944; one s. three d.; ed. Colegio Americano, Bogotá and Escuela Militar de Cadetes.
Director and Prof.. Escuela Militar de Cadetes 65; Chief of Staff and Commdr. of the Army 68; C.-in-C. of Armed Forces 69; Minister of Nat. Defence 70-74; Amb. to Portugal 75-; several decorations and medals.
Leisure interests: golf, photography.
c/o Embassy of Columbia, Praca Jose Fontana, 10 Dto. 5, Lisbon, Portugal.

Currie, George Bale, B.A.; Canadian business executive; b. 11 Jan. 1925, Hamilton, Ont.; s. of John Ferguson and Marie (Allen) Currie; m. Martha Bernice Home Brown 1955; two s.; ed. Hamilton Collegiate Inst., McMaster Univ., Harvard Graduate School of Business.
Assistant Man. Canadian Bank of Commerce 52-55, Asst. Gen. Man. Ont. Branches 55, European Rep., Zurich 59, Regional Gen. Man. B.C. and Yukon Branches, Canadian Imperial Bank of Commerce 63; Asst. Vice-Pres. Finance, MacMillan Bloedel Ltd. 65, Vice-Pres. Strategic Planning and Devt. 68, Vice-Pres. Finance and Strategic Planning and Devt. 69, Exec. Vice-Pres. Finance and Admin. 72, Chair. 74.
Leisure interests: golf, music.
MacMillan Bloedel Ltd., 1075 West Georgia Street, Vancouver, B.C. V6E 3R9; Home: 1680 West 40th Avenue, Vancouver, B.C. V6M 1V9, Canada.
Telephone: (604) 683-6711 (Office); (604) 263-6080 (Home).

Curti, Merle, A.B., PH.D.; American historian; b. 15 Sept. 1897, Papillion, Neb.; s. of John Eugene Curti and Alice Hunt Curti; m. 1st Margaret Wooster 1925 (deceased), 2nd Frances Becker 1968; two d.; ed. Harvard.
Dwight Morrow Prof. of History Smith Coll. 36-37; visiting Prof. Chicago and Calif. Univs. and Inst. of Technology Calif.; Prof. Columbia Univ. 37-42, Wisconsin 42-68; Frederick Jackson Turner Prof. of History, Univ. of Wis. 47-68, Emeritus Prof. 68-; Visiting Prof. Univ. of Tokyo 59-60; Hon. Consultant, Library of Congress 69-72; Hon. Fellow Truman Inst. 75-; mem. Board of Advisers American Council Learned Socs., mem. Social Science Research Princeton Univ.

Advisory Council 18; awarded Pulitzer Prize 44; Pres. Miss. Valley Historical Asscn. 51-52; and American Historical Asscn. 53-54; Fellow, Inst. for Behavioral Sciences 55-56: A.C.L.S. Prize for extraordinary scholarly achievement" $10,000 60; Knight Order of Northern Star (Sweden); Hon. L.H.D., Hon. Lit.D.
Publs. *Austria and the United States 1848-1852* 26, *Bryan and World Peace* 27, *American Peace Crusade 1815-1861* 29, *War or Peace: The American Struggle 1636-1936* 36, *The Social Ideas of American Educators* 35, *American Issues* 41, *Growth of American Thought* 44 (Pulitzer Prize), *The Roots of American Loyalty* 46, *American Scholarship in the Twentieth Century* (jointly), *Prelude to Point Four* (jointly) 54, *Probing Our Past* 55, *An American Paradox* 56, *The Making of an American Community* 59, *Rise of the American Nation* (with Paul Todd) 60, *American Philanthropy Overseas: a History* 63, *Philanthropy in the Shaping of American Higher Education* (with Roderick Nash) 65, *Rise of the American Nation* 66, *Human Nature in American Historical Thought* 69, etc.
2015 Van Hise Avenue, Maidstone, Wis. 53705, U.S.A.

Curtin, David Yarrow, A.B., PH.D.; American chemist; b. 22 Aug. 1920, Philadelphia, Pa.; s. of Ellsworth F. Curtin and Margaretta Cope Curtin; m. Constance O'Hara 1950; one s. two d.; ed. Swarthmore Coll. and Univ. of Illinois.
Private Asst. (with L. F. Fieser), Harvard Univ. 45-46; Instructor in Chem., Columbia Univ. 46-49, Asst. Prof. 49-51; Asst. Prof. Univ. of Illinois 51-52, Assoc. Prof. 52-54, Prof. 54-, Head, Div. of Organic Chem. 63-65, Head, Div. of Chem. 68-; mem. Nat. Acad. of Sciences.
Leisure interests: music, photography.
Publs. Many scientific papers.
Department of Chemistry and Chemical Engineering, University of Illinois, Urbana, Ill. 61801; 3 Montclair Road, Urbana, Ill. 61801, U.S.A.
Telephone: 217-344-5149.

Curtis, Ellwood F., B.A., C.P.A.; American accountant and business executive; b. 14 May 1914; ed. Dartmouth Coll.
With Haskins & Sells, Certified Public Accountants 35-39; with Deere & Company (manufacturers of agricultural and industrial equipment) 39-, Comptroller 44, Dir. 51-, Vice-Pres. 56-59, Exec. Vice-Pres. 59-64, Pres. 64-.
Deere & Company, John Deere Road, Moline, Ill., 61265, U.S.A.

Curzon, Clifford, C.B.E., D.MUS., F.R.A.M.; British concert pianist; b. 18 May 1907, London; m. Lucille Wallace 1931; two s.; ed. Royal Acad. of Music, London, and studied in Berlin under Schnabel and in Paris under Wanda Landowska and Nadia Boulanger.
Recent tours throughout the world; coast-to-coast tours U.S.A. 37-72, including engagements with the N.Y. Philharmonic Orchestra, the Philadelphia Orchestra, etc.; Hon. D.Litt. (Sussex Univ. 73).
Leisure interest: gardening.
The White House, Millfield Place, London, N.6, England.

Cusack, Cyril James; Irish actor and writer; b. 26 Nov. 1910, Durban; s. of Alice Violet Cole and James Walter Cusack; m. Mary Margaret Kiely 1945; two s. four d.; ed. Univ. Coll., Dublin and Nat. Univ.
Joined Abbey Theatre, Dublin 32; Leading Actor, Nat. Theatre, Dublin 32, 45, 46, Assoc. and Shareholder 66-; Producer, Gaelic Players 35-36; Man. Dir. Cyril Cusack Productions 46-61; first London appearance in *Ah Wilderness* 36; Produced *Tareis an Aifrinn*, Gate Theatre, Dublin 42; Man. Gaiety Theatre, Dublin 45; has played leading roles in many stage plays in Ireland, U.K., and Broadway notably: *The Playboy of the*

Western World, The Moon for the Misbegotten, Julius Caesar (Cassius), *The Physicists, Andorra, The Cherry Orchard, Mr. O, Arms and the Man* (Int. Critics' Award 61), *Krapp's Last Tape* (Int. Critics' Award 61); since first film appearance in *Knocknagow* 37, other films have included: *The Small Back Room, Odd Man Out, The Elusive Pimpernel, The Man Who Never Was, Ill Met by Moonlight, A Terrible Beauty, The Blue Veil* (Oscar nomination 52), *Johnny Nobody, The Waltz of the Toreadors, I Thank a Fool, 80,000 Suspects, One Spy Too Many, The Spy Who Came in from the Cold, The Taming of the Shrew, Oedipus Rex, Galileo Galilei, King Lear, David Copperfield, Country Dance, Day of the Jackal, Juggernaut, The Temptation of Mr. O*; also appears in television plays and series.
Publ. *Timepieces* (poetry) 70.
Cluan Chaoin, Deilginis, Dublin; Mont Alto, Deilginis, Dublin, Ireland; 2 Vincent Terrace, London, N.1, England.
Telephone: 01-278-2681; Dublin 809707.

Cushman, Gen. Robert E., Jr.; American government official; b. 1914, St. Paul, Minnesota; *m.* Audrey Boyce 1940; one *s.* one *d.*
Commanded U.S. Marine Infantry battalion in Pacific; after war various command and staff assignments in U.S. and Europe; Asst. to Vice-Pres. Nixon for Nat. Security Affairs 57-61; Commdr. 3rd Marine Div. 62, G-2 and G-3 H.Q. 62-64, Camp Pendleton, Calif. and 5th Marine Div. 64-67, III Marine Amphibious Force, Viet-Nam 67-69; Deputy Dir. of Central Intelligence Agency (CIA) 69-72; Commdt. Marine Corps. 72-75.
c/o Headquarters, U.S. Marine Corps, Washington, D.C. 20380, U.S.A.

Cutler, Sir (Arthur) Roden, V.C., K.C.M.G., K.C.V.O., C.B.E., K.ST.J., B.EC.; Australian public servant and diplomatist; b. 24 May 1916, Sydney; *s.* of Arthur and Ruby (née Pope) Cutler; *m.* Helen Morris 1946; four *s.*; ed. Sydney High School and Univ. of Sydney.
Justice Dept. N.S.W. (Public Trust Office) 35-42; State Sec. Retd. Servicemen's League N.S.W. 42-43; mem. of Aliens' Classification and Advisory Cttee. to advise Commonwealth Govt. 42-43; Asst. Dep. Dir. of Security Service N.S.W. 43; Commonwealth Asst. Commr. of Repatriation 43-46; High Commr. in New Zealand 46-52; High Commr. in Ceylon 52-55; Minister to Egypt 55-56; Sec.-Gen. SEATO 57; Chief of Protocol, Dept. of External Affairs, Canberra 57; State Pres. Retd. Servicemen's League, Australian Capital Territory; Australian High Commr. in Pakistan 59-61; Australian Rep. to the Independence of the Somali Repub. 60; Australian Consul-Gen., New York 61-65; Del. to UN Gen. Assembly 63-64; Australian Amb. to the Netherlands 65-66; Gov. New South Wales 66-; 2/5th Field Regt., A.I.F., Middle East 40-42; Hon. LL.D. (Sydney Univ.), Hon. D.Sc. (Univ. of N.S.W., Univ. of Newcastle); Hon. Col. Royal N.S.W. Regt., Sydney Univ. Regt.; Hon. Air Commodore No. 22 Sqdn. R.A.A.F.
Leisure interests: sailing, swimming, shooting, photography.
Government House, Sydney, N.S.W., Australia.

Cutler, Walter Leon, M.A.; American diplomatist; b. 25 Nov. 1931, Boston, Mass.; *s.* of Walter Leon Cutler and Esther Dewey; *m.* Sarah Gerard Beeson 1957; two *s*; ed. Wesleyan Univ. and Fletcher School of Int. Law and Diplomacy.
Vice-Consul, Yaoundé, Cameroon 57-59; Staff Asst. to Sec. of State 60-62; Political-Econ. Officer, Algiers 62-65; Consul, Tabriz, Iran 65-67; Political-Mil. Officer, Seoul, Republic of Korea 67-69; Political Officer, Saigon, Repub. of Viet-Nam 69-71; Special Asst., Bureau of Far Eastern Affairs, Dept. of State 71-73, mem. Senior Seminar on Foreign Policy 73-74,

Dir. Office of Cen. Africa 74-75; Amb. to Zaire Dec. 75-.
Leisure interests: sports, ornithology.
American Embassy, Kinshasa, Zaire.

Cutts, Trevett Wakeham, LL.B.; Australian diplomatist; b. 28 May 1914, Mildura, Victoria; *m.* Maidie Phyllis Stuhmcke 1945; two *s.*; ed. Melbourne High School and Melbourne Univ.
Naval war service; joined Dept. of External Affairs 46; mem. Mission Singapore and Indonesia 46-50; Official Sec. High Comm. in Canada 52-54; Counsellor UN 54-57; Chargé d'Affaires Moscow 59-60; Consul-Gen. San Francisco 60-62; Ambassador to the Philippines 63-65; High Commr. to Pakistan 66-68; Amb. to S. Africa 68-72; High Commr. to Malta 72-75.
Leisure interests: golf sailing.
c/o Ministry of Foreign Affairs, Canberra, Australia.

Cyrankiewicz, Józef; Polish politician; b. 23 April 1911, Tarnów; ed. Jagiellonian Univ., Cracow.
Served in the artillery from the outbreak of war, captured by the Germans, escaped and organized resistance in the Cracow district; arrested and imprisoned in Auschwitz and Mauthausen concentration camps 41-45; mem. of the Polish Socialist Party 32-48, Polish United Workers' Party 48-; Sec.- Gen. of the P.S.P. Central Exec. Cttee. 45-48; mem. of the Central Cttee. 48-75, of the Political Bureau of the PUWP Central Cttee. 48-71; Minister without Portfolio 46; Deputy to the Seym 47-72; Premier 47-52, Vice-Premier 52-54, Premier 54-70; Chair. of the Econ. Cttee. of the Council of Ministers 57-69; Chair. of the Union of Former Political Prisoners 46-49, Union of Fighters for Freedom and Democracy 49-72; Chair. Council of State 70-72; mem. Presidium, All-Polish Cttee. of Nat. Unity Front 75; Chair. All-Polish Peace Cttee. 73-75; Order of Polonia Restituta First Class 49; Order of Banner of Labour First Class 51; Order of Builders of People's Poland 64, and other awards.
Ogólnopolski Komitet Pokoju, ul. Rajców 10, 00-220 Warsaw, Poland.

Cziffra, Georges; French concert pianist; b. 5 Nov. 1921, Budapest, Hungary; *s.* of Julius Cziffra and Helen Nagy; *m.* Soleyka Abdin 1942; one *s.* one *d.*; ed. Conservatoire of Music, Budapest.
Cabaret pianist in Hungary 38-50; came to Paris 56; recitals and concerts in U.S.A., U.K., Canada, France, Israel, Belgium, Netherlands, Italy, Switzerland, Japan and South America; plays Liszt, Grieg, Tchaikovsky, Beethoven, Schumann, etc.; f. Festival de la Chaise Dieu 68 and also Biennial Concours Int. de Piano, Versailles, for young pianists 68; records for HMV; Chevalier Légion d'Honneur 73.
16 rue Ampère, 75017 Paris, France.

Czinege, Lajos; Hungarian politician; b. 24 March 1924, Karczag; *s.* of József Czinege and Mária Andrási; *m.* Maria Völgyi 1949; two *s.* one *d.*
Agricultural labourer; official Communist Party 47-51; Lieut.-Col. 51-54; Lieut.-Gen. 60; Col.-Gen. 62; mem. Central Cttee., Hungarian Socialist Workers' Party 59-, Substitute mem. Political Cttee. 61-70; Minister of Defence 60-.
Leisure interests: mountaineering, wild game shooting.
Ministry of Defence, H-1885 Budapest V, Pálffy György utca 7/11, Hungary.
Telephone: 114-200.

Czottner, Sándor; Hungarian politician; b. 12 May 1903, Csokonya; *s.* of Antal Czottner and Erzsébet Kappel; *m.* Katalin Barics 1925; one *s.*; ed. Technical Univ.
Engine fitter; Minister of Mining and Power 51, of Heavy Industry 61-63.
Leisure interests: gardening, rose-breeding.
Bimbó ut 168, 1026 Budapest II, Hungary.
Telephone: 364-791.

Czubiński, Lucjan, D.JUR.; Polish lawyer; b. 21 July 1930, Dobrzelin, near Kutno; ed. A. Mickiewicz Univ., Poznań.

Army 49-; Officer of Public Prosecutor 51-; Chief Mil. Prosecutor 68-72; Brig.-Gen. 70-; mem. Cen. Appeal Comm., later Presidium mem. 71-; Procurator Gen. 72-; Deputy mem. Cen. Cttee. Polish United Workers' Party Dec. 75-; Order of Banner of Labour, 1st Class; Officer's Cross, Order of Polonia Restituta; Gold Cross of Merit;

J. Krasicki Gold Award; Medal of 30th Anniversary of People's Poland.

Publs. *Niektóre problemy odpowiedzialności karnej żołnierzy* 68, *Istota rozkazu wojakowego* 69, *Kodeks karny, Cześć wojskowa* 69, *Wychowawcze treści prawa wofskowego i regulaminów* 70.

Prokuratura Generalna, ul. Krakowskie Przedmieście 25, 00-071 Warsaw, Poland.

Telephone: 26-05-05 (Office).

D

Daane, James Dewey; American banker and educator; b. 6 July 1918, Grand Rapids, Mich.; *m.* 1st Blanche M. Tichenor 1941 (dissolved), 2nd Onnie B. Selby 1953 (deceased), 3rd Barbara W. McMann 1963; three *d.*; ed. Duke Univ. and Harvard Univ.
Federal Reserve Bank of Richmond 39-60, Monetary Economist 47, Asst. Vice-Pres. 53, Vice-Pres., Dir., Research Dept., 57; Chief, Int. Monetary Fund Mission to Paraguay 50-51; Vice-Pres., Econ. Adviser, Federal Reserve Bank of Minneapolis May-July 60; Asst. to Sec. of U.S. Treasury, Principal Adviser to Under-Sec. for Monetary Affairs 60-61; Dep. Under-Sec. of Treasury for Monetary Affairs and Gen. Dep. to Under-Sec. for Monetary Affairs 61-63; mem. Board of Govs., Federal Reserve System 63-74; Vice-Chair. Commerce Union Bank 74-; Vice-Chair. Tennessee Valley Bancorp, Inc. 75-; Frank K. Houston Prof. of Banking and Finance, Graduate School of Management, Vanderbilt Univ. 74-; Dir. Whittaker Corpn., Calif. 74-; mem. American Finance Asscn., American Econ. Asscn.
Commerce Union Bank, 4th and Union, Nashville, Tenn. 37219; Home: 102 Westhampton Place, Nashville, Tenn. 37205, U.S.A.

Dacko, David; Central African Republic politician; b. 30; ed. Ecole Normale, Brazzaville.
Minister of Agriculture, Stockbreeding, Water and Forests, Central African Govt. Council 57-58; Minister of Interior, Economy and Trade, Central African Provisional Govt. 58-59; Premier, Central African Republic 59-66, Minister of Nat. Defence, Guardian of the Seals 60-66; Pres. of Central African Republic 60-66; mem. Mouvement pour l'Evolution Sociale de l'Afrique Noire (MESAN); under house arrest July 69-.
Bangui, Central African Republic.

da Cunha Sottomayor Corrêa d'Oliveira, Jose Gonçalo; Portuguese lawyer and politician; see *The International Who's Who 1975-76.*

Daddah, Moktar Ould; Mauritanian politician; b. 20 Dec. 1924; ed. secondary school, Senegal and Paris.
Interpreter; studied law; with firm Boissier Palun, Dakar; territorial councillor 57; Premier, Islamic Republic of Mauritania 58-; Pres. of the Republic 61-, also Minister of Nat. Defence and Foreign Affairs; Pres. Org. Commune Africaine et Malgache 65; Leader Parti du Peuple.
Office of the President, Nouakchott, Mauritania.

Dadzie, Emmanuel Kodjoe, LL.B.; Ghanaian diplomatist and lawyer; b. 16 March 1916, Sekondi; *m.* Irma St. Rose; two *s.* three *d.*; ed. Achimota Coll., Accra, King's Coll., London and Lincoln's Inn, London.
Served in Gold Coast Civil Service 36-42; Royal Air Force 42-47; in private legal practice, Accra 51-59; Head, Legal and Consular Services Div., Ministry of Foreign Affairs 59; Amb. to Romania 62-66; Resident Rep. of Ghana to IAEA 63-66; mem. Board of Govs. 63; Amb. to France and Perm. Rep. to UNESCO 65-67; Amb. Ministry of Foreign Affairs, Accra 68; Amb. to U.S.S.R. 69; Dir. Policy Planning Div., Ministry of Foreign Affairs 70; Principal Sec., Ministry of Foreign Affairs 71; Dir. of Protection, UN High Comm. for Refugees, Geneva, 72; del. to various UN, OAU and other int. confs. and several sessions of UN Gen. Assembly.
Leisure interests: motoring, golfing.
Chemin de la Tourelle 12, 1211 Geneva 19, Switzerland. Telephone: 98-41-56.

Dagnino Pastore, José María, D.ECON., PH.D.; Argentine economist; b. 19 Nov. 1933, Buenos Aires; *s.* of Lorenzo Dagnino Pastore and Elida Josefina Locci de Dagnino Pastore; *m.* Irene Lipka 1959; two *d.*; ed. Escuela Argentina Modelo, Nacional San Martín,

Universidad de la Plata, and Univ. of California and Harvard Univ.
Member of teaching and research bodies, Univs. of La Plata, Buenos Aires and Harvard; adviser at univs., secretariats and to Ministries of Executive Control; Chief Investigator, Torcuato di Tella Inst.; Dir. of Investigations FIEL; Prof., Faculty of Econ. Science, Univ. of Buenos Aires and Argentine Catholic Univ.; Minister of Economy, Province of Buenos Aires 66-68; Sec. to Nat. Devt. Council 68-69; Minister of Economy and Labour June 69-June 70; recipient of awards from Inst. of Int. Educ., UN, OAS and Rockefeller Foundation; Ovidio Gimenez Foundation Prize 64.
Publs. *Argentine Economic Policy* 70, books and articles in economic journals.
Valentín Vergara 1834, Florida, Provincia de Buenos Aires, Argentina.
Telephone: 791-1083.

Dahanayake, Wijeyananda; Ceylonese politician; b. 22 Oct. 1902; ed. Richmond Coll. Galle and St. Thomas' Coll. Mount Lavinia.
Trained teacher; elected mem. Galle Municipal Council 35-59, Mayor of Galle 39, 40 and 41; elected to the State Council for Bibile 44; M.P. 48-; Minister of Education 56-59; Prime Minister, Sept. 59-March 60; Minister of Home Affairs 65-June 70; mem. Nat. State Assembly 72-; founded Ceylon Dem. Party 59; Hon. LL.D. (Vidyalankara Univ.), Hon. D.Litt. (Vidyodaya Univ.).
c/o National State Assembly, Colombo; Home: 225 Richmond Hill Road, Galle, Sri Lanka.
Telephone: 09-2403 (Home).

Dahl, Charles Raymond; American business executive; b. Brooklyn, N.Y.; ed. Cooper Union School of Engineering, New York and Stanford Graduate School of Business.
Joined Crown Zellerbach Corpn. 50, Man. pulp and paper mill, Bogalusa La. 61-64, Vice-Pres. 64, Exec. Vice-Pres. 69, Pres. and Chief Exec. Officer Feb. 70-; mem. Board of American Paper Inst.; mem. Nat. Industrial Pollution Control Council.
Crown Zellerbach Corporation, One Bush Street, San Francisco, Calif. 94119, U.S.A.

Dahl, Odd; Norwegian research engineer; b. 3 Nov. 1898, Drammen; *s.* of Laurits Dahl and Olga Sørensen; *m.* Vesse Mathiesen 1927; one *s.*
Air pilot and photographer, Roald Amundsen Arctic *Maud* Expedition 22-25, photograph travel, Amazon Basin 26; Research Asst. Carnegie Inst., Washington 27, Asst. Physicist 28-36, magnetic field work, Asia 28; Research Engineer, Chr. Michelsens Inst. Norway 37-68, Consultant 68-; mem. of the Institute 43-; in charge design and construction, Norwegian-Dutch Nuclear Reactor, Kjeller, Norway 48; Group Dir. European Council for Nuclear Research (C.E.R.N.) 52-55; in charge design and construction Norwegian boiling heavy water reactor project (H.B.W.R.) 55; mem. Norwegian Academy of Science; awarded prize, American Asscn. for the Advancement of Science (jointly with Tuve and Hafstad) 31; awarded prize, Norwegian Engineering Soc. 51; Commdr. St. Olav (Norway) and Commdr. of Orange-Nassau; Hon. D.Phil. (Univ. of Bergen).
Leisure interest: building sailing-ship models.
Chr. Michelsens Institut, Nygardsgaten 114, Bergen, Norway.
Telephone: Bergen 217633.

Dahl, Robert Alan, PH.D.; American professor of political science; b. 17 Dec. 1915; *s.* of Peter I. Dahl and Vera Lewis Dahl; *m.* 1st Mary Louise Barlett 1940, (deceased 1970), three *s.* one *d.*; *m.* 2nd Ann Goodrich

Sale 1973; ed. Univ. of Washington, Div. of Economic Research, Nat. Labor Relations Board and Yale Univ. Management Analyst, U.S. Dept. of Agriculture 40; Economist, Office of Production Management, O.P.A.C.A. and War Production Board 40-42; U.S. Army 43-45; Yale Univ., successively Instructor, Asst. Prof., Assoc. Prof. and now Sterling Prof. of Political Science 46-; Chair. Dept. of Political Science 57-62; Ford Research Prof. 57; Lecturer in Political Science, Flasco, Santiago, Chile 67; Guggenheim Fellow 50; Fellow, Center for Advanced Study in the Behavioral Sciences 55-56 and 67; Fellow, American Acad. of Arts and Sciences, American Philosophical Soc., Nat. Acad. of Sciences; Trustee, Center for Advanced Study in the Behavioral Sciences; mem. Educ. Advisory Board, Guggenheim Foundation.
Publs. *Congress and Foreign Policy* 50, 64, *Domestic Control of Atomic Energy* (with R. Brown) 51, *Politics, Economics and Welfare* (with C. E. Lindblom) 53, *A Preface to Democratic Theory* 56, *Social Science Research on Business* (with Haire and Lazarsfeld) 59, *Who Governs?* 61, *Modern Political Analysis* 63, *Political Oppositions in Western Democracies* 66, *Pluralist Democracy in the United States* 67, *After the Revolution* 70, *Polyarchy: Participation and Opposition* 71, *Regimes and Opposition* 72, *Democracy in the United States* 72.
Department of Political Science, Brewster Hall, Yale University, New Haven, Conn. 06520, U.S.A.

Dahlbeck, Eva; Swedish actress and author; b. 8 March 1920, Nacka; d. of Edvard Dahlbeck and Greta Österberg; m. Col. Sven Lampell 1944; two s.; ed. Royal Dramatic Theatre School, Stockholm.
Films acted in include: *The Counterfeit Traitor* 61, *Biljett till Paradiset* 61, *För att inte tala om alla dessa Kvinnor* 64, *Alskande par* 64, *Kattorna* 65, *Les Créatures* 65, *Den Röda Kappan* 66.
Plays acted in include: *Candida* 61, *Ändå älskar vi varavdra* 63, *Tchin-Tchin* 63, *The Balcony* 64, *Doctors of Philosophy* 64.
Leisure interests: reading, music.
Publs. *Dessa mina minsta* (play) 55, *Hem till Kaos* (novel) 64, *S'is'ta Spegeln* (novel) 65, *Den S'junde Natten* (novel) 66, *Domen* (novel) 67, *Med Seende Ögon* (novel) 72, *Hjrätslagen* (novel) 74, *Saknadens Dal* (novel) 76.
Home: 35 Chemin Pont du Centenaire, CH 1213 Onex, Switzerland; Office: c/o Svenska Filminstitutet, Kungsgatan 48, Stockholm C, Sweden.
Telephone: 924452.

Dahlgaard, Tyge; Danish economist and politician; b. 8 April 1921, Copenhagen; s. of Bertel Dahlgaard (q.v.); m. Karen Joergensen 1947; two d.; ed. Copenhagen Univ.
Junior Economist, Ministry of Agriculture 47-49; Perm. Rep. to UN, Geneva 49-50; Asst. Head of Section (Multilateral Econ. Problems), Ministry for Foreign Affairs 50-54; Danish Sec.-Gen. Nordic Cttee. for Econ. Co-operation 54-57; Counsellor, Danish Perm. Del. to OEEC, Paris 57-59; Counsellor (Econ. Affairs), Danish Embassy, Washington, D.C. 59-64; Amb. and Perm. Rep. to EEC, ECSC and Euratom, Brussels 64-66; Minister of Commerce and European Market Relations 66-Oct. 67; Amb. to Yugoslavia 68-72; Amb. to Japan and Korea 72-.
Leisure interests: music, piano playing, reading political and historical literature.
c/o Danish Embassy, Denmark House, 6th Floor, 17-35 Minami Aoyama 4-chome, Minato-ku, Tokyo 107, Japan.
Telephone: 404-2331.

Dahl-Iversen, Erling, M.D., D.M.SC.; Danish surgeon; b. 30 Nov. 1892, Copenhagen; s. of Anders Dahl-Iversen and Catherine Pedersen; m. Inga Margrethe

Thortsen 1925; two s.; ed. Univ. of Copenhagen and Copenhagen hospitals.
Professor of Surgery, Univ. of Copenhagen 35-63, Emeritus 63-; Surgeon-in-Chief, Univ. Clinic C, Rigshospitalet, Copenhagen 35-63; Hon. Fellow American Coll. of Surgeons, Royal Coll. of Surgeons (U.K. and Ireland); Hon. mem. Soc. int. de chirurgie; Foreign Assoc. Académie de Chirurgie, Paris.
Publs. *Etude expérimentale de l'influence de la cholécystectomie sur les voies biliaires et la sécrétion gastrique* 24, *Operative Surgery* 39, *Special Urological Diagnostics* 42, *Physical Signs in Surgery* 44, *Clinical Surgery I* 52, *II* 55, *The Importance of Sex-Hormones in the Physiological and Pathological Conditions of the Breast* 35, *The Influences of Endocrines in the Post-operative Period* 55, *Surgery in Denmark in the 19th Century* 60, *Surgery in Denmark in the 18th Century* 65, and numerous surgical papers.
Leisure interest: painting.
Tranegaardsvej 24, Copenhagen-Hellerup, Denmark.
Telephone: Hellerup 7820.

Dahrendorf, Ralf Gustav, DR.PHIL., PH.D.; German sociologist and politician; b. 1 May 1929, Hamburg; s. of Gustav Dahrendorf and Lina Witt; m. Vera Banister 1954; three d.; ed. Hamburg Univ. and London School of Economics.
Assistant 54, Privatdozent in sociology at Univ. of Saar, Saarbrücken 57; Fellow, Center for Advanced Study in the Behavioral Sciences, Palo Alto, U.S.A. 57-58; Prof. of Sociology, Hamburg 58, Tübingen 60, Constance 66 (on leave since 69); First Dean of the Faculty of Social Science, Univ. Constance 66-67; Visiting Prof. at several European and North Amer. univs.; Vice-Chair. of Founding Cttee. of Univ. Constance 64-66; Adviser on educational questions to the Land Govt. of Baden-Württemberg 64-68; Chair. of the Comm. on Comprehensive Univ. Planning 67-68; mem. German Council of Educ. 66-68; mem. Free Dem. Party (FDP) 67, Fed. Exec. 68-74; mem. Land Diet of Baden-Württemberg and Vice-Chair. FDP Parl. Party 68-69; mem. Fed. Parl. (Bundestag) and Parl. Sec. of State in Foreign Office 69-70; mem. Comm. of the European Communities 70-74; Pres. German Sociological Soc. 67-70; Chair., Royal Univ. of Malta Comm. 72-74; Dir. European Centre for Research and Documentation in Social Sciences 66-; mem. German PEN Centre 71-, Hon. Presidium of the Anglo-German Soc. 73-; Senator Max-Planck-Gesellschaft 75-; Dir. London School of Economics 74-; BBC Reith Lecturer 74; Hon. Fellow, London School of Economics 73; Fellow, Imperial Coll., London, 74; Hon. mem. Royal Irish Acad. 74; Foreign Hon. mem. American Acad. of Arts and Sciences 75; Grand Croix de l'Ordre du Mérite du Sénégal 71; Grand Croix de l'Ordre du Mérite du Luxembourg 74; Grosses Bundesverdienstkreuz mit Stern und Schulterband (Fed. Republic of Germany) 74; Grosses goldenes Ehrenzeichen am Bande (Austria) 75; Grand Croix de l'Ordre de Léopold II (Belgium) 75; Hon. D.Litt. (Univ. Reading) 73, LL.D. (Univ. Manchester) 73, D.Sc. (New Univ. of Ulster) 73, D. Univ. (Open Univ.) 74, D.H.L. (Kalamazoo Coll.) 74, Litt.D. (Trinity College, Dublin) 75; Journal Fund Award for Learned Publications 66.
Publs. include: *Marx in Perspective* 53, *Industrie- und Betriebssoziologie* 56, *Homo Sociologicus* 59, *Soziale Klassen und Klassenkonflikt* 57 and 59, *Die angewandte Aufklärung* 63, *Gesellschaft und Demokratie in Deutschland* 65, *Pfade aus Utopia* 67, *Essays in the Theory of Society* 68, *Konflikt und Freiheit* 72, *Plädoyer für die Europäische Union* 73, *The New Liberty: Survival and Justice in a Changing World* (Reith Lectures) 75.
London School of Economics and Political Science, Houghton Street, London, WC2A 2AE, England.
Telephone: 01-405-7686.

Daiches, David, M.A. (EDIN.), D.PHIL (OXON.), PH.D. (CANTAB.); British university professor and writer; b. 2 Sept. 1912, Sunderland; s. of Dr. Salis and Flora (née Levin) Daiches; m. Isobel J. Mackay 1937; one s. two d.; ed. George Watson's Coll., Edinburgh, Edinburgh Univ. and Balliol Coll., Oxford.
Bradley Fellow, Balliol Coll., Oxford 36-37; Asst. Prof. of English, Univ. of Chicago 40-43; Second Sec. British Embassy, Washington 44-46; Prof. of English, Cornell Univ. 46-51; Univ. Lecturer in English, Cambridge Univ. 57-61, Fellow of Jesus Coll., Cambridge 57-62; Dean, School of English Studies, Univ. of Sussex 61-67, Prof. of English 61-; Hon. Litt.D. (Brown Univ., Edinburgh Univ.); Dr. h.c. (Sorbonne); many awards and prizes.
Leisure interests: music, talking.
Publs. 35 books including: *The Novel and the Modern World* 39, *A Study of Literature* 48, *Robert Burns* 50, *Two Worlds* 56, *Critical Approaches to Literature* 56, *Literary Essays* 56, *Milton* 57, *A Critical History of English Literature* 60, *More Literary Essays* 68, *Scotch Whiskey* 69, *Sir Walter Scott and his World* 71, *A Third World* (autobiography) 71, *Robert Burns and his World* 71, *Prince Charles Edward Stuart* 73, *Robert Louis Stevenson and his World* 73, *Was* 75, *Moses* 75, *James Boswell and His World* 76.
Downsview, Wellhouse Lane, Burgess Hill, RH15 OBN, Sussex, England.

Dainton, Sir Frederick Sydney, Kt., F.R.S., M.A., B.SC., PH.D., SC.D.; British scientist and university administrator; b. 11 Nov. 1914, Sheffield; s. of George Whalley and Mary Jane Dainton; m. Barbara Hazlitt, PH.D., 1942; one s. two d.; ed. Central Secondary School, Sheffield, St. John's Coll., Oxford and Sidney Sussex Coll., Cambridge.
University Demonstrator in Chemistry, Cambridge Univ. 44, H. O. Jones Lecturer in Physical Chem. 46; Prof. of Physical Chem. Leeds Univ. 50-65; Vice-Chancellor, Univ. of Nottingham 65-70; Prof. Dept. of Physical Chem., Univ. of Oxford 70-73; Visiting Prof. Univ. of Toronto 49; Mass. Inst. of Technology 59; Tilden Lecturer Chemical Soc. 50; Lecturer, Univ. of Notre Dame, Indiana 52; Cornell Univ. 61, Univ. of Alberta 62; Fellow, St. Catharine's Coll., Cambridge 45, Praelector 46; Chair., Asscn. for Radiation Research 64-66, Advisory Cttee. for Scientific and Technical Information 66-; Pres. Faraday Soc. 65-67, Chemical Soc. 72-73, Asscn. for Science Educ. 67; mem. Council for Scientific Policy 65-, Chair. 70-73; Cen. Advisory Council for Science and Technology 67-; Chair. Advisory Board for Research Councils 72-; Chair. Univ. Grants Cttee. 73-; Trustee British Museum (Nat. Hist.); Hon. mem. Royal Soc. of Science, Uppsala, American Acad. of Arts and Sciences; Göttingen Acad. of Sciences; Hon. Fellow, St. Catharine's Coll., Cambridge 61, St. John's Coll., Oxford 68; Hon. Sc.D., Lódz and Trinity Coll., Dublin; many hon. degrees from British and foreign Univs.; Sylvanus Thompson Medal, British Inst. of Radiology 58; Davy Medal, Royal Soc. 69, Faraday Medal, Chemical Soc. 73.
Leisure interests: walking, colour photography.
Publs. *Chain Reactions* 56, 2nd edn. 66, *Photochemistry and Reaction Kinetics* 68; numerous papers in scientific journals on reaction kinetics, especially photo and radiation chemistry, polymer chemistry and on scientific policy and education.
University Grants Committee, 14 Park Crescent, London, W1N 4DH; Home: Fieldside, Water Eaton Lane, Kidlington, Oxford, England.
Telephone: 01-636-7799 (Office).

Dakin, Allin Winston, M.A., M.B.A.; American educational administrator; b. 2 June 1905, Mason City, Iowa; s. of Channing E. and Norra Allin Dakin; ed. State Univ. of Iowa and Harvard Univ.

Instructor in Commerce, State Univ. of Iowa 26-29; J. & W. Seligman & Co. and Tri-Continental Corpn. (investment bankers and investment trust), New York 31-34; Bursar and Commerce Dept., Robert Coll., Istanbul 34-39; Bursar, American Coll. for Girls, Istanbul 35-39; Controller, Pomona, Scripps and Claremont Colls. 40-44; Admin. Dean, State Univ. of Iowa 44-73, Dean Emeritus 73-; Fellow, Archaeological Inst. of America, Nat. Geographical Soc., Amer. Geographic Soc., Inst. Int. de Ideales Americanistas (Mexican Section), Nat. Council, Boy Scouts; District Gov., Vice-Pres. and Dir. Rotary Int.; Chair. Rotary Convention Cttee. 60; Chair. Rotary Int. Finance Cttee. 63, Program Planning 66, Public Relations 67 and numerous other cttees.; Pres. UN Asscn., Iowa, Dir. and Pres. 62-70; Dir. Partners for the Alliance 65-; Hon. LL.D., Westmar; Kt. Scottish Rite Masonry.
Leisure interests: travel, music.
Publs. *Foreign Securities in the American Money Market* 32, *Adventuring Around Africa.*
Home: 329 Ellis Avenue, Iowa City, Iowa, U.S.A.
Telephone: 319-338-8687 (Home).

Dakov, Mako; Bulgarian politician; b. 5 Dec. 1920, Pleven; m. Milka Stefanova 1951; two d.; ed. studies in forestry engineering.
Director of Scientific Research, Inst. of Forestry 50-51; Prof. Higher Forestry and Technical Inst. 51-57; Deputy Minister of Agriculture and Forestry 57, subsequently Chair. Cttee. for Forestry; Minister for Forestry and Forest Industry 66-71; Deputy Chair. Council of Ministers July 71-.
Leisure interest: sport (especially tennis).
Publs. more than 120 publications on politics, economics and forestry.
Council of Ministers, Sofia, Bulgaria.
Telephone: 87-61-51.

Dalai Lama, The (Tenzin Gyatso); Tibetan ruler and religious leader; Fourteenth Incarnation; b. 6 July 1935.
Born of Tibetan peasant family at Taktser in Amdo Prov.; enthroned at Lhasa 40; rights exercised by regency 34-50; assumed power 50; fled to Chumbi in S. Tibet after abortive resistance to Chinese 50; negotiated agreement with China 51; Vice-Chair. Standing Cttee., mem. Nat. Cttee. CCPCC 51-59; Hon. Chair. Chinese Buddhist Asscn. 53-59; Del. to Nat. People's Congress 54-59; Chair. Preparatory Cttee. for the Autonomous Region of Tibet 55-59; Dr. of Buddhist Philosophy 59; Supreme Head of all Buddhist sects in Tibet.
Publs. *My Land and People* 62, *Losar Migje* (The Opening of the Wisdom Eye) 63, *Umai Dhemig* (Key to the Middle Way) 71.
Thekchen Choling, Dharmsala Cantt., Kangra District, Himachal Pradesh, India.

Dale, William B.; American financial official; b. 24 March 1924; ed. Wayne High School, Michigan, Univ. of Michigan and Fletcher School of Law and Diplomacy.
Assistant U.S. Treasury Rep., Brussels 48-50, Acting U.S. Rep. 51-52; Deputy Chief, British Commonwealth and Middle East Div., U.S. Treasury Dept. 52-53; U.S. Treasury Rep. in Middle East 53-55; Program Man., Int. Research, Stanford Research Inst., Washington 56-61; Dir. Bureau of Int. Programs, U.S. Dept. of Commerce 61-62; Deputy Asst. Sec. for Int. Affairs, U.S. Dept. of Commerce 62; U.S. Exec. Dir. Int. Monetary Fund 62-74, Man. Dir. March 74-.
6008 Landon Lane, Bethesda 14, Md., U.S.A.

Daley, Richard J.; American lawyer and politician; b. 1902, Chicago; m. Eleanor Guilfoyle; four s. three d.; ed. Nativity of Our Lord Grammar School, De La Salle High School and De Paul Univ.
Member, Illinois House of Representatives 36-38; mem.

Illinois Senate 39-43, Floor Leader 42; Tax Dir. of Illinois 49-52; Clerk of Cook County 53-55; Mayor of Chicago 55-; several decorations; Democrat.
Leisure interest: fishing.
Room 507, City Hall, Chicago, Illinois, U.S.A.

Dalhousie, 16th Earl of; Simon Ramsay, Kt., G.B.E., M.C., D.L., LL.D.; British politician and Governor-General; b. 17 Oct. 1914; ed. Eton Coll., and Oxford Univ.
Served in Black Watch 36-45; Mem. of Parl, 45-50; Conservative Whip 46-48; Gov. Gen. Fed. of Rhodesia and Nyasaland 57-63; Lord Lieut. County of Angus 67-; Hon. LL.D. (Dundee Univ.) 67.
Brechin Castle, Brechin, Scotland.

Dali, Salvador; Spanish painter; b. 11 May 1904; ed. Acad. of Fine Arts, Madrid and Paris.
Impressionist, Futurist, Constructivist and Surrealist; designer of film scenarios, scenery and costumes for ballet and opera; lecturer in Museum of Modern Art, New York 35; Exhbn. of Jewels, London 60; retrospective exhbn., Rotterdam 70-71.
Publs. *Babaoua, Secret Life of Salvador Dali, Hidden Faces, Fifty Secrets of Magic Craftmanship, Dali on Modern Art, The World of Salvador Dali, Le Mythe Tragique de l'Angélus de Millet, Diary of A Genius.*
c/o Carstairs Gallery, 11 East 57th Street, New York 22; Hotel St. Regis, Fifth Avenue and 55th Street, New York 22, New York, U.S.A.; Port-Lligat, Cadaqués, Spain.

Dalldorf, Gilbert, M.D., D.SC.; American experimental pathologist and administrator; b. 12 March 1900, Davenport, Iowa; s. of Julius and Hulda (Leisner) (Dalldorf) Goos; m. Frances Elizabeth Barnhart 1926; one s. one d.; ed. Univs. of Iowa and Freiburg, New York Univ. and Cornell Univ. Medical Coll.
Pathologist, New York Hospital 26-30; Dir. of Laboratories, Grasslands Hospital 30-45; Dir. Div. of Laboratories and Research, N.Y. State Dept. of Health and Prof. of Pathology, Albany Medical Coll. 45-57; Prof. Univ. of Buffalo Medical School 50-57, Graduate School of Cornell Univ. 58-67; retd.; mem. Sloan-Kettering Inst. 58-67, Nat. Acad. of Sciences, Asscn. of American Physicians, Asscn. of Immunology, Soc. of Experimental Pathology, Asscn. of Public Health Labs. (Pres. 42); research, in vitamin deficiency diseases 26-37, in virus diseases 37-57, and in neoplastic diseases 58-69; Dr. h.c., Albert Ludwigs Univ. and Bowdoin Coll.; Fisher Memorial Award 51, Distinguished Service Award, New York Univ. Alumni 56, Albert Lasker Award 59; Medal of New York Acad. of Medicine 64.
Leisure interest: sailing.
Publs. *Avitaminoses* (with Walter Eddy) 37-41, *Introduction to Virology* 55, *Fungi and Fungous Diseases* 62.
Oxford, Maryland 21654, U.S.A.
Telephone: 301-226-5357.

Dalle, François Léon Marie, L. EN D.; French business executive; b. 18 March 1918, Hesdin; s. of Joseph and Jeanne (née Dumont) Dalle; m. Sophie Camplez; two s. two d.; ed. Saint-Joseph de Lille and Faculté de Droit, Paris.
Former advocate, Court of Appeal; Deputy Dir.-Gen. Société Monsavon 45; Pres.-Dir.-Gen. Société Monsavon-L'Oréal 57; Pres.-Dir.-Gen., L'Oréal 61-; mem. Exec. Council, Conseil National du Patronat Français; Vice-Pres. Admin. Council, Inst. Pasteur; Admin. INSEAD, Philips, Saipo, Lancôme, Nestlé, Banque Nat. de Paris, Union des Annonceurs, Centre Européen d'Education Permanente, Institut de l'Entreprise; mem. Exec. Council Entreprise et Progrès; Pres.-Dir.-Gen. Mennen France; Légion d'Honneur, Médaille de la Résistance, Officier des Palmes Académiques; Commendator della Repubblica Italiana.
Leisure interests: writing, hunting.
Publs. *L'Entreprise du Futur* (with J. Bounine-Cabale)

71, *Quand l'Entreprise s'Eveille a la Conscience Sociale* (with J. Bounine-Cabale) 75.
L'Oréal, 14 rue Royale, 75008 Paris; Home: 11 rue de Chanaleilles, 75007 Paris, France.
Telephone: 260-35-80 (Office); 551-17-25 (Home).

Dalley, Christopher Mervyn, C.M.G., M.A., M.I.MECH.E., F.INST.PET.; British oil executive; b. 26 December 1913, U.K.; s. of late Christopher Dalley; m. Elizabeth A. Gammell 1947; one s. three d.; ed. Epsom Coll., Surrey and Queens' Coll., Cambridge.
Served in Royal Navy 39-45; joined British Petroleum Co. 46; Iranian Oil Producing Co. 54-62; Iraq Petroleum Co. and assoc. cos., Man. Dir. 63-70, Chair. 70-73; Dir. Viking Resources Trust 73-; Chair. Oil Exploration (Holdings) 73-, Viking Jersey Equipment Ltd. 73; Order of Homayoun (Iran).
Home: Mead House, Woodham Walter, near Maldon, Essex and 6 Godfrey Street, London, S.W.3, England.
Telephone: Danbury 2404 (Essex); 01-352-8260.

Dalrymple, Ian Murray, B.A., F.R.S.A.; British writer, film producer and director; b. 26 Aug. 1903, Johannesburg, S. Africa; s. of late Sir William Dalrymple and Lady Dalrymple; m. 2nd Joan Magaret Craig 1939; three s. one d.; ed. Rugby School and Trinity Coll., Cambridge.
Film Editor 27-35; writer of screen plays 35-40; Exec. Producer, Crown Film Unit, Ministry of Information 40-43; Assoc. Exec. Producer, M.G.M.-London Films 43-46; Producer and Man. Dir. Wessex Film Productions Ltd. 46-; Advisory Producer, British Lion Film Corpn. Ltd. 52-54; Chair. British Film Academy 57-58; Fellow, Royal Soc. of Arts.
Leisure interests: reading, weeding.
Principal productions: *A Cry from the Streets, The Admirable Crichton, A Hill in Korea, Raising a Riot, The Heart of the Matter, Bank of England, The Changing Face of Europe* (a series of six short films in colour on European recovery), *The Wooden Horse, All over the Town, Once a Jolly Swagman, Dear Mr. Prohack, Esther Waters, The Woman in the Hall, Western Approaches, Target for To-night, London Can Take It, Chaucer's Tale;* as writer of screen plays: *South Riding, The Citadel, Storm in a Teacup, Pygmalion,* etc.
3 Beaulieu Close, Cambridge Park, Twickenham, TW1 2JR, England.

Dalton, Jack; American librarian; b. 21 March 1908, Holland, Virginia; s. of John Preston and Selma (Butler) Dalton; m. Mary Armistead Gochnauer 1933; one s.; ed. Virginia and Michigan Univs.
Instructor in English, Virginia Polytechnic Inst. 30-34; Reference Librarian, Univ. of Virginia 34-42, Assoc. Librarian 42-50, Librarian 50-56; Dir. Int. Relations Office, American Library Asscn. 56-59; Dean, School of Library Service, Columbia Univ. 59-70; Dir. Library Devt. Center, Columbia Univ. 70-.
School of Library Service, Columbia Univ., New York 27, N.Y.; Home: 445 Riverside Drive, New York, N.Y. 10027, U.S.A.
Telephone: MO3-3359.

Daly, John (Charles), Jr.; American (b. South Africa) broadcaster; b. 20 Feb. 1914; s. of John Charles and Helen Grant (Tennant) Daly; m. Margaret Criswell Neal 1937 (deceased), Virginia Warren 1960; four s. two d.; ed. Boston Coll.
Schedule Engineer, Capital Transit Co., Washington 35-37; Corresp. and News Analyst, Columbia Broadcasting System 37-49; Special Events Reporter and White House Corresp. 37-41, service in U.S.A., Europe and South America for C.B.S. 45-49; Corresp.-Analyst, American Broadcasting Co., also Moderator, television programmes on all networks; Vice-Pres. American Broadcasting Co., in charge of News, Special Events and Public Affairs 53-60; mem. Water Pollution Control Advisory Board 60-62; Dir. Voice of America 67-68.
1070 Park Avenue, New York, N.Y. 10028, U.S.A.

Dam, (Carl Peter) Henrik, DR. PHIL.; Danish biochemist; b. 21 Feb. 1895, Copenhagen; s. of Emil Dam and Emilie Peterson; m. Inger Olsen 1924; ed. Polytechnic Inst., Copenhagen and Univ. of Copenhagen. Instructor in Chemistry, School of Agriculture and Veterinary Medicine, Copenhagen 20, Physiological Laboratory, Univ. of Copenhagen 23; Assoc. Prof. Inst. of Biochemistry, Univ. of Copenhagen 29-41; Prof. of Biochemistry and Nutrition, Polytechnic Inst. Copenhagen 41-65, Prof. emeritus Polytechnic Inst. Copenhagen 65-; Dir. Biochemical Div. of Danish Fat Research Inst. 56-63; mem. Royal Danish Acad. of Sciences and Letters, Danish Acad. of Tech. Sciences; Pres. Danish Nutrition Soc. 67-71, 75-; Fellow, American Inst. of Nutrition; mem. of several other scientific socs.; studied Microchemistry with F. Pregl Graz 25, Metabolism of Sterols in Rudolf Schönheimer's Laboratory, Freiburg 32-33 (Rockefeller Fellow), worked with P. Karrer, Zürich 35, and later; lectured in U.S. and Canada 40-41 and 49; research work, Woods Hole Marine Biological Laboratories 41; Senior Research Assoc. Univ. of Rochester, N.Y. 42-45; Assoc. mem. Rockefeller Inst. for Medical Research 45-48; Joint Hon. Pres. Int. Union of Nutritional Sciences; awarded Nobel Prize 43 (for discovery of Vitamin K); Hon. F.R.S. (Edinburgh), Hon. D.Sc. (St. Louis Univ.).
Leisure interests: travel, history of science and culture.
Office: Østervoldgade 10 III, 1350 Copenhagen K; Home: Jagtvej 229, 2100 Copenhagen Ø, Denmark.

Damas-Aléka, Georges; Gabonese politician; b. 18 Nov. 1902, Libreville; m.; eight c.; ed. Mission Catholique de Libreville, Ecole Universelle (correspondence course) Paris, diplomatic training course, Quai d'Orsay, Paris.
Worked in bank 24-39; Chief Accountant, Compagnie Maritime des Chargeurs Réunis, Libreville 39-59; del. Conseil d'Admin., Gouvernement Gén. dé l'Afrique Equatoriale Française 43-46; deputy mem. Privy Council to Gov. of Gabon 48-54; Town Councillor, Libreville 56-63; employee of Gabonese Admin. 60; Civil servant Jan. 61-; Amb. to EEC, Belgium, Netherlands and Luxembourg 61, to Fed. Repub. of Germany 63; M.P. (Gabon) April 64-; Pres. of Nat. Assembly April 64-; Vice-Pres. Comm. of Parl. Conf. of CEEEAMA Asscn. Dec. 64-Dec. 65, Pres. Dec. 65-Dec. 66, Vice-Pres. Dec. 66-; Admin., Shell-Gabon Co., Port Gentil 60-; Composer of *La Concorde* (Gabon Nat. Anthem); Chevalier, Légion d'Honneur, Etoile Noire du Bénin, Ordre des Arts et Lettres de la Repub. Française, Grand Officier, Etoile Equatoriale, Ordre Nat. Gabonais, Ordre du Mérite Centrafricaine, etc.
Publs. *L'Homme Noir, Recueil des Allocutions prononcées par M. Georges Damas-Aléka.*
Office of the President of the National Assembly, National Assembly Buildings, Libreville, Gabon.

Dambe, Amos Manyangwa; Botswana diplomatist; b. 30 March 1911, Nswazwi, Francistown; m. Grace Dambe 1951; three s. five d.; ed. Tati Training Inst. and Adams Coll.
Primary school teacher until 62; Party Organizer, Botswana Democratic Party, then Asst. Gen. Sec. until 68; mem. Parl. for Mmadinare 65-; Minister of Commerce, Industry and Mines 65-66, of Home Affairs 66-68, of Works and Communications, of Agriculture; Amb. to U.S.A. 72-; British Empire Medal 48, Presidential Order of Honour (Botswana) 75.
Leisure interests: football, tennis, cricket, bowling.
Embassy of Botswana, 4301 Connecticut Avenue, N.W., Washington, D.C. 20008; Home: 3560 Brandywine Street, N.W., Washington, D.C. 20008, U.S.A.
Telephone: (202) 244-4990-1 (Office).

Damon, Roger Conant, B.A.; American banker; b. 4 Aug. 1906, Fitchburg, Mass.: s. of Isaac and Marion (Conant) Damon; m. Ruth T. Hawley 1931; one d.;
ed. Hotchkiss School, Yale Coll, and Stonier Graduate School of Banking.
Joined First Nat. Bank of Boston 29, Asst. Cashier 36-41, Asst. Vice-Pres. 41-43, Vice-Pres. 43-52, Senior Vice-Pres. 52-59, Dir. 56-, Pres. and Chair. of Exec. Cttee. 59-71, Chair. of Board and Chief Exec. Officer 66-71; Chair. First Nat. Boston Corpn. 70-71; Dir. Edison Co., New England Mutual Life Insurance Co., Raytheon Co., Massachusetts Bay United Fund Inc., Eastern Air Lines Inc., Howard Johnson Co., Liberty Mutual Insurance Co., and other companies; official of other financial and educational orgs.
Leisure interests: golf, duck-shooting, salt-water fishing.
172 Beacon Street, Boston, Mass. 02116, U.S.A.

Dănălache, Florian; Romanian politician; b. 9 July 1915, Bucharest; m. Virginia Dănălache; one s. one d.; ed. Acad. of Economic Studies, Bucharest.
Member Romanian Communist Party 44; mem. Central Cttee. 55-; alt. mem. Exec. Cttee. of Central Cttee. of R.C.P. 65-67, mem. Exec. Cttee. 67-; First Sec., Bucharest Town Cttee. of the R.C.P. 54-66; Minister of Railroads 66-69; Chair. Romanian Gen. Trade Union 69-71; Minister of Transport and Telecommunications Feb. 71-72; Chair. Central Union of Handicraft Co-operatives 72-; Deputy to Grand Nat. Assembly 52-; mem. of Grand Nat. Assembly Presidium 58-61; Chair. Comm. for Defence of Grand Nat. Assembly 61-66; Hero of Socialist Labour.
UCECOM, Calea Plennei 46, Bucharest, Romania.

Danckwerts, Rt. Hon. Sir Harold Otto, Kt., P.C., M.A.; British lawyer; b. 23 Feb. 1888, London; s. of W. O. Danckwerts, K.C. and Mary Lowther; m. 1st Florence Pride 1918 (died 1969), one s. one d.; m. 2nd Ella Hamilton Marshall 1969; ed. Winchester Coll., Balliol Coll., Oxford, and Harvard Law School, U.S.A.
Called to Bar Lincoln's Inn 13; served in First World War 14-19; practised as Barrister until May 49, also Tutor and Reader to the Law Society 14-41; Bencher of Lincoln's Inn 41; Junior Counsel to the Treasurer and Board of Trade in Chancery Matters and Counsel to the Attorney-Gen. in Charity Matters 41-49; apptd. Judge of the High Court of Justice (attached to the Chancery Div.) 49-61; knighted July 49, Lord Justice, Court of Appeal 61-69; Treasurer of Lincoln's Inn 62; retd. 69.
Leisure interests: making model ships, wood-carving, photography.
4 Stone Buildings, Lincoln's Inn, London, W.C.2, England.

Danckwerts, Peter Victor, M.A., S.M., G.C., M.B.E., F.R.S.; British chemical engineer; b. 4 Oct. 1916, Southsea; s. of Vice-Admiral V. H. Danckwerts, C.M.G. and Joyce Middleton; m. Lavinia Anne MacFarlane 1960; ed. Winchester Coll. School, Balliol Coll., Oxford, Mass. Inst. of Technology.
Served in Royal Navy (Lieut.) 40-46; Graduate Student, Mass. Inst. of Tech. 46-48; Lecturer, Cambridge Univ. 48-54; Deputy Dir. of Research and Devt., U.K. Atomic Energy Authority, Industrial Group 54-56; Prof. of Chem. Eng. Science, Imperial Coll. of Science and Tech. 56-59; Shell Prof. of Chem. Eng. 59-; E. V. Murphree Award of American Chem. Soc.; Hon. Foreign Fellow, American Acad. of Arts and Sciences.
Publs. *Gas-Liquid Reactions* 70, numerous scientific papers.
Department of Chemical Engineering, Pembroke Street, Cambridge, England.
Telephone: 58231.

Dange, Shripad Amrit, M.P.; Indian trade union leader; b. 10 Oct. 1899; m. 1928; two d.
Took a prominent part in organizing Textile Workers' Unions in Bombay; one of the founders of Indian

Communist Party 24; arrested on many occasions for trade union and political activity; sentenced to twelve years' transportation in the Meerut conspiracy trial; released 36; imprisoned 39-43; Pres. Girni Kamgar Union; Pres. All-India T.U.C. 43-45; Del. to W.F.T.U. Paris 45, Moscow 46; Vice-Pres. W.F.T.U. 48; Editor and Founder of *Socialist* 22, first Marxist paper in India; Editor and Founder of *Kranti,* first working-class paper in Marathi language; mem. Legislative Assembly, Bombay 46-51; imprisoned 48-50; Gen. Sec. All-India Trade Union Congress 49-; mem. Legislative Assembly, New Delhi 57-61, 67-; Chair. Indian Communist Party 62-.
Leisure interests: history, philosophy, literature.
Publs. *Gandhi versus Lenin* 21, *Hell Found* 27, *Literature and the People* 45, *India from Primitive Communism to Slavery* 49, *One Hundred Years of our Trade Unions* 52, *Mahatma Gandhi and History* 68, *When Communists Differ* 70, etc.
9 Kohinoor Road, Dadar, Bombay 14, India.

Danialov, Abdurakhman Danialovich; Soviet politician; b. 1908; ed. Moscow Inst. of Water Economy and Higher Party School.
Member C.P.S.U. 28-; State and party work 37-40; Chair. Council of Ministers, Dagestan Autonomous Republic 40-48, First Sec. Dagestan Regional Cttee. C.P.S.U. 48-67; Cand. mem. Central Cttee. C.P.S.U. 52-56, mem. 56-; Chair. Presidium, Dagestan A.S.S.R. Supreme Soviet 67-; Deputy Supreme Soviet U.S.S.R.; mem. Presidium Supreme Soviet 66-.
Presidium of the Dagestan A.S.S.R. Supreme Soviet, Makhachkala, Dagestan A.S.S.R., U.S.S.R.

Daniel, (Elbert) Clifton, Jr.; American newspaperman; b. 19 Sept. 1912, Zebulon, N.C.; s. of Elbert and Elvah Daniel; m. Margaret Truman 1956; four s.; ed. Univ. of North Carolina.
Associate Editor *Daily Bulletin,* Dunn, N.C. 33-34; Reporter *News and Observer,* Raleigh, N.C. 33-37; Associated Press, New York City, Washington, Berne, London 37-43; *New York Times* 44-, London SHAEF Headquarters, Paris, Middle East, Germany, U.S.S.R. 44-55, New York City 55-, Asst. to Managing Editor 57-59, Asst. Managing Editor 59-64, Managing Editor 64-69, Assoc. Editor 69-; D.Litt. 70.
Leisure interests: reading, swimming.
New York Times, 229 W. 43rd Street, New York City 36, N.Y., U.S.A.

Daniel, Glyn Edmund, M.A., PH.D., LITT.D.; British archaeologist; b. 23 April 1914, Lampeter Velfrey; s. of late John Daniel and Mary Jane Edmunds; m. Ruth Langhorne 1946; ed. Barry County School, Univ. Coll. of S. Wales (Cardiff), and St. John's Coll., Cambridge.
In Cambridge 32-, except for service in R.A.F. during Second World War (Photo Intelligence: Wing Commdr. in Charge Air Photographic Interpretation, India and S.E. Asia Command); Fellow, St. John's Coll., Cambridge 38-, Univ. Lecturer in Archaeology 45-74, Disney Prof. of Archaeology 74-; Dir. of Studies in Archaeology and Anthropology, St. John's Coll., Cambridge; Dir. Anglia Television Ltd.; Editor *Antiquity* and *Ancient Peoples and Places* series 57-.
Leisure interests: travelling, walking, writing detective stories.
Publs. *The Three Ages* 42, *A Hundred Years of Archaeology* 50, *The Prehistoric Chamber Tombs of England and Wales* 50, *The Megalith Builders of Western Europe* 56, *The Prehistoric Chamber Tombs of France* 60, *New Grange* (with S. P. O'Riordain) 64, *Man Discovers his Past* 67, *The Origins and Growth of Archaeology* 68, *The First Civilisations* 68, *Archaeology and the History of Art* 70, *Megaliths in History* 73, *France before the Romans* 74.

St. John's College, Cambridge; Home: The Flying Stag, 70 Bridge Street, Cambridge, England.
Telephone: 61621 (College); 56082 (Home).

Daniel-Lesur, J. Y.; French composer; b. 19 Nov. 1908, Paris; s. of Robert and Alice (née Thiboust) Lesur; m. Simone Lauer 1943; one s. one d.; ed. Paris Conservatoire.
Musical Adviser to Radiodiffusion-Télévision Française; Principal Insp. of Music at Ministry of Cultural Affairs; Admin. de la Réunion des Théâtres Lyriques Nationaux; Insp.-Gen. of Music, Ministry of Cultural Affairs; contrib. to *Arts La Gazette des Lettres, Polyphonie, La Revue Musicale* and other publs.; teaches, and writes film music; Dir. hon. Schola Cantorum, mem. Conseil Supérieur de l'Enseignement musical, French Comm. UNESCO; Officier, Légion d'Honneur, Commdr. Ordre Nat. de Mérite, Officier Ordre des Arts et des Lettres; Grand Prix du Conseil Général de la Seine, Grand Prix de Paris, Lauréat Acad. des Beaux Arts.
Leisure interest: Racing Club de France.
Works include: *Suite Française pour Orchestre* 35, *Passacaille* 37, *Pastorale pour Petit Orchestre* 38, *Ricercare pour Orchestre* 39, *Quatre Lieder pour Chant et Orchestre* 33-39, *Trio d'Anches* 39, *Trois Poèmes de Cécile Sauvage* 39, *Quatuor à Cordes* 41, *L'Enfance de l'Art* 42, *Variations pour piano et orchestre à Cordes* 43, *Clair comme le Jour* 45, *Suite pour Trio à Cordes et Piano* 43, *Suite Médiévale pour Flûte, Harpe et Trio à Cordes* 44, *Chansons Cambodgiennes* 46, *Berceuses à tenir éveillé* (chant) 47, *Pastorale variée pour piano* 47, *Ballade pour piano* 48, *Andrea del Sarto* (symphonic poem) 49, *Dix chansons populaires à trois voix égales* 50, *Ouverture pour un festival* 51, *Chansons françaises à quatre voix mixtes* 51, *L'Annonciation* (cantata) 52, *Cantique des Cantiques, pour 12 voix mixtes* 53, *Concerto da Camera pour piano et Orchestre de Chambre* 53, *Cantique des Colonnes pour ensemble vocal féminin et orchestre* 54, *Sérénade pour orchestre à Cordes* 54, *Le Bal du Destin* (ballet), *Elégie pour deux guitares* 56, *Symphonie de Danses* 58, *Messe du Jubilé pour choeur mixte, orchestre et orgue* 60, *Fantaisie pour deux pianos, Trois études pour piano* 62, *Chanson de mariage pour choeur de voix de femmes* 64, *Deux Chansons de Marins pour choeur d'Hommes* 64, *Deux Chansons de bord pour choeur mixte* 64, *Andrea del Sarto* (2-act opera) 68, *Contre-Fugue pour deux pianos* 70, *Symphonie* 74, *Nocturne pour hautbois et orchestre à cordes* 74.
82 Boulevard Flandrin, 75116 Paris, France.
Telephone: 727-49-86.

Daniels, John Hancock; American business executive; b. 28 Oct. 1921, St. Paul Minn.; s. of Thomas L. Daniels and Frances Hancock Daniels; m. Martha Hill Williams 1942; two s. two d.; ed. St. Paul Acad., Phillips Exeter Acad., Yale Univ., and Harvard Univ.
Archer Daniels Midland Co. 46, Flax Buyer, and Sales Management, Linseed Oil Div., Asst. Vice-Pres. 55-57, Dir. of Production and Procurement, Dehydrated Alfalfa Div. 56-57, Vice-Pres., Dir. and Manager Formula Feed Div. 57-58, Pres. and Chief Exec. Officer 58-68, Chair. of Board 68-72; Chair. National City Bancorpn. 72-; Pres. Mulberry Resources Inc. 72-; Dir. SOO Line Railroad, Nat. City Bank of Minneapolis, Warwick Electronics Inc.; Trustee of Cttee. for Econ. Devt.; mem. Business Council; Dir. Masters of Foxhounds Asscn. of America.
Leisure interest: foxhunting.
75 South Fifth Street, Minneapolis, Minn. 55402; Home: 2472 Parkview Drive, Hamel, Minn. 55340, U.S.A.
Telephone: 612-340-3186 (Office).

Danielsson, Bengt Emmerik, PH.D., Swedish anthropologist and writer; b. 6 July 1921, Krokek; m. Marie-Thérèse Sailley 1948; one s. one d.; ed. Univ. of Uppsala, Sweden and Univ. of Washington, Seattle.
Field research among Jibaro Indians, Upper Amazonas

6-47, in Tuamotu Archipelago, French Polynesia 49-51, Australia 55-56; mem. Kon-Tiki Expedition 47; Assoc. Anthropologist Bernice P. Bishop Museum Honolulu, ꓷ2-; mem. Pacific Science Board expedition to Tuamotu Archipelago 52; Leader George Vanderbilt expedition ꓕo Society Islands 57, Swedish TV expedition to South ꓢeas 62; technical adviser for film *Mutiny on the Bounty* 61; Producer series *Terry's South Sea Adventures*; ꓢwedish Consul French Polynesia 60-67, 71-; Dir. Nat. Museum of Ethnography, Stockholm 67-71.
Publs. *The Happy Island* 51, *The Forgotten Islands of ꓕhe South Seas* 52, *Love in the South Seas* 54, *Work and Life on Raroia* 55, *From Raft to Raft* 59, *What Happened ꓳn the Bounty* 62, *Gauguin in the South Seas* 65; Children's Books: *Terry in the South Seas* 57, *Terry in Australia* 58, *Terry's Kon-Tiki Adventure* 63, *La découverte de la Polynésie* 72, *Moruroa, mon amour* 74.
Papehue, Paea, Tahiti; Box 558, Papeete.
Telephone: 82474; 82320.

Daninos, Pierre; French writer; b. 26 May 1913, Paris; m. 1st Jane Marrain 1942, 2nd Marie-Pierre Dourneau 1968; one s. two d.; ed. Lycée Janson de Sailly.
Began as journalist 31; liaison agent to the British Army, Flanders 40; Columnist for *Le Figaro*.
Leisure interests: loafing, tennis, collecting British hobbies.
Publs. *Les Carnets du Bon Dieu* (Prix Interallié) 47, *Sonia, les autres et moi* (Prix Courteline) 52, *Les Carnets du Major Thompson* 54, *Vacances à Tous Prix* 58, *Un Certain Monsieur Blot* 60, *Le Jacassin* 62, *Snobissimo* 64, *Le 36e Dessous* 66, *Le Major Tricolore* 68, *Le Plus que Parfait* 70, *Le Pyjama* 72, *Les Touristocrates* 74.
81 rue de Grenelle, Paris 7e, France.

Dankevich, Konstantin Fyodorovich; Soviet composer; b. 1905, Odessa; ed. Odessa Conservatoire.
Professor, Odessa Conservatoire 48-53, Kiev Conservatoire 53-; mem. C.P.S.U. 46-; mem. Ukrainian and U.S.S.R. Composers' Unions; Honoured Worker of the Arts of the Ukrainian S.S.R. 41, People's Artist of the U.S.S.R. 54; Orders of Red Banner of Labour 51, of Lenin 60.
Principal compositions: Festival Overture 28, *Night of the Tragedy* (opera) 33, *No Pasarán* (suite for symphony orchestra) 36, *Othello* (symphonic poem) 37, First Symphony (for 20th Anniversary of October Revolution) 37, *Taras Shevchenko* (symphonic poem) 38, *Lily* (ballet) 40, Second Symphony (dedicated to heroic mothers of First World War) 45, *Bogdan Khmelnitsky* 53, *1917* (symphonic poem) 56, *Youth Greets Moscow* 56, *October* (oratorio).
Composers' Union of the Ukrainian S.S.R., 3 Ulitsa Chekistov, Kiev, U.S.S.R.

Dannay, Frederic (co-writer with late Manfred B. Lee under *pseudonym* **Ellery Queen**); American writer and editor; b. 20 Oct. 1905, Brooklyn, New York; s. of Meyer H. Nathan and Dora Wallerstein; m. Hilda Wiesenthal 1947 (deceased); two s.; ed. Boys High School, Brooklyn.
Editor *Ellery Queen's Mystery Magazine* 41-; Editor 70 anthologies; Visiting Prof., Univ. of Texas 58-59; owner of Ellery Queen Collection of First Editions of mystery short stories and Sherlock Holmes in Library of Univ. of Texas; many awards including 5 "Edgars", Grand Master 60 and Columba Mystery Award, Iona Coll. 68.
Leisure interests: book and stamp collecting, reading, theatre, television and spectator sports.
Publs. include 63 crime and mystery novels (34 about Ellery Queen), 7 books of short stories (about Ellery Queen), 3 books of criticism, history and bibliography, 4 novels under pseudonym Barnaby Ross, biographical novel, as by Daniel Nathan, *The Golden Summer*. 53
29 Byron Lane, Larchmont, New York 10538, U.S.A.

Danson, Hon. Barnett (Barney) Jerome, P.C.; Canadian politician; b. 8 Feb. 1921, Toronto; s. of Joseph and Saidie Eleanor Wolfe Danson; m. Isobel Bull 1943; four s.; ed. Public and High Schools, Toronto.
Served Queen's Own Rifles of Canada 39-45; joined Joseph B. Danson & Sons Ltd., insurance brokers 45; Sales Man. Maple Leaf Plastics Ltd. 50-53; Chair. Danson Corpn. Ltd. 53; mem. Parl. for York North 68-; mem. Standing Cttee. on Finance, Trade and Econ. Affairs, Vice-Chair. Standing Cttee. on External Affairs and Nat. Defence; Parl. Sec. to Prime Minister Trudeau 70-72; Minister of Urban Affairs Aug. 74-; mem. Canadian NATO Parl. Asscn., Canadian Group Inter-Parl. Union; Co-Chair. Canada/U.S. Interparl. Group; Del. to Interparl. Conf. on European Co-operation and Security 73; fmr. Chair. Soc. of Plastics Industry in Canada; mem. Board Soc. of Plastics Industry in New York, Canadian Mfrs. Asscn., Canadian Chamber of Commerce; Liberal.
Leisure interest: fishing.
Ministry of Urban Affairs, Ottawa, Ont.; Home: 111 Harrison Road, Willowdale, Ont.; Summer: Carling Bay, Nobel, Ont., Canada.

Danton, J. Periam, B.A., B.L.S., M.A., PH.D.; American professor and librarian; b. 5 July 1908, Palo Alto, California; s. of George Henry and Annina Periam; m. Lois King 1948; one s. one d.; ed. Leipzig, Columbia and Chicago Univs., and Oberlin and Williams Colls.
Served in N.Y. Public Library 28-29; Williams Coll. Library 29-30, American Library Asscn. 30-33; Librarian and Assoc. Prof. Colby Coll. Library 35-36; Librarian and Assoc. Prof. Temple Univ. 36-46; Del. Int. Fed. of Library Asscns. meetings 39, 64, 66, 67, 68, 69, 70, 71, 72; Visiting Prof., Univs. of Chicago 42 and Columbia 46; Lt., Lt.-Commdr., U.S.N.R. 42-45; Prof. Librarianship 46-, and Dean, School of Librarianship, Calif. Univ. 46-61; Pres. Asscn. American Library Schools 49-50; Fulbright Research Scholar (Univ. Göttingen) 60-61, (Vienna) 64-65; Guggenheim Fellow 71-72; U.S. Dept. of State, American Specialist, Ethiopia 61; Ford Foundation Consultant on Univ. Libraries in Southeast Asia 63; UNESCO Library Consultant, Jamaica 68; Surveyor and Consultant, numerous libraries; Dir. U.S. Dept. of State-American Library Asscn. Multi-Area Group Librarian Program 63-64; Guest Lecturer, The Hague 61, Univ. Toronto 63, Hebrew Univ. Jerusalem 65, Univ. Belgrade, Ljubljana and Zagreb 65, Univ. of British Columbia 68, McGill Univ. 69, Univ. Puerto Rico 70; Hon. Research Fellow, Univ. London 74-75.
Leisure interests: classical music, tennis, swimming, skiing, travel.
Publs. *Library Literature, 1921-32* 34, *Education for Librarianship* 49, *United States Influence on Norwegian Librarianship 1890-1940* 57, *The Climate of Book Selection: Social Influences on School and Public Libraries* 59, *Book Selection and Collections: A Comparison of German and American University Libraries* 63, *Jamaica: Library Development* 68, *Index to Festschriften in Librarianship* 70, *Between M.L.S. and Ph.D.: A Study of Sixth-Year Specialist Programs in Accredited Library Schools* 70, *The Dimensions of Comparative Librarianship* 73; mem. Board of Editors Asscn. of Coll. and Research Libraries *Monographs* 66-70, *Library Quarterly* 68-, *International Library Review* 68-.
School of Librarianship, University of California, Berkeley, Calif. 94720, U.S.A.
Telephone: 642-0924.

Dantzig, George Bernard, M.A., PH.D.; American professor of operations research and computer science; b. 8 Nov. 1914, Portland, Ore.; s. of Tobias and Anna G. Dantzig; m. Anne Shmuner 1936; two s. one d.;

ed. Univs. of Maryland, Michigan and California (Berkeley).
Junior Statistician, U.S. Bureau of Labor Statistics 37-39; Chief, Combat Analysis Branch, U.S.A.F. Headquarters Statistical Control 41-46; Mathematical Adviser, U.S.A.F. Headquarters 46-52; Research Mathematician, Rand Corpn., Santa Monica, Calif. 52-60; Chair. Operations Research Center and Prof., Univ. of Calif. (Berkeley) 60-66; Prof. of Operations Research and Computer Science, Stanford Univ. 66, C. A. Criley Chair. of Transportation Sciences; Int. Inst. for Applied Systems Analysis, Head of Methodology Project 73-74; mem. Nat. Acad. of Sciences.
Publs. *Linear Programming and Extensions* 63, *Compact City* (with Thomas L. Saaty) 73; over 100 published technical papers.
Department of Operations Research, Encina Commons, Stanford University, Calif. 94305, U.S.A.
Telephone: 415-497-4095.

Dantzig, Rudi Van; Netherlands choreographer; b. 4 Aug. 1933, Amsterdam; s. of Murk van Dantzig and Berendina Homburg; ed. High School and Art Coll. Took ballet lessons with Sonia Gaskell; joined Sonia Gaskell's co. Ballet Recital (later Netherlands Ballet), soloist 59; won Prix de la Critique (Paris) for choreography in *Night Island* 55; joint artistic dir. and principal choreographer Netherlands Nat. Ballet 68-; has also worked for London Dance Theatre, Ballet Rambert, The Royal Ballet, Harkness Ballet (New York), Bat-Dor (Tel-Aviv), Ballet d'Anvers (Antwerp) and Nat. Ballet of Washington; Ridder Oranje-Nassau 69.
Leisure interests: "The world, life, living, and everything concerned with that."
Choreography for: *Night Island* 55, *Jungle* 61, *Monument for a Dead Boy* 65, *Romeo and Juliet* 67, *Moments* 68, *Epitaaf* 69, *Astraal* 69, *The Ropes of Time* 70, *On Their Way* 70, *Painted Birds* 71, *Are Friends Delight or Pain* 72, *The Unfinished* 73.
1e Looiersdwarsstraat 27, Amsterdam, Netherlands.
Telephone: 245067.

Daoud, Lt.-Gen. Mohammad; Afghan army officer and politician; b. 18 July 1909; ed. Habibia Coll., Kabul, Pre-cadet School, Kabul, and in France.
Governor of Kandahar 32; Gov. and C.-in-C. Eastern Provinces 34; C.-in-C. Central Forces and Military Schools 37; suppressed revolt of 45; Prime Minister 53-63, concurrently Minister of Defence and of the Interior; led coup deposing King Mohammed Zahir Shah July 73; Pres., Prime Minister Repub. of Afghanistan 73-, also Minister of Foreign Affairs and Nat. Defence.
Office of the President, Kabul, Afghanistan.

Daphtary, Chandra Kisan; Indian lawyer; b. 1 April 1893, Bombay; s. of Kisanlal Daphtary; m. Sushila Chatterjee 1924; one s. two d.; ed. St. Paul's School, London, and Magdalene Coll., Cambridge.
Advocate-General, Bombay State 45-51; Solicitor-Gen. of India 51-63; Attorney-Gen. 63-68; Chair., Bar Council of India 63-68; mem. Rajya Sabha.
A-8 Maharani Bagh, Ring Road, New Delhi 14, India.
Telephone: 631066.

Darby, Harry, B.S., M.E.; American industrialist, farmer-stockman; b. 23 Jan. 1895, Kansas City, Kansas; s. of Harry and Florence Isabelle (Smith) Darby; m. Edith Marie Cubbison 1917; four d.; ed. local public schools Kansas, and Univ. of Illinois.
With Missouri Boiler Works Co. 11-15; Shop Supt. 15-17; Vice-Pres. 17-19; with The Darby Corpn. since 20; Pres. 23-45; at present Chair. of Board and owner; Dir. Commercial Nat. Bank, Kansas Heart Asscn. Inc., Navy League of U.S., Washington, D.C., Univ. of Kansas Research Foundation; mem. Advisory

Cttee. Nat. Rivers and Harbours Congress, Washington; Chair. State Highway Comm., Kan. 33-37, *Kansas City Post*, Soc. of American Mil. Engineers; Fellow, American Soc. of Mechanical Engineers; Chair. Emer. Board of Govs., American Royal Livestock and Horse Show; Dir. and mem. several other livestock asscns.; Nat. Conventions 40, 44 and 48; mem. Republican Del. to Republican Nat. Cttee. for Kansas 40-64, Exec. Cttee. of 15 of Republican Nat. Convention since June 44; U.S. Senator from Kansas 49-51; U.S. Army First World War; Chair. Board Eisenhower Foundation, Abilene, Kansas; Hon. LL.D. (Kansas and Missouri).
Office: First and Walker Avenue, Kansas City, Kan. 66110; Home: 1220 Hoel Parkway, Kansas City, Kan. 66102, U.S.A.

Darby, William Jefferson, M.D., PH.D.; American professor of nutrition; b. 6 Nov. 1913, Galloway, Ark.; s. of William J. and Ruth (Douglass) Darby; m. Elva Louise Mayo 1935; three s.; ed. Univs. of Arkansas and Michigan.
Assistant Professor, Biochemistry, Vanderbilt Univ. School of Medicine 44-46, Asst. Prof. Medicine 44-46, Asst. Prof. Biochemistry and Medicine 46-48, Prof. Biochemistry, Chair. Dept., Dir. Div. of Nutrition 49-71, Prof. Medicine in Nutrition 65-; mem. Council on Foods and Nutrition, American Medical Asscn. 48-62, Chair. 60-62; WHO expert panel on nutrition, consultant Yugoslavia, Austria, Indonesia, Egypt, Southern Rhodesia, Basutoland, Guatemala and other Central American countries 50-; mem. Cttee. of Consultants Interdepartmental Cttee. on Nutrition for Nat. Defense and Dir. of Surveys in the Philippines, Ethiopia, Ecuador, Lebanon, Jordan and Nigeria 55-63; Chair. Advisory Cttee. on Nutrition to the office of the Surgeon Gen., U.S. Army 59-72; mem. Panel on Nutrition, Space Science Board, Nat. Acad. of Sciences 62-72; Nat. Consultant to the Surgeon Gen., U.S. Air Force 67-72; mem. Scientific Advisory Cttee. the Nutrition Foundation Inc. 67-71, Pres. 72-; Public Trustee, Food and Drug Law Inst.; Co-Chair. Hazardous Materials Advisory Cttee., Environmental Protection Agency 71-; mem. or fmr. mem. of numerous other professional and public bodies; Hon. mem. El Colegio de Guatemala 50, Austrian Public Health Asscn. 51, Nat. Medical Society of Panama 51, Philippine Dietetic Asscn. 57, Serbian Acad. of Science 59; Conrad. A. Elvehjem Award for Public Service in Nutrition, American Inst. of Nutrition 72; Thomas Jefferson Award, Vanderbilt Univ. 69; Order of the Cedars of Lebanon 72, Star of Jordan 63, Order of Rodolfo Robles, Guatemala 59; numerous other awards.
Leisure interests: bibliophily, history of nutrition.
Publs. (with J. S. McLester) *Nutrition and Diet in Health and Disease* 52, (with V. N. Patwardhan) *The State of Nutrition in the Arab Middle East*, numerous other contributions to medical books, numerous articles.
The Nutrition Foundation Inc., 99 Park Avenue, New York, N.Y. 10016; Home: Route 2, Box 165 Thompson Station, Tenn. 37170, U.S.A.
Telephone: 212-687-4832 (Home); 615-794-6888.

D'Arcy, Rev. Martin Cyril, S.J., M.A.; British Roman Catholic priest; b. 15 June 1888, Bath; s. of Martin Valentine d'Arcy and Madeline Keegan; ed. Stonyhurst Coll., and Oxford.
Lecturer in Philosophy, Oxford Univ. 27-45; Master of Campion Hall, Oxford 33-45; English Provincial of the Society of Jesus 45-50; Hon. D.Litt. (Nat. Univ. of Ireland, Fordham Univ.), Hon. LL.D. (Georgetown Univ.).
Publs. *Thomas Aquinas* 30, *Mirage and Truth* 35, *Nature of Belief* 37, *Death and Life* 42, *The Mind and Heart of Love* 45, *Communism and Christianity* 56, *The Meeting of Love and Knowledge* 57, *The Sense of History* 59, *No*

Absent God 63, *Facing God* 66, *Facing the People* 68, *Humanism and Christianity* 69, *Facing the Truth* 69.
14 Mount Street, London, W.1, England.
Telephone: 01-493-7811.

Daridan, Jean-Henri; French diplomatist; b. 15 Aug. 1906; ed. Collège de Juilly, Ecole des Chartes and Univ. de Paris à la Sorbonne.
Entered French Ministry of Foreign Affairs 32; Third Sec. Rome, Prague 33-38; war and resistance services 42-44; Counsellor Chungking 45-46; Chargé d'Affaires Bangkok 47; Minister-Counsellor Washington 48-54; Deputy High Commr. French Indochina 54; Deputy Dir.-Gen. Political and Econ. Affairs, Paris 55, Dir.-Gen. 56; Ambassador to Japan 59-62; Diplomatic Adviser to French Govt. 63-65; Ambassador to India 65-70, concurrently to Nepal 65-67; Adviser to Cie. Schlumberger Ltd., Paris 70; two prizes from Académie Française; Commdr. Légion d'Honneur, Croix de Guerre, Hon. K.B.E. (U.K.).
Publs. *John Law, Père de l'Inflation* 38, *Abraham Lincoln* 62, *Noirs et Blancs, de Lincoln à Johnson* 65.
36 rue Sainte-Croix-de-la-Bretonnerie, Paris 4e, France.

Darken Lawrence Stamper, PH.D.; American physical chemist; b. 18 Sept. 1909, Brooklyn, N.Y.; s. of William H. Darken and Gertrude Stamper Darken; m. Margaret Fitzgerald 1939; three s. three d.; ed. Hamilton Coll., Clinton, N.Y. and Yale Univ.
Chemist with H. Kohnstamm Co., N.Y. 34-35; Physical Chemist, U.S. Steel Corpn. 35-54, Asst. Dir. 54-56, Asst. Dir. Fundamental Research Lab. 56-57, Assoc. Dir. 57-62, Dir. of Fundamental Research 62-71; Prof. of Mineral Sciences, The Pa. State Univ. 72-; Williams Lecturer, M.I.T. 56, Howe Lecturer, A.I.M.E. 61; Campbell Lecture, American Soc. for Metals 61, Jeffries and Carnegie Lectures 63, Sauveur Lecture 68; mem. Nat. Acad. of Sciences; Fellow, N.Y. Acad. of Sciences, American Asscn. for Advancement of Science, Metallurgical Soc. of A.I.M.E. and American Inst. of Chemists; Clamer Medal, Franklin Inst. 66, Hunt Award, A.I.M.E. 68; 20th Hatfield Memorial Lecturer, Sheffield Univ. 69; American Soc. for Metals Gold Medal 71.
Publs. *Physical Chemistry of Metals* (with R. W. Gurry) 53; numerous articles in professional journals.
248 Deike Building, The Pennsylvania State University, University Park, Pa. 16802, U.S.A.
Telephone: 814-865-9063.

Darling, Sir Frank Fraser (*see* Fraser Darling, Sir Frank).

Darling, Sir James Ralph, Kt., C.M.G., O.B.E., M.A.; British teacher and broadcasting official; b. 18 June 1899, Tonbridge, Kent; s. of Augustine M. Darling and Jane Baird (née Nimmo); m. Margaret Dunlop Campbell 1935; one s. three d.; ed. Repton School and Oriel Coll., Oxford.
Served in First World War; Schoolmaster, Liverpool 21-24, Charterhouse, Godalming 24-29; Headmaster, Geelong Church of England Grammar School, Australia 30-61; mem. Commonwealth Universities Comm. 42-51, Australian Broadcasting Control Board 55-61; Chair. Australian Broadcasting Comm. 61-67; Hon. Fellow and Past Pres. Australian Coll. of Educ.; Chair. Australian Road Safety Council 61-71; Chair. Australian Frontier Comm. 62-71, Pres. 71-, Immigration Publicity Council; mem. Melbourne Univ. Council 33-71; Vice-Pres. Australian Elizabethan Theatre Trust 64, now Pres.
Publs. *The Education of a Civilised Man, Timbertop,* etc.
3 Myamyn Street, Armadale, Victoria 3143, Australia.
Telephone: Melbourne 20-6262.

Darlington, Charles Francis, A.B.; American diplomatist; b. 13 Sept. 1904, New York City; s. of Charles Francis Darlington and Letitia Craig O'Neill; m. Alice N. Benning 1931 (died 1973); two s. one d.; ed. Harvard Univ., New Coll., Oxford and Inst. des Hautes Etudes Int., Geneva.
Worked in the Secr., LN, Geneva 29-31; with Bank of Int. Settlements, Basle 31-34; Asst. Chief, Div. of Trade Agreements, Washington 35-39; Foreign Exchange Man., Gen. Motors Overseas Operations 39-42; Lt. Commdr. U.S.N.R. 43-44; Sec. Exec., Steering and Co-ordination Cttees. UN, San Francisco 45; with Socony Mobil Oil Co., Iraq Petroleum Co., Near East Devt. Co. 46-61; Ambassador to Gabon 61-65.
Leisure interests: gardening, reading.
Publ. (with Alice B. Darlington) *African Betrayal* 68.
30 East 72nd Street, New York, N.Y. 10021, U.S.A.
Telephone: 212-861-8193.

Darlington, Cyril Dean, D.SC., F.R.S.; British scientist; b. 19 Dec. 1903, Chorley, Lancs.; two s. (one deceased) three d.; ed. St. Paul's School and Wye Coll.
Director, John Innes Institute 39-53; Emeritus Prof. of Botany, Oxford Univ. 53-71; Keeper, Oxford Botanic Garden 53-71; Hon. Fellow of Magdalen Coll.; foreign mem. Royal Danish Acad. and Accad. Nazionale dei Lincei; awarded Royal Medal of Royal Society for research in Cytology and Genetics 46; founder (with Sir Ronald Fisher) of *Heredity* 47.
Leisure interest: gardening.
Publs. *Chromosomes and Plant Breeding* 32, *Recent Advances in Cytology,* 3rd edn. 65, *The Handling of Chromosomes* (with L. F. La Cour) 5th edn. 69, *The Conflict of Science and Society* 48, *The Dead Hand on Discovery* 49, *Elements of Genetics* 49, *Genes, Plants and People* (with K. Mather) 50, *The Facts of Life* 53, (transl. French, German, Italian, Japanese), *Chromosome Botany and the Origins of Cultivated Plants* 3rd edn. 73, *Chromosome Atlas of Flowering Plants* (with A. P. Wylie) 2nd edn. 56, *Evolution of Genetic Systems* 2nd edn. 58, *Darwin's Place in History* 59, *Genetics and Man* 64, *Teaching Genetics* (co-editor) 63, *Chromosomes Today* (co-editor) 64-72, *Evolution of Man and Society* 69 (trans. in seven languages).
Botany School, Oxford, England.
Telephone: Oxford 53394.

Darlington, William Aubrey, C.B.E., M.A.; British dramatic critic, dramatist and writer; b. 20 Feb. 1890, Taunton, Somerset; s. of Thomas Darlington and Edith Bainbridge; m. Marjorie Sheppard 1918 (deceased); two d. (one deceased).
Shrewsbury School and St. John's Coll., Cambridge.
Served with Northumberland Fusiliers Great War 14-19; contrib. to *Punch* and other publs.; Editor *The World* 19; joined *Daily Telegraph* 20, Dramatic Critic 20-68; London Drama Corresp. *N.Y. Times* 39-60.
Leisure interests: theatre, reading, cricket and golf.
Publs. Plays: *Alf's Button, Carpet Slippers, The Key of the House, The Streets of London* (burlesque version); Novels: *Alf's Button, Wishes Limited, Egbert, Alf's Carpet, Mr. Cronk's Cases, Alf's New Button;* Criticism: *Through the Fourth Wall, Literature in the Theatre, Sheridan, J. M. Barrie, The Actor and his Audience, The World of Gilbert and Sullivan, Six Thousand and One Nights, Olivier;* also *I Do What I Like* (autobiography) and *A Knight Passed By* (translation of play by Jan Fabricius); contributor to *Encyclopaedia Britannica.*
Monksdown, Bishopstone, Sussex, England.
Telephone: 01-589-4918 and Seaford 892657.

Darmojuwono, H.E. Cardinal Justine; Indonesian ecclesiastic; b. 2 Nov. 1914, Godean.
Ordained Priest 47; Archbishop of Semarang 63-; created Cardinal by Pope Paul VI 67; Chair. Conf. of Indonesian Bishops; Bishop of the Indonesian Armed Forces; mem. of Congregation for Sacraments and Divine Worship; mem. Secr. for Non-Christians; mem. Presidium of Asian Bishops' Conf.
Jalan Pandanaran 13, Semarang, Java, Indonesia.
Telephone: Semarang 20348.

13

Darrieux, Danielle; French actress; b. 1 May 1917, Bordeaux; m. Georges Mitsinrides 1948; one s.; ed. Paris Univ.

Chevalier Légion d'Honneur.

Has played important roles in the following films: Le Bal, Mayerling, Un mauvais garçon, Battement de coeur, Premier rendez-vous, Ruy Blas, Le Plaisir, Madame de . . ., Le Rouge et le Noir, Bonnes à tuer, Le Salaire du péché, L'Amant de Lady Chatterley, Typhon sur Nagasaki, La Ronde, Alexander the Great, Marie Octobre, L'Homme à femmes, Les lions sont lâchés, Le Crime ne paie pas, le Diable et les Dix Commandements, Le Coup de grâce, Patate, Greengage Summer, Les demoiselles de Rochefort, 24 heures de la vie d'une femme, Divine.

Has acted in the following plays: la Robe mauve de Valentine 63, Gillian 65, Comme un oiseau 65, Secretissimo 65, Laurette 66, CoCo 70, Ambassador (musical) 71, Folie Douce 72.

2 Villa de la Tour, Paris 16e, France.

Dart, Justin; American business executive; b. 17 Aug. 1907; ed. Northwestern Univ.

Walgreen Co. 29-41, rose to Gen. Manager and Dir.; United Drug Co. (now Dart Industries Inc.) 41-, Pres. 46-, Chair., Pres. and Chief Exec. Officer 66-; Dir. United Air Lines 42-; Trustee, Univ. of Southern California 61-; Vice-Chair. Board of Trustees, Univ. of Southern California; Dir. Conles Communications.

8480 Beverly Boulevard, Los Angeles, Calif. 90048, U.S.A.

Dart, Raymond Arthur, M.SC., M.D., CH.M.; Australian anatomist; b. 4 Feb. 1893, Toowong, Brisbane, Queensland; s. of Samuel Dart and Eliza Ann Brimblecombe; m. Marjorie Frew 1936; one s. one d.; ed. Queensland and Sydney Univs.

House Surgeon, Royal Prince Alfred Hospital, Sydney 17-18; Capt. Australian Army Medical Corps 18-19; Senior Demonstrator in Anatomy, Univ. Coll., London 19-20; Fellow Rockefeller Foundation 20-21; Senior Demonstrator in Anatomy and Lecturer in Histology, Univ. Coll., London 21-22; Prof. of Anatomy 23-59, Dean Faculty of Medicine 25-43, Univ. of the Witwatersrand, Johannesburg; mem. Int. Comm. on Fossil Man 29-; Fellow Royal Society of South Africa 30-, mem. Council 38; mem. Board South African Inst. for Medical Research 34-46; mem. South African Medical Council 34-48; mem. S. African Nursing Council 44-50; Pres. S. African Soc. of Physiotherapy 59-68, Anthropological Section, Pan-African Congress of Prehistory 47-51, Vice-Pres. 59-63; Pres. S. African Asscn. for the Advancement of Science 52-53, Pres. Anthropological Section 25, Gold Medallist 39; Guest Lecturer, Viking Fund Seminar, N.Y. 49; Lowell Lecturer, Boston Oct. 49; John Hunter Memorial Lecturer, Sydney 50; Robert Broom Memorial Lecturer (Durban) 51; Senior Capt. Scott Medal, South African Biological Soc. 55; Hon. D.Sc. (Natal, Witwatersrand and La Salle Univs.); Viking Medal and Award for Physical Anthropology (New York) 57; Woodward Lecturer (Yale) 58; Simon Biesheuvel Medal 63; Pres. Asscn. Scientific and Technical Socs. of S. Africa 63-64; Fellow Inst. Biology, Foreign Fellow Linnaean Soc., London 74; Drennan Memorial Lecturer (Cape Town) 66; United Steelworkers Prof. of Anthropology in The Inst. of Man, in The Insts. for the Achievement of Human Potential 66-; Gold Medal, S. African Nursing Asscn. 70; Silver Medal, Medical Asscn. of S. Africa 72, L. S. B. Leakey Foundation Award 73, 80 year tribute for Human Evolution Nov. 73.

Publs. include: Australopithecus Africanus: the Man-Ape of South Africa 25, Racial Origins in the Bantu speaking Tribes of South Africa 37, African Serological Patterns and Human Migrations 51, The Osteodontokeratic Culture of Australopithecus Prometheus 57, Adventures with the Missing Link 59, Africa's Place in the Emergence of Civilisation 60, Beyond Antiquity 65.

20 Eton Park, Eton Road, Sandhurst, Johannesburg, South Africa.

Das, Sudhi Ranjan, B.A., LL.B.; Indian judge; b. 1 Oct. 1894, Calcutta; s. of late Rakhal Chandra and Binodini Das; m. Swapana Das 1919; two s. one d.; ed. Tagere's School, Santiniketan, Bangabasi Coll., Calcutta and Univ. Coll., London.

Called to Bar, Gray's Inn 18, to Calcutta Bar 19; Lecturer Univ. Law Coll., Calcutta; Additional Judge, High Court, Calcutta 42, Puisne Judge 44; Chief Justice East Punjab High Court (Simla) 49-50; Judge Fed. Court of India 50; Judge Supreme Court of India 50-55; Chief Justice of India 56-59; Vice-Chancellor, Visva-Bharati Univ. 59-66; Vice-Pres. Indian Council for Cultural Relations 64-65; Chair. Statesman Ltd. 68-; edited Mulla's Transfer of Property Act.

Leisure interests: reading and writing books.

Office: Swapanpuri, Kalimpong, West Bengal; Home: 118 Netaji S. C. Bose Road, P.O. Regent Park, Calcutta 40, India.

Telephone: Calcutta 46-3103.

Das Gupta, Bimal; Indian artist; b. 27 Dec. 1917; ed. Krishnalth Collegiate School, Berhampore, W. Bengal, and Govt. Coll. of Arts and Crafts, Calcutta.

Originally painted landscapes in water colours; is now avant-garde painter in oils; Senior Lecturer in Painting, Coll. of Art, Delhi 63-; paintings in Nat. Gallery of Modern Art, New Delhi, Nat. Gallery of Poland, Warsaw, Berlin Museum, Pilnitz Gallery, Dresden, Hermitage Gallery, Leningrad; one-man exhbns. in Delhi, Calcutta, Bombay, Madras, Amritsar, Mysore, Berlin, Poland, London, New York, Cairo, Moscow, Belgrade and Paris; exhibited at São Paulo Bienal, and int. exhbns. in Japan, New York and U.S.S.R.

Das Gupta, Prodosh Kusum, B.A.; Indian sculptor and writer; b. 10 Jan. 1912, Dacca; s. of late Nalini Nath Das Gupta and Charubala Das Gupta; m. T. C. Kamala 1940; two s.; ed. Univ. of Calcutta Government Schools of Arts and Crafts, Lucknow and Madras, Royal Acad. of Arts, London and Ecole de Grand Schaumère, Paris.

Founder, Calcutta Group (pioneer org. of modern art in India) 43, Sec. 43-51; Reader and Head, Dept. of Sculpture, Baroda Univ. 50; Prof. of Sculpture, Govt. Coll. of Arts and Crafts, Calcutta 51-57; Dir. Nat. Gallery of Modern Art, New Delhi 57-70; Pres. Third Congress, Int. Asscn. of Arts, Vienna 60; mem. Indian Artists' Dels. to U.S. and U.S.S.R.; represented India in int. sculpture competition The Unknown Political Prisoner, Tate Gallery, London; works in Nat. Gallery of Modern Art, New Delhi, Madras Museum, Acad. of Fine Arts Gallery, Calcutta and in private collections in India and abroad.

Leisure interests: music, photography, poetry, writing on art.

Publs. My Sculpture, Temple Terracottas of Bengal, Fallen Leaves, and numerous articles on art.

K-5 Jangpura Extension, New Delhi 14; Home: Umaramam, Trichur-4, Kerala, India.

Telephone: New Delhi 616123.

Dashti, Ali; Iranian writer, politician and diplomatist; b. 95; ed. Iraq.

Former mem. Majlis; fmr. Editor Shafaq Soekh (Red Dawn); Ambassador to Egypt 50, Amb. to Lebanon 60-63; Senator 63-.

Publs. novels, short stories, essays, analytical works on poetry of Hafez, Saadi, Rumi, Omar Khayam and Khaghani.

The Senate, Teheran, Iran.

Daskalakis, Apostolos; Greek university professor; b. 1903, Sparta; *s.* of Vassilios and Maria Daskalakis; *m.* Hellen Vranicus 1935; two *d.*; ed. Athens Univ. and Univ. de Paris à la Sorbonne.

Began career as journalist 21; Foreign Corresp. of various Athens newspapers 27-32; Prof. of Medieval and Modern History, Athens Univ. 39, of Ancient Greek History 50-54, and of Modern Greek History 55; Rector, Athens Univ. 53-55; Cultural Counsellor, Ministry of Foreign Affairs 50; Perm. Rep. of Greece to Council of Cultural Co-operation, Council of Europe, 52-73, Pres. 65; Hon. Prof. of many European univs.

Publs. *The Causes of the Greek War of Independence* 27, *Chypre hellénique à travers quarante siècles d'histoire* 32, *History of Modern Greece* 52, *The Hellenism of the Ancient Macedonians* 60, *La Bataille des Thermopyles* 62, *Alexander the Great* 63, *Rhigas Velestinlis* 64, *Texts and Sources of the History of Greek War of Independence* (6 vols.) 68, *The Greek People under the Turkish Empire* 70 and many other books and articles.

Apostolos Evrou 3, Athens 611, Greece.

Telephone: 7770151.

Dassault, Marcel; French aeronautical engineer; b. 22 Jan. 1892, Paris; *m.* Madeleine Minckès; two *s.* (Serge Dassault, *q.v.*); ed. Lycée Condorcet, Paris, and Ecole Nat. Supérieure de l'Aéronautique.

Responsible for prototypes of numerous civil and mil. aircraft 18-39; Partner Soc. d'études Marcel Dassault; Engineering Adviser and Technical Dir. Soc. des avions Marcel Dassault; Dir. Dassault Belgique Aviation 68-; fmr. Pres. Union syndicale des industries aéronautiques; Editor-in-Chief *Jours de France*; sole partner Soc. Régie—Jours de France 67-; Editor *Vingt-quatre heures* (daily) 65-66; Partner Soc. immobilière du rond-point des Champs-Elysées 68-; Deputy 51-55, 58-; Senator 57-58; Union des démocrates pour la République.

Assemblée Nationale, Paris 7e; Villa Dassault, avenue du Roi-Albert, 06 Cannes, France.

Dassault, Serge; French engineer; b. 4 April 1925, Paris; *s.* of Marcel Dassault (*q.v.*) and Madeleine Minckès; *m.* Nicole Raffel 1950; ed. Lycée Janson-de-Sailly, Ecole Polytechnique, Ecole Nat. Supérieure de l'Aéronautique, Centre de Perfectionnement dans l'Administration des Affaires and Inst. des Hautes Etudes de la Défense Nationale.

Director of Flight Testing, Avions Marcel Dassault 55-61, Export Dir. 61-63; Asst. Dir.-Gen. Electronique Marcel Dassault 63-67, Pres. Dir.-Gen. 67-; Pres. Fondation des Oeuvres Sociales de l'Air; Commissaire Général des Salons Internationaux de l'Aéronautique et de l'Espace; Pres. Asscn. Française pour la Participation dans les Entreprises; Chevalier de la Légion d'Honneur; Médaille de l'Aéronautique.

Leisure interests: golf, hunting.

55 quai Carnot, 92214 Saint-Cloud, France.

Telephone: 602-50-00.

Dassin, Jules; American film director; b. 12 Dec. 1911; *m.* Melina Mercouri (*q.v.*); ed. Morris High School. Attended drama school in Europe 36; Asst. Dir. to Alfred Hitchcock 40; films directed in U.S. include *Brute Force, Naked City, Night and the City*; settled in France 54 and directed *Rififi, Celui qui doit mourir, La Loi, Never on Sunday* 60, *Phaedra* 61, *Topkapi* 63, *10.30 p.m. Summer* 66, *Up Tight* 68, *Promise at Dawn* 70, *The Rehearsal* 74, etc.; Director's Prize, Cannes Film Festival 55 for *Rififi*.

c/o Alain Bernheim, 16 avenue Hoche, Paris 8e, France.

Datcu, Ion; Romanian diplomatist; b. 20 Feb. 1930, Brasov; *s.* of Ion and Maria Datcu; *m.* Viorica Datcu 1956; ed. history and philosophy.

Cultural Attaché, Romanian Embassy, Moscow 57-59; Press Attaché, Rome 59-61; Dir., Div. of Int. Organizations and mem. of the Board, Min. of Foreign Affairs 61-66; Del to UN Gen. Assembly 61-65; Rep. at confs.

of the ILO, Econ. Comm. for Europe and UNESCO; Amb. to Japan 66-69 and Australia 67-69; Rep. at sessions of Econ. Comm. for Asia and the Far East, Tokyo 67, Canberra 68 and Singapore 69; Rep. to UN Office and specialized agencies in Geneva, Del. to Cttee. on Disarmament Conf. and Rep. to ILO Governing Body 69-71; Perm. Rep. to UN 72-.

Leisure interests: theatre, classical music, tennis.

Permanent Mission of Romania to United Nations, 60 East 93rd Street, New York, N.Y. 10028, U.S.A.

Daube, David, D.IUR., PH.D., D.C.L., F.B.A.; university professor; b. 8 Feb. 1909, Freiburg-im-Breisgau; *s.* of Jakob Daube and Selma Daube (née Ascher); *m.* 1936, divorced 1964; three *s.*; ed. Berthold-gymnasium, Freiburg, and Univs. of Freiburg, Göttingen and Cambridge. Fellow of Caius Coll., Cambridge 38-46; Lecturer in Law, Cambridge; C-51; Prof. of Jurisprudence, Aberdeen 51-55; Regius Prof. of Civil Law, Oxford, and Fellow of All Souls Coll. 55-70, Emeritus Regius Prof. 70; Dir. Robbins Hebraic and Roman Law Collections and Prof.-in-Residence, School of Law, Univ. of Calif., Berkeley 70-; Senior Fellow, Yale Univ. 62; Gifford Lecturer, Edinburgh 62, 63; Lecturer at Uppsala Univ. 63; Ford Prof. of Political Science, Univ. of Calif., Berkeley 64; Riddell Lecturer, Newcastle 65; Gray Lecturer, Cambridge 66; Pope John XXIII Lecturer, Catholic Univ. of America, Washington 66; Messenger Lecturer, Cornell Univ. 71; Visiting Prof., Univ. of Constance 66-; Charles Inglis Romson Prof. of Law, Univ. Colorado 74; Fellow, British Acad. and Amer. Acad. of Arts and Sciences; Pres. Classical Asscn. of Great Britain 1976-77; Hon. Fellow, Oxford Univ. Centre for Postgraduate Studies 73, Gonville and Caius Colls., Cambridge; Corresp. mem. Göttingen and Bavarian Acads. of Sciences, Royal Irish Acad.; Hon. LL.D. (Edinburgh and Leicester); Dr. h.c. (Paris Sorbonne), Hebrew Union Coll.; Dr. Jur. h.c. (Munich).

Publs. *Studies in Biblical Law* 47, *The New Testament and Rabbinic Judaism* 56, *Forms of Roman Legislation* 56, *The Exodus Pattern in the Bible* 63, *The Sudden in the Scriptures* 64, *Collaboration with Tyranny in Rabbinic Law* 65, *Roman Law* 69, *Civil Disobedience in Antiquity* 72, *Ancient Jewish Law* (with Reuven Yaron) 76.

School of Law, University of California, Berkeley Calif. 94720, U.S.A.

Dauben, William Garfield, A.M., PH.D.; American professor of chemistry; b. 6 Nov. 1919, Columbus, Ohio; *s.* of H. J. Dauben and Leilah Stump; *m.* Carol Billings Hyatt 1947; two *d.*; ed. Ohio State, Harvard and Oxford Univs., and Eidgenössische Technische Hochschule, Zurich.

Postdoctoral Fellow, Harvard Univ. 44; at. Univ. of Calif., Berkeley 45-, Prof. of Chem. 58-; Editor-in-Chief *Organic Syntheses, Organic Reactions*; Consultant to U.S. Public Health Service, Nat. Science Foundation, Amer. Chem. Soc.; mem. Nat. Acad. of Sciences, American Chem. Soc., Chem. Soc. (London), Swiss Chem. Soc.

Leisure interests: golf, skiing.

Publs. scientific research articles in *Journal of the American Chemical Society* and *Journal of Organic Chemistry*.

20 Eagle Hill, Berkeley, Calif. 94707, U.S.A.

Telephone: 415-524-2142.

Daultana, Mian Mumtaz Muhammad Khan; Pakistani politician; b. 23 Feb. 1916; *s.* of the late Mian Ahmad Yar Khan Daultana; ed. Punjab Univ. and Corpus Christi Coll. Oxford Univ.

President Indian Majlis, Oxford Univ. 36-37; called to the Bar 39; Punjab Legislative Assembly, Muslim League Party Rep. 43, re-elected 51, Rep. from Sialkot Mohammedan Rural Constituency 46; Gen.-Sec., Punjab Provincial Muslim League 44-47; mem.

All-India Muslim League Cttee. of Action 46; mem. Indian Constituent Assembly 46, and first Pakistan Constituent Assembly 47; Finance Minister, Punjab 47; Pres., Punjab Muslim League 48; Chief Minister of the Punjab 51-53; Minister for Defence, Central Govt. Oct.-Dec. 57; Pres. Council Muslim League 67-72; participated Round Table Conf. as a mem. Democratic Action Cttee. 69; mem. Nat. Assembly 70; Amb. to the U.K. 72-.
Embassy of Pakistan, 35 Lowndes Square, London, SW1X 9NJ, England.

Daux, Georges; French Hellenist; b. 21 Sept. 1899, Bastia, Corsica; s. of Louis Daux and Célestine Digoy; m. Vida Pirjevec 1926; ed. Univ. of Paris.
Member French Archaeological School, Athens 20-24; Cultural Counsellor, French Embassy, Istanbul 24-26; Prof., Dean of the Faculty of Letters and Pres. of Dijon Univ. 27-45; Prof. of Greek History, Sorbonne and Dir. of French Archaeological School at Athens 45-69; mem. of Security Council's Comm. of Inquiry in the Balkans 47; mem. Inst. for Advanced Studies, Princeton 47-48; visiting Prof. Harvard 49-50; Sather Prof. Berkeley 56-57; Geddes-Harrower Prof., Aberdeen 70; mem. Deutsches Archäologisches Inst., Berlin, Accademia Pontificale, Rome, Yugoslav Acad., Zagreb, Deutsche Akademie der Wissenschaften, Berlin, American Philosophical Soc., Philadelphia, Accademia dei Lincei, Rome, Académie des Inscriptions, Paris, British Acad.; hon. life mem. Society for Promotion of Hellenic Studies, London, Archaeological Institute of America, New York, Société Archéologique, Athens and others; Dr. h.c. (Brussels and Liège).
Leisure interests: skiing, tennis, zoology.
6 avenue Paul Appell, Paris 14e, France.
Telephone: Paris 540-4928.

Davico, Oskar; Yugoslav poet and novelist; b. 1909; ed. Belgrade Univ.
Imprisoned for working with Resistance 41; escaped and joined partisans 43; mem. Fed. Cttee. on Film Censorship 58; recipient of several literary awards.
Publs. *With the Partisans of Markos, Poetry and Resistance, The Poem* (novel), *A Man's Man* (poetic drama), *Gedichte* 65.
c/o Serbian Writers' Association, Belgrade, Yugoslavia.

David, Donald Kirk, A.B., M.B.A.; American former foundation executive; b. 15 Feb. 1896; ed. Idaho and Harvard Univs.
Instructor Harvard Univ. Business School 19-21, Asst. Dean 20-27, Asst. Prof. of Marketing 21-26, Assoc. Prof. of Marketing 26-27; Vice-Pres. and Pres. of Royal Baking Powder Co. 27-30; Vice-Pres. Great Island Holding Corpn. 30-41; Pres. American Maize Products Co. 32-41; William Ziegler Prof. of Business Admin., Harvard Univ. Graduate School of Business Admin. and Assoc. Dean 42, Dean 42-55; Vice-Chair. of the Ford Foundation 56-66; Dir. of Aluminium Ltd., Ford Motor Co., Pan American World Airways, Inc., R. H. Macy & Co., Ind.; Trustee, The Rockefeller University; Dir. The Great Atlantic and Pacific Tea Co., Sinclair Oil Corp., City Investing Co.; Chair. Board of Cttee. for Econ. Devt. 57-62; Orders of Orange-Nassau and St. Olaf; Hon. LL.D. (Idaho Univ. 41, St. Lawrence Univ. 46, Harvard 48, Washington and Lee Univs. 49, Northeastern Univ. 51, Carleton Coll. 52, Colgate Univ. 54, Univ. of California 64); Hon. Litt.D. (Univ. of Western Ontario 51, Ohio Univ. 62).
Publs. *Retail Store Management Problems* 22, *Problems in Retailing* (with M. P. McNair) 26.
200 East 66th Street, New York, N.Y. 10022; also Osterville, Mass., U.S.A.

David, Edward Emil, Jr., SC.D.; American scientist; b. 25 Jan. 1925, Wilmington, N.C.; s. of the late Edward Emil and Beatrice Liebman David; m. Ann

Hirshberg 1950; one d.; ed. Georgia Inst. of Technology and Mass. Inst. of Technology (M.I.T.).
Joined Bell Telephone Laboratories 50; specialized in field of underwater sound and communication acoustics 50-63, in research in computing science 63-70; Science Adviser to Pres. Nixon and Dir. Office of Science and Technology (Exec. Office of the Pres.) Aug. 70-73; Exec. Vice-Pres. Gould Inc. 73-; Pres. Gould Laboratories 73-; Chair. Board of Trustees, Aerospace Corpn.; mem. Nat. Acad. of Sciences, Nat. Acad. of Engineering; Fellow, American Acad. of Arts and Sciences, Acoustical Soc. of America, Audio Engineering Soc., Amer. Asscn. for the Advancement of Science and Inst. of Electrical and Electronics Engineers; hon. degrees: Stevens Inst. of Technology, Polytechnic Inst. of Brooklyn, Carnegie-Mellon Univ., Univ. of Michigan, etc.
Leisure interests: tennis, skiing, minerals, photography, travel.
Publs. Co-author of *Man's World of Sound* 58, *Waves and the Ear* 60, *The Man-made World* 69; over 100 technical articles.
Gould Center, Rolling Meadows, Ill. 60008, U.S.A.

David, Václav; Czechoslovak politician and diplomatist; b. 23 Sept. 1910, Studený; ed. Commercial Coll., Prague.
Worked for ČKD Libeň 29-32; mem. of the illegal Central Cttee. of the Communist Party of Czechoslovakia 44-45; mem. of the Nat. Assembly 45-69; Minister of Foreign Affairs 53-68; Amb. to Bulgaria 69-71; mem. of Central Cttee. of the C.P. of Czechoslovakia 45-; Deputy to House of the People, Fed. Assembly 69-, Chair. 71-; mem. Presidium, House of the People, Fed. Assembly 71-, Deputy Chair. Fed. Assembly 71-; Deputy Chair. of Cen. Cttee. Czechoslovak-Soviet Friendship Union 53-72, Chair. 72-; several decorations for part in Resistance Movement during World War II; Order of the Republic 55; Klement Gottwald Order 60; Order of Victorious February 73.
Federal Assembly, Prague, Czechoslovakia.

Davidson, Alfred E.; American international lawyer; b. 11 Nov. 1911; s. of Maurice P. Davidson and Blanche Reinheimer; m. Claire H. Dreyfuss 1934; two s.; ed. Horace Mann School, Harvard Univ. and Columbia Law School.
Legislative Counsel, Exec. Office of President of U.S.A. 41; Gen. Counsel, Foreign Econ. Admin. 44-45, UNRRA 45, Int. Refugee Org. (Preparatory Comm.), Geneva 47; Dir. for Europe, Middle East and Africa, UNICEF 47; Econ. Adviser to UN Sec.-Gen. 51; Gen. Counsel Korean Reconstruction Agency, UN, New York 52; Exec. Asst. to Chair. of Board, Riotinto of Canada, N.Y.C. 55; int. law practice, including Dir. Channel Tunnel Study Group; Int. Econ. Adviser, Co. for Establishment of the Great Belt Bridge (Denmark) 59-69; Special Rep. of IFC in Europe, Paris 70-72; Counsel, Wilmer, Cutler & Pickering (law firm) 72-75; mem. Bars of N.Y.C. and D.C.; Dir. American Asscn. for Residents Abroad; co-founder, Asscn. for the Promotion of Humor in Int. Affairs.
Leisure interests: politics, reading, tennis, bridge.
Publs. articles in journals.
5 rue de la Manutention, Paris 16e, France.
Telephone: 7235168.

Davidson, George F., PH.D., LL.D., L.H.D.; Canadian public official; b. 18 April 1909, Bass River, Nova Scotia; s. of late Oliver Wendell Davidson and Emma Jane Sullivan; m. Elizabeth Ruth Henderson 1935; two s. one d.; ed. Univs. of British Columbia and Harvard.
Superintendent of Welfare and Neglected Children for British Columbia 34; Exec. Dir. Vancouver Welfare Fed. and Council of Social Agencies 35; Dir. of Social Welfare, British Columbia 39; Exec. Dir. of Canadian Welfare Council 42; Deputy Minister of Nat. Welfare

44-60, of Citizenship and Immigration 60-63; Dir. Bureau of Government Organization 63, Sec. of Treasury Board 64-67; Pres. Canadian Broadcasting Corpn. 68-72; Under-Sec.-Gen. of UN for Administration and Management 72-; has served since 46 as Canadian Rep. or mem. Canadian dels. to various sessions of UN Gen. Assembly, Economic and Social Council and Social Comm. and Chair. of the Social, Humanitarian and Cultural Cttee. 53; Pres. Inst. of Public Admin. of Canada 51; Pres. of the UN Economic and Social Council 58; Pres. Int. Conf. of Social Work 56-60; Chair. Nat. Joint Council of Public Service 54-60.
Leisure interests: music, travel, swimming, people.
United Nations, New York, N.Y. 10017; 400 East 54th Street, Apt. 24C, New York, N.Y. 10022, U.S.A.
Telephone: 754-1234, ext. 2181 (Office); 371-9087 (Home).

Davidson, Norman Ralph, PH.D.; American professor of chemistry; b. 5 April 1916, Chicago, Ill.; s. of Bernard R. Davidson and Rose Lefstein; m. Annemarie Behrendt 1942; three s. one d.; ed. Univ. of Chicago and Oxford Univ.
Professor of Chem., Calif. Inst. of Technology 67-; mem. Nat. Acad. of Sciences.
Publs. *Statistical Mechanics* 62, and numerous scientific articles.
Division of Chemistry and Chemical Engineering, California Institute of Technology, Pasadena, Calif. 91125; Home: 318 East Laurel Avenue, Sierra Madre, Calif. 91024, U.S.A.
Telephone: 213-795-6811 (Office); 213-355-1969 (Home).

Davidson, Ralph P.; American magazine publisher; b. 17 Aug. 1927, Santa Fe, N.M.; s. of Clarence and Doris Parsons Davidson; m. Jeanne Skidmore 1951; two s.; ed. Stanford Univ.
European Advertising Dir. Time-Life Int., London 64; Man. Dir. Time Int., New York 67; Asst. Publr. *Time* 68, Assoc. Publr. 69, Publr. 72-; Vice-Pres. Time Inc. 72-.
Leisure interests: reading, tennis, skiing.
Time Inc., Time & Life Building, Rockefeller Center, New York, N.Y.; Home: 494 Harbor Road, Southport, Conn., U.S.A.
Telephone: 212-556-3456 (Office); 203-259-3861 (Home).

Davie, Alan, C.B.E.; British painter; b. 1920, Grangemouth, Stirlingshire; s. of James W. Davie and Elizabeth Turnbull; m. Janet Gaul 1947; one d.; ed. Edinburgh Coll. of Art.
Jazz musician and maker of jewellery; Gregory Fellowship, Leeds Univ. 56-59; first one-man exhbn. Edinburgh 46; one-man exhbns. in Europe and U.S.A. 49-; rep. at Dunn Int. Exhbn., London 63; Prize for the best foreign painter at his one-man exhbn. at the 7th Bienal de São Paulo, Brazil 63; Gulbenkian Painting and Sculpture of a Decade Exhbn., Tate Gallery, London 64; several exhbns. at the Salon de Mai; one-man exhbns. at Gimpel Galleries in London, New York and Zürich 49-; exhbns. at Rome, Munich, Montreal, Texas, California 70, Switzerland, Los Angeles, Norway, Poland, Geneva, Cologne 71, New York 72; first public music recital, Tate Gallery and Gimpel Fils, London 71; three recordings 72; restropective exhbn. Edinburgh Festival, R.S.A. Galleries 72; music concerts 72, concerts and broadcasts 74; C.B.E. 72.
Leisure interests: gliding, music, photography, underwater swimming.
The Bottoms, St. Buryan, Penzance, Cornwall, England.

Davies, David Arthur, M.SC., F.INST.P.; British meteorologist; b. 11 Nov. 1913, Barry, Wales; m. Mary Shapland 1938; one s. two d.; ed. Univ. of Wales.
Meteorological Office, Air Ministry 35-39, R.A.F. 39-47; Principal Scientific Officer, Meteorological Office, Air Ministry 47-49; Dir. East African Meteorological Dept.,

Nairobi 49-55; Pres. W.M.O. Regional Asscn. for Africa 51-55; mem. Royal Inst. of Public Admin. 50-; Hon. mem. American Meteorological Soc. 70; Sec.-Gen. World Meteorological Org. 55-; Dr. h.c. (Physics) (Univ. of Bucharest) 70.
Leisure interests: music, reading.
Publs. include meteorological papers and articles on international co-operative efforts through meteorology.
World Meteorological Organization, 41 Avenue Giuseppe Motta, Geneva; Home: Chemin des Rojalets, 1296 Coppet, Vaud, Switzerland.
Telephone: 34-64-00 (Office); 76-18-26 (Home).

Davies, Rev. Jacob Arthur Christian, B.SC.; Sierra Leonean diplomatist; b. 24 May 1925; m.; ed. Univ. of Reading, Selwyn Coll., Cambridge Univ., Imperial Coll. of Tropical Agriculture.
Served in various capacities at Min. of Agriculture and Natural Resources and later became Perm. Sec.; Co-Man. of a project of the UN Development Programme, FAO 67-69, and later apptd. Chair. of the Public Service Comm.; fmr. Amb. to U.S.A.; High Commissioner to the U.K. and non-resident Amb. to Denmark, Sweden and Norway 72-74; Asst. Dir.-Gen. UN Food and Agriculture Org., Rome 74-75.
Leisure interests: philately, sports.
c/o Ministry of Foreign Affairs, Freetown, Sierra Leone.

Davies, Rt. Hon. John Emerson Harding, P.C., M.B.E., F.C.A., M.P.; British politician; b. 8 Jan. 1916, London; s. of Arnold Davies and Edith Harding; m. Vera Georgina Bates 1943; one s. one d.; ed. St. Edward's School, Oxford.
Trained as an accountant; Combined Operations experimental establishment Second World War; joined Anglo-Iranian Oil Co. 46; Svenska B.P. Stockholm 47-48, Paris 53-55 and London; Dir. S.F.B.P., Paris 51-60; Dir. B.P. Trading Ltd. 60-61; Vice-Chair. and Man. Dir. Shell-Mex and B.P. Ltd. 61-65; mem. Nat. Econ. Devt. Council (N.E.D.C.) 64-69, Council of Industrial Design 65-70, British Productivity Council 65-69, British Nat. Export Council 65-70; Dir.-Gen. Confederation of British Industry 65-69; Dir. Hill, Samuel Group Ltd. 69-70, 74-; mem. Parl. for Knutsford 70-; Minister of Technology July-Oct. 70; Sec. of State for Trade and Industry and Pres. of Board of Trade 70-72; Chancellor, Duchy of Lancaster, Minister for European Affairs 72-74.
Leisure interests: travel, music.
House of Commons, London, S.W.1, England.
Telephone: 01-628-8011.

Davies, Paul Lewis, B.S.; American manufacturer; b. 27 July 1899; ed. Univ. of California and Graduate School of Business Harvard Univ.
Clerk, Nat. Bank of Commerce, N.Y. 22; Asst. Cashier, Asst. Vice-Pres., Vice-Pres. Wells Fargo Bank, San Francisco 29-33; Vice-Pres. and Treas. Food Machinery Corpn. 29-33, Exec. Vice-Pres. 33-40; Pres. FMC Corpn. (fmrly. Food, Machinery and Chemical Corpn.) 40, Chair. of Board 56-66, Senior Dir. 67-72, Senior Dir. Emeritus 72-; Dir. Stanford Research Inst., etc.; Senior Man. Dir. Lehman Brothers Inc. 66-73, Senior Consultant 73; Bechtel and Davies 73-; mem. Business Council; Trustee, Cttee. for Econ. Devt.; mem. Advisory Council, School of Business Admin., Univ. of Calif.; Dir. Nat. Industrial Conf. Board, Int. Business Machines Corpn.
1598 University Avenue, San José, Calif. 92110, U.S.A.

Davies, Percy Richmond, M.B.E., M.R.S.L.; Sierra Leonean lawyer; b. 18 Sept. 1911, Freetown; ed. Govt. Model School, Council of Legal Educ. School of Law, London.
Official Administrator 52-54; part-time Lecturer in Law, Fourah Bay Coll., Univ. of Durham 53, 57; Admin., Registrar-Gen. 54-66; Master, Registrar, Supreme Court of Sierra Leone; Commr. for Oaths 53;

Public Notary 54; Puisne Judge 66; Justice of Appeal 71; Chancellor, Diocese of Sierra Leone and Prov. of West Africa (Anglican Communion) 69; has served as chair. various govt. inquiry comms.; Speaker House of Parl. 73-.

House of Parliament, Tower Hill, Freetown; Home: 29 Old Railway Line, Brookfields, Freetown, Sierra Leone.

Davies, Peter Maxwell, B.MUS.; British composer; b. 8 Sept. 1934, Manchester; s. of Thomas Davies and Hilda Howard; ed. Leigh Grammar School, Royal Manchester Coll. of Music, Manchester Univ.

Studied with Goffredo Petrassi 57; Dir. of Music, Cirencester Grammar School 59-62; lecture tours in Europe, Australia and New Zealand 65; Composer in Residence Univ. of Adelaide 66; Dir. Pierrot Players 67-70, Fires of London 70-; Olivetti Prize 59; Koussevitsky Award 64, Koussevitsky Recording Award 66.

Compositions include, *St. Michael* sonata for 13 wind instruments 57, *Prolation* for orchestra 58, *O Magnum Mysterium* for chorus, instruments and organ 60, *String Quartet* 61, *Leopardi Fragments* for soprano, contralto and chamber ensemble 61, *First Fantasia on John Taverner's In Nomine* 62, *Veni Sancte Spiritus* for chorus and orchestra 63, *Seven In Nomine* 63-65, *Second Fantasia on John Taverner's In Nomine* 64, *Shepherd's Calender* for young singers and instrumentalists 65, *Revelation and Fall* for soprano and instrumental ensemble 65, *Ecce Manus Tradentis* for mixed chorus and instruments 65, *Antechrist* for chamber ensemble 67, *L'homme armé* 68, revised 71, *Stedman Caters* for instruments 68, *St. Thomas Wake-Foxtrot* for orchestra 69, *Worldes Blis* 69, *Vesalii Icones* 69, *Eram quasi Agnus* (instrumental motet) 69, *Eight Songs for a Mad King* 69, *Points and Dances from Taverner* 70, *From Stone to Thorn* for mezzo-soprano and instrumental ensemble 71, *Taverner* (opera) 72, *Blind Man's Buff* (masque) 72, *Hymn to Saint Magnus* for chamber ensemble and soprano 72, *Stone Litany* for mezzo-soprano and orchestra 73, *Miss Donnithorne's Maggot* for mezzo-soprano and chamber ensemble 74; *Ave Marisstella* for chamber ensemble 75; *The Blind Fiddler* for mezzo soprano and chamber ensemble 75; has written music for films, *The Devils, The Boyfriend,* and many piano pieces, works for choir, instrumental works and realisations of fifteenth and sixteenth century composers.

c/o Boosey and Hawkes, 295 Regent Street, London, W1A 1BR, England.

Telephone: 01-580 2060.

Davies, Richard Townsend, A.B.; American diplomatist; b. 28 May 1920, Brooklyn, N.Y.; s. of late John W. A. Davies and of Laura (née Townsend) Davies; m. Jean Stevens 1949; four s.; ed. Columbia Univ., Ohio State Univ., Middlebury Coll., Vt.

Diplomatic posts in Warsaw and Moscow 47-53; Political Officer, Int. Staff, NATO 53-55; Second Sec., American Embassy, Kabul 55-58; Public Affairs Adviser, Office of E. European Affairs, Dept. of State 58-59, Office of Soviet Union Affairs 59-61; First Sec., American Embassy, Moscow 61-62, Political Counsellor 62-63; Fellow Foreign Service Inst. 63-64; Deputy Exec. Sec., Dept. of State 64; Asst. Dir. for U.S.S.R. and E. Europe, U.S. Information Agency 65-68; Consul-Gen. Calcutta 68-69; mem. Planning and Coordination Staff, Dept. of State 69-70, Deputy Asst. Sec. of State for European Affairs 70-72; Amb. to Poland 72-.

Leisure interests: reading, tennis, paddle tennis.

American Embassy, Aleje Ujazdowskie 29-31, Warsaw, Poland.

Telephone: 28-30-41.

Davies, Rt. Hon. Sir (William) Arthian, Kt., P.C., D.L., M.A.; British judge; b. 10 May 1901, London; s. of

Arthian and Claudia Davies; m. Mary Bailey Liptrot 1933; one d.; ed. Dulwich Coll., and Trinity Coll., Oxford.

Called to the Bar (Inner Temple) 25; Junior Counsel to Ministry of Labour and Nat. Service 34-47; Recorder of Merthyr Tydfil 46-49; K.C. 47; Recorder of Chester 49-52; J.P. (Buckinghamshire) 48; Deputy Chair. Quarter Sessions 51-61, Chair. 61-71; Deputy Chair. Cardiganshire Quarter Sessions 49-52; Judge, High Court of Justice 52-61; Deputy Chair. Parl. Boundary Commission for Wales 59-61; Lord Justice of Appeal 61-74; Privy Councillor 61; Hon. Fellow Trinity Coll., Oxford 69.

Publ. *The Arbitration Acts* 34.

Ballinger Lodge, Great Missenden, Bucks., England.

Davignon, Viscount Etienne, LL.D.; Belgian diplomatist; b. 4 Oct. 1932, Budapest, Hungary; m. Françoise de Cumont 1959; one s. two d.

Head of Office of Minister of Foreign Affairs 63, Political Dir. 69-; Chair. Gov. Board, Int. Energy Agency Nov. 74-.

Leisure interests: golf, skiing, tennis.

12 avenue des Fleurs, Brussels, Belgium.

Davin, Jean; Gabon diplomatist; b. 23 March 1922, Libreville; m.; two c.

Director of External Relations, Ministry of Foreign Affairs 60-61, Sec.-Gen. 61-64; Counsellor, Bonn 64-65; Deputy Rep. to EEC 65-66; has represented Gabon at OAU confs. and many inter-governmental meetings; mem. Gabon del. to UN Gen. Assembly 63, 64; del to ECOSOC sessions, Geneva 65, 66; Perm. Rep. to UN 69-73; Amb. to Italy 73-.

Embassy of Gabon, Via XX Settembre 40, Rome, Italy.

Davis, Artemus Darius; American business executive; b. 22 Nov. 1905, Henderson, Ark.; s. of William M. and Ethel Chase Davis; m. Pauline K. McCormick 1970; two s. (by previous marriage); ed. Univ. of Idaho.

Manager, Table Supply Store, Little River, Fla. 25-29, Vice-Pres. Table Supply Stores Inc. 29-34, Pres. 34-39; Pres. and Dir. Winn-Dixie Stores Inc., Jacksonville, Fla. 39-65, Chair. Exec. Cttee. 54-70, Vice-Chair. of Board 65-.

Leisure interests: hunting, ranching.

5050 Edgewood Court, Jacksonville, Fla., U.S.A.

Telephone: 904-384-5511.

Davis, Bernard D(avid), A.B., M.D.; American professor of microbiology; b. 7 Jan. 1916, Franklin, Mass.; s. of Harry and Tillie Davis; m. Elizabeth Menzel 1955; two s. one d.; ed. Harvard Univ. and Harvard Medical School.

At Johns Hopkins Hospital 40-41; with U.S. Public Health Service 42-54; Prof. of Pharmacology, New York Univ. Medical School 54-57; Prof. of Bacteriology and Immunology, Harvard Medical School 57-68; Adele Lehman Prof. of Bacterial Physiology, Harvard Medical School 68-; mem., Nat. Acad. of Sciences, American Acad. of Arts and Sciences, World Acad. of Art and Science, American Soc. Biological Chem., American Soc. Microbiology.

Leisure interest: piano.

Publs. *Microbiology* (co-author) 67 (2nd edn. 73); and numerous scientific articles.

Harvard Medical School, Boston, Mass. 02115; Home: 23 Clairemont Road, Belmont, Mass. 02178, U.S.A.

Telephone: 617-RE4-3300 (Office); 617-IV4-0460 (Home).

Davis, Bette (Ruth Elizabeth); American actress; b. 5 April 1908, Lowell, Mass.; d. of Harlow M. and Ruth E. Davis; m. 1st Harmon O. Nelson 1932 (dissolved), 2nd Arthur Farnsworth 1940 (died 1943), 3rd William G. Sherry 1945 (dissolved), one d.; 4th Gary Merrill 1950 (dissolved), one s. one d.; ed. Cushing Acad. Ashburnham, Mass.

Motion Picture Acad. Award as best actress of year, in *Dangerous* 35, *Jezebel* 38.
Films acted in include: *Of Human Bondage, Bordertown, Dangerous, The Petrified Forest, Jezebel, Dark Victory, Juarez, The Old Maid, The Private Lives of Elizabeth and Essex, The Great Lie, The Bride Came C.O.D., All About Eve, Payment on Demand, Phone Call from a Stranger, The Star, The Virgin Queen, Storm Center, The Catered Affair, John Paul Jones, The Scapegoat, What Ever Happened to Baby Jane, Hush . . . Hush, Sweet Charlotte, ·The Nanny, The Anniversary, Connecting Rooms, Bunny O'Hare, Madam Sin, The Game, Miss Moffatt* (musical) 74.
Publ. *The Lonely Life* (autobiography) 62.
c/o Gottlieb Schiff Fabricant & Sternklar, P.C., 555 Fifth Avenue, New York, N.Y. 10017, U.S.A.
Telephone: 212-MU2-4717.

Davis, Colin Rex, C.B.E.; British musician; b. 25 Sept. 1927, Weybridge, Surrey; *m.* 1st April Cantelo 1949 (dissolved 1964), one *s.* one *d.*; *m.* 2nd Ashraf Naini 1964, two *s.*; ed. Christ's Hospital and Royal Coll. of Music.
Assistant Conductor, BBC Scottish Orchestra 57-59; Conductor, Sadler's Wells Opera House 60, Musical Dir. 61-65; Chief Conductor, BBC Symphony Orchestra 67-71, Chief Guest Conductor 71-; Musical Dir. Covent Garden Sept. 71-; Principal Guest Conductor, Boston Symphony Orchestra 72-.
Leisure interests: reading, cooking, gardening.
Office: c/o Pears-Phipps Management, 8 Halliford Street, London, N1 3HE, England.

Davis, Deane Chandler; American lawyer and politician; b. 7 Nov. 1900; ed. Boston Univ.
Practised law, Barre, Vt. 22-31, 36-40; City Attorney, Barre 24-26, 28-30; State Attorney, Washington County, Vt. 26-28; Superior Judge, State of Vt. 31-36; mem. law firm, Barre, Vt., and Chelsea, Vt. 36-40; Gen. Counsel, Nat. Life Insurance Co. 40-50, Vice-Pres. 43-50, Pres. 50-66, Chair. Board 67-68; Gov. of Vermont 69-73; Pres., Man. Dir. Co-operative Health and Information Center, Vermont 73-; Republican.
5 Dyer Avenue, RD1, Montpelier, Vt., U.S.A.

Davis, Jacob E.; American business executive; b. 31 Oct. 1905; ed. Ohio State Univ., and Harvard Univ.
Admitted to Ohio Bar 30; legal practice 30-37; mem. Ohio Gen. Assembly 35-37; Judge, Court of Common Pleas, Pike County, Ohio 37-40; mem. U.S. House of Reps. 41-43; Special Asst. Sec. Navy, Asst. Gen. Counsel, Navy Dept. 43-44; Vice-Pres. Kroger Co. 45, Dir. 49-, Exec. Vice-Pres. 61-62, Pres. 62-70; Dir. Anchor Hocking Corpn., Cincinnati Milacron Inc., Ohio Nat. Life Insurance Co. 70-, Dir. Overhead Door Corpn. 73-.
5685 Kugler Mill Road, Cincinnati, Ohio, U.S.A.

Davis, Jerome, PH.D.; American sociologist; b. 2 Dec. 1891, Kyoto, Japan; *s.* of Jerome and Frances Davis; *m.* Mildred Rood 1920; one *s.* one *d.*; ed. Oberlin Coll., Union Theological Seminary and Columbia Univ.
Lecturer, extension courses, N.Y. City 14; Sec. to Sir Wilfred Grenfell, Labrador 15; Russian war work 16-18; Asst. Prof. of Sociology, Dartmouth Coll. 21-24; Gilbert L. Stark Prof. of Practical Philanthropy, Yale Univ. 24-37; mem. Board of Trustees, Oberlin Coll.; Dir. Promoting Enduring Peace Inc.; Pres. American Fed. of Teachers 36-39, Eastern Sociological Society 36, 37; Chair. Conn. Legislative Comm. on Jails 31-39; Dir. of work in P.O.W. camps for all Canada for World's Cttee., Y.M.C.A. 40-43; made survey on Arab-Israel situation 53; Visiting Prof. Univ. of Colorado 50, Fisk Univ. 54, Japanese Univs. 55, 65; Hon. D.D. (Oberlin), LL.D. (Hillsdale Coll.), D.Litt. (Fla. Southern); directed American-European Seminars to Russia and other European countries 57, 59-64, 66, 68, 69, Around the World Seminar 67; directed Seminar to Moscow 70, to Eastern European countries 71, 72, 73, to China and to Europe and England 74; Winner of the Gandhi Peace Award 67.
Leisure interests: lecturing, tennis, horse shoes, shuffle board.
Publs. *The Russians and Ruthenians in America* 21, *The Russian Immigrant* 22, *Christian Fellowship among the Nations* (with R. B. Chamberlin) 25, *Adventuring in World Co-operation* 25, *Business and the Church* 26, *Introduction to Sociology* (with H. E. Barnes) 27, *Readings in Sociology, Christianity and Social Adventuring* 27, *Labor Speaks for Itself on Religion* 29, *Contemporary Social Movements* 30, *The New Russia* 33, *The Jail Population of Connecticut, Capitalism and its Culture* 35, *Labor Problems in America* (with E. Stein) 40, *Behind Soviet Power* 46, *Character Assassination* 51, *Peace, War and You* 52, *Religion in Action* 55, *On the Brink* 59, *Citizens of One World* 61, *World Leaders I Have Known* 63, *Disarmament—a World View* 64, *A Life Adventure for Peace* 67, *Peace or World War III* 68.
Friends House, Sandy Spring, Md. 20860, U.S.A.
Telephone: 301-774-4609.

Davis, Sir John Henry, Kt., F.C.I.S.; British industrialist; b. 10 Nov. 1906, London; *s.* of Sydney Myering Davis and Emily Harris; *m.* dissolved 1965; one *s.* two *d.*; ed. City of London School.
Chairman, Rank Org. Ltd. 62 (March 77), Chief Exec. 62-74; Chair. of principal subsidiary cos. in U.K. and abroad principally concerned with films, leisure activities, television, manufacturing, property devt. and technology; Joint Pres. Rank Xerox Ltd. 72-; Chair. Southern Television Ltd., Children's Film Foundation Ltd.; Dir. Eagle Star Insurance Co. Ltd.; Gov. British Film Inst.; Pres. Advertising Asscn.; Hon. D.Tech. (Loughborough) 75; Commdr. de l'Ordre de la Couronne 74.
Leisure interests: farming, gardening, reading, travel, music.
Office: 38 South Street, London, WIA 4QU; Home: Crowhurst Place, Lingfield, Surrey, RH7 6LY, England.
Telephone: 01-629-7454 (Office); Lingfield 56 (Home).

Davis, Kingsley, PH.D., M.A., A.B., A.M.; American sociologist; b. 20 Aug. 1908; ed. Univ. of Texas and Harvard Univ.
Instructor in Sociology, Smith Coll., 34-36; Asst. Prof. Clark Univ. 36-37; Assoc. Prof. Pennsylvania State Univ. 37-42, Prof. 42-44, Head, Sociology Div. 37-42; Research Assoc. Office of Population Research, Princeton Univ. 42-48; Assoc. Prof. Princeton 44-48; Prof. of Sociology, Graduate Faculty of Political Science, Columbia 48-55; Assoc. Dir. Bureau of Applied Social Research 48-49, Dir. 49-52; Prof. of Sociology, Univ. of California at Berkeley 55-; Pres. American Sociological Asscn., Population Asscn. of America.
Publs. *Modern American Society* (with Bredemeier and Levy) 49, *Human Society* 49, *The Population of India and Pakistan* 51, *World's Metropolitan Areas* (with others) 59, *World Urbanization, Vol. I* 69, *Vol. II* 72.
7 Selbourne Drive, Piedmont, Calif. 94611, U.S.A.

Davis, Nathanael Vining; Canadian businessman; b. 26 June 1915, Pittsburgh, Pennsylvania; *s.* of late Edward Kirk and Rhea (Reineman) Davis; *m.* Lois Howard Thompson 1941; one *s.* one *d.*; ed. Harvard Univ., London School of Economics and Political Science.
Joined Alcan Group 39; Pres. and Dir. Alcan Aluminium Ltd. 47-72, Chair. Chief Exec. Officer and Dir. 72-; Dir. Aluminum Co. of Canada Ltd. and other subsidiaries in the Alcan group, Bank of Montreal and Canada Life Assurance Co.; Gov., The Canadian Asscn. for Latin America; Trustee, American School of Classical Studies, Athens.
Box 6090, Montreal, Quebec, Canada H3C 3H2.
Telephone: 514/877-2340.

Davis, Nathaniel, M.A., PH.D.; American diplomatist; b. 12 April 1925, Boston, Mass.; s. of Harvey Nathaniel Davis and Alice Marion Rohde; m. Elizabeth Kirkbride Creese 1956; two s. two d.; ed. Phillips Exeter Acad., Brown Univ., Fletcher School of Law and Diplomacy, Cornell Univ., Middlebury Coll., Columbia Univ., Univ. Central de Venezuela.

Assistant in History, Tufts Univ. 47; Lecturer in History, Howard Univ. 62-65, 66-68; Third Sec., U.S. Embassy, Prague 47-49; Vice-Consul, Florence 49-52; Second Sec., Rome 52-53, Moscow 54-56; Deputy Officer-in-Charge, Soviet Affairs, Dept. of State 56-60; First Sec., Caracas 60-62; Special Asst. to Dir. of Peace Corps 62-63; Deputy Assoc. Dir. 63-65; Minister to Bulgaria 65-66; Senior Staff, Nat. Security Council, White House 66-68; Amb. to Guatemala 68-71, to Chile 71-73; Dir.-Gen. U.S. Foreign Service 73-75; Asst. Sec. of State for African Affairs April-Dec. 75; Amb. to Switzerland Dec. 75-; Hon. LL.D. (Brown Univ.) 70; Hartshorn Premium 42, Caesar Hirsch Premium 42; Cinco Aguilas Blancas Alpinism Award 62. Leisure interests: skiing, mountain climbing, white water canoeing, water-colour painting.

U.S. Embassy, Jubiläumsstrasse 93-95, Berne, Switzerland.
Telephone: 251260.

Davis, Owen Lennox, B.A., LL.B., O.B.E.; Australian diplomatist; b. 12 April 1912, Sydney; s. of late Henry Davis; m. Alison Mary Nicholas 1940; ed. King's School, Sydney and Sydney Univ.

Barrister-at-Law 38-40; Australian Forces (Capt.) 40-45; joined Australian Dept. of External Affairs 46; First Sec., Washington 48-51, Karachi 52-53; Acting High Commr., Wellington, N.Z. 54-55; Senior External Affairs Rep. London 57-59; Australian High Commr. to S. Africa 59-61, Amb. 61-62; Australian Amb. to Brazil 62-64; Asst. Sec. Ministry of External Affairs 65-66, First Sec. 67-69; Amb. to Belgium and EEC 69-72, and Luxembourg 70-72; Amb. to Mexico 72-74; Perm. Rep. to the UN Office at Geneva 74-. Leisure interests: history, tennis, golf.

Permanent Mission of Australia to the Office of the UN at Geneva, 56-58 rue de Moillebeau, 1211 Geneva 19, Switzerland.
Telephone: 34-62-00.

Davis, Shelby Cullom; American diplomatist; b. 1 April 1909; ed. Princeton and Columbia Univs., and Univ. of Geneva.

Managing Partner, Shelby Cullom Davis & Co. 47-; mem. N.Y. Stock Exchange 41-; Econ. Adviser to T. E. Dewey Presidential Campaigns 40, 44; Amb. to Switzerland 69-74.

c/o State Department, Washington, D.C., U.S.A.

Davis, Hon. William Grenville, Q.C., M.P.; Canadian lawyer and politician; b. 30 July 1929, Brampton, Ont.; ed. Univ. of Toronto.

Called to the Bar 55; partner in family law firm, Brampton; mem. Ontario Legislature 59-; Minister of Educ., Provincial Govt. of Ont. 62-71, also of Univ. Affairs 64-71; Premier of Ontario and Pres. of Council March 71.-

Office of the Premier of Ontario, Toronto, Ont., Canada.

Davitadze, Levan Mikhailovich; Soviet politician; b. 1916; ed. Shota Rustaveli State Pedagogical Inst., Batumy and Higher Party School of C.P.S.U. Central Committee.

Teacher, School Dir., Insp., then Head of a district dept. of educ. 37-42; Sec. Khulo District Cttee. of the Party, Chair. Khulo District Soviet, Official of Communist Party of Georgia 42-53; Sec. Adzhar Regional Cttee. C.P. of Georgia 53-61; Chair. Council of Ministers, Adzhar Autonomous S.S.R. 61-; mem. Central Cttee. C.P. of Georgia; Deputy to U.S.S.R. Supreme Soviet 62-; mem. Comm. for Educ., Science and Culture, Soviet of Nationalities; mem. C.P.S.U. 39-; Hero of Socialist Labour, Order of Lenin, Hammer and Sickle Gold Medal, etc.

Council of Ministers, Adzhar Autonomous S.S.R., Batumi, U.S.S.R.

Davy, Georges Ambroise, D. ès L.; French university professor; b. 31 Dec. 1883, Bernay; m. Marie-Rose Vial 1918; four c.; ed. Ecole Normale Supérieure and Univ. de Paris.

Professor of Literature and Dean, Dijon 19-30; Rector, Rennes Univ. 31-38; Insp.-Gen. Public Instruction 39-44; Prof. Faculty of Letters, Paris 44-55, Dean 50-56; mem. Inst. of Acad. of Political and Moral Sciences 52, Pres. 65; Pres. Int. Inst. of Political Philosophy 53-67; Pres. Cttee. Sociological Study Centre; mem. Dir. C.N.R.S. until 63, Nat. Cttee. C.N.R.S. 63-; fmr. Vice-Pres. Int. Sociological Asscn., Int. Council of Social Sciences of UNESCO; Hon. Dean, Faculty of Letters, Paris; Dir. Thiers Foundation; Prof. h.c. Univ. of Brazil; Dr. h.c. Brussels Univ.; Assoc. mem. Royal Acad. of Belgium; mem. French Inst.; Hon. K.B.E. (England), Grand Officier Légion d'Honneur; Commdr. numerous foreign orders.
Leisure interests: travel, agriculture.

Publs. include: *La Foi jurée* 22, *Le Droit, l'idéalisme et l'Expérience* 23, *Sociologie politique* 25, *Sociologues d'Hier et d'Aujourd'hui* 35, *l'Homme: le fait social et le fait politique* 73, and numerous articles.

Fondation Thiers, 5 rond-point Bugeaud, Paris 16e, France.
Telephone: PAS-03-33.

Dawnay, Lt.-Col. Christopher Payan, C.B.E., M.V.O.; British business executive; s. of late Maj.-Gen. Guy P. Dawnay and Mrs. Dawnay; m. Patricia Wake 1939; two s. two d.; ed. Winchester and Magdalen Coll., Oxford.

Dawnay Day & Co. Ltd., Merchant Bankers 33-39, 46-50; Army service 39-45; Partner, Edward de Stein & Co., Merchant Bankers 51-60; Managing Dir., Lazard Bros. & Co. 60-74; Chair. Guardian Assurance Co. 67-68, Guardian Royal Exchange Assurance Co. 70-74, Dalgety & New Zealand Loan Ltd., Philblack Ltd.; Dir. other cos.; Legion of Merit.

Longparish House, Andover, Hampshire, England.

Day, J. Edward, A.B., LL.B.; American lawyer and politician; b. 11 Oct. 1914; ed. Univ. of Chicago and Harvard Univ.

Admitted Illinois Bar 38, in private law practice 39-40, 45-49; served U.S. Navy 40-45; Legal and Legislative Asst. to Gov. Adlai Stevenson 49-50; Commr. of Insurance, Illinois 50-53; with Prudential Insurance Co., America 53-61, Vice-Pres. Western Operations, Los Angeles 57-61; Postmaster-Gen. of U.S. 61-63; Partner, Sidley and Austin 63-73, Cox, Langford and Brown, Washington, D.C. 73-; Democrat.

Publs. *Bartholf Street, Descendants of Christopher Day of Bucks County, Pennsylvania, My Appointed Round—929 Days as Postmaster General, Speeches Don't Have to be Dull, Humor in Public Speaking.*

21 DuPont Circle, N.W., Washington, D.C. 20036, U.S.A.

Day, Robin; British television and radio journalist; b. 24 Oct. 1923, London; s. of William and Florence Day; m. Katherine May (née Ainslie) 1965; one s.; ed. Bembridge School, Oxford Univ.

Army Service 43-47; Pres. Oxford Union 50; called to the Bar 52; BBC radio journalist 54-; Independent Television News newscaster and political correspondent 55-59; BBC television political interviewer and reporter specializing in current affairs 59-; Introducer of *Panorama* 67-72; mem. Phillimore Cttee. on Law of Contempt 71-74; Richard Dimbleby Award, Soc. of Film and TV Arts 74.
Leisure interests: talking, skiing, reading.

Publs. *Television—A Personal Report* 61, *The Case for*

Televising Parliament 63 (pamphlet), *Troubled Reflections of a TV Journalist* (article in "Encounter") May 70, *Day by Day* 75.
c/o BBC Studios, Lime Grove, London, W.12, England.

Dayal, Rajeshwar, M.A.; Indian diplomatist; b. 12 Aug. 1909, Naini Tal, U.P.; s. of the late Mr. and Mrs. D. Dayal; m. Susheela Srivastara 1938; ed. P.S. Coll., Naini Tal, U.P. Allahabad Univ., and New Coll., Oxford. Entered Indian Civil Service 32; Deputy Secretary, Civil Supplies Dept., U.P. Govt. 43-46, Home Sec. 46-48; Minister-Counsellor and Chargé d'Affaires Moscow 48-50; Special Commr. to Indian Govt. and Joint Sec. to Govt. External Affairs Dept. 50; Alternate Rep. Security Council 50-51, Permanent Rep. to U.N. 52-54, mem. U.N. Peace Observation Comm., U.N. Comm. of Twelve on Disarmament, U.N. Comm. for Relief and Rehabilitation of Korea, U.N. Trusteeship Council, U.N. Human Rights Comm.; Amb. to Yugoslavia 55-58, concurrently Minister to Bulgaria and Romania; High Commr. to Pakistan 58-60, May 61-63; Personal Rep. of Sec.-Gen. of UN in the Congo Sept. 60-May 61; Special Sec. Ministry of External Affairs 63-65; Commonwealth Sec. Ministry of External Affairs 65; Amb. to France 65-67; Sec.-Gen. Ministry of Foreign Affairs 67-Nov. 68; Chair. UN Cttee. for Eradication of Racial Discrimination 69-; Visiting Prof. Princeton Univ. 69-70; Scholar in Residence, Aspen Inst. for Humanistic Studies 72; Woodrow Wilson Fellow, Smithsonian Inst. 71, 73; Fellow, St. Antony's Coll., Oxford 76; Padma Vibhushana 69.
Leisure interests: shooting, riding, music, gardening, reading.
Publ. *Mission for Hammarskjöld (The Congo Crisis)* 76.
17 Palam Marg, New Delhi 57, India.
Telephone: 671-446.

Dayan, Lt.-Gen. Moshe, LL.B.; Israeli soldier and politician; b. 20 May 1915, Degania; s. of Dvora and Shmuel Dayan; m. 1st Ruth Schwartz 1935 (divorced 1972), 2nd Rachel Corem 1973; ed. agricultural high school, Nahalal, Staff Coll., Camberley, U.K. and Tel-Aviv Univ.
Trained in Haganah (Jewish militia) 29; second in command to Capt. Orde Wingate 37; imprisoned by British when Haganah declared illegal 39; released to lead reconnaissance and commando troops Vichyst Syria, wounded, losing eye 41; intelligence work in Haganah 41-48; Jordan Valley Front, "Dany" campaign 48; promoted to Sgan-Aluf (Lt.-Col.) and named Commander, Jerusalem front 48; represented Israel Defence Forces at Rhodes armistice talks with Jordan 49; promoted to Aluf (Maj.-Gen.) and Commander, Southern Region Command 50; after military studies in U.K. appointed Commander Northern Region Command 51; Head of Gen. Staff Branch at G.H.Q. 52; Chief of Gen. Staff 53-58; studied at Faculty of Law, Tel-Aviv Univ. and in Jerusalem 58-59; Minister of Agriculture 59-64; resigned from Govt. 64; joined RAFI party 65; mem. of Knesset Nov. 65-; joined Unity Govt. as Minister of Defence 67; Knesset "Maarach" (Alignment) list 69; Minister of Defence 69-74.
Leisure interest: archaeology.
Publs. *Diary of the Sinai Campaign* 66, *Mapa Kadasha, Yahassim Aherim* (New Map, Other Relations) 69, various articles on Vietnam etc.
11 Yoav Street, Zahala, Israel.
Telephone: 427-318.

Deacon, Sir George E. R., Kt., C.B.E., D.SC., F.R.S., F.R.S.E., F.R.A.S., F.R.G.S.; British physicist; b. 21 March 1906, Leicester; s. of late George R. Deacon; m. Margaret E. Jeffries 1940 (died 1966); one d.; ed. City of Leicester Boys' School and King's Coll., London.
Joined Discovery Investigations 27; Royal Navy Scientific Service 39; Dir. Nat. Inst. of Oceanography 49-71;

Fellow, King's Coll., London; Fellow, Royal Inst. of Navigation, Pres. 61-64; Vice-Pres. Royal Geographical Soc. 65-70; Polar Medal 42; Alexander Agassiz Medal, U.S. Nat. Acad. of Sciences 62, Royal Medal, Royal Soc. 69, Prince Albert I of Monaco Medal 70, Inst. of Navigation Bronze Medal 70; Founder's Medal, Royal Geographical Soc. 71; Scottish Geographical Medal 72; Hon. D.Sc. (Liverpool, Leicester).
Leisure interests: walking, gardening, history, history of science.
Publs. publications on the Southern Ocean in *Discovery Reports;* papers on waves, currents and general oceanographic topics in scientific and professional journals.
Flitwick House, Milford, Surrey, England.
Telephone: Godalming 5929.

Deakin, Sir Frederick William Dampier, Kt., D.S.O., M.A.; retired British university official; b. 3 July 1913, London; s. of Albert Whitney and Bertha Mildred Deakin; m. 1st Margaret Beatson Bell 1935 (dissolved); 2nd Livia Stela Nasta 1943; two s.; ed. Westminster School and Christ Church, Oxford.
Fellow and Tutor, Wadham Coll., Oxford 36-49, Research Fellow 49, Hon. Fellow 52; with Queen's Own Oxfordshire Hussars 39-41; seconded to Special Operations, War Office 41; led first British Mil. Mission to Marshal Tito 43; First Sec. Embassy, Belgrade 45-46; Warden of St. Antony's Coll., Oxford 50-69; Hon. Fellow 69; D.S.O. 43; Russian Order of Valour 44, Chevalier Légion d'Honneur 53, Bundes Ehrenkreuz (Fed. Germany) 58, and two Yugoslav mil. orders.
Leisure interests: travel, writing.
Publs. *The Brutal Friendship: Mussolini, Hitler and the Fall of Italian Fascism* 62, *The Case of Richard Sorge* 64, *The Embattled Mountain* 71.
Le Castellet, 83 Var, France.
Telephone: 98-73-21.

Dean, Antony Musgrave; British broadcaster; b. 7 Jan. 1921, Loose, Kent; s. of Arthur Edis Dean, C.B.E., M.A., M.LITT. and Elsie Georgina Dean (née Musgrave-Wood); m. 1st Anne Virginia Batcup 1943, 2nd Sheila Francis Whittingham 1956; three s. three d.; ed. The King's School, Canterbury.
Commissioned Queen's Bays (2nd Dragoon Guards) 41, wounded Western Desert 42; Forces Broadcasting Service Kenya 45-46; Recording, feature film work and BBC news stringer 47-52; Broadcasting Officer, Kenya Govt. 52-59; Controller of Programmes, Kenya Broadcasting Service 59-61, Operations Exec. 62-64; Dir. of Radio Programme Dept. and Sec. Radio Programme Cttee. of European Broadcasting Union 64-.
Leisure interests: music, skiing.
Villa Chania, 1295 Mies, Vaud, Switzerland.
Telephone: (022) 55-19-63.

Dean, Arthur Hobson, A.B. LL.B., LL.D.; American lawyer; b. Oct. 1898, Ithaca, New York; s. of William Cameron and Maud J. J. Dean; m. Mary Marden 1932; one s. one d.; ed. Cornell Univ.
Admitted to New York Bar 23, practised with Sullivan & Cromwell, N.Y., partner of firm since 29; general counsel to various corpns.; Dir. and Trustee numerous cos. including El Paso Co., American Bank Note Co., Nat. Union Electric Corpn., Bank of New York; Trustee, Cornell Univ.; mem. American Bar Asscn.; Hon. Dir. Council on Foreign Relations and Japan Soc. Inc.; Dir. Netherland-America Foundation, etc.; Chair. of Board, The Spanish Inst. Inc.; Rep. for U.S. and 16 nations contributing troops at Panmunjom negotiations; special U.S. Amb. to Korea 53-54; Amb. to UN Conf. on Law of the Sea, Geneva 58, 60, to Nuclear Test Ban Negotiations, Geneva 61-62 to Disarmament Conf., Geneva 62; American Soc. of Int. Law 56-59, Pres. 61-62, Hon. Vice-Pres. 62-; mem. Acad. of Political Science, and Political and Social Science, American

Econ. Asscn., American Law Inst., American Judicature Soc., Int. Law Asscn., etc.; Hon. LL.D. (Hamilton, Allegheny, Rutgers, Washington, Brown, Dartmouth, Bowdoin and C.W. Post Colls. and Adelphi Univ.); Hon. D.C.L. (Hofstra Coll.); Hon. D.Hum. (Washington Coll.); Hon. D.Litt. (Lafayette Coll.); Officier Légion d'Honneur.
Publs. include: *Investment Banking in a Changing World* 51, *Can Conventional Accounting Cope with Inflation?* 51, *The Relation of Law and Economics to the Measurement of Income* 52, *Investment Banking and the Antitrust Laws* 52, *Test Ban and Disarmament: The Path of Negotiation* 66.
Office: 48 Wall Street, New York, N.Y. 10005; Home: Mill River Road, Oyster Bay, L.I., N.Y. 11771, U.S.A.

Dean, Basil, C.B.E.; British theatre and film director and producer; b. 27 Sept. 1888, Croydon.
Member Horniman Repertory Co. 07-10; first Dir. Liverpool Repertory Theatre 11-13; Man. Dir. Reandean Productions 19-25; Joint Man. Dir. Theatre Royal, Drury Lane 24-25; Gov. Dir. Basil Dean Productions 26-64, Basil Dean Enterprises 39-; Chair. and Man. Dir. Radio Keith Orpheum Ltd. 30-32, Shute Lecturer, Liverpool Univ. 32-33; Chair. and Man. Dir. Associated Talking Pictures Ltd., A.T.P. Studios Ltd. 28-38; Founder and Dir.-Gen. Entertainment Nat. Service Asscn. (ENSA) 39-46; Dir. Nat. Service Entertainment 41-46.
Productions include : *Bill of Divorcement* 21, *Loyalties* 23, *Hassan* 23, *A Midsummer Night's Dream* 24, *Constant Nymph* 26, *Autumn Crocus* 28, *Call it a Day* 30, *When we are married* 38, *An Inspector Calls* 46, *The Diary of a Nobody* 54, *Touch it Light* 58; films: *Sally in our Alley, Constant Nymph, Escape, Sing As We Go.*
Publs. *Theatre at War* 56, *Seven Ages* (autobiography), Vol. I 70, *Mind's Eye*, Vol. II 73.
102 Dorset House, Gloucester Place, London, N.W.1, England.
Telephone: 01-935-6154.

Dean, John Gunther, PH.D.; American diplomatist; b. 24 Feb. 1926, Germany; s. of Dr. Joseph and Lucy Dean; m. Martine Duphénieux 1952; two s. one d.; ed. Harvard Coll., Harvard and Paris Univs.
Entered Govt. Service 50; diplomatic posts in France, Belgium, Viet-Nam, Laos, Togo, Mali and in U.S. Dept. of State; Dir. Pacification Programme in Mil. Region 1, Viet-Nam 70-72; Deputy Chief of Mission, American Embassy, Laos 72-74; Amb. to Khmer Repub. 74-75; various U.S. and foreign decorations for service in Africa and Viet-Nam.
Leisure interest: tennis.
Embassy of America, Dag Hammarskjölds Allé 24, 2100 Ø, Copenhagen, Denmark.

Dean, Sir Patrick Henry, G.C.M.G.; British diplomatist; b. 16 March 1909, Berlin, Germany; s. of Prof. Henry Roy and Irene Dean (née Wilson); m. Patricia Wallace Jackson 1947; two s.; ed. Rugby School and Gonville and Caius Coll., Cambridge.
Called to Bar at Lincoln's Inn 34; legal practice 34-39; Asst. Legal Adviser, Foreign Office 39-45, Head, German Political Dept. 45-50, Minister in Rome 50-51; Senior Civilian Instructor Imperial Defence Coll. 52; Asst. Under-Sec. Foreign Office 53-56, Deputy Under-Sec. 56-60; Perm. Rep. to UN 60-64; Amb. to U.S.A. 65-69; Chair. ESU Dec. 72-; Dir. Taylor Woodrow Ltd., Ingersoll Rand Holdings Ltd.; Int. Adviser to American Express; Hon. LL.D. (Columbia, Lincoln, Wesleyan Univs., Chattanooga, William and Mary Coll., Hofstra); Hon. Bencher Lincoln's Inn; Hon. Fellow Clare Coll. and Gonville and Caius Coll., Cambridge.
Leisure interests: shooting, fishing, walking.
5 Bentinck Mansions, Bentinck Street, London, W.1, England.
Telephone: 01-935-0881.

Dean, Robert Halladay, B.A.; American food executive; b. 27 June 1916; ed. Grinnell Coll.
Manager, Checkerboard Elevator Co., Buffalo 41-43; Man. Ralston Purina Co., Ohio 43-45, Grain Div., St. Louis 45-48, Pres. Int. Div., St. Louis 58-, Vice-Pres. Asst. to Pres. 58-61, Exec. Vice-Pres., Dir. 61-63, Chief Operating Officer 63-66, Pres. 66-69, Chair., CEO 66-.
Office: 835 South 8th Street, St. Louis, Mo.; Home: 4 Devon Road, Glendale 22, Mo., U.S.A.

Dearden, H. E. Cardinal John, S.T.D.; American ecclesiastic; b. 15 Oct. 1907, Valley Falls, R.I.; s. of John S. Dearden and Agnes Gregory Dearden; ed. Holy Trinity School, Central Falls, St. Philomena Elementary School, Cleveland, Cathedral Latin School, Cleveland, St. Mary Seminary, Cleveland, N. American Coll., Rome and Pontifical Gregorian Univ., Rome.
Ordained priest 32; Papal Chamberlain with title of Very Rev. Monsignor 45; Coadjutor Bishop of Pittsburgh 48-50, Bishop of Pittsburgh 50-58; Asst. to Pontifical Throne 57; Archbishop of Detroit 58-; held various posts on Nat. Catholic Welfare Conf. and Vatican Council; Pres. Nat. Conf. of Catholic Bishops 66-71; cr. Cardinal 69.
Leisure interest: reading.
1234 Washington Boulevard, Detroit, Mich. 48226, U.S.A.
Telephone: 237-5816.

de Aréchaga, Eduardo Jimenez (*see* Jiménez de Aréchaga, Eduardo.)

De Backer-van Ocken, Rika; Belgian politician; b. 1 Feb. 1923, Anvers; seven c.; ed. Ecole Ste. Lutgarde, Anvers and Catholic Univ. of Louvain.
Worked on *Winkler Prins voor de Vrouw* encyclopaedia; Editor KAV (Christian league of working women); Vice-Pres. Christian Social Party, Anvers; mem. Provincial Senate for Anvers 71-74; mem. Senate 74-, mem. Comms. for Nat. Educ., Culture, Justice; Minister of Dutch Culture and Flemish Affairs 74-.
Ministry of Dutch Culture and Flemish Affairs, Rue de la Loi 151, 1040 Brussels, Belgium.

DeBakey, Michael Ellis, B.S., M.D., M.S.; American surgeon; b. 7 Sept. 1908, Lake Charles, Louisiana; s. of Shaker M. DeBakey and Raheega Zerba; m. 1st Diana Cooper 1936 (died 1972); four s.; m. 2nd Katrin Fehlhaber 1975; ed. Tulane Univ., New Orleans.
Instructor Tulane Univ. 37-40, Asst. Prof. of Surgery 40-46; War Service, Colonel, ultimately Dir. Surgical Consultant Div., Office of the Surgeon Gen. 42-46; U.S. Army Surgical Consultant to Surgeon-General 46-; Assoc. Prof. Tulane Univ. 46-48; Prof. and Chair. Dept. of Surgery, Baylor Coll. of Medicine, Houston 48-, Pres. 69-; Dir. Nat. Heart and Blood Vessel Research and Demonstration Center, Houston Methodist Hospital; Surgeon-in-Chief, Ben Taub Gen. Hospital; Senior Attending Surgeon, Methodist Hospital and Consultant in Surgery, Veterans Administration Hospital, Houston; consultant surgeon to many hospitals in Texas; mem. Nat. Advisory Heart Council 57-61, Program Planning Cttee. and Cttee. on Training 61-, Nat. Advisory Council on Regional Medical Programs 65-; Chair. Pres. Comm. on Heart Disease, Cancer and Stroke 64-; implanted first artificial heart in man April 66; editorial staff of numerous medical journals and editor of *General Surgery: Vol. II, History of World War II*, co-editor *American Lectures in Surgery*; mem. numerous Amer. and foreign medical socs. and asscns. and holder of numerous advisory appointments; many awards and hon. degrees.
Publs. over 940 articles.
Baylor College of Medicine, Texas Medical Center, 1200 Moursund Avenue, Houston, Texas 77025, U.S.A.
Telephone: 797-9353.

De Beer, Zacharias Johannes, M.B., CH.B.; South African business executive; b. 11 Oct. 1928, Woodstock, Cape; s. of the late Dr. Z. J. De Beer and Jean De Beer;

m. 1st Maureen Strauss 1952, 2nd Mona Schwartz 1965; one *s.* two *d.*; ed. Diocesan Coll., Rondebosch and Univ. of Cape Town.

House Surgeon, Groote Schuur Hosp. 52; Medical Practitioner 53-59; mem. Parl. 53-61; Dir. P. N. Barrett Co. (S. African Advertising Contractors) 62-67; joined Anglo American Corpn. of S. Africa 68, Man. 70-72, mem. Board 74-; Chair. Anglo American Corpn. of Cen. Africa Ltd. 72-; Chair. LTA Ltd.; Exec. Dir. Anglo American Corpn. (South Africa) Ltd.; Dir. Nchanga Consolidated Copper Mines Ltd. and other cos.

Leisure interests: bridge, politics, tennis.

Publ. *Multi-Racial South Africa: the Reconciliation of Forces* 60.

Office: Box 61587, Marshalltown, Transvaal; Home: 39 Cotswold Drive, Saxonwold, Johannesburg, South Africa.

Telephone: 838-8111 (Office); 42-9778 (Home).

De Benedetti, Giulio; Italian journalist; b. 1890, Asti Piemonte; *m.* Maria Bignami; one *d.*

Foreign Corresp. of *La Stampa*, Turin 15-18; Special Corresp. in Germany 19-30; Chief Editor and Dir. of the *Gazzetta del Popolo*, Turin; Dir. of *L'Opinione* (Liberal Party), Turin 45; Chief Editor and Dir. of *La Stampa* and *Stampa Sera*, Turin 48-70; Grande Ufficiale della Repubblica.

94 corso Giovanni Lanza, Turin, Italy.

de Besche, Hubert W. A.; Swedish diplomatist; b. 7 July 1911, Frösö; *s.* of Col. Hubert and Mrs. Ebba de Besche; *m.* Eva D. K. H. Rhedin 1946; two *d.*; ed. Univ. of Stockholm and Grenoble and Heidelberg.

Ministry of Foreign Affairs 36-, served in London and Stockholm 36-47, Head Comm. of Trade and Commerce 47-49, Economic Counsellor, Washington; Head, Trade Dept., Ministry of Foreign Affairs 53-56, Deputy Sec.-Gen. Ministry of Foreign Affairs 56-63; Ambassador to U.S.A. 64-73, to Denmark 73-; mem. Steering Board for Trade, OEEC 56-60; Vice-Chair. Trade Cttee., OECD 60-63; Chair. EFTA Negotiations 59; del. to numerous trade negotiations; Grand Cross North Star (Sweden), Grand Cross Dannebrog (Denmark), Grand Cross Homayoun (Iran), Grand Cross Order of Christ (Portugal), Order of the Sun (Peru), Order of Merit (Chile); Hon. K.B.E., etc.

Leisure interests: fencing, fishing, skiing.

Embassy of Sweden, Skt. Annae Plads 15, 1250 Copenhagen, Denmark.

de Beus, J. G., LL.D.; Netherlands diplomatist; b. 1909; *m.* Louise G. Broussard 1960; one *d.*; ed. Univ. of Leyden.

Entered foreign service; served Brussels 36-38, Copenhagen 38-39, Berlin 39-40; Sec. to Foreign Office and to Prime Minister (London) 40-45; Counsellor, Washington 45-49; Perm. Del. to UN 48-49; Alternative Del. to Third Gen. Assembly of UN; Head, Far-Eastern Office 49; Deputy High Commr. Jakarta 50; Minister, Washington 50-54; Amb. to Pakistan 55-57; Amb. to the U.S.S.R. 57-60; Amb. to Australia 60-63; Perm. Rep. of Netherlands to UN 64-67; Amb. to Fed. Repub. of Germany 67-74; Asst. Sec.-Gen. UN 75-; Exec. Dir. UN Fund for Drug Abuse Control 75-; Commdr. Order of Orange-Nassau, Knight Order of Netherlands Lion, Grand Cross, Order of Merit, Fed. Republic of Germany.

Leisure interests: tennis, squash, skiing.

Publs. *The Jurisprudence of the General Claims Commission, U.S.A. and Mexico* 38, *De Wedergeboorte van het Koninkrijk* 43, *The Future of the West* 53, *In Rusland* 64.

c/o UN Fund for Drug Abuse Control, Palais des Nations, Geneva, Switzerland.

Debeyre, Guy Edouard Pierre Albert; French university professor; b. 6 Nov. 1911; ed. Lille Univ.

Prof. Faculty of Law and Economic Sciences, Univ. of Lille 45-55, Dean 50-55, Rector 55-72; Prof. Univ. Paris; Conseiller d'Etat 72; Pres.-Gen. Cttee. for Econ. Expansion of the North and Pas de Calais 56-; Vice-Pres. Nat. Council of Regional Economies and of Productivity 69-; Commdr. Légion d'Honneur, Croix de Guerre (39-45), Hon. C.B.E.

Publs. *La Responsabilité de la puissance publique en France et en Belgique* 36, *Le Conseil d'Etat Belge* 47, *Traité de Droit Administratif* 54, *Le Droit public des Français* 56.

12 place du Panthéon, 75005 Paris; place de Palais-Royal, 75001 Paris; Home: 112 rue Meurein, 59000 Lille, France.

Telephone: 572156 (Home).

De Boor, Helmut, DR. PHIL.; German literary scholar; b. 24 March 1891, Bonn; *s.* of Prof. Dr. Carl de Boor; *m.* Ellen Siebs 1920; two *d.*; ed. Univs. of Freiburg, Marburg, Leipzig.

Lector in Gothenburg 19-22; lecturer Greifswald 21-26; Extra. Prof. Leipzig 26-30; Prof. in Berne 30-45; Prof. Free Univ. of Berlin 49-59, Emer. 59-; Corresp. mem. Bavarian Academy of Sciences 63-.

Publs. *Das Nibelungenlied* 40, *Geschichte der deutschen Literatur von den Anfängen bis zur Gegenwart* Vols. I and II 57, Vol. III 62, *Kleine Schriften* Vol. I 64, Vol. II 66, *Die deutsche Literatur; Texte und Zeugnisse* Vol. I, 1-2 65, *Die Textgeschichte der lateinischen Osterfeiern* 67. Bachstelzenweg 11, Berlin-Dahlem, Germany.

Telephone: Berlin 761813.

Debré, Michel, D. en D.; French politician; b. 15 Jan. 1912, Paris; *m.* Anne Marie Lemaresquier 1936; four *s.*; ed. Ecole des Sciences Politiques, Paris.

Auditeur, Conseil d'Etat 34; Commr. de la République, Angers region 44; mem. Comm. for Reform of the Civil Service 45; attached to Saar Economic Mission 47; Sec. Gen. German and Austrian Affairs, Ministry of Foreign Affairs 48; elected Senator from Indre et Loire 48, re-elected 55, Deputy from St. Denis, Réunion 63-, re-elected 67, 68-73; Garde des Sceaux June 58-59; Prime Minister Jan. 59-April 62; Minister of Economic Affairs and Finance 66-68, of Foreign Affairs 68-69, of Defence 69-73; Officier Légion d'Honneur, Croix de Guerre, Union des Democrates pour la République (UDR).

Publs. *Refaire la France* 44, *Demain la paix* 45, *La République et son pouvoir* 50, *La République et ses problèmes* 53, *La Mort de l'état républicain, Ces Princes qui nous gouvernent* 57, *Refaire une démocratie, un Etat, un pouvoir* 58, *Au Service de la Nation* 63, *France, quelle jeunesse te faut-il?* 65, *Sur le gaullisme* 67, *A la jeunesse* 69, *Lettres à des militants sur la continuité, l'ouverture et la fidélité* 70, *Une certaine idée de la France* 72, *Combat pour les élections de 1973* 73, *Une politique pour la Réunion* 75.

18 rue Spontini, 75116 Paris, France.

Debrot, Nicolaas, LL.D., M.D.; Netherlands physician, writer and fmr. governor; b. 4 May 1902; ed. primary and secondary schools in Curaçao and Nijmegen and Univs. of Utrecht and Amsterdam.

Lived in France and U.S.A. 28-32; practised medicine, Amsterdam and Curaçao 42-50; official and governmental posts 50-70; successively mem. Exec. Council Netherlands Antilles, Gen. Rep. of Netherlands Antilles in The Hague, Dir. of Cabinet of Minister of Netherlands Antilles, mem. Council of State; Gov. of Netherlands Antilles 62-70; Knight Order of Netherlands Lion; Grand Cross in the Order of Vasco Nuñez de Balboa.

Publs. (Prose): *My Sister the Negro* 35, *Pray for Camille Willocq* 46, *Clouded Existence* 48, *Pages from a Diary in Geneva* 62; (Poetry): *Confession in Toledo* 44, *Poignant Summer* 45, *Those Absent* 52.

c/o Council of State, Netherlands Antilles.

Debu-Bridel, Jacques, L. EN D.; French writer and politician; b. 22 Aug. 1902; *s.* of Gabriel Debu and

Ernestine Bridel; *m.* Adélaide Plusanski 1927; two *d.*; ed. Colls. of Lausanne and Dreux, Faculty of Law, Sorbonne, Paris, and Ecole Libre des Sciences Politiques.

Journalist with *l'Eclair* 22; then with various publs.; notably *l'Avenir* and *Comédia*; co-founder of Federalist review *Latinité*; wrote for *l'Ordre* for six years; mem. of **Ligue des Patriotes** and **l'Union pour la Nation; Chief Sec. to Minister for Merchant Marine 39; French Army 40; Leader of Resistance in Occupied Zone; mem. of l'Organisation Civile et Militaire and of Front National; rep. of Nat. Republicans to Council of Resistance 43-45; Provisional Sec.-Gen. for Navy 45; mem. of Provisional Consultative Assembly and of Comms. for National Defence, Propaganda and Information; Dir. of journal *Front National*, resgnd. because of Communist domination 45; mem. of R.P.F. (Gaulliste); Vice-Pres. Organizing Cttee. R.P.F. for the Seine; Paris Municipal Councillor 47-48; Senator for the Seine 48, re-elected 52-58; mem. Paris Municipal Council 53; founder Union Démocratique du Travail 58; Chair. of Budget Cttee. for Fine Arts, Council of the Republic; Dir. of Paris Services, Radio Monte Carlo 60-66, Dir. of Information 66-69; Dir. of weekly *Notre République* 66; Médaille de la Resistance, Croix de Guerre, Officier de la Légion d'Honneur.

Leisure interests: horses, dogs, knitting.

Publs.: Novels: *Jeunes Ménages* 35 (Prix Interallié), *Exil au Grand Palais* 48, *Déroute* 45, *Sous la Cendre* 51, *Frère esclave* (new edn. 57); Essays: *Alphonse Daudet et la Famille* 29, *Alger* 30, *La Grande tragédie du Monde animal* 55; Biographies: *La Fayette* 45, *Emily Brontë* 50, *Journées Révolutionnaires de Paris, Vol. I* 60, *Vol. II* 61, *Conjuration d'Amboise* 63.

Home: 15 rue des Barres, 75004 Paris, France.

de Bunsen, Sir Bernard, Kt., C.M.G., M.A.; British administrator; b. 1907, Cambridge; *s.* of the late L. H. G. de Bunsen and Victoria (née Buxton) de Bunsen; *m.* Joan Harmston 1975; ed. Leighton Park School and Balliol Coll., Oxford.

Schoolmaster, Liverpool Public Elementary Schools 31-34; Asst. Dir. of Education, Wiltshire County Council 34-38; H.M. Inspector of Schools, Ministry of Education 38-46; Dir. of Education, Palestine 46-48; Prof. of Education, Makerere Univ. Coll. 48, Act. Principal Aug. 49, Principal 50-63; Vice-Chancellor, Univ. of East Africa 63-65; Principal, Chester Coll., England 66-71; Chair. Africa Educ. Trust 66-, Africa Bureau 71-; Vice-Pres., Anti-Slavery Soc. 75-; Hon. LL.D. (Univ. of St. Andrews).

Leisure interests: African and international affairs.

3 Prince Arthur Road, London, N.W.3, England. Telephone: 01-435-3521.

Debus, Kurt Heinrich, PH.D., M.S.; American (b. German) engineer; b. 29 Nov. 1908, Frankfurt-am-Main, Germany; *s.* of Heinrich P. J. Debus and Melly Graulich; *m.* Irmgard Helene Brueckmann 1937; two *d.*; ed. Technische Hochschule, Darmstadt.

Assistant Prof. Technische Hochschule, Darmstadt 39-42; Test Engineer, Flight Test Dir., Peenemuende Rocket Centre, Germany 42-45; Deputy Dir. Guidance and Control Div., and Staff Asst. to Wernher von Braun, Army Ballistic Missile Agency, Huntsville, Ala. 45-52; U.S. citizen 50-; Dir. Missile Firing Lab., Army Ballistic Missile Agency, Cape Canaveral (later Cape Kennedy), Florida 60-62; Dir. Launch Operations Center, Nat. Aeronautics and Space Admin. (NASA), Cape Canaveral 62-63; Dir. John F. Kennedy Space Center, NASA Kennedy Space Center 63-74; retd. from govt. service 74; Chair. of Board OTRAG 75-; mem. Nat. Acad. of Engineering 75-, Advisory Board, British Interplanetary Soc., Hon. mem. Hermann Oberth Gesellschaft, German Soc. for Rocket Technology and Space Flight, Instrument Soc. of America; Ex-Officio mem.

Florida Council of 100; numerous decorations and medals including Exceptional Civilian Service Award, U.S. Army 59, NASA Distinguished Service Medal 69, U.S. Space Hall of Fame Award 69, Bundesverdienstkreuz (Fed. Germany); many hon. degrees.

Leisure interest: music.

Publs. Numerous works, designs, etc. on launch of ballistic missiles and space vehicles 39-.

280 Bahama Boulevard, Cocoa Beach, Fla. 32931, U.S.A.

De Butts, John D.; American communications executive; b. 10 April 1915, Greensboro, N.C.; *s.* of Sydnor and Mary Ellen De Butts; *m.* Gertrude Willoughby Walke 1939; two *d.*; ed. Virginia Military Inst.

Joined Chesapeake and Potomac Telephone Co. of Virginia 36. Subsequently held assignments with American Telephone and Telegraph Co. (AT & T) and New York Telephone; Vice-Pres. C & P Companies 59; Pres. Illinois Bell Co. 62; Exec. Vice-Pres. AT & T 66, Vice-Chair. 67-72, Dir. 67-, Chair. and Chief Exec. Officer April 72-; Dir. Citicorp, Kraftco Corpn., U.S. Steel Corpn., United Fund of Greater N.Y.; Vice-Chair. and Trustee Duke Endowment.

Leisure interests: hunting, fishing, golf.

American Telephone & Telegraph Co., 195 Broadway, New York, N.Y. 10007, U.S.A. Telephone: 201-393-3412.

Decaris, Albert Marius Hippolyte; French artist; b. 6 May 1901, Sotteville-les-Rouen; *m.*; one *d.*; ed. Ecole Estienne, Ecole Nationale Supérieure des Beaux-Arts.

Frescoes, Int. Exhibition, Paris 37, New York 38, Town Hall, Vesoul; engravings and book illustrations; design of French and French Overseas postage stamps; Premier Grand Prix de Rome 19; mem. Acad. des Beaux Arts, Pres. 60, 66; Pres. Inst. de France 60; Officier Légion d'Honneur; Croix de Guerre (1939-45).

3 quai Malaquais, 75006 Paris, France. Telephone: 0338261.

de Chirico, Giorgio; Italian painter; b. 10 July 1888; ed. Acad. of Fine Arts, Munich.

Went to Paris 11; creator of Metaphysical School of painting 14; first exhibited in Rome 19; visited U.S. 36-38; executed numerous designs for the theatre.

Works include: *The Enigma of an Autumn Afternoon, Nostalgia of the Infinite, Joys and Enigmas of a Strange Hour, Departure of a Poet, Mystery of a Street, The Departure of the Knight Errant, Mysterious Bathing.*

Publs. include: *Hebdomeros* (novel) 29, *Gustave Courbet* 25, *Piccolo trattato di tecnica pittorica* 28, *Commedia dell'arte moderna* (jointly) 45, *Memorie della mia vita* (autobiography) 45.

31 Piazza di Spagna, Rome, Italy.

Decker, William Conway, B.S., M.B.A.; American business executive; b. 26 Dec. 1900, York, Pa.; *s.* of Jacob E. and Laura F. Decker; *m.* 1st Helen E. Rich 1929, 2nd Sylvia B. Sundstrom 1945; one *s.* one *d.*; ed. Pennsylvania State Univ., Columbia Univ., and Harvard Business School.

Engineering Dept. Western Electric Co. N.Y. 22; Sales Dept. Brown Co. Portland, Maine 27; Sales Manager Corning Glass Works, Corning, N.Y. 30, Chief Cost Accountant 34, Treas. 36, Controller and Asst. to Pres. 39, Vice-Pres. 41, Pres. and Dir. 46-61, Chief Exec. Officer 57-60, Chair. of Board and Chief Exec. Officer 61-64, Chair. of Exec. Cttee. 64-65, Hon. Vice-Chair. 65-71, Hon. Chair. 71-; Trustee, Corning Glass Works Foundation; Dir. Pittsburgh Corning Corpn., Corning Glass Works; Hon. LL.D. (Alfred Univ.); Hon. D.Eng. (Clarkson Coll.).

Leisure interests: golf, bridge.

5 East Fifth Street, Corning, N.Y., U.S.A. Telephone: 607-962-0123.

Dédéyan, Charles, D. ès L.; French university professor; b. 4 April 1910, Smyrna, Turkey; s. of Prince and Princess Dédéyan (née Emma Elisabeth Ekisler); *m.* Phyllis Sivrisarian 1938; four s. one d.; ed. Coll. Notre Dame de Ste. Croix, Neuilly and Sorbonne.
Reader in French Literature, Univ. of Rennes 42; Prof. of French and Comparative Literature, Univ. of Lyons 45; Prof. of Comparative Literature at the Sorbonne 49-; Sec.-Gen. Int. Fed. of Modern Languages and Literature 46-54; Dir. Inst. of Comparative Modern Literature, Sorbonne 55-68, 71; Editor of *Encyclopédie permanente Clartés* 61-, and *Revue des Etudes Gaulliennes.*
Leisure interest: fine arts.
Publs. *La Sophonisme de Mairet* 45, *Montaigne chez ses amis anglo-saxons* 46, *Essai sur le Journal de Voyage de Montaigne* 46, *Le Journal de Voyage de Montaigne* 47, *Argile* 47, *Studies in Marivaux, Stendhal, Du Fail, Balzac, V. Hugo* 50-53, *Le Thème de Faust dans la Littérature Européenne* 54-67, *Madame de Lafayette, La Nouvelle Héloïse, Stendhal et les Chroniques italiennes* 55, *Voltaire et la Pensée anglaise* 56, *Le "Gil Blas" de La Sage* 56, 65, *Gérard de Nerval et l'Allemagne* 57-59, *L'Angleterre dans la pensée de Diderot* 59, *Dante en Angleterre* 58-66, *"Le Roman Comique" de Scarron* 59, *Rilke et la France* 61, *L'Influence de Rousseau sur la sensibilité européenne à la fin du XVIIIe. siècle* 61, *Stendhal Chroniqueur* 62, *Victor Hugo et l'Allemagne* 63, 65, *L'Italie dans l'oeuvre romanesque de Stendhal* 63, *Le Cosmopolitisme littéraire de Charles Du Bos* 68, 70, *Racine et sa "Phèdre"* 68, *Le Nouveau Mal du Siècle de Baudelaire à nos Jours* 68-72, *Une guerre dans le mal des hommes* 71, *Chateaubriand et Rousseau* 72, *Le Cosmopolitisme européen sous la Révolution et l'Empire* 75, *L'Arioste en France* 75.
27 rue de la Ferme, Neuilly-sur-Seine; and Manoir de La Motte, 35 La Richardais, France.
Telephone: 747-83-84 and 46-21-12.

Dedijer, Vladimir, DR.IURIS, M.A.; Yugoslav writer; b. 4 Feb. 1914, Belgrade; *m.* 1st Olga Popović 1943, 2nd Vera Križman 1944; one s. two d.; ed. Belgrade Univ.
Lieut.-Col. in Tito's army, Second World War; Yugoslav Del. to U.N. Gen. Assemblies 45, 46, 48, 49, 51, 52; mem. Yugoslav Del. to Peace Conf., Paris 46; mem. Central Cttee. League of Communists of Yugoslavia 52-54; Prof. of Modern History, Belgrade Univ. 54-55; defended right of M. Djilas to free speech 54; expelled from Central Cttee. of League of Communists 54; sentenced to 6 months on probation 55; Simon Senior Fellow, Manchester Univ. 60-62 now Hon. Fellow; Fellow of St. Antony's Coll., Oxford 62-63; Research Assoc., Harvard Univ. 63-64; Visiting Prof. Cornell Univ. 64-65, Mass. Inst. of Technology 69, Brandeis Univ. 70-71; Pres. Bertrand Russell's Int. War Crimes Tribunal 64-; mem. Serbian Acad. of Sciences 68; Order of Liberation of Yugoslavia.
Leisure interests: ping-pong, fortune-telling.
Publs. *Partisan Diary* 45, *Notes from the United States* 45, *Paris Peace Conference* 48, *Yugoslav-Albanian Relations* 49, *Tito* 52, *The Beloved Land* 62, *Sarajevo* 63; *The Battle Stalin Lost* 69, *History of Yugoslavia* 73.
Gorkičeva 16/V, Ljubljana, Yugoslavia.

de Duve, Christian René, M.D., M.SC.; Belgian scientist; b. 2 Oct. 1917, Thames Ditton, England; s. of Alphonse de Duve and Madeleine Pungs; *m.* Janine Herman 1943; two s. two d.; ed. Univ. of Louvain.
Professor of Physiol. Chemistry, Univ. of Louvain Medical School 47-; Prof. of Biochemistry, Rockefeller Univ., New York City 62-; Pres. Int. Inst. of Cellular and Molecular Pathology, Brussels; mem. Royal Acad. of Medicine (Belgium), Royal Acad. of Belgium, American Chem. Soc., Biochem. Soc., American Soc. of Biol. Chem., Pontifical Acad. of Sciences, American Soc. of

Cell Biology, Deutsche Akademie der Naturforsches, Leopoldina, Koninklijke Akademie voor Geneeskunde van België, etc.; Foreign mem. American Acad. of Arts and Sciences; Foreign assoc. Nat. Acad. of Sciences, U.S.A.; Prix des Alumni 49; Prix Pfizer 57; Prix Franqui 60; Prix Quinquennal Belge des Sciences Médicales 67; Gairdner Foundation Int. Award of Merit (Canada) 67; Dr. H. P. Heineken Prijs (Netherlands) 73; Nobel Prize for Medicine 74.
Leisure interests: tennis, skiing, bridge.
80 Central Park West, New York City, N.Y. 10023, U.S.A.; Le Pré St. Jean, 5988 Nethen, Belgium.
Telephone: (212)-724-8048 (U.S.A.); (010)-866628 (Belgium).

Deedes, Rt. Hon. William Francis, P.C., M.C.; British fmr. politician and newspaper editor; b. 1 June 1913, Aldington, Kent; *m.* Evelyn Hilary Branfoot 1942; two s. (one deceased) three d.; ed. Harrow School.
Member of Parliament for Ashford (Kent) 50-Sept. 74; Parl. Sec., Ministry of Housing and Local Govt. 54-55; Parl. Under-Sec. Home Dept. 55-57; Minister without Portfolio (Information) July 62-64; mem. Advisory Cttee. on Drug Dependence 67-74; Chair. Select Cttee. on Immigration and Race Relations 70-74; Editor *Daily Telegraph* 75-.
New Hayters, Aldington, Kent, England.
Telephone: Aldington 269.

Deer, William Alexander, M.SC., PH.D., F.R.S.; British mineralogist and petrologist; b. 26 Oct. 1910. Manchester; s. of William Deer and the late Davina Cunningham; *m.* 1st Margaret Marjorie Kidd 1939 (died 1971), 2nd Rita Tagg 1973; two s. one d.; ed. elementary and Central High School, Manchester, and Univs. of Manchester and Cambridge.
Assistant Lecturer, Univ. of Manchester 37-39; Senior 1851 Research Fellow 39-40; Research Fellow, St. John's Coll., Cambridge 39-47; Demonstrator, Mineralogy Dept., Cambridge Univ. 46-50; Tutor, St. John's Coll. 48-50; Prof. of Geology, Manchester Univ. 50-61; Prof. of Mineralogy and Petrology, Cambridge Univ. 61-; Master of Trinity Hall, Cambridge 66-75; Vice-Chancellor, Cambridge Univ. 71-73; mem. Natural Environment Research Council 68-71; Pres. Mineralogical Soc. 68-70; Pres. Geological Soc. 69-71; Greenland expeditions 35, 36, 53, 66; Hon. Fellow, St. John's Coll., Cambridge; Trustee, British Museum 66-75; Daniel Pigeon Prize and Murchison Medal of Geological Soc., London; Bruce Medal of Royal Soc. of Edinburgh.
Leisure interest: gardening.
Publs. *Carsphairn Igneous Complex* 35, *Petrology of the Skaergaard Intrusion, East Greenland* (with L. R. Wager) 39, *Rock Forming Minerals* 5 vols. (with R. A. Howie and J. Zussman) 62-63, *Petrology and Mineralogy of the Kangerdlugssuaq Alkaline Intrusion* (with Dr. C. Kempe) 70.
Department of Mineralogy and Petrology, Downing Place, Cambridge; Steading, Church Street, Great Shelford, Cambs., England.
Telephone: 51741 (Downing Place); Shelford 3671.

Dees, Bowen Causey, PH.D.; American science administrator; b. 20 July 1917, Batesville, Miss.; s. of John S. and Ida Lea (Causey) Dees; *m.* Sarah E. Sanders 1937; one d.; ed. Mississippi High Schools, Mississippi Coll., N.Y. Univ.
Graduate Asst., N.Y. Univ. 37-42, Instructor in Physics, N.Y. Univ. 42-43; Prof. of Physics, Mississippi Coll. 43-44; Instructor in Electrical Communications, Radar School, Mass. Inst. of Technology 44-45; Asst. Prof. of Physics, Rensselaer Polytechnic Inst. 45-47; Physicist to Div. Dir., Scientific and Technical Div., Gen. H.Q., Supreme Commdr. for the Allied Powers, Tokyo 47-51; Program Dir. for Fellowships, Nat. Science Foundation 51-56; Deputy Asst. Dir. for Scientific Personnel and Educ. 56-59, Asst. Dir. 59-63; Assoc. Dir. for Educ.

63-64, for Planning 63-66; Vice-Pres. Univ. of Ariz. 66-68, Provost for Academic Affairs 68-70; Pres. The Franklin Inst. Feb. 70-.

Leisure interests: photography, handicrafts.

Publs. *Fundamentals of Physics* 45; articles in educational and scientific journals.

The Franklin Institute, 20th and Benjamin Franklin Parkway, Philadelphia, Pa. 19103; Home: 8208 Seminole Avenue, Chestnut Hill, Philadelphia, Pa. 19118, U.S.A.

de Faria, Antonio Leite; Portuguese Ambassador to United Kingdom 68-73; see *The International Who's Who 1975-76.*

de Ferranti, Basil Reginald Vincent Ziani, M.A., C.ENG., F.I.E.E., F.B.C.S.; British business executive; b. 2 July 1930, Alderley Edge, Cheshire; s. of Sir Vincent (*q.v.*) and Lady de Ferranti (née Wilson); brother of Sebastian Ziani de Ferranti, *q.v.*; m. 1st Susan Sara Gore, three s.; m. 2nd Simone Nangle, one d.; m. 3rd Hilary Mary Laing; ed. Eton and Trinity Coll., Cambridge.

Graduate Apprenticeship Course, D. Napier & Sons, Acton 53-54; Manager of Domestic Appliances, Ferranti Ltd. 54-57; Dir. of Overseas Operations, Ferranti Ltd. 57-62; Dep. Managing Dir., Int. Computers & Tabulators Ltd. 63-64, Managing Dir. ICT 64-68; Dir. International Computers (Holdings) Ltd. 68-72; Deputy Chair., Ferranti Ltd. 72-; M.P. 58-64; Parl. Sec. Ministry of Aviation July-Oct. 62; mem. Econ. and Soc. Cttee. of EEC 73-; Conservative.

Ferranti Ltd., Millbank Tower, Millbank, London, S.W.1; Home: 19 Lennox Gardens, London, S.W.1, England.

Telephone: 01-834-6611 (Office); 01-584-2256 (Home).

de Ferranti, Sebastian Ziani; British electrical engineer; b. 5 Oct. 1927, Alderley Edge, Cheshire; s. of Sir Vincent (*q.v.*) and Lady de Ferranti (née Wilson); brother of Basil Reginald Vincent Ziani de Ferranti, *q.v.*; m. Mona Helen Cunningham 1953; one s. two d.; ed. Ampleforth Coll.

Commissioned in 4th/7th Dragoon Guards; Brown Boveri, Switzerland and Alsthom, France 48-50; Transformer Dept., Ferranti Ltd. 50, Dir. 54-, Man. Dir. 58-, Chair. Feb. 63-; Pres. BEAMA 69-70, Manchester Technology Asscn. 72-, Manchester and Region Centre for Educ. in Science, Educ. and Technology 72-; Chair. Int. Electrical Asscn. 70-72; mem. Nat. Defence Industries Council 69-; Trustee, Tate Gallery 71-; Hon. D.Sc. (Salford Univ.); Hon. Fellow, Manchester Univ. Inst. of Science and Technology; Granada Guildhall Lecture 66; Royal Inst. Discourse 69; Louis Blériot Lecture, Paris 70; Faraday Lecture 70, 71; Hon. D.Sc., Cranfield Inst. of Technology 73.

Ferranti Ltd., Hollinwood, Lancashire; Home: Kerfield House, Knutsford, Cheshire, England.

Telephone: 061-681-2000 (Office).

de Ferranti, Sir Vincent Ziani, Kt., M.C., LL.D., D.ENG·, F.I.E.E., F.R.A.E.S.; British electrical engineer; b. 16 Feb. 1893; m. Dorothy H. C. Wilson 1919; two s. (Basil and Sebastian, *q.v.*), three d.; ed. Repton School.

Served First World War 14-19; Man. Transformer Dept., Ferranti Ltd. 21-30, Chair. Ferranti Ltd. 30-63; Chair. British Electrical and Allied Manufacturers' Asscn. 38-39, Vice-Pres. 46-57, Pres. 57-59; served Second World War 39-40; Hon. Col. 123 Field Engineer Regt., R.E., T.A. 48-57; Pres. Inst. of Electrical Engineers 46-47; Chair. British Nat. Cttee. and Chair. Int. Exec. Council of World Power Conf. 50-62; Pres. British Electrical Power Convention 49-50; Pres. Television Society 54-57.

Henbury Hall, Macclesfield, Cheshire, SK11 9PJ, England.

Telephone: Macclesfield 22400.

Defferre, Gaston, LIC. en D.; French lawyer, politician and journalist; b. 14 Sept. 1910; ed. Coll. de Nîmes, Aix-en-Provence Univ.

Legal practice in Marseilles before the second World War, resistance activity in the "Brutus" organisation 40-44; Dir. *Le Provençal* 44-; Pres. Municipal Resistance Del., Marseilles 44; Mayor of Marseilles April-Oct. 45, May 53-; Dep. from Bouches du Rhône to Constituent Assemblies 45-46, Nat. Assembly 46-58; Sec. of State, Présidence du Conseil Jan.-June 46; Under-Sec. of State for Overseas France Dec. 45-Jan. 46; Minister of the Merchant Marine July 50-August 51; Minister of Overseas France Jan. 56-May 57; Senator 59-62; Deputy to Nat. Assembly 62-; Socialist Candidate for President of the Republic 64-65, 69; Officier, Légion d'Honneur, Croix de Guerre, Rosette de la Résistance, King's Medal for Courage in the Cause of Freedom; fmr. mem. Dir. Cttee. Parti Socialiste (S.F.I.O.).

Publ. *Un nouvel horizon.*

Assemblée Nationale, Paris; Mairie de Marseille, Marseille, France.

De Filippo, Eduardo (brother of Peppino De Filippo, *q.v.*); Italian playwright, actor and producer; b. 1900. Worked as actor, producer and writer with Compagnia Vincenzo Scarpetta and Compagnia Teatro Nuovo; founder of Il Teatro Umoristico I De Filippo 31-44; Dir. and Owner Teatro San Ferdinando, Naples 53-; many prizes as playwright, actor and producer.

Publs. *Natale in Casa Cupiello, Non ti Pago, Napoli Milionaria, Filumena Marturano, Questi Fantasmi, Le Voci di Dentro, Le Bugie con le gambe lunghe, Sabato, Domenica e Lunedi,* and many other one-act plays, operas, TV scripts and films; three books of poetry.

Via Aquileia 16, Rome, Italy.

De Filippo, Giuseppe (Peppino De Filippo) (brother of Eduardo De Filippo, *q.v.*); Italian playwright, actor and producer; b. 24 Aug. 1903.

Debut 09; with brother Edward founded variety company 31; Founder and Dir. Italian Theatre Co. of Peppino de Filippo 44-, Company toured Russia May 65; writer of over sixty farces, musical *Le metamorfosi di un suonatore ambulante,* and numerous poems and songs; also appears in films and on television.

Viale Parioli 96, Rome, Italy.

de Fischer Reichenbach, Henry-Béat, DR. JUR.; Swiss diplomatist; b. 22 July 1901, Berne; s. of Henry and Marie Caroline de Fischer Reichenbach (née Falck-Crivelli); m. Madeleine de Graffenried 1949; three d.; ed. Stella Matutina, Feldkirch, Univs. of Berne, Fribourg, Munich and Paris.

Entered Swiss Diplomatic Service 29, The Hague, Buenos Aires, Warsaw, Riga and Helsinki; Counsellor, Bucharest 42-47; Asst. to Head of Mission, Cairo 47-49, Minister, Cairo 49-54, Addis Ababa 52-54, Lisbon 54-59; Ambassador to Austria 59-64; Ambassador to United Kingdom 64-66; Pres. Fondation pour l'histoire des Suisses à l'étranger; Pres. Swiss Asscn. of Knights of the Sovereign Order of Malta; Pres. Comité international exécutif de l'Ordre de Malte pour l'assistance aux lépreux 70; Pres., Fédération Européenne des Associations contre La Lèpre 72-73; Camões Prize 61.

Leisure interests: architecture, history, psychology.

Publs. *Contributions à la connaissance des relations suisses-égyptiennes* 56, *Dialogue luso-suisse* 60, *Les Suisses en Grande-Bretagne au XVIIIe siècle* 68.

Le Pavillon, Thunplatz 52, 3000 Berne; Clos Soleil, Vufflens-le-Château, (Vaud), Switzerland.

Telephone: 031-44-15-09 (Berne).

Defraigne, Jean, D. en DROIT; Belgian politician; b. 19 April 1929, Roosendael, Netherlands; m.; two c.; ed. Univ. of Liège.

Lawyer and Deputy Magistrate; mem. City Council, Liège 65-, Alderman 71-73; mem. Chamber of Reps.

65-74, Senator 74-; Sec. of State for Walloon Regional Economy 73-74; Minister of Public Works 74-; Freedom and Progress Party.
Ministry of Public Works, rue de la Loi 155, 1040 Brussels, Belgium.

de Freitas, Rt. Hon. Sir Geoffrey Stanley, K.C.M.G., M.P.; British barrister, politician, and diplomatist; b. 7 April 1913; s. of Sir Anthony Patrick and Lady de Freitas (née Maud Short); m. Helen Graham Bell 1938; three s. one d.; ed. Haileybury, Clare Coll., Cambridge (Hon. Fellow) and Yale Univ. (Mellon Fellow).
Borough Councillor in Shoreditch 36-39; mem. Gen. Council of the Bar 39; served Royal Air Force 40-45; Labour M.P. for Central Nottingham 45-50, for Lincoln 50-61, for Kettering 64-; Parl. Private Sec. to Prime Minister 45-46; Under-Sec. of State for Air 46-50; Del. to UN Assembly 49, 64; Under-Sec. of State Home Office 50-51; Del. to Council of Europe 51-54, 65-70 (Leader of Del. 65-66), to NATO Parl. Conf. 55-60 (Treas. 58-60), (Leader of Del. 65-66, 74-); Chair. Soc. Labour Lawyers 56-58, Labour Party Housing Cttee. 51-54, Air Cttee. 55-60, Agriculture Cttee. 60-61, Defence Cttee. 64-; mem. Select Cttee. on Privileges 64-66; Chair. Labour Cttee. for Europe 64-72; High Commr. in Ghana 61-63, in Kenya 63-64; Pres. Assembly of Council of Europe 66-69; mem. European Parliament (Vice-Pres.) 75-; Chair. Select Cttee. on Overseas Devt. 74-76; Dir. Laporte Industries Ltd. 68-.
Office: House of Commons, London, S.W.1; Home: 11 Trumpington Road, Cambridge, England.
Telephone: 01-219-4571 (Office); Cambridge 58477 (Home).

Dega, Wiktor, M.D.; Polish surgeon, orthopaedist and educator; b. 7 Dec. 1896, Poznań; s. of Wiktor and Zofia D.; m. Maria Zelewska 1928; one s. two d.; ed. Berlin, Warsaw and Poznań Univs.
Assistant-resident, Orthopaedic Clinic of Poznań Univ. 24-30; Chief Asst., Orthopaedic Inst., Poznań 30-38; Head, Orthopaedic Dept. Municipal Hospital, Bydgoszcz 38-39; Head, Children's Surgery Dept., Karol and Maria Hospital, Warsaw 40-45; Dir. Orthopaedic Clinic, Univ. and Medical Acad., Poznań 46-67, Prof. Emer. 67-; mem. Presidium All-Polish Cttee. of Nat. Unity Front June 71-; Chair. Polish Soc. for Fight against Disablement; mem. Polish Acad. of Sciences, Vice-Chair. Cttee. for Rehabilitation and Adaptation of Man 72-; mem. Int. Soc. of Orthopaedics and Traumatology, Int. Soc. of Surgeons, Fed. German Orthopaedic Asscn.; Hon. mem. Austrian, Czechoslovak, Finnish, French, G.D.R., Hungarian, Soviet, Polish, Yugoslav, Bulgarian Socs. of Orthopaedics and Traumatology, Polish Soc. of Rheumatology, Polish Medical Soc., Polish Medical Alliance U.S.A.; corresp. mem. American Acad. of Orthopaedic Surgery, Italian Soc. Orthopaedics and Traumatology; foreign mem. French Acad. Surgeons; Expert on Rehabilitation Affairs WHO; Dr. h.c. Medical Acad., Poznań, Cracow and Wrocław; State Prizes 51, 68; Albert Lasker Prize 66; Alfred Jurzykowski Award, U.S.A. 73; Order of Builders of People's Poland, Officer's and Commdr.'s Cross with Star of Order Polonia Restituta, Order of Banner of Labour 1st Class.
Publs. numerous articles in professional journals.
Home: ul. Dzierżyńskiego 135, Poznań, Poland.

de Gaay Fortman, Wilhelm Friedrich; Netherlands politician; b. 8 May 1911, Amsterdam; m.; two s. three d.; ed. Gymnasium Dordrecht, Calvinist Gymnasium, Amsterdam and Free Univ. Amsterdam.
Special Agricultural Office, Ministry of Econ. Affairs 34-38; with Ministry of Social Affairs, later Head, Industrial Relations Div. 38-47; Prof. of Civil Law and Labour Law, Free Univ. of Amsterdam 47, Rector 62-63, 65-72; mem. Parl. (First Chamber) 60, Party Leader in Chamber 71, Second Vice-Chair. First

Chamber 69; Minister for Home Affairs May 73-; mem. State Comm. on Civil Law 47, European Comm. on Human Rights 65, Vice-Chair. 72; mem. Board Netherlands Org. for the Advancement of Fundamental Research (ZWO) 60; Chair. Netherlands Section, Kingdom Comm.; Principal, Nat. Protestant Trade Union Cadre Training Centre 48-72; Vice-Pres. Netherlands Univs. Council; numerous church activities; Gentleman-in-Waiting (Extraordinary) to the Queen 55; Knight, Order of Netherlands Lion 59, Commdr. Order of Orange-Nassau 72.
Publs. *De onderneming in het arbeidsrecht* 36, *De arbeider in de nieuwe samenleving* 52, *De vakbeweging* 54, *Recht doen* 72.
Ministry of Home Affairs, The Hague, Netherlands.

de Gale, Sir Leo Victor, G.C.M.G., C.B.E.; Grenadan administrator; b. 28 Dec. 1921, St. Andrew's; s. of George Victor and Marie Leonie de Gale; m. Brenda Mary Helen Scott; five s. two d.; ed. Grenada Boys' Secondary School, Univ. of Sir George Williams, Montreal, Canada.
Chairman, mem. Public Service Comm. 60-74; mem. Judicial and Legal Services Comm. 70-73; Chair. Grenada Cadets Comm. Board 71-74; Gov.-Gen. of Grenada 74-; Chair. and mem. Board of Govs. Grenada Boys' Secondary School 60-65; mem. Board of Govs., Grenada Teachers' Coll. 66-67; First Dir. Grenada Branch, British Red Cross Soc. 60-65; Deputy Chair. Grenada Co-operative Banana Soc.
Leisure interests: golf, tennis, billiards.
Governor-General's House, St. George's, Grenada.
Telephone: 2401.

de Geer, Carl, LL.B.; Swedish business executive; b. 20 Sept. 1918, Stockholm; s. of Louis de Geer and Beth (Tersmeden) de Geer; m. Maud Mörner af Morlanda 1942; two s.; ed. Uppsala Univ. and Stockholm School of Econs.
Joined Stockholms Enskilda Bank 47, Asst. Dir. 51, Dir. 54; Vice-Man. Dir. AB Investor 56-70, Man. Dir. 70-; Chair. of Board AB Nordiska Kompaniet, Eurocard Nord AB, HNJ Intressenter, AB Navigare, Rederi AB Motortank, Svenska Ostasiatiska Kompaniet, Finansierings AB Vendor, AB Vendax, Återförsäkrings AB Atlas; Vice-Chair. KemaNord AB, Nitro Nobel AB; mem. Board Skandinaviska Enskilda Banken, Gen. Reinsurance Corpn., U.S.A. and others; mem. Advisory Board U.S. Trust Investment Fund.
Leisure interests: hunting, tennis.
Office: AB Investor, P.O. Box 16 174, 5-103 24 Stockholm; Home: Stora Wäsby, 5-194 01 Uplands Väsby, Sweden.

De Geer, Jan Gustaf Gérard; Swedish international official; b. 7 Sept. 1918.
Swedish Red Cross Liaison Officer with British Red Cross in Germany 46, with British Red Cross Comm. for N.W. Europe and Control Comm. for Germany 47; A.D.C. to Count Bernadotte, Palestine 48; Chief, Swedish Red Cross Mission to Berlin 48-49; Chief, Foreign Relations Dept., Swedish Red Cross 49-56, Acting Sec.-Gen. (ex officio) 56-57; Sec.-Gen., World Fed. of United Nations Asscns. 63, now Hon. Treas.; several foreign decorations.
World Federation of United Nations Associations, Centre International, Geneva; 20 Chemin Colladon, 1211 Geneva, Switzerland.

Degerbøl, Magnus, DR. PHIL.; Danish zoologist; b. 8 July 1895, Sjørring; s. of Jens Hansen Jensen and Mette Sørensen; m. Ellen Marie K. Jürgensen 1924; one s. one d.; ed. Københavns Universitet.
Curator of Mammals, Zoological Museum, Univ. of Copenhagen 24-43, Keeper of Vertebrate Dept. 43-50, Dir. Quaternary-Zoological Laboratory 56-66; Univ. of Copenhagen Lecturer Quaternary-Zoology 50-56, Prof. 56-66; Pres. Danish Natural History Soc. 44-49, and

Zootopografical Investigations of Denmark 46-62; Editor *Videnskabelige Meddelelser Dansk Naturhistorisk Forening* 31-44, *Danmarks Fauna* 40-46, and *Acta Arctica* 43-60; mem. Royal Danish Acad. of Sciences and Letters; Hon. mem. American Soc. of Mammalogists 62; Corresp. Fellow Arctic Inst. N. America 67; Knight Order of Dannebrog.
Expeditions: Blossevilles Coast, East Greenland 32, Equatoria, Central Africa Expedition 47, Subantarctic Seas, Galathea Expedition 52, Andes Mountains 54, Pres. Danish Thule-Ellesmere Island Expedition 39-41.
Publs. *The Prehistoric Vertebrates of Denmark* 33-70, *Mammals, Fifth Thule Expedition Arctic North America* 35, *Mammals of Denmark* 35, *Mammalia Zoology of the Faroes* 40, and works on evolution, domestication, Norse culture and Eskimo habitation in Greenland.
Fuglevadsvej 4, Kgs. Lyngby, Denmark.
Telephone: 870529.

De Groote, Jacques, M.A.(ECON.); Belgian international finance official; b. 25 May 1927, Klerken; *m.*; ed. Cambridge and Louvain Univs.
Adviser Nat. Bank of Belgium 57-65; Adviser to Gov. of Nat. Bank of Zaire 66-69; Financial Adviser to Belgian Del. to OECD 65-71; Chief Adviser, Research Dept., Nat. Bank of Belgium 71-73; Exec. Dir. Int. Bank for Reconstruction and Devt. (World Bank) and Int. Monetary Fund 73-; Knight Order of Leopold (Belgium).
700 19th Street, N.W., Washington, D.C. 20431, U.S.A.; Home: 11 avenue de Mercure, 1180 Brussels, Belgium.
Telephone: (202) 393-6362 (Office).

Degtyar, Dmitry Danilovich; Soviet diplomatist and politician; b. 1904; ed. Moscow Planning Inst.
Trade Union activity 35-38; State Exec. 38-39; Chair. State Planning Cttee. of the R.S.F.S.R. 39-47; Vice-Chair. U.S.S.R. State Planning Comm. 49-53; Vice-Chair. Council of Ministers of the R.S.F.S.R. 39-47; mem. later Deputy Chair. State Cttee. for Foreign Econ. Affairs 57-62; Ambassador to Guinea 62-64; Dep. Chair. State Cttee. for Foreign Econ. Affairs 65-.
State Cttee. for Foreign Economic Affairs, Ovchinnikovskaya nab. 18/1, Moscow, U.S.S.R.

de Guingand, Major-General Sir Francis W., K.B.E., C.B., D.S.O.; Business executive and fmr. army officer; b. 28 Feb. 1900, London; s. of late Francis Julius de Guingand; *m.* Arlie R. Stewart 1942 (dissolved 1957); one *d.*; ed. Ampleforth Coll., Royal Military Coll., Sandhurst, Staff Coll., Camberley.
Joined Army 20, served in King's African Rifles 26-31; Military Asst. to Sec. of State for War 39-40; Dir. Military Intelligence, Middle East 42; Chief of Staff 8th Army 42-44, 21st Army Group 44-45, retd. 47; Chair. Rothmans of Pall Mall Ltd., London 61-, Rothmans in S. Africa 61-, Carreras Ltd. 67-68; Dir. and Int. Dir. Rothmans Group.
Publs. *Operation Victory* 47, *African Assignment* 53, *Generals at War* 64.
c/o Rothmans Carreras Ltd., 27 Baker Street, London, W.1, England.
Telephone: 01-486-1244.

Dehlavi, Samiulla Khan; Pakistani diplomatist; b. 14 Sept. 1913, Mangrol; s. of Sir A. M. K. Dehlavi; *m.* Begum Geneviève Chantrenne; two s.; ed. Univs. of Bombay and Oxford.
Joined Indian Civil Service 38, served in Province of Bengal, later District Magistrate, Tipperah and Chittagong, E. Pakistan; later in Pakistani Foreign Office; Deputy Sec. Ministry of Foreign Affairs and Commonwealth Relations 50; Chargé d'Affaires *a.i.*, Paris 50-53; Joint Sec. Ministry of Foreign Affairs and Commonwealth Relations 53-57; Amb. to Italy, concurrently to Tunisia 57-61; Foreign Sec. 61-63; Amb. to U.A.R., also

to Libya and Yemen 63-65, to Switzerland, concurrently to Albania 65-66; High Commr. in U.K. and concurrently Amb. to Ireland 66-68; Amb. to France 68-72, to U.S.S.R., concurrently to Finland and Mongolia 72-75, to Fed. Repub. of Germany 75-; Sitara-i-Pakistan; Grand Cross of Merit (Italy).
Leisure interests: riding, big game hunting, collecting antiques.
Embassy of Pakistan, Bonn-Bad Godesberg, Rheinallee 24, Federal Republic of Germany.

Dehnkamp, Willy; German politician; b. 22 July 1903, Hamburg; s. of Arthur and Anna Dehnkamp (née Griebel); *m.* Helene Kömmpel 1927; two s.; ed. elementary school.
Apprenticeship as locksmith 18-22; mem. Social Democrat Party 20-; mem. Blumenthal County Council 29-33; persecuted by Nazis 33-36; Army Service 42-45; Prisoner-of-War in U.S.S.R. 45-48; Municipal Official Bremen-Blumenthal 49-51; Senator for Educ., Bremen 51-65, Pres. of Senate and Mayor of Bremen 65-67; Deputy mem. Bundesrat 52-63, mem. 63-67; Pres. Standing Conf. of Ministers for Cultural Affairs of German Federal Republic 54-55, 62-63; mem. German Scientific Council 57-65, German Educ. Council 68-72, Exec. Board of German UNESCO Comm. 68-; Chair. Gerhard-Marcks-Stiftung, Bremen 70-.
Leisure interest: gardening.
282 Bremen-Blumenthal, Rönnebeckerstrasse 87a, Federal Republic of Germany.
Telephone: 60-22-86.

De Hoffmann, Frederic, M.A., PH.D.; American scientist and industrialist; b. 8 July 1924, Vienna, Austria; s. of Otto and Marianne de Hoffmann; *m.* Patricia Lynn Stewart 1953; no *c.*; ed. Harvard Univ.
Scientific mem. Los Alamos Lab., U.S. Atomic Energy effort 44-45, Alt. Asst. Dir. 50-51; founded Gen. Atomic Div. of Gen. Dynamics Corpn. 55; founded Gen. Atomic Europe 60; Vice-Pres. and Senior Vice-Pres. Gen. Dynamics 55-67, also Pres. Gen. Atomic and Gen. Atomic Europe; Pres. Gulf Gen. Atomic and Gulf Gen. Atomic Europe 67-69; Vice-Pres. Gulf Oil Corpn. 67-69; Chancellor The Salk Inst. 70-72, mem. Board 70-, Pres. 72-; mem. Board, Gulf Mineral Resources Co. 68-73, S. Calif. First Nat. Bank 71-75; Pres. Conf. on future of Science and Technology, Govt. of Austria 72-; trustee various academic institutions, etc.; Grand Silver Cross of Merit and Cross of Science and Arts (Austria).
Leisure interests: skiing, photography.
The Salk Institute, P.O. Box 1809, San Diego, Calif. 92112; Home: 9736 La Jolla Farms Road, La Jolla, Calif. 92037, U.S.A.
Telephone: 714-453-4100 (Office); 714-453-0454 (Home).

Deif, Nazir; Egyptian international finance official; b. 4 March 1923; *m.*; four *c.*; ed. Univs. of Cairo and Chicago.
Member Expert Group on Industrialization of U.A.R. 53-54; Dir. Econ. Planning Comm. 57-58, Dir.-Gen. 58-61; Under-Sec. Ministry of Planning 61-64; Gov. IMF 64-66; Minister of Treasury 64-68; Prof. Inst. of Statistical Studies and Research, Cairo Univ. 68; Special Sequestrator American Univ. in Cairo 69-70; Exec. Dir. IMF 70-; mem. UN Cttee. for Devt. Planning 66; Consultant UN Industrial Devt. Org. 68; Adviser Arab Centre for Industrial Devt. 69.
International Monetary Fund, 19th and H Streets, N.W., Washington, D.C. 20431, U.S.A.

Deighton, Len; British author; b. 1929, London.
Publs. *The Ipcress File, Horse under Water* 63, *Funeral in Berlin* 64, *Billion Dollar Brain* 66, *An Expensive Place to Die* 67, *Action Cook Book, Où est le Garlic, Len Deighton's London Dossier* (guide book), *Only When I Larf* 68, *Bomber* 70, *Declarations of War* (short stories) 71, *Close-Up* 72, *Spy Story* 74, *Yesterday's Spy* 75.

c/o Jonathan Cape Ltd., 30 Bedford Square, London, W.C.1, England.
Telephone: 01-636-9395.

Deinoff, Rolf, B.SC.(ECON.); Swedish business executive; b. 6 Feb. 1917, Örebro, Sweden; s. of Josef and Elisabeth Deinoff; m. Britta Danielson 1938; three s. one d.; ed. Higher Commercial School, Örebro, Stockholm School of Economics, and Inst. of Business Studies.
Assistant, Dept. of Prices for Mil. Deliveries, Nat. Swedish Industry Comm. 41-43; Financial Man. AB Pumpindustri, Mölndahl 43-47; Stockholms Enskilda Bank 47-67, Deputy Man. Dir. 60-67; Deputy Man. Dir. Svenska Tändsticks Aktiebolaget (Swedish Match Co.), Jönköping Jan.-June 68, Man. Dir. June 68-; Chair., Vice-Chair. and mem. of the Board of a number of Swedish and foreign companies; Commdr. Royal Order of Vasa; Grand' Ufficiale dell' Ordine al Merita della Repubblica Italiana.
Leisure interest: golf.
Svenska Tändsticks Aktiebolaget, Box 16100, S-103 22 Stockholm; Home: Strandvägen 27, 114 56 Stockholm, Sweden.
Telephone: 08/22-06-20 (Office); 08/63-34-35 (Home).

De Jager, Cornelis; Netherlands astronomer; b. 29 April 1921, Texel; s. of Jan de Jager and Cornelia Kuyper; m. Duotsje Rienks 1947; two s. two d.; ed. Univ. of Utrecht.
Assistant in theoretical physics, Univ. of Utrecht 46; Asst. in Astronomy, Univ. of Leiden, Asst. Astron. Inst., Utrecht; Assoc. Prof. of Stellar Astrophysics, Univ. of Utrecht 57, Ordinary Prof. in Gen. Astrophysics 60-; Extraordinary Prof., Univ. of Brussels and founder, Space Research Lab., Utrecht Astron. Inst. 61; Man. Dir. Utrecht Astron. Inst. 63-; Asst. Gen. Sec. Int. Astron. Union 67-70, Gen. Sec. 70-73; Pres. Netherlands Astron. Asscn. 75-; mem. Exec. Council Cttee. on Space Research (COSPAR) 70-72, Pres. 72-; mem. Exec. Council, ICSU 70-; Aggregate Prof., Univ. of Brussels 70-; mem. Royal Netherlands Acad. of Art and Sciences, Royal Belgium Acad. of Art and Sciences; Assoc. mem. Royal Astron. Soc. (London); Corresp. mem. Soc. Royale de Science, Liège, Int. Acad. Astronautics; Dr. h.c. Univ. of Wrocław, Poland 75.
Leisure interests: wild life, bird observation, cinematography, participation in cross-country races.
Publs. About 200 publications including: The Hydrogen Spectrum of the Sun 52, Structure and Dynamics of the Solar Atmosphere 59, The Solar Spectrum 65, Solar Flares and Space Research 69, Reports on Astronomy 70, Highlights in Astronomy 70, Image Processing Techniques in Astronomy (with H. Nieuwenhuyzen) 75.
Offices: Utrecht, Observatory, Zonnenburg 2; Space Research Laboratory, Beneluxlaan 21, Utrecht; Home: Zonneburg 1, Utrecht, Netherlands.
Telephone: 312841, 937145 (Offices); 314253 (Home).

Dejean, Maurice; French diplomatist; b. 30 Sept. 1899, Clichy; m. Marie-Claire Giry 1953; one d.; ed. Sorbonne.
Served Ministry of Foreign Affairs 26, Berlin 29-39; Chef de Cabinet (for Foreign Affairs) to Daladier and Reynaud 39-40; collaborated with Coulondre in editing French Yellow Book 40; Nat. Commr. for Foreign Affairs French Nat. Cttee. 41-42; Diplomatic Adviser to French Cttee. of Nat. Liberation 42-43; Minister Plenipotentiary to Allied Governments in London 43-44; Gen. Dir. for Political Affairs Foreign Office 44-45; Del. San Francisco Conf. 45, U.N. Gen. Assembly N.Y. 46; French Ambassador to Czechoslovakia Dec. 45-Dec. 49; French Del. Int. Ruhr Authority May 49-Feb. 50; Head of French Mission, SCAP, Tokyo (rank of Ambassador) 50-52, Ambassador to Japan 52-54; Commr.-Gen. in Indo-China 54-55; Amb. to U.S.S.R. 55-64; Ambassadeur de France 45-; Dir. Shell française

65-72, Soc. des bains de mer et du Cercle des étrangers de Monaco 66-73; Pres. Soc. franco-soviétique de coopération industrielle (SOFRACOP) 66-68; Commdr. Légion d'Honneur.
110 boulevard de Courcelles, 75017 Paris, France.

Dejmek, Kazimierz; Polish actor and theatre director; b. 17 May 1924; m. 1925; two c.; ed. State Theatrical Acad., Łódź.
Actor, Rzeszów, Jelenia Góra Companies 45; Actor, Teatr Wojska Polskiego 46-49; Founder and Gen. Dir. Teatr Nowy, Łódź 49-61; Head, State Theatrical Acad., Łódź 52-55; Gen. Manager and Artistic Dir., Teatr Narodowy, Warsaw 61-68, Teatr Nowy, Łódź 69-; Assoc. Man. Teatr Dramatyczny, Warsaw 72-; numerous decorations.
Principal productions: Winkelried's Day (Andrzejewski and Zagórski) 56, Measure for Measure, Julius Caesar (Shakespeare) 56, 60, Darkness Covers the Earth (Andrzejewski) 57, Agamemnon (Aeschylus), Electra (Euripides), The Frogs (Aristophanes) 61, 63, The Story of the Glorious Resurrection of Our Lord (Nicolai of Wilkowieck) 61, 62, Word about Jacob Szela (Bruno Jasieński) 62, The Life of Joseph (Nicolai Rej) 65, Kordian (Słowacki) 65, Der Stellvertreter (Hochhuth), Dziady (A. Mickiewicz) 67, Uncle Vanya (Chekhov) 68, Jeux de Massacre (Ionesco) 71, Baths and Bed-Bug (Mayakovsky) 71, Trial Against Nine from Catonsville 71, Controller (Gogol) 71, La Passione 72, Acting About Resurrection 72, opera Henry VI at the Chase (Karol Kurpiński) 72, Philemon (Dürrenmatt) 73, opera Magic Flute (Mozart) 73, Electra (Giraudoux) 73, opera Devils of Loudun (Penderecki) 74, Operetta (Gąbrowicz) 75.
Ul. Rajców 8, 00-220 Warsaw, Poland.

de Jongh, Theunis Willem, M.SC., M.A., D.COM.; South African banker; b. 15 Dec. 1913, Gouda; s. of Petrus Johannes de Jongh and Rachel E. Wium; m. Anna F. Visser 1941; three s. two d.; ed. Stellenbosch, Pretoria and Columbia Univs.
Chief Statistician, Industrial Devt. Corpn. of S. Africa 42-45; Head, Econ. Research, S. African Reserve Bank 46-62, Exec. Asst. 62-67, Gov. and Chair. 67-; Chair. Nat. Finance Corpn. of S. Africa 67-; Alt. Gov. IBRD, IFC and IDA 67-72, Gov. 72-; mem. of Prime Minister's Econ. Advisory Council 67-; Decoration for Meritorious Service, S. Africa 75.
Leisure interests: golf, tennis; keen follower of rugby and cricket.
Publ. An Analysis of Banking Statistics in South Africa 47.
South African Reserve Bank, P.O. Box 427, Pretoria 0001; 134 Eastwood Street, Arcadia, Pretoria 0002, South Africa.
Telephone: 2-9581 (Office); 74-2231 (Home).

Dekeyser, Willy Clément, D.SC.; Belgian university professor; b. 16 Feb. 1910, Ostend; s. of Georges and Eugenie Vanderputte; m. Marie Madeleine Vandenberge 1943; one d.; ed. Albert School and Athénée Royal, Ostend, Ghent Univ.
Teacher, Athénée Royal, Ghent 31; Asst. Ghent Univ. 38, Lecturer 44, Prof. of Crystallography 48-; mem. Scientific and Technical Cttee. Euratom, Advisory Panel NATO, Flemish Acad. of Sciences; mem. Board Soc. Belge d'Optique et Instruments de Précision (OIP); Croix de Guerre, Commdr. Ordre de Léopold.
Leisure interest: French literature.
Publs. Les dislocations et la croissance des cristaux (with S. Amelinckx) 55, The structure and properties of grain boundaries (with S. Amelinckx) in Solid State Physics Vol. 8.
Laboratorium voor Kristallografie en Studie van de Vaste Stof, Krijgslaan 271, B-9000 Ghent; Home: Rijsenbergstraat 57, B-9000 Ghent, Belgium.
Telephone: 091-22-57-15.

de Kiewiet, Cornelis Willem, M.A., PH.D., LL.D., L.H.D., LITT.D.; American (b. Netherlands) historian; b. 21 May 1902; ed. Jeppe High School, Johannesburg, and Univs. of Witwatersrand, London, Paris and Berlin.
Teaching Asst. in History, Univ. of Witwatersrand 23; Teacher of Afrikaans and History, Prince Edward High School, Salisbury, S. Rhodesia 23-25; Asst. Prof. of History, State Univ. of Iowa 29-35; Assoc. Prof. 35-37; Prof. 37-41; Prof. of Modern European History, Cornell Univ. 41-48; Dean of Coll. of Arts and Sciences, Cornell Univ. 45-48, Provost 48-49; acting Pres. 49-51; Pres. Rochester Univ. June 51-61, Emer. 61-; Special Consultant to Navy Dept. and Dir. of Army Specialized Training Programmes in Area and Language, Cornell Univ. 43-45; Sec.-Treas. Asscn. American Univs. 51-54, Vice-Pres. 54-56, Pres. 56-58; Council Higher Educ., N.Y. State 58-; Nat. Acad. of Sciences Advisory Comm. for Africa 58-; Comm. for Education Liaison between U.S. and Sub-Sahara Africa 59-; Special Cttee. on Sponsored Research A.E.E. 58.
Publs. *British Colonial Policy and the South African Republics* 29, *The Imperial Factor* 37, *A History of South Africa* 41, *The Anatomy of South African Misery* 56; collaborator in many works, including *Cambridge History of the British Empire*.
22 Berkeley Street, Rochester, N.Y., U.S.A.

de Klerk, Albert; Netherlands organist and composer; b. 4 Oct. 1917; ed. Amsterdamsch Conservatorium under Dr. Anthon van der Horst.
Organist St. Joseph's Church, Haarlem 33-; City Organist Haarlem 56-; Prof. of Organ and Improvization, Amsterdamsch Conservatorium 64-; Dir. of Catholic Choir, Haarlem 46-; numerous gramophone records for Telefunken; Prix d'Excellence, Amsterdam 41, Prix du Disque, Prix Edison (for *Die Kleinorgel*) 62.
Compositions: several works for organ including two concertos for organ and orchestra, chamber-music, and liturgical music (seven masses).
Crayenesterlaan 22, Haarlem, Netherlands.
Telephone: 023-280654.

De Kooning, Willem; American (b. Netherlands) artist; b. 1904; ed. Rotterdam Acad. of Fine Arts.
Display work, dept. stores in the Netherlands 20-24; worked in Belgium 24-25, America 26, housepainter, muralist, New York 26, Mural, Hall of Pharmacy, New York World's Fair 39; Teacher, Black Mountain Coll. 48, Yale 50-51; One-man shows Egan Gallery 48, 50, Sidney Janis Gallery 53; Knoedler & Co., Manhattan 67; retrospective exhbn. at Tate Gallery, London 68; pictures in Museum of Modern Art, New York, St. Louis Museum, Chicago Art Inst. and in private collections.
Woodbine Drive, The Springs, East Hampton, N.Y. 11973, U.S.A.

Delacombe, Sir Rohan, K.C.M.G., K.C.V.O., K.B.E., C.B., D.S.O., K.ST.J.; British administrator and fmr. army officer; b. 25 Oct. 1906, Malta; s. of the late Lieut.-Col. and Mrs. A. Delacombe; m. Eleanor J. Foster, C.ST.J. 1941; one s. one d.; ed. Harrow, Royal Mil. Acad., Sandhurst, and Staff Coll., Camberley.
Served in Egypt, North China, India, active service Palestine, South-East Asia 37-39, France, Norway, Normandy, Italy 39-45; Deputy Mil. Sec., War Office 53-55; Major-Gen. 56; G.O.C., Berlin 59-62; retd. 62; Gov. Victoria, Australia 63-74; Administrator of Australia on four occasions; Pres. Royal British Legion, Wiltshire; mem. Victoria Promotion Council (Europe); Freeman of Melbourne; Hon. LL.D. Univs. of Melbourne and Monash.
Leisure interests: normal.
Shrewton Manor, Salisbury, Wilts., England.
Telephone: Shrewton 253.

de la Flor Valle, Gen. Miguel; Peruvian army officer and politician; b. 11 March 1924, Ferreñafe, Lambayeque; s. of Guillermo E. De la Flor Zevallos and Manuela M. Valle Urtega; m. María L. Illich Remott 1959; two s. two d.; ed. Colegio Nacional San José de Chiclayo, Escuela Militar Chorrillos, Escuela de Infantería, Escuela Superior de Guerra and Ecole Supérieure de Guerre, France.
Entered army 42, commissioned 46, Gen. 71; Pres. Board of Dirs. Compañía Peruana de Teléfonos 70, 71; Minister of Foreign Affairs Jan. 72-; Orden Militar de Ayacucho, Cruz del Mérito Militar and decorations from Belgium and Argentina.
Leisure interests: badminton, football.
Ministerio de Relaciones Exteriores, Lima, Peru.

de la Fuente y de la Fuente, Licinio; Spanish politician and lawyer; b. 7 Aug. 1923, Noez, Toledo; m.; six c.; ed. Univ. of Madrid.
Called to the Bar 49; lawyer in Ciudad Real 50-54, Segovia 54-56; Civil Gov. of Caceres 56-60; lawyer, Supreme Court 63-65; Nat. Adviser to Toledo Movement 61-64, Chief. of Secr. of Nat. Council of Toledo Movement 64-68, First Sec. 68-69; Dir.-Gen. Servicio Nacional de Cereales 65-68; mem. Parl. 64-71; Minister of Labour 69-75, Third Vice-Pres. 73-75.
Ministerio de Trabajo, Madrid, Spain.

Delage, Emile Jean-Baptiste, D. ès L.; French university professor; b. 23 July 1890, Paris; s. of Emile Jules and Emma (née Schmieder) Delage; m. Marguerite Martin 1921 (died 1970); ed. Univ. of Paris.
Lecturer Faculty of Letters Bordeaux 29-31, Prof. 31-32, Prof. of Greek Language and Literature 32-46; Dean of Faculty of Letters 41-46; Rector Académic de Clermont-Ferrand 46-50; Rector Acad. de Bordeaux 50-60, Hon. Rector 60-; served in First and Second World Wars; Croix de Guerre, Officier de la Légion d'Honneur, Commdr. des Palmes Académiques.
Leisure interest: music (violin).
Publs. *Biographie d'Apollonios de Rhodes* 30, *La Géographie dans les "Argonautiques" d'Apollonios de Rhodes* 30, *Les "Argonautiques" d'Apollonios de Rhodes* (trans., Vol. I) 74.
100 rue Chevalier, Bordeaux, France.
Telephone: 48-75-82.

de la Mare, Sir Arthur, K.C.M.G., K.C.V.O.; British diplomatist; b. 15 Feb. 1914; m.; three d.; ed. Victoria Coll., Jersey, and Pembroke Coll., Cambridge.
Diplomatic Service, served Tokyo and Seoul 36-42, Washington 42-43, Foreign Office 43-47; Consul, San Francisco 47-50; First Sec., Tokyo 50-53; Counsellor, Foreign Office 53-56, Washington 56-60; Head of Far Eastern Dept., Foreign Office 60-63; Amb. to Afghanistan 63-65; Asst. Under-Sec. of State, Foreign Office 65-68; High Commr. in Singapore 68-70; Amb. to Thailand 70-73; Int. Business Consultant 75-.
The Birches, Onslow Road, Burwood Park, Walton-on-Thames, Surrey, KT12 5BB, England.

de la Mare, Richard Herbert Ingpen, M.A.; British publisher; b. 4 June 1901; s. of Walter de la Mare, O.M., C.H. (poet) and Constance Elfrida Ingpen; m. Amy Catherine Donaldson 1930; three s. one d.; ed. Oxford Univ.
Faber and Gwyer Ltd. 25-29, Dir. 27; Dir. Faber & Faber Ltd. 29, Vice-Chair. 46, Chair. 60-71; Pres. Faber & Faber (Publishers) Ltd. 71-.
Leisure interests: listening to music, oriental art, gardening.
Faber & Faber Ltd., 3 Queen Square, London, W.C.1; Much Hadham Hall, Hertfordshire, England.
Telephone: 01-278-6881 (Office); Much Hadham 2663 (Home).

de Lancey, William J.; American steel executive; b. 2 June 1916, Chicago, Ill.; m. Sally (née Roe) 1940; ed. Elgin High School, Ill., Michigan Univ. and Law School.
Navy service in World War II, Lieut. Junior Grade,

mmendation ribbon; with Cravath, Swaine and Moore w firm; joined Repub. Steel Corpn. as Asst. Counsel 2, Asst. Gen. Counsel 54, Gen. Counsel 59, Vice-Pres. nd Gen Counsel 61, mem. Board of Dirs. 68, Exec. ice-Pres. 71, Pres. 73-74, Pres. and Chief Exec. fficer Feb. 74-; Dir. Cleveland Trust Co., Standard il Co., Sherwin-Williams Co., Ohio Bell Telephone Co., eserve Mining Co., Liberia Mining Co. Ltd., Beatrice ocahontas Co.

epublic Steel Corporation, Republic Building, Cleveand, Ohio 44104, U.S.A.

Delaney, James J.; American politician; b. 19 March 901, New York City; *m.* Lola Mathis (deceased); one .; ed. St. John's Univ. (New York).

ormer mem. Danahy & Delaney Law Firm, Brooklyn; mr. Asst. District Attorney, District Attorney's Office, ueen's County, N.Y.; mem. U.S. House of Reps. 45-46, 9-76; Democrat; Hon. LL.D. (St. John's Univ., N.Y.). uite 2267, Rayburn House Office Building, Washington, D.C. 20515, U.S.A.

Telephone: 202-225-3965.

Delano, William A., B.A., LL.B.; American lawyer and ormer government official; b. 25 May 1924, Kalamazoo, Mich.; *s.* of Hubert W. Delano and Edna L. Draper; *m.* Georgia Heigelmann 1946; three *s.* one *d.*; ed. Yale Coll. and Yale Law School.

American Friends' Service Cttee. in Germany 48-50; Law Practice Winthrop, Stimsom, Putman and Roberts, New York City 53-61; Chair. Cttee. on Bill of Rights Asscn. of Bar of City of New York City; mem. Special Cttee. to Study Commitment Procedures, Special Cttee. on Passport Procedures, Cttee. on Foreign and Comparative Law; fmr. Nat. Dir. American Civil Liberties Union; Legal Adviser during formation of U.S. Peace Corps 61, first Gen. Counsel, U.S. Peace Corps 61-63, Special Asst. to Dir. U.S. Peace Corps 63-64; Sec.-Gen. Int. Secretariat for Volunteer Service 64-67; mem. Board of Dirs. Nat. Cttee. on U.S.-China Relations, Crossroads Africa; Pres. Gale Associates; Vice-Pres. Center for War/Peace Studies.

Leisure interests: reading, conversation, politics, tennis, skiing.

Publs. *Freedom to Travel* 58, *Mental Illness and Due Process.*

114 East 10th Street, New York City, N.Y., U.S.A.

Telephone: 212-982-3274.

De Laurentiis, Dino; Italian film producer; b. 8 Aug. 1919, Torre annunziata, Naples; *s.* of Aurelio and Giuseppina (née Salvatore) De Laurentiis; *m.* Silvana Mangano 1949; one *s.* three *d.*

Founded Real Ciné, Turin 41; Exec. Producer Lux Film 42; acquired Safir Studios and founded Teatri della Farnesina 48; co-founder Ponti-De Laurentiis S.p.A. 50; numerous awards and prizes include Oscars for *La Strada* 57, *Le Notti di Cabiria* 58, Golden David Awards for *Le Notti di Cabiria* 58, *The Tempest* 59, Silver Ribbon (Italian Film Critics) for *La Strada* 54, Venice Silver Lion for *Europa 51* 52.

Films produced include: *La Figlia del Capitano, Il Bandito, Molti Sogni per la Strada, Anna, Bitter Rice, La Strada, Le Notti di Cabiria, Ulysses, War and Peace, The Tempest, This Angry Age, Europa 51, The Gold of Naples, The Great War, Five Branded Women, I Love, You Love, The Best of Enemies, Barabbas, To Bed or not to Bed, The Bible, The Three Faces of a Woman, Barbarella, A Man Called Sledge, Waterloo, The Valachi Papers, Serpico, Mandingo.*

Office: Viale Libano 28, Rome; Casella Postale 10780, Rome, EUR, Italy.

Telephone: 5915551 (Office).

Delay, Jean, DR. en MED., DR. ès L.; French psychologist; b. 14 Nov. 1907; ed. Paris Univ.

Professor of Mental Diseases and Encephalography,

Dir. Inst. of Psychology, Sorbonne 51-70; Pres. 1st World Congress of Psychiatry 50; mem. Acad. de Médecine 55-, Acad. Française 59-; Commandeur, Légion d'Honneur; Dr. h.c. Zürich and Montreal Univs.

Publs. *Les Dissolutions de la Mémoire, Les Dérèglements de l'Humeur, La Psychophysiologie humaine, Aspects de la Psychiatrie Moderne;* novels: *La Cité Grise* 46, *Hommes sans Nom* 48; *La Jeunesse d'André Gide.*

53 avenue Montaigne, Paris 8e, France.

Delbarre, Florian François, D. en MED.; French professor of medicine; b. 7 Sept. 1918, Paris; *s.* of Florian and Marguerite Delbarre; *m.* 2nd Jeanne Dacheux; two *c.* (of 1st *m.*); ed. Lycée Michelet, and Faculties of Science and Medicine, Paris.

Served as intern in Paris Hospitals 43-49; Head of Clinic of Faculty of Medicine, Paris 49-55; Fellow of the Faculty of Medicine, physician, Paris Hospitals 55-60, Prof. of Rheumatology at the Faculty of Medicine 60-, Prof. Clinic of Rheumatology 67-; Dir. Research Centre on Osteo-Articular Diseases at l'Hôpital Cochin; Dean of the Faculty of Medicine, Paris-Cochin; Pres. of Medical Scientific Cttee. of the Nat. Centre of Scientific Research; Consultant to the World Health Org.; Vice-Pres. Paris-René Descartes Univ.; fmr. Pres. French League against Rheumatism; Officier de la Légion d'Honneur, Officier du Mérite Chevalier de l'Ordre de la Santé Publique, Chevalier de l'Orde des Palmes Académiques, Officier du Mérite de la République Italienne, Médaille d'Or des Hopitaux de Paris, Lauréat de l'Académie Nationale de Médecine.

Publs. *L'insuffisance alimentaire* (with Prof. C. Richet) 50, *Les Stimulines hypophysaires* (with Profs. Lemaire and Michard) 50, *Cortisone et cortico-stimuline en Rheumatologie* (with Profs. F. Coste and J. Cayla) 52.

64 boulevard Arago, Paris 13, France.

Telephone: 587-3403.

Delbart, Georges, D. ès sc.; French engineer; b. 11 April 1899, Anzin; *s.* of Charles Delbart and Thérèse Verriez-Delhalle; *m.* Nelly Laurent; one *s.* one *d.*; ed. Lycée de Valenciennes, Faculty of Science, Lille Univ.

Laboratory Chief Société Escaut et Meuse 22-27; entered Anciens Etablissements Cail and was successively Laboratory Service Chief, Head of the steelworks and Chief Metallurgist; engaged in manufacture of armaments, especially of tanks; Scientific Adviser to the "Armoured Vehicles" service Ministry of Armaments 39-40; missions to England 40, Germany 46, Western Europe 51, U.S.A. and Canada 52, Brazil 54, 58, Argentina, Chile 59, Peru, Brazil 60, India 64, Brazil 66, Mexico 66, Australia 67, Japan 67; Hon. Dir. of the French Iron and Steel Research Inst.; Hon. Pres., Dir.-Gen. of *Revue de Métallurgie;* Hon. Dir. standardization office, French Steel Industry; Officier Légion d'Honneur; Commdr. de l'Ordre National du Mérite.

Leisure interests: sculpture, painting, literature.

35 rue de Lorraine, 78100 Saint-Germain-en-Laye, France.

Telephone: 963-5220.

Del Bo, Rinaldo; Italian politician and lawyer; b. 19 Nov. 1916; ed. Inst. Leo XIII, Milan, Law School, Univ. of Milan (Doctor of Laws), and Univ. of Pavia.

Member Camera dei Deputati 48; Under-Sec. of State, Ministry of Labour 51-56, Foreign Office 56-57; Minister for Relations between Govt. and Parl. 57-Jan. 59, of Foreign Trade Feb. 59-60; Pres., High Authority of European Coal and Steel Community 63-67; Chair. Italian Del. at the Int. Conf. of Labour at Geneva; Commdr. de la Légion d'Honneur; Viareggio Prize for a Literary Essay 57.

Publs. *Problema dell'egualianza nello Stato contemporaneo* 48, *Nuovi aspetti della sovranità degli Stati* 50, *La Volontà dello Stato* 57.

Via Eleonora Duse 53, Rome, Italy.

Delbrück, Max; American (b. German) biologist; b. 4 Sept. 1906, Berlin; s. of Hans Delbrück; ed. Univs. of Tübingen, Berlin, Bonn and Göttingen.
Went to U.S. 37, naturalized 45; Prof. of Biology, Calif. Inst. of Technology 47-; Visiting Prof. 56 and Acting Prof. 61-63, Cologne Univ.; mem. Nat. Acad. of Sciences; Fellow Leopoldina Acad., Halle, Royal Danish Acad., Foreign mem. Royal Soc. (U.K.); Kimber Gold Medal (Genetics), U.S. Nat. Acad. of Sciences; Hon. Ph.D. (Copenhagen, Chicago); Nobel Prize for Medicine (jointly with S. Luria, q.v.) 69.
California Institute of Technology, Pasadena, Calif. 91109, U.S.A.

del Campo, Juan Domingo; Uruguayan diplomatist; b. 20 Oct. 1919, Montevideo; s. of Juan Domingo del Campo and Paulina Mañé; m. Esther Pastorino 1969; one s. one d.; ed. Univ. of Law and Social Sciences.
Held various diplomatic posts in Brazil 38-40, Colombia 48-49, Venezuela 58-59, Argentina 61-67; Amb. to Italy 70-72, to U.K. 72-75; mem., leader of dels. on OAS, Inter-American Council of Jurists, Latin American Free Trade Asscn. and other int. orgs., mem. negotiations for Latin American integration; Adviser to Pres. Jorge Pacheco Areco on Econ. Trade.
Leisure interests: history, philosophy, horse racing.
Publs. *An Experience in the Application of the Right of Political Asylum* 56, *The Uruguayan Policy in LAFTA* 68, *The Uruguayan Policy in the River Plate Basin* 69, *Prevailingness of J. E. Rodó's Thought* 71, *Political Realism of Talleyrand* 71.
c/o Ministerio de Asuntos Exteriores, Montevideo, Uruguay.

De Leeuw, Ton; Netherlands composer; b. 16 Nov. 1926, Rotterdam; m. Arlette Reboul 1952; one s. three d.; ed. musical colls. in Netherlands and France and under Jaap Kunst, Amsterdam.
With Radio Hilversum 54-, responsible for annual radio programmes of Contemporary and non Western Music 56-; Prof. Composition Conservatoires of Amsterdam and Utrecht 59-; Lecturer, Univ. of Amsterdam 62-; Dir. Conservatoire of Amsterdam 72-; Study of Indian classical music and dance 61; numerous prizes including Prix Italia 56 and Prix des Jeunesses Musicales 61.
Compositions: *Hiob* (Radiophonic Oratorio) 56, *Mouvements Rétrogrades* 57, *First String Quartet* 58, *Antiphonie* (chamber music with 4 electronic sound-tracks) 60, *Symphonies for Wind Instruments* 63, *The Dream* (Opera) 63, *Men go their ways* (piano) 64, *Second String Quartet* 65, *Syntaxis I* (Electronic) 66, *Spatial music I-IV* 66-68, *Haiku II* (Sopr. and orch.) 68, *Lamento Pacis* (vocal and instr.) 69, *Litany of our Time* (Television play) 70, *Music for Strings* 70.
Publ. *The Music of the 20th Century* 64.
Costeruslaan 4, Hilversum, Netherlands.
Telephone: 02150-15783.

Delfim Netto, Antonio, D.ECON.; Brazilian economist; b. 5 May 1928, São Paulo; s. of José Delfim and Maria Delfim; ed. School of Econs. and Management, São Paulo State Univ.
São Paulo State Univ., Asst. Prof. 52-54, Assoc. Prof. 54-59, Prof. 63, fmr. Dir. Insts. of Management and Econ. Research, School of Econs. and Man.; mem. São Paulo State Planning Comm. for Devt. 65; Sec. of Finance, São Paulo State Govt. 66-67; Minister of Finance 67-74; Consultant and Technical Adviser to several orgs. in São Paulo; Order of Merit of the Brazilian Armed Forces; Order of Boyaca (Colombia); Order of Christ (Portugal); Order of Merit (Italy); Legion of Hon. (France).
Leisure interest: reading.
Publs. *O Mercado de Açucar no Brasil* 58, *O Problema do Café no Brasil* 59, *O Trigo no Brasil* 60, *Alguns Aspectos da Inflação Brasileira* 63, *Agricultura e*

Desenvolvimento 66, *Planejamento para o Desenvolvimento* 66.
503 Av. Aclimação, São Paulo 01531, Brazil.

Delfini, Delfo; Italian international civil servant; b. 6 July 1913, Rome; ed. Univ. of Rome.
Captain in Army Reserve 39-45; with Shell, Rome 45-49; expert for econ. questions, Ministry of Foreign Affairs, mem. Italian Del. to OECD 50-59; Head of Div., Econ. and Social Cttee., European Communities 60, Dir. 69, Acting Sec.-Gen. 71, Sec.-Gen. March 73-, Economic and Social Committee of the European Community, rue Ravenstein 2, 1000 Brussels, Belgium.
Telephone: 12-39-20, 13-95-95.

Delfont, Sir Bernard, Kt.; British impresario and film executive; b. 5 Sept. 1909, Tokmak, Russia; s. of Isaac and Olga Winogradsky; brother of Sir Lew Grade (q.v.); m. Carole Lynne 1946; one s. two d.
Entered theatrical management in Britain 41; first London production 42, has since presented very many shows in London; re-introduced variety to the West End at the London Casino 47-48, presenting Laurel and Hardy, Sophie Tucker, Lena Horne, Olsen and Johnson, Mistinguette, etc.; presents summer shows in many seaside resorts; presenter with Louis Benjamin of the annual Royal Variety Performance; assumed management of London theatres: Wimbledon 42, Whitehall 43, St. Martin's 43, Winter Garden (with Mala de la Marr) 44, Saville 46, New Royalty 60, Comedy and Shaftesbury theatres 64; took over lease of Prince of Wales Theatre 58, New London Theatre 73; converted London Hippodrome into Talk of the Town theatre restaurant 58; Chair. and Chief Exec. EMI Film and Theatre Corpn., EMI Television Films Ltd.; Chair. EMI Cinemas Ltd., EMI Leisure Enterprises Ltd., EMI Elstree Studios, EMI Film Productions Ltd., Associated British Cinemas Ltd.; Dir. Grade Org., Bernard Delfont Org., Forte's (Holdings) Ltd., Central Beach Amusements Ltd., Lewenstein-Delfont Productions Ltd., Bernard Delfont Ltd., Theatre Restaurants Ltd., and many other companies; Pres. Variety Artistes' Fed.; Past Chief Barker, Variety Club of Great Britain.
Recent productions, alone or with others, include: *The Roar of the Greasepaint—The Smell of the Crowd*, *Pickwick*, both in N.Y. (with David Merrick), *Barefoot in the Park*, *The Killing of Sister George*, *The Matchgirls*, *Funny Girl*, *The Odd Couple*, *Martha Graham Dance Co.*, *Sweet Charity*, *The Four Musketeers*, *Golden Boy*, *Hotel in Amsterdam*, *Time Present*, *Mame*, *Your Own Thing*, *What the Butler Saw*, *Cat Among the Pigeons*, *Carol Channing with her 10 Stout-Hearted Men*, *The Great Waltz*, *Kean*, *Rabelais*, *Applause*, *The Threepenny Opera*, *The Good Old Bad Old Days*, *The Unknown Soldier and His Wife*, *A Doll's House*, *The Wolf*, *Brief Lives*, *Henry IV*, *A Streetcar Named Desire*, *Cinderella*, *The Good Companions*, *The Danny La Rue Show*, *Harvey*, *A Little Night Music*, *Dad's Army*, *The Plumber's Progress*, *The Exciting Adventures of Queen Daniella*, *Great Expectations*, *Mardi Gras*.
30-31 Golden Square, London, W1R 4AA, England.
Telephone: 01-437-9234.

Delforge, Marc, D. EN D.; Belgian journalist; b. 2 Dec. 1909, Heusy; s. of René Delforge and Marie-Elise Laroche; m. Lucie Attout 1935; three s. four d.; ed. Coll. Notre Dame de la Paix, Namur and Univ. of Louvain.
Barrister Namur 32-34 and 40-42; Asst. Editor *Vers l'Avenir* 32-34, Editor-in-Chief 34-; Chef de Cabinet to Belgian Minister of Information, London 42-44; Lecturer, Univ. of Louvain 46; Dr. h.c. (Univ. of Montreal, Canada); Officer, Order of Leopold of the Crown and of Leopold II, Commdr., Order of St. Gregory the Great, Resistance Medal, etc.

Leisure interests: travelling and reading.
22 Rue de la Falise, Namur, Belgium.
Telephone: 081/121064.

Delgado, Pedro Abelardo; Salvadorian economist;
b 3 Nov. 1919; ed. Univ. de San Carlos, Guatemala and
American Univ., Washington, D.C.
Director Econ. Studies Dept. 53-55; Prof. Econ. Theory
and Econ. Problems, Univ. of El Salvador 54-55, 59-60;
Commercial Attaché, Bonn 57-59; Sec. Central Ameri-
can Econ. Co-operation Cttee. (UN Econ. Comm. for
Latin America) 57-59, 60-61; Deputy and Acting
Minister of Economy 59-60; Sec.-Gen. Central American
Common Market 61-66; Gov. Inter-American Bank for
Devt., Washington, D.C. 59-60; del. at Punta del Este
Meeting 61 and UN Conf. on Trade and Devt., Geneva
64; Adviser to Pres. of IDB 66-70; Dir. Special Pro-
gramme on Trade Expansion and Econ. Integration
among Developing Countries (UNCTAD), Geneva 70-.
c/o UNCTAD, Palais des Nations, 1211 Geneva 10;
Home: 26 rue du 31 Décembre (App. 50), 1207 Geneva,
Switzerland.

Delhaye, Jean, D. ÈS SC.; French astronomer; b.
25 Feb. 1921, Lourches; s. of Parfait Delhaye and Rosa
Duc; m. Jeanne Guézel 1944; four c.; ed. Facultés des
Sciences, Rennes and Paris and Univs. of Leiden and
Stockholm.
Astronomer, Observatoire de Paris 43-57; Prof. and
Dir. of Observatory, Univ. of Besançon 57-64; Deputy
Dir. Observatoire de Paris 64-67, Dir. 68-71; Dir. Inst.
National d'Astronomie et de Géophysique 71-; corresp.
mem. Acad. des Sciences; mem. Bureau des Longitudes.
Publs. various articles on astronomy.
Institut National d'Astronomie et de Géophysique,
place Janssen, 92190-Meudon; Home: 2 rue de la
Pléiade, 94240 L'Hay les Roses, France.
Telephone: (1) 027-75-30 (Office); (1) 660-45-42 (Home).

De L'Isle, 1st Viscount, cr. 56, 6th Baron De L'Isle
and Dudley; **William Philip Sidney,** V.C., K.G., P.C.,
G.C.M.G., G.C.V.O., K.ST.J., M.A., D.L.; British Peer of the
Realm; b. 23 May 1909, London; s. of late 5th Baron
De L'Isle and Dudley and late Winifred Bevan; m. 1st
Hon. Jacqueline Corinne Yvonne Vereker 1940 (died
1962); one s. four d.; 2nd Margaret Lady Glanusk 1966;
ed. Eton and Magdalene Coll., Cambridge.
Fellow of Inst. of Chartered Accountants 34; with
Barclays Bank 36-39; commissioned Grenadier Guards
(Reserve) 29; served France and Belgium 39-40, Italy
43-44; Conservative M.P. for Chelsea 44-45; Parl. Sec.
to Ministry of Pensions 45; Joint Treas. Conservative
Party 48; Sec. of State for Air 51-55; Exec. with
Schweppes (Home) Ltd. 58-61; Gov.-Gen. of Australia
61-65; Chair. Phoenix Assurance Co. Ltd.; Dir. Save
and Prosper Group Ltd., Yorkshire Bank Ltd., Phoenix
Assurance Co., New York, The Glen Falls Insurance
Co., New York; Pres. British Heart Foundation 76;
Trustee of the Winston Churchill Memorial Trust; Trus-
tee R.A.F. Museum; Chancellor, Order of St. Michael
and St. George 68.
Leisure interests: fishing, shooting, oil painting, gar-
dening, reading biographies.
Phoenix Assurance Co. Ltd., Phoenix House, King
William Street, London, E.C.4; Home: Penshurst Place,
near Tonbridge, Kent, England.
Telephone: 01-626-9876 (Office); Penshurst 223 (Home).

Delivanis, Dr. Dimitrios J.; Greek university teacher;
b. 3 April 1909, Vienna; s. of John D. Delivanis and
Helen J. Triantaphyllidis; m. Maria Negreponti 1959;
one d.; ed. Univs. of Athens, Paris, Berlin and London
School of Economics.
Assistant Prof. Econs., Univ. of Athens 38-44; Sec.-
Gen. Ministry of Welfare 39-41; Greek Co-ordinator,
Joint Relief Cttee. for Greece 43-45; Assoc. Prof. of
Econs. Salonika Univ. 44-47, Prof. 48-74; mem. Exec.

Cttee. Centre of Econ. Research, Athens 61-64, Centre
of Social Sciences, Athens 60-67; Vice-Pres. Greek Econ.
Asscn. 61-70, Pres. 71-75, Hon. Pres. 75-; mem. Exec.
Cttee. Int. Econ. Asscn. 59-65, Treas. 65-68; mem.
Board of Mediterranean Social Sciences Research Cen-
tre 61, Pres. 65-69; mem. Board Inst. of Balkan Studies
60-73, Exec. Dir. 71-72, Pres. 74-; Vice-Rector, Univ.
of Salonika 64-65, Rector 65-66, Pro-Rector 66-67; Pres.
Centre of Planning and Econ. Research 68-73; mem.
Board of Asscn. Française de Science Economique 75-;
Guest Prof. at foreign univs. 49-; Orders of Phoenix
(First Class) and George I (Second Class), Greece;
Officier Légion d'Honneur, France.
Leisure interests: mountaineering, travel.
Publs. *La politique des banques allemandes en matière de
crédit a court terme* 34, *Greek Monetary Developments
1939-48* 49, *L'économie sous-développée* 63, *Die inter-
nationale Liquidität* 65, *Economics* (in Greek), six edns.
52-71. *L'Influence de L'Inflation Sévissant depuis 1939*
70, *Economic and Monetary Policy* (in Greek) 5th edn.
74, numerous articles in Greek, French, German and
English.
Jan Smuts 50, Athens; and Morgenthaou 1, Thessalonika, Greece.
Telephone: Athens 613209; Thessalonika 229-977.

Dell, Rt. Hon. Edmund, P.C., M.A.; British politician;
b. 15 Aug. 1921, London; s. of Reuben and Frances
Dell; m. Susanne Gottschalk 1963; ed. Owen's School,
London, The Queen's Coll., Oxford.
Lecturer, The Queen's Coll., Oxford 47-49; Exec.
Imperial Chemical Industries Ltd. 49-63; mem. Man-
chester City Council 53-60, Pres. Manchester and Sal-
ford City Council 58-61; mem. Parl. for Birkenhead 64-,
Parl. Sec. Ministry of Technology 66-67, Parl. Under-
Sec. of State, Dept. of Econ. Affairs 67-68, Minister of
State, Board of Trade 68-69, Minister of State, Dept. of
Employment 69-70, Chair. Public Accounts Cttee. of
House of Commons 72-74, Paymaster-Gen. 74-76; Sec.
of State for Trade April 76-; Labour.
Leisure interest: listening to music.
Publ. *Political Responsibility and Industry* 73.
4 Reynolds Close, London, NW11 7EA, England.
Telephone: (01) 455-7197.

Della Casa-Debeljevic, Lisa (*see* Casa-Debeljevic).

Del Mar, Norman Rene, C.B.E., F.R.C.M., F.G.S.M.;
British conductor; b. 31 July 1919, London; m. Pauline
Mann 1947; two s.; ed. Marlborough and Royal Coll. of
Music.
Assistant to Sir Thomas Beecham, Royal Philharmonic
Orchestra 47; Principal Conductor English Opera Group
49; Prof. of Conducting Guildhall School of Music 53;
Conductor BBC Scottish Orchestra 60-65; Principal
Guest Conductor Gothenburg Symphony Orchestra
69-73; Conductor Royal Acad. of Music; Conductor and
Prof. of Conducting, Royal Coll. of Music; Principal
Conductor Acad. of the BBC 74-(77); freelance conductor
in U.K. and abroad; Hon. mem. Royal Acad. of Music;
Hon. D. Mus. (Glasgow).
Publ. *Richard Strauss* (3 vols.) 62-72.
Witchings, Hadley Common, Herts., England.

Del Monaco, Mario; Italian singer; b. 1919; ed. Scuola
d'Arte, Pesaro.
Début in *Madame Butterfly* (Teatro Puccini, Milan) 40;
La Scala début in *La Bohème* 43; foreign début Royal
Opera House, Covent Garden (London) 45; American
début in *Manon Lescaut* (New York Metropolitan Opera
House) 50; South American début in *Otello* (Teatro
Colón, Buenos Aires) 50; has appeared in numerous
films; Arena d'Oro 55, Orfeo d'Oro 57, Maschera
d'Oro 58.
c/o Metropolitan Opera Association, 147 West 39th
Street, New York City 18, N.Y., U.S.A.

de Loës, Charles, LL.D.; Swiss businessman and banker; b. 30 Aug. 1895; ed. Mulhouse Coll., and Univs. of Geneva and Berne.
Partner, Hentsch and Co., Bankers, Geneva 30-; Vice-Chair. Helvetia-Vie, Life Insurance Co., Geneva 32, Vice-Chair Société Générale pour l'Industrie, Geneva 43; Dir. Helvetia Accident Insurance Co., Zürich 47; Dir. Crédit Foncier Suisse, Zürich 49; Chair. of Board Swiss Bankers' Asscn., Basle 50; Dir. Int. Chamber of Commerce, Paris 51; Chair. Soc. Int. pour Participations Industrielles et Commerciales S.A., Basle 58.
Ch. Belle-Fontaine 10, Cologny, Geneva, Switzerland.

Delon, Alain; French actor; b. 8 Nov. 1935, Sceaux; *m.* Nathalie Delon (dissolved); one *s.*
With French Marine Corps 52-55; independent actor-producer under Delbeau (Delon-Beaume) Productions 64- and Adel Productions 68-.
Films include: *Christine* 58, *Faibles Femmes* 59, *Le Chemin des Ecoliers* 59, *Purple Noon* 59, *Rocco and His Brothers* 60, *Eclipse* 61, *The Leopard* 62, *Any Number Can Win* 62, *The Black Tulip* 63, *The Love Cage* 63, *L'Insoumis* 64, *The Yellow Rolls Royce* 64, *Once a Thief* 64, *Les Centurions* 65, *Paris Brûle-t-il?* 65, *Texas Across the River* 66, *Les Aventuriers* 66, *Le Samourai* 67, *Histoires extraordinaires* 67, *Diaboliquement votre* 67, *Adieu l'ami* 68, *Girl on a Motorcycle* 68, *La Piscine* 68, *Jeff* 68, *Die Boss, Die Quietly* 69, *Borsalino* 70, *Madly* 70, *Doucement les Basses* 70, *Le Cercle Rouge* 71, *L'Assassinat de Trotsky* 71, *La Veuve Couderc* 71, *Un Flic* 72, *Le Professeur* 72, *Scorpio* 72, *Traitement de Choc* 72, *Les Granges Brûlées* 73, *Deux Hommes dans la Ville* 73, *Borsalino & Co.* 73, *Les Seins de Glace* 74, *Creezy* 75, *Zorro* 75, *Le Gitan* 75. Stage performances: *'Tis Pity She's a Whore* 61, 62, *Les Yeux Crevés* 67.
4 rue Chambiges, 75008 Paris, France.

Delorme, Jean; French engineer and businessman; b. 25 Oct. 1902, Paris; *m.* Sabine Kablé 1937; three *c.*; ed. Ecole Nat. Supérieure des Mines, Paris.
President and Dir.-Gen. Air Liquide 45-, Soc. d'Oxygène et d'Acétylène d'Extrême-Orient; Pres. La Soudure Autogène Française; Chair. Air Liquide Canada Ltée.; Pres. American Air Liquid Inc., Società per l'Industria dell'Ossigeno e di altri gas; Vice-Pres. L'Air Liquide "Hellas" (Greece) 70; Chair. Union Liquid Air Co. (Pty.) Ltd., Liquid Air Corpn. of N. America; Vice-Pres. La Oxigeno S.A. (Buenos Aires); mem. Board Sociedad Española del Oxigeno S.A., Teikoku Sanso Kabushiki Kaisha, Soc. Chimique de la Grande Paroisse, Soc. Lyonnaise Industrielle Pharmaceutique "Lipha", Comp. Générale des Eaux, etc.; Pres. Eurospace, Institut Océanographique; mem. Board French Nat. Cttee. Int. Chamber of Commerce, Inst. France-Canada, Asscn. Française d'Action Artistique, Comité Parlementaire Français du Commerce; Croix de Guerre, Médaille de la Résistance, Commdr. Légion d'Honneur.
Leisure interest: yachting.
Publ. *La Mer et l'Espace, Nouvelles conquêtes dans l'espace et la mer.*
Office: 75 quai d'Orsay, 75007 Paris; Home: 1 Avenue du Maréchal Manoury, 75016 Paris, France.

De Los Angeles, Victoria; Spanish soprano singer; b. 1 Nov. 1923, Barcelona; *m.* Enrique Magriñá Mir 1948; two *s.*; ed. Univ. and Conservatoire of Barcelona.
Barcelona début 45, Paris Opera and La Scala, Milan 49, Royal Opera House, Covent Garden, London 50, Metropolitan Opera House, New York 51, Vienna State Opera 57; numerous appearances at other opera houses, concert tours and recordings; 1st Prize, Geneva Int. Competition 47; Cross of the Order of Isabel the Catholic and numerous other orders and decorations.
Avenida de la Victoria 57, Barcelona 17, Spain.

Delouvrier, Paul; French civil servant; b. 25 June 1914; ed. Collège Saint-Etienne, Strasbourg, Faculté de Droit and Inst. d'Etudes Politiques, Paris.
Inspector, Ministry of Finance 41; Dir. Finance Division, Monnet Plan Commissariat General 46-47; Dir. du Cabinet, Ministry of Finance 47-48, Dir.-Gen. of Taxes 48-53; Sec.-Gen. Interministerial Cttee. on European Economic Co-operation; Dir. of Finance, European Iron and Steel Community 55-58; Delegate Gen. in Algeria Dec. 58-60; Prof. Inst. of Political Studies, Paris; Del.-Gen. Paris Region 61-; Prefect of Paris Region 66-69; Pres. Inst. of Housing and Town Planning, Paris Region 62-; Pres. Conseil d'Admin., Electricité de France Jan. 69-; Pres. West Atlantic Asscn. 70; Pres. Plan-Construction 71; Croix de Guerre, Grand Officier Légion d'Honneur.
32 rue de Mouceau, Paris 8e; Home: 7 avenue de Ségur, 75007 Paris, France.
Telephone: ALM 94-00 (Office); INV 14-64 (Home).

del Portillo, Albaro; Spanish priest; b. 11 March 1914, Madrid; ed. Higher Technical School of Civil Eng., Madrid, Univ. of Madrid, Angelicum Univ., Rome.
Trained as engineer; ordained Roman Catholic priest 44; Procurator Gen. Opus Dei 44, Sec.-Gen. 40-47, 56-75, Pres.-Gen. 75-; Consultant to the Sacred Congregation of the Religious, Vatican Curia 54, to the Sacred Congregation of the Council 59; Pres. Preparatory Comm. for the Laity, Vatican Council II 60, Sec. Comm. for the Clergy, 62-65; Consultant to Conciliar Comm. for Bishops, also to Pontifical Comm. for Reform of the Code of Canon Law 63; Consultant to the Congregation for the Doctrine of the Faith 65; Grand Chancellor, Univs. of Navarra (Spain) and Piura (Peru) 75; Kt. of Honour and Devotion of the Supreme Order of Malta 58; Grand Cross of St. Raymond of Pennafort 67.
Publs. *Discovery and Explorations of the Coasts of California* 47, *Faithful and Laity in the Church* 69, *On the Priesthood* 70, *Ethics and Law* 71, *Associations for Priests* 75.
Viale Bruno Buozzi 73, 00197 Rome, Italy.
Telephone: 879042.

Delprat, Daniel Apollonius, DR. JUR.; Netherlands shipowner; b. 10 Jan. 1890, Amsterdam; *s.* of Dr. Constant Charles Delprat and Catharina Elisabeth Reynvaan; *m.* 1st Saskia Veth 1915, 2nd Martine L. A. Labouchere 1973; ed. Amsterdam High School and Univ. of Amsterdam.
Joined Nederland Line Royal Dutch Mail 15, apptd. rep. in Neths. East Indies 20, Man. Dir. 27-, Chair. 57, Dir. 58; Chair. Shareholders Trust Comm., Royal Netherlands Navigation Co.; Hon. Chair. Amsterdam Chamber of Commerce, Hon. Chair. Sea Transport Cttee., Int. Chamber of Commerce; Knight, Order of Netherlands Lion; Grand Officer Order of Orange-Nassau; Commdr. Légion d'Honneur; 1st Class Order of Vasa; 1st Class Order of Merit, Austria.
Leisure interest: historical studies.
Publs. *Treatise on Through Bills of Lading* 15, *Treatise on Flag Discrimination* 52, *Aperire Terram Gentibus: Reminiscences Last Decade Suez Canal Company* 72.
Museumplein 7, Amsterdam, Netherlands.
Telephone: 73-66-90.

De Lullo, Giorgio; Italian actor and theatre producer; b. 24 April 1921; ed. Accad. Nazionale d'Arte Drammatica, Rome.
Joined Compagnia Ninchi-Pagnani 45; founder-mem. Piccolo Teatro, Milan and Rome; founded Compagnia dei Giovani with R. Falk, R. Valli and A. M. Guarnieri 55; numerous tours in Europe including World Theatre Season, London 65, 66; produces open-air theatre seasons in Florence, Capri and Verona; St. Vincent

Prize 58 for production *D'amore si muore* (Patroni-Griffi); Gold Medal 60.
Via Appia Antica 140, Rome, Italy.

Delvaux, Louis, D.IUR.; Belgian lawyer; b. 21 Oct. 1895.
Law practice at Jodoigne; Catholic Deputy 36-46; Min. of Agriculture 45; Judge, Court of the ECSC 52-58. Judge, Court of the European Communities 58-67; legal adviser, Banque Nat. de Belgique 48-.
Home: 30 Boulevard d'Avranches, Luxembourg, Grand Duchy of Luxembourg; and 11 avenue des Commandants, Borlée, Jodoigne, Belgium.
Telephone: 264-36 (Luxembourg); 811-22 (Jodoigne).

Delvaux, Paul; Belgian artist; b. 1897; ed. Brussels Acad. of Fine Arts.
Began as a painter of portraits, land- and sea-scapes; after travel in France and Italy adopted the surrealistic style; has executed murals in the Kursaal, Ostend, Institut de Zoologie, Liège, and in private houses in Brussels; Prof. Inst. Nat. Supérieur d'Architecture et des Arts Décoratifs, Brussels; mem. Acad. Royale des Sciences, des Lettres et des Beaux Arts de Belgique; exhbn. at Piccadilly Gallery, London 66.
c/o Académie Royale des Sciences, des Lettres et des Beaux Arts de Belgique, Palais des Académies, 1 rue Ducale, Brussels, Belgium.

de Maizière, General Ulrich; German army officer; b. 24 Feb. 1912, Stade; s. of Walther de Maizière and Elisabeth Dückers; m. Eva Werner 1944; two s. two d.; ed. Humanistisches Gymnasium, Hanover.
Army service 30, commissioned 33; Battalion and Regimental Adjutant, 5th Prussian Infantry Regt.; Gen. Staff Coll., Dresden 40; during Second World War Gen. Staff Duties with 18th Motorized Infantry Div., G3 of 10th Mechanized Div., wounded 44, at end of war G3 in Operations Div. Army Gen. Staff; Prisoner-of-war 45-47; dealer in books and sheet music 47-51; Office of Fed. Commr. for Nat. Security Affairs 51; Col. and Chief of Ops. Branch, Fed. Armed Forces Staff 55; Commdr. of Combat Team A1 and Commdr. 2nd Brigade 58; Deputy Commdr. 1st Armoured Infantry Div. 59; Commandant, Fed. Armed Forces School for Leadership and Character Guidance 60-62, Fed. Armed Forces Command and Staff Coll. 62-64; Chief of Army Staff 64-66; Chief of Fed. Armed Forces Staff 66-72; Commandeur Légion d'Honneur 62, Freiherr-von-Stein-Preis 64, Commdr. Legion of Merit 65 and 69, Grand Officier Légion d'Honneur 69, Grosses Bundesverdienstkreuz mit Stern und Schulterband 70; retd.
Leisure interests: classical music, literature.
Publs. *Die Landesverteidigung im Rahmen der Gesamtverteidigung* 64, *Soldatische Führung heute* 66, *Bekenntnis zum Soldaten* 71, *Führen im Frieden* 74, *Verteidigung in Europa* 75.
53 Bonn-Bad Godesberg, Eschenweg 37, Federal Republic of Germany.
Telephone: 02221/321972.

Demant, Rev. Vigo Auguste, B.SC.(ENG.), D.LITT.; British theologian; b. 8 Nov. 1893, Newcastle upon Tyne; s. of T. and E. Demant; m. Marjorie Doris Tickner 1925; one s. two d.; ed. Univs. of Durham and Oxford and Ely Theological Coll.
Assistant Curate St. Thomas's, Oxford 19-23, St. Silas, Kentish Town, London 29-33; Dir. of Research, The Christian Social Council, London 29-33; Vicar of St. John the Divine, Richmond, Surrey 33-42, Canon of St. Paul's, London 42-49; Gifford Lecturer (St. Andrews) 56-58; Prof. of Moral and Pastoral Theology and Canon of Christ Church, Oxford 49-71.
Leisure interest: carpentry.
Publs. *God, Man and Society* 33, *Christian Polity* 36 *The Religious Prospect* 39, *Theology of Society* 47 *What is Happening to Us* (Broadcast Talks) 49, *Religion* and the Decline of Capitalism 52, *A Two-Way Religion* 57, *Christian Sex Ethics* 63.
31 St. Andrew's Road, Old Headington, Oxford, England.

Demarteau, Joseph, DR. en DROIT; Belgian journalist; b. 1919, Liège; m. Françoise Beer 1944; one s. four d.; ed. Coll. Saint Servais, Liège, and Univ. of Liège.
Assistant, Univ. of Liège 42; barrister 42; Sec. *Gazette de Liège* 44, Dir. and Editor-in-Chief 59-; Dir. *Libre Belgique-Gazette de Liège* 67; medal *Pro Ecclesia et Pontifice*, Officier Ordre Mérite Civil Espagnol, Officier Ordre Léopold II, and other foreign orders.
Leisure interest: music.
26 Boulevard d'Avroy, Liège; Home: 5 place Emile Dupont, Liège, Belgium.
Telephone: 23-70-03.

de Martino, Ciro; Italian banker; b. 12 Dec. 1903; m. Renata Cametti; two d.; ed. Università degli Studi, Rome.
Joined Banca d'Italia, Cosenza br. 27, Sec. to Vice Gen. Man. 31, Asst. Insp. 40; Rep. to Banca d'Italia at Interdepartmental Comm. on change of currency; Chair. Interbanks Cttee., negotiating re-establishment of Italian bank brs. in East Africa 48; Adviser to Somali authorities on Italian banking in the territory 50; Senior Insp. in charge of Gen. Inspectorate, Banca d'Italia 51, Head of Org. Dept. 53, Gen. Insp. and Head of Banking Supervision Dept. 60; resigned 65; Chair. Board of Dirs., Banco di Sicilia, Palermo, 65-; Knight of Grand Cross; Order of Merit of the Republic of Italy.
Via Generale Magliocco 1, Palermo, Sicily; Home: Via Dei Colli Della Farnesina 118, Rome, Italy.

De Martino, Francesco; Italian university professor and politician; b. 31 May 1907; ed. Liceo Gianbattista Vico, Naples, and Univ. degli Studi, Naples.
Professor of History of Roman Law, Univ. of Naples 34-38, Univ. of Messina 38-40, Univ. of Bari 40-50, Univ. of Naples 50; mem. Chamber of Deputies 48-; Sec. Partito Socialista Italiano 64-66; Joint Sec. Unified Italian Socialist Party 66-70; Sec.-Gen. Partito Socialista Italiano (PSI) 72-; Deputy Prime Minister 68-69, 70-72.
Publs. *Storia della Costituzione Romana*, Vol. 5, and numerous legal, historical and political articles.
Partito Socialista Italiano, Via del Corso 476, Rome, Italy.

Demas, William Gilbert, M.A.; Trinidadian economist and civil servant; b. 14 Nov. 1929, Port-of-Spain; s. of late Herman and Audrey (née Walters) Demas; m. Norma Taylor 1958; one d.; ed. Queen's Royal Coll., Trinidad and Emmanuel Coll., Cambridge.
Head, Econ. Planning Div., Govt. of Trinidad and Tobago 59-66; Perm. Sec. Ministry of Planning and Devt. 66-68; Econ. Adviser to the Prime Minister 68-69; Sec.-Gen. Commonwealth Caribbean Regional Secr. 70-74; Pres. Caribbean Devt. Bank 74-; Humming Bird Gold Medal (for public service).
Leisure interests: films, listening to all kinds of music.
Publs. *Economics of Development in Small Countries* 65, *Planning and the Price Mechanism in the Context of Caribbean Economic Integration* 66.
Colgrain House, 205 Camp Street, Georgetown, Guyana.

de Mayo, Paul, PH.D., D. ÈS SC., F.R.S.C., F.R.S.; British chemist; b. 8 Aug. 1924, London; s. of S. N. de Mayo and A. B. Juda; m. Mary Turnbull 1949; one s. one d.; ed. Univ. of Exeter, Birkbeck Coll. and Univ. of London.
Assistant Lecturer, Birkbeck Coll. 54-55; Lecturer, Univ. of Glasgow 55-57, Imperial Coll. of Science and Technology 57-59; Prof., Univ. of W. Ontario 59-, Dir. Photochemistry Unit 69-72; Merck, Sharp & Dohme Lecture Award 66; Centennial Medal (Canada) 67.

Publs. Ed. *Molecular Rearrangements, Vol. I* 63, *Vol. II* 64; Monographs: *Mono and Sesquiterpenoids* 59, *The Higher Terpenoids* 59; over 160 publications in scientific journals.
Photochemistry Laboratory, University of Western Ontario, London, Ont.; Home: 436 St. George Street, London, Ont. N6A 3B4, Canada.
Telephone: 519-679-2473 (Office); 519-679-902 (Home).

Dementyev, Pyotr Vasilevich; Soviet government official; b. 1907; ed. Zhukovsky Air Force Engineering Acad.
With Aircraft Industry 31-53; Minister Aviation Industry 53-57; Chair. State Cttee. Aircraft Industry 57-65; Minister of Aircraft Industry 65-; mem. Central Cttee. Soviet Communist Party 56-; Deputy to U.S.S.R. Supreme Soviet 54-; Order of Lenin (five times), Order of Red Banner, Order of Red Banner of Labour; Hero of Socialist Labour, Gold Medal *Hammer and Sickle*, etc.
Ministry of Aircraft Industry, Moscow, U.S.S.R.

Demetriadis, Phokion; Greek journalist and cartoonist; b. 18 Nov. 1894, Istanbul; *m.* Melpo Theodoridou 1924; one *d.*; ed. National School of Languages and Commerce, Istanbul.
Journalist 22-; regular contributor to Athens *To Vima*, *Ta Nea* and to *Makedonia* of Thessaloniki; European and World first prizes in World Political Cartoonists' Competition, Los Angeles 61; Acad. of Athens Award 69.
Publs. *Shadows over Athens* 45, *The Spotted Goat* 50, *With the Cartoonist's Eye* 59, illustrated modern Greek *Homer's Odyssey* 69.
3rd September Street 174, Athens, Greece.
Telephone: 871381.

Demicheli Lizaso, Pedro Alberto; Uruguayan lawyer and politician; b. 7 Aug. 1896, Rocha; *m.* Sofia Alvarez Vignoli de Demicheli, 1925; one *s.*
Minister of Public Education; Minister of Interior and Vice-Pres. of Uruguay 30-35; Pres. of Council of State and Vice-Pres. of Uruguay 74-; prizes from Univs. of Montevideo and Buenos Aires for various books.
Publs. *Los Entes Autónomos* 25, *Gobierno Local Autónomo* 29, *Lo Contencioso Administrativo* 34, *Formación Constitucional Rioplatense* (3 vols.) 50, *Origen Federal Argentino* 66, *Formación Nacional Argentina* (2 vols.) 72.
Juan Benito Blanco 1275, Piso 10, Montevideo, Uruguay.
Telephone: 79-50-54.

Demichev, Pyotr Nilovich; Soviet politician; b. 1918; ed. Moscow Mendeleev Chemical and Technological Inst.
Soviet Army 37-44; Instructor, Moscow Mendeleev Chemical and Technological Inst. 44-45; Party Work 45-56; Sec. Moscow Regional Cttee. C.P.S.U. 56-58; Business-Man. U.S.S.R. Council of Ministers 58-59; First Sec. Moscow Regional Cttee., C.P.S.U. 59-60; First Sec. Moscow City Cttee., C.P.S.U. 60-61; Sec. C.P.S.U. Central Cttee. 62-74, mem. 61-, Alt. mem. Politburo C.P.S.U. Central Cttee. 64-74; Minister of Culture 74-; Deputy to U.S.S.R. Supreme Soviet; Order of Lenin 68.
Ministry of Culture, Moscow, U.S.S.R.

Demiéville, Paul; French orientalist; b. 13 Sept. 1894, Lausanne; *m.* 1927; two *c.*
Mem. Ecole française d'Extrême-Orient, Hanoi 19-24; Prof. Univ. of Amoy, China 24-26; mem. Maison Franco-Japonaise, Tokyo 26-30; Prof. School of Oriental Languages, Paris 31-45; Dir. of Studies, Ecole des Hautes Etudes, Paris 45; Prof. of Chinese Language and Literature, Coll. de France 46-64; mem.

Inst. de France (Acad. des Inscriptions et Belle Lettres) 51-.
234 boulevard Raspail, 75014 Paris, France.
Telephone: 033-41-84.

Demirel, Suleiman; Turkish engineer and politicia[n], b. 1924; ed. Istanbul Technical Univ.
Qualified engineer; worked in U.S.A. 49-51, 54-55; wit[h] Dir.-Gen. of Electrical Studies, Ankara 50-52; in charg[e] of building various hydro-electric schemes 52-54; Hea[d] of Dept. of Dams; Dir.-Gen. of Water Control 54-5[?]; first Eisenhower Fellow for Study in U.S.A. 55; Di[r.] State Hydraulics Admin. 55-60; Teacher of Engineerin[g] Middle East Technical Univ. 60-64; in private practic[e] 61-65 (consultant to Morrison-Knudsen); Pres. Justic[e] Party 64-; Deputy Prime Minister Feb.-Oct. 65; Prim[e] Minister 65-71, April 75-.
Office of the Prime Minister, Ankara, Turkey.

De Mita, Luigi Ciriaco; Italian politician; b. 2 Fe[b.] 1928, Nusco, Avellino.
Former mem. Catholic Action; mem. Chamber o[f] Deputies for Benevento-Avellino-Salerno 63, 72-; Nat[.] Councillor Partito Democrazia Cristiana (Christia[n] Democrats) 64, later Political Vice-Sec.; Under-Sec. fo[r] the Interior; Minister of Industry and Commerce 73-74[,] of Foreign Trade Nov. 74-76; Christian Democrat.
c/o Ministry of Foreign Trade, Rome, Italy.

Demus, Otto, DR. PHIL., M.A.; Austrian art historian[;] b. 4 Nov. 1902, Harland; *s.* of Dr. Karl and Paula[?] Demus; *m.* Margarethe Demus 1950; two *s.*; ed. Univ[.] of Vienna.
Assistant, Inst. for History of Art, Univ. of Vienna 28-29; keeper of monuments in Carinthia 29-36; monu[-]ments officer in Fed. Monuments Office 36-39; voluntary emigration to England 39; returned to Austria 46[;] Pres. Fed. Monuments Office 46-; lecturer on histor[y] of Art, Univ. of Vienna 37-39, 46-51, Prof. 51-; Slad[e] Prof. Art, Cambridge 68-69; mem. Vienna Acad. o[f] Science and Inst. of Archaeology, Mainz Acad. o[f] Sciences, Académie des inscriptions et belles lettres[,] Acad. Palermo, British Acad., Acad. of Serbia; Austrian Cross of Honour for Science and Art (1st Class) 59[,] Grosses Ehrenzeichen der Republik Österreich 65[;] Fellow, Soc. of Antiquaries 60; mem. Ateneo Veneto[;] Commendatore dell'Ordine di Merito della Repubblica Italiana 65, Dr. h.c. (Munich).
Leisure interests: reading, music, walking, travel.
Publs. *Byzantine Mosaics in Greece* (with E. Diez) 31[,] *Die Mosaiken von San Marco in Venedig 1100-1300* 35[,] *Byzantine Mosaic Decoration* 47, *Sicilian Mosaics of* *the Norman Period* 49, *The Church of San Marco in Venice* 60, *Romanische Wandmalerei* 68, *Byzantine Art and the West* 70.
Prinz Eugenstrasse 27, 1030 Vienna III, Austria.
Telephone: 73-49-094.

Demuth, Richard H., A.B., LL.B.; American lawyer and financier; b. 11 Sept. 1910, New York; *s.* of Leopold and Dora Holzman Demuth; *m.* Eunice Burdick 1947; one *d.*; ed. Princeton Univ. and Harvard Law School.
Law Clerk to Fed. Circuit Judge 34-35; practised law in New York with firm of Simpson, Thacher and Bartlett 35-39; Special Asst. to U.S. Attorney-Gen., Office of Solicitor-Gen. 39-42; Asst. to Chief of Procurement Div., Air Technical Service Command 42-45; Legal Adviser, Industry Division, U.S. Mil. Govt. in Germany, mem. Central German Admin. Departments (Economic) Cttee. Allied Control Council 45-46; Asst. to Pres., Int. Bank for Reconstruction and Development 46-47, Asst. to Vice-Pres. 47-51, Dir. Technical Assistance and Liaison 51-61, Dir. Devt. Services Dept. 61-73; Asst. to Pres. Int. Finance Corpn. 56-57; Partner law firm of Surrey, Karasik and Morse, Wash. March 73-; led Bank missions to Brazil 49, Surinam 51, Burma 53, Spain 58, Turkey 65; mem. of President's Council; Chair. Int.

oard for Plant Genetic Resources; fmr. Chair. Con-
ltative Group on Int. Agricultural Research; fmr.
em. Governing Board, Int Inst. for Educational
lanning.
eisure interests: tennis, golf.
o Surrey, Karasik and Morse, 1156 15th Street, N.W.
Washington, D.C. 20005; Home: 5404 Bradley Boule-
ard, Bethesda, Maryland 20014, U.S.A.

Demy, Jacques; French film director; b. 5 June 1931;
. Agnès Varda (*q.v.*); ed. Collège de Nantes and Ecole
ationale de Photographie et Cinématographie, Paris.
rix Louis Delluc 64, Palme d'Or Festival de Cannes
4.
hort films: *Le sabotier du Val de Loire* 57, *Le Bel
ndifférent* 58, *Ars* 59; full-length films: *Lola* 60, *La Baie
es Anges* 62, *Les Parapluies de Cherbourg* 63, *Les
Demoiselles de Rochefort* 66, *Model Shop* 68, *Peau d'Ane*
o, *Pied Piper of Hamelin* 71, *L'Evènement le Plus
mportant depuis que l'Homme a Marché sur la Lune* 73.
6 rue Daguerre, 75014 Paris, France.
Telephone: 734-57-17.

Deneuve, Catherine (Catherine Dorléac); French
ctress; b. 22 Oct. 1943, Paris; d. of Maurice Dorléac
nd Renée Deneuve; m. David Bailey (divorced); one
.; ed. Lycée La Fontaine, Paris.
ilm debut in *les Petits Chats* 59; films include: *Les
ortes claquent* 60, *l'Homme à femmes* 60, *le Vice et la
Vertu* 62, *Et Satan conduit le bal* 62, *Vacances portu-
aises* 63, *les Parapluies de Cherbourg* 63 (Golden Palm
t Cannes Festival 64), *les Plus Belles Escroqueries du
monde* 63, *la Chasse à l'homme* 64, *Un monsieur de
ompagnie* 64, *la Costanza della Ragione* 64, *Repulsion
4, le Chant du monde* 65, *la Vie de château* 65, *Liebes
Karusell* 65, *les Créatures* 65, *les Demoiselles de Rochefort
6, Belle de jour* 67 (Golden Lion at Venice Festival 67),
Benjamin 67, *Manon 70* 67, *Mayerling* 68, *la Chamade
8, Folies d'Avril* 69, *Belles d'un soir* 69, *la Sirène du
Mississippi* 69, *Tristana* 70, *Peau d'âne* 71, *Ça n'arrive
qu'aux autres* 71, *Liza* 71, *Un flic* 72, *L'Evènement le
Plus Important depuis que l'Homme a Marché sur la
Lune* 73, *Touche pas la Femme Blanche* 74, *La Femme
aux Bottes Rouges* 75, *La Grande Bourgeoisie* 75, *Hustle*
76.
c/o Artmedia, 37 rue Marbeuf, 75008 Paris; Home: 36
ave. Georges-Mandel, 75116 Paris, France.

Den Hartog, Jacob Pieter, E.E., PH.D.; American
engineer; b. 23 July 1901, Java, Indonesia; s. of
Maarten Den Hartog and Elisabeth Schol; m. Elisabeth
Stolker 1926; two s.; ed. Delft Univ. of Technology,
Netherlands and Univ. of Pittsburgh, Pa.
Moved to Netherlands 16; came to U.S. 24; Engineer,
Westinghouse Research Laboratory, Pittsburgh 24-32;
Asst. Prof. and Assoc. Prof. Harvard Univ. 32-41;
Lieut.-Commdr. to Capt., U.S. Naval Reserve; U.S.
Navy 41-45; Prof. of Mechanical Engineering, Mass.
Inst. of Technology 45-67, Head, Dept. of Mechanical
Engineering 54-58, Prof. Emer. 67-; also Consulting
Engineer; Fellow, American Inst. of Aeronautics and
Astronautics, Inst. of Mechanical Engineers, London;
mem., Nat. Acad. of Sciences, American Inst. of
Consulting Engineers, Royal Inst. of Engineers,
Netherlands; Hon. mem. American Soc. of Mechanical
Engineers, Japan Soc. of Mechanical Engineers; Hon.
A.M. Harvard Univ., Hon. Dr. Eng. Carnegie Inst. of
Technology, Pittsburgh, Hon. Dr. Applied Sc. Univ.
of Ghent, Hon. Dr. Tech. Sc. Delft Univ. of Technology,
Hon. Sc.D. Salford Univ., Hon. Sc.D. Univ. of New-
castle-upon-Tyne.
Publs. *Mechanical Vibrations* (trans. in ten languages)
1st U.S. edn. 34, 4th U.S. edn. 56; also three other
books and 35 papers.
Massachusetts Institute of Technology, Cambridge,

Mass. 02139; Home: Barnes Hill Road, Concord, Mass.
01742, U.S.A.
Telephone: 617-253-3298 (Office); 617-369-2907 (Home).

den Hollander, Franciscus Querien; Netherlands
mechanical engineer; b. 1893, Goes; ed. Delft Univ. of
Technology.
Trained with Holland Railway Co. 16-17; employed by
Netherlands Indies State Railways 18-37; Asst. Man.
Govt. Artillery Establishments, Hembrug 38-40, Gen.
Man. 40; Perm. Under-Sec., Min. of Econ. Affairs
45; Man. Dir. of Traffic, Ministry of Transport 45-46;
Gen. Man. and Acting Pres. of Netherlands Railway
46-47, Pres. 47-59; Hon. Life Fellow Perm. Way Inst.;
F.R.S.A.; hon. mem. Inst. of Transport, Inst. of
Railway Signal Engineers, Inst. of Mechanical Engineers
London, Royal Inst. of Engineers The Hague; Knight
Order of Netherlands Lion; Grand Officer Order of
Orange-Nassau; Officier Légion d'Honneur (France);
Hon. Dr. Tech. Sc (Delft Univ. of Technology).
9A Amersfoortseweg, Maarn, The Netherlands.

Denholm, John Ferguson, C.B.E.; British shipowner;
b. 8 May 1927, Glasgow; s. of Sir William and Lady Den-
holm (née Ferguson); m. Elizabeth Murray Stephen
1952; two s. two d.; ed. Loretto School, Midlothian.
Chair. Denholm Line of Steamers Ltd., Denholm Ship
Management Ltd.; Pres. Chamber of Shipping of U.K.
73-74; mem. Board P. & O. Steam Navigation Co. 74-.
Leisure interests: sailing, skiing, shooting.
Newton of Belltrees, Lochwinnoch, Renfrewshire,
Scotland.
Telephone: Lochwinnoch 406.

Deniau, Jean François, D. EN D., L. ÈS L.; French
economist and diplomatist; b. 31 Oct. 1928, Paris; ed.
Institut d'Etudes Politiques de Paris, Ecole Nationale
d'Admin.
Ecole Nationale d'Administration 50-52; Finance Insp.
52-55; Sec.-Gen. Inter-Ministerial Cttee. on European
Econ. Co-operation 55-56; Del. to OEEC. 55-56; Del. to
Inter-Govt. Conf. on the Common Market and Euratom
56; Head of Mission, Cabinet of Pres. of Counsel 57-58;
Technical Adviser, Ministry of Industry and Commerce
58-59; Dir. Comm. on countries seeking association
with EEC 59-61; Head of Del., Conf. with States seek-
ing membership of EEC 61-63; Dir. External Econ.
Relations, Ministry of Finance and Econ. Affairs
(France) 63; Amb. to Mauritania 63-66; Pres. Comm.
Franco-Soviétique pour la télévision en couleur; mem.
Combined Comm. of EEC, ECSC, and Euratom July
67-73; Commr. for Devt. Aid, European Communities
69-73; Sec. of State for Foreign Affairs 73-74, for
Agricultural and Rural Devt. 74, for Agriculture 75-76.
Publ. *Le Marché Commun* 58, 60.
37 rue de Chézy, 92 Neuilly-sur-Seine, France.

Deniau, Xavier; French politician; b. 24 Sept. 1923,
Paris; s. of Marc Deniau and Marie-Berthe Loth-
Simmonds; m. Irène Ghica-Cantacuzène 1953; five c.;
ed. Univ. of Paris and Ecole nationale de la France
d'Outre-mer.
Successively Dir. of External Affairs, Cameroon, and
Political Adviser to the Gen. High Commr. of Dakar
44-55; mem. French del. to UN 55-58 and to NATO
60-62; Technical Adviser, Cabinet of the Minister for
Armed Forces 60-62; Maître des Requêtes, Council of
State 62-; Deputy for the fourth constituency of the
Loiret 62-; Chair. for Cultural Relations and Technical
Co-operation, Foreign Affairs Comm., Nat. Assembly
62-68, Vice-Pres. Foreign Affairs Comm. 68-72, 73-;
Mayor of Escrignelles 65-; Sec. of State in charge of
Overseas Depts. and Territories 72-73; mem. Comm.
nationale pour l'éducation, la science et la culture 68-;
Sec.-Gen. Association internationale des parlemen-
taires de langue française 67-; Vice-Pres. Asscn.
nationale France-Canada 66-69; Pres. Association

France-Québec 69-72; Pres. friendship groups France-Cameroun 63-72, France-Québec and France-Canada 67-72; mem. Société française d'onomastique; Officier Légion d'Honneur; Croix de guerre 39-45 and Croix de guerre des Théâtres d'Opérations Extérieurs; Commdr. Ordre du Christ; allied to Union des Démocrates pour la République (U.D.R.).
14 rue Saint Guillaume, 75007 Paris, France.

Denis, Maurice Thimotée Ghislain; Belgian politician; b. 18 Sept. 1916, Namur; s. of Maurice Denis and Marie Masson; m. Blanche Debois 1943; one d.; ed. Athénée Provincial du Centre à Morlanwelz and Ecole des Hautes Etudes Commerciales et Consulaires, Liège.
Professor and Head, Dept. of Political Economy, Ecole des Hautes Etudes Commerciales et Consulaires de Liège; Sec. Office of the Prime Minister 46-47; mem. Liège City Council 46-; mem. Chamber of Reps. 56-; Minister of the Budget Feb. 71-Jan. 72; Officier de l'Ordre de Léopold, de l'Ordre de la Couronne, Académie de France; Croix de Guerre avec Palmes, Médaille Militaire, Croix Civique.
Leisure interests: theatre, shows, travel.
Chamber of Representatives, 1040 Brussels; Home: 16 avenue Rogier, 4000 Liège, Belgium.

Denisse, Jean-François; French astronomer; b. 16 May 1915, Saint-Quentin, Aisne; s. of Jean Julien Denisse and Marie Nicolas; m. Myriam Girondot 1948; two d.; ed. Ecole Normale Supérieure.
Teacher at Lycée, Dakar 42-45; at Centre Nat. de la Recherche Scientifique (C.N.R.S.) 46-47; Guest Worker, Nat. Bureau of Standards, U.S.A. 48-49; Head of Research of C.N.R.S. at Ecole Normale Supérieure 50-51, Dir. of Studies, Inst. des Hautes Etudes, Dakar 52-53; Asst. Astronomer, Paris Observatory 54-56, Astronomer 56-63, Dir. 63-68; Chair. of Board of Nat. Space Research Centre 68-73; Dir. Institut National d'Astronomie et de Géophysique 68-71; Pres. Bureau des Longitudes 74-75; mem. Acad. des Sciences 67-; Officier Légion d'Honneur.
Leisure interests: tennis, sailing, skiing, golf.
Observatoire de Paris, Section d'Astrophysique, 92190 Meudon; 177 rue Marceau, 91120 Palaiseau, France. Telephone: 626-16-30.

Denkstein, Vladimir, PH.D., D.SC.; retd. Czechoslovak National Museum director; b. 3 Feb. 1906, Dobřany; m. Zdenka Vondrášková 1940; two s.; ed. Charles Univ., Prague.
Assistant, Inst. of Art History, Charles Univ., Prague 30-32; Asst. Curator, Regional Museum, České Budějovice 32-40; Asst. Curator, Dept. of Historical Archaeology, Nat. Museum, Prague 40-45, Head Curator 45-56, Dir. of the Nat. Museum, Prague 56-70; Editor *Acta Musei Nationalis Pragae* 56-73; Chair. Czechoslovak Nat. Cttee. of Int. Council of Museums 58-69, Central Museums Council 59-69; Chair. Czechoslovak Nat. Cttee. of Int. Asscn. for the History of Glass; dist. for Merits in Construction 66.
Publs. *Jihočeská gotika* (South Bohemian Gothic Art) 53, *Lapidarium Národního muzea* (Lapidary of the National Museum) 58, *Pavises of the Bohemian Type* I, 62, II, 64, III, 65.
Kyjevská 9, 16000, Prague 6, Czechoslovakia.

Denktaş, Rauf R.; Cypriot politician; b. 27 Jan. 1924; s. of Judge M. Raif bey; m. Ayden Munir 1949; two s. two d.; ed. The English School, Nicosia, and Lincoln's Inn, London.
Law practice in Nicosia 47-49; Jr. Crown Counsel 49, Crown Counsel 52; Acting Solicitor-Gen. 56-58; Pres. Fed. of Turkish Cypriot Asscns. 58-60; Pres. Turkish Communal Chamber 60, re-elected 70; Vice-Pres. of Cyprus 73-; Pres. Turkish Federated State of Cyprus 75-.
Leisure interests: reading, writing, sea sports, shooting.
Publs. *Secrets of Happiness* (1st edn. 43, 2nd edn. 73),

Hell Without Fire 44, *A Handbook of Criminal Cases* 55 *Five Minutes to Twelve* 66, *The AKRITAS Plan* 72 *A Short Discourse on Cyprus* 72, *The Cyprus Problem* 73 The Office of the President, Turkish Federated State c Cyprus, Mershin 10, Turkey.

Dennery, Etienne Roland; French diplomatist; b 20 March 1903, Paris; s. of Georges and Amélie Denner (née Meyer); m. Denise Fenard 1949 (died 1967); one s. ed. Ecole Normale Supérieure, Univ. of Paris.
Economic expert L.N. Study Comm., Manchuria 32 Prof. Ecole Libre des Sciences Politiques, Paris 32-39 Sec.-Gen. Centre d'Etudes de Politique Etrangère Paris 35-39; Dir. of Information, Fighting French H.Q. London 41-42; Capt. Artillery, Fighting French Force Libya and Italy 43-44; Dir. American Section, Ministry of Foreign Affairs, Paris 45-50; Amb. to Poland 50-54 to Switzerland 54-61, to Japan 61-64; Gen. Admin. o Nat. Library and Dir. French Libraries and Public Reading 64-; mem. UNESCO Exec. Council 66-; mem du Comité de direction du Centre national du lettres 74-.
Leisure interests: golf, reading.
Publ. *Foules d'Asie* 30.
8 rue des Petits-Champs, 75002 Paris; and Bibliothèque Nationale, 58 rue de Richelieu, Paris 2e, France.
Telephone: Richelieu 32-03.

Denning, Baron (Life Peer), cr. 57, of Whitchurch; **Alfred Thompson Denning,** P.C., M.A.; British lawyer; b. 23 Jan. 1899; ed. Magdalen Coll., Oxford.
Called to the Bar, Lincoln's Inn 23; K.C. 38; High Court Judge 44; Lord Justice of Appeal 48-57; Nominated Judge for War Pensions Appeals 45-48; Chair. Cttee. on Procedure in Matrimonial Causes 46-47; Lord of Appeal in Ordinary 57-62; Master of the Rolls 62-; Chair. Cttee. on Legal Educ. for Students from Africa 62-; Pres. Birkbeck Coll.; Treas. Lincoln's Inn 64; Head of Security Enquiry 63; Hon. D.C.L. (Oxford) 65.
Publs. *Freedom under the Law* 49, *The Changing Law* 53, *The Road to Justice* 55.
The Lawn, Whitchurch, Hants., England.

Dennis, Charles Cecil, Jr., A.B., LL.B.; Liberian lawyer and politician; b. 21 Feb. 1931; s. of Charles and Isabel Thomson Dennis; m. Agnes Cooper 1956; three c.; ed. Coll. of W. Africa, Lincoln Univ., Penn. and George Washington Univ., U.S.A.
Legal Counsel, Dir. Legislative Drafting Service, Liberian Senate; admitted to Bar of Supreme Court of Liberia 60; with Morgan Grimes and Harmon, law firm 62; established C. Cecil Dennis, Jr., law firm 65; Prof. Louis Arthur Grimes School of Law, Univ. of Liberia; mem. Liberian Codification Comm.; Chair. Board of Dirs. Bank of Liberia; Vice-Pres. LAMCO 72-73; Hon. Consul-Gen. of Repub. of Korea; Minister of Foreign Affairs 73-; Commdr. Order of the Star of Africa, Knight Great Band of Humane Order of African Redemption, Knight Grand Commdr. of Most Venerable Order of Pioneers, Grand Cross Commdr. Order of Orange-Nassau.
Ministry of Foreign Affairs, Monrovia, Liberia.

Dennison, David Mathias, A.B., PH.D.; American professor of physics; b. 26 April 1900, Oberlin, Ohio; s. of Walter and Anna (Green) Dennison; m. Helen Johnson 1924; two s.; ed. Swarthmore Coll. and Univ. of Michigan.
General Educ. Board Fellow, studied under Prof. Niels Bohr, Copenhagen 24-26; further study under Prof. Schrodinger, Zürich 26-27; Asst. Prof., Univ. of Michigan 27-30, Assoc. Prof. 30-35, Prof. 35-, Chair. Physics Dept. 55-65, Harrison M. Randall Univ. Prof. of Physics 66-70, Prof. Emer. 70-; mem. Nat. Acad. of Sciences.
Publs. 45 scientific articles dealing with molecular structure, specific heat of hydrogen, quantum theory, etc. 24-.

Department of Physics, University of Michigan, Ann Arbor, Mich.; Home: 2511 Hawthorn Road, Ann Arbor, Mich. 48104, U.S.A.
[*Died April* 1976.]

Dennison, Admiral Robert Lee, B.S., M.S., D.ENG.; American naval officer; b. 13 April 1901, Warren, Pennsylvania; *m.* Mildred Fenton Mooney Neely 1937; one *s.* one *d.*; ed. U.S. Naval Acad., Pennsylvania; State Coll., Johns Hopkins Univ.
Ensign 23, promoted through grades to Admiral 59; commanded U.S.S. *Ortolan* 35-37, *Cuttlefish* 37-38, *John D. Ford* 40-41, *Missouri* 47-48; Chief of Staff, Pacific Fleet Amphibious Forces 42-43, 9th Amphibious Fleet 43; mem. Joint War Plans Cttee. (Joint Chiefs of Staff) 44-45; Asst. Chief of Naval Operations (Politico-Mil. Affairs) 45-47; Naval Aide to Pres. of U.S. 48-53; Commdr. 4th Cruiser Div. Atlantic Fleet 53-54; Dir. Strategic Plans Div., Asst. Chief of Naval Operations, mem. Joint Strategic Plans Cttee. 54-56; Commdr. 1st Pacific Fleet 56-58; Dep. Chief of Naval Operations (Plans and Policy) 58-59; C.-in-C. U.S. Naval Forces, Eastern Atlantic and Mediterranean 59-60; C.-in-C. Atlantic Command, Atlantic Fleet and N.A.T.O. Supreme Allied Commdr. Atlantic 60-63; Vice-Pres. and mem. Board Copley Press Inc. 63-74; Dir. Atlantic Council 66-; numerous American and overseas decorations.
5040 Westpath Terrace, Washington, D.C. 20016, U.S.A.

Dennler, William H.; American business executive; b. 30 Sept. 1910; ed. Iowa State Univ.
Joined Gen. Electric Co. 33; Gen. Man. Major Appliance Div. 60; Vice-Pres. 62; Vice-Pres. and Group Exec. of Components and Construction Materials Group Jan. 66; Exec. Vice-Pres. and mem. President's Office, Jan. 68; Dir., Vice-Chair. of Board and Exec. Officer, Dec. 68-.
General Electric Co., 570 Lexington Avenue, New York, N.Y. 10022, U.S.A.

Denson, John Boyd, C.M.G., O.B.E.; British diplomatist; b. 13 Aug. 1926, Sunderland, Co. Durham; only *s.* of late George Denson and Alice Denson; *m.* Joyce Myra Symondson 1957; ed. Perse School and St. John's Coll., Cambridge.
Army Service, Royal Artillery and Intelligence Corps 44-48; St. John's Coll., Cambridge 48-51; joined British Foreign Service 51, served Hong Kong 51-52, Tokyo 52-53, Peking 53-55, London 55-57, Helsinki 57-59, Washington 60-63, Laos 63-65; Asst. Head of Far Eastern Dept., Foreign Office, London 65-68; Chargé d'Affaires a.i., Peking 69-71, Chargé d'Affaires en titre 71; Royal Coll. of Defence Studies, London 72; Counsellor and Consul-Gen., Athens 73-.
Leisure interests: looking at pictures, the theatre and wine.
19 Gainsborough Court, College Road, Dulwich, London, S.E.21, England.
Telephone: 01-693-8361.

Dent, Frederick; American government official; b. 17 Aug. 1922, Cape May, N.J.; *s.* of late Magruder Dent and of Edith Baily Dent; *m.* Mildred C. Harrison 1944; two *s.* three *d.*; ed. St. Paul's School, Concord, N.H., Yale Univ.
U.S. Navy, Pacific Theater, World War II, with rank of Lieut.; joined Mayfair Mills, Arcadia 47, Pres. 58; Chair. Spartanburg South Carolina, County Planning and Devt. Comm. 60-73; fmr. Dir. Mayfair Mills, Gen. Electric Co., S.C. Nat. Bank, Scott Paper Co., Mutual Life Insurance Co. of N.Y.; fmr. mem. Business Council, Commerce Dept. Int. Business Advisory Comm. and Labor Management, Labor Textile Advisory Comm.; ex-officio Dir. S.C. Textile Mfg. Asscn., American Textile Mfg. Inst.; fmr. mem. Gates Comm. on All-Volun-

teer Armed Force 69-70; Sec. of Commerce 73-75; Special Rep. of U.S. Govt. for Trade Negotiations March 75-.
Leisure interests: golf, tennis, bowls, swimming.
Office of the Special Representative for Trade Negotiations, 1800 G Street, N.W., Washington, D.C. 20506; and 2964 University Terrace, N.W., Washington, D.C. 20016, U.S.A.
Telephone: (202) 395-5114 (Office).

Den Uyl, Joop; Netherlands politician; b. 1919, Amsterdam; *m.*; seven *c.*; ed. Univ. of Amsterdam.
Formerly Councillor, Municipal Council of Amsterdam; Minister of Econ. Affairs April 65-Nov. 66; Leader of the Opposition, Second Chamber 67-73; Prime Minister and Minister of Gen. Affairs 73-; Partij van de Arbeid (Labour).
Office of the Prime Minister, The Hague; and Partij van de Arbeid, Tesselschadestraat 31, Amsterdam-West, Netherlands.

de Oliveira Campos, Roberto; Brazilian diplomatist; b. 17 April 1917, Cuiabá, Mato Grosso; *s.* of Waldomiro de Oliveira Campos and Honorina de Oliveira Campos; *m.* Maria Stella Tambellini de Oliveira Campos; two *s.* one *d.*; ed. Catholic Seminaries of Guaxupé and Belo Horizonte; George Washington Univ., Columbia Univ., N.Y., and New York Univ.
Entered Brazilian Foreign Service 39; Econ. Counsellor to Brazil–U.S.A. Econ. Devt. Comm. 51-53; Dir.-Gen., Man. and Pres. of Nat. Econ. Devt. Bank 52-59; Sec.-Gen. Nat. Devt. Council 56-59; Prof. of Money and Banking and Business Cycles, School of Econs., Univ. of Brazil 56-61; Roving Amb. for Financial Negotiations in W. Europe 61; Amb. to U.S.A. 61-63; Minister of State for Planning and Co-ordination 64-67; Amb. to U.K. March 75-; mem. Inter-American Cttee. for the Alliance for Progress 64-67; Pres. Inter-American Council of Commerce and Production 68-70; mem. Board of Govs. Int. Devt. Research Centre, Board of Dirs. Resources for the Future, Inc.; numerous Brazilian and foreign orders and decorations.
Publs. *Ensaios de História Ecenômica e Sociologia, Economia, Planejamento e Nacionalismo, A Moeda, O Govêrno e o Tempo, A Técnica e o Riso, Reflections on Latin American Development, Do outro lado da cerca, Temas e Sistemas, Ensaios contra a maré, Política Econômica e Mitos Políticos;* co-author: *Trends in International Trade* (GATT report), *Partners in Progress* (report of Pearson Cttee., IBRD), *A Nova Economia Brasileira, Formas Criativas No Desenvolvimento Brasileiro;* technical articles and reports in journals.
Embassy of Brazil, 32 Green Street, London, W.1; Residence: 54 Mount Street, London, W.1, England.
Telephone: 629-0507 and 629-5435.

de Oliveira Figueiredo, João Baptista; Brazilian army officer; b. 15 Jan. 1918, Rio de Janeiro; *s.* of Euclydes and Valentina de Oliveira Figueiredo; *m.* Dulce Maria de Castro Figueiredo 1942; two *s.*; ed. Colégio Militar de Porto Alegre, Colégio Militar do Rio de Janeiro, Acad. Militar das Agulhas Negras.
Instructor, Escola Militar do Realengo, Acad. Militar das Agulhas Negras, Escola de Aperfeiçoamento dos Oficiais, Escola de Comando e Estado-Maior do Exército, Escola Superior de Guerra 54-55, 61-64; mem. Mil. Mission to Paraguay 55-57; Commdr. Fôrça Pública, State of São Paulo 66-67; Commdr. 1st Regiment, Guards' Cavalry 67-69; Gen. and Chief of Staff, 3rd Army 69; Chief of Pres. Mil. Household 69-74; Sec.-Gen. Council of Nat. Security; many orders and medals incl. Medalha Militar, Medalha de Guerra, Medalha Honorífica (Paraguay), etc.
Leisure interest: horse racing.
Granja do Torto, Brasília, D.F., Brazil.
Telephone: 23-7755.

de Oriol y Urquijo, Antonio María; Spanish lawyer and politician; b. 15 Sept. 1913; ed. Stonyhurst Coll., England, and Universidad Central de Madrid.
Captain in civil war; later in private business; Dir.-Gen. of Charities and Social Works 57-65; fmr. Pres. Supreme Assembly of Spanish Red Cross; Minister of Justice 65-74; President of the Council of State 74-; Gran Cruz del Mérito Civil and other decorations.
Finca Valgrande, El Plantío (Madrid), Spain.

De Peyer, Gervase, A.R.C.M.; British clarinettist and conductor; b. 11 April 1926; s. of Esme Everard Vivian de Peyer and Edith Mary Bartlett; m. Sylvia South-combe 1950 (divorced 1971), one s. two d.; m. 2nd Susan Rosalind Daniel 1971; ed. King Alfred's School, London, Bedales School and Royal Coll. of Music, London.
Studied in Paris 49; Int. soloist 49-; Founder-mem. and Dir. Melos Ensemble; Principal Clarinet, London Symphony Orchestra 55-72; Musical Dir. Melos Sinfonia; Dir. London Symphony Wind Ensemble; recording artist with all major companies; gives recitals and master classes throughout the world; Gold Medallist Worshipful Company of Musicians 48; Charles Gros Grand Prix du Disque 61, 62; Plaque of Honor for Acad. of Arts and Sciences of America for the recording of Mozart concerto 62; appears with Chamber Music Soc., Lincoln Center, New York 69-.
Leisure interests: theatre, good food, anything danger-ous.
16 Langford Place, St. John's Wood, London, N.W.8, England.
Telephone: 01-624-4098.

De Pous, Jan Willem; Netherlands politician; b. 23 Jan. 1920, Aalsmeer; s. of Theunis de Pous and Aagje Maarse; m. Greta van Itterzon 1951; one s. two d.; ed. Amsterdam Univ.
On staff of Trouw 43-46; mem. Board, Christian Nat. Press Org. for Neths. 45-; Sec. and Econ. Adviser, Protestant Employers' Org. in the Netherlands 49-59; Lecturer Econ. Theory, Free Univ. of Amsterdam 53-59; mem. Council of State 58-59; Minister of Econ. Affairs May 59-63; Adviser Govts. of Surinam and Dutch Antilles 66-74; Pres. Del. Dutch-Belgian Joint Venture Baalhoek canal 69-75; Christian-Historical Union; Pres. Social-Econ. Council 64-, Cen. Cttee. on Hospital Tariffs 64; Mining Council 67-; Pres. of Supervisory Board, K.L.M. Royal Dutch Airlines 64-; mem. Board of Dirs. Philips, R.S.V. Engineering Works and Shipyards, B.A.M. Batavian Contracting Co., I.C.U. Information and Communication Co.; numerous decorations.
c/o Social-Economic Council, Bezuidenhoutseweg 60, The Hague; Home: Van Zaeckstraat 65, The Hague, Netherlands.
Telephone: 070-814341 (Office); 070-241575 (Home).

Depreux, Edouard Gustave; French lawyer and politi-cian; b. 31 Oct. 1898, Viesly (Nord); m. Françoise Monroy 1927; one s. one d.; ed. Faculties of Letters and Law, Paris.
Delegate to Provincial Consultative Assembly 44; Mayor of Sceaux 44-59; Deputy to Constituent Assembly 46-58, Minister of the Interior 46-47, of Nat. Educ. Feb.-April 48, Pres. Socialist Party, Nat. Assembly 46-56; formerly Pres. of High Court of Justice; Nat. Sec. Parti Socialiste Unifié 60-67, Hon. Nat. Sec. 67-; Croix de Guerre (14-18 and 39-45); Médaille de la Résistance avec rosette.
Publs. Renouvellement du socialisme, La Chine Nouvelle et son héritage, Souvenirs d'un militant 72, Servitude et grandeur du P.S.U. 74.
13 rue Linois, Apartment 2202, Paris 15, France.

Dequae, André, L. ès SC.ECON.; Belgian politician; b. 3 Nov. 1915, Kortrijk; m. Agnes Vandemoortele 1940; three s. three d.; ed. Louvain Univ.

Member Chamber of Representatives 46-, Vice-Pres. 58-60, First Vice-Pres. 65-74, Pres. 74-; Minister o Reconstruction 50, of Colonies 50-54, of External Trade 58, of Econ. Co-ordination 60-61, of Finance 61-65 mem. Council of Europe and WEU; Christian Socia. Party; Commdr. de l'Ordre de Léopold, Médaille de la Résistance, Médaille du Souvenir.
Leisure interests: books, swimming.
St. Elooidreef 36, Kortrijk, Belgium.
Telephone: 056-221999.

De Quay, Jan Eduard, D.LITT.; Netherlands politician; b. 1901, s'Hertogenbosch; m. Maria Van der Lande 1927; five s. four d.; ed. Utrecht Univ.
Lecturer and later Prof. Tilburg Roman Catholic Univ. 34-46; Labour Organisation Commr. 40; leader Nether-lands Union 40-41; Prov. Governor North Brabant 46-59; Minister for War in second Gerbrandy cabinet; Prime Minister and Minister of General Affairs 59-63; Chair. of Board of Dirs. K.L.M. 64; mem. of the First Chamber; Commdr. Order Orange-Nassau, Commdr. Order Netherlands Lion, etc.
Leisure interests: history, psychology.
c/o K.L.M., Schiphol Airport, The Netherlands.

De Ranitz, Jonkheer Johan Antoni; Netherlands diplomatist; b. 30 June 1915; ed. Univ. of Leiden.
Entered diplomatic service 40; has served in Canberra, Batavia, Berne, and Cairo; Deputy Perm. Rep. to N. Atlantic Council 57; Amb. and leader of del. negotiating admission of new members to EEC 62; Amb. to U.A.R. 63; Dir.-Gen. Dept. of Political Affairs, Ministry of Foreign Affairs, The Hague 64-70; Amb. to France 70-.
Ambassade des Pays-Bas, 85 rue de Grenelle, Paris 7e, France.

Dereli, Cevat; Turkish artist; b. 1900; ed. Ecole des Beaux Arts, Paris.
Lived in Paris 24-28; Prof. of Painting, Istanbul Acad. of Fine Arts; rep. at numerous exhibitions, including the Venice Biennale 56 and the Brussels Int. Exhbn. 58.
Academy of Fine Arts, Istanbul; Home: Bagdat Cad, Çinar Dibi, Çinar Palas, D11 Erenköy, Istanbul, Turkey.

Dernesch, Helga; Austrian opera singer; b. 3 Feb. 1939, Vienna; m.; two c.
Sang many operatic roles in Bern 61-63, Wiesbaden 63-66, Cologne 66-69; guest appearance with Deutsche Oper Berlin; regular appearances at Bayreuth Festival 65-69, at Salzburg Easter Festival 69-73; has sung in operas and concerts throughout Europe and U.S.A.; many recordings.
Leisure interests: riding, hunting, literature.
c/o Emil Jucker, Tobelhofstrasse 2, 8044 Zurich, Switzerland.

De Robertis, Eduardo Diego Patricio, M.D.; Argentine histologist, cytologist and embryologist; b. 11 Dec. 1913; ed. Univ. of Buenos Aires.
Rockefeller Fellow, Chicago and Johns Hopkins Univs. 40, 44; at Biophysical Laboratory, Rio de Janeiro 43; Dir. Dept. of Cellular Ultrastructure, Inst. de In-vestigaciones de Ciencias Biológicas 46; Lecturer in Physiology, Texas Univ. 52; Walker-Ames Prof. Univ. of Washington (Seattle) 53; Prof. Histology, Univ. of Buenos Aires 57, now Prof. Cytology, Histology and Embryology; Dir. Inst. de Anatomía Gen. y Embriolo-gía 57, now Dir. Inst. of Cell Biology, Faculty of Medi-cine, Univ. of Buenos Aires; mem. Argentine Acad. of Sciences, Argentine Research Council, American Acad. of Neurology, American Soc. for Neurochemistry; Fellow, New York Acad. of Sciences; Mitre Inst. Award, Van Meeter Award; Argentine Nat. Prize; Buenos Aires Gold Medal; Shell Foundation Prize 69; Dr. h.c. (Loyola Univ.); Hon. mem. American Coll. of Physicians, Nat. Acad. of Sciences, Pan American Medical Asscn.

ubls. *Citologia General* 46, 52, 55 (English trans. 48, ., Japanese trans. 55, Russian trans. 62; since 65 ppears as *All Biology*); *Histophysiology of synapses and eurosecretion* 64 (French trans.), *Cell Biology* 5th edn. ranslated into Spanish, Italian, Russian, Hungarian, olish); more than 200 papers on cytology, thyroid and, electromicroscopy, neurology and neurochemis- ry.
nstitute of Cell Biology, Facultad de Medicina, Para- uay 2155, 2° piso, Buenos Aires, Argentina.
elephone: 83-9180 and 83-8989.

Deroy, Henri, L. ès L., D. en D.; French banker and ompany director; b. 12 June 1900, Paris; s. of Léon nd Camille (née Mouillefarine) Deroy; m. Marie- hérèse Toulouse 1928; two s. two d.; ed. Faculty of Law, Paris, and Ecole Libre des Sciences Politiques.
ntered Gen. Inspectorate of Finance 23; became Deputy Dir. of Budget 26, Asst. Dir. 29; Head of various epts. in same org. 30-35; Dir.-Gen. Caisse des Dépots t Consignations 35-45, Gov. of Crédit Foncier de rance 45-55, mem. Council of Admin. La Banque de rance 36-55; Hon. Gov. Crédit Foncier de France; Ion. Pres. Cie. Financière de Paris et des Pays-Bas, ompagnie Int. des Wagon-Lits; Vice-Chair. Bank for nt. Settlements; Dir. Banque Ottomane, Crédit Foncier le France, Crédit Foncier Franco-Canadien, Paribas nt., Hachette, Soc. des Raffineries de Sucre de Saint- Louis; Prof. of Budgetary Legislation, Ecole des ciences Politiques 26-47; Grand Officier de la Légion l'Honneur.
Publs. *Œuvres du Moulin-Vert* 27, *Les Hôtels du crédit oncier en France* 52.
6 avenue Foch, 75116 Paris, France.
Telephone: 727-27-61.

Derthick, Lawrence Gridley, Snr., B.A., M.A., LL.D.; American administrator and educationist; b. 23 Dec. 906, Hazel Green, Kentucky; s. of Henry J. and Pearl S. Derthick; m. Helda L. Hannah 1927; two s. one d.; ed. Univs. of Tennessee, Columbia and Chattanooga.
Has held many educational appointments since 27; United States Commr. of Educ., Dept. of Health, Educ. and Welfare 56-61; Asst. Exec. Sec. for Pro- fessional Devt. and Instructional Services, Nat. Educ. Asscn. of U.S. 61-71; Educ. Consultant 72-.
Leisure interests: travel, volunteer service in civic and international activities.
Publs. *Be Safe and Live* (co-author); numerous educ. and other works.
Box 817, 121 North Washington Street, Alexandria, Va. 22314, U.S.A.
Telephone: (703) 836-7572.

Déry, Tibor; Hungarian author; b. 18 Oct. 1894, Budapest; ed. Grammar school and Commercial Acad., Budapest.
As a young office clerk early joined the revolutionary movements, organized strikes; took part in 18-19 revolution; spent several years in exile; in prison 57-60; Kossuth Prize 48; Banner of Order of Hungarian People's Republic.
Leisure interest: literature.
Publs. Poetry: *Ló Buza Ember, Énekelnek és meghalnak, Szemtelnezve, Felhőállatok*; Novels: *Országuton, Szemtöl- szembe, A Tengerparti Gyár, A Befejezetlen Mondat, Felelet, Niki, Pesti felhőjáték, G.A. ur X-ben, A Kiközö- sitö, A Kéthangu Kiáltás, Képzelt riport egy amerikai popfesztivälról, Kedves bópeer, A félfülü, Kyvagiokén*; Short stories: *Alvilági Jatékok, Jókedv és Buzgalom, Simon Menyhért születése, Hazáról emberekröl, A ló meg az oregasszony, Utkaparo, Szerelem, Theokritosz Ujpesten* I, II; Theatre: *Tanuk, Tukör, Itthon, A csodacsecsemö,* etc.; Autobiography: *Itélet nincs.*
Lotz Karoly u. 20, H-1026 Budapest II, Hungary.

De Saeger, Jozef; Belgian accountant and politician; b. 1911, Boom, Province of Antwerp.

Former accountant; Christian Social Deputy 49; Minister of Public Works 65-66, 68-70, 72-73, of Public Health and Environment Jan.-Sept. 73, of Public Health, Environment and Family 73-74, of Public Health and Family Affairs 74-.
Ministry of Public Health and Family Affairs, Brussels, Belgium.

Desai, Hitendra Kanaiyalal, B.A., LL.D.; Indian politi- cian; b. 9 Aug. 1915 in Surat; ed. Bombay Univ. Faculties of Economics and Law.
Took part in anti-British political activities; imprisoned 30, 41, 42-43; set up private legal practice in Surat 39; elected mem. Surat Municipal Council 39-57; mem. Bombay Legislative Asscn. 57-60; Minister of Educ., Bombay 57-60; Minister of Revenue, Gujarat State 60, later Home Minister; Leader of the House Gujarat Assembly 60-; Chief Minister of Gujarat 65-72; mem. Congress Party, elected to Supreme Exec. 68.
1 Shahibaug, Ahmedabad 4, Gujarat, India.

Desai, Khandubhai Kasanji; Indian politician; b. 23 Oct. 1898 Bulsar Gujarat; ed. High School Bulsar and Wilson Coll.
Joined Non-co-operation Movement under Gandhi 20; graduated from Gujarat Vidyapith Nat. Inst. and taught for some time; with Labour Union, Ahmedabad 21; Asst. Sec. Textile Labour Asscn., now Gen. Sec.; spread a network of unions throughout Gujarat; imprisoned 32-33; elected to Bombay Assembly 37 and to Constituent Assembly 46; served with many cttees. in the Ministries of Commerce, Industries, Railways and Labour; mem. of Congress Working Cttee., In- dustrial Finance Corpn. and Employers' State In- surance Corpn.; founded Indian Nat. Trade Union Congress 47, Pres. for three years, and fmr. Gen. Sec.; Minister of Labour 54-57; mem. Fiscal Cttee. 48; Chair. Oil India Ltd. 61-68; mem. first Nat. Defence Council, Board of Trade, Gujarat Devt. Corpn.; Gov. of Andhra Pradesh 68-75.
Raj Bhavan, Hyderabad-41, Andhra Pradesh, India.

Desai, Shri Morarji Ranchhodji; Indian politician; b. 29 Feb. 1896; ed. Bulsar and Wilson Coll., Bombay.
Served in the Provincial Civil Service in the Bombay Presidency 18-30; joined Civil Disobedience Movement led by Mahatma Gandhi 30, and was convicted for it; mem. of All-India Congress Cttee. since 31; Sec. Gujerat Provincial Congress Cttee. 31-37, 39-46; Min. for Revenue and Forests 37-39; imprisoned in the Quit India Movement for about five years; Home and Revenue Minister, Bombay 46-52; Chief Minister of Bombay 52-56; Union Minister for Commerce and Industry 56-58, Finance Minister 58-63; Deputy Prime Minister and Minister of Finance 67-July 69; mem. All India Congress Cttee. until 69; Chair. Parl. Group, Congress Party (Opposition) 69-; mem. Congress Party Parl. Board 63; Treas. of Congress 50-58; Chair. Admin. Reforms Comm. 66; mem. Working Cttee. A.I.C.C.; Hon. Fellow, Coll. of Physicians and Sur- geons, Bombay; Hon. LL.D. Karnatak Univ.
5 Dupleix Road, New Delhi, India.

Desailly, Jean; French actor; b. 24 Aug. 1920, Paris; ed. Paris Ecole des Beaux Arts.
Pensionnaire, Comédie Française 42-46; mem. Renaud- Barrault Company 47-68; Dir. Théâtre Jacques Hébertot 72-; mem. Council for Cultural Devt. 71-; plays include: *La Nuit du Diable, Le Bossu, Malatesta, Le Procès, On ne badine pas avec l'Amour, Le Château, Madame Sans-Gêne, Tête d'Or, La Cerisaie, Le Marchand de Venise, Comme il vous plaira, Hamlet, Andromaque, le Soulier de Satin, Il faut passer par les nuages, Le Mariage de Figaro, Brève Rencontre, Un ami imprévu, Double Jeu, Le Légume*; Co-Dir. *Tout dans le jardin*; films include *Le Père Goriot, La Symphonie Pastorale, Le Point du Jour, Occupe-toi, d'Amélie, Si Versailles m'était conté, Les Grandes Manoeuvres, Maigret tend un*

Piège, Les Grandes Familles, Le Baron de l'Ecluse, Plein Soleil, la Mort de Belle, Un soir sur la plage, les Sept Péchés capitaux, les Amours célèbres, l'Année du bac, La Peau douce, Le Doulos, Les Deux Orphelines, Le Franciscain de Bourges, L'Ardoise, Comptes à rebours, L'Assassinat de Trotsky, Un flic.
53 quai des Grands Augustins, 75006 Paris, France.

Desbordes, Joseph-Noël; French steel executive; b. 23 Dec. 1898; ed. Ecole Polytechnique.
President-Director-General Havre Drawing and Rolling Mills until 62; Vice-Pres. Dir.-Gen. Tréfimétaux (merger of Havre Drawing and Rolling Mills and French Metal Co.) 62-67, Pres. 67, Hon. Pres. 70-; Man. Cie. Péchiney 70-, Soc. Péchiney-Ugine-Kuhlmann 72-; Officier, Légion d'Honneur.
Péchiney-Ugine-Kuhlmann, 23 rue Balzac, Paris 8e; Home: 17 Avenue Paul Doumer, 78 Chatou (Seine-et-Oise), France.

Desbrière, Georges; French business executive; b. 25 Nov. 1901; ed. Ecole Centrale des Arts et Manufactures and Ecole Supérieure d'Electricité.
Engineer, Compagnie Française des Métaux 25-32, Sec.-Gen. 32-38, Dir. Gen. 38-47, Administrator Dir.-Gen. 47-52, Vice-Pres. Dir.-Gen. 52-56, Pres. Dir.-Gen. 56-62, Pres. of Société Tréfimétaux (merger of Tréfileries et Laminoirs du Havre and Compagnie Française des Métaux) 62-67, now Hon. Pres. Seichimé; Vice-Pres. of Péchiney 67; Vice-Pres. Soc. Péchiney-Ugine-Kuhlmann 71-75, Pres.-Dir.-Gen. 67-72; Administrator Tréfimétaux GP, Cegedur GP and Scal GP, of Crédit Industriel et Commercial, Sidelor, Comptoir Lyon-Alemand, Pres. Chamber of Commerce and Industry, Paris 60-63; mem. Conseil Economique et Social; Commdr. Légion d'Honneur, Commdr. du Mérite Commercial et du Mérite Touristique.
6 rue de d'Amiral-Courbet, 75116 Paris, France.

Descamps, Albert Louis; Belgian theologian and university official; b. 27 June 1916, Escanaffles; s. of Fidèle Descamps and Mélanie Dumonchaux; ed. Collège St.-Léon, Bruges, Petit Séminaire de Bonne-Espérance, Catholic Univ. Louvain and Institut Biblique Pontifical, Rome.
Professor, Great Seminary of Tournai 47-55; Lecturer, Catholic Univ., Louvain 52; Prof., Faculty of Theology, Catholic Univ., Louvain 53-60, 69-; Pres. Holy Ghost Coll. 56-60; Pres. Institut Supérieur des Sciences Religieuses 54-60; Rector, Catholic Univ. of Louvain 62, Rector Magnificus 64, Hon. Rector Magnificus 70-; Titular Bishop of Tunis 60-; mem. Studiorum Novi Testamenti Societas, Cambridge 57-; mem. Société des Sciences, des Arts et des Lettres du Hainaut, Société scientifique de Bruxelles; Commandeur Ordre de Léopold.
Leisure interest: history.
Publs. books and numerous articles.
13 Oude Markt, B-3000 Louvain, Belgium.
Telephone: 016-220431.

Desch, Kurt; German publisher; b. 2 June 1903; ed. Oberrealschule.
Formerly in advertising and journalism, including *Frankfurter Zeitung* and *Dortmunder General-Anzeiger*; expelled from Reichsschrifttumskammer 36; with Zinnen-Verlag, Vienna and Munich 41-44; escaped to Tirol 44; took over Zinnen-Verlag and founded his own firm, Kurt Desch, Munich, and Theaterverlag Kurt Desch Nov. 45 (branches in Basle and Vienna 53); founded Deutscher Laienspielverlag, Weinheim 47, Welt im Buch 53, Kurt Desch Film G.m.b.H., Munich 57.
Desch-Insel an der Romanstrasse 7-9, Munich 19, Federal Republic of Germany.

Deschamps, Hubert; French colonial governor and university professor; b. 22 July 1900, Royan; s. of Jules Deschamps and Ernestine Quod; m. 2nd Paule Poggi 1940; one s.; ed. Univ. de Paris à la Sorbonne.

Professor, Casablanca 21-22; Colonial Administrate Madagascar 26-36; Asst. to Léon Blum 36-38; Pro Ecole Nat. des Langues Orientales Vivantes 36-3 Gov. 38-50; Asst. to Sec. of State for France Overse 54-55; Research Posts 50-62; Prof. of Modern Afric̀ History, Univ. of Paris 62-70.
Leisure interests: swimming, walking, reading ar writing.
Publs. *Madagascar, Les Méthodes et les doctrin coloniales de la France, Histoire de Madagasc̀ L'Afrique au XXe siècle, L'Europe découvre l'Afriqu Histoire Générale de l'Afrique Noire, Histoire de la Traı des Noirs, Mémoires* (Roi de la Brousse), and mar others.
30 rue Jacob, Paris 6e, France.
Telephone: 633-39-88.

Desguin, Georges Maurice; Belgian journalist; 1913; ed. in France.
With *Aero*, Paris, before 39; imprisoned during Secon World War; Sec. to Editor *Le Matin*, Antwerp 44-5 Chief Editor 50-53, Man. Dir. 53-; Order of Mer (Italy).
Home: Beau Soleil, 6-8 Eikendreef, Kapellen, nea Antwerp; Office: *Le Matin*, 29 Vieille Bourse, Antwer Belgium.

Deshmukh, Chintaman Dwarkanath, B.A.; Indiá administrator and banker; b. 14 Jan. 1896 Nata District Kolaba Maharashtra; s. of Dwarkanaţ Ganesh Deshmukh and Bhagirathi Deshmukh; m. 1 Rosina Silcox 1920 (died 1949); 2nd G. Durgabai 195̈ one d.; ed. Elphinstone Coll., Bombay, and Jesus Coll Cambridge.
Served in Central Province and Berar as Asst. Comm Under-Sec. to Govt.; Deputy Commr. and Settlemen Officer 19-30; Sec. to second Round Table Conf. 3̈ Revenue and Financial Sec. Govt. of Central Provinc and Berar 32-39; Joint Sec. Dept. of Education; Healt and Lands Officer on Special Duty, Finance Dept Custodian Enemy Property April-Oct. 39; Sec. Centrà Board of the Reserve Bank of India 39-41; Deput Gov. Reserve Bank of India 41-43; del. World Monetar Conf. 44; Gov. Reserve Bank of India 43-49; Gov. fc India on Int. Monetary Fund and Int. Bank for Re construction and Development 46-49, Pres. Indiá statistical Inst., 45-64; Financial Rep. of Govt. of Indiá in Europe and America 49-50; mem. Planning Comm Minister of Finance Govt. of India 50-56; Chair. Inı Monetary Fund and Int. Bank for Reconstruction an Development 50; Chair. Univ. Grants Comm. 56-61 Chair. Nat. Book Trust 57-60; Hon. Fellow, Jesȕ College, Cambridge 52; Chair. Admin. Staff Coll. o India, Hyderabad 60-73; Pres. India Int. Centre, Ne̊ Delhi 59-; Vice-Chancellor, Univ. of Delhi 62-67; men Board of Trustees, UN Inst. for Training and Researcİ 65-70, Vice-Chair. 66-70; Chair. Central Sanskrit Boar̀ 67-68; Ramon Magsaysay Award 59; Pres. Indiá Inst. of Econ. Growth 65-74; Pres. Council for Sociá Devt. 66-; Pres. Population Council of India 70-Barrister at Law; Hon. LL.D. (Univs. Princeton, Neẁ Jersey, Leicester and 13 Indian univs.).
Leisure interests: social work, gardening.
Publs. *The Course of My Life* 74, *Bhagavadgita* 76 *Gems from the Amara Kosha* 76.
"Rachana", 2-2-18/50 Central Training Institute Hyderabad 500768, Andhra Pradesh, India.
Telephone: 71323.

Desio, Ardito, F.D.S., F.R.G.S., F.M.G.S.; Italian geolo gist, geographer and explorer; b. 18 April 1897, Pal manova, Udine; s. of Antonio Desio and Caterinȧ Zorzella; m. Aurelia Bevilacqua 1932; one s. one d.; ed Dept. of Natural Science, Univ. of Florence (Dı Natural Science).
Lecturer of Geology, Univ. of Milan 26-31; Prof. o Geology, Univ. of Milan 31; Dir. Inst. of Geology, Univ

Milan, now Emeritus Prof.; led seventeen overseas exploratory expeditions and scientific missions in Libya, Sahara, Ethiopia, Jordan, Iran, Afghanistan, Pakistan (Karakoram), India, Philippines, Burma, Antarctica; leader of the successful expedition to K2 (28,250 feet), second highest peak in the world 54; Patron's Medal (U.K.), Antarctic Service Medal (U.S.A.); Knight Grand Cross (Italy); mem. Italian Nat. Acad.; numerous other awards.

Leisure interests: mountaineering, photography.

Publs. about 350 vols. including a number of vols. about the geology and geography of Libya, Aegean Islands, Eastern Alps, Karakoram Range (Himalaya), Hindu Kush Range, Afghanistan, a monograph on the glaciers of Ortles-Cevedale massif, a treatise of geology applied to engineering, a vol. on the geology of Italy, scientific reports on expeditions, etc.

Istituto di Geologia, Piazza Gorini 15, 20133 Milan; Home: Viale Maino 14, 20129, Milano, Italy.
Telephone: 292813 (Office); 709845 (Home).

de Sitter, Lamoraal Ulbo, D.SC.; Netherlands geologist; b. 6 March 1902, Groningen; s. of Prof. Dr. Willen de Sitter and E. Suermondt; m. 1st Ingrid Frick 1926; 2nd C. M. Koomans 1942; three s. two d.; ed. Universität Zürich, Univ. de Lausanne and Rijksuniversiteit te Leiden.

Military service 25-26; field geologist, Bataafse Petroleum Mij. (Royal Dutch Shell), Borneo 26-29; field geologist Shell Oil Co., Venezuela 29-31; in Hague Office, Shell 32; Chief Geologist, Java, Bataafse Petroleum 33-34; Univ. of Leiden 34-, Prof. of Structural and Applied Geology 48-68; mem. Royal Netherlands Acad. of Science; Hon. mem. Royal Irish Acad. (Science Section); Foreign mem. Geol. Soc. of London; Hon. mem. Soc. Belge de Géologie, de Paléontologie et d'Hydrologie, Geol. Soc. of America.

Leisure interests: wood carving and sculpture, gardening.

Publs. *Structural Geology* (2nd edn.) 64, *Geology of the Bergamasc Alps* 49, *Geologic Maps of Central Pyrenees* (1 : 50,000, sheets 1, 2, 3, 4, 5, 6, 7, 8), *Geologic Maps of the Paleozoic of the Cantabrian Mountains* (1 : 50,000, 4 sheets), *Variation in Tectonic Style* 63, *Hercynian and Alpine Orogenies in N. Spain* 65.

Geological Institute, University of Leiden, Garenmarkt 1B, Leiden, and Maxend 66, Nistelrode (N. Br.), Netherlands.
Telephone: 04124-444.

Desnuelle, Pierre Antoine Edouard; French biochemist; b. 8 Aug. 1911; ed. Lycée Ampère, Lyons, and Univs. of Lyons, Heidelberg and Cambridge.

Professor of Biochemistry, Univ. of Marseilles 46-, Dir. Inst. of Biochemistry, Faculty of Sciences, Marseilles 61-; mem. Nat. Cttee. on Scientific Research 48-; Pres. of Soc. of Biochemistry 60-; Sec. Gen. Int. Union of Biochemistry; Chevalier de la Légion d'Honneur, Officier de l'Ordre Nat. du Mérite, Chevalier des Palmes Académiques.

17 avenue du Colonel-Sérot, 13 Marseilles (8e), France.

De Souza, Wilfred Raoul Eugène; Benin diplomatist; b. 18 April 1935, Ouidah; s. of Pierre E. de Souza and Angèle Ninaggioli; m. Francine Antonini 1963; one d.; ed. Univ. of Paris.

Diplomatic intern, French Ministry of Foreign Affairs and French Embassy, Vienna 60; Second Sec. Embassy of Dahomey, Bonn 61-64; First Sec., Paris 64-68; Sec.-Gen. Dahomey Ministry of Foreign Affairs (with rank of Minister Plenipotentiary) 68-70; Chief, Dahomey del. to Franco-Dahomey Comm. on Econ. Co-operation 67; del. to various int. confs. including sessions of Council of Ministers of OAU, and UN Gen. Assembly; Perm. Rep. to UN, concurrently Amb. to U.S.A. 70-73; Amb. to France March 73-, also accred. to Algeria,

Italy, Malta, Spain and U.K.; Chevalier Ordre Nat. du Dahomey, Légion d'Honneur and other hons.

rue du Cherche-Midi 89, Paris 6e; Residence: 15 rue Alphonse de Neuville, 75017 Paris, France.
Telephone: 553-50-45/6 (Office); 924-32-67 (Home).

Dessau, Einar; Danish industrialist and mechanical engineer; b. 17 July 1892, Tuborg, Hellerup; s. of late Benny and Paula Dessau (née Heyman); m. Johanne Holtermann 1926; two s. one d.; ed. Copenhagen Royal Technical Univ.

With firm of Melchior, Armstrong and Dessau Inc., New York City 16-17; own export business, New York 18-20; Dir. United Breweries and Tuborg Breweries, Copenhagen 20-63; Dir. Tuborg Harbour Crane Co., Crystal Icework Ltd., Danish Brewers' Asscn.; Chair. Vitamon A-S; Pres. Danish Mineral Water Manufacturers' Asscn. -63; Vice-Chair. Royal Danish Aero Club -64, Hon. mem. 69; Dir. Danish Refrigeration Research Inst ; mem. Cttee. of Soc. of Friends of Danish Technical Museum; Vice-Chair. Danish Coll. Cité Universitaire, Paris, etc.; on Cttee. of Denmark-America Foundation -68 and of Dano-Belgian Soc.; Chair. Nordisk Saenksmede Industry -73; mem. New York Acad. of Science; Hon. mem. Copenhagen Radio Club, Danish Soc. of Radio Listeners and Tele. Viewers 62; Hon. Dipl. Fédération Aéronautique Internationale 58; Chevalier 1st Class, Order of Dannebrog, Denmark; Officier, Ordre de la Couronne, Belgium; Officier, Légion d'Honneur, France; Officier de l'Instruction Publique, France.

Leisure interests: technology, electronics, acoustics, photography.

Baunegårdsvej 50, Hellerup, Denmark.
Telephone: Copenhagen: GEntofte 3520.

Dessau, Paul; German composer; b. 19 Dec. 1894; m. Ruth Berghaus (q.v.); ed. High School and Music School Klindworth-Scharwenka.

Conductor in Hamburg, Cologne, Mainz and Berlin; three Nat. Prizes; Vaterländischer Verdienstorden in Gold; Karl Marx Orden.

Works include: *Lilo Hermann, Thälmann-Kolonne, Lukullus* (opera), *Puntila* (opera), two symphonies, *In Memoriam Bertolt Brecht, Six Vietnam Choruses, Five Vietnam Melodramas, Lanzelot* (opera), *Lenin—Orchestral Music No. 3, The "U.S.A."—Company of My Son, Gespräch mit einem Kind über Lenin.*

1615 Zeuthen, Karl Marx Strasse 20, German Democratic Republic.

De Staercke, Roger; Belgian industrial official; b. 1902.

President, Fed. of Belgian Industries 62-70; fmr. Vice-Pres. Gen. Council of Econs.. Nat. Council of Labour; Hon. Regent Nat. Bank of Belgium; fmr. Pres. Board of Dirs., Belgian Office of Foreign Trade; fmrly. Administrator Office of Nat. Export Credits Guarantee; Chair. Econ. and Social Cttee., European Econ. Community and Euratom 58-60, Vice-Chair. 60-62; Hon. Pres. Fed. of Belgian Industries 70-.

Fédération des Entreprises de Belgique, 4 rue Ravenstein, Brussels 1, Belgium.
Telephone: (02) 11-58-80.

Destrée, Jacques (*pseudonym* of Marcel Renet), D. en M.; French doctor, journalist and politician; b. 16 Jan. 1905, Paris; s. of Louis and Marie-Valérie (née Ameeuw) Renet; m. Wilhelmina Maurice; one s. two d.; ed. Lycée Français, Mainz, the Sorbonne, l'Ecole des Hautes Etudes Historiques and Faculty of Medicine, Paris.

Worked in Paris hospitals and then practised medicine in Montrouge and Paris 33-43; research on stammering 34; active in Resistance Movement from 40; Founder and Dir. of clandestine journal *Résistance;* founded Clandestine Press Federation which later became French

Press Federation 43; in German concentration camps 43-45; on return became Gen. Man. of *Résistance*, later of *Ce Matin* and finally Pol. Dir. of *Aurore* 45-67; Senator (R.P.F., Gaulliste) for the Seine 46-52; mem. of Foreign Affairs Comm. and Vice-Pres. of Press Comm.; Commdr. de la Légion d'Honneur; Croix de Guerre (39-45); Rosette de la Résistance; Officier de la Santé publique; Croix du Combattant volontaire.
30 rue de Miromesnil, Paris 8e, France.
Telephone: 265-74-58.

de Strycker, Cecil A. J. F. J. M., D.S.C.; Belgian banker; b. 2 Feb. 1915, Derby, England; s. of Joseph de Strycker and Jeanne André Dumont; m. Elisabeth Braffort, 1948.
Director, Caisse Générale d'Epargne et de Retraite 71; mem. Comm. Bancaire 71; Gov. Banque Nationale de Belgique Feb. 75-; Pres. Office Central de la Petite Epargne Feb. 75-, Conseil des Institutions publiques de Crédit Feb. 75-, Institut Belgo-Luxembourgeois du Change Feb. 75-; Dir. Bank for Int. Settlements Feb. 75-; mem. Cttee. of Cen. Bank Govs. of EEC Feb. 75-, Dir. European Fund for Monetary Co-operation Feb. 75-; Gov. Int. Monetary Fund Feb. 75-, Alt. Gov. Int. Bank for Reconstruction and Devt. Feb. 75-; Officier de l'Ordre de Léopold; Grand Officier de l'Ordre de Léopold II.
14 avenue Bois du Dimanche, B-1150 Brussels, Belgium.
Telephone: 219-46-00 (Office).

Deswarte, Willem; Belgian lawyer and public servant; b. 6 Sept. 1906; m. Irene Tesch 1940; ed. Univs. of Brussels and Geneva.
Practising lawyer, assoc. with Bâtonnier Soudan till 33; then entered S.A. Grands Magasins "A l'Innovation," became Sec.-Gen., Dir. and Admin. Dir.-Gen.; Pres. Tribunal Maritime Belge à Londres 45; Counsellor Ministère des Finances 46; Private Sec. to Prime Minister and later to Minister of Interior 47; Dir.-Gen. Soc. Anonyme Belge d'Exploitation de la Navigation Aérienne (SABENA) 49-71; Pres. Belgian Section, World Asscn. of World Federalists; Commdr. Ordre de Léopold.
Leisure interest: chess.
Publs. *La Limitation des Dividendes* 42, *L'Impôt sur le Capital Appliqué aux Sociétés par Actions* 46.
Chaussée de Charleroi 133, 1060 Brussels, Belgium.

de Terra, Helmut, PH.D.; American (b. German) anthropologist; b. 11 July 1900, Guben; s. of Otto Albert de Terra and Margarethe Günther; m. 1st Rhoda Hoff 1929, 2nd Eleanore Muller 1939, 3rd Elizabeth Pschorr 1964; one s. one d.; ed. public school, Marburg (Hesse) and Univ. of Munich.
Assistant, Inst. of Geology, Univ. of Munich 25-27; Instructor and Asst. Prof. Yale Univ. 30-36; Research Assoc. Carnegie Inst. of Washington, D.C. 36-50; Geographer, U.S. Dept. of Interior 42-44; Research Assoc. Wenner-Gren Foundation for Anthropological Research 45-50; Research Assoc. and Adjunct Prof., Columbia Univ. 52-61; Guest Prof. Univ. of Munich 62-63; Dir. Werner Reimers Foundation for Anthropogenetic Research, Frankfurt (Main) 63-66; Silliman Fellow, Yale Univ.; Fellow, Geological Soc. of America; special research: pleistocene geology of early man in Asia and Mexico and biographical studies of leaders in natural science; mem. of numerous expeditions.
Leisure interests: reading, hiking.
Publs. *Geologische Forschungen in K'un-lun und Karakorum Himalaya* 30, *Geological Studies in the Northwest Himalayas* 35, *Studies on the Ice Age in India and Associated Human Cultures* 39, *Durch Urwelten am Indus* 40, *The Pleistocene of Burma and Java* 44, *Tepexpan Man (Mexico)* 49, *The Life and Times of Alexander von Humboldt* 55, *Man and Mammoth in Mexico* 56, *Studies of the Documentation of Alexander*

von Humboldt 58-60, *Memoirs of P. Teilhard de Chardin* 64.
Chalet Montclair, CH 1837, Château d'Oex, Switzerland
Telephone: 029-47169.

Dethier, Vincent Gaston, A.B., A.M., PH.D.; American professor of biology; b. 20 Feb. 1915, Boston, Mass. s. of Jean Vincent Dethier and Marguerite Frances (Lally); m. Lois Evelyn Check 1960; two s.; ed. Harvard Coll. and Harvard Univ.
Instructor, Biology and Asst. Prof., John Carroll Univ. 39-41; Lieut. to Major SNC, Army Air Corps 42-46; Active Reserve, Lieut.-Col., Office of the Surgeon-Gen. 46-62; Prof. of Zoology and Entomology, Ohio State Univ. 46-47; Assoc. Prof. and Prof. of Biology, Johns Hopkins Univ. 47-58; Prof. of Zoology and Psychology, and Assoc. of Neurological Inst. of School of Medicine, Univ. of Pa. 58-67; Prof. of Biology, Princeton Univ. 67-75; Prof. of Zoology, Univ. of Mass. 75-; Pres. American Soc. of Zoologists 67; Fellow, American Acad. of Arts and Sciences, Nat. Acad. of Sciences; mem. Entomological Soc. of America; Hon. Sc.D. (Ohio State Univ. and Providence Coll.); Hon. Fellow, Royal Entomological Soc., London; Fellow, Royal Soc. of Arts.
Leisure interests: skiing, boating.
Publs. *Chemical Insect Attractants and Repellents, Animal Behaviour* (with E. Stellar), *To Know a Fly, The Physiology of Insect Senses, Fairweather Duck, Biological Principles and Processes* (with C. Villee) 71, *Man's Plague, The Hungry Fly*; and numerous scientific papers.
Department of Zoology, University of Massachusetts, Amherst, Mass. 01002, U.S.A.
Telephone: 413-545-2046.

Deulofeu, Venancio, DR. CHEM.; Argentine chemist; b. 1 April 1902, Buenos Aires; s. of Tomas and Camila (née Gascons) Deulofeu; m. Irene Escasanay 1928; no c.; ed. Univ. of Buenos Aires.
Assistant, Instituto Bacteriológico, Buenos Aires; Head, Organotherapeutic Section 32-44; Asst. Prof. of Biochemistry, Rosario Univ. 25; Asst. Prof. of Organic Chemistry, Buenos Aires 29, Prof. 39-68, Head of Dept. 63-69, Prof. Emer 68-; Asst. Prof. of Biochemistry 31-48; Pres. Argentine Asscn. for the Advancement of Science 52-57; mem. Bureau IUPAC 47-51, 63-69, Cttee. on Science and Technology (COSTED), ICSU 68-, Council for Scientific and Technological Research (Argentina) 58-67; Vice-Pres. 64; Vice-Pres. Nat. Inst. for Technological Research 58-69, and mem. of many scientific societies, including Nat. Acad. of Sciences, and Nat. Acad. of Medicine, Buenos Aires; Dr. h.c. Paris, Santiago (Chile), Cordoba (Argentina).
Leisure interests: reading history and economics.
Publs. *Enseñanza e Investigación Científicas* 47, *Curso de Química Biológica* with A. D. Marenzi) (9th edn.) 67, and many research papers in the fields of carbohydrates, hormones, alkaloids, flavonols, amino acids, etc.
Parera 77, Buenos Aires, Argentina.
Telephone: 44-1422.

Deuss, Hanns, DR.RER.POL.; German banker; b. 18 Feb. 1901, Wuppertal-Barmen; ed. Univ. of Cologne. Trained with Barmer Bank-Verein and Dresdner Bank; with Commerzbank, Berlin 42, with Bankverein Westdeutschland, Düsseldorf 45-, Dir. 55-; Partner, Heydt-Kersten & Söhne; Chair. Supervisory Board Commerzbank A.G. (Düsseldorf, Frankfurt/Main, Hamburg), Buderus'sche Eisenwerke (Wetzlar); Vice-Chair. Karstadt AG (Essen), Chair. Supervisory Board July 75-; mem. Supervisory Board Hochtief Aktiengesellschaft für Hoch-und Tiefbauten (Essen, fmrly. Gebr. Helfmann); Deputy Chair. Atlantic Hotel GmbH (Hamburg).
4005 Meerbusch 1, Am Wald 1, Federal Republic of Germany.

Deutekom, Cristina; opera singer; b. Holland. First major appearance at Munich State Opera 66, then at Vienna Festwochen; sang at Metropolitan Opera, N.Y. 67; has sung in all the major opera houses in Europe, especially Italy, and U.S.A.; specializes in *bel canto* operas by Rossini, Bellini and Donizetti; recordings for EMI, Decca and Philips; Grand Prix du Disque 69, 72.
c/o S.A. Gorlinsky Ltd., 35 Dover Street, London, W1X 4NJ, England.

Deutsch, Babette; American writer; b. 22 Sept. 1895, New York; d. of Michael Deutsch and Melanie Fisher; m. Avrahm Yarmolinsky 1921; two s.; ed. Barnard Coll.
Lecturer, Columbia Univ. 44-71; Hon. Litt.D. (Columbia Univ.); mem. Nat. Inst. of Arts and Letters, American Acad. of Arts and Letters, Acad. of American Poets, PEN.
Leisure interests: friendship, the arts, modest cooking.
Publs. *Banners* 19, *Honey Out of the Rock* 25, *A Brittle Heaven* 25, *In Such a Night* 27, *Fire for the Night* 30, *Epistle to Prometheus* 31, *Mask of Silenus* 33, *This Modern Poetry* 35, *One Part Love* 39, *Heroes of the Kalevala* 40, *Walt Whitman: Builder for America* 41, *It's a Secret* 41, *Rogue's Legacy* 42, *The Welcome* 42, *Take Them, Stranger* 44, *The Reader's Shakespeare* 46, *Poetry in Our Time* 52, 56, 63, 64, *Tales of Faraway Folk* (with A. Yarmolinsky) 52, *Animal, Vegetable, Mineral* 54, *Poetry Handbook* 57, 62, 69, 74, *Coming of Age: New and Selected Poems* 59, *Collected Poems 1919-62*, 63, *More Tales of Faraway Folk* (with A. Yarmolinsky) 64, *The Steel Flea* (with A. Yarmolinsky) 64, *Eugene Onegin* (with A. Yarmolinsky) 65; trans. *Poems from The Book of Hours*, by Rilke 41, *Two Centuries of Russian Verse* (with A. Yarmolinsky) 66, *I Often Wish* 66, *Poems of Samuel Taylor Coleridge* 67, *The Collected Poems of Babette Deutsch* 69, *There Comes a Time* (trans. from E. Borchers).
300 West 108th Street, New York 25, N.Y. 10025, U.S.A.
Telephone: 749-1324.

Deutsch, John James, C.C., LL.D., B.COM., F.R.S.C.; Canadian university administrator; b. 26 Feb. 1911; ed. Queen's Univ., Kingston.
Research Asst., Bank of Canada 36; Asst. Dir. of Research, Rowell-Sirois Comm. 37; Special wartime Asst. to Under-Sec. of State for External Affairs 42; mem. Editorial Dept., Winnipeg Free Press 45; Dir. Int. Econ. Relations Div., Dept. of Finance, Ottawa 46; Asst. Deputy Minister of Finance 53; Sec. Treasury Board, Govt. of Canada 54; Head. Dept. of Econs. and Political Science, Univ. of B.C. 56; Vice-Principal (Admin.) and Prof. of Econs., Queen's Univ., Kingston 59, Vice-Principal 62, Principal and Vice-Chancellor 68-; Chair. Econ. Council of Canada 63; Dir. Canadian Imperial Bank of Commerce, Int. Nickel Co. of Canada Ltd.; mem. numerous comms. and advisory cttees.; several hon. degrees.
Queen's University, Kingston, Ont., Canada.

de Valois, Dame Ninette, D.B.E.; British choreographer; b. 6 June 1898.
Prima Ballerina, Royal Opera Season, Covent Garden 19 and 28; British Nat. Opera Company 18; mem. The Diaghileff Russian Ballet 23-26; Choreographic Dir. to the Old Vic, Festival Theatre, Cambridge, and the Abbey Theatre 26-30; Dir. The Royal Ballet and the Royal Ballet School from its foundation in 31 until 63, now Gov. Royal Ballet; Hon. Mus. Doc. (London) 47; Hon. D.Mus. (London, Sheffield, Trinity Coll. Dublin); Chevalier de la Légion d'Honneur 50; Hon. D.Litt. (Reading, Oxford); D.F.A. Smith Coll. Mass. 57; Hon. LL.D. Aberdeen 58; Erasmus Prize 74.
Choreographic works include: *Job, The Rake's Progress, Checkmate, The Prospect Before Us, Don Quixote.*

Publs. *Invitation to the Ballet* 37, *Come Dance with Me* 57.
c/o Royal Ballet School, 153 Talgarth Road, London, W.14, England.

De Vaucouleurs, Gerard Henri, DR. DE L'UNIV. (Paris), D.SC. (Canberra); American (b. French) astronomer; b. 25 April 1918; ed. Univ. of Paris.
Assistant astronomer, Peridier Observatory 39, 41-42; C.N.R.S. research student Physics Research Laboratory, Sorbonne 43-45; Research Fellow, Astrophysics Inst. C.N.R.S., Paris 45-49; Science programme, BBC London 50-51; Research Fellow, Australian Nat. Univ. at Commonwealth Observatory, Mt. Stromlo 51-54; Observer-in-Charge, Yale-Columbia Southern Station, Mt. Stromlo 54-57; Astronomer Lowell Observatory, Flagstaff, Ariz. 57-58; Research Assoc. Harvard Coll. Observatory, Cambridge, Mass. 58-60; Assoc. Prof. Astronomy Univ. of Texas 60-64; Prof. Univ. of Texas 65-; mem. Int. Astronomical Union, and several astronomical asscns. in U.S.A., U.K., France and Australia.
Publs. *Astronomie* (with L. Rudaux) 48, English, Spanish and Italian trans. 59-67, *Physique de la planète Mars* 51, English trans. 54, Russian trans. 56, *Discovery of the Universe* 56, *Manuel de Photographie Scientifique* 56, *L'exploration des galaxies voisines* 58, *Astronomical Photography* 61 (Russian trans. 75), *Reference Catalogue of Bright Galaxies* (with A. de Vaucouleurs) 64, *Survey of the Universe* (with D. Menzel and F. Whipple) 70, *New Reference Catalogue of Bright Galaxies* (with A. de Vaucouleurs and H. G. Corwin, Jr.) 76, and about 300 papers.
Department of Astronomy, University of Texas, Austin, Texas 78712, U.S.A.
Telephone: 471-4488.

Devaux, Louis Armand; French metals executive; b. 5 April 1907, Tananarive, Madagascar; m. 1927; one s.; ed. Lycée Louis-le-Grand and Univ. de Paris à la Sorbonne.
With Banque de Paris et des Pays-Bas 27-29; Cartier S.A. 29-46, Pres. 44-46, Chair. Board Cartier Inc., New York 46-49; Pres. Pétroles Toneline S.A. 49-51; Asst. Dir.-Gen. Compagnie des Produits Chimiques et Raffineries de Berre 49-51; Asst. Dir.-Gen. Shell Française 52-60, Pres. Dir.-Gen. 60-67; Pres. Soc. des Pétroles Shell Berre 60-67; Pres. Dir.-Gen. Soc. Le Nickel 67-71; Pres. Conseil de Direction, Centre Français du Commerce Extérieur 72-; Vice-Pres. Société Le Nickel, Soc. Minière et Métallurgique de Penarroya; Dir. Shell Française, Cie. de Mokta, Soc. Générale de Fonderie, The Rio Tinto Zinc Corpn.; Commdr. Ordre Nat. du Mérite, Officier Légion d'Honneur, Croix de Guerre.
1 rue de la Paroisse, 7800 Versailles, France.

de Venot de Noisy, Jack; French international lawyer; b. 29 July 1916, Orleans; m. Lilian Marie Harel de la Coutancière; one s. one d.; ed. Ecole Saint-Grégoire, Pithiviers.
President Int. Fed. of Judicial and Fiscal Counsellors; Sec.-Gen. Int. Council of Space Law; Pres. Fed. of Latin Nations; Hon. Pres. Order of Int. Lawyers of France; Vice-Pres. Int. Confed. of Asscns. of Experts and Advisers (UNO); Chevalier Légion d'Honneur; Croix de Guerre.
Leisure interests: riding, hunting.
11 avenue d'Jéna, Paris 16e, France.
Telephone: 723-65-70.

De Villiers, Willem Johannes, PH.D.; South African engineer; b. 4 April 1921, Jacobsdal, Orange Free State; m. Francina Maria Meyer 1949; two s. one d.; ed. Grey Coll., Bloemfontein and Univ. of Cape Town.
Engineer, Pretoria Power Station 45-49; joined Anglo American Corpn. 50, successively Engineer, Power Station Supt., Technical Research and Devt. Engineer,

Engineering Supt., Asst. Man. and Man., Rhokana Corpn., Kitwe, Zambia 50-60; Consulting Mechanical Engineer responsible for method and work studies at the gold mines, Anglo American Corpn., Johannesburg and at Welkom 61-65; played an important part in the planning of the Cabora-Bassa project; Man. Dir. L.T.A. Engineering 65-68; Industrial Adviser to Sanlam 68-70; Deputy Man. Dir., Gen. Mining and Finance Corpn. 70-71, Man. Dir. 71-.
Leisure interests: tennis, water-skiing.
General Mining and Finance Corporation Ltd., 6 Holland Street, Johannesburg, South Africa.

Devitt, Edward James; American judge; b. 5 May 1911, St. Paul, Minnesota; m. Marcelle LaRose MacRae 1939; one s. one d.; ed. Univ. of North Dakota.
Private legal practice, East Grand Forks, Minnesota 35-39, Municipal Judge 35-39, Asst. Attorney-Gen., Minnesota 39-42, Instructor in Law, Univ. of North Dakota 35-39; St. Paul Coll. 45-; mem. U.S. House of Reps. 47-48; Probate Judge, Ramsey County, St. Paul 50-54, Judge, U.S. District Courts, Minnesota 54-, Chief Judge 58-.
730 Federal Courts Building, St. Paul, Minnesota 55101, U.S.A.
Telephone: 612-228-7178.

Devletoglou, Evangelos A., PH.D.; Greek economist and politician; ed. Univ. of Athens, Columbia Univ., N.Y.
Reserve Officer Greek Navy; with Bank of Greece 60-67; Senior Economist, Int. Monetary Fund 69; with IMF, Geneva 72; Under-Sec. of Co-ordination and Planning July-Nov. 74; mem. Parl. Nov. 74-; Minister of Finance Nov. 74-; New Democracy Party.
Ministry of Finance, Athens, Greece.

Devlin, Baron (Life Peer, cr. 61), of West Wick in the County of Wiltshire, **Patrick Devlin,** Kt., P.C., F.B.A.; British lawyer; b. 25 Nov. 1905; ed. Stonyhurst Coll., and Christ's Coll., Cambridge.
Called to the Bar 29, K.C. 45; Attorney-Gen. to the Duchy of Cornwall 47-48; Justice of the High Court 48-60; Master of the Bench of Gray's Inn 47; Pres. of Restrictive Practices Court 57-60, British Maritime Law Asscn. 62-; Chair. Cttee. Inquiry into Dock Labour Scheme 56, into decasualisation of Dock Labour 64, Nyasaland Inquiry Comm. 59; Lord Justice of Appeal 60-61; Lord of Appeal in Ordinary 61-63; Chair. the Press Council 64-69; High Steward of Cambridge Univ. 66-; Hon. LL.D. (Glasgow) 62, (Toronto) 62, (Cambridge) 66; Hon. D.C.L. (Oxford) 65.
Publs. *Trial by Jury* 56, *Criminal Prosecution in England* 58, *Samples of Lawmaking* 62, *The Enforcement of Morals* 65, *Inside Journalism* 67, *Too Proud to Fight* 74.
West Wick House, Pewsey, Wilts., England.

Devons, Samuel, PH.D., F.R.S.; British professor of physics; b. 30 Sept. 1914, Bangor, N. Wales; s. of David I. Devons and Edith Edlestein; m. Celia Ruth Toubkin 1938; four d.; ed. Trinity Coll., Cambridge.
Scientific Officer, Air Ministry 39-45; Fellow, Dir. of Studies, Lecturer in Physics, Trinity Coll., Cambridge 46-49; Prof. of Physics, Imperial Coll. of Science 50-55, Acting Dir. of Laboratory 53-54; Langworthy Prof. of Physics and Dir. of Physical Laboratories, Manchester Univ. 55-60; Visiting Prof. of Physics, Columbia Univ. New York 59-60, Prof. 60-, Chair. Dept. of Physics 63-67; Visiting Prof., Barnard Coll., History of Physics 69; mem. UNESCO Technical Aid, Argentina 57; Royal Soc./Leverhulme Visiting Prof., India 68-69; Racah Visiting Prof., Hebrew Univ., Jerusalem 73-74; Balfour Visiting Prof., Weizmann Inst., Rehovot 73; Rutherford Prize and Medal, Physical Soc. 70.
Publs. *Excited States of Nuclei* 49, *Biology and the Physical Sciences* (Editor) 69, *High Energy Physics and Nuclear Structure* (Editor) 70.

Physics Department, Columbia University, New York N.Y. 10027; Home: Lewis Road, Irvington, New York N.Y. 10533, U.S.A.
Telephone: 212-280-4124/5102 (Office); 914-LY1-768: (Home).

De Vries, Peter, A.B.; American writer; b. 27 Feb 1910; m. Katinka Loeser; three c.; ed. Calvin Coll. Michigan, and Northwestern Univ.
Free-lance writer 31-; Assoc. Editor *Poetry* 38, co-Editor 42; joined editorial staff of *New Yorker* 44; mem. National Inst. of Arts and Letters.
Publs. *No but I saw the Movie* 52, *The Tunnel of Love* 54, *Comfort me with Apples* 56, *The Mackerel Plaza* 58 dramatization of *The Tunnel of Love* (with Joseph Fields) 57, *The Tents of Wickedness* 59, *Through the Fields of Clover* 61, *The Blood of the Lamb* 62, *Reuben Reuben* 64 (dramatized as *Spofford* by Herman Shumlin 67), *Let Me Count the Ways* 65, *The Vale of Laughter* 67, *The Cat's Pyjamas and Witch's Milk* 68, *Mrs. Wallop* 70, *Into Your Tent I'll Creep* 71, *Without A Stitch in Time* 72, *Forever Panting* 73, *The Glory of the Hummingbird* 74, *I Hear America Swinging* 76.
170 Cross Highway, Westport, Conn., U.S.A.

Devyatkov, Nikolai Dmitrievich; Soviet electronics specialist; b. 11 April 1907, Vologda; ed. Leningrad Polytechnical Inst.
Junior, then senior scientific assoc. A.F. Ioffe Inst. of Physics and Technology and other research insts. 25-54; Head of Dept., Inst. of Radio Engineering and Electronics, U.S.S.R. Acad. of Sciences 54-60; Chair. of Dept., Moscow Physics and Technology Inst. 60-; corresp. mem. U.S.S.R. Acad. of Sciences 53-68, Academician 68-; Lenin Prize; U.S.S.R. State Prize; Hero of Socialist Labour; Order of Lenin (twice), Hammer and Sickle Gold Medal, etc.
Publs. numerous works on theoretical and experimental problems of electronics.
U.S.S.R. Academy of Sciences, 14 Leninsky Prospekt, Moscow, U.S.S.R.

de Waart, Edo; Netherlands conductor; b. 1 June 1941, Amsterdam; s. of M. de Waart and J. Rose; m. Roberta Alexander 1974; one s. one d.; ed. Amsterdam Music Lyceum.
Assistant Conductor, Concertgebouw Orchestra, Amsterdam 66; Permanent Conductor, Rotterdam Philharmonic 67, Musical Dir. and Principal Conductor 73-; Principal Guest Conductor, San Francisco Symphony Orchestra 75-; First Prize Dimitri Mitropoulos Competition, New York 64.
Essenlaan 68, Rotterdam 3016, Netherlands.
Telephone: 010-124391.

Dewar, Michael James Steuart, B.A., D.PHIL., M.A., F.R.S.; British professor of chemistry; b. 24 Sept. 1918, Ahmednagar, India; s. of Francis Dewar and Nan Balfour Dewar; m. Mary Williamson 1944; two s.; ed. Winchester Coll. and Balliol Coll., Oxford.
ICI Fellow, Oxford Univ. 45; Physical Chemist, Courtaulds Ltd. 45-51; Prof. of Chem. and Head of Dept., Univ. of London, Queen Mary Coll. 51-59; Prof. of Chem., Chicago Univ. 59-63; Robert A. Welch Prof. of Chem., Univ. of Texas in Austin 63-; Fellow, Royal Soc. and American Acad. of Arts and Sciences; Reilly Lecturer, Notre Dame Univ. 51; Tilden Lecturer, Chemical Soc. 54; Visiting Prof., Yale Univ. 57; Hon.-Sec. Chemical Soc. 57-59; Harrison Howe Award, American Chem. Soc. 61; Falk-Plaut Lecturer, Columbia Univ. 63; Daines Lecturer, Univ. of Kansas 63; Glidden Co. Lecturer, Western Reserve Univ. 64; William Pyle Philips Visitor, Haverford Coll. 64; Arthur D. Little Visiting Prof. Mass. Inst. of Technology 66; Marchon Visiting Lecturer, Newcastle upon Tyne, England 66; Glidden Company Lecturer, Kent State Univ. 67; Barton Lecturer, Univ. of Oklahoma 69; Benjamin Rush Lecturer, Univ. of Pennsylvania 70;

Kahlbaum Lecturer, Univ. of Basle 70; William Pyle Philips Visitor, Haverford Coll. 70; Kharasch Visiting Prof., Chicago 71; Venable Lecturer, Univ. of N.C. 71; Phi Lambda Upsilon Speaker, Johns Hopkins Univ. 72; Firth Visiting Prof., Sheffield Univ., England, 72; Foster Lecturer, State Univ. of N.Y. at Buffalo, 73; Five College Chemistry Lecturer, Mt. Holyoke, Hampshire, Amherst, Smith Colls., Univ. of Mass., 73, Robert Robinson Lecturer of the Chem. Soc. 74; Special Lecturer, Univ. London 74; Sprague Lecturer Univ. Wis. 74; Hon. Fellow Balliol Coll., Oxford 74.
Leisure interests: numerous and varied.
Publs. *The Electronic Theory of Organic Chemistry* 49, *Hyperconjugation* 62, *Introduction to Modern Chemistry* 65, *The Molecular Orbital Theory of Organic Chemistry* 69, *Computer Compilation of Molecular Weights and Percentage Compositions of Organic Compounds* 70, *The PMO Theory of Organic Chemistry* 75; frequent contributions to scientific journals.
Department of Chemistry, University of Texas, Austin, Texas 78712; Home: 6808 Mesa Drive, Austin, Tex. 78731, U.S.A.
Telephone: 512-345-0147 (Home).

Dewdney, Duncan Alexander Cox, C.B.E.; British company director; b. 22 Oct. 1911, Hampton-on-Thames, England; s. of Claude Felix Dewdney and Annie Ross; m. Edith Marion Riley 1935; two d.; ed. Bromsgrove School, Worcs., and Birmingham Univ. Chemist, British Petroleum Co. 32-36; Technical Asst., Standard Oil Devt. Co. 36-40; R.A.F. 40-45; Research and Devt. Adviser, Anglo-American Oil Co. Ltd. 46-47; Man. Devt. Dept., Esso Devt. Co. 47-49; Man. Esso European Laboratories 49-51; with Refining Dept. Esso Petroleum Co. 51-57, Dir. 57-63, Man. Dir. 63-68, Vice-Chair. 68; Chair. Board Irish Refining Co. Ltd. 57-65; Chair. Mechanical Eng. Econ. Devt. Comm. 64-68, of Anglesey Aluminium Ltd. 68-71, of RTZ Metals Ltd. 68, of RTZ (Britain) 69, of RTZ Devt. Enterprises Ltd. 70; Exec. Dir. Rio Tinto-Zinc Corpn. Ltd. 68-72; mem. Nat. Prices and Incomes Board 65-69; Chair. Welsh Industrial Devt. Board 72-; Deputy Chair. Manpower Services Comm. 74-; Legion of Merit.
Salters, Harestock, Winchester, England.
Telephone: 0962-2034.

de Wendel, Henri; French industrialist; b. 9 Sept. 1913; ed. Ecole centrale des arts et manufactures.
Administrator of Metallurgical Soc. of Senelle-Maubeuge, Slate Quarries of Angers, J. J. Carnaud Establishments and Forges de Basse-Indre; Pres. Compagnie Lorraine Industrielle et Financière, Profilés et Tubes de l'Est; Vice-Pres. SACILOR; Chevalier Légion d'Honneur.
9 avenue du Maréchal-Manoury, Paris 16e, France.

De Wet, Dr. Carel, B.SC., M.B., B.CH.; South African physician, politician and diplomatist; b. 25 May 1924, Memel, Orange Free State; m. Rina Maas 1949; one s. three d.; ed. Vrede High School, Orange Free State, Pretoria Univ., and Univ. of Witwatersrand.
Medical practice, Boksburg, Transvaal, Winburg, Orange Free State, and Vanderbijlpark, Transvaal; Mayor of Vanderbijlpark 50-52; mem. Parl. 53-63; Amb. to U.K. 64-67; Minister of Planning and Mines 67-May 70, and Health 68-72; Amb. to U.K. 72-.
Leisure interests: farming, shooting, golf, trees.
South African Embassy, Trafalgar Square, London, WC2N 5DP, England.

de Windt, Edward Mandell; American business executive; b. 31 March 1921, Great Barrington, Mass.; s. of Delano de Windt and Ruth Church; m. Betsy Bope 1941; three s. two d.; ed. Berkshire School and Williams Coll.
Production Clerk, Valve Plant, Eaton Corpn. 41, Vice-Pres. and Dir. of Sales 60, Group Vice-Pres. Inter-

national 61, Exec. Vice-Pres. 67, Pres. 67-69, Chair. of Board Sept. 69-.
Leisure interests: golf, tennis.
Eaton Corporation, 100 Erieview Plaza, Cleveland, Ohio 44114, U.S.A.

De Winter, August; Belgian barrister and politician; b. 12 May 1925, Grimbergen; m. Marcelle Janssens; one s. one d.
Barrister; Sec. of State, Regional Econ., Brussels; mem. Chamber of Reps. 63; mem. Belgian Del. to UN 63; Mayor of Grimbergen 64-71; Nat. Rep. at symposium of European Liberal Parties 64; Pres. Parti pour la liberté et le progrès (PLP) Fed. of Brussels 62-66; Minister for External Trade 66-68; Chair. Board of Govs. Vrije (Free) Univ. Brussels 69-72; Pres. PLP-PVV faction Chamber of Reps. 73-74; Pres. PVV Brussels district 73-.
180 G. Van Haelen Avenue, 1190 Brussels, Belgium.
Telephone: 02/344-91-65.

Dexter, John; British theatre and opera director.
Actor in repertory, television and radio until 57; directed 15 plays at Royal Court Theatre 57-72; Assoc. Dir. Nat. Theatre 63-73, directed 14 plays; directed 13 plays elsewhere 59-74; Dir. of Production, Metropolitan Opera, New York 74-.
Plays directed in 63-66 include *Chips With Everything, Do I Hear a Waltz?, Royal Hunt of the Sun, Black Comedy and White Lies, The Unknown Soldier and his Wife* (all in New York); in 71-73 include *Woman Killed With Kindness, Tyger, The Good Natur'd Man, The Misanthrope, Equus, The Party* (all National Theatre); *The Old Ones* 72 (Royal Court), *Pygmalion* 74. Film directed: *The Virgin Soldiers* 68; Operas directed: *Benvenuto Cellini* (Covent Garden) 66, *House of the Dead, Boris Godunov, Billy Budd, Ballo in Maschera, I Vespri in Siciliani* (Hamburg), *The Devils* (Sadler's Wells), *I Vespri Siciliani* (Metropolitan, N.Y. and Paris), *La Forza del Destino* (Paris) 75, *La Gioconda* 75, *Aïda* (new production) 76, *Le Prophète* (new production) 76 (all Metropolitan Opera).
Leisure interest: work.
c/o Metropolitan Opera, Lincoln Center, New York, N.Y. 10023, U.S.A.

Dextraze, Gen. Jacques Alfred, C.B.E., C.M.M., D.S.O., C.D.; Canadian army officer; b. 15 Aug. 1919, Montreal; s. of Alfred and Amanda Dextraze; m. Francis Helena Pare; four s. (one deceased); ed. St. Joseph de Bethier, Montreal, MacDonald Business Coll. and Univ. of Columbia.
With Dominion Rubber Co. 38-40; Fusiliers Mount Royal 39-45, Lt.-Col. and Commdg. Officer 44-45; Commdg. Officer Hastings and Prince Edward Regt. 45; with Singer Mfg. Co. 45-50, Man. Forest Operations 47-50; Commdg. Officer 2nd Battalion, Royal 22e Regt. 50-52; Officer in charge of Admin., E. Quebec Area 52-54; Gen. Staff Officer, Quebec 54-55, Col. and Chief of Staff, Quebec 56-57; Commdt. Royal Canadian School of Infantry 57-60, Camp Valcartier 60-62; Brig., Commdr. E. Quebec Area 62; Chief of Staff, H.Q., UN Operations in Congo 63-64; Commdr. 2 Canadian Infantry Brigade Group 64-66; Chief of Staff for Operations and Training, H.Q. Mobile Command 66-67, Maj.-Gen., Deputy Commdr. Operations 67; Deputy Chief of Personnel, Canadian Forces H.Q. 69, Lt.-Gen., Chief of Personnel 70-72, Gen., Chief of Defence Staff 72-; mem. Canadian Comm. to Tripartite Mil. Confs. 57; mem. Int. Cttee. for Standardization of Arms and Nat. Mil. Resources 57-60; Hon. Aide-de-Camp to H.E. the Gov.-Gen. 58; Commdr. Canadian Order of Mil. Merit, Canadian Forces Decoration.
Leisure interests: reading, bridge, golf, editing military papers.
National Defence Headquarters, Ottawa, Ont. K1A 0K2, Canada.

Dey, Bishnu; Bengali poet; b. 18 July 1909, Calcutta; s. of late Abinash Ch. Dey and Mrs. M. Dey (née Bhose); m. Pranati Raychaudhuri 1934; one s. two d.; ed. Calcutta Univ.

Professor of English, Central Calcutta Coll., now retd. Leisure interests: music, painting, drama, sculpture.

Publs. *Urbasi-o-Artemis* 32, *Chorābāli* 36, *Purbolékh* 41, *22nd June* 42, *Sāt Bhāi Champā* (poems) 45, *Roochi-o-Pragatee* (essays) 46, *Sandipér Char* (poems) 47, *The Art of Jamini Roy* (with John Irwin) 45, *Samundrér Mauno* 45, *Caramel Doll* (English trans. of *Rabindranath Tagore's Story*) 46, *Introducing Nirode Mazumdar* 46, *Bengal Painters' Testimony* 46, *Anwista* (poems) 50, *Sahityér Bhabisyat* (essays) 52, *Elioter Kabita* (translations of T. S. Eliot's poems) 53, *Nām Rékhéchhi Komal Gāndhar* (poems) 53, *An Introduction to Jamini Roy* 53, *Hé Bidéshi Phul* (trans. of poems of various countries) 57, *Paintings of Rabindranath Tagore, India and Modern Art; Alekhya* (poems) 58, *Tumi Shudhu Panchisé Baisakh* (poems) 58, *Mao Tse-tung* (translations in verse) 58, *Prodosh Das Gupta—His Sculpture* 61, *Élo-mélo-jiban o Silpa-sahitya* (essays) 58, *Sāhityér Désh Bidésh* (essays) 63, *Smriti Sattā Bhabisyat* (poems) 63, *Ékalér Kabitā* 63, *Satyendranath Bose, A Legend in His Lifetime* 63, *Sei Andhakār chāi* (poems) 66, *Rabindranath-o-Adhunikatār Samasyā* (essays) 66, *Michael, Rabindranath-o-anyānya-jijnānsa* (critical essays) 67, *Rushati Panchāsati* (poems) 67, *Sambad Mulata Kabya* (poems) 70, *Itihasér Tragic Ullyāsé* (poems) 70, *In the Sun and the Rain* (essays in English) 72, *History's Tragic Exultation* (translations of poems into English) 73, *Rabi Karojjal Nija Déshé* (poems on Bangladesh) 73, *Ishā Bāshya Dibā Nishā* (poems) 74.

9/17 Fern Road, Calcutta 19, West Bengal, India.

Dey, Surendra Kumar, M.SC.; Indian electrical engineer and politician; b. 15 Sept. 1906, Sylhet (now in Bangladesh); s. of late P. L. Dey and late B. Dey; m. Aruna Dey 1933; two s. three d.; ed. Zilla School, Rangpur, Bengal Engineering Coll., Purdue and Michigan Univs., U.S.A.

Rose from position of Sales Engineer to Divisional Man. for India, Burma and Ceylon with Victor X-ray Corpn. (India) Ltd. 32-47; Hon. Technical Adviser, Ministry of Rehabilitation 47-52; built township of Nilokheri, a pilot experiment in agro-industrial development; mem. of Exec., United Council for Relief and Welfare 49-53; Admin., Community Projects Admin., mem. Central Board, Bharat Sewak Semaj 52-56; Minister for Community Development 56-58 and Co-operation 59-66; Minister of Mines and Metals 66-67; resigned office in Govt. of India early 67; then worked as Special Adviser to Administrator UNDP on global mission of rural devt. in continents; Pres. All India Panchayat Parishad 68-73; Special Consultant UNROD, Dacca, Bangladesh 72-73; awarded Padma Bhushan 55; Hon. LL.D. (Univ. of Michigan).

Leisure interests: reading, gardening.

Publs. *The Quest, Fragments Across, Missing Link, Planning for Life, Random Thoughts I, II and III, Community Development, Community Development—A Bird's Eye View, Sahakari Samaj—A Cooperative Commonwealth, Panchayati Raj, Nilokheri, Community Development: A Chronicle, Power to the People?—A Chronicle of India* 47-67.

Residence: "Bul Bul", 5-Lajpatrai Marg, Lajpatnagar IV, New Delhi 24; Office: A-23, Kailash Colony, New Delhi 48, India.

Telephone: 624836 (Office); 74151 (Residence).

Dey-Deva, Mukul Chandra, M.C.S.E. (U.S.A.), F.R.S.A., A.R.C.A. (London), F.I.A.L. (Germany), I.E.S. and B.S.E.S.; Indian artist and writer; b. 23 July 1895, Sridharkhola village, District Dacca; s. of Kula Chandra Dey and Purnasasi Basu; m. Srimati Bina Roy 1932; one d.; ed. Santiniketan School (West Bengal).

Studied art with Dr. Abanindranath Tagore (Calcutta) and in Japan, Chicago and London; exhibited Indian Soc. of Oriental Art, Calcutta 13, Tokyo 16, Art Int. Chicago 16; studied Slade School of Art, London 20; scholarship Royal Coll. of Art, London 20-22; Art Teacher King Alfred School, Hampstead 20-21; Lecturer Indian Art, L.C.C. London 25-27; Royal Acad. 22-23; paintings and drypoint-etchings in perm. collection, British Museum, London 24-28; 1st one-man show, London 27; executed murals Wembley Exhbn., London 25; exhibited Philharmonic Hall, Berlin 26, Indian Soc. of Oriental Art, Calcutta 28; Principal Govt. Coll. of Art, Calcutta; Officer-in-Charge Art Section and Keeper Govt. Art Gallery, Indian Museum, Calcutta; Trustee Indian Museum 28-43; Founder Kalika Art Gallery 44; Fulbright Visiting Prof. of Art in U.S.A. 53-54; Curator Nat. Gallery of Modern Art, Govt. of India, New Delhi 55-57; exhbn., Commonwealth Inst., London 60; works accepted for Australian National Collection previously in New Australian Art Gallery, Canberra 69, Bengal School of Indian Art, Tetsuro and I. Sugimoto Museum, Kyoto, Japan 68-70; Award and Certificate of Honour, Rabindra Bharati Univ., Calcutta 72.

Works include paintings, portraits, drypoint-etchings, engravings, copies of frescoes in Ajanta and Bagh Caves, Pollonaruwa temples, Ceylon, Sittanavasal caves, S. India, British Museum, London, U.S.A., etc.

Leisure interests: painting, drawing, writing, gardening, photography.

Publs. *12 Portraits* 17, *My Pilgrimages to Ajanta and Bagh* 25 and 51, *My Reminiscences* 38, *15 Drypoints* 39, *20 Portraits* 43, *Portraits of Mahatma Gandhi* 48, *Birbhum Terracottas* 57, *Indian Life and Legends* (10 vols.) 74-.

Kalika Art Gallery, P.O. Santiniketan, West Bengal, India.

DeYoung, Russell; American businessman; b. 3 April 1909, New Jersey; m. Lois Bishop 1937; two s. one d.; ed. Akron Univ., and Mass. Inst. of Technology.

Joined Goodyear Tire & Rubber Co. 28-; Vice-Pres. (Production) 47-56; Exec. Vice-Pres. 56-58, Pres. 58-64, Chair. of Board 64-74, Chief Exec. Officer 64-73; Dir. Lykes-Youngstown Corpn., Kennecott Copper Corpn., Continental Can Co., Ward Foods Inc.

910 Eaton Avenue, Akron, Ohio 44303, U.S.A.

Dhavan, Shanti Swarup; Indian judge and diplomatist; b. 2 July 1905; s. of Beli Ram Dhavan and Saraswati Dhavan (née Chopra); m. Shakuntala Kapur 1935; two s. one d.; ed. Government Coll., Lahore, Forman Christian Coll., Lahore, Emmanuel Coll., Cambridge, Middle Temple, London, and Univs. of Bonn and Heidelberg.

Former Pres. Cambridge Union; Advocate, Allahabad High Court; Senior Standing Counsel, Govt. of Uttar Pradesh 56-58; Puisne Judge, Allahabad High Court 58-67; High Commr. of India in U.K. 68-69; Governor of W. Bengal 69-71; Lecturer in Law, Univ. of Allahabad 40-54; Pres. Uttar Pradesh Section, Indo-Soviet Cultural Soc. 65-67; mem. Law Comm. of India 72-; Sastri Memorial Lecturer, Kerala Univ., Trivandrum 73.

Publs. several articles on Indian jurisprudence and the legal and judicial systems of Ancient India.

15 Safdarjang Road, New Delhi; Home: 28 Tashkent Marg, Allahabad, Uttar Pradesh, India.

Dhebar, Uchhrangrai Navalshankar; Indian politician; b. 21 Sept. 1905; m. 1922; one s. one d.; ed. Rajkot and Bombay.

Lawyer, W. India States Agency Court 29-36; joined Indian Nat. Congress 36; Pres. Viramgam Taluka Congress Cttee. 36; Sec. Kathiawar Political Conf. 37-48; Chief Minister, Saurashtra 48-54; Pres. Indian Nat. Congress 54-59; mem. Lok Sabha 62-63; Head, Khadi

and Village Industries Comm. 63-; Padma Vibhushan Award 73.
Leisure interest: books.
3 Irla Road, Bombay 56, India.
Telephone: 571323.

Dhillon, Gurdial Singh; Indian politician; b. 6 Aug. 1915, Amritsar; *s.* of Hardit Singh; ed. Govt. Coll., Lahore, and Univ. Law Coll., Lahore.
Army Service; became active worker of Congress and Akali Dal; imprisoned twice during freedom struggle; with Pratap Singh Kairon started Punjabi daily *Virman* 47-52; Chief Editor Urdu daily *Sher-e-Bharat*; Man. Dir. Nat. Sikhs Newspaper Ltd.; mem. Punjab Univ. Senate; elected to Punjab Legislative Assembly 52; Deputy Speaker Punjab Vidhan Sabha 52-54, Speaker 54-62; Minister of Transport 65, of Shipping and Transport Nov. 75-; Speaker Lok Sabha 69-75; Pres. Inter-Parliamentary Union 74-75; Chair. Cttee. on Public Undertakings 69-; mem. Exec. Cttee. Congress Party.
Publs. several brochures on current affairs.
Ministry of Transport, New Delhi, India.

Dia, Mamadou; Senegalese politician; b. 18 July 1910, Kombole; ed. William Ponty School, Dakar.
Councillor, Senegal 46-52; Grand Councillor, French West Africa 52-57; Founder mem. Bloc Démocratique Sénégalais (BDS), later Sec.-Gen; Senator for Senegal 49-55; Dep. to Nat. Assembly, Paris 56-59; Dep. to Legislative Assembly, Senegal 59; Vice-Pres., Council of Ministers Senegal 57-58, Pres. 58-59; Vice-Pres., Mali Fed. 59-60; Pres. Council of Ministers, Senegal 60-62, concurrently Minister of Defence and Security 62; Govt. overthrown Dec. 62, sentenced to life detention May 63, sentence reduced to 20 years imprisonment 72, released 74; Chevalier, Palmes Académiques.
Publs. *Réflexions sur l'économie de l'Afrique Noire* 53, *Contributions à l'étude du mouvement coopératif en Afrique Noire* 57, *L'économie africaine* 57, *Nations Africaines et solidarité mondiale* 60.
Dakar, Senegal, West Africa.

Diaconescu, Gheorghe; Romanian lawyer and diplomatist; b. 12 March 1915; ed. School of Law, Iași Univ.
In Supreme Court and Gen. State Prosecuting Magistracy until 54; with Ministry of Justice 51-61; Amb. to Poland 61-66; Perm. Rep. of Romania to UN 66-72; Dir., Ministry of Foreign Affairs 72-73, Deputy Dir. 73-; Prof. of Law, Bucharest Univ.
Publs. several works and studies in field of law.
Ministerul Afacerilor Externe, Bucharest, Romania.

Diah, Burhanudin Mohamad (husband of Herawati Diah, *q.v.*); Indonesian journalist and diplomatist; b. 1917; ed. Taman Siswa High School, Medan, Sumatra and Ksatrian School for Journalism, Bandung, Java.
Asst. Editor daily *Sinar Deli*, Medan 37-38; free-lance journalist 38-39; Chief of Indonesian Information Desk, British Consulate-Gen. 39-41; Editor-in-chief Indonesian monthly *Pertjaturan Dunia dan Film* 39-41; radio commentator and editorial writer daily *Asia Raya* 42-45; Editor-in-chief daily *Merdeka* 45-49, 68-; Pres. Merdeka Press Ltd., Masa Merdeka Printing Presses; active in political movement, especially during Japanese occupation; Chair. New Youth (underground) movement and jailed by Japanese in 42 and again in 45; active in forcing proclamation of Indonesian Independence Aug. 45; mem. Provisional Nat. Cttee., Republic of Indonesia 45-49; mem. Provisional Indonesian Parl. 54-56; mem. Nat. Council 57-59; Amb. to Czechoslovakia 59-62, to U.K. 62-64, to Thailand 64-66; Minister of Information 66-68; Vice-Chair., Press Council of Indonesia 70-.
Office: Jalan M. Sangadi 11, Jakarta; Home: Jalan Diponegoro, Jakarta, Indonesia.

Diah, Herawati, B.A. (wife of Burhanudin Mohamad Diah, *q.v.*); Indonesian journalist; b. 1917; ed. Barnard Coll. (Columbia Univ.).
Announcer and feature writer, Indonesian Radio 42; Sec. to Minister of Foreign Affairs, Republic of Indonesia Sept.-Dec. 45; reporter daily *Merdeka* 46; Editor Indonesian Sunday paper *Minggu Merdeka* Jan.-July 47 (when it was banned by Dutch authorities); reporter *Merdeka* Aug. 47-Jan. 48; Editor illustrated weekly *Madjalah Merdeka* 48-51, of *Minggu Merdeka* May 51; Editor of women's monthly magazines, *Keluarga* (Family) 53-59, of daily, *Indonesian Observer* 55-59; Founder, Dir. Foundation for Preservation of Indonesian Art and Culture 67-.
Jalan Diponegoro, Jakarta, Indonesia.

Diakité, Moussa; Guinean government official; b. 1927; ed. Ecole Primaire Supérieure, Ecole Technique Supérieure.
Treasury 54; Dep. Mayor of Kankan 56; Vice-Pres. Grand Council of West Africa 58; Sec. of State, Grand Council of West Africa 58; Gov. Central Bank of Guinea and Minister of Finance 60-63; Minister of Foreign Trade and Banking 63-68; Sec. of State for Industry, Mines and Power 68-71; Minister of the Interior 72-; Compagnon de l'Indépendance.
Ministry of the Interior, Conakry, Republic of Guinea.

Diamand, Peter, C.B.E.; Netherlands (b. Austrian) musical administrator; b. 8 June 1913; *m.* Sylvia Rosenberg; one *s.*; ed. Schiller-Real-gymnasium, Berlin, and Friedrich Wilhelm Univ., Berlin.
Studied law in Berlin until Nazi laws made this impossible; emigrated to Holland 33; Private Sec. to Artur Schnabel 34-39; Asst. Dir. Netherlands Opera 46-48; Gen. Man. Holland Festival 48-65, Artistic Adviser 65-73; co-founder Netherlands Chamber Orchestra and mem. of Board 55-; Dir. Edinburgh Festival 65-; Knight Order of Orange-Nassau; Grand Cross of Merit Austria; Commdr. Order of Merit Italy; Hon. LL.D., Univ. of Edinburgh.
Edinburgh Festival Society, 29 St. James's Street, London, S.W.1, England.

Diamond, Baron (Life Peer), cr. 70, of the City of Gloucester; **John Diamond,** F.C.A.; British politician; b. 1907, Leeds; *s.* of Solomon Diamond and Henrietta Beckerman; two *s.* two *d.*; ed. Leeds Grammar School.
Chartered Accountant; Labour M.P. for Blackley, Manchester 45-51, Gloucester 57-70; mem. Gen. Nursing Council and Chair. of its Finance and Gen. Purposes Cttee. 47-53; Hon. Treas. Fabian Soc. 50-64; Dir. Sadler's Wells Trust 57-64; Hon. Treas. Labour Cttee. for Europe 61-64; Chief. Sec. to the Treasury 64-70; mem. Cabinet 68-70; Hon. Treas. The European Movt.; Deputy Chair. of Cttees., House of Lords 74; Chair. Royal Comm. on Distribution of Income and Wealth 74-.
Publs. *Public Expenditure in Practice* 75, co-author: *Socialism the British Way* 48.
Leisure interests: music, golf and skiing.
House of Lords, London, S.W.1; and 44 Chenies, nr. Rickmansworth, Herts., England.

Diamond, William, PH.D.; American international finance official; b. 1917, Baltimore, Md.; *m.* Lois Wilhelm 1946; ed. Johns Hopkins Univ.
With U.S. Board of Econ. Warfare and U.S. Foreign Econ. Admin. 42-44; Economist on U.S. missions to Turkey and Czechoslovakia 44-46; Econ. Adviser to UNRRA mission to Czechoslovakia, later in London; joined Loan Dept. of World Bank 47; Deputy Dir. of Foreign Trade Admin. of Greece 47-48; various posts, World Bank 48-55; Econ. Devt. Inst. 55-58; Adviser to Industrial Credit and Investment Corpn. of India 59-60; Asst. Dir. Operations, Western Hemisphere, World

Bank 60-62; Dir. Devt. Finance Companies Dept., Int. Finance Corpn. 62-68; Dir. Devt. Finance Companies Dept., World Bank 68-72, Dir. S. Asia Dept. 72-.
Publs. *The Economic Thought of Woodrow Wilson, Czechoslovakia between East and West, Development Banks, Development Finance Companies: Aspects of Policy and Operations.*
South Asia Department, International Bank for Reconstruction and Development, 1818 H Street, N.W., Washington, D.C. 20433; Home: 3315 Garfield Street, N.W., Washington, D.C. 20008, U.S.A.
Telephone: 333-1863 (Home).

Dias, Anthony Lancelot, B.A., B.SC.(ECON); Indian civil servant; b. 13 March 1910, Poona; s. of late Dr. and Mrs. E. X. Dias; m. Joan J. Vas 1939; four d.; ed. Deccan Coll., Poona, London School of Econs. and Magdalene Coll., Cambridge.
Entered Indian Civil Service 33; Sec. Educ. Dept. 52-55, Agricultural Dept. 55-57, Home Dept. 57-60; Chair. Bombay Port Trust 60-64; Sec. Dept. of Food, Ministry of Food and Agriculture 64-70; Lieut.-Gov. of Tripura 70-71; Gov. of West Bengal Aug. 71-; mem. Board of Govs., Int. Dept. Research Centre, Ottawa, Canada; Padma Vibhushan 70.
Leisure interests: golf, photography.
Publ. *Feeding India's Millions.*
Raj Bhavan, Calcutta, West Bengal, India.
Telephone: 23-5641.

Dias, Felix (Bandaranaike); Ceylonese politician; b. 1931.
Minister of Finance and Parl. Sec. to Minister of Defence and of External Affairs July 60-62; Minister without Portfolio Nov. 62-May 63, of Agriculture, Food and Co-operatives May 63-65; Minister of Public Admin., Local Govt. and Home Affairs May 70-75, of Justice 72-, of Finance Sept. 75-.
Ministry of Justice, Colombo; Mahanuga Gardens, Colombo 3, Sri Lanka.
Telephone: 95738 (Office); 27343 (Home).

Diaz-Casanuevo, Humberto, DR.PHIL.; Chilean Permanent Representative to UN 71-73; see *The International Who's Who 1975-76.*

Díaz de Molina, Afredo Hugo Florencio, D.JUR. AND SC.S.; Argentine writer; b. 27 Oct. 1901; ed. Nat. Univ. of Buenos Aires.
Minister of Government, Justice and Education, Jujuy 43; Head of Monopolies Department, Ministry of Industry and Commerce 43-49; Legal Adviser 50-52; Lawyer Vialidad 55-63; mem. Nat. Comm. on Anniversary of Sovereign Assembly of 13, 63; Teacher at Reconquista Nat. Coll.; hon. mem. Co-operative Asscn. 50-64; Santiago Derquix and José Figueroa Alcorta Colls.; Prof. Civil Law, Univ. of La Plata 55-62; Prof. History of Argentine Insts., Univ. of Buenos Aires 58-63; Founder and Dean of Faculty of Economics at the Free Univ. of Morón 61·63, Rector 63; Vice-Pres. Argentine Inst. of Genealogical Science; Founder and Editor first Argentine *Heraldic Review* 40; Pres. Argentine-Cuban Cultural Inst.; Vice-Pres. Bolívar Soc. of Argentina; mem. chief historical and genealogical institutes of Europe and America; Chevalier Légion d'Honneur.
Publs. include: *El Poema del Olimpo* 19, *Ja, ja, ja,* 23, *El genio epónimo del Libertador José de San Martín* 50, *Los orígenes constitucionales argentinos* 55; *La constitución cordobesa de 1821 y su influencia institucional* 58, *El sindicato y los derechos sindicales en la reforma constitucional de 1957* 60, *La oligarquía argentina Córdoba* 65.
3931 Juan María Gutiérrez, Buenos Aires, Argentina.

Díaz Ordaz, Gustavo; Mexican lawyer and politician; b. 1911; ed. Instituto de Ciencias y Artes Oaxaca and Colegio del Estado de Puebla.

Legal and judicial posts, Puebla, Tlatlangui and Tehuacán 37; Dep. to Fed. Legis. Assembly and Senator 46-52; fmr. Prof. of Admin. and Labour Law, Puebla Univ.; Chief Officer, Secretariat of the Govt. 52-58; Sec. of the Govt. 58, later Minister of the Interior; Pres. of Mexico 64-70; Partido Revolucionario Institucional.
c/o Partido Revolucionario Institucional, Insurgentes Norte 59, Mexico, D.F., Mexico.

Diba, H.I.M. Queen Farah (see Pahlavi, H.I.M. Queen Farah Shahbanou).

Dibba, Sherrif Mustapha; Gambian politician; b. 1937; ed. govt. and mission schools.
Clerk, United Africa Co. -59; mem. Nat. Assembly (People's Progressive Party) 60-; Minister of Local Govt. -66; Minister of Works and Communications 66; of Finance, of Trade and Devt. until 70; Vice-Pres. 70-72; Amb. to European Communities 72-74; Minister of Econ. Planning and Industrial Devt. July 74-.
Ministry of Economic Planning and Industrial Development, Marina Parade, Banjul, The Gambia.

di Belgiojoso, Lodovico Barbiano; Italian architect; b. 1 Dec. 1909; ed. School of Architecture, Milan.
Architect 32; Prof. of Architecture 49; Prof. Venice Univ. Inst. of Architecture 56-63; Prof. of Architectural Composition, School of Architecture, Milan Polytechnic 63-; private practice with Peressutti and Rogers in town planning, architecture, interior decoration and industrial design; mem. Nat. Council of Italian Town Planning Inst.; mem. Acad. di S. Luca, Rome.
Works include houses, factories, pavilions; Italian Merchant Navy Pavilion, Paris Int. Exhbn. 37; health resort for children, Legnano 39; Post Office, Rome 39; monument to the dead in German concentration camps, Milan cemetery 46; U.S. Pavilion at Triennale 51; Olivetti Showroom, Fifth Avenue, New York, and Labyrinth at the Tenth Triennale 54; restoration and re-arrangement of Castello Sforzesco Museums 56; skyscraper Torre Velasca, Milan 57; Canadian Pavilion, Venice Biennale; collaborator Italian Pavilion, Brussels Exhbn. 58; Hispano Olivetti Building, Barcelona 65.
Publs. (in collaboration with Banfi, Peressutti and Rogers): *Piano regolatore della Val d'Aosta* 37, *Piano A.R.* 46, *Stile* 36, etc.
Studio Architetti B.B.P.R., 2 via dei Chiostri, Milan, Italy.

Dichter, Ernest, PH.D.; American psychologist; b. 14 Aug. 1907, Vienna; s. of William Dichter and Matilde Schneider; m. Hedy Langfelder 1935; one s. one d.; ed. Univs. of Paris and Vienna.
Consultant Psychologist on Programs, Columbia Broadcasting System 42-46; developed application of social science to advertising, public service, politics (motivational research); Pres. Ernest Dichter Creativity Ltd.
Leisure interests: gardening, painting, bee-keeping.
Publs. *Successful Living* 47, *Strategy of Desire* 60, *Handbook of Consumer Motivations* 64, *Motivating Human Behavior* 71, *The New World of Packaging* 73, *Why Not: Management Problems of the 70s* 73.
P.O. Box 217, Albany Post Road, Croton-on-Hudson, N.Y. 10520, U.S.A.
Telephone: (914) CR-1-8774.

Dicke, Robert H(enry), A.B., PH.D.; American physicist; b. 6 May 1916; ed. Princeton Univ. and Univ. of Rochester.
Microwave Radar Devt., Mass. Inst. of Technology 41-46; Physics Faculty, Princeton Univ. 46-, Cyrus Fogg Brackett Prof. of Physics 57-, Chair. Physics Dept., Princeton Univ. 67-70; mem. Advisory Panel for Physics, Nat. Science Foundation 59-61; Chair. Advisory Cttee. on Atomic Physics, Nat. Bureau of Standards 61-63; mem. N.A.S.A. Cttee. on Physics 63-; Chair. 63-66; Chair. Physics Panel, Advisory to Cttee.

on Int. Exchange ot Persons (Fulbright-Hays Act) 64-66; Nat. Lecturer, Sigma Xi 67; mem. Visiting Cttee. Nat. Bureau of Standards 74-; Fellow American Physical Soc., American Geophysical Union, American Acad. of Arts and Sciences; mem. American Astronomical Soc., Nat. Acad. of Sciences, Nat Science Board 70-; Assoc. Royal Astronomical Soc.; Hon. D.Sc. (Univ. of Edinburgh) 72; Rumford Medal, American Acad. of Arts and Sciences 67, Nat. Medal of Science 70, Comstock Prize, Nat. Acad. of Sciences 73, Cresson Medal, Franklin Inst. 74.
Publs. (with Montgomery and Purcell) *Principles of Microwave Circuits* 48 (with J. P. Wittke), *An Introduction to Quantum Mechanics* 60, *The Theoretical Significance of Experimental Relativity* 64, *Gravitation and the Universe* 70.
Joseph Henry Laboratories, Princeton Univ., Princeton, N.J. 08540, U.S.A.
Telephone: 609-452-4317.

Dickel, Maj.-Gen. Friedrich; German army officer and politician; b. 9 Dec. 1913; ed. elementary school. Former moulder; mem. Kommunistische Partei Deutschlands until 45, Sozialistische Einheits Partei (S.E.D.) 45-; in Saar, France, Netherlands 33-36; fought in Spanish Civil War 36-37; in U.S.S.R. 37-46; Maj. Gen. Regular People's Police 53-56, Maj.-Gen. People's Army 56-63; Minister of Interior and Chief of People's Police (Volkspolizei) 63-.
Innenministerium, Berlin; Home: Mauerstrasse 29/31, 108 Berlin, German Democratic Republic.

Dickens, Frank, M.A., D.SC., PH.D., F.INST.BIOL., F.R.S.; British biochemist; b. 1899, Northampton; s. of John William and Elizabeth Ann Dickens; m. Molly Jelleyman 1925; two d.; ed. Northampton Grammar School and Magdalene Coll., Cambridge.
Lecturer in Biochemistry, Middlesex Hospital Medical School, at same time working for Medical Research Council 29-31; mem. Scientific Staff, Medical Research Council 31-33; Research Dir. North of England Council of British Empire Cancer Campaign 33-46; Research for Naval Personnel Cttee. of Medical Research Council, Nat. Inst. for Medical Research 43-44; mem. Scientific Advisory Cttee. of British Empire Cancer Campaign 34-; an Editor of *Biochemical Journal* 37-47; Philip Hill Prof. of Experimental Biochemistry, Middlesex Hosp. Medical School, Univ. of London 46-67; Chair. British Nat. Cttee. for Biochemistry 64-66; fmrly. Dir. Tobacco Research Council's Laboratories 67-69; Hon. D.Sc. Univ. of Newcastle-upon-Tyne 72; Hon. mem. Biochem. Soc. 67-.
Leisure interests: fishing, photography.
Publs. *Chemical and Physical Properties of the Internal Secretions* (with E. C. Dodds), translation of *The Metabolism of Tumours* (by O. Warburg), Editor *Oxygen in the Animal Organism* (with E. Neil), *Carbohydrate Metabolism and its Disorders* (with P. Randle and W. J. Whelan), *Essays in Biochemistry* (with P. N. Campbell).
Home: 15 Hazelhurst Crescent, Findon Valley, Worthing, Sussex BN14 0HW, England.
Telephone: Findon 2022.

Dickey, James, B.A., M.A.; American poet; b. 2 Feb. 1923; ed. Clemson Coll. and Vanderbilt Univ.
Served Second World War with U.S. Army Air Force and U.S. Air Force in Korea; Consultant in Poetry, Library of Congress, Washington 66-68; *Sewanee Review* Fellow 54-55, Guggenheim Fellow 62-63; writer in residence and Prof. of English, Univ. of S. Carolina 68-; Vachel Lindsay Award and Longview Award 59; Prix Médicis 71.
Publs. Poems: *Into the Stone* 60, *Drowning with Others* 62, *Helmets* 64, *Two Poems of the Air* 64, *Buckdancer's Choice* 65, *Poems 1959-1967* 67, *The Eye-Beaters* 70,

Self-Interviews 70, *Sorties* 71; Criticism: *The Suspect in Poetry* 64; novel: *Deliverance* 70.
c/o University of South Carolina, Columbia, South Carolina 29208, U.S.A.

Dickey, John Sloan, A.B., J.D.; American college president and lawyer; b. 4 Nov. 1907, Lock Haven, Pa.; s. of John W. Dickey and Gretchen Sloan Dickey; m. Christina M. Gillespie 1932; one s. two d.; ed. Dartmouth Coll., and Harvard Law School.
Began practice in Boston 32; Asst. to Asst. Sec. of State and Asst. to legal adviser, U.S. Dept. of State 34-36; law practice with Gaston, Snow, Hunt, Rice & Boyd, Boston 36-40; Special Asst. to Sec. of State 40; Special Asst. to Co-ordinator of Inter-American Affairs 40-44, and detailed to U.S. Dept. of State as Chief, Div. of World Trade Intelligence; Dir. Office of Public Affairs, Dept. of State 44-45, and served as public liaison officer U.S. del., UN Conf. on Int. Org., San Francisco 45; Pres. of Dartmouth Coll. 45-70, Pres. Emer. and Bicentennial Prof. of Public Affairs 70-.
Leisure interests: fishing, hunting, conservation.
Publs. Contributor to *The Secretary of State* 60, Editor *The United States and Canada* 64.
Dartmouth College, Hanover, New Hampshire; Home: 11 Lyme Road, Hanover, New Hampshire 03755, U.S.A.
Telephone: 603-646-3578 (Office); 603-643-3034 (Home).

Didriksen, Jan, LL.M.; Norwegian lawyer and business executive; b. 15 May 1917; m. Dagmar Mellgren 1946; ed. Oslo Univ. and Harvard Business School.
District Commdr. Underground Mil. Forces 41-42; Judge 46-54; Chief, Law Dept., Norwegian Employers' Fed. 54-62, Del. to Int. Labour Org. (ILO) 56-62; Dir. Fed. of Norwegian Industries 63-65, Dir.-Gen. 65-.
Norges Industriforbund, Drammensveien 40, P.O. Box 2435 Solli, Oslo 2; Home: Sörkedalsveien 94, Oslo 3, Norway.
Telephone: Oslo 56-43-90 (Office); Oslo 14-48-52 (Home).

Diebenkorn, Richard; American artist; b. 22 April 1922, Portland, Ore.; s. of Richard Diebenkorn and Dorothy Stephens; m. Phyllis Gilman 1943; one s. one d.; ed. Stanford Univ., Univs. of Calif. and New Mexico and Calif. School of Fine Arts.
Teacher, Calif. School of Fine Arts 47-50, Univ. of Illinois 52-53, Calif. Coll. of Arts and Crafts 55-60, San Francisco Art Inst. 61-66; Prof. of Art, Univ. of Calif. at Los Angeles 66-73; Artist-in-residence Stanford Univ. 63-64; Tamarind Fellowship 62; mem. Nat. Council on the Arts 66-69; first one-man exhbn. San Francisco 48; numerous one-man exhbns. in cities throughout U.S.A. 48-, Tate Gallery, London 64; has exhibited in many group shows at Guggenheim Museum, Carnegie Internationals, Museum of Modern Art, San Francisco Museum of Art, etc.; Venice Biennale 68.
Publ. *Drawing* 65.
334 Amalfi Drive, Santa Monica, Calif. 90402, U.S.A.

Diebold, John, M.B.A., LL.D., SC.D., D.ENG.; American management consultant; b. 8 June 1926, Weehawken, N.J.; s. of William and Rose (Theurer) Diebold; m. Doris Hackett 1951; one d.; ed. Swarthmore Coll. and Harvard Business School.
With Griffenhagen & Assocs., management consultants, New York City, also Chicago 51-57, owner 57-, merged with Louis J. Kroeger and Assocs. to become Griffenhagen-Kroeger Inc. 60; established Diebold Group Inc., New York City 54, Pres., Chair. Board, Los Angeles, San Francisco, Washington, Chicago 54-; established Urwick Diebold Ltd., England 58, Co-Chair. 58-; established Raadgevend Bur. Berenschot-Diebold, N.V. 58, Diebold Europe, S.A., Pres. 60-; Chair. Diebold Computer Leasing Inc. 67-, Gemini Computer Systems Inc. 68-, Intermodel Transport Systems Inc. 69-; Dir.

Genesco 69-; U.S. Council Trusteeship, Int. Chamber of Commerce 72-; Dir. Acad. for Educ. Devt. 72-; Order of Merit, Italy; Grand Cross 71; coiner of word *automation*. Publs. *Automation—The Advent of the Automatic Factory* 52, *Beyond Automation* 64, *Man and the Computer Technology as an Agent of Social Change* 69, *Business Decisions and Technological Change* 70; Editor *World of the Computer* 73.

John Diebold and Assoc., 430 Park Avenue, N.Y. 10022, U.S.A.

Diederichs, Georg, DR.RER.POL.; German politician; b. 1900; ed. Univs. of Göttingen and Rostock.
Soldier 18-19; mem. German Democratic Party 26-30, Social Democratic Party 30-; in pharmaceutical industry 30-45; concentration camp and prison for illegal resistance work 35, 36; soldier 39-45; Mayor, Northeim 45-46; M.P. Council 48-49; mem. Landtag, Lower Saxony 47-; Vice-Pres. Lower Saxony Landtag 55-57, Minister for Social Affairs 57-61, Prime Minister 61-70; mem. (Federal) Bundesrat 62-, Dep. Pres. 62-63, Pres. 63-64.
Leinerandstrasse 23, Laatzen near Hanover, Federal Republic of Germany.

Diederichs, Nicolaas, M.A., D.LITT. et PHIL.; South African economist and politician; b. 17 Nov. 1903, Ladybrand, Orange Free State; *m.* Margaretha Potgieter 1932; one *s.* two *d.*; ed. Boshof High School, Grey Univ. Coll., Univs. of Munich, Cologne and Leiden.
Former Chair. Economic Inst., Decimal Coinage Comm.; fmr. Prof. Free State Univ.; M.P. for Randfontein 48-58, Losberg 58-74, for Overvaal 74-75; Minister for Econ. Affairs 58-67, also of Mines 61-64, of Finance 67-75; Chancellor Randse Afrikaanse Universiteit 68; Pres. of South Africa April 75-; Hon. D.Comm., Orange Free State and Stellenbosch Univs.; Order of Merit, Paraguay; Knight of the Great Cross, Order of Merit, Italy.
Leisure interests: reading, golf.
Publs. *Vom Leiden und Dulden, Die Volkebond, Nasionalisme as Lewensbeskouing, Die Kommunisme* and numerous articles and brochures.
Office of the President, Pretoria, Transvaal, Republic of South Africa.

Diefenbaker, Rt. Hon. John George, C.H., P.C., Q.C., M.A., LL.B., F.R.S.C., M.P.; Canadian lawyer and politician, b. 18 Sept. 1895, Grey County, Ont.; *s.* of William and Mary (Bannerman) Diefenbaker; *m.* 1st Edna Brower 1929 (deceased), 2nd Olive Palmer (née Freeman) 1953; ed. Saskatchewan Univ.
Served overseas with Canadian Army 16-17; called to Bar of Saskatchewan 19; King's Counsel 29; Vice-Pres. Canadian Bar Asscn. 39-42; mem. Canadian Parl. 40-; Leader Progressive Cons. Party Dec. 56-Sept. 67; Prime Minister of Canada June 57-April 63; Fellow Royal Soc. of Arts, Fellow Royal Soc. of Canada; Fellow Royal Architectural Inst. of Canada; Hon. Bencher, Gray's Inn, London; 35 hon. degrees; Hon. Fellow (Bar-Ilan Univ., Israel); Hon. Freeman of City of London 63; Scottish Rite Mason; Chancellor of Univ. Saskatchewan 69-.
House of Commons, Ottawa, Ont.; 246 19th Street West, Prince Albert, Sask.; 115 Lansdowne Road South, Rockcliffe Park, Ottawa, Ont., Canada.

Diehl, Günter; German diplomatist; b. 8 Feb. 1916, Cologne; *m.* Helga von Rautenstrauch 1939; three *s.* one *d.*; ed. Univ. of Cologne, and Université de Bordeaux.
Entered Diplomatic Service 39; Foreign Office 45; Foreign Editor *Hamburger Abendblatt* 48; Foreign Dept. Press Office 50; Foreign Office Spokesman 52; Counsellor German Embassy Santiago 56; Head of Foreign Dept. Press and Information Service 60; Head Planning Div. Foreign Office 66; Chief, Press and Information

Office, Fed. Repub. of Germany 67-69; Amb. to India 70-.
Leisure interests: painting, shooting, fishing.
Embassy of the Federal Republic of Germany, P.O. Box 613, New Delhi, India.

Diehl, Val B.; American business executive; b. 1917, Mitchell, S. Dakota; ed. Dakota Wesleyan Univ.
Joined Nabisco Inc. 42; U.S. Navy; various sales posts, Nabisco Inc. until 54, Asst. Dir. of Int. Operations 54-56; Chair. Nabisco Foods Ltd., U.K. 56-61; Asst. to Pres., Nabisco Inc. 61, Vice-Pres. Int. Div. 62, Exec. Vice-Pres., Dir., mem. Exec. Cttee. 68, Pres., Chief Operating Officer 73-.
Nabisco Inc., East Hanover; New Jersey 07936, U.S.A.
Telephone: (212) 751-5000.

Dieminger, Walter E., DR. RER. TECH.; German aeronomist; b. 7 July 1907, Würzburg; *s.* of Ludwig and Anna (née Kraus) Dieminger; *m.* Dr. Ilse Günther 1935; two *s.* one *d.*; ed. Humanistisches Gymnasium, Würzburg and Technische Hochschule, Munich.
Research Scientist, German Air Force Test Centre 34-43; Head, Advisory Org. for Radio Propagation 43-45; Head, Inst. for Ionospheric Research 45-56; Man. Dir. Max-Planck-Inst. für Aeronomie 56-65, now Dir.; Hon. Pres. German Nat. Cttee. URSI; mem. Finnish Acad. of Sciences, Acad. Leopoldina, Int. Acad. of Astronautics; Vice-Pres. URSI 66-69, Pres. 69-72; F. C. Gauss-Medal 72.
Leisure interests: amateur radio, model railway, photography.
Publs. about 100 articles on radio propagation, aeronomy and space research; contribs. to encyclopaedias (including *Brockhaus*).
3411 Elvese, Berlinerstrasse 12, Federal Republic of Germany.
Telephone: (05503) 1089.

Dienesch, Marie-Madeleine; French politician; b. 1914, Cairo, Egypt; ed. Coll. Sainte Marie, Neuilly, Coll. Sévigné and Sorbonne, Paris.
Professor, Lycée de Saint-Brieuc; Founder and Sec. Syndicat Général de l'Education Nationale des Côtes-du-Nord (S.G.E.N.) 44; Founder and Pres. Union Féminine Civique et Sociale des Côtes-du-Nord 44; Rep. to Nat. Constituent Assembly 45-46; Rep. to Nat. Assembly 46-, Vice-Pres. 58-59; Int. Vice-Pres. Union of European Women 62; Sec. of State for Educ. June-July 68, for Social Affairs 68-69, for Social Welfare 69; Sec. of State at Ministry of Health, responsible for Social Welfare 72-74.
Home: 79 avenue de Breteuil, Paris 15e, France.

Dieng, Diakha; Senegalese international official; b. 16 Aug. 1933, Saint Louis; *m.* Danièle Egretaud 1961; one *s.* two *d.*; ed. Lycée Faidherbe, St. Louis, Université de Dakar, Université de Paris, Ecole des Impôts, Paris.
Registry Office, France 60, Dakar 61; Sec., later First Sec., Embassy of Senegal, Brussels 62-63; First Sec. Embassy of Senegal, Paris 63-64; Sec.-Gen. Union Africaine et Malgache de Coopération Economique (UAMCE), Yaoundé 64-65, Organisation Commune Africaine et Malgache, Yaoundé (OCAM) 64-68; Amb. to Egypt 68-70, concurrently accred. to Syria, Sudan, Jordan; Dir. of the Cabinet of the Prime Minister 70-; Officier, Ordre National Sénégalais; Commandeur, Ordre National de la Côte d'Ivoire; Commandeur, Ordre National Malgache; Officier, Ordre du Léopard (Zaire); Commandeur, Ordre de la Valeur du Cameroun; Officier, Légion d'Honneur.
Office of the Prime Minister, Dakar, Senegal.

Diesel, Jurgen, DR.JUR.; German diplomatist; b. 4 Jan. 1926, Berlin; *m.* Elenore von Dungern 1954; one *s.* two *d.*; ed. Univs. of Erlangen and Munich.
Diplomatic Acad., Speyer 52-54; Attaché, German Embassy, Santiago 54-56, First Sec., Caracas 56-60;

Disarmament Section, Ministry of Foreign Affairs 60-64; Disarmament Negotiations, Geneva 64-68; Head, E. European Div., Ministry of Foreign Affairs 68-73; Amb. to Switzerland 73-; decorations from Chile, Romania, Sweden, Venezuela.
Leisure interests: filming, mountains, travelling.
Embassy of Federal Republic of Germany, Brunnadernrain 31, 3006 Berne, Switzerland.
Telephone: 440831, 446088.

Dietrich, Helmut; German banker; b. 23 March 1922; ed. Hochschule für Ökonomie, Berlin.
Former Branch Dir., Deutsche Notenbank, fmr. Area Dir., Pres. Deutsche Notenbank 64-68; now Vice-Pres. Staatsbank der Deutschen Demokratischen Republik; Pres. Deutsche Investitionsbank; Vaterländischer Verdienstorden, Verdienstmedaille der Deutschen Demokratischen Republik, etc.
108 Berlin, Charlottenstrasse 33, German Democratic Republic.

Dietrich, Marlene; German-born American actress and singer; b. 27 Dec. 1902; ed. Augusta Victoria School, Berlin.
Début in Berlin; worked with Max Reinhardt; emigrated to U.S. 30; has appeared in numerous films including *Golden Earrings, Foreign Affair, Stage Fright, Rancho Notorious, The Blue Angel, Scarlet Empress, Shanghai Express, Witness for the Prosecution,* etc.; also numerous stage and cabaret appearances; Officier, Légion d'Honneur 72, U.S. Medal of Freedom.
c/o Capitol, 1750 Vine Street, Hollywood, Calif. 90028, U.S.A.

Dietz, David (Henry), A.B., LITT.D., LL.D.; American newspaper editor and author; b. 6 Oct. 1897, Cleveland, Ohio; s. of Henry and Hannah (Levy) Dietz; m. Dorothy Cohen 1918; one s. two d.; ed. Western Reserve Univ.
Member Editorial staff of The Cleveland Press 15-; Science Editor of the Scripps-Howard Newspapers 21-; Lecturer in General Science, Western Reserve Univ. 27-; Visiting Lecturer on the Science of Modern War at Yale Univ. 42; Science Commentator, Nat. Broadcasting Co. 45-50; Winner Pulitzer Prize in Journalism 37; Westinghouse Award for Distinguished Science Writing 45; Lasker Medical Journalism Award 54; James T. Grady Award 60; was Consultant to the Surgeon-General of the U.S. Army during Second World War, newspaper corresp. and radio commentator, atomic bomb tests, Bikini 46; Hon. Litt.D. (Western Reserve Univ.) 48; Hon. LL.D. (Bowling Green State Univ.) 54.
Leisure interests: violin, golf, book-collecting.
Publs. *The Story of Science* 31, *Medical Magic* 37, *Atomic Energy in the Coming Era* 45; article on "The Atomic Bomb" in the 1946 edition of the *Encyclopædia Britannica, Atomic Science, Bombs and Power* 54, *All about Satellites and Space Ships* 58, *All About Great Medical Discoveries* 60, *All About the Universe* 65, *Stars and the Universe* 69, *The New Outline of Science* 72.
2891 Winthrop Road, Shaker Heights, Ohio 44120, U.S.A.
Telephone: 991-3834.

Dietzfelbinger, Hermann; German ecclesiastic; b. 14 July 1908; ed. Friedrich-Alexander-Univ. zu Erlangen-Nürnberg, Eberhard-Karls Univ., Tübingen, and Ernst Moritz Arndt-Univ., Greifswald.
Protestant Bishop of Bavaria 55-; Pres. Council of German Evangelical Church 67-73.
8 Munich 37, Meiserstrasse 13, Federal Republic of Germany.

Dieudonné, Jean Alexandre, D. ès sc.; French university professor; b. 1 July 1906, Lille (Nord); s. of Ernest Dieudonné and Léontine Lebrun; m. Marie Odette Clavel 1935; one s. one d.; ed. Ecole Normale Supérieure and Inst. of Advanced Study, Princeton.

Assistant Prof., Univ. of Rennes 33-37, Univ. of Nancy 37-48; Prof., Univ. of Nancy 48-52, Univ. of Michigan 52-53, Northwestern Univ. 53-59, Inst. des Hautes Etudes Scientifiques, Paris 59-64, Univ. of Nice 64-70; retd. 70; mem. French Acad. of Sciences; Pres. Soc. Mathématique de France 64-65; Chevalier Légion d'Honneur.
Leisure interests: music, cooking, gardening.
Publs. *La géométrie des groupes classiques* 55, *Foundations of Modern Analysis* 60, *Eléments d'Analyse II* 68, *III* 70, *IV* 71, *Calcul infinitésimal* 68, *Introduction to the Theory of Formal Groups* 73, *Cours de Géométrie Algébrique* (2 vols.) 74; 120 papers in mathematical journals.
Villa Nancago, Corniche Fleurie, 06 Nice; 10 rue du Général Camou, Paris 7e, France.
Telephone: 83-29-43 (Nice); 551-14-56 (Paris).

Diez de Medina, Raúl; Bolivian diplomatist; b. 1914, La Paz; s. of Eduardo Diez de Medina and Etelvina Guachalla; m. Mary Leudinskas 1950; two s. three d.; ed. Colegio Nacional Ayacucho, La Paz, and School of Foreign Service, Georgetown Univ., Washington, D.C.
Diplomatic Service, Washington 30; Latin American Editor *Sunday Star*, Washington 30-37; Sec., Counsellor and Minister Washington 37-46; Del. of Bolivia to UN Relief and Rehabilitation Admin. 46; Ambassador of Bolivia to UN Palestine Comm. 48; Dir. Dept. of Public Information, Pan American Union 48; Bolivian Del. to fifth UN Assembly 50; Pres. COPESA, La Paz 55-58; Dir. Pan American Union Office, Bolivia 58-64; Ambassador of Bolivia to Council of Org. of American States 64-69, Vice-Chair. Council of OAS 66-67; Bolivian Del. to tenth, eleventh and twelfth meetings of Ministers of Foreign Affairs of American Republics 65-69; OAS rep. in Argentina 69-.
Publs. *Autopsy of the Monroe Doctrine* 34, *The U.S. versus Europe in Latin America* 37.
Oficina OEA, Avenida de Mayo 760 (1er piso), Buenos Aires, Argentina.

Dijoud, Paul Charles Louis; French politician; b. 25 July 1938, Neuilly-sur-Seine; s. of Jules-Raoul Dijoud and Andrée Claquin; m. Catherine Cochaux 1968; one s. one d.; ed. Lycée Condorcet, Faculté de Droit de Paris, Inst. d'Etudes politiques de Paris.
Student at Ecole Nat. d'Admin. 64-66; Commercial attaché, dept. of external econ. relations in Ministry of Econ. and Finance; mem. Parl. for Hautes-Alpes 67-; Asst. Sec.-Gen. Ind. Republican Party 67-69; Conseiller Général for canton of Embrun 68-; Pres. Ind. Republican Exec. Cttee. for Provence-Côte d'Azur 68-; Mayor of Briançon 71-; Sec. of State attached to Prime Minister's Office 73-, later to Minister of Cultural Affairs and the Environment, to Minister of Employment with Responsibility for Immigrant Workers May 74-.
Immeuble "la Durance", 05200 Embrun, France.

Dike, Kenneth Onwuka, PH.D.; Nigerian historian; b. 17 Dec. 1917; ed. Dennis Memorial Grammar School (Onitsha), Achimota Coll. (Ghana), Fourah Bay Coll. (Sierra Leone), Univs. of Durham, Aberdeen and London.
Lecturer in History, Univ. Coll. Ibadan 50-52, Senior Lecturer 54-56, Prof. History 56-60, Principal 58-60; Vice-Chancellor, Univ. of Ibadan 60-Dec. 66; Senior Research Fellow, West African Inst. of Social and Econ. Research 52-54; Founder-Dir. Nigerian Nat. Archives 51-64; Chair. Nigerian Antiquities Comm. 54-; Pres. Historical Soc. of Nigeria 55-69; Dir. Inst. of African Studies, Univ. of Ibadan 62-67; Chair. Planning Cttee., Univ. of Port Harcourt 67-70; Fellow Royal Historical Soc.; Hon. LL.D. (Aberdeen, Leeds, Northwestern, London, Columbia, Princeton, Ahmadu Bello Univs.); Hon. D.Litt. (Boston and Birmingham), Hon. D.Sc. (Moscow).

Publs. *Report on the Preservation and Administration of Historical Records in Nigeria 53, Trade and Politics in the Niger Delta 1830-1890 56, A Hundred Years of British Rule in Nigeria 57, The Origins of the Niger Mission 58*; numerous articles in learned journals on Nigerian and West African history.
P.O.B. 59, Awka, Via Enugu, Eastern Region, Nigeria.

Dikshit, Umar Shankar; Indian politician and journalist; b. 12 Jan. 1901, Ugo, Uttar Pradesh; *s.* of late Ram Swarup Dikshit; *m.* Shiva Pyari Dikshit; one *s.*; ed. Govt. School and Christchurch Coll., Kanpur. Secretary, Kanpur City Congress Cttee. and mem. Uttar Pradesh Congress Cttee. 20-25; imprisoned for participation in Non-Co-operation Movt. 21-23; Pres. Uttar Bharatiya Sabha and Hindi Bhashi Sammedan 25-30; active in underground movt. 32, imprisoned 30, 32-33; Hon. Sec. Hindustani Prachar Sabha, Bombay 34-41; joined Quit India Movt. 42, detained until 44; Custodian, Evacuee Property, New Delhi 48-52; Hon. Adviser, Nat. Small Industries Corpn. 56; Man. Dir. Associated Journals Ltd., Lucknow 57-; mem. Rajya Sabha 61-; Minister of Health and Family Planning 71-73, of Home Affairs 73-74, without Portfolio Oct. 74-Feb. 75, of Shipping and Transport Feb.-Nov. 75; Gov. of Karnataka 75-.
Leisure interests: reading, swimming, badminton.
Office of The Governor, Bangalore, Karnataka, India.

Dikushin, Vladimir Ivanovich; Soviet mechanical engineer; b. 8 Aug. 1902, Kuibyshev; ed. Moscow Higher Technical School.
Experimental Scientific Research Inst. of Metal Cutting Lathes 33-; Chief engineer of plan of first automatic factory in U.S.S.R.; specialist in field of machine-tool engineering; mem. Acad. of Sciences of the U.S.S.R. 53-; State prizewinner 41, 51; Hero of Socialist Labour 69; Order of Lenin (three); Hammer and Sickle Gold Medal, etc.
Publs. include *Ultrasonic Erosion and its Dependence on Vibration Characteristics of Tool 58.*
Experimental Scientific Research Institute of Metal Cutting Lathes, 21b Donskoi Proyezd, Moscow, U.S.S.R.

Dilhorne, 1st Viscount, cr. 65, 1st Baron, cr. 62; **Reginald Edward Manningham-Buller,** Bt., Kt., P.C., Q.C., B.A.; b. 1 Aug. 1905, Latimer, Bucks.; *s.* of Sir Mervyn Manningham-Buller, Bt. and the Hon. Lilah Cavendish; *m.* Lady Mary Lindsay 1930; one *s.* three *d.*; ed. Eton Coll. and Magdalen Coll., Oxford.
Called to Inner Temple Bar 27, Treas. 75; mem. Parl. 43-62; Solicitor-Gen. 51-54; Attorney-Gen. 54-62; Lord Chancellor 62-64; Lord of Appeal in Ordinary 69-.
Leisure interests: shooting, fishing.
6 King's Bench Walk, Temple, London, E.C.4; Horninghold Manor, Market Harborough, Leics., England.
Telephone: 01-583 0022 (London); Hallaton 641 (Home).

Dillard, Hardy Cross, B.S., LL.D.; American judge and former professor; b. 23 Oct. 1902, New Orleans, La.; *s.* of James Hardy Dillard and Avarene Budd Dillard; *m.* 1st Janet Schauffler 1934 (died 1970), one *s.* one *d.*; *m.* 2nd Valgerdur Dent 1972; ed. U.S. Military Acad., Univs. of Va. and Paris and Inst. des Hautes Etudes Internationales.
Assistant and Assoc. Prof., Univ. of Va. Law School 27-29, 32-38, Prof. 38-58, James Monroe Prof. of Law 58-70, Dean 63-68; private law practice 29-30; Carnegie Endowment Fellow 30-31; Dir. Inst. of Public Affairs (Univ. of Va.) 39-42; served U.S. Army 43-46; Dir. of Studies Nat. War Coll. 46-47; Board of Consultants 51-54; mem. Comm. to revise constitution of Va. 68-69; Advisory Council U.S. Air Force Acad. 66-70, and various consultancy work to public and private orgs. until 70; Judge, Int. Court of Justice, The Hague 70-; mem. Arbitral Tribunal in Beagle Channel case between

Argentina and Chile 71-; Lecturer, Oxford Univ. 53, Hague Acad. of Int. Law 57, Sibley Lecturer, Univ. of Georgia 62, Visiting Prof. Columbia Univ. Law School 62-63, Tucker Lecturer, Washington and Lee Univ. 65, Bailey Lecturer La State Univ. 66, Strong Lecturer Cornell Univ. 71; Pres. Amer. Soc. of Int. Law 63; mem. Council Amer. Law Inst., and Editorial Boards of *American Journal of International Law* and *Virginia Quarterly Review*; Raven and Thomas Jefferson Awards of Univ. of Va., Bronze Star Medal and Legion of Merit with Oak Leaf Cluster, Distinguished Civilian Award of U.S. Air Force.
Leisure interests: reading, grandchildren.
Publs. *Some Aspects of Law and Diplomacy*; about 110 articles and reviews in technical and non-technical journals.
International Court of Justice, Peace Palace, The Hague, Netherlands; 1221 Rugby Road, Charlottesville, Va. 22903, U.S.A.
Telephone: 070-92-44-41 (Peace Palace); 804-295-5992 (Home).

Diller, Hans, PH.D.; German professor of classics; b. 8 Sept. 1905, Worms; *s.* of the late Gustav and Klara (née Tent) Diller; *m.* Inez Sellschopp 1932; two *s.*; ed. Univs. of Frankfurt/Main, Hamburg, Munich and Florence.
Lecturer, Leipzig Univ. 32; Lecturer, Hamburg Univ. 33; Prof. at the Univ. of Rostock 37; Prof. Univ. of Kiel 42-; mem. Akademie der Wissenschaften und der Literatur, Mainz, 52; Editor *Hermes* and *Zetemata*; Dr. Phil. h.c. Athens; Dr. Med. h.c. Kiel.
Leisure interests: history and art of Schleswig-Holstein.
Publs. *Die Überlieferung der hippokratischen Schrift*, etc. 32, *Wanderarzt und Aitiologe* 34, *Göttliches und menschliches Wissen bei Sophokles* 50, *Die Bakchen und ihre Stellung im Spätwerk des Euripides* 55, *Hippokrates, Schriften: Die Anfänge der abendländischen Medizin* 62, *Die dichterische Form von Hesiods Erga* 62, *Sophokles-Wege der Forschung* 67, *Hippocrates, De aere aquis locis edidit et in linguam Germanicam vertit*, CMG I 1, 2 70, *Kleine Schriften zur antiken Literatur* 71, *Zur Periodisierung des geschichtlichen Ablaufs in der griechischen Antike* 72, *Kleine Schriften zur griechischen Medizin* 73.
Sternwartenweg 18, 23 Kiel, Federal Republic of Germany.
Telephone: Kiel 85194.

Dillon, Brendan, M.A.; Irish diplomatist; b. 30 Nov. 1924, Dublin; *s.* of William Dillon and Pauline Kerrigan; *m.* Alice O'Keeffe 1949; four *s.* one *d.*; ed. Blackrock Coll. and Univ. Coll., Dublin.
Chief of Protocol, Ministry of Foreign Affairs 68; Amb. to Denmark, concurrently to Norway and Iceland 70; Asst. Sec.-Gen., Ministry of Foreign Affairs 72; Perm. Rep. to European Communities Aug. 73-.
Permanent Representation of Ireland to the European Communities, avenue Galilée 5, 1030 Brussels, Belgium.
Telephone: 218-06-05.

Dillon, C. Douglas, A.B.; American investment banker and diplomatist; b. 21 Aug. 1909, Geneva; *s.* of Clarence and Anne (Douglass) Dillon; *m.* Phyllis Elsworth 1931; two *d.*; ed. Groton School and Harvard Coll.
Member N.Y. Stock Exchange 31-36; with U.S. and Foreign Securities Corpn. and U.S. and Int. Securities Corpn. 37-53, Pres. 46-53, 67-, Dir. 38-53, 67-; Dir. Dillon, Read & Co. Inc. 38-53, Chair. of Board 46-53, Chair. of Exec. Cttee. 71-; served as Ensign, advancing to Lieut.-Commdr. U.S.N.R. 41-45; awarded Air Medal, Legion of Merit with Combat Device; American Amb. to France Jan. 53-57; Under-Sec. of State for Economic Affairs 57-59; Under-Sec. of State 59-61; Sec. of the Treasury 61-65; Chair. Rockefeller Foundation; Pres. Metropolitan Museum of Art 70-; LL.D. (Harvard, Columbia, New York, Hartford, Rutgers, Pennsylvania

and Princeton Univs., Lafayette, Williams and Middlebury Colls.); Republican.
767 Fifth Avenue, New York, N.Y. 10022, U.S.A.
Telephone: 18 06 05.

Dillon, Ian Birt Harper; Rhodesian politician; b. 18
April 1915, Salisbury; s. of Charles and Ivy Dillon; m.
Maureen M. Comley 1939; three s. two d.; ed. Gatooma
and Hartley Schools and St. George's Coll., Salisbury.
Mine manager 54-59; Councillor, Belingwe/Shabani
Road Council 54-59; M.P. for Shabani Constituency
58-; Chief Govt. Whip 62-64; Parl. Sec. (subsequently
Deputy Minister) to Minister of Mines and Lands 64-68;
Minister of Mines Jan. 69-.
Leisure interests: golf, fishing.
Ministry of Mines, P/Bag 7709, Causeway; Home: 92
Baines Avenue, Salisbury, Rhodesia.
Telephone: 703781.

Dillon, James Mathew; Irish farmer, merchant and
barrister-at-law; b. 1902; s. of John Dillon and Eliza-
beth Mathew; m. Maura Phelan 1942; one s.; ed. Mount
St. Benedict and Nat. Univ. of Ireland.
Studied business org. in London and Chicago; barrister,
King's Inns 31; mem. Daíl for Co. Donegal 32-37, for
Co. Monaghan 37-69; Minister of Agriculture 48-51 and
54-57; Leader of Fine Gael and of Opposition 59-65;
mem. Council of State; Knight Commdr. Order of St.
Gregory the Great 75.
Ballaghaderreen, Co. Mayo, Ireland.

Dime, Jim; American artist; b. 1935, Cincinnati,
Ohio; m. Nancy Minto 1957; three s.; ed. Cincinnati
Art Acad.
First one-man exhbn. Reuben Gallery, New York 60;
has subsequently held numerous one-man exhbns. in
U.S.A. and throughout Europe including Palais des
Beaux Arts, Brussels 63, 70, Sidney Jannis Gallery,
N.Y. 63, 64, 67, Robert Fraser Gallery, London 65, 66,
69, Stedelijk Museum, Amsterdam (drawings) 67,
Museum of Modern Art, Munich 69, Berlin Festival,
Sonnabend Gallery, N.Y., and Whitney Museum of
American Art, N.Y. 70; exhbn. of Designs for *A Mid-
summer Night's Dream*, Museum of Modern Art, N.Y.
67; has participated in numerous group exhbns. in-
cluding *Painting and Sculpture of a Decade*, Tate
Gallery, London 64, Venice Biennale 64, *A Decade of
American Drawings* 65, *Young America* 65, and *Art of
the United States 1670-1966* 66 (all three at Whitney
Museum of American Art), U.S. Pavilion, *Expo 67*,
Montreal, and Hayward Gallery, London 69; work
appears in many public collections including Guggenheim Museum, Moderna Museet, Stockholm, Museum
of Modern Art, N.Y., Dallas Museum of Fine Arts,
Tate Gallery, and Whitney Museum of Modern Ameri-
can Art.
Publs. *Welcome Home, Lovebirds* 69 (also illustrator);
co-author and illustrator *The Adventures of Mr. and
Mrs. Jim & Ron* 70.
c/o Sonnabend Gallery, 924 Madison Avenue, New York
City, N.Y. 10021, U.S.A.

Dimechkié, Nadim, B.A., M.A.; Lebanese diplomatist;
b. 5 Dec. 1919, Lebanon; m. Margaret Alma Sherlock
1946; two s.; ed. American Univ. of Beirut.
Entered Ministry of Supply 43, Dir. Econ. Affairs 44;
entered Foreign Service 44; served London 44-49,
Ottawa 49-51; Dir. Econ. and Social Dept., Ministry of
Foreign Affairs 51-52; Chargé d'Affaires, Cairo 52,
Minister and Chargé d'Affaires 53-55; Minister to
Switzerland 55-57; Amb. to U.S.A. 58-62; Dir. Econ.
Affairs, Ministry of Foreign Affairs 62-66; Amb. to
U.K. 66-; awards include Ordre du Cèdre, Egyptian
Order of Ismail, Greek Order of Phoenix.
Leisure interest: swimming.
Lebanese Embassy, 21 Kensington Palace Gardens,
London, W.8, England.
Telephone: 01-229-7265.

Dimény, Dr. Imre, DR.AGR.; Hungarian agronomist
and politician; b. 3 Aug. 1922, Komolló; s. of János
Dimény and Anna Illyés; m. Erzsébet M. Buzgó 1947;
one d.
Agronomic Engineer; rural, county and ministry official
45-55; Dept. Head, later Vice-Pres. Nat. Planning
Bureau 55-62; Alt. mem. Central Cttee. and Leader
Agricultural Dept. Hungarian Socialist Workers' Party
62-66, mem. 66-; Minister of Agriculture and Food 67-
75; Rector Univ. of Horticulture, Budapest 75-.
Leisure interest: reading.
Publs. *Determinants of the power machine requirement
in domestic agriculture* 61, *Economy of mechanization in
agriculture* 72, *Agriculture and technological development* 73, *Economy of mechanization in animal husbandry*
74, *Economy of development of mechanization in agriculture* 75.
University of Horticulture, Budapest XI, Villányi ut
35-41; Home: Budapest II, Szilágyi Erzsébet Fasor 79,
Hungary.

Dimitrios I, (Dimitrios Papadopoulos); Archbishop of
Constantinople and Ecumenical Patriarch; b. 8 Sept.
1914, Istanbul; ed. Theological School of Halki,
Heybeliada-Istanbul.
Ordained Deacon 37; Ordained Priest 42; Preacher in
Edessa, Greece 37-38; Preacher, Parish of Feriköy-
Istanbul 39-45; Priest of the Orthodox Community,
Teheran 45-50; Head Priest, Feriköy 50-64; Bishop of
Elaia, Auxiliary Bishop of the Patriarch Athenagoras
in Istanbul 64-72; Metropolitan of Imvros and Tenedos
72; Archbishop of Constantinople and Ecumenical
Patriarch July 72-.
Rum Ortoks Patrikhanesi, H. Fener, Istanbul,
Turkey.
Telephone: 23-98-50; 21-19-21; 21-25-32.

Dimitriou, Nicos George, F.C.C.S.; Cypriot merchant
banker, diplomatist and politician; b. 16 July 1920;
m.; three d.; ed. Larnaca Commercial Lyceum, Greek
Gymnasium, Athens, and Maiden Erlegh Private
School, Reading, England.
Manager and Sec. N. J. Dimitriou Ltd., Merchant
Bankers 52-62, Man. Dir. 62-; Man. Dir. Larnaca Oil
Works Ltd. 63-73; Dir. several Cyprus companies; Dir.
Bank of Cyprus Ltd. 58-61; Chair. Cyprus Chamber of
Commerce 60-63; Pres. Chamber of Commerce and
Industry, Larnaca 63-68, Pezoporicos Club, Larnaca
57-68; Pres. Cyprus Soc. of Inc. Secretaries 68; Consul-
Gen. of Denmark 61-; mem. Council, Cyprus Chamber
of Commerce and Industry 63-68; Chair. Cyprus Devt.
Corpn. Ltd. 66-68; Minister of Commerce and Industry
68-70; Chair. Electricity Authority of Cyprus 70-73,
Advisory Board Nat. and Grindlays Bank Ltd. 70-73;
Amb. to U.S.A. 74-; Commdr. Order of Cedar of
Lebanon, Order of the Dannebrog (Denmark).
Leisure interests: photography, riding, swimming,
writing, golf.
Publ. *Chambers of Commerce, their objects and aims.*
Embassy of Cyprus, 2211 R Street, N.W., Washington,
D.C., U.S.A.; Artemis Avenue 39, Larnaca, Cyprus.

Dinesen, Erling; Danish trade unionist and politician;
b. 25 Feb. 1910; ed. Public School, Naestved, and
Commercial School, Naestved.
President Roskilde Branch, Commercial and Office
Employees' Union 37; Sec. Danish Commercial and
Office Employees' Union 43-45, Business Manager 45-49,
Pres. 49-63; mem. Exec. Board Danish Fed. of Trade
Unions 50-63, mem. Apprentice Council 50-63; mem.
Industrial Council of Labour Movement 50-63, Cttee.
of Productivity of Ministry of Commerce 53-63, Labour
Council 54-63, Nat. Assessment Cttee. 57-63, Cttee. of
Social-Democratic Press in Denmark 58-63, Exec. Cttee.
of Int. Fed. of Commercial, Clerical and Technical
Employees, Amsterdam 52-63; Minister of Labour

63-68, 71, 75-; mem. Exec. Board Social-Democratic Party 65-, Vice-Chair. 69-72, Chair. 72-73.
Ullasvej 3, Bagsvaerd, Denmark.
Telephone: 98-22-78.

Dingle, Herbert, D.I.C., A.R.C.S., D.SC., F.R.A.S.; British physicist; b. 2 Aug. 1890, London; *s.* of James and Emily (née Gorddard) Dingle; *m.* Alice Law (née Westacott) 1918 (died 1947); one *s.* (died 1975); ed. Plymouth Technical School and Royal Coll. of Science. Emeritus Prof. of History and Philosophy of Science, University College, London.
Publs. *Relativity for All* 22, *Modern Astrophysics* 24, Portions of *Life and Work of Sir Norman Lockyer* 28, *Science and Human Experience* 31, *Through Science to Philosophy* 37, *The Special Theory of Relativity* 40, *Mechanical Physics* 41, *Sub-atomic Physics* 42, *Science and Literary Criticism* 49, *Practical Applications of Spectrum Analysis* 50, *The Scientific Adventure* 52, *The Sources of Eddington's Philosophy* 54, (with Viscount Samuel) *A Threefold Cord* 61, *Science at the Crossroads* 72, *The Mind of Emily Brontë* 74.
104 Downs Court Road, Purley, Surrey CR2 1BD, England.
Telephone: 01-660-3581.

Dinitz, Simcha, M.SC.; Israeli diplomatist; b. 23 June 1929, Tel Aviv; *s.* of Josef and Bruria Dinitz; *m.* Vivian Dinitz 1954; two *d.* one *s.*; ed. Herzeliah High School, Tel Aviv, Univ. of Cincinnati and Georgetown Univ. School of Foreign Service.
Israel Defence Forces 48-50; Asst. to Dir. of Information Embassy of Israel, Washington 54-58; Dept. of Information, Ministry for Foreign Affairs, Jerusalem 58-61; Dir. of Bureau of Dir.-Gen. of Ministry for Foreign Affairs 61-63; Dir. of Bureau and Political Sec. to Foreign Minister 63; mem. Israel Del. to UN 63-66; Minister to Rome 66-68; Minister in charge of Information, Washington 68-69; Political Adviser to Prime Minister 69-73, also Dir.-Gen. of Prime Minister's Office 72-73; Amb. to U.S.A. 73-.
Leisure interests: music, sports, reading.
Israeli Embassy, 1621 22nd Avenue, N.W., Washington, D.C., U.S.A.; and 40 Nayot, Jerusalem, Israel.
Telephone: 32314.

Di Nola, Raffaello; Italian business executive; b. 10 Aug. 1912, Naples; *s.* of Enrico di Nola and Maria Luisa de Rosa; *m.* Liliana Carisch 1942; three *c.*; ed. Milan Univ.
Commenced career with Rumanica (chemicals firm); joined the Pirelli Group 39, subsequently became Gen. Man. and Man. Dir. and Dir. of other companies in the group; Man. Dir. Alfa Romeo S.p.A. 62-74, Vice-Pres., and Man. Dir. Alfa Romeo Alfasud S.p.A.; Pres. Alfa Romeo Int. S.A.; Pres. Spica S.p.A.; Pres. Breda Termomeccanica S.p.A.; Pres. Termosud S.p.A.; Cavaliere di Gran Croce della Repubblica Italiana.
Alfa Romeo S.p.A., Via Gattamelata 45, Milan, Italy.
Telephone: 3977.

Diori, Hamani; Niger politician; b. 16 June 1916; ed. Victor Ballot School, Dahomey, and Ecole William Ponty, Senegal.
Deputy, Niger Territory, French Nat. Assembly 46-51, 56-58; Vice-Pres. Nat. Assembly 57; Prime Minister, Republic of the Niger 58-60; Pres. of the Republic of Niger 60-74, Council of Ministers 60-74, also Minister of Foreign Affairs until 74; ousted by coup April 74; mem. Rassemblement Démocratique Africain (RDA); Chair. OCAM 67-70; fmr. Pres. Conseil d'Entente.

Diouf, Abdou, L. en D., L. ès SC.; Senegalese politician; b. 7 Sept. 1935, Louga; ed. Lycée Faidherbe, St. Louis, Dakar and Paris Univs.
Joined the Senegalese Progressive Union (U.P.S.) 61; now mem. Political Bureau and Deputy Admin. Sec. U.P.S.; Dir. of Technical Co-operation and Minister of Planning 60; Asst. Sec.-Gen. to Govt. until 61, Sec.-

Gen. 64-65; Gov. Sine-Saloum Region 61-62; Dir. de Cabinet of Pres. of Repub. 63-65; fmr. Chair. Council of Ministers Org. of Senegal River Basin States; Minister of Planning and Industry 68-70; Prime Minister Feb. 70-; mem. Parl. 73-.
Office of the Prime Minister, Dakar, Senegal.

Diplock, Baron (Life Peer), cr. 68, of Wansford; **(William John) Kenneth Diplock,** P.C.; British judge; b. 8 Dec. 1907, Croydon; *s.* of W. J. H. Diplock; *m.* Margaret S. Atcheson 1938; no *c.*; ed. Whitgift School, Univ. Coll., Oxford and Middle Temple, London.
Called to the Bar 32; King's Counsel 48; Recorder of Oxford 50-56; Judge of the High Court 56-61; Pres. Restrictive Practices Court 60-61; Lord Justice of Appeal 61-68; Lord of Appeal in Ordinary 68-; Chair. Security Comm. 71-, Inst. of Advanced Legal Studies 73; Hon. Fellow American Bar Foundation 69; Hon. LL.D. (Alberta) 72.
1 Crown Office Row, Temple, London, E.C.4; Wansford-in-England, Peterborough, England.
Telephone: 01-219-3110 (Office).

Dirac, Paul Adrien Maurice, O.M., F.R.S., B.SC., PH.D.; British physicist; b. 8 Aug. 1902; ed. Bristol, Cambridge Univ.
Fellow St. John's Coll., Cambridge; Lucasian Prof. of Mathematics, Cambridge Univ. 32-68, now Prof. Emer.; Prof. of Physics Florida State Univ. 71-; Nobel Prize for Physics 33; awarded Royal Medal of Royal Soc. for devt. of new quantum mechanics 39; Copley Medal of Royal Soc.); Dr. h.c. (Moscow Univ.).
Publ. *Principles of Quantum Mechanics* 30.
Department of Physics, Florida State University, Tallahassee, Florida 32306, U.S.A.

Dirzhinskaite-Pilyushenko, Leokadia Yuozovna; Soviet politician; b. 20 Jan. 1921, Laukis-Vilkovish, Lithuania; ed. Higher Party School.
Komsomol worker 40-51; Party worker 51-53; Sec., later First Sec. Shyaulyai City Cttee. of C.P. of Lithuania 53-61; Vice-Chair. Council of Ministers and Minister of Foreign Affairs of Lithuanian S.S.R. 61-; mem. Central Cttee. of C.P. of Lithuania; mem. C.P.S.U. 50-; Order of the Red Banner of Labour (twice).
Council of Ministers of Lithuanian S.S.R., Vilnius, U.S.S.R.

DiSalle, Michael Vincent, LL.B.; American government official; b. 6 Jan. 1908, New York; *m.* Myrtle E. England 1929; one *s.* four *d.*; ed. Georgetown Univ.
Assistant District Counsel, Home Owners' Loan Corpn. 33-35; mem. Ohio Legislature 37-38; Asst. City Law Dir. Toledo 39-41; Councilman Toledo 42-50, Vice-Mayor 44-48, Mayor 48-50; Founder and first Chair. Labour-Management-Citizens Cttee., Toledo; Dir. Office of Price Stabilisation, Washington, D.C. 50-52; nominated Democratic candidate for U.S. Senate from Ohio 52; Dir. Economic Stabilisation Agency Dec. 52-Jan. 53; Gov. of Ohio 58-62; law practice, Columbus, Ohio 63-66; Partner Chapman, DiSalle and Friedman 66-.
Leisure interests: golf, reading.
Office: Chapman, DiSalle and Friedman, Pennsylvania Building, 932 Pennsylvania Building, Washington, D.C. 20004, U.S.A.

Ditchburn, Robert William, M.A., PH.D., F.R.S., M.R.I.A.; British physicist; b. 14 Jan. 1903, Lancashire; *s.* of William and Martha Ditchburn; *m.* Doreen May Barrett 1929; one *s.* three *d.*; ed. Liverpool and Cambridge Univs.
Fellow of Trinity Coll., Dublin 28-46; Prof. of Natural Philosophy (Physics), Dublin Univ. 29-46; Principal Experimental Officer, Admiralty 42-45; Prof. of Physics, Reading Univ. 46-68, Emer. 68-; Tech. Consultant; Senior Scholar, Hooper Prize, Yeats Prize (Trinity Coll., Cambridge); Isaac Newton Student, Cambridge Univ.

Leisure interests: music, the social implications of science.

Publs. *Light* 52 (revised 63, 76); *Eye-Movements and Visual Perception* 73.

9 Summerfield Rise, Goring, Reading, RG8 0DS, England.

Telephone: Goring 3470.

Diwakar, Ranganath, LL.B., M.A.; Indian author and politician; b. 30 Sept. 1894, Dharwar; s. of Rama-chandra and Sita Diwakar; m. Radha Diwakar 1918; one s.; ed. Bombay Univ.

Teacher and Prof. of English 16-20; founded *Karmaveer* (Kannada weekly paper) 21, editor until 30, now sole trustee of People's Education Trust, Hubli, controlling *Karmaveer* and *Samyukta Karnatak* (Kannada daily paper) and *Kasturi* (monthly Kannada digest); Pres. Karnatak Provincial Congress Cttee. 30-34; mem. Constituent Assembly 46; Min. of Information and Broadcasting 48-52; Gov. of Bihar 52-57; Chair. Gandhi Smarak Nidhi 57-, and Peace Foundation, New Delhi 59-; imprisoned for sedition (during freedom movement) 21-23, 24-26, 30-32, 40, 44; mem. Rajya Sabha 62-69.

Leisure interests: reading, writing, swimming, walking, gardening.

Publs. In English: *Glimpses of Gandhiji* 49, *Satyagraha in Action* 49, *Upanishads in Story and Dialogue* 50, *Satyagraha—Pathway to Peace* 50, *Mahayogi* (biography of Aurobindo Ghose), *Saga of Satyagraha* 70, and 20 books in Kannada and Hindi on religion, philosophy, and other subjects.

c/o Sri Arvind Krupa, 233 Sadashiv Nagar, Bangalore 560006, Karnataka, India.

Dixey, Sir Frank, K.C.M.G., O.B.E., D.SC., F.R.S., F.G.S., F.R.G.S.; British geologist; b. 7 April 1892; ed. Univ. of Wales.

Lecturer in Geology, Univ. of Wales 14-15; mil. service, R.G.A., Western Front 15-18; Govt. Geologist, Sierra Leone 18-21; Dir. Geological Survey of Nyasaland 21-39; Dir. Water Development Dept. Northern Rhodesia 39-44; Dir. Geological Survey, Nigeria 44-47; Geological Adviser to Colonial Sec. and Dir. of Overseas Geological Surveys 47-59; Murchison Medal, Geological Society, London; Draper Medal, Geological Society, S. Africa; Hon. mem. Geological Society, Belgium and Geological Soc. South Africa; Hon. M.I.M.M.

Publ. *Practical Handbook of Water Supply, London,* and papers on geology, mineral resources, and geomorphology of African territories.

Woodpecker Cottage, Bramber, Sussex, England.

Telephone: Steyning 81-2313.

Dixey, Paul Arthur Groser; British underwriter; b. 13 April 1915, Herts.; s. of the late Neville Dixey and Marguerite Groser; m. Mary Margaret Baring 1939; one d. four s.; ed. Stowe School and Trinity Coll., Cambridge Univ.

Served Royal Artillery, 39-45; mem. London Insurance Market Del. to Indonesia 58; mem. Dunmow R.D.C. 58-64, Cttee. of Lloyd's Underwriters' Asscn. 62-, Cttee. of Salvage Asscn. 62- (Chair. 64-65), Cttee. of Lloyd's 64-70, 72-, Gen. Cttee. Lloyd's Register of Shipping 64-; Deputy Chair. of Lloyd's 67, 69, 72, Chair. 73, 74; mem. Council, Morley Coll. 52-62; Chair. Govs., Vinehall School 66-73.

Leisure interests: riding, fly-fishing.

Easton Glebe, Little Easton, near Great Dunmow, Essex, England.

Telephone: Great Dunmow 2840.

Dixon, Frank James; American medical scientist; b. 9 March 1920, St. Paul, Minnesota; s. of Frank James and Rose Augusta (Kuhfield) Dixon; m. Marion Edwards 1946; two s. one d.; ed. Univ. of Minnesota, U.S. Naval Hospital, Great Lakes, Ill.

Research Asst., Dept. of Pathology, Harvard Medical School, 46-48; Instructor, Dept. of Pathology, Washington Univ. Medical School 48-50; Asst. Prof. Dept. of Pathology 50-51; Prof. and Chair. Dept. of Pathology, Univ. of Pittsburgh School of Medicine 51-61. Chair. Biomedical Research Depts. 70-74; Chair. Dept. of Experimental Pathology, Scripps Clinic and Research Foundation 61-74, Dir. 74-; Prof. in Residence, Dept. of Pathology, Univ. of California at San Diego 68-; mem. National Acad. of Sciences, Asscn. Amer. Physicians; Harvey Society Lecturer 62; Theobald Smith Award in Medical Sciences from AAAS 52, Parke-Davis Award from the American Society for Experimental Pathology 57, Award for Distinguished Achievement from Modern Medicine 61, Martin E. Rehfuss Award in Internal Medicine 66, Von Pirquet Medal from Annual Forum on Allergy 67, Bunim Gold Medal from the American Rheumatism Asscn. 68, Mayo Soley Award from the Western Society for Clinical Research 69, Gairdner Foundation Award 69.

Publs. Co-editor *Advances in Immunology, Tumors of the Male Genital System, Atlas of Tumor Pathology* (Section VIII—Fascicle 32, Armed Forces Institute of Pathology) 52; and 300 papers.

Office: Scripps Clinic and Research Foundation, 476 Prospect Street, La Jolla, California 92037; Home: 2355 Avenida de la Playa La Jolla, California, 92037, U.S.A.

Telephone: 714-459-2390, Ext. 365 (Office).

Dixon, Thomas F., B.S.ENG., B.S. and M.S. CHEM.ENG., M.S.AERO.ENG.; American executive and aerospace engineer; b.15 March 1916;ed. Vanderbilt and Michigan Univs., and California Inst. of Technology.

Research Engineer, N. American Aviation 46-54, Dir. Propulsion Center, Rocketdyne Div. N. American Aviation 54-55, Chief Engineer 55-60, Vice-Pres. Research and Engineering 60-63, Vice-Pres. 63-; Dep. Assoc. Administrator Nat. Aeronautics and Space Admin. 61-63; Chair. of the Board, Airtronics Inc. 68-74; Exec. Vice-Pres. Teledyne McCormick Selph 75; Fellow, Amer. Rocket Soc., Amer. Inst. Aeronautics and Astronautics; Robert M. Goddard Memorial Award 57; shared Louis W. Hill Space Transportation Award 61.

Teledyne McCormick Selph, 3601 Union Road, Hollister, Calif. 9502, U.S.A.

Telephone: 408-637-3731.

Diz, Adolfo Cesar, C.P.A., D.ECON., M.A., D.PHIL.; Argentine economist; b. 12 May 1931, Buenos Aires; s. of Agustín Diz and Elisa Aristizábal; m. Martha Solari 1959; four s.; ed. Univ. de Buenos Aires and Univ. of Chicago.

Instructor of Statistics, Univ. of Buenos Aires 51-55, 58-59; Prof. of Statistics, Univ. of Tucumán 59-60, Dir. Inst. of Econ. Research 59-65, Prof. of Statistics and Econometrics 60-61, 64, Prof. of Monetary Theory 62, 65-66; Exec. Dir. Int. Monetary Fund (IMF) 66-68; Envoy extraordinary and Minister plenipotentiary, Argentine Financial Rep. in Europe 69-; mem. of Argentine socs. and of Directive Cttee., Argentine Branch, Inst. of Applied Econ. Science, Paris, American Econ. Asscn. and Econometric Soc.

Publs. *Money and Prices in Argentina 35-62, Varieties of Monetary Experience,* and numerous economic articles.

Argentine Financial Representative in Europe, 93 rue de la Servette, Geneva; Home: Villa 7, Chemin de la Fin, Commugny (Vaud), Switzerland.

Telephone: (022)-34-45-85 (Office); (022)-76-11-77 (Home).

Djerassi, Carl, A.B., PH.D.; American chemist; b. 29 Oct. 1923, Vienna; s. of Dr. Samuel Djerassi and Dr. Alice Friedmann; m. Norma Lundholm; one s. one d.; ed. Kenyon Coll. and Univ. of Wisconsin.

Research Chemist, Ciba Pharmaceutical Co., Summit;

N.J. 42-43, 45-49; Assoc. Dir. of Research, Syntex, S.A., Mexico City 49-51, Research Vice-Pres. 57-60, Pres. Syntex Research 68-72; Assoc. Prof. of Chemistry Wayne State Univ., Detroit 52-54, Prof. 54-59, Stanford Univ. 59-; Chair. of the Board Synvar Associates 66-; Pres. and Chair. of the Board Zoecon Corp. 68-; Dir. Cetus Corpn. 72-; British Chemical Soc. Centenary Lecturer 64; Royal Swedish Acad. of Engineering Sciences thirteenth Chemical Lecturer 69; Swedish Pharmaceutical Soc. Scheele Lecturer 72; mem. Editorial Board *Journal of the American Chemical Society* 68-, *Journal of Organic Chemistry* 55-58, *Tetrahedron* 58-, *Steroids* 63-, *Proceedings* of Nat. Acad. of Sciences 64-70; mem. Nat. Acad. of Sciences Board on Science and Technology for Int. Devt 67-, Chair. 72-; mem. American Pugwash Cttee. 67-; mem. Nat. Acad. of Sciences, Brazilian Acad. of Sciences, American Acad. of Arts and Sciences; Foreign mem. German Acad. of Natural Scientists (Leopoldina), Royal Swedish Acad. of Sciences 73; Hon. Fellow, British Chemical Soc. 68, Amer. Acad. of Pharmaceutical Science; Hon. D.Sc., Nat. Univ. of Mexico, Kenyon Coll., Ohio, Fed. Univ. of Rio de Janeiro, Worcester Polytechnic Inst. and Wayne State Univ.; Award in Pure Chemistry 58, Baekeland Medal 59, Fritzche Medal 60, Creative Invention Award 73, Amer. Chemical Soc.; Intra-Science Research Award 69, Freedman Foundation Patent Award 71, Chemical Pioneer Award 73, Perkin Medal 75, Amer. Inst. of Chemists; Nat. of Medal Science 73.

Leisure interests: cattle ranching, skiing.

Publs. (author or co-author) over 800 articles and *Optical Rotatory Dispersion* 60, *Steroid Reactions* 63, *Interpretation of Mass Spectra of Organic Compounds* 64, *Structure Elucidation of Natural Products by Mass Spectrometry* (2 vols.) 64, *Mass Spectrometry of Organic Compounds* 67.

Department of Chemistry, Stanford University, Calif. 94305, U.S.A.

Djilas, Milovan; Yugoslav writer and politician; b. 1911; ed. Belgrade Univ.

Member Communist Party 32, imprisoned 32-35; mem. Central Cttee. Communist Party 38, Politburo 40; successively Minister, Head of Parliament, Vice-Pres. of Yugoslavia until 54; expelled from Communist Party 54; imprisoned 56-61, May 62-Dec. 66; 1969 Freedom Award (U.S.) 68.

Publs. *Essays 1941-46* 47, *Struggle of the Communist Party of Yugoslavia* 48, *On National History as an Educational Subject* 49, *Lenin and the Relations Between Socialist States* 50, *On New Roads to Socialism* 50, *Reflections on Various Questions* 51, *On the Aggressive Pressure of the Soviet Bloc against Yugoslavia* 51, *The Legend of Njegoš* 52, *The New Class* 57; in English: *Land without Justice* (autobiography vol. 1) 58, *Montenegro* 64, *The Leper* 65, *The Unperfect Society: Beyond the New Class* 69, *Memoir of a Revolutionary* (autobiography vol. 2) 73.

Belgrade, Yugoslavia.

Djojohadikoesoemo, Soemitro; Indonesian politician; b. 29 May 1917, Kebumen, Central Java; ed. Econ. Univ., Rotterdam and the Sorbonne, Paris.

Assistant to Prime Minister of Indonesia 46; Pres. Indonesian Banking Corpn. 47; Chargé d'Affaires, Washington, D.C. 49-50; Minister of Econ. Affairs 50-51; Minister of Finance 52-53, 55-56; Prof. and Dean, Faculty of Econs., Univ. of Indonesia, Jakarta 51-57; left the country after the PRRI/Permesta armed rebellion 58; Minister of Trade 68-73; Minister of State for Research 73-.

Ministry of State for Research, Jakarta, Indonesia.

Dlamini, Hon. Kanyakwezwe Henry; Swazi politician; b. Manzini District; *m.*; eight *c.*; ed. Matsapha Nat. School and in Cape Province.

Agricultural Demonstrator 49; Rural Devt. Officer 60-64; studied advanced agricultural techniques in Taiwan 64-65; Extension Officer, Swaziland Milling Co., Manzini 65; mem. House of Assembly 67-; Minister of Foreign Affairs 71-72, of Establishments and Training 72-73, for Civil Service 73-; del. to UN Gen. Assembly, OAU and other int. confs.

Ministry for the Civil Service, Mbabane, Swaziland.

Dlamini, Rt. Hon. Prince Makhosini, LL.D.; Swazi politician; b. 1914, Enkhungwini; *s.* of Prince Majozi Inkhosikati Lasimelane; *m.*; ten *c.*; ed. Franson Christian Memorial School, Swazi National School, Matsapa, and Umphumulo Training Inst., Natal.

Headmaster, Bethel Mission School 39; teacher, Franson Christian High School 41-42, Matsapa Swazi Nat. High School 43-46; Principal, Swazi Nat. High School, Lobamba 46-47; Chair. Hlatikulu Branch, Swaziland Teachers' Asscn., Sec.-Gen. Swaziland Teachers' Asscn.; mem. Swazi Nat. Council 47; Rural Devt. Officer 49-62; Chief of Enkungwini 50; acted as Sec. to Swazi Nation several times 50-; studied in Europe 59-60; Leader Imbokodvo Nat. Movement 64-; mem. Swazi Legislative Council 64-67; mem. self-govt. Cttee. 65-66; led del. to Independence Conf., London 68, to Land Alienation Talks 68; Prime Minister April 67-; Grand Commdr., Order of the Niger 70; Nat. Security Merit First Class (S. Korea) 71; Nat. Order of the Brilliant Star (China) 71.

Leisure interests: reading, farming, politics.

Office of the Prime Minister, Box 395, Mbabane, Swaziland.

Telephone: 2251.

Doan, Charles Austin, B.S., M.D., SC.D. (HON.), M.A.C.P.; American physician; b. 5 June 1896; ed. Hiram Coll., Johns Hopkins Medical School, Univ. of Cincinnati and Harvard Medical School.

Assistant, Dept. of Anatomy, Johns Hopkins Medical School 24; Asst., Dept. of Medicine, Harvard Medical School; Asst. Physician, Boston City Hospital and Asst., Thorndike Memorial Laboratory 25; Assoc. in Medical Research, Rockefeller Inst. for Medical Research 25-30; Prof. of Medicine and Dir., Dept. of Medical and Surgical Research, Ohio State Univ. 30-36; Chair. and Prof. Dept. of Medicine and Dir. of Medical Research 36-44; Dean, Coll. of Medicine, Dir. Univ. Health Centre, Ohio State Univ. 44-61, Prof. of Medicine and Dir. Medical Research 44-61, Dir. Division of Hematology, Dept. of Medicine, Coll. of Medicine; Pres. American Soc. of Hematology 62-63; Pres. Ohio Public Health Asscn. 38-40; Dir.-at-large, Nat. Tuberculosis Asscn., Medical Dir. Columbus Cancer Clinic 47, mem. Asscn. American Physicians, American Society for Experimental Pathology, American Asscn. for Advancement of Science; Gov. for Ohio of F.A.C.P.; Chair. Board of Govs., Vice-Pres. M.A.C.P. 57-59; A.M.A. Dist. Service Citation, Gold Medal Award 60.

Home: 4935 Olentangy Boulevard; Office: 3600 Olentangy River Road, Columbus, Ohio, U.S.A.

Doan, Herbert D., B.CH.E.; American chemical executive; b. 5 Sept. 1922, Midland, Mich.; *s.* of Leland and Ruth Doan; two *s.* two *d.*; ed. Cornell Univ.

Manager, Chemicals Dept., Dow Chemical Co. 56-60, Exec. Vice-Pres. Dow Chemical Co. 60-62, Pres. 62-71, now Dir.; Partner Doan Assocs.; Chair. Doan Resources Corpn.; Dir. Chemical Bank and Trust Co., Midland, Mich., Centennial Corpn., Dow Corning Corpn.; Pres. Mich. Foundation for Advanced Research; Incorporator, Neurosciences Research Foundation, Brookline, Mass.; Trustee, Dow Foundation; mem. Amer. Inst. of Chemical Engineers, Cornell Univ. Engineering Coll. Council, Amer. Chem. Soc., Board of Fellows Saginaw Valley Coll., Advisory Council of Michigan State Univ., Graduate School of Business

Admin., East Lansing, Mich., Advisory Board, Dept. of Chemical Eng., Univ. of Calif. Berkeley.
Leisure interests: skiing, sailing, reading.
Doan Associates, 110 E. Grove Street, Midland, Michigan 48640; Home: 3801 Valley Drive, Midland, Mich. 48640, U.S.A.
Telephone: (517) 631-2471 (Office).

Dobb, Maurice Herbert, M.A., PH.D., F.B.A.; British economist; b. 1900, London; s. of Walter Herbert Dobb and Annie Elsie Moir; m. Barbara Marian Nixon 1931; ed. Charterhouse and Pembroke Coll., Cambridge. Research Student London School of Economics 22-24; Lecturer in Economics in Cambridge Univ. 26 and Lecturer and Fellow of Trinity Coll. 48; Visiting Lecturer (Russian Economic and Social History) Univ. of London School of Slavonic Studies 43-46; Visiting Prof. Univ. of Delhi School of Economics 51; Reader in Econs., Cambridge Univ. 59-67, Emeritus Reader 67-; Alfred Marshall Lecturer, Cambridge Univ. 73; Hon. Dr.Econ.Sc. (Charles Univ., Prague) 64, Hon. D.Litt. (Univ. of Leicester) 72.
Leisure interests: reading, music, walking.
Publs. Wages 28, *Political Economy and Capitalism* 37, 40, *Studies in the Development of Capitalism* 46, *Soviet Economic Development since 1917* 47, 67, *Economic Theory and Socialism, Collected Papers* 55, *An Essay on Economic Growth and Planning* 60, *Papers on Capitalism, Development and Planning* 67, *Welfare Economics and the Economics of Socialism* 69, *Theories of Value and Distribution since Adam Smith* 73; collaborated in editing Royal Econ. Soc.'s edn. *Works and Correspondence of David Ricardo* 48-54.
Trinity College, Cambridge, and College Farmhouse, Fulbourn, Cambridgeshire, England.
Telephone: Cambridge 58201 (College).

Dobbs, Mattiwilda; American singer; ed. Spelman Coll., Atlanta, and Columbia Univ.
Studied with Lotte Leonard 46-50; Marian Anderson scholarship, soloist at Mexico Univ. Festival 47; studied at Mannes Music School and Berkshire Music Center 48, with Pierre Bernac, Paris 50-52; 1st Voice Prize, Geneva Int. Competition 51; concert tour Netherlands, France and Sweden 52; debut La Scala (Milan) in *L'Italiana in Algeri* 53; sang at Glyndebourne 53, 54, 56, 61, Royal Opera House, Covent Garden (London) 54, 55, 56, 59, San Francisco Opera 55, Metropolitan Opera (New York) 56-; Stockholm Royal Opera 57-; Hamburg State Opera 61-63; concert appearances in Europe, U.S.A., Mexico, Israel, Australia, New Zealand and U.S.S.R.; Order of the North Star (Sweden).
Vastmannagatan 50, Stockholm, Sweden.
Telephone: 34-83-00.

Dobles Sánchez, Lic. Luis; Costa Rican diplomatist; b. 1925; m.; five c.; ed. McDonogh School, Baltimore, U.S.A., and Univ. of Calif.
Secretary, Costa Rican Legation, Paris 48; Chargé d'Affaires, Rio de Janeiro 49-51; Dir. of Protocol, Ministry of Foreign Affairs 51-53; Amb. to Brazil 53-55; Man. Dir. Coffee Office, Costa Rica 58-60; Amb. to Peru 60-62, to Bolivia 61-62, to France 75-; Vice-Minister, Ministry of Foreign Affairs 66-68; Perm. Rep. to UN 68-70; Pres. Corpn. Euro-Costarricense S.A. (COERSA).
P.O. Box 1518, San José, Costa Rica.

Dobozy, Imre; Hungarian writer; b. 30 Oct. 1917, Vál; s. of Dániel Dobozy and Ilona Kukucska; m. Ilona Horvát 1939; one s. one d.
General Sec., Asscn. of Hungarian Writers; Kossuth Prize; Labour Order of Merit Golden Degree 70.
Leisure interest: travel.
Publs. *New Seed in Cumenia* (novel), *Spring Wind*

(short story), *Storm* (play and film), *Continuation Tomorrow* (play), films: *Yesterday, Dawn, The Song of the Swain, Corporal and the Others, Eljött a Tavasz* (Spring has Come) 68.
Hungarian Writers' Asscn., H-1062 Budapest VI, Bajza u. 18, Hungary.
Telephone: 201-013.

Dobrynin, Anatoly Fedorovich, M.SC.; Soviet diplomatist; b. 16 Nov. 1919, Krasnaya Gorka; ed. technical coll.
Engineer at aircraft plant, Second World War; joined diplomatic service 44; Counsellor, later Minister-Counsellor, Soviet Embassy, Washington 52-55; Asst. Deputy Minister of Foreign Affairs 55-57; Under-Sec.-Gen. for Political and Security Council Affairs UN 57-60, Head American Dept., U.S.S.R. Ministry of Foreign Affairs 60-61; Amb. to U.S.A. 62-; Alt. mem., C.P.S.U. Central Cttee. 66-71, mem. 71-.
Embassy of the U.S.S.R., 1125 16th Street, N.W., Washington, D.C. 20036, U.S.A.

Dobrzański, Dr. Bohdan; Polish soil scientist; b. 3 March 1909, Strutynka; ed. Lwów Polytechnic.
Docent 39-50, Assoc. Prof. 50-56, Prof. 56-; Corresp. mem. Polish Acad. of Sciences 60-69, mem. 69-, Presidium mem. 66-68, Deputy Sec. 69-71, Sec. Dept. V 72-; Chair. Establishment for Protection of Environment of Industrial Regions; Prof. Higher School of Agriculture 46-69; Dir. Inst. of Soil Science and Rural Chem., Agricultural Acad., Warsaw 69-; Editor-in-Chief *Polish Journal of Soil Science*; mem. Int. Soc. of Soil Science; Vice-Chair. FAO Working Party on Soil Classification and Survey; foreign mem. All-Union V. I. Lenin Acad. of Agricultural Sciences, Moscow; Dr. h.c. (Higher School of Agriculture, Lublin); Knight's Cross, Order of Polonia Restituta 52, Officer's Cross 54, Commdr.'s Cross 72; Medal of 30th Anniversary of People's Poland 74.
Publs. *Gleby i ich wartosc użytkowa* (Soils and their Usefulness) 61, *Zarys geografii gleb* (Outline of Geography of Soils) 66, *Gleboznawstwo* (Soil Science) 66; many articles, some in English.
Ul. Marszałkowska 84/92 m. 111, 00-514 Warsaw, Poland.

Dobson, Sir Richard Portway, Kt., M.A.; British business executive; b. 11 Feb. 1914, Bristol; s. of Prof. J. F. Dobson and Dina Portway; m. E. M. Carver (née Herridge) 1946; one d.; ed. Clifton Coll., Bristol and King's Coll., Cambridge.
Joined British-American Tobacco 35, appointments in China 36-40, 46-50; served R.A.F. 41-45; Dir. British-American Tobacco 55, Deputy Chair. 62, Vice-Chair. 68-70, Chair. 70-76, Pres. April 76-; Chair. British Leyland Ltd. April 76-; Dir. Tobacco Securities Trust Co., Chair. 76-; Dir. Commonwealth Devt. Finance Co. Ltd. 74, SIFIDA Investment Co. S.A. 74, Exxon Corpn. 75, Lloyds Bank Int. 76-, etc.
Leisure interests: golf, fishing.
British Leyland Ltd., Leyland House, 174 Marylebone Road, London, NW1 5AA; 16 Marchmont Road, Richmond, Surrey, England.
Telephone: 01-486 6000 (Office); 01-940-1504 (Home).

Dobson, William Arthur Charles Harvey, M.A., D.LITT., F.R.S.C.; Canadian sinologist; b. 8 Aug. 1913, London; two s.; ed. Christ Church, Oxford.
Service with Argyll and Sutherland Highlanders, rising to rank of Lieut.-Col. 40-45; lecturer in Chinese, Oxford Univ. 48-52; Prof. of Chinese, Toronto Univ. 52-, Head, Dept. of East Asian Studies 52-64; Order of Cloud and Banner, Fifth Class (China), Canada Council Molson Prize.
Publ. *Civilisations of the Orient* 55, *Late Archaic Chinese* (grammar) 59, *Early Archaic Chinese* 62, *Mencius* 63, *Late Han Chinese* 64 *The Language of the*

Book of Songs 67, *A Dictionary of the Chinese Particles* 74.
47 Queen's Park Crescent East, University of Toronto, Toronto M5S 2C3, Ontario, Canada.
Telephone: 928-2902.

Docking, Robert; American banker and politician; b. 9 Oct. 1925, Missouri; *s.* of George Docking and Mary Virginia Blackwell; *m.* Meredith Gear 1950; two *s.*; ed. Univ. of Kansas and Graduate School of Banking, Univ. of Wisconsin.
With Union State Bank, Arkansas City, Kansas 56-59, Pres. 59-; Mayor of Arkansas City 63-66; Gov. of Kansas 67-74; mem. Amer. Asscn. of Criminology; fmr. Chair. of Interstate Oil Compact Comm. 69; State Co-Chair. of the Ozarks Regional Comm. 69; fmr. Chair. American Red Cross; Fmr. Pres. Arkansas City Chamber of Commerce; mem. American and Kan. Bankers' Asscns., Ind. Oil and Gas Asscn. and numerous other nat. and regional socs.; Fellow, Harry Truman Library Inst. for Nat. and Int. Affairs; Democrat; Hon. LL.D. (Benedictine Coll.) 73.
925 North 2nd Street, Arkansas City, Kan., U.S.A.

Dodd, Edwin Dillon; American business executive; b. 26 Jan. 1919, Point Pleasant, W. Va.; *s.* of David Rollin and Mary G. (Dillon) Dodd; *m.* Marie Marshall 1942; one *d.*; ed. Upper Arlington High School, Columbus, O., Ohio State Univ. and Harvard Graduate School of Business Admin.
Joined Owens-Illinois Inc. 46, Dir. of Public Relations 49, Production Man. Libbey Glass Div. 54, Factories Man. 56; joined Forest Products Group 58, Gen. Man. 61; Vice-Pres. Owens-Illinois Inc. 59, Exec. Vice-Pres. 64, Dir. 66, Pres. 68-, Chief Operating Officer 68-72, Chief Exec. Officer 72-; Dir. Ohio Bell Telephone Co., Nat. Petro-Chemicals Corpn., Goodyear Tire and Rubber Co., Toledo Trust Co.; Distinguished Citizens Award; Legion of Merit; Military Medal (Philippines Govt.).
Leisure interests: fishing, hunting, golf.
Owens-Illinois Inc., P.O. Box 1035, Toledo, Ohio 43666. Home: 5029 Corey Road, Toledo, Ohio 43623, U.S.A.
Telephone: 419-242-6543 (Office); 419-882-2669 (Home).

Dodds, Eric Robertson, M.A., F.B.A.; British classical scholar; b. 26 July 1893, Banbridge, N. Ireland; *m.* Annie Edwards Powell 1923; ed. Campbell Coll., Belfast, and Univ. Coll., Oxford.
Lecturer in Classics Univ. Coll. Reading 19-24; Prof. of Greek, Birmingham Univ. 24-36; Regius Prof. of Greek, Oxford Univ. 36-60; Sather Visiting Prof. Univ. of Calif. 49; Pres. Classical Asscn. 63; corresp. mem. Bavarian Acad.; mem. Inst. Français; Hon. mem. American Acad. of Arts and Sciences; Hon. D.Litt. (Manchester, Belfast, Edinburgh and Birmingham); Hon. Litt.D. (Dublin Univ.); Hon. Fellow, Univ. Coll., Oxford; Hon. Student, Christ Church, Oxford.
Leisure interest: psychical research.
Publs. *Select Passages Illustrative of Neoplatonism* 23 and 24, *Thirty-two Poems* 29, *Proclus' Elements of Theology* 33, *Journal and Letters of Stephen MacKenna* 36, *Euripides' Bacchae* 44, *The Greeks and the Irrational* 51, *Plato's Gorgias* 59, *Pagan and Christian in an age of Anxiety* 65, *The Ancient Concept of Progress and other Essays* 73.
Cromwell's House, Old Marston, Oxford, England.
Telephone: Oxford 41024.

Dodds, Harold Willis, A.M., PH.D., LL.D., LITT.D.; American educationist; b. 28 June 1889; ed. Princeton and Pennsylvania Univs.
Instructor Purdue Univ. 14-16; Asst. Prof. Western Reserve Univ. 19-20; Prof. of Politics Princeton Univ. 27-34 and Pres. 33-57; Electoral Adviser to Nicaraguan Govt. 22-24; Trustee, Union Theological Seminary, Danforth Foundation; mem. American Philosophical Soc.;

Technical Adviser to Pres. Tacna-Africa Plebiscitary Comm. 25-26; Chief Adviser to Pres. Nat. Board o Elections of Nicaragua 28; Consultant in Election Law and Procedure, Cuban Govt. 35; Chair. American Dele gation, Anglo-American Conf. on Refugee Problem Bermuda 43; Chair. President's Comm. on Integration of Govt. Medical Services 45; mem. President's Advisory Comm. on Universal Training 47; Chair. Task Force on Personnel, 2nd Hoover Comm. 54-55.
Publs. *Out of this Nettle . . . Danger* 43, *The Academic President—Educator or Caretaker?* 62.
87 College Road West, Princeton, N.J., U.S.A.

Dodge, Cleveland E., A.B., LL.D., PH.D.; American company director and executive; b. 5 Feb. 1888; ed. Princeton, New York and Columbia Univs.
Phelps Dodge Corpn. 10-, Vice-Pres. 24-61, now Hon. Dir.; Officer First World War 17-19; Pres. YMCA New York City 25-35, Mining and Metallurgical Society of America 37, and Woodrow Wilson Foundation 50; Alumni Trustee, Princeton Univ. 41-45; Dir. Emeritus Int. House, New York City, Int. Cttee. YMCA; Board of Trustees, Teachers' Coll., Columbia Univ.; Dir. Near East Foundation, Council of Churches, City of New York; Hon. Trustee, American Museum of Natural History; Trustee, Grant Foundation; Dir. Atlantic Mutual Insurance Co.; Grand Commdr. Order of George I of Greece; Order of Homayoun (Iran).
Dodgewood Road, Riverdale, New York City, N.Y. 10471; Office: 641 Lexington Avenue, New York, N.Y. 10022, U.S.A.

Dodge, John Vilas; American editor; b. 25 Sept. 1909, Chicago; *s.* of George Dodge and Helen Porter; *m.* Jean Plate 1935; two *s.* two *d.*; ed. Northwestern Univ., Illinois and Univ. of Bordeaux.
Freelance writer 31-32; Editor *Northwestern University Alumni News*, and Official Publications of Northwestern Univ. 32-35; Exec. Sec. Northwestern Univ. Alumni Asscn. 37-38; Asst. Editor *Encyclopaedia Britannica*, and Assoc. Editor *Britannica Book of the Year* 38-43, Assoc. Editor *Ten Eventful Years* (4 vol. History 37-46) 47; Asst. Editor *Encyclopaedia Britannica* 46-50, Man. Editor 50-60, Exec. Editor 60-64, Senior Vice-Pres. Editorial 64-65, Senior Editorial Consultant 65-70, 72-; Editor *Britannica World Language Dictionary* 54; Editorial Adviser *Encyclopaedia Universalis* (Paris) 68-.
Office: 425 N. Michigan Avenue, Chicago, Illinois 60611; Home: 1499 Shermer Road, Northbrook, Illinois 60062, U.S.A.
Telephone: 312-321-7183 (Office); 312-272-0254 (Home).

Doell, Richard Rayman, PH.D.; American geophysicist; b. 28 June 1923, Oakland, Calif.; *s.* of Raymond A. and Mabel L. Doell; *m.* Ruth G. Jones 1950; two *d.*; ed. Univ. of Calif. (Berkeley).
Assistant Prof. of Geophysics, Massachusetts Inst. of Technology (M.I.T.) 56-59; Geophysicist U.S. Geological Survey 59-; mem. Nat. Acad. of Sciences.
Leisure interests: sailing, hiking.
Publs. *Paleomagnetism* 61, *Geomagnetic reversals* 63, *History of the geomagnetic field* 69.
U.S. Geological Survey, 345 Middlefield Road, Menlo Park, Calif. 94025, U.S.A.
Telephone: 415-325-6761, ext. 434.

Doerflinger, Raymond, L. EN D., D. ÈS SC.; French international navigation official; b. 17 May 1929, Nlivange/Moselle; *m.*; one *c.*; ed. Univ. of Nancy.
Assistant in Econ. Sciences, Univ. of Nancy; Sec. Council of European Communities; Asst. Sec.-Gen. Cen. Comm. for Navigation of the Rhine, Sec.-Gen. Jan. 70-.
Central Commission for the Navigation of the Rhine, Palais du Rhin, Strasbourg, France.
Telephone: 32-35-84.

Doering, William von Eggers, PH.D.; American professor of chemistry; b. 22 June 1917, Fort Worth, Tex.; s. of Carl Rupp Doering and Antoinette Mathilde von Eggers; m. 1st Ruth Haines 1947 (divorced 1954), two s. one d.; m. 2nd Sarah Cowles 1969; ed. Shady Hill School, Cambridge, Mass., Belmont Hill School, Belmont, Mass. and Harvard Univ.

With Office of Scientific Research and Devt. 41, Nat. Defense Research Cttee. 42, Polaroid Corpn. 43 (all in Cambridge, Mass.); Instructor, Columbia Univ. 43-45, Asst. Prof. 45-48, Assoc. Prof. 48-52; Prof. Yale Univ. 52-56, Whitehead Prof. of Chem. 56-67; Prof. Harvard Univ. 67-68, Mallinckrodt Prof. of Chem. 68-; Consultant Upjohn Co. 56-; Chair. Council for a Livable World, Washington, D.C. 64-73, Pres. 73-; mem. Nat. Acad. of Sciences, Amer. Acad. of Arts and Sciences; John Scott Award 45, Amer. Chem. Soc. Award in Pure Chem. 53, A. W. von Hoffman Medal (Gesellschaft Deutscher Chemiker) 62, and other awards from Amer. Chem. Soc.; Hon. D.Sc. (Texas Christian Univ.).
Leisure interests: music, theatre, tennis, hiking.
Publs. *Quinine* 44, *Tropolone* 50, *Tropylium Ion* 54, *Carbenes* 54, *Bullvalene* 62, *Thermal Rearrangements* 66.
Harvard University Dept. of Chemistry, 12 Oxford Street, Cambridge, Mass. 02138; Home: 53 Francis Avenue, Cambridge, Mass. 02138, U.S.A.

Dogramaci, Ihsan, M.D., LL.D., F.R.C.P., F.A.A.P.; Turkish pediatrician and educator; b. 3 April 1915, Erbil; s. of Ali Dogramaci and Ismet Kirdar; m. Ayser Hikmet Suleyman 1942; two s. one d.; ed. Istanbul and Wash. Univs.
Assistant Prof. of Pediatrics, Ankara Univ. 47-49, Assoc. Prof. 49-54, Prof. and Head of Dept. 54-63; Dir. Research Inst. of Child Health, Ankara 58-; Prof. of Pediatrics and Head of Dept., Hacettepe Faculty of Medicine 63-, Dean of Faculty June 63-Nov. 63; Pres. Ankara Univ. 63-65; Pres. Hacettepe Medical Centre, Ankara 65-; Rector, Hacettepe Univ. 67-; mem. UNICEF Exec. Board 60-, Chair. 67-70; Pres. Int. Pediatric Asscn. 68-; Pres. Union of Middle-Eastern and Mediterranean Pediatric Socs. 71-73; mem. of Standing Conf. of Rectors and Vice-Chancellors of the European Univs. 69-; Hon. Fellow Amer. Acad. Pediatrics 59; Hon. mem. Amer. Pediatric Soc., Deutsche Gesellschaft für Kinderheilkunde 73, Soc. de Pédiatrie de Paris 58, British Ped. Asscn. 64, Finnish Pediatric Asscn. 71, etc.; Corresp. mem. Acad. Nat. de Médecine, France 73; Hon. LL.D. Nebraska Univ. 65; Dr. h.c. Nice Univ. 73; Fellow, Royal Coll. of Physicians (London) 71; Chevalier Légion d'Honneur 73.
Publs. *Annenin Kitabi—Mother's Handbook on Child Care* 52-74, *Premature Baby Care* 54, articles and monographs on child health, pediatrics and medical education; Editor of *Turkish Journal of Pediatrics,* and consulting editor of *Clinical Pediatrics* (Philadelphia).
Hacettepe University, Ankara, Turkey.
Telephone: 11-94-42.

Dohnanyi, Klaus von, DR.JUR.; German politician; b. 23 June 1928, Hamburg; s. of Johann-Georg and Christine (née Bonhoeffer) von Dohnanyi; m. Christa Gross 1966; two s. one d.; ed. Munich, Columbia, Stanford and Yale Univs.
Formerly with Ford Motor Co., Detroit, Mich. and Cologne; Dir. Planning Div. Ford-Werke, Cologne 56-60; Dir. Inst. für Marktforschung und Unternehmensberatung, Munich 60-67; Sec. of State, Fed. Ministry of Economy 68; mem. Bundestag 69-; Parliamentary Sec. of State, Ministry of Educ. and Science 69-72; Minister of Educ. and Science 72-74; Social Democrat.
5300 Bonn-Ippendorf, Am Lappenweiher 20, Federal Republic of Germany.
Telephone: 636434.

Doi, Masaharu; Japanese chemical executive; b. 1 May 1894, Amagasaki, Hyogo; s. of Yataro and Taki Doi; m. Tae Shimizu 1922; three s. one d.; ed. Tokyo Imperial Univ.
Sumitomo Chemical Co. 20-, Gen. Man. 42, Dir. 44-, Pres. 47-63, Chair. 63-75, Adviser 75-; Chair. Nippon Telephone and Telegraph Public Corpn., Japan-Italy Econ. Cttee.; Chair. and Trustee, Kansai Nikkan Kyokai; Vice-Chair. Fed. of Econ. Orgs.; Dir., Japan Atomic Industries Forum, Sumitomo Chiba Chemical Co. Ltd., Sumitomo Bakelite Co. Ltd., Mainichi Broadcast Co. Ltd., Seitetsu Kagaku Co. Ltd., Kansai Econs. Fed.; Consultant, Japan Chemical Industries Asscn., Kansai Electric Power; Adviser, Ministry of Int. Trade and Industry, Osaka Chamber of Commerce and Industry, Kansai Chemical Industries Asscn.; mem. Advisory Board on Social Devt., Advisory Board of Hokkaido and Tohoku Devt. Corpn., Int. Chamber of Commerce.
Leisure interest: Kouta (Japanese traditional song).
2-21 Kumoi-cho, Nishinomiya, Hyogo Prefecture, Japan.
Telephone: 0798-22-3979.

Doi, Shozaburo; Japanese banking executive; b. 23 Dec. 1907, Yonago City; s. of Chikao Doi and Toshie Miyoshi; m. Mikiko Mikamo 1929; two s. two d.; ed. Aoyama Gakuin Univ.
Joined The Mitsui Trust & Co. Ltd. 29; Dir. The Mitsui Trust & Banking Co. Ltd. 58, Pres. 68, Chair. 71-; Dir. Mitsui Petroleum Devt. Co. Ltd. 69-, Mitsui Ocean Devt. Co. Ltd. 70-, Mitsui Devt. Co. 71-; Auditor Developer Sanshin Co. Ltd. 71-, Mitsui Alumina Co. Ltd. 72-; Inspector Japan Medical Foods Asscn. 72-.
Leisure interests: reading, golf, gardening.
The Mitsui Trust and Banking Co. Ltd., 1-1, Nihombashi Muromachi 2-chome, Chuo-ku, Tokyo 103, Japan.

Doisy, Edward Adelbert, A.B., M.S., PH.D.; American university professor; b. 13 Nov. 1893; ed. Univ. of Illinois and Harvard Univ.
Asst. in Biochemistry, Harvard Medical School 15-17; Army service 17-19; Instructor, Assoc. and Assoc. Prof. in Biochemistry, Washington Univ. School of Medicine 19-23; Prof. of Biochemistry, and Dir. of Dept., St. Louis Univ. School of Medicine 23-65; Distinguished Service Prof. Emeritus of Biochemistry and Dir. Emer. of Edward A. Doisy Dept. of Biochemistry 65-; mem. Pontifical Acad. of Science 48, Amer. Acad. of Arts and Sciences, Nat. Acad. Sciences, Amer. Philosophical Soc.; awarded gold medal, St. Louis Medical Soc. 35; Willard Gibbs Medal 41; Squibb award 44; shared the Nobel Prize in Physiology and Medicine for 43 with Dr. Henrik Dam; Barren Medal 73; Hon. Sc.D. Washington Univ., Yale, Chicago, Central Coll., Illinois Univ., Gustavus Adolphus Coll.; Dr. h.c. Paris; LL.D. (Hon.) St. Louis Univ.
Office: 1402 South Grand Boulevard, St. Louis, Missouri 63104, U.S.A.
Telephone: 664-9800.

Doke, Clement Martyr, M.A., D.LITT.; South African philologist; b. 16 May 1893, Bristol, England; s. of Rev. J. J. Doke and Agnes Biggs; m. Hilda Lehman 1919 (deceased 1948); one s. four d.; ed. Transvaal Univ. Coll., Pretoria, and London Univ.
Missionary S. Africa Baptist Missionary Soc. 14-21; Lecturer in Bantu Languages, Univ. of Witwatersrand, Johannesburg 23; Prof. and Head of Dept. of Bantu Studies 31-53; Editor *South African Baptist* 22-47; Joint Editor *Bantu Studies* 31-41 and *African Studies* 42-53; has conducted research trips to Lamba, Ila, Shona, the Bushman tribes, etc.; Pres. Baptist Union of S. Africa 49-50; Acting Principal, Baptist Theological Coll. of

Southern Africa 51 and 55; Hon. D.Litt. (Rhodes), Hon. LL.D. (Witwatersrand).

Leisure interest: biblical studies.

Publs. *Ukulayana Kwawukumo* (translation of New Testament in Lamba) 21, *Lamba Folklore* 27, *Text Book of Zulu Grammar* 27, *Unification of the Shona Dialects* 31, *The Lambas of Northern Rhodesia* 31, *Comparative Study in Shona Phonetics* 31, *Bantu Linguistic Terminology*, *Lamba-English Dictionary* 37, 2nd edn. 73, *Text Book of Lamba Grammar* 38, (with the late Dr. B. W. Vilakazi) *Zulu-English Dictionary* 48, *The Southern Bantu Languages* 54, *Textbook of Southern Sotho Grammar* 57 (with the late Dr. S. M. Mofokeng), *English-Zulu Dictionary* 58 (with the late Dr. D. McK. Malcolm and J. M. A. Sikakana), *Amasiwi Awalesa* (trans. of Bible in Lamba) 59, *Contributions to the History of Bantu Linguistics* 61 (with D. T. Cole), *English-Lamba Vocabulary* 63.

Flat 19, Marina Hills, Kearn Road, Baysville, East London 5201, South Africa.

Telephone: East London 20433.

Doko, Toshio; Japanese business executive; b. 15 Sept. 1896; ed. Tokyo Inst. of Industrial Science, Univ. of Tokyo.

With K.K. Tokyo Ishikawajima Shipyard 20; with Ishikawajima Shibaura Turbine Co. Ltd. 36, Pres. 46; elected Pres. Ishikawajima Heavy Industries Co. Ltd. 50, Chair. of Board 64-74 (now Ishikawajima-Harima Heavy Industries); Dir. Tokyo Shibaura Electric 57, Pres. 65-; Ishikawajima do Brasil Estaleiros S.A. 59-; Vice-Pres. Fed. of Econ. Orgs. (Keidanren), Pres. 74-; Medal of Honour with Blue and Navy Ribbons, Order of Southern Cross (Brazil), First Class Order of the Sacred Treasure.

Tokyo Shibaura Electric Co. Ltd., 1-6 1-chome, Chiyodaku, Tokyo, Japan.

Dolanc, Stane; Yugoslav politician; b. 1925.

Held various positions in the Army, Ljubljana Univ. and the Slovene League of Communists; now Sec. Exec. Bureau of the Presidium, League of Communists of Yugoslavia.

League of Communists of Yugoslavia, Bulevar Lenjina 6, Novi Beograd, Yugoslavia.

Dolci, Danilo; Italian writer and social worker; b. 28 June 1924, Sesana (Trieste); ed. Faculty of Architecture, Milan Polytechnic.

Collaborated with Saltini, founder of Christian community Nomadelfia; social work in Sicily 52-; opened centres for study on problem of providing organic development for a traditionally under-employed population 58; Premio della Bontà, Milan 54, Lenin Peace Prize 58, Laurea philosophiae h.c. (Univ. of Berne) 68, Sonning Prize 71.

Publs. *Banditi a Partinico* 55 (English trans. 60), *To Feed the Hungry* 59, *Spreco* 60 (English trans. 63), *Conversazioni* 62, *Verso un mondo nuovo* 64 (English trans. 65), *Chi gioca solo* 66 (English trans. *The Man who Plays Alone* 69), *Inventare il futuro* 68, *Il limone lunare* 70, *Non sentite l'odore del fumo?* 71, *Chissà sei pesci piangono* 72, *Poema umano* 73.

Centro Studi e Iniziative, Largo Scalia 5, Partinico (Palermo), Sicily, Italy.

Telephone: 781905.

Dole, Robert; American politician: b. 22 July 1923, Russell, Kan.; s. of Mr. and Mrs. Doran R. Dole; one d.; ed. Russell public schools, Univ. of Kansas and Washbourn Municipal Univ.

Member Kansas Legislature 51-53; Russell County Attorney 53-61; mem. House of Reps. 60-68; U.S. Senator from Kansas 68-; Chair. Republican Nat. Cttee. 71-72; Adviser, U.S. Del. to FAO Conf., Rome 65; mem. Congressional Del. to India 66, Middle East 67;

Trustee, William Allen White Foundation, Univ. of Kan.; mem. Nat. Advisory Cttee., The John Wesley Colls.; mem. American Bar Asscn.; mem. Nat. Advisory Cttee. on Scouting for the Handicapped, Kan. Asscn. for Retarded Children, Advisory Board of United Cerebral Palsy, Kan.; Hon. mem. Advisory Board of Kidney Patients Inc.; Republican.

New Senate Office Building, Washington, D.C. 20510, U.S.A.

Telephone: 202-225-6521.

Dolgoplosk, Boris Alexandrovich; Soviet organic chemist; b. 12 Nov. 1905, Lukoml, Byelorussia; ed. Moscow Univ.

At synthetic rubber plants 32-46; Instructor, later Prof. Yaroslavl Technical Inst. 44-46; Assoc., All-Union Research Inst. of Synthetic Rubber 46-; Assoc. Inst. of High Molecular Compounds, U.S.S.R. Acad. of Sciences; Inst. of Petrochemical Synthesis, U.S.S.R. Acad. of Sciences 62-; mem. C.P.S.U. 45-; Corresp. mem. U.S.S.R. Acad. of Sciences 58-64, mem. 64-; State Prize (twice); Order of Lenin (twice) and other awards.

Leninsky Prospekt 29, Moscow V-71, U.S.S.R.

Dolin, Anton (Patrick Healey-Kay); British ballet dancer and choreographer; b. 27 July 1904; ed. privately.

Actor and dancer 15-21; Diaghilev's Russian Ballet Co. 21-27, 28-29, created roles in *Le Train Bleu, Le Bal, Zepher and Flore, Le Facheaux, Fils Prodigue, Les Biches*; created Nemchinova-Dolin Co. of Ballet 26, 27; associated with Camargo Soc.; Guest Dancer, Vic-Wells Ballet Co. 31-35, Markova-Dolin Ballet Co. 35-37; founded as Artistic Dir. and Premier Dancer London Festival Ballet 50-59; Rome Opera Dir. of Ballet 60, now artistic adviser to Les Grands Ballets Canadiens and Vice-Pres. of the Royal Acad. of Dancing; Co-Chair. Ballet Dept., Indiana Univ.; Order of the Sun (Peru), Queen Elizabeth II Coronation Award 58; choreographic works: *David, Job, Nightingale and the Rose, Rhapsody in Blue, Quintet, Capriccioso, Pas de Quatre, Hymn to the Sun, Espagnol, Giselle, Variations for Four, The Swan of Tuonela*.

Publs. *Divertissement* 30, *Ballet Go Round* 39, *Pas de Deux* 50, *Markova* 53, *Autobiography* 59, *The Sleeping Ballerina* 66.

99 Madison Street, New Bedford, Mass. 02740, U.S.A.

Doll, Sir William Richard Shaboe, Kt., O.B.E., F.R.S., M.D., D.SC., F.R.C.P.; British epidemiologist and medical researcher; b. 28 Oct. 1912, Hampton; s. of William and Kathleen Doll; m. Joan Faulkner (née Blatchford) 1946; one s. one d.; ed. Westminster School and St. Thomas's Hospital Medical School, Univ. of London.

Military Service 39-45; with Medical Research Council's Statistical Research Unit 48-69, Dir. 61-69; mem. Advisory Cttee. on Medical Research WHO 63, Council of Int. Epidemiological Asscn. 61, Scientific Cttee. Int. Agency for Cancer Research 65-70, 75, Hebdomadal Council, Oxford Univ. 75-; Regius Prof. of Medicine, Oxford 69-; mem. Royal Comm. on Environmental Pollution 73-; David Anderson Berry Prize, Royal Soc. of Edinburgh (jointly) 58, Hon. Assoc. Physician Central Middx. Hospital 49-69; Bisset Hawkins Medal, Royal Coll. of Physicians, London 62, UN Award for Cancer Research 62, Rock Carling Fellow, Nuffield Provincial Hospitals Trust, London 67, Gairdner Award 70, Buchanan Medal, Royal Soc. 72, Presidential Award, N.Y. Acad. of Sciences 75.

Leisure interests: conversation, good food.

Publs. Articles on aetiology of lung cancer, leukaemia, epidemiology, effects of ionizing radiations, oral contraceptives, treatment of gastric ulcers, etc.

13 Norham Gardens, Oxford, England.

Telephone: Oxford 55207.

Dölle, Hans, Dr. Jur., Dr. h.c.; German lawyer; b. 25 Aug. 1893, Berlin; s. of Emil and Maria (née Hils) Dölle; m. Else Vorwald 1920; one s.; ed. Berlin, Freiburg and Lausanne Univs.

Professor of Law, Hamburg; Vice-Pres. Max Planck Soc. 61-.

Publs. *Kernprobleme des internationalen Rechts der freiwilligen Gerichtsbarkeit* 61, *Familienrecht, mit rechtsvergleichenden Hinweisen* 2 vols. 64-65, *Der Beitrag der Rechtsvergleichung zum deutschen Recht, Hundert Jahre deutsches Rechtsleben 1860-1960* 62, *Internationales Privatrecht* 68, 2nd edn. 72.

2 Hamburg 76, Schöne Aussicht 16, Federal Republic of Germany.

Telephone: 220-60-19.

Dollezhal, Nikolay Antonovich; Soviet academician and power engineering scientist; b. 27 Oct. 1899, Omelnik, Ukraine; ed. Moscow Higher Technical School.

Lecturer, Inst. of Nat. Economy, and Moscow Higher Technical School 23-32; Technical Dir. Leningrad Inst. of Nitrogen Production Equipment 32-34; Chief Eng. Kiev "Bolshevik" plant 35-38; Dir. Moscow Research Inst. of Chemical Machinery 42-53; Dir. Scientific Research Inst. 53-; mem. Bureau of Dept. of Physico—Technical Problems of Energy of U.S.S.R. Acad. of Sciences 53-62; mem. Dept. Technical Science, U.S.S.R Acad. of Sciences 60-; State Prize (four), Lenin Prize 57, Hero of Socialist Labour, Order of Lenin (four), Hammer and Sickle Gold Medal, etc.

Publs. *The Principles of Designing Steam Operated Power Units* 33, *Theory of Compressor Valves* 41, *Reactor of Atomic Power Station of U.S.S.R. Academy of Sciences* 56; *Uranium-graphite reactors in power stations with steam heating* 57.

U.S.S.R. Academy of Sciences, 14 Leninsky Prospekt, Moscow, U.S.S.R.

Dollfus, Audouin, D. ès SC.; French astronomer; b. 12 Nov. 1924, Paris; s. of Charles Dollfus and Suzanne Soubeyran; m. Catherine Browne 1959; four c.; ed. Univ. de Paris.

Joined Observatoire de Meudon (astrophysical div. of Observatoire de Paris) 46, now Head of Lab. for Physics of the Solar System; Astronomer, Observatoire de Paris 65-; mem. Int. Acad. of Astronautics; Prize of Acad. des Sciences.

Leisure interest: ballooning.

Publs. 140 scientific publications on astrophysics.

77 rue Albert Perdroux, 92-Chaville, France.

Telephone: 926-97-43.

Dollinger, Werner, DR. RER. POL.; German politician and industrialist; b. 10 Oct. 1918, Neustadt/Aisch; s. of Richard and Lisette (née Hösch) Dollinger; m. Herta Dehn 1945; one s. two d.; ed. School of Commerce, Nuremberg and Frankfurt Univ.

Military service 43-45; Chair. Neustadt Chamber of Commerce and Industry 48; founder mem. of CSU and Neustadt Town Councillor 46-; Dist. Chair. CSU 51; Dist. Councillor 52-; mem. Bundestag and CDU/CSU Parl. group 53-; mem. ECSC Common Assembly 56-58; Dep. Chair. CSU Land chapter in Bundestag 57-62; Chair. CDU/CSU working cttee. on budget, finance and taxes 57-62; Deputy Chair. CSU and Minister of Fed. Property 62-66; Minister of Posts and Telecommunications 66-69; Deputy Chair. CSU Land Chapter in Bundestag; Chair. CSU working group foreign affairs and defence.

Leisure interests: tennis, skiing, swimming, walking.

Office: Bundeshaus, 53 Bonn; Home: 30 Hampfergrundweg, 853 Neustadt/Aisch, Federal Republic of Germany.

Telephone: Bonn 163641.

Dolman, Claude Ernest, M.B., B.S., D.P.H., PH.D., F.R.C.P. (London), F.R.C.P. (Canada), F.R.S.C.; Canadian medical bacteriologist and writer; b. 23 May 1906, Porthleven, Cornwall, England; s. of John E. Dolman and Peternal E. Holloway; m. 1st Ursula Coray 1931, 2nd Clarisse Askanazy 1955; four s. two d.; ed. Wallingford Grammar School, Christ's Hospital, St. Mary's Hospital Medical School and several other London hospitals.

Research and Clinical Assoc., Connaught Labs., Univ. of Toronto 31-35, Research mem. 35-72, Consultant 72-73; Dir. Div. of Labs., Provincial Dept. of Health of British Columbia 35-56; Prof. and Head of Dept. of Bacteriology and Preventive Medicine, Univ. of British Columbia 36-51, Dept. of Bacteriology and Immunology 57-65, Research Prof. Dept. of Microbiology 65-71; Prof. Emer. of Microbiology 71-; Hon. Lecturer Dept. of History of Medicine and Science 64-72; Acting Head Dept. of Nursing and Health, Univ. of B.C. 35-43, Prof. and Head 43-51; Assoc. Editor *Journal of Immunology* 46-57; Pres. Canadian Asscn. of Medical Bacteriologists 64-66; Pres. Royal Soc. of Canada 69-70; Cheadle Gold Medal for Medicine (St. Mary's Hospital) 29, Coronation Medal 53.

Leisure interests: antiquarian, gardening.

Publs. *Bacterial Food Poisoning* 43, *Report on a Survey of Medical Education in Canada and the United States* 46, *Science and the Humanities* 50, *The Epidemiology of Meat-Borne Diseases* 57, *Type E Botulism: its Epidemiology, Prevention and Specific Treatment* 63, *Water Resources of Canada* (Editor) 67, *Bacteriophages of Clostridium botulinum* 72, *Science as a Way of Life* 74; also numerous articles in scientific and medical journals on staphylococcus toxins, botulinus toxins and botulism, salmonella infections, brucellosis, etc., general public health and the history of microbiology.

1611 Cedar Crescent, Vancouver 9, B.C. V6J 2P8, Canada.

Telephone: 604-738-8374 (Home).

Dolmatovsky, Yevgeny Aronovich; Soviet poet; b. 5 May 1915, Moscow; s. of Aron and Adel Dolmatovsky; ed. Moscow Literature Inst.

State Prizewinner 49; Orders of Great Patriotic War (1st Class), of Red Star, Badge of Honour, Red Banner of Labour (twice), and other decorations.

Leisure interest: driving.

Publs. Anthologies: *Lyrics* 34, *Song of the Dnieper* 42, *Notes on the Steppes* 45, *A Word About the Future* 59, *African Poems* 61; Novel in verse *Volunteers* 56, 69, *Selected Works* 59, *Years and Songs* 63, *Poems about Us* 64, *Life of Lyrics* 65, *Selected Works* 65, *The Last Kiss* 67, *The Girl in White* 68, *Selected Works* (2 vols.) 71, *Victory Autographs* 72, *Stories of your Songs* 73, *It Was . . .* 73, *I Ask the Floor* 74.

Writers' Union, Ul. Vorovskogo 52, Moscow, U.S.S.R.

Dolmetsch, Carl Frederick, C.B.E., HON. F.T.C.L., HON. F.L.C.M.; British musician; b. 23 Aug. 1911, Fontenay-sous-Bois, France; s. of Arnold Dolmetsch and Mabel Johnston; m. (dissolved); one s. two d.; ed. privately.

First public concert performance at age of 7, and first concert tour aged 8; toured Alaska and South America, Australia, Austria, Belgium, Canada, France, Germany, Holland, Italy, Japan, New Zealand, Sweden, Switzerland and the U.S.A.; Dir. Soc. of Recorder Players 37-; Dir. Haslemere Festival of Early Music and Instruments 40-; Man. Dir. Arnold Dolmetsch Ltd. (musical instrument makers); mem. Art Workers' Guild, I.S.M.; Hon. D.Litt. (Univ. of Exeter).

Leisure interests: ornithology, natural history.

Publs. Many editions of recorder music; books on recorder playing 57, 62, and 70.

Jesses, Haslemere, Surrey, England.

Telephone: Haslemere 3818.

Dombrovskaya, Yulia Fominichna; Soviet pediatrician; b. 11 Dec. 1891, Elets; ed. Medical Institute for Women, St. Petersburg (Leningrad).

Pediatrician at a hospital 13-16; Intern, Asst., Lecturer, Prof., Head of Dept. First Moscow Medical Inst. 16-; Corresp. mem. U.S.S.R. Acad. of Medical Sciences 45-53, mem. 53-; Chair. of Boards of All-Union and Moscow Pediatric Socs.; mem. Purkyně Medical Soc. (Czechoslovakia) and Bulgarian Pediatric Soc.; Order of Lenin 53, 61, 65; Red Banner of Labour 45; Lenin Prize 70.
Publs. Over 160 works on child pathology, classification of pneumonia and role of vitamins in child physiology and pathology.
First Moscow Medical Institute, 19 Bolshaya Pirogovskaya ul., Moscow, U.S.S.R.

Domenici, Pete V., B.S., LL.B.; American senator; b. 7 May 1932; s. of Choppo and Alda Domenici; m. Nancy Burk 1958; two s. six d.; ed. Univs. of Albuquerque, New Mexico, Denver.
Elected to Albuquerque City Comm. 66, Chair. 67; mem. nat. league of cities revenue and Finance Steering Cttee. and the Resolutions Cttee. of the 1969 Annual Conf. of Mayors; served on Governor's Policy Board for Law Enforcement and on Middle Rio Grande Conf. of Govts.; elected U.S. Senator from New Mexico 72-.
Leisure interests: hunting, fishing.
Russell Office Building, Washington, D.C., U.S.A.

Dominick, Peter Hoyt, A.B., LL.B.; American lawyer and politician; b. 7 July 1915; ed. Yale Univ. and Yale Law School.
U.S. Army Air Corps 42-45; Partner, law firm Holland and Hart, Denver, Colorado 46-61; mem. Colorado House of Reps. 57-61; mem. U.S. Congress 61-63; U.S. Senator from Colorado 63-74; Amb. to Switzerland 75-; Republican.
American Embassy, Berne, Switzerland; and 5050 East Quincy Street, Englewood, Colorado, U.S.A.

Domoto, Hisao; Japanese painter; b. 1928; ed. Kyoto Acad. of Fine Arts.
First Prize, Acad. of Japan 51 and 53; studied in France, Italy and Spain 52; settled in Paris 55; abandoned traditional Japanese style and exhibited abstract paintings Salon des Indépendants, Salon de Mai, Paris 56, 57; rep. at Rome/New-York Art Foundation first exhbn. Rome, "Otro Arte" Exhbn. Madrid, Facchetti and Stadler Galleries, Paris 57; First Prize of Musée d'Art Moderne for foreign painters in Paris 58; one-man exhbn. Martha Jackson Gallery, New York 59.
9 rue St. Didier, Paris 16e, France.

Donaldson, Hon. Sir John Francis, Kt.; British judge; b. 6 October 1920, London; s. of Dr. M. Donaldson and Mrs. E. M. H. Maunsell; m. Dorothy M. Warwick 1945; one s. two d.; ed. Charterhouse School and Trinity Coll., Cambridge.
Called to the Bar, Middle Temple 46; Queen's Counsel 60; Judge of the High Court of Justice, Queen's Bench Div. 66-; Pres. Nat. Industrial Relations Court (NIRC) 71-74.
Leisure interest: sailing.
Royal Courts of Justice, Strand, London, W.C.2, England.

Donat-Cattin, Carlo; Italian journalist and politician; b. 26 June 1919, Finale Ligure.
Trained as journalist; wrote for *L'Italia* until 40, then *Popolo Nuovo*, Turin; joined Christian Democrat Regional Cttee. of Piedmont, Turin Provincial Cttee. and Nat. Council; helped organize Fed. of Independent Labour Unions; fmr. mem. Gen. Council L.C.G.I.L., C.I.S.L., Italian Catholic Action; organized Christian Democrat Party; represented Christian Democrat Party on Nat. Ctee. of Liberation at Ivrea and in Canavese district; elected to Chamber of Deputies 58, 63, 68 for Turin constituency; Under-Sec. for State Participations in 1st, 2nd and 3rd Moro govts.; fmr.

mem., Parl. Comm. to investigate Mafia; Minister of Labour and Social Security 69-73; Minister without Portfolio in charge of Southern Devt. 73-74; Minister of Industry Nov. 74-.
Camera dei Deputati, Rome, Italy.

Donath, Helen; American opera and concert singer; b. 10 July 1940, Corpus Christi, Tex.; d. of Jimmy Erwin and Helen Hamauei; m. Klaus Donath 1965; one s.; ed. Roy Miller High School, Del Mar Coll., Tex.
Studied with Paola Nivikova, later with husband Klaus Donath; debut at Cologne Opera House 62, at Hanover Opera House 63-68, Bayerische Staatsoper, Munich 68-72; guest appearances in Vienna, Milan, San Francisco, Lisbon, etc.; has given concerts in all major European and American cities; major roles include, Pamina in *Die Zauberflöte*, Zerlina in *Don Giovanni*, Eva in *Die Meistersinger*, Sophie in *Der Rosenkavalier*; many recordings 62-; Pope Paul Medal; Salzburg 50 Year Anniversary Medal; Bratislava Festival Award.
Leisure interests: playing with son, swimming, filming.
3001 Brelingen, Federal Republic of Germany.

Donati, Antigono; Italian banker; b. 20 Jan. 1910, Rome; s. of Giacomo and Olga Fano Donati; m. Margherita Flora; one s. one d.; ed. Liceo Tasso, Rome and Univs. of Rome and Padua.
Member First Republican Parl. 48-53; Pres. Italian Nat. Cttee. for Int. Econ. and Technical Co-operation, Ministry of Foreign Affairs 60-67; Pres. Cttee. of Technical Co-operation, OECD 63-66; Pres. Nat. Inst. for Foreign Trade 65-69; Pres. Banca Nazionale del Lavoro 67-; Pres. Ente Finanziario Interbancario Efibanca 68-; Pres. Comm. for Labour, Social Welfare and Co-operation, Consiglio Nazionale dell'Economia e del Lavoro (CNEL) 61-; Pres. Int. Asscn. of Insurance Law, Luxembourg 60-; mem. of Board Nat. Inst. of Insurance 60-, and le Assicurazioni d'Italia S.p.A.; Dr. jur. h.c. (Hamburg) and hon. degrees from Univs. of Calif. (Los Angeles) and Phoenix, Ariz.; Gold Medal for Culture and Arts 60; INA Prize, Accad. Nazionale dei Lincei 62; Cavaliere del Lavoro, Cavaliere di Gran Groce dell'Ordine al merito; honours from Argentina, Brazil, Chile, Finland, France, Federal Germany, Greece, Luxembourg, Mexico, Peru, Portugal and Spain.
Publs. *Il Contratto di assicurazione in abbonamento* 35, *L'assicurazione per conto di chi spetta* 37, *L'invalidità delle deliberazioni di assemblea di società anonime* 37, *L'assicurazione nel Codice Civile, nel Commentario D'Amelio* 43, *Trattato di diritto delle assicurazioni private* (3 vols.) 52-56, *Manuale del Diritto delle assicurazioni* 56, *Codice delle assicurazioni* 60, *L'assicurazione nei Paesi del MEC* 63.
Via Cassia 1951, Rome, Italy.
Telephone: 6998193.

Donatoni, Franco; Italian professor of musical composition; b. 9 June 1927, Verona; s. of Silvio Donatoni and Dolores Stefannuci; m. Susan Park 1958; one s. one d.; ed. Bologna and Rome.
Professor of Composition, Bologna 53-55, Milan 55-67, Turin 67-69, Milan 69-; Docente, Advanced Course in Composition, Accademia Chigiana di Siena 70; Marzotto Prize 66, Koussevitsky Prize 68 and other prizes for composition.
Works include: *Puppenspiel* 51, *Sezioni* 60, *Per Orchestra* 62, *Quartetto IV* 63, *Asar* 64, *Puppenspiel (2)* 65, *Souvenir* 67, *Etwa ruhiger im Ausdruck* 67, *Doubles II* 69-70, *Questo* 70.
Via Bassini 39, 20133 Milan, Italy.
Telephone: (02) 293408.

Donegan, Patrick Sarsfield; Irish businessman, farmer and politician; b. 29 Oct. 1923, County Louth; s. of Thomas F. and Roseanne Donegan; m. 1955; two s. two d.; ed. St. Vincent's, Castleknock.

ine Gael M.P. for Louth 54-; fmr. Del. to Inter-Parliamentary Union; mem. Council of Europe; Vice-Pres. Fine Gael Party; Minister of Defence March 73-.
Leisure interests: hunting, boating, football, shooting, tennis, badminton.
"St. Etchen's", Monasterboice, Co. Louth, Ireland.
Telephone: (041) 8944.

Donen, Stanley; American film producer and director; b. 13 April 1924.
Director of films including *Fearless Fagan, Give the Girl a Break, Royal Wedding, Love is Better Than Ever, Deep in My Heart, Seven Brides for Seven Brothers, Funny Face, Kiss Them for Me;* co-dir. *Singin' in the Rain, It's Always Fair Weather, On the Town;* producer-dir. *Pajama Game, Indiscreet, Damn Yankees, Once More with Feeling, Surprise Package, The Grass is Greener, Charade, Arabesque, Two for the Road, Bedazzled, Staircase, The Little Prince, Lucky Lady.*
c/o Edward Traubner, Suite 504, 1800 Century Park East, Los Angeles, Calif. 90067, U.S.A.

Dönhoff, Gräfin (Countess) **Marion,** DR. RER. POL.; German journalist; b. 2 Dec. 1909, Friedrichstein, East Prussia; d. of August Graf Dönhoff and Ria (née von Lepel); unmarried; ed. in Potsdam, Königsberg, Frankfurt/Main and Basel Univ.
Engaged in admin. of various agricultural estates in East Prussia 36-45; joined *Die Zeit* 46, Political Editor 55, Chief Editor of *Die Zeit* 68-72, Publisher 72-; Hon. Dr. Smith Coll., U.S.A.; Joseph E. Drexel Prize, Theodor Heuss Prize, Peace Prize of German Book Trade 71.
Leisure interest: art (painting and graphic art).
Publs. *Namen, die keiner mehr nennt* 62, *Die Bundesrepublik in der Ära Adenauers* 63, *Reise in ein fernes Land* (co-author) 64, *Welt in Bewegung* 65, *Deutsche Aussenpolitik von Adenauer bis Brandt* 70.
Hamburg-Blankenese, Am Pumpenkamp 4, Federal Republic of Germany.

Donini, Ambrogio, PH.D.; Italian historian, politician and diplomatist; b. 8 Aug. 1903, Lanzo Torinese; s. of the late Pier Luigi and of Giaccone Irene; m. Olga Jahr 1930; one s.; ed. Univ. of Rome and Harvard Univ.
Reader in History of Christianity, Univ. of Rome 26; obliged to emigrate to U.S.A. in 28 because of opposition to Fascist régime; research for Th.D. at Harvard Univ. Theological School 28-30; Lecturer in Italian Literature, Brown Univ., Providence 29; Asst. Prof. of Italian, Smith Coll., Northampton, Mass. 30; anti-fascist political activity in Europe 32-39; Editor of anti-fascist daily *La Voce degli Italiani*, Paris; in U.S.A. as Editor of Italian anti-fascist weekly *L'Unità del Popolo* 39-45; Lecturer of History of Religion, Jefferson School, New York 43-45; returned to liberated Italy after 17 years' exile 45; Free Prof. of History of Christianity, Univ. of Rome; Dir. of Gramsci Cultural Institute, Rome 49; joint editor of Rome review *Ricerche Religiose;* elected to Rome City Council Nov. 46; Ambassador to Poland 47-48; mem. World Peace Council 50; elected to the Senate 53, 58; mem. Communist Party of Italy since 27; elected to Central Cttee. 48, to Central Control Cttee. 56; Prof. History of Christianity, Univ. of Bari 60.
Leisure interests: chess and classical music.
Publs. *Ippolito di Roma, Polemiche teologiche e controversie disciplinari nella Chiesa di Roma agli inizi del III secolo* 25, *Manuale introduttivo alla Storia del Cristianesimo* (joint author) 26, *Per una storia del pensiero di Dante in rapporto al movimento gioachimita* (Dante Prize, Harvard Univ.) 30, *Le basi sociali del Cristianesimo primitivo* 46, *L'Italia al bivio* 55, *I Manoscritti ebraici del Mar Morto e le origini del Cristianesimo* 57, *Chiesa e Stato nell'Italia d'oggi* 58, *Lineamenti*

di Storia delle Religioni 59, *Lezioni di Storia del Cristianesimo*, vol. I, *Le Origini* 64.
Contrada S. Sisinio, 00068 Rignano Flaminio, Rome, Italy.
Telephone: 0761-50027.

Donleavy, James Patrick; American author; b. 23 April 1926, New York City; s. of Patrick and Margaret Donleavy; m. Mary Wilson Price; one s. one d.; ed. Preparatory School, New York, and Trinity Coll., Dublin.
Served in the U.S.N. during the Second World War; Brandeis Univ. Creative Arts Award; Evening Standard Drama Award; American Acad. and Nat. Inst. of Arts and Letters Award.
Publs. *The Ginger Man* (novel) 55, (play) 59, *Fairy Tales of New York* (play) 60, *A Singular Man* (novel) 63, (play) 64, *Meet My Maker the Mad Molecule* (short stories and sketches) 64, *The Saddest Summer of Samuel S* (novella) 66, (play) 68, *The Beastly Beatitudes of Balthazar B* (novel) 68, *The Onion Eaters* (novel) 71, *The Plays of J. P. Donleavy* (collection) 72, *A Fairy Tale of New York* (novel) 73, *The Unexpurgated Code: A Complete Manual of Survival and Manners* 75.
Levington Park, Mullingar, Co. Westmeath, Ireland.
Telephone: 044-8903.

Donnay, J(oseph) D(ésiré) H(ubert), E.M., PH.D.; American university professor; b. 6 June 1902, Grandville, Belgium; s. of Joseph Donnay and Marie Doyen; m. 1st Marie Hennin 1931, 2nd Gabrielle Hamburger 1949; three s. one d.; ed. Liège and Stanford Univs.
Engineer and geologist, Société financière franco-belge de colonisation, French Morocco 29-30; Research Assoc. and Teaching Fellow, Stanford Univ. 30-31; Assoc. in Mineralogy and Petrography, Johns Hopkins Univ. 31-39; Prof. Laval Univ. Quebec 39-45; Research Chemist, Hercules Powder Co. 42-45; Visiting Prof. Johns Hopkins Univ. 45; Prof. Univ. of Liège 46-47; Prof. of Crystallography and Mineralogy, Johns Hopkins Univ. 46-71; Chargé de cours, Univ. of Montreal 70-72, Guest Prof. 72-; Sec.-Treas. American Soc. for X-ray and Electron Diffraction 44-46; Vice-Pres. Soc. géologique Belgique 46-47; Vice-Pres. Mineralogical Soc. of America 49 and 52, Pres. 53; Vice-Pres. Crystallographic Soc. of America 46 and 48, Pres. 49; Corresp. mem. Société Royale des Sciences de Liège; Vice-Pres. Société française de Minéralogie 49; Vice-Pres. Geological Society of America 54; Hon. Prof. Univ. of Liège 48-; Pres. American Crystallographic Asscn. 56; Fulbright Lecturer, Sorbonne 58-59; Vice-Pres. Asscn. française de Cristallographie 59-60, Visiting Prof. Univ. Marburg 66, 68; Corresp. mem. Soc. géologique, Belgium 66, Hon. mem. 72; Roebling Medal 71.
Leisure interest: philology.
Publs. *Spherical Trigonometry* 45, *Crystal Data* 54, 63, 72-73, *Space Groups and Lattice Complexes* 73.
320 Côte Saint-Antoine, Montreal, Quebec H3Y 2J4, Canada.

Donnell, James C., II, A.B., LL.D., D.S., L.H.D.; American business executive (retd.); b. 30 June 1910, Findlay, Ohio; s. of Otto Dewey Donnell and Glenn McClelland; m. Dolly Louise De Vine 1932; one d.; ed. Princeton Univ.
Director Marathon Oil Co. 36-, Vice-Pres. 37-48, Pres. 47-72, Chair. 72-75; Dir. Mountain Fuel Supply Co. 35-72, Chair. of the Board 72-74; Dir. Nat. City Bank of Cleveland, First Nat. Bank of Findlay, Armco Steel Corpn., Phelps Dodge Corpn., American Petroleum Inst., Libbey-Owens-Ford Co., New York Life Insurance Co.; mem. Nat. Petroleum Council, World Alliance of YMCA's, Nat. Board YMCA.
539 South Main Street, Findlay, Ohio, U.S.A.
Telephone: 419-422-2121.

Donner, Andreas Matthias, D.IUR.; Netherlands jurist; b. 15 Jan. 1918; s. of Jan Donner (*q.v.*) and Golida van den Burg; *m.* Dina A. Mulder 1946; three *s.* six *d.*; ed. Amsterdam Free Univ.
Legal Adviser Assoc. of Christian Schools in the Netherlands 41-45; Prof. of Constitutional Law Free Univ. of Amsterdam 45-58; Pres. Court of Justice of the European Communities 58-64, Judge 64-, alt. Pres. of First Chamber; Hon. Dr. Iur. (Univ. of Louvain), Fellow, Royal Netherlands Acad. of Sciences and Art.
Publs. *Nederlands Bestuursrecht* (Netherlands Administrative Law) 53, 4th edn. 74, *Handboek van het Nederlandse Staatsrecht* 9th edn. 72.
Cour de Justice des Communautés Européennes, Kirchberg; and Route de Thionville 235, Hespérange, Luxembourg.
Telephone: 47621.

Donner, Frederic G., B.A.; American businessman; b. 1902; ed. Michigan Univ.
Joined General Motors Corpn. 26, Asst. Treas. 34-37, Gen. Asst. Treas. 37-41, Vice-Pres. 41-56, Exec. Vice-Pres. 56-58, Chair. and Chief Exec. Officer 58-Oct. 67, remains mem. Board and mem. Finance Cttee.; Chair. Board of Trustees, Alfred P. Sloan Foundation 68-.
630 Fifth Avenue, New York, N.Y. 10020, U.S.A.

Donner, Jan, DR. JUR., DR. RER. POL.; Netherlands jurist; b. 1891, Assen; *m.* Golida van den Burg 1916 (died 1965); six *c.*; ed. Univs. of Utrecht and Leiden.
Adviser of the Minister of Justice 22-26; Minister of Justice 26-33; mem. of Supreme Court 33-46, Pres. 46-61; Minister of State 71.
Scheveningseweg 86b, The Hague, Netherlands.
Telephone: 070-551056.

Donner, Jörn Johan, B.A.; Finnish film director and writer; b. 5 Feb. 1933, Helsinki; s. of Dr. Kaj Donner and Greta von Bonsdorff; *m.* 1st Inga-Britt Wik 1954 (divorced), two *s.*; *m.* 2nd Jeanette Bonnier 1974; ed. Helsinki Univ.
Worked as writer and film director in Finland and Sweden, writing own film scripts; contributor and critic to various Scandinavian and int. journals; Dir. Swedish Film Inst., Stockholm 72-; Man. Dir. Jörn Donner Productions; mem. Board Marimekko Textiles and other cos.; Opera Prima Award Venice Film Festival 63.
Films: *A Sunday in September* 63, *To Love* 64, *Adventure Starts Here* 65, *Rooftree* 67, *Black on White* 68, *Sixtynine* 69, *Portraits of Women* 70, *Anna* 70, *Images of Finland* 71, *Tenderness* 72, *Baksmalla* 74.
Leisure interest: fishing.
Publs. novels, short stories and non-fiction including: *Report from Berlin* 58, *The Personal Vision of Ingmar Bergman* 62.
Pohjoisranta 12, 00170 Helsinki 17, Finland; Fredrikshovsgatan 10, S-11522, Stockholm; and The Swedish Film Institute, Filmhuset, Box 27126, S-10252 Stockholm, Sweden.
Telephone: 652675 (Helsinki); 677333, 661212 (Stockholm).

Donoso, José, A.B.; Chilean writer; b. 5 Oct. 1924; s. of José and Alicia Donoso; *m.* María P. Serrano 1961; one *d.*; ed. The Grange School, Santiago, Instituto Pedagógico (Universidad de Chile), and Princeton Univ., U.S.A.
Worked as shepherd in Patagonia before going to Univ.; later lived in Buenos Aires; Doherty Foundation Scholarship to Princeton Univ.; Prof. of English Conversation, Catholic Univ. of Chile 52, later Teacher of Techniques of Expression, School of Journalism, Univ. of Chile; journalist on *Revista Ercilla*, Santiago 59-64; Visiting Lecturer, Writers' Work..hop, English Dept., Univ. of Iowa, U.S.A. 66-67; Premio Municipal de Santiago 55; Chile-Italia Prize for Journalism 60;

William Faulkner Foundation Prize (for *Coronación*) 62; Guggenheim Fellow.
Publs. *Veraneo y otros Cuentos* 55, *Coronación* 58, *E Charleston* (short stories) 60, *Este Domingo* (novel) 66, *El Lugar sin Límites* (novel) 66, *El obsceno pájaro de la noche* (novel) 71, *Cuentos* (short stories) 71, *Historia Personal del "Boom"* (essay) 72.
Calaceite, Province of Teruel; also c/o Carmen Balcells Urgel 241, Barcelona 11, Spain.
Telephone: Calaceite 78.

Donovan, Hedley Williams; American journalist; b. 24 May 1914, Brainerd, Minn.; s. of Percy Williams and Alice Dougan Donovan; *m.* Dorothy Hannon 1941; two *s.* one *d.*; ed. Univ. of Minnesota and Hertford Coll., Oxford.
Reporter, *Washington Post* 37-42, U.S. Naval Reserve 42-45; Writer and Editor *Fortune* 45-53, Managing Editor 53-59; Editorial Dir. Time Inc. 59-64, Editor-in-Chief 64-; Trustee New York Univ., Mount Holyoke Coll., Carnegie Endowment for Int. Peace, Univ. of Minnesota Foundation; Dir. Council on Foreign Relations; Fellow, Amer. Acad. of Arts and Sciences; Order of the Yugoslav Flag 71.
Time Inc., Time and Life Building, Rockefeller Center, New York, N.Y. 10020, U.S.A.
Telephone: 212-556-3701

Donskoi, Mark Semyonovich; Soviet film producer and scenario writer; b. 8 March 1901, Odessa.
Film Producer 26-; mem. C.P.S.U. 45-; State Prize-winner (for *Gorky's Childhood* 41, *Rainbow* 46, *Village School* 48, *Mother's Fidelity* 68); Richard Winnington Award 55, Honoured Art Worker of Turkmen S.S.R.; People's Artist of the U.S.S.R. 66; Hero of Socialist Labour 71; Order of Lenin (twice), Hammer and Sickle Gold Medal, etc.
Principal productions: *Gorky's Childhood* 38, *My Apprenticeship* 39, *My Universities* 40 (Trilogy); *The Rainbow* 46, *Village School* 47, *At A High Price, Mother* 55, *Foma Gordeev* 60, *Good Day, Children* 61, *Mother's Heart* 65, *Mother's Fidelity* 66.
Union of Cinematographists of the U.S.S.R., 14 Vassilievskaya ul., Moscow, U.S.S.R.

Doob, Joseph Leo, M.A., PH.D.; American professor of mathematics; b. 27 Feb. 1910, Cincinnati, Ohio; s. of Leo Doob and Mollie Doerfler Doob; *m.* Elsie Haviland Field 1931; two *s.* one *d.*; ed. Harvard Univ.
University of Illinois 35-, Prof. of Maths 45-; mem. Nat. Acad. of Sciences, American Acad. of Arts and Sciences.
Leisure interest: recorder.
Publ. *Stochastic Processes*.
Department of Mathematics, University of Illinois, Urbana, Ill. 61801, U.S.A.
Telephone: 333-1261.

Doob, Leonard W., PH.D.; American psychologist; b. 3 March 1909, New York; s. of William and Florence Doob; *m.* Eveline Bates 1936; three *s.*; ed. Dartmouth Coll., Duke Univ., Univ. of Frankfurt, and Harvard Univ.
Department of Psychology, Yale University 34-, Prof. of Psychology 50-; Psychologist, War Dept., 42-43; Policy Co-ordinator, Overseas Branch, Office of War Information 44-45; Chair. Council of African Studies, Yale Univ. 61-67, 72-; Visiting Research Prof. Univ. Coll. of Dar es Salaam, Tanzania 67-68, Univ. of Ghana 71; Editor *Journal of Social Psychology* 65-; Dir. of Social Sciences, Yale 63-66; Fellow John Simon Guggenheim Foundation 60-61.
Publs. *Propaganda* 35, *Frustration and Aggression* 39, *The Plans of Men* 40, *Public Opinion and Propaganda* 48, *Social Psychology* 52, *Becoming More Civilised* 60, *Communication in Africa* 61, *Patriotism and Nationalism* 64, *Ants will not Eat Your Fingers* 66, *A Crocodile has*

e by the Leg 67, Resolving Conflict in Africa 70, atterning of Time 72.
eisure interests: music, cycling, gardening.
ale University, 333 Cedar Street, New Haven, Con-ecticut, U.S.A.
elephone: 203-436-1596.

Doolittle, Lieut.-Gen. James H., B.A., D.SC.; American viator and business executive; b. 14 Dec. 1896; ed. Univ. of Calif., and Mass. Inst. of Technology.
Enlisted in U.S. Army Signal Corps as aviation cadet 7; commissioned as Second Lieut.; flight and gunnery instructor; served in Army as Second and First Lieut. 7-30; established a number of air records, including the following: (1) first flight across U.S. in less than 24 ours; (2) won Schneider Cup Race 25; (3) first man to do outside loop; (4) first man to fly over 300 m.p.h. in a and plane; retd. from Army with a reserve commission to become Manager of Aviation for Shell Oil Co. 30; warded Harmon trophy of Ligue Internationale des Aviateurs for pioneering work in blind flying 31; estab-lished new transcontinental flight record 31; new world peed record for land planes 32; recalled to active duty with U.S. Army 40; as Lieut.-Col. led famous Tokyo aid April 42; later commanded 12th and 15th Air Forces, and, in Jan. 44, 8th Air Force, retd. Air Force Feb. 59; Vice-Pres. of Shell Oil Co. 46-58, Dir. of Corpn. April 46-67; Chair. Exec. Cttee., Vice-Chair. Board of Trustees Aerospace Corpn. 65-70; Chair. Board, Space Technology Laboratories 59-62, Consultant 62-66; Dir. TRW Inc. 62-69; Dir. Mutual of Omaha Insurance Co. 61-, United Benefit Life Insurance Co. 64-, Tele-Trip Co., Inc. 66-; Dir. Companion Life Insurance Co. 58-, Mutual of Omaha Growth and Income Funds 68-; adviser to govt. boards; decorations include Con-gressional Medal of Honor, D.F.C., and D.S.M. with Oak-Leaf Clusters, Air Medal with three Oak-Leaf Clusters, Silver Star, Bronze Star, and many foreign awards, including Hon. K.C.B. (U.K.).
Office: 5225 Wilshire Boulevard, Los Angeles 90036, Calif.; Home: 233 Marguerita Avenue, Santa Monica, Calif., U.S.A.
Telephone: 213-936-8109.

Dooyeweerd, Herman, LL.D.; Netherlands lawyer and philosopher; b. 1894, Amsterdam; s. of Hermen Dooyeweerd and Maria Spaling; m. Jantiena Fernhout 1924 (died 1963); three s. six d.; ed. Reformed Gym-nasium and Free Univ., Amsterdam.
Chief Juridical Officer, Dept. of Labour 19; Dir. Dr. A. Kuyper Foundation, The Hague 22; Senior Prof. of Legal Theory, Philosophy and History of Law, Free Univ. of Amsterdam 26-67; Fellow and fmr. Sec. Royal Dutch Acad. of Sciences and Humanities (Humanities Section); fmr. Pres. Dutch Asscn. for Philosophy of Law; fmr. Vice-Pres. Board of Trustees, Inst. of Social Studies, The Hague; Vice-Pres. of the Int. Asscn. for Reformed Philosophy; Editor-in-Chief *Philosophia Reformata*; Knight of the Order of the Lion of the Netherlands and of the Order of Orange-Nassau.
Leisure interests: piano, belles-lettres.
Publs. *De Ministerraad in het Ned. Staatsrecht* 17, *De Crisis in de Humanistische Staatsleer* 31, *De Wijsbegeerte der Wetsidee* (three vols.) 35-36, *Grond-problemen in de leer der Rechtspersoonlijkheid* 37, *Recht en Historie* 38, *Reformatie en Scholastiek in de Wijsbegeerte* (Vol. I) 49, *Transcendental Problems of Philosophical Thought* 48, *De Strijd om het Souvereiniteitsbegrip in de Moderne Rechts- en Staatsleer* 50, *A New Critique of Theoretical Thought* (four vols.) 53-58, 2nd edn. 69, *Conférences Parisiennes* 59, *Encyclopedie der Rechts-wetenschap* 60, *In the Twilight of Western Thought* 61 (2nd edn. 65; Japanese and Spanish trans. 69), *Verken-ningen* 62, *Vernieuwing en Bezinning* 64 (2nd edn.), *Die Bedeutung der Philosophie der Gesetzesidee für die Rechts- und Sozialphilosophie* 67, *Het juridisch wilsbegrip*

en de juridisch normatieve uitlegging van rechtshande-lingen 73.
Oranje Nassaulaan 13, Amsterdam O.Z., Netherlands.
Telephone: 020-791430.

Döpfner, H.E. Cardinal Julius; German ecclesiastic; b. 26 Aug. 1913.
Ordained priest 39; Bishop of Würzburg 48-57, of Berlin 57-61, Archbishop of Munich 61-; created Cardinal by Pope John XXIII 58; mem. of the Congre-gations of the Oriental Church, for the clergy, and of the Propagation of the Faith among the peoples, and of the commission for revision of Canon Law; Chair. Bavarian Bishops Conf.
Archbishop's House, Kardinal-Faulhaber-Strasse 7, 8 Munich 2, Federal Republic of Germany.
Telephone: 29-69-55.

Dorati, Antal; American conductor and composer; b. 9 April 1906, Budapest, Hungary; ed. Franz Liszt Acad. of Music, Budapest, and Univ. of Vienna.
Assistant conductor Royal Opera, Budapest 24-28; First conductor Opera House, Münster 29-32; Musical Dir. de Ballet Russe de Monte Carlo 33-39, Ballet Theatre of N.Y. 39-41, New Opera Co., N.Y. 42-43, Dallas Sym-phony Orchestra 45-49, Minneapolis Symphony Orches-tra 49-60; Principal Conductor B.B.C. Symphony Orchestra 62-66, Stockholm Philharmonic Orchestra 66-74; Musical Dir. Washington Nat. Symphony Orchestra 70-(77); Principal Conductor Royal Philharmonic Orchestra 75-; Hon. Pres. Philharmonia Hungarica; mem. Royal Acad. Sweden; guest conductor of several American and European Orchestras and at numerous festivals; has made over 200 symphonic recordings; 10 Grand Prix du Disque and other record awards, Bruckner Medal, Mahler Medal, George Washington Award, etc.; Hon. Dr. Macalester Coll., Minn.; Commdr. of Royal Vasa Order, Sweden; Chevalier des arts et lettres, France; Ehrenkreuz litteris et artibus, Austria.
Compositions: *Concerto for cello and orchestra, Concerto for piano and orchestra, The Way* (Dramatic Cantata), *Missa Brevis* (for chorus and percussion), *The Two Enchantments of Li-Tai-Pe* (Chamber Cantata), *Noc-turne and Capriccio* (for Oboe and String Quartet), *Magdalena* (Ballet), *Symphony, Octet for Strings, Largo Concertato* (for string orchestra), *Chamber Music* (song cycle), *Madrigal Suite* (chorus and small orchestra), *Seven Pieces for Orchestra, Contours* (for large orchestra), *Nightmusic* (flute and chamber orchestra), *Chamber-music* (song cycle with small orchestra), violin and piano pieces, ballet arrangements, etc.
c/o Ibbs & Tillett, 124 Wigmore Street, London, W.1, England; c/o Hurok Attractions, 1370 Avenue of the Americas, New York, N.Y. 10019, U.S.A.

Dorazio; Italian artist; b. 1927, Rome; ed. Rome, Paris.
Played major role in the revival of Italian Futurist and Abstractionist tradition, published manifesto *Forma I* 47; has exhibited throughout Europe, U.S.A., S. America and Australia; established Fine Arts Dept. of School of Fine Arts, Univ. of Pennsylvania 60-61, Prof. 60-69; included in main avant-garde exhbns. of 50s and 60s; one-man exhbns. mainly in Venice Biennale 60, 66, Düsseldorf 61, San Marino Int. 67, Bennington, U.S.A., Cologne, Berlin 69, Museum of Modern Art, Belgrade 70, and at Marlborough Galleries in Rome 64, 68, 72, New York 65, 69, London 66; Venice Biennale Prize 60, Paris Biennale Prize 61, Prix Kandinsky 61, Premio Int. Lissone 65, Int. Prize, Cracow 70.
c/o Marlborough Galleria d'Arte, Rome, Italy.

Dorenfeldt, Lauritz Jenssen; Norwegian attorney-general (retired); b. 1909.
Assistant Judge 37; Prosecutor, Oslo 47; Attorney-Gen. 68-74.
c/o Tinghuset, Grubbegate 1, Oslo, Norway.
Telephone: 33-22-70.

Doriot, Georges Frederic, B.S.; American educator and business executive; b. 24 Sept. 1899, Paris, France; s. of Auguste and Berthe Doriot; m. Edna Allen 1930; ed. Lynton Coll., Kent, England, Paris Univ., Harvard Graduate School of Business Admin.
Prof. of Industrial Management, Harvard Graduate School of Business Admin. 29-66, Prof. Emer. 66-; Brigadier Gen., U.S. Army 41-47, serving as Dir. of Military Planning (Office of the Quartermaster-Gen.), Deputy Dir. for Research and Development (War Dept. Gen. Staff) and Deputy Admin., War Assets Admin. (Office of Asst. Chief of Staff G-4); Dir. Amer. Research and Devt. Corpn. 46-72, Chair. 72-; Hon. Pres. European Enterprise Devt. (EED) S.A.; Advisory Dir. Nat. Shawmut Bank of Boston; Dir. The Boston Co.; Digital Equipment Corpn., Sun Life Assurance Co. of Canada (U.S.), Technical Studies, Canadian Enterprise Devt. (CED) and other cos.; Conseiller, Institut Européen d'Administration des Affaires, Paris; Trustee, Vice-Pres. Franklin Foundation; Trustee Inst. for the Future; public mem. Hudson Inst.; Distinguished Service Medal (U.S.), Commdr. Légion d'Honneur (France), C.B.E. (U.K.), Grand Officier du Mérite, Recherche et Invention (France).
Leisure interests: photography, painting.
12 Lime Street, Boston, Mass. 02108, U.S.A.
Telephone: 742-3838.

Dorival, Bernard; French museum curator and writer; b. 14 Sept. 1914; ed. Lycées Carnot and Condorcet, Paris and Ecole normale supérieure.
Professor Ecole du Louvre 41-; Curator Musée Nationale de l'Art Moderne, Paris 41-65, Chief Curator 65-68; Curator Musée Nat. des Granges de Port-Royal 55-68; Chargé de recherches at Centre National de la Recherche Scientifique 68-.
Publs. *La Peinture française* 42, *Les Etapes de la peinture française contemporaine* 43-46, *Du Côté de Port-Royal* 46, *Les Peintres du XXe siècle* 55, *L'Ecole de Paris au Musée national d'art moderne* 61; monographs on Cezanne and Rouault.
78 rue Notre-Dame-des-Champs, Paris 6e, France.

Dorman, Sir Maurice Henry, G.C.M.G., G.C.V.O., M.A.; British administrator (retd.); b. 7 Aug. 1912, Stafford; s. of the late John Ehrenfried Dorman and Madeleine Bostock; m. F. Monica Churchward Smith 1937; one s. three d.; ed. Sedbergh School, Magdalene Coll., Cambridge.
Administration Officer, Tanganyika Territory 35, Clerk of Council 40-45; Asst. to Lieut.-Gov., Malta 45; Principal Asst. Sec., Palestine 47; seconded to Colonial Office as Asst. Sec., Social Services Dept. 48; Dir. Social Welfare and Community Devt., Gold Coast 50; Chief Sec., Trinidad and Tobago 52, Acting Gov., Trinidad 54, 55; Gov., C.-in-C. and Vice-Admiral of Colony and Protectorate of Sierra Leone 56-61, Gov.-Gen. Independent State of Sierra Leone 61-62; Gov. and C.-in-C. State of Malta 62-64, Gov.-Gen. 64-71; Deputy Chair. Pearce Comm. on Rhodesia 72; Dir. MLH Consultants, Ramsbury Building Soc.; Chair. Wiltshire Area Health Authority; Trustee, Imperial War Museum Lambeth; Pres. Anglo-Sierra Leone Soc.; Chief Commdr., St. John's Ambulance; Chair. Board of Govs., Badminton School, Bristol; Hon. D.C.L. (Durham), Hon. LL.D. (Royal Univ. of Malta), K.St.J. 57; Gran Croce al Merito Melitense (Sov. Ordine Militaire di Malta) 66.
Leisure interests: house, garden, golf, reading.
The Old Manor, Overton, Marlborough, Wiltshire; 42 Lennox Gardens, London, S.W.1, England.
Telephone: Lockeridge 600; 01-584-8698.

Dorodnitsyin, Anatoliy Alekseyevich; Soviet geophysicist; b. 2 Dec. 1910, Bashino; ed. Grozny Petroleum Inst.
Instructor, higher educational and research establishments, Moscow, Leningrad 36-41; Central Aerodynamics Inst. Moscow 41-55; Mathematics Inst. U.S.S.R. Aca of Sciences 45-55; Prof. Moscow Physics-Technical Ins 47-; mem. U.S.S.R. Acad. of Sciences 53-; Dir. Computing Centre, U.S.S.R. Acad. of Sciences 55-; Sta Prizes 46, 47, 51; Hero of Socialist Labour 70-; Ord of Lenin (thrice), Hammer and Sickle Gold Medal, etc.
Publs. *The Boundary Layer in Compressible Gas* 4 *The Effects of the Earth's Surface Topography on A Currents* 50, *Asymptotic Laws of Distribution of Prop Meanings for Some Special Types of Second Order 5 Solution of Mathematical and Logical Problems wi Help of Fast Electronic Computers* 56, *Laminar Bord Layer in Compressible Gas* 57, *Some Cases of Axi Symmetric Supersonic Current of Gas* 57, *A Contributio to Solution of Mixed Problems of Transonic Aero dynamics* 59, *A Method of Solution of Equation Laminar and Border Layer* 60.
Computing Centre, U.S.S.R. Academy of Sciences, 2 Ul. Vavilova, Moscow, U.S.S.R.

Dorolle, Pierre-Marie, M.D., F.R.C.P.; French inter national health official (retd.); b. 14 Nov. 1899, Wassy s. of Maurice and Marie Luce Dorolle; m. Mary A Andrew 1953; two d.; ed. Univs. of Marseilles, Paris an Bordeaux and Post-Graduate School of Tropica Medicine, Marseilles.
Overseas Army Medical Corps, later with Govt. Medica Service, French Indochina 25-37; Rapporteur, Leagu of Nations Intergovernmental Conf. of Rural Hygiene Far East 37; Chief Medical Expert, Rep. of Sec.-Gen. League of Nations Technical Co-operation with China 37-40; successively Dir., Health Services Saigon-Cholon Dir., Health Services, Annam Protectorate, Dir. Healtb Services, Office of High Commr. 40-50; Dep. Dir.-Gen World Health Org. 50-73; Officier Légion d'Honneur Croix de guerre avec palme; Médaille d'argent des Epidémies; Médaille d'honneur du Service de Santé Grand Cross of Merit, Order of Malta; Grand Cross Order of Merit, Fed. Repub. of Germany; numerous other awards; Hon. Fellow, Royal Soc. of Health Laureate of French Nat. Acad. of Medicine (Prix de la ville de Paris); Lord Cohen Gold Medal, Royal Soc. of Health; Dr. h.c.
Leisure interest: natural sciences.
Publs. Articles and books on tropical medicine, preventive and social medicine, public health.
Le Chazal, 11 Chemin des Ramiers, 1245 Collonge-Bellerive, Switzerland.
Telephone: (022) 52-1966 (Home).

Doronina, Tatiana Vasilyevna; Soviet actress; b. 1933; ed. Studio School of Moscow Art Theatre.
At Leningrad Lenin Komsomol State Theatre 56-59; at Leningrad Maxim Gorky State Bolshoi Drama Theatre 59-66; Moscow Art Theatre 66-71; Majakovski Theatre 71-; Honoured Artist of R.S.F.S.R.
Main roles include: Zhenka Shulzhenko (*Factory Girl* by Volodin), Lenochka (*In Search of Happiness* by Rozov), Sophia (*Wit Works Woe* by Griboyedov), Nadya Rozoyeva (*My Elder Sister* by Volodin), Nadezhda Polikarpovna (*The Barbarians* by Gorky), Lashka (*Virgin Soil Upturned* by Sholokov), Nastasya Filippovna (*The Idiot* by Dostoyevsky), Valka (*Irkutsk Story* by Arbuzov), Oxana (*Loss of the Squadron* by Korneichuk).
Majakovski Theatre, 3 Proyezd Khudozhestvennogo Teatra, Moscow, U.S.S.R.

Doroszewski, Witold Jan; Polish linguist; b. 1 May 1899, Moscow; s. of Antoni and Maria Doroszewski; m. Janina Rogowska 1927; two s.; ed. Moscow and Warsaw Universities, Ecole Nationale des Langues Orientales Vivantes, Paris.
Head, Polish Language Dept., Warsaw Univ. 29; mem. Warsaw Scientific Soc. 30-51, Polish Acad. of Knowledge 47-51, Polish Acad. of Sciences 52-; Head, Linguistics Inst. Polish Acad. of Sciences 54-70; Editor-

-Chief *Dictionary of the Polish Language* (11 vols.) -69; Editor-in-Chief *Dictionary of Correct Polish* 68-; hair. Int. Cttee. of Slavists 68-, Asscn. for Culture of e Language; Hon. mem. Polish Linguistics Soc. 74-; em. Soc. de Linguistique de Paris, Amer. Linguistics oc.; Foreign mem. Bulgarian Acad. of Sciences 63, rbian Acad. of Sciences 72, Austrian Acad. of iences 74; Dr. h.c. Univ. of Łódź and Humboldt Univ. rlin 60, Univ. of Prague 68; State Prize 54; Officer d Commdr., Polonia Restituta, Légion d'Honneur; der of Banner of Labour First Class 59; Title of eritorious Teacher of People's Poland 70. eisure interest: sailing. ubls. Over 500 works on history of Polish language, ord-formation, phonetics, dialects, vocabulary, mantics and semiotics. ome: ul. Sewerynów 6 m.20, 00331 Warsaw, Poland.

Dorrance, John Thompson, Jr.; American business xecutive; b. 7 Feb. 1919; *m.*; two *s.* one *d.*; ed. St. eorge's School and Princeton Univ. ssistant Treasurer, Campbell Soup Co. 50-55, Asst. to he Pres. 55-62, Chair. of Board 62-; mem. Board of irs. Campbell Soup Co. 47-, Morgan Guaranty Trust o. 55-, Penn. Mutual Insurance Co. ampbell Soup Co., Campbell, Camden, New Jersey 8101, U.S.A.

Dorsey, Bob Rawls; American oil executive; b. 27 ug. 1912, Rockland, Texas; *m.* Angelina Johnapelus 941; two *s.* one *d.*; ed. Univ. of Texas. ith Gulf Oil Corpn., Port Arthur Refinery 34-38; niv. of Texas 38-40; Port Arthur Refinery, Gulf Oil orpn. 40-48; Man. Venezuela Gulf Refining Co., Puerto a Cruz, Venezuela 48-55; Gen. Office, Gulf Oil Corpn. 5-58, Admin. Vice-Pres. 58-61, Senior Vice-Pres. 61, xec. Vice-Pres. 61-65, Pres. 65-72, Dir. 64-76, Chair. of he Board and Chief Exec. Officer 73-76; Charter rustee, Univ. of Pittsburgh; Dir. American Petroleum nst., Gen. Foods Corpn., Tex-Ex Corpn.; mem. Presi-ent's Council, Calif. Inst. of Technology; Hon. .Sc. Univ. of Tampa; Distinguished Graduate ward in Engineering, Univ. of Texas 65; Distinguished lumnus of Univ. of Texas 68. eisure interests: hunting, fishing, modern art, horti-ulture, football, baseball, reading (especially geo-raphy). ulf Oil Corporation, P.O.B. 1166, Pittsburgh, Pa. 5230, U.S.A.

Dorticós Torrado, Osvaldo; Cuban lawyer and politi-ian; b. 17 April 1919; ed. Havana Univ. Leader of Castro revolutionary movement in Cien-uegos 57-58; arrested and imprisoned Dec. 58; escaped and fled to Mexico; returned upon success of revolution; Minister of Revolutionary Laws Jan.-July 59; Pres. of Cuba July 59-; Minister of Economy and Chair. Central Board of Planning 64-; Vice-Pres. Cuban Nat. Bar Asscn. Palacio Presidencial, Havana, Cuba.

Dos Santos, Marcelino; Mozambique poet and nation-alist leader; b. 1931, Lourenço Marques; ed. Lisbon and Paris. Secretary of External Affairs, Presidential Council of Frente de Libertação de Moçambique (FRELIMO) Feb. 69-; Vice-Pres. FRELIMO May 70-; Minister of Devt. and Econ. Planning, FRELIMO Government June 75-; audience with Pope Paul VI, Rome July 70. FRELIMO, Maputo (Lourenço Marques), Mozambique.

Dostrovsky, Israel, PH.D.; Israeli scientist; b. 1918, Odessa, U.S.S.R.; *m.* Daphne Wormald; one *s.* one *d.*; ed. Univ. Coll., London. Engaged in research work, Univ. Coll., London 40-43; Lecturer in Chem., Univ. Coll. of N. Wales 43-48; Joined staff of Weizmann Inst. of Science 48; Head of Isotope Research Dept., Weizmann Inst. 48-65; mem.

Isra Atomic Energy Comm. and first Dir. of Research 53-57; Chair. Nat. Council of Research and Devt. 59-61; Senior scientist, Brookhaven Nat. Laboratory, U.S.A. 61-64; Dir.-Gen. Israel Atomic Energy Comm. 65-71; Vice-Pres. Weizmann Inst. 71-73, Pres. 73-; Ramsay Medal, U.K. 44; Weizmann Prize, Israel 52; Dr. h.c. (Tel Aviv Univ.) 73. Neve Weizmann, Rehovot, Israel.

Doty, Paul Mead, B.S., M.A., PH.D.; American bio-chemist and specialist in science policy and arms control; b. 1 June 1920; ed. Pennsylvania State Coll., Columbia and Cambridge Univs. Instructor and Research Associate, Polytechnic Inst., Brooklyn 43-45, Asst. Prof. Chemistry 45-46; Asst. Prof. Chemistry, Univ. of Notre Dame 46-48; Asst. Prof. Harvard 48-50, Assoc. Prof. Chemistry 50-56; Prof. 56-; Pres. Science Advisory Cttee. 61-65; Mal-linckrodt Prof. of Biochemistry 68-; Consultant to the Arms Control and Disarmament Agency, Nat. Security Council; Dir. of Program for Science and Int. Affairs, Harvard Univ. 73-; Fellow, Amer. Acad. of Arts and Science, Nat. Acad. of Sciences, Philosophical Soc. Harvard University, Cambridge, Mass. 02138, U.S.A. Telephone: 617-495-1554.

Douce, William C., B.SC. (CHEM. ENG.); American business executive; b. 9 Dec. 1919, Kingman, Kan.; *s.* of William Thew and Grace Clark Douce (née Griswold); *m.* Willene Magruder; one *c.*; ed. Univ. of Kansas. Chairman Operating Cttee., Phillips Petroleum Co. 63, Man. Chemical Dept. 66, Senior Vice-Pres., Dir. 69, Exec. Vice-Pres. 71, Chair. Exec. Cttee. 71, Pres. and Chief Exec. Officer 74-. Leisure interests: hunting, fishing, golf. 3425 S.E. Hawthorn Court, Bartlesville, Okla. 74003, U.S.A. Telephone: (918) 333-1553.

Doudoroff, Michael, M.A., PH.D.; American bacteri-ologist; b. 14 Nov. 1911, Petrograd, Russia; *s.* of Boris and Natalie Doudoroff; *m.* Olga Fowlks 1953; one *s.*; ed. Stanford Univ. Professor of Bacteriology and Molecular Biology, Univ. of Calif., Berkeley 52-; Guggenheim Fellow, Pasteur Inst., Paris 60-62; Prof. Miller Inst. for Basic Research 62; mem. Nat. Acad. of Sciences. Publs. *The Microbial World* (with others) 70 (3rd edn.); numerous research articles in scientific journals. Leisure interests: fishing, lepidoptera. Department of Bacteriology and Immunology, Uni-versity of California, Berkeley, Calif. 94720, U.S.A.

Dougan, Robert Ormes, M.A., F.L.A.; American (b. British) librarian; b. 21 Aug. 1904; ed. Univ. Coll., London. Librarian, Royal Historical Soc. London 25-35; Cataloguer and Bibliographical Research Worker, E. P. Goldschmidt & Co. (London antiquarian booksellers) 26-40; service with R.A.F. 41-45; Librarian, Sandeman Public Library, Perth 45-52; Organizer, Scottish Books Exhibitions (Edinburgh and Glasgow), Festival of Britain 50-51; Dep. Librarian, Trinity Coll. Dublin 52-58; Lecturer on Book of Kells for Forás Eireann 56-58; Keeper, Archbishop Marsh's Library, Dublin 57-58; Librarian, Henry E. Huntington Library, San Marino (Calif.) 58-72; Hon. D.Lit. Publ. *Scottish Tradition in Photography* 49. Leisure interests: early photography, travel. 855 South Orange Grove Boulevard, Pasadena, Calif. 91105, U.S.A. Telephone: (213) 799-6732.

Douglas, David Charles, M.A., F.B.A., D.LITT.; British historian; b. 5 Jan. 1898, London; *s.* of Dr. John and Margaret (née Peake) Douglas; *m.* Evelyn Wilson 1932; one *d.*; ed. Sedbergh and Keble Coll., Oxford.

Lecturer in Medieval History Glasgow Univ. 24-34; Prof. of History Univ. Coll. of the South-West 34-39; mem. Council Royal Historical Society 35-38, Vice-Pres. 49-54; Prof. of Medieval History, Leeds Univ. 39-45; Prof. of History Bristol Univ. 45-63; Dean Faculty of Arts 58-60; Ford's Lecturer, Oxford Univ. 62-63; Trustee London Museum 45-70; Hon. Fellow Keble Coll., Oxford 59-.

Publs. *The Norman Conquest* 26, *The Social Structure of Medieval East Anglia* 27, *The Age of the Normans* 28, *Feudal Documents from the Abbey of Bury St. Edmunds* 32, *The Development of Medieval Europe* 35, *English Scholars* (awarded James Tait Black Memorial Prize) 39, *Domesday Monachorum* 45, *William the Conqueror* 64; *The Norman Achievement* 69; Gen. Editor *English Historical Documents* 53- (in progress).

4 Henleaze Gardens, Bristol, England.

Douglas, Donald W., B.SC.; American engineer; b. 6 April 1892; ed. U.S. Naval Acad., and Mass. Inst. of Technology.

Chief Engineer Glenn L. Martin Co. 15-16 and 17-20; Chief Civilian Engineer U.S. Signal Corps for Aviation 16-17; Pres. Douglas Co., Santa Monica, Calif. 20-28; Pres. Douglas Aircraft Co. Inc. 28-57, Chair. Board, Chief Exec. Officer 57-67; Hon. Chair. McDonnell Douglas Corpn. 67-; Commdr. Order of Orange-Nassau 50; Chevalier, Légion d'Honneur 50.

4 Crest Road East, Rolling Hills, Calif. 90274, U.S.A.

Douglas, Donald Wills, Jr.; American businessman, b. 3 July 1917, Washington D.C.; s. of Donald Wills Douglas and Charlotte (Ogg) Douglas; m. 1st Molly McIntosh 1939 (died), 2nd Jean Cooper 1947; two d.; ed. Stanford Univ. and Curtiss-Wright Technical Inst. Joined Douglas Aircraft Co. Inc., Santa Monica, Calif. 39, Chief, Flight Test Group in charge of testing models 43-, Dir. Contract Admin. 48, in charge, Research Laboratories, Santa Monica Div. 49, Vice-Pres. Mil. Sales 51-57, Dir. 53-, Pres. 57-67; Corporate Vice-Pres., McDonnell Douglas Corpn. 67-71, Senior Corp. Vice-Pres. 71-72; Pres. and Chief Exec. Officer Douglas Devt. Co. 72-; Govt. Aerospace Industries Asscn.; Air Force Asscn.; Trustee Air Force Museum Foundation; Asscn. of the U.S. Army; Conquistadores del Cielo; Nat. Defense Transportation Asscn.; Nat. Industrial Conf. Board; American Inst. of Aeronautics and Astronautics; Nat. Security Industrial Asscn.; Dir. Hilton Corpn. Hotels; Dir. Nat. Advisory Cttee., Youth Opportunity Campaign; Knight Legion of Honour (France) 61; Officer of the Order of Merit (Italy) 62; mem. various clubs and yachting clubs.

Leisure interests: hunting, fishing, yachting.

Douglas Development Company, 2121 Campus Drive, Irvine, Calif. 92664; Home: 26341 Calle Roberto, San Juan Capistrano, Calif. 92675, U.S.A.

Douglas, Kirk, A.B.; American actor; b. 9 Dec. 1916; ed. St. Lawrence Univ., and American Acad. of Dramatic Arts.

President Bryna Productions 55-; Dir. Los Angeles Chapter, UN Asscn.; Acad. Awards 48, 52, 56; New York Film Critics Award, Hollywood Foreign Press Award, etc.; Hon. Dr. of Fine Arts (St. Lawrence Univ.) 58.

Appeared on Broadway in *Spring Again, Three Sisters, Kiss and Tell, The Wind is Ninety, Alice in Arms, Man Bites Dog*; films include *The Strange Love of Martha Ivers, Letters to Three Wives, Ace in the Hole, The Bad and the Beautiful, 20,000 Leagues under the Sea, Ulysses, Lust for Life, Gunfight at O.K. Corral, Paths of Glory, The Vikings, Last Train from Gun Hill, The Devil's Disciple, Spartacus, Strangers When We Meet, Seven Days in May, Town without Pity, The List of Adrian Messenger, In Harms Way, Cast a Giant Shadow, The Way West, War Waggon, The Brotherhood, The Arrangement, There Was a Crooked Man, Gunfight* 71, *Light at the Edge of the World, Catch Me a Spy, A Man to Respect* 72, *Cat and*

Mouse, Scalawag (dir.) 73, *Once Is Not Enough* 7, *Posse* (prod., actor) 75.

707 North Canon Drive, Beverly Hills, Calif., U.S.A.

Douglas, Paul Howard, A.M., PH.D.; American polit cian and university professor; b. 26 March 1892; e Bowdoin Coll., Columbia and Harvard Univs.

Instructor in Economics, Univ. of Ill. 16-17; Instructc and Asst. Prof. Reed Coll., Portland, Oregon 17-18 Asst. Prof. of Economics, Univ. of Washington 19-2 Asst. Prof. of Industrial Relations, Univ. of Chicag 20-23, Assoc. Prof. 23-25, Prof. 25; Acting Dir. Swarth more Unemployment Study 30; Sec. Pa. Comm. o Unemployment, and Adviser to the N.Y. Comm. 3 mem. Consumers' Advisory Board Nat. Recover Admin. 33-35; mem. Advisory Cttee. to U.S. Senate an Social Security Board 37; U.S. Senator from Illinoi 48-66; Chair. Board of Trustees, Freedom House 67-6c served in U.S. Marine Corps, Second World Wai Fellow Econometric Soc., American Acad. Arts an Sciences; mem. American Philosophical Soc., America Econ. Asscn. (Pres. 47), American Statistical Asscn. hon. degrees from William and Mary, Bates, De Pau Oberlin, Tulane, Rollins, Bowdoin, Rochester, etc Democrat.

Publs. *American Apprenticeship and Industrial Educa tion* 21, *Worker in Modern Economic Society* (with others 23, *Wages and the Family* 25, *Adam Smith, 1776-192e* (with others) 28, *Real Wages in the United States, 1890 1926* 30, *Movement of Real Wages 1926-1928* (co author) 30, *The Problem of Unemployment* (co-author 31, *Standards of Unemployment Insurance* 33, *Th Theory of Wages* 34, *Controlling Depressions* 35, *Socia Security in the United States* 36, *Economy in the Nationa Government* 52, *Ethics in Government* 52.

2909 Davenport Street, N.W., Washington, D.C. 20008 U.S.A.

Douglas, William Orville, A.B., LL.B.; American jurist b. 16 Oct. 1898; ed. Whitman Coll., Columbia Univ. New York.

Instructor, Yakima High School, Washington 20-22 with law firm Cravath, de Gersdorff, Swaine and Wood New York 25-27; Lecturer in Law, Columbia Univ. Law School 24-28; collaborated with U.S. Dept. of Com merce, bankruptcy studies 29-32; Dir. Bankruptcy Studies, Inst. of Human Relations, Yale Univ. 29-32 Sec. to Cttee. on Study of Business of Federal Courts (Nat. Comm. on Law Observance and Enforcement) 30-32; Prof. of Law, Yale Law School 28-32, Sterling Prof. of Law 32-39; Dir. Protective Cttee. Study, Securities and Exchange Comm., Washington, D.C. 34-36, Commr. Securities and Exchange Comm. 36-39, Chair. 37-39; mem. Temporary Nat. Economic Cttee. 38-39; Associate Justice, Supreme Court of U.S. 39-75.

Publs. *Democracy and Finance* 40, *Being an American* 48, *Of Men and Mountains* 50, *Strange Lands and Friendly People* 51, *Beyond the High Himalayas* 52, *North from Malaya* 53, *An Almanac of Liberty* 54, *We the Judges* 56, *Russian Journey* 56, *The Right of the People* 58, *West of the Indus* 58, *Exploring the Himalaya* (*Landmark*) 58, *My Wilderness: East to Kathadin* 61, *A Living Bill of Rights* 61, *America Challenged* 60, *Muir of the Mountains* 61, *Democracy's Manifesto* 62, *Anatomy of Liberty* 63, *Mr. Lincoln and the Negroes* 63, *Freedom of the Mind* 63, *A Wilderness Bill of Rights* 65, *The Bible and the Schools* 66, *Towards a Global Federalism* 68, *Points of Rebellion* 69, *Hemispheric Co-op.* 71, *The Three Hundred Year War* 72, *Go East, Young Man* 74.

U.S. Supreme Court, Washington, D.C. 20543, U.S.A.

Doulatram, Jairamdas, B.A., LL.B.; Indian politician; b. 21 July 1891.

Joined Indian Home Rule Movement 16; took part in Gandhi's Satyagraha Movement 19; mem. All-India Congress Cttee. 27-40; Editor *The Bharatvasi* 19-20; partici-

ated in Gandhi's Non-Co-operation Movement 20-21; imprisoned for sedition 21-23; Editor *The Hindustan Times* Delhi 25-26, Gandhi's *Young India* 30; mem. Bombay Legislative Council 27-29; joined Satyagraha Movement for Indian Freedom 30; imprisoned twice during Civil Disobedience Movement 30-32, released 34; Gen. Sec. Indian Nat. Congress 31, Acting Pres. I. N. Congress 34, mem. Congress Working Cttee. 29-40; Chair. Textile Labour Wage Enquiry Cttee. 38; detained in prison during "Quit India" movement 42-45; mem. All-India Village Industries Board 41-46; Indian Constituent Assembly 46-50; Gov. of Bihar 47; Minister of Food and Agriculture Govt. of India 48-50; Gov. of Assam 50-56; Chief Editor *Collected Works of Mahatma Gandhi* 57-59; mem. Governing Body Gandhi Peace Foundation 58-70; mem. Indian Parliament 59-.
Rajya Sabha, Parliament House, New Delhi 1; Home: 14 Tughlak Road, New Delhi 11, India.

Dours, Jean, L. ès D.; French administrator; b. 14 Jan. 1913; ed. Lycée d'Auch, Coll. de Saint-Gaudens and Faculté de Droit, Paris.
Adviser, Council of Prefecture of Rouen 39; Asst. Prefect, Albertville 43; Asst. Chief, Office of Central Admin. 45; Asst. Dir. Private Office, Prefect of Seine 47-57; Technical Adviser, Private Office of René Billères, Minister of Educ.; Adviser, Head Office of Nat. Defence 58, Dir. 59; Prefect, Bône Dec. 61-May 62; Dir. Private Office of Christian Fouchet, High Commr. of France in Algeria April 62-June 62, Private Office of Christian Fouchet, Minister of Information 62, then of Nat. Educ. 62-66; Dir. Gen. Sûreté Nationale 67; Dir.-Gen. of Nat. Police 69-72; Mayor of Auch 68-; Officier Légion d'Honneur, Croix de Guerre, Commdr. des Palmes Académiques, and other awards.
81 boulevard Suchet, Paris 16e, France.

Dovali Jaime, Antonio: Mexican civil engineer and business executive; b. 3 Oct. 1905, Zacatecas, Zac.; *m.* María Ramos Elorduy; two *c.*; ed. Nat. Preparatory School and Nat. Engineering School, Univ. of Mexico.
Director, Railway Construction, Ministry of Public Works 43-48; Under-Sec. for Public Works 49-52; Dir. Gen. Mexican Petroleum Inst. 66-70; Dir. Gen. Petróleos Mexicanos Dec. 70-; Nat. Engineering Award.
Publ. *Situación y Tendencias de la Industria Petrolera Nacional 71.*
Marina Nacional 329, 12°, México 17, D.F., Mexico.
Telephone: 531-61-65.

Dow, John Christopher Roderick, B.SC. (Econ.); British economist; b. 1916, Harrogate; *s.* of Warrender Begernie and Amy Dow; *m.* Clare Keegan 1960; one *s.* three *d.*; ed. Bootham School, York, Brighton, Hove and Sussex Grammar School, and Univ. Coll., London.
Drummond-Fraser Research Fellow, Dept. of Economics Univ. of Manchester 38-39; R.A.F. 40-43; Ministry of Aircraft Production 43-45; Econ. Section, Cabinet Office, later Treasury successively Econ. Asst., Econ. Adviser, Senior Econ. Adviser 45-54, 62-63; Research in Management of British Economy, Cambridge Univ. 54-55; Nat. Inst. of Econ. and Social Research, London 55-62, Dep. Dir. 57-62; Asst. Sec.-Gen. (Econ. and Statistics) OECD 63-73; Exec. Dir. Bank of England 73-.
c/o Bank of England, Threadneedle Street, London, E.C.2, England.

Dowell, Anthony, C.B.E.; British ballet dancer; b. 16 Feb. 1943, London; *s.* of Arthur H. Dowell and late Catherine E. Dowell; unmarried; ed. Royal Ballet School.
Principal dancer, The Royal Ballet 66, now Senior Principal dancer; created the following ballets: *The Dream* 64, Benvolio in *Romeo and Juliet* 65, *Shadow*

Play 67, *Monotones* 69, *Triad* 72, *Manon* 74, *Encounters* 75.
Leisure interests: painting, paper sculpture, theatrical costume design.
c/o The Royal Ballet, Covent Garden, London, WC2E 7QA, England.
Telephone: 01-240-1200.

Dowell, Dudley, LL.D.; American insurance executive (retired); b. 24 Aug. 1903; ed. Little Rock High School, and Univ. of Arkansas.
New York Life Insurance Co. 21-, Clerk, Little Rock 21-25, Cashier, Jackson, Mississippi 25-27, Asst. Manager Little Rock 27-29, Manager Butte, Montana 29-36, Seattle 36-39, Supervisor Allegheny Dept. Pittsburg 39-41, Inspector of Agencies 41, Superintendent, Home Office 41, Asst. Vice-Pres. 42, Vice-Pres. 43-45, Vice-Pres. in charge Agencies New York City 45-54, Exec. Vice-Pres. 54-62, Dir. 58-, Chair. Exec. Cttee. 59-69, Pres. and Chief Admin. Officer 62-69; Dir. J. Henry Schroder Banking Corpn. and Schroder Trust Co.; Pres. of numerous Insurance Asscns.
Route 2, Box 338c, Eden Isle, Heber Springs, Ark. 72543, U.S.A.

Dowling, Geoffrey Barrow, M.D., F.R.C.P.; British physician; b. 1891, Cape Town, S. Africa; *s.* of Thomas Barrow Dowling and Minna (née Crump); *m.* Mary Elizabeth Kelly 1923; two *s.* two *d.*; ed. Diocesan Coll. School, Cape, Exeter Cathedral School, Dulwich Coll., Guy's Hosp.
Served in ranks in France 15-17; Medical Registrar, Guy's Hosp. 20-23, Asst. Physician in Dept. of Dermatology 28-33, Physician in Charge 33-56; Dir. of Studies at Post-Graduate Inst. of Dermatology, St. John's Hosp. for Diseases of the Skin 50-56 (retd.); Hon. M.D. (Utrecht, Pretoria); Hon. mem. British, European and American Dermatological Socs.
Leisure interest: mainly general reading.
Publs. contributions to dermatological literature.
52 Ravenscourt Gardens, London, W.6, England.
Telephone: 01-748-9796.

Down, Alastair Frederick, O.B.E., M.C., T.D., C.A.; British oil executive; b. 23 July 1914, Kirkcaldy, Fife, Scotland; *s.* of Frederick Edward Down and Margaret Isobel Hutchison; *m.* Maysie Hilda Mellon 1947; two *s.* two *d.*; ed. Marlborough Coll.
British Petroleum (then Anglo-Iranian Oil Co.) 38-; Army Service 40-45; with BP in Iran 45-47, London 47-54; Chief Rep. of BP, Canada 54, later Pres. The British Petroleum Co. of Canada Ltd., BP Canada Ltd., BP Refinery Canada Ltd., BP Exploration Co. of Canada Ltd.; Man. Dir. The British Petroleum Co. Ltd. 62-75, Deputy Chair. 69-75; Chair., Chief Exec. Burmah Oil Co. Ltd. Jan. 75-; mem. Soc. of Chartered Accountants of Scotland.
Leisure interests: golf, fishing, shooting.
Burmah Oil Co. Ltd., Burmah House, Pipers Way, Swindon, Wilts., England.
Telephone: (0793) 30151.

Downer, Hon. Sir Alexander Russell, K.B.E., M.A., F.R.S.A., BAR.-AT-LAW; Australian diplomatist; b. 7 April 1910, Adelaide; *s.* of the late Hon. Sir John Downer, K.C.M.G., K.C.; *m.* Mary Isobel, *d.* of the late Sir James Gosse, 1947; one *s.* three *d.*; ed. Geelong Grammar School, Victoria, Brasenose, Coll., Oxford, and Inner Temple, London.
Served with Australian Imperial Forces 40-45; prisoner of war of Japanese 42-45; Liberal Mem. Australian House of Representatives 49-64; mem. Parl. Foreign Affairs Cttee. 52-58; mem. of Constitutional Review Cttee. 56-59; Rep. of the Australian Parl. at the Coronation of H.M. Queen Elizabeth II 53; Minister of State for Immigration 58-63; High Commr. for Australia in

the United Kingdom 64-72; a Gov. English Speaking Union 73; Freeman of City of London 65; Hon. LL.D. (Birmingham Univ.) 73.
Leisure interests: reading, country life, travel, collecting antiques.
26-27 Queens Gate Gardens, London, S.W.7, England; Martinsell, Williamston, South Australia, Australia.

Downes, Ralph (William), C.B.E., K.S.G., M.A., B.MUS., F.R.C.M.; British organist; b. 16 Aug. 1904, Derby; s. of James and Constance Downes; m. Agnes Rix 1929; one s.; ed. Derby Municipal Secondary School, Royal Coll. of Music, Keble Coll., Oxford, and Pius X School of Liturgical Music, New York.
Director of Music, Univ. Chapel, Princeton Univ. 28-35; Concert organist and Organist, the London Oratory 36-; Organ Consultant to L.C.C., Royal Festival Hall 49-53, Govt. of Malta 60-62, Corpn. of Croydon 61-64; Curator of Organs, Royal Festival Hall 54-, and Fairfield Hall, Croydon; Prof. of Organ, Royal Coll. of Music 54-75; Jury-mem. Int. Organ Festivals, Haarlem, Munich, St. Albans; designer of organs; organ, choral and piano compositions and articles on organ design and its musical significance; Hon. R.A.M., Hon. F.R.C.O.
c/o The Oratory, London, S.W.7, England.
Telephone: 01-567-6330.

Downs, Brian Westerdale, M.A., D.LITT.; British university professor; b. 4 July 1893, Hull; s. of James and Ethel Downs (née Wilson); m. Evelyn Faith Marion Wrangham 1946; ed. Abbotsholme School and Christ's Coll., Cambridge.
Fellow of Christ's Coll. 19-50, 63-; Lecturer in English, Cambridge Univ. 26-50; British Council Rep. in the Netherlands 45-46; Master of Christ's Coll. 50-63 and Prof. of Scandinavian Studies 50-60; Vice-Chancellor, Cambridge Univ. 55-57; Commdr. of the Royal Swedish Order of the North Star; Officier Légion d'Honneur; Ridder (1st Class) Order of Dannebrog (Denmark).
Publs. *Richardson* 28, *Ibsen, the intellectual Background* 46, *Six Plays by Ibsen* 50, *Strindberg* (in collaboration with Miss Mortensen) 49, *Norwegian Literature 1860-1918* 66.
Christ's College, Cambridge; Home: 75 Long Road, Cambridge, England.
Telephone: Cambridge 59601.

Dowson, Graham Randall; British business executive; b. 13 Jan. 1923, Southend; s. of late Cyril James and Dorothy Celia Dowson (née Foster); m. Fay Valerie Weston 1954 (dissolved 1974); two d.; ed. City of London School, Ecole Alpina, Switzerland.
War service 39-45, Pilot, Squadron Leader R.A.F. 41-46; Sales, U.S. Steel Corpn. (Columbia Steel), Los Angeles 46-49; Mid-South Network (MBS), Radio U.S.A. 49-52; Dir. A. C. Nielsen Co., Oxford 53-58, Southern T.V. Ltd., London 58-59; Dir. Rank Organisation 60, Deputy Chief Exec. 72, Chief Exec. 74-75; Chair. Mooloya Investments, Erskine House Investment Trust; Pres. of Appeals, Nat. Playing Fields Asscn. 71-73; Chair. British Section, European League for Econ. Co-operation 72-.
Leisure interest: sailing.
Rank Organisation Ltd., 38 South Street, London, W1A 4QU, England.

Doyenin, Vasily Nikolayevich; Soviet politician; b. 1909; ed. Far Eastern Polytechnical Inst.
Director of a works making light motor vehicles 48-50; later Chair. Econ. Council of R.S.F.S.R.; Minister of Machine-Building for Light and Food Industry and Household Articles 65-, mem. C.P.S.U. 40-, Alt. mem. Central Cttee. C.P.S.U. 66-; Deputy to U.S.S.R. Supreme Soviet 66-.
Ministry of Machine-Building for Light and Food Industry and Household Articles, 17 Presnensky val, Moscow, U.S.S.R.

Doyle, Hon. Chief Justice Brian André, B.A., LL.B.; Zambian judge; b. 10 May 1911, Moulmein, Burma; ed. Douai School and Trinity Coll., Dublin.
Magistrate, Trinidad and Tobago 37; Resident Magistrate Uganda 42; Solicitor-Gen. Fiji 48, Attorney-Gen. 49; Attorney-Gen. N. Rhodesia 56, Attorney-Gen. and Minister of Legal Affairs 59-65; Justice of Appeal Zambia 65; Chief Justice of Zambia 69-75.
P.O. Box R.W. 67, Lusaka, Zambia.

Drabble, Bernard J., B.A.; Canadian international financial official; b. 20 May 1925, Portsmouth, England; s. of James C. W. Drabble and Mary Buchanan Simpson; ed. Portsmouth Grammar School, and McGill Univ.
Deputy Chief, Research Dept., Bank of Canada 64; Assoc. Adviser 66, Adviser to the Govs. 71, Deputy Gov. 74; Exec. Dir. Int. Monetary Fund Nov. 74-; Allan Oliver Gold Medal, McGill Univ.
Leisure interests: tennis, swimming, music.
International Monetary Fund, Washington, D.C. 20431; Home: 4701 Willard Avenue, Apartment 531, Chevy Chase, Md. 20015, U.S.A.

Drabble, Margaret; British author; b. 1939, Sheffield; m. Clive Swift; three c.; ed. Newnham Coll., Cambridge.
Publs. *A Summer Bird-Cage* 63, *The Garrick Year* 64, *The Millstone* 65, (John Llewelyn Rhys Memorial Prize 66), *Jerusalem the Golden* 67, *The Waterfall* 69, *The Needle's Eye* 72, *Arnold Bennett: A Biography* 74, *The Realms of Gold* 75, *The Genius of Thomas Hardy* (Editor) 76.
c/o A. D. Peters & Co., 10 Buckingham Street, London W.C.2, England.
Telephone: 01-839-2556.

Dracos, George; Greek business executive; b. 1916; ed. Economic Univ. of Athens.
Managing Dir. Isola Manufacturing Co. 38-, Pres. 63-; Dir. P. Dracos S.A. Trading Co., 37-; Pres. VES Trading Co. 62-; Pres. Federation of Greek Industries 58-; mem. Board, Athens Technological Inst.; High Order of Phoenix.
22 Homer Street, Athens, Greece.

Drăgan, Dr. Joseph Constantin; Romanian industrialist (lives in Italy); b. 1917; ed. Univs. of Bucharest and Rome.
Founder-Manager Dacia Co. 40, Dacia Inc. 47, Banca Gallia & Co. and Butane-Gas 48, Dragochimica Co. 52, Traschimici Shipping Co. 52; and various companies in Europe and Africa, all controlled by Dragofina Petroleum Investment Trust Reg. Lugano, Switzerland and Vaduz, Liechtenstein; founded *Romanian Catholic Monitor* and *European Bulletin* 49 and *Eastern Europe Monitor* 54; Chair. N. Italy Marketing Asscn., Spanish Marketing Asscn.; mem. Int. Chamber of Commerce; Vice-Chair. for Europe of Int. Marketing Fed.
9 via Larga, Milan, Italy.

Drăgănescu, Emil; Romanian politician; b. 18 Dec. 1919, Galați; m. Ofelia Drăgănescu; one s. one d.; ed. Polytechnic School, Bucharest.
Engineer in Bucharest 42-48; Deputy Minister of Building and of Building Materials Industry 52-55; Vice-Chair., State Control Cttee. 55-61; Vice-Chair. State Planning Cttee. 61-65; Minister of Electric Power 65-68; Vice-Chair. Council of Ministers 68-; Minister of Transport and Tele-communications 72-74; Chair. Nat. Council for Physical Educ. and Sport 73-; Chair. State Planning Cttee. 74-75; mem. of C.P. 46; mem. Central Cttee. of R.C.P. 65-, alt. mem Exec. Cttee. 68-, mem. Exec. Cttee 69-; Deputy to Grand Nat. Assembly 69-; mem. Defence Council 74-; Order of Labour 69.
Central Committee of the Romanian Communist Party, Bucharest, Romania.

Dragstedt, Lester R., M.S., PH.D., M.D.; American physiologist and surgeon; b. 2 Oct. 1893, Anaconda, Mont.; s. of John A. and Caroline Seline Dragstedt; m.

Gladys Shoesmith 1922; two s. two d.; ed. Rush Medical Coll., Chicago and Univs. of Chicago, Vienna and Budapest.

Instructor in Pharmacology, State Univ. of Iowa 16-17, Asst. Prof. of Physiology 17-19; Asst. Prof. of Physiology, Univ. of Chicago 20-23, Assoc. Prof. of Surgery 25-30, Prof. 30-48, Chair. and Thomas D. Jones Distinguished Service Prof. of Surgery 48-59; Prof. of Physiology and Pharmacology and Head of Dept. of Physiology and Pharmacology, Northwestern Univ. Medical School 23-25; Research Prof. of Surgery, Univ. of Florida 59-, Prof. of Physiology 66-; Hon. mem. Royal Coll. of Surgeons of England, Royal Coll. of Physicians and Surgeons of Canada, Swedish Surgical Soc., German Surgical Soc., Acad. of Surgery of France, Acad. of Science and Asscn. of Gastroenterologists of Mexico; corresp. mem. Royal Acad. of Arts and Sciences, Uppsala; Fellow Amer. Acad. of Arts and Sciences; Hon. D.Sc. (Florida); Dr. h.c., Univs. of Lyons, Uppsala and Guadalajara; Royal Order of North Star of Sweden 67, Distinguished Service Award of Amer. Medical Asscn. 63, Julius Friedenwald Medal, Amer. Gastroenterological Asscn. 64, Henry Jacob Bigelow Medal, Boston Surgical Soc. 64, First Distinguished Service Award from Amer. Surgical Asscn. 69.
Leisure interests: golf, fishing, travel.
Publs. 350 articles in scientific and medical journals, including papers on thyroid and parathyroid glands, peptic, duodenal and gastric ulcers and lipocaic hormone discovery 19-.
2224 N.W. Eleventh Avenue, Gainesville, Fla. 32601; Summer: Rapid City, Mich., U.S.A.
Telephone: 904-372-4503.

Drake, Sir (Arthur) Eric (Courtney), Kt., C.B.E., M.A., F.C.A.; British business executive; b. 29 Nov. 1910, Rochester, Kent; s. of Dr. A. W. Courtney Drake and Ethel Davidson; m. 1st Rosemary Moore 1935; two d.; m. 2nd Margaret E. Wilson 1950; two s.; ed. Shrewsbury School and Pembroke Coll., Cambridge.
Anglo-Persian Oil Co. Ltd. (now The British Petroleum Co. Ltd.) 35-75; Man. Dir. The British Petroleum Co. Ltd. 58-75, Deputy Chair. 62-69, Chair. 69-75; Pres. Chamber of Shipping of U.K. 64; Dir. P & O Co., Hudson's Bay Co.; Hon. Petroleum Adviser to British Army 71-; mem. Cttee. on Invisible Exports; mem. Gen. Cttee. of Lloyd's Register of Shipping; mem. Gov. Body of Shrewsbury School; Hon. D.Sc. (Cranfield) 71; Hon. Fellow Manchester Inst. of Science and Technology 74; Freeman of City of London 74; H.M. Lieut. for City of London; Hambro Award for Businessman of the Year 71; Commdr. Ordre de la Couronne (Belgium); Kt. Grand Cross, Order of Merit (Italy); Officer Légion d'Honneur (France); Order of Homayoun II (Iran) 74; Commdr. Order of Leopold (Belgium) 75; Hon. Elder Brother, Trinity House; Hon. Co. Master Mariners.
Leisure interests: sailing, shooting.
c/o The British Petroleum Co. Ltd., Britannic House, Moor Lane, London, E.C.2; Home: The Old Rectory, Cheriton, Alresford, Hants., England.
Telephone: 01-920-8301 (London Office).

Drake, Frank Donald, B.ENG.PHYS., M.A., PH.D.; American astronomer; b. 28 May 1930, Chicago; s. of Richard C. Drake and Winifred Thompson Drake; m. Elizabeth B. Bell 1953; three c.; ed. Cornell and Harvard Univs.
United States Navy 52-55; Harvard Radio Astronomy Project 55-58; Ewen-Knight Corpn. 57-58; Scientist, Head Scientific Services and Telescope Operations on Nat. Radio Astron. Observatory 58-63; Chief, Lunar and Planetary Science Section, Jet Propulsion Laboratory 63-64; Prof. of Astronomy, Cornell Univ. 64-; Dir. Arecibo Ionospheric Observatory 66-68; Assoc. Dir. Center for Radiophysics and Space Research, Cornell

Univ. 67-; Chair. Dept. of Astronomy, Cornell Univ. 68-71; Dir., Nat. Astronomy and Ionosphere Center 71-; Vice Pres. American Asscn. for the Advancement of Science 72-73; mem. Nat. Acad. of Sciences 72-.
Leisure interests: swimming, sailing.
Publ. *Intelligent Life in Space* 62.
Center for Radiophysics and Space Research, Cornell University, Ithaca, N.Y. 14850, U.S.A.
Telephone: 256-3734.

Drake-Brockman, Hon. Thomas Charles; Australian politician; b. May 1919, Toodyay, W. Australia; s. of Mr. and Mrs. R. J. Drake-Brockman; m. Edith M. Sykes; one s. four d.; ed. Guildford Grammar School, Perth.
Served with R.A.A.F. 41-45; Pres. Wool Exec., Farmers Union of W. Australia; Vice-Pres. Australian Wool and Meat Producers Fed. 57-58; mem. Senate 58-; Minister of State for Air Nov. 69-72, for Aboriginal Affairs and Admin. Services Nov. 75-; Distinguished Flying Cross.
Leisure interest: golf.
Ministry of Aboriginal Affairs and Administrative Services, Canberra, Australia.

Drapeau, Jean, C.C., Q.C., LL.B.; Canadian lawyer and politician; b. 18 Feb. 1916, Montreal; s. of late Joseph-Napoléon Drapeau and Berthe Martineau; m. Marie-Claire Boucher 1945; three s.; ed. Jean-de-Brébeuf and Le Plateau Schools, Montreal, and Univ. of Montreal.
Admitted to Montreal Bar 43; practised law in Criminal and Civil Courts, specializing in commercial and corpn. law; Mayor of Montreal 54-57, 60-; founded Montreal Civic Party 60; Senior Canadian rep. at the Int. Bureau of Exhbns., Paris 67-71; Hon. degrees from Univ. of Moncton 56, Univ. of Montreal 64, McGill Univ. 65, Boswell Inst., Loyola Univ. 66, Sir George Williams Univ. and Laval Univ. 67; Hon. mem. American Bar Asscn.; Gold Medal, Royal Architectural Inst. of Canada 67.
Mayor's Office, City Hall, Suite 104, Montreal, Canada.
Telephone: 872-3100.

Draper, Charles Stark, B.A., B.S., M.S., PH.D.; American aeronautical engineer; b. 2 Oct. 1901, Windsor, Mo.; s. of Charles A. and Martha W. Draper (née Stark); m. Ivy Hurd Willard 1938; three s. one d.; ed. Univ. of Missouri, Stanford Univ., and Mass. Inst. of Technology.
Assistant Prof. of Aeronautical Engineering, M.I.T. 35-38, Assoc. Prof. 38-39, Prof. 39-, Dir. Instrumentation Laboratory 40-69; Head of Dept. of Aeronautics and Astronautics 51-66; Vice-Dir. Charles Stark Draper Laboratory 70-, Pres. 71-; research and devt. on fire control, flight control and inertial guidance systems for U.S. Air Force and Navy, consulting engineer to many aeronautical companies and instrument manufacturers; mem. several advisory groups connected with military services; Pres. Int. Acad. of Aeronautics; Medal of Merit (presidential citation) 46, Exceptional Civilian Service Award (Dept. of Air Force) 51, 68 and 69, Navy Distinguished Public Service Award 56, 60, Holley Medal (American Soc. of Mech. Engrs.) 57, American Hon. Fellowship for 58 of Inst. of Aeronautical Sciences 59, Potts Medal Award, Franklin Inst. 60, Nat. Medal of Science 65; Hon. degree Eidgenössische Technische Hochschule, Switzerland; Guggenheim Award 67; N.A.S.A. Distinguished Public Service Medal 67; N.A.S.A. Public Service Award, Apollo Achievement Award 69; Founder's Medal, Nat. Acad. of Engineering 69, Distinguished Civilian Service Medal, Dept. of Defence; Hon. degree, Univ. of Portland, Ore., and many other national awards.
Leisure interests: sports cars, gliding.
Publs. *Instrument Engineering* (with W. McKay and S. Lees) Vol. I 52, Vol. II 53, Vol. III 55, and numerous papers in the fields of instrumentation and control.

Office: Massachusetts Institute of Technology, Charles Stark Draper Laboratory, 68 Albany Street, Cambridge, Mass. 02139; Home: 62 Bellevue Street, Newton, Mass., U.S.A.
Telephone: 464-0670.

Drees, Willem, (father of Willem Drees, q.v.); Netherlands politician; b. 5 July 1886, Amsterdam; s. of Johannes M. and Anna S. Drees; m. Catharina Hent 1910; two s. one d.; ed. Commercial School.
Joined Twentsche Bank; stenographer to States-Gen. 07; Chair. Hague Federation of the S.D.A.P. (Social Democratic Workers' Party) 11-31; mem. Hague Municipal Council 13; mem. Provincial States of Zuid Holland 19, and in 33 mem. Second Chamber; mem. S.D.A.P. party executive since 27; filled many other Social posts; during the occupation Chair. of Convention of Political Parties and Central Cttee. Resistance Movement; mem. Gov. Advisory Council; Min. Social Affairs in Schermerhorn's Govt. June 45-46, and Beel's Govt. June 46-48; introduced Old Age Pensions Act 47; Prime Minister Aug. 48-Dec. 58; awards include, Hon. G.C.M.G., Grand Cross of Order of Léopold (Belgium), of Order of Crown of Oak (Luxembourg), Grand Croix Légion d'Honneur and Order of Dannebrog, Grand Cross Order of the Netherlands Lion, Hon. Minister of State, etc.; Hon. Citizen, The Hague; Hon. D.Econ.; Hon. Dr. Jur.
Beeklaan 502, The Hague, Netherlands.
Telephone: 070-335424.

Drees, Willem, DR.ECON.; Netherlands politician; b. 24 Dec. 1922, The Hague; s. of Dr. Willem Drees (q.v.) and Catharina Hent; m. Anna E. Gescher 1947; one s. four d.; ed. grammar school, The Hague and Netherlands School of Econs., Rotterdam.
Economist, International Monetary Fund, Washington, D.C. 47-50; Financial Counsellor, Netherlands Embassy, Jakarta 50-53; Deputy Dir. Central Planning Bureau, The Hague 55; Dir. of the State's Budget, Ministry of Finance, 56-69; Treasurer-Gen. Ministry of Finance 69-71; Prof. of Public Finance, Netherlands School of Econs. 63-71; mem. Second Chamber of Parl. May-July 71, Sept. 72-; Minister of Transport and Public Works 71-72; mem. Int. Inst. of Public Finance; Knight, Order of Netherlands Lion 61; Commdr. Order of Orange-Nassau 72.
Leisure interests: animal watching.
Publs. On the level of government expenditure in the Netherlands after the war 55, Moving the capital city 59, Efficiency in government spending 66, Financing higher education 66, Dutch public expenditure (co-author) 68.
Second Chamber of Parliament, Binnenhof 1A, The Hague; Home: Wildhoeflaan 35, The Hague, Netherlands.
Telephone: 070-61-49-11 (Office); 070-680118 (Home).

Drell, Sidney David; American professor of physics b. 13 Sept. 1926, Atlantic City, N.J.; s. of Tulla and Rose White Drell; m. Harriet Stainback 1952; one s. two d.; ed. Princeton Univ. and Univ. of Illinois.
Research Assoc. Univ. of Illinois 49-50; Physics Instructor Stanford Univ. 50-52; Research Assoc. Mass. Inst. of Technology 52-53; Asst. Prof. 53-56; Assoc. Prof. Stanford Univ. 56-60, Prof. of Physics 60-63; Prof. Stanford Linear Accelerator Center 63-, Deputy Dir. and Exec. Head of Theoretical Physics 69-; Visiting Scientist and Guggenheim Fellow, CERN 61-62; Visiting Prof. and Loeb Lecturer, Harvard Univ. 62, 70; Consultant to Office of Science and Technology, Exec. Office of the Pres., President's Science Advisory Cttee. 66-70, Arms Control and Disarmament Agency, etc.; Chair. High Energy Physics Advisory Panel, ERDA 74-; mem. numerous advisory cttees. and editorial boards; mem. Nat. Acad. of Sciences, American Acad. of Arts and Sciences; Fellow American Physical Soc.; Guggen-

heim Fellow, Rome 72; E. O. Lawrence Memorial Award 72.
Leisure interest: music.
Publs. Relativistic Quantum Mechanics, Relativistic Quantum Fields (both with J. D. Bjorken) and numerous articles in The Physical Review and other professional journals.
Stanford Linear Accelerator Center, P.O. Box 4349 Stanford, Calif. 94305; Home: 570 Alvarado Row Stanford, Calif. 94305, U.S.A.
Telephone: 415-854-3300 (Office); 415-325-0565 (Home)

Drese, Claus Helmut, DR.PHIL.; German theatre director; b. 25 Dec. 1922, Aachen; s. of Karl Drese and Helene Drese; m. Helga Lautz 1950; two c.; studied German studies, philosophy and history in Cologne, Bonn and Marburg.
Theatre Literary Man., Mannheim 52-59; Theatre Dir. Heidelberg 59-62, Wiesbaden 62-68, Cologne 68-.
Publs. Various contributions to newspapers, radio and television.
5000 Köln-Dellbrück, Schluchterheide 13, Federal Republic of Germany.
Telephone: 68-48-47.

Drew, Jane Beverly, F.R.I.B.A., F.I.ARB., F.S.I.A.; British architect; b. 24 March 1911, Thornton Heath, Surrey; d. of Harry Guy Radcliffe Drew and Emma Spering Jones; m. Edwin Maxwell Fry 1942; two d.; ed. Croydon High School, Architectural Asscn.
In partnership with J. T. Alliston 34-39; private practice 39-45; Partner, Fry, Drew & Partners 46-73, Fry, Drew, Knight & Creamer 73-; Asst. Town Planning Adviser to Resident Minister, West African Colonies 44-45; Senior Architect Capital Project of Chandigarh, Punjab, India 51-54; Beamis Prof. Mass. Inst. of Technology 61; Visiting Prof. of Architecture Harvard Univ. 70; Bicentennial Prof., Utah Univ.; mem. Council Royal Inst. of British Architects; mem. Council, Pres. Architectural Asscn. 69; Hon. LL.D. (Ibadan Univ.), Dr. h.c. (Open Univ.).
Major work includes housing, hospitals, schools, colls. in U.K., West Africa, Middle East, India; town planning, housing and amenity bldgs. in Iran, West Africa, India; a section of Festival of Britain 51; current work in office planning, industrial housing, hospitals and Open Univ.
Leisure interests: reading, writing, friends.
Publs. Architecture for Children (with Maxwell Fry) 44, Village Housing in the Tropics (with Maxwell Fry and Harry Ford) 45, Founder Editor Architects' Year Book 45-, Architecture in the Humid Tropics (with Maxwell Fry), Tropical Architecture 56.
63 Gloucester Place, London W.1, England.
Telephone: 01-935-3318.

Dreyfus, Pierre; French business executive; b. 18 Nov. 1907.
Inspector-Gen. of Industry and Commerce, Chief of Gen. Inspectorate, and Dir. of Cabinet to Minister of Industry and Commerce 47-49; Pres. Houillères de Lorraine 50, Charbonnages de France 54; Pres. of Energy Comm. of the Plan, and Dir. of Cabinet to Minister of Industry and Commerce 54; Vice-Pres. Régie nationale des usines Renault 48-55, Pres., Dir. Gen. 55-; Pres. Société des Aciers fins de l'Est; Commdr. Légion d'Honneur.
Régie Nationale des Usines Renault, B.P. 103, 92 Boulogne-Billancourt (Seine); Home: 51 avenue des Champs-Elysées, Paris 8e, France.

Dreyfus, Pierre; French industrialist; b. 2 Nov. 1907, Mulhouse; m. Colette Schwob 1933; three c.; ed. Lycée de Mulhouse, Ecole de Filature et Tissage, Mulhouse.
Joined Etablissement Dreyfus Frères, Mulhouse 29, Admin. Dir. 33, Man. Dir. 49-65; Président-directeur-général, P. Dreyfus et Cie, Mulhouse 65-; Président du

Directoire de Schaeffer-Impression, Vieux-Thann; Chevalier Légion d'Honneur.
Grand-Rue, 68 Vieux-Thann, France.

Drick, John, E., B.S.; American banker; b. 26 Nov. 1911, Williamsport, Pa.; ed. Phillips Acad., Andover, Mass., and Sheffield Scientific School, Yale Univ. Assistant Cashier, The First National Bank of Chicago 44-46, Asst. Vice-Pres. 47-50, Vice-Pres. Petroleum and Term Loans Divs. 50-63, Senior Vice-Pres. 64, Exec. Vice-Pres. 65, Head of Commercial Banking Dept. 68, Pres. 69-74, Dir. 69-, Chair. Exec. Cttee. 74-; Dir. Stepan Chemical Co., MCA Inc., Oak Industries Inc., Cen. Ill. Public Service Co., Transportation Asscn. of America.
1 First National Plaza, Chicago, Ill. 60670; Home: 1039 Miami Road, Wilmette, Ill., U.S.A.

Drickamer, Harry George, B.S.E., M.S., PH.D.; American professor of physical chemistry and chemical engineering; b. 19 Nov. 1918, Cleveland, Ohio; s. of George H. and Louise S. Drickamer; m. Mae Elizabeth McFillen 1942; two s. three d.; ed. Univ. of Michigan. Pan American Refining Corpn. Texas City 42-46; Asst. Prof. of Chemical Engineering, Univ. of Illinois 46-49, Assoc. Prof. 49-53, Prof. 53-, Head, Div. of Chemical Engineering 55-58, Prof. of Physical Chem. and Chemical Engineering 58-, mem. Center for Advanced Study 63-; mem. Nat. Acad. of Sciences, American Acad. of Arts and Sciences; Allan P. Colburn Award, American Inst. of Chemical Engineers 47; Ipatieff Prize, American Chem. Soc. 56; Oliver E. Buckley Solid State Physics Award, American Physical Soc. 67; Alpha Chi Sigma Award, American Inst. of Chemical Engineers 67, Walker Award 72; Vincent Bendix Award, American Soc. of Engineering Educ. 68, William Walker Award, American Inst. of Chemistry 72; Langmuir Award in Chemical Physics, American Chemical Soc. 74.
Leisure interests: reading of medieval and 18th-century history, walking.
Publs. Over 200 papers in scientific journals.
105 R. Adams Laboratory, East Chemistry Building, University of Illinois, Urbana, Ill. 61801; Home: 304 East Pennsylvania Street, Urbana, Ill. 61801, U.S.A. Telephone: 217-333-0025 (Univ.).

Drijver, Alexander, M.MECH.ENG.; Netherlands mechanical engineer; b. 17 Nov. 1904, Bodegraven; m. 1930; five s. one d.; ed. Technische Hogeschool te Delft.
Mechanical Engineer, Koninklijke Nederlandsche Hoogovens en Staalfabrieken N.V., IJmuiden 28, Chief, Engineering Dept. 45-50, Dir. of Engineering 50-59, Asst. Man. Dir. 59-61, Man. Dir. 61-67, Chair. of Board of Man. Dirs. 67-70, deputy mem., Supervisory Board 70-; Vice-Pres. Centre Nat. de Recherches Métallurgiques, Liège 60-70; Dir. Int. Iron and Steel Inst. 67-70; mem. State Council of Ministry of Waterworks 67-; Board mem. Royal Soc. of Engineers (Holland), mem. Iron and Steel Inst. (U.K.), Verein Deutscher Eisenhüttenleute; Hon. mem. Iron and Steel Inst. of Japan; Gold Medal of Honour of Mech. Eng. and Shipbuilding Section of Royal Netherlands Soc. of Engineers; Knight Order of Netherlands Lion; Dr. h.c.
Leisure interests: yachting, swimming, cycling, ice-skating; nature-lover.
Publs. Articles and papers on technical and econ. devt. in iron and steel industry in nat. and int. magazines.
Koninklijke Nederlandsche Hoogovens en Staalfabrieken N.V., IJmuiden; Home: Zomerzorgerlaan 4, Bloemendaal, Netherlands.
Telephone: IJmuiden 99111 (Office); 023-252801 (Home).

Driss, Rachid; Tunisian journalist and diplomatist; b. 27 Jan. 1917, Tunis; m. Jeanine Driss 1953; one s.; ed. Sadiki Coll., Tunis.

Joined Neo-Destour party 34; journalist exiled in Cairo, and with Pres. Bourguiba founder mem. Bureau du Maghreb Arabe; returned to Tunisia 55; Editor *El Amal*; Deputy, Constitutional Assembly 56; Sec. of State Post Office and Communications 57-58; mem. National Assembly 58, 69-; Amb. to the U.S.A. and Mexico 64-68; mem. Political Bureau of Council of the Repub. 69-; Perm. Rep. to UN 70-; Vice-Pres. Econ. and Soc. Council 70, Pres. 71; Grand Cordon de l'Ordre de l'Indépendance de la République Tunisienne and many foreign decorations.
Permanent Mission of Tunisia to the United Nations, 40 East 71st Street, New York, N.Y. 10021; Home: 35 East 85th Street, New York, U.S.A.
Telephone: 988-7200 (Office); 744-3693 (Home).

Driver, William J., B.B.A., LL.B.; American government official; b. 9 May 1918; s. of John J. Driver and Bridget A. Farrell; m. Marian R. McKay 1947; two s.; ed. Niagara Univ., Rochester, N.Y., and George Washington Univ., Washington, D.C.
Executive and Admin. Officer, H.Q., Adjutant-Gen., European Theatre of Operations, U.S. Army 42-46; Office of Asst. Chief of Staff, U.S. Army 51-53; Chief Benefits Dir., Veterans Administration 59-61; Deputy Admin., Veterans Admin. 61-65, Admin. of Veterans Affairs 65-69; Pres. Mfg. Chemists Asscn. 69-; numerous awards.
1825 Connecticut Avenue, N.W., Washington, D.C. 20009; Home: 215 West Columbia Street, Falls Church, Va. 22046, U.S.A.

Drobnis, Alexandras Antonovich; Soviet politician; b. 26 March 1912, Pilkaraistis, Lithuania; s. of Antanas Drobnis and Stephania Petrushkevichiute; m. Lidija Kupstaite 1944; two d.; ed. Vilnius State Univ.
Chief of State Bank office 40-42; Deputy People's Commissar of Finance, Lithuanian S.S.R., later People's Commissar 42-47; Vice-Chair. Council of Ministers and Chair. State Planning Cttee. of Lithuanian S.S.R. 57-; mem. Central Cttee. of C.P. of Lithuania; mem. C.P.S.U. 44-; Order of Lenin (twice), Order of Red Banner of Labour (three times).
State Planning Committee of Lithuanian SSR, Lenin al. 38/2, Vilnius, U.S.S.R.

Drogheda, 11th Earl of, cr. 1661; **Charles Garrett Ponsonby,** K.G., K.B.E.; b. 23 April 1910; British newspaper executive and arts administrator; ed. Eton and Trinity Coll., Cambridge.
Joined staff of *Financial News* 32; worked for Ministry of Production 42-45; Man. Dir. *Financial Times* 45-70, Chair. and Chief Exec. 71-75; Chair. Industrial & Trade Fairs Ltd.; Dir. Economist Newspaper Ltd.; Chair. Royal Opera House, Covent Garden Ltd. 58-74, Newspaper Publrs.' Asscn. Ltd. 68-70; Gov. The Royal Ballet; Pres. Inst. of Dirs. 75-; Pres. Country Dance Theatre; Joint Chair. Youth and Music; Grand Officer Order of Léopold II.
Parkside House, Wick Lane, Englefield Green, Surrey; and 8 Lord North Street, London, S.W.1, England.
Telephone: Egham 2800.

Droit, Michel; French journalist and writer; b. 23 Jan. 1923, Vincennes; s. of Jean Droit; m. Janine Bazin 1947; one s. one d.; ed. Lycée Louis le Grand, Paris, Univ. of Paris, and Ecole Libre des Sciences Politiques.
Resistance Movement 42-44; War Correspondent and Reporter for press, radio and TV 44-56; Foreign Affairs Commentator, French TV 56-60; Editor-in-Chief *Tribunes et Débats*, French TV 60-61; Editor-in-Chief *Le Figaro Littéraire* 61-71; Advisory Editor to *La Librairie Plon* 68; Management Adviser to *Le Figaro* 71; Producer TV Programme *A propos* 61-; Chair. Safaris de la Ouandjia-Vakaga, Central African Republic; Prix Max Barthou 55; Prix Carlos de Lazerme 61, Grand Prix

du Roman de l'Académie Française 64; Chevalier, Légion d'Honneur; Médaille Militaire.

Leisure interests: big game hunting, karate, skin-diving.

Publs. novels: *L'Ecorché, Pueblo, Le Retour, Les Compagnons de la Forêt-Noire, L'Orient Perdu, La Ville Blanche;* travel: *Jours et nuits d'Amérique du Sud, J'ai vu vivre le Japon, Panoramas mexicains;* essays: *André Maurois, La Camargue;* biography: *De Lattre Maréchal de France, L'Homme du Destin* (5 vols.); short stories: *La Fille de l'Ancre Bleue;* film: *Un Français Libre.*

29 avenue d'Eylau, Paris 16e, France.

Telephone: Kleber 23-10.

Droogleever Fortuyn, Jan, M.D., M.SC.; Netherlands neurologist; b. 12 April 1906; ed. Univs. of Utrecht, Amsterdam.

Department of Neurology, Amsterdam 39-51; Prof. of Neurology, Groningen 51-; Montreal Neurological Inst. 46-47; Dutch Central Inst. for Brain Research 47-51.

Publs. *Experimental Study on Cortico-Thalamic Relationships* 38, *Studies in Epilepsy* 47, *Studies on Topographical Relationships in the Brain* 56, *Petit Mal* 57, *Geometrical properties of the neurons in general and of the lateral geniculate body of the rabbit in particular* 64, *Forms of Muscle Fatigue* 70, *On the State of the Nervous System and Related Subjects* 71-73.

Department of Neurology, University Hospital, Oostersingel 59, Groningen, Netherlands.

Telephone: 050-139123.

Drozdenko, Vasily Ivanovich; Soviet diplomatist; b. 1924; ed. Engineering Inst., Dnepropetrovsk and C.P.S.U. Higher Party School.

Member, C.P.S.U. 44-, cand. mem. Cen. Cttee. 66-71, mem. 71-; army service 42-45; party and Komsomol work 46-52; Sec. Cen. Cttee. Ukrainian C.P. 52-54, Second Sec. 54-55, First Sec. 55-60; First Sec., Kiev City Cttee., Ukrainian C.P. 60-62; First Sec., Regional C.P. Cttee., Kiev 62-66; Sec. Cen. Cttee., C.P. of Ukrainian S.S.R. 66-71; Amb. to Romania 71-.

Soviet Embassy, Şoseaua Kiseleff 6, Bucharest, Romania.

Drucker, Peter Ferdinand, LL.D.; American management consultant and teacher; b. 19 Nov. 1909, Vienna, Austria; s. of Adolph and Caroline Drucker; m. Doris Schmitz 1937; one s. three d.; ed. gymnasium, Vienna and Univ. of Frankfurt.

Professor of Political Philosophy, Bennington Coll., Bennington, Vt. 42-49; Prof. of Management, Graduate School of Business Admin. 50-72; Clarke Prof. of Social Science, Claremont Grad. School, Claremont, Calif. 71-; Management Consultant (own firm) 45-; Fellow, American Asscn. for Advancement of Science, American Acad. of Management, Int. Acad. of Management; Hon. Fellow, British Inst. of Management; eight hon. degrees from univs. in U.S.A., U.K., Japan, Belgium and Switzerland.

Publs. *The End of Economic Man* 39, *The Future of Industrial Man* 42, *Concept of the Corporation* 46, *The New Society* 50, *The Practice of Management* 54, *America's Next Twenty Years* 57, *Landmarks of Tomorrow* 59, *Managing for Results* 64, *The Effective Executive* 66, *The Age of Discontinuity* 69, *Technology, Management and Society* 70, *The New Markets and other essays* 71, *Management: Tasks, Responsibilities, Practices* 74.

Claremont Graduate School, Claremont, Calif. 91711; Home: 636 Wellesley Drive, Claremont, Calif., U.S.A.

Telephone: 0714-621-1488 (Home).

Drumalbyn, 1st Baron, cr. 63, of Whitesands; **Niall Malcolm Stewart Macpherson,** P.C., K.B.E.; British politician; b. 3 Aug. 1908, Gaya, India; s. of Sir (Thomas) Stewart Macpherson, C.I.E., I.C.S.; m. Margaret Phyllis Runge 1937; two d.; ed. Edinburgh Acad., Fettes Coll., and Trinity Coll., Oxford.

With Reckitt & Colman Ltd. 31-39; Major, Queen's Own Cameron Highlanders 39-45; M.P. for Dumfries 45-63; Joint Under-Sec. of State for Scotland 55-60, Parl. Sec. Board of Trade 60-62; Minister of Pensions and Nat. Insurance 62-63; Minister of State, Board of Trade 63-64; Chair. Advertising Standards Authority 65-70, 74-; Chair. Overseas Cttee., Asscn. of British Chambers of Commerce 68-70; Minister without Portfolio 70-74; Conservative.

Leisure interests: music, sport.

High Larch, Iver Heath, Bucks., England.

Telephone: 0753-653021.

Drummond, Roscoe, B.S.J.; American writer; ed. Syracuse Univ.

Reporter with *Christian Science Monitor*, Boston 24, later editorial writer, Chief, Washington News Bureau; on leave as Dir. of Information, E.C.A. (Paris) 49-51; Chief, Washington Bureau *New York Herald Tribune* 53-55; Washington columnist for Publishers' Newspaper Syndicate 55-; Hon. Litt.D. Dartmouth Coll. 47, Hon. D.D.L. Principia Coll. 54.

Publ. *Duel at the Brink: John Foster Dulles' Command of American Power* (with Gaston Coblenz) 60.

3029 Cambridge Place, N.W., Washington, D.C., U.S.A.

Drummond de Andrade, Carlos; Brazilian writer; b. 30 Oct. 1902.

Head of Private Office of Minister of Educ. and Culture 34-45; Head of History Section, Office of Nat. and Artistic Heritage 45-62; Historian of *Correio da Manhã* (Rio de Janeiro) 54-.

Publs. Poetry includes: *Alguma Poesia* 30, *Brejo das Almas* 34, *Sentimento do Mundo* 40, *A Rosa do Povo* 45, *Claro Enigma* 51, *Fazendeiro do Ar* 53, *Lição de Coisas* 62; prose: *Contos de Aprendiz* 51, and four vols. of history.

Rua Conselheiro Lafaiete 60, Ap. 701, Rio de Janeiro, R.J., Brazil.

Druon, Maurice Samuel Roger Charles; French author; b. 23 April 1918, Paris; m. Madeleine Marignac 1968; ed. Lycée Michelet and Ecole des Sciences Politiques, Paris.

War Corresp. Allied Armies 44-45; mem. Académie Française 66-; Minister for Cultural Affairs 73-74; Prix Goncourt for novel *Les Grandes Familles* 48; Prix de Monaco 66; Officier, Légion d'Honneur; Commdr. des Arts et Lettres; Commdr. Order of Phoenix (Greece); Commdr. Ordre de la République de Tunisie; Grand Cross of Merit (Italy); Grand-Croix Ordre du Lion du Sénégal; Grand Cross of the Aztec Eagle (Mexico); Grand Officer, Order of Merit (Malta).

Leisure interest: riding.

Publs. *Lettres d'un Européen* 43, *La Dernière Brigade* 46, *La Fin des Hommes* (3 vols. *Les Grandes Familles* 48, *La Chute des Corps* 50, *Rendez-vous aux Enfers* 51), *La Volupté d'être* 54, *Les Rois Maudits* 55-60 (6 vols. *Le Roi de Fer, La Reine Etranglée, Les Poisons de la Couronne, La Loi des Mâles, La Louve de France, Le Lis et le Lion), Tistou les pouces verts* 57, *Alexandre le Dieu* 58, *Des Seigneurs de la plaine à l'hôtel de Mondez* 62, *Les Mémoires de Zeus* (2 vols. *L'aube des dieux* 63, *Les jours des hommes* 67), *Bernard Buffet* 64, *Paris, de César à Saint Louis* 64, *Le Pouvoir* 65, *Les Tambours de la Mémoire* 65, *Le Bonheur des uns . . .* 67, *Discours de Réception à l'Académie française* 68, *L'Avenir en Désarroi* 68, *Vezelay, colline éternelle* 68, *Nouvelles Lettres d'un Européen* 43-70, *Une Eglise qui se trompe de siècle* 72, *La Parole et le Pouvoir* 74; plays: *Mégarée* 42, *Un Voyageur* 53, *La Contessa* 62.

73 rue de Varenne, Paris 7e, France.

Drury, Allen Stuart, B.A.; American writer; b. 2 Sept. 1918; ed. Stanford Univ.

Editor *Tulare Bee* 40-41; County Editor *Bakersfield Californian* 42; army service 42-43; Senate Staff, United

Press 43-45; freelance corresp. Washington 46-47; Nat. Editor *Pathfinder Magazine* 47-52; Nat. Staff, *Washington Evening Star* 52-54; Senate Staff, *New York Times* 54-59; contrib. *Readers' Digest* 60-; Pulitzer Prize for novel *Advise and Consent* 60.
Publs. *Advise and Consent* 59, *A Shade of Difference* 62, *A Senate Journal* 63, *That Summer* 65, *Three Kids in a Cart* 65, *Capable of Honor* 66, *A Very Strange Society, Courage and Hesitation* 71, *The Promise of Joy: The Presidency of Orrin Know, Come Nineveh, Come Tyre* 74.
Box 927, Maitland, Florida, U.S.A.

Drury, Hon. Charles Mills, P.C., C.B.E., D.S.O., E.D.; Canadian politician; b. 17 May 1912; ed. McGill Univ., Royal Military Coll., Kingston, Ontario, and Univ. of Paris.
Chief, UNRRA Mission, Poland 45-47; Dep. Minister, Dept. of Nat. Defence 49-55; Pres. Provincial Transport Co. 56-60; Pres. Avis Transport of Canada Ltd. 58-63, Needco Frigistors Ltd. 60-63; Dir. Livingstone Range Syndicate Ltd. 61-63; Minister of Defence Production and Industry 63-68; Pres. of Treasury Board 68-74; Minister of Science and Technology and of Public Works Aug. 74-; Chevalier de la Légion d'Honneur; Order of Polonia Restituta (Poland); Liberal.
Ministry of Science and Technology, Ottawa, Ont.; 23 Mackay Street, Ottawa, Ontario, Canada.

Druzhinin, Nikolai Mikhailovich; Soviet historian; b. 13 Jan. 1886, Kursk; s. of Mikhail and Nadezhda (Khudokormova) Druzhinin; m. Elena Ioasafovna Druzhnina (née Chistyakova); ed. Moscow Univ.
Officer in World War I 16-18; Educ. Officer, Red Army 19-21; gen. educ. work 19-29; Prof. Moscow Univ. 34-48; research work Historical Inst. of U.S.S.R. Acad. of Sciences 38-; mem. U.S.S.R. Acad. of Sciences 53-; State Prize, Order of Lenin (three), Order of Red Banner of Labour (two).
Publs. include: *Decembrist Nikita Muravjev* 33, *On Periods of History of Capitalist Economic System in Russia* 49, *State Peasantry and P. D. Kiselev's Reform*, Vols. 1-2 46-58, *Conflict Between Productive Forces and Feudal Economic System Before 1861 Reform* 57, *Memoirs and Thoughts of an Historian* 67, *Besonderheiten der Genesis des Kapitalismus in Russland* 73, *The Effect of the Agrarian Reforms of the 1860s upon the Economy of the Russian Village* 75.
U.S.S.R. Academy of Sciences, Department of History, 19 Ul. Dmitry Ulyanov, Moscow, U.S.S.R.

Drysdale, Sir (George) Russell, Kt.; British-born Australian artist; b. 7 Feb. 1912; ed. Geelong Grammar School, Victoria, Australia.
Art studies in Melbourne, London and Paris; works in New York Metropolitan Museum of Art, Nat. Gallery, London, Tate Gallery, London, Nat. Galleries of New South Wales, Victoria, South Australia, etc.; mem. Commonwealth Art Advisory Board 62-; Dir. Pioneer Sugar Mills Ltd.
Publ. (with Jock Marshall) *Journey Among Men* 62.
Bouddi Farm, Kilcare Heights, Hardy's Bay, N.S.W., Australia.

Dua, Indardev, B.A., LL.B.; Indian judge; b. 4 Oct. 1907, Mardan (now in Pakistan); s. of Amirchand and Parbati Devi; m. Sheila Dua 1915; one s.; ed. Christian Coll., Lahore, Law Coll., Punjab and Punjab Univ.
Practised at the Bar, Lahore High Court 33-47, Punjab High Court 47-58; Judge, Punjab High Court 58, Delhi High Court 66; Chief Justice, Delhi High Court 67-69; Judge of the Supreme Court 69-73; Lokayukta (Ombudsman), State of Rajasthan.
Leisure interests: studies in development of rule of law and liberal-democratic movement; interested in promoting egalitarian system of society.
Lokayukta, 11 Civil Lines, Jaipur, India.
Telephone: 67265.

Duarte, Paulo; Brazilian writer, journalist, and anthropologist; b. 1899; ed. Institut Champagnat, France and Faculty of Law, São Paulo, Institut d'Ethnologie and Musée de l'Homme, Paris.
Former Deputy 34-37; Editor of *Diario Nacional, O Estado de São Paulo*, and Dir. of Editora Anhambi; during the 1932 revolution commanded the Frente de Bianor and Trem Blindado which fought and took part in the retreat of Cruzeiros; exiled, returned to Brazil 34; elected State Legislature; exiled again 37, returned 46; Pres. Cttee. for Prehistory, São Paulo Inst. of Prehistory and Ethnology; worked at Musée de l'Homme, Paris, and Museum of Modern Art, New York; founded the periodical *Anhambi*; Pres. Sociedade de Escritores and Sec.-Gen. Institut Français des Hautes Etudes Brésiliennes, Paris; Dir. Inst. of Prehistory, Univ. of São Paulo.
Publs. *Sob as Arcadas* 27, *Agora Nos* 27, *Versos de Trilussa* 28, *Que e que há* 31, *Contra o Vandalismo e o Exterminio* 36, *Variações sobre a gastronomia* 42, *Lingua Brasileira* 42, *Prisão, Exilio e Luta* 45, *Palmares pelo Avesso* 47, *Trilussa* 55, *O Espirito das Catedrais* 58, *Paul Rivet, por ele mesmo* 60, *O resto não é silencio* 66, *O Sambaqui Visto atraves de alguns Sambaquis* 68.
Cuidade Universitaria, caixa Postal 11.133, São Paulo, Brazil.

Dubček, Alexander, D.SC.S.; Czechoslovak politician; b. 27 Nov. 1921, Uhrovec; ed. Communist Party Coll., Moscow, and Law Faculty, Comenius Univ., Bratislava.
Chief Sec. of Regional Cttee. of C.P. of Slovakia in Banská Bystrica 53-55; Chief Sec. Regional Cttee. of C.P. of Slovakia, Bratislava 58-60; mem. Presidium and Sec. of Central Cttee. of C.P. of Slovakia 62-68; mem. Presidium Central Cttee. of C.P. of Czechoslovakia 63-69; First Sec. Central Cttee. of C.P. of Slovakia 63-68; First Sec. Central Cttee. C.P. of Czechoslovakia 68-69; Chair. Central Cttee. of Slovak Nat. Front 63-68; mem. Presidium of Central Cttee. of Nat. Front; Deputy to Nat. Assembly 48, 60, 64-69, and to Slovak Nat. Council 64-70; mem. Exec. Cttee. of Presidium Central Cttee. C.P. of Czechoslovakia 68-69; Deputy to House of the People 69-70; Chair. Fed. Assembly April-Oct. 69; Amb. to Turkey 69-70; Inspector, Forestry Admin., Bratislava 70-; Order of 25 Feb. 1948, 49; Award for Merits in Construction 58; Czechoslovak Peace Prize 68.
Forestry Enterprise, Bratislava, Czechoslovakia.

Dubinin, Mikhail Mikhailovich; Soviet physical chemist; b. 1 Jan. 1901, Moscow; ed. Moscow Higher Technical School.
In Moscow Higher Technical School 21-32, Prof. 33-; Head of Laboratory of Sorbtion Processes, Inst. of Physical Chemistry, U.S.S.R. Acad. of Sciences 46-; mem. U.S.S.R. Acad. of Sciences 43-; Pres. Mendeleyev Chemical Soc. 46-50; Head Chemical Section U.S.S.R. Acad. of Sciences 48-57; Editor-in-Chief *Bulletin of U.S.S.R. Academy of Sciences, Chemical Series*; Hon. mem. Hungarian Acad. of Sciences: State Prize 42, 50; Hero of Socialist Labour; Order of Lenin (twice); Order of the Patriotic War; Order of the Red Star (twice), Hammer and Sickle Gold Medal, etc.
Publs. *Fiziko-khimicheskie osnovy sortsionnoi tekhniki* 35, 39, *Theory of Volume Filling for Vapor Adsorption* 66, *Porous Structure and Adsorption Properties of Active Carbons* 66, *Adsorption in Micropores* 67, *Porous Structure of Adsorbents and Catalysts* 67, *Surface of Non-Porous and Porous Adsorbents* 70, 73, 74, *Physical Adsorption of Gases and Vapors in Micropores* 75.
c/o U.S.S.R. Institute of Physical Chemistry, Academy of Sciences, Leninsky Prospekt 31, Moscow 117071, U.S.S.R.

Dubinin, Nikolai Petrovich; Soviet biologist; b. 4 Jan. 1907, Kronstadt; s. of Petr Fedorivich and Anna Gerasimovna Dubinin; m. Lydia Georgievna Dubinina 1962; one d.; ed. Moscow Univ.
At Moscow Zootechnical Inst. 28-32; at Inst. of

Cytology, Histology and Embryology, U.S.S.R. Acad. of Sciences 32-48; at Inst. of Forestry 49-55, Inst. of Biophysics 55-58; Dir. Inst. of Cytology and Genetics, Siberian Dept., U.S.S.R. Acad. of Sciences 58-60; Dir. Inst. of Gen. Genetics, U.S.S.R. Acad. of Sciences 66-; mem. C.P.S.U. 69-; Presidium mem. Siberian Dept., U.S.S.R. Acad. of Sciences 58; Corresp. mem. U.S.S.R. Acad. of Sciences 46-66, mem. 66-; Chair. of "Man and Environment" Section of State Cttee. for Science and Technology of U.S.S.R. Council of Ministers; Darwin Medal 50; Lenin Prize 66; Order of October Revolution 75; 30th Anniversary of Victory Medal.
Leisure interests: fishing, hunting.
Publs. *General Genetics* 70, *Horizons of Genetics* 70, *Vesnoe Dvizhenie* 73.
Institute of General Genetics, U.S.S.R. Academy of Sciences, 7 Profsoyuznaya Street, 117312 Moscow, U.S.S.R.
Telephone: 135-62-13.

Dubinsky, David; Polish-born American trade unionist; b. 22 Feb. 1892.
Emigrated to U.S.A. 11, naturalised 16; Man. Sec. Local Branch Int. Ladies' Garment Workers' Union 21-29; Vice-Pres. Int. Ladies' Garment Workers' Union 22-29, Gen. Sec. and Treas. 29-32, Pres., Gen. Sec. and Treas. 32-59, Pres. 59-66; Vice-Pres. and mem. Exec. Council A.F.L. 34-36 (resigned), 45-55, A.F.L.-C.I.O. 55-; a founder of the American Labor Party 36; founder Vice-Chair. Liberal Party 44; founder Americans for Democratic Action 47.
24 Fifth Avenue, New York City, N.Y. 10011, U.S.A.

Dubois, Jacques-Emile, D.SC.; French university professor; b. 13 April 1920, Lille; s. of Paul Dubois and Emilienne Chevrier; m. Bernice Claire Shaaker 1952; one s. one d.; ed. Univs. of Lille and Grenoble.
Member Liberation Cttee., Isère 43-47; Ramsay Fellow, Univ. Coll., London 48-50; Scientific Adviser to French Cultural Counsellor, London 48-50; Prof. of Physical Chemistry and Petrochemistry, and Dir. of Chemistry Inst., Univ. of Saar 49-57, Dean of Science Faculty 53-57; Prof. of Physical Organic Chemistry, Univ. of Paris 57-; Research Fellow, Columbia Univ., New York 56; Guest Prof. of Physical Chemistry, Univ. of Saar 58; Scientific Adviser to French Minister of Educ. 62-63; Joint Dir. of Higher Educ. 63-65; Dir. of Research for Ministry of Defence 65-; Chair. IUPAC Interdivisional Cttee. on Machine Documentation 70-; Vice-Pres. French Physical Chem. Soc. 72-74, Pres. 74-; French Nat. Del. to Codata; mem. Directorate Nat. Research Council 63-71; mem. Council French Chemical Soc. 65-71; mem. Faraday Soc.; Officier Légion d'Honneur, Officier Ordre National du Mérite, Médaille de la Résistance, Commdr. des Palmes Académiques; Jecker Prize and Berthelot Medal (Acad. of Sciences); Le Bel and Ancel Prizes (French Chemical Soc.); Stas Medal (Belgian Chemical Soc.); Grand Prix Technique, City of Paris 75.
Leisure interests: skiing, water skiing.
Publs. works in field of kinetics, fast reaction rates, electro-chemistry, automation applied to chemistry and coding of organic compounds by use of matrixes, and a systematic approach by these methods to correlations between structure and reactivity of organic compounds; the whole comprising the topological system D.A.R.C.
100 rue de Rennes, 75006 Paris, France.
Telephone: 222-45-16.

Dubos, René Jules, PH.D.; American bacteriologist; b. 20 Feb. 1901, Saint Brice, France; ed. Coll. Chaptal and Inst. Nat. Agronomique (Paris).
Assistant Editor Int. Inst. of Agronomy, Rome 22-24; settled in U.S.A. 24 (naturalized U.S. citizen 38); Research Asst. Rutgers Univ. N.J. Experimental Station 24-27; Fellow, Rockefeller Univ. for Medical Research 27-28, Asst. 28-30, Assoc. 30-38, Assoc.

mem. 38-41, mem. 41-42; Fabyan Prof. of Comparative Pathology and Tropical Medicine, Harvard Univ Medical School 42-44; mem. Rockefeller Univ. for Medical Research 44-56, Prof. 56-71, Emer. 71-; mem. Nat. Acad. of Sciences, American Philosophical Soc. Nat. Research Council; numerous awards include John Phillips Memorial Award (American Coll. of Physicians) 40, George Wilson Medal (American Clinical and Climatological Asscn.) 46, Lasker Award (American Public Health Asscn.) 48, Hitchcock Award (Univ. of Calif.) 54; Scientific Achievement Award (American Medical Asscn.); Arches of Science Award 66; Pulitzer Prize for Non-Fiction for *So Human an Animal* 69; Inst. of Life Prize 72; numerous hon. degrees.
Publs. include: *The Bacterial Cell* 45, *Bacterial and Mycotic Infections of Man* 48, *Louis Pasteur* 50, *The White Plague—Tuberculosis, Man and Society* 52, *Biochemical Determinants of Microbial Disease* 54, *Mirage of Health* 59, *The Unseen World* 63, *Health and Disease* 65, *Man Adapting* 65, *Man, Medicine & Environment* 68, *So Human an Animal* 68, *Reason Awake: Science for Man* 70, *A God Within* 72, *Only One Earth* (co-author Barbara Ward) 72.
Office: Rockefeller University, 1230 York Avenue, New York, N.Y. 10021; Home: Old Albany Post Road, Garrison, New York, N.Y. 10524, U.S.A.

DuBridge, Lee Alvin, M.A., PH.D.; American physicist and educator; b. 21 Sept. 1901, Terre Haute, Indiana; s. of Frederick A. and Elizabeth (née Browne) DuBridge; m. Doris M. Koht 1925; one s. one d.; ed. Cornell Coll., and Univ. of Wisconsin.
Instructor in Physics, Univ. of Wisconsin 25-26; Fellow Nat. Research Council at Calif. Inst. of Technology 26-28; Asst. Prof. of Physics, Washington Univ. St. Louis, Missouri 28-33; Assoc. Prof. 33-34; Prof. of Physics and Chair. of Dept., Univ. of Rochester 34-46; Dean of Faculty of Arts and Science 38-42; on leave of absence, Univ. of Rochester, for war service as Dir. of Radiation Lab. at M.I.T., under the Nat. Defense Research Cttee. 40-45; Pres. of Calif. Institute of Technology 46-69; Scientific Adviser to Pres. Nixon 69-70; mem. Scientific Advisory Cttee., Gen. Motors 71-; mem. Gen. Advisory Cttee. U.S. Atomic Energy Comm. 46-52; Chair. Science Advisory Cttee., Office of Defense Mobilisation 52-56; mem. Nat. Academy of Sciences, American Philosophical Society; Pres. American Physical Society 47; mem. Governing Board, American Inst. of Physics 41-46; Fellow, American Asscn. for Advancement of Science; mem. Board of Trustees, Carnegie Endowment for Int. Peace 51-57, Nat. Science Foundation Board 50-54, 58-64; mem. Board of Trustees, Rockefeller Foundation 56-67; mem. Board of Trustees Mellon Inst. 58-67; Trustee, U.S. Churchill Foundation 60-68, Thomas Alva Edison Foundation, Inc. 60-68, Henry E. Huntington Library and Art Gallery, San Marino, Calif.; various directorships; Benjamin Franklin Fellow, Royal Soc. of Arts, London, England 62-; Research Corpn. award 47; Medal for Merit 48; King's Medal for Service in Cause of Freedom 46; Hon. Fellow and Gold Medal award American Coll. of Cardiology 66; numerous hon. degrees.
Publs. *Photoelectric Phenomena* (with A. L. Hughes) 32, *New Theories of the Photoelectric Effect* 35, *Introduction to Space* 60.
Home: Apartment 3A, 2355 Via Mariposa West, Laguna Hills, Calif. 92653, U.S.A.

Dubuffet, Jean; French artist; b. 31 July 1901; ed. Paris art schools.
Worked alternately as painter and commercial traveller 24-42; free-lance artist 42-; travels in the Sahara 47-49; settled at Venice 55; has made extensive study of "Art Brut"—the work of criminals, mental defectives, etc.; has experimented widely in the production of

works from unusual materials such as sand, sponges, nails, tar and glass; retrospective exhbn., Tate Gallery, London 66, Guggenheim Museum, N.Y. 67.

Publs. *Prospectus et tous écrits suivants* Vol. I 68, Vol. II 8.

1 rue de Verneuil, Paris 73; Home: 06-Vence, France.

Dubuisson, Marcel Georges V. C.; Belgian university professor; b. 1903, Olsene, E. Flanders; s. of Georges Dubuisson and Adeline Maudens; m. Adèle Brouha 1934; one s. one d.; ed. Liège Univ.
Director Dept. of Zoology, Ecole des Hautes Etudes 25-31; Dir. Dept. of Anatomy, Ghent Univ. 28-31; Dir. Biology, Liège Univ., Prof. Faculty of Science 36-71, Rector and Pres. 53-71; mem. Royal Acad. of Sciences, Pres. 60-61.
Publs. 140 papers on physiology, biochemistry and biophysics of muscular contraction.
c/o Department of General Biology, University of Liège, Quai Van Beneden 22, Liège, Belgium.

du Cann, Col. the Rt. Hon. Edward Dillon Lott, P.C. M.A., M.P.; British politician and banker; b. 28 May 1924, Beckenham; s. of C. G. L. du Cann; m. Sallie Murchie 1962; two d. one s.; ed. Woodbridge School, Suffolk, and St. John's Coll., Oxford.
M.P. 56-; Founder and Chair. Unicorn Group of Unit Trusts 57-62, 64-72; Chair. Asscn. Unit Trust Mans. 61; Econ. Sec. to the Treasury 62-63; Minister of State, Board of Trade 63-64; Chair. of Conservative Party 65-67; Chair. 1922 Cttee. 72-; Chair. First Select Cttee. on Public Expenditure 70-72, Public Accounts Cttee. 72-; Chair. Keyser Ullmann Ltd. 68-75, Cannon Assurance Ltd. 72-; Visiting Fellow, Univ. of Lancaster Business School; Patron, Asscn. of Insurance Brokers 73-; Hon. Col. 155 Regiment (Wessex) Volunteers.
Leisure interests: sailing, country pursuits, travel.
Publ. *Investing Simplified* 59.
19 Lord North Street, London, S.W.1, England.

Ducci, Roberto, LL.D.; Italian diplomatist; b. 8 Feb. 1914, Florence; s. of Gino Ducci and Virginia Boncinelli; m. Wanda Matyjewicz 1951; two s.; ed. Rome Univ.
Entered Foreign Service 37; served Ottawa 38, Newark N.J. 40; Italian del. to Peace Conf. 46, Warsaw 47, Rio 49, Italian del. to N.A.T.O. and O.E.E.C. 50-55; mem. del. Brussels Six-Power Conf. 55-57; Chair. Drafting Cttee. Rome Treaties 56-57; Asst. Dir.-Gen. Economic Affairs, Ministry of Foreign Affairs 55-58; Ambassador to Finland 58-62; mem. of Board, European Investment Bank 58-68; Head, Italian Del. to Brussels U.K.-EEC Conf. 61-63; Deputy Dir.-Gen. for Political Affairs 63-64, Dir.-Gen. 70-; Amb. to Yugoslavia 64-67, to Austria 67-70; Grand Cross, Italian Order of Merit.
Leisure interests: poetry, collecting old glass.
Publs. *Prima Età di Napoleone* 33, *Questa Italia* 48, *L'Europa Incompiuta* 71, *D'Annunzio Vivente* 73, and numerous political essays and articles.
c/o Ministry of Foreign Affairs, Rome, Italy.
Telephone: 3871.

Duchesne, Lucien R.; French international official; b. 9 March 1908, Paris; m.; two d.
Member Staff, Int. Chamber of Commerce 32-, later Asst. Sec.-Gen. and Admin. Dir.; Sec. Int. Congresses 33-; Sec. of Council, Exec. Cttee. and Budget Comm.; Sec. Int. Bureau of Chambers of Commerce 50-56; mem. Soc. for Accountancy and French Inst. of Expert-Accountants 36-; mem. Ecole Nouvelle d'Organisation Economique and Sociale 45-; Mayor of La Celle Saint-Cloud 59-; Gen. Councillor of Yvelines district 64-; Chevalier, Légion d'Honneur, and numerous other French and foreign honours and medals.
15 Allée Corot, 78170 La Celle Saint-Cloud, France.
Telephone: 969:70:33.

Duckmanton, Talbot Sydney, C.B.E.; Australian broadcasting executive; b. 26 Oct. 1921, South Yarra, Victoria; s. of S. J. Duckmanton; m. Florence Sim-

monds 1947; one s. three d.; ed. Newington Coll., Stanmore, New South Wales, Sydney Univ., and Australian Administrative Staff Coll.
Australian Army and Air Force Service; Australian Broadcasting Comm. 39-, Man. for Tasmania 53-57, Controller of Admin. 57-59, Asst. Gen. Man. (Admin.) 59-64, Deputy Gen. Man. 64-65, Gen. Man. 65-; Vice-Pres. Asian Broadcasting Union 70-73, Pres. 73-; Pres. Commonwealth Broadcasting Asscn. 75-; Trustee, Visnews Ltd. 65-; mem. Council, Australian Admin. Staff Coll. 69-, Australian Film Devt. Corpn. 70-75, Australian Council for the Arts 73-75, Australia Council 75-.
Australian Broadcasting Commission, 145-153 Elizabeth Street, Sydney, 2000 New South Wales, Australia.
Telephone: 31-0211.

Ducreux, Louis Raymond; French theatrical and operatic manager; b. 22 Sept. 1911.
Artistic Man. Theatrical Company *Le Rideau Gris* 31-35, Co.-Dir. with André Roussin 35-40; Stage Dir. *Compagnie Claude Dauphin*, Cannes 40-42; Actor-Man. *La Comédie de Lyon* 42-43; playwright, actor, composer and stage dir. in Paris 44-61; Man. Opéra de Marseille 61-65, 68-72, Opéra de Monte Carlo 65-72, Grand Théâtre de Nancy 73-; Officier Légion d'Honneur, Officier des Arts et Lettres.
Publs. Plays: *La Part du Feu, Un Souvenir d'Italie,* French version of *The Heiress* and *Bell, Book and Candle*; Musical Plays: *L'Amour en papier, Le Square du Pérou*; Libretto of *L'Héritière.*
10 rue Hégé Sippe Moreau, Paris 9, France.

Dudinskaya, Natalya Mikhailovna; Soviet ballerina; b. 21 Aug. 1912; ed. Leningrad School of Choreography.
Prima Ballerina Kirov Academic Opera and Ballet Theatre, Leningrad; theatre coach in the Kirov Theatre 51-; principal parts include all ballets by Tchaikovsky, *Raimonda* by Glazunov, *Giselle, Les Sylphides, Don Quixote* and *The Bayadere* by Mincous; has created leading roles in *Laurencia* by Krein, *Gayane* by Khachaturyan, *Cinderella* by Prokofiev, *The Bronze Horseman* by Gliere, *Shuralé* by Yarullin, the Polish Maiden in *Taras Bulba* by Soloviev-Sedoy 56, Sarie in *The Path of Thunder* by Kara Karayev 58, Baroness Strahl in *The Masquerade* by Laputin 60, Titania in *A Midsummer Night's Dream* 63, The Wicked Fairy in the film *The Sleeping Beauty* 64, *The Spanish Suite* by Viana López Gerardo 66, *Miniature* by Krein 67; guest artist in many foreign countries; People's Artist of U.S.S.R.; State Prizewinner 41, 47, 49, 51; Order Red Banner of Labour, etc.
Kirov Opera and Ballet Theatre, Ploshchad Iskusstv, 1, Leningrad, U.S.S.R.

Dudintsev, Vladimir Dmitrievich; Soviet writer; b. 29 June 1918, Kupyansk, Ukraine; s. of Claudia and Dmitry Dudintsev; m. Natalia Gordeeva 1942; one s. three d.; ed. Moscow Legal Inst.
Soviet Army 41-45; Feature Writer of *Komsomolskaya Pravda* 46-51; mem. Union of Soviet Writers.
Leisure interest: sailing.
Publs. *With Seven Brothers* (collected stories) 52, *In His Place* 54, *Not By Bread Alone* 56, *Tales and Stories* 59, *A New Year's Tale* 60, *Stories* 63; trans. Suvra Golovanivsky's *Poplar on the other Bank* 67 and twenty other books 57-74.
Lomonosovsky Prospekt 19, KW 74, Moscow W311; U.S.S.R. Union of Writers, Ul. Vorovskogo 52, Moscow, U.S.S.R.
Telephone: 130-21-68 (Home).

Dudley, Guilford, Jr.; American diplomatist; b. 23 June 1907, Nashville; s. of Guilford and Anne (Dallas) Dudley; m. Jane Anderson; two s. one d.; ed. Loomis Inst., Peabody Coll. and Vanderbilt Univ.
Formerly insurance exec., Pres., Dir. Life and Casualty Insurance Co., WLAC-TV, WLAC Radio, Casualty

Insurance Co. of Tenn.; Chair., Dir. World-Wide Life Assurance Co. Ltd., London; Dir. Life Insurance Investors Inc.; Dir. Third Nat. Bank, Nashville, Bank of Palm Beach and Trust; mem. Nat. Planning Asscn.; Amb. to Denmark 69-71; Chair. of Board, Life & Casualty Co. of Tennessee 71-.

Harding Place at Hillsgoro Road, Nashville, Tenn. 37215, U.S.A.

Duesenberry, James Stembel, B.A., M.A., PH.D.; American economist; b. 18 July 1918; ed. Univ. of Michigan.

Teaching Fellow in Econs., Univ. of Michigan 39-41; in U.S. Air Force 42-45; Instructor, Mass. Inst. of Technology 46; Teaching Fellow in Econs., Harvard Univ. 46-48, Asst. Prof. of Econs. 48-53, Assoc. Prof. 53-57, Prof. 57-; Fulbright Research Prof., Cambridge Univ. 54-55; Ford Foundation Research Prof. 58-59; Consultant, Cttee. of Econ. Devt. 56; mem. President's Council of Econ. Advisers 66-.

Publs. *Income, Saving and the Theory of Consumer Behavior* 49, *Business Cycles and Economic Growth* (with Lee Preston) 58, *Cases and Problems in Economics* 59, *Money and Credit: Impact and Control* 64.

4521 Cumberland Avenue, Chevy Chase, Maryland 20015; and 25 Fairmont Street, Belmont, Mass., U.S.A.

Dufek, Rear-Admiral George J.; American naval officer and polar explorer; b. 10 Feb. 1903 Rockford, Ill.; *s.* of Frank and Mary B. Dufek; *m.* Muriel Thomson 1947; two *s.* two *d.*; ed. U.S. Naval Acad.

Served with U.S. Navy 25-59; commanded destroyers and naval air stations in Japan, Kwajalein and the State of Washington during Second World War; commanded aircraft carrier *Antietam* during Korean War; accompanied two arctic and six antarctic expeditions; Chief Staff Officer, Arctic Task Force 46; Commdr. of a group of ships in Antarctic Operation *Highjump* 46-47; headed Task Force 80 in the Arctic 47-48; Commdr. U.S. Naval Support Force, Antarctica 54-59 (retd.); **Commdr.** Task Force 43 for Operation *Deep Freeze*, U.S.N. Antarctic Expedition 55-59; U.S. Antarctic Projects Officer; Director Mariners Museum, Newport News, Va. 60-73; Distinguished Service Medal 57, and Gold Star 59, Legion of Merit (with two gold stars), Antarctic Expedition Medal, Croix de Guerre, Chevalier of the Legion of Honour, André Medal of the Swedish Geographical Society, Hubbard Medal 59; Hon. Comp. Most Hon. Order of the Bath 59, Commdr. Ordre de la Couronne, Belgium 59; several honorary degrees.

Leisure interests: fishing, hunting, walking, gardening, reading.

Publs. *Operation Deep Freeze, Through the Frozen Frontiers.*

101 Museum Parkway, Newport, News, Va. 23606, U.S.A.

Telephone: 804-596-3315.

Duff, Sir (Arthur) Antony, K.C.M.G., C.V.O., D.S.O., D.S.C.; British diplomat; b. 1920.

Ambassador to Nepal 64-65; with Commonwealth Office and subsequently with F.C.O. 65-69; Deputy High Commr., Kuala Lumpur 69-72; High Commr. to Kenya 72-75; Deputy Under-Sec. Foreign and Commonwealth Office 75-.

30 Park Mansions, Prince of Wales Drive, London, S.W.11, England.

Telephone: 01-720-2883.

Dufourcq, Norbert, D. ÈS L.; French musicologist and organist; b. 21 Sept. 1904, Saint Jean de Braye, Loiret; *s.* of Albert Dufourcq; *m.* Odette Latron 1926; one *s.* five *d.*; ed. Collège Stanislas and Lycée Henri IV, Paris, Sorbonne and Ecole Nationale des Chartes.

Teacher of History Coll. Stanislas, Paris 35-45; Prof. of History of Music and Musicology at Paris Conservatoire 41-75; Organist Eglise Saint-Merry 23-; Sec.-Gen., then Vice-Pres. of Soc. of Friends of Organ 27-; mem. c Comm. for Historic Organs 32-; Editor-in-Chief reviev *L'Orgue* 29-; Prof. Sweet Briar Coll. (Paris) 49; Pres Société Française de Musicologie 56-58; Prof. Ecol Normale de Musique de Paris 58-63; Pres. Soc. d l'Ecole des Chartes 75-76; Dir. Conservatoire Municipa du Luxembourg, Paris 75-; Dir. *Orgue et Liturgie, le Grands Heures de l'Orgue, L'Orgue, Cahiers et Mémoires d L'Orgue*; Lecturer, Jeunesses Musicales de Franc 42-61.

Leisure interests: archaeology, travel.

Publs. *Documents inédits relatifs à l'Orgue français XIVe-XVIIIe siècles* 34-35, *Esquisse d'une histoire d l'Orgue en France du XIIIe au XVIIIe siècles* 35, *Le musique d'orgue française de J. Titelouze à J. Alai* 41-49, *Orgues comtadines et provençales, Les Clicquot César Franck, Le Clavecin, L'Orgue, Petite Histoire de la Musique en Europe, Bach, génie allemand, génie latin? Bach, le Maître de l'Orgue* 48-74, *La musique française* 48, 2nd edn. 70, *Autour de Coquard, Nicolas Lebègue* 54, *Notes et références . . . sur Michel R. Delalande* 57, *Jean de Joyeuse et la pénétration de la facture parisienne dans le Midi de la France au XVIIe siècle* 58, *J. B. de Boesset* 62, *Le Grand Orgue du Prytanée Militaire de la Flèche* 64, *Le Livre de l'Orgue française*, Vol. II: *Le Buffet* 69, Vol. I: *Les Sources* 71, Vol. IV: *La Musique* 72, Vol. III: *La Facture I* 75; *César Franck et la genèse des premières oeuvres d'orgue* 73; preface to organ compositions of G. Jullien, N. de Grigny, A. Raisons, Clérembault, G. C. Nivers (3 vols.), F. Couperin (3 vols.), A. Dornel, M. Lanes, A. Boely (3 vols.); *Pièces de Clavecin de N. Lebègue* 57, *L'orgue parisien sous le règne de Louis XIV* 57; edited *La Musique, des origines a nos jours* 48, *Histoire de France*, 2nd edn. 71, *Larousse de la Musique* 57-58 (2 vols.), *La Vie Musicale en France sous les Rois Bourbons* (22 vols.), *Recherches sur la Musique Classique Française* (15 vols.) 60-75, musical section of *Que Sais-Je?* (40 vols.), *La Musique, les Hommes, les Instruments, les Oeuvres* 65 (2 vols.); Gen. Editor *Le lys d'or, Les Neuf Muses* (30 vols.).

14 rue Cassette, Paris 6e, France.

Telephone: 222-53-29.

Dufournier, Bernard Alfred Eusèbe; French diplomatist; b. 23 March 1911; ed. Lycée Janson de Sailly, Sorbonne, Ecole des Sciences Politiques, Paris.

Counsellor in Brussels 54-56; Amb. to Pakistan 57-60, to Chile 60-63, to Libya 63-66, to Finland 66-69, to Lebanon 69-72, to Switzerland 72-75.

Ministère des Affaires Etrangères, Quai d'Orsay, Paris, France.

Dugersuren, Mangalyn; Mongolian diplomatist; b. 15 Feb. 1922, Galuut Somon, Bayanhonger Aymag (Porvince); ed. Inst. of International Relations, Moscow.

Schoolmaster 41-44; studies in Moscow 46-51; Deputy Head, later Head of Dept., Ministry of Foreign Affairs, Mongolia 51-53; Sec. of Central Cttee. of Mongolian Revolutionary Youth League 53-54; Deputy Minister of Justice 54-56; Deputy Minister of Foreign Affairs 56-58; Amb. to India 58-62; First Deputy Minister of Foreign Affairs 62-63, Minister of Foreign Affairs 63-68; Perm. Rep. to UN 68-72; Perm. Rep., UN Office at Geneva and other int. orgs. Aug. 72-; mem. Central Cttee. of Mongolian People's Revolutionary Party.

Permanent Mission of Mongolian People's Republic, 5 chemin des Crettets, Conches, 1231 Geneva, Switzerland.

Duhamel, Jacques; French politician; b. 24 Sept. 1924; *s.* of Jean Duhamel and Hélène (née Rochut); *m.* Collette Rousselot 1947; four *c.*; ed. Lycée Janson de Sailly, Faculté de Droit et des Lettres, Univ. de Paris, Ecole libre des Sciences politiques and Ecole Nat. d'Administration.

Civil Servant 49-62, Dir.-Gen. Nat. Centre of Foreign Trade 60-62; Deputy for Jura 62-69, 73-; Parl. Leader

Progress and Modern Democracy Parl. Group 67-69; Mayor of Dole 69-; Minister of Agriculture June 69-Jan. 71; Minister of Culture Jan. 71-73; Parl. Leader Union centriste 73-74; Officier Légion d'Honneur; Croix de Guerre 39-45; Médaille de la Résistance.
Leisure interests: music, modern painting.
3, quai de la Tournelle, Paris 5e, France.

Duisenberg, Willem Frederik, D.ECONS.; Netherlands economist; b. 9 July 1935, Heerenveen; m. Tine Stelling 1960; two s. one d.; ed. State Univ. of Groningen.
Scientific Asst., State Univ., Groningen 61-65; with Int. Monetary Fund 66-69; Special Adviser De Nederland-andsche Bank N.V. 69-70; Prof. of Macro-econs., Univ. of Amsterdam 70-73; Minister of Finance 73-.
Leisure interests: sailing, tennis, photography.
Publs. *Economic Consequences of Disarmament* 65, *The IMF and the International Monetary System* 66, *The British Balance of Payments* 69, *Some Remarks on Imported Inflation* 70.
Ministry of Finance, Korte Voorhout 7, The Hague; Home: Couperuslaan 13, Uithoorn, Netherlands.
Telephone: 070-767767 (Office); 02975-63401 (Home).

Dukakis, Michael S.; American politician; b. 1933, Brookline, Mass.; m. Katharine Dickson); one s. two d.; ed. Brookline High School, Swarthmore Coll., Harvard Law School.
Army service in Korea 55-57; mem. Town Meeting, Brookline 59, Chair. Town Cttee. 60-62; alt. Del. Democratic Nat. Convention 68; mem. Mass. House of Reps. for Brookline 62-70, later Chair. Cttee. on Public Service and mem. Special Comm. on Low Income Housing; founded a research group for public information 70; moderator of radio public affairs debate programme *The Advocates*; Gov. of Massachusetts 74-.
State House, Boston, Mass. 02133, U.S.A.

Duke, Angier Biddle; American diplomatist; b. 30 Nov. 1915, New York City; s. of Cordelia Drexel Biddle and Angier B. Duke; m. Robin Chandler Lynn 1962; three s. one d.; ed. St. Paul's School, Concord, N.H., and Yale Univ.
Major U.S. Army Air Force, Second World War; entered American Foreign Service 49, Sec. and Consul, Buenos Aires 49-51; Special Asst. to Stanton Griffis, Amb. in Madrid 51-52; Amb. to El Salvador 52-53; Pres. Int. Rescue Cttee. 54-61; Vice-Pres. CARE 55-58; Chair. Exec. Cttee. American Friends of Viet-Nam 57-60; Chief of Protocol, Dept. of State, Washington, D.C. 61-65, and Chief of Protocol for White House with rank of Amb. 61-65, 68; Amb. to Spain 65-68, to Denmark 68-69; Commr. of Civic Affairs, N.Y. 74-; Pres. American Immigration and Citizenship Conf. 59-64; Trustee, Inst. for American Univs., Aix-en-Provence, France, Westminster Coll., Fulton, Mo.; Commdr. Nat. Order of Viet-Nam, Grand Cross of Merit of Order of Malta (Austria), Order of Honour and Merit (Haiti); Commdr. Order of George I (Greece); Hon. L.H.D. (Long Island Univ.); Hon. LL.D. (Iona Coll.); Hon. LL.D. (Duke Univ.).
Leisure interests: skiing, golf.
Department of Civic Affairs, 521 Fifth Avenue, New York, N.Y. 10017, U.S.A.

Duke, Charles M., Jr.; American astronaut; b. 3 Oct 1935, Charlotte, N. Carolina; ed. U.S. Naval Academy and Mass. Inst. of Technology.
Commissioned in U.S. Air Force 57; completed flight training 58, later assigned to 526 Fighter Interceptor Squadron, Ramstein, Germany (served three years), later Instructor in Control Systems, Air Force Aerospace Research Pilot School; selected as astronaut by NASA April 66; Lunar module pilot, *Apollo XVI*, April 72.
NASA Johnson Space Center, Houston, Texas 77058, U.S.A.

Duke-Elder, Sir William Stewart, G.C.V.O., M.A., D.SC., M.D., CH.B., PH.D., LL.D., F.R.C.S. (Eng.), F.A.C.S., F.R.A.C.S., F.R.C.P., F.R.S., K.G.ST.J.; Scottish ophthalmic surgeon; b. 1898, Dundee; s. of Rev. Neil Elder and Isa Duke; m. Phyllis Mary Edgar 1928; ed. St. Andrews, Edinburgh and London Univs.
Practised Ophthalmic Surgery London 27-; Ophthalmic Surgeon Moorfields Eye Hospital 28, St. George's Hospital 29; Howe Lecturer Harvard 30; Brig. R.A.M.C. 40-46; Surgeon-Oculist to Their Majesties King Edward VIII, George V and Queen Elizabeth 52-65; Extra Surgeon-Oculist to Queen Elizabeth 65-73; Hon. Consulting Surgeon to the R.A.F.; Pres. Inst. of Ophthalmology, Univ. of London; Fellow Univ. Coll.; Con. Surgeon Moorfields Eye Hospital and St. George's Hospital; Pres. Int. Council of Ophthalmology 50-62 and 16th Int. Congress. Life Pres. 62-; Examiner in Ophthalmology, Royal Coll. of Surgeons 47-51; fmr. Pres. Faculty of Opthalmologists, Opthalmological Soc. U.K.; Life Pres. Opthalmological Soc. of Greece: Editor *British Journal of Opthalmology* 48-73 and *Opthalmic Literature*; numerous awards, including British Asscn. Medal 15, B.M.A. Middlemore Prize 28, Mackenzie Medal (Glasgow) 32, Nettleship Medal 33, Howe Medal (U.S.A.) 46, Research Medal, American Medical Asscn. 47, Donders Medal (Netherlands) 47, Doyne Medal (Oxford) 48, Gullstrand Medal (Stockholm) 52, Craig Prize (Belfast) 52, Gonin Medal 54, Lister Medal 56, Bowman Medal 57; Fothergillian Gold Medal 62; Star of Jordan (1st Class); Bronze Star (U.S.A.); Proctor Medal (U.S.A.) 60; Lang Medal 65; Commdr. Royal Order of the Phoenix (Greece) 65; numerous hon. degrees.
Leisure interests: writing, literature.
Publs. *Textbook of Ophthalmology*, Vols. I-VII 32-54, *Recent Advances in Ophthalmology*, 4th edn. 51, *Century of International Ophthalmology* 58, *Diseases of the Eye*, 15th edn. 69, *System of Ophthalmology* (13 vols.) 58-73, *The Practice of Refraction*, 8th edn. 69.
63 Harley Street, London, W.1; 28 Elm Tree Road, London, N.W.8, England.
Telephone: 01-580-1264.

Dulbecco, Renato; American virologist; b. 22 Feb. 1914, Cantanzaro, Italy; s. of Leonardo and Maria Dulbecco; m. 1st Guiseppina Salva 1940 (divorced 1963); m. 2nd Maureen Muir 1963; one s. two d.; ed. Università degli Studi, Turin.
Assistant Prof. of Pathology, Univ. of Turin 40-46, of Experimental Embryology 47; Research Assoc. Dept. of Bacteriology, Indiana Univ. 47-49; Senior Research Fellow California Inst. of Technology 49-52, Assoc. Prof. 52-53, Prof. 54-63; Senior Fellow, Salk Inst. for Biological Studies 63-; Asst. Dir. of Research, Imperial Cancer Research Fund Labs. (London) 72-74, Deputy Dir. March 74-; mem. Genetics Soc. of America, Amer. Asscn. for Cancer Research, Amer. Asscn. for the Advancement of Science; mem. Nat. Acad. of Sciences, Amer. Acad. of Arts and Sciences; Foreign mem. Royal Soc., London 74; Hon. LL.D. Glasgow 70; Hon. D.Sc. Yale 68; several awards, including Ehrlich Prize, Ludovic Gross Horwitz Prize 73, Selman A. Waksman Award in Microbiology, Nat. Acad. of Sciences, U.S.A. 74, Nobel Prize in Medicine (Physiology) 75.
Imperial Cancer Research Fund, Lincoln's Inn Fields, London, W.C.2; Home: Hedgerows, Wilderness Road, Chislehurst, Kent, England.
Telephone: 01-242 0200 (Office); 467 5228 (Home).

Dultzin, Leib (Leon Aryeh); Israeli business executive; b. 31 March 1913, Minsk, Russia; m. Annette Gutman Hanow 1962; one s. (by previous marriage), one d.
Lived in Mexico 28-56, Israel 65-; mem. of the executive, Jewish Agency, Treas. 68; Minister without Portfolio, Govt. of Israel 70-73; Chair. Exec. Cttee. Jewish Agency 73-; Gov. Pal Land Devt. Co. Ltd.,

Bank Leumi Le Israel; Dir. Rassco Ltd., Yakhim Hakal Co. Ltd., Otzar Hataasiya; mem. World Directorate, Keren Hayesod; mem. of numerous Zionist orgs. The Jewish Agency for Israel, P.O. Box 92, Jerusalem; and 11 Mapu Street, Tel-Aviv, Israel.

Dumas, Pierre, L. ES D.; French politician; b. 15 Nov. 1924; ed. Ecole Libre des Sciences Politiques.
Sales Man. Box Co., La Rochette; Mayor of Chambéry 59-; Dep. 58-; Sec. of State for Public Works April-Oct. 62, Sec. of State for Relations with Parl., responsible for Tourism 62-67; Sec. of State to Prime Minister, in charge of Tourism 67-68; Sec. of State for Social Affairs 68-69; Deputy 69-; Pres., Groupe des Députés-Maires; Pres. Soc. française pour le Tunnel Routier du Fréjus; Pres. Conseil d'Admin., Office Nat. des Forêts; Union pour la Nouvelle République.
Home: 17 rue de Boigne, 73 Chambéry, France.

du Maurier, Dame Daphne (Lady Browning), D.B.E.; British writer; b. 13 May 1907; d. of Sir Gerald du Maurier and Muriel Beaumont; m. Sir Frederick Browning 1932 (died 1965); one s. two d.; ed. privately, Paris.
Leisure interests: walking, swimming.
Publs. *The Loving Spirit* 31, *I'll Never be Young Again* 32, *The Progress of Julius* 33, *Gerald, a Portrait* 34, *Jamaica Inn* 36, *The du Mauriers* 37, *Rebecca* 38, *Frenchman's Creek* 41, *Hungry Hill* 43, *The Years Between* (play) 45, *The King's General* 46, *September Tide* (play) 48, *The Parasites* 49, *My Cousin Rachel* 51, *The Apple Tree* 52, *Mary Anne* 54, *The Scapegoat* 57, *The Breaking Point* 59, *The Infernal World of Branwell Brontë* 60, *Castle Dor* (continuation of MS. left by late Sir A. Quiller-Couch) 62, *The Glass-Blowers* 63, *Flight of the Falcon* 64, *Vanishing Cornwall* 67, *The House on the Strand* 69, *Not After Midnight* 71, *Rule Britannia* 72, *Golden Lads* 75.
Kilmarth, Par, Cornwall, England.
Telephone: Par 2706.

Duminy, Jacobus Petrus, B.SC., M.A.; South African university professor and administrator; b. 16 Dec. 1897, Bellville, Cape; s. of J. A. Duminy and Maria Zeederberg; m. Gwendoline Ellen Finnemore 1930; two s. one d.; ed. Cape Town Univ., Oxford Univ., and Univ. of Paris.
Professor of Mathematics, Univ. of Pretoria 30-42; Principal, Pretoria Technical Coll. 42-58; Principal and Vice-Chancellor, Univ. of Cape Town 58-67; Pres. S.A. Asscn. for the Advancement of Science 62; First Vice-Pres. Rotary International 69-70; Hon. LL.D. Natal, Rhodes, Cape Town; Commdr. Order of St. John.
Leisure interests: music, art appreciation, Rotary, reading, writing, travel, tennis, gardening.
The Cotswolds, Kenilworth, Cape 7700, South Africa.
Telephone: 71-0507.

Dumitriu, Petru; Romanian novelist and essayist; b. 8 May 1924, Bazias, Romania; s. of the late Lt.-Col. Petre Dumitriu and Theresia von Debretzy; m. Irene Medrea 1955; two d.; ed. Ludwig-Maximilians-Universität, Munich.
Chief Editor *Viata Romaneasca* (literary monthly), Bucharest 53-55; Man. State Publishing House for Literature and Art, Bucharest 55-58; Chair. Council of Publishing Houses, Ministry of Culture, Bucharest 58-60; in W. Europe 60-; Editor, S. Fischer Verlag, Frankfurt am Main, German Federal Republic 63-67; Romanian State Prize for Literature 49, 52, 56; Star of the Republic; Order of Labour, etc. (Romania).
Publs. Novels: *The Boyars* (3 vols., Romanian) 56, *Meeting at the Last Judgement* 61, *Incognito* 62, *The Extreme Occident* 64, *Die Transmoderne* (essay, German) 65, *Les Initiés* (French) 65, *The Sardinian Smile* 67, *L'Homme aux Yeux Gris* (French) 68, *Retour à Milo* (French) 69, *Le Beau Voyage* (French) 69.

Seilerstrasse 12, Frankfurt am Main, German Federal Republic.
Telephone: Frankfurt 29:12:14.

Dummett, Robert Bryan, C.B.E.; British oil executive; b. 1912; m. Mary Grieve 1936; one s. one d.; ed. Rugby School and Univs. of Cambridge and Göttingen.
With British Petroleum Co. (B.P.) (then Anglo-Iranian Oil Co.) 36-, Area Man. (Switzerland, Italy and Malta) Distribution Dept. 48-53; Man. Dir. Commonwealth Oil Refineries Ltd. (now B.P. Australia Ltd.) 53; Man. Dir. B.P. 57-67, Deputy Chair. 67-72; mem. London Board Commercial Bank of Australia 72-; Grande Ufficiale dell' Ordine al Merito, Italy 67; Cavaliere di Gran Croce 70.
4 Audley Square, London, W.1., England.

Du Mond, Jesse William Monroe, B.S., M.S. in E.E. PH.D.; American emeritus professor of physics; b. 1 July 1892, Paris, France; s. of Frederick Melville Dumond and Louise Adèle (née Kerr); m. Louise Marie Baillet 1944; two d.; ed. Calif. Inst. of Technology and Union Coll. Schenectady, New York.
Teaching Fellow, Physics, Calif. Inst. of Technology 21-29, Research Fellow 29-31, Research Assoc. 31-38, Assoc. Prof. 38-46, Prof. 46-63, Prof. Emer. 63-; mem. Editorial Board *Annual Tables of Physical Constants*, mem. Cttee., Fundamental Physical Constants and Conversion Factors, Nat. Research Council, Chair. Sub-Cttee. on Atomic Constants; with Office of Scientific Research and Devt., U.S. Navy 44; Visiting Prof. Utah State Univ. 64, 65; Consultant Physicist Los Alamos Scientific Laboratory 65-; mem. Nat. Acad. of Sciences; Hon. Ph.D. Univs. of Uppsala and Manitoba.
Leisure interests: travel, music.
Publs. *Fundamental Constants of Physics* (with E. R. Cohen and K. Crowe) 56; approx. 150 scientific articles on researches in atomic and nuclear physics and instrumentation; also numerous reports and encyclopaedia articles.
Room 163, West Norman Bridge Laboratory, California Institute of Technology, Pasadena, Calif.; Home: 530 S. Greenwood Avenue, Pasadena, Calif., U.S.A.
Telephone: 213-795-6841, Ext. 1280 (Office); 213-449-3802 (Home).

Dumont, Donald, B.S., M.A.; American diplomatist; b. 6 Dec. 1911, Boston, Mass.; s. of Joseph Henry Dumont and Emma Hayward; m. Marie Paris 1945; three s.; ed. Oberlin Coll., Trinity Coll., and Yale Univ. School of International Relations.
History and Science Master, Brent School, Philippines 35-37; Instructor in English, Trinity Coll. 37-39; Clerk and Vice-Consul, American Foreign Service 40, Dakar 41-42, Rabat 43-46, Tunis 46-50, Consul, Istanbul 50-51, Stuttgart 51-54; Officer in Charge Sub-Saharan Affairs, Dept. of State 54-57; Consul-Gen., Dakar 58-60, Chargé d'Affaires, Fed. of Mali 60; UN Adviser, Bureau of African Affairs, Dept. of State 61, Dep. Dir. of African and Malagasy Union Affairs 61-62; U.S. Minister to Burundi 62-63, Amb. 63-66; Visiting Prof. and Diplomat-in-Residence, Univ. of Tenn. 66-67; Foreign Affairs Research Council, Dept. of State 67-70; UN Resident Rep. to Repub. of Mali 70-.
Leisure interest: sailing.
Publs. *Brief History of Philippines* 40, *Ivory Coast Chapter* in *The Legislature in Transitional Societies* 68.
B.P. 120, Bamako, Mali; Home: 1661 Crescent Place, N.W., Washington, D.C. 20009, U.S.A.

Dumont, René; French agronomist; b. 13 March 1904, Cambrai; s. of Remy Dumont; m. Suzanne Philippon 1928; one d.; ed. Institut National Agronomique, Ecole Supérieure d'Agriculture Tropicale.
Adviser in agronomy, rural economy and agricultural planning to numerous govts. throughout the world, to UN, UNESCO, FAO, etc.; Prof. of Agriculture, Inst.

at. Agronomique 33-; candidate, French Presidential
ection 74.
eisure interests: antiques, painting, wife.
ubls. 28 works including: *Terres vivantes* 61, *L'Afrique*
ire est mal partie 62, *Kolkhoz, Sovkhoz* 64, *Cuba,*
cialisme et développement 64, *Chine surpeuplée* 65,
ous allons à la famine 66, *Développement et socialisme*
9, *Cuba, est-il socialiste?* 70, *Paysanneries aux abois* 72,
'Utopie ou la mort 73, *Agronome de la faim* 74, *La*
roissance de la Famine 75, *La Chine, Révolution*
ulturale 76.
avenue Roosevelt, 94 Fontenay-sous-Bois, France.
elephone: TRE-46-85.

Dunant, Yves, DR.CHEM.; Swiss pharmaceuticals
xecutive; b. 8 Sept. 1912, Emmen; s. of Georges
)unant and Denyse (née Schumacher); m. 1st Chantal
e Rivoyre 1949 (deceased), 2nd Claudine Guyonnet
974; two d.; ed. Eidgenössische Technische Hoch-
chule, Zürich, Inst. Pasteur, Univ. of Paris.
oined Sandoz Ltd., Basle 38; Asst. mem. Board of
Man. Laboratoires Sandoz, Paris 46, mem. Board of
Man. 48; Head of Marketing Dept. of Pharmaceutical
)iv., Sandoz Ltd. 63, Head of Pharmaceutical Div.,
nem. Exec. Cttee. 67, Man. Dir. 69, Vice-Chair. and
Man. Dir. 73-.
eisure interests: travel, modern art, literature, music,
ports.
iandoz Ltd., CH-4002 Basle; Home: 51 Rennweg,
CH-4052 Basle, Switzerland.
Telephone: 43 95 53 (Office); 42 94 83 (Home).

Duncan, Admiral Charles Kenney; American naval
officer; b. 7 Dec. 1911, Nicholasville, Ky.; s. of late
Charles W. Duncan and late May Kenney; m. Sheila A.
Taylor 1941; ed. Univ. of Kentucky, U.S. Naval Acad.
and Armed Forces Staff Coll.
Executive Officer, *U.S.S. Hutchins* 42; Commdg.
Officer *U.S.S. Wilson* 43; Dir. of Naval Officer Procure-
ment, Bureau of Naval Personnel 44; Exec. Officer,
U.S.S. *Wisconsin* 46; Commdr. Destroyer Div. 62, 51;
Admin. Aide to chief of Naval Personnel 53; Commdg.
Officer, *U.S.S. Chilton* 55; Commdr. Amphibious Group
One 58, Amphibious Training Command, Pacific 59;
Commdr. Naval Base, Subic Bay, Philippines 61; Asst.
Chief of Naval Personnel 62; Commdr. Cruiser-Des-
troyer Force Atlantic 64, Amphibious Force Atlantic
65, Second Fleet and NATO Striking Fleet Atlantic 67;
Chief of Naval Personnel and Deputy Chief of Naval
Operations (Manpower and Naval Reserve) 68; C.-in-C.
Atlantic 70-72; C.-in-C. U.S. Atlantic Fleet 70-72;
Supreme Allied Commdr. Atlantic 70-72; C.-in-C. W.
Atlantic Area 70-72; mem. Sec. Navy's Advisory Board
on Educ. and Training 76-; Distinguished Service
Medal, Legion of Merit, Grand Cross of Order of Orange-
Nassau, and many other awards.
Route 1, Box 160, Waterford, Va. 22190, U.S.A.

Duncan, John Spenser Ritchie, C.M.G., M.B.E., M.A.;
British diplomatist; b. 26 July 1921, Glencarse,
Scotland; s. of late Rev. J. H. Duncan, D.D., and
Sophia Playfair Ritchie; m. Sheila Grace Fullarton
Conacher, D.R.C.O.G. 1950; one d.; ed. George Watson's
Boys' Coll., Glasgow Acad., Dundee High School,
Edinburgh Univ.
Sudan Political Service 41-56; Deputy Dir.-Gen.
British Information Services, U.S.A. 59-63; Consul-
Gen. Muscat 63-65; Head of Personnel, Foreign and
Commonwealth Office 65-69; Minister, Camberra 69-71;
High Commr. in Zambia 71-74; Amb. to Morocco 75-.
Leisure interests: golf, music.
Publs. *The Sudan: A Record of Achievement* 52, *The*
Sudan's Path to Independence 57.
c/o Foreign and Commonwealth Office, King Charles
Street, London, SW1A 2AH, England.

Duncan, Ronald, M.A.; British poet and playwright;
b. 6 Aug. 1914, Salisbury, Rhodesia; s. of Reginald

John and Ethel Duncan; m. Rose Marie Theresa
Hansom 1940; one s. one d.; ed. Switzerland and
Cambridge Univ.
Founded English Stage Co. with George Devine 56.
Leisure interest: farming.
Publs. *The Dull Ass's Hoof* 41, *Postcards to Pulcenella*
42, *Journal of a Husbandman* 44, *This Way to the Tomb*
46, *The Rape of Lucretia* 46, *Home Made Home* 47, *Ben
Jonson* 47, *Songs and Satires of the Earl of Rochester* 48,
Stratton 48, *Jan's Journal* 48, *Tobacco Cultivation in
England* 48, *The Typewriter* 48, *Beauty and the Beast* 48,
The Cardinal 49, *The Mongrel and Other Poems* 50, *Our
Lady's Tumbler* 51, *Selected Writings of Mahatma
Gandhi* 61, *The Blue Fox* 51, *Jan at the Blue Fox* 52,
The Last Adam 52, *Where I Live* 53, *Don Juan* 54, *The
Death of Satan* 55, *The Catalyst* 57, *Christopher Sly* 59,
The Solitudes 60, *Blind Man's Buff, Saint Spiv* 60,
Judas 60, *Abelard and Heloïse* 60, *The Rabbit Race* 63,
All Men are Islands (autobiog. Vol. I) 64, *O-B-A-F-G*
65, *The Rebel* 65, *The Trojan Women* 66, *How to Make
Enemies* (autobiog. Vol. II) 68, *The Perfect Mistress* 69,
Unpopular Poems 69, *Man* (Parts I-V) 70-74, *The Gift*
70, *Collected Plays* 70, *A Kettle of Fish* 71, *Dante's De
Vulgari Eloquentia* 73, *The Tale of Tails* 75, *The Edge
of Knowledge* 76, *Autobiography* (Vol. III) 76.
Mead Farm, Welcombe, Nr. Bideford, N. Devonshire,
England.
Telephone: Morwenstow 375 and 215.

Duncan-Sandys, Baron (Life Peer), cr. 74; **Duncan
Edwin Duncan-Sandys,** P.C., C.H.; British politician;
b. 24 Jan. 1908; s. of Capt. George and Mildred
(Cameron) Sandys; m. 1st Diana Churchill, d. of the late
Rt. Hon. Sir Winston Churchill, 1935 (dissolved 1960),
one s. two d.; m. 2nd Marie-Claire Schmitt 1962, one d.;
ed. Eton and Magdalen Coll., Oxford.
Diplomatic Service 30-33; served at Foreign Office and
British Embassy, Berlin; M.P. (Cons.) for Norwood Div.
of Lambeth 35-45, for Streatham Div. of Lambeth
50-74; Lieut. Territorial Army 37; political columnist,
Sunday Chronicle 37-39; mem. Conservative Party Nat.
Exec. 38-39; served in Norway 40; Lieut.-Col. 41;
disabled on active service 41; Finance mem. of Army
Council 41-43; Parl. Sec. to Ministry of Supply 43-44;
Chair. of Cabinet Cttee. for defence against German
"V" weapons 43-45; Minister of Works 44-45; founded
European Movement 47, Chair. Int. Exec. 48-50, Chair.
Parl. Council 50-51, 68-70; mem. Parl. Assembly of
Council of Europe 50-51, 65-; mem. Gen. Advisory
Council of BBC 47-51; Dir. Ashanti Goldfields Corpn.
47-51, 66-72; Minister of Supply 51-54; Minister of
Housing and Local Govt. 54-57; Minister of Defence
57-59; Minister of Aviation 59-60; Sec. of State for
Commonwealth Relations 60-62, Sec. of State for
Commonwealth Relations and Sec. of State for Colonies
62-64; Founder Civic Trust, Pres. 56-; Chair. Lonrho
Ltd. 72-; Pres. Europa Nostra 69-; mem. WEU
Assembly; Joint Pres. Franco-British Council 72-;
Chair. Int. Org. Cttee. for Architectural Heritage Year
75; Hon. Fellow, Royal Inst. of British Architects;
Hon. mem. Royal Town Planning Inst.; Grand Cross of
the Order of Merit of Italy; Medal of City of Paris 74;
Order of Sultanate of Brunei 74; Gold Cup of European
Movement 75; Goethe Gold Medal of Hamburg Founda-
tion 75; Grand Cross of Order of Crown of Belgium 75.
Leisure interest: abstract painting.
86 Vincent Square, London, SW1P 2PG, England.
Telephone: 01-834-5886.

Dunckel, Wallis Bleecker, B.A.; American banker;
b. 9 May 1901, New York; s. of Dr. Walter Adams
Dunckel and Amalie Jean Inglis Young; m. Margaret
Lindsay Sutherland 1928; two s. one d.; ed. Trinity
School, New York City, and Yale Univ.
Joined Bankers Trust Co. 23, Head, Pension Div. 38-57,
mem. Senior Management 57-60, Pres. and Dir. 60-66;

Pres. BT New York Corpn. (now Bankers Trust New York Corpn.) 66-68, Dir. 66-74; Dir. American Bank Note Co.
320 Valley Road, Easton, Conn. 06612, U.S.A.

Dundee, 11th Earl of, cr. 1660 (Scot.), **Henry James Scrymgeour-Wedderburn,** P.C., J.P., D.L., LL.D.; British politician; b. 3 May 1902; ed. Winchester and Balliol Coll., Oxford.
President, Oxford Union 24; M.P. 31-45; Parl. Under-Sec. of State for Scotland 36-39; Additional Parl. Under-Sec. of State, Scottish Office 41-42; Minister without Portfolio 58-61; Minister of State for Foreign Affairs 61-64; Deputy Leader House of Lords 62-64; Hereditary Royal Standard bearer for Scotland; Hon. LL.D. St. Andrews Univ.; Conservative.
Birkhill, Cupar, Fife, Scotland.

Dunham, Katherine; American dancer and choreographer; ed. Chicago and Northwestern Univs.
Debut, Chicago World's Fair 34; with Chicago Opera Co. 35-36; Julius Rosenwald Travel Fellowship 36-37; Dance Dir. Labor Stage 39-40; has appeared in numerous films 41-; founded Katherine Dunham School of Cultural Arts and Katherine Dunham Dance Co. 45; numerous tours and personal appearances in North and South America and Europe.
Publs. *Journey to Accompong, Form and Function in Primitive Dance, Form and Function in Educational Dance,* etc.
c/o Lee Mosell, 608 Fifth Avenue, New York City, N.Y. 10020, U.S.A.

Dunham, Sir Kingsley C., Kt., F.R.S., PH.D., D.SC., M.S., S.D.; British geologist; b. 2 Jan. 1910, Sturminster Newton, Dorset; s. of Ernest Pedder and Edith Agnes Dunham; m. Margaret Young 1936; one s.; ed. Johnston School, Durham, Univ. of Durham and Harvard Univ.
Temporary Geologist, New Mexico Bureau Mines 35; Geologist, Geological Survey of Great Britain 35-45, Head of Petrographical Dept. 46-50; Prof. of Geology and Head of Dept. Univ. of Durham 50-66, Prof. Emer. 68, Sub-Warden 59-61; Consulting Geologist, Laporte Industries Ltd. 53-66, Consolidated Gold Fields Ltd. 54-66; Geological Adviser Imperial Chemical Industries Ltd. 61-66; Dir. Inst. of Geological Sciences (Natural Environment Research Council) 66-75; Chair. Council for Environmental Science and Engineering 72-75; Pres. Yorks. Geological Soc. 58-60, British Asscn. for the Advancement of Science (Section C 61, Asscn. 72-73), Inst. of Mining and Metallurgy 63-64, Geological Soc. of London 66-68, Int. Union of Geological Sciences 69-72; mem. Council, Royal Soc. 64-66, Foreign Sec., Vice-Pres. 71-; mem. Council for Scientific Policy, Dept. of Educ. and Science 64-66; Bigsby Medal of Geological Soc. 54; Gold Medal of Inst. of Mining and Metallurgy 68; Murchison Medal 66; Royal Medal of the Royal Soc. 70; D.Sc. h.c. (Durham, Liverpool, Birmingham, Illinois, Leicester, Michigan, Kent, Edinburgh, Exeter), Hon. Sc.D. (Cambridge).
Leisure interests: music (piano, organ, opera, ballet), gardening.
Publs. *Geology of the Organ Mountains of New Mexico* 36, *Geology of the Northern Pennine Orefield* 49, *Fluorspar* 52, *Geology of North Skye* (with F. W. Anderson) 66; Editor *Symposium on the Paragenesis and Reserves of the Ores of Lead and Zinc* 48.
Charleycroft, Quarryheads Lane, Durham, DH1 3DY, England.
Telephone: (0385) 3997.

Dunlop, John T., A.B., PH.D., LL.D.; American economist and industrial relations expert; b. 5 July 1914, Placerville, Calif.; s. of John and Antonia Dunlop, née Forni; m. Dorothy Webb 1937; two s. one d.; ed. Univs. of California and Chicago.

Instructor Harvard Univ. 38, Assoc. Prof. 45, Chair. Wertheim Cttee. on Industrial Relations 45-, Prof. 50-Chair. Dept. of Econs. 61-66, Dean Faculty of Arts and Sciences 70-73; Chair. Board for Settlement of Jurisdictional Disputes 48-57; mem. Atomic Energy Labo. Relations Panel 48-53; mem. Sec. Labor's Advisor. Cttee. on Labor-Management Relations in Atomi. Energy Installations 54-57; mem. Kaiser Steel Steelworkers' Comm. 60-68, Presidential Railroad Comm. 60-62, Missiles Sites Labor Comm. 61-67; Chair. Nat. Manpower Policy Task Force 68-69; mem. President's Nat. Comm. on Productivity 70-73, Chair. 73-; Chair. Manpower Inst. 70-; Dir. Cost of Living Council 73-74; Co-ordinator President's Labor-Management Cttee. 74-; U.S. Sec. of Labor 75-; Chair. Construction Industry Joint Conf. 59-68; mem. Construction Industry Collective Bargaining Comm. 69-; Chair Construction Industry Stabilization Cttee. 71-73, mem. 73-74; Pres. Industrial Relations Research Asscn. 60. Int. Industrial Relations Research Asscn. 73-; mem Amer. Acad. of Arts and Sciences, Amer. Philosophica. Soc.; Louis K. Comstock Award, Nat. Electrica. Contractors' Asscn. 74.
Publs. *Wage Determination under Trade Unions* 44. *Cost Behaviour and Price Policy* 44, *Collective Bargaining: Principles and Cases* (with James J. Healy) 49, *The Wage Adjustment Board* (with Arthur D. Hill) 50, *The Theory of Wage Determination* (Editor) 57, *Industrial Relations Systems* 58, *Industrialism and Industrial Man* 60, *Potentials of the American Economy* (Editor) 61, *Economic Growth in the United States* (Editor) 61, *Automation and Technological Change* (Editor) 62, *Frontiers of Collective Bargaining* (Editor) 67, *Labor and the American Community* (with Derek Bok) 70, *Inflation and Incomes Policies: the Political Economy of Recent U.S. Experience* 74, *Industrialism and Industrial Man Reconsidered* 75.
Department of Labor, 14th Street and Constitution Avenue, N.W., Washington, D.C. 20210; Home: 509 Pleasant Street, Belmont, Mass. 02178, U.S.A.

Dunlop, Sir John Wallace, K.B.E.; Australian company director; b. 1910; ed. Geelong Grammar School (Australia).
Chairman, CSR Ltd., Edwards Dunlop and Co. Ltd.; Dir. Australian Industry Devt. Corpn., Rothmans of Pall Mall (Australia) Ltd., Lansing Bagnall (Australia) Pty. Ltd.
275 George Street, Sydney, N.S.W. 2000, Australia.
Telephone: 2-0222.

Dunlop, Robert Galbraith; American Chairman and Chief Executive Officer of Sun Oil Co. 71-74; see *The International Who's Who 1975-76.*

Dunn, Halbert Louis, M.D., M.A., PH.D.; American statistician; b. 17 May 1896, New Paris, Ohio; s. of Louis and Irene (Halbert) Dunn; m. 1st Katherine Brandner 1920, three s.; m. 2nd Elizabeth Phelps 1941; ed. Univ. of Minnesota.
Instructor of Anatomy, Univ. of Minnesota 22-23; Asst. in Medicine, Presbyterian Hospital, N.Y. 23-24; Fellow in Medicine, Mayo Clinic, Rochester, Minn. 24-25; Assoc. Prof., Johns Hopkins Univ. 25-29; Head, Dept. of Statistics, Mayo Clinic 29-32; Dir., Univ. Hospital and Prof. of Medical Statistics, Univ. of Minn. 32-53; Chief Statistician and Chief of Vital Statistics Div., Bureau of the Census, Dept. of Commerce, Washington 35-46; Chief of Nat. Office of Vital Statistics, Dept. of Health, Education and Welfare 46-60, Special Asst. on Ageing, U.S. Public Health Service 60-61; Sec.-Treas. Public Health Conf. on Records and Statistics 49-58, Chair. 58-60; Charter mem. Inter-American Statistical Inst. 40-, Sec.-Gen. 42-52, Consultant to its Exec. Cttee. 52-54, Hon. Pres. 55-; Consultant and Lect. High-Level Wellness 62-, Consultant on Ageing,

.S. Office of Educ. 62-66; Fellow, American Public Health Asscn., American Statistical Asscn., American sscn. for the Advancement of Science.
eisure interests: music (library of tape recordings).
ubls. *Creative Destiny, Your World and Mine, High-level Wellness, Positive Health, Man and the Environ-ment,* and numerous articles.
637 Edelmar Terrace, Rossmoor Silver Spring, Md. 0906, U.S.A.
Telephone: 301-598-6221.

Dunnett, Alastair MacTavish; British journalist; b. 6 Dec. 1908, Kilmacolm; s. of David Sinclair Dunnett and Isabella Crawford MacTavish; m. Dorothy Halliday 946; two s.; ed. Overnewton School and Hillhead High School, Glasgow.
Entered Commercial Bank of Scotland Ltd. 25; co-ounder, The Claymore Press 33-34; with *Glasgow Weekly Herald* 35-36, *The Bulletin* 36-37, *Daily Record* 7-40; Chief Press Officer, Sec. of State for Scotland 0-46; Editor *Daily Record* 46-55, *The Scotsman* 56-72; Man. Dir. Scotsman Publications Ltd. 62-70, Chair. 0-74; Chair. Thomson Scottish Petroleum Ltd., Edinburgh 72-; mem. Exec. Board Thomson Org. Ltd. 3; Dir. Scottish Television 75-; Gov. Pitlochry Festival Theatre; mem. Press Council 59-62; mem. Scottish Tourist Board 62-70; mem. Council of Nat. Trust for Scotland 62-70; mem. Scottish Int. Educ. Trust, Scottish Int. Information Cttee., Scottish Theatre Ballet Cttee., Scottish Opera Cttee.
Leisure interests: sailing, riding, walking.
Publs. *Treasure at Sonnach* 35, *Heard Tell* 46, *Quest by Canoe* 50, *Highlands and Islands of Scotland* 51; Plays: *The Original John Mackay* 56, *Fit to Print* 62.
Office: Thomson Scottish Petroleum Ltd., 17 Charlotte Square, Edinburgh EH2 4DJ; 87 Colinton Road, Edinburgh EH10 5DF, Scotland.
Telephone: 031-225-4285 (Office); 031-337-2107 (Home).

Dunphy, John Englebert, M.D.; American surgeon and physician; b. 31 March 1908, Northampton, Mass.; s. of Dr. M. M. Dunphy and Kathryn Duggan; m. Nancy S. Stevenson 1936; one s. three d.; ed. Coll. of the Holy Cross, Harvard Medical School.
Peter Bent Brigham Hosp. 33-59, Surgeon 49-57, Assoc. Staff 59; Harvard Medical School 36-59, Asst. Prof. 47-50, Clinical Prof. 53-55, Prof. 55-59; Mil. Service 40-46, Medical Corps 40-45 (Lt.-Col. 44), Consultant Oise Intermediate Section E.T.O. 45; Chief Consultant in Surgery for Veterans' Admin., New England area 46-59; Consultant to the Surgeon-Gen., Educ. and Training Div., Dept. of the Army 54-; mem. Advisory Cttee. on Trauma 70-; Dir. Fifth Surgical Service and Sears Surgical Laboratory, Boston City Hosp. 55-59; Surgeon, New England Deaconess Hosp. 56-59; Kenneth A. J. Mackenzie Prof. of Surgery and Chair. of Dept., Univ. of Ore. Medical School 56-64; Prof. of Surgery and Chair. of Dept., Univ. of Calif. School of Medicine 64-75; now Assoc. Chief of Staff for Educ., Veterans Admin. Hosp.; Pres. Lahey Clinic Foundation, Soc. of Univ. Surgeons, Soc. for Surgery of the Alimentary Tract; mem. American Acad. of Arts and Sciences, A.A.A.S., A.M.A., Asscn. of Surgeons of Great Britain and Ireland, Soc. Int. de Chirurgie, Royal Soc. of Medicine and many other asscns.; mem. editorial board *Annals of Surgery, American Journal of Surgery, Journal of Surgical Research, Cancer, California Medicine*; many hon. fellowships and memberships; many lectureships and visiting professorships; five hon. degrees.
Leisure interests: tennis, travel.
Publs. about 300 articles in journals; co-author *Physical Examination of the Surgical Patient* (4th edn.) 74.
Veterans' Administration Hospital, 4150 Clement Street, San Francisco, Calif. 94121; Home: 2821

Steiner Street, San Francisco, Calif. 94123, U.S.A.
Telephone: (415) 221-4810, Ext. 613 (Office); (415) 931-9510 (Home).

Dunsheath, Percy, C.B.E., M.A., D.SC.(ENG.), D.ENG., LL.D., M.I.E.E.; British engineer; b. 16 Aug. 1886; ed. Sheffield, Cambridge and London Univs.
General Post Office Engineer 08-19; served in First World War 15-18; Dir. of Research W. T. Henley's Telegraph Works Co. Ltd. 19-29, Chief Engineer 29-34, Dir. 36-60; Chair. Cambridge Instrument Co. 56-64; mem. Senate Univ. of London; Chair. of Convocation London Univ. 49-61; Pres. Electrical Development Asscn. 52-53 Pres. Inst. of Electrical Engineers 46, Hon. mem. 64-; Pres. ASLIB 49-50; Leader Univs./Industry Team visiting U.S.A. 51; Chair. Special F.B.I. Cttee. on shortage of Science Teachers; Pres. Int. Electro-technical Comm. 55-58; LL.D. h.c. London Univ.; Hon. Fellow, Univ. Coll., London 67.
Leisure interest: watercolour painting.
Publs. *Industrial Research* (Advisory Editor) 47, *The Graduate in Industry* 48, *Century of Technology* (editor) 51, *The Electrical Current* 51, *Convocation in the University of London* 58, *Electricity, How it Works* 60, *A History of Electrical Engineering* 61, *Giants of Electricity* 67, *Dordogne Days* 72, *Nearly Ninety* 75.
Wotton Cottage, Wescott, Dorking, Surrey, RH4 3NP, England.
Telephone: Dorking 81552.

Dunsmore, Robert Lionel, M.C., B.SC., D.C.S., F.E.I.C.; Canadian executive; b. 2 Sept. 1893, Seaforth, Ont.; s. of Robert Johns Dunsmore and Margaret Paisley; m. Rosabel Voaden 1916; one s.; ed. Queen's Univ., Kingston, Ont.
Engineer Imperial Oil Co., Sarnia, Ont. 19-22; Asst. Supt. Calgary Refinery, Imperial Oil Ltd. 22-25; Gen. Supt. Talara (Peru) Refinery, Int. Petroleum Co. Ltd. 26-30, 46-49; Supt. Halifax Imperial Oil Ltd. 30-43; Man. Montreal Refinery 44-46; Co-ordinator Mfg. Int. Petroleum Co. Ltd.; Pres. Champlain Oil Products Ltd. 49-58, Dir. 58-63; Pres. Montreal Board of Trade 56-57; Chair. of Board, Canadian Broadcasting Corpn. 58-63; mem. Board of Trustees, Queen's Univ., Kingston, Ont. 51-73; Dir. and Vice-Chair. of Board BNP (Canada) Ltd. 74; Fellow Eng. Inst. of Canada; Montreal Medal, Queen's Univ.
Leisure interests: tennis, painting.
Home: 4 Centre Street, Kingston, Ontario, Canada.
Telephone: 544-6860.

Dunstan, Donald Allan, Q.C., LL.B., M.P.; Australian solicitor and politician; b. 21 Sept. 1926, Fiji; s. of Vivian Dunstan and Ida May Hill; m. Gretel Ellis 1949; two s. one d.; ed. Collegiate School of St. Peter, Adelaide, and Univ. of Adelaide.
Labour mem. of Parl. 53-; Attorney-Gen. of South Australia 65, Attorney-Gen., Treas., Minister of Housing and Premier of South Australia 67-68, Leader of Opposition 68-70, Premier 70-.
15 Clara Street, Norwood, South Australia 5067.
Telephone: 380-5204 (Home).

Dunton, Arnold Davidson, D.SC., LL.D.; Canadian university president; b. 4 July 1912; ed. Lower Canada Coll., Montreal, McGill Univ., Univ. of Grenoble, Cambridge Univ., Univ. of Munich.
Reporter *Montreal Star* 34; Assoc. Editor 37; Editor *Montreal Standard* 38; Wartime Information Board 42, Gen. Man. 44; Chair. Board of Govs. Canadian Broadcasting Corpn. 45; Pres. and Vice-Chancellor Carleton Univ. 58-.
410 Maple Lane, Rockcliffe, Ottawa, Ont., Canada.

Dunworth, John Vernon, C.B., C.B.E.; British nuclear physicist; b. 24 Feb. 1917; s. of late John Dunworth and Susan Ida (née Warburton); m. Patricia Noel

Boston 1967; one *d.*; ed. Manchester Grammar School and Clare Coll., Cambridge.

Twisden Studentship and Fellowship, Trinity Coll., Cambridge 41; War Service with Ministry of Supply on Radar Devt. 39-44; Nat. Research Council of Canada, on Atomic Energy Devt. 44-45; Univ. Demonstrator in Physics, Cambridge 45; joined Atomic Energy Research Est., Harwell 47; Dir. Nat. Physical Laboratory 64-; Alt. Mem., Organizing Cttee. of UN Atoms for Peace Conf., Geneva 55, 58; Vice-Pres. Int. Cttee. of Weights and Measures 68-; Fellow, American Nuclear Soc. 60; Chair. British Nuclear Energy Soc. 64-70; Commdr. with Star, Order of Alfonso X el Sabio (Spain) 60.

Bushy House, Teddington, Middx., TW11 0LW, England.

Telephone: 01-977-1070.

Duong Van Minh, Lieut.-Gen.; Head of State, Republic of Viet-Nam, Jan.-Nov. 64, President April 75; see *The International Who's Who 1975-76.*

Dupong, Jean; Luxembourg lawyer and politician; b. 18 May 1922, Luxembourg; ed. Athenée de Luxembourg, Loyola Coll., Montreal, Canada, and Univs. of Lausanne and Paris.

Lawyer at Court of Appeal, Luxembourg 48-; Deputy for S. Constituency 54-; Minister of Justice, Nat. Educ., Family Affairs and Population 67-69, of Nat. Educ., Labour and Social Security 69-72, of Nat. Educ., Youth, Labour and Social Security 72-74; Pres. Christian Social Party 65-72; Bronze Star (U.S.A.); Croix de Guerre, Luxembourg; Chevalier de la Couronne de Chêne, Luxembourg.

c/o Ministry of National Education, Luxembourg, Grand Duchy of Luxembourg.

Dupont, Clifford Walter, G.C.L.M., I.D., M.A.; Rhodesian solicitor, farmer and politician; b. 6 Dec. 1905, London; s. of Alfred Walter and Winifred Mary Dupont; m. Armenell Mary Betty Bennet 1963; ed. Bishops Stortford Coll., and Clare Coll., Cambridge.

Solicitor, London 29-39, 45-48; Royal Artillery, rose to Major 40-45; emigrated to Rhodesia 48; M.P. in Fed. Assembly 58-62; mem. S. Rhodesian Parl. 62-; Minister of Justice and Minister of Law and Order, S. Rhodesia 62-64; Minister without Portfolio June-Aug. 64; Deputy Prime Minister and Minister of External Affairs 64-65; Deputy Prime Minister and Minister of External Affairs and of Defence 65; appointed Head of State (with title of "Officer Administering the Govt.") by Prime Minister of Rhodesia, Mr. Ian Smith Nov. 65; appointed Acting President of Rhodesia March 70; Pres. of Repub. of Rhodesia April 70-Dec. 75; Independence Decoration 70.

Leisure interests: shooting, fishing, horse breeding.

Home: P.O. Box 2078, Salisbury, Rhodesia.

Du Pont, Edmond; American businessman; b. 23 Aug. 1906; ed. Andover Acad., Princeton Univ., and Oxford Univ.

Partner, Francis I. du Pont & Co. 33-70, F.I. du Pont, Glore Forgan & Co. 70-71; Dir. Continental Amer. Life Insurance Co. 64-72; Dir. Winterthur Corpn.; Dir. Episcopal Church Foundation.

2106 Grant Avenue, Wilmington, Del. 19806, U.S.A.

duPont, Irénée, Jr.; American engineer; b. 8 Jan. 1920; ed. Dartmouth Coll., Massachusetts Inst. of Technology.

Fairchild Engine & Airplane Corpn. 43-46; E. I. du Pont de Nemours & Co. 46-, Supervisor Parkersburg, W. Va., 48-51, Charleston, W. Va. 51-53, Wilmington, Del. 53-, mem. Cttee. on Audit 64-, Dir. and Laboratory Dir., polychemicals technical services; Dir. Wilmington Trust Co.

Box 38, Montchanin, Delaware 19710, U.S.A.

Dupont, Jacques-Bernard; French inspector of finances and diplomatist; b. 5 April 1922; s. of Louis

Dupont and Alice Perisse; m. Marianne Ederle 195[?]; two s. one d.; ed. Univ. of Toulouse and Ecole National[?] d'Administration, Paris.

Lecturer, Tübingen Univ. 46-49; with French Hig[?] Comm., Germany 49-52; Ecole Nat. d'Administratio[?] 52-54; Insp. of Finances 54-; with Financial Counsello[?] Saarbrücken 57, Technical Adviser, Ministry of Foreig[?] Affairs 58, Head Office, Insp.-Gen. of Finances 61 Ambassador to Dahomey 61-64; Dir.-Gen. O.R.T.F[?] 64-68; Vice-Pres. European Broadcasting Union 66-67 Dir.-Gen. Man., Cie. Int. des Wagons-Lits et d[?] Tourisme 70-; Pres.-Dir.-Gen. Soc. Européenne d[?] Restauration (EUREST) 71-.

40 rue de l'Arcade, Paris 8e; Home: 1 rue du Maréchal de-Lattre-de-Tassigny, 92-Neuilly-sur-Seine, France.

Dupont, Pierre, L. ès D.; Swiss lawyer and diplomatist b. 1912, Geneva; s. of Eugène Dupont and Mari[?] Deruaz; m. Georgette Grillet 1939; one s. one d.; ed legal studies in Geneva.

Swiss Political Dept., Berne; legations in Paris and Brussels; fmr. mem. Swiss Del. to OECD; fmr. Head Finance Section of Swiss Political Dept.; fmr. Head Swiss del. to Perm. Franco-Swiss Comm. on free Zones in Haute-Savoie and Pays de Gex; Minister Plen. and Envoy Extraordinary to Venezuela and Panama 57; Amb. to Poland 61; Amb. to Netherlands 65-67, to France 67-.

Ambassade de Suisse, 142 rue de Grenelle, 75007 Paris, France.

Telephone: 551-6292.

du Pont, Pierre Samuel, III; American business executive; b. 1 Jan. 1911; ed. Tower Hill School, Phillips Exeter Acad., M.I.T.

E. I. du Pont de Nemours & Co. 34-, Development Dept. 40-41, Nylon Div. 42-45, Trade Analysis Div. 45-47, Dir. 48, Sec. 54-63, mem. Finance Cttee. 59-63, Vice-Pres. and mem. Cttee. 63-65; Dir. Wilmington Trust Co. 51-66; mem. Amer. Chemical Soc.

Rockland, Delaware 19732, U.S.A.

Dupont-Sommer, André Louis; French university professor; b. 23 Dec. 1900, Marnes-La-Coquette, Hauts-de-Seine; m. 1971; two c.; ed. Univ. de Paris à la Sorbonne.

Secretary, Collège de France 34-40; Dir. of Studies, School of Higher Studies 38-; Prof. Univ. of Paris 45-63; Pres. of Inst. of Semitic Studies, Univ. of Paris 52-; Prof. Collège de France 63-71, Hon. Prof. 72-; mem. Institut de France (Secrétaire Perpétuel de l'Académie des Inscriptions et Belles-Lettres) 61-; Foreign mem. Accademia dei Lincei 72-; Corresp. mem. Austrian Acad. of Sciences; Officier Légion d'Honneur, Commdr. Ordre des Palmes académiques.

Leisure interests: cars, travelling.

Publs. *La Doctrine gnostique de la lettre waw . . .* 46, *Les Araméens* 49, *Les inscriptions araméennes de Sfiré* 48, *Aperçus préliminaires sur les manuscrits de la Mer Morte* 53, *Les Ecrits esséniens découverts près de la Mer Morte* 59, 60, 64, etc.

Palais Mazarin, 25 quai de Conti, Paris 6e, France.

Telephone: Paris 326-02-92.

Dupouy, Gaston, D. ès sc.; French scientist; b. 7 Aug. 1900, Marmande (Lot et Garonne); s. of Joseph Dupouy; m. Jeanne Duzan 1928.

Research at Sorbonne Laboratory 22; taught at Ecole Normale Supérieure de Jeunes Filles, Sèvres; in charge of research, Caisse Nationale des Sciences; joint Dir. of Ecole Pratique des Hautes Etudes 33; research at electro-magnetic laboratory Bellevue; Dir. of Lectures, Faculty of Science, Rennes Univ. 35; Sec. Société Française de Physique; Prof. of Faculty of Science, Toulouse Univ. 37, Dean; mem. New York Acad. of Sciences 51; Dir. Laboratoire d'Optique Electronique, Nat. Centre for Scientific Research (C.N.R.S.), Tououse, Hon. Dir. 70; Dir.-Gen. C.N.R.S. 50, Hon. Dir.-Gen. 57; mem. Nat. Comm. of UNESCO; mem. consultative Cttee. of Univs.; mem. Inst. de France 50; mem. Atomic Energy Cttee., Cttee. of Scientific Action for Nat. Defence 54; research work in fields of magnetism, electron-optics and high voltage electron microcopy, constructed first 1.5 MV Electron Microscope 60, and first 3.5 MV Electron Microscope 69; Hon. Fellow several Socs.; Pres. Int. Fed. of Socs. for Electron Microscopy 68; Commdr. de la Légion d'Honneur, Ordre de Léopold I, Order of Orange-Nassau, Order of Sacred Treasure (Japan), Grand Officier de l'Ordre Nat. du Mérite.

Laboratoire d'Optique Electronique, rue Jeanne-Marvig, B.P. 4007, 31055 Toulouse (Haute-Garonne), France.

Telephone: 52-65-96.

du Pré, Jacqueline, O.B.E.; British violoncellist; b. 1945; m. Daniel Barenboim (q.v.) 1967; ed. London Cello School, Guildhall School of Music under William Pleeth, under Paul Tortelier in Paris and Rostropovich in Moscow.

Debut at Wigmore Hall at sixteen; has been soloist with principal English orchestras and conductors at Royal Festival Hall, Royal Albert Hall and Bath and Edinburgh Festivals; has given concerts in Berlin, Paris, Rotterdam, Stavanger, U.S.A., U.S.S.R. and Australia; Fellow of Guildhall School of Music 75.

c/o Harold Holt Ltd., 122 Wigmore Street, London, W.1, England.

Dupuis, Raymond, Q.C.; Canadian lawyer and company director; b. 2 Aug. 1907; ed. Univ. of Montreal. Called to Province of Quebec Bar 30; Dir. Dupuis Frères 33, Pres. 45-61; Dir. Royal Bank of Canada, Canadian Broadcasting Corpn., Dominion Tar and Chemical Co. Ltd., Burns & Co. Ltd., Canada Life Assurance Co., Globe Indemnity Co. of Canada, Hudson Bay Insurance Co., Western Assurance Co., British America Assurance Co., Compagnie d'Assurance du Quebec, Soc. Nationale de Fiducie; Nat. Pres. Canadian Chamber of Commerce 56-57; official of numerous civic and philanthropic orgs.

Office: 612 St. James Street, West Montreal, Quebec; Home: 21 Messier Street, Sainte-Hilaire, Quebec, Canada.

Durand, Bernard Raymond Amédée; French diplomatist; b. 4 Dec. 1911, Besançon; s. of Col. Jean Durand and Jeanne d'Arces; m. Anne Chatin 1947; one s. two d.; ed. Coll. Saint-Michel, Saint Etienne and Faculté de Droit, Paris.

Attaché, French Embassy, Madrid 39, Rabat 43; First Sec., Cairo 47; Counsellor, Lisbon 51-55; Private Sec. to Antoine Pinay, Minister of Foreign Affairs 55-56; First Counsellor, Athens 56-61; Deputy Dir. to Maurice Couve de Murville, Minister of Foreign Affairs 62-65, Chief of Protocol to the Presidency and Ministry of Foreign Affairs 65-69; Amb. to Greece 69-73, to Portugal 73-; Officier Légion d'Honneur; Commdr., Ordre du Mérite.

Leisure interests: riding, golf.

French Embassy, Rua dos Santos-o-Velho 5, Lisbon, Portugal.

Durant, Will, A.M., PH.D.; American writer; b. 5 Nov. 1885; ed. St. Peter's Coll., and Columbia Univ.

Publs. *The Story of Philosophy* 26, *Transition* 27, *The Mansions of Philosophy* 29, *Adventures in Genius* 31, *The Story of Civilisation:* Vol. I *Our Oriental Heritage* 35, Vol. II *The Life of Greece* 39, Vol. III *Caesar and Christ* 44, Vol. IV *The Age of Faith* 50, Vol. V *The Renaissance* 53, Vol. VI *The Reformation* 57, Vol. VII *The Age of Reason Begins* (with Ariel Durant) 61, Vol. VIII *The Age of Louis XIV* (with Ariel Durant) 63, Vol. IX *The Age of Voltaire* (with Ariel Durant) 65, Vol. X *Rousseau*

and Revolution (with Ariel Durant) 67 (Pulitzer Prize 68), *The Lessons of History* 68, *Interpretations of Life* (with Ariel Durant) 70.

5608 Briarcliff Road, Los Angeles, Calif. 90028, U.S.A.

Duras, Marguerite; French writer; b. 4 April 1914, Giadinh, Indo-China; ed. Sorbonne.

Graduated in law; Sec. Ministry of Colonies 35-41; writer 43-.

Publs. *Les Impudents* 43, *La Vie Tranquille* 44, *Un Barrage contre le Pacifique* 50, *Le Marin de Gibraltar* 52, *Les Petits Chevaux de Tarquinia* 53, *Des Journées entières dans les Arbres* 54 (short stories), *Le Square* 55, *Moderato Cantabile* 58, *Les Viaducs de la Seine-et-Oise* 60, *Hiroshima Mon Amour* (film), *Dix Heures et demie du Soir en Eté* 60 (film 67), *L'Après-Midi de Monsieur Andesmas* 62, *Le Ravissement de Lol. V. Stein, Des Journées Entières dans les Arbres* (play) 64, *La Música* (play) 65, (film) 67, *Les Eaux et les Forêts* (play) 65, *Le Vice-Consul* 66, *L'Amante Anglaise* 67, *Yes, peut-être* and *Le Shaga* (two plays) 68, *Détruire, dit-Elle* 69, *Susanna Andler* (play) 69, *Abaha Sabana David* 71, *L'Amour* 72, *Jaune le Soleil* (film) 71, *Nathalie Granger* (film) 72, *La femme du Gange* (film) 73.

5 rue Saint-Benoît, 75006 Paris, France.

Durkin, John Anthony, B.A., LL.B.; American lawyer; b. 29 March 1936, Brookfield, Mass.; s. of Joseph Durkin and Charlotte Dailey; m. Patricia Moses 1965; one s. two d.; ed. Holy Cross Coll., Worcester, Mass., Georgetown Univ. Law Center, Washington, D.C.

Served in U.S. Navy 59-61, Lieut.-Commdr. in Corps Reserve; Asst. to Admin. of Nat. Banks, Washington, D.C. 63-66; Asst. Attorney-Gen., New Hampshire 66-68; New Hampshire Insurance Commr. 68-73; mem. Exec. Cttee. of Nat. Asscn. of Insurance Commrs. 70-73; Senator for New Hampshire 75-.

Leisure interests: reading, travelling.

60 Lenz Street, Manchester, New Hampshire 03102, U.S.A.

Telephone: (603) 669-4089; (603) 627-4435.

Durrani, Shakirullah; Pakistani investment banker and airline executive; b. 20 Sept. 1928, Sheikh-Kale, Tehsil Charsadda, Peshawar; s. of late Maj. Mohd. Zaman Khan; m. Samina Hayat 1951; one s. five d.; ed. Government Coll., Lahore, Indian Military Acad., Dehradun, and Pakistan Military Acad., Kakul.

Regular Officer Pakistan Army until 51; Lloyds Bank Ltd., training in U.K. and service in Karachi, Rawalpindi, Lahore and Dacca branches 52-60; Chief of Operations, Pakistan Industrial Credit and Investment Corpn. 60-63, Deputy Man. Dir. 63-66; Man. Dir. Investment Corpn. of Pakistan 66-68; Man. Dir. Pakistan Int. Airlines Corpn. 68-71; Gov. State Bank of Pakistan 71; under house arrest Dec. 72; Sitara-e-Khidmat 65, Sitara-e-Quaid-e-Azam 69, Grand Cordon, Order of Independence First Class (Jordan) 70.

c/o State Bank of Pakistan, P.O. Box 4456, McLeod Road, Karachi, Pakistan.

Durrell, Gerald Malcolm, F.R.S.L., F.R.G.S., F.Z.S.; British zoologist and writer; b. 7 Jan. 1925, Jamshedpur, India, s. of Lawrence Samuel and Louisa Florence (née Dixie) Durrell; m. Jacqueline Sonia Rasen 1951; ed. private tutors.

Student keeper, Whipsnade Park 45-46; zoological collecting expeditions: British Cameroons 47 and 48, British Guiana 49, Argentina and Paraguay 53, British Cameroons 56, Trans-Argentine 58, New Zealand, Australia and Malaysia 61, Sierra Leone 64, Mexico 68; established own zoo in Jersey 59, founded Jersey Wildlife Preservation Trust 64; contributes to many magazines and dailies; numerous lectures, B.B.C. broadcasts and 4 major T.V. series on animals; mem. Inst. of Biology, British Ornithologists Union.

Leisure interests: reading, photography, drawing,

swimming, history and maintenance of zoological gardens.
Publs. *The Overloaded Ark* 52, *Three Singles to Adventure* 53, *The Bafut Beagles* 53, *The Drunken Forest* 55, *My Family and Other Animals* 56, *Encounters with Animals* 59, *A Zoo in My Luggage* 60, *The Whispering Land* 62, *Menagerie Manor* 64, *Two in the Bush* 66, *Rosy is My Relative* (novel) 68, *Birds, Beasts and Relatives* 69, *Fillets of Plaice* 71, *Catch Me a Colobus* 72; Childrens' Books: *The New Noah* 56, *Island Zoo* 61, *Look at Zoos* 61, *My Favourite Animal Stories* 63, *The Donkey Rustlers* 68, *Beasts in My Belfry* 73, *The Talking Parcel* 74.
Jersey Wildlife Preservation Trust, Les Augres Manor, Trinity, Jersey, Channel Islands.
Telephone: North 949-1454.

Durrell, Lawrence George, F.R.S.L.; British author and official; b. 27 Feb. 1912; ed. Coll. of St. Joseph, Darjeeling, India, and St. Edmund's Coll., Canterbury, England.
Formerly Foreign Service Press Officer (Athens and Cairo), Press Attaché (Alexandria and Belgrade), Dir. of Public Relations (Dodecanese Islands), Dir. of British Council Institutes (Kalamata, Greece, and Cordoba, Argentina), and Dir. of Public Relations (Govt. of Cyprus); James Tait Black Memorial Prize 74.
Publs. Poetry: *A Private Country* 43, *Cities, Plains and People* 46, *On Seeming to Presume* 48, *The Tree of Idleness* 55, *Selected Poems* 56, *Collected Poems* 60, 68, *The Ikons* 66, *The Red Limbo Lingo* 71, *Vega and Other Poems* 73; Verse drama: *Sappho* 50, *Acte* 62, *An Irish Faustus* 64; Prose: *Panic Spring* 37, *The Black Book* 38, *Prospero's Cell* 45, *Cefalu* (*The Dark Labyrinth*) 47, *Reflections on a Marine Venus* 53, *Bitter Lemons* 57, *The Alexandria Quartet: Justine* 57, *Balthazar* 58, *Mountolive* 58, *Clea* 60; *Tunc* 68, *Spirit of Place* 69, *Nunquam* 70, *The Big Supposer* 73, *Monsieur* 74; Humour: *Esprit de Corps* 57, *Stiff Upper Lip* 58, *Sauve Qui Peut* 66; Juvenile: *White Eagles Over Serbia* 57; Trans. *Four Greek Poets* 46, *Pope Joan* 48; Letters: *A Private Correspondence* (with Henry Miller) 62.
c/o The National and Grindlay's Bank Ltd., 13 St. James's Square, London, S.W.1, England.

Dürrenmatt, Friedrich; Swiss writer; b. 5 Jan. 1921; s. of Reinhold and Hulda (née Zimmermann) Dürrenmatt; m. Lotti Geissler 1946; one s. two d.; ed. Univs. of Berne and Zürich.
Leisure interest: painting.
Publs. Plays: *Der Blinde, Die Ehe des Herrn Mississippi, Romulus der Grosse, Ein Engel kommt nach Babylon, Der Besuch der alten Dame, Es steht geschrieben, Die Physiker, Der Meteor, Portrait of a Planet, Die Wiedertäufer, Frank V, König Johann und Titus Andronicus nach Shakespeare, Play Strindberg, Der Mitmacher*; radio plays: *Der Doppelgänger, Stranitzky und der Nationalheld, Nächtliches Gespräch mit einem verachteten Menschen, Herkules und der Stall des Augias, Das Unternehmen der Wega, Abendstunde im Spätherbst, Der Prozess um des Esels Schatten, Die Panne*; novels: *Der Richter und sein Henker, Der Verdacht, Grieche sucht Griechin, Das Versprechen*; short stories: *Die Stadt, Die Panne, Der Sturz*; essay: *Theater-Probleme, Theaterschriften und Reden I, II*.
Pertuis du Sault 34, 2000 Neuchâtel, Switzerland.
Telephone: (038) 25-63-23.

Dürrenmatt, Peter Ulrich; Swiss journalist; b. 29 Aug. 1904; ed. Univs. of Berne and Geneva.
Began career as teacher; mem. staff *Schweizer Mittelpresse* 34; Editor Swiss Section *Basler Nachrichten* 43-49. Chief Editor 49-; mem. Nat. Council 59.
Publs. *Die Bundesverfassung, ihr Wert und ihre Bewährung* 48, *Kleine Geschichte der Schweiz im zweiten Weltkrieg* 49, *Zerfall und Wiederaufbau der Politik* 51,

Schweizergeschichte 57, *Die Welt zwischen Krieg und Frieden* 59, *Europa will leben* 60, *50 Jahre Weltgeschichte* 62, *In die Zeit gesprochen* 65.
Basler Nachrichten, Dufourstrasse 40, Basle, Switzerland.

Duruflé, Maurice; French organist and composer; b 11 Jan. 1902; ed. Paris Conservatoire.
Prize for organ (Conservatoire) 22; prize for harmony 24; prize for accompaniment 26; prizes for fugue and for composition 28; Prix des "Amis de l'Orgue" 30; Organist of Saint-Etienne-du-Mont; Asst. Prof. at Conservatoire Paris 42; Prof. d'harmonie, Conservatoire de Paris 43-.
Works include: Organ: *Prélude, Adagio et Choral Varié sur le Veni Creator* 29; *Suite* 33; *Prélude et Fugue* 42; Chamber Music: *Trio pour Flûte, Alto et Piano; Quatre Motets* 60; Orchestra: *Trois Danses* 35, *Andante et Scherzo* 40, *Requiem pour Solo, Choeurs, Orchestre et Orgue* 47, *Messe: Cum jubilo* 66.
6 Place du Panthéon, Paris, 5e, France.
Telephone: 326-45-02.

Dushkin, Alexei Nikolaevich; Soviet architect; b.1903, Alexandrovka; ed. Architectural Dept. of Kharkov Building Inst.
Builder 24-28; Architect in Moscow; Chief Architect, Metropolitan Designing Inst. 33-43, 59-; Chief Architect, Ministry of Railways 43-59; Lecturer, Moscow Inst. of Architecture 47-, Prof. 66-; State prizewinner (three times); awarded Order of Lenin (twice), Order of Red Banner of Labour.
Works include: help with design of 'Kropotkinskaya', Square of the Revolution, Mayakovsky, Avtozavodskaya, Novoslobodskaya (Moscow underground stations), one of designers of building at Lermontov Square (former Red Gates), department stores, Moscow, and several railway stations.
Union of Architects of the U.S.S.R., Ul. Shchuseva 3, Moscow, U.S.S.R.

Dutilleux, Henri; French composer; b. 22 Jan. 1916, Angers; s. of Paul and Thérèse (née Koszul) Dutilleux; m. Geneviéve Joy 1946; ed. Conservatoire national de Musique, Paris.
Career devoted to music 45-; Dir. service *Créations Musicales* Radiodiffusion française 45-63; Prof. of Composition Ecole Normale de Musique, Paris 61-, Pres. 69-, Assoc. Prof. Conservatoire National Supérieur de Musique, Paris 70-71; Vice-Pres. Syndicat Nat. des Auteurs et Compositeurs 62-; fmr. mem. UNESCO Music Council; 1st Grand Prix de Rome 38, Grand Prix du Disque 57, 58, 66 and 68, Grand Prix du Conseil Général de la Seine 59, Grand Prix National de la Musique 67.
Compositions: *Sonata for Piano* 48, *First Symphony* 51, *Le Loup* (Ballet) 53, *Second Symphony* (*Le Double*) 59, *Métaboles* 64, *Cello Concerto: Tout un monde lointain* 70, *Figures de Résonances* (for two pianos) 71.
12 rue Saint-Louis en l'Ille, 75004 Paris, France.
Telephone: 326-3914.

Duval, Charles Gaëtan, BAR.-AT-LAW; Mauritius politician; b. 9 Oct. 1930, Rose Hill; s. of Charles R. and Rosina M. Duval; divorced; one s.; ed. Royal Coll., Curepipe, Lincoln's Inn, London and Faculty of Law, Univ. of Paris.
Entered politics 58; mem. Town Council, Curepipe 60, re-elected 63, Legislative Council, Curepipe 60, re-elected 63; mem. Municipal Council, Port Louis 69-; mem. "Le Centre Culturel Français"; Chair. Town Council, Curepipe 60-61, 63-Feb. 68; Rep. Curepipe at Nice 60; Minister of Housing, Lands and Town and Country Planning 64-Nov. 65; attended London Constitutional Conf. 65; Leader, Parti Mauritien Social Démocrate (P.M.S.D.) 66-; first M.L.A. for Grand River North-West and Port Louis West 67; Leader of

the Opposition 67-Nov. 69; Minister of External Affairs, Tourism and Emigration 69-73; Mayor, City of Port Louis 69-71; Lord Mayor of Port Louis 71-; Pres. Asscn. Touristique de l'Océan Indien (A.T.O.I.) 73; Chair. S. African Regional Tourism Council 73.
Leisure interests: horse-riding, farming.
Poste Lafayette; and Grand Gaube, Mauritius.
Telephone: 35-551; 39-518.

Duval, H.E. Cardinal Léon-Etienne, D.THEOL.; Algerian (b. French) ecclesiastic; b. 9 Nov. 1903, Chenex, Haute-Savoie, France; s. of François Duval and Joséphine Saultier; ed. Petit Séminaire, Roche-sur-Foron, Grand Séminaire Annecy, Séminaire français Rome, and Pontificia Universitas Gregoriana.
Ordained priest 26; Prof. Grand Séminaire Annecy 30-42; Vicar-Gen. and Dir. of works, Diocese of Annecy 42-46; consecrated Bishop of Constantine and Hippo 46; Archbishop of Algiers 54-; created Cardinal 65; Officier Légion d'Honneur.
Publs. *Paroles de Paix* 55, *Messages de Paix 1955-1962* 62, *Laïcs, Prêtres, Religieux dans l'Eglise* 67.
Archbishop's House, 13 rue Khelifa-Boukhalfa, Algiers, Algeria.
Telephone: 63-42-44; 64-05-82.

Duvalier, Jean-Claude; Haitian Head of State; b. 3 July 1951, Port-au-Prince; s. of late Pres. François Duvalier and Simone (née Ovide), *q.v.*; ed. Coll. of St. Louis de Gonzague, Port-au-Prince and faculty of law Univ. of Haiti.
Named political heir to Pres. François Duvalier Jan. 71; Life Pres. April 71-.
Palais National, Port-au-Prince, Haiti.

Duvalier, Simone; First Lady of Haiti; b. 19 March 1913, Léogane, Port-au-Prince; d. of Jules Faine; m. late Pres. François Duvalier 1939; one s. (Jean-Claude, *q.v.*) three d.; ed. secondary school, Port-au-Prince.
Trained as nurse; First Lady of Haiti Oct. 57-.
Palais National, Port-au-Prince, Haiti.

Duverger, Maurice; French political scientist; b. 5 June 1917, Angoulème; m. Odile Batt 1949; ed. Bordeaux Univ.
Prof. of Political Sociology, Paris Univ. 55-; Dir. of Dept. of Political Science (Sorbonne); Dir. of Study and Research, Fondation Nat. des Sciences Politiques; contributor to *Le Monde*.
Leisure interest: theatre.
Publs. *Les Partis Politiques* 51, *La Participation des Femmes à la Vie Politique* 55, *Les Finances publiques* 56, *Demain, la République . . .* 58, *Méthodes de la Science Politique* 59, *De la Dictature* 61, *La Vième République et le Régime Présidentiel* 61, *Introduction to the Social Sciences* 64, *Introduction à la Politique* 64, *Sociologie politique* 66, *La démocratie sans le peuple* 67, *Institutions politiques* 70, *Janus: les deux faces de l'Occident* 72, *Sociologie de la Politique* 73, *La monarchie républicaine* 74.
24 rue des Fossés Saint-Jacques, Paris 5e, France.

Duvieusart, Jean Pierre, D. EN D.; Belgian lawyer and politician; b. 10 April 1900, Frasnes lez Gosselies; s. of Léopold Duvieusart and Maria Boval; m. Alexandrine Blanche Dijon 1930; three s. one d.; ed. Collège des Pères Jésuites, Charleroi, and Univ. of Louvain.
Mayor of Frasnes lez Gosselies 27-47; Provincial Judge, Hainault 33-36; mem. House of Reps. 44-49, Senator 49-; Minister of Econ. Affairs and of the Middle Classes 47-50, 52-54; Prime Minister 50; Del. to UN Gen. Assembly 50; Pres. European Parl. 64-65; lawyer, Charleroi; Commdr. Ordre de Léopold, numerous other decorations.
Leisure interest: history.
2 boulevard Joseph II, 6000-Charleroi, Belgium.
Telephone: 31 41 43.

du Vigneaud, Vincent, PH.D.; American university professor; b. 18 May 1901, Chicago, Ill.; s. of Mary Theresa O'Leary and Alfred Joseph du Vigneaud; m. Zella Zon Ford 1924; one s. one d.; ed. Univs. of Illinois and Rochester.
Assistant Prof. Univ. of Ill. 30-32; Prof. and Head Dept. of Biochemistry George Washington Univ. 32-38; same at Cornell Univ. Medical Coll. 38-67, Emer. 67-; Prof. of Chemistry, Cornell Univ. 67-75; awarded Hillebrand Prize of Chemical Society of Washington 36; mem. Nat. Acad. of Sciences; Foster Lecturer Univ. of Buffalo 39; Mead-Johnson Vitamin B Complex Award, American Inst. of Nutrition 43; Hitchcock Prof. Univ. of California 44; Nichols Medal, New York Section of the American Chemical Society 45; Julius Stieglitz Memorial Lecturer 48; Lasker Award 48; Eastman Lecturer 49; Lecturer, Univ. of London 49, Messenger Lecturer Cornell 50, Harvey Society Lecturer 42 and 54, Dakin Memorial Lecturer 56, etc.; Osborne and Mendel Award 53, Passano Award 55, American Coll. of Physicians Award 65, Dohme Lectures Johns Hopkins Medical School 68; Eli Lili Lecture Award 67, Endocrine Soc., etc.; Nobel Prize for Chemistry 55; Hon. Sc.D. (Yale and New York Univs.) 55; Hon. Sc.D. (Univ. of Ill.) 60; Hon. Sc.D. (Univs. St. Louis and Rochester) 65, (George Washington Univ.) 68.
Leisure interests: horseback riding, bridge.
Home: 200 White Park Road, Ithaca, N.Y. 14850; Office: Department of Chemistry, Cornell University, Ithaca, N.Y., U.S.A.
Telephone: 607-272-7469.

Duvillard, Henri; French politician; b. 3 Nov. 1910. Journalist, Dir. *La Dépêche du Loiret* 47-52; on staff of Gen. Koenig (Minister of Nat. Defence) 54, 55; on staff of H. Ulvet (Minister of Industry and Commerce) 54-55; on staff of Maurice Lemaire (Sec. of State for Industry and Commerce) 56-57; Deputy for Loiret; fmr. Vice-Pres. U.N.R. Group in Nat. Assembly; fmr. Public Relations Officer, Papeteries de France; Minister for Ex-Servicemen 67-72; Médaille Militaire, Croix de Guerre (39-45), Médaille de la Résistance.
12 rue du Grenier-à-sel, 45000 Orléans, France.

Duwaerts, Leon-Louis; Belgian journalist; b. 13 Jan. 1905; ed. Athénée de Saint-Gilles-lez-Bruxelles.
Sec.-Gen. Union professionelle de la presse belge 28-35, Association générale de la presse belge 35-58, Pres. 58-60; Pres. Association professionnelle de la presse cinématographique belge 35-37, 40-50, now Hon. Pres.; Editor-in-Chief Agence Belga; Hon. Pres. Fédération Int. de la presse cinématographique; Pres. Belgian Journalists' Inst.; Commdr. Ordre de Léopold, etc.
Publs. *Le Statut du Journaliste professionnel de la presse filmée* 35, *Droits et Devoirs du Journaliste* 52.
120 avenue Henri Jaspar, Brussels 6, Belgium.
Telephone: 02/37-57-27.

Duwez, Pol E., D.SC.; American professor of materials science; b. 11 Dec. 1907, Mons, Belgium; m. Nera Faisse 1935; one d.; ed. School of Mines, Mons and Univ. of Brussels.
Research Fellow Physics, Calif. Inst. of Technology 33-35; Prof., School of Mines, Mons 35-40; Calif. Inst. of Technology, Research Engineer 41-45, Chief Materials Section, Jet Propulsion Laboratory 45-54, Prof. of Materials Science 47-; mem. Science Advisory Board to Chief of Staff, U.S.A.F. 45-55; mem. Nat. Acad. of Sciences 72-; Charles B. Dudley Award, American Soc. for Testing Materials 51; C. H. Matthewson Gold Medal, American Soc. Mining and Metallurgical Engineers 64; Campbell Memorial Lecturer, American Soc. of Metals 67; F. J. Clamer Medal, Franklin Inst. 68; A. Sauveur Achievement Award, Amer. Soc. of Metals 73; Gov. Cornez Prize, Belgium 73; Paul Lebeau Medal, Paris 74.
Leisure interest: chamber music.

Publs. numerous papers on: plastic deformation and wave propagation, heat transfer, powder metallurgy, titanium and its alloys, high temperature refractory materials, alloy systems.
1535 Oakdale Street, Pasadena, Calif. 91106, U.S.A.

Dvořák, Richard; Czechoslovak politician; b. 28 Dec. 1913, Křešice on Elbe; ed. Commercial Coll., Teplice. Imprisoned by Gestapo 39-45; mem. Nat. Assembly 48; Minister, Foreign Trade 53-59; Ambassador, U.S.S.R. 59-63; Head, Central Board for Dev. of Local Economy 63; Minister of Finance Sept. 63-66; Amb. to India and Nepal 67-71, to German Democratic Repub. 71-; mem. of Comm. of Central Cttee. of C.P. of Czechoslovakia for questions of Living Standards 63-66; Deputy to Nat. Assembly 60-64; Alt. mem. Central Cttee. of C.P. of Czechoslovakia 58-62, mem. 62-66; Order of Labour 63, Order of Victorious February 73.
Czechoslovak Embassy, Schönhauser Allee 10-11, 1054 Berlin-Prenzlauer Berg, German Democratic Republic.

Dy, Francisco Justiniano, M.D., M.P.H.; Philippine public health administrator; b. 17 Sept. 1912, Manila; m. Fé L. de la Fuente 1941; two s. two d.; ed. Univ. of Philippines and School of Hygiene and Public Health, Johns Hopkins Univ., U.S.A.
Research Asst. and Instructor, Inst. of Hygiene, Univ. of Philippines 38-41; U.S. Army 42-45; Senior Surgeon, U.S. Public Health Service 45-46; Consultant and Chief of Malaria Division, U.S. Public Health Service Rehabilitation Programme in Philippines 46-50; Prof. of Malariology and Chair. Dept. of Parasitology, Inst. of Hygiene, Univ. of Philippines 50-52; Deputy Chief, Malaria Section, World Health Org. (WHO), Geneva 50-51; Regional Malaria Adviser, WHO, for W. Pacific Region 51-57; Dir. of Health Services, WHO Regional Office for W. Pacific 58-66, Regional Dir. of WHO for W. Pacific July 66-; mem. Nat. Research Council of Philippines; Distinguished Service Star (Philippines); Legion of Merit, with Oak Leaf Cluster (U.S.A.).
Leisure interest: gardening.
Regional Office for the Western Pacific, World Health Organization, P.O. Box 2932, Manila, Philippines.
Telephone: 59-20-41.

Dykes Bower, Sir John, Kt., C.V.O.; British organist; b. 13 Aug. 1905; ed. Cheltenham Coll., and Corpus Christi Coll., Cambridge.
Organist and Master of the Choir, Truro Cathedral 26-29, Succentor 29; Organist, New Coll., Oxford 29-33, Durham Cathedral 33-36; Fellow, Corpus Christi Coll., Cambridge 34-37; Organist, St. Paul's Cathedral, London 36-67; Pres. Inc. Asscn. of Organists 49-50, Royal Coll. of Organists 60-62, Hon. Sec. 68-; Hon. D.Mus. (Oxford), and several hon. diplomas.
4Z Artillery Mansions, Westminster, London, S.W.1, England.
Telephone: 01-222-6147.

Dylan, Bob; American composer and singer; b. Robert Zimmerman 24 May 1941, Duluth, Minn.; m.
Best known for composition and interpretation of pop, country and folk music; numerous songs include: Blowin' in the Wind, Don't think twice, it's all right, A hard rain's a-gonna fall, She belongs to me, It's all over now baby blue, The times they are a-changing, Just like a woman, I'll be your baby tonight, I shall be released, Lay, lady, lay, If not for you, Mr. tambourine man, etc.; has acted in films, Don't Look Back, Eat the Document, Pat Garrett and Billy the Kid; Hon. D.Mus. (Princeton Univ.) 70.
Publ. Tarantula 66-71, Writings and Drawings by Bob Dylan.
P.O. Box 264, Cooper Station, New York, N.Y. 10003, U.S.A.

Dymshyts, Veniamin Emmanuilovich; Soviet engineer and politician; b. 1910; ed. Higher Technical School, Moscow.
Member C.P.S.U. 37-; in metallurgical construction 31-50; Deputy Minister construction enterprises in metallurgical and chemical industries 50-57; Chief Engineer (Construction), Bhilai Steel Plant, India 57-59; Chief of Dept., State Planning Cttee. 59-61, First Dep. Chair. 61-62, Chair. 62; Chair. Econ. Council U.S.S.R. 62-65; Chair. U.S.S.R. State Cttee. for Material and Technical Supplies 65-; Deputy Chair. U.S.S.R. Council of Ministers 62-; mem. Central Cttee. C.P.S.U. 61-; Deputy to Supreme Soviet 62-; State Prize 46, 50; Order of Lenin; Order of the Red Banner of Labour (twice), State Committee for Material and Technical Supplies.
5 Orlikov pereulok, Moscow, U.S.S.R.

Dyson, Freeman John, F.R.S.; American physicist; b. 15 Dec. 1923, Crowthorne, England; s. of late Sir George Dyson and Lady Mildred (Atkey) Dyson; m. 1st Verena Huber 1950 (divorced 1958), 2nd Imme Jung 1958; one s. five d.; ed. Cambridge and Cornell Univs.
Fellow of Trinity Coll., Cambridge 46; Warren Research Fellow, Birmingham Univ. 49; Prof. of Physics, Cornell Univ. 51-53; Prof., Inst. for Advanced Study, Princeton 53-; Chair. Fed. of American Scientists 62; mem. U.S. Nat. Acad. of Sciences 64-; Heineman Prize, American Inst. of Physics 65; Lorentz Medal, Royal Netherlands Acad. 66, Hughes Medal, Royal Soc. 68, Max Planck Medal, German Physical Soc. 69.
Publs. Papers in The Physical Review, Journal of Mathematical Physics, etc.
Institute for Advanced Study, Princeton, N.J. 08540, U.S.A.
Telephone: 609-924-4400.

Dzerzhinsky, Ivan Ivanovich; Soviet composer; b. 9 April 1909, Tambov; ed. Gnesin Inst., Moscow and Leningrad Conservatoire.
Studied piano under Prof. B L. Yavorsky, and composition under Profs. M. G. Gnesin, P. B. Ryazanov, B. Asafyevch; composer of operas; mem. C.P.S.U. 42; mem. Board of Union of Soviet Composers 36-48; State Prize 50; Order of Lenin 39; Hon. Art Worker of R.S.F.S.R. 57.
Works include, operas: Quiet Don 35, Virgin Soil Upturned 37, Days of Volochaevsk 39, Thunderstorm 40, Blood of the People 41, Nadezhda Svetlova 42, Prince Lake 47, The Snow Storm 46, Far from Moscow 54; symphonic poem Ermak; three piano concertos; piano cycles: Spring Suite and Russian Painters; song cycles: First Love 43, The Flying Bird 45, Earth 49, To a Woman Friend 50, The New Village 50, The Northern Bojan 55, Leningrad 57, Destiny of a Man (opera) 61, The Whirlwind (opera) 65-66, Grigory Melexov (opera, cont. Quiet Don) 66-67, Native Rivers (song cycles) 66.
Union of Soviet Composers, R.S.F.S.R., 8/10 Ul. Nezhdanovoy, Moscow, U.S.S.R.

Dzotsenidze, Georgi Samsonovich, D.SC.; Soviet scholar and politician; b. 10 Feb. 1910, Kutaisi, Georgian S.S.R.; ed. Tbilisi Univ.
Dozent, then Prof. of Geology, State Pedagogical Inst., Kutaisi 33-34; mem. C.P.S.U. 40-; Dozent, Prof., later Dean, Tbilisi Univ. 34-59; Deputy Sec. Acad. of Sciences, Georgia 51-55, Vice-Pres. 55-58; Rector, Tbilisi Univ. 58-59; Deputy to U.S.S.R. Supreme Soviet 58-76 (retd.); Chair. Presidium Supreme Soviet Georgia 59-76; Deputy Chair. Presidium Supreme Soviet U.S.S.R. 60-76; mem. Cen. Auditing Cttee. C.P.S.U. 61-73; mem. Political Bureau Cen. Cttee. of Georgian C.P., Academician, U.S.S.R. Acad of Sciences 68-; Lenin Prize, U.S.S.R. State Prize.
Presidium of the Supreme Soviet of the Georgian S.S.R., Tbilisi, U.S.S.R.

Dzur, Col.-Gen. Martin, ING.; Czechoslovak army officer and politician; b. 12 July 1919, Ploštín, Czechoslovakia; ed. School of Wood Processing, V. M. Molotov Military Acad. of Rear Echelon Services, Kalinin, U.S.S.R., and Military Staff Acad. of Armed Forces, U.S.S.R.

Technical clerk, Slovak Paper Mills, Ružomberok 39-41; Army service 41-43; joined 1st Czechoslovak Independent Brigade, Soviet Army, U.S.S.R.; served in U.S.S.R. 43-45; Div. Gen. Staff Officer, State Sec.'s A.D.C., A.D.C. to Chief of Mil. Office of Pres. of Czechoslovakia 45-49; various important posts in Army and Ministry of Nat. Defence 53-58; Deputy Minister of Nat. Defence 58-68, Minister 68; Minister of Nat. Defence, Fed. Govt. of Č.S.S.R. 69-; mem. Central Cttee. C.P. of Czechoslovakia 68-; Deputy to House of the People, Fed. Assembly 71-; Army-Gen. 72; Order of Labour 69, Soviet, Czechoslovak and Polish Medals including Award for Strengthening Friendship in Arms, 1st Class 72, Commdr.'s Cross with Star of Order of Polish Revival 72, Order of Victorious February 74.
Ministry of National Defence, Prague, Czechoslovakia.

Dzuverovic, Nikola; Yugoslav politician; b. 1917, Prokuplje; s. of Arsenije and Jelisaveta Dzuverovic; m. Nada Dzuverovic 1946; two d.; ed. Secondary School of General Education.
Former Sec. Regional Cttee. of Communist Party for Prokuplje, Dir.-Gen. of Machine Building Directorate, Serbia, mem. Exec. Council, Serbia, Pres. Board of Management, Fed. Chamber of Industry; Fed. Sec. for Foreign Trade 62-67; mem. of the Praesidium of the Socialist Alliance of the Working Peoples of Yugoslavia; Deputy on the People's Council of the Fed. Assembly.
Leisure interest: fishing.
Koste Jovanovica 49, Belgrade, Yugoslavia.
Telephone: 648-044.

E

Eagle, Harry, A.B., M.D.; American researcher in cell biology; b. 13 July 1905, New York City; *m.* Hope Whaley 1928; one *d.*; ed. Johns Hopkins Univ. and Johns Hopkins Medical School.
Assistant, Instructor Dept. Medicine, Johns Hopkins Medical School 28-32; Nat. Research Fellow, Harvard 32-33; Asst. Prof. Microbiology, Univ. of Pa. Medical School 33-36; U.S. Public Health Service 36-61; Dir. Venereal Disease Research Lab. and Lab. of Experimental Therapeutics, Johns Hopkins School of Hygiene and Public Health, and the Public Health Service 36-48, Adjunct Prof. of Bacteriology, Johns Hopkins School of Hygiene and Public Health 46-48; Scientific Dir., Research Branch, Nat. Cancer Inst. 47-49; Chief, Section on Experimental Therapeutics at Nat. Microbiological Inst., Nat. Inst. of Health 49-59, Laboratory of Cell Biology at Nat. Inst. of Allergy and Infectious Diseases 59-61; Prof. and Chair., Dept. of Cell Biology, Albert Einstein Coll. of Medicine, N.Y. 61-71, Div. of Biological Sciences 68-71, Univ. Prof. 71-, Dir. Cancer Research Center 71-, Assoc. Dean for Scientific Affairs 74-; Harvey Lecturer 59; Trustee, Microbiological Foundation (Waksman); mem. numerous advisory cttees.; mem. numerous socs. including Nat. Acad. of Sciences, American Acad. of Arts and Sciences, Soc. of American Microbiologists (Pres. 57-58), Amer. Acad. of Microbiology, Amer. Asscn. of Immunologists (Pres. 64-65), Amer. Asscn. of Cancer Research (on Board of Dirs. 63-66); Hon. M.Sc. Yale Univ., Hon. D.Sc. Wayne Univ.; Eli Lilly Award in Microbiology 36, Presidential Certificate of Merit 48, Borden Award, Amer. Asscn. of Medical Colls. 64, Albert Einstein Commemorative Award 68, Modern Medicine Award 72, Louisa Gross Horwitz Award 73.
Publs. Studies relating to: Bacterial physiology; Immunochemistry: serodiagnosis of syphilis, blood coagulation; Chemotherapy: syphilis, trypanosomiasis and tropical diseases; Detoxification of metal poisoning; Mode of action of antibiotics; Cell and tissue culture.
Albert Einstein College of Medicine, Eastchester Road and Morris Park Avenue, Bronx, N.Y. 10461; Home: 370 Orienta Avenue, Mamaroneck, N.Y. 10543, U.S.A. Telephone: 212-430-2302 (Office); 914-OW 8-8218 (Home).

Eagleton, Thomas Francis, LL.B.; American lawyer and politician; b. 4 Sept. 1929; ed. Amherst Coll. and Harvard Univ.
Admitted to Mo. Bar 53; private law practice St. Louis 53-56; Circuit Attorney, St. Louis 57-60; Attorney-Gen., State of Mo. 61-65, Lieut.-Gov. 65-68; Senator from Mo. 69-; selected as candidate for Vice-Presidency but later resigned 72; Democrat.
U.S. Senate, Washington, D.C., U.S.A.

Eames, Charles; American designer; *m.* Ray Kaiser 1941.
Independent designer of furniture, toys, films, exhibits, including *The World of Franklin and Jefferson* 75-76, etc.; in partnership with wife, Ray Eames.
Office: 901 Washington Boulevard, Venice, Calif.; Home: 203 Chautauqua Boulevard, Pacific Palisades, Calif., U.S.A.

Earle, Arthur Frederick, PH.D.; Canadian economist and business executive; b. 13 Sept. 1921, Toronto, Ont.; *s.* of Frederick Charles Earle and Hilda Mary (née Brown); *m.* Vera Domini Lithgow 1946; two *s.* one *d.*; ed. Univ. of Toronto and London School of Economics.
Royal Canadian Navy 39-46; Canada Packers Ltd. 46-48; Aluminium Ltd. in British Guiana, West Indies and Canada 48-53; Treas. Alumina Jamaica Ltd. 53-55;

Sales Exec., Aluminium Union, London 55-58; Vice-Pres. Aluminium Ltd. Sales Inc., New York 58-61; Deputy Chair. Hoover Ltd. 61-65, Man. Dir. 63-65, Dir. 61-74; Principal, London Graduate School of Business Studies 65-72; Pres. Int. Investment Corpn. for Yugoslavia 72-74; Pres. Boyden Consulting Group Ltd.; Assoc., Boyden Associates 74-; mem. The Consumer Council 63-68; Gov. and mem. of Council of Management of Ditchley Foundation; Gov. Nat. Inst. of Econ. and Social Research 68-74; Gov. London School of Econs.; Fellow, London Business School.
Leisure interest: hill climbing.
Publs. Numerous economic and management publications.
Suite 2701 Commerce Court North, P.O. Box 389, Toronto, Ont. M5L 1G3; Apartment 804 Old Mill Towers, 39 Old Mill Road, Toronto, Ont. M8X 1G6, Canada.
Telephone: 416-869-3848 (Office); 416-231-4505 (Home).

Earle, Ion, B.A., T.D.; British discount banker; b. 12 April 1916, Neath, Glamorgan; *s.* of Stephen Earle and Beatrice (née Blair White); *m.* Elizabeth Dain Stevens 1946; one *s.* one *d.*; ed. Stowe School, Univ. Coll., Oxford and Univ. of Grenoble.
Head of Regional Org., Fed. of British Industries 52-60; Chief Exec., Export Council for Europe 60-64; Dir. British Nat. Export Council 64-66, Deputy Dir.-Gen. 66-71; joined Kleinwort Benson Ltd. 72; Clive Discount Co. Ltd. 73-.
Leisure interests: golf, gardening, travel.
5 McKay Road, London, S.W.20, England.

Eason, Henry, C.B.E., J.P., B.COM., F.I.B.; British banking administrator; b. 12 April 1910, Middlesbrough; *s.* of late H. and F. J. Eason; *m.* Florence Isobel Stevenson 1939; one *s.* two *d.*; ed. Yarm and King's Coll., Univ. of Durham.
Barrister; Lloyds Bank Ltd. until 39; Royal Air Force (Wing Commdr.), Second World War; Sec.-Gen. Inst. of Bankers 59-71, a Vice-Pres. 69-75.
Leisure interests: golf, travel, reading.
12 Redgate Drive, Hayes Common, Bromley, Kent, BR2 7BT, England.

Eastland, James O.; American politician; b. 28 Nov. 1904; ed. Univs. of Mississippi and Alabama and Vanderbilt Univ.
Admitted to Mississippi Bar 27; practised law; mem. Mississippi House of Reps. 28-32; Senator from Miss. 43-; Pres. of Senate 72-; Democrat.
United States Senate, Washington, D.C.; and 5116 Macomb Street, Washington, D.C. 20016, U.S.A.

Easum, Donald B., M.P.A., PH.D.; American diplomatist; b. 27 Aug. 1923, Culver, Ind.; *s.* of Chester and Norma Brown Easum; *m.* Augusta Pentecost 1954; three *s.* one *d.*; ed. Univ. of Wisconsin, Princeton and London Univs.
Reporter *New York Times* 49; joined Foreign Service 53; held diplomatic posts in Nicaragua 55-57, Indonesia 57-59, Senegal 63-66, Niger 66-67; Exec. Sec. Agency for Int. Devt., Dept. of State 61-63; Staff Dir. Interdept. Group for Inter-American Affairs 69-71; Amb. to Upper Volta 71-73; Asst. Sec. of State for African Affairs 74-75; Amb. to Nigeria March 75-.
Leisure interests: singing, tennis, table tennis, gardening.
Publ. article in *Race and Politics in South Africa* 75.
American Embassy, Lagos, Nigeria.

Eaton, Cyrus Stephen, A.B., D.C.L., LL.D.; American industrialist and railroad executive; b. 27 Dec. 1883; ed. McMaster Univ., Toronto.

Co-founder Cliffs Corpn.; founder Republic Steel Corpn.; fmr. Dir. Cleveland Trust Co., Republic Steel Corpn., Youngstown Sheet and Tube Co., Inland Steel, Nat. Acme; Chair. and Dir. Chesapeake and Ohio Rly., now Chair. Emeritus; Chair. Chessie System Inc. until 73; Chair. Steep Rock Iron Mines Ltd., West Kentucky Coal Co.; Chair. Pres. and Dir. Portsmouth Steel Corpn.; fmr. Dir. Sherwin-Williams Co., Cleveland Electric Illumination Co., Kansas City Power and Light Co.; Trustee, Denison Univ., Univ. of Chicago, Cleveland Museum of Natural History; mem. American Council of Learned Socs., American Historical Asscn., American Philosophical Asscn.; Dir. Harry S. Truman Library Inst. of Nat. and Int. Affairs; mem. Atlantic Province Econ. Council, Royal Norwegian Acad. of Sciences, American Acad. of Arts and Sciences; Hon. LL.D. (Eotvoes Lorand Univ., Budapest); Lenin Peace Prize.
Publs. *The Third Term "Tradition"* 40, *Financial Democracy* 41, *The Professor Talks to Himself* 42, *Investment Banking—Competition or Decadence?* 44, *A New Plan to Re-open the U.S. Capital Market* 45, *A Capitalist Looks At Labor* 47, *Is the Globe Big Enough for Capitalism and Communism?* 58, *Canada's Choice* 59, *The Engineer as Philosopher* 61.
Terminal Tower, Cleveland, Ohio 44113; Home: Acadia Farms, Northfield, Ohio 44067, U.S.A.
Telephone: 216-861-2200 (Office); 216-467-7125 (Home).

Eban, Abba; Israeli politician; b. 2 Feb. 1915, Cape Town, S. Africa; *s.* of Avram Eban and Alida Solomon; *m.* Susan Ambache 1945; one *s.* one *d.*; ed. Univ. of Cambridge.
Research Fellow and Tutor for Oriental Languages, Pembroke Coll. 38; apptd. Liaison Officer of Allied H.Q. with the Jewish population in Jerusalem for training volunteers 42; Chief Instructor at the Middle East Arab Centre in Jerusalem 44; entered service of Jewish Agency 46; apptd. Liaison Officer with UN Special Comm. on Palestine 47; apptd. by the Provisional Govt. of Israel as its rep. in the UN 48, Perm. Rep. 49 59, Vice-Pres. Gen. Assembly 53; Amb. to U.S.A. 50-59; elected to Knesset 59, Minister without Portfolio 59-60, Minister of Educ. and Culture 60-63, Deputy Prime Minister 63-66, Minister of Foreign Affairs 66-74; Guest Prof. Columbia Univ. 74, Haifa Univ. 75; Pres. Weizmann Inst. of Science 58-66; Vice-Pres. UN Conf. on Science and Technology in Advancement of New States 63, mem. UN Advisory Cttee. on Science and Technology for Devt.; M.A. (Cambridge); Hon. Dr. (Univs. of New York, Boston, Maryland, Cincinnati, Temple, etc.); Fellow World Acad. of Arts and Sciences, Fellow American Acad. of Arts and Sciences.
Publs. *The Modern Literary Movement in Egypt* 44, *Maze of Justice* 46, *Social and Cultural Problems in the Middle East* 47, *The Toynbee Heresy* 55, *Voice of Israel* 57-9, *Tide of Nationalism* 59, *Chaim Weizmann: A Collective Biography* 62, *Reality and Vision in the Middle East (Foreign Affairs)* 65, *Israel in the World* 66, *My People* 68, *My Country* 73; numerous articles in English, French, Hebrew and Arabic.
The Knesset, Jerusalem, Israel.

Eberhard, Wolfram, PH.D.; American professor of sociology; b. March 1909, Potsdam, Germany; *s.* of Prof. Gustav and Gertrud (née Müller) Eberhard; *m.* Alide Roemer 1934; two *s.*; ed. School of Oriental Languages, Berlin, and Univ. of Berlin.
Professor of Chinese History and Language Ankara Univ., Turkey 37-48; Prof. of Sociology, Univ. of Calif. (Berkeley) 48-; Guggenheim Fellow; Corresp. mem. Acad. of Sciences and Literature, Mainz, Bavarian Acad. of Sciences, Munich, and the China Acad., Taiwan; Fellow American Folklore Asscn.
Leisure interest: ranching.

Publs. *Settlement and Social Change in Asia* 67, *Moral and Social Values of the Chinese* 71, *The Chinese Silver Screen* 72, *Studies in Hakka Folktales* 74, *History of China* (revised edition) 76.
Department of Sociology, University of California, Berkeley, Calif. 94720, U.S.A.

Eberhart, Richard, M.A., LITT.D.; American poet; b. 5 April 1904, Austin, Minn.; *s.* of late Alpha La Rue Eberhart and late Lena Lowenstein; *m.* Helen Elizabeth Butcher 1941; one *s.* one *d.*; ed. Univ. of Minnesota, Dartmouth Coll., St. John's Coll., Cambridge and Harvard Univ.
United States Naval Reserve World War II, rose to Lieut.-Commdr.; Asst. Man. Butcher Polish Co. 46, now Hon. Vice-Pres. and mem. of Board of Dirs.; Master of English, St. Mark's School, Southborough Mass. 33-41, Cambridge School, Kendal Green, Mass., 41-42; Visiting Prof. of English and Poet in residence, Univ. of Washington 52-53; Prof. of English, Univ. of Connecticut 53-54; inaugural Visiting Prof. of English, Poet in residence, Wheaton Coll., Norton, Mass. 54-55; Resident Fellow in Creative Writing, Christian Gauss Lecturer, Princeton 55-56; Prof. of English, Poet in residence, Dartmouth 56-, Class of 1925 Prof. 68-, Emer. 70; Distinguished Visiting Prof., Univ. of Florida, Gainesville 74; Adjunct Prof., Colombia Univ. 75; Visiting Prof., Univ. of California, Davis 75; mem. Advisory Cttee. on Arts for Nat. Cultural Center, Washington (now John F. Kennedy Center for Performing Arts) 59; Consultant in Poetry, Library of Congress 59-61; mem. Nat. Inst. Arts and Letters 60, Peace Corps Mission to Kenya Aug. 66, Amer. Acad. Arts and Sciences 67; Founder and Pres. Poets' Theatre Inc., Cambridge, Mass. 51; D.Lit., Dartmouth 54, Skidmore 66, Wooster 69, Colgate 74; Harriet Monroe Memorial Prize 50; Shelley Memorial Prize 51, Bollingen Prize 62; Pulitzer Prize 66; Fellow of Acad. of Amer. Poets 69; Hon. Consultant in Amer. Letters, Library of Congress 63-66, 66-69; Hon. Pres. Poetry Society of America 72, London Poetry International 73.
Leisure interests: cruising on coast of Maine and swimming.
Publs. *A Bravery of Earth* 30, *Reading the Spirit* 37, *Song and Idea* 42, *Poems New and Selected* 44, *Burr Oaks* 47, *Brotherhood of Men* 49, *An Herb Basket* 50, *Selected Poems* 51, *Undercliff* 53, *Great Praises* 57, *Collected Poems 1930-60* 60, *Collected Verse Plays* 62, *The Quarry* 64, *Selected Poems 1930-65* 65, *New Directions* 65, *Thirty One Sonnets* 67, *Shifts of Being* 68, *Fields of Grace* 72, *New Collected Poems* 75.
5 Webster Terrace, Hanover, New Hampshire 03755, U.S.A.
Telephone: 643:2938.

Eberle, Josef; German newspaper publisher; b. 1901, Rottenburg, Neckar; *s.* of Josef and Berta (née Entress) Eberle; *m.* Else Lemberger 1929; ed. Grammar School, Rottenburg.
Former bookseller; with Radio Stuttgart until 33; served American consulate, Stuttgart until 42; publisher *Stuttgarter Zeitung* 45-71, Pres. of the Board; Pres. Württemberger Bibliotheksgesellschaft, Stuttgart; Vice-Pres. Deutsche Schillergesellschaft, Stuttgart-Marbach; mem. Deutsche Akad. Darmstadt, PEN Club; Prof. Dr. phil. h.c. Tübingen.
Leisure interests: collecting antique bronzes, Latin poetry, incunabula.
Publs. *Interview mit Cicero, Laudes, Stunden mit Ovid, Ovid, Heilmittel* (translation), *Amores* (Latin poetry), *Sal Niger* (100 Epigrams, Latin and German), *Lateinische Nächte* (essays), *Aller Tage Morgen* (autobiography).
Rosengartenstrasse 9, Stuttgart-Frauenkopf, Federal Republic of Germany.
Telephone: 21401.

Eberle, William Denman; American building equipment executive and government official; b. 5 June 1923, Boise, Ida.; *s.* of J. Louis and Clare (née Holcomb) Eberle; *m.* Jean C. Quick 1947; three *s.* one *d.*; ed. Stanford Univ., Harvard Univ. Graduate School of Business and Harvard Law School.

Admitted Ida. bar 50; partner Richards, Haga and Eberle (law firm) 50-60; Dir. Boise Cascade Corpn. 52-68, Sec. 60-65, Vice-Pres. 61-66; Pres., Chief Exec. Officer and Dir. American Standard Inc. 66-71; Special Rep. of U.S. Govt. for Trade Negotiations 71-74; Exec. Dir. Council on Int. Econ. Policy 74; Dir. Atlantic Group of Insurance Cos., PPG Industries, Fed. Reserve Bank of N.Y., Nat. Industrial Conf. Board; mem. Ida. House of Reps. 53-63; mem. Amer. and Ida. Bar Asscns.; Trustee, Stanford Univ.; Co-Chair. Nat. Urban Coalition.

85 Club Road, Riverside, Conn. 06878, U.S.A.

Ebert, Carl (Anton Charles), C.B.E.; American opera director; b. 20 Feb. 1887, Berlin, Germany; *s.* of Wilhelm and Maria Ebert; *m.* 1st Lucie Splisgarth 1912 (dissolved 1923), one *s.* (Peter Ebert, *q.v.*) one *d.* (died 1946); *m.* 2nd Gertrude Eck 1924, one *s.* two *d.*; ed. Max Reinhardt's School of Dramatic Art, Berlin.

Began career as actor at Max Reinhardts Deutsches Theater, Berlin 09-14; Schauspielhaus, Frankfurt a.M. 15-22, Staatstheater, Berlin 22-27; Founder, Dir., teacher in Schools of Dramatic Art in Frankfurt 19, and Berlin (Prof.) 25; acted in silent films, recited European Literature; parts included Faust, Egmont, Lear, Brutus, Petruchio, Peer Gynt, etc.; Gen. Dir. and Producer, Hess. Landestheater 27-31, Städtische Oper, Berlin, 31-33; left Germany because of Nazi régime March 33, acted Zürich and Basle, Guest Producer Basle, Salzburg Festival, State Opera and Burgtheater Vienna, Arena Verona 32-38; Maggio Musicale Florence 33-37, Teatro Colon Buenos Aires 33-36; Artistic Dir. and Producer Glyndebourne Opera 34-59, of Glyndebourne productions at Edinburgh Festivals 47-55; Adviser to Turkish Ministry of Educ., Founder Dir. (and teacher) Turkish State School of Opera and Drama, Ankara 36- and Turkish Nat. Theatre, Ankara 39-47; Prof. and Head Opera Dept., Univ. of Southern Calif., Los Angeles 48-54; Artistic Dir. and Producer Guild Opera Co., Los Angeles 50-; Gen. Dir. and Producer Städtische Oper, Berlin 54-61; Pres. German section of Int. Theatre Inst., Berlin 56-61; Guest Producer London, Milan, Ankara, Venice, Paris, New York, Copenhagen 47-59; Biennale world première Stravinsky's *The Rake's Progress;* Producer Metropolitan Opera New York, Glyndebourne Opera England, also Zürich, Ireland, Copenhagen, Deutsche Oper, Berlin 61-67; Master Class in Opera, B.B.C. TV London 65, 67; Hon. mem. Deutsche Oper Berlin, Staatstheater Darmstadt; Board of Dirs. Opera Guild of S. California, Int. Theatre Inst.; Hon. Mus.D., Edinburgh Univ. 54; Hon. D. Fine Arts, Univ. of Southern Calif. 55; Ernst Reuter Plakette, Berlin 57; Knight of Dannebrog, Denmark 59; Grosses Verdienstkreuz mit Stern, Germany 59; Grosses Ehrenzeichen, Austria 59; Hon. C.B.E. 60; Commendatore Ordine Al Merito, Italy 66. Leisure interests: travel, gardening.

809 Enchanted Way, Pacific Palisades (Los Angeles), Calif.; and c/o Huttenback Artist Bureau, Philharmonic Auditorium, Los Angeles 13, Calif., U.S.A.

Ebert, Friedrich; German politician; b. 18 Sept. 1894; ed. elementary and secondary schools.

Book printer by trade; war service in First World War; Editor of *Brandenburger Zeitung* 25-33; mem. of Reichstag 28-33; imprisoned in concentration camps; official of Social Democratic Party 45; elected to Brandenburg Diet as mem. of Socialist Unity Party (SED) 46, mem. Politburo 50-; mem. German-Soviet Friendship Soc. 50-58; mem. State Council 60-, now Vice-Chair.; Pres. of Diet 64; elected to German People's Council March 48; Lord Mayor of Berlin (Eastern Sector) Nov. 48-July 67; mem. of the Volkskammer 50-.

Wahnschaffestrasse 11, Berlin-Pankow, German Democratic Republic.

Ebert, James David, PH.D.; American embryologist; b. 11 Dec. 1921, Bentleyville, Pa.; *s.* of Alva Charles Ebert and Anna Frances Brundege; *m.* Alma Christine Goodwin 1946; one *s.* two *d.*; ed. Washington and Jefferson Coll. and Johns Hopkins Univ.

Adam T. Bruce Fellow in Biology, Johns Hopkins Univ. 49-50; Instructor in Biology, Mass. Inst. of Technology 50-51; Asst. Prof. of Zoology, Indiana Univ. 51-54, Assoc. Prof. 54-55; Dir. Dept. of Embryology at Carnegie Inst. of Washington, Prof. of Biology at Johns Hopkins Univ. and Prof. of Embryology at Johns Hopkins Univ. School of Medicine 56-; Dir. Marine Biological Lab. 70-; Visiting Assoc. Scientist, Medical Dept., Brookhaven Nat. Lab. 53, 54; Trustee, Jackson Lab., Marine Biological Lab.; Dir. Oak Ridge Associated Univs.; mem. Nat. Acad. of Sciences; mem. Amer. Philosophical Soc.; mem. Inst. of Medicine; Fellow, Amer. Acad. of Arts and Sciences; First Distinguished Service Award, Washington and Jefferson Coll.; Hon. Sc.D., Yale Univ.

Leisure interests: sport, especially swimming, writing fiction.

Publs. *The Biology of Ageing* (Co-editor) 60, *Interacting Systems in Development* 65, 70, *Biology* 73; Contributor to: *The Chick Embryo in Biological Research* 52, *Molecular Events in Differentiation Related to Specificity of Cell Type* 55, *Aspects of Synthesis and Order in Growth* 55, *The Cell* 59, *Major Problems in Developmental Biology* 66, *The Neurosciences: A Study Program*; and about 140 professional articles.

Department of Embryology, Carnegie Institution of Washington, 115 West University Parkway, Baltimore, Md. 21210; Home: 6728 Glenkirk Road, Baltimore, Md. 21239, U.S.A.

Telephone: 301-467-1414 and 1415 (Office).

Ebert, Peter; British (naturalized) opera director; b. 6 April 1918, Frankfurt-am-Main, Germany; *s.* of Carl Ebert (*q.v.*) and Lucie Oppenheim; *m.* 1st Kathleen Havinden 1944, two *d.*; *m.* 2nd Silvia Ashmole 1951, five *s.* three *d.*; ed. Salem School, Germany, and Gordonstoun, Scotland.

Intendant, Stadttheater Bielefeld, Germany 73-75, Intendant, Wiesbaden State Theatres 75-; Dir. of Productions, Scottish Opera 65-76; Producer, Guild Opera Co., Los Angeles 62-.

Leisure interests: raising a family.

Hessisches Staatstheater, 62 Wiesbaden, Federal Republic of Germany.

Telephone: Wiesbaden 39331.

Ebtehaj, Abol Hassan; Iranian banker and administrator; b. 29 Nov. 1899, Rasht, Iran; *s.* of Ebrahim and Fatima Ebtehaj; *m.* 1st Mariam Nabavi 1929, 2nd Azarnoosh Sani 1956; one *s.* one *d.*; ed. Paris and Beirut.

Joined Imperial Bank of Iran 20; Govt. Inspector Agricultural Bank and Controller of State-owned Cos. 36; Vice-Gov. Bank Melli Iran 38; Chair. and Man. Dir. Mortgage Bank 40; Gov. Bank Melli Iran (National Bank of Persia) 42-50; Chair. Persian Del. Middle East Financial and Monetary Conf., Cairo 44; Chair. Persian Del. Bretton Woods Conf. 44; Ambassador to France 50-52; Adviser to Man. Dir. Int. Monetary Fund 52; Dir. Middle East Dept., Int. Monetary Fund 53; Man. Dir. Plan Organization (Devt. Board), Teheran 54-59; Chair. and Pres. Iranians' Bank (private bank) 59-.

Leisure interests: golf, tennis.

Iranians' Bank, Takht Jamshid Avenue, Teheran, Iran.

Telephone: 834341/2 (Office); 628272 (Home).

Eccles, 1st Viscount (cr. 64), of Chute, 1st Baron (cr. 62); **David McAdam Eccles,** K.C.V.O., P.C., M.A.; British politician; b. 18 Sept. 1904, London; s. of William McAdam Eccles M.S., F.R.C.S. and Anna Coralie Anstie; m. Hon. Sybil Frances Dawson 1928; two s. one d.; ed. Winchester and New Coll., Oxford.
Member staff Central Mining and Investment Corpn. 23-39; joined Ministry of Econ. Warfare Sept. 39; Econ. Adviser to H.M. Ambs. in Madrid and Lisbon 39-42; Ministry of Production 42-43; Conservative M.P. for Chippenham Div. of Wilts. Aug. 43-62; Minister of Works 51-54, of Educ. 54-57; Pres. Board of Trade 57-59; Minister of Educ. 59-62; Paymaster-Gen. with responsibility for the Arts 70-73; Chair. Trustees of British Museum until 70, of British Library 73-; Pres. World Crafts Council 74.
Leisure interest: collecting antiques and books.
Publs. *Wages on the Farm* 45, *Half-Way to Faith* 66, *Life and Politics* 67, *On Collecting* 68.
Dean Farm, Chute, nr. Andover, Hampshire, England.

Eccles, Sir John Carew, Kt., M.B., B.S., D.PHIL., F.R.A.C.P., F.R.S.N.Z., F.A.A., F.R.S.; Australian research physiologist; b. 27 Jan. 1903, Melbourne; s. of William James and Mary (née Carew) Eccles; m. 1st Irene Frances Miller 1928 (divorced 1968), 2nd Helena Táboříková 1968; four s. five d.; ed. Melbourne Univ., Magdalen Coll., Oxford.
Rhodes Scholar 25; Junior Research Fellow, Exeter Coll., Oxford 27-32, Staines Medical Fellow 32-34; Fellow and Tutor, Magdalen Coll., Oxford, lecturer in physiology 34-37; Dir. Kanematsu Memorial Inst. of Pathology, Sydney, Australia 37-43; Prof. of Physiology, Otago Univ., New Zealand 44-51, Australian Nat. Univ., Canberra 51-66; AMA/ERF Inst. for Biomedical Research, Chicago 66-68; at State Univ. of New York at Buffalo 68-75; Waynflete Lecturer, Oxford 52; Herter Lecturer, Johns Hopkins Univ., Baltimore 55; Foreign Hon. mem. American Acad. of Arts and Sciences, Accademia Nazionale dei Lincei, Deutsche Akad. der Naturforscher (Leopoldina); Cothenius Medal; mem. Pontifical Acad. of Sciences, American Philosophical Soc., National Acad. of Sciences, Indian Acad. of Sciences, Royal Acad. of Belgium; Ferrier Lecturer, Royal Soc. 60; Pres. Australian Acad. of Science 57-61; Hon. Fellow Exeter Coll. and Magdalen Coll. Oxford, Hon. Fellow New York Acad. of Sciences; Hon. Sc.D. (Cambridge, Tasmania, Univ. British Columbia, Gustavus Adolphus Coll., Marquette, Loyola, Yeshiva, Oxford), Hon. M.D. (Charles Univ., Prague), Hon. LL.D. (Melbourne); Royal Medal, Royal Soc. 62, Nobel Prize for Medicine 63.
Leisure interests: philosophy, art, European travel.
Publs. *Reflex Activity of the Spinal Cord* (in collaboration) 32, *Neurophysiological Basis of Mind* 53, *Physiology of Nerve Cells* 57, *Physiology of Synapses* 64, *The Cerebellum as a Neuronal Machine* 67, *Inhibitory Pathways of the Central Nervous System* 69, *Facing Reality* 70, *The Understanding of the Brain* 73, *The Self and its Brain* (with Sir Karl Popper)76.
Ca' a la Gra', CH 6611 Contra, Ticino, Switzerland.
Telephone: 093-67 29 31.

Eccles, Marriner Stoddard; American financier and business executive; b. 9 Sept. 1890, Logan, Utah; s. of David and Ellen (Stoddard) Eccles; m. 1st May Campbell Young 1913, 2nd Sara Madison Glassie 1951; two s. (one deceased) one d.; ed. in district schools and at Brigham Young Coll.
Organized Eccles Investment Co. 16, Vice-Pres. and Gen. Man. 16-29, Pres. 29-72; Pres. First Nat. Bank of Ogden, Ogden Savings Bank, Successor Banks 20-34, Utah Bankers' Asscn. 24-25; organized First Security Corpn., a bank holding co., Pres. 28-34, Chair. 51-; Chair. Amalgamated Sugar Co.; Dir. First Security Bank of Utah, N.A.; Dir. Utah Construction & Mining

Co. (now Utah Int. Inc.), Chair. of Board 40-71; Pres. Eccles Investment Co. 29-; Dir. many companies; Asst. to Sec. of Treasury 34; Gov. Fed. Reserve Board 34-36; mem. Board of Govs. Fed. Reserve System 34-51, Chair. 36-48; U.S. Del. Bretton Woods 44; mem. Board of Econ. Stabilization 42-46, Nat. Advisory Council on Int. Monetary and Financial Problems 45-48, Advisory Board of Export-Import Bank 45-48; mem. of Comm. on Money and Credit 58-61, Advisory Comm. on Econ. Policy of Dem. Advisory Council 57-60; Hon. Dir. Planned Parenthood-World Population 60-; Hon. Chair., Dir. Utah Construction & Mining Co. (now Utah Int. Inc.); mem. Nat. Comm. on U.S.-China Relations; sponsor, The Atlantic Council 62-; Hon. LL.D. (Univ. of Utah, Utah State Univ.); Trustee, American Assembly of Columbia Univ. 59-.
Publ. *Beckoning Frontiers.*
P.O. Box 390, Salt Lake City, Utah 84110, U.S.A.
Telephone: 364-7211.

Ecevit, Bülent, B.A.; Turkish journalist and politician; b. 1925, Istanbul; s. of late Prof. Fahri Ecevit, M.P. and Nazli Ecevit; m. Rahsan Ecevit 1946; ed. Robert Coll., Istanbul, Ankara, London and Harvard Univs.
Government official 44-50, Turkish Press Attaché's Office, London 46-50; Foreign News Editor, Man. Editor, later Political Dir. *Ulus* (Ankara) 50-61, Political Columnist, *Ulus* 56-61; M.P. (Republican People's Party) 57-60, Oct. 61-; mem. Constituent Assembly 61; Minister of Labour 61-65; Political Columnist *Milliyet* 65; Prime Minister Jan.-Nov. 74; Sec.-Gen. Republican People's Party 66-71, Chair. 72-; mem. Int. Asscn. of Art Critics.
Leisure interests: art and literature.
Publs. *Left of Center* 66, *The System Must Change* 68, *Atatürk and Revolution* 70, *Conversations* 74, *Democratic Left* 75, *Foreign Policy* 75; Trans. (into Turkish) *Gitanjali* (R. Tagore) 41, *Straybirds* (R. Tagore) 43, *Cocktail Party* (T. S. Eliot) 63.
Home: Or-An, Ankara, Turkey.
Telephone: 27-68-76 (Party Headquarters), 25-18-76 (Parliament).

Echandi Jiménez, Mario, LL.D.; Costa Rican diplomatist and politician; b. 1915; ed. Univ. of Costa Rica.
Legal career 38-47; Sec.-Gen. Partido Unión Nacional 47; Ambassador to U.S.A. 50-51, 66-68; Minister for Foreign Affairs 51-53; Presidential candidate 53; mem. Nat. Assembly 53-58; Pres. of Costa Rica 58-62; defeated candidate in Pres. election Feb. 70.
San José, Costa Rica.

Echavarria Velez, Luis Fernando; Colombian industrialist and politician; b. 10 March 1928, Medellín; m. Stella Uribe; eight c.; ed. Colegio de San Ignacio, Medellín, Worcester Acad., Mass., Brown and Wisconsin Univs.
Worked in glass works, Cristalería Pedlar S.A., Vice-Pres. 51-55, Pres. 66-73; Vice-Pres. Cervecería Union S.A. 55-58; Vice-Pres. Fabricato 58-61; private business and investment 61-63; Minister, Colombian Embassy, Washington D.C. 63-66; Alt. Dir. Inter-American Devt. Bank; Advance Management Program, Harvard Business School 71; Minister of Finance 73-74.
Apartado Aéreo 3543, Medellín, Colombia.

Echeverría Alvarez, Lic. Luis; Mexican lawyer and politician; b. 17 Jan. 1922; ed. Univ. Nacional Autónoma de México.
Private Sec. to Pres. of Exec. Cttee. of Partido Revolucionario Institucional (PRI) 40-52, also Dir. of Press and Propaganda, PRI 49-52; Dir. of Accounts and Admin., Sec. of Marine 52-54; Senior Official, Sec. of Public Educ. 54-57; Senior Official, Central Exec. Cttee. of PRI 57; Under-Sec. of Interior 58-63, Sec. of Interior 63-70; Asst. Prof. of Law, Univ. Nac. de México; Pres. of Mexico 70-.
Palacio de Gobierno, México, D.F., Mexico.

Eckerberg, Per, PH.D.; Swedish civil servant; b. 17 Aug. 1913; *m.* Dr. Inga Folin 1947; two *c.*; ed. Univ. of Lund.

Secretary, Public Comm. on Population 44-46; Ministry of Social Affairs 48-50, Under-Sec. of State 50-56; Gov., Province of Ostergötland 56-; Pres. of Bd., Swedish Broadcasting Corpn. 56-; Rep. to ILO Confs. 51-57; Pres. Bank of Sweden 56-57; Pres. of Board, Göta Canal 57-; Pres. Swedish Savings Bank Asscn. 61, Nat. Supplementary Pensions Fund 60-, Cttee. for Labour Market Policy 61, Cttee. for Public Information 68, Cttee. for Industrial Policy 69, Cttee. for Multinational Enterprises 74; Editor *Tiden* 47-49.

Leisure interests: fishing, sailing.

c/o Sverges Radio A.B., Oxenstiernsgatan 20, 105 10, Stockholm; Castle of Linköping, Linköping, Sweden.

Telephone: 013-120011.

Eckert, J. Presper, Jr., M.A.; American engineer; b. 9 April 1919; ed. William Penn Charter School and Univ. of Pennsylvania.

Research Assoc., Moore School of Electrical Eng., Univ. of Pa. 41-46; co-designer, co-inventor Electronic Numerical Integrator and Calculator—ENIAC (with Dr. J. W. Mauchly) 42-46; Co-designer, co-inventor automatic computers BINAC 46-49, UNIVAC 48-51; Partner, Electronic Control Co. 46-47; Vice-Pres. Eckert-Mauchly Computer Corpn. 47-50; Dir. of Eng., Eckert-Mauchly Div. Remington Rand Inc. 50-54; Vice-Pres. (Eng.) Remington Rand Inc. 54-55; now Vice-Pres. UNIVAC Div., Sperry Rand Corpn.

P.O. Box 500, Blue Bell, Pa. 19422, U.S.A.

Eckhardt, Felix, D.IUR.; German businessman; b. 13 Nov. 1896; ed. Jena and Munich Univs.

Law practice in Cologne 30-; mem. of Board, Dortmunder Union-Brauerei Aktiengesellschaft 38-42, Chair. 42-; Pres. Deutscher Brauer-Bund 49-51, Dir. 51-; mem. of Board, Bundesverband der Deutschen Industrie 52-58; Chair. Kurfürsten-Bräu Aktiengesellschaft, Bonn, Apollinaris Brunnen Aktiengesellschaft, Bad-Neuenahr, Apollinaris Overseas Ltd., London, Dortmunder Hotelgesellschaft, Presta Overseas Ltd., Grubenvorstand der Gewerkschaft Philippine, Dortmund 50-; mem. of Board, Dortmund-Hörder Hüttenunion A.G., Markenverband 52-, Siepmann-Werke A.G., Belecke-Möhne 58-.

Rote Beckerstrasse 31, Dortmund, Federal Republic of Germany.

Eckstein, Otto, PH.D.; American economist; b. 1 Aug. 1927, Ulm, Germany; *m.* Harriett Mirkin 1954; one *s.* two *d.*; ed. Princeton and Harvard Univs.

U.S. Army 46-47; Instructor, Harvard Univ. 55-57, Asst. Prof. 57-60, Assoc. Prof. 60-63, Prof. of Econs. 63-; Technical Dir., Study of Employment, Growth and Price Levels, Joint Econ. Cttee., U.S. Congress 59-60; mem. Council of Econ. Advisers, Exec. Office of the Pres. 64-66; mem. Nat. Advisory Council on Econ. Opportunity 67-69; Pres. Data Resources Inc. 69-.

Publs. *Water Resource Development: The Economics of Project Evaluation* 58, *Multiple Purpose River Development* (with J. V. Krutilla) 58, *Staff Report on Employment, Growth, and Price Levels* (with others) 59, *Economic Policy in Our Time: An International Comparison* (with others) 64, *Public Finance: Budgets, Taxes, Fiscal Policy* 64.

Department of Economics, Littauer Center, Harvard University, Cambridge, Mass. 02138, U.S.A.

Eco, Umberto; Italian university professor; b. 5 Jan. 1932; *s.* of Giulio Eco and Giovanna Bisio; *m.* Renate Ramge 1962; two *c.*; ed. Univ. degli Studi, Turin.

With Italian Television 54-59; Asst. Lecturer in Aesthetics, Univ. of Turin 56-63, Lecturer 63-64; Lecturer Faculty of Architecture, Univ. of Milan 64-65; Prof. of Visual Communications, Univ. of Florence 66-69; Prof. of Semiotics, Milan Polytechnic 70-71; Univ. of Bologna 71-75; Columnist on *L'Espresso* 65-.

Publs. *Il Problema Estetico in San Tommaso* 56, *Sviluppo dell'Estetica Medioevale* 59, *Opera Aperta* 62, *Diario Minimo* 63, *Apocalittici e Integrati* 64, *L'Oeuvre Ouverte* 65, *La Struttura Assente* 68, *Il Costume di Casa* 73, *Trattato di Semiotica Generale* 75, *A Theory of Semiotics* 75.

Via Melzi d'Eril 23, Milan, Italy.

Telephone: 34-78-06.

Edberg, Rolf; Swedish journalist, diplomatist and administrator; b. 14 March 1912, Lysvik; *s.* of C. F. and Madnis Edberg; *m.* Astrid Persson 1937; one *s.* two *d.*

Chief Editor *Oskarshamns Nyheter* 34-37; Asst. Editor *Östgöten*, Linköping 38-40, Chief Editor 41-45; Chief Editor *Ny Tid*, Gothenburg 45-46; mem. Parl. 41-44 and 49-56; Del. to UN 52-61; Amb. to Norway 56-67; Gov. Province of Värmland 67-; Rep. to Council of Europe 49-52, to Scandinavian Council 53-56; Pres. Swedish Press Club 51-53; Del. Disarmament Conf. 62-65; Pres. Stockholm Int. Peace Inst. 74-; Hon. Ph.D. 74.

Publs. *On the Shred of a Cloud* 66, *At the Foot of the Tree* 72, *Letters to Columbus* 73, *On Earth's Terms* 74, *A House in the Cosmos* 74, and several works on political subjects.

Länsstyrelsen, Karlstad, Sweden.

Telephone: 115040.

Edel, (Joseph) Leon, M.A., D. ès L.; American writer and teacher; b. 9 Sept. 1907, Pittsburgh, Pa.; *s.* of Simon Edel and Fanny Malamud; *m.* Roberta Roberts 1950; ed. Yorkton Collegiate Inst., Saskatchewan, McGill Univ. and Univ. of Paris.

Graduate Asst. in English, McGill Univ. 27-28; Asst. Prof. Sir George Williams Univ., Montreal 32-34; journalism and broadcasting 34-43; U.S. Army 43-47; Adjunct Prof., New York Univ. 50-53, Assoc. Prof. 53-55, Prof. of English 55-66; Henry James Prof. of English and American Letters 66-73, Citizens Prof. of English, Hawaii Univ. 72-; Fellow, American Acad. of Arts and Sciences, Sec. Nat. Inst. of Arts and Letters 65-67, Pres. U.S. PEN 57-59, Council Authors' Guild 66-68; Pres. Authors' Guild 69-71; Fellow, Royal Soc. of Literature 70, American Acad. of Arts and Letters 72; mem. Soc. of American Historians, Modern Humanities Research Asscn., Educational Advisory Board Guggenheim Foundation 67-(77); Advisory Cttee. Metropolitan Museum Centenary 69-70; Hon. mem. William Alanson White Psychoanalytic Soc. 67-; Hon. D.Litt. (Union Coll., Schenectady, N.Y., and McGill Univ.); Pulitzer Prize (biography) 63, Nat. Book Award (non-fiction) 63.

Leisure interests: music, book collecting, swimming.

Publs. *The Life of Henry James* (I *The Untried Years* 53, II *The Conquest of London* 62, III *The Middle Years* 62, IV *The Treacherous Years* 69, V *The Master* 72), *Willa Cather* (with E. K. Brown) 53, *The Psychological Novel* 55, *Literary Biography* 57; Editor: *The Complete Plays of Henry James* 49, *Selected Letters of Henry James* 55, *The Complete Tales of Henry James* (12 vols.) 62-65, *The Diary of Alice James* 64, *Literary History and Literary Criticism* 64, *The American Scene* 68, *Henry D. Thoreau* 70, *Henry James: Letters* (I and II) 74-75, *Edmund Wilson: The Twenties* 75.

Department of English, University of Hawaii, Honolulu, Hawaii 96822, U.S.A.

Telephone: 948-8805.

Edelman, Gerald Maurice, M.D., PH.D.; American molecular biologist; b. 1 July 1929, New York; *s.* of Edward and Anna Freedman Edelman; *m.* Maxine Morrison 1950; two *s.* one *d.*; ed. Ursinus Coll., Univ. of Pennsylvania, and The Rockefeller Univ.

Medical House Officer, Mass. Gen. Hospital 45-55; Capt., U.S. Army Medical Corps. 55-56; Asst. Physician, Hospital of The Rockefeller Univ. 57-60; Asst. Prof. and Asst. Dean of Graduate Studies, The Rockefeller

Univ. 60-63, Assoc. Prof. and Assoc. Dean of Graduate Studies 63-66, Prof. 66-74; Vincent Astor Distinguished Prof. 74-; Vice-Pres. The Harvey Society 74-75, Pres. 75-; mem. Nat. Acad. of Sciences, American Acad. of Arts and Sciences; Fellow, New York Acad. of Sciences; Trustee, Rockefeller Brothers Fund; mem. Board of Trustees, Salk Inst. for Biological Studies; mem. Genetics Soc.; mem. American Chem. Soc.; mem. Advisory Board, The Basel Inst. for Immunology; mem. Board of Governors, Weizmann Inst. of Science, Israel; mem. American Soc. of Biological Chemists; mem. American Asscn. of Immunologists; Annual Alumni Award, Ursinus Coll. 69; Eli Lilly Award in Biological Chem., American Chemical Soc. 65; Spencer Morris Award, Univ. of Pa. 54; Nobel Prize for Physiology or Medicine 72 (with R. Porter *q.v.*); Albert Einstein Commem. Award of Yeshiva Univ. 74; Buchman Memorial Award., Calif. Inst. of Tech. 75; Hon. D.Sc. Univ. of Pennslyvania 73; Hon. Sc.D. Ursinus Coll. 74; Hon. M.D. Univ. of Siena, Italy 74; Hon. D.Sc. Adolphus Coll., Minn. 75.
Leisure interests: violin, chamber music.
Publs. About 150 articles in professional journals.
The Rockefeller University, 66th Street (and York Avenue), New York, N.Y. 10021, U.S.A.
Telephone: 212-360-1542.

Edelmann, Otto Karl; Austrian opera singer; b. 5 Feb. 1917, Vienna; *m.* Ilse-Maria Straub 1960; two *s.* one *d.*; ed. Realgymnasium and State Acad. of Music, Vienna.
First opera appearances 38; P.O.W. in U.S.S.R. two years during Second World War; mem. Vienna State Opera 48-; with Salzburg Festival 48-; perm. mem. Metropolitan Opera New York 54-; took part in first Bayreuth Festival 51; world-famous as *Sachs* in Meistersinger; Knight Order of Dannebrog.
Leisure interests: painting and boxing.
Vienna 1237, Breitenfurterstrasse 547, Austria.
Telephone: 86-17-404.

Eden, Rt. Hon. Sir John, Bt., M.P.; British politician; b. 15 Sept. 1925.
Member of Parl. for Bournemouth 54-; Minister of State, Ministry of Technology July-Oct. 70; Minister for Industry, Dept. of Trade and Industry Oct. 70-April 72; Minister for Posts and Telecommunications 72-74; Dir. Chesham Amalgamations and Investments; mem. Board Cen. and Sherwood; Del. to Council of Europe and WEU 60-62; mem. House of Commons Expenditure Cttee.; Pres. Wessex Area Conservatives; Conservative.
41 Victoria Road, London, W8 5RH, England.

Edenman, Ragnar H. L., PH.D.; Swedish politician; b. 1 April 1914, Uppsala; *m.* Karin Hook 1941; two *s.*
Member Municipal Council of Uppsala 43-50; M.P. 49-68; Pres. of Cttees. on wider access to higher educ. 46-48, support to good literature 48-52, secondary schools 54-55, devt. of the univs. 55-57, comprehensive schools 57-61; Minister of Church Affairs and Educ. 57-67; Gov. Prov. of Uppsala 67-.
Home: The Castle, 75125 Uppsala, Sweden.
Telephone: 018-133451 (Home).

Edgerton, Harold Eugene, B.S., M.S., D.SC.; American scientist, inventor and teacher; b. 6 April 1903, Fremont, Neb.; *s.* of Frank Eugene Edgerton and Mary (Coe) Edgerton; *m.* Esther May Garrett 1928; two *s.* one *d.*; ed. Univ. of Neb. and Mass. Inst. of Technology.
Research Asst. Mass. Inst. of Technology 27-28, Instructor 28-32, Asst. Prof. of Electrical Eng. 32-38, Assoc. Prof. 38-48, Prof. 48-66, Inst. Prof. Emer. 66-; Inventor of electronic flash (strobe) 31; Co-Founder, E.G. & G. (fmrly. Edgerton, Germeshausen and Grier), Vice-Pres. 47, Chair. of Board 55-66, Hon. Chair. of Board 66-; three expeditions to Einewetok for Atomic Energy Comm.; underwater camera devt.

for Nat. Geographic Soc., Capt. Jacques Y. Cousteau, and Bathyscaphes FNRS III, Trieste and Archimede; Fellow, Inst. of Electrical and Electronic Engineers, Photographic Soc. of America, Royal Photographic Soc. of Great Britain, Soc. of Motion Pictures and T.V. Engineers; mem. of numerous scientific insts. including Amer. Acad. of Applied Science, Acad. of Underwater Arts and Sciences, Amer. Acad. of Arts and Sciences, Nat. Acad. of Sciences, Nat. Acad. of Engineering, Woods Hole Oceanographic Inst.; Hon. Dr. Eng. (Univ. of Nebraska), Hon. LL.D. (Doane Coll., Univ. of S. Carolina) 69; 28 awards including U.S. Camera Achievement Gold Medal 51, E. I. duPont Gold Medal of Soc. of Motion Picture and TV Engineers 62, Richardson Medal of Optical Soc. of America 68, John Oliver LaGorce Gold Medal of Nat. Geographic Soc. 68, Holley Medal, Amer. Soc. of Mechanical Engineers 73, Nat. Medal of Science 73.
Leisure interests: nature photography (particularly humming-birds), deep-sea studies, guitar music.
Publs. *Flash, Seeing The Unseen* (with J. R. Killian) 54, *Electronic Flash, Strobe* 70, and 144 technical articles 30-.
Massachusetts Institute of Technology, Room 4-405, Cambridge, Mass. 02139; Home: 100 Memorial Drive, Cambridge, Mass. 02142, U.S.A.
Telephone: 617-494-8783 (Office); 617-864-4790 (Home).

Edinburgh, H.R.H. The Prince Philip, Duke of, Earl of Merioneth and Baron Greenwich of Greenwich in the County of London (all titles cr. 47), created Prince of the United Kingdom of Great Britain and Northern Ireland 57, K.G., K.T., O.M., G.B.E.; b. 10 June 1921, Corfu; *s.* of H.R.H. the late Prince Andrew of Greece and Denmark, G.C.V.O. and of H.R.H. the late Princess (Victoria) Alice Elizabeth Julia Marie, R.R.C., elder *d.* of 1st Marquis of Milford Haven, G.C.B., G.C.V.O., K.C.M.G.; ed. Cheam School, Salem (Baden), Gordonstoun School and Royal Naval Coll., Dartmouth.
Served 39-45 war with Mediterranean Fleet in Home Waters and with British Pacific Fleet in S.E. Asia and Pacific; renounced right of succession to the Thrones of Greece and Denmark and was naturalized a British subject 47, adopting the surname of Mountbatten; *m.* 20 Nov. 1947 H.R.H. Princess Elizabeth (now H.M. Queen Elizabeth II), elder daughter of H.M. King George VI; Personal A.D.C. to H.M. King George VI 48-52; Privy Councillor 51-; Chancellor, Univ. of Wales 48-, Univ. of Edinburgh 52-; Admiral of the Fleet, F.M. and Marshal of the R.A.F. 53-; Patron and Chair. of Trustees, Duke of Edinburgh's Award Scheme 56-; Privy Councillor of Canada 57-; Visitor, Royal Coll. of Art 67-; Pres. numerous bodies, including English-Speaking Union of the Commonwealth 52-, Royal Soc. of Arts 52-, Commonwealth Games Federation 55-, Royal Agricultural Soc. of the Commonwealth 58-, British Medical Asscn. 59-60, Wildlife Trust 60-65, 72-77, World Wildlife Fund British Nat. Appeal 61-, Council for Nat. Academic Awards 65-75, Scottish Icelandic Asscn. 65-, The Maritime Trust 69-79, Nat. Council of Social Service 70-73, Australian Conservation Foundation 71-76; numerous awards and decorations from many countries; Hon. LL.D. (Univs. of Wales, London, Edinburgh, Cambridge, Karachi and Malta); Hon. D.C.L. (Univs. of Durham and Oxford); Hon. D.Sc. (Univs. of Delhi, Reading, Salford, Southampton and Victoria); Hon. Degree (Eng. Univ., Lima, Peru); Hon. Dr. of Law (Univ. of Calif. at Los Angeles).
Publs. *Birds from Britannia* 62, *Wildlife Crisis* (with late James Fisher) 70.
Buckingham Palace, London, S.W.1, England.

Edmund-Davies, Baron (Life Peer), cr. 74; **Herbert Edmund-Davies,** LL.D., B.C.L.; British judge; b. 15 July 1906, Mountain Ash, Glam.; *s.* of Morgan John and Elizabeth Maud Davies (née Edmunds); *m.* Eurwen

Williams-James 1935; three d.; ed. Mountain Ash Grammar School, King's Coll., London and Exeter Coll., Oxford.

Lecturer and Examiner, London Univ. 30-31; Army Officers' Emergency Reserve 38, Infantry OCTU, later commissioned Royal Welch Fusiliers 40; Q.C. 43, Bencher 48, Treas. 65, 66; Asst. Judge Advocate-Gen. 44-45; Recorder Merthyr Tydfil 42-44, Swansea 44-53, Cardiff 53-58; Judge of High Court of Justice, Queen's Bench Div. 58-66; Lord Justice of Appeal 66-74; Lord of Appeal in Ordinary 74-; Chair. Lord Chancellor's Cttee. on Limitation of Actions 61, Tribunal of Inquiry into Aberfan Disaster 66, Council of Law Reporting 67-72, Home Sec.'s Criminal Law Revision Cttee.; Life mem. Canadian Bar Asscn.; Trustee, CIBA Foundation; Hon. mem. Royal Soc. of Medicine (Library and Lay); Pres. Univ. Coll. of Swansea 65-75; Pro-Chancellor Univ. of Wales 74-; Life Gov. and Fellow, King's Coll., London; Hon. Fellow, Exeter Coll., Oxford; Hon. LL.D. (Univ. of Wales).

House of Lords, London, S.W.1; Home: 5 Gray's Inn Square, London, WC1R 5EU, England.

Edlén, Bengt, DR.PHIL.; Swedish university professor; b. 2 Nov. 1906, Gusum; s. of Gustaf and Maria Edlén (née Rundberg); m. 1st Ruth E. Grönwall 1935, 2nd Elfriede I. Mühlbach 1940; one s. three d.; ed. Uppsala Univ.

Assistant Physics Dept., Uppsala Univ. 28, Asst. Prof. 34; Prof. of Physics, Lund Univ. 44-73, Emer. Prof. 73-; mem. Swedish, Danish, Norwegian Acads. of Sciences, Académie des Sciences, Paris, American Acad. of Arts and Sciences, etc.; Commandeur de l'Ordre des Palmes Académiques; Hon. D.Sc.(Kiel); awards in recognition of research on atomic spectra with applications to astrophysical problems, including the solar corona, include: Arrhenius Gold Medal of Swedish Acad. of Sciences, Gold Medal of Royal Astronomical Soc., London, H. N. Potts Medal of Franklin Inst., Philadelphia, Mees Medal of Optical Soc. of America, Henry Draper Medal of Nat. Acad. of Sciences, Washington.

Leisure interests: spectroscopy, gardening.

Physics Department, University of Lund, Lund, Sweden. Telephone: 046-111037.

Edsall, John Tileston, A.B., M.D.; American professor of biological chemistry; b. 3 Nov. 1902, Philadeplhia; s. of David Linn Edsall and Margaret Harding Tileston; m. Margaret Dunham 1929; three s.; ed. Harvard Coll., Harvard Medical School and Cambridge Univ.

Assistant Prof. of Biological Chem., Harvard Univ. 32-38, Assoc. Prof. 38-51, Prof. 51-73, Prof. Emer. 73; Editor-in-Chief *Journal of Biological Chemistry* 58-67; Visiting Fulbright Lecturer, Cambridge 52, Tokyo 64; Visiting Prof., Coll. de France, Paris 55; Spiers Memorial Lecturer, Faraday Soc., Cambridge 52; Visiting Lecturer, Australian Nat. Univ., Canberra 70; Scholar, Fogarty Int. Center, Nat. Insts. of Health, Bethesda, Md. 70-71; Guggenheim Fellow, Calif. Inst. of Technology 40-41; Pres. American Soc. of Biological Chemists 57-58, Sixth Int. Congress of Biochemistry, New York 64; mem. Nat. Acad. of Sciences, American Philosophical Soc., American Acad. of Arts and Sciences, Deutsche Akad. der Naturforscher (Leopoldina), Royal Danish Acad. of Sciences; Hon. Sc.D. (Western Reserve Univ., New York Medical Coll. and Univs. of Chicago and Mich.); Passano Foundation Award for Medical Research 66, Willard Gibbs Medal (American Chemical Soc.) 72; foreign mem. Royal Swedish Acad. of Sciences; Hon. Dr.Phil. Univ. of Gotëburg 72.

Leisure interests: travel, photography, walking.

Publs. *Proteins, Amino Acids and Peptides* (with E. J. Cohn) 43, *Biophysical Chemistry* (with J. Wyman) Vol. 1 58, *Aspects actuels de la biochimie des acides aminés et des proteines* 58, *Advances in Protein Chemistry*

(Co-Editor) Vols. 1-30; numerous papers on chemistry of amino acids, proteins, and enzymes in *Journal of American Chemical Soc.*, *Journal of Biological Chemistry*, etc.

The Biological Laboratories, Harvard University, Cambridge, Mass. 02138; Home: 985 Memorial Drive, Cambridge, Mass. 02138, U.S.A.

Telephone: 617-495-2314 (Office); 617-876-5007 (Home).

Edu, Chief Alhaji Shafi Lawal; Nigerian businessman and administrator; b. 7 Jan. 1911, Epe, Lagos State; s. of Lawal Edu and Raliatu Seriki; m. 1934; five s. three d.; ed. Epe Govt. School and privately.

Worked as teacher; clerk, African Oilnut Co. 36; local manager, Holland W. Africa Lines 45; ship's chandler 45, later food contractor for Nigerian army, Lagos; mem. W. House of Assembly 51-54, later mem. for W. House of Reps. 54-; Vice-Pres. Lagos Chamber of Commerce and Industry 58-63, Pres. 63-; Commr. in charge of Health, W. Nigeria 62; Vice-Pres., Commonwealth Chamber of Commerce 65-66, Pres. 66; Pres. Asscn. of Chambers of Commerce, Industry and Mines of Nigeria; Dir. Nigerian Oil Refinery Co., First City Investment Co., B.P. (Nigeria); Chair. African Alliance, Niger Petroleum Co., Alumaco (Nigeria) Ltd., Blackwood Hodge, Slee Investment Co. and assoc. cos.; Officer of Order of Orange Nassau (Netherlands).

Leisure interests: golf and swimming.

Association of Chambers of Commerce, Industry and Mines of Nigeria, P.O. Box 109, Lagos, Nigeria; Home: 5 Williams Street, Lagos, Nigeria.

Telephone: 25858.

Edwards, Corwin D.; American politician and university professor; b. 1 Nov. 1901, Nevada, Mo.; s. of Granville Dennis Edwards and Ida May Moore Edwards; m. 1st Janet Morris Ward 1924, 2nd Gertrud Berta Greig 1948; one s. one d.; ed. Univ. of Missouri, Oxford (England) and Cornell Univs.

Assistant Prof. of Econs., New York Univ. 26-33; Economist and Technical Dir. Consumers Advisory Board, Nat. Recovery Administration 33-35, Coordinator, Trade Practice Studies 35; Economist President's Cttee. on Industrial Analysis 36; Asst. Chief Economist, Fed. Trade Comm. 37-39; Chief of Staff, American Technical Mission to Brazil 42-43; Economist, Chair. Policy Board, Anti-Trust Div., Dept. of Justice 39-44; Consultant on Cartels, Dept. of State 43-48; Prof. of Econs. Northwestern Univ. 44-48; Head Mission on Japanese Combines 46; Dir. Bureau of Econs., Fed. Trade Comm. U.S.A. 48-53; U.S. Rep. ad hoc Cttee. on Restrictive Practices of ECOSOC 51-52; Pitt Prof. Univ. of Cambridge 53-54, Prof. of Econs., Univ. of Virginia 54-55, Prof. of Business and Govt., Graduate School of Business, Univ. of Chicago 55-63, Prof. of Econs., Univ. of Oregon 64-71; Consultant, President's Asst. for Consumer Affairs 66-67; mem. Consumers' Advisory Council 67-69; Assoc. Editor *Antitrust Bulletin* 69-.

Leisure interests: sailing, swimming and travel.

Publs. Co-author *Economic Behavior* 31, *Economic Problems in a Changing World* 39, *A Cartel Policy for the United Nations* 45, *The United States and International Markets* 72; author *Maintaining Competition* 49, *Big Business and the Policy of Competition* 56, *The Price Discrimination Law: A Review of Experience* 59, *Cartelization in Western Europe* 64, *Trade Regulation Overseas: The National Laws* 66, *Control of Cartels and Monopolies: An International Comparison* 67.

11 New Jersey Avenue, Lewes, Del., U.S.A.

Telephone: 645-9015.

Edwards, Edwin Washington, LL.D.; American politician; b. 7 Aug. 1927, Marksville, La.; s. of Clarence W. Edwards and Agnes Brouillette Edwards; m. Elaine Schwartzenburg 1949; two d. two s.; ed. Louisiana State Univ.

Naval Cadet 45-46; practiced law in Crowley, La. 49-66, senior partner in law firm of Edwards, Edwards and Broadhurst; mem. Crowley City Council 54-62, La. State Senate 64-66; House of Reps. 65-72, Public Works Cttee. 65-68, Whip to La. and Miss. Dels., Judiciary Cttee. and Cttee. on Internal Security; Gov. of La. 72-; Chair. Interstate Oil Compact Comm. 74-, Ozarks Regional Comm. 74-, Educ. Comm. of Task Force on State, Institutional and Fed. Responsibilities May 75-; mem. Nat. Resources and Environmental Man. Cttee. of Southern Govs.' Conf., Rural and Urban Devt. Cttee. of Nat. Govs.' Conf.; mem. Crowley Chamber of Commerce, Crowley Industrial Foundation, American Legion; Democrat.
Governor's Mansion, Baton Rouge, La. 70801, U.S.A.

Edwards, Sir George Robert, O.M., C.B.E., F.R.S.; British aeronautical designer and executive; b. 9 July 1908; ed. London Univ.
Design Staff, Vickers Armstrong, Weybridge 35, Experimental Man. 40, Chief Designer 45, Gen. Man. and Chief Engineer 53; Man. Dir. British Aircraft Corpn. Ltd. 60-76; Pro-Chancellor Univ. of Surrey 64-; Daniel Guggenheim Medal 59; Taylor Gold Medal; Fellow, Royal Soc.; Albert Medal 72; Royal Soc. Royal Medal 74; Hon. F.R.Ae.S., Hon. F.A.I.A.A.
Albury Heights, White Lane, Guildford, Surrey, England.

Edwards, Gordon; American food products executive; b. 29 May 1907, Franklin, Va.; s. of Claude Joseph and Marion Lee (Lawless) Edwards; m. Alida Beamon 1932; one s. two d.; ed. Virginia Polytechnic Inst., and George Washington Univ.
Kraftco Corpn. (fmrly. Nat. Dairy Products Corpn.), Washington 27-35, New York City 35-36, Zone Controller, Chicago 36-49, with Kraft Foods Div., Chicago; Dir. Kraftco Corpn. 62, Pres. 65, Chief Exec. Officer 66, Chair. and Chief Exec. Officer 68-72; Dir. Cluett, Peabody & Co. Inc., B. F. Goodrich Co., Irving Trust Co., Communications Satellite Corpn., Pitney Bowes Inc.
Leisure interest: golf.
74 Winding Lane, Greenwich, Conn. 06830, U.S.A.

Edwards, Air Commodore Sir Hughie Idwal, V.C., K.C.M.G., C.B., D.S.O., O.B.E., D.F.C.; Australian administrator; b. 1 Aug. 1914, Fremantle, W. Australia; s. of late Hugh Edwards; m. 1st Cherry Kyrle Beresford 1942 (died 1966), 2nd Dorothy Carew Berrick 1972; one s. one d.; ed. Fremantle Boys' School.
Cadet R.A.A.F. 35-36; R.A.F. Officer (mentioned in despatches) 36-63; Dir. Australian Selection (Pty.) Ltd. 64-73; Gov. of W. Australia Jan. 74-.
Leisure interests: reading, horse racing.
Government House, Perth, Western Australia 6000.
Telephone: 25 3222.

Edwards, Robert John; British journalist; b. 26 Oct. 1925, Farnham, Surrey; s. of Gordon and Margaret (née Grain) Edwards; m. Laura Ellwood 1952 (dissolved 1972); two s. two d.; ed. Ranelagh School.
Editor *Tribune* 51-55; Deputy Editor *Sunday Express* 57-59; Editor *Daily Express* 63-65; Editor *The Sunday People* (fmrly. *The People*) 66-72; Editor *The Sunday Mirror* 72-.
Leisure interest: boating.
Flat 331, Cromwell Tower, The Barbican, London, E.C.2, England.

Edwards, Sir Sam(uel Frederick), Kt., F.R.S., F.INST.P., F.I.M.A.; British physicist and administrator; b. 1 Feb. 1928, Swansea; s. of Richard and Mary Jane Edwards; m. Merriell E. M. Bland 1953; one s. three d.; ed. Swansea Grammar School, Gonville and Caius College, Cambridge, Harvard Univ.
Member, Inst. for Advanced Study, Princeton 52-53; staff mem. Birmingham Univ. 53-58, Manchester Univ. 58-72; Prof. of Theoretical Physics, Manchester Univ.

63-72; John Humphrey Plummer Prof. of Physics, Cambridge Univ. 72-; mem. Council, Inst. of Physics 67-73, Vice-Pres. of Inst. 70-73, Chair. Publ. Div. 70-73; mem. Science Board, Science Research Council 70-73, mem. Physics Cttee. 68-70, Polymer Science Cttee. 68-73, Chair. Physics Cttee. 70-73, Science Research Council 73-; mem. Council European Physical Soc. 69-71, Univ. Grants Cttee. 71-73, Scientific Advisory Council, Min. of Defence 73-, Advisory Board for the Research Councils, Dept. of Ed. and Science 73-, Metrology and Standards Requirements Board, Dept. of Ind. 74-, Advisory Council on Research and Devt., Dept. of Energy 74-, Senatsausschusses fur Forschungspolitik und Forschungsplanung du Max Planck Gesellschaft 75-; Fellow Gonville, Caius Colls., Cambridge; Hon. D.Tech, Loughborough 75; Hon. D.Sc., Edinburgh 76; Maxwell Medal and Prize, Inst. of Physics 74.
Science Research Council, State House, High Holborn, London, WC1R 4TA, England.
Telephone: 01-242-1262.

Edwards, William Philip Neville, C.B.E., M.A.; British industrialist; b. 5 Aug. 1904; ed. Rugby, Corpus Christi Coll., Cambridge, and Princeton Univ. (Davison Scholar).
Public Relations Officer, London Passenger Transport Board 39-41; Asst. to Chair. of Supply Council, Ministry of Supply 41-43; Head of Industrial Information Div., Ministry of Production, and alternate Dir. of Information, British Supply Council, Washington 43-45; Dir. Overseas Information Div., Board of Trade, London 45-46; Counsellor, British Embassy, Washington, D.C., in charge of British Information Services 46-49; Deputy Overseas Dir. Federation of British Industries (F.B.I.) 49-51, Dir. Promotion and Information, F.B.I. 51-65, Confederation of British Industry (C.B.I.) 65-66; Dir. of British Overseas Fairs Ltd. 53-66, Chair. 66-68; U.K. Assoc. Dir. Business International S.A. 69-75; Chair. Burton Sheen Ltd. 71-75; Chair. P.R.I. Group.
Hill House, Brockham Lane, Betchworth, Surrey, England.

Eeg-Henriksen, Haakon; Norwegian company director and civil engineer; b. 17 March 1892; ed. Norwegian Univ. of Technology.
Began engineering career abroad 15-17; with Christiania Cementstöperi 17-19, with Solbergfossen Hydro-Electric Power Plant 19-22; managed own contracting firm 22-29; Partner, Eeg-Henriksen & Diderich Lund Ltd. 30-52, Dir. and Owner 52-; Dir. Construction Directorate, Ministry of Defence 52-54; Dir. H. Eeg-Henriksen Ltd. 54-; mem. Board Sigyn Life Insurance Co.; mem. Cttee. Norwegian Life Insurance Co.; fmr. Pres. Norwegian Defence Asscn.; Chair. Hausmannsgatens Industribygg; Commdr. Order of St. Olav.
Havna Allé 11, Oslo 3, Norway.

Efanov, Vasili Prokofievich; Soviet painter; b. 23 Nov. 1900, Kuibyshev; ed. Samara Industrial Arts Technicum and in Moscow.
Teacher in V. Suzikov Art Inst. 48-57, Prof. 49-; Moscow Pedagog. Inst. 60-; paintings exhibited in the Moscow Tretiakov Gallery, Leningrad Russian Museum; mem. C.P.S.U. 54-; mem. U.S.S.R. Acad. of Arts 47-; People's Artist of R.S.F.S.R. 51 and U.S.S.R. 65, State prizewinner 41, 46, 48, 50, 52; Order of Lenin, etc.; mem. editorial collegium *Iskusstvo*.
Academy of Arts of the U.S.S.R., 21, Kropotkinskaya ulitsa, Moscow, U.S.S.R.

Etholm, Mogens; Danish business executive; b. 20 May 1910, Copenhagen; s. of Christian Christensen and Ingeborg (née Ohlsson); m. Birgitte Jensen 1947; ed. univ., and commercial studies in England, Germany and France.
Copenhagen trade agencies 30-45; Managing Dir. Emil Warthoe & Soenner A/S 45-50, Nordisk Andelsforbund (Scandinavian Co-operative Wholesale Soc.) 51-64,

"National" Co. 53-57, Nordisk Andels-Eksport (Scandi-navian Co-operative Export) 54-64; mem. Central Cttee. Int. Co-operative Alliance, London 61-64; mem. the "Maritime and Commercial Court" 61-; Chair. Nordisk Andelsforbund, Calif., Inc., San Francisco 62-64; Sec.-Gen. European Co-operative Wholesale Cttee. for Developments in Production and Marketing Fields 63-64; Commercial Adviser 64-; Knight Order of Dannebrog.
Leisure interests: literature and philosophy.
65B Strandvejen, Copenhagen Ø, Denmark.
Telephone: 01-29-36-46.

Efimov, Anatoly Nikolaevich; Soviet economist; b. 1908 Troitsk, Chelyabinsk Region; ed. The Urals Indus-trial Inst.
Lecturer, The Urals S. M. Kirov Polytechnical Inst. 37-48; Head, Section of Econ. Investigation, Urals Div. of U.S.S.R. Acad. of Sciences 48-55; Dir. Econ. Re-search Inst., U.S.S.R. State Planning Comm. 55-; corresp. mem. U.S.S.R. Acad. of Sciences 64-70, Academician 70-; mem. C.P.S.U. 48-; U.S.S.R. State Prize 68; Order of Red Banner of Labour and medals.
U.S.S.R. State Planning Commission, Moscow, U.S.S.R.

Efon, Vincent; Cameroonian politician; b. 28 Aug. 1927, Mbos; ed. Paris, Toulouse.
Directeur de Cabinet, Minister of Nat. Educ. July 60-July 62; Chief, Produce Dept. 62-63; Asst. Dir., then Dir. Econ. Orientation March 63-Jan. 66; Dir. of Foundation Products 66-67; Dir. CHOCOCAM and Soc. Franco-Camerounaise des Tabacs (SFCT); Minister of Commerce and Industry May 67-Aug. 68; Minister of Planning and Devt. 68-70, of Transport 70-72, of Foreign Affairs July 72-75.
Ministry of Foreign Affairs, Yaoundé, United Republic of Cameroon.

Efremov, Mikhail Timofeyevich; Soviet politician; b. 1911; ed. Industrial Inst., Kuibyshev.
Member C.P.S.U. 32-; party work 42-; Sec. Kuibyshev District Cttee. C.P.S.U. 51-59; Perm. Staff, Central Cttee. of C.P.S.U. 59-61; mem. Central Cttee. C.P.S.U. 56-; First Sec. Cheliabinsk District Cttee., C.P.S.U. 61-63; First Sec. Gorky District Cttee., C.P.S.U. 63-65; Deputy Chair. U.S.S.R. Council of Ministers 65-71; Amb. to German Democratic Repub. 71-75; Deputy to U.S.S.R. Supreme Soviet 54-.
c/o Ministry of Foreign Affairs, Moscow, U.S.S.R.

Efremov, Oleg Nikolaevich; Soviet actor and director; b. 1 Oct. 1927, Moscow; ed. Moscow Arts Theatre Studio.
Studio School of Moscow Art Theatres 45-49; Actor and producer at Cen. Children's Theatre 49-56; Chief Pro-ducer Sovremennik Theatre 56-70; Chief Stage Man. Moscow Art Theatre 70-; has produced many plays at Sovremennik Theatre; film work 55-; Merited Art Worker of R.S.F.S.R. 57, R.S.F.S.R. People's Actor 69, U.S.S.R. State Prize 69.
Moscow Art Theatre, Proezd Khudozhestvennogo Teatra 3, Moscow, U.S.S.R.

Egal, Mohamed Ibrahim; Somali politician; b. 1921, Berbera; ed. Koranic School, Sheikh Intermediate School, and in U.K.
Secretary, Berbera Branch, Somali Nat. League Party 56; Sec.-Gen. Somali Nat. League Party 58-60; Prime Minister of Somaliland 60; Minister of Defence, Somali Repub. 60-62, of Educ. 62-63; re-elected to Parl. March 64; mem. Somali Youth League Party 66; Prime Minister and Minister of Foreign Affairs, Somali Repub. 67-69; in detention following coup 69, released Oct. 75.

Egami, Fujio, D.SC.; Japanese biochemist; b. 21 Nov. 1910, Tokyo; s. of Shimao and Mitsuko Egami; m. Yuki Yoneta 1939; two d.; ed. Univ. of Tokyo and in Stras-bourg and Paris.
Associate Prof. of Biochem., Nagoya Univ. 42-43, Prof.

of Biochem. 43-60; Prof. of Biochem., Univ. of Tokyo 58-71, Saitama Univ. 68-71; mem. Science Council of Japan 49-72, Vice-Pres. 66-69, Pres. 69-72; Dir. Mitsubishi-Kasei Inst. of Life Sciences 71-; Chemical Soc. of Japan Prize 54; Officier de l'Instruction Publique (French Govt.) 54; Asahi Culture Prize 67, Japan Acad. Prize 71; Légion d'Honneur 71.
Leisure interest: Esperanto.
Publs. *Biochemistry of Nucleic Acids, Biochemistry of Heteropolysaccharides, Enzyme Biochemistry, Micro-biological Chemistry, Minor Elements and Evolution, Discovery of Ribonuclease* T_1, T_2 *and* U_2.
Mitsubishi-Kasei Institute of Life Sciences, 11 Mina-miooya, Machidashi, Tokyo; Nukui-minami-cho III-1-7, Koganei-shi, Tokyo, Japan.
Telephone: 0427-26-1211 (Office); 0423-81-9212 (Home).

Egeberg, Roger Olaf, M.D.; American physician; b. 13 Nov. 1903, Chicago, Ill.; m. Margaret McEchron Chahoon; one s. two d.; ed. Cornell and Northwestern Univs.
Intern, Wesley Hospital, Chicago; Resident Univ. Hospital, Ann Arbor, Mich.; practised medicine (specializing in internal medicine) Cleveland, Ohio 32-42; Chief Medical Service, Veterans' Admin. Hospital, Los Angeles 46-56; Medical Dir. L.A. County Hospital 56-58; L.A. County Dept. Charities 58-64; mem. staff Los Angeles County Gen. Hospital, and Rancho Los Amigos Hospital, Downey, Calif.; Prof. of Medicine Univ. of Calif. at Los Angeles (U.C.L.A.) 48-64, Coll. of Medical Evangelists 56-64; Prof. of Medicine, Univ. of S. Calif. 56-69, Dean School of Medicine 64-69; mem. Nat. Advisory Cancer Council, Special Medical Advisory Group to the Veterans' Admin., Calif. Board of Public Health; Asst. Sec. for Health, Educ. and Welfare 69-71, Special Asst. to Sec. for Health Policy 71-; Co-Chair. U.S.-U.S.S.R. Comm. for Health Co-operation 72-; Fellow, American Coll. of Physicians; mem. American Medical Asscn., American Clinical and Climatological Asscn.; Bronze Star, Legion of Merit, St. Olaf's Medal (Norway).
Publs. Numerous articles in professional journals.
Department of Health, Education and Welfare, 330 Independence Avenue, S.W., Washington, D.C. 20201, U.S.A.

Egeland, Leif, M.A., B.C.L.; South African diplomatist and businessman; b. 19 Jan. 1903, Durban; m. Marguerite Doreen de Zwaan 1942; one d.; ed. Durban High School, Natal Univ. Coll., and Trinity Coll., Oxford.
Rhodes Scholar for Natal 24, Harmsworth Scholar Middle Temple 27; Barrister 30; Fellow Brasenose Coll. 27-30; Advocate Supreme Court S. Africa 31; M.P. Durban 33-38, Zululand 40-43; with 6th S. African Armoured Div., Middle East 43; Union Minister to Sweden 43-46, to Neths. and Belgium 46-48; High Commr. for Union of South Africa in London 48-50; S. African Del. to San Francisco Conf. 45; leader of S. African Del. to Final Assembly L.N., Geneva 46; S. African Del. to First and Third Gen. Assemblies of UN, Paris, to Paris Peace Conf. 46 and Pres. Comm. for the political and territorial questions in the draft Peace Treaty with Italy at that Conf.; Chair. Standard Gen. Insurance Co. Ltd., Smuts Memorial Trust; a Vice-Pres., Exec. Trustee of the South Africa Founda-tion; Pres. South African Guide Dogs Asscn.; Hon. Bencher Middle Temple; Hon. LL.D. (Cambridge Univ.); Knight Commdr. with Star of St. Olav (Norway), Knight Grand Cross of the North Star (Sweden).
Leisure interests: tennis, gardening, bridge.
Home: 11 Fricker Road, Illovo, Johannesburg, South Africa.
Telephone: 421642 (Home).

Eggan, Fred Russell, PH.D.; American anthropologist; b. 12 Sept. 1906, Seattle, Wash.; s. of Alfred J. Eggan

and Olive M. Smith; *m.* 1st Dorothy Way 1938 (deceased), 2nd Joan Rosenfels 1969; no. *c.*; ed. Univ. of Chicago.
Instructor, Univ. of Chicago 35-40, Asst. Prof. 40-44, Assoc. Prof. 45-48, Prof. of Anthropology and Chair. Dept. of Anthropology 48-; Visiting Fellow, All Souls' Coll., Oxford 70; mem. Nat. Acad. of Sciences, American Philosophical Soc., American Acad. of Arts and Sciences; Viking Fund Medal, L. H. Morgan Lecturer; Frazer Lecturer 71.
Leisure interests: travel, photography.
Publs. *Social Organization of the Western Pueblos* 50, *The American Indian* 68; Editor of *Social Anthropology of North American Tribes* 37 (2nd edn. 55).
Department of Anthropology, 1126 East 59th Street, Chicago, Ill. 60637; Home: 5752 South Harper Avenue, Chicago, Ill. 60637. U.S.A.
Telephone: 753-3707 (Office); Butterfield 8-5140 (Home).

Eghbal, Manouchehr, M.D.; Iranian physician and politician; b. 13 Oct. 1909, Khorassan; ed. Persia and Univs. of Montpellier and Paris.
Professor, Infectious Diseases, Medical Faculty, Univ. of Teheran 40-53; from 43-50 successively apptd. Under-Sec. of State for Public Health, Minister for Public Health, Minister of Posts, Telegraph and Telephones, Minister of Nat. Educ., of Roads and Communications, of Interior; Gov.-Gen. Azerbaidjan (Northern Region of Iran) 50-51; Chancellor, Univ. of Tabriz 50; Senator 53; Dean of Faculty of Medicine, Chancellor, Teheran Univ. 55-57; Minister to the Imperial Court 56; Prime Minister 57-60; Prof. Teheran Univ. 60-61; mem. of Parl. 61-; Perm. Iranian Rep. to UNESCO 61-; Chair. of Board and Gen. Man. Dir. Nat. Iranian Oil Co. Oct. 63-; Pres. Iranian Medical Council; Chair. Board of Trustees Teheran Univ., Bou Ali Sina Univ.; Assoc. Mem. Soc. of Exotic Pathology, Pasteur Inst., Acad. of Medicine, Paris; mem. Board of Trustees of several insts., Board of Dirs. of numerous nat. companies and socs.; Hon. Dr. (Lafayette Coll., U.S.A., Paris Univ., Bordeaux Univ., Univ. of Pubjab, Pahlavi Univ., Univ. of Bucharest, Univ. of Stellenbosch, Nat. Univ. of Seoul, Univ. of Southern Calif.); 54 decorations including Grand Croix, Légion d'Honneur; Grand Cross, Order of Danebrog; Order of Merit (China); Order of the Rising Sun (Japan); Das Grossverdienstkreuz mit Schulterband; hon. G.B.E.
Office: National Iranian Oil Co., Ave. Takhte Jamshid, P.O. Box 1863; Home: Elahieh, Teheran, Iran.
Telephone: 6151 (Office); 261080 (Home).

Egk, Werner; German composer; b. 17 May 1901, Auchsesheim bei Donauwörth; *s.* of Joseph Egk and Maria Buck; *m.* Elisabeth Karl 1923; one *s.* (deceased); ed. Univ. of Munich.
Conductor, Prussian State Opera, Berlin 36-40; Dir Hochschule für Musik, Berlin (West) 50-53; Hon. Pres. of *Cisac* (Confédération Internationale des Sociétés d'Auteurs et Compositeurs); mem., Music Section of the Bayerische Akademie der Schönen Künste, Akademie der Künste Berlin; Pres. of *Deutscher Komponistenverband*; Pres. of *Deutscher Musikrat* 54-72.
Publs. Operas: *Zaubergeige* 35, *Peer Gynt* 38, *Columbus* 41, *Irische Legende* 55, *Revisor* 57, *Die Verlobung in San Domingo* 63, *17 Tage und 4 Minuten* 66; ballets: *Joan von Zarissa* 40, *Abraxas* 48, *Sommertag* 49, *Chinesische Nachtigall* 53, *Danza* 60, *Casanova in London* 69; concert works: *Furchtlosigkeit und Wohlwollen* (oratorio) 31, *La Tentation de Saint Antoine* 46, *Orchestersonate* 48, *Französische Suite* 50, *Chanson et Romance* 53, etc.
Ch-5726 Unterkulm am Bohler, Munich, Federal Republic of Germany.

Eglevsky, André; American (b. Russian) ballet dancer and producer; b. 21 Dec. 1917; ed. Nice, Paris and London.
With René Blum's Ballet de Monte Carlo 36; went to United States 37; Grand Ballet du Marquis de Cuevas 47; New York City Ballet Co. 50-58; with wife founded André Eglevsky School of Ballet 55; Teacher and Artistic Dir. André Eglevsky Ballet Co. 60-.
20 Unqua Road, Massapequa, N.Y. 11758, U.S.A.

Eglin, Colin Wells; South African politician and quantity surveyor; b. 14 April 1925, Cape Town; *s.* of Carl Eglin and Elsie Mary Wells; *m.* Joyce Cortes 1949; three *d.*; ed. De Villiers Graaff High School and Univ. of Cape Town.
Army service in Egypt and Italy 43-45; mem. Pinelands Municipal Council 51-54, Cape Provincial Council 54-58; mem. Parl. for Pinelands Constituency 58-61, for Sea Point Constituency 74-; Chair. Progressive Party of S.A. for Cape Province 59-66, Chair. Nat. Exec. 66-70, Nat. Leader 70-75; Nat. Leader S.A. Progressive Reform Party 75-; Partner, Bernard James and Partners (Quantity Surveyors) 52-.
Leisure interests: tennis, golf, travel.
P.O. Box 1475, Cape Town; 10 Southway, Pinelands, Cape, South Africa.
Telephone: 451068, 434636 (Office); 531978 (Home).

Egorov, Anatoli Grigorievich; Soviet journalist; b. 25 Oct. 1920, Skopin, Ryazan Region; ed. Moscow Pedagogical.
Soviet army service 41-46; mem. C.P.S.U. 44-; Teacher, Pedagogical Inst., Vladivostok 46-48; Deputy Editor, then Editor, *Kommunist* 52-56, 65-; Chief Editor, *V Pomoshch Politicheskomu Samoobrazovaniu* (Political Self-Education Guide) 56-60; Perm. staff Cen. Cttee. C.P.S.U. 61-66; mem. Cen. Auditing Comm. C.P.S.U. 61-66; Alt. mem. Cen. Cttee. C.P.S.U. 66-; Corresp. mem. U.S.S.R. Acad. of Sciences 62-; several decorations.
c/o U.S.S.R. Academy of Sciences, 14 Leninsky Prospekt 14, Moscow V-71, U.S.S.R.

Egorov, Boris Borisovich, M.SC.(MED.); Soviet cosmonaut; b. 1937, Moscow; *s.* of Boris Grigorievich Egorov; ed. Moscow Medical Inst.
Scientist in field of aviation and cosmic medicine; doctor in team of spacecraft *Voskhod I* in flight Oct. 64; Hero of Soviet Union; Order of Lenin, Golden Star Medal; Pilot-Cosmonaut of U.S.S.R.
Zvezdny Gorodok, Moscow, U.S.S.R.

Egorychev, Nikolai Grigorievich; Soviet politician and diplomatist; b. 1920; ed. Moscow Higher Technical Inst.
Member C.P.S.U. 42-; army service 41-46; Sec. Bauman Regional Cttee. (Moscow) C.P.S.U. 54-60; Perm. staff Central Cttee. 60-61; First Sec. Moscow City Cttee. C.P.S.U. 61-67; Deputy Minister of Tractor and Agricultural Machinery Building Oct. 67; mem. Central Cttee. of C.P.S.U. 61-; mem. Bureau for R.S.F.S.R.; Deputy to U.S.S.R. Supreme Soviet; mem. Presidium Supreme Soviet of U.S.S.R. 66-67; Amb. to Denmark 70-.
Embassy of the U.S.S.R., Kristianiagade 5, Copenhagen, Denmark.

Ehard, Hans, DR. JUR.; German lawyer and politician; b. 10 Nov. 1887, Bamberg; *s.* of August Georg Ehard and K. Konrad; *m.* 1st Annelore Maex 1916 (died 1957), 2nd Dr. Sieglinde Odörfer; one *s.*; ed. Univs. of Munich and Würzburg.
Served in Bavarian Ministry of Justice, rising to rank of Ministerial Counsellor 33; Asst. State Prosecutor in Hitler trial, Munich 24; seconded to Reich Ministry of Justice 25-28; owing to non-membership of Nat. Socialist Party was transferred to Oberlandesgericht, Munich, as Senate Pres. 33; State Counsellor in Bavar-

ian Ministry of Justice Oct. 45; as State Sec. became mem. of Bavarian State Govt.; Minister-Pres. of Bavaria 46-54, 60-62, Minister of Justice 62-66; Pres. Bavarian Parl. 54-60; mem. Christian Social Union; Pres. Bavarian Red Cross 55-69; Hon. Pres. Bavarian Red Cross 69-; numerous decorations.
Leisure interests: archaeology, astronomy.
8 Munich 90, Am Schilcherweg 4A, Federal Republic of Germany.
Telephone: 649554.

Ehmke, Horst Paul August; German lawyer and politician; b. 4 Feb. 1927, Danzig; s. of Dr. med. Paul Ehmke and Hedwig (née Hafften); m. 1st Theda Baehr, 2nd Maria Hlavacova 1972; one s. two d.; ed. High School, Danzig, Univ. of Göttingen and Princeton Univ., U.S.A.
Research Assoc., Law School, Berkeley, U.S.A. 58; graduated in Bonn 60; Prof. of Law Univ. of Freiburg 61-67, Dean of Law and Govt. Faculty 66-67; Deputy of Fed. Minister of Justice 67-69; Fed. Minister of Justice March-Oct. 69; Head of Fed. Chancellor's Office and Minister 69-72; Fed. Minister for Research and Technology, Posts and Telecommunications 72-74; Social Democrat.
Leisure interests: history, modern literature, modern art, sport, gardening.
Publs. *Grenzen der Verfassungsänderung* 53, *"Ermessen" und "unbestimmter Rechtsbegriff" im Verwaltungsrecht* 60, *Wirtschaft und Verfassung* 61, *Prinzipien der Verfassungsinterpretation* 63, *Politik der praktischen Vernunft* 69, *Politik als Herausforderung* 74, *Tribunregelung und Grundgesetz* 75.
Adenauerstrasse 19, 534 Rhöndorf, Federal Republic of Germany.
Telephone: Bonn 163429.

Ehrenberger, Vlastimil, ING.C.SC.; Czechoslovak politician; b. 16 Feb. 1935, Svojanov, Olomouc Dist.; ed. Mining Coll., Ostrava.
Foreman, Chief Foreman, Zárubek Mine, Ostrava 55-61; Chair. Communist Party Works Cttee. in Stachanov Mine until 63; mem. Czechoslovak C.P. Regional Cttee. in N. Moravia, Sec. 70; Dept. for Heavy Industry, Cen. Cttee. of Czechoslovak C.P. 67-68; Deputy Gen. Man. of Construction of Ostrava-Karviná Mines 68; mem. Nat. Econ. Comm. of Cen. Cttee. of Czechoslovak C.P. 70-; Vice-Premier of Czechoslovakia 73-74; Minister of Fuel and Power 74-.
Ministry of Fuel and Power, Prague, Czechoslovakia.

Ehrlich, Julius; German-born American conductor; b. 3 Feb. 1894; ed. Staatliche Hochschule für Musik, Frankfurt-am-Main, Germany.
Dir. "Stadthallen" Concerts and Radio Station, Hanover 23-28; Prof. Leningrad Conservatory, Conductor Leningrad Opera 30-33; Conductor, Royal Flemish Opera, Antwerp 34-36; emigrated to U.S.A. 37; Conductor Milwaukee Symphony Orchestra, Milwaukee Sinfonietta 39-47; Dir. Milwaukee Annual Brotherhood Week Concerts; Grand Prix du Disque 34; regular guest conducting tours to Europe 47-67.
Garten Strasse 8, 8 Munich 40, Federal Republic of Germany.
Telephone: 3001538.

Ehrlich, Paul Ralph, M.A., PH.D.; American population biologist; b. 29 May 1932, Philadelphia, Pa.; s. of William and Ruth (Rosenberg) Ehrlich; m. Anne Fitzhugh Howland 1954; one d.; ed. Univs. of Pennsylvania and Kansas.
Associate investigator, U.S.A.F. research project, Alaska and Univ. of Kansas 56-57; Research Assoc. Chicago Acad. of Sciences and Univ. of Kansas Dept. of Entomology 57-59; mem. Faculty, Stanford Univ. 59-, Prof. of Biology 66-; Hon. D.Hum.Litt. (Univ. of the Pacific) 70.
Leisure interests: collecting primitive art.

Publs. *How to Know the Butterflies* 61, *Population Resources and Environment* 70, 72 (both with A. H. Ehrlich); *The Population Bomb* 68, 71; *How to be a Survivor* (with R. L. Harriman) 71; co-editor: *Man and the Ecosphere* (with J. P. Holdren and R. W. Holm) 71, *Global Ecology* (with J. P. Holdren) 71, *Human Ecology* (with A. H. Ehrlich and J. Holdren) 73, *Ark II* (with D. Pirages) 74, *The Process of Evolution* (with R. W. Holm and D. R. Parnell) 74, *The End of Affluence* (with A. H. Ehrlich) 74, *Biology and Society* (with R. W. Holm and I. Brown) 76, and numerous other books; over 200 scientific and popular articles.
Department of Biological Sciences, Stanford University, Stanford, Calif. 94305, U.S.A.

Ehrlich, S. Paul, Jr., M.P.H., M.D.; American physician; b. 4 May 1932, Minn.; s. of S. Paul Ehrlich and Dorothy E. Fiterman; m. Geraldine McKenna 1959; three d.; ed. Univs. of Minnesota and Calif.
Staff Physician, Grants and Training Branch, Nat. Heart Inst., Nat. Insts. of Health, Bethesda 59-60; Chief, Epidemiology Field Training Station, Heart Disease Control Program, Wash., D.C. 61-66, Deputy Chief Heart Disease Control Program 66-67; Lecturer in Epidemiology, School of Public Health, Univ. of Calif. 63-; Clinical Assoc. Prof., Dept. of Community Medicine and Int. Health, Georgetown Univ. School of Medicine, Wash., D.C. 67-; Adjunct Prof. of Int. Health, Univ. of Texas; Assoc. Dir. for Bilateral Programs, Office of Int. Health, 67-68; Deputy Dir. Office of Int. Health 68-69; Acting Dir. Office of Int. Health, Dept. of Health, Educ. and Welfare Dec. 69-70, Dir. 70-; Asst. Surgeon-Gen., USPHS 70, Acting Surgeon-Gen. 73-; U.S. Rep. to World Health Org. (WHO) 74-; Diplomate, American Board of Preventive Medicine; Chair. Exec. Board of WHO.
Publs. Articles on Chronic Disease Control, Coronary Disease Risk Factors, and the Relationship of the Stroke to Other Cardiovascular Diseases.
Office of International Health, PHS, Department of Health, Education and Welfare, 5600 Fishers Lane, Rockville, Md. 20852, U.S.A.
Telephone: 301-443-1774.

Ehrlichman, John Daniel, LL.B., J.D.; American attorney; b. 20 March 1925, Tacoma, Wash.; s. of late Rudolph I. Ehrlichman and Lillian Danielson; m. Jeanne Fisher 1949; three s. two d.; ed. Univ. of Calif. (Los Angeles) and Standford Univ.
Served with U.S. Army Air Corps during Second World War; fmrly. with Hullin Ehrlichman Roberts and Hodge (law firm) Seattle; Dir. of Convention Activities subsequently Tour Dir. Presidential Campaign 68; Counsel to Pres. Nixon Nov. 68-69; Asst. to Pres. for Domestic Affairs Nov. 69-March 73 (resigned over the Watergate case); convicted for Watergate related charges July 74, Feb. 75.

Eichfeld, Johan Hansovich; Soviet botanist and government official; b. 25 Jan. 1893, Paide Town, Estonia; ed. Leningrad Agricultural Inst.
Assistant at polar research station Kola Peninsular until 40; Dir. All Union Research Inst. Plant Growing, Leningrad 40-46; Pres. Estonian Acad. of Sciences 50-65; corresp. mem. U.S.S.R. Acad. of Sciences 53-; Chair. Presidium Estonian Supreme Soviet 58-61; State Prize for agricultural experimental work in the Polar regions and four Orders of Lenin.
National Academy of Sciences, 14 Leninsky Prospekt, Moscow, U.S.S.R.

Eichler, Irena; Polish actress; b. 19 April 1908, Warsaw; ed. Theatrical School, Warsaw, student of Aleksander Zelwerowicz.
Began career in Vilnius, Lvov, Krakow and Lódź; later with Polish and Nat. Theatres in Warsaw; abroad 39-45; went to Brazil, helped organize Brazilian Nat. Theatre and Dramatic School; Warsaw theatres 45-;

Rozmaitości, Nowy, Współczesny, Ludowy; Teatr Narodowy 58-; State Prize, 1st Class 55; Order of Banner of Labour, 1st Class 59; Ministry of Culture and Arts Prize 65; Officer's Cross, Order of Polonia Restituta.

Roles include: Salome (Wilde), Cleopatra (Norwid), Chimène (Corneille), Judith (Giraudoux), Balladyna (Słowacki), Mrs. Warren (Shaw), Rosita (Lorca), Maria Stuart (Schiller), Phèdre (Racine), Maria Tudor (V. Hugo).

Ul. Odyńca 27, 02-606 Warsaw, Poland.

Eickhoff, Gottfred; Danish sculptor and professor; b. 11 April 1902, Copenhagen; s. of Gudfred Eickhoff and Asa Brandt; m. Gerda Arensbach Andersen 1927; ed. Københavns Universitet, and Paris under Charles Despiau.

Professor of Sculpture, Acad. of Fine Arts, Copenhagen 55-72, Pro-rector 56-66; mem. Council of Art 56-73, extraordinary mem. 74-; exhbns. and works in museums in Europe and U.S.A., monuments in Denmark, Sweden and Belgium; Knight, Order of Dannebrog; Kai Nielsen Prize 42, Henri Nathansens Prize 51, Eckersberg Medal 44, Viggo Jarls Prize I 62, II 74, Haslund Prize 71.

Leisure interests: writing on art, travel.

Frederiksholms Kanal 28A, Copenhagen, Denmark.

Telephone: (01)131418.

Eigen, Manfred, DR. RER. NAT.; German physical chemist; b. 9 May 1927; ed. Georg-August-Univ. zu Göttingen.

Max-Planck Inst. of Physical Chem., Göttingen, as Asst., later as Prof. and Head of Dept. 53-, Dir. 64-; Otto Hahn Prize 62; Nobel Prize for Chem. (with Norrish and Porter) for investigation of extremely rapid chemical reactions by means of disturbing the (molecular) equilibrium by the action of very short energy pulses 67; Foreign hon. mem. American Acad. of Arts and Sciences; mem. Akad. der Wissenschaften, Göttingen; Assoc. mem. Nat. Acad. of Sciences, U.S.A.; Foreign mem. Royal Soc., U.K.; Hon. Dr. Univ. of Washington, St. Louis Univ., Harvard Univ. and Cambridge Univ.

Max-Planck-Institut für Biophysikalische Chemie, Karl-Friedrich-Bonhoeffer-Institut, Am Fassberg, 3400 Göttingen-Nikolausberg, Federal Republic of Germany.

Telephone: 0551-20-14-32.

Eika, Hallvard; Norwegian farmer and politician; b. 5 Dec. 1920, Torquay, Sask., Canada; s. of Ketil and Kari (née Landsverk) Eika; m. Aslaug Vethe 1959; two s. one d.; ed. Agricultural Coll. of Norway and abroad.

Scientific Asst., Inst. for Agricultural Economy, Agricultural Coll. of Norway 46-48; Consultant, Norwegian Farmers' Union 48-50, Royal Soc. for Rural Devt. of Norway 50-52; Farmer, Bø 52-; Chair. Norwegian Farmers' Union 55-66; mem. Board Norwegian Forest Owners Fed. 55-65, Bøndernes Bank A/S 62-, Forenede Liv Insurance Comp. 56-; mem. Presidium, Cen. Council of Nordic Agricultural Orgs. 56-66; Vice-Pres. Int. Fed. of Agricultural Producers 64-67; Mayor of Bø 67-70, 76-; mem. Parl. 69-; Minister of Agriculture 70-71; Minister of Commerce and Shipping 72-73; Chair. Bø Hotel A/S 68-; Chair. Telemark Distriktshøgskole 71-.

Bø, Telemark; Sig. Seyrsgt. 1, Oslo, Norway.

Telephone: Bø 83 Oslo 44-86-45.

Eilenberg, Samuel, PH.D.; American mathematician; b. 30 Sept. 1913; ed. Univ. of Warsaw.

Instructor, Univ. of Michigan 40-41, Asst. Prof. 41-45, Assoc. Prof. 45-46; Prof. Indiana Univ. 46-47; Prof. Columbia Univ. 47-; Visiting Prof. Univ. of Paris 50-51, and 66-67; mem. Nat. Acad. of Sciences, Amer. Acad. of Arts and Sciences; hon. mem. London Math. Soc.; fmr. Vice-Pres. Amer. Math. Soc.

Leisure interest: Indian and S.E. Asian art.

Publs. *Foundations of Algebraic Topology* (with N. E. Steenrod) 52, *Homological Algebra* (with H. Cartan) 56, *Recursiveness* (with C. C. Elgot) 70, *Automata, Languages and Machines*, vol. A 74, vol. B 76; numerous articles in professional journals.

Department of Mathematics, Columbia University, New York, N.Y. 10027, U.S.A.

Eilers, Louis Kenneth, PH.D.; American business executive; b. 11 April 1907, Gillespie, Ill.; s. of William H. and Minnie (née Luken) Eilers; m. C. Frances Wampler 1930; three s. two d.; ed. Blackburn Coll., Univs. of Illinois and Virginia, and Northwestern Univ.

Superintendent Roll Coating Finishing Dept. Eastman-Kodak Co. 46-50; Asst. to Man. Film Mfg. 50-52, Asst. Man. 52-53; Admin. Asst. to Gen. Man. Kodak Park 53, Asst. Gen. Man. 54-56; Vice-Pres. and Asst. Gen. Man. Eastman Kodak Co. 56-59; Pres. Eastman Chemical Products Inc. 59-61; First Vice-Pres. Tennessee Eastman Co. and Texas Eastman Co. 59-61, Pres. 61-63; Pres. Carolina Eastman Co. 61-63; Exec. Vice-Pres. Eastman Kodak Co. 63-67, Dir. and mem. Exec. Cttee. 63-, Pres. 67-70, Chair. Exec. Cttee. 67-69, Chief Exec. Officer 69-72, Chair. of Board of Dirs. 70-72; Hon. Sc.D. (Blackburn Coll.); Assoc. Fellow Soc. of Photographic Scientists and Engineers.

Leisure interests: golf, bowling.

57 Knollwood Drive, Rochester, N.Y. 14618, U.S.A.

Eilts, Hermann Frederick, M.A., LL.D.; American (b. German) diplomatist; b. 23 March 1922, Germany; m. Helen Brew Eilts 1948; two s.; ed. Ursinus Coll., Johns Hopkins Univ., Univ. of Pennsylvania.

Several diplomatic posts in Teheran 47-48, Jeddah 48-51, Aden 51-54, Baghdad 54-56, Washington, D.C. 56-61; First Sec., American Embassy, London 62-64; Counsellor, Deputy Head of Mission, American Embassy, Tripoli 64-65; Amb. to Saudi Arabia 65-70; Diplomatic Adviser to U.S. Army War Coll. 70-73; Amb. to Egypt 73-; Arthur Fleming Award for Distinguished Govt. Service, U.S. Army Decoration for Distinguished Civilian Service.

Leisure interests: coins, stamps, reading, hiking, tennis.

5 America El Latina St. (Garden City), Cairo, Egypt.

Telephone: Cairo 28219.

Einaudi, Giulio; Italian publisher; b. 2 Jan. 1912, Turin; s. of Prof. Luigi Einaudi and Ida Pellegrini; m. Renata Aldrovandi 1950; three s. three d.; ed. Liceo Massimo d'Azeglio and Univ. of Turin.

Founder Publishing House, Giulio Einaudi Editore 33, Gen. Man. 54-.

Leisure interests: mountaineering, paintings, rare books.

Via Umberto Biancamano 1, 10121 Turin, Italy.

Telephone: 533653.

Einem, Gottfried von; Austrian professor and composer; b. 24 Jan. 1918, Berne, Switzerland; s. of William and Gerta Louise von Einem; m. Lotte Ingrisch; one s.; ed. Gymnasium at Ratzeburg and musical studies with Boris Blacher.

Coach, State Opera in Berlin 39-44; Musical Adviser to Dir. of Dresden State Opera, Coach Bayreuth Festival 38-39; mem. Board of Salzburg Festival 48-; mem Acad. of Arts, Berlin, Vienna Konzerthaus Gesellschaft 63-; Prof. Hochschule für Musik, Vienna 65; numerous awards and prizes including Austrian State Prize 65.

Compositions: Operas *Death of Danton* (Büchner), *The Trial* (Kafka), *Der Zerrissene* (Nestroy), *Visit of the Old Lady* (Dürrenmatt), five Ballets and various other works for orchestra including a piano and a violin concerto.

Vienna III, Marokkanergasse 11, Austria.

Telephone: 731457.

Einem, Herbert Günter von, DR. PHIL.; German art historian; b. 16 Feb. 1905; ed. High Schools in Erfurt and Göttingen, and Univs. of Göttingen, Berlin and Munich.

Assistant at Landesmuseum, Hanover 29-36; Art History studies, Göttingen 36; Prof. of Art History, Greifswald Univ. 43-46, Univ. of Frankfurt 46-47, Univ. of Bonn 47-70, Emer. 70-; mem. Acad. of Sciences of North Rhine-Westphalia, Acad. of Science and Literature, Mainz; Corresp. mem. Acad. of Sciences, Göttingen, Acad. of Sciences, Munich, German Archaeological Inst.; Foreign mem. Royal Swedish Acad.; Hon. mem. Int. Cttee. on History of Art; Commendatore al Merito della Repubblica Italiana.
Publs. *Karl Ludwig Fernow* 35, *Caspar David Friedrich* 38, 3rd edn. 50, *Beiträge zu Goethes Kunstauffassung* 56, *Michelangelo* 59, *Stil und Überlieferung* 71, *Goethe-Studien* 71.
Home: 34 Göttingen-Geismar, Charlotten-burgerstrasse 19, App. C 912, Federal Republic of Germany.

Eisen, Herman N(athaniel), A.B., M.D.; American immunologist and microbiologist; b. 15 Oct. 1918, Brooklyn, N.Y.; s. of Joseph M. Eisen and Lena M. (Karush) Eisen; m. Natalie Aronson 1948; three s. two d.; ed. New York Univ.
Professor of Medicine (Dermatology), Washington Univ., St. Louis 55-61, Prof. of Microbiology and Head of Dept. 61-73; Prof. of Immunology, Mass. Inst. of Technology 73-; Harvey Lecturer 64; Consultant to Surgeons-Gen. of Public Health Service, Dept. of the Army; Chair. Study Section for Allergy and Immunology, Nat. Insts. of Health 64-68; mem. editorial boards of Journal of Immunology, Bacteriological Reviews, Physiological Reviews, Proceedings of the Nat. Acad. of Sciences of U.S.A., American Soc. for Clinical Investigation (Vice-Pres. 63-64), American Asscn. of Immunologists (Pres. 68-69), American Soc. for Biological Chemists, American Assch. of Physicians, Nat. Acad. of Sciences, American Acad. of Arts and Sciences; New York Univ. Medical Science Achievement Award 68.
Leisure interests: reading, tennis.
Publs. *Methods in Medical Research* Vol. 10 (Editor) 64, *Microbiology* (co-Author) 67, *Immunology* 74; about 100 scientific articles.
E17-128 Center for Cancer Research, Massachusetts Institute of Technology, Cambridge, Mass. 02139; Home: 9 Homestead Street, Waban, Mass., U.S.A. Telephone: 617-253-6406.

Eisenhower, John Sheldon Doud, B.S., M.A.; American author and diplomatist; b. 3 Aug. 1922, Denver, Colo.; s. of late Gen. Dwight D. Eisenhower and Mamie Doud Eisenhower; m. Barbara Jean Thompson 1947; one s. three d.; ed. Stadium High School, Tacoma, Wash., U.S. Military Acad., West Point, Columbia Univ. and Armored Advance Course and General Staff Coll., U.S. Army.
Assigned to First Army, Second World War; Instructor in English, U.S. Mil. Acad., West Point 48-51; served as Battalion Operations Officer, Div. Asst. Operations Officer and Div. Intelligence Officer, Korea; C.O. 1st Battalion, 30th Infantry 53-54; Instructor in Infantry Tactics, Engineer School, Fort Belvoir 55-57; Joint War Plans Div., Army Staff, Pentagon 57-58; Asst. Staff Sec. in White House 58-61; researcher and editor on Eisenhower memoirs *The White House Years*; Amb. to Belgium 69-71; Consultant to President Nixon; Chair. Interagency Classification Review Cttee. 73; Brig.-Gen. U.S. Army Reserve 74; mem. Nat. Archives Advisory Cttee. 74-; Chair. Pres.'s Advisory Cttee. on Refugees 75; Legion of Merit, Bronze Star, Army Commendation Ribbon, Combat Infantry Badge, Grand Cross, Order of the Crown (Belgium).
Leisure interests: golf and military history.
Publs. *The Bitter Woods* 69, *Strictly Personal* 74.
Valley Forge, Pa. 19481, U.S.A.

Eisenhower, Dr. Milton Stover; American public official and educationist; b. 15 Sept. 1899, Abilene,

Kan.; s. of David J. Eisenhower and Ida Stover Eisenhower; brother of late Dwight D. Eisenhower; m. Helen Elsie Eakin 1927 (deceased); one s. one d.; ed. Kansas State Univ. and Univ. of Edinburgh, Scotland.
Vice-Consul, Edinburgh 24-26; Dir. of Information U.S. Dept. of Agriculture 28-41; Land Use Co-ordinator 37-42; Pres. Kansas State Univ. 43-50; Pres. Pa. State Univ. 50-56; Pres. The Johns Hopkins Univ. 56-67, 71-72; Special Amb. and Personal Rep. of Pres. of U.S. on Latin American Affairs 53, 57, 59, 60; Chair. President's Comm. to Examine Violence June 68-Dec. 69; hon. degrees many univs. U.S. and abroad; decorations from Colombia, Bolivia, Venezuela, Korea, Ecuador, Mexico and Chile.
Leisure interests: painting, music, swimming, English croquet, reading.
Publs. *The Wine is Bitter* 63, *The President is Calling* 74.
4545 North Charles Street, Baltimore, Md. 21210, U.S.A. Telephone: 301-366-3300.

Eisenstadt, Shmuel N., M.A., PH.D.; Israeli professor of sociology; b. 10 Sept. 1923, Warsaw, Poland; s. of Michael Eisenstadt and Rosa Boruchin; m. Shulamit Yaroshevski 1948; two s. one d.; ed. Hebrew Univ., Jerusalem and London School of Econs. and Political Science.
Chairman, Dept. of Sociology, Hebrew Univ., Jerusalem 51-68, Prof. of Sociology 59-, Dean, Faculty of Social Sciences 66-68; Visiting Prof., Univ. of Oslo 58, Univ. of Chicago 60, Harvard Univ. 66, 68-69, Michigan 70, Chicago 71, Harvard 75; Carnegie Visiting Prof., Mass. Inst. of Technology 62-63; Hon. Fellow, London School of Econs.; Foreign Fellow American Anthropological Asscn.; Fellow Netherlands Inst. of Advanced Studies 73; mem. Israel Acad. of Sciences and Humanities, Int. Sociological Soc., American Sociological Asscn.; Foreign mem. American Philosophical Soc.; Foreign Hon. mem. American Acad. of Arts and Sciences; McIver Award, American Sociological Asscn. 64, Rothschild Prize in the Social Sciences 69, Israel Prize in the Social Sciences 73.
Publs. *The Absorption of Immigrants* 54, *From Generation to Generation* 56, *Essays on Sociological Aspects of Economical and Political Development* 61, *The Political Systems of Empires* 63, *Essays on Comparative Institutions* 65, *Modernization, Protest and Change* 66, *Israeli Society* 68, *The Protestant Ethic and Modernization* 68, *Political Sociology of Modernization* (in Japanese) 68, *Comparative Perceptives on Social Change* (editor) 68, *Charisma and Institution Building: Selections from Max Weber* (editor) 68, *Modernizicão e Mudança Social* 69, *Political Sociology* (editor) 70, *Social Differentiation and Stratification* 71, *Tradition, Change and Modernity* 73, *Collection of Essays in Spanish* 73, *Post-traditional Societies* (editor) 74.
The Hebrew University, Jerusalem; Home: Rechov Radak 30, Jerusalem, Israel.
Telephone: 32467.

Eisenstaedt, Alfred; American photographer; b. 6 Dec. 1898, Dirschau, Germany; s. of Joseph and Regina Eisenstaedt; m. Kathy Eisenstaedt (died 1972); ed. Hohenzollern Gymnasium Berlin.
Emigrated to U.S.A. 35; with Time Inc. 36-, staff photographer *Life* magazine 36-72, *People* magazine 72-; freelance work including advertising, promotion and giving lectures throughout U.S.A.; Photographer of the Year 51, Culture Prize in Photography (German Soc. of Photographers), Int. Understanding Award 67, Clifton Edom Award, Univ. of Missouri Joseph Sprague Award, and many others.
Leisure interests: music, hiking, greenhouse gardening.
Publs. *Witness to our Time, Martha's Vineyard, The Eye of Eisenstaedt, Witness to Nature, Wimbledon: A Celebration, People.*

Time Inc., Time & Life Building, Room 2850, Rockefeller Center, New York, N.Y. 10020, U.S.A.
Telephone: (212) 556-2342.

Eisner, Thomas, B.A., PH.D.; American professor of biology; b. 25 June 1929, Berlin, Germany; s. of Hans E. Eisner and Margarete Heil-Eisner; m. Maria L. R. Löbell 1952; three d.; ed. High School and Preparatory School, Montevideo, Uruguay, Champlain Coll., Plattsburgh, N.Y. and Harvard Univ.
Research Fellow in Biology, Harvard Univ. 55-57; Asst. Prof. of Biology, Cornell Univ. 57-62, Assoc. Prof. 62-65, Prof. of Biology 65-; Lalor Fellow 54-55, Guggenheim Fellow 64-65, 72-73; Dir. Nat. Audubon Soc. 70-; Fellow, Amer. Acad. of Arts and Sciences, Royal Acad. of Arts and Sciences, Animal Behaviour Soc.; mem. Nat. Acad. of Sciences 69, Nat. Council for Nature Conservancy 69; Newcomb-Cleveland Prize (with E. O. Wilson) of A.A.A.S. 67, Founders Memorial Award of Entomological Soc. of America 69, Outstanding Teacher Award, Cornell Univ. 73.
Leisure interests: harpsichord, piano, conservation.
Publs. Over 100 technical papers and two books on animal behaviour, chemical ecology, comparative physiology, chemical communication in animals.
Section of Neurobiology and Behaviour, Division of Biological Sciences, Cornell University, Ithaca, N.Y. 14850, U.S.A.
Telephone: 607-256-4464.

Ejbye-Ernst, Arne; Danish journalist and editor; b. 16 Dec. 1927, Århus; s. of Niels Ejbye-Ernst and Agnete Ejbye-Ernst (née Steckhahn); m. Birgit Møller 1951; two s.; ed. Marselisborg Gymnasium, and Danish Coll. of Journalism.
Journalist Danish Labour Press 49-56; Editor Ny Tid, Aalborg 56-59; Editor-in-Chief Aktuelt, Copenhagen 59-64, Editor-in-Chief Politiken, Copenhagen 66-71; Editor of the publishers' magazine 72-; Lecturer and Leader, Danish Coll. of Journalism, Aarhus 64-66; Adviser to Danish Newspaper Asscn. 64-66; Chair. Copenhagen Editors' Soc. 62-64, 67-69; Chief Principal of Inst. for Press Research 71; Dean of School of Journalism 74.
Publ. Masscommunication as Business 73, Study of Local Monopoly Press: "Aalborg Stiftstidende" in the Local Community 75.
Office: Halmstadgade 11, 8100 Aarhus N, Denmark.
Telephone: 06-161122.

Ejoor, Maj-Gen. David Akpode; Nigerian Army Chief of Staff 72-75; see The International Who's Who 1975-76.

Ekangaki, Nzo; Cameroonian politician; b. 22 March 1934, Nguti; ed. Bali Coll., Hope Waddle Training Inst., Calabar, Nigeria and Univs. of Ibadan, Nigeria, London, Oxford and Bonn.
Served in several posts in Cameroon admin. 59-60; Deputy Minister of Foreign Affairs 62-64; Minister of Public Health and Population 64-65, of Labour and Social Welfare 65-72; Sec.-Gen. Org. of African Unity 72-74; Sec.-Gen. Kamerun Nat. Democratic Party (KNDP) 62-66; mem. of Political Bureau, Cameroon Nat. Union Party (CNU) 66-; mem. Parl. S. Cameroon 61-62, mem. first Nat. Federal Assembly 62-65, 65-70; del. to many int. confs., to WHO Conf., Geneva 64, to several Int. Labour Confs.; rep. on many missions abroad.
c/o Cameroon National Union Party, Yaoundé, Cameroon.

Eke, Abudu Yesufu, M.A., B.SC.; Nigerian educational administrator; b. 7 Sept. 1923, Benin City; s. of Yesufu O. and Barikisu A. Eke; m. Clara Noyogiere Eke 1956; three s. three d.; ed. Higher Coll., Yaba, Univ. Coll., Ibadan and Sidney Sussex Coll., Cambridge.
Various posts in Public Relations Dept. 48-54; Information Officer, Fed. Information Services 54-55; Asst.

Registrar, Univ. Coll., Ibadan 55-58; Principal Information Officer, subsequently Chief Information Officer, Western Nigeria Information Services 59-61; Registrar, Univ. of Ife 61-62; Commr. for Information, W. Region Govt. June-Aug. 62; Registrar, Univ. of Lagos 62-71; Commr. for Finance and Economic Development, Midwest State Govt. 67-71; Fed. Commr. for Educ. 71-74; Educ. and Econ. Consultant 75-; Hon. LL.D.
Publs. History of Group Divergence in Physical Anthropology, One Nigeria (one-act play), Problems of Decolonization in Africa, The Future of the OAU, A New Policy on Education in Nigeria, The Eradication of Illiteracy in Nigeria.
28A Cameron Road, Ikoyi, Lagos, Nigeria.
Telephone: 24029 (Home).

Eker, Bjarne Reidar, DR. MED.; Norwegian doctor; b. 26 Nov. 1903, Oslo, Norway; m. 1953; ed. Universitet i Oslo.
Scientific Asst., Anatomy Inst., Oslo Univ. 32-36; Pathologist, Univ. Hospital 36-39; Chief Pathologist, Norwegian Radium Hospital 39-, Dir. 47-; Dir. Norsk Hydros Inst. of Cancer Research; Pres. Norwegian Cancer Soc. 50-66; Chair. Radiation Hygiene Advisory Council 56-.
Leisure interests: fishing, skiing.
Publs. about 50 scientific publications in the field of genetics, radiobiology and tumour pathology.
The Norwegian Radium Hospital, Montebello, Oslo 3, Norway.

Ekloh, Herbert H.; German retail executive; b. 3 March 1905, Bochum; s. of Albrecht Ekloh and Grete Ekloh (née Küderling); ed. High School.
Retailer 28-; opened first self-service store in Europe 38; opened first European Supermarket—Rheinlandhalle, Cologne 57; Owner Ekloh Food Chain 28-59; Dir. Kaufhof AG, Cologne 35-40; Pres. Görlitzer AG, Dresden 41-45; Pres. Supermercados Ekloh, Havana, Cuba 54-57; Pres. Hussel AG 63-69, Deputy Chair. 70-73, Chair. 74-; Hon. Consul for Mexico in Bonn 73-; Pres. German Aero Club Section for North Rhine-Westphalia 64-70.
Leisure interest: flying.
Oberländer Ufer 94, 5 Cologne, Federal Republic of Germany.
Telephone: 02331-3901 (Office); 0221-384035 (Home).

Eklund, (Arne) Sigvard, D.S.; Swedish nuclear physicist; b. 19 June 1911, Kiruna; s. of Severin Eklund and Vilhelmina Pettersson; m. Anna-Greta Johansson 1941; one s. two d.; ed. Univ. of Uppsala.
Nobel Inst. for Physics 37-45; Asst. Prof. of Nuclear Physics, Royal Inst. of Technology, Stockholm 46; Senior Scientist, Research Inst. for Nat. Defence, Stockholm 46-50; Dir. of Research AB Atomenergi, Stockholm 50-56, Deputy to Man. Dir. 50-61, Dir. of Reactor Devt. Div. 57-61; Sec.-Gen. Second UN Conf. on Peaceful Uses of Atomic Energy 58; Dir.-Gen. Int. Atomic Energy Agency (IAEA) Dec. 61-; mem. Royal Swedish Acad. of Eng. Sciences 53, Royal Swedish Acad. of Sciences 72; Fellow, American Nuclear Soc. 61; Hon. mem. British Nuclear Eng. Soc. 63; Atoms for Peace Award 68; Gold Medal, Province of Vienna 71; Dr. h.c. (Graz Univ.) 68, (Acad. Mining and Metallurgy, Cracow, Poland) 71, (Bucharest Univ., Romania) 71, (Chalmers Inst. of Tech., Gothenburg, Sweden) 74.
International Atomic Energy Agency, Kaerntnerring, A-1010, Vienna I; Home: Krapfenwaldgasse 48, 1190 Vienna, Austria.
Telephone: 52-45-11 (Office); 32-24-24 (Home).

Ekman, Wilhelm; Swedish steel executive; b. 13 Nov. 1912, Korsnäs; s. of Wilhelm Ekman and Martha Gerdts; m. Birgitta Lübeck 1940; two s. three d.; ed. Royal Inst. of Technology, Stockholm.
Blast Furnace and Open Hearth Engineer, Fagersta Bruks AB 37-43, Man. 43-51; Technical Dir. Steel-

works, Uddeholms AB 52-56, Man. Dir. 56, Pres. -75; Pres. Tuolluvaara Gruv AB; mem. Board of Swedish Employers' Confederation, Fed. of Swedish Industries (Pres. 65-66), Skandinaviska Enskilda Banken; Pres. Swedish Ironmasters' Asscn., Scandinaviska Enskilda Banken; Commdr. 1st Class, Royal Order of Vasa.
Leisure interests: skiing, tennis.
Bruksdisponent Wilhelm Ekman, Uddeholms AB, 68305 Hagfors, Sweden.
Telephone: 0563-11400.

Ekwensi, Cyprian; Nigerian pharmacist and writer; b. 26 Sept. 1921, Minna, Northern Nigeria; ed. Achimota Coll., Ghana, School of Forestry, Ibadan and Univ. of London.
Lecturer in Biology, Chem. and English, Igbobi Coll., Lagos 47-49; Lecturer, School of Pharmacy, Lagos 49-56; Pharmacist, Nigerian Medical Service 56; Head of Features, Nigerian Broadcasting Corpn. 56-61; Dir. of Information, Fed. Ministry of Information, Lagos 61-66; Dir. of Information Services, Enugu 66; Chair. East Cen. State Library Board, Enugu 71-; Dir. Reveille Printing and Publishing Co. Ltd., East Cen. State; Visiting lecturer, Iowa Univ.; mem. Soc. of Nigerian Authors, Inst. Public Relations Nigeria and U.K.; Dag Hammarskjöld Int. Award for Literary Merit 68.
Leisure interests: photography, Adire Tie-Die.
Publs. *When Love Whispers, Ikolo the Wrestler 47, The Leopard's Claw 50, People of the City 54, Passport of Mallam Ilia, The Drummer Boy 60, Jagua Nana 61, Burning Grass, An African Night's Entertainment, Yaba Round about Murder 62, Beautiful Feathers 63, Great Elephant Bird, Rainmaker 65, Lokotown, Juju Rock, Trouble in Form VI, Iska, Boa Suitor 66, Coal Camp Boy 73, Samankwe in the Strange Forest 74, Samankwe and the Highway Robbers, Restless City, Christmas Gold 75.*
P.O. Box 317, Enugu, Nigeria; Ia. University, Ia. City, Ia. 52242, U.S.A.
Telephone: Enugu 3149.

Elahi Chaudhri, Fazal, B.SC., M.A.(ECONS.), LL.B.; Pakistani politician; b. 1904, Punjab Province; ed. Muslim Univ., Aligarh.
Joined Gujarat District Bar 29; mem. Gujarat District Board 31-53; Head District Muslim League 44; mem. Punjab Legislative Assembly 45-56; Parl. Sec. Punjab Govt., later Minister for Educ. and Health 47-56; Speaker W. Pakistan Assembly 56-58; mem. Nat. Assembly 62-, Deputy Speaker 65-70, Speaker 71-73; Pres. of Pakistan Aug. 73-.
The Presidency, Rawalpindi, Pakistan.

Elath, Eliahu, B.A., M.A., PH.D.; b. 30 July 1903, Snowsk, Russia; s. of Menahem and Rivka Epstein; m. Zehava Zalel 1931; ed. Hebrew Univ. of Jerusalem and American Univ. of Beirut.
Jewish Agency 34; Jewish Agency Observer to San Francisco Conf. 45; Head of Jewish Agency's Political Office in Washington, D.C. and Special Representative of Provisional Council of Govt. of Israel 48; Israel Ambassador to U.S.A. 48-50; Minister to Great Britain 50-52, Ambassador 52-59; Adviser, Ministry of Foreign Affairs 59-60; Pres. Hebrew Univ., Jerusalem 61-67; Pres. Israel Oriental Soc.; Vice-Pres. Jewish Colonization Asscn. (ICA). Hon. Ph.D.; Chair. Afro-Asian Inst., Tel-Aviv.
Leisure interests: music and reading.
Publs. *Bedouin, their Life and Manners 34, Trans-Jordan 35, Israel and her Neighbours 59, San Francisco Diary 71, Britain's Routes to India 71, Zionism and the Arabs 74.*
17 Bialik Street, Beth Hakerem, Jerusalem, Israel.
Telephone: 524615.

Elazar, Lieut.-Gen. David; Israeli army officer; b. 1925, Yugoslavia; m.; two s. one d.; ed. Hebrew Univ.

Went to Israel 40; entered Palmach 46; served in War of Liberation, Sinai Campaign; Commdr. Armoured Corps 61; Officer-in-Charge, Northern Command 64; commanded forces of Northern Command during six-day War June 67; Chief, Gen. Staff Branch 69; Chief of Staff and C.-in-C. Israeli Army 71-74; Pres., Chair. of Board, ZIM (Israel Navigation Co. Ltd.) 74-.
[*Died 14 April 1976.*]

Eldin, Gérard; French international civil servant; b. 21 March 1927, Cannes; s. of Charles and Elise Eldin; m. Marie-Cécile Bergerot 1960; two s. two d.; ed. Univ. d'Aix-en-Provence and Ecole Nationale d'Administration.
Inspector of Finances 54-58; served in the Treasury 58-63; Adviser to Minister of Finance and Econ. Affairs 63-65; Deputy Dir. Dept. of Planning 65-70; Deputy Sec.-Gen. OECD 70-; Chevalier, Ordre Nat. du Mérite.
Leisure interests: tennis, music, local history, archaeology.
63 bis rue de Varenne, 75007 Paris, France.
Telephone: 551-51-86.

Eldjárn, Dr. Kristján, M.A., PH.D.; Icelandic academic and politician; b. 6 Dec. 1916, Tjorn, Iceland; ed. Univ. of Copenhagen, Univ. of Iceland.
Assistant, Nat. Museum of Iceland 45-47; Curator 47-68; mem. Council of Archaeological Soc. of Iceland 45-; mem. Council of Icelandic Literary Soc. 61-68; mem. Perm. Comm. of Union Internationale des Sciences Préhistoriques et Protohistoriques 62-; Chair. Cttee. on Icelandic Place Names; mem. Icelandic Soc. of Arts and Sciences 50-; Pres. of Iceland 68-.
Publs. *The ruins of Stong 47, Twelve articles on archaeological finds in Iceland 48, The Cathedral of Holar 50, The Church at Grof, Archaeological finds from Pagan Times in Iceland, History of the National Museum 62;* editor of *Journal of Archaeological Society 49-.*
Office of the President, Reykjavík, Iceland.

Eley, Sir Geoffrey (Cecil Ryves), C.B.E.; British company director; b. 18 July 1904, East Bergholt, Suffolk; s. of Charles Eley; m. Penelope Hughes Wake-Walker 1937; two s. two d.; ed. Eton, Trinity Coll., Cambridge and Harvard Univ.
On editorial staff of *Financial News* 26-28; int. banking and finance in England, France, Switzerland and U.S.A. 28-32; London Man. of Post and Flagg N.Y. 32-39; Naval Intelligence Div. Admiralty 39-40; Capital Issues Cttee. 40-41; Dir. of Contracts Min. of Supply 41-46; Dir. of Overseas Disposals 46-47; Chair. British Drug Houses Ltd. 48-65, Brush Group Ltd. 53-58, Richard Thomas and Baldwins Ltd. 59-64; mem. London Electricity Board 48-58; Dir. Bank of England 49-66; High Sheriff of Greater London 66-67; Chair. Thomas Tilling & Co. Ltd., Heinemann Group of Publishers Ltd.; Vice-Chair. BOC Int. Ltd. (fmrly. British Oxygen Ltd.); Deputy Chair. British Bank of the Middle East; Dir. Equity and Law Assurance Soc.; Dir. Airco Inc.; mem. Council Royal U.K. Benevolent Asscn.; Vice-Pres. Middle East Asscn.
Leisure interests: gardening, the arts, foreign travel.
27 Wynnstay Gardens, Allen Street, London, W8 6UR, England.
Telephone: 01-748-2020.

Elfving, Gösta; Swedish journalist and politician; b. 2 Sept. 1908, Ludvika; s. of Oscar E. Signe Jonsson-Elfving; m. A. L. Ljungkvist 1933; one d.
On staff of *Värmlands Folkblad* 25; Editor of same 34-40; Editor-in-Chief *Västgöta-Demokraten* Borås 40-44; Editor-in-Chief *Morgon-Tidningen* Stockholm (leading Swedish Labour daily) 44-57; mem. Exec. Social Democratic Party 44-58, State Youth Cttee. 39-51, State Tourist Cttee. 48-51, of Parl. 54-57; Chair. or

mem of several Royal Comms.; Gov. Kopparbergs Län) 57-73.
Leisure interest: photography.
Uppsala, Sweden.

Elias, Taslim Olawale, Q.C., B.A., LL.M., PH.D., LL.D.; Nigerian lawyer and politician; b. 11 Nov. 1914; ed. C.M.S. Grammar School, Lagos, Igboli Coll., Lagos, Univ. Coll., London, and Inst. of Advanced Legal Studies, London.
Yarborough Anderson Scholar of Inner Temple 46-49; called to the Bar 47; Simon Research Fellow, Univ. of Manchester 51-53; Oppenheim Research Fellow, Inst. of Commonwealth Studies, Nuffield Coll. and Queen Elizabeth House, Oxford 54-60; Visiting Prof. in Political Science, Delhi Univ. 56; mem. Del. to Nigerian Constitutional Conf., London 58; Fed. Attorney-Gen. and Minister of Justice, Nigeria 60-66, Attorney-Gen. Oct. 66-71, mem. Federal Exec. Council 66-71; Commr. for Justice June 67-71, Chief Justice of Supreme Court 72-75; mem. Int. Court of Justice Feb. 76-; mem. UN Int. Law Comm. 61-; mem. Governing Council, Univ. of Nigeria 59-66; Gov. School of Oriental and African Studies, London Univ. 58-61; Chair. UN Cttee. of Constitutional Experts to draft Congo Constitution 61, 62; Prof. of Law and Dean of Faculty of Law, Univ. of Lagos, Nigeria 66-73; Chair. Governing Council, Nigerian Inst. of Int. Affairs 72-; Chair. Cttee. of UN Conf. on Law of Treaties 68, 69; Pres. Nigerian Soc. of Int. Law; Chair. African Inst. of Int. Law; Assoc. mem. Inst. of Int. Law 69-; Hon. LL.D. (Dakar), D.Litt. (Ibadan) 69.
Publs. *Nigerian Land Law and Custom* 51, *Nigerian Legal System* 54, *Ghana and Sierra Leone: Development of their Laws and Constitutions* 62, *British Colonial Law: A Comparative Study* 62, *Government and Politics in Africa* 2nd ed. 63, *Nature of African Customary Law* 2nd edn. 62, *Nigeria: Development of its Laws and Constitution* 65; Co-author of *British Legal Papers* 58, *International Law in a Changing World* 63, *Sovereignty Within the Law* 65, *African Law: Adaptation and Development* 65, *Law, Justice and Equity* 67, *Nigerian Press Law* 69, *Nigerian Prison System* 68, many articles.
20 Ozumba Mbadiwe, Victoria Island, Lagos, Nigeria.
Telephone: 27549.

Elias IV Moawad; Arab ecclesiastic; b. 1914, Arsoun, Metn, Lebanon; ed. Theological Inst. of Halki, Instanbul.
Greek Orthodox Patriach of Antioch and the Whole Orient Sept. 70-.
P.O. Box 9, Damascus, Syria.
Telephone: 116329-110329

Eliel, Ernest L., M.SC., PH.D.; American professor of chemistry; b. 28 Dec. 1921, Cologne, Germany; s. of Oskar Eliel and Luise Tietz; m. Eva Schwarz 1949; two d.; ed. Univs. of Edinburgh, Havana and Illinois.
Assistant, Laboratorios Vieta-Plasencia 43-46; Instructor, Univ. of Notre Dame 48-50, Asst. Prof. 50-53 Assoc. Prof. 53-60, Prof. 60-72, Head Dept. of Chem. 64-66; W. R. Kenan, Jr. Prof. of Chem., Univ. of N. Carolina, Chapel Hill 72-; Summer Consultant, Standard Oil of Indiana Inc. 56; Nat. Science Foundation Senior Postdoctoral Fellow, Harvard Univ. 58, Calif. Inst. of Technology 58-59, Eidgenössische Technische Hochschule, Zurich 67-68; Guggenheim Fellow 75-76; mem. Nat. Acad. of Sciences; Lavoisier Medal 68 and other awards.
Leisure interests: photography, travel, swimming, hiking.
Publs. *Stereochemistry of Carbon Compounds* 62, *Conformational Analysis* (co-author) 65, *Elements of Stereochemistry* 69 and over 200 articles in professional journals; co-editor: *Topics in Stereochemistry* 67-.

Department of Chemistry, University of North Carolina, Chapel Hill, N.C. 27514; Home: 725 Kenmore Road, Chapel Hill, N.C. 27514, U.S.A.
Telephone: 919-933-6197 (Office); 919-929-7966 (Home).

Eliot, Martha May, A.B., M.D.; American pediatrician; b. 7 April 1891; ed. Radcliffe Coll. and Johns Hopkins School of Medicine.
Instr. in Pediatrics Yale Univ. School of Medicine 21-27, Asst. Clinical Prof. 27-32, Associate Clinical Prof. 32-35, Lecturer 35-49; attending pediatrician New Haven Hospital and Dispensary 23-34; Dir. Div. Child and Maternal Health, U.S. Children's Bureau 24-34, Asst. Chief 34-41, Assoc. Chief 41-49; Asst. Dir.-Gen. WHO 49-51; Chief U.S. Children's Bureau, Washington, D.C. 51-56; Prof. of Maternal and Child Health, Harvard School of Public Health 57-60, Emer. 60-; U.S. Rep. Exec. Board UN Children's Fund 52-57; Consultant in Maternal and Child Health to WHO 60-61.
21 Francis Avenue, Cambridge, Mass. 02138, U.S.A.

Eliseev, Alexey Stanislavovich; Soviet cosmonaut; b. 13 July 1934; ed. Moscow Higher Technical School and Moscow Physical-Technical Inst.
Engineer-designer 62-64; joined cosmonaut training unit 66; mem. C.P.S.U. 67-; engineer of spacecraft *Soyuz 5* which formed first manned orbital station with *Soyuz 4* Jan. 69; engineer of *Soyuz 8* which accomplished a group flight together with *Soyuz 6* and *Soyuz 7*; Engineer of *Soyuz 10* April 71; Hero of Soviet Union (twice), Gold Star (twice), Order of Lenin (twice), Pilot-Cosmonaut of U.S.S.R., K. Tsiolkovsky Gold Medal of U.S.S.R. Acad. of Sciences, Y. A. Gagarin Gold Medal of F.A.I. and other awards.
Zvezdny Gorodok, Moscow, U.S.S.R.

Eliseev, Georgy Ivanovich; Soviet sports administrator; b. 1913; ed. Leningrad Builders' School and Leningrad Inst. of Physical Culture.
Technician, then building engineer 35-37; Chief Training Sports Dept., then Asst. Chair. Regional Council Sporting Soc. *Burevestnik*, Leningrad 37-39; mem. C.P.S.U. 44; engineer for sporting constructions, Regional Council Sporting Soc. *Burevestnik*, Leningrad 47-49; Chair. Central Council Sporting Soc. *Burevestnik* 49-53, 55-56, 62-; Section Chief of Physical Culture and Sports Dept. of U.S.S.R. Central Council of Trade Unions 53-55, Chief 56-61; Pres. U.S.S.R. Council Voluntary Sporting Socs. of Trade Unions 61-; Deputy Pres. Central Council U.S.S.R. Union of Sporting Socs. and Orgs. 65-; U.S.S.R. Cttee. for Sports and Physical Culture 68-; Order Red Banner (twice), Alexander Nevsky, Great Patriotic War, Red Star, Red Banner of Labour.
U.S.S.R. Committee for Physical Culture and Sports, 4 Skatertny pereulok, Moscow, U.S.S.R.

Elistratov, Pyotr Matveyevich; Soviet politician; b. 1917; ed. Higher Party School of the Central Cttee., C.P. Ukraine.
Komsomol and party work 37-41; mem. C.P.S.U. 39-; Sec., then First Sec. Vladivostok City Cttee., Komsomol 41-42; Third Sec. Vladivostok City Cttee. C.P.S.U. 42-43; Soviet army service 43-46; Second Sec. Odessa, then First Sec. Kherson Regional Cttee., Komsomol Ukraine 46-49; First Sec. Kakhovka City Cttee. C.P. Ukraine 52-54; Sec., Second Sec., then First Sec. Kherson Regional Cttee. C.P. Ukraine 54-61; Second Sec. Central Cttee. C.P. Azerbaijan 61-68; First Sec. Mordovian Regional Cttee. C.P.S.U. 68-71; mem. Cen. Auditing Comm. C.P.S.U. 61-66; Candidate mem. C.P.S.U. Cen. Cttee. 66-71; Ministry of Foreign Affairs 71-; Deputy to U.S.S.R. Supreme Soviet 58-; mem. Comm. for Legislative Proposals, Soviet of Union.
Ministry of Foreign Affairs, 32-34 Smolenskaya-Sennaya ploschchad, Moscow, U.S.S.R.

Elizabeth II; Queen of Great Britain and Northern Ireland and of her other Realms and Territories (*see under Reigning Royal Families at front of book for full titles*); b. 21 April 1926.
Succeeded to the Throne following death of her father, George VI, 6 Feb. 1952; married, Nov. 1947, H.R.H. the Prince Philip, Duke of Edinburgh, b. 10 June 1921; children: Prince Charles Philip Arthur George, Prince of Wales (heir apparent), b. 14 Nov. 1948; Princess Anne Elizabeth Alice Louise, Mrs. Mark Phillips, b. 15 Aug. 1950; Prince Andrew Albert Christian Edward, b. 19 Feb. 1960; Prince Edward Antony Richard Louis, b. 10 March 1964.
Buckingham Palace, London; Windsor Castle, Berkshire, England; Balmoral Castle, Aberdeenshire, Scotland; Sandringham, Norfolk, England.

Elizabeth Angela Marguerite; H.M. Queen Elizabeth the Queen Mother, Lady of the Order of the Garter, Lady of the Order of the Thistle, C.I., G.C.V.O., G.B.E.; member of the British Royal Family; b. 4 Aug. 1900; m. 1923 H.R.H. The Duke of York, later H.M. King George VI (died 1952); reigned as Queen 36-52.
Clarence House, London, S.W.1; Royal Lodge, Windsor Great Park, Berks., England; Castle of Mey, Caithness, Scotland.

Elkes, Joel, M.B., CH.B., M.D.; American physician; b. 12 Nov. 1913; Koenigsberg, Germany; s. of Elkanan and Miriam Elkes; m. 1st Dr. Charmian Bourne 1943; one d.; m. 2nd Josephine Rhodes 75; ed. Univ. of London and Birmingham Medical School, England.
Sir Halley Stuart Research Fellow in Pharmacology, Univ. of Birmingham 42-45, Lecturer in Pharmacology 45-48, Senior Lecturer and Act. Dir. Dept. of Pharmacology 48-50, Prof. and Chair. Dept. of Experimental Psychiatry 51-57; Consultant Psychiatrist, Birmingham Hospitals and Scientific Dir. Birmingham Regional Psychiatric Early Treatment Centre 53-57; Chief, Clinical Neuropharmacology Research Centre, Nat. Inst. of Mental Health (U.S. Nat. Insts. of Health) 57-63; Dir. of Behavior and Clinical Studies Center, St. Elizabeth's Hospital 57-63, Clinical Prof. of Psychiatry, George Washington Univ. School of Medicine 57-63; Henry Phipps Prof. and Dir. Dept. of Psychiatry and Behavioral Sciences, The Johns Hopkins Univ. School of Medicine, Psychiatrist-in-Chief, The Johns Hopkins Hospital 63-73; Distinguished Service Prof. The Johns Hopkins Univ. 73-; Samuel McLaughlin Visiting Prof.-in-Residence, McMaster Univ., Ont. 75; Editor *Psychopharmacologia*, Assoc. Editor *Journal of Psychiatric Research*; Org. Sec. 1st Int. Neurochemical Symposium; fmr. mem. Central Council Int. Brain Research Org. Research Cttee.; mem. Mental Health Research Fund; Fellow, American Acad. of Arts and Sciences, American Psych. Asscn., American Coll. of Psychiatry, Royal Coll. of Psychiatry, U.K., American Coll. Neuropsychopharmacology; Benjamin Franklin Fellow, Royal Soc. Arts; Harvey Lecturer 62, Salmon Lecturer 64; First Pres. Amer. Coll. of Neuropsychopharmacology; Pres. Amer. Psychopathological Asscn. 68, etc.
Leisure interests: painting, clubs.
Publs. *Effects of Psychosomimetic Drugs in Animals and Man* 56, *Drug Effects in Relation to Reactor Specificity within the Brain* 58, *Ataractic and Hallucinogenic Drugs in Psychiatry* 58, *Psychopharmacology: The Need for some Points of Reference* 59, *Schizophrenic Disorder in Relation to Levels of Neural Organisation: The Need for Some Conceptual Points of Reference* 61, *Subjective and Objective Observation in Psychiatry* 62, *Behavioral Pharmacology in relation to Psychiatry* 67.
Hopkins House, 110 West 39th Street, Baltimore 17021210, Md., U.S.A.
Telephone: 366-1930.

Elkins, Sir Anthony Joseph, Kt., C.B.E.; British business executive; b. 30 May 1904; s. of late Dr. and Mrs. F. A. Elkins; m. 1st Mabel Brenda Barker 1930 (deceased), three s. one d.; m. 2nd Ines Erna Miller 1944 (dissolved); m. 3rd Nora Christiane Elliot 1969; ed. Haileybury Coll.
Honorary Presidency Magistrate, Bombay 28; mem. Advisory Cttee. E. India and E. Bengal Railways 38-40; Controller of Supplies, Bengal Circle, Dept. of Supply, India 41-45; Chair. Darjeeling Himalayan Railway 45-47; Chair. Gillanders Arbuthnot & Co. Ltd., Calcutta 45-54; Chair. Bryant and May Ltd. 55-64; Dep. Chair. British Match Corpn. 55-64, Chair. 64-72; Chair. Airscrew-Weyroc Ltd. 59-64; Chair. Gestetner Ltd. 64-72; Vice-Chair. and Dir. Army and Navy Stores 65-72; Pres. Inst. of Export 67-68; retd. 72.
"Malindia", 23 Clontarf Street, Sorrento, W. Australia 6020.

Ellicott, Robert James, Q.C.; Australian lawyer and politician; b. 15 April 1927, Moree, N.S.W.; m.; two s. two d.; ed. Fort Street Boys' High School and Univ. of Sydney.
Admitted to Bar in N.S.W. 50, Victoria 60; appointed Q.C. 64; Commonwealth Solicitor-Gen. 69-73; mem. House of Reps. for Wentworth, N.S.W. 74-; Opposition spokesman on Consumer Affairs and Commerce 74-75; Attorney-Gen. Dec. 75-.
Leisure interests: tennis, farming.
Parliament Buildings, Canberra, A.C.T., Australia.

Elliot, Sir John, Kt.; British business executive; b. 1898, London; ed. Marlborough and Sandhurst.
Served 3rd Hussars 17-20; journalist 20-24; joined Southern Railway (public relations and advertising) 25, Traffic Development Officer 30, Asst. Traffic Man. 33; many visits to U.S.A. and Canada to study rail, road and air services; Deputy Gen. Man., Southern Railway 37, Acting Gen. Man. 47; Chief Regional Officer, Southern Region, British Railways 48-49, London Midland Region 50-51; Chair. Railway Exec. 51-53; Chair. London Transport 53-59; Chair. Thos. Cook and Son Ltd. 59-67, Pullman Car Co. Ltd. 59-62, Sleeping Car Co. (Wagons Lits) 62-71, Willing and Co. Ltd. 59-70; Dir. Commonwealth Devt. Corpn. 59-66, Thos. Tilling and Co. Ltd. 59-70, British Airports Authority 65-69; Pres. Inst. of Transport 53-54; Vice-Pres. Union Internationale des Chemins de Fer 47 and 51-53; Chair. London and Provincial Posters Group 66-71, Australian Posters (Pty.) Ltd. 70-73; transport adviser to Govt. of Victoria, Australia 49, 66, 70; mem. World Bank Survey (Transport), East Africa 69; High Sheriff of London 70-71; Officier Légion d'Honneur, Amer. Medal of Freedom.
Leisure interests: military history, gardening, shooting.
Publs. *The Way of the Tumbrils* 58, *Early Days of the Southern Railway* 60, *Where Our Fathers Died* 64, *Speaking of That* 64.
Stonyfield, Great Easton, Dunmow, Essex, England.

Elliott, Sir Norman Randall, Kt., C.B.E., M.A.; British electricity executive; b. 19 July 1903, London; s. of William Randall Elliott and Catherine Dunsmore; m. Phyllis Clarke 1963; ed. privately and St. Catharine's Coll., Cambridge.
Called to Bar, Middle Temple, London 32; Col., Deputy Dir. of Works, 21 Army Group 39-44; mem. North of Scotland Hydro Electric Board, London Passenger Transport Board, London and Home Counties Joint Electricity Authority; Chair. South-Eastern Electricity Authority; Chair. South-Eastern Electricity Board 48-62, South of Scotland Electricity Board 62-67; Dir. James Howden & Co. Ltd. 67-68, Chair. Howden Group 73-; Chair. The Electricity Council 68-72; Dir. Newarthill & McAlpine Group 72-; Chair. British Nat. Cttee. Union Int. des Producteurs et Distributeurs d'Energie Electrique.

eisure interests: ball games, theatre.
Publs. *Electricity Statutes, Orders and Regulations* 51, 67.
Herbrand Walk, Cooden, Sussex, England.

Elliott, Osborn, A.B.; American journalist; b. 25 Oct.
924, New York City; s. of John and Audrey N.
Osborn) Elliott; m. 1st Deirdre M. Spencer 1948,
divorced 1972; three d.; m. 2nd the fmr. Mrs. Inger A.
McCabe; two step d., one step s.; ed. The Browning
School (N.Y.), St. Paul's School (Concord) and Harvard
Univ.
Reporter N.Y. *Journal of Commerce* 46-49; Contributing
Editor *Time* 49-52, Assoc. Editor 52-55; Senior Busi-
ness Editor *Newsweek* 55-59, Man. Editor 59-61, Editor
61-69, 72-75, Editor-in-Chief 69-72, 75-, Vice-Chair. 70,
Pres. and Chief Exec. Officer 71-72, Chair. of Board 72-;
Dir. Washington Post Co. 61-; Trustee, American
Museum of Natural History, Asia Soc., New York
Public Library 68-72, St. Paul's School 69-73, Winston
Churchill Foundation of the U.S. Ltd. 70-73; mem.
Council on Foreign Relations; mem. Board of Overseers
of Harvard Coll. 65-71; Fellow American Acad. of Arts
and Sciences; served with U.S. Naval Reserve 44-46.
Publ. *Men at the Top* 59; Editor *The Negro Revolution
in America* 64.
444 Madison Avenue, New York, N.Y. 10022, U.S.A.

Elliott, Roger James, D.PHIL.; British physicist; b.
8 Dec. 1928, Chesterfield; s. of James Elliott and
Gladys Elliott (née Hill); m. Olga Lucy Atkinson 1952;
one s. two d.; ed. Swanwick Hall School, Derbyshire
and New Coll., Oxford.
Research Assoc. Univ. of Calif., Berkeley 52-53;
Research Fellow, Atomic Energy Research Est.,
Harwell 53-55; Lecturer, Univ. of Reading 55-57;
Lecturer, Oxford Univ. 57-65, Reader 65-74, Fellow,
St. John's Coll. 57-74, Wykeham Prof. of Physics 74-;
Visiting Prof. Univ. of Calif., Berkeley 60-61; Miller
Visiting Prof. Univ. of Ill., Urbana 66; Maxwell Medal
(Physical Soc.) 68.
Leisure interests: tennis, squash.
Publs. *Magnetic Properties of Rare Earth Metals* 72,
Solid State Physics and its Applications 73; articles in
learned journals.
11 Crick Road, Oxford, England.
Telephone: Oxford 58369.

Elliott, Thomas Anthony Keith, C.M.G., M.A.; British
diplomatist; b. 27 May 1921, Burford, Oxon.; s. of Sir
Ivo Elliott, Bt. and Margery Carey; m. Alethea
Richardson 1951; one s. three d.; ed. Eton Coll. and
Balliol Coll., Oxford.
Army service in East Africa 41-46; joined diplomatic
service 47; Third Sec., Belgrade 49, Second Sec. 50;
First Sec., Peking 57, Athens 60; Counsellor, Foreign
Office 64; Political Adviser, Hong Kong 65; Counsellor,
Washington, D.C. 68, Minister 70; Amb. to Finland
72-75, to Israel Aug. 75-; Head of U.K. Del. to Conf. on
Security and Co-operation in Europe (Stage II), Geneva
73-74.
Leisure interests: music, travel, historical research.
British Embassy, 192 Hayarkon Street, Tel-Aviv,
Israel.

Ellis, Sir Charles Drummond, Kt., B.A., PH.D., F.R.S.;
British physicist; b. 11 Aug. 1895, London; s. of Isabella
Carswell and Charles Ellis; m. Paula Dantziger 1925;
no c.; ed. Harrow, Royal Military Acad. Woolwich,
Trinity Coll., Cambridge.
Formerly Fellow and Lecturer Trinity Coll., Cambridge,
Lecturer Physics Dept. Cambridge Univ.; Wheatstone
Prof. of Physics King's Coll. London Univ. 36-46;
External Prof. of Physics at all Canadian universities
38-39; Scientific Adviser to Army Council 43-46; Dir.
Finance Corpn. for Industry 45-69; Gov. Harrow
School; mem. Nat. Coal Board 46-55; Pres. British Coal
Utilisation Research Asscn. 46-55; Consultant to Gas

Council, to Battelle Inst., to British American Tobacco
Co. Ltd. and to Tobacco Research Council.
Leisure interests: golf, cooking.
Publ. *Radiations from Radioactive Substances* (with Sir
Ernest Rutherford and James Chadwick) 30.
Seawards, Cookham Dean, Berkshire, England.
Telephone: Marlow 3166.

Ellis, Elmer, B.A., A.M., PH.D.; American historian;
b. 27 July 1901, McHenry County, N. Dakota; s. of
Thomas Clarkson and Lillie Jane (Butterfield) Ellis;
m. Ruth Clapper 1925; ed. Univ. of N. Dakota and
State Univ. of Iowa.
Instructor N. Dakota State Teachers' Coll. 25-28;
Lecturer in History, State Univ. of Iowa 28-30; Asst.
Prof., Assoc. Prof. and Prof. of History, Univ. of
Missouri 30-; Acting Dean of Graduate School, Univ. of
Missouri, summers 36, 39, 41, Vice-Pres. in charge of
Extra Divisional Educational Activities 45-46, Dean of
Faculty Coll. of Arts and Science 46-55, Acting Pres.
54-55, Pres. 55-66; Pres. Emer. Univ. of Missouri
66-; Pres. Nat. Council for Social Studies 37; U.S.
Army History Branch, War Dept. Gen. Staff 43-45
mem. History Advisory Cttee., U.S. Army and
Chair. 57-59; Pres. Miss. Valley Hist. Asscn. 50; mem.
Board of Editors *Mississippi Valley Historical Review*
47-50, Board of Dirs. Social Science Research Council
46-51; Fulbright Visiting Lecturer, Univ. of Amsterdam
51-52; Pres. Board of Dirs. Harry S. Truman Inst. for
Nat. and Int. Affairs 57-; mem. Board of Foreign
Scholarships, U.S. Dept. of State 58-61, Civil Rights
Advisory Cttee. U.S. Dept. of Agriculture 65-68; Pres.
Nat. Comm. on Accrediting 62-64; Pres. Nat. Asscn.
State Univs. and Land-Grant Colls. 64-65; Consultant
Educ. comm. of States 67-71, Rockefeller Foundation
67; Educational Consultant on Admin., Univ. of Del
Valle, Calif., Colombia 67, Texas Technological Univ.
68-69; mem. Board of Curators, Stephens Coll. 67-73;
Consultant on Admin. Structure, Orissa Agric. and
Tech. Univ., Bhubaneswar, India 70; Pres. Mo. State
Historical Soc. 74-; Hon. LL.D. (Univ. of N. Dakota 46,
Central Coll., Fayette, Missouri 55, Drury Coll.,
Springfield, Missouri 56, Washington Univ. 60); Hon.
Litt.D. (Culver-Stockton Coll., Canton, Mo. 61); D.Litt.
(St. Louis Univ. 66))
Publs. *Education Against Propaganda* 37, *Mr. Dooley
at his Best* 38, *Henry Moore Teller, Defender of the
West* 41, *Mr. Dooley's America, a Life of Finley Peter
Dunne* 41, *Toward Better Teaching in College* 54.
Office: 323 Jesse Hall, University of Missouri, Columbia,
Missouri; Home: 107 W. Brandon Road, Columbia,
Missouri, U.S.A.
Telephone: 314-882-4269 (Office).

Ellis, Howard S., B.A., M.A., PH.D., LL.D.; American
economist; b. 2 July 1898, Denver, Colo.; s. of Sylvester
B. Ellis and Nellie B. Young; m. Hermine Hoerles-
berger 1935; three d.; ed. Univs. of Iowa, Michigan,
Harvard, Heidelberg and Vienna.
Instructor and later Prof., Univ. of Michigan 20-22,
24-38, of Calif. 38-43, 46-50 and 51-65; Visiting Prof.,
Columbia 44-45, 49-50, Tokyo 51, Wisconsin 72; econ.
analyst, Fed. Reserve Board, Washington 43-44; Asst.
Dir. of Research and Statistics 44-45; Econ. Policy
Cttee., U.S. Chamber of Commerce 45-46; Dir. Marshall
Aid Research Project Council on Foreign Relations
49-50; Pres. American Econ. Asscn. 49; Pres. Int. Econ.
Asscn. 53-56, mem. Exec. Cttee. 56-62; Visiting Prof.,
Univ. of Bombay 58-59; Head, UNESCO Mission on
Econs. in Latin America 60, Econ. Research Center,
Athens 63; U.S. Aid Mission, Rio de Janeiro 65-67;
IV Semana Económica Internacional, Barcelona 73.
Leisure interests: music, garden.
Publs. *German Monetary Theory 1905-1933* 34, *Exchange
Control in Central Europe* 41, *The Economics of Freedom:
The Progress and Future of Aid to Europe* 50, *Approaches*

to Economic Development 55, *Private Enterprise and Socialism in the Middle East* 70; Editor *The Economy of Brazil* 69.
936 Cragmont Avenue, Berkeley, Calif., 94708, U.S.A.
Telephone: 525-2734.

Ellison, Rt. Rev. Gerald Alexander, P.C., M.A., D.D.; British ecclesiastic; b. 19 Aug. 1910, Windsor, Berks; s. of John Henry Joshua Ellison and Sara Dorothy Graham Crum; m. Jane Elizabeth Gibbon 1947; one s. two d.; ed. Westminster School, New Coll., Oxford and Westcott House, Cambridge.
Curate Sherborne Abbey 35-37; Domestic Chaplain to Bishop of Winchester 37-39, to Archbishop of York 43-46; Chaplain to R.N.V.R. 40-43; Vicar St. Mark's Portsea and Hon. Chaplain to Archbishop of York 46-50; Canon of Portsmouth 50; Bishop of Willesden 50-55, of Chester 55-73, of London 73-.
Leisure interests: oarsmanship, walking.
London House, 19 Cowley Street, Westminster, SW1P 3LZ London, England.
Telephone: 01-930-0661/2.

Ellison, Ralph (Waldo); American writer; b. 1 March 1914, Okla.; ed. Tuskegee Inst.; m. Fanny McConnell 1946.
Writer of reviews, short stories, articles and criticism 39-; Fellow, American Acad. Rome 55-57; subsequently taught at Bard Coll. 58-61; Alexander White Visiting Prof., Univ. of Chicago 61; Visiting Prof. of Writing, Rutgers Univ. 62-64; Albert Schweitzer Prof. in Humanities, N.Y. Univ. 70-; mem. Nat. Inst. of Arts and Letters, American Acad. of Arts and Sciences, American Acad. of Arts and Letters, and others; Rosenwald Fellowship; Nat. Book Award and Russwurm Award for first novel *Invisible Man*; lecturer on American culture and literature and Negro folklore at several American universities and at Salzburg Seminar 54; several hon. degrees; Medal of Freedom 69; Chevalier de l'Ordre des Arts et Lettres 70.
Publs. *Invisible Man* 52, *Shadow and Act* (essays) 64.
730 Riverside Drive, New York, N.Y. 10031, U.S.A.; also c/o Secker and Warburg, 14 Carlisle Street, London, W.1, England.

Ellscheid, Robert, D.IUR.; German lawyer and business executive; b. 19 Feb. 1900; s. of Michael Ellscheid and Maria Zens; m. Hertha Hiedemann 1926; two d.; ed. Cologne and Bonn Univs.
Served First World War; lawyer 24-; Chair. Advisory Econ. Council, British Zone 46-47; Lecturer on Industrial Rights, Cologne Univ. 47-52, Prof. 52; Chair. of Supervisory Board, Zanders Feinpapiere GmbH, Felix Heinrich Schoeller GmbH; mem. Supervisory Board Kaufhof AG, Schwäbische Zellstoff AG, BASF Farben und Fasern AG; Chair. of Advisory Council Gerolsteiner Sprudel KG, Lindgens und Söhne, Herbol-Werke GmbH; mem. of Advisory Council Rhein. Erz- und Metallhandel GmbH, Atlas Copco Deutschland GmbH, Atlas Copco MCT, J. W. Zanders KG, ITS Int. Tourist Services Länderreisedienste GmbH KG; mem. of joint Advisory Council of Allianz Versicherungs AG and Allianz Lebensversicherungs AG; mem. Cen. Cttee. Dresdner Bank AG; lawyer at Provincial Court of Cologne; Prof.h.c. Univ. of Cologne, Senator h.c. 70; Pres. h.c. of German Asscn. for Industrial Patents and Copyright, Berlin.
Office: Köln 1, Habsburgerring 9; Home: Köln-Marienburg, Eugen-Langen-Strasse 2, Federal Republic of Germany.

Ellsworth, Ralph E., A.B., B.S. in L.S., PH.D., LL.D.; American librarian and professor; b. 22 Sept. 1907, Forest City, Iowa; s. of H. E. Wallace and C. G. Helma m. Theda Chapman 1931; two s.; ed. Oberlin Coll., Western Reserve Univ., Chicago Univ.
Librarian, Adams State Coll. 31-34; Dir. Libraries, Colorado Univ. 37-43; Dir. Libraries, Iowa Univ. 44-58;

Dir. Libraries and Prof. of Library Science, Colorad Univ. 58-72, Prof. Emer. 72-.
Leisure interests: travel, angling, music, library archi tecture.
Publs. (with D. E. Bean) *Modular Planning for Colleg and Small University Libraries* 48, *Library Buildings* 60 *The American Right Wing* 60, *Planning College an University Buildings* 60 (2nd edn. 68), *The Schoo Library: Facilities for Independent Study* 64, *The Schoo Library* 65, *The Economics of Book Storage* 69, *Academi Library Buildings* 73.
860 Willowbrook Road, Boulder, Colo. 80302, U.S.A.
Telephone: 303-443-2592.

Elmandjra, Mahdi, PH.D.; Moroccan internationa official; b. 13 March 1933, Rabat; s. of M'Hamed Elmandjra and Rabia Elmrini; m. Amina Elmrini 1956 two d.; ed. Lycée Lyautey, Casablanca, Putney School Vermont, U.S.A., Cornell Univ., London School o Economics and Faculté de Droit, Univ. de Paris.
Head of Confs., Law Faculty, Univ. of Rabat 57-58 Adviser, Ministry of Foreign Affairs, and to Moroccan Del. to UN 58-59; Dir.-Gen., Radiodiffusion Télévision Marocaine 59-60; Chief of African Div., Office of Relations with Mem. States, UNESCO 61-63; Dir. Exec. Office of Dir.-Gen. of UNESCO 63-66; Asst. Dir.-Gen. of UNESCO for Social Sciences, Human Sciences and Culture July 66-Dec. 69; Visiting Fellow, Centre of Int. Studies, London School of Econs. and Political Science 70; Asst. Dir.-Gen. of UNESCO for Pre-Programming 71-74; Special Adviser to Dir.-Gen. of UNESCO 75-; Vice-Chair. Devt. Sciences Information Systems Steering Cttee.; Chevalier, Ordre des Arts et Lettres (France).
Leisure interests: reading, skiing.
Publs. *The League of Arab States* 57, *Nehru and the Modern World* 68, *Relations between Japanese and Western Arts* 68, *Economie et Culture* (in Economie et Société Humaine) 72, *Informatics in Government* (IBI World Conf. on Informatics) 72, *Globalidad Interdisciplinaria y Exigencias Sociales Cualitativas* 72, *The United Nations System: An Analysis* 73, *Global Co-operation as an Operational Concept* (with John E. Fobes) 75, *Devsis* (mem. of study team) 75.
Office: UNESCO, place de Fontenoy, Paris 7e; Home: 12 rue Dufrenoy, Paris 16e, France, and 20 rue Chenier, Casablanca, Morocco.
Telephone: 577-1610 (UNESCO).

Elmendorff, Wilhelm, DR. RER. POL.; German accountant; b. 3 Sept. 1903; ed. Univs. of Freiburg (Breisgau), Berlin and Cologne, and London School of Economics.
With Economic Statistical Insts. and commercial press 27-34; Chartered Accountant 34-; Chair. Supervisory Board Preussag, VTG (Vereinigte Tanklager und Transportmittel G.m.b.H.) until 72, Hamburg, Schachtbau Thyssen G.m.b.H., Mülheim-Ruhr; Adviser on Accounting to European Communities 74-; fmr. Pres. German Inst. of Certified Public Accountants, Düsseldorf; fmr. Pres. Union Européenne des Experts Comptables Economiques et Financiers.
4 Düsseldorf, Klosterstrasse 58, Federal Republic of Germany.

Elsasser, Walter M., PH.D.; American theoretical physicist and geophysicist; b. 20 March 1904, Mannheim, Germany; s. of Moritz and Johanna (Masius) Elsasser; m. 1st Margaret Trahey 1937, 2nd Susanne Rosenfeld 1964; one s. one d.; ed. Univs. of Heidelberg, Munich and Göttingen.
Assistant, Technical Univ. of Berlin 28-30; Instructor in Physics, Frankfurt 30-33; Research Fellow, Inst Henri Poincaré, Sorbonne 33-36; Asst. Meteorologist, Calif. Inst. of Technology 36-41; Research Assoc., Blue Hill Meteorological Observatory, Harvard Univ. 41-42; War Research Signal Corps Labs. 42-44; mem. Radio Wave Cttee. of Nat. Defense Research Cttee. 44-45;

ndustrial Researcher, Radio Corpn. of America, N.J. 5-47; Assoc. Prof. of Physics, Univ. of Pa. 47-50; rof., Univ. of Utah 50-56, Univ. of Calif., San Diego 6-62; Geophysicist, Princeton Univ. 62-68; Research rof., Univ. of Maryland 68-; Guest Lecturer, Sorbonne, aris 35, 36, Lecturer, Mass. Inst. of Technology 38; ellow, Physical Soc.; mem Nat. Acad. of Sciences, eophysical Union, Physical Soc.; German Physical oc. Prize 32, Bowie Medal of Geophysical Union 59, leming Medal 71.

ubls. *The Physical Foundation of Biology* 58, *Atom and rganism* 66; numerous works on the physics of the earth. nstitute for Fluid Dynamics and Applied Mathenatics, University of Maryland, College Park, Md. 0740; Home: 3450 Toledo Terrace, Hyattsville, Md. 0782, U.S.A.

elephone: 301-454-4129 (Office); 301-559-3524 (Home).

Elslande, Renaat van; Belgian lawyer, university professor and politician; b. 21 Jan. 1916, Boekhoute; n. Ghislaine Van Acker 1945; one s. three d.

Professor, Univ. of Louvain; mem. Chamber of Reps. 49-; Minister, Under-Sec. of State for Cultural Affairs 50, later Minister for Culture and Educ.; Minister for European Affairs and Flemish Culture 66-68; Minister for Home Affairs 72-73, for Foreign Affairs 73-; Christian Social Party.

39 Kerkstraat, Lot, Belgium.
Telephone: 02-376-32-39.

Eltester, Walther, D.THEOL.; German theologian; b. 18 April 1899, Hohenlandin; s. of late Rev. Ernest Eltester and late Martha Diestel; m. Dr. Renate Berger 1935; two s. two d.; studied theology in Jena and Berlin.

Scientific Asst. Prussian Acad. of Science 31-40; Scientific Officer and Prof. 40-45; Reader in Ecclesiastical History, Univ. of Berlin 40-45; Extraordinary Prof. of Ecclesiastical History and Dean of Theological Faculty, Univ. of Berlin 45-49, Ordinary Prof. 47-49; Ordinary Prof. of New Testament and Old Church History, Univ. of Marburg 49-55; Prof. of Church History, Univ. of Tübingen 55-; mem. of Comm. for History of Religion, German Acad. of Sciences, Comm. for Patristic Studies in the German Federal Republic, Soc. Novi Testamenti Studiorum.

Editor *Zeitschrift für neutestamentliche Wissenschaft* and *Beihefte* (until 70) and *Arbeiten zur Kirchengeschichte* (until 69).

Waldeckstrasse 23, 47 Tübingen-Lustnau, Federal Republic of Germany.
Telephone: Tübingen 23717.

Elton, Charles Sutherland, F.R.S.; British zoologist; b. 29 March 1900, Manchester; s. of late Oliver Elton and Letitia Maynard MacColl; m. 1st Rose Montague 1928, no c.; m. 2nd Edith J. Scovell 1937, one s. one d.; ed. Liverpool Coll. and New Coll., Oxford.

Ecologist, Oxford Univ. Expedition to Spitzbergen 21, Merton Coll. Arctic Expedition 23, Oxford Univ. Arctic Expedition 24, Oxford Univ. Lapland Expedition 30; Dir. Bureau of Animal Population, Dept. of Zoological Field Studies, Oxford Univ. 32-67; Reader in Animal Ecology, Oxford Univ. 36-67; Hon. Fellow, Corpus Christi Coll., Oxford 67-; mem. Nature Conservancy 49-56; Foreign Hon. mem. Amer. Acad. of Arts and Sciences 68-; Gold Medal, Linnean Soc. 67; Darwin Medal, Royal Soc. 70.

Leisure interests: natural history, reading, gardening.
Publs. *Animal Ecology* 27, *Animal Ecology and Evolution* 30, *The Ecology of Animals* 33, *Exploring the Animal World* 33, *Voles, Mice and Lemmings* 42, *The Ecology of Invasions by Animals and Plants* 58, *The Pattern of Animal Communities* 66.

61 Park Town, Oxford, England.
Telephone: Oxford 57644.

Elvin, Herbert Lionel, M.A.; British educationist; b. 7 Aug. 1905, Buckhurst Hill, Essex; s. of Herbert

Henry Elvin (Pres. T.U.C. 1938) and Mary Jane Elvin; m. Mone Bedortha Dutton 1934; one s.; ed. Trinity Hall, Cambridge, and Yale Univ.

Fellow of Trinity Hall, Cambridge, and mem. of Faculty of English, Cambridge, 30-45; temporary civil servant, Air Ministry 40-42, Ministry of Information (American Div.) 42-45; Principal, Ruskin Coll., mem. Faculty of English, Oxford 45-50; mem. Univ. Grants Cttee. 46-50; Dir. Dept. of Education, UNESCO 50-56; Prof. Education (Tropical Areas) London Univ., Inst. of Education 56-58; Dir. Inst. of Education, London Univ. 58-73; Chair. Commonwealth Educ. Liaison Cttee. 65-73; mem. Govt. of India Educ. Comm. 65-66; Emer. Prof. of Educ. (London).

Leisure interests: reading, golf.
Publs. *Men of America* 41, *An Introduction to the Study of Poetry* 49, *Education and Contemporary Society* 65.
4 Bulstrode Gardens, Cambridge, England.
Telephone: 58309.

Elvin, Violetta (Violetta Prokhorova); British ballerina; b. 3 Nov. 1925, Moscow; d. of Vassili Prokhorov and Irena T. Grimusinskaya; m. Fernando Savarese 1959; one s.; ed. Bolshoi Theatre School, Moscow.

Member, Bolshoi Theatre Ballet 42; evacuated to Tashkent 43; ballerina, Tashkent State Theatre; rejoined Bolshoi Theatre as soloist 44; joined Sadler's Wells Ballet, Royal Opera House, Covent Garden (now the Royal Ballet) as guest soloist 46, and later as regular mem., prima ballerina 51-56; guest artist, Stanislavsky Theatre, Moscow 44, Sadler's Wells Theatre 47; guest prima ballerina, La Scala 52-53; guest artist, Cannes 54, Copenhagen 54, Teatro Municipal, Rio de Janeiro 55, Festival Hall 55; guest prima ballerina, Royal Opera House, Stockholm 56; Royal Opera House, Covent Garden 56 (concluded her stage career); film appearances: *The Queen of Spades, Twice Upon a Time, Melba.*

Leisure interests: reading, walking, swimming.
c/o British Consulate-General, Via Crispi, Naples, Italy.

Elworthy, Baron (Life Peer), cr. 72; **Marshal of the R.A.F. (Samuel) Charles Elworthy,** G.C.B., C.B.E., D.S.O., M.V.O., D.F.C., A.F.C.; British air force officer and businessman; b. 23 March 1911, Timaru, New Zealand; s. of late Percy Elworthy (Capt. 1st Life Guards); m. Audrey Hutchinson 1936; three s. one d.; ed. Marlborough Coll. and Trinity Coll., Cambridge.

Reserve of Air Force Officers 33; Called to Bar (Lincoln's Inn) 35 (Bencher 70); R.A.F. 36-, Bomber Command 39-45, Commandant R.A.F. Staff Coll. 57-59; Deputy Chief of Air Staff 59-60; C.-in-C. Middle East 60-63; Chief of Air Staff Sept. 63-67; Chief of Defence Staff 67-71; Chair. Board of Management, Royal Comm. for Exhbn. of 1851; Dir. Nat. Bank of New Zealand 71-, British Petroleum Ltd. 71-, Plessey Co. 71-; Chair. Scientific Control Systems (Holdings) 72-; Constable and Gov. of Windsor Castle; H.M. Lieut. for Greater London 73-.

Leisure interests: shooting, fishing.
Norman Tower, Windsor Castle, Berks., England.
Telephone: Windsor Castle 68286.

Elwyn-Jones, Baron (Life Peer), cr. 74, of Llanelli in the County of Carmarthen and of Newham in Greater London; **(Frederick) Elwyn Jones,** M.A., Q.C.; British lawyer and politician; b. 24 Oct. 1909 Llanelli; s. of Frederick and Elizabeth Jones; m. Pearl Binder 1937; one s. two d.; ed. Llanelli Grammar School, Univ. Coll. of Wales, Aberystwyth, and Gonville and Caius Coll., Cambridge.

Called to Bar, Gray's Inn 35; Deputy Judge Advocate 43-45; M.P. 45-74; Recorder of Merthyr Tydfil 49-53, of Swansea 53-60, of Cardiff 60-64, of Kingston-upon-Thames 68-74; Parl. Private Sec. to Attorney-Gen. 46-51; Attorney-Gen. 64-70; Pres. Univ. Coll., Cardiff; Fellow of King's Coll., London; mem. Bar Council 56-59; Chair. of Soc. of Labour Lawyers 57-60; Treas,

of Justice, British Section, Int. Comm. of Jurists 59-64. 70-74; Lord Chancellor March 74-; Hon. LL.D. (Wales); Labour.
Leisure interests: travelling, walking.
Publs. *Hitler's Drive to the East* 37, *The Battle for Peace* 38, *The Attack from Within* 39.
House of Lords, London, SW1A oPW, England.

Elytis, Odysseus; Greek poet and essayist; b. 1911, Heracleion, Crete; ed. Univs. of Athens and Paris. Contributed first to review *Nea Grammata* 35; became expounder of surrealism; art critic for newspaper *Kathimerini* 46-48; Broadcasting and Programme Dir. Hellenic Nat. Broadcasting Inst. 45-46 and 53-54; represented Greece at Rencontres Int. de Genève 48 and Congrès de l'Association des Critiques d'Art 49; Councillor of the Arts Theatre; Councillor of the Nat. Theatre 74.
Leisure interests: trying home painting and collage.
Publs. *Orientations* 36, *Clepsydras of the Unknown* 37, *Sporades* 38, *Sun the First* 43, *Heroic and Funeral Song for the Lost Sub-lieutenant in Albania* 45, *Six and One, Regrets for Heavens* 60, *Axion Esti* 59, *The Light-Tree and the Fourteenth Beauty* 71, *The Monogram* 71, *The Painter Theophilos* 73, *The Siblings* 74.
23 Skoufa Street, Athens, Greece.
Telephone: 626458.

Elyutin, Vyacheslav Petrovich, DR.TECH.SC.; Soviet scientist and politician; b. 11 March 1907, Saratov; ed. Moscow Steel Inst.
Instructor, Moscow Steel Inst. 30-35; Dean, Deputy Dir. All-Union Industrial Acad., Moscow 35-41; Soviet Army 41-45; Dir. Moscow Steel Inst. 45-51; mem. C.P.S.U. 29-; Deputy Minister of Higher Educ. of the U.S.S.R. 51-54, Minister of Higher Educ. 54-59; Minister of Higher and Secondary Special Educ. 59-; corresp. mem. Soviet Acad. of Sciences; Alternate mem., Cen. Cttee., Communist Party of the Soviet Union 56-61, mem. 61-; Deputy to U.S.S.R. Supreme Soviet 62-; State Prize 52; Order of Lenin (twice); Order of the Red Banner of Labour, Badge of Honour (twice).
Ministry of Higher and Secondary Specialized Education, 11 Ulitsa Zhdanova, Moscow, U.S.S.R.

Emanuel, Nikolai Markovich; Soviet physical chemist; b. 1 Oct. 1915, Tim, Kursk Region; ed. Leningrad Industrial (Polytechnical) Inst.
Scientific worker at Inst. of Chemical Physics, U.S.S.R. Acad. of Sciences 38-; Asst. Prof. Moscow Univ. 44-50, Prof. 50-; mem. C.P.S.U. 48-; Corresp. mem. U.S.S.R. Acad. of Sciences 58-66, mem. 66-, Head, Dept. of Kinetics of Chemistry and Biological Processes at Inst. of Chemical Physics, U.S.S.R. Acad. of Sciences 60-, Academician-Sec. Dept. of General and Technical Chemistry 75-; Chair. Nat. Cttee. of Soviet Chemists 72-; Editor-in-Chief of Journal *Uspekhi Khimii* 73-; Foreign mem. Royal Swedish Acad. of Sciences 74, Acad. of Sciences of German Democratic Republic 75; mem. New York Acad. of Sciences 74-; Dr. h.c. Szeged Univ. (Hungary) 74; Lenin Prize for research into properties and particular features of chain reactions 58; Order of Red Banner of Labour 65 and 71, Order of Lenin 75, Order of Peace and Friendship (Hungary) 75, and other decorations.
Publs. *Intermediate products of complex gaseous reactions* 46, *The inhibition of fat oxidation processes* 67, *Liquid Phase Oxidation of Hydrocarbons* 67, *Clinical oncology— a quantitative approach* 72, *Chemical Kinetics, Homogeneous Reactions* 62, 69, 74 (English edn. 74).
U.S.S.R. Academy of Sciences V-71 Leninsky Prospekt 14, Moscow; Institute of Chemical Physics, Academy of Sciences of U.S.S.R., Vorob'evskoe shosse 2b, Moscow 117334, U.S.S.R.

Emanuels, Severinus D.; Netherlands Surinam lawyer and politician; b. 27 Feb. 1910, Rotterdam; *m.* Helena

Geertruida Hitzel; one *s.*; ed. Univs. of Leyden an Utrecht, Ecole de Droit, Paris.
District Attorney's Office, Magelang, Indonesia 37-38 Acting Judge, Court of Justice, Makassar 38-42 Royal Netherlands Army Service 42-45; Chief, Bureau: of Law, Dean of Law School, Celebes 46-48; Sec.-Gen Dept. of Justice, Celebes 48-51; District Attorney Paramaribo 51-52; Minister of Finance, Surinam 52-55 Counsellor, Netherlands Embassy, U.S.A. 56-58; Prim Minister of Surinam, Minister of General Affairs an Interior Affairs 58-63; Minister Plenipotentiary at Th Hague 63-64; Counsellor for Press and Cultural Affairs Netherlands Embassy in Mexico 65-68; Netherlands Amb. to Trinidad and Tobago, Barbados and Guyana 68-.
Leisure interests: home movies, reading, golf.
90 Independence Square, Port of Spain, Trinidad, West Indies.
Telephone: 51722.

Emeleus, Harry, D.SC., C.B.E., F.R.S.; British professor of chemistry; b. 22 June 1903, London; *s.* of Karl H. and Ellen Emeleus; *m.* Mary C. Horton 1931; two *s.* two *d.*; ed. Imperial Coll., London, Technische Hochschule, Karlsruhe and Princeton Univ.
Member of staff, Imperial Coll., London 31-45; Prof. of Inorganic Chem., Cambridge Univ. 45-70, now Prof. Emer.; Davey Medal, Royal Soc., Lavoisier Medal, French Chem. Soc., Stock Medal, German Chem. Soc.
Leisure interests: fishing, gardening.
Publ. *Modern Aspects of Inorganic Chemistry* (with J. S. Anderson) 38.
149 Shelford Road, Trumpington, Cambridge, England.
Telephone: Trumpington 2374.

Emelyanov, Vasily Semyonovich; Soviet metallurgist; b. 12 Feb. 1901, Khvalynsk, Saratov Region; ed. Moscow Mining Acad.
Director Cheljabin Mining Plant 35-37; Defence Cttee. 37-40; Dir. Standards Cttee. 40-46; metallurgist in tank factory in Urals during Second World War, designed gun turret, Dept. Head Moscow Engineering and Physics Inst. 46-; Dir. Admin. for Peaceful Uses of Atomic Energy 58-60; Chair. State Cttee. for Atomic Energy 60-62, Deputy Chair. 62-65; Editor-in-Chief *Atomic Energy* 58; Corresp. mem. Soviet Acad. of Sciences 53; Alt. mem. C.P.S.U. Central Cttee. until 66; mem. UN Consultative Cttee. 55-65, UN Int. Agency for Atomic Energy 57-65; Chair. Comm. on Scientific Problems of Disarmament under Presidium of U.S.S.R. Acad. of Sciences; State prizewinner; Hero of Socialist Labour; Order of Lenin (four), October Revolution and other awards.
Publs. include; *On Production of Manganese Steel* 34, *Influence of Nitrogen on Properties of Steel* 35, *Mechanical Properties of Dual and Triplet Alloys of Zirconium with Tantalum and Niobium at Normal and High Temperatures* 58.
U.S.S.R. Academy of Sciences, 14 Leninsky Prospekt, Moscow, U.S.S.R.

Emeneau, Murray Barnson, M.A., PH.D.; American university professor; b. 28 Feb. 1904, Lunenburg, Nova Scotia, Canada; *s.* of Archibald and Ada Emeneau; *m.* Katharine Fitch Venter 1940; two stepdaughters; ed. Dalhousie, Oxford and Yale Univs.
Instructor in Latin, Yale Univ. 26-31; Fellowships, Yale Univ. and American Council of Learned Societies 31-40; research in India 35-38; Asst. Prof. of Sanskrit and Gen. Linguistics, Univ. of Calif. 40-43, Assoc. Prof. 43-46, Prof. 46-71, Prof. Emer. 71-; Guggenheim Fellowship 49, 56-57, 58; Vice-Pres. Linguistic Soc. of America 49, Pres. 50; Assoc. Editor American Oriental Soc. 40-47, Editor 47-52, Pres. 54-55, Western Branch 64-65; Hermann Collitz Prof. of Indo-European Comparative Linguistics, Indiana Univ. 53; Faculty Research Lecturer, Berkeley, Univ. of Calif. 55-56, Chair.

Dept. of Linguistics 53-58, Chair. Dept. of Classics 59-62; mem. American Philosophical Soc. 52; hon. mem. Nat. Inst. of Humanistic Sciences, Vietnam 57, Linguistic Soc. of India 64, Linguistic Research Group of Pakistan 71; Hon. Fellow Royal Asiatic Soc. 69; mem. American Acad. of Arts and Sciences 70; Vice-Pres. Int. Asscn. for Tamil Research 66; Presented with *Studies in Indian Linguistics* by Centres of Advanced Study in Linguistics, Deccan Coll. and Annamalai Univ., and Linguistic Soc. of India 68; Lucius Wilbur Cross Medal Yale Graduate School Asscn. 69; Hon. L.H.D. (Univ. of Chicago) 68, Hon. LL.D. (Dalhousie Univ.) 70; Berkeley Citation 71. Leisure interests: ballet, opera, travel.
Publs. *Jambhaladatta's Version of the Vetālapañcaviṅśati* 34, *A Union List of Printed Indic Texts and Translations in American Libraries* 35, *Kota Texts* 44-46, *Studies in Vietnamese (Annamese) Grammar* 51, *Kolami, a Dravidian Language* 55; *Vedic Variants* Vol. III (with M. Bloomfield & F. Edgerton) 34; *A Dravidian Etymological Dictionary* (with T. Burrow) 61, *Dravidian Borrowings from Indo-Aryan* (with T. Burrow) 62, *Brahui and Dravidian Grammar* 62, *Kālidāsa's Sakuntalā* translated from the Bengali Recension 62, *Dravidian Linguistics, Ethnology and Folktales* (collected papers) 67, *A Dravidian Etymological Dictionary: Supplement* (with T. Burrow) 68, *Toda Songs* 71, *Ritual Structure and Language Structure of the Todas* 74.
Department of Linguistics, University of California, Berkeley, Calif. 94720; Home: 909 San Benito Road, Berkeley, Calif. 94707, U.S.A.

Emerson, Alfred E(dwards), B.A., M.A., PH.D.; American scientist; b. 31 Dec. 1896, Ithaca, N.Y.; s. of Alfred Emerson and Alice Louisa Edwards Emerson; m. 1st Winifred Jelliffe 1923 (deceased), 2nd Eleanor Fish 1950 (deceased); one s. one d.; ed. Cornell Univ.
Instructor and Assoc. Prof. of Zoology, Univ. of Pittsburgh 22-29; Assoc. Prof. of Biology, then Prof., Univ. of Chicago 29-62, Prof. Emer. 62-; Visiting Prof., Univ. of Calif. 49, Mich. State Univ. 60; John Simon Guggenheim Fellow 26-27, Belgian-American Foundation Fellow 48; Pres. Ecological Soc. of America 41, Ill. Acad. of Science 46, Soc. of Systematic Zoology 58, Soc. for the Study of Evolution 60; Research Assoc., Assoc.-Founder, Benefactor, American Museum of Natural History; Research Assoc., Field Museum of Natural History; mem. Nat. Acad. of Sciences; Hon. Sc.D.
Leisure interests: music, travel, scientific research.
Publs. *Principals of Animal Ecology* (Co-Author) 49, *Ecology and Evolution* 55; about 150 articles on biology and science, also chapters in books.
Huletts Landing, N.Y. 12841, U.S.A.
Telephone: 518-499-0937.

Emerson, Ralph, PH.D.; American professor of botany; b. 19 April 1912, New York City; s. of Haven and Grace Parrish Emerson; m. Enid Merle Budelman 1942; one s. one d.; ed. Fieldston High School, N.Y.C., Harvard Coll. and Harvard Univ.
National Research Council Fellow in Botany, Cambridge 37-39; Research Fellow in Biology, Harvard 39-40; Instructor in Botany, Univ. of Calif. (Berkeley) 40-44, Asst. Prof. 44-48, Assoc. Prof. 48-53, Prof. 53-; Chair. Dept. of Botany 67-71; Guggenheim Fellow, Harvard 48-49, Costa Rica 56-57; mem. Nat. Acad. of Sciences, A.A.A.S., Mycological Soc. of America, Botanical Soc. of America, British Mycological Soc., American Inst. of Biological Sciences, Asscn. of Tropical Biology, Calif. Acad. of Sciences, etc.; Fellow, American Acad. of Arts and Sciences.
Leisure interests: sailing, photography, gardening.
Publs. articles in learned journals.
Department of Botany, University of California,

Berkeley, Calif. 94720; Home: 454 Beloit Avenue, Berkeley, Calif. 94708 U.S.A.
Telephone: 415-642- 11 (Office); 415-526-9215 (Home).

Emery, Kenneth O., PH.D.; American oceanographer. b. 6 June 1914, Saskatchewan, Canada; s. of Clifford A; and Agnes B. Emery; m. Caroline Alexander 1941; two d.; ed. N. Texas Agricultural Coll., Arlington, Univ. of Illinois and Scripps Inst. of Oceanography.
Associate Geologist, Illinois State Geological Survey 41-43; Assoc. Marine Geologist, Univ. of Calif. Div. of War Research 43-45; Asst., Assoc. and Prof. of Geology, Univ. of S. Calif. 45-62; Geologist, U.S. Geological Survey (summer only) 46-60; Senior Scientist, Woods Hole Oceanographic Inst. 62-, Dean of Educ. 67, Henry Bryant Bigelow Chair., Oceanography 75; Guggenheim Fellowship 59; mem. Nat. Acad. of Sciences, American Acad. of Arts and Sciences; Shepard Prize in Marine Geology 69, Médaille Commémorative du Prince Albert Ier de Monaco, Compass Distinguished Achievement Award 74, A.A.A.S.—Rosenstiel Award in Oceanography 75.
Leisure interest: stock market.
Publs. *Bikini and adjacent atolls* 54, *The Sea off Southern California* 60, *The Dead Sea* 67, *Oyster Pond* 70, *The Western North Atlantic Ocean* (with Elazar Uchupi) 72.
74 Ransom Road, Falmouth, Mass. 02540, U.S.A.

Emilio (*see* Pucci di Barsento, Marchese Emilio).

Emmanuel, Pierre; French writer; b. 3 May 1916, Gan (Pyrénées-Atlantiques); s. of Emile Mathieu and Maria Juge-Boulogne; m. 1st Jeanne Crépy 1938, one d.; m. 2nd Janine Loo 1952, one d.
Director of the English Service 45-47, North-American Service 47-59, Radiodiffusion Française; Visiting Prof. Harvard, Johns Hopkins, Brandeis, Buffalo, Queen's Univs.; mem. Acad. Française 68-; Pres. Int. PEN 69-71; Pres. French PEN; Chair. Comm. pour les Affaires Culturelles du VIe Plan Conseil de Développement Culturel 71-73, Comm. pour la Réforme de l'Enseignement du Français; Pres. Nat. Inst. de l'audio-visuel, Fondation d'Hautvillers; Administrator, Cité Internationale des Arts; Officier de la Légion d'Honneur, Grand Officier de l'Ordre Nat. du Mérite, Commdr. des Arts et Lettres, Commdr. of Yugoslav Flag, Grand Prix de Poésie de l'Académie Française; Dr. h.c. (Oxford and Neuchâtel).
Publs. Poetry: *Tombeau d'Orphée* 41, *Combats avec tes Défenseurs* 42, *Sodome* 44, *Le poète fou* 44, *Babel* 51, *Visage Nuage* 56, *Versant de l'âge* 58, *Evangéliaire* 61, *La Nouvelle Naissance* 63, *Ligne de Faîte* 68, *Jacob* 70, *Sophia* 73; novel: *Car enfin je vous aime* 49; autobiography: *Qui est cet homme* 48, *L'ouvrier de la onzième heure* 54; essays: *Le Goût de l'Un* 63, *La face humaine* 65, *Baudelaire devant Dieu* 67, *Le Monde est intérieur* 67, *Autobiographies* 70, *Choses Dites* 70, *Pour une Politique de la Culture* 71, *La révolution parallèle* 75.
61 rue de Varenne, Paris 7e, France.
Telephone: 551-91-06.

Emmet, Dorothy Mary, M.A.; British university professor; b. 29 Sept. 1904, London; d. of late Rev. Cyril W. Emmet and late Gertrude Julia (née Weir); ed. Lady Margaret Hall, Oxford.
Adult education work Maesyrhaf Settlement 27-28, 31-32; Commonwealth Fellowship in U.S. 28-30; Research Fellow, Somerville Coll., Oxford 30-31; Lecturer in Philosophy, King's Coll., Newcastle-on-Tyne 32-38; Lecturer in Philosophy of Religion, Univ. of Manchester 38-45; Reader in Philosophy 45-46; Sir Samuel Hall Prof. of Philosophy, Univ. of Manchester 46-66, Emer. Prof. 66-; Hon. Fellow Lady Margaret Hall, Oxford; Fellow Emer. Lucy Cavendish Coll., Cambridge; Hon. D.Litt. (Glasgow).
Leisure interests: walking, gardening, reading.
Publs. *Whitehead's Philosophy of Organism* 32, *Philo-*

sophy and Faith 36, *The Nature of Metaphysical Thinking* 45, *Function, Purpose and Powers* 58, *Rules, Roles and Relations* 66; Editor (with A. MacIntyre) *Sociological Theory and Philosophical Analysis* 70.
11 Millington Road, Cambridge, England.
Telephone: Cambridge 50822.

Emmett, Paul H., PH.D.; American chemist; b. 22 Sept. 1900, Portland, Ore.; s. of John and Vina Emmett; m. Mrs. Leila Jones 1930; ed. Washington High School, Portland, Oregon State Coll. and Calif. Inst. of Technology.
Instructor, Oregon State Coll. 26-27; Asst. Chemist to Senior Chemist, Fixed Nitrogen Research Lab., U.S. Dept. of Agriculture 26-37; Prof. of Chemical Engineering, Johns Hopkins Univ. 37-44; Manhattan project, Columbia Univ. 43-44; Multiple Petroleum Fellowship, Mellon Inst. of Industrial Research 44-55; W. R. Grace Prof. of Chem., Johns Hopkins Univ. 55-70; mem. Nat. Acad. of Sciences; Pittsburgh Award, American Chem. Soc. 53, Kendall Award 58, Consejo Superior, Madrid 64; Dr. h.c. (Univ. de Lyon).
Leisure interests: fishing, golf.
Publs. *Catalysis* Vols. I-VII (Editor) 54-61; about 150 scientific articles in technical journals.
Portland State University, Portland, Oregon 97207, U.S.A.

Emminger, Otmar; DR.OEC.PUBL.; German banker; b. 2 March 1911, Augsburg; m. two s.; ed. Berlin, Munich, Edinburgh and London Univs.
Member and Div. Chief, German Inst. for Business Research 35-39; at Bavarian Ministry of Economic Affairs 47-49; mem. German del. to O.E.E.C. Paris 49-50; Dir. Research and Statistics Dept. Bank Deutscher Länder 51-53; mem. Board of Govs. Bank Deutscher Länder (now Deutsche Bundesbank) 53-, mem. Board of Dirs. Deutsche Bundesbank 57-69, Deputy Gov. and Vice-Chair. Board of Dirs. 70-; Exec. Dir. Int. Monetary Fund 53-59; Vice-Chair. EEC Monetary Cttee. 58-; Chair. of Deputies of "Group of Ten" (important mems. of Int. Monetary Fund) 64-67; German Rep. on Econ. Policy Cttee. of OECD; Chair. Working Party III of OECD, Paris 69-.
Publs. *Die englischen Währungsexperimente der Nachkriegszeit* 34, *Die Bayerische Industrie* 47, *Deutschlands Stellung in der Weltwirtschaft* 53, *Währungspolitik im Wandel der Zeit* 66, *Zwischenbilanz der DM-Aufwertung* 70, *Inflation and the International Monetary System* 73.
Hasselhorstweg 36, Frankfurt/Main, 10 Federal Republic of Germany.
Telephone: 1581 (Office); 653476 (Home).

Emmons, Howard Wilson, M.E., M.S., SC.D.; American professor of mechanical engineering; b. 30 Aug. 1912, Morristown, N.J.; s. of Peter Emmons and Margaret Lang Emmons; m. Dorothy Allen 1937; two s. one d.; ed. Stevens Inst. of Technology and Harvard Univ.
Research Engineer, Westinghouse Electric and Manufacturing. Co 38-39; Prof., Univ. of Pennsylvania 39-40; Prof., Harvard Univ. 40-; Chair. Fire Research Cttee., Nat. Acad. of Sciences 68-70, *ad hoc* Fire Panel, Nat. Bureau of Standards 71-; Fellow, Amer. Soc. of Mechanical Eng.; mem. Nat. Acad. of Sciences; Hon. Dr. Eng. (Stevens Inst. of Technology); Gold Medal Int. Combustion Symposium; Centenary Award Stevens Inst. of Technology; Timoshenko Medal ASME.
Leisure interests: tennis, town government.
Publs. numerous articles in scientific journals.
Department of Engineering and Applied Physics, Pierce Hall 308, Harvard University, Cambridge, Mass. 02138; Home: 233 Concord Road, Sudbury, Mass. 01776, U.S.A.
Telephone: 617-495-2847 (Office); 617-443-6623 (Home).

Empson, William, M.A.; British literary critic and poet; b. 27 Sept. 1906, Yorefleet Hall, near Goole, Yorks; s. of Arthur Reginald Empson and Laura Micklethwait; m. Hester Henrietta Crouse 1941; two s.; ed. Winchester Coll. and Magdalene Coll., Cambridge.
Professor of English Literature at Bunrika Daigaku Tokyo 31-34; Prof. of English Literature, Peking Nat. Univ., then part of Combined South-Western Univs. 37-39, and, after its return, at Peking 47-52; Chinese Editor, BBC 41-47; Prof. of English Literature, Sheffield Univ. 53-71, Prof. Emeritus 71-.
Publs. *Seven Types of Ambiguity* 33, 62, *Some Versions of Pastoral* 35, *Poems* 35, *The Gathering Storm* (verse) 40, *The Structure of Complex Words* 51, *Collected Poems* 55, *Milton's God* 61, Editor (with D. Pirie) *Selected Poems of Coleridge* 72.
Studio House, 1 Hampstead Hill Gardens, London, N.W.3, England.

Enahoro, Chief Anthony; Nigerian politician; b. 22 July 1923, Uromi Ishan Division, Mid-Western State; s. of late Chief Okotako Enahoro; m. Helen Ediae 1954; four s. one d.; ed. Govt. Schools, Uromi and Owo and King's Coll., Lagos.
Journalist 42-50; Editor *Southern Nigeria Defender* 44-46, *Daily Comet* 46-49, concurrently Assoc. Editor *West African Pilot*; Editor-in-Chief *Morning Star* 50; foundation mem. Action Group, Sec. and Chair. of Ishan Div. Council; mem. Western House of Assembly and Fed. House of Reps. 51, later Minister of Home Affairs (Western Region); Opposition spokesman on Foreign Affairs and Legislative Affairs 59-63; moved motion for self-government and attended all constitutional talks preceding independence 60; detained during Emergency period in Western Nigeria 62, fled to Britain 63; extradited from Britain and imprisoned in Nigeria for treason; released by Mil. Govt. 66; Leader of Mid-West del. to *ad hoc* Constitutional Conf. and mem. *ad hoc* Constitutional Cttee. 66; Fed. Commr. for Information and Labour June 67-75; Fed. Commr. with Special Duties Jan.-July 75; Hon. D.Sc. (Benin) 72; Pres.World Festival of Negro Arts and Culture 72-75.
Leisure interests: golf, current affairs.
Publ. *Fugitive Offender* (autobiography).
c/o Federal Executive Council, Lagos, Nigeria.

Enckell, (Carl Fredrik) Ralph (Alexander), M.A.; Finnish diplomatist; b. 13 May 1913, Helsinki; s. of Carl Enckell and Lucy Ponsonby-Lyons; m. Laura Virkkunen, five s. two d.
Second Secretary, Finnish Legation, Stockholm 44-45; First Sec., Paris 45-50, Moscow 50-55; Head, Political Dept., Foreign Office, Helsinki 55-59; Permanent Rep. to UN, New York 59-65, Amb. to Sweden 65-69; Amb. to OECD 69-; roving Amb. for the Conf. on Security and Co-operation in Europe 70-72; Amb. to France 72-.
Leisure interest: history.
Finnish Embassy, 2 rue Fabert, Paris 7e, France.

Endacott, Paul; American petroleum executive (retd.); b. 13 July 1902, Lawrence, Kansas; s. of Frank Charles Endacott and Rebecca Lucinda Herning; m. Lucille Easter 1930; two s.; ed. Kansas Univ.
Joined Phillips Petroleum Co. as engineer 23, worked in Philgas Div., Detroit 27-34, Dir. Sales Research, Bartlesville 34-38, Asst. to Exec. Vice-Pres. 38-43 also Vice-Chair. Operating Cttee. (later Chair.), Vice-Pres. 43-49, and Dir., mem. Exec. Cttee. 43-, Exec. Vice-Pres. and Asst. to Pres. 49-51, Pres. 51-62, Vice-Chair. 62-67; Hon. Dir. American Petroleum Inst.; and official of many civic and charitable orgs.
320 Delaware Avenue, Bartlesville, Okla. 74003; Home: 916 Cherokee Avenue, Bartlesville, Okla. 74003, U.S.A.
Telephone: 336-5766 (Office); 336-1620 (Home).

Endeley, E. M. L., O.B.E.; Nigerian medical doctor and politician; b. 10 April 1916, Buea (then in Nigeria); s. of late Chief Mathias Liffafe Endeley and of Mariana Mojoko Liombe; *m.* 1st Ethel Mina Green (divorced 1961), 2nd Fanny Ebenye Njoh 1965; eight *s.* three *d.*; ed. Buea Govt. School, Catholic Mission, Bojongo, Govt. Coll. Umuahia, Higher Coll., Yaba.

Qualified as doctor 42; entered Govt. service 43; served Lagos, Port Harcourt, etc.; in charge of Cottage Hospital, Buea; trade union leader 47; formed Cameroons Nat. Fed. (afterwards Kamerun Nat. Congress) 49; Pres. Bakweri Co-op. Marketing Union 55; led South Cameroons Del. to Constitutional Conf., London 57; first Premier of South Cameroons 58-59; Leader of the Opposition 59-61; Leader Nat. Convention Party (later Cameroon People's Nat. Convention Party), West Cameroon 61-66; Asst. Treas. and mem. Cameroon Nat. Union Political Bureau 66-74, mem. Central Cttee. 75; mem. Nat. Ass., Yaoundé; Chair. House Cttee. on Production, Town Planning, Agriculture, Stock-farming, Rural and Civil Engineering.

Leisure interests: mountaineering, gardening, wild game hunting.

P.O. Box 5, Buea, Southwest Province, United Republic of Cameroon.

Telephone: Buea 32-42-26.

Enderby, Keppel Earl, Q.C., LL.M.; Australian lawyer and politician; b. 25 June 1926, Dubbo, N.S.W.; *s.* of Alfred Charles and Daisy Kathleen Enderby; *m.* two *c.*; ed. Dubbo High School, Univs. of Sydney and London.

Practising barrister; Lecturer, Examiner in Commercial Law, Sydney Technical Coll. 55-62; Senior Lecturer in Law, Australian Nat. Univ. 63-65; mem. Parl. for A.C.T. 70-74, for Canberra 74-75; Minister for A.C.T. and Northern Territory 72-74; Minister for Supply and for Secondary Industry 74-75; Attorney-Gen. Feb.-Nov. 75, Minister for Customs and Excise Feb.-June 75; Chair. Privileges Cttee. of House of Representatives.

Leisure interests: reading, farming, flying, golf.

Publ. *Courts Martial Appeals in Australia* (Fed. Law Review) 64.

32 Endeavour Street, Red Hill, A.C.T., Australia.

Telephone: 733811.

Enderl, Kurt, D.IUR.; Austrian diplomatist; b. 12 April 1913, Budweis; *s.* of Hugo and Karoline Enderl (née Stegmann); *m.* Adele Leigh 1967; ed. Univ. of Vienna.

War-work, London 39-46; Third Sec., Austrian Legation, London 46-47; Vice-Consul, New York 47-48; Ministry of Foreign Affairs 48-50; Chargé d'Affaires Austrian Legation, New Delhi 50-53; Ministry of Foreign Affairs 53-55; Minister, Austrian Legation, Israel 55-58; Head, Multilateral Dept. Ministry of Foreign Affairs 58-61, Chef de Protocol 72-74; Amb. to Poland 62-67, to Hungary 67-72, to U.K. 75-; several decorations.

Leisure interests: music, tennis, skiing.

Austrian Embassy, 18 Belgrave Square, London, SW1X 8HU, England.

Telephone: 01-235-3731.

Enders, John Franklin, PH.D., D.SC., LL.D., L.H.D.; American bacteriologist; b. 10 Feb. 1897, West Hartford, Conn.; *s.* of John Ostrom Enders and Harriet Goulden Whitmore; *m.* 1st Sarah F. Bennett 1927, 2nd Carolyn Keane 1951; one *s.* one *d.*, one stepson; ed. Yale and Harvard Univs.

Assistant Dept. of Bacteriology and Immunology, Harvard Medical School 29-30, Instructor 30-32, Faculty Instructor 32-35, Asst. Prof. 35-42, Assoc. Prof. 42-56, Prof. 56-62, Univ. Prof. (Harvard) 62-67, Emeritus 68; Chief Research Div., Infectious Diseases, Children's Hospital Medical Center 47-72; Chief ,Virus Research Unit, Div. of Infectious Diseases, C.H.M.C.; mem. Nat. Acad. of Sciences; Foreign mem. Royal Soc. (U.K.); Foreign mem. Acad. des Sciences Inst. de France;

Passano Award 53; Lasker Award 54; Nobel Prize in Physiology and Medicine 54, Cameron Prize in Practical Therapeutics 60, Robert Koch Medal 63, Presidential Freedom Medal 63.

Leisure interests: fishing, gardening, playing the piano.

The Children's Hospital Medical Center, 300 Longwood Avenue, Boston, Mass. 02115; Home: 64 Colbourne Crescent, Brookline, Mass., U.S.A.

Enders, Thomas O., M.A.; American economist; b. 28 Nov. 1931, Hartford, Conn.; *m.* Gaetana Marchegiano; four *c.*; ed. Yale, Paris and Harvard Univs.

With Dept. of State 59-; Research Specialist, Div. of Research and Analysis for Far East 59-60; Econ. Officer, Stockholm 60-63; Supervisory Int. Economist, Bureau of European Affairs 63-66; Special Asst. Office of Under Sec. of State for Political Affairs 66-68; Deputy Asst. Sec. of State for Int. Monetary Affairs 68-69; Deputy Chief of Mission, Belgrade 69-71, Phnom Penh 71-73; Asst. Sec. of State for Econ. and Business Affairs 74-75; Amb. to Canada 75-; Arthur S. Flemming Award 70.

American Embassy, 100 Wellington Street, Ottawa K1P 5TI, Canada.

Endicott, Kenneth Milo, M.D.; American physician; b. 6 June 1916, Canon City, Colo.; *s.* of James Milo Endicott and Florence Violet Doran Endicott; *m.* Frances Ann Clarke 1950; one *s.* two *d.*; ed. Univ. of Colorado.

Intern, U.S. Marine Hospital 39-40; U.S. Public Health Service 39-, Medical Dir. 51; Experimental Pathology, Nat. Insts. of Health 42-51, Scientific Dir. Div. of Research Grants 51-55, Chief, Cancer Chemotherapy Nat. Service Center 55-58, Assoc. Dir. Nat. Insts. of Health 58-60; Asst. Surgeon General 60, Dir. Nat. Cancer Inst. 60-69; Dir. Bureau of Health Manpower Educ. 69-73; Administrator, Health Resources Admin. 73-; mem. Amer. Medical Asscn., Amer. Asscn. of Pathologists and Bacteriologists, Amer. Soc. for Experimental Pathology, American Asscn. for Advancement of Science, Soc. for Experimental Biology and Medicine, American Asscn. for Cancer Research, Washington Acad. of Sciences.

Health Resources Administration, DHEW, Rockville, Md. 20852; Home: Beall Mount River Road Potomac, Md. U.S.A.

Engel, Albert Edward, M.A., PH.D.; American professor of geology; b. 17 June 1916, St. Louis, Mo.; *s.* of Louis and Louise Engel; two *s.*; ed. Univ. of Missouri and Princeton Univ.

Geologist, U.S. Geol. Survey 42-47; Prof. of Geology, Calif. Inst. of Technology 48-58; Prof. of Geology and Environmental Sciences, Univ. of Calif. at San Diego and Scripps Inst. of Oceanography; mem. Nat. Acad. of Sciences, American Acad. of Arts and Sciences etc.; Guggenheim Fellow 53.

Leisure interests: horticulture, architecture, archaeology, ecology, painting, the environment of the earth, politics.

Publs. approximately 150 articles and two books discussing the origin and evolution of the Earth and its life.

Division Geological Research, Scripps Institution of Oceanography, P.O. Box 109, La Jolla, Calif. 92037, U.S.A.

Engel, Ir. Antonie Jacobus; Netherlands industrialist; b. 1896, Oosthuizen; *s.* of Frederik Engel and Marie Antoinette Allan; *m.* P. C. Goudswaard 1922; three *s.* one *d.*; ed. Elementary School, Hillegom, Secondary School, Leiden, Univ. of Delft.

State Mines, Limburg; Algemene Kunstzijde Unie N.V. (rayon and synthetic yarns and fibres) 24-, Mechanical Engineer, Plant Manager Chief. Gen. Engineering Dept., Man. Staple Fibre Plant, Vice-Pres. 47-54, Pres. 54-62, Deputy Chair. Supervisory Council 62-67;

Chair. Technical Coll., Arnhem; mem. Royal Inst. of Engineers; Knight in the Order of the Netherlands Lion; Officer Order of Orange-Nassau; Peter Stuyvesant Award (U.S.A.).
Leisure interests: music, photography, gardening.
Home: Rozenhagelaan 4, Velp (Gld.), Netherlands.
Telephone: 08302-3118.

Engelhardt, Vladimir Alexsandrovitch; Soviet biochemist; b. 4 Dec. 1894, Moscow; s. of Alexander and Vera Engelhardt; m. Militza Liubimova 1927; two d.; ed. Moscow Univ.
Public Health Biochemical Inst. 21-29; Prof. Kazan Univ. 29-34, Leningrad Univ. 34-40, Moscow Univ. 39-59; Head of Laboratory, Inst. of Biochemistry, Moscow 35-59; Academic Sec. Biological Dept., Acad. of Sciences 55-59; Dir. Inst. of Molecular Biology, Moscow 59-; mem. Bureau, Vice-Pres. I.C.S.U. 55-63; mem. U.S.S.R. Acad. of Sciences; Hon. Foreign Mem. Royal Inst., London, Nat. Acad. of Sciences, U.S.A., American Acad. of Arts and Sciences, Indian Nat. Science Acad., Leopoldina Acad. of Nat. Sciences, German Acad. of Sciences, Berlin; Fellow Royal Soc., Edinburgh; Editor Biochimia 36-; Hon. D.Sc. (Cambridge, Vienna, Marseille, Berlin); State Prize; Order of Lenin (three times), Hero of Socialist Labour 69; Order of the Red Banner of Labour; Gold Medals: Lomonossov, Kothenius.
Leisure interests: mountaineering, photography.
Institute of Molecular Biology, U.S.S.R. Academy of Sciences, Vavilov Street 32, Moscow B-312, U.S.S.R.

Engellau, Gunnar Ludvig; Swedish civil engineer; b. 11 Nov. 1907; m. Margit Höckert 1933; one s. five d.; ed. Kung. Tekniska Högskolan, Stockholm.
With Swedish State Railways, Gothenburg, Orebro, Stockholm 32-34; Dept. Head, AB Motala Verkstad, Motala 35-37, Purchase and Sales Man. 37-39; Head, Technical Sales Dept., Electrolux 39-43; Man. Dir. Svenska Flygmotor AB, Trollhättan 43-56; Man. Dir. AB Volvo, Gothenburg and Head, Volvo Corpn. 56-71; Chair. of Board, AB Volvo 71-, Sâfveåns AB, Uddeholms AB, Volvo BM AB, Eskilstuna and AB Volvo Flygmotor, Trollhättan; mem. Board of Dirs. SKF, Skandinaviska Enskilda Banken, AB Electrolux, Rederi AB Transatlantic, Sukab AB, AB Hevea, Gen. Export Asscn. of Sweden, Swedish Acad. of Engineering Sciences, Park Avenue Hotel AB.
AB Volvo, 405 08 Gothenburg; Home: Dicksonsgat 6, 412 56 Gothenburg, Sweden.

Engen, René Léopold Alexis; Belgian civil engineer; b. 13 Dec. 1918, Brussels-Etterbeek; s. of Léopold Engen and Louise Etienne; m. Madeleine Lekeu 1942; one d.; ed. Free Univ. of Brussels.
Engineer with ACEC 42-45; Engineer Verreries de Mariemont 45, Chief Eng. 49, Dir. 50; Dir. Verreries Réunies Val St. Lambert et Momignies 54; Man. Verlica-Momignies 60, Man. Dir. 61, Admin. Del. 68; Man. Dir. Electrorail 69-, Schneider 72-; Dir. Elican, Spie-Batignolles, Jeumont-Schneider, Jeumont-Industrie, Cie. Financière de l'Union Européene, Creusot-Loire, Arbed, Salem, Marine-Schneider, Intercom, Interbrabant, Cofibel; mem. Exec. Cttee. Creusot-Loire; Officier Ordre de la Couronne, Ordre de Léopold; Médaille de la Résistance; Médaille Civique (1st Class).
Schneider, 42 rue d'Anjou, 75008 Paris, France; and Electrorail, 23 avenue de l'Astronomie, 1030 Brussels, Belgium.
Telephone: 260-36-72 (Paris); 218-61-70 (Brussels).

Engman, Lewis August, A.B., LL.B.; American lawyer and government official; b. 6 Jan. 1936, Grand Rapids, Mich.; s. of H. Sigurd and Florence C. Lewis Engman; m. Jacqueline Ransford Graham 1961; three s.; ed. Univ. of Mich., Univ. of London (Univ. Coll.), London School of Econs. and Harvard Law School.
Associate, Warner, Norcross & Judd, law firm, Grand

Rapids 61-65, Partner 65-70; Dir. of Legis. Affairs, President's Cttee. on Consumer Interests 70; Gen. Counsel Office of Consumer Affairs 70-71; Asst. Dir. Domestic Council 71-73; Chair. Fed. Trade Comm. Feb. 73-; mem. Council, Admin. Conf. of U.S. 74-.
Federal Trade Commission, Pennsylvania Avenue, at 6th Street, Washington, D.C. 20580, U.S.A.

Engstrom, Elmer W.; American electronics executive; b. 25 Aug. 1901, Minneapolis, Minn.; s. of Emil and Anna (Nilssen) Engstrom; m. Phoebe Leander 1926; one s.; ed. elementary schools, St. Paul, Minn. and Univ. of Minnesota.
Joined Radio Engineering Dept., Gen. Electric Co. 23; G.E.C. radio engineering activities transferred to Radio Corpn. of America (RCA) 30, Div. Engineer in charge of Photophone 30, research into television and colour television; Dir. of Gen. Research RCA 42-43, Dir. of Research of RCA Labs. 43-45, Vice-Pres. (Research, RCA Labs. Div.) 45-51, Vice-Pres. (RCA Labs. Div.) 51-54, Exec. Vice-Pres. (Research and Engineering) 54-55, Senior Exec. Vice-Pres. RCA 55-61, Pres. RCA 61-65, Chief Exec. Officer and Chair. Exec. Cttee. 66-Dec. 67, Chair. Exec. Cttee. 68-71.
Apartment 31-01, Meadow Lakes, Hightstown, N.J. 08520, U.S.A.
Telephone: 609-448-4100, extension 551.

Ennals, Rt. Hon. David Hedley, P.C., M.P.; British politician; b. 19 Aug. 1922; m. Eleanor Caddick 1950; three s. one d.; ed. St. Mary's Grammar School, Loomis Inst.
War service; Labour Party Overseas Sec. 57-64; M.P. for Dover 64-70, for Norwich North 74-; Minister of State, Dept. of Health and Social Security 68-70, Foreign and Commonwealth Office 74-76; Sec. of State for Social Services April 76-; Labour.
House of Commons, Westminster, London, S.W.1, England.

Enright, Dennis Joseph, M.A., D.LITT.; British teacher and writer; b. 11 March 1920 Leamington Spa, Warwicks.; s. of George and Grace (née Cleaver) Enright; m. Madeleine Harders 1949; one d.; ed. Leamington Coll., and Downing Coll., Cambridge.
Lecturer in English, Farouk I Univ. Alexandria 47-50; Org. Tutor, Birmingham Univ. Extra-Mural Dept. 50-53; Visiting Prof. Konan Univ. (Japan) 53-56; Gastdozent, English Seminar, Berlin Free Univ. 56-57; British Council Prof. Chulalongkorn Univ. Bangkok 57-59; Johore Prof. of English, Univ. of Singapore 60-70; Co-editor Encounter Magazine Sept. 70-Feb. 73; Editorial adviser, Chatto and Windus 72-74, Dir. 74-; contributor to Scrutiny, Essays in Criticism, New York Review of Books, New Statesman, Encounter, Listener.
Leisure interests: reading, films, listening to music.
Publs. The Laughing Hyena and Other Poems 53, Academic Year 55, The World of Dew: Aspects of Living Japan 56, Bread rather than Blossoms: Poems 56, The Poetry of Living Japan: An Anthology 57, The Apothecary's Shop: Essays on Literature 57, Insufficient Poppy 60, Some Men are Brothers: Poems 60, Addictions: Poems 62, Figures of Speech 65, The Old Adam (poetry) 65, Conspirators and Poets: literary criticism 66, Unlawful Assembly (poetry) 68, Selected Poems 69, Memoirs of a Mendicant Professor 69, Shakespeare and the Students 70, The Typewriter Revolution and Other Poems 71, Daughters of Earth (poetry) 72, Man is an Onion (literary criticism) 72 The Terrible Shears (poetry) 73, Rhyme Times Rhyme (children's poems) 74, A Choice of Milton's Verse 75, Sad Ires (poetry) 75.
c/o Chatto and Windus Ltd., 40-42 William IV Street, London, W.C.2, England.

Enrique y Tarancón, H.E. Cardinal Vicente; Spanish ecclesiastic; b. 14 June 1907, Burriana, Castellón; s. of

Manuel E. Urios and Vincenta T. Fandos; ed. Seminario Conciliar Rortosa, Tarragona and Universidad Pontificia Valencia.
Administrative Asst. of Vinaroz 30-33, Archpriest 38-43; Archpriest, Villarreal 43-46; Bishop of Solsona 46-64; Gen. Sec. Spanish Bishopric 56-64; Archbishop of Ovopie 64-69; Archbishop of Toledo, Primate of Spain 69-71; Archbishop of Madrid Dec. 71-; Cardenal del Tit. de S. Juan Crisóstomo, Monte Sacro 69-; mem. Sacred Congregations for Bishops, Divine Worship, and Reform of Canon Law; mem. Spanish Acad. 69.
Leisure interests: musical composition, listening to classical music, particularly Bach.
Publs. *La Renovación Total de la Vida Cristiana* 54, *Los Seglares en la Iglesia* 58, *Sucesores de los Apóstoles* 60, *La Parroquia, Hoy* 61, *El Misterio de la Iglesia* 63, *Ecumenismo y Pastoral* 64, *La Iglesia en el Mundo de Hoy* 65, *El Sacerdocio a la Luz del Concilio Vaticano 11* 66, *La Iglesia del Posconcilio* 67, *La Crisis de Fe en el Mundo Actual* 68, *Unidad y pluralismo en la Iglesia* 69, *Liturgia y lengua del pueblo* 70, *El magisterio de Santa Teresa* 70.
Palacio Arzobispal, S. Justo 2, Madrid 12, Spain.
Telephone: 24-14-804.

Enters, Angna; American mime artist, painter and sculptor; b. 28 April 1907; ed. privately.
Presented *Composition in Dance Form* (later called *Theatre of Angna Enters*), which combined mime, dance, music, etc., in solo performance, in N.Y. 24; London debut 28; Paris debut 29, rep. U.S.A. in Berlin Arts Festival 51; 10th London season 56; presented mime *Pagan Greece* under auspices N.Y. Metropolitan Museum of Art 43; Guggenheim Foundation Fellowships for research in Mime and Art in Greece, Egypt 34-35; Painting: N.Y. debut 33; various exhibitions Newhouse Galleries N.Y.; London debut 34; exhibition Brook Street Galleries 50; 3rd London exhibition at Foyle Gallery 56; Sculpture: N.Y. debut 45; work exhibited in N.Y. Metropolitan Museum of Art and other museums and private collections; composed scores for own play and mimes; play-within-play for Commedia dell'Arte sequence, choreography and dance for *Scaramouche* (film) 52; author of *Lost Angel* (film) 44, *10th Avenue Angel* (film) 46, and *You Belong to Me* (film) 48-49; first work in ceramics exhibited 52; exhibition in New York 58; 32nd annual Lecture Tour of U.S. and Canada in her one-woman theatre 60; directed and designed sets and costumes for *Yerma* 58; 22nd Broadway season solo theatre 60; Fellow Center for Advanced Studies, Wesleyan Univ., Middletown, Conn. 62-.
Publs. *First Person Plural* (own illustrations) 37; *Love Possessed Juana* (play) 39; *Silly Girl* (autobiography) 44; *A Thing of Beauty* (novel) 48; and stories for screen; *Among the Daughters* 55, *Artist's Life* (sequel to *First Person Plural*) 57; author of article on *Pantomime* for *Encyclopaedia Britannica*, adaptor-translator of Edmond Rostand's *Chantecler* 60, *The Loved and the Unloved* 61; *Angna Enters on Mime* 65.
35 West 57th Street, New York City, N.Y. 10019, U.S.A.

Enwonu, Benedict Chuka, M.B.E.; Nigerian sculptor; b. 21; ed. Holy Trinity School, Onitsha, Govt. Colls. Umu-Ahia and Ibadan, Univ. Coll., London.
First One-Man Show, Lagos 42; on the strength of this he was given a special scholarship by Shell-Mex to study in England; rep. UNESCO Exhibition, Paris 46; first One-Man Exhibition, London 48, subsequent exhibitions 50, 52, 55; exhibition U.S. 50; commissioned to execute statue of H.M. Queen Elizabeth, Doors, Panels and Speaker's Chair, Lagos House of Representatives, and the group *The Risen Christ* for the Chapel, Univ. Coll., Ibadan; Art Adviser to the Federal Govt. of Nigeria 68-72; fmr. Prof. of Fine Arts, Univ. of Ife; his works have been purchased by H.M. Queen

Elizabeth II, the late Sir Jacob Epstein and others; R. B. Bennett Empire Art Prize 57.
University of Ife, Ile-Ife, Nigeria.

Enzensberger, Hans Magnus, DR. PHIL.; German poet and writer; b. 11 Nov. 1929, Kaufbeuren; *m.* Maria Aleksandrovna Makarova; one *d.*; ed. Univs. of Erlangen, Freiburg im Breisgau, Hamburg and Paris.
Third Programme Editor, Stuttgart Radio 55-57; Lecturer, Hochschule für Gestaltung, Ulm 56-57; Literary Consultant to Suhrkamp's (publishers), Frankfurt 60-; mem. "Group 47"; Editor *Kursbuch* (review) 65-75, Publisher 70-; Hugo Jacobi Prize 56; Kritiker Prize 62; Georg Büchner Prize 63.
Publs. *Verteidigung der Wölfe* (poems) 57, *Landessprache* (poems) 60, *Clemens Brentanos Poetik* (essay) 61, *Einzelheiten* (essays) 62, *Blindenschrift* (poems) 64, *Politik und Verbrechen* (essays) 64, *Deutschland, Deutschland unter Anderen* 67, *Das Verhör von Habana* (play) 70, *Freisprüche* 70, *Gedichte 1955-1970* (poetry) 71, *Durruti* (film) 71; English edn. of Poems: *Poems for People Who don't Read Poems* 68; *Der kurze Sommer der Anarchie* (novel) 72, *Gespräche mit Marx und Engels* 73, *Palaver* 74, *Mausoleum* (poetry) 75; Edited *Museum der Moderner Poesie* 60, *Allerleirauh* 61, *Andreas Gryphius Gedichte* 62.
c/o Suhrkamp Verlag, Fach 2446, Frankfurt/Main, Federal Republic of Germany.

Ephrussi, Boris; French (b. Russian) geneticist; b. 9 May 1901, Moscow; ed. Univ. de Paris à la Sorbonne.
Associate Prof. of Biology, Johns Hopkins Univ., U.S.A. 41-44; Prof. of Genetics, Univ. of Paris 45-68; Dir. Laboratory of Physiological Genetics, Centre Nat. de la Recherche Scientifique (France) 46-70; Exchange Prof. Harvard Univ. 54, Calif. Inst. of Technology 59; F. H. Herrick Distinguished Prof. of Biology, Western Reserve Univ., U.S.A. 61-67; mem. Royal Danish Acad.; Foreign Assoc. Nat. Acad. of Sciences (U.S.A.); Légion d'Honneur; Dir. Centre de Génétique Moléculaire du C.N.R.S. 67-70, Hon. Dir. 70-.
Publs. *La Culture des Tissus* 32, *Nucleo-cytoplasmic Relations in Micro-organisms* 53, *Hybridization of Somatic Cells* 72.
Centre de Génétique Moléculaire, 33 rue Gustave-Vatonne, 91190 Gif-sur-Yvette, France.
Telephone: 907-78-28.

Epishev, Gen. Alexei Alexeyevich; Soviet politician and Army Officer; b. 19 May 1908, Astrakhan; ed. Red Army Acad. of Mechanisation.
Member C.P.S.U. 29-; First Sec. Kharkov Regional and City Cttees. C.P. Ukraine, Plenipotentiary Rep. Military Council, Stalingrad Front, Dep. People's Commissar for Medium Machine Building U.S.S.R. 38-43; Soviet army service 43-46; Sec. Central Cttee. C.P. Ukraine 46-51; Dep. Minister of State Security U.S.S.R. 51-53; First Sec. Odessa Regional Cttee. C.P. Ukraine 53-55; Ambassador to Romania 55-61, to Yugoslavia 61-62; Head, Political Dept., Soviet Army and Navy 62-; Cand. mem. Central Cttee. C.P.S.U. 52-64, mem. of the Central Cttee. of C.P.S.U. 64-; Gen. of the Army 62-; Deputy to U.S.S.R. Supreme Soviet 38-46, 50-; Military Attaché U.K. 75-; mem. Comm. for Foreign Affairs, Soviet of Union; Awarded Order of Lenin (twice), Order of the Red Banner (thrice), Red Star, Bogdan Khmelnitsky (first class) and others.
Embassy of the Union of Soviet Socialist Republics, 16 Kensington Palace Gardens, London, W.8, England.
Telephone: 01-229 6451.

Epley, Marion Jay, Jr., LL.B.; American oil executive; b. 17 June 1907; *s.* of Marion Jay and Eva (née Quin) Epley; *m.* Jane Dudley 1927; two *s.* one *d.*; ed. Tulane Univ. and Tulane Law School, New Orleans, Louisiana.
Private law practice, New Orleans 30-42, 45-47; U.S. Navy 42-45; Gen. Attorney, Texaco Inc. Louisiana and

New York 48-57, Asst. to Chair. of Board of Dirs. 58-60, Vice-Pres. 58-60, Senior Vice-Pres. 60-61, Exec. Vice-Pres. 61-65, Pres. 65-70, Chair. 70-71; Board of Dirs. Texaco Inc. and American Petroleum Inst.; Vice-Chair. Supervisory Board Deutsche Erdöl-Aktiengesellschaft, Hamburg.
810 South Ocean Boulevard, Palm Beach, Fla. 33480, U.S.A.

Eppelsheimer, Hanns W., DR. PHIL.; German librarian and literary historian; b. 17 Oct. 1890; ed. Univs. of Freiburg, Munich and Marburg.
Director, Hesse Land Library 29-33, 45; Dir. Univ. Library, Frankfurt 46-58; Founder and Dir. Deutsche Bibliothek 47-59; Prof. of Univ. Frankfurt for Library Science 47; mem. German UNESCO Comm. 51-66; mem. German Acad. of Languages and Poetry, Darmstadt 53, Vice-Pres. 58-62, Pres. 63-66, Hon. mem. 66-; Grosses Bundesverdienstkreuz mit Stern.
Publs. *Petrarca* 27, *Handbuch der Weltliteratur* 37, 47-50, 60, *Schild des Aeneas* 55, *Bibliographie der Deutschen Literaturwissenschaft* 45- (5 vols. 64).
Untermainkai 15, Frankfurt am Main, Federal Republic of Germany.
Telephone: 281607.

Eralp, Orhan, B.A., LL.B., PH.D.; Turkish diplomatist; b. 28 Jan. 1915, Izmir; m. Jalé Mizanoglu 1956; two s.; ed. Robert Coll., Istanbul, Univ. Coll., London, and London School of Economics.
Ministry of Foreign Affairs 39-; Sec. Washington 42-48; Adviser to Turkish Del., UN Conciliation Comm. for Palestine 49-51; Perm. Rep. to European Office of UN, Geneva 51; Counsellor, London 52; Dir.-Gen. Second Dept., Ministry of Foreign Affairs 52-56; Ambassador to Sweden 57-59, to Yugoslavia 59-64; Perm. Rep. of Turkey to UN, New York 64-69; Sec.-Gen. Ministry of Foreign Affairs 69-72; Perm. Rep. of Turkey to NATO 72-.
Leisure interests: golf, tennis, bridge.
Permanent Delegation of Turkey to NATO, 1110 Brussels, Belgium.
Telephone: 414400.

Erbakan, Necmettin; Turkish politician; b. 1926, Sinop; ed. Inst. of Mechanics, Technical Univ. of Istanbul and Technische Universität, Aachen, Germany.
Assistant Lecturer, Inst. of Mechanics, Technical Univ. of Istanbul 48-51; Engineer, Firma Deutz 51-54; Prof. Technical Univ. of Istanbul 54-66; Chair. Industrial Dept., Turkish Asscn. of Chambers of Commerce 66-68, Chair. of Asscn. 68; mem. Nat. Assembly 69-; f. Nat. Order Party 70 (disbanded 71); Chair. Nat. Salvation Party Oct. 72-; Deputy Prime Minister and Minister of State Jan.-Sept. 74, Deputy Prime Minister March 75-.
Office of the Deputy Prime Minister, Ankara, Turkey.

Erban, Evžen; Czechoslovak politician; b. 18 June 1912, Vsetin; s. of Hugo Erban and Marie (née Splíchalová); m. Zora Doskočilová 1966; ed. Charles Univ., Prague.
Trade Union Sec. 36-45; Gen. Sec. Central Council of Trade Unions 45-50; Minister of Labour and Social Welfare 48-51; Chair. State Social Security Office 52-62; Chair. Board of State Material Reserves 63-68; Gen. Sec. Central Cttee. Nat. Front 68; Chair. Central Cttee. of Nat. Front 68-71; mem. Central Cttee. and Presidium of Central Cttee. (Deputy Chair.) Czechoslovak Social Dem. Party 45-48; mem. Central Cttee. and Presidium of Central Cttee. of C.P. of Czechoslovakia 48-51, 68-71; mem. Exec. Cttee. of Presidium of Central Cttee., C.P. of Czechoslovakia 68-69; Deputy to Nat. Assembly 45-52; Deputy to Czech Nat. Council 68; Deputy to House of Nations 69-, and mem. Presidium of Fed. Assembly 69; Chair Czech Nat. Council 69-; mem. Bureau of Central Cttee. C.P. of Czechoslovakia for directing Party work in the Czech lands Jan. 70-; mem. Plenum State

Planning Comm. 66-68; mem. Presidium of Int. Asscn. of Social Security 57-62; mem. Exec. Board, Int. Labour Office. Geneva 58-61; numerous decorations, including Order of the Repub. 62, Klement Gottwald Order 68, Hon. award of 3rd Guard Tank Brigade, U.S.S.R., Order of Victorious February 73.
Leisure interests: culture, sport, hunting.
Czech National Council, Prague; Sněmovní 4, Malá Strana, Prague 1, Czechoslovakia.
Telephone: 2105.

Erdélyi, Miklós; Hungarian conductor; b. 9 Feb. 1928, Budapest; s. of Ernő Erdélyi and Ida Friedrich; m. Kata Miklós 1952; ed. Music Acad. of Budapest under János Ferencsik and Rezső Kokai.
Started career as conductor in 47; helped found Hungarian Radio chorus 49, acted as their second conductor 51; joined staff of Hungarian State Opera 51-; conductor, touring throughout Europe 51-, and in U.S.A. 72; gave first performance of numerous Hungarian 20th-century works; has conducted everything from 17th-century opera (Monteverdi: Poppea's Coronation) to contemporary oratorio (E. Petrovics: The Book of Jonah); Kossuth Prize 75.
Leisure interests: travel, architecture.
Publs. *Franz Schubert* (biography) 63, numerous studies in musical journals.
H-1062 Budapest, Délibáb-utca 19, Hungary.
Telephone: 428-182.

Erdey-Grúz, Tibor, PH.D.; Hungarian physico-chemist; b. 1902, Budapest; s. of Aladár Erdey-Grúz and Olga Heuffel; m. 1st Magda Berg 1934 (died 1946), 2nd Maria Haban 1947; one s. two d.; ed. Péter Pázmány Univ., Budapest.
Professor of Physical Chemistry R. Eötvös Univ., Budapest; Sec. of Chemistry Section Hungarian Acad. of Sciences 48-50, 59-64, Gen. Sec. 50-53, 56-57, 64-70; Minister of Educ. 52-56; Pres. of the Council for Science and Higher Educ. 62-64; mem. Hungarian Acad. of Sciences 43, Pres. 70-; mem. German Acad. of Sciences, Berlin 62; Hon. mem. Romanian Acad. of Sciences 65; Foreign mem. of the Soviet Acad. of Sciences 66; Corresp. mem. Austrian Acad. of Sciences 69; foreign mem. Bulgarian Acad. of Sciences 69, Serbian Acad. of Arts and Sciences 75; Kossuth Prize 50, 56; Gold Degree, Labour Order of Merit 70; Red Banner Order of Labour 72.
Publs. *The Practice of Physical Chemistry* 34, 62, 65, 67-68 (with János Proszt), *Atoms and Molecules* 45, 66, *Theoretical Physical Chemistry* 52-54, 62-64 (with Géza Schay), *The Foundations of Physical Chemistry* 58, 63, 69, 72, *The Foundations of the Structure of Matter* 61, 67, *The Knowledge of Chemicals* 43, 64, *Matter and Motion* 62, *Philosophical Gleaning in the Natural Sciences* 65, *The Material Structure of the World* 66, *The Chemical Sources of Energy* 67, 71, 74, *The Kinetics of Electrode Reactions* 69, 72, 75, *Transport Processes in Solutions* 71, 74, *The Hungarian Chemical Nomenclature.*
Roosevelt tér 9, Budapest V, and Lékai J. tér 2, H-1124 Budapest XII, Hungary.
Telephone: 121-087 and 355-452.

Erfurth, Ulrich; German theatre director; b. 22 March 1910, Elberfeld; m. Ingeborg Brose 1934; two d.; ed. Univs. of Cologne and Berlin.
Actor and Producer, Municipal Theatre, Wuppertal 31-34; Chief Producer, Koblenz 34-35; Producer, Staatstheater, Berlin 34-35; Producer, Hamburg, and Artistic Dir. Real-Film G.m.b.H. 46-49; Chief Producer, City Theatres, Düsseldorf, and Schauspielhaus, Hamburg 49; Production Dir., Düsseldorf 51-55; Chief Producer, Hamburg 55-62; Dir. Volkstheater, Vienna, and Chief Producer, Schauspielhaus, Hamburg 62-64; Dir. Kammerspiele, Hamburg, and Deutsche Kammerspiele, Santiago 64; Ord. Prof., Folkwanghochschule,

Essen 64; Deutsche Kammerspiele, Buenos Aires 65, Burgtheater, Vienna 65; Bad Hersfeld Festival 66; Gen. Supt. City Theatres, Frankfurt 67-.
Leisure interest: music.
Zickzackweg 12a, 2 Hamburg-Othmarschen, Federal Republic of Germany.

Ergin, Sait Naci; Turkish civil servant and politician; b. 1908, Niğde; *m.*; two *c.*; ed. Faculty of Political Sciences, Istanbul.
Joined Ministry of Interior, later Ministry of Finance; studied public finance in France; later Under-Sec., Ministry of Finance, Ankara; mem. Constituent Assembly responsible for drafting 1961 Constitution; Minister of Finance March 71-April 72.
Ankara, Turkey.

Erhard, Ludwig; German economist and politician; b. 4 Feb. 1897, Fuerth, Bavaria; *s.* of Wilhelm and Auguste (née Hassold) Erhard; *m.* Luise Lotter 1923; one *d.*; ed. Handelshochschule, Nuremberg, and Univ. of Frankfurt.
War service 16-19; on staff of Handelshochschule Nuremberg, rising to be Head of Institut für Wirtschaftsbeobachtung 28-42; Head of Institut für Industrieforschung, Nuremberg 43-45; Bavarian State Minister of Economics 45-46; Chair. Sonderstelle Geld und Kredit (Special Agency entrusted with task of preparing plan for currency reform) Oct. 47; Dir. of Dept. of Economics in United Economic Territory, Frankfurt-Höchst March 48-Sept. 49; mem. Bundestag 49-; Federal Minister of Econ. Affairs 49-63; Deputy Fed. Chancellor 57-63, Fed. Chancellor 63-66; Chair. of Christian Democrat Party 66-67, Hon. Chair. Christian Democrat Party 67; Hon. Prof. Univ. of Munich 47, Univ. of Bonn 49; mem. Council of Ministers of the European Econ. Community (EEC) 58-63; Hon. LL.D. (Harvard, Columbia and others).
Leisure interests: classical music and sport.
Publs. *Germany's Comeback in the World Market, Prosperity Through Competition* 58, *The Economics of Success* 63.
53 Bonn, Johanniterstrasse 8, Federal Republic of Germany.
Telephone: Bonn 23-13-43.

Erickson, Arthur Charles, O.C., B.ARCH., F.R.A.I.C., A.R.C.A.; Canadian architect; b. 14 June 1924, Vancouver; *s.* of late Oscar and of Myrtle Erickson; ed. Univ. of British Columbia, McGill Univ.
Travel study in Mediterranean countries and N. Europe; Asst. Prof. Univ. of Oregon 55-56; Assoc. Prof. Univ. of British Columbia 61; Canada Council Fellowship for architectural research in Asia 61; with Erickson, Massey 63-72; mem. many architectural insts., asscns.; Fellow Royal Architectural Inst. of Canada; Academician Royal Canadian Acad. of Arts; mem. Science Council of Canada Cttee. on Urban Devt. 71, mem. Board, Canadian Conf. of the Arts 72, Canadian Council on Urban Research, Board of Trustees, Inst. for Research on Public Policy, Design Council of Portland Devt. Comm.; life mem. Vancouver Art Gallery; Hon. D. Eng. (Nova Scotia Technical Coll.) 71, Hon. LL.D. (Simon Fraser Univ.) 73, (McGill Univ.) 75; won First Prize in competition for Simon Fraser Univ., First Prize for design of Canadian Pavilion at Expo '70, Osaka, Pan Pacific Citation, American Inst. of Architects, Hawaiian Chapter 63, Molson Prize, Canada Council for the Arts 67, Architectural Inst. of Japan Award for Best Pavilion Expo '70, Royal Bank of Canada Award 71, Tau Sigma Delta Gold Medal, American Architectural Fraternity 73, Auguste Perret Award, Int. Union of Architects 74, Canadian Housing Design Council Awards for Residential Design 75.
Publ. *The Architecture of Arthur Erickson* 75.
Arthur Erickson Architects, 2412 Laurel Street,

Vancouver, B.C. and Suite M15-17, 4 New Street, Toronto, Ont.; Home: Vancouver, B.C., Canada.
Telephone: 879-0221 (Office, Vancouver); 924-7728 (Toronto).

Ericson, Admiral Stig H:son; Swedish naval officer; b. 12 July 1897, Stockholm; *s.* of Rear-Admiral and Cabinet Minister Hans Ericson and Elin Gadelius; *m.* Barbro Almström 1921; one *d.*; ed. Stockholm.
Joined Navy 15, Commodore 43, Rear-Admiral 45; Commanding Active Fleet 50-53; Vice-Admiral 53; Commdr.-in-Chief 53-61, Admiral 61; Grand Marshal of the Royal Court 62-69; Grand Marshal of the Realm 70-; Pres. and mem. of Board Carnegie Foundation of Sweden, AB Marabou, Waldemarsudde Foundation.
Leisure interests: writing and painting.
Publs. books on naval affairs and memoirs.
Royal Palace, Stockholm C, Sweden.
Telephone: 11-06-07

Ericsson, John August; Swedish politician; b. 6 April 1907; *m.* Anna Ingeborg Karlström 1928; two *d.*; ed. privately.
Member of Parl. 37-; Head of Div. and Vice-Chair. State Labour Comm. 43; Minister without Portfolio 45-48; Minister of Commerce 48-55, of Social Affairs, Labour and Housing 55-57; Pres. Standing Cttee. of Ways and Means 59-70; Man. Dir. AB Vin- and Spritcentralen 57-; Chair. Sveriges Riksbank 70-74; Social Democrat.
Reimersholmsgatan 5, Stockholm, Sweden.

Erikson, Erik Homburger; American psychoanalyst; b. 15 June 1902, Frankfurt am Main, Germany; *m.* Joan Mowat Serson; two *s.* one *d.*; ed. Vienna Psychoanalytic Inst., Univ. of Vienna, Harvard Univ.
Research Fellow, Harvard Medical School 35-36; Research Asst., Instructor, Asst. Prof. in Psychoanalysis Yale School of Medicine 36-39; Research Assoc. Child Devt., Lecturer in Psychiatry, Prof. of Psychology Univ. of Calif. 39-51; psychoanalytic training, San Francisco 42-; Senior Staff mem. Austen Riggs Center, Stockbridge, Mass. 51-60; Visiting Prof. Psychiatry Univ. of Pittsburgh Medical School 51-60; Visiting Prof. Int. Studies M.I.T. 58-60; Prof. of Human Devt., Lecturer in Psychiatry Harvard Univ. 60-70, Prof. Emer. 70; Sr. Consultant in Psychiatry Mount Zion Hosp., San Francisco 72-; mem. Int. Psychoanalytic Asscn. (Vienna) 33, American Psychoanalytic Asscn. (Boston) 34, Life mem. 64, Nat. Acad. of Educ., American Acad. of Arts and Sciences; Fellow Center for Advanced Studies in the Behavioral Sciences, Stanford, Calif. 62, 65, Davie Lecturer (Cape Town) 68, Godlein Lecturer (Harvard) 72, Jefferson Lecturer Nat. Endowment for the Humanities 73; hon. M.A. (Harvard), LL.D. (Brown, Calif.), Sc. D. (Loyola), Soc. Sc. D. (Yale); Foneme Prize (Milan) 69, Nat. Book Award 70, Pulitzer Prize 70, Melcher Award 70, Aldrich Award American Acad. of Pediatrics 71, Research Award Nat. Assoc. For Mental Health 74.
Publs. *Childhood and Society* 50, 63, *Young Man Luther: A Study in Psychoanalysis and History* 58, *Insight and Responsibility* 64, *Identity: Youth and Crisis* 68, *Gandhi's Truth: On the Origins of Militant Non-Violence* 69, *Life History and the Historical Moment* 75.
Tiburon, Calif. 94920, U.S.A.
Telephone: 415-435-2008.

Erikson, Richard John, M.A., J.D., PH.D.; American officer, lawyer and educator; b. 21 June 1943, Alexandria, Va.; *s.* of Theodore John Erikson and Helen Anita (née Whisnant); *m.* Joan Kathryn Harmony 1970; one *d.*; ed. Florida State Univ., Univ. of Michigan Law School and Univ. of Virginia.
Graduate Asst. Fla. State Univ. 64-65; Visiting Prof. Univ. of Detroit 70; Asst. Staff Judge Advocate, Headquarters Air Univ., Maxwell Air Force Base 71-73; Project Researcher, Office of The Judge Advo-

cate-Gen., U.S.A.F. 71-75; U.S. Expert at Geneva Conf. on the Reaffirmation and Devt. of Int. Humanitarian Law in Armed Conflict 72; Editor-in-Chief *Air Force Law Review* 73-75; Faculty mem., The Judge Advocate-Gen.'s School, U.S.A.F., Maxwell Air Force Base 73-75; Deputy Dir. Int. Law Div. HQ U.S.A.F., Europe, Ramstein Air Base, Fed. Repub. of Germany 75-; Meritorious Service Medal.

Leisure interests: bridge, chess, bowling.

Publs. *International Law and the Revolutionary State* 72; articles in *Air University Review, Air Force Law Review, Alabama Lawyer.*

Headquarters U.S.A.F.E./JAI, APO 09012, Federal Republic of Germany.

Telephone: 06371-47-6941 (civilian).

Erim, Nihat, PH.D.; Turkish politician; b. 1912, Kandira, Kocael Province; *m.*; two *c.*; ed. Lycée of Galatasaray, Istanbul, and Univ. of Istanbul Law School and Univ. of Paris.

Professor of Constitutional and Int. Law, Univ. of Ankara and Legal Adviser, Ministry of Foreign Affairs 42; mem. Parl. 45-50; Minister of Public Works, concurrently Deputy Prime Minister 48-50; Publr. and Editor *ULUS* (organ of the Republican People's Party) 50, subsequently Publr. and Editor of *Halkçi*; mem. for Turkey, European Human Rights Comm.; mem. Parl. 61-; Deputy Chair. Republican People's Party Nat. Assembly Group 61-71; mem. Turkish Parl. Group, European Council 61-70; Prime Minister March 71-April 72; Senator 72-.

Publs. several books on law.

The Senate, Ankara, Turkey.

Erkin, Feridun Cemal; Turkish diplomatist; b. 1899; ed. Galatasaray Lyceum and Univ. of Paris (Law Faculty).

First Sec. Turkish Embassy London 28-29; Counsellor in Berlin 34-35; Consul-Gen. Beirut 35-37; Head of Commercial Dept. of Min. of Foreign Affairs 37-38; Head of Political Dept. Ministry of Foreign Affairs 39-42; Asst. Sec.-Gen. with rank of Minister 42-45; Sec.-Gen. with rank of Ambassador 45; Turkish del. at UN Conf. San Francisco 45; Head of Turkish del. final meeting of League of Nations 46; Ambassador to Italy 47-48, to U.S.A. June 48-55, to Spain 55-57, to France 57-60, to U.K. 60; Minister of Foreign Affairs March 62-65; mem. Turkish Nat. Assembly; mem. Int. Diplomatic Acad., Geneva; mem. Acad. of Political Sciences, New York; mem. Inst. de France (Academy of Moral and Political Sciences).

Disisien Bakanliği, Ankara, Turkey.

Erlander, Tage Fritiof, B.A.; Swedish politician; b. 13 June 1901; ed. elementary school, public high school of Karlstad, and Univ. of Lund.

Graduated 28; on the Editorial Staff of *Svensk Upplagsbok* (Swedish Encyclopaedia) 28-38; mem. of Parl. Second Chamber 33-44, First Chamber 45-48, Second Chamber 49-70, Unicameral. Parl. 71-73; Under-Sec. of State of Ministry of Social Affairs 38; Minister without Portfolio 44-45, of Educ. 45-46; Prime Minister Oct. 46-Sept. 69; Social Democratic Labour Party.

Fyrverkarbacken 21, 11260 Stockholm, Sweden.

Erlanger, Philippe; French writer and international art organizer; b. 11 July 1903, Paris; *s.* of late Camille Erlanger; ed. Lycée Janson de Sailly, Université de Paris à la Sorbonne and Ecole libre des sciences politiques.

Organizer of about 500 exhbns. and over 1,000 theatrical and musical presentations; Dir. French Asscn. for Artistic Affairs 38-68; Head, Artistic Exchange Dept., Ministry of Foreign Affairs 46-68; Inspector-Gen. Ministry of National Education 60-; Minister Plenipotentiary 68; Founder and Hon. Pres. Cannes Int. Film Festival 46; Grand Prix du Rayonnement

Français 62, Grand Prix Littéraire du Départment de la Seine 63, Prix des Ambassadeurs 66; Grand Prix Gobert (Acad. Française) 69; Commdr. Légion d'Honneur, Hon. C.B.E., and numerous other French and foreign decorations.

Publs. include *Henri III* 35, *Le Régent* 38, *Monsieur, Frère de Louis XIV* 53, *Diane de Poitiers* 55, *L'étrange mort de Henri IV* 57, *Le Massacre de la Saint-Barthélemy* 60, *Cinq Mars* 62, *Louis XIV* 65, *Clemenceau* 68, *Richelieu* 69, *Margaret d'Anjou* 70, *La Reine Margot* 72, *La France sans Etoile* 74.

Home: Résidence du Grand Hotel, 45 Croisette, Cannes 06, France.

Telephone: 38-13-00.

Ermini, Giuseppe, DR.JUR.; Italian lawyer and politician; b. 20 July 1900.

Prof. of History of Italian Law, Urbino Univ., Fellow 26; Prof. of Univ. of Cagliari 27, subsequently of Perugia Univ.; Rector of Perugia Univ. 45-; Christian Democrat deputy 46-; Pres. of Comm. for Educ. and Fine Arts; Under-Sec. Entertainments Office 54; Minister of Educ. 54-55; now Senator.

Università degli Studi, Perugia, Italy.

Ermolyeva, Zinaida Vissarionovna; Soviet biologist; b. 27 Oct. 1898, Frolovo, Volgograd; ed. Rostov Univ. Director and Lecturer, Bacteriology Dept., Inst. of Bacteriology, Rostov Univ. 21-25; Dir. Microbial Biochemistry Dept., All-Union Inst. for Experimental Medicine, Moscow 25-44; Dir. Inst. for Biological Prevention of Infections, Moscow 45-47; Dir. Dept. of Experimental Chemotherapy, Antibiotics Research Inst., Moscow 47-; Dir. Dept. of Microbiology, Central Postgraduate Med. Inst., Moscow 52-; Pres. Cttee. for Antibiotics, U.S.S.R. Ministry of Public Health; Editor journal *Antibiotiki* 56-; mem. U.S.S.R. Acad. Medical Sciences 65; Order of Lenin (twice), State Prize 43, Badge of Honour; Honoured Worker of Science 70; and various medals.

Publs. *Cholera* 43, *Penicillin* 46, *Antibiotics and their Applications* 54, *Streptomycin Therapy* 58, *Antibiotics, Experimental and Clinical Investigations* Vol. I 56, Vol. II 59, *Biological Active Substances of Natural Origin* 64, *Antibiotics, Interferous and Microbial Polysaccharides* 65.

Department of Microbiology, Central Postgraduate Medical Institute, 1/2 Ploshchad Vosstanya, Moscow, U.S.S.R.

Erni, Hans; Swiss painter; b. 21 Feb. 1909, Lucerne; *m.* Doris Kessler 1949; one *s.* two *d.*; ed. Académie Julien, Paris and Vereinigte Staatsschulen für freie und angewandte Kunst, Berlin.

Member Groupe Abstraction-Création, Paris; mem. S.W.B.; Exhbns. Lucerne, Paris, Basle, Oxford, Liverpool, London, Cambridge, Leicester, Zürich, Milan, Rotterdam, Prague, Stockholm, Chicago, New York, Rome, Copenhagen, Tokyo, San Francisco, Los Angeles, Washington, Mannheim, Cologne; abstract mural picture Swiss section Triennale Milan, frescoes Lucerne; great mural *Switzerland* for Swiss Nat. Exhbn. Zürich 39; Great Murals Exposition internationale de l'Urbanisme et de l'Habitation Paris 47, Mural in Bernese hospital Montana; mem. Alliance Graphique Int.; Int. Prize at the Biennale del Mare 53; great mural at the Musée Ethnographique, Neuchâtel 54; has illustrated bibliophile edns. of classics by Plato, Pindar, Sophocles, Virgil, Buffon, Renard, Valéry, Homer (*Odyssey*), Albert Schweitzer (*La Paix*), Voltaire (*Candide*), Paul Eluard, etc.; murals for Int. Exhbn. in Brussels 58; mosaics for the Abbey of St. Maurice 61, for Swiss T.V. and Radio Building, Berne 64; Engraved glass panels "Day and Night" and "Towards a Humanistic Future" for the Société des Banques Suisses, Geneva, 63; exhibitions in Japan and Australia 63, 64, Pro Juventute stamps 65; murals in Rolex Foundation, Union de Banques

Suisses, Sion 66, for Swissair Zürich, and La Placette Geneva 67; exhbns. in Chicago, New York, Geneva 66-68. Leisure interest: art.
Publs. *Wo steht der Maler in der Gegenwart?* 47, *Erni en Valais* 67, *Israel Sketchbook* 68.
6045 Meggen, Lucerne, Switzerland.
Telephone: 041-371382.

Ernst, Max; French painter and sculptor; b. 2 April 1891, Brühl; *m.* 1st Louise Strauss 1918, 2nd Marie-Berthe Aurenche 1926, 3rd Dorothea Tanning 1946; ed. Gymnasium, Brühl, Univ. of Bonn.
Joined Rheinische Expressionisten group of poets and painters 11; Art Critic *Volksmund*, Bonn 12; participated in *Erster Deutscher Herbstsalon*, Der Sturm, Berlin 13; joined Das Junge Rheinland group 18; produced lithographs, engravings and collages, f. Cologne Dada movt. with Baargeld 19; first one-man exhbn. in Paris 21, exhibited at first surrealist exhbn. 25; developed frottage technique 25; first one-man exhbn. in U.S.A. 32, *Europe after Rain I* 33, *Europe after Rain II* 40-42; first sculpture 34; adopted decalcomania technique 36; lived in U.S.A. 41-53, in France 53-; major exhbns. include retrospective exhbns. in Paris 45, 50, Brühl 51, at Musée Nat. d'Art Moderne 59, at Museum of Modern Art, N.Y. 61, *Inside the Sight*, touring exhbn. 70; has collaborated on many films and ballets; Grand Prix for *The Polish Rider* Venice Biennale 54, Stephan Lochner Medal, City of Cologne 61; Hon. Ph.D. Univ. of Bonn 72; Officier Légion d'Honneur 74.
Publs. collage-novels: *La Femme 100 Têtes* 29, *Rêve d'un Petite Fille Qui Voulut Entrer au Carmel* 30, *Une Semaine de Bonté ou Les Septs Éléments Capitaux* 34; *Beyond Painting* 48, *Maximilliana ou L'Exercise Illégal de l'Astronomie* 64.
[*Died* 1 *April* 1976.]

Ernstberger, Anton, DR.IUR.; German banker; b. 20 August 1910, Munich; *s.* of Adolf and Therese (née Reiner) Ernstberger; *m.* Angela Lorenz 1938; one *d.*; ed. Univ. of Munich.
Assessor, Bavarian Ministry of Interior 36-37; with Bankhaus Merck, Finck & Co., Munich 37-56, Exec. Man. 50; Man. Dir. Bankhaus Hardy & Co. G.m.b.H., Frankfurt 56-60; Partner, Bankhaus August Lenz & Co., Munich 58-60, Gen. Partner 60-; mem. Exec. Board, Bayerische Hypotheken- und Wechselbank, Munich 60-, Chief Spokesman 68-; mem. Exec. Board, Deutscher Kanal- und Schiffahrtsverein, Rhein-Main-Donau e.v.; Chair. of Board, AGROB AG, Ismaning, Paulaner-Salavator-Thomasbräu, Munich, August Lenz & Co. (Canada) Ltd., Papierwerke Waldhof-Aschaffenburg AG, Munich, Carl Steiner & Co. AG, Salzburg, United Ceramics Ltd., Toronto and Salzburger Kredit-und Wechselbank; Chair. of Board, Dortmunder Union-Schultheiss Brauerei AG, Dortmund und Berlin; Deputy Chair. of Board, Karl Wenschow G.m.b.H., Munich Westfalen bank AG, Bochum, Wicküler-Küpper-Brauerei K.G.a.A., Wuppertal, Held und Francke Bau AG, Munich; mem. Board Board of Dirs. Bayerische Versicherungsbank, Magirus Deutz AG (Ulm), Rhein-Main-Donau AG, Anton Steinecker Machinen-fabrik G.m.b.H., Freising; mem. Board Bank für Kärnten AG, Klagenfurt, and several other admin. and consultative boards; Royal Swedish Consul General.
Leisure interests: family life, religious activities, gardening, hiking, swimming and collecting old jugs.
8000 Munich 2, Theatinerstrasse 11, Federal Republic of Germany.
Telephone: 23661.

Erofeyev, Vladimir Ivanovich; Soviet diplomatist; b. 9 Oct. 1920, Leningrad; ed. First Moscow State Inst. of Foreign Languages.
Diplomatic Service 42-; Asst. to Minister of Foreign Affairs 55; Counsellor, Paris 55-59; Deputy Head, First European Dept., U.S.S.R. Ministry of Foreign Affairs 59-62; Amb. to Senegal 62-66; on staff Ministry of Foreign Affairs 66-70; Asst. Dir.-Gen. UNESCO 70-75.
c/o Ministry of Foreign Affairs, Moscow, U.S.S.R.

Erofeyev, Vladimir Yakovlevich; Soviet diplomatist; b. 24 May 1909, Moscow; ed. Moscow Machine Tool Inst.
Diplomatic Service 39-; Deputy Dir. and Chief of Consular Dept., State Cttee. for Foreign Affairs 39-40; Counsellor to Turkey 40-42; Deputy Chief, Second European Dept., Ministry of Foreign Affairs 42-48; Head of Dept. for Latin American Countries 48-49; Counsellor, London 49-52; Counsellor Ministry of Foreign Affairs 52-54; Minister Counsellor, Paris 54-55; Chief of Second European Dept., Ministry of Foreign Affairs 55-58, of Near East Dept. 58-59; Amb. to the U.A.R. 59-65; on staff Ministry of Foreign Affairs 65-68; Amb. to Iran 68-.
U.S.S.R. Embassy, Teheran, Iran.

Erroll of Hale, 1st Baron (cr. 64) of Kilmun in the County of Argyll; **Frederick James Erroll,** P.C., M.A., C.ENG., F.I.E.E., F.I.MECH.E.; British politician; b. 27 May 1914, London; *s.* of late George Murison Erroll; *m.* Elizabeth Sowton Barrow 1950; ed. Oundle School and Trinity Coll., Cambridge.
Served in engineering industry 36-39; war service, Tank Div., reached rank of Col. 39-45; M.P. for Altrincham and Sale 45-64; Parl. Sec. Ministry of Supply 55-56, Board of Trade 56-58; Econ. Sec. Treasury 58-59; Minister of State, Board of Trade 59-60; Privy Counsellor 60-; Pres. Board of Trade 61-63; Minister of Power 63-64; mem. Nat. Econ. Development Council 62-63; Chair. Bowater Corpn. 73-, Harland Simon 75-, Consolidated Gold Fields 76-, Chair. and Dir. of several other cos. 65-; Pres. London Chamber of Commerce 66-69, Vice-Pres. 69; mem. of the Council of Inst. of Dirs., Chair. 73-; Deputy Chair. Decimal Currency Board 66-71; Pres. of the British Export Houses Asscn. 68-72, Hispanic and Luso-Brazilian Councils 69-73; Chair. Cttee. on Liquor Licensing 71-72, Automobile Assen. 74-; Conservative.
21 Ilchester Place, London, W.14, England.
Telephone: 01-602-2195.

Erskine, Ralph, A.R.I.B.A., A.M.T.P.I., S.A.R.; British architect; b. 24 Feb. 1914, Mill Hill, London; *s.* of George Erskine and Mildred (née Gough); *m.* Ruth Monica Francis 1939; one *s.* two *d.*; ed. Friends' School, Saffron Walden, Essex, Regent Street Polytechnic, London, and Konst. Akad., Stockholm.
Own practice in Sweden since 39, branch office in Byker, Newcastle upon Tyne 69-; engaged in city renewal plans, new library for Stockholm Univ., town planning, designs for flats, private houses, housing estates, industrial buildings, churches, shopping centres, and homes for the elderly; designed Hall of Residence, Clare Coll., Cambridge, England; studies and research in architectural problems on building in subarctic regions, sketches: town site, Resolute, N.W.T., Canada; Guest Prof. at Technical School, Zürich; lectures in Holland, Japan, Canada, Sweden, Finland, Poland, Denmark, Switzerland, England and America; has participated in exhbns. in Sweden, Canada, Holland, Denmark and Switzerland; Hon. A.I.A., Dr. Tech. (Lund Univ.) 75; Kasper Salin Prize (Sweden), Ytong Prize 74; foreign mem. Royal Swedish Acad. of Arts.
Leisure interests: skiing, skating, sailing.
Gustav III's väg, 170 11 Drottningholm, Sweden.
Telephone: 7590352, 7590050 (Office).

Erskine, Sir (Robert) George, Kt., C.B.E., B.L.; British merchant banker; b. 5 Nov. 1896; ed. Kirkcud-bright Acad. and Edinburgh Univ.
On staff of Nat. Bank of Scotland 13-29; served First World War 14-18; joined Morgan Grenfell & Co. Ltd. 29, Dir. 45-67, later mem. Advisory Cttee.; Dir. London & Provincial Trust Ltd., Alan Paine Ltd.;

Master of Glaziers Co. 60-61; High Sheriff of Surrey 63-64; Pres. Inst. of Bankers 54-56; Deputy Chair. Navy, Army and Air Force Inst. 41-52; mem. Jenkins Cttee. on Company Law 59-62, Council R.A.F. Benevolent Fund, London Advisory Cttee. Scottish Council (Devt. and Industry).
Busbridge Wood, Godalming, Surrey, England.
Telephone: Hascombe 378.

Erskine of Rerrick, 1st Baron (cr. 64); **John Maxwell Erskine,** Bart., G.B.E., Kt., K.ST.J., D.L., J.P., F.R.S.E.; British public servant; b. 14 Dec. 1893; ed. Kirkcudbright Acad. and Edinburgh Univ.
Governor of Northern Ireland 64-68; Gen. Man. Commercial Bank of Scotland Ltd. (now incorporated in Royal Bank of Scotland), Edinburgh 32-53, Dir. 51-69; fmr. Dir. Caledonian Insurance Co., Guardian Assurance Co. Ltd. and other cos.; official of numerous commercial and civic orgs.; Hon. LL.D. (Glasgow and Belfast), Hon. F.R.C.P.(E.).
69 Eaton Square, London S.W.1, England.

Ertl, Josef; German politician; b. 7 March 1925, Oberschleissheim; ed. Technical Univ. of Munich.
Joined Bavarian State Ministry of Food, Agriculture and Forests 52; Dir. Youth Advisory Service until 59; Head, Agricultural School, Miesbach 59; Dir., Office of Agriculture, Miesbach 60; Senior Agricultural Counsellor 60; mem. Bundestag 61-; Land Vice-Chair. 63; Vice-Chair. Parl. Free Democrats 68-; Fed. Minister of Food, Agriculture and Forestry 69-; Free Democrat.
Bundesministerium für Landwirtschaft, 53 Bonn-Duisdorf, Bonner Strasse 85, Federal Republic of Germany.

Ervin, Samuel James, Jr., A.B., LL.B.; American politician and lawyer; b. 27 Sept. 1896, Morganton, N. Carolina; m. Margaret Bruce Bell 1924; one s. two d.; ed. Univ. of N. Carolina and Harvard Univ.
Served in France with First Div., First World War; practised law, Morganton 22-, except for service on bench; Rep. in N. C. Gen. Assembly 23, 25, 31; Judge, Burke County Criminal Court 35-37, N.C. Superior Court 37-43; Rep. from 10th N.C. District, 79th Congress 46-47; Assoc. Justice, N. C. Supreme Court 48-54; Senator from N. Carolina 54-74; Chair. Senate Watergate Cttee. 73; Democrat.
Morganton, North Carolina 28655, U.S.A.

Esaki, Leo, PH.D.; Japanese scientist; b. 12 March 1925, Osaka; s. of Soichiro Esaki and Niyoko Ito; m. Masako Araki 1959; one s. two d.; ed. Univ. of Tokyo.
With Sony Corpn. 56-60, conducted research on heavily-doped Ge and Si which resulted in the discovery of tunnel diode; with IBM Corpn., U.S.A. 60-, IBM Fellow, IBM T. J. Watson Research Center, N.Y., 60-, Man. Device Research 62-; major field of research is non-linear transport and optical properties on semiconductors, junctions, thin films, etc., currently involved on a man-made semiconductor lattice grown by a sophisticated ultra-high vacuum evaporation system: a computer-controlled molecular-beam epitaxy; mem. Japan Acad. 75; Nishina Memorial Award 59; Asahi Press Award 60; Toyo Rayon Foundation Award 61; Morris N. Liebmann Memorial Prize 61; Stuart Ballantine Medal, Franklin Inst. 61; Japan Acad. Award 65; Nobel Prize for Physics 73; Order of Culture, Japanese Govt. 74.
Publs. numerous articles in professional journals.
IBM T. J. Watson Research Center, P.O. Box 218, Yorktown Heights, N.Y. 10598; Home: 16 Shady Lane, Chappaqua, N.Y. 10514, U.S.A.
Telephone: (914) 945-2342 (Office); (914) 238-3329 (Home).

Esaki, Masumi; Japanese politician; b. 1915.
Member, House of Reps. for Aichi prefecture, elected 11 times; twice head, Defence Agency, implementing controversial fourth defence strengthening programme; fmr. Parl. Vice-Minister for Construction; fmr. Deputy Sec.-Gen. and Chair. Liberal Dem. Party Diet Policy Cttee.; Minister of Home Affairs and Chair. Nat. Public Safety Comm. 72-73; Liberal Dem. Party.
House of Representatives, Tokyo, Japan.

Esau, Katherine, PH.D.; American botanist; b. 3 April 1898, Yekaterinoslav, Ukraine (now Dnepropetrovsk, U.S.S.R.); d. of John Esau and Margarethe Toews; ed. Coll. of Agriculture, Moscow, in Berlin and Univ. of Calif. at Berkeley.
Instructor and Junior Botanist, Univ. of Calif. at Davis 31, other ranks 31-49, Prof. and Botanist 49-65 (transferred to Santa Barbara Campus 63), Prof. of Botany, Emer. 65-; continuing research in plant anatomy, ultrastructure and effects of viruses on plants; Pres. Botanical Soc. of America 51; Faculty Research Lecturer Univ. of Calif. at Davis 46, Prather Lecturer in Biology Harvard Univ. 60, John Charles Walker Lecturer Univ. of Wis. 68; Fellow John Simon Guggenheim Foundation 40; mem. American Acad. of Arts and Sciences, Nat. Acad. of Sciences, American Philosophical Soc.; Hon. D.Sc. (Mills Coll., Oakland, Calif.), Hon. LL.D. (Univ. of Calif.); Merit Award Certificate, 50th Anniversary of Botanical Soc. of America 56, Eleventh Int. Botanical Congress Medal 69; Foreign mem. Swedish Royal Acad. of Sciences 71-.
Publs. *Plant Anatomy* 53, 2nd edn. 65, *Anatomy of Seed Plants* 60, *Plants, Viruses, and Insects* 61, *Vascular Differentiation in Plants* 65, *Viruses in Plant Hosts. Form, Distribution and Pathologic Effects* 68, *The Phloem* Vol. 5, Part 2 of *Handbuch der Pflanzenanatomie* 69; and numerous research articles.
Department of Biological Sciences, University of California, Santa Barbara, Calif. 93106; Home: 8 West Constance Apt. 8, Santa Barbara, Calif. 93105, U.S.A.
Telephone: 805-961-2645 (Office); 805-687-0830 (Home).

Escande, Leopold, D. ès SC. PHYS.; French university professor; b. 1 June 1902, Toulouse; s. of Gabriel Escande and Jenny Desmazures; m. Renée Setzes 1924; one d.; ed. Inst. Electrotechnique et de Mécanique Appliquée Toulouse and Toulouse Univ.
Professor of Hydraulics, Toulouse Univ.; Chair. Institut Nat. Polytechnique de Toulouse; Scientific Adviser to Délégation Générale à la Recherche Scientifique; mem. Acad. des Sciences (Paris) and corresp. mem. Acad. of Coimbra (Portugal), of Rio de Janeiro, of Bologna, Bogotá, Madrid, Barcelona, Lima, also at Mexico, Belgrade, Milan, Padua, Buenos Aires, Caracas, Warsaw, Genoa, Zagreb, Naples, Sofia; Grand Officier Légion d'Honneur; Dr. h.c. (Univs. of Recife, São Paulo, Lisbon, Liège, Porto Alegre, Lima, Rio de Janeiro, Vienna, Ghent, Buenos Aires, Berlin, Cracow, Salonica, Sherbrooke, Genoa, Bath, Sarajevo).
Leisure interests: painting, poetry, travel.
Publs. *Etude Théorique et Expérimentale sur la Similitude des Fluides Incompressibles Pesants* 29, *Barrages* 37, *Etudes des Veines de Courant* 40, *Hydraulique Générale* 41-43, *Recherches Théoriques et Expérimentales sur les Oscillations de l'Eau dans les Chambres d'Equilibre* 43, *Compléments d'Hydraulique* Vol. I 47, Vol. II 51, *Méthodes Nouvelles pour le Calcul des Chambres d'Equilibre* 49, *Nouveaux Compléments d'Hydraulique* Vol. I 53, Vol. II 55, Vol. III 58, Vol. IV 63, *Rêves et Souvenirs* Vol. I 73, Vol. II 74.
"Enseeiht", 2 rue Camichel, 31 Toulouse; and 8 rue Claire Pauilhac, 31 Toulouse, France.

Eschenmoser, Albert, DR. SC. NAT.; Swiss chemist; b. 5 Aug. 1925, Erstfeld; s. of Alfons and Johanna Eschenmoser (née Oesch); m. Elizabeth Baschnonga 1954; two s. one d.; ed. Collegium Altdorf, Kantonsschule St. Gallen, Swiss Federal Inst. of Technology, Zurich.
Privatdozent, Organic Chemistry, Swiss Fed. Inst. of

Technology 56, Prof. of Organic Chemistry 60, **Prof. Gen.** Organic Chemistry 65; Arthur D. Little Visiting Prof. Mass. Inst. of Technology 61; Brittingham Visiting Prof. Univ. of Wisconsin 65; Visiting Prof. Israel Inst. of Technology 69; Morris S. Kharasch Visiting Prof. Univ. of Chicago 70; Foreign Hon. mem. American Acad. of Arts and Sciences 66; Foreign Assoc. Nat. Acad. of Sciences, U.S.A. 73; Hon. Dr. rer. nat. (Univ. of Fribourg) 66, Hon. D.Sc. (Univ. of Chicago) 70; Kern Award, Swiss Fed. Inst. of Technology 49, Werner Award, Swiss Chemical Soc. 56, Ruzicka Award, Swiss Fed. Inst. of Technology 58, Fritzsche Award, American Chemical Soc. 66, Marcel Benoist Prize 73, R. A. Welch Award in Chemistry (Houston, Texas) 74, Kirkwood Medal (Yale) 76.
Publs. numerous articles in professional journals.
Bergstrasse 9, 8700 Küsnacht (ZH), Switzerland.
Telephone: 90 73 92.

Escher, Alfred Martin, DR. JUR.; Swiss diplomatist; b. 23 March 1906; ed. Univs. of Zürich, Berlin and Kiel, Acad. for Int. Law, The Hague.
Entered service of Fed. Political Dept. 31; Attaché, Bangkok 32; Sec. of Legation, Warsaw 35, Berlin 39; First Sec., Berlin 41, Ankara 41; Consul, Baghdad 42, Athens 44; Counsellor, London 45; Commr. Int. Cttee. of the Red Cross for Refugees in Palestine 48; Minister to Iran 51-54, concurrently to Afghanistan 53-54; mem. Neutral Nations Supervisory Comm. for Armistice, Korea 54; Minister to Italy 55-57, Amb. to Italy 57-59; Amb. to German Fed. Republic, May 59-64, to Austria 64-72; Representative of UN Sec.-Gen. responsible for Namibia (S.W. Africa) 72-73.
c/o Office of the Secretary-General of the United Nations, UN Secretariat, New York, N.Y. 10017, U.S.A.

Escherich, Rudolf Johann, DR.RER.POL.; German business executive; b. 27 Oct. 1923, Wegscheid, Bavaria; m. Helga Koch 1959; one s. one d.; ed. Univ. of Munich.
Chairman Managing Board Vereinigte Aluminium-Werke AG; mem. Man. Board VIAG Vereinigte Industrie-Unternehmungen AG.
Leisure interests: flying, golf, tennis, skiing.
Vereinigte Aluminium-Werke AG, 5300 Bonn, Gerichtsweg 48; Home: 5205 St. Augustin 2, Drachenfelsstrasse 13, Federal Republic of Germany.
Telephone: 552215 (Office); Siegburg 22596 (Home).

Escobar, Maria Luisa; Venezuelan composer; b. 5 Dec. 1909; ed. Curaçao and Paris.
Founder and Pres. until 43 Ateneo de Caracas; founder and Dir.-Gen. Asociación Venezolana de Autores y Compositores (A.V.A.C.) 47; Artistic Dir. the Ballet-Theatre of Caracas; rep. Venezuela at Int. Congress on Musical Education, Paris 37, Int. Conf. of Society Authors and Composers, Buenos Aires 48, Rome 62, 25th Int. Congress Nat. Fed. of Music Clubs, U.S.A. 49, First Inter-American Music Conf., U.S.A. 49; awarded medals and diplomas of honour by Venezuela, France, Cuba, Mexico, U.S.A., and India.
Leisure interests: journalism, radio and T.V. announcing.
Works include *Orquideas azules* (symphony and ballet), *La Princesa Girasol* (operetta), *Guaicaipuro* (ballet), *Vals Sentimental* (piano and orchestra), *El Rey Guaicaipuro* (opera), *Canaimé* (musical drama), *Concierto Sentimental* (piano and orchestra), *Pajaro de Siele Colores* (violin and piano) and many folksongs, etc.
Apartado Postal 10, 233, Caracas; Home: Guaicaipuro, Calle Baruta, Bello Monte (Norte), Caracas, Venezuela.

Escobar Cerda, Luis; Chilean economist; b. 1927; ed. Univ. of Chile and Harvard Univ.
Director of School of Econs., Univ. of Chile 51-55, Dean of Faculty of Econs. 55-64; Minister of Econ. Devt. and Reconstruction 61-63; mem. Inter-American Cttee. for Alliance for Progress 64-66; Exec. Dir. Int. Monetary Fund 64-66, 68-70, IBRD 66-68; Special Rep. for Inter-American Orgs. IBRD 70-; Trustee of Population Reference Bureau 68-73; mem. Advisory Cttee. on Population and Devt. OAS 68-73; mem. Council Soc. for Int. Devt. 69-72.
Publs. *The Stock Market* 59, *Organization for Economic Development* 61, *A Stage of the National Economic Development* 62, *Considerations on the Tasks of the University* 63, *Organizational Requirements for Growth and Stability* 64, *The Role of the Social Sciences in Latin America* 65, *The Organization of Latin American Government* 68, *Multinational Corporations in Latin America* 73, *International Control of Investments* 74.
International Bank for Reconstruction and Development, 1818 H Street, N.W., Washington, D.C. 20433, U.S.A.; Los Tulipanes 2979, Santiago, Chile.

Escovar Salom, Ramón; Venezuelan politician; b. 1926, Lara State.
Member Nat. Congress 47; Minister of Justice; Rep. to Lara State Legis. Assembly; mem. Senate; Sec.-Gen. of the Presidency 74-75; Minister of Foreign Affairs 75-.
Ministerio de Relaciones Exteriores, Caracas, Venezuela.

Eshpai, Andrei Yakovlevich; Soviet composer; b. 15 May 1925, Kozmademyansk, Mary A.S.S.R.; ed. Moscow Conservatoire.
Secretary R.S.F.S.R. Composers' Union; Honoured Worker of Arts of Mari Autonomous S.S.R. 61, Honoured Worker of Arts of Yakutsk Autonomous S.S.R. 64, Order of Red Star 46, Badge of Honour 67.
Principal compositions: *Symphonic Dances on Mari Themes* 52, *Hungarian Melodies* (for violin and orchestra) 52, Concerto for Piano and Orchestra 54, Concerto for Violin and Orchestra 56, Symphony 59; Piano Pieces, Sonatina, Six Preludes, suite romances, folk song arrangements, film music.
R.S.F.S.R. Composers' Union, 8-10 Ulitsa Nezhdanovoi, Moscow, U.S.S.R.

Espie, Frank Fletcher, O.B.E.; Australian mining engineer; b. 1917, Bawdwin, Burma; m.; four c.; ed. St. Peter's Coll., Adelaide, Adelaide Univ.
Served 9th Div., AIF, N. Africa and New Guinea rising to rank of Capt. 40-45; Underground Man., then Mine Supt., Zinc Corpn.-New Broken Hill Consolidated Mines 43-57, Asst. Gen. Man. for Production 57-61; Gen. Man. Comalco Products, Yennora, Sydney 61-62, Gen. Man. Industrial Div. 64-65; successively Exec. Dir., Man. Dir., Chair. of Dirs., Bougainville Copper Ltd. 65-; Exec. Dir. Conzinc Riotinto of Australia Ltd. 68-, Deputy Chair. 74-; Chair. Australian Mining and Smelting Co. Ltd.; Dir. Broken Hill Assoc. Smelters Pty. Ltd. 72, Rio Tinto Zinc Corpn. Ltd., London; Pres. Australian Mines and Metals Asscn.; Vice-Pres. Australian Mining Industry Council; Councillor Australian Mineral Industries Research Asscn.; mem. Australasian Inst. of Mining and Metallurgy (Pres. 75).
Leisure interests: golf, surfing.
Bougainville Copper Ltd., 95 Collins Street, Melbourne, Australia.

Espinosa-San Martin, Juan José; Spanish Minister of Finance 65-69; see *The International Who's Who 1975-76.*

Espy, R. H. Edwin, B.A., PH.D., B.D.; American church executive; b. 30 Dec. 1908, Portland, Oregon; s. of Harry Albert and Helen Medora (Richardson) Espy; m. Cleo Lovace Mitchell 1944; ed. Univ. of Redlands, California, Union Theological Seminary, Univs. of Tübingen and Heidelberg and Yale Univ.
Youth Secretary, Universal Christian Council for Life and Work, and World Alliance for Int. Friendship through the Churches, Geneva 36-39; Sec. First World Conf. of Christian Youth Amsterdam 39; Sec. European Student Relief Fund, New York 40; Gen. Sec. Student

Volunteer Movement for Foreign Missions 40-43; Exec. Sec. Nat. Student Council, Y.M.C.A., New York 43-35; Assoc. Exec. Sec. Div. of Christian Life and Work, Nat. Council of Churches, New York 55-57; Assoc. Gen. Sec. Nat. Council of Churches 58-63, Gen. Sec. 63-; Dir. World University Service 43-57; del. to numerous Int. Religious Confs.; mem. Joint Working Group World Council of Churches and Roman Catholic Church 65-; Hon. D.D. (Univ. of Redlands), L.H.D. (Oberlin Coll.), Litt.D. (Keuka Coll.).
Publ. *The Religion of College Teachers* 51.
475 Riverside Drive, New York, N.Y. 10025, U.S.A.

Essaafi, M'hamed; Tunisian diplomatist; b. 26 May 1930, Kelibia; s. of Boubaker Essaafi and Fatma Sfaxi; m. Hedwige Klat 1956; one s. one d.; ed. Collège Sadiki and Univ. of Paris.
Secretariat of State for Foreign Affairs, Tunis 56; Tunisian Embassy, London 56-57; First Sec., Washington 57-60; Dir. of American Dept., Secr. of Foreign Affairs, Tunis 60-62, American Dept. and Int. Conf. Dept. 62-64; Amb. to U.K. 64-69; Sec.-Gen. at the Ministry for Foreign Affairs, Tunis 69-70; Amb. to U.S.S.R. 70-74, to Fed. Repub. of Germany 74-; Grand Officier, Ordre de la République Tunisienne.
Leisure interests: shooting, reading.
Tunisian Embassy, 103 Kölnerstrasse, Bonn-Bad Godesberg, Federal Republic of Germany.
Telephone: 376981.

Essonghe, Jean-Baptiste; Gabonese diplomatist; b. 1927, Setté-Cama, Gabon; m.; two c.; ed. Ecole Nat. de la France d'Outre-Mer, Paris.
Entered civil service, later Sec.-Gen. Nat. Assembly; First Counsellor, Embassy in France 67-68, later in U.S.A., Perm. Mission to UN Office, Geneva, and Embassy in Canada; Amb. to Tunisia 74-75; Perm. Rep. to UN Sep. 75-.
Permanent Mission of Gabon to the United Nations, 820 Second Avenue, Room 902, New York, N.Y. 10017, U.S.A.

Estang, Luc; French writer; b. 12 Nov. 1911, Paris; s. of Lucien Achille Marie Bastard and Marie Eugénie Peyroux; m. Suzanne Madeleine Bouchereau-Boisgontier 1939; ed. Artois and in Belgium.
Journalist and literary and dramatic critic, *La Croix* (Paris) 34-55; Editorial Sec. of *Editions du Seuil*, Paris, weekly collaboration in *Figaro*, and on radio; Chevalier de la Légion d'Honneur, Grand Prix de Littérature de l'Académie Française 62, Prix Guillaume-Appolinaire 68.
Publs. Novels: *Les Stigmates, Cherchant qui dévorer, Les Fontaines du grand abîme, L'Interrogatoire, L'Horloger du Cherche-Midi, Le Bonheur et le Salut, Que ces mots répondent, L'Apostat, La Fille à l'Oursin, Il était un P'tit Homme;* poetry: *Les Quatre Eléments, Les Béatitudes, D'une Nuit Noire et Blanche;* essays: *Le Passage du Seigneur, Présence de Bernanos, Saint-Exupéry par lui-même, Ce que je crois, Invitation à la poésie;* play: *Le Jour de Cain.*
28 rue de l'Université, Paris 7e, France.
Telephone: 548-29-91.

Estes, Joe Ewing; American judge; b. 24 Oct. 1903; ed. East Texas State Teachers Coll. and Univ. of Texas.
Admitted to Texas Bar 27, partner Crosby and Estes 28-30, Phillips, Trammell, Estes, Edwards & Orn 30-45, Sanford, King, Estes & Cantwell 46-52, Estes & Cantwell 52-55; U.S.N.R. 42-45; U.S. District Judge, Dallas 55-60, Chief Judge, U.S. District Court, Texas, Northern District 60-72, Judge, Temporary Emergency Court of Appeals 72-; mem. Advisory Cttee. on Rules of Evidence of Jud. Conf. of U.S., Co-ordinating Comm. for Multiple Litigation of Jud. Conf. of U.S., Fed. American Dallas Bar Asscns., State Bar of Texas, American Judicature Soc., Nat. Lawyers Club, Philosophical Soc. of Texas, Newcomen Soc., American

Legion; Trustee mem. Exec. Comm. S.W. Legal Foundation, American Law Inst., Cttee. on Trial Practice and Technique of the Jud. Conf. of the United States; Fellow and Chair. Judicial Section, American Bar Asscn. 61-62; now Research Fellow; Hon. LL.D. (East Texas Univ.) 74; Hatton W. Sumners Award (South Western Legal Foundation) 72.
Publs. co-author of *Handbook for Effective Pre-Trial Procedure, Handbook for Newly Appointed U.S. Dist. Judges, Manual for Complex Litigation* (Co-Editor).
U.S. Court House, Dallas, Tex. 75202; 5846 Desco Drive, Dallas, Texas 75225, U.S.A.

Estes, William K., B.A., PH.D.; American behavioural scientist; b. 17 June 1919, Minneapolis, Minn.; s. of Dr. George D. Estes and Mona Kaye; m. Katherine Walker 1942; two s.; ed. Univ. of Minn.
Medical Officer U.S. Army 44-46; Faculty mem. Indiana Univ. 46-62; Prof. of Psychology Stanford Univ. 62-68; Editor *Journal of Comparative and Physiological Psychology* 62-68; Prof., Rockefeller Univ. 68-; Pres. Experimental Div., American Psychological Asscn. 58; mem. Soc. of Experimental Psychologists, Nat. Acad. of Sciences, etc.; Distinguished Scientific Contribution Award of American Psychological Asscn. 62, Warren Medal for Psychological Research 63.
Leisure interest: music.
Publs. *An Experimental Study of Punishment* 44, *Modern Learning Theory* (with S. Koch and others) 54, *The Statistical Approach to Learning Theory* 59, *Studies in Mathematical Learning Theory* (with R. R. Bush) 59, *Stimulus Sampling Theory* (with E. Neimark) 67, *Learning Theory and Mental Development* 70, *Handbook of Learning and Cognitive Processes* (ed.) 75.
The Rockefeller University, New York, N.Y. 10021, U.S.A.
Telephone: 212-360-1740.

Estreicher, Karol, PH.D.; Polish art historian; b. 4 March 1906, Cracow, Poland; s. of Stanislas and Helena Estreicher; m. Teresa Lasocka 1945; ed. Cracow Univ.
Assistant Lecturer, Jagiellonian Univ., Cracow 31-39, Docent 45-50, Assoc. Prof. 52-72, Prof. 72-, Dir. Univ. Museum 52-; Polish Rep. in Germany for Restitution of Looted Works of Art, Munich 45-49; Chief Conservator of the reconstruction of Collegium Maius, Cracow 46-64; Pres. Soc. of Friends of the Fine Arts, Cracow 51; Editor *Rocznik Krakowski*; numerous decorations.
Publs. *Miniatury kodeksu Behema* (The Miniatures of Behem's Codex) 30, *Tryptyk Świętej Trójcy* (The Triptych of the Holy Trinity) 36, *Katalog Strat Kultury Polskiej pod Okupacją Niemiecką* (Catalogue of Polish Cultural Losses Under the German Occupation) 39-44, *Nie Odrazu Kraków Zbudowano* (Cracow wasn't built in a day) 44, *Krystianna* (novel) 57, *Collegium Maius* 68, *Łańcuch Aleksandy* (The Chain of Princess Alexandra) 70, *Leon Chwistek* (biography) 71, *An Outline of Art History* (in Polish) 73, *Bartolomeo Berrecci Italian Architect in Poland* 73, *Nineteenth Century Polish Bibliography* 57-73 (2nd edn.), *Copernican Relics in the Jagiellonian University* 73, *The Collegium Maius of the Jagiellonian University in Cracow* 73.
Jagiellonian University, Ul. Gołębia 24, Cracow; 30-220 Sarnie Uroczysko, 30-225 Cracow, Poland.
Telephone: 228-12 (Home).

Etaix, Pierre; French film director and actor; b. 23 Nov. 1928, Roanne; m. Annie Fratellini 1969; ed. lycée.
Apprenticed as stained-glass designer; Asst. film producer 49-55; small part in Robert Bresson's *Pickpocket* 59; leading role in Jacques Tati's *Jour de Fête*, Paris Olympia 60; directed first short film *Rupture* 61; other short films: *Heureux Anniversaire* 62 (Acad. Award ("Oscar") for best short film 63), *Insomnie* (First Prize, Oberhausen Festival 65); full-length films: *Le Soupirant* 63 (Prix Louis Delluc, Prize for best

humorous film, Moscow Festival 63), *Yoyo* 64 (Grand Prix de L'O.C.I.C., Grand Prix pour la Jeunesse, Cannes 65), *Tant qu'on a la santé* 66 (Coquille d'Argent, Saint-Sebastian Festival), *Le Grand Amour* 69 (Grand Prix du Cinéma Français, Grand Prix de l'O.C.I.C. 69), *Les Clowns* 70.
Compagnie Artistique de Productions et d'Adaptations Cinématographiques, 29 rue de Constantine, Paris 7e; Home: 39 rue des Vignes, Paris 16e, France.
Telephone: 224-77-19.

Ete, Muhlis, M.A., PH.D.; Turkish economist; b. 23 Oct. 1904.
Asst. Instructor 30, later Asst. Prof. Faculty of Law and Economics, Istanbul Univ.; Teacher of Statistics, School of Political Science, Istanbul, and of Money and Exchange, Higher School of Commerce and Economics Istanbul; Prof. of Business Economics, later of Gen. Principles of Economics, Ankara School of Political Science 40-50; Minister of State Enterprises 50-51; Minister of Economy and Commerce 51-52; Vice-Pres. of the Council of Europe 53; Pres. Prime Minister's High Control Board 58-61; Minister of Commerce 62-63; mem. of Parl.; fmr. Chief Ed. *Türk Ekonomisi*; Pres. Turkish Econ. Asscn.; Dir. School of Econs. and Commerce, Istanbul 67.
Publs. *Transportation, Money and Exchange, Lessons in Business Economics, Administration of Temporary and Permanent Exhibits, Commerce, Banking and Exchanges, Probleme der Assozierung der Türkei mit der Europäischen Wirtschaftsgemeinschaft*, and numerous translations.
Istanbul, Göztepe, Yeşil Çeşme Sok. 30/8, Turkey.
Telephone: 554832.

Eteki a Mbumua, William-Aurélien, LIC. EN DROIT; Cameroonian politician; b. 20 Oct. 1933, Douglas; *s.* of Joseph Mbumua and Mana Kutta; *m.* Naimi Betty Eyewe; one *s.* one *d.*; ed. Ecole Nat. d'Admin., Paris.
Prefect for Nkam 59, for Sanage Maritime 60-61; Minister of Educ., Youth and Culture 61-68; Pres. of Conf., UNESCO 68-70; Special Adviser, with rank of Minister, to Pres. of United Republic of Cameroon 71-74; Sec.-Gen. Org. of African Unity June 74-; Commdr. des Palmes Académiques, and many other decorations.
Leisure interests: literature, poetry, painting, tennis, football, swimming.
Publs. *Un Certain Humanisme* 70, *Démocratiser la Culture* 74, and many articles on education and African culture.
Organization of African Unity, P.O. Box 3243, Addis Ababa, Ethiopia.
Telephone: 157700.

Etemadi, Nour Ahmad; Afghan diplomatist and politician; b. 1920; ed. Istiqlal Lyceum and Kabul Univ.
Former diplomatic posts in London and Washington; Econ. Section, Ministry of Foreign Affairs 53-64, Deputy Minister of Foreign Affairs 63, Minister 65-71; Amb. to Pakistan 64; Prime Minister 67-71; Amb. to Italy 72-73, to U.S.S.R. (also accred. to Finland and Romania) 74-.
Embassy of Afghanistan, Skaterny per. 25, Moscow, U.S.S.R.

Etherington, Edwin Deacon, B.A., LL.B.; American attorney and executive; b. 25 Dec. 1924, Bayonne, N.J.; *s.* of late Charles Kenneth Etherington and Ethel Bennett; *m.* Katherine Colean 1953; three *s.* one *d.*; ed. Lawrenceville School, N.J., Wesleyan Univ. and Yale Law School.
Instructor and Asst. to Dean, Wesleyan Univ. 48-49; Law Clerk, Hon. Henry W. Edgerton, U.S. Court of Appeal, Washington, D.C. 52-53; Attorney, Wilmer and Broun, Washington, D.C. 53-54, Milbank, Tweed, Hadley, New York City 54-56; Sec. New York Stock Exchange 56-58, Vice-Pres. 58-61; Partner, Pershing

Co., New York City 61-62; Trustee, National Urban Coalition, Alfred P. Sloan Foundation, etc.; Dir. Connecticut Gen. Life Insurance Co., American Express Co., American Can Co., American Stock Exchange, Automatic Data Processing, Inc., Norton Co., Southern New England Telephone Co., United States Trust Co. of New York, etc.; Pres. American Stock Exchange 62-66; Pres. Wesleyan University 67-70; Pres. Nat. Center for Voluntary Action, Washington, D.C. 71-72, Chair. 72-; Counsel, Reid and Riege, P.C., Hartford, Conn. (law firm); Chair. Nat. Advertising Review Board 73-; Chair. Governor's Comm. on Services and Expenditures (for State of Conn.) 71; mem. and official of several civic socs. and orgs.; Hon. LL.D. (Wesleyan Univ. and Amherst Coll. Mass.) 65, (Trinity) 67, (Amherst) 68; Hon. L.H.D. (American Int. Coll.) 67.
Leisure interests: golf and other clubs.
Old Lyme, Conn. 06371, U.S.A.

Ethridge, Mark Foster; American newspaper publisher; b. 22 April 1896; ed. Univ. of Mississippi, and Mercer Univ., Georgia.
Began career as reporter; with N.Y. Sun and Consolidated Press 23-24, Associated Press 33; Asst. Gen. Man. *Washington Post* 33-34; Pres. and publisher *Richmond* (Va) *Times Dispatch* 34-36; Vice-Pres. and Gen. Man. *Courier Journal and Louisville Times* 36-42; Publisher 42-62, Chair. Board 62-63; Vice-Pres., Editor *Newsday*, Long Island, N.Y. 63-65, Consultant to Editor and Dir. 65-; mem. of President's Farm Tenancy Comm. 36; elected Pres. of Nat. Asscn. of Broadcasters 38; Chair. Fair Employment Practices Comm. 41-43; U.S. mem. of UN Comm. of Inquiry in the Balkans 47; Chair. U.S. Advisory Comm. on Information 48, mem. until 51; Trustee, Ford Foundation.
Route 1, Moncure, N.C., U.S.A.

Etiang, Paul Orono, B.A.; Ugandan diplomatist; b. 15 Aug. 1938, Tororo; *s.* of Kezironi Orono and Esta Adacat Adeke; *m.* Zahra A. Foum 1967; two *s.*; ed. Busoga Coll. and Makerere Univ. Coll.
District Officer, Provincial Admin. 62-64; Asst. Sec., Ministry of Foreign Affairs 64-65; Second Sec., Uganda Embassy, Moscow 65-67; mem. Uganda Mission to UN 67-68; First Sec. 68; High Commr. to U.K. 69-71; Chief of Protocol and Marshal of Diplomatic Corps, Uganda 71-; Perm. Sec. Ministry of Foreign Affairs 71-73, Acting Minister of Foreign Affairs May-Oct. 73; Acting Minister of State for Foreign Affairs at Pres. Office 73-75; Minister of State March 75-.
Leisure interests: billiards, badminton, music, theatre.
Office of the President, Kampala, Uganda.

Etiemble, René, D. ès L.; French professor of literature; b. 26 Jan. 1909, Mayenne; *m.* Jeannine Kohn 1963; ed. Lycée de Laval, Lycée Louis le Grand, Ecole Normale Supérieure and Fondation Thiers; Faculté de droit, Ecole des langues orientales.
Professor, Univ. of Chicago 37-43, Univ. of Alexandria, Egypt 44-48, Univ. of Montpellier 49-55; Prof. of Gen. and Comparative Literature, Univ. of Paris (Sorbonne) 56-; numerous travels abroad.
Publs. include: *Rimbaud* (with Y. Gauclère) 36, *L'Enfant de choeur* 37, *Peaux de Couleuvre* 48, *Le Mythe de Rimbaud* (3 vols. 52-61—Prix Saint Beuve 52), *Supervielle* 60, *Blason d'un corps* 61, *Parlez-vous franglais?* 64, *Hygiène des Lettres* (5 vols.) 52-67, *Le Sonnet des Voyelles* 68, *Retours du monde* 69, *Deux "lectures" du Kyoto de Kawabata* 72; on China: *Confucius* 56, *Le Nouveau Singe pélerin* 58, *Connaissons-nous la Chine* 64, *Le Jargon des Sciences* 66, *Les Jésuites en Chine* 66, *Yun Yun, l'Erotique Chinoise* 69, *Essais de littérature (vraiment) générale* 74, *Mes contre-poisons* 74.
Institut de Littérature Générale et Comparée, Université de Paris III (Nouvelle Sorbonne), 75230 Paris; Home: Vigny 28500 Vernouillet, France.

Etoungou, Simon Nko'o; Cameroonian diplomatist and politician; b. 14 Feb. 1932; ed. secondary and post-secondary schools, and diplomatic training in France. Head of Office in Ministry of Econ. Planning 56-57; Cabinet Attaché, Ministry of Finance 58-59; First Sec., Cameroon Embassy, Paris 60; Minister-Counsellor 60-61; Amb. to Tunisia 61-64; led numerous Cameroon dels. 63-64; concurrently Amb. to Algeria July-Nov. 64; Amb. to U.S.S.R. 64-65; Minister of Foreign Affairs 65-66, 68-70; Minister of Finance 66-68; Amb. to Belgium, Netherlands and Luxembourg and Perm. Rep. to EEC 71-; Knight of Nat. Order of Merit (Cameroon), and decorations from Senegal, Tunisia, Fed. Repub. of Germany and Gabon.
131-133 ave. Brugmann, Brussels 1060, Belgium.
Telephone: 45-18-70.

Etter, Philipp; Swiss lawyer and politician; b. 21 Dec. 1891; ed. Einsiedeln Gymnasium and Zürich Univ. Examining Judge, Zug canton 17; mem. Zug cantonal Govt. 23; Deputy to Council of States 30; mem. Fed. Council 34-59; Pres. Swiss Confederation 39, 42, 47, 53; fmr. Dir. Fed. Department of the Interior; Dr. h.c. Neuchâtel Univ. and Zürich Fed. Inst. of Technology; Hon. Senator Freiburg Univ.; Conservative.
Publs. *Reden an das Schweizervolk* 39, *Sens et Mission de la Suisse* 42, *Stimmrecht der Geschichte* 53.
Dalmazirain 6, Berne, Switzerland.

Ettinghausen, Richard, PH.D.; American art writer and curator; b. 5 Feb. 1906, Frankfurt am Main, Germany; s. of Edmund Ettinghausen and Selma (née Stern); m. 1st Basia Grulion 1935 (died 1936), 2nd Elizabeth Sgalitzen 1945; two s.; ed. Univs. of Munich, Cambridge and Frankfurt a.M.
Asst. Islamic Dept., State Museum, Berlin 31-33; Asst. to Editor *A Survey of Persian Art* 33-34; Research Assoc., American Inst. for Persian Art and Archæology, N.Y. 34-37; Lecturer on Islamic Art, Inst. of Fine Arts, N.Y. Univ. 37-38; mem. Inst. of Advanced Study, Princeton, N.J. 37-38; Assoc. Prof. of Islamic Art, Univ. of Mich., Ann Arbor 38-44; Assoc. in Near Eastern Art, Freer Gallery of Art, Smithsonian Inst., Washington, D.C. 44-58; Research Prof. of Islamic Art, Mich. Univ. 48-, Curator of Near Eastern Art, Freer Gallery of Art 58-61, Adjunct Curator of Near Eastern Art, Los Angeles County Museum of Art, Head Curator 61-66; Adjunct Prof. of Fine Arts, New York Univ. 60-67, Prof. 67-; Editor *Ars Islamica* 38-54; Near Eastern Editor *Ars Orientalis* 51-57; mem. Consultative Cttee. *Ars Orientalis* 58-; Editorial Board *The Art Bulletin* 40-, *Kairos* 59-; Consultative Chair. Islamic Dept. Metropolitan Museum of Art, New York 69-.
Leisure interests: nature walks, hiking.
Publs. *The Unicorn (Studies in Muslim Iconography I)* 50, *Paintings of the Sultans and Emperors of India in American Collections* 61, *Persian Miniatures in the Bernard Berenson Collection* 61, Preface to *Turkey, Ancient Miniatures* 61, *Arab Painting* 62, *Turkish Miniatures* 65; Editor and Contributor: *A Selected and Annotated Bibliography of Books and Periodicals in Western Languages dealing with the Near and Middle East, with special emphasis on Medieval and Modern Times* 52, *Aus der Welt der islamischen Kunst* 59.
Institute of Fine Arts, New York University, 1 East 78th Street, New York, N.Y. 10021; Home: 24 Armour Road, Princeton, N.J. 08540, U.S.A.
Telephone: 609-924-7362 (Home); 212-988-5550 (Office).

Etzdorf, Hasso von, LL.D.; German diplomatist; b. 2 March 1900; ed. Univs. of Berlin, Göttingen and Halle.
Held various posts at Foreign Office and diplomatic appointments in Tokyo, Rome, Genoa, etc.; Chief of German Del. to Interim Cttee. for European Defence Community (EDC), Paris 53; Deputy Sec.-Gen. Western European Union (WEU), London 55; Amb. to Canada 56-58; Deputy Under-Sec. of State, Foreign Office 58-61; Amb. to U.K. 61-65; Vice-Pres. Int. Nuclear S.A., Brussels; Adviser to Board, Gutehoffnungshütte, AG, Oberhausen; Hon. G.C.V.O.
8019 Eichtling, Post Moosach, Obb., Federal Republic of Germany.
Telephone: GLONN-08093-1402.

Evang, Karl, M.D.; Norwegian health official; b. 19 Oct. 1902, Oslo; m. Dr. Gerda Sophie Moe 1929; one s. one d.; ed. Universitetet i Oslo.
General practitioner 29-32; on staff of Municipal Hospital, Oslo 32-34; Norwegian Govt. Service 37-, Dir.-Gen. Norwegian Health Services 39-72; Pres. World Health Assembly 49; Chair. Exec. Board, World Health Org. 65; Visiting Prof. Social Medicine 73; Léon Bernard Medal and Prize, World Health Org. 66, Bronzman Prize, American Public Health Asscn. 70.
Leisure interests: fishing, tennis, skiing.
Publs. include: *Sexual Education* 51, *Health Service Society and Medicine* 58, *Health Services in Norway* 60, *Use and Abuse of Drugs* 66, *Current Narcotic Problems* 67, *Narcotics, the Generations and Society* 70, *Health and Society* 74, *Health Services in Norway* 76.
Maaltrostun 11B, Oslo 3, Norway.
Telephone: 142460.

Evans, Daniel Jackson, M.S.; American politician; b. 16 Oct. 1925, Seattle, Wash.; s. of Daniel Lester Evans and Irma (Ide) Evans; m. Nancy Ann Bell 1959; three s.; ed. Roosevelt High School, Seattle, and Univ. of Washington.
United States Naval Reserve 43-46; Lieut. on active duty Korean War 51-53; Asst. Man. Mountain Pacific Chapter, Assoc. Gen. Contractors 53-59; State Rep., King County 56-64; Partner, Gray & Evans, structural and civil engineers 59-64; inaugurated Gov. Washington State 65, re-elected 68, 72; Chair. Western Govs. Conf. 68-69; Chair. Constitutional Revision and Exec. Re-organization Cttee. of Nat. Govs. Conf.; Republican Floor Leader of the House 61-65; Chair. Cttee. on Exec. Management and Fiscal Affairs 69; Chair. Transportation, Commerce and Technology, Cttee. of Nat. Govs. Conf. 69-; Keynote speaker, Republican Nat. Convention 68; mem. Steering Cttee. Urban Coalition 69-; mem. Republican Governors' Advisory Board to Pres. 69; Chair. Policy Cttee. of Republican Govs. Asscn. 70-71; mem. Comm. of the Cities in the 70s 71-72; mem. Advisory Board on Intergovernmental Relations 72; Public Official of the Year 70; several hon. degrees; Human Rights Award 67.
Leisure interests: skiing, sailing, mountain climbing.
Office of the Governor, Legislative Building, Olympia, Washington 98501, U.S.A.
Telephone: 753-6780.

Evans, Earl Alison, Jr., PH.D.; American biochemist; b. 11 March 1910, Baltimore, Md.; s. of Earl Alison Evans and Florence (Lewis) Evans; ed. Baltimore Polytechnic Inst., Johns Hopkins and Columbia Univs.
Assistant in Pharmacology, School of Medicine, Johns Hopkins Univ. 31-32; Asst. endocrine research 32-34; Univ. Fellow in Biochemistry, Columbia Univ. 34-36; Instructor in Biochemistry, Chicago Univ. 37-39, Asst. Prof. 39-41, Assoc. Prof. and Acting Chair. of Dept. 41-42, Prof. 42-, Chair. of Dept. 42-72; Reserve Officer, U.S. Foreign Service, Chief Scientific Officer, American Embassy, London 47-48; Consultant to Sec. of State 51-53; mem. Board of Scientific Counsellors, Nat. Inst. of Arthritis and Metabolic Diseases, Nat. Insts. of Health 60-63; mem. Div. Cttee. for Biological and Medical Sciences, Nat. Science Foundation 63-66; Chair. Postdoctoral Fellowship Cttee., Div. of Biology and Agriculture, Nat. Acad. of Sciences, Nat. Research Council 63-65; mem. Air Force Office of Scientific Research Fellowship Board 66-, Advisory Board American Foundation for Continuing Educ. 62-;

Rockefeller Fellow, Univ. of Sheffield, England 40-41; Fellow, All Souls Coll., Oxford 68-69; Fellow, Pierpont Morgan Library 69-, Welch Lecturer (Houston) 72; Eli Lilly Medal of American Chemical Soc. 41; mem. American Chemical Soc., American Asscn. for Advancement of Science (Fellow), Soc. for Experimental Biology and Medicine, British Biochemical Soc., American Soc. of Biological Chemists, American Soc. of Bacteriologists; Hon. mem. Asociacion Quimica Argentina.
Publs. *Biochemical Studies of Bacterial Viruses* 52; co-author: *Biological Symposia V* 41, *Symposium of Respiratory Enzymes* 42; Editor: *Biological Action of the Vitamins* 42.
12 East Scott Street, Chicago, Illinois 60610, U.S.A.
Telephone: 312-753-3960 (Office); MOhawk 4-4866 (Home).

Evans, Dame Edith (Mary), D.B.E.; British actress; b. 8 Feb. 1888; ed. St. Michael's School, Chester Square, London.
First appearance as Cressida in *Troilus and Cressida* at King's Hall, Covent Garden 12; later roles include Agatha Payne in *The Old Ladies* New Theatre 35, Arcadina in *The Seagull* New Theatre 36, Kit Markham in *Old Acquaintance* Apollo Theatre 42, Hesione Hushabye in *Heartbreak House* Cambridge Theatre 43; Lady Pitts in *Daphne Laureola* Wyndham's 49, Helen in *Waters of the Moon* Haymarket Theatre 51-53; The Countess in *The Dark is Light Enough* 54; Mrs. St. Maugham in *The Chalk Garden* 56, Queen Katherine in *Henry VIII* 58; Stratford-upon-Avon: Countess of Rousillion in *All's Well that Ends Well*, Volumnia in *Coriolanus* 59, Margaret in *Richard III*, Nurse in *Romeo and Juliet* 61; Violet in *Gentle Jack* 64, Judith in *Hay Fever* 64, Mrs. Forrest in *The Chinese Prime Minister* 65; gave a dramatic reading of Shaw's *The Black Girl in Search of God*, Mermaid Theatre 68, *Edith Evans and Friends* 74; films: *The Queen of Spades* 48, *The Last Days of Dolwyn* 48, *The Importance of Being Earnest* 52, *The Nun's Story*, *Look Back in Anger* 59, *Tom Jones* 63, *Chalk Garden* 64, *Young Cassidy* 65, *The Whisperers* 66, *Fitzwilly* 66, *Prudence and the Pill* 67, *The Madwoman of Chaillot* 69, *Crooks and Coronets* 69, *David Copperfield* 70, *Scrooge* 70, *A Doll's House* 73, *Craze* 74, *The Slipper and the Rose* 76; Hon. D.Lit. (London Univ.) 50; Hon. Litt.D. (Cambridge Univ.), Hon. D.Litt. (Oxford Univ., Univ. of Hull); numerous acting awards.
Gatehouse, Kilndown, Cranbrook, Kent, England.

Evans, Sir Francis Edward, G.B.E., K.C.M.G., D.L.; British diplomatist; b. 4 April 1897, Canterbury; s. of Thomas Edward Evans and Amy Harriet Alwood; m. Mary Dick 1920; ed. Belfast Royal Acad. and London School of Economics.
Service, First World War; Consular Service 20, New York 20-26, Boston 26-29, Panama 29-32, Boston 32-34, Los Angeles 34-39; Foreign Office 39-43; Consul, New York 43, Consul-Gen. 44-50; Under-Sec. of State 51; Minister to Israel 51; Amb. to Israel 52-54, to Argentina 54-57; Deputy Chair. N. Ireland Development Council 57-63; Agent, Govt. of N. Ireland in Great Britain 62-66; Pres. of Council, *Ulster 71* Festival; Hon. LL.D. (Queen's Univ., Belfast), Hon. D.C.L. (Ripon Coll., Wisconsin), Hon. D.Litt. (New Univ. of Ulster, Coleraine); Knight of St. John.
Leisure interests: military history, painting.
Home: 180 Upper Malone Road, Dunmurry, Belfast, N. Ireland.
Telephone: Belfast 614188.

Evans, Sir Geraint Llewellyn, Kt., C.B.E.; British opera singer; b. 16 Feb. 1922, Pontypridd, Wales; m. Brenda Evans Davies 1948; two s.; ed. Guildhall School of Music.
Principal baritone, Royal Opera House, Covent Garden 48-; has sung leading roles at: Glyndebourne Festival Opera, Vienna State Opera, La Scala (Milan), Metropolitan Opera (New York), San Francisco Opera, Lyric Opera (Chicago), Salzburg, Edinburgh Festival, Paris Opera, Teatro Colon (Buenos Aires), Mexico City, Welsh National Opera, Scottish Opera, Berlin Opera, Teatr Wielki (Warsaw); Gov. London Opera Centre; Dir. Harlech Television; F.G.S.M.D. 60; Hon. D.Mus. (Wales) 65 (Leicester); Hon. F.R.A.M. 69; Worshipful Co. of Musicians Sir Charles Santley Memorial Award 63, Harriet Cohen Int. Music Award (Opera Medal) 67.
34 Birchwood Road, Petts Wood, Kent, England.
Telephone: Orpington 20529.

Evans, Harold J., PH.D.; American plant physiologist; b. 19 Feb. 1921, Franklin, Ky.; s. of James H. and Allie Evans; m. Elizabeth Dunn 1946; two d.; ed. Univ. of Kentucky and Rutgers Univ.
Assistant Prof., Assoc. Prof., Prof. of Botany, N. Carolina State Univ. 48-61; Post-doctoral Fellow, Johns Hopkins Univ. 52; Prof. of Plant Physiology, Oregon State Univ. 61-; Visiting Prof. Univ. of Sussex 67; George A. Miller Visiting Prof. Univ. of Ill. 73; Pres. American Soc. of Plant Physiologists 71-; mem. Nat. Acad. of Sciences; Hoblitzelle Nat. Award 65, Oregon State Univ. Alumni Distinguished Prof. Award 73, Univ. of Ky. Distinguished Alumnus Award 75.
Publs. numerous articles in professional journals.
2939 Mulkey Street, Corvallis, Ore. 97330, U.S.A.
Telephone: 503-754-1214 (Office); 503-752-3227 (Home).

Evans, Harold Matthew, M.A.; British newspaper editor; b. 28 June 1928; one s. two d.; ed. Durham Univ.
Commonwealth Fund Fellow, Univ. of Chicago 56-57; Editor *Sunday Times*, London 67-; mem. Exec. Board, Times Newspapers Ltd. 68-, Int. Press Inst. 74-; Journalist of the Year Prize 73, Int. Editor of the Year Award 75.
Leisure interests: music, table tennis, skiing.
Publs. *Active Newsroom* 64, *Editing and Design, Newsman's English* 70, *Newspaper Design* 71, *Newspaper Headlines* 73, *Newspaper Text* 73, *We Learned to Ski* (co-author) 74, *Freedom of the Press* 74.
c/o Sunday Times, 200 Gray's Inn Road, London, W.C.1. England.
Telephone: 01-837-1234.

Evans, Joan, D.LITT., D.LIT., F.S.A., F.R.HIST.S., F.R.S.L.; British archaeologist; ed. Berkhamsted Girls' School, Oxford and London Univs.
Librarian, St. Hugh's Coll., Oxford 17-22; Travelling Fellow, Anglo-Swedish Society 22; Suzette Taylor Fellow, Lady Margaret Hall, Oxford 37-39; Hon. Fellow, St. Hugh's Coll. 36-, Supernumerary Fellow 51-58; Fellow, Univ. Coll., London 50; Pres. Royal Archaeological Inst. 48-57, Treas. 59-63; Dir. Soc. of Antiquaries 54-59, Pres. 59-64, now Hon. Vice-Pres.; Trustee, London Museum 51-66, British Museum 63-67; mem. Advisory Cttee. Victoria and Albert Museum 53-68; Hon. LL.D. (Edinburgh Univ.), Hon. D.Litt. (Cambridge Univ.), Hon. A.R.I.B.A.; Chevalier of the Legion of Honour, Gold Medal, Soc. of Antiquaries 73, and numerous other awards and honours.
Publs. *Magical Jewels of the Middle Ages and Renaissance* 22, *Life in Medieval France* 25, 58, *Pattern: a Study of Decorative Art, Monastic Life at Cluny* 31, *Romanesque Architecture of the Order of Cluny* 38, *Taste and Temperament* 39, *Time and Chance—the story of Arthur Evans and his Forbears* 43, *Art in Medieval France* 48, *English Art 1307-1461* (Oxford History of English Art, Vol. V) 49, *Cluniac Art of the Romanesque Period* 50, *A History of Jewellery* 53, *John Ruskin* 54, *A History of the Society of Antiquaries* 56, *Diaries of John Ruskin* 56-59, *The Lamp of Beauty* 59, *Madame Royale* 59, *Monastic Architecture in France from the Renaissance to the Revolution* 64, *Prelude and Fugue* (autobiography) 64, *The Victorians* 66, *The Conways* 67, *Later Monastic*

Architecture in France 67, *Later Monastic Iconography in France* 70.

Thousand Acres, Wotton-under-Edge, Glos., England.

Evans, John Robert; Canadian university administrator; b. 1 Oct. 1929; s. of William Watson Evans (deceased) and Mary Evelyn Lucille (née Thompson) (deceased); m. Jean Gay (née Glassco) 1954; four s. two d.; ed. Univ. of Toronto and Univ. Coll., Oxford. Resident in clinical medicine and Hon. Registrar, Nat. Heart Hosp., London, England 55-56; Asst. Resident in medicine, Sunnybrook Hosp., Toronto 56-57; Asst. Resident in medicine Toronto Gen. Hosp. 57-58; Ontario Heart Foundation Fellow, Hosp. for Sick Children, Toronto 58-59; Chief Resident in medicine, Toronto Gen. Hosp. 59-60; Univ. of Toronto, Markle Scholar in Academic Medicine 60-65; Research Fellow, Baker Clinic Research Lab., Harvard Medical School 60-61; Univ. of Toronto, Assoc. Dept. of Medicine and Physician, Toronto Gen. Hosp. 61-65, Pres. Univ. of Toronto 72-; Dean, Faculty of Medicine and Prof. Dept. Medicine 65-72, Vice-Pres. (Health Sciences) McMaster Univ. 67-72; Chair. Nat. Health Grants, Dept. of Nat. Health and Welfare 69-74; Pres. Assoc. of Canadian Medical Colls. 71; Fellow, Royal Coll. of Physicians and Surgeons of Canada, American Coll. of Physicians, American Council on Clinical Cardiology; mem. numerous medical cttees. and socs.

Leisure interests: farming, conservation.

Office of the President, University of Toronto, Toronto 5, Ontario, Canada.

Evans, Luther Harris, M.A., PH.D.; American political scientist and librarian; b. 13 Oct. 1902, Sayersville, Tex.; s. of George Washington Evans and Lillie Johnson; m. Helen Murphy 1925; one s. ed. Univ. of Texas and Stanford Univ.

Instructor in citizenship Stanford Univ. 24-27, in government New York Univ. 27-28, and in political science Dartmouth Coll. 28-30; Asst. Prof. of Politics Princeton Univ. 30-35; Dir. Historical Records Survey, Work Projects Administration 35-39; Dir. Legislative Reference Service, Library of Congress 39-40; Chief Asst. Librarian of Congress 40-45, Librarian June 45-53; Adviser UNESCO London 45; mem. U.S. Nat. Comm. for UNESCO 46-52 (Chair. 52), 59-63; Adviser or Del. to UNESCO Gen. Confs. 47-53 (mem. Exec. Board 49-53); Dir.-Gen. of UNESCO 53-58; Senior Staff mem. Brookings Inst., Washington, D.C. 59-61; Dir. Project on Educ. Implications of Automation, Nat. Educ. Assen., Washington D.C. 61-62; Dir. Int. and Legal Collections Columbia Univ., N.Y. 62-71; Pres. World Federalists U.S.A. 71-; numerous hon. degrees and decorations; Democrat.

Leisure interests: reading, travel.

Publs. *The Virgin Islands from Naval Base to New Deal* 45, *Automation and the Challenge to Education* 62, *Federal Department Libraries* 63, *The Decade of Development: Problems and Issues* 66, *The U.S. and UNESCO* 71.

25 Claremont Ave., New York City, N.Y. 10027, U.S.A. Telephone: 212-666-4289.

Evans, Maurice; American actor-manager; b. 3 June 1901, Dorchester, Dorset, England; s. of Alfred Herbert and Laura Evans; ed. Grocers' Company School, London. In America 36-; U.S. Army 42-45; Artistic Supervisor, New York City Center Theatre 49-51; Pulitzer and Critics Prizes for production of *Teahouse of the August Moon* 53.

Plays acted in include: *Richard II, Hamlet* 38-39, *Henry IV, Part I* 39, *Twelfth Night* 40-41, *Macbeth* 41-42, *Hamlet* 45-47; produced and acted in *Man and Superman* 47-49, *The Browning Version* 49, *The Devil's Disciple* 50, *Richard II* 51, *Dial "M" for Murder* 52-54, *The Apple Cart* 56-57, *Heartbreak House* 59-60, *Tenderloin* (musical) 60-61, *The Aspern Papers*

61-62, *Shakespeare Revisited, A Program for Two Players* (with Helen Hayes) 62-63.

Films include *Kind Lady* 50, *Androcles and the Lion, Gilbert and Sullivan, Macbeth* 60, *Warlord* 65, *Jack of Diamonds, Planet of the Apes* 67, *Rosemary's Baby, Thin Air* 68, *Beneath the Planet of the Apes* 70.

c/o Charles H. Renthal and Co., 641 Lexington Avenue, New York, N.Y. 10022, U.S.A.

Evans, Robert Beverley; American business executive and financier; b. 19 March 1906; ed. Virginia Episcopal School, Univ. of Michigan and Univ. of Lausanne, Switzerland.

Former Dir. and Vice-Pres. Evans Products Co.; fmr. Pres. Precision Science Co.; fmr. Dir. Detroit-Windsor Freedom Festival; fmr. Vice-Commodore Yachtsmen's Assen. of America and Commodore and Chair. Finance Cttee. Detroit Int. Regatta Assen.; Chair. Board American Motors Corpn., until 67, Staudacher Marine Industries; mem. Board of Dirs. M.B. Corpn., Automobile Manufacturers Assen.; Pres. Ready Power Co., La Coquille Real Estate Corpn.; Patron, Detroit Symphony; mem. Founders Soc. Detroit Inst. of Arts; Dir. Detroit City Center Comm.; inventor of industrial and marine equipment.

American Motors Corporation, 14250 Plymouth Road, Detroit, Michigan 48232, U.S.A.

Evans, Ronald E., M.SC.; American astronaut; b. 10 Nov. 1933, St. Francis, Kan.; s. of Clarence E. and Marie A. Evans; m. Janet Merle Pollom; one s. one d.; ed. Highland Park High School, Univ. of Kansas and U.S. Naval Coll. Postgraduate School.

Commissioned through Naval Reserve Officers Training Corps; completed flight training 57; carrier duty, two cruises; Combat Flight Instructor with VF-124 61, 62; later flew F8 aircraft on carrier duty, Viet-Nam, selected by NASA as astronaut 66; support crew for *Apollo VII* and *XI*; backup command module pilot for *Apollo XIV*; prime command module pilot for *Apollo XVII* mission. Viet-Nam Service Medal, Navy Commendation Medal (66), Johnson Space Center Superior Achievement Award (70), Navy Distinguished Service Medal (73), NASA Distinguished Service Medal (73), Republic of Senegal's National Order of the Lion (73), etc.

Leisure interests: hunting, fishing, camping, sailing, boating, golfing.

NASA Johnson Space Center, Houston, Tex. 77058, U.S.A.

Evans, Russell Wilmot, M.C., LL.B.; British business executive; b. 4 Nov. 1922, Birmingham; s. of William Henry Evans and Ethel Williams Wilmot; m. Pamela Muriel Hayward 1956; two s. one d.; ed. King Edward's School, Birmingham, Univ. of Birmingham.

Infantry commander in Italy during war service; qualified as solicitor 49; Asst. Sec. at Harry Ferguson 51, Sec. of Massey-Ferguson (Holdings) and its U.K. subsidiaries after merger of Ferguson and Massey-Harris, resigned 62; on Parent Board of group of private companies in construction industry; joined Rank Org. 67, Deputy Sec. 67-68, Sec. 68-72, Dir. 72-, Man. Dir. 75-; Dir. of principal subsidiary cos., incl. Rank Xerox and Southern Television.

Leisure interests: tennis, squash, photography.

Walnut Tree, Roehampton Gate, London, S.W.15, England.

Evans, Thomas Mellon, B.A.; American business executive; b. 8 Sept. 1910; ed. Shadyside Acad. and Yale Univ.

President, H. K. Porter Co. Inc. 39-56, Chair. 56-; Chair. Crane Co. 59-; Dir. H. K. Porter France Usines de Marpent (France), H. K. Porter (Nederland) N.V., H. K. Porter Co. (Great Britain) Ltd., Fed. Wire and Cable Co. Ltd. (Canada), Société d'Applications Hydrauliques et Electriques (France); Chair. and Dir. Crane Canada Ltd., Dir. Crane Ltd. (England), Crane

S.A. France, N.V. Nederlands-Amerikaanse Fitting-fabriek (Holland), Orion Petro-Chimica S.p.A. Round Hill Road, Greenwich, Conn., U.S.A.

Evans of Hungershall, Baron (Life Peer) cr. 67, of the Borough of Royal Tunbridge Wells; **B. Ifor Evans,** M.A., D.LIT., HON. D. ÈS L. (Paris), HON. LL.D. (Manchester), F.R.S.L.; British writer and educationist; b. 19 Aug. 1899; ed. Stationers' Co. School and Univ. Coll., London.
Lecturer in English Literature Manchester Univ. 21-24; Prof. of English Language and Literature Univ. Coll. Southampton 25-26; Prof. of English Literature Sheffield Univ. 26-33; Albert Kahn Travelling Fellowship 24; Univ. Prof. of English Language and Literature Queen Mary Coll. Univ. of London 33-44, Principal 44-51; Provost of Univ. Coll. London 51-66; Fellow Univ. Coll. London; Vice-Chair. A.C.G.B. 46-51; with Ministry of Information 39-41; Educational Dir. to British Council 41-44; Public Orator, Univ. of London 47-52; mem. of Exec. British Council 50-54; Chair. *Observer* Trustees 57-66, Nat. Insurance Advisory Cttee. 57; Trustee of the British Museum; Consultant Wates Foundation; Chair. Rediffusion Educational Council, Educational Advisory Council—Thames Television, Cassel Trust; Hon. LL.D. (Univ. of Manchester); Officer Legion of Honour (France); Knight of the Order of the Crown (Belgium); Commdr. of the Order of Orange Nassau.
Publs. *William Morris and his Poetry* 24, *Encounters* 26, *Keats and the Chapman Sonnet* 30, *English Poetry in the Later Nineteenth Century* 33, *The Limits of Literary Criticism* 33, *Keats* 34, *Romanticism and Tradition* 39, *A Short History of English Literature* 40, *In Search of Stephen Vane* 46, *The Shop in the King's Road* 47, *Literature Between the Wars* 47, *Short History of British Drama* 48, *The Church in the Markets* 48, *The Arts in England* (with Mary Glasgow) 48, *The Use of English* 49, *A Victorian Anthology* (with Marjorie R. Evans) 49, *The Language of Shakespeare's Plays* 51, *Literature and Science* 54, *English Literature: Values and Traditions* 62.
1317 Minster House, St. James Court, Buckingham Gate, London, S.W.1, England.

Evensen, Jens, LL.D.; Norwegian lawyer and politician; b. 5 Nov. 1917, Oslo; ed. law schools and Harvard Univ., U.S.A.
Junior partner, law firm 41-45; Legal Counsel to Solicitor-Gen. 48-49; Advocate, Supreme Court 51; Rockefeller Fellowship 52-53; Dir.Gen. Legal Dept., Ministry of Foreign Affairs 61; Chair. Norwegian Petroleum Council 64-, Fishery Limits Comm. 67-69, many other cttees.; Amb. for negotiating Trade Agreement with European Communities 72; Minister of Commerce 73-74; Minister without Portfolio (Law of the Sea Min.) 74-.
c/o Ministry of Foreign Affairs, Oslo, Norway.

Everingham, Douglas Nixon, M.B., B.S.; Australian politician and medical practitioner; b. 25 June 1923, Wauchope, N.S.W.; s. of Herman Clifford and Hilda Mary Everingham; m. Beverley May Withers 1948; one s. two d.; ed. Fort Street School, Univ. of Sydney.
Resident Medical Officer in gen. and mental hospitals 46-53; gen. practice 53-67; mem. Fed. Parl. 67-75; Minister for Health 75; Vice-Pres. World Health Assembly 75-.
Leisure interests: semantics, interlinguistics, pasigraphy, spelling reform, humanism.
Publs. *Chemical Shorthand for Organic Formulae* 43, *Critique of Bliss Symbols* 56, *Braud Inglish Speling* 66.
Parliament House, Canberra, A.C.T.; Home: 50 Corberry Street, Rockhampton, Queensland, Australia. Telephone: 733 144 (Canberra), 24408 (Home).

Everton, John Scott, B.A., B.D., PH.D., D.D.; American educationist and diplomatist; b. 7 March 1908; ed.

Colgate-Rochester Divinity School, Yale Univ. and Cambridge Univ.
Minister, Central Baptist Church, Pennsylvania 37-41; Dean of Chapel and Prof. Philosophy and Religion, Grinnell Coll. 41-49; Pres. Kalamazoo (Mich.) Coll. 49-53; rep. Ford Foundation, Burma 53-56, Exec. Assoc., New York City 56-59, Assoc. Dir. Int. Training and Research Program 59-61; former Lecturer, External Examiner in Philosophy, Univ. of Rangoon; Ambassador to Burma 61-63; Vice-Pres. Educ. and World Affairs 63-68; Exec. Dir. of the Overseas Educational Service 63-68; Pres. Robert Coll., Istanbul, Turkey 68-72; Chair. Burma Council Exec. Cttee. of the Asia Soc. 63-; Rep. The Rockefeller Foundation, Indonesia 72-; mem. numerous cttees.; Hon. D.D. (Grinnell Coll.) 49, Hon. LL.D. (Univ. of Redlands) 63, Hon. D.Hum.Litt. (Univ. of Chattanooga) 64.
P.O. Box 63, Jogjakarta, Indonesia.

Evtushenko, Evgeny Alexandrovich; Soviet poet; b. 18 July 1933, Zima, Irkutsk Region; ed. Moscow Literary Inst.
Geological expeditions with father to Kazakhstan 48, the Altai 50; literary work 49-; visits to France, Africa, U.S.A., Cuba, U.K., Germany 60-63; mem. Editorial Board of *Yunost* magazine; U.S.S.R. Cttee. for Defence of Peace Award 65, Order of Red Banner of Labour.
Publs. verse: *Scouts of the Future* (collected verse) 52, *The Third Snow* (lyric verse) 55, *The Highway of Enthusiasts* 56, *Zima Junction* 56, *The Promise* (collected verse) 59, *Conversation with a Count, Moscow Goods Station, At the Skorokhod Plant, The Nihilist, The Apple* 60-61, *A Sweep of the Arm* 62, *Tenderness* 62, *A Precocious Autobiography* 63, *Cashier, Woman, Mother, On the Banks of the Dniepr River, A Woman and a Girl, Do the Russians Want War?, Bratskaya Hydro-Electric Power Station* 65, *A Boat of Communication* 66, *Collection of Verses* 67, *That's what is happening to me* 68, *Under the Skin of the Statue of Liberty* (play) 72.
Union of U.S.S.R. Writers, ul. Vorovskogo 52, Moscow, U.S.S.R.

Ewald, Paul P., F.R.S.; British physicist; b. 23 Jan. 1888, Berlin; m. Ella Philippson 1913; two s. two d.; ed. Univs. of Cambridge, Göttingen and Munich.
Lecturer in Theoretical Physics, Univ. of Munich 18-21; Prof. of Theoretical Physics, Technische Hochschule Stuttgart 21-37; Research Fellow, Univ. of Cambridge 37-39; Lecturer, later Prof. in Mathematical Physics, Queen's Univ., Belfast 39-49; Head, Dept. of Physics, Polytechnic Inst. of Brooklyn 49-57, Prof. 57-59, Prof. Emer. 59-; Corresp. mem. Akad. der Wissenschaften, Göttingen, Bayerische Akad. der Wissenschaften; mem. American Acad. of Arts and Sciences, Deutsche Akad. der Naturforscher (Leopoldina); Hon. mem. Soc. Française de Minéralogie et de Cristallographie, Deutsche Mineralogische Gesellschaft, Cambridge Philos. Soc.; Dr. h.c. (Stuttgart, Paris, Adelphi, Munich and Polytechnic Inst. of Brooklyn).
Publs. *Kristalle und Röntgenstrahlen* 23, *Fifty Years of X-Ray Diffraction* 62.
108 Sheldon Road, Ithaca, N.Y. 14850, U.S.A.

Ewaldsen, Hans Lorenz, DIPL.SC.POL.; German business executive; b. 6 Sept. 1923, Lunden, Schleswig Holstein; s. of Lorenz and Marie (née Kröger) Ewaldsen; m. Marianne Paulsen 1951; two s.; ed. Univ. of Kiel.
Member, Man. Board, Deutsche Babcock & Wilcox AG 60, Chair. 67-.
Leisure interests: hunting, tennis.
Deutsche Babcock & Wilcox AG, 4200 Oberhausen, Duisburger Strasse 375, Federal Republic of Germany.

Ewertsen, Harald Wind; Danish ear, nose and throat specialist; b. 17 April 1913, Hjorring; m. Bodil Knipschildt 1942; three s. two d.; ed. Københavns Universitet.

Doctor's dissertation, Univ. of Copenhagen 46; Ear, nose and throat specialist 49; Dir. State Hearing Rehabilitation Centre of Copenhagen 51-; Asst. Prof. Danmarks Larerhojskole 65; Vice-Pres. Int. Soc. of Audiology 62-66; Pres. Danish Medical Audiological Soc. 67-72; Co-editor *International Audiology* 62-66; Vald. Klein Prize 74; many specialist publs.
Leisure interests: magic conjuring tricks, horse-riding, photography.
208 Virum Stationsvej, Virum, Denmark.
Telephone: 01-85-6100.

Exeter, 6th Marquess of; **David George Brownlow Cecil,** K.C.M.G., LL.D., D.L., J.P.; British politician, businessman and sportsman; b. 9 Feb. 1905; ed. Eton and Cambridge.
Winner Olympic 400 metres hurdles 28, three British Empire and eight British championships, etc.; Conservative M.P. 31-43; Parl. Private Sec. to Parl. Sec. Minister of Supply 39-41; Lt.-Col., Asst. Dir. Tank Supply 41; Controller Repairs and Overseas Supplies of Aircraft, Ministry of Aircraft Production 41-43; Gov. and Commdr.-in-Chief Bermuda 43-45; Chair. Organizing and Exec. Cttee. of 1948 Olympic Games, London; Rector, St. Andrews Univ. 49-52; Leader of U.K. Industrial dels. to Pakistan 50, and Burma 54; Pres. Radio Industry Council 52; Mayor of Stamford 61; Pres. Int. Amateur Athletic Fed., Amateur Athletic Asscn.; Pres. British Olympic Asscn.; mem. Int. Olympic Cttee. (Vice-Pres. 56-68); Pres. British Horse Soc. 63; Empire Chambers of Commerce 52-54; Chair. Birmid Qualcast Ltd.; Dir. Nat. Westminster Bank, Firestone Tyre & Rubber Co., Lands Improvement; Pres. British Travel Asscn. 66-69; Hereditary Grand Almoner; Hon. LL.D., Hon. F.R.C.S.
Burghley House, Stamford, Lincolnshire, England.
Telephone: Stamford 3131.

Exon, John James; American state governor; b. 9 Aug. 1921, Geddes, S. Dakota; s. of John J. and Luella (Johns) Exon; m. Patricia Pros 1943; one s. two d.; ed. Univ. of Omaha.
Vice-Chairman, Nebraska State Democratic Cen. Cttee. 64-68; mem. Neb. Democratic Party Exec. Cttee. 64-; Neb. Democratic Nat. Cttee. Man 68-70; Gov. of Nebraska Jan. 71-; mem. Lincoln Chamber of Commerce, Nat. Stationers and Office Equipment Asscn.
Office of the Governor, State Capitol, Lincoln, Neb.; Governor's Mansion, 1425 H Street, Lincoln, Neb., U.S.A.
Telephone: 402-471-2244 (Office); 402-432-3123 (Home).

Eyadéma, Gen. Gnassingbe; Togolese army officer and politician; b. 1935, Pya, Lama Kara District.
Served with French Army 53-61, especially in Indo-China, Dahomey, Niger and Algeria; commissioned 63; Army Chief of Staff (Togo) 65-; led army coup Jan. 67; Pres. of Togo and Minister of Defence April 67-; f. Rassemblement du Peuple Toglais, Paris 69-; Grand Officier, Ordre National de Mono; Mil. Cross; Chevalier, Légion d'Honneur (France).
Leisure interest: hunting.
Office of the President, Lomé, Togo.

Eyebu-Bakand'asi, Ipoto; Zaire diplomatist; b. 8 Aug. 1933, Kinshasa; m.; seven c.; ed. Inst. Universitaire de Hautes Etudes Internationales, Geneva.
Director of Cabinet, Ministry of Foreign Affairs of the Congo (Leopoldville) 60-63; OAU assignments 64, 65; Deputy to Special Commr. for Central Basin of Congo 65; Technical Adviser, Ministry of Foreign Affairs 66; Counsellor, London 66; Amb. to Algeria 67-69, India 70, Ethiopia 70-72; Perm. Rep. to UN 72-74.
c/o Ministry of Foreign Affairs, Kinshasa, Zaire.

Eyre, Dean Jack; New Zealand High Commissioner in Canada 68-73; see *The International Who's Who 1975-76.*

Eyring, Henry, M.S., PH.D.; American professor of chemistry; b. 20 Feb. 1901, Colonial Juarez, Chihuahua, Mexico; s. of Edward Christian and Caroline Romney Eyring; m. 1st Mildred Bennion 1928 (died 1969), 2nd Winifred Brennan 1971; three s. four d.; ed. Univ. of Arizona, Univ. of Calif.
Instructor in Chemistry, Univ. of Arizona and Wisconsin 24-28; Research Assoc. Univ. of Wisconsin 28-29; Nat. Research Fellow, Kaiser Wilhelm Inst., Berlin 29-30; Lecturer in Chemistry, Univ. of Calif. 30-31; Asst. and Assoc. Prof. of Chemistry, Princeton Univ. 31-38, Prof. 38-46; Dean of Graduate School Univ. of Utah 46-66, Distinguished Prof. of Chemistry and Metallurgy 66-; research work for the Army, Navy and OSRD on the theory of smokes and of high explosives, during Second World War; Dir. of the fundamental research programme of the Textile Foundation, Princeton 44-46; Editor of Annual Reviews of Physical Chemistry; mem. of U.S. Acad. of Arts and Sciences, Utah Acad. of Arts and Science, Arts and Letters, Amer. Philosophical Soc., Int. Acad. of Quantum Molecular Science 69, Deutsche Akademie der Naturforscher 75, Nat. Science Board 62-68, Amer. Asscn. Adv. of Sciences, Pres. 65, Dir. 61-66, Amer. Chem. Soc., Pres. 63, Nat. Acad. of Science 45-, Amer. Phil. Soc. Rheology, Vice-Pres. 46; Dir. of Annual Reviews 54-71; Hon. mem. of the Chemical Soc. (London); award from Research Corpn. for outstanding contribution to science 49, Bingham Medal (Amer. Chemical Soc.) 51, Theodore William Richards Medal, N.E. Section of ACS, Nat. Medal of Science 66, Irving Langmuir Award 67, Willard Gibbs Medal 67, Cresson Medal, Franklin Inst. 69, Linus Pauling Medal, Puget Sound Section of ACS 69, Willard Gardner Award, Utah Acad. of Sciences, Arts and Letters 73, Joseph Priestly Celebration Award, Dickinson Coll. 74, Theodore William Richards Medal, N.E. Section of ACS 74; Joseph Priestley Medal, American Chemical Soc. 75; Hon. D.Sc., Utah State Univ., Univ. of Arizona 71, Univ. of Notre Dame 69, Marquette Univ. 69, Seoul Nat. Univ. 63, Princeton Univ. 56, Northwestern Univ. 53.
Leisure interests: application of quantum mechanics and statistical mechanics; theory of reaction rates, theory of liquids, molecular biology, rheology, radioactivity, optical rotation, theory of flames.
Publs. with others: *The Theory of Rate Processes* 41, *Quantum Chemistry* 44, *The Kinetic Basis of Molecular Biology* 54, *Modern Chemical Kinetics* 63, *Statistical Mechanics and Dynamics* 64, *Significant Liquid Structures* 69, *The Theory of Optical Activity* 71, *The Theory of Rate Processes in Biology and Medicine* 74, *Deformation Kinetics* 75, and over 530 papers in national scientific journals.
Department of Chemistry, University of Utah, Salt Lake City, Utah 84112; 1922 East 9th South, Salt Lake City, Utah, U.S.A.

Eysenck, Hans Jurgen, PH.D., D.SC.; British psychologist; b. 4 March 1916, Berlin, Germany; s. of Edward Eysenck and Ruth Werner; m. Sybil Bianca Giuletta Rostal 1950; four s. one d.; ed. Univs. of Dijon, Exeter and London.
Research Psychologist, Mill Hill Emergency Hospital 42-45; Psychologist, Maudsley Hospital, London 45; Reader and Dir., Psychological Dept., Inst. of Psychiatry, Univ. of London 50-55, Prof. of Psychology 55-.
Publs. *Dimensions of Personality* 47, *The Scientific Study of Personality* 52, *The Structure of Human Personality* 53, *Uses and Abuses of Psychology* 53, *The Psychology of Politics* 54, *Sense and Nonsense in Psychology* 56, *The Dynamics of Anxiety and Hysteria* 57, *Perceptional Processes and Mental Illness* 57, *Manual for the Maudsley Personality Inventory* 59, *Experiments in Personality* (2 vols.) 60, *Behaviour Therapy and the Neuroses* 60, *Handbook of Abnormal*

Psychology 60, *Manual for the Eysenck Personality Inventory* 63, *Experiments with Drugs* 63, *Crime and Personality* 64, *Experiments in Motivation* 64, *Causes and Cures of Neuroses* 65, *Experiments in Behaviour Therapy* 65, *Fact and Fiction in Psychology* 65, *Smoking, Health and Personality* 65, *The Biological Basis of Personality* 67, *Structure and Measurement of Personality* 69, *The Structure of Human Personality* 70, *Readings in Introversion/Extraversion* 71, *Race, Intelligence and Education* 71, *Psychology is about People* 72, *Encyclopaedia of Psychology* (ed.) 72-, *Measurement of Intelligence* 73, *Experimental Study of Freudian Theories* 73, *The Inequality of Man* 73, *Eysenck on Extraversion* 73, *Case Histories in Behaviour Therapy* 75, *Introduction to Psychology* 75, *Know Your Own Personality* (with Glenn Wilson)75.
Leisure interests: tennis, squash, photography.
Department of Psychology, Institute of Psychiatry, Maudsley Hospital, Denmark Hill, London, S.E.5; Home: 10 Dorchester Drive, London, S.E.24, England.

Eyskens, Gaston, M.S., DR. RER. POL., DR. SC.COM., LIC. SC.ECON.; Belgian economist and politician; b. 1 April 1905, Lierre, Prov. of Antwerp; ed. Univ. of Louvain and Columbia Univ.
Professor Univ. of Louvain 31; Cabinet Dir., Ministry of Labour 34-35; mem. of Parl. 39-73; Minister of Finance 45 and 47-49; Gov. Int. Bank for Reconstruction and Devt. 47-49; Prime Minister 49; Minister of Econ. Affairs 50; Vice-Pres. Econ. and Social Council UN 51; Prime Minister 58-61, June 68-Nov. 72; Minister of State; Minister of Finance 65-66; Hon. Dr. Econ. (Cologne), Hon. Dr. of Laws (Columbia), Hon. Dr. Phil. (Jerusalem); mem. Christian Social Party.
Leisure interests: landscape and portrait painting.
Publs. *Le Port de New York dans son rôle économique* 29, *De Arbeider en de Bedrijfsleiding in Amerika* 31, *La conjoncture économique du Congo Belge* 34, *Les Finances Publiques Belges* 55, *Economische Theorie en Economische Politiek* 56, *Geld en Financiewezen* 56, etc.
60 rue de Namur, Louvain, Belgium.
Telephone: 224-43.

Eytan, Walter, M.A.; Israeli civil servant; b. 24 July 1910, Munich, Germany; s. of Dr. Maurice Leon Ettinghausen and Hedwig Kahn; m. Beatrice Levison; two s. one d.; ed. St. Paul's School, London, and Queen's Coll., Oxford.
Lecturer in German, Queen's Coll., Oxford 34-46; Principal, Public Service Coll., Jerusalem 46-48; Dir.-Gen. Ministry for Foreign Affairs, Israel 48-59; Amb. to France 60-70; Political Adviser to Foreign Minister 70-72; Chair. Israel Broadcasting Authority 72-.
Publ. *The First Ten Years* 58.
18 Rehov Balfour, Jerusalem, Israel.
Telephone: 02-31268.

Eyuboğlu, Bedri Rahmi; Turkish painter and poet; b. 1913; ed. Académie des Beaux Arts, Constantinople, and André Lhote Atelier, Paris.
Exhibited in Turkey with advanced painters' *Group D*

33-37; influenced by Anatolian handicraft designs 41-45; worked on block printing, serigraphy, engraving and textile printing 45-50; mosaic work since 57; Ford Foundation Grant for travel in Europe and U.S.A. 61-63; Prof. Acad. of Fine Arts, Istanbul; has also written poems, essays and travel notes in books, magazines and newspapers; Prize at São Paulo Bienal 56, Gold Medal, Brussels Fair 58; exhbns. in several cities of Europe and U.S.A.
Major works: Panel at Brussels Fair 58, Mosaic panel for NATO Building in Paris 59, Christmas Card for UNICEF 61, mosaic murals in Ankara, Izmir and Istanbul 63-65.
29/3 Manolya Sokak, Kalamis, Kızıltoprak, Istanbul, Turkey.

Ezhov, Leonid Savvich; Soviet foreign trade official; b. 28 Feb. 1916; ed. Moscow Inst. of Mechanical Engineering and Acad. of Foreign Trade.
Member C.P.S.U. 44-; U.S.S.R. Trade Rep., Italy 49-51; Commercial Attaché, later, U.S.S.R. Commercial Rep. in Lebanon 51-56; Official, Ministry of Foreign Trade 56-62; Commercial Rep. in Belgium 62-66; Chief of Dept., Ministry of Foreign Trade 66-; Badge of Honour.
Ministry of Foreign Trade, 32-34 Smolenskaya-Sennaya ploshchad, Moscow, U.S.S.R.

Ezhov, Valentin Ivanovich; Soviet screen-play writer; b. 21 Jan. 1921, Kuibyshev; ed. All-Union State Inst. of Cinematography.
Member C.P.S.U. 51-; Lenin Prize for script of *Ballad of a Soldier*; co-author scripts for *Our Champions* 54, *World Champion* 55, *Liana* 56, *A Man from the Planet Earth* 58, *The House of Gold* 59, *The Volga Flows* 62, *Story of a Woman Flier* 64, *Wings* 66.
Mosfilm Studios, 1 Mosfilmovskaya ulitsa, Moscow, U.S.S.R.

Ezpeleta, Mariano; Philippine Ambassador to Australia and Chief of Mission to New Zealand 60-71; see *The International Who's Who 1975-76*.

Ezra, Sir Derek, Kt., M.B.E.; British business executive; b. 23 Feb. 1919; s. of David and Lillie Ezra; m. Julia Elizabeth Wilkins 1950; ed. Monmouth School and Magdalene Coll., Cambridge.
Military service 39-47; rep. of Nat. Coal Board at Cttees. of OEEC and ECE 48-52; mem. U.K. Del. to High Authority of European Coal and Steel Community 52-56; Regional Sales Man. Nat. Coal Board 58-60, Dir.-Gen. of Marketing 60-65; mem. Nat. Coal Board 65-, Deputy Chair. 65-71, Chair. 71-; Chair. (des.) of British Inst. of Management Oct. 76-; Deputy Chair. Confed. of British Industry Overseas Cttee. 75-; Chair. CBI Europe Cttee., European Trade Cttee. of the British Overseas Trade Board; mem. British Overseas Trade Board.
The National Coal Board, Hobart House, Grosvenor Place, London, S.W.1, England.
Telephone: 01-235-2020 (Office).

F

Fabbri, Diego; Italian playwright; b. 2 July 1911. Former lawyer; Nat. Theatre Prize for *Inquisizione* 50; Marzotto Int. Prize for *Portrait of a Young Man*. Plays include: *Orbite* 41, *Paludi* 42, *La Libreria del Sole* 43, *Inquisizione* 50, *Rancore* 50, *Il Seduttore* 51, *Processo di famiglia* 54, *Processo a Gesù* 55, *La Bugiarda* 56, *Veglia d'armia* 57, *Delirio* 58, *Figli d'arte* 59, *Processo Karamazov* 61, *Portrait of a Young Man* 62, *The Confidant* 64, libretto for *L'Avventuriero* 68.
Santa Prisca 15, Rome, Italy.

Fabiani, Dante Carl; American industrialist; b. 13 Aug. 1917; ed. Tri-State Coll. and Purdue Univ.
Auburn Rubber Corpn., Indiana 38-42; Gen. Electric Co., Ind. 42-45; Continental Can Co., Ohio 45-47; Controller, Asst. Man. Standard Products Co. Ohio, 48-51; Dir., Sec.-Treas. Townsend Co., Pa. 51-59; Vice-Pres. Finance, H. K. Porter Co. Inc. 59-60; Dir., Vice-Pres. Finance, McDonnell Aircraft Corpn., Missouri 60; Pres. and Dir. Crane Co., New York 60-; Dir. Sawhill Tubular Products 67-; Chair. C.F.I. Steel Corpn. 70-; Republican.
300 Park Avenue, New York, N.Y. 10022; Home: 15 North Avenue, Westport, Conn., U.S.A.

Fabiani, Simonetta (*see* under Simonetta).

Fabinyi, Andrew, D.PHIL., O.B.E., F.R.S.A.; Australian publisher; b. 27 Dec. 1908, Budapest, Hungary; s. of Dr. Imre Fabinyi and Margaret Nagel; m. Elisabeth Clare Robinson 1940; three s. two d.; ed. Minta Gymnasium and Pazmany Univ., Budapest, Hungary.
British Publishers Rep. in Hungary 33-39; Publishing Manager, F. W. Cheshire Pty. Ltd. 39-54; Australian Army Educ. Service 42-46; Publishing Dir. F. W. Cheshire Pty. Ltd. 54-; Pres. Australian Book Fair Council 55-60, Victorian Branch of Library Asscn. of Australia 55, 59, 65, 66, Public Libraries Div. of Library Asscn. of Australia 62; Dir. Lansdowne Press Pty. Ltd. 62-69; Pres. Australian Book Publishers' Asscn. 65, 66; mem. Exec. Cttee. for Econ. Devt. of Australia 65-; Gen. Councillor, Library Asscn. of Australia 66-67; Pres. of Australian Inst. of Int. Affairs 67-69, Pres. N.S.W. branch 71-73; Chair. Australian Book Trade Advisory Cttee. 67-68, Chair. Press and Publs. Cttee. Australian UNESCO Nat. Cttee. 68-69; mem. Australian UNESCO Cttee. for Communications 70-, Chair. Australian Nat. Comm. for UNESCO 72-; Chair. Int. Book Year Cttee. 72; mem. Int. Advisory Cttee. on Documentation, Libraries and Archives (Paris) 71-73; Chair. Cheshire Group Publishers and Booksellers 68-69; Dir. La Trobe Univ. Bookshop Board 70-; Chair. Australian Book Publishers Asscn. Book Export Cttee. 71-; Man. Dir. Pergamon Press Australia 69-75, Dir. 75-; Redmond Barry Award, Library Asscn. of Australia 74; Research Fellow, Univ. of N.S.W. 75-.
Leisure interest: reading.
Publs. *Social and Cultural Issues of Migration, Living in Cities*; articles in *Meanjin, Australian Book Review, Hemisphere, The Australian Author, The Bulletin*; Chapters in *Literary Australia, Adult Education in Australia, Librarianship in Tomorrow's World, Introducing Australia, The Development of Australian Children's Book Publishing*.
116 Grosvenor Road, Lindfield, New South Wales 2070, Australia.
Telephone: 465783.

Fabre, Robert; French pharmacist and politician; b. 21 Dec. 1915, Villefranche de Rouergue; s. of Georges Fabre and Louise Feille; m. Christiane Dutilh 1942; ed.

Faculté de Médecine et Pharmacie de Toulouse. Mayor of Villefranche de Rouergue, Aveyron 53; Conseiller Général for Aveyron 55; mem. Parl. for Aveyron 62-; Vice-Pres. Regional Council for Midi-Pyrénées 73; Pres. Mouvement des Radicaux de Gauche; Palmes Académiques; Médaille de Jeunesse et des Sports; Chevalier de la Santé Publique; Officier, Ordre Nat. du Sénégal.
Leisure interest: painting.
13 rue Marcellin Fabre, 12200 Villefranche de Rouergue; 31 rue Raynouard, 75016 Paris, France.
Telephone: 45-09-47 (Villefranche); 525-13-95 (Paris).

Fábri, Zoltán; Hungarian film director; b. 1917; ed. grammar school, Acad. of Fine Arts, Budapest, and Acad. of Dramatic Art, Budapest.
Former painter, later actor at Nat. Theatre 41; Army Service, Second World War; joined Artists' Theatre, Budapest, after Second World War; later Head of Youth Theatre; joined State Film Production Org. 50, film dir. 52-; Chair. Union of Hungarian Film Artists; Grand Prix, Carlovy-Vary Film Festival for *Professor Hannibal* 56; Grand Prix, Moscow Film Festival for *Twenty Hours* 65, Kossuth Prize 53, 55, 70.
Films: *The Storm* 52, *Fourteen Lives Saved* 54, *Merry-Go-Round* 55, *Professor Hannibal* 56, *April Fool* 57, *Anna* 58, *The Beast* 59, *Two Half-Times in Hell* 61, *Darkness in Daytime* 63, *Twenty Hours* 64, *Late Season* 67, *Boys of Pal-Street* 69, *The Unfinished Sentence* 75.
c/o Hungarofilm, H-1054 Budapest 5/5, Báthori-utca 10, Hungary.
Telephone: 116-650.

Fabricius, Johan; Netherlands writer; b. 1899, Bandung, Java; s. of Jan Fabricius and Minke Dornseiffen; m. 2nd Anna Bleeker 1968; two s. one d. (from previous marriage); ed. Batavia, Leyden, and The Hague.
Former war corresp. on Austro-Italian front; B.B.C. and *The Times* corresp. in Indonesia 45-46.
Leisure interests: painting, illustrating, piano.
Publs. include: *De scheepsjongens van Bontekoe* 24, *Hans de klokkeluider* (play) 25, *Het meisje met de blauwe hoed* 27, *Charlotte's grote reis* 28, *Mario Ferraro's ijdele liefde* 29, *Komedianten trokken voorbij* 31 (awarded Van der Hoogt Prize 32), *Melodie der verten* 32, *Leeuwen hongeren in Napels* 34, *De dans om de galg* 34, *Flipje* 36, *Kasteel in Carinthië* 38, *Eiland der Demonen* 40, *Nacht over Java* 42, *De kraton* 45, *Halfbloed* 46, *Hoe ik Indie terugvond, Hotel Vesuvius* 47, *De Grote Geus* 48, *De Grote Beproeving* 50, *Mijn Huis staat achter de Kim* (memoirs) 51, *De Ontvoering van Europa* 52, *Langs de Leie* 52, *Een Wereld in Beroering* (memoirs) 52, *Gordel van Smaragd* 53, *De Nertsmantel* 53, *Het Duistere Bloed* (play) 53, *Idylle 1871* (play) 53, *Toernooi met de Dood* 54, *Nacht zonder Zegen* 55, *Setoewo de Tijger* 56, *Nuit Maudite, Die heiligen Pferde, Ma Rosalie, Hopheisa in regen en wind* (memoirs) 64, *Wat u nodig hebt, mevrouw, is een vriend* 64, *Dag Leidse Plein* 65, *Dromen is ook leven* 65, *Weet je nog, Yoshi?* 66, *Wij Tz'e Hsi, Keizerin van China* 67, *Het Water Weet van niets* 68, *Wittebroodsweken met Mama* 69, *Voorrijden, mevrouw?* 69, *Shock Treatment* (play) 69, *Onder de hete Caraibische zon* (short stories) 70, *De kop van Jut* 70, *Sentimental Journey* 71, *Met klein orkest* 71, *De duivel in de toren* 71, *Partnerruil niet uitgesloten* 72, *Hanneke's Bruiloft* 72, *Carlinho, mijn kleinzoon* 73, *Het gordijn met de ibissen* 74, *Het Portret* 74, *Barcarolle* 75, *De wijze Goeroe's van Benares* 75, *De Oorlog van de kleine paardjes* 75, *Er zijn*

geen echte gekken meer in Capri 76, *Gringo, een reis naar Paraguay in 1921* 76.
Uitgeberij Leopold N.V., Badhuisweg 232, The Hague; 15 Meentweg 7, Glimmen (gem. Haren, Groningen), Netherlands.
Telephone: 05906-1606.

Facio Segreda, Gonzalo J.; Costa Rican lawyer and diplomatist; b. 28 March 1918; ed. National Univ. of Costa Rica, New York Univ. School of Law, and Inst. of Inter-American Law, New York.
Founder Law Firm of Facio, Fournier and Cañas; Prof. Philosophy of Law, Nat. Univ. of Costa Rica 44-47, Prof. Admin. Law 47-51, Prof. Econ. and Social Org. 59-61, Prof. Admin. Law 59-62; founder-mem. Nat. Liberation Party 48, mem. Exec. Cttee. 48-56, Chair. Planning Board 59-62; Ambassador, Rep. to the Org. of American States (OAS) 56-58, 62, Vice-Chair. Council 57-58, Chair. Council OAS 62-63; Ambassador to U.S.A. 62-66; Minister of Foreign Affairs May 70-75; Editor magazine *Surco* 42-45, weekly *Democratic Action* 45-48, daily *La República* 55-56; Pres. Security Council UN 75-.
Calle, 31-33 Avenida 13, San José, Costa Rica.

Fack, Robbert; Netherlands diplomatist; b. 1 Jan. 1917, Amsterdam; *m.* Patricia H. Hawkins 1943; four *s.*; ed. Univ. of Amsterdam.
Military service 37-45; entered diplomatic service 45; served in Ministry of Foreign Affairs and UN 46-48, Rome 50-54, Canberra 54-58; Minister Plenipotentiary, Bonn 58-63; Amb. at Large 68-70; Perm. Rep. to UN 70-74; Amb. to U.K. 76-; Head dels. to int. confs.; decorations include Kt. Netherlands Lion, Officer Order of Orange-Nassau, Kt. (military div.), Croix de Guerre avec Etoile d'Argent (France).
Leisure interests: water sports, winter sports, gardening.
Royal Netherlands Embassy, 38 Hyde Park Gardens, London, SW7 5DP, England.
Telephone: 01-584-5040.

Fadeyechev, Nikolai Borisovich; Soviet ballet dancer; b. 27 Jan. 1933; ed. Bolshoi Theatre Ballet School.
Bolshoi Theatre Ballet Company 52-; People's Artist of R.S.F.S.R.
Chief roles: Siegfried (*Swan Lake*), Albert (*Giselle*), Jean de Brien (*Raimonde*), Harmodius (*Spartacus*), Frondoso (*Laurensia*), Danila (*Stone Flower*), Romeo (*Romeo and Juliet*), Prince Desire (*Sleeping Beauty*).
State Academic Bolshoi Theatre of U.S.S.R., 1 Ploshchad Sverdlova, Moscow, U.S.S.R.

Fagerholm, Karl-August; Finnish politician; b. 1901; ed. Helsinki.
Barber 17-23; Chair. Finnish Barbers T.U. 20-23; Mem. of Parl. 30-66; mem. Presidential electorate 31; Minister of Social Affairs 37-43; mem. of Castren Govt. 44; Speaker of the Diet 45-48, 50-56, 59-61, 65-66; Prime Minister July 48-Mar. 50, Mar. 56-May 57, Aug. 58-Jan. 59; Chair. Shopworkers' Union 30-42, Hon. Chair. 43-; Workers' Rep. at Labour Conf. Geneva 30, Govt. Rep. 38 and 39; Dir.-Gen. State Alcohol Monopoly 52-; Spokesman for several professional workers' unions; mem. Exec. Cttee. Social Democratic Party.
Temppelik 15, Helsinki, Finland.

Fahd ibn Abdul Aziz, Crown Prince; Saudi Arabian politician; b. 1922; brother of the late King Faisal.
Minister of Educ. 53, of the Interior 62-75; Second Deputy Prime Minister 68-75, First Deputy Prime Minister 75-; became Crown Prince 75.
Office of the Deputy Prime Minister, Riyadh, Saudi Arabia.

Fahlström, Öyvind Axel Christian; Swedish artist and writer; b. 28 Dec. 1928, São Paulo, Brazil; *s.* of Frithiof and Karin (née Kronvall) Fahlström; *m.* Barbro Östlihn 1960.

Former critic for periodicals and *Expressen* Stockholm; manifesto for *Concrete poetry* 52, increasingly active as painter since mid-'fifties; One-man exhbns. Galerie Daniel Cordier, Paris 59 and 62, Sidney Janis Gallery, New York 63, 67, 69, 71, 73, Cologne 70; Rep. of Sweden, Venice Biennale 66; author of plays, dir. two short films, one feature (*Du Gamla Du Fria*) 69.
Leisure interests: politics, music.
Publs. *Minneslista till Dr. Schweitzer's sista uppdrag* (poetry) 64, *Den Helige Torsten Nilsson* (novel for tape) 65, *Bord* (poetry) 66, *Om Livskonst ø.a.* (essays) 70.
121 Second Avenue, New York 10003, U.S.A.; and Köpmangatan 8, Stockholm C, Sweden.

Fahmy, Ismail; Egyptian diplomatist and politician; b. 1922; ed. Cairo Univ.
Entered diplomatic service 45; Counsellor to Egyptian Del. to UN 57, and later in charge of UN Affairs, Ministry of Foreign Affairs; Chair. Political Cttee. of UN, New York until 68; Amb. to Austria 68-71; Under-Sec. of State for Foreign Affairs 71-72; Amb. to Fed. Repub. of Germany 72-73; Minister of Tourism March-Oct. 73, of Foreign Affairs Oct. 73-; Vice-Pres. Council of Ministers April 75-.
Ministry of Foreign Affairs, Cairo, Egypt.

Fairfax, Sir Vincent Charles, Kt., C.M.G.; Australian business executive; b. 26 Dec. 1909, Cambooya, Queensland; *s.* of John H. F. Fairfax and Ruth B. Dowling; *m.* Nancy Heald 1939; two *s.* two *d.*; ed. Geelong Grammar School, Victoria and Brasenose Coll., Oxford.
Military service 40-46; Royal Flying Doctor Service 54-71; Dir. Bank of N.S.W. 53, John Fairfax Ltd. 56; Dir. Australian Mutual Provident Soc. 56, Chair. 66; Chair. Stanbroke Pastoral Co. Pty. Ltd. 64; Chair. Australian Section, Commonwealth Press Union 50-73; Chair. Boys Brigade 50, Press 73; Chief Commr. Scout Asscn. N.S.W. 58-68, for Australia 69-73; mem. Council Royal Agricultural Soc., N.S.W. 50-, Treas. 59, Pres. 73; Deputy Pres. Royal Agricultural Soc. of Commonwealth 66; mem. Church of England Property Trust 50-71, Council Art Gallery Soc. of N.S.W. 53-69, Glebe Admin. Board 62-73; Trustee, Walter and Eliza Hall Trust 53.
Leisure interests: tennis, golf, trout fishing.
Home: 550 New South Head Road, Double Bay, N.S.W. 2028; Office: 2 Castlereagh Street, Sydney, N.S.W. 2000, Australia.

Fairfax, Sir Warwick (Oswald), Kt., M.A.; Australian journalist; b. 1902; *s.* of Sir James Oswald Fairfax and Mabel Hixson; *m.* 1st Marcie Elizabeth Wilson 1928, one *s.* one *d*; *m.* 2nd Hanné Anderson Bendixsen 1948, one *d.*; *m.* 3rd Mary Wein 1959, one *s.*; ed. Geelong Grammar School and Sydney and Oxford Univs.
Joined staff John Fairfax and Sons Ltd. (*Sydney Morning Herald, The Sun, The Sun-Herald, The Australian Financial Review*, etc.) 25, Dir. 27, Man. Dir. 30, Chair. of Dirs. 36; Chair. Assoc. Newspapers Ltd.; Dir. David Syme and Co. Ltd.; Vice-Pres. Board Australian Elizabethan Theatre Trust; mem. Council Australian Nat. Univ.
Leisure interests: the arts, philosophy, motoring and vintage cars.
Publs. Ed. *A Century of Journalism* (the Sydney Morning Herald) 31; *Men, Parties and Policies* 43, *The Triple Abyss: towards a modern synthesis* 65; plays: *A Victorian Marriage, Vintage for Heroes, The Bishop's Wife*.
John Fairfax and Sons Ltd., P.O. Box 506, G.P.O. Sydney; Home: Fairwater, 560 New South Head Road, Double Bay, Sydney, N.S.W. 2028; Harrington Park, Narellan, N.S.W. 2567, Australia.
Telephone: 2-0944 (Office); 36-4161 (Home).

Faizi, Djaudat Kharisovich; Soviet composer; b. 4 Jan. 1910, Orenburg; ed. Kazan Univ., and Tatar Opera Studio of Moscow Conservatoire.

Executive mem. Composer's Union of Tatar Autonomous S.S.R.; Honoured Worker of Arts of the Tatar Autonomous S.S.R. 44, and of the R.S.F.S.R. 57, People's Artist of the Tatar Autonomous S.S.R. 64.
Principal works: *Bashmachki* (Slippers) 42, *Seagulls* 44, *On the Banks of the Volga* 49 (all musical comedies); *Undispatched Letters* (opera) 59; over 150 songs and romances, instrumental music and theatre music.
Composers' Union of the Tatar A.S.S.R., Kazan, U.S.S.R.

Fajon, Etienne; French politician and journalist; b. 11 Sept. 1906.
Member of the Central Cttee., French C.P. 32; Deputy for Courbevoie 36-40; Del. to Provisional Assembly 44-45; mem. Constituent Assembly 45-46; Deputy for Seine 46-58, 62-67; Deputy for Seine-baint-Denis 67-; mem. of Party Political Bureau 45-, Party Sec. 54-56, 70-; Dir. *L'Humanité* 58-74.
Publs. *L'Union est un combat* 75, *Mémoires* 76.
Comité Central du Parti Communiste Français, 2 place Colonel Fabien, 75940 Paris Cédex 19, France.
Telephone: 202-70-10.

Falcao, Armando Ribeiro; Brazilian lawyer and politician; b. 1920, Ceará State.
Leader Chamber of Deputies 59; Minister of Justice 60-61, 74-.
Ministério de Justica, Brasflia, Brazil.

Falin, Valentin Mikhailovich; Soviet diplomatist; b. 3 April 1926, Leningrad; ed. Moscow State Inst. of International Relations.
Official in Soviet Control Comm. in Germany 50-52; mem. staff U.S.S.R. Ministry of Foreign Affairs 52-56; Head, Second European Dept., Ministry of Foreign Affairs 66-68, Third European Dept. 68-71; Amb. to Fed. Repub. of Germany 71-.
U.S.S.R. Embassy, Bonn, Federal Republic of Germany.

Falk, Isidore Sydney, PH.D.; American medical economist, social security expert; b. 30 Sept. 1899, Brooklyn, N.Y.; s. of Samsin and Rose (Stolzberg) Falk; m. Ruth Hill 1925; two s.; ed. Yale Univ.
Assistant Dept. of Public Health 15-20; Instructor Yale Univ. 20-23; Asst. Prof. of Hygiene and Bacteriology 23-26, Associate Prof. 26-29 and Prof. 29 Univ. of Chicago; Associate Dir. Cttee. on Costs of Medical Care 29-33; Research Associate Milbank Memorial Fund 33-36; Statistical Consultant U.S. Public Health Service 36; Chief of Health Studies Social Security Board 36-38, Asst. Dir. Bureau (later Division) of Research and Statistics 38-40, Dir. 40-54; mem. Int. Bank Mission to Malaya 54; Consultant on Public Health and Social Security to Govt. of Panama 55 and 56; Consultant on Health to Panama Canal Zone Govt. 57; Consultant on Health Services to United Steelworkers of America 58-; Prof. of Public Health (Medical Care), Yale Univ. 61-68; Prof. Emer. and Lecturer in Public Health 68-; Vice-Chair. and Exec. Dir. Community Health Center Plan.
Publs. *Laboratory Outlines in Bacteriology and Immunology* (with J. F. Norton) 26; co-Editor *The Newer Knowledge of Bacteriology and Immunology* 28, *The Costs of Medical Care* (with C. R. Rorem and M. D. Ring) 33, *Security Against Sickness* 36, *Disability Among Gainfully Occupied Persons* (with Barkev S. Sanders and David Federman) 45, *Medical Care Insurance, A Social Insurance Program for Personal Health Services* (with staff) 46, *Social Insurance Program for Haiti* 52, *The Social Services* (in *Economic Development of Malaya*) 55, *A Review of the Social Security Program of Panama* (English and Spanish texts) 56, *Health in Panama: A Survey and a Program* (English and Spanish texts) 57, *A Survey of Health Services and Facilities in the (Panama) Canal Zone* 58, *Medical Care Program for Steelworkers and their Families* (with others) 60, *Development of the*

Community Health Center Plan in New Haven, Conn. 1969-1973 3 vols. (with others) 73, *Standards for Good Medical Care* 4 vols. (with H. K. Schonfeld and J. F. Heston) 75; numerous papers.
Route 2, Stonington, Conn.; 150 Sargent Drive, New Haven, Conn. 06511 (Office); 472 Whitney Avenue, New Haven, Conn. 06511, U.S.A.
Telephone: 787-3141 (Office); 776-6537 (Home).

Falkenhausen, Gotthard Freiherr Von, DR.IUR.; German banker; b. 20 Jan. 1899, Lübben; ed. Humboldt-Universität zu Berlin, Georg-August-Universität zu Göttingen and Martin Luther-Universität Halle-Wittenberg.
Attorney, Königsberg 26-28; Legal Adviser, Disconto Gesellschaft (later Deutsche Bank) 38-; Partner, Burkhardt & Co., Essen (bankers) 38-; Vice-Chair. Admin. Board Bankhaus C. G. Trinkaus & Burkhardt 72; mem. Essen City Council 48-68; Hon. Chair. Supervisory Board, Kundenkreditbank (Consumer Credit Bank), Düsseldorf; mem. Supervisory Board Klöckner-Werke, Duisburg (iron and steel); Pres. German Bankers' Asscn.; Vice-Pres. Chamber of Commerce for Cities of Essen, Mülheim and Oberhausen; Hon. Pres. German-French Chamber of Commerce, Paris; Hon. Chair. Atlantic Bridge Org., Hamburg; Hon. Pres. German Bankers Asscn.; mem. Board of Management German Council, European Movement, Bonn, Centre d'Etudes de Politique Etrangère, Paris, Rheinisch-Westfälische Börse, Düsseldorf.
Essen-Bredeney, Brachtstrasse 21, Federal Republic of Germany.
Telephone: 190201 (Office); 441764 (Home).

Falkenheim, Ernst, G.P.; German businessman; b. 7 May 1898, Starnberg/Obb.; s. of Dr. Hugo and Rosa Falkenheim (née Jaeger); m. Gertrud Heddrich 1945; one d.; ed. Univ. of Munich.
Served in First World War; worked for Hugo Stinnes Concern; joined Deutsche Shell 36; mem. of the Board of Deutsche Shell until 1963; Chair. of the Board of Fichtel und Sachs, A.G., Schweinfurt, and other companies; Hon. Senator Tübingen Univ.; Grosses Bundesverdienstkreuz Deutschland; Bayerischer Verdienstorden.
Leisure interests: philosophy, history, golf.
Hagrainerstrasse 15, 8183 Rottach-Egern Obb., Postfach 20, Federal Republic of Germany.
Telephone: 08022-6238.

Falkner, Sir (Donald) Keith, Kt., F.R.C.M.; British musician; b. 1 March 1900, Sawston, Cambs.; s. of John Charles Falkner; m. Christabel Margaret Fullard 1930; two d.; ed. New Coll. School, Oxford, Perse School, Cambridge and Royal Coll. of Music, London.
Pilot R.N.A.S. 17-18; professional singer 23-46; Sub-Lt. R.A.F.V.R. 40-45; Music Officer, British Council in Italy 46-50; Assoc. Prof. Cornell Univ. 52, Prof. 56-60; Dir. Royal Coll. of Music 60-74; Hon. R.A.M., Hon. G.S.M. (Guildhall School of Music), Hon. F.T.C.L. (Trinity Coll. of Music, London), Hon. D.Mus.(Oxon.).
Leisure interests: golf, cricket, squash racquets, walking, reading.
Low Cottages, Ilketshall St. Margaret's Road, Bungay, Suffolk, England.

Fall, Cheikh Ibrahima; Senegalese diplomatist and administrator; b. 4 Feb. 1930, Dakar; six s. one d.; ed. Lycée Faidherbe Saint-Louis, and Univs. of Dakar and Rennes.
Agent of Gen. Admin. and Justice; Chief Asst. Office of Econ. Affairs, Haut-Commissariat of French West Africa 56-57; Technical Counsellor, Ministry of Econ. Affairs and Planning 57-59; Dir. de Cabinet of Sec. of State of Commerce and Industry 59-60; Dir. of Commerce, Ministry of Commerce, Industry and Crafts; Dir of External Finance, Ministry of Finance and Econ.

Affairs; Amb. to Fed. Germany and Netherlands 64-65,
o U.S.S.R., Poland 65-68, to U.S.A., Canada, Mexico,
Trinidad and Tobago, Haiti 68-73; Sec.-Gen. West
African Econ. Community 73-; del. to many countries,
to UN and affiliated orgs., Vice-Pres. del. to World
Conf. on Commerce and Devt., Geneva 64; Trustee,
Port of Commerce, Dakar, Crédit Populaire Sénégalais,
Soc. d'Armement à la Peche; numerous orders and
decorations.
Rue Destenave, Ouagadougou, Upper Volta.
Telephone: 30-00 (Office); 20-22 (Home).

Fall, Medoune; Senegalese diplomatist; b. 21 July
1919, St. Louis, Senegal; ed. Ecole supérieure, Dakar.
Secretary, Territorial Assembly, Senegal 52-56; Dir. of
Social Insurance, Louga 56-59; District Chief, Podor
and Bambey 59-60; Head, Diourbel Regional Devt.
Assistance Centre 60-61; Gen. Dir. Nat. Board for
Farm Produce Purchases, later Gov. of Diourbel
Region 61-63; Amb. to France 64-66, concurrently to
Spain, and Rep. to UNESCO 65-66; Amb. to Belgium
and Perm. Rep. to EEC 66-68; Amb. to U.S.S.R. 68-71;
Perm. Rep. to UN 71-.
Permanent Mission of Senegal to United Nations, 51
East 42nd Street, 17th Floor, New York, N.Y. 10017,
U.S.A.

Fälldin (Nils Olof) Thorbjörn; Swedish farmer and
politician; b. 24 April 1926, Högsjö; s. of N. J. and
Hulda (Olsson) Fälldin; m. Solveig Oberg 1956; two
s. one d.; ed. secondary school.
Member, Second Chamber of Parl. 58-64, First Chamber
67-70; mem. Parl. (Riksdag) 71-; Chair. Centre Party
(largest opposition party) 71-.
Leisure interests: fishing, athletics.
Ås, 870 16 Ramvik, Sweden.
Telephone: 0612/43097.

Falle, Sir Samuel, K.C.V.O., C.M.G., D.S.C.; British
diplomatist; b. 19 Feb. 1919; ed. Victoria Coll., Jersey,
Channel Islands.
Served in Royal Navy 37-48; Diplomatic Service 48-;
Consul-Gen., Gothenburg, Sweden 61-63; Head of UN
Dept., Foreign Office 63-67; Deputy High Commr. in
Malaysia 67-69; Amb. to Kuwait 69; High Commr. in
Singapore 70-74; Amb. to Sweden 74-.
British Embassy, 8 Skarpögatan, 115 27 Stockholm,
Sweden; and c/o Foreign and Commonwealth Office,
London, S.W.1, England.

Fallon, Walter A., M.S.; American business executive;
b. Schenectady, N.Y.; m.; two d.; ed. Union Coll. and
Rensselaer Polytechnic Inst.
Joined Eastman Kodak Co. 41, Vice-Pres. 70, Dir. 70-,
Gen. Man. U.S. and Canadian Photographic Div., Dir.
Kodak-Pathe 70, Dir. Kodak Ltd. 72, mem. Exec
Cttee. 71, Dir. Eastman Chemical Products Inc. 71,
Pres. and Chief Exec. Officer, Chair. Operations and
Finance Cttees. 72-; Hon. D.Sc. (Union Coll.) 72; mem.
of Business Council, Trustee Cttee. of Econ. Devt., Dir.
General Motors Corpn., Lincoln First Banks Inc., etc.
Eastman Kodak Company, 343 State Street, Rochester,
N.Y. 14650; Home: 35 Edgewater Lane, Irondequoit,
New York, U.S.A.

Faluvégi, Lajos; Hungarian economist and politician;
b. 22 Oct. 1924, Mátraderecske; ed. Univ. of Political
Economy.
Joined the working-class movt. 47, Hungarian Socialist
Workers' Party 62; held various posts at Ministry of
Finance, Deputy Minister 68-71; Minister of Finance
71-; mem. State Planning Cttee. 73-; mem. Board of
Political Econ. attached to HSWP Cen. Cttee. 75-.
Ministry of Finance, H-1369 Budapest V, József nádor
tér 2/4, Hungary.
Telephone: 182-660.

Fan Tzu-yu; Chinese politician.
On Long March in Dept. of Supplies, 2nd Front Army
34-35; Champion of Swimming Contest for Generals in
People's Liberation Army Units 60; Maj.-Gen., Gen.
Logistics Dept., PLA 64; Minister of Commerce 71-.
People's Republic of China.

Fanfani, Amintore; Italian economist and politician;
b. Feb. 1908.
Fellow, Catholic Univ. of Milan 32, Titular Prof. in
Economic History 36, later Prof. Univ. of Rome 54;
mem. Constituent Assembly for XVI District 46, M.P.
for same district 48-68; Minister of Labour and Social
Security in 4th, 5th and 6th De Gasperi Cabinets 47-50;
Minister of Agriculture and Forestry, 8th De Gasperi
Cabinet July 51, Minister of the Interior 53 and Prime
Minister Jan. 54; Sec. Christian Democrat Party July
54-59; Prime Minister July 58-Jan. 59, July 60-
April 63; Minister of Foreign Affairs 65, 66-68; Pres. of
Senate 68-73, Life Senator 72-; Pres. UN Gen. Assembly
65-66; Sec. Democrazia Cristiana 73-75; Chair. April 76-.
Publs. Le origini dello spirito capitalistico 32, Catto-
licesimo e protestantesimo nella formazione storica del
capitalismo 34, Storia delle dottrine economiche 38-71,
Indagini sulla rivoluzione dei prezzi 39, Storia economica
40-71, Storia del lavoro 43, Colloqui sui poveri 41,
Persona, beni, società 45, Le tre città 46, Poemi Omerici
ed Economia Antica 60, Una Pieve in Italia 64.
Home: E.U.R. Piazzale Luigi Sturzo 15, Rome, Italy.

Fang, Roland Chung, B.A., M.A.; Chinese scholar;
b. 1902; ed. Tsing Hua Coll., Peking, Calif. and Stanford
Univs.
Professor of English Literature, Central Univ. Nanking
28-30; Prof. of English Literature and Head of English
Dept., Wuhan Univ. 31-44; Visiting Prof. Trinity
Coll. Cambridge Univ. 44-46; Prof. of English and Head
of Dept. of Foreign Languages, Chekiang Univ. 47-51,
Chekiang Teachers' Coll. 51-52; Prof. Anhwei Univ.,
Wuhu 52-53, East China Teachers' Univ. Shanghai 53-
54, Futan Univ., Shanghai 54-56; Head, English Dept.,
Shanghai Inst. of Foreign Languages 57-.
Publs. Book of Modern English Prose (2 vols.) 34, Studies
in English Prose and Poetry 39, A Chinese Verse Trans-
lation of Shakespeare's Richard III 59, Complete Works
of Chaucer translated into Chinese 62, Chaucer's Canterbury Tales (revised edn.) 63.
Shanghai Institute of Foreign Languages, Shanghai,
People's Republic of China.

Fang Yi; Chinese politician; b. 1909, Fukien.
Editor Commercial Press, Shanghai 30; on Long March
34; Sec.-Gen. N. China People's Govt. 48; Vice-Gov. of
Shantung 49, of Fukien 49-52; Deputy Mayor of
Shanghai 52-53; Vice-Minister of Finance 53-54; with
Embassy of People's Repub. of China, Hanoi 54-61;
Alt. mem. 8th Cen. Cttee. of CCP 56; Dir. of Bureau for
Econ. Relations with Foreign Countries, State Council
61-64; Chair. Comm. for Econ. Relations with Foreign
Countries 64-68; Alt. mem. 9th Cen. Cttee. of CCP 69;
Minister of Econ. Relations with Foreign Countries 69-;
mem. 10th Cen. Cttee. of CCP 73.
People's Republic of China.

Fannin, Paul Jones, B.A.; American politician; b.
29 Jan. 1907, Ashland, Ky.; m. Elma Addington 1934;
three s. one d.; ed. Arizona and Stanford Univs.
Partner Fannin Brothers (Industrial Developments);
fmr. Pres. Maricopa County Better Business Bureau;
Gov. of Arizona 58-65; Chair. Western Govs. Conf. 63;
mem. President's Civil Defense Advisory Council 63-64;
Senator from Arizona 64-; del. to Mexico-U.S. Interparl.
Conf. 65, 66, 67; del. to Int. Labor Org., Geneva 66;
mem. several Senate Cttees.
Leisure interest: golf.
U.S. Senate, Washington, D.C., U.S.A.

Farah, Abdulrahim Abby; Somali diplomatist; b. 1919; ed. Univ. of Exeter and Balliol Coll., Oxford. Ambassador to Ethiopia 61-65; Perm. Rep. of Somalia to United Nations 65-69, 70-74; Minister of Agriculture 69-70; UN Commr. for Technical Co-operation 72-73; UN Asst. Sec.-Gen. for Special Political Questions 73-.
Office of the Assistant Secretary-General, United Nations Secretariat, New York, N.Y., U.S.A.

Farhan, Ishaq Ahmad, M.SC., M.A., ED.D.; Jordanian educationalist; b. 1934, Ein Karem; m.; ed. American Univ., Beirut, and Columbia Univ., New York .
Science teacher 58-64; with Ministry of Educ., Amman 64-, Dir. of Pedagogical Services and Head, Syllabi Section 69, Dir. of Syllabi 69-70; Minister of Educ. 70-73, of Endowments and Islamic Shrines 73; Consultant for scientific and educational affairs, Royal Scientific Soc. 74, Dir.-Gen. 75.
Publs. several school textbooks and articles in scientific and pedagogical journals.
Royal Scientific Society, Amman, Jordan.

Faria Lima, Floriano Peixoto; Brazilian naval officer; b. 15 Nov. 1917, Guanabara; s. of João Soares de Lima and Castorina Faria Lima; m. Hilda de Faria Lima 1941; one d.; ed. Naval Acad.
Officer in Navy; Rear-Adm. 66; Vice-Adm. 69; Deputy Head of Office of Minister for the Navy; Naval Attaché, Brazilian Embassy, Washington, D.C., Ottawa; del. to Inter-American Defence Council (Junta Interamericana de Defesa); mem. Joint Comm. for Brazilian-U.S. Defence; Dir. Petrobrás 69-74; Gov. Rio de Janeiro State 75-; Portuguese Mil. Merit Medal, Spanish Merit Medal, Medal of Legion of Mil. Merit of U.S.A., and many Brazilian decorations.
Leisure interests: soccer, volleyball, collecting watches.
Palacio Guanabara, Rio de Janeiro, Brazil.

Faricy, William Thomas, LL.B.; American railroad executive; b. 7 March 1893, St. Paul, Minn.; s. of John I. and Thecla Brown Faricy; m. Norma Hauser 1918; two d.; ed. St. Paul Coll. of Law.
Attorney, C., St. P. M. & O. Railway Co. 14; gen. practice St. Paul 16-17, 19-20; gen. attorney C., St. P. M. & O. Railroad Co., St. Paul 20-24; commerce attorney, C. & N. W. Railway Co., Chicago 24-25; Vice-Pres. Hauser Securities Co. and Asst. to Pres. Hauser Construction Co., Portland, Oregon, and Long Beach, Calif. 25-27; Minn. attorney, C. & N. W. Railway Co., St. Paul 27-29; gen. solicitor C. St. P. M. & O. Railway Co., St. Paul 29-33, C. & N. W. Railway System, Chicago 33-42; Gen. Counsel, C. & N. W. Railway Co. 42-44; Vice-Pres. and Gen. Counsel C. St. P. M. & O. Railway Co. 42-47, C. & N. W. Railway Co. 44-47; Chair. Western Conf. of Railway Counsel 44-46; Pres. Asscn. of American Railroads 47-57, Chair. of Board 57-58; Advisory Dir. Riggs Nat. Bank, Washington, D.C.; Chair. Civilian Components Policy Board, Dept. of Defense 49-50; Chair. U.S. Nat. Comm. Pan American Railway Congress Asscn. 49-58, mem. 59-68; fmr. Pres. Hauser Securities Co. of Portland, Oregon; fmr. Pres. and Trustee, Grant Smith & Co. & McDonnell Ltd., Vancouver, B.C. 60-; Life Trustee, Northwestern Univ. Leisure interests: golf, travel.
Association of American Rail-Roads, 1920 L Street, N.W., Washington, D.C.; Home: 4914 Glenbrook Road, N.W., Washington, D.C. 20016, U.S.A.
Telephone: 202-293-4021 (Office).

Faris, Mustapha, DIPL.ING.; Moroccan economist; b. 17 Dec. 1933; ed. Ecole Nat. des Ponts et Chaussées, Paris.
Government Civil Engineer, Dept. of Public Works 56-61; Dir. of Supply, Nat. Irrigation Office 61-65; Dir.-Gen. of Hydraulic Engineering 65-69; Sec. of State for Planning attached to Prime Minister's Office 69-71;

Minister of Finance 71-72; Pres., Dir.-Gen. Banque Nationale pour le Développement Economique Dec. 72-; fmr. Vice-Pres. Int. Comm. on Large Dams; Gov. IBRD (World Bank), African Devt. Bank; Ordre du Trône.
Banque Nationale pour le Développement Economique, B.P. 407, Rabat, Morocco.

Farland, Joseph S., A.B., LL.B.; American diplomatist; b. 11 Aug. 1914; ed. West Virginia Univ. and Coll. of Law.
Attorney and counsellor to private cos. 38-42; Govt. service 42-44; U.S. Navy 44-45; Pres. of coal cos. 46-; Consultant to Special Asst. to Under-Sec. of State for Mutual Security Affairs 56; Amb. to Dominican Repub. 57-60, to Panama 60-63, to Pakistan 69-72, to Iran 72-73; Consultant on Latin American Affairs, *Reader's Digest.*
c/o Department of State, Washington, D.C. 20520, U.S.A.

Farley, James A., HON. D.C.L., LL.D.; American politician; b. 30 May 1888; ed. Stony Point High School and Packard Commercial School, N.Y. City.
Book-keeper 06; for many years Sales Man. for Universal Gypsum Co., N.Y. City; founded James A. Farley & Company Inc. 26; President and Director General Builders' Supply Corporation 29-33, 49-, Chairman 57; Chairman Coca-Cola Export Corporation September 40; Dir. Coca-Cola Co. of Canada Ltd.; Town Clerk Stony Point 12-19; Port Warden, N.Y. City 18-19; Chair. N.Y. State Athletic Comm. 25-33; Postmaster-Gen. in Roosevelt's Cabinet Mar. 33-Aug. 40; Sec. N.Y. Dem. State Cttee. 28-30, Chair. 30-July 44; Chair. Dem. Nat. Cttee. 32-40; Dir. Nat. Foreign Trade Council; mem. American Acad. of Political and Social Science, New York State Banking Board; holds many Hon. Degrees of American Colls. and Univs.
Publs. *Behind the Ballots* 38, *Jim Farley's Story* 49.
301 Park Avenue, New York City, N.Y., U.S.A.

Farmanfarmaian, Khodadad, M.A., PH.D.; Iranian economist and banker; b. 8 May 1928, Teheran; s. of Abdol Hossein and Hamdam Farmanfarmaian; m. Joanna Parkhurst 1949; one s. two d.; ed. American Univ. of Beirut, and Stanford and Colorado Univs.
Instructor and Research Asst., Dept. of Econs., Colorado Univ. 52-53; Instructor, Dept. of Econs., Brown Univ. 53-55; Research Fellow, Center for Middle Eastern Studies, Harvard Univ. 55-57; Research Assoc., Dept. of Econs. and Oriental Studies, Princeton Univ. 57-58; Dir. Econ. Bureau, Plan Org. 58-61; mem. Tax Comm., Ministry of Finance 58-60; mem. High Econ. Council 64-; Deputy Man. Dir. Plan Org. 61-62; Man. Dir. 70-73; Deputy Gov., Bank Markazi Iran (Central Bank of Iran) 64-69, Gov. 69-70; Chair. Board Dirs., Bank Sanaye Iran 73-; medals from govts. of Iran and Belgium.
Leisure interests: reading, tennis.
Publs. *Social Change and Economic Behaviour in Iran, Exploration in Entrepreneurial History* 56, *How Can the World Afford OPEC Oil?* (co-author) 75; has contributed to *Middle Eastern Journal.*
c/o Bank Sanaye Iran, Avenue Sepahbod Zahedi, No. 106, Teheran, Iran.

Farmer, James Leonard; American civil rights leader; b. 1920, Marshall, Texas; s. of late James Leonard Farmer, PH.D. and late Pearl Marion Houston Farmer; m. Lula A. Peterson 1949; two d.; ed. Wiley Coll. and Howard Univ.
Former Program Dir., Nat. Assoc. for the Advancement of Coloured People (NAACP); fmr. Int. Rep. State, County and Municipal Employees Union; Dir. Congress of Racial Equality 61-March 66; Pres. Center for Community Action Educ. 65-; Prof. of Social Welfare, Lincoln Univ. 66-68; Adjunct Prof. N.Y. Univ. 68;

Asst. Sec. for Admin., U.S. Dept. of Health, Educ. and Welfare 69-Dec. 70.
Leisure interests: detective stories, fishing.
Publ. *Freedom—When?* 66.
5129 Chevy Chase Parkway, N.W., Washington, D.C. 20008, U.S.A.
Telephone: 202-363-2611 (Home).

Farmer, Sir (Lovedin) George (Thomas), Kt., LL.D., M.A., F.C.A., J.DIP.M.A.; British motor executive; b. 13 May 1908, Bridgnorth, Shropshire; s. of Lovedin Thomas Farmer and Florence Webb; m. Editha Mary Fisher; ed. Oxford High School.
Chairman Rover Ltd. 63-73; Deputy Chair. British Leyland Motor Corpn. Ltd. 72-73; Dir. Newall Machine Tool Co. Ltd.; Pres. Birmingham Chamber of Commerce 60-61, Soc. of Motor Manufacturers and Traders 62-64, Deputy Pres. 64-65, Chair. of its Exec. Cttee. 68-72; Chair. Zenith Carburettor Co. 73-; mem. Court of Worshipful Co. of Coach and Coach Harness Makers; Gov. Chair. of Exec. Council and Finance Cttee. of Royal Shakespeare Theatre until 75, Deputy Chair. 75-; Pres. Loft Theatre, Leamington Spa; Pro-Chancellor Univ. of Birmingham 66-75.
Leisure interests: theatre, golf, fishing.
Fairford, 8 Hill Park, Ballakillowey, Colby, Isle of Man, England.
Telephone: Port St. Mary 2573.

Farner, Donald S., PH.D., D.SC.; American zoophysiologist; b. 2 May 1915, Waumandee, Wis., s. of John and Lillian S. Farner; m. Dorothy S. Copps 1940; one s. one d.; ed. Hamline Univ. and Univ. of Wisconsin.
Instructor in Zoology, Univ. of Wisconsin 41-43; Asst. Prof. of Zoology, Univ. of Kansas 46-47; Assoc. Prof. of Zoophysiology, Washington State Univ. 47-52, Prof. of Zoophysiology 52-65, Dean of Graduate School 60-64; Prof. of Zoophysiology, Univ. of Washington 65-, Chair. Dept. of Zoology 66-; Fulbright Research Fellow and Hon. Lecturer Univ. of Otago 53-54; Guggenheim Fellow and Hon. Lecturer in Zoology, Univ. of W. Australia 58-59; Pres. Int. Union of Biological Sciences 67-73; Chair. Div. of Biology and Agriculture Nat. Acad. of Sciences, Nat. Research Council 68-73, Div. Biological Sciences 73-74; Nat. Sigma Xi Lecturer 63; mem. American Soc. of Zoologists, American Physiol. Soc., American Chem. Soc. Ecological Soc. of America, American Soc. of Naturalists, American Ornithologists Union, Soc. for Endocrinology, American Asscn. for Advancement of Science, American Soc. for Photobiology, Deutsche Ornithologen Gesellschaft; Brewster Medal, American Ornithologists Union 62.
Publs. Approx. 200 research and review publs. 41-.
Department of Zoology, University of Washington, Seattle, Washington 98195, U.S.A.
Telephone: 206-543-1620.

Farrar, Frank L., LL.B.; American politician; b. 2 April 1929, Britton, S. Dak.; s. of Virgil and Venetia Farrar; m. Pat Henley; one s. four d.; ed. Univ. of South Dakota Business School and Univ. of South Dakota School of Law.
Service in Korean War, retd. Capt. U.S. Army Reserve; Internal Revenue Agent 55-57; Marshall Co. Judge; Marshall Co. State's Attorney; Attorney-Gen. of S. Dakota 62-68; Gov. of S. Dakota 69-71; Marshall Co. Republican Chair.
Home: P.O. Box 190, Britton, S. Dak. 57430, U.S.A.
Telephone: 605-448-2274.

Farrell, Eileen; American opera singer; b. 1920.
Debut with Columbia Broadcasting Co. 41, own programme for six years; opera debut with San Francisco Opera; toured throughout the U.S.A. and in other parts of the world.
72 Louis Street, Staten Island, N.Y. 10304, U.S.A.

Farrell, James Augustine, Jr.; American shipping executive; b. 13 Jan. 1901; ed. Yale Univ.
Shipping business 24-; Chair. of the Board and Dir. Farrell Lines Inc.; Dir. Nat. Foreign Trade Council Inc., Maritime Asscn. of Port of New York, Canterbury School, Argonaut Line; mem. American Soc. of Mechanical Engineers, American Soc. of Naval Architects; U.S. Naval Reserve 41-44; Fellow Royal Soc. of Arts and Design; Hon. Dr. Commercial Science (Duquesne Univ.); Commdr. Star of Africa; Grand Cross Humane Order of Africa Redeemed; Naval Order of the U.S.
Farrell Lines Inc., 1 Whitehall Street, New York, N.Y. 10004; 25 Old Farm Road, Darien, Conn., U.S.A.

Farrell, James Thomas; American writer and columnist; b. 27 Feb. 1904, Chicago, Ill.; s. of James Fraser and Marjory Farrell; one c.; ed. Chicago Univ.
Cigar store clerk, filling-station attendant, part-time journalist; Guggenheim Fellow 36-37; mem. Nat. Inst. of Arts and Letters; Hon. degrees Oxford and Ohio Univs.
Leisure interests: has no time for these.
Publs. *Young Lonigan—a boyhood in Chicago Streets* 32, *Gas House McGinty* 33, *The Young Manhood of Studs Lonigan* 34, *Calico Shoes* 34, *Judgement Day* 35, *Guillotine Party and Other Stories* 35, *A Note on Literary Criticism* 36, *A World I Never Made* 36, *Can All This Grandeur Perish* 37, *Collected Short Stories* 37, *No Star is Lost* 38, *Tommy Gallagher's Crusade* 39, *Father and Son* 40, *Ellen Rogers* 41, *$1,000 a week and other stories* 42, *My Days of Anger* 43, *To Whom It May Concern* 44, *The League of Frightened Philistines* 45, *Bernard Clare* 46, *When Boyhood Dreams Come True* 46, *Literature and Morality* 47, *The Life Adventurous* 47, *The Road Between* 49, *An American Dream Girl and Other Stories* 50, *This Man and this Woman, Yet Other Waters* 52, *The Face of Time* 53, *Reflections At Fifty* 54, *French Girls are Vicious* 55, *A Farrell Omnibus* 56, *A Dangerous Woman and Other Stories* 57, *My Baseball Diary* 57, *It Has Come to Pass* 58, *Side Street and Other Stories* 61, *Boarding House Blues* 61, *Sound of the City* 62, *The Silence of History* 63, *What Time Collects* 64, *Lonely for the Future* 65, *The Collected Poems of James T. Farrell* 65, *When Time was Born* 66, *New York's Eve 1929* 67, *A Brand New Life* 68, *Judith* 69, *Christmas Is Not Forever* 69, *Invisible Swords* 70, *Judith and Other Stories* 73.
c/o Doubleday & Co., 277 Park Avenue, New York, N.Y. 10017, U.S.A.

Farrer-Brown, Leslie, C.B.E., J.P.; British public servant; b. 2 April 1904, London; s. of the late Sydney and Annie Brown; m. Doris Evelyn Jamieson 1928; two s.; ed. London School of Economics.
Assistant Registrar, London School of Econs. 27-28; Admin. Staff, Univ. of London 28-36; Sec. Cen. Midwives Board 36-44; Ministry of Health 41-44; Dir. The Nuffield Foundation 44-64; Chair. Overseas Visual Aid Centre 58-70, Centre for Educational Television Overseas 64-70, Inst. of Race Relations 64-68; Cttee. for Research and Devt. in Modern Languages 65-70; Centre for Information on Language Teaching 66-72; Nat. Council for Social Service 60-73; Voluntary Cttee. on Overseas Aid and Devt. 66-, Inst. of Child Health (Univ. of London) 66-; Vice-Pres. Royal Commonwealth Soc. 69-; Trustee, Commonwealth Foundation; Chair. Alliance Building Soc.; Gov. and Hon. Fellow, London School of Econs., Vice-Chair. of Council, Univ. of Sussex; Hon. LL.D. (Birmingham and Witwatersrand), Hon. D.Sc. (Keele), Hon. F.D.S., R.C.S.
Leisure interests: travel, painting.
Dale House, Keere Street, Lewes, Sussex, England.
Telephone: Lewes 2007.

Farrow, Mia; American actress; b. 9 Feb. 1946, Calif.; d. of Maureen O'Sullivan and John Villiers Farrow; m. 1st Frank Sinatra (*q.v.*) 1966 (divorced 1968), 2nd André Previn (*q.v.*) 1970; three s. two d.

Stage debut in *The Importance of Being Earnest*, N.Y. 63; French Acad. Award for best actress 69, David Donatello Award (Italy) 69, Rio de Janeiro Film Festival Award 69, San Sebastian Award.

Stage appearances in London *Mary Rose, The Three Sisters, House of Bernardo Alba* 72-73, RSC production of *The Marrying of Ann Leete* 75; films include *Guns at Batasi* 64, *Rosemary's Baby* 68, *Secret Ceremony* 69, *John and Mary* 69, *See No Evil* 70, *The Great Gatsby* 73; TV appearances in *Peyton Place* 64-66, *Johnny Belinda* 65, *Peter Pan* 75.

Leisure interests: reading, mind wandering, listening to music and certain people.

c/o Paul Kohna, 9169 Sunset Boulevard, Hollywood, Calif. 90069, U.S.A.

Telephone: (213) 271-5165.

Fasi, Mohammed El; Moroccan university rector; b. 2 Sept. 1908, Fez; *m.* Malika El Fasia 1935; three *s.* three *d.*; ed. Al Qarawiyin Univ., Fez, Univ. de Paris à la Sorbonne and Ecole des Langues Orientales, Paris.

Teacher, Inst. des Hautes Etudes Marocaines 35-40; Head Arab manuscript section, Bibliothèque Gén., Rabat 40; Tutor to Prince Moulay Hassan 41-44, 47-52; Rector Al Qarawiyin Univ. 42-44, 47-52; Vice-Pres. Conseil des Uléma 42-; Founder-mem. Istiqlal Party 44; under restriction 44-47, 52-54; Minister of Nat. Educ. 55; Rector of the Univs. of Morocco 58- (Mohammed V Univ. until 70, Al Qarawiyin Univ. 70-); Pres. Moroccan Del. to Gen. Conf. of UNESCO 56, 58, 60, 64, Vice-Pres. 62, leader of numerous UNESCO Confs. in the Arab World, Pres. Exec. Board of UNESCO 64-; Minister of State for Cultural Affairs and Nat. Educ. 68; Pres. Admin. Council of the Asscn. of partially or entirely French-speaking Univs. (AUPELF) 66; Pres. Asscn. of African Univs. 67; Pres. Exec. Board of Asscn. of Islamic Univs. 69; mem. Acad. of Arabic Language, Cairo 58, Acad. of Iraq; Dr. h.c. Univ. of Bridgeport 65, Univ. of Lagos 68, Univ. of Jakarta 68.

Leisure interests: painting (has held exhibitions).

Publs. Numerous works in Arabic and French including *L'évolution politique et culturelle au Maroc* 58, *La Formation des Cadres au Maroc* 60, *Chants anciens des Femmes de Fes* 67.

Centre de Coordination entre les Commissions nationales arabes pour l'UNESCO, B.P. 702, Rabat-Agdal; Home: 18 zenkat Saadiyyin, Rabat, Morocco.

Telephone: 702-82/79, 705-55; 307-13 (Home).

Fast, Howard; American writer; b. 11 Nov. 1914, New York City; *s.* of Berney Fast and Ida (née Miller); *m.* Bette Cohen 1937; one *s.* one *d.*; ed. Nat. Acad. of Design.

Began writing 31; translated into 82 languages; film has been made of *Spartacus* (with Kirk Douglas); Bread Loaf Literary Award 34, Schomburg Award for Race Relations 44, Newspaper Guild Award 47, Int. Peace Prize 54, Screenwriters Award 60, Secondary School Book Award 62, Emmy Award 74.

Leisure interests: gardening, working about my country place.

Publs. Novels: *The Children* 35, *Place in the City* 37, *Conceived in Liberty* 39, *The Last Frontier* 41, *The Unvanquished* 42, *Citizen Tom Paine* 43, *Freedom Road* 44, *The American* 46, *Clarkton* 47, *My Glorious Brothers* 48, *The Proud and the Free* 50, *Spartacus* 51, *The Passion of Sacco and Vanzetti* 53, *Silas Timberman* 54, *Moses, Prince of Egypt* 58, *The Winston Affair* 59, *April Morning* 61, *Power* 62, *Agrippa's Daughter* 64, *Torquemada* 66, *The Hunter and the Trap* 67, *The Hessian* 72; Short stories: *Patrick Henry and the Frigate's Keel, Departure and Other Stories, The Last Supper*; History: *Romance of a People, Peekskill: U.S.A., The Naked God, The Jews* 69, *The Crossing* 70, *The Hessian* 72, *A Touch of Infinity* 73; Plays: *The Crossing, The Hill,*

The Ambassador (for T.V.) 74; Screenplays: *Spartacus* 59, *The Hill* 63, *Martian Shop* 64, *Torquemada* 66, *The Hunter and the Trap* 67, *The Jews* 68, *The General Zapped an Angel* 70.

c/o Paul Reynolds Inc., 599 Fifth Avenue, New York, N.Y. 10017, U.S.A.

Fatayi-Williams, Atanda, M.A., LL.B., F.R.S.A.; Nigerian judge; b. 22 Oct. 1918, Lagos; *s.* of Alhaji Issa Williams and Alhaja Ashakun Williams; *m.* Irene Violet Lofts 1948; three *s.*; ed. Methodist Boys' School, Lagos, Trinity Hall, Cambridge, Middle Temple, London.

Private practice, Lagos 48-50; Crown Counsel, Lagos 50-55; Deputy Commr. for Law Revision, W. Nigeria 55-58; Chief Registrar, High Court of W. Nigeria 58-60, Judge 60-67; Justice of Appeal, W. State 67-69; Justice, Supreme Court of Nigeria 69; Chair. Ports Arbitration Board 71, All Nigeria Law Reports Cttee. 72-, Board of Trustees, Van Leer Nigerian Educ. Trust 73-; mem. Nigerian Inst. of Int. Affairs 69, Body of Benchers, Nigerian Law School 74-, Legal Practitioners Privileges Cttee. 75-.

Leisure interests: speedboats, swimming, walking, travel.

Publs. *Revised Laws of Western Nigeria* (with Sir John Verity) 59, Editor *Western Nigeria Law Reports 1955-1958*.

Supreme Court, Lagos; Home: 4 Inner Crescent, Ikoyi, Lagos, Nigeria.

Telephone: 21670, 22622 (Home).

Faulkner, Rt. Hon. (Arthur) Brian (Deane); British (N.Ireland) politician; b. 18 Feb. 1921; *s.* of late James A. Faulkner, O.B.E.; ed. Elm Park, Co. Armagh, N. Ireland, and Coll. of St. Columba, Rathfarnum, Co. Dublin.

Director Belfast Collar Co. 41-63; M.P. (N. Ireland) 49-73, mem. N. Ireland Assembly 73-74; Govt. Chief Whip, Parl. Sec. Ministry of Finance, N. Ireland 56-59; Minister of Home Affairs 59-63, of Commerce 63-Jan. 69; Minister of Devt., N. Ireland, 69-71; Prime Minister 71-72; Chief Exec. N. Ireland Admin. Jan.-May 74; Leader Ulster Unionist Party 71-74, Leader Unionist Party of N. Ireland 74-; mem. N. Ireland Constitutional Convention 75; Unionist.

Highlands, Seaforde, Co. Down, N. Ireland.

Faulkner, Arthur James; New Zealand politician; b. 20 Nov. 1921; ed. Otahuhu District High School.

Member Parl. for Roskill 57-; undertook fact finding missions to Repub. of Viet-Nam, Indonesia, Malaysia, Thailand, Singapore and the Philippines 63, 67; visited U.S.A. 65; study tour of Britain to discuss EEC 69; Minister of Defence, concurrently in charge of War Pensions and Rehabilitation 72-74; Minister of Labour and State Services 74-75.

c/o Parliament Buildings, Wellington; Home: Inverness Avenue, Mount Roskill, Auckland 4, New Zealand.

Faulkner, Sir Eric Odin, Kt., M.B.E.; British banker; b. 21 April 1914, St. Albans, Herts.; *s.* of Sir Alfred Edward Faulkner, C.B., C.B.E. and Lady Florence Edith Faulkner; *m.* Joan Mary Webster 1939; one *s.* one *d.*; ed. Bradfield Coll. and Corpus Christi Coll., Cambridge.

Joined Glyn, Mills & Co. (Bankers) 36; Army Service, Royal Artillery (Lt.-Col.) 39-46; rejoined Glyn, Mills & Co. 46, Local Dir. 47, Man. Dir. 50, Deputy Chair. 59, Chair. 63-68; Deputy Chair. Lloyds Bank Ltd. Dec. 68-March 69, Chair. Lloyds Bank Ltd. 69-75; Dir. Union Discount Co. of London Ltd. 49-53, Chair. 53-70; Dir. Hudsons Bay Co. 50-72, Vickers Ltd. 57-; Dir. Bank of London and South America 69-71, Lloyds Bank Int. Ltd. 71-; Deputy Chair. Cttee. of London Clearing Banks, Chair. 72-74; Pres. British Bankers' Asscn. 72-73.

Leisure interests: walking, fishing, fmrly. playing cricket and Asscn. Football.
71 Lombard Street, London, E.C.3, England.
Telephone: 01-626-1500.

Faulkner, Rt. Hon. J. Hugh, P.C.; Canadian politician; b. 9 March 1933, Montreal; *m.* Jane Meintjies; ed. Lakefield Coll. School, McGill Univ., Le Centre d'Etudes Industrielles and Carleton Univ.
Former teacher, Peterborough; mem. Parl. for Peterborough 65-; Chair. Standing Cttee. on Labour and Employment 66; Deputy Speaker of Parl. 68; Parl. Sec. to Sec. of State 70; Sec. of State 72-.
House of Commons, Ottawa, Ontario, Canada.

Faulkner, Padraig; Irish Minister of Education 69-73; see *The International Who's Who 1975-76.*

Faure, Edgar, D. EN D.; French lawyer and politician; b. 18 Aug. 1908; ed. Ecole des Langues Orientales, Paris. Advocate at Paris Court of Appeal; Dir. of Legislative Services to the Presidency of the Council of the French Cttee. of National Liberation 43-44; took part, as asst. del., in War Crimes Trials Nuremberg 45; Deputy for the Jura (Radical-Socialist) 46-58; Vice-Pres. of Comm. of Enquiry into Events in France between 33-45; Vice-Pres. of High Court of Justice; Sec. of Finance Comm. of National Assembly; Sec. of State for Finance 49-50; Minister of Budget 50-51, of Justice 51-52; Prime Minister Jan.-Feb. 52; Minister of Finance and Econ. Affairs 53-54, of Foreign Affairs Feb. 55; Prime Minister Feb. 55-Jan. 56; Minister of Finance, May-June 58; Senator 59-; Prof. of Law, Univ. of Dijon 62-66; Minister of Agriculture 66-68, of Educ. 68-69; Minister of State for Social Affairs 72-73; Pres. of Nat. Assembly 73-; Hon. Pres. Mouvement pour le socialisme par la participation 71-; Pres. Asscn. for the Preservation and Devt. of Eastern France 70-; Dir. of Research, Faculté de Droit, Besançon 70-; Pres. Int. Comm. on Devt. of Educ. 71-.
Publs. *La Politique française du pétrole, M. Langois n'est pas toujours égal à lui-même* (novel), *Le Serpent et la Tortue* (study of China) 61, *La Disgrâce de Turgot* 61, *Etude sur la capitation de Dioclétien d'après le panégyrique VIII, Prévoir le présent* 66, *Education nationale et la Participation* 68, *Philosophie d'une réforme* 69, *l'Ame du combat* 70, *Ce que je crois* 71.
83 avenue Foch, Paris 16e, France.

Faure, Maurice Henri, D. EN D.; French politician; b. 2 Jan. 1922; *m.* Andrée Guillemain 1945; two *s.*; ed. Lycée de Périgueux, Faculty of Law and Letters, Bordeaux and Toulouse Univs.
Deputy to Nat. Assembly (Lot) 51-; Sec. of State for Foreign Affairs (Mollet Cabinet) Jan. 56-June 57, (Bourgès-Manoury Cabinet) June-Nov. 57, (Gaillard Cabinet) Nov. 57-May 58; Minister for European Institutions May-June 58; Pres. French del. Common **Market and Euratom Conf.,** Brussels 56; mem. del. 11th Session U.N. Gen. Assembly, New York 56; Special Asst. Minister for Foreign Affairs on Morocco and Tunisia Nov. 56-June 57; mem. European Coal and Steel Community Assembly; fmr. Mayor of Prayssac (Lot); Conseiller Général, Salviac canton (Lot) 57-58; Pres. Departmental Asscn. of Mayors of Lot, Mouvement Européen; Pres. Entente Démocratique of the Nat. Assembly 60-62; Pres., later Leader, Parti Republicain Radical et Radical-Socialiste 61-65, 69-71; Pres. Rassemblement Démocratique Group, Nat. Assembly 62; Pres. Econ. Devt. Comm. for Midi-Pyrénées 64-70; Mayor of Cahors 65-; Pres. du Conseil Général du Lot 70-.
Assemblée Nationale, Paris 7e; 28 boulevard Raspail, Paris 7e, France.

Fauteux, Rt. Hon. Joseph Homoré Gérald, P.C., C.C., LL.L., D.C.L., LL.D.; Canadian judge; b. 22 Oct. 1900, St. Hyacinthe, Quebec; *s.* of Homère Fauteux and Héva

Mercier; *m.* Yvette Mathieu 1929; two *s.* three *d.*; ed. Coll. Ste. Marie, Montreal and Univ. of Montreal.
Called to the Bar of Quebec 25; practised law in Montreal; Crown Attorney 29; cr. K.C. 33; Asst. Senior Crown Prosecutor, Montreal 30-36; Chief Crown Prosecutor 39-44; Justice Superior Court, Quebec 47; Justice, Supreme Court of Canada 49; Legal Adviser, Royal Comm. on spying activities in Canada 46; mem. Comm. on Revision of Criminal Code in Canada; fmrly. Legal Adviser Royal Canadian Mounted Police; Pres. Cttee. of Inquiry into Remission Br., Dept. of Justice 53; Vice-Pres. Conf. on the Family 63; Chief Justice of Canada 70-73; Prof. of Law, McGill Univ. 36-50, Dean 49; Dean, Faculty of Law, Ottawa Univ. 53-62; Chair. Board of Govs. 65-66, Chancellor 70; mem. Canadian Bar Asscn. (Hon. Sec. 41-47); Hon. LL.D. (Univs.) of Ottawa 53, Laval 57, Sudbury 58, Montreal 62); Hon. D.C.L. (McGill Univ. 55); Companion, Order of Canada 74; Catholic.
Leisure interests: gardening, fishing, outdoor sports.
937 St. Clare Road, Town of Mount Royal, Quebec, H3R 2M8, Canada.

Fauvet, Jacques, L. en D.; French editor; b. 9 June 1914, Paris; *s.* of Pierre Fauvet and Andrée (née Meunieur-Pouthot); *m.* Claude Decroix 1939; five *c.*; ed. Lycée St. Louis, Paris, and Faculté de Droit, Univ. de Paris.
An editor, *l'Est Républicain,* Nancy 37-39; joined *Le Monde* 45, Head of Domestic Politics Dept. 48-58, Asst. Editor-in-Chief 58-63, Editor-in-Chief of *Le Monde* 63-, Gen. Editor 68, Dir.-Gen. 69-; Officier Légion d'Honneur, Croix de Guerre (39-45).
Publs. *Les partis politiques dans la France actuelle* 47, *Les Forces politiques en France* 51, *La France déchirée* 57, *La politique et les paysans* 58, *La IVe République* 59, *La fronde des généraux* 61, *Histoire du parti communiste français,* Vol. I 64, Vol. II 65.
Le Monde, 5 rue des Italiens, Paris 9e; 5 rue Louis-Boilly, Paris 16e, France.
Telephone: 770-91-29.

Favre, Alexandre Jean Auguste; French scientist; b 23 Feb. 1911, Toulon; *m.* Luce Palombe 1939; three *c*; ed. Univs. Aix-Marseille and Paris.
Assistant Lecturer, Faculty of Science, Univ. of Marseilles 32-38, Lecturer 38-41, Asst. Prof. 41-45, Assoc. Prof. 45-51, Prof. 51-, Dir. Inst. of Mechanical Statistics of Turbulence 60-; Scientific Asst. Ministry of Air 32; Scientific Counsellor, Nat. Office of Aerospacial Studies and Research 47, Atomic Energy Commissariat 58; mem. Nat. Cttee. for Scientific Research 63, Nat. Cttee. for Univs. 72-75, Mathematical Soc. of France, Physical Soc. of France, American Physical Soc.; Pres. Fédération Universitaire de Mécanique; Chevalier Légion d'Honneur, Officier des Palmes Académiques; corresp. mem. of Académie des Sciences, mem. Académie des Sciences, Lettres, Arts de Marseille.
Major Research includes: hypersustentation 34, hyperconvection 51; inventor of centrifugal sub-transsupersonic compressor 40; inventor of apparatus for statistical measurement of time correlation 42, and of appliance for detection of random noise 52; research on turbulence of fluids and space-time correlations 42-75, and on statistical equations of turbulent compressible gas 48-75.
Leisure interests: international trips, relations.
Institut de Mécanique Statistique de la Turbulence, 12 avenue Général Leclerc, 13 Marseilles; Home: La Cadenelle, 122 Rue Ct. Rolland, Marseilles (8), France.
Telephone: 641650 (Office); 776586 (Home).

Favre, Antoine, LL.D.; Swiss judge; b. 1897, Sion, Valais; ed. Univs. of Paris, Fribourg (Switzerland) and Berlin.
Professor of Law, Fribourg Univ. 30-52; mem. Valais **Gra**nd Council 45-52; Deputy Nat. Council 43-52; mem.

Fed. Court 52; Judge, European Court of Human Rights 63-.

Publs. include: *The Evolution of Personal Rights in the Federal Constitution* 36, *Notes on the Condition of the Free Man in a Strong State* 43, *The Universal Declaration of Human Rights* 48, *The New (Swiss) Law of Nationality* 52, *The Objectivist Interpretation of International Treaties* 62, *Swiss Constitutional Law*, 2nd edn., 70.

5 Chemin des Collines, 1950 Sion, Switzerland.

Fawcett, Don Wayne, M.D.; American anatomist; b. 14 March 1917, Springdale, Iowa; s. of Carlos J. Fawcett and Mary Mabel Kennedy; m. Dorothy Secrest 1941; two s. two d.; ed. Harvard Coll., Harvard Medical School.

Captain, Medical Corps, U.S. Army 43-46; Research Fellow in Anatomy, Harvard Medical School 46, Instructor 46-68, Assoc. 48-51, Asst. Prof. 51-55; Prof. and Chair. Dept. of Anatomy, Cornell Medical Coll. 55-59; Hersey Prof. of Anatomy and Head of Dept., Harvard Medical School 59-, Curator, Warren Anatomical Museum 61-70, James Stillman Prof. of Comparative Anatomy 62-, Sr. Assoc. Dean for Preclinical Affairs 75; Pres. American Asscn. of Anatomists 65-66, American Soc. for Cell Biology 61-62, Int. Fed. of Socs. for Electron Microscopy 76-80; mem. Nat. Acad. of Sciences, American Soc. of Zoologists, American Soc. of Mammalogists, Electron Microscope Soc. of America, Int. Soc. for Cell Biology, etc.; Fellow, American Asscn. for the Advancement of Science, American Acad. of Arts and Sciences, New York Acad. of Sciences, etc.; Dr. h.c. Univ. of Siena 74, N.Y. Medical Coll. 75.

Leisure interests: photography of wild animals, shell collecting, zoological research.

Publs. over 100 papers and two textbooks on histology, cell biology and reproductive biology.

Department of Anatomy, Harvard Medical School, 25 Shattuck Street, Boston, Mass. 02115, U.S.A.

Fawcett, James Edmund Sandford, M.A.; British barrister-at-law; b. 16 April 1913, Didcot; s. of Joseph and Edith Fawcett; m. Frances B. Lowe 1937; one s. four d.; ed. Rugby School, and New Coll., Oxford.

Practised at the Bar 37-39, 50-55, 72-; Asst. Legal Adviser, Foreign Office 45-50; Gen. Counsel, IMF 55-60; Fellow, All Souls Coll., Oxford 38, 60-69; mem. European Comm. of Human Rights 62-, Pres. 72-; Dir. of Studies, Royal Inst. of Int. Affairs 69-72.

Leisure interests: astronomy, piano.

Publs. *British Commonwealth in International Law* 63, *Application of the European Convention on Human Rights* 68, *The Law of Nations* 69.

23 Hanover House, St. John's Wood High Street, London, NW8 7DX, England.

Fawzi, Ahmad Muhammad Al-Salem; Jordanian civil engineer and politician; b. 1927, Amman; m.; ed. Baghdad Coll. and in U.S.A.

Engineer, Amman 50-51; District Engineer, Maa'n 51-53; Chief of Technical Section for Buildings June-Oct. 53; Asst. Under-Sec., Ministry of Public Works Nov. 53, Under-Sec. 59; apptd. responsible for all aspects of road design and construction Dec. 55; mem. Devt. Board and Chief of Exec. Ctte. of Cen. Water Authority July 59; Govt. Rep. at Potash Co. 59-61; mem. Exec. Cttee. of Hejaz Railway Redevt. Scheme 62; Mayor of Amman 64-; Minister of Municipal and Rural Affairs and Minister of State to Prime Minister July 67-68; Minister of Public Works April 68-69; Al Kawkab Medal (2nd Grade), Al Nahda Medal (2nd Grade), Alawi Medal of Morocco.

c/o Municipality of Amman, Amman, Jordan.

Fawzi, Mahmoud; Egyptian politician; b. 1900; ed. Univs. of Cairo, Rome, Liverpool and Columbia Univ.

Vice-Consul, N.Y. and New Orleans 26-29; Consul, Kobe, Japan 29-36; 2nd Sec. Athens 36-37; Consul then Consul-Gen. Liverpool 37-40; Dir. Dept. of Nationalities, Ministry of Foreign Affairs 40-41; Consul-Gen., Jerusalem 41-44; Egyptian rep. Security Council, UN 46; alternate rep. UN Gen. Assembly, N.Y. 46; later perm. rep. of Egypt to U.N.; Ambassador to Great Britain 52; Minister of Foreign Affairs Dec. 52-58; Minister of Foreign Affairs, United Arab Republic 58-64; mem. Presidency Council 62-64; Dep. Prime Minister for Foreign Affairs 64-67; President's Asst. for Foreign Affairs 67-68; Prime Minister Oct. 70-Jan. 72; Vice-Pres. of Egypt 72-74.

c/o Office of the Vice-President, Cairo, Egypt.

Fayat, Henri, D.LL.; Belgian lawyer and politician; b. 28 June 1908, Molenbeek-Saint-Jean; ed. Royal Athenaeum, Brussels and Univ. of Brussels.

Advocate, Brussels 35-73; Legal Attaché, Belgian Foreign Office, London 42-43; Chief Assistant to the Belgian Ministry of the Interior, London 43, and in Brussels 44; Chief Asst. to Deputy Prime Minister 44-45; mem. House of Reps. 46-71; Prof. Faculty of Law, Univ. of Brussels 48-; mem. Consultative Assembly of the Council of Europe 49-50, Common Assembly of the European Coal and Steel Community 54-57; Minister of Foreign Trade 57-58, 68-71; Deputy Foreign Minister 61-66; Sec. of State for Foreign Trade 72-73, for Ports Policy 73; Chair. Brussels Conf. on British application for membership of European Econ. Community 63.

51A Aarlenstraat, 1040 Brussels, Belgium.

Faye, Jean Pierre; French writer; b. 19 July 1925; ed. Univ. de Paris à la Sorbonne.

Teacher, Lycée de Reims 51-54; Exchange Fellow Univ. of Chicago 54-55; Asst. Prof. Univ. de Lille 55-56, Univ. de Paris à la Sorbonne 56-60; Research, Centre Nat. de la Recherche Scientifique 60-64; Founder of the *Collectif Change* and *Centre d'Analyse et de Sociologie des Langages* (C.A.S.L.); Prix Renaudot 64.

Publs. Novels: *Entre les Rues* 58, *La Cassure* 61, *Battement* 62, *Analogues* 64, *L'Ecluse* 64, *Les Troyens* 70; Poems: *Fleuve Renversé* 59, *Théâtre* 64, produced in Odéon Théâtre de France by Roger Blin 65, *Couleurs Pliées* 65; Essays: *Le Récit Hunique* 67, *Langages totalitaires, Théorie du récit* 72, *La Critique de Langage et son Economie* 73, *Migrations de Récit sur le Peuple Juif* 74, *Inferno* 75, *Versions* 75, *L'Ovale* 75; Editor of the review *Change* 68.

Editions Seghers-Laffont, 6 place Saint Sulpice, Paris 6e, France.

Fayez, Akef Mithqal Al-; Jordanian politician; b. 1924; ed. Aleh Univ., Lebanon.

President Jordanian Agricultural Asscn. 45; Chief of Protocol for Tribes, Royal Palace 46; Co-founder Jordanian People's Party; mem. House of Reps. 47-, Speaker 62-68, successively Minister of Agriculture Development and Construction, Defence, Communications, and Public Works 57-62; Chair. Nat. Group, Inter-Parl. Union 64-; Deputy Prime Minister and Minister of the Interior 69; Minister of State for Affairs of Presidency Council June 70-Sept. 70.

House of Representatives, P.O. Box 72, Amman, Jordan.

Fazekas, János; Romanian politician; b. 16 Feb. 1926, Lupeni, Hunedoara County; s. of János and Zsuzsánna Fazekas; m. Erzsébet Fazekas 1949; two s.

Member of Union of Communist Youth 44, Sec. for Odorhein-Secuiesc District 44, for Braşov and then for Mureş 46-47, mem. of Bureau 46, Sec. of Central Cttee. 49-54; Deputy to Grand Nat. Assembly 50; mem. Central Cttee. R.C.P. 54-, Sec. 54-61; Minister of Food Industry 61-65; Vice-Chair. Council of Ministers 65-; Minister of Internal Trade 74-; Alt. mem. of Exec. Cttee. of Cen. Cttee. 65, mem. 67; mem. of Exec. Bureau, Nat. Cttee. of Socialist United Front 68; mem. Acad. of

Social and Political Sciences 70; Hero of Socialist Labour.

Leisure interests: political science, economics, history and literature.

Central Committee of the Romanian Communist Party, Bucharest, Romania.

Feather, Baron (Life Peer), cr. 74, of the City of Bradford; **Victor (Grayson Hardie) Feather,** C.B.E.; British trade union official; b. 10 April 1908, Bradford; s. of Harry and Edith Feather; m. Alice Helena Fernyhough Ellison 1930; one s. one d.; ed. Hanson, Bradford. Co-operative employee 23-37; joined Trades Union Congress (TUC) staff 37, Asst. Sec. 47-60, Asst. Gen. Sec. 60-69, Gen. Sec. 69-73; a Gov. BBC May 73-; Vice-Pres. Int. Confed. of Free Trade Unions; Pres. European Trade Union Confederation 73-74; Chair Standing Advisory Comm. on Human Rights in N. Ireland 73; Special Adviser on Trade Union Affairs, Nat. Econ. Council 73; Adviser on Social Responsibility to SKF 74; mem. Arts Council 74-, Royal Dockyards Policy Board 75-; Hon. D.Tech. (Bradford), Hon. LL.D. (Manchester) 74.

Leisure interests: painting, reading, cricket.

Publs. *Trade Unions, True or False* 51, *How do the Communists Work?* 53, *Essence of Trade Unionism* 63.

43 Shelley Crescent, Heston, Middx., England.

Telephone: 01-570-6241.

Feather, Norman, LL.D., F.R.S., F.R.S.E., PH.D.; British physicist and university professor; b. 16 Nov. 1904, Crimsworth, Yorks.; s. of Samson and Lucy (née Clayton) Feather; m. Kathleen Grace Burke 1932; one s. two d.; ed. Bridlington School and Trinity Coll., Cambridge.

Fellow Trinity Coll. Cambridge 29-33, 36-45; Assoc. in Physics Johns Hopkins Univ. 29-30; Fellow and Lecturer in Physics, Liverpool Univ. 35-36; Lecturer in Physics, Cambridge Univ. 36-45; Prof. of Natural Philosophy Edinburgh Univ. 45-75; Pres. Royal Soc. of Edinburgh 67-70.

Publs. *An Introduction to Nuclear Physics* 36, *Lord Rutherford* 40, *Nuclear Stability Rules* 52, *Mass, Length and Time* 59, *Vibrations and Waves* 62, *Electricity and Matter* 68, *Matter and Motion* 70; about 100 scientific papers and review articles.

9 Priestfield Road, Edinburgh, EH16 5HJ, Scotland.

Telephone: 031-667-2631.

Federspiel, Per T., C.B.E.; Danish barrister; b. 9 April 1905, Berlin, Germany; s. of Holger Federspiel and Asta (née Nutzhorn); m. Elin Zahle 1934; three s.; ed. Harrow School and Copenhagen Univ.

London corresp. to Danish newspapers 31-32; Secretary to Danish Counsel in the East Greenland sovereignty case at the Int. Court at The Hague 32-33; Counsel at the Danish Courts of Appeal 37; Hon. Legal Adviser to the British Embassy Copenhagen; Min. of Special Affairs 45-47; mem. Danish Parl. 47-73; Del. to the UN Assembly 46-49; mem. UN Palestine Comm. 47-48. Consultative Assembly, Council of Europe 49-71, Chair. 60-63; Chair. Econ. Cttee. 53-60; mem. European Parl. 73; Vice-Pres. Int. Comm. of Jurists, mem. Exec. Cttee. 63-; Hon. Gov. Atlantic Inst. 63-; Liberal.

Leisure interests: history, antiques, game shooting.

38 Dyrehavegaardsvej, DK-2800, Lyngby, Denmark.

Telephone: 01-135800 (Office); 01-880009.

Fedin, Konstantin Alexandrovich, D.PHIL.; Soviet novelist; b. 24 Feb. 1892, Saratov; m.; one d.; ed. Moscow Commercial Inst.

Interned in Germany 14-18; returned to Russia 18; with Commissariat of Educ.; later journalist and war corresp.; mem. Secretariat, Union of Soviet Writers 53-; Chair. Moscow Union of Soviet Writers 55-59; mem. Acad. of Sciences, U.S.S.R. 58-; Corresp. mem. Deutsche Akad. der Künste 54-; Chair. Soviet-German

Cultural and Friendship Soc. 58-70; First Sec. Writers' Union of U.S.S.R. 59-72, Chair. 72; Deputy to U.S.S.R. Supreme Soviet; mem. Comm. for Foreign Affairs Union of Soviets; Order of Lenin (four times), Order of Red Banner of Labour (twice), Order of October Revolution, Hero of Socialist Labour 67; Dr. h.c. Humbolt Univ.; awarded Silver Medal of World Peace Council.

Publs. *Anna Timofevna* 22, *The Waste Land* 23, *Cities and Years* 24, *Transvaal* 26, *Brothers* 28, *I Was an Actor* 37, *Rape of Europe* 34, *Bakunin in Dresden* (play) 22, *Sanatorium Arktur* 40, *Gorky among Us* 43-44 (enlarged edn. 67), *Return to Leningrad* 45, *Early Joys* 46, *No Ordinary Summer* 48, *Die Flamme* 62; collected works in 6 vols. 52-54, in 9 vols. 59-62, in 10 vols. 69-73, *Dichter, Kunst, Zeit* 57.

U.S.S.R. Writers' Union, 52 Ul. Vorovskogo, Moscow, U.S.S.R.

Fedorenko, Nikolai Prokofievich; Soviet economist; b. 28 April 1917, Preobrazhenskoe Village, Zaporozhye Region; m. Dljacina Nina Fedorenko; one d.; ed. Moscow M. V. Lomonosov Inst. of Fine Chemical Technology and Higher Party School of C.P.S.U. Central Committee.

Soviet Army 42-45; Instructor, Head of Dept., Moscow M. V. Lomonosov Inst. of Fine Chemical Technology 46-62; Deputy Academician-Sec. Dept. of Econs., U.S.S.R. Acad. of Sciences 62-63; Dir. Central Econ.-Mathematical Inst., U.S.S.R. Acad. of Sciences 63-; Corresp. mem. U.S.S.R. Acad. of Sciences 62-64, Academician 64-; State Prize 70.

Leisure interests: Russian and foreign painting.

Publs. numerous works on economics of chemical industry.

V-333 ul. Vavilova 44, bld. 2, Moscow, U.S.S.R.

Telephone: 135-88-30.

Fedorenko, Nikolai Trofimovich, D.PHIL.; Soviet sinologist and diplomatist; b. 22 Nov. 1912, Pyatigorsk, Stavropol; s. of Matrena and Trofim Fedorenko; m. Alla Fedorenko 1943; three d.; ed. Moscow Inst. of Oriental Studies.

Diplomatic service 39-; Counsellor, Soviet Embassy, Chungking 46; Chargé d'Affaires, Nangking 48, Peking 52; Head, First Far East Dept. (China); mem. Policy Planning Board, Ministry of Foreign Affairs 50-55; Deputy Foreign Minister 55; Amb. to Japan 58-62; Perm. Rep. to UN 62-68; on staff of Ministry of Foreign Affairs 68-69; Senior Assoc. Inst. of Peoples of Asia, U.S.S.R. Acad. of Sciences 68-; Editor-in-Chief *Foreign Literature* monthly 70; Sec. Board of Writers Union of U.S.S.R. 70; Corresp. mem. U.S.S.R. Acad. of Sciences 58-; Hon. mem. Accademia Fiorentina.

Publs. fifteen books and over 100 articles on Chinese literature.

Institute of Oriental Studies, Armyansky pereulok 2, Moscow, U.S.S.R.

Telephone: 233-5147, 157-3895.

Fedorov, Evgeny Konstantinovich; Soviet geophysicist; b. 10 April 1910, Bendery, Moldavian S.S.R.; ed. Leningrad Univ.

Polar station, Franz Joseph Land 32-33, Cape Chelyuskin 34-35; Geophysicist and Astronomer, Soviet Drifting Station *North Pole 1* 37-38; Chief of Board Hydrometeorological Service, U.S.S.R. Council of Ministers 39-47; Geophysical Inst., U.S.S.R. Acad. of Sciences 47-55; Dir. Inst. of Applied Geophysics, U.S.S.R. Acad. of Sciences 55-; Chief Scientific Sec. Presidium of U.S.S.R. Acad. of Sciences 60-62; Head of Chief Board Hydrometeorological Service of the Council of Ministers 63-; mem. C.P.S.U.; Academician 60-; State Prize 46; Order of Lenin (four times), Hero of the Soviet Union, Order of Kutuzov 2nd Class, Order of Patriotic War 1st Class (2), Order of the Red Banner of Labour.

Publs. *Astronomical Measurements* 40, *Meteorological Instruments and Observations* 41-45, *Principal Problems of Hydrometeorological Service* 46, *Influence of Atomic Blasts on Meteorological Processes* 56, *Physical Methods of Influence on Weather* 59, *Some Problems of Developments of Sciences of Earth* 62, *Active Influence on Meteorological Processes* 62, etc.
Chief Board of the Hydrometeorological Service, per. Pavlika Morozova 12, Moscow, U.S.S.R.

Fedorov, Nikolai Alexandrovich; Soviet haemotologist; b. 11 Jan. 1904, Voronezh; ed. Voronezh Univ.
Senior Research Assoc. Central Inst. of Haemotology and Blood Transfusion 29-33; Head of Laboratory 33, Head of Dept., Moscow Stomatology Inst. 43-; Corresp. mem. U.S.S.R. Acad. of Medical Sciences 57-, mem. 63-; mem. Board Int. Soc. of Haemotologists; Order of Red Banner of Labour.
Publs. Over 100 works on blood transfusion and conservation, new blood and plasma substitutes, especially heteroproteoseones; established existence and duration of burn putoantigens thus creating a new trend in haemotology (immunchemotherapy).
Central Institute of Blood Transfusion, U.S.S.R. Ministry of Public Health, 4 Novozykovsky pereulok, Moscow, U.S.S.R.

Fedorov, Victor Stepanovich; Soviet politician; b. 12; ed. Grozny Oil Inst.
Member C.P.S.U. 39-; Dir. Grozny Oil Inst. 37-40; in oil industry 40-46; First Deputy Minister of Oil Industry U.S.S.R. 46-57; Chair. of Council for Nat. Economy of Bashkir Econ. Region 57-58; Chair. of State Cttee. for Oil Refining and Petro-Chemicals for Gosplan U.S.S.R. 58-64; Minister of Oil Refining and Petro-Chemicals 65-; Deputy Supreme Soviet, U.S.S.R. 58-; Hero of Socialist Labour, Order of Lenin (twice), *Hammer and Sickle* Gold Medal and other awards; State Prize U.S.S.R.; alternating mem. Central Cttee. C.P.S.U. 61-.
Ministry of Oil Refining and Petro-Chemicals, 1 Ulitsa Marx-Engels, Moscow, U.S.S.R.

Fedoseyev, Pyotr Nikolayevich; Soviet philosopher; b. 22 Aug. 1908, Starinskoe Village, Gorky Region; ed. Gorky Teachers' Inst. and Moscow Inst. of History, Philosophy and Literature.
Director U.S.S.R. Acad. Inst. of Philosophy 55-62, Dir. Inst. of Marxism-Leninism 67-73; mem. U.S.S.R. Acad. of Sciences 60-, Vice-Pres. and Chair. section of Social Sciences, U.S.S.R. Acad. of Sciences 62-; mem. Int. Social Sciences Council; mem. C.P.S.U. 39-; mem. C.P.S.U. Central Cttee. 62-; Deputy to U.S.S.R. Supreme Soviet 61-; mem. U.S.S.R. Parl. Cttee.; Foreign mem. of G.D.R. and Polish Acads. of Sciences; Hon. mem. Hungarian, Bulgarian and Czechoslovakian Acads. of Sciences; Chair. U.S.S.R.-Hungarian Friendship Soc.; Order of Lenin (three times); Order of Patriotic War, Order of Red Banner of Labour (twice).
Publs. *How Did Human Society Appear?* 34, *Historical Materialism as a Science About the Laws of Society Development* 54, *Productive Forces and Relations of Production of Socialist Society* 55, *Socialism and Humanism* 58, *Communism and Philosophy* 62, 72, *Marxism in XX Century* 72, *Dialectics of the Contemporary Epoch* 66, 72.
U.S.S.R. Academy of Sciences, 17 Leninsky Prospekt, Moscow, U.S.S.R.

Fehér, Lajos; Hungarian politician; b. 1917; ed. Univ. of Debrecen.
Secondary school teacher; Deputy Chief, Political Police; Man. Editor *Szabad Föld*; mem. Editorial Board *Szabad Nép*; mem. Central Cttee. Hungarian Socialist Workers' Party 56-, Sec. 59-62, mem. Political Cttee. 56-March 75; Deputy Prime Minister 62-74; mem. Govt. Econ. Cttee. 62-73; mem. State Planning Cttee. 73-74; Pres. Hungarian Fed. of Partisans.

Partisan Federation, Szabadsag tér 16, Budapest V, Hungary.
Telephone: 111-480.

Feichtinger, Arne Ferdinand, M.S. IN ENG.; Swedish electrical executive; b. 29 Oct. 1906, Örby, Älvsborgs Län; s. of Ferdinand Feichtinger and Alma (née Andersson); m. Ruth Inez Krutmeijer 1934.
Electrical Engineer, Siemens & Halske A.G., Berlin-Siemensstadt 28-29; Sales Manager, Svenska Siemens AB, Stockholm 30-38, Dir. 39-51, Vice-Pres. 52-54, Pres. 55-69, Chair. and Chief Exec. Officer 70-72; mem. Board of Dirs., Siemens Corpn., New York 70-, Elema-Schönander AB, Stockholm 70-72, Telub AB, Växjö 67-69, ELIF, Stockholm 56-72; mem. R.S.A., and many asscns.; del. to numerous int. confs.; Knight (1st Class) Order of Vasa.
Leisure interest: travelling.
Office: Siemens, Floragatan 2, S-114 31 Stockholm; Home: 27 Villavägen, S-182 75 Stocksund, Sweden.

Feiffer, Jules; American cartoonist and writer; b. 26 Jan. 1929, New York; ed. Art Students League, Pratt Inst.
Assistant to syndicated cartoonist Will Eisner 46-51; cartoonist, author, syndicated Sunday page, Clifford, engaged in various art jobs 53-56; contributing cartoonist *Village Voice*, New York City 56-; cartoons published weekly in *The Observer* (London) 58-66, 72-, monthly in *Playboy* (magazine); cartoons nationally syndicated in U.S. 59-; sponsor Nat. Cttee. for Sane Nuclear Policy; U.S. Army 51-53; Acad. Award for Animated Cartoon, Munro 61; Special George Polk Memorial Award 62.
Publs. books: *Sick, Sick, Sick* 59, *Passionella and other stories* 60, *The Explainers* 61, *Boy, Girl, Boy, Girl,* 62, *Hold Mei* 62, *Harry, The Rat With Women* (novel) 63, *Feiffer's Album* 63, *The Unexpurgated Memoirs of Bernard Mergendeiler* 65, *The Great Comic Book Heroes* 67, *Feiffer's Marriage Manual* 67, *Pictures at a Prosecution* 71; plays: *Crawling Arnold* 61, *Little Murders* 66, *God Bless* 68, *The White House Murder Case* 70; screen plays: *Little Murders* 71, *Carnal Knowledge* 71.
c/o Hall Syndicate, 30 East 42nd Street, New York, N.Y. 10017, U.S.A.

Feiling, Sir Keith Grahame, Kt., O.B.E., D.LITT., M.A.; British writer and historian; b. 1884; ed. Marlborough and Balliol Coll., Oxford.
Fellow, All Souls Coll. 06; Lecturer, Toronto Univ. 07-09, Lecturer 09, Student and Tutor 11-36; Research Student, Christ Church, Oxford 36-46; served with Black Watch 15, Sec. Central Recruiting Board India 17; Lecturer in Modern History 28-36, Ford Lecturer in English History 31-32, Chichele Prof. of Modern History, Oxford 46-50, Emeritus 50-; Hon. Student, Christ Church; Hon. Mem. Massachusetts Historical Society; founded Oxford Univ. Conservative Asscn. 24; contributor to *The Observer, The Times* and *English Historical Review.*
Publs. *History of the Tory Party 1640-1714* 24, *England under the Tudors and Stuarts* 26, *British Foreign Policy 1660-1672, Sketches in Nineteenth Century Biography* 30, *The Second Tory Party 1714-1832* 38, *Life of Neville Chamberlain* 46, *A History of England* 50, *Warren Hastings* 54, *In Christ Church Hall* 60.
c/o Christ Church, Oxford, England.

Feinberg, Evgeny Lvovich; Soviet physicist; b. 27 June 1912, Baku; s. of Dr. L. B. Feinberg and T. A. Feinstein; m. Valentine Konen 1932; one d.; ed. Moscow Univ.
Postgraduate, Moscow Univ. 35-38; Research Assoc., Lebedev Inst. of Physics U.S.S.R. Acad. of Sciences 38-, Head of Sector 52-; Lecturer, Asst. Prof. Moscow

Power Inst. 35-39; Prof. Gorky Univ. 44-45; Prof. Moscow Engineering Physics Inst. 46-54; Corresp. mem. U.S.S.R. Acad. of Sciences 66-.
Leisure interests: chess, history of art, science.
Publs. Works on radiophysics, nuclear physics, cosmic rays, statistical acoustics and elementary particles.
P. N. Lebedev Institute of Physics, 53 Leninsky Prospekt, Moscow B-333, U.S.S.R.

Feinberg, Nathan, DR.JUR.UTR.; Israeli emeritus professor; b. 6 June 1895, Kovno, Russia; s. of Leon Feinberg and Henia (née Ratner) Feinberg; m. 1st Judith Ostrovsky-Mevorach 1925 (deceased), 2nd Anna Hirshowitz 1974; ed. Univ. of Zürich and Graduate Inst. of Int. Studies, Geneva.
Head of Dept., Ministry of Jewish Affairs, Lithuania 19-21; Sec. Cttee. of Jewish Dels., Paris 22-24; law practice in Palestine 24-27 and 34-45; Lecturer, Univ. of Geneva 31-33; Lecturer, Hebrew Univ., Jerusalem 45-49, Assoc. Prof. 49-52, Prof. of Int. Law and Relations 52-66, Emer. Prof. 66-, Dean of Faculty of Law 49-51; mem. Perm. Court of Arbitration; mem. Inst. Int. Law; mem. Board of Govs. Hebrew Univ.
Publs. *La Question des Minorités à la Conférence de la paix de 1919-1920 et l'action juive en faveur de la Protection Internationale des Minorités* 29, *La Juridiction de la Cour Permanente de Justice Internationale dans le Système des Mandats* 30, *La Juridiction de la Cour Permanente de Justice dans le Système de la Protection Internationale des Minorités* 31, *La Pétition en Droit International* 33, *Some Problems of the Palestine Mandate* 36, *L'Admission de Nouveaux Membres à la Société des Nations et à L'Organisation des Nations Unies* 52, *The Jewish Struggle against Hitler in the League of Nations—the Bernheim Petition* (in Hebrew) 57, *The Legality of a 'State of War' after the Cessation of Hostilities* 61, *Palestine under the Mandate and the State of Israel—Problems in International Law* (in Hebrew) 63, *The Jewish League of Nations Societies* (in Hebrew) 67, *The Arab-Israel Conflict in International Law* 70, *On an Arab Jurist's Approach to Zionism and the State of Israel* 71; co-editor *The Jewish Year Book of International Law* 49; editor *Studies in Public International Law in Memory of Sir Hersch Lauterpacht* (in Hebrew) 62.
6 Ben Labrat Street, Jerusalem 92307, Israel.
Telephone: 33345.

Feki, Ahmed Hassan el-; Egyptian Ambassador to United Kingdom 67-71; see *The International Who's Who 1975-76.*

Feldberg, Wilhelm Siegmund, C.B.E., M.A., M.D., F.R.S.; British physiologist; b. 19 Nov. 1900, Hamburg, Germany; s. of Emil Daniel and Amalie (née Bacharach) Feldberg; m. Katherine Scheffler 1925; one s. (deceased) one d.; ed. Univ. of Berlin.
Reader in Physiology, Cambridge Univ. until 49; Head of Physiology and Pharmacology Div., Nat. Inst. for Medical Research, London 49-65, Hon. Head 65-66; Head, Lab. of Neuropharmacology, Nat. Inst. for Medical Research 66-74, Grant Holder 74-; Hon. Lecturer, Univ. of London 50-; Fellow, Royal Soc. 47-; Ferrier Lecturer 74; Hon. mem. Physiological Soc., British Pharmacological Soc., Royal Soc. of Medicine, German Physiological Soc., German Pharmacological Soc.; Grand Cross, Order of Merit, German Fed. Repub. 61; Baly Medal 63; Schmiedeberg Plakette 69; Hon. M.D. (Freiburg, Berlin, Cologne, Liège); Philip Stöhr Medal 70, Hon. D.Sc. (Bradford Univ.) 73, Hon. LL.D. (Bradford).
Leisure interests: women's fashions, collecting antique furniture.
Publs. *Histamin* (with E. Schilf), *A Pharmacological Approach to the Brain from its Inner and Outer Surface* 63; numerous articles in medical and scientific journals.

Office: National Institute for Medical Research, Mill Hill, London, NW7 1AA; Home: Lavenham, Marsh Lane, Mill Hill, London, NW7 4NT, England.

Feldman, Myer, B.S.(ECON.), LL.B.; American lawyer and politician; b. 22 June 1917, Philadelphia, Pa.; s. of Israel and Bella Kurland Feldman; m. Silva Moskovitz 1941; one s. one d.; ed. Univ. of Pennsylvania.
Gowen Fellow, Univ. of Pennsylvania 38-39, Prof. of Law, 40-42; Special Counsel, S.E.C., Exec. Asst. to Chair., S.E.C. 49-53; Counsel, Senate Banking and Currency Cttee. 55-57; Prof. of Law, American Univ. 56-59; Legislative Asst., Senator John F. Kennedy 58-61; Dir. of Research, Democratic Nat. Cttee. 60; Deputy Special Counsel to Pres. of the United States 61-64, Counsel 64-65; Gov. Weizmann Inst., Israel 62-; Overseer Coll. of the Virgin Islands 63-; Trustee, Eleanor Roosevelt Foundation 63-76, United Jewish Appeal 65-, Jewish Publication Soc. 65-; Chair. Board Speer Publications, Capital Gazette Press Ind., Bay Publs. 68-75; Contributor to *The Saturday Review* 65-71; partner Ginsburg and Feldman 65-; Dir. Flying Tiger Line 66-; Flame of Hope, Inc. 67-; Del. to Democratic Nat. Convention 68; Chair of Board of Dirs. of WWBA Inc., WOCN Inc., WLLH Inc. and WADK Inc.; Vice-Chair. Congressional Leadership for the Future 70; Pres. New York Int. Art Festival 73-; Pres. McGovern for Pres. Cttee. 72; Chair. and Treas. Birch Bayh for Pres. Cttee. 75-76; Democrat.
Leisure interests: tennis, swimming.
Publs. *Standard Pennsylvania Practice* (4 vols.).
1700 Pennsylvania Avenue, N.W., Washington, D.C. 20006, U.S.A.
Telephone: 223-3800.

Feldt, Kjell-Olof, PH.D.; Swedish politician; b. 8 Aug. 1931, Holmsund; ed. Univs. of Uppsala and Lund.
Under-Secretary, Ministry of Finance 67-70; Minister of Trade 70-75; Minister without Portfolio 75-; Social Democratic Labour Party.
Ministry of Finance, Fack S-10310, Stockholm 2, Sweden.

Felek, Burhan, L. en D.; Turkish journalist; b. 1889; ed. Scutari Lycée and Istanbul Univ.
Civil servant 08; served in Army Reserve First World War; sports journalist and photographer 19; Editor *Milliyet* (Istanbul daily) 25-; Pres. Asscn. of Turkish Journalists; Pres. Turkish Olympic Cttee.; Hon. O.B.E. (U.K.); mem. Int. Press Inst.; NATO medal, Diplôme Olympique.
Publs. Works on photography, sport and travel; two collections of humorous stories and one play; translations of novels into Turkish, including *Il Piccolo Mondo di Don Camillo, Il Compagno Don Camillo.*
Home: Dost apt. 8/9 M. Kemal cad., Nişantaş, Istanbul
Office: *Milliyet*, Istanbul, Turkey.
Telephone: 481436.

Felici, H.E. Cardinal Pericle; Italian ecclesiastic; b. 1 Aug. 1911.
Ordained Priest 33; Titular Archbishop of Samosata 60-; also Co-Chair. Commission on Revision of Canon Law; created Cardinal by Pope Paul VI 67.
Via Pfeiffer 10, 10093 Rome, Italy.

Felli, Col. Roger Joseph; Ghanaian army officer and politician; b. 2 May 1941, Navrongo; m.; two c.; ed. Govt. Secondary School, Tamale and Royal Mil. Acad., Sandhurst.
Joined Ghanaian Army 60, Regular Officer 63; mil. training courses in U.K. 64, 69 and Ghana Mil. Acad., Teshie 67; successively Adjutant, No. 1 Signal Regt., Staff Officer II, Operations and Training Section, Communications Directorate, Dir. of Communications, Act. Commdr. No. 1 Signal Regt.; Commr. for Works and Housing, then Commr. for Trade 72-74, for Econ.

Planning 74-75, for Foreign Affairs Oct. 75-; mem. Nat. Redemption Council.

Department of Foreign Affairs, Accra, Ghana.

Fellini, Federico; Italian film director; b. 20 Jan. 1920; m. Giulietta Masina (q.v.).

Screen writer: *Quarta pagina* 42, *Roma città aperta* 44-45, *Paisa* 46, *Il delitto di Giovanni Episcopo* 47, *In nome della legge* 48-49, *La città si difende* 51, *Il brigante di Tacca di Lupo* 53, etc.; Director *Lo sceicco bianco* 52, *I vitelloni* 53, *La strada* (Oscar) 54, *Il bidone* 55, *Le notti di Cabiria* (Oscar) 57, *Fortunella* 58, *La Dolce Vita* (Cannes 1st Prize) 60, *The Temptation of Dr. Antonio* (from *Boccaccio* 70) 62, 8½ (Oscar) 63, *Giulietta degli spiriti* (Golden Globe, Hollywood) 64, *Satyricon* 69, *Never Bet the Devil Your Head* (from *Spirits of the Dead*) 69, *I Clowns* (television film) 71, *Roma* 72, *Amarcord* (N.Y. Film Critics' Circle Award 74) 73, *I Remember* 74, has always written scripts for his own films.

141a Via Margutta 110, Rome, Italy.

Fellner, William John; American economist; b. 31 May 1905, Hungary; m. Valerie Korek 1936; one d.; ed. Budapest Univ., Fed. Inst. of Technology, Zürich and Berlin Univ.

Industrial management 29-38; mem. Dept. of Econs. Univ. of Calif., Berkeley 39-52; Prof. of Econs. Yale Univ. 52-; Chair. Dept. of Econs. 62-64; Consultant U.S. Treas. Dept. 45, 49-52, 69-73; Resident Scholar Amer. Enterprise Inst. 72-73; mem. Council of Econ. Advisers 73-75; mem. Cttee. of Independent Experts OEEC 59-60; Fellow, Amer. Acad. of Arts and Sciences; Fellow, Econometric Soc.; Pres. Amer. Econ. Asscn. 69.

Publs. *Monetary Policies and Full Employment* 46, *Competition Among the Few* 49, *Trend and Cycles in Economic Activity* 56, *Emergence and Content of Modern Economic Analysis* 60, *Probability and Profit* 65, *Economic Policies and Inflation* 72, *A New Look at Inflation* 73.

Home: 131 Edgehill Road, New Haven, Conn.; Office: Department of Economics, Yale University, New Haven, Conn., U.S.A.

Telephone: 436-3310 (Office); 777-4186 (Home).

Feng Yu-lan; Chinese philosopher; b. 1895, Tang-ho, Honan; ed. China Acad., Shanghai, Peking Univ. and Columbia Univ., U.S.A.

Professor of Philosophy Chung-chou Univ., Kaifeng 23, Tsinghua Univ. 25-52; Dean, Coll. of Arts, Tsinghua Univ. 33; Visiting Prof. Univ. of Pennsylvania, U.S.A. 46-47; Dir. Research Dept. of History of Chinese Philosophy, Peking Univ. 54; Prof. Peking Univ. 61-68.

Publs. *The Philosophy of Life* 24, *A Kind of Outlook on Life* 24, *A History of Chinese Philosophers* (3 parts) 30, 33, 36, *The New Neo-Confucianism* 38, *The New World* 39, *The New Teachings of the World* 40, *The New Origin of Men* 42, *The New Origin of Truth* 42, *The New Understanding of Speech* 48, *A Short History of Chinese Philosophy* 48.

People's Republic of China.

Feng Yung-shun; Chinese army officer.

Major-General People's Liberation Army 57; Deputy Dir., Gen. Ordinance Dept., PLA 57; Deputy Dir., Gen. Logistics Dept., PLA 69-.

People's Republic of China.

Fenn, Ingemund; Norwegian newspaper editor; b. 18 Sept. 1907, Stryn, Nordfjord; m. Elsa Reinertsen 1941; one s.; univ. education.

Journalist 28-; on staff of *Bergens Tidende* 36-, editor Oslo office and parl. corresp. 46-56, Chief Editor 56-; Pres. Parl. Corresp. Asscn. 51-56; Chair. Norwegian Liberal Press Asscn. 59-71; mem. board Norwegian Editors' Asscn., Norwegian Press Asscn., Chair. Board Norwegian News Bureau; mem. Town Council; Liberal.

Bergens Tidende, P.O. Box 873, 5001 Bergen; Home: Starefossvei 58B, 5000 Bergen, Norway.

Telephone: 310900.

Fenner, Frank John, M.B.E., M.D., F.A.A., F.R.S.; Australian research biologist; b. 21 Dec. 1914, Ballarat, Victoria; s. of Dr. and Mrs. Charles Fenner; m. E. M. Roberts 1943; one d.; ed. Thebarton Technical High School, Adelaide High School, Adelaide Univ.

Medical Officer, Hospital Pathologist, Australian Forces 40-43, Malariologist 43-46; Francis Haley Research Fellow, Walter and Eliza Hall Inst. for Medical Research, Melbourne 46-48; Travelling Fellow, Rockefeller Inst. for Medical Research 48-49; Prof. of Microbiology, Australian Nat. Univ. 49-73; Dir. John Curtin School of Medical Research, Australian Nat. Univ. 67-73, Dir. Centre for Resource and Environmental Studies 73-; David Syme Prize, Melbourne Univ. 49; Harvey Lecturer, Harvey Soc. of N.Y. 58; Overseas Fellow, Churchill Coll., Cambridge 61-62; Mueller Medal 64; Britannica Australia Award 67, Flinders Lecture 67, David Lecture 73.

Leisure interests: gardening, fishing.

Publs. about 100 scientific papers, mainly on acidfast bacilli and pox viruses, *The Production of Antibodies* (with F. M. Burnet) 49, *Myxomatosis* (with F. N. Ratcliffe) 65, *The Biology of Animal Viruses* 68, 2nd edn. 74, *Medical Virology* (with D. O. White) 70, 2nd edn. 76.

Centre for Resource and Environmental Studies, Australian National University, Canberra, Australia.

Telephone: 49-4588.

Fenoaltea, Sergio; Italian Ambassador to United States 61-67; see *The International Who's Who 1975-76.*

Fenton, Beatrice; American sculptor; b. 12 July 1887, Philadelphia, Pa.; d. of Thomas H. Fenton, M.D. and Lizzie S. (Remak) Fenton; ed. School of Industrial Art and Pennsylvania Acad. of Fine Arts.

Works include: Seaweed Fountain, Fairmount Park, Philadelphia 22, Schmitz Memorial Tablet, Acad. of Music 26, Gate Post Figures at Children's Hospital, Philadelphia 32, Garden Figure, Danby Park, Wilmington, Del. 31, Bust of Wm. Penn for Penn Club, Philadelphia 32, Fountain, Brookgreen Gardens, S.C. 32, Bust of Felix E. Schelling, Furness Library, Univ. of Pa. 35, Bust of Thomas H. Fenton, M.D., Art Club of Philadelphia 37, Ariel Sun-Dial, Shakespeare Garden, Univ. of Pa. 38, Drinking Fountain, Hahnemann Medical Coll., Philadelphia 42, Lizette Woodworth Reese Memorial, Pratt Library, Baltimore, Md. 43, Evelyn Taylor Price Memorial Sun-Dial, Rittenhouse Square Philadelphia 48; winning design for Vice-Pres. Barkley Congressional Medal 50; bust of Joseph Moore for Moore Inst., Philadelphia 54; Two Fountain groups *Fish on Coral Reef*, Fairmount Park, Pa. 64; Da Vinci Bronze Medal 54; Fellowship of Pa. Acad. of Fine Arts Exhbn. 67; Percy M. Owens Prize.

Leisure interests: playing the piano, horse-back riding.

Home: 621 Westview Street, Philadelphia 19, Pa., U.S.A.; Studio: 311 West Duval Street, Philadelphia 44, Pa., U.S.A.

Telephone: 848-8587 (Studio); 844-4945 (Home).

Fenton, Roy Pentelow, C.M.G.; British banker; b. 1 July 1918, Salford, Lancs.; s. of Heber Fenton; m. Daphne Cheason 1941; one s.; ed. Salford Grammar School.

War Service 39-46; Bank of England 46-58; Governor, Central Bank of Nigeria 58-63; Dep. Chief, Central Banking Information Dept., Bank of England 63-65, Chief Overseas Dept. 65-75; Vice-Chair. European Monetary Agreement 68-72; Chief Exec. Keyser Ullman Ltd. 75.

Keyser Ullman Ltd., 25 Milk Street, London, EC2V 8JE, England.

Telephone: 01-606-7070.

Feoktistov, Konstantin Petrovich, D.SC.; Soviet cosmonaut; b. 1926; ed. Moscow Higher Technical School. Injured in World War II; group instructor for cosmonauts; the scientific mem. of the team aboard the first-ever multi-seater space ship "Voskhod I" (12 Oct. 64); mem. C.P.S.U.; Hero of the Soviet Union; Pilot-Cosmonaut of U.S.S.R.

Zvezdny Gorodok, Moscow, U.S.S.R.

Ferencsik, János; Hungarian musician; b. 18 Jan. 1907; ed. Conservatoire, Budapest.

General Musical Dir. Hungarian State Opera House until 73; Gen. Musical Dir. Hungarian State Concert Orchestra; Pres., Chief Conductor Budapest Philharmonic Orchestra; Asst. Bayreuth Festival 30-31; guest conductor Vienna Opera House 48-50; Hon. Prof. Hungarian Acad. of Music; has given concerts in numerous European countries, Japan, Australia, Argentina, U.S.A., and U.S.S.R.; Kossuth Prize 51, 61, Eminent Artist.

Leisure interest: photography.

Csopaky-u. 12, H-1022 Budapest, Hungary.

Telephone: 312-550.

Ferguson, Clarence Clyde, Jr., A.B., J.D., D.I.L.; American diplomatist and professor of law; b. 4 Nov. 1924, Wilmington, N.C.; s. Clarence Clyde Ferguson and Georgeva Owens Ferguson; m. Dolores Zimmerman Ferguson 1954-1969; three d.; ed. Ohio State Univ., Harvard Law School and Havana Univ.

Called to Bar 51; Teaching Fellow, Law School 51-52; associated with Baltimore, Paulson and Canudo 52-54; Asst. U.S. Attorney 54-55; Professor of Law, Rutgers Univ. 55-63; Howard Univ. 63-June 70; U.S. expert, UN sub-comm. on discrimination 64-; U.S. Amb. to Uganda 70-72; Deputy Asst. Sec. of State for Internal Affairs 72-; U.S. Rep. on the UN Econ. and Social Council 73-; fmr. Special Co-ordinator for Relief to Civilian victims of the Nigerian Civil War; Hon. LL.D.

Leisure interests: art, music.

Publs. *Desegregation and the Law* 57, 62, 70, *Trial Presentation* 57, *Enforcement Judgements and Liens* 61, *Secured Transactions* 61, *Racism and American Education* 70, numerous articles and book reviews.

United States Mission to the United Nations, 799 UN Plaza, New York, N.Y. 10017, U.S.A.

Telephone: 212-573-6485.

Ferguson, Glenn Walker, B.A., M.B.A., J.D., D.S., LL.D.; American university president; b. 28 Jan. 1929, Syracuse, N.Y.; s. of Forrest E. Ferguson and Mabel W. Ferguson; m. Patricia Lou Head 1950; two s. one d.; ed. Cornell Univ., Georgetown Univ., Univ. of Santo Tomas (Manila), George Washington Univ., Univ. of Chicago and Univ. of Pittsburgh.

Staff Associate, Governmental Affairs Inst., Washington, D.C. 54-55; Asst. Editor and Asst. Sec.-Treas., American Judicature Soc., Chicago 55-56; successively Admin. Asst. to Chancellor, Asst. Dean and Asst. Prof. Graduate School of Public and Int. Affairs, Assoc. Dir., Coordinated Educ. Center, Univ. of Pittsburgh 56-60; Management Consultant 60-61; Special Asst. to Dir., U.S. Peace Corps 61, Peace Corps Dir. in Thailand 61-63, Assoc. Dir. 63-64; Dir. Vista Volunteers, Office of Econ. Opportunity, Washington, D.C. 64-66; Amb. to Kenya 66-69; Chancellor, Long Island Univ. 69-70; Pres. Clark Univ. 70-73, Univ. of Connecticut 73-; U.S. Air Force 51-53; mem. Pres. Task Force on Poverty 64, Fed. Bar Asscn., Council on Foreign Relations, Amer. Political Science Asscn.; mem. Board of Trustees, Cornell Univ., Board of Dirs. Private Export Funding Corpn., Board of Dirs., Foreign Policy Asscn., New England Board of Higher Educ.

University of Connecticut, Storrs, Conn. 06268, U.S.A.

Ferguson, Homer, J.D.; American lawyer and politician; b. 25 Feb. 1889, Harrison City, Pa.; s. of Samuel and Margaret (Bush) Ferguson; m. Myrtle Jones 1913; one d.; ed. Pittsburgh Univ., Michigan Univ. Law School.

Law practice Detroit 13-29; Circuit Judge Wayne County, Mich. 29-41; One-man grand jury, Wayne County, Mich. 39-42; U.S. Senator from Mich. 43-55; Chair. Republican Policy Cttee. 83rd Congress; mem. Foreign Relations Cttee. and Appropriation Cttee. 83rd Congress; mem. 2nd Hoover Comm.; Amb. to the Philippines 55-56; resigned 56 to accept presidential appointment; Judge, U.S. Court of Military Appeals 56-72, Senior Judge 72-; mem. Michigan and American Bar Asscns.; mem. American Judicature Soc., Washington Inst. of Foreign Affairs, Metropolitan Club, World Peace Thru Law Center; Hon. mem. Interparliamentary Union; Republican.

Leisure interests: painting, gardening.

Home: 5054 Millwood Lane, N.W., Washington 20016, D.C.; Office: U.S. Court of Military Appeals, Washington, D.C. 20442, U.S.A.

Telephone: OX3-1903 (Office).

Ferguson, James L.; American business executive; ed. Hamilton Coll. and Harvard Business School.

Served U.S. Army Corps of Engineers in Pacific Theater, World War II; Assoc. Advertising Man. Procter & Gamble Co.; joined Gen. Foods Corpn. 63, Gen. Man. Birds Eye Div. 67, Vice-Pres. 68, Group Vice-Pres. 70, Exec. Vice-Pres. 72, Chief Operating Officer 72, Pres., Dir. 72-, Chief Exec. 73-, Chair. 74-; Dir. Union Carbide Corpn., Grocery Mfrs. of America Inc.; Trustee, Hamilton Coll.; mem. Steering Cttee. Juillard School.

General Foods Corporation, 250 North Street, White Plains, N.Y. 10625, U.S.A.

Ferguson, Wallace Klippert, PH.D., LITT.D., F.R.S.C.; Canadian historian; b. 23 May 1902; ed. Univ. of Western Ontario and Cornell Univ.

Instructor, New York Univ. 28-30, Asst. Prof. 30-40, Assoc. Prof. 40-45, Prof. 45; Chair. History Dept., Univ. of W. Ontario 56, Senior Prof. 65-; Pres. Canadian Historical Asscn. 60-61, Renaissance Soc. of America 65-67, Council of American Historical Asscn. 64-68; Social Science Research Council Fellowship 27-28; Guggenheim Fellowship 39-40; Canada Council Medal 67.

Publs. *Opuscula Erasmi (A Supplement to the Omnia Opera)* 33, *A Survey of European Civilization* (with G. Bruun) 36, *The Renaissance* 40, *The Renaissance in Historical Thought* 48, *Europe in Transition 1300-1520* 62, *Renaissance Studies* 63.

1061 Waterloo Street, London, Ontario, Canada.

Telephone: 519-432-4751.

Ferlinghetti, Lawrence; American writer; b. circa 1920, Yonkers, N.Y.

Publs. include *Pictures of the Gone World* (poems), *Selections from Paroles by Jacques Prévert, A Coney Island of the Mind* (poems), *Her* (novel), *Starting from San Francisco* (poems), *Unfair Arguments with Existence* (7 plays), *Routines, After the Cries of the Birds* (poem) *Moscow in the Wilderness, Segovia in the Snow* (poem broadside), *The Secret Meaning of Things* (poems), *Tyrannus Nix?* (poem), *Back Roads to Far Places* (poems), *Open Eye, Open Heart* (poems), *The Mexican Night* (travel journal); also translations, film-scripts and phonograph records.

c/o City Lights Bookshop, 261 Columbus Avenue, San Francisco, Calif. 94133; c/o J. B. Lippincott Company, East Washington Square, Philadelphia, Pa. 19105, U.S.A.

Fernand-Laurent, Jean; French diplomatist; b. 3 Nov. 1917; Paris; s. of Camille Jean Fernand-Laurent; m. Anne-Marie Le Saint 1952; three d.; ed. Sorbonne, Paris, Lyons and Peterhouse, Cambridge.

Third Sec., Belgrade 45-48; First Sec., Moscow 48-51; Counsellor, Tel-Aviv 54-58; Consul-Gen., Hamburg 58-62; First Counsellor, Algiers 62-64; Perm. Del. to UNESCO 66-70; Amb. and Perm. Rep. to European

Office of UN, Geneva June 70-; Officier, Légion d'Honneur, Croix de Guerre, Commdr. Ordre du Mérite.
Leisure interest: social sciences.
Publ. *Morale et Tyrannie* (essay) 67.
Les Ormeaux, 36 Route de Pregny, 1292 Chambésy, Geneva, Switzerland.
Telephone: 58-15-12.

Fernandes, Gil Vicente Vaz, M.A.; Guinean diplomatist; b. 10 May 1937, Bolama, Guinea-Bissau; s. of Anibal Vaz Fernandes and Teresa Pereira Fernandes; ed. Univ. of New Hampshire, The American Univ.
Involved for several years in the struggle for nat. liberation of Guinea-Bissau and the Cape Verde Islands; Perm. Rep. of Partido Africano da Indepêndencia da Guiné e Cabo Verde (PAIGC) to Egypt 68-72, Scandinavia 72-75; Perm. Rep. of Guinea-Bissau to UN 75-; Amb. to U.S.A. 75-.
211 East 43rd Street, Suite 604, New York, N.Y. 10017, U.S.A.
Telephone: (212) 661-3977.

Fernández-Cuesta Illana, Nemesio; Spanish lawyer, economist and politician; b. 24 May 1928, Madrid; m. María Victoria Luca de Tena y Brunet 1955; seven s. three d.; ed. Cen. Univ., Madrid
Deputy Dir.-Gen. Banco Exterior de Espana; Under-Sec. for Trade 69-73; Deputy Gov. Bank of Spain 73; Minister of Trade 73-75; Adviser to Spanish del., 23rd UN Gen. Assembly 68; Journalism Prize (Madrid Chamber of Commerce); Grand Cross of Civil Merit, Order of Isabel la Católica, foreign decorations.
Leisure interests: football, horse racing.
Guisando, 26-5°C, Ciudad Puerto de Hierro, Madrid 35, Spain.
Telephone: 216-54-13 (Home).

Fernández González, Jaime Manuel, LL.D.; Dominican politician; b. 4 Sept. 1920; m. María Altagracia Rodríguez; one d.; ed. Univ. Autónoma de Santo Domingo and Univ. of New York.
Former school teacher, later journalist; law officer, Dept. of the Interior and Police; Supt. of Banks; Auditor-Gen. Univ. Autónoma de Santo Domingo; Admin. Sec. Office of the President; Pres. Partido Movimiento de Consiliación Nacional; presidential candidate 70; Sec. of State for Foreign Affairs 70-72, for Educ., Fine Arts and Worship 72; has represented Dominican Repub. at numerous int. confs.; head of del. to XXV session of UN Gen. Assembly; holds several nat. and foreign decorations.
Calle Elvira de Mendoza No. 11, Santo Domingo, Dominican Republic.
Telephone: 682-4237 (Home).

Fernández Maldonado, Gen. Jorge; Peruvian army officer and politician; b. 29 May 1922, Ilo, Moquegua; m. Estela Castro Faucheux; two s. two d.; ed. Chorillos Mil. School.
Head of Army Intelligence Service; Dir. of Army Intelligence Service School, also of Mariscal Ramon Castilla Mil. School, Trujillo; Mil. Attaché, Argentina; mem. Pres. Advisory Cttee. (COAP); Minister of Energy and Mines 68-75; Army Chief of Staff 75-76; Prime Minister, Minister of War, Commdr. Gen. of Army Feb. 76-.
Oficina del Primer Ministro, Lima, Peru.

Fernández Miranda, Torcuato; Spanish politician; b. 10 Nov. 1915, Gijón; m.; seven c.; ed. Univs. of Oviedo and Madrid.
Director, Senior Coll. of Valdés Salas, Univ. of Oviedo 49-51, Rector, Univ. of Oviedo 51-53; Dir.-Gen. of Intermediate Educ. 54-55; Dir.-Gen. of Univ. Educ. 56-62; Dir.-Gen. Social Promotion, Ministry of Labour 62-66; Prof. of Political Law, Central Univ.; mem. Parl. and Nat. Adviser to Chief of State; Minister and Sec.-Gen. Nat. Movement 69-74; Deputy Prime Minister of Spain 73-74; Pres. Cortes Dec. 75-.

Publs. *La justificación del Estado, El Concepto de lo social y otros ensayos, El problema político, Situación social y libertad, Estado y Constitución*, etc.
c/o General ORÁA, 16-Madrid-6, Spain.

Fernández-Muro, José Antonio; Argentine painter; b. 1 March 1920.
Director, Nat. School of Fine Arts, Buenos Aires 57-58; travelled and studied in Europe and America on UNESCO Fellowship of Museology 57-58; lives in New York 62-; one-man exhbns. in Buenos Aires, Madrid, Washington, New York, Rome and Detroit; represented in numerous Group Shows including *50 ans de Peinture Abstraite*, Paris and *The Emergent Decade*, Guggenheim Museum 65; prizes include Gold Medal, Brussels World Fair 58, Guggenheim Int. and Di Tella Int. awards.
Major works: *Superimposed circles* 58, *In Reds*, Di Tella Foundation, Buenos Aires 59, *Horizonte terroso*, Museum of Modern Art, Caracas 61, *Circulo azogado*, Museum of Modern Art, New York 62, *Lacerated Tablet*, Rockefeller, New York 63, *Elemental Forms*, Massachussetts Inst. of Technology 64, *Silver Field*, Guggenheim Museum 65, *Summit*, Bonino Gallery, N.Y.
353 East 50th Street, New York, N.Y., U.S.A.

Fernández Retamar, Roberto, DR. en FIL.; Cuban writer; b. 9 June 1930, Havana; s. of José M. Fernández Roig and Obdulia Retamar; m. Adelaida de Juan 1952; two d.; ed. Univ. de la Habana, Univ. de Paris à la Sorbonne and Univ. of London.
Professor, Univ. of Havana 55-; Visiting Prof. Yale Univ. 57-58; Dir. *Nueva Revista Cubana* 59-60; Cultural Counsellor of Cuba in France 60; Sec. Union of Writers and Artists of Cuba 61-65; Dir. of Review *Casa de las Américas* 65-; Visiting Lecturer Columbia Univ. 57, Univ. of Prague 65; Nat. Prize for Poetry, Cuba 52.
Leisure interests: reading, swimming.
Publs. Poetry: *Elegía como un Himno* 50, *Patrias* 52, *Alabanzas, Conversaciones* 55, *Vuelta de la Antigua Esperanza* 59, *Con las Mismas Manos* 62, *Poesía Reunida 1948-1965* 66, *Buena Suerte Viviendo* 67, *Cuaderno paralelo* 73; studies: *La poesía Contemporánea en Cuba* 54, *Idea de la Estilística* 58, *Papelería* 62, *Ensayo de otro mundo* 67, *Introducción a Cuba: la historia* 68, *Que veremos arder* 70, *A quien pueda interesar* 70, *Caliban* 71, *Lectura de Martí* 72, *El son de Vuelo popular* 72.
Calle H 508, Vedado, Havana, Cuba.
Telephone: 32-3587.

Fernández Sordo, Alejandro, LL.B.; Spanish lawyer; b. 4 Sept. 1921, Oviedo; m. María de la Concepción Capal Vega; two s. three d.
President, Nat. Press, Radio, T.V. and Publicity Syndicate 64-65; Nat. del. State Press and Radio Org. 65-69; Dir.-Gen. of Press 69-73; Sec.-Gen. Syndical Org. 73; Minister of Syndical Relations Jan. 74-Dec. 75; Grand Cross of Cisneros, of Political Merit, of Mil. Merit, of Aeronautical Merit, of Civil Merit, and other decorations.
Leisure interests: camping, mountaineering.
Paseo del Prado, 18-20, Madrid, Spain.
Telephone: 227 83 18; 230 93 72.

Fernando, Hugh Norman Gregory, O.B.E., B.A., B.C.L.; Ceylonese judge; b. 17 Nov. 1910; ed. St. Joseph's Coll., Colombo, Trinity Coll., Kandy, and Balliol Coll., Oxford.
Barrister of Gray's Inn (London); Legal Draftsman, Ceylon 50-54; Commr. of Assizes and Puisne Justice, Supreme Court 54-66; Chief Justice of Sri Lanka (fmrly. Ceylon) 66-; Leader, Ceylon Del. to Afro-Asian Legal Consultative Cttee. 62; Chair. Cheshire Homes Foundation, Sri Lanka; Chair. Appeal for Children Fund, Sri Lanka; Hon. Master of Bench (Middle Temple), Master of Bench (Gray's Inn).
[*Died March* 1976.]

Fernando, Thusew Samuel, C.B.E., Q.C., LL.B.; Ceylonese judge; b. 5 Aug. 1906, Ambalangoda; s. of late T. O. Fernando; m. Malini Wickramasuriya 1943; one s.; ed. Royal Coll., Colombo, Univ. Coll., Colombo, Univ. Coll., London, and Lincoln's Inn, London. Crown Counsel 36-52; Solicitor-Gen., Ceylon 52-54; Attorney-Gen. 54-56; Justice of Supreme Court of Ceylon 56-68; mem. Judicial Service Comm. 62-68; Pres. Int. Comm. of Jurists, Geneva 66-; mem. Int. Cttee. of Inst. on Man and Science, New York; Pres. Asian-African Legal Consultative Cttee. 71; Pres. Court of Appeal 71-73; High Commr. in Australia and N.Z. 74-; mem. Constitutional Court 72.
Leisure interest: social service.
Sri Lanka High Commission, Canberra, Australia.

Fernig, Leo; British educationist; b. 1915; ed. Univ. Coll. of the Province of Natal.
Teacher, Natal Dept. 37-40; served in Army Educ. Corps. 40-46; Editor, Oxford Univ. Press 46-48; Programme Specialist, Educational Clearing House, UNESCO 48-52, Chief of Div. 52-61; Asst. Dir. Int. Co-operation for the Study and Advancement of Educ., Dept. of Educ., UNESCO 61-66, Dir. of Operational Services, Educational Sector 66, Acting Dir., Dept. of School and Higher Educ. Aug. 67, Dir. Dept. for Advancement of Educ. Oct. 67-70, Dir. Int. Bureau of Educ. (IBE) 70-.
Publs. articles in journals.
International Bureau of Education, Palais Wilson, 1211 Geneva 14, Switzerland.

Ferniot, Jean; French journalist; b. 10 Oct. 1918, Paris; s. of Paul and Jeanne (née Rabu) Ferniot; m. 1st Jeanne Martinod 1942 (divorced), 2nd Christiane Servan-Schreiber 1959; three s. two d.; ed. Lycée Louis-le-Grand.
Head, Political Dept., *France-Tireur* 45-47; Political Columnist, *L'Express* 57-58; Chief Political Correspondent *France-Soir* 59-63; Editor *L'Express* 63-66; on staff Radio Luxembourg and Political Commentator *France-Soir* Dec. 66-; Prix Interallié 61; Croix de Guerre.
Publs. *Les Ides de Mai* 58, *L'Ombre Porté* 61, *Pour le Pire* 62, *Derrière la Fenêtre* 64, *De Gaulle et le 13 Mai* 65, *Mort d'une Révolution* 68, *Paris dans mon assiette* 69, *Complainte contre X* 73, *De de Gaulle à Pompidou* 73, *Ça suffit!* 74, *Pierrot et Aline* 74, *La Petite Légume* 74.
62 rue Singer, Paris 16e, France.
Telephone: 288-08-18.

Ferrari, Alberto, LL.D., M.A.; Italian banker; b. 16 Dec. 1914, Parma; ed. Univ. di Pisa, Yale Univ., and Univ. Bocconi, Milan.
With Banca Commerciale Italiana 38-51, with Presidency of Cabinet as Financial Expert 47, Italian Del. to European Co-operation Cttee., Paris 47, Italian Perm. Rep. to European Payments Cttee., Paris 48-50; Gen. Sec. Bank for Int. Settlements, Basle 51-61; Gen. Man. Consorzio di Credito per le Opere Pubbliche and Istituto di Credito per le Imprese di Pubblica Utilità, Rome 61-66; Gen. Man. Banca Nazionale del Lavoro, Rome 66-, Man. Dir.; Vice-Chair. Associazione Bancaria Italiana; Chair. Capitalfin Int.; mem. Board of Asscn. of the Italian Stock Companies, Board of Dirs. of Efibanca and INSUD, Comm. Permanente du Bareme de la Ligue des Sociétés; Kt. Gran Croce of the Italian Repub., Commdr. Belgian Order of the Crown, Officier Légion d'Honneur.
Publs. *La Gestione del Credito* 47, *Politica Monetaria* 59, *Politica monetaria en su perspectiva historica* 61.
Banca Nazionale del Lavoro, Via Vittorio Veneto 119, Rome, Italy.
Telephone: 4661.

Ferrari, Enzo; Italian racing car executive; b. 20 Feb. 1898.
Entered motor racing 20-, driver with Alfa Romeo 20-31; founder Ferrari Ltd. 29-, began building own cars 40-; cars have won numerous Grand Prix and Championship Races.
Publ. *Le mie gioie terribili* (autobiog.).
Ferrari Works, Maranello, Modena, Italy.

Ferrazzi, Ferruccio; Italian painter; b. 15 March 1891, Rome; m. Orizia Randone 1922; three s.
Titular Prof. of Decoration, Inst. of Fine Arts, Rome 29-; Instructor, American Acad., Rome 35-36; Dir. Scuola Vaticana del Mosaico 67; mem. Acad. d'Italie 32, Accad. del Disegno Firenze 35-, Accad. Naz. S. Luca 25, Accad. Pontificia Virtuosi al Pantheon 50, First Int. Prize Carnegie Inst. 26.
Leisure interests: poetry, sculpture.
Works include: *Focolare* (Rome Modern Art Gallery) 10, *Genitrice* (Rome) 12, *Presagio* (Bologna Municipal Gallery) 14, *Vita gaia* (Galleria Capitolina, Rome) 21, *Festa notturna, Adolescente* 22, *Horitia* (Florence Modern Art Gallery) 23, *Caratteri della famiglia* (New York) 23, *Viaggio tragico* (Pittsburgh), *Idolo* (Coll. Wedekind) 25, *Tempesta* (Jeu de Paume, Paris) 25, *La Monta* 29, *Il toro romano* (Rome Modern Art Gallery) 30, Seven tapestries (Palace of Corpns., Rome) 32, *Sabaudia* (mosaic) 35, *Clemenza di Traiano* (Palace of Justice, Milan) 38, *Fabiola e Ninetta che parlano* (Art Gallery, Bucharest) 33; frescoes for churches: S. Eugenio, Rome, S. Rita, Cascia 51, Univ. of Padua, etc.; encaustic paintings for S. Benedetto Church, Rome 49; mosaic *Dell' Apocalisse* 27-54, Acqui; frescoes: *Risurrezione*, Amatrice 53-55; *l'Ultima Cena di Cristo*, Assisi 56, *Le Opere e i Giorni*, Mausoleo Acqui 54-60; four sculptures *Nella Villa di S. Liberata* 59-65; mosaic, Propaganda Fide Coll., Rome 65-66; mosaic, apse of the Church of S. Antonio, Taranto 70; seven paintings on *Illuminazione della Memoria* 72.
Studio: Strada del Pianone 15, "Giardino delle Sculture", Santa Liberata, Grosseto 58010; and Piazza delle Muse, Via G. G. Porro 27, Rome 00197, Italy.
Telephone: Santa Liberata 814327; Rome 801270.

Ferré, Luis A., M.A.; Puerto Rican politician and administrator; b. 17 Feb. 1904, Ponce; s. of Antonio Ferré; m. Lorencita Ramirez de Arellano 1931; one s. one d.; ed. Morristown School, Morristown, N.J. and Mass. Inst. of Technology.
Worked for Puerto Rico Iron Works 25-41; founded Ponce Cement Corpn. with father and brothers 41; assisted in merger of government-owned plants with Ferre Enterprises 50; mem. Ponce Constitutional Convention to draft constitution of Puerto Rico 52; mem. House of Reps. 52-; appointed to U.S.-Puerto Rico Comm. on Status of Puerto Rico 65; Pres. New Progressive Party Aug. 67-; Gov. of Puerto Rico 68-72; mem. and Hon. Sec. Mass. Inst. of Technology; mem. American Acad. of Arts and Sciences, Citizens' Advisory Cttee. of Govt. Security Comm. and numerous other socs.; Order of Vasa (Sweden) 58; Knight, Order of the Holy Sepulchre 59; Hon. Ph.D. (Springfield Coll., Mass. and Catholic Univ. of Puerto Rico).
Partido Nuevo Progresista, San Juan, Puerto Rico.

Ferreira, Herculano de Amorim, C.ENG., D.SC.; Portuguese physicist; b. 22 Oct. 1895, S. Miguel, Azores; s. of Dr. J. B. Carreiro Ferreira and Maria I. de M. Amorim; m. Jorgina do C. Monjardino 1934; two s. two d.; ed. Univs. of Lisbon and London.
Served in First World War 17-18; Lecturer, Univ. of Lisbon 20, Prof. 30-65; Visiting Prof., Univ. of London 33-34; Physicist, Lisbon Inst. for Cancer 34-37; Under-Sec. of State for Nat. Educ. 44-46; Dir.-Gen. of Meteorological and Geophysical Services 46-65; Chair. Nat. Cttee. for Int. Radio-Science Union 48-65; mem. Exec. Cttee. WMO 51-59, Vice-Pres. 55-59; Pres. Academia das Ciencias de Lisboa 63-; Chair. Nat. Cttee. for Int. Hydrological Decade 67-, Int. Geog. Union 68-; Foreign mem. Royal Spanish Acad., Brazilian Acad. of Letters,

Nat. Acad. of Sciences (Argentina); Hon. mem. Acad. du Mérite Scientifique, Paris; Hon. C.B.E. (U.K.); Order for Scientific Merit (Portugal and Spain). Leisure interests: music, fencing.
Publs. *The Double Refraction of Quartz along the Optic Axis* 30, *The Thermal Ionization of Sodium by Tungsten* 34, *The Climate of Portugal*, 17 vols. 42-66, *El Mapa Magnético de la Peninsula Ibérica* 51-61, *Carte Seismotectonique du Portugal* 60, *Hydrology as one of the Earth Sciences* 62, *Science, Technology and Humanities* 63, *Dynamic Climatology of Southern Africa* 65, etc.
Rua Academia das Ciencias 19, Lisbon 2; Home: Casa da Grota, Estoril, Portugal.
Telephone: 33866 (Office); 260180 (Home).

Ferrier, Johan Henri Eliza; Surinam politician; b. 12 May 1910, Paramaribo.
Member of Surinam Parl. 46-48; Dir. Dept. of Educ. Paramaribo 51-55; Prime Minister, Minister of Gen. Affairs, of Home Affairs 55-58; Counsellor, Ministry of Educ., Arts and Science, Netherlands 59-65; Man. Dir. Billiton Mining Co., Surinam 66-67; Gov. of Surinam 68-75; Pres. Repub. of Surinam Nov. 75-; Dr. of Arts and Philosophy, Netherlands 50.
Office of the President, Paramaribo, Surinam.

Ferry, John Douglass, A.B., PH.D.; American professor of chemistry; b. 4 May 1912, Dawson, Canada (of U.S. parents); s. of Douglass Hewitt Ferry and Eudora Beaufort Bundy; m. Barbara Norton Mott 1944; one s. one d.; ed. Stanford Univ. and Univ. of London.
Instructor, Harvard Univ. 36-38, Soc. of Fellows, Harvard 38-41; Assoc. Chemist, Woods Hole Oceanographic Inst. 41-45; Research Assoc., Harvard 42-45; Asst. Prof., Univ. of Wisconsin 46; Assoc. Prof. 46-47; Prof. 47-; Chair. Dept. of Chemistry 59-67; Pres. Soc. of Rheology 61-63; Chair. Int. Cttee. on Rheology 63-68; mem. Nat. Acad. of Sciences; Fellow, American Acad. of Arts and Sciences, Hon. mem. Groupe Français de Rhéologie; Special Lecturer, Kyoto Univ., Japan 68, Université de Grenoble (Ecole d'Eté) 73; Farrington Daniels Research Prof. 73-; Eli Lilly Award, Amer. Chem. Soc. 46; Bingham Medal, Soc. of Rheology 53; Kendall Award, Amer. Chem. Soc. 60; High Polymer Physics Prize, Amer. Physical Soc. 66; Colwyn Medal, Inst. of the Rubber Industry (London) 71; Witco Award, Amer. Chem. Soc. 74.
Leisure interest: travel.
Publ. *Viscoelastic Properties of Polymers* 61, 70.
Department of Chemistry, University of Wisconsin, Madison, Wis. 53706; Home: 137 N. Prospect Avenue, Madison, Wis. 53705, U.S.A.
Telephone: 608-262-1485 (Office); 608-233-4936 (Home).

Fery, John Bruce, M.B.A.; American business executive; b. 12 Feb. 1930, Bellingham, Wash.; s. of Carl S. and Margaret Fery; m. Delores Carlo 1953; three s.; ed. Univ. of Washington and Stanford Univ. Graduate School of Business.
Assistant to Pres., Wester Kraft Corpn. 55-56, Production Man. 56-57; Asst. to Pres., Boise Cascade Corpn. 57-58, Gen. Man. Paper Div. 58-60, Vice-Pres. 60-67, Exec. Vice-Pres. and Dir. 67-72, Pres. June 72-, Chief Exec. Officer Oct. 72-.
Boise Cascade Corporation, One Jefferson Square, Boise, Ida. 83701, U.S.A.
Telephone: 208-384-8560.

Feshbach, Herman, PH.D.; American professor of physics; b. 2 Feb. 1917, New York, N.Y.; s. of David and Ida Feshbach; m. Sylvia Harris 1940; two s. one d.; ed. City Coll., New York, N.Y. and Mass. Inst. of Technology.
Tutor in Physics, City Coll., New York, N.Y. 37-38; Asst. Prof., Mass. Inst. of Technology (MIT) 45-47, Assoc. Prof. 47-54, Prof. of Physics 54-; Dir. Center for

Theoretical Physics, MIT 67-73; Head, Dept. of Physics MIT 73-; Guggenheim Fellow 54-55, Ford Foundation Fellow 62-63; Vice-Pres. Amer. Acad. of Arts and Science 73-; mem. Nat. Acad. of Sciences; Navy Ordnance Award 43; Bonner Prize, American Physical Soc. 73.
Publs. *Methods of Theoretical Physics* (with Philip M. Morse) two vols. 53, *Theoretical Nuclear Physics* (with Amos de Shalit) 74, *Reaction Dynamics* (with F. S. Levin) 73.
Center for Theoretical Physics, 6-307, Massachusetts Institute of Technology, 77 Massachusetts Avenue, Cambridge, Mass.; Home: 5 Sedgwick Road, Cambridge, Mass., U.S.A.
Telephone: 864-6900, Ext. 4821 (Office); 354-2721 (Home).

Fessard, Alfred Eugène, D.SC.; French neurophysiologist; b. 28 April 1900, Paris; m. Denise Albe 1942; one s. one d.; ed. Paris Univ.
Professor of Gen. Neurophysiology, Coll. de France (retd.); Dir. Inst. Marey 47-71; mem. Acad. des Sciences, Acad. de Médicine and numerous foreign acads. and socs.; Prix Lallemant 35, Prix Roy-Vaucouloux 54; Officier Légion d'Honneur, Chevalier Ordre de Léopold II, Commdr. Palmes Académiques, Commdr. Ordre National du Mérite.
Publs. A large number of scientific works on basic neurophysiology, electro-encephalography, electric fish etc.
Office: 4 avenue Gordon Bennett, Paris 16e; Home: 51 rue Molitor, Paris 16e, France.
Telephone: 527-2837.

Fessler, Ernst; German banker; b. 23 Aug. 1908; s. of Hans and Amalie (née Spancken) Fessler; m. Auguste Massenberg 1939; three s.; ed. Univs. of Freiburg and Cologne.
Ministry of Justice 34; Supervisory Office for Banking 35-45; mem. Board of Management, Landeszentralbank of Lower Saxony 48-51, Vice-Pres. 51-53; Vice-Pres. Landeszentralbank of North-Rhine Westphalia 53-56, Pres. 56-; mem. Central Bank Council Deutsche Bundesbank 56-; mem. Board of Trustees, Rheinisch-Westfälisches Inst. für Wirtschaftsforschung 56-72, Deputy Chair. 73-; Deputy Chair, Supervisory Board, Stahlwerke Bochum 66-; mem. Energy-Council of North-Rhine Westphalia 67-.
Poststrasse 56, 4005 Meerbusch-Büderich, Federal Republic of Germany.

Festinger, Leon, M.A., PH.D.; American professor of psychology; b. 8 May 1919, New York; s. of Alex and Sarah Solomon Festinger; m. Trudy Bradley 1968; two s. two d.; ed. City Coll. of New York and State Univ. of Iowa.
Research Assoc. in Psychology, Univ. of Iowa 41-43; Senior Statistician, Cttee. on Selection and Training of Aircraft Pilots, Univ. of Rochester 43-45; Asst. Prof. of Social Psychology, Mass. Inst. of Technology 45-48; Assoc. Prof. and Program Dir. Research Center for Group Dynamics, Univ. of Mich. 48-51; Prof. of Psychology, Univ. of Minnesota 51-55; Prof. of Psychology, Stanford Univ. 55-68; Else and Hans Staudinger Prof., Graduate Faculty Dept. of Psychology, New School for Social Research 68-; mem. Nat. Acad. of Sciences; Distinguished Scientific Contribution Award, American Psychol. Asscn.
New School for Social Research, 66 West 12th Street, New York, N.Y. 10011; Home: 37 West 12th Street, New York, N.Y. 10011, U.S.A.
Telephone: 675-2700, 273-2777 (Office); 675-8325 (Home).

Fetscher, Iring, DR. PHIL.; German political scientist; b. 4 March 1922, Marbach; s. of Prof. Rainer Fetscher; m. Elisabeth Götte 1957; two s. two d.; ed. König-

Georg-Gymnasium, Dresden, Eberhard-Karls-Universität, Tübingen, Université de Paris, and Johann Wolfgang Goethe-Universität, Frankfurt.
Editor *Marxismusstudien* 56-; radio commentator on political, philosophical and sociological questions; Prof. of Political Science, Johann Wolfgang Goethe-Universitat, Frankfurt 63-; Theodor-Heuss Prof. New School for Social Research, New York 68-69; Guest Prof. Tel-Aviv Univ. 72; Fellow, Netherlands Inst. for Advanced Study in the Humanities and Social Sciences 72-73; Extraordinary Prof. for Social and Political Philosophy, Catholic Univ. of Nijmegen 74-75.
Leisure interests: collects autographed letters and manuscripts.
Publs. include *Von Marx zur Sowjetideologie* 56 (18th edn. 73), *Uber dialektischen und historischen Materialismus* (Commentary of Stalin) 56, 62, *Rousseaus, politische Philosophie* 60, 68, 75, *Der Marxismus, seine Geschichte in Dokumenten* Vol. I 62, Vol. II 64, Vol. III 65, *Marx-Engels Studienausgabe* 4 vols. 66, *Introduction to Hobbes' Leviathan* 66, *Karl Marx und der Marxismus* 67, *Der Rechtsradikalismus* 67, *Der Sozialismus* 68, *Der Kommunismus* 69, *Hegel: Grosse und Grenzen* 71, *Modelle der Friedenssicherung* 72, *Wer hat Dornröschen wachgeküsst?—das Märchenverwirrbuch* 72, 74, *Marxistische Porträts* Vol. I 75, Vol. II 76.
Institut für Politikwissenschaft, Mertonstrasse 17, 6 Frankfurt-am-Main; Home: Ganghoferstrasse 20, Frankfurt-am-Main, Federal Republic of Germany.
Telephone: 52-15-42.

Feuillère, Edwige; French actress; b. 29 Oct. 1910, Vesoul; *m.* Pierre Feuillère (divorced); ed. Conservatoire National de Paris.
Appeared for two years at the Comédie Française, at Théâtre National Populaire 65; has played leading parts in *La dame aux camélias, Sodome et Gomorrhe, L'Aigle à deux têtes, Partage de Midi, La Parisienne, Phèdre, Constance, Rodogune, La Liberté est un dimanche, Pour Lucrèce, Lucy Crown, Eve et Line, La Folle de Chaillot, A Delicate Balance, Les Bonshommes, Sweet Bird of Youth*; films include: *Sans Lendemain, De Mayerling à Sarajevo, J'étais une aventurière, L'Idiot, Olivia, Cap de l'Espérance, Adorables créatures, Le Blé en herbe, Les Fruits de l'été, En Cas de Malheur, La Vie à Deux, Les Amours Célèbres, Le Crime ne paie pas, Si la vie nous sépare, La chair de l'orchidée*; Chevalier de la Légion d'Honneur, Commdr. des Arts et Lettres.
Leisure interest: reading.
19 rue Eugène Manuel, Paris 16e, France.

Feyide, Chief Meshach Otokiti, A.C.S.M., D.I.C., C.ENG., M.I.M.M., F.INST.PET.; Nigerian chartered engineer; b. 31 March 1926, Ipele, Owo Div., W. State; *s.* of Chief Samuel Otokiti and Juliana Elebe Otokiti (née Adeola); *m.* Christiana Oluremi 1954; one *s.* two *d.*; ed. Govt. Coll., Ibadan, Camborne School of Mines, U.K., Imperial Coll. of Science and Technology, London.
Mines Ranger, Sub-Insp. of Mines, Mines Dept. 46-49; Insp. of Mines 54-59; Petroleum Engineer, Ministry of Mines and Power 60; attached to B.P. Sunbury Research Centre and Eakring Oil Fields, U.K. 60-61; Ministry of Petroleum and Mines, Trinidad and Tobago 61; Senior Petroleum Engineer, Ministry of Mines and Power 62-64, Chief Petroleum Engineer, Head of Petroleum Div. 64-70, Dir. Petroleum Resources, Head of Dept. of Petroleum Resources 70-74; Sec.-Gen. Org. of Petroleum Exporting Countries 75-76.
Leisure interests: music, reading.
Organization of Petroleum Exporting Countries, Dr. Karl Lueger Ring 10, 1010 Vienna, Austria.
Telephone: 63-97-80.

Feynman, Richard Phillips, PH.D.; American physicist; b. 11 May 1918; ed. Massachussetts Inst. of Technology and Princeton Univ.
Member staff atomic bomb project, Princeton 42-43, Los Alamos 43-45; Assoc. Prof. of Theoretical Physics, Cornell Univ. 45-50; Prof. of Theoretical Physics, Calif. Inst. of Technology 50-; mem. American Physical Soc., American Asscn. for Advancement of Science; Foreign mem. Royal Soc. (U.K.); Einstein Award 54; Nobel Prize for Physics 65.
Physics Department, California Institute of Technology, Pasadena, California 91109, U.S.A.

Feyzioğlu, Turhan, LL.D.; Turkish university professor and politician; b. 19 Jan. 1922, Kayseri; *s.* of Sait Azmi Feyzioğlu and Neyyire Feyzioğlu; *m.* Leyla Firdevs 1949; one *d.*; ed. Galatasaray Lycée, Istanbul Univ., and Ecole Nationale d'Administration, Paris.
Assistant Prof. Ankara Political Science School 45-47, Assoc. Prof. 47-54; Research, Nuffield Coll., Oxford 54; Co-editor *Forum* 54-58; Prof. Ankara Univ. 55; Dean, Political Science School, Ankara 56; M.P. 57, 61, 65-; mem. Nat. Exec. Cttee. Republican People's Party 57-61, Vice-Pres. 65, 66; Pres. Middle East Technical Univ. 60; mem. Constituent Assembly 60; Minister of Education 60; Minister of State 61; Deputy Prime Minister 62-63; mem. Turkish High Planning Council 61-63; Turkish Rep. Consultative Assembly Council of Europe 64-66, 72; Leader Reliance Party 67-; Deputy Prime Minister April 75-.
Leisure interest: gardening.
Publs. *Administrative Law* 47, *Judicial Review of Unconstitutional Laws* 51, *Les Parties Politiques en Turquie* 53, *The Reforms of the French Higher Civil Service* 55, *Democracy and Dictatorship* 57, *Communist Threat* 69.
Office: T.B.M.M., Ankara; Home: Farabi Sokak 9/3, Ankara, Turkey.
Telephone: 18-31-01 (Office); 270619 (Home).

fforde, Sir Arthur Frederic Brownlow, Kt., G.B.E., M.A., LL.D.; British solicitor and educationist; b. 23 Aug. 1900, Watford; *s.* of Arthur Brownlow fforde and Mary Alice Storer Branson; *m.* Mary Alison MacLehose 1926; two *s.* one *d.*; ed. Rugby School, and Trinity Coll., Oxford.
Admitted as solicitor 25; partner Linklaters and Paines, London 28-48; mem. Council of Law Society 37-48; Deputy Dir.-Gen. Ministry of Supply 40-41; Under-Sec. Ministry of Supply 43; Under-Sec. Treasury 44-45; Headmaster Rugby School 48-57; Chair. Board of Governors, B.B.C. 57-64, Central Board of Finance, Church of England 60-65; Dir. Equity and Law Life Assurance, Nat. Westminster Bank 57-70.
Wall's End, Wonersh, Guildford, Surrey, England.

Fforde, John Standish, M.A.; British banker; b. 16 Nov. 1921, Broadstone, Dorset; *s.* of late F. C. Fforde; *m.* Marya Retinger; three *s.* one *d.*; ed. Rossall School and Christ Church, Oxford.
Assistant, Prime Minister's Statistical Branch 51-53; Fellow in Econs., Nuffield Coll. 53-56; Adviser Bank of England 57-59, Deputy Chief Central Banking Information Dept. 59-64, Adviser to Govs. 64-66, Chief Cashier 66-70, Dir. March 70-.
Leisure interests: travel, walking.
Publs. *The Federal Reserve System 1945-49* 53, *An International Trade in Managerial Skills* 57.
106 Hawtrey Road, London, N.W.3, England.

Fichtner, Kurt; German politician; b. 1916.
Formerly Deputy Chair. Econ. Advisory Council of D.D.R.; Deputy Chair. Council of Ministers 69-74; Deputy Chair. State Planning Comm. 74-; cand. mem. Cen. Cttee. Sozialistiche Einheitspartei Deutschlands (SED); Vaterländischer Verdienstorden.
Ministerrat, Berlin, German Democratic Republic.

Fiedler, Leslie A., PH.D.; American professor of English and literary critic; b. 8 March 1917, Newark, N.J.; *s.* of Jacob Fiedler and Lillian Rosenstrauch; *m.* 1st Margaret Shipley 1939 (until 1972), three *s.* three *d.*;

m. 2nd Sally Andersen, two step-*s.*; ed. Univ. of Wisconsin and New York Univ. (Heights).
Member of Staff, Montana State Univ. 41-63, Chair. Dept. of English 54-56; Prof. of English State Univ. of N.Y. at Buffalo 64, Chair. Dept. of English 74-77; Assoc. Fellow, Calhoun Coll., Yale Univ.; teaches at vacation courses at univs. in many parts of Europe and U.S.A.; Rockefeller Fellow 46-47, Fulbright Fellow 51-53, 61-62; Kenyon Review Fellowship in Criticism and Christian Gauss Fellowship, Princeton Univ. 56; Guggenheim Fellowship 70-71; Furioso Poetry Prize 57, Award of Nat. Inst. of Arts and Letters 57.
Leisure interests: swimming and/or meditation.
Publs. include: *An End to Innocence: Essays on Culture and Politics* 55, *The Art of the Essay* 58 (revised edn. 69), *Love and Death in the American Novel* 60, 66, *No! In Thunder: Essays on Myth and Literature* 60, *Pull Down Vanity and Other Stories* 62, *The Second Stone: A Love Story* 63, *Waiting for the End* 64, *Back to China* 65, *The Last Jew in America* 66, *The Return of the Vanishing American* 68, *Nude Croquet and Other Stories* 69, *Being Busted* 70, *Collected Essays* 71, *The Stranger in Shakespeare* 72, *The Messengers Will Come No More* 74, *In Dreams Awake* 75.
Department of English—Annex B, State University of New York at Buffalo, Buffalo, N.Y. 14214; Home: 154 Morris Avenue, Buffalo, N.Y. 14214, U.S.A.
Telephone: 716-831-2330 (Office); 716-838-4105 (Home).

Field, Henry, B.A., M.A., D.SC.; American anthropologist; b. 15 Dec. 1902, Chicago, Ill.; *m.* Julia Rand Allen 1953; one *d.* (one *d.* by previous marriage); ed. Eton Coll. and New Coll., Oxford.
Asst. Curator of Physical Anthropology, Field Museum of Natural History (Chicago) 26-34, Curator 34-41; engaged in Govt. research work in Washington 41-45; Research on Anthropology of S.W. Asia 46-47; Univ. of Calif. African Expedn. 47-48; Peabody Museum-Harvard Expedn. to Near East 50, West Pakistan 55, Siberia and Mongolia 74; Research Fellow, Peabody Museum, Harvard 50-; Adjunct Prof. of Anthropology, Univ. of Miami 66-.
Publs. *Arabs of Central Iraq, their History, Ethnology and Physical Characters* 35, *Contributions to the Anthropology of Iran* 39, *The Anthropology of Iraq, Part I:* No. 1 40, Nos. 2-3 49, *Part II,* No. 1 51, Nos. 2, 3 52, *Contributions to the Anthropology of the Faiyum, Sinai, Sudan and Kenya* 52, *The Track of Man* 53, *Contributions to the Anthropology of the Caucasus* 53, *Bibliography on S.W. Asia,* I-VII 53-64, *Ancient and Modern Man in S.W. Asia* (vol. I) 56, (vol. II) 61, *Anthropological Reconnaissance in W. Pakistan* 59, *North Arabian Desert Archaeological Survey* 25-50, 60, "M" Project for F.D.R.: *Studies on Migration and Settlement* 62, Editor *Peabody Museum Russian Translation Series* Vols. I-III, V 59-70, *Contributions to the Physical Anthropology of the Peoples of India* 70, *Contributions to the Anthropology of Saudi Arabia* 73.
Office: Peabody Museum, Cambridge 38, Mass.; Home: 3551 Main Highway, Coconut Grove, Miami 33133, Fla., U.S.A.
Telephone: Miami 1-305-443-8306.

Fieser, Louis Frederick, A.B., PH.D.; American chemist; b. 7 April 1899; ed. Williams College and Harvard University.
Travelling Fellow to Univs. of Frankfurt-on-Main and Oxford 25; Assoc. and Assoc. Prof. at Bryn Mawr 25-30; Asst. Prof. Harvard 30-34; Assoc. Prof. 34-37; Prof. 37-39; Sheldon Emery Prof. of Organic Chem. 39-68, Prof. Emer. 68-; Scholar in Residence, State Univ. of New York 69; mem. Nat. Acad.; received K. Berkham Judd prize 41; Hon. D.Pharm. (Paris); Hon. D.Sc. (Williams Coll.).
Publs. *Experiments in Organic Chemistry* 35, *Chemistry in Three Dimensions* 63, *The Scientific Method* 64,

Organic Experiments, 2nd edn. 68; with Mary Fieser: *Organic Chemistry* 44, *Natural Products Related to Phenanthrene,* 3rd edn. 49, *Introduction to Organic Chemistry* 57, *Basic Organic Chemistry* 59, *Steroids* 59, *Style Guide for Chemists* 60, *Reagents for Organic Synthesis,* Vol. I 67, Vol. II 69.
27 Pinehurst Road, Belmont, Mass. 02178, U.S.A.

Figgures, Sir Frank, K.C.B., C.M.G.; British retd. civil servant; b. 5 March 1910; ed. Oxford and Yale Univs. Called to Bar 36; Mil. Service (R.A.) 40-46; Treasury 46-71; Dir. Trade and Finance, O.E.E.C. 48-51; Under-Sec. Treasury 55-60; Sec.-Gen. European Free Trade Asscn. (EFTA) 60-65; Third Sec. Treasury 65-68; Second Perm. Sec. (Finance Group) 68-71; Dir.-Gen. Nat. Econ. Devt. Office 71-73; Chair. Pay Board 73-74; Dir. Julius Baer Inst. 75-.
31 South View, Uppingham, Rutland, England.
Telephone: Uppingham 3250.

Figini, Luigi; Italian architect; b. 27 Jan. 1903, Milan; *s.* of Alessandro F. and Pia Jardini; *m.* Gege Bottinelli 1934; ed. Politecnico di Milano.
Active collaborator with *Gruppo 7* of Milan, later with *Architetti di Quadrante;* collaborates mainly with Gino Pollini; mem. Accad. di S. Luca, Accad. Tiberina, Movimento Italiano per l'Architettura Moderna; numerous prizes.
Major works: numerous offices, villas, artists' studios and factories including Offices for De Angeli Frua, Milan 31; Olivetti works 34-57, nursery school 39-41, and "Fascia Servizi Sociali", Olivetti, Ivrea Church Madonna dei poveri, Milan 52-54, Ina Casa quarter Via Harrar, Milan 51, House and garden terrace, Hoepli 55-57, Pozzi Ceramic Works, Sparanise 60-63, drawings for Borgo Porto Conte 51, House in Via Circo, Milan 56, working on church SS. Giovanni e Paolo 66.
Leisure interests: horticulture, ornithology, zoophily.
Publs. *L'elemento verde e l'abitazione* 50, numerous expos. and articles in architectural magazines.
Studio: Via Manin 3, Milan; Home: Via Perrone di S. Martino 8, Milan, Italy.
Telephone: 650-162 (Studio); 690-326 (Home).

Figueres Ferrer, José; Costa Rican politician; b. 25 Sept. 1906; *m.* 2nd Karen Olsen; six *c.;* ed. Costa Rica, Mexico Univs., Massachusetts Inst. of Technology.
Coffee planter and rope maker in Costa Rica until 42; exiled to Mexico 42-44; became Junta Pres. of the Repub. after 48, resigned 49; worked on economic problems 49-52; Pres. 53-58; Visiting Prof., Harvard Univ. 63-64; Pres. of Costa Rica 70-74; Pres. Nat. Liberation Party.
Publs. *Cartas a un Ciudadano, La Pobreza de las Naciones* 73, and numerous articles.
Apartado No. 4820, San José, Costa Rica.
Telephone: 25-16-68.

Filali, Abd al-Latif, LL.D.; Moroccan politician and diplomatist; b. 1928, Fez; ed. Univ. of Paris.
Ambassador, Ministry of Foreign Affairs 57; Chargé d'Affaires UN 58-59; Head, Royal Cabinet 59-60; Chargé d'Affaires, Paris 61; Amb. to China (People's Republic) 65, to Algeria 67; Minister of Higher Educ. 68-69; Amb. to Spain 69-71; Minister of Foreign Affairs 71-72.
c/o Ministry of Foreign Affairs, Rabat, Morocco.

Filatov, Antonin Nikolayevich; Soviet surgeon and haemotologist; b. 17 Aug. 1902, Kamenka, Kaluga Region; ed. Moscow Univ.
Intern, Research Assoc. Inst. of Medicine 25-36; Asst. Prof. 36-39; Asst. Prof. Inst. of Postgraduate Medical Training, Leningrad 39-42; Deputy Dir. and Head of Research Inst. of Blood Transfusion, Leningrad 42-; Corresp. mem. U.S.S.R. Acad. of Medical Sciences 53-66, mem. 66-; mem. Int. Asscn. of Surgeons, Int. Soc. of Haemotologists; mem. Board U.S.S.R. and

R.S.F.S.R. Socs. of Surgeons; Hon. mem. Pirogov Surgical Soc.; Order of Red Star; Badge of Honour; Red Banner of Labour; State Prize 53; Merited Scientist R.S.F.S.R.

Publs. About 200 works on surgical treatment of vascular derangements, transplantation and substitution of tissues and organs, application of biological haennostatic methods.

Institute of Blood Transfusion, R.S.F.S.R. Ministry of Public Health, 16 Vtoraya Sovietskaya ulitsa, Leningrad, U.S.S.R.

Filbinger, Hans Karl, D. IUR.; German lawyer and politician; b. 15 Sept. 1913, Mannheim; *m.* Ingeborg Breuer 1950; one *s.* four *d.*; ed. Albert-Ludwigs-Univ., Freiburg im Breisgau, Ludwig-Maximilians-Univ., Munich, and Univ. de Paris à la Sorbonne.

Teacher, Univ. of Freiburg 37-40; War Service and Prisoner-of-War 40-46; lawyer, Freiburg 46-60; mem. Landtag of Baden-Württemberg 60-; Minister of Interior, Baden-Württemberg 60-66; Minister-Pres. of Baden-Württemberg Dec. 66-; Pres. Bundesrat (Upper House) 73-74; mem. Comm. on Decartelization Questions 47; Founder mem. German-French Soc., Freiburg, Soc. for Supra-national Co-operation; mem. NATO Parl. Conf.; Chair. Baden-Württemberg Democrat (CDU) Federation; Deutsches Grosskreuz and other awards.

Richard Wagnerstrasse 15, 7 Stuttgart-1, Federal Republic of Germany.

Filer, John H.; American insurance executive; b. New Haven, Conn.; ed. De Pauw and Yale Univs.

Joined Gumbart, Corbin, Tyler and Cooper (law firm), New Haven 51; mem. Connecticut Senate 57-58; Chair. Farmington Board of Education 61-67; Asst. Counsel Aetna Life and Casualty Co. 58; Gen. Counsel 66, Admin. Asst. to Chair. and Pres. 67, Exec. Vice-Pres. 68, Vice-Chair. Jan. 72, Chair. and Chief Exec. Officer July 72-; Dir. U.S. Steel Corpn., Vice-Chair. Connecticut Business and Industry Asscn., Dir. Insurance Asscn. of Connecticut, Inst. of Life Insurance, Greater Hartford Chamber of Commerce; Aetna Life and Casualty Co.

151 Farmington Avenue, Hartford, Conn. 06115, U.S.A.

Filip, Jan, PH.D., D.SC.; Czechoslovak historian; b. 25 Dec. 1900, Chocnějovice; ed. Charles Univ., Prague.

Professor of Pre-History and of Early History, Charles Univ.; corresp. mem. of the Czechoslovak Acad. of Sciences 52, Academician 55; Chair. History Section of the Czechoslovak Acad. of Sciences 55-57; Vice-Pres. Acad. of Sciences 57-61, mem. Presidium 62; Dir. Archaeological Inst., Acad. of Sciences 63-; Pres. Int. Union of Prehistoric and Protohistoric Sciences 63-69; mem. Scientific Collegium on History, Czechoslovak Acad. of Sciences; Laureate of the State Prize 57; Order of Labour 61; foreign mem. Royal Danish Acad. of Sciences and Art 65; Royal Acad. of Sciences, Belgium 69, Akad. der Wissenschaft, Göttingen 66, Swedish Acad. 72; Polish Order of the Gold Cross 49; Medal of Swedish Acad. of Literature, Art and Antiquities 68; Gottfried Herder Prize of Vienna Univ. 70; Gold Plaque for Services to Science and Mankind, Czechoslovak Acad. of Sciences 70.

Publs. *Historic Beginnings of the Český ráj, an area in North-Eastern Bohemia, Pre-history of Czechoslovakia, The Beginnings of Slav Settlements in Czechoslovakia, The Celts in Central Europe, The Urnfields in Bohemia, Celtic Civilization and its Heritage, Encyclopaedia of Pre- and Early European History, Frühe Stufen der Kunst.*

Archaeological Institute, Letenská 4, Prague 1, Czechoslovakia.

Telephone: 533-406.

Filipchenko, Col. Anatoly Vasilievich; Soviet cosmonaut; b. 26 Feb. 1928, Davydkovo village, Voronezh Region; ed. School of Military Pilots, Chuguev and Military Air Force Acad.

Turner 43-47; Air Force Fighter Pilot 50-53; mem. C.P.S.U. 52-; with Cosmonaut Training Unit 63-, Commdr. of space ship *Soyuz-7*, made a group flight with *Soyuz-6* and *Soyuz-8* Oct. 69, Commdr. of *Soyuz-16* Dec. 74; awards include Hero of Soviet Union, Gold Star, Order of Lenin, Pilot-Cosmonaut of U.S.S.R., K. Tsiolkovsky Gold Medal of U.S.S.R. Acad. of Sciences.

Zvezdny Gorodok, Moscow, U.S.S.R.

Filliozat, Jean, D. en MED., D. ès L.; French professor; b. 4 Nov. 1906, Paris; *m.* Anne Surugue 1930; three *c.*; ed. Univ. of Paris.

Department of Manuscripts, Nat. Library, Paris 36-41; Lecturer in Modern Indian Languages, Ecole Nat. des Langues Orientales 37-39; temporary Lecturer, Ecole Pratique des Hautes Etudes 37-39, and 41; Dir. of Studies, Indian Philology 41-; Prof. Coll. de France 52-; Dir. Institut français d'Indologie, Pondicherry 55-, Ecole française d'Extrême-Orient, Paris 56-; mem. Académie des Inscriptions et Belles Lettres 66-; Sec. Société Asiatique de Paris.

Leisure interest: horseback riding.

Publs. *Etude de démonologie indienne, Le Kumaratantra de Ravana* 37, *Catalogue du fonds sanskrit de la Bibliothèque nationale* 41, *Magie et médecine* 43, *Fragments de textes koutchéens de médecine et de magie* 48, *La doctrine classique de la médecine indienne, ses origines et ses parallèles grecs* 49, *L'Inde classique, Manuel des Etudes indiennes* (in collaboration) 47-53, *Inde, nation et traditions* 61, *Les Philosophies de l'Inde* 70, *Un texte tamoul de dévotion Vishnouite, le Tiruppavai* 72, *Un texte de la religion kaumāra* 73, *Laghupravandhāh* 74.

35 rue François Rolland, 94130-Nogent-sur-Marne, France.

Finch, Robert Hutchison, LL.B., J.D.; American lawyer and government official; b. 9 Oct. 1925, Tempe, Arizona; *s.* of Robert L. and Gladys Hutchison Finch; *m.* Carol Crothers 1946; one *s.* three *d.*; ed. Occidental Coll. Calif. and Univ. of Southern Calif.

Served in U.S. Marine Corps 43-45 and during Korean War; has been senior partner in Inglewood law firm; fmr. instructor and trustee Palos Verdes Coll. and Marymount Coll., Calif.; Admin. Asst. to Vice-Pres. Nixon 58-60; Los Angeles District Attorney's Advisory Counsel 65; Lieut.-Gov. State of Calif. (Republican) 67-68; Sec. of Health, Educ. and Welfare Jan. 69-June 70; Counsellor to the Pres. 70-72; Partner, McKenna, Fitting & Finch 72-; fmrly. mem. Board of Regents, Univ. of Calif., Board of Trustees Calif. State Colls. and Occidental Coll.; mem. Statewide Cttee. of YMCA Youth and Govt. 67.

Publs. *The New Conservative Liberal Manifesto* (editor) 68.

McKenna, Fitting & Finch, 3435 Wilshire Boulevard, Los Angeles, Calif. 90010; Home: 1449 St. Albans Drive, San Marino, Calif. 91108, U.S.A.

Finch, William G. H.; American radio engineer; b. 28 June 1895; ed. Woodward High School, Cincinnati, Marconi Inst. N.Y., and Columbia Univ.

With Cleveland Illuminating Co. 16-17; Nat. District Telegraph Co. (N.Y.) 17-19 and Royal Indemnity Co. 19-21; Radio Engineering Editor *Int. News Service* 21-; established first radiotypewriter press circuit between New York and Chicago 32, between New York and Havana 33; Chief Radio Consulting Engineer and Technical Dir. Hearst Newspapers; Chief Engineering Sec. Amer. Radio News Corp. 29-34; Asst. Chief Fed. Communications Comm. 34-35; Founder and Pres. Finch Telecommunications Inc. 35-41; Chief Engineer 74th Congress Investigation Cttee.; served U.S. Navy 41-44 and 49, now Special Asst. Electronics to Asst. Chief Bureau of Shipping for Electronics; inventor automatic highspeed radio printing system, radio relay and recorder, and high fidelity transmission system;

holds 160 patents; mem. Int. Radio Consulting Cttee., Tech. Commission on radio and cable communications to Amer. Publishers Asscn. 24-; Fellow A.I.E.E., etc. Legion of Merit, Wisdom Award 71, etc.
Home: "Elfin", Newtown, Conn., U.S.A.

Fini, Leonor; Italian painter; b. 30 Aug. 1918, Buenos Aires, Argentina; d. of Erminio Fini and Malvina Braun; ed. Trieste.
Galérie Altmann-Carpentier, Paris; numerous one-man exhbns. in Paris, Rome, London, New York, retrospective exhbn. Knokke-le-Zoute, Belgium 65; created numerous décors for La Scala, Milan, Paris Opera, Comédie française, Compagnie Madeleine Renaud, Jean-Louis Barrault etc.; has participated in numerous group exhbns. including Venice Biennale and Salon de Mai, Paris; has illustrated numerous books; Dott. h.c. Free Univ. of Trieste.
8 rue de la Vrillière, Paris 1er, France.

Finland, Maxwell, M.D., D.SC.; American physician; b. 15 March 1902, Russia; s. of Frank and Rebecca (Povza) Finland; unmarried; ed. Boston public schools, Harvard Coll. and Harvard Medical School.
Postdoctoral hosp. training, Boston City Hosp. 26-29; fellowships in medicine, Harvard and Boston City Hosp. 28-38; Prof. of Medicine, Harvard 40-64, Prof. Emer. 64-; Dir. Thorndike Memorial Lab. 63-68; Harvard Medical Services, Boston City Hosp. 63-68; Epidemiologist, Boston City Hosp. 68-72, Hon. Physician 72-; Consultant, Veterans Admin. Hosp. 45-73, Distinguished Physician 73-; Charles V. Chaplin Award 60, Bristol Award 66, John Phillips Memorial Award 71, Oscar B. Hunter Award 71, Sheen Award, American Medical Asscn. 71.
Leisure interests: music, theatre-going.
Publs. more than 750 articles on infectious diseases, bacteriology, immunology and chemotherapy of infections.
Veterans Administration Hospital, 150 South Huntington Avenue, Boston, Mass. 02130; and Channington Laboratory, Boston City Hospital, Boston, Mass. 02118, U.S.A.

Finlay, Allan Martyn, PH.D., LL.M., Q.C.; New Zealand lawyer and politician; s. of David Finlay and Emma Matilda (Thomson) Finlay; m. Zelda May Crosby 1957; one s. two d.; ed. Otago Boys High School, Otago Univ., London School of Economics and Harvard Law School.
Research Asst., League of Nations 38; Private Sec. to various N.Z. Govt. Ministers 39-43; M.P. 46-49, 63-; Dir. Tasman Empire Airways Ltd. 58-61; Vice-Pres. N.Z. Labour Party 56-59, Pres. 60-64; Attorney-Gen., Minister of Justice, Civil Aviation and Meteorological Services 72-75; Minister in Charge of Publicity 74; Head of Del. to Int. Court of Justice to put case against atmospheric nuclear testing by France in the Pacific 73, 74; Queen's Counsel 73.
Leisure interests: music, tramping, argument.
Publs. *Third Party Contracts* 39, *Social Security in New Zealand* 40.
9 Central Terrace, Kelburn, Wellington, New Zealand. Telephone: 767-739.

Finletter, Thomas K(night), B.A., LL.B., LL.D.; American lawyer; b. 11 Nov. 1893, Philadelphia, Pa.; m. 1st Gretchen Damrosch 1920 (deceased), two d.; m. 2nd Eileen Wechsler Geist 1973, one s. one d.; ed. Episcopal Acad., Philadelphia, and Univ. of Pennsylvania.
Special Asst. to U.S. Sec. of State, Washington 41-44; Consultant U.S. del. to U.N. Conf. San Francisco 45; Chair. President's Air Policy Comm. 47; Min.-in-Charge Economic Co-operation Admin. Mission to U.K. 48-49; Sec. of the Air Force 50-53; partner, Coudert Bros. (lawyers), New York 26-41, 44-48, 49-50, 53-61, of counsel 65-70; U.S. Perm. Rep. to NATO 61-July 65.
Publs. *Principles of Corporate Reorganisation* 37, *Cases*

on Corporate Reorganisation 38, *Law of Bankruptcy Reorganisation* 39, *Can Representative Government do the Job?* 45, *Power and Policy* 54, *Foreign Policy: The Next Phase* 58, *Foreign Policy: The Next Phase, the 1960s* 61, *Interim Report* 68.
Leisure interests: work.
151 East 79 Street, New York City, U.S.A.

Finley, David Edward, A.B., LL.B.; American museum director (retired); b. 13 Sept. 1890, York, South Carolina; m. Margaret M. Eustis 1931; ed. Univ. of South Carolina and George Washington Law School.
U.S. Army 17-18; Asst. Counsel, War Finance Corpn. 21-22; mem. War Loan Staff, U.S. Treasury 22-27; Special Asst. to Sec. of Treasury 27-32; Dir. Nat. Gallery of Art 38-56; Vice-Chair. American Comm. for Protection and Salvage of Artistic and Historic Monuments in War Areas 43-46; Pres. American Asscn. of Museums 45-49; mem. The Comm. of Fine Arts 43-63, Chair. 50-63; Chair. Nat. Trust for Historic Preservation 49-62, Chair. Emeritus 62, Hon. Trustee 94-; Trustee, Corcoran Gallery of Art 57-; Chair. White House Historical Asscn. 61-73; mem. Smithsonian Art Comm.; mem. Nat. Portrait Gallery Comm. 63-; hon. mem. American Inst. of Architects; Theodore Roosevelt Distinguished Service Medal 57; Henry Medal, Smithsonian Inst. 67; Hon. D.Litt. (Univ. of South Carolina), Hon. LL.D. (George Washington Univ.), Hon. L.H.D. (Georgetown Univ.), Hon. D.F.A. (Yale).
Leisure interests: museums, gardening, reading.
Home: 3318 "O" Street, Washington, D.C. 20007, U.S.A.

Finley, James Danielly, B.S.; American textile executive; b. 14 July 1916, Jackson, Ga.; m. Nancy Butler 1941; three s.; ed. Georgia Inst. of Technology and Harvard Business School.
Military Service, Second World War; Textile Engineer, Firestone Tyre and Rubber Co.; joined J. P. Stevens and Co., Inc. 45, Dept. Man., Woollen and Worsted Div. 51-56, Asst. to Vice-Pres. for Sales and Merchandising, Cotton Div. 56-58, Vice-Pres. (of Company) 58-61, Vice-Pres. in Charge of Cotton Div. Sales and Merchandising 61, mem. Exec. Cttee. 59, Exec. Vice-Pres. and mem. Mfg. Advisory Cttee. 64-65, Chair. of the Board July 65-; Chief Exec. Officer 69-.
Office: J. P. Stevens and Co., Inc., 1185 Avenue of the Americas, New York, N.Y. 10036; Home: 12 Blossom Cove Road, Red Bank, N.J., U.S.A.

Finney, Albert; British actor; b. 9 May 1936; m. Anouk Aimée 1970; ed. Salford Grammar School and Royal Academy of Dramatic Art.
Birmingham Repertory Co. 56-58; Shakespeare Memorial Theatre Co. 59; Nat. Theatre 65, 75; formed Memorial Enterprises 66.
Plays acted in include: *Julius Caesar, Macbeth, Henry V, The Beaux Stratagem, The Alchemist, The Lizard on the Rock, The Party, King Lear, Othello, A Midsummer Night's Dream, The Lily-White Boys, Billy Liar, Luther, Much Ado About Nothing, Armstrong's Last Goodnight, Miss Julie, Black Comedy, Love for Love, A Flea in her Ear, A Day in the Death of Joe Egg, Alpha Beta, Krapp's Last Tape, Cromwell, Chez Nous, Hamlet, Tamburlaine;* Dir. *Loot* 75.
Films acted in include: *The Entertainer, Saturday Night and Sunday Morning, Tom Jones, Night Must Fall, Two for the Road, Scrooge, Gumshoe* 71, *Murder on the Orient Express* 74; Directed and acted in *Charlie Bubbles.*
Memorial Enterprises Ltd., Aspen House, 25 Dover Street, London, W.1, England.
Telephone: 01-491-7621.

Finney, David John, M.A., SC.D., F.R.S., F.R.S.E.; British professor of statistics; b. 3 Jan. 1917, Latchford, Warrington; s. of Robert George Stringer Finney and

Bessie Evelyn Finney (née Whitlow); *m.* Mary Elizabeth Connolly 1950; one *s.* two *d.*; ed. Univs. of Cambridge and London.
Statistician, Rothamsted Experimental Station 39-45; Lecturer in the Design and Analysis of Scientific Experiment, Univ. of Oxford 45-54; Reader in Statistics, Univ. of Aberdeen 54-64; Prof. of Statistics, Univ. of Aberdeen 64-66; Prof. of Statistics, Univ. of Edinburgh 66-; Dir. Agricultural Research Council's Unit of Statistics 54-; Chair. Computer Board for Univs. 70-74; Pres. Royal Statistical Soc. 73-74; Hon. D. ès Sciences agronomiques (Gembloux).
Publs. *Probit Analysis* 47, 52, 71, *Biological Standardization* (with J. H. Burn and L. G. Goodwin) 50, *Statistical Method in Biological Assay* 52, 64, *Introduction to Statistical Science in Agriculture* 53, 62, 72, *Experimental Design and its Statistical Basis* 55, *Técnica y Teoría en el Diseño de Experimentos* 57, *Introduction to the Theory of Experimental Design* 60, *Statistics for Mathematicians* 68; about 170 papers.
Department of Statistics, The University, Edinburgh; Home: 43 Cluny Drive, Edinburgh EH10 6DU, Scotland.
Telephone: 031-667-1011 (Univ.); 031-447-2332.

Finniss, Guillaume Max, D.C.L.; French civil servant; b. 4 Oct. 1909, Lille; *s.* of Robert Finniss and Elisabeth Finniss (née Lenfant); *m.* Huguette Bichon 1935; one *d.*; ed. Lycée Buffon, and Faculté de Droit, Paris, Ecole des Hautes Etudes Commerciales.
Inspector of Industry and Commerce 47; Technical Adviser to Sec. of State for Commerce 48-49; Dir. Inst. of Industrial Property 50-65; Insp.-Gen. of Industry 53; Pres. Cttee. of Co-ordination for the harmonization of legislative procedures in Industrial Property in the countries of European Econ. Community 59-; Pres., Dir.-Gen. Int. Patent Inst. 65-; Pres. Cttee. Council of Europe 60-; Officier de la Légion d'Honneur, Commdr. de l'Ordre du Mérite, Chevalier de l'Ordre de Malte; numerous other honours and decorations from France and elsewhere.
Leisure interest: applied arts.
2 Patentlaan, Rijswijk (Z.H.), Netherlands; 40 boulevard des Invalides, Paris 7e, France.

Finniston, Sir (Harold) Montague, Kt., PH.D., B.SC., F.R.S., F.R.S.A.; British metallurgist; b. 15 Aug. 1912, Glasgow, Scotland; *s.* of Robert Finniston and Esther (née Diamond) Finniston; *m.* Miriam Singer 1936; one *s.* one *d.*; ed. Allen Glen's School, Glasgow, Glasgow Univ. and Royal Coll. of Science and Technology, Glasgow.
Joined Stewarts & Lloyds 34; Chief Research Officer, Scottish Coke Research Cttee. 37; metallurgist, Atomic Energy of Canada, Chalk River 45-46; U.K. Atomic Energy Authority, Harwell 48-58; Research Dir. C. A. Parsons & Co. and Man. Dir. Int. Research and Devt. Co. Ltd., 59-67; Deputy Chair. British Steel Corpn. 67-73, Chief Exec. 71-73, Chair. 73-76; Gen. Sec. British Assen. for Advancement of Science 70-73; mem. Board Nat. Research Devt. Corpn. 63-73; Chair. Int. Research Devt. Co. Ltd. 68-, Political and Econ. Planning 74-; Redpath, Dorman, Long 72-74; Pres. Metals Soc. 74-75; Vice-Pres. Royal Soc.; Vice-Pres. Iron and Steel Inst.; Vice-Pres. ASLIB 74-; Assoc. of Royal Coll. of Science and Technology; mem. Nat. Econ. Devt. Council 74-; Fellow, Inst. of Metallurgists, Pres. 75-76; Fellow, Inst. of Physics; Hon. mem. American Iron and Steel Inst., Indian Inst. of Metals; Hon. D.Sc. (Strathclyde) 68; D.Univ. (Surrey) 69; Hon. D.Sc. (Birmingham) 71, (City Univ., London) 74; Bessember Medal, Tawara Gold Medal 75, A. A. Griffiths Silver Medal 76, Eichner Medal 76, Glazebrook Medal 76.
Leisure interests: walking, reading, spectator sports.
British Steel Corporation, 33 Grosvenor Place, London. S.W.1; Home: Flat 72, 33 Prince Albert Road, St. John's Wood, London, N.W.8. England.
Telephone: 01-235-1212 (Office).

Firestone, Leonard Kimball, B.A.; American business executive and diplomatist; b. 10 June 1907, Akron, O.; *s.* of Harvey S. Firestone, Sr.; *m.* 1st Polly Curtis (deceased), 2nd Barbara K. Heatley 1966; two *s.* one *d.*; ed. Hill School, Pottstown, Pa., Princeton Univ.
Sales Dept., Firestone Tire & Rubber Co. 31-41, Vice-Pres. 32-35, Sales Man., Akron 35-39, Dir. 39-73; Pres. Firestone Aviation Products Co. 41-43; Lt. U.S. Navy 41-43; Pres., Gen. Man. Firestone Tire & Rubber Co. of Calif. 43-70; Amb. to Belgium June 73-; Dir. Nat. Council on Alcoholism Inc.; mem. Nat. Board of Assocs., Smithsonian Inst.; Hon. Chair. Deafness Research Foundation; Past Pres. World Affairs Council; mem., Past Chair. Board of Trustees, Univ. of S. Calif.; Hon. LL.D. (Univ. of S. Calif.) 65, (Pepperdine Univ.) 71, Hon. D.Hum. (Okla. Christian Coll.) 70; Grand Band, Order of the Star of Africa 69.
American Embassy, 27 boulevard du Regent, 1000 Brussels, Belgium; and 515 South Flower Street, Suite 4470, Los Angeles, Calif. 90071, U.S.A.
Telephone: 513-38-30 (Embassy); (213) 680-28-85·

Firestone, Raymond Christy, B.A.; American businessman; b. 6 Sept. 1908, Akron, Ohio; *s.* of Harvey S. Firestone and Idabelle Smith; *m.* 1st Laura Lisk 1935 (deceased 1960), 2nd Jane Allen Messler 1962; two *d.*; ed. Princeton Univ.
Joined Sales Div., The Firestone Tire and Rubber Co. 33; Gen. Man., Memphis, Tenn. plant 36-37; Pres. Firestone Tire and Rubber Co. of Tennessee 37-49; Dir. The Firestone Tire and Rubber Co. 42-, Vice-Pres. (Research and Development) 49-54, Exec. Vice-Pres. 54-57, Pres. 57-64, Chair. Exec. Cttee. and Chief Exec. Officer 64-66, Chair. of the Board 66-, Chief Exec. Officer 66-73; Dir. The Firestone Bank; Vice-Pres. Board of Dirs. Nat. 4-H Service Cttee. 58-; mem. numerous civic and business orgs. and recipient of several awards including: Hon. LL.D. (Akron), Hon. D. Hum. Univ. of Liberia).
Leisure interests: foxhunting, golf.
Office: The Firestone Tire and Rubber Co., 1200 Firestone Parkway, Akron, Ohio 44317; Home: Lauray Farms, Bath, Ohio 44210, U.S.A.

Firkušný, Rudolf; American pianist; b. 11 Feb. 1912; Napajedla, Czechoslovakia; *m.* Tatiana Nevolova 1965; one *s.* one *d.*; ed. Conservatoires of Music, Brno and Prague.
First appeared with Czechoslovak Philharmonic Orchestra 22; world-wide concert tours including tours of Europe 30-39, South America 43-, annual tours of Europe and U.S.A. since 43, tours of Australia, New Zealand 59, 67.
Staatsburg, New York 12580, U.S.A.

Firnberg, Hertha, DR. PHIL.; Austrian politician; b. 18 Sept. 1909, Vienna; *d.* of Dr. Josef and Anna Firnberg; *m.* 1932; ed. Univs. of Vienna and Freiburg i. Br.
Employed by Prokura (publishers) 41-45; Asst. Inst. for Econ. and Cultural History, Univ. of Vienna 46; Head of Statistical Dept., Chamber for Blue and White-Collar Workers, Lower Austria 48-69; mem. Bundesrat 59, Nationalrat 63; Chair. Socialist Party's Fed. Women's Cttee. 56-; Deputy to Chair. Fed. Socialist Party 66-; Minister without Portfolio April 70; Minister for Science and Research July 70-; Körner-preis; Förderungspreis der Stadt Wien.
Leisure interests: reading, swimming, walking.
Publs. various sociological studies.
1100 Vienna, Altdorferstrasse 5, Austria.

Firth, Sir Raymond William, Kt., M.A., PH.D., F.B.A.; British social anthropologist; b. 25 March 1901, Auckland, N.Z.; *s.* of Wesley Hugh Bourne Firth and Marie Elizabeth Jane Firth (née Cartmill); *m.* Rosemary

Upcott 1936; one *s.*; ed. Auckland Univ. Coll. and **London School of Economics.**
Field Research in Anthropology, Tikopia, British Solomon Islands Protectorate 28-29; Lecturer in Anthropology Univ. of Sydney 30-31, Acting Prof. 31-32; Lecturer in Anthropology London School of Econs. 32-35, Reader 35-44, Prof. 44-68; Emer. Prof. Univ. of London 68-; Prof. Pacific Anthropology, Hawaii Univ. 68-69; Visiting Prof. Univ. of B.C. 69, Cornell Univ. 70, Univ. of Chicago 70-71, Graduate Center City Univ. of N.Y. 71-72; Hon. Sec. Royal Anthropological Inst. 36-39, Pres. 53-55; research in peasant econs. and anthropology in Malaya as Leverhulme Research Fellow 39-40; served with Naval Intelligence Div. Admiralty 41-44; Sec. of Colonial Social Science Research Council Colonial Office 44-45; research surveys in West Africa 45, Malaya 47, New Guinea 51; field research in Tikopia 52, 66; Visiting Prof. Univ. of Chicago 55; Fellow Center for Advanced Study in the Behavioral Sciences, Stanford, Calif. 59; Foreign Hon. mem. American Acad. of Arts and Sciences, American Philosophical Soc., Royal Soc. of New South Wales, Royal Soc. of New Zealand, Royal Danish Acad. of Sciences and Letters; Viking Fund Medal 59; Huxley Memorial Medal 59; Hon. Ph.D. (Oslo) 65, Hon. LL.D. (Michigan) 67, Hon. D.Litt. (East Anglia) 68, (Australian Nat. Univ.) 69, (Exeter) 72, Hon. D.Hum. Letters (Chicago) 68, Hon. D.Sc. (British Columbia) 70.
Leisure interests: Romanesque art, 15th-18th century music.
Publs. *The Kauri Gum Industry* 24, *Primitive Economics of the New Zealand Maori* 29, *Art and Life in New Guinea* 36, *We, The Tikopia: A Sociological Study of Kinship in Primitive Polynesia* 36, *Human Types* 38, *Primitive Polynesian Economy* 39, *The Work of the Gods in Tikopia* 40, *Malay Fishermen: Their Peasant Economy* 46, *Elements of Social Organization* 51; Ed. *Two Studies of Kinship in London* 56, Ed. *Man and Culture: An Evaluation of the Work of Malinowski* 57, *Social Change in Tikopia* 59, *History and Traditions of Tikopia* 61, *Essays on Social Organisation and Values* 64, Ed. *Themes in Economic Anthropology* 67, *Tikopia Ritual and Belief* 67, *Rank and Religion in Tikopia* 70, *Families and their Relatives* (with Jane Hubert and Anthony Forge) 70, *Symbols Public and Private* 73.
33 Southwood Avenue, London, N.6, England.
Telephone: 01-348-0768.

Firyubin, Nikolai Pavlovich; Soviet diplomatist; b. 4 April 1908, Ulyanovsk; ed. Ordzhonikidze Aviation Inst., Moscow.
Member C.P.S.U. 29-; engineer, aircraft industry 35-38; party and Soviet work 38-53; Sec. Moscow Regional Cttee. C.P.S.U. 40-49; Diplomatic Service 53-, Minister-Counsellor, U.S.S.R. Embassy, Czechoslovakia 53, Amb. 54-55, to Yugoslavia 55-57; Deputy Minister of Foreign Affairs U.S.S.R. 57-; Cand. mem. Central Cttee. C.P.S.U. 55-66; Orders of Lenin, Red Banner of Labour, Great Patriotic War (1st Class), Red Star, etc.
Ministry of Foreign Affairs, 32-34 Smolenskaya-Sennaya ploshchad, Moscow, U.S.S.R.

Fischer, Annie; Hungarian pianist; b. 1914; widow of Aladár Toth; ed. Budapest Acad. of Music.
Studies with Arnold Székely and Ernő von Dohnányi; concert debut in Beethoven's C Major Concerto 22; numerous concerts, tours and recordings 26-; 1st Prize, Int. Liszt Competition, Budapest 33; Kossuth Prizes 49, 55 and 65; Hon. Prof. of Acad. of Music, Budapest 65; decorated Eminent Artist; Red Banner Order of Labour 74.
Szent Istvan Park 14, H-1137 Budapest XIII, Hungary.

Fischer, Ernst Otto, DR.RER.NAT., DIPL.CHEM.; German professor of chemistry; b. 10 Nov. 1918, Müchen-Solln; *s.* of late Dr. Karl Tobias Fischer and Valentine Danzer; ed. Theresiengymnasium and Technische Hochschule, Munich.
Lecturer in Chemistry, Technische Hochschule 54-57; Prof. of Inorganic Chemistry, Munich Univ. 57-64, Technische Hochschule (now Technische Univ.) 64-; Univ. of Jena 59, Univ. of Marburg 60; Firestone Lecturer Univ. of Wisconsin 69; Visiting Prof. Univ. of Florida 71; Inorganic Chemistry Pacific West Coast Lecturer U.S.A., Canada 71; Arthur D. Little Visiting Prof. Mass. Inst. of Technology 73; Visiting Distinguished Lecturer Univ. of Rochester 73; mem. Bayerische Akad. der Wissenschaften 64, Deutsche Akad. der Naturforscher Leopoldina 69; Hon.Dr.rer.nat. (Munich Univ.) 72, Hon. D.Sc. (Strathclyde) 75; Göttinger Acad. Prize for Chemistry 57, Alfred-Stock-Gedächtnis Prize 59, Nobel Prize for Chemistry 73.
Leisure interests: history, arts, mountaineering.
Publs. 370 scientific publs., $Fe(C_5H_5)_2$ Structure 52, $Cr(C_6H_6)_2$ 55, *Metal-Complexes Vol. I* (with H. Werner) 66, *Übergangsmetall-Carbin-Komplexe* 73.
Sohnckestrasse 16, 8 Munich 71, Federal Republic of Germany.
Telephone: 794623.

Fischer, Gottfried Bermann, DR.MED., DR.PHIL. h.c.; American publisher; b. 31 July 1897, Gleiwitz, Silesia; *m.* Brigitte Fischer 1926; three *d.*; ed. Univs. of Breslau, Freiburg and Munich.
Assistant Surgeon in Berlin hospital 23-25; with S. Fischer Verlag 25-, Owner and Pres. 34, firm moved to Vienna 36, to Stockholm 38; emigrated to U.S.A. 40, founded L. B. Fischer Corpn., New York (now S. Fischer Corpn.); re-established S. Fischer Verlag in Frankfurt/Main 50, later Chair. of Board S. Fischer Verlag G.m.b.H., retd. 72; founded Fischer Bücherei, Frankfurt (paperback publishers) 52; Editor *Neue Rundschau* (literary periodical); Goethe Plakette (Frankfurt) 57, Grosses Bundesverdienstkreuz 58.
Leisure interests: sculpturing, tennis.
Publs. Autobiography *Bedroht-Bewahrt*, Fischer Verlag 67; *Correspondence with Thomas Mann 1932-1955.*
Casa Fischer, 1-55041 Camaiore (Lucca), Italy; 6 Daffodil Lane, Cos Cob, Conn.; P.O. Box 237, Old Greenwich, Conn. 06807, U.S.A.
Telephone: Camaiore 0584 689088 (Italy); 203-661-5226 (U.S.A.).

Fischer, Hanns, DR.RER.NAT.; German professor of chemistry; b. 21 July 1935, Darmstadt, Fed. Germany; *s.* of Karl Fischer and Irma (née Schrauth); *m.* Irmelin Walter 1964; one *s.* one *d.*; ed. Tech. High School, Darmstadt, Univ. of Munich.
Lecturer, Tech. High School, Darmstadt 66; Deputy Head of Dept., Kunststoff-Institut, Darmstadt 66; Prof. Extraordinary, Univ. of Zurich 69, Prof. of Physical Chem. 71-; J. S. Stas Medal 71, Centenary Lectureship 74.
Leisure interests: recorder playing, walking on mountains.
Publs. *Magnetic Properties of Free Radicals* 65, about 100 articles on free radicals, structure and reaction kinetics 59-75.
Physikalisch-Chemisches Institut, Rämistrasse 76, CH-8001, Zürich; Talstrasse 18, CH-8125 Zollikerberg, Switzerland.
Telephone: 01/32-62-41 (Office); 01/63-93-83 (Home).

Fischer, John; American editor; b. 27 April 1910, Texhoma, Okla.; *s.* of John and Georgia Caperton Fischer; *m.* Elizabeth Wilson 1935; two *d.*; ed. Oklahoma Univ. and Oxford Univ.
Reporter, *Daily Oklahoma* 32-33; U.S. Dept. of Agriculture 36; Washington Corresp. for Associated Press 37; Board of Econ. Warfare, Intelligence Div. 39; **Chief of Econ. Intelligence, Lend-Lease for Foreign Econ. Admin., India 43;** Assoc. Editor, *Harper's Magazine* 44-47, Editor-in-Chief Gen. Book Dept.

Harper's 46; Editor-in-Chief *Harper's Magazine* 53-67, Contrib. Editor July 67-, mem. Board of Trustees Brookings Inst. and Nat. Educational Television Network; Visiting Fellow Yale Univ.; mem. Comm. on Environmental Policy for State of Connecticut; mem. Exec. Cttee., American Soc. of Magazine Editors; Dr. h.c. Kenyon Coll. 53, Massachusetts Univ. 50, Bucknell Univ. 59.
Leisure interests: sailing, gardening.
Publs. *Why they Behave like Russians* (English title *Scared Men in the Kremlin*) 47, *Master Plan U.S.A.* 51, *The Stupidity Problem* 64, *Six in the Easy Chair* 74, *Vital Signs, U.S.A.* 75.
c/o Harper's Magazine, 2 Park Avenue, New York, N.Y. 10016, U.S.A.

Fischer, Josef; German business executive; b. 11 July 1912, Oberhausen, Rheinland: s. of Johann J. and Karoline Fischer; m. Martha Kückelhaus 1932; four s. three d.; ed. Demag AK, Duisberg.
Hauptrevision Vereinigte Stahlwerke until 54; Dir. of Finance, Deutsche Kohlenbergbau-Leitung 46; mem. Exec. Board Altenessener Bergwerks AG 52, Harpener Bergbau AG 57, Hoesch AG 65, Estel NV 72; Deputy Chair. Estel NV Hoesch-Hoogovens 73-; Chair. of Board Hoesch AG, Hoesch Werke AG 73-; mem. supervisory boards of various other cos.
Leisure interests: golf, swimming, walking, books, music.
Estel NV Hoesch-Hoogovens, Nijmegen, Netherlands; Home: 4307 Kettwig/Ruhr, Am Stammensberg 38, Federal Republic of Germany.
Telephone: 02144-4720 (Home).

Fischer, Paul; Danish diplomatist; b. 24 March 1919, Copenhagen; s. of Ernst Fischer and Ellen Dahl; m. Jytte Kalckar 1945; one s.; ed. Lyceum Alpinum, Zuoz, Switzerland and Univ. of Copenhagen.
Foreign Service 44-, Stockholm, The Hague, Ministry of Foreign Affairs 44-60; Ambassador to Poland 60-61; Perm. Under-Sec. of State for Foreign Affairs 61-71; Amb. to France 71-; Commdr. Order of Dannebrog (1st Class).
Embassy of Denmark, avenue Marceau 77, Paris 16e, France.

Fischer, Robert James (Bobby); American chess player; b. 9 March 1943, Chicago.
Started to play chess aged 6; mem. Manhattan Chess Club 55; U.S. Junior Chess Champion 56, 57; winner, U.S. Open Championship 57, 59, 60, 62, 63; participated in Interzonal Tournament, Portoroz, Yugoslavia 58; named International Grand Master (the youngest ever) 58; has participated in numerous int. chess tournaments 58-; defeated Boris Spassky (*q.v.*) to become World Chess Champion 72-75; City of New York Gold Medal 72.
Publ. *Games of Chess* 59.
560 Lincoln Plaza, Brooklyn, N.Y., U.S.A.

Fischer-Dieskau, Dietrich; German baritone; b. 28 May 1925, Berlin; s. of Dr. Albert Fischer-Dieskau and Dora Klingelhöffer; m. 1st Cellistin Irmgard Poppen 1949 (died 1963), 2nd Ruth Leuwerik 1965 (divorced 1967), 3rd Kristina Pugell 1968; three s. by first marriage; ed. high school in Berlin, singing studies with Prof. Georg Walter and Prof. Hermann Weissenborn.
Military service 43-45; prisoner of war in Italy until 47; First Lyric and Character Baritone, Berlin State Opera 48-; mem. Vienna State Opera Co. 57-; numerous concert tours in Europe, U.S.A. and Asia; has appeared at a number of festivals: Bayreuth, Salzburg, Lucerne, Montreux, Edinburgh, Vienna, Holland, Munich, Berlin, Coventry, etc.; best-known roles in *Falstaff, Don Giovanni, Le nozze de Figaro*, etc.; first performances of contemporary composers Britten, Henze, Tippett, etc.; mem. Akad. der Künste, Int. Mahler-Gesellschaft

(Vienna) and German Section, Int. Music Council, Hon. mem. Wiener Konzerthausgesellschaft 63, Royal Acad. of Music (London), Royal Acad. (Stockholm;) Int. Recording Prizes 55, 57, 58, 60, 63, 64, 65, 67, 69, 70; Berlin Kunstpreis 50, Mantua Golden Orpheus Prize 55; Bundesverdienstkreuz, 1st Class 58; Edison Prize 60, 62, 64, 65, 67, 70; Mozart Medal 62; Golden Orpheus 67; Grosses Verdienstkreuz des Verdienstordens der Bundesrepublik Deutschland 74.
Leisure interest: painting.
Publs. *Texte Deutscher Lieder, Auf den Spuren der Schubert-Lieder, Wagner und Nietzsche, der Mystagoge und sein Abtrünniger* 74.
Lindenallee 22, 1 Berlin 19, Germany.

Fishbein, Morris, M.D., B.S.; American physician; b. 22 July 1889, St. Louis, Mo.; s. of Benjamin Fishbein and Fannie (Glück) Fishbein; m. Anna Mantel 1914; two s. (one deceased) two d.; ed. Univ. of Chicago and Rush Medical Coll.
House Physician Durand Hospital of McCormick Inst. for Infectious Diseases 12-13; Asst. Editor *Journal of American Medical Assцn.* 13-24, Editor 24-49; Prof. Emeritus, School of Medicine, Univ. of Chicago; Prof. Emeritus, Medical Coll., Univ. of Illinois; Consultant Medical Editor, Doubleday & Co., New York City; Medical Editor *Britannica Book of the Year* 38-72; Editor *Medical World News* 60-74, *Excerpta Medica* 49-71; Consulting Editor *Postgraduate Medicine* 50-70, *Family Health* 69-; Fellow, American Medical Assцn., etc.
Leisure interests: reading, bridge, music, travel.
Publs. *Medical Writing: Its Art and Technic, Tonics and Sedatives, Handbook of Therapy, Your Weight and How to Control it, Why Men Fail* (with Dr. William A. White), *The Medical Follies, The New Medical Follies, Shattering Health Superstitions, The Human Body and its Care, An Hour on Health, Doctors and Specialists, Fads and Quackery in Healing, Modern Home Medical Adviser, Syphilis, Your Diet and Your Health, Do You Want to Become a Doctor? The National Nutrition, First Aid Training* (co-author), *Successful Marriage, Medical Uses of Soap, Doctors at War, Health and First Aid* (co-author), *Common Ailments of Man, Popular Medical Encyclopaedia, A History of the American Medical Association, Handy Home Medical Adviser, Crusading Obstetrician* (with S. T. DeLee), *Medical Progress, Children for the Childless, New Advances in Medicine, Illustrated Medical and Health Encyclopaedia, Modern Marriage and Family Living, Modern Family Health Guide, Heart Care, Morris Fishbein, M.D.: An Autobiography, Ask the Doctor.*
5454 South Shore, Chicago Ill. 60615, U.S.A.

Fisher, Adrian Sanford; American government official; b. 21 Jan. 1914; ed. Univs. of Princeton and Harvard.
U.S. Army service 42-46; Law Secretary to Associate Justices of U.S. Supreme Court 38-39; Attorney, Bonneville Power Admin. 39, Securities and Exchange Comm. 39-40, Tennessee Valley Authority 40-41; Asst. to Legal Adviser Dept. of State 41, Asst. Chief, Foreign Funds Control Div. 41-42; Solicitor, Dept. of Commerce 46-48; Gen. Counsel, Atomic Energy Comm. 48-49; Legal Adviser, Dept. of State 49-53; private legal practice 53-54; Prof. of Int. Law and Trade, Georgetown Univ. 53-58, Dean 69-; mem. U.S. Panel on Perm. Court of Arbitration 53-59; Vice-Pres. and Counsel, The Washington Post Co. 55-61; Deputy Dir. U.S. Arms Control and Disarmament Agency 61-69.
600 New Jersey Avenue, N.W., Washington, D.C. 20001; Home: 2721 N Street, N.W., Washington, D.C. 20007, U.S.A.

Fisher, Ernest M(cKinley), A.M., PH.D., LL.D.; American economist; b. 15 May 1893, Macedonia, Ill.; s. of Marshall Duff and Ada C. (Vise) Fisher; m. Ethel Moore 1922; one s.; ed. McKendree Coll., Coe Coll. and Northwestern and Wisconsin Univs.

Instructor American Univ. Beirut 14-17, Wisconsin Univ. 19-22; Dir. of Research Nat. Asscn. of Real Estate Boards 23-26; Prof. of real estate management, Univ. of Michigan 26-34; economic adviser Federal Housing Admin. 34-40; Chair. Housing Census Advisory Cttee., Bureau of the Census 39-42, 59-63, 65-71; dir. of mortgage and real estate finance and dep. man. American Bankers Asscn. 40-45; Prof. of Urban Land Econs., Columbia Univ. 45-61, Emer. 61-; Special Lecturer, School of Architecture 61-64; Special Lecturer in Planning, Yale Univ. 62; Chair. Admin. Board and Dir. of the Institute for Urban Land Use and Housing Studies, Columbia Univ. 47-55; Consultant Board of Govs. Fed. Reserve System 50-53; Dir. First Fed. Savings and Loan Asscn. of New York 54-68; Consultant to Ford Foundation 61, 64-, and to Fed. Deposit Insurance Corpn. 65-66; Consultant to Worcester County Inst. for Savings 55-68, to Small Business Admin. 66-71, to First Nat. Mortgage Bank Ltd., Nassau 66-67; mem. American Econ. Asscn.; Fellow American Statistical Asscn.; one-time Fellow American Geographical Soc. and American Asscn. for the Advancement of Science; Cert. for distinguished service, Bureau of Census 69.
Leisure interests: gardening, photography, folk music, carpentry, travel.
Publs. *Advanced Principles of Real Estate Practice* 30; *European Housing Policy and Practice* (with Richard U. Ratcliff) 36, *Urban Real Estate Markets: Characteristics and Financing* 51, *Urban Real Estate* (with Robert Moore Fisher) 54, *The Mutual Mortgage Insurance Fund* (with Chester Rapkin) 56, *U.S. Housing and Congressional Goals* 75, *Urban Housing Market Performance in America 1870-1970* (with C. J. Stokes) 75; Editor *Home Mortgage Lending, Home Mortgage Loan Manual*, etc.
199 Hillcrest Avenue, Leonia, N.J. 07605, U.S.A., Telephone: 201-944-3302.

Fisher, Max Henry; British journalist; b. 30 May 1922, Berlin; *s.* of Friedrich Fischer and Sophia Baks; *m.* Rosemary Margaret Maxwell 1952; two *s.* one *d.*; ed. Rendcomb Coll. and Lincoln Coll., Oxford.
Army service 42-46; German War Documents Project, Foreign Office Library 49-56; Visiting Lecturer, Melbourne Univ. 56; *Financial Times*, successively Diplomatic Corresp., Foreign Editor, Asst. Editor, Deputy Editor 57-73; Editor, *Financial Times* 73-.
Leisure interests: music, history, playing bad golf.
Publs. With Prof. N. Rich, ed. *The Holstein Papers* (4 vols.).
16 Somerset Square, Addison Road, London W.14, England.

Fisher, William Bayne, B.A., DR. DE L'UNIV. (Paris); British university professor; b. 24 Sept. 1916, Darwen, Lancs.; ed. Univs. of Manchester, Louvain, Caen and Paris.
Research Fellow 37-40; served in Royal Air Force 40-46, commissioned 41, O.C. R.A.F. Liaison Unit, Syria and Lebanon 44-45; Lecturer, Univ. of Manchester 46; Lecturer, Dept. of Geography, Aberdeen Univ. 47-53; Reader and Head of Dept. of Geography, Univ. of Durham 54-56, Prof. 56-; Dir. Centre of Middle Eastern and Islamic Studies 62-65; Principal, Graduate Soc. 65-; Consultant, H.M. Govt., Govt. of Libya and Harvard Univ., U.S.A.; Leader Univ. Expedition to Libya 51; Murchison Award Royal Geographical Soc. 73.
Leisure interests: travel, music, geographical gastronomy.
Publs. *The Middle East—a Physical, Social and Regional Geography* 50 (5th edn. 71), *Spain* (with H. Bowen-Jones) 58, *Malta* (with H. Bowen-Jones and J. C. Dewdney), Editor Vol. I *The Cambridge History of Iran* (land and people) 68, *Populations of the Middle East and North Africa* (with J. I. Clarke) 72.

Home: 42 South Street, Durham, DH1 4QP; Office: Department of Geography, South Road, Durham, DH1 3LE, and 38 Old Elvet, Durham, DH1 3JD, England.
Telephone: 64291 (Home); 64971 and 64466 (Office).

Fisk, James Brown, B.S., PH.D.; American physicist; b. 30 Aug. 1910, West Warwick, R.I.; *s.* of Henry James Fisk and Bertha Brown; *m.* Cynthia Hoar 1938; three *s.*; ed. Mass. Inst. of Technology and Trinity Coll. Cambridge.
Junior Fellow of Soc. of Fellows, Harvard Univ. 36-38; Assoc. Prof. of Physics, Univ. of N. Carolina 38-39; electronics research engineer and later Asst. Dir. Physical Research, Bell Telephone Laboratories 39-47; Dir. other cos.; Gordon McKay Prof. of Applied Physics, Harvard Univ. (resigned 49), Dir. Physical Research 49-52, Dir. of Research, Physical Sciences 52-54, Vice-Pres. Research 54-55, Exec. Vice-Pres. 55-59, Pres. 59-73, Chair of Board 73-74, Bell Telephone Laboratories, Dir. 55-74; Fellow, Amer. Acad. of Arts and Sciences; mem. American Philosophical Soc.; mem. Nat. Acad. of Sciences; Fellow, American Physical Soc.; Fellow, Inst. of Electrical and Electronics Engineers; Dir. of Research Div., U.S. Atomic Energy Comm. (resigned 48); mem. Pres. Science Advisory Cttee. 52-60, Consultant 60-73; mem. Gen. Advisory Cttee. to U.S. Atomic Energy Comm. 52-58; Dir. Neptune Int. Co., Gen. Amer. Investors, Sloan-Kettering Inst. for Cancer Research, The Equitable Life Assurance Soc. of the U.S., Amer. Cyanamid Co., Amer. Nat. Bank & Trust Co. Ltd.; Hon. Sc.D. (Carnegie Inst. of Technology) 56, (Williams Coll.) 58, (Newark Coll. of Eng.) 56,; Hon. M.A. (Harvard Univ.) 47; Hon. Sc.D. (Columbia Univ.) 60, (Colby Coll.) 62, (New York Univ.) 63, (Rutgers State Univ.) 67, Hon. LL.D. (Fairleigh-Dickinson) 73, (Drew Univ. 68; Hon. LL.D. (Lehigh Univ.) 68, (Ill. Inst. of Technology) 68; Hon. Dr. of Engineering (Univ. of Michigan) 63, (Univ. of Akron 63); Hon. D.Litt. (Newark State Coll.) 69; Hon. D.Sci. (Harvard Univ.) 69; Life mem. Mass. Inst. of Technology Corpn.; mem. Board of Overseers of Harvard Coll. 61-67, Nat. Acad. Eng.; Trustee, John Simon Guggenheim Memorial Foundation, Alfred P. Sloan Foundation; Dir. Cummins Engine Co., Corning Glass Works.
Leisure interests: mountain climbing, gardening, golf.
Publs. Articles in *Proceedings of Royal Society* 33-34, *Physical Review* 34-40, *Bell System Technical Journal* 46.
Lees Hill Road, Basking Ridge, N.J., U.S.A.; Office: Bell Telephone Laboratories, Inc., Murray Hill, New Jersey 07974, U.S.A.
Telephone: 201-582-4471.

Fistoulari, Anatole; British conductor; b. 20 Aug. 1907; ed. Kiev, Berlin and Paris.
First Symphony Concert, Kiev 14, later conducted all over Russia; concerts in Western Europe 20; conducted Grand Opera Russe, Paris, with Chaliapin 31; conducted Ballet de Monte Carlo with Massine in England, France, Italy and U.S.A.; first symphony concert with London Symphony Orchestra 42, Principal Conductor, London Philharmonic Orchestra 43-44; Founder and Principal Conductor of London International Orchestra 46-; numerous engagements in Europe, Israel, South Africa and the Americas; numerous recordings.
65 Redington Road, London, N.W.3, England.

Fitch, Val Logsdon, B.ENG., PH.D.; American physicist; b. 10 March 1923, U.S.A.; *s.* of Fred B. Fitch and Frances M. Logsdon Fitch; *m.* Elise Cunningham 1949 (deceased 1972); two *s.*; ed. McGill and Columbia Univs.
United States Army 43-46; Instructor, Columbia Univ. 53-54, Princeton Univ. 54, rising to Prof., Princeton Univ. 60-; Sloan Fellow 60-64; mem. Nat. Acad. of Sciences, American Acad. of Arts and Sciences, President's Science Advisory Cttee. 70-73; Research

Corpn. Award 68; Ernest Orlando Laurence Award 68. Leisure interest: conservation.
Publs. Major publs. in area of Meson Physics.
Joseph Henry Laboratories, P.O. Box 708, Princeton University, Princeton, N.J., U.S.A.
Telephone: 609-452-4374.

Fitouri, Mohamed, L. EN D.; Tunisian politician; b. 4 April 1925, Kairouan; *m.*; two *c.*; ed. Lycée Carnot, Tunis, Inst. des Hautes Etudes, Tunis and Faculté de Droit, Paris.
Called to the bar 52; mem. Council, Nat. Assen. of Lawyers 60; Advocate, Court of Cassation 62; mem. Econ. and Social Council; City Counsellor, Tunis 69; Deputy to Nat. Assembly Nov. 69-; Minister of Justice 70-71, of Finance Oct. 71-.
Ministry of Finance, Tunis, Tunisia.

Fitt, Hon. Gerard; British politician; b. 9 April 1925, Belfast; *s.* of George Patrick Fitt and Mary Ann Fitt; *m.* Ann Doherty 1947; five *d.*
Entered local politics in Belfast 55; mem. Northern Ireland Parl., Stormont, for Dock Constituency 62-72; mem. U.K. Parl., Westminster, for W. Belfast 66-; Deputy Chief Exec., N. Ireland Assembly 74-May 75; Leader, Social Democratic and Labour Party (SDLP).
85 Antrim Road, Belfast, Northern Ireland; Irish Club, 82 Eaton Square, London, S.W.1, England.

Fitzgerald, Ella; American singer; b. 25 April 1918. Sang with Chick Webb Band 34-39; toured with Jazz at the Philharmonic troupe in United States, Japan, and Europe 48-; appeared in film *Pete Kelly's Blues* 55; numerous night club and television appearances 56-; toured with An Evening of Jazz troupe in Sweden, Norway, Denmark, France, Belgium, Germany, Italy, Switzerland 57; many awards from musicians' polls and *Downbeat* and *Metronome* magazines; recordings for Decca 36-55, Verve 56-.
c/o Salle Productions Inc., 451 North Canon Drive, Beverly Hills, Calif., U.S.A.

Fitzgerald, Dr. Garret; Irish economist and politician; b. 1927; *s.* of late Desmond Fitzgerald; ed. Belvedere Coll. and Univ. Coll. Dublin.
Called to the Bar 46; fmrly. Research and Schedules Man. Aer Lingus, Lecturer in Political Econ. Univ. Coll. Dublin, mem. Nat. Univ. of Ireland Senate, Econs. Corresp. and Hon. Sec. Inst. of Transport; fmr. mem. Seanad Eireann; mem. Dáil for Dublin South-East and Fine Gael Front Bench mem. 69-; Minister for Foreign Affairs March 73-; leading mem. European Movement.
Publs. include *Towards a New Ireland.*
Ministry for Foreign Affairs, Iveagh House, 80 St. Stephen's Green, Dublin 2, Ireland.

Fitzgerald, Stephen; Australian scholar and diplomatist; b. 1938; ed. Australian Nat. Univ., Canberra.
With Dept. of Foreign Affairs until 66; Fellow Dept. of Far Eastern History, Australian Nat. Univ., Deputy Head Contemporary China Centre until 73; Amb. to People's Repub. of China April 73-.
Ministry of Foreign Affairs, Canberra, A.C.T., Australia.

FitzGibbon, (Robert Louis) Constantine (Lee-Dillon), F.R.S.L.; Irish author; b. 8 June 1919; *s.* of Commdr. Francis Lee-Dillon FitzGibbon and Georgette Folsom; *m.* Marjorie Steele 1967; one *s.* (by previous *m.*) one *d.*; ed. Univ. of Munich, Sorbonne and Exeter Coll., Oxford.
Vice-President, Irish Acad. of Letters; Hon. Fellow, Royal Soc. of Literature; Fellow, Guggenheim Memorial Foundation 66.
Publs. *The Arabian Bird* 49, *The Iron Hoop* 50, *Dear Emily* 52, *Miss Finnigan's Fault, Norman Douglas, The Holiday* 53, *The Little Tour* 54, *The Shirt of*

Nessus 55, *In Love and War* 56, *The Blitz* 57, *Paradise Lost and More* 59, *When the Kissing had to Stop* 60, *Going to the River* 63, *Random Thoughts of a Fascist Hyena* 63, *The Life of Dylan Thomas* 65, *Selected Letters of Dylan Thomas* (editor) 66, *Through the Minefield* 67, *Denazification* 69, *High Heroic* 69, *Out of the Lion's Paw* 69, *Red Hand: The Ulster Colony* 71, *A Concise History of Germany* 72, *In the Bunker* 73, *The Life and Times of Eamon de Valéra* 73, *The Golden Age* 74, *Maxims of la Rochefoucauld* 74, *Secret Intelligence in the Twentieth Century* 76, *Music Far Away* 76; translations from French, German and Italian; contributions to periodicals in Britain, America and elsewhere.
St. Ann's, Killiney Hill Road, Co. Dublin, Ireland.

Fitzhugh, Gilbert Wright; American insurance executive; b. 8 July 1909, New York; *s.* of Herbert W. Fitzhugh and Ethel Gilbert Fitzhugh; *m.* Léa Van Ingh 1933; one *s.* one *d.*; ed. Princeton Univ.
Metropolitan Life Insurance Co. 30-73, Asst. Gen. Man. Canadian Head Office 46, 47, Vice-Pres. in charge of Planning and Devt., New York City 58-60, Vice-Pres., Gen. Man. for Canada 60-61, Exec. Vice-Pres. New York City 62, Pres. 63-66, Chair. of Board and Chief Exec. Officer 66-73; Dir. Metropolitan Life Insurance Co., Lloyds Bank Calif., Singer Co., Metromedia, ARA Services; Trustee, Calif. Inst. of Technology; Fellow, Soc. of Actuaries; Trustee of Hosp. of Scripps Clinic.
Leisure interests: hiking, golfing, travelling, photography.
Box 1452, Rancho Santa Fe, Calif. 92067, U.S.A.
Telephone: 714-756-3585.

Fitzmaurice, Sir Gerald (Gray), G.C.M.G., Q.C., B.A., LL.B.; British lawyer and international judge; b. 24 Oct. 1901, Storrington, Sussex; *s.* of Vice-Adm. Sir Maurice and Mabel Gertrude (Gray) Fitzmaurice; *m.* Alice Evelina Alexandra Sandberg 1933; two *s.*; ed. Malvern and Gonville and Caius Coll., Cambridge.
Called to Bar, Gray's Inn 25, Bencher 61; legal practice 25-29, 73-; Third Legal Adviser, Foreign Office 29; Legal Adviser, Ministry of Econ. Warfare 39-43; Second Legal Adviser, Foreign Office 45-53, Legal Adviser 53-60; Legal Adviser to U.K. Dels., San Francisco UN Charter Conf. 45, Paris Peace Conf. 46, UN Assembly 46, 48-59, Japanese Peace Conf., San Francisco 51, Berlin and Manila Confs. 54, Law of the Sea Confs. 58, 60; Judge, Int. Court of Justice 60-73; Judge of the European Court of Human Rights 74-; mem. UN Int. Law Comm. 55-60, Pres. 59; mem. Inst. Int. Law, Pres. 67-69; Pres. Grotius Soc. 56-60; Hon. Fellow, Caius Coll. 61, Hon. LL.D. (Edin.) 70, (Cambridge) 72.
Leisure interests: gardening, drawing.
2 Hare Court, Temple, London, E.C.4; Home: 3 Gray's Inn Square, London, W.C.1, England.
Telephone: 01-242-4339, 01-353-0076 and 01-583-2574.

Fitzpatrick, Gen. Sir (Geoffrey Richard) Desmond, G.C.B., D.S.O., M.B.E., M.C.; British army officer; b. 14 Dec. 1912, Ash Vale, Hants.; *s.* of late Brig.-Gen. Sir Richard Fitzpatrick, C.B.E., D.S.O., and Lady Fitzpatrick; *m.* Mary Campbell 1944; one *s.* one *d.*; ed. Eton Coll. and Royal Military Coll., Sandhurst.
Commissioned 32; served in Palestine 38-39; served in Middle East, Italy and N.W. Europe 39-45; A.D.C. to H.M. The Queen 59; Asst. Chief of Defence Staff, Ministry of Defence 59-61; Dir. Mil. Operations, War Office 62-64; Chief-of-Staff, British Army of the Rhine (B.A.O.R.) 64-65; G.O.C.-in-C., N. Ireland 65-66; Vice-Chief of Gen. Staff 66-68; promoted Gen. 68; C.-in-C. B.A.O.R. and Commdr. Northern Army Group 68-70; Deputy Supreme Allied Commdr., Europe 70-73; A.D.C. (Gen.) to the Queen 70-73; Lieut.-Gov. and C.-in-C. of Jersey 74-.
Government House, Jersey, Channel Islands.

Fitzpatrick, Thomas J.; Irish politician and solicitor; b. 1918, Scotstown, Co. Monaghan; ed. St. Macartan's Coll., Monaghan, and Univ. Coll., Dublin.
Solicitor 39-; Councillor, Cavan Co. Council 50-, Chair. 60 and 61, fmr. mem. various local authority cttees.; mem. Seanad Eireann 60-64; mem. Dáil 65-; fmr. mem. Fine Gael Front Bench and Nat. Exec.; Fine Gael Spokesman on Local Govt. 69-73; Minister for Lands March 73-.
Ministry of Lands, Government Buildings, Dublin 2, Ireland.

Fitzsimmons, Frank Edward; American trade union official; b. 7 April 1908, Jeannette, Pa.; s. of Frank and Ida May (Stanley) Fitzsimmons; m. Mary Patricia Fitzsimmons 1952; one s. one d.
Bus driver, Detroit Motor Co. 26; truck driver Nat. Transit Corpn. and 3-C Highway Co.; joined Teamster's Union 34, Business Agent for local union branch 37, Vice-Pres. 40, Sec.-Treas. 43; mem. Exec. Board and Int. Vice-Pres. Teamster's Union 61, Gen. Vice-Pres. 66-71, Gen. Pres. 71-; founded Alliance for Labour Action 69.
Leisure interests: golf, poker, watching baseball.
International Brotherhood of Teamsters, Chauffeurs, Warehousemen and Helpers of America, 25 Louisiana Avenue, N.W., Washington, D.C. 20001, U.S.A.

Fjeldstad, Öivin; Norwegian violinist and conductor; b. 2 May 1903; ed. Oslo Conservatoire under Gustav Fr. Lange, Leipzig Conservatoire under Walther Davisson, and Berlin Conservatoire under Clemens Kraus.
Debut as violinist 21; violinist, Oslo Philharmonic Orchestra 23-45; debut as conductor with Oslo Philharmonic Orchestra 31; Chief Conductor, Norwegian State Broadcasting 45-62, Norwegian State Opera Orchestra 58-59; Musical Dir. and Chief Conductor Oslo Philharmonic Orchestra 62-; has appeared as guest conductor in Austria, Belgium, British Columbia, Czechoslovakia, Denmark, Finland, France, German Federal Republic, Great Britain, Greece, Israel, Italy, Netherlands, Poland, Sweden, Turkey, U.S.A., U.S.S.R. and Yugoslavia; Knight, Order of St. Olav, Order of Finland's Lion, Ordre de la Couronne, Order Orange-Nassau; Golden Honour Medal of Norwegian King, Honour Medal of Norwegian Musicians, Arnold Schoenberg Diploma (Salzburg) 52.
Damfaret 59, Bryn-Oslo 6, Norway.

Flahiff, H.E. Cardinal George Bernard; Canadian ecclesiastic; b. 26 Oct. 1905, Paris, Ontario; s. of John J. Flahiff and Eleanor Fleming.
Ordained 30; Archbishop of Winnipeg 61-; cr. Cardinal 69.
Chancery Office, 50 Stafford Street, Winnipeg, Manitoba R3M 2V7, Canada.
Telephone: 204-474-2361.

Flamand, Paul; French publisher; b. 25 Jan. 1909; ed. Collège Saint-Paul, Angoulême.
Founder and Dir. of Editions du Seuil, Paris.
Editions du Seuil, 27 rue Jacob, Paris 6e, France.

Flamson, Richard J., III; American banker; b. 2 Feb. 1929, Los Angeles, Calif.; s. of Richard J. and Mildred Jones Flamson; m. Arden Black 1951; three s. one d.; ed. Claremont Men's Coll., Univ. of Washington.
Joined Security Pacific Nat. Bank 55, Vice-Pres. Adminstrator, Instalment Loan Div. 62, Nat. Banking Dept. 65, Int. Banking Dept. 68, Senior Vice-Pres. 69, Exec. Vice-Pres. 70, Vice-Chair. of Board 73-; Pres. Security Pacific Corpn. 73-; Dir., Officer several subsidiary cos.
Leisure interests: boating, tennis, golf, reading.
Security Pacific National Bank, 333 South Hope Street, Los Angeles, Calif. 90017; Home: 2000 Kewamee Drive, Corona del Mar, Calif. 92625, U.S.A.
Telephone: (213) 613-6526 (Office); (714) 673-8593 (Home).

Flanagan, Seán, B.A.; Irish politician; b. 26 Jan. 192? Co. Mayo; s. of Martin S. Flanagan and Annie Spelmar m. Patricia Doherty 1950; two s. five d.; ed. Uni Coll., Dublin.
Qualified solicitor 46; mem. Irish Parl. del. to Counc of Europe 52-53 and 57-59; Parl. Sec. to Minister fo Industry and Commerce 65-66; Minister for Health 66-69; Minister for Lands 69-73; T.D. Mayo South 51 69; T.D. Mayo East 69-; Fianna Fáil (Republica Party).
Leisure interests: golf, swimming, music.
65 St. Lawrence Road, Clontarf, Dublin 3, Ireland.

Flavin, Joseph Bernard, M.S.; American busines executive; b. 16 Oct. 1928, St. Louis, Mo.; s. of Josepl B. Flavin and Mary Toomey; m. Melisande Barillon one s. one d.; ed. Univ. of Massachusetts, Columbia Univ. Graduate School of Business.
Management positions, IBM World Trade Corpn. 53-65 Controller 65-67; with Xerox Corpn. 67-75, Vice-Pres and Man. Control Dept. 67-68, Group Vice-Pres. and Man. Corporate Services 68-69, Senior Vice-Pres. Finance and Planning 69-70, Exec. Vice-Pres. 70-72, Exec. Vice-Pres. and Pres. Int. Operations 72-75; Chair. and Chief Exec. Officer, The Singer Co. 75-.
Leisure interests: skiing, golf.
30 Rockefeller Plaza, New York, N.Y. 10020, U.S.A.
Telephone: (212) 581-4800.

Fleckenstein, Günther; German theatre director; b. 13 Jan. 1924, Mainz; m. Heike Kaase 1965; two d.; ed. Realgymnasium, Mainz, and Univ. Mainz.
Producer of plays and operas, Theater Ulm 54-55, theatre in Essen/Gelsenkirchen 55-57; Chief Producer of Plays, theatre in Münster 57-59; Producer and Dir. Landestheater, Hanover 59-65; Dir. Deutsches Theater, Göttingen 66-; Guest Dir. for theatres in Berlin, Hamburg and Stuttgart; Guest Dir. TV in Munich and Stuttgart; has dramatized for stage and TV Der Grosstyrann und das Gericht (Bergengruen); stage production in German of Les jeux sont faits (Sartre), Im Räderwerk (Sartre), Ehen werden im Himmel geschlossen, Dramatisierungen für das Kinder- und Jugendtheater.
Deutsches Theater in Göttingen, 34 Göttingen, Theaterplatz; Home: 34 Göttingen-Geismar, Meininger Weg 8, Federal Republic of Germany.
Telephone: 5-94-71 (Home).

Flegel, Manfred; German economist and politician; b. 3 June 1927, Magdeburg; ed. Univs. of Rostock and Berlin.
Member and Sec. Central Cttee., Nat.-Demokratische Partei Deutschlands 48-; mem. Volkskammer 50-; mem. Econ. Cttee. 50-54; mem. Finance Cttee. 54-; Deputy Chair. Council of Ministers of D.D.R. and Minister for Materials Supply 69-74; Deputy Chair. Council of Ministers and Chair. State Treaty Comm. 74-; Vaterländischer Verdienstorden; Ernst-Moritz-Arndt Medaille.
Ministerrat, Berlin, German Democratic Republic.

Fleischman, Théo; Belgian writer; b. 1893, Antwerp; m. Jeanne Bourtembourg 1930; one s. one d.
On editorial staff of La Gazette, Brussels 20; Dir. of Talks, Radio-Belgique 24; Dir. of Talks in French, Belgian Nat. Broadcasting Inst. (I.N.R.) 30-37; Dir.-Gen. 37; Dir.-Gen. of Belgian Nat. Broadcasting in London 42; Director-General of Broadcasting (French), I.N.R. 45-53; Hon. Admin. Dir. of the Musical Chapel of Queen Elizabeth of Belgium; Président d'Honneur Université Radiophonique et Télévisuelle Internationale; Corresp. mem. Inst. de France; Commdr. Order of the Crown, Chevalier Order of Léopold, Officer of Léopold II, Croix de Guerre with Palm, Commdr. Légion d'Honneur; Commdr. Order of Polonia Restituta, etc.
Leisure interests: literature, history.

ubls. *Ce vieil enfant* (poems) 22, *Archipel* (poems) 23, *'Aventure (1914-18)* 24, *Anthologie des Poètes de l'Yser* 5, *Ici Londres—le Message du Jour* 45, *Un curieux cit de Waterloo* 46, *Icare* 47, *Le Roi de Gand, Napoléon u bivouac, Un qui vevient de loin, Bruxelles pendant la ataille de Waterloo, Tapin tambour de Bonaparte en gypte, Le Peuple aux Yeux Clairs, En écoutant parler 'apoléon, En écoutant parler les grognards de Napoléon, 'apoléon et la Musique, L'Epopée impériale racontée ar la Grande Armée, L'Evadé de Sainte-Hélène, His-ires singulières;* has written many radio features.
3 Avenue Hamoir, 1180 Brussels (Uccle), Belgium.
'elephone: 374-09-72.

Fleischmann, Rudolf, DR.RER.NAT.; German physi-ist; b. 1 May 1903, Erlangen; *s.* of Dr. Albert and 'ranziska Fleischmann (née Kiefl); *m.* Marianne lüller 1963; ed. Univs. of Erlangen, Munich.
nstitute of Physics, Göttingen 30-32, Heidelberg 32-34; Kaiser Wilhelm Physical Inst., Heidelberg 34-41; Extra-rdinary Prof. of Physics, Univ. of Strasbourg 41-44; 'rof. of Physics, Univ. of Hamburg, and Dir. of State 'hysical Inst. 47-53; Prof. of Physics, Head of Physics Dept., Univ. of Erlangen 53-69.
9 Langemarickpl., 852 Erlangen, Federal Republic of Germany.
Telephone: 09131 26221.

Fleming, Allan Percy, O.B.E.; Australian librarian; b. 5 March 1912; ed. State School, Scotch Coll. and Univ. of Melbourne.
Journalist 32-39; War Service as Lt.-Col. 39-46; Dir. Joint Intelligence Bureau, Dept. of Defence 47-48; Asst. Joint Sec. and Controller Joint Service Orgs. 48-58; Trade Commr., Paris 59-62; First Asst. Sec. Dept. Trade and Industry, Canberra 62-66; Special Commercial Adviser, London 67; Del. to GATT Conf. 61 and UNCTAD Confs. 63-66; Pres. UNCTAD Board Sept. 65; Commonwealth Parl. Librarian 67-70; Nat. Librarian 70-73.
60 Gellibrand Street, Campbell, Canberra, A.C.T. 2601, Australia.

Fleming, Charles Alexander, O.B.E., F.R.S., F.R.S.N.Z., D.SC.; New Zealand naturalist and paleontologist; b. 9 Sept. 1916, Auckland; *s.* of George Fleming and Winifred Hardy; *m.* Margaret Alison Chambers 1941; three *d.*; ed. Kings Coll., Auckland and Auckland Univ. Coll.
Joined N.Z. Geological Survey as Asst. Geologist 40, becoming Paleontologist and later Chief Paleontologist (Dept. of Scientific and Ind. Research); published research on geological and biological topics, mainly on history of life in N.Z.; has taken part in expeditions to subantarctic islands; Pres. Royal Soc. N.Z. 62-66; Pres. Australian and N.Z. Asscn. for Advancement of Science 69; Pres. Ornithological Soc. of N.Z. 45; mem. Nat. Parks Authority, N.Z.; mem. Nat. Museum of N.Z. Council; Corresp. Fellow, American Ornithologists Union; Foreign mem. American Philosophical Soc.; Hon. mem. Geological Soc. of London; William Smith Lecturer 68; Hector and Hutton Medals of Royal Soc. of N.Z.; Walter Burfitt Medal of Royal Soc. of New South Wales; ANZAAS Medal of Australian and N.Z. Asscn. for Advancement of Science.
Leisure interests: New Zealand cicadas, recorded music, fishing for New Zealand whitebait.
Publs. *Checklist of New Zealand Birds* (editor) 53, Hochstetter's *Geology of New Zealand* (translator and editor) 59, *Stratigraphic Lexicon: New Zealand* (editor) 59, *Marwick's Illustrations of New Zealand Shells* 66, and over 200 research papers on N.Z. geology, paleon-tology, zoology and biogeography.
Office: New Zealand Geological Survey, P.O.B. 30368, Lower Hutt; Home: "Balivean", 42 Wadestown Road, Wellington, New Zealand.
Telephone: 699-059 (Office); 737288 (Home).

Fleming, Hon. Donald Methuen, P.C., Q.C., B.A., LL.B., D.C.L., LL.D.; Canadian barrister; b. 23 May 1905, Exeter, Ont.; *s.* of Louis Charles Fleming and Maud Margaret Wright Fleming; *m.* Alice Mildred Watson 1933; two *s.* one *d.*; ed. Univ. of Toronto and Osgoode Hall Law School.
Called to Bar 28; created King's Counsel 44; M.P. for Toronto-Eglinton 45-63; Minister of Finance of Canada 57-62; Gov. Int. Bank, Monetary Fund, Int. Finance Corpn., Int. Devt. Agency 57-63; Minister of Justice and Attorney-Gen. of Canada 62-63; Man. Dir. Bank of Nova Scotia Trust Co. (Bahamas) Ltd. and its sub-sidiaries; Dir. Gore Mutual Insurance Co., Empressas Sudamericanas Consolidades S.A., M. & G. (Cayman) Ltd., and many other companies; Gen. Counsel to Bank of Nova Scotia in Bahamas and Caribbean.
Leisure interest: sports.
P.O. Box N3016, Nassau, Bahamas.
Telephone: 21025 (Office); 34616 (Home).

Fleming, Robben Wright, LL.D.; American university administrator; b. 18 Dec. 1916, U.S.A.; *s.* of Edmund P. and Jeanette Wheeler Fleming; *m.* Aldyth L. Quixley; one *s.* two *d.*; ed. Beloit Coll., Wis. and Univ. of Wisconsin.
Attorney. Securities and Exchange Comm., Washing-ton, D.C. 41-42; Mediator, Nat. War Labor Board 42; Dir. Industrial Relations Center, Univ. of Wis. 47-52; Dir. Inst. of Labor and Industrial Relations, Univ. of Illinois 52-58; Prof. of Law, Univ. of Wis. 58-67, Chancellor 64-67; Prof. of Law, Pres. Univ. of Michigan, Ann Arbor 68-; fourteen hon. degrees.
Leisure interests: sports, crafts, reading.
Publs. *The Politics of Wage Price Decisions* (with M. Edelman) 65, *The Labor Arbitration Process* 65.
815 South University Avenue, Ann Arbor, Mich. 48104, U.S.A.

Fleming, Rt. Rev. William Launcelot Scott, M.A., M.S., D.D., F.R.S.E.; British ecclesiastic and explorer; b. 7 Aug. 1906; ed. Rugby School, Trinity Hall and Westcott House, Cambridge, and Yale Univ.
Ordained deacon 33, priest 34; Fellow and Chaplain Trinity Hall 33-49, Dean 37-49; expeditions to Ice-land and Spitzbergen 32-33; Chaplain and Geologist, British Graham Land Expedition 34-37; Chaplain, R.N.V.R. 40-44; Dir. Service Ordination Candidates 44-46; Dir. Scott Polar Research Inst. Cambridge 46-49; Bishop of Portsmouth 49-59; Bishop of Norwich 59-71; Dean of Windsor, Domestic Chaplain to H.M. Queen Elizabeth II, Register of the Order of the Garter 71-; Chair. Church of England Youth Council 50-61; Chair. Archbishops' Advisers on Needs and Resources of the Church of England 63-; Vice-Chair. Parl. Group for World Govt. 70; mem. Royal Comm. on Environmental Pollution 70-73; Hon. Chaplain R.N.V.R. (now R.N.R.) 50; Hon. Fellow, Trinity Hall, Cambridge 56; Hon. Vice-Pres. Royal Geographical Soc. 61.
The Deanery, Windsor Castle, Windsor, Berks., England.
Telephone: Windsor 65561.

Flemming, Arthur Sherwood, A.M., LL.B.; American educator and government official; b. 12 June 1905; *m.* Bernice Virginia Moler 1934; five *c.*; ed. Ohio Wesleyan, American and George Washington Univs.
Instructor, American Univ. 27-30, Dir. School of Public Affairs 34-39, Exec. Officer 38-39; mem. U.S. Civil Service Comm. 39-48; Int. Civil Service Advisory Board 50-64; Nat. Advisory Cttee. of Peace Corps 61-; Pres. Ohio Wesleyan Univ. 48-58 (on leave 51-57); Asst. to Dir. Office of Defense Mobilisation 51-53, Dir. 53-57; statutory mem. Nat. Security Council, participating by invitation of the Pres. of the U.S. in Cabinet meetings 53-57; Sec. of Health, Educ. and Welfare 58-61; Pres. Univ. of Oregon 61-68; Pres.

Macalester Coll., St. Paul 68-71; Chair. Board of Trustees, Citizenship Clearing House 59-62; Pres. Nat. Council of Churches in America 67-70; Fed. Commr. on Ageing; mem. U.S. Comm. on Civil Rights, Chair. 74-; numerous hon degrees; Republican.
Commission on Civil Rights, 1121 Vermont Avenue, N.W., Washington, D.C. 20425, U.S.A.

Flerov, Georgy Nikolayevich; Soviet physicist; b. 2 March 1913, Rostov-on-Don; ed. Leningrad Industrial Inst.
Scientific Work, Leningrad Inst. of Physics and Technology 38, later Chief Laboratory of Multicharged Ions, Kurchatov Inst. of Atomic Energy, Moscow; Dir. Nuclear Reaction Laboratory, Joint Inst. for Nuclear Research, Dubna 60-; mem. C.P.S.U. 55-; Corresp. mem. U.S.S.R. Acad. of Sciences 58-68, Academician 68-; Hero of Socialist Labour, State Prize (three times), Lenin Prize 67, etc.
Publs. *The Absorption of Slow Neutrons by Cadmium and Mercury* 39, *The Spontaneous Fission of Uranium* (with K. A. Petrzhak) 40, *Experiments on the Fission of Uranium* (with L. I. Russinov) 40, *On the Proton Decay of Radioactive Nuclei* (with others) 64, *Synthesis of Transuranic Elements* (with others) 57, 64, *Elements of the Second Hundred* (with I. Zvara) 71, *Experiments on the Synthesis of and Search for Transuranic Elements at the JINR* 71.
Laboratory of Nuclear Reactions, Joint Institute for Nuclear Research, Dubna, Moscow Region, U.S.S.R.

Fletcher, Douglas Valmore, C.B.E.; Jamaican lawyer and diplomatist; b. 22 May 1917, Kingston; s. of Reginald H. Fletcher and Edith Simpson; m. Hazel Rose 1940; two s. three d.; ed. Jamaica Coll.
Attorney-at-Law 38; mem. Legis. Council 53-62; Minister without Portfolio and Leader of Govt. Business 59-62; Senator and Leader of Opposition 62-67; Amb. to U.S.A. 72-; Dir. of various insurance, banking and mortgage financing companies.
Leisure interest: golf.
Embassy of Jamaica, Washington, D.C., U.S.A.; Home: 21 East Street, Kingston, Jamaica.
Telephone: (202) 387-1010 (Office); 922-5860 (Home).

Fletcher, Harvey, B.S., PH.D.; American physicist; b. 11 Sept. 1884; s. of Charles E. and Elizabeth Meller Fletcher; m. 1st Lorena Chipman 1908, five s.; m. 2nd Fern Eyring 1970; ed. Brigham Young Univ. and Univ. of Chicago.
Head of Dept. of Physics, Brigham Young Univ. 11-16; on engineering staff of Research Dept. of Bell Telephone Laboratories 16-49, Dir. Physical Research 33-49; Prof. of Electrical Engineering Columbia 49-52; Dir. Research, Brigham Young Univ. 52-. Dean Coll. Physics and Engineering Sciences 53-60; Pres. Utah Acad. of Science 15-16, Fellow American Physical Soc. (Pres. 45) and Acoustical Society of America, co-organizer and First Pres. 29; mem. Nat. Acad. of Sciences 33; Fellow American Asscn. for the Advancement of Science (Chair. Section B. 37); Pres. American Fed. of Organizations for the Hard of Hearing 29-30; Hon. Sc.D. (Columbia and Utah Univs., Kenyon Coll., Stevens Inst. of Technology, Brigham Young Univ. and Case School of Applied Science).
Leisure interest: fishing.
Publs. *Speech and Hearing* 29, *Speech and Hearing in Communications* 53.
1615 N. Willow Lane, Provo, Utah 84601, U.S.A.

Fletcher, James Chipman, PH.D.; American scientific administrator; b. 5 June 1919, Millburn, N.J.; m. Fay Lee; one s. three d.; ed. Columbia Univ. and Calif. Inst. of Technology.
Research physicist, U.S. Navy Bureau of Ordnance 40; Special Research Assoc., Cruft Lab. of Harvard Univ. 41; Teaching Fellow, Princeton Univ. 42, later In-

structor and Research Physicist; Teaching Fellow Calif. Inst. of Technology 45; Instructor, Univ. c Calif., Los Angeles 48; Dir. Theory and Analysis Lab Electronics Div., Hughes Aircraft Co. 48; Assoc. Dir Ramo Woolridge Corpn. 54, subsequently Dir. o Electronics, Guided Missile Div. (later bacame Spac Technology Labs.); organized Space Electronics Corpn (with F. W. Lehan) 58, subsequently Pres. Space Gen Corpn. (following merger of Space Electronics Corpn and Aerojets Gen. Corpn.) 61, Chair. of Board until 64 Pres. Univ. of Utah 64-71; Admin. NASA 71-.
National Aeronautics and Space Administration 400 Maryland Avenue, S.W., Washington, D.C. 20546 U.S.A.

Fletcher-Cooke, Sir John, Kt., C.M.G., M.A.; British colonial official (retd.) and writer; b. 8 Aug. 1911 Burnham, Bucks.; s. of the late Charles Arthur Fletcher-Cooke and Gwendolen May (née Bradford); two s. one d.; ed. Malvern Coll., Paris and Oxford Univs.
Colonial Office, Private Sec. to Perm. Under-Sec. 34-37; Malayan Civil Service 37-42; Served in R.A.F. and taken P.O.W. by Japanese 42-46; Sec. to Constitutional Comm. Malta 46; Under-Sec. to Palestine Govt. 46-49; Counsellor, U.K. Del. to UN 49-51; Colonial Sec., Cyprus 51-55; Minister for Constitutional Affairs, Tanganyika 56-59; Chief Sec. to Govt. 59-60; Deputy Gov. of Tanganyika 60-61; M.P. (Southampton Test) Oct. 64-66; Commonwealth Parliamentary Asscn. Del. to Nigeria 65; Visiting Prof. Colorado Univ. 61-62, 66, 73, 74; mem. Kenya Constituencies Delimitation Comm. 62; Adviser to Ottoman Bank 62-64; mem. Exec. Cttee. Overseas Employers' Fed. 63-65; Vice-Chair. Int. team to review structure and org. of FAO, Rome 67; Dir. Programmes in Diplomacy, Carnegie Endowment, New York 67-68; Official Mission for British Govt. to New Hebrides 69.
Publs. *Parliament as an Export* (co-author) 66, *The Emperor's Guest* 71; numerous articles on the United Nations, Commonwealth, Middle East and African affairs; short stories.
c/o Lloyds Bank, 3 Broad Street Place, London, E.C.2, England.

Flindt, Flemming Ole; Danish ballet dancer and choreographer; b. 30 Sept. 1936; ed. Royal Danish Ballet School.
Ballet dancer 55-; solo dancer Royal Theatre, Copenhagen 57-60; Danseur Etoile Théâtre Nat. de l'Opéra, Paris 60-; Dir. Royal Danish Ballet 65-; guest artist Royal Ballet Covent Garden 63; guest choreographer Metropolitan Opera House, New York and La Scala, Milan 65; Grand Prix Italia (*La Leçon*) 63.
Choreography: *La Leçon*, (Ionesco) 63; *Jeune Homme à Marier*, Ionesco 64, *The Three Musketeers* 66, *The Miraculous Mandarin* 66, *The Triumph of Death*, *Dreamland* 74; choreography and libretto: *Felix Luna* 73.
Bülowsvej 26, Copenhagen, Denmark.
Telephone: 144665.

Flitner, Andreas, DR. PHIL., M.A.; German educationist; b. 28 Sept. 1922, Jena; s. of Wilhelm Flitner and Elisabeth Czapski; m. Sonia Christ 1950; one s. six d.; ed. "Christianeum" Gymnasium, Hamburg, and Univs. of Hamburg, Heidelberg, Basle and Oxford.
Lecturer in German, Univ. of Cambridge 50-51; Tutor, Leibniz-Kolleg, Tübingen and High School Teacher 51-54; Dozent in Educ., Tübingen 55; Extraordinary Prof. of Education, Erlangen 56-58; Prof. of Education, Univ. of Tübingen 58-; Visiting Prof. Evanston, Ill. 67.
Leisure interest: modern art.
Publs. *Erasmus im Urteil seiner Nachwelt* 52, *Die politische Erziehung in Deutschland—Geschichte und Probleme* 57, *Glaubensfragen im Jugendalter* 61, *Wege zur pädagogischen Anthropologie* 63, *Die Jugend und die überlieferten Erziehungsmächte* (with G. Bittner) 65,

Soziologische Jugendforschung – Darstellung und Kritik aus pädagogischer Sicht 63, *Goethe an W. von Humboldt, Goethe—Jb.* 65, *Der Streit um die Vorschulerziehung* 67, *Brennpunkte gegenwärtiger Pädagogik, Studien zur Schul-und Sozialerziehung* 69, *Das Basler Winckelmann-Portrait* 71, *Spielen-Lernen, Praxis und Deutung des Kinderspiels* 72; Editor *Erasmus, Briefe* (3rd edn.) 56, *J. A. Comenius, Grosse Didaktik* 54, *Wilhelm v. Humboldt, Works* in 5 vols. (with K. Giel) 60-, *Einführung in pädagogisches Sehen und Denken* (with H. Scheuerl) 67, *Erziehung in Wissenschaft und Praxis* (23 vols.) 67-, *Das Kinderspiel, Texte* 73; Co-Editor *Anthropologie und Erziehung* 59-, *Sozialpädagogik* (10 vols.) 68-, *Zeitschrift für Pädagogik* 62- (Chair. 69-).
Im Rotbad 43, 74 Tübingen, Federal Republic of Germany.
Telephone: 292407.

Flores-Avendaño, Guillermo; Guatemalan politician and diplomatist.
President of Guatemala 57-58; Ambassador to Costa Rica, Mexico and Italy 58-61; Perm. Rep. of Guatemala to UN 61-63.
c/o Ministry of Foreign Affairs, Guatemala City, Guatemala.

Florin, Peter; German diplomatist; b. 2 Oct. 1921, Cologne; s. of Wilhelm Florin; m. three c.; ed. Mendeleyev Coll. of Chemistry, Moscow.
Assistant, later Editor, Nat. Cttee. for a Free Germany weekly magazine; Vice-Pres. Wittenberg District 45; Editor-in-Chief, Halle 45-48; Head of Dept., Ministry of Foreign Affairs, G.D.R. 49-52; Head of Foreign Affairs and Int. Relations Dept., Cen. Cttee., Socialist Unity Party 53-66, mem. Cen. Cttee. 58-; mem. People's Chamber (Volkskammer) 54-; Amb. to Czechoslovakia 67-69; State Sec., First Deputy Minister of Foreign Affairs 69-73; Perm. Rep. to UN Sept. 73-; Order of Red Star, Patriotic Order of Merit, Order of Banner of Labour, Medal for Anti-Fascist Fighters.
Permanent Mission of German Democratic Republic to United Nations, 58 Park Avenue, New York, N.Y. 10016, U.S.A.

Florit, H.E. Cardinal Ermenegildo; Italian ecclesiastic; b. 5 July 1901, Fagagna, Udine; ed. Seminario Diocesano di Udine, Pontificia Univ. Lateranense and Univ. Gregoriana.
Ordained Priest 25; Chaplain at Palmanova 27-29; Canon of San Marco 33; Prof. of Theology, Pontificia Univ. Lateranense 29-51, Pro-Rector 51-54; Pro-Rector Pontificium Institutum Utriusque Juris 51-54; Domestic Prelate to His Holiness 50-; Coadjutor Archbishop of Florence 54-62, Archbishop 62-; created Cardinal 65; mem. Pontifical Comm., on Bishops and Diocesan Org. for Ecumenical Council 60-, for Revision of Code of Canon Law 65-; mem. Catholic Biblical Asscn. of America.
Founded magazine *Lateranum* and published various books on biblical culture, in particular *Il Metodo della Storia delle Forme, Ispirazione biblica*.
Arcivescovado, Piazza S. Giovanni 3, Florence, Italy.
Telephone: 29-88-13.

Florkin, Marcel, M.D.; Belgian biochemist; b. 15 Aug. 1900; ed. Univ. de Liège.
Professor of Biochem., Univ. of Liège 34; Pres. Int. Union of Biochemistry 58; Pres. Biochemical Section, Int. Union of Biological Sciences; mem. Exec. Cttee. Int. Council of Scientific Unions 59; Pres. Council for Int. Orgs. of Medical Sciences 64-70, Int. Acad. of History of Medicine 62-; Pres. of Biology Working Group, Cttee. on Space Research (COSPAR) 63-; mem. Exec. Cttee. Int. Biological Programme 63-, Int. Cell Research Org. 62-; mem. Belgian Del. to Gen. Confs. of UNESCO 46-66; Visiting Prof. of Physiology, Duke Univ., U.S.A. 59-60; Walker-Ames Prof., Univ. of Washington 63; Visiting Prof. Univ. of Oregon 66;

mem. Acad. Royale de Belgique, Acad. Royale de Médecine de Belgique; Hon. mem. Royal Inst. (U.K.); Hon. Fellow Royal Soc. of Edinburgh; mem. Leopoldina Acad., Halle; Prix Francqui 46, Prix K. Jonckheere 60, Prix Henri de Parville 66; Dr. h.c. (Montpellier, Bordeaux, Rio de Janeiro, Gembloux).
Publs. *Biochemie générale* 43, *L'évolution biochimique* 44, *Introduction biochimique à la Médecine* 59, *Comparative Biochemistry* (Editor) 60-64, *Comprehensive Biochemistry* (Editor) 62-, *Aspects moléculaires de l'adaptation et de la phylogénie* 66, *A molecular approach to phylogeny* 66; *Médecine et Médecins au Pays de Liège* 54, *Un Prince, Deux Préfets* 57, *Naissance et Déviation de la Théorie cellulaire dans l'oeuvre de Théodore Schwann* 60, *Lettres de Théodore Schwann* 61, *Médecins, Libertins et Pasquins* 64.
6 rue Naimette, Liège, Belgium.

Flory, Paul John, PH.D.; American professor of chemistry; b. 19 June 1910, Sterling, Ill.; m. Emily C. Tabor 1936; one s. two d.; ed. Manchester Coll., Ind., Ohio State Univ.
Research Chemist E. I. Dupont de Nemours & Co. 34-38; Research Assoc., Univ. of Cincinnati 38-40; Research Chemist, Esso Lab. 40-43; Section Head, Research Lab., Goodyear Tire and Rubber Co. 43-48; Prof. Cornell Univ. 48-56; Exec. Dir. of Research, Mellon Inst. 56-61; Prof. of Chem., Stanford Univ. 61-; mem. Nat. Acad. of Sciences, American Chemical Soc., American Physical Soc., American Acad. of Arts and Sciences, Nat. Research Council; Fellow American Asscn. for the Advancement of Science; Hon. Ph.D. (Manchester Coll., Ind., and Polytechnic Inst., Milan), Hon. Sc.D. (Univ. of Manchester (Eng.), Ohio State Univ.); Nobel Prize for Chem. for work in molecular science 74, and many other prizes.
Department of Chemistry, Stanford University, Stanford, Calif. 94305, U.S.A.

Flowers, Sir Brian Hilton, Kt., M.A., D.SC., F.INST.P., F.R.S.; British physicist; b. 13 Sept. 1924, Blackburn, Lancs.; s. of late Rev. Harold J. Flowers and of Marion V. (née Hilton) Flowers; m. Mary Frances Behrens 1951; two step s.; ed. Gonville and Caius Coll., Cambridge, and Univ. of Birmingham.
Anglo-Canadian Atomic Energy Mission (Tube Alloys) at Montreal and Chalk River, Canada 44; Scientific Officer, Nuclear Physics Div., Atomic Energy Research Establishment, Harwell 46; transferred to Theoretical Physics Div. 48; Head of Theoretical Physics Div. 52; Chief Research Scientist 58; Prof. Theoretical Physics, Manchester Univ. 58-60; Langworthy Prof. of Physics 60-72; Pres. Inst. of Physics 72-; Fellow, Physical Soc. 56, mem. Council 60; mem. Council Inst. of Physics and the Physical Soc. 61, Vice-Pres. 62-66; mem. Advisory Council on Scientific Policy 62-64, Council on Scientific Policy 65-67, Advisory Board for the Research Councils 72-73; Del. Pugwash Conf. Cambridge 62, Dubrovnik 63, Karlovy Vary 64, Venice 65, Oxford 72; Chair. Steering Cttee. of the Nat. Physical Laboratory 65-68; Chair. Computer Board for Univs. and Research Councils 66-70, Science Research Council 67-73; Rector, Imperial Coll., Univ. of London 73-; Chair. Royal Comm. on Environmental Pollution 73-; Gov. Weizmann Inst. 69-; mem. Advisory Council, Science Policy Foundation 75-; Chevalier Légion d'Honneur 75; Hon. D.Sc. (Sussex) 68, (Wales) 72, (Leicester) 73.
Leisure interests: music, painting, walking.
Publs. Editor *Advances in Physics* 59, 63, *Cambridge Monographs in Physics* 61 and numerous scientific papers in the journals of learned societies on nuclear reactions and the structure of atomic nuclei, and on science policy.
Imperial College, London, SW7 2AZ, England.
Telephone: 01-589-5111.

Fobes, John Edwin; American diplomatist and international official; b. 16 March 1918, Chicago, Ill.; *s.* of Wilfred Franklin Fobes and Mabel Skogsberg; *m.* Hazel Ward Weaver 1941; one *s.* one *d.*; ed. Northwestern Univ., Fletcher School of Law and Diplomacy and School for Advanced International Studies, Johns Hopkins Univ.
U.S. Army Air Force 42-45; UN Secretariat, London and New York 45-46; Admin. Analyst, U.S. Bureau of the Budget 47-48; Asst. Dir. Technical Assistance, U.S. Marshall Plan, Washington 48-51; Dep. Dir. Organization and Planning, Mutual Security Agency, Washington 51-52; Adviser, U.S. Del. to NATO and European Regional Orgs., Paris 52-55; Dir. Office of Int. Admin., Dept. of State 55-59; (elected) mem. UN Advisory Cttee. on Admin. and Budgetary Questions 55-60; Senior Adviser, U.S. Del. to the 10th, 11th, 12th, 13th, 14th sessions of UN Gen. Assembly; Special Adviser to Asst. Sec. of State Washington 59-60; Program Officer and Dep. Dir. U.S. Agency for Int. Devt. Mission to India 60-64; Asst. Dir.-Gen. (Admin.), UNESCO, Paris 64-70, Deputy Dir.-Gen. 71-; Pres. American Library in Paris 68-70; visiting scholar Indiana and Harvard Univs. 70; D.H. Bucknell Univ. 73.
Leisure interests: community service, walking, reading, writing.
UNESCO, 7/9 place de Fontenoy, Paris 7e, France.
Telephone: 577-1610 (Office).

Foccart, Jacques; French civil servant; b. 31 Aug. 1913; ed. Collège de l'Immaculée Conception, Laval.
Exporter; Adviser, Rassemblement du Peuple Français (R.P.F.) Group, Council of the Republic 52-58; Sec.-Gen. R.P.F. 54; Technical Adviser, Gen. de Gaulle's office (Pres. of the Council) 58-59; Technical Adviser in Secretariat-Gen. of Presidency of Republic 59; Sec.-Gen. Presidency for French Community and African and Malagasy Affairs 60-69, 69-74; Commdr., Légion d'Honneur, Croix de Guerre 39-45, Rosette de la Résistance.
Villa Charlotte, 95 Luzarches, France.

Fock, Jenő; Hungarian politician; b. 17 May 1916, Budapest.
Mechanic; Nat. Youth Cttee. Communist Party 37; Dep. Minister, Metallurgy and Engineering 51-54; Sec. Nat. Council of Trade Unions 55-57; Sec. Central Cttee. Hungarian Socialist Workers' Party 57-61, mem. Political Cttee. 57-; Dep. Prime Minister 61-67, Prime Minister 67-May 75.
Leisure interests: literature, fine arts, watching football, playing tennis.
Parliament Building, H-1357, Budapest, Hungary.

Focke, Katharina, DR.PHIL.; German journalist and politician; b. 8 Oct. 1922, Bonn; *d.* of Ernst Friedlander and Dr. Franziska (née Schulz) Friedlander; *m.* Dr. Ernst Günter Focke 1954 (deceased 1961); ed. Hamburg Univ.
Journalist 46-54; joined Social Democratic Party 64; mem. North Rhine Westphalia Diet 66; mem. Bundestag 69-; Parl. State Sec. of Fed. Chancellor 69; Fed. Minister for Youth, Family Affairs and Health 72-; Social Democrat.
Publs. *Europa über den Nationen* 62, *Europäer in Frankreich* 65.
Ministerium für Jugend, Familie und Gesundheit, 53 Bonn-Bad Godesberg 1, Kennedy allee 105-107; and 5 Köln 51, Pferdmengesstrasse 34, Federal Republic of Germany.
Telephone: 0221-38-80-85.

Fog, Mogens, M.D.; Danish professor of neurology; b. 9 June 1904; ed. Københavns Universitet.
Chief Prof. of Neurology, Univ. of Copenhagen 38-, Rector of Copenhagen Univ. 66-72; mem. Danish Freedom

Council during German occupation 43-45, Minister for Repatriation and Compensation 45, mem. of Folketing 45-50; Klein's Prize 62; Dr. h.c. Oslo Univ., Hon. mem. Royal Soc. of Medicine and Asscn. British Neurologists. Publs. *Aphasia* (with Knud Hermann) 41, *Neurology for Psychologists* 55 and numerous other articles on scientific and political themes.
Neuromedicinsk Afdeling Rigshospitalet, Tagensvej 18, Copenhagen N, Denmark.

Fogg, Gordon Elliott, B.SC., PH.D., SC.D., LL.D., F.I.BIOL., F.R.S.; British botanist; b. 26 April 1919, Langar, Notts.; *s.* of Rev. Leslie Charles Fogg and Doris Mary Fogg (née Elliott); *m.* Elizabeth Beryl Llechid Jones 1945; one *s.* one *d.*; ed. Dulwich Coll., Queen Mary Coll., Univ. of London, and St. John's Coll., Cambridge.
Assistant for Seaweed Survey of Britain, Marine Biological Asscn. 42; Plant Physiologist, Pest Control Ltd. 43-45; Asst. Lecturer, Dept. of Botany, Univ. Coll. London 45-47, Lecturer 47-53, Reader 53-60; Prof. of Botany in Univ. of London at Westfield Coll. 60-71; Prof. of Marine Biology, Univ. Coll. of N. Wales 71-; Rockefeller Fellow 54; Hon. Sec. Inst. of Biology 53-56, Vice-Pres. 61-62, Pres. 76-; Botanical Sec., Soc. for Experimental Biology 57-60; Pres. British Phycological Soc. 62-63; Pres. Int. Phycological Soc. 64; Joint Hon. Sec. Xth Int. Botanical Congress, Edin. 64; Visiting Research Worker, British Antarctic Survey 66, 74; Gen. Sec. British Asscn. 67-72; Royal Soc./Leverhulme Visiting Prof. Univ. of Kerala 70; Chair. of Council, Freshwater Biol. Asscn. 74-.
Leisure interests: water-colour painting, walking, listening to music, photography.
Publs. *The Metabolism of Algae* 53, *The Growth of Plants* 63, *Algal Cultures and Phytoplankton Ecology* 65, *Photosynthesis* 68, *The Blue-Green Algae* (with W. D. P. Stewart, P. Fay and A. E. Walsby) 73.
Marine Science Laboratories, Menai Bridge, Anglesey, Gwynedd, LL59 5EH, Wales.
Telephone: 0248712-641.

Fogh-Andersen, Poul, M.D., DR. MED.; Danish plastic surgeon; b. 7 Dec. 1913, Copenhagen; *s.* of late Vagn Fogh-Andersen and Lili Fogh-Andersen (née Nielsen); *m.* Birgit Duelund 1943; one *s.* two *d.*; ed. St. Jörgen's High School and Copenhagen Univ.
Scientific Asst., Univ. Inst. of Human Genetics, Copenhagen 39-40; Asst., various Copenhagen hospitals 41-45; Asst. Surgeon, Copenhagen Municipal Hospital 46-49; First Asst. Surgeon, Univ. Hospital 50-53, Deaconess Hospital 54-55; Chief Surgeon, Dept. of Surgery A (Plastic Surgery), Deaconess Hospital, Copenhagen 56-; Consultant Plastic Surgeon, Univ. Hospital 56-62; Plastic Surgeon, Dronning Louise's Children's Hospital, Copenhagen 59-71; Consultant Surgeon, State Inst. for Defective Speech 56-; Cofounder and Pres. Danish Soc. of Plastic and Reconstructive Surgery 64-69; Pres. Org. Danish Plastic Surgeons 66-; Pres. Scandinavian Asscn. of Plastic Surgeons 66-68; Corresp. mem. American Soc. of Plastic and Reconstructive Surgery 55-; Swedish Asscn. of Plastic Surgeons 66-; British Asscn. of Plastic Surgeons 73-; Danish Editor *Scandinavian Journal of Plastic and Reconstructive Surgery* 67-; Gen. Sec. 2nd Int. Congress on Cleft Palate, Copenhagen, Aug. 73.
Leisure interest: history of plastic surgery.
Publs. *Inheritance of Harelip and Cleft Palate* (Thesis) 42, chapters in textbooks and articles in scientific periodicals on surgery and plastic surgery.
Dronningensvej 12, Copenhagen F., Denmark.
Telephone: Fasan 6516.

Fojtík, Jan, PH.D., C.SC.; Czechoslovak politician; b. 1 March 1928, Milotice nad Bečvou; ed. Charles Univ. Prague, and Acad. of Social Sciences of Cen. Cttee. of C.P.S.U., Moscow.

Editor of journal Soviet Science-philosophy, Czecho-slovak-Soviet Inst. 50-51; Editor *Rudé právo* 51-68; Editor-in-Chief of *Nová mysl* (New Thought); Rector of School of Political Studies Cen. Cttee., C.P. of Czechoslovakia 69; Alt. mem. Cen. Cttee., C.P. of Czechoslovakia 66-69, mem. 69-, Sec. 69-; mem. Cen. Cttee. Secr. 70-; Deputy to House of People, Fed. Assembly 69-71; Chair. Cultural Cttee., House of the People 69; Deputy to House of Nations, Fed. Assembly 71-; Award for Merits in Construction 63, State Journalists' Prize 65, Friendship Medal (Mongolia) 72, Order of Victorious February 73.
Office: Central Committee of C.P. of Czechoslovakia, Prague 1, nábr. Kyjevské brigády, 12, Czechoslovakia.

Folchi, Alberto Enrico; Italian lawyer and politician; b. 17 June 1897, Rome; s. of Pio Folchi and Emma Cruciani Alibrandi; m. Laura di Lorenzo 1919; one s. one d.; ed. Nazarene Coll. of the Scolopi Order and Univ. of Rome.
Served in 14-18 and 39-45 wars; active mem. Christian Democratic Party of Rome, Sec. 48-49; mem. Nat. Council Christian Democratic Party 48-50, 60; mem. Chamber of Deputies 53-; Under-Sec. for Foreign Affairs 55-60; Minister of Sports and Tourism 60-63; Prof. of Law, Univ. of Rome and Parma, and fmr. Pres. Nat. Inst. for Welfare of Employees of Local Boards (INADEL); Pres. Inst. of Parl. Studies; Vice-Pres. Conseiller Credito Italiano, Rome, 69-71, Credito Fondiario 72; Knight Order of Malta.
Publs. *I Mandati Coloniali* 36, *Sull'Ordinamento Giuridico della Tunisia* 40, *Democrazia Politica e Democrazia Economica* 46, *L'Occidente di Fronte al Comunismo* 55, *Europa unita: i trattati per l'Euratom e il mercato comune* 57, *Politica Europea ed energia atomica* 57, *Le Nazioni Unite nella presente situazione internazionale* 58, *Incontro al Vertice* 59, *Somalia Indipendente* 60.
Via Nizza 36, Rome, Italy.

Folcini, Enrique E.; Argentine international finance official; b. 21 Aug. 1936; ed. Univ. of Buenos Aires.
Joined Argentinian civil service 55; Nat. Council for Devt. 63-67; Nat. Dir. Econ. and Financial Policy, Ministry of Labour, and Under-Sec. of Econs. and Labour 69-70; Sec. of Finance 70; Exec. Dir. for Argentina and Peru, Inter-American Devt. Bank 70-72. Presidencia de la Nación, Buenos Aires, Argentina.

Foldes, Andor; American concert pianist; b. 21 Dec. 1913, Budapest, Hungary; s. of Emil Foldes and Valerie Ipolyi; m. Lili Rendy 1940; ed. Classical Gymnasium, Budapest, and under Dohnányi, Liszt Acad. of Music, Budapest.
Debut with Budapest Philharmonic Orchestra 21; First Prize, Int. Franz Liszt Piano Competition, Budapest 33; numerous world tours; resident in U.S. 39-61, Switzerland 61-; Grosses Bundesverdienstkreuz (German Fed. Repub.), Ordre du Mérite Culturel et Artistique (France); Médaille d'Argent (City of Paris) 70; records for HMV.
Leisure interests: art collecting, literature, hiking, swimming.
Publs. *Keys to the Keyboard* 50, *Gibt es einen zeitgenössischen Beethoven-Stil?* 63.
Herrliberg, near Zürich, Switzerland.

Foley, Maurice; British politician; b. 9 Oct. 1925; ed. St. Mary's Coll., Middlesbrough.
Worked as electrical fitter; mem. Electrical Trades Union 41-46; Transport and Gen. Workers' Union 48-; mem. Parl. 63-73; Joint Parl. Under-Sec. Home Office 66-67; Minister of State, Foreign Office 68-70; EEC Deputy Dir.-Gen. for Devt. 73-.
Directorate-General for Development, 200 rue de la Loi, Brussels, Belgium.

Foley, Milton Joseph, B.A.; Canadian business executive; b. 1910, Kentwood, La., U.S.A.; s. of Jeremiah S. and Marie V. Foley; m. Kathryn Robuck 1935; one s. one d.; ed. Duval and Robert E. Lee High Schools, Florida, Notre Dame Univ.
Vice-Pres. Brooks-Scanlon Corpn. 38-41, Pres. 41-46; Vice-Pres. Brooks-Scanlon Inc. 46-48; Exec. Vice-Pres. Powell River Co. Ltd., Vancouver 48-55, Pres. 55-60; Pres. MacMillan, Bloedel & Powell River, Vancouver 60-61; Vice-Pres. and Dir. Anglo-Canadian Pulp and Paper Mills Ltd., Quebec 61-; Dir. Brooks-Scanlon, SuInc., wanne Lumber Mfg. Co., Florida Forest Products.
Leisure interests: golf and swimming.
A-4 600 Laurier Avenue, Quebec 4, P.Q., Canada.
Telephone: 418-522-3713.

Folger, John Clifford, B.S., M.S.; American investment banker and diplomatist; b. 28 May 1896, Sheldon, Ia.; s. of Homer Folger and Emma Funston; m. Kathrine Dulin 1929; two s.; ed. State Coll. of Washington.
Chairman Board of Folger, Nolan, Fleming, Douglas, Inc. 41-; Pres. Investment Bankers Assen. of America 43-45, Piedmont Mortgage Co.; Chair. Virginia Industries Inc.; Dir. Int. Business Machines, World Banking Corpn. Ltd., Hilton Hotels Corpn.; Amb. to Belgium 57-59; Gov. N.Y. Stock Exchange; Chair. Republican Nat. Finance Cttee. 55-57, 60-61; mem. Nat. Inst. of Social Science, The Pilgrims; mem. Exec. Cttee. District Chapter American Red Cross; Washington Cathedral Chapter; mem. Georgetown Board of Regents, Georgetown Univ.; Republican.
Home: 2991 Woodland Drive, N.W., Washington 8; Office: 725 15th Street, N.W., Washington 5, D.C., U.S.A.

Folkers, Karl, PH.D.; American professor of chemistry; b. 1 Sept. 1906, Decatur, Ill.; s. of August W. Folkers and Laura Black Folkers; m. Selma Johnson 1932; one s. one d.; ed. Univs. of Illinois and Wisconsin and Yale Univ.
With Merck and Co. Inc., Rahway, N.J. 34-62, in Lab. of Pure Research 34, Asst. Dir. of Research 38, Dir. of Organic and Biochemical Dept. 45, Assoc. Dir. of Research and Devt. Div. 51, Dir. of Organic and Biological Chemical Research 53, Exec. Dir. of Fundamental Research 56, Vice-Pres. for Exploratory Research 62; Pres. and Chief Exec. Officer Stanford Research Inst., Menlo Park, Calif. 63; Prof. of Chem. and Dir. of Inst. for Biomedical Research, Univ. of Texas 68-; Harrison-Howe Recipient and Lecturer 49; Pres. American Chemical Soc. 62; mem. Nat. Acad. of Sciences; Foreign mem. Royal Swedish Acad. of Engineering Sciences; mem. Board of Trustees Gordon Research Confs., Council of Board of Trustees Stanford Research Inst.; Hon. mem. Società Italiana di Scienze Farmaceutiche; Hon. D.Phar. (Univ. of Uppsala, Sweden), Hon. D.Sc. (Univs. of Wisconsin and Illinois, and Philadelphia Coll. of Pharmacy and Science); numerous awards including Mead Johnson Co. Award (co-recipient) 40, Presidential Certificate of Merit 48, Perkins Medal 60, Nichols Medal 67, Von Meter Prize of American Thyroid Assen. (co-recipient), first Robert A. Welch Award and Medal for research in the life processes 72, Acad. of Pharmaceutical Sciences Research Achievement Award in Pharmaceutical and Medicinal Chem. 74.
Publs. *Vitamins and Coenzymes* (Arthur F. Wagner and K. Folkers) 64; and 476 publs. in the field of vitamins, antibiotics, hormones and drugs, 140 of which are on Coenzyme Q.
Institute for Biomedical Research, The University of Texas at Austin, Austin, Tex. 78712; Home: 6406 Mesa Drive, Austin, Tex. 78731, U.S.A.
Telephone: 512-471-7174 and 512-471-7292 (Office).

Follett, Sir David Henry, Kt., M.A., PH.D.; British scientist and civil servant; b. 5 Sept. 1907, Wimbledon, London; s. of Septimus Follett and Rose Annie Follett (née Ford); m. Helen Alison Wilson 1932; three s. (deceased); ed. Rutlish School, Brasenose Coll., Oxford and Birkbeck Coll., London.
With Adam Hilger Ltd. (optical instrument manufacturers) 29-37; Asst. Keeper Dept. of Physics, Science Museum, London 37-39, 45-49; with Meteorological Branch, R.A.F. Volunteer Reserve 39-45; Dep. Keeper Dept. of Physics, Science Museum 49-57, Keeper Dept. of Electrical Engineering and Communications 57-60, Dir. and Sec. 60-73; Vice-Pres. Inst. of Physics and Physical Soc. 65-69.
Leisure interests: gardening, sailing.
3 Elm Bank Gardens, Barnes, London, S.W.13, England.
Telephone: 01-876-8302

Folsom, Marion Bayard; American business executive; b. 23 Nov. 1893; ed. Georgia and Harvard Univs.
Joined Eastman Kodak Co. 14, Treas. 35-53, Dir. 47-53; 58-68; served U.S. Army, First World War; helped draft Social Security Act 34; helped to organise Cttee. for Economic Development 42; Staff Dir. House Cttee. on Postwar Economic Policy and Planning 44-46; Under-Sec., Treasury 53-55; Sec. of Health, Education and Welfare July 55-58; Vice-Chair. White House Conf. on Health; Chair. Governor's Cttee. on Hospital Cost; mem. Fed. Advisory Council for Employment Security 66-70, Nat. Health Advisory Council 70-.
106 Oak Lane, Rochester, N.Y. 14610, U.S.A.

Fomin, Andrei Andronovich; Soviet diplomatist; b. 5 Dec. 1918, Leningrad; ed. Nicolayevsk Shipbuilding Inst.
Soviet Foreign Ministry 46-; Adviser to Soviet Del. UN 54-59; Chargé d'Affaires (a.i.) Congo (Léopoldville) 60; Counsellor for American Countries, U.S.S.R. Ministry of Foreign Affairs 60-61; Minister-Counsellor, Rio de Janeiro 61-62; Amb. to Brazil 62-65; Deputy Sec.-Gen. Ministry of Foreign Affairs 65-67; Head, Dept. for S. Asia, Ministry of Foreign Affairs 67-.
Ministry of Foreign Affairs, 32-34 Smolenskaya-Sennaya ploshchad, Moscow, U.S.S.R.

Foncha, John Ngu; Cameroonian politician; b. 21 June 1916.
Member House of Assembly 51-65; Prime Minister and Minister of Local Govt., Southern Cameroons 59-61; Prime Minister, Western Cameroon 61-65; Vice-Pres., Fed. Republic of Cameroon 61-70; Leader, Kamerun Nat. Democratic Party (KNDP) 55-66; United Cameroon Nat. Union (CNU) 66-72.
Cameroon National Union, P.O.B. 964, Yaoundé, United Republic of Cameroon.
Telephone: 23-70.

Fonda, Henry; American actor; b. 16 May 1905; m. 1st Margaret Sullivan 1931 (deceased); m. 2nd Frances Seymour Brokaw 1936 (died 1950), one s. (Peter Fonda) one d. (Jane Fonda, q.v.); m. 3rd Susan Blanchard 1950 (divorced 1956), one d.; m. 4th Afdera Franchetti 1957 (divorced 1962); m. 5th Shirlee Adams 1965; ed. Univ. of Minnesota.
Debut in Omaha 25; first appearance in New York 34; films 35-; U.S. Navy 42-45; Bronze Star; Presidential Citation.
Has appeared in the plays: *The Farmer Takes a Wife* 34, *Blow ye Winds* 37, *Mr. Roberts* 48, *Point of No Return* 51, *The Caine Mutiny Court Martial* 53, *Two for the Seesaw* 58, *Silent Night, Lonely Night* 59, *Critics' Choice* 60, *A Gift of Time* 62, *Generation* 65, *Our Town* 68, *The Smith Family* (TV Series) 71, *The Trial of A. Lincoln* 71, *The Time of Your Life* 72, *Red Pony* (TV) 73, *Clarence Darrow* 74.
Films include: *The Farmer Takes a Wife* 35, *Way*

Down East 35, *The Trail of the Lonesome Pine* 36, *You Only Live Once* 37, *Young Mr. Lincoln* 39, *Drums Along the Mohawk* 39, *The Grapes of Wrath* 40, *The Lady Eve* 41, *The Big Street* 41, *Male Animal* 41, *The Ox-Bow Incident* 42, *My Darling Clementine* 46, *The Fugitive* 47, *Fort Apache* 48, *Mister Roberts* 55, *War and Peace* 56, *The Wrong Man* 57, *The Tin Star* 57, *Twelve Angry Men* 57, *Warlock* 59, *Advise and Consent* 62, *The Longest Day* 62, *How the West was Won* 63, *Fail Safe* 63, *The Best Man* 64, *Sex and the Single Girl* 64, *The Rounders* 64, *In Harm's Way* 65, *A Big Hand for a Little Lady* 66, *The Dirty Game* 66, *The Battle of the Bulge* 66, *Welcome to Hard Times* 67, *Stranger on the Run* 67, *Madigan* 68, *Yours, Mine and Ours* 68, *The Boston Strangler* 68, *Once Upon a Time in the West* 69, *Too Late the Hero* 70, *There Was a Crooked Man* 70, *The Cheyenne Social Club* 70, *Sometimes a Great Notion* 72, *Ash Wednesday* 73, *The Serpent* 73, *My Name is Nobody* 74, *The Last Days of Mussolini*.
c/o CMA, 600 Madison Avenue, New York, N.Y. 10022, U.S.A.

Fonda, Jane; American actress; b. 21 Dec. 1937; d. of Henry Fonda (q.v.) and Frances (née Seymour); m. 1st Roger Vadim (q.v.) 1967 (dissolved 1973), 2nd Tom Hayden 1973; two c.; ed. Vassar Coll.
Active anti-war campaigner; broadcast Hanoi radio 72.
Films include: *Tall Story* 60, *A Walk on the Wild Side* 62, *Period of Adjustment* 62, *Sunday in New York* 63, *The Love Cage* 63, *La Ronde* 64, *Histoires Extra-ordinares* 67, *Barbarella* 68, *They Shoot Horses Don't They?* 69, *Steelyard Blues*, *Klute* 70, *Tout Va Bien* 72, *A Doll's House* 73; dir., appeared in *Viet-Nam Journey*, *The Blue Bird* 75; Acad. Award for Best Actress 72.
Ashley Famous Agency, 9255 Sunset Boulevard, Los Angeles, Calif. 90069, U.S.A.

Fong, Hiram, LL.B., LL.D.; American attorney and politician; b. 1 Oct. 1907; ed. Kalihi Waena Grammar School, St. Louis Coll. and McKinley High School, Univ. of Hawaii and Harvard Law School.
Former Deputy City Attorney, Honolulu, and Speaker Hawaii Territorial House of Representatives; Founder of law firm of Fong, Miho, Choy and Robinson; Pres. Finance Factors, Grand Pacific Life Insurance Co., Finance Realty, Finance Investment Co., and Market City, Ltd.; U.S. Senator from Hawaii 59-; Republican; Hon. LL.D. (Tufts and Hawaii Univs., Lafayette Coll., Long Island Univ.).
1313 New Senate Office Building, Washington, D.C.; 1102 Alewa Drive, Honolulu 96817, Hawaii, U.S.A.

Fontaine, Maurice Alfred, D. ès SC.; French physiologist; b. 28 Oct. 1904, Savigny-sur-Orge; s. of Emile Fontaine and Lea Vadier; m. Yvonne Broca 1928; one s.; ed. Lycée Henri IV, Paris, and Faculty of Sciences and Faculty of Pharmacy, Univ. of Paris.
Various posts at Faculty of Sciences, Paris, and Faculty of Pharmacy, Paris; Dir. of Institut Océanographique, Paris; Pres. Soc. Européenne d'Endocrinologie comparée 69-; Dir. of Museum Nat. d'Histoire Naturelle, Paris 66-71; lectures on comparative and ecological physiology, particularly of marine animals; specializes in comparative endocrinology and fish migration; Dir. of Research in these fields and also the study of ectocrine substances in sea water and marine pollution; Pres. Acad. des Sciences; mem. Acad. Nat. de Médecine, Acad. agriculture; Officier Légion d'Honneur; Commdr. Ordre de Sahametrei (Cambodia), Commdr. Ordre de St. Charles (Monaco).
Leisure interest: the sea.
Publ. *Physiologie* (collection La Pléïade) 69.
Académie des Sciences, Institut de France, 23 quai de Conti, 75006 Paris; 25 rue Pierre Nicole, 75005 Paris, France.

Fontana Codina, Enrique; Spanish politician; b. 17 Oct. 1921, Reus, Tarragona; *m.*; three *c.*; ed. Univ. of Barcelona.
Commissar-Gen. of Supplies and Transport 65-69; mem. of Council of Agricultural Credit Bank; fmr. adviser to Bank of Spain; Pres. Olive Oil Exporters' Group 59; mem. Spanish Del. to Int. Oleic Council; Technical Dir. for Consumers, Commissary of Supplies; Joint Pres. Food Industries Comm.; mem. of Falange; mem. of Cortes; Minister of Commerce Oct. 69-73.
c/o Ministerio de Comercio, Madrid, Spain.

Fontanet, Joseph, D. EN D.; French politician; b. 9 Feb. 1921, Frontenex (Savoy); *s.* of Joseph Fontanet and Marthe Blanchard; *m.* Hélène Pouliquen 1940; six *c.*
In Secret Army, Second World War, joined French forces in N. Africa 43; on staff of Sec. of State for Public Health and Population 50-51; Conseiller Général, Moutiers (Savoy) 51-, Vice-Pres. Conseil Général 61; Counsellor, French Union 56-; Deputy for Savoy 56-58, 62-69, 73; Sec. of State for Industry and Commerce 59; for Internal Commerce 59-61; Minister of Public Health and Population 61-62; Sec.-Gen. Mouvement Républicain Populaire (M.R.P.) 63-66; Minister of Labour 69-72, of Educ. 72-74; Croix de Guerre (39-45). Leisure interests: sailing, swimming, hunting.
54 avenue de Saxe, 75015 Paris; Home: 36 boulevard Emile-Augier, 75016 Paris, France.
Telephone: 504-70-99; 567-16-85.

Fontanne, Lynn; British actress; b. 6 Dec. 1887, Woodford, Essex; *m.* Alfred Lunt (*q.v.*).
Began as child in pantomime, Drury Lane; small parts, various London companies with Lewis Waller, Beerbohm Tree, Lena Ashwell; played in touring companies with Weedon Grossmith for few seasons, playing name part in *Young Lady of 17*, and other small parts in various curtain-raisers; on tour in *Milestones*, then revival in London; small parts in *My Lady's Dress;* U.S.A.: many plays with Laurette Taylor; name part in *Dulcy*, followed by many leads, including *Goat Song, Strange Interlude, Arms and the Man, Second Man, Caprice, At Mrs. Beams, Pygmalion, In Love with Love, The Guardsman, Meteor, Reunion in Vienna, Design for Living, Point Valaine, Taming of the Shrew, Idiots' Delight, The Seagull, Amphytrion 38, There Shall Be No Night* by Robert Sherwood, *Love in Idleness* by Terence Rattigan, *I Know My Love* (adapted from Achard's *Auprès de ma Blonde*); played in *Quadrille* 52-53, *The Great Sebastian, The Visit*; many hon. degrees.
c/o Theatre Guild, 245 West 52nd Street, New York City, N.Y., U.S.A.

Fonteyn, Margot (*see* Arias, Señora doña Margot Fonteyn de).

Fontoura, Gen. Carlos; Brazilian army officer and politician; b. 1912, Cachoeira, Rio Grande do Sul; *s.* of Graciliano Pôrto da Fontoura and Otília Neves da Fontoura; ed. Colégio Militar, Pôrto Alegre, Escola Militar do Realengo, Escola das Armas, Escola de Comando e Estado-Maior do Exército.
Commander 8th Regiment Cavalry; Chief of Staff 2nd Cavalry Div.; Chief of Staff 6th Infantry Div.; Chief of Staff 3rd Army Div. 68; Head, Nat. Information Service (Serviço Nacional de Informações) 69-.
Serviço Nacional de Informações, Rio de Janeiro, Brazil.

Foot, Rt. Hon. Sir Dingle Mackintosh, Kt., P.C., Q.C. (brother of Lord Caradon, *q.v.*, and Michael Foot, *q.v.*); British politician; b. 24 Aug. 1905; ed. Balliol Coll., Oxford.
Queen's Counsel; fmr. Pres. Oxford Union; Liberal M.P. for Dundee 31-45; Parl. Sec. to Min. of Economic Warfare 40-45; mem. British Delegation San Francisco Conf. 45; mem. Royal Comm. on Justices of the Peace 46, Cttee. on Intermediaries 49; Bencher of Gray's Inn

52; Chair. of *Observer* Trustees Board 53-55; joined Labour Party 56; M.P. 57-June 70; Solicitor-Gen. Oct. 64-Aug. 67.
2 Paper Buildings, Temple, London, E.C.4, England.
Telephone: 01-353 9119.

Foot, Rt. Hon. Michael Mackintosh, P.C., M.P.; (brother of Lord Caradon, *q.v.*, and Sir Dingle Foot, *q.v.*); British journalist and politician; b. 23 July 1913; ed. Forres School, Swanage, Leighton Park School, Reading, and Wadham Coll. Oxford Univ.
President, Oxford Union 33; contested Monmouth 35; Asst. Editor *Tribune* 37-38, Joint Editor 48-52, Editor 52-59, Man. Dir. 52-74; mem. staff *Evening Standard* 38, Acting Editor 42-44; political columnist *Daily Herald* 44-64; mem. Parl. for Plymouth, Devonport 45-55, for Ebbw Vale 60-; Opposition spokesman on European Policy; Sec. of State for Employment 74-76; Lord Pres. of Council, Leader of House of Commons April 76-; Spanish Republican Order of Liberation 73; Labour.
Publs. *Armistice 1918-1939* 40, *Trial of Mussolini* 43, *Brendan and Beverley* 44, *Still At Large* 50, part author *Guilty Men* 40 and *Who Are the Patriots?* 49, *Full Speed Ahead* 50, *The Pen and the Sword* 57, *Parliament in Danger* 59, *Aneurin Bevan* Vol. I 62, Vol. II 73, *Harold Wilson: A Pictorial Biography* 64.
House of Commons, Westminster, London, S.W.1, England.

Foote, Emerson; American advertising executive; b. 13 Dec. 1906; ed. public schools.
Clerk 23-31; Leon Livingston Advertising, San Francisco 31-35; Yeomans and Foote (own advertising business) 35-36; with J. Stirling Getchell Inc., New York 36-38; Vice-Pres., Dir. and Exec. Vice-Pres. Lord & Thomas 38-42; Pres. and Dir. Foote, Colne & Belding 42-50; Vice-Pres. and Dir. McCann-Erickson Inc. 51, Exec. Vice-Pres. 52-57, Senior Vice-Pres. 58-60, Pres. 60-63, Chair. of Board 62-64; Pres. Kastor Foote Hilton & Atherton Inc. 64-67; Chair. Emerson Foote Inc. 67; Consultant and Dir. Bozell & Jacobs Inc. 67-; official of philanthropic orgs.
Gypsy Trail, Carmel, N.Y. 10512, U.S.A.

Foots, Sir James (William), Kt., B.M.E., M.AUS., I.M.M.; Australian mining engineer and company director; b. 12 July 1916; ed. Coburg and Univ. High Schools, Melbourne and Univ. Melbourne.
Mining engineer 38-45, with North Broken Hill Ltd. 38-43, Allied Works Council 43-44, Lake George Mines Ltd. 44-45, Zinc Corpn Ltd. 46-54; Asst. Gen. Man. Zinc Corpn. and New Broken Hill Consolidated Ltd. 53-54; Gen. Man. Mount Isa Mines Ltd. 55-56, Dir. 56-, Man. Dir. 66-70, Chair. 70-; Chair. and Chief Exec. M.I.M. Holdings Ltd. 70-; Dir. Bank of New South Wales 71-, Thiess Holdings Ltd. 71-; mem. Senate Queensland Univ. 70-; Pres. Australian Mining Industry Council 74, 75; Pres. Australasian Inst. of Mining and Metallurgy 74.
M.I.M. Holdings Limited, G.P.O. Box 1433, Brisbane, Q. 4001; and M.I.M. Holdings Limited, M.I.M. Building, 160 Ann Street, Brisbane, Q. 4000, Australia.

Forbes, Hon. Alexander James, M.C., D.PHIL.; Australian politician; b. Dec. 1923, Hobart, Tasmania; *m.* Margaret Allison Blackburn 1952; two *s.* three *d.*; ed. Knox Grammar School, Sydney, St. Peter's Coll., Adelaide, Royal Mil. Coll., Duntroon, and Univ. of Adelaide and Univ. of Oxford.
Served with 2nd Australian Mountain Battery, New Guinea and Bougainville 42; mem. British Occupation Forces, Japan 46, on attachment to British Army 46-47; student, Adelaide Univ. 47-50; a resident tutor, St. Mark's Coll., Adelaide 51; travelling scholarships until 54; Lecturer in Political Science, Univ. of Adelaide 54-56; Liberal mem. Parl. for Barker 56-; Minister for

the Army and Minister Assisting the Treas., also responsible for Navy 63-64; Minister for Health 66-71, for Immigration 71-72; Opposition spokesman for Defence 73-75; mem. Council, Australian Nat. Univ. 61-63; Pres. Australian Inst. of Int. Affairs (South Australian Branch) 60-62.
AMP Building, King William Street, Adelaide; Home: Walkerville, Adelaide, S. Australia.

Forbes, Sir Archibald Finlayson, G.B.E., Kt.; British chartered accountant and business executive; b. 6 March 1903; s. of Charles and Elizabeth Forbes; m. late Angela Gertrude Ely 1969; one s. two d.; ed. Paisley and Glasgow Univ.
Chartered accountant 27; fmr. mem. firm of Thomson McLintock & Co.; Exec. Dir. Spillers Ltd. 35-73; Dir. of Capital Finance, Air Ministry 40; Deputy Sec. Ministry of Aircraft Production 40-43; Controller of Repair, Equipment and Overseas Supplies 43-45; mem. Aircraft Supply Council 43-45; Chair. Iron and Steel Board 46-49; Chair. The Debenture Corpn. 49-; Pres. Fed. of British Industries 51-53; Chair. Iron and Steel Board 53-59; Chair. Cen. Mining and Investment Corpn. 59-64; Chair. Midland Bank 64-75, Pres. 75-; Chair. Spillers Ltd. 65-68, now Pres.; Chair. Cttee. of London Clearing Banks 70-72; Deputy Chair. Thomas Cook Group 75; Dir. Samuel Montagu and Co. Ltd., Bland Payne Holdings Ltd.
Leisure interests: golf, fishing.
40 Orchard Court, Portman Square, London, W.I. England.
Telephone: 01-935-9304.

Forbes, Bryan; British film executive, director and screenwriter; b. July 1926, Stratford-atte-Bow, London; m. Nanette Newman 1955; two d.; ed. West Ham Secondary School.
Studied at Royal Acad. Dramatic Art, first stage appearance 42; served in Intelligence Corps 44-48; entered films as actor 48; wrote and co-produced The Angry Silence 59; Dir. Whistle Down the Wind 61; Writer and Dir. The L-Shaped Room 62, Seance on a Wet Afternoon 63, King Rat 64; Producer and Dir. The Wrong Box 65; Writer, Producer and Dir. The Whisperers 66, Deadfall 67, The Madwoman of Chaillot 68, The Raging Moon (Long Ago Tomorrow in U.S.A.) 70; Writer, Producer and Dir. filmed biography of Dame Edith Evans for Yorkshire TV 73; filmed documentary on life style of Elton John for ATV 74; The Stepford Wives 74, The Story of Cinderella 75; Head of Production, Assoc. British Picture Corpn. 69-71, subsequently became EMI Film Productions Ltd.; mem. Gen. Advisory Council of BBC 66-69, Experimental Film Board of British Film Acad.; Govt. Nominee BBC Schools Broadcasting Council 72-; Trustee, Writers' Guild of Great Britain; British Film Acad. Award for The Angry Silence; Best Screenplay Awards for Only Two Can Play, Seance on a Wet Afternoon; United Nations Award for The L-Shaped Room; many Film Festival prizes.
Leisure interests: collecting books, running a bookshop, landscape gardening, collecting Napoleonic relics, avoiding bores.
Publs. Truth Lies Sleeping (short stories) 51, The Distant Laughter (novel) 72, Notes for a Life (autobiog.) 74.
c/o The Bookshop, Virginia Water, Surrey, England.
Telephone: Wentworth 2463.

Ford, Alexander; Polish film director; b. 24 Jan. 1908, Łódź.
Directed short, later full length films, Poland, 28-39; worked in U.S.S.R. film studios during Second World War making documentary and educational films in Novosibirsk and Tashkent; organized Polish Army Film Command 43; Man. Dir. Film Polski 45-47; Artistic Dir. film production group Studio 55-; emi-

grated to Israel 68; Gold Medal, Venice Festival 48; Nat. Award, First Class 52; Cannes Festival Award 54; Nat. Award, First Class 60.
Films include: Early Morning, Polish Manchester (Droga Młodych), Street Legion (Legion Ulicy), Na Start, Battle at Lenino (Bitwa Pod Lenino), Majdanek, Cmentarzysko Europy, Border Street, (Ulica Graniczna) 48, The Youth of Chopin (Młodość Chopina), Five from Barska Street (Piątka z Ulicy Barskiej) 54, The Eighth Day of the Week 58, Knights of the Teutonic Order (Krzyżacy) 60, The First Circle 72.
Israeli Film Service, P.O. Box 2090, Jerusalem, Israel.

Ford, Benson; American business executive; b. 20 July 1919, Detroit; s. of Edsel B. Ford and Eleanor Clay Ford; m. Edith McNaughton Ford 1941; one s. one d.; ed. Detroit Univ. School, Hotchkiss School, Princeton Univ.
Joined Ford Co. 40; currently Vice-Pres., Chair. Dealer Policy Board; Dir. Seaboard Properties Co.; Trustee, the Edison Inst., Ford Foundation; Chair. and Chief Exec. Officer Henry Ford Hosp., Detroit; Dir. Ford Motor Co.; Pres. Ford Motor Co. Fund.
Leisure interests: reading, golf, boating, photography.
Ford Motor Co., The American Road, Dearborn, Mich. 48121; Home: 635 Lake Shore Road, Grosse Pointe Shores, Mich. 48236, U.S.A.

Ford, Edmund Brisco, M.A., D.SC., F.R.S.; British professor emeritus; b. 23 April 1901, England; s. of Harold Dodsworth Ford and Gertrude Emma Bennett; ed. Wadham Coll., Oxford.
Demonstrator in Zoology and Comparative Anatomy, Oxford 28; Reader in Genetics, Oxford 38, subsequently Prof. of Ecological Genetics, now Prof. Emer.; Fellow of All Souls Coll., Oxford to 71; Pres. Genetical Soc. of Great Britain 46-49; Hon. Fellow, Wadham Coll., Oxford; Hon. F.R.C.P.; Darwin Medal of Royal Soc. 54; Weldon Medal and Prize, Oxford Univ. 59; Medal of Helsinki 67; Hon. D.Sc. (Liverpool).
Leisure interests: archaeology, travel, study of paintings.
Publs. Mendelism and Evolution (8th edn.) 65, The Study of Heredity (2nd edn.) 50, Genetics for Medical Students (7th edn.) 73, Butterflies (5th edn.) 67, Moths (3rd edn.) 72, Ecological Genetics (4th edn.) 75, Genetic Polymorphism.
Genetic Laboratories, Department of Zoology, Parks Road, Oxford; All Souls College, Oxford; Home: 5 Apsley Road, Oxford, England.
Telephone: 56787 (Laboratory); 22251 (All Souls Coll.); 58147 (Home).

Ford, Gerald Rudolph; American politician and lawyer; b. 14 July 1913, Omaha, Nebraska; s. of Gerald R. Ford, Sr. and Dorothy Gardner Ford; m. Elizabeth (Betty) Bloomer 1948; three s. one d.; ed. Univ. of Michigan and Yale Univ. Law School.
Partner, law firm Ford and Buchen 41-42; U.S. Navy service 42-46; mem. law firm Butterfield, Keeney and Amberg 47-49; mem. U.S. House of Reps. 49-73; House Minority Leader 65-73; Vice-Pres. of U.S.A. 73-74, Pres. of U.S.A. Aug. 74-; mem. Interparl. Union, Warsaw 59, Brussels 61, Belgrade 63; mem. U.S.-Canadian Interparl. Group, Chair. House of Repub. Conf. 63; mem. Warren Comm.; American Political Science Distinguished Congressional Service Award; Republican.
Publ. Portrait of the Assassin (with John R. Stiles).
The White House, Washington, D.C., U.S.A.
Telephone: (202) 456-1414.

Ford, Henry, II; American industrialist; b. 4 Sept. 1917, Detroit; s. of Edsel B. and Eleanor (Clay) Ford; m. 1st Anne McDonnell 1940 (divorced), one s. two d.; m. 2nd Maria Cristina Vettore Austin 1965; ed. Hotchkiss School, Yale Univ.
Dir. Ford Motor Co. 38; spent one year at Ford Motor

Co. 40; joined Navy 41; released because of his father's death and rejoined Ford Motor Co. 43; Vice-Pres. 43-44; Exec. Vice-Pres. 44; succeeded his grandfather as Pres. Sept. 45-60, Chair. and Chief Exec. Officer 60-; Alt. Del. to UN 53; Chair. Trustees, Ford Foundation 43-46, Trustee 56-; Chair. Nat. Alliance of Businessmen 68-69; mem. Business Council; Chair. Nat. Center for Voluntary Action 70-72; Chair. Presidential Election Campaign Fund Advisory Board; Co-Chair. Detroit Renaissance.
Ford Motor Co., The American Road, Dearborn, Mich. 48121; Home: Grosse Pointe Farms, Mich., U.S.A.

Ford, John Archibald, C.M.G., M.C., M.A. (OXON.); British diplomatist; b. 19 Feb. 1922, Newcastle under Lyme; ed. St. Michael's Coll., Tenbury, Sedbergh School, Oriel Coll., Oxford.
Served in Royal Artillery, rank of Major 42-46; joined Foreign Service (later Diplomatic Service) 47; Third Sec. British Legation, Budapest 49-52, Third Sec. and Resident Clerk, Foreign Office 52-54, Private Sec. to Perm. Under-Sec. of State, F.O. 54-56; Consul, San Francisco 56-59; seconded to H.M. Treasury 59; attended course at Admin. Staff Coll., Henley 59; First Sec. and Head of Chancery British Residency, Bahrain 59-61; Asst., F.O. Personnel Dept. 61-63, Head of Establishment and Org. Dept., Diplomatic Service 64-66; Counsellor (Commercial), British Embassy, Rome 66-70; Asst. Under-Sec. F.C.O. 70-71; H.B.M. Consul-Gen., New York and Dir.-Gen. British Trade Devt. in U.S. 70-75; Amb. to Indonesia May 75-.
British Embassy, Jalan M. H. Thamrin 75, Jakarta, Indonesia; Foreign and Commonwealth Office (Jakarta), London, S.W.1, England.

Ford, Robert Arthur Douglass, M.A., C.C.; Canadian diplomatist; b. 8 Jan. 1915, Ottawa; s. of Arthur Rutherford Ford and May Lavinia Scott; m. Maria Thereza Gomes 1946; ed. Univ. of Western Ontario and Cornell Univ.
Instructor, History Dept., Cornell Univ. 39-40; Dept. of External Affairs 40-; served Rio de Janeiro, Moscow, London 40-51; Chargé d'Affaires, Moscow 51-54; Head of European Div., Dept. of External Affairs 54-57; Amb. to Colombia 57-58, to Yugoslavia 59-61, to United Arab Republic 61-63, to U.S.S.R. 64-; Gov.-General's Award for Poetry 56; Hon. D.Litt., Univ. Western Ontario 65, Gold Medal of Professional Inst. of Public Service of Canada 71.
Leisure interests: travel, poetry, translations (Russian, Portuguese).
Publs. *A Window on the North* (poetry) 56, *The Solitary City* (poetry) 69.
c/o Department of External Affairs, Ottawa, Canada.

Ford, William Clay, B.S.(ECON.); American businessman; b. 14 March 1925; s. of Edsel Ford; ed. Yale Univ.
Dir. Ford Motor Co. 48; mem. of Sales and Advertising Staff 48 and of the Industrial Relations Staff 49; quality control Man. Lincoln-Mercury Div. Jet Engine Defence Project 51; Man. Special Product Operations 52; Vice-Pres. Ford Motor Co. and Gen. Man. Continental Div. 53; Group Dir. Continental Div. 55; Vice-Pres. Product Planning and Design 57-; Chair. Planning and Design Cttees.
Ford Motor Co., The American Road, Dearborn, Mich. 48121, U.S.A.

Forde, Rt. Hon. Francis Michael, P.C.; Australian schoolteacher, electrical engineer, politician and diplomatist; b. 18 July 1890, Mitchell, Queensland; s. of late John Forde and Ellen Forde; m. Veronica Catherine O'Reilly 1925; one s. three d.; ed. Christian Brothers Coll., Toowoomba.
Member Queensland Legislature 17-22; Fed. M.P. 22-46; mem. Royal Comm. on Motion Picture Industry 27-28; Minister for Trade and Customs 30-31 and 32; Act.

Minister for Markets and Transport 30-31; Dep.-leader Fed. Labour Party and of Opposition 31-41; Dep. Prime Minister, Deputy Leader Federal Labour Party and Minister for the Army 41-46; Minister for Defence 46; Act. Prime Minister 44-45; Leader Australian Del. to Commonwealth Minister's Conf. March-April 45; Prime Minister July 45; Leader, Australian Del. to San Francisco Conf. April 45; Australian High Commr. in Canada Nov. 46-53; Dean of the Diplomatic Corps., Ottawa 52-53; mem. for Flinders, Queensland Legislature 55-57; Rep. Australia at Gen. MacArthur's Funeral, U.S.A. 64; Hon. LL.D. (Ottawa, Montreal, Laval and Queensland Univs.).
Leisure interests: tennis, golf, bowls, reading.
44 Highland Terrace, St. Lucia, Brisbane, Queensland 4067, Australia.
Telephone: Brisbane 70-9447.

Foreman, Carl, C.B.E., F.R.S.A.; American cinema writer, producer and director; b. 1914; s. of Isidore and Fanny (Rozin) Foreman; m. Evelyn Smith 1965; ed. Crane Coll., Univ. of Illinois and Northwestern Univ.
Managing Dir., Exec. Producer, Open Road Films Ltd.; Commdr. Order of the Phoenix (Greece); mem. Board of Govs. British Film Inst. 65-71; mem. Exec. Council, Film Production Asscn. of Great Britain 67-; Pres. Writers' Guild of Great Britain 67-; mem. Board of Govs., Nat. Film School; Writers' Guild of America Award; Best American Drama: *High Noon* 52, Writers' Guild of Great Britain Laurel Award for Distinguished Service to Writers 68; Writers' Guild of America Laurel Award 69; Variety Club of Great Britain Show Business Writer Award 72.
Film Scripts: *So This is New York* 48, *Champion* 49, *Home of the Brave* 49, *The Men* 50, *Cyrano de Bergerac* 50, *The Bridge on the River Kwai* 57; Film Writer-Producer: *High Noon* 52, *The Key* 57, *The Guns of Navarone* 61; Film Writer-Producer-Director: *The Victors* 63; Exec. Producer: *Born Free* 65, Writer-Producer *Mackenna's Gold* 67; Exec. Producer *Otley* 68, *The Virgin Soldiers* 69, *Living Free* 71, *Young Winston* 72.
25 Jermyn Street, London, S.W.1, England.
Telephone: 01-437-4534.

Forgeot, Jean; French business executive; b. 10 Oct. 1915, Paris; s. of P. E. Forgeot and Aydée Lefebvre; m. Sylviane Busck 1948; one d.; ed. Faculté de Droit, Paris.
Formerly Insp., Ministry of Finance; Adviser to the Cabinet of Vincent Auriol; Sec.-Gen. to Pres. of Repub. 47-54; fmr. Pres. Dir.-Gen. Schneider S.A.; Vice-Pres. Chrysler-France; Pres. Dir.-Gen. Cie. Financière de l'Union Européenne, Esso-Standard, Cie. Maritime des Chargeurs Réunis, Imprimerie Georges Lang; Pres. Creusot-Loire; Officier, Légion d'Honneur, Croix de Guerre (39-45).
Leisure interests: tennis, golf.
80 boulevard Flandrin, Paris 16e, France.

Forlani, Arnaldo; Italian politician; b. 8 Dec. 1925, Pesaro; s. of Luigi and Caterina Forlani; m. Alma Ioni; two s.; ed. Univ. of Urbino.
Deputy Sec. of Christian Democrat Party 62-69, Political Sec. 69-73; Minister of State Undertakings 69-70, of Defence Nov. 74-.
Leisure interests: politics, journalism.
Via Sallustiana, 53 Rome, Italy.
Telephone: 470-240 (Home).

Forman, Miloš; Czechoslovak film director; b. 18 Feb. 1932, Čáslav; ed. Film Faculty, Acad. of Music and Dramatic Art, Prague.
Director of Film Presentations, Czechoslovak Television 54-56; of Laterna Magika, Prague 58-62; mem. Artistic Cttee., Šebor-Bor Film Producing Group; Czechoslovak Film Critics' Award for *Peter and Pavla* 63; Grand

Prix 17th Int. Film Festival, Locarno, for *Peter and Pavla* 64, Prize Venice Festival 65; Grand Prix of French Film Acad. for *A Blonde in Love* 66; Klement Gottwald State Prize 67; Acad. Award (Best Dir.) for *One Flew Over the Cuckoo's Nest* 76.
Films include: *Talent Competition, Peter and Pavla, The Knave of Spades, A Blonde in Love, Episode in Zruč, Like a House on Fire (A Fireman's Ball), Taking Off* 71, *One Flew Over the Cuckoo's Nest* 75, Co-Dir. *Visions of Eight* 73.
Living in U.S.A.

Formentini, Paride, DR.ECON. and COMM.SC.; Italian businessman; b. 12 June 1899, Cremona; ed. Genoa Univ.
Held diplomatic posts 21-24; Personal Sec. to Dr. Alberto Pirelli of Società Italiana Pirelli (Milan) 24-25; Dep. Man., Sec. Board of Dirs. and Exec. Cttee. Central Management, Banco di Roma 26-31; Dep. Gen. Man. Istituto Mobiliare Italiano (IMI) 32-33; Gen. Man. Società Torinese Esercizi Telefonici (S.T.E.T.) 34-36; Gen. Man. Società Finanziaria Marittima Finmare 37-47; Dep. Gen. Man. Banca d'Italia 47-48, Gen. Man. 48-59; Chair. and Pres. European Investment Bank 59-70, Hon. Pres. 70-; Chair. of Board Fonditalia Management Co. 70-.
c/o Fonditalia Management Co., boulevard de la Pétrusse 134, Luxembourg.

Formica, Gianni, P.H.D.; Italian space research administrator; *m.*; one *d.*; ed. Milan Polytechnic.
Director CGE—Gen. Electric, Milan 59-69; Prof. of Hydraulics, Faculty of Agronomy, Catholic Univ. of Milan 62-70; Dir. Società Italiana Sistemi Informativi Elettronici 69-73, Head, Milan office 70-73; Prof. of Hydraulics, Faculty of Engineering, Univ. of Ancona 71-73; Dir. European Space Operations Centre 73-.
Publs. numerous works on digital computing, the scientific applications of computers and related subjects.
European Space Operations Centre, 5 R. Bosch Strasse, Darmstadt, Federal Republic of Germany.

Forna, Alpha George Sembu; Sierra Leonean politician; b. 11 April 1932; *s.* of Alhaj Mendé and Fatu Forna; *m.* 1958; six *s.* two *d.*; ed. Fourah Bay Coll., Univ. Coll., Sierra Leone, London and Antwerp.
Assistant Social Devt. Officer, Ministry of Social Welfare 55-58; Diamond Valuer, London 58-62, Sierra Leone 62-69; Minister of Transport and Communications 69, of Finance 70-71, of Agriculture and Natural Resources 71-73, of Health 73-74, of Tourism and Culture 74-.
Leisure interests: farming, boating, game hunting, table tennis, lawn tennis.
P.O. Box 788, 121 Wilkinson Road, Freetown, Sierra Leone.
Telephone: 23043 (Office); 30534 (Home).

Fornari, Giovanni, DR. JUR.; Italian diplomatist; b. 21 May 1903, Rome, Italy; *s.* of Giuseppe Fornari and M. Concetta de Ferrante dei baroni di San Paolo; *m.* Maretta Arnaldi 1934; two *s.* one *d.*; ed. Univ. of Rome.
Vice-Consul, France 26-30; Ministry of Foreign Affairs 30-34; Del. to League of Nations 32; First Sec., Madrid, Morocco, Athens 34-40; Missions to Turkey 33, Yugoslavia 40; Min. Foreign Affairs 41-42, 44-45; Chargé d'Affaires, Netherlands 43, Argentina 46-47; Ambassador to Chile 48-49; Gov. of Italian Somaliland 50-53 (with rank of Ambassador); Ambassador to Brazil 53-55, to U.A.R. 55-61; Dir.-Gen. of Political Affairs, Ministry of Foreign Affairs, Rome 61-64; Amb. to France 64-69; Pres. Electroconsult (ELC); Pres. Italia-Francia Asscn.; Pres. FUNDUS.
Leisure interests: golf, gardening.
Via Cassia 1951 (Olgiata), Rome, Italy.
Telephone: 699-80-35.

Fornasetti, Piero; Italian painter, designer, manufacturer of large line of household articles and decorative arts consultant; b. 1913; one *s.*; ed. Brera Acad. of Arts.
Designer of textiles, mosaics, furniture, decorations and porcelain; Editor of books in limited editions, etc.; Perm. Exhbn., Milan; Sarfatti Scholarship, Neiman Marcus Award.
Principal works: screens, furniture, panels, porcelain and ceramic items, decorating accessories, etc.; exhbns. in stores, fairs and museums: Zürich and Basle; Bolide design, Musée des Arts Décoratifs, Palais du Louvre, Paris 70; Interior decoration: Padua Univ., Hilton Hotel, Istanbul; Hotel Duomo (Milan); interior decoration for ships: *Giulio Cesare, Conte Grande, Andrea Doria, Australia, Oceania,* and for hotels, etc.
Leisure interests: collection of documents, stands, decorative arts.
Via Antonio Bazzini 14, Milan, Italy.
Telephone: 292-662.

Foroughi, Mahmoud; Iranian diplomatist; b. 8 Aug. 1915; ed. Teheran Univ.
Iranian Foreign Service 39-, London 43-48, Ministry of Foreign Affairs 48-50; Consul-Gen. in New York, Del. to UN Gen. Assembly 50-56; Ambassador to Brazil 57-62; Under-Sec. for Political Affairs, Ministry of Foreign Affairs 62; Ambassador to Switzerland 62-63, to U.S.A. 63-65, to Afghanistan 66-72; Dir. Inst. of Int. Affairs 74-.
Institute of International Affairs, Ministry of Foreign Affairs, Teheran, Iran.

Forrest, Sir James Alexander, Kt.; Australian industrialist; b. 10 March 1905, Kerang, Victoria; *s.* of J. Forrest; *m.* Mary C. Armit 1939; three *s.*; ed. Melbourne Univ.
Partner, Hedderwick Fookes & Alston, Solicitors 33-70, Consultant 70-73; served R.A.A.F. and Dept. Aircraft Production 42-45; Chair. Australian Consolidated Industries Ltd. 53-, Nat. Bank of Australasia Ltd. 59-, Chase-N.B.A. Group Ltd. 69-, Alcoa of Australia Ltd. 70-; Dir. Australian Mutual Provident Soc. 61-, Chair. Victorian Branch Board 57-; Dir. Western Mining Corpn. Ltd. 70-; mem. Council Monash Univ. 61-71, Royal Children's Hosp. Research Foundation and Victoria Law Foundation.
Leisure interests: golf, fishing.
19th Floor, AMP Tower, 535 Bourke Street, Melbourne, Victoria 3000; Home: 11 Russell Street, Toorak, Victoria 3142, Australia.

Forster, Isaac; Senegalese international judge; b. 14 Aug. 1903; ed. Lycée Hoche, Versailles, and Univ. of Paris.
General State Counsel's Dept. for French West Africa 30; Dep. Judge, Dakar 33; Dep. to Prosecutor, Conakry, Guinea 33; Judge, St. Denis, Réunion, then Madagascar 41; Judge of Court, Guadeloupe 45, French West Africa 47; Pres. of Chamber, Dakar 57; Sec.-Gen. of Govt., Senegal 58-60; Prosecutor-Gen., Dakar 59; First Pres. Supreme Court of Senegal 60-64; Judge, Int. Court of Justice, The Hague 64-; assoc. mem. Inst. of Int. Law; numerous decorations.
International Court of Justice, Peace Palace, The Hague 2012, Netherlands.

Forsyth, William Douglass, O.B.E., M.A., B.LITT., DIP.ED.; Australian diplomatist; see *The International Who's Who 1975-76.*

Fortas, Abe; American lawyer, government official and fmr. judge; b. 19 June 1910, Memphis, Tenn.; *s.* of William and Ray Fortas; *m.* Carolyn E. Agger 1935; ed. Southwestern Coll., Memphis, and Yale Univ.
Assistant Prof. of Law, Yale 33-37; Asst. Chief, Legal Div., Agricultural Adjustment Admin. 33-34; Asst. Dir.

orporate Reorganization Study, Securities and xchange Comm. 34-37; Consultant 37-38; Asst. Dir. ublic Utilities Div. 38-39; Gen. Counsel, Public Works dmin. 39-40, Bituminous Coal Div. 39-41; Dir. Div. : Power, Dept. of Interior 41-42; Under-Sec. of the nterior 42-46; mem. law firm Arnold, Fortas and Porter, Vashington, D.C. 46-65; Judge, U.S. Supreme Court 5-May 69; law practice 69-.
054 31st Street, N.W., Washington, D.C. 20007, U.S.A. elephone: 337-5700.

Forte, Sir Charles, Kt., F.H.C.I.; British hotelier and aterer; b. 26 Nov. 1908, Monteforte Casalattico, rosinone, Italy; s. of Rocco and Maria Luigia Forte; ı. Irene Mary Chierico 1943; one s. five d.; ed. Alloa ıcad., Dumfries Coll., and Mamiani, Rome.
ame to London and opened first milk bar 35; acquired riterion Restaurant 53, Monico Restaurant, Café Royal, Slater and Bodega chain 54, Hungaria Restaur- nt 56, Waldorf Hotel 58, Fuller's Ltd. 59; Chair. forte's (Holdings) Ltd., Les Grands Hotels Associés td., Paris, Hotel George V, Paris, British Hotels, Restaurants and Caterers Asscn.; Deputy Chair. and Chief Exec. Trust Houses Forte Ltd.; Dir. TraveLodge nt. Inc., TraveLodge Australia; Dir. Forte's and Co. Ltd., Italian Int. Bank, London, Nat. Sporting Club, Theatre Restaurants Ltd., etc.; Consul-Gen. of San Marino in London; Pres. Italian Chamber of Commerce for Great Britain 52-; mem. British Inst. of Florence, Italy; Board mem. British Travel Asscn.; Grand Officer of the Order of the Italian Repub.; Cavaliere di Gran Croce della Republica Italiana; Knight of Magistral Grace of Sovereign and Mil. Order of Malta.
Leisure interests: literature, music, fishing, shooting.
166 High Holborn, London, W.C.1, England.
Telephone: 01-836 1213.

Fortier, Claude, C.C., M.A., M.D., PH.D., F.R.C.P.(C.)., F.R.S.C.; Canadian physiologist; b. 11 June 1921, Montreal, Canada; s. of Carolus Fortier and Flore- Edith Lanctôt; m. Elise Gouin 1953; four d.; ed. Univs. of Montreal, Lausanne and London.
Lecturer in Neurophysiology, Univ. of Montreal 47-51, Asst. Prof. of Experimental Medicine and Surgery 50-52; Research Assoc., Dept. of Neuroendocrinology, Univ. of London 53-55; Assoc. Prof. of Physiology and Dir. Lab. of Neuroendocrinology, Baylor Univ. Coll. of Medicine, Houston, Tex. 55-60; Dir. Endocrine Labs., Laval Univ. 60-, Prof. of Experimental Physiology 61-, Chair. Dept. of Physiology 64-; Vice-Chair. Medical Research Council of Canada 65-67; Vice-Chair. Medical Research Advisory and Co-ordinating Cttees, Defence Research Board 67-70; Chair. Advisory Cttee. on Medical Research, Govt. of Quebec 68-70; Vice-Chair. Science Council of Canada 75-; mem. Canadian Physio- logical Soc. (Pres. 66-67), American Physiological Soc., New York Acad. of Sciences, American Asscn. for Advancement of Science, etc.; Chair. of Board of Canadian Fed. of Biological Socs. 73-74, Pres. Royal Soc. of Canada 74-75; mem. Advisory Cttee. to Comm. on Canadian Studies 73-, Advisory Council of the Order of Canada 74-75; Trustee, Inst. for Research on Public Policy 74-; and of several govt. agencies and editorial boards; Companion Order of Canada 70-; Archambault Research Award of French Canadian Asscn. for the Advancement of Sciences 72; Science Award of Govt. of Quebec 72.
Leisure interests: sailing, skiing.
Publs. over 180 publications in physiology and related subjects.
Département de Physiologie, Faculté de Médecine, Université Laval, Quebec G1K 7P4; Science Council of Canada, 150 Kent, Ottawa, Ontario K1P 5PY; Home: 1014 De Grenoble, Ste-Foy, Quebec G1V 2Z9, Canada.
Telephone: 418-656-3259 (Office); 418-653-9656 (Home).

Fortier, Jean-Marie; Canadian ecclesiastic; b. 1 July 1920, Quebec; s. of Joseph Fortier and Alberta Jobin; ed. Petit Séminaire de Québec, Laval Univ., Univ. of Louvain, Belgium.
History Teacher, Grand Séminaire de Québec 50-60; Auxiliary Bishop of Ste.-Anne-de-la-Pocatière 60; Bishop of Gaspé 65; Archbishop of Sherbrooke 68-; mem. Vatican's Sacred Congregation for Sacraments and Divine Worship 75-.
Archevêché de Sherbrooke, C.P. 430, Sherbrooke, Quebec, Canada.

Fortner, Wolfgang; German composer; b. 12 Oct. 1907; ed. Univ. of Leipzig and Leipzig Conservatory of Music.
Lecturer Evangelical Church Music Inst., Heidelberg 31-53; Prof. of Composition N.W. German State Acad. of Music, Detmold 54-57, State High School for Music, Freiburg 57-; Founder and Dir. Heidelberg Chamber Orchestra 35-41; Founder and Dir. *Musica Viva* Heidelberg 46, Freiburg 58, Munich 64; Pres. German Section Int. Soc. for Contemporary Music; several awards.
Compositions: Opera: *Bluthochzeit* 57, *In seinem Garten liebt Don Perlimphin Belisa* 62; Ballet: *Die weisse Rose* 53; Cantata: *Die Pfingstgeschichte* 63; Orchestral works: *Capriccio* 38, *Sinfonie* 47, *Phantasie über B-A-C-H* 50, *Impromptus* 57, *Triplum*, etc.; and many other works.
Mühltalstrasse 122D, Heidelberg, Federal Republic of Germany.

Foss, Lukas; American composer, conductor, pianist and professor of music; b. 15 Aug. 1922, Berlin, Germany; s. of Martin Fuchs and Hilda Schindler; m. Cornelia B. Brendel 1955; one s. one d.; ed. Lycée Pasteur, Paris, Curtis Inst. of Music, Yale Univ. Music School.
Professor of Conducting and Composition, Univ. of Calif. at Los Angeles 51-62; Founder Dir. Center for Creative and Performing Arts, Buffalo Univ. 63-; Musical Dir., Conductor Buffalo Philharmonic Orchestra 62-70; Musical Adviser, Conductor Brooklyn Philharmonic Orchestra 71-, Jerusalem Symphony Orchestra 72-; Dir., Conductor Ojai Festival, Calif. 55, 56, 57, Festival of the Arts Today, Buffalo Philharmonic 64, 67, Franco-U.S. Festival 64, Stravinsky Festival 65; Visiting Prof. Harvard Univ. 69-70, Manhattan School of Music 72-73; mem. Nat. Inst. of Arts and Letters; Dr. h.c.; N.Y. Music Critics' Circle Awards; Prix de Rome; Ditson Award 74, and nine composition awards.
Compositions include *Time Cycle*, *Echoi*, *Baroque Variations*, *Paradigm*, *Geod*, *Cave of the Winds*, *Orpheus*, *Map*, *Percussion Concerto*, *String Quartet*.
17 East 96th Street, New York, N.Y. 10028, U.S.A.

Foster, Kenneth C.; American insurance executive; b. 31 Jan. 1913, Augusta, Me.; s. of Earle Browne and Glenys Young Foster; m. Alice Good 1942; two d.; ed. Univ. of Maine, Columbia and Newark Univs.
With Prudential Insurance Co. of America 38-, Dir. of Agencies 47-50, Vice-Pres. 50-58, Senior Vice-Pres. 58-65, Vice-Pres. in charge of Western operations 65-66, Exec. Vice-Pres. 67-70, Pres. and Dir. 70-.
Leisure interests: gardening, boating, golf.
Publs. articles in insurance handbooks and periodicals.
The Prudential Insurance Co. of America, Prudential Plaza, Newark, N.J. 07101, U.S.A.
Telephone: 201-336-1234.

Foster, Sir Robert Sidney, G.C.M.G., K.C.V.O., K.ST.J.; British official; b. 11 Aug. 1913, London; s. of the late Sidney Charles Foster and Jessie Edith (née Fry) Foster; m. Margaret Walker 1947; ed. Eastbourne Coll. and Peterhouse, Cambridge.
Cadet, Northern Rhodesia Administrative Service 36-38, Dist. Officer 38-40; Military Service 40-43; Dist. Officer, N. Rhodesia 43-53, Senior Dist. Officer

53-57, Provincial Commr. 57-60, Sec., Native Affairs 60-61; Chief Sec., Nyasaland 61-63, Dep. Gov. 63-64; High Commr., Western Pacific June 64-Dec. 68; Gov. and C.-in-C. Fiji Dec. 68-70, Gov.-Gen. 70-72; Officier Légion d'Honneur 66.
Leisure interest: do-it-yourself.
"Kenwood", 16 Ardnave Crescent, Southampton, Hants, SO1 7FJ, England.
Telephone: Southampton 69412.

Foster, William Chapman; American retd. government official; b. 27 April 1897, Westfield, N.J.; s. of J. S. Foster and Anna L. Chapman; m. Beulah Robinson 1925; one s.; ed. Massachusetts Inst. of Technology.
With Pressed and Welded Steel Products Co. 22-46, Pres. 46; resigned to become Under Sec. of Commerce 46-48; Deputy U.S. Representative abroad to E.C.A. 48-49, Deputy Administrator 49-50, Administrator 50-51; Deputy Sec. of Defense 51-53; Pres. Manufacturing Chemists Asscn. 53-55, Exec. Vice-Pres. and Dir. Olin Mathieson Chemical Corpn., Chair. and mem. Board of Dirs. Reaction Motors Inc. 55-58; Vice-Pres. and Senior Adviser, Olin Mathieson 58-61; Chair. of Board and Pres. United Nuclear Corpn. 61; Dir. U.S. Arms Control and Disarmament Agency 61-69; Chair. Porter Int. Co.; served U.S. Army World War I and War Dept. World War II; U.S. Medal for Merit; Hon. mem. A.S.M.E. 69; numerous hon. degrees.
Leisure interests: yachting, golf.
3304 R Street, N.W., Washington, D.C. 20007, U.S.A.
Telephone: 202-338-2440.

Foster-Sutton, Sir Stafford William Powell, Kt., K.B.E., C.M.G., O.B.E. MIL., Q.C.; British lawyer; b. 24 Dec. 1898, Philadelphia, U.S.A.; s. of G. W. Foster-Sutton and Florence Mary Sutton; m. Linda Dorothy Allwood 1919; one s. (deceased) one d.; ed. St. Mary Magdalen School and private tutor.
Served in army 14-26; active service, R.F.C. and R.A.F. First World War 14-18; called to the Bar (Gray's Inn) 26; private practice 26-36; Solicitor-Gen. Jamaica 36; Attorney-Gen. Cyprus 40; Col. Commdg. Cyprus Volunteer Force and Inspector Cyprus Forces 41-44; mem. for Law and Order and Attorney-Gen. Kenya 44-48, Acting Gov. Aug.-Sept. 47; Attorney-Gen. Malaya 48-50; Chief Justice Fed. of Malaya 50; Officer Administering the Govt., Fed. of Malaya Sept.-Dec. 50; Pres. West African Court of Appeal 51-56; Chief Justice, Fed. of Nigeria 56-58; Act. Gov.-Gen. May-June 57; Pres. Pensions Appeal Tribunals for England and Wales 58-73; Chair. Zanzibar Comm. of Inquiry 61, Regional Boundaries and Constituencies Delimitation Comms., Kenya 62, Referendum Observers, Malta 64, Council of Britain/Nigeria Asscn., Exec. Cttee. Overseas Service Pensioner's Asscn.
7 London Road, Saffron Walden, Essex, England.
Telephone: Saffron Walden 2246 (Home).

Fostervoll, Alf Jakob; Norwegian politician; b. 20 Jan. 1932, Kristiansund; s. of Alv Kr. and Astrid Fostervoll; m. Gerd Klinge 1967; two c.; ed. Teachers' Coll. of Norway.
Teacher, Gomalandet School, Kristiansund 56-57, Headmaster 67; mem. Kristiansund Municipal Council, Alderman 60-, Deputy Chair. 67-69; mem. Møre and Romsdal County Council 67; mem. Board Møre and Romsdal County Steamship Co. 67; mem. Storting 69-; Chair. Nordmøre Labour Party 65-69; Minister of Defence 71-72, Oct. 73-76.
Tiriltunga 2, 1346 Gjettum, Norway.

Fou Ts'ong; Chinese pianist; b. 10 March 1934; m. 1st Zamira Menuhin 1960 (dissolved 1970), 2nd Hijong Hyun 1973; ed. Shanghai and Warsaw.
First performance, Shanghai 53, concerts in Eastern Europe and U.S.S.R. 53-58; London debut 59, concerts

in Europe, North and South America, Australia an Far East.
c/o Wilfred van Wyck Ltd., Troon, Old Mill Lan Bray, Berks., England.

Fouché, Jacobus Johannes, D.M.S.; South Africa politician; b. 6 June 1898, Wepener, O.F.S.; s. Jacobus Johannes Fouché and Maria Elizabeth (n Steynberg); m. Letta Rhoda McDonald 1920; one ed. Victoria Coll., Stellenbosch.
M.P. for Smithfield 41-50, for Bloemfontein West 60-6 Administrator, Orange Free State 51-59; Minister Defence 59-66, of Agricultural Technical Services an Water Affairs 66-68; State Pres. of S. Africa 68-7. Decoration for Meritorious Service 71.
Leisure interest: farming.
c/o Office of the State President, Pretoria, Transvaa Republic of South Africa.
Telephone: 74-3131.

Fouchet, Paul Jacques; French diplomatist; b. 25 Ja 1913; ed. Lycée Condorcet and Faculty of Law, Pari French Consulate, Addis Ababa 38-39, Third Sec Ankara 41, French Consulate, Baghdad 41-42, resigne 42; recalled by Vichy Govt. 43, Civil and Militar Command, Algeria 43; Allied Military Govt., Italy 43 44, mem. French Del. to Consultative Council on Italia Affairs 44-45, Consul, Milan 45-46; Office of Foreig Affairs, Paris 46-47; First Sec. New Delhi 47-49; mem French Del. to UN Special Comm. on Balkans 49-50 First Sec Athens 50-52, Second Counsellor, Vienn 54-59; Head of Dept. for Technical Co-operation 59-62 Amb. to Niger 62-64, to Dominican Repub. 64-66, t Libya 66-69; Deputy Gen. Dir., Cultural, Scientific an Technical Dept., Ministry of Foreign Affairs 69-71 Amb. to Brazil 72-75, to Sweden 75-; Officier Légio d'Honneur.
French Embassy, 28 Narvägen, 115 23 Stockholm Sweden; and 2 rue de Noisel, Paris 16e, France.

Foulkes, Nigel Gordon, M.A., F.B.I.M., F.R.S.A.; Britis business executive; b. 29 Aug. 1919, London; ed Gresham's School and Balliol Coll., Oxford.
Production Man., H. P. Bulmer & Co., Ltd. 47-51 Management Consultant, P.E. Consulting Group Ltd 51-56; Senior Personnel Officer, Birfield Ltd. 57-58 Dir. Greaves and Thomas Ltd. 59-61; Exec. Asst. to Chair., Int. Nickel Ltd. 61-64; Man. Dir. Rank Xerox Ltd. 64-70; Chair. F.O.B.A.S. Ltd. 70, British Airports Authority 72-; Dir. Imagic Holdings 71, Charterhouse Group 72, Bekaert Group (Belgium) 73, Council, British Inst. of Management 72, Stone-Platt Industries 75; mem. Court, Brunel Univ., London 75.
British Airports Authority, 2 Buckingham Gate, London, S.W.1, England.
Telephone: 01-834-6621.

Fourcade, Jean-Pierre; French politician; b. 18 Oct. 1929, Marmande; s. of Raymond and Germaine (née Raynal) Fourcade; m. Odile Mion 1958; ed. Coll. de Sorèze, Bordeaux Univ. Faculté de Droit, Inst. des Etudes politiques.
Student, Ecole Nat. d'Admin. 52-54; Insp. des Finances 54-73; Chargé de Mission to Sec. of State for Finance (later Minister of Finance) 59-61, Conseiller technique 62, Dir. adjoint du Cabinet 64-66; Asst. Head of Service, Inspection gén. des Finances 62; Head of Trade Div., Directorate Gen. of Internal Trade and Prices 65, Dir.-Gen. 68-70; Asst. Dir.-Gen. Crédit industriel et commercial 70, Dir.-Gen. 72-74, Admin. 73-74; Admin., later Pres. and Dir.-Gen. Soc. d'Epargne mobilière 72-74; Admin. Banque transatlantique 71-74, Soc. commerciale d'Affrètement et de Combustibles 72-74; Minister of Econ. and Finance 74-; Mayor of Saint-Cloud 71-; Conseiller gén., canton of Saint-Cloud 73-; Officier, Ordre Nat. du Mérite.

inistère de l'Economie et des Finances, 93 rue de
ivoli, 75001 Paris; Home: 8 Parc de Bearn, 92210
aint-Cloud, France.

Fourest, Henry-Pierre; French ceramist; b. 22 Dec.
)11, Paris; s. of Georges Fourest and Valentine Fourest
uée Noe); m. Françoise Labayle-Paranaud 1946; one
three d.; ed. Ecole du Louvre and Institut d'Art et
rchéologie.
ssistant in Dept. of Paintings, Musée du Louvre; Asst.
a Musée Céramique de Sèvres; Chief Curator of Musée
at. Céramique de Sèvres, Musée Nat. Adrien Du-
ouché; Lecturer Ecole Nationale Supérieure Céramique
e Sèvres; fmr. Prof. Ecole du Louvre; Pres. Asscn. de
Ecole du Louvre; Chevalier Légion d'Honneur,
fficier des Arts et des Lettres, Officier Ordre Nat. du
Iérite.
eisure interests: music, ichthyology.
6 rue de Liège, Paris 9e, France.
elephone: 874-19-81.

Fourie, Bernardus Gerhardus, M.A., B.COM.; South
African diplomatist; b. 1916, Wolmaransstad; s. of
N. P. Fourie; m. Daphne Madeleine Doyle 1962; one s.
ne d.; ed. Pretoria and New York Univs.
On staff of Berlin Embassy 39, Brussels 40, London
High Comm. 39, 40-45; Del. to San Francisco Conf. 45,
UN Prep. Comm. and 1st Gen. Ass. 46; with Dept. of
External Affairs Int. Orgs. Div. 52-57, Asst. Sec.
African Div. 57-58; Perm. Rep. to UN 58-62; Under
Sec. African Div., Dept. of Foreign Affairs 62-63;
Sec. for Information 63-66; Sec. for Foreign Affairs 66-.
Leisure interests: tennis, gardening.
Department of Foreign Affairs, Union Buildings,
Private Bag X141, Pretoria, Republic of South
Africa.
Telephone: Pretoria 48-6912.

Fournier, Pierre Léon Marie; French concert cellist
and teacher; b. 24 June 1906, Paris; s. of Gen. Gaston
Fournier and Gabrielle (née Morice) Fournier; m. Lydia
Antik 1936; one s.; ed. Coll. Saint-Louis-de-Gonzague,
Conservatoire nat. supérieure de musique.
Professor, Ecole normale de musique 37-39, Conservatoire nat. supérieure de musique 41-49; concert tours
in Europe, North and South America, South Africa and
Far East 26-; has transcribed numerous works for
cello; Officier de la Légion d'Honneur, Commdr. de
l'Ordre national du Mérite, Officier des Arts et des
Lettres, Commdr. de l'Ordre de Léopold II.
14 parc Château-Banquet, Geneva, Switzerland.

Fournier-Acuña, Fernando, LL.D.; Costa Rican
lawyer and diplomatist; b. 13 Sept. 1916, San José; ed.
Univ. of Costa Rica and Harvard Univ.
Founding mem. Facio, Fournier & Cañas (law firm),
San José 42-; Prof. of History of Law, Univ. of Costa
Rica 47-48; Prof. of Roman Law 59-; mem. Constituent
Assembly 49-; Deputy Minister of Foreign Affairs
53-54; Minister 55; Amb. to U.S.A. and Perm. Rep. to
OAS 55-56; Del. Inter-American Council of Jurists 61-;
mem. Exec. Cttee. Inter-American Fed. of Lawyers
61-69, Pres. 67; mem. Int. Acad. of Trial Lawyers 69-.
Facultad de Derecho, Universidad de Costa Rica,
Apdo. 3979, San José, Costa Rica.

Fourquet, Gen. Michel Martin Léon; French air force
officer; b. 9 June 1914, Brussels, Belgium; m. Micheline
Roger 1939; five c.; ed. Lycée Louis-le-Grand and Ecole
Polytechnique, Paris.
Air Force Officer 43-44; Commdt. First Tactical Air
Group 60-61, 5th Air Region, Algiers 61-62; Chief
Commdt. Forces in Algeria 62; Sec.-Gen. of Nat.
Defence 62-66; Perm. Under-Sec. for Armaments 66-68;
Chief of Staff of Armed Forces 68-71; mem. Higher Air
Council 62-68; mem. Atomic Energy Cttee. 66-71; Pres.
Supervisory Council Soc. Nat. Industrielle Aérospatiale
75-; Pres. and Dir. Gen. Soc. des Autoroutes Paris-Est-

Lorraine 72-; Pres. Groupement pour le Financement
de Fos 72-; Grand Croix Légion d'Honneur, Compag-
non de la Libération, Croix de Guerre, Croix de la
Valeur Militaire, Médaille de l'Aéronautique, D.F.C.
(U.K.), etc.
Leisure interests: riding, hunting.
Home: 5 Villa Sainte-Foy, 92200 Neuilly-sur-Seine,
France.

Fowden, Leslie, PH.D., F.R.S.; British plant chemist;
b. 13 Oct. 1925, Rochdale, Lancs.; ed. Univ. Coll.,
London.
Member, Scientific Staff, Human Nutrition Research
Unit. Medical Research Council 47-50; Lecturer in
Plant Chem., Univ. Coll., London 50-55, Reader 56-64,
Prof. of Plant Chem. 64-73 and Dean of Faculty of
Science 70-73; Dir. Rothamsted Experimental Station
73-; mem. Council of Royal Soc. 70-72.
Office: Rothamsted Experimental Station, Harpenden,
Herts.; Home: 7 Ferncroft, 15 Basire Street, London,
N.1; and 1 West Common, Harpenden, Herts., England.

Fowler, Edward Michael Coulson, M.ARCH., F.N.Z.I.A.,
A.R.I.B.A.; New Zealand architect; b. 19 Dec. 1929,
Marton; s. of William Coulson and Faith Agnes Fowler
(née Netherclift); m. Barbara Hamilton Hall 1953;
two s. one d.; ed. Christ's Coll., Christchurch, Auckland
Univ.
With Ove Arup & Partners, London 54-55; Partner,
Gray Young, Morton Calder & Fowler, Wellington 59;
Senior Partner, Calder, Fowler & Styles 65-; travelled
abroad to study cen. banking systems security methods;
work includes Overseas Terminal, Wellington, Reserve
Bank, Wellington, Dalmuir House, Wellington Club,
office bldgs., factories, houses, churches; mem. Welling-
ton City Council 68-; Chair. NZIA Educ. Cttee. 67-73;
Mayor of Wellington 74-.
Leisure interests: sketching, writing.
Publs. *Country Houses of New Zealand* 72, *Wellington
Sketches: Folios I, II* 73.
Calder, Fowler, Styles & Partners, P.O. Box 2692,
Wellington; Home: 31 Hobson Crescent, Thorndon,
Wellington, New Zealand.
Telephone: 726916 (Office); 721117 (Home).

Fowler, Henry Hamill, A.B., LL.B., J.S.D.; American
lawyer, investment banker and government official; b.
5 Sept. 1908, Roanoke, Va.; s. of Mack Johnson Fowler
and Bertha (née Browning) Fowler; m. Trudye Pamela
Hathcote 1938; one s. (deceased) two d.; ed. Roanoke
Coll. and Yale Univ.
Admitted to Virginia Bar 33, D.C. Bar 46; Counsel
Tennessee Valley Authority 34-38, Asst. Gen. Counsel
39; Asst. Gen. Counsel O.P.M. 41, War Production
Board 42-44; Econ. Adviser, U.S. Mission Econ. Affairs,
London 44; served Foreign Econ. Admin. 45; Adminis-
trator Nat. Production Authority 51-52; Administrator
Defense Production Admin.; Dir. Office of Defense
Mobilization and mem. Nat. Security Council 52-53;
senior mem. law firm, Fowler, Leva, Hawes and Sym-
ington, Wash. D.C., 46-51, 53-61, 64-65; Under Sec.
U.S. Treasury 61-64, Sec. 65-68; Gen. Partner Goldman,
Sachs, New York 69-; Dir. Corning Glass Works, U.S.
Industries Inc., U.S. & Foreign Securities, Norfolk and
Western Railway Co., Foreign Policy Asscn.; Trustee,
Alfred P. Sloan Foundation, Carnegie Endowment for
Peace; Chair. Inst. of Int. Educ., Atlantic Council of
U.S., U.S. Treasury Advisory Cttee. on Reform of Int.
Monetary System; Trustee, Roanoke Coll., Lyndon B.
Johnson Foundation; Dir. Japan Soc.; Democrat.
Leisure interests: tennis, bridge, books.
Office: Goldman, Sachs & Co., 55 Broad Street, New
York, N.Y. 10004; Home: 209 South Fairfax Street,
Alexandria, Va., and 200 East 66th Street, New York,
N.Y. 10021, U.S.A.
Telephone: 676-8322 (Office).

Fowler, Peter Howard, D.SC., F.R.S.; British physicist; b. 27 Feb. 1923, Cambridge; *s.* of Sir Ralph Howard Fowler, F.R.S. and Eileen Rutherford; *m.* Rosemary Hempson (née Brown) 1949; three *d.*; ed. Winchester Coll. and Univ. of Bristol.
Flying Officer in R.A.F., Radar and Tech. Officer 42-46; Asst. Lecturer in Physics, Univ. of Bristol 48, Lecturer 51, Reader 61, Royal Soc. Research Prof. 64-; Visiting Prof. Univ. of Minn. 56-57; Hughes Medal, Royal Soc. 74.
Leisure interests: gardening, meteorology.
Publs. co-author: *The Study of Elementary Particles by the Photographic Method* 59.
H. H. Wills Physics Laboratory, Tyndall Avenue, Bristol, BS8 1TL, England.
Telephone: Bristol 24161, Ext. 113.

Fowler, Sir Robert William Doughty, K.C.M.G.; British diplomatist; b. 6 March 1914, Sutton-in-Ashfield, Notts.; *s.* of William and Martha Louise Fowler; *m.* Margaret MacFarquhar MacLeod 1939; one *s.* one *d.*; ed. Queen Elizabeth's Grammar School, Mansfield and Emmanuel Coll., Cambridge.
Burma Civil Service 37-48, Military Admin., Burma Army 44-46; Additional Sec. to Gov. of Burma 47; Commonwealth Relations Office (C.R.O.) 48; mem. U.K. Delegation to UN 50-53; Head of Fed. of Rhodesia and Nyasaland and High Comm. Territories Dept., C.R.O. 54-56; Deputy High Commr. Pakistan 56-58, Canada 60-62, Nigeria 63-64; High Commr. in Tanzania 64-66; Under-Sec. (African Affairs) Commonwealth Office 66; Amb. to Sudan Oct. 66-June 67; Referendum Admin., Gibraltar Sept.-Oct. 67; Amb. to Sudan Feb. 68-70; Panel of Chairmen, Civil Service Selection Board, London 72-.
Leisure interests: photography, painting.
7 Leicester Close, Henley-on-Thames, Oxfordshire, England.
Telephone: Henley 2404.

Fowler, William Alfred, B.ENG.PHYSICS, PH.D.; American professor of physics; b. 9 Aug. 1911, Pittsburgh, Pa.; *s.* of John McLeod and Jennie Summers (née Watson) Fowler; *m.* Ardiane Foy Olmsted 1940; two *d.*; ed. Ohio State Univ. and Calif. Inst. of Technology.
Research Fellow in Nuclear Physics, Calif. Inst. of Technology 36-39, Asst. Prof. of Physics 39-42, Assoc. Prof. 42-46, Prof. 46-70; Inst. Prof. of Physics 70-; Research Staff mem., Section T, and Div. 4, Nat. Defense Research Cttee. (N.D.R.C.) 41, Asst. Dir. of Research, Section L, Div. 3, N.R.D.C. 41-45; Technical Observer, Office of Field Services and New Devts. Div., War Dept. in South and Southwestern Pacific Theaters 44; Act. Supervisor, Ord. Div., R and D NOTS 1945; Science Dir., Project Vista, Dept. of Defense 51-52; Walker-Ames Prof. of Physics, Univ. of Wash. 63; Visiting Prof. of Physics, Mass. Inst. of Technology 66; Fulbright Lecturer and Guggenheim Fellow, Univ. of Cambridge 54-55; Lecturer at numerous univs. and socs. in U.S. and abroad; Guggenheim Fellow, St. John's Coll. and Dept. of Applied Maths. and Theoretical Physics, Univ. of Cambridge 61-62, Visiting Fellow, Inst. of Theoretical Astronomy, Univ. of Cambridge 68, 69, 70, 71, 72; Chair. Joint Discussion on Nucleogenesis, 10th Gen. Assembly of Int. Astronomical Union, Moscow 58; Del. to numerous int. confs. on astronomy, nuclear physics, astrophysics and cosmology; Fellow, American Physical Soc. (mem. Board of Editors 53-55, of Council 58-61, Vice-Pres. 75, Pres. 76), American Acad. of Arts and Sciences, Royal Astronomical Soc., London, Assoc. 75; mem. Int. Astronomical Union, American Asscn. for the Advancement of Sciences, American Astronomical Soc., American Asscn. of Univ. Profs. (Pres. Calif. Inst. of Technology Chapter 63-67), Nat. Acad. of Sciences, British Assn. for the Advance-

ment of Science, Royal Soc. of Arts, etc.; Chair. Physic Section, Nat. Acad. of Sciences 71-74, Int. Soc. o Gen. Relativity and Gravitation 74-; mem. Nat Science Board, Nat. Science Foundation 68-74, Spac Science Board, Nat. Acad. of Sciences 71-74; Corresp mem. Soc. Royale des Sciences de Liège, Atheneum Pasadena; Naval Ordnance Devt. Award 45, Medal fo: Merit 48, Lamme Medal, Ohio State Univ. 52, Liège Medal, Univ. of Liège 55, Calif. Co-Scientist of th Year 58, Barnard Medal of Meritorious Service t Science, Columbia Univ. 65; Apollo Achievemen Award, NASA 69; Bonner Prize, Amer. Physical Soc 70; G. Unger Vetlesen Prize, Columbia Univ. 73, Nat Medal of Science 74.
Publs. Contributions to numerous scientific books and journals.
Kellogg Radiation Laboratory, California Institute o: Technology, 1201 E. California Boulevard, Pasadena, Calif. 91125, U.S.A.
Telephone: 213-795-6841, Ext. 1272.

Fowles, John; British author; b. 31 March 1926, Essex; *s.* of Robert J. Fowles and Gladys M. Richards; *m.* Elizabeth Whitton 1954; no *c.*; ed. Bedford School and Univ. of Oxford.
PEN Silver Pen Award 69, W. H. Smith Literary Award (for *The French Lieutenant's Woman*) 69.
Leisure interests: gardening, natural history.
Publs. *The Collector* 63, *The Aristos* 64, *The Magus* 65, *The French Lieutenant's Woman* 69, *The Ebony Tower* 74.
c/o Anthony Sheil Associates Ltd., 52 Floral Street, London, W.C.2, England.

Fox, Rev. Adam, M.A., D.D.; British ecclesiastic and educationist; b. 15 July 1883, Kensington, London; *s.* of William Henry and Ellen (née Frost) Fox; ed. Winchester Coll. and Univ. Coll. Oxford.
Asst. Master Lancing Coll. 06-18, Diocesan Coll. Rondebosch, Cape Province 25-29; Warden of Radley Coll. 18-24; Fellow and Dean of Divinity Magdalen Coll. 29-42; Canon of Chichester 36-42; Prof. of Poetry Oxford 38-43; Canon of Westminster 42-63, Archdeacon of Westminster 51-59, Sub-Dean 59-63, Treas. 46-59, retired 63.
Leisure interests: poetry, Greek.
Publs. *Old King Coel* 33, *Dominus Virtutum* 36, *Plato for Pleasure* 46, *English Hymns and Hymn Writers* 47, *Meet the Greek Testament* 52, *John Mill and Richard Bentley* 54, *Plato and the Christians* 57, *God is an Artist* 57, *Dean Inge* 60, *English Well Used* (with Sir Andrew Claye) 68, *Sacred and Secular: A Companion* (with G. amd G. Keene) 75.
4 Little Cloister, London, SW1P 3PL, England.
Telephone: 01-222-5821.

Fox, Bertrand, PH.D.; American economist; b. 28 Feb. 1908, Williams Bay, Wis.; *s.* of Philip Fox and Ethel L. Snow; *m.* 1st Mary K. Ziegler 1935 (divorced 1950), 2nd Patricia N. O'Neill 1951; four *s.* two *d.*; ed. Northwestern Univ. and Harvard Univ.
Instructor and Tutor in Economics, Harvard Univ. 31-35; Asst. Prof. of Economics, Williams Coll. 35-40, Assoc. Prof. 40-45; Dir. Military Div., War Production Board 41-45; Prof. of Economics, Williams College 45-49; Admin., Merrill Foundation 47-62; Edsel Bryant Ford Prof. of Business Admin., Harvard Business School 55-67, Dir. of Research 53-68, Jacob H. Schiff Prof. of Investment Banking 67-; Research Dir. and Chief of Staff, Comm. on Money and Credit 58-61; Dir. Eberstadt Fund 66-, Harvard Univ. Press 66-, Cambridge Research Inst. 71-, Chemical Fund 71-; mem. American Finance Assn., American Economic Assn.
Publ. *Monetary and Fiscal Policy 1919-1939* 48.
Harvard Business School, Soldiers Field, Boston, Mass. 02163; Home: 18 Edgewood Road, Lexington, Mass. 02173, U.S.A.
Telephone: 617-495-6288.

Fox, Sir (Henry) Murray, G.B.E., M.A., D.LITT.; British chartered surveyor; b. 7 June 1912; s. of Sir Sidney Fox; m. Helen Isabella Margaret Crichton; one s. two d.; ed. Malvern and Emmanuel Coll., Cambridge.
Senior Partner, Chestertons; Chair. Trehaven Trust Group; Dir. City and Metropolitan Building Soc., Robert Marriott Ltd., Henley Forklift Co. Ltd.; Sheriff, City of London 71-72; Lord Mayor of London 74-75.
Leisure interests: golf, walking, reading.
Compter House, 9 Wood Street, London, E.C.2; Home: Flat 2, 43 Beech Street, London, E.C.2; Bradden Lodge, Bradden, Nr. Towcester, Northants., England. Telephone: 606-3055 (Office).

Foy, Lewis Wilson; American steel executive; b. 8 Jan. 1915, Somerset County, Pa.; s. of George M. and Nellie (Speicher) Foy; m. Marjorie Werry 1942; two d.; ed. Duke Univ., George Washington Univ. and Lehigh Univ.
Served U.S. Army 41-46; Joined Bethlehem Steel Corpn. 36, Buyer 50-52, Asst. to Purchasing Agent 52-55, Asst. Purchasing Agent 55-61; Asst. to Vice-Pres. (Purchasing) 61-63; Vice-Pres. Purchasing 63-70; Dir. 63-, Exec. Vice-Pres. 70, Pres. 70-74, Chair. and Chief Exec. Officer Aug. 74-; Dir. J. P. Morgan & Co. Inc., Morgan Guaranty Trust Co. of N.Y., Prospecciones Geologico Mineras, S.A., Brinco Ltd., Fluoruros S.A., Bituminous Coal Operators Asscn., Amer. Iron & Steel Inst.; Trustee, Moravian Coll., and Council of the Americas; mem. Newcomen Soc. in N. America, Business Council, Econ. Club of N.Y., Business Roundtable, Pennsylvania Soc., Board of Govs. United Way of America; Hon. LL.D. (Moravian Coll. and Lehigh Univ.), Hon. D.C.L. (Univ. of Liberia); Knight Great Band, Humane Order of African Redemption of Repub. of Liberia.
Martin Tower, Bethlehem, Pa. 18016; Home: Kenridge Farm, East Macada Road, Bethlehem, Pa. 18017, U.S.A.
Telephone: 215-694-3885 (Office).

Foyer, Jean, D. EN D.; French civil servant; b. 27 April 1921.
Professor, Paris Univ.; Deputy for Maine-et-Loire, Mayor of Contigné; Sec. of State for Relations with Member States of the French Community (Debré Cabinet) 60; Minister of Co-operation 61-62, of Justice 62-67; Pres. Nat. Assembly Comm. on Constitutional Laws of Legislation and Gen. Admin. of the Repub. 68-72, 73-; Minister of Public Health 72-73; Chevalier du Mérite Agricole.
49 Contigné (Maine-et-Loire), France.

Foyle, Christina; British bookseller; b. 1911; ed. Parliament Hill School and Aux Villas Unspunnen, Switzerland.
Entered book trade 28; Man. Dir. W. & G. Foyle Ltd., Foyle's Libraries Ltd. 63-, Dir. John Gifford Ltd., Foyle's Gallery, The Book Club, Foyle's Literary Luncheons.
W. & G. Foyle Ltd., 121 Charing Cross Road, London, W.C.2; and Beeleigh Abbey, Maldon, Essex, England.

Frachon, Benoît; French politician and trade union leader; b. 13 May 1893.
Factory worker and militant trade union leader at early age; served French Army 14-18; joined Socialist Party 19; worked for adhesion of party to Communist International; Sec. of Syndicat des Métaux du Chambon 22-24; Sec. of Union Départementale des Syndicats de la Loire 24-26; Sec. of regional organisation of Communist Party and mem. of Central Cttee. 26-; Nat. Sec. of party 28-33; Sec. of Confédération Générale du Travail Unitaire 33-36; Sec. of Confédération Générale

du Travail 36-39, Gen. Sec. 45-67; Pres. Confédération Générale du Travail 67-; clandestine activity 39-44. 213 rue Lafayette, Paris 10e, France.

Fraenkel, Gottfried Samuel, PH.D.; American professor of entomology; b. 23 April 1901, Munich, Germany; s. of Dr. Emil Fraenkel and Flora (née Weil); m. Rachel Sobol 1928; two s.; ed. Univ. of Munich.
Fellow Int. Educ. Board (Rockefeller Foundation) Zoological Station, Naples 26-27; Asst., Hebrew Univ., Jerusalem 28-30; Privatdozent, Zoology, Univ. of Frankfurt-am-Main 31-33; Research Assoc., Univ. Coll., London 33-35; Lecturer, Imperial Coll. of Science and Technology, London 36-48; Prof. of Entomology, Univ. of Ill. 48-; mem. Nat. Acad. of Sciences; Hon. Fellow, Royal Entomological Soc., London; Research Career Award, Nat. Insts. of Health 62-72.
Leisure interests: working-travel, marine biological laboratories, the Mediterranean, playing chamber music, singing madrigals, old editions of music, old engravings.
Publs. *The Orientation of Animals* (with D. L. Gunn) 40, new edn. 61, *Decorative Title Pages of Music, 200 Examples from 1500 to 1800* 68; about 200 scientific papers in learned journals, mostly on subjects concerning the physiology of insects.
Department of Entomology, University of Illinois, Urbana, Ill. 61801; Home: 606 W. Oregon, Urbana, Ill. 61801, U.S.A.
Telephone: 217-333-3736 (Office); 217-344-6581 (Home).

Fraga Iribarne, Manuel; Spanish writer, diplomatist and politician; b. 23 Nov. 1922, Villalba, Lugo; m. Maria del Carmen Estévez 1948; two s. three d.; ed. Santiago and Madrid Univs.
Professor of Political Law, Valencia Univ. 45; Diplomatic Service 45-; Prof. Theory of State and Constitutional Law, Madrid Univ. 48-; Gen. Sec. Inst. of Hispanic Culture 51; Gen. Sec. Nat. Educ. Ministry 55; Dir. Inst. of Political Studies 61; Minister of Information and Tourism 62-Oct. 69; also Sec.-Gen. of Cabinet Oct. 67-Oct. 69; Amb. to U.K. 73-75; Minister of the Interior and Deputy Premier for Internal Affairs Dec. 75-; mem. Cttee. for Defence of Christian Civilization, Union of Family Orgs.
Leisure interests: hunting, fishing.
Publs. thirty books on press, art, constitutional and social subjects.
Ministerio de Asuntos Interiores, Madrid, Spain.

Fragoso, José Manuel; Portuguese Ambassador to Brazil 67-72; see *The International Who's Who 1975-76*.

Frame, Janet; New Zealand writer; b. 1924, Dunedin; ed. Oamaru North School, Waitaki Girls' High School, Dunedin Training Coll. and Otago Univ.
Hubert Church Award for New Zealand Prose; New Zealand Scholarship in Letters 64, Burns Fellow Otago Univ. Dunedin.
Publs. *Lagoon* 51, *Owls do Cry* 57, *Faces in the Water* 61, *The Edge of the Alphabet* 62, *Scented Gardens for the Blind* 63, *The Reservoir* (stories), *Snowman, Snowman* (fables), *The Adaptable Man* 65, *A State of Siege* 67, *The Pocket Mirror* (poetry), *Yellow Flowers in the Antipodean Room* 68, *Mona Minim and the Smell of the Sun* (children's book) 69, *Intensive Care* (novel) 71, *Daughter Buffalo* (novel) 72.
c/o W. H. Allen & Co., 43 Essex Street, London, W.C.2; 61 Evans Street, Dunedin, Otago, New Zealand.

França, José-Augusto, D. ès L., D.HIST.; Portuguese writer and art historian; b. 16 Nov. 1922, Tomar; s. of José M. França and Carmen França; m. 2nd Marie-Thérèse França; one d. (by previous marriage); ed. Lisbon Univ., Ecole des Hautes Etudes and Univ. of Paris.
Travels in Africa, Europe and Americas 45-; Editor Lisbon literary review *Unicornio* 51-56, Co-Editor *Cadernos*

de Poesia 51-53; Founder-Dir. Galeria de Marco, Lisbon 52-54; art critic 46-; film critic 48-; lexicographical publisher 48-58; lived in Paris 59-63; Prof. Cultural History and History of Art, Dir. Inst. of Art History, New Univ. of Lisbon; Editor *Pintura & Não* 69-70; Editor *Colóquio Artes* 70-; Vice-Pres. Int. Asscn. of Art Critics 70-73, Acad. Nacional Belas Artes, Lisbon 75-; City Councillor, Lisbon 74-75; mem. Int. Asscn. of Art Critics, Int. Cttee. of Art History, Int. Asscn. for Cultural Freedom, PEN Club (Portuguese section), Academia Nacional de Belas Artes, Acad. das Ciencias de Lisboa, Acad. Portuguesa de Historia; Chevalier Ordre des Artes et Lettres (France).
Leisure interest: travel.
Publs. *Natureza Morta* (novel) 49, *Charles Chaplin—the Self-Made Myth* (essay) 52, *Azazel* (play) 57, *Amadeo de Souza-Cardoso* (essay) 57, *Despedida Breve* (short stories) 58, *Situação da Pintura Ocidental* (essay) 59, *Da Pintura Portuguesa* (essays) 60, *Dez Anos de Cinema* (essays) 60, *Une Ville des Lumières: La Lisbonne de Pombal* (essay) 63, *A Arte em Portugal no Século XIX* (essay) 67, *Oito Ensaios sobre Arte Contemporânea* (essays) 67, *Edgard Pillet: L'Artiste et L'Oeuvre* (essay) 67, *Le Romantisme au Portugal* (essay) 72, *Jérome Bosch* (essay) 72, *Almada, o Português sem Mestre* (essay) 72, *A Arte na Sociedade Portuguesa no Século XX* (essay) 72, *Antonio Carneiro* (essay) 73, *A Arte em Portugal no século XX* (essay) 74, *Zé Povinho* (essay) 75, *Millares* (essay) 75.
Mailing address: Rua Escola Politecnica 49/4 Lisbon 2; Fundacão C. Gulbenkian, Avenida Berne, Lisbon 1, Portugal; 9 Villa Virginie, Paris 75014, France.
Telephone: 362028 (Lisbon); 540-49-19 (Paris).

Francescatti, Zino; French concert violinist; b. 9 Aug. 1902, Marseilles; *m.* Yolande Potel de la Brière 1930; ed. privately.
Has played with most of the world's leading orchestras; frequently mem. of jury in int. musical contests; Hon. mem. Paris Conservatoire Orchestra, Philadelphia Orchestra, etc.; Commdr., Légion d'Honneur 75, Commdr. de l'Ordre de Léopold de Belgique 67; Commdr. de l'Ordre des Arts et des Lettres.
Leisure interests: chess problems, stamp collecting, driving, gardening.
Salle Pleyel, 252 rue du Faubourg-Saint-Honoré, Paris 8e; Summer Residence: La Ciotat-13, France; and 165 West 57th Street, New York, N.Y., U.S.A.

Francfort, Pierre Jean; French diplomatist; b. 28 Oct. 1908, Paris; *m.* Nadine Labey 1946; two *s.* one *d.*; ed. Lycée Carnot and Ecole des Sciences politiques.
Third Sec., Peking 35, Madrid 38-39; with Free French Govt. in London 42-45, Counsellor, London 45-48, Moscow 48-50, Washington 51-53; Minister, Romania 54-57; Private Sec. to Minister for Foreign Affairs 57-58; at Ministry of Foreign Affairs 60-62; Amb. to Hungary 62-65, to Yugoslavia 65-70, to Sweden 70-72; Ministry of Foreign Affairs; Officier Légion d'Honneur.
Leisure interest: history of art.
44 Avenue de la Bourdonnais, 75007 Paris, France.
Telephone: 551-63-66.

Francis, Sir Frank Chalton, K.C.B., M.A., F.S.A., F.L.A., F.M.A.; British librarian; b. 5 Oct. 1901, Liverpool, Lancs.; *s.* of Frank William Francis and Elizabeth Chalton; *m.* Katrina Florence McClennon 1927; two *s.* one *d.*; ed. Liverpool Inst., Liverpool and Cambridge Univs.
Classical Master, Holyhead County School 25-26; Asst. Keeper, British Museum 26-46; Sec. of British Museum 46-48; Keeper Dept. of Printed Books 48-59; Dir. and Principal Librarian, British Museum 59-Oct. 68; Hon. Fellow, Emmanuel Coll., Cambridge; Hon. Sec. Bibliographical Society; Lecturer in Bibliography, Univ. Coll., London; Chair. Council of British

Nat. Bibliography, Int. Relations Cttee., ASLIB (Asscn. Special Libraries and Information Bureaux), Executive Cttee., Library Asscn., Univ. and Research Section, Library Asscn., Nat. Cttee. for ICOM (Int. Council of Museums); mem. Library Advisory Council, England; Editor of *The Library* 36-53; Joint Editor *Journal of Documentation* 47-68; Advisory Editor *Library Quarterly*; Assoc. Editor *Libri*; Vice-Pres. Int. Advisory Cttee. on Bibliography, UNESCO; Pres. ASLIB 57-59, Int. Fed. of Library Asscns. 63-69, Bibliographical Soc. 64-66, Library Asscn. 65; Pres. Museums Asscn. 65-66; Chair. Int. Conf. on Cataloguing Principles, Paris 61, Anglo-Swedish Soc.; Consultant Council on Library Resources, Washington 68-; Master Worshipful Co. of Clockmakers 74; Hon. F.L.A.; Hon. D.Lit. (Dublin, Liverpool Exeter, British Columbia, Leeds, New Brunswick, Oxford, Cambridge, Wales Univs.); Corresp. mem. Massachusetts Historical Soc., Acad. des Beaux-Arts, Paris; Foreign Hon. mem. American Acad. Arts and Sciences; Hon. mem. Gustav Adolfs Akademien, Sweden.
Leisure interests: bibliography and gardening.
The Vine, Nether Winchendon, Aylesbury, Bucks., England.
Telephone: Haddenham 290184.

Francis, Sam, M.A.; American artist; b. 1923; ed. Univ. of California at Berkeley.
First exhbn. 47; subsequent exhbns. include San Francisco 48, Paris 51, 55, 56, New York 56, London, Berne, Tokyo, Osaka 57, Brussels 58, Dunn Int. Exhbn., London 63, Centre for Nat. Contemporary Arts, Paris 69, Tokyo Prize for American Artists in Japan; rep. in permanent collections of Museum of Modern Art and Guggenheim Foundation, New York, Tate Gallery, London; three mural panels, Kunsthalle, Basle, Switzerland 56-57, mural, Sōfu School Tokyo 57.
345 West Channel Road, Santa Monica, Calif. 90402, U.S.A.

François-Poncet, André, LL.D.; French politician and diplomatist; b. 13 June 1887; ed. Ecole Normale Supérieure.
Director, Société des Etudes et Informations Economiques; mem. Cttee. Republican Party; Deputy 24-31; Under-Sec. of State for Fine Arts 28-29; Under-Sec. for Nat. Economy in Tardieu Cabinet 30; Under-Sec. of State to the Prime Minister's Office in Laval Cabinet 31; Amb. to Germany 31-38, to Italy 38-40; mem. Nat. Council 41; arrested by Gestapo 43; liberated by Allies May 45; Special diplomatic counsellor to Ministry of Foreign Affairs Dec. 48; French High Commr. in Germany 49-55; Pres. French Red Cross 55-67; Grand Croix de la Légion d'Honneur; mem. Acad. Française 52-, Acad. des Sciences morales et politiques 61; Chancellor Institut de France 61-64.
Publs. *Les Affinités électives de Goethe, Ce que pense la Jeunesse allemande, La France et le problème des réparations, Discours français, Réflexions d'un républicain moderne, De Versailles à Potsdam, Souvenirs d'une Ambassade à Berlin, Carnets d'un Captif, Au Fil des Jours, Propos d'un Libéral—Au Palais Farnèse.*
92 rue du Ranelagh, Paris 16e, France.

Frangatos, Gerassimos, D.SC.; Greek scientist; b. 1923, Monoplata; *m.*; ed. Univ. of Athens, McGill Univ., and Nat. Council for Research, Ottawa, Canada.
Director of various important companies engaged in chemical production and research, Canada and U.S.A. 56-65; Prof. of Organic Chemistry, Athens Polytechnic 65; Scientific Adviser to Prime Minister; Pres. Hellenic Centre for Atomic Research; Minister of Nat. Education and Religion 72.
Publs. various scientific articles.
c/o Ministry of National Education, Athens, Greece.

Frangulis, A. F.; Greek diplomatist; b. 8 Nov. 1888; ed. Univs. of Athens, Geneva, Lausanne, Berlin and Paris.

Mem. of Greek Del. to Supreme Council, London, to negotiate peace with Turkey 20-21; subsequently del. to League of Nations 20-46; co-founder of Académie Diplomatique Internationale 26, now its Permanent Sec.-Gen. (with rank of Ambassador).

Publs. *Dictionnaire Diplomatique*, Vols. I-VIII, *La Conception Nouvelle de la Neutralité, Une ligue des Nations comme garantie d'une Paix durable, Wilson, sa vie, son oeuvre, Les Précurseurs de la S.d.N., La Norvège et le droit des gens, Le principe des nationalités et le droit de libre disposition, Les Sanctions contre les responsables de la Guerre, L'Albanie et l'Empire du Nord, La question du proche Orient, La Grèce et la crise mondiale* (2 vols.), *Théorie et Pratique des Traités Internationaux, La Grèce, son Histoire International, son Statut International* (Vols. I-III), etc.

4 *bis* avenue Hoche, Paris 8e, France.

Franjieh, Suleiman; Lebanese politician; b. 14 June 1910, Zgharta; *m.*; five *c.*; ed. coll. at Antoura, near Beirut.

Elected to Parl. as Independent mem. 60 and 64; Minister of Posts, Telegraphs and Telephones and Minister of Agriculture 60-61; Minister of the Interior 68; Minister of Justice, Minister of Econ., Minister of Public Works, Minister of Nat. Econ. 69-70; head, trade delegation to negotiate Soviet-Lebanese trade and payments agreement; Pres. of Lebanon Sept. 70-76.

c/o Office of the President, Beirut, Lebanon.

Franju, Georges; French film director; b. 12 April 1912.

Stage Designer; then Co-Founder, Cinémathèque française 37, and of journal *Cinématographe* 38; Exec. Sec. Int. Fed. of Film Archives 38-45; Gen. Sec. Inst. of Scientific Cinematography 45-52; Dir. of short films 49-, full-length films 58-; Gen. Sec. Acad. du Cinéma; Officier des Arts et des Lettres, Chevalier Légion d'Honneur 71.

Short films include: *Le Sang des bêtes, En passant par la Lorraine, Hôtel des Invalides, Le Grand Méliès, M. et Mme Curie, A propos d'une rivière, Mon chien, Les Poussières, La Première nuit, Le Théâtre nationale populaire, Notre-Dame, Cathédrale de Paris*; Full-length films: *La Tête contre les murs* 58, *Les Yeux sans visage* 59, *Pleins feux sur l'assassin* 60, *Thérèse Desqueyroux* 62, *Judex* 63, *Thomas l'Imposteur* 65, *Les Rideaux Blancs* 66, *La Faute de l'Abbé Mouret* 70, *Nuits Rouges* 74.

13 quai des Grands-Augustins, Paris 6e, France.

Frank, Frederick Charles, O.B.E., D.PHIL., F.INST.P., F.R.S.; British professor of physics; b. 6 March 1911, Durban, S. Africa; *s.* of Frederick Frank and Medora Celia Emma Frank (née Read); *m.* Maia Maita Asché 1940; ed. Thetford Grammar School, Ipswich School and Lincoln Coll., Oxford.

Kaiser Wilhelm Institut für Physik, Berlin-Dahlem 36-38; Colloid Science Laboratory, Cambridge 39-40; Chemical Defence Research Establishment, Porton 40; Air Ministry, A.D.I. (Science) 40-46; H. H. Wills Physics Laboratory, Univ. of Bristol 47-76, Research Fellow 48-51, Reader 51-54, Prof. 54-69, Henry Overton Wills Prof. and Head of Dept., Univ. of Bristol 69-76; Visiting Prof. Univ. of Calif., San Diego 64-65; Vice-Pres. Royal Soc. 67-69; Holweck Prize 63; Bakerian Lecturer 73; Hon. D.Sc. (Ghent) 55, (Bath) 74.

Leisure interests: gardening, walking.

Publs. articles in various learned journals, mostly dealing with either dielectrics or the physics of solids.

H. H. Wills Physics Laboratory, Tyndall Avenue, Bristol, BS8 1TL; Home: Orchard Cottage, Grove Road, Coombe Dingle, Bristol 9, Avon, England.

Telephone: 0272-24161 (Office); 0272-681708 (Home).

Frank, Gleb Mikhailovich; Soviet biophysicist; b. 24 May 1904, Gorky; ed. Simferopol Univ.

Associate Leningrad Physico-technical Inst., later All-Union Inst. of Experimental Medicine 29-43; Dir. Laboratory of U.S.S.R. Head of Medical Sciences 43-52; Head, Lab. of the Biophysics of Animate Structures and Deputy Scientific Dir. Inst. of Biophysics of U.S.S.R. Acad. of Medical Sciences 52-60; Dir. Inst. of Biophysics U.S.S.R. Acad. of Sciences 60-; Prof. of Biophysics, Moscow Univ.; Corresp. mem. U.S.S.R. Acad. of Sciences 46-66, mem. 66-; mem. C.P.S.U. 47-; State Prize 51.

Institute of Biophysics, Academy of Sciences of the U.S.S.R., 142292, Pushchino, Moscow Region, U.S.S.R.

Frank, Ilya Mikhailovich; Soviet physicist; b. 23 Oct. 1908, Leningrad; ed. Moscow Univ.

Fmr. Asst. to Prof. S. I. Vavilov 28; worked at Leningrad Optical Inst. (Laboratory of Prof. A. N. Terenin) 30-34; at Lebedev Inst. of Physics (U.S.S.R. Acad. of Sciences) 34-; Prof. of Physics, Moscow Univ. 44-, Head of Laboratory 57-; Corresp. mem. U.S.S.R. Acad. of Sciences 46-68, Academician 68-; Nobel Prize for Physics (with Tamm and Cherenkov) 58, State Prize 46, Order of Lenin (twice), Order of the Red Banner of Labour, etc.

Publs. *Function of Excitement and Curve of Absorption in Optic Dissociation of Tallium Ioclate* 33, *Coherent Radiation of Fast Electron in a Medium* 37, *Pare Formation in Krypton under Gamma Rays* 38, *Doppler Effect in Refracting Medium* 42, *Neutron Multiplication in Uranium-Graphite Systems* 55, *On Group Velocity of Light in Radiation in Refracting Medium* 58, *Vavilov-Cherenkov Radiation* 60, *Optics of Light Sources* 60, *On Some Peculiarities of Elastic Deceleration of Neutrons* 64.

P.N. Lebedev Institute of Physics, Academy of Sciences of the U.S.S.R., 53 Leninsky Prospekt, Moscow, U.S.S.R.

Frank, Paul, DR. RER. POL.; German foreign office official; b. 4 July 1918, Hilzingen; *s.* of Josef and Anna Frank; *m.* Irma Sutter 1950; two *s.*; ed. Volksschule, Realgymnasium and Univs. of Freiburg i. Br., Zürich and Fribourg (Switzerland).

Vice-Consul, Paris 50, First Sec. 55; Chief, West European Desk, Foreign Office, Bonn 57; Counsellor, Observer Mission to UN, New York 60; mem. Planning Staff, Foreign Office 63, Dir. W. European Dept. 65, Dir. of Political Affairs 68, Sec. of State 70-, Chief of the President's Office 74-; various decorations.

Leisure interests: painting, architecture.

Bundespräsidialamt, 53 Bonn, Kaiser-Friedrich-Strasse 16, Federal Republic of Germany.

Franke, Egon; German politician; b. 11 April 1913, Hanover.

Co-founder of S.P.D.; in charge of Org. Dept. of Party Exec. until 52; District Chair., Hanover; Land Chair., Lower Saxony; mem. Bundestag for Hanover 51-; mem. Party Exec. 64-; Alderman, Hanover 45-47; mem. Landtag Hanover 46-47, Lower Saxony 47-51; Chair. All-German Cttee. 67-69; Minister of Intra-German Affairs Oct. 69-.

Bundesministerium für innerdeutsche Beziehungen, 53 Bonn-Bad Godesberg 1, Kölner Strasse 140, Federal Republic of Germany.

Franke, Herbert, PH.D., LL.D.; German university professor; b. 27 Sept. 1914; *m.* Ruth Freiin von Reck 1945; one *s.*; ed. Univs. of Cologne, Bonn and Berlin.

Reader Cologne Univ. 49; British Council Fellow, Cambridge 51; Prof. of Far Eastern Studies Univ. of Munich 52-, Dean Faculty of Letters 58-59; Sec.-Gen. XXIVth Int. Congress of Orientalists 57; Sec. 53, Pres. 65-71; Pres. Deutsche Morgenländische Gesellschaft, Editor of its *Zeitschrift* 60-65; Vice-Pres. Deutsche Forschungsgemeinschaft 74-; Visiting Prof. Univ. of

Washington 64-65, 69-70; Prix Stanislas Julien (Acad. des Inscriptions et Belles-Lettres, Paris) 53; mem. Bavarian Acad. of Sciences.

Publs. *Beiträge zur Wirtschaftsgeschichte Chinas unter der Mongolenherrschaft* 49, *Sinologie* 53, *Beiträge zur Kulturgeschichte Chinas unter der Mongolenherrschaft* 56, etc.

Institut für Ostasienkunde, Universität München, Munich; Home: Fliederstrasse 23, 8035 Gauting, Federal Republic of Germany.

Telephone: Munich 850-29-07.

Frankel, Sir Otto Herzberg, Kt., D.SC., D.AGR., F.R.S., F.A.A., F.R.S.N.Z., F.W.A.A.S.; Australian geneticist; b. 4 Nov. 1900, Vienna; *m.* Margaret Anderson 1939; ed. Agricultural Univ. of Berlin.

Chief, Div. of Plant Industry, Commonwealth Scientific and Industrial Research Organization 51-62, mem. of Exec. 62-66, Senior Research Fellow Div. 66-.

Leisure interests: skiing, fishing, gardening.

C.S.I.R.O., P.O. Box 1600, Canberra City, A.C.T. 2601; Home: 4 Cobby Street, Campbell, A.C.T. 2601, Australia.

Frankel, Sally Herbert, M.A., PH.D., D.SC.; British economist; b. 22 Nov. 1903, Johannesburg, S. Africa; *s.* of late Jacob and Mathilde (née Buxbaum) Frankel; *m.* Ilse J. Frankel 1928; one *s.* one *d.*; ed. St. John's Coll., Johannesburg, Univ. of Witwatersrand and London School of Economics.

Prof. of Economics and Head of Dept. of Economics and Economic History, Univ. of Witwatersrand 31-46; Chair. Comm. to report on Rhodesia Railways Ltd. 42-43; Chair. Comm. of Enquiry into Mining Industry of S. Rhodesia 45; mem. Royal Comm. on East Africa 53-55; Emer. Prof. in Economics of Underdeveloped Countries, Oxford; Emer. Fellow, Nuffield Coll. (Prof. and Professorial Fellow 46-71); Visiting Prof. Univ. of Va. 67, 68, 70, 71, 72, 73; Hon. D.Litt. (Rhodes Univ.), Hon. D.Sc.(Econ.) (Univ. of the Witwatersrand).

Leisure interests: gardening, chess.

Publs. *Co-operation and Competition in the Marketing of Maize in South Africa* 26, *The Railway Policy of South Africa* 28, *Coming of Age: Studies in South African Citizenship and Politics* 38, *Capital Investment in Africa: Its Course and Effects* 38, *The Concept of Colonisation* 49, *The Economic Impact on Under-Developed Societies* 53, *Investment and the Return to Equity Capital in the South African Gold Mining Industry 1887-1965: An International Comparison* 67, *Gold and International Equity Investment* 69.

The Knoll House, Hinksey Hill, Oxford, England.

Telephone: Oxford 735345.

Frankenthaler, Helen, B.A.; American artist; b. 1928, New York; *m.* Robert Motherwell 1958 (separated 1971); ed. Bennington Coll., Vt.

Trustee Bennington Coll. 67; Fellow Calhoun Coll., Yale Univ. 68; one man exhbns. throughout U.S.A. and Europe, particularly at André Emmerich Gallery, Whitney Museum of American Art, and Metropolitan Museum of Art, New York 51-; mem. Nat. Inst. of Arts and Letters 74, Corpn. of Yaddo; Hon. D.Hum.Litt. (Skidmore Coll.) 69, Hon. D.F.A. (Smith Coll.) 73, (Moore Coll. of Art) 74; First Prize, Paris Biennale 59, Joseph E. Temple Gold Medal Award, Pennsylvania Acad. of Fine Arts 68, Spirit of Achievement Award, Albert Einstein Coll. of Medicine 70, Gold Medal of the Commune of Catania, Florence 72, Garrett Award, Art Inst. of Chicago 72, Creative Arts Award, Amer. Jewish Congress 74.

c/o André Emmerich Inc., 41 East 57th Street, Fifth Floor, New York, N.Y. 10022; Studio: 117½ East 83rd Street, New York, N.Y., U.S.A.

Frankfurt, Stephen Owen, B.A.; American advertising executive; b. 17 Dec. 1931; ed. New York Univ. and Pratt Inst.

Joined Young & Rubicam 55, Art and Copy Supervisor 57, Vice-Pres. and Dir. of Special Projects 60, Senior Vice-Pres. and Co-Creative Dir. of Agency 64, Creative Dir. Jan. 67-, Pres. Jan. 68-; Gold Medal, N.Y. Art Dirs. Club 58, 59, 61, 62, 63; Special Gold Medal Outstanding TV Advertising 61, Winner TV Category Venice Film Festival 64, Achievement Award, N.Y. Art Dirs. Club April 68.

Young & Rubicam U.S.A., 285 Madison Avenue, New York City, N.Y., U.S.A.

Telephone: 576-8608.

Franklin, Norman Laurence, C.B.E., PH.D., C.ENG., F.I.C.E.; British chemical engineer; b. 1 Sept. 1924, Leeds, Yorks.; *s.* of William Alexander Franklin and Beatrice Franklin; *m.* Bessie Coupland 1949; one *s.* one *d.*; ed. Batley Grammar School, Univ. of Leeds.

Deputy Man. Dir. United Kingdom Atomic Energy Authority (UKAEA) 64-67, performed Special Duties 68, mem. for Production 69-71; Chief Exec. British Nuclear Fuels Ltd.; Chair. and Man. Dir. Nuclear Power Co. Ltd. May 75-.

Leisure interest: walking.

Publs. *Statistical Analysis in Chemistry and the Chemical Industry* 54, *The Transport Properties of Fluids*, Vol. 4, *Chemical Engineering Practice* 57, *Heat Transfer by Conduction*, Vol. 7, *Chemical Engineering Practice* 63, *Papers in Translation* (Inst. of Chemical Engineers) 53-66.

1 Greenacre Close, Knutsford, Cheshire, WA16 8NL, England.

Telephone: Knutsford (0565) 3045.

Franklin, William Henry; American business executive; b. 30 Jan. 1909, Chicago, Ill.; *m.* Mary Haas 1937; two *s.* two *d.*; ed. Phillips Exeter Acad. and Princeton Univ.

Auditor, Price Waterhouse & Co., Chicago 34-41; Asst. Controller Caterpillar Tractor Co. 41-44, Controller 44-52, Vice-Pres. 52-62, Exec. Vice-Pres. 62-66, Pres. 66-72, Chair. of Board 72-75; mem. Nat. Asscn. Accountants, Amer. Inst. of Accountants and other orgs.

500 Miller Road, Peoria, Ill. 61614, U.S.A.

Franks, Baron (Life Peer) cr. 62, of Headington in the County of Oxford; **Oliver Shewell Franks,** P.C., G.C.M.G., K.C.B., C.B.E., M.A.; British college principal; b. 16 Feb. 1905, Birmingham; *s.* of Rev. S. Franks and Katharine Shewell; *m.* Barbara Mary Tanner 1931; two *d.*; ed. Bristol Grammar School and Queen's Coll., Oxford.

Fellow and Praelector in Philosophy, Queen's Coll. Oxford 27-37; Prof. of Moral Philosophy Univ. of Glasgow 37-45; Civil Servant (temporary) Ministry of Supply 39-46; Perm. Sec. Ministry of Supply 45-46; Provost Queen's Coll. Oxford 46-48; Hon. Fellow of Queen's Coll., Oxford 48, Wolfson Coll., Oxford, St. Catharine's Coll., Cambridge; British Amb. to U.S.A. 48-52; Chair. Lloyds Bank 54-62; Provost, Worcester Coll., Oxford 62-76; Chancellor, Univ. of E. Anglia 65-; Chair. Friends' Provident and Century Life Office 55-62; Chair. Cttee. of London Clearing Bankers 60-62; mem. Nat. Econ. Devt. Council (NEDC) 62-64; Hon. D.C.L. Oxford and other hon. degrees.

The Provost's Lodgings, Worcester College, Oxford, England.

Telephone: Oxford 47777.

Franz Josef II, Prince of Liechtenstein, Duke of Troppau and of Jägerndorf, Count of Rietberg; b. 16 Aug. 1906, Schloss Frauenthal; *s.* of Prince Alois and Princess Elisabeth of Liechtenstein; *m.* Georgine (Gina), Gräfin von Wilczek 1943; four *s.* one *d.*; ed. Schotten Gymnasium and Forestry and Agricultural Univ., Vienna.

Ruler Principality of Liechtenstein, succeeded July 38.

Schloss Vaduz, Principality of Liechtenstein.

Telephone: 075-21212.

Franzen, Ulrich J., B.A., B.ARCH.; American architect; b. 15 Jan. 1921; ed. Williams Coll., and Harvard Univ. Head of Ulrich Franzen and Assocs., New York City; Lecturer Yale and Cornell Univs., Univs. of Cincinnati and Illinois, etc.; Visiting Prof. Yale, Harvard and Washington Univs. and Carnegie Inst. of Technology; Chair. Architectural Board of Review, City of Rye 58-63, Urban Design Review Board, City of Cincinnati 64-65, Nat. Council on Schoolhouse Construction and U.S. Navy Review and Advisory Panel on Architecture 65-; Pres. Architectural League of New York 66; mem. Amer. Inst. of Architects; numerous awards for design and construction including Brunner Memorial Prize, Nat. Inst. of Arts and Letters 62, Thomas Jefferson Award 70, 71, 72.
Works include: Barkin Levin Co., Long Island City 58, Philip Morris Research Center, Richmond, Va. 59, Plans for Helen Whiting Inc., Pleasantville, N.Y. 62, Philip Morris Operations Center 63, Agronomy Building for Cornell Univ. and New Alley Theatre, Houston, Texas, Residence and Dining Halls, Univ. of N.H., housing for elderly, Torrington, Conn. 72, First City Nat. Bank of Binghamton, N.Y. 73.
Office: 555 Madison Avenue, New York, N.Y. 10022; Home: 975 Park Avenue, New York City 28, N.Y., U.S.A.

Fraser, Lady Antonia, B.A.; British author; b. 27 August 1932, London; d. of the Earl and Countess of Longford (q.v.); m. Rt. Hon. Hugh Fraser, M.P. (q.v.) 1956; three s. three d.; ed. Dragon School, Oxford, St. Mary's Convent, Ascot and Lady Margaret Hall, Oxford.
Publs. King Arthur 54 (revised edn. 70), Robin Hood 55 (revised edn. 71), Dolls 63, History of Toys 66, Mary, Queen of Scots 69 (James Tait Black Memorial Prize), Cromwell: Our Chief of Men 73, King James VI and I 74, Scottish Love Poems, A Personal Anthology 74, Kings and Queens of England 75.
52 Campden Hill Square, London, W.8, England; Eilean Aigas, Beauly, Inverness-shire, Scotland.

Fraser, Sir Hugh, 2nd Bt.; British business executive; b. 18 Dec. 1936; m. 1st Patricia Bowie 1962 (dissolved 1971), 2nd Aileen Ross 1973; ed. St. Mary's, Melrose, and Kelvinside Acad.
Director, House of Fraser Ltd. 58-65, Deputy Chair. 65-66, Chair. 66-; Chair. Harrods Ltd., John Barker & Co. Ltd., Binns Ltd., Scottish and Universal Investments Ltd., George Outram & Co. Ltd.; Chair. House of Fraser (Northern Management) Ltd. 62-; Dir. Highland Tourist (Cairngorm Devt.) Ltd.; succeeded to father's Baronetcy (Lord Fraser of Allander, Bt.) 66, and disclaimed Barony.
Dineiddwg, Mugdock, nr. Milngavie, Stirlingshire, Scotland.
Telephone: Milngavie 1182.

Fraser, Rt. Hon. Hugh Charles Patrick Joseph, P.C., M.B.E., M.P.; British politician; b. 23 Jan. 1918; m. Lady Antonia Pakenham (Lady Antonia Fraser q.v.) 1956; three s. three d.; ed. Ampleforth Coll., Balliol Coll., Oxford, and Univ. of Paris.
With Lovat Scouts, Phantom and Special Air Service, Second World War; Cons. M.P. 45-; Parl. Private Sec. to Sec. of State for the Colonies 51-54; Parl. Under Sec. of State and Financial Sec., War Office 58-60; Parl. Under-Sec. of State for Colonies 60-62; Sec. of State for Air 62-64; Minister of Defence for the Royal Air Force 64; Dir. Ionian Bank 64-, Sun Alliance.
52 Campden Hill Square, London, W.8, England.

Fraser, James Campbell, B.COM., F.B.I.M.; British business executive; b. 2 May 1923, Dunblane, Scotland; s. of Alexander Ross and Annie McGregor Fraser; m. Maria Harvey (née McLaren) 1950; two d.; ed. Glasgow Univ. and Dundee School of Econs.

Served in R.A.F. 41-45; Raw Cotton Comm. 50-52; Economist Intelligence Unit 52-57; with Dunlop Rubber Co. Ltd. 57-, Public Relations Officer 58, Group Marketing Controller 62, Man. Dir. Dunlop New Zealand Ltd. 67, Exec. Dir. 69, Joint Man. Dir. 71, Man. Dir. 72-; Chair. Scottish TV 75-; mem. Council Confed. of British Industry, NEDC; Chair. CBI Econ. Situation Cttee.; Pres. Soc. of Business Economists.
Leisure interests: athletics, reading, theatre, cinema, gardening, walking.
Dunlop House, 25 Ryder Street, St. James's, London, S.W.1; Home: Silver Birches, 4 Silver Lane, Purley, Surrey, England.
Telephone: 01-660-1703.

Fraser, Rt. Hon. (John) Malcolm, P.C., M.A. (OXON.); Australian politician; b. 21 May 1930, Melbourne; s. of the late J. Neville Fraser and of Una Fraser; m. Tamara Beggs 1956; two s. two d.; ed. Melbourne Grammar School and Oxford Univ.
Member of Parl. for Wannon 55-; mem. Joint Parl. Cttee. of Foreign Affairs 62-66; Chair. Govt. Members' Defence Cttee.; Sec. Wool Cttee.; mem. Council of Australian Nat. Univ., Canberra 64-66; Minister for the Army 66-68; Minister for Educ. and Science 68-69; Minister for Defence 69-71; Minister for Educ. and Science 71-72; Leader of Liberal Party March 75-; Prime Minister Nov. 75-.
Leisure interests: fishing, photography, vintage cars, motorcycles.
Parliament House, Canberra, A.C.T., Australia.

Fraser, Sir Robert Brown, Kt., O.B.E., B.A., B.SC.; British television administrator; b. 26 Sept. 1904, Adelaide, Australia; s. of Reginald Fraser and Thusnelda Homburg; m. Betty Harris 1931; one d.; ed. St. Peter's School, Adelaide, Univs. of Melbourne and London.
Leader Writer, Daily Herald 30-39; Empire Div., Min. of Information, London 39-41; Dir. Publications Div., M.O.I. 41-45; Controller of Production M.O.I. 45-46; Dir.-Gen. Central Office of Information 46-54; Dir.-Gen. Independent Television Authority 54-70; Chair. Independent Televison News 71-74; Hon. Fellow, London School of Econs. 65; Hon. Life mem. Royal Inst. of Public Admin.; Gold Medal Royal TV Soc. 70.
Flat 5M, Portman Mansions, Chiltern Street, London, W.1, England.

Fraser, William, C.B.E., B.SC., C.ENG., F.I.E.E.; British business executive; b. 1911, Glasgow; m. Kathleen Mary Moore 1938 (died 1971); two s. two d.; ed. Glasgow High School and University Coll., London.
Joined Joseph Lucas Ltd. and rose to Production Engineer 37; joined Scottish Cables Ltd. 37, Dir. 38, Man. Dir. 48, Chair. 58; Chair. Scottish Cables (South Africa) Ltd. 57; Chair. Scottish Council Fed. British Industries 59-61; Exec. Dir. British Insulated Callender's Cables Ltd. 59, Vice-Chair. Phillips Cables (Canada) 61-70, Exec. Dir. Overseas Cos. 62-70, Deputy Chair. Metal Manufactures Ltd. (Australia) 63-70, Man. Dir. Overseas 64-68, Man. Dir. Overseas and Construction Group 68-70, Chair. BIC Construction Co. Ltd. 68-69, Chair. Balfour Beatty & Co. Ltd. 69-70, Deputy Chair. and Chief Exec. British Insulated Callender's Cables Ltd. (now BICC Ltd.) 71-73, Chair. May 73-; Dir. Clydesdale Bank Ltd. 74-, Anglesey Aluminium Ltd. 71-74.
Leisure interests: fishing, shooting, golf.
21 Bloomsbury Street, London, WC1B 3QN; Home: Fenwick Lodge, Ewenfield Road, Ayr, Scotland; and 87 Whitehall Court, London, SW1A 2EP, England.
Telephone: 01-637-1300 (Office).

Fraser Darling, Sir Frank, Kt., D.SC., PH.D., LL.D., F.R.S.E.; British biologist; b. 23 June 1903, United Kingdom; m. 1st Marian Fraser 1925 (divorced), 2nd Averil Morley 1948 (died 1957), 3rd Christina Macinnes;

three *s.* one *d.*; ed. privately and Univ. of Edinburgh. Chief Officer, Imperial Bureau of Animal Genetics 30-33; Leverhulme Research Fellow 33-36; Carnegie Research Fellow 36-40; Dir. West Highland Survey 44-50; Rockefeller Special Research Fellow 50; Senior Lecturer in Ecology and Conservation, Univ. of Edinburgh 52-58; Vice-Pres. Conservation Foundation, Washington, D.C. 58-72, Hon. Trustee 72-; Mungo Park Medal, Royal Scottish Geographical Soc. 47; BBC Reith Lecturer 69; U.S. Nat. Parks Service Medal 72; Commdr. Order Golden Ark (Netherlands) 73; Browning Award (U.S.A.) 73.
Leisure interests: gardening, English literature, natural history, fine art.
Publs. include: *A Herd of Red Deer* 37, *Bird Flocks and the Breeding Cycle* 38, *A Naturalist on Rona* 39, *Natural History in the Highlands and Islands* 47, *West Highland Survey* 55, *Pelican in the Wilderness* 56, *The Unity of Ecology* 63, *Wilderness and Plenty* 70; many papers and articles.
Lochyhill, Forres, Moray, Scotland; The Conservation Foundation, 1717 Massachusetts Avenue, N.W., Washington, D.C. 20036, U.S.A.
Telephone: Forres 2664 (Home).

Fraser of Kilmorack, Baron (Life Peer), cr. 74, of Rubislaw in the County of the City of Aberdeen; **(Richard) Michael Fraser,** Kt., C.B.E.; British politician, businessman and consultant; b. 28 Oct. 1915, Nottingham; *s.* of the late Dr. Thomas Fraser, C.B.E., D.S.O.; *m.* Elizabeth Chloë Drummond 1944; two *s.* one *d.*; ed. Aberdeen Grammar School, Fettes Coll., Edinburgh, and King's Coll., Cambridge.
Royal Artillery 39-46; Conservative Research Dept. 46-64, Head of Home Affairs Section 50-51, Joint Dir. 51-59, Dir. 59-64; Sec. Conservative Party's Advisory Cttee. on Policy 51-64, Deputy Chair. Conservative Party 64-75; Sec. to Conservative Leader's Consultative Cttee. 64-70, 74-75; Chair. Conservative Research Dept. 70-74; Dir. Glaxo Holdings Ltd. 75-; Smith-Mundt Fellowship, U.S.A. 52; M.B.E. (Mil.) 45.
Leisure interests: reading, music, opera, ballet, travel.
18 Drayton Court, London, S.W.10, England.
Telephone: 01-370-1543.

Fraser of Tullybelton, Baron (Life Peer), cr. 74; **Walter Ian Reid Fraser,** B.A., LL.B.; British judge; b. 3 Feb. 1911, Glasgow; *s.* of Alexander Reid Fraser and Margaret Russel MacFarlane; *m.* Cynthia MacDonell 1943; one *s.*; ed. Repton School, Balliol Coll., Oxford, Glasgow Univ.
Advocate, Scotland 36; Lecturer in Constitutional Law, Glasgow Univ. 36-39, 45-46, Edinburgh Univ. 46-48; Queen's Counsel 53; Dean of Faculty of Advocates 59-64; Senator Coll. of Justice in Scotland 64-74; Lord of Appeal in Ordinary 75-; Army (Royal Artillery) Service 39-45; Hon. LL.D. (Glasgow Univ.).
Leisure interests: walking, shooting.
House of Lords, London, S.W.1; and Tullybelton House, Bankfoot, Perthshire, Scotland.
Telephone: Bankfoot 312.

Frazão, Sergio Armando, B.A., LL.B.; Brazilian diplomatist; b. 26 Feb. 1917, Rio de Janeiro; *s.* of Felix Armando de Morais Frazão and Zelia Halbout de Amorin Carrão; *m.* Lice de Faria Frazão 1939; one *s.*; ed. Colegio Pedro Segundo, Univ. of Brazil Law School.
Entered diplomatic service 42; served in Paris, Vienna, with Perm. Mission to UN, New York, Santiago, Lisbon and Washington, D.C. 46-61; Amb. to Egypt 64-66, to Uruguay 66-69; Head Brazilian Del. to UN, Geneva 69; Amb. to Fed. Repub. of Germany 69-71; Perm. Rep. to UN 71-75; Amb. to Spain 75-; Pres. Brazilian Coffee Inst. 61; mem. del. to UN Gen. Assembly 53, 54, 71-74; Pres. ECOSOC 73, and rep. to numerous other int. confs.; Grand Officer of Mil. Merit; Grand Officer Ordem de Cristo (Portugal); Order of

Merit (Argentina); Grand Cross, Ordem do Rio Branco; Commdr. Order of Merit (Italy).
Publs. *The Autonomy of the Will*; many articles on political and econ. subjects.
Brazilian Embassy, Fernando del Santo 6, Madrid, Spain.

Freccia, Massimo; American (b. Italian) conductor; b. 19 Sept. 1906; ed. Cherubini Royal Conservatoire, Florence.
Guest conductor New York Philharmonic Orchestra 38, 39, 40; Musical Dir. and Conductor, Havana Philharmonic Orchestra 39-43, New Orleans Symphony Orchestra 44-52, Baltimore Symphony Orchestra 52-59; Chief Conductor Rome (R.A.I.) Orchestra 59-; frequent appearances as Guest Conductor of famous orchestras in Europe and U.S.; tours in Australia 63, Japan 67, South Africa 69; appeared at various int. festivals, including Vienna, Prague, Berlin, Lisbon, Montreux; Hon. D.Mus. Tulane Univ., New Orleans; Order of the Star of Italian Solidarity.
c/o Ibbs and Tillett, 124 Wigmore Street, London, W1H 0AX; Home: 25 Eaton Square, London, S.W.1, England.

Fred, Edwin Broun, B.S., M.S., PH.D.; American professor emeritus of bacteriology; b. 22 March 1887, Middleburg, Va.; *s.* of Samuel Rogers and Catherine Conway (Broun); *m.* Rosa Helen Parrott 1913; two *d.*; ed. Randolph Macon Acad., Front Royal, Va., Virginia Polytechnic Inst. and Univ. of Göttingen.
Assistant Prof. of Bacteriology, Virginia Polytechnic Inst. 12-13; Asst. Prof., Univ. of Wis. 13-14, Assoc. Prof. 14-18, Prof. 18-58, Dean of Graduate School 34-43, Dean Coll. of Agriculture and Dir. Agricultural Experiment Station 43-45, Pres. Univ. of Wis. 45-58, Pres. Emer. and Prof. Emer. 58-; Hon. LL.D. (Lawrence Coll., Northwestern Univ., Mich. State Coll.), Hon. D.Sc. (Marquette Univ., Beloit Coll., Univ. of N. Carolina, Northland Coll., Wis., Univ. of Wis.); Medal of Merit for service in Second World War.
Publs. *Textbook of Agricultural Bacteriology* (with F. Löhnis) 23, *Laboratory Manual of Microbiology* (with S. A. Waksman) 28, *Root Nodule and Bacteria and Leguminous Plants* (with Baldwin and McCoy) 32.
1636 Van Hise Hall, University of Wisconsin, Madison, Wis. 53706; Home: 10 Babcock Drive, Madison, Wis. 53706, U.S.A.
Telephone: 608-262-3682 (Office); 608-255-1244 (Home).

Frédéricq, (Baron) Louis Paul Simon; Belgian lawyer and university professor; b. 25 Nov. 1892, Ghent; *m.* Marie-Thérèse Varlez 1920; five *c.*; ed. Univ. of Ghent.
Lecturer, Univ. of Ghent 24, Prof. 29, and Rector 36-38; Gov. of Eastern Flanders 38; Chef de Cabinet to the King June 39; returned to Univ. of Ghent and to practise at the Bar 45-; Prof. Univ. of Brussels 46; mem. Royal Acad. of Science, Letters and Fine Arts of Belgium; Past Pres. Int. Acad. of Comparative Law; Hon. Dr. Univs. of Rennes, Lille, Paris and Utrecht.
Leisure interest: golf.
Publs. *Traité de Droit Commercial belge* (10 vols.), *Handboek van Belgisch Handelsrecht* (3 vols.).
Gontrode Heirweg 112, 9220, Merelbeke, Belgium.
Telephone: 306212.

Frederiksen, Emil; Danish literary critic; b. 2 June 1902; *s.* of Emil Frederiksen and Johanna Rapp; *m.* Karen Trier 1927; three *s.* one *d.*; ed. St. Andreas Kollegium (Charlottenlund), Univs. of Copenhagen, Uppsala, Lund, Berlin and Paris.
Lecturer in Danish Language and Literature, Univ. of Paris 29, Univs. of Stockholm, Gothenburg and Lund 30-36; Literary critic, *Kristeligt Dagblad*, Copenhagen 36-44, *Berlingske Tidende* Copenhagen 44-; Editor *Gads Danske Magasin* 42-55.
Leisure interest: wandering.
Publs. *Modern Dansk Literatur* (in Swedish) 31, *Fra*

Saxo til Hjalmar Gullberg 44, *Ung Dansk Literatur* 45, 52, *Johannes Jørgensens Ungdom* 46, *Den unge Grundtvig og andre Essays* 48, *Dante* 65, *Jacob Paludan* 66, *H. C. Branner* 67, *W. A. Linneman* 69, *Knuth Becker* 70.
H. A. Clausens V. 24, 2820 Gentofte, Denmark.
Telephone: GE 798.

Frederiksen, Ib Christian; Danish farmer and politician; b. 9 Aug. 1927, Svenstrup J.; s. of Thøger Frederiksen and Theodora G. Sørensen; m. Betty Hammer 1951; two s. one d.; ed. Himmerland Youth School, Rodding Folk High School and Borris Agricultural School.
Member, Mariager Town Council 66-71, Mayor 70-71; mem. Aarhus County Council 70-71; Minister of Agriculture 71-73; Social Democrat.
Home: Midtbjerg, 9550 Mariager, Denmark.
Telephone: (08) 54 11 76.

Fredga, Arne, DR.CHEM.; Swedish organic chemist; b. 18 July 1902, Uppsala; s. of Dr. Carl Fredga and Elin (née Cassel) Fredga; m. Brita Öhlin 1931; two s. two d.; ed. Univ. of Uppsala.
Assistant at the Chemical Inst. Uppsala Univ. 30-35; Asst. Prof. of Chem. 35-39; Prof. of Organic Chem. 39-69; mem. of the Swedish Royal Acad. of Sciences 43-; mem. various other scientific socs.; Hon. mem. Société Chimique Belge, Finska Kemistsamfundet; mem. Nobel Cttee. of Chem. 44-75, Nat. Science Research Council 52-54, Nat. Cttee. for Chem. 56-62; Pres. Swedish History of Science Soc. 67-, Nobel Cttee. of Chem. 72-75, Board of Trustees of Nobel Foundation 72-75, Nat. Cttee. History of Science 74-.
Leisure interests: botany, history of science.
Publs. about 180 papers on stereo-chemistry, organic compounds of sulphur and selenium, plant growth regulators and chemical biography.
Börjegatan 3 A, Uppsala, Sweden.
Telephone: 018-13-57-34.

Freed, Louis Franklin, M.A., D.PHIL., M.B., C.H.B., M.D., D.P.M., D.P.H., D.T.M. and H., D.LITT. ET PHIL., D.I.H., F.R.S.S.A.F., F.S.S., F.R.A.I., F.R.G.S., F.R.C.PSYCH.; South African sociologist and social philosopher; b. 1903, Libau, Balticum; s. of Nahum and Hannah Freed; m. Silvia Sidersky 1933; two s.; ed. Univs. of St. Andrews, Pretoria, Witwatersrand, Stellenbosch, Orange Free State and South Africa and Tara Hosp., Johannesburg.
Former South African Ed. of *International Journal of Sexology*; former Medical Officer, Tara Neuro-Psychiatric Hospital, Johannesburg 57; Medical Officer, Sterkfontein Mental Hospital, Krugersdorp 56-57; Lecturer on Social Medicine 49-; Lecturer in Dept. of Psychiatry and in Dept. of Sociology, Univ. of Witwatersrand, Johannesburg 53-; Guest Lecturer, Inst. of Criminology, Cambridge, Inst. of Criminology, Hebrew Univ. of Jerusalem, Oxford Univ. Mental Health Soc. 65; D.Phil. Univ. of Orange Free State 58; fmr. mem. New York Acad. of Sciences, S. African Asscn. for the Advancement of Science, Exec. Cttee. of Convocation, Univ. of Witwatersrand; Pres. Mental Health Soc., Witwatersrand, Exec. Cttee. South African PEN, Exec. Cttee. of Inst. for the study of Man in Africa, Exec. Cttee. Inst. of Adult Educ., Exec. Cttee. Johannesburg Youth Council, Exec. Cttee. S. African Nat. Epilepsy League; medical sociologist, Tara Neuro-Psychiatric Hospital, Johannesburg; Hon. D.Phil. (Orange Free State Univ.), Ph.D. (Natal Univ.).
Leisure interests: bowls, walking.
Publs. *The Problem of European Prostitution in Johannesburg* 49, *Sex Education in Transvaal Schools* 38, *The Philosophy of Sociological Medicine* 48, *Findings of an Investigation into a Group of Patients presenting the Symptoms of Schizophrenia* 53, *The Social Aspect of Venereal Disease* 51, *The Psychosociology of Neoplasia*

58, *A Methodological Approach to the Problem of Mental Disorder* 56, *The Use of Methodological Principles in the Investigation of a Case of Trichomoniasis* 57, *The Problem of Crime in the Union of South Africa: An Integralistic Approach, An Enquiry into the Causality of Cancer* (with G. Giannopoulos), *Cancer-Killer No. 1* 60, *The Problem of Alcoholism: An Integralist Approach* 61, *A Critical Analysis of R. F. A. Hoernle's Contributions to Philosophy with Special Reference to his Synoptic Treatment of Diverse Dimensions of Reality* 65, *The Problem of Suicide in Johannesburg Examined from the standpoint of Incidence, Causality and Control* 67, *The Psychopath: A Social Challenge, A Case of Temporal Lobe Epilepsy, Aspects of Human Disorganisation* 68, *Medico-social Aspects of Epilepsy* 69, *The Social Aspects of Alcoholism* 68, *Commentary on the Report of the Committee of Enquiry into Drug Abuse* 72, *The Phenomenon of Guilt and Guilt Feelings with Special Reference to the Buberian Approach* 72, *Who is Martin Buber?* 73, *Martin Buber: The Humanist Emphasis in his Philosophy* 75, *The Problem of Human Rehabilitation: An Integralist Approach* 75.
15 Lystanwold Road, Saxonwold, Johannesburg, South Africa.
Telephone: 23-0009 (Office); 41-8877 (Home).

Freeman, Gaylord Augustus, Jr., B.A., LL.B.; American banker; b. 19 Jan. 1910; ed. Morgan Park High School, Dartmouth Coll., Harvard Law School.
Attorney, First Nat. Bank of Chicago 40-50, Vice-Pres. 50-59, Pres. 60-62, Vice-Chair. of the Board 62-69, Chair. and Chief Exec. Officer 69-; Dir. Borg-Warner Corpn., Central Coal & Coke Co., Chicago & North Western Railway Co., Clearing Industrial District, Container Corpn., Caterpillar Tractor Co., Time Inc.; Trustee, Northwestern Univ.
White Thorn Road, Wayne, Illinois, U.S.A.

Freeman, H.E. Cardinal James Darcy; Australian ecclesiastic; b. 19 Nov. 1907, Sydney; s. of Robert Freeman and Margaret Smith; ed. Christian Brothers' High School, Sydney, St. Columba's Coll., Springwood and St. Patrick's Coll., Manly.
Ordained Priest 30; Private Sec. to H.E. Cardinal Gilroy, Archbishop of Sydney 40-46; Auxiliary Bishop of Sydney 57: Bishop of Armidale 68; Archbishop of Sydney 71-; created Cardinal by Pope Paul VI 73; Knight of the Holy Sepulchre.
St. Mary's Cathedral, Sydney, N.S.W., Australia.
Telephone: 232-3788.

Freeman, Rt. Hon. John, P.C., M.B.E.; British journalist and diplomatist; b. 19 Feb. 1915; ed. Westminster School and Brasenose Coll., Oxford.
Advertising Consultant 37-40; active service in North Africa, Italy and North-West Europe 40-45; M.P. (Lab.) Watford 45-55; Financial Sec. to the War Office 46-47; Under-Sec. of State for War 47-48; Parl. Sec. to the Ministry of Supply 48-51 (resgnd.); retd. from politics 55; Deputy Editor *New Statesman* 58-61, Editor 61-65; British High Commr. in India 65-68; Amb. to U.S.A. 69-71; mem. Board, ITN (Independent Television News) 71-, Ind. Television Publs. 71-; Chair. and Chief Exec. London Weekend Television 71-.
London Weekend Television Ltd., The South Bank Television Centre, Kent House, London, S.E.1, England.

Freeman, Nelson Wright; American business executive; b. 6 Aug. 1908, Charleston, Ill.; s. of Ernest and Mabel Freeman (née Wright); m. Norma Greenlese 1928; two d.; ed. Univ. of Illinois.
Branch Man. Universal Credit Corpn., Detroit 29-34; Pres. and Gen. Man. Freeman & Riesen Motors Co. Milwaukee 34-38; Man. Assocs. Investment Co., Houston 38-42; Personnel and Safety Dir. Lummus Co. Houston 42-43; with Tenneco Inc. Houston (then

named Tennessee Gas Transmission Co.) 43-61, as Man. Personnel Dept., Asst. to Pres. 47, Vice-Pres. 50, Senior Vice-Pres. 54; Pres. Midwestern Gas Transmission Co. Houston 54-61; natural gas consultant, banker and rancher 62-64; Pres. Houston Nat. Bank 64-66; Dir. Tenneco Inc. 66-, Pres. 66-72, Chief Exec. Officer 68-74, Chair. of the Board 71-; Chair. of Board Tenneco Corpn. and Tenneco Int. Inc., of Exec. Cttee. J. I. Case Co., of Operating Policy Cttee. Walker Man. Co.; Dir. of numerous other Tenneco Inc. divisions, subsidiaries and affiliates.
Tenneco Inc., P.O.B. 2511, Houston, Texas 77001; Homes: Route 5, Box 31, Brenham, Texas, and 1233 Post Oak Park Drive, Houston, Texas 77027, U.S.A.
Telephone: 713-229-2131.

Freeman, Orville L., A.B., LL.B.; American lawyer and politician; b. 9 May 1918, Minneapolis, Minn.; s. of Orville E. Freeman and the late Frances (née Schroeder) Freeman; m. Jane C. Shield 1942; one s. one d.; ed. Central High School, Minneapolis, Minnesota Univ. Law School.
Chairman, Civil Service Comm., Minn. 46-48; admitted to Minn. Bar 47; partner in law firm 47-55; Gov. State of Minn. 55-61; nominated John F. Kennedy at Dem. Nat. Convention, L.A. 60; Sec. of Agriculture 61-69; Pres. EDP Technology Int. Inc. 69-70; Pres. Business Int. Corpn. 70-, Chief Exec. Officer 71-; mem. Council on Foreign Relations, Int. Club of Washington, D.C., Univ. Club of N.Y. City; Hon. mem. Soil Conservation Soc. of America; mem. Board of Trustees Nat. Recreation and Parks Asscn., Board of Dirs. Cttee. for the Future, KMS Industries Inc., Natomas Corpn., Franklin Mint, U.S. Tree Farms System Inc., Coalition for Rural America, Multinational Agribusiness Systems Inc., Rural America Marketing, Exec. Cttee. of Advisory Council on Japan-U.S. Econ. Relations, U.S.-EEC Businessmen's Council; Faculty mem. Salzburg Seminar Feb. 74; Hon. Ph.D. (Univ. Seoul, American Univ., Washington, D.C., Fairleigh Dickinson Univ., Rutherford, N.J., St. Joseph's Coll., Philadelphia, Pa.).
Leisure interests: skiing, squash, swimming, sailing.
Publs. *World Without Hunger* and many articles.
1 Dag Hammarskjöld Plaza, New York, N.Y. 10017, U.S.A.

Freeman, Sir Ralph, C.V.O., M.B.E., M.A., F.I.C.E., F.R.S.A., F.C.I.T., F.A.S.C.E.; British chartered engineer; b. 3 Feb. 1911, Finchley, London; s. of late Sir Ralph Freeman and Mary Freeman (née Lines); m. Joan E. Rose 1939; two s. one d.; ed. Uppingham School and Worcester Coll., Oxford.
Construction Engineer, Dorman Long and Co., South Africa, Rhodesia and Denmark 32-36, 37-39, Braithwaite and Co. 36-37; on staff of Freeman, Fox & Partners 39-46; served with Royal Engineers, Experimental Bridging Est. 43-45, later bridging adviser to Chief Engineer 21 Army Group H.Q., N.W. Europe Campaign; mem. Council, Inst. of Civil Engineers 51-55, 57-61, Vice-Pres. 62-66, Pres. 66-67; mem. Nat. Con. Council to Ministry of Works 52-56, Board of Govs., Westminster Hosp. 63-69, Advisory Council on Scientific Research and Devt. 66-69, Defence Scientific Advisory Council 69-72, Royal Fine Art Comm. 68-; Consulting Engineer to H.M. the Queen for Sandringham Estate 49-76; Senior Partner, Freeman, Fox & Partners 62-; Chair. Asscn. Consulting Engineers 75-76; Pres. Welding Inst. 75-(77); mem. gov. body, Imperial Coll. of Science and Tech. 75-; Order of Orange-Nassau (Netherlands) 45; Hon. Fellow, Rhodesian Inst. of Engineers 69, Hon. Fellow, Inst. of Mechanical Engineers 70.
Leisure interests: golf, carpentry, sailing.
Publs. several papers in *Proceedings Inst. of Civil Engineers.*
Freeman, Fox & Partners, 25 Victoria Street, London,

S.W.1.; Lombarden, Limpsfield Chart, Oxted, Surrey, England.
Telephone: 01-222-8050 (Office); Limpsfield Chart 3284 (Home).

Freeth, Gordon, LL.B.; Australian politician; b. 6 Aug. 1914, S. Australia; s. of Rt. Rev. Evelyn and Gladys M. (née Snashall) Freeth; m. Joan C. C. Baker 1939; one s. two d.; ed. Univ. of Western Australia.
Barrister and Solicitor of Supreme Court of W. Australia; Solicitor Katanning, W. Australia 39-49; Royal Australian Air Force 42-45; mem. Parl. 49-69; Minister for Interior and Works 58-63; Minister assisting the Attorney-Gen. 61-63; Minister for Shipping and Transport 63-68, for Air and Minister assisting the Treas. 68-69, for External Affairs Feb.-Oct. 69; Amb. to Japan 70-73; Liberal.
Leisure interests: golf, squash, reading.
142 Victoria Avenue, Dalkeith 6009, Western Australia.

Frei, Ephraim Heinrich, D.PHIL.; Israeli professor of electronics; b. 2 March 1912, Vienna, Austria; s. of Dr. Siegmund Frei and Franziska Frei (née Wiener); m. Yael Fanny Rosenfeld 1948; one s. one d.; ed. Vienna and Hebrew Univs.
Broadcasting Engineer, British Army; attached to British Embassy, Athens 44-46; mem. staff Scientific Dept., Ministry of Defence 48-50; Prof. and Head, Dept. of Electronics, Weizmann Inst. of Science 53-; mem. Inst. for Advanced Study, Princeton, N.J. 52; Int. Research Fellow, Stanford Research Inst. Calif. 60; Board of Dirs. Yeda; Advisory Board, Jerusalem Coll. of Technology; Editorial Board, Medical Progress through Technology; Fellow, I.E.E.E.; Weizmann Prize 57.
Leisure interest: archaeology.
Publs. scientific papers on electronics, physics and biomedical engineering.
3 Klausner Street, Jerusalem-Talpiot, Israel.
Telephone: 02-262949.

Frei Montalva, Eduardo, LL.D.; Chilean lawyer and politician; b. 16 Jan. 1911, Santiago; s. of Eduardo Frei Schlins and Victoria Montalva; m. María Ruiz-Tagle 1935; three s. four d.; ed. Public School, Lentue, Inst. of Humanities, Santiago and Catholic Univ. of Chile.
Former mem. Chamber of Deputies, now mem. Senate; fmr. Minister of Public Works; founder-mem. Nat. Falange, later Christian Democrat Party 35, Pres. of Party on three occasions, and fmr. Chair.; Pres. of Chile 64-70; Editor *El Tarapacá* (daily) 35-37; Knight Grand Cross Order of the Bath.
Leisure interests: reading, sport.
Publs. *The Regime of Fixed Salaries and its Possible Abolition, Unknown Chile, Now is the Time, Politics and the Spirit, The History of Chilean Political Parties, Truth Has Its Hour, Political Meaning and Form, Thought and Action.*
c/o Partido Demócrata Cristiano, Santiago, Chile.

Freihsler, Gen. Johann; Austrian army officer and politician; b. 4 Dec. 1917, Vienna; m.; one s. two d.; ed. Military Acad.
General Staff Officer during Second World War; Ministry of the Interior 45; later Departmental Chief, Fed. Ministry of Defence; Inspectorate-Gen. of the Forces; Head, Operations Group, Fed. Ministry of Defence; Fed. Minister of Defence 70-71; Socialist Party.
c/o Bundesministerium für Landesverteidigung, Vienna Austria.

Freitas-Cruz, João de; Portuguese diplomatist; b. 27 March 1925, Lisbon; s. of José A. and Maria Amelia de Freitas-Cruz; m. Maria de Lourdes Salazar Antunes 1955; three s.; ed. Lisbon Univ.
Attaché, Ministry of Foreign Affairs 48; subsequently held posts with Perm. Del. of Portugal to NATO, and

the Portuguese Embassies in London, Pretoria and Tananarive; Consul-Gen., subsequently Minister Pleni-potentiary, New York 64; Consul-Gen., Salisbury, Rhodesia 65-70; Perm. Rep. of Portugal to OECD Oct. 70-71; Amb. to Fed. Repub. of Germany 71-73; Dir.-Gen. of Political Affairs, Ministry of Foreign Affairs 73; Perm. Rep. to NATO Aug. 74-.
Leisure interests: golf, hunting.
Avenue de l'Armée 76, 1040 Brussels, Belgium.

Frelek, Ryszard, PH.D.; Polish politician; b. 30 May 1929, Parysów near Garwolin; ed. Cen. School of Foreign Service, Warsaw.
Member Peasant Youth Union, then Polish Youth Union to 50, Polish United Workers' Party (PZPR) 50-; Corresp. in India, PAP (Polish Press Agency) 57-59, later Deputy Editor-in-Chief of Foreign Dept., Deputy Editor-in-Chief of PAP 68-69; Head of Polish Inst. of Int. Affairs 69-71; Docent, Warsaw Univ. for many years; Head of Foreign Dept. of Cen. Cttee., PZPR 71, mem. Secr. of Cen. Cttee. 71-75, Sec. Cen. Cttee. Dec. 75-; Deputy to Seym 72-; Order of Banner of Labour, 1st Class; Knight's Cross, Order of Polonia Restituta.
Polska Zjednoczona Partia Robotnicza, Ul. Nowy Świat 6, 00-497 Warsaw, Poland.

French, Charles Stacy, S.B., M.A.; American scientist; b. 13 Dec. 1907, Lowell, Mass.; s. of Charles Ephraim French and Helena Stacy French; m. Margaret Wendell Coolidge 1938; one s. one d.; ed. Loomis School and Harvard Univ.
Research Fellow, Biology, Calif. Inst. of Technology, Pasadena, Calif. 34-35; Guest Worker, Kaiser Wilhelm Inst. Berlin-Dahlem 35-36; Austin Teaching Fellow, Biochemistry, Harvard Medical School, Boston 36-38; Instructor (Research), Chem., Univ. of Chicago 38-41; Asst., Assoc. Prof., Botany, Univ. of Minn. 41-47; Dir. Dept. of Plant Biology, Carnegie Inst. 47-73, Dir. Emer. 73-; Prof. (by courtesy) Biology, Stanford Univ.; Chair. Western Section, Amer. Soc. Plant Physio-logists 54; mem. Nat. Acad. of Sciences, Amer. Acad. of Arts and Sciences, Deutsche Akad. der Naturforscher Leopoldina; Award of Merit, Botanical Soc. of America 73; Hon. Ph.D. (Univ. of Göteborg) 74.
Leisure interests: mountaineering, conservation of natural areas, development of instruments for plane table plotting for maps.
Publs. Numerous articles and reviews in technical journals on photosynthesis and the spectroscopy and functions of plant pigments; annual reports in Carnegie Inst. of Washington *Year Book* 48-.
Carnegie Institution, Stanford, Calif.; Home: 11970 Rhus Ridge Road, Los Altos Hills, Calif., U.S.A.
Telephone: (415) 325-1521 (Office); (415) 948-8318 (Home).

Freni, Mirella; Italian opera singer; b. Moderna.
Debut 55, debut at La Scala, Milan 62, Glyndebourne Festival 61, Royal Opera House, Covent Garden 61, Metropolitan Opera, N.Y. 65; has sung at Vienna State Opera and at Salzburg Festival and leading opera houses throughout the world.
Major roles include: Nanetta in *Falstaff*, Mimi in *La Bohème*, Zerlina in *Don Giovanni*, Susanna, Adina in *L'elisir d'amore*, Violetta in *La Traviata*, Desdemona in *Otello*.
c/o John Coast Concerts, 1 Park Close, London, S.W.1, England.

Frère, Jean; Belgian diplomatist and banker; b. 1919, Chatou, Seine-et-Oise, France; s. of Maurice Frère; m. Marie-Rose Vanlangenhove 1949; one s. three d.; ed. Germany, Austria, Brussels Univ.
With Solvay & Cie. (Chemical Industries), Brussels 41-46; entered diplomatic service 46, Attaché (Commercial and Econ.), Belgian Legation, Prague 48-51; Political Div., Ministry of Foreign Affairs 51-52; First Sec. (Econ.), Belgian Embassy, Rome 52-58; Gen. Sec. European Investment Bank 58-; mem. Belgian del. Conf. between EEC mem. countries and Britain 62; Conseiller Banque Lambert 62-, Man. Partner Banque Lambert 67-; Conseiller Général Banque Bruxelles Lambert S.A. 75-; mem. of the Board, Banco di Roma (Belgique) S.A., Gruppo Finanziario Tessile (GFT) Turin; Chair. Comm. on Int. Investments and Econ. Devt., Int. Chamber of Commerce; Chair. of Board S.A. Belge AEG-Telefunken, Brussels; many Belgian and foreign decorations.
Leisure interests: violin, painting, photography, elec-tronics.
Banque Bruxelles Lambert S.A., 24 avenue Marnix, 1050 Brussels; Home: 106 avenue de l'Observatoire, 1180 Brussels, Belgium.
Telephone: (02) 513-81-81 (Office); (02) 374-08-56 (Home).

Freud, Anna, C.B.E., LL.D., SC.D. (daughter of late Sigmund Freud); British (naturalized) psychoanalyst; b. 3 Dec. 1895.
Member Vienna Psycho-Analytic Soc.; Chair. Training Inst. of the Vienna Psycho-Analytic Society; Chair. of the Vienna Psycho-Analytic Society 25-38; Organizer of a Residential War Nursery for Homeless Children, London 40-45; mem. of the British Psycho-Analytic Society and Inst. of Psycho-Analysis 38-; Dir. of the Hampstead Child-Therapy Course and Clinic 38-; Vice-Pres. Int. Psycho-Analytic Asscn. 38-; Hon. LL.D. Clark Univ., Worcester, Mass. 50, Sheffield Univ. 66, Hon. Sc.D., Jefferson Medical Coll., Phila., Pa. 64, Univ. of Chicago 66, Yale Univ. 68.
Publs. *Introduction to Psychoanalysis for Teachers* 31, *The Ego and the Mechanisms of Defence* 37, *The Psycho-Analytical Treatment of Children* 46, *Normality and Pathology in Childhood* 65, *Indications of Child Analysis*, and other papers 69, *Difficulties in the Path of Psycho-analysis* (U.S.A.) 69, *Research at the Hampstead Child Therapy Clinic*, and other papers 1956-65 70, *Problems of Psychoanalytic Technique and Therapy* 73, *The Writings of Anna Freud Vols. I-VII* (U.S.A.) 73; and, with Dorothy Burlingham, *Young Children in War-time* 42, *Infants Without Families* 43.
20 Maresfield Gardens, London, N.W.3, England.

Freud, Lucian; British painter; b. 8 Dec. 1922; ed. Central School of Art, Goldsmiths' Coll., London.
Teacher at Slade School of Art, London 48-58; first one-man exhibition 44, subsequently 46, 50, 52, 58, 63, 68, 72; works have been acquired by New York Museum of Modern Art, Melbourne Nat. Gallery, Tate Gallery, London, etc.; rep. at Dunn Int. Exhibition, London 63.
c/o Anthony d'Offay, 9 Dering Street, London, W.1, England.

Freudenberg, Karl Johann, DR.PHIL.; German chemist; b. 29 Jan. 1886, Weinheim (Baden); s. of Hermann and Helene Freudenberg (née Siegert); m. Doris Nieden 1910 (deceased); two s. (killed in 2nd World War) three d.; ed. Realprogymnasium Weinheim, Goethe-Gymnasium Frankfurt, Univ. of Bonn, and Univ. of Berlin.
Worked with Emil Fischer, Berlin 08-13; Privatdozent, Univ. of Kiel 14; First World War (Iron Crosses) 14-20; Privatdozent, Univ. of Munich 20; Extraordinary Prof. Univ. of Freiburg 21; Full Prof. and Dir. Chemical Laboratory, Technical Univ. Karlsruhe 22-26; Full Prof. and Dir. Chemical Laboratory, Univ. of Heidel-berg 26-56, Rector of Univ. of Heidelberg 49; Dir. of Research Inst. for Chemistry of Wood and Poly-saccharides, Chemical Inst., Heidelberg 46-69; Carl Schurz Memorial Prof., Univ. of Wis. 31; Dohme Lec-turer, Univ. of Baltimore 31; Cooch Behar Prof. Lecturer, Indian Asscn. for Cultivation of Science, Jadavpur, Calcutta 58; mem. Acads. of Heidelberg,

Göttingen, Munich, Uppsala, Stockholm, Lund, Helsinki; Foreign mem. Royal Soc., London; Hon. mem. Acad. Leopoldina, Halle, Int. Acad. Wood Science, Swiss Chemical Soc., Japanese Chemical Soc., Japanese Agricultural Chemical Soc., Spanish Soc. of Physics and Chem., Soc. of Austrian Chemists, Chemical Soc. London, Gesellschaft Deutscher Chemiker, Societas Scientiarum Fennica, etc.; Dr. h.c. Technical Univs. of Graz and Darmstadt, Univs. Basle and Berlin, Humboldt Univ.; Grosses Bundesverdienstkreuz mit Stern, Emil Fischer and Alex. Mitscherlich Medals.
Publs. *Chemie der natürlichen Gerbstoffe* 20, *Stereochemistry* 33, *Tannin, Cellulose, Lignin* 33, *Organische Chemie* (with Plieninger—12th edn.) 70 (trans. into Spanish, English, Japanese); *Constitution and Biosynthesis of Lignin* (with Neish) 68; papers on stereochemistry, natural organic high molecular substances; tannins, sugars, etc., cellulose, starch, proteins, lignin.
6900 Heidelberg, Wilckensstrasse 34, Federal Republic of Germany.
Telephone: 41948.

Freund, Mrs. Miriam Kottler, M.A., PH.D.; American Zionist organizer; b. 17 Feb. 1906, New York City; d. of Harry Kottler and Rebecca Zindler; m. Milton Freund 1927; two s.; ed. Hunter Coll., New York Univ. Teacher high schools, N.Y.C. to 44; Nat. Board Hadassah, Women's Zionist Organisation 40-, Vice-Pres. 53-56, Pres. 56-60; Chair. Nat. Youth Aliyah 53-56; mem. Actions Cttee., World Zionist Organisation 56-; Chair. Exec. American Zionist Council 60-; mem. Nat. Board Jewish Nat. Fund 47-; Del. 21st Orientalist Congress, Moscow 60; mem. American Asscn. Univ. Women, Jewish History Soc., Assembly of Jewish Agency 71-, Board United Israel Appeal 65-; H. Spold Centennial Lecturer, Historical Soc. and Hebrew Univ.; Nat. Asscn. Chair. State of Israel Bonds, Women's Div. 75; Exec. World Council of Synagogues; Editor Hadassah Magazine, Nat. Educ. Chair.
Leisure interests: travel, painting, writing.
Publs. *Jewish Merchants in Colonial America* 36, *Jewels for a Crown* 63.
575 Park Avenue, New York, N.Y. 10021, U.S.A.
Telephone: 838-4900; (612) 224-1355.

Frey, Roger; French politician; b. 11 June 1913, Nouméa, New Caledonia; s. of François and Anne-Marie (née Brun) Frey; m. Lucienne Bernier 1936; one s. one d.; ed. Coll. Stanislas, Paris and Ecole des Sciences Politiques.
Counsellor of the French Union 52; Sec. Gen. Parti Républicain Social 54, U.N.R. 58; Minister of Information 59-Feb. 60: Minister attached to Prime Minister's Office 60-62; Minister of the Interior 62-67; Minister of State responsible for relations with Parl. 67-71, Minister of State responsible for Admin. Reforms 71-72; Pres. Constitutional Court 74-; Croix de Guerre, Légion d'Honneur; Union pour la Nouvelle République (U.N.R.).
56 boulevard Flandrin, 75116 Paris, France.

Frey-Wyssling, Prof. Albert, DR.SC.NAT.; Swiss university professor; b. 8 Nov. 1900, Küsnacht-Zürich; s. of Dr. Hans Frey and Clara Hoepfner; m. Margrit Wyssling; two s. two d.; ed. Swiss Federal Inst. of Technology (ETH), and Univs. of Geneva, Jena and Paris.
Rockefeller Fellow, Univ. of Jena 25, at Paris 26; Teacher of Gen. Botany at ETH 27; Plant Physiologist, Experimental Station AVROS, Sumatra, Indonesia 28-32; Asst. and Lecturer, Gen. Botany, ETH Zürich 32-38, Prof. Gen. Botany and Plant Physiology, Eidgenössische Technische Hochschule (ETH) 38-70, Prof. Emer. 70-, Rector ETH 57-61; Dr. h.c. (Utrecht, Münster, Rennes, Vancouver, Nijmegen, Fribourg); Foreign mem. Royal Society, London 57, Foreign Assoc. Nat. Acad. of Sciences of U.S.A. 70.

Publs. *Stoffausscheidung der höheren Pflanzen* 35, *Submikroskopische Morphologie des Protoplasmas* 38, *Submicroscopic Morphology of Protoplasm* 48 and 53, *Submikroskopische Struktur des Cytoplasmas* 55, *Macromolecules in Cell Structure* 57, *Die pflanzliche Zellwand* 59, *Ultrastructural Plant Cytology* (with K. Mühlethaler) 65, *Comparative Organellography of the Cytoplasm* 73, *The Plant Cell Wall* 76.
Schiltrain, 8706 Meilen, Switzerland.

Freymond, Jacques, D. ès L.; Swiss professor of history; b. 5 Aug. 1911, Lausanne; m. Antoinette Cart 1940; two s. one d.; ed. Univs. of Lausanne, Munich and Paris. Teacher in various secondary schools 35-42; Prof. of Modern and Contemporary History, Univ. of Lausanne 43-55; Prof. of Diplomatic History, Ecole des Sciences sociales et politiques, Univ. of Lausanne 46-55; Diplomatic Chronicler, *Gazette de Lausanne* 46-55; Rockefeller Fellow in U.S. for studies, especially Yale and Columbia Univs. 49-50; Prof. of History at Graduate Inst. of Int. Studies, Geneva 51-, Dir. Graduate Inst. of Int. Studies 55-; Prof. History of Int. Relations, Univ. of Geneva 58-; corresp. mem. Académie des Sciences Morales et Politiques 61; mem. Int. Red Cross Cttee. 59-72, Vice Pres. 65-66, 69-70; Pres. Int. Political Science Asscn. 64-67.
Leisure interest: music.
Publs. *La politique de François Ier à l'égard de la Savoie* 39, *Lénine et l'Impérialisme* 51, *De Roosevelt à Eisenhower: la politique étrangère américaine* 53, *Le conflit Sarrois* 59, *La Première Internationale, recueil de documents* (Editor) 62, *Etudes et documents sur la Première Internationale en Suisse* 64, *Western Europe since the War* 64, *Contributions à l'étude du Comintern* 65.
Office: 132 rue de Lausanne, c/o Institut Universitaire de Hautes Etudes Internationales, 1211 Geneva; Home: 1294 Genthod, Geneva, Switzerland.
Telephone: 311730.

Freyre, Gilberto de Mello, B.A., M.A., D.LITT., POL.SC.D.; Brazilian writer and social anthropologist; b. 1900; ed. Colegio Americano, Recife, Baylor and Columbia Univs., U.S.A.
Research in England, France, Germany and U.S. 22, 31, 36, 37; Prof. of Sociology, Pernambuco State Normal School 28-30; Prof. of Sociology and Founding Prof. of Social Anthropology, Rio de Janeiro Univ. 35-38; Supervisor North East Brazil Social and Educational Research Centre 57-; M.P. 46-50; del. UN Gen. Assembly 49, 64; Technical Adviser, Dept. for Protection of Historical and Artistic Monuments, UN Cttee. on Race Relations in South Africa 54; founded Recife Inst. for Research in Social Sciences 49; mem. Fed. Council of Culture of Brazil 67-; Visiting Prof. and Lecturer at many univs.; Hon. mem. American Sociological Soc., Brazilian Historical and Geographical Inst., American Acad. of Arts and Sciences, World Acad. of Arts and Sciences, French Acad. of Sciences; Hon. Prof., Recife and Bahia Univs.; mem. Portuguese, Ecuadorean and Colombian Historical Acads., American Anthropological Asscn., Lisbon Geog. Soc., American Philosophical Soc., Hispanic Soc. of America, Portuguese Acad. of Sciences; Hon. Aggregatus of Sociology, Buenos Aires Univ.; Dr. h.c. (Columbia, Sussex, Coimbra, Sorbonne, Münster Univs.); Dir. *Diogène* and *Cahiers Internationaux de Sociologie* (Paris), Inst. Int. de Civilisations Différentes (Belgium); Filipe d'Oliveira Award 34, Amsfield-Wolf Award (Princeton) 57, Brazilian Acad. of Letters Award for high literary merit 59; Great Cross of Military Merit 60, Great Cross of the Brazilian Order of Baron of Rio Branco (Diplomacy) 66, and numerous other awards.
Publs. *Casa-Grande e Senzala* (in English as *The Masters and the Slaves*) 34, *Sobrados e Mucambos* (in English as *The Mansions and the Shanties*) 36, *Sociologia, Problemas brasileiros de Antropologia* (Brazil: An Interpretation) 45, *Ingleses no Brazil* 48, *Aventura e Rotina* 53, *Vida*

Social no Brasil nos Meados do Século XIX 64, *Dona Sinká e o Filho Padre* (in English as *Mother and Son*), *Talvez Poesia.*
Apipucos, Recife, Brazil.

Friberg, Sten Axel, M.D.; Swedish orthopaedic surgeon; b. 5 Sept. 1902, Stockholm; *s.* of Axel and Teresia Friberg; *m.* 1st Gertrud Thomasson 1928, one *d.*; *m.* 2nd Gudrun Modéen 1932, two *s.* two *d.*; ed. Karolinska Institutet, Stockholm.
Professor 43-, Head of Univ. Clinic of Orthopaedic Surgery 43-, Rector of Karolinska Institutet 53-69; mem. Board of Nobel Foundation 53-69; Chair. Nobel Prize for Medicine Cttee. 60-69; mem. Scientific Council at Nat. Swedish Social Welfare Board; mem. Nat. Swedish Industrial Injuries Insurance Court; Editor *Acta Orthopaedica Scandinavica* 47-71; Pres. Soc. Int. de Chirurgie Orthopédique et de Traumatologie; mem. Acad. de Chirurgie, France; Hon. or Corresp. mem. Orthopaedic Asscns. in Argentina, Austria, France, Germany, Great Britain, Italy, Scandinavia, U.S.A.; Corresp. mem. Soviet Acad. of Medical Sciences.
Leisure interests: literature, bridge, golf.
Publs. Approx. 60 works, mainly on orthopaedics.
Las Colondrinas, Rio Verde, Marbella, Spain.
Telephone: Malaga 811314.

Frick, Alexander; Liechtenstein politician; b. 1910, Schaan, Liechtenstein; *s.* of Alexander and Theresia Frick-Wanger; *m.* Hildegard Kranz 1939; five *s.* four *d.*; ed. Training Coll. for Teachers.
Began career as teacher 29; official in Tax Dept. 30-36, Chief of Dept. 36; Head of Govt. 45-62; Pres. of the Diet 69; awarded Grand Cross of Liechtenstein Order of Merit, Great Silver Insignia of Honour (Bande der Republik Österreich); Hon. Dr. (Univ. Freiburg); Grosskreuz des Piusordens; mem. Bürgerpartei.
Im Ganser 121, Schaan, Principality of Liechtenstein.
Telephone: 2-18-02.

Frick, Gottlob; German bass opera singer; b. 1906; ed. Stuttgart Opera Chorus and under Neudörfer-Opitz.
First small part in Bayreuth Festival 30; with Coburg Opera 34, then Freiburg-im-Breisgau and Königsberg Opera; with Dresden Opera 40-50; joined West Berlin City Opera 50; regular commitments with Vienna State Opera, Bavarian State Opera and guest artist at Covent Garden and Metropolitan, New York; chiefly known for Wagnerian roles including Daland, Hermann, King Heinrich, King Mark, Pogner, Gurnemanz and bass parts in *The Ring* especially Fasolt, Hunding and Hagen; also sings in Oratorio; Verdienstkreuz (1st Class), Grosse Bundesverdienstkreuz, Österreichische Ehrenkreuz für Wissenschaft und Kunst (1st Class).
Enzkieis-Pforzheim, Eichelberg-Haus Waldfrieden, 7531 Olbronn-Dürrn, Federal Republic of Germany.
Telephone: 07043-6508.

Fricker, Peter Racine, F.R.C.O., A.R.C.M.; British musician; b. 5 Sept. 1920, Wood Green, London; *s.* of Edward Racine and Deborah Alice Fricker (née Parr); *m.* Helen Clench 1943; ed. St. Paul's School and Royal Coll. of Music.
Served R.A.F. 39-45; worked in London as composer, conductor and music administrator 46-64; Dir. of Music, Morley Coll. 52-64; Prof. of Music, Univ. of Calif. 64-, Hon. D.Mus. (Leeds) 58; W. German Order of Merit 65; Hon. mem. Royal Acad. of Music, Hon. Prof. Fellow, Univ. of Wales, Cardiff.
Leisure interest: travel.
Works: *First String Quartet* 48, *First Symphony* 49, *First Violin Concerto* 50, *Violin Sonata* 50, *Second Symphony* 51, *Viola Concerto* 53, *Second String Quartet* 53, *Second Violin Concerto* 53, *Piano Concerto* 54, *Dance Scene for Orchestra* 54, *Horn Sonata* 55, *Litany for Double String Orchestra* 55, *Musick's Empire* (Chorus and Orchestra) 55, *'Cello Sonata* 56, *The Vision of*

Judgement (Oratorio) 57, *Octet* 58, *Comedy Overture* 58, *Toccata for Piano and Orchestra* 59, *Serenade No. 1 for Six Instruments* 59, *Serenade No. 2 for Flute, Oboe and Piano* 59, *Third Symphony* 60, *12 Studies for Piano* 61, *Cantata for Tenor and Chamber Ensemble* 62, *O Longs Désirs* (song cycle for soprano and orchestra) 63, *Ricercare for Organ* 65, *Four Dialogues for Oboe and Piano* 65, *Four Songs, Voice and Piano, Texts by Andreas Gryphius* (also with Orchestra) 65, *Fourth Symphony* 66, *Fantasy for Viola and Piano* 66, *Three Scenes for Orchestra, The Day and the Spirits* (soprano and harp) 67, *Seven Counterpoints for Orchestra* 67, *Ave Maris Stella* (male voices and piano) 67, *Refrains for Solo Oboe* 68, *Magnificat for Soloists, Chorus and Orchestra* 68, *Episodes for Piano* 68, *Concertante No. 4 for Flute, Oboe, Violin and Strings* 68, *Set No. I for organ* 68, *Toccata Gladius Domini for organ* 68, *Some Superior Nonsense for tenor and chamber ensemble* 69, *Serenade No. 3 for four saxophones* 69, *Episodes II for piano* 69, *Praeludium for organ* 69, *Paseo for guitar* 70, *The Roofs for soprano and percussionist* 70, *Concertante No. 5 for piano and string quartet* 71, *Intrada for Organ* 71, *Nocturne for orchestra* 71, *Ballade for flute and piano* 72, *Seven Little Songs* (Hölderlin) *for chorus* 72, *Introitus for Orchestra* 72, *The Groves of Dodona for six flutes* 73, *Two Petrarch madrigals for chorus* 74, *Spirit Puck for clarinet and percussion* 74, *Trio Sonata for organ* 74, *Third String Quartet* 75, *Fifth Symphony, for Organ and Orchestra* 75.
Office: Department of Music, University of California, Santa Barbara, California 93106; Home: 5423 Throne Court, Santa Barbara, Calif. 93111, U.S.A.
Telephone: 805-964-3737.

Friday, William Clyde, B.S., LL.B., LL.D.; American educator; b. 13 July 1920, Raphine, Va.; *s.* of David Latham and Mary Elizabeth Rowan Friday; *m.* Ida Willa Howell 1942; three *d.*; ed. Wake Forest Coll., North Carolina State Coll. and Univ. of N. Carolina Law School.
Assistant Dean of Students, Univ. of N. Carolina at Chapel Hill 48-51, Acting Dean of Students 50-51, Admin. Asst. to Pres. Univ. of N. Carolina 51-54, Sec. of Univ. of N. Carolina 54-55, Acting Pres. of Univ. of N. Carolina 56, Pres. Oct. 56-; Hon. LL.D. (Wake Forest Coll., Belmont Abbey, Duke Univ., Princeton Univ., Elon Coll., Davidson Coll. and Univ. of Kentucky).
Leisure interests: gardening, golf, reading.
University of North Carolina, General Administration, Chapel Hill, North Carolina 27514, U.S.A.
Telephone: 919-933-6981.

Friderichs, Hans, DR.RER.POL.; German politician; b. 16 Oct. 1931, Wittlich; *m.* Erika Wilhelm; two *d.*
Manager, Rhineland-Hesse Chamber of Industry and Trade 59-63; Deputy Business Man. FDP 63-64, Business Man. 64-69; mem. Bundestag 65-69; Sec. of State, Ministry of Agriculture, Viniculture and Protection of the Environment for Rhineland Palatinate 69-72; Fed. Minister of Econs. 72-; Deputy Chair. FDP 74-.
Leisure interests: art, sport.
Wirtschaftsministerium, 53 Bonn-Duisdorf, Villemombler Strasse, Federal Republic of Germany.
Telephone: 762356.

Fridh, Gertrude; Swedish actress; b. 26 Nov. 1921; ed. Gothenburg School of Dramatic Art.
Gothenburg Theatre 44-49; Intima Theatre, Stockholm 50; Allé Theatre, Stockholm 55-57; Royal Dramatic Theatre, Stockholm 58-.
Plays acted in include: *Ett Dockhem* 53, *Som ni behagar* 54, *Le Misanthrope* 57, *Anna Karenina* 58, *Hedda Gabler* 64 (London 68).
Films acted in include: *Skepp till indialand* 47, *Tvd*

trappor över gåaden 49-50, *Hjärter Knekt* 50, *Smul-trunstället* (Wild Strawberries) 57, *Ansiktet* (The Face) 58, *Djävulens Öga* 60.
c/o Svenska Filminstitutet, Kungsgatan 48, Stockholm C, Sweden.

Fried, Josef, PH.D.; American organic chemist; b. 21 July 1914, Poland; s. of Abraham and Frieda Fried; m. Erna M. Werner 1939; one d.; ed. Univs. of Leipzig and Zurich and Columbia Univ.
Research Assoc., Squibb Inst. for Medical Research 44-47, Head of Dept. 47-49, Dir., Div. of Organic Chem. 59-63; Prof. Depts. of Chem. and Biochem. and Ben May Lab. for Cancer Research 63-; mem. Nat. Acad. of Sciences; Amer. Chemical Soc. Award in Medical Chem. 74.
Leisure interests: violin (chamber music), skiing, sailing.
Publs. concerning chemistry and bio-chemistry of steroids, prostaglandins, carcinogenic hydrocarbons.
Department of Chemistry, University of Chicago, 5735 S. Ellis Avenue, Chicago, Ill. 60637, U.S.A.
Telephone: 312-947-5079.

Friedan, Betty; American feminist leader; b. 4 Feb. 1921, Illinois; m. Carl Freidan 1947 (divorced 1969); two s. one d.
Founder Nat. Org. for Women 66, first Pres. 66-70, Chair. 70-72; Organizer Nat. Women's Political Caucus 71, Int. Feminist Congress 73, First Women's Bank & Trust Co. 73; Visiting Prof. of Sociology, Temple Univ. 72, Yale Univ. 74, Queen's Coll. 75; numerous lectures in U.S.A. and Europe; mem. PEN; American Humanist Award 75.
Publs. *The Feminine Mystique* 63, *It Changed My Life* 76; articles in McCall's, Harper's, etc.
One Lincoln Plaza, New York, N.Y. 10023, U.S.A.

Friedel, Jacques; French physicist; b. 11 Feb. 1921, Paris; s. of Edmond Friedel and Jeanne Friedel (née Bersier); m. Mary Winifred Horder 1952; two s.; ed. Ecole Polytechnique, Ecole des Mines de Paris, Bristol Univ.
Mining engineer, Ecole des Mines de Paris 48-56; Maître de Conférences, Univ. de Paris 56-59; Prof. of Solid State Physics, Univ. de Paris (later Paris Sud) 59-; Chevalier, Légion d'Honneur; Officier, Ordre du Mérite; Hon. mem. American Acad. of Sciences and Letters, Inst. of Physics.
Leisure interest: gardening.
Publ. *Dislocations* 56.
2 rue Jean François, Gerbillon, Paris 6e, France.
Telephone: 222-2585.

Frieden-Kinnen, Madeleine; Luxembourg politician; b. 4 Oct. 1915, Esch-sur-Alzette; m. Pierre Frieden (who became Prime Minister 58 and died 59) 1946.
President of Luxembourg Women's Catholic Action 60-66; Pres. Auxilia-Equipes sociales de malades (Asscn. to help chronic sick, disabled and prisoners) 57-66; Pres. Asscn. des Villages d'Enfants SOS de Luxembourg (org. to form an orphans' village) 63-66; Editor of Women's Page in *Luxemburger Wort* 65-66; Pres. Women's Section of Christian Social Party 66-; Sec. of State for Family, Youth, Population, Social Security and Nat. Educ. 67-69; Minister of Family, Youth, Social Security, Public Health and Cultural Affairs Feb. 69-Sept. 72.
c/o Ministère de la Famille, Luxembourg City, Luxembourg.

Friedenthal, Richard, DR. PHIL.; British writer; b. 9 June 1896, Munich; s. of Prof. Dr. Hans Friedenthal and Martha (née Elster) Friedenthal; m. Elisabeth C. Bach-Güttermann 1950; ed. Gymnasium, Berlin, Humboldt-Universität zu Berlin, Friedrich-Schiller-Universität, Jena, and Ludwig-Maximilians-Universität, Munich.
Former Reader and Editor, Knaur Verlag, Berlin;

writer and editor in England 38-; mem. German Acad., Darmstadt; Hon. Pres. PEN Centre, Fed. Repub. of Germany; Grosses Bundesverdienstkreuz (Fed. Repub. of Germany).
Leisure interests: collecting books, music.
Publs. include poetry, novels, short stories; biographies: *Der Eroberer* 32, *Leonardo da Vinci* 59, *G. F. Handel* 59, *Goethe—His Life and Times* 65; travel books: *Die Party bei Herrn Tokaido* 58, *London zwischen gestern und morgen* 60; Editor *Knaurs Lexikon* 31, *Facts* (4 vols.) 34, *Letters of the Great Artist* (2 vols.) 64, *Luther—His Life and Times* 67, *Entdecker des Ich* (*Montaigne, Pascal, Diderot*) 69, *Jan Hus, Heretic and Rebel* 72.
15 Burgess Hill, London, N.W.2, England.
Telephone: 01-435-8783.

Friedman, Irving S., A.B., M.A., PH.D.; American economist; b. 31 Jan. 1915; m. Edna Friedman; two s. one d.; ed. Columbia Univ., N.Y.
Member Office of Sec. of Treasury, U.S. 41-46; Chief Int. Monetary Fund (IMF) 46-48; Asst. for Policy Matters to Deputy Man. Dir. IMF 48-50; Dir. Exchange Restrictions Dept., IMF 50-64; Econ. Adviser to Pres. of Int. Bank for Reconstruction and Devt. (World Bank) 64-70; Chair. Econ. Cttee.; mem. President's Council; Visiting Fellow, All Souls Coll., Oxford 70-71; Prof. in Residence, World Bank 71-74; Senior Adviser for Int. Operations, First Nat. City Bank, N.Y. 74-; Chair. Center of Concern 71-; Vice-Pres. and Treas. Soc. for Int. Devt.; mem. Amer. Econ. Soc., Council on Foreign Relations; Order of Sacred Treasure, Japan.
Leisure interests: golf, sailing, tennis, astronomy.
Publs. *Inflation: A Worldwide Disaster* 73, and numerous books and articles on international economics.
Home: 6620 Fernwood Court, Bethesda, Md.; and 860 UN Plaza, New York, U.S.A.
Telephone: EM-5-5023 (Home).

Friedman, Milton, B.A., M.A., PH.D.; American economist; b. 31 July 1912, New York; s. of Jeno Saul and Sarah Esther Friedman; m. Rose Director 1938; one s. one d.; ed. Rutgers Univ., Chicago and Columbia Univs.
Associate Economist, Nat. Resources Cttee. 35-37, Nat. Bureau of Economic Research 37-45 (on leave 40-45), 48-; Principal Economist, Div. of Tax Research, U.S. Treasury Dept. 41-43; Assoc. Dir. Statistical Research Group, Div. of War Research, Columbia Univ. 43-45; Prof. of Economics, Univ. of Chicago 48-; Board of Editors *Econometrica*; Pres. American Econ. Asscn. 67; mem. President's Comm. on an All-Volunteer Armed Force; mem. President's Comm. on White House Fellows 71; Pres. Mont Pelerin Soc. 70-72; mem. Nat. Acad. of Sciences 73-; numerous hon. degrees.
Leisure interests: tennis, carpentry, talk.
Publs. *Income from Independent Professional Practice* (with Simon Kuznets) 46, *Sampling Inspection* (with others) 48, *Essays in Positive Economics* 53, *A Theory of the Consumption Function* 57, *A Program for Monetary Stability* 59, *Capitalism and Freedom* 62, *Price Theory: a provisional text* 62, *A Monetary History of the United States 1867-1960* (with Anna J. Schwartz) 63, *Inflation: Causes and Consequences* 63, *The Balance of Payments: Free Versus Flexible Exchange Rates* (with Robert V. Roosa) 67, *Dollars and Deficits* 68, *Optimum Quantity of Money and Other Essays* 69, *Monetary Statistics of the United States* (with Anna J. Schwartz) 70, *A Theoretical Framework for Monetary Analysis* 72, *Social Security: Universal or Selective?* (with Wilbur J. Cohen) 72, *An Economist's Protest* 72 (2nd edn. 75), *Money and Economic Development* 73, *Milton Friedman's Monetary Framework* 74; econ. columnist with *Newsweek*.
1126 East 59th Street, Chicago, Ill. 60637, U.S.A.
Telephone: MI 3-0800, Extension 4523.

Friedmann, Georges Philippe; French university professor and sociologist; b. 13 May 1902, Paris; s. of Adolphe and Elisabeth (née Nathan) Friedmann; m.

1st Hania Olszewska 1937-57, 2nd Marcelle Rémond. Inspector-Gen. of Technical Education 45; Prof. Conservatoire Nat. des Arts et Métiers 46-62; Dir. d'Etudes, Ecole Pratique des Hautes Etudes (Sorbonne) 48-76; Dir. du Centre d'Etudes Sociologiques 49-51; Pres. Int. Sociological Asscn. 56-59; Pres. Latin-American Faculty of Social Science, Santiago 58-64; Joint Editor of the revue *Annales* 47-; Officier Légion d'Honneur, Médaille de la Résistance.
Leisure interests: tennis, swimming.
Publs. *La Crise du Progrès* 36, *De la Sainte Russie à l'U.R.S.S.* 38, *Leibniz et Spinoza* 46, *Problèmes Humains du Machinisme Industriel* 46, *Où va le travail humain?* 50, *Villes et Campagnes* (edited) 53, *Le Travail en miettes* 56, *Problèmes d'Amérique Latine* (2 vols.) 59, 61, *Traité de Sociologie du Travail* (2 vols.) 61, 62, *Fin du Peuple Juif?* 65, *Sept Etudes sur l'homme et la technique* 66, *La Puissance et la Sagesse* 70.
11 rue François Ponsard, Paris 16e, France.

Friedmann, Herbert, PH.D.; American zoologist and fmr. museum director; b. 22 April 1900, New York City; s. of Uriah M. Friedmann and Mary Behrmann; m. Karen Juul Vejlo 1937; one d.; ed. Coll. of City of New York and Cornell Univ.
Instructor in Biology, Brown Univ. 26-27, Amherst Coll. 27-29; Curator of Birds, U.S. Nat. Museum, Smithsonian Inst. 29-57, Head Curator of Zoology 57-61; Dir. Los Angeles County Museum of Natural History 61-70; Prof. of Zoology in Residence, Univ. of Calif. at Los Angeles 64-70, Past Pres. Amer. Ornithologists Union; Past Vice-Pres. Amer. Asscn. for Advancement of Science; Emer. mem. Amer. Soc. of Zoologists; mem. Nat. Acad. of Sciences 62; Hon. mem. Deutsche Ornith. Gesellschaft 64-, S. African Ornith. Union 73-; fmr. Research Fellow, Guggenheim Foundation; Leidy Medal, Acad. of Natural Sciences, Phila. 55; Elliot Medal Nat. Acad. of Sciences 59; Brewster Medal, Amer. Ornithologists Union 64.
Leisure interests: symbolism in medieval and renaissance art of Europe.
Publs. 16 books and several hundred papers including *The Cowbirds, a Study in the Biology of Social Parasitism* 29, *Birds of the Frick Expedition to Ethiopia and Kenya*, 2 vols., 30, 37; *The Symbolic Goldfinch* 46, *The Honeyguides* 55, *The Parasitic Weaverbirds* 60, *Host Relations of the Parasitic Cowbirds* 63, *Distributional List of the Birds of Mexico*, 2 vols. (with others) 50, 57, *Check List of North American Birds*, 5th edn. (with A. Wetmore and cttee.) 57, *Evolutionary History of the Avian Genus Chrysococcyx* 68.
350 South Fuller Avenue, Apt. 12H, Los Angeles, Calif. 90036, U.S.A.

Friedrich, Carl Joachim; American (born German) professor of political science; b. 5 June 1901; ed. Marburg, Frankfurt, Vienna and Heidelberg Univs. Emigrated to U.S.A. 22; Lecturer in Govt. Harvard 26-27, Asst. Prof. 27-31, Assoc. Prof. 31-36. Prof. of Govt. 36-71, Eaton Prof. Science of Govt. 55-71, Prof. Emer. 71-; Prof. of Political Science Heidelberg 56-66, Prof. Emer. 66-.
Publs. *Studies in Federalism* 54, *The Philosophy of Law in Historical Perspective* 56, 58, *The Age of the Baroque* 62, *Man and His Government* 63, *Transcendent Justice* 64, *Totalitarian Dictatorship and Autocracy* 65, *Introduction to Political Theory* 67, *Federalism* 68, *Constitutional Government and Democracy* 68, *Europe: An Emergent Nation?* 69, *The Pathology of Politics* 72, *Tradition and Authority* 72.
14 Hawthorn Street, Cambridge, Mass. 02138, U.S.A.

Friedrich, Johannes, DR. PHIL.; German orientalist; b. 27 Aug. 1893, Leipzig; ed. Leipzig Univ.
Privat Dozent Leipzig Univ. 24, Extra. Prof. 29, Prof. of Oriental Philology 35, Rector 48-49; Prof. Ancient Oriental Philology, Berlin Free Univ. 50, Emer. 61;

Ord. mem. Saxon Acad. of Sciences; Hon. mem. Deutsche Morgenländische Gesellschaft, Linguistic Soc. of America; Corresp. mem. Oriental Inst., Prague, German Archaeological Inst. (Istanbul Section), Ex Oriente Lux Asscn., Leiden, Istituto Lombardo, Milan, and Societas Orientalis Fennica, Helsinki; Co-Editor *Zeitschrift der Deutschen Morgenländischen Gesellschaft.*
Publs. *Staatsverträge des Hatti-Reiches in hethitischer Sprache* (Vol. I 26, Vol. II 30), *Kleinasiatische Sprachdenkmäler* 32, *Einführung ins Urartäische, Ras Schamra* 33, *Kleine Beiträge zur churritischen Grammatik* 39, *Entzifferungsgeschichte der hethitischen Hieroglyphenschrift* 39, *Hethitisches Elementarbuch* (Vol. I 40, 2nd edn. 60, Vol II 46, 2nd edn. 67), *Phönizisch-punische Grammatik* 51, *Hethitisches Wörterbuch* 52, 57, 61, 66, *Entzifferung verschollener Schriften und Sprachen* 54 (2nd edn. 66), *Kurze Grammatik der alten Quiché-Sprache im Popol Vuh* 55, *Hethitische Gesetze* 59, *Zwei russische Novellen in neusyrischer Übersetzung* 60, *Hethitisches Keilschrift-Lesebuch* 60, *Geschichte der Schrift* 66.
Schloss-Strasse 49, 1 Berlin 41, Germany.

Friendly, Alfred, A.B.; American journalist; b. 30 Dec. 1911, Salt Lake City, Utah; m. Jean Ulman 1937; three s. two d.; ed. Amherst Coll.
Reporter, *Washington Daily News* 36-38; Reporter, *Washington Post* 39-51, Asst. Man. Editor 52-55, Man. Editor 55-65, Assoc. Editor 66-71, Vice-Pres. and Dir. 63-66; Asst. to Trustee, Associated Gas and Electric Corpn. 40; served in Air Force Intelligence 42-45, Legion of Merit; Chief European Information Branch, Econ. Co-operation Admin. 48-49; Dir. American Soc. of Newspaper Editors 61-65; Trustee, Amherst Coll. 61-67; Pulitzer Prize 68; Sydney Hillman Award 72; Hon. L.H.D. (Amherst Coll.) 58.
Leisure interest: archaeology.
Publs. *The Guys on the Ground* 44, *Crime and Publicity* (Co-Author) 67.
47 Cheyne Place, London, SW3 4HL, England.
Telephone: 01-351-0606.

Friendly, Fred W., H.L.D.; American broadcaster and journalist; b. 30 Oct. 1915, New York City; s. of Samuel Wachenheimer and Therese Friendly; m. 1st Dorothy Greene, 2nd Ruth W. Mark 1968; five s. one d.; ed. Cheshire Acad., Connecticut, and Nichols Coll., Dudley, Massachusetts.
Began broadcasting career writing, producing and narrating series *Footprints in the Sands of Time* on local radio station 38; U.S. Army 41-45 as lecturer in Educ. section and corresp. for China, Burma and India on Army newspaper *Roundup*; commenced long professional partnership with Edward R. Murrow with historical gramophone record *I Can Hear It Now*; then Columbia Broadcasting System (C.B.S.) Radio Series *Hear It Now* and TV Series *See It Now* 51; Exec. Producer C.B.S. Reports 59-64; Pres. C.B.S. News 64-66; Edward R. Murrow Prof. of Journalism, Columbia Univ. 66-; Adviser on Television to Ford Foundation 66-; Soldiers Medal of Heroism; Legion of Merit with four battle stars; ten George Foster Peabody Awards; Hon. D.Hum.Litt. (Grinnell Coll., Iowa and Brown Univ., Rhode Island); mem. Rhode Island Heritage Hall of Fame; Chair. Mayor Lindsay's Task Force on CATV and Telecommunications 68.
Publs. *See It Now* (co-author) 55, *Due to Circumstances Beyond Our Control* 67.
Ford Foundation, 320 East 43rd Street, New York, N.Y. 10017; 4614 Fieldston Road, Riverdale, N.Y. 10471, U.S.A.
Telephone: 202-573-4848 (Office).

Friis, Henning Kristian; Danish social research executive; b. 11 Oct. 1911, Copenhagen; s. of Prof. Aage Friis and Benedicte Blichfeldt; m. Britt Hallberg 1937; two s. one d.; ed. Københavns Universitet.
Social Science Adviser, Ministry of Social Affairs 41-58;

Sec.-Gen. Danish Govt. Youth Comm. 45-52, Cttee. on Scientific and Technical Personnel 56-59; Chair. OECD Cttee. for Scientific and Technical Personnel 58-65; Exec. Dir. Danish Nat. Inst. of Social Research 58; Chair. Board of Trustees, Danish Schools of Social Work 66-71; Chair. European Social Research Cttee., Int. Gerontological Asscn. 54-60; mem. Exec. Cttee. Int. Sociological Asscn. 59-65; Vice-Chair. Danish Social Science Council 68-, European Centre for Co-ordination in the Social Sciences 68-; mem. Board of Trustees, UN Inst. on Training and Research 65-; mem. Exec. Cttee. Int. Social Science Council; Editor *Scandinavia between East and West* 50, and *Family and Society* 64.
Leisure interests: tennis, reading newspapers.
Publs. *Social Policy and Social Trends* 58, *Longstanding Public Assistance Clients* 60, *Old People in a low-income Area in Copenhagen* 61, *Institutional Means of Collaboration between the Social Sciences* 62, *Development of Social Research in Ireland* 65, *Social Policy and Social Research in India* 68.
28 Borgergade, DK-1300 Copenhagen K, Denmark.
Telephone: (01) 13-98-11.

Friis, Torben; Danish banker; b. 1 Dec. 1904.
With Aarhus Privatbank 21-26; Banque des Pays du Nord, Paris 26-27; Sec. Danish Consulate-Gen., Paris 27-28, 31-33; with Danish company 29-31; joined Danmarks Nationalbank 34, special foreign responsibilities, Man. 58-74; Perm. Del., Payments Cttee., Org. for European Econ. Co-operation (OEEC) 48-50; with Int. Monetary Fund (IMF) 54-58, 66-68, Alt. Exec. Dir. 54-56, Exec. Dir. 56-58 and 66-68; mem. Nordic Financial and Currency Cttee. 60-65, Chair. 65-66; Rep. in Scandinavia for Standard Chartered Bank Ltd. 75; Legion of Honour and Order of Dannebrog.
Frdbg. Allé 74, 1820 Copenhagen V, Denmark.

Friis Johansen, Knud, PH.D.; Danish archaeologist; b. 1 Nov. 1887; ed. Copenhagen Univ.
Assistant Keeper Copenhagen Nat. Museum 11 and Keeper 22; Prof. of Archaeology Copenhagen Univ. 27-56.
Publs. *Les Vases Sicyoniens* 23, *Hoby-Fundet* 23, *De forhistoriske Tider i Europa* 27, *Corpus Vasorum Antiquorum, Copenhague, Musée National, Iliaden i tidlig graesk Kunst* 34, *Thésée et la danse à Délos* 45, *The Attic Grave Reliefs* 51, *Exochi* 58, *Eine Dithyrambos-Aufführung* 59, *Ajas und Hector* 61, *The Iliad in Early Greek Art* 67.
Egernvej 27, Copenhagen F, Denmark.

Frimpong-Ansah, Jonathan Herbert; Ghanaian banker; b. 22 Oct. 1930, Mampong, Ashanti; s. of Hammond Owusu-Ansah and Elizabeth Achiaa; m. Selina Agyemang 1954; one d. three s.; ed. Univ. of Ghana and London School of Econs.
Statistician, Ghana Govt. 54-59; Bank of Ghana, Dir. of Research 61-65, Deputy Gov. 65-68, Gov. 68-73; Chair. Ghana Diamond Marketing Board 69-72; Dir. Volta River Authority 72-; Chair. Ashanti Goldfields Corpn. Ltd. 73-; Vice-Chair. Deputies of the Cttee. of the Board of Govs. on Reform of the Int. Monetary System and Related Issues, IMF, Wash. 73-74; Consultant World Bank 75; Chair. Standard Bank Ghana Ltd., Accra 75-.
Leisure interest: art.
Publs. articles in *Economic Bulletin* (Ghana) and *Bulletin of the Inter Credit Bank* (Geneva), contribs. in *International Monetary Reform-Documents of the Committee of Twenty* 74.
31 Brookdene Drive, Northwood, Middx., England; 3 Liberation Link, Accra, Ghana.
Telephone: Northwood 27907; Accra 23314.

Frings, H.E. Cardinal Joseph, DR. THEOL.; German ecclesiastic; b. 6 Feb. 1887, Neuss; s. of Heinrich Frings and Maria Sels; ed. Gymnasium, Neuss, and Univs. of Innsbruck, Bonn and Freiburg im Breisgau, and Priests' Seminary of Cologne.

Ordained 10; Auxiliary Priest in Köln-Zollstock; went to Papal Biblical Inst., Rome 13-14; Rector in Köln-Fühlingen and Neuss; Parish Priest in Köln-Braunsfeld; Regent of Priests' Seminary of Bensberg; Archbishop of Cologne 42-69; created Cardinal by Pope Pius XII 46; mem. Praesidium, 2nd Vatican Council 62; mem. Sacred Congregations of the Council, of Religious Orders, of Rites, for the Eastern Church, of Seminaries and Univs. of Study, for the Propagation of the Faith; Dr. Phil. h.c.
Leisure interests: Mozart, Shakespeare.
Eintrachstrasse 164, 5 Cologne, Federal Republic of Germany.
Telephone: 20821.

Frink, Elisabeth, C.B.E.; British sculptor; b. 14 Nov. 1930, Thurlow; m. 1st Michael Jammet 1956 (dissolved 1962), one s.; m. 2nd Edward Pool 1968 (dissolved 1974); m. 3rd Alexander Csáky 1974; ed. Convent of the Holy Family, Exmouth, and Guildford and Chelsea Schools of Art.
Taught sculpture at Chelsea School of Art 53-60, St. Martin's School of Art 55-64; Visiting Lecturer, part-time, Royal Coll. of Art 65-67; exhibited regularly at Waddington Galleries 55- and also abroad; lived in France 67-72; now living and working in London.
Leisure interests: music, riding, outdoor occupations.
Publs. (illustrated) *Aesop's Fables* 67, *Canterbury Tales* 71, *The Odyssey* 74, *The Iliad* 75; *The Art of Elisabeth Frink* 72.
c/o Waddington Galleries, 2 Cork Street, London, W.1, England.

Frisch, Karl von; German zoologist and university professor; b. 20 Nov. 1886, Vienna; s. of Anton and Marie von Frisch (née Exner); m. Margarete Mohr 1917; one s. three d.; ed. Univs. of Vienna and Munich.
Privatdozent, Munich Univ. 12; Prof. and Dir. Zoological Inst., Rostock Univ. 21, Breslau 23, Munich 25, Graz 46, Munich 50-58; mem. Acad. of Science (Munich, Vienna, Göttingen, Washington, Uppsala, Boston, Stockholm, etc.); foreign mem. Royal Society, London; hon. mem. Royal Entomological Society, London, and American Physiological Soc.; Hon. Ph.D. (Univs. of Berne, Graz, Harvard, Tübingen and Rostock); Hon. D.Sc. (Fed. Tech. Inst., Zürich); Magellan Prize of American Philosophical Soc., Kalinga Prize 59, Nobel Prize for Medicine or Physiology (jointly with K. Lorenz *q.v.* and N. Tinbergen *q.v.*) 73; Orden pour le Mérite.
Leisure interest: collecting insects.
Publs. *Aus dem Leben der Bienen* 27 (The Dancing Bees 54), *Du und das Leben* 36 (Man and the Living World 63), *Bees* 50 (revised edn. 71), *Biologie* 52-53 (Biology 64), *Erinnerungen eines Biologen* 57 (A Biologist Remembers 67, 73), *Tanzsprache und Orientierung der Bienen* 65 (The Dance Language and Orientation of Bees 67), *Animal Architecture* 74.
Über der Klause 10, 8000 Munich 90, Federal Republic of Germany.
Telephone: 644948.

Frisch, Max; Swiss writer and architect; b. 15 May 1911, Zurich; ed. Zürich Univ. and Technical High School.
Worked as foreign corresp. for newspapers throughout Europe and the Near East; diploma in architecture 41; designs executed include the Zürich Recreation Park; first play published 45; abandoned architecture for full-time writing 55; Rockefeller Grant for Drama 51, mem. Amer. Acad. of Arts and Letters 74; Prize of the German Acad. 58, Jerusalem Prize, Ehrenpreis des Schillergedächtnispreises des Landes Baden-Württemberg 65, Grosser Schillerpreis Zürich 74.
Publs. Plays and novels: *Blätter aus dem Brotsack* 40, *J'adore ce qui me brûle oder Die Schwierigen* 45, *Bin oder Die Reise nach Peking* 45, *Nun singen sie wieder* 45,

Tagebuch mit Marion 47, *Die Chinesische Mauer* 47, *Als der Krieg zu Ende war* 49, *Tagebuch 1946-1949* 50, *Graf Oederland* 51, *Don Juan oder Die Liebe zur Geometrie* 53, *Stiller* 54 (translated into 17 languages), *Homer faber* 57 (translated into 15 languages), *Biedermann und die Brandstifter* 58, *Die grosse Wut des Philipp Hotz* 58, *Andorra* 61 (translated into 11 languages), *Mein Name sei Gantenbein* 64, *Biografie: Ein Spiel* 67, *Oeffentlichkeit als Partner* 68, *Wilhelm Tell für die Schule* 71, *Tagebuch 66-71* 72, *Dienstbüchlein* 74, *Montauk* 75.
CH-6611 Berzona, Switzerland; c/o Suhrkamp-Verlag, Frankfurt/Main, Federal Republic of Germany.
Telephone: 093-85-11-20.

Frisch, Otto Robert, O.B.E., DR. PHIL., F.R.S.; British experimental physicist; b. 1 Oct. 1904, Vienna; s. of Dr. Justinian Frisch; m. Ulla Blau 1951; one s. one d.; ed. Vienna Univ.
Engaged in Physics Research at Berlin 27-30, Hamburg 30-33, London 33-34, Copenhagen 34-39, Birmingham and Liverpool 39-43, Los Alamos, N.M., U.S.A. 43-46, Atomic Energy Establishment Harwell 46-47; Jacksonian Prof. of Natural Philosophy, Cambridge 47-72; Fellow of Trinity Coll., Cambridge.
Leisure interest: music.
Publs. *Meet the Atoms* 47, *Atomic Physics Today* 61, *Working with Atoms* 65, *The Nature of Matter* 72.
Trinity College, Cambridge, England.

Frische, Carl Alfred, PH.D.; American scientist and business executive; b. 13 Aug. 1906; ed. Miami Univ., Ohio, and Univ. of Iowa.
Physicist, Research Fellow, Columbia Univ. 32-33; Sperry Gyroscope Co. 33-68, Chief Research Div. 43-45, Vice-Pres. (Engineering) 45-54, Vice-Pres. (Operations) 54-57; Exec. Vice-Pres. Sperry Gyroscope Div., Sperry-Rand Corpn. 57-58, Pres. 58-68, Consultant 68-71; Dir. other companies.
6642 Praying Monk Road, Scottsdale, Ariz. 85253, U.S.A.

Fritzhand, Marek, PH.D.; Polish philosopher; b. 12 Oct. 1913, Buczacz; ed. Lwów Univ.
Doctor 51-54, Assoc. Prof. 54-65, Prof. 65-; Dean, Faculty of Philosophy, Warsaw Univ. 62-65; Head, Moral Science Dept., Warsaw Univ.; Editor-in-Chief *Etyka* 66-71, mem. of Editorial Staff 73-, mem. Polish Philosophical Soc.; mem. Cttee. of Philosophical Sciences, Polish Acad. of Sciences 66-72, Chair. 72-; Corresp. mem. Polish Acad. of Sciences 73-; Gold Cross of Merit (twice), Cross of Valour, Cross of Grunwald, 3rd Class, Knight's Cross, Order of Polonia Restituta.
Publs. include *Myśl etyczna młodego Marksa*; monograph *Wprowadzenie do metaetyki*.
Al. Wyzwolenia 2 m. 3, 00-570 Warsaw, Poland.

Froehlke, Robert F.; American government official; b. 15 Oct. 1922, Neenah, Wis.; m. Nancy J. Barnes; two s. two d.; ed. Marshfield Senior High School, Wis. and Univ. of Wisconsin Law School.
Associate, McDonald & McDonald (Law firm), Madison, Wis. 49-50; mem. faculty, Univ. of Wis. Law School 50-51; Asst. Gen. Counsel, Legal Dept., Sentry Insurance, Stevens Point, Wis. 51; Exec. Vice-Pres., Sentry Life Insurance Co. 59-69; Vice Pres. (Sales), Sentry Insurance Cos. 67; Resident Vice-Pres. Sentry Insurance, Boston, Mass. 68-69; Asst. Sec. of Defense 69-71; Sec. of the Army 71-73; Pres. Sentry Corpn. 73-.
1201 500 Marie Avenue, Stevens Point, Wis. 54481, U.S.A.

Frølund, Hakon; Danish forester; b. 10 Sept. 1916, Frederiksberg; s. of Thomas Frølund (fmr. Chief Justice of Denmark) and Stella (née Fleischer) Frølund; m. Else E. Rasmussen 1941; five c.; ed. Kgl. Veterinaer- og Landbohøjskole, Copenhagen.

Assistant Forest Officer Danish State Forest Service 42-53, Chief Commercial Div. 53-58; Inspector, Price Directorate 44-53; Chair. Danish Soc. of Forest Engineers 55-59; Dir. Danish State Forest Service 58-; mem. Danish FAO Cttee. 54-; Chair. FAO/ECE/ILO Study Group on Forest Workers' Training, Health, Safety 54-72; mem. Nordic Forest Union 55-59, Chair. Safety 54; mem. Nordic Forest Union 55-59, Chair. Danish Cttee. 59-; Pres. Nordic Forest Union 62-67; Chair. Danish Forest Research Comm. 58; Vice-Chair. Danish Forestry Soc. 58-67, FAO European Forestry Comm. 63-67; mem. Danish Council Nature Conservation 59-72, Internordic Forest Research Cttee. 68-; Chair. Danish Cttee. Overseas Forestry Devt. 68-72; mem. Danish Council for Overseas Devt. 72-; leader FAO/DANIDA Forestry Mission to Nigeria 71; Commdr. of Dannebrog (Denmark), Commdr. de Mérite Agricole (France).
Skovstyrelsen, Strandvejen 863, 2930 Klampenborg; Enghavevej 4, 2930 Klampenborg, Denmark.
Telephone: 01-63-11-66 (Office); 01-OR 3127 (Home).

Fromm, Erich, PH.D.; American (b. German) psychoanalyst; b. 23 March 1900; ed. Univs. of Frankfurt, Heidelberg and Munich, and Berlin Inst. of Psychoanalysis.
Guest Lecturer, Columbia Univ. 35-39; Lecturer, New School for Social Research 38-54; mem. Faculty Bennington Coll. 42-50; Prof. Michigan State Univ. 58-62; Dir. Mexican Inst. of Psychoanalysis, affiliated with Nat. Univ. of Mexico 55-67; Adj. Prof. of Psychology, New York Univ. 62-; Diplomate of American Psychological Asscn.
Publs. *Man for Himself* 47, *Fear of Freedom* 41, *Psychoanalysis and Religion* 50, *The Forgotten Language* 51, *The Sane Society* 55, *The Art of Loving* 56, *Sigmund Freud's Mission* 59, *Zen Buddhism and Psychoanalysis* (with D. T. Suzuki and R. de Martino) 60, *Marx's Concept of Man* 61, *May Man Prevail?* 61, *Beyond the Chains of Illusion* 62, *The Dogma of Christ and other Essays* 63, *The Heart of Man* 64, *You shall be as Gods* 66, *The Revolution of Hope* 68, *The Nature of Man* (Ed. with R. Xirau) 69, *The Crisis of Psychoanalysis* 70, *Social Character in a Mexican Village* (with M. Maccoby) 70, *The Anatomy of Human Destructiveness* 73.
180 Riverside Drive, New York 24, N.Y., U.S.A.; Patricio Sanz 748-5, México 12, D.F., Mexico.

Frommel, Gerhard; German composer and music teacher; b. 7 Aug. 1906, Karlsruhe; s. of Otto Frommel and Helene Helbing; m. Gertrud Neuhaus 1930; three s.; ed. Leipzig Musikhochschule and Prussian Acad. of Arts, Berlin.
Teacher of music since 29, Prof. of Composition, Frankfurt Hochschule für Musik 60-.
Compositions: Two symphonies, *Sinfonietta* for string orchestra, *Symphonisches Vorspiel*, piano concerto (with string orchestra and clarinet), *Suite* and *Variationen* for orchestra, *Herbstfeier* for baritone, chorus and orchestra, six-part mass, *36 Lieder nach St. George*, seven piano sonatas, two violin sonatas, two operas, ballet and chamber music.
Leisure interests: poetry, philosophy.
Publs. *Der Geist der Antike bei R. Wagner* 33, *Neue Klassik in der Musik* 35, *Drei Maximen von Stefan George über Dichtung* 69.
Werderplatz 10, Heidelberg, Federal Republic of Germany.
Telephone: 06221/40102.

Frondel, Clifford, PH.D., M.A.; American mineralogist; b. 8 Jan. 1907, New York; s. of George Frondel and Martha Kinderman; m. Judith Weiss 1949; two d.; ed. Mass. Inst of Technology, Columbia Univ. and Colo. School of Mines.

Teaching Fellow, M.I.T. 37-39; Research Assoc. Harvard Univ. 39-42; Senior Physicist, U.S. War Dept. 42-43; Dir. of Research, Reeves Sound Laboratories 43-45; Assoc. Prof. of Mineralogy, Harvard Univ. 46-54, Prof. 54-, Chair. Dept. of Geological Sciences 65-; Pres. Mineralogical Society of America 56; Fellow A.A.A.S., Geological Soc. America and American Acad. of Arts and Sciences; Foreign mem. Austrian Acad. of Sciences, Accademia Nazionale dei Lincei, Deutsche Akademie der Naturforscher; Becke Medal, Mineralogical Soc. of Austria; Roebling Medal, Mineralogical Soc. of America; Boricky Medal, Charles Univ., Prague. Leisure interest: gardening.
Publs. *Dana's System of Mineralogy* (co-editor), 3 vols., 43, 51, 62, *Systematic Mineralogy of Uranium and Thorium* 58, *Minerals of Franklin and Sterling Hill* 73. 12 Geological Museum, 24 Oxford Street, Cambridge, Mass. 02138; Home: 20 Beatrice Circle, Belmont, Mass. 02178, U.S.A.
Telephone: 617-484-4719 (Home).

Frondistis, Athanassios; Greek army officer and politician; b. 26 Sept. 1900, Island of Skiathos; s. of Ioannis Frondistis and Stamatia Frondistou; m. Frosso Lemonidou 1939; one d.; ed. Univ. of Athens, Military School and Higher School of War.
Held various military positions and fought in wars of 22, 40-41 and in guerilla warfare; participated actively in nat. opposition movement during German occupation 41-44; Chief of Defence Gen. Staff 59-62; in Reserves 62-; Deputy for Nat. Radical Union 63, 64-67; Minister for Communications 67.
Leisure interests: reading, literature.
46 King Constantinou Avenue, Athens 516, Greece.
Telephone: 724-652.

Frondizi, Arturo, D.IUR.; Argentine lawyer and politician; b. 1908; ed. Buenos Aires Univ.
Formed a resistance movement as a student and imprisoned 30; in law practice 32-; mem. Metropolitan Convention Radical Party, Prof. Buenos Aires Univ. 32; Radical deputy 46; Pres. Parliamentary Radical Party 46-50; candidate for Vice-Presidency 52; Pres. Nat. Cttee. Radical Party 54; Pres. of Argentina 58-62; now leader of Movimiento de Integración y Desarrollo.
Publs. *Petroleum and Politics* 55, *Los intereses de los trabajadores y el destino de la nacionalidad* 57, *Política económica nacional* 63, *Política exterior argentina* 63, *Petróleo y Nación* 64, *Estrategia y Táctica del Movimiento Nacional* 65, *El problema Agrario Argentino* 65.
Luis Maris Campos 665, Buenos Aires, Argentina.

Frondizi, Risieri, PH.D.; Argentine professor of philosophy; b. 20 Nov. 1910, Posadas; s. of Julio Frondizi and Isabel Ercoli; m. Josefina Barbat 1938; one s. one d.; ed. Instituto Nacional, Buenos Aires, and Harvard, Michigan and Mexico Univs.
Prof. Philosophy, Tucuman Univ. 38-46; Visiting Prof. Venezuela 47-48, Pennsylvania 48-49, Yale 49-50, Puerto Rico 50-52, Columbia 55, Texas 65, California (Los Angeles) 66-68; mem. Inst. for Advanced Study, Princeton 64; Prof. Ethics, Buenos Aires Univ. 56-66; Rector 57-62; Prof. Phil. Southern Ill. Univ. 70-; Pres. Inter-Amer. Union of Latin Amer. Univs. 59-62; mem. Admin. Board Int. Asscn. of Univs. 60-70; mem. Inst. International de Philosophie (Paris); mem. gov. cttee. International Federation Philosophical Socs. (Brussels).
Publs. *Philosophy's Point of Departure* 45, *The Nature of the Self* 52, *What is Value?* 58, *Descartes* 67, *El yo como estructura dinámica* 70, *The University in a World of Tensions* 71, *Man and Values in 20th Century Latin American Philosophy* 75, and more than 50 scholarly articles.
Junin 1925, Buenos Aires, Argentina.
Telephone: 44-2700.

Fronius, Hans; Austrian artist; b. 12 Sept. 1903, Sarajevo, Bosnia (now Yugoslavia); s. of Dr. and Mrs. Fronius (née Passini); m. Christine Lauberger 1951; four s. one d.; ed. Mittelschule, Graz, and Akad. der Bildenden Künste, Vienna.
Professor of Fine Arts, Fürstenfeld 29-60, Mödling 60-64; over eighty one-man exhbns., including Prague 37, Vienna (Albertina) 52, 72, 73, Paris 55, 74, Mexico City 57, Venice Biennale 58, Madrid (Biblioteca Nacional) 67, Mainz (Gutenberg Museum) 68, and in many German, French and Austrian cities; army service, Russia and Italy 43-45; has illustrated 75 books and portfolios; Staatspreismedaille 37, Meisterpreis für Malerei und Graphik 50; Grosser Österreichischer Staatspreis für Malerei und Graphik 66; Ehrenmedaille in Gold der Stadt Wien 68; Würdigungspreis des Landes Steiermark 74; Grosses Ehrenzeichen für Kunst und Wissenschaft, 1st Class.
Leisure interests: literature, history, music, travel.
A2380 Perchtoldsdorf bei Wien, Guggenberggasse 18, Austria.
Telephone: (Vienna) 86-25-83.

Frost, David Paradine, O.B.E.; British television personality and writer; b. 7 April 1939, Beccles, Suffolk; s. of Rev. W. J. Paradine Frost; ed. Gillingham and Wellingborough Grammar Schools and Caius Coll., Cambridge.
Appeared in *That Was The Week That Was*, B.B.C. Television 62; other programmes with B.B.C. included *A Degree of Frost* 63, 73, *Not So Much A Programme More A Way of Life* 64-65, *The Frost Report* 66-67, *Frost Over England* 67 (Golden Rose Award, Montreux 67); appeared in *The Frost Programme*, I.T.A. 66-67, 67-68, 72; formed London Weekend Consortium with Aidan Crawley 67; Chair. and Chief Exec. David Paradine Ltd. 66-; Joint Deputy Chair. Equity Enterprises 73- (Chair. 72-73); host in programmes *Frost on Friday, Frost On Saturday, Frost On Sunday* 68-69, *David Frost Show*, U.S.A. 69-72, *David Frost Revue*, U.S.A. 71-73, *That Was The Year That Was*, U.S.A. 73, *The Frost Interview* 74, *We British* 75.
Publs. include: *That Was The Week That Was, How To Live Under Labour, Talking With Frost, To England With Love* (with Antony Jay), *The Americans, Whitlam and Frost.*
46 Egerton Crescent, London, S.W.3, England.

Früh, Eugen; Swiss painter and illustrator; b. 22 Jan. 1914, St. Gallen; s. of Huldreich and Teresa Früh; m. Erna Yoshida Blenk (artist) 1934; ed. Zürich School of Art and in Paris and Rome.
C. F. Meyer Foundation Fine Arts Prize 43, Fine Arts Prize, Kanton Zürich 67.
Works include: *Die kleine Stadt* 41, *Pastorale d'été* 46, *La comédie et la musique* 47, *Capricci* 48, *Spanisches Gespräch* 51, *Notturno* 57, *Château d'Artiste* 62, *Gartenfest* 64, *Bambuswald* 72, *Lotus* 73-74; also murals and book illustrations.
Leisure interests: literature, music, travel.
Römergasse 9, 8001 Zürich, Switzerland.
Telephone: 01-478863.

Frühauf, Hans, DR. ING., DR. ING. E.h.; German scientist; b. 4 Jan. 1904, Pforzheim, Baden; ed. Eberhard-Ludwigs-Gymnasium, Stuttgart, and Technische Hochschule, Stuttgart.
Professor, Technical Univ. of Dresden 50-, Pro-rector Technical Univ. Dresden; Dir. of Inst. of High Frequency Technology and Electronics, Technical Univ. of Dresden 50-; Vice-Pres. German Acad. of Sciences 57-63, mem. German Acad. of Sciences, mem. of the Forschungsrat (Vice-Pres. until 62), mem. Wissenschaftrat; Pres. D.D.R. Nat. Cttee. of the URSI; Editor and Editor-in-Chief *Elektrische Informations- und Energie-Technik*, Leipzig; Editor *Bucherei der Hoch-*

Frequenztechnik, Leipzig; Editor *Über Wissenschaftliche Grundlagen der modernen Technik*, Berlin; Editor *Elektronisches Rechnen und Regeln*, Berlin; Nat. Prize, Second Class 51, First Class 61.
Akademie der Wissenschaften der D.D.R., 108 Berlin, Otto-Nuschke-Strasse 22-23; Karl-Marx-Allée 48, 102 Berlin, German Democratic Republic.
Telephone: Dresden 483-2433 (Office); Dresden 42-6-92, Berlin 27-9-41-06 (Home).

Frühbeck de Burgos, Rafael; Spanish conductor; b. 15 Sept. 1933, Burgos; s. of Wilhelm and Stephanie (née Ochs) Frühbeck; m. María Carmen Martínez 1959; one s. one d.; ed. music academies in Bilbao, Madrid, and Munich, and Univ. of Madrid.
Chief conductor, Municipal Orchestra, Bilbao 58-62; Music Dir. and Chief Conductor, Spanish Nat. Orchestra, Madrid 62-; Music Dir. of Düsseldorf and Chief Conductor Düsseldorf Symphoniker 66-70; Music Dir. Montreal Symphony Orchestra 74-; Gran Cruz al Mérito Civil, Orden de Alfonso X, Orden de Isabel la Católica.
c/o Harold Holt Ltd., 122 Wigmore Street, London, W1H 0DJ, England; Home: Madrid 7, Reyes Magos 20, Spain.
Telephone: 252-04-16 (Home).

Frumkin, Alexander Naumovich; Soviet physical chemist; b. 24 Oct. 1895, Kishinev; m. Prof. Perevalova Emiliya Georgievna 1968; ed. Univ. of Odessa.
Professor at Inst. of Educ., Odessa 22; Prof. at Karpov Inst. of Physical Chemistry 22-46; read course of lectures on Colloidal Chemistry at Inst. of Wisconsin, U.S.A. 28-29; Dir. Inst. of Physical Chemistry of U.S.S.R. Acad. of Sciences 39-49; concurrently Head of the Chair. of Electrochemistry at the Univ. of Moscow 30-; Dir. Inst. of Electrochemistry, U.S.S.R. Acad. of Sciences 58-; mem. U.S.S.R. Acad. of Sciences 32, Polish Acad. of Sciences 45, Akad. Deutscher Naturforscher Leopoldina 56, Bulgarian Acad. of Sciences, Royal Acad. of Sciences of the Netherlands 65; Hon. F.N.I. Delhi 65; Foreign mem. Deutscher Akad. Wiss., Berlin 56; Corresp. mem. Saxon Acad. of Sciences, Leipzig 66; Hon. mem. All-Union Mendeleev Chemical Soc. 65, Yugoslav Acad. of Sciences and Arts 65, U.S. Acad. of Arts and Sciences 70, Belgian Chem. Soc. 70, French Chem. Soc. 72, Polish Chem. Soc. 74; Foreign Assoc. Nat. Acad. of Sciences of U.S.A. 69; Dr. rer. nat. h.c. (Tech. Univ., Dresden) 58, Dr. Chem. Sc. h.c. (J. E. Purkine Univ., Brno) 72; awarded State Prize (three times); Lenin Order 45, 65, 75; Palladium Medal Electrochemical Soc., U.S.A. 59; Hero of Socialist Labour 65.
Leisure interest: mountain touring.
Institute of Electrochemistry, Academy of Sciences of the U.S.S.R., 31 Leninsky Prospekt, Moscow, U.S.S.R.
Telephone: 232-46-48 (Office).

Fruton, Joseph Stewart, B.A., M.A., PH.D.; American biochemist; b. 14 May 1912, Czestochowa, Poland; s. of Charles Fruton and Ella Eisenstadt; m. Sofia Simmonds 1936; ed. Columbia Univ.
Associate, Rockefeller Inst. for Medical Research 34-45; Assoc. Prof. of Physiological Chemistry, Yale Univ. 45-50, Prof. of Biochemistry 50-57, Chair. Dept. of Biochemistry 51-67, Eugene Higgins Prof. of Biochemistry 57-, Dir. Div. of Science 59-62; Assoc. Editor *Journal of Biological Chemistry* and *Biochemistry*; Harvey Lecturer 55, Dakin Lecturer 62; Visiting Prof. Rockefeller Univ. 68-69; Sarton Lecturer 76; Benjamin Franklin Fellow, Royal Soc. of Arts; mem. American Philosophical Soc., Nat. Acad. of Sciences, American Acad. of Arts and Sciences, Harvey Soc., American Chemical Soc., American Soc. of Biological Chemists, Biochemical Soc., History of Science Soc.; Eli Lilly Award in Biological Chem. 44; Pfizer Award in History of Science 73.
Leisure interests: history of science, music.

Publs. *General Biochemistry* (with S. Simmonds) 53 (2nd edn. 58), *Molecules and Life* 72, *Selected Bibliography of Biographical Data for the History of Biochemistry since 1800* 74; numerous scientific articles in *Journal of Biological Chemistry*, *Biochemistry*, *Journal of Amer. Chemical Soc.*, *Proceedings* of Nat. Acad. of Sciences, and other journals.
350 Kline Biology Tower, Yale University, New Haven, Conn. 06520, U.S.A.
Telephone: 203-436-2644.

Fry, Christopher, F.R.S.L.; British dramatist; b. 18 Dec. 1907, Bristol; s. of Emma Marguerite Hammond and Charles John Harris; m. Phyllis Marjorie Hart 1936; one s.; ed. Bedford Modern School.
Actor, Citizen House, Bath 27; Teacher, Hazelwood Preparatory School 28-31; Dir. Tunbridge Wells Repertory Players 32-35; Dir. Oxford Repertory Players 40 and 44-46; at Arts Theatre, London 45; Fellow of the Royal Soc. of Literature; Awarded The Queen's Gold Medal for Poetry 62; Hon. Dip. Arts (Manchester) 62.
Leisure interest: gardening.
Publs. *The Boy with the Cart* 39, *The Firstborn* 46, *A Phoenix too Frequent* 46, *The Lady's Not for Burning* 49, *Thor, with Angels* 49, *Venus Observed* 50, *A Sleep of Prisoners* 51, *The Dark is Light Enough* 54, *Curtmantle* (R. S. L. Heinemann Award) 62, *A Yard of Sun* 70, *The Brontës of Haworth* (four plays for television) 73; Trans. *Ring Round the Moon* 50, *The Lark* (Anouilh) 54, *Tiger at the Gates* 55, *Duel of Angels* 58, *Judith* (Giraudoux) 62, *Peer Gynt* 70, *Cyrano de Bergerac* 75; Film Scripts: *The Beggar's Opera, The Queen is Crowned, Ben Hur, Barabbas, The Bible*.
The Toft, East Dean, nr. Chichester, Sussex, England.

Fry, Donald William, C.B.E., M.SC.; British physicist; b. 30 Nov. 1910, Weymouth, Dorset; s. of William J. and Mary J. (née Symonds) Fry; m. Jessie Florence Wright 1934; three s.; ed. King's Coll., London Univ.
Research Physicist, G.E.C. Research Laboratories 32-40; with Air Ministry Research Establishment at Swanage and Malvern 40-46; on staff of Atomic Energy Research Establishment 46-49; Head, Gen. Physics Div. 50-54, Chief Physicist 54-58, Deputy Dir. 58, A.E.R.E., Harwell; Dir. Atomic Energy Establishment, Winfrith 59-73; awarded Duddell Medal of the Physical Soc. 50; Fellow King's Coll., London 60; Fellow of the Inst. of Physics, Inst. of Electrical Engineers, Inst. of Electrical and Electronics Engineers; Chartered Eng.
Leisure interests: travel, photography.
Coveway Lodge, Overcombe, Weymouth, Dorset, England.
Telephone: Preston 833276.

Fry, E. Maxwell, C.B.E., LL.D., B.ARCH., R.A.R.A., F.R.I.B.A., M.T.P.I.; British architect; b. 2 Aug. 1899, Wallasey, Cheshire; s. of Ambrose and Lily Fry; m. Jane Drew (q.v.) 1942; three d.; ed. Liverpool Inst., and Liverpool Univ. School of Architecture.
Studied in Europe and New York; partner Adams, Thompson & Fry 27-34; with Prof. Walter Gropius 34-36, served R.E.'s 39-45; Town Planning Adviser to Resident Minister W. Africa 43-45; in partnership with Jane Drew (q.v.) 45-; a Senior Architect to Chandigarh, Punjab Govt. Capital Project 51-54; now consultant to Fry, Drew, and Partners; work includes Impington Village Coll., Ibadan Univ. in Nigeria, Govt. Centre, Mauritius, Schools and Colls. for Gold Coast Govt., Flats and Houses at Harlow New Town, Engineering and Veterinary Buildings, Liverpool Univ. Headquarters, Rolls-Royce Ltd. and Pilkington Brothers Ltd.; Senior Royal Academician; Royal Gold Medal for Architecture 64.
Leisure interests: reading, drawing, gardening.
Publs. *Fine Building* (with Jane B. Drew) 45, *Architecture for Children, Architecture in Humid Tropics*,

Tropical Architecture (with Jane B. Drew) 64, *Art in a Machine Age* (68 R.A. Lectures) 69, *Maxwell Fry: Autobiographical Sketches* 75.
63 Gloucester Place, London, W.1, England.
Telephone: 01-935-3318.

Fry, Thornton Carl, A.M., PH.D.; American mathematician; b. 7 Jan. 1892; ed. Findlay Coll. and Wisconsin Univ.
Mathematics Instructor, Wisconsin Univ. 12-16; with Western Electric Co. 16-24; on staff of Bell Telephone Laboratories 24-56, Dir. mathematical research 40-44, switching research 44-47 and engineering 47-49, Asst. to Exec. Vice-Pres. 49-51, to Pres. 51-56; Vice-Pres. and Dir. Univac Engineering Division, Remington Rand 57-60; Vice-Pres. Research and Engineering Remington Rand Division of Sperry Rand Corpn. 60; Consultant to Dir., Nat. Center for Atmospheric Research 61-67; Consultant and mem. board of directors, Granville-Phillips Co. 63-70; Consultant, The Boeing Co. 64-70; Fellow, American Physical Society, American Asscn. for Advancement of Science, American Inst. of Electrical Engineers, etc.; mem. Amer. Math. Society, Amer. Astronomical Society, etc.; Presidential Certificate of Merit; Hon. D.Sc. Findlay Coll. 58.
Publs. *Elementary Differential Equations, Probability and its Engineering Uses*; numerous articles.
500 Mohawk Drive, Boulder, Colo. 80303, U.S.A.

Frydenlund, Knut; Norwegian politician; b. 31 March 1927, Drammen.
Joined Foreign Service 53; Sec., Norwegian Embassy, Bonn 53-55; Sec., then Counsellor, Foreign Ministry 56-62; Press Counsellor, Norwegian Embassy, Brussels 62-63; Perm. Rep. to Council of Europe 63-65; Head of Section, Ministry of Foreign Affairs 66-69; Consultant, Labour Party Research Office 67-69; mem. Labour Party Oslo Exec. 68-74, Chair. Int. Cttee. 71-73; mem. Parl. for Oslo 69-; mem. del. to Consultative Assembly, Council of Europe 70-73; Minister of Foreign Affairs Oct. 73-.
Ministry of Foreign Affairs, Oslo Dep., Norway.

Frye, Herman Northrop, C.C., M.A.; Canadian university professor; b. 14 July 1912, Sherbrooke, Quebec; s. of Herman and Catherine Frye (née Howard); m. Helen Kemp 1937; ed. Univ. of Toronto, Emmanuel Coll., and Univ. of Oxford.
Department of English, Victoria Coll., Univ. of Toronto 39-, Chair. of Dept. 52, Principal of Victoria Coll. 59, Univ. Prof. and Prof. of English in Victoria Coll. 67-; Lorne Pierce Medal, Royal Soc. of Canada 58; Canada Council Medal 67; Pierre Chauveau Medal, Royal Soc. of Canada 70; Molson Prize 70; Hon. Fellow Merton Coll. 73; 24 hon. degrees.
Leisure interest: Canadian Radio-Television Comm.
Publs. *Fearful Symmetry: A Study of William Blake* 47, *Anatomy of Criticism* 57, *The Well-Tempered Critic* 63, *The Educated Imagination* 63, *T. S. Eliot* 63, *Fables of Identity* 63, *A Natural Perspective* 65, *The Return of Eden* 65, *Fools of Time* 67, *The Modern Century* 67, *A Study of English Romanticism* 68, *The Stubborn Structure* 70, *The Bush Garden* 71, *The Critical Path* 71.
University of Toronto, Toronto 181, Ont. M5S 1A1, Canada.
Telephone: 928-2011.

Frye, Richard Nelson, PH.D.; American orientalist; b. 10 Jan. 1920, Birmingham, Ala.; s. of Nels Frye and Lillie Hagman; m. Barbara York 1948 (divorced 1973); two s. one d.; ed. Univ. of Ill., Harvard Univ., and School of Oriental and African Studies, London.
Junior Fellow, Harvard 46-49; Visiting Scholar, Univ. of Teheran 51-52; Aga Khan Prof. of Iranian, Harvard 57-; Visiting Prof., Oriental Seminary, Frankfurt Univ. 58-59; Visiting Prof. Hamburg Univ. 68-69; Assoc. Editor *Central Asian Journal, Indo-Iranica* (Calcutta);

Hon. mem. German Archaeol. Soc.; Dir. Asia Inst., Pahlavi Univ., Shiraz.
Leisure interests: fencing, bookbinding.
Publs. *Notes on the early coinage of Transoxiana* 49, *History of the Nation of the Archers* 52, *Narshakhi, The History of Bukhara* 54, *Iran* 56, *Heritage of Persia* 62, *Bukhara, The Medieval Achievement* 65, *The Histories of Nishapur* 65, *Persia* 68, *Inscriptions from Dura Europos* 69, *Excavations at Qasr-i-Abu-Nasr* 73, *The Arabs in the East* 75; Editor vol. 4 *Cambridge History of Iran* 75.
546 Widener Library, Cambridge 38, Mass., U.S.A.

Fthenakis, Emmanuel, M.S.; Greek civil engineer and politician; b. 4 Aug. 1921, Athens; s. of Col. Anastasios Fthenakis and Irene Magoulakis; m. Alkystis Kassandras 1955; two d.; ed. Nat. Technical Univ. of Athens, and Massachusetts Inst. of Technology.
Private practice in Civil Engineering 46-50; Testing and Research Engineer, Building Materials Lab., Ministry of Public Works, Athens 50-56; Exec., Doxiades Assocs. 56-65; Founder and Dir. Building Materials and Methods of Construction Research Center, Iraq 57; Consultant to Govts. of Ghana and Nigeria and director of operations and projects in the field of housing planning, town, regional and national physical and econ. planning and devt. 59-63; Dir. of Research and mem. Board of Dirs. Doxiadis Assocs. 63-65; Founder and Dir. Doxiadis Assocs. Computer Center 63-65; Man. Dir. of own int. consulting firm and planning and devt. consultant to govts. of Nigeria, Ghana, Sierra Leone and int. orgs. (including FAO) and banks; Minister for Communications Feb. 69; alt. Minister for Econ. Co-ordination June 69; Gov. for Greece IBRD 69; Minister without Portfolio Aug. 71-Aug. 72; Minister of Mercantile Marine, Transport and Telecommunications 72-73; mem. American Concrete Inst., World Soc. of Ekistics, American Asscn. for Advancement of Science.
Leisure interests: hiking, reading, golf.
Publs. a number of reports and papers on development projects.
42 Anagnostopoulou Street, Athens 136, Greece.
Telephone: 634340, 635772.

Fuchs, Hans; German international finance official; ed. Technische Hochschule, Stuttgart.
With Maschinenfabrik Augsburg-Nurnberg A.G.; joined IBRD (World Bank) as engineer 56; Asst. Chief, Industry Div. 63; Deputy Asst. Dir., Industry Div. 64; Deputy Dir., Dept. of Investments, Latin America, Europe, Australasia, Int. Finance Corpn. (IFC) 65; Dir. Engineering Dept. IFC 68-69; Dir. Industrial Projects Dept. IBRD 69-.
International Bank for Reconstruction and Development, 1818 H Street, N.W., Washington, D.C. 20433, U.S.A.

Fuchs, Sir Vivian Ernest, M.A., PH.D., F.R.S.; British geologist and explorer; b. 11 Feb. 1908, Freshwater, Isle of Wight; s. of Ernest and Violet Anne Fuchs (née Watson); m. Joyce Connell 1933; one s. one d. (one d. deceased); ed. St. John's Coll., Cambridge.
With Cambridge East Greenland Expedition 29, Cambridge Expedition to East African Lakes 30-32; Leader, Lake Rudolf Rift Valley Expedition 33-34; Leader, Lake Rukwa Expedition 37-38; served Second World War; Commdr. Falkland Islands Dependencies Survey (Antarctica) 47-50; Dir. Falkland Islands Dependencies Scientific Bureau 51-60; Dir. British Antarctic Survey 60-73; Leader, Trans-Antarctic Expedition 55-58; Founder's Gold Medal (Royal Geog. Soc.) 51, Polar Medal 53, Clasp and Bar, Special Gold Medal (Royal Geog. Soc.) 58; Silver Medal (R.S.A.), Gold Medal (Royal Scottish Geog. Soc.); Richthofen Gold Medal (Berlin Geog. Soc.), Kirchenpauer Gold Medal (Hamburg Geog. Soc.), Gold Medal (Paris Geog. Soc.) 58, Hubbard Gold Medal

(Amer. Nat. Geog. Soc.), Gold Medal (Royal Nether-
lands Geog. Soc.) 59, Hans Egede Medal (Royal Danish
Geog. Soc.) 61, Prestwick Medal (Geological Soc.,
London) 60; Hon. LL.D. (Edinburgh and Birmingham
Univs.), Hon. D.Sc. (Durham Univ.) 58, (Cambridge
Univ.) 59, (Wales Univ.) 71, (Leicester Univ.) 72; Hon.
Fellow, Wolfson Coll., Cambridge 70.
Leisure interests: squash racquets, swimming.
Publs. *The Crossing of Antarctica* (with Sir Edmund
Hillary) 58, *Antarctic Adventure* 59; Editor *Great
Explorers, The Forces of Nature* 76, various geological
and geographical papers.
78 Barton Road, Cambridge, England.
Telephone: 0223-59238.

Fuentes, Carlos; Mexican author and diplomatist; b.
1928, Mexico City; s. of Rafael Fuentes Boettiger and
Berta Macías Rivas; m. 1st Rita Macedo 1959, 2nd
Sylvia Lemus 1973; one s. two d.; ed. Univ. of Mexico,
Inst. des Hautes Etudes Internationales, Geneva.
Member, Mexican Del. to Int. Labour Organization
(ILO), Geneva 50-52; Asst. Head, Press Section,
Ministry of Foreign Affairs, Mexico 54; Asst. Dir.
Cultural Dissemination, Univ. of Mexico 55-56; Head
Dept. of Cultural Relations, Ministry of Foreign
Affairs 57-59; Editor *Revista Mexicana de Literatura*
54-58, Co-Editor *El Espectador* 59-61, Editor *Siempre*
and *Política* 60-; Amb. to France 75-; Fellow, Woodrow
Wilson Int. Center for Scholars, Washington, D.C. 74.
Publs. *Los días enmascarados* 54, *La región más trans-
parente* 58, *Las buenas conciencias* 59, *Aura* 62, *La
muerte de Artemio Cruz* 62, *Cantar de ciegos* 65, *Zona
sagrada* 67, *Cambio de piel* (Biblioteca Breve Prize 67),
París, La Revolución de Mayo 68, *La Nueva Novela
Hispanoamericana* 69, *Cumpleaños* 69, *Le Borgne est
Roi* 70, *Casa con Dos Puertos* 70, *Todos los gatos son
pardos* 70, *Tiempo Mexicano* 71, *Don Quixote or the
Critique of Reading* 74, *Terra Nostra* 74.
Ambassade du Mexique, 20 avenue du Président
Wilson, Paris 16e, France; and Editorial Joaquín
Mortiz, Tabasco 106, México 7, D.F., Mexico; also c/o
Gallimard, 5 rue Sébastien-Bottin, Paris 7e, France.
Telephone: 727-2924; 727-1329 (Paris).

Fugard, Athol; South African actor and playwright;
m.; one d.
Plays: *The Blood Knot, Hello and Goodbye, People are
Living Here, Boesman and Lena* 70, *Sizwe Banzi is
Dead* 73, *The Island* 73, *Statements after an Arrest under
the Immorality Act* 74, *No Good Friday* 74, *Nongogo* 74.
P.O. Box 5090, Walmer, Port Elizabeth, South Africa.

Fuglsang-Damgaard, Hans, D.D.; Danish ecclesiastic;
b. 29 July 1890, Oersted; s. of Laurids and Maria
Fuglsang-Damgaard; m. Caroline Wagner 1926; three s.
one d.; ed. Copenhagen Univ.
Professor of Theology 25; Dean of Copenhagen Cathedral
33; Bishop of Copenhagen and Primate of Denmark
34; mem. Cttee. of Fourteen, preparing World Council
of Churches 38; Vice-Pres. World Council of Chris-
tian Educ. 47; mem. Publ. Board *Lutheran World
Review* 48; mem. Central Cttee. World Council of
Churches 48; Vice-Pres. The Mission to Lepers 49; Pres.
Internationale Gesellschaft für Religionspsychologie
52; Chair. Church of Denmark Council of Inter-Church
Relations 54; Pres. Danish Church abroad 61-; Hon.
D.D. Sopron Univ.; Knight Grand Cross of the Order
of Dannebrog; Grand Officier, Légion d'Honneur; Grand
Cross, Ordre de St. Lazare; Frankenhuis Medal;
Centenary Medal, Leprosy Mission 74.
Leisure interests: flowers, paintings, pictures.
Publs. *Videnskabelig og Kristelig Livstydning* 25,
Pariseyskolens Teologi 30, *Religionspsykologi* 33, *Privat-
skriftemaalets Fornyelse* 33, *Oxford Gruppen* 36, *Land,
Land, her Herrens Ord* 40, *Gud er vor Tilflugt og
Styrke* 41, *Taler ved Bispevielser* 42, *Fest og Alvor i*

Danmarks Kirke 46, *Kirken og Tiden* 46, *The Problem
of South Schleswig and the Christian Church* 46, *Guds-
ordet i Atomalderen* 47, *Der stander et Hus* 47, *Kirken
og de Sociale Problemer* 56, *Kirken og Diakonien* 57,
Menighedsraadene og Folkekirken 58, *Pascals Gudsbegreb*
68, *Kirke og Synagoge* 70, *Pascal, den Evigt Aktuelle* 71,
Fra Freud Til Frankl 72, *Fra Skyttegrav Til Bispestol*
75.
Österbrogade 114, Copenhagen Ø, Denmark.
Telephone: Öbro 8723.

Fujii, Shinzo, LL.B.; Japanese business executive;
b. 13 Dec. 1893, Osaka; m. 1924; three s.; ed. Tokyo
Imperial Univ.
Mitsubishi Shipbuilding and Engineering Co. Ltd.
18-45; Gen. Manager Kobe Shipyard and Engine Works,
Mitsubishi Heavy Industries Ltd. 45-46, Dir. and Gen.
Manager Kobe Shipyard 46-49, Managing Dir. 49-50;
Pres. Shin Mitsubishi Heavy Industries Ltd. 50-59,
Chair. Board of Dirs. 59-62, Pres. 62-64; Pres. Mitsubishi
Heavy Industries Ltd. 64-65, Chair. Board of Dirs. 65-
69, Counsellor 69-; Blue Ribbon Medal; Second Order
of Merit with the Order of the Sacred Treasure.
Leisure interests: fishing, mahjong, Go.
Mitsubishi Heavy Industries Ltd., 5-1, Marunouchi
2-chome, Chiyoda-ku, Tokyo, Japan.
Telephone: 03-212-3111.

Fujimoto, Ichiro, B.ENG.; Japanese iron and steel
executive; b. 21 Jan. 1909; ed. Tokyo Univ.
Joined Kawasaki Dockyard Co., Ltd. 32, Man. Rolling
Dept. No. 1, Fukiai Works 45; Dir. Kawasaki Steel
Corpn. (a breakaway company of Kawasaki Dockyard)
and Asst. Gen. Man. of Fukiai Works 53-55, Gen. Man.
of Fukiai Works 55-57, Man. Dir. Kawasaki Steel
Corpn. 57-62, Senior Man. Dir. 62-64, Exec. Vice-Pres.
64-66, Pres. July 66-; Hattori Award for contribution
to devt. of Japanese iron and steel industry 64.
Kawasaki Steel Corporation, Kitahonchodori, Fukiaku,
Kobe, Japan.

Fujioka, Shingo; Japanese oil executive; b. 27 June
1901; ed. Keio Univ. Tokyo.
Director and Gen. Man. Kawasaki Refinery, Mitsubishi
Oil Co. Ltd. 50-55, Managing Dir. Mitsubishi Oil Co.
Ltd. 55-61, Pres. 61-; mem. Cttee. World Petroleum
Conf. 61-, Petroleum Deliberative Council 63-; Chair.
Japan Petroleum Asscn.; Blue Ribbon Award 63.
Mitsubishi Oil Co. Ltd., 1 Shiba-Kotohiracho, Minato-
ku, Tokyo, Japan.

Fujisaki, Akira, LL.B.; Japanese business executive;
b. 1 May 1917, Kagoshima; s. of Kokichi Fujisaki and
Misako Morita; m. Sakae Ishida 1951; one d.; ed. Tokyo
Imperial Univ.
Joined Sumitomo Mining Co. Ltd. (later Sumitomo
Metal Mining Co. Ltd.) 41, Controller 64, Dir. 67, Man.
Dir. 70, Pres. 73-.
Leisure interest: golf.
Sumitomo Metal Mining Co. Ltd., 11-3, 5-chome,
Shimbashi, Minato-ku, Tokyo; Home: 2-7-14, Nishi-
Kamakura, Kamakura-shi, Kanagawa Prefecture,
Japan.
Telephone: 03-434-221 (Office); 0467-32-6233 (Home).

Fujisawa, Tokusaburo; Japanese business executive;
b. 13 Sept. 1907, Tokyo; s. of Miki and Yoshiyasu
Fujisawa; m. Kazuko Kanai 1934; two s.; ed. Tokyo
Univ. of Commerce.
Bank of Japan 30-62, Chief of Admin. Dept. 52-54, of
Foreign Exchange Dept. 54-56, Bank of Japan Rep.,
New York 56-58, Chief of Bank Relations and Super-
vision Dept. 58-59, Dir. Bank of Japan, concurrently
Man. Osaka Branch 59-62; Vice-Pres. The Export-
Import Bank of Japan 62-70; Pres. Tokyo Small
Business Investment Co. 70-.
Leisure interests: Go, haiku, golf.

Office: Tokyo Small Business Investment Co., 2-47 Kabuto-cho, Nihonbashi-ku, Tokyo; Home: 13-10, No. 3 Naka-ochiai, Shinzyuku-ku, Tokyo, Japan. Telephone: 952-0760.

Fujiyama, Aiichiro; Japanese businessman and politician; b. 22 May 1897, Tokyo; s. of Raita Fujiyama and Mine Fujiyama; m. Hisako Yuki; one s. one d.; ed. Keio Univ.
Pres. Dai Nippon Sugar Manufacturing Co. 34 and Nitto Chemical Industry 37; Pres. Japan Air Lines 51, Adviser 53-; Pres. Japan and Tokyo Chambers of Commerce 51-57; Pres. Japan Fed. UNESCO Asscns. 51-; Pres. Advertising Fed. 53-; Dir. Int. Telegraph and Telephone Co. 53-; mem. Council of Int. Chamber of Commerce 54-; Pres. Soc. for Econ. Co-operation in Asia 54-61; Minister for Foreign Affairs 57-60; mem. House of Reps. 58-; State Minister in charge of Econ. Planning Board 61-62, 65-66; Pres. Asscn. for the Promotion of Int. Trade 73.
Leisure interest: painting.
Publs. *Shacho gurashi Sanju-nen* 52, *Okyaku-shobai* 53, *Kuchibeni-kara kikansha-made* 53.
21-1-1, Shirogane-dai, Minato-ku, Tokyo, Japan.

Fujiyoshi, Tsuguhide; Japanese business executive; b. 24 Jan. 1913, Fukuaka; s. of late Kiichi and of Haruko Fujiyoshi; m. Yukho 1941; three s. two d.; ed. Tokyo Univ.
Joined Toyo Rayon Co. Ltd. (now Toray Industries Inc.) 35, Hamburg Office 60-61, Man. Nagoya Plant 61, Dir. 62, Man. Dir. 64, Exec. Vice-Pres. 66, Pres. 71-.
Leisure interest: golf.
Room 605 Takanawa Sky Mansion, 8-6 Takanawa 4-chome, Minoto-ku, Tokyo 108, Japan.
Telephone: 03-445-6511.

Fukuda, Chisato; Japanese business executive; b. 20 Oct. 1896; ed. Kyoto Imperial Univ.
Fujitomo Bill-Broker Bank (later The Fujimoto Securities Co. Ltd.) 21-43; Dir. Daiwa Securities Co. Ltd. 43, Exec. Vice-Pres. 54-57, Pres. 57-63, Counsellor 63-; Gov. Fed. of Econ. Organizations 58-, Tokyo Stock Exchange 60-; Tokyo Securities Dealers' Asscn.
4-13-1, Denenchofu, Ota-ku, Tokyo, Japan.

Fukuda, Hajime; Japanese politician; b. 1902; ed. Tokyo Univ.
Reporter, Political Editor, Kyodo News Service; mem. House of Reps. for Fukui Pref. 49-; fmr. Parl. Vice-Minister of Labour; Minister of Int. Trade and Industry 62, for Home Affairs 72-73, Dec. 74-; Liberal-Democratic Party.
c/o House of Representatives, Tokyo, Japan.

Fukuda, Takeo; Japanese politician; b. 14 Jan. 1905; ed. Tokyo Imperial Univ.
With Ministry of Finance 29-50, Deputy Vice-Minister 45-46, Dir. of Banking Bureau 46-47, Dir. Budget Bureau 47-50; mem. House of Reps. 52-; Chair. Policy Board Liberal-Democratic Party, later Sec.-Gen.; fmr. Minister of Agriculture and Forestry; Minister of Finance 65-Dec. 66; Sec.-Gen. Liberal Democratic Party Dec. 66-68; Minister of Finance 68-71, 73-74, of Foreign Affairs 71-72; Dir.-Gen. Admin. Management Agency 72-73; Deputy Prime Minister, Dir. of Econ. Planning Agency Dec. 74-.
Economic Planning Agency, 3-1 Kasumigaseki 1-chome, Chiyoda-ku, Tokyo; and 1-247 Nozawa-machi, Setagaya-ku, Tokyo, Japan.

Fukuhara, Nobusaku, D.SC.; Japanese business executive; b. 12 Nov. 1911, Ginza, Chuo-ku, Tokyo; s. of Shinichi and Yone Fukuhara; m. Minae Yamawaki 1934; one s. two d.; ed. Yokohama Technical Coll. (now Yokohama Nat. Univ.) and Duke Univ., U.S.A.
Joined Shiseido Co. Ltd. 32, Dir. 52, Man. Dir. 62, Senior Man. Dir. 73, Pres. 75-; Dir. Fed. of Econ. Orgs.

75-; Exec. Dir. Japan Fed. of Employers' Asscns. 75-Counsellor, Japan Chemical Industry Asscn. 75-; mem. Presidium, Int. Fed. of Socs. of Cosmetic Chemists 73-Leisure interests: photography, golf, tennis.
Shiseido Company Ltd., 7-5-5 Ginza, Chuo-ku, Tokyo; Home: 2-18-5 Minami-senzoku, Ohta-ku, Tokyo, Japan.
Telephone: 572-5111 (Office); 727-3902 (Home).

Fulbright, James William, LL.B., M.A.; American politician; b. 9 April 1905; m. Elizabeth Kremer Williams 1932; two d.; ed. Univ. of Arkansas, Oxford Univ. and George Washington Univ.
Special Attorney Anti-Trust Div., U.S. Dept. of Justice 34-35; Instructor in Law, George Washington Univ. 35-36; Lecturer in Law Univ. of Arkansas 36-39 Pres. 39-41; mem. 78th Congress (43-45), 3rd District Arkansas; U.S. Senator from Arkansas 45-74; Chair. Senate Cttee. Foreign Relations 59-74; Legal Counsel for United Arab Emirates 76-; Japan Foundation Award 74, Hon. K.B.E. 75; Democrat.
Publs. *Old Myths and New Realities* 64, *Prospects for the West* 65, *The Arrogance of Power* 67, *The Crippled Giant* 72.
Fayetteville, Ark., U.S.A.

Fulla, Ludovit; Czechoslovak painter; b. 27 Feb. 1902, Ružomberok; ed. School of Fine and Applied Arts, Prague.
Professor at School of Arts and Crafts, Bratislava 29-38, Dir. 38-39; schoolteacher, Bratislava 49-52, Asst. Prof. Art Coll., Bratislava 49-52; over 800 works, including stage designs, paintings, designs for tapestries, graphic works and book illustrations; exhibited at Venice Biennials 34, 42, 54, 56, 62, Brussels Int. Exhbn. 35, 58, Milan Triennial 36, Paris World Fair 37, São Paulo Biennial 57, Moscow 58-59, Second Int. Tapestry Biennial, Lausanne 56; Grand Prix and Silver Medal, Paris 37; Gold Medal and Diploma, Int. Brussels Exhbn. 58; Order of Labour 62, Nat. Artist 63, State Prize 66, 69, Order of the Repub. 72.
Union of Slovak Artists, Ružomberok, Galeria, Czechoslovakia.

Fuller, Richard Buckminster; American geometer, educator, architect-designer; b. 12 July 1895, Milton, Mass.; s. of Richard Buckminster and Caroline Wolcott (Andrews) Fuller; m. Anne Hewlett 1917; two d. (one deceased); ed. Milton Acad. Harvard Univ., Annapolis Naval Acad.
Asst. Export Man. Armour & Co. 19-21; Nat. Accounts Sales Man. Kelly-Springfield Truck Co. 22; Pres. Stockade Building System 22-27; Founder Pres. 4-D Co., Chicago 27-32; Founder, Dir. and Chief Engineer Dymaxion Corpn. 32-35; Asst. to Dir. of Research and Development, Phelps Dodge Corpn. 36-38; Technical Consultant *Fortune* magazine 38-40; Vice-Pres. and Chief Engineer, Dymaxion Co. Inc. 41-42; Chief, Mechanical Engineering Section, Board of Economic Warfare, Special Asst. to Dir. Foreign Economic Admin. 42-44; Chair. Dymaxion Dwelling Machines 44-46; Pres. Geodesics Inc. 54-, Synergetics Inc. 54-59, Plydomes Inc. 57-; Prof. of Generalised Design Science Exploration, Southern Ill. Univ. 59-68, Distinguished Prof. 68-; The Charles Eliot Norton Prof. of Poetry, Harvard Univ. 61-62; Fellow and life mem. A.A.A.S.; World Fellow in Residence Univ. of Pa., Bryn Mawr, Haverford and Swarthmore Colls., Univ. City Science Center; hon. life mem. American Inst. of Architects; inventor-discoverer of energetic-synergetic geometry and of geodesic and tensegrity structures; built domes for U.S. Marine Corps and U.S. Navy (in all over 100,000 geodesic domes in 100 countries, including geodesic dome for Expo '67, Montreal 67); 39 hon. degrees in Design, Arts, Science, Humane Letters, Laws, Fine Arts, Literature, Eng. and Architectural Eng. 54-75; Gold Medal for Architecture, Royal Inst. of

British Architects 68, Gold Medal, American Inst. of Architects 70.

Publs. *Nine Chains to the Moon* 38, *No More Second-Hand God* 62, *Untitled Epic of Industrialization* 63, *Education Automation* 63, *Ideas and Integrities* 63, *Operating Manual for Spaceship Earth* 69, *Utopia or Oblivion: the Prospects for Humanity* 70, *Intuition* 72, *Earth, Inc.* 73, *Synergetics: Explorations in the Geometry of Thinking* 75.

3500 Market Street, Philadelphia, Pa. 19104, U.S.A. Telephone (215) 387-2255.

Fuller, Roy Broadbent, c.b.e., f.r.s.l.; British solicitor and author; b. 11 Feb. 1912, Failsworth, Lancashire; s. of Leopold Charles Fuller and Nellie Broadbent; m. Kathleen Smith 1936; one s.

Assistant Solicitor, Woolwich Equitable Building Soc. 38, Solicitor 58-69; Dir. 69; war service in Royal Navy 41-46; mem. Arts Council Poetry Panel 55-59; Chair. Building Socs. Asscn. Legal Advisory Panel 58-69; Vice-Pres. Building Socs. Asscn.; mem. Board Poetry Book Soc. 60-76; Prof. of Poetry, Univ. of Oxford 68-73; Gov. BBC 72-; mem. Arts Council 76-; Duff Cooper Memorial Prize 68; Queen's Medal for Poetry 70.

Publs. Verse: *The Middle of a War* 42, *A Lost Season* 44, *Epitaphs and Occasions* 49, *Counterparts* 54, *Brutus's Orchard* 17, *Collected Poems* 62, *Buff* 65, *New Poems* 68, *Seen Grandpa Lately?* 72, *Tiny Tears* 73, *From the Joke Shop* 75; Novels: *The Second Curtain* 53, *Fantasy and Fugue* 54, *Image of a Society* 56, *The Ruined Boys* 59, *The Father's Comedy* 61, *The Perfect Fool* 63, *My Child, My Sister* 65, *The Carnal Island* 70; Edited: *The Building Societies Acts*; Criticism: *Owls and Artificers* 72, *Professors and Gods* 73.

37 Langton Way, London, S.E.3, England. Telephone: 01-858-2334.

Fullerton, Lt.-Col. Charles G., m.sc.; American astronaut; b. 11 Oct. 1936, Rochester, N.Y.; s. of Mr. and Mrs. Charles R. Fullerton; m. Marie J. Buettner; one d.; ed. U.S. Grant High School, Portland, Ore., Calif. Inst. of Technology, and U.S.A.F. Aerospace Research Pilot School.

Mechanical design engineer, Hughes Aircraft Co., Culver City Calif.; entered active service in U.S. Air Force July 58; joined Aeronautical Systems Div., Wright-Patterson Air Force Base, Ohio 65; flight crew mem. U.S.A.F. Manned Orbiting Lab.; selected as NASA astronaut Sept. 69.

Leisure interests: woodworking, boating, volleyball, tennis.

NASA Johnson Space Center, Houston, Texas 77058, U.S.A.

Fulton, Baron (Life Peer), cr. 66, of Falmer; **John Scott Fulton,** Kt.; British administrator; b. 27 May 1902, Monifieth, Angus, Scotland; s. of Prof. A. R. Fulton and Annie Alexander Scott; m. Jacqueline Wilkinson 1939; three s. one d.; ed. Dundee High School, St. Andrews Univ. and Balliol Coll., Oxford.

Assistant in Logic and Scientific Method, London School of Econs. 26-28; Fellow, Balliol Coll., Oxford 28-47, Tutor in Philosophy 28-35, in Politics 35-47; Jowett Lecturer 35-38, Jowett Fellow 45-47; Faculty Fellow, Nuffield Coll. 33-47; Principal Asst. Ministry of Fuel and Power 42-44; Principal, Univ. Coll. of Swansea 47-59; Vice-Chancellor, Univ. of Wales 52-54, 58-59; Vice-Chancellor, Univ. of Sussex 59-67; Chair. Board for Mining Qualifications 50-62, Univs. Council for Adult Education 52-55, Univs. Central Council on Admissions 61-64, B.B.C. Liaison Advisory Cttee. on Adult Educ. 62-65, I.T.A. Adult Educ. Advisory Cttee.; Chair. Inter-Univ. Council on Higher Educ. Overseas 64-68, Exec. Vice-Chair. 68-; Gov. and Vice-Chair. B.B.C. 65-67; Chair. of Cttee. to examine Structure, Recruitment, Training and Management of Home Civil Service 66-68; Chair. British Council 68-71; Chair.

Council, London Univ. Inst. of Educ. 67-; Chair. Tavistock Inst. of Human Relations 68-, Manpower Soc. 73-.

Leisure interests: golf, gardening, hill-climbing.

Publs. *In Defence of Democracy* (with C. R. Morris) 35, various articles in learned journals.

Brook House, Priestman's Lane, Thornton-le-Dale, Pickering, Yorkshire, England. Telephone: Thornton-le-Dale 221.

Fulton, Rt. Hon. Edmund Davie, p.c., q.c.; Canadian Minister of Justice and Attorney-General 57-62; see *The International Who's Who 1975-76.*

Fumagalli, Guido; Italian businessman; b. 12 Oct. 1902; ed. Istituto Tecnico C. Cattaneo, Milan.

Commission Agent Stock Exchange, Milan 46-56; Stockbroker, Milan 56-; mem. Stock Exchange Cttee. 63-64, Pres. 65-70; Pres. Union of Italian Stock Exchange Cttees. 65-; Cavaliere Ufficiale della Corona d'Italia.

Via Meravigli 16, Milan; and Viale Romagna 5, Milan, Italy.

Funahashi, Masao; Japanese business executive; b. 3 May 1913, Aichi Pref.; s. of Azuma and Suzu Funahashi; m. Keiko Matsubara 1946; one s. one d.; ed. Tokyo Univ.

Manager of Purchasing Dept., Furukawa Electric Co. Ltd. 59, of Finance and Accounting Dept. 61, Man. Dir. 68, Exec. Dir. 71, Vice-Pres. 73, Pres. 74-.

Leisure interest: golf.

6-1, Marunouchi 2-chome, Chiyoda-ku, Tokyo, Japan. Telephone: Tokyo (03) 213-0811 (Office).

Funcke, Friedrich, d.iur.; German business executive; b. 27 Sept. 1903, Kamen, Hamm; m. Elisabeth Sasse 1955; one s. two d.; ed. Univs. of Freiburg, Berlin and Erlangen.

Joined Gelsenkirchener Bergwerks-Aktien-Gesellschaft (coal mining) 31, mem. Man. Board 45-67; Chair. of Man. Board Gelsenberg AG, Essen 66-69; Chair. Advisory Board Ruhrgas AG, Essen, Gelsenwasser AG, Gelsenkirchen; mem. Advisory Board Gelsenberg AG, Essen, Westdeutsche Wohnhäuser AG, Essen; mem. Board Aktionsgemeinschaft deutsche Steinkohlenreviere G.m.b.H., Düsseldorf.

Leisure interests: shooting and golf.

43 Essen-Ruhr, Brucker Holt 27, Federal Republic of Germany.

Füncke, Liselotte; German politician; b. 20 July 1918, Hagen; d. of Oscar Füncke and Bertha (née Osthaus) Füncke; ed. commercial studies in Berlin.

Formerly employed in industry and commerce, Hagen and Wuppertal; mem. Diet of North-Rhine-Westfalia 50-61; mem. Bundestag 61-, Vice-Pres. Bundestag 69-; Chair. Bundestag Finance Cttee. 72-; mem. Presidium, Freie Demokratische Partei (FDP) 68-.

Bundestag, 53 Bonn; Home: 58 Hagen, Stadtgarten-Allee 1, Federal Republic of Germany. Telephone: Hagen 24055.

Funès, Louis de; French actor; b. 31 July 1914.

Plays include *Winterset, Un Tramway Nommé Désir, Ornifle, Les Belles Bacchantes*; films include *Le Blé en Herbe, Mam'zelle Nitouche, Papa, Maman, la Bonne et Moi, L'Impossible Monsieur Pipelet, Courte Tête, La Traversée de Paris, Un Cheveu sur la Soupe, Ni Vu ni Connu, La Vie à Deux, Certains l'Aiment Froide, Mon Pote le Gitan, Chair à Poisson, Candide, Les Dix Commandements, Le Gendarme de Saint-Tropez, Le Corniaud, les Bons Vivants, le Gendarme à New York, Fantomas se déchaine, le Grand Restaurant, la Grande Vadrouille, Oscar, Les Grandes Vacances, Fantomas contre Scotland Yard, Le Petit Baigneur, Le Tatoué, le gendarme se marie, Un coup fumant, Hibernatus, L'homme orchestre, Le Gendarme en ballade, Sur un arbre perché, Les Aventures de Rabbi Jacob.*

45 rue de Monceau, Paris 8e, France.

Funke, Gösta Werner, PH.D.; Swedish scientist and administrator; b. 27 Oct. 1906, Stockholm; s. of Oscar Werner Funke and Sofia Carlsson; m. Gunborg Blomquist 1935; two d.; ed. Univ. of Stockholm, and Technische Hochschule, Darmstadt.
Lecturer in Physics, Univ. of Stockholm 37-41; Prof. Technical Coll., Norrköping 39-43, Bromma Coll. 43-45; Sec.-Gen. Swedish Atomic Cttee. 45-59; mem. Swedish Nat. Cttee. for UNESCO 57-60; Sec.-Gen. Swedish Nat. Science Research Council 45-72, Swedish Atomic Research Council 59-72; mem. Joint Cttee. for the Nordic Research Councils 48-72; Swedish Rep. to CERN 53-72; Pres. of Finance Cttee. 61-64, Pres. of Council 66-69; Swedish Rep., European Southern Observatory (ESO) 61-72, Pres. of Council 66-68; Swedish rep. on many cttees. concerning Nordic or int. collaboration in different fields of science; mem. Swedish Acad. of Engineering Sciences 68-; Riddare av Vasaorden, Kommendör av Nordstjärneorden, Commdr. Ordre Nat. du Mérite (France).
Leisure interest: gardening.
Publs. *Text Book of Mathematics* 40, *Sverige inför atomåldern* 56, *Introduktion till naturvetenskaplig forskning i Sverige* 63; articles in specialized journals.
San Rafael 89, Alfaz del Pí, Alicante, Spain.

Funston, George Keith; American executive; b. 12 Oct. 1910; ed. Sioux Falls High School, Trinity Coll., Hartford, Conn., and Harvard School of Business Admin.
Asst. to Vice-Pres. in Charge of Sales, American Radiator and Standard Sanitary Corpn. 35-38, Asst. to Treas. 38-40; Sales-Planning Dir., later Dir. of Purchases, Sylvania Electric Products, Inc. 40; War Production Board 41-44; Lieut.-Commdr. U.S. Navy 44-45; Pres. Trinity Coll., Hartford, Conn. 44-51; Pres. New York Stock Exchange 51-67; Chair. Olin Mathieson Chemical Corpn. 67-72; Dir. Metropolitan Life Insurance Co., and several other companies; has 22 hon. degrees from Amer. univs.
Vineyard Lane, Greenwich, Conn. 06830, U.S.A.

Fuoss, Raymond Matthew, PH.D.; American chemist; b. 28 Sept. 1905, Bellwood, Pa.; s. of Jacob Z. Fuoss and Bertha M. Zimmerman Fuoss; m. 1st Rose E. Harrington 1926, one d.; m. 2nd Ann M. Stein 1947; ed. Harvard Univ., Brown Univ., and Univs. of Leipzig, Munich and Cambridge.
Research Instructor, Brown Univ. 32-33; Int. Postdoctoral Research Fellow, Leipzig and Cambridge 33-35; Research Prof. Brown Univ. 35-36; Research, Gen. Electric Co., Schenectady, N.Y. 36-45; Sterling Prof. of Chem., Yale Univ. 45-74, Emer. Prof. 74-; mem. Nat. Acad. of Sciences, Amer. Acad. of Arts and Sciences, and Amer. Chem. Soc. (Pure Chem. Award 35).
Leisure interests: languages, music.
Publs. over 250 research papers on electrolytes, polymers and dielectrics 25-.
Sterling Chemistry Laboratory, Yale University, New Haven, Conn. 06520; 57 Mill Rock Road, New Haven, Conn. 06511, U.S.A.
Telephone: 201-436-8139 (Office); 201-787-2392 (Home).

Fuoss, Robert; American editor; b. 16 Dec. 1912; ed. Michigan Univ.
Editor Saline *Observer* 33; salesman Vick Chemical Co.; Batten, Barton, Durstine and Osborn, Inc., advertising; Promotion Manager *Country Gentleman* 37-39; Promotion Manager *Saturday Evening Post* 39-42, Man. Editor 42-55, Exec. Editor 55-62, Vice-Pres., Public Relations 62-64; Senior Editor *Reader's Digest* 64-65, Exec. Vice-Pres. 65-, mem. Man. Cttee. 65-; Trustee Dickenson Coll., Pennsylvania 66-; Board of Dirs. Presbyterian Life. Philadelphia 65-; Dir.-at-Large, Nat. Retail Merchants' Asscn. 67-; Distinguished Service Award, Overseas Press Club 61.

c/o Reader's Digest, Pleasantville, N.Y. 10570, U.S.A.

Fürer, Arthur Carl Othmar, D.IUR., D.ECON.; Swiss lawyer and business executive; b. 18 Dec. 1920, Gossau; s. of Carl and Clara Fürer (née Staub); m. Bea Hofer 1951; one s.; ed. Gymnasium Feldkirch, Austria, Univs. of Fribourg, Berne and St.-Gall.
Practised as Attorney in St.-Gall 44-46; joined Société pour le Développement de l'Economie Suisse, Zurich 46-47; Legal Adviser and Man. Sec. to Georg Fischer AG, Schaffhausen 47-54; with Nestlé Alimentana S.A., Vevey 54-, Gen. Man. 69, Man. Dir. 75-; mem. Board Soc. pour le Développement de l'Economie Suisse, Soc. Suisse des Industries Chimiques, Fed. Comm. for Trade Policy; Dir. Swiss Nat. Bank.
Nestlé Alimentana S.A., Avenue Nestlé, 1800 Vevey; Home: Chemin des Roches, CH-1803 Chardonne, Switzerland.
Telephone: 021-51-01-12 (Office); 021-51-47-94 (Home).

Furgler, Kurt, DR.IUR.; Swiss politician; b. 24 June 1924, St.-Gall; m. Ursula Stauffenegger; two s. four d.; ed. Univs. of Fribourg, Zurich, Geneva, Grad. Inst. for Int. Studies, Geneva.
Lawyer, St.-Gall 50-71; mem. Nat. Council 55-71; Leader of Christian Democratic Party Group in Swiss Parl.; mem. Fed. Council 72-, Head of Dept. of Justice and Police 72-; Vice-Pres. Jan. 76-.
Leisure interests: sport, music, literature.
Muri, Parkweg 6, Switzerland.
Telephone: 52-25-00.

Furstenberg, H.E. Cardinal Maximilian van; Netherlands ecclesiastic; b. 23 Oct. 1904.
Ordained Priest 31; Titular Archbishop of Palto 49-; also Apostolic Nuncio in Portugal until 68; Head of Sacred Congregation for the Eastern Churches 68-; created Cardinal by Pope Paul VI 67.
00193 Rome, Via della Conciliazione 34, Italy.
Telephone: 69-84-662.

Furth, Warren Wolfgang, A.B., J.D., American lawyer and international official; b. 1 Aug. 1928, Vienna, Austria; s. of John W. Furth and Hedwig von Ferstel; m. Margaretha F. de la Court 1959; one s. one d.; ed. Harvard Coll., and Harvard Law School.
Law Clerk, Palmer, Dodge, Gardner, Bickford & Bradford, Boston, Mass. 51; admitted to New York Bar 52; Law Clerk to Hon. H.M. Stephens, Chief Judge, U.S. Court of Appeals, District of Columbia Circuit 52-53; U.S. Army 54-57; Assoc. Cravath, Swaine & Moore (law firm) 57-58; with Int. Labour Office (ILO), Geneva 59-70, Exec. Asst. to Dir.-Gen. 64-66, Chief of Technical Co-operation Branch and Deputy Chief, Field Dept. 66-68, Deputy Chief, later Chief, Personnel and Admin. Services Dept. 68-70; Asst. Dir.-Gen. WHO 71-; mem. American Bar Asscn.
World Health Organization, avenue Appia, 1211 Geneva; Home: 13 route de Presinge, 1249 Puplinge (Geneva), Switzerland.
Telephone: 50-14-22.

Furukawa, Susumu, B.A.; Japanese banker; b. 19 Aug. 1913, Saga Prefecture; m. Kimiko Furukawa; four s.; ed. Kyoto Univ.
Entered Nomura Bank (now Daiwa Bank) 38, Gen. Man. Business Dept. 61, Dir. 61, Man. Dir. 63, Senior Man. Dir. 66, Deputy Pres. 68, Pres. 73-.
Leisure interests: haiku (seventeen-syllabled poem), golf.
Daiwa Bank Ltd., 21 Bingo-machi, 2-chome, Higashi-ku, Osaka 541; Home: 13-7, 2-chome, Furuedai, Suita City, Osaka, Japan.
Telephone: (06) 871-9621 (Home).

Fusco, Dott. Stanislao; Italian banker; b. 13 July 1894, Naples.
Associated with Banca Commerciale Italiana 24-48;

Gen. Man. Banco di Napoli 48-65, Chair. 65-75; Vice-Pres. Azienda Tabacchi Italiani (ATI), Inst. for the Econ. Devt. of Southern Italy (ISVEIMER); Dir. Italian Section, Int. Chamber of Commerce; Dir. and mem. Board, Associazione Bancaria Italiana, Assicurazioni Generali; Dir. Instituto Mobiliare Italiano (IMI); Dir. Soc. Storia di Napoli, Centro Azione Latina, Anciennes Institutions de Crédit Italiennes; Cavaliere del Lavoro, Cavaliere Mauriziano, Gran Croce Magistrale dell'Ordine di Malta, Grande Ufficiale della Corona d'Italia, Cavaliere di Gran Croce al Merito della Repubblica, Chevalier, Légion d'Honneur (France), Commdr. Ordre Nat. du Mérite.
c/o Banco di Napoli, Via Roma 177, Naples, Italy.

Fuson, Reynold Clayton, M.A., D.SC., PH.D.; American chemist; b. 1 June 1895; ed. Univ. of Montana, Univ. of Calif., Univ. of Minnesota.

Nat. Research Fellow, Harvard Univ. 24-26, Instructor 26-27; Assoc. in Chemistry, Univ. of Illinois 27-28, Asst. Prof. 28-30, Assoc. Prof. 30-32, Prof. of Organic Chemistry 32-63, Prof. Emer. 63-; Prof. of Chemistry, the Rice Inst. 47-48; Visiting Prof. Univ. of Nevada 63-66, Prof. Emer. 66-; mem. Nat. Acad. of Sciences, Center for Advanced Study; awarded William H. Nichols Medal 53, College Chemistry Teacher Award, Manufacturing Chemists' Asscn. 60, John R. Kuebler Award 64, Distinguished Achievement Award, Univ. of Minnesota 51.
Publs. *A Brief Course in Organic Chemistry* (with others) 41, 59, *Advanced Organic Chemistry* 50, *Organic Chemistry* (with H. R. Snyder) 55, *The Systematic Identification of Organic Compounds* (with others) 56, *Reactions of Organic Compounds* 62.
1442 Hillside Drive, Reno, Nevada 89503, U.S.A.
Telephone: 786-6974.

G

Gabaldón, Arnoldo; Venezuelan malariologist; b. 1 March 1909, Trujillo; *s.* of Joaquín Gabaldón and Virginia Carrillo de Gabaldón; *m.* María Teresa Berti 1937; two *s.* three *d.*; ed Universidad Central de Venezuela, Hamburg Inst. of Tropical Diseases and Johns Hopkins Univ.
Hospital Intern, Caracas 28-30; Lab. Asst. Bacteriological and Parasitological Lab., Caracas 30-32; Health Officer, San Fernando, Apure 32-33; Rockefeller Fellow, Johns Hopkins Univ. 34-36; Chief, Div. of Malariology, Ministry of Health 36-50; Technical Consultant, WHO Anti-Malaria Operations, India 50; Dir. Inst. of Aphtous Fever, Ministry of Agriculture, Venezuela 50; Consultant Div. of Malariology, Ministry of Health and Social Assistance 51-59; Technical Consultant, Panamerican Sanitary Org. 54, Panamerican Sanitary Office Anti-Malaria Campaign, Trinidad 57; Minister of Health and Social Assistance, Venezuela 59-64; mem. Venezuelan Nat. Acad. of Medicine; Consultant, Bureau of Malariology and Environmental Health, Ministry of Health and Social Assistance, Venezuela 64-73; Simón Bolívar Prof. of Latin American Studies, Univ. of Cambridge 68-69; Dir. Laboratory for Malaria Studies, Nat. Inst. of Hygiene, Caracas.
Leisure interests: hunting, fishing.
Publs. Numerous studies on malaria, public health and parasitology, *Una política Sanitaria* 65.
P.O. Box 5387, Caracas 101, Venezuela.

Gaballah el-Sayed, Sayed; Egyptian politician; ed. Cairo and Wisconsin Univs.
Teacher, Cairo Univ., Head Agricultural Econ. Section; Under-Sec. of State for Planning 63-71; Minister for Planning 71-74.
c/o Ministry of Planning, Cairo, Egypt.

Gabin, Jean (*pseudonym* of Jean-Alexis Moncorgé); French actor; b. 17 May 1904.
Fmr. labourer and delivery boy; began stage career at Folies Bergères; film debut in *Chacun sa Chance* 30; Best Actor Award, Berlin Film Festival 71.
Films include *Gloria, Coeur de Lilas* 31, *Adieu les Beaux Jours, Le Tunnel* 33, *Maria Chapdelaine* 34, *La Bandera* 35, *Pépé le Moko, La Grande Illusion, Le Messager* 37, *Quai des Brumes, La Bete Humaine* 38, *Le Jour se lève* 39, *Moontide* 42, *Martin Roumagnac* 46, *Au-dela des Grilles* 48, *La Marie du Port* 50, *La Traversée de Paris, French Can Can, Le sang et la tête, Crime et Châtiment, Sans douleur, The Possessors, Ne Touchez Pas Au Grisbi, Le Rouge est Mis, Les Grandes Familles, Le Président, The Big Snatch, Le cave se rebiffe, Un singe en hiver, le Gentlèman d'Epsom, Mélodie en sous-sol, Monsieur, le Deuxième Souffle, le Tonnerre de Dieu, Du rififi a Paname, le Jardinier d'Argenteuil, Le Soleil des voyous, Le Pacha, Le Tatoué, Le Chat, Le drapeau noir flotte sur la marmite, L'Affaire Dominici* 73, *Deux Hommes dans la Ville* 73, *The Verdict* 74; Co-Producer (with Fernandel) *L'Age Ingrat* 64.
Office: c/o Bernheim, 55 avenue George V, Paris 8e; Home: "la Pichonnière", 61 Bonnefoi (Orne), France.

Gabo, Naum, K.B.E.; American sculptor; b. 5 Aug. 1890, Briansk, Russia; *s.* of Boris and Fannie (née Azyerskaya) Pevsner; *m.* Miriam Israels 1936; one *d.*; ed. Munich, Paris and Oslo.
Worked in Russia in asscn. with Kandinsky, Malevitch and Tatlin 17-21; exponent of Constructivist Art; issued Realist Manifesto 20; lived in Berlin 21-32, Paris 32-36, England 36-46, U.S.A. 46-; rep. at numerous exhbns., including the Brussels Int. Exhbn. 58, and

Coolsingel, Rotterdam, Tate Gallery, London 66; mem. American Inst. of Arts and Letters; Dr. h.c. Royal Coll. of Art (U.K.); Fellow American Acad. of Arts and Sciences; foreign mem. Swedish Royal Acad. of Fine Arts.
Leisure interest: chess.
Publs. *Gabo 57, Of Divers Arts* 62.
Breakneck Hill Road, Middlebury, Conn., U.S.A.
Telephone: 203-758-9487.

Gabor, Dennis, C.B.E., D.SC., DR.ING., F.INST.P., F.I.E.E., M.I.E.E., F.R.S.; British electrical engineer; b. 5 June 1900; *s.* of Bertalan Gabor and Ady Jakobovits; *m.* Marjorie L. Butler 1936; ed. Technical Univ., Budapest, and Technische Hochschule, Charlottenburg.
Research engineer in German Research Asscn. of High Voltage Plants 26-27; Siemens and Halske, Berlin-Siemensstadt 27-33; British Thomson Houston Co. Research Lab., Rugby 34-48; Reader in Electronics, Imperial Coll. of Science and Technology, Dept. of Electrical Engineering 49-58; Prof. Applied Electron Physics at Imperial Coll., Univ. of London 58-67; Senior Research Fellow 67-; Staff Scientist, CBS Labs., Stamford, Conn., U.S.A. 67; mem. Club of Rome; Foreign Assoc. U.S. Nat. Acad. of Sciences; Hon. mem. Hungarian Acad. of Sciences; inventor of holography; Cristoforo Colombo Prize of Int. Inst. of Communications, Genoa 67; Medal of Honor, Inst. of Electrical and Electronic Engineers 70; Rumford Medal, Royal Soc. 68; Nobel Prize for Physics 71; Holweck Prize, French Physics Soc. 71; Kulturpreis, German Photographic Soc. 71; Hon. D.Sc. (Southampton Univ. 70, Bridgeport Eng. Inst. 72, Univ. of Surrey 72, City Univ., London 72), Hon. Dr. (Delft Technical Univ.) 71, Hon. LL.D. (Univ. of London) 73.
Leisure interest: writing on social matters, especially on the future.
Publs. *Inventing the Future* 63, *Innovations: Scientific, Technological and Social* 70, *The Mature Society* 72; about eighty papers on high-speed oscillography of transients, gas discharges and plasmas, electron optics and electron microscopy, physical optics (diffraction and interference microscopes), communication theory and communication techniques (television).
Imperial College, London, S.W.7, England (forwarding address); "La Margioretta", Viale dei Gigli, Lavinio pr. Anzio, Italy (summer).
Telephone: 01-589-5111 (England); 98-21-146 (Italy).

Gábor, Miklós; Hungarian actor; b. 7 April 1919, Zalaegerszeg; *s.* of Béla Gábor and Ilona Czuckelter; ed. Budapest Coll. of Dramatic Art.
Member Hungarian Nat. Theatre 45-54, Madách Theatre, Budapest 54-75; Katona József Theatre, Kecskemét 75-; best-known roles include Hamlet, King Richard III, Ferdinand (in Schiller's *Kabale und Liebe*), Ruy Blas, John Tanner (in Shaw's *Man and Superman*) and George (*Who's Afraid of Virginia Woolf*); has appeared in numerous films; Kossuth Prize 62, Merited Artist 62, Eminent Artist 67.
Leisure interest: writing.
Publ. *With The Pen.*
Katona József Szinhaz, Kecskemét, Hungary.
Telephone: 220-677.

Gabre-Sellassie, Zewde, M.A., PH.D.; Ethiopian diplomatist; b. 12 Oct. 1926, Metcha, Shoa; ed. Haile Selassie I Secondary School, Coll. des Frères and St. George School, Jerusalem, Coll. des Frères and American

Mission, Cairo, Univ. of Exeter, Oxford Univ. and Lincoln's Inn, London.
Economic Attaché, later Head of Press, Information and Admin. Div., Ministry of Foreign Affairs 51-53; Dir.-Gen. Maritime Affairs 53-55; Deputy Minister, Ministry of Public Works, Transport and Civil Aviation 55-57; Mayor and Gov. of Addis Ababa 57-59; Amb. to Somalia 59-60; Minister of Justice 61-63; Senior mem. St. Anthony's Coll., Oxford 63-71; Perm. Rep. to the UN 72-74; Minister of Interior March-May 74, of Foreign Affairs May-Dec. 74; Deputy Prime Minister July-Sept. 74; Visiting lecturer, Univ. of Calif., U.S.A. 55; Vice-Pres. ECOSOC 74; Officer of Menelik II (Ethiopia); Grand Cross, Order of Phoenix (Greece), of Istiqlal (Jordan); Grand Officer Flag of Yugoslavia, Order of Merit (Fed. Repub. of Germany); Commdr. Order of St. Olav (Norway), of Orange-Nassau (Netherlands).
Ministry of Foreign Affairs, Addis Ababa, Ethiopia.

Gabriel, Ralph Henry, PH.D., LITT.D.; American historian; b. 29 April 1890, Reading, N.Y.; s. of Cleveland and Alta Monroe Gabriel; m. Christine Davis 1917; two s. one d.; ed. Yale Univ.
Member staff Yale Univ. 15 and Prof. 28-58; mem. staff U.S. War Dept. School of Military Govt. 43-46; mem. American Historical Asscn.; mem. Newcomen Society; Visiting Prof. Sydney Univ. Australia 46; Prof. American History Cambridge Univ. 51-52; Prof. of American Civilisation, American Univ. 58-64; Visiting Prof. Tokyo Univ. 64, George Washington Univ. 65; U.S. Del. at Tenth Session of UNESCO 58; mem. of U.S. Nat. Comm. for UNESCO 58-63; Editor *Pageant of America* (15 vols.) 24-29; Joint-Editor *The American Mind* 37; Editor Library of Congress Series in American Civilisation.
Leisure interests: hiking, canoeing.
Publs. *Evolution of Long Island* 22, *Toilers of Land and Sea* 26, *Lure of the Frontier* 29, *The Course of American Democratic Thought* 40, 56, *Religion and Learning at Yale* 58, *American Values, Continuity and Change* 74.
484 Whitney Avenue, New Haven, Conn. 06511, U.S.A.

Gadda Conti, Piero, LL.D.; Italian writer; b. 13 Feb. 1902, Milan; s. of Giuseppe and Matilde Gadda Conti; m. Anna Maria Castellini 1939; one s.; ed. Pavia Univ.
Novelist and journalist; Italian Literary Prizewinner 30; Bagutta Prize for Literature for *La Paura* 71.
Publs. *L'Entusiastica Estate* 24, *Liuba* 26, *Verdemare* 27, *Mozzo* 30, *A Gonfie Vele* 31, *Gagliarda* 32, *Orchidea* 34, *Festa da Ballo* 37, *Nuvola* 38, *Moti del Cuore* 40, *Vocazione Mediterranea* 40, *Incomparabile Italia* 47, *Beati Regni* 54, *Vita e melodie di Giacomo Puccini* 55, *Adamira* 56, *Vanterie Adolescenti* 60, *Cinema e civiltà* 60, *Cinema e Giustizia* 61, *Cinema e Sesso* 62, *Cinema e Libertà* 63, *La Milano dei Navigli* 65, *Cinema e Società* 65, *La Brianza* 66, *La Paura* 70, *Confessioni di Carlo Emilio Gadda* 74; plays: *La Veste d'Oro* 24, *Dulcinea* 27.
Piazza Castello 20, Milan, Italy.
Telephone: 873-771.

Gaddafi, Col. Mu'ammar Muhammad al-; Libyan army officer and political leader; b. 1941, Misurata; s. of Mohamed Abdussalam Abuminiar and Aisha Abuminiar; three s.; ed. Univ. of Libya, Benghazi.
Served with Libyan Army 65-; Chair. Revolutionary Command Council and C.-in-C. of Armed Forces of Libya Sept. 69-; Prime Minister 70-72; Minister of Defence 70-72; mem. Pres. Council, Fed. Arab Repubs. 71-.
Revolutionary Command Council, Tripoli, Libya.

Gaddafi, Wanis; Libyan politician.
Head of Exec. Council in Cyrenaican Provincial Govt. 52-62; Fed. Minister of Foreign Affairs Jan. 62-63, of Interior 63-64, of Labour 64; Ambassador to the Fed. German Repub. 64-65; later Minister of Planning

and Devt.; later Minister of Foreign Affairs; Prime Minister 68-69; imprisoned for two years Nov. 71.
Tripoli, Libya.

Gaetano, Cortesi; Italian industrial executive; b. 8 May 1912, Mesenzana, Varese; s. of late Giuseppe Gaetano and Angela (née Ferrini); m. Fiorella Lello 1946; three s.; ed. Univ. Bocconi, Milan.
Research at London School of Econs., Berlin Handelshochschule and Yale; joined econ. agency Istituto per la Riconstruzione Industriale (IRI) working in Stabilimenti Tessili Italiana and later in Banca Commerciale Italiana, New York and Italy 40-45, in Cen. Inspectorate 45-57; Gen. Dir. of Finmeccanica 57-60, of IRI 60-66; Chair. and Gen. Man. Italcantieri (Trieste) 66-71, Gen. Man. Fincantieri 71-74; Chair. and Gen. Man. Alfa Romeo S.p.A. 74-, now also to Alfa Romeo Alfasud S.p.A.; Pres. Studi Impianti Consulenze Automotoristiche S.r.l.; mem. Board of Dirs. and Exec. Cttee., Assoc. Sindacale Intersind (employers' asscn. for state-controlled firms).
Leisure interest: mountains.
Publ. *Pianificazione Programmazione e Controlli Industriale* 55.
Alfa Romeo S.p.A., Via Gattemelata 45, 20149 Milan, Italy.
Telephone: 02-93391.

Gafurov, Bobojan Gafurovich, D.SC.; Soviet historian and orientalist; b. 31 Dec. 1908, Ispisar Village, Tajik S.S.R.; ed. Samarkand Law School and All-Union Inst. of Journalism.
Member C.P.S.U. 32-; Head of Dept., Deputy Editor-in-Chief, Editor-in-Chief *Krasny Taikistan* (Red Tajikistan) 35-41; Sec. Central Cttee. of C.P. of Tajikistan 41-46, First Sec. 46-56; Dir. Inst. of Oriental Studies 56-; mem. Tajik S.S.R. Acad. of Sciences; Corresp. mem. U.S.S.R. Acad. of Sciences 58-68, Academician 68-; mem. Polish Soc. of Orientalists; mem. Indian Council on Cultural Relations; Vice-Chair. Board of Afro-Asian Solidarity Funds; Vice-Chair. Soviet Cttee. of Solidarity with Countries of Asia and Africa; Vice-Chair. Soviet Cttee. of Peace Defence; Honoured Scientist, Tajik S.S.R.; Order of Lenin (six times); Order of Red Banner, etc.
Publs. Scientific works on history, ideology, civilization and culture of Middle East and Central Asia.
Institute of Oriental Studies, U.S.S.R. Academy of Sciences, Moscow, U.S.S.R.

Gaganova, Valentina Ivanovna; Soviet textile spinner and politician; b. 1932; ed. technical textile inst.
Turner, factory at Kovrov 47-48; Apprentice Spinner, Vyshny Volochok 48-49, Spinner 49-50, Foreman Planner 50-; mem. Central Cttee. of C.P.S.U. 61-71; Hero of Socialist Labour 59.
Cotton Plant, Vyshny Volochok, Kalinin Region, U.S.S.R.

Gage, Harlow W., B.A.; American motor company executive; b. 6 Feb. 1911, Springfield, Mass.; ed. Norwich Univ., Northfield, Vt.
With Gen. Motors Ltd. (starting as Messenger, Overseas Div. in New York) 34-, Asst. to Man. Dir. Gen. Motors Near East S.A., Alexandria, Egypt 36-40, Sales Corresp. for Foreign Distributors' Div. of Gen. Motors, New York Jan. 41-Dec. 41, at Overseas Operations Div., Washington 42-45, Sales Man. Gen. Motors New Zealand Ltd., Wellington Sept. 45-54, Man. Dir. GM New Zealand Ltd. 54-56, Asst. to Man. Dir. of Gen. Motors-Holden's Pty. Ltd., Melbourne 56-58, Asst. Man. Dir. GM-Holden's June 58, Man. Dir. 59-62, Regional Group Exec. GM Overseas Div. 62-63, Feb. 68-Oct. 68, Dir. Opel, Holden's group with responsibility for GM vehicle mfg. subsids. 63-68, Gen. Man. GM Overseas Div. and Vice-Pres. and mem. of Admin. Cttee. of Gen. Motors Corpn. Oct 68-; Trustee, Council

for Latin America Inc., U.S. Council of Int. Chamber of Commerce; Dir. American-Australian Asscn.; mem. Board of Dirs. of Nat. Foreign Trade Council Inc., The Council on Foreign Relations.
General Motors Corporation, General Motors Building, Detroit, Mich. 48202, U.S.A.

Gaggero, Sir George, Kt., O.B.E., J.P.; British industrialist; b. 5 April 1897; s. of Joseph Gaggero and Mary Dassoy; m. Mabel Andrews-Speed 1925; two s. two d.; ed. Gibraltar, Germany and England.
Chairman, M. H. Bland & Co. Ltd 14-70, Hon. Pres. 70-; Chair. Bland Group of Companies, incl. Rock Hotel Ltd., Bland Cable Cars Ltd., Bland Line, Thomas Mosley & Co. Ltd., M. H. Bland & Co. (U.K.) Ltd.; Pres. Gibraltar Airways Ltd. (Chair. 47-66); Pres. Gibraltar Employers Fed. 28-40; Dir. Gibraltar Chamber of Commerce 18-22, The Rock Fire Assurance Co. Ltd. 27-52, Gibraltar Transporters Ltd. 30-66, Mackintosh & Co. (Gibraltar) Ltd. 43-67; Chair. Gibraltar Shipping Asscn. 56-60, Gibraltar Stevedoring Co. Ltd. 48-59, Stevedoring & Cargo Handling Co. Ltd. 59-65; City Councillor 21-24; unofficial mem. Exec. Council 24-30, 36-43; Chair. Bench of Justices 49-59; Chief A.R.P. Warden, Gibraltar 38-40; Chair. Board of District Commrs. 40-43; mem. Public Service Comm. 56-58; Chair. Merchant Navy Welfare Cttee. 42-47, mem. 22-70; served on many local cttees.; Swedish Consul 39; Swedish Consul-Gen. 54-66; F.R.S.A.; Coronation Medals 37, 53; Chevalier (1st class) Royal Swedish Order of Vasa.
75 Prince Edward's Road, Gibraltar.
Telephone: A5643.

Gagnebin, Albert P., B.S., M.S.; American mining executive; b. 23 Jan. 1909, Torrington, Conn.; m. Genevieve Hope; two d.; ed. Yale Univ.
Research Engineer, Int. Nickel Co. Inc. 32-49, Ductile Iron Group Leader 49-54, Asst. Man. of Nickel Sales 55-56, Man. 56-61, Asst. Vice-Pres. 57-58, Vice-Pres. 58-64, Vice-Pres. Int. Nickel Co. of Canada Ltd. 60-64, Exec. Vice-Pres. Int. Nickel Co. of Canada Ltd. and Int. Nickel Co. Inc. 64-67, Dir. Int. Nickel Co. 64-, Int. Nickel Co. of Canada 65-, Pres. Int. Nickel Co. of Canada Ltd. and Int. Nickel Co. Inc. 67-72, Chair. and Chair. Exec. Cttee. 72-74; Dir. Int. Copper Research Asscn.; Trustee, Atlantic Mutual Insurance Co., Bank of New York; Dir. Abex Corpn., American-Swiss Asscn., Inc., Ingersoll-Rand Co., Centennial Insurance Co., Toronto-Dominion Bank, Illinois Central Industries, Bank of N.Y., N. American Advisory Board of Swissair; Yale Eng. Asscn., Councillor French Chamber of Commerce in U.S.; co-inventor of Ductile Iron; Hon. Life mem. American Foundrymen's Soc; mem. Nat. Acad. of Eng., Wash.; Awards 52, 65 and 67.
Publs. *Fundamentals of Iron and Steel Castings* 57, and numerous articles.
143 Grange Avenue, Fair Haven, N.J. 07701, U.S.A.
Telephone: 201-747-0139.

Gainza Paz, Alberto; Argentine journalist; b. 16 March 1899; ed. Nat. Univ. of Buenos Aires Law School.
Editor *La Prensa*, Buenos Aires, which he joined in 33; Dr. h.c. of Columbia Univ. New York and Northwestern Univ. Ill.
La Prensa, Avenida de Mayo 567, Buenos Aires, Argentina.

Gairbekov, Muslim Gairbekovich; Soviet politician; ed. Kabardino-Balkar State Univ.
Member C.P.S.U. 32; Teacher 32-35; Exec. Party and Local Govt. posts 36-40; People's Commissar for Educ. and Vice-Chair. Council of People's Commissars of the Chechen-Ingush Autonomous S.S.R. 40-57; Chair. Council of Ministers of the Chechen-Ingush Autonomous S.S.R., Deputy to U.S.S.R. Supreme Soviet 57-;

mem. Educ., Science and Cultural Cttee., Soviet of Union.
Council of Ministers, Chechen-Ingush Autonomous S.S.R., Grozny, U.S.S.R.

Gairdner, Lieut.-Gen. Sir Charles Henry, G.B.E., K.C.M.G., K.C.V.O., C.B., K.G.ST.J.; British administrator; b. 20 March 1898, Batavia, Java; s. of C. A. Gairdner and Theodora A. Bergsma; m. Hon. Evelyn Handcock (d. of 5th Baron Castlemaine) 1925; ed. Repton and Royal Military Acad., Woolwich.
Gazetted 2nd Lieut., Royal Artillery 16; served in France and Flanders; transferred to 10th Royal Hussars 26, Major 31, Lieut.-Col. 37, Col. 40, Major-Gen. 42, Lieut.-Gen. 44; commnd. 10th Royal Hussars 37-40; Col. 49-52; Gen. Staff Officer, 1st Grade, 7th Armoured Div. 40-41; Deputy Dir. of Plans, Middle East 41; G.O.C. 6th and 8th Armoured Divs. 42; Chief of Gen. Staff, N. Africa 43; Maj.-Gen. Armoured Fighting Vehicles, India 44; Personal Rep. of Prime Minister of U.K. in Far East and Head of U.K. Liaison Mission 45-48; retd. 48; Gov. of Western Australia 51-63, Tasmania 63-68; Medal of Freedom with Silver Palm (U.S.A.); Hon. D.Litt. (W. Australia); Hon. LL.D. (Tasmania).
Leisure interests: polo, golf, yachting.
24 The Esplanade, Peppermint Grove, Western Australia.
Telephone: 316756.

Gaiser, Gerd, DR. PHIL.; German writer; b. 15 Sept. 1908, Oberriexingen, Württemberg; ed. Art Academies at Stuttgart and Königsberg, and Univ. of Tübingen.
Studied painting and the history of art; served German Air Force in Second World War; Fontane Prize of City of Berlin 51, Literature Prize of Bavarian Fine Arts Acad. 55 etc.; mem. Acad. of Arts, Berlin, Bavarian Fine Arts Acad., Munich.
Publs. *Zwischenland* (short stories) 49, *Eine Stimme hebt an* 50, *Das Schiff im Berg* 53, *Die Sterbende Jagd* 54, *Einmal und Oft* 56, *Schlussball* 57, *Sizilianische Notizen* 59, *Gib acht in Domokosch* 59, *Am Pass Nascondo* 60, *Klassiker der Modernen Malerei* 62, *Alte Meister der Moderne* 62, *Aktuelle Malerei* 63, *Gazelle Grün* 65, *Umgang mit Kunst* 74.
Robert Koch-Str. 39, Reutlingen, Württemberg, Federal Republic of Germany.
Telephone: 41637.

Gaitonde, Vasudeo; Indian artist; b. 1924; ed. Sir J. J. School of Art, Bombay.
Exhibited in London, New York, Paris, São Paulo, Tokyo; one man shows in New Delhi and Bombay; John D. Rockefeller Third Fund Grant 64; First Prize, Young Asian Artists' Exhibition, Tokyo 57.
Works in: Nat. Gallery of Modern Art and Lalit Kala Akademi, New Delhi, Tata Inst. of Fundamental Research and Atomic Energy Establishment, Bombay, Museum of Modern Art, New York.
89 Bhulabhai Desai Road, Bombay 26, India.

Gaivorontsev, Ivan Petrovich; Soviet politician; b. 1928; ed. Azov-Black Sea Inst. of Agriculture.
Agronomist 49-58; Party Official, Sec. of Chelyabinsk Regional Cttee. of C.P.S.U. 58-65; Chair. Chelyabinsk Regional Soviet 65-; Deputy to U.S.S.R. Supreme Soviet 66-; mem. Comm. for Nature Protection, Soviet of Union; mem. C.P.S.U. 55-.
Chelyabinsk Regional Soviet of Working People's Deputies, Chelyabinsk, U.S.S.R.

Gaja, Roberto, LL.D.; Italian diplomatist; b. 27 May 1912, Turin; s. of Guido Gaja and Carlotta Pia Galliani; m. Carla Travaglini 1937; one s. two d.; ed. Univ. of Turin law faculty.
Entered diplomatic service 37; First Sec. and Chargé d'Affaires, Vienna 46-47; Italian Rep. and later Chargé d'Affaires, Tripoli 49-52; Counsellor, Paris 55; Asst.

Dir. of Personnel, Ministry of Foreign Affairs 57, Gen. Dir. for Political Affairs 64-69, Sec.-Gen. of Ministry 69-75; Minister, Sofia; rank of Amb. 67; Amb. to U.S.A. 75-.
Publs. *Discorsi sul Mondo Oscuro* 37, *The Political Consequences of the Atomic Bomb* 59, *Foreign Policy and Nuclear Weapons* 69, *An Inquiry into Italian Foreign Policy* 70.
Italian Embassy, 1601 Fuller Street, N.W., Washington, D.C. 20009, U.S.A.
Telephone: AD4-1935.

Gajendragadkar, Pralhad Balacharya, M.A., LL.B; Indian judge; b. 16 March 1901, Satara, Maharashtra State; *m.* Shalina Pralhad Gajendragadkar 1925; two *d.*; ed. Karnatak Coll., Dharwar, Deccan Coll., Poona, Law Coll., Poona, and Univ. of Bombay.
Joined Bombay Appellate Side Bar 26; Edited *Hindu Law Quarterly*; Chair. Bank Award Comm. 55; Judge of the Bombay High Court 45-57; Judge, Supreme Court of India 57-64, Chief Justice 64-66; Vice-Chancellor, Bombay Univ. 66-71; Pres. S. P. Mandali, Poona; Pres. Swastik League, Bombay; Visiting Lecturer, U.S. univs. 65; leader dels. Indian Jurists to U.S.S.R. and Australia 65; Chair. Dearness Allowance Comm., Govt. of India 66-67; Chair. Nat. Comm. on Labour 67-69; Chair. Jammu and Kashmir Comm. of Inquiry 67-68; Pres. Asiatic Soc. of Bombay; mem. Univ. Grants Comm.; mem. Man. Council Nat. Centre for the Performing Arts; Chair. Banaras Hindu Univ. Inquiry Cttee. 68-69; Chair. Board of Visitors, J.J. Group of Hospitals, Bombay 67-; Pres. Ramkrishna Mission, Bombay; Vice-Pres. The Centre of Applied Politics, New Delhi; Trustee, India Int. Centre New Delhi, mem. Board of Govs. Shri Ram Centre for Industrial Relations, New Delhi; mem. Nat. Integration Council; Pres. Inst. of Public Undertakings; Sir Lallubhai Shah Lectures 50, Patel Memorial Lectures 66, Nagpur Univ. Extension Lectures 67, Fourth J. N. Tata Lecture 68, Gandhi Memorial Lecture, Nairobi 68, Telang Memorial Lectures 70; Hon. LL.D. (Karnatak); Sir Jehangir Ghandy Medal for Industrial Peace 69; Hon. Chair. Law Reforms Comm., Govt. of India 71-; Padma Vibhushan 72.
Publs. Sanskrit Text of Nanda Pandit's *Dattaka Mimamsa* and its English translation, *Law, Liberty and Social Justice, Kashmir—Retrospect and Prospect, Jawaharlal Nehru—A Glimpse of the Man and His Teachings, The Constitution of India: Its Philosophy and Basic Postulates.*
Law Reforms Commission, Government of India, Shastri Bhavan, Dr. Rajendra Prasad Road, New Delhi 1; Home: Vice-Chancellor's Lodge, University Sports Pavilion, Marine Lines, Bombay 20, India.
Telephone: 259887 (Office); 291750 (Home).

Gajewski, Wacław, PROF. DR.; Polish geneticist; b. 28 Feb. 1911, Kraków; ed. Warsaw Univ.
Doctor 37-46, Docent 46-54, Assoc. Prof. 54-64, Prof. 64-; Corresp. mem. Polish Acad. of Sciences 58-69, mem. 69-, Chair. Botanical Cttee. 68-, now Dir. Inst. of Biochemistry and Biophysics; head, Dept. of Taxonomy and Geography of Plants and Prof. Inst. of Botany, Warsaw Univ.; Editor-in-Chief *Acta Societatis Botanicorum Poloniae*; mem. Int. Asscn. for Plant Taxonomy, Int. Soc. for the Study of Evolution, American Soc. of Naturalists, American Genetics Asscn.; Knight's Cross, Order of Polonia Restituta 57, Officer's Cross 73.
Publs. popular scientific books: *Symbioza* (Symbiosis) 46, *Tajemnice liścia* (Secrets of the Leaf) 49, *Jak poznawano prawa dziedziczności* (How they Learned the Laws of Heredity) 58, *W poszukiwaniu istoty dziedziczeniz* (In Search of the Essence of Heredity) 66; numerous articles.
Ul. J. Dąbrowskiego 75 m. 201, 02-586 Warsaw, Poland.

Gałaj, Dyzma; Polish politician and scientist; b. 15 Jan. 1915, Mystkowice, Łowicz district; *s.* of Kazimierz and Maria Gałaj; *m.* 1944; one *s.* one *d.*; ed. Univ. of Łódź.
Teacher 36; combatant in Peasants' Battalions 42-45; active mem. Rural Youth Union ("Wici") 38-48; after liberation scientific worker, agricultural acads. in Łódź, Olsztyn and Warsaw 48-64; Editor-in-Chief *Wieś Współczesna* 57-64; Head, Inst. for Research on Regions being industrialized, Polish Acad. of Sciences 64-72, Deputy Head 72-; Dir. Inst. for Rural and Agricultural Devt., Polish Acad. of Sciences, 71-; mem. Peasants' Party 48; mem. Cen. Cttee. United Peasants' Party 49-, mem. Presidium, Cen. Cttee. 69-, Vice-Pres. Cen. Cttee. 71-73; Deputy to Seym 65-, Marshal of Seym Feb. 71-March 72; mem. State Council March 72-; Prof. of Sociology Ruralis, Polish Acad. of Sciences; Order of Banner of Labour Second Class, Commdr. Cross of same, Order of Polonia Restituta, Cross of Valour, Partisans' Cross and other decorations.
Publs. Books on agriculture and peasants' political movt.; numerous articles in professional journals.
Institute for Rural and Agricultural Development, Nowy Swiat 72, Warsaw; Home: Zuravia 2/13, Warsaw, Poland.
Telephone: 26-94-36 (Office); 29-00-75 (Home).

Galambos, Robert, M.A., PH.D., M.D.; American professor of neurosciences; b. 20 April 1914, Lorain, Ohio; *s.* of John and Julia Galambos; *m.* 1st Jeannette Wright 1939; three *d.*; *m.* 2nd Carol Armstrong 1971; ed. Harvard Univ. and Univ. of Rochester School of Medicine.
Teaching Fellow, Physiology, Harvard Univ. 39-41, Tutor in Biochemistry 41-42, 47-48, Research Fellow, Psycho-Acoustic Laboratory 47-51; Instructor in Physiology, and Junior Investigator, Office of Scientific Research and Devt., Harvard Univ. Medical School 42-43; Intern, Emory Univ. Hospital 46, Asst. Prof. Anatomy, Emory Univ. Medical School 46-47; Chief, Dept. of Neurophysiology, Walter Reed Army Inst. of Research 51-62; Eugene Higgins Prof. of Psychology and Physiology, Yale Univ. 62-68; Prof. Neurosciences, Univ. of Calif., San Diego 68-.
Publs. *The Avoidance of obstacles by Flying Bats: Spallanzani's ideas (1794) and later theories,* in *Isis* (34) 42, *Inhibition of activity in single auditory nerve fibers by acoustic stimulation,* in *Journal of Neurophysiology* (7) 44, *A Glia-neural theory of brain function,* in *Proceedings* of Nat. Acad. of Sciences (47) 61, *An Electroencephalograph study of classical conditioning* (with Guy C. Sheatz), in *American Journal of Physiology* (203) 62, *Suppression of auditory nerve activity by stimulation of efferent fibers to cochlea,* in *Journal of Neurophysiology* (19) 65, and 125 others.
Department of Neurosciences, University of California, La Jolla, Calif. 92037; Home: 8826 La Jolla Scenic Drive, La Jolla, Calif. 92037, U.S.A.
Telephone: 453-2000, Ext. 2154 (Office); 453-0151 (Home).

Galanshin, Konstantin Ivanovich; Soviet politician; b. 1912; ed. Urals Industrial Inst.
Electrical Fitter 30-37; Engineer, Central Relay Service of "Uralenergo" Power System, Deputy Chief, then Chief of Relay Service of "Permenergo" Power System, Dir. of Perm Region Hydro-electric Power Station 37-50; First Sec. Berezniki Town Cttee. of C.P.S.U. 50-54; Party Official 54-60; First Sec. Perm. Regional Cttee. of C.P.S.U. 60-68; U.S.S.R. Minister of Pulp and Paper Industry 68-; Deputy to U.S.S.R. Supreme Soviet; mem. C.P.S.U. 44-, mem. Cen. Cttee. 61-; Order of Lenin.
U.S.S.R. Ministry of Pulp and Paper Industry, 13/5 Bolshoi Kiselny Pereulok, Moscow, U.S.S.R.

Galbraith, J. Kenneth, B.S., M.S., PH.D.; American economist, diplomatist and writer; b. 15 Oct. 1908; ed. Toronto, California and Cambridge (England) Univs. Research fellow, Calif. Univ. 31-34; Instructor, Harvard Univ. 34-39; Lecturer 48-49, Prof. of Econs. 49-; Amb. to India 61-63; B.B.C. Reith Lecturer 66; Asst. Prof. Princeton Univ. 39-42; Dep. Administrator, Office of Price Admin. 41-43; mem. Board of Editors *Fortune* magazine 43-48; Dir. Office of Econ. Security Policy, State Dept. 45; Nat. Chair. Americans for Democratic Action 69; Pres. Amer. Econ. Asscn. 71; Fellow Amer. Acad. of Arts and Sciences; Freedom Medal 46.
Publs. *Theory of Price Control, American Capitalism* 52, *The Great Crash, Economics and the Art of Controversy* 55, *The Affluent Society* 58, *Journey to Poland and Yugoslavia* 59, *The Liberal Hour* 60, *Made to Last* 64, *The New Industrial State* 67, *The Triumph* (novel) 68, *Ambassador's Journal* 69, *Indian Painting* (co-author) 69, *A Contemporary Guide to Economics, Peace and Laughter* 71, *Economics and the Public Purpose* 74.
30 Francis Avenue, Cambridge, Mass., U.S.A.

Galbraith, Vivian Hunter, M.A., F.B.A.; British historian; b. 15 Dec. 1889; m. Georgina R. Cole-Baker 1921; one s. two d.; ed. Highgate School, Manchester Univ., and Balliol Coll., Oxford.
Assistant Lecturer Manchester Univ. 20-21; Asst. Keeper Public Records 21-28; Fellow and Tutor in Modern History Balliol Coll. and Univ. Reader in Diplomatic History 28-37; Prof. History, Edinburgh Univ. 37-44, London Univ. 44-47, Dir. Inst. Hist. Research 44-47; Regius Prof. of Modern History Oxford Univ. 47-57; mem. Royal Comm. Ancient and Hist. Monuments England and Scotland; Hon. D.Litt. (Belfast, Edinburgh and Manchester).
Leisure interest: golf.
Publs. *Anonimalle Chronicle of St. Mary's Abbey York* 27, *Introduction to use of the Public Records* 34, *Literacy of Medieval English Kings* 35, *St. Albans Chronicle 1406-1420* 37, *Roger Wendover and Matthew Paris* 44, *Studies in the Public Records* 48, *Herefordshire Domesday* 50, *Historical Research in Medieval England* 51, *The Making of Domesday Book* 61, *The Historian at Work* 62, *An Introduction to the Study of History* 64, *The Administrative Importance of Domesday Book* 74.
20A Bradmore Road, Oxford, OX2 6QP, England. Telephone: Oxford 59318.

Gale, Ernest Frederick, PH.D., SC.D., F.R.S.; British professor of chemical microbiology; b. 15 July 1914, Luton, Beds.; s. of Ernest Francis Edward Gale and Nellie Annie Gale; m. Eiry Mair Jones 1937; one s.; ed. Weston-super-Mare Grammar School and St. John's Coll., Cambridge.
Research in chemical microbiology, Cambridge 37-; Senior Student, Royal Comm. for Exhbn. of 1851 39-41; Beit Memorial Fellow 41-43; mem. Staff, Medical Research Council 43-60, Dir. M.R.C. Unit for Chemical Microbiology 48-60; Prof. of Chemical Microbiology, Univ. of Cambridge 60-; Fellow, St. John's Coll., Cambridge 40-; Meetings Sec. Soc. for Gen. Microbiology 52-58, Int. Rep. 63-67, Pres. 67-69; Herter Lecturer, Baltimore 48; Hanna Lecturer, Western Reserve Univ. 51; Harvey Lecturer, N.Y. 55; Malcolm Lecturer, Syracuse Univ. 67; Linacre Lecturer, St. John's Coll., Cambridge Univ. 73; Fellow of Royal Soc. 53-; Leeuwenhoek Lecturer, Royal Soc. 56.
Leisure interests: reading, cine-photography.
Publs. *Chemical Activities of Bacteria* 47, *Organisation and Synthesis in Bacteria* 59, *Promotion and Prevention of Synthesis in Bacteria* 68, *The Molecular Basis of Antibiotic Reaction* 72; scientific papers and reviews in journals of biochemistry and microbiology.
Sub-Department of Chemical Microbiology, Department of Biochemistry, University of Cambridge, Cambridge; Home: 25 Luard Road, Cambridge, England. Telephone: 0223-51781 (Univ.); 0223-47585 (Home).

Gale, General Sir Richard, G.C.B., K.B.E., D.S.O., M.C.; British army officer; b. 25 July 1896; ed. Merchant Taylors School, Aldenham and Royal Military Coll.
Commissioned Worcestershire Regt. 15; served through all ranks to General 44; Commdr. 6th Airborne Div. 42-44, 1st British Airborne Corps 44-45; Deputy Commdr. 1st Allied Airborne Army; G.O.C. 1st Infantry Div., Palestine 46-47, British Troops Mediterranean 48-49; Lieut.-Gen. 47; Dir.-Gen. Mil. Training 49; Gen. 52; Commdr. Northern Army Group and C.-in-C. British Army of the Rhine 52-56; Deputy Supreme Allied Commdr. Europe 58-60; Commdr. Legion of Merit and Légion d'Honneur, Croix de Guerre, Grand Officer de la Couronne.
Publs. *With 6th Airborne Division in Normandy, The Worcestershire Regiment, Battles of the Bible* 63, *Call to Arms* (autobiography) 68, *Kings at Arms* 71.
Hampton Court Palace, Surrey, England.

Galea, Joseph, M.B.E., M.D., D.P.H., M.F.C.M., R.C.P.; British doctor and writer; b. 1902, Qormi, Malta; s. of Louis Galea and Maria Cilia; m. Hilda Portelli 1932; two d.; ed. St. Aloysius Coll., Univs. of Malta and Edinburgh.
Port Health Officer, Malta 30-37; M.O.H. Valletta 37-48; Senior Health Officer, Ministry of Health 48-51; Chief Govt. M.O. and Superintendent of Public Health of Malta 51-61; Prof. and Examiner, Royal Univ. Malta; Pres. Acad. of Maltese Writers, Soc. Welfare of Mentally Handicapped, Royal Soc. of Health (Malta Branch), Asscn. Maltese Writers, Qormi Civic Cttee., Malta Horticultural Soc.; mem. Govt. Contracts Comm. of Malta, Malta Relief Fund, Industrial Injuries Board, Malta Historical Society; holds Medal and Prizes for Maltese literary work; Officer of the Order of St. John of Jerusalem; Knight of Grace of the Sovereign Order of Malta, Grand Officer of Merit Order of Malta.
Leisure interests: travelling, book-collecting.
Publs. include: *First Aid to War Casualties, Health and Design of Dwelling Houses, The Sources of Maltese Literature, Zmien-I-Ispanjoli, Ragel Bil Ghaqal, Grajja Tal Gwerra, San Guan, Id-Dinja Rota, Bla Habi, Fiex Nasalna, History of Malta since 1530, The Health Conditions of the Maltese Islands, Short History of the Sovereign Order of Malta, Fire at the Opera House, Stories of the War in Malta.*
34 Strait Street, Valletta, Malta; and St. John Club, 50 Eaton Place, London, London, S.W.1, England. Telephone: 24311 (Malta).

Galichon, Georges, L.EN.D.; French administrator and fmr. airline executive; b. 3 Nov. 1915; ed. Lycée Janson-de-Sailly and Ecole des Sciences Politiques.
Auditeur au Conseil d'Etat 41, Maître des Requêtes 47; Dir. at the Presidency of the Council 49-55; Gen. Sec. High Cttee. of the Youth of France and Overseas Territories at the Presidency of the Council 55-58; Dir. du Cabinet, to Pierre Chatenet, Minister of the Interior 59, to the Pres. of the Repub. 61-67; Councillor of State 63-; Pres. Air France 67-75; Commdr. Légion d'Honneur, Croix de Guerre.
Home: 6 rue de Seine, Paris 6e, France.

Galili, Israel; Israeli politician; b. May 1911, Brailov, Ukraine (now U.S.S.R.); ed. Ahad Ha'am Primary School.
Went to Palestine 14; later worked on buildings and in printing; f. Asscn. of Working Youth 24; helped establish Kibbutz Na'an 30; Haganah activities 35-48; Deputy Minister of Defence, Israel Govt. 48; mem. Knesset; Minister without Portfolio (in charge of Information Services) 66; Minister without Portfolio, 69-; mem. Achdut Ha'Avoda Party.
The Knesset, Jerusalem; Kibbutz Na'an, Israel.

Galindo Pohl, Reinaldo; Salvadorian diplomatist; b. 18 Oct. 1918; m. Esperanza Vélez 1954; one s.; ed. Univ. of El Salvador.

President Nat. Constitutional Assembly 50; Minister of Educ. 50-56; Amb. in special mission to Chile 52; Prof. Constitutional Law and Philosophy of Law, Univ. of El Salvador 59-68; Dir. Bureau of Relations with Mem. States, UNESCO 57-59; mem. Inter-American Comm. n Human Rights 60-64; Perm. Rep. of El Salvador to UN 67-; mem. Inter-American Juridical Cttee. 72-74, Pres. 74-.
Leisure interest: hiking.
Permanent Mission of El Salvador to the United Nations, 211 East 43rd Street, Suites 1302-1303, New York, N.Y. 10017, U.S.A.

Gall, Joseph Grafton, PH.D.; American professor of biology; b. 14 April 1928, Washington, D.C.; s. of late John C. and Elsie (Rosenberger) Gall; m. Dolores M. Hogge 1955; one s. one d.; ed. Yale Univ.
Instructor, Asst. Prof., Assoc. Prof., Prof., Dept. of Zoology, Univ. of Minnesota 52-64; Prof. of Biology and Molecular Biophysics and Biochemistry, Yale Univ. 64-; mem. Cell Biology Study Section, Nat. Insts. of Health 63-67, Chair. 72-; mem. Nat. Acad. of Sciences, American Acad. of Arts and Sciences.
Leisure interest: collecting books on the history of biology.
Publs. scientific articles on chromosome structure, nucleic acid biochemistry, cell fine structure, organelles of the cell.
118 Kline Biology Tower, Yale University, New Haven, Conn.; Home: 3 Crestview Drive, North Haven, Conn., U.S.A.

Gallagher, Francis George Kenna, C.M.G., LL.B.; British diplomatist; b. 25 May 1917, London; s. of George and Joanna Gallagher; ed. London Univ.
Entered civil service 35; active service, R.A.F. 41-45; entered diplomatic service 45; Vice-Consul, Marseilles 48; Second-Sec., Paris 48; First Sec., Western Orgs. Dept., Foreign Office 50; Head of Chancery, Damascus 53; Asst. Head, Northern Dept. 56, Mutual Aid Dept. 59; Head, European Econ. Orgs. Dept. 60; Commercial Counsellor, Berne 63; Head, Western Economic Dept., C.R.O. 65; Asst. Under-Sec. of State, Foreign Office 68; Amb., Head of Del. to OECD 71-.
Leisure interests: music, chess.
Organization for Economic Co-operation and Development, Château de la Muette, 2 rue André Pascal, Paris 16e, France.
Telephone: 524 9821.

Galley, Robert; French engineer and politician; b. 11 Jan. 1921; ed. Lycée Louis-le-Grand, Paris, Lycée Hoche, Versailles, École centrale des arts et manufactures and Ecole Nat. Supérieure du pétrole et des moteurs.
Compagnie Chérifienne des Pétroles 50-54; in Commissariat à l'Energie atomique 55-66; Pres. of Perm. Comm. for Electronics, Dept. of the Plan 66-; Minister of Supply and Housing May-July 68, of Scientific Research and Atomic Energy 68-69, of Posts 69-72, of Transport 72-73, of the Armed Forces 73-74, of Supply 74-; Commdr. Légion d'Honneur; Compagnon de la Libération, Croix de Guerre (39-45).
1 place de la Porte-de-Passy, Paris 16e, France.

Gallico, Paul William, B.S.; American writer; b. 26 July 1897, New York City; s. of Paolo Gallico and Hortense Erlich; m. Baroness Virginia von Falz-Fein (née Curtis-Bennett) 1963; two s. (of previous marriage); ed. Clinton High School, and Columbia Univ.
Seaman Gunner in U.S. Naval Reserve during First World War; Sports Editor *New York Daily News* 22-36; freelance writer 36-; War Corresp. *Cosmopolitan* magazine during Second World War; contributor to *Saturday Evening Post, Cosmopolitan, Vanity Fair, Red Book, Esquire,* etc.
Leisure interests: fencing, deep-sea fishing.
Publs. *The Snow Goose* 41, *The Lonely* 47, *Confessions*

of a Story Writer 48, *Jennie* 50, *The Small Miracle* 51, *Snowflake, Trial by Terror* 52, *The Foolish Immortals* 53, *Love of Seven Dolls* 54, *Ludmila* 55, *Thomasina* 57, *The Steadfast Man, Flowers for Mrs. Harris, The Hurricane Story* 59, *Mrs. Harris Goes to New York* 60, *Too Many Ghosts* 61, *Further Confessions of a Story-Teller* 61, *Scruffy* 62, *Coronation* 62, *The Day the Guinea Pig Talked, Love, Let Me Not Hunger* 63, *The Hand of Mary Constable* 64, *The Silent Miaow* 64, *The Day Jean Pierre was Pignapped* 64, *Mrs. Harris M.P.* 65, *The Day Jean Pierre went round the World* 65, *The Man who was Magic* 66, *The Story of a Silent Night* 67, *Manxmouse* 68, *The Poseidon Adventure* 69, *The Day Jean-Pierre joined the Circus* 69, *Matilda* 70, *The Zoo Gang* 71, *Honourable Cat* 72, *The Boy who Invented the Bubble Gun* 74, *Mrs. Harris Goes to Moscow* 74, *Miracle in the Wilderness* 75.
Apt. 7, Le Ruscino, Quai Antoine Premier, Monaco.

Gallien, Louis; French embryologist and university professor; b. 2 Jan. 1908, Cherbourg, Manche; s. of Louis V. and Eugenie Gallien; m. Andrée Guéguen 1932; one s. one d.; ed. Lycée de Cherbourg, Univ. de Caen and Univ. de Paris à la Sorbonne.
Assistant Prof. Univ. of Paris 32-37; Prof. Fac. Sc. Univ. of Rennes-Caen 38-44; Prof. Univ. of Paris 45; Dir. Laboratoire Embryologie 54; mem. Institut de France, Acad. of Arts, Science and Letters, Padua; assoc. mem. Académie Royale de Belgique; Foreign mem. Accad. Nazionale dei Lincei; Grand Prix des Sciences Physiques de l'Académie des Sciences; Dr. h.c. Univ. de Louvain, Officer Légion d'Honneur.
Leisure interests: poetry, philosophy.
Publs. *La Sexualité* 41, *Le Parasitisme* 43, *La Sélection animale* 46, *L'insémination artificielle chez les animaux domestiques* 48, *Problèmes et Concepts de l'Embryologie expérimentale* 58, *Sexe détermination* 59, *L'Embryologie* 65, *Différenciation et Organogenèse Sexuelle des Métazoaires* 73, *Bases Cytologiques et Génétiques de la Sexualité* 73.
31 rue Gazan, Paris 14, France.
Telephone: 588-42-97.

Gallimard, Claude; French publisher; b. 10 Jan. 1914, Paris; ed. Faculté de Droit, Paris.
Joined Editions Gallimard 37, Asst. Dir.-Gen. 66-.
Editions Gallimard, 5 rue Sébastien-Bottin, Paris 7e, France.

Galliner, Peter; British publisher; b. 19 Sept. 1920, Berlin, Germany; s. of Dr. Moritz Galliner and Hedwig Isaac; m. Edith Marguerite Goldschmidt 1948; one d.; ed. in Berlin and London.
Worked for Reuters, London 42-45; Foreign Man. *Financial Times*, London 45-61; Chair. of Board and Man. Dir. Ullstein Publishing Group, Berlin 61-64; Vice-Chair. and Man. Dir. British Printing Corpn. Publishing Group, London 67-70; Int. Publishing Consultant 65-67, 70-75; Dir. Int. Press Inst.; Fed. Cross of Merit, First Class (Fed. Germany).
Leisure interests: reading, music.
27 Queen's Grove, St. John's Wood, London, N.W.8, England.
Telephone: 01-722-0361.

Gallopin, Roger Edouard, D.IUR.; Swiss lawyer; b. 14 Dec. 1909, Geneva; s. of Edouard Gallopin and Marie Coulin; m. Monica Speitel de Cussy 1959; one s. one d.; ed. Munich and Geneva Univs., London School of Economics.
Barrister, Geneva 35-37; Head of P.O.W. section, Int. Red Cross Cttee., Second World War; Dep. Sec.-Gen. Int. Cttee. of the Red Cross 43-50, missions in Europe, Africa, Asia, America, Exec. Dir. 50-; Del. to Int. Red Cross Confs., Stockholm, Toronto, Delhi, Vienna, Istanbul; mem. and Dir.-Gen., Pres. Exec. Council 73-; mem. Int. Lawyers' Club, Geneva; several foreign distinctions awarded by govts. or nat. Red Cross Socs.

Leisure interests: reading, various outdoor sports. Publ. *Le Conflit anglo-irlandais considérémente spécial depuis les articles d'accord de 1921* 35.
50 Quai Gustave Ador, Geneva, Switzerland.
Telephone: 35-65-25.

Gallup, George Horace, M.A., PH.D., LL.D.; American statistician; b. 18 Nov. 1901, Jefferson, Iowa; m. Ophelia Smith Miller 1925; two s. one d.; ed. Univ. of Iowa.
Lecturer Univ. of Iowa 23-29; Head, Dept. of Journalism, Drake Univ. 29-31; Prof. of Journalism, Northwestern Univ. 31-32; Dir. of Research, Young and Rubicam Advertising Agency 32-47, Vice-Pres. 37-47; Prof. Pulitzer School of Journalism, Columbia Univ. 35-37; founded American Inst. of Public Opinion 35, Dir. 35-; founded British Inst. of Public Opinion 36; Pres. Nat. Municipal League 52-56; Chair. of Council, Chair. All-America Cities Award Cttee.; Chair. of Board, The Gallup Org. Inc., Chair. Gallup Int. Research Insts. Inc.; Hon. D.Sc. (Tufts Univ.), Hon. LL.D. (Drake, Boston, Chattanooga, Northwestern, Colgate, Rider and Iowa Univs.); numerous awards.
Publs. include: *Public Opinion in a Democracy* 39. *Guide to Public Opinion Polls* 44, 48, *The Miracle Ahead* 64, *The Sophisticated Poll Watcher's Guide* 72.
The Great Road, Princeton, New Jersey, U.S.A.

Galsworthy, Sir Arthur Norman, K.C.M.G.; British diplomatist; b. 1 July 1916; s. of the late Capt. Arthur and the late Violet (née Harrison) Galsworthy; m. Margaret Agnes Hiscocks 1940 (died 1973); two s.; ed. Emanuel School and Corpus Christi Coll., Cambridge.
Entered Colonial Office 38; on active service 39-45; returned to Colonial Office 45-51; Chief Sec., West African Inter-Territorial Secr., Accra 51-54; Colonial Office 54-66; Deputy Under-Sec. of State, Commonwealth Office (later Foreign and Commonwealth Office) 66-69; British High Commr. in New Zealand 69-72, also to Tonga and Western Samoa (both non-resident) 70-72; Gov. Pitcairn Islands 70-72; Amb. to Ireland 73-76.
Leisure interests: bird-watching, riding, fishing.
c/o Foreign and Commonwealth Office, King Charles Street, London, S.W.1., England.

Galsworthy, Sir John, K.C.V.O., C.M.G.; British diplomatist; b. 19 June 1919, London; s. of Arthur Galsworthy and Violet Gertrude (Harrison) Galsworthy; m. Jennifer Ruth Johnstone 1942; one s. three d.; ed. Emanuel School, and Corpus Christi Coll., Cambridge.
Served in H.M. Forces 39-41; Foreign Office 41-46; Third Sec., Madrid 46; Second Sec., Vienna 49; First Sec., Athens 51; Foreign Office 54; Bangkok 58; counsellor, British del. to EEC, 62; Econ. Counsellor, Bonn 64-67, Paris 67-70; Minister (European Economic Affairs), Paris 70-71; Amb. to Mexico 72-.
Leisure interest: fishing.
British Embassy, Lerma 71, Cuauhtémoc, México, D.F., Mexico.

Galuška, Miroslav; Czechoslovak journalist and diplomatist; b. 9 Oct. 1922, Prague; m. Milena Galuška 1949; two s.
Foreign Editor *Rudé Právo* 45-48; Editor *Tvorba* 48-52; Head, Press Dept., Foreign Ministry 52-58; Amb. to U.K. 58-61; Deputy Editor-in-Chief *Rudé Právo* 61-62; Editor-in-Chief *Kulturni Tvorba* 63-64; Chair. British Cttee. of Czechoslovak Soc. for Int. Relations, Prague 63-66; Amb. and Commr.-Gen., Czechoslovak participation at World Exhbn., Montreal 64-67, Osaka 69-71; Minister of Culture and Information April-Dec. 68; Minister of Culture Jan.-July 69; Deputy to Czech Nat. Council 68-69.
Leisure interests: culture, sport.
Na Ostrohu 17, Prague 6, Czechoslovakia.
Telephone: 32-30-96.

Galvêas, Ernane; Brazilian economist and banker; b. 1 Oct. 1922, Cachoeiro do Itapemirim; s. of Jose Galvêas and Maria de Oliveira; m. Odaléa dos Santo 1948; one s. one d.; ed. Coll of Economics and Finance Rio de Janeiro, Centro de Estudios Monetarios Latino Americanos, Mexico and Yale Univ.
Formerly Prof. of Banking and Finance, Coll. o Economics and Finance, Rio de Janeiro, subsequently Prof. of Int. Trade, of Monetary Policy and of Int Monetary Policy; Assoc. Chief, Econs. Dept., Supervisory Council for Finance and Credit (SUMOC) 53-61; Econ. Consultant to Minister of Finance 61-63; Financial Dir. Merchant Marine Comm. 63-65; Dir. Foreign Trade Dept., Banco do Brasil 66-68; Pres. Banco Central do Brasil 68-74.
Publs. Numerous articles on economic and financia topics.
Avenida Atlântica, 2492 Apt. 301, Rio de Janeiro, Brazil.

Gálvez-Barnes, Roberto; Honduran aeronautica engineer, politician and diplomatist; b. 18 May 1925, Puerto Cortes; s. of Juan Manuel Gálvez and Laura Barnes de Gálvez; m. Lucía Cristina Montes de Gálvez 1948; two s. three d.; ed. Louisiana State Univ. and Mass. Inst. of Technology, U.S.A.
Captain in charge of Ground School for Pilots, Honduran Air Force 49-50; Dir.-Gen. of Civil Aeronautics 50-55; Man. Honduran Cotton Co-operative and Honduras Industrial S.R.L. 55-56; Minister of Communications and Public Works Jan.-Oct. 56; mem. Mil. Junta 56-57; Man. Honduras Industrial, S.R.L. 57-58; Vice-Pres. and Gen. Man. TAN airlines 58-70; Amb. to U.S.A. 70-74; Medal of Merit, First Class (Ministry of Defence, Honduras); Order of Morazán (Honduras); Order of Vasco Nuñez de Balboa (Panama); Order of the Propitious Cloud (China).
Leisure interests: music, fencing.
9A Calle 516, Tegucigalpa, D.C., Honduras.
Telephone: 2-9156 (Home).

Galvin, Robert W.; American executive; b. 9 Oct. 1922, Marshfield, Wis.; m. Mary Barnes 1944; two s. two d.; ed. Univs. of Notre Dame and Chicago.
Motorola, Inc. Chicago 40-, Chair. of Board; Dir. Harris Trust and Savings Bank, Chicago; Trustee Illinois Inst. of Technology; Fellow, Univ. of Notre Dame; Dir. Junior Achievement of Chicago; mem. President's Comm. on Int. Trade and Investment; Electronic Industries Asscn. Medal of Honour 70.
Leisure interests: skiing, water-skiing, tennis, horse-riding.
5725 East River Road, Chicago, Ill. 60631, U.S.A.

Gamazi, Lt.-Gen. Muhammad Abdul Ghani; Egyptian army officer; b. 1920; ed. Egyptian Mil. Acad., Cairo, and in U.S.A. and U.S.S.R.
Commander of Armoured Battalion 59; Chief of Mil. Operations of Land Forces 66; Chief of Staff of Second Army 67; in charge of army training 71; Deputy Chief of Staff 73; Commdr. Suez Front Oct. 73; Chief of Staff Dec. 73-; negotiated disengagement agreement Jan. 74; Deputy Premier, Minister of War Dec. 74-; Second Deputy Prime Minister 75-.
Ministry of War, Cairo, Egypt.

Gamba, Pierino; Italian conductor; b. 16 Sept. 1936, Rome.
First concert Opera House, Rome 45; has conducted a total of over 120 orchestras in concerts throughout Europe, America and Africa; guest conductor with Philharmonia Orchestra, Accademia di Santa Cecilia, Rome, Danish State Radio Orchestra, Belgian Nat. Orchestra and numerous other orchestras; Hon. Dir. nine symphony orchestras; Arnold Bax Medal 62.
c/o Symphonicum Europae, B.P.1, Monte Carlo, Monaco.

Gambrell, David Henry; American politician; b. 20 Dec. 1929, Atlanta, Ga.; *s.* of E. Smythe Gambrell and Kathleen Hagood; *m.* Luck Flanders; one *s.* three *d.*; ed. Davidson Coll. and Harvard Law School.
Practising lawyer, Atlanta 52-, Partner Gambrell & Mobley 63-; Chair. Georgia Democratic Party; Senator from Georgia 71-73; Pres. Atlanta Bar Asscn. 65, Georgia Bar Asscn. 67.
3820 Castlegate Drive, N.W., Atlanta, Ga. 30327, U.S.A.

Gamedze, Dr. A. B., M.A.; Swazi teacher, theologian and diplomatist; b. 3 April 1921, Shiselweni District; *s.* of Rev. John Mbulawa Gamedze and Sarah Mavosho (née Shongwe) Gamedze; *m.*; three *s.* three *d.*; ed. at Mhlosheni and at Matsapa, Swaziland, at Umphumulo Inst., Natal, Adams Coll., Natal, and Wheaton Coll., Ill., U.S.A.
Head Teacher, Jerusalem School 42, transferred to Franson Christian High School 43; Head Teacher, Makhonza School 46-47; started first rural market for Jerusalem and New Haven Farmers Asscn.; at Wheaton Coll., Ill., studying education, Christian education and theology 47-51; Lecturer, Evangelical Teacher Training Coll., Natal 51-56; Founder and Editor *Africa's Hope* 55-61; Pres. African Teachers' Christian Fellowship 56; ordained Minister of Evangelical Church 56; assisted Organizing Insp. of Religious Educ. in Secondary Schools, Transvaal 58; Lecturer in Divinity and Educ. and Chaplain of Univ. of Fort Hare 60-61; joined staff of Franson Christian High School 62; Superintendent (Grantee) of all Evangelical Church Schools 62-65; Vice-Pres. Evangelical Church; Vice-Pres. Swaziland Conf. of Churches 64; Senior Liaison Officer, Swaziland 65-67; mem. Senate 67-; Minister of Educ., Swaziland 67-71; High Commr. in U.K., concurrently Amb. to France, Belgium and Federal Germany 71-72; Sec. to Swazi nation 73-74, then private sec. to King Sobhuza II, then Chief of Protocol, Dept. of Foreign Affairs; Editor *Imbokodvo Bulletin* 69-70; Dir. of Church Extension in northern Swaziland; dir. of various cos.; Hon. LL.D. Wheaton Coll., U.S.A. 68.
Leisure interests: writing, walking, Evangelical Church in Swaziland, indoor games.
P.O. Box 868, Mbabane, Swaziland.
Telephone: 2661 (Office), 2427 (Home).

Gamzatov, Rasul Gamzatovich; Soviet poet and politician; b. 8 Sept. 1923, Tsadasa, Daghestan, A.S.S.R.; ed. Moscow A. M. Gorky Literary Inst.
National poet of Dagestan; mem. Communist Party of Soviet Union 44-; Chair. of Board of Union of Dagestan Writers 51-; Deputy of Supreme Soviet of U.S.S.R. 62-; State Prize 52, Lenin Prize 63, Orders of Lenin 60, of Red Banner of Labour (2), etc.
Publs. *High Stellars* 62, *Mountains and Valleys* 63, *And Stars are Talking* 64, *Selected Lyrics* 65, *Sick Teeth* (poetry) 67, *My Daghestan* 68.
Daghestan A.S.S.R. Union of Writers, Makhachkala, U.S.S.R.

Ganao, David-Charles; Congolese politician; b. 20 July 1928, Djambala; *m.* Shirley O'Hayes 1964; four *s.*; ed. Teachers Training Coll.
Teacher, then Headmaster; Diplomatic training in France 60; Head of Political Affairs, Congolese Foreign Ministry 60-63; Minister of Foreign Affairs 63-68, of Co-operation, Tourism and Civil Aviation 66-68; Amb. and Perm. Rep. to the UN, Geneva 69-73; Amb. to Switzerland 70-73; Minister of Foreign Affairs 73-75.
c/o Ministry of Foreign Affairs, Brazzaville, People's Republic of the Congo.

Gance, Abel; French film director and writer; b. 25 Oct. 1889; ed. Collège Chaptal, Paris.
President Television Cttee. Radiodiffusion-Télévision française 58; Théatre de l'Empire (renamed Théatre Abel Gance) 61; Officier Légion d'Honneur, Commdr. des Arts et Lettres; Grand Prix Nat. du Cinéma 74.
Invented triple screen 26, sound perspective 32, pictoscope 33.
Director of numerous films including: *La Folie du Docteur Tube* 16, *Barberousse* 16, *Les Gaz Mortels* 16, *J'accuse* 18, *La Roue* 22, *Napoléon* 26, *La Fin du Monde* 30, *Mater Dolorosa* 32, *Le Maître de forges* 33, *La Dame aux camélias* 34, *Lucrèce Borgia* 35, *Un Grand Amour de Beethoven* 36, *Paradis Perdu* 39, *Vénus aveugle* 40, *La Capitaine Fracasse* 42, *La Tour de Nesle* 54, *Austerlitz* 60, *Cyrano et d'Artagnan* 62.
Publs. *Un Doigt sur le clavier* (poetry), *La Victoire de Samothrace* (play), *J'accuse* 22, *La beauté à travers le cinéma* 26, *Prisme* 30.
22 rue de l'Yvette, Paris 16e, France.

Gandar, Leslie Walter; New Zealand sheep farmer and politician; b. 26 Jan. 1919, Wellington; *s.* of Max Gandar; *m.* Monica Justine Smith 1944; four *s.* two *d.*; ed. Wellington Coll. and Victoria Univ., Wellington.
War service in R.N.Z.A.F. 40-44; sheep farming 45-; mem. Pohangina County Council 52-69, Chair. 59-69; mem. M'tu Catchment Board 56-68; mem. Massey Univ. Council 63, Chancellor 70-75; Minister of Educ., Science and Technology Dec. 75-.
Parliament Buildings, Wellington; Home: Moorlands, No. 6 RD, Feilding, New Zealand.

Gandhi, Indira Priyadarshini; Indian politician; b. 19 Nov. 1917, Allahabad; *d.* of late Pandit Jawaharlal and Kamala Nehru; *m.* Feroz Gandhi 1942 (died 1960); two *s.*; ed. in India, Switzerland and Somerville Coll., Oxford.
Founded Vanar Sena, a children's organization to aid Congress non-co-operation movement 29; joined Congress 38; imprisoned for thirteen months 42; hostess for her father 46-64; worked in riot areas under Mahatma Gandhi 47; Minister for Information and Broadcasting, New Delhi 64-66, Prime Minister 66-, also in charge of Planning Ministry 67; Minister of Atomic Energy 67-, of External Affairs 67-69, of Finance 69-70, of Home Affairs 70-73, of Information and Broadcasting 71-, of Space 72-, of Planning Jan. 75-, of Defence Nov.-Dec. 75; mem. Rajya Sabha 64-67, mem. Lok Sabha 67-, leader Congress Parl. Party 67-; Founder-Pres. Bal Sahayog, New Delhi; Pres. Training Centre for Vagrant Boys, Allahabad; Vice-Pres. Indian Council of Child Welfare; Chair. Standing Cttee., Children's Film Soc.; mem. Standing Cttee. Cen. Social Welfare Board, Children's Book Trust; mem. Working Cttee., All-India Congress Cttee., Pres. Women's Dept., mem. Cen. Electoral Board, Youth Advisory Board; Pres. All-India Congress Party 59-60; mem. UNESCO Exec. Board 60; Deputy Pres. Int. Union of Child Welfare; Howland Memorial Prize, Yale Univ. 60; Hon. D.Litt. (Agra.) Hon. D.C.L. (Oxford), Bharat Ratna Award 71.
Leisure interests: folk and classical music, folk dances, bird-watching.
Publ. *India: The Speeches and Reminiscences of Indira Gandhi* 75.
Office of the Prime Minister, New Delhi, India.

Gandhi, Manmohan Purushottam, M.A., F.R.ECON.S., F.S.S.; Indian businessman; b. 5 Nov. 1901, Junagad; *m.* Rambhaben Sukhlal 1926; ed. Bahauddin Coll., Junagad, Gujerat Coll., Ahmedabad, Bombay Univ., Hindu Univ., Benares.
Statistical Asst. Govt. of Bombay Labour Office 26; Asst. Sec. Indian Currency League, Bombay 26; Sec. Indian Chamber of Commerce 26-36; Officer-in-Charge Credit Dept., Nat. City Bank of New York, Calcutta 36-37; Chief Commercial Man. Rohtas Industries Ltd., Dalmia Cement Ltd.; Editor *Major Industries of India* and *Indian Textile Industry* (annuals) 37-; Dir. Indian

Sugar Syndicate Ltd., Indian Link Chain Manufacturers Ltd., E. India Cotton Assen. Ltd., Saru Eng. Corpn. Ltd. 59-; mem. All India Council Technical Educ., Advisory Council on Trade, All India Handloom Board, Small Scale Industries Board 66-, Senate and Syndicate, Bombay Univ. 62-70, Fed. Of Indian Chambers of Commerce and Industry 29-30; Sec. Indian Nat. Cttee. Int. Chamber of Commerce, Calcutta 29-31; Sec. Indian Sugar Mills Assoc. 32-36; Adviser Indian Tariff Board 47; mem. E. Indian Railway Advisory Cttee. 39-41; Controller of Supplies for Bengal 41-43; Hon. Prof. Sydenham Coll. of Commerce and Econs. 43-49; Dean Faculty of Commerce, Bombay Univ. 68-69; Hon. Presidency Magistrate and J.P., Greater Bombay 49-69.
Leisure interests: verse-making, tennis, badminton.
Publs. *A Mercantile Marine for India* 25, *Foreign Capital in India* 26, *Economic Planning in India* 35, *A Revised Tariff Policy for India* 37, *Unemployment in India* 38, *Problems of the Indian Sugar Industry* 45, *Handloom Weaving Industry Annual* 52-53, *Some Impressions of Japan* 55, *Indian Sugar Industry Annual* 34-64.
Nanabhay Mansion, Pherozeshah Mehta Road, Fort, Bombay, India.
Telephone: 261047 (Office); 358805 (Home).

Ganilau, Sir Ratu Penaia Kanatabatu, C.M.G., C.V.O., K.B.E., D.S.O., E.D.; Fijian politician; b. 28 July 1918; ed. Queen Victoria School, Fiji.
With Fiji Civil Service 37-41; Capt. 4th Battalion, Fiji Mil. Forces 40-46; Asst. Rehabilitation Officer 46; District Officer 48-53; Fiji Mil. Forces, Malaya 53-56; Commdg. Officer 1st Battalion, Malaya 56, Roko 57; mem. Legislative Council 58-63; Sec. for Fijian Affairs 65-70; Minister for Home Affairs 70-72; Leader of Govt. in Senate 70-72; Minister for Communications, Works and Tourism 72-; Deputy Prime Minister 73-.
Ministry of Communications, Works and Tourism, Suva, Fiji.

Gannon, Rev. Robert Ignatius, S.J., A.B., LITT.D., A.M., S.T.D., L.H.D., LL.D.; American ecclesiastic and educationist; b. 20 April 1893, St. George, Staten Island, N.Y.; *s.* of Frank S. and Marietta Burrows Gannon; ed. Georgetown and Gregorian Univs., and Christ's Coll., Cambridge.
Entered Society of Jesus 13; Ordained Priest 26; Instructor in English and Philosophy Fordham Univ. 19-22, in English 22-23; Dean St. Peters' Coll. Jersey City 30-36, Hudson Coll. of Commerce and Finance 32-35; Pres. Fordham Univ. 36-49; Dir. Mt. Mauresa House of Retreats 49-52; Rector, St. Ignatius Loyola Church of New York 52-58; Superior Jesuit Missions House 58-64; Pres. Emeritus Fordham Univ. 64-; Hon. Life Mem. Newcomen Soc.; F.R.S.A.; Hon. Vice-Pres. Pan-American Soc.; Trustee Free Europe Univ. in Exile; Trustee Netherlands America Foundation; Knight Order of Orange-Nassau (Netherlands), Knight Commdr. with Star, Order of Polonia Restituta, Knight of Sovereign Military Order of Malta.
Publs. *The Technique of the One-Act Play* 25, *After Black Coffee* 47, *The Poor Old Liberal Arts* 61, *Cardinal Spellman: a Biography* 62, *After More Black Coffee* 64, *The Story of Fordham* 66.
St. Ignatius House of Retreats, Searingtown Road, Manhasset, N.Y. 11030, U.S.A.
Telephone: 516-621-8300.

Ganshof, François Louis, LL.D., D.LIT.; Belgian professor of history and law; b. 14 March 1895, Bruges; *s.* of Arthur Ganshof and Louise van der Meersch; *m.* Nelly Kirkpatrick 1920; one *s.* three *d.*; ed. Royal Athenaeum, Bruges, and Univs. of Ghent and Paris.
Served at the Bar in Brussels 22-23; Lecturer 23-29, and Prof. 29-61, of Medieval History and Legal History, Univ. of Ghent; served in Belgian Army in both World Wars; Hon. Major; mem. Royal Flemish Acad. of Sciences of Belgium; corresp. F.B.A. and F.R.H.S. Dr. h.c. Glasgow, London, Cambridge.
Publs. *Etudes sur les Ministériales* 26, *Recherches sur le tribunaux de châtellenie* 32, *Etude sur le développement des villes entre Loire et Rhin* 43, *La Flandre sous le Premiers Comtes* 49, *Feudalism* 54, *La Belgique Carolingienne* 58, *Recherches sur les capitulaires* 58, *Charlemagne et les institutions de la monarchie franque* 65, *Frankish institutions under Charlemagne* 68, *Histoire des relations internationales*, Vol. I, *Le moyen âge* 69, *Droit romain dans les capitulaires* 69, *The Carolingians and the Frankish Monarchy* 71.
Rue Jacques Jordaens 12, 1050 Brussels, Belgium.
Telephone: 481565.

Ganshof van der Meersch, Viscount Walter, LL.D.; Belgian jurist; b. 1900, Bruges; *m.* Elizabeth Orts 1923; one *s.* one *d.*; ed. King's Coll., Wimbledon, England, Royal Athenaeum, Bruges, and Univs. of Paris and Brussels.
Professor of Constitutional Law 38, European Law 58, Comparative Law 60, Univ. of Brussels; Pres. Inst. of European Studies, Brussels, and Inter-university Centre of Public Law; Pres. Inter-Univ. Centre of Comparative Law; Judge Advocate-Gen. 40; Served in Belgian Army in both World Wars; Lieut.-Gen. High Commr. for Security of the Realm 43; mem. Supreme Court of Justice 47-; Minister of Gen. Affairs in Africa 60; Judge ad hoc, Int. Court of Justice, the Hague 60-68; Attorney-Gen. 68-; Judge, European Court of Human Rights, Strasbourg 73-; Lecturer, Hague Acad. of Int. Law 75; Francqui Chair., Univ. Louvain 75; Hon. Bencher Gray's Inn, London; mem. Académie Internationale de Droit comparé, Académie Royale des Sciences d'Outremer, Académie Royale des Sciences de Belgique; Hon. C.B. (U.K.); Grand Cross Order of Crown (Belgium); Grand Cross Order of Léopold (Belgium); Commdr. Legion of Merit (U.S.A.); Commdr. Légion d'Honneur; Grand Officier Order Crown of Oak (Luxembourg); Belgian and French Croix de Guerre and other war medals.
Publs. *Pouvoir de fait et règle de droit dans le fonctionnement des institutions politiques* 56, *Fin de la souveraineté belge au Congo* 63, *Le droit des organisations européennes* 64, *Le droit des communautés européennes* 69.
33 avenue Jeanne, 1050 Brussels, Belgium.
Telephone: 02-6472914.

Gaponov-Grekhov, Andrei Victorovich; Soviet physicist; b. 7 June 1926, Moscow; ed. Gorky State Univ.
Postgraduate student, Gorky State Univ. 49-52; Instructor, Gorky Polytechnical Inst. 52-55; Senior Scientific Assoc., Head of Dept. of Radio Physics, Research Inst., Gorky State Univ. 55-; Corresp. mem. U.S.S.R. Acad. of Sciences 64-68, Academician 68-; State Prize 67.
Publs. numerous theoretical and experimental works in field of inducted cyclotronic radiation, which led to development of a new class of electronic instruments—masers with cyclotronic resonance.
Gorky State University, Gorky, U.S.S.R.

Garango, Lieut. Marc Tiémoko, L. en D.; Upper Voltan army officer and politician; b. 27 July 1927, Gaoua; ed. Univs. of Dakar, Paris, Aix-en-Provence.
Completed mil. training at Bingerville, Ivory Coast; served in French Army in Indochinese and Algerian campaigns; promoted to Lieut. 61, Capt. 63 Supply Officer, Upper Volta Army 65-66; Minister of Finance and Commerce 66-76; Amb. to China (Taiwan) June 66; Pres. Banque Centrale des Etats de l'Afrique de l'Ouest; Pres. Nat. Monetary Cttee. (BCEAO); Gov. Int. Monetary Fund (IMF).
c/o Ministry of Finance and Commerce, Ouagadougou, Upper Volta; 29 rue du Colisée, Paris 8e, France.

Garba, John Mamman; Nigerian civil servant and banking official; b. 25 Sept. 1918, Maiduguri; s. of late Alimji Garba Katsina and Mairo Garba; m. Amina Kumbo 1956; four s. two d.; ed. Igbobi Coll. Yaba, Agricultural School, Zaria and London School of Economics. Department of Agriculture, Nigeria 37-56; Asst. Sec. Office of Nigerian Commissioner, London 57-58; Second Sec. Office of U.K. High Commr., Ottawa 58; Acting Senior Asst. Sec., Office of Nigerian Commr., London 58-59; Asst. Pilgrim Officer, Nigerian Pilgrim Office, Khartoum 59-60; Chargé d'Affaires, later Minister, Washington, D.C. 60-61; Acting Deputy Perm. Sec., Ministry of Finance, Nigeria 61, Deputy Perm. Sec. 62; Deputy Sec. to Council of Ministers 63; Exec. Dir. Int. Bank for Reconstruction and Devt., Int. Devt. Asscn., and Int. Finance Corpn. 63-66; Amb. to Italy 66-72, concurrently accred. to Spain, Greece and Cyprus 70-72, to U.S.A. 72-75.
c/o Ministry for External Affairs, Lagos, Nigeria.

Garba, Col. Joseph Nanven; Nigerian army officer and politician; b. 17 July 1943, Langtang; m. Evelyn Okon Edem; two d.; ed. Sacred Heart School, Shendam, Nigerian Mil. School, Zaria, Men's Officer Cadet School, Aldershot, Staff Coll., Camberley, England.
Platoon Command, 4th Bn. 63, Company Command 63-64, Mortar Platoon Command 64; Second in Command Fed. Guards 64-65; Gen. Staff Officer, 3 HQ, Second Brigade 65; UN Observer, India and Pakistan 65-66; Officer Commanding Fed. Guards 66-68; Commdr. Brigade of Guards 68-75; mem. Supreme Mil. Council Aug. 75-; Commr. for External Affairs Aug. 75-.
Leisure interests: basketball, photography.
Supreme Military Council, Lagos, Nigeria.

Garbo, Greta Lovisa; American (b. Swedish) film actress; b. 18 Sept. 1905.
National Theatre 24; star of first film *Gösta Berlings Saga* in Sweden 24; went to U.S.A. 25.
Films include *Joyless Streets, The Torrent, The Temptress, Flesh and the Devil, Love, The Divine Woman, The Mysterious Lady, The Woman of Affairs, Wild Orchids, The Single Standard, The Kiss, Romance, Inspiration, Mata Hari, Grand Hotel, Queen Christina, The Painted Veil, Anna Karenina, Camille, Conquest, Ninotchka, Two Faced Woman.*
450 East 52nd Street, New York, N.Y., U.S.A.

Garbuzov, Vassili Fyodorovich; Soviet politician; b. 1911; ed. Finance and Economics Inst., Kharkov.
Dozent, Finance and Econs. Inst., Kharkov 33-42; Commissariat for Finance, Kirghizia, later All-Union Commissariat for Finance 42-44; Dir. Finance and Econs. Inst., Kiev 44-50; Chair. Ukraine State Plan 50-52; Deputy then First Deputy Minister of Finance, U.S.S.R. 52-60, Minister of Finance 60-; mem. C.P.S.U. 39-, mem. Central Cttee., C.P.S.U. 61-; Deputy to Supreme Soviet U.S.S.R. 58-; Order of Lenin, Order of the Red Banner of Labour.
Ministry of Finance, 9 Ulitsa Kuibysheva, Moscow, U.S.S.R.

García, Francisce Javier Conde; Spanish lawyer and diplomatist; b. 3 Dec. 1908; ed. Madrid Univ.
Professor Faculty of Law, Univ. of Madrid 41; Prof. Political Law, Univ. of Santiago de Compostela 43; Prof. Political Law, Univ. of Madrid 49; Prof. of Sociology; entered Diplomatic Corps 47; Dir. Inst. Political Studies 48; Nat. Adviser for Educ. 52; Pres. Spanish Cttee. of Labour and Social Sciences at UNESCO 55; fmr. Amb. to Philippines, later to Uruguay, and to Canada; Visiting Prof. Univ. of Ottawa; mem. Real Academia de Ciencias Morales y Políticas de Madrid; Gran Cruz de la Orden de Cisneros, Cruz de Isabel la Católica, Cruz de Caballero de la Real y muy distinguida Orden de Carlos III, etc.

Publs. *El Pensamiento Político de Bodino* 35, *Introducción al Derecho Político Actual* 42, *Teoría y sistema de las formas políticas* 44, *Representación política y régimen español* 45, *El saber político en Maquiavelo* 48, *Sobre los modos actuales de historiar el pensamiento político* 48, *Misión política de la inteligencia* 50, *Los supuestos históricos de la Sociología* 51, *La Revolución* 52, *El teorema político de la concurrencia en Rousseau, Introducción a la antropología de Xavier Zubiri* 53, *El Hombre-animal político* 57.
Office: 124 Springfield Road, Ottawa 2, Ont.; Home: 11 Crescent Road, Rockliffe Park, Ottawa, Ont., Canada.
Telephone: 745-7064 (Office); 749-9782 (Home).

García-Baxter, Tomás Allende; Spanish politician; b. 4 Feb. 1920, Madrid; m.; nine c.; ed. Univ. of Madrid.
President, Cámara Oficial Sindical Agraria de Guadalajara 53, subsequently Pres. Central Econ. Section of Joint Nat. Council of Hermandades Sindicales de Labradores y Ganaderos 62-65; fmr. Pres. Cttee. of Econ. Problems, European Agricultural Confed., now Adviser; Vice-Pres. Agricultural Comm.; mem. Cortes; mem. Govt. Comm. on Fundamental Law and Presidency; sub-commissary, Econ. and Social Devt. Plan 65; Minister of Agriculture 69-75; Cruz de Guerra and several awards for services to agriculture.
Publs. works on agricultural economics.
c/o Ministerio de Agricultura, Madrid, Spain.

García Hernández, José; Spanish lawyer and politician; b. 1915.
Called to the Bar 41; Civil Gov. Lugo 47-48, Gran Canaria 48-51; Dir.-Gen. Local Admin. 51; mem. Parl. during eight admins.; Man. Banco Exterior de España; Pres. Parl. Budgetary Comm.; Minister of the Interior, First Vice-Pres. 73-75; Grand Cross of Civil Merit.
c/o Ministerio de la Gobernación, Madrid, Spain.

García Marquez, Gabriel; Colombian writer; b. 1928; m.; two s.
Worked as journalist in Colombia and in Europe; started writing books 46; now lives in Spain; contributes to *Mundo Nuevo, Casa de las Américas, etc.*; Rómulo Gallegos Prize 72.
Publs. include novels: *La hojarasca* 55, *El coronel no tiene quien la escriba* 61, *Los funerales de la Mamá Grande* 62, *La mala hora* 62, *Cien años de soledad* 67 (English trans. *A Hundred Years of Solitude* 70), *Relato de un Náufrago* 70, *Leafstorm and other stories* 72.
Editorial Seix-Barral, Provenza 219, Barcelona, Spain.

García Mata, Rafael; Argentine agronomist and politician; b. 12 March 1912; ed. Colegio del Salvador, Buenos Aires, and Faculty of Agronomy and Veterinary Science, Univ. de Buenos Aires.
On staff of *Revista de Economía Argentina* 29-30; First Sec. Ministry of Finance and Public Works, Province of Santa Fé 30-31; Editorial Sec. *Revista de Economía Argentina* 31-35, mem. Board of Dirs. 36-53; Technical Sec., Office of Econ. Studies of Argentine Industrial Fed. 32-35; Head of Econ. Service of Nat. Cotton Council 35-36, Dir.-Gen. 36-43; Dir.-Gen. of Agriculture, Ministry of Agriculture 43-45, Dir.-Gen. of Agric. Research 45-52; Titular Prof. of Econs. and Agrarian Org., Univ. of Buenos Aires 47-56; Dir. and Vice-Pres. Nat. Bank of Argentina 49-50; Under-Sec. for Agric. and Livestock 58-62; Minister to Spain 66-67; Sec. of State for Agric. and Livestock 67-69; mem. numerous dels. and missions.
Publs. include: *Geografía Económica Argentina* 36, *Argentina Económica* 39, 42, 43, *El Problema Agrario Argentino* 50.
c/o Secretaría de Estado de Agricultura y Ganadería, Buenos Aires, Argentina.

García Peláez, Raúl, LL.D.; Cuban lawyer, politician and diplomatist; b. 15 Jan. 1922; ed. Univ. of Havana. Former mem. July 26th Revolutionary Cttee.; later

Prosecutor at Camaguey Court of Appeal, then Chair. Camaguey Municipal Council for Co-ordination and Inspection; then Gen. Treas. Revolutionary Forces in Camaguey Province, Rep. of Nat Inst. of Agrarian Reform in Nuevitas, and Gen. Sec. Matanzas Provincial Cttee. of United Party of Cuban Socialist Revolution; mem. Cen. Cttee. of Cuban C.P. 65-, Head of Revolutionary Orientation Comm. of Cen. Cttee. of Cuban C.P. until 67; Amb. to U.S.S.R. 67-74.
Partido Comunista, Havana, Cuba.

García-Peña, Roberto; Colombian journalist; b. 1910; ed. Externado de Colombia, Bogotá, and Univ. of Chile.
Reporter *El Tiempo* 29; Private Sec. to Minister of Govt. 30; Sec. Colombian Embassy, Peru 34, Chile 35, Chargé d'Affaires 37; Sec.-Gen. Ministry of Foreign Affairs 38; Editor *El Tiempo* 39-; mem. Council of Dirs., Inter-American Press Soc.
Avenida Jimenez 6-77, Bogotá, Colombia.

García Robles, Alfonso, LL.D.; Mexican diplomatist; b. 20 March 1911; ed. Universidad Nacional Autónoma de México, Univ. of Paris, and Acad. of International Law, The Hague.
Foreign Service 39-, Sweden 39-41; Head, Dept. of Int. Orgs., later Dir.-Gen. of Political Affairs and Diplomatic Service 41-46; Dir. of Div. of Political Affairs, UN Secretariat 46-57; Head of Dept. for Europe, Asia and Africa, Mexican Ministry of Foreign Affairs 57-61; Amb. to Brazil 62-64; Under-Sec. for Foreign Affairs 64-71; Perm. Rep. to UN 71-75; Sec. for Foreign Affairs Dec. 75-; Pres. Preparatory Comm. for the Denuclearization of Latin America 64-67; several decorations from various countries.
Publs. *Pan-Americanism and the Good Neighbour Policy* 40, *The Sorbonne Yesterday and Today* 43, *Post-War Mexico* 44, *Mexican International Policy* 46, *Echoes of the Old World* 46, *The Post-War World: From the Atlantic Charter to the San Francisco Conference* (2 vols.) 49, *The Geneva Conference and the Extent of Territorial Waters* 59, *The Denuclearization of Latin America* 67, *The Tlatelolco Treaty* 67, *Mexico in the United Nations* (2 vols.) 70.
Secretaría de Relaciones Exteriores, México, D.F.; Sierra Vertientes 691, México 10, D.F., Mexico.

Gardent, Paul; French mining executive; b. 10 July 1921, Grenoble; m. Janine Robert 1958; one s.; ed. Ecole Polytechnique.
Mining Engineer, Valenciennes 44-48; Asst. Chief Mining Engineer, Lille 48-49, Chief Mining Engineer 50; Technical Adviser to J. M. Louvel (Minister of Industry and Commerce) 50-52; Dir. of Gen. Studies, Charbonnages de France 52-58; Dir. of Gen. Studies and Financial Services, Houillères du bassin de Lorraine 58-63; Asst. Dir., then Dir.-Gen. Houillères du bassin du Nord et du Pas-de-Calais 63-68; Dir.-Gen. Charbonnages de France 68-.
Charbonnages de France, 9 avenue Percier, Paris 8e; Home: 5-7 rue de la Chaise, Paris 75007, France.
Telephone: 544-03-43 (Home).

Gardiner, Baron (Life Peer) cr. 63, of Kittisford, in the County of Somerset; **Gerald Gardiner,** P.C., C.H., Q.C., M.A.; British barrister; b. 30 May 1900; ed. Harrow School and Magdalen Coll., Oxford.
President Oxford Union and Oxford Univ. Dramatic Soc. 24; called to Bar 25; mem. Cttee. on Supreme Court Practice and Procedure 47-53; Q.C. 48; mem. Lord Chancellor's Law Reform Cttee. 52-63; Master of Bench of Inner Temple 55; Chair. General Council of the Bar 58, 59; Lord Chancellor 64-June 70; mem. Int. Comm. of Jurists 71-; Chancellor, The Open Univ. 72-; Hon. LL.D. (Birmingham, London, Southampton).
Publs. *Capital Punishment as a Deterrent and the Alternative* 56, *Law Reform Now* (Jt. Editor) 63.
House of Lords, London, S.W.1, England.

Gardiner, Robert Kweku Atta, B.SC., M.A.; Ghanaian civil servant and international administrator; b. 29 Sept. 1914, Kumasi; s. of Phillip H. D. Gardiner and Nancy T. Ferguson; m. Linda Charlotte Edwards 1942, one s. two d.; ed. Fourah Bay Coll., Sierra Leone, Selwyn Coll., Cambridge, and New Coll., Oxford.
Lecturer in Econs. Fourah Bay Coll. 43-46; Area Specialist UN Trusteeship Dept. 47-49; Dir. Dept. of Extra-Mural Studies, Univ. Coll. Ibadan, Nigeria 49-53; Dir. Dept. of Social Welfare and Community Development, Ghana 53-55; Chair. Kumasi Coll. of Technology Council, Ghana 54-58; Perm. Sec. Ministry of Housing, Ghana 55-57; Establishment Sec. and Head of Civil Service 57-59; Deputy Exec. Sec. UN Economic Comm. for Africa, Addis Ababa 59-61, Exec. Sec. 63-75; Minister of Econ. Planning, Ghana Oct. 75-; Chair. Commonwealth Foundation 70-73; David Livingstone Visiting Prof. of Econs., Strathclyde Univ. 70-71; Sec. Ghana Presidential Comm. and Council of States; Special Envoy of UN Sec.-Gen. to the Congo 61; Dir. UN Div. for Public Admin. 61; UN Special Rep. to the Congo 62-63; BBC Reith Lecturer 65; Hon. D.C.L. (East Anglia), Hon. LL.D. (Bristol, Ibadan, East Africa, Strathclyde), Hon. Ph.D. (Uppsala).
Leisure interests: golf, reading, music, walking.
Publ. *Development of Social Administration* 54 (jointly).
Ministry of Economic Planning, Accra, Ghana.

Gardner, Ava; American actress; b. 24 Dec. 1922, Smithfield, North Carolina; m. 1st Mickey Rooney 1942, 2nd Artie Shaw 1945, 3rd Frank Sinatra (*q.v.*) 1951 (divorced).
Films include: *Lost Angel, Three Men in White, Singapore, One Touch of Venus, Great Sinner, East Side West Side, My Forbidden Past, Show Boat, Love Star, The Snows of Kilimanjaro, Ride Vaquero, Mogambo, The Barefoot Contessa, Bhowani Junction, The Little Hut, The Sun also Rises, Naked Maja, On the Beach, 55 Days to Peking, Night of the Iguana, The Bible, Mayerling, Tam-Lin, The Life and Times of Judge Roy Bean, Earthquake, The Bluebird.*
Jess S. Morgan & Co. Inc., 6300 Wilshire Boulevard, Suite 1100, Los Angeles, Calif. 90048, U.S.A.

Gardner, Dame Helen Louise, D.B.E., M.A., D.LITT., F.B.A., F.R.S.L.; British teacher and author; b. 13 Feb. 1908, London; d. of Charles Henry and Helen Mary Roadnight Gardner (née Roadnight Cockman); ed. North London Collegiate School, and St. Hilda's Coll., Oxford.
Lecturer, Royal Holloway Coll. 31-34, Univ. of Birmingham 34-41; Tutor, St. Hilda's Coll. Oxford 41-54, Fellow 42-66, Hon. Fellow 66-; Reader in Renaissance English Literature, Oxford Univ. 54-66; Merton Prof. of English Literature, Oxford Univ. 66-75; Fellow, Lady Margaret Hall, Oxford 66-75; Hon. Fellow 75-; Del. Oxford Univ. Press 59-75; Visiting Prof. Univ. of Calif. 54; Riddell Lecturer, Univ. of Durham 56; Alexander Lecturer, Univ. of Toronto 62; Ewing Lecturer, Univ. of Calif. 66; Messenger Lecturer, Cornell Univ. 67; Eliot Memorial Lecturer, Univ. of Kent 68; mem. Cttee. for Higher Educ. 61, Council for Nat. Academic Awards 64-67; Trustee, Nat. Portrait Gallery 67-.
Leisure interests: travel, gardening.
Publs. *The Art of T. S. Eliot* 49, *The Divine Poems of John Donne* (editor) 52, *The Metaphysical Poets* (editor) 57, *The Business of Criticism* 59, *The Elegies and the Songs and Sonnets of John Donne* 65, *A Reading of 'Paradise Lost'* 65, *Religion and Literature* 71, *The Faber Book of Religious Verse* (editor) 72, *The New Oxford Book of English Verse* (editor) 72, *The Composition of "Four Quartets"* 76.
Myrtle House, Eynsham, Oxford, England.
Telephone: (0865) 881497.

Gardner, John William, PH.D., LL.D.; American writer and social worker; b. 8 Oct. 1912; s. of William and Marie Gardner; m. Aida Marroquin 1934; two d.; ed. Stanford Univ., and Univ. of Calif.
Teaching Asst. in Psychology, Univ. of Calif. 36-38; Instructor in Psychology, Conn. Coll. 38-40; Asst. Prof. Mount Holyoke Coll. 40-42; Head Latin-American Section, Foreign Broadcasting Intelligence Service, Fed. Communications Comm. 42-43; served U.S. Marine Corps 43-46; staff mem. Carnegie Corpn. of New York 46-47, Exec. Assoc. 47-49, Vice-Pres. 49-55, Pres. 55-65, Consultant 68-; Pres. Carnegie Foundation 55-65; U.S. Secretary of Health and Education and Welfare 65-68; Head of Urban Coalition (Campaign to transform cities of America) 68-70; Dir. N.Y. Telephone Co. 61-65, Shell Oil Co. 62-65, Time Inc. 68-72, Amer. Airlines 68-71; Chair. Common Cause (Citizen's Lobby) 70-; Fellow, American Psychological Asscn., American Acad. of Arts and Sciences; Chair. Soc. Sciences Panel, Scientific Advisory Board, U.S. Air Force 51-55; Dir. N.Y. School of Social Work 49-55, Metropolitan Museum of Art 57-65, Stanford Univ. 68-, Rockefeller Brothers Fund 68-, N.Y. Foundation 70-76, Senior Exec. Council, Conf. Board 70-75; mem. Pres. Kennedy's Task Force on Educ. 60; Chair. U.S. Advisory Comm. on Int. Educational and Cultural Affairs 62-64, Pres. Johnson's Task Force on Educ. 64, White House Conf. on Educ. 65; Hon. degrees from numerous American colls. and univs.; U.S.A.F. Exceptional Service Award 56, Presidential Medal of Freedom 64, Nat. Acad. of Sciences Public Welfare Medal 66, UAW Social Justice Award 68, AFL-CIO Murray Green Medal 70, Christopher Award 71, American Inst. for Public Service Award 73, Robert F. Kennedy Humanitarian Award 74, Clark Kerr Educ. Award 74.
Publs. *Excellence* 61, *Self-Renewal* 63, *No Easy Victories* 68, *The Recovery of Confidence* 70, *In Common Cause* 72, *Know or Listen to Those Who Know* (with Francesca Gardner Reese) 75; Editor *To Turn the Tide* (by John F. Kennedy).
Office: 2030 M Street N.W., Washington, D.C. 20036; Home: 5325 Kenwood Avenue, Chevy Chase, Md. 20015, U.S.A.

Gardner, Kenneth Burslam, B.A., A.L.A.; British orientalist and librarian; b. 5 June 1924, London; s. of Douglas V. Gardner and Dora V. Bowden; m. Cleone Winifred Adams 1949; two s. two d.; ed. Univ. Coll., London, and School of Oriental and African Studies, Univ. of London.
Assistant Librarian, School of Oriental and African Studies, Univ. of London 50-54; Asst. Keeper, Dept. of Oriental Printed Books and MSS., British Museum 55-57, Keeper 57-70, Principal Keeper of Printed Books 70-74; Deputy Keeper of Oriental Printed Books and MSS, British Library 74-.
Leisure interests: gardening, reading, mountain walking.
1 Duncombe Road, Bengeo, Hertford, England.
Telephone: 0092-53591.

Gardner, Stephen Symmes, M.B.A.; American banker and government official; b. 26 Dec. 1921, Wakefield, Mass.; s. of George F. Gardner and Mildred Edmands; m. Consuelo Andonegui 1943; three s. two d.; ed. Harvard Coll. and Business School.
With Girard Bank, Philadelphia, Pa. 49-74, Pres. 66-71, Chair. 71-74; Deputy Sec. U.S. Treasury Dept. 74-76; Vice-Chair. Board of Govs., Fed. Reserve System Feb. 76-; Bronze Star, U.S. Army, Alexander Hamilton Award (Treasury Dept.) 76.
Leisure interests: tennis, sailing.
Federal Reserve System, Washington, D.C. 20551; 700 New Hampshire Avenue, N.W., Washington, D.C. 20037; Old Baltimore Pike and Wawa Road, Wawa, Pa. 19063, U.S.A.
Telephone: 202-452-3000 (Office); 202-965-0480 (Washington, D.C.); 215-459-5375 (Pa.).

Garin, Vasco Vieira; Portuguese diplomatist; see *The International Who's Who 1975-76.*

Garland, George David, PH.D., F.R.S.C.; Canadian geophysicist; b. 29 June 1926, Toronto; s. of N. L. Garland and Jean McPherson; m. Elizabeth MacMillan 1949; two s. one d.; ed. Univ. of Toronto and St. Louis Univ.
Geophysicist, Dominion Observatory, Ottawa 50-54; Prof. of Geophysics, Univ. of Alberta, Edmonton 54-63; Prof. of Geophysics, Univ. of Toronto 63-; Deputy Gen. Sec. Int. Union of Geodesy and Geophysics 60-63, Gen. Sec. 63-73.
Leisure interests: canoeing, history of Canadian exploration, early maps.
Publs. *The Earth's Shape and Gravity* 65, and papers in scientific journals dealing with gravity, terrestrial magnetism, structure of the earth's crust, electrical conductivity of the crust, heat flow from the earth.
Department of Physics, University of Toronto, Toronto 5; Home: 1 Forest Glen Crescent, Toronto 12, Canada. Telephone: 928-3159 (Office); 488-5127 (Home).

Garland, Hon. Ransley Victor, M.P., F.C.A., F.C.I.S., A.A.S.A.; Australian politician; b. 5 May 1934, Perth; m. Lynette Jamieson 1960; two s. one d.; ed. Hale School and Univ. of W. Australia.
In practice as Chartered Accountant 58-70, incl. univ. tutoring; Dir. of various cos. 60-67; Councillor, Claremont Town Council 63-70; Deputy Mayor of Claremont 69; Fed. Councillor 64-69; Senior Vice-Pres. Liberal Party of W. Australia 65-69; mem. House of Reps. April 69-; Minister of State for Supply 71-72; Minister Assisting the Treasurer March-Dec. 72, Dec. 75-Feb. 76; Acting Minister of Customs and Excise June-July 72; Leader Australian Del. to IPU 71; Parl. Adviser to 28th Gen. Assembly of UN 73; Minister for Posts and Telecommunications Dec. 75-Feb. 76 (resigned); Fellow, Inst. of Chartered Accountants; Assoc. Australian Soc. of Accountants, Inst. of Chartered Secs.
Leisure interests: golf, squash, music, reading.
Parliament House, Canberra, A.C.T. 2600; 191 St. George's Terrace, Perth, W.A. 6000; Richardson Avenue, Claremont, W.A. 6010, Australia.
Telephone: 726535 (Canberra); 222400 (Perth); 313632 (Claremont).

Garner, Baron (Life Peer), cr. 69; **(Joseph John) Saville Garner,** G.C.M.G.; British civil servant; b. 14 Feb. 1908, London; s. of Joseph and Helena M. (Culver) Garner; m. Margaret Beckman 1938; two s. one d.; ed. Jesus Coll., Cambridge.
Appointed Dominions Office 30; Private Sec. to successive Secs. of State 40-43; Senior Sec. Office of High Commr. Ottawa 43-46, Deputy High Commr. 46-48; Asst. Under-Sec. Commonwealth Relations Office 48-51; Deputy High Commr. in India 51-53; Deputy Under-Sec. Commonwealth Relations Office 53; High Commr. in Canada 56-61; Perm. Under-Sec. of State, Commonwealth Relations Office (C.R.O.) 62-66; Commonwealth Office 66-68; Head of Diplomatic Service 65-68; Chair. Commonwealth Inst. 68-74, Commonwealth Scholarship Comm., Royal Postgraduate Medical School, Inst. of Commonwealth Studies, London Board of Dirs. Bank of Adelaide; mem. Council Voluntary Service Overseas 69-, Security Comm. 68-73; hon. degrees from several universities.
Leisure interest: gardening.
Publ. Translated from German: *The Books of the Emperor Wu Ti* 30.
23 Kennington Palace Court, London, S.E.11, England. Telephone: 01-735-7408.

Garner, Wendell Richard, A.B., A.M., PH.D.; American psychologist; b. 21 Jan. 1921, Buffalo, N.Y.; s. of Richard Charles and Lena Cole Garner; m. Barbara Chipman Ward 1944; one s. two d.; ed. Franklin and Marshall Colls. and Harvard Univ.

Instructor, rising to Prof., Johns Hopkins Univ. 46-67, Chair. Dept. of Psychology 54-64; James Rowland Angell Prof. of Psychology, Yale Univ. 67-, Dir. of Social Sciences 72-73, Chair. Dept. of Psychology 74-; mem. Nat. Acad. of Sciences; Distinguished Scientific Contribution Award of the American Psychological Assen. 64.
Leisure interests: gardening, boating.
Publs. *Applied Experimental Psychology* (with A. Chapanis and C. T. Morgan) 49, *Uncertainty and Structure as Psychological Concepts* 62, *The Processing of Information and Structure* 74.
Department of Psychology, Yale University, New Haven, Conn. 06510; Home: 48 Yowago Avenue, Branford, Conn. 06405, U.S.A.
Telephone: 203-436-0343 (Office); 203-481-0007 (Home).

Garnett, David, C.B.E.; British novelist; b. 9 March 1892, Brighton, Sussex; s. of Edward and Constance Garnett; m. 1st Rachel Alice Marshall 1921 (died 1940), two s.; m. 2nd Angelica Vanessa Bell 1942, four d.; ed. Imperial Coll. of Science, South Kensington.
Educated as biologist; Fellow, Imperial Coll. of Science and Technology.
Leisure interests: fishing, travel.
Publs. *Lady into Fox* (Hawthornden and Tait-Black Prizes) 22, *A Man in the Zoo* 24, *The Sailor's Return* 25, *Go She Must* 27, *The Old Dove-cote* 28, *No Love* 29, *The Grasshoppers Come* 31, *A Rabbit in the Air* 32, *Pocahontas* 33, *Beany-Eye* 35, *The War in the Air* 41, *The Golden Echo* 53, *Flowers of the Forest, Aspects of Love* 55, *A Shot in the Dark* 58, *A Net for Venus* 59, *The Familiar Faces* 62, *Two by Two* 63, *Ulterior Motives* 66, *A Clean Slate* 71, *The Sons of the Falcon, Purl and Plain* 73, *Plough Over the Bones* 73, *The Master Cat* 74; Editor: *The Letters of T. E. Lawrence, The Novels of Thomas Love Peacock, The Essential T. E. Lawrence, The Garnett-White Letters* 68, *Carrington: Letters and Extracts from her Diaries* 70
Le Verger de Charry, 46 Montcuq, France.

Garnham, Percy Cyril Claude, C.M.G., M.D., D.SC., F.R.C.P., F.I.BIOL., F.R.S.; British medical protozoologist; b. 15 Jan. 1901, London; s. of late Lieut. P. C. Garnham, R.N.D. and late Edith Garnham; m. Esther Long Price 1924; two s. four d.; ed. St. Bartholomew's Hospital, London.
Colonial Medical Service 25-47; f. Div. of Insect Borne Diseases, Nairobi, Kenya 44; Reader in Medical Parasitology, London School of Hygiene and Tropical Medicine 47-51, Prof. of Medical Protozoology and Dir. Dept. of Parasitology, London School of Hygiene and Tropical Medicine 52-68; Prof. Emer. and Snr. Research Fellow, Imperial Coll. of Science and Technology, London 68-; Fogarty Int. Scholar 70; Pres. Royal Soc. of Tropical Medicine and Hygiene 67-69; Pres. British Soc. of Parasitologists 70-72, European Fed. of Parasitologists 71-; Pres. 2nd Int. Conf. on Protozoology; Pontifical Academician, Acad. of Sciences, Vatican; Assoc. mem. Acad. Royale de Médecine, Belgium, Acad. Nat. de Médecine, France; Foreign mem. Acad. Royale des Sciences d'Outre-Mer de Bruxelles and Accad. Lancisiana, Rome; Hon. mem. Polish, Mexican and British Socs. of Parasitologists, Soc. of Protozoologists, Soc. Pathologie Exotique, Paris, Brazilian, British and American Socs. of Tropical Medicine, Soc. de Protistologues de la Langue française, Soc. de Geografia de Lisboa; Univ. of London Gold Medal 28, Darling Medal and Prize WHO 52, Bernhardt Nocht Medal, Hamburg 58, Gaspar Vianna Medal, Brazil 62, Manson Medal 66, Emile Brumpt Prize (Paris) 70, Médaille d'Or, Soc. de Pathologie Exotique 71, Médaille de Vermeil, Acad. Nat. de Médecine, France 72; Mary Kingsley Medal, Liverpool 73, Rudolf Leuckart Medal (Germany) 74; Hon. F.R.C.P. (Edinburgh), Hon. Dr. (Bordeaux).
Leisure interests: chamber music, European travel.

Publs. *Immunity to Protozoa* (with Pierce and Roitt) 63, *Malaria Parasites* 66, *Progress in Parasitology* 71.
Imperial College of Science and Technology Field Station, Ashurst Lodge, Ascot, Berks.; Home: Southernwood, Farnham Common, Bucks., England.
Telephone: 0990-23911 (Office); Farnham Common 3863 (Home).

Garnier, E. L. M. René, DR. ès SC.; French scientist; b. 16 Jan. 1887, Chalon-sur-Saône; s. of Commandant Edouard Garnier and Clémence Boutonnet; m. Germaine Queyrat 1913 (deceased); two s. three d. (one deceased); ed. Externat St. Michel (Moulins) and Univ. de Paris.
Professor Faculté des Sciences, Poitiers 13-27; Prof. Faculté des Sciences, Paris 28-58, Hon. Prof. 59-; Lecturer, Ecole Polytechnique, Paris 43-52, Examiner of students 52-58; mem. Acad. of Sciences (Institut de France) 52-, Accad. Naz. Lincei (Rome), Acad. Royale de Belgique; Commdr. Légion d'Honneur.
Publs. *Cours de Mathématiques générales, Leçons d'Algèbre et de Géométrie, Cours de Cinématique,* and numerous articles in scientific journals.
21 rue Decamps, Paris 16e, France.
Telephone: 553-27-78.

Garofalides, Theodore; Greek doctor and airline executive; b. 17 Nov. 1898; ed. Univs. of Athens and Paris.
Assistant, First Surgery Clinic, Athens Univ. 24-29; Resident Surgeon "Evangelismos" Clinic 33-40; Asst. Prof. of Orthopaedics, Athens Univ. 35-48, Special Prof. 48-59, Perm. Prof. 56; Dir. Voula "Asclipeion" Hospital 38-; Dir. Konialidian Orthopaedic Clinic 50-; Prof. of Orthopaedics, Physiotherapeutic School 56-; Pres. Greek Soc. of Surgeons 60; Publisher *Orthopaedic Chronicle* 50-; Chair. of Board of Olympic Airways and Olympic Cruises; numerous decorations.
37 King George II Avenue, Glyfada, Athens; Office: 24 Hòmere Street, Athens, Greece.
Telephone: Glyfada 04101 (Home); 611340 (Office).

Garran, Sir (Isham) Peter, K.C.M.G.; former British diplomatist; b. 15 Jan. 1910, Melbourne, Australia; s. of the late Sir Robert Randolph Garran, G.C.M.G., Q.C.; m. Mary Elisabeth Stawell 1935; two s. one d.; ed. Melbourne Grammar School, and Trinity Coll., Melbourne Univ., Australia.
British Diplomatic Service 34-70; Belgrade 37-41, Lisbon 41-44, Berlin 47-50, The Hague 50-52; Insp. of Foreign Service Establishments 52-54; Commercial Minister, Washington 55-60, Ambassador to Mexico 60-64, to Netherlands 64-70; Dir. Lend Lease Corpn. (Australia), U.K. Branch of Australian Mutual Provident Soc., Associated Resources Ltd.
Leisure interest: gardening.
Roanoke, Bosham Hoe, Sussex, England.
Telephone: Bosham 57-2347.

Garrels, Robert M., B.S., M.S., PH.D.; American professor of geology; b. 24 Aug. 1916, Detroit, Mich.; s. of John C. Garrels and Margaret Anne Garrels; m. 1st Jane M. Tinen 1940 (divorced 1969), one s. two d.; 2nd Cynthia A. Hunt 1970; ed. Univ. of Mich. and Northwestern Univ.
Instructor, Asst., Assoc. Prof., Northwestern Univ. 41-52, Prof. of Geology 65-69; Chief of Solid State Group, Geochemistry and Petrology Branch, U.S. Geological Survey 52-55; Assoc. Prof., Harvard Univ. 55-57, Prof. of Geology 57-63, Chair. Dept. of Geological Sciences 63-65; Henri Speciale Chair of Applied Science, Univ. of Brussels 62-63; Prof. of Geology Scripps Inst. of Oceanography 69-71; Captain James Cook Prof. of Oceanography, Univ. of Hawaii 72-74; Prof. of Geology Northwestern Univ. 74-; mem. Nat. Acad. of Sciences; Petroleum Research Fund of American Chemical Soc. Type C Award 63, Best Paper Award (with F. T. Mackenzie) in *Journal of*

edimentary Petrology 66, Arthur L. Day Medal of Geological Soc. of America 66; V. M. Goldschmidt Award, Geochem. Soc. 73; Hon. D.Sc. (Brussels) 69. Leisure interest: athletics.
Publs. *A Textbook of Geology* 51, *Mineral Equilibria at Low Temperature and Pressure* 60, *Solutions, Minerals and Equilibria* (with C. L. Christ) 65, *The Evolution of Sedimentary Rocks* (with F. T. Mackenzie) 71, *Water, The Web of Life* (with Cynthia Hunt) 72, *Chemical Cycles and the Global Environment* (with F. T. Mackenzie and Cynthia Hunt) 75.
Department of Geological Sciences, Locy Hall, Northwestern University, Evanston, Ill. 60201, U.S.A.
Telephone: (312) 492-5097.

Garrett, Lieut.-Gen. Sir Ragnar, P.S.C., K.B.E., C.B.; Australian officer; b. 12 Feb. 1900; ed. Guildford Grammar School, Perth, and Duntroon Royal Military Coll.
Lieutenant, Australian Staff Corps 21; served in Middle East and South West Pacific in Second World War; mentioned in despatches; Lieut.-Col. 40, Brigadier 43; Commandant, Australian Staff Coll. 50-51; Maj.-Gen. 51; G.O.C. Western Command Australia 51-53; Deputy Chief of Gen. Staff 53-54; Lieut-Gen. 54; G.O.C. Southern Command 54-58; Chief Australian Gen. Staff 58-60; Principal Australian Admin. Staff Coll. 60-64; Chair. West Australian Shipping Service 65-70.
16 Blake Court, Mount Eliza, Victoria, Australia.

Garrett, Ray, Jr., A.B., LL.B.; American lawyer and government official; b. 11 Aug. 1920, Chicago, Ill.; s. of Ray and Mabel May Garrett; m. Virginia R. Hale 1943; one s. three d.; ed. Yale Univ., Harvard Law School.
Captain, U.S. Army Field Artillery, European Theater 42-46; Teaching Fellow, Harvard Law School 49-50; Asst. Prof. N.Y. Univ. School of Law 50-52; private practice, Gardner, Carton & Douglas (Attorneys), Chicago 52-54, 58-73; Dir. Corporate Regulation Div., U.S. Securities and Exchange Comm. 54-58, Chair. 73-76; Chair. Corpn., Banking and Business Law Section, American Bar Asscn. 64-65.
Leisure interests: fishing, travel.
Publs. *Commentaries on Model Debenture Indentures* (Chair. of Advisory Cttee.) 67, and articles in various legal publs.
Home: 182 Myrtle Street, Winnetka, Ill. 60093, U.S.A.
Telephone: (202) 755-1130 (Office); (312) 446-1768 (Home).

Garrido Diaz, Luis, LL.D., D.ECON.; Mexican lawyer and educationist; b. 1898; ed. Univ. Nacional Autónoma de México.
Lawyer, Prof. Col. de San Nicolás de Hidalgo, Pres. of Supreme Tribunal of Michoacán State and Rector Univ. of Michoacán 24-28; Prof. Schools of Law and Economics, Univ. Nacional Autónoma de México 29-, Rector 48-50; mem. Comm. for drafting new Penal Code; fmr. Head Diplomatic Dept., Ministry of Foreign Affairs; co-founder Mexican Asscn. of Univs. and Insts. of Higher Education; Hon. Pres. Nat. Acad. of History and Geography; Vice-Pres. Nat. Athenaeum of Science and Art; Pres. Latin American Univ. Union; mem. Exec. Council, Int. Asscn. of Univs., Int. Asscn. for Penal Law; Treas. Mexican Acad. of Languages; many Mexican and foreign hon. degrees and decorations.
Publs. *Los Apólogos de mi Breviario* 22, *El Amor Inglosable* (novel) 26, *Meditaciones de un Idealista* 28, *La Reforma de Nuestra Constitución Política* 32, *El Plan Sexenal ante la Doctrina Administrativa* 33, *La Ley Penal Mexicana* 34, *La Delincuencia Infantil de México* (with J. Angel Ceniceros) 36, *En Torno a la Paradoja* (short stories) 37, *La Doctrina Mexicana de Nuestro Derecho Penal* 41, *El Valor Doctrinario de la Revolución Mexicana* 46, *Notas de un Penalista* 46,

El Espíritu de Francia 46, *Ensayos Penales, Discursos y Mensajes.*
Patricio Sanz 725, Mexico D.F., Mexico.

Garrigues Sánchez Díaz-Cañabate, Dr. Antonio, LIC. EN DER.; Spanish lawyer, diplomatist and politician; b. 9 Jan. 1904, Madrid; s. of Joaquín Garrigues and Isabel Díaz-Cañabate; m. Hellen Anne Walker 1944 (deceased); ed. Univ. of Madrid.
Practised law 25-31; Dir.-Gen. of Legal Registers 31; private practice 31-62; Amb. to U.S.A. 62-64, to Vatican City 64-73; Minister of Justice Dec. 75-; Pres. and Dir. of numerous commercial and industrial cos.
Publs. many books and articles on legal, political, economic and financial topics.
Ministerio de Justicia, Madrid, Spain.

Garriott, Owen K.; American astronaut; b. 22 Nov. 1930, Enid, Okla.; s. of Mr. and Mrs. Owen Garriott; m. Helen Mary Walker; three s. one d.; ed. Univ. of Oklahoma and Stanford Univ., Calif.
Electronics Officer, U.S. Navy 53-56; fmr. consultant to Manned Space Science Div., NASA Office of Space Sciences and Applications; fmr. Sec. U.S. Comm., Int. Scientific Radio Union; fmr. Regional Editor *Planetary and Space Sciences*; taught electronics, electromagnetic theory and ionospheric physics, Stanford Univ., and research into ionospheric physics 61-65; selected by NASA as astronaut June 65; completed flight training, Williams Air Force Base, Ariz. 66; Science Pilot for 2nd Skylab space mission July-Sept. 73; mem. American Geophysical Union, Inst. of Electrical and Electronic Engs., American Astronomical Soc.; NASA Distinguished Service Medal 73.
NASA Johnson Space Center, Houston, Tex. 77058, U.S.A.

Garrone, H.E. Cardinal Gabriel Marie, D.PHIL., D.THEOL.; French ecclesiastic; b. 12 Oct. 1901, Aix-les-Bains, Savoie; s. of Jean Garrone and Joséphine Mathieu; ed. Inst. Notre-Dame de la Villette, Univ. de Grenoble and Pontificia Universitas Gregoriana, Rome.
Professor, Grand Seminary, Chambéry 45; Archbishop Coadjutor, Toulouse 47; Archbishop, Toulouse and Narbonne, Primate of Narbonne 56-66; Vice-Pres. Perm. Council of Plenary Assembly of French episcopate 64-66; Pro-Prefect, Congregation of Seminaries and of Univs., Rome 66-67; Prefect, Congregation for Catholic Educ. 67-; cr. Cardinal by Pope Paul VI 67; Grand Croix Légion d'Honneur; Croix de Guerre (39-45).
Publs. *Psaumes et Prières, Invitation à la prière, Leçons sur la foi, La Morale du Credo, La Porte des Ecritures, Panorama du Credo, Sainte Eglise notre Mère, Morale chrétienne et valeurs humaines, Que faut-il croire?, La Religieuse présente à Dieu et au Monde, Seigneur, dis-moi ton nom, Le Concile, orientations, Qu'est-ce que Dieu?, Ce que croyait Thérèse de Lisieux, Religieuse aujourd'hui? Oui mais . . . , L'Eucharistie au secours de la Foi, Voilà ta mère, L'Action catholique, Foi et Pédagogie, L'Eucharistie, Pourquoi Prier?, La Religieuse, Signe de Dieu dans le Monde, Les Psaumes, prière pour aujourd'hui, La profession de Foi de Paul VI, Ce que croyait Pascal, Le Goût de Pain, Les Ecrits spirituels du Cardinal Saliège, Présentation de "Gaudium et spes", Le secret d'une vie engagée: Mgr. Guerry, L'Eglise: 1965-72, Que faut-il faire?, La foi en 1973, Pour vous, qui suis-je?, La foi au fil des jours, Le Credo lu dans l'Historie, Aller . . . jusqu'à Dieu, Prêtre, Ce que croyait Jeanne Jugan.*
Largo del Colonnato 3, 00193 Rome, Italy.
Telephone: 698-39-56.

Garvey, Sir Terence (Willcocks), K.C.M.G.; British diplomatist; b. 7 Dec. 1915, Dublin; s. of Francis Willcocks Garvey and Ethel Margaret Ray; m. 1st Barbara Tomlinson, 2nd Rosemary O'Neill; two s. one d.; ed. Felsted School and Univ. Coll., Oxford.

Entered Foreign Service 38, served U.S.A., Chile, Germany, Egypt, Yugoslavia; Chargé d'Affaires in China 62-65; Amb. to Mongolia 63-65; Asst. Under-Sec. of State, Foreign Office 65-68; Amb. to Yugoslavia 68-71; High Commr. to India 71-73; Amb. to U.S.S.R. 73-75.
Leisure interest: fishing.
c/o Foreign and Commonwealth Office, Downing Street, London, S.W.1, England.

Garvin, Clifton C., Jr.; American business executive b. 22 Dec. 1921; *m.* Thelma Volland 1943; one *s.* three *d.*; ed. Virginia Polytechnical Inst.
Army service until 47; joined Exxon 47, Process Engineer, Baton Rouge Refinery, Man. Product Supply and Distribution Exxon Co. U.S.A. (fmrly. Humble Oil & Refinery Co.) 61, Vice-Pres. Exxon Co. U.S.A. Central Region 63, Pres. Exxon Chemical Co., Exec. Vice-Pres., Dir. Exxon Corpn. 68, Chair. of Board, Chief Exec. Officer 72-; Dir. N.Y. Urban Coalition, American Petroleum Inst., Econ. Devt. Council, First Nat. City Bank, Citicorp, PepsiCo; mem. American Chemical Soc., American Inst. of Chemical Engs., The Business Council; Trustee, Joint Council on Econ. Educ., Cttee. for Econ. Devt.; mem. Board Alfred P. Sloan Foundation, Sloan-Kettering Inst. for Cancer Research.
Leisure interest: golf.
Exxon Corporation, 1251 Avenue of the Americas, New York, N.Y. 10020, U.S.A.

Garwin, Richard L., M.S., PH.D.; American physicist; b. 19 April 1928, Cleveland, Ohio; *s.* of Robert and Leona S. Garwin; *m.* Lois E. Levy 1947; two *s.* one *d.*; ed. public schools in Cleveland, Case Western Reserve Univ. and Univ. of Chicago.
Instructor and Asst. Prof. of Physics, Univ. of Chicago 49-52; mem. staff, IBM Watson Lab., Columbia Univ. 52-65, 66-70; Adjunct Prof. of Physics, Columbia Univ. 57-; Dir. of Applied Research, IBM T. J. Watson Research Center 65-66, IBM Fellow 67-; mem. Defense Science Board 66-69; mem. President's Science Advisory Cttee. 62-66, 69-72; mem. IBM Corporate Technical Cttee. 70-71; mem. Council on Foreign Relations; mem. Nat. Acad. of Sciences, Inst. of Medicine 75-; Fellow, American Physical Soc.; Fellow, American Acad. of Arts and Sciences; Ford Foundation Fellow, CERN, Geneva 59-60; Hon. doctorate (Case Western Reserve Univ.) 66.
Leisure interests: skiing, military technology, arms control, social use of technology.
Publs. 70 published papers and 22 U.S. patents.
IBM Corporation, Research Division, Thomas J. Watson Research Center, P.O. Box 218, Yorktown Heights, New York, N.Y. 10598, U.S.A.
Telephone: 914-945-2555.

Gary, Romain; French writer and diplomatist; b. 8 May 1914; ed. Lycée de Nice and Paris Univ.
Served as pilot with Free French Air Force squadron "Lorraine" in Africa, Palestine and Russia 40-45; attached to Foreign Ministry 45-56; Consul-Gen. in Los Angeles (U.S.) 56-60; attached to Ministry of Information 67-; Officier de la Légion d'Honneur; Compagnon de la Libération; Croix de Guerre; Prix des Critiques 45, Prix Goncourt 56.
Publs. many works including *Education Européenne* 43, *Tulipe* 46, *Le Grand Vestiaire* 49, *Les Couleurs du Jour* 52, *Les Racines du Ciel* (Prix Goncourt 56), *Promesses de l'Aube* 59, *Madame L* 59, *The Ski Bum* 65, *Frère Océan* 65, *Pour Sganarelle* 65, *La danse de Gengis Cohn* 67, *La Tête coupable* 68, *Le Mangeur d'étoiles, Adieu, Gary Cooper* 69, *Chien Blanc* 70, *Les Enchanteurs* 73, *The Gasp* 73, *La nuit sera calme, Les Têtes de Stéphanie* 74; *Direct Flight to Allah* 75 (under pseudonym René Deville); for the theatre: *Johnie Couer, Gloire à nos*

illustres pionniers; directed film, *Les Oiseaux von mourir au Pérou* 68.
c/o Editions Gallimard, 5 rue Sébastien-Bottin, Paris 7e, 108 rue du Bac, Paris 7e, France.

Gasanova, Shamama Makhmudalikizi; Soviet agriculturalist and politician; b. 1923; ed. Kirovobad Agricultural Inst.
Farmer in cotton-growing "1st May Day" collective farm 39-53; Chair. "1st May Day" collective farm 53-; Deputy to U.S.S.R. Supreme Soviet 54-; Vice-Chair. Soviet of Union, U.S.S.R. Supreme Soviet 70-75; Hero of Socialist Labour, Order of Lenin, Hammer and Sickle Gold Medal (twice).
"1st May Day" Collective Farm, Fizuli District, Azerbaijan, U.S.S.R.

Gascar, Pierre; French writer; b. 13 March 1916, Paris; *m.* 2nd Alice Simon 1958; two *s.* (of first marriage).
Army service in France and Scotland 39-40; captured, twice escaped, recaptured and sent to Rawa-Ruska concentration camp (Ukraine); formerly journalist, journeys in Europe, China, S.E. Asia, America and Africa; Prix des Critiques, Prix Goncourt 53, Grand Prix de Littérature (Acad. Française) 69.
Leisure interest: travel.
Publs. *Les Meubles* 49, *Les Bêtes, Le Temps des Morts* 53, *Les Femmes* 55, *La Graine, Chine Ouverte* 56, *L'Herbe des Rues, Voyage chez les Vivants* 58, *La Barre de Corail, Soleils, Les Pas Perdus* 59, *Le Fugitif* 61, *Vertiges du Présent, Les Moutons de Feu* 63, *Le Meilleur de la Vie* 64, *Les Charmes* 65, *Auto* 68, *Les Chimères* 69, *L'Arche* 71, *Le Présage* 73, *L'Homme et l'Animal* 74, *Les Sources* 75.
Abbaye de Baume-les-Messieurs, Jura-39, France.

Gaskill, William; British theatre director; b. 24 June 1930; ed. Salt High School, Shipley, and Hertford Coll., Oxford.
Director, Granada Television 56-57; Asst. Artistic Dir. Royal Court Theatre, London 58-60; Dir. Royal Shakespeare Company 61-62; Assoc. Dir. Nat. Theatre, London 63-65; Artistic Dir. English Stage Company, Royal Court Theatre 65-72.
Stage productions include: (Royal Court Theatre) *Epitaph for George Dillon, One Way Pendulum, Saved, Early Morning, Man is Man, Lear, Big Wolf, The Sea*; (National Theatre) *The Recruiting Officer, Mother Courage, Philoctetes, Armstrong's Last Goodnight, The Beaux Stratagem*; (Royal Shakespeare Co.) *The Caucasian Chalk Circle, Richard III, Cymbeline*; other productions include, *Baal, Snap, The Speakers, The Kitchen, Love's Labour Lost*.
c/o Barclay's Bank, 55 England's Lane, London, N.W.3, England.

Gáspár, Sándor; Hungarian politician; b. 15 April 1917, Pánd; *s.* of János Gáspár and Julianna Kiss; *m.* Lenke Hajdu 1940; one *s.*
Motor mechanic; mem. Communist Party 36-, several posts in C.P. 45-; formerly high posts in Iron and Metal Workers' Trade Union; Asst. Gen. Sec. Central Council of Trade Unions 52, Gen. Sec. 56-59, 65-; First Sec. Budapest Cttee. of Hungarian Socialist Workers' Party 59-60, 62-65; mem. Central Cttee. Hungarian Socialist Worker's Party 58-, Sec. 61, mem. Political Cttee. 59-; Deputy Pres. Hungarian Presidential Council 63-.
Leisure interests: wild-game shooting, angling.
Central Council of Trade Unions, H-1415 Budapest VI, Dózsa Gy. ut 84/b, Hungary.

Gaspard, Roger Germain Charles; French business executive; b. 27 April 1902, Brest; *m.* Suzanne Guichemerre 1935; ed. Lycée Henri-IV, Paris and Ecole Polytechnique.
Director-Gen. Electricité de France 46-62, Pres. 62-63, Hon. Pres. 64-; Vice-Pres. Compagnie Nat. du Rhône

46-62; Vice-Pres. Conseil Général des Ponts et Chaussées 63, Assoc. Partner Schneider S.A. 63, Vice-Pres. 64, Pres., Dir.-Gen. 66-May 69; Pres., Dir.-Gen. Forges et Ateliers du Creusot (Usines Schneider) 64-69; Dir. CGEE Alsthom 70; Pres. Dir.-Gen. Brévatome 71; Pres. French Cttee. World Energy Conf. 70-74, Int. Exec. Council, World Energy Conf. 74-; Dir. Crédit Lyonnais 66-73, Soc. minière et métallurgique de Penarroya 68-73; Pres. Ligue Nat. française contre le cancer; Grand Officier de la Légion d'Honneur, Médaille de la Résistance.

10 boulevard de Port Royal, 75005 Paris, France.
Telephone: 707-23-65.

Gass, Sir Michael David Irving, K.C.M.G., M.A.; British overseas administrator (retd.); b. 24 April 1916, Wareham, Dorset; s. of George I. Gass and Norah E. Mustard; m. Elizabeth Periam Ackland-Hood 1975; ed. King's School, Bruton, Christ Church, Oxford and Queens' Coll., Cambridge.
Appointed to Colonial Admin. Service, Gold Coast 39; war service 39-45; District Commr., Gold Coast 45; Asst. Regional Officer, Ashanti 53; Perm. Sec., Ministry of Interior, Ghana 56; Chief Sec. to Western Pacific High Comm. 58; Colonial Sec. Hong Kong 65; High Commr. for Western Pacific 69-73.
Leisure interest: ornithology.
Broadway, Butleigh Wootton, Glastonbury, Somerset, England.
Telephone: Street 2856.

Gassman, Vittorio; Italian actor and director; b. 1 Sept. 1922; ed. Law Univ. of Rome and Dramatic Acad. of Rome.
Plays acted in include: *Hamlet, Othello, As You Like It, Troilus and Cressida, Oedipus Rex, Prometheus Bound, Ghosts, Peer Gynt, Orestes, Rosencrantz and Guildenstern are Dead, Richard III,* etc.; has directed his own group since 51; Films acted in include: *Bitter Rice, Anna, Rhapsody, War and Peace, The Miracle, I Soliti Ignoti,* etc.; Dir. *Kean* 56 and *The Great War,* Venice Festival winner; Dir. musical-play *Irma la Douce;* four awards for the best Italian theatre actor of the year, four for the best film actor; created Teatro Popolare Italiano (mobile theatre, 3,000 seats); dir. and played Agamemnon in production of Aeschylus' *Oresteia,* Syracuse 60.
Piazza S. Alessio 32, Rome, Italy.

Gastambide, Raymond, L. EN D., DIP.SC.POL.; French diplomatist; b. 10 Dec. 1910; s. of Maurice Gastambide and Marthe Kullmann; m. Marie-José Dugueyt 1968; one s. two d. (from previous marriage); ed. Ecole des Roches, Verneuil sur Avre.
Embassy Attaché, Vienna 37, Berne 38, Barcelona 40-42; with Govt. of Algiers Nov. 42, until recalled by Vichy Mar. 43; Résidence Générale, Rabat, Morocco 43-47; Consul-Gen., San Sebastian 47-50; attached to UN Headquarters 50-55; mem. of French Del. UN Gen. Assembly 51 and 52; Head of Dept. of UNHCR 55-58; Political Attaché French Del. to UN 58; Sec.-Gen. of French Del. UN Gen. Assembly 59-60; Head of the Disarmament Service 63; Amb. to Hungary 65-71, to Sweden 72-75; Officier Légion d'Honneur; Commandeur Ordre de Léopold (Belgium).
Leisure interests: tennis, swimming.
c/o Ministère des Affaires Etrangères, Paris; 6 Square Henry Pathé, 75-Paris 16e, France.
Telephone: 288-20-39 (Home).

Gastaut, Henri Jean; French biologist; b. 5 April 1915, Monaco; s. of Jean-Baptiste Gastaut and Marie-Louise Manceau; m. Yvette Reynaud 1935; two s. one d.; ed. Monaco and Nice Lycées, Marseilles Univ.
Head, Nervous Anatomy Laboratory 39, Nervous Diseases Clinic 44, Tit. Prof. Pathological Anatomy 52-, Marseilles Univ. Medical Faculty; Head, Marseilles Hospitals Neurobiological Laboratory 53-, Marseilles region Centre for Epileptic Children 60-; Dir. Neuro-

biological Research Unit, Inst. Nat. de la Santé Marseilles 61-; Marseilles Hospitals Biologist 63-; Dir. Medical Tropical Inst., Dean of the Medical Faculty, Marseilles 67; Rector Acad. of Aix-Marseilles 70, Titular Prof. Clinical Neurophysiology 72-; Sec., later Pres., Int. Fed. of Socs. for Electroencephalography and Clinical Neurophysiology, Int. League against Epilepsy; Hon. mem. or corresp. Soc. de Neurologie Française, American Acad. of Neurology, Royal Medico-Psychological Asscn. (U.K.), Royal Soc. of Medicine (U.K.), etc.; Dr. h.c. (Ottawa, Liège, Bologna); Prix Monthyon (French Acad. des Sciences) 57; Chevalier Légion d'Honneur, Officier Ordre du Mérite, Palmes Académiques, Officier Saint Charles de Monaco, Commandeur Ordre National, Ivory Coast.
Leisure interest: collection of ethnographical art.
Publs. books and monographs on applied neurophysiology.
87 boulevard Périer, Marseilles 8, France.
Telephone: 33-44-82.

Gat, Dr. Joel R., M.SC., PH.D.; Israeli professor of isotope research; b. 17 Feb. 1926, Munich, Germany; m.; two c.; ed. Hebrew Univ., Jerusalem.
Department of Physical Chem., Hebrew Univ. 49-50; Ministry of Defence Laboratories, Jerusalem 50-52; Israel Atomic Energy Comm., Rehovot 52-59; Fellow, ISNSE, Argonne Nat. Laboratories and Enrico Fermi Inst., Univ. of Chicago, Ill. 55-56; Fellow, Scripps Inst. of Oceanography, Univ. of Calif. San Diego at La Jolla 64-65; Acting Head, Isotopes Dept., Weizmann Inst. of Science 66-70, 74-; Prof. Isotope Research 71-; Deputy Chair. Scientific Council 72-; Walter P. Reuther Chair in the Peaceful Uses of Atomic Energy 68.
3 Hagrast, Rehovot, Israel.

Gates, Marshall De Motte, Jr.; American professor of chemistry; b. 25 Sept. 1915, Boyne City, Mich.; s. of Marshall D. Gates and Virginia Orton Gates; m. Martha L. Meyer 1941; two s. two d.; ed. Rice and Harvard Univs.
Assistant Prof. of Chem., Bryn Mawr Coll. 41-46, Assoc. Prof. 47-49; Tech. Aide, Nat. Defense Research Council 43-46; Lecturer in Chem. Univ. of Rochester 49-52, part-time Prof. 52-60, Prof. 60-68, Charles Houghton Prof. of Chemistry 68-; mem. Cttee. on Drugs Addiction and Narcotics, Div. of Medical Sciences, Nat. Research Council 56-69; mem. Nat. Acad. of Sciences, American Chem. Soc.; Fellow, American Acad. of Arts and Sciences, N.Y. Acad. of Sciences; Asst. Editor *Journal of American Chemical Society* 49-62, Editor 63-69; Max Tishler Lecturer, Harvard 53, Welch Foundation Lecturer 60; mem. President's Cttee. on Nat. Medal of Science 68-70, Advisory Board, Chem. Abstract Services 74-76; E. P. Curtis Award 60.
Leisure interests: skiing, sailing.
Department of Chemistry, University of Rochester, Rochester, N.Y. 14627; Home: 41 West Brook Road, Pittsford, New York, U.S.A.

Gates, Thomas Sovereign, Jr.; American politician; b. 10 April 1906; ed. Univ. of Pennsylvania.
Associated with Drexel and Co. 28-, partner 40-53; Under-Sec. for Navy 53-57; Sec. for Navy 57-59; Sec. of Defense 59-61; Head U.S. Liaison Office, Peking 76-; Naval Reserve Officer 42-45; Chair. Exec. Cttee. Morgan Guaranty Trust 61-62, 65-68, 69-71, Pres. 62-65, Dir. 71-; Dir. Bethlehem Steel Corpn. 70-, Campbell Soup Co., Cities Service Co., Gen. Electric Co., Insurance Co. of North America, Scott Paper Co. and Smith Kline & French Laboratories; Trustee, Univ. of Pa. and Acad. of Political Science; Bronze Star, Yale; Hon. LL.D., Columbia and Yale Univs., and Univ. of Pa.
U.S. Liaison Office, Peking, People's Republic of China; Home: Mill Race Farm, Devon, Pa. 19333, U.S.A.

Gatto, Eugenio; Italian lawyer and politician; b. 1911, Zenson di Piave.
Former mem. Catholic Action; appointed to Nat. Liberation Cttee. of Venice; as rep. of Christian Democrat Party signed surrender of Venice and negotiated withdrawal of German troops; Commr. of Justice and Internal Affairs, regional Nat. Cttee. of Liberation April 45; fmr. Provincial Sec. of Christian Democrat Party; fmr. local Councillor; fmr. Pres. Provincial Fed. of the "Coldiretti"; elected to Chamber of Deputies 48, 53, 58; Under-Sec. for Industry, 2nd Fanfani and 2nd Segni govts.; Under-Sec. for State Participations, 3rd and 4th Fanfani govts.; elected to Senate 63, 68, Under-Sec. for State Participations, 1st Leone govt.; Under-Sec. to Ministry of the Treasury, 2nd and 3rd Moro govts.; Minister for Bureaucratic Reform; Minister without Portfolio responsible for problems of Regional Devt. March 70-Jan. 72.
Camera dei Deputati, Rome, Italy.

Gaud, William Steen, B.A., LL.B.; American lawyer and government official; b. 9 Aug. 1907; ed. Yale Univ. and Law School.
Instructor Yale Law School 31-33; law practice, N.Y. 35-41; Special Asst. to Sec. of War 45-46; mem. Carter, Ledyard and Milburn law firm 46-61; Asst. Administrator (in charge of the Middle East and South Asia Region) Agency for Int. Development 61-64; Dep. Administrator, Agency for International Development 64-66, Administrator 66-70; Exec. Vice-Pres. Int. Finance Corpn. 69-74; Consultant to World Bank Group 74-.
International Bank for Reconstruction and Development, 1818 H Street, N.W., Washington, D.C. 20433, U.S.A.

Gaudry, Roger, D.SC.; Canadian university administrator; b. 1913, Quebec City; s. of Joseph-Marc Gaudry and Marie-Ange Frenette; m. Madeleine Vallée 1941; two s. three d.; ed. Laval Univ.
Rhodes Scholar, Oxford Univ. 37-39; Lecturer in Organic Chem., Faculty of Medicine, Université Laval 40, Assoc. Prof. 45-50, Prof. 50-54; Guest Speaker at La Sorbonne under the auspices of the Institut Scientifique Franco-Canadien; Asst. Dir. of Research, Research Laboratories, Ayerst McKenna and Harrison Ltd. 54, Dir. of Research 57-65 (and of Ayerst Laboratories, N.Y.), Vice-Pres. 63-65; Rector, Université de Montréal 65-75; Vice-Chair. Science Council of Canada 66-72, Chair. 72-75; Chair. Council, UN Univ. 74-76; Fellow, Royal Soc. of Canada 54; Pres. Chemical Inst. of Canada 55-56, Canadian Asscn. of Rhodes Scholars 60-61; mem. Board Société de Chimie Industrielle de France 60-, Board of Govs. and Exec. Cttee. Université de Montréal 61-65, Defence Research Board of Canada 62-68, Board Nat. Research Council of Canada 63-68, Nat. Cancer Inst. of Canada 63-, Board Association des Universités Partiellement ou Entièrement de Langue Française 65- (Vice-Pres. 72-75); mem. Académie du Monde latin 67, Institut de la Vie, Paris 68-; Pres. Asscn. of Univs. and Colls. of Canada 69-71; mem. of the Board Int. Asscn. of Univs. 70-, Pres. 75-; Gen. Trust of Canada 70-75; mem. Econ. Council of Canada 70-73; Pres. Conf. of Rectors and Principals of Quebec Univs. 70-72; hon. life mem. Corpn. of Professional Chemists of Quebec 64, Association professionnelle des pharmaciens d'industrie du Québec 72; hon. mem. Royal Coll. of Physicians and Surgeons of Canada 71; Hon. LL.D. (Univ. of Toronto) 66, D.Sc. (Royal Mil. Coll. of Kingston) 66, D.Sc. (Univ. of B.C.) 67, LL.D. (McGill Univ.) 67, Doctorate (Université de Clermont-Ferrand, France) 67, LL.D. (St. Thomas Univ., Fredericton, N.B.) 68, LL.D. (Brock Univ., St. Catherines, Ont.) 69, LL.D. (Bishop's Univ.) 69, D.Sc. (Univ. of Sask., Regina) 70; Province of Quebec Science Award (three times); Pariseau Medal, Association canadienne-française pour l'avancement des sciences 58; Companion of the Order of Canada 68.
Publs. numerous scientific papers on organic and biological chemistry.
Université de Montréal, 2910 boulevard Edouard-Montpetit, app. 6, CP 6128, Montreal H3C 3J7, Quebec, Canada.

Gaus, Günter; German Secretary of State, journalist, diplomatist and politician; b. 23 Nov. 1929, Braunschweig; s. of Willi and Hedwig Gaus; m. Erika Butzengeiger 1955; one d.; ed. Oberrealschule Braunschweig and Munich Univ.
Journalist with various daily and weekly newspapers, and Second German TV 53-65; Programme Dir. Südwestfunk 65-69; Chief Editor *Der Spiegel* 69-73; Sec. of State, Chancellery of Fed. Repub. of Germany, Bonn 73-; Head of Perm. Representation of Fed. Repub. of Germany, Berlin (G.D.R.) 74-; Adolf Grimme Prize, Bronze 64, Silver 65.
Publs. *Zur Person* (two vols.), *Bonn ohne Regierung* 65, *Gespräch mit Herbert Wehner* 66, *Zur Wahl gestellt* 69.
Ständige Vertretung der Bundesrepublik Deutschland, 104 Berlin, Hannoversche Strasse 30, German Democratic Republic.
Telephone: 282-5261.

Gautier, Georges Armand Léon; French overseas administrator; b. 11 April 1901, Boulogne-sur-Mer; m. Marie-Louise Cailleau 1923; ed. Univ. de Paris, Ecole Nationale de la France d'Outre-Mer.
Administrator in the Civil Service in Indo-China 25; Sec.-Gen. Indo-China Government 41; Governor of the Colonies 42; Sec.-Gen. of Madagascar 50; Gov.-Gen. of France Overseas 51; Sec.-Gen. of the High Comm. of France in Indo-China 51; High Comm. of the French Republic of Vietnam 51; Pres. Conseil d'Administration de l'Institut d'Emission de l'A.E.F. et du Cameroun 55; Pres. of the Administrative Council of Central Bank of the States of Equatorial Africa and of the Cameroon 59-73; Commdr. Légion d'Honneur.
35 rue de la Ferme, 92 Neuilly-sur-Seine (Seine), France.
Telephone: SAB-26-88.

Gautier, Jean-Jacques; French dramatic critic; b. 4 Nov. 1908, Essômes, Aisne; m. Gladys Leigh 1946; ed. Collège de Dieppe, Lycée de Laon, and Univ. of Paris.
Journalist *L'Echo de Paris* 35; Editorial Staff *L'Epoque* until 39; Dramatic Critic *Figaro* 44-; Sec.-General Comédie Française until 46; mem. Acad. Française 72-; Officer Légion d'Honneur; Croix de Guerre; Prix Goncourt 46, Grand Prix de la Nouvelle 57, Grand Prix Littéraire de Monaco 70.
Leisure interest: walking.
Publs. *Histoire d'un fait divers* 46 (Prix Goncourt), *Vous aurez de mes nouvelles* 57 (Grand Prix de la Nouvelle), *Si tu ne m'aimes pas je t'aime* 60, *C'est pas d'jeu* and *Deux fauteuils d'orchestre* 62, *Une femme prisonnière* 68, *La Chambre du Fond* 70, *Cher Untel* 74, and other novels.
25 quai d'Anjou, Paris 4e, France.

Gauvin, Michel, D.S.O., B.A.; Canadian diplomatist; b. 7 April 1919, Quebec; s. of Raymond Gauvin and Stella McLean; divorced; two s.; ed. St. Charles Garnier Coll., Laval and Carleton Univs.
Ambassador to Ethiopia 66-69, to Portugal 69-70, to Greece 70-; Head of Canadian del. to Int. Comm. for Control and Supervision, Viet-Nam Jan.-Aug. 73.
Leisure interests: golf, sailing, bridge.
Publ. *La Geste du Régiment de la Chaudière*.
Canadian Embassy, 4 Ioannou Ghenadiou, Athens, Greece.

Gavazzeni, Gianandrea; Italian musician and writer; b. 1919, Bergamo; ed. Milan Conservatory (under Renzo Lorenzoni) and under Ildebrando Pizzetti and Mario Pilati.

Early compositions included *Concerto bergamasco* (for orchestra), *Paolo e Virginia* (opera, first perf. at Bergamo 35) and *Il furioso nell'isola di San Domingo* (ballet, first perf. at San Remo 40); conductor 40-; associated with La Scala, Milan 48-, Artistic Dir. 66-68; has participated in many festivals with La Scala including the Edinburgh Festival 57, World Fair, Brussels 57, *Expo* 67, Montreal and also at the Bolshoi and Kremlin theatres, Moscow 64; has directed numerous operatic recordings with La Scala; as a music critic has written studies of Donizetti, Pizzetti, Mascagni, Mussorgsky and guides to the operas of Mozart, Wagner, etc.; other compositions include *Il canto di S. Alessandro*, *Canti d'operai lombardi* (for orchestra), three *Concerti di Cinquando* (for orchestra), violin and 'cello concertos, piano pieces and numerous songs with words by Bacchelli, Cardarelli, Rilke, etc.
Via Porta Dipinta 5, Bergamo, Italy.

Gavin, Lieut.-Gen. James M., D.S.O.; American army officer, diplomatist and business executive; b. 22 March 1907, New York, N.Y.; s. of Martin Thomas and Mary (Terrel) Gavin; m. 2nd Jean Emert Duncan 1948; one d. (first marriage), four d. (second marriage); ed. U.S. Military Acad. at West Point.
Enlisted as Private 24, Lieut. 29, Lt.-Gen. 44; Commanded 505th Paratroop Combat Team, landing in Sicily and Salerno 43; Asst. Div. Commdr. 82nd Airborne Div. landing in Normandy 44, Div. Commdr. 82nd Airborne Div. landing in Nijmegen 44; Ardennes 45; Deputy Chief of Staff for Plans and Research 55; Chief Research and Devt. 55-59; Amb. to France 61-62; mem. American Acad. Sciences; Pres. Arthur D. Little, Inc. 60-61, 63-64, Chair. of the Board 64-; Dir. American Electric Power Co. Inc., John Hancock Life Insurance Co.; Advisory Dir. New England Merchants Nat. Bank.
Leisure interests: reading, golf, tennis, painting.
Publs. *Airborne Warfare* 47, *War and Peace in the Space Age* 58, *France and the Civil War in America* 64, *Crisis Now* 68.
c/o Arthur D. Little Inc., 25 Acorn Park, Cambridge, Mass. 02140, U.S.A.
Telephone: 617-864-5770, Ext. 2601 (Office).

Gawrysiak, Jerzy; Polish politician; b. 1928, Rybno, near Wołcławek; ed. Leningrad Univ.
Scientific worker, Poznań Polytechnic till 58; Sec. Poznań-Wilda District Cttee. of Polish United Workers' Party (PZPR) 58-61; Deputy Head of Org. Dept., Poznań Voivod Cttee. of PZPR 61-63, Econ. Sec. 64-70; Deputy Chair. Praesidium of Poznań Voivod Nat. Council 63-64; Under-Sec. of State, Ministry of Internal Trade 71-72; Head of Econ. Dept., Cen. Cttee. of PZPR 72; First Sec. Rzeszów Voivod Cttee. of PZPR 72-75; Minister of Internal Trade and Services May 75-; Knight's and Officer's Cross, Order of Polonia Restituta; Order of Banner of Labour, 2nd Class 74.
Ministerstwo Handlu Węwnetrznego i Usług, Plac Powstańców Warszawy 1, 00-030 Warsaw, Poland.

Gaxotte, Pierre; French writer; b. 19 Nov. 1895; ed. Ecole Normale Supérieure.
Taught history 20-22; Editor-in-chief of *Candide* 24-40; now writes for *Figaro*; mem. Acad. Française 53-.
Publs. *La Révolution Française* 28, *Le Siècle de Louis XV* 33, *Frédéric II* 38, *La France de Louis XIV* 46, *Histoire des Français*, 2 vols. 51, *Thèmes et variations* 57, *Histoire de France* 61, *Histoire de L'Allemagne*, 2 vols. (Prix des Ambassadeurs 63) 63, *Aujourd'hui* 65, *L'Académie française* 65, *Paris au XVIIIe siècle* 68, *Mon village et moi* 68, *Le Nouvel Ingénu* 70, *Louis XIV* 74.
23 rue Froidevaux, Paris 14e, France.

Gay, Geoffrey Charles Lytton, F.R.I.C.S.; British real estate consultant; b. 14 March 1914; s. of Charles Gay and Ida Lytton; m. Dorothy Ann Rickman 1947; one s. two d.; ed. St. Paul's School.

Served World War II, Durham Light Infantry B.E.F. 40, Staff Coll. Camberley and India, Lieut.-Col., Chief of Staff, Sind District 43; joined Knight Frank and Rutley 29, Senior Partner 73-75; Gen. Commr. for Inland Revenue 53-; mem. Westminster City Council 62-71; World Pres. Int. Real Estate Fed. (FIABCI) 73-75; mem. St. John Council for London; Gov. Benenden School; Liveryman, Worshipful Co. of Broderers; Chevalier Ordre de l'Economie Nationale 60; Officer Order of St. John of Jerusalem.
Leisure interests: photography, painting, music, theatre, fishing.
C2 Albany, Piccadilly, London, W.1. England.
Telephone: 734-6330.

Gazenko, Oleg Georgievich, PH.D., M.D.; Soviet physiologist; b. 12 Dec. 1918, Nikolaevka, Stavropol; m.; one s. one d.; ed. Moscow Medical Inst.
Service in the Army 41-46; Research Assoc. Kirov Mil. Medical Acad. 46-47; U.S.S.R. Acad. of Sciences Inst. of Experimental Medicine 47-69, Dir. Inst. of Medical and Biological Problems 69-; mem. C.P.S.U. 53; Corresp. mem. U.S.S.R. Acad. of Sciences 66-; mem. Int. Acad. of Astronautics, Aerospace Medical Asscn.; Order of Lenin; Daniel and Florence Guggenheim Int. Astronautics Award 75.
Leisure interests: mountaineering, canoeing.
Publs. Works on experimental physiology and space medicine; Co-editor *Foundations of Space Biology and Medicine* (U.S.A.-U.S.S.R. joint publ.).
U.S.S.R. Academy of Sciences, 14 Leninsky Prospekt, Moscow V-71, U.S.S.R.

Gazier, Albert, L. EN D.; French politician; b. 16 May 1908, Valenciennes; m. Marie-Louise Elter 1945.
Employed by Presses Universitaires de France, Paris; joined Socialist Party; Sec.-Gen. of Chambre des Employés de la Région Parisienne; active in Resistance during Occupation; came to England and later returned to France; mem. of Bureau de Confédération Générale du Travail (C.G.T.); C.G.T. delegate to Provisional Constituent Assemblies Algiers 43-44, Paris 44-45; later Sec. of C.G.T. Bureau; Deputy for Seine; Under-Sec. for Nat. Economy in Gouin Govt.; Under-Sec. for Public Works and Transport in Bidault Govt.; Sec. to Presidency of Council in Blum Govt.; Minister of Information in Pleven and Queuille Govts. 50-51; Minister of Social Affairs 56-57; Minister of Information May 58; mem. of Exec. French Socialist Party.
12 avenue du Parc, 92 Vanves, France.
Telephone: 642-23-08.

Gazit, Maj.-Gen. Shlomo; Israeli army officer; b. 1926, Turkey; m.; three c.; ed. Tel Aviv Univ.
Joined Palmach 44, Co. Commdr. Hazel Brigade 48; Dir. Office of Deputy Chief of Staff; Dir. Office of Chief of Staff 53; Liaison Officer with French Army Del., Sinai Campaign 56; Instructor Israel Defence Forces Staff and Command Coll. 58-59; Gen. Staff 60-61; Deputy Commdr. Golani Brigade 62; Instructor Nat. Defence Coll.; with Intelligence Branch, IDF 64-67; Dir. Dept. of Mil. Govt., Gen. Staff and Co-ordinator of Activities in Administered Areas, Ministry of Defence 67-74; rank of Maj.-Gen. 73; Head of Mil. Intelligence April 74-.
Military Intelligence Headquarters, Israel Defence Forces, Tel Aviv, Israel.

Gazzar, Abdel Hadi el; Egyptian artist; b. 1925; ed. Cairo and Rome Acad. of Fine Arts.
Professor of Painting, Cairo Faculty of Fine Arts; rep. at numerous exhibitions, including the 28th and 30th Venice Biennale, Brussels Int. Exhibition 58 and São Paulo Bienal 61; Exhibitions in Cairo, Alexandria and Rome; First Prize "10 Years of the Revolution" Exhibition 62.
Faculty of Fine Arts, Cairo University, Cairo, Egypt.

Gedda, Nicolai; Swedish operatic tenor; b. 11 July 1925; ed. Musical Acad., Stockholm.
Debut, Stockholm 52; Concert appearances Rome 52, Paris 53, 55, Vienna 55, Aix-en-Provence 54, 55; first operatic performances in Munich, Lucerne, Milan and Rome 53, Paris, London and Vienna 54; Salzburg Festival 57-59, Edinburgh Festival 58-59; with Metropolitan Opera, N.Y. 57-; world-wide appearances in opera, concerts and recitals; numerous recordings.
c/o Lies Askonas, 19A Air Street, London, W.1, England.
Telephone: 01-734 5459.

Geddes, Sir (Anthony) Reay (Mackay), K.B.E.; British business executive; b. 7 May 1912; ed. Rugby and Cambridge Univ.
Chairman Dunlop Holdings Ltd. 68-; Dir. Pirelli S.p.A. 71-, Soc. Int. Pirelli S.A., Shell Transport & Trading Co. Ltd. 68-, Midland Bank Ltd. 67-, Rank Org. 75-; Chair. Shipbuilding Inquiry Cttee. 65-66, British Nat. Cttee. of Int. Chamber of Commerce 74-; mem. Int. Advisory Cttee., Chase Manhattan Bank 74-.
Dunlop House, 25 Ryder Street, St. James's, London, S.W.1, England.

Geddes, Ford Irvine, M.B.E.; British business executive; b. 17 Jan. 1913; s. of I. C. Geddes; m. Barbara Gertrude Parry-Okeden 1945; one s. four d.; ed. Loretto School and Gonville and Caius Coll., Cambridge.
Anderson Green and Co. Ltd., London 34, Dir. 47-68; Army Service 39-45; Man. Dir. P. & O. Steam Navigation Co. 63-72, Deputy Chair. 68-71, Chair. 71-72; Dir. Equitable Life Assurance Soc., Pres. 63-71; Dir. Bank of New South Wales (London Advisory Board), Chair. Technical Cttee., Chamber of Shipping of U.K. 60-65; Chair. British Shipping Fed. 65-68; Chair. Container Fleets Ltd. 67-71; Pres. Int. Shipping Fed. 67-69.
The Manor, Berwick St. John, Shaftesbury, Dorset SP7 0EX, England.

Geddes of Epsom, Baron (Life Peer), cr. 58, of Epsom; **Charles John Geddes,** C.B.E.; British trade unionist; b. 1 March 1897; ed. Blackheath School.
Member Exec. Council Union of Post Office Workers 28, Asst. Gen. Sec. 41, Gen. Sec. 45-57; Chair. Post Office Departmental Whitley Council, Staff Side; mem. Civil Service Nat. Whitley Council; mem. Gen. Council, Trades Union Congress 46-58, Chair. 54-55; mem. Exec. Board ICFTU; Pres. European Regional Org. of ICFTU; Pres. Postal, Telegraph and Telephone Int. 56-58; Chair. Polyglass Group Cos.; Dir. Telesign Ltd.; mem. Royal Inst. Int. Affairs; mem. Labour Party.
28 Parkhill Court, Addiscombe Road, Croydon, CR0 5PJ, England.
Telephone: 01-681-1188.

Geertsema, Willem Jacob, LL.M.; Netherlands politician; b. 18 Oct. 1918, Utrecht; m. Adolfine Schoonenberg 1947; three s.; ed. classical grammar school and State Univ., Leiden.
Private tutor in Civil Law 47-53; mem. Leiden Municipal Council 50-53; Burgomaster of Warffum 53-57; Head, Gen. Affairs Dept. under the State Sec. for Home Affairs 57-59; Burgomaster of Wassenaar 61-71; mem. Second Chamber of Parl. 59-71, Leader of Liberal Party in Second Chamber 64-66, 69-71; Chair. Netherlands Soc. for Prevention of Rheumatism and Nat. Rheumatism Fund until June 71; Second Deputy Prime Minister and Minister for Home Affairs July 71-May 73; Minister for Surinam and Netherlands Antilles Affairs Jan.-May 73; Cross of Merit, Netherlands Red Cross 67, Knight, Order of the Netherlands Lion 70.
Leisure interests: cricket, hockey.
c/o Ministry of Home Affairs, The Hague; Home: Konijnenlaan 47, Wassenaar, Netherlands.
Telephone: 01751-8260.

Gegesi Kiss, Pál, M.D.; Hungarian pediatrician; b. 11 Feb. 1900, Nagyszöllös; s. of Ernö Gegesi Kiss and

Mariska Nagy; m. Anna Vadnay 1947; two s. three d. two adopted s.
Rector of Budapest Medical Univ. 55-61; Dir. Budapest Clinic of Pediatrics No. 1 46-71, Prof. Emer. 71-; mem. Hungarian Acad. of Sciences; Pres. Hungarian Nat. Red Cross; Hon. mem. Soviet Soc. of Pediatrics 57, Purkyné Medical Soc. of Czechoslovakia 63; Kossuth Prize 57; Order of Labour Gold Medal, Liberation Medal, Order of the Red Banner, Gold Medal, Hungarian Acad. of Sciences.
Leisure interest: fine arts.
Publs. *Diabetes Mellitus in Newborns and Infants* 56; (co-author) *Cardiac and Circulatory Diseases in Infancy and Childhood* 53, 60, *Disease and Medical Treatment* 65, *Bases of Clinical Psychology* 68, *Personality Disorders in Childhood* 65, *Psychopathology in Childhood* 72.
No. 1 Clinic of Pediatrics, Semmelweis University Medical School, Bókay János-u. 53, H-1083 Budapest VIII, Hungary.
Telephone: 343-186.

Geghman, Yahya Hamoud; Yemeni diplomatist; b. 24 Sept. 1934; ed. Law Schools, Cairo, Paris, Damascus and Boston and Columbia Univs.
Teacher of Arabic Language and Literature, Kuwait 57-59; Dir.-Gen. Yemen Broadcasting System, Special Adviser, Ministry of Foreign Affairs 62-63; Deputy Perm. Rep. to UN 63-66, 67-68; Minister Plenipotentiary, Yemen Arab Repub. (Y.A.R.) Embassy to U.S.A. 63-67; Minister of Foreign Affairs 68-69; Minister of State, Personal Rep. of the Pres. 69; Deputy Prime Minister 69-71; Perm. Rep. to UN 71-73; Amb. to U.S.A. 73-74; Pres. Supreme Council for Youth's Welfare and Sport 70; Gov. for Y.A.R., Int. Bank for Reconstruction and Devt., Int. Monetary Fund 70-71; mem. of del. to Conf. of Arab Heads of Govts. 65, 69, to U.S.S.R. 68, to UN General Assembly 62-; has represented Y.A.R. at many int. functions.
Publs. articles on politics, economics and literature in various Arabic journals.
c/o Ministry of Foreign Affairs, Sana'a, Yemen Arab Republic.

Gehlhoff, Walter, M.D.; German diplomatist; b. 6 May 1922, Berlin; s. of Kurt Gehlhoff and Elsbeth Legies; m. Dr. Eva Biegel 1949; one s. two d.
Held several diplomatic posts in Bonn 51-53, 58-60, Cairo 53-56, Beirut 56-58, Teheran 60-66; Dir. Middle East Affairs Desk, Foreign Office, Bonn 66; Deputy Asst. Sec. of State for Political Affairs 69, Acting Asst. Sec. of State 70; Amb. and Perm. Observer of Fed. Germany to UN 71-73, Amb. and Perm. Rep. 73-74; State Sec., Foreign Office, Bonn 74-.
Leisure interests: ornithology, astronomy.
c/o Auswärtiges Amt, 53 Bonn, Adenauerallee 99-103, Federal Republic of Germany.
Telephone: (02221) 17-2068.

Geijer, (Johan) Lennart; Swedish lawyer and politician; b. Sept. 1909, Ystad; m. Ninnie Löfgren 1944; two s. two d.; ed. Univs. of Lund and Stockholm.
Secretary and legal adviser, Swedish Union of Clerical and Technical Employees in Industry 39-57, Central Org. of Salaried Employees in Sweden 57-66; mem. Consultative Assembly, Council of Europe 64-66; mem. Riksdag 62-; Minister without Portfolio 66-69, Minister of Justice 69-.
Publ. *Employer and employees as judges in the Labour Court* 58.
Ministry of Justice, Fack, 103 10 Stockholm 2, Sweden.

Geijer, Karl Arne; Swedish trade union executive; b. 7 May 1910; ed. Trade Union Coll.
Metal worker until 38; Educational Sec., Swedish Metal Workers' Union 38-45, Sec. 45-49, Pres. 49-56; Pres. Confederation of Swedish Trade Unions 56-73; fmr. Pres.

Int. Confederation of Free Trade Unions (ICFTU); M.P., Social Democratic Party 55-.
Barnhusgatan 18, S-10553 Stockholm C, Sweden.

Geijer, Per, PH.D.; Swedish geologist; b. 7 May 1886, Stockholm; s. of Maj.-Gen. Gottschalk Geijer and Ketty Glosemeyer; m. Ester Hagström 1910 (died 1969); three s. one d.; ed. Uppsala Univ.
Lecturer Stockholm Univ. 10-14; Geologist Geological Survey of Sweden 14-31, Dir. 42-51; Prof. of Mineralogy and Geology, Royal Technological Inst. 31-41; retd.; Foreign mem. Nat. Acad. of Sciences, U.S.A., Geological Soc., U.K., American Geological Soc.
Publs. in various series and journals on geology and mineralogy, mainly on ore deposits 08-.
Stockholmsv. 96, 182 74 Stocksund, Sweden.
Telephone: 08-755 1189.

Geill, Torben, M.D.; Danish physician; b. 14 Aug. 1896, Aarhus; m. Luise Christine Haberda 1926; one s.; ed. Københavns Universitet.
Medical Asst., Univ. Medical Clinic, Copenhagen 26-28; Medical Asst., Bispebjerg Hospital, Copenhagen 30-36; Medical Dir. De Gamles By (Geriatric Unit), Copenhagen 36-66; mem. State Disablement Court 43-; Pres. Danish Gerontological Soc. 50-62, Int. Asscn. of Gerontology 63-66; Hon. mem. Italian Gerontological Soc., Argentine Gerontological Soc., Danish Gerontological Soc.; Knight Order of Dannebrog, 1st degree. Leisure interests: literature, music, paintings and engravings, archaeology, history of medicine, genealogy, philately.
Publs. *Studies on Albumin and Globulin in Serum and Urine* 28, *Textbook on Geriatrics* (with S. Eckerstrom), *Alderdomsproblemer* (Problems of Ageing), numerous papers on internal medicine, geriatrics, history of medicine and philately.
18 Barsehøj, Copenhagen-Hellerup, Denmark.
Telephone: GE 2717.

Geisel, Gen. Ernesto; Brazilian army officer, business executive and politician; b. 3 Aug. 1907, Bento Gon- calves, Rio Grande do Sul; s. of Augusto Geisel; brother of Orlando Geisel (q.v.); m. Amália Markus Geisel; one d.; ed. Military Colleges at Realengo, Armas, Estado Maior e Superior de Guerra and Army Staff Coll., U.S.A.
Served in various army units; numerous appts. included: chief artillery instructor, mil. coll.; Mil. Attaché, Brazilian Embassy, Uruguay; mem. perm. staff, Escola Superior de Guerra; Deputy Chief Mil. Cabinet of the Presidency 55, Chief 64-67; Sec.-Gen. Council for Nat. Security; Sec. of Public Works for State of Paraíba; Supt. of Pres. Bernardes Refinery 55; mem. Nat. Petroleum Council 57-58, 59-61; Minister, Supreme Mil. Court 67-69; Pres. of Petrobrás 69-73; Pres. candidate, ARENA Party 73; Pres. of Brazil March 74-; numerous decorations.
Office of the President, Brasília, Brazil.

Geisel, Orlando; Brazilian army officer and politician; b. 5 Sept. 1905, Rio Grande do Sul; s. of Augusto Geisel; brother of Gen. Ernesto Geisel (q.v.); ed. Colégio Militar de Porto Alegre, Escola Militar do Realengo.
Captain 30, Commdr. 32; Mil. Attaché, U.S.A. 50; Commdr. 3rd Army 66; Chief of Staff, Army 66; Chief of Staff of the Armed Forces 69-74; Minister of the Army 69-74.
c/o Ministério de Exército, Brasília, Brazil.

Gelb, Ignace Jay, PH.D.; American university professor; b. 14 Oct. 1907; ed. Univ. of Rome.
Travelling Fellow, later Instructor, Univ. of Chicago 29-41, Asst. Prof. 41-43, Assoc. Prof. 43, 46-47, Prof. of Assyriology 47-65, Frank P. Hixon Distinguished Service Prof. 65-; U.S. Army 43-45; Guggenheim Fellow 60-61; Colvin Research Prof. 62-63; Editor *Chicago Assyrian Dictionary* 47-; Hon. mem. Société Asiatique,

Paris, Societas Orientalis Fennica, Helsinki, Indian Oriental Soc., Hyderabad; Foreign mem. Accad. Nazionale dei Lincei, Rome; Fellow of the American Academy of Arts and Sciences; Pres. American Name Soc. 63-; Pres. American Oriental Soc. 65-.
Publs. *Hittite Hieroglyphs I-III* 31-42, *Inscriptions from Alishar* 35, *Hittite Hieroglyphic Monuments* 39, *Hurrians and Subarians* 44, *A Study of Writing* 52, *Sargonic Texts from the Diyala Region* 52, *Old Akkadian Writing and Grammar* 52, *Glossary of Old Akkadian* 57, *Sequential Reconstruction of Photo-Akkadian* 69.
Oriental Institute, University of Chicago, Chicago, Ill. 60637; and 5454 Woodlawn Avenue, Chicago, Ill., U.S.A.

Gelbard, José Ber; Argentine (b. Polish) business executive; b. 14 April 1917, Poland; m. Dina Haskel; one s. one d.
President Exec. Council of CAPIC; Pres. Gen. Econ. Fed. 53-55, 66-68, 70-73, mem. Nat. Consultative Comm. 53-55, Pres. Inst. of Econ. and Financial Inves- tigations 62-66; Minister of Finance May-Aug. 73, of the Economy 73-74; Pres. Nat. Productivity and Social Welfare Congress 55; Head of Employers' Asscn.; Head of del. to ILO Confs. 65, 71, Head of econ. dels. to Spain, Poland, Hungary, Czechoslovakia, U.S.S.R., Cuba, Venezuela, Peru and Chile 73-74, and del. to many other int. confs.; many foreign decorations.
Publs. numerous publications on socio-economic topics.
Arribeños 1697, 4° piso, Buenos Aires, Argentina.

Gélin, Daniel Yves; French actor; b. 19 May 1921; ed. Lycée de St. Malo, Paris Conservatoire.
Member Théâtre Nat. Populaire Company 60-; films in- clude *La Ronde, Dieu a Besoin des Hommes, Les Mains Sales, Paris-Canaille, Les Amants du Tage, En Effeuil- lant la Marguerite, Mort en Fraude, Charmants Garçons, Suivez-moi Jeune Homme, Ce Corps Tant Désiré, Austerlitz, Monsieur Masure, La Morte Saison des Amours, La Proie pour l'Ombre, Le Testament d'Orphée, Carthage en flammes, Peur panique, Le Jour le plus long, Règlements de compte, La Bonne Soupe, Vacances Portu- gaises, Le Soleil Noir* 66, *Duel à la vodka* 67, *Le Mois le plus beau* 68, *Slogan, Hallucinations sadiques, Détruite dit-elle* 69, *La Servante* 70, *Le Souffle au Coeur* 70, *Un linceul n'a pas de poches* 75.
Publ. *Fatras* (verse).
92 boulevard Murat, 75016 Paris; 28 Boutigny-sur- Opton, France.

Gell-Mann, Murray, PH.D.; American physicist; b. 15 Sept. 1929, New York City; s. of the late Arthur and Pauline Gell-Mann; m. J. Margaret Dow 1955; one s. one d.; ed. Yale Univ. and Massachusetts Inst. of Tech.
Member Inst. for Advanced Study, Princeton 51, 55; Instructor, Asst. Prof., and Assoc. Prof., Univ. of Chicago 52-55; Assoc. Prof., Calif. Inst. of Technology 55-56, Prof. 56-66, R. A. Millikan Prof. of Theoretical Physics 67-; Research Assoc. Univ. of Illinois 51, 53; Visiting Assoc. Prof. Columbia Univ. 54; Visiting Prof. Collège de France and Univ. of Paris 59-60, Mass. Inst. of Technology 63; mem. Nat. Acad. of Sciences, American Physical Soc., American Acad. of Arts and Sciences; Fellow and Chair. Western Center, American Acad. of Arts and Sciences 70-; Consultant, Inst. for Defense Analyses, Arlington, Va. 61, Rand Corpn., Santa Monica, Calif. 56-; mem. N.A.S.A. Physics Panel 64-, President's Science Advisory Cttee. 69-; Consultant to Los Alamos Scientific Laboratory, Los Alamos, N.M. 56-; Dannie Heineman Prize, American Physical Soc. 59; Ernest O. Lawrence Award 66, Franklin Medal 67, John J. Carty Medal (Nat. Acad. of Sciences) 68, Nobel Prize in Physics 69; Hon. Sc.D. (Yale) 59, (Chicago) 67, (Illinois) 68, (Wesleyan Univ.) 68; Dr. h.c. (Turin, Italy) 69.
Major works: Developed strangeness theory, theory of neutral K mesons, eightfold way theory of approximate

symmetry, current algebra; contributed to theory of dispersion relations, and knowledge of structure of weak interaction.

Leisure interests: historical linguistics, wilderness trips.

Publ. (with Yuval Ne'eman *q.v.*) *The Eightfold Way* 64.

Lauritsen Laboratory of Physics, California Institute of Technology, Pasadena, Calif. 91109, U.S.A.

Telephone: 213-795-6841, Ext. 2686.

Gellhorn, Martha; American writer and war correspondent; b. St. Louis, Mo.; one *s.*; ed. John Burroughs School and Bryn Mawr Coll.

War Corresp., covering Spanish Civil War, Finnish-Russian War, Sino-Japanese War, Second World War, Java, Vietnam and Arab-Israeli Wars; now occasional journalism in Europe and Africa.

Publs. *The Trouble I've Seen* 36, *A Stricken Field* 39, *The Heart of Another* 40, *Liana* 43, *The Wine of Astonishment* 48, *The Honeyed Peace* 53, *Two by Two* 58, *The Face of War* 59, *His Own Man* 61, *Pretty Tales for Tired People* 65, *The Lowest Trees Have Tops* 67.

c/o Morgan Guaranty Trust Co., 31 Berkeley Square, London, W.1, England.

Gelzer, (Carl Otto) Michael, D.IUR.; Swiss diplomatist; b. 23 July 1916, Schaffhausen; *s.* of Heinrich Gelzer and Charlotte Lüdecke; *m.* Marie Christiane Sarasin 1964; two *s.*; ed. Univ. of Basle.

Deputy Attorney-Gen. of Canton of Basle City 43-45; Fed. Political Dept., Berne 46; Second Sec. Legation in Bucharest 51; First Sec. Del. in Berlin, Deputy Chief of Mission 55; Chief of Section, Fed. Political Dept. 57; Counsellor of Embassy and later Deputy Chief of Mission, Washington, D.C. 61; Deputy Chief of Div. for Political Affairs, Fed. Political Dept. 66, Deputy Dir., Chief of Div. for Political Affairs (Africa, Asia and Latin America) 73-75; Amb. to Fed. Repub. of Germany 75-.

Embassy of Switzerland, Goethestrasse 66, 5 Köln 51, Federal Republic of Germany.

Telephone: 38-06-41.

Gemayel, Sheikh Pierre; Lebanese politician; b. 1905; ed. Univ. St. Joseph, Beirut and Cochin Hospital, Paris.

Trained as a pharmacist; founded Parti Démocrate Social Libanais (Les Phalanges) 36, Leader 37-; imprisoned 37, 43; organized general strike 43; established the first Labour Code 44; Minister of Public Works 60, of Finance 60-61, of Communications 60, of Public Health 60, 61; Minister of Public Works 61-64, of the Interior 66-67; Deputy for Beirut 60-; Lebanese, Polish and Egyptian decorations.

Phalanges Libanaises, P.O. Box 992, Place Charles Hélou, Beirut, Lebanon.

Geneen, Harold Sydney, B.S.; American business executive; b. 22 Jan. 1910, Bournemouth, England; *s.* of Alexander and Aida (DeCruciani) Geneen; *m.* June Elizabeth Hjelm 1949; ed. New York Univ., Harvard Business School.

Worked for Wall Street brokers 26-32; Accountant, Mayflower Associates Inc. 32-34, Lybrand, Ross Bros. & Montgomery 34-42; American Can Co. 42-46; Bell & Howell Co., Chicago 46-50; Jones & Laughlin Steel Corp., Pittsburgh (Vice-Pres. and Controller) 50-56; Exec. Vice-Pres. and Dir. Raytheon Manufacturing Co., Waltham 56-59; Pres. and Chief Exec. Officer, Dir. Int. Telephone and Telegraph Corpn. 59-73, Chair. 64-; Pres., Chief Operating Officer 73-; mem. Board Int. Rescue Cttee.; U.S. Chair. Advisory Cttee. European Inst. Business Admin.; Grand Officer, Order of Merit for Distinguished Service, Peru; Commdr. of Belgian Order of the Crown; Great Cross Civil Merit, Grand Cross of Isabella (Spain); Doctor of Laws, PMC Colls., Lafayette Coll.

320 Park Avenue, New York, N.Y. 10022, U.S.A.

Genet, Jean; French writer; b. 19 Dec. 1910, Paris.

Publs. include: *Le Condamné à mort* 42, *Notre-Dame-des Fleurs* 43 (revised edn. 51), *Chants secrets* 45, *Miracle de la rose* 46, *les Bonnes* 47, *Pompes funèbres* 47, *Querelle de Brest* 47, *l'Enfant criminel et 'Adame Miroir* 49, *Haute Surveillance* 49, *le Journal du voleur* 49, *le Balcon* 56, *les Nègres* 58, *les Paravents* 61, *le Condamné à mort*, *la Galère, le Parade, Un chant d'amour, le Pêcheur du Suquet* (poems); *les Bonnes* 46, *Haute Surveillance* 49, *les Nègres* 58, *le Balcon* 59, *les Paravents* 61 (plays), *L'étrange mot d'* . . . , *Ce qui est resté d'un Rembrandt déchiré en petits carrés, Lettres à Roger Blin, Comment jouer "Les Bonnes", Comment jouer "Le Balcon"*.

c/o Rosica Colin, 4 Hereford Square, London, SW7 4TU, England; and Editions Gallimard, 5 rue Sebastien Bottin, Paris 7e, France.

Genevoix, Maurice; French novelist; b. 29 Nov. 1890, Decize, Nièvre; *s.* of Gabriel and Camille Balichon; *m.* Suzanne Neyrolles 1943; two *d.*; ed. Ecole Normale Supérieure.

Prix Goncourt winner 25; mem. Acad. Française 46-, Permanent Sec. 58-; mem., Conseil de la Radiodiffusion Française 58-; Hon. Pres. of the Librairie Académique Perrin 60-; mem. Conseil Supérieur des Gens de Lettres; Grand Croix de la Légion d'Honneur, Croix de Guerre, Commdr. des Arts et des Lettres, Commdr. Palmes Académiques; Grand Prix National des Lettres 70.

Leisure interest: painting.

Publs. *Sous Verdun* 14, *Nuits de guerre* 17, *Au seuil des guitounes* 18, *Jeanne Robelin* 20, *La boue* 21, *Rémi des Rauches* 22, *Les Eparges* 23, *La joie* 24, *Euthymos, vainqueur olympique* 24, *Raboliot* 25, *La boîte a pêche* 26, *Les mains vides* 28, *Cyrille* 28, *L'assassin* 30, *Rroû* 31, *H.O.E.* 32, *Forêt voisine* 33, *Gai l'amour* 32, *Marcheloup* 34, *Tête baissée* 37, *La dernière harde* 38, *Les compagnons de l'Aubepin* 38, *L'hirondelle qui fit le printemps* 41, *La framboise et Belhumeur* 42, *Canada* 45, *Eva Charlebois* 44, *Sanglar* 46, *L'écureuil du bois bourru* 47, *Afrique blanche, Afrique noire* 49, *Ceux de 14* 50, *L'Aventure est en nous, Fatou Cissé, Routes de L'Aventure, Au Cadran de mon clocher, Vaincre à Olympie, Jeux de Glaces* 61, *La Loire, Agnès et les Garçons* 62, *Derrière les Collines* 64, *Beau-François* 65, *La Fôret Perdue* 67, *Le Roman de Renard, Jardins sans murs* 68, *Tendre Bestiare* 68, *Bestiaire Enchanté* 69, *Bestiaire Sans Oubli* 71, *La Grèce de Caramanlis* 72, *La Mort de Près* 72, *La Perpétuité* 74.

17 rue Davioud, 75016 Paris; "Les Vernelles", 45 Saint-Denis-de-l'Hôtel, France.

Genovés, Juan; Spanish artist; b. 1930, Valencia; ed. Escuela Superior de Bellas Artes, Valencia.

Has taken part in numerous group exhbns.; one-man exhbns. in Spain, Portugal, U.S.A., Italy, Germany, Netherlands, Japan, U.K. and S. America 56-; took part in Paris Biennale 61, Venice Biennale 62, 66, São Paulo Biennale 65, etc.; Gold Medal, San Marino Biennale 67; Premio Marzotto 68.

c/o Marlborough Fine Art, 6 Albemarle Street, London, W.1, England.

Genscher, Hans-Dietrich; German politician; b. 21 March 1927, Reideburg, Saale; ed. Leipzig and Hamburg Univs.

Scientific Asst., Parl. Free Democratic Party (FDP) 56, later Sec.; Fed. Party Man. 62-64; Vice-Chair. 68-74, Chair. 74-; Deputy in Bundestag 65-; Fed. Minister of the Interior 69-74; Vice-Chancellor, Minister of Foreign Affairs May 74-.

Auswärtiges Amt, Adenauerallee 99-103, Bonn, Federal Republic of Germany.

Gensous, Pierre; French trade union official; b. 25 July 1925; Mont-de-Marson; one *s.* one *d.*; ed. Ecole Nationale Professionnelle, Tarbes.

Official, Union départementale des Hautes Pyrenées

des syndicats CGT, Sec. Féd. des Métaux CGT 54; Pres. Int. Union of Metal Workers' Trade Unions 61-62, Sec.-Gen. 64; Asst. Sec.-Gen. WFTU 65-69, Sec.-Gen. 69-.
World Federation of Trade Unions, Nam. Curieovych 1, Prague 1, Czechoslovakia.
Telephone: 67856.

Gentil, Paul; French railway executive; b. 20 Dec. 1921, Bourbon l'Archambault (Allier); s. of Julien Gentil and Anna Raynal; m. Marise Marfaing 1947; two d.; ed. Lycée d'Aurillac, Lycée de Clermont-Ferrand, Ecole Polytechnique and Ecole Nat. Supérieure des Mines, Paris.
Mining Engineer, Clermont-Ferrand 48-54; Railway Engineer, Soc. Nat. des Chemins de Fer Français (SNCF-French Nat. Railways), Dir. of Movement 66-71, Deputy Dir.-Gen. 71-74, Dir.-Gen. Oct. 74-; Chevalier, Légion d'Honneur.
88 rue Saint-Lazare, 75436 Paris Cedex 09, France.
Telephone: 874-73-00, 874-91-73, 522-96-00.

Georgadze, Mikhail Porfiryevich; Soviet government official; b. 1912; ed. Moscow Inst. of Mechanization of Agriculture.
Worked as tractor driver 29-34; mem. C.P.S.U. 42-; Engineer and subsequently Chief Engineer and Dept. Chief at U.S.S.R. Ministry of Agriculture 41-51; Chief Transcaucasian Motor Tractor Stations Admin. 51-53; Minister of Agriculture, Georgia, and Deputy Chair. Georgia Council of Ministers 53-54; Deputy to U.S.S.R. Supreme Soviet 54-; Sec. Central Cttee. Georgian C.P. 54-56; First Deputy Chair. Georgian Council of Ministers 56-57; Alt. mem. C.P.S.U. Central Cttee. 66-; Sec. Presidium U.S.S.R. Supreme Soviet 57-; Order of Lenin, etc.
Presidium of Supreme Soviet of U.S.S.R., The Kremlin, Moscow, U.S.S.R.

George, André, D.L.; French critic, essayist and physicist; b. 31 July 1890, Blida, Algeria; s. of Gaston George and Berthe Constant-François; m. Paule d'Izarny-Gargas 1937; two stepsons, two stepdaughters; ed. Paris Univ.
Member Comité du Langage Scientifique (founded by Acad. des Sciences); mem. Editorial Cttee. and Dir. Science Page, *Nouvelles Littéraires* 45-71; Dir. series *Sciences d'aujourd'hui* and *Les Savants et le Monde;* Science corresp. for *Figaro;* Pres. Sociéte Scientifique de Bruxelles 51-53; Air Commandant 40; Awarded Métais-Larivière Prize of Acad. Française for *Pasteur;* Grand Prix Broquette-Gonin Acad. Française for Collected Works 62; Prix Binoux de l'Acad. des Sciences pour écrits scientifiques 69, Grand Prix Métais-Larivière de l'Acad. Française 75; Officier de la Légion d'Honneur, Croix de Guerre, Officier des Arts et des Lettres.
Publs. *Henri Poincaré* (critical essay), *Arthur Honegger* 26, *Tristan et Isolde de Wagner* 27, *L'oratoire* 28, *L'oeuvre de Louis de Broglie et la Physique d'aujourd'hui* 31, *Mécanique quantique et Causalité* 32, *Les Conséquences générales de la Physique contemporaine* 33, *Pierre Termier* (awarded Bordin Prize of Acad. Française) 33, *Les Nébuleuses spirales et l'Univers en expansion* 34, *Paris* (essay) 37, *Le Véritable Humanisme* 42, *Dimensions du Temps* 43, *Les Grands Appels de l'Homme Contemporain* (ouvrage collectif) 46, *Pasteur* 58, trans. and complementary chapter of *Einstein, his Life and Time* (by Ph. Frank) 52-68, trans. and introduction of *Scientific Autobiography and Last Papers* (Max Planck) 60, *Science et Foi* 62, *Napoléon et les Sciences* (in *Napoléon,* ouvrage collectif) 68, *Vue d'ensemble de l'oeuvre de Louis de Broglie* 73, *Louis de Broglie, créateur de la Mécanique Ondulatoire* 75; numerous magazine and lecture writings.
Château de Gargas, Fronton, Haute-Garonne, 31620, France.
Telephone: (61) 84-95-16.

George, Thomas Neville, D.SC., PH.D., SC.D., D. ES SC., LL.D., F.R.S., F.R.S.E.; British university professor; b. 13 May 1904, Swansea, Wales; s. of T. Rupert George; m. Sarah Davies 1932; ed. Dynevor School and Grammar School, Swansea, Univs. of Wales, Cambridge and London.
Fellow, Univ. of Wales 26; Geologist on H.M. geological survey 30-33; Prof. of Geology, Univ. of Wales 33-46; Prof. of Geology, Univ. of Glasgow 47-74, Emer. Prof. 74-; Woodward Lecturer, Yale Univ. 56; Senior Foreign Fellow, Northwestern Univ. 64; Visiting Prof., Univs. of Witwatersrand, Cape Town and Natal 67; Distinguished Visiting Lecturer, Univ. Saskatchewan 74; Pres. Asscn. of Univ. Teachers 59-60, Palaeontological Asscn. 62-64, Scottish Field Studies Asscn. 65-68, Geological Soc. of London 68-70, Asscn. of Teachers of Geology 70-71; Corresp. mem. Geol. Soc. Belgium; Lyell Medal, Geological Soc. of London 63; Clough Medal, Edinburgh Geological Soc. 73; Kelvin Prize, Royal Philosophical Soc. 75.
Publs. *Evolution in Outline* 48, *British Regional Geology: North Wales* 61, *University Instruction in Geology* 65, *The British Caledonides* 66, *The Geology of Scotland* 67, *British Regional Geology: South Wales* 70.
Department of Geology, University of Glasgow, Glasgow, W.2, Scotland.
Telephone: 041-339-8855, Ext. 224.

George, William Henry Krome; American chemical engineer and business executive; b. 27 March 1918, St. Louis, Mo.; m. Jean Murphy 1946; three s.; ed. Edwardsville Public School, Ill., Virginia Mil. Inst. and Mass, Inst. of Technology (MIT).
Joined Aluminum Co. of America (Alcoa) 42; Plant Technical Div., Baton Rouge 42-44; Cost and Tech. Adviser, East St. Louis 44-51; Senior Staff Accountant, Pittsburgh 51-56; Chief Cost Accountant 56-60; Admin. Asst. Controller's Div. 60-63; Man. Econ. Evaulation Div. 63-64; Man. and Vice-Pres. Econ. Analysis and Planning 64-65; Vice-Pres. (Finance) 65-67, Exec. Vice-Pres. 67-70, Dir. 67-, Pres. 70-75, Chief Operating Officer 72-75, Chair. of Board and Chief Exec. Officer 75-; Dir. PPG Industries Inc., Pullman Inc., Mellon Bank N.A., Nat. Center for Resource Recovery; mem. MIT Corpn., World Affairs Council of Pittsburgh, Council on Foreign Relations, Management Executives Soc., Nat. Industrial Energy Council, U.S. Council of the Int. Chamber of Commerce; mem. Advisory Council Aluminium Soc.; Trustee Univ. of Pittsburgh.
Aluminum Company of America, 1501 Alcoa Building, Pittsburgh, Pennsylvania; Home: 642 Grove Street, Sewickley, Pennsylvania, U.S.A.

George-Brown, Baron (Life Peer), cr. 70, of Jevington in the County of Sussex; **George Alfred George-Brown,** P.C.; British politician; b. (as George Alfred Brown) 2 Sept. 1914, Lambeth; s. of George Brown; m. Sophie Levene 1937; two d.
Member of Parl. 45-70; Parl. Private Sec. to Minister of Labour and Nat. Service 45-47, to Chancellor of Exchequer 47; Joint Parl. Sec. Ministry of Agriculture and Fisheries 47-51; Minister of Works April-Oct. 51; Deputy Leader, Labour Party 60-70; First Sec. of State and Sec. of State for Econ. Affairs 64-66; Sec. of State for Foreign Affairs and Deputy Prime Minister 66-68; Productivity Counsellor, Courtaulds Ltd. 68-73; Dir. Diebold Computer Leasing 73-, First Fortune Holdings 74-; Chair. Council for Int. Contact Trust 74-, Stewart Title (U.K.) Ltd. 74-; Order of Cedar of Lebanon 71; Biancamano Prize 72; Labour (to 76).
Publ. *In My Way* (memoirs) 71.
House of Lords, London, S.W.1, England.

Georges, Chief Justice Philip Telford; West Indian Chief Justice of Tanzania 65-71; see *The International Who's Who 1975-76.*

Georges-Picot, Guillaume, L. en D.; French diplomatist and business executive; b. 10 Aug. 1898, Etretat; *m.* Nadya Biske 1932; three *d.*

Served French Army First World War; entered diplomatic service as Embassy Attaché 24, Ministry of Foreign Affairs Paris, placed on reserve list at his own request 26, rejoined service 28; Sec. Moscow 28-30; Ministry of Foreign Affairs Paris 30; took part in Int. Conf. Lausanne 32; successively Sec. Sofia, Sec. Bangkok, Sec. Peking, Sec. Mexico City; at disposal of Residency-Gen. Tunisia 40-41; sent to Washington 41; joined Free French and became Dir. of Civil Services French Mission to Washington 42; served Free French Forces 43-44; later at Commissariat of Foreign Affairs; after Liberation at Ministry of Foreign Affairs, Paris; sent on mission to China; Minister to Albania 46; Ambassador to Venezuela 46-48; Ambassador to Argentina 48-51; Asst. Sec.-Gen. of U.N. 51-54; Ambassador to Mexico 54-57; Permanent Rep. to U.N. and to Security Council 57-59; Dir., then Pres. Compagnie industrielle maritime 62-; Vice-Pres. Soc. d'investissements métropolitains et d'outre-mer (SIMER) 59-, Soc. des plantations réunies de Mimot 59-; Dir. of other companies; Hon. Chair. Franco-American Cttee. 68-; Commdr. de la Légion d'Honneur; Croix de Guerre.

Leisure interests: gardening, hiking, reading.

66 avenue Foch, Paris 16e, France.

Telephone: 704-23-07.

Georges-Picot, Jacques Marie Charles; French company director; b. 16 Dec. 1900; ed. Lycée Janson-de-Sailly, Ecole Libre des Sciences Politiques and the Sorbonne.

Inspector of Finance 25; Deputy Head of Secretariat, Ministry of Air 28; Head of Secretariat, Ministry of Budget 29; Deputy Dir. of Budget 31; Dir. of Taxes 35; Asst. Man., Suez Canal Co. 37, Pres. and Dir.-Gen. 57-70, Hon. Pres. 70- (renamed Suez Finance Co. 58); Pres. Crédit Industriel del' Ouest 57-71, Hon. Pres. 71-; Vice-Pres. Compagnie de Pont-à-Mousson 66-70, Compagnies d'assurances La Providence; Dir. Saint-Gobain, Compagnie française des pétroles, etc.; Dir. Fondation Nationale des Sciences Politiques 61, Institut Catholique de Paris; Commdr. de la Légion d'Honneur, Hon. K.B.E.

2 Square Mignot, Paris 16e, France.

Georgi, Rudi; German economist and politician; b. 1928. Candidate mem. Cen. Cttee. Sozialistische Einheitspartei Deutschlands; Minister for Heavy Engineering and Plant Construction 69-72, for Machine and Transport Manufacturers 72-73, for Processing-Machine and Vehicle Construction 73-.

Ministerrat, Berlin, German Democratic Republic.

Georgiev, Vladimir Ivanov; Bulgarian university professor; b. 1908, Gabare; *s.* of Ivan G. Grazdana and Janka Zeljazkova; *m.* Magdalena A. Obreimova 1953; ed. Univs. of Sofia, Vienna, Paris, Berlin and Florence. Professor Univ. of Sofia since 31; Dean Faculty of Letters 47-48; Rector 51-56; Dir. Inst. for Linguistics Acad. of Science; mem. Presidium Bulgarian Acad. of Science; Hon. Pres. Asscn. Int. des Etudes; Vice-Pres. Int. Cttee. of Slavists; mem. Acad. des Inscriptions et Belles Lettres, Paris, Sächsische Akad. der Wissenschaft, Leipzig, Soc. Finno-Ougrienne, Helsinki, Soc. Linguistique de Paris; Dr. h.c. (Univs. of Berlin and Prague).

Publs. many works, including *Vorgriechische Sprachwissenschaft* 41, *Issledovanija po sravniteljno-istoricheskomu jezykoznaniyu* 58, *Les deux langues des inscriptions crétoises* 63, *Vokalnata sistema v riazvoja na slavjanskite ezici* 64, *Introduzione alla storia delle lingueindeuropee* 66, *Osnovni problemi na slavjanskata diahronna morfologija* 69, etc.

c/o Bulgarian Academy of Sciences, 7 Noemvri 1, Bulgaria.

Georgy, Guy-Noël; French diplomatist; b. 17 Nov. 1918, Paris; *m.* Odette Bonhomme 1944; two *s.* one *d.*; ed. Faculty of Law, Bordeaux and Paris.

Chief of Cabinet and Head of Information Dept., Cameroun 45-49; Attaché, Ministry for French Overseas Territories 50; Head of North-Cameroun District, Maroua 51-55; Chief of Cabinet, Ministry for French Overseas Territories 55; Gen. Sec. to Gabon 56; Gen. Manager of Econ. Affairs and Plan, Equatorial Africa 57, West Africa 58; High Commr. in Congo 59; High Commr. Congo (Brazzaville) 60; Ambassador to Bolivia 61-64, to Dahomey 64-69, to Libya 69-.

c/o Ministère des Affaires Etrangères, Paris; 9 avenue Franco-Russe, Paris 7e, France.

Telephone: 551-87-50 (Paris).

Géraldy, Paul (*pseudonym* of Paul Lefèvre-Géraldy); French writer; b. 6 March 1885, Paris; ed. Lycée Henri IV, Lycée Buffon, Paris.

Commdr. Légion d'Honneur.

Publs. include *Toi et Moi*, *Vous et Moi* (verse), *Les Noces d'Argent*, *Les Grands Garçons*, *Aimer*, *Duo* (adapted from Colette), *Christine*, *Robert et Marianne* (plays), *Clindindin* (for children), *L'Homme et l'Amour* (essay), *Trois Comédies Sentimentales*, *Vous qui passez* (plays).

3 rue de Martignac, Paris and La Colline, 83 Beauvallon, Var, France.

Gerasimov, Innokentii Petrovich, D.GEOG.; Soviet geographer and pedologist; b. 9 Dec. 1905, Kostroma; *s.* of P. V. Gerasimov and M. P. Gerasimova; *m.* R. P. Zimina 1951; two *d.*; ed. Univ. of Leningrad.

Dokuchaev Inst. of Soil Science 30-56; Chief, Div. of Geography and Cartography of Soils 50-56; Dir. Inst. of Geography, Acad. of Sciences of U.S.S.R. 56-; Prof. Faculty of Geography, Lomonosov State Univ. of Moscow 46-56; Editor-in-Chief *Proceedings of the Academy of Sciences of U.S.S.R.*; mem. Acad. of Sciences 53-; Pres. All-Union Soc. of Soil Science 64-72; Vice-Pres. All-Union Geographical Soc. 56-, Int. Geographical Union 58-66; mem. Acads. of Science of Bulgaria, German Dem. Repub., Hungary; Hon. mem. Geographical Socs. of Poland, Finland, Serbia, Austria, Italy, Colombia, Cuba, France, Hungary, German Dem. Repub., Bulgaria, Royal Geographical Socs. of England and Scotland; Order of Lenin, Order of Red Star, Badge of Honour, etc.; State Prize Winner.

Leisure interests: art, music.

Publs. *Lednikovyi period na teritorii S.S.S.R.* (Glacial Period of the U.S.S.R. Territory) 39, *Ocherki po fizicheskoi geografii zarubezhnykh stran* (Essays on the Physical Geography of Foreign Countries) 59, *Osnovy pochvovedenia i geografii pochy* (Principles of Soil Science and Geography of Soils) 60, *Pochvite v Bolgaria* (Soils of Bulgaria) 60, *Strukturnye cherty reliefa S.S.S.R.* (Structural Features of the Relief of the U.S.S.R.) 58, *Pochvy tsentralnoi Yevropy* (Soils of Central Europe) 60, Soviet Geography (Editor-in-Chief) 60, *Physico-Geographical Atlas of the U.S.S.R.* 64, *Preobrazovanie prirody i razvitije geograficheskoj nauki v S.S.S.R.* (Transformation of Nature and Development of Geographical Science in the U.S.S.R.) 67, *Resursy biosfery na teritorii S.S.S.R.* (Resources of the Biosphere in the U.S.S.R. Territory) 71, *National Atlas of Cuba* 72, *Chelovek, obshchestvo, sreda* (Man, Society, Environment) 73.

Institute of Geography, Academy of Sciences of the U.S.S.R., 29 Staromonetny perenlok, Moscow, 109017, U.S.S.R.

Telephone: 2-31-61-44.

Gerasimov, Sergei Appolinarievich; Soviet film director and dramatist; b. 21 May 1906, Sverdlovsk; ed. State Inst. of Scenic Arts, Leningrad.

Began work in films as an actor 24; acted in films *The Overcoat* 26, *S.V.D.* 27, *One* 30, *The Border* 35, *Mas-*

querade 41; organized Leningrad Actor's Workshop and directed films *Seven Brave People* 35, *Komsomolsk* 37, *The Teacher* 39; other films *The Unvanquished* 42, *Great Land* 44, *The Young Guard* 48, *Liberated China* 50, *Country Doctor* 52, *Quiet Flows the Don* 58, *The Sputnik Speaks* 59, *Men and Beasts* 62, *The Journalist* (First Prize, Moscow Film Festival 67), *At the Lake* 70 (State Prize 71); mem. Praesidium Soviet Peace Cttee., Praesidium Union of Soviet Socs. of Friendship and Cultural Relations with Foreign Countries, Editorial Board of *Foreign Literature*; People's Artist of U.S.S.R.; State prizes for films *The New Teacher* 41, *The Young Guard* 49, *Liberated China* 51; Prof. and Head of the Directors' and Actors' Studios of the All-Union State Inst. of Cinematography; Sec. Asscn. of Film Makers of the U.S.S.R.; mem. C.P.S.U. 43-; Deputy to Supreme Soviets of U.S.S.R. 50-58, R.S.F.S.R. 67-; Order of Lenin (twice) and numerous decorations.
Publs. screenplays *The Teacher* 39, *Our Days* 40, articles on cinema.
Union of Cinematographists of the U.S.S.R., 14 Vasilevskaya, Moscow, U.S.S.R.

Gerdener, Theo J. A.; South African politician; b. 19 March 1916, Cape Town; s. of late Dr. G. B. A. Gerdener; m. Martha van Rensberg 1943; three c.; ed. Univ. of Stellenbosch.
Former mem. editorial staff, *Die Burger* and *Die Huisgenoot*; freelance journalist 49-; Leader, Nat. Party, Natal Provincial Council 54; Dir. and editor *Die Nataller* (Afrikaans newspaper), Durban 54-59; Senator 61; Administrator of Natal 61; Deputy Minister of Bantu Devt. May 70; Minister of the Interior Nov. 70-July 72 (resigned); f. and Dir. Action South and Southern Africa 72-; Founder, Leader Democratic Party 73-.
Leisure interests: sport, reading.
160 Anderson Street, Lynnwood, Pretoria, South Africa.

Gere, Mihai; Romanian politician; b. 2 Sept. 1919, Timişoara; m. Maria Gere; one s. one d.
Member R.C.P. 40-; political imprisonment 40-44; Alt. mem. Exec. Cttee. of Central Cttee. of Romanian C.P. 65-; Vice-Pres. State Council 65-67; Chair. State Cttee. for Local Admin. Problems 67-69; Deputy to Grand Nat. Assembly 65-; Alt. mem. Central Cttee. 66-; Sec. Nat. Council of Socialist Unity Front 72-; Hero of Socialist Labour.
Central Committee of the Romanian Communist Party, Bucharest, Romania.

Gerentz, Sven; Swedish journalist; b. 3 Sept. 1921, Visby, Sweden; s. of Thure and Elin (née Hemström) Gerentz; m. Kerstin Blix 1945; one s. one d.; ed. Stockholm School of Economics.
Secretary to Board of Trade 45-52, Chamber of Commerce 52-57; Man. Dir. Swedish Automobile Manufacturers' Asscn. 57-59, Chair. 60-; Deputy Man. Dir. *Svenska Dagbladet* 60-62, Man. Dir. 62-73, Chief Editor 69-73; Man. Dir. Tidningarnas Telegrambyraa 74-; Vice-Chair. Board of Swedish News Agency (TT) 65-72, Chair. 72-73; mem. Board, Stockholm Chamber of Commerce 65-.
Publs. *The Stockholm Mercantile Marine Office 1748-1948* 48, *The Swedish Board of Commerce and the Economy* 51.
Tidningarnas Telegrambyraa 105 12 Stockholm; Home: Johannesgatan 28, 111 38 Stockholm, Sweden.
Telephone: 22-44-80 (Office); 11-77-39 (Home).

Gerhardie, William Alexander, O.B.E., F.R.S.L., M.A.; British writer; b. 21 Nov. 1895, St. Petersburg (now Leningrad), Russia; s. of Charles Alfred Gerhardie and Clara Wadsworth; ed. St. Petersburg schools and Worcester Coll., Oxford.

Fought in the First World War as trooper, cadet and capt.; with Mil. Attaché, British Embassy, Petrograd, and British Mil. Mission to Siberia 16-20; with European Div., B.B.C. 42-45; First Editor of *English by Radio*; formed own company, Gerhardie Players, to produce own plays 75.
Leisure interest: creative idleness.
Publs. *Futility* 22, *The Polyglots* 25, *Doom* 28, *Pending Heaven* 30, *Resurrection* 34, *Of Mortal Love* 36, *My Wife's the Least of It* 38 (novels); *Pretty Creatures* (short novels) 27; a critical study of Chekhov 23, and an autobiography *Memoirs of a Polyglot* 31; *The Romanovs* (a biography of the dynasty) 39; *My Literary Credo: an Introduction to the Collected Revised Uniform Edition of the Works* 47, *Highlights of Russian History* 50; *Donna Quixote* 27, *I Was A King In Babylon* 46, *Rasputin* 60, *The Fool of the Family* (with C. P. Snow) 66 (plays); *Works, 2nd Collected Uniform Definitive Edn.,* 10 vols. 70-74; *Lip Service: Prognosis Dramatica Chronicling a Month in Mid-Next Century* 75; Essays in *Encounter*, *Books and Bookmen* and *Twentieth Century* 71.
19 Rossetti House, 106 Hallam Street, London, W.1, England.
Telephone: 01-580-4878.

Gerhardsen, Einar; Norwegian politician; b. 10 May 1897.
Road worker 14-22; Chair. Road Repairers' Union 19; Sec. Norwegian Municipal Asscn. 22-23; Sec. Oslo Labour Party 25-35; Sec. Norwegian Labour Party 34-45; mem. Oslo Town Council 32-45; Mayor of Oslo 40, dismissed by Germans; worked as road repairer; mem. Secret Central Cttee.; arrested 41; deported to Germany 42; held in Gestapo Headquarters in Oslo as hostage against British Mosquito raids 44; again Mayor of Oslo 45; Chair. Labour Party 45-65; Prime Minister 45-51; Leader Labour Party in Parl. 51-55; Pres. of Parl. 54-55; Prime Minister 55-Aug. 63 and Sept. 63-Oct. 65; mem. Parl. 65-.
Stortinget, Oslo, Norway.

Gerlach, Manfred, DR. JUR.; German politician; b. 8 May 1928, Leipzig.
Joined Liberal-Democratic Party 45; co-founder F.D.J. (Free German Youth), Leipzig; mem. of Central Cttee. of F.D.J.; Mayor of Leipzig 50-53; Editor *Liberal-Demokratische Zeitung*, Halle; Gen. Sec. Central Cttee. Liberal-Demokratische Partei Deutschlands (L.D.P.D.) 54-67, Chair. 67-; mem. Volkskammer 49-, Nat. Council of Nat. Front 54-; Deputy Chair. of the State Council (Staatsrat) 60-; Vice-Pres. German-British Soc. 67-68.
Leisure interests: literature and gardening.
L.D.P.D., Johannes-Dieckman-Strasse 48/49, 108 Berlin, German Democratic Republic.
Telephone: 2202171.

Gerlach, Walther, DR. RER. NAT.; German physicist; b. 1 Aug. 1889, Biebrich am Rhein; m. Dr. Ruth Probst 1939; ed. Univ. of Tübingen.
Lecturer at Tübingen 16, Göttingen 17, Frankfurt 20; Extraordinary Prof. Univ. of Frankfurt 21-25; Prof. of Physics, Tübingen Univ. 25 and Munich Univ. 29-57; mem. Bavarian Acad. of Science, Göttingen Acad. of Science, Acad. Leopoldina Halle; Hon. mem. Int. Acad. for History of Science, Paris; Dr. Med. h.c.; Dr. Rer. h.c.
Leisure interest: history of science.
Publs. *Grundlagen der Quantentheorie* 21, *Atombau und Atomabbau* 23, *Materie, Elektrizität, Energie* 23, *Die chemische Spektralanalyse* 30, Part II 33, Part III 36, *Magnetismus* 31, *Foundations and Methods of Chemical Analysis by the Emission Spectrum* 34, *Methoden der naturwissenschaftlichen Erkenntnis* 36, *Max Planck-Werk und Wirkung* 48, *Akademische Provinz* 49, *Humaniora und Natur* 50, *Physik des täglichen Lebens* 56,

Physik (Fischer Lexikon) 60, 67, *Humanität und Natur-wissenschaftliche Forschung* 62, *Die Sprache der Physik* 62, *Physik in Geistesgeschichte und Pädagogik* 64, *Johannes Kepler* 66, *Der Natur die Zunge lösen, Leben und Leistung grosser Forscher* 67, *Otto Hahn* 69, *Johannes Kepler, Dokumente* 71, *Zeichen der Natur, Naturerscheinungen* 72, *Kepler und die Copernicanische Wende* 73.
15 Franz Joseph Strasse, 8000 Munich 40, Federal Republic of Germany.

Gerling, Hans, DR. RER. POL.; German insurance executive; b. 6 June 1915, Cologne; s. of Robert and Auguste (Hoffmeister) Gerling; m. Irene Uhrmacher 1942; one s. three d.; ed. Universität zu Köln.
With Gerling-Konzern Versicherungsgesellschaften (insurance cos.) 37-; Chair. Board Gerling-Konzern Rheinische Versicherungs-Gruppe AG, Cologne, Gerling-Global Gen. and Reinsurance Co. Ltd., Gerling Insurance Service Co. Ltd., London, Gerling Global Gen. Insurance Co., Reinsurance Co., Life Insurance Co., Toronto, Gerling Global Offices Inc., N.Y., Gerling Global Reinsurance Co. of S. Africa Ltd.; holds top positions in numerous other companies.
Leisure interest: history of science.
Home: Cologne, Gereonshof; Office: Cologne, von-Werth-Strasse 14, Federal Republic of Germany.
Telephone: 20521.

Germain, Hubert; French politician; b. 6 Aug. 1920, Paris; s. of Gen. and Mrs. Germain; m. Simone Millon 1945; one s. two d.; ed. Lycée Saint-Louis, Paris and Lycée Michel Montaigne, Bordeaux.
Sub-Lieutenant, French Foreign Legion, Libya 41-42; Attaché to Cabinet of the C.-in-C. Forces of Occupation in Germany 45; Mayor of Saint-Chéron 53-65; Chargé de mission, Cabinet of the Minister of Armed Forces 60-62, Technical Adviser 67-68; Deputy for the fourteenth constituency of Paris 62-67, 68-73; Founder and Pres. parl. asscn. Présence et Action du Gaullisme 69-72; Minister of Post and Telecommunications 72-74, of Parl. Relations March-May 74; Union des Démocrates pour la République (U.D.R.).
1 place du Palais-Bourbon, Paris 7e, France.

Germain, Paul, D. ès SC.; French professor of theoretical mechanics; b. 28 Aug. 1920, Saint-Malo; s. of Paul Germain and Elisabeth Frangeul; m. Marie-Antoinette Gardent 1942; one s. one d.; ed. Ecole Normale Supérieure de Paris and Univ. of Paris.
Research Engineer, Office Nat. d'Etudes et de Recherches Aérospatiales (O.N.E.R.A.) 46-49; Assoc. Prof. Univ. of Poitiers 49-54; Prof. Univ. of Lille 54-58; Prof. of Theoretical Mechanics Univ. of Paris 58-; Visiting Prof., Brown Univ. 53-54, Stanford Univ. 69-70; Dir. O.N.E.R.A. 62-68; Fellow, A.I.A.A.; mem. Acad. des Sciences 70-, Perm. Sec. 75; mem. Int. Acad. of Astronautics; Dr. h.c. (Louvain) 61, (Strathclyde) 75.
Leisure interests: hiking, swimming, skiing.
Publs. *Mécanique des Milieux Continus* 62, *Cours de Mécanique des Milieux Continus* 73 and more than eighty papers on theoretical aerodynamics, magnetohydrodynamics, shock wave theory and mechanics of continua.
University of Paris VI—Tour 66, 9 quai Saint Bernard, Paris 5e; Home: 3 Avenue de Champaubert, Paris 15e, France.
Telephone: 336-25-25 (Office); 306-35-53 (Home).

German, His Holiness; Yugoslav ecclesiastic; b. 1899, Jošanička Banja, Central Serbia; ed. Theological Faculty, Univ. of Belgrade.
Bishop of Moravitza 51, of Budapest 52, of Žiča 56; Patriarch, Serbian Orthodox Church 58-.
Serbian Patriarchate, P.O. Box 182, 11001 Belgrade, Yugoslavia.

Germani, Gino; Argentine sociologist; b. 4 Feb. 1911, Rome, Italy; s. of Luigi Germani and Pasqualina G. Catalini; m. Celia Carpi 1954; one s. one d.; ed. Univs. of Rome and Buenos Aires.
Research Assoc., Inst. of Sociology, Univ. of Buenos Aires 41-45; Prof. of Sociology, Colegio Libre de Estudios Superiores, Buenos Aires and Rosario (Argentina) 46-55; Prof., Dept. of Sociology, Univ. of Buenos Aires 55-66, Head of Dept. 57-62, Dir. Inst. of Sociology 55-66; Research Program Dir., Centro de Sociología Comparada, Inst. Torcuato Di Tella, Buenos Aires 64-66; Visiting Prof. of Sociology, Univ. of Chicago 59, Columbia Univ., N.Y. 64-65; First Monroe Gutman Prof. of Latin American Affairs, Harvard Univ. 66-; Vice-Pres. Int. Sociological Asscn. 62-66; mem. Int. Social Science Council 61-68; Pres. Asociación Sociológica Argentina 60-66; Hon. Fellow American Acad. of Arts and Sciences; mem. Exec. Cttee. Latin American Social Science Council 67-; mem. Consiglio italiano per le scienze sociali 74-.
Leisure interests: music, hi-fi, science fiction.
Publs. *La Sociología Científica* 56, 62, *Estudios de Psicología Social* 56, *Estructura Social de la Argentina* 55, *Política y Massa* 61, *Política y Sociedad en una Epoca de Transción* 62, 64, 66, 68, 72, 74 (trans. Portuguese 73), *La Sociología en la América Latina* 64, 65, *Estudios de Sociología y de Psicología Social* 66, 71, *Sociología de la Modernización* 69, 73 (trans. Italian 71, 75), *Politique et Société* 72, *El concepto de Marginalidad* 73, *Urbanization, Modernization and the Urban Crisis* 74 (trans. Italian, Spanish 75), *Autoritarismo, Fascismo e Classi Sociali* 75.
Office: William James Hall 568, Harvard University, Cambridge, Mass. 02138, U.S.A.; Homes: via delle Terme Deciane II, 00153 Rome (winter and spring); via delle Azalee 35, Numana (Ancona), Italy.
Telephone: 495-3849 (Office); 573788 (Home, Rome), 950352 (Home, Ancona).

Germani, Fernando; Italian musician; b. 5 April 1906; ed. Rome Conservatoire and Pontifical Inst. of Sacred Music.
Professor of Organ Music at the Rome Conservatoire, Chigiana Music Acad. (Siena), Curtis Inst. (Philadelphia); recitals in the Americas, Australasia, South Africa, Europe; Commdr. Order of St. Gregorius Magno; Commdr. Order of St. Sylvester; Knight Crown of Italy.
Publs. Revision of works of Girolamo Frescobaldi 36, *A Method of Organ Playing* 42.
Via delle Terme Deciane 11, Rome, Italy.

Germanus, Gyula (Julius); Hungarian orientalist; b. 1884, Budapest; m. 1st Rose Hajnóczy (died 1944), 2nd Kate Kajari 1949; ed. Univs. of Budapest, Istanbul, Vienna and Leipzig.
Lecturer at Oriental Acad. of Commerce 12, Univ. of Political Economy, Dept. of Oriental Sciences 29, Univ. of Santiniketan, Bengal 29-32; Sec. Hungarian P.E.N. Club 26-44; Prof. of Arab Language, Budapest Univ. 48-65; numerous journeys in Near East; pilgrimage to Mecca 34; Visiting Lecturer Syrian, Egyptian, Moroccan and Indian Univs.; Corresp. mem. Arab Acad. of Cairo, Arab Acad. of Baghdad, Arab Acad. of Damascus, Indian Inst. of Islamic Studies, Delhi; mem. Accad. del Mediterraneo (Italy), Accad. Leonardo da Vinci (Rome); Fellow, Inst. for Cultural Research (London).
Leisure interest: reading.
Publs. *Evliya Celebi on 17th Century Guilds in Turkey* 07, *The Role of the Turks in Islam* 33-34, *Allah Akbar* 36, *Sulle orme di Maometto* 38, *Az arab szellemiség megujhodása* (The Rebirth of Arab Mentality) 44, *Dichtkunst Ibn Rúmis* 57, Autobiography: *A félhold fakó fényében* (The Half-Moon's Dim Light) 58, *Kelet Fényei Felé* (Towards the Light of the East), *Modern*

Poetry of South Arabia, The New Palestinian Poetry under Crossfire; and many treatises on Arabic literature.
Petöfi tér 3, H-1052 Budapest V, Hungary.
Telephone: 184-680.

Gerstacker, Carl A.; American chemical executive; b. 16 Aug. 1916; ed. Univ. of Michigan.
Accounting Dept., Dowell Div. Dow Chemical Co. 38-40; U.S. Army 40-46; Chemical Eng., Dow Chemical Co. 46-48, Dir. 48-, Treas. 49-59, Vice-Pres. 55, mem. Exec. Cttee. 57, Chair. Finance Cttee. 59-, Chair. Board of Dirs. 60-; fmr. Pres. Synthetic Organic Chemical Mfrs.' Asscn.; fmr. Chair. Mfg. Chemists' Asscn.; Vice-Pres. United Presbyterian Church in U.S.A. Inc.; Chair. Export Expansion Council, U.S. Dept. of Commerce 66-73; Chair. Advisory Council on Japan-U.S. Econ. Relations; mem. Int. Advisory Council Chase Manhattan Bank; Dir. Carrier Corpn., Eaton Corpn., Dundee Cement Co.; mem. U.S. Comm. UNESCO 67-70; mem. Council, Rockefeller Univ.; Dr. h.c. (Cen. Mich. Univ., Albion Coll.); President's E Award for Export Services 71.
Dow Chemical Co., P.O. Box 1682, Midland, Mich. 48640, U.S.A.
Telephone: 517-6360010.

Gerstenberg, Richard C.; American motor executive; b. 24 Nov. 1909, Little Falls, N.Y.; m. Evelyn Hitchingham; one s. one d.; ed. Univ. of Mich.
Joined Gen. Motors Corpn. 32; Asst. Comptroller 49; Treas. 56; Vice-Pres. in charge of Financial Staff 60, in charge of Finance 67; mem. Board of Dirs. Nov. 67-; Vice-Chair. of Board and Chair. Finance Cttee. April 70-71, Chair. and Chief Exec. Officer 72-74; Dir. of several Gen. Motors subsidiaries including Gen. Motors Acceptance Corpn. and Motors Insurance Corpn.; mem. Visiting Cttee. Harvard Business School and Univ. of Mich. Graduate School of Business Admin.; mem. numerous civic and community orgs.
1000 Stratford Lane, Bloomfield Hills, Mich. 48013, U.S.A.

Gerstenmaier, Eugen Karl Albrecht, D. THEOL.; German politician and theologian; b. 25 Aug. 1906, Kirchheim-Teck; s. of Albrecht Gerstenmaier and Albertine Lauffer; m. Brigitte von Schmidt 1941; two s. one d.; ed. Univs. of Tübingen, Zürich and Rostock.
Priv. dozent Berlin Univ. 38; Prof. staff Foreign Section, Evangelical Church; took part 20th July Plot 44, imprisoned, released by Allies 45; organized relief work of the Evangelische Kirche Deutschlands 45; mem. Synod 45-73; mem. Bundestag 49-69, Pres. 54-69; mem. Council of Europe 50; Vice-Pres. CDU 55-69; Pres. Deutsche-Afrika Gesellschaft 71, Evangelisches Siedlungswerk in Deutschland, Deutsche Sozialpolitische Gesellschaft; several hon. degrees.
Publs. *Die Kirche und die Schöpfung* 37, *Hilfe für Deutschland* 46, *Die Evangelische Kirche und ihre Sozialpolitik* 52, *Reden und Aufsätze* (Vol. 1 56, Vol. 2 61), *Neuer Nationalismus?* 65.
5486 Oberwinter, Rheinhöhenweg 90, Federal Republic of Germany.
Telephone: 02228/285.

Gestrin, (Lars Olof) Kristian, B.L.; Finnish lawyer and politician; b. 10 April 1929, Helsinki; s. of Lars Gestrin and Mary Cabell; m. Monica Eddina Furuhjelm 1962; one s. two d.; ed Helsinki Univ.
Lawyer, Ane Gyllenberg Banking Co. 54-65, mem. Board 58-; mem. Parl. 62-; Chair. Swedish People's Party 73-74; Minister of Defence 70-71, 72-74, of Trade and Industry 74-75, of Justice 75-.
Leisure interest: literature.
Oikeusministeriö, Ritarikatu 2, Helsinki 17; Home: Tammitie 10, Helsinki 33, Finland.
Telephone: 1601 (Office); 484816 (Home).

Getty, Jean Paul; American oil executive; b. 15 Dec. 1892, Minneapolis, Minn.; s. of George Franklin Getty and Sarah Catherine McPherson Risher; m. 1st Jeannette Dumont 1923 (divorced), one s.; m. 2nd Allene Ashby 1926 (divorced); m. 3rd Fini Helmle 1928 (divorced), one s.; m. 4th Ann Rork 1932 (divorced), two s.; m. 5th Louise Dudley Lynch 1939 (divorced), one s. (deceased); ed. South California, California and Oxford Univs.
Industrial Oil Producer 14; Pres. and Gen. Man. George F. Getty Inc. 30-33; Dir. Petroleum Corp. 32-34, Tidewater Assoc. Oil Co. 32-36; Pres. and Gen. Man. Spartan Aircraft Co. 42-61; Pres. Pacific Western Oil Corp. 47, Mission Corp. 56; Pres., Dir. and Principal Owner Getty Oil Co. 56-; mem. N.Y. and Calif. Chamber of Commerce; Founder, Trustee J. Paul Getty Museum 53-; Officer Légion d'Honneur, Grande Médaille, City of Paris (Silver), Benjamin Franklin Fellow R.S.A.; Hon. LL.D., Ogio Northern Univ.
Leisure interests: travel, reading, art.
Publs. *History of the Oil Business of George Franklin and J. Paul Getty 1903-39* 41, *Europe in the 18th Century* 49, *Collector's Choice* (with Ethel LeVane) 56, *My Life and Fortunes* 63, *Joys of Collecting* 65, *How to be rich* 66, *The Golden Age* 68, *How to be a Successful Executive* 71.
Sutton Place, nr. Guildford, Surrey, England; and 17985 Pacific Coast Highway, Malibu, Calif. 90265, U.S.A.

Gevers, Baron Willem J. G.; Netherlands diplomatist; b. 16 Jan. 1911; s. of late Baron W. A. F. Gevers; m.; two s. one d.; ed. Univ. of Leyden.
Entered Netherlands diplomatic service 37; served in Warsaw, The Hague, Madrid and London 37-54; Envoy, later Amb. to Iran 54-60; Amb. to Israel 60-64; Chief of Protocol and Deputy Sec. Gen., Ministry of Foreign Affairs, The Hague 64-70; Amb. to U.K. 71-76, also accred. to Iceland; retd. 76; Order of Netherlands Lion, Order of Orange-Nassau and various foreign decorations.
c/o Ministry of Foreign Affairs, Amsterdam, Netherlands.

Ghaffari, Abolghassem, D.SC., PH.D.; Iranian mathematician; b. 1909, Teheran; s. of Hossein Ghaffari and Massoumeh Shahpouri; m. Mitra Meshkati 1967; two d.; ed. Darolfonoun School, Teheran, and Univs. of Nancy, Paris, London, and Oxford.
Assoc. Prof. Teheran Univ. 37-42, Prof. of Mathematics 42-; Mathematics Research Asst. King's Coll. London 47-48; Research Fellow, Harvard 50-51, Research Assoc. Princeton 51-52; mem. Inst. for Advanced Study, Princeton 51-52; Senior mathematician, Nat. Bureau of Standards, Washington, D.C. 56-57; Aeronautical research scientist 57-64; Aerospace scientist NASA, Goddard Space Flight Center, Greenbelt, Md. 64-; Professorial Lecturer in Mathematics and Statistics, American Univ. Wash., D.C. 58-62, and other American Univs.; mem. American, French and London Mathematical Socs.; American Astronomical Soc., Philosophical Soc. of Washington; Fellow, N.Y. Acad. of Sciences 61 and Wash. Acad. of Sciences 63; American Asscn. for Advancement of Science 65; Orders of Homayoun, Danesh (1st class) and Sepass (1st class), U.S. Special Apollo Achievement Award.
Leisure interests: walking and gardening.
Publs. *Sur l'Equation Fonctionnelle de Chapman-Kolmogoroff* 36, *The Hodograph Method in Gas Dynamics* 50.
7109 Connecticut Avenue, Washington, D.C. 20015, U.S.A.; and Shah Reza Avenue, 31 Ladan Street, Teheran, Iran.
Telephone: 301-657-4358.

Ghaidan, Gen. Saadoun; Iraqi army officer and politician; b. 1930; m.; five c.; ed. secondary educ. in Ramadi and Military Coll.

Commissioned 2nd Lieut. 53; Commdr. Repub. Body-Guard Forces 68; mem. Revolutionary Command Council 68-; Minister of the Interior 70-74, of Communications 74-.
Ministry of Communications, Baghdad, Iraq.

Ghaleb, Mohamed Mourad; Egyptian diplomatist; b. 1 April 1922, Cairo; m. Shoukreya Ali Mohamed 1953; two d. Under-Sec. Foreign Affairs, Cairo 59-60; Amb. to Congo Repub. (Léopoldville) 60, to U.S.S.R. 61-71; Minister of State for Foreign Affairs 71-72; Minister of Foreign Affairs Jan.-Sept. 72, of Information 73-74; Amb. to Yugoslavia June 74-.
Leisure interests: swimming, tennis, reading, camping.
Embassy of Egypt, Andre Nikolića 12, Belgrade, Yugoslavia; 78 El Nil Street, Gueza, Cairo, Egypt.

Ghanem, Gen. Iskander A.; Lebanese army officer; b. 1 Jan. 1913, Saghbine; s. of Assaad Ghanem and Marie Khoury; m. Laurice Khoury 1941; three s.; ed. Coll. du Sacré Coeur, Mil. Acad., Homs, and Gen. Staff Coll., Leavenworth, Kansas, U.S.A.
Promoted to rank of Capt. in Lebanese Army 45; Artillery Battalion Commdr., Artillery Inspector 47-58; Lt.-Col. 53, Col. 59; Deputy Chief of Staff 59-66; Brig. 64; Commdr. Northern Region 66, 68; Armed Forces Attaché, Washington D.C. 66-67; Head Mil. Court 67; Commdr. Beirut Region 67-68, 68-69; C.-in-C. Lebanese Army 71-Sept. 75, on leave of absence Sept. 75-; Gen. 71; Minister of Hydro-electric Resources and Defence May-June 75; has attended various mil. tours in Lebanon and abroad; War Medal, Lebanese Merit Medal, Cedars Medal of High Ranking Officers, The Highest Mil. Cedars Medal, French Proficiency Medal, Portuguese Proficiency Medal, and several other decorations.
Leisure interest: reading.
Mar Takla Hazmieh, Beirut, Lebanon.

Ghanem, Ismail, D. en D. Egyptian lawyer; b. 24 May 1924, Alexandria; m. 1st Moyna Kathleen McGrath 1951 (deceased), 2nd Martje Schotanus 1959; four c.; ed. Alexandria Univ., Faculté de Droit, Paris and Inst. of Comparative Law, New York Univ.
Member Staff, Faculty of Law, Alexandria Univ. and Ein-Shams Univ. 51-; Dean Faculty of Law, Arab Univ. of Beirut, Lebanon 62-63; Dean, Faculty of Law, Ain-Shams Univ. 66-68, Vice-Rector 68-70, Rector 71-74; Perm. Del. to UNESCO, Paris 70-71; Minister of Culture May-Sept. 71, of Higher Educ. and Scientific Research 74-75; mem. Exec. Board, Cairo Governorate; mem. Board Acad. for Scientific Research; Chair. Council for the Social Sciences 71.
Publs. *Le Droit du Travail* 62, *La Vente* 63, *Le Droit Subjectif* 63, all in Arabic; *Les Droits réels principaux*, 2 vols., 62, *La Théorie générale des Obligations* 66-67.
c/o Ministry of Higher Education, Cairo, Egypt.

Ghanem, Mohamed Hafez, PH.D.; Egyptian lawyer and government official; b. 28 Sept. 1925; ed. Cairo Univ. and Univ. de Paris.
Lecturer, Faculty of Law, Alexandria Univ. 49; Prof. of Public Int. Law and Vice-Dean, Faculty of Law, Ain Shams Univ. 60-68; Minister of Tourism 68-69, of Educ. 69-71; Sec.-Gen. Arab Socialist Union 73-75; Deputy Prime Minister, Minister of Higher Educ. 75-; Hon. Sec. Egyptian Soc. of Int. Law; mem. Arbitration, Conciliation and Mediation Comm. of Org. of African Unity 66-71; mem. Legal Consultative Comm. for Afro-Asian Countries 58-65; State Prize for best publ. in field of Int. Law and Political Science 60.
Publs. *Public International Law* (Arabic) 64, *International Organization* 67.
3 Sharia El Bergass, Garden City, Cairo, Egypt.

Ghenima, Mohamed; Tunisian banker; b. 15 May 1929, Akouda; m. Anissa Smida 1961; three c.
Member Destour Socialist Party; fmr. Asst. Dir.-Gen.

Nat. Bank of Tunisia, Pres., Dir.-Gen.; now Gov Central Bank of Tunisia.
Banque Centrale de Tunisie, Tunis, Tunisia.

Gherab, Mohamed Habib; Tunisian diplomatist; b. 8 May 1926, Tunis; m. Fawzia Ladjimi 1958; one s. one d.; ed. School of Law, Paris.
Ambassador to Spain 65-67; Special Adviser to Tunisian Sec. of State for Foreign Affairs 67-69; mem. del. to XXIII session of UN Gen. Assembly; Asst. Sec.-Gen of UN and Dir. of Personnel March 69-.
Office of Personnel, UN Secretariat, New York, N.Y. 10028; Home: 45 East 89th Street, New York, N.Y. 10028, U.S.A.

Ghiaurov, Nicolai; Bulgarian singer; b. 13 Sept. 1929, Velingrad; ed. Sofia Music Acad., Moscow Conservatoire.
Played violin, piano and clarinet from an early age; debut at Sofia Opera House as Don Basilio in *Barber of Seville* 55, debut in Bologna 58, debut at La Scala, Milan as Varlaam in *Boris Godunov* 59; regular appearances at La Scala, Metropolitan Opera, N.Y., Vienna State Opera; major roles include title role in *Boris Godunov*, Mephistopheles in *Faust*.
c/o John Coast Concerts, 1 Park Close, London S.W.1, England.

Ghika, Nicolas; Greek painter and designer; b. 1906; s. of Adm. Alexander Hadjikyriacos and Helen Ghika; m. Barbara Warner (née Hutchinson) 1961; ed. Athens and Acad. Ranson, Paris.
Represented at numerous group exhbns., museums and art galleries in Europe, U.S.A. and Australia; nineteen one-man exhbns. in Europe and U.S.A., and three retrospectives (British Council, Athens 46, Whitechapel Gallery, London 61, Nat. Pinacotheka, Athens 73); has given lectures, designed décors, costumes and masks for plays and ballets, incl. Stravinsky's *Persephone*, Covent Garden, London 61; Prof. School of Architecture, Athens; mem. Acad. of Athens 72; First Prize Acad. of Athens.
Publs. lithographs, engravings, articles on art, etc.; has illustrated books.
27 Blomfield Road, London W.9, England; and 3 Kriezotou Street, Athens, Greece.

Ghikas, Solon; Greek politician and retd. army officer; b. 1898, Trikala; ed. Cadet School, Athens, Ecole de Saumur, France.
Army service on Macedonian Front, World War I and World War II 40-41; Mil. Attaché, Greek Embassy, Washington, D.C.; Commdr. Third Army Corps; Chief of Army Gen. Staff; retd. with rank of Lt.-Gen. 53; mem. Parl. for Nat. Radical Union; Minister of Communications and Public Works; Minister of Public Order July 74-; Medal for Outstanding Action; Knight Commdr. Order of George I, Order of the Phoenix.
Ministry of Public Order, Odos Tritis Septemvriou 48, Athens 103, Greece.

Ghilarov, Merkury Sergeyevich; Soviet entomologist; b. 7 March 1912, Kiev; s. of Sergei Alexeyevich Ghilarov and Elizaveta Sergeyevna; m. Irina Ivanovna Blokhintseva 1936; one s.; ed. Kiev Univ.
Research Assoc., U.S.S.R. Inst. of Sugar Industry 33-34, Ukrainian Research Station *Kauchukonos* 34-36, Inst. of Rubber-bearing Plants 36-44, Inst. of Morphology of Animals, U.S.S.R. Acad. of Sciences 44-, Prof. 49-; Laboratory Leader, Inst. of Animal Evolutionary Morphology and Ecology 56-; Corresp. mem. U.S.S.R. Acad. of Sciences 66-, Academician 74; Vice-Pres. Acad. of Zoology (Agra, India) 60-; Pres. All-Union Entomological Soc. 70-; Academician, Akademie Leopoldina 74-; Vice-Pres. Perm. Cttee. Int. Congress Entomology; mem. Int. Soil Science Soc.; Hon. mem. Accad. Italiana di Entomologia 73-, and Entomological Socs. of Czechoslovakia, France, Finland, Helsingfors, Lund, Hungary; State Prizes 51, 67.

Leisure interests: reading (memoirs, poetry), classical music, skiing.

Publs. Works on insect and arthropod evolution, soil zoology and insect larvae morphology.

Institute of Animal Evolutionary Morphology and Ecology, Leninsky Prospekt 33, Moscow 117071, U.S.S.R.

Telephone: 232-20-88; 137-60-71.

Ghiringhelli, Antonio; Italian theatre director; b. 1903, Brunello (Varese); ed. Univ. of Genoa.

Became Dir. and eventually owner of factories; career with Teatro alla Scala, Milan 45-; appointed to solve problems facing theatre following the war; in less than one year theatre was rebuilt and orchestra and chorus reorganized; Toscanini inaugurated reconstructed auditorium 46; Extraordinary Commr. Teatro alla Scala 45-48, Supt. 48-72; created Piccola Scala 55; Medaglia d'Oro, City of Milan 52; Croix de l'art et de la culture, French Govt. 67.

c/o Teatro alla Scala, Milan, Italy.

Ghirshman, Roman, D. ès L.; French archaeologist; b. 3 Oct. 1895, Karkov, Russia; m. Antoinette Tania Levienne 1925; ed. Sorbonne, Ecole des Hautes Etudes and Ecole du Louvre.

Honorary Dir. French Archaeological Del. in Iran and Afghanistan; Hon. Prof. Univ. of Aix-en-Provence; mem. Acad. des Inscriptions et Belles Lettres; Corr. Fellow of British Acad.; Commdr. Légion d'Honneur, Grand Officer of Orders of Tadj and Homayoun (Iran); Medal of Freer Gallery of Art, Washington; Dr. h.c. (Univ. of Teheran).

Leisure interests: violin, guitar, singing, history.

Publs. *Fouille de Tepe Giyan* 36, *Fouilles de Sialk* (2 vols.) 38, 39, *Bégram-Histoire des Kouchans* 46, *Les Chionites-Hephtalites* 48, *Iran, des origines à l'Islam* 50, *Bîchapour I* and *II* 56, 71, *Iran, Parthes et Sassanides* 62, *Perse, Proto-iraniens, Mèdes, Achéménides* 63, *Tchoga Zanbil I* and *II* 66, 68, *Terrasses sacrées de Bard-è Néchandeh et Masjid-i Solaiman* 76.

96 rue La Fontaine, Paris 16e, France.

Telephone: 224 80-25.

Ghizikis, Gen. Phaidon; Greek army officer; b. 16 June 1917, Volos; widower; one s.; ed. Mil. Acad., War Coll. and Nat. Defence Coll.

Promoted to rank of Lieut.-Col. 57, Col. 66, Brig.-Gen. 68, Maj.-Gen. 69, Lieut.-Gen. 71, Gen. 73; Commdr. of Raiding Force, Dept. of Hellenic Army Command 70; Deputy Commdr. of Hellenic Army Command 71; Commdr. C Corps 72; Commdr. of First Army 73; Pres. of Repub. of Greece 73-74; Knight Commdr. Royal Order of George 1st; Grand Cross of the Redeemer.

c/o Office of the President, Athens, Greece.

Ghorbal, Ashraf, PH.D.; Egyptian diplomatist; ed. Washington Univ.

Joined Egyptian Del. to UN 49; Head Egyptian Interests Section, Indian Embassy, Washington 68-73; Press Adviser to the Pres. Feb.-Nov. 73; Amb. to U.S.A. Nov. 73-.

Egyptian Embassy, 2310 Decatur Place, N.W., Washington, D.C. 20008, U.S.A.

Ghorra, Edward; Lebanese diplomatist; b. 1913, Zahle; s. of Abdallah Ghorra and Linda Abou-Kkeir; m. Olgo Elkouri 1947; ed. Univ. de Saint-Joseph, Beirut.

Consul-General, New York 45-50, Sydney 50-55; mem. Lebanese Del. to UN 47-49, 58, 63; Alt. Rep. UN Econ. and Social Council 48; Head Western Affairs Dept., Ministry of Foreign Affairs 56-57, Dir. Political Affairs Dept. 57-58; Amb. to U.S.S.R. 59-63; Dir. Dept. of Lebanese Overseas, Ministry of Foreign Affairs 63-65; Amb. to Czechoslovakia and Poland 65-68; Perm. Rep. to UN 68-, Rep. to Human Rights Comm. 69-, to Social Comm. 69-71, to Econ. and Social Council 71-73; Vice-

Pres. of UN Gen. Assembly 68, 74, ECOSOC 73; Rep. to UNDP 72-74; Chair. 1st Cttee., UN Gen. Assembly, 30th Session 75.

Leisure interests: golf, philately.

Permanent Mission of Lebanon to the United Nations, 866 United Nations Plaza, Room 533-535, New York, N.Y. 10017, U.S.A.

Ghosh, Amalananda, M.A.; Indian archaeologist; b. 3 March 1910, Banaras; s. of U. N. Ghosh; m. Sudha De 1938; one s. one d.; ed. A.B. High School, Banaras, Queen's Coll., Banaras, and Univs. of Allahabad and London.

Assistant Supt., Archaeological Survey of India 37-44, Superintendent 44-50; Deputy Dir.-Gen. for Exploration, Archaeological Survey of India 50-52; Joint Dir.-Gen. of Archaeology in India, Archaeological Survey of India 52-53, Dir.-Gen. 53-68; UNESCO Archaeological Consultant to Govts. of Qatar 68, Bahrain 68, Saudi Arabia 69, Yemen 70; Hon. Mem. Int. Congress for Prehistoric and Protohistoric Sciences; Corresp. mem. Int. Council on Museums, Int. Cttee. on Monuments, Artistic and Historical Sites and Archaeological Excavation; Hon. Fellow, Soc. of Antiquaries of London, Deutsches Archäologisches Inst.; Vice-Pres. Royal India, Pakistan and Ceylon Soc.; Hon. Corresp., Archaeological Survey of India; Fellow, Indian Inst. of Advanced Study 68-71; Award of Padma Sri 62; Visiting Prof. of Indian Culture, Indonesian Univ. 73-74.

Leisure interest: reading fiction.

Bankuli, Gurgaon Road, New Delhi 110037, India.

Telephone: 39-2318.

Ghosh, Parimal, M.A.; Indian business executive and politician; b. 15 March 1917; ed. St. Paul's Coll., Univ. of Calcutta.

Dir. Himalay Paper & Board Mills Private Ltd., Himalay Paper (Machinery) Ltd., P. Ghosh & Co., Card Board and Printing & Processing Industries Ltd. until 67; mem. Lok Sabha 67-; Minister of State for Railways 67-69; Minister of State for Health, Family Planning, Works, Housing and Urban Devt. 69-71; Man. Dir. Himalay Paper and Board Mills Pte. Ltd. 71-.

46c Chowringhee Road, Everest House, Calcutta 16, India.

Ghosh, Tushar Kanti, B.A.; Indian journalist; b. 21 Sept. 1898, Calcutta; s. of Mahatma Sisir Kumar Ghosh and Sm. Kumudini Ghosh; m. 1st Tushar Kanti Ghosh 1920, 2nd Bibha Rani Ghosh; one s. one d.; ed. Calcutta Univ.

Editor *Amrita Bazar Patrika*; former Pres. Indian Journalists' Asscn; Pres. Andhra Journalists' Conf., Guntur 37; All-India Printers' Conf., Poona 39; former Pres. Indian and Eastern Newspaper Society, All-India Newspaper Editors' Conf., Audit Bureau of Circulation, United Press of India; fmr. Vice-Pres. Int. Press Inst.; Chair. Press Trust of India; founder *Jugantar*, Calcutta, *Northern Indian Patrika*, Allahabad and *Amrita* (Bengali weekly); Chair. Commonwealth Press Union, Indian Section; mem. Exec. Cttee., Int. Press Inst.; Padma Bhusan 64.

Leisure interest: reading.

Amrita Bazar Patrika City Office, 3 Chittaranjan Avenue, Calcutta 13, India.

Telephone: 23-2838.

Ghoussein, Talat Al-; Kuwaiti diplomatist; b. 16 May 1924; ed. American Univ. of Cairo.

Foreign News Editor *As-Shaab* (Jaffa, Palestine) 46-47; Controller, Arab Bank Ltd., Jaffa, Palestine 47-48; Editor Foreign News and Dir. of English Section, Broadcasting Station of Jordan 48-49; Dir. Press and Public Information, Ministry of Foreign Affairs, Yemen 49-53; Sec.-Gen., Development Board, Kuwait 53-60; Deputy Private Sec. to Emir of Kuwait 60-61;

Minister-Counsellor, Kuwait Embassy, Washington 62-63, Ambassador of Kuwait to U.S.A. 63-70, to Morocco 70-71, to Japan 71-.
Embassy of Kuwait, 13-12, Mita 4-chome, Minato-ku, Tokyo, Japan.

Ghozali, Sid Ahmed; Algerian industrialist; b. 31 March 1937, Marnia; ed. Ecole des Ponts et Chaussées, Paris.
Formerly Dir. of Energy, Ministry of Industry and Energy; Adviser, Ministry of the Economy 64; Under-Sec., Ministry of Public Works 64-65; Pres., Dir.-Gen. Société nationale pour la recherche, la production, le transport, la transformation et la commercialisation des hydrocarbures (SONATRACH) 66-; mem. Org. technique de mise en valeur des richesses du sous-sol saharien 62-.
SONATRACH, Immeuble Maurétania, Agha, Algiers, Algeria.

Giacconi, Riccardo, PH.D.; American astrophysicist; b. 6 Oct. 1931, Genoa; s. of Antonio Giacconi and Elsa Giacconi Canni; m. Mirella Manaira 1957; one s. two d.; ed. Univ. of Milan.
Assistant Prof. of Physics, Univ. of Milan 54-56; Research Assoc. Indiana Univ. 56-58, Princeton Univ., 58-59; joined American Science & Engineering Inc. 59-73, mem. Board of Dirs. 66, Exec. Vice-Pres. 69-73; Assoc. Harvard Coll. Observatory 70-72; Assoc. Dir. Center for Astrophysics 73-; Prof. of Astronomy, Harvard Univ. 73-; mem. Asscn. of Univs. for Research in Astronomy 71-75; mem. Nat. Acad. of Sciences, American Acad. of Arts and Sciences, A.A.A.S., American Astron. Soc., American Physical Soc., Italian Physical Soc., Int. Astron. Union; mem. various scientific panels etc.; Fulbright Fellow 56-58; Helen B. Warner Award, American Astron. Soc. 66; Como Prize, Italian Physical Soc. 67; Röntgen Prize in astrophysics, Physikalisch-Medizinische Gesellschaft, Würzburg 71; NASA Medal for Exceptional Scientific Achievement; NASA Distinguished Public Service Award 72.
Leisure interests: skiing, scuba diving, painting.
Publs. X-ray Astronomy (co-editor) 74; also numerous articles in professional journals.
60 Garden Street, Cambridge, Mass. 02138; Home: 26 Craigie Street, Cambridge, Mass. 02138, U.S.A.
Telephone: 617-495-7207 (Office); 617-492-7289 (Home).

Giaever, Ivar, PH.D.; American physicist; b. 5 April 1929, Bergen, Norway; s. of John A. Giaever and Gudrun M. Skaarud; m. Inger Skramstad 1952; one s. three d.; ed. Norwegian Inst. of Technology, Rensselaer Polytechnical Inst., N.Y.
Norwegian Army 52-53; Patent Examiner, Norwegian Patent Office 53-54; Mechanical Engineer, Canadian Gen. Electric Co. 54-56; Applied Mathematician, Gen. Electric Co. 56-58; Physicist Gen. Electric Research and Devt. Center 58-; Oliver E. Buckley Prize 65, Guggenheim Fellowship 70, Nobel Prize for Physics 73.
Leisure interests: skiing, sailing, tennis, hiking, camping.
Publs. in Physics Review Letters: Energy Gap in Superconductors Measured by Electron Tunneling 60, Study of Superconductors by Electron Tunneling 61, Detection of the AC Josephson Effect 65, Magnetic Coupling Between Two Adjacent Superconductors 65; The Antibody-Antigen Reaction: A Visual Observation 73.
Research and Development Center, P.O. Box 8, Schenectady, N.Y. 12301; Home: 2080 Van Antwerp Road, Schenectady, N.Y. 12309, U.S.A.
Telephone: 518-FR4-9708 (Home).

Giambruno, Dr. Carlos, LL.D., D.SC.S., J.D.; Uruguayan diplomatist; b. 3 Sept. 1928, Montevideo; m.; three c.; ed. univs. of Montevideo and Rome.
Administrative Official, Library of the Cabildo and later Dept. of Diplomatic Treaties and Archives, Min. of Foreign Affairs 44-48; Sec., Legation to the Holy See 48-52; Consul, Civitavecchia, Italy, in charge of emigration plans carried out in collaboration with the Intergovernmental Cttee. for European Migration 52-63; Minister Counsellor, Italy 63-68, acted as Chargé d'Affaires ad interim and Permanent Rep. to FAO; Dir. Dept. of Foreign Policy, Min. of Foreign Affairs 69-70, Dir. Dept. of Int. Organizations 70-72; Permanent Rep. and Chair. Third Cttee. (Social, Humanitarian and Cultural), UN 72-; served as Pres. of the nat. comm. for study of the boundary problems in the Rio de la Plata and as del. to several sessions of the Gen. Assembly and to the Organization of American States; fmrly. Prof. of Int. Public Law, Univ. of Montevideo, Mil. Inst. for Higher Studies and Command School, Uruguayan Air Force.
Publs. several works in the fields of law and diplomacy.
Permanent Mission of Uruguay to United Nations, 301 East 47th St., Room 16J, New York, N.Y. 10017, U.S.A.
Telephone: (212) 757-8240.

Giap, Gen. Vo Nguyen (see Vo Nguyen Giap, Gen.).

Giauque, William Francis, B.S., PH.D.; American chemist; b. 12 May 1895, Niagara Falls, Ont., Canada; s. of William Tecumseh Sherman Giauque and Isabella Jane (Duncan) Giauque; m. Muriel F. Ashley 1932; two s.; ed. Univ. of Calif.
Instructor in Chemistry Univ. of California 22-27, Asst. Prof. 27-30, Assoc. Prof. 30-34, Prof. of Chemistry 34-; mem. Nat. Acad. of Sciences 36-, American Acad. of Arts and Sciences 50-; mem. American Philosophical Society 40; awarded Chandler Medal of Columbia Univ. 36 for invention and first application of adiabatic demagnetization method of producing temperatures below $1°$ absolute, Elliott Cresson Medal of Franklin Inst. 37; discovered with H. L. Johnston, oxygen isotopes 17 and 18 by means of absorption of sunlight in earth's atmosphere; Nobel Prize for Chemistry 49; Willard Gibbs Medal 51; Gilbert N. Lewis Medal 55; Hon. D.Sc. (Columbia), Hon. LL.D. (Calif.).
Department of Chemistry, University of California, Berkeley, Calif. 94720, U.S.A.

Gibberd, Sir Frederick, Kt., C.B.E.; British architect; b. 7 Jan. 1908; ed. King Henry VIII School, Coventry.
Architectural town-planning and landscape design practice in London 30-, Harlow New Town 56; fmr. Principal, Architectural Asscn. School of Architecture; Mem. Royal Acad.; Fellow, Royal Inst. of British Architects, Soc. of Industrial Artists, Royal Town Planning Inst., Inst. Landscape Architects; fmr. mem. Royal Fine Art Comm.; Architect-Planner Harlow New Town 47-; Planning Consultant Nuneaton 48-, Doncaster and Hull 54-, Leamington Spa 57-, Swindon 57-, Santa Teresa, Venezuela 59-.
Works include: Somerford Estate (Hackney), Scunthorpe steel works, technical colls. at Hull, Huddersfield and numerous schools, London Airport, Belfast Hospital, Nat. Dock Labour Board offices (London), civic centres for Doncaster, Harlow, Hull, Leamington Spa and St. Albans, nuclear power stations at Hinkley Point and Sizewell; landscape design includes Queen's Gardens, Hull, reservoirs at Derwent, Kielder and Tryweryn and potash mine at Boulby; new monastery, Douai Abbey; winner of open competitions for Metropolitan Roman Catholic Cathedral, Liverpool 60 (opened 67), mosque, Regent's Park, London 69, Inter-Continental Hotel, Arundel Great Court and Coutts Bank, London.
Publs. The Architecture of England 38, Town Design 53, Metropolitan Cathedral of Christ the King 68.
Office: 8 Percy Street, London, W.1; Home: The House, Marsh Lane, Old Harlow, Essex, England.

Gibbons, James; Irish politician; b. 3 Aug. 1924, Kilkenny; s. of Martin Gibbons and Agnes Bowe; m. Margaret O'Neill 1950; five s. six d.; ed. Univ. Coll., Dublin.
Member of Kilkenny County Council 54-57; Parl. Sec. to Minister of Finance 65-69; Minister of Defence July 69-70, Minister of Agriculture 70-73; mem. Fianna Fáil.
Dunmore, Ballyfoyle, Co. Kilkenny, Ireland.

Gibbons, Stella Dorothea, F.R.S.L.; British poet and novelist; b. 5 Jan. 1902, London; d. of C. J. P. T. Gibbons, M.D. and Maude Phoebe Standish Gibbons; m. Allan Charles Webb 1931 (died 1959); one d.; ed. North London Collegiate School and Univ. Coll., London.
Journalist 22-33, British United Press, *Evening Standard, The Lady.*
Leisure interests; listening to classical music, reading.
Publs. *The Mountain Beast* (poems) 30, *Cold Comfort Farm* (Femina Vie Heureuse Prize 33) 32, *Bassett* 34, *The Priestess* (poems) 34, *Enbury Heath* 35, *The Untidy Gnome* 35, *Miss Linsey and Pa* 36, *Roaring Tower* (short stories) 37, *Nightingale Wood* 38, *The Lowland Venus* (poems) 38, *My American* 39, *Christmas at Cold Comfort Farm* (short stories) 40, *The Rich House* 41, *Ticky* 43, *The Bachelor* 44, *Westwood* 46, *The Matchmaker* 49, *Conference at Cold Comfort Farm* 49, *Collected Poems* 50, *The Swiss Summer* 51, *Fort of the Bear* 53, *Beside the Pearly Water* (short stories), 54, *The Shadow of a Sorcerer* 55, *Here Be Dragons* 56, *White Sand and Grey Sand* 58, *A Pink Front Door* 59, *The Weather at Tregulla* 62, *The Wolves were in the Sledge* 64, *The Charmers* 65, *Starlight* 67, *The Snow Woman* 69, *The Woods in Winter* 70.
19 Oakeshott Avenue, Highgate, London, N.6, England.
Telephone: 01-340-2566.

Gibbs, Hon. Sir Geoffrey Cokayne, K.C.M.G.; British banker; b. 20 July 1901; ed. Eton Coll., and Christ Church, Oxford.
With Ministry of Econ. Warfare 39-45; Dir. and Past Chair. Antony Gibbs & Sons Ltd., Australia and New Zealand Bank Ltd., and Barclays Overseas Devt. Corpn. Advisory Council Export Credits Guarantee Dept., Chair. Managing Trust Nuffield Foundation 51-73, Imperial Relations Trust, Nat. Corpn. for Care of the Aged; mem. Court of Grocers' Company (Master 38-39); Hon. D.C.L. (Oxford).
[*Died 6 July* 1975].

Gibbs, Rt. Hon. Sir Humphrey Vicary, P.C., G.C.V.O., K.C.M.G., K.ST.J., O.B.E.; b. 22 Nov. 1902; m. Dame Molly Peel Nelson 1934; five s.; ed. Eton Coll. and Trinity Coll., Cambridge.
Farmer, Bulawayo 28-; Gov. Rhodesia (fmrly. S. Rhodesia) 60-June 69; Acting Gov.-Gen. Fed. of Rhodesia and Nyasaland 63; Dir. of cos.; Hon. LL.D. (Birmingham); Hon. D.C.L. (E. Anglia).
Bonisa Farm, Private Bag 5583W, Bulawayo, Rhodesia.
Telephone: 69002 Bulawayo.

Gibbs, Oswald Moxley, C.M.G., B.SC.; Grenadian diplomatist; b. 15 Oct. 1927, Snug Corner; s. of Michael "McKie" Gibbs and Emelda Mary Cobb; m. Dearest Agatha Mitchell 1955; two s. two d.; ed. Grenada Boys' Secondary School and City of London Coll.
Solicitor's Clerk 48-51; Refinery Operator, Curaçao 51-55; Civil Servant 55-57; Welfare Officer, E. Caribbean Comm., London 65-67, Trade Sec. 67-72, Deputy Commr. 72-73, Acting Commr. 73-; High Commr. in U.K. Nov. 74-.
Leisure interests: photography, coin collecting, fishing.
High Commission for Grenada, Kings House, 10 Haymarket, London, SW1Y 4DA; Home: 16 Hazlebury Road, London, SW6 2NB, England.
Telephone: 01-930 7902 (Office); 01-736 2164 (Home).

Gibbs, R. Darnley, M.SC., PH.D.; British botanist; b. 30 June 1904, Ryde, Isle of Wight; s. of Frank Ernest Gibbs and Edith Beatrice Wills; m. Avis Patricia Cook 1961; one s.; ed. Univ. Coll., Southampton, and McGill Univ.
Member McGill Univ. staff, Demonstrator to Assoc. Prof. of Botany 25-55, Prof. of Botany 55-65, Macdonald Prof. of Botany 65-71, Prof. Emer. 71-; fmr. Pres. Fraser-Hickson Inst. Montreal; Fellow, Royal Society of Canada (Pres. Section V 53-54); Fellow, Linnean Society of London.
Leisure interest: gardening.
Publs. *A Modern Biology* (with E. J. Holmes) 37, *Botany, An Evolutionary Approach* 50, *Chemotaxonomy of Flowering Plants* 74.
32 Orchards Way, Southampton SO2 1RE, England.
Telephone: 554452.

Gibbs, Gen. Sir Roland Christopher, K.C.B., C.B.E., D.S.O., M.C.; British army officer; b. 22 June 1921, Barrow Gurney; s. of Guy Melvil Gibbs and Margaret Olivia St. John; m. Davinia Jean Merry 1955; two s. one d.; ed. Eton Coll. and Royal Mil. Coll., Sandhurst.
Commissioned into 60th Rifles 40; Served in N. Africa, Italy, N.W. Europe 39-45; Commanded Parachute Bn. 60-62; British Army Staff, Washington, D.C. 62-63; Commanded Parachute Brigade 63-66; Chief of Staff, HQ Middle East 66-67; Commdr. British Forces, Gulf 69-71, British First Corps 72-74; C.-in-C. U.K. Land Forces 74-76.
Leisure interests: pictures, country pursuits.
Shaldon Lodge, Alton, Hampshire, England.
Telephone: Alton 82391.

Gibbs, Timothy Durant; Rhodesian farmer and politician; b. 27 Dec. 1938, Nyamandhlovu; s. of Sir Humphrey Gibbs (q.v.); ed. Ruzawi, Marandellas, Diocesan Coll., Rondebosch, S. Africa.
President Matabeleland branch, Rhodesian Nat. Front Union (RNFU) 69-71; Dir. of cos.; Pres. The Rhodesia Party 74-.
Private Bag W. 5583, Bulawayo; Home: Bonisa Farm, Redbank, Nyamandhlovu, Rhodesia.

Gibiński, Kornel, PROF. DR.; Polish physician; b. 7 Sept. 1915, Crakow; ed. Medical Dept. of Jagellonian Univ., Crakow.
Held in Gross Rosen concentration camp during World War II; Organizer, 3rd Clinic of Internal Diseases in Wrocław 45; Doctor 45-49, Docent 49-54, Assoc. Prof. 54-62, Prof. 62-; Organizer and Dir. Inst. of Internal Diseases, Silesian Medical Acad. in Katowice 53-; Corresp. mem. Polish Acad. of Sciences 65-73, mem. 73-, now Chair. Cttee. of Experimental Therapy; mem. Int. Soc. of Internal Medicine, New York Acad. of Sciences, Polish Soc. of Physicians, Polish Cardiological Soc.; Vice-Pres. Polish Soc. of Internists; Dr. h.c. (Poznań Medical Acad.) 75; Gold Cross of Merit 55, Knight's Cross, Order of Polonia Restituta 58, Officer's Cross 64; Order of Banner of Labour, 2nd Class 74; Order of Builders of People's Poland 74.
Publs. about 230, mainly on physiology and gastrology, many in translations.
Ul. Zawadzkiego 63A, 40-128 Katowice, Poland.

Giblin, E. Burke, LL.B., M.B.A., C.P.A.; American business executive; b. 23 Dec. 1913, Brooklyn; m.; c.; ed. St. John's Univ. and Harvard Business School and Boston Univ. School of Law.
Joined Haskins & Sells (Public Accountants), New York 37; U.S. Navy 40-46; with General Foods Corpn. 46-67, successively in marketing, financial and gen. management positions, and Exec. Vice-Pres. for operations and business devt.; admitted to Mass. Bar 51; Pres. and Dir. Warner-Lambert Co. 67-73, Chair. and Chief Exec. Officer 73-; mem. of the Board, Fidelity

Union Trust Co.; dir. numerous educ. and philanthropic insts.

Warner Lambert Co., Morris Plains, N.J. 07950, U.S.A.

Gibrat, Robert Pierre Louis, LIC. ÈS SC., DR. EN DROIT; French engineer; b. 23 March 1904, Lorient, Morbihan; s. of Jean Gibrat and Jeanne Decebecke; m. Iseult Viel 1928; three d.; ed. Ecole Polytechnique, Ecole Nat. Supérieure des Mines and the Sorbonne.

Dir. of Electricity, Ministry of Public Works 40-42; Sec. of State for Communications March-Sept. 42; Consulting Engineer Electricité de France (Tidal Energy Plants) 42-68; Dir.-Gen. Groupement pour l'Industrie Atomique 55-; Chair. Société pour l'Industrie Atomique, SOCIA; Consulting Engineer Centrales Thermiques 42-; fmr. Pres. Soc. Française des Electriciens; mem. Int. Inst. of Statistics; Fellow, Int. Econometric Soc.; mem. Scientific Cttee., Commissariat Energie Atomique; fmr. Pres. Soc. des Ingénieurs Civils; fmr. Pres. Assen. technique pour l'Energie nucléaire; fmr. Pres. Scientific and Technical Cttee. Euratom; fmr. Pres. Soc. de Statistique de Paris; fmr. Pres. Soc. de Météorologie de France; Pres. French branch, American Nuclear Soc.

Leisure interests: languages, archaeology.

Publs. *Les Inégalités Economiques, L'énergie des marées.*

SOLMER, 32 rue de Lisbonne, 75008 Paris; Creusot Loire, 42 rue d'Anjou, 75008 Paris; Home: 101 ave. de Villiers, 75017 Paris, France.

Telephone: 924-9870 (Home).

Gibson, Baron (Life Peer), cr. 75, of Penn's Rocks in the County of East Sussex; **Richard Patrick Tallentyre Gibson;** British company director; b. 5 Feb. 1916, London; s. of Thorneley Carbutt Gibson and Elizabeth Anne Augusta Wetzler-Coit; m. Elisabeth Dione Pearson 1945; four s.; ed. Eton Coll., Magdalen Coll., Oxford.

Vice-Chairman Westminster Press Ltd. 53-76; Chair. Pearson Longman Ltd. 67-; Deputy Chair. S. Pearson & Son Ltd. 69-75, Exec. Deputy Chair. 75-; Chair. Arts Council of Great Britain 72-, Financial Times Ltd. 75-.

Leisure interests: music, architecture, gardening.

Penn's Rocks, Groombridge, Sussex; and 4 Swan Walk, London, S.W.3, England.

Telephone: Groombridge 244; 01-351-0344.

Gibson, Alexander Drummond, C.B.E., L.R.A.M., A.R.C.M., A.R.C.O.; British conductor; b. 11 Feb. 1926, Motherwell; s. of James McClure Gibson and Wilhelmina Gibson; m. Ann Veronica Waggett; three s. one d.; ed. Dalziel School, Glasgow Univ., Royal Scottish Acad. of Music, Royal Coll. of Music, London, Mozarteum, Salzburg, and Accademia Chigiano, Siena.

Royal Corps of Signals 44-48; studied Royal Coll. of Music 48-51; Asst. Conductor B.B.C. Scottish Orchestra 52-54; Staff Conductor Sadler's Wells Opera 54-56, Musical Dir. 57-59; Guest Conductor Royal Opera House, Covent Garden 57-58; Musical Dir. and Principal Conductor Scottish Nat. Orchestra 59-; Founder, Artistic Dir. and Principal Conductor of Scottish Opera 62-; Guest Conductor all major symphony orchestras of Great Britain and many in Europe and America; Hon. LL.D. (Aberdeen and Stirling), Hon. D.Mus. (Glasgow), Hon. R.A.M.

15 Cleveden Gardens, Glasgow, G12 oPU, Scotland.
Telephone: 041-339-6668.

Gibson, Col. the Hon. Colin William George, P.C. (Can.), Q.C., M.C., V.D.; Canadian jurist; b. 16 Feb. 1891, Hamilton, Ont.; s. of Hon. Sir John and Lady Gibson; m. Florence Kerr 1917; four s.; ed. Royal Military Coll., Kingston, Osgoode Hall, Toronto.

Served Royal Fusiliers 14-19; awarded Ordre de Léopold and Croix de Guerre; practised Law in Hamilton, Ontario; commanded Royal Hamilton Light Inf. 29-34; 4th Inf. Brigade 35-38, Hamilton Garrison 39-40;

six times mem. of Canadian rifle team to Bisley; Hon. A.D.C. to Lords Bessborough and Tweedsmuir when Govs.-Gen. of Canada; elected M.P. 40, 45 and 49; Min. of Nat. Revenue 40-45; Min. of Nat. Defence for Air 45-46; Sec. of State of Canada 46-49; Minister of Mines and Resources 49-50; Judge of Court of Appeal, Ont. 50-65; Commdr. Order of Polonia Restituta 46; Chair. of Council, Dominion of Canada Rifle Assen. 28-48, Pres. 52-54; Pres. Canadian Citizenship Council 52-54; Vice-Pres. Nat. Rifle Assen. (G.B.) 51-; Hon. LL.D. (Royal Mil. Coll.) 65.

"Oxley", Ancaster, Ontario, Canada.

Gibson, Edward G.; American astronaut; b. 8 Nov. 1936, Buffalo, N.Y.; s. of Mr. and Mrs. Calder A. Gibson; m. Julia Ann Volk 1959; two s. two d.; ed. Univ. of Rochester and Calif. Inst. of Technology.

Research asst. specializing in jet propulsion and plasma physics while studying at Calif. Inst. of Technology; later did aerospace research with Philco Corpn. Applied Research Laboratories, Newport Beach, Calif. and solar physics research; selected by NASA as astronaut 65; completed flight training at Williams Air Force Base, Ariz. 66; scientific pilot *Skylab III* mission 72.

Leisure interests: long distance running, swimming.

Publ. *The Quiet Sun.*

NASA Johnson Space Center, Houston, Tex. 77058, U.S.A.

Telephone: 713-483-2311.

Gibson, Eleanor Jack, M.A., PH.D.; American psychologist; b. 7 Dec. 1910, Peoria, Ill.; d. of William and Isabel Grier Jack; m. James Gibson 1932; one s. one d.; ed. Smith Coll. and Yale Univ.

Instructor, Smith Coll., Northampton, Mass. 33-40, Asst. Prof. 40-49; Research Assoc. in Psychology, Cornell Univ. 49-65; Prof. of Psychology 65-; Visiting Prof. Mass. Inst. of Technology 73; mem. Nat. Acad. of Sciences; Distinguished Scientist Award, American Psychological Assen. 68, Guggenheim Fellow 72-73, Wilbur Cross Medal, Yale 73.

Publs. *Principals of Perceptual Learning and Development* 69; articles in all psychological journals.

Department of Psychology, Cornell University, Ithaca, N.Y. 14850; Home: 111 Oakhill Road, Ithaca, N.Y., U.S.A.

Telephone: 256-4371 (Office); 273-0412 (Home).

Gibson, Quentin Howieson, M.D., PH.D., D.SC., F.R.S.; American (b. British) professor of biochemistry; b. 9 Dec. 1918, Aberdeen, Scotland; s. of William H. Gibson, O.B.E., D.SC.; m. Audrey J. Pinsent 1951; one s. three d.; ed. Repton School and Queen's Univ. Belfast.

Demonstrator in Physiology, Queen's Univ., Belfast 41-47; Lecturer in Physiology, Univ. of Sheffield 47-55; Prof. and Head of Dept. of Biochemistry 55-63; Prof. of Biophysical Chem., Johnson Foundation, Univ. of Pennsylvania 63-65; Prof. of Biochemistry, Cornell Univ. 65-; mem. Physiological Soc. (London) and American Soc. of Biological Chemists; Fellow American Acad. of Arts and Sciences; Editor *Biochemical Journal* 53-59; Editor *Journal of Biological Chemistry* 65-70, Assoc. Editor 75-.

Leisure interest: sailing.

Publ. *Rapid Mixing and Sampling Methods in Biochemistry* (Editor) 64.

Department of Biochemistry and Molecular Biology, Cornell University, Ithaca, N.Y.; Home: 98 Dodge Road, Ithaca, New York 14850, U.S.A.

Gibson, Roy; British space administrator; b. 4 July 1924, Manchester; m. Inga Elgerus 1971; one s. one d. (by previous marriage); ed. Chorlton Grammar School, Wadham Coll., Oxford, London School of Econs.

Colonial Administrative Service, Malaya 48-58; U.K. Atomic Energy Authority, London 59-67; Deputy Dir.

Technical Centre, European Space Research Org. (ESRO) 67-71, Dir. of Admin. ESRO 71-74, Acting Dir.-Gen. 74-75; Dir.-Gen., European Space Agency April 75-.
Leisure interests: music, languages, bridge, walking.
European Space Agency, 114 ave. Charles de Gaulle, 92522 Neuilly-sur-Seine, France.
Telephone: 637-7400.

Gichuru, James Samuel; Kenyan teacher and politician; b. 1914, Thogoto, Kiambu District; ed. Church of Scotland Missionary School, Kikuyu High School and Makerere Coll., Uganda.
Teacher, Kikuyu High School 35-40; Headmaster, Church of Scotland Mission School, Dagoretti 40-50; Pres. Kenya African Union 44-47; Chief, Dagoretti location 50-52; under restriction order during state of emergency 55-60; Teacher, Roman Catholic Secondary School, Githunguri 58-60; Pres. Kenya African Nat. Union (KANU) 60-61, Vice-Pres. 66-; M.P. 61-; Minister of Finance April 62-63, of Finance and Econ. Planning 63, and Dec. 64; mem. of Govs. Kenyatta Foundation 66; Vice-Pres. for Central Province 66-69; Minister of Defence Dec. 69-.
Ministry of Defence, Nairobi; Thogoto, Kiambu, Kenya.

Gielen, Michael Andreas; Austrian conductor and composer; b. 20 July 1927, Dresden, Germany; m. Helga Augsten 1957; one s. one d.; ed. Univ. of Buenos Aires; studied composition under E. Leuchter and J. Polnauer.
Pianist in Buenos Aires; on music staff of Teatro Colón 47-51; with Vienna State Opera 51-60, perm. conductor 54-60; First Conductor, Royal Swedish Opera, Stockholm 60-65; Conductor and composer in Cologne 65-69; Musical Dir. Nat. Orchestra of Belgium 69-73; Chief Conductor Netherlands Opera 73-75.
D-6246 Glashütten/TS, Wiesengrund 22, Federal Republic of Germany.

Gielgud, Sir (Arthur) John, Kt., D.LITT., LL.D. (brother of Val Gielgud, q.v.); British actor and theatrical producer; b. 14 April 1904, London; s. of Frank Gielgud and Kate Lewis; ed. Westminster.
First stage appearance at Old Vic 21; Plays acted in include: Shakespeare's plays, Restoration comedies, *The Constant Nymph, The Good Companions, Richard of Bordeaux, The Potting Shed, Ivanov, Forty Years On; The Battle of Shrivings, Home, Caesar and Cleopatra, Veterans, The Tempest, Bingo, No Man's Land;* Productions include: Shakespeare, Restoration drama, *The Importance of Being Earnest, The School for Scandal, The Three Sisters, Dear Brutus, The Circle, The Heiress, The Lady's not for Burning, Ivanov;* Plays directed include: *A Day by the Sea, The Chalk Garden, Nude with Violin, Five Finger Exercise, The Last Joke, Big Fish, Little Fish, School for Scandal, Halfway Up the Tree, Private Lives, The Constant Wife;* Films played in include: *The Barretts of Wimpole Street, St. Joan, Julius Ceasar, Richard III, Becket, The Loved One, Chimes at Midnight, Mister Sebastian, The Charge of the Light Brigade, The Tempest, Eagle in a Cage, Lost Horizon, 11 Harrowhouse, Murder on the Orient Express;* Operas directed: *The Trojans* (Berlioz), *A Midsummer Night's Dream* (Britten); Shakespeare recital: *Ages of Man* in Europe, America and Australasia; Best supporting Actor (*Murder on the Orient Express*), Soc. of Film and TV Arts 74.
Leisure interests: reading, music.
Publs. *Early Stages* 38, *Stage Directions* 63, 64, *Distinguished Company* 72.
16 Cowley Street, London, S.W.1, England.

Gielgud, Val Henry, C.B.E. (brother of Sir John Gielgud, q.v.); British writer; b. 28 April 1900; ed. Rugby and Oxford Univ.
Actor, free-lance journalist, private sec. 21-28; joined

staff of *Radio Times* 28; Head of Drama BBC 29-52, of Sound Drama 52-63.
Publs. *Black Gallantry* 28, *Chinese White* (a play) 28, *Gathering of Eagles* 29, *Imperial Treasure* 30, *Under London* 30, *The Broken Men* 31, *How to Write Broadcast Plays* 32, *Death at Broadcasting House* 33 (with Eric Maschwitz), *Gravelhanger* 34, *Death as an Extra* 35 (with Eric Maschwitz), *Outrage in Manchukuo* 37, *Death in Budapest* 37 (with Eric Maschwitz), *The Red Account* 38, *Punch and Judy* (a play) 38, *The First Television Murder* 40, *Beyond Dover* 41, *Confident Morning* 43, *Radio Theatre* 46, *Years of the Locust* 47, *The Right Way to Radio Playwriting* 48, *Fall of a Sparrow* 49, *Special Delivery* 50, *One Year of Grace* 50, *Party Manners* (play) 50, *Iron Curtain* (play) 51, *Poison in Jest* (play), *The High Jump* 53, *The Bombshell* (play) 53, *Cat* 55, *Mediterranean Blue* (play) 56, *British Radio Drama, 1952-1956* 57, *Gallows' Foot* 58, *To Bed at Noon* 60, *And Died So?* 61, *The Goggle-Box Affair* 63, *Years in a Mirror* 65, *Prinvest-London* 65, *Cats, A Personal Anthology* 66, *Conduct of a Member* 67, *A Necessary End* 69, *The Candle-Holders* 70, *The Black Sambo Affair* 72, *My Cats and Myself* 72, *In Such a Night* 74, *A Fearful Thing* 75.
Wychwood, Barcombe, Lewes, Sussex, England.
Telephone: Barcombe 268.

Gienow, Herbert Hans Walter, D.JUR.; German business executive; b. 13 March 1926, Hamburg; s. of Günther and Margarethe Gienow; m. Imina Brons 1954; one s. one d.; ed. Hamburg Univ.
Head Clerk Deutsche Warentreuhand AG, mem. Board of Management 59; mem. Hamburg Bar; chartered accountant 61; mem. Board of Management Klöckner-Werke AG 62, Chair. Oct. 74-.
Leisure interests: books, sailing, model soldiers.
Klöckner-Werke AG, 41 Duisburg, Mülheimer Strasse 50; Home: 4033 Hösel, Am Adels 7; and 2 Hamburg 52, Charlotte-Niese-Strasse 17, Federal Republic of Germany.
Telephone: (02131) 3961 (Office); (02102) 60692 (Hösel); (040) 827717 (Hamburg).

Gierek, Edward; Polish politician; b. 6 Jan. 1913, Porąbka, Bedzin district; m. Stanisława Gierek; two s.; ed. Cracow Acad. of Mining and Metallurgy.
Lived in France 23-34 and in Belgium 37-48; one of the organizers and leaders of Belgian resistance movement during German occupation in World War II; after the war Chair. Nat. Council of Poles in Belgium and one of the organizers of the Polish Workers' Party and Union of Polish Patriots in Belgium; returned to Poland 48; mem. Polish United Workers' Party (P.Z.P.R.) 48-, Sec. Voivodship Cttee. Katowice 49-54, First Sec. 57-70, mem. Cen. Cttee. 54-, Head Dept. of Heavy Industry, Cen. Cttee. 54-56, mem. Politburo Cen. Cttee. 56-, First Sec. Cen. Cttee. 70-; Deputy to Seym (Parl.) 52-; mem. Presidium All-Polish Cttee. of Nat. Unity Front 71-; Order of Banner of Labour First Class, Order of Builders of People's Poland, Order of Lenin 73, Order of Great Yugoslav Star 73, Frederic Joliot-Curie Gold Medal 74, José Marti Nat. Order (Cuba) 75, etc.
Polska Zjednoczona Partia Robotnicza, Nowy Świat 6, 00-497 Warsaw, Poland.

Gierowski, Stefan; Polish painter; b. 21 May 1925, Częstochowa; s. of Józef and Stefania (Wasilewska) Gierowski; m. Anna Golka 1951; one s. one d.; ed. Acad. of Fine Arts, Crakow.
Docent, Acad. of Fine Arts, Warsaw, Dean of Painting Dept. 75-; mem. Polish Asscn. of Plastic Artists, Sec.-Gen. 57-59, Pres. of Painting Section 59-61, 63-66; Knight's Cross, Order of Polonia Restituta.
One-man shows: Warsaw 55, 57, 60, 67, 72, Galerie la Cloche, Paris 61, 65, Auverrier Galerie Numaga, Switzerland 68; exhibited in group shows: Contemporary

Art Exhbn., Warsaw 57, Carnegie Inst., Pittsburgh 64, 67, 34th Biennale, Venice 68, Triennale of India, New Delhi 68.

Ul. Gagarina 15, 00-595 Warsaw, Poland.

Gierster, Hans; German musical director; b. 12 Jan. 1925; ed. Musikhochschule, Munich, and Mozarteum, Salzburg.

Formerly Musical Dir. Freiburg-im-Breisgau Municipal Theatres; Gen. Musical Dir. Municipal Theatres Nuremberg 56-, Musical Theater 71-; guest conductor at State operas of Hamburg, Munich and Vienna; guest appearances at festivals in Munich 64, Edinburgh (with Bavarian State Opera, *Cosi Fan Tutte*) 65, Glyndebourne (presented *The Magic Flute*) 66, Zurich 71, Vienna 72; concerts with Philharmonic Orchestras of Bamberg, Berlin, Munich, Vienna, London, Mexico. Musiktheater Nürnberg, 8500 Nuremberg, Richard-Wagner-Platz 1, Federal Republic of Germany.

Gieysztor, Aleksander; Polish historian; b. 17 July 1916, Moscow; s. of Aleksander and Barbara (Popiel) Gieysztor; m. Irena Czarnecka 1938; one s. one d.; ed. Warsaw Univ.

Adjunct and Docent Warsaw Univ. 45-49, Prof. 49-, Dir. of Research into origins of Polish State 49-53, Pro-Rector 56-59, Dir. Historical Inst. 55-75; Pres. Univ. Comm. of State Educ. Council 60-69; mem. Bureau Int. Cttee. of Historical Sciences 65- (Vice-Pres. 75-); Assoc. Prof. Collège de France 68; Corresp. fellow, Medieval Acad. of America 68-; Visiting Fellow, All Souls Coll., Oxford 68-69; Chair. Scientific Council of Historical Inst., Polish Acad. of Sciences 72-; Chair. Scientific Council of Nat. Library 72-; Corresp. mem. Polish Acad. of Sciences 71, Koninklijke Akademie voor Wetenschappen, Brussels 72; Dr. h.c. (Aix-Marseille, Bordeaux, Paris IV- Sorbonne and Budapest Univs.); Silver Cross Virtuti Militari, Order Polonia Restituta Commdr. Class, Chevalier Légion d'Honneur, Gold Cross of Merit 53, Ordine al Merito della Repubblica italiana 75.

Publs. *Wzadza Karola Wielkiego* (Rule of Charles the Great) 38, *Genesis of the Crusades* 50, *History of Poland* (co-author) 68, *Zarys dziejów pisma łacińskiego* (Outline of the History of Latin Alphabet) 73, *Thousand Years of Poland* (with S. Herbst and B. Lesnodorski) 76, numerous articles on medieval history.

Ul. Wilcza 8 m. 20, 00-532 Warsaw, Poland.

Telephone: 28-41-38.

Giffen, Albert Egges van, DR.SS.; Netherlands archaeologist; b. 1884; ed. State Univ. of Groningen.

Assistant, State Univ. of Groningen 11; Keeper State Museum of Antiquities, Leyden 12-14; Keeper Zoological Lab., State Univ. of Groningen, Provincial Museum of Drenthe and Municipal and Provincial Museum, Groningen 17; Dir. Biological-Archaeological Inst., State Univ. of Groningen 20, Lecturer in Pre-history and Germanic Archaeology 30, Extra. Prof. 39, Ord. Prof. 43-45, Extra. Prof. Univ. of Amsterdam 41-43 and 46-54; Govt. Adviser 55-; Gold Medal, Soc. of Antiquaries, London 51; Knight of Netherlands Lion; Chevalier de la Légion d'Honneur.

Publs. *De hunebedden in Nederland*, I 25, II 27, *Atlas*, I and II 25, *Die Bauart der Einzelgräber: Beitrag zur Kenntnis der älteren individuellen Grabhügelstrukturen in der Niederlanden* 30, *Jaarverslagen van de Vereniging voor Terpenonderzoek 1-37*, 17-53, *Oudheidkundige aantekeningen over Drentse vondsten, Nieuwe Drentse Volksalmanak* 18-54, *Opgravingen in Drente, een handboek voor het kennen van het Drentse leven in voorbije eeuwen* (pp. 393-628) 44.

Zwolle, Weteringpark 7, Zalnéflat 62, Netherlands.

Telephone: 0-5200-13943.

Gil Robles, José Maria; Spanish lawyer and politician; b. 1899.

Leader, Spanish Christian Democrat Party; mem. Privy Council of Don Juan, Pretender to Spanish Throne; exiled 62; returned to Spain 69; led prosecution in Matesa case.

Gilbert, Carl Joyce; American lawyer and business executive; b. 3 April 1906; ed. Univ. of Virginia and Harvard Univ.

Admitted to Massachusetts Bar 31, with Ropes, Gray, Boyden and Perkins 31-48; U.S. Army 41-46; Vice-Pres. The Gillette Co., Boston 48-56, Pres. 56-58, Chair. of Board 58-66, Chair. Exec. Cttee. 66-69; Special Rep. for Trade Negotiations of Pres. of U.S.A. 69-71.

Strawberry Hill, Dover, Mass. 02030, U.S.A.

Gilbert, Ian H. G.; British business executive; b. 25 Nov. 1910, Chingford, Essex; s. of Claude Edward Gilbert and Ethel Mary Dolleymore; m. Violet Edith Heelas 1938; one s. two d.; ed. Bradfield Coll., Berkshire.

Deloitte, Plender, Griffiths & Co. (Chartered Accountants) 30-38; Accountant and later Sec. The Leopoldina Railway Co. Ltd., London 38-51; Dir. Bryant & May Ltd. 51-55, Managing Dir. 55-64, Chairman 64-72; Dir. British Match Corpn. Ltd. 53-64, Deputy Chair. 64-72, Chair. 72-75; Chair. Bryant & May (Latin America) Ltd. 64-73, Airscrew-Weyroc Ltd. 65-72; Dir. Baker Perkins Holdings Ltd. 72-75, Chair. 75-; Chair. Anglo-Brazilian Soc. 70.

Leisure interests: golf, reading.

Adams Cottage, Bramshott, Liphook, Hants, England.

Telephone: Liphook 72-3075.

Gilbert, Milton, M.A., PH.D.; American economist; b. 8 April 1909; ed. Temple Univ., and Univ. of Pennsylvania.

Editor *Survey of Current Business*, U.S. Dept. of Commerce 38-41; Chief Nat. Income Div., U.S. Dept. of Commerce 41-51; Dir. of Statistics and Nat. Accounts, OEEC 51-55, Dir. of Economics and Statistics 55-60; Bank for International Settlements, Econ. Adviser 60-75, also Head, Monetary and Econ. Dept.; private econ. consultant 75-; Fellow, American Statistical Asscn.

Publs. *Currency Depreciation and Monetary Policy* 39, *U.S. National Income Supplement* (with associates) 47, *An International Comparison of National Products and the Purchasing Power of Currencies* (with Irving B. Kravis) 54, *The Problem of Rising Prices* (with associates) 61, *The Gold Dollar System: Conditions of Equilibrium and the Price of Gold* 68, *The Discipline of the Balance of Payments and the Design of the International Monetary System* 70.

Bank for International Settlements, Centralbahnstr. 7, Basle, Switzerland.

Gilbert, Pierre-Eugène, L. ÈS L., L. EN D.; French diplomatist; b. 12 Jan. 1907; m. Catherine Bembo 1944; one s.; ed. Univ. de Paris à la Sorbonne and Ecole des Langues Orientales.

Ministry of Foreign Affairs Paris 32-33; Sec. Interpreter Far East, successively at Foochow, Yünnanfu, Peking and Nanking 33-37; mem. of French Del. Brussels Conf. 37, Embassy Shanghai 37-39; Ministry of Foreign Affairs Paris 39; later at Vancouver and Helsinki, joined Free French 40, Lieut.-Commdr. R.N. 40-44; dismissed and deprived of nationality by Vichy; Commissariat of Foreign Affairs Algiers 44; after Liberation mem. Purge Comm. Ministry of Foreign Affairs, Paris; Govt. Commr. at sessions of Council of State 45-47; Minister to Thailand 47-49; Ambassador to Peru 49-52; Ambassador to Israel 53-59; Diplomatic counsellor 59-61; Pres. and Dir.-Gen. Soc. Française des Techniques Pye (S.F.T.P.), Immobilière Franco-Allemande (I.F.R.A.); Administrator Schneider Radio-Télévision S.A.; Commandeur de la Légion d'Honneur, Croix de Guerre, Médaille de la Résistance.

Leisure interests: sailing, shooting, farming.

48 rue Boissière, Paris 16e; and Saint Nicolas de Bliquetuit 76, France.
Telephone: 553-79-14 (Paris).

Gilchrist, Sir Andrew Graham, K.C.M.G.; British diplomatist (retd.); b. 19 April 1910, Lesmahagow, Scotland; s. of late J. G. Gilchrist; m. Freda Grace Slack 1946; two s. one d.; ed. Edinburgh Acad., and Exeter Coll., Oxford.
Siam Branch, British Consular Service 33-36, 38-41, also served Paris, Marseilles, Morocco; Army service, S.E. Asia 44-46; Foreign Office 46-51; Consul-Gen., Stuttgart 51-54; Foreign Office Counsellor, Staff of U.K. Commr.-Gen. for S.E. Asia, Singapore 54-56; Ambassador to Iceland 56-59; Consul-Gen., Chicago 60-63; Amb. to Indonesia 63-66; Asst. Under-Sec. Commonwealth Office 66-67; Amb. to Ireland 67-70; Chair. British Highlands and Islands Devt. Board, Inverness 70-.
Publ. *Bangkok Top Secret* 70.
Pett Conachie, Avoch, Ross-shire, Scotland.
Telephone: Fortrose 655.

Gilels, Emil Grigorevich; Soviet pianist; b. 19 Oct. 1916, Odessa; m. Farizet Gilels 1948; one d.; ed. Odessa Musical and Dramatic Inst. and Moscow Conservatoire.
First Prize, All-Russia Music Competition 33; Prof. Moscow Conservatoire 52; concert tours in Europe, U.S.A., Japan, etc.; has recorded for DGG, EMI and RCA; People's Artist of the U.S.S.R.; State Prize 46, Lenin Prize 62; Hon. Prof., Budapest Conservatoire, Royal Acad. of Music, London.
Moscow State Conservatoire, Ul. Gerzena 13, Moscow, U.S.S.R.

Gillard, Francis (Frank) George, C.B.E., B.SC., F.R.S.A.; British broadcasting and communications consultant; b. 1 Dec. 1908, Tiverton, Devon; s. of Francis Henry and Emily Jane Gillard; ed. St. Luke's Coll., Exeter.
Schoolmaster 31-41; B.B.C. War Corresp. 41-45; B.B.C. W. Region Programme Dir. 45-55; Chief Asst. Dir. of Sound Broadcasting 55-56; Controller W. Region 56-63; Dir. of Sound Broadcasting Aug. 63-69, Man. Dir. Radio 69; Consultant EMI Ltd. 70-, Corpn. for Public Broadcasting, U.S.A. 70-.
Leisure interests: country life, reading, travel.
Trevor House, Poole, Wellington, Somerset, England.
Telephone: Wellington 2890.

Gillemot, László, D.SC.; Hungarian mechanical engineer; b. 7 Oct. 1912, Budapest; s. of Ferenc Gillemot and Olga Sugár; m. Eva Kovácsi 1937; two s. one d.
Rector of Budapest Technical Univ. 54-57; Dir. of Research Inst. for Non-Ferrous Metals 48-69; Dir. of Research Inst. for Iron and Steel 49-52; Prof. Technical Univ. of Budapest; mem. Hungarian Acad. of Sciences; Corresp. mem. Yugoslav Acad. of Sciences; Kossuth Prizes 49, 57; Labour Order of Merit, Golden Degree; Commdr.'s Degree of Medal of Merit for Scientific Research, France 66.
Major subjects of study: material testing; structure of metals with reference to fracture energy; welding technology; plastic deformation of metals; high energy rate forging.
Leisure interests: sport, music, cats.
Technical University of Budapest, Bertalan Str. 7, H-1521 Budapest XI; Home: Tarcali Str., 2, H-1113, Budapest XI, Hungary.
Telephone: 658-793.

Gillen, Stanley James, B.B.A.; American motor executive; b. 10 Aug. 1911, Ohio; s. of Bernard J. Gillen and Johanna P. Spillane; m. Mary Elizabeth Marks 1935; three d.; ed. St. Fredrick's High School, Pontiac, Mich., and Univ. of Detroit.
Financial Analyst, Fisher Body Division, Gen. Motors Corpn. 33-47; Contract Administrator, Defense Pro-

ducts, Ford Motor Co., U.S.A. 47-48, Controller, Steel Div. 48-55, Controller, Tractor and Implement Div. 55-56, Asst. Gen. Man. Steel Div. 56-60, Gen. Man. Steel Div. 60-61, Gen. Parts Div. 61-65; Chair. Autolite Motor Products Ltd. 62-65; Man. Dir. and Chief Exec. Officer, Ford of Britain 65-67, Dir. 65-71; Vice-Pres. (Manufacturing) Ford of Europe 67-69, Chair. and Chief Exec. Officer 69-71; Dir. Ford of Europe Inc. 67-71; Vice-Pres. Ford Motor Co. U.S.A. 67-71; Dir. Ford Credit Co. 65-67, Henry Ford and Son Ltd., Cork, Ireland 65-67, Ford Werke AG, Cologne, 70-71; Dir. American Chamber of Commerce (U.K.) 67-; Dir. Sangamo Weston Ltd., Enfield 71-, Sangamo Electric, U.S.A. 72-; mem. Soc. of Automotive Engineers, Nat. Advisory Council for Motor Manufacturing Industry 66-67; Lord Wakefield Gold Medal 71.
Leisure interests: golf, skiing, shooting, horology.
58 Campden Hill Court, Campden Hill Road, London, W8 7HU, England.
Telephone: 01-937-3479 (Office).

Gillès, Daniel; Belgian writer; b. 1917, Bruges; m. Simone Lambinon 1948; one d.; ed. law studies.
Prix Rossel (Belgium); Grand prix de la critique littéraire (France) 67.
Leisure interests: travel, tennis, painting.
Publs. include: *Jetons de présence, le Coupon* 44, *les Brouillards de Bruges, l'Etat de grâce, la Termitière, Mort-la-Douce, La Rouille* (stories), *Le Festival de Salzbourg;* biographies: *Tolstoï, D. H. Lawrence ou le puritain scandaleux, Tchékhov.*
161 avenue Churchill, Brussels 18, Belgium.
Telephone: 341-71-55.

Gillespie, Hon. Alastair William, M.A., M.COM.; Canadian business executive and politician; b. 1 May 1922, Victoria, B.C.; s. of Errol Pilkington and Catherine B. Gillespie; m. Diane C. Clark 1947; one s. one d.; ed. Univs. of British Columbia, McGill, Oxford and Toronto.
Served, Royal Canadian Volunteer Reserve 41-45; Pres. Welmet Industries Ltd., Welland & Canada Chromalox Co., Rexdale; Vice-Pres. and Dir. Canada Corporate Management Co. Ltd., Toronto; Chair. Exec. Cttee. Canadian Inst. of Public Affairs 62-64 (Dir. 54-65); mem. Parl. 68-; Chair. Exec. Cttee. of Commons Finance, Trade and Econ. Affairs Cttee. 68-70; Parliamentary Sec. to Pres. of Treasury Board 70-71; Minister of State for Science Aug. 71-72; Minister of Industry, Trade and Commerce 72-; Liberal.
78 John Street, Ottawa, Ontario K1M 1N4, Canada.

Gillet, Guillaume; French architect; b. 20 Nov. 1912; ed. Ecole Nat. Supérieure des Beaux Arts, Paris.
Premier Grand Prix de Rome 46; Chief Architect, Bâtiments Civils et Palais Nationaux 54-; Prof., Ecole nationale supérieure des beaux-arts 53-; Consulting Architect to Ministry of Building; Head Architect, French Section, Brussels Int. Exhibition 58; Head of UNESCO Town-Planning Mission to Israel; mem. Acad. des Beaux Arts 68; Commdr. Ordre des Arts et Lettres 66, Ordre de la Couronne (Belgium) 58, Chevalier Légion d'Honneur 59, etc.
17 rue Bonaparte, Paris 6e, and 10 rue des Nonnains-d'Hyère, Paris 4e, France.
Telephone: ARC 44-17 and ARC 85-36.

Gillet, Renaud; French industrialist; b. 14 Dec. 1913, Lyon; s. of Charles Gillet; m. Marie Colcombet 1939; two s. one d.; ed. Ecole Supérieure de Chimie Industrielle, Lyon.
With Soc. Rhodiacéta 35, Cie. Industrielle des Textiles Artificiels et Synthétiques (CTA) 42; Gen. Man. Textil 61; Pres. Dir.-Gen. Pricel 66; Vice-Pres. Rhône-Poulenc S.A. 72, Pres. Dir.-Gen. 73-.
Rhône-Poulenc S.A., 22 avenue Montaigne, 75008 Paris; Home: 3 place Vauban, 75007 Paris, France.

Gillet, Robert, L. ès L., L. en D.; French diplomatist; b. 17 April 1912; ed. Ecole Libre des Sciences Politiques, and Oxford Univ.

Attaché, Ankara 41-43; Deputy Dir. at Ministry of Foreign Affairs (Econ. and Finance Section) 45-51; Counsellor, Madrid 51-53, Cairo 53-55; Minister Tunis 55-57; Technical Counsellor Minister of Foreign Affairs 57-58; Dir. Office of M. Couve de Murville, Ministry of Foreign Affairs 58-64, Deputy Dir. Political Affairs, Ministry of Foreign Affairs 64; Ambassador to Morocco 65-70; Amb. to Spain 70-; Officier Légion d'Honneur, Hon. K.C.M.G., and other honours.

French Embassy, Héroes del Diez de Agosto 9, Madrid, Spain; 21 *bis* avenue d'Iéna, Paris 16e, France.

Gilliatt, Penelope, F.R.S.L.; British author and film critic; b. London; *d.* of Cyril and Mary (Douglass) Conner; *m.* 1st Prof. R. W. Gilliatt (divorced), 2nd John Osborne (*q.v.*) 1963 (divorced); one *d.*; ed. Queen's Coll. Univ. of London, Bennington Coll. Vt., U.S.A.

Film critic, *The Observer* 61-67, theatre critic 65; guest film critic, *The New Yorker* 67, regular film critic (six months each year) 68-; awards for writing, American Acad., Nat. Inst. of Arts and Letters 72; awards for screenplay *Sunday, Bloody Sunday* from Writers' Guild of America, Writers' Guild of England, Nat. Soc. of Film Critics (New York), New York Film Critics' Soc.

Publs. Novels: *One by One* 65, *A State of Change* 68; Short stories: *What's It Like Out?* 68 (*Come Back if it Doesn't Get Better*, U.S.A. 67), *Nobody's Business* 72, *Penguin Modern Short Stories* 70; plays, films: *Property* 70, *Sunday, Bloody Sunday* (screenplay) 71; TV play: *The Flight Fund* 74; non-fiction: *Unholy Fools: Film and Theatre* 72; *Jean Renoir, Essays, Conversations, Reviews* 75; *Tati* 76.

The New Yorker, 25 West 43rd Street, New York, N.Y. 10036, U.S.A.

Gilligan, John Joyce, M.A.; American politician; b. 22 March 1921, Cincinnati, Ohio; *s.* of Harry J. and Blanche D. J. Gilligan; *m.* Mary K. Dixon 1945; two *s.* two *d.*; ed. Notre Dame Univ. and Univ. of Cincinnati.

Instructor in literature, Xavier Univ., Cincinnati 48-53; mem. Cincinnati City Council 53-64, 67; mem. House of Reps., U.S. Congress 64-67; unsuccessful candidate for U.S. Senate 68; Gov. of Ohio 71-74; Democrat.

Leisure interests: tennis, sailing.

c/o Office of the Governor, The State House, Columbus, Ohio 43215, U.S.A.

Telephone: 614-469-3526.

Gillon, Etienne, L. ès L., L. en D., C.P.A.; French editor; b. 21 March 1911; ed. Ecole Libre des Sciences Politiques.

Librairie Larousse 32-, Man. Dir. 52-; Pres. Syndicat National des Editeurs; Vice-Pres. Asscn. for Graphic and Plastic Arts; Croix de Guerre; Chevalier Légion d'Honneur.

17 rue du Montparnasse, 75006 Paris; 23 avenue Emile-Deschanel, 75007 Paris, France.

Gillon, Mgr. Luc-Pierre-A., D.SC.; Belgian ecclesiastic and scientist; b. 15 Sept. 1920, Rochefort.

Research physicist, Inst. Interuniversitaire des Sciences Nucléaires 48; guest staff mem. Brookhaven Nat. Laboratory, New York 53; Rector Lovanium Univ. 54; Dean of Science Faculty and Prof. of Nuclear Engineering, Catholic Univ. of Louvain 72.

Leisure interest: flying (private aeroplane).

Université de Louvain, Institut de Physique Corpusculaire, chemin du Cyclotron, 1348 Louvain La Neuve, Belgium.

Telephone: 010-41-72-43 (Office); 010-41-70-59 (Home).

Gilman, Alfred, B.S., PH.D.; American professor of pharmacology; b. 5 Feb. 1908, Bridgeport, Conn.; *s.* of Joseph Gilman and Frances Zack; *m.* Mabel Schmidt 1934; one *s.* one *d.*; ed. Yale Univ.

Research Fellow in Biochemistry, Yale School of Medicine 31-32, Research Fellow in Pharmacology 32-35, Asst. Prof. of Pharmacology and Toxicology 35-43; U.S. Army 43-46; Assoc. Prof. of Pharmacology, Coll. of Physicians and Surgeons, Columbia Univ. 46-48, Prof. 48-56; Prof. and Chair. Dept. of Pharmacology, Albert Einstein Coll. of Medicine 56-73, part-time Prof. 73-, Assoc. Dean for Graduate Studies 64-69; Lecturer Dept. of Pharmacology, Yale Univ. School of Medicine 73, Visiting Prof. of Pharmacology, Univ. of Va. School of Medicine 73; Fellow, American Asscn. for Advancement of Science, American Acad. of Arts and Sciences; mem. Nat. Acad. of Sciences, American Physiological Soc., Soc. for Experimental Biology and Medicine, Harvey Soc., American Soc. for Pharmacology and Experimental Therapeutics, N.Y. Acad. of Sciences, N.Y. Acad. of Medicine; Hon. Fellow, American Acad. of Allergy; mem. Pharmacology and Experimental Therapeutics Study Section, U.S. Public Health Service 46-49, 50-55, Chair. 55-60; Pres. American Soc. for Pharmacology and Experimental Therapeutics 60-61; official of other medical orgs.

Leisure interests: fishing, boating.

Publ. Co-Author and Co-Editor (with Dr. Louis S. Goodman) *The Pharmacological Basis of Therapeutics.*

Department of Pharmacology, Yale University School of Medicine, 333 Cedar Street, New Haven, Conn. 06510; Home: 123 York Street, New Haven, Conn. 06511, U.S.A.

Telephone: (203) 436-1333 (Office); (203) 624-5344 (Home).

Gilman, Henry, B.S., M.A., PH.D.; American professor of chemistry; b. 9 May 1893, Boston, Mass.; *s.* of David Gilman and Jane (Gordon) Gilman; *m.* Ruth Shaw 1929; one *s.* one *d.*; ed. Harvard Univ., Eidgen. Technische Hochschule, Zürich, Sorbonne, Paris and Oxford Univ.

Instructor, Harvard Univ. 18-19; Assoc., Univ. of Ill. 19; Asst. Prof. Iowa State Coll. 19, Prof. of Chem. 23, Distinguished Prof. of Sciences and Humanities, Iowa State Univ. 62-; Research Dir. and Adviser for various Govt. Agencies including Atomic Energy Comm., Office of Scientific Research and Devt. and Nat. Defence Research Cttee., U.S. Air Force; Firestone Int. Lecturer, Int. Symposia Lecturer, Bordeaux 68, Moscow 71, Madison 72 and numerous other lectureships in U.S. and abroad; Official Visitor and Lecturer, U.S.S.R. 63; mem. of Editorial Boards of various scientific books and periodicals; Trustee, Carver Research Foundation; Fellow, American Asscn. for the Advancement of Science (Vice-Pres.; Section Chair. 30); Hon. Fellow, Chemical Soc., London; mem. American Chemical Soc. (Councillor-at-Large 39-41, 42-44, Chair. Organic Div.), Nat. Acad. of Sciences, Org. Cttee. of Int. Symposia in Organometallic Chem.; Foreign mem. Royal Soc., London 75; F. S. Kipping Award in Organosilicon Chem., Int. Organometallic Lecture Award, Mid-West Gold Medal, Merit Award by Iowa Acad. of Sciences.

Leisure interests include: non-professional reading, travel, hiking, tennis, badminton.

Publs. *Catenated Organic Compounds of Group IV-B* (with W. H. Atwell and F. K. Cartledge), *Organic Substituted Cyclosilanes* (with G. L. Schwebke), *Introduction to Organometallic Chemistry* (with F. K. Cartledge) 69, *Organic Chemistry—An Advanced Treatise,* 4 vols. (Editor), Collective Vol. I of *Organic Syntheses, More that One-half Century of Organometallic Chemistry,* introductory lecture at Third Int. Organosilicon Symposium; research articles in standard scientific journals on various subjects including organometallic and organosilicon chemistry, organofluorine chemistry and contribs. to encyclopaedias and other books.

Department of Chemistry, Iowa State University, Ames, Ia. 50010; Home: 3221 Oakland Street, Ames, Ia. 50010, U.S.A.
Telephone: 294-6342 (Office); 292-1171 (Home).

Gilmore, Voit; American government official; b. 13 Oct. 1918, Winston-Salem, N.C.; s. of John Merriman Gilmore and Helen Hensel; m. Kathryn Kendrick 1945; two s. three d.; ed. Univ. of N. Carolina.
With Senator Josiah Bailey; Pan American World Airways; Navy Air Transport Service, Second World War; took over family lumber business, Southern Pines 48; Pres. N. Carolina Travel Council 57-59; observer on four polar expeditions; Dir. U.S. Travel Service 62-64; Pres. Holly Corpn. 64-; mem. N. Carolina State Senate 65, 67; Pres. N. Carolina Symphony Soc. 65-68; Chair. N. Carolina Comm. on Educ. and Employment of Women 66-72; Dir. Southern Nat. Bank 72-; Pres. Amer. Forestry Asscn. 73-76; mem. Explorers' Club of New York City, Bohemian Club of San Francisco.
Leisure interest: exploration.
700 East Indiana Avenue, Southern Pines, N.C., U.S.A.
Telephone: 692-2811.

Gilroy, His Eminence Cardinal Sir Norman Thomas, K.B.E.; Australian ecclesiastic (retd.); b. 22 Jan. 1896; ed. St. Columba's Coll., Springwood, and Urban Coll., Rome.
Ordained priest 23; Bishop of Port Augusta 34-37; Coadjutor Archbishop of Sydney 37-40; Archbishop of Sydney, Metropolitan 40-71; created Cardinal Feb. 46.
St. John Vianney Villa, Market Street, Randwick, N.S.W. 2031, Australia.

Gilruth, Robert Rowe, B.S., M.S.; American engineer; b. 8 Oct. 1913, Nashwauk, Minn.; s. of Henry A. Gilruth and Frances M. (Rowe) Gilruth; m. 1st Esther Jean Barnhill 1937 (died 1972), 2nd Georgene Hubbard Evans 1973; one s. one d.; ed. Univ. of Minnesota.
With Nat. Advisory Cttee. for Aeronautics (later Nat. Aeronautics and Space Admin.—N.A.S.A.) 37-, Dir. Space Task Group (Project Mercury) 58; Dir. N.A.S.A. Manned Spacecraft Center (Projects Mercury, Gemini and Apollo) 61-72; Dir. Key Personnel Development, NASA 72-73, retd. 73; Consultant to NASA Administrator 74-; Fellow, American Rocket Soc., Institute of Aerospace Sciences, American Astronautical Soc.; Gov. Nat. Rocket Club; Sylvanus Albert Reed Award 50, Outstanding Achievement Award (Univ. of Minn.) 54, Louis W. Hill Space Transportation Award 62, NASA Distinguished Service Medal 62, U.S. Chamber of Commerce Great Living American Award 62, Dr. Robert H. Goddard Memorial Award of American Rocket Society 62; Hon. Fellow, Inst. of Aerospace Sciences 63; Spirit of St. Louis Medal by American Soc. of Mechanical Engineers 65; Americanism Award by China-Burma-India Veterans Asscn. 65; mem. Int. Acad. of Astronautics 65-; mem. Houston Philosophical Soc. 66-; Daniel Florence Guggenheim Award, Int. Acad. of Astronautics 66, 1966 Space Flight Award of American Astronautical Soc.; mem. Nat. Acad. of Engineering 68, Nat. Acad. of Sciences 74; NASA Distinguished Service Medal 69; Rockefeller Public Service Award 69; Hon. Fellow, Royal Aeronautical Soc.; U.S. Nat. Space Hall of Fame Award 69; American Soc. of Mech. Engineers Medal 70; Inst. of Mechanical Engineers James Watt Int. Medal 71; Nat. Aviation Club Award for Achievement 71; Robert J. Collier Trophy (Nat. Aeronautics Asscn. and Nat. Aviation Club) 72; four hon. degrees.
Leisure interests: boating and boat building.
Office: NASA, Johnson Space Center, Houston, Texas 77058; Home: 5128 Park Avenue, Dickinson, Texas 77539, U.S.A.
Telephone: 713-483-3438 (Office).

Gilson, Etienne, D.LITT., PH.D., LL.D.; French historian and philosopher; b. 13 June 1884; ed. Sorbonne. Professor, Lille Univ. 13 and Strasbourg Univ. 19; Prof. of Medieval Philosophy in Sorbonne 21-32; Prof. Coll. de France 32-50; Dir. Inst. of Medieval Studies at Toronto 29; Prof. Harvard Univ. 26-28; mem. Acad. Française 46-; Corresp. mem. British Acad., Royal Acad. of Netherlands; Counseiller de la République; Commdr. Légion d'Honneur, Croix de Guerre; Dr. h.c. Oxford, Aberdeen, St. Andrews, Glasgow.
Publs. La philosophie au Moyen-Age 22, Le Thomisme 22, La philosophie de St. Bonaventure 24, Introduction à l'étude de St. Augustin 29, L'esprit de la philosophie médiévale 32, La théologie mystique de St. Bernard 34, Le réalisme méthodique 35, Christianisme et philosophie 36, The Unity of Philosophical Experience 37, Héloïse et Abélard, Reason and Revelation in the Middle Ages 38, Dante et la Philosophie 39, God and Philosophy 41, L'être et l'essence 48, L'école des muses 50, La Philosophie de St. Augustin, Jean Duns Scot, Le Philosophie et le Théologien, Peinture et réalité, Introduction aux artsud, beau, Matières et formes 64, The Spirit of Thomism 64, Recent Philosophy 66, D'Aristote à Darwin et retour 71.
9 rue Saint-Romain, Paris 6, France.

Gimbel, Bruce A.; American businessman; b. 28 July 1913; m. Barbara Poulson 1945; two s. one d.; ed. Choate School and Yale Univ.
Joined Gimbel Bros. Inc. 35, Pres. 53-; joined Saks Fifth Avenue 36, Vice-Pres. 46-53, Chair. of Board, Chief Exec. Officer 73-.
Leisure interest: flying.
Home: 435 East 52nd Street, New York, N.Y.; 1275 Broadway, New York, N.Y., U.S.A.

Gimenez-Arnau y Gran, José Antonio; Spanish diplomatist; b. 8 May 1912, Laredo, Santander; ed. Univ. of Bologna.
Entered diplomatic service 42; held posts in Buenos Aires, Dublin 43-53; Dir.-Gen. for Econ. Co-operation, Ministry of Commerce 53; Counsellor for Foreign Trade, Montevideo 56; Minister Plenipotentiary 60; Amb. to Nicaragua 61, to Guatemala 62; Perm. Rep. to Int. Orgs in Geneva 64; Amb. to Brazil 67-69, to Portugal 69-73, to Italy 73-; decorations from Spain, Guatemala, Italy, Brazil, Germany and France.
Publs. De pantalón largo, Murió hace 15 años, El Puente, La canción del jilguero, La cárcel sin puertas, etc.
Spanish Embassy, Largo Fontenella Borghese 19, Rome, Italy.

Ginastera, Alberto; Argentine composer; b. 11 April 1916; ed. Conservatorio Nac. de Música y Arte Escénico.
Director Instituto Torcuato di Tella, Centro Latinoamericano de Altos Estudios Musicales.
Works include: Ollantay (symphonic poem) 48, Music for film Cabailito Criollo 54, Variaciones concertantes 57, Obertura para el Fausto Criollo (orchestra), two symphonies, Panambí (ballet), Estancia (ballet), Don Rodrigo (opera), Bomarzo (opera) 67, Beatrice Cenci (opera) 71.
Instituto Torcuato di Tella, Superí 1502, Buenos Aires, Argentina.

Gingrich, Arnold, A.B.; American editor and author; b. 5 Dec. 1903, Grand Rapids, Mich.; s. of John Hembling Gingrich and Clara Alice Speare; m. 1st Helen Mary Rowe 1924 (deceased), 2nd Jane Kendall 1955; three s.; ed. Michigan Univ.
Advertising copy writer 25; Editor Apparel Arts, Vice-Pres. Apparel Arts Publications Inc. 31-45; Editor Esquire, Vice-Pres. Esquire Inc. 33-45; Editor Coronet 36-45, Ken 38-39; European Editor Esquire and Coronet 45-49; Gen. Man. Flair, Vice-Pres. Cowles Magazines Inc. 49-51; Senior Vice-Pres. and Publisher, Esquire 52-74, Editor in Chief, Senior Vice-Pres. 74-.
Leisure interests: fly fishing and collecting violins.

Publs. *Cast Down the Laurel* 35, *The Well-Tempered Angler* 65, *Toys of a Lifetime* 66, *Business and the Arts* 69, *A Thousand Mornings of Music* 70, *Nothing But People: The Early Days at Esquire* 71, *The Joys of Trout* 73, *The Fishing in Print* 74.
Office: 488 Madison Avenue, New York 22; Home: 605 East Saddle River Road, Ridgewood, New Jersey, 07450, U.S.A.
Telephone: PLaza 9-3232; 652-8582 (Home).

Ginsberg, Allen; American poet; b. 3 June 1926, Newark, N.J.; s. of Louis Ginsberg and Naomi Levy; ed. Grammar High School, Paterson, N.J. and Columbia Coll.
Travelled to Mexico and Europe during fifties; interest in Gnostic-mystical poetry and politics led to residence in Far East 62-63; experiments with poetic effects of psychedelic drugs 52-, Cambridge experiments with Dr. Timothy Leary 61; visited Africa and Arctic, South America 60, Russia and E. Europe 65; elected Kral Majales (King of May), Czechoslovakia 65; participated in college poetry readings and conventions 58-61, also Flower Power marches and anti-war rallies; Contributing Editor, *Black Mountain Review*, Advisory Guru, *The Marijuana Review*; attended first Human Be-in, San Francisco 67, Yippie Life Festival, Chicago 68; arrested several times during various anti-war protests; Co-Dir. Jack Kerouac School of Disembodied Poetics, Naropa Inst., Colo. (Buddhist Studies Inst.); mem. Nat. Inst. of Arts and Letters 74; has recorded *Songs of Innocence and of Experience by William Blake, Tuned by Allen Ginsberg*; now learning music and dairy farming.
Leisure interests: meditation, blues music, drugs.
Publs. Poetry: *Howl and Other Poems* 56, *Kaddish and Other Poems* 61, *Empty Mirror* 61, *Reality Sandwiches* 63, *Ankor Wat* 68, *Airplane Dreams* 68, *Planet News* 68, *The Fall of America* 73; prose: *Yage Letters* 63, *Indian Journals* 70, *Gay Sunshine Interview* 73, *Allen Verbatim* 74, *The Vision of the Great Rememberer* 74, *First Blues* (songs) 75 and many contributions to anthologies.
c/o City Lights Books, 1562 Grant Avenue, San Francisco, Calif. 94133, U.S.A.

Ginsburg, Marcel; Belgian diamond merchant; b. 1891, Moscow; m. Rosalia Zagorodzka 1954; two d.
Former Pres. Belgian Diamond Exchange, Treas. of Diamond Office, Pres. of the Fed. of Belgian Diamond Exchanges, Vice-Pres. of the World Federated Diamond Exchanges; Hon. Pres. Antwerp Diamond Exchange; Gold Medal of Lauréat du Travail; Officer of the Order of Léopold; Commdr. Order of the Crown.
Leisure interest: music.
65 Avenue de Belgique, Antwerp, Belgium.
Telephone: 30-64-07.

Ginzburg, Natalia; Italian writer; b. 1916, Palermo; m. 1st L. Ginzburg, 2nd Gabriele Baldini.
First short stories published at age 17; works now translated into several languages; Strega Prize (for *Lessico famigliare*) 63; Marzotto Prize (for *L'Inserzione*).
Publs. novels include: *La Strada che va in Città* 42, *E'stato così, Valentino, Sagittario, Le voci della sera, Le Piccole Virtù* 62, *Lessico famigliare* 63, *Tutti i nostri ieri, Caro Michele* 73; dramatic works include: *Ti ho sposato per allegria, L'Inserzione*; other writings include *Mai devi domandarmi*.
Piazza Camp Marzio 3, Rome, Italy.

Ginzburg, Vitaly Lazarevich, DR. SC.; Soviet physicist; b. 4 Oct. 1916, Moscow; s. of Lazar and Augusta Ginzburg; m. Nina Ginzburg 1946; one d.; ed. Moscow Univ.
At Inst. of Physics, U.S.S.R. Acad. of Sciences 40-; Prof. Gorky Univ. 45-68, Moscow Tech. Inst. of Physics 68-; mem. C.P.S.U. 44-; Corresp. mem. U.S.S.R. Acad. of Sciences 53-66, mem. 66-; Lomonosov Prize 62, U.S.S.R. State Prize 53; Lenin Prize 66; Hon. D.Sc. (Univ. of Sussex) 70; Order of Lenin, etc.

Publs. Works on theoretical physics (superconductivity, etc.), astrophysics and radiophysics.
U.S.S.R. Academy of Sciences, 14 Leninsky Prospekt, Moscow, U.S.S.R.

Ginzton, Edward Leonard, B.S.E.E., M.S.E.E., PH.D.; American electrical engineer; b. 27 Dec. 1915, Ukraine, Russia; s. of Leonard Louis and Natalie (Philipova) Ginzton; m. Artemas A. McCann 1939; two s. two d.; ed. Univ. of Calif. at Berkeley and Stanford Univ.
During Second World War, developed art of microwave measurements and high-power klystron; later directed construction of several large linear accelerators including the design of the two-mile long SLAC; Teaching and research, Stanford Univ. 46-61; Co-Founder Varian Assocs., Palo Alto, Calif. 48, mem. of Board 48-, Chair. of Board 59-, Pres. 64-68; mem. Nat. Acad. of Eng. Council 74-, NRC Comm. on Nuclear and Alternative Energy Systems 75-, NAS Cttee. on Solar Energy Research Inst. 75-; mem. Nat. Acad. of Engineering, Nat. Acad. of Sciences; Inst. of Electrical and Electronic Engineers awards: Morris Liebmann Memorial Prize, Medal of Honor 69; Calif. Mfr. of the Year Award 74.
Leisure interests: photography, skiing, sailing, hiking, restoring old motor-cars.
Publs. *Microwave Measurements* 57; and numerous papers, technical articles and patents.
Varian Associates, 611 Hansen Way, Palo Alto, Calif.; Home: 28014 Natoma Road, Los Altos Hills, Calif., U.S.A.
Telephone: 493-4000 (Office); 948-5362 (Home).

Gioia, Niccolò; Italian engineer and motor executive; b. 23 Dec. 1914, Florence; s. of Antonio Gioia and Elisa Martini; m. Laura Camino 1946; two d.
Head of Dept., Fiat 45; Deputy Head of Iron and Steel Dept. and Asst. to Dir.-Gen. 58; Head of a Div. 66; Deputy Dir.-Gen. 67-69, Dir.-Gen. 69-; and mem. Directing Cttee.; mem. Consultative Cttee. ECSC.
Fiat S.p.A., Corso Marconi 10, 10100 Turin, Italy.

Giolitti, Antonio; Italian politician; b. 12 Feb. 1915; ed. Univ. of Rome.
Member Constituent Assembly 46; Under-Sec. of Foreign Affairs June-Oct. 46; mem. Chamber of Deputies 48-, Pres. Commission for Industry and Trade Chamber of Deputies 63, 64-70; Minister of the Budget and Econ. Planning 63-64, 70-74.
Publs. *Riforme e rivoluzione* 57, *Il Comunismo in Europa* 60, *Un socialismo possibile* 67.
Camera dei Deputati, Rome, Italy.

Giovannetti, Rt. Rev. Mgr. Alberto; Italian ecclesiastic and diplomatist; b. 20 July 1913, Rome; ed. Pontifical Gregorian Univ. and Pontifical Acad. of Rome.
Ordained priest 35; Teacher of Classical Languages 36-40; Editor Catholic weekly 36-40; lectured on Pius XII's Vatican diplomacy during World War II; entered Vatican diplomatic service 44; served at the Holy See Secr. of State, Germany and at UN H.Q., New York; rep. of the Vatican to several int. confs.; fmr. Permanent Observer of the Holy See to the UN 64; Dr. h.c. (St. John's Univ., Manhattan Coll.).
Leisure interests: classical music, gardening.
Publs. *The Red Book of the Persecuted Church* 56 (under pseudonym of Alberto Galter), *The Vatican and the War* 60, *Rome Open City* 62, *We Have a Pope* 58, *Il Palazzo è di Vetro* 71; articles in *America, Catholic Encyclopaedia, L'Osservatore Romano*.
323 East 47th Street, New York, N.Y. 10017, U.S.A.
Telephone: 212-752-1763.

Girard de Charbonnières, Guy de, L. en D.; French diplomatist; b. 7 Jan. 1907; m. Countess Marianne de Rumerskirch 1948; one s. one d.; ed. Lycée Janson de Sailly, Ecole des Sciences politiques.
Attaché French Embassy, Brussels 30; Third Sec. London 33, Second Sec. 38, First Sec. 41; joined Gen.

.e Gaulle's Comité National 43, Second Counsellor
.3, Dir. du Cabinet, Commissariat, later Ministry of
Foreign Affairs 43; First Counsellor 44; Minister to
Copenhagen 45, Amb. 47-51, to Argentina 51-55, to
Greece 57-64, to Switzerland 64-65; Diplomatic Coun-
ellor to the French Govt. 66-72; retd. 73; Commdr.
Légion d'Honneur; Grand Cross Order of Dannebrog
Denmark), etc.
55 Avenue Foch, Paris 16e, France.
Telephone· Passy 66-04.

Giraudet, Pierre; French civil engineer and airline
executive; b. 5 Dec. 1919, Koléa, Algeria; s. of Pierre
Giraudet and Irma Basset-Villéon; m. Mireille Bou-
gourd 1947; one s. two d.; ed. Collège Notre Dame
l'Afrique, Lycée Bugeaud, Science Faculty, Algiers.
Head of Hydraulic Eng. Services, Moyen Cheliff,
Algeria 46-53; Head of Technical Service, Algerian
Dept. of Hydraulic Eng. 54-56; Head of Algiers Port
Devt. 56-60; Dir. of Works, Independent Port of Le
Havre 61-67; Dir. of Investments, Paris Airport 67-71,
Deputy Gen. Man. 71; Gen. Man. Régie Autonome des
Transports Parisiens 72; Chair. Air France Nov. 75-;
Chevalier, Légion d'Honneur, Officier, Ordre Nat. du
Mérite.
Leisure interest: yachting.
1 square Max Hymens, 75015 Paris; Home: 78 avenue
de Suffren, 75015 Paris, France.

Giri, Dr. Tulsi; Nepalese politician; b. Sept. 1926.
Deputy Minister of Foreign Affairs 59; Minister of
Village Development 60; Minister without Portfolio 60;
Minister of Foreign Affairs, the Interior, Public Works
and Communications 61; Vice-Chair. Council of Minis-
ters and Minister of Palace Affairs 62; Chair. Council of
Ministers and Minister of Foreign Affairs 62-65; mem.
Royal Advisory Cttee. 69-74; Adviser to the King 74-;
Prime Minister Dec. 75-.
Jawakpurdham, District Dhanuka, Nepal.

Giri, Varahagiri Venkata; Indian barrister-at-law and
diplomatist; b. 10 Aug. 1894, Berhampur; m. Saraswathi
Bai 1917; four s. seven d.; ed. Kallikote Coll., Berham-
pur and Nat. Univ. of Ireland.
Trade Union leader for many years; fmr. Gen. Sec. and
Pres. All-India Railwaymen's Fed.; twice Pres. All-
India Trade Union Congress; Indian workers' del. to
Int. Labour Conference Geneva 26; workers' rep. Second
Round Table Conf., London 31; mem. Central Legisla-
tive Assembly for several years; Minister of Labour,
Industries, Commerce and Co-operation, Madras 37-39;
Minister in Madras Govt. again 46-47; High Commr. for
India in Ceylon 47-51; Minister of Labour, Govt. of
India 54 (resigned Sept. 54); Gov. Uttar Pradesh 57-60,
Kerala 60-65, Mysore 65-67; Vice-Pres. of India 67-69,
Acting Pres. May-Aug. 69, Pres. 69-74; Pres. Indian
Conf. of Social Works 58-60; Hon. D.Litt. (Banaras
Hindu, Lucknow and Andhra Univs.), Hon. LL.D.
(Agra, Moscow, Sofia and Bratislava Univs.).
Publs. *Industrial Relations, Labour Problems in Indian
Industry, Jobs for Our Millions.*
No. 1 Third Block, Jayanagar, Bangalore 11, India.

Giroud, Françoise; French journalist and politician;
b. 21 Sept. 1916; ed. Lycée Molière, Coll. de Groslay.
Editor *Elle* 45-52, *L'Express* 53, mem. Gov. Bd. 71-74;
Minister for Women's Affairs July 74-; Vice-Pres. Parti
Radical 75-; Médaille de la Résistance.
Publs. *Le Tout Paris* 52, *Nouveaux Portraits* 53, *La
Nouvelle Vague: portrait de la jeunesse* 58, *Si je Mens* 72,
Une Poignée d'Eau 73; films: *Antoine et Antoinette* 47,
La Belle que voilà 50, *l'Amour, Madame* 51, *Julietta* 53.
Secrétariat d'Etat auprès du Premier Ministre, 72 rue
de Varenne, 75007 Paris, France.

Giscard d'Estaing, Edmond, L. ès L., D. en D.; French
financier; b. 29 March 1894, Clermont-Ferrand; s. of
Valéry Giscard d'Estaing and Louise Monteil-Ansaldi;

m. May Bardoux 1923; two s. (q.v. Valéry Giscard
d'Estaing), three d.; ed. Univs. de Clermont-Ferrand
and Paris.
Served French Army 14-19; Inspector of Finances 19-
30; numerous financial missions abroad; Dir. of Finances
to French High Commissariat Rhineland 21-26; Hon.
Pres. Société Financière pour la France et les Pays
d'Outre-Mer; Hon. Pres. Société du Tunnel du Mont-
Blanc; Dir. Air France, Bergougnan, Crédit Foncier
Immobilier, Kléber-Colombes; Hon. Pres. Secours
Catholique; mem. Institut de France (Acad. des Sciences
Morales et Politiques); Grand Officier de la Légion
d'Honneur; Chevalier de l'Ordre de Malte; Commdr.
de l'Ordre de Saint Grégoire le Grand; Commdr. de la
Couronne de Belgique; Commdr. Grosses Verdienst-
kreuz (Austria); Commdr. Order of Dannebrog,
Commdr. Order of Merit (Fed. Germany), Commdr.
Order of Merit (Italy); Officier de Saint-Maurice et
Saint-Lazare (Italy), Croix de Guerre (14-18), Grand
Officer Order of Isabel la Católica.
Publs. *Misère et Splendeur des Finances Allemandes* 24,
Capitalisme 30, *La Maladie du Monde* 33, *Le Chemin
de la Pauvreté* 47, *La France et l'Unification Economique
de l'Europe* 53, *Réfractions* 57, *Les Finances: Terre
inconnue* 59, *Le Cahier beige* 73.
Home: 101 avenue Henri Martin, Paris 16e; and
Château de Varvasse, Chanonat (Puy de Dôme); Office:
23 rue de l'Amiral d'Estaing, Paris 16e, France.
Telephone: 553-62-90 (Office); 870-69-53 (Home).

Giscard d'Estaing, François, L. en DR.; French civil
servant; b. 17 Sept. 1926; ed. Ecole Nat. d'Administration, Inst. d'Etudes Politiques.
Deputy Inspector of Finance 52, Inspector 54; Tech-
nical Adviser to Minister of Agriculture 55-56, 58-59, to
Sec. of State for the Budget 56-57; Head of Cen. Admin.
Ministry of Agriculture 57; Dir. Banque Cen. des Etats
d'Afrique Equatoriale et du Cameroun 59-68; Dir.
Banque française du commerce extérieur 70-, Dir.-Gen.
74-; Mayor of Saint-Amant-Tallende 65-71; Croix de
Guerre; Chevalier de la Légion d'Honneur.
Leisure interest: big-game hunting.
6 rue Adolphe Yvon, 75116 Paris, France.
Telephone: 504-8268.

Giscard d'Estaing, Valéry, K.C.B.; French civil servant
and politician; b. 2 Feb. 1926, Koblenz, Germany; s. of
Edmond Giscard d'Estaing (q.v.) and May Bardoux;
m. Anne-Aymone de Brantes 1952; two s. two d.; ed.
Ecole Polytechnique, Ecole Nat. d'Administration.
Official, Inspection des Finances 52, Inspecteur 54;
Deputy Dir. du Cabinet of Prés. du Conseil June-Dec.
54; Deputy for Puy de Dôme 56-58, re-elected for
Clermont 58, for Puy de Dôme 62, 67; Sec. of State for
Finance 59, Minister for Finance and Econ. Affairs
62-66, 69-74; Pres. Comm. des Finances, de l'Economie
général et du plan 67-68, 73-74; Pres. of France May
74-; Founder-Pres. Fed. Nat. des Républicains Indé-
pendants 65; Del. to UN Gen. Assembly 56, 57, 58;
Chair. OECD Ministerial Council 60; Croix de Guerre;
Chevalier de l'Ordre de Malte; Grand Croix Isabel la
Católica, etc.
Leisure interests: shooting, skiing.
Palais de l'Elysée, 55 et 57 rue du Faubourg-Saint-
Honoré, 75008 Paris; Varvasse, Chanonat (Puy de
Dôme), France.

Gish, Lillian Diana; American actress; b. 14 Oct. 1896,
Ohio.
Began acting at the age of five, in the theatre, and has
appeared in many plays and films; Lecture tours of
Europe and America 69, 70, 71.
Leisure interests: travel, reading.
Plays include *Camille, Dear Octopus, Hamlet* (when she
played Ophelia), *Crime and Punishment, Life with
Father, The Curious Savage, The Trip to Bountiful, The
Chalk Garden, The Family Reunion, All the Way*

Home, A Passage To India, Too True to be Good, Romeo and Juliet (nurse) 65, *Anya* (musical) 65, *I Never Sang for My Father* 68, *Uncle Vanya*, N.Y. 73, *A Musical Jubilee* (musical comedy) 75; films include *Birth of a Nation, Hearts of the World, True Heart Susie, Orphans of the Storm, The Scarlet Letter, Annie Laurie, The Swan, Duel in the Sun, The Night of the Hunter, The Cobweb, The Unforgiven,* Walt Disney's *Follow Me Boys* 66, *Warning Shot* 66, *The Comedians* 67, *Arsenic and Old Lace* (television) 69.
Publs. *Lillian Gish: an Autobiography* 68, *The Movies, Mr. Griffith and Me* 69, *Dorothy and Lillian Gish* 73.
430 East 57th Street, New York, N.Y. 10022, U.S.A.

Gislason, Gylfi Th., DR. RER. POL.; Icelandic economist and politician; b. 17 Feb. 1917, Reykjavík; s. of Thorsteinn Gislason and Thórunn Pálsdóttir; m. Gudrún Vilmundardóttir 1939; three s.; ed. Reykjavík Coll., Univs. of Frankfurt am Main and Vienna.
Lecturer of Econs., Univ. of Iceland 41-46, Prof. 46-56; mem. of Parl. 46-; Minister of Educ. and Industries 56-58, of Educ. and Commerce 58-71, Prof. of Econs. 72-; mem. Central Cttee. Social-Democratic Party 42-, Sec. 46-65, Vice-Chair. 65-68, Chair. 68-74; Chair. Social-Democratic Parl. Group 74-; Pres. of Parl. 74; Gov. for Iceland, Int. Monetary Fund 56-65; Gov. for Iceland Int. Bank for Reconstruction and Devt. 65-71; mem. Board of Govs. Iceland Bank of Devt. 53-66, Devt. Fund of Iceland 66-71, Nat. Theatre 54-; Chair. State Research Council 65-71; mem. Icelandic Science Soc.; Dr. Oecon. h.c.
Leisure interest: music.
Publs. *General Business Theory* 41, *Bookkeeping* 42, *Finance of Private Business Enterprises* 45, *Management of Industrial Enterprises* 53, *Accountancy* 55, *The Marshall Plan* 48, *Socialism* 49, *Capitalism, Socialism and the Co-operative Movement* 50, *The Foreign Policy of Iceland* 53, *The Problem of Being an Icelander* 73, *Enterprise and Society* 74, *Fishery Economics* 75, *Essays on Business Administration* 75.
Office: Althing Building, Reykjavík; Home: Aragata 11, Reykjavík, Iceland.
Telephone: 11560 (Office); 15804 (Home).

Gislason, Vilhjalmur, M.A.; Icelandic educationist and writer; b. 16 Sept. 1897, Reykjavík; s. of Thorsteinn Gislason and Thórunn Pálsdóttir; m. Inga Arnadottir 1927; one s. two d.; ed. Reykjavík Univ.
Former Dir.-Gen. State Broadcasting Corpn.; Chair. Nat. Theatre, etc.
Publs. *Islensk endurreisn* 23, *Islensk Thjothfraethi* 24, *Eggert Olafsson* 26, *Snorri Sturluson og godafraedin* 42, *Jon Sigurdsson i raedu og riti* 44, *Sjómannasaga* 45, *Eirikur a Brunum* 46, *Bessastadir* 47, *Reyjavik fyrrum og nú* 48, *Reyjavik i myndum* 48, *Brautryojendur* 50, *Allingisrimur* 51, *Mannfundir* 54, *Gamlar myndir* 55, *Islenzk verziun* 55, *Tbúinadarbálkur* 68, *Blöd og Bladamenn 1773-1943* 72; translated Victor Hugo, Dostoievsky and others into Icelandic.
Starhagi 2, Reykjavík, Iceland.

Giulini, Carlo Maria; Italian conductor; b. 9 May 1914; ed. Accademia S. Cecilia, Rome.
Debut as conductor, Rome 44; fmr. Dir., Italian Radio Orchestra; Principal Conductor, La Scala, Milan 53-55; Conductor, Philharmonia Orchestra, London (renamed New Philharmonia Orchestra); Edinburgh Festival 65; Principal Conductor Vienna Symphony Orchestra.
Via Jacopo da Ponte 49, Rome, Italy.

Giuranna, Bruno; Italian viola player; b. 6 April 1933, Milan; ed. Coll. S. Giuseppe and Conservatorio di Musica Santa Cecilia, Rome, and Conservatorio di Musica S. Pietro a Maiella, Naples.
Founder mem. I Musici 51-61; Prof. Conservatorio G. Verdi, Milan 61-65, Conservatorio S. Cecilia, Rome 65-; Prof. Acad. Chigiana 66-; Prof. Nordwest-

deutsche Musikakademie, Detmold, Germany 69 mem. Int. Music Competition jury, Munich 61-62, 6 69, Geneva 68, Budapest 75; soloist at concerts i festivals including Edinburgh Festival, Hollan Festival and with orchestras including Berlin Philha monic Orchestra, Amsterdam Concertgebouw Orchestr and Teatro alla Scala, Milan; Academician of Sant Cecilia 74.
Via Misurina 71, 00135 Rome, Italy.
Telephone: 325575.

Gjaerevoll, Dr. Olav; Norwegian politician an scientist; b. 24 Sept. 1916, Tynset; s. of Gunnar an Kristine Gjaerevoll; m. Astri Skaar 1944; one s. one d. ed. Uppsala Univ. and in U.S.A. and Canada.
Teacher; Curator, Royal Scientific Soc. Museum 47 joined staff, Teachers Training Coll., Trondheim 47 Prof. of Botany Univ. of Trondheim 58-; Minister o Social Affairs 63-65; Rep. to Storting 65-69; Ministe of Prices and Wages March 71-72; Minister of th Environment 72; mem. Trondheim Town Counci 52, Deputy Chair. 55-58, Chair. 58-63; Chair. Trond heim United Labour Party 49-51; mem. State Natur Conservation Council 58-, Chair. 60-; mem. Roya Scientific Soc. 51-, Acad. of Sciences 58-.
Leisure interests: mountain walking and skiing.
Valentinlystvn 9, Trondheim, Norway.

Gjerde, Bjartmar; Norwegian politician; b. 6 Nov 1931, Sande, Sunnemøre.
Journalist *Sunnmøre Arbeideravis* 48-53; Editor *Frit Slag* 53-58; Chair. Labour League of Youth 58-61; mem State Youth Council; Sec. Labour Parl. Group 61-62 Chief. Sec. Workers' Educ. League 62-71; mem Council on Broadcasting 63-, UNESCO Comm. 64-66 Norwegian Cultural Council 65-, Council on Adul Educ. 66-71; Minister of Church and Educ. 71-72, 73-76 for Industries Jan. 76-; mem. Labour Party Nat. Exec 73-.
Ministry of Industries, Oslo, Norway.

Gladstone, Sir (Erskine) William, Bt., M.A.; Britisl scout and former schoolmaster; b. 29 Oct. 1925, Eton s. of Charles A. and Isla M. (née Crum) Gladstone; m Rosamund A. Hambro 1962; two s. one d.; ed. Etor and Christ Church, Oxford.
Royal Navy 43-46; Asst. Master, Shrewsbury Schoo 49-50, Eton Coll. 51-61; Headmaster, Lancing Coll 61-69; Deputy Lieut. of Flintshire 69, Clwyd 74; Chie Scout, U.K. and Overseas branches 72-.
Leisure interests: reading history, gardening, shooting Hawarden Castle, Deeside, Clwyd, CH5 3PB; Fasque Laurencekirk, Kincardineshire; The Scout Association 25 Queensgate, London, SW7 5JS, England.
Telephone: Hawarden 532210; Fettercairn 341 01-584-6896 (Scout Association).

Gladwyn, 1st Baron (cr. 60), of Bramfield; **Hubert Miles Gladwyn Jebb,** G.C.M.G., G.C.V.O., C.B.; Britisl diplomatist; b. 25 April 1900; s. of Sydney and Rose (née Chichester) Jebb; m. Cynthia Noble 1929; one s two d.; ed. Eton and Magdalen Coll., Oxford.
Entered Diplomatic Service 24; served in Teheran and Rome; Private Sec. to Parl. Under-Sec. of State 29-31; Private Sec. to Permanent Under-Sec. of State 37-40; appointed to Ministry of Economic Warfare 40; Acting Counsellor in Foreign Office 41; Head Reconstruction Dept., Foreign Office 42-45; Counsellor 43 appointed Exec. Sec. of Preparatory Comm. of U.N. Aug. 45; Acting Sec.-Gen. of U.N. Feb. 46; Asst. Under-Sec. of State in Foreign Office, May 46-49; Deputy Under-Sec. of State 49-50; U.K. Rep. on Permanent Comm. of Treaty of Brussels, April 48; Permanent Rep. of U.K. to U.N. 50-54; Ambassador to France 54-60; Deputy Leader Liberal Party, House of Lords; mem. European Parl.; Pres. Campaign for a European Political Community; Vice-Chair. European

Iovt. U.K.; Ex-Pres. Atlantic Treaty Asscn.; Hon.
'res. Atlantic Inst.; Grand Croix de la Légion d'Hon-
eur 57; Hon. D.C.L. (Univs. of Syracuse 51, Oxford 54,
Essex 74); Liberal.
Publs. *The European Idea* 66, *Halfway-Way to 1984* 67,
De Gaulle's Europe, or Why the General Says No 69,
Europe After De Gaulle 70, *The Memoirs of Lord
Gladwyn* 72.
2 Whitehall Court, London, S.W.1; Bramfield Hall,
Halesworth, Suffolk, England.
Telephone: 01-930-3160 (Office).

Glasbergen, Willem; Netherlands prehistorian; b.
24 July 1923, Noordwyk; s. of Abraham Glasbergen
and Hendrika B. Anker; m. Ernestine Duyvis 1952;
two s. five d.; ed. State Univ. of Groningen.
Assistant, Inst. for Biological Archaeology, State Univ.
of Groningen 43-47, Conservator 50-60; Asst., State
Service for Archaeological Investigations in the Nether-
lands 47-49; Curator Archaeological Dept., Groningen
Museum of Antiquities 55-56; Curator Archaeological
Dept., Provinciaal Museum van Drenthe, Asscn. 55-56;
Extra. Prof. Univ. of Amsterdam and Dir. Inst. of
Pre- and Protohistory 56-60, Ordinarius 60-; mem.
Royal Netherlands Acad. of Sciences and Letters 59.
Leisure interest: gardening.
Publs. *Barrow Excavations in the Eight Beatitudes* 54, *De
Voorgeschiedenis der Lage Landen* 59.
Instituut voor Prae- en Protohistorie, Herengracht
256/IV, Amsterdam-C; Home: Dr. Abraham Kuyper-
laan 25, Amersfoort, Netherlands.
Telephone: 020-246671 (Office); 03490-16179 (Home).

Glaser, Donald Arthur, B.S., PH.D.; American physi-
cist; b. 21 Sept. 1926, Cleveland, Ohio; s. of William
Joseph and Lena Glaser; m. Ruth Louise Thompson
1960 (divorced 1969); one s. one d.; ed. Case Inst. of
Technology, Calif. Inst. of Technology.
University of Michigan 49-59; Univ. of California 59-;
Henry Russell Award 55, Charles Vernon Boys Prize
(The Physical Soc.) 58, Nobel Prize 60; Nat. Science
Foundation Fellow 61; Guggenheim Fellow 61-62; Bio-
physicist, Univ. of Calif., Berkeley 62-64; Prof. of
Physics and Molecular Biology, Univ. of Calif. 64-;
mem. Nat. Acad. of Sciences; Hon. Sc.D.; several
awards.
Leisure interests: skiing, sailing, skin diving, music.
Publs. *Some Effects of Ionizing Radiation on the Forma-
tion of Bubbles in Liquids* 52, *A Possible Bubble
Chamber for the Study of Ionizing Events* 53, *Bubble
Chamber Tracks of Penetrating Cosmic-Ray Particles* 53,
Progress Report on the Development of Bubble Chambers
55, *Strange Particle Production by Fast Pions in Propane
Bubble Chamber* 57, *Weak Interactions: Other Modes,
Experimental Results* 58, *The Bubble Chamber* 58,
*Development of Bubble Chamber and Some Recent
Bubble Chamber Results in Elementary Particle Physics*
58, *Decays of Strange Particles* 59, *Computer identification of bacteria by colony morphology* 72, *Effect of nali-
dixic acid on DNA replication by toluene-treated E. coli*
73, *The isolation and partial characterization of mutants
of E. coli and cold-sensitive synthesis of DNA* 74, *Rates
of chain elongation of ribosomal RNA molecules in E. coli*
74, *Chromosomal sites of DNA-membrane attachment in
E. coli* 74, *Effect of growth conditions in DNA-membrane
attachment in E. coli* 75, *Characteristics of cold-sensitive
mutants of E. coli K12 defective in Deoxyribonucleic acid
replication* 75; many papers written jointly with other
physicists.
229 Molecular Biology-Virus Laboratory, University of
California, Berkeley, Calif. 94720, U.S.A.

Glass, David Victor, PH.D., F.B.A., F.R.S.; British
professor of sociology; b. 2 Jan. 1911, London; s. of
Philip and Dinah Glass; m. Ruth Durant 1942; one s.
one d.; ed. Raine's Foundation School, and London
School of Econs.

Research Sec., Population Investigation Cttee. 36;
Reader in Demography, London School of Econs. 46,
Prof. of Sociology 49-; Chair. Population Investigation
Cttee.; Hon. Pres. Int. Union for Scientific Study of
Population; mem. Int. Statistical Inst.; Foreign Assoc.
mem. U.S. Nat. Acad. of Sciences 73; Hon. Foreign
mem. American Acad. of Arts and Sciences; Hon. D.Sc.
(Univs. of Mich, Edinburgh), Hon. D.Sc.Econ. (Queen's,
Belfast).
Publs. *The Town in a Changing World* 35, *The Struggle
for Population* 36, *European Population Movements and
Policies* 40, *Introduction to Malthus* (editor) 53, *Social
Mobility in Britain* 54, *The Trend and Pattern of
Fertility in Britain* (with E. Grebenik) 54, *Society:
Approaches & Problems for Study* (co-editor) 62,
Population in History (co-editor) 65, *Population and
Social Change* (co-editor) 72, *Numbering the People* 73,
The Population Controversy (editor) 73, *The Develop-
ment of Population Statistics* (editor) 73.
10 Palace Gardens Terrace, London, W.8, England.
Telephone: 01-229-1556.

Glass, H(iram) Bentley, M.A., PH.D.; American pro-
fessor of biology; b. 17 Jan. 1906, Laichowfu, Shantung,
China; s. of Wiley B. and Eunice (Taylor) Glass; m.
Suzanne G. Smith 1934; two c.; ed. Baylor Univ. and
Univ. of Texas.
Teacher, Timpson High School, Timpson, Tex. 26-28,
Stephens Coll., Columbia, Mo. 34-38, Goucher Coll.,
Baltimore, Md.; Assoc. Prof. of Biology, Johns Hopkins
Univ. 47-52, Prof. 52-65; Acad. Vice-Pres. (65-71) and
Distinguished Prof. of Biology, State Univ. of New
York at Stony Brook 65-; Asst. Editor *Quarterly Review
of Biology* 45-48, Assoc. Editor 49-57, Editor 58-; mem.
Advisory Cttee. on Biology and Medicines, Atomic
Energy Comm. 56-63, Chair. 62-63; mem. Nat. Acad.
of Sciences Cttee. on Genetic Effects of Atomic Radia-
tion 55-64; mem. Continuing Cttee. Pugwash-COSWA
Confs. 58-64; Chair. Biological Sciences Curriculum
Study 59-65, Board Chair. Cold Spring Harbor Labora-
tory 67-73; Lecturer at numerous orgs.; Pres. Fund for
Overseas Research and Educ. 66-, American Asscn. for
Advancement of Science 69, Nat. Asscn. Biology
Teachers 71, American Asscn. of Univ. Profs. 58-60,
American Soc. of Naturalists 65, American Inst. of
Biological Sciences 54-56, American Soc. of Human
Genetics 67, Phi Beta Kappa 67-70; Vice-Pres. Genetic
Soc. of America 60; Chair. Section of Zoology and
Anatomy, Nat. Acad. of Sciences 64-67, Class II (Bio-
logical Sciences) 68-71; mem. Nat. Acad. of Sciences,
American Acad. of Arts and Sciences, American
Philosophical Soc.; Foreign mem. Czechoslovak Acad.
of Sciences; numerous hon. degrees.
Leisure interests: music, philately (China).
Publs. *Genes and the Man* 43, *Science and Liberal
Education* 60, *Science and Ethical Values* 65, *Genetic
Continuity: A Laboratory Block* 65, *Genetic Continuity:
A Laboratory Block, Teacher's Supplement* 65, *The
Timely and the Timeless* 70; Editor of numerous
symposia and surveys, and collaborator on other books;
numerous articles.
State University of New York at Stony Brook, Stony
Brook, N.Y. 11790, U.S.A.
Telephone: 516-246-5027.

Glasser, Georges Charles; French industrialist; b.
24 Aug. 1907, Paris; m. Huguette Farjon 1934; three d.
President and Man. Dir. Soc. Alsthom 59-; Hon. Pres.
Soc. Nat. Sud-Aviation, Union Syndicale des Industries
Aéronautiques; Commdr. Légion d'Honneur, Chevalier
du Mérite Agricole, Grand Officer, Order of Orange-
Nassau, Médaille de l'Aéronautique, Commdr. Order
of the Lion (Finland).
Leisure interests: tennis, golf.
130 avenue Victor Hugo, Paris 16e, France.
Telephone: 727-51-39.

Glasspole, Florizel; Jamaican politician; b. 25 Sept. 1909; ed. Ruskin Coll., Oxford.
General Sec., Jamaica United Clerks Asscn. 37-38, Jamaica Trades Union Congress 38-52; Pres. Jamaica Printers and Allied Workers Union 42-48; Gen. Sec. Water Comm. and Manual Workers Asscn. 41-48; Pres. Machado Employees Union 52-55; mem. House of Reps. 44-; Minister of Labour 55-57, of Education 57-62, 72-73; Leader House of Reps. 55-62, 72-73; mem. House of Reps. Cttee. examining Jamaica's independence constitution; mem. Del. agreeing Constitution with British Govt. 62; Gov.-Gen. of Jamaica 73-.
Governor-General's House, Kingston, Jamaica.

Glazer, Nathan, PH.D.; American educationist; b. 25 Feb. 1923, New York City; s. of Louis and Tillie (Zacharevich) Glazer; m. 1st Ruth Slotkin 1943 (divorced 1958), 2nd Sulochana Raghavan 1962; three d.; ed. City Coll. of New York, Univ. of Pennsylvania and Columbia Univ.
Member of staff, *Commentary Magazine* 44-53; Editor and Editorial Adviser, Doubleday Anchor Books 54-57; Visiting Lecturer, Univ. of Calif., Berkeley 57-58; Instructor, Bennington Coll., Vermont 58-59; Visiting Lecturer, Smith Coll. 59-60; Prof. of Sociology, Univ. of Calif., Berkeley 63-69; Prof. of Educ. and Social Structure, Harvard Univ. 69-; Fellow, Center for Advanced Study in the Behavioural Sciences, Stanford, Calif. 71-72; mem. American Acad. of Arts and Sciences, American Sociological Asscn.; Guggenheim Fellow 54, 66; Hon. LL.D. (Franklin and Marshall Coll.) 71, LL.D. (Colby Coll.) 72.
Publs. *American Judaism* 57, 72, *The Social Basis of American Communism* 61, *Remembering the Answers* 70, *Affirmative Discrimination* 76; Co-author: *The Lonely Crowd* 50, *Faces in the Crowd* 52, *Studies in Housing and Minority Groups* 60, *Beyond the Melting Pot* 63 (2nd edn. 70); Co-editor: *The Public Interest* 73-.
Graduate School of Education, Harvard University, Gutman Library, 6 Appian Way, Cambridge, Mass. 02138, U.S.A.
Telephone: 617-495-4671.

Glazur, Adam, M.SC.; Polish engineer and politician; b. 1933, Kołaczyce near Jasło; ed. Electrical Faculty, Mining Acad., Cracow.
Chief Power Eng., later Chief Eng., then Dir., Glass Works at Krosno 54-64; Head of Dept. in Ministry of Construction and Construction Materials Industry 64-69, Under-Sec. of State 69-74, First Deputy Minister 74-75, Minister of Construction and Construction Materials Industry May 75-; Knight's Cross, Order of Polonia Restituta.
Ministerstwo Budownictwa i Przemysłu Materiałów Budowlanych, ul. Wspólna 2, 00-505 Warsaw, Poland.

Gleason, Andrew Mattei, B.S.; American mathematician; b. 4 Nov. 1921, Fresno, Calif.; s. of Henry Allan Gleason and Eleanor Theodalinda Mattei; m. Jean Berko 1959; three d.; ed. Yale Univ.
United States Navy 42-46, 50-52; Junior Fellow of Soc. of Fellows, Harvard Univ. 46-50, Asst. Prof. of Mathematics 50-53, Assoc. Prof. 53-57, Prof. of Mathematics 57-69, Hollis Prof. of Mathematicks and Natural Philosophy 69-; mem. Nat. Acad. of Sciences; Hon. M.A.; Newcomb-Cleveland Prize of A.A.A.S. 52.
Publ. *Fundamentals of Abstract Analysis* 66.
Department of Mathematics, Harvard University, Cambridge, Mass. 02138; Home: 110 Larchwood Drive, Cambridge, Mass. 02138, U.S.A.
Telephone: 495-4316 (Office); 864-5095 (Home).

Glemser, Oskar Max, DR.-ING., German chemist; b. 12 Nov. 1911, Stuttgart; s. of Karl Glemser and Amalie Gogel; m. Ida-Maria Greiner 1938; one s. one d.; ed. Gymnasium Bad-Canstatt and Technische Hochschule, Stuttgart.

Senior Engineer, Inst. for Inorganic Chemistry and Electro Chemistry, Technische Hochschule, Aachen 39-41, Dozent 41-48, Extra-Mural Prof. 48-52; Prof and Dir. of the Inst. of Inorganic Chemistry, Univ. o: Göttingen 52-; Pres. of Acad. of Sciences, Göttingen 62-70; mem. Bureau IUPAC; mem. Leopoldina German Acad. for Scientific Research, Halle, Austrian Acad. o: Sciences, Centro Superiore di Logica e Scienze Comparate, Bologna; Pres. German Chemical Soc.; Liebig Medal of German Chemical Soc. 70; Silver Medal o: Univ. of Helsinki 72.
Leisure interests: archaeology, literature, skiing, swimming.
Office: Anorganisch-Chemisches Institut der Universität Göttingen, Tammannstrasse 4, 34 Göttingen; Home: Richard-Zsigmondy Weg 10, 34 Göttingen, Federal Republic of Germany.
Telephone: 0551-393002 (Office); 0551-57814 (Home).

Glen, Sir Alexander Richard, K.B.E., D.S.C.; British business executive; b. 18 April 1912; ed. Fettes Coll., and Balliol Coll., Oxford.
Organizer and Leader, Oxford Univ. Arctic Expedition 33, 35-36; Banking, New York and London 36-39; R.N.V.R. 39-59; Pres. H. Clarkson & Co. Ltd.; Deputy Chair. Export Council for Europe 60-64, Chair. 64-66; mem. Council Royal Geographical Soc. 45-47, 54-57, 61-62; mem. Council, Mount Everest Foundation 55-57; Chair. British Tourist Authority 69-; numerous medals and decorations.
Publs. *Young Men in the Arctic* 35, *Under the Pole Star* 37, *Footholds Against a Whirlwind* 75.
46 Wilton Crescent, London, S.W.1, England.

Glen, Robert, O.C., B.SC., M.SC., PH.D., F.R.S.C.; Canadian entomologist and research administrator; b. 20 June 1905, Paisley, Scotland; s. of James Allison Glen and Jeannie Blackwood Barr; m. Margaret Helen Cameron 1931; two s.; ed. Univs. of Saskatchewan and Minnesota.
Junior and Asst. Entomologist, Dominion Entomological Laboratory, Saskatoon, Saskatchewan 28-35, in charge wireworm investigations, Dominion Entomological Laboratory 35-45; Research Co-ordinator, Entomology Div., Canada Dept. of Agriculture, Ottawa 45-50, Chief, Entomology Div. 50-57; Assoc. Dir. Science Service, Canada Dept. of Agriculture 57-59; Dir.-Gen. Research Branch, Canada Dept. of Agriculture 59-62, Asst. Deputy Minister (Research) 62-68; Sec. Commonwealth Scientific Cttee. 68-72; Fellow, Agricultural Inst. of Canada, Royal Soc. of Canada; Pres. E. Ontario Branch, Agricultural Inst. of Canada 50-51, Entomological Soc. of Canada 57, Entomological Soc. of America 62; Caleb Dorr Fellowship, Univ. of Minnesota 31-32; Shevlin Fellowship, Univ. of Minnesota 32-33; mem. Science Council of Canada 66; Foreign Assoc. Nat. Acad. of Sciences (U.S.A.) 67; Outstanding Achievement Award, Univ. of Minnesota 60; Entomological Soc. of Canada 64, Medal of Service Order of Canada 67, etc.; Hon. LL.D. (Univ. of Saskatchewan) 59, Hon. D.Sc. (Univ. of Ottawa) 60; Hon. mem. Canadian Seed Growers Asscn. 68 (for life), Entomological Soc. of America 72, of Canada 75.
Leisure interests: sports, gardening.
Publs. include: *Elaterid larvae of the tribe Lepturoidini* 50, and reports on Canadian entomology 54-56.
4523 Juniper Place, Victoria, B.C., V8N 3KI, Canada.
Telephone: 477-5924.

Glenkinglas, Baron (Life Peer) cr. 74, of Cairndow; **Michael Antony Cristobal Noble,** P.C.; British politician; b. 19 March 1913; s. of Sir John Noble, Bt.; m. Anne Pearson 1940; four d.; ed. Eton Coll. and Magdalen Coll., Oxford.
Served with R.A.F.V.R. 41-45; M.P. 58-74; Scottish Whip 60-62; Sec. of State for Scotland 62-64; Chair. Associated Fisheries Ltd. 66-70; Chair. Glendevon

Farms (Winchburgh) 69-; Minister for Trade June 70-Oct. 72; Chair. British Agricultural Export Council 73-; Dir. John Brown Engineering 73, D.A. Monteith Holdings Ltd. 74; Conservative.
Strone, Cairndow, Argyll, Scotland.

Glenn, Frank, M.D., F.A.C.S.; American surgeon; b. 7 Aug. 1901, Marissa, Ill.; s. of Charles Glenn and Minnie McMurdo Glenn; m. Esther Child 1938; two s. one d.; ed. Washington Univ.
Intern in Medicine, Strong Memorial Hosp. 27-28; First Asst. Resident Surgeon, New York Hosp. 32-33, Surgeon-in-Chief 47-67, Consultant in Surgery 67-; Asst. in Surgery, Cornell Univ. Medical Coll. 32-33, Assoc. Prof. 41-47, Prof. of Surgery 47-67, Emer. 67-; Consultant in Gen. Surgery to Veterans' Admin. 46-; Advisory Consultant to New York Branch 46-50; Consultant in Surgery, Memorial Hosp., New York 68-; Editorial Consultant to Medical Dept. of Macmillan Co., New York; served with Medical Corps, U.S. Army (Lieut.-Col., Bronze Star) as Surgical Consultant to 6th Army and to 6th Service Command 42-46; mem. American Medical Assen., American Surgical Assen., Editorial Board *Annals of Surgery*, many medical socs. in U.S.A.; Consultant Editor, *Surgery, Gynaecology and Obstetrics*.
The New York Hospital, 525 East 68th Street, New York, N.Y. 10021; Home: 200 East 66th Street, New York, N.Y. 10021, U.S.A.

Glenn, Lt.-Col. John Herschel, Jr., D.F.C. (8 times) and Air Medal with 18 clusters; American politician, aviator and astronaut; b. 18 July 1921; ed. Muskingum Coll., Univ. of Maryland.
Naval aviation cadet 42; commissioned Marine Corps 43; Marine Fighter Squadron 155 in Marshall Islands 44 (59 combat missions); mem. Fighter Sq. 218 North China Patrol; Instructor Corpus Christi, Texas 48-50; Marine Fighter Sq. Korea (63 missions); Fighter Design Branch, Navy Bureau of Aeronautics, Washington 56; speed record Los Angeles–New York (3 hr. 23 min.) 57; training for space flight 60-61, completed 3 orbits of the earth in Spaceship *Friendship VII*, 20th February 62; resigned from U.S. Marine Corps 65; Dir. Royal Crown Cola Co. 65-; Consultant to NASA; U.S. Senator from Ohio Jan. 75-; NASA Distinguished Service Medal 62; U.S. Nat. Space Hall of Fame Award 69.
Publ. (co-author) *We Seven* 62.
U.S. Senate, Washington, D.C. 20510; and 203 Sleepy Hollow Court, Timbercove, Seabrook, Texas, U.S.A.

Glenn, Sir (Joseph Robert) Archibald, Kt., O.B.E., B.C.E., F.I.E. (AUST.), M.I.CHEM.E.; Australian chemicals executive and engineer; b. 24 May 1911, Sale, Victoria; s. of Joseph Robert Glenn; m. Elizabeth M. M. Balderstone 1939; one s. three d.; ed. Scotch Coll., Melbourne, Melbourne and Harvard Univs.
Chief Engineer I.C.I. Australia Ltd. 47-49, Gen. Man. 49-53, Man. Dir. 53-73, Chair. 63-73; Dir. Imperial Chem. Industries Ltd. 70-75; Chair. Fibremakers Ltd. 63-73; Dir. Bank of New South Wales 67-; Chair. IMI Australia Ltd. 70-, Collin Wales Pty. Ltd. 73-; Dir. Alcoa Australia Ltd. 73-, Hill Samuel Australia Ltd. 73-, Tioxide Australia Ltd. 73-; Chair. IC Insurance Australia Ltd. 74-; Gov. Atlantic Inst. of Int. Affairs; Chair. Council, Scotch Coll.; Chancellor, La Trobe Univ., Melbourne 66-72.
Leisure interests: tennis, golf, farming.
Home: 3 Heyington Place, Toorak 3142, Victoria, Australia.
Telephone: 6620201 (Office); 204453 (Home).

Glennan, T. Keith, B.S.; American engineer and administrator; b. 8 Sept. 1905, Enderlin, N.D.; s. of late Richard Henry Glennan and Margaret Laing Pauline; m. Ruth Haslup Adams 1931; one s. three d.; ed. Eau Claire (Wis.) High School, Eau Claire State

Teachers' Coll., and Yale Univ. Sheffield Scientific School.
Western Electric Co. Ltd. 28-30; Electrical Research Products Co. 30-35; Paramount Pictures Inc. 35-41; Studio Man. Samuel Goldwyn Studios 41-42; Admin., later Dir. U.S. Navy Underwater Sound Laboratories (Columbia Univ. Div. of War Research), New London, Conn. 42-45; exec. with Ansco, Binghamton (New York) 45-47; Pres. Case Inst. of Technology, Cleveland 47-66; mem. Atomic Energy Comm. 50-52; First Admin. Nat. Aeronautics and Space Admin. (N.A.S.A.) 58-61; Pres. Associated Universities Inc. 65-68; Dir. Republic Steel Corpn., and other companies; U.S. Rep. (rank of Amb.) to IAEA 70-73; Consultant, U.S. Dept. of State 73-; Trustee Rand Corpn. 63-73, Aerospace Corpn. 69-70, 74-; Case Western Reserve Univ. 71-; Fellow, American Acad. of Arts and Sciences, Nat. Acad. of Eng.; Medal for Merit; Hon. LL.D. (Tulane Univ., Miami Univ., Western Reserve Univ., Columbia Univ.); Hon. D.Sc. (Oberlin Coll., Clarkson Coll. of Technology, John Carroll Univ., Akron Univ., Univ. of Toledo, Muhlenberg Coll., Cleveland State Univ.); Hon. D.Eng. (Stevens Inst. of Technology, Case Institute of Technology, Fenn Coll.); Hon. M.A. (Yale Univ.); Univ. Medal of Honor (Rice Univ.), N.A.S.A. Distinguished Service Medal 66, U.S. State Dept. Distinguished Honor Award 73; Benjamin Franklin Fellow (Royal Soc. of Arts, London).
Leisure interests: woodworking, public service, new towns.
11483 Waterview Cluster, Reston, Va. 22090, U.S.A.
Telephone: 703-471-4210.

Gleske, Leonhard, DR.RER.POL.; German banker; b. 18 Sept. 1921.
President, Landeszentralbank in Bremen; mem. Central Bank Council, Deutsche Bundesbank; Dir. Bank for Int. Settlements.
28 Bremen, Am Wall 122, Federal Republic of Germany.

Gligorov, Kiro; Yugoslav politician; b. 3 May 1917, Štip; s. of Blagoje and Katarina Gligorov; m. Nada Gligorov; one s. two d.; ed. Faculty of Law, Univ. of Belgrade.
Member, Presidium of Antifascist Assembly of People's Liberation of Macedonia during Second World War; Deputy Sec.-Gen. to Govt. of Yugoslavia 46-47; Deputy Dir. Exec. Council for Gen. Econ. Affairs 55-62; Fed. Sec. for Finance 62-67; Vice-Pres. Fed. Exec. Council 67-69; mem. Exec. Bureau of Presidency of League of Communists of Yugoslavia 69-74; mem. Presidency of Socialist Fed. Repub. of Yugolsavia 71-72; Pres. Parl. 74-; holder of many Yugoslav and foreign honours.
Leisure interests: tennis, hunting.
Publs. many articles and studies in finance and economics.
Bulevar Oktobarske revolucije 14, Belgrade, Yugoslavia.
Telephone: 640-687; 339-396 (Office).

Glistrup, Mogens; Danish lawyer; b. 28 May 1926, Rønne; s. of Lektor Lars Glistrup; m. Lene Borup Svendsen 1950; one s. three d.; ed. Rønne, Copenhagen Univ.
Training in American law Univ. of Berkeley Calif. 51-52; teacher in income tax law Univ. of Copenhagen 56-63; law practice 50-, own firm 56-; founded Progress Party 72; mem. Parl. 73-; on trial for alleged tax evasion and fraud 74.
Leisure interests: chess, bicycling, bridge, football.
Publ. *Skatteret* 57.
100 Skovbrynet, DK2800 Kongers Lyngby, Denmark.
Telephone: 01-878545.

Glob, Peter Vilhelm, DR.PHIL.; Danish archaeologist and museum director; b. 20 Feb. 1911, Kalundborg; ed. Univ. of Copenhagen.

Archaeological expedition, Greenland 32-33, 53; Chief of Danish Archaeological Expeditions, Bahrein 53-65, Qatar 57-64, Kuwait 58-62; Prof. of Archaeology and Prehistory of Europe, Aarhus Univ. 49-60; Danish Rigsantikvar (Dir.-Gen. of Central Office and of Museum of National Antiquities in Denmark) 60-.
Publs. *Eskimo Settlements in Kempe Fjord and King Oscar Fjord* 35, *Études sur la civilisation des sépultures individuelles de Jutland* 45, *Eskimo Settlements in North East Greenland* 46, *Ard and Plough* 51, *Danish Antiquities II* 52, *Grauballemanden* 59, *Hommes des tourbières* 65, *Vorzeitdenkmäler Dänemarks* 68, *Al-Bahrain* 68, *Rock Carvings in Denmark* 69, *The Mound People* 74.
National Museum, Frederiksholms Kanal 12, 1220 Copenhagen K, Denmark.
Telephone: 01-134411.

Glock, Sir William Frederick, Kt., C.B.E.; British musician; b. 3 May 1908, London; *s.* of William G. Glock and Gertrude Maltby; *m.* Anne Balfour (née Geoffroy-Dechaume) 1952; ed. Christ's Hospital, West Horsham, Gonville and Caius Coll., Cambridge and under Artur Schnabel, Berlin.
Music Critic, *Daily Telegraph* 34, *The Observer* 34-45, *New Statesman* 58-59; served with Royal Air Force 41-46; Dir. Summer School of Music, Bryanston 48-52, Dartington Hall, Devon 53-; Founder and Editor *The Score* 49-61; Chair. British Section, Int. Soc. of Contemporary Music 54-58; Controller of Music, BBC 59-72; mem. Board of Dirs. Royal Opera House, Covent Garden 68-73; Dir. Bath Festival 75-; Chair. London Orchestral Concert Board 75-; Hon. mem. Royal Philharmonic Soc.; Gold Medal of R.S.A.; mem. Arts Council of G.B. 72-75; Hon. D.Univ. (York); Hon. D.Mus. (Nottingham Univ.).
Sudbury House, Faringdon, Oxon., England.
Telephone: 036-72-0381.

Glocker, Richard, PH.D.; German physicist; b. 21 Sept. 1890; ed. Munich Univ.
Lecturer, Stuttgart Technical Univ. 19, and Extra. Prof. 23; Prof. for Röntgen-Technique 25; Head of X-Ray Laboratory and mem. Council of Max Planck Inst. for Metal Research (retd. 61); Hon. mem. Deutsche Röntgen-Gesellschaft, Deutsche Gesellschaft für Metallkunde, Gesellschaft für Biophysik, Deutsche Gesellschaft für Medizinische Physik; Co-Editor *Fortschritte auf dem Gebiet der Röntgenstrahlen und der Nuklearmedizin*; Dr. Med. h.c.
Publs. *Materialprüfung mit Röntgenstrahlen* 27 (5th edn. 70 with Macherauch), *Röntgen- und Kernphysik für Mediziner und Biophysiker* 65.
Robert Boschstrasse 10, Stuttgart-N., Federal Republic of Germany.

Glossbrenner, Alfred S.; American businessman; b. 6 June 1901, Indianapolis, Ind.; *s.* of Alfred M. Glossbrenner and Minnie M. Stroup; *m.* 1923; two *s.*; ed. Univ. of Wisconsin.
With tin plate plant, American Sheet and Tin Plate Co. 30-31; Foreman, South Chicago plant, Ill. Steel 32-35; Asst. Supt. Campbell hot strip mill, Youngstown Sheet and Tube Co. 35-36, Supt. 36-42, Supt. Brier Hill Works 42-43, Gen. Supt. Youngstown Dist. 43-47, Asst. Vice-Pres. 47-50, Vice-Pres. (Operations) 50-56, Pres. 56-65, Dir 53-, Chief Exec. Officer 60-66, Chair. Exec. Cttee. 63-, Chair. of Board 65-; Dir. Youngstown Steel Door Co., Dollar Savings and Trust Co., Nat. City Bank of Cleveland, Ohio Bell Telephone Co., Lykes Youngstown Corpn.; mem. Board Y.M.C.A., Youngstown Community Chest; official of other business and educational orgs.
Leisure interest: golf.
Office: Box 900, Youngstown, Ohio 44501; Home: 2782 Logan Road, Youngstown, Ohio, U.S.A.

Glossop, Peter; British opera singer (baritone); b. 6 July 1928, Sheffield; *s.* of Cyril Glossop and Violet

Elizabeth Wright; *m.* Joyce Blackham 1955; ed. High Storrs Grammar School, Sheffield.
Joined Sadler's Wells Opera 52; with Covent Garden Opera Co. 62-66; freelance singer 66-; First Prize Bulgarian First Competition for Young Opera Singers 61; debut at La Scala, Milan as Rigoletto 65; Hon. D.Mus. (Univ. of Sheffield) 70.
Leisure interests: antiquities and squash racquets.
Kenlade, 11 The Bishops Avenue, London, N.2, England.

Glubb, Lieut.-Gen. Sir John Bagot, K.C.B., C.M.G., D.S.O., O.B.E., M.C.; British officer; b. 16 April 1897, Preston, Lancs.; *s.* of Maj.-Gen. Sir Frederic Manley Glubb and Frances Letitia (née Bagot); *m.* Muriel Forbes 1938; two *s.* two *d.*; ed. Cheltenham and Royal Military Acad., Woolwich.
2nd Lieut. Royal Engineers 15, served France; served Iraq 20; Admin. Insp. Iraq Govt. 26; Officer Commdg. Desert Area, Transjordan 30; Officer Commdg. Arab Legion, Transjordan (now Jordan) 38-56.
Leisure interests: religion, motoring, reading, travel.
Publs. *Story of the Arab Legion* 48, *A Soldier with the Arabs* 57, *Britain and the Arabs* 59, *War in the Desert* 60, *The Great Arab Conquests* 63, *The Empire of the Arabs* 63, *The Course of Empire* 65, *The Lost Centuries* 67, *Syria, Lebanon and Jordan* 67, *A Short History of the Arab Peoples* 68, *The Life and Times of Muhammad* 70, *Peace in the Holy Land* 71, *Soldiers of Fortune, the Story of the Mamelukes* 73, *The Way of Love* 74, *Haroon Al Rasheed and the Great Abbasids* 76.
West Wood St. Dunstan, Mayfield, Sussex, England.
Telephone: 04-355-3136.

Glueck, Sheldon, LL.M., PH.D.; American criminologist; b. 15 Aug. 1896, Warsaw, Poland; *s.* of Charles and Anna (Steinhardt) Glueck; *m.* Eleanor Touroff 1922 (deceased 1972); one *d.* (deceased); ed. George Washington Univ., Nat. Univ. Law School and Harvard Univ.
Instructor, Dept. of Social Ethics, Harvard Univ. 25-29; Asst. Prof. of Criminology, Harvard Univ. Law School 29-31, Prof. 31-50, Roscoe Pound Prof. of Law 50-63, Emer. 63-; Dir. Basic Researches into Causes, Management and Prevention of Juvenile Delinquency, Harvard Law School 25-; fmr. mem. U.S. Supreme Court Advisory Cttee. on Revision of Rules of Criminal Procedure; fmr. mem. American Law Inst., Cttee. on Youth Correction Authority and Model Penal Code; mem. American Bar Asscn. Cttee. on Juvenile Delinquency, Nat. Council on Crime and Delinquency, Int. Acad. of Law and Sciences, Int. Soc. of Criminology, American Soc. of Criminology, German Soc. of Criminology; Fellow American Acad. of Arts and Sciences, American Psychiatric Asscn., American Asscn. for Advancement of Science (fmr. Joint Vice-Pres.); Hon. LL.D. (Univ. of Salonika) 48, Hon. S.D. (Harvard Univ.) 58, Hon. S.S.D. (George Washington Univ.) 68; numerous awards including Isaac Ray Award (American Psychiatric Asscn.) 61.
Leisure interests: travel, theatre (as playwright, director and actor).
Publs. *Mental Disorder and the Criminal Law* 25, *War Criminals: their Prosecution and Punishment* 44, *The Nuremberg Trial and Aggressive War* 46, *The Problem of Delinquency* (Editor) 59, *Law and Psychiatry: Cold War or Entente Cordiale?* 62, *Roscoe Pound and Criminal Justice* (Editor) 65, *Continental Police Practices* 74; and books on delinquency and crime with Eleanor T. Glueck.
Harvard Law School, Cambridge, Mass. 02138, U.S.A.

Glushko, Valentin Petrovich; Soviet rocket scientist and designer; b. 2 Sept. 1908, Odessa; *m.* Magda Emsin 1947; two *s.* two *d.*; ed. Leningrad Univ.
Founder and Chief designer, Gas Dynamics Laboratory-Experimental Design Bureau (GDL-OKB), working on devt. of liquid-propellant, electrical rockets and rocket engines 29-; designed world's first electrothermal jet

engine 29-33, first Soviet liquid-propellant rocket engines 30-31; Corresp. mem. U.S.S.R. Acad. of Sciences 53-58, mem. 58-; Bureau mem. Dept. of Physical-Technical Problems in Energetics, U.S.S.R. Acad. of Sciences 60-; mem. C.P.S.U. 56-; Deputy to U.S.S.R. Supreme Soviet 66-; Hero of Socialist Labour (twice); Lenin Prize 57; State Prize 67; Order of Lenin (three times); Hammer and Sickle Gold Medal (twice); Order of October Revolution; Red Banner of Labour; Tsiolkovsky Gold Medal, etc.

Publs. *Pioneers of Rocketry* (Selected Works 1929-45) 72, *Development of Rocketry and Space Technology in the U.S.S.R.* 73, *GDL-OKB Rocket Engines* 75.

U.S.S.R. Academy of Sciences, 14 Leninsky Prospekt, Moscow, U.S.S.R.

Glushkov, Viktor Mikhaylovich; Soviet mathematician; b. 24 Aug. 1923, Rostov on Don; *m.* Valentina Mikhaylovna Glushkova; two *d.*; ed. Rostov on Don Univ.

Ural Timber Inst. 48-55; Head, Computer and Mathematics Laboratory, Kiev Inst. of Mathematics 56; Dir. Computer Centre, Ukrainian Acad. of Sciences 57-62; Dir. Inst. of Cybernetics, Ukrainian Acad. of Sciences 62; Corresp. mem. Ukrainian Acad. of Sciences 58-60, mem. 61, Vice-Pres. 62-; mem. U.S.S.R. Acad. of Sciences 64-; State Cttee. for Science and Technology, Moscow Mathematical Soc.; mem. C.P.S.U., Cen. Cttee. C.P. of Ukraine; Deputy U.S.S.R. Supreme Soviet; Hero of Socialist Labour; Lenin Prize 64; State Prize 68; Order of Lenin (three times); Hammer and Sickle Gold Medal, etc.

Leisure interests: poetry, classical music, angling.

Publs. over 300 scientific papers and books, incl. *Introduction to Cybernetics, Synthesis of Digital Automata, Introduction to AMS.*

Institute of Cybernetics, Ukrainian Academy of Sciences, 252207 Kiev 207, U.S.S.R.

Telephone: 662-008 (Office).

Gnägi, Rudolf; Swiss lawyer and politician; b. 3 Aug. 1917, Schwadernau; ed. Progymnasium and Gymnasium, Bienne, and Universität Bern.

Lawyer 43-46; Sec. Farmers', Tradesmen' and Burghers' Party of Berne 46, also Peasants' Fed. of Berne 46; Sec. of Farmers', Tradesmen' and Burghers' Party of Switzerland 47; Govt. Councillor for Canton of Berne 52; Nat. Councillor 53; mem. Fed. Council 66-; Head of Communications and Power Dept. 66-68; Head of Fed. Military Dept. July 68-; Vice-Pres. of Fed. Council 70, Pres. (Head of State) Jan.-Dec. 71, Jan. 76-.

Spiegel-Berne, Steingrubenweg 8, Switzerland.

Gnatt, Poul Rudolph; New Zealand (b. Danish) dancer, choreographer and producer; b. 24 March 1923, Vienna, Austria; *s.* of late Kai Gnatt and Kaja (née Olsen); *m.* Rigmor Strøyberg 1951; four *s.*; ed. Royal Danish Ballet School.

Joined Royal Danish Ballet School 29, Principal Dancer 49; Principal Dancer, Ballettes des Champs Elysées 46-47, Metropolitan Ballet 47-49 Ballet Russe 50-51, Borovansky Ballet 51-53; Founder and Artistic Dir. New Zealand Ballet 53-63; guest performances and short return to Royal Danish Ballet 63-64; Resident Teacher, Australian Ballet School and Producer/Ballet-master, The Australian Ballet 64; Founder of Dance Theatre, Philippines, Manila 68; Guest Producer, New Zealand Ballet Co. 15 year birthday season.

Leisure interests: tennis, handicraft, opera.

Choreography: *Satan's Wedding* 55, *Sonata* (Beethoven) 55, *Valse Triste* 55, *Peer Gynt* 56, *Prismatic Variations* (with Russell Kerr) 58, *The Miraculous Mandarin, Peter and the Wolf* 68.

Niles Julesgate 40, Oslo 2, Norway.

Telephone: 44-67-10.

Goad, Sir Edward Colin Viner, K.C.M.G.; British int. civil servant; b. 21 Dec. 1914, Cirencester, Glos.; *s.* of the late Maurice G. V. and Caroline (née Masters) Goad; *m.* Joan O. Bradley 1939; one *s.*; ed. Cirencester Grammar School and Cambridge Univ.

Ministry of Transport 37-63, Asst. Sec. 48, Under-Sec. 63; Deputy Sec.-Gen. (and Sec. Maritime Safety Cttee.) UN Inter-Governmental Maritime Consultative Organization 63-67, Sec.-Gen. 68-73, retd. 73; mem. Advisory Board, Int. Bank, Washington D.C.

Leisure interests: gardening, 18th-century English furniture.

The Paddock, Ampney Crucis, Cirencester, Glos., England.

Telephone: Poulton 353.

Goba, Maj. Louis Sylvain; Congolese army officer and politician; ed. Versailles and Saint-Cyr.

Assistant Dir. of Mil. Engineers until 68; Chief of Staff of Congolese People's Nat. Army 68-, promoted Capt. 68; mem. Parti Congolais du Travail (PCT) 69-, Cen. Cttee. 70-, Special Gen. Staff of Revolution 74-, Political Bureau; Sec. of State for Defence 69-70; Minister of Public Works and Transport 70-74; promoted Maj. 73; Chief of Gen. Staff of Armed Forces 74-; Prime Minister, responsible for Plan Dec. 75-; mem. Council of State 75-.

Office of the Prime Minister, Brazzaville, Congo People's Republic.

Gobbi, Tito; Italian baritone opera singer; b. 24 Oct. 1915, Bassano del Grappa, Vicenza; *s.* of Giovanni Gobbi and Enrica Weiss; *m.* Matilde de Rensis 1937; one *d.*; ed. Padua Univ.

Opera début in *La Traviata*, Rome 38; has sung in numerous operas in major theatres throughout the world; also in a number of films; also produces operas, incl. *Simon Boccanegra*, Covent Garden 65; master classes, lectures in England, U.S.A., Italy, Portugal.

Leisure interests: reading, painting, driving, boating.

Via Valle della Moletta 47, 00 123 La Storta, Rome, Italy.

Telephone: 6990996.

Gočár, Jiři; Czechoslovak architect; b. 12 June 1913, Prague; ed. Faculty of Civil and Structural Engineering, Czech Technical Univ.

Own practice until 48; *Stavoprojekt*, Prague 49-54; Union of Architects affil. to Union of Czechoslovak Artists 54-56; Union of Architects of Czechoslovakia 56-59, Chair. 59-69; Head of Architects' *Atelier* 65; mem. Council for Reconstruction of Prague Castle 59-68; Deputy Chair. Fed. Cttee. for Technical Devt. and Investment 69-70; architect with Investis 70-; Chair. Union of Czech Architects 69-70; mem. Exec. Cttee. Union Int. des Architectes, Chair. Czechoslovak Section 67; Chair. Co-ordination Cttee., Federal Ministry for Technical Devt. and Investment, for Housing Environment 72; work on housing, public and industrial buildings; mem. Cen. Cttee. C.P. of Czechoslovakia 66-70; Order of Labour 63.

Investis, Prague 1, Břehová 1, Czechoslovakia.

Godard, Jean-Luc; French film director; b. 3 Dec. 1930; ed. Lycée Buffon.

Journalist and film critic; film director 58-; Prix Jean Vigo for *A Bout de Souffle* 60, Jury's Special Prize and Prix Pasinetti, Venice Festival 62, Diploma of Merit, Edinburgh Film Festival 68 for *Weekend*.

Films: *Opération Béton* 54, *Une Femme Coquette* 55, *Tous les garçons s'appellent Patrick* 57, *Charlotte et son Jules* 58, *Une Histoire d'eau* 58, *A bout de souffle* 59, *Le Petit Soldat* 60, *Une Femme est une Femme* 61, *Les Sept Péchés capitaux* (episode) 61, *Vivre sa vie* 62, *RoGoPaG* (episode) 62, *Les Carabiniers* 63, *Le Mépris* 63, *Les Plus Belles Escroqueries du monde* (episode) 63, *Paris vu par* . . . (episode) 63, *Bande à part* 64, *Une Femme mariée* 64, *Alphaville* 65, *Pierrot le fou* 65, *Masculin-féminin* 66, *Made in U.S.A.* 66, *Deux ou trois choses que*

je sais d'elle 67, *La Chinoise* 67, *Loin du Vietnam* (episode) 67, *Weekend* 67, *Le Plus Vieux Métier du monde* (episode) 67, *Vangelo '70* (episode) 67, *Le Gai Savoir* 68, *Un Film comme les autres* 68, *One Plus One* 68, *One American Movie-1 a.m.* 69, *British Sounds* 69, *Le Vent d'Est* 69, *Lotte in Italia* 70, *Vladimir et Rosa* 71, *Tout va bien* 72, *Numéro Deux* 75.
80 rue des Archives, 75003 Paris, France.

Godber, 1st Baron, cr. 56, of Mayfield in the County of Sussex; **Frederick Godber,** Kt.; British director of oil companies; b. 6 Nov. 1888, London; s. of Edward and Marion Louise Godber; m. Violet E. B. Lovesy 1914; two d.
In U.S.A. 19-29; Dir. Shell Union 22, Chair. 37-46; Chair. Shell Transport and Trading Co. Ltd. 46-61; **fmr.** Chair. Anglo-Saxon Petroleum Co. Ltd., **Shell Petroleum Co. Ltd.** and of associated companies; Chair. Commonwealth Devt. Finance Co. Ltd. 53-68, Retail Consortium Mar. 76-; Trustee, Churchill Coll. Trust Fund, Cambridge 58-.
Leisure interests: gardening and farming.
50 Kingston House, Princes Gate, London, S.W.7; and Ganesden, Mayfield, Sussex, England.
[*Died* 10 *April* 1976].

Godber, Rt. Hon. Joseph Bradshaw, P.C., M.P.; British politician; b. 17 March 1914, Bedfordshire; s. of Isaac and Bessie Godber; m. Miriam Sanders 1936; two s.; ed. Bedford School.
Family Business 32; Beds. County Councillor 46-52; M.P. 51-; Parl. Private Sec. to Parl. Sec. to Ministry of Labour 52-55; Asst. Govt. Whip 55-57; Joint Parl. Sec., **Ministry of Agriculture, Fisheries and Food** 57-60; Joint Parl. Under-Sec. of State, Foreign Office 60-61; Minister of War 63; Minister of Labour 63-64; Minister of State, Foreign and Commonwealth Office 70-72, of Agriculture, Fisheries and Food 72-74; Chair. Sidney C. Banks 74-; Dir. Booker McConnell 74-, Tricentrol Ltd. 75-; Consultant, Beecham (Food & Drink) Ltd. 74-; Conservative.
Leisure interest: gardening.
House of Commons, London, S.W.1; and Willington Manor, nr. Bedford, England.
Telephone: 02-303-284.

Goddard, David R., M.A., PH.D.; American professor of biology; b. 3 Jan. 1908, Carmel, Calif.; s. of Pliny Earle Goddard and Alice Rockwell Goddard; m. 1st Doris Martin 1933 (deceased), 2nd Katharine Evans 1952; one s. one d.; ed. Univ. of Calif. at Berkeley.
Instructor to Prof., Univ. of Rochester 35-46; Chair. Dept. of Botany 38-46; Prof. of Botany, Univ. of Pennsylvania 46-58; Chair. Dept. of Botany 52-57; Dir. Div. of Biology 57-61; Gustave C. Kuemmerle Prof. of Botany 58-64, Provost, Univ. of Pennsylvania 61-71, Prof. of Biology 64-71; Univ. Prof. of Science and Public Policy 71-72; Univ. Prof. of Biology 72-75; Nat. Research Council Fellow, Rockefeller Univ. 33-35; Guggenheim Fellow, Univ. of Chicago 42-43, Cambridge Univ. 50; mem. Nat. Acad. of Sciences (Home Sec. 75-), American Acad. of Arts and Sciences, American Philosophical Soc.; Pres. American Soc. of Plant Physiologists 58, Soc. of Gen. Physiologists 48; official numerous other socs.; Stephen Hales Award, American Soc. of Plant Physiologists 48, Certificate of Merit, Botanical Soc. of America 62.
Leisure interest: gardening.
Publs. *Physical Chemistry of Cells and Tissues* (with Hober and others) 45; articles on enzymes, cellular respiration, cellular growth and physiology of infection.
National Academy of Sciences, 2101 Constitution Avenue, Washington, D.C. 20418; Home: 490 East Abington, Philadelphia, Pa. 19118, U.S.A.
Telephone: (202) 389-6209 (Office); (215) 247-6681 (Home).

Goddard, Samuel Pearson, A.B., LL.B.; American lawyer and politician; b. 8 Aug. 1919, Clayton, Missouri; s. of Samuel Pearson Goddard Sr. and Florence Goddard; m. Julia Hatch Goddard 1944; three s.; ed. Harvard Coll., and Univ. of Arizona Law School.
U.S. Army Air Corps 41-46; law firm Terry and Wright 46; former senior partner, law firm, Goddard and Ahearn, later partner; Chair. Tucson United Community Campaign 59, Pres. 60-62; Pres. Western Conf. of Community Chests, United Funds and Councils 61-63; mem. Nat. Board Dirs. United Community Funds and Councils of America 63-69, Exec. Cttee. 66-69, Vice-Pres. 68-69; Chair. Democratic Party of Arizona 60-62, Democratic Nominee for Governor 62, 68, Gov. of Arizona 65-67; Democratic Nat. Ctteeman. 72-75; mem. White House Conference Cttee., Children and Youth 59, Phoenix Symphony Board 68-76, Board of Governors, United Way of America 72-; Chair. Task Force, "Making People a Part of the System" 71, UWA Nat. Acad. for Volunteerism 73-75; officer of numerous business, civic and academic organizations; Unitarian.
Suite 410 Arizona Title Building, 111 West Monroe, Phoenix, Arizona 85003, U.S.A.
Telephone: 1-602-258-6629.

Godden, Rumer (Mrs. Margaret Rumer Haynes Dixon); British author; b. 10 Dec. 1907; d. of Arthur L. Godden and Katherine N. Hingley; m. 1st Laurence S. Foster 1949, 2nd James L. Haynes-Dixon; ed. privately.
Leisure interests: family, travel, ballet, pekinese dogs.
Publs. *Chinese Puzzle* 35, *The Lady and the Unicorn* 37, *Black Narcissus* 39, *Breakfast with the Nikolides* 41, *Fugue in Time* 44, *The River* 46, *A Candle for St. Jude* 48, *Kingfishers Catch Fire* 52, *An Episode of Sparrows* 55, *The Greengage Summer* 59, *China Court* 61, *The Battle of the Villa Fiorita* 63, *In This House of Brede* 69; trans. *Prayers from the Ark* 62; *Two Under the Indian Sun* (autobiography) 65, *Swans and Turtles* 68, *The Raphael Bible* 70, *Shiva's Pigeons* (with Jon Godden) 72, *The Peacock Spring* 75; poems, children's books, films.
4 Mermaid Street, Rye, Sussex, England.

Gödel, Kurt, PH.D.; American logician; b. 28 April 1906, Brno, Czechoslovakia; s. of Rudolf and Marianne (Handschuh) Gödel; m. Adele Porkert 1938; ed. Universität Wien.
Dozent, Univ. of Vienna 33-38; mem. Inst. for Advanced Study, Princeton, N.J. 33, 35, 38-53, Prof. 53-; mem. Nat. Acad. of Sciences, American Philosophical Soc., American Acad. of Arts and Sciences; Foreign mem. Royal Soc. (U.K.); Hon. mem. London Mathematical Soc.; Corresp. mem. Acad. des Sciences Morales et Politiques (Paris); Corresp. Fellow British Acad., Einstein Award (co-recipient) 51; Hon. Litt.D. (Yale Univ.), Hon. Sc.D. (Harvard Univ.), Amherst Coll., Rockefeller Univ.); Nat. Medal of Science 74.
Leisure interest: ancient history.
Publs. *Ueber formal unentscheidbare Saetze* 31, *The Consistency of the Continuum Hypothesis* 40, *Rotating Universes in General Relativity Theory* 50.
Institute for Advanced Study, Princeton, N.J., U.S.A.
Telephone: 609-WA4-4400.

Godley, George McMurtrie; American diplomatist; b. 23 Aug. 1917, New York City; s. of Frederick A. and Anne Franchot Godley; m. Elizabeth McCray 1966; two s.; ed. Yale and Chicago Univs.
U.S. Naval Reserve 39-41, U.S. Marine Corps 45-46; Foreign Service Officer 41-, served Marseilles, Berne, Paris, Pnom Penh 41-55; Foreign Affairs Officer, Dept. of State 57-60; Staff Co-ordinator, Dept. of State 60; Counselor, Consul, Léopoldville 61-62; Dir., Office of Central African Affairs, Dept. of State

2-64; Amb. to Repub. of Congo (Kinshasa) 64-66; Career Minister 66; Foreign Service Insp. 67; Deputy Asst. Sec. State for E. Asian and Pacific Affairs 68-69; Amb. to Laos 69-73, to Lebanon 74-.
American Embassy, Avenue de Paris (Corniche), Amm. Ali Reza, Beirut, Lebanon.

Godwin, Sir Harry, Kt., M.A., PH.D., SC.D., F.G.S., R.L.S., F.R.S.; British botanist; b. 9 May 1901, Rother-am, Yorks.; s. of Charles William Thomas Godwin and Mary Jane Grainger; m. Margaret Elizabeth Daniels 1927; one s.; ed. Long Eaton County Secondary School and Clare Coll., Cambridge.
Fellow of Clare Coll., Cambridge 25-; Univ. Demon-trator in Botany 23-, Univ. Lecturer 34-48, Reader 48-60; Head of Univ. Sub-Dept. of Quaternary Re-search 48-66; Prof. of Botany 60-68; Pres. British Ecological Soc. 43; Pres. 10th Int. Botanical Congress, Edin. 64; Pres. Botanical Section, British Asscn. 56; mem. Nature Conservancy 49-54, 65-72; co-Editor *New Phytologist* 31-61; Editor *Journal of Ecology* 58-65; mem. Svenska Växtgeografiska Salskapet 37-; Corresp. mem. Botanical Soc., Gothenburg 53; Hon. Fellow, Royal Irish Acad. 55, Botanical Soc. of Edinburgh 61; Corresp. mem. Botanical Soc. of America 66; Foreign mem. Royal Scientific Soc., Uppsala 61; Foreign mem. German Acad. of Sciences, Leopoldina 62; Foreign mem. Royal Danish Acad. of Science and Letters 62; Prestwich Medal, Geological Soc. of London 51; Croonian Lecturer Royal Soc., London 60; Gold Medal, Linnean Soc., London 66; Medal of Univ. of Helsinki 66; Hon. Sc.D. (Trinity Coll., Dublin) 60, (Univ. of Lancaster) 68, (Univ. Durham) 74.
Leisure interests: the country, gardening, and the visual arts.
Publs. *Plant Biology* 30, *History of the British Flora* 56 (revised edn. 75); also scientific papers on ecology of bogs and fens 29-41; on vegetational history, pollen-analysis, radiocarbon dating in context of Quaternary history 35-; pollen-grain ontogeny 66-.
30 Barton Road, Cambridge, CB3 9LF, England.
Telephone: 50883.

Goebel, Walther F., A.B., A.M., PH.D.; American pro-fessor of biochemistry; b. 24 Dec. 1899, Palo Alto, Calif.; s. of Julius Goebel and Kathryn Vreeland; m. Cornelia Van Rensselear Robb 1930; two d.; ed. Univs. of Ill. and Munich.
Research Asst., Rockefeller Univ. (fmrly. Rockefeller Inst.) 24-27, Research Assoc. 27-34, Assoc. mem. 34-44, mem. 44-57, Prof. of Biochemistry 57-70, Prof. Emeritus 70-; mem. Nat. Acad. of Sciences; Hon. D.Sc. (Middle-bury Coll., Vt.); Avery-Landsteiner Award, Gesellschaft für Immunologie 73.
Leisure interests: music, photography, painting.
Publs. Numerous scientific articles on biochemistry, microbiology and chemical immunology in *Journal of American Chemical Soc.*, of *Experimental Medicine*, of *Biochemistry* and of *General Physiology*; *Annales* of Inst. Pasteur, *Proceedings* of Nat. Acad. of Sciences, etc.
Rockefeller University, New York, N.Y. 10021; Home: Vineyard Lane, Greenwich, Conn. 06830, U.S.A.

Goehr, Alexander; British composer; b. 10 Aug. 1932, Berlin; s. of Walter Goehr; m. 1st Audrey Baker 1954, 2nd Anthea Felicity Staunton 1972; three d.; ed. Berk-hamstead School, Royal Manchester Coll. of Music, Paris Conservatoire (with Oliver Messiaen), and privately with Yvonne Loriod.
Composer, teacher, conductor 56-; held classes at Morley Coll., London; part-time post with B.B.C., being responsible for production of orchestral concerts 60-; works performed in Darmstadt, Prague, Venice, Zagreb, Warsaw, Cologne, Donaueschingen, Lucerne and other cities in Europe and America; Hon. Fellow Royal

Manchester Coll. of Music; awarded Churchill Fellow-ship 68; Composer-in-Residence, New England Con-servatory, Boston, Mass. 68-69; Assoc. Prof. of Music, Yale Univ. 69-70; now Prof. West Riding Chair. of Music at Univ. of Leeds; Hon. D.Mus. Univ. of South-ampton 73.
Works include: *Songs of Babel* 51, *Sonata* 52, *Fantasias* 54, *String Quartet* 56-57, *Cappriccio* 57, *The Deluge* 57-58, *La Belle Dame Sans Merci* 58, *Variations* 59, *Four Songs from the Japanese* 59, *Sutter's Gold* 59-60, *Suite* 61, *Hecuba's Lament* 59-61, *A Little Cantata of Proverbs* 62, *Concerto for Violin and Orchestra* 61-62, *Two Choruses* 62, *Virtutes* 63, *Little Symphony* 63, *Little Music for Strings* 63, *Five Poems and an Epigram of William Blake* 64, *Three Pieces for Piano* 64, *Pastorals* 65, *Piano Trio* 66, *Arden muss sterben* (Arden Must Die—opera) 66, *Quartet* 67, *Romanza* 68, *Naboth's Vineyard* 68, *Symphony in One Movement, Opus 29* 70, *Shadowplay-2* 70, *Sonata about Jerusalem* 70, *Piano Concerto* 72, *Clarinet Monologue* 73, *Metamorphosis Dance* 74.
Department of Music, University of Leeds, 14 Cromer Terrace, Leeds 1; East Lodge, Farnley, Nr. Otley, West Yorkshire, England.
Telephone: Otley 51366 (Home).

Goenka, Ramanath; Indian newspaper director; b. 11 May 1902, Dharbhanga; s. of Basantillal Goenka; m. Moongibai Goenka (died 1966); one s. two d.; ed. Dharbhanga, Bihar.
Started own textile business, Madras 26; mem. Madras Legislative Council 26-30; Sec. Independent Party in Council 27, supported many nationalist causes; mem. Constituent Assembly of India 46-50; Pres. Indian and Eastern Newspaper Soc. (IENS) 51; Man. Dir. *Indian Express* Group of Newspapers; Del. to Empire Press Union Conf. 51; Chair. Press Trust of India 52-53 and 68; Chair. Punjab Nat. Bank Ltd. 62-63.
Hick's Bungalow, Express Estates, Mount Road, Madras 2, India.
Telephone: 83151.

Goes, Albrecht; German writer; b. 22 March 1908; s. of Eberhard Goes and Elisabeth (née Panzerbieter); m. Elisabeth Schneiter 1933; three d.; ed. Tübingen Univ.
Evangelical pastor, Württemberg 30-52; writer 53-; Lessing Prize, Hamburg 53, mem. Berliner Akad. für Künste, Deutsche Akad. für Sprache und Dichtung.
Publs. *Unruhige Nacht, Von Mensch zu Mensch* 49, *Gedichte* 50, *Das Brandopfer* 53, *Freude am Gedicht* 54, *Vertrauen in das Wort* 55, *Ruf und Echo* 56, *Genesis* 57, *Hagar am Brunnen* 58, *Rede auf Goethes Mutter* 58, *Ravenna* 59, *Aber im Winde das Wort* 63, *Das Löffelchen* 65, *Im Weitergehen* 66, *Der Knecht macht keinen Lärm* 68, *Die guten Gefährten* 69, *Kanzelholz* 71.
c/o Akademie der Künste, Hanseatenweg 10, Berlin 21, Federal Republic of Germany.

Goetze, Roger; French business executive; b. 6 Dec. 1912, Paris; ed. Lycée Carnot and Faculté des Lettres et des Sciences de Paris.
Inspector of Finances 37; Dir. Gen. of Finance, Algeria 42-49; Dir. of Budget 49-57; Pres. S.N. Repal 46-66; Dep. Gov. Crédit Foncier de France S.A. 57, Gov. 67-; Grand Officer de la Légion d'Honneur.
Crédit Foncier de France S.A., 19 rue des Capucines, Paris 1er, France.

Goff, Abe McGregor, LL.B.; American lawyer and government official; b. 21 Dec. 1899, Cofax, Wash.; s. of Herbert W. Goff and Mary Dorsey; m. Florence L. Richardson 1927; one s. one d.; ed. Univ. of Idaho.
Army Service, First World War; Law Practice, Idaho 24, Prosecuting Attorney 26-34; State Senator, Idaho 40-41; Pres. Idaho State Bar 40-41; army service, Africa, Europe, Pacific, Japan, Second World War; mem.

U.S. Congress 47-48; Law Practice 48-54; Gen. Counsel, U.S. Post Office Dept. 54-58; U.S. Interstate Commerce Comm. 58-67, Chair. 64-67; Legion of Merit and other awards; Republican.
Leisure interests: books, walking.
503 East C Street, Moscow, Idaho 83843, U.S.A.
Telephone: 208-882-2627.

Gogoleva, Elena Nikolaevna; Soviet actress; b. 7 April 1900; ed. Moscow Philharmonic School of Music and Drama.
Acted at Maly Theatre 18-; People's Artist of the U.S.S.R.; State prizewinner (thrice).
Principal roles: plays by Ostrovsky, Gorky and contemporary playwrights.
Maly Theatre, 1/6 Ploshchad Sverdlova, Moscow, U.S.S.R.

Goguel, Jean, D.SC.; French geologist; b. 2 Jan. 1908, Paris; s. of Dr. Maurice Goguel; m. Micheline Vernes 1931; three s. three d.; ed. Ecole Polytechnique, Ecole des Mines, Paris.
Entered Service de la Carte Géologique 31, Dir. 53-67; Prof. Ecole Nat. Supérieure des Mines 35-, Ecole des Ponts et Chaussées 41-55; Vice-Pres. Bureau des Recherches Géologiques et Géophysiques 67-; Foreign Hon. mem. American Acad. of Arts and Sciences (Boston), Nat. Acad. of Sciences (Washington); Prix James Hall 38, Prix Cuvier 48, Prix Prestwich (Soc. Géologique).
Publs. *Introduction à l'étude mécanique des déformations de l'écorce terrestre* 43, 2nd edn. 49, *L'Homme dans l'univers* 47, *Traité de tectonique* 52, 2nd edn. 65, *Application de la géologie aux travaux de l'ingénieur* 59, 2nd edn. 67, *La Géothermie.*
74 rue de la Fédération, Paris 15e; Home: 100 rue du Bac, Paris 7e, France.
Telephone: SUF 94-00 (Office); LIT 76-13 (Home).

Goh Keng Swee, B.A., B.SC.(ECON.), PH.D.; Singapore politician; b. 6 Oct. 1918, Malacca; ed. Raffles Coll., London Univ.
Vice-Chairman People's Action Party; elected Legislative Assembly from Kreta Ayer Div. and Minister for Finance 59-65; initiated Singapore's industrialization plan, the establishment of Econ. Devt. Board; Minister of Defence 65-67, of Finance 67-70, of Defence Aug. 70-, concurrently Deputy Prime Minister 72-; mem. Governing Council, Asian Inst. for Econ. Devt. and Planning, Bangkok 63-66; Ramon Magsaysay Award for Govt. Service 72.
Publs. *Urban Incomes and Housing; a report on the Social Survey of Singapore, 1953-54* 58, *Economics of Modernization and Other Essays* 72.
Ministry of Defence, Minden Road, Tanglin, Singapore 10.

Goheen, Robert Francis, B.A., M.A., PH.D., LITT.D., LL.D.; American professor and administrator; b. 15 Aug. 1919, Vengurla, India; s. of Robert H. H. and Anne (Ewing) Goheen; m. Margaret M. Skelly 1941; two s. four d.; ed. Lawrenceville School and Princeton Univ.
Instructor, Princeton Univ. 48-50, Asst. Prof. 50-57, Prof. 57-; Senior Fellow in Classics, American Acad. in Rome 52-53; Dir. Nat. Woodrow Wilson Fellowship Programme 53-56; Pres. Princeton Univ. July 57-72; Chair. Council on Foundations, Inc. 72-; mem. Board Carnegie Foundation for Advancement of Teaching, Rockefeller Foundation, American Acad. in Rome; mem. Council on Foreign Relations, American Acad. of Arts and Sciences; Dir. Equitable Life Assurance Soc. of U.S., Dreyfus Third Century Fund; Hon. LL.D., Litt.D., L.C.D., L.H.D., degrees from some 25 univs. and colls. including Harvard, Yale, Madras, North Carolina, Notre Dame.
Leisure interests: golf, tennis, reading.

Publs. *The Imagery of Sophocles' Antigone, The Hum Nature of a University.*
Council on Foundations, Inc., 888 7th Avenue, N York, N.Y. 10019, U.S.A.
Telephone: 212-489-7120.

Gokhale, Hari Ramachandra; Indian politician; 1917; ed. at Baroda and Bombay.
Former political worker and trade unionist; subs quently practised law and was Judge of Bombay Hi Court until 66; mem. Lok Sabha 71-; Minister of La Justice and Company Affairs, Govt. of India March 7 Shastri Bhavan, Dr. Rajendra Prasad Road, New Del 1, India.

Gold, Joseph, LL.M., S.J.D.; British lawyer; b. 12 Ju 1912, London, England; m. Ruth Schechter 1939; one two d.; ed. London and Harvard Univs.
Lecturer in Law, London Univ. 37-39; mem. Briti Govt. Mission to Washington 42-46; with IMF 46-, Ge Counsel, Dir. Legal Dept. 60-.
Publs. *Fund Agreement in the Courts* 62, *The Stand-E Arrangements of the IMF* 70, *Voting and Decisions i the IMF* 72, *Membership and Nonmembership in t IMF* 74, and contributions to professional journa
International Monetary Fund, 700 19th Street, N.W Washington, D.C. 20431, U.S.A.

Gold, Thomas, F.R.S., SC.D.; American (fmrly. Britis astronomer; b. 22 May 1920, Vienna, Austria; s. c Mr. and Mrs. Max Gold; m. 1st Merle Eleanor Tuber 1947, 2nd Carvel Lee Beyer 1972; four d.; ed. Zuo Coll., Switzerland, and Trinity Coll., Cambridge.
Experimental Officer, British Admiralty (radar re search) 43-46; Fellow, Trinity Coll., Cambridge 47 Chief Asst. to Astronomer Royal, Royal Greenwic Observatory 52-56; Prof. of Astronomy, Harvard Univ 57-59; Prof. of Astronomy, Cornell Univ. 59-; Di Cornell Univ. Centre for Radiophysics and Space Re search 59-; Fellow, A.A.A.S., mem. Nat. Acad. o Sciences, American Philosophical Soc.
Leisure interests: skiing, water skiing.
Publs. *The Steady State Theory of the Expandin Universe* 48, *The Alignment of Galactic Dust* 52, *Th Field of a Uniformly Accelerated Charge* 54, *Instabilit of the Earth's Axis of Rotation* 55, *The Lunar Surface* 65 *Cosmic Rays from the Sun* 57, *Plasma and Magneti Fields in the Solar System* 59, *The Origin of Solar Flare* 60, *Rotating Neutron Stars as the Origin of the Pulsatin Radio Source* 68, *Rotating Neutron Stars and the Natur of Pulsars* 69, *Apollo 12 Seismic Signal: Indication of Deep Layer of Powder* 70, etc.
Center for Radiophysics and Space Research, Space Sciences Building, Cornell University, Ithaca, N.Y 14853, U.S.A.
Telephone: 607-256-5284.

Goldberg, Arthur Joseph, B.S. IN L., DR.JUR.; Ameri can lawyer and politician; b. 8 Aug. 1908, Chicago, Ill. s. of Joseph Goldberg and Rebecca Perlstein; m. Dorothy Kurgans 1931; one s. one d.; ed. City Coll. Chicago and Northwestern Univ.
Private Law Practice 29-48; Gen. Counsel, Congress of Industrial Workers 48-55; Gen. Counsel, United Steelworkers 48-61; Special Counsel, American Federa tion of Labor-Congress of Industrial Organisations 55- 61; Gen. Counsel, Industrial Union Dept., A.F.L.- C.I.O. 55-61; Sec. of Labor 61-62; Justice of U.S. Supreme Court 62-65; Perm. Rep. of U.S. to UN 65-68; Prof. of Law and Diplomacy, American Univ., Wash ington 72-73; Charles Evans Hughes Prof., Woodrow Wilson School, Princeton Univ. 68-69; Distinguished Prof. School of Int. Relations, Columbia Univ. 69-70; Visiting Distinguished Prof. Hastings Coll. of the Law, San Francisco 74-; Democrat.

ubls. *Civil Rights in Labor-Management Relations: a labor Viewpoint* 51, *A.F.L.-C.I.O.—Labor United* 56, *nions and the Anti-Trust Laws* 56, *Management's eserved Rights* 56, *Ethical Practices* 58, *A Trade nion Point of View* 59, *Suggestions for a New Labor olicy* 60, *The Role of the Labor Union in an Age of igness* 60, *The Annals of The American Academy of olitical and Social Science* (Vol. 339) 62, *The Defenses Freedom: The Public Papers of Arthur J. Goldberg* 66, *qual Justice: the Warren Era of the Supreme Court* 72. ιoι 17 Street, N. W. Washington, D.C. 20036, .S.A. elephone: 202-293-3900.

Goldberg, Leo, M.A., PH.D.; American astronomer; b. ɓ Jan. 1913, Brooklyn, N.Y.; s. of Harry and Rose Ambush) Goldberg; m. Charlotte B. Wyman 1943; wo s. one d.; ed. Harvard Univ. .esearch Fellow, Harvard Univ. 38-41; Asst. Research ssoc. and Research Physicist, Univ. of Mich. 41-46, Pir. of Observatory and Chair. Dept. of Astronomy 46-60; staff mem. Smithsonian Astrophysical Observaɔry 60-66; Higgins Prof. of Astronomy, Harvard Univ. ɔ-73, Higgins Prof. Emeritus 73-; Chair. Dept. of stronomy 66-71; Dir. Harvard Coll. Observatory 66-ı, Kitt Peak Nat. Observatory 71-; Ed. *Annual Review f Astronomy and Astrophysics* 61-73; mem. Nat. Acad. f Sciences, Soc. Royale des Sciences de Liège, American Philosophical Soc.; Foreign Assoc. Royal Astronomical oc., London; Hon. mem. Royal Astronomical Soc. of .anada; Past Pres. American Astronomical Soc.; fmr. ʿice-Pres. Int. Astronomical Union, Pres. 73-; Hon. .c.D. (Univ. of Mass., Amherst 70, Univ. of Mich. 74); Russell Lecturer Citation, American Astronomical Soc. 3; NASA Distinguished Service Medal 73. Publs. Numerous technical and scientific articles in strophysical journals. Office: Kitt Peak National Observatory, P.O. Box °6732, 950 N. Cherry Avenue, Tucson, Ariz. 85726; Iome: 3425 Via Guadalupe, Tucson, Ariz. 85716, U.S.A. Telephone: 602-327-5511 (Office); 602-881-0677 (Home).

Goldberger, Marvin Leonard, PH.D.; American pro-essor of physics; b. 22 Oct. 1922, Chicago, Ill.; s. of Joseph and Mildred Sedwitz Goldberger; m. Mildred C. Ginsburg 1945; two s.; ed. Carnegie Inst. of Technology and Univ. of Chicago. Research Assoc. Radiation Lab., Univ. of Calif. (Berkeley) 48-49, M.I.T. 49-50; Asst. Prof., Prof., Univ. of Chicago 50-57; Eugene Higgins Prof. of Physics, Princeton Univ. 57-, Chair. Physics Dept. 70-; Chair. Fed. of American Scientists 71-72; mem. Nat. Acad. of Sciences, American Acad. of Arts and Sciences; Dannie Heineman Prize for Mathematical Physics 61. Leisure interests: skin diving, spectator sports. Publ. *Collision Theory* (with K. M. Watson) 64. The Joseph Henry Laboratories, Jadwin Hall, Prince-ton University, Princeton, N.J. 08540, U.S.A.

Goldfinger, Ernő, A.R.A., F.R.I.B.A.; British architect; b. 11 Sept. 1902, Budapest, Hungary; s. of Dr. Oscar Goldfinger and Regine Haiman; m. Ursula Ruth Blackwell 1933; two s. one d.; ed. Ecole Nat. et Supérieur des Beaux Arts, Paris and Inst. d'Urbanisme, Sorbonne, Paris. Member, Congrès Int. de l'Architecture Moderne 28-59; Sec. British Section of Réunion Int. des Architectes 35-45; mem. Foreign Relations Cttee., R.I.B.A. 46; mem. Architectural Registration Council of the U.K. 41-50, Council of Industrial Design 61-65; now working privately; mem. Modern Architectural Research (MARS) group 34-60; mem. Building Requirements sub-cttee. of Scientific Advisory Cttee., Ministry of Works 43-45; mem. Council, Royal Acad. 74; mem. Council, Architectural Asscn. 60-65, 65-68. Leisure interests: architecture, travel.

Publs. articles in *Architectural Review, County of London Plan Explained* 45. 2 Willow Road, London, NW3 1TH.

Goldhaber, Gertrude Scharff, PH.D.; American physi-cist; b. 14 July 1911, Mannheim, Germany; d. of Otto Scharff and Nelly Steinharter; m. Maurice Goldhaber (q.v.) 1939; two s.; ed. Univs. of Freiburg, Zurich, Berlin and Munich. Research Assoc. in Physics, Imperial Coll., London 35-39; Physicist, Univ. of Illinois 39-48; Consultant, Argonne National Laboratory 46-50; Asst. Prof., Univ. of Illinois 48-50; Assoc. Physicist, Brookhaven National Laboratory 50-58, Physicist 58-62, Senior Physicist 62-; Consultant, Los Alamos Scientific Laboratory 53-; mem. Nat. Acad. of Sciences, Board of Trustees, Fermi Nat. Accelerator Laboratory 72-(78), Forum Cttee. of Nat. Acad. of Sciences (NAS) 74-76, Report Review Cttee., NAS 73-; Consultant Arms, Control and Disarmament Agency 74-. Leisure interests: history of science, literature and art, recent results in neuroendocrinology, tennis, swimming, hiking. Publs. author and co-author of many articles on physics subjects. Department of Physics, Brookhaven National Labora-tory, Upton, N.Y. 11973; Home: 91 South Gillette Avenue, Bayport, N.Y. 11705, U.S.A. Telephone: 516-345-3912 (Office); 516-HR2-0651.

Goldhaber, Maurice, PH.D.; American physicist; b. 18 April 1911, Lemberg, Austria; s. of Charles Gold-haber and Ethel Frisch Goldhaber; m. Gertrude Scharff (Goldhaber q.v.) 1939; two s.; ed. Berlin Univ. and Cambridge Univ., U.K Professor of Physics, Univ. of Illinois 38-50; Senior scientist, Brookhaven Nat. Lab. 50-60, Chair. Dept. of Physics 60-61, Dir. 61-73; mem. Nat. Acad. of Sciences, American Philosophical Soc.; Fellow, American Acad. of Arts and Sciences, American Asscn. for the Advance-ment of Science; Tom W. Bonner Prize in Nuclear Physics of American Physical Soc. 71, Associated Univs. Inc. Distinguished Scientist 73; U.S. Atomic Energy Comm. Citation for Meritorius Contributions 73; Hon. Ph.D. (Univ. of Tel-Aviv) 74. Leisure interests: tennis, hiking. Publs. Numerous articles in professional scientific journals on neutron physics, radioactivity, nuclear isomers, nuclear photo-electric effect, nuclear models, fundamental particles. Brookhaven National Laboratory, Upton, N.Y. 11973, U.S.A. Telephone: 516-345-3494.

Goldin, Nikolai Vasilyevich; Soviet engineer and poli-tician; b. 1910; ed. Kharkov Electrical Engineering Inst. Engineer, Head of Design Office, Man. of Trust, Dir. of Board of Assembly of Electrical Equipment, U.S.S.R. Ministry of Construction of Heavy Industry Plants 37-50; Head of reconstruction works on many iron and steel plants devastated in Second World War, par-ticularly Zaporozhstal Iron and Steel Works 43-50; Deputy Minister for Construction of Heavy Industry Plants, then for Construction of Metallurgical and Chemical Industries Plants 50-57; Chief Engineer, Bhilhai Iron and Steel Works, India 58-61; Econ. Counsellor, U.S.S.R. Embassy, Cuba 62-63; Deputy Minister of Assembly and Special Construction Works 63-67; Minister for Construction of Heavy Industry Enterprises 67-; Deputy to U.S.S.R. Supreme Soviet 67-; mem. C.P.S.U. 29-, mem. Cen. Cttee. 71-; Order of Lenin (thrice) and several other decorations. Ministry for Construction of Plants of Heavy Industry, 19/21, 5 Ulitsa Yamskogo Polya, Moscow, U.S.S.R.

Golding, William (Gerald), M.A., C.B.E.; British writer; b. 19 Sept. 1911; ed. Marlborough Grammar School, and Brasenose Coll., Oxford.

F.R.S.L. 55; Hon. Fellow, Brasenose Coll., Oxford 66; Hon. D.Litt. (Sussex Univ.) 70.
Leisure interests: music, sailing, Greek.
Publs. *Lord of the Flies* 54 (film 63), *The Inheritors* 55, *Pincher Martin* 56, *Free Fall* 59, *The Spire* 64, *The Hot Gates* 65, *The Pyramid* 67, *The Scorpion God* 71; play *Brass Butterfly* 58.
Ebble Thatch, Bowerchalke, Wiltshire, England.

Goldman, Eric F., M.A., PH.D., D.C.L., LITT.D., LL.D., L.H.D.; American historian and writer; b. 17 June 1915, Washington, D.C.; s. of Harry E. Goldman and Bessie Chapman; m. Joanna R. Jackson 1952; ed. Baltimore City Coll., and Johns Hopkins Univ.
Professor, Princeton Univ. 40-, Rollins Prof. of History 62-; Special Consultant to Pres. Johnson 63-66; Moderator NBC TV Discussion Panel 59-67; Guest essayist CBS Morning News 75-; Bancroft Prize 52, Emmy Award 62, 66, Library of Congress Fellow 47, Guggenheim Fellow 56, McCosh Fellow 62; Pres. Soc. of American Historians 62-69.
Leisure interests: fishing, gardening.
Publs. incl. *Charles J. Bonaparte, John Bach McMaster, Rendezvous with Destiny: A History of Modern American Reform, The Crucial Decade, America 1945-55, The Crucial Decade—and After, America 1945-60, The Tragedy of Lyndon Johnson* 69.
213 Palmer Hall, Princeton University, Princeton, N.J., U.S.A.
Telephone: 609-924-6444.

Goldman, Sir Samuel, K.C.B.; British banker and fmr. civil servant; b. 10 March 1912, London; s. of late Philip and Sarah Goldman; m. Patricia Rosemary Hodges 1943; one s.; ed. Raines Foundation School, Davenant Foundation School and London School of Economics.
Moody's Economist Services 34-38; Sebag and Co. 38-39; Bank of England 40-47; joined Civil Service as statistician, Central Statistical Office Jan. 47, transferred to Treasury 47, Chief Statistician 48, Asst. Sec. 52, Under-Sec. 60, Third Sec. 62; Second Perm. Sec., Treasury 68-72; Man. Dir. Orion Bank Ltd.; Chair. Covent Garden Market Authority.
Leisure interests: gardening, music.
The Old Orchard, Danes Hill, Oxshott, Surrey, England.
Telephone: Oxshott 2052.

Goldmann, Nahum; Israeli (fmrly. American) Zionist leader; b. 10 July 1895, Wisznewo, Poland; s. of Salomon and Rebecca Goldmann; m. Alice Gottschalk 1934; two s.; ed. Heidelberg, Berlin and Marburg Univs.
Editor and Publisher German Hebrew Encyclopedia 22-34; mem. Zionist Political Comm. 27; Act. Chair. Zionist Action Cttee. 33; escaped from Germany 34; Rep. of Jewish Agency to L. of N.; in U.S. 40-46; Pres. World Jewish Congress 51-, World Zionist Org. 56-68, Conf. on Jewish Claims against Germany; Chair. Cttee. on Jewish Claims against Austria 50-, Memorial Foundation for Jewish Culture.
18 Ahad Haam, Jerusalem, Israel; 12 avenue Montaigne, Paris, France.

Goldmark, Peter Carl, PH.D.; American scientist; b. 2 Dec. 1906, Budapest, Hungary; ed. Univs. of Vienna and Berlin.
Went to U.S. 33; joined Columbia Broadcasting System as Chief Engineer, Television Research Dept. 36, Vice-Pres. (Engineering) 50, Pres. and Dir. of Research, C.B.S. Laboratories (Div. of Columbia Broadcasting System) 54-72; Visiting Prof. of Medical Electronics, Univ. of Pennsylvania Medical School; Pres., Dir. of Research Goldmark Communications Corpn. 72-; mem. Nat. Acad. of Engineering 72-; Morris Liebmann Memorial Prize for Electronic Research 46; Television Broadcasters Asscn. Medal (for work on colour tele-

vision) 54; Vladimir K. Zworykin Television Prize 6; David Sornoff Gold Medal 71; Elliott Cresson Medal 7; Carnegie-Mellon Inst. Award 72; Industrial Researc Inst. Medallist 72; Golden Omega Award 73.
Major works: developed first practical colour televisio system (field-sequential system) 40; developed lon playing record 48; transmission of Lunar Orbiter' photographs of the lunar surface; contributed t development of special electron tubes, audio and acous tical systems, magnetic recording, and data storage an display; supervised development of Linotron (computer tape-driven, ultra high speed photocomposing system) supervised development of Electronic Video Recordin (E.V.R.).
Publ. *Autobiography* 73.
Goldmark Communications Corporation, 1 Communica tion Plaza, Stamford, Connecticut, U.S.A.

Goldreich, Peter, PH.D.; American professor o planetary science and astronomy; b. 14 July 1939, Nev York City; s. of Paul Goldreich and Edith Rosenfield Goldreich; m. Susan Kroll 1960; two s.; ed. Cornel Univ.
Post-Doctoral Fellow Cambridge Univ. 63-64; Asst Prof. Astronomy and Physics, Univ. of Calif. (Los Angeles Campus) 64-66, Assoc. Prof. 66; Assoc. Prof Planetary Science and Astronomy Calif. Inst. Techno logy 66-69, Prof. 69-; mem. Nat. Acad. of Sciences 72-Leisure interest: competitive athletics, e.g. running wrestling, basketball and bicycling.
Publs. on planetary dynamics, pulsar, theory, radic emission from Jupiter, galactic stability and inter stellar masers.
California Institute of Technology, Pasadena, Calif. 91109; Home: 2827 N. Holliston Avenue, Altadena, Calif. 91001, U.S.A.

Golds, Anthony Arthur, C.M.G., M.V.O.; British diplomatist; b. 31 Oct. 1919, Macclesfield, Cheshire; s. of Arthur O. and Florence (née Massey) Golds; m. Suzanne Macdonald Young 1944; one s. one d.; ed. King's School, Macclesfield and New Coll., Oxford.
Served, Royal Armoured Corps 39-46; Commonwealth Relations Office (C.R.O.) 48-51; First Sec., Calcutta and Delhi 51-53; S. Asia Dept., C.R.O. 53-56; First Sec. Ankara 57-59, Karachi 59-61; Counsellor, Head of Malaysia/Indonesia Dept., Foreign Office/C.R.O. 61-65; Counsellor, Rome 65-70; Amb. to Cameroon, Gabon and Equatorial Guinea 70-72; High Commr. to Bangladesh 72-74; Senior Civilian Instructor, Royal Coll. of Defence Studies 75-.
Leisure interests: literature, cricket, rugby, golf.
Royal College of Defence Studies, c/o Foreign and Commonwealth Office, King Charles Street, London, S.W.1, England.

Goldschmidt, Bertrand, DR. ès SC.; French scientist; b. 2 Nov. 1912, Paris; m. Naomi de Rothschild 1947; one s. one d.; ed. Ecole de Physique et de Chimie, Univ. of Paris.
Assistant, Curie Laboratory, Paris 35-40; Section Leader Anglo-Canadian Atomic Project 42-45, Head, Chemis try Div. 46; Head, Chemistry Div. Commissariat à l'Energie Atomique 46-59, Head, External Relations Div. 53-59, Head, External Relations and Planning 59-70, Head Int. Relations Div. 70-; Gov. for France IAEA 57; Prof. Inst. d'Etudes Politiques 60-65; Exec. Vice-Pres. European Atomic Energy Soc. 55-58; Pres. Soc. Industrielle des Minerais de l'Ouest 55-61; Commdr. Légion d'Honneur; Atoms for Peace Award 67; mem. Scientific Advisory Cttee. to IAEA 59.
Publs. *L'Aventure atomique* 62, *Les Rivalités atomiques* 67.
Commissariat à l'Energie Atomique, 29-33 rue de la Fédération, Paris 15e; Home: 11 boulevard Flandrin, Paris 16e, France.
Telephone: 504-11-93 (Home).

Goldsmith, James Michael; British financier and industrialist; b. 26 Feb. 1933, Paris; s. of Frank Goldsmith and Marcelle Mouiller; m. 1st Isabel Patino 1954, 2nd Ginette Lery 1958; five c.; ed. Eton College.

Chairman and founder, Cavenham Ltd. 65-; Chair. and founder Générale Occidentale S.A. 69-; Chair. Anglo-Continental Investment and Finance Co. Ltd. 72-; Chair. Slater Walker Securities Ltd.; Dir. Soc. des Hotels Réunis; Dir. Banque Rothschild; Dir. Banque Occidentale pour l'Industrie et le Commerce.

65-68 Leadenhall Street, London, EC3A 2BA, England; 10 Avenue des Champs Elysées, 75008 Paris, France. Telephone: 480-5676 (England); 359-9922 (France).

Goldstein, Abraham S., M.A.; American professor of law; b. 27 July 1925, New York, N.Y.; s. of Isidore and Zetta (Crystal) Goldstein; m. Ruth Tessler 1947; one s. one d.; ed. City Coll. N.Y., Yale Law School and Cambridge Univ., England.

Associate, Cook and Berger, Washington, D.C. 49; Law Clerk to Circuit Judge David Bazelon (q.v.), U.S. Court of Appeals 49-51; Partner, Donohue and Kaufman 51-56; Assoc. Prof., Yale Law School 56-61, Prof. 61-, Dean 70-; Fellow, Branford Coll., Yale Univ. 62-; Visiting Prof. of Law, Stanford Law School 63; Visiting Fellow, Christ's Coll. 64-65; mem. Comm. to Revise Criminal Statutes of Comm. 66-70; Consultant, President's Comm. on the Administration of Criminal Justice 67; mem. Gov.'s Planning Comm. of Criminal Admin. 67-71, mem. Conn. Board of Parole 68-70; mem. Judicial Council of Conn. 70-; Hon. M.A. (Cambridge and Yale Univs.).

Publs. *The Insanity Defence* 67, *Crime, Law and Society* (with J. Goldstein) 71, *Criminal Procedure* (with L. Orland) 74; articles and book reviews in professional journals.

Yale Law School, New Haven, Conn. 06520; Home: 845 Ellsworth Avenue, New Haven, Conn. 06511, U.S.A.

Goldstein, Rabbi Israel, M.A., D.D., D.H.L., LITT.H.D., PH.D., LL.D.; American Rabbi; b. 18 June 1896, Philadelphia, Pa.; s. of David and Fannie Goldstein; m. Bertha Markowitz 1918; one s. one d.; ed. Univ. of Pennsylvania, Jewish Theological Seminary of America, and Columbia Univ.

Rabbi Congregation B'nai Jeshurun N.Y. City 18-60, Rabbi Emeritus 61-; Pres. Jewish Conciliation Board of America 29-68 (now Hon. Pres.), Jewish Nat. Fund of America 33-43 (now Hon. Pres.), Synagogue Council of America 42-44, Zionist Organisation of America 44-46; Assoc. Consultant to U.S. Del. UN Conf. San Francisco 45; Chair. World Confed. of Gen. Zionists 46-71 (now Hon. Pres.), United Palestine Appeal 47-49; Co-Chair. United Jewish Appeal 47-49; Treas. Jewish Agency 47-49; Pres. Amidar Israel Nat. Housing Co. for Immigrants 48-49; mem. World Jewish Congress Exec. 48- and Chair. of its Western Hemisphere Exec. 50-60, Hon. Vice-Pres. 59-; Pres. American Jewish Congress 51-58, now Hon. Pres.; Pres. World Hebrew Union; mem. Jewish Agency for Israel Exec. 48-71; World Chair. Keren Hayesod-United Israel Appeal 61-71; Chair. Jerusalem Artists' House 63-68; Deputy Chair. Board of Govs. Hebrew Univ. of Jerusalem; mem. Board of Govs. Weizmann Inst. of Science, World Directorate of Jewish Nat. Funds, Univ. of Haifa; Hon. Pres. Israel Interfaith Comm., Int. Synagogue, Kennedy Int. Airport, N.Y.; Vice-Pres. Conf. Jewish Organizations on Material Claims v. Germany 51-70; mem. Joint Exec. Board Jewish Claims on Austria 52-65; Pres. Jewish Restitution Successor Org. 50-61; Chair. Jerusalem Council Israel-America Friendship League; Hon. Vice-Chair. Liberal Party 50-; Founder Brandeis Univ. 46; Hon. degrees from New York Univ., Brandeis Univ., Dropsie Univ., Hebrew Univ. of Jerusalem; Israel Goldstein Chair in Zionism at Hebrew Univ. of Jerusalem; Israel Goldstein Chair in Practical Theology, Jewish Theological Seminary of America, Israel Goldstein Synagogue Hebrew Univ.; Israel Goldstein Youth Village, Jerusalem.

Publs. *A Century of Judaism in New York* 30, *Towards a Solution* 40, *Mourner's Devotions* 41, *Brandeis University* 51, *American Jewry Comes of Age* 55, *Transition Years* 62, *Israel at Home and Abroad* 73.

12 Pinsker Street, Jerusalem, Israel. Telephone: 36020, 30907.

Goldstein, Sydney, PH.D., M.A., F.R.S.; British university professor; b. 3 Dec. 1903, Hull; s. of Joseph Abraham and Hilda (Jacobs) Goldstein; m. Rosa R. Sass 1926; one s. one d.; ed. Bede Collegiate School, Sunderland, Univs. of Leeds and Cambridge.

Rockefeller Research Fellow Univ. of Göttingen 28-29; Lecturer in Applied Mathematics, Univ. of Manchester 29-31, Univ. of Cambridge 31-45; Fellow, St. John's Coll., Cambridge 29-32, 33-45, Hon. Fellow 65-; Leverhulme Research Fellow, Calif. Inst. of Technology 38-39; Aerodynamics Div., Nat. Physical Laboratory 39-45; Beyer Prof. of Applied Mathematics, Univ. of Manchester 45-50; Chair. Aeronautical Research Council of Great Britain 46-49; Prof. of Applied Mathematics, Technion Israel Inst. of Technology, Haifa 50-55, Chair. Aeronautical Engineering 50-54, Vice-Pres. 51-54; Gordon-McKay Prof. of Applied Mathematics, Harvard Univ. 55-70, Emer. Prof. 70-; foreign mem. Royal Netherlands Acad. of Sciences; Dr. h.c. of Engineering (Purdue Univ. 67), of Science (Case Inst. of Technology 67, Technion Israel Inst. of Technology 69, and Univ. of Leeds 73); Timoshenko Medal (American Soc. Mech. Eng.) 65; Hon. F.R.Ae.S.; Hon. Fellow Weizmann Inst. of Sciences, British Inst. of Mathematics and Its Applications.

Publs. *Lectures on Fluid Mechanics* 60; Editor: *Modern Developments in Fluid Dynamics* 38 (Dover edn. 65); papers on mathematics, mathematical physics, hydrodynamics and aerodynamics.

28 Elizabeth Road, Belmont, Mass. 02178, U.S.A.

Goldstücker, Eduard, PH.D.; Czechoslovak university professor; b. 30 May 1913, Podbiel, Czechoslovakia; ed. Charles Univ., Prague, and Oxford Univ., England.

Secretary of League for Human Rights, Prague 36-38; secondary school teacher 38-39; in U.K. 39-45, worked at Czechoslovak Ministry of Foreign Affairs in London 43-44; Ambassadorial Sec., Paris 44-45; Deputy Amb. in London 47-49; Envoy to Tel-Aviv 50-51; political imprisonment 51-55; Dept. of German Literature, Faculty of Philosophy, Charles Univ., Prague 56-69, Prof. 63-69, Pro-Rector of Charles Univ. 66-69; Chair. Union of Czechoslovak Writers 68-69; Deputy to Czech Nat. Council 68-69; Visiting Prof. of Comparative Literature, Univ. of Sussex 69-71, Prof. 71-; Visiting Fellow, Center for the Study of Democratic Institutions, Santa Barbara, Calif. 72-73; several awards including Goethe Gold Medal of Goethe Inst., Munich 67, Klement Gottwald Award 68.

Publs. History of German literature, especially German literature in Prague; *Rainer Maria Rilke und Franz Werfel* 60, *Franz Kafka* 64 (Prize of Publishing House of Czechoslovak Writers), *Libertà e Socialismo* 68, *The Czech National Revival, the Germans and the Jews* 72.

c/o University of Sussex, Brighton, Sussex, England.

Goldwater, Barry; American politician; b. 1 Jan. 1909; ed. Staunton Military Acad., Univ. of Arizona.

Republican Senator from Ariz. 52-64, 69-; Republican candidate for Pres. of United States 64; Goldwater's Inc. 29-, Pres. 37-53, Chair. Board 53-; U.S. Army Air Force 41-45.

Publs. *Arizona Portraits* 40, *Journey Down the River of Canyons* 40, *Speeches of Henry Ashurst: The Conscience of a Conservative* 60, *Why Not Victory?* 60, *Where I Stand* 64, *The Face of Arizona* 64, *People and*

Places 67, *Conscience of a Majority* 70, *Delightful Journey* 71.
United States Senate, Washington, D.C. 20510, U.S.A.

Gołubiew, Antoni; Polish novelist; b. 25 Feb. 1907, Wilno; *s.* of Mikołaj and Antonina Gołubiew; *m.* Janina 1933; two *s.* two *d.*; ed. Univ. of Wilno. Literary début 26; Editor, bi-weekly *Pax* 34-36; co-editor *Tygodnik Powszechny* (weekly publ.); Cracow Regional prize for historical cycle 48, Readers' Prize of Odra-weekly 48, Pietrzak Prize 51, Knight's and Commdr.'s Cross, Order of Polonia Restituta 55, 75. Publs. Cycle of historical novels *Bolesław Chrobry*: *Puszcza* (The Forest), *Szło Nowe* (The Coming of the New), *Złe dni* (Bad Days), *Rozdroża* (Crossroads), *Wnuk* (The Grandson) 74; Essays: *Listy do Przyjaciela* (Letters to a Friend), *Poszukiwania* (Searches), *Unoszeni Historią* (Carried by History), *Świadkowie przemian* (The Witnesses of Change) 74; Short stories: *Na Drodze* (The Road), *Spotkanie na Świętokrzyskiej* (Encounter in Świętokrzyska Street) 74.
Leisure interest: fishing.
Ul. Jaskółcza 4, 31-105 Cracow, Poland.
Telephone: 5-0202.

Golzio, Silvio; Italian statistician and business executive; b. 2 Feb. 1909; ed. Università degli Studi, Turin.
University lecturer, Florence and Turin Univs.; deported to Germany 43-45; Head, Research Office Comitato Interministriale per la Ricostruzione 47-50; Dir. Istituto Nazionale delle Assicurazioni; Gen. Manager then Pres. Società Idroelettrica Piemonte; Pres. and Managing Dir. Società Finanziaria Telefonica (STET) 61-; Dir.-Gen. Istituto Ricostruzione Industriale 64-; Chair. Credito Italiano; Pres. Italian Business Press Asscn.; two war decorations.
Piazza Solferino 11, Turin, Italy.

Gombault, Charles Henri; French journalist; b. 25 Aug. 1907; *m.* Primrose Bordier 1966; one *s.* one *d.*; ed. Lycée Condorcet, Paris.
Journalist *Le Soir*, later *Le Populaire* 27; Soc. and Political Journalist, *Paris-Midi, Paris-Soir* 28-39; Asst. Editor-in-Chief *Match* 39; Ed. and co-founder, *France London* 40-45; Sec.-Gen., later Editor-in-Chief, *France-Soir* 45, Man. Dir. 60-70; Officier, Légion d'Honneur.
Home: 17 avenue des Sycomores, Paris 16e, France.

Gombrich, Sir Ernst (Hans Josef), Kt., C.B.E., PH.D., M.A., F.B.A., F.S.A., F.R.S.L.; British art historian; b. 30 March 1909, Vienna, Austria; *s.* of Dr. Karl Gombrich and Prof. Leonie (née Hock); *m.* Ilse Heller 1936; one *s.*; ed. Theresianum, Vienna, and Vienna Univ.
Research Asst., Warburg Inst., Univ. of London 36-39; B.B.C. Monitoring Service, Second World War; Senior Research Fellow, Warburg Inst. 46-48, Lecturer 48-54, Reader 54-56, Special Lecturer 56-59, Dir. 59-; Prof. of History of the Classical Tradition, Univ. of London 59-; Slade Prof. of Fine Art, Univ. of Oxford 50-53; Durning-Lawrence Prof. of History of Art, Univ. Coll., London 56-59; Visiting Prof. Harvard Univ. 59; Slade Prof. of Fine Art, Univ. of Cambridge 61-63; Hon. Fellow, Jesus Coll., Cambridge 63; Prof. at Large, Cornell Univ. 70-76; Trustee, British Museum 74-; mem. Standing Comm. on Museums and Galleries 76-; Corresp. mem. Turin, Uppsala and Netherlands Acads.; Hon. mem. American Acad. of Arts and Sciences; Foreign mem. American Philosophical Soc.; Hon. Fellow, Royal Inst. of British Architects; Hon. D.Lit. (Queen's Univ., Belfast), Hon. LL.D. (St. Andrews), Hon. D. Litt. (Leeds, Oxford), Hon. Litt.D. (Cambridge, Manchester), Hon. D. Hum. Litt. (Chicago) 75; W. H. Smith and Son Annual Literary Award 64; Medal of N.Y. Univ. 70; Erasmus Prize 75.
Leisure interest: music.

Publs. *Caricature* (with E. Kris) 40, *The Story of Art* 5 *Art and Illusion* 59, *Meditations on a Hobby Horse* 6 *Norm and Form* 66, *In Search of Cultural History* 6 *Aby Warburg* 70, *Symbolic Images* 72, *Illusion in Natu and Art* (ed. with R. L. Gregory) 73, *Art History a the Social Sciences* 74.
19 Briardale Gardens, London, N.W.3, England.
Telephone: 01-435-6639.

Gomes, Gen. Francisco da Costa; Portuguese arm officer; b. 30 June 1914, Chaves; *s.* of António Jo Gomes and Idalina Júlia Monteiro da Costa Gomes; *1* Maria Estela née Furtado de Antas Varejao 195: one *s.*; ed. Military Coll., Cavalry School, Univs. Coimbra and Oporto and Inst. de Altos Estude Militares.
Chief of Staff, Military Command, Macau 49-51; mer H.Q. staff, NATO, Norfolk, U.K., 54-56; Under-Sec. Army Staff 59-61; 2nd-in-Command Military Force Mozambique 65-68; C.-in-C. Military Forces, Mozan bique 68-69; C.-in-C. Military Forces, Angola 70-7: Chief of Staff, Armed Forces of Portugal 72-74, Ma 74-; mem. Junta Nacional de Salvação 74-75; Pre of Portugal Sept. 74-; mem. Supreme Revolutionar Council of Armed Forces Movt. 75-; Grand Office Ordem Nacional do Cruzeiro do Sul do Brasil, Medalb de Mérito Militar 1st Class, Campaign Medals Mozan bique, Angola, and numerous other awards.
Leisure interests: riding, swimming.
Palácio de Belém, Lisbon, Portugal.

Gómez Bergés, Victor; Dominican lawyer and pol tician; b. 25 Feb. 1940, Santiago de los Caballeros; ec Universidad de Santo Domingo.
Assistant legal officer, Dept. of Formal Complaints Secr. for Admin., Control and Reclamation of Nationa Resources 62, Head, Dept. of Complaints 63, Deput Sec. of State for Admin., Control and Reclamation o Nat. Resources 63, for Agriculture 64; Sec. of State fo Interior and Police 65; Sec. Gen. Dominican Municipa League 66; Sec. of State for Educ., Fine Art an Culture 70-72; Sec. of State for Foreign Affairs 72-75 mem. Nat. Devt. Comm.; del. to numerous int. confs. Orden de Duarte, Sánchez y Muella.
Secretaría de Estado de Relaciones Exteriores, Sant Domingo, Dominican Republic.

Gomory, Ralph Edward, PH.D.; American mathe matician and business executive; b. 7 May 1929 Brooklyn, N.Y.; *s.* of Andrew L. Gomory and Maria Schellenberg; *m.* Laura Secretan Dumper 1954 (di vorced 1968); two *s.* one *d.*; ed. Williams Coll., King' Coll. Cambridge Univ. and Princeton Univ.
Lieutenant, U.S. Navy 54-57; Higgins Lecturer an Asst. Prof., Princeton Univ. 57-59; joined IBM 59 Fellow 64, filled various managerial positions including Dir. Mathematical Science Dept., mem. Corp. Technica Cttee. 70, Dir. of Research 70, Vice-Pres. 73-; Andrew D. White Prof.-at-Large, Cornell Univ. 70; mem. Nat. Acad. of Sciences, Nat. Acad. of Eng.; Fellow, Econo metric Soc., American Acad. of Arts and Sciences 73 Lanchester Prize, Operations Research Soc. of America 64; Hon. D.Sc. (Williams Coll.) 73.
Leisure interests: history, skiing, sailing, tennis.
Publs. many papers in mathematical journals.
IBM T.J. Watson Research Center, Box 218, Yorktown Heights, N.Y. 10598; 260 Douglas Road, Chappaqua, N.Y., U.S.A.
Telephone: (914) 945-2122 (Office); (914) 238-8522 (Home).

Gomułka, Władysław (Wiesław); Polish politician; b. 6 Feb. 1905, Krosno.
Was Sec. of several Trade Union Organizations 27, and leader of Polish working class for many years; impri soned twice by the Sanacja regime for his anti-Fascist activities; took active part in Defence of Warsaw 39;

ned ranks of Polish Workers' Party immediately it
is formed; organized detachments and groups People's
my in Sub-Carpathian district; Sec. Warsaw group
lish Workers' Party 42; Sec. Central Cttee. 43-48;
initiator of armed opposition against Germans and
organizer of Nat. Council of Poland; first Deputy
ime Minister, Polish Gov. of Nat. Unity June 45;
ce-Premier and Minister for Regained Territories 45-
n. 49; Vice-Pres. Supreme Nat. Control Chamber
n.-Sept. 49; expelled from United Workers' Party
ov. 49; arrested 51, released Dec. 54; First Sec.
ntral Cttee. Polish United Workers' Party Oct.
-70; Deputy to Seym 57-72; mem. Council of State
-71; retd. 71; numerous Polish and foreign decora-
ons.

Gonçalves, Brig.-Gen. Vasco dos Santos; Portuguese
my officer; b. 3 May 1921, Lisbon; *m.*; one *s.* one *d.*;
. Mil. Coll., Army School.

ined Portuguese Army 42; mem. teaching staff,
ridges and Roads Section, Army School; promoted to
nk of Lt. 46, Capt. 54, Maj. 63, Lt.-Col. 67, Brig.74;
rious commissions in Eng. Branch of Army, later
em. Directorate, Eng. Branch; mem. Armed Forces
ovt. 74-75, Junta of Nat. Salvation 74-75, Supreme
evolutionary Council March-Sept. 75; Prime Minister
ly 74-Sept. 75; several awards and decorations.
o Office of the Prime Minister, Lisbon, Portugal.

Gonçalves Cerejeira, H.E. Cardinal Manuel; Portuguese
clesiastic; b. 29 Nov. 1888, Lousado; ed. Braga
minary and Univ. of Coimbra.

tudent of Braga Seminary 06-09; Univ. of Coimbra
)-12; ordained Priest 11; Prof. Univ. of Coimbra 19;
rchbishop of Mitylene 28; Patriarch of Lisbon 29-71;
reated Cardinal by Pope Pius XI 29; mem. Sacred
ongregations de Propaganda Fide, of Rites and of
minaries and Univs. of Study; Dr. h.c. Rio de Janeiro,
razilian Fed. and Montpellier Univs.

ubls. *O Renascimento em Portugal* (2 vols.) 18; *Do
alor Histórico de Fernão Lopes* 25, *Notas Históricas
bre os Ordenados dos Lentes da Universidade* 27, *A
lma de S. Francisco de Assis* (2nd edn.) 43, *Cartas
os Novos* (2nd edn.) 43, *Vinte Anos de Coimbra* 43,
bras Pastorais* (7 vols. 36-70), *A Idade Media* (2nd
dn.) 44, *A Igreja e o Pensamento Contemporaneo*
5th edn.) 53, *Cartas de Roma* 66, *Na Hora do Diálogo
7, Aos Homens de Boa Vontade* 71, *Clenardo e a Soc-
dade Portuguesa do seu tempo* (4th edn.) 74.
ampo Santana 45, Lisbon 1, Portugal.

Gonda, Jan, PH.D.; Netherlands Sanskrit scholar; b.
4 April 1905, Gouda; *s.* of Jan Gonda and Martha J.
Derksema; *m.* Henriette Wijnholt 1962; ed. State Univ.
Jtrecht and Leyden.

xtra. Prof. Sanskrit State Univ. Utrecht 32-41, Prof.
anskrit and Indo-European Linguistics 41-75; mem.
oyal Dutch Acad. of Sciences; Hon. Fellow Royal
siatic Society; Hon. Foreign Mem. Amer. Acad. of
rts and Sciences.
eisure interest: walking, music.
ubls. *Oud-Javaans Brahmanda Purana* (2 vols.) 32,
imiles in Sanskrit Literature* 39, *Ursprung und Wesen
es indischen Dramas* 40, *Sanskrit in Indonesia* 52,
epetition in the Veda* 59, *Die Religionen Indiens
Vol. I)* 60, (Vol. II) 63, *Visnuism and Sivaism* 70, *Old
ndian* 71, *The Vision of the Vedic Poets* 63, *The
avayajñas* 65, *Dual Deities* 74, *Vedic Literature* 75 and
many other works on Sanskrit and Indo-European lin-
uistics.
ffice: Institute of Oriental Languages, Nobelstraat, 2B,
Jtrecht; Home: 13 van Hogendorpstraat, Utrecht,
Netherlands.
elephone: 030-319143 (Office); 030-516531 (Home).

Gonella, Guido; Italian lawyer, journalist and poli-
ician; b. 18 Sept. 1905; ed. Univs. of Milan, Rome,
Paris, London and Berlin.

Assistant in Faculty of Philosophy of Law, Univ. of
Rome 25; Prof. of Philosophy of Law, Bari and Pavia;
Editor *Osservatore Romano* 32; founder of clandestine
newspaper *Popolo* 43; Dir. of *Popolo* (official organ of
Christian Dem. Party) 44-46; mem. of Constituent
Assembly; Minister of Education 46-51; Minister with-
out Portfolio 51-53; Minister of Justice 53-54, 57-58,
July 58-Jan. 59, Feb. 59-Feb. 60, March 60-62, June 68-
Dec. 68; mem. of Parl. 48-; Vice-Pres. Chamber of
Deputies 66-; fmr. Sec.-Gen. Christian Democratic
Party.
Pubis. *La valutazione del machiavellismo nell' etica
di B. Croce* 30, *I dualismi nella dottrina eticogiuridica di
Hegel* 32, *Al di qua del bene e del male* 32, *La filosofia del
diritto secondo Antonio Rosmini* 34, *La dottrina della
personalità ed alcuni suoi riflessi sociali* 34, *Etudes
critiques* 36, *Schopenhauer—Studien in Rom* 37, *La
persona nella filosofia del diritto* 38, *La crisi del con-
trattualismo* 38, *La nozione di bene comune* 38, *Principi
di un ordine sociale* 42, *Presupposti di un ordine internazionale* 43, *Pace romana e pace cartaginese* 47.
Camera dei Deputati, Rome, Italy.

Gonseth, Ferdinand; Swiss professor; b. 22 Sept. 1890,
Sonviliers; *s.* of Ferdinand Gonseth and Marie Gonseth-
Bourquin; *m.* Marguerite Jacot 1917; one *s.* one *d.*; ed.
Swiss Fed. Inst. of Technology, Zürich.
Lecturer at the Swiss Fed. Inst. of Technology 15-17
and at Univ. of Zürich 17-19; extraordinary Prof. Univ.
of Zürich 19-20; ordinary Prof. Univ. of Berne 20-30;
ordinary Prof. Swiss Fed. Inst. of Technology, Zürich
30-60, Hon. Prof. 61-; Dir. Int. Review of Philosophy
of Knowledge *Dialectica*; organizer of *Entretiens de
Zurich*; Pres. Int. Acad. of Philosophy of Science;
Patron of l'Association Ferdinand Gonseth and of
l'Institut de la Méthode à Bienne; Corresp. mem.
Inst. de France; Officier Légion d'Honneur; Hon.
Dr. ès Lettres (Univ. de Lausanne).
Publs. *Qu'est-ce que la logique?* 37, *Les mathématiques et
la réalité* 36, *La géométrie et le problème de l'espace* 45-55,
Philosophie scolastique et philosophie ouverte 54, *Chroni-
ques de philosophie des sciences de l'Institut international
de philosophie* 58, *Le problème du Temps, essai sur la
méthodologie de la recherche* 64 (Eng. trans. *Time and
Method*), *Le référentiel, univers obligé de médiatisation* 75
and various publs. on human sciences.
Leisure interest: music.
Chemin du Muveran 12, 1012 Lausanne, Switzerland.
Telephone: 021-224657.

González Casanova, Pablo; Mexican sociologist and
university administrator; b. 11 Feb. 1922, Toluca; *s.*
of Pablo González Casanova and Concepción del
Valle; *m.* Natalia Henríquez Ureña 1947; three *s.*; ed.
El Colegio de México, Escuela Nacional de Antropología,
Univ. Nacional Autónoma de México and Univ. de
Paris.
Assistant Researcher, Inst. de Investigaciones Sociales,
Univ. Nacional Autónoma de México (UNAM) 44-50,
Researcher 50-52; Researcher, El Colegio de México
50-54; Sec. Gen. Asscn. of Univs. 53-54; Titular Prof.
of Mexican Sociology, Escuela Nacional de Ciencias
Políticas y Sociales, UNAM 52-66, of Gen. Sociology
54-58; Dir. Escuela Nacional de Ciencias Políticas y
Sociales 57-65, Full-time Titular Prof. 64-65, Titular
Prof. of Research Planning 67-; Dir. Instituto de
Investigaciones Sociales, UNAM 66-70; Rector, Uni-
versidad Nacional Autónoma de México 70-72; Pres.
Admin. Cttee. Facultad Latinoamericana de Ciencias
Sociales, Santiago and Centro Latinoamericano de
Investigaciones Sociales, Rio de Janeiro, UNESCO
59-65; mem. Asscn. Internationale de Sociologues de
Langue Française, Comité Int. pour la Documentation
des Sciences Sociales, Acad. de la Investigación
Científica; Pres. Asociación Latinoamericana de
Sociología 69-72.

Publs. *El misoneísmo y la modernidad cristiana* 48, *Satira del Siglo XVIII* (with José Miranda) 53, *Una utopía de América* 53, *La literatura perseguida en la crisis de la Colonia* 58, *La ideología norteamericana sobre inversiones extranjeras* 55, *Estudio de la técnica social* 58, *La Democracia en México* 65, *Las categorías del desarollo económico y la investigación en ciencias sociales* 67, *Sociología de la explotación* 69.
Av. San Jerónimo No. 742 (Antes 92), México 20, D.F., Mexico.
Telephone: 548-65-00.

González Martín, H.E. Cardinal Marcelo; Spanish ecclesiastic; b. 16 Jan. 1918, Villanubla, Valladolid. Ordained 41; consecrated Bishop of Astorga 61; titular Archbishop of Case Mediane 66; auxiliary Archbishop of Barcelona 67; Archbishop of Toledo and Primate of Spain 71-; created Cardinal by Pope Paul VI 73.
Arco de Palacio 1, Toledo, Spain.
Telephone: 224 100.

Gonzi, Most Rev. Michael, K.B.E., D.D., J.C.D., B.LITT.; Maltese ecclesiastic; b. 13 May 1885, Vittoriosa; s. of Joseph Gonzi and Maria Anna Tonnei; ed. Seminary and Royal Univ., Malta, and Beda Coll., Rome.
Ordained priest 08, Prof. Holy Scripture and Hebrew, Malta Univ. 15; Senator Malta Legislature 21; Canon Theologian Malta Cathedral Chapter 23; Bishop of Gozo 24, of Malta 43, Archbishop and Metropolitan of Malta 44- (duties to be performed by Apostolic Admin. 75-); Asst. at the Pontifical Throne 49.
Archbishop's Palace, Valletta, Malta.
Telephone: Central 26317.

Goodale, Sir Ernest William, Kt., C.B.E., M.C.; British solicitor; b. 6 Dec. 1896, Mortlake, Surrey; s. of William Thomas Goodale and Frances Mary Wheatley; m. 1st Gwendolen Branscombe Warner 1924 (died 1972); one s. one d.; m. 2nd Pamela J. Bone 1973; ed. Richmond Secondary School.
Legal Exec. and partner in firm Minet Pering Smith & Co., Solicitors 20-28; Sec. and Dir. Warner & Sons Ltd. 28-30, Man. Dir. 30-61, Chair. 49-70, Dir. 70-; Hon. Vice-Pres. Int. Silk Asscn. 49-68; Vice-Pres. British Man-Made Fibres Fed. 43-73; Pres. Textile Inst. 39-40, 57-59; Vice-Pres. Inst. of Exports 56-66; Chair. Furnishing Fabric Fed. 45-68, Furnishing Fabric Export Group 42-67; Hon. Pres. Furnishing Fabric Manufacturers' Asscn., etc.; Pres. British Colour Council 53-70; mem. Council Royal Soc. of Arts 35-, Chair. 49-51, Vice-Pres. 50-; mem. Nat. Advisory Council on Art Educ. 59-66; Hon. Fellow, Soc. Industrial Artists.
Leisure interest: philately.
"Branscombe", Nutcombe Lane, Dorking, Surrey, England.
Telephone: 0306-2718.

Goodell, Charles Ellsworth, LL.B., M.GOVT.; American politician; b. 16 March 1926, Jamestown, N.Y.; s. of Dr. Charles E. Goodell and Francesca Bartlett; m. Jean Rice 1954; five s.; ed. Williams Coll. and Yale Univ.
Instructor, Quinnipiac Coll., New Haven 50-51; admitted to Conn. Bar 51, N.Y. Bar 54; Congressional Liaison Asst., Dept. of Justice 54-55; Partner law firm Van Vlack, Goodell & McKee, Jamestown, N.Y. 55-59, Roth, Carlson, Kurt, Spengler & Goodell, New York 71-; mem. U.S. House of Reps. 59-68; Senator from N.Y. 68-71; Head of Clemency Board for Vietnam Resisters 74; Republican.
Leisure interests: golf, skiing, swimming, tennis.
Publ. *Political Prisoners in America* 73.
12 Elm Rock Road, Bronxville, N.Y. 10708, U.S.A.

Goodenough, Ward Hunt, PH.D.; American anthropologist; b. 30 May 1919, Cambridge, Mass.; s. of Erwin R. Goodenough and Helen M. Lewis; m. Ruth A. Gallagher 1941; two s. two d.; ed. Groton School, Cornell and Yale Univs.

Instructor in Anthropology, Univ. of Wisconsin 48-4 Asst. Prof. of Anthropology, Univ. of Pennsylvan 49-54, Assoc. Prof. 54-62, Prof. and Curator of Oceania Ethnology, Univ. Museum 62-; Visiting Prof. of Anthropology, Cornell Univ. 61-62; Board Chair., Huma Relations Area Files Inc. 71-; mem. Board of Dir American Asscn. for the Advancement of Science 72-7 Pres. American Ethnological Soc. 63, Soc. for Applie Anthropology 64; mem. American Philosophical Soc American Acad. of Arts and Sciences, Nat. Acad. o Sciences; Editor *American Anthropologist* 66-70.
Leisure interests: music, stamp collecting.
Publs. *Property, Kin and Community on Truk* 5 *Co-operation in Change* 63, *Explorations in Cultura Anthropology* 64, *Description and Comparison in Cult ural Anthropology* 70, *Culture, Language and Society* 7 University Museum, Philadelphia, Pa. 19104; 204 Fo Lane, Wallingford, Pa. 19086, U.S.A.
Telephone: 215-594-7461 (Museum); 215-565-108 (Home).

Goodeve, Sir Charles Frederick, Kt., O.B.E., D.SC. F.R.S., F.R.I.C.; British scientist; b. 21 Feb. 1904 Canada; s. of Canon F. W. Goodeve and Emma (Hand Goodeve; m. Janet I. Wallace 1932; two s.; ed. Univ of Manitoba, London.
Lecturer and Reader in Chem., Univ. Coll., Londo 29-39; Officer, Royal Naval Volunteer Reserve 23-45 active service 39-45; Dir. British Iron and Stee Research Asscn. 45-69; Consultant to British Stee Corpn. 69-; Vice-Pres. Royal Soc. 68-70; Dir. Londo and Scandinavian Metallurgical Co.; U.S. Medal o Freedom 45, Bessemer Gold Medal 62, Carl Lueg Gol Medal 62, Silver Medal of Operational Research Soc 64.
Leisure interests: ice-skating, swimming.
Publs. Numerous articles in scientific journals o physical chemistry, operational research, proces metallurgy.
38 Middleway, London, N.W.11, England.
Telephone: 01-455-7308.

Goodhart, Arthur Lehman, K.B.E., Q.C., LL.D., D.C.L. F.B.A.; American jurist; b. 1 March 1891; ed. Yale Cambridge and Oxford Univs.
Barrister 15; Asst. Corpn. Counsel, New York 15-17 Counsel to American Mission to Poland 19; Fellow anc Lecturer Corpus Christi Coll., Cambridge Univ. 19 and Sec. to Vice-Chancellor of Univ. 21; Editor *Cambridge Law Journal* 21; Chair. Cambridge Law Examiners 23 Prof. of Jurisprudence Oxford Univ. 31-51, Emeritus 51-; Master of Univ. Coll. 51-63, Hon. Fellow 63- Fellow Nuffield Coll. Oxford and Hon. Fellow Corpus Christi Coll. and Trinity Coll., Cambridge; Editor *Law Quarterly Review*; Chair. S. Region Local Price Regulation Cttee.; mem. Law Revision Cttee., Supreme Court Procedure Cttee., Company Law Revision Cttee. Royal Commission on the Police, etc.; Curator Bodleian Library; Pres. Int. Asscn. of Univ. Profs. 48; Vice-Pres Int. Law Asscn.; hon. mem. American Acad. of Arts and Sciences; Hon. LL.D. (Edinburgh, Yale, Calif. Harvard, Princeton, Columbia, London, Pennsylvania, Belfast, Melbourne, Williams and Wesleyan Univs.).
Publs. *Poland and the Minority Races* 20, *Law and the Needs of Society* 25, *The General Strike* 27, *Essays in Jurisprudence and the Common Law* 31, *Precedent in English and Continental Law* 34, *The Government of Great Britain* 46, *English Contributions to the Philosophy of Law* 49, *Five Jewish Lawyers on Common Law* 50, *English Law and the Moral Law* 53, *Law of the Land* 66.
c/o University College, Oxford; and Whitebarn, Boars Hill, Oxford, England.

Goodison, Nicholas Proctor, M.A., F.S.A., F.R.S.A.; British stockbroker; b. 16 May 1934, Radlett; s. of Edmund Harold Goodison and Eileen Mary Carrington Proctor; m. Judith Abel Smith 1960; one s. two d.; ed.

Marlborough Coll. and King's Coll., Cambridge. Joined H. E. Goodison & Co., members of The Stock Exchange (now named Quilter, Hilton, Goodison & Co.) 58, Partner 62, Senior Partner 75-; mem. Council of The Stock Exchange 68-, Chair. various standing cttees. 71-76, Chair. of The Stock Exchange 76-; Hon. Keeper of Furniture, Fitzwilliam Museum, Cambridge. Leisure interest: history of furniture and decorative arts.
Publs. *English Barometers 1680-1860* 68, *Ormolu: the Work of Matthew Boulton* 74; many papers and articles on the history of furniture, clocks and barometers.
Garrard House, Gresham Street, London, E.C.2; and The Stock Exchange, Old Broad Street, London, E.C.2, England.

Goodman, Baron (Life Peer) cr. 65, of the City of Westminster; **Arnold Abraham Goodman,** C.H., M.A., LL.M.; British solicitor and public official; b. 21 Aug. 1913; ed. Univ. Coll., London, and Downing Coll., Cambridge.
Partner, Goodman Derrick & Co., Solicitors; Chair. Arts Council of Great Britain 65-72, British Lion Films (Holdings) 65-72; mem. South Bank Theatre Board 68-, Industrial Reorganization Comm. 69-71; Fellow, Univ. Coll., London; Chair. Board of Trustees of newspaper *The Observer*; mem. Exec. Cttee. The British Council; Chair. Cultural Cttee. British UNESCO; Chair. Newspaper Publishers' Asscn. 70-; Pres. Nat. Book League 72-; mem. Board of Dirs. Royal Opera House, Covent Garden 72-; Pres. Theatres Advisory Council 72-; Chair. Housing Corpn. and Nat. Building Agency 73-; Vice-Chair. British Council 74-; appointed Master of Univ. Coll., Oxford 76-; Dimbleby Memorial Lecture 74, Hon. LL.D. (Bath Univ.) 76.
Publ. *Not for the Record* 72.
Goodman Derrick & Co., 4 Little Essex Street, London, W.C.2, England.

Goodman, Benny; American musician; b. 30 May 1909.
With the Ben Pollack Band, Los Angeles 25-29; radio and recording work, New York 29-34; formed Benny Goodman Orchestra 35; also formed smaller groups for "chamber jazz"; recorded commissioned works by Bartok, Copland and Hindemith 40; European tour 50; new orchestra formed 57, toured American Univs. 56-57, the Far East, Europe 59, South America 61, U.S.S.R. 62, Japan 64, Europe 70, 71, (with British musicians) 72; guest soloist with various symphony orchestras; numerous recordings; has appeared in the films *Hollywood Hotel, Sweet and Low Down, Stage Door Canteen*, etc.; recorded the soundtrack of *The Benny Goodman Story* 56; Hon. LL.D. Ill. Inst. of Technology.
Publ. *Kingdom of Swing* (with Irving Kolodin).
200 East 66th Street, New York, N.Y., U.S.A.

Goodman, Julian; American broadcasting executive; b. 1 May 1922, Glasgow, Ky.; s. of Charles A. and Clara (Franklin) Goodman; m. Betty Davis 1946; three s. one d.; ed. Western Kentucky and George Washington Univs.
Vice-President, NBC News 61-65; Senior Exec. Vice-Pres. Nat. Broadcasting Co. Inc. 65, Pres. and Chief Admin. Officer 66-70, Pres. and Chief Exec. Officer 70-74, Chair. Board and Chief Exec. Officer 74-; Hon. LL.D. (William Jewell Coll., Liberty, Mo.), Hon. D. Hum. Litt. (Florida Univ.) 73; Gold Medal, Int. Radio and TV Soc. 72; Distinguished Communications Medal, Radio and TV Comm., Southern Baptist Convention 70, Paul White Memorial Award, Int. Conf. of Radio and TV News Dirs. 73.
Leisure interests: sailing, golf.
National Broadcasting Co. Inc., 30 Rockefeller Plaza, New York, N.Y. 10020, U.S.A.
Telephone: CI 7-8300.

Goodman, Raymond John; British international civil servant; b. 26 Oct. 1916, London; s. of J. S. Goodman and Helena Taylor; m. Dorothy Bruchholz (U.S.) 1953; two s. two d.; ed. London School of Economics and Univs. of Copenhagen and Oslo.
War Service, R.N.V.R. 40-46; Dir. Political and Econ. Planning (P.E.P.), London 46-53; Asst. to Chair. of Marks and Spencer Ltd. 53-56; joined World Bank as Loan Officer 56, Asst. Dir. of Admin. 62-65, Deputy Dir. Far East (later Asia) Dept. 65-68, Dir. E. Asia and Pacific Dept. 68-74, Dir. Financial Policy 75-; Hon. Vice-Pres. Consumers Asscn. of Great Britain 57-; Pres. Group Health Asscn. of Washington, D.C. 62-63.
International Bank for Reconstruction and Development (World Bank), 1818 H Street, N.W., Washington, D.C. 20433; Home: 2946 Macomb Street, N.W., Washington, D.C. 20008, U.S.A.
Telephone: 477-3606 (Office); EM2-2946 (Home).

Goodpaster, Gen. Andrew Jackson, B.S., M.S.E., M.A., PH.D.; American army officer; b. 12 Feb. 1915, Granite City, Ill.; s. of Andrew Jackson Goodpaster and Teresa Mary (Mrovka) Goodpaster; m. Dorothy Anderson 1939; two d.; ed. McKendree Coll., Lebanon, Ill., U.S. Mil. Acad., Command and Gen. Staff School, Fort Leavenworth, Kan., and Princeton Univ.
Commanding Officer 48th Engineer Battalion, Italy 43; Staff Officer, War Dept. 44-47; Graduate study, Princeton Univ. 47-50; Special Asst. to Chief of Staff, Supreme H.Q. Allied Powers Europe (SHAPE) 50-54; District Engineer, San Francisco 54; Staff Sec. to Pres. of U.S.A. 54-61; Asst. Div. Commdr. 3rd Infantry Div., 61; Commdg. Gen. 8th Infantry Div., Europe 61-62; Asst. to Chair. Joint Chiefs of Staff 62-66; Dir. Joint Staff, Org. of Joint Chiefs of Staff 66-67; Commandant, Nat. War Coll., Washington, D.C., with added duty as U.S. Army Rep., UN Mil. Staff Cttee. Aug. 67-July 68; mem. U.S. Del to Paris talks on Viet-Nam April-June 68; Deputy Commdr. U.S. Mil. Assistance Command, Viet-Nam June 68-May 69; C.-in-C. U.S. European Command 69-74; Supreme Allied Commdr. Europe (NATO) 69-74; Fellow, Woodrow Wilson Int. Center for Scholars, Washington, D.C. 74-; Distinguished Service Cross, Defense Distinguished Service Medal; Army Distinguished Service Medal with Three Oak Leaf Clusters; Navy Distinguished Service Medal; Air Force Distinguished Service Medal; Silver Star; Legion of Merit with Oak Leaf Cluster; Purple Heart with Oak Leaf Cluster; numerous other U.S. and foreign decorations from Italy, Repub. of Korea, Repub. of Vietnam, Netherlands, Belgium, Luxembourg, Fed. Repub. of Germany, Turkey and Portugal.
SHAPE Liaison Office, 1A711, Pentagon, Washington, D.C. 20310, U.S.A.
Telephone: OX 77946 (Office).

Goodwin, Sir Reg(inald), Kt., C.B.E.; British local government official; b. 3 July 1908, London; s. of Thomas William Goodwin and Lydia (née Warn); m. Penelope Mary Thornton 1943; two s. one d.; ed. Grammar School.
Leader, Bermondsey Borough Council 46-64; mem. London County Council, Chair. Finance, Housing, Gen. Purposes and Establishment Cttees. 46-64; mem. Greater London Council 64-, Deputy Leader 64-67, Chair. Finance Cttee. 64-67, Leader of Opposition 67-73, Leader of Council 73-; mem. Basildon Devt. Corpn. 65-, Deputy Chair. 70-; Man. Trustee, Municipal Insurance Co. 75-; mem. Court, Univ. of London 66-; Asst. Gen. Sec., Nat. Asscn. of Boys' Clubs 34-45, Gen. Sec. 45-73; Deputy Lieut. of Greater London; Labour.
Leisure interests: gardening, walking.
Room 133, The County Hall, London, S.E.1; Home: Twitten Cottage, Marlhill, Pulborough, West Sussex, England.
Telephone: 01-633 6153 (Office); 0798 22202 (Home).

Goodwin, Richard N.; American lawyer and fmr. government official; b. 7 Dec. 1931; ed. Brookline High School, Tufts Univ., and Harvard Law School.
Law Clerk for Justice Felix Frankfurter, U.S. Supreme Court 58-59; Special Counsel for House Sub-cttee.'s Legislative Oversight Cttee. 59; worked for Senator Kennedy during Pres. election campaign 59-60; mem. President's Task Force on Latin American Affairs 60-61; Asst. Special Counsel to Pres. 61; Dep. Asst. Sec. of State for Inter-American Affairs 61-63; Sec.-Gen. Int. Peace Corps Secr. 63-64; Special Asst. to Pres. 64-65; Fellow, Center for Advanced Studies, Wesleyan Univ. 65-67.
Publs. *The Sower's Seed* 65, *Triumph or Tragedy: Reflections on Vietnam* 66.
14 Chestnut Street, Boston, Mass., U.S.A.

Gookin, R(alph) Burt, B.SC., M.B.A.; American business executive; b. 23 June 1914, Chariton, Iowa; s. of Albert Brisbine and Maude Mary McFarland Gookin; m. Mary Louise Carroll 1948; one s. one d.; ed. Northwestern Univ. and Harvard Business School.
With Firestone Tire and Rubber Co. 35-40, Forest Lawn Co. 40-41, Los Angeles Shipbuilding and Drydock Co. 42-43, Consolidated Steel Co. 44-45, Exec. Accountant H. J. Heinz Co. 45, Controller 51, Dir. and Vice-Pres. Finance 59, Exec. Vice-Pres. 64, Pres. and Chief Exec. Officer 66, Vice-Chair. and Chief Exec. Officer 73; Chair. Universal Grocery Product Code Ad Hoc Cttee.; mem. Board of Dirs. Bank of America, Westinghouse Electric Corpn., Allegheny Gen. Hosp., WQED-TV-Public Broadcasting Service, etc.; fmr. Pres. of Financial Exec. Research Foundation and Pittsburgh Chapter of Financial Execs. Inst.; Presidential Task Force on Int. Devt.
Leisure interest: golf.
H. J. Heinz Company, P.O. Box 57, Pittsburgh, Pa. 15230; Park Mansions, 5023 Frew Avenue, Pittsburgh, Pa. 15213, U.S.A.
Telephone: 412-237-5434 (Office); 412-621-5720 (Home).

Gooneratne, Tilak Eranga, B.A.; Ceylonese civil servant and lawyer; b. 27 March 1919; s. of Thomas Edwin Gooneratne and Dona Sophia Athulathmudali; m. Pamela Jean Rodrigo 1947; two d.; ed. St. John's Coll., Panadura, Ceylon, Ceylon Univ., and Ceylon Law Coll.
Joined Ceylon Civil Service 43; Asst. Sec. Ministry of External Affairs 47-51; Controller of Immigration and Emigration 49-51; Govt. Agent, Trincomalee 51-54, Matra 54-56; Registrar Gen. Marriages, Births and Deaths 56-58; Dir.-Gen. of Broadcasting and Dir. of Information, Ceylon 58-60; Commr. Co-operative Devt. 60-63; Acting Perm. Sec. Ministry of Commerce and Trade 63; Dir. of Econ. Affairs 63; Deputy Sec. to Treasury 63-65; Pres. Colombo Plan Council for Technical Co-operation in South and South East Asia 64-65; Del. to UN Gen. Assembly 64-65; Deputy Sec.-Gen. Commonwealth Secr. 65-70; High Commr. to U.K. 70-, Amb. to European Communities 74-, also Amb. to Belgium, Netherlands, Luxembourg 75-.
Leisure interests: tennis, table tennis, travel.
Publs. *An Historical Outline of the Development of the Marriage and Divorce Laws of Ceylon, An Historical Outline of the Development of the Marriage and Divorce Laws Applicable to Muslims in Ceylon, Fifty Years of Co-operative Development in Ceylon.*
Embassy of Sri Lanka, 21-22 avenue des Arts, 1040 Brussels; Home: 6 Kennedy Park, 171 avenue Montjoie, Uccles, 1180 Brussels, Belgium.
Telephone: 5139891 (Office); 3449309 (Home).

Goonetilleke, Sir Oliver Ernest, G.C.M.G., K.C.V.O., K.B.E., K.ST.J., B.A., LL.D., F.R.S.A., F.R.E.S.; Ceylonese politician; b. 20 Oct. 1892, Trincomalee; m. Phyllis Mary Miller 1967; ed. London Univ.
Assistant Auditor for Railways Ceylon 21; Asst. Colo-

nial Auditor 24-31; Colonial Auditor 31; Auditor-Gen. July 31; Ceylon Govt. Del. to Int. Railway Congress, Cairo 33; Chair. Retrenchment Comm. Ceylon 38; Civil Defence and Food Commr. 42; mem. Ceylon War Council 42; Financial Sec. Govt. of Ceylon 45-47; Home Minister 47; High Commr. in U.K. 48-51; Minister of Home Affairs 51-52, of Agriculture and Food 52-53, of Civil Defence 53, also Leader of the Senate; Minister of Finance 54; Gov.-Gen. of Ceylon 54-62; Vice-Pres. Royal Inst. of Int. Affairs; Dir. of numerous companies; Underwriting mem. Lloyd's, London; sentenced *in absentia* to four years' imprisonment by Ceylonese court Feb. 76.
14 Albion Gate, Hyde Park Place, London, W.2, England.
Telephone: 01-723-5814.

Goormaghtigh, John Victor, D. en DROIT; Belgian lawyer and public servant; b. 15 March 1919, Ghyverinchove; s. of S. Norbert Goormaghtigh and Mable Lawrence; m. Eliane Weber 1945; two s. one d.; ed. Brussels Univ.
Admitted to the Bar 42; Advocate, Court of Appeal 45; Dir. Belgian Inst. of Int. Affairs 47-52, then mem. Board and Hon. Sec.; Joint Sec. Int. Academic Union 49; Consultant to UNESCO 50; Sec. Preparatory Cttee. Int. Political Science Asscn. 49, Sec.-Gen. 55-60; Dir. European Centre, Carnegie Endowment for Int. Peace 50-; Prof. of Political Science, Univ. of Geneva 61-62; Chair. Board Int. School of Geneva 61-66; Chair. Int. Baccalaureate Office (fmrly. Int. Schools Exam. Syndicate) 65-; Dir. Centre for Research on Int. Insts. 74-; Prof. Grad. Inst. of Int. Studies, Geneva 75-76; Editor *Chronique de Politique Etrangère* 48-52; Chevalier Order of the Crown; Croix de Guerre (Belgium and France), Médaille de la Résistance, Chevalier Ordre de la Valeur du Cameroun.
Leisure interests: painting, gardening.
Office: 11A avenue de la Paix, 1211 Geneva 20; Home: 1249 Malval/Dardagny, Geneva, Switzerland.
Telephone: 34-23-50 (Office); 54-14-44 (Home).

Goossens, Léon Jean, C.B.E., F.R.C.M., HON. R.A.M.; British oboist; b. 12 June 1897; ed. Christian Brothers Catholic Inst., Liverpool, Liverpool Coll. of Music and Royal Coll. of Music, London.
Principal Oboist Queen's Hall Orchestra 13-15; war service 15-18, wounded; Principal Oboist, Queen's Hall until 24, Royal Opera House, Covent Garden and London Philharmonic Orchestra until 38; Principal Oboist Royal Philharmonic Orchestra; world-wide oboe recitals since 27; Prof. Royal Coll. of Music and Royal Acad. of Music; numerous lecture recitals; encouraged a new school of oboe-playing with oboe as solo instrument; Cobbett Medal for Chamber Music 54; numerous int. tours.
7A Ravenscourt Square, London, W.6, England.

Gopal-Ayengar, Anekal Ramaswamiengar, M.SC., M.A., PH.D., F.A.SC., F.N.I.; Indian biologist; b. 1 Jan. 1909; ed. Univs. of Mysore and Toronto.
Lecturer in Botany, Mysore Univ. 33-38; Vincent Massey Fellow, Univ. of Toronto 38-39; Senior Instructor, Univ. of Toronto 41-45, Kettering Research Fellow, Barnard Skin and Cancer Hospital and Research Assoc., Washington Univ., St. Louis, Mo. 45-47; Chief Research Cytologist, Tata Memorial Hospital, Bombay 47-51; Head, A.E.C. Unit on Cell Biology 48-51; Senior Int. Research Fellow, Lady Tata Trust and Research Assoc., Chester Beatty Research Inst., London and Inst. for Cell Research, Karolinska Inst., Stockholm 51-53; Expert, Radiation Cttee. of World Health Org. (WHO) 58-73; Chief Scientific Officer and Head, Biological and Medical Divs., Atomic Energy Establishment, Trombay (AEET) 60-62; Dir. Biology Group (AEET) 62-67; mem. Indian Nat. Cttee. for Co-operation with UNESCO (Natural Sciences) 61-71; Chair. Nat. Cttee. for Biophysics 62-; Indian Rep. on

UN Scientific Cttee. on Effects of Atomic Radiation (UNSCEAR) 62-, Chair. 66-67; Pres. Indian Soc. of Genetics and Plant Breeding 63-64; mem. Int. Asscn. for Radiation Research (IARR) 63-66; Rep. for South-East Asia on Genetics Section of Int. Union of Biological Sciences (IUBS) and Int. Cell Research Org. (ICRO) 63-66; mem. Exec. Cttee. and Council ICRO 63-71; Pres. Comm. on Radiation Biophysics of Int. Union for Pure and Applied Physics (IUPAB) 65-69; IUPAB's rep. on SCIBP 66-72; mem. Indian Nat. Cttee. for Biological Sciences 65-; Dir. Bio-Medical Group Atomic Energy Comm. (AEC) 68-71, Emer. Dir. and Bio-Medical Adviser 71-; mem. and Sec. Int. Comm. on Radiation Biophysics of IUPAB 69-72; Pres. Indian Asscn. for Radiation Protection (IARP) 69-72; mem. Int. Cttee. on Experimental Studies on Human Cancer, Comm. for Experimental Oncology; Fellow Indian Acad. of Sciences; associated with New York Acad. of Sciences for Cancer Research; Hon. Prof. of Cell Biology Madurai Univ. 69-; J. H. Bhabha Prize 48; Padma Shri 67.
8B Atomic Energy Officers Apartments, Little Gibbs Road, Malabar Hill, Bombay 400006, India.
Telephone: 359346.

Gopalan, A. K., M.P.; Indian politician; b. 1 Oct. 1904, Mavilai, Cannanore; s. of Shri Ryru Nambiar; m. C. K. Suseela; one d.; ed. Cannanore, Malabar and Kerala.
Deputy Leader Communist Group in Parl. 57, Leader 52, 62, 67; Main Opposition Group Leader in Parl. 71; Sec. Nat. Council C.P. of India; Pres. All India Kisan (Peasants) Sabha; mem. Polit Bureau CPI(M), Exec. Cttee. of Trade Union Int. of Agricultural Forestry and Plantation Workers (detained July 75).
Leisure interests: reading and writing.
Publs. *Kerala, Past and Present, Autobiography, I Saw a New World.*
4 Ashoka Road, New Delhi, India.
Telephone: 382870.

Gopallawa, William, M.B.E.; President of Sri Lanka; b. 17 Sept. 1897, Dullewa, Matale; s. of Tikiri Banda Gopallawa and Dullewa Gopallawa Kumarihamy; m. Seila Rambukwella 1928; two s. two d.; ed. Dharmarajah Coll., St. Anthony's Coll., Kandy and Law Coll., Colombo.
Enrolled as Attorney-at-Law of Supreme Court 24; mem. Matale Urban Council 27-39, Chair. 28-34; Municipal Commr. Kandy 39-52, Colombo 52-57; Amb. to People's Repub. of China 58-61, to U.S.A., Cuba and Mexico 61-62; Gov.-Gen. of Ceylon 62-72; Pres. Repub. of Sri Lanka (fmrly. Ceylon) 72-; Chancellor, Univ. of Sri Lanka; Hon. LL.D. (Univs. of Sri Lanka and Vidyalankara); Hon. D.Litt. (Vidyodaya Univ.).
Leisure interests: cricket, tennis, golf.
President's House, Colombo, Sri Lanka.
Telephone: Colombo 27821.

Goppel, Alfons; German lawyer and politician; b. 1 Oct. 1905, Regensburg; s. of Ludwig and Barbara Goppel; m. Gertrud Wittenbrink 1935; five s.; ed. Humanistisches Gymnasium, Regensburg, and Ludwig Maximilians Univ., Munich.
State Attorney 34, Judge 38; Vice-Mayor of Aschaffenburg 52; State Sec. of Justice (Bavaria) 57; Minister of Interior (Bavaria) 58-62; Minister-Pres. of Bavaria 62-; mem. Bavarian Land Diet 54-; numerous decorations.
8 Munich 22, Prinzregentenstrasse 7; Home: 8033 Krailling, Sommerweg 2, Federal Republic of Germany.
Telephone: 21651 (Office).

Goray, Narayan Ganesh, B.A., LL.B.; Indian politician; b. 15 June 1907, Hindala, Maharashtra; s. of Ganesh Govind Gore and Saraswati; m. Sumati Kirtane 1935; one d.; ed. Fergusson Coll., Poona.
Congress Socialist Party 30, mem. Nat. Exec. 34, Mayor of Poona; imprisoned for political activities before independence; Joint Sec. Socialist Party 48; Gen. Sec. Praja Socialist Party 49-54, 54-65, Chair. 65-; led first batch of Satyagrahis against Portuguese Govt. in Goa; mem. Lok Sabha 57-62, Rajya Sabha 70.
Leisure interests: music, painting, writing.
Publs. *History of the United States of America,* etc.
1813 Sadashiv Peth, Poona 30, Maharashtra State, India.
Telephone: 56614.

Gorbatko, Col. Viktor Vasiliyevich; Soviet cosmonaut; b. 3 Dec. 1934, Krasnodar Region; ed. School o; Military Pilots in Bataisk and Zhukovsky Air Force Engineering Acad.
Air Force Fighter Pilot 56-63; mem. C.P.S.U. 59-; with cosmonaut training unit 61; Engineer-investigator of spaceship *Soyuz*-7, which made a group flight with *Soyuz*-6 and *Soyuz*-8 Oct. 69; Hero of Soviet Union, Gold Star, Order of Lenin and other awards; Pilot-Cosmonaut of the U.S.S.R., K. Tsiolkovsky Gold Medal of the U.S.S.R. Acad. of Sciences.
Zvezdny Gorodok, Moscow, U.S.S.R.

Gordey, Michel; French journalist and writer; b. 17 Feb. 1913, Berlin, Germany; s. of Samuel Rapaport and Eugenia Gourvitch; m. Beverly Bronstein 1950; one s. one d.; ed. Lycée Janson de Sailly, Law Faculty of Sorbonne and Ecole des Sciences Politiques, Paris.
Lawyer, Paris 33-37; French Army 37-40; U.S. Office of War Information, French Editor, Voice of America 41-45, Chief Editor 44-45; U.S. Corresp. *Paris-Presse* 45; U.S. and UN Corresp., Agence-France-Presse, New York and Washington 45-46; Roving Foreign and Diplomatic Corresp. *France-Soir,* Paris 45-56, Chief Foreign Corresp. 56-73; assignment to China 71-72; Roving Foreign and Diplomatic Corresp., *L'Express,* Paris 73-; articles have been published in magazines and newspapers in U.K., U.S.A., German Federal Republic, Japan, Italy and Switzerland; TV and radio broadcasts in U.K., U.S.A., Canada and German Federal Republic; several journalistic awards.
Leisure interests: reading, high mountains, walking.
Publ. *Visa pour Moscou* 51.
16 rue de Savoie, Paris 6e, France.
Telephone: 033-7982.

Gordillo, Pedro Antonio; Argentine politician and civil engineer; b. 30 April 1921, Córdoba; s. of Ing. Pedro N. Gordillo and María Amelia Montes; m. María Rosa Hombravella 1948; six s.; ed. Colegio Jesuita San José, Colegio Nacional Monserrat and Universidad Nacional de Córdoba.
Under-Secretary of Public Works, Province of Córdoba 55-56; Minister of Public Works, Tourism and Agriculture 62-63, subsequently Ministry of Finance and Econ.; Mayor of Córdoba 66-67; Pres. Council of Admin. Services of Radio and Television, Córdoba 67; Minister of Public Works and Services, Govt. of Argentina 71-73.
Avenida Hipólito Yrigoyen 468, 3er piso, Córdoba, Argentina.
Telephone: 26403.

Gordimer, Nadine; South African writer; b. 20 Nov. 1923; d. of Isidore Gordimer and Nan Myers; m. Reinhold Cassirer 1954; one s. one d.; ed. convent school.
Recipient of W. H. Smith Literary Award 61 and Thomas Pringle Award (English Acad. of S.A.) 69, James Tait Black Memorial Prize 71, Booker Prize (co-winner) 74, Grand Aigle d'Or Prize (France) 75, CNA Literary Award (S. Africa) 75.
Publs. *The Soft Voice of the Serpent* (stories), *The Lying Days* (novel) 53, *Six Feet of the Country* (stories) 56, *A World of Strangers* (novel) 58, *Friday's Footprint* (stories) 60, *Occasion for Loving* (novel) 63, *Not For*

Publication (stories) 65, *The Late Bourgeois World* (novel) 66, *A Guest of Honour* (novel) 70, *Livingstone's Companions* (stories) 72, *The Conservationist* (novel) 74, *Selected Stories* 75; co-editor *South African Writing Today* 67.

7 Frere Road, Parktown, Johannesburg, South Africa.

Gordis, Robert, B.A., PH.D.; American rabbi and biblical scholar; b. 6 Feb. 1908, Brooklyn, N.Y.; *m.* Fannie Jacobson 1928; three *s.*; ed. Coll. of City of New York, The Dropsie Coll., Philadelphia and Jewish Theological Seminary.

Mayer Sulzberger Fellow in Biblical Philology, Dropsie Coll. 26-29; Instructor in Bible and Jewish History, Hebrew Teachers' Training School for Girls 28-30; Instructor, Teachers' Inst. of Jewish Theological Seminary 30-31; Rabbi, Temple Beth-El, Rockaway Park, L.I. 31-68, Rabbi Emer. 68-; Seminary Prof. of Bible, Jewish Theological Seminary 37-; Pres. Rabbinical Assembly of America 44-46; Vice-Pres. Synagogue Council of America 46-48, Pres. 48-49; Adjunct Prof. in Religion, Columbia Univ. 49-57; Lecturer in Old Testament, Union Theological Seminary 53-54; Prof. of Bible, Jewish Theological Seminary of America 61-; Consultant to Center for Study of Democratic Insts. of Fund for Repub. 60-; Prof. of Religion, Temple Univ. 67-74; Prof. of Philosophies of Religion, Jewish Theological Seminary 74-; Assoc. Editor Dept. of the Bible and contrib. to *Universal Jewish Encyclopaedia*; Chair. Board of Editors *Judaism*, Editor 70-; Hon. D.D. (Jewish Theological Seminary) 50.

Publs. *Biblical Text in the Making* 37, *The Jew Faces a New World* 41, *The Wisdom of Ecclesiastes* 45, *Conservative Judaism—An American Philosophy* 45, *Koheleth—The Man and His World* 51, *Song of Songs* 54, *Judaism and the Modern Age* 55, *A Faith for Moderns* 60, *The Root and the Branch—Judaism and the Free Society* 62, *The Book of God and Man: A Study of Job* 65, *Judaism in a Christian World* 66, *Sex and the Family in Jewish Tradition, Leave a Little to God* 67, *Poets, Prophets and Sages—Essays in Biblical Interpretation* 71, *Faith and Reason, Essays in Judaism* 73, *The Book of Esther* 74, *Song of Songs—Lamentations* 74, *The Book of Job—Commentary and Translation* 75, *The Word and the Book* (*Studies in Biblical Language and Literature*) 76.

15 East 84th Street, New York City, N.Y. 10028; Home: 150 West End Avenue (Apt. 24M), New York, N.Y. 10023, U.S.A.

Telephone: 212-RI9-8000 (Office); 212-877-1484 (Home).

Gordon, Hon. John Bowie (Peter); New Zealand politician; b. 1921, Stratford; *s.* of Dr. William P. Gordon, C.B.E. and Dr. Doris C. Gordon, M.B.E.; *m.* Dorothy Morton 1943; two *s.* one *d.*; ed. St. Andrew's Coll., Christchurch, Lincoln Coll.

Served as pilot in R.N.Z.A.F. 41-44, mentioned in dispatches; Pres. West Otago Branch Federated Farmers; mem. first Nat. Hydatids Council; Chair. Dir. of Heriot Transport 51-54; Dir. Farmers' Mutual Insurance 51-60, N.Z. Board Shaw Savill 56-60; toured Britain, Scandinavia and U.S. under Nuffield Scholarship 54; visited U.S. under U.S. State Dept. Foreign Leadership Award 64; M.P. for Clutha 60-; Minister of Transport and Railways 66-72; Minister of Marine and Fisheries 72, of Labour and of State Services 75-National Party.

Leisure interests: golf, cooking.

Parliament House, Wellington, New Zealand.

Gordon, Kermit; American economist; b. 3 July 1916, Philadelphia, Pa.; *s.* of H. B. Gordon and Ida E. Robinson; *m.* Mary King Grinnell 1941; one *s.* two *d.*; ed. Swarthmore Coll., Univ. Coll., Oxford, and Harvard Univ.

Research Asst. Econs., Swarthmore Coll. 39-40; Admin.

Fellow, Harvard 40-41, Teacher of Econs. 50, 54; Office of Price Admin. 41-43; Special Asst. to Sec. for Econ. Affairs, State Dept. 45-46; Consultant 46-53; Econs. Faculty, Williams Coll. 46-, Prof. of Econs. 55-62, David A. Wells Prof. of Political Econ. 61-62; mem. Council of Econ. Advisers 61-62; Dir. of Budget 62-65; Vice-Pres. Brookings Inst. 65-67, Pres. 67-; mem. several econ. orgs; mem. Board of Trustees Ford Foundation 67-75, mem. Exec. Cttee. 70-75; Trustee, Cttee. for Econ. Development 68-; Fellow, American Acad. of Arts and Sciences 67-; mem. Gen. Advisory Cttee., U.S. Arms Control and Disarmament Agency 69-72; mem. American Philosophical Soc. 71-, U.S. Fed. Pay Board 71-72.

The Brookings Institution, 1775 Massachusetts Avenue, N.W., Washington, D.C. 20036, U.S.A.

Telephone: 202-797-6200.

Gordon, Lincoln, B.A., D.PHIL.; American political economist and diplomatist; b. 10 Sept. 1913, New York; *s.* of Bernard and Dorothy Gordon; *m.* Allison Wright 1937; two *s.* two *d.*; ed. Harvard Univ. and Balliol Coll., Oxford.

Instructor in Govt., Harvard Univ. 36-40; Prof. of Govt. and Admin., Harvard Business School and Graduate School of Public Admin. 46-50; Govt. service with Nat. Resources Planning Board 39-40; Nat. Defense Advisory Cttee. 40-41; W.P.B. 42-45; Deputy Programme Vice-Chair., W.P.B. 44, Programme Vice-Chair. 45; Consultant, Dept. of State in development of European Recovery Programme 47-48; Dir. Programme Div. ECA in Office of Special Rep. in Europe 49-50; Economic Adviser to Special Asst. to the Pres. (W. A. Harriman) 50-51; Asst. Dir. for Programme, Office of Dir. for Mutual Security 51-52; Minister for Economic Affairs and Chief of MSA Mission to U.K. Oct. 52-55; William Ziegler Prof. of Int. Economic Relations, Harvard Univ. Graduate School of Business Administration July 55-61; Ambassador to Brazil 61-66; Asst. Sec. of State for Inter-American Affairs 66-67; Pres. The Johns Hopkins Univ. 67-71; Visiting Prof. of Political Econs., Johns Hopkins School of Advanced Int. Studies 71-72; Fellow Woodrow Wilson Int. Center for Scholars, Washington 72-75; Senior Fellow Resources for the Future, Washington 75-.

Leisure interests: music ('cellist), woodworking.

Publs. *The Public Corporation in Great Britain* 38, *Government and the American Economy* (with M. Fainsod) 41; Editor *International Stability and Progress: United States Interests and Instruments* 57; *United States Manufacturing Investment in Brazil* (with E. L. Grommers) 61, *O Progresso Pela Aliança* 62, *A New Deal for Latin America* 63.

1755 Massachusetts Avenue, Washington D.C., 20036 (Office); 3069 University Terrace, N.W. Washington D.C., 20016, U.S.A. (Home).

Telephone: 202-462-4400 (Home).

Gordon, Richard F., Jr.; American football manager and former astronaut; b. 5 Oct. 1929, Seattle, Wash.; *m.* Barbara Field; four *s.* two *d.*; ed. Univ. of Washington.

Entered U.S. Navy 51; received naval aviator wings 53; attended All-Weather Flight School; later at Naval Air Station, Jacksonville, Fla.; attended Navy's Test Pilot School, Patuxent River 57; first project test pilot for F4H Phantom II; won Bendix Trophy Race 61; selected by NASA as astronaut Oct. 63; pilot of backup crew for *Gemini VIII* flight; pilot of *Gemini XI* mission Sept. 66; Command module pilot, *Apollo XII* Nov. 69; retd. USN/NASA 72; Exec. Vice-Pres. New Orleans Saints professional football team 72-; NASA Exceptional Service Medal, NASA Distinguished Service Medal, USN Distinguished Service Medal.

New Orleans Saints Professional Football Team, New Orleans, La. 70130, U.S.A.

Gordon, Hon. Walter Lockhart, P.C., F.C.A., LL.D.; Canadian politician (retd.); b. 27 Jan. 1906; ed. Upper Canada Coll., Toronto, and Royal Military Coll., Kingston.
Partner, Clarkson, Gordon & Co., Toronto, Chartered Accountants 35-63; Partner, Woods, Gordon & Co., Management Consultants, Toronto 40-63; Special Asst. to Dep. Minister of Finance, Canada 40-42; M.P. 62-68; Minister of Finance and Receiver Gen. of Canada 63-65; Minister without Portfolio Jan. 67-April 67; Pres. of Privy Council April 67-68; Chair. Canadian Corporate Management Co. Ltd. 68-; Chancellor, York Univ., Toronto; Chair. several Royal Comms.; Liberal.
Office: Suite 2080, Commerce Court West, Toronto, Ontario; Home: 22 Chestnut Park Road, Toronto 5, Ontario, Canada.

Gordon, William Edwin, M.A., M.S., PH.D.; American radio physicist; b. 8 Jan. 1918, Patterson, N.J.; s. of William and Mary Scott Gordon; m. Elva Freile 1941; one s. one d.; ed. Montclair State Coll., N.J. and New York and Cornell Univs.
Associate Dir. Electrical Engineering Research Lab., Univ. of Texas 46-48; Research Assoc., Cornell Univ. 48-53, Assoc. 53-59, Prof. 59-65, Distinguished Prof. 65-66; Dir. Arecibo Ionospheric Observatory, Puerto Rico 60-66; Vice-Pres., Rice Univ. 69-72; Dean of Science & Eng., Rice Univ. 66-75; Dean School of Natural Sciences 75-; Prof. of Electrical Eng. and Space Physics & Astronomy, Rice Univ. 66-; Chair., Board of Trustees, Upper Atmosphere Research Corpn. 71-72, 73-; Vice-Pres. Int. Scientific Radio Union 75-; mem. NSF Research Advisory Cttee. 73-, Nat. Acad. of Sciences Cttee. on Solar Terrestrial Research 66-74, NAS Panel on Jicamarca Radio Observatory 69-74, Board of Trustees, Univ. Corpn. for Atmosphere Research 75-, Nat. Acad. of Sciences, Nat. Acad. of Eng., American Meteorological Soc., American Asscn. for Advancement of Science; Fellow I.E.E., American Geophysical Union, Guggenheim Fellow. Balth Van der Pol Gold Medal for distinguished research in radio sciences 63-66, 50th Anniversary Medal of American Meteorological Soc. 70.
Leisure interests: sailing, swimming, music.
Publs. Numerous articles in learned journals.
12422 Mossycup Drive, Houston, Tex. 77024, U.S.A. Telephone: 713-522-5953.

Gordon-Lazareff, Hélène; French journalist; b. 21 Sept. 1909.
Director and Editor-in-Chief *Elle* (weekly) 45-; mem. Television Programme Cttee. of O.R.T.F. 65.
Publ. *L'U.R.S.S. à l'heure Malenkov* (with P. Lazareff).
Office: 100 rue Réaumur, Paris 2e; Home: Château de la Grille Royale, 78 Louveciennes (Yvelines), France.

Gordon-Smith, Ralph; British business executive; b. 22 May 1905; ed. Bradfield Coll.
Smiths Industries Ltd. 27-, Dir. 33, Group Man. Dir. 47-, Chair. 51-, Chief Exec. 67-, non-exec. Chair. 68-, Pres. 73.
Office: Smiths Industries Ltd., Cricklewood Works, London, N.W.2; Home: "The Old Ship", Bosham, Sussex, England.
Telephone: 01-452-3333 (Office).

Gordon-Walker, Baron (Life Peer), cr. 74, of Leyton in Greater London; **Patrick Chrestien Gordon Walker,** P.C., C.H., M.A., B.LITT.; British politician; b. 7 April 1907, Worthing, Sussex; s. of Judge A. L. Gordon Walker and Dora M. Chrestien; m. Audrey M. Rudolf 1934; two s. three d.; ed. Wellington Coll., and Christ Church, Oxford.
Student and History Tutor, Christ Church 31-40; BBC European Service 40-44; Chief Editor Radio Luxembourg 44; Asst. German Service Dir., BBC 45; M.P. (Labour) for Smethwick 45-64, for Leyton 66-74; P.P.S.

to Mr. Morrison 46; Parl. Under-Sec. of State for Commonwealth Relations 50-51; Foreign Sec. Oct. 64-Jan. 65; Minister without Portfolio Jan.-Aug. 67; Sec. of State for Educ. and Science 67-68; Chair. British Film Inst. 46; Adviser to Initial Teaching Alphabet Foundation 65-67; Chair. Book Devt. Council 65-67.
Leisure interests: reading, writing, painting.
Publs. *History of Europe in the Sixteenth and Seventeenth Centuries* 35, *Outline of Man's History* 39, *The Lid Lifts* 45, *Re-statement of Liberty* 51, *The Commonwealth* 62, *The Cabinet* 70.
105 Frobisher House, Dolphin Square, London, S.W.1, England.

Gordy, Walter, B.A., M.A., PH.D.; American professor of physics; b. 20 April 1909, Lawrence, Miss.; s. of Walter Kalin Gordy and Gertrude (Jones) Gordy; m. Vida Brown Miller 1935; one s. one d.; ed. Mississippi Coll., Clinton, and Univ. of N. Carolina, Chapel Hill.
Associate Prof. of Mathematics and Physics, Mary Hardin-Baylor Coll., Belton, Tex. 35-41; Nat. Research Fellow, Calif. Inst. of Technology, Pasadena 41-42; mem. Staff, Radiation Lab., Mass. Inst. of Technology 42-46; Assoc. Prof. of Physics, Duke Univ., Durham, N.C. 46-48, Prof. 48-; James B. Duke Prof. 58-; Visiting Prof. of Physics, Univ. of Tex. 58; mem. Nat. Research Council 54-57, 68-74; Fellow, American Physical Soc., Chair. S.E. Section 53-54, mem. Council 67-71, 73-; Fellow, American Asscn. for the Advancement of Science (Council 55); mem. Radiation Research Soc. (Council 61-64); mem. Nat. Acad. of Sciences; Assoc. Editor *Journal of Chemical Physics* 55-58, *Spectrochimica Acta* 57-60; mem. Editorial Board *Radiation Research* 69-72; Science Research Award, Oak Ridge Inst. of Nuclear Studies 48, Jesse W. Beams Medal, Amer. Physical Soc. (Southeastern Section) 74; Dr. h.c. (Univ. of Lille) 55; Hon. LL.D. (Miss. Coll.) 59.
Publs. *Microwave Spectroscopy* (with W. V. Smith and R. F. Trambarulo) 53, *Chemical Applications of Spectroscopy* (with others) 56, *Microwave Molecular Spectra* (with R. L. Cook) 70; research papers on infra-red spectroscopy, microwave spectroscopy, magnetic resonance, millimetre and submillimetre wave radiation, nuclear moments, molecular structures, chemical physics.
Office: Department of Physics, Duke University, Durham, N.C. 27706; Home: 2521 Perkins Road, Durham, N.C. 27706, U.S.A.
Telephone: 919-684-8112 (Office); 919-489-4206 (Home).

Gore-Booth, Baron (Life Peer), cr. 69, of Maltby in the West Riding of the County of Yorkshire; **Paul Henry Gore-Booth,** G.C.M.G., K.C.V.O.; British diplomatist; b. 3 Feb. 1909, Doncaster; s. of Mordaunt Gore-Booth and Evelyn Mary Scholfield; m. Patricia Mary Ellerton 1940; two s. two d.; ed. Eton and Balliol Coll., Oxford.
Third Sec. Foreign Office 33, Vienna 36, Tokyo 37; Second Sec. Tokyo 38, Shanghai Oct.-Nov. 41, Washington Dec. 42, acting First Sec. Nov. 43; mem. U.K. del. to Int. Food Conf. Hot Springs 43, UNRRA Conf. Atlantic City 43, Civil Aviation Conf., Chicago 44, U.N. Preparatory Confs., Dumbarton Oaks 44, San Francisco 45; transferred to Foreign Office 45; Sec. to U.K. Del. to first meeting of U.N. Gen. Assembly, London Jan. 46; promoted to Foreign Service Officer, Grade 6, as Head of Refugee and U.N. Economic and Social Depts. July 47; Head of European Recovery Dept., Foreign Office 48; Dir.-Gen. British Information Services, Washington 49-53; Ambassador to Burma 53-56; Deputy Under-Sec. of State, Foreign Office 56-60; High Commr. in India 60-65; Perm. Under-Sec. of State Foreign Office (later Foreign and Commonwealth Office) 65-Feb. 69; Head of Diplomatic Service March 68-Feb. 69; Dir. Grindlays Bank Ltd. (fmrly. Nat. and Grindlays Bank), U.K. Provident Inst.; Chair. Save the Children Fund,

Windsor Music Festival 71-73; Chair., Governing Body, School of Oriental and African Studies, London Univ. 75-.
Leisure interests: Sherlock Holmes, music, theatre, camping, languages.
Publ. *With Great Truth and Respect* (memoirs) 74.
70 Ashley Gardens, Westminster, London, S.W.1, England.

Górecki, Henryk; Polish composer; b. 6 Dec. 1933, Czernica, near Rybnik; studied composition in Warsaw State Higher School of Music under B. Szabelski.
Docent, Faculty of Composition, State Higher School of Music, Katowice, Rector 75-; First Prize, Young Composers' Competition, Warsaw, for *Monologhi* 60, Paris Youth Biennale, for *1st Symphony* 61; Prize, UNESCO Int. Tribune for Composers for *Refrain* 67, for *Ad Matrem* 73; First Prize, Composers' Competition, Szczecin, for *Kantata* 68; Prize of Union of Polish Composers 70, of Cttee. for Polish Radio and TV 74, of Minister of Culture and Arts 65, 69, 73.
Ul. Feliksa Kona 4 m.1, 40-133 Katowice, Poland.

Goren, Maj.-Gen. Shlomo; Israeli rabbi; b. 1917, Poland; *m.*; one *s.* two *d.*; ed. Hebrew Univ.
Settled in Palestine 25; Co-founder Kfar Hassidim; Chief Chaplain, Israel Defence Forces; Chief Rabbi of Tel-Aviv (elected June 68); Ashkenazi Chief Rabbi of Israel Oct. 72-; Rabbi Kook Prize.
Publs. *Nezer Hakodesh* (on Maimonides), *Shaarei Tahara*, *Talmud Yerushalmi Meforash*, *Torath Ha Moadim*, etc., as well as works on religion in military life, prayers for soldiers etc.
Chief Rabbinate, Hechal Shlomo, Jerusalem, Israel.

Goret, Pierre; French veterinary researcher; b. 27 Aug. 1907, Rosières en Santerre; *s.* of Lucien Goret and Henriette Bouffette; *m.* Yvonne Boulet 1931; one *s.* two *d.*; ed. Coll. Providence, Amiens, Ecole de Médecine, Amiens, and Ecole Vétérinaire, Alfort.
Professor, Ecole Vétérinaire Lyon 46-55, Ecole Vétérinaire Alfort 55-; Asst. Lecturer, Univ. de Paris à la Sorbonne, l'Institut Pasteur, l'Institut Agronomique, etc.; mem. Académie de Médecine and Académie Vétérinaire; Fellow Ecoles Vétérinaires 45; Officier Légion d'Honneur; Foreign Corresp. mem. Royal Soc. of Medicine, London; Expert, WHO Zoonoses Cttee.
Leisure interests: philately, reading.
Publs. on various subjects dealing with comparative pathology and microbiology, especially with reference to virus ailments in animals and zoonoses.
31 rue Faidherbe, 94160 Saint-Mandé (Val-de-Marne), France.
Telephone: 328-26-70.

Gorev, Nikolay Nikolayevich; Soviet pathologist; b. 21 April 1900, Kazan; ed. Irkutsk Univ.
Asst. of Pathological Chair., Irkutsk Univ. 26-31; Head of Chair., Khabarovsk Med. Inst. 31-34; Head of Dept. Inst. of Experimental Biology and Pathology 34-53; Corresp. mem. U.S.S.R. Acad. of Medical Sciences 45-53 mem. 53-; Head of Chair. Kiev Stomatological Inst. 45-55; Head of Laboratory, Kiev Inst. of Physiology 53-60, Kiev Inst. of Tuberculosis 55-58; Dir. Inst. of Gerontology and Experimental Pathology 58-61, Head of Lab. 61-; mem. of Board, U.S.S.R. Socs. of Pathophysiologists, Gerontologists, Cardiologists; has participated in congresses and symposiums in Norway, Britain, Czechoslovakia, Hungary, etc.; Order of Lenin, Badge of Honour, Merited Scientist of Ukrainian S.S.R.
Publs. About 120 works on pathology of cardiovascular system, shock, hypertension, gerontology.
Institute of Gerontology, 67 Vyshgorodskaya Street, Kiev, U.S.S.R.

Goring, Marius; British actor; b. 23 May 1912, Newport, Isle of Wight; *m.* Lucie Mannheim; ed. Perse School, Cambridge and Univs. of Frankfurt, Munich and Paris.

Studied for the stage under Harcourt Williams and Old Vic Dramatic School; first London stage appearance 27; joined Old Vic and appeared in many leading Shakespearian and other classical roles; has appeared throughout Europe and acted in German and French; founded the company of Shakespeare Comedians 57, subsequently undertook Arts Council tour of Paris, Netherlands, Finland and India with them; now appears frequently in the London theatres, at the Royal Shakespeare Theatre, Stratford-upon-Avon and other theatres in U.K.; Vice-Pres. British Actors' Equity Assen. 75-; recent stage appearances include: *The Apple Cart* (Cambridge), *The Devil's Disciple* (Yvonne Arnaud Theatre), *The Bells* (Derby and London), *Sleuth* (London), *The Wisest Fool* (Yvonne Arnaud Theatre); television: *The Expert*, *Year of the Crow*, *The Gamekeeper*, *Fall of Eagles*.
Films include: *The Red Shoes*, *A Matter of Life and Death*, *So Little Time*, *Up from the Beach*, *Subterfuges* 68, *First Love* 69.
c/o Film Rights Ltd., 113/117 Wardour Street, London, W1V 4EH, England.

Gorizontov, Pyotr Dmitrievich; Soviet pathophysiologist; b. 3 Sept. 1920, Petropavlovsk; *m.* 1928; one *d.*; ed. Omsk Medical Inst.
Junior Research Assoc., Omsk Medical Inst. 27-30; Senior Research Assoc., Lenin Acad. of Agricultural Sciences 30-32; Head of Laboratory, Deputy Dir. Inst. of Public Health, Magnitogorsk 32-34; Junior Research Assoc., Asst. Prof., Head of Chair, First Moscow Medical Inst. 34-52; Head of Chair, Cen. Inst. of Postgraduate Medical Training 53-60; Head of Laboratory, Deputy Dir., Dir. Inst. of Biophysics, U.S.S.R. Ministry of Public Health 52-; mem. C.P.S.U. 57-; Corresp. mem. U.S.S.R. Acad. of Medical Sciences 52-62, mem. 62-; mem. of Hon. U.S.S.R. Soc. of Röntgenologists and Radiologists; mem. Board U.S.S.R. Soc. of Pathophysiologists; Order of Lenin (three times), Red Banner of Labour, Badge of Honour, Lenin Prize 63.
Leisure interest: nature photography.
Publs. Over 100 works, including monographs *Effect of brain on cholesterine metabolism*, *Pathological physiology of acute radiation sickness resulting from external ionizing radiation*.
Institute of Biophysics, U.S.S.R. Ministry of Public Health, 46 Zhivopisnaya ulitsa, Moscow; Apartment 120, 24 Kutuzovsky prospekt, Moscow, U.S.S.R.
Telephone: 249-31-18 (Home).

Gorkin, Alexandr Fyodorovich; Soviet politician and lawyer; b. 5 Sept. 1897, Rameshki, Kalinin; ed. Tver High School.
Held Party and Soviet Exec. posts 17-37; mem. C.P.S.U. 16-; mem. Presidium and Sec. to Cen. Exec. Cttee. of U.S.S.R. 37; Sec. of Presidium of Supreme Soviet of the U.S.S.R. 38-53, Deputy Sec. 53-56, Sec. 56; Chair. of the Supreme Court of the U.S.S.R. 57-72; Deputy to the Supreme Soviet of the U.S.S.R. 37-; mem. Auditing Comm. C.P.S.U.; awarded Order of Lenin (three times), Hero of Socialist Labour, Hammer and Sickle Gold Medal.
Supreme Court of the U.S.S.R., 15 Ulitsa Vorovskogo, Moscow, U.S.S.R.

Goronwy-Roberts, Baron (Life Peer), cr. 74, of Caernarvon and of Ogwen; **Goronwy Owen Roberts,** P.C.; British politician; b. 20 Sept. 1913, Rhos, Wrexham; *s.* of Edward and Amelia Roberts; *m.* Marian Ann Evans 1942; one *s.* one *d.*; ed. Ogwen Grammar School, Univ. Coll. of N. Wales, Bangor, and Univ. of London.
Infantry, Army Reserve 41; Youth Education Officer, Caerns. Educ. Authority 41-44; M.P. 45-74; Minister of State, Welsh Office 64-66, Dept. of Education and Science 66-67, Foreign Office 67-69, Board of Trade 69-70; Parl. Under-Sec. of State for Foreign and Com-

monwealth Affairs 74-75; Minister of State for Foreign and Commonwealth Affairs 75-; mem. House of Commons Panel of Chairmen 63-64; Chair. Regional Econ. Cttee. for Wales 65; fmr. Chair. Hughes & Son Ltd., Publishers, Wrexham; fmr. Lecturer in Education, Univ. Coll., Swansea; Leader, U.K. del. UN Human Rights Conf., Teheran 68, Commonwealth Parl. Conf., Nassau 68; mem. Court of Govs., Univ. Coll. of Wales, Nat. Museum of Wales; mem. Fabian Soc.; Trustee, Oppenheimer Trust for Ex-Servicemen; Fellow, Royal Soc. of Arts 67; Freeman Royal Borough of Caernarvon; Hon. Fellow Univ. Coll., Aberystwyth; Labour.
Leisure interests: walking, music, collecting year books.
Foreign and Commonwealth Office, Downing Street, London, SW1A 2AH; Homes: Plas Newydd, Pwllheli, Gwynedd, Wales; 5 Oakover Manor, North Side, London, S.W.4, England.

Gorresio, Vittorio, D.IUR.; Italian writer; b. 18 July 1910, Modena; s. of Marco Gorresio and Teresa Silvestro; m. Alessandra E. Bolis 1958; ed. Rome Univ.
Rome corresp. of *La Stampa* (Turin) 48-; Liberal.
Leisure interests: riding, golf.
Publs. *Un Anno di Libertà* 45, *I Moribondi di Montecitorio* 47, *I Carissimi Nemici* 49, *I Bracci Secolari* 51, *Risorgimento Scomunicato* 58, *L'Italia a Sinistra* 63, *La Nuova Missione (Il Papato di Giovanni XXIII)* 68, *Roma Ieri e Oggi* 70, *Il Sesto Presidente* 72, *Il Papa e il Diavolo* 73.
Piazza Navona 106, Rome, Italy.
Telephone: 561468.

Gorse, Georges; French diplomatist; b. 15 Feb. 1915; ed. Lycée Louis-le-Grand and Ecole Normale Supérieure (Agrégé de Lettres).
Prof. French Lycée at Cairo 39-40; Prof. Fouad I Univ. 40; joined Gen. de Gaulle 40; Dep.-Chief Cabinet of Gen. de Gaulle at Algiers 44 and at Paris 45; Mem. of the Consultative and Constituent Assemblies; Dep. of la Vendée 46; Under Sec. of State for Moslem Affairs 47; Under Sec. of State for French territories overseas 49; Mem. of the Assembly of the Union Française 51-; Del. UN sessions at San Francisco and New York; Ambassador to Tunisia 57-61; Sec. of State for Foreign Affairs (relations with African States of *Expression Française*) 61-62; Minister of Co-operation May-Nov. 62; Amb. to Algeria 63-67; Minister of Information April 67-May 68, of Labour, Employment and Population 73-74.
11 rue Magellan, Paris 15e, France.

Gorshkov, Admiral Sergei Georgievich; Soviet naval officer; b. 26 Feb. 1910, Kamenets-Podolsk, Ukraine; ed. Naval School, Frunze.
Flotilla Commdr. Black Sea. Sea of Azov. and Danube 41-44; Squadron Commdr. Black Sea Fleet 44-48, Chief of Staff 48-51, Commdr. Black Sea Fleet 51-55; First Deputy C.-in-C. U.S.S.R. Fleet 55-56; Deputy Minister of Defence of U.S.S.R. 56-; Commdr.-in-Chief U.S.S.R. Fleet 56-; Admiral of the Fleet 62-; Admiral of the Fleet of the Soviet Union 67-; mem. C.P.S.U. 42-; Deputy to Supreme Soviet U.S.S.R. 54-, mem. Planning and Budgetary Comm., Soviet of Nationalities; Candidate mem. Central Cttee., C.P.S.U. 56-61, mem. 61-; Hero of the Soviet Union; awarded Order of Lenin (thrice), October Revolution, "Gold Star" Medal, Kutuzov (1st class), Ushakov (1st and 2nd class), Red Banner (twice), Red Star, Sword of Honour with a Coat-of-Arms in Gold, and other awards.
Ministry of Defence, Naberezhnaya M. Thoreza, 34 Moscow, U.S.S.R.

Gorter, Cornelis Jacobus, PH.D., D.SC., LL.D.; Netherlands physicist; b. 14 Aug. 1907, Utrecht; s. of H. J. Gorter and Anne C. van Eck; m. Lilla C. E. C. von Krogh 1938; two s. two d.; ed. Univ. of Leiden.
Lecturer, Univ. of Groningen 36-40; Prof. Univ. of

Amsterdam and Dir. of Zeeman Laboratory 40-46; Prof. Univ. of Leiden and Dir. Kamerlingh Onnes Laboratory 46-73; Vice-Pres. Int. Union of Pure and Applied Physics 46-51 and 60-66; mem. Royal Neths. Acad. of Sciences 46-, Vice-Pres. 50-60, Pres. 60-66; Foreign mem. Royal Swedish Acad. of Sciences, Royal Flemish Acad. of Sciences, Finnish Acad. of Sciences, Royal Norwegian Soc. of Sciences, American Acad. of Arts and Sciences, American Philosophical Soc.; Foreign Assoc. Nat. Acad. of Sciences (U.S.A.) 67-; Dr. h.c. Grenoble, Sorbonne, Canterbury, Córdoba (Argentina), Trondheim; discovered paramagnetic relaxation 36.
Leisure interests: walking, skiing.
Publs. *Paramagnetische Eigenschaften von Salzen* 32, *Paramagnetic Relaxation* 47, *Progress in Low Temperature Physics* (six vols., 55-70).
Burggravenlaan 3, Leiden, Netherlands.
Telephone: 071-124785.

Gorton, Rt. Hon. John Grey, C.H., M.P., M.A.; Australian politician; b. 9 Sept. 1911, Melbourne; s. of J. R. Gorton; m. Bettina Brown 1935; two s. one d.; ed. Geelong Grammar School and Brasenose Coll., Oxford.
Served Royal Australian Air Force during Second World War, severely wounded; Councillor Kerang Shire 47-52, and Pres. of Shire; Senator for State of Victoria 49-68, Govt. Leader in Senate 67-68; Minister for Navy 58-63; Minister Assisting Minister for External Affairs 60-63; Minister-in-Charge of Commonwealth Scientific and Industrial Research Org. (C.S.I.R.O.) 62-68; Minister for Works and under-Prime Minister, Minister-in-Charge of Commonwealth Activities in Educ. and Research 63-66; Minister for Interior 63-64, for Works 66-67; Minister for Educ. and Science 66-68; Prime Minister of Australia Jan. 68-March 71; Minister of Defence and Deputy Leader of Liberal Party March-Aug. 71; mem. Parl. Liberal Party Exec.; Spokesman on Environment and Conservation, Urban & Regional Devt.; Deputy Chair. of Joint Parl. Cttee. on Prices 73-74; mem. House of Reps. Feb. 68-; fmrly. Liberal, Independent May 75-.
Leisure interests: reading, swimming.
Parliament House, Canberra, A.C.T. 2600, Australia.

Goryachkin, Alexander Vasilyevich; Soviet politician; b. 1910; ed. Moscow Engineering and Economics Inst.
Director, later Chief Engineer of textile mill in Kostroma 30-39; mem. C.P.S.U. 39-; Deputy People's Commissar of Textile Industry of Byelorussian S.S.R. 40-45; Minister of Textile Industry of Byelorussian S.S.R. 45-52; Chair. Council of Producers' Co-operatives of Byelorussian S.S.R. 52-54; Deputy Minister of Light Industry of U.S.S.R. 55-56; Perm. Rep. of Byelorussian S.S.R. Council of Ministers to U.S.S.R. Council of Ministers 56-; mem. Central Cttee. of C.P. of Byelorussia 56-; Deputy to Supreme Soviet of Byelorussian S.S.R.
Permanent Representation of Byelorussian S.S.R. Council of Ministers to U.S.S.R. Council of Ministers, ulitsa Bogdana Khmelnitskogo, Moscow, U.S.S.R.

Goryunov, Dmitry Petrovich; Soviet journalist and diplomatist; b. 30 Sept. 1915, Kovrov, Vladimir; s. of Petre Guerassimovich Goryunov and Aleksandra Federovna; m. Veronika Gabrielevna 1947; one d.; ed. Higher Party School.
Worked as lathe-turner in Kovrov and Ivanovo 30-40; mem. C.P.S.U. 40-, mem. Central Auditing Comm.; Editor youth paper *Leninetz* 34; Leader, Ivanovo District Komsomol Cttee. (youth organization) 40-42; in charge of propaganda, Central Cttee. H.Q. of Komsomol, Moscow 42-45; training at Party school 46-49; Editor *Komsomolskaya Pravda* 49-57; Asst. Editor *Pravda* 57-60; Dir.-Gen. *Tass* Agency 60-67; Amb. to Kenya 67-73, to Morocco 75-; Deputy to Supreme Soviet U.S.S.R. until 70; Alt. mem. of

C.P.S.U. Cen. Cttee.; Order of Red Banner of Labour.
Leisure interest: history of literature.
Embassy of the U.S.S.R., 20 Avenue Annegai, Rabat,
Morocco.

Gosline, James E., PH.D.; American President of
Standard Oil Co. of California 67-69; see *The International Who's Who 1975-76*.

Gošnjak, Ivan, Gen. of the Army; Yugoslav soldier
and politician; b. 1909; ed. Grammar School in Pakrac.
Sometime carpenter and local trade union leader in
Sisak; joined (illegal) Communist Party 33; in U.S.S.R.
35-37; fought with Spanish Republican Army 37-39;
imprisoned in concentration camp in France 39-41;
fought with Nat. Liberation Army in Yugoslavia
42-45; commanded 1st Croatian Corps; Commdr. Gen.
Headquarters of Croatia; Commdr. Zagreb Army
after 45; Mem. of Parl. 45-63; Deputy Minister of
Defence 48-53; mem. of Fed. Exec. Council of Yugoslavia and Sec. of State for Defence 53-67; mem.
Praesidium of Cen. Cttee. of the Communist League of
Yugoslavia; mem. Council of the Fed.; decorations
include Orders of Freedom, of the National Hero,
and Spanish (Republican), French, Greek, Soviet,
Czechoslovak, Romanian, Polish, Albanian, Egyptian,
Ethiopian and other honours.
Kneza Miloša 33, Belgrade, Yugoslavia.

Goss, Richard John; South African chartered accountant; b. 8 July 1928, Cape Town; *m.*; one *s.* two *d.*; ed.
Rondebosch Boys' High School and Cape Town.
Joined S.A. Breweries as Management Accountant,
Head Office, Johannesburg 52, Chief Accountant 54-57,
Asst. Admin. Man. 57-60, Group Commercial Man. 60-
64; attended Harvard Business School, U.S.A. 64; Gen.
Man., Beer Div., S.A. Breweries 65-67, Group Man. Dir.
67-; Board mem. of all major cos. of S.A. Breweries
Group; Dir. Netherlands Bank of S. Africa Ltd. and
Southern Life Asscn.
Leisure interest: tennis.
The South African Breweries Ltd., P.O. Box 1099,
2 Jan Smuts Avenue, Johannesburg, South Africa.

Gosse, Edmund Barr, M.A. (CANTAB.); Australian
company director; b. 14 July 1915, Perth; *s.* of late Sir
James Gosse; *m.* Christel Gebhardt 1939; one *s.* one *d.*;
ed. St. Peter's Coll., Adelaide, Trinity Hall, Cambridge.
Manager Lysaght's Works, Newcastle 53-63; Chair.
John Lysaght (Aust.) Ltd. 67-; Dir. Guest, Keen and
Nettlefolds (Overseas) Ltd.; mem. Iron & Steel Inst.,
U.K.; Dir. ICI Australia Ltd.
Leisure interests: gardening, squash.
27 Sutherland Crescent, Darling Point, NSW 2027,
Australia.

Gosztonyi, Dr. János; Hungarian politician; b. 1925;
ed. Univ. of Economic Sciences, Budapest.
Member of Parl. 47-; Head of Editorial Board *Népszabadság* 65-70; Deputy Minister of Cultural Affairs 70-;
State Sec. of Educ. 74-; mem. Central Cttee. Hungarian
Socialists Workers' Party.
Ministry of Education, H-1884 Budapest V, Szalay-u.
10/14, Hungary.
Telephone: 118-600.

Gott, Edwin Hays; American steel executive; b.
22 Feb. 1908, Pittsburgh, Pa.; *s.* of Leonard Hays and
Isabel Dalzell; *m.* Mary L. Carr 1934; one *s.* two *d.*; ed.
Lehigh Univ.
With U.S. Steel Corpn. 37-; beginning as Industrial
Engineer, Ohio Works; Vice-Pres. (Operations-Steel)
56-58, Vice-Pres. (Production-Steel Producing Divs.)
58-59, Admin. Vice-Pres. (Cen. Operations) 59, Exec.
Vice-Pres. (Production) 59-67, Pres. and Chief Admin.
Officer, U.S. Steel Corpn. 67-68, Chair. and Chief Exec.
Officer 69-73, Dir., mem. Exec. Cttee. 73-; official and
mem. of civic and business orgs.

Leisure interests: hunting, fishing.
U.S. Steel Corporation, 600 Grant Street, Pittsburgh, Pa. 15230, U.S.A.
Telephone: 412-433-1191.

Gott, Rodney Cleveland; American business executive;
b. 11 Sept. 1911, Brooklyn, N.Y.; *s.* of Charles C. D.
Gott and Florence Hutchinson; *m.* Lydia G. McAdam
1933; three *s.*; ed. U.S. Military Acad.
American Radiator and Standard Sanitary Corpn. 35-41;
AMF Inc. (fmrly. American Machine & Foundry Co.),
New York City 46-, Vice-Pres. 46-54, Exec. Vice-Pres.
54-62, Pres. 62-70, 73-, also Chair. and Chief Exec.
Officer 68-.
Leisure interests: tennis, water sports.
AMF Inc., 777 Westchester Avenue, White Plains,
N.Y. 10604, U.S.A.
Telephone: 914-694-9000.

Gotta, Salvatore; Italian novelist and dramatist; b.
18 May 1887.
Publs. *Pia* 12, *Il figlio inquieto* 17, *La più bella donna
del mondo* 19, *L'amante provinciale* 19, *Tre mondi* 21,
Il primo re 22, *La donna mia* 24, *Lula—misticismo e
sensualità* 25, *Ombra la moglie bella* 26, *Il nome tuo* 27,
La sagra delle virgini 28, *Il peccato originale* 29, *Tu, la
mia ricchezza* 30, *L'amica dell'ombra* 32, *Il gioco dei
colori* 32, *I figli degli amanti* 33, *Lilith* 34, *Il paradiso
terrestre* 35, *L'angelo ferito* 36, *Portofino* 37, *I giganti
innamorati* 38, *Amina* 39, *La sposa giovane* 40, *I sensitivi* 46, *Piccolo alpino* 26, *Il diavolo in provincia* 29,
Serenata alle vergini 30, *Bella figlia dell'amore* 34, *La
signora di tutti* 35, *A bocca nuda* 37, *Tre donne innamorate* 39, *Un fiore sull'autostrada* 40, *Ottocento* 43,
Di là dal fiume c'è una donna 44, *Il volto dell'umano
amore* 44, *Ingrid, l'amica delle nuvole* 44, *Quartetto in
paradiso* 45, *Macerie a Portofino* 46, *Signore salvaci, ci
perdiamo* 47, 72, *Lo specchio dei sensi* 48, *Domani a Te* 50,
Tempo della Regina Margherita 51, *La Saga dei Vela*
(3 vols.) 55, *Ilaria* 56, *L'Almandco di Gotta* 58, *Orgasmo*
60, *Due Donne a Sirmione* 61, *Le Signore della Villa
Antica* 62, *I Diavoli del Gran Paradiso* 62, *Zaira ragazza
del Cirro* 63, *Aria del mio Paese* 64, *L'ultimo dei Vela* 65,
Il progresso si diverte 67, *L'indemoniata* 69, *Murat* 70, *Il
fiore di Matisse* 72, *Corradino di Svevia* 73, *Prendersi e
Casciarsi*.
Villa Aranci, Portofino (Genoa), Italy.

Götze, Heinz, DR. PHIL.; German publisher; b. 8 Aug.
1912, Dresden; ed. Univs. of Leipzig, Munich and Naples.
Partner (Co-Proprietor) Springer-Verlag, Berlin, Heidelberg, New York 57-, J. F. Bergmann Verlagsbuchhandlung, Munich 57-; Lange & Springer, Scientific Bookshop, Berlin 57-; Pres. of Springer-Verlag New York
Inc. 64-; mem. Board of Dirs. Universitätsdruckerei
H. Stürtz A.G., Würzburg 65-; Corresp. mem. German
Archaeological Inst. 56-; Dr. Med. h.c. Univs. of
Heidelberg and Erlangen 72.
Home: Ludolf Krehl-Strasse 41, D-69 Heidelberg;
Springer-Verlag, D-69 Heidelberg, Neuenheimer Landstr. 28-30, Federal Republic of Germany.
Telephone: 487225 (Office).

Goudsmit, Samuel Abraham, O.B.E., PH.D.; American
physicist; b. 11 July 1902, The Hague, Netherlands;
s. of Isaac Goudsmit and Marianne Gompers; *m.* 1st
Jaantje Logher 1927, one *d.*, 2nd Irene B. Rothschild
1960; ed. Univs. of Leyden and Amsterdam.
Published theory of electron spin (with George Uhlenbeck) 25; Rockefeller Fellowship 26; Lecturer in
Physics, Univ. of Michigan 27-32, Prof. 32-46; Guggenheim Fellowship 38; Visiting Prof. Harvard Univ. 41;
mem. radar research team at Mass. Institute of Technology and in England 42-46; Head of Scientific
Intelligence Mission in Europe 44-45; Prof. of Physics,
Northwestern Univ. 46-48; Senior Scientist, Brookhaven Nat. Laboratory 48-70, Head of Physics Dept.

52-60; corresp. mem. Royal Netherlands Acad. of Sciences; mem. American Acad. of Arts and Sciences, American Philosophical Soc.; Fellow Amer. Physical Soc., Netherlands Physical Soc., Nat. Acad. of Science, Amer. Nuclear Soc.; Editor-in-Chief American Physical Soc. 51-74; Founder and Editor *Physical Review Letters*; Medal of Freedom 46, Research Corpn. Science Award 54, Max-Planck Medal, German Physical Soc. 65; Karl T. Compton Award for Distinguished Statesmanship in Science, Amer. Inst. of Physics 74; Hon. D.Sc. Case Inst. Tech. 58, Univ. Chicago 72, Utah State Univ. 72.
Leisure interest: Egyptology.
Publs. *Also* 47 and numerous articles on the structure of atoms.
Brookhaven National Laboratory, Upton, N.Y. 11973, U.S.A.
Telephone: 516-345-2543.

Gough, Rt. Rev. Hugh Rowlands, C.M.G., O.B.E., T.D., M.A., D.D.; British ecclesiastic; b. 19 Sept. 1905, Pakistan; s. of Rev. Charles Massey Gough; m. Madeline Elizabeth Kinnaird 1929; one d.; ed. Cambridge Univ., London Coll. of Divinity.
Deacon 28, Priest 29; Curate St. Mary Islington 28-31; Perpetual Curate St. Paul, Walcot, Bath 31-34; Vicar St. James Carlisle 34-39, St. Matthew Bayswater 39-46; of Islington and Rural Dean 46-48; Prebendary St. Paul's Cathedral 48; Archdeacon West Ham 48-58; Suffragan Bishop of Barking 48-59; Archbishop of Sydney 59-66, Primate of Australia 59-66; retd. 72; mem. Council London Coll. of Divinity, Clifton Theological Coll., Haileybury Coll., Monkton Combe School, St. Lawrence Coll., Chigwell School, Stowe School, Kingham Hill Trust; war service 39-45, O.B.E. (Mil.), mentioned in despatches; Hon. Chaplain to the Forces 2nd Class; Hon. D.D. (Wycliffe, Toronto), Hon. Th.D. (Australia).
20 Sion Hill, Bath, Avon, England.
Telephone: Bath 313660.

Gouhier, Henri Gaston; French university professor and writer; b. 5 Dec. 1898, Auxerre; m. Marie-Louise Dufour; one d.; ed. Ecole normale supérieure and Faculté des lettres de Paris.
Professor, Faculty of Literature, Lille Univ. 29-41, Univ. of Paris 41-68; mem. Acad. des Sciences morales et politiques 61-, Royal Acad. of Belgium; Officier Légion d'Honneur; Grand Prix de littérature de l'Acad. Française 65.
Leisure interest: theatre.
Publs. *La Pensée religieuse de Descartes* 24, *La Vocation de Malebranche* 26, *La Philosophie de Malebranche et son expérience religieuse* 26, *Notre ami Maurice Barrès* 28, *La Vie d'Auguste Comte* 31, *L'Essence du théâtre* 43, *La jeunesse d'Auguste Comte et la formation du positivisme* (3 vols.) 33, 36, 41, *Les Conversions de Maine de Biran* 47, *la Philosophie et son histoire* 44, *L'Histoire et sa philosophie* 52, *Le Théâtre et l'existence* 52, *Les Premières Pensées de Descartes* 58, *L'Oeuvre théâtrale* 58, *Bergson et le Christ des Evangiles* 61 (Prix Lecomte de Nouy 62), *La Pensée métaphysique de Descartes* 62, *Pascal, Commentaires* 66, *Benjamin Constant* 67, *Les Méditations Métaphysiques de J. J. Rousseau* 70, *Le Combat de Marie Noel* 71, *Renan, auteur dramatique* 72, *Pascal et les Humanistes Chrétiens: L'Affaire Saint-Ange* 74, *Antonin Artaud et l'essence du théâtre* 74.
21 boulevard Flandrin, Paris 16e, France.
Telephone: 504-16-09.

Goulart, Dr. João Belchior Marques; Brazilian politician; b. 1 March 1918; ed. Rio Grande do Sul Univ.
Joined Partido Trabalhista 45, National Party Dir. 51; Minister of Labour, Industry and Commerce 53-54; elected Vice-Pres. of Brazil 56, re-elected 61; Pres. of Brazil 61-64.
Montevideo, Uruguay.

Gould, Beatrice Blackmar, B.A., M.S.; American magazine editor and writer; b. Emmetsburg, Iowa; d. of H. E. Blackmar and Mary K. Fluke; m. Charles Bruce Gould 1923; one d.; ed. State Univ. of Iowa and Columbia Univ.
Newspaper reporter and woman's editor *N.Y. Sunday World* 26-29; writer for magazines 29-35; Editor (with husband) *Ladies' Home Journal* 35-62; various journalistic awards (with husband).
Leisure interests: theatre, books, sailing, swimming, dancing.
Publs. *Man's Estate* 27, *The Terrible Turk* 34, *American Story* 68 (two plays and autobiography, with husband).
Bedensbrook, Hopewell, N.J., U.S.A.
Telephone: 609-466-0170.

Gould, Glenn; Canadian composer and pianist; b. 1932, Toronto; ed. Royal Toronto Conservatory of Music.
Studied with Alberto Guerrero; Assoc. of Conservatory of Music at age of twelve; played at Eaton Auditorium in Casavant series 46; debut with Toronto Symphony Orchestra 46, debut in U.S.A. 55; concert performances throughout the world including in Moscow, Leningrad 57; gave up public performances 64; recordings 64-; fmr. Lecturer Toronto Univ.; Founder, Musical Dir. New Music Assocs. of Toronto; recordings for Columbia Records (CBS) 55-; recordings, TV, radio programmes for Canadian Broadcasting Comm.; has written articles on music, and documentary *The Idea of the North*.
c/o Canadian Broadcasting Commission, 1500 Bronson Avenue, Ottawa Ont., K1G 3J5, Canada.

Gould, Kingdon, Jr., A.B., LL.B.; American diplomatist; b. 3 Jan. 1924, N.Y.; s. of Kingdon and Annunziata (Lucci), Gould; m. Mary Bunce Thorne 1945; four s. five d.; ed. High School in Millbrook, N.Y., Yale Univ. and Yale Law School.
Director Consolidated Coal Co. 45-50; Organizer and Principal, A & G Partnership, Parking Man. Inc. 53-69; Amb. to Luxembourg 69-72, to The Netherlands 73-; Founder and Chair. Glenelg Country School 54-; Dir. Butler Bros. 55-57; Incorporator and Dir. State Bank of Laurel, Md. 56-63; Org. White Mountain Nat. Bank 62; Org. and Dir. Madison Nat. Bank 63-69; Chair. Murray Corpn. 64-69; mem. Maryland Board of Natural Resources 68-69.
Leisure interests: riding, swimming, fly fishing, tennis, golf, skiing, chess.
Tobias Asserlaan, The Hague, Netherlands; Home: Overlook Drive, Laurel, Md. 20810, U.S.A.
Telephone: 070-624911 (The Hague).

Gould, Laurence McKinley, LL.D., SC.D., L.H.D., LITT.D., B.S., M.A.; American geologist; b. 22 Aug. 1896; ed. Univ. of Michigan.
Professor of Geology, Univ. of Michigan 21-32; Prof. of Geology Carleton Coll., Northfield 32-45; Chief Arctic Section, U.S. Army Air Force 42-44; Pres. Carleton Coll. 45-62; Prof. of Geology, Univ. of Arizona 63-; Dir. U.S. Antarctic Programme for Int. Geophysical Year; Trustee Ford Foundation; mem. Nat. Science Board; Trustee Carnegie Foundation for the Advancement of Teaching; Sc.D. h.c.
Publs. *Geological and Geographical Results of Putnam Baffin Island Expedition, Geographical Results of Byrd Antarctic Expedition* 31, *The Geology of La Sal Mountains, Utah* 36, *Glaciers of Antarctica, Structure of Queen Maud Mountains, Antarctica, Cold—The Record of an Antarctic Sledge Journey*.
9451 East Rosewood, Tucson, Ariz. 85710, U.S.A.

Gould, Samuel Brookner, A.B., A.M.; American university chancellor; b. 11 Aug. 1910, New York; s. of Nathaniel Gould and Lina Brookner; m. Laura J. Ohman 1936; one s.; ed. Bates Coll., New York Univ., Oxford, Cambridge and Harvard Univs.

Instructor, William Hall High School, W. Hartford, Conn. 32-38; Head, Dept. of Speech, Brookline, Mass. Schools 38-47; Prof. of Radio, Speech, Dir. of Div. of Radio, Speech and Theatre, Boston Univ. 47-50; Asst. to Pres., Boston Univ. 50-53; Senior Assoc., Cresap, McCormick & Paget 53-54; Pres. Antioch Coll. 54-59; Chancellor, Univ. of Calif. at Santa Barbara 59-62; Pres. Educational Broadcasting Corpn. 62-64; Chancellor, State Univ. of New York 64-70, Emeritus 70-; Dir. McKinsey and Co. Inc. 70-71; Vice-Pres. Educ. Testing Service and Pres. Inst. for Educ. Devt. 71-74; mem. numerous educational and civic cttees.; Hon. LL.D. (Bates Coll., Wilberforce Univ., Union Coll., New York Univ., Alfred Univ., Univ. of California, Colgate Univ.), Hon. L.H.D. (Alfred Univ.), Hon. Litt.D. (Univ. of Akron).
Leisure interest: golf.
Publs. *Knowledge is Not Enough* 59, *Training the Local Announcer* (with S. A. Diamond) 50, *Explorations in Non-Traditional Study* (co-editor) 72, *Diversity by Design* (co-author) 73.
1055 Bogey Lane, Sarasota, Fla. 33577, U.S.A.
Telephone: 813-388-2996.

Goulden, Mark; British journalist and publisher; *s.* of Morris and Eve Goulden; *m.* Jane Moore 1932; two *s.* one *d.*; ed. Clifton, Bristol.
Reporter on *Cambridge Daily News* 13; Managing Editor and Dir. *Eastern Morning News* and *Hull Evening News* 23-30; Managing Editor *Yorkshire Evening News*, Leeds 30-32; Managing Editor *Sunday Referee* 32-36; fmr. Managing Editor *Cavalcade*, etc.; Chief Editor Argus Press Ltd.; Dir. Illustrated Publications Ltd. and Macfadden's Magazines Ltd. 36-41; Chair. W. H. Allen & Co. 39-; Dir. Howard and Wyndham 70-(76).
Leisure interests: pioneer of British flying, speaking and writing on press and publishing.
14 Carlos Place, London, W.1, England; and 295 Madison Avenue, New York, N.Y. 10017, U.S.A.
Telephone: 01-491-7646.

Goulian, Mehran, A.B., M.D.; American physician; b. 31 Dec. 1929, Weehawken, N.J.; *s.* of Dicran Goulian and Shamiram Mzrakjian; *m.* Susan Hook 1961; three *s.*; ed. Columbia Coll. and Columbia Coll. of Physicians and Surgeons.
Fellow in Medicine (Hematology), Yale Univ. School of Medicine 59-60; Research Fellow in Medicine (Hematology), Harvard Univ. July-Dec. 60, 62-63, Instructor in Medicine 63-65; Clinical and Research Fellow in Medicine (Hematology), Mass. Gen. Hospital July-Dec. 60, 62-63, Asst. in Medicine 63-65; Fellow in Biochemistry, Stanford Univ. School of Medicine 65-67; Research Assoc. in Biochemistry, Univ. of Chicago and Argonne Cancer Research Hospital 67-69, Assoc. Prof. of Medicine 67-70, Assoc. Prof. of Biochemistry 69-70; Prof. of Medicine, Univ. of California, San Diego 70-.
Leisure interest: music.
Department of Medicine, University of California, San Diego, La Jolla, Calif. 92037, U.S.A.
Telephone: 714-452-3016.

Goulli, Slaheddine El, LL.D.; Tunisian diplomatist; b. 22 June 1919, Sousse; *m.* 1958; one *d.*; ed. Collège de Sousse and Université de Paris.
In private industry 47-56; active in Tunisian Nat. Liberation Movement, Europe 47-56; Gen. Consul, Marseilles 56-58; Counsellor, Washington 58, Minister, Washington 59-62; Alt. Exec. Dir. World Bank 61-62; Amb. to Belgium, also accred. to Netherlands and Luxembourg 62, concurrently Perm. Rep. to EEC; Perm. Rep. to UN 69; Amb. to U.S.A. 69-74, also accred. to Mexico 70-74 and Venezuela 72-74; Grand Cordon de l'Ordre de la République Tunisienne 66, also decorations from Belgium and Luxembourg.
5 Rue Zeroud, Gammarth-La Marsa, Tunisia.
Telephone: 270-989.

Gouyon, H.E. Cardinal Paul; French ecclesiastic; b. 24 Oct. 1910, Bordeaux.
Ordained priest 37; consecrated Bishop 57; Bishop of Bayonne 57; Titular Archbishop of Pessinonte 63; Archbishop of Rennes 64-; cr. Cardinal 69.
Archevêché, 3 contour de la Motte, 35-Rennes, France.

Gowon, Gen. Yakubu; Nigerian army officer; b. 19 Oct. 1934, Lur Pankshin Div., Benue Plateau State; *s.* of Yohanna and Saratu Gowon; *m.* Victoria Hansatu 1969; one *s.*; ed. St. Bartholomew's School, Wusasa, Zaria, Govt. Coll., Zaria, Royal Military Acad., Sandhurst, Staff Coll., Camberley and Joint Services Coll., Latimer, England.
Adjutant, Nigerian Army March 60; with UN peacekeeping force, Congo Nov. 60-June 61, 63; promoted Lieut.-Col. and appointed Adjutant-Gen. Nigerian Army June 63; Chief of Staff 66; Maj.-Gen. June 67; promoted General Oct. 71; Head of Fed. Mil. Govt. and C.-in-C. of Armed Forces of Fed. Repub. of Nigeria 66-75 (deposed in coup); studying at Warwick Univ. 75-; Chair. Assembly of Heads of State, Org. of African Unity 73-74.
Leisure interests: squash, tennis, cinematography, pen-drawings.
University of Warwick, Coventry, CV4 7AL, England.

Goyer, Hon. Jean-Pierre, P.C., B.A., LL.B., Canadian lawyer and politician; b. 17 Jan. 1932, St. Laurent, Quebec; *s.* of Gilbert and Marie-Ange Goyer; *m.* Michelle Gascon 1960; three *d.*; ed. Univ. of Montreal.
Member of Parliament 65-; Parl. Sec. to Sec. of State for External Affairs 68-70; Solicitor-Gen. Dec. 70-; Minister of Supply and Services and Receiver Gen. for Canada Nov. 72-; Liberal.
300 The Driveway, Townhouse 6, Ottawa, Ontario, K1S 3M6, Canada.

Graaff, Sir de Villiers, Bart., M.B.E., M.P.; South African politician; b. 8 Dec. 1913; ed. Univs. of Cape Town, Oxford and Leyden (Holland).
Served Second World War; M.P. 48-April 58, June 58-; Chair. United Party, Cape Province 56-58; Leader of the Opposition (United South African Nat. Party) 56-.
De Grendel, Pte. Bag G.P.O. Cape Town, Cape Province, South Africa.

Grabar, André, D. ès L.; (brother of Pierre Grabar, *q.v.*); French art historian and archaeologist; b. 26 July 1896, Kiev, U.S.S.R.; *s.* of Nicolas Grabar and Elizabeth Baronne Prittwitz; *m.* Julie Ivanova 1923; two *s.*
Former Prof. of History of Art, Strasbourg Univ., Ecole des Hautes Etudes 37; Prof. of Early Christian and Byzantine Archaeology, Coll. de France 46-66; mem. Acad. des Inscriptions et Belles Lettres 55-, Dumbarton Oaks Inst., Deutsches Archäologisches Inst. and of other Acads. in U.K., U.S.A., Austria, Bulgaria, Denmark, Norway, Serbia, Italy; founded *Cahiers Archéologiques*; Dr. h.c. (Princeton, Edinburgh and Uppsala Univs.).
Leisure interest: painting.
Publs. *La Peinture Religieuse Bulgare* 28, *L'Empereur dans l'Art Byzantin* 36, *Martyrium* 46, *La Peinture Byzantine* 54, *Le Haut Moyen-Age* 57, *La Peinture Romane* 58, *L'Iconoclasme Byzantin* 58, *Sculptures Byzantines* 63, *Byzance* 63, *Le Premier Art Chrétien* 66, *Le Siècle d'Or de Justinien* 66, *L'Art du Moyen Age en Europe Orientale*, *L'Art de la Fin de l'Antiquité et du Moyen Age* 68, *Christian Iconography, a Study of its Origins* 68.
2 avenue Dode de la Brunerie, Paris 16, France.
Telephone: AUT 3656.

Grabar, Pierre, (brother of André Grabar, *q.v.*); French immunologist; b. 10 Sept. 1898, Kiev, U.S.S.R.; *s.* of Nicolas Grabar and Elizabeth Prittwitz; *m.* Nina Ivanova 1929 (died 1974); one *d.*; ed. Lycée Kiev and Univs. of Strasbourg and Paris.

Lecturer, Univ. of Strasbourg 28-38; Chief of Laboratory, Institut Pasteur 38-45, Chief of Dept. 45-68, Emer. Chief of Dept. 69; Dir. Cancer Research Inst., Nat. Centre for Scientific Research 61-68, Emer. Dir. 69-; mem. French Acad. of Medicine; mem. or hon. mem. numerous int. learned socs.; Officier Légion d'Honneur, Commdr. des Palmes académiques; Behring Int. Prize; Gairdner Award, Univ. of Toronto; Grande Médaille de la Ville de Lille and several other awards; Prizes of the French Acad. of Science; Dr. h.c. (Copenhagen); Great Medal of First Int. Congress of Immunology 70.
Leisure interests: gardening, stamps, music.
Publs. More than 300 publications (incl. 3 monographs) on immunochemistry, proteins, ultrafiltration, ultrasonics, electrophoresis, etc.
Institut Pasteur, 28 rue du Dr. Roux, Paris 15e; Home: 192 bis, rue de Vaugirard, 75015 Paris, France.
Telephone: 567-85-45 (Home).

Graber, Pierre; Swiss politician; b. 6 Dec. 1908, La Chaux-de-Fonds; s. of Paul and Blanche (née Vuilleumier) Graber; m. Pierrette Meilland; ed. gymnasiums in Neuchâtel and Berne and Univs. of Neuchâtel and Vienna.
Lawyer, Lausanne 33-46; mem. Lausanne Legislative Council 33-46; mem. Great Council of Vaud 37-46; Mayor of Lausanne 46-49; mem. Lausanne City Council and Dir. Dept. of Finance 49-62; mem. Council Canton Vaud, Dir. Dept. of Finance 62-70, Pres. 68; mem. Nat. Council 42-69, Pres. 66; Leader of Socialist Group in Fed. Assembly 67-69; mem. Fed. Council 70-, Head of Fed. Political (Foreign Affairs) Dept. 70-; Vice-Pres. Fed. Council Jan.-Dec. 74; Pres. of Swiss Confed. Jan.-Dec. 75; Social Democrat.
Département Politique Fédéral, 3003 Berne; Alter Aargauerstalden 9, 3000 Berne, Switzerland.

Grabowski, Franz; German business executive; b. 25 Dec. 1897.
Member Supervisory Board, Commerzbank A.G., Düsseldorf; mem. Advisory Board, HGI-Hess. Gesellschaft f. industrielle Unternehmungen F. Flick G.m.b.H., Wetzlar; Hon. Senator Technische Hochschule Darmstadt, Justus-Liebig-Universität Giessen; Grosses Bundesverdienstkreuz mit Stern des Verdienstordens der B.R.D.; Dr. Ing. (Hon.).
Vogelsang 40, 633 Wetzlar, Federal Republic of Germany.
Telephone: 4-36-81.

Grace, Her Serene Highness Princess, (Grace Patricia Kelly); b. 12 Nov. 1929; d. of John Brendan and Margaret (Majer) Kelly; m. His Serene Highness Prince Rainier III of Monaco (q.v.) 1956; one s. two d.; ed. Acad. of the Assumption and Stevens School (Philadelphia) and American Acad. of Dramatic Arts, New York.
Began stage career in Philadelphia; appeared on Broadway in the play *The Father* 49; films 51-55 include *Fourteen Hours, High Noon, Dial M For Murder, Rear Window, The Country Girl* (Oscar), *Bridges at Toko-Ri, To Catch a Thief, The Swan, High Society, Mogambo, Green Fire;* Pres. of Monégasque Red Cross 58-; Hon. Pres. Monaco U.S.A., Girl-Guides of Monaco, Asscn. des Amis de l'Enfance, Irish-American Cultural Inst.; Pres. Garden Club of Monaco, Princess Grace Foundation; Chair. Organizing Cttee. Centennial of Monte Carlo; Grand Croix Order of St. Charles, Grand Cordon Order of Greece, Grand Croix of the Equestrian Order of the Holy Sepulchre of Jerusalem, Lady of the Sovereign Order of Malta, Gold Medals of French, Italian and Austrian Red Cross.
Leisure interests: cultural and social activities of the Principality.
Palais Princier, Monaco-Ville, Monaco.
Telephone: 30-18-31.

Grace, J. Peter; American business executive; b. 25 May 1913, Long Island, N.Y.; s. of Joseph P. and Janet Macdonald Grace; m. Margaret Fennelly 1941; five s. four d.; ed. Yale Univ.
Joined W. R. Grace & Co. 36, Sec. 42-43, Dir. 43-, Vice-Pres. 45, Pres. and Chief Exec. Officer 45-71, 74-, Chair. and Chief Exec. Officer 71-74; Dir. Kennecott Copper Corpn., First Nat. City Bank, Ingersoll-Rand Co., Citicorp. Centennial Insurance Co., Omega Fund Inc. Deering Miliken Inc., Brascan Ltd., Stone & Webster Inc.; Chair. of Board Chemed Corpn.; Trustee, Atlantic Mutual Insurance Co.; Trustee, U.S. Council for Int. Chamber of Commerce; active in many fields of public service; Hon. LL.D. from several colls., and univs.; many foreign decorations.
Office: W.R. Grace & Co., Grace Plaza, 1114 Avenue of the Americas, New York, N.Y. 10036; Home: 41 Shelter Rock Road, Manhasset, L.I., N.Y., U.S.A.
Telephone: (212) 764-5555 (Office).

Grace, William Edwin; American trailer manufacturer; b. 27 April 1908, Fort Worth, Tex.; s. of James Grace and Anna Christelles; m. Mary Corinne Funderburk 1931; one s.; ed. public schools.
Bookkeeper, Hobbs Manufacturing Co., Fort Worth 30, Office Manager 31-33, Credit Manager 33-35, Sales Manager 35-37, Vice-Pres. and Gen. Manager 37-41, Exec. Vice-Pres. (Operations) 41-55; Vice-Pres. (Hobbs Trailer Div. and Southwestern Div.) Fruehauf Trailer Co. (now named Fruehauf Corpn.) 55-58, Pres. and Chief Exec. Officer 58-73, Chair. of Board 73-; Pres. W. E. Grace Finance Co. 34-; official of numerous other corpns.
Fruehauf Corporation, 10900 Harper Avenue, Detroit, Michigan 48232, U.S.A.
Telephone: 313-921-2410.

Gracias, H.E. Cardinal Valerian, D.D., M. AGG.; Indian ecclesiastic; b. 23 Oct. 1900; ed. St. Patrick's High School, Karachi, St. Joseph's Seminary, Mangalore, Papal Seminary, Kandy, and Gregorian Univ., Rome.
Sec. to the Archbishop 29-36; Chancellor of the Archdiocese 29; Editor *Messenger of the Sacred Heart* 35; Co-editor *The Examiner* 38; Rector of the Pro-Cathedral, Bombay 41; Titular Bishop of Tannis and Auxiliary to the Archbishop of Bombay 46-50; Archbishop of Bombay 50-; created Cardinal by Pope Pius XII 53; mem. Sacred Congregations for the Oriental Church, of Sacraments and De Propaganda Fide; fmr. Pres. Catholic Bishops' Conf. of India; mem. Council for Implementation of the Constitution on the Sacred Liturgy, and Comm. for Revision of Code of Canon Law; mem. Secr. for Non-Christians; awarded "Padma Vibhushan" by Pres. of India 66.
Publs. *Features of Christian Life, Heaven and Home, The Vatican and International Policy, The Decline of Public Morals, The Chief Duties of Christians as Citizens.*
Archbishop's House, Nathalal Parekh, Marg 8, Bombay, 400 039, India.
Telephone: 213131-32-33.

Gracq, Julien; French professor and writer; b. 27 July 1910, St. Florent le Vieil, Maine et Loire; ed. Ecole Normale Supérieure and Ecole des Sciences Politiques, Paris (Prof. agrégé d'histoire).
Prof. d'histoire 35-47; Prof. d'histoire Lycée Claude Bernard, Paris 47-70; retd.
Leisure interest: chess.
Publs. *Au château d'Argol* 39, *Un Beau Ténébreux* 45, *Le Roi Pêcheur* 47, *Liberté Grande* 47, *André Breton* 47, *La littérature à l'estomac* 50, *Le Rivage des Syrtes* 51, *Un Balcon en Forêt* 58, *Préférences* 61, *Lettrines* 67, *La Presqu'île* 70, *Lettrines 2* 74.
61 rue de Grenelle, Paris 7e, France.
Telephone: 222-00-12.

Grad, Harold, PH.D.; American professor of mathematics; b. 14 Jan. 1923, New York, City; s. of Herman Grad and Helen Selinger; m. Betty J. Miller 1949; one s. one d.; ed. Cooper Union and New York Univ.
Assistant Prof., New York Univ. 48, Assoc. Prof. 52, Prof. of Mathematics 57-, Dir. Magneto-Fluid Dynamics Div. 59-; Chair. Fluid Dynamics Div. 63, American Courant Inst. of Mathematical Sciences Physical Soc. Plasma Physics Div. 69; mem. Nat. Acad. of Sciences; Fellow, American Physical Soc., A.A.A.S.; N.Y. Acad. of Science award in Nuclear Physics and Engineering 70. Publs. articles and chapters in books on kinetic theory of gases, plasma physics, controlled thermonuclear research.
Courant Institute of Mathematical Sciences, 251 Mercer Street, New York, N.Y. 10012; Home: 248 Overlook Road, New Rochelle, N.Y. 10804, U.S.A.
Telephone: 212-460-7204 (Office); 914-636-7969 (Home).

Grade, Sir Lew, Kt.; British television executive; b. 25 Dec. 1906; s. of Isaac and Olga Winogradsky; brother of Bernard Delfont (q.v.); m. Kathleen Sheila Moody 1942; one s.; ed. Rochelle Street School.
Joint Man. Dir. theatrical agents—Lew and Leslie Grade Ltd. -55; Deputy Man. Dir. Assoc. Television Ltd. 55-; Man. Dir. Inc. Television Co. Ltd.; Chief Exec. and Deputy Chair. Assoc. Television Corpn. Ltd., Chief Exec. and Chair. 73-; Deputy Chair. and Man. Dir. ATV Network Ltd. until 73, Chair. 73-; Chair. Stoll Theatres Corpn., Moss Empires 73-, A. P. Films Ltd.; Dir. Assoc. Television Corpn. (Int.) Ltd., Independent Television Corpn. (U.S.A.), Canastel Broadcasting Corpn. (Canada), New World Music Ltd., Ambassador Bowling Ltd., Planned Holdings Ltd., Bermans (Holdings) Ltd., Bentray Investments Ltd., Pye Records Ltd.
ATV House, Great Cumberland Place, London, W.1, England.

Gradl, Johann Baptist, DR. RER.POL.; German politician; b. 25 March 1904, Berlin; m. Marianne Brecour 1931; two s. two d.; ed. Kaiser-Wilhelm-Realgymnasium, Berlin, Humboldt-Universität zu Berlin, and Martin Luther-Universität, Halle-Wittenberg.
On staff of Germania, Berlin 26-30; mem. Exec. Board Deutsche Sparkassen-und Giroverband (Union of German Savings and Deposit Banks) 31-38; mem. Reichsgruppe Banken 38-45; newspaper publisher, W. Berlin 48-65; mem. Centre Party until 33; mem. Christian Democratic Union (C.D.U.) 45-, mem. Fed. Board of Dirs. of C.D.U. 53-71; mem. Bundestag 57-; Fed. Minister for Expellees, Refugees, War Victims and All-German Affairs 65-66; Grosses Bundesverdienstkreuz mit Stern und Schulterband.
Leisure interest: classical music.
Publ. The History of Reparation Payments, For German Unity.
Office: Bonn, Bundeshaus; Home: Zerbster Strasse 28, 1 Berlin 45-Lichterfelde, Federal Republic of Germany.
Telephone: (West Berlin) 7116087.

Graffman, Gary; American pianist; b. 14 Oct. 1928; ed. Curtis Inst. of Music, Philadelphia under Mme. Isabelle Vengerova.
Professional début with Philadelphia Orchestra 47; concert tours all over the world; appears annually in America with major orchestras; gramophone recordings for Columbia Masterworks and RCA Victor including concertos of Tchaikovsky, Rachmaninoff, Brahms, Beethoven, Chopin and Prokofiev.
c/o Beal Management, 119 West 57th Street, New York, N.Y. 10019, U.S.A.

Graham, Billy (see Graham, William Franklin).

Graham, Donald Martin, LL.D.; American banker; b. 10 Sept. 1913, Pittsburgh, Pa.; s. of the late Robert T. and Jane M. Graham; m. Josephine D. Hall 1936; two s. one d.; ed. Northwestern Univ.

Associated with law firm Mayer, Meyer, Austrian & Platt (now Mayer, Brown & Platt) 36-44, Partner 45-52; Vice-Pres. Continental Illinois Nat. Bank and Trust Co. of Chicago 53, Senior Vice-Pres. 59, Vice-Chair. Board of Dirs. 60, Chair. of Board and Chief Exec. Officer 69-73; Hon. Litt.D. (DePaul Univ.) Hon. L.D. (MacMurray Coll.) and other honours.
Leisure interests: fishing and reading.
2247 Orrington Avenue, Evanston, Ill. 60201, U.S.A.
Telephone: 312-DA8-7554.

Graham, Gerald Sandford, M.A., PH.D., F.R.HIST.S.; Canadian university professor emeritus; b. 27 April 1903, Sudbury, Ont.; s. of Rev. H. S. Graham and Florence M. Chambers; m. Constance M. Greey 1950; two s. two d.; ed. Queen's Univ. (Ontario) and Harvard, Cambridge, Berlin and Freiburg Univs.
Instructor in History and Tutor, Harvard Univ. 30-36; Lecturer, Asst., Assoc. and later Prof., Queen's Univ. 36-46; served R.C.N.V.R. 42-44; Reader in History, Birkbeck Coll., Univ. London 46-48, Rhodes Prof. of Imperial History, King's Coll. 49-70; Visiting Prof. Univ. of Western Ontario 70-72; Montague Burton Visiting Prof. Univ. of Edinburgh 74; Hon. D.Litt. (Univ. of Waterloo, Ont.)
Leisure interests: travel, food and wine.
Publs. British Policy and Canada 1774-91 30, Sea Power and British North America 1783-1820 41, Canada, A Short History 50, Empire of the North Atlantic 50, 58, The Walker Expedition to Quebec, 1711 54, The Navy and South America 1807-1823 (with R. A. Humphreys) 62, The Politics of Naval Supremacy 65, Britain in the Indian Ocean 1810-1850 67, A Concise History of Canada 68, A Concise History of the British Empire 69, Tides of Empire 72, The Royal Navy in the American War of Independence 76; Editor Imperial Studies Series (auspices Royal Commonwealth Soc.) 58-70, West Africa History Series 56-70; contributor to Newfoundland, Economic, Diplomatic and Strategic Studies 46, Cambridge History of the British Empire (Vol. III) 59.
The Athenaeum, Pall Mall, London, S.W.1; Home: Hobbs Cottage, Beckley, Rye, Sussex, England.
Telephone: Beckley 308 (Home).

Graham, Katharine; American newspaper executive; b. 16 June 1917, New York City; d. of Eugene and Agnes Meyer; m. Philip L. Graham 1940 (died 1963); three s. one d.; ed. Madeira School, Vassar Coll., and Univ. of Chicago.
Reporter San Francisco News 38-39; various depts. The Washington Post 39-45; Pres. The Washington Post Co. (owns The Washington Post, Washington, Newsweek magazine, and several radio and TV stations) 63-73, Chair. of Board and Chief Exec. Officer 73-; Publisher, The Washington Post 68-; Trustee, Univ. of Chicago George Washington Univ. Cttee. for Econ. Devt., The Urban Inst., Fed. City Council; mem. Advisory Cttee. to the John Fitzgerald Kennedy School of Govt., Inst. of Politics, Harvard, The Conf. Board; mem. Board Newspaper Advertising Bureau, Inc., Allied Chemical Corpn., Amer. Newspaper Publrs.' Asscn., Assoc. Press, American Press Inst.; John Peter Zenger Award 73.
Office: 1150 15th Street, N.W., Washington, D.C. 20071; Home: 2920 R Street, N.W., Washington, D.C. 20007, U.S.A.

Graham, Martha, LL.D.; American dancer and choreographer; b. 11 May 1894, Pittsburgh; ed. Bard Coll.
Studied with Ruth Denis; Soloist Denishawn Co. 20, Greenwich Village Follies 23; choreographer-dancer 48th Street Theatre, N.Y. 26; Founder, Artistic Dir. Martha Graham Dance Co., Martha Graham School of Contemporary Dance; solo performances with leading orchestras of U.S.; has choreographed for foreign dance cos. and toured with co. abroad; Guggenheim

Fellow 32, 39, Capegio Award 59, Aspen Award 65, Creative Arts Award, Brandeis Univ. 68, Distinguished Service to Arts Award, Nat. Inst. of Arts and Letters 70, Handel Medallion of New York 70.
Works include: *Appalachian Spring, Letter to the World, Cave of the Heart, Diversion of Angels, Acrobats of God, Dark Meadow, Night Journey, Clytemnestra, Phaedra, Legend of Judith, Errand into the Maze, Seraphic Dialogue, Mendicants of the Evening, Myth of a Voyage, Holy Jungle, Stone of Destiny.*
Publ. *The Notebooks of Martha Graham* 37.
Martha Graham School of Contemporary Dance, 316 East 63rd Street, New York, N.Y. 10021, U.S.A.

Graham, Pierre Robert, M.A.; American diplomatist; b. 10 Aug. 1922, France; s. of William R. Graham and Jeanne Augereau; m. Dr. Helgard Planken 1968; three d.; ed. Coll. Aristide Briand, U.S. Merchant Marine Acad. and Univ. of Chicago.
Third Sec., Morocco 51-54; Second Sec., Lebanon 54-57; France 57-58; First Sec., Senegal 58-61; Chief of Personnel for Latin America, Dept. of State 62-64; Counsellor and Chargé d'Affaires, Guinea 64-66; Deputy Dir. Office of Int. Econ. and Social Affairs, Dept. of State 67-69; Perm. Rep. to UNESCO 69-73; Counsellor and Chargé d'Affaires, Amman, Jordan 73-74; Amb. to Upper Volta 74-.
American Embassy, Ouagadougou, Upper Volta.

Graham, William Franklin (Billy), B.S., D.D., D.HUM., LL.D., D.LITT.; American evangelist; b. 7 Nov. 1918, Charlotte, N.C.; s. of William Franklin and Morrow Graham; m. Ruth M. Bell 1943; two s. three d.; ed. Florida Bible Seminary, Tampa and Wheaton Coll.
Ordained to Baptist Ministry 39; Broadcaster on *Songs in the Night* 43-45; Founder, Suburban Professional Men's Club, Chicago 43; Vice-Pres. Youth for Christ International 46-; Pres. Northwestern Schools, Minneapolis 47-51; evangelistic campaigns 46-; weekly broadcast *Hour of Decision* 50-; *My Answer* (syndicated column in 176 U.S. daily newspapers); founder and editor-in-chief *Decision* magazine; Pres. Billy Graham Evangelistic Asscn.; numerous hon. degrees.
Publs. *Calling Youth to Christ* 47, *Revival in our Time* 50, *America's Hour of Decision* 52, *I saw your Sons at War* 53, *Peace with God* 53, *The Secret of Happiness* 55, *My Answer* (book) 54, *World Aflame* 65, *The Challenge, The Jesus Generation.*
Office: 1300 Harmon Place, Minneapolis, Minn.; Home: Montreat, N. Carolina 28757, U.S.A.
Telephone: 612-332-8081 (Office).

Graham-Douglas, Nabo Bekinbo, LL.M., PH.D.; Nigerian Attorney-Gen. and Commr. for Justice 72-75; see *The International Who's Who 1975-76.*

Grainger, Isaac B.; American banker; b. 15 Jan. 1895, Wilmington, N.C.; s. of John V. and Katie R. Grainger; m. Catherine Garrett 1917; three s.; ed. Woodberry Forest School, Orange, Va., and Princeton Univ.
Formerly Vice-Pres. Murchison Nat. Bank, Wilmington, North Carolina; Exec. Vice-Pres. North Carolina Bank and Trust Co. 29-34; Pres. Montclair Trust Co. 34-43; Vice-Pres. Chemical Bank (New York) Trust Co. 43-50, Exec. Vice-Pres. 50-56, Pres. 56-60; Dir. Fort Myers Southern Railroad Co., Hartford Fire Insurance Co., Hartford Accident and Indemnity Co., American Manufacturing Co., Shearson Capital Fund Inc., Shearson Appreciation Fund; Adviser Dir. Union Electric Co.; Trustee, Inst. for Crippled and Disabled; mem. New York Chamber of Commerce; mem. North Carolina Soc., Soc. of Colonial Wars in State of New York, Pilgrims of U.S., Newcomen Soc. (England); Infantry Capt. in First World War.
Leisure interests: golf, bridge, fishing, backgammon.
Chemical Bank, 11 West 51st Street, New York, N.Y.; Home: 200 East 66th Street, New York, N.Y., U.S.A.
Telephone: 212-922-6252 (Office).

Granado, Donald Casimir; Trinidadian trade unionist, politician and diplomatist; b. 14 March 1915, Trinidad; s. of Grecorio and Octavia Granado; m. Anne-Marie Faustin (Lanbard) 1959; one s. one d. and one d. by previous marriage.
Former School Teacher; Sec. Union of Commercial and Industrial Workers 50-54; Sec./Treas. Trinidad and Tobago Fed. of Trade Unions 53-54; Pres. C.G.A. Credit Union 54-56; Sec./Treas. People's Nat. Movement 56; Minister of Labour and Social Services 56-61; Minister of Health and Housing and Dep. Leader of House of Reps. 61-63; Trinidad and Tobago Ambassador to Venezuela 63-64; High Commr. in Canada 64-69; Amb. to Brazil and Argentina 64-69; High Commr. to U.K. 69-71; resigned 71; fmr. Amb. to France, Germany, Italy, Belgium, Luxembourg, Netherlands, Switzerland; awarded Trinity Cross (Trinidad and Tobago's highest honour).
Leisure interests: cricket, environmental improvement, bridge, gardening, golf.
"Chadenam G," 20 Grove Road, Valsayn Park North, Curepe, Trinidad.
Telephone: 662-5905.

Granatkin, Valentin Alexandrovich; Soviet sports administrator; b. 16 July 1908, Moscow; s. of Alexandr Mihailovich and Evdokia Iacovlevna Granatkin; m. Valentina Nikolaevna Dokuchaeva 1933; one d.; ed. Moscow technical school.
Electrical engineer until 42; on staff of Central Cttee. of Communist Party of Soviet Union 42-50; Chair. Moscow Regional Cttee. of Physical Culture and Sport 51-53; Deputy Chair. of Cttee. for Physical Culture and Sport, R.S.F.S.R. Council of Ministers 54-59; mem. Central Presidium of Soviet Union Sports Socs. and Orgs. 59-64; Pres. Football Federation of U.S.S.R. 50-64, 68-; Vice-Pres. Int. Football Fed. 46-.
Leisure interests: music, record collecting.
U.S.S.R. Committee for Physical Culture and Sports, 4 Skatertny pereulok, Moscow, U.S.S.R.
Telephone: 2915794.

Grandetzka, Willi; German agriculturist and politician; b. 1927.
Chairman, Erfurt District Exec., Demokratische Bauernpartei Deutschlands 65-; mem. Presidum DBD Cen. Exec. 68-; mem. Volkskammer 67-; Deputy Chair. Cttee. for Citizens' Complaints, Volkskammer; mem. Council of State 71-; Vaterländischer Verdienstorden, and other decorations.
Staatsrat, Marx-Engels-Platz, Berlin 102, German Democratic Republic.

Grandgeorge, René Jean; French engineer and businessman; b. 27 Feb. 1899, Geneva; s. of Henri Grandgeorge and Georgine Excoffier; m. Simone Christin 1926; one s. four d.; ed. Ecole Centrale de Paris.
Honorary Gen. Man. Compagnie de Saint-Gobain; Dir. La Pierre Synthétique; Commdr. Légion d'Honneur, Grand Ordre Ordine al Merito (Italy).
Leisure interests: golf, sailing.
Home: La Mougine, 06-Mougins (A.M.); Office: Compagnie de Saint-Gobain, 62 boulevard Victor Hugo, 92 Neuilly-sur-Seine (Seine), France.

Grandi, Dino, Count (di Mordano); Italian lawyer, politician and diplomatist; b. 4 June 1895; ed. Bologna Univ.
Served Italian Army First World War (decorated); led Fascist movement in Northern Italy and took part in March on Rome as Chief of Gen. Staff of the Quadrumvirate; mem. Gen. Council of Fascist Party; mem. Gen. Council of Italian Nat. Trade Unions 20-23; elected to Chamber of Deputies 21; Vice-Pres. 24; Under-Sec. of State for Home Affairs 24; for Foreign Affairs 25-29; Ministry of Foreign Affairs 29-32; Ambassador to

Great Britain 32-39; Head of Italian Del. to Locarno Conf. 25; to Confs. for Settlement of War Debt 25, 26, and 29; to Financial Conf., Paris and London 31; to Naval Conf. in London 30 and 36; to Reparations Conf. Lausanne 32; to Disarmament Conf. Geneva 32; Permanent Italian Del. to L.N. Council and Assembly 25-32; Italian Representative on Non-Intervention Cttee. 36-39; Ministry of Justice 39-43; Pres. of the Chamber of the Fasci and Corporations 39-43; Prof. of Law in Rome Univ. during Second World War; involved in overthrow of Mussolini 43; now in retirement.
Publs. *Origins of Fascism* 29, *Italian Foreign Policy* 31, *The Spanish War in the London Committee* 39, *The Frontiers of the Law* 39, *Humanity and Law* 41, and other legal works.
Albareto Di Modena, Italy.

Grandval, Gilbert Yves Edmond; French government official and politician; b. 12 Feb. 1904; ed. Lycée Condorcet.
Chemical Industry 27-40, Head of Resistance in Eastern France 43-44, Military Gov. Saar 45-48, French High Commr. Saar 48-52, Ambassador 52-55; Resident-Gen. in Morocco 55; Sec.-Gen. Merchant Marine 58; Sec. of State for External Trade April-May 62; Minister of Labour 62-66; Pres. Compagnie des Messageries Maritimes 66-72; Pres. Union Travailliste 71-; mem. Conseil, Ordre de la Libération.
Publs. *Ma Mission au Maroc* 56, *La Libération de l'Est de la France* 74.
9 rue Armengaud, 92210 Saint-Cloud (Hauts-de-Seine), France.

Grandy, Marshal of the R.A.F. Sir John, G.C.B., K.B.E., D.S.O.; British air force officer; b. 8 Feb. 1913, Northwood, Middx.; s. of the late Francis Grandy and Nellie Lines; m. Cecile Elizabeth Florence Rankin 1937; two s.; ed. Univ. Coll. School, London.
Pilot Officer 31; served Second World War; Deputy Dir. Operational Training, Air Ministry 46-49; Air Attaché, Brussels 49-50; Commdr. Northern Sector Fighter Command 50; Air Staff H.Q. Fighter Command 52-54; Commandant Central Fighter Establishment 54-57; Imperial Defence Coll. 57; Commdr. Task Force Grapple 57-58; Asst. Chief of Air Staff 58-61; C.-in-C. R.A.F. Germany, Commdr. 2nd Allied Tactical Air Force 61-63; A.O.C.-in-C. Bomber Command 63-65; C. in C. British Forces Far East and U.K. Military Rep. to SEATO 65-67; Air Commodore 56; Air Vice-Marshal 58; Air Marshal 61; Air Chief Marshal 65; Marshal of the R.A.F. 71; Chief of Air Staff 67-April 71; Gov. and Commdr.-in-Chief of Gibraltar Oct. 73-; Hon. Panglima Mangku Negara; Hon. Liveryman of the Haberdashers' Company; Trustee Imperial War Museum, R.A.F. Church St. Clements Dane; mem. Management Cttee. of Royal Nat. Lifeboat Inst.; Vice-Pres. Nat. Asscn. of Boys Clubs; Knight of the Order of St. John.
Leisure interests: sailing, golf, shooting.
The Convent, Gibraltar.

Granfil, Toma; Yugoslav diplomatist; b. 31 Aug. 1913, Vrsac; s. of Dr. Djoka and Jelena Granfil; m. Anica Aldan 1940; no c.; ed. Belgrade Law School.
Practising lawyer 36-41; participated in Nat. Liberation Struggle 41-45; Minister for Trade and Supplies, Serbia 48-49; Chair. Yugoslav Section, Int. Chamber of Commerce (ICC), Paris 54-65; Man. Dir. and Pres., Yugoslav Bank for Foreign Trade 55-65; Vice-Pres. Exec. Council of Serbia 65-67; Pres. Yugoslav-Italian Econ. Comm. 67-71; mem. Fed. Exec. Council in charge of econ. relations with foreign countries 67-71; Chief of Yugoslav delegation for negotiations with EEC 68-71; Amb. to U.S.A. 71-75; several Yugoslav and foreign decorations.
Publs. several articles and studies in econ. policy.
Secretariat of Foreign Affairs, Belgrade, Yugoslavia.

Granick, Sam, M.S., PH.D.; American professor of biochemistry; b. 16 Feb. 1909, New York City; s. of Aaron and Dora (Ustin) Granick; m. Elsa Bachman 1938; one s. one d.; ed. Univ. of Michigan.
Member of Staff, Rockefeller Univ. 38-, Prof. of Biochemistry 64-; mem. Nat. Acad. of Sciences, American Acad. of Arts and Sciences, American Soc. of Naturalists (Vice-Pres. 63), American Soc. of Biological Chemists, American Chemical Soc., Soc. for Developmental Biology (Pres. 67), American Soc. of Plant Physiologists, Botanical Soc.; Harvey Lecturer 49; research on chloroplasts, free radicals of redox dyes, ferritin and iron metabolism and on heme and chlorophyll biosynthesis.
Rockefeller University, New York, N.Y. 10021, U.S.A.

Granier de Lilliac, René; French business executive; b. 1919, Nantes; ed. Ecole Polytechnique.
Joined Compagnie Française des Pétroles 54, responsible for Middle East Operations 54, Sec.-Gen. 60, Dir. 63; Pres. Cie. Française de Raffinage 66; Admin. Cie. Française des Pétroles 68, Vice-Pres. 70, Deputy Dir.-Gen. Feb. 71, Pres.-Dir. Gen. July 71-.
Compagnie Française des Pétroles, 5 rue Michel-Ange, Paris 16e, France.

Granier-Doyeux, Marcel Alfredo; Venezuelan pharmacologist and diplomatist; b. 14 March 1916, Caracas; m.; six c.; ed. Central Univ. of Venezuela, Yale Univ., U.S.A., Univ. of Basle, Switzerland.
Held several teaching and medical posts in Venezuela 36-43; Prof. of Pharmacology, Faculty of Medical Sciences, Cen. Univ. of Venezuela 43-, Faculty of Pharmacy and Chemistry 48-53; Head Inst. for Experimental Medicine, Caracas 45-46; Head Pharmacological Service, Venezuelan Inst. for Social Security 48-49; Librarian Acad. of Physical, Mathematical and Natural Sciences 49-; Vice-Pres. Nat. Acad. of Medicine 64, Pres. 64-68; Amb. to France 69-73; Perm. Rep. to UN 73-74; has attended numerous int. confs., and served on many int. bodies dealing with narcotics and other drugs incl. Int. Narcotics Control Board, Vice-Pres. 68-, Expert Cttee. on Drug Dependence, WHO, Vice-Chair. 68.
Publs. over 216 articles in national and foreign scientific journals on physiology, pharmacology, toxicology, etc., and six textbooks.
c/o Ministerio de Relaciones Exteriores, Caracas, Venezuela.

Granit, Ragnar Arthur, MAG. PHIL., M.D.; Swedish neurophysiologist; b. 30 Oct. 1900, Helsinki, Finland; s. of Arthur W. Granit and Albertina H. Malmberg; m. Baroness Marguerite Bruun 1929; one s.; ed. Swedish Normallyceum, Helsinki, and Helsinki Univ.
Docent, Helsinki Univ. 29-37, Prof. of Physiology 37-40; Fellow, Univ. of Pennsylvania 29-31; Invited Royal Caroline Inst., Stockholm 40, Prof. of Neurophysiology 46-67; Dir. Nobel Inst. for Neurophysiology 45-67; Visiting Prof. Rockefeller Inst. 56-66, St. Catherine's Coll., Oxford 67, Fogarty Int. Cen., Nat. Inst. of Health, Bethesda, U.S.A. 71-72, 75, Univ. Düsseldorf 74; Pres. Royal Swedish Acad. of Science 63-65; foreign mem. Royal Soc., London, Nat. Acad. of Sciences, Washington, and several other acads.; hon. mem. American Acad. of Arts and Sciences; several prizes and hon. degrees; Nobel Prize for Physiology or Medicine 67.
Leisure interests: sailing, gardening.
Publs. *Ung Mans Väg till Minerva* 41, *Sensory Mechanisms of the Retina* 47, *Receptors and Sensory Perception* 55, *Charles Scott Sherrington, An Appraisal* 66, *Basis of Motor Control* 70, *Mechanisms Regulating the Discharge of Motoneurons* 72.
Nobel Institute for Neurophysiology, Karolinska Institutet, Stockholm 60; 14 Eriksbergsgatan, 11430 Stockholm, Sweden.
Telephone: 213728 (Home).

Grano, H.E. Cardinal Carlo; Italian ecclesiastic; b. 14 Oct. 1887.
Ordained Priest 12; Titular Archbishop of Salonica 58-; Apostolic Nuncio in Italy; created Cardinal by Pope Paul VI 67.
[*Died March* 1976.]

Granö, Olavi Johannes, PH.D.; Finnish professor of geography; b. 27 May 1925, Helsinki; s. of Prof. Dr. Johannes G. Granö and Hilma Ekholm; two d.; ed. Turku, Helsinki and Copenhagen Univs.
Assistant Prof. of Geography, Helsinki Univ. and Helsinki School of Econs. 48-57; Assoc. Prof. of Geography, Turku Univ. 58-61, Prof. 62-; Pres. Archipelago Research Inst. 65-; Pres. Finnish Nat. Research Council for Sciences 64-69; Pres. Central Board of Research Councils (Acad. of Finland) 70-73; Pres. Geographical Soc. of Finland; mem. Finnish Acad. of Science and Letters.
Publs. scientific publications on geography, geology and science policy.
Department of Geography, Turku University, Turku; Home: Sirppitie 1A, 20540 Turku, Finland.
Telephone: 335599 (Office); 370640 (Home).

Grant, Cary; British-born American actor; b. (as Archibald Alexander Leach) 18 Jan. 1904, Bristol, England; s. of Elias and Elsie (Kingdom) Leach; m. 1st Virginia Cherrill 1934 (divorced 1934), 2nd Barbara Hutton 1942 (divorced 1945), 3rd Betsy Drake 1949 (divorced), 4th Dyan Cannon 1965 (divorced 1968); one d.; ed. Fairfield Acad., Somerset.
Moved to U.S.A. 21; began acting New York 21; film actor since 32; naturalized U.S. citizen 42; exec. dir. Fabergé.
Leisure interest: riding.
Films include *Blonde Venus* 33, *She Done Him Wrong* 33, *Alice in Wonderland* 33, *I'm No Angel* 33, *Sylvia Scarlett* 35, *Suzy* 36, *The Awful Truth* 37, *Topper* 37, *Bringing Up Baby* 38, *Holiday* 38, *Gunga Din* 39, *Only Angels Have Wings* 39, *In Name Only* 39, *My Favourite Wife* 40, *His Girl Friday* 40, *The Philadelphia Story* 40, *Penny Serenade* 41, *Suspicion* 41, *The Talk of the Town* 42, *Once upon a Honeymoon* 42, *Destination Tokyo* 43, *Mr. Lucky* 43, *Once upon a Time* 44, *None but the Lonely Heart* 44, *Arsenic and Old Lace* 44, *Night and Day* 45, *Notorious* 46, *The Bachelor and the Bobbysoxer* 47, *The Bishop's Wife* 48, *Every Girl Should Be Married* 48, *Mr. Blandings Builds His Dream House* 48, *I Was a Male War Bride* 49, *Crisis* 50, *People Will Talk* 51, *Monkey Business* 52, *Room for One More* 52, *Dream Wife* 53, *To Catch a Thief* 55, *The Pride and the Passion* 57, *An Affair to Remember* 57, *Kiss Them for Me* 57, *Indiscreet* 58, *Houseboat* 58, *North by Northwest* 59, *Operation Petticoat* 59, *The Grass is Greener* 60, *That Touch of Mink* 62, *Charade* 63, *Father Goose* 64, *Walk, Don't Run* 66.
West Pico Blvd., Los Angeles, Calif. 90064, U.S.A.

Grant, Duncan James Corrowr; British artist; b. 1885, Rothiemurchus, Inverness; s. of Maj. Bartle Grant and Ethel Isobel McNeil; ed. St. Paul's School; studied painting in Paris, Italy and London.
Apart from painting, has designed costumes and décor for ballet and opera, textiles; decorated houses, churches, furniture; mem. Camden Town Group 11-, London Group 19-, London Artists Assoc. 29-31; worked with Roger Fry at Omaga Workshop, London 13-19; exhbns. in London (Grafton Galleries, Whitechapel Gallery, Agnew & Sons, etc.), Paris, Zurich, Tokyo 31, Venice Biennale 26, 32; one-man exhbns. at Carfax Gallery, London 20, Leicester Galleries, London 45; retrospective exhbn. London 29; pictures in Tate Gallery, London, Walker Art Gallery, Liverpool, Bucharest.
Works include: decorations for Borough Polytechnic, *Football*, *Bathers* 11, decorations for parish church,

Berwick, Sussex (with Vanessa and Quentin Bell) 43, *Cinderella* decorations, Children's Restaurant, Tottenham (with Vanessa Bell) 46, etc.
Leisure interest: travel.
Charleston, Firle, Sussex, England.

Grant, Verne E., PH.D.; American biologist; b. 17 Oct. 1917, San Francisco, Calif.; s. of Edwin E. and Bessie C. (Swallow) Grant; m. 1st Alva Day 1946, 2nd Karen S. Alt 1960; one s. one d. and one adopted d.; ed. Univ. of California (Berkeley).
Visiting Investigator, Carnegie Inst. of Washington, Stanford, Calif. 49-50; Geneticist and experimental taxonomist, Rancho Santa Ana Botanic Garden, Claremont, Calif. 50-67; Prof. of Biology, Inst. of Life Science, Texas A. & M. Univ. 67-68; Prof. of Biological Sciences, Univ. of Arizona 68-70; Dir. Boyce Thompson Arboretum, Ariz. 68-70; Prof. of Botany, Univ. of Texas 70-; Nat. Research Council Fellowship 49-50; Phi Beta Kappa Award in Science 64; Certificate of Merit, Botanical Soc. of America 71; mem. Nat. Acad. of Sciences; Fellow American Acad. of Arts and Sciences.
Leisure interests: hiking, watching trains, classical music.
Publs. *Natural History of the Phlox Family* 59, *The Origin of Adaptations* 63, *The Architecture of the Germplasm* 64, *Flower Pollination in the Phlox Family* (with Karen Grant) 65, *Hummingbirds and Their Flowers* (with Karen Grant) 68, *Plant Speciation* 71, *Genetics of Flowering Plants* 75; numerous papers on plant genetics and plant evolution.
Department of Botany, University of Texas at Austin, Austin, Tex. 78712; Home: 2811 Fresco Drive, Austin, Tex. 78731, U.S.A.
Telephone: 512-471-5858 (Office).

Grant, Walter Lawrence, PR.ENG., D.SC., M.SC., C.E. and M.I.MECH.E., A.F.R.AE.S., M.(S.A.)I.M.E.; South African engineer; b. 22 Aug. 1922, Potchefstroom, Transvaal; s. of Walter W. Grant and Petronella Peters; m. Anna Catharina Christina van Deventer; ed. Witwatersrand Technical Coll., Univs. of the Witwatersrand and Pretoria.
Head, Thermodynamic Div., Nat. Mechanical Engineering Research Inst. (N.M.E.R.I.), S. African Council for Scientific and Industrial Research (C.S.I.R.) 52-57; Dir. N.M.E.R.I. 57-59; Chief Engineer, S.A. Atomic Energy Board 59-64, Deputy Dir.-Gen. and Dir. of Reactor Engineering 64-67; Dir.-Gen. S.A. Atomic Energy Board 67-70, Deputy Pres. 70-; Gen. Man. Uranium Enrichment Corpn. of S.A. Ltd. 71; Gold Medal, Inst. of Mechanical Engineering 58; Havenga Prize 66, Co-recipient Henrik Verwoerd Award 71 and other awards; Hon. D.Sc. (Univ. Pretoria) 74.
Leisure interests: photography, target shooting.
Publs. 18 scientific publs. 53-70.
Uranium Enrichment Corporation of South Africa Ltd., P.O. Box 4587, Pretoria, Transvaal, South Africa.

Grantham, Don L., C.P.A.; American business executive; b. Mattoon, Ill.; m. Mary E. Grantham; two s. two d.; ed. Mattoon High School, Eastern Illinois Coll. and Univ. of Illinois.
Joined Beatrice Foods Co. 34, Regional Vice-Pres. 61, Dir. 63, Gen. Man. Dairy Operations 64, Exec. Vice-Pres. 66, Pres. and Chief Operating Officer 72-, Dir. La Salle Nat. Bank, Chicago.
Beatrice Foods Co., 120 La Salle Street, Chicago, Ill. 60603; Home: 201 North Green Bay Road, Lake Forrest, Ill. 60045, U.S.A.
Telephone: 312-234-1942 (Home).

Granville, Sir Keith, Kt., C.B.E., M.INST.T.; British airline executive; b. 1 Nov. 1910, Faversham; m. 1st Patricia Capstick 1933, 2nd Truda Belliss 1946; two s. five d.; ed. Tonbridge School.

Trainee, Imperial Airways 29, served in Italy, Tanganyika, Southern and Northern Rhodesia, Egypt, India; then Man. African and Middle East Div., British Overseas Airways Corpn. (B.O.A.C.) 47, Commercial Dir, B.O.A.C. 54, Deputy Man. Dir. 58-60; Chair. B.O.A.C. Associated Companies Ltd. 60-64; Deputy Chair. B.O.A.C. 64-71, Deputy Chair. and Man. Dir. Jan. 69, Chair. 71-72; mem. Exec. Cttee. IATA 72-74, Pres. 72-73; Deputy Chair. British Airways Board 72-74; mem. Maplin Devt. Authority 73-74.
Exbury, Sea Road, Westgate-on-Sea, Kent, England.
Telephone: Thanet 31415 (Westgate-on-Sea).

Granville, Maurice F., M.SC.; American oil executive; b. 26 Oct. 1915, La Grange, Tex.; s. of Maurice F. and Dorathea (née von Rosenburg) Granville; m. Janet Knotts 1945; one s. one d.; ed. Univ. of Texas and Mass. Inst. of Technology.
Joined Texaco Inc. 39, Supervisor of operations at Westville 50, Asst. Plant Man. 51, Man. of Texaco's chemical activities at Port Arthur 55, Gen. Man. Petrochemical operations, New York 58, Vice-Pres. in charge of Petrochemical Dept. 60; Vice-Pres. in charge of Strategic Planning and Asst. to Chair. of Board 67; Pres. and Dir. Texaco Inc. 70, Chair. Board of Dirs. 71-, Chief Exec. Officer Jan. 72-; Chair. Board of Dirs., American Petroleum Inst.; mem. Board of Dirs., Metropolitan Opera Asscn., Gov. Board of Corpn. of MIT, Board of Trustees, Presbyterian Hosp., New York; Dir. Fed. Reserve Bank of New York.
Texaco Inc., 135 East 42nd Street, New York, N.Y. 10017, U.S.A.

Grass, Günter; German artist and writer; b. 16 Oct. 1927, Danzig (now Gdańsk, Poland); ed. art school.
Lyric Prize, Süddeutscher Rundfunk 55, Group 47 Prize 59, Literary Prize, Asscn. of German Critics 60, Georg-Büchner Prize 65.
Publs. *Die Vorzüge der Windhühner* (poems and drawings) 55, *Die Blechtrommel* 59, *Gleisdreieck* (poems and drawings) 60, *Katz und Maus* 61 (film 67), *Hundejahre* 63, *Ausgefragt* (poems), *Über das Selbstverständliche* 68, *Ortlich Betäubt* 69, *Aus dem Tagebuch einer Schnecke* 72, *Dokumente zur politischen Wirkung* 72; plays: *Hochwasser* 56, *Noch 10 Minuten bis Buffalo* 58, *Onkel, Onkel* 58, *Die Bösen Köche* 61, *Die Plebejer proben den Aufstand* 65, *Davor* (Beforehand) 68.
Niedstrasse 13, 1 Berlin 41, Federal Republic of Germany.

Grassberger, Roland, LL.D.; Austrian criminologist; b. 1905, Vienna; s. of Dr. Roland Grassberger and Mathilde Rabl; m. Isabella Hiess 1933; two s.; ed. High School and Univ. of Vienna.
Practice at Criminal Court 29-30, at Police Office 31-32; Asst. Lecturer in Criminology, Univ. of Vienna 30, Lecturer 31-46, Director, Inst. of Criminology, Univ. of Vienna 46-, Prof. of Criminal Law and Criminology 48-, Dean, Faculty of Law 54-55, 60-61, Rector of Univ. of Vienna 62-63; Sworn Expert for Criminology at Austrian Courts 31-.
Leisure interest: history.
Publs. *Die Brandlegungskriminalität* 28, *Die Strafzumessung* 32, *Gewerbs-und Berufsverbrechertum in den U.S.A.* 33, *Die Lösung kriminalpolitischer Probleme durch die mechanische Statistik* 46, *Psychologie des Strafverfahrens* 50, 68, *Die Kriminalität des Wohlstandes* 62, *Die Unzucht mit Tieren* 68.
Tendlergasse 17, 1090 Vienna, Austria.
Telephone: 42-50454.

Grassé, Pierre, D. ès SC.; French biologist; b. 27 Nov. 1895, Périgueux; m. 1947; three c.; ed. Paris Univ.
Specialized in research on cellular structure, cytology, animal sociology, evolution; Prof. Faculty of Science, Paris; Dir. Laboratoire d'Evolution des Etres Organisés; Founder of Laboratoire de Primatologie et écologie des

Forêts equatoriales (Gabon); mem. scientific council, Nat. Council for Scientific Research; corresp. mem. Belgian Royal Acad. of Arts and Sciences; mem. Acad. of Sciences (Anatomy and Zoology) 48, Pres. 67; Dr. h.c. (Brussels Univ. 46, Basle Univ. 60, Univ. of Ghent 65, Univ. Madrid 68, Univ. Bonn 68, Univ. São Paulo 68); Commdr. de la Légion d'Honneur.
Publs. *Parasites et Parasitisme, La Réproduction Sexuée et L'Analyse Expérimentale de la Fécondation, Précis de Biologie animale* (8th edn.); *Précis de Zoologie* (2 vols.); *Biologie générale;* Dir. and Editor *Traité de Zoologie* (34 vols), *Toi, ce Petit Dieu* (essay) 71, *L'Évolution du Vivant* 73.
Laboratoire d'évolution des êtres organisés, Faculté des Sciences, 105 boulevard Raspail, Paris 6e; 61 boulevard Saint-Michel, Paris 5e, France.

Grassi, Paulo; Italian theatre director.
Director, Teatro Piccolo, Milan 46-72; Superintendent, La Scala, Milan 72-76.
c/o Teatro alla Scala, Milan, Italy.

Grasso, Ella Tambussi, M.A.; American state governor; b. 10 May 1919, Windsor Locks, Conn.; d. of James and Maria Oliva Tambussi; m. Dr. Thomas A. Grasso 1942; one s. one d.; ed. Mount Holyoke Coll.
Member Connecticut Gen. Assembly 53-55; Sec. of State, Conn. 58-69; mem. House of Reps. 70-74; Gov. of Conn. Jan. 75-; Dr. h.c. (Holyoke Coll., Sacred Heart Univ.); Knight Order of Merit of the Italian Repub.
Leisure interests: reading, gardening, hiking.
State Capitol, Hartford, Conn.; Residence: 990 Prospect Street, Hartford, Conn.; Home: 2 Woodland Hollow, Windsor Locks, Conn., U.S.A.
Telephone: 623-3424.

Gratz, Leopold; Austrian politician; b. 4 Nov. 1929, Vienna; ed. Faculty of Law, Univ. of Vienna.
Served in Fed. Ministry for Social Admin. 52-53; mem. Secr. Socialist Parl. Party 53, Sec. 57; Sec. Socialist Party Exec. 63; mem. Bundesrat 63-66, Nationalrat 66-; Chair. Educational Policy Comm. of Exec. of Socialist Party 68; Minister of Educ. 70-71; Mayor of Vienna 73-.
Rathaus, 1082 Vienna, Austria.

Graur, Alexandru; Romanian philologist; b. 9 July 1900, Botoşani, Romania; m. Neaga Sion; one s.; ed. Bucharest Univ., and the Sorbonne, Paris.
Prof. of Philology, Univ., Bucharest (Dean of Philological Faculty 54-56); mem. of Praesidium of Acad. of Socialist Repub. of Romania; Gen. Manager Publishing House of the S.R.R. Acad.; State Prize 53; Star of Socialist Repub. of Romania, Fourth Class, Order of Labour, First Class.
Publs. include *Les consonnes géminées en latin* 29, *I et V en latin* 29, *Nom d'agent et adjectif en roumain* 29, *Incercare asupra fondului principal lexical al limbii române* 54, *Studii de lingvistică generală* 60, *Etimologii românesti* 63, *The Romance Character of Romanian* 67, *Tendinţele actuale ale limbii române* 68; contributions to *Gramatica Limbii române* (Vols. I-II) 63; numerous articles in newspapers and learned periodicals in Romania, France, U.S.S.R., Great Britain, China, etc.
Office: Academia R.S.R., Calea Victoriei 125, Bucharest; Home: Boul. A. Ipătescu 12, Bucharest (22), Romania.
Telephone: 50.52.08.

Grave, Walter Wyatt, M.A., PH.D.; British educationist; b. 16 Oct. 1901, King's Lynn; s. of the late Walter and Annie Grave; m. Kathleen Margaret Macpherson 1932; two d.; ed. Emmanuel Coll., Cambridge.
Fellow of Emmanuel Coll., Cambridge 26-66, 72-, Tutor 36-40; Lecturer in Spanish, Cambridge Univ. 36-40, Senior Proctor 38-39, Admin. Officer, Ministry of Labour and Nat. Service 40-43; University Registrary

43-52; Principal, Univ. Coll. of West Indies 53-58; Censor, Fitzwilliam House, Cambridge, Jan. 59-66; Master, Fitzwilliam Coll., Cambridge 66-71, Hon. Fellow 71-; Hon. LL.D. (Cambridge and McMaster Univs.).
18 Luard Road, Cambridge, England.
Telephone: 47415.

Gravel, Mike; American politician; b. 13 May 1930, Springfield, Mass; *s.* of Alphonse and Maria Gravel; *m.* Rita Martin 1959; one *s.* one *d.*; ed. Columbia Univ. Real estate developer; mem. Alaska House of Reps. 62-66; Speaker, Alaska House of Reps. 65; U.S. Senator from Alaska 69-; Democrat.
Publs. *Jobs and More Jobs, Citizen Power, The Pentagon Papers* (editor).
U.S. Senate, Washington, D.C., U.S.A.

Graves, Harold N., Jr., A.B., M.S.; American journalist; b. 20 Jan. 1915, Manila, Philippines; *s.* of Harold N. Graves and Florida Tolbert; *m.* Alta F. Judy 1937; three *s.*; ed. Princeton and Columbia (School of Journalism) Univs.
Editorial Research Asst. for *Literary Digest* 36; Assoc. Ed. *Pathfinder* 36-39; Dir. Princeton Listening Center 39-41; Asst. to Dir. Foreign Broadcast Intelligence Service, Fed. Communications Comm., Washington 41-43; attached to U.S. Navy, Office of Strategic Services, Washington, Ceylon and Thailand 43-45; Washington correspondent Providence (Rhode Island) *Evening Bulletin* 46-50; Dir. of Information, Int. Bank for Reconstruction and Devt. 50-67, Int. Devt. Asscn. 59-67, Int. Finance Corpn. 60-67; Assoc. Dir. Devt. Services Dept. IBRD and IDA 67-73; Exec. Sec. Consultative Group on Int. Agricultural Research 72-.
Leisure interest: golf.
4816 Grantham Avenue, Chevy Chase, Maryland 20015, U.S.A.
Telephone: OLiver 4-1694.

Graves, Robert Ranke, F.R.A.I.; British writer; b. 24 July 1895; ed. Charterhouse and St. John's Coll., Oxford.
Served France with Royal Welch Fusiliers; Prof. of English Literature Egyptian Univ. 26; Prof. of Poetry, Oxford Univ. 61-66; Queen's Gold Medal for Poetry 68; Hon. mem. American Acad. of Arts and Sciences 70-; Hon. Fellow, St. John's Coll., Oxford 71-; now residing in the Balearic Islands.
Publs. include *Goodbye to All That* 29, *But It Still Goes On* 30, *No Decency Left* (with Laura Riding) 32, *The Real David Copperfield* 33, *I, Claudius* 34 (awarded Hawthornden Prize), *Claudius the God* (awarded James Tait Black Prize) 34, *Antigua, Penny Puce* 36, *Count Belisarius* 38 (awarded Femina-Vie-Heureuse Stock Prize 39), *Collected Poems* 38, *T. E. Lawrence to his Biographers* (with Liddell Hart) 39, *Sergeant Lamb of the Ninth* 40, *Proceed, Sergeant Lamb* 41, *The Long Week End* (with Alan Hodge) 41, *Wife to Mr. Milton* 43, *The Reader Over Your Shoulder* (with Alan Hodge) 43, *The Golden Fleece* 44, *King Jesus* 47, *Poems 1938-1947* 47, *The White Goddess* 48, *Watch the North Wind Rise* 49, *The Common Asphodel* 49, *The Golden Ass* (translation) 49, *The Islands of Unwisdom* 49, *Poems and Satires* 51, *The Nazarene Gospel Restored* (with Joshua Podro) 54, *Poems* 53, *The Greek Myths* 54, *Homer's Daughter* 55, *Adam's Rib* 55, *The Infant with the Globe* (translation) 55, *Winter in Majorca* 55, *The Cross and the Sword* 55, *The Crowning Privilege* 55, *Catacrok!* 56, *Lucan's Civil Wars* (translation) 56, *Suetonius' Twelve Cæsars* (translation) 56, *Jesus in Rome* (with Joshua Podro) 56, *They Hanged My Saintly Billy* 57, *Steps: A Miscellany* 58, *Collected Poems, The Anger of Achilles* (adapted translation of *The Iliad* 59 (awarded Alexander Droutzkoy Gold Medal of the Nat. Poetry Society of America and the William Foyle Award for Poetry, London 60), *Food for Centaurs* 60, *The Penny Fiddle* 61, *More Poems* 61,

Six Oxford Addresses 62, *Comedies of Terence* (translation) 62, *New Poems* 62, *Hebrew Myths* (with Dr. Raphael Patai) 63, *Man Does, Woman Is* (poetry) 64, *Love Re-spelt* (poetry) 65, *Collected Poems* 65, *Majorca Observed* 65, *Mammon and the Black Goddess* 65, *Poetic Craft and Principle* 67, *Arrive at Highwood Hall* 67, *The Rubaiyyat of Omar Khayaam* (with Omar Ali-Shah) 68, *The Poor Boy Who Followed His Star* 68, *Poems about Love* 68, *Poems 1965-68* 68, *The Crane Bag and Other Disputed Subjects* (essays) 69, *Poems 1968-1970* 70, *Poems 1970-1972* 72, *Difficult Questions, Easy Answers* 72, *Timeless Meeting* (poems) 73, Editor *Song of Songs* 73, *At the Gate* (poems) 75, *Collected Poems* 75.
c/o A. P. Watt & Son, 26-28 Bedford Row, London, W.C.1, England; Deya, Mallorca, Balearic Islands, Spain.

Gray, Elisha, II; American businessman; b. 7 Sept. 1906; ed. Mass. Inst. of Technology.
With Sears, Roebuck & Co. 28-33; Vice-Pres., Gen. Operating Man. Cutler Shoe Co., Chicago 33-38; joined Whirlpool Corpn., St. Joseph, Mich. 38, Vice-Pres. 40, Dir. 43, Exec. Vice-Pres. 47, Pres. 49-58, Chair. 58-71, Chair. Finance Cttee. 71-; Dir. Gen. Foods Corpn., Warwick Electronics Inc. 67-; fmr. Dir. Gen. Sears Bank and Trust Co.; mem. Business Council, Mass. Inst. of Technology.
400 Nickerson Avenue, Benton Harbour, Mich., U.S.A.

Gray, Gordon, A.B., LL.D.; American lawyer and politician; b. 30 May 1909; ed. Univ. of North Carolina and Yale Law School.
Admitted to N.Y. Bar 34; with Carter, Ledyard & Milburn 33-35; admitted N.C. Bar 36; with Manly, Hendron & Womble 35-37, Chair. Board 61-; mem. N.C. Senate 38-42, 46-47; Asst. Sec. of Army 47-49, Under-Sec. 49, Sec. 49-50; Special Asst. to Pres. April-Nov. 50; Pres. Univ. of N. Carolina 50-55; Asst. Sec. of Defense for Int. Security Affairs 55-57; Dir. Psychological Strategy Bd. 51-52; Chair. Nat. Comm. in Financing of Hospital Care 51-54; Dir. Office of Defense Mobilisation 57-58; mem. Presidential Cttee. on U.S. overseas information policy 60; Special Asst. to Pres. for Nat. Security Affairs 58-61; mem. President's Foreign Intelligence Adv. Board 61; Chair. Summit Communications Inc.; Chair. Emeritus Nat. Trust for Historic Preservation; mem. Boards American Security and Trust Co., R. J. Reynolds Tobacco Co.; Trustee Emeritus Corcoran Gallery of Art; Democrat.
1616 H Street, N.W., Washington, D.C., U.S.A.

Gray, H.E. Cardinal Gordon Joseph, M.A.; British ecclesiastic; b. 10 Aug. 1910, Leith, Edinburgh, Scotland; *s.* of Francis W. Gray and Angela Gray; ed. Holy Cross Acad., Edinburgh, St. Joseph's Coll., Mark Cross, St. John's Seminary, Wonersh and St. Andrews Univ., Scotland.
Ordained 35; Curate St. Andrews 35-41; Parish Priest Hawick 41-47; Rector St. Mary's Coll. (Nat. Junior Seminary for Scotland) 47-; Archbishop of St. Andrews and Edinburgh 51-; created Cardinal 69; Hon. D.D. (St. Andrews Univ.) 67.
Leisure interests: gardening, carpentry, liturgy.
Archbishop's House, 42 Greenhill Gardens, Edinburgh, EH10 4BJ, Scotland.
Telephone: 031-447-3337.

Gray, Harry Barkus, PH.D.; American chemist; b. 14 Nov. 1935, Kentucky; *m.* Shirley Barnes 1957; two *s.* one *d.*; ed. Univ. of W. Kentucky, Northwestern Univ. and Univ. of Copenhagen.
Assistant Prof. of Chemistry, Columbia Univ. 61-63, Assoc. Prof. 63-65, Prof. 65-66; Prof. of Chem. Calif. Inst. of Technology 66-; mem. Nat. Acad. of Sciences; Franklin Award 67, Fresenius Award 70, American Chem. Soc. Award in Pure Chem. 70, Harrison Howe Award 72, MCA Award 72, Guggenheim Fellow 72-73.
Leisure interests: tennis, music.
Publs. *Electrons and Chemical Bonding* 65, *Molecular*

Orbital Theory 65, *Ligand Substitution Processes* 66, *Basic Principles of Chemistry* 67, *Chemical Dynamics* 68, *Chemical Principles* 70, *Models in Chemical Science* 71, *Chemical Bonds* 73.
Noyes Laboratory of Chemical Physics, California Institute of Technology, Pasadena, Calif. 91109; Home: 2015 Glen Springs Road, Pasadena, Calif. 91107, U.S.A.
Telephone: 213-795-6841 Ext. 2500 (Office); 213-798-1496 (Home).

Gray, Harry J., M.SC.; American business executive; b. 1919 Milledgeville Crossroads, Georgia; *m.*; two *c.*; ed. Univ. of Illinois.
Served as Capt. in Army in 2nd World War; formerly Exec. Vice-Pres., Gen. Man. Greyhound Movers (div. of Greyhound Corpn.) and Vice-Pres. and Gen. Man. Greyhound Storage Inc.; joined Litton Industries Inc. 54, corporate Vice-Pres. 58, Group Vice-Pres. 61, mem. Board Dirs. 66-71, Senior Exec. Vice-Pres. 69-; Pres. and Chief Admin. Officer, United Aircraft Corpn. (now United Technologies Corpn.) 71-, also mem. Board of Dirs. and Exec. Cttee., Chief Exec. Officer 72-, Chair. Jan. 74-; Dir. Essex Int. Inc., Turbo Power and Marine Systems, Inc., Pratt & Whitney Aircraft of West Virginia, Inc., United Technologies Int. Inc. Pratt & Whitney Aircraft of Canada Ltd., all subsidiaries of United Technologies Corpn., Citicorp., First Nat. City Bank of New York, Aetna Life and Casualty Co., Hartford; Silver Star and Bronze Star for gallantry in action.
United Technologies Corporation, United Technologies Building, Hartford, Conn. 06101, U.S.A.

Gray, Hon. Herbert E.; Canadian politician; b. 25 May 1931, Windsor, Ont.; *s.* of Harry and Fannie Gray; *m.* Sharon Sholzberg 1967; one *s.* one *d.*; ed. Victoria Public School, Kennedy, Coll. Inst. Windsor, McGill Univ. and Osgoode Hall Law School, Toronto. Member of Parl. 62-; Chair. of House of Commons Standing Cttee. on Finance, Trade and Econ. Affairs 66-68; Parl. Sec. to Minister of Finance 68-69; Minister without Portfolio 69-70, Minister of Nat. Revenue 70-72; Minister of Consumer and Corporate Affairs 72-74; Govt. Observer Inter-American Conf. of Ministers of Labour, Bogotá 63; Vice-Chair. Del. to NATO Parl. Conf., Paris 63; mem. Del. to Canada-France Interparl. Conf. 66; mem. Canadian Del. to IMF and IBRD meeting 67, Canada-U.S. Interparl. Conf. 67-68; Liberal.
1253 Victoria Avenue, Windsor, Ontario, Canada.

Gray, Sir John Archibald Browne, M.A., M.B., B.CHIR., SC.D., F.R.C.P., F.R.S.; British physiologist and administrator; b. 30 March 1918, Highgate, London; *s.* of Sir Archibald Gray, K.C.V.O., C.B.E., and Elsie Cooper; *m.* Vera K. Mares 1946; one *s.* and *d.*; ed. Cheltenham Coll., Clare Coll., Cambridge and Univ. Coll. Hospital, London.
Service Research for M.R.C. 43-45; Surgeon Lieut., R.N.V.R. 45-46; M.R.C. Scientific Staff, Nat. Inst. for Medical Research 46-52; Reader in Physiology, Univ. Coll. London 52-58, Prof. of Physiology 58-66; Second Sec. Medical Research Council 66-68, Sec. 68-.
Leisure interests: sailing, painting, tennis.
Publs. numerous papers on sensory receptors and sensory nervous system.
Medical Research Council, 20 Park Crescent, London, W1N 4AL, England.
Telephone: 01-636-5422.

Gray, Louis Patrick, B.SC., JU.D.; American lawyer and civil servant; b. 18 July 1916, St. Louis, Mo.; *m.*; four *c.*; ed. U.S. Naval Acad. Annapolis Wash. and George Washington Univ. Law School, Wash. D.C.
Served U.S. Navy World War II, Korean War, rose to Capt. and post of Military Asst. to Chair., Joint Chiefs

of Staff and Asst. to Sec. of Defence for Legal and Legislative Affairs; retd. from Navy 60; admitted to bar D.C. 49, Conn. 58, and has practised before U.S. Court of Military Appeals, Supreme Court, Court of Claims Court of Appeals for D.C. Circuit; joined Suisman, Shapiro & Wool 61, Partner Suisman, Shapiro, Wool Brennan & Gray 67-69, 70, Suisman, Shapiro, Wool & Brennan 73-; Founded Capital for Technology Corpn.; Exec. Asst. to Sec. of Health, Education and Welfare 69-70; Special Consultant to President's Cabinet Cttee. on Education 70; Asst. Attorney General for Civil Division of Justice Dept. 70, Head of Civil Division 71; Acting Dir., Federal Bureau of Investigation 72-73 (resgnd. over Watergate case); mem. American Bar Asscn.; active in numerous civil and community affairs; Distinguished Service Award; Navy Commendation Medal with combat "V", American Defense Service Medal with bronze "A", United Nations Service Medal, Submarine Combat Pin (3 stars).
Suisman, Shapiro, Wool & Brennan, 325 State Street, New London, Conn. 06320, U.S.A.

Graylin, John Cranmer, C.M.G.; British (Rhodesian) lawyer and politician; b. 12 Jan. 1921, Stow Maries, Essex; *s.* of George John and Evelyn Gertrude (née Hull) Graylin; *m.* Sibella Margaretha Alheit 1946; two *s.* three *d.*; ed. Mid-Essex Technical Coll., Chelmsford, England, and Law Society School of Law, London.
Royal Air Force, Second World War; Solicitor 49; settled in Rhodesia 50; law practice, Livingstone 51-; Livingstone Municipal Councillor 52; mem. Fed. House of Parl. 53-63; Deputy Chair. of Cttees. 54; Minister of Agriculture 59-August 63 (resigned); Chair. Tobacco Export Promotion Council of Rhodesia 64-67; Chair. Nat. Export Council 67-69, Transportation Comm. 69; Chief Exec. Asscn. Rhodesian Industries 69-; mem. of Board Agricultural Finance Corpn., Agricultural Research Council.
Leisure interests: golf, bird watching, growing orchids, raising pheasants.
c/o Association of Rhodesian Industries, ARNI House, 109 Rotten Row, Salisbury, Rhodesia.

Greatbatch, Sir Bruce, Kt., K.C.V.O., C.M.G., M.B.E.; British colonial administrator; b. 10 June 1917, Warwicks.; ed. Malvern Coll. and Brasenose Coll., Oxford.
Appointed to Colonial Service, N. Nigeria 40; service with Royal W. African Frontier Force 40-45; resumed colonial service, N. Nigeria 45, Resident 56, Sec. to Gov. and Exec. Council 57, Senior Resident, Kano 58; Sec. to Premier of N. Nigeria and Head of Regional Civil Service 59; Deputy High Commr. in Kenya 64; Gov. and C.-in-C. of the Seychelles and Commr. for the British Indian Ocean Territory 69-73; Head of British Devt. Div. in the Caribbean 73-.
c/o National Provincial Bank Ltd., Cornmarket Street, Oxford, England.

Grechko, Marshal Andrei Antonovich; Soviet army officer; b. 17 Oct. 1903, Kuibyshevka; ed. Frunze Military Acad., Moscow, and General Staff Military Acad.
In First Cavalry Army 19; Officers' School 22, later Platoon Commdr. and Squadron Commdr.; at Frunze Mil. Acad. until 36, later Regimental Commdr. and Chief-of-Staff of Cavalry Div.; graduated from Gen. Staff Mil. Acad. 41; Commdr. 34th Cavalry Div., Southwest Front 41, later Commdr. of Cavalry Corps, Army, and Second-in-Command of Front; took part in liberation of N. Caucasus and Ukraine, Poland and Czechoslovakia; Commdr. Kiev Mil. Area 45-53; Commdr.-in-Chief Soviet Army Group in Germany 53-57; C.-in-C., Land Forces 57-60; First Deputy Minister of Defence and C.-in-C. Warsaw Pact Forces 60-67; Minister of Defence 67-; mem. C.P.S.U. 28-; mem. Central Cttee. C.P.S.U.; mem. Politburo 73-;

Deputy to U.S.S.R. Supreme Soviet 46-; Hero of Soviet Union; Order of Lenin (five times), Gold Star Medal and numerous other decorations.
Ministry of Defence, Moscow, U.S.S.R.
[Died 26 April 1976.]

Greco, Emilio; Italian sculptor; b. 11 Oct. 1913, Catania; *m.* Anna Greco 1969; ed. Accad. di Belle Arti, Palermo.
Professor of Sculpture Accad. di Belle Arti, Rome; mem. Accad. Nazionale di San Luca; first sculpture exhbn., Catania 33; one-man exhbns. in Rome, Milan, Naples, London, San Francisco, Rhode Island; represented in numerous group exhbns. in Italy and abroad including 4th Rome Quadriennale, 28th Venice Biennale, Bienal São Paulo 57, Palazzo Barberini 58, Zwerge Garden Salzburg 59; works in public and private collections in Rome, Milan, Venice, Florence, Trieste, Città del Capo, London, Leeds, Monaco, Hamburg, Cologne, St. Louis and Pinacoteca Vaticana; engaged on monument to Pope John XXIII 65-67; Medaglia d'Oro of Italian Pres. 61, Comune di Venezia prize, Venice Biennale 56.
Major works: *Monumento a Pinocchio in Collodi* 53-56, *Grande Bagnante I* (Tate Gallery, London) 56, *Grande Bagnante 3* (Musée National d'Art Moderne, Paris) 57, *Testa di Donna* (Pinacoteca Vaticana) 57, *Grande Figura Accoccolata* (Museum of Modern Art, Kyoto, Japan) 61, three bronze doors, Cathedral of Orvieto 61-64, Monument to Pope John XXIII 65-67.
Leisure interest: music.
Viale Cortina d'Ampezzo 132, Rome, Italy.
Telephone: 32-41-48.

Gredal, Eva; Danish social worker and politician; b. 1927
Chairman Nat. Asscn. of Social Workers 59-67; Vice-Chair. Nat. Asscn. of Women; mem. several social welfare cttees.; mem. Board Mental Health Asscn.; mem. Parl. 71-75; Minister for Social Affairs 71-73, of Welfare and Social Affairs Feb. 75-; Social Democrat.
Ministry of Welfare and Social Affairs, Copenhagen, Denmark.

Gredler-Oxenbauer, Willfried Andreas Kolomann, DR.JUR.; Austrian diplomatist; b. 12 Dec. 1916, Vienna; *s.* of Richard and Bertha (née Kiticsan); *m.* Elfriede Jirgl 54; three *d.*; ed. Vienna, Berlin and Harvard Univs.
Entered foreign service 42, served in Berlin and Belgrade 42-45; with Österreichische Vermögensschutzgesellschaft, Vienna (banking concern) 45-63; mem. Austrian Parliament 53-63 (Liberal Party); Perm. Rep. to Council of Europe 63-70; Amb. to Federal Germany Dec. 70-; Grosskreuz (Fed. Germany), Grosses Silbernes Ehrenzeichen (Austria), Grand Officer's Cross, Order of Knights of Malta.
Leisure interests: bibliophile, modern history, breeding snakes.
Publs. various articles on European and minority problems and also on human rights.
Österreichische Botschaft, 53 Bonn, Poppelsdorfer Allee 55; 53 Bonn, Friedrich-Wilhelm-Strasse 14, Federal Republic of Germany.
Telephone: 22-60-97/98 (Office); 23-11-12 (Home).

Green, David Ezra, B.A., A.M., PH.D.; American professor of enzyme chemistry; b. 5 Aug. 1910, New York N.Y.; *s.* of Herman L.and Jennie Green; *m.* Doris Cribb, 1936; two *d.*; ed. Washington Square Coll. and Cambridge School of Biochemistry.
Beit Memorial Research Fellow 34-38, Senior Beit Memorial Research Fellow 38-40; Fellow, Harvard Univ. 40-41; Assoc. in Biochemistry, Columbia Univ. Coll. of Physicians and Surgeons 41-46, Asst. Prof. of Biochemistry, and Dir. of Enzyme Chem. Laboratory 46-48; Prof. of Enzyme Research, and Co-Dir. Inst. for

Enzyme Research, Univ. of Wis. 48-; mem. Nat. Acad. of Sciences, American Acad. of Arts and Sciences; Paul-Lewis Laboratories Award in Enzyme Chem. of the American Chemical Soc.
Leisure interests: dancing, jogging.
Publs. *Mechanisms of Biological Oxidations* 39, *Molecular Insights into the Living Process* 67.
Institute for Enzyme Research, 1710 University Avenue, Madison, Wis. 53706; Home: 1525 Sumac Drive, Madison, Wis. 53705, U.S.A.
Telephone: 608-262-3361 (Office); 608-233-6329 (Home).

Green, (James) Maurice Spurgeon, M.B.E., M.A.; British newspaper editor; b. 8 Dec. 1906, Padiham, Lancs., England; *s.* of Col. J. E. and Constance Green; *m.* Janet G. Norie 1936; two *s.*; ed. Rugby School and Univ. Coll., Oxford.
Editor *The Financial News* 34-38; Royal Artillery 39-44; Financial and Industrial Editor *The Times* 38-39, 44-53, Asst. Editor 53-61; Deputy Editor *The Daily Telegraph* 61-64, Editor 64-74; Pres. Inst. of Journalists 76.
Leisure interests: music, fishing, shooting.
15 Sloane Avenue, London, S.W.3, England.

Green, Julien American (b. French) novelist; b. 6 Sept. 1900, Paris, France; ed. France and Univ. of Virginia.
Member Académie Française 71-, Acad. Royale de Belgique, American Acad. 71-, Conseil Littéraire de Monaco; Prix Nat. des Lettres (France) 66, Grand Prix de l'Académie Française 70.
Publs. *Adrienne Mesurat* (crowned by Acad. Française) 27, *Leviathan* 29, *L'autre Sommeil* 30, *Le Voyageur sur la Terre* 25, *Suite Anglaise* 26, *Les Clefs de la Mort, Épaves* 32, *Le Visionnaire* 34, *Minuit* 36, *Journal* 38, *Varouna* 40, *Memories of Happy Days* 42, *Journal* 46, *Si j'étais vous . . .* 47, *Journal* 49, *Moira* 50, *Journal* 51, *Journal* 55, *Le Malfaiteur* 56, *Le Bel Aujourd'hui* 58, *Chaque Homme dans sa Nuit* 60, *Partir avant le Jour* 63, *Mille Chemins Ouverts* 64, *Journal 28-58, Terre Lointaine* 66, *Vers l'invisible* 67, *Les Années Faciles* 70, *L'Autre* 71, *Ce Qui Reste de Jour* (memoirs) 72, *Qui Sommes-Nous* 72, *Oeuvres Complètes, Pleiade I, II, III* 73, *IV* 75, *Jeunesse* (memoirs) 74, *Liberté* (essay) 74; plays: *Sud* 53, *L'Ennemi* 54, *L'Ombre* 56.
c/o Plon, 8 rue Garancière, Paris 6e, France.

Green, Marshall, B.A.; American diplomatist; b. 27 Jan. 1916, Holyoke, Mass.; *s.* of Addison Loomis Green and Gertrude Metcalf; *m.* Lispenard Seabury Crocker 1942; three *c.*; ed. Groton School, and Yale Univ.
Private Sec. to American Ambassador to Japan 39-41; Lieut. U.S. Navy 42-45; U.S. Foreign Service 45-; Third Sec., Wellington, N.Z. 46-47; Japanese Desk Officer, State Dept., Washington 47-50; Second, later First Sec., Stockholm 50-55; Nat. War Coll. 55-56; Policy Planning Adviser, Far East, State Dept. 56-59; Minister-Counsellor, Seoul 60-61; Consul-Gen., Hong Kong 61-63; Deputy Asst. Sec. of State, Far East 63-65; Amb. to Indonesia 65-69; Asst. Sec. of State for E. Asian and Pacific Affairs 69-73; Amb. to Australia 73-; Meritorious Service Award, Nat. Civil Service League Career Service Award.
Leisure interests: music, travel, conservation, sports.
American Embassy, Yarralumla, Canberra, A.C.T., Australia; and Department of State, Washington, D.C. 20520, U.S.A.

Green, Maurice (*see* Green, James Maurice S.).

Green, Paul, A.B., LITT.D.; American playwright; b. 17 March 1894, Lillington, N.C.; *s.* of William A. Green and Betty Byrd Green; *m.* Elizabeth Atkinson Lay 1922; one *s.* three *d.*; ed. Univ. of North Carolina and Cornell Univ.
Second Lieut. American Expeditionary Force 18-19; Instructor in and Prof. of Philosophy, Univ. of North

Carolina 23-32; Pulitzer Prizewinner 27, Guggenheim Fellow 28-30; Prof. of Dramatic Art, Univ. of North Carolina 35-50; Pres. National Folk Festival 34-35, National Theatre Conference 40-42; Lecturer in Asia on American Theatre for Rockefeller Foundation and UNESCO 51; mem. Nat. Inst. of Arts and Letters; many hon. doctorates.

Publs. *The Lord's Will* 25, *In Abraham's Bosom and The Field God* 27, *Lonesome Road* 26, *Wide Fields* 28, *In the Valley and Other Plays* 28, *The House of Connelly and Other Plays* 31, *The Laughing Pioneer* 32, *Roll Sweet Chariot* 34, *Shroud My Body Down* 35, *This Body the Earth* 35, *Hymn to the Rising Sun* 36, *Johnny Johnson* 37, *The Lost Colony* 37, *The Enchanted Maze* 39, *Out of the South* 39, *The Highland Call* 41, *Native Son* (with Richard Wright) 41, *The Hawthorn Tree* 43, *Forever Growing* 45, *Salvation on a String and Other Stories* 46, *The Common Glory* 48, *Dog on the Sun* 49, *Peer Gynt* (adaptation) 51, *Dramatic Heritage* 53, *Wilderness Road* 56, *The Founders* 57, *Drama and the Weather* 58, *Wings for to Fly, The Confederacy* 59, *The Stephen Foster Story* 60, *Five Plays of the South* 63, *Plough and Furrow* 63, *Cross and Sword* 66, *The Sheltering Plaid* 65, *Texas* 67, *Sing All a Green Willow* 68, *Home to My Valley* 70, *Trumpet in the Land* 72, *The Honeycomb* 72, *Drumbeats in Georgia* 73, *Land of Nod and Other Stories* 76, *Louisiana Cavalier* 76, *We the People* 76; also numerous screen plays.
Old Lystra Road, Chapel Hill, N.C. 27514, U.S.A. Telephone: 919-933-8581.

Greenberg, Joseph Harold, PH.D.; American professor of anthropology; b. 28 May 1915, Brooklyn, N.Y.; s. of Jacob Greenberg and Florence Pilzer Greenberg; m. Selma Berkowitz 1940; ed. Columbia Coll. and Northwestern Univ.
Army service in Signal Intelligence Corps 40-45; Instructor and Asst. Prof. Univ. of Minn. 46-48; Asst., Assoc., then Prof., Columbia Univ. 48-62; Prof. of Anthropology, Stanford Univ. 62-, Ray Lyman Wilbur Distinguished Prof. of Social Sciences 71; First Distinguished Lecturer, American Anthropological Asscn. 70; mem. Nat. Acad. of Sciences, Amer. Acad. of Arts and Sciences 72-; Haile Sellassie I Prize for African Research 67.
Leisure interest: playing the piano.
Publs. *The Languages of Africa* 63, 2nd edn. 66, *Universals of Language* (Editor) 63, *Anthropological Linguistics: An Introduction* 68, *Language Universals— A Research Frontier* (in *Science*) 69, *The Indo-Pacific Hypothesis* (in *Current Trends in Linguistics* Vol. 8, Editor Thomas Sebeok) 70, *Language, Culture and Communication* 71.
Department of Anthropology, Stanford University, Stanford, Calif. 94305; Home: 860 Mayfield, Stanford, Calif. 94305, U.S.A.
Telephone: 415-321-2300, Ext. 4547 (Office); 415-321-0488 (Home).

Greenborough, Hedley Bernard, C.B.E., F.B.I.M., F.INST.PET.; British oil executive; b. 7 July 1922, Kingston-upon-Thames; s. of William and Elizabeth Marie Greenborough (née Wilson); m. Gerta Ebel 1951; one s.; ed. Wandsworth School and U.S. Navy, Pensacola, Florida, U.S.A.
Joined Asiatic Petroleum Co., London 39; with Shell Oil Calif., U.S.A. 46-47; with Shell Brazil 47-57; Exec. Vice-Pres. Shell Argentina 60-66; Far East Area Co-ordinator, Shell Int., London 66-69; Man. Dir. of Marketing, Shell-Mex and B.P. Ltd. 69-71, Chief Exec., Man. Dir. 71-75; Deputy Chair. and Man. Dir. Shell U.K. Ltd. Jan. 76-; Vice-Chair. British Chamber of Commerce, Argentina 62-66, British Road Fed. 69-; Chair. U.K. Oil Pipelines Ltd. 71-, U.K. Oil Industry Emergency Cttee. 71-, U.K. Petroleum Industry Advisory Cttee. 71-; Gov. Ashridge Management Coll.

72-; mem. CBI Council and Econ. Policy Cttee. 72-; Pres. Elect Inst. of Petroleum 76-.
Leisure interests: golf, travel, music.
Shell-Mex House, Strand, London, W.C.2; Home: 30 Burghley House, Oakfield, Somerset Road, Wimbledon Common, London, S.W.19, England.
Telephone: 01-438-3111 (Office); 01-946-0095 (Home).

Greene, Graham (brother of Sir Hugh Greene, *q.v.*), C.H.; British writer; b. 2 Oct. 1904; ed. Berkhamsted School and Balliol Coll., Oxford.
Sub-Editor *The Times* 26-30; Lit. Editor *Spectator* 40-41; Foreign Office 41-44; Dir. Eyre and Spottiswoode (Publishers) Ltd. 44-48; Dir. of Bodley Head 58-68; Chair. Nat. Book League 74-; Hon. Litt.D. (Cambridge) 62, Hon. D. Litt. (Edinburgh) 67; Hon. Fellow, Balliol Coll., Oxford 63, Chevalier de la Légion d'Honneur 69, Shakespeare Prize (Hamburg) 68.
Publs. *Babbling April* 25, *The Man Within* 29, *The Name of Action* 30, *Rumour at Nightfall* 31, *Stamboul Train* 32, *It's a Battlefield* 34, *England made me* 35, *Journey without Maps, A Gun for Sale* 36, *Brighton Rock* 38, *The Lawless Roads* 39, *The Confidential Agent* 39, *The Power and the Glory* 40 (Hawthornden Prize), *British Dramatists* 42, *The Ministry of Fear* 43, *Nineteen Stories* 47, *The Heart of the Matter* 48, *The Lost Childhood and Other Essays* 51, *The End of the Affair* 51, *Essais Catholiques* 53, *Twenty-one Stories* 54, *Loser Takes All* 55, *The Quiet American* 55, *Our Man in Havana* 58, *A Burnt-Out Case* 61, *In Search of a Character: Two African Journals* 61, *A Sense of Reality* 63, *The Comedians* 66, *May We Borrow Your Husband? And Other Comedies of the Sexual Life* (short stories) 67, *Collected Essays* 69, *Travels with my Aunt* 69, *A Sort of Life* (autobiography) 71, *The Honorary Consul* 73, *Lord Rochester's Monkey* (biography) 74.
Plays: *The Living Room* 53, *The Potting Shed* 57, *The Complaisant Lover* 59, *Carving a Statue* 64, *The Return of A. J. Raffles* 75.
Screen plays: *Brighton Rock* 48, *The Fallen Idol* 48, *The Third Man* 49, *Our Man in Havana* 60, *The Comedians* 67.
Children's Books: *The Little Train* 47, *The Little Fire Engine* 50, *The Little Horse Bus* 52, *The Little Steam-roller* 53.
c/o The Bodley Head, 9 Bow Street, London, W.C.2, England.

Greene, Sir Hugh (Carleton), K.C.M.G., O.B.E.; British publisher and broadcasting official; b. 15 Nov. 1910, Berkhamsted; s. of the late Charles and Marion Greene; brother of Graham Greene (*q.v.*); m. 1st Helga Guinness 1934, two s.; m. 2nd Elaine Shaplen 1951, two s.; m. 3rd Tatjana Sais 1970; ed. Berkhamsted School and Merton Coll., Oxford.
Newspaper correspondent in Germany 34-39; expelled from Germany 39; correspondent in Poland 39; R.A.F. 40; Head of German Service, B.B.C. 40-46; Controller of Broadcasting, British Zone, Germany 46-48; Head of East European Service, B.B.C. 49-50; Head of Emergency Information Service, Malaya 50-51; Asst. Controller Overseas Service, B.B.C. 52-55, Controller 55-56; Dir. of Admin., B.B.C. 56-58; Dir. of News and Current Affairs 58-59; Dir.-Gen., B.B.C. Jan. 60-March 69; mem. Board of Govs., B.B.C. July 69-Aug. 71; Chair. The Bodley Head July 69-, Greene King Brewery 71-; Vice-Pres. European Broadcasting Union 63-68; Hon. D.C.L. (Univ. of East Anglia) 69, Dr. h.c. (Open Univ. and York Univ. 73).
Publs. *The Spy's Bedside Book* 57, *The Third Floor Front* 69, *The Rivals of Sherlock Holmes* (Editor) 70, *More Rivals of Sherlock Holmes* (Editor) 71, *The Future of Broadcasting in Britain* 72, *The Crooked Counties* (Editor) 73.
Earls Hall, Cockfield, Bury St. Edmunds, Suffolk, England.

Greene, James Edward; Liberian politician; b. 6 July 1915, Greenville, Sinoe County; s. of late James E. Greene and Mary L. Greene-Severe; m. Minnie L. Frazier 1944; three c.; ed. Liberia Coll. (also Univ. of Liberia).
Teacher, Sinoe High School 41-49, Principal 49-52; Supt. Sinoe County 52-61; Senator from Sinoe County 61-72; Nat. Vice-Chair. True Whig Party 63-67, Chair. 67-72; Vice-Pres. of Liberia 72-; numerous nat. and foreign decorations.
Leisure interests: hunting, swimming.
Office of the Vice-President, Monrovia; Greenville, Sinoe County, Liberia.

Greene of Harrow Weald, Baron (Life Peer), cr. 74, of Harrow in Greater London; **Sidney Francis Greene,** Kt., C.B.E.; British trade unionist; b. 12 Feb. 1910, London; s. of Frank J. Greene and Alice Kerrod; m. Masel E. Carter 1936; three d.; ed. in London.
General Sec. Nat. Union of Railwaymen 57-74; mem. Gen. Council, TUC 57-, Chair. 69-70; mem. Nat. Econ. Devt. Council 62-; mem. Advisory Council, Export Credits Guarantee Dept. 67-70; Dir. Bank of England 70-, Times Newspapers Ltd. 74-, Rio Tinto Zinc Corpn. 75-, Nat. Freight Corpn., Southern Electricity Bd., Trade Union Unit Trust.
Leisure interests: cricket, gardening.
26 Kynaston Wood, Boxtree Road, Harrow Weald, Middx., England.

Greenewalt, Crawford Hallock, B.S.; American executive; b. 16 Aug. 1902, Cumington, Mass.; s. of Frank Lindsay and Mary Hallock Greenewalt; m. Margaretta Lammot du Pont 1926; two s. one d.; ed. William Penn Charter School, Philadelphia and Massachusetts Inst. of Technology.
Joined E. I. du Pont de Nemours and Co. 22; Pres. du Pont de Nemours 48-62, Chair. of Board 62-67, Chair. of Finance Cttee. 67-74; Dir. Morgan Guaranty Trust Co. 63-72, Boeing Co. 64-74; Fellow, American Acad. of Arts and Sciences; mem. Nat. Acad. of Sciences, American Philosophical Soc., Business Advisory Council, Mass. Inst. of Technology Corpn.; Trustee, Carnegie Inst., Wash.; Regent, Smithsonian Inst. 56-74; many hon. degrees; Chemical Industry Award 52, William Proctor Prize (American Asscn. for the Advancement of Science) 57, Medal for Advancement of Research (American Soc. of Metals) 58, Poor Richard's Club Gold Medal for Achievement 59.
Publs. *The Uncommon Man* 59, *Hummingbirds* 60, *Bird Song: Acoustics and Physiology* 69.
Home: Greenville, nr. Wilmington, Del., U.S.A.

Greenfield, James Lloyd; American newspaper executive; b. 16 July 1924; ed. Harvard Univ.
Cleveland Press 39-41; Voice of America 49-50; Corresp. for *Time* Magazine, Korea and Japan 51-55, Bureau Chief, New Delhi 56-57, Deputy Bureau Chief London 58-61; Chief Diplomatic Corresp. *Time-Life*, Washington, D.C. 61-62; Deputy Asst. Sec. of State, Public Affairs 62-64; Asst. Sec. of State, Public Affairs 64-66; Asst. Vice-Pres. Continental Air Lines, L.A., Calif. 66-68; Vice-Pres. Westinghouse Broadcasting Co. 68-69; Foreign Editor *New York Times* 69-.
850 Park Ave., New York, N.Y. 10021, U.S.A.

Greenfield, Julius Macdonald, C.M.G., Q.C., LL.B., B.C.L.; British (Rhodesian) retd. lawyer and politician; b. 13 July 1907, Boksburg, Transvaal, S. Africa; s. of Rev. C. E. and Mrs. Greenfield; m. Florence M. Couper 1935; two s. one d.; ed. Milton School, Bulawayo, and Univs. of Cape Town and Oxford.
Rhodesian Rhodes Scholar 29; admitted to practise as advocate of High Court of S. Rhodesia 33, practised at Bulawayo till 50; elected to S. Rhodesia Parl. (United Party) 48; Minister of Justice and Internal Affairs 50-53; elected to Parl. of Fed. of Rhodesia and

Nyasaland (Fed. Party) 53; Minister of Home Affairs and Education 53-55; Minister of Education and Law 55-58; Minister of Law 58-62, of Law and Home Affairs 62-63; returned to law practice 64; Puisne Judge of High Court of Rhodesia 68-74.
Leisure interest: building in stone.
17 Retzia Road, Hoheisen, Bellville, Cape, South Africa.

Greenhill of Harrow, Baron (Life Peer), cr. 74, of the Royal Borough of Kensington and Chelsea; **Denis Arthur Greenhill,** G.C.M.G., O.B.E.; British diplomatist; b. 7 Nov. 1913, Woodford, Essex; s. of James and Susie Greenhill; m. Angela McCulloch 1941; two s.; ed. Bishop's Stortford Coll. and Christ Church, Oxford.
Served in Second World War in Egypt, N. Africa, Italy, India and S.E. Asia, demobilized with rank of Col.; in British Foreign Service 46-; in Sofia 47-49, Washington 49-52; at Foreign Office 52-54; at Imperial Defence Coll. 54; U.K. Del. to NATO, Paris 55-57, to Singapore 57-59; Counsellor, Washington, D.C. 59-62, Minister 62-64; Asst. Under-Sec. of State, Foreign Office 64-66; Deputy Under-Sec. of State 66-69; Perm. Under-Sec. of State for Foreign and Commonwealth Affairs 69-73; Gov. BBC 73-; led British mission to Rhodesia Feb. 76; Dir. British Petroleum, S. G. Warburg, Clerical, Medical and Gen. Assurance, Wellcome Foundation, British-American Tobacco 74, Hawker Siddeley Group 74; mem. Security Comm., British Leyland.
25 Hamilton House, Vicarage Gate, London, W.8, England.
Telephone: 01-937-8362.

Greenspan, Alan, B.S., M.A.; American economist; b. 6 March 1926, N.Y.; s. of Herbert Greenspan and Rose Goldsmith; ed. New York and Columbia Univs.
President, Townsend-Greenspan & Co. Inc., econ. consultants 54-74; mem. Nixon for Pres. Cttee. 68-69; mem. Task Force for Econ. Growth 69, Comm. on an All-Voluteer Armed Force 69-70, Comm. on Financial Structure and Regulation 70-71; Consultant to Council of Econ. Advisers 70-74, to U.S. Treasury 71-74, to Fed. Reserve Board 71-74; Chair. Council of Econ. Advisers Sept. 74-; mem. Sec. of Commerce's Econ. Advisory Board 71-72, Securities and Exchange Comm.'s Cen. Market System Cttee. 72, G.N.P. Review Cttee. of Office of Management and Budget, *Time* Magazine's Board of Economists 71-74; Senior Adviser Brookings Inst. Panel on Econ. Activity 70-74; Past Pres., Fellow, Nat. Asscn. of Business Economists; Dir. Trans World Financial Co. 62-74, Dreyfus Fund 70-74, Gen. Cable Corpn. 73-74, Sun Chemical Corpn. 73-74.
Leisure interest: golf.
860 United Nations Plaza, New York, N.Y. 10017; and Watergate East, 2500 Virginia Avenue, N.W., Washington, D.C. 20037, U.S.A.

Greenstein, Jesse Leonard, PH.D.; American astronomer; b. 15 Oct. 1909, New York; s. of Maurice Greenstein and L. Feingold; m. Naomi Kitay 1934; two s.; ed. Horace Mann School for Boys and Harvard.
Engaged in real estate and investments 30-34; Nat. Research Fellow 37-39; Assoc. Prof., Yerkes Observatory, Univ. of Chicago 39-48; Research Assoc. McDonald Observatory, Univ. of Texas 39-48; Mil. Researcher under Office of Scientific Research and Devt. (optical design), Yerkes 42-45; Prof. and Exec. Officer for Astronomy 48-72, Calif. Inst. of Technology, Lee A. DuBridge Prof. 70- and staff mem. Mount Wilson and Palomar Observatories (now Hale) 48-, mem. Owens Valley Radio Observatory staff; Chair. Faculty of Inst. 65-67; Visiting Prof. Inst. for Advanced Studies, Princeton 64 and 68-69; mem. Nat. Acad. of Sciences, American Philosophical Soc., Int. Astronomical Union, Board of Overseers, Harvard Coll. 65-71, Editorial Board *Astrophysical Journal*; Chair. Board Assoc.

Univ. Research in Astronomy 74-; Consultant to Nat. Science Foundation, Nat. Aeronautics and Space Admin.; Chair. Nat. Acad. of Sciences Survey of Astronomy; Russell Lecturer; Amer. Astronomical Soc.; California Scientist of Year Award 64; Bruce Medal, Astronomical Soc. of Pacific; Distinguished Public Service Award; Gold Medal, Royal Astronomical Soc.
Leisure interests: art, travel, wine.
Publs. *Stellar Atmospheres* (Editor), many technical papers.
California Institute of Technology, Pasadena, California, U.S.A.
Telephone: 213-795-6811.

Greenwald, Joseph Adolph, LL.B.; American economist and diplomatist; b. 18 Sept. 1918, Chicago, Ill.; s. of Jacob and Lena (née Corman) Greenwald; m. Mary V. Doyle 1942; two s. one d.; ed. Univ. of Chicago and Georgetown Univ. Law School.
Economist, War Production Board 42-43; Int. Economist, Dept. of State 47; admitted D.C. Bar 51; U.S. Resident Rep., Int. Econs. Orgs., Geneva 52-55; Chief, Commercial Policy Branch, Dept. of State 55-58; First Sec. American Embassy, London 58-63; Dir. Office Int. Trade, Dept. of State 63-65; Deputy Asst. Sec. of State for Int. Trade Policy and Econ. Defense 65-68; Leader U.S. Del., 2nd UN Conf. on Trade and Devt., New Delhi 68; Acting Asst. Sec. of State for Econ. Affairs 68-69; U.S. Perm. Rep. to OECD 69-72; Amb. to EEC 72-75; Asst. Sec. of State for Econ. and Business Affairs 76-.
EB (Room 6828), Department of State, Washington, D.C. 20520; Home: 1661 Crescent Place, N.W., Washington, D.C. 20009, U.S.A.

Greenwood, Allen, C.B.E., J.P.; British business executive; b. 4 June 1917, London; ed. Cheltenham Coll. and Coll. of Aeronautical Engineering.
Joined Vickers-Armstrongs Ltd. 39; R.N.V.R. (Fleet Air Arm) 42-46; Service Man., Vickers-Armstrongs (Aircraft) Ltd. 53, Dir. 60; Sales and Service Man., British Aircraft Corpn. Ltd. 61, Deputy Chair. 72-75 Chair. 76-; one of Airframe Dirs. for Concorde 61 Dir. British Aircraft Corpn. (Operating) Ltd. 64, British Aircraft Corpn. (U.S.A.) Inc. 64, SEPECAT S.A. 66, Remploy Ltd. 68 (Vice-Chair. 72), Panavia Aircraft G.m.b.H. 69 (Chair. 69-72), British Aircraft Corpn. (Australia) Pty. Ltd. 72, Europlane Ltd. 73, Industrial Advisers to the Blind 74; Pres. Soc. of British Aerospace Cos. Ltd. 70-72, Assn. Européenne des Constructeurs de Materiel Aerospatiel 74.
British Aircraft Corporation Ltd., Weybridge, Surrey, England.
Telephone: Weybridge 45522.

Greenwood, Ivor John, Q.C., LL.B.; Australian politician; b. 15 Nov. 1926, Melbourne; m.; two c.; ed. Scotch Coll., Melbourne.
Admitted to Victorian Bar 51; Vice-Pres. Victorian State Exec. of Liberal Party 66-68; Senator from Victoria 68-; Minister for Health March-Aug. 71; Attorney-Gen. 71-72; Deputy Leader of Opposition in the Senate 72-75; Attorney-Gen. and Minister for Police and Customs Nov.-Dec. 75, Minister for Environment, Housing and Community Devt. Dec. 75-; Deputy Leader of the Govt. in the Senate; Liberal.
4 Treasury Place, Melbourne 3000, Australia.
Telephone: 63-6494.

Greenwood of Rossendale, Baron (Life Peer), cr. 70, of East Mersea in the County of Essex; **Anthony Greenwood,** P.C., J.P., M.A.; British politician; b. 14 Sept. 1911; m. Gillian Crawshay-Williams 1940; two d.; ed. Kingston Grammar School, Merchant Taylors' School, and Balliol Coll., Oxford.
Member of Parl. 46-70; Vice-Chair. Parl. Labour Party 50-51; mem. Nat. Exec. Cttee. Labour Party 54-, mem.

Bureau, Socialist Int. 60-; Nat. Vice-Chair. Labour Party 62-63, Chair. 63-64; Sec. of State for the Colonies 64-65; Minister of Overseas Devt. 65-66; Minister of Housing and Local Govt. 66-May 70; Pro-Chancellor, Univ. of Lancaster 72-; Trustee of several educ. trusts; Dir. several companies; Vice-Pres. Building Socs. Asscn., Commonwealth Parl. Asscn. (British branch). Cen. Council for the Rehabilitation of the Disabled (Chair. 75-), British Waterworks Asscn., etc.; Pres. River Thames Soc. 72-, London Soc. 72-, British Trust for Conservation Volunteers 75-; Chair. U.K. Housing Asscn. 72-, Local Govt. Staff Comm. for England 72-, Housing Centre 73-75, Pres. 75-; Deputy Chair. Housing Corpn. 74-; Chair. Local Govt. Training Board 75-; Conciliator Int. Centre for Settlement of Investment Disputes 75; mem. of Board, Commonwealth Devt. Corpn., of Court of Univ. of Essex, Cen. Lancashire Devt. Corpn., of Advisory Board on Redundant Churches 75-; Deputy-Lieut. for Essex 75-; Fellow, Royal Society of Arts, Ancient Monuments Soc., Royal Commonwealth Soc.
38 Downshire Hill, Hampstead, London, N.W.3; The Old Ship Cottage, East Mersea, Colchester, England.
Telephone: 01-435-3276; 020638-3249.

Greer, Germaine Australian feminist and author; b. 29 Jan. 1939, Melbourne; ed. Melbourne and Sydney Univs. and Cambridge Univ., England.
Lecturer in English, Warwick Univ. 68-73; numerous television appearances and public talks including discussion with Norman Mailer (q.v.) in The Theatre of Ideas, New York.
Publs. *The Female Eunuch* 70; articles for *Listener*, *Spectator*, *Esquire*, *Harper's Magazine*, *Playboy* and other journals.
c/o Curtis Brown Ltd., 1 Craven Hill, London, W2 3EW, England.

Gregh, François-Didier; French public servant; b. 26 March 1906, Paris; s. of Fernand Gregh (mem. Acad. Française) and Harlette Hayem; m. Adé Barbier 1947; ed. Lycée Janson-de-Sailly, Faculty of Law and Letters, Ecole Libre des Sciences Politiques, Paris.
Inspector of Finances 30-35; Financial Controller 35-43; Dir. of the Budget, Ministry of Finance 44-49; Dir. Crédit Lyonnais 49-53; Dir. of Int. Bank for Reconstruction and Development (Asian and Middle East Div.) 53-55; Asst. Sec.-Gen. for Economy and Finance, NATO 55-59, Deputy Sec.-Gen. 59-67; Insp.-Gen. of Finances (French Govt.) 59-69, 72-; Minister of State, Principality of Monaco 69-72; Commdr. Légion d'Honneur, several foreign decorations.
9 rue Michel-Ange, Paris 16e, France.
Telephone: AUT 79-24.

Grégoire, Henri; Belgian classical and Byzantine scholar.
Prof. of Greek and Byzantine History, Brussels Univ.; Sather Prof. Univ. of Calif. 38; Co-Founder Ecole Libre des Hautes Etudes N.Y.; Vice-Dean Faculty of Letters 41-45, Pres. 44; Asst. Prof. of History, New School for Social Research, N.Y.; Pres. Asscn. Int. des Byzantinistes; Editor *Byzantion*, *Corpus Bruxellense Historiae Byzantine*, *La Nouvelle Clio*, *Ta Kyprin*; Co-Founder and Joint Editor of *Le Flambeau* 18-; *Renaissance* 42-; Pres. Centre Nat. de Recherches byzantines, and Editor of its publs.; assoc. mem. Acad. des Inscriptions et Belles Lettres, Paris, and Accad. Nazionale dei Lincei, Rome; mem. Brussels, Bucharest, Copenhagen, Mainz, Munich and Palermo Acads., Medieval Acad. of America, Slav Insts. of Prague and of Belgrade; Chair. Acad. of Mythological and Religious Research, Bulgarian Historical Society, Byzantine Insts. of Providence, R.I., Paris and Istanbul, etc.; Dr. h.c. (Paris, Athens, Thessalonika, Algiers, Sofia. Cairo).
Publs. *Digenis Akritas, the Byzantine Epic in History and Poetry* (with P. Morphopoulos) 42, *Dans la mon-*

tagne grecque 48, *Asklepios, Apollon Smintheus et Rudra* (with R. Goossens and M. Mathieu), *La base historique de l'épopée médiévale* 50, *Les Persécutions dans l'Empire romain* (with P. Orgels, J. Moreau and A. Maricq) 51, *Euripides Tragédies* III-VII, *Les Perles de la Poésie Slave* 60.
45 rue des Bollandistes, Brussels, Belgium.

Grégoire, Pierre; Luxembourg politician; b. 9 Nov. 1907; ed. secondary and higher education, Luxembourg. Administrative career 29-33; Editorial staff *Luxemburger Wort* 33-59; mem. Govt. 59; fmr. Minister of Foreign Affairs, Armed Forces and Cultural Affairs; Pres. Asscn. of Catholic Writers; in concentration camp 40-45; Pres. Chamber of Deputies until 74; numerous Luxembourg and foreign decorations.
Publs. *Drucker, Gazettisten und Zensoren* (4 vols.) 64, *Le Baiser d'Europe* 67, and about thirty other works (literary, poetry, history, criticism, etc.).
Strassen, 177 route d'Arlon, Luxembourg-Ville, Luxembourg.
Telephone: Luxembourg 478-461.

Gregor, Ján, ING.; Czechoslovak economist; b. 10 May 1923, Turčianska Štiavnička; ed. School of Economics, Bratislava.
Head of Dept., Commissioner's Office for Light Industry 51-52; Deputy Commr. of Trade 53-54; Deputy Commr. of Consumer Goods Industry 56-60; Head of Dept., Slovak Planning Comm. 60-63, Deputy Chair. 63-69; Deputy Minister of Planning, Slovak Socialist Repub. 69-70; Minister of Industry, Slovak Socialist Repub. 70-71; Deputy Prime Minister of Č.S.S.R. 71-; Deputy to House of Nations, Fed. Assembly 71; Chair. Czechoslovak-Romanian Govt. Comm. for Econ. and Scientific Technical Co-operation 73; Order of Labour 70, Order of Victorious February 73.
Office of Government Presidium of Č.S.S.R., nábř. kpt. Jaroše 4, Prague 1, Czechoslovakia.

Gregorios, Bishop Paul, M.DIV., S.T.M., TH.D., F.I.I.C.S. (fomerly **Verghese, Rev. Thadikkal Paul**); Indian ecclesiastic; b. 9 Aug. 1922, Tripunithura, India; s. of T. P. Piely and Mrs. Aley Piely; ed. Goshen Coll., Princeton and Yale Univs., Keble Coll., Oxford.
Taught in govt. schools in Ethiopia 47-50; studied in U.S.A. 50-54; Gen. Sec. Orthodox Christian Student Movement of India 55-57; Hon. Lecturer in Religion, Union Christian Coll., Alwaye 54-56; Special Staff Asst. H.I.M. Haile Sellassie I 56-59; Chief Adviser, Haile Sellassie Foundation 59; Assoc. Gen. Sec. and Dir. of the Div. of Ecumenical Action, World Council of Churches, Geneva 62-67; Principal, Syrian Orthodox Theological Seminary, Kottayam, Kerala 67-; consecrated as Bishop; Chair. Life and Action Unit, Christian Conf. of Asia; Vice-Chair. Kerala Philosophers' Congress, Theological Comm., Christian Peace Conf., Prague; Senator, Kerala Univ.; mem. various World Council of Churches' and Christian Peace Conf. comms. and cttees.; fmr. leader WCC del. to UNESCO
Leisure interests: boating, mountain hikes.
Publs. *Joy of Freedom* 67, *The Freedom of Man* 70, *Be Still and Know* 71, *Koptisches Christentum* 73, *Die Syrischen Christen in Indien* 74, *Authority and Freedom* 74.
Orthodox Theological Seminary, Kottayam, Kerala, India.
Telephone: Kottayam 3526.

Gregory, Bernard Paul, PH.D.; French physicist; b. 19 Jan. 1919, Bergerac, Dordogne; s. of Paul Gregory and Cécile Aeschlimann; m. Florence Volk; two s. two d.; ed. Ecole Polytechnique, Paris, and Massachusetts Inst. of Technology, U.S.A.
Professor of Physics, Ecole des Mines, Paris 53-58; Prof. of Physics, Ecole Polytechnique, Paris, also Deputy Dir. of Physics Laboratory 59-65; Directorate mem. for Research, European Org. for Nuclear Research (CERN)

64-65; Dir.-Gen. of CERN Jan. 66-Dec. 70; Prof. of Physics and Dir. Physics Laboratory, Ecole Polytechnique, Paris 71-; Croix de Guerre 39-45; Chevalier, Légion d'Honneur; Ordre du Mérite.
Publs. articles on high-energy nuclear physics, in particular works on the discovery of new particles by means of cosmic rays and high-energy accelerators.
Laboratoire de Physique Nucléaire de Hautes Energies, Ecole Polytechnique, 17 rue Descartes, 75 Paris 5e, France.
Telephone: 033-99-17.

Gregory, Horace Victor, B.A.; American writer; b. 10 April 1898, Milwaukee, Wis.; s. of Henry Bolton Gregory and Anna Catherine Henkel; m. Marya Zaturenka (poet, winner of Pulitzer Prize for Poetry 1938) 1925; one s. one d.; ed. Milwaukee and Univ. of Wisconsin.
Freelance in New York 24-; awarded Young Poet's Prize for Poetry (Chicago) 28, Helen Haire Levinson Poetry Award 34, Russell Loines Award (American Inst. Arts and Letters) 42, Guggenheim Fellowship 51, Union League Civic and Arts Foundation Prize for Poetry (Chicago) 51; Acad. of American Poets Award 62, Bollingen Prize Yale 65; elected mem. Inst. of Arts and Letters 64; mem. English Faculty, Sarah Lawrence Coll., Bronxville 34-62; Lecturer New School for Social Research 55-56; contrib. to *New Republic, New Masses, Herald Tribune, Poetry, Saturday Review of Literature, Partisan Review, New York Times, Book Review, The Commonweal,* etc.
Leisure interests: travel, classical music, painting, history.
Publs. *Rooming House* (poems) 32, *Poems of Catullus* (translation) 33, *D. H. Lawrence: Pilgrim of the Apocalypse* 33, *No Retreat* (poems) 33, *Chorus for Survival* (poems) 35, *Poems 1930-40* 41, *The Shield of Achilles, Essays on Beliefs in Poetry* 44, *A History of American Poetry 1900-1940* (with Marya Zaturenska) 46, *Selected Poems of Horace Gregory* 51; *Ovid's Metamorphoses: an adaptation into modern verse* 58, *Amy Lowell: An Historical Portrait* 58, *The World of James McNeill Whistler* 59, *Medusa in Gramercy Park* (poems) 61, *Collected Poems* 64; Editor: *New Letters in America* 37, *The Triumph of Life* (anthology of devotional and elegaic verse) 43, *The Portable Sherwood Anderson* 49, *The Snake Lady and Other Stories* by Vernon Lee 54, *Robert Browning's Selected Poems* 56, *The Mentor Book of Religious Verse* 56; *The Crystal Cabinet* (with Marya Zaturenska) 62, *Love Poems of Ovid* (new English verse adaptation) 64, *The Silver Swan: An Anthology* (with Marya Zaturenska) 66, *Dorothy Richardson: An Adventure in Self-Discovery* 67, *The House on Jefferson Street: A Cycle of Memories* (autobiography) 71, *Spirit of Time and Place: Collected Essays of Horace Gregory* 73.
Palisades, Rockland County, N.Y., 10964, U.S.A.
Telephone: 914-EL9-4362.

Gregory, Roderic Alfred, C.B.E., M.SC., PH.D., D.SC., M.R.C.S., L.R.C.P., F.R.S.; British physiologist; b. 29 Dec. 1913, London; s. of Alfred and Alice Gregory; m. Alice Watts 1939; one d.; ed. George Green's School, London, and Univ. Coll. and Hospital, Univ. of London.
Sharpey Scholar, Univ. Coll., London 36-39; Rockefeller Travelling Medical Fellow 39-41; Lecturer in Physiology, Univ. Coll., London 41-45; Senior Lecturer in Physiology, Univ. of Liverpool 45-48; George Holt Prof. of Physiology, Univ. of Liverpool 48-; mem. Medical Research Council of Great Britain 67-71; Hon. mem. American Gastroenterological Soc. 67, British Soc. of Gastroenterology 74; Vice-Pres., Royal Soc. 72-73; Fellow, Univ. Coll., London; Hon. D.Sc. (Univ. of Chicago); Baly Medal Royal Coll. of Physicians, London; Feldberg Prize; Anniversary Medal, Swedish Medical Soc.; Hunter Medal and Triennial Prize, Royal Coll. of Surgeons of England 69.

Leisure interest: music.
Publs. Various articles in journals of physiology and gastroenterology.
Department of Physiology, University of Liverpool, Liverpool, England.
Telephone: 051-709-9306.

Greindl, Josef; German singer; b. 23 Dec. 1912.
Studies with Paul Bender and Anna Bahr-Mildenburg 32-36; with Krefeld Stadttheater 36, Städtische Bühnen, Düsseldorf 38, Berlin State Opera 42, Deutsche Oper Berlin 48-, Vienna State Opera 56-59, 65-; sang at Bayreuth Festival 43, 44, 52-70, Salzburg Festival 49-52, Lucerne Festival 51, Zürich Festival 51-54, Easter Festival (Salzburg) 69-70; Dir. Opera and Music School, Saarbrücken 61-; has frequently sung at foreign opera houses, including Metropolitan Opera, New York, La Scala, Milan and in Rome, Naples, Venice, Paris, Lisbon, Amsterdam, Tokyo, Buenos Aires, San Francisco and Mexico City, numerous European concert tours and recordings; Berlin Art Prize 55; Bundesverdienstkreuz (1st Class).
Küchelstrasse 1a, 8000 Munich 70, Federal Republic of Germany.
Telephone: 744506.

Grendys, Michal, M.JUR.; Polish politician; b. 25 Sept. 1912, Witkowice, Rzeszów Voivod; ed. Łódź Univ.
Member, Democratic Party (SD) 44-, Sec. of District Cttee. in Rzeszów, later Vice-Chair.; Sec. of SD Voivod Cttees. in Rzeszów 46-50, Łódź 50-53, Crakow 53-55; active in Nat. Councils and Nat. Unity Front in Rzeszów, Łódź, Crakow 46-55; mem. Cen. Cttee. of SD, Head of Organizational Team, later of Team for Nat. Councils 55-65, mem. of Secr. 65-69, Sec. Cen. Cttee. 71-; Deputy to Seym (Parl.) 57-; mem. Council of State 72-; Order of Banner of Labour, 1st Class, Knight's Cross and Officer's Cross, Order of Polonia Restituta, Gold Cross of Merit.
Kancelaria Rady Państwa PRL, ul. Wiejska 4/6/8, 00-489 Warsaw, Poland.

Grenfell, Joyce Irene, O.B.E.; British entertainer and writer; b. 10 Feb. 1910, London; d. of Paul Phipps and Nora Langhorne; m. Reginald P. Grenfell 1929.
Radio Critic *Observer* 36-39; first stage appearance in Farjeon's *Little Revue* April 39-April 40; appeared in *Diversion* Wyndham's Theatre Oct. 40-April 41, *Light and Shade* Ambassadors Theatre Sept. 41; Welfare Officer Canadian Red Cross 41-43; entertained troops, and in hospitals in N. Africa, the Middle East, India and Italy 44-45; appeared in Noel Coward's revue *Sigh No More* 45-46, *Tuppence Coloured* 47-48, *Penny Plain* 49-50, *Joyce Grenfell Requests the Pleasure*, London 54-55, New York 55; Toured U.S. and Canada with solo programme 56, 58, 60, and in Sydney, Australia 59, Switzerland and Canada 63, London 65, Australia, Hong Kong 69; mem. Pilkington Cttee. on Radio and TV 60-62; appeared in Australia, New Zealand, Hong Kong and Singapore 63; toured Australia 66, 69, U.S.A. 70, G.B. 70, 71; Pres. Soc. of Women Writers and Journalists; Council mem. Winston Churchill Memorial Fellowship Trust; Hon. Fellow Lucy Cavendish Coll. Cambridge, Manchester Polytechnic; films include: *Poet's Pub, The Happiest Days of Your Life, Stage Fright, Galloping Major, Laughter in Paradise, The Magic Box, The Pickwick Papers, Genevieve, The Million Pound Note, Forbidden Cargo* 53, *Belles of St. Trinians* 54, *The Pure Hell of St. Trinians, The Americanisation of Emily* 63, *The Yellow Rolls-Royce* 64; Radio: own series *A Note With Music, The How Series* in collaboration with Stephen Potter, and frequent broadcasts on *Ten to Eight* and *Women's Hour*; TV: solo spectaculars for B.B.C. 67-69, 71-72; appearances in *Face the Music* (quiz) 71-75.

Leisure interests: music, painting, birdwatching, writing.
c/o Hutton Management Ltd., 33 Sloane Street, London, S.W.1, England.
Telephone: 01-235-3197.

Grenfell, Hon. Julian Pascoe Francis St. Leger; British international civil servant; b. 23 May 1935, London; s. of Lord Grenfell of Kilvey; m. 1st Loretta Reali 1961 (dissolved 1970), one d.; 2nd Gabrielle Raab 1970, one d.; ed. Eton Coll., King's Coll., Cambridge.
Second Lieut., Kings Royal Rifle Corps 54-56; Capt. Queen's Royal Rifles (Territorial Army) 63; television journalist 60-64; joined IBRD 65, Chief of Information and Public Affairs in Europe 69-72, Deputy Dir. European Office 73-74; Special Rep. for UN Orgs. 74.
Leisure interests: tennis, winetasting.
United Nations, Room 2245, New York, N.Y. 10017, U.S.A.
Telephone: 754-1234.

Gresford, Guy Barton, B.SC., F.R.A.C.I.; Australian science administrator; b. 7 March 1916, Sydney; m. Bettine Attiwill 1948; one s. two d.; ed. Hobart High School, Royal Melbourne Technical Coll., Trinity Coll., Univ. of Melbourne, and School of Administration, Harvard Univ.
Officer in Charge, Australian Scientific Liaison Office, London 42-46; Asst. Sec. (Australian) Commonwealth Scientific and Industrial Research Org. 47-52, Sec. (Physical Sciences) 52-59, Sec. 59-66; Dir. for Science and Technology, UN 66-73; Sec. UN Advisory Cttee. for Application of Science and Technology to Development 66-73; Senior Adviser on Science, Technology and the Environment, Australian Dept. of Foreign Affairs 73-; Harkness Fellow, Commonwealth Fund of New York 57.
Leisure interests: books, walking, gardening.
Department of Foreign Affairs, Canberra, A.C.T., Australia.
Telephone: 613622.

Gressitt, J(udson) Linsley, B.S., M.S., PH.D., F.R.E.S.; American entomologist; b. 16 June 1914, Tokyo, Japan; s. of James F. and Edna Linsley Gressitt; m. Margaret Kriete 1941; four d.; ed. Stanford and California Univs.
Asst. in Zoology Cal. Univ.; Instructor Lingnan Univ. (Canton and Hong Kong) 39-41; interned 41-43; Lieut. U.S.N. Medical Research Unit No. 2 45-46; Asst. Prof. Lingnan Univ. 46. Assoc. Prof. 48-51; mem. U.S. Nat. Research Council (Pacific Science Board) 51-52; Entomologist Bishop Museum, Honolulu 53-, Chair. Dept. of Entomology 56-72; L. Allen Bishop Distinguished Chair. of Zoology 63-; Chair. Standing Cttee. on Pacific Entomology (Pacific Science Asscn.) 53-57; field work in Far East 29-51, South Pacific 51-, Antarctica 59-66; Guggenheim Fellowship 55-56, Fulbright Fellowship (Australia) 60-61; Polar Research Cttee. Nat. Acad. of Sciences 65-69, Chair. Governor's Cttee. on Conservation 69-70; Chair. State Comm. Natural Area Reserves 70-73; Dir. Wau Ecology Inst., Wau, New Guinea 71-; Gregory Medal, Pacific Science 75.
Leisure interests: hiking, skiing, gardening.
Publs. *Longicorn Beetles of Hainan Island* 40, *Longicorn Beetles of China* 51, *Filth-inhabiting Flies of Guam* (with G. Bohart) 51, *Tortoise-beetles of China* 52, *Coconut Rhinoceros Beetle* 53, *Insects of Micronesia—Introduction* 54, *Cerambycidae* 56, *Hispine Beetles from the South Pacific* 57, *Longicorn Beetles from New Guinea* Vol. I 59, *Bibliographic Introduction to Antarctic-Subantarctic Entomology* 60, *Problems in the Zoogeography of Pacific and Antarctic Insects* 61, *Chrysomelidae of China and Korea* (with S. Kimoto) 61, 63, *Insects of Campbell Island* 64, *Land Arthropods of Antarctica* 65, *Bibliography of New Guinea Entomology* (with J. Szent-

Ivany) 68, Editor *Entomology of Antarctica* 67, *Sub-antarctic entomology* 70, *Cerambycid-beetles of Laos* 70, *Advances in Antarctic entomology* 71, *Entomology Islands south of New Zealand* 71, *Pacific Insects, Journal of Medical Entomology.*
Bishop Museum, Honolulu, P.O. Box 6037, Hawaii 96818, U.S.A.; and Wau Ecology Institute, Box 77, Wau, Papua New Guinea.
Telephone: Wau 44-6341, 44-6206.

Grewe, Wilhelm G.; German university professor and diplomatist; b. 16 Oct. 1911; ed. Univs. of Berlin, Freiburg, Frankfurt and Hamburg, and The Acad. of International Law, The Hague.
Taught in Berlin and Göttingen Univs. 41-47; Prof. of Law, Freiburg Univ. 47-55; Chief of Legal Division, Foreign Office 53-54, of the Political Division 55-58; Ambassador to U.S.A. 58-62, Perm. Rep. to North Atlantic Treaty Organisation (NATO) 62-71; Amb. to Japan 71-; mem. Perm. Court of Arbitration, The Hague.
Publs. *Gnade und Recht* 36, *Ein Besatzungsstatut für Deutschland* 48, *Deutsche Aussenpolitik der Nachkriegszeit* 60, *Spiel der Kräfte in der Weltpolitik* 70.
CPO Box 955, Tokyo, Japan.
Telephone: 473-0151.

Grey, Beryl Elizabeth, C.B.E.; British prima ballerina; b. 11 June 1927, London; d. of Arthur and Annie Groom; m. Dr. Sven Gustav Svenson 1950; one s.; ed. Dame Alice Owens School, London, Madeline Sharp School, Royal Ballet School, and de Vos School of Dance.
Debut Sadler's Wells Co. 41; Prima Ballerina with Royal Ballet until 57; freelance int. prima ballerina since 57; first full-length ballet *Swan Lake* on 15th birthday; has appeared since in leading roles of classical and numerous modern ballets including *Giselle, Sleeping Beauty, Sylvia, Casse Noisette, Les Sylphides, Checkmate, Donald of the Burthens, Dante Sonata, Three Cornered Hat, Ballet Imperial, Lady and the Fool, Les Rendezvous*; American, Continental, African, Far Eastern tours with Royal Ballet since 45; guest artist European Opera Houses in Norway, Finland, Sweden, Denmark, Belgium, Romania, Germany, Italy, etc.; guest artist South and Central America, Middle East, Union of South Africa, Rhodesia, Australasia; first foreign guest artist ever to dance with the Bolshoi Ballet in Russia 57-58 (Moscow, Leningrad, Kiev, Tiflis) and first to dance with Peking Ballet and Shanghai Ballet 64; Dir.-Gen. of Arts Educational Trust, London 66-68; Artistic Dir. of London Festival Ballet 68; Hon. D.Mus. (Leicester), Hon. D.Litt. (London).
Leisure interests: music, painting, reading, swimming.
Publs. *Red Curtain Up* 58, *Through the Bamboo Curtain* 65.
78 Park Street, London, W.1, England.
Telephone: 01-629-0477.

Grey, John R.; American oil executive; b. Burbank, Calif.; ed. Stanford Univ.
Joined Standard Oil Co. of Calif. 44, Man. Salt Lake Refining Co. 57, Vice-Pres. Chevron Oil (Western Div.) 61, Pres. Salt Lake Pipe Line Co., Man. Operations, Richmond, Calif. 62, Chief Engineer Standard Oil Co. of Calif. 65, Vice-Pres. Mfg., Western Operations Inc. 66, Vice-Pres. 69, Dir. 70-, Pres. 74-.
Standard Oil Co. of California, 225 Bush Street, San Francisco, Calif. 94104, U.S.A.

Grey of Naunton, Baron (Life Peer), cr. 68; **Ralph Francis Alnwick Grey,** G.C.M.G., G.C.V.O., O.B.E., LL.B.; British civil servant; b. 15 April 1910, Wellington, New Zealand; s. of Francis A. Grey and Mary W. Spence; m. Esmé Burcher 1944; two s. one d.; ed. Wellington Coll., Auckland Univ. Coll., Pembroke Coll., Cambridge
Barrister and Solicitor, Supreme Court of New Zealand 32; Judge's Assoc. N.Z. 32-36; Cadet, Colonial Admin. Service, Nigeria 37, Asst. Financial Sec. 48, Admin.

Officer (First Class) 51, Development Sec. 52, Sec. to the Gov.-Gen. and Council of Ministers 54; Chief Sec. Fed. of Nigeria 55-57; Deputy Gov.-Gen. 57-59; mem. Council of Ministers, Fed. of Nigeria 55-57, and mem. Council of Ibadan Univ. Coll.; Gov. and C.-in-C. British Guiana 59-64; Gov. and C.-in-C. Bahamas 64-68, also Gov. Turks and Caicos Islands 65-68; Gov. of N. Ireland 68-73; Deputy Chair. Commonwealth Devt. Corpn. July 73-; Bristol Regional Board, Lloyds Bank Ltd. 73-; Chair. Royal Overseas League 76-; Hon. LL.D. (Queen's Univ., Belfast); Hon. Bencher, Inn of Court Northern Ireland; Bailiff of Egle, Order of St. John 75; Hon. Freeman, City of Belfast, Borough of Lisburn.
Leisure interests: golf, reading, cinematography.
Overbrook, Naunton, Glos., England.
Telephone: Guiting Power 263.

Grezel, Pierre Louis Charles, L.en D.; French business executive; b. 1 Dec. 1901, Tunis; ed. Ecole Polytechnique and Ecole des Mines, Paris.
Director, subsequently Asst. Dir.-Gen. Electricité de France 46-55; Pres. Cie. Générale d'Electro-Céramique, Société des Accumulateurs Fixes et de Traction 55; Assoc. Man. MM. Lazard Frères et Cie. 57; fmr. Hon. Pres., Pechiney Ugine Kuhlmann; Admin. Cie. Française Thomson-Houston Hotchkiss Brandt, Thomson-C.S.F., Simca Automobiles, Aluminium de Grèce, Greece, Ugina-Casablanca, Morocco, Mines de Fer de Mekambo, Gabon, Forces Motrices de Mauvoisin, Switzerland and other companies; Officier, Légion d'Honneur.
c/o Ugine Kuhlmann, 10 rue Général-Foy, Paris 8e; Home: 34 rue Guynemer, Paris 6e, France.

Gribachov, Nikolai Matveyevich; Soviet poet and journalist; b. 19 Dec. 1910, Lopush Village, Bryansk Region; two s.; ed. Coll. of Land Reclamation, Gorky Literary Inst.
Land Surveyor in Northern regions; Editor-in-Chief *Soviet Union* 50-; mem. C.P.S.U. 43-; Sec. of Board, U.S.S.R. Union of Writers 53-54, 59-; alternate mem. Central Cttee. C.P.S.U. 61-; Deputy R.S.F.S.R. Supreme Soviet 67-; State Prizewinner 48, 49; Lenin Prize 60, Order of Lenin (twice), Hero of Socialist Labour, Hammer and Sickle Gold Medal, Red Banner, Red Star (twice), October Revolution, Patriotic War 1st Class.
Publs. *The Bolshevik Collective Farm* 47, *Spring in the Pobeda* 48, *Poems and Verses* 51, *After Thunderstorm* 52, *My Dear Fellow-Countrymen* 54, *Thoughtful Mood* 55, *Face to Face with America* 61, *Orbit of Century* 61, *Selected Works* (3 vols.) 61, *America, America* 61, *I am Going* 62, *Night Thunderstorm* (novel) 64, *White-Black* (poetry) 65, *Love and Anxiety and Battle* (poetry) 67.
U.S.S.R. Union of Writers, Ulitsa Vorovskogo 52, Moscow, U.S.S.R.

Griera, Antoni, LITT.D.; Spanish philologist; b. 1887; ed. Univs. of Halle, Zürich and Paris.
Professor of History of Spanish Literature, Gran Seminario de Barcelona; Prof. of Christian Culture, Escuela Superior de Bellas Artes de Barcelona; Prof. of Romance Philology, Univ. of Barcelona; mem. Higher Council of Scientific Research, Madrid; mem. Real Acad. de Buenas Letras, Barcelona, Real Acad. de Bellas Artes de San Jorge, Barcelona; Royal Gustav Adolfus Acad., Uppsala, Royal Literary and Royal Historic and Ancient Literature Acads. Stockholm; Accad. di Scienze, Bologna, Pontificia Accad. Romana di Archeologia; Dr. h.c. (Würzburg and Louvain).
Publs. *Tresor de la Llengua, de les Tradicions et de la Cultura popular de Catalunya,* 14 vols. 35-47, *Atlas linguístic de la Catalunya,* 8 vols., *Boletín de Dialectología catalana-española.* 50 vols., 13-70, *Atlas linguístic d'Andorra* 60, *Vocabulario Vasco* 60, *Memories* 63, *Consueta jueva* 66, *Liturgia Popular* 67, *Homonímies* 67, *Els Ormeigs de pescar dels rius i costes de Catalunya* 68,

Homonimies d'Andorra 68, *Los Atlas lingüísticos y la interpretación de sus mapas* 68, *La Casa Catalana* 73, *Trilogia de la Vida* 70, *Aling Arán* 73.
Instituto Internacional de Cultura Románica, Abadía de San Cugat del Vallés, Barcelona, Spain.

Griesmeier, Hans Heinz, DR., DIPL.RER.POL.; German business executive; b. 6 Feb. 1925, Munich; s. of Prof. Dr. Josef and Katharina (née Gerlsberger) Griesmeier; m. Dr. Ellen Ausserbauer 1953; one s. one d.; ed. Dillmann Gymnasium, Stuttgart and Univ. Tübingen. Deputy mem. Man. Board, Standard Elektrik Lorenz A.G., Stuttgart 52-66; Chair. Loewe Opta G.m.b.H., Kronach and Berlin 67-71; Chair. Man. Board, Grundig A.G. 71-.
Grundig A.G., D-8510 Fürth, Kurgartenstrasse 37, Federal Republic of Germany.
Telephone: 0911-7031.

Griffin, Admiral Sir Anthony (Templer Frederick Griffith), G.C.B.; British naval officer and shipbuilding executive; b. 24 Nov. 1920, Peshawar, India (now Pakistan); s. of Col. Forrester Metcalfe Griffith Griffin, M.C., and Beryl Alice Beatrix Griffith Griffin; m. Rosemary Ann Hickling 1943; two s. one d.; ed. Royal Naval Coll., Dartmouth.
Entered Royal Navy 34; war service H.M.S. *Gloucester, Fury, Talybont, Implacable, Empress* 39-45, mentioned in dispatches 43, 45; Lieut.-Commdr. 49, Commdr. 51; Application Commdr., H.M.S. *Mercury II* 52-54; Exec. Officer H.M.S. Eagle 55-56; Capt. 56; Deputy Dir. of Navigation and Direction, Admiralty 57-59; Command H.M.S. *Woodbridge Haven* and Capt. Inshore Flotilla 59-60; Deputy Dir. of Plans 60-62; Command H.M.S. *Ark Royal* 64-65; Rear-Adm. 66; Naval Sec. 66; Asst. Chief of Naval Staff (Warfare) 66-68; Vice-Adm. 68; Flag Officer Second-in-Command, Far East Fleet 68-69; Flag Officer, Plymouth, Adm. Supt., Devonport, Commdr. Cen. Sub Area, E. Atlantic, Commdr. Plymouth Sub Area, Channel 69-71; Controller of the Navy 71-75; Adm. 71; Chair. Organizing Cttee. and Chair. Designate of British Shipbuilders Dec. 75-.
Leisure interest: sailing.
12-18 Grosvenor Gardens, London, S.W.1; Candles Copse, Cranleigh, Surrey, GU6 8LG, England.
Telephone: 01-730 9600 (Office); Cranleigh 3314 (Home).

Griffin, Charles Donald; American naval officer; b. 12 Jan. 1906, Philadelphia, Pa.; s. of Joseph R. Griffin and Mande L. Spicknall; m. 1st Camilla Y. Ganteaume 1934 (died 1963), 2nd Marion H. Schaefer; one s. two d.; ed. U.S. Naval Acad., and Univ. of Michigan.
U.S. Navy 27-, Vice-Adm. 60, Adm. 63; Duty in Battleships and Destroyers 27-30, U.S.S. *Enterprise* 37-40, Flight Test Officer, Naval Air Station, Anacostia 40-42, Commdr. Carrier Air Group 9, U.S.S. *Essex* 42-43; mem. Joint War Plans Cttee., Joint Chiefs of Staff 44, Commanding Officer, U.S.S. *Croatan* 45-46, Plans Officer, U.S. Atlantic Fleet 46-47, Strategic Plans Div., Operations Navy 48-50, Plans Officer, U.S. Pacific Fleet 51-54 Commanding Officer, U.S.S. *Oriskany* 53-54, Special Asst. to Chair., Joint Chiefs of Staff 55-56, Commdr. Carrier Div. 4, 57-58, Dir. Strategic Plans, Navy Dept. 59-60, Commdr. Seventh Fleet 60-Oct. 61, Dep. Chief of Naval Operations for Fleet Operations and Readiness Dec. 61-63, C.-in-C. U.S. Naval Force in Europe 63-65; C.-in-C. Allied Forces, Southern Europe 65-68.
Leisure interests: sport events, golf, gardening, hunting.
4610 Dexter Street, N.W., Washington, D.C. 20007, U.S.A.

Griffin, Donald (Redfield), M.A., PH.D.; American biologist; b. 3 Aug. 1915, Southampton, N.Y.; s. of late Henry F. Griffin and Mary W. Redfield; m. 1st Ruth Castle 1941 (dissolved 1965), 2nd Jocelyn Crane

1965; one s. three d.; ed. Harvard Coll. and Graduate School of Arts and Sciences, Harvard Univ.
Junior Fellow, Harvard Univ. 40-46, Research Assoc. 42-45; Asst. Prof. of Zoology, Cornell Univ. 46-47 Assoc. Prof. 47-52, Prof. 52-53; Prof. of Zoology Harvard Univ. 53-65, Chair. Dept. of Biology 62-65 Prof. The Rockefeller Univ. 65-; mem. Nat. Acad. of Sciences, American Philosophical Soc.; Elliott Medal 60 Leisure interest: sailing.
Publs. *Listening in the Dark* 58, *Echoes of Bats and Men* 59, *Animal Structure and Function* 62, *Bird Migration* 64.
The Rockefeller University, New York, N.Y. 10021; Home: 52 Willow Street, Belmont, Massachusetts 02178, U.S.A.

Griffin, James Bennett, PH.D.; American anthropologist and archaeologist; b. 12 Jan. 1905, Atchison, Kan.; s. of Charles Bennett and Maude (Bostwick) Griffin; m. Ruby Fletcher 1936; three s.; ed. Univs. of Chicago and Michigan.
Research Assoc. Musuem of Anthropology, Univ. of Mich. 36-41, Asst. Curator, Archaeology 36-42, Assoc. Curator 42-45, Curator 45-76, Dir. 46-75, Assoc. Prof. of Anthropology, Univ. of Mich. 45-49, Prof. 49-76, Prof. Emer. 76-, Henry Russel Lecturer 71-72; Chair. Dept. of Anthropology 72-75; mem. Perm. Council, Int. Union of Prehistoric and Protohistoric Sciences 48-, mem. Exec. Cttee. 62-; Pres. Cttee. on Anthropology, Pan American Inst. of Geography and History 54-59; Fellow, Amer. Asscn. for the Advancement of Science, American Anthropological Asscn.; mem. Soc. for American Archaeology (Asst. Editor 36-46, Assoc. Editor 46-50, First Vice-Pres. 45-46, mem. Exec. Cttee. 45-46, 50-53, Pres. 51-52), Nat. Acad. of Sciences, Sociedad Mexicana de Antropología; Sec. American Quarternary Asscn. 70-72; mem. Exec. Cttee. Asscn. of Field Archaeology 71-; Viking Fund Medal and Award in Archaeology 57; Hon. D.S. (Indiana Univ.) 71.
Leisure interest: travel.
Publs. *The Fort Ancient Aspect* 43, *Archaeological Survey in the Lower Mississippi Alluvial Valley* 40-47 (Co-Author) 50, *Archaeology of Eastern United States* 52; and over 200 professional articles.
Museum of Anthropology, 4017 University Museums Building, Ann Arbor, Mich. 48104; Home: 360 Evergreen Place, Ann Arbor, Mich, 48104, U.S.A.
Telephone: 764-0482 (Office); 663-5371 (Home).

Griffin, Robert P., A.B., B.S., J.D.; American lawyer and politician; b. 6 Nov. 1923, Detroit, Michigan; s. of J. A. and Mrs. Griffin; m. Marjorie J. Anderson 1947; three s. one d.; ed. Central Mich. Univ., and Univ. of Mich. Law School.
Admitted to Mich. Bar; mem. law firm Williams, Griffin, Thompson and Coulter, Traverse City 50-56; mem. U.S. House of Reps. 56-66; U.S. Senator from Mich. 66-; Minority Whip in Senate 69-; mem. Senate Commerce, Foreign Relations and Rules and Admin. Cttees.; mem. Amer. Bar Asscn.; Hon. LL.D. (Univ. of Mich. and Detroit Coll. of Law); Republican.
Leisure interests: golf, camping.
U.S. Senate, Washington D.C., U.S.A.

Griffith, Ernest Stacey; American political scientist and research director; b. 28 Nov. 1896, Utica, New York; s. of George Griffith and Elizabeth Stacey; m. Margaret Davenport 1929; two s. three d.; ed. Hamilton Coll., and Univ. of Oxford.
Instructor in Economics, Princeton 20-21; Warden, Univ. Settlement and David Lewis Club, Liverpool 23-28; Lecturer in Social Studies, Univ. of Liverpool 26-28; Assoc. Prof., Syracuse Univ. 28-29; Visiting Prof., Harvard 29-30; Dean and Prof. of Political Science, Syracuse 30-35, and American Univ., Washington 35-40; Dir. Legislative Reference Service, Library of Congress 40-58; Fulbright Prof., Oxford 51-52, and

Lecturer Int. Christian Univ. and Rikkyo Univ., Tokyo 66-67 and at Birmingham, Manchester, Swansea and Oslo; Dean, School of Int. Service, American Univ., Wash. 58-65; Consultant Editor Praeger Series U.S. Govt. Depts. and Agencies 66-; Pres. Nat. Acad. of Econs. and Political Science 58-63; Hon. mem. Nat. Acad. of Public Admin.
Leisure interests: tennis, wilderness, mountain climbing.
Publs. *The Impasse of Democracy* 39, *The Modern Government in Action* 42, *Research in Political Science* 48, *Congress: Its Contemporary Role* 51, 61, 67, 75, *The American System of Government* 54, 59, 62, 67, 76, *History of American City Government* (four vols.) 38, 74, 76, *The Institutional Presidency* 76.
Home: 1941 Parkside Drive N.W., Washington, D.C. 20012, U.S.A.
Telephone: RA6-5638.

Griffith, Harold Melvin; American steel executive; b. 4 July 1904, Clinton, Ill.; *m.* Fredrica Schneider 1927; two *d.*; ed. Chicago Technical Coll. and Harvard Univ.
Steel works metallurgist, Bethlehem Steel Co. 26-30; Jones & Laughlin Steel Co. 30-36; with Steel Co. of Canada Ltd. 36-, Vice-Pres. 53-64, Exec. Vice-Pres. 64-66, Pres. 66-71, Chief Exec. Officer 68-73, Chair. of Board 71-; Dir. and mem. Exec. Cttee. of Int. Iron and Steel Inst.; Dir. Toronto, Hamilton & Buffalo Railway Co., Canadian General Electric Co. Ltd., Toronto Dominion Bank, Steetley Industries Ltd., Steetley of Canada (Holding) Ltd., Rockwell Int. of Canada Ltd.; mem. Board of Govs., Ontario Research Foundation; mem. American Iron and Steel Inst., American Inst. of Mining, Metallurgical and Petroleum Engineers.
Leisure interests: golf, curling, lapidary.
Steel Company of Canada Ltd., P.O. Box 205, Toronto Dominion Centre, Toronto M5K 1J4, Ontario; Home: 1404 Old Mill Towers, 39 Old Mill Road, Toronto, Ontario M8X 1G6, Canada.
Telephone: 416-362-2161.

Griffith, Thomas, A.B.; American editor; b. 30 Dec. 1915, Tacoma, Wash.; *s.* of Thomas Griffith and Anne O'Reilly; *m.* Caroline Coffman 1937; ed. Univ. of Washington.
Reporter, then Asst. City Editor *Seattle Times* (Wash.) 36-41; Nieman Fellow, Harvard 42; Contributing Editor, then Assoc. Editor *Time* magazine 43-46, Senior Editor 46, Nat. Affairs Editor 49-51, Foreign Editor 51-60, Asst. Man. Editor, *Time* 60-63; Senior Staff Editor, all Time Inc. Publs. 63-67; Editor *Life* magazine 68-73; Staff contributor, *Time, Fortune* magazines, columnist, *Atlantic Monthly* 74-.
Publs. *The Waist-High Culture* 58, *How True?—a Sceptic's Guide to Believing the News* 74.
Time & Life Building, Rockefeller Center, New York, N.Y. 10020; Home: 25 East End Avenue, New York, N.Y. 10028, U.S.A.
Telephone: JU 61212 (Office); RE4-7625 (Home).

Griffith-Jones, Sir Eric (Newton), K.B.E., C.M.G., Q.C.; British company director and former colonial civil servant; b. 1 Nov. 1913, Singapore; *s.* of O. P. and Edith S. Griffith-Jones; *m.* Mary P. Rowland Heagerty 1946; two *s.* (one deceased) two *d.*; ed. Cheltenham Coll.
Barrister-at-Law 34; Advocate and Solicitor, Straits Settlements and Johore 35, Crown Counsel, Straits Settlements 39, Malayan Union 46; Senior Federal Counsel, Fed. of Malaya 48; Legal Adviser, Selangor 48-49, Perak 49-51; Solicitor-Gen., Kenya 52-55; Dep. Speaker and Chair. of Cttees. Kenya Legislative Council 54-55; Attorney-Gen. and Minister for Legal Affairs, Kenya 55-61 (at times Acting Chief Sec. and Acting Gov.), Deputy Gov. 61-63 (at times Acting Gov.); Chair. The Guthrie Corpn. Ltd. and Assoc. Cos. 65-, Property Holdings (Pennine) Ltd. 66-, Sutcliffe

Mitchell (Insurances) Ltd. 66-; Dir. Provident Mutual Life Assurance 64-; Dir. Perak River Hydro-Electric Power Co. 70-72, Vice-Chair. 73-; Deputy Chair. Commonwealth Devt. Corpn. 71-72, Chair. 72-; Mil. Service 41-46.
Leisure interests: private forestry, shooting, tennis, water-skiing, golf.
Office: 52-54 Gracechurch Street, London, EC3V 0BD; Home: The Combe, Rogate, Near Petersfield, Hants., England.
Telephone: 01-626-5052 (Office).

Grigorov, Mitko; Bulgarian politician and diplomatist; b. 1920, Trin; *s.* of Grigor Dimitrov and Raina Grigorova; *m.* Stanka Grigorova 1956; one *d.*; ed. Sofia Univ.
Member of Workers' Youth Union 39; worked for Bulgarian Communist Party 40; political imprisonment 42-44; Head Dept. of and Sec. of Sofia City Cttee. of C.P.; Head, Propaganda and Agitation Dept. Central Cttee. of C.P. 50-54, 57; First Sec. Varna Regional Cttee. of C.P. 54-57; mem. Central Cttee. of Bulgarian C.P. 57-, Sec. 58, mem. of Politburo 61-66; Minister, Bulgarian P.R. 62-66; mem. Prague Editorial Board *Problems of Peace and Socialism*; Amb. to U.K. 69-71; mem. State Council 71-, Vice-Pres 74-; Order of Georgi Dimitrov.
Leisure interest: walking.
c/o Durzhaven Suvet, Dondoukov Street 82, Sofia, Bulgaria.

Grigorovich, Yuri Nikolayevich; Soviet ballet-master; b. 1 Jan. 1927; ed. Leningrad Choreographic School and Lunarcharski Inst. of Theatrical Art, Moscow.
Troupe of Kirov Theatre 46, Soloist until 62, Ballet-Master, Kirov Theatre 62-63; Chief Ballet Master, Bolshoi Theatre, Moscow 64-; People's artist of R.S.F.S.R.; Lenin Prize 70; Ballets include *Spartacus, Ivan The Terrible.*
State Academic Bolshoi Theatre, 1 Ploshchad Sverdlova, Moscow, U.S.S.R.

Grigson, Geoffrey; English poet; b. 2 March 1905, Pelynt, Cornwall; *s.* of Canon W. S. Grigson and Mary B. Boldero; *m.*; one *s.* three *d.*; ed. Univ. of Oxford.
Founder and one-time Editor of the English periodical *New Verse:* Duff Cooper Memorial Prize 71.
Publs. *Several Observations: Thirty-five Poems* 39, *Under the Cliff and Other Poems* 43, *Henry Moore* 43, *The Isles of Scilly and other Poems* 46, *Samuel Palmer* (biography) 47, *The Harp of Aeolus* (criticism) 48, *Places of the Mind* 49, *Poems of John Clare's Madness* 49, *The Crest on the Silver* (autobiography) 50, *The Victorians* 50, *Selected Poems of William Barnes* 50, *Selected Poems of John Clare* 50, *Essays from the Air* 51, *Gardenage* 52, *Freedom of the Parish* 54, *The Englishman's Flora* 55, *English Drawings* 55, *Painted Caves* 57, *The Three Kings, Art Treasures of the British Museum* 58, *A Herbal of All Sorts* 59, *The Cherry Tree* 59, *English Excursions* 60, *Samuel Palmer's Valley of Vision* 60, *Christopher Smart* 61, *Collected Poems* 63, *Poems of Walter Savage Landor* 64, *Shapes and Stories* (with Jane Grigson) 64, *The Shell Country Alphabet* 66, *A Skull in Salop and Other Poems* 67, *The English Year* 67, *Poems and Poets, Ingestion of Ice-Cream and Other Poems* 68, *A Choice of William Morris's Verse* (Editor) 69, *Notes from an Odd Country* 70, *Discoveries of Bones and Stones: Poems* 71, *Faber Book of Popular Verse* 71, *Penguin Book of Unrespectable Verse* 71, *Rainbows, Fleas and Flowers* 71, *Shapes and Creatures* 72, *Sad Grave of an Imperial Mongoose and other Poems* 73, *Faber Book of Love Poems* (Editor) 73, *The Contrary View* 74, *Dictionary of English Plant Names* 74, *Angles and Circles* 74, *Britain Observed* 75, *Penguin Book of Ballads* 75, *Poet to Poet: Cotton* 75, *The Goddess of Love* 76, *Faber Book of Epigrams* 76.
Broad Town Farm, nr. Swindon, Wiltshire, England.

Grimes, Joseph Rudolph, B.A., M.I.A., LL.D., J.D.; Liberian lawyer, diplomatist and politician; b. 31 Oct. 1923, Monrovia, Liberia; s. of Louis Arthur and Victoria Elizabeth Grimes; m. Doris Delicia Duncan 1954; ed. Coll. of West Africa, Liberia Coll., Law School Harvard Univ. and Columbia Univ.

Cadet, Bureau of Public Health and Sanitation 38-42; Clerk, Exec. Mansion 42-47; Counsellor, Dept. of State 51-56; Dir. Louis Grimes School of Law, Liberia Univ. 54-58; Under-Sec. of State 56-60, Sec. of State 60-72; Dir. Nat. Port Authority, W. African Explosives and Chemical Co., Liberia Tractor and Equipment Co., Liberian Amusements Ltd.; Chair., Board of Dirs., P.P.P. Timber Industries Ltd., Stevfor; Chancellor Episcopal Diocese of Liberia; mem. Board of Trustees, Univ. of Liberia, Coll. of W. Africa; mem. Liberian Del. to Asian African Conf., Bandung 55, to Heads of African States Conf. 61, to 15th-26th Sessions of UN Gen. Assembly; Grand Officier, Légion d'Honneur, Most Venerable Order of the Pioneers, Knight Great Band, Humane Order of the African Redemption, Hon. K.B.E., and other honours; Hon. LL.D. (Columbia Univ.) 71.

Leisure interests: reading, croquet.

P.O. Box 1588, Monrovia, Liberia.

Telephone: 26220.

Grimes, William Francis, C.B.E., D.LITT., F.S.A., F.M.A.; British archaeologist; b. 31 Oct. 1905; ed. Univ. of Wales.

Assistant Keeper of Archaeology, National Museum of Wales 26-38; Asst. Archaeology Officer, Ordnance Survey Office 38-45, Acting Archaeology Officer 45; seconded to Ministry of Works, Ancient Monuments Dept., for investigation of historic monuments threatened with destruction 39-45; Dir. of London Museum 45-56; Hon. Dir. of Excavations, Roman and Medieval London Excavation Council 47-; Sec. Council for British Archæology 49-54, Pres. 55-59; Pres. London and Middlesex Archæological Society 50-59; Vice-Pres. Society of Antiquaries of London 53-57; Vice-Pres. Prehistoric Soc. 57-60, Soc. for Medieval Architecture 57-64; Pres. Royal Archaeological Inst. 57-60; Chair., London Topographical Society 61-73; Dir. Inst. of Archaeology and Prof. of Archaeology, Univ. of London 56-73; Chair. Faculty of Archaeology, History and Letters, British School at Rome 63-66; Pres. Cambrian Archaeological Asscn. 63-64; Chair. Royal Comm. on Ancient Monuments (Wales and Monmouthshire) 67-.

Publs. Holt, Denbighshire: The Works-Depot of the Twentieth Legion at Castle Lyons (Y Cymmrodor, Vol. XLI, 1931), The Prehistory of Wales, Charterhouse (with Prof. M. D. Knowles), Excavations in Defence Sites 1939-45, 1 Brooke House, Hackney (with W. A. Eden, M. Draper, A. Williams), The Excavation of Roman and Medieval London 68.

2 Bryn Road, Swansea, West Glamorgan, Wales.

Grimond, Rt. Hon. Joseph, P.C., M.P., LL.D., D.C.L., T.D.; British politician; b. 29 July 1913, St. Andrews, Scotland; s. of Joseph B. Grimond and Helen L. Richardson; m. Laura Bonham Carter 1938; two s. one d.; ed. Eton and Balliol Coll., Oxford.

Barrister; served Fife and Forfar Yeomanry 39-45; fmr. Dir. of Personnel, European Office of UNRRA; Sec. Nat. Trust for Scotland 47-49; Liberal M.P. for Orkney and Shetland 50-; Liberal Chief Whip 51-57, Leader of Parl. Party 57-67, May-(July) 76; Rector, Edinburgh Univ. 61-64; Rector, Aberdeen Univ. 69-72; Chancellor, Univ. of Kent 70-.

Publs. The Liberal Future 59, The Liberal Challenge 63.

Old Manse of Firth, Kirkwall, Orkney, Scotland; The House of Commons, London, S.W.1, England.

Telephone: 01-219-4580.

Grin, Edmond, DR.THEOL.; Swiss theologian; b. 11 Sept. 1895, Suchy, Switzerland; s. of François and Bertha (née Voruz) Grin; ed. Lausanne, theological faculties Lausanne, Zürich, Strasbourg and Marburg, philosophical faculty, Paris.

Pastor, Chesalles-sur-Moudon 22-26, Echallens 26-32; Extraordinary Prof. of Theology, Lausanne Univ. 32-38, Prof. 38-66, Dean of the Faculty 38-40, 46-50, Rector 56-58, Hon. Prof. 66-; Pres. Conf. of Swiss Rectors 58, Comm. théologique des Eglises protestantes de la Suisse 63; Lauréat de l'Université de Lausanne; Dr. h.c. Basle Univ.; Diploma Hautes Etudes de philosophie Univ. de Paris à la Sorbonne.

Publs. Charles Secrétan et la philosophie de Schelling 25, La morale chrétienne sur la base de la foi réformée 29, Les origines et l'évolution de la pensée de Charles Secrétan 30, Morale de la conscience et morale de la grâce 33, La notion protestante des oeuvres 37, Le salut par la foi et les oeuvres du chrétien 38, Expérience religieuse et témoignage du Saint-Esprit 47, Les exigences de l'Evangile et la question sociale 50, J. Chr. Blumhardt 52, Existentialisme et morale chrétienne 56, La pensée théologique de Bonhoeffer 60, De Calvin à Ch. Secrétan 60, La Christologie de D. Bonhoeffer 61, D. Bonhoeffer et l'interprétation "non-religieuse" des notions bibliques 62, L'actualisation du message biblique chez D. Bonhoeffer 63, Une discipline ecclésiastique aujourd'hui? 64, Théologie systématique en Suisse romande, continuité d'une tradition 66, Ein Jahrhundert ethischer Theologie in französischer Sprache: von Charles Secrétan zu Jacques Ellul (1880-1965), 66, Un grand théologien méconnu: Emile Brunner 67, La pensée d'un prophète contemporain: D. Bonhoeffer, d'après A. Dumas 69.

Florybel, 4 Longeraie, 1006 Lausanne, Switzerland.

Telephone: (021) 20-77-31.

Griñan Núñez, Alba; Cuban Ambassador to U.K. 65-73; see The International Who's Who 1975-76.

Grishin, Ivan Timofeyevich; Soviet foreign trade official; b. 18 July 1911; ed. Higher Party School.

Member C.P.S.U. 31-; Party and Komsomol Leader 35-41; Chair. Novosibirsk Regional Cttee. of C.P. 41-45; Second, later First, Sec., Volgograd Regional Cttee. of C.P. 48-55; Amb. to Czechoslovakia 55-59; Deputy Minister of Foreign Trade 59-; Order of Lenin (three times), Order of Red Banner of Labour (three times).

Ministry of Foreign Trade, 32/34 Smolenskaya-Sennaya Ploshchad, Moscow, U.S.S.R.

Grishin, Viktor Vasilievich; Soviet politician; b. 1914; ed. Moscow Railway Inst.

Fmr. railway engine driver and locomotive depot chief; mem. C.P.S.U. 39-; Sec. Serpukhov City Cttee. C.P.S.U. 42-50; Sec. Moscow Region Cttee. C.P.S.U. 50-56, Cand. mem. Pres. Central Cttee. of C.P.S.U. 61-66, Alt. mem. Politburo 66-71, mem. 71-; Chair. All-Union Cen. Council of Trade Unions 56-67; First Sec. Moscow City Cttee. of C.P.S.U. 67-; Deputy to Supreme Soviet 50-; mem. Pres. U.S.S.R. Supreme Soviet; mem. Soviet Parl. Del. to U.K. 56; Order of Lenin, Badge of Honour.

Moscow City Committee of C.P.S.U., 6 Staraya Ploshchad, Moscow, U.S.S.R.

Grishmanov, Ivan Aleksandrovich; Soviet engineer and politician; b. 1906; ed. Leningrad Inst. of Civil Engineers.

Member C.P.S.U. 29-; Deputy to Supreme Soviet of R.S.F.S.R. 55; Head Construction Dept., Central Cttee. of Communist Party of U.S.S.R. 56-61; Chair. State Cttee. for Construction Materials, Council of Ministers, U.S.S.R. 61-65; Minister of Building Materials Industry 65-; mem. Central Cttee. C.P.S.U. 61-; Deputy, U.S.S.R. Supreme Soviet 62-; Order of Red Banner of Labour and other decorations.

U.S.S.R. Ministry of Building Materials Industry, 2-5 Ploshchad Nogina, Moscow, U.S.S.R.

Grist, Reri; American coloratura soprano; ed. Music and Art High School, New York City and Queen's Coll. First major part Consuelo in *West Side Story* 57; with Santa Fé Opera Co. and New York City Opera 59, Washington Opera Soc. 60, 62, Vancouver Opera Asscn. 62, 64, San Francisco Opera 63, 64, 65, 66, Chicago Lyric Opera 64, Montreal debut as Gilda, *Rigoletto* 66, Metropolitan Opera debut as Rosina, *Barber of Seville* 66; has sung in numerous opera houses and festivals in Europe including debut as Queen of the Night, *Magic Flute* in Cologne, Glyndebourne 62 as Despina, *Cosi Fan Tutti* and Zerbinetta, *Ariadne*, Naples 63, Holland Festival 63, Piccola Scala, Milan 63, Bordeaux Opera 64, Munich State Opera 65; regular appearances with Zurich Opera 60-, Covent Garden 62, 66, Vienna State Opera 63-, Salzburg Festival 64-.
c/o Metropolitan Opera Association, 147 West 39th Street, New York, N.Y. 10018, U.S.A.

Griswold, Erwin Nathaniel, A.M., LL.D., S.J.D., L.H.D., D.C.L.; American lawyer; b. 14 July 1904, East Cleveland, Ohio; s. of James H. Griswold and Hope Erwin; m. Harriet A. Ford 1931; one s. one d.; ed. Oberlin Coll., and Harvard Law School.
Worked in the office of the Solicitor Gen. 29-34; Asst. Prof. of Law, Harvard Law School 34-35, Prof. of Law 35-46, Dean and Langdell Prof. of Law 46-67; mem. U.S. Civil Rights Comm. 61-67; Pres. Asscn. American Law Schools 57-58; Dir. American Council of Learned Socs. 62-68; Solicitor Gen. of the U.S. 67-73; Pres. American Bar Foundation 71-; mem. American Philosophical Soc., Corresp. F.B.A., Hon. Bencher Inner Temple, etc.
Leisure interests: golf, reading.
Publs. *Spendthrift Trusts* 36, 47, *Cases on Federal Taxation* 40-66, *Cases on Conflict of Laws* (with others) 64 (5th edn.), *The Fifth Amendment Today* 54, *Law and Lawyers in the United States* 64.
Office: 1100 Connecticut Avenue N.W., Washington, D.C. 20036; Residences: 36 Kenmore Road, Belmont, Mass. 02178; 3900 Watson Place N.W., Washington, D.C. 20016, U.S.A.
Telephone: 202-293-2030.

Grobbelaar, James Arthur; South African trade union leader; b. 24 Aug. 1925, Pretoria, S.A.; s. of Evert J. and Doris (née Greenwood) Grobbelaar; m. Gwendoline W. Thewlis 1949; two d.; ed. Pretoria Junior High School and Observatory Boys' High School, Cape.
Boilermaker by trade; Branch Official of S. African Boilermakers' Soc. 49-55, Nat. Organizer 55-59, Area Sec. 59-62, Admin. Sec. 62-64; Gen. Sec. Trade Union Council of S. Africa 64-; Editor *Labour Mirror*.
Leisure interests: swimming, golf, gardening, reading.
4th Floor, Vulcan House, 88 Anderson Street, Johannesburg; Home: 15 Bonifay Court, 21 Pendoring Road, Blackheath, Johannesburg, Transvaal, South Africa.
Telephone: 838-3824 (Office); 678-1080 (Home).

Grochowiak, Stanisław; Polish writer; b. 24 Jan. 1934, Leszno Wielkopolskie; s. of Bronisław and Pelagia Grochowiak; m. Anna Grochowiak; two s. two d.; ed. Univs. of Poznań and Wrocław.
Co-Editor *Współczesność* 58-60, *Nowa Kultura* 61-63, *Kultura* 63-72; mem. Polish Writers' Asscn. 60-; Prize of Minister of Culture and Art 62, 73, Gold Cross of Merit 64, Knight's Cross of Order Polonia Restituta 74.
Publs. Poetry: *Ballada rycerska* 56, *Menuet z pogrzebaczem* 56, *Rozbieranie do snu* 59, *Agresty* 63, *Kanon* 65, *Totentanz in Polen* 69, *Nie było lata* 70, *Polowanie na cietrzewie* 72; Novels: *Plebania z magnoliami* 56, *Lamentnice* 58, *Trismus* 63, *Karabiny* 65; Drama: *Rzecz na głosy* 66, *Okapi* 73.
Ul. Czerniakowska 56 m. 47, 00-717, Warsaw, Poland.
Telephone: 42-25-50.

Groebe, Hans, DR. JUR.; German business executive; b. 29 Sept. 1916, Breslau; ed. Univ. of Freiburg and Kiel.

Commercial apprenticeship AEG, Erfurt 35-37; mil. service 37-45; rejoined AEG 50; Commercial Man., Münster 55-58, Hanover 58-64; Man. Technical Products Group 64; mem. Man. Board, AEG-Telefunken 66, Chair. June 70-.
AEG-Telefunken, 6 Frankfurt 70, AEG-Hochhaus, Federal Republic of Germany.
Telephone: (0611) 600-35-82.

Groeben, Hans von der, DIP.JUR.; German retd. Common Market commissioner; b. 14 May 1907, Langheim, Ostpreussen; s. of Georg von der Groeben and Eva von Mirbach; ed. Charlottenburg Engineering Coll., Berlin, Bonn and Göttingen Univs.
With Ministry of Agriculture, Berlin 33-39; mil. service 39, 42-45; Lower Saxony Ministry of Finance 45-52; Dir. ECSC Div., Fed. Ministry of Economic Affairs 52-58; Co-rapporteur Spaak Report (on setting up of EEC); Chair. working party for drawing up EEC Treaty 56; mem. Comm. of EEC 58-67; mem. Comm. European Communities 67-70; Dr. h.c. rer pol.; Grosses Bundesverdienstkreuz mit Schulterband und Stern, and other decorations.
Leisure interests: sociology, philosophy, music.
Publs. *Europa–Plan und Wirklichkeit* 69, *Kommentar zum Europäischen Wirschafts-Gemeinschaft Vertrag* 74.
5308 Rheinbach, Federal Republic of Germany.
Telephone: 02226-2525.

Groenman, Sjoerd, LITT.D., PHIL.D.; Netherlands sociologist; b. 28 Nov. 1913, Roosendaal; s. of Berend Groenman and Anna Margaretha Joustra; m. Lucie Limborgh Meijer 1939; three s. one d.; ed. Gymnasium Winschoten and Universiteit van Amsterdam.
Sociologist, Community at Emmen 38, Northern Econ. Technological Org. 40, Econ. Technological Inst., Overijssel 41, Board of North-Eastern Polder (Zuiderzeeworks) 43; Prof. of Sociology, Utrecht State Univ. 48, Dean, Faculty of Social Sciences 63-67; Prof., Applied Sociology, Univ. of Leiden 56-60; Chair. Int. Social Science Council 60-70; mem. Int. Cttee. on Documentation of Social Sciences 64-70; mem. Board of Dirs. European Centre for Coordination and Documentation in Social Sciences, Vienna 63-70; Chair. Advisory Cttee. Ministry of Social Work 56-66; Rector (Magnificus), Utrecht Univ. 71-76; Officer, Order of Orange Nassau 63.
Leisure interest: publishing in different journals and newspapers.
Publs. *Methoden der Sociografie* (Methods of Social Research) 50, 66, *Kolonisatie op nieuw land* (Colonisation on New Land) 53, *Ons deel in de ruimte* (Our Part in Space) 59, *Sociaal gedrag en omgeving* (Social Behaviour and Surroundings) 71.
Anna Paulownalaan 188, Zeist near Utrecht, Netherlands.
Telephone: 03404-15385.

Grollet, Louis Jean Alfred, M.D.; French doctor; b. 14 July 1899; ed. Univ. de Paris à la Sorbonne.
Former urologist, Faculty of Medicine, Paris, and Medical Asst., Hopital Broca; Medical Superintendent, Ecole Nationale Vétérinaire d'Alport (Seine); Sec.-Gen. Soc. of Comparative Pathology and Int. Cttee. of Congress of Comparative Pathology; Founder Sec.-Gen. of Asscn. for Clean Air 56; Founder Sec.-Gen. of Medical Centre specialising in biological and electronic research; Editor-in-Chief *Revue de Pathologie Comparée* 31- (*Revue de Pathologie Comparée et de Médecine Expérimentale* since 67); mem. New York Acad. of Sciences; Officier Légion d'Honneur and other decorations.
4 rue Théodule-Ribot, Paris 17e, France.

Gromashevsky, Lev Vasilievich; Soviet epidemiologist; b. 13 Oct. 1887, Nikolaev, Ukraine; s. of Vasilij L. Gromashevsky and Anna A. Gromashevskaya; m.

Lubov L. Gromashevskaya 1950; two *s.* two *d.*; ed. Novorossiysk Univ., Odessa.

Practising epidemiologist 11-14; Army surgeon 14-17; Junior Research Assoc., Head of Chair, Rector Medical Inst., Odessa 18-27; Dir. Sanitary-Bacteriological Inst., Dniepropetrovsk 28-31; Prof. Cen. Inst. of Post-graduate Medical Training, Moscow 31-48; Dir. Cen. Inst. of Epidemiology and Microbiology 31-33; Head Sanitary-Epidemiological Laboratory 33-38; Soviet Army 41-42; Dir. Inst. of Infectious Diseases, Kiev 48-51; Head of Chair, Medical Inst., Kiev 51-63; Inst. of Epidemiology, Microbiology and Parasitology 63-; mem. C.P.S.U. 05-; mem. U.S.S.R. Acad. of Medical Sciences 44-; Hero of Socialist Labour 67, Orders of Lenin, Order of October Revolution, Badge of Honour (twice) and medals.

Leisure interest: literature.

Publs. Over 200 works on epidemiology of various infectious diseases.

Institute of Epidemiology, Microbiology and Parasitology, 4 Spusk Razina, Kiev; Home: Pereulok Marjanenko 11/12, Flat 14, Kiev, U.S.S.R.

Telephone: 937757 (Home).

Gromyko, Andrey Andreyevich, D.ECON.; Soviet diplomatist; b. 18 July 1909, Starye Gromyky, Byelo-russia; ed. Minsk Agricultural Inst. and Moscow Inst. of Economics.

Member C.P. 31-; worked as senior research scientist at Acad. of Sciences; in charge of American Div. of Nat. Council of Foreign Affairs 39; Counsellor at Washington Embassy 39-43; Amb. to U.S.A. and Minister to Cuba 43-46; Soviet Rep. on UN Security Council 46-49; Deputy Foreign Minister 46-49; 1st Deputy Minister of Foreign Affairs 49-52, 53-57, Min-ister of Foreign Affairs 57-; Ambassador to Great Britain 52-53; Deputy to Supreme Soviet 46-50, 58-; Alt. mem. C.P.S.U. Cen. Cttee. 52-56, mem. 56-, mem. Politburo 73-; took part in Teheran, Yalta and Potsdam Confs., Chair. Del. to Dumbarton Oaks Conf. on Post-War Security 44; Chair. Comm. for Publ. of Diplomatic Documentation; Hero of Socialist Labour; Orders of Lenin (four times), Hammer and Sickle Gold Medal and other decorations.

Ministry of Foreign Affairs, 32-34 Smolenskaya-Sennaya Ploshchad, Moscow, U.S.S.R.

Gronchi, Giovanni; Italian politician; b. 10 Sept. 1887; ed. Pisa Univ.

Early mem. of Don Sturzo's movement; active in re-organization of Italian trade unionism; served in army 14-18; a founder of Italian Popular Party; Mem. Parl. 19-; Under-Sec. of State for Industry and Commerce 22-23; retired from public life 23-42; Sec. of State for Commerce, Industry and Labour 44-46; Pres. Christian Democrat Parl. Group 46-48; Speaker, Chamber of Deputies 48-55, President of Italian Republic 55-62.

Publ. *Autobiography* 62.

Senato della Repubblica, Rome; and Via Carlo Fea 7, Rome, Italy.

Groningen, Bernhard A. van, D.LITT., PH.D.; Nether-lands university professor; b. 20 May 1894, Voorst; *s.* of Rudolf van Groningen and Johanna Roskam; *m.* Elisabeth M. van der Poel 1934; ed. Athénée Royal and Brussels and Groningen Univs.

Classics Teacher 19-26; Rector, Assen Gymnasium 26-29; Asst. Prof. of Greek Papyrology, Univ. of Gron-ingen 25-29; Prof. of Greek Language, Literature and Greek Antiquities, Univ. of Leiden 29-64; mem. Royal Acad. of Netherlands 35-, Pres. 49-63; Knight Order of the Lion, Commdr. Order Orange-Nassau (Netherlands); Hon. D.Litt. (Belfast) and Ph.D. (Thessaloniki).

Leisure interest: music.

Publs. *Le Gymnasiarque des métropoles de l'Egypte romaine* 24, *Aristote, le second livre de l'Economique* 33,

Papyrological Primer (in collaboration with M. David) 40, 46, 52, 64, *Short Manual of Greek Palaeography* 40, 55, 63, 67, *Basileus* 41, *The Warren Papyri* (in collabora-tion) 41, *Herodotus, with commentary in Dutch* 45-55, *A Family Archive from Tebtunis* 50, *In the Grip of the Past* 53, *La Poésie verbale grecque* 53, *Homerus* 54, *La compo-sition littéraire archaïque grecque* 58, *Le Dyscolos de Ménandre, Etude critique du texte* 60, *Traité d'Histoire et de Critique des Textes Grecs* 63, *Théognis I, Commentaire* 66, *Aristote, les 3 economiques* 68, *Euphorion* 70, *Carmina et Epigrammata Graece* 72.

Cronesteinflat 50, Leiden, Netherlands.

Telephone: 071-767118.

Gronouski, John Austin, PH.D.; American economist and government official; b. 26 Oct. 1919, Wisconsin; *s.* of John A. and Mary R. Gronouski; *m.* Mary Louise Metz 1948; two *c.*; ed. Oshkosh State Teachers Coll., Oshkosh, Wis., and Univ. of Wisconsin.

U.S. Army Air Corps 42-45; Prof. Univ. of Maine 48-50; Research Assoc. Fed. Tax Administrators 52-56; Research Assoc. Univ. of Wisconsin 56-57; Prof. Wayne State Univ. 57-59; Research Dir. Wisconsin Dept. of Taxation and Univ. of Wisconsin Tax Impact Study 59; Exec. Dir. Revenue Survey Comm., Wisconsin 59-60; Commr. of Taxation, Wisconsin 60-63; Post-master-Gen. of the United States 63-65; Ambassador to Poland 65-68; Dean, Lyndon B. Johnson School of Public Affairs, Univ. of Texas, Austin 69-74, Prof. of Econ. and Public Affairs 74-; mem. Nat. Acad. of Public Administrators; mem. Presidential Comm. on Int. Radio Broadcasting 72-73; Pres. Polish Inst. of Arts and Sciences 74-; Democrat.

Leisure interests: swimming, golf, politics.

Lyndon B. Johnson School of Public Affairs, University of Texas, Austin, Tex. 78712; Home: 610 East 43rd Street, Austin, Tex. 78751, U.S.A.

Telephone: 512-471-5711 (Office); 454-2435 (Home).

Groote, Paul De; Belgian engineer and politician; b. 1905; ed. Athénée Royal de Bruxelles and Univ. of Brussels.

Gen. Sec. of Permanent Cttee. for Co-ordination of Transport in Congo 27, Chief Engineer for Otraco operation 30; Lecturer Brussels Univ. 34; Prof. 45; Adviser to Min. of Communications 44; Vice-Chair. Nat. Office for Transport Regulation 44; mem. Board of Belgian Railways 44; mem. Exec. Board E.C.I.T.O. 45; Min. of Economic Co-ordination and Nat. Re-equipment Mar. 47-49; mem. Euratom Comm. 58-67; Pres. Brussels Univ. 60-61; Belgian Labour Party.

Publs. *La Co-ordination des Transports en Belgique* 45, *Unité d'exploitation des Transports* 46.

249 Dieweg, Brussels, Belgium.

Gropper, William; American artist; b. 3 Dec. 1897; *s.* of Harry and Jenny Gropper; *m.* Sophie Frankle 1925; two *s.*; ed. Nat. Acad. of Design and New York School of Fine and Applied Arts.

16 one-man shows New York 36-58; further one-man shows Paris, Detroit, Warsaw, Moscow, Mexico City, etc.; rep. in perm. collections of New York Metro-politan Museum of Art and Museum of Modern Art, Chicago Art Inst., Whitney Museum of American Art, Paul Sachs Collection, Library of Congress, Walker Art Center, Pushkin Museum, Moscow, Nat. Museum, Prague, etc.; mem. American Nat. Inst. of Arts and Letters; awards include Young Israel Prize, John Herron Prize for Lithography, Guggenheim Fellowship, Carnegie Int. Painting Prize, etc.

Publs. *Gropper* (drawings), *The Little Tailor, Capriccios, Caucasian Studies, Lest We Forget*; also much book illustration.

Hickory Hickory Drive, Great Neck Estates, N.Y. 11021, U.S.A.

Gros, André; French judge at International Court of Justice; b. 19 May 1908, Douai, France; s. of Maurice Gros and Adèle Berr; m. Dulce Simoes-Correa 1940; two s.; ed. Univs. of Lyon and Paris.

Assistant Law Faculty Paris 31, Asst. Prof. Univ. Nancy 35, Toulouse 37, Univ. Prof. Public Law 38-; seconded to Ministry of Foreign Affairs 39; Prof. Political Science Rio de Janeiro Univ. 39, 41-42; served France 40; legal Counsellor to French Embassy in London; French rep. on War Crimes Comm., London 45; legal adviser to French Del. Council of Foreign Ministers and Peace Conf. Paris 46; Legal Adviser Ministry of Foreign Affairs 47-; Prof. Ecole Nationale d'Administration Paris 47-; mem. Permanent Court of Arbitration, The Hague 50; del. to Comm. for the Rhine 50; Agent to Int. Court of Justice 50-60; Conseiller d'Etat 54-; Judge, Int. Court of Justice 64-; mem. Inst. of Int. Law 65; mem. UN Int. Law Comm. 61-; mem. Court of Arbitration in Beagle Channel case between Argentina and Chile 71; Commdr. Légion d'Honneur, Croix de Guerre (39-45), Hon. Mem. of the Bench (Inner Temple) 72.

Leisure interests: reading, golf.

Publs. *Survivance de la Raison d'Etat* 32, *Problèmes Politiques de l'Europe* 42-44 (Spanish trans. 43), *La Convention de Genève sur les pêcheries* 59, *Traités et Documents diplomatiques* (with Paul Reuter) 60, 3rd edn. 70, *La protection diplomatique* (in *Encyclopédie française*) 64.

International Court of Justice, Peace Palace, The Hague, Netherlands; and 12 rue Beaujon, Paris 8e, France.

Gross, Bernhard, DIPL.ING., DR. RER. NAT.; Brazilian physicist; b. 1905, Stuttgart; s. of Wilhelm and Sophie Gross; m. Gertrud Gunz 1935; two s.; ed. Tech. Univ. Stuttgart, and Univ. of Berlin.

Research asst. Dept. of Physics, Stuttgart 31-33; staff mem. Nat. Inst. of Technology, Rio de Janeiro 34-; Dir. Electricity Div. 46-47; Dir. Physics Div. Brazilian Nat. Research Council 51-54; Prof. of Physics Univ. of Federal District, Brazil 34-37; Prof. of Electrical Measurements Catholic Univ., Rio de Janeiro 55; fmr. mem. Scientific Advisory Cttee. I.A.E.A.; Brazilian rep. to U.N. Scientific Advisory Cttee. 58-60; mem. Brazilian Del. to UN Scientific Cttee. on Effects of Atomic Radiation 57-59; Dir. Div. of Scientific and Technical Information, Int. Atomic Energy Agency, Vienna 61-67; Dir. of Research, Nat. Nuclear Energy Comm. of Brazil 67-69; Visiting Prof., Technical Univ., Karlsruhe, Germany 69; Scientist, Laboratoire Recherches Physiques, Veyrier, Switz. 70; Research Prof. Inst. of Physics and Chem., Univ. of São Paulo in São Carlos 72-; Consultant, Bell Laboratory, Murray Hill, N.J.

Publs. *Mathematical Structure of Theories of Viscoelasticity* 53, *Singularities of Linear System Functions* 61, *Charge Storage Effects in Solid Dielectrics* 64, and over 100 papers on cosmic radiation, radiation effects and dosimetry, electrets, viscoelasticity, electrical network theory.

Sternwartestrasse 55, A-1180 Vienna, Austria. Telephone: 34-77-932 (Home).

Gross, Courtlandt S.; American businessman; b. 21 Nov. 1904; ed. Harvard Univ.

Clerk and Salesman, Lee Higginson & Co., Boston 27-29; Buyer, Dir. Viking Flying Boat Co., New Haven 29-32; Eastern Rep., Lockheed Aircraft Corpn., New York City 32-40, Vice-Pres., Gen. Man., Dir., Burbank 43-52, Exec. Vice-Pres. 52-56, Pres. 56-61, Chair. 61-67, Chair. Finance Cttee. 67-; Pres., Dir. Vega Aircraft, Burbank 40-43; Dir. Lockheed Air Terminal, Burbank, Southern Calif. Gas Co.; Overseer, Harvard Coll.

2 Bryn Mawr Avenue, Bryn Mawr, Pa. 19010; Home: 1230 Arrowmink Road, Villanova, Pa. 19085, U.S.A.

Gross, Ludwik, M.D.; American cancerologist; b. 11 Sept. 1904, Cracow, Poland; s. of Dr. Adolf and Augusta Gross; m. Dorothy L. Nelson 1943; one d.; ed. Uniwersytet Jagiellonski, Cracow.

Intern and Resident St. Lazar Hospital, Cracow 29-32; clinical training, Salpêtrière Hospital, Univ. de Paris à la Sorbonne 32-39; cancer research, Pasteur Inst., Paris 32-39, Christ Hospital, Cincinnati, Ohio, U.S. 41-43; Capt. to Major, Medical Corps, U.S. Army 43-46; Chief, Cancer Research Unit, Veterans' Admin. Hospital, New York 46-; Consultant, Sloan-Kettering Inst. 53-56, Assoc. Scientist 57-60; Research Prof., Mount Sinai School of Medicine, City Univ. of N.Y. 71-; Dir. American Assen. for Cancer Research 73-76; mem. Nat. Acad. of Sciences, American Medical Assen., American Soc. of Hematology and other socs.; Fellow American Coll. of Physicians, New York Acad. of Sciences, American Assen. for the Advancement of Science, Int. Soc. of Haematology; Diplomate, American Board of Internal Medicine; awards include Prix Chevillon, Acad. Médecine, Paris 37, R. R. de Villiers Int. Award for Leukemia Research 53, Walker Prize, Royal Coll. Surgeons, England 62, Pasteur Silver Medal, Pasteur Inst., Paris 62, L. W. James Award, James Ewing Soc., N.Y. 62, WHO UN Prize 62, Bertner Foundation Award, Univ. of Texas 63, Albert Einstein Centennial Medal, Philadelphia 65, Albion O. Bernstein M.D., Award, N.Y. State Med. Soc. N.Y. 71, Special Virus Cancer Program Award, Nat. Cancer Inst. 72, William S. Middleton Award, Veterans' Admin. 74, Albert Lasker Basic Medical Research Award, N.Y. 74; Award for Cancer Immunology, Cancer Research Inst., N.Y. 75.

Leisure interests: music, piano.

Publs. *Oncogenic Viruses* 61 (2nd revised edn. 70), and over 200 papers on experimental cancer and leukemia.

Veterans Administration Hospital, 130 West Kingsbridge Road, Bronx, New York 10468, U.S.A. Telephone: 212-LU4-9000, Ext. 227.

Grosul, Yakim Sergeyevich; Soviet historian; b. 21 Sept. 1912, Karagashe, Moldavia; ed. Tiraspol State Pedagogic Inst.

Member C.P.S.U. 39-; secondary school teacher 41-44; Lecturer, Moldavian Pedagogic Inst. 44-46; Chair. Moldavian U.S.S.R. Acad. of Sciences 47-50; Vice-Chair. and later Chair. Presidium of Moldavian Branch of U.S.S.R. Acad. of Sciences 50-61; mem. and Pres. Moldavian Acad. of Sciences 61-; Corresp. mem. U.S.S.R. Acad. of Sciences 66-; Deputy to U.S.S.R. Supreme Soviet; mem. U.S.S.R. Parl. Group Cttee.; mem. Central Cttee. Moldavian C.P.; Order of Lenin (twice) and other awards.

Moldavian S.S.R. Academy of Sciences, 1 Leninsky Prospekt, Kishinev, U.S.S.R.

Groszkowski, Janusz, DR.ING., F.I.E.E.E.; Polish university professor, radio-electronics specialist; b. 21 March 1898, Warsaw; m. Mary Groszkowski 1921; one d.

Lecturer, Warsaw Technical Univ. 22-29, Prof. 29-68; Dir. Radio Inst. (later State Inst. of Telecommunications), Warsaw 29-50; mem. Polish Acad. of Sciences 52-, Vice-Pres. 57-62, Pres. 63-72, mem. Presidium 72-; Chair. Govt. Council Science and Technology 63-72; Chair. Nat. Comm. Int. Scientific Radio Union 59-72; Vice-Pres. Int. Scientific Radio Union 66-72; Chair. Comm. of Nat. Prizes 70-; Vice-Chair. All-Polish Cttee. of Nat. Unity Front 68-71, Chair. 71-; Deputy Chair. State Council 72-; Deputy to Seym 72-; mem. Bulgarian, Cuban, Czechoslovak, Hungarian, Romanian, U.S.S.R. Acads. of Sciences, American Vacuum Soc.; Hon. mem. Soc. Française Electronique et Radioélectrique; Fellow, I.E.E.E. (U.S.A.); Dr. h.c. Warsaw, Gdańsk and Łódź Tech. Univs.; State Prizes 1st Class 51, 52, 68; Commdr. Cross of Order of Polonia Restituta 37, 54;

Order of Banner of Labour 1st Class 58, Order of Builders of People's Poland 64, and other mil., Polish and foreign awards.

Publs. *The Interdependence of the Frequency Variation and Harmonic Content and Constant Frequency Oscillators* 32, *On the Temperature Coefficient of Inductance* 35, *The Fundamentals of Frequency Stabilization* 38, *Frequency Generation and Stabilization* (in Polish, Russian, Romanian, Chinese) 47, 58, *High Vacuum Technology* (in Polish, Russian) 48, 57, *Frequency of Self-Oscillations* (in English) 63, *High Vacuum Engineering* (in Polish) 72 (in Russian 75), and about 300 other short publications.

Ogólnopolski Komitet FJN, Aleje Ujazdowskie 13, Warsaw; Home: ul. Nowowiejska 22 m. 7, 00-665, Warsaw, Poland.

Grotowski Jerzy; Polish theatre director and teacher of acting; b. 11 Aug. 1933, Rzeszów; s. of Marian Grotowski and Emilia Kozlowska; ed. Faculty of Acting of Państwowa Wyzsza Szkola Teatralna (National Theatrical Acad.) Cracow, Faculty of Stage-directing in Moscow and Cracow.

One of the leading exponents of audience involvement, has directed at Teatr Stary (Old Theatre), Cracow 57-59; Lecturer Nat. Theatrical Acad., Cracow 59-; Dir. Teatr 13 Rzedow (Theatre Laboratory), Opole 59-64, later called Inst. for Research on Actor's Method-Laboratory Theatre, moving to Wrocław 65-; worked with Royal Shakespeare Co., London 66, and at N.Y. Univ.; Dir. Prof. Ecole Supérieure d'Art Dramatique, Aix-en-Provence; has run Pan-Scandinavian courses for actors at Odin Teatret, Holstebro, Denmark 66, 67, 68 69 and at Stockholm 66; Golden Prize, Int. Festival of Theatres in Belgrade 67; Ministry of Culture of Poland Award for Research into Pedagogics 67; Drama Desk Award, N.Y. for *Apocalypsis cum Figuris* 69-70; Award of Polish Ministry of Foreign Affairs 70; Main Polish State Award of Research and for *Apocalypsis cum figuris* 72.

Productions include *Cain* 60, *Dziady* 61, *Kordian* 62, *Acropolis* 62, *Faustus* 63, *Hamlet* 64, *The Constant Prince* 65, *Apocalypsis cum Figuris/colage* 68-69, 72 (version II).

Leisure interest: travelling.

Publ. *Towards A Poor Theatre* 68.

Teatr Laboratorium, 50-101 Wrocław, Rynek Ratusz 27, Poland.

Telephone: 342-67.

Grouès, Henri (called **Abbé Pierre**); French ecclesiastic and philanthropist; b. 5 Aug. 1912; ed. Collège des Jésuites and Univ. of Lyons.

Entered Capuchin Order 30; left for health reasons 38; almoner at the hospital of La Mure and in charge of the Groupements de Jeunesse and the Orphanage of the Cote Ste. André 40, vicar of Grenoble 41; founded an escape organization through the Alps and the Pyrenees, founded the cttee. against forced labour; joined Free French Forces in Algiers as Almoner to the Fleet 44; Dep. for Meurthe-et-Moselle 46-51; organized help for the destitute and the homeless and created the Centre d'Emmaüs through an appeal to public opinion; founded the revue *Faim et Soif* 54; Chevalier de la Légion d'Honneur, Croix de Guerre (2 citations avec palmes), Médaille de la Résistance, Médaille des Evadés, Médaille des Combattants Volontaires, Médaille des Maquisards Belges.

Publs. *23 mois de vie clandestine, Vers l'Homme, Feuilles Eparses* (poems), *L'Abbé Pierre vous Parle, Emmaüs* 59, *Pleine Vie, Le Scandale de la Faim Inter pelle l'Eglise.*

2 avenue de la Liberté, Charenton (Val de Marne 94), France.

Telephone: 368-62-44.

Groussard, Serge, L. ès L.; French writer and journalist; b. 18 Jan. 1921, Niort; s. of Col. Georges Groussard and Vera Bernstein; m. Monique Berlioux 1956; two d.; ed. Lycée La Rochelle and Lycée Gourand, Rabat, Ecole Nat. d'Administration, Ecole Libre des Sciences Politiques, and Univ. de Paris.

Chief Reporter *Le Figaro* 54-62, *L'Aurore* 62-69; Special Contributor *Le Figaro* 69-; Chevalier Légion d'Honneur, Croix de Guerre, Médaille de la Résistance, Croix de la Valeur Militaire; Prix Claude Blanchard 48, Prix International du Grand Reportage 48, Prix du Roman populiste 49, Prix Fémina 50, Grand Prix de la Nouvelle 55.

Leisure interest: sport.

Publs. *Crépuscule des vivants* 46, *Pogrom* 48, *Solitude Espagnole* 48, *Des gens sans importance* 49, *La Femme sans passé* 50, *Talya* 51, *La Ville de joie* 52, *Un officier de tradition* 54, *Une chic fille* 56, *La Belle Espérance* 58, *Quartier chinois* 58, *La Passion du Maure* 59, *Jeunesse sauvage* 60, *Une espionne doit mourir* 62, *Les Chacals* 64, *Mektoub* 68, *Tu es Soleil* 70, *Taxi de Nuit* 71, *L'Algérie des Adieux* 72, *La Médaille de Song* 73, *La Guerre Oubliée* 74.

5 rue de Koufra, Boulogne-sur-Seine 92, France.

Telephone: 825 17-43.

Grover, Amar Nath, M.A., LL.B.; Indian judge; b. 15 Feb. 1912, Shwebo (British Upper Burma); s. of G. L. and S. D. Grover; m. Mrs. Kanth Grover 1937; three s. one d.; ed. Univs. of Punjab, Lahore, Christ's Coll., Cambridge and Middle Temple, London.

Called to Bar 36; Barrister, High Court, Lahore 36-47, later at High Court of E. Punjab, Simla and Chandigarh; Judge, High Court, Punjab 57-68; mem. Punjab Bar Council 54-57, Law Comm. (Punjab) 57; Judge, Supreme Court of India 68-73; Chair. Finance Cttee. Indian Branch Int. Law Asscn.; mem. Governing Body Indian Law Inst. 70-73.

Leisure interests: golf, reading, fine arts, music (Indian, and Western), comparative laws.

Publs. several articles on various branches of law.

132 Sunder Nagar, New Delhi 3, India.

Telephone: 70118.

Grover, Sir Anthony Charles, Kt.; British underwriter; b. 13 Oct. 1907, Harrow, Middx.; s. of Frederick J. and Ruby E. Grover; m. Marguerite B. Davies 1931; one s. one d.; ed. Westminster School.

Served in Coldstream Guards, rising to rank of Major (mentioned in despatches) 40-45; Chair. Lloyd's Underwriters' Asscn. 54-56; Deputy Chair. and Treas. Lloyd's Register of Shipping 56-57, Chair. 63-73; Deputy Chair. Lloyd's 58, Chair. 59-60; Chair. Lifeguard Assurance Ltd., Anglo-Swedish Development Co. Ltd., Arne Glucksman (U.K.) Ltd.; Dir. Risdon-Beazley Marine Ltd., Lynbridge Securities Ltd., Grover-Bolton & Co. Ltd.; Commdr. Order of Léopold II, Order of Orange-Nassau, Order of Dannebrog.

Leisure interest: golf.

Dial Cottage, Firbank Lane, St. John's, Woking, Surrey, England.

Telephone: Woking 73928.

Groves, Sir Charles, Kt., C.B.E., F.R.C.M.; British musician and conductor; b. 10 March 1915, London; s. of Frederick Groves and Annie Whitehead; m. Hilary Barchard 1948; one s. two d.; ed. St. Paul's Cathedral Choir School, Sutton Valence School, Kent and Royal Coll. of Music.

Conductor, BBC Northern Symphony Orchestra 44-51, Bournemouth Symphony Orchestra 51-61, Welsh Nat. Opera Co. 61-63; Conductor, Dir. of Music, Royal Liverpool Philharmonic Orchestra 63-; Assoc. Conductor Royal Philharmonic Orchestra 68-; has toured Europe, U.S.A., S. America, Australia, S. Africa; numerous television and radio recordings; conducts all

major orchestras in U.K. including opera; Pres. Nat. Fed. of Music Socs. 72-; Hon. D.Mus. (Liverpool), Hon. R.A.M.
Leisure interests: reading, cricket, country walking.
23 Fulwood Park, Liverpool, L17 5AD; 191 St. Andrews House, Barbican, London, EC2 Y8BA; and The Athenaeum, 107 Pall Mall, London S.W.1, England.
Telephone: 051-727-1121 (Home); 01-628-6550.

Groves, Wallace, M.A., B.SC., LL.B., LL.M.; American financier; b. 20 March 1901, Norfolk, Va.; s. of James S. Groves and Lillie Edwards; m. Georgette Cusson; three s. two d.; ed. Georgetown Univ., Washington, D.C. Admitted Maryland Bar 25; private legal practice 25-31; fmr. Pres. and Chair. Phoenix Securities Corpn.; Founder of Freeport, Bahamas; fmr. Chair. Grand Bahama Port Authority; Hon. LL.D. (Ursinus Coll., Pa.).
Leisure interests: yachting, tennis.
P.O. Box 5, Freeport, Grand Bahama, Bahamas.
Telephone: 809-352-6377 (Office).

Groza, Maria; Romanian professor and politician; b. 1 Sept. 1918, Deva, Hunedoara County; ed. Bucharest Acad. of Economics.
Civil Servant, Ministry of Foreign Affairs 48-55; Asst. Acad. of Econs., Bucharest 49-55, lecturer in Social Sciences 55-; mem. and Vice-Pres. Grand Nat. Assembly 65-; Sec. Nat. Council of Women of S.R.R. 58-64, Vice-Pres. 64-; del. to numerous women's int. congresses, UNESCO and UN congresses and confs. on social problems in Montreal 60, Grenoble 64, Helsinki (Vice-Pres.) 68, Iaşi (Pres.) 69; mem. of Romanian del. to UN Gen. Assembly Sessions XVIII, XX-XXIII.
Publs. Papers on the social position of Romanian women, and the education of youth in Romania in *Femmes du Monde Entier* (UNESCO) and Romanian periodicals.
Consiliul National al Femeilor, Str. Polonă 19, Bucharest; 69 Bulevardul Aviatorilor, Bucharest, Romania.

Grozev, Guero; Bulgarian diplomatist; b. 13 April 1921, Strelcha; m.; two c.; ed. studies in political and social science, Sofia.
Former Chair. Cen. Cttee. Union of People's Youth and Deputy Minister for Educ. and Culture; entered diplomatic service 60; Amb. to Czechoslovakia 60-63; First Deputy Minister for Foreign Affairs 63-71; Perm. Rep. to UN Jan. 71-; Deputy to Bulgarian Nat. Assembly; mem. Del. to UN Gen. Assembly 70.
Permanent Mission of Bulgaria to United Nations, 11 East 84th Street, New York, N.Y. 10028, U.S.A.

Grubb, Louis Edward, B.A.; American business executive; b. 17 April 1912, Passaic, N.J.; s. of William H. Grubb and Nettie Ralph Arnold; m. Catherine A. Swartz 1936; one s. one d.; ed. Wesleyan Univ., Middletown, Conn.
Joined International Nickel, Inc. (U.S. subsidiary) 34, Vice-Pres. 61; Man. Dir. and later Chair. Henry Wiggin & Co. Ltd., Hereford, U.K. 64; Man. Dir. and later Chair. Int. Nickel Ltd., London 67; Exec. Vice-Pres. and Dir., Int. Nickel Co. of Canada Ltd. 71, Pres. and Chief Exec. Officer 72-74, Chair. and Chief Officer 74-.
Leisure interests: sailing, golf.
One New York Plaza, New York, N.Y. 10004, U.S.A.; Home: 619 Avenue Road, Toronto, Ont., M4V 2K6, Canada.
Telephone: (212) 742-4740 (New York); Home: (416) 486-1731 (Toronto).

Grübel, Albert, DR.IUR.; Swiss lawyer; b. 22 March 1918, Basle; s. of Wilhelm and Clara Grübel (née Baumann); m. Jona Bach 1951; ed. High School, Basle and Basle Univ.
Commerce Div., Fed. Dept. of Econ. 43-51; Swiss Fed. of Trade and Industry 51-66; Amb., Del. of Swiss Fed. Council for trade agreements 66-67; Dir. Fed. Office for

Industry and Labour 68-74; Perm. Rep. to OECD 74-. Swiss Delegation to Organisation of Economic Co-operation and Development, 28 rue de Martignac, 75007 Paris, France.
Telephone: 551-62-92.

Grüber, Arthur; German conductor; b. 21 Aug. 1910; ed. Hochschule für Musik, Cologne.
Conductor in Frankfurt-am-Main 32-38; Dir. Opera Wuppertal 38-39; Conductor, Berlin Opera House, 39-44; Dir. of Music, Halle 44-47; Chief Conductor, Hamburg State Opera 47-51 and Komische Opera, Berlin 47-53; Gen. Music Dir. in Brunswick 55-62; Gen. Music Dir. in Karlsruhe and Dir. of Conductors' Section, Badische Hochschule für Musik 62-.
Compositions: comic opera, *Trotz wider Trotz*, first performed 48, *Hölderlin-Ode* 54.
Badisches Staatstheater, Karlsruhe, Federal Republic of Germany.

Grüber, Heinrich K. E., D.D., PH.D., L.H.D.; German ecclesiastic; b. 24 June 1891, Stolberg; s. of Ernst Grüber and Alwine Cleven; m. Margarete Vits 1920; two s. one d.; ed. Univs. of Bonn, Berlin and Utrecht.
Clergyman in Dortmund 20, Dir. Inst. for Juvenile Delinquents; Clergyman in Düsseldorf 25, Templin 26; dismissed by Nazis 33; Clergyman in Berlin-Kaulsdorf 34; Founder and Dir. "Buro Grüber" (Relief Cttee. for Victims of Nuremberg Laws) 37; inmate of Sachsenhausen and Dachau Concentration Camps 40-43; Dean of Berlin 45-; mem. Berlin City Council; Rep. Council of Protestant Church of Germany; Pres. Protestant Relief Cttee. for Victims of Nuremberg Laws; Vice-Pres. British-German Fellowship; Rep. Protestant Relief Comm. of Berlin and East Zone of Germany; Rep. Council of Protestant Church to Govt. of German Democratic Republic 48-58; Pres. Deutsch-Israelische Gesellschaft; hon. degrees; Ossietzky Medal 65; Commdr. Orange-Nassau 66; Albert Schweitzer Prize 67.
Publs. *Dona Nobis Pacem* 51, *Leben in Spannungen* 58, *An der Stechbahn* 60, *Durchkreuzter Hass* 61, *Fürchtet euch nicht* 62, *Pro Israel* 63, *Leben an der Todeslinie-Dachauer Predigten, Der Gerechte unter den Nationen* 66, *Erinnerungen aus sieben Jahrzehnten* 68.
1 Berlin 37, Teltower Damm 124; Home: 1 Berlin 33, Im Winkel 5, Germany.
Telephone: 815-14-95 (Office).

Gruber, Karl J., DR. JUR.; Austrian politician; b. 3 May 1909, Innsbruck, Austria; ed. Univs. of Innsbruck and Vienna.
Austrian resistance leader 38-45; Gov. of the Tyrol May-Oct. 45; State Sec. for Foreign Affairs 45-46; Minister of Foreign Affairs 46-53; Amb. to U.S.A. 54-57; mem. of Parl. 46; Lecturer in Econs., Vienna Univ. 46-61; fmr. Vice-Pres. OEEC; Special Adviser to Int. Atomic Energy Agency 58-60; Amb. to Spain 61-66, to German Fed. Repub. 66; Sec. of State 66-69; Amb. to U.S.A. 70-73, to Switzerland 73-75; Hon. LL.D. (Univ. of S. Calif.) 46; Austrian People's Party.
Publs. *Die Politik der Mitte* 45, *Voraussetzungen der Vollbeschäftigung* 46, *Zusammenhang zwischen Grösse, Kosten und Rentabilität industrieller Betriebe* 48, *Zwischen Befreiung und Freiheit* 53.
c/o Ministry of Foreign Affairs, Vienna; Home: Rennweg 6A, 1030 Vienna, Austria.

Grubiakov, Vasily Fedorovich; Soviet diplomatist; b. 5 May 1911, Kustanai, Kazakhstan; ed. Saratov Univ., Higher Diplomatic School.
Second, First Sec., Soviet Embassy in Turkey 43-45; Consul-Gen. in Istanbul 45-47; Adviser and Senior Adviser, Soviet Del. at UN 53-57; Chief First European Dept., Foreign Ministry 62-65; Amb. to Belgium 67-69, to Turkey 69-74.
c/o Ministry of Foreign Affairs, Moscow, U.S.S.R.

Grudzień, Gen. Mieczysław, M.A.; Polish politician; b. 1922, Majki, Płock district; ed. Coll. of Political Officers and Military Political Acad.

Lived in France and Belgium 22-47; during World War II activist in French Resistance; returned to Poland and joined the Polish People's Army 47; various posts in the military party-political machine, recently First Assistant Chief, Political Headquarters of Polish Army; divisional General Oct. 71-; deputy mem. Cen. Cttee. PZPR/Polish United Workers Party Dec. 71-; Minister for Combatants' Affairs June 72-; Vice-Pres. Chief Council of Union of Fighters for Freedom and Democracy 74-; mem. Presidium Cen. Board, Soc. for Polish-Soviet Friendship 74-.

Ministerstwo d/s Kombatantów, Aleje Ujazdowskie 6a, 00-461 Warsaw, Poland.
Telephone: 29-32-81.

Grudzień, Zdzisław; Polish politician; b. 6 Oct. 1924, Escaudain, France; ed. Acad. of Mining and Metallurgy, Cracow.

Mine-Worker, coal-mines in Belgium and France; activist of leftist labour movt.; mem. French Communist Party 42-46; during Second World War participated in French resistance; returned to Poland 46; mem. Polish Workers' Party (PPR) 46-48, Polish United Workers' Party (PZPR) 48-; active mem. Rural Youth Union 49 and Polish Youth Union 49-56; Head, Propaganda Dept., Voivodship Cttee. PZPR, Katowice 57-60, Sec. Voivodship Cttee., Katowice 60-Dec. 70, First Sec. Dec. 70-; mem. Cen. Cttee. PZPR 64-, Deputy mem. Politburo Cen. Cttee. 71-75, mem. 75-; Deputy to Seym 65-; Chair. Seym Comm. of Nat. Defence March 72-; Chair. Voivodship Nat. Council, Katowice 73-; Order of Banner of Labour 1st and 2nd class and other decorations.

Polska Zjednoczona Partia Robotnicza, Komitet Wojewódzki, Katowice, Poland.

Gruen, Victor; American architect; b. 18 July 1903, Vienna, Austria; s. of Dr. Adolph Gruenbaum and Elisabeth Levy; m. Kemija Salihefendic 1963; one s. one d. (from previous marriage); ed. Vienna Technological Inst., and Acad. of Fine Arts.

Designer, Supervisor and Co-ordinator with Melcher & Steiner, Vienna 24-33; independent practice in Vienna, executing a large number of residential and commercial projects 33-38; designer in New York and Los Angeles 38-48; in independent practice as Senior Partner, Victor Gruen Associates 48-68; f. Victor Gruen Center for Environmental Planning 68, Zentrum für Umweltplanung 73; planning and architectural consultant in France (Préfecture de la Région Parisienne), Belgium (Université Catholique de Louvain), Austria (City of Vienna), Scandinavian countries, Italy, Switzerland, Fed. Repub. of Germany, Spain; has lectured at many univs. and colls. in the U.S.A. and Europe; Fellow, American Inst. of Architects; affiliate mem. American Inst. of Planners, etc.; has exhibited in Washington, Brussels (World Fair), New York, Mexico City, Moscow, Berlin, etc.

Projects include: about 50 regional shopping centres, including Detroit and Minneapolis, Midtown Plaza, Rochester, N.Y.; revitalization plans for Fort Worth, Fresno, Boston and the City of Vienna.

Leisure interest: photography.

Publs. *Shopping Towns U.S.A.* (with Larry Smith), *The Heart of Our Cities, Centers for the Urban Environment, Das Überleben der Städte, Die lebenswerte Stadt* (The Livable City) 75, *Is Progress a Crime* 75; numerous articles on design, architecture and planning.

Zentrum für Umweltplanung, 1030 Vienna (Office); Traungasse 7, 1030 Vienna, Austria.
Telephone: 72-15-35 (Office).

Gruenther, Gen. Alfred M.; American army officer (retd.); b. 3 March 1899, Nebraska; s. of Christian and Mary Gruenther; m. Grace Elizabeth Crum 1922; two s.; ed. U.S. Military Acad.

Routine peacetime assignments 19-41; Chief of Staff, Third Army 41-42; Deputy Chief of Staff, Allied Force H.Q. (London, North African campaign, Algiers) 42-43; Chief of Staff, Fifth Army (Italian campaign) 43-44; Chief of Staff, 15th Army Group (Italian campaign) 44-45; Deputy Commanding Gen. U.S. Forces in Austria 45; Deputy Commandant, Nat. War Coll. 45-47; Dir. Joint Staff, Joint Chiefs of Staff 47-49; Deputy Chief of Staff for Plans and Combat Operations, Army Gen. Staff 49-51; Chief of Staff, SHAPE 51-53; Gen. Aug. 51; Supreme Allied Commdr. Europe 53-56; Pres. American Red Cross 57-64; Chair. English-Speaking Union of U.S. 66-68; mem. President's Comm. on Arms Control and Disarmament 66-69; mem. President's Comm. on Heart Disease, Cancer, Stroke 64-66; Dir. Pan American World Airways, N.Y. Life Insurance Co., Dart Industries Inc., Federated Dept. Stores Inc., Inst. for Defense Analyses; mem. The Business Council; mem. President's Comm. on an All-Volunteer Armed Force 69-70; mem. Visiting Cttee. School of Med., Univ. of Miami, Exec. Cttee. Atlantic Council, Electoral Coll.; D.S.M. (with two Oak Leaf Clusters) (U.S.); Hon. C.B. (U.K.); Grand Cross Légion d'Honneur, Médaille Militaire (France); Grand Cordon, Order of Leopold (Belgium), and numerous other int. decorations; Hon. degrees from 38 univs. including Harvard, Yale, Dartmouth, Columbia, Holy Cross.

Leisure interest: contract bridge (Hon. Pres. World Bridge Fed.).

Publs. *The Referee's Analysis of the Decisive Hands of the Lenz-Culbertson Match* 31, *Duplicate Contract Bridge Complete* 33.

Cathedral Apartments, 4101 Cathedral Avenue, N.W., Washington, D.C. 20016, U.S.A.
Telephone: 202-244-7693.

Gruijters, Johannes Petrus Adrianus; Netherlands politician; b. 30 June 1931, Helmond; m. Jannetje Mol 1936; one s.; ed. Augustinianum, Eindhoven, Municipal Univ. of Amsterdam.

Company Sec. de Wit's Textiel Nijverheid, Helmond (now incorporated in Hatema Texoprint/Gamma) 53-58; studied 58-60; Chief Foreign Editor *Algemeen Handelsblad* 60-67; Councillor Amsterdam Municipal Council 62-66; Co-Founder Democraten 66; mem. State Advisory Cttee. for the Constitution and Electoral Law 67-71; mem. Provincial States of N. Holland 70-71; Editor-in-Chief, Het Spectrum, Publrs. 71-72; mem. Second Chamber 72-73; Minister of Housing and Physical Planning 73-.

Publs. *De doortrekking van het Wilhelminakanaal-Daarom D'66, Experimenten in democratie, Nixon-McGovern.*

Van Alkemadelaan 85, The Hague, Netherlands.
Telephone: 070-246524.

Grumiaux, Arthur; Belgian violinist.

Has appeared at international music festivals at Glyndebourne, Salzburg, Lucerne, Aix-en-Provence, Strasbourg, and Vienna; soloist with most leading European orchestras, has made tours of America, Japan and Middle East; repertoire includes all the great classical and romantic works for the violin and many modern works including the concertos of Bartok, Berg, Stravinsky and Walton; noted exponent of works of Mozart; records for Philips; Grand Prix du Disque (several), and awards from German and Italian critics.

c/o Ibbs and Tillett, 124 Wigmore Street, London, W1H 0AX, England.
Telephone: 01-486-4021.

Grumman, Leroy Randle; American aeronautical engineer; b. 4 Jan. 1895, Huntingdon, New York; s. of George Tyson Grumman and Grace (Conklin

Grumman; *m.* Rose Werther 1921; one *s.* three *d.*; ed. Cornell Univ.

Aeronautical Engineer, Loening Aeronautical Engineering Corpn., N.Y.C. 20-29; Pres. Grumman Aircraft Corpn. 30-46, Chair. Board of Dirs. 46-66, Hon. Chair. 66-; Presidential Medal for Merit 45. Daniel Guggenhiem Medal 48, Frank M. Hawks Memorial Award 58, enshrined in Aviation Hall of Fame 72; Hon. Eng. D. Brooklyn Polytechnic Inst., Hon. LL.D. Adelphi Coll. Grumman Corporation, South Oyster Bay Road, Bethpage, Long Island, New York; Home: 77 Bayview Road, Plandome, N.Y. 11030, U.S.A.
Telephone: 516-575-0574.

Grümmer, Elisabeth; German soprano opera singer; b. 1921; ed. drama school, Meiningen and musical studies in Aachen.

Engaged at Stadttheater, Aachen 41, Städtische Oper, Duisburg 41, Staatsoper, Berlin 48, Deutsche Oper, Berlin 61-; has made appearances at many foreign opera houses; Prof. Staatliche Hochschule für Musik und Darstellende Kunst, Berlin; awarded title of Kammersängerin; Berliner Kunstpreis 65.
Deutsche Oper, 1 Berlin, Richard Wagnerstrasse 10, Germany.

Grünbaum, Henry; Danish economist and politician; b. 27 July 1911; ed. Københavns Universitet.

Former engraver; Sec. Econ. Council Danish Labour Movement 38-40; Statistician of Trade Unions Congress 40-48; mem. Resistance Movements Liaison Cttee., Stockholm 44-45; Econ. and Political Columnist on *Social-Demokraten* (daily, now *Aktuelt*) 49-56; Econ. Adviser to Danish Gen. Workers Union 56-64, and Editor-in-Chief of Danish Gen. Workers Union biweekly periodical 62-64; Minister of Econ. and Scandinavian Affairs 64-65, Minister of Finance 65-68, Oct. 71-73; mem. of Parl. Nov. 66; mem. Board Econ. Soc. 59-65.
Publs. *Industrial Democracy, Consumers Price-Index and Wages.*
Torvegade 47, 1400 Copenhagen, Denmark.

Grüneberg, Gerhard; German politician; b. 29 Aug 1921; ed. elementary school and building studies.

Builder 39-41, 45-46; war service and prisoner-of-war 41-45; official in Socialist Unity Party, (S.E.D.) 46-; First Sec. Frankfurt/Oder District Cttee. 52; mem. and Sec. Central Cttee. S.E.D. 58-, Candidate mem. Politburo 63-66, mem. 66-; mem. Agricultural Council of Council of Ministers 63-; mem. Volkskammer 58-, mem. Comm. for Foreign Affairs 58-63; mem. Nat. Council of Nat. Front 58-; Vaterländischer Verdienstorden in Silver 59, in Gold 64.
Sozialistische Einheitspartei Deutschlands, 102 Berlin, 2 Werderscher Markt, German Democratic Republic.

Grünewald, Herbert, DR.RER.NAT.; German chemical industry executive; b. 12 Sept. 1921, Weinheim; *m.* Ilse Cramer 1956; four *c.*; ed. Univs. of Heidelberg and Frankfurt am Main.

With Bayer AG, Leverkusen 56-, Production Man. and Dir. Intermediate Div. 64, mem. Management Board, Head of Personnel and Social Welfare 68, Chair. Management Board July 74-; Chair. Management Board Carl-Duisberg-Gesellschaft G.m.b.H. 71; mem. Advisory Board Agfa Gevaert AG 73, Schloemann Siemag AG 73, DEGUSSA 74, Erdölchemie 74.
509 Leverkusen-Bayerwerk; Home: Rudolf-Girtler-Strasse 11, 509 Leverkusen, Federal Republic of Germany.
Telephone: (2172) 30-67-72 (Office).

Grunfeld, Henry, LL.D.; British (b. German) banker; b. 1 June 1904, Breslau, Germany; *s.* of Max Grunfeld and Rosa Grunfeld (née Haendler); *m.* Berta Lotte Oliven 1931; one *s.* one *d.*; ed. law studies in Berlin.
Partner in family firm 27; Man. New Trading Co. Ltd.

38; joined S. G. Warburg & Co. Ltd. 46, Dir. 51-, Chair. 69-74, Pres. 74-; Chair. Mercury Securities Ltd. 64-74, Pres. 74-.
30 Gresham Street, London, EC2P 2EB, England.
Telephone: (01) 600-4555.

Grunwald, Ernest, PH.D.; American professor of chemistry; b. 2 Nov. 1923, Wuppertal, Germany; ed. Univ. of Calif., Los Angeles.

Research Chemist, Portland Cement Asscn. 47; Research Fellow, Columbia Univ. 48; Assoc. Prof., later Prof. Florida State Univ. 49-60; Research Chemist, Bell Telephone Labs. 60; Prof. of Chemistry, Brandeis Univ. 64-; mem. Nat. Acad. of Sciences, American Acad. of Arts and Sciences; Chaim Weizmann Fellowship, Alfred P. Sloan Fellowship; American Chem. Soc. Award in Pure Chem.
Department of Chemistry, Brandeis University, Waltham, Mass. 02154, U.S.A.

Grushin, Pyotr Dmitriyevich; Soviet aviation specialist; b. 28 Jan. 1906, Volsk; ed. Moscow Aviation Inst.

Member C.P.S.U. 31-; leading engineer in aircraft industry 32-; Dean of Dept. Moscow Aviation Inst. 48-51; Dir. Aircraft Plant 53-; mem. Cen. Cttee. C.P.S.U. 66-; corresp. mem. U.S.S.R. Acad. of Sciences 62-66, mem. 66-; Hero of Socialist Labour; Lenin Prize.
Publs. Works on aerodynamics and aircraft construction.
U.S.S.R. Academy of Sciences, 14 Leninsky Prospekt, Moscow, U.S.S.R.

Grut, Aage, M.D., D.P.H., D.I.H.; Danish health officer; 23 Dec. 1906, Holte; *s.* of Gen. Chamberlain Torben Grut, K.C.V.O.; *m.* Ulla Schultz 1946; no *c.*; ed. Copenhagen Univ.

Medical Inspector of Factories 40-48; Chief Industrial Hygiene Division and Industrial Hygiene Adviser, I.L.O., Geneva, 48-53; Medical Officer of Health 54; Senior Medical Inspector of Labour 55-; Asst. Sec.-Gen. Int. Conf. of Experts on Pneumoconiosis, Sydney 50-; Chair. Int. Cttee. on Carbon Monoxide; Univ. Medal 36, Hon. mem. Argentine Soc. of Industrial Medicine 51, Cuban Soc. of Industrial Medicine 53.
Leisure interests: violin and gardening.
Publs. Many papers in medical periodicals.
Hambros allé 20, Hellerup, Denmark.
Telephone: HE 1628.

Grützner, Erich; German chemical worker, social scientist and politician; b. 1910.

Member Communist Party 32-46, Sozialistische Einheitspartei Deutschlands 46-; mem. Volkskammer 58-; Chair. Leipzig District Council 59-74; mem. Council of State 60-; Vaterländischer Verdienstorden in Gold, and other decorations.
Staatsrat, Marx-Engels-Platz, 102 Berlin, German Democratic Republic.

Gscheidle, Kurt; German engineer and politician; b. 16 Dec. 1924, Stuttgart; *s.* of Georg and Emma Maria Gscheidle (née Schloz); *m.* Elisabeth Scharnhorst 1953; one *s.*; ed. REFA Inst., Sozialakademie.

Telecommunications technician, Fed. Postal Service 48; Head, Secr. for Technology and Econs., Postal Workers' Union 53-57, Vice-Pres. Postal Workers' Union 57-; mem. Parl. (Bundestag) 61-; Sec. of State, Fed. Ministry of Posts 69-74; Fed. Minister of Traffic, Posts and Telecommunications May 74-.
Leisure interests: cooking, tennis.
Publs. books on industrial organization and personnel management.
53 Bonn-Bad Godesberg, Kennedy Allee 72, Federal Republic of Germany.
Telephone: 02221-86200; 02221-145500.

Guayasamin Calero, Oswaldo; Ecuadorean painter; b. 1919; ed. School of Fine Arts, Quito.

First exhibition 40; toured United States 42; visited

Russia and China; paints portraits and murals; Bienal de España Prize 55, Mexican prize 60.
c/o School of Fine Arts, Quito, Ecuador.

Guazzugli Marini, Giulio, DR. PH.; Italian atomic energy administrator; b. 1914; *m.* Maria Fantozzi 1940; one *s.* one *d.*; ed. Rome Univ.
Assistant Professor of Philosophy, Rome Univ. 37-47; Personal Sec. to Signor Carlo Sforza, Minister of Foreign Affairs 47-49; official at Council of Europe, Strasbourg 49-53; Dir., Secretariat, Council of Coal and Steel Community 53-57; Exec. Sec. Euratom Commission 58-67; Dir.-Gen. European Community Joint Research Centre 68-71; Special Adviser to the Commission of the European Communities 71-.
Leisure interest: sailing.
19 Passeggiata di Ripetta, Rome, Italy.
Telephone: 87-87-98.

Gucwa, Stanisław; Polish politician; b. 18 April 1919, Przybysławice; *s.* of Jan Gucwa and Maria Opita; *m.* Maria Gucwa 1946; two *d.*; ed. Acad. of Political Science, Warsaw.
Managerial posts in Cen. Board of Flour Milling Industry and in Ministry of Food 48-56; Under-Sec. of State Ministry of Agriculture 57-68; Minister of Food Industry April 68-Feb. 71; Vice-Chair. State Council 71-72; mem. Peasant Party 45-49, United Peasant Party 49-; mem. Pres. Cen. Cttee. 59-71, Chair. Feb. 71-; Deputy to Seym (Parl.) 61-, Marshal 72-; mem. Pres. All-Polish Cttee. of Nat. Unity Front June 71-; Order of Banner of Labour 1st Class, Commdr. Cross, Order Polonia Restituta, Gold Cross of Merit, Medal of Georgi Dymitrov, Order of Builders of People's Poland 74, and other decorations.
Zjednoczone Stronnictwo Ludowe, ul. Grzybowska 4, 00-131 Warsaw, Poland.

Güden, Hilde; Austrian opera singer; b. 15 Sept. 1922; ed. High School, and Acad. of Music.
Member, Vienna State Opera, La Scala, Milan 47-, Metropolitan Opera, New York 51-, Deutsche Oper Berlin, West Berlin; Festivals Salzburg, Edinburgh, Glynebourne, etc.; toured Europe, U.S.A., Canada, Japan; awarded title of "Kammersängerin" by the Pres. of Austria 50; Grand Cross for Science and Art 59; Cross of Order of Dannebrog 62; awarded Decca Golden Record 58, Vienna Phil. Orch. Silver Rose 59, Golden Oscar of Acad. du Disque Français 61; Hon. mem. of Vienna State Opera 72; Grand Cross of Honour 72; Golden Orpheus, Acad. de Lyrique, Paris.
c/o Staatsoper, Vienna, Austria.

Gudmundsson, Gudmundur I., CAND. IURIS; Icelandic lawyer and politician; b. 17 July 1909, Hafnarfjordur; *m.* Rosa Ingolfsdóttir 1942; five *s.*; ed. Reykjavík Coll., and Univ. of Iceland.
Law practice 34-45; Supreme Court Attorney 39-45; District Judge, Hafnarfjordur 45-56; mem. Althing 42-65; Minister for Foreign Affairs 56-65, Minister of Finance 58-59; Amb. to U.K., Netherlands, Spain and Portugal 65-71, to Nigeria 71, to U.S.A., Canada, Mexico, Brazil, Argentina, Cuba 71-73, to Sweden, Finland, Austria 73-; Commdr. with Star, Order of Icelandic Falcon, Grand Cross White Rose (Finland), Grand Cross St. Olav (Norway), Hon. K.B.E., and many other decorations; Labour.
Icelandic Embassy, Kommendörsgatan 35, 114 58 Stockholm; Home: Kungsvägen 16, 182 75 Stocksund, Sweden.
Telephone: 08-62 4016 (Office); 08-85 8080 (Home).

Gudmundsson, Kristmann; Icelandic writer; b. 23 Oct. 1901, Borgarfjördur; *s.* of Sigridur Björnsdottir and Gudmundur Jonsson; *m.* Holmfridur H. Mariasdottir; four *d.*
Writes in Icelandic and Norwegian; his novels have been translated into 36 languages; Icelandic Falcon Order.

Leisure interests: philosophy, religion, history, astronomy, botany and literature.
Publs. *Poems of Twilight* 22, *Icelandic Love* 26, *The Bridal Gown* 27, *Armann and Vildis* 28, *Morning of Life* 29, *Sigmar* 30, *The Blue Coast* 31, *The Sacred Mountain* 32, *Early Spring* 33, *White Nights* 34, *Children of Earth* 35, *The Lamp* 36, *The Goddess and the Bull* 38, *The Sneering Stonemonster* 43, *Comrade Woman* 47, *An Evening in Reykjavík* 48, *Scarlet Mist* (2 vols.) 50-52, *The Tragedy at Osterby* 55, *Poems from Kristmann* 55, *History of World Literature* (2 vols.) 55-56, *The Little Café* 58, *A Voyage to the Stars* 59, *Adventures in Space* 59, *Autobiography* (4 vols.), *The Black Isolde* 59, *Norwegian Idyll* 60, *My Botanical Garden* 61, *The White Flame* 61, *The Golden Isolde* 62, *Playthings* 62, *The Centre* 65, *Winter Days* 66, *Blue Eyes* (short story collection) 68, *The Great Carpenter* 69, *Summer in Selavik* 70, *The Smile.*
P.O. Box 615, Tomasarhaga 9, Reykjavík, Iceland.
Telephone: 15048.

Guebeily, Mohammed Abdel Maaboud El-, B.SC. (HONS.); Egyptian nuclear scientist; b. 5 Feb. 1921; ed. Cairo Univ. and Curie Laboratory, Paris.
Chemist in Chemical Dept., then Demonstrator in Faculty of Science, Cairo Univ. 46-52; at Inst. for Atomic Energy, Norway 56; Asst. Prof. of Nuclear Chem., U.A.R. Atomic Energy Establishment 57, Head of Nuclear Chem. Dept. 58, Dir. of Technical Bureau of Nuclear Power Reactor Project 63, Dir. Egyptian Atomic Energy Establishment 65, also Chair. of Supreme Cttee. for Nuclear Power Reactor; Chair. Joint Arab Scientific Council for Utilization of Atomic Energy for Peaceful Purposes; mem. Supreme Council for Scientific Research; mem. Scientific Advisory Cttee. of Int. Atomic Energy Authority (IAEA); attended numerous UN confs. on atomic energy; Hon. D. ès Sc.
Publs. Many scientific papers.
Atomic Energy Establishment, Cairo, Egypt.

Guéhenno, Jean (*pseudonym* of Marcel Guéhenno); French writer and educationist; b. 25 March 1890; ed. Ecole Normale Supérieure.
Served French Army 14-18; teacher, various Paris lycées. Chief Editor of review *L'Europe* until 36; supervised collection *Ecrits* for Librairie Grasset; Dir. of weekly *Vendredi* 36; after Liberation wrote for *Figaro* and *Figaro Littéraire*; Gen. Insp. of Nat. Educ. 45-61, Hon. Insp. 61-; Commdr. de la Légion d'Honneur, Croix de Guerre, Médaille de la Résistance, Prix des Ambassadeurs, Paris Literature Prize, Eve Delacroix Prize; mem. Académie Française 62-; Cino del Duca Prize 73.
Publs. *L'Evangile Eternel, Caliban Parle, La Conversion à l'Humain, Le Journal d'un Homme de Quarante Ans* 34, *Journal d'une Révolution* 38, *Dans la Prison, La France et le Monde* 46, *Journal des Années Noires* 47, *Jean Jacques, en Marge des Confessions* 48, *La Part de la France* 49, *Jean Jacques: roman et vérité* 50, *Voyages: tournée américaine, tournée africaine* 52, *Jean Jacques: grandeur et misère d'un esprit* 52, *Aventures de l'esprit, La France et les Noirs, La part de la France, La foi difficile, Sur le Chemin des Hommes, Changer La Vie, Ce que je crois* 64, *La Mort des autres* 68, *Caliban et Prospero* 69, *Carnets du Vieil Ecrivain* 71.
35 rue Pierre-Nicole, Paris 5e, France.

Guéna, Yves René Henri; French politician; b. 6 July 1922, Brest; *m.* Oriane de la Bourdonnaye 1945; five *s.* two *d.*; ed. Ecole Nat. d'Administration.
Official in Morocco 47; Maître des Requêtes, Conseil d'Etat 57; Dir. de Cabinet to M. Debré (Minister of Justice) 58-59, Dep. Dir. de Cabinet to M. Debré (Prime Minister) Jan.-July 59; High Commr. Ivory Coast 59-60, Envoy Extraordinary (Dean of Diplomatic Corps) 60-61; Deputy for Dordogne 62-; Minister of Posts and Telecommunications 67-68, 68-69, of Information May-July 68, of Transport 73-74, of

Industrial and Scientific Devt. March–May 74; Deputy Sec.-Gen. U.D.R. 74-75, Del.-Gen. 75-; Mayor of Périgueux (Dordogne) March 71-; Conseiller d'Etat 72; Commdr. Légion d'Honneur, Croix de Guerre, Médaille de la Résistance.

Publs. *Historique de la Communauté* 62, *Maintenir l'Etat* 70.

186 avenue Victor Hugo, Paris 16e, France.

Guérin, André Paul; French journalist; b. 1 Dec. 1899; ed. Collège de Flers, Lycée de Rennes, Caen Univ., and Ecole Normale Supérieure, Univ. of Paris.

On staff of *L'Oeuvre* 22-39; Editor *L'Aurore* 46-; Officier de la Légion d'Honneur, Croix de Guerre.

Publs. *Manuel des Partis Politiques en France* 28, *Normandie Champ de Bataille de la Libération* 54, *Vacances en Normandie* 57, *Opération Bergère* 61, "*1871*" *La Commune* 66, *La Folle Guerre de 1870* 70, *La Vie Quotidienne en Normandie au Temps de Madame Bovary* 75.

8 place de l'Abreuvoir, 78 Marly-le-Roi, France.
Telephone: 958-47-75.

Guérin, Daniel; French writer; b. 19 May 1904, Paris; s. of Marcel and Juliette Guérin; m. Marie Fortwängler 1934; one d.; ed. Lycée Louis-le-Grand, Ecole des Sciences Politiques.

Journalist, writer, sociologist, historian; Founder, Centre laïque des Auberges de jeunesse; Cultural Adviser, Théâtre des Nations; mem. French Inst. de Sociology, Comm. d'Histoire Economique et Sociale de la Revolution Française.

Leisure interests: reading, travel, theatre, cinema.

Publs. *Le Livre de la dix-huitième année* 22, *L'enchantement du Vendredi-Saint* 25, *La Vie selon la chair* 28, *La Peste brune a passé là* 33, *Fascisme et grand capital* 36, *La Lutte de classes sous la 1ère République* 46, *Où va le peuple américain?* 51, *Au service des colonisés* 54, *Kinsey et la sexualité* 55, *Les Antilles décolonisées* 56, *Jeunesse du socialisme libertaire* 59, *Shakespeare et Gide en correctionnelle?* 59, *Eux et Lui* 62, *Front Populaire révolution manquée* 63, *Décolonisation du Noir américain* 63, *Sur le fascisme* 65, *Un jeune homme excentrique* 65, *L'Anarchisme* 65, *L'Algérie qui se cherche, L'Algérie caporalisée* 64, 65, *Ni Dieu ni Maître* 66, *Le Mouvement ouvrier américain 1867-1967* 68, *Pour un Marxisme libertaire* 69, *Essai sur la révolution sexuelle* 69, *La révolution française et nous* 70, *La concentration économique aux U.S.A.* 71, *Rosa Luxemburg et la spontanéité révolutionnaire* 71, *Autobiographie de Jeunesse* 72, *De l'oncle Tom aux panthères, Bourgeois et bras nu, Ci-gît le colonialisme* 73; Editor: *Rosa Luxemburg le socialisme en France* 71, *Trotsky sur la deuxième guerre mondiale, Gauguin Oviri écrits d'un sauvage* 74, *Fourier vers la Liberté en Amour* 75, *Les assassins de Ben Barka* 75; Plays: *Le Grain sous la Neige* 61, *Vautrin* 62.

13 rue des Marronniers, 75016 Paris, France.
Telephone: 224-67-08.

Guéron, Jules; French atomic scientist; b. 2 June 1907, Tunis; s. of Lazare Guéron and Louise Bornstein; m. Geneviève Bernheim; three s.; ed. Lycée Charlemagne, Paris, and Univ. de Paris à la Sorbonne.

Lecturer, Univ. of Strasbourg 38, Asst. Prof. 46-69 (on leave since 47); with Tube Alloys 41-46; Head of Service Commissariat of Atomic Energy 46-49, Dir. Commissariat of Atomic Energy 49-58, Dir. Centre de Saclay 51-54, Dir. of Gen. Programme 54-58, Head Physical-Chemistry Dept. 49-58; Dir.-Gen. Research EURATOM 58-68; Lecturer, Conservatoire Nat. des Arts et Métiers 51-61; Prof. Faculté des Sciences d'Orsay 69-; mem. and Sec. Comm. on Atomic Weights, Int. Union of Pure and Applied Chem. 60-69; Chevalier Légion d'Honneur; Prix Adrian, Chemical Soc. of France 35.

Publs. About 100 scientific and gen. publications.

15 rue de Siam, Paris 16e, France.
Telephone: 504-09-89.

Guerrero, Dr. Gustavo A.; Nicaraguan economist and banker; b. 26 Aug. 1923; ed. Univ. of Texas and American Univ., Washington, D.C.

Chief of Econ. Studies, Ministry of Economy, Nicaragua 49-55; training at Int. Monetary Fund 52; Dir. of Budget, Nicaragua 55-57; Dir. of Internal Revenue 57-60; Vice-Minister of Economy 60-63, Minister of Economy 62-63; Vice-Minister of Finance 63-65; Pres. Central American Bank for Econ. Integration 65-68; Pres. and Gen. Man. Inst. de Fomento Nacional 68; Dir. Nat. Devt. Inst. (Nicaragua) 53-65, Central Bank of Nicaragua 60-65 (Pres. 68), Corinto Port Authority 63-65, Booth Nicaragua (commercial fishing) 62-65, Hercasa (chemical enterprise) 64-65; mem. Central Customs Cttee. of Nicaragua 56-65; Exec. Sec. Nat. Econ. Council of Nicaragua 60-63; mem. Board of Dirs. Latin American Planning Inst. 65-67, 67-69; Del. to numerous int. confs.; Commdr. Order of Quetzal (Guatemala); Grand Cross Nat. Order of Jose Matías Delgado (El Salvador).

Instituto de Fomento Nacional, Managua, Nicaragua.

Guerrero, Leon Maria; Philippine diplomatist; b. 24 March 1915, Manila; s. of Alfredo L. Guerrero and Filomena Francisco; m. 1st Anita Corominas (deceased), 2nd Margaret Burke; ed. Ateneo de Manila, Philippine Law School, Manila.

Associate Editor, Philippines Free Press 35-40; Office of Solicitor-Gen. 40; served army 40-45; Chief of Protocol, Dept. of Foriegn Affairs 46; Legal and Legislative Counsel, Philippines Senate 48; Under-Sec. of Foreign Affairs 54; Amb. to Great Britain (concurrently Minister to Norway, Sweden, Finland and Denmark) 54-61, to Spain 61-66, to India (concurrently to Nepal, Afghanistan) 66-72, to Mexico (also accred. to Colombia, Costa Rica, El Salvador, Venezuela, etc.) 73-; Chair. Philippine Trade Mission and Minister to German Federal Republic 55; Amb. Extraordinary to Independence Celebrations of Ghana 57; Del. UN Gen. Assembly 59; Vice-Chair. Int. Sugar Council 59, Chair. 60; Chair. Philippine Del. to Int. Sugar Confs. 58, 62, 68; Vice-Chair. Philippine Del. to UNCTAD 68.

Publs. *Twilight in Tokyo* 46, *Passion and Death of the USAFFE* 47, *Report from Europe* 50, *The Young Rizal* 52, *Our Foreign Relations* 52, *Alternatives for Asians* 58, *An Asian on Asia* 58, *Noli Me Tangere* 60, *El Filibusterismo* 61, *El Si y El No* 63, *The First Filipino* 63, *The Philippine Revolution* 69, *Prisoners of History* 72, *Today Began Yesterday* 75.

Philippine Embassy, 125 Sierra Torrecillas, Lomas de Chapultepec, Mexico 10, Mexico.

Guerrero, Manuel Flores León; American (Guam) politician; b. 25 Oct. 1914, Agaña, Guam; s. of José L. G. León Guerrero and María Luján Flores; m. Delfina T. León Guerrero 1934; three s. and four d.; ed. Guam schools.

Guam Government 30-48, 50-; Asst. Sec. Guam 56-60, Sec. 61-63; Gov. of Guam 63-71; Vice-Pres. Guam Commercial Corpn. 46-48; Fiscal Adviser, Controller 48-49; Chair. Finance Cttee. 48-50; Alt. U.S. Commr. S. Pacific Comm. 62-64, U.S. Commr. 64; Pres. Guam Capital Investment Corpn. 72-73; Prof., Lecturer Univ. of Guam; hon. degrees from Virginia Inst. of Technology and Colorado State Coll.

P.O. Box 223, Agaña, Guam.
Telephone: 777-9212.

Guerrero Cienfuegos, Francisco José; Salvadorian Minister of Foreign Affairs 68-72; see *The International Who's Who 1975-76.*

Guerrero Gutiérrez, Lorenzo, M.D.; Nicaraguan Minister of Foreign Affairs 67-74; see *The International Who's Who 1975-76.*

Guerri, H.E. Cardinal Sergio; Italian ecclesiastic; b. 25 Dec. 1905, Tarquinia.
Ordained 29; cr. Cardinal 69; Pro-Pres. Pontifical Comm. for the State of the Vatican City.
00120 Stato Città del Vaticano, Rome, Italy.

Guest, Baron (Life Peer), cr. 61; **Rt. Hon. Christopher William Graham Guest,** M.A., LL.B.; British lawyer; b. 7 Nov. 1901, Edinburgh; s. of Edward G. and Mary C. Guest; m. Catherine Geraldine Hotham 1941; four s. one d.; ed. Merchiston Castle School, Edinburgh, Clare Coll., Cambridge and Univ. of Edinburgh.
Advocate, Scottish Bar 25; Barrister, Inner Temple 26; K.C. 45; Sheriff of Ayr and Bute 51, of Perth and Angus 53; Dean, Faculty of Advocates 55; Senator, Coll. of Justice 57; Lord of Appeal in Ordinary 61-71; Hon. Fellow, Clare Coll., Cambridge.
Leisure interests: fishing, golf, reading.
3 Ainslie Place, Edinburgh, Scotland.

Guest, Douglas, C.V.O., M.A., MUS.B., F.R.C.M., HON. R.A.M., HON. F.R.C.O., F.R.S.C.M.; British organist and conductor; b. 9 May 1916, Mortomley, Yorkshire; s. of Harold and Margaret Guest; m. Peggie Falconer 1941; two d.; ed. Reading School, Royal Coll. of Music and King's Coll., Cambridge (Organ Scholar).
War Service as Major, Royal Artillery 39-45; Dir. of Music, Uppingham School 45-50; Organist and Master of Choristers, Salisbury Cathedral 50-57, Worcester Cathedral 57-63; Conductor of The Three Choirs Festival 57-63; Organist and Master of Choristers Westminster Abbey 63-; Prof. Royal Coll. of Music 63-.
Leisure interest: fly-fishing.
Composition: *Missa Brevis* 57.
8 The Little Cloister, Westminster Abbey, London, S.W.1, England.
Telephone: 01-222-6222.

Guggenheim, Paul, LL.D.; Swiss international lawyer; b. 15 Sept. 1899, Zurich; m. Hélène Guggenheim-Sachs 1931; two s.; ed. Coll. for Classical Studies, Zürich, and Univs. of Geneva, Rome and Berlin.
Lecturer Geneva Univ. 28-31; Asst. Prof. 31-40 and full Prof. 40, Graduate Inst. of Int. Studies; Prof. of Int. Public Law Geneva Univ. 55; mem. of the Permanent Court of Arbitration, The Hague 51-; Agent and Counsel for Switzerland and other countries in different cases before the Int. Court of Justice and European Court of Human Rights, mem. and Pres. several Conciliation Comms.; Lecturer at The Hague Acad. of Int. Law 32, 49, 52 and 58; mem. of the UN Cttee. for elaborating the Constitution of Erythrae 51-52; Pres. Swiss Soc. of Int. Law 64-69; Hon. mem. American Soc. of Int. Law; mem. Inst. of Int. Law, four Int. Conciliation Comms.; mem. of the Acad. of Political and Econ. Sciences of the Repub. of Venezuela 64; Legal Adviser of the European Conf. of Molecular Biology 67-68; Dr. h.c. (Univs. of Louvain, Dijon, Kiel, Paris and Rome); Manley Hudson Gold Medal of the American Soc. of Int. Law 70, Award of the City of Geneva 71.
Publs. *Traité de droit international public*, Vol. I 53, 67, Vol. II 54, and many publs. on international law.
1 route de Bout du Monde, 1206 Geneva, Switzerland.
Telephone: 46-50-97.

Guggenheim, Peggy; American art collector; b. 26 Aug. 1898; ed. Jacobi School, New York.
Opened Guggenheim Jeune Art Gallery, London 38-39; Art of this Century Gallery, New York 42-46; Museo Palazzo Venier dei Leoni, Venice 51-; exhibitions of private collection throughout Europe 51-, London 65.
Publs. *Out of this Century* 46, *Una Collezionista Ricorda* 56, *Confessions of an Art Addict* 60.
Palazzo Venier dei Leoni, 701 San Gregorio, Venice, Italy.

Guha, Mrs. Phulrenu, D.LITT.; Indian social worker; b. 13 Aug. 1911; d. of the late Surendranath and Abala Bala Datta; m. the late Dr. Biresh Chandra Guha 1943; ed. Calcutta Univ. and Univ. de Paris à la Sorbonne Participated in Freedom Movement since early days social worker, West Bengal, for over forty years actively assoc. with relief, social and children's welfare family planning, defence aid, moral and social hygiene undertook relief work during Bengal famine 43 Noakhali 46, Calcutta 47-; Sec. United Council o Relief and Welfare, West Bengal; Chair. W. Benga Social Advisory Board 59-67, Cttee. on Status of Women in India; Gen. Sec. and Vice-Pres. All India Women's Conf.; mem. Rajya Sabha 64-70; Union Minister of State for Social Welfare 67-70; Pres. Indian Council for Child Welfare; Adviser Sanyal Inst. of Social Welfare and Business Management; mem. Cen. Social Welfare Board 71-, All India Congress Cttee., Gov. Bodies of Colls. in Delhi, Calcutta.
Leisure interests: travelling, music, handicrafts, reading.
55/5 Purna Das Road, Calcutta 700 029, India.

Gui, Luigi; Italian politician; b. 26 Sept. 1914, Padova; s. of Corinto Gui and Angelina Pinzan; m. Alessandra Volpi 1947; three s.
War service, Italy and Russia 41-43; Christian Democrat underground movement 43-45; elected to Constituent Assembly 46, re-elected 48, 53, 58, 63, 68, 72; fmr. Sec. of the Parl. Comm. on Agriculture and Under-Sec. Ministry of Agriculture and Forestry; Minister of Labour 57-58, of Educ. 62-68, of Defence 68-70, of Health 73-74, of Civil Service Reform March-Nov. 74, of Interior Dec. 74-Feb. 76; Pres. Christian Democrat Deputies Parl. Group June 58-Feb. 62.
Palazzo Viminale, via A. De Pretis, Rome, Italy.
Telephone: 4667.

Guibert, Roger, D. EN D.; French railways executive; b. 15 April 1907, Paris; s. of André Guibert and Louise née Hallopeau; m. Yvonne Thillaye 1928; two s. four d.; ed. Ecole Polytechnique.
Engineer for Roads and Bridges, Highways Dept.,Strasbourg 31-34; Principal Engineer, Chemins de fer du Nord 35; Chief Engineer, Commercial Service of Société Nationale des Chemins de fer Français (SNCF) 44; Dir. Western Region, SNCF 58; Deputy Dir.-Gen. SNCF 58, Dir.-Gen. 66-74; Commdr. Légion d'Honneur.
Publs. *Le Nouveau Statut des Transports Routiers* 39. *Service Public et Productivité* 56, *La SNCF: cette inconnue* 69.
103 rue du Faubourg-Saint-Honoré, 75008 Paris, France.

Guichard, Baron Olivier Marie Maurice; French politician; b. 27 July 1920; ed. Univ. de Paris and Ecole libre des sciences politiques.
Member Rassemblement du peuple français, and Principal Sec. Gen. de Gaulle 47-48; Press Officer Atomic Energy Commissariat 55-58; Asst. Dir. Office of Gen. de Gaulle 58, Technical Adviser to the Pres. 59-60; Del. Gen. of Org. des régions sahariennes 60-63; Gen. Asst. Office of the Prime Minister 63-66; Del. for Regional and Territorial Affairs 63-67; mem. Nat. Assembly 67, 74-; Minister of Industry 67-68, of Econ. Planning May 68-69, of Educ. June 69-72, of Supply July 72-73, of Planning Equipment and Housing 73-74, of Transport March-May 74; Dir. Compagnie nationale du Rhône 66-; mem. Council of Admin. Radiodiffusion-Télévision française 64-67; Médaille militaire, Chevalier Légion d'Honneur, Croix de Guerre.
Publs. *Aménager la France* 65, *Education nouvelle* 71, *Un chemin tranquille* 75.
12 avenue Bugeaud, Paris 16e, France.

Guidotti, Salvatore, D.ECON.; Italian politician; b. 1 Oct. 1912, Naples; ed. Naples Univ.
Economic consultant to Soc. Meridionale di Elettricita 36-44; prof. of statistics 45; Counsellor for statistics, Treasury Dept., 45-46; Bank of Italy, Chief Economic

Research Dept., rising to Central Manager and Econ-mic Counsellor to the Governor 47-65; General Manager, Banco di Napoli 65; asstd. in drawing up Vanoni Plan and Five-Year Economic Development Plan; mem. Commission for Study of Public Expen-iture, Public Savings and the Money Market 66-; ounder mem. and Vice-Pres. ISCO (Italian Institute or the Study of the Current Economic Situation); talian Rep. to OECD Cttee. on Political Economy and Vice-Pres. Joint Policy Cttee. of EEC; Dir. European nvestment Bank.

Publs. Numerous books and articles on statistics, economics and finance.

Banco di Napoli, Via Roma 177, Naples, Italy.

Guiga, Driss, L. EN D.; Tunisian politician; b. 21 Aug. 1924, Testour; *m.* four *c.*; ed. Sadiki Coll., Tunis. Called to the Bar, Tunis; Chef de Cabinet, Ministry of Public Health 52; Dir. Nat. Security until 63; Dir.-Gen. of Tourism and Thermal Affairs 63; Sec. of State for Public Health Sept.-Nov. 69; Minister of Public Health 69-73, of Nat. Educ. 73-; mem. Destour Socialist Party 43-, has held several party posts, currently mem. Cen. Cttee.

Ministère de l'Education Nationale, Tunis, Tunisia.

Guilford, Joy Paul, PH.D., LL.D., SC.D.; American psychologist; b. 7 March 1897, Marquette, Neb.; *s.* of Edwin Augustus Guilford and Arvilla Monroe; *m.* Ruth Sheridan Burke 1927; one *d.*; ed. Aurora (Nebraska) High School, Univ. of Nebraska and Cornell Univ. Instructor in Psychology, Univ. of Illinois 26-27; Asst. Prof. of Psychology, Kansas Univ. 27-28; Assoc. Prof. and Prof., Univ. of Nebraska 28-40; Dir. Bureau of Instructional Research, Univ. of Nebraska 38-40; Prof. of Psychology, Univ. of S. Calif. (on leave 42-46) 40-67; Aviation Psychologist, U.S. Army Air Forces, Dir. of Psychological Research Units 42-46; Dir. Aptitudes Research Project, Univ. of S. Calif. 49-69; mem. Nat. Acad. of Sciences 54-; Pres. American Psychological Asscn. (A.P.A.) 49-50; Bingham Memorial Lecturer 59; Distinguished Scientific Contribution Award, A.P.A. 64, Richardson Creativity Award, A.P.A. 66, Founders Medal, Creative Educ. Foundation 70, Award for Contributions to Educ. and Psychological Measure-ment, Educ. Testing Service 74.

Leisure interests: gardening, colour photography.

Publs. *Psychometric Methods* 36, 54, *General Psychology* 40, 52, *Fundamental Statistics in Psychology and Educa-tion* 42, 50, 56, 65, 73, *Personality* 59, *The Nature of Human Intelligence* 67, *The Analysis of Intelligence* 71.

Box 1288, Beverly Hills, Calif. 90213, U.S.A.

Telephone: 213-271-2369.

Guillabert, André; Senegalese lawyer, politician and diplomatist; b. 15 June 1918; ed. Lycée Faidherbe, St. Louis-du-Sénégal, Faculté des Lettres, Bordeaux, and Faculté de Droit, Toulouse.

Lawyer, Dakar Court of Appeal 45-; Vice-Pres., Conseil Général du Sénégal 47-52; First Vice-Pres. Territorial Assembly, Senegal 52; Counsellor, Assembly of French Union 57-58; Senator (France) 58-59, Senator (French Community) 59-61; Vice-Pres. Constituent Assembly, Senegal 58-59, First Vice-Pres. Legislative Assembly 59, Nat. Assembly 60-62; Amb. to France (also accred. to Denmark, Finland, Norway, Sweden and Spain) 60-62, 66-; Minister of Foreign Affairs, Senegal 62; Keeper of the Seals and Minister of Justice 62-63; Deputy and Vice-Pres. Nat. Assembly, Senegal 63-66; Grand Officier Légion d'Honneur and many other decorations.

Ambassade du Sénégal, 14 avenue Robert Schuman, 75007 Paris, France; 47 avenue de la République, Dakar, Senegal.

Guillaumat, Pierre L. J.; French civil servant; b. 5 Aug. 1909; ed. Prytanée Militaire, La Flèche and Ecole Polytechnique.

Chef du Service des Mines, Indochina 34-39, Tunisia 39-43; Dir. o)Carburants 44-51; Admin.-Gen. Atomic Energy Comm. 51-58; Pres. Petroleum Research Bureau 45-58; Minister of the Armies, de Gaulle Cabinet, June 58-Jan. 59, Debré Cabinet Jan. 59-Feb. 60; Minister attached to Prime Minister's Office Feb. 60-April 62; Minister of Education (*a.i.*) Nov. 60-Feb. 61; Pres. Union Générale des Pétroles 62-65, Electricité de France 64-66, Entreprise de Recherches et d'Activités Pétrolières 66-75, Soc. Nat. des Pétroles d'Aquitanie 66-75, Pres. of Soc. Nat. ELF-Aquitaine Jan. 76-; Pres. Conseil d'Administration de l'Ecole Polytechnique 71-74; Grand Officier de la Légion d'Honneur, Croix de Guerre.

7 rue Nélaton, Paris 15e, France.

Guillemin, Henri; French writer and university professor; b. 19 March 1903; ed. Ecole Normale Supérieure, Paris.

Teaching posts, various lycées, France 28-36; Prof. of French Literature, Univ. of Cairo, Egypt 36-38; Prof. of French Language and Literature, Univ. of Bordeaux 38-42; Cultural Counsellor, French Embassy, Berne 45-62; Prof., Univ. of Geneva 63-; Chevalier, Légion d'Honneur; Grand Prix de la Critique, Paris 65.

Publs. Over thirty volumes of literary history and history.

58 faubourg de l'Hôpital, Neuchâtel, Switzerland.

Guillén, Nicolás; Cuban poet; b. 10 July 1902, Camagüey; *s.* of Nicolas Guillen and Argelia Batista; ed. Camagüey Inst.

Legal studies 21; poet and author 22-; Spanish war correspondent for *Mediodía* magazine 37-38; Mayoral Candidate for Camagüey 40 (Popular Socialist, later Cuban C.P.); Candidate for Senate, La Habana Province 48; Pres. Cuban Union of Writers and Artists (UNEAC); Amb. of Cuba; Lenin Peace Prize 54; Order of Merit of Haiti.

Poetry: *Motivos de son* 30, *Sóngoro cosongo* 31, *West Indies Ltd.* 34, *España* 37, *Cantos para soldados y sones para turistas* 37, *El son entero* 47, *La paloma de vuelo popular* 58, *Elegías* 58, *Tengo* 64, *Poemas de Amor* 64, *El Gran Zoo* 67, *La rueda dentada* 72, *El diario que a diario* 72; essays on violinist Brindis de Salas 35; chronicles: *Prosa de Prisa* 62.

Unión de Escritores y Artistas de Cuba, Calle 17 No. 351, Vedado, Havana; Calle O No. 2, piso 22, Edificio Someillán, Vedado, Havana, Cuba.

Telephone: 32-4551 (Office); 32-1079 (Home).

Guinness, Sir Alec, Kt., C.B.E.; British actor; b. 2 April 1914, London; *m.* Merula Salaman 1938; one *s.*; ed. Pembroke Lodge, Southbourne and Roborough, Eastbourne.

Entered Advertising Agency as Copywriter 33; Scholar-ship to Fay Compton Studio of Dramatic Art 34; First Stage appearance April 34; played in seasons for John Gielgud and Old Vic Theatre Co.; *Hamlet* in modern dress 38; served R.N.V.R. 40-44; began film career 45; Hon. Dr. Fine Arts (Boston Coll.); films include: *Great Expectations* 46, *Oliver Twist* 47, *Kind Hearts and Coronets* 48, *The Lavender Hill Mob* 51, *The Man in the White Suit* 51, *The Bridge on the River Kwai* 57, (Oscar 58), *The Horse's Mouth* 58, *Our Man in Havana* 59, *Tunes of Glory* 60, *Lawrence of Arabia* 62, *Dr. Zhivago* 66, *The Comedians* 67, *Oliver Cromwell* 69, *Hitler, the Last Ten Days* 72; plays include: *The Prisoner* 54, *Hotel Paradiso* 56, *Ross* 57, *Exit the King, Dylan* 63, *Macbeth* 65, *Wise Child* 67, 68, *A Voyage Round My Father* 71, *Habeas Corpus* 73, *A Family and a Fortune* 75.

Kettlebrook Meadows, Steep Marsh, Petersfield, Hants., England.

Guiringaud, Louis de; French diplomatist; b. 12 Oct. 1911; *s.* of Pierre and Madeleine (née de Catheu) de Guiringaud; *m.* Claude Mony 1955; one *s.*; ed. Lycée

Buffon, Lycée Saint Louis, Univ. de Paris à la Sorbonne, and Ecole des Sciences Politiques.
Staff of Minister for Foreign Affairs 36; entered Diplomatic Service 38-; Attaché Ankara 38-39; with French forces 39-40; assigned to French High Comm., Beirut 40-41; with Resistance in France 42; Special Asst. to French Commr. for Foreign Affairs, de Gaulle's Provisional Govt., Algiers 43-44; with French forces Italy and France 44-45; First Sec., London 46-49; Political Dir. French High Commission in Germany 49-52; Consul-Gen. San Francisco 52-55; Deputy Rep. to UN Security Council 55-57; Amb. to Ghana 57; Dir. Dept. of Moroccan and Tunisian Affairs, Ministry for Foreign Affairs 60; Deputy High Commr. in Algeria 62; Gen.-Inspector Diplomatic Posts 63-66; Ambassador to Japan 66-72; Perm. Rep. to UN 72-; Commdr. Légion d'Honneur, Croix de Guerre, Grand Cross of Rising Sun (Japan), etc.
Permanent Mission of France to United Nations, One Dag Hammarskjöld Plaza, 245 East 47th Street, New York, N.Y. 10017, U.S.A.

Guirola, Carlos Alberto; Salvadorian banker; b. 1894; ed. Hitchcock Military Acad., California, Univ. of California, Coll. of Agriculture, Davis, California, and Heald's Business Coll., San Francisco.
President, El Salvador Nat. Legislative Assembly 31; Dir. Banco Salvadoreño 28-35, Pres. 36, 38, 40, 42, 44, 46-.
Banco Salvadoreño, 2A Ave. Norte 129, San Salvador, El Salvador.

Guitton, Jean Marie Pierre; French university professor; b. 18 Aug. 1901; ed. Ecole Normale Supérieure.
Former teacher in schools at Troyes, Moulins, Lyon, and Univs. of Montpellier and Dijon; Prof. of Philosophy and History of Philosophy, Univ. of Paris 55-68; mem. Programmes Cttee. Radiodiffusion et Télévision Française (ORTF) 65-; mem. Académie Française 61-; Observer at 2nd Vatican Council 63.
Leisure interest: painting.
Publs. *Le temps et l'éternité chez Plotin et Saint Augustin, La philosophie de Newman, L'existence temporelle, Essai sur l'Amour humain, Le Problème de Jésus, Le Nouvel Art de Penser, Le travail intellectuel, Portrait de Monsieur Pouget, Jésus, Apprendre à vivre et à penser, Le Cardinal Saliège, La vocation de Bergson, L'Eglise et l'Evangile, Problème et Mystère de Jeanne d'Arc, Journal Oecuménique, Le Clair et l'Obscur Vers l'Unité, Dialogue avec Paul VI, Profiles paralleles, Histoire et Destinée, Oeuvres completes* (3 vols.), *Ce que je crois, la Famille et l'Amour,* etc.
1 rue de Fleurus, 75006 Paris; La Pensée,Champagnat, 23190 Bellegarde-en-Marche, France.

Gujral, Inder Kumar, M.A.; Indian politician; b. 4 Dec. 1919, Jhelum (now in W. Pakistan); s. of Shri Avatar Narain Gujral and Shrimati Pushpa Gujral; m. Shrimati Sheil Gujral 1944; two s.; ed. Forman Christian Coll. and Hailey Coll. of Commerce in Lahore, Punjab Univ.
Jailed for participation in freedom fight 30-31 (and again during Quit India movement 42); helped nat. effort for rehabilitation of displaced persons; Minister of State for Communications and Parl. Affairs March 67-69, for Information, Communications and Broadcasting 69-71, Minister of State for Works, Housing and Urban Devt. 71-72, for Information and Broadcasting 72-75, for Planning 75-; mem. Rajya Sabha 70-; Vice-Pres. New Delhi Municipal Cttee. for five years; helped organize Citizens Cttee. for Civil Defence; mem. All India Cen. Citizens Council, Sec. Resources Sub-Cttee.; mem. All India Congress Cttee.; represented India at Inter-Parl. Union Conf. in Canberra; Founder-Pres. Delhi Arts Theatre; Treas. Fed. of Film Socs. of India;

Vice-Pres. Lok Kalyan Samiti; Co-Chair. Asian Regional Conf. of Rotary Int. 58.
Leisure interests: theatre, poetry.
9 Motilal Nehru Marg, New Delhi 110011; 67 Model Town, Jullundur City, Punjab, India.

Guldberg, Ove; Danish civil engineer, lawyer and politician; b. 2 Dec. 1918, Nysted; s. of Frede and Else Guldberg (née Richter); m. Else Guldberg (née Christiansen) 1942; three s.
Employed by Vejle City Admin. 42; with Civil Engineering Contractor, K. Hindhede 43; at City of Copenhagen's City Engineer's Office 44; at Research Laboratory, Ministry of Fisheries 46-47; mem. Cen. Cttee., Inst. of Danish Engineers 46-48, Sec. 48, Dir. 52-65; Sec. Asscn. of Consultant Engineers 56, Dir. 65; Man. of the building of the Inst. of Danish Engineers 57; Liberal mem. Folketing (Parl.) 64-; Minister for Transport and Communications 68-71; mem. European Parl. 73-, Vice-Pres. 75; Minister for Foreign Affairs 73-75; Sec. Conf. of Reps. from Engineering Socs. of W. Europe and U.S.A. (EUSEC) 55-58; Pres. Civil Defence Union 62-65; mem. Civil Defence Council 62-68; Commdr. Order of Dannebrog First Class, Knight Grand Cross St. Michael and St. George, Grand Cross (Fed. Repub. of Germany), Grand Cross St. Olav (Norway), Grand Cross of the Yugoslav Flag.
Skovvangen 18, 2920 Charlottenlund, Denmark.

Gülek, Kasim, B.SC.(COM.), PH.D.; Turkish politician, economist and farmer; b. 20 Dec. 1910, Adana; s. of Mustafa Rifat and Tayyibe; m. Nilufer Devrimel 1967; one s. one d.; ed. Robert Coll., Ecole des Sciences Politiques, Paris, Columbia, Cambridge, London, Berlin and Hamburg Univs.
Member of Parl. 40-; Chair. Cttee. on Commerce 43; Minister of Public Works 47; Minister of Communications 48; Minister of State 49; Del. to Council of Europe 49, 50, 51, 58, 60, 61, 62; Chair. UN Comm. on Korea; fmr. Sec.-Gen. People's Republican Party 51-59; mem. Constituent Assembly 60; Vice-Pres. Council of Europe 61-62; expelled from Republican People's Party for one year Dec. 62; Pres. North Atlantic Assembly 68; Gov. Atlantic Inst. 69; Senator 69.
Leisure interests: archaeology, photography.
Publs. *Development of Economically Backward Countries* 32, *Development of Banking in Turkey* 33, *Democracy Takes Root in Turkey* 51.
B. Evler, 50 Sosak no. 3, Ankara, Turkey.
Telephone: 13-25-63 (Ankara); 45-30-46 (Istanbul).

Gullion, Edmund Asbury, A.B., LL.D.; American diplomatist; b. 2 March 1913, Lexington, Ky.; s. of the late Maj.-Gen. W. Gullion and Ruth Matthews Gullion; m. Patricia Palmer 1961; ed. Princeton Univ.
Vice-Consul, Marseilles 37; Dept. of State 38; Vice-Consul, Salonika 39; Third Sec. London 42-43; Algiers 42; Chargé d'Affaires, Helsinki 43; Second Sec. Stockholm 44; Dept. of State, Washington 45; Counsellor, Saigon 50; Dept. of State, Washington 52-56; Foreign Service Insp. 57; Dept. of State 60; Acting Dep. Dir. U.S. Disarmament Admin. 60, Dep. Dir. 61; Ambassador to the Congo (Léopoldville) 61-64; Career Minister, Dean Fletcher School of Law and Diplomacy 62, Tufts Univ. 64-; mem. American Foreign Service Asscn., American Acad. of Arts and Sciences, Council on Foreign Relations (N.Y.); Dir. World Peace Foundation, World Affairs Council (Boston), Inst. of Strategic Studies (London).
Tufts University, Fletcher School of Law and Diplomacy, Medford, Mass. 02155, U.S.A.

Gullotti, Antonino; Italian politician; b. 14 Jan. 1929, Ucria, Messina.
Provincial Sec., Partito Democrazia Cristiana (Christian Democrats), Messina 51, then Regional Sec., Sicily;

Nat. Councillor, DC 54-, mem. Cen. Cttee. 60, Vice-Sec. DC; mem. Chamber of Deputies 58-; Vice-Pres. Comm. of Enquiry investigating the Mafia; Minister of Public Works 72-73, for State Participation 73-74, of Health Nov. 74-; Christian Democrat.
Ministry of Health, viale dell'Industria 20, 00144 Rome, Italy.

Guna-Kasem, Pracha; Thai diplomatist; b. 29 Dec. 1934, Bangkok; *m.*; one *s.*; ed. Dhebsirinda School, Bangkok, Marlborough Coll., Hertford Coll., Oxford and Yale Univ.
Joined Ministry of Foreign Affairs 59; Chief of Section, Political Div. of Dept. of Int. Org. 60-61, Second Sec. SEATO Div. 62-63; Alt. Mem. for Thailand, SEATO Perm. Working Group 62-63; Embassy in Egypt 64-65; Chief of Foreign News Analysis Div. of Information Dept. and concurrently in charge of Press Affairs 66-69, Chief of Press Div. 70-71, Dir.-Gen. of Information Dept. 73-75; Consul-Gen. in Hong Kong 71-73; Perm. Rep. to UN Sept. 75-; fmrly. Special Lecturer, Thammasat Univ.; mem. del. to UN Gen. Assembly 62, 68, 70, 74, to 2nd Afro-Asian Conf., Algeria 65, to SEATO Council 66.
Permanent Mission of Thailand to the United Nations, 20 East 82nd Street, New York, N.Y. 10028, U.S.A.

Gunaratne, Victor Thomas Herat, L.M.S., D.T.M. & H., D.P.H., M.R.C.P.(E.), F.R.C.P.(E.); Ceylonese international health official; b. 11 March 1912, Mellowagara; *s.* of the late H. M. G. Herat Gunaratne; *m.* Clarice Gunaratne 1937; one *s.* two *d.*; ed. Ceylon Medical College, London School of Hygiene and Tropical Medicine, and Univ. of Edinburgh Medical School.
Acting Deputy Dir. Public Health Services, Ceylon 59-61; Deputy Dir. Ceylon Medical Services 61-64; Dir. Health Services, Govt. of Ceylon 64-67; Pres. World Health Assembly 67; Dir. WHO Regional Office for S.E. Asia; Hon. Fellow Indian Acad. of Medical Sciences 75.
Publs. Articles in professional journals.
WHO Regional Office for South-East Asia, World Health House, Ring Road, Indraprastha Estate, New Delhi 1, India.
Telephone: 270181.

Gundelach, Finn Olav; Danish diplomatist; b. 23 April 1925, Vejle; *s.* of Albert and Jenny Hobolt; *m.* Vibeke Rosenvinge 1953; two *s.*; ed. Aarhus Univ.
Secretary, Danish Ministry of Foreign Affairs 53; Perm. Rep. to UN, Geneva 55; Dir. Dept. of Commercial Policy, GATT 59; Asst. Gen. Sec. GATT 59, Asst. Gen. Dir. 65; Amb. to EEC 67-72; mem. Comm. of European Communities 73-; Knight, Order of Dannebrog; Grand Cross (Brazil).
Publs. articles in foreign trade journals.
36 rue Cardinal Micara, 1050 Brussels, Belgium.
Telephone: 02-72-07-54.

Gundersen, O. C., CAND. JUR.; Norwegian lawyer and politician; b. 17 March 1908, Oslo; *m.* Ragna Lorentzen 1937; one *d.*; ed. Oslo Univ.
Qualified as solicitor 31, High Court barrister 39; Town Councillor, Trondheim 38, dismissed by Nazis 41; escaped to Sweden, attached to Norwegian Legation, Stockholm; summoned to London 42 and apptd. Dir. of State Insurance Office and Chair. Insurance Council; Town Councillor and Alderman Trondheim; Minister of Justice Nov. 45-53; Chair. Norwegian del. to UN 49, 51, 52; Chair. UN Observer Group (Hungarian Question) 56; Justice of the Supreme Court; Chair. UN Special Advisory Board 57-; Amb. to U.S.S.R. 58-61; Minister of Commerce and Shipping 62-63, of Justice 63-65; Chair. EFTA Ministerial Council 53; Judge of Supreme Court 67-.
The Supreme Court, Oslo; Home: Olav Kyrresgate 11B, Oslo 2, Norway.
Telephone: 56-51-19 (Home).

Gunn, Thom(son William), M.A.; British poet; b. 29 Aug. 1929, Gravesend; *s.* of Herbert Smith Gunn and Ann-Charlotte Gunn; ed. Trinity Coll., Cambridge.
Taught English at Univ. of Calif., Berkeley 58-66; Levinson Prize 55, Somerset Maugham Prize 59; grants from Nat. Inst. of Arts and Letters 64, Rockefeller Foundation 66, Guggenheim Foundation 72.
Publs. *Fighting Terms* 54, *The Sense of Movement* 57, *My Sad Captains* 61, *Positives* (with Ander Gunn) 66, *Touch* 67, *Moly* 71.
1216 Cole Street, San Francisco, Calif. 94117, U.S.A.

Gunn, Sir William Archer, K.B.E., C.M.G.; Australian grazier and company director; b. 1 Feb. 1914, Goondiwindi, Queensland; *s.* of the late Walter Gunn and Doris Isabel Gunn; *m.* Mary Phillipa Haydon 1939; one *s.* two *d.*; ed. The King's School, Parramatta, New South Wales.
Chairman Australian Wool Board 63-72, Int. Wool Secr. Board 61-73, Queensland Advisory Board, Devt. Finance Corpn. 62-72; Chair. Gunn Devt. Pty. Ltd., Eagle Corpn. Ltd., Cattle Investments Ltd., Livestock Management Pty. Ltd.; Dir. Rothmans of Pall Mall (Australia) Ltd., Grazcos Co-operative Ltd., Clausen Steamship Co. (Australia) Pty. Ltd., Walter Reid & Co. Ltd., Moline Pastoral Co. Pty. Ltd., Roper Valley Pty. Ltd., Coolibah Pastoral Co. Pty. Ltd., Mataranka Pty. Ltd., Unibeef Australia Pty. Ltd., Gunn Rural Management Pty. Ltd.; mem. Commonwealth Bank Board 52-59, Faculty of Veterinary Science, Univ. of Queensland 53-, Reserve Bank Board 59-, Australian Meat Board 53-66, Australian Wool Bureau 51-63 (Chair. 58-63), Australian Woolgrowers Council 47-60 (Chair. 55-58), Graziers Fed. Council of Australia 50-60 (Pres. 51-54), Australian Woolgrowers and Graziers Council 60-65, Export Devt. Council 62-65, Exec. Council, United Graziers Asscn. of Queensland 44-69 (Vice-Pres. 47-51, Pres. 51-59), Australian Wool Testing Authority 58-63, C.S.I.R.O. State Cttee. 51-68, Australian Wool Corpn. 73; Chair. The Wool Bureau Inc. New York 62-69, etc.; Trustee Queensland Cancer Fund; Golden Fleece Achievement Award (Nat. Asscn. of Wool Manufacturers of America) 62; Award of the Golden Ram (Nat. Wool Growers' Asscn. of S. Africa) 73.
Office: Wool Exchange, 69 Eagle Street, Brisbane, Queensland 4000; Home: 98 Windermere Road, Ascot, Brisbane, Queensland 4007, Australia.
Telephone: Brisbane 221-4044 (Office); Brisbane 268-2688 (Home).

Gunneng, Arne, LL.B.; Norwegian diplomatist; b. 1 Dec. 1914, Oslo; *m.* Ingrid Fleischer 1939; three *d.*; ed. Oslo Katedralskole, Oslo Univ.
First Sec. Embassy, Washington 45-48; Ministry of Foreign Affairs, Oslo 48-50; Chargé d'Affaires, Warsaw 50-51; Counsellor, Stockholm 51-52; Dep. Perm. Rep. North Atlantic Council, Paris 52-55; Ambassador to Canada 55-59; Dir.-Gen. of Political Affairs, Ministry of Foreign Affairs, Oslo 59-62; Ambassador to Sweden 62-66, to U.S.A. 66-73, to Italy 73-.
Norwegian Embassy, Via delle Terme Deciane 10, 00153 Rome, Italy.

Gunness, Robert Charles, B.S., D.SC.; American oil executive; b. 28 July 1911, Fargo, North Dakota; *m.* Beverly Osterberger; two *s.* one *d.*; ed. Univ. of Massachusetts and Massachusetts Inst. of Technology.
Assistant Dir. of Research, Standard Oil Co. (Indiana) 43-45, Assoc. Dir. 45-47, Man. of Research 47-52, Asst. Gen. Man. of Mfg. 52-54, Dir. 53-, Gen. Man. Supply and Transportation 54-56, Exec. Vice-Pres. 56-65, Pres. 65-74, Vice-Chair. 74-75; Vice-Chair. Research and Devt. Board, Dept. of Defense, Washington, D.C. 51; Dir. Harris Trust and Savings Bank, Inland Steel Co.,

The John Crerar Library; Trustee, Univ. of Chicago; life mem. of Corpn., Mass. Inst. of Technology.
Leisure interests: golf, skiing.
Standard Oil Company (Indiana), 200 East Randolph Drive, Chicago, Ill. 60601, U.S.A.
Telephone: 312-856-6310.

Gunsalus, Irwin Clyde, M.S., PH.D.; American biochemist and author; b. 29 June 1912, Sully Co., S. Dak.; s. of I. C. and Anna (Shea) Gunsalus; m. 1st Carolyn F. Foust 1951 (died 1970), 2nd Dorothy Clark 1970; four s. three d.; ed. Cornell Univ.
Assistant Bacteriologist, Cornell Univ. 35-37, Instructor 37-40, Asst. Prof. 40-44, Assoc. Prof. 44-46, Prof. 46-47; Prof. Univ. of Indiana 47-50; Prof. Univ. of Illinois 50-55, Prof. of Biochemistry 55-, Head of Dept. 55-66; Editor, *Biochemical and Biophysical Research Communications, Bacteriological Reviews*; mem. Advisory Boards *Analytical Biochemistry, Biochemistry*; Guggenheim Memorial Foundation Fellow 49, 59, 68; mem. Nat. Acad. of Sciences; Mead Johnson Award 46.
Leisure interests: gardening, music, art, viniculture.
Publs. Over 300 scientific papers.
Biochemistry Division, University of Illinois, Urbana, Ill. 61801; Home: 1709 Pleasant Circle, Urbana, Ill. 61801, U.S.A.
Telephone: 217-333-2010 (Office); 217-344-5541 (Home).

Gupta, Chandra Bhanu, M.A., LL.B.; Indian politician; b. 14 July 1902; s. of late Sri Hiralal; ed. Lucknow Univ.
Joined Indian Nat. Congress 21; law practice 25; mem. All India Congress Cttee. 26-; mem. Court, Lucknow Univ. 27, Council 29, Treasurer 46-58; Pres. Lucknow City Congress Cttee. 28-46; mem. Uttar Pradesh Congress Cttee. 33-39, Treasurer 46-, Vice-Pres. 58, Pres. 60, 64; mem. Legislative Assembly, Uttar Pradesh 37, 46, 52, 61, 67, 69-74; Parl. Sec. to Chief Minister 46; Minister of Food and Civil Supplies, Health, Planning and Industry 47-57; Chief Minister of Uttar Pradesh 60-62, 62-63, 67, 69-70; Leader of Opposition 67-68; Leader Congress Legislature Party (Opposition) 70-74; Pres. Motilal Memorial Soc. 61-, Bharat Seva Sansthan, Shiksha Samiti, Ganga Prasad Verma Memorial Soc. 64-, Hon. Fellow Indian Acad. of Medical Sciences 75.
Seva Kutir, Pan Dariba, Lucknow, Uttar Pradesh, India.

Gur, Lieut.-Gen. Mordechai; Israeli army officer; b. 5 May 1930, Jerusalem; m.; two s. two d.; ed. Hebrew Univ., Jerusalem.
Served in Haganah; Co. Commdr. during Independence War 48-49; Paratroop Battalion Commdr., Sinai Campaign 56; Deputy Commdr. Paratroop Forces 57; Instructor, Command and Staff Coll. 58; studies at Ecole de Guerre, Paris 58-60; C.O. Golani Brigade 61-63; in charge of Command and Staff Coll. 65-66; C.O. Paratroop Brigade during Six-Day War 67; mem. Israeli Del. to UN Emergency Session 67; C.O. Israeli Forces in Gaza and N. Sinai, Northern Command 67-72; Mil. Attaché, Washington 72-73; C.O. Northern Command during Yom Kippur War Oct. 73; Chief Mil. Negotiator at Geneva Peace Conf. Dec. 73; Chief of Staff April 74-; Medal of Valour 55.
Publs. several children's books.
Ministry of Defence, Jerusalem, Israel.

Gürler, Gen. Faruk; Turkish army officer; b. 1913, Üsküdar, Istanbul; ed. War School, War Acad. for Land Forces.
Commander, Artillery and Infantry Units; Staff Officer, High Defence Council; Instructor War School and War Acad., later Acting Commdr.; Intelligence Officer, NATO; Deputy Chief of Staff of Army Corps., Deputy Artillery Commdr. of Div. and Army Corps., later Army Corps. Commdr.; Chief of Staff of Land Forces Command; Acting Under-Sec. of State, then Under-Sec. of

State, Ministry of Nat. Defence; promoted to rank of Gen. 68; Deputy Chief of Gen. Staff, Commdr. of Land Forces 68-72; Chief of General Staff 72-73; Senator and unsuccessful Presidential candidate 73.
The Senate, Ankara, Turkey.

Gürün, Kâmuran; Turkish diplomatist; b. 1924, Çengelköy (Istanbul); m. 1967; ed. studied political science.
Entered diplomatic service 48; posted to Turkish Embassy, Bonn 51; subsequently held various posts at Ministry of Foreign Affairs and diplomatic missions abroad; Dir.-Gen. Dept. for Admin. Affairs 61, subsequently Perm. Sec. to the Inter-Ministerial Cttee. on External Econ. Relations, Dir.-Gen. Dept. for Econ. and Commercial Affairs, Deputy Sec.-Gen. for Econ. Affairs and Sec.-Gen. Inter-Ministerial Econ. Council; Amb. to Romania 67-70; Perm. Rep. of Turkey at OECD 70-72; Amb. to Greece 74-.
Embassy of Turkey, 8 Odos Vassileos, Gheorghiou II, Athens, Greece.

Gurupadaswamy, M. S., M.A., LL.B.; Indian journalist and politician; b. 8 Jan. 1923; ed. Univs. of Mysore and Lucknow.
Practising lawyer 46-48; Editor *Prajamatha*, Bangalore 47-52; Pres. Mysore State Journalists Asscn. 50-51; mem. House of People 52-57; mem. Nat. Exec. Praja Socialist Party 57-63; Chair. Mysore State Praja Socialist Party 58-60; Sec. Parl. Group Praja Socialist Party 52-64; mem. Council of Studies 60-; Editor *Parliament Studies* 55-67; Union Minister of State for Atomic Energy 67, later Minister of State for Food and Agriculture, resigned Oct. 69.
Publs. *International Studies, Political Pilgrimage, Communalism.*
Ministry of Food and Agriculture, New Delhi, India.

Gustafson, Torsten, PH.D.; Swedish physicist; b. 8 May 1904, Falkenberg; s. of Albin Gustafson and Hulda Bramstång; m. Karin Lindskog 1935; one s. three d.; ed. Lund, Göttingen and Copenhagen Univs.
Professor of Theoretical Physics, Lund Univ. 39-70; mem. Swedish Atomic Energy Research Council 45-64, Swedish Atomic Energy Del. 56-70; del. European Org. for Nuclear Research, CERN 53-64; Dir. Nordic Inst. for Theoretical Atomic Physics 57-58, Chair. 63-69; Govt. Advisory Del. on Research 63-68; mem. of numerous Scandinavian Acads. of Science; Hon. Dr. Helsinki 69.
Leisure interest: bird-watching.
Publs. Papers on flow round airfoil-like bodies 27-36, on inertia currents in the oceans 36, on divergencies in quantum electrodynamics 37-47, on atomic nuclei 47-, on flight altitudes of birds.
Gyllenkroks allé 13, Lund, Sweden.

Gustafsson, Carl Åke Torsten, PH.D.; Swedish geneticist; b. 8 April 1908, Stockholm; s. of Emil and Anna Gustafsson; m. Madeleine Berggren 1932; two s. three d.; ed. Lunds Universitet, and in Stockholm and U.S.
Docent, Univ. of Lund 35, Research Assoc. 44; Prof. and Head, Inst. of Forest Genetics; Royal Coll. of Forestry, Stockholm 47, Prefect 67-68, Head, Inst. of Genetics, Lund Univ. 68, Prefect 68; Guest Lecturer at various institutes and universities throughout Europe, and in U.S.A., Thailand, India, Philippines, etc.; mem. Royal Physiographic Soc., Royal Acad. of Forestry and Agriculture, Royal Acad. of Sciences (all in Sweden), and Leopoldina Acad. of Natural Sciences (Germany), Royal Acad. of Sciences (Denmark), Nat. Acad. of Sciences (U.S.), etc.
Leisure interests: poetry, art, mystery of life.
Publs. 200 scientific articles; books of prose and poetry.
Institute of Genetics, Lund University, Sölvegatan 29, 223 62 Lund, Sweden.
Telephone: 046-124620 (Office); 046-149900 (Home).

Guth, Paul; French author, journalist and radio & television broadcaster; b. 5 March 1910, Oasun; ed. Coll. de Villeneuve sur Lot, Lycée Louis le Grand. Teacher of French, Latin and Greek, Lycée de Dijon, Lycée de Rouen, then Lycée Janson de Sailly; journalist, contributor to several newspapers and journals including, *Spectator, Figaro Littéraire, L'Album du Figaro, La Gazette des Lettres, La Revue de Paris,* etc. contrib. to numerous radio programmes; regular appearance on TV programme, *Premières Nouvelles;* Grand Prix du Théâtre 46, Grand Prix littéraire, Paris 64, Grand Prix littéraire, Monaco 73; Officier Légion d'Honneur, Commdr. des Arts et Lettres.
Publs. *Quarante contre Un, Autour des Dames du Bois de Boulogne, Les Sept Trompettes, Le Pouvoir de Germaine Calban, Naïf* series including, *Les Mémoires d'un Naïf* (Prix Courtline 53), *Le Naïf Locataire* (Grand Prix du Roman 56), *Jeanne la Mince* series; children's books: *La Locomotive Joséphine, Le fin mot de l'Histoire, Moustique et le Marchand de Sable, Moustique et Barbe Bleue, Moustique dans la Lune, Si ces Grands Hommes étaient morts à vingt ans, Le Naïf dans la Littérature, Comment j'ai crée le personnage du Naïf, Une Bombe Littéraire au temps des années folles: dadaïsme, Saint Louis roi de France, Henri IV, Histoire de la Littérature française* 2 vols. 67, *Lettre ouverte aux idoles* 68, *L'Histoire de la douce France* 68-70, *Mazarin* 72.
24 rue Desbordes Valmore, 75016 Paris, France.

Guthrie, Sir Giles Connop McEacharn, Bt., o.b.e., d.s.c., j.p.; British merchant banker and businessman; b. 21 March 1916; s. of the late Sir Connop Guthrie and Lady Mary Islay McEacharn; m. Rhona Stileman 1939; two s.; ed. Eton and Magdalene Coll., Cambridge. Winner (with C. W. A. Scott) Portsmouth-Johannesburg Air Race 36; Traffic Officer, British Airways 38-39; Fleet Air Arm, Second World War 39-46; fmr. Managing Dir. Brown Shipley and Co. Ltd.; fmr. Dep. Chair. North Central Finance Ltd.; fmr. Dir. Prudential Assurance Co. Ltd., Radio Rentals Ltd. and other companies; Chair. and Chief Exec. B.O.A.C. 64-Dec. 68; Dir. B.E.A. 59-68; Chair. Air Transport Insurance Ltd. Bermuda 69-71; Dir. several Jersey Cos.
Leisure interests: dendrology, sailing, walking.
Rozel, Jersey, Channel Islands.

Guthrie, Randolph Hobson, b.s., ll.b.; American lawyer and business executive; b. 1905, Richmond, Va.; s. of Mr. and Mrs. Joseph H. Guthrie; m. Mabel E. Welton 1934; two s. one d.; ed. The Citadel, Charleston and Harvard Law School.
Senior Partner of Mudge, Rose, Guthrie and Alexander and predecessor firms since 43; Chair. Board of Studebaker-Worthington Inc. 63-71, Chair. Exec. Cttee. 71; Chair. Board of UMC Industries Inc. 69-.
Leisure interest: golf.
Office: 20 Broad Street, New York, N.Y. 10005; Home: South Beach Lagoon, Hilton Head, S.C., U.S.A. Telephone: 212-422-6767.

Gutiérrez, Julio César, dr. econ.; Paraguayan economist and banker; b. 11 Feb. 1920; s. of Emilo and Amalia Gutiérrez; m. Beatriz Ferrari 1963; three s. and two d.; ed. Escuela Nacional de Comercio, Asunción, Universidad Nacional, Asunción, and Centro de Estudios Monetarios Latinamericano, Mexico.
Superintendent of Banks, Paraguay 50-56; Financial Adviser to Ministry of Finance 57-58; Nat. Financial Controller, Paraguay 59-62; Dir. of Seminary, Faculty of Econ. Sciences, Asunción 57-60, Univ. Prof. 60-62; Econ. Counsellor, Paraguayan Embassy, Washington 62-69; Exec. Dir. Inter-American Devt. Bank (IDB) 64-70; Rep. of the IDB in Lima, Peru, 71-73; Exec. Dir. IDB and Minister of Paraguayan Embassy, Washington 74-.
Leisure interests: fishing and golf.
Inter-American Development Bank, 808 17th Street,

N.W., Washington, D.C. 20577; Home: 5504 Surrey Street, Chevy Chase, Md., U.S.A.
Telephone: 986-1278.

Gutiérrez, Mario R.; Bolivian politician and diplomatist; b. 19 Oct. 1917, Santa Cruz de la Sierra; m.; five c.; ed. Catholic Univ. of Chile and Gabriel René Moreno Univ., Santa Cruz.
Mem. Bolivian Socialist Falange; Minister for Foreign Affairs 71-73; six times interim President of Bolivia; served as Deputy and Senator for La Paz in Nat. Congress; Amb. to UN June 75-.
Publs. *Alegato Histórico de los Derechos de Bolivia al Pacífico, Predestinación Histórica de Bolivia, Sangre y Luz de Dos Razas, Soberania y Entreguismo, Presencia Internacional de Bolivia.*
Permanent Mission of Bolivia to the United Nations, 211 East 43rd Street, 11th Floor, New York, N.Y. 10017, U.S.A.

Gutiérrez Cano, Joaquín; Spanish international bank official; b. 1920; ed. Univ. of Madrid.
Spanish Diplomatic Service 47-57; Pres. Spanish Fruit Producers' and Exporters' Asscn. 58; M.P. 58-; mem. Council of Inst. of Fiscal Studies 60-; Perm. Counsellor, National Economy; mem. Board Bank of Spain 62-, Bank of Industrial Credit 62-; Exec. Dir. for Spain, Italy, Greece and Portugal, International Bank for Reconstruction and Devt. (World Bank) 63-68; Minister of Devt. Planning Jan. 74-.
Ministry of Development Planning, Madrid, Spain.

Gutiérrez Gomez, José, d.iur., d.rer.pol.; Colombian diplomatist; b. 1909; ed. Antioquia Univ.
Man. Cali Agricultural, Industrial and Mining Credit Bank 32-35, Uribe Angel Laboratories, Medellín 35-46; Chair. Nat. Asscn. of Industrialists (ANDI) 46-57; mem. Govt. Economic Cttee. 47-48, Economic Mission to Washington 48; del., with rank of Ambassador, Ninth Gen. Assembly of U.N. 52, Fourth Extraordinary Session, Inter-American Economic and Social Council, Rio de Janeiro 54; Mayor of Medellín 57; Ambassador to U.S. and to Council of the Organization of American States 57-60; Dir. Corporación Financiera Nacional 61-, now Pres.; Hon. D.Econ. (Antioquia Univ.).
Corporación Financiera Nacional, Medellín, Colombia.

Gutmann, Viktor, dip. ing., dr. tech., dr. phil., sc.d.; Austrian chemist; b. 10 Nov. 1921, Vienna; s. of Viktor Gutmann and Margarete Lehmann; m. Elisabeth Schuster 1968; two s. two d.; ed. Technical Univ. of Vienna.
Assistant in research, Technical Univ. of Vienna 46-48, 50-52, Dozent 53-57, Prof. of Inorganic Chemistry 57-, Head of Dept. 60-; Post-Doctoral Fellow, Cambridge 48-50; Prof. of Inorganic and Analytical Chemistry, Baghdad Univ. 52-53; mem. Göttingen Acad. of Science, Austrian Acad. of Science, Leopoldina Acad. of Science (Halle); Carl Friedrich Gauss Medal.
Leisure interests: mountaineering, skiing, gardening.
Publs. *Halogen Chemistry* (Ed.), *Halides as Ionizing Solvents,* 56 *Polarography in Non-Aqueous Solvents* 60, *The Role of the Donor Number* 66, *Co-ordination Chemistry in Non-Aqueous Solvents* 68, *Chemical Functionality* 71, *Phenomenological Approach to Lotion-Solvent Interactions* 72, *Thermochemistry of the Chemical Bond* 73, *Redox-Properties, Changes effected by Co-ordination* 73, *Effects of Ligands on the Kinetics of Substitution and Redox Reactions* 74, *Empirical Approach to Molecular Interactions* 75, *Empirical Parameters for Donor and Acceptor Properties of Solvents* 76, *Solvent Effects on the Reactivities of Organometallic Compounds* 76; 320 research papers.
Technische Hochschule, Getreidemarkt 9, A 1060 Vienna; Home: Trinksgellgasse 16, A 2380 Perchtoldsdorf, Austria.
Telephone: 0222-571651-116 (Office); 0222-869519 (Home).

Gutowski, Armin Ferdinand; German professor and economist; b. 14 July 1930, Nuremberg; s. of Adam and Meta Gutowski; m. Dr. Renate Merklein 1973; ed. Univs. of Nuremberg, Hamburg and Mainz.
Research Assoc., Research Inst. of Political Econs., Univ. of Mainz 52-66; Rockefeller Research Fellow, Calif., Princeton and Chicago Univs. 60-61; Deputy Chief Economist, Kreditanstalt für Wiederaufbau, Frankfurt (Main) 66-67, Chief Econ. Adviser 67-; Prof. of Econs. and Devt., Univ. of Giessen 67-70; Chair. and Dir. Tropeninstitut, Giessen 69-70; Prof. of Econs. (Money and Int. Finance) Univ. of Frankfurt 70-; mem. Council of Econ. Experts on Devt. in Fed. Repub. of Germany 70-; mem. Board of Advisers, Fed. Ministry of Economy 70-; mem. Mont Pelerin Soc., Dir. 70-74; Co-Editor *Wirtschaft und Wettbewerb* 73-.
Publs. books: *Konstruktions- und Entwicklungsaufträge* 60, *Wirtschaftliche Weinbaupolitik* 62, *Konglomerate Unternehmungsgrösse und wirtschaftliche Macht* 71, *International Monetary Problems* (co-author) 72; papers: *Theoretische Ansätze zu einem Konzept von Anbieterpolitik* 73, *How the World can Afford OPEC Oil* (co-author) 75, *Chances for Price-level Stability in Various International Monetary Systems* 75.
Kreditanstalt für Wiederaufbau, 6000 Frankfurt-am-Main, Palmengartenstrasse 5-9; Home: 6242 Kronberg 3, Parkstrasse 25, Federal Republic of Germany.
Telephone: 0611/74311 (Office); 06173/3858 (Home).

Gutowsky, Herbert Sander, A.B., M.S., PH.D.; American physical chemist; b. 8 Nov. 1919, Bridgman, Mich.; s. of Otto Gutowsky and Hattie Meyers; m. Barbara Joan Stuart 1949; three s.; ed. Indiana and Harvard Univs. and Univ. of Calif. (Berkeley).
Instructor, Univ. of Ill. 48, Asst. Prof. 51-55, Assoc. Prof. 55-56, Prof. of Physical Chem. 56-, Head, Div. of Physical Chem. 56-62, Head, Dept. of Chem. and Chemical Engineering 67-70, Dir. School of Chemical Sciences, Head, Dept. of Chem. 70-, Assoc. mem. Center for Advanced Study, Univ. of Ill. 62-63; Guggenheim Fellow 54-55; Walker Ames Visiting Prof. at Univ. of Wash. 57; mem. Nat. Acad. of Sciences, American Acad. of Arts and Sciences; American Chemical Soc. awards: unrestricted grant for petroleum research 65, Irving Langmuir Award in Chemical Physics 66-, Midwest Award of St. Louis Section 73, Peter Debye Award in Physical Chem. 75; Award of the Int. Soc. of Magnetic Resonance 74.
Leisure interests: gardening, photography, science fiction, bowling, girl-watching, philately.
Publs. Scientific articles, mainly in *Journal* of American Chemical Soc., *Journal of Chemical Physics*, *Physical Review*, *Discussions* of Faraday Soc., *Journal of Physical Chemistry*.
School of Chemical Sciences, University of Illinois, Urbana, Ill. 61801, U.S.A.
Telephone: 217-333-0710.

Guttmann, Sir Ludwig, Kt., C.B.E., M.D., F.R.C.P., F.R.C.S.; British neurosurgeon and spinal cord specialist; b. 3 July 1899, Tost, Silesia, Germany; s. of Bernhard and Dorothy (née Weissenberg) Guttmann; m. Else Samuel 1927; one s. one d.; ed. Gymnasium, Königshutte, Silesia, and Univs. of Breslau (now Wrocław, Poland), Freiburg and Würzburg.
Assistant to Prof. O. Foerster, Neurological and Neurosurgical Dept., Wenzel Hancke Krankenhaus, Breslau 23-28, Assoc. of Prof. Foerster's Clinic 30; Neurosurgeon, Psychiatric Dept., Univ. of Hamburg-Friedrichsberg 28-29; Dozent Univ. of Breslau 30; Dir. Neurological and Neurosurgical Dept., Jewish Hosp., Breslau 33-39; Research Fellow, Neurosurgical Dept., Univ. of Oxford 39-44; Dir. Nat. Spinal Injuries Centre, Stoke Mandeville Hosp. 44-46, now Emer. Consultant to Hosp.; Dir. Stoke Mandeville Sports Stadium for the

Disabled 69-; Prof. Emer. (Cologne); Hon. Dr., D.Sc., D.Chir., LL.D.; Hon. Freeman of Aylesbury, Bucks.; Hon. F.R.C.P. (Canada); decorations from 19 countries; Hon. mem. medical and other asscns.
Leisure interests: bowling, travelling.
Publs. Vol. *Surgery, Official British Medical History of World War II* 53, *Comprehensive Management and Research of Spinal Cord Injuries* 73, *Textbook on Sport for the Disabled* 76; 172 publs. in medical and scientific journals.
Stoke Mandeville Sports Stadium for the Paralysed and Other Disabled, Aylesbury, Buckinghamshire; 26 Northumberland Avenue, Aylesbury, Buckinghamshire, England.
Telephone: 84848 (Office); 4901 (Home).

Gutton, André Henry Georges; French architect and town planner; b. 8 Jan. 1904, Fontenay-sous-Bois; s. of Henry B. Gutton; m. Elisabeth Lafargue 1927; two s. one d.; ed. Ecole nationale supérieure des beaux arts and Inst. d'Urbanisme de l'Univ. de Paris.
Architect for private buildings and nat. palaces 36-; Prof. Inst. of Town Planning, Sorbonne 43-49; Prof. of Theory of Architecture, Nat. School of Fine Arts 49-58, of Town Planning 58-; Technical Counsellor, Govt. of Syria 51; mem. Exec. Cttee. Union internationale des architectes 49-, Pres. Town Planning Comm. 51; Consultant Town-Planner Canton of Geneva 60; Pres. Parisian Order of Architects 61-; Vice-Pres. Congress of Architects 65; mem. Acad. of Architecture, Royal Acad. of Belgium; Hon. Fellow American Inst. of Architects; Int. Prize for plan for Place des Nations, Geneva 58; Officier Légion d'Honneur, Knight, Order of Orange-Nassau, of Dannebrog; Officier des Arts et Lettres.
Major works: Architectural Plans for Institut de France 43, Post Office Buildings, Paris 44, The Opera 50, Post Office Buildings at Versailles, Nancy, Besançon, Chateauroux, Roanne, 92 Neuilly-sur-Marne and schools and offices in France; Town Planning: Plans for Nancy 38, Dakar (Senegal), Boulogne, Issy 45, Aleppo (Syria) 52, Sihanoukville (Cambodia) 60.
Publs. *Charte de l'Urbanisme* 41, *Conversations sur l'Architecture*: (*L'edifice dans la cité, La maison des hommes, les églises et les temples, les universités, L'urbanisme au service de l'homme*).
Office: Institut de France, 1 rue de Seine, Paris 6e; Home: 23 bis quai Conti, Paris 6e, France.
Telephone: Danton 59-56.

Guttuso, Renato; Italian painter; b. 2 Jan. 1912.
Mem. of the "Corrente" group 40-42; one of the founders of the group "Fronte Nuovo delle Arti" 47; rep. at Dunn Int. Exhbn., London 63; Prize for Young Artists 24th Biennale, Venice, one-man show at 26th Biennale, Second Int. Prize for "La Spiaggia" 28th Biennale; Titular Prof. of Design, Liceo Artistico Rome; mem. Lenin Peace Prize Cttee.; Lenin Peace Prize 72.
Ciancaleoni 1, Rome, Italy.

Guy, Michel; French horticulturist and politician; b. 28 June 1927, Paris; s. of late Georges Guy and Aline Charon; ed. Ecole Bossuet, Paris.
Managing Dir. Etablissements Guy-Charon (horticulture firm) 50-70; Artistic Adviser, Int. Festival of Dance 64-71; Founder and Dir.-Gen. Paris Autumn Festival 72-74; Sec. of State for Culture June 74-.
Leisure interest: collecting modern paintings.
3 rue de Valois, 75001 Paris; Home: 156 rue de Rivoli, 75001 Paris, France.

Guy, William Lewis, B.S., M.S.; American farmer and politician; b. 30 Sept. 1919, Devils Lake, N. Dakota; m. Elizabeth J. Mason 1942; two s. three d.; ed. North Dakota State Univ., Minnesota Univ.

Lieutenant U.S. Navy 42-45; Asst. County Agent, Cass County 47; Livestock Salesman 47; co-owner Guy-Bean Farm Supply 48; farmer 48-60; State Rep. Cass County 59-61; Gov. N. Dakota 61-73; U.S. Senator for N. Dakota Jan. 75-; Chair. Missouri River States Comm. 61, 62; Founder and First Chair. of 15-State Midwest Governors' Conf. 62, 63; President's election observer, South Viet-Nam 67; Chair. Nat. Governors' Conf. 67; mem. President's Cttee. on Health Facilities 68; Democrat.
U.S. Senate, Washington, D.C. 20510; and Casselton, North Dakota, U.S.A.

Guyard, Marius-François, D. ès L.; French university official; b. 18 March 1921, Paris; s. of Marius Guyard and Jeanne Chabrillat; m. Françoise Bordier 1947; two s. two d.; ed. Ecole Normale Supérieure and the Sorbonne.
Professor, Univ. of Athens 55-57; Strasbourg Univ. 57-63; Cultural Counsellor, French Embassy, U.K. 63-65; Prof. of French Literature, Sorbonne 65-67; Vice-Chancellor, Univ. of Montpellier 67-69, of Amiens 69-70, of Strasbourg Univs. 70-; Chair. Conf. des Recteurs Français 75-; Chevalier, Légion d'Honneur, Officier, Ordre National du Mérite, Palmes Académiques, Chevalier des Arts et Lettres, Commdr. Orange-Nassau.
Publs. *La Grande-Bretagne dans le Roman Français* 54, *Recherches Claudéliennes* 64, editions of Lamartine, and Hugo, numerous contributions to revues and critical anthologies.
6 rue de la Toussaint, Strasbourg, Bas-Rhin, France. Telephone: 32-49-80.

Guyer, Roberto E., LL.D.; Argentine UN official; b. 10 March 1923, Buenos Aires; m. María Julia Mackinlay 1962; ed. Buenos Aires School of Law, Acad. of Int. Law, The Hague, and Oxford and Columbia (N.Y.) Univs.
Entered Argentine Foreign Service 56; served in Washington, Bonn, The Hague (with rank of Amb.) and as mem. of Argentine del. to UN and OAS; also held various senior posts in Argentine Ministry of Foreign Affairs; fmr. Prof. of Int. Law, Univ. of Buenos Aires and Nat. War Coll.; UN Under-Sec.-Gen. for Special Political Affairs March 71-.
United Nations, New York, N.Y. 10017, U.S.A.

Guyot, H.E. Cardinal Jean, D.THEOL.; French ecclesiastic; b. 7 July 1905, Bordeaux; ed. Univ. of Bordeaux, Grand Séminaire and Collegium Angelicum, Rome.
Ordained Priest 32; Priest, Bordeaux 32; served as Diocesan Chaplain, Collège Saint-Genès and later in youth insts. for eight years; Founder, Séminaire Saint-Maurice pour les Vocations d'Aînés 38; Vicar-Gen. 44-49; Coadjutor to Bishop of Coutances 49; Bishop of Coutances 50-67; Pres. Commission épiscopale du Clergé et des Séminaires and mem. of the Board, Conseil Permanent, Gen. Synod 64; Archbishop of Toulouse 66-; created Cardinal by Pope Paul VI 73; Keeper Acad. des Jeux Floraux de Toulouse; Officier Légion d'Honneur; Grand Croix Ordre de Malte.
Archevêché, 24 rue Perchepeinte, 31073 Toulouse Cedex, France.
Telephone: 52-32-01.

Guzhenko, Timofei Borisovich; Soviet politician; b. 15 Feb. 1918, Tatarinovo, Kursk Region; ed. Odessa Inst. of Marine Transport and Acad. of Merchant Marine.
Engineer, Murmansk Port 42-49; Dir. Kholmsk and Korsakov ports 51-55; Pres. Sakhalin Steamship Co. 55-60; Head of Main Dept., U.S.S.R. Ministry of Merchant Marine 60-62; Deputy Head of Dept., C.P.S.U. Central Cttee. 62-66; First Vice-Minister,

U.S.S.R. Ministry of Merchant Marine 66-70, Minister 70-; Deputy to U.S.S.R. Supreme Soviet 70-; Orders of Lenin, Red Banner of Labour, Red Star, etc.
Ministry of Merchant Marine, 1/4 Ulitsa Zhdanova, Moscow, U.S.S.R.

Guzmán, Martín Luiz; Mexican writer, journalist and politician; b. 6 Oct. 1887; s. of Martín L. Guzmán and Carmen Franco Terrazas; m. Anita West Villalobos 1909; three s.; ed. Escuela Nacional Preparatoria and Mexico Univ.
Editorial Staff, *El Imparcial* 08; took part in Mexican Revolution 13; Co-founder *El Honor Nacional* 13; Counsellor to Minister of War 14; exile 14-20; Editor-in-Chief *El Heraldo de México* 20; Founder *El Mundo* 22; mem. Chamber of Deputies 22-24; lived in Spain 24-30; Founder and Man. Dir. *Tiempo* (Mexico) 42-; Amb. to UN 51; Pres. Comisión Nacional de los Libros de Texto Gratuitos 64-.
Publs. *La querella de México* 15, *A orillas del Hudson* 22, *El águila y la serpeinte* 28, *Aventuras democráticas* 29, *La sombra del caudillo* 29, *Javier Mina* 32, *Filadelfia, paraíso de conspiradores* 33, *El hombre y sus armas* 38, *Campos de batalla* 39, *Panoramas políticos y la causa del pobre* 40, *Memorias de Pancho Villa* 51, *Muertes históricas* 58, *Otras páginas* 59, *Academia e Islas Marías* 59, *Axhaná González en las elecciones* 60, *Maestros rurales y Piratas y Corsarios* 60, *Necesidad de cumplir las leyes de Reforma* 63, *Febrero de 1913* 63, *Crónicas de mi destierro* 63.
Tiempo, Barcelona 32, Apdo. 1122, Mexico, D.F., Mexico.

Guzmán Neyra, Alfonso; Mexican politician and judge; b. 1906, Pánuco, Ver.; s. of Alfonso Víctor Guzmán Rodríguez; m. Adelaida Rodríguez Quiroz de Guzmán 1936; one s.; ed. National Univ. of Mexico.
President, Supreme Tribunal of Justice, Veracruz; Dep. for First District, Veracruz; Pres. Fed. Cttee. for Conciliation and Arbitration; Dir. Govt. Works in Fed. District; Pres. Regional Cttee. of Partido Revolucionario Institucional (P.R.I.); Pres. Supreme Court of Justice 59-64; Judge Fourth Chamber 65-69; Pres. Supreme Court of Justice 69-74.
Leisure interest: shooting.
Alejandro Dumas 15, Col. Polanco, Mexico 5, D.F., Mexico.
Telephone: 5-20-04-79.

Gvati, Chaim; Israeli farmer and politician; b. 29 Jan. 1901, Pinsk, Russia; s. of Shmuel and Esther Gvati; m. Luba Laskov 1925; one d.; ed. Vilna, Poland, and Russian university.
Emigrated to Israel 24; mem. Kibbutz 24-, mem. Kibbutz Meuchad Central Cttee. 42-45; Chair. Security and Farming Cttees. of The Agricultural Centre 45-49; Dir.-Gen. Ministry of Agriculture 50-57; Sec. Ichud Hakvutzot Veakibbutzim 59-62; Sec. Federation of Kibbutz Movement 63-64; Minister of Agriculture 64-74; Mapai.
Leisure interest: Israeli agriculture.
Kibbutz Yifat, Israel.

Gwinn, William Persons; American aircraft executive; b. 22 Sept. 1907, New York; s. of Frederick W. Gwinn and Clare Persons; m. 1st Joyce Clark 1934 (died 1957), two s. one d.; m. 2nd Mary Berry Devoe 1958 (died 1969); m. 3rd Rachel Coleman Witman 1970; ed. Gunnery Preparatory School, Washington, Conn.
Joined Pratt & Whitney Aircraft Div. of United Aircraft Corpn. 27, Sales Dept. 27-34, W. Coast rep. 34-39, Asst. Sales Man. 39-42, Asst. Gen. Man. 42, Acting Gen. Man. 43-44, Gen. Man. 44-56, Vice-Pres. United Aircraft Corpn. 46-56, Pres. and Chief Admin. Officer 56-67, Pres. and Chief Exec. Officer 68, Chair. and Chief Exec. Officer 68-72; Dir. Conn. Mutual Life Insurance

Co., Shell Oil Co., F. & M. Schaefer Corpn., Trustee, Rensselaer Polytechnic Inst. of Connecticut, Aviation Museum Asscn., Trinity Coll. (Life); mem. Industry Advisory Council; Hon. Dr. Eng. (Rensselaer Polytechnic Inst.) 56, D.Sc. (Trinity Coll.) 61.

Leisure interests: golfing, yachting.

3060 South Ocean Boulevard, Palm Beach, Florida 33480, U.S.A.

Telephone: 305-582-7189.

Gyani, Lt.-Gen. Prem Singh, O.B.E.; Indian army officer; b. 1910; ed. Rashtra Indian Military Coll., Dehra Dun, and R.M.A., Woolwich.

Commissioned and joined Regt. of Artillery 32; passed Staff Coll., Quetta 41; commanded Field Regt. Burma theatre 44-46; Dir. of Artillery, Army H.Q. 47-50; attended Imperial Defence Coll., London 51; commanded Infantry Brigade 52-54; alternate del. (military), Int. Comm. for Truce Supervision and Control, Laos 54-55; Commdt. Defence Services Staff Coll., Wellington, India 55-59; G.O.C. Infantry Div. 59; Commdr. UN Emergency Force Gaza Dec. 59-64; UN Observer in Cyprus 64; Commdr. UN Cyprus Force March-June 64; Pres. Birla Inst. of Technology, Ranchi 65-67; mem. Punjabi Univ. Syndicate 71-73; Trustee *The Tribune*, Chandigarh 72-.

25 Sector 5, Chandigarh, Punjab, India.

Gyenes, András; Hungarian politician; b. 1923, Kisbecskerek; ed. Communist Party Acad., Moscow.

Joined Communist Party 45; held various trade union positions 44-58; Vice-Pres. Hungarian Council for Physical Training and Sports until 62; Deputy Head, Foreign Dept., Cen. Cttee., Hungarian Socialist Workers' Party (HSWP) 62-69, Head 69-70, 71-74; Deputy Minister of Foreign Affairs 70-71; Amb. to German Democratic Repub. 74-75; Sec. Cen. Cttee., HSWP 75-.

Hungarian Socialist Workers' Party, 1387 Budapest, Széchenyi rakpart 19, Hungary.

Telephone: 111-400.

Gyllenhammar, Pehr Gustaf; Swedish business executive; b. 28 April 1935, Gothenburg; m. Christina Gyllenhammar; four c.; ed. Univ. of Lund and Centre d'Etudes Industrielles, Geneva.

Employed by Amphion Insurance Co. 60; Asst. Admin, Head, Skandia Insurance Co. 65, Deputy Man. Dir. 68. Pres. Skandia Co. 70; Pres. Volvo Group May 71-.

AB Volvo, S 40508, Gothenburg, Sweden.

Győri, Imre; Hungarian politician; b. 1924.

Successively Section Head of Hungarian Socialist Workers' Party Cen. Cttee., Deputy Leader of Agitation and Propaganda Dept., First Sec. of Municipal Party Cttee. of Szeged; mem. of Parl. 63-; mem. Cen. Cttee., HSWP 66-, Sec. 74-; Labour Order of Merit 58, 65, 70; Jubilee Commemorative Medal of Liberation 70.

Hungarian Socialist Workers' Party, 1387 Budapest, Széchenyi rakpart 19, Hungary.

Telephone: 111-400.

Gysi, Klaus; German journalist and diplomatist; b. 1912.

Joined Communist Party 31; Minister of Culture 73-; Amb. to Italy 73-.

Embassy of the German Democratic Republic, Viale Castro Pretorio 116, Rome, Italy.

H

Haack, Robert William; American financial executive; b. 15 Feb. 1917; ed. Hope Coll. and Harvard Business School.
Naval service, Second World War; with Robert W. Baird & Co. (Milwaukee securities firm) until 64, Partner 50-64; Pres. Nat. Asscn. of Securities Dealers, Washington 64-67; Pres. New York Stock Exchange 67-72; Interim Chair. Lockheed Aircraft Corpn. Feb. 76-.
c/o New York Stock Exchange, 11 Wall Street, New York 5, N.Y., U.S.A.

Haagen-Smit, Arie Jan, PH.D.; Netherlands scientist; b. 22 Dec. 1900, Utrecht; s. of Jan Willem Adrianus Haagen-Smit and Maria G. Van Maanen; m. Maria W. Bloemers 1935; one s. three d.; ed. Univ. of Utrecht.
Chief Asst. in Organic Chem., Univ. of Utrecht 29-36, Lecturer, Chem. of Natural Products 33-36; Lecturer, Chem. of Natural Products, Harvard Univ. 36-37; Assoc. Prof., Calif. Inst. of Technology 37-40, Prof. in Bio-organic Chem. 40-71, Prof. Emer. 71-; Chair. State of Calif. Air Resources Board 68-, President's Task Force on Pollution 70-; mem. Nat. Acad. of Sciences, Royal Acad. of Sciences, Netherlands; Knight, Order of Orange-Nassau; Fritzsche Award, American Chem. Soc., Frank Chambers Award, Air Pollution Control Asscn., Hodgkins Medal, Smithsonian Inst., Morrison Award, U.S. Dept. of Agriculture, Cottrell Award, N.A.S., Monsanto Award, A.C.S., National Medal of Science, U.S. Pres., Tyler Ecology Award.
Leisure interests: orchid horticulture, photography, hiking.
Publs. articles in professional journals.
California Institute of Technology, 1201 East California, Pasadena, Calif.; Home: 416 South Berkeley, Pasadena, Calif., U.S.A.
Telephone: 213-795-6811, Ext. 1912 (Office); 213-796-8208 (Home).

Haak, Jan Friedrich Wilhelm; South African lawyer and politician; b. 20 April 1917, Prince Albert; m. Maria Theron 1944; three c.; ed. Prince Albert School and Univ. of Stellenbosch.
Attorney, Bellville, Cape Town 45-48; Advocate, Cape Bar 60; Mayor of Bellville 49-51; M.P. 53-; Deputy Minister of Econ. Affairs 61-64, Deputy Minister of Mines June 62-64, Deputy Minister of Planning Dec. 62-64; Minister of Mines and Planning Aug. 64-67, of Econ. Affairs Jan. 67-May 70; mem. Chief Council of Nat. Party 51-, Prime Minister's Econ. Advisory Council; Dir. ISCOR, Trust Bank, Transterra Mining; Pres. Afrikaans Handelsinstituut.
8 Governer Street, Welgemoed, Bellville, Republic of South Africa.
Telephone: Cape Town 973569.

Haavikko, Paavo Juhani, PH.D.; Finnish writer and publisher; b. 25 Jan. 1931, Helsinki; s. of Heikki Adrian Haavikko and Rauha Pyykönen; m. 1st Marja-Liisa Vartio (née Sairanen) 1955 (died 1966), one s. one d.; m. Ritva Rainio (née Hanhineva) 1971; ed. Univ. of Helsinki.
Worked in real estate concurrently with career as writer 51-67; mem. board Finnish Writers' Asscn. 62-66; mem. State Cttee. for Literature 66-67; mem. board of Yhtyneet Kuvalehdet magazine co. and Suuri Suomalainen Kirjakerho (Great Finnish Book Club) 69; Literary Dir. Otava Publishing Co. 67-; six state prizes for literature; Pro Finlandia Medal.
Publs. Tiet Etäisyyksiin 51, Tuuliöinä 53, Synnyinmaa 55, Lehdet Lehtiä 58, Talvipalatsi 59, Runot 62, Puut Kaikki Heidän Vihreytensä 66, Neljätoista Hallitsijaa

70, Puhua vastata opettaa 72, Runoja Matkalta Salmen Yli 73, Kaksiky m mentä ja yksi 74 (poems); Poésie 65, Selected Poems 68 (translations); Münchausen, Nuket 60, Ylilääkari 68, Sulka 73, Ratsumies 74, Harald Pitkäikäinen 74 (plays); Yksityisiä Asioita 60, Toinen Taivas Ja Maa 61, Vuodet 62, Lasi Claudius Civiliksen Salaliittolaisten Pöydällä 64 (prose).
Tamminiementie 15, 02940 Espoo 94, Finland.

Habakkuk, Sir Hrothgar John, Kt., M.A., F.B.A.; British economic historian; b. 13 May 1915, Barry, Glam.; s. of Evan Guest Habakkuk and Anne Bowen; m. Mary Richards 1948; one s. three d.; ed. Barry County School, Univ. Coll., Cardiff, St. John's Coll., Cambridge.
Fellow, Pembroke Coll., Cambridge 38-50, Dir. of Studies in History 46-50; Lecturer, Faculty of Econs., Cambridge 46-50; Chichele Prof. of Econ. History, Fellow All Souls Coll., Oxford 50-67; Principal Jesus Coll., Oxford 68-; Vice-Chancellor Univ. of Oxford 73-; Pres. Univ. Coll. of Swansea 75-; Hon. Fellow, St. John's and Pembroke Colls., Cambridge; Foreign mem. American Acad. of Arts and Sciences, American Philosophical Soc.; Hon. D.Litt. (Cambridge, Wales, Pa.).
Publs. American and British Technology in the Nineteenth Century 62, Population Growth and Economic Development 71, Editor, Cambridge Economic History of Europe Vol. VI.
The Lodgings, Jesus College, Oxford, England.
Telephone: Oxford 48140.

Habashi, Wadie; Sudanese agricultural economist and politician; b. 14 Aug. 1917, Merowe; s. of late Yousef Habashi and Moawwad Safina; m. Ratiba Boutros 1944; no c.; ed. Univ. of Khartoum and Oxford Univ.
Worked on the Al Aalyab, Burgaeg and White Nile devt. schemes; Agricultural Insp. for Khartoum Province and later for Merowe, Dongla and Halfa; Technical Adviser to the Minister of Agriculture; Asst. Dir. for Planning and Devt., Dept. of Agriculture, Dir. 55-66; Rep. of Sudan to FAO Conf. 56, to Int. Tobacco Conf., Rhodesia 63; Chair. Board of Dirs., Elgash Corpn.; Dir. Production Div., Equatoria Projects Board; Head, Advisory Comm. for Agricultural Research; mem. Gezira Scheme Admin. Council; mem. Board of Faculty of Agriculture, Univ. of Khartoum; with FAO 66-71, joined Int. Bank and Kuwait Fund of Arab Devt. Oct. 71; Minister of Agric. 71-73, of Agric., Food and Natural Resources 73-74; Pres. Nat. Council for Research 74-; mem. Council, Univ. of Khartoum, Nat. Council for Higher Educ.; Chair. Nat. Cttee. for Man, Environment and Devt.
Leisure interests: photography, horse riding, hunting, reading, testing modern agricultural technology on a small private farm.
National Council for Research, P.O. Box 2404, Khartoum, Sudan.
Telephone: 70701, 79381 (Office); 42515 (Home).

Habe, Hans; American writer; b. 12 Feb. 1911, Budapest, Hungary; s. of Imre Habe and Bianca Bekessy; m. Licci Balla 1957; one s.; ed. Franz Joseph Gymnasium, Vienna, and Univs. of Vienna and Heidelberg.
Former newspaperman and reporter, Vienna; fmr. Editor-in-Chief Der Morgen, Vienna; fmr. League of Nations Corresp. Prager Tagblatt, Geneva; served in French and U.S. Armies, Second World War; Editor-in-Chief Die Neue Zeitung after Second World War, later Founder and Editor-in-Chief Münchner Illustrierte and Echo der Woche (Munich); Columnist, Welt

am Sonntag (Hamburg); numerous decorations; Herzl Prize, Israel; Fellow, Boston Univ.; Gov. Univ. of Haifa.

Leisure interests: boating, collecting netsukes.

Publs. *Three Over the Frontier* 36, *A Time Collapses* 38, *Sixteen Days* 39, *A Thousand Shall Fall* (film *Cross of Lorraine*) 41, *Kathrine* 43, *Aftermath* 47, *Walk in Darkness* (also play) 48, *Black Earth* 52, *Our Love Affair with Germany* 52, *All My Sins* 55, *Off Limits* 56, *The Devil's Agent* 57, *Ilona* 60, *The Countess* 62, *Anatomy of Hatred* 64, *The Mission* 65, *Im Jahre Null* 66, *Christopher and his Father* 67, *Gentlemen of the Jury* 67, *The Poisoned Stream* 69, *Wie einst David* 71, *Erfahrungen* 73, *Palazzo* 75.

Casa Acacia, Via Muraccio, Ascona, Ticino, Switzerland.

Telephone: Ascona 352383.

Habeck, Fritz, DR.IUR.; Austrian writer; b. 8 Sept. 1916, Neulengbach; s. of late Dr. Karl and Marianne H. (née Adelsmayr) Habeck; m. Gerda Vilsmeier 1951; two s. two d.; ed. Univ. of Vienna.

Served in German Army during Second World War; Asst. Man. Josefstadt Theatre, Vienna 46; radio producer in Vienna 53-; Goethe Award of City of Vienna, City Prize of Vienna, Austrian State Prize, Handel-Mazzetti Prize, Vienna Children's Book Prize 60, 61, 63, 67, 70, 73, State Children's Book Prize 63, 67, Wildgans Prize of Austrian Industry 64, Stifter Prize 73.

Leisure interests: gardening, chronicle of the family.

Publs. Novels: *Der Scholar vom linken Ga'gen* 41, *Der Tanz der sieben Teufel* 50, *Das Boot kommt nach Mitternacht* 51, *Das zerbrochene Dreieck* 53, *Ronan Gobain* 56, *Der Ritt auf dem Tiger* 58, *Der Kampf um die Barbacane* 60, *Die Stadt der grauen Gesichter* 61, *Der verliebte Oesterreicher* 61, *Der eindugige Reiter* 63, *In eigenem Auftrag* (Selections) 63, *Der Piber* 65, *Die Insel über den Wolken* 65, *König Artus* 65, *Aufstand der Salzknechte* 67, *Salzburg-Spiegel* 67, *Marianne und der wilde Mann* 68, *François Villon* 69, *Doktor Faustus* 70, *Johannes Gutenberg* 71, *Schwarzer Hund im goldenen Feld* 73; *Der schwarze Mantel meines Vaters* 76; Plays: *Zwei und swei ist vier* 48, *Baisers mit Schlag* 50, *Marschall Ney* 54.

Grillparzerstrasse 6, A-2500 Baden, Austria.

Telephone: 02252-39-695.

Habel, Karl, M.D.; American medical researcher; b. 28 Sept. 1908, Philadelphia, Pa.; s. of Charles Habel and Claire Ward; m. Ruth J. Carter 1934; one s. one d.; ed. Univ. of Pennsylvania and Jefferson Medical Coll.

Intern, Philadelphia Gen. Hospital 35; Resident, then Asst. Chief Resident, Phila. Gen. Hospital for Pediatrics 36; Asst. Chief Resident, Phila. Hospital for Contagious Diseases 38; Commissioned Officer, U.S. Public Health Service (U.S.P.H.S.) 38-67; Chief of various Depts. at Microbiological Inst. 48-67; mem. Dept. of Experimental Pathology, Scripps Clinic and Research Foundation, La Jolla, Calif. 67-75; at Reading Inst. of Rehabilitation, Pa. 75-; Editor, *Proceedings* of the Soc. for Experimental Biology and Medicine 54-63, *Virology* 62-, *Journal of Immunology* 66-; Consultant to Comm. on Immunization, Armed Forces Epidemiological Board 56-; mem. Advisory Cttee. Pan American Health Org. 76-, Expert Cttee. Rabies, WHO 68-, and mem. numerous other cttees.; mem. Nat. Acad. of Sciences, A.A.A.S., New York Acad. of Science, American Acad. of Microbiology and others; Distinguished Service Medal U.S.P.H.S. 66.

Publs. 115 scientific articles and WHO pamphlets.

Room 108E, Reading Institute of Rehabilitation, RD 1, Box 252, Reading, Pa. 19607, U.S.A.

Haberler, Gottfried, DR.RER.POL., D.IUR.; Austrian-born American economist; b. 20 July 1900; ed. Vienna Univ.

Graduate student London, Harvard and other Univs.

27-29; lecturer, later Prof. of Economics and Statistics, Vienna Univ. 28-36; Visiting lecturer, Harvard Univ. 31-32; attached to Financial Section, League of Nations, Geneva 34-36; settled in U.S.A. 36; Prof. of Int. Trade Harvard Univ. 36-71; Prof. Emer. Harvard Univ.; Resident Scholar, American Enterprise Inst.; Assoc. Board of Govs., Fed. Reserve System, Washington 43; Pres. Int. Economic Asscn. 50-51, Hon. Pres. 53-; Pres. Nat. Bureau of Economic Research 55; mem. American Economic Asscn. (Vice-Pres. 48), Royal Economic Soc.; Charter mem. Econometric Soc.; Pres. American Econ. Asscn. 63-.

Office: American Enterprise Institute, 1150 17th Street N.W., Washington, D.C. 20036; Home: 4108 48th Street, N.W., Washington, D.C. 20016, U.S.A.

Telephone: 202-296-5616 (Office); 202-244-1774 (Home).

Habermeier, Walter O.; German international finance official; b. 24 Jan. 1931, Heilbronn; m.; two s.; ed. Univs. of Tübingen and Munich.

With German Fed. Bank, Dept. of Int. Orgs. and Agreements 57-60; mem. German Perm. Del., OEEC, Paris 60-61; Asst. to Pres. European Monetary Agreement 60-61; Alternate Exec. Dir., IMF 62-65; Special Adviser, German Fed. Bank 66; Deputy Treas., IMF 66. Treas. 69-.

International Monetary Fund, 19th and H Street, N.W., Washington, D.C. 20431, U.S.A.

Habgood, Rt. Rev. Dr. John Stapylton, D.D., M.A., PH.D.; British ecclesiastic; b. 23 June 1927, Stony Stratford; s. of Arthur Henry Habgood and Vera Chetwynd-Stapylton; m. Rosalie Mary Anne Boston 1961; two s. two d.; ed. Eton Coll., King's Coll. Cambridge Univ. and Cuddesdon Coll. Oxford.

Demonstrator in Pharmacology, Cambridge Univ. 50-53; Fellow, King's Coll. Cambridge Univ. 52-55; Curate, St. Mary Abbott's Church, Kensington 54-56; Vice-Principal, Westcott House, Cambridge 56-62; Rector, St. John's Church, Jedburgh, Scotland 62-67; Principal, Queen's Coll., Birmingham 67-73; Bishop of Durham 73-.

Leisure interests: carpentry, caravanning.

Publ. *Religion and Science* 64.

Auckland Castle, Bishop Auckland, Co. Durham DL14 7NR, England.

Telephone: Bishop Auckland 2576.

Habib-Deloncle, Michel, L. ès L., L. en D.; French lawyer and politician; b. 26 Nov. 1921; ed. Ecole libre des Sciences Politiques, Paris and Faculties of Law and Letters (Sorbonne), Univ. of Paris.

Resistance Movement 41-45; Journalist, *France Catholique* 45-53; Sec.-Gen. Parl. Group Rassemblement du Peuple Français 48-54; mem. Asscn. of the French Union 54-58; Deputy 58-73; Sec. of State to the Ministry of Foreign Affairs 62-66, to the Ministry of Educ. 66-67; mem. European Parl. 67, Vice-Pres. 72; Int. Relations Del., Exec. Cttee. Union Démocratique pour la Ve République 68-71; Deputy Sec.-Gen. UDR 71; Political Editor, *La Nation* 68.

17 rue de l'Yvette, Paris 16e, France.

Haby, René Jean, D. ÈS L.; French educator and politician; b. 9 Oct. 1919, Dombasle; s. of René Haby and Marguerite (née Demangeon); m. Paulette Masson 1945; one s. two d.; ed. Ecole Normale d'Instituteurs de Nancy, Faculté des Lettres de Nancy.

History teacher, Lycées of Lons-le-Saunier 47, Toul 49, Nancy 52; Proviseur, Lycées of St. Arold 54, Avignon 58, Metz 60, Montgeron 62; Dir. of Teaching, Ministry of Nat. Educ. 62-64; Insp. Gén. de l'Instruction Publique 63-; Asst. Dir.-Gen. of Teacher Training 64-65; Lecturer, Faculty of Letters and Human Sciences, Nancy 65, Paris IV 70; Dir. du Cabinet to Minister of Youth and Sports 66-68; Rector, Acad. de Clermont-Ferrand 72-74; Minister of Educ. May 74-; Chevalier, Légion

'Honneur, Commdr. Ordre Nat. du Mérite; Officier
es Palmes Académiques.
.eisure interest: tennis.
Publs. *La Région des Houillères lorraines* 65, *Déforma-
ions rocheuses au-dessus des Excavations souterraines* 70;
nany articles on the economy of N.E. France and on
ducation.
.e Nouzet, 4 Chemin du Dessus-des-Vignes, 91230
Montgeron, France.

Habyalimana, Maj.-Gen. Juvénal; Rwandan poli-
:ician; b. 3 Aug. 1937, Rambura, Gisenyi; ed. Coll.
St. Paul, Bukavu, Zaire, Lovanium Univ., Kinshasa
and Officers' School, Kigali.
Joined Nat. Guard as Platoon Leader, became Co.
Commdr. and later Asst. Staff Officer to Commdr. of
Nat. Guard; Chief of Staff 63-65; promoted Maj. 64;
Minister for the Nat. Guard and Chief of Staff of Police
65-73; Lieut.-Col. 67, Col. 70, Maj.-Gen. 73; Pres. of
Rwanda 73-, Minister of Nat. Defence 73-, Prime
Minister 74-; Pres. Comité pour la Paix et l'Unité Nat.
73-75, leader Mouvement révolutionnaire national pour
la développement 75-; Chair. OCAM Conf. of Heads of
State and Govt. 75.
Office of the President, Kigali, Rwanda.

Hachette, Jean-Louis, LIC. en DR.; French publisher;
b. 30 June 1925, Paris; m. Y. de Bouillé 1954; one s.
two d.; ed. Collège Stanislas, Paris, and Faculté de
Droit, Paris.
Joined Librairie Hachette (founded by great-grand-
father in 1826) 46; entire career spent with Librairie
Hachette, now Admin.; Pres. Libraire Gen. Française.
Leisure interests: polo, golf, skiing.
Office: 79 boulevard Saint-Germain, 75006 Paris; Home:
8 rue de Presbourg, 75116 Paris, France.
Telephone: 325-22-11 (Office); 704-64-75 (Home).

Hachisuka, Kunio, LL.B.; Japanese government
official; b. 1920; ed. Tokyo Univ.
Ministry of Railways (now Transport) 42-; Chief, Goods
Transport Section, Transport Div., Bureau of Road
Transport, Ministry of Transport 55; Chief, Planning
Section, Bureau of Tourism 57-58; Chief, Admin.
Section, Private Railways Div., Railway Supervision
Bureau 59; Chief, Gen. Affairs Section, Bureau of Road
Transport 60; Chief, Planning Section, Secretariat to the
Minister 61; Dir. Nagoya District Land Transport
Bureau 62, Osaka District Bureau 63-64; Dir. Private
Railways Div., Railway Supervision Bureau 65; Dir.
Transport Div., Bureau of Road Transport 66-67; Dir.
Div. of Tourism, Secretariat to the Minister 68-.
Division of Tourism, Secretariat to the Minister,
Ministry of Transport, 2-1-3, Kasumigaseki, Chiyoda-
ku, Tokyo, Japan.

Hacker, Louis Morton, M.A., LL.D.; American univer-
sity professor and administrator; b. 17 March 1899,
New York City; s. of Morris H. and Celia (née Waxel-
baum) Hacker; m. 1st Lillian Lewis 1921, 2nd Beatrice
Larson 1953; one s. one d.; ed. Columbia Univ.
Taught history and econs. at Ohio State, Wis., Hawaii,
Pa. State, Cambridge, Yeshiva, Fairleigh Dickinson
Univs., Utah State Agricultural, Army War, Nat. War
Colls., and New School for Social Research, New York;
Lecturer, Columbia Univ. 35-48, Prof. of Econs. 48-67,
Prof. Emer. 67-; Dean, School of Gen. Studies 49-58;
Harmsworth Prof. of American History, Oxford Univ.
and Fellow, Queen's Coll. 48-49; Editor and contributor
of *New International Encyclopaedia*, *Encyclopaedia of
Social Sciences*, *Columbia Encyclopaedia*; Editor *The
American Century* Series; Hon. LL.D. (Hawaii), Hon.
L.H.D. (Columbia).
Leisure interests: travel, walking, bridge, conversation.
Publs. *The United States since 1865* (with B. B.
Kendrick) 32, *The Farmer is Doomed* 33, *A Short
History of the New Deal* 34, *The United States: A Graphic

History 37, *American Problems of Today* 39, *Triumph
of American Capitalism* 40, *The United States and its
place in World Affairs* (with others) 43, *Shaping of the
American Tradition* 47, *New Industrial Relations* (with
others) 49, *The United States in the Twentieth Century*
(with H. S. Zahler) 52, *Government Assistance to Universities in Great Britain* (with others) 52, *Capitalism
and the Historians* (with others) 53, *Alexander Hamilton
in the American Tradition* 57, *American Capitalism* 57,
Larger View of the University 61, *Documents in American
Economic History* (2 vols.) 61, *The World of Andrew
Carnegie, 1865-1901* 68, *The Course of American
Economic Growth and Development* 70.
430 West 116th Street, New York, N.Y. 10027; and
Columbia University, New York, N.Y. 10027, U.S.A.
Telephone: 212-666-9252.

Hackett, Gen. Sir John Winthrop, G.C.B., C.B.E.,
D.S.O. AND BAR, M.C., B.LITT., M.A., LL.D.; retd. British
army officer; b. 5 Nov. 1910, Perth, Australia; s. of Sir
John Winthrop Hackett; m. Margaret Frena 1942;
three d.; ed. Geelong Grammar School (Australia) and
New Coll. Oxford.
Commissioned 31; Palestine 36; Transjordan Frontier
Force 37-40, Syria 41; Sec. Comm. of Control, Syria
and Lebanon; G.S.O. 2, 9th Army; Western Desert 42;
G.S.O. 1, Raiding Forces, G.H.Q., Middle East Land
Forces; Commdr. 4th Parachute Brigade 43; Italy 43;
Arnhem 44; Commdr. Transjordan Frontier Force 47;
D.Q.M.G., British Army of the Rhine (B.A.O.R.) 52;
Commdr. 20th Armoured Brigade 54; G.O.C. 7th
Armoured Div. 56-58; Commandant, Royal Mil. Coll.
of Science 58-61; G.O.C. in C., Northern Ireland
Command 61-63; Deputy Chief of Imperial Gen. Staff
63-64; Deputy Chief of Gen. Staff, Ministry of Defence
64-66; C.-in-C. British Army of the Rhine (B.A.O.R.)
and Commdr. Northern Army Group 66-68; Lees
Knowles Lecturer, Cambridge 61; Kermit Roosevelt
Lecturer, U.S.A. 67; Harmon Memorial Lecturer,
U.S.A.F. 70; Principal, King's Coll., London 68-75; Pres.
Classical Assen. of U.K. 70-71, English Assen. of U.K.
73-74; Fellow, King's Coll., London; Hon. Fellow, St.
George's Coll., Univ. of Western Australia, New Coll.,
Oxford.
Leisure interests: travel, country pursuits and music.
Coberley Mill, Cheltenham, Gloucestershire, England;
and Loughros, Ardara, Co. Donegal, Eire.

Haddon-Cave, Charles Philip, C.M.G., M.A.; British
overseas administrator; b. 6 July 1925; ed. Univ. of
Tasmania, King's Coll., Cambridge.
With Overseas Admin. Service 52-; successively posted
in Kenya, Seychelles and Hong Kong; Financial Sec.
Hong Kong 71-.
Colonial Secretariat, Central District, Hong Kong;
Home: 45 Shouson Hill, Hong Kong.

Haddow, Alexander John, C.M.G., D.SC., M.D., F.R.C.P.,
F.R.S., F.R.S.E.; British professor of medicine; b. 27
Dec. 1912, Glasgow; s. of Alexander and Margaret
Blackburn Haddow; m. Margaret Ronald Scott Orr
1946; two s.; ed. Hillhead High School, Glasgow, Glas-
gow Univ. and London School of Hygiene and Tropical
Medicine.
Medical Research Council Junior Research Fellow in
Tropical Medicine 38-41; Entomologist, Yellow Fever
Research Inst., Entebbe 42-45; staff mem. Int. Health
Div., Rockefeller Foundation 45-49; Overseas Research
Service 50-65; Epidemiologist, East African Virus
Research Inst. 50-52, Acting Dir. 52-53, Dir. 53-65;
Senior Lecturer in Epidemiology, Univ. of Glasgow
65-70, also Dir. Cancer Registration Bureau, West of
Scotland Hosp. Region 66-70; Assoc. Dean, Faculty of
Medicine and Titular Prof. of Tropical Medicine, Univ.
of Glasgow 70-71, Prof. of Admin. Medicine and Admin.
Dean Faculty of Medicine 71-; Chalmers Gold Medal,
Royal Soc. of Medicine and Hygiene 57, Stewart Prize,

British Medical Asscn. 62, Keith Prize, Royal Soc. of Edinburgh 68.
Leisure interests: various.
Publs. over 100 scientific papers.,
Medical Faculty Office, The University, Glasgow G12 8QQ; Home: 16 Hamilton Drive, Glasgow G12 8DR, Scotland.
Telephone: 041-339-8855 (Office); 041-339-7187 (Home).

Hadithi, Murtada al-; Iraqi politician; b. 1939, Ramadi; ed. Higher Teachers' Training Inst. and Univ. of Baghdad.
School Teacher, Fallouja 66-67; mem. Revolutionary Command Council 67; Chair. Kurdish Affairs Bureau and Peace Cttee. 67; mem. World Peace Cttee.; Minister of Labour 70-71, of the Economy June-Oct. 71, of Foreign Affairs 71-74; Amb. to U.S.S.R. 74.
c/o Ministry of Foreign Affairs, Baghdad, Iraq.

Hadiwidjaja, Tojib; Indonesian agriculturalist and politician; b. 12 May 1919, Tjiamis, W. Java; ed. Middelbare Landbouwschool and Faculty of Agriculture, Bogor.
Chairman, Pasundan Obor Foundation 36-40; Asst. Plant Pathologist, Inst. for Plant Diseases, Dept. of Agriculture, Bogor 39-48; Student, and concurrently Instructor of Plant Pathology, Faculty of Agriculture, Univ. of Indonesia, Bogor 48-55, Asst. Prof. 55-56, Prof. 56-, Dean 57-62; mem. Regional Representative Council, W. Java 60-62; Minister of Higher Learning and Science 62; Amb. to Belgium 65-66; Minister of Plantations 67; Chair. Indonesian Nat. Inst. for Science and Research 67; Minister of Agriculture 68-; mem. numerous advisory cttees., etc.; del. to several int. confs.
Ministry of Agriculture, Jakarta, Indonesia.

Hadley, Morris, A.B., LL.B.; American lawyer; b. 21 March 1894, New Haven, Conn.; s. of Arthur Twining Hadley and Helen (Morris) Hadley; m. Katherine C. Blodgett 1919; two s. two d.; ed. Groton School, Yale Univ., and Harvard Law School.
Army service (Major) in Europe 17-19; legal practice in New York City 21-; Trustee, Carnegie Corpn. 47-67 (Chair. 55-66); Partner, Milbank, Tweed, Hadley & McCloy; Trustee, N.Y. Public Library (Pres. 43-58); Hon. LL.D. (Yale, Univ. of Nevada).
Publs. *The Citizen and the Law* 41, *Arthur Twining Hadley* 48.
1 Chase Manhattan Plaza, New York, N.Y. 10005; Home: 71 East 71st Street, New York, N.Y. 10021, U.S.A.
Telephone: 212-422-2660.

Hadow, Sir Michael, K.C.M.G.; British diplomatist; b. 17 Aug. 1915, Shillong, Assam, India; s. of Malcolm McGregor Hadow and Constance Mary Lund; ed. Berkhamsted School and King's Coll., Cambridge.
Indian Civil Service 37-48; Foreign Office 48-52; Private Sec. to Minister of State for Foreign Affairs 49-52; Head of Chancery, Mexico City 52-54; Foreign Office 55, Head of Levant Dept. and Counsellor 58; Counsellor, Paris 59-62; Head of News Dept., Foreign Office 62-65; Amb. to Israel 65-69, to Argentina 69-72; Dir. Anglo-Israel Asscn. 73-.
Leisure interests: country pursuits.
Anglo-Israel Association, 9 Bentinck Street, London, W1M 5RP, England.

Hadson-Taylor, Hon. Joseph Charles Ojumiri; Sierra Leonean politician; b. 2 Aug. 1931, Freetown; m.; two c.; ed. Cathedral Boys' and Prince of Wales Schools.
Civil Servant, Colonial Sec.'s Office and Public Service Comm.; established own trading and transport co., Hadson-Taylor and Co.; Councillor, Freetown City Council 63, First Alderman and Chair. Finance and Gen. Purposes Cttee. 64, Deputy Mayor 65; mem. Parl. for Freetown Central 67-; Minister of Information and

Broadcasting 68-69; Minister of State and Leader of the House, later Minister of Health 69-73; Minister of Labour 73-74, of Health 74-; Del. to WHO Assembly, Geneva 72, ILO and OAU Confs. 73; attended many Commonwealth Parl. and African Regional confs.; African Regional Rep., Exec. Cttee., Gen. Council of Commonwealth Parl. Asscn.
Leisure interests: lawn tennis, walking, barbecue.
Ministry of Health, Freetown, Sierra Leone.

Haedens, Kléber Gustave; French writer and critic; b. 11 Dec. 1913, Equeurdreville; s. of Gustave Haedens and Edith Boucheau; m. Caroline Carloni 1951 (died 1972); ed. Prytanée Militaire de La Flèche, Inst. Montesquieu de Libourne and Ecole Supérieure de Commerce et d'Industrie de Bordeaux.
Literary and Film Critic *Présent*; Drama Critic *Paris-Soir*; Sport Critic *Action Française* and *Figaro* 37-45; Theatre and Film Critic *L'Epoque*; Literary Editor *Samedi-Soir*; Literary Critic *Paris-Presse* 51-, *Nouveau Candide* 62-, *le Journal du Dimanche* 68-, *Radio-télé Luxembourg*, *France-Soir* and *Elle* 70-; Prix Interallié 66, Grand Prix de la Critique de l'Acad. Française 71, Grand Prix du Roman de l'Acad. Française for *Adios* 74.
Leisure interests: rugby, tennis, music, opera, gastronomy.
Publs. Essays: *Gérard de Nerval* 39, *Paradoxe sur le roman* 41, *Une histoire de la littérature francaise* 43, *L'Air du Pays* 63; Novels: *l' Ecole des parents* 37, *Magnolia Jules* 38, *Une jeune Serpente* 40, *Salut au Kentucky* 47, *Adieu à la rose* 55, *L'été finit sous les tilleuls* 66, *Adios* 74.
La Bourdette, Dureville, 31320 Castaner-Tolosan, France.
Telephone: 08-22-61.

Haekkerup, Per; Danish politician; b. 25 Dec. 1915, Ringsted; s. of Hans K. Haekkerup; m. Grete Haekkerup; three s.; ed. Univ. of Copenhagen.
Member, City Council of Copenhagen 46-50; mem. *Folketing* (Parl.) 50-; Pres. Social-Democratic Youth Movement 46-52; Gen. Sec., Int. Union of Socialist Youth 46-54; mem. Consultative Assembly, Council of Europe 53-62; Econ. Editor *Aktuelt* 56-61; Minister of Foreign Affairs 62-66, of Econ. Affairs 71-73, 75; Parl. Spokesman and Floor Leader of Social Democratic Party Nov. 66-71.
Leisure interests: yachting and keeping his summer residence in good condition.
Publ. *Danmarks Udenrigs-politik* 65.
Home: Niels Juelsgade 13, Copenhagen K, Denmark.
Telephone: Minerva 301.

Haensel, Vladimir, M.S., PH.D., D.SC.; American catalytic chemist; b. 1 Sept. 1914, Freiburg, Germany; s. of Paul Haensel and Anna Tugenhold; m. Mary Magraw 1939; two d.; ed. Northwestern Univ. and Mass. Inst. of Technology.
Research Chemist, UOP Inc. 37-45; Dir. Crkg Research 45-55, Dir. Refining Research 55-59, Dir. Process Research 60-63, Vice-Pres. and Dir. of Research 64-72, Vice-Pres. Science and Technology 72-; mem. Nat. Acad. of Sciences, Nat. Acad. of Engineering; several awards including the American Chem. Soc. Award in Industrial and Engineering Chem. 64, Perkin Medal for outstanding work in Applied Chem., Nat. Medal of Science 73.
Leisure interests: tennis, gardening.
Publs. over 50 articles and chapters in books on various scientific subjects.
UOP World Headquarters, Ten UOP Plaza, Des Plaines, Ill. 60016; Home: 706 West North Street, Hinsdale, Ill. 60521, U.S.A.
Telephone: 312-391-3131 (Office); 312-323-3273 (Home).

Haertl, Karl, DR.IUR.; Austrian government official; b. 8 Jan. 1912, Aspang an Wechsel; s. of Karl Haertl; m. Dagmar Haertl-Hermann 1968; one d.; ed. Vienna Univ.

egal practice 38-39; military service Second World War 40-45; Judge, Vienna 45-46; Asst. Man. Nat. Theatre 49-57, Man. 57-63; Perm. Sec. Ministry of Educ. 63-65; Dir.-Gen. for Fine Arts 65-.
Leisure interest: art.
Strozzigasse 2, 1080 Vienna; Home: 1090 Vienna, Widerhofergasse 7, Austria.
Telephone: 3489-554.

Haferkamp, Wilhelm; German Common Market official and politician; b. 1 July 1923 Duisburg; ed. Universität zu Köln.
Head of Social Policy Dept. of Deutscher Gewerkschaftsbund (German Trade Union Fed.) 50, mem. Exec. Cttee. and Head of Econ. Dept. 62-67; Socialist mem. Landtag of North Rhine-Westphalia 58-66, 67; mem. Combined Comm. of European Communities July 67-70, Vice-Pres. 70-.
Commission of the European Communities, 200 rue de la Loi, 1040 Brussels, Belgium.
Telephone: Brussels 35-00-40.

Hafez, Maj.-Gen. Amin El; Syrian army officer and politician; b. 1911.
Former Military Attaché in Argentina; took part in the revolution of March 1963; Deputy Prime Minister, Mil. Gov. of Syria and Minister of Interior March-Aug. 63; Minister of Defence and Army Chief of Staff July-Aug. 63; Pres. of Revolutionary Council and C.-in-C. of Armed Forces July 63; Prime Minister Nov. 63-May 64, Oct. 64-Sept. 65; Chair. of Presidency Council 65-66; sentenced to death in absentia Aug. 71; living in exile.

Hafstein, Jóhann; Icelandic politician; b. 19 Sept. 1915; ed. Univ. of Iceland.
Law studies in England 38-39; Man., later Gen. Man., Independence Party 39-52; Gen. Man. Fisheries Bank of Iceland 52-63; Town Councillor, Reykjavík 46-58; mem. Althing 46-; Minister of Justice and Industry 63-70; Prime Minister July 70-71; Leader, Independence Party until 73.
Sjálfstaedisflokkurinn, Laufásvegi 46, Reykjavík, Iceland.

Haftmann, Werner, DR. PHIL.; German art historian and writer; b. 28 April 1912, Glowno; ed. Univs. of Berlin and Göttingen.
First Asst. Inst. of History of Art, Florence 35-40; Dozent in Art History, State High School for Fine Arts, Hamburg 51-55; Freelance writer 56-66; Dir. Nat. Gallery, Berlin 67-; Lessing Prize, City of Hamburg 62; Goethe-Plakette (Hesse) 64; Reuter-Plakette (Berlin) 74.
Publs. Das italienische Säulenmonument 39, Paul Klee Wege bildnerischen Denkens 50, 61, Malerei im XX. Jahrhundert (2 vols.) 54, 56, 62, 65, Emil Nolde 58, E. W. Nay 60, Skizzenbuch: Zur Kultur der Gegenwart 61, Nolde-Ungemalte Bilder 63, Wols-Aufzeichnungen 63, Guttuso, Autobiographische Bilder 70, Marc Chagall 72, Jorge Castillo 75, Marc Chagall, Gouachen, Zeichnungen, Aquarelle 75, Hans Uhlmann 75.
Gmund a. Tegernsee, Bernöckerweg 22, Federal Republic of Germany.

Hagelstange, Rudolf; German author; b. 14 Jan. 1912, Nordhausen/Harz; s. of Wilhelm Hagelstange and Helene (née Struchmann); m. Karola Dittel 1939; two s. three d.; ed. Humanistisches Gymnasium, Nordhausen.
Journalist 35-40; war corresp. 40-45; professional author 45-; mem. Munich Bavarian Acad., Darmstadt Acad. of Speech and Poetry; mem. PEN; German Critics' Prize 52; German Schiller Stiftung 55; Julius Campe Prize 58; Grosses Verdienstkreuz 59; Olympic Diploma 64.
Publs. Es spannt sich der Bogen 43, Venezianisches Credo 45, 75, Strom der Zeit 48, Meersburger Elegie 50, Ballade vom verschütteten Leben 51, Zwischen Stern und Staub 53, Tragödie des Orpheus 55, Die Nymphe von Fiesole (poetry) 57, Die Nacht 54, Es steht in unserer Macht 53, How do you like America? 57, Lied der Muschel 58, Spielball der Götter 59, Nacht Mariens 59, Viel Vergnügen 60, Huldigung 60, Römisches Olympia 61, Lied der Jahre 61, Reise nach Katmandu 62, Farbiges Deutschland 62, Die Puppen in der Puppe (Eine Russlandreise) 63, Corazón (Gedichte aus Spanien) 63, Zeit für ein Lächeln, Heitere Prosa 66, Der schielende Löwe (U.S.A.) 67, Der Krak in Prag (poetry) 69, Altherren Sommer 69, Alleingang 70, Gespräche über Bäume (poetry) 71, Venus im Mars 72, Gast der Elemente (poetry) 72, Fünf Ringe (Anthology) 72, Der General und das Kind 74, Der grosse Filou 75, Reisewetter 75.
6122 Erbach, Am Schlehdorn, Federal Republic of Germany.
Telephone: 06062-2128.

Hagen, Uta Thyra; American actress; b. 12 June 1919, Göttingen, Germany; d. of Oskar F. L. Hagen and Thyra Leisner; m. 1st José V. Ferrer 1938, 2nd Herbert Berghof 1951; one d.; ed. Univ. of Wisconsin High School, Royal Acad. of Dramatic Art, London, and Univ. of Wisconsin.
Debut as Ophelia in Hamlet, Dennis, Mass. 37; Teacher (and Co-Founder) Herbert Berghof Studio (School of Acting) 47-.
Leisure interests: gardening, cooking, needlework.
Plays acted in include: The Seagull, Arms and the Man, The Latitude of Love, The Happiest Days, Key Largo, Othello, The Master Builder, Angel Street, A Streetcar Named Desire, The Country Girl, Saint Joan, Tovarich, In Any Language, The Lady's not for Burning, The Deep Blue Sea, Cyprienne, A Month in the Country, The Good Woman of Setzuan, The Affairs of Anatol, The Queen and the Rebels, Who's Afraid of Virginia Woolf?, The Cherry Orchard, The Other 72.
Publ. Respect for Acting 73.
Herbert Berghof Studio, 120 Bank Street, New York City, N.Y., U.S.A.

Hager, Kurt; German politician; b. 10 Aug. 1912; ed. Oberrealschule, Stuttgart.
Member Kommunistische Partei Deutschlands (K.P.D.) until 45, Sozialistische Einheitspartei Deutschlands (S.E.D.) 45-; fmr. journalist; fought in Spanish Civil War 37-39, Dir. of Radio Madrid; interned in U.K. in Second World War; posts in S.E.D. 45-54; Prof. of Philosophy, Humboldt Universität zu Berlin 49; mem. Central Cttee. S.E.D. 54-, Sec. for Propaganda of Central Cttee. 55-, mem. Politburo 63-, Sec. and Leader of Ideological Comm., Politburo 63-; mem. Volkskammer 58-; Vaterländischer Verdienstorden in Silber.
Sozialistische Einheitspartei Deutschlands, 102 Berlin Am Mark-Engels-Platz 2, German Democratic Republic.

Hagerty, James C.; American radio and television executive; b. 9 May 1909, Plattsburg, N.Y.; s. of James and Katharine Hagerty; m. Majorie Lucas 1932; two s.; ed. Blair Acad., New Jersey, and Columbia Univ.
Became reporter on New York Times 34; Legislative Corresp in Albany 38-43; appointed Press Sec. by Gov. Thomas E. Dewey 43; joined Eisenhower forces 52; appointed Press Sec. to Gen Eisenhower, after Eisenhower's nomination as Pres candidate, and served in that capacity during the 52 campaign and until 61; Vice-Pres. for news, American Broadcasting Co. 61-63; Vice-Pres. (Corporate Relations) American Broadcasting Companies Inc. 63-.
Leisure interests: music, ballet, golf.
American Broadcasting Companies Inc., 1330 Avenue of the Americas, New York, N.Y.; Home: 7 Rittenhouse Road, Bronxville, N.Y. 10708, U.S.A.
Telephone: LT1-7777 (Office); Deerfield 7-5424.

Hägg, Gunnar, DR. PHIL.; Swedish university professor; b. 14 Dec. 1903, Stockholm; s. of Erik and Hertha Hägg (née Trägårdh); m. Gunnel Margareta

Silfwerbrand 1934; four s. one d.; ed. Univs. of Stockholm, London and Jena.
Lecturer, Univ. of Stockholm 29-36; Prof. of Gen. and Inorganic Chem., Univ. of Uppsala 36-69; mem. Royal Swedish Acad. of Science 42, Royal Soc. of Science of Uppsala 40, Royal Physiographical Soc. of Lund 43, Royal Neths. Acad. of Science 50, Royal Danish Society of Science 56, Royal Swedish Acad. of Engineering Sciences 57, Leopoldina German Acad. of Scientists 60, Norweg. Acad. of Science 61; Vice-Pres. Int. Union of Crystallography 60; mem. Nobel Cttee. for Chemistry, Royal Swedish Acad. of Science 65, Chair. 76.
Publs. *Kemisk Reaktionslära* 40, *Die Theoretischen Grundlagen der Analytischen Chemie* 50, *Teoría de la Reacción Química* 62, *Allmän och Oorganisk kemi* 63, *General and Inorganic Chemistry* 69; and numerous works mainly dealing with X-ray crystallography and its applications to inorganic chemistry.
Institute of Chemistry, The University, Uppsala; Home: Thunbergsvägen 24, Uppsala, Sweden.
Telephone: 018-139460 (Office); 018-136989 (Home).

Hägglöf, Gunnar; Swedish diplomatist; b. 15 Dec. 1904; m. Anna Folchi Vici; ed. Uppsala Univ.
Entered diplomatic service 26, served Paris, London, Moscow; Minister without Portfolio 39; led dels. to Berlin and London during 39-45 war; Minister to Belgian and Dutch Govts. 44, to Moscow 46; Perm. Del. to UN 47; Amb. to Great Britain 48-67, to France 67-71.
Publ. *Diplomat* 72.
Ministry of Foreign Affairs, Stockholm, Sweden.

Hägglöf, Ingemar; Swedish diplomatist; b. 20 April 1912, Stockholm; s. of Richard Hägglöf and Sigrid (née Ryding); m. Baroness Ingegerd Beck-Friis; one s.; ed. Uppsala Univ.
Bachelor of Laws 34; joined Ministry of Foreign Affairs 34; served in London 35, Paris 36, Berlin 38, Stockholm 41, Moscow 43, Stockholm 45-49; Counsellor Embassy, Washington 49-51, Deputy Head, Commercial Dept. 51-53; Del. to OEEC, Paris 53; Council of Europe 53; EFTA, Geneva 60; Perm. Swedish Rep. to OEEC, Paris 53-61; Amb. 57-61, to OECD 61-63; Amb. to Finland 64-71, to France 71-.
Leisure interests: horses and music.
Ambassade de Suède, 17 rue Barbet de Jouy, 75 Paris 7e, France.
Telephone: 555-92-15.

Hagihara, Yusuke, DR. SC.; Japanese astronomer; b. 28 March 1897, Osaka; s. of Sutejiro Hagihara and Teru Fukuoka; m. Yuiko Fukai 1926; two s. one d.; ed. Tokyo, Cambridge, Paris, Göttingen and Harvard Univs.
Assistant, Tokyo Univ. 21, Asst. Prof. 23, Prof. of Astronomy 35-57; Rockefeller Fellowship 28-29; Harvard Observatory Research Assoc. 38; Dir. of Tokyo Astronomical Observatory 46-57 (Visiting Prof. Chicago Univ. 52), Emeritus 57; Prof. of Astronomy, Tohoku Univ. 57-60; Consultant Smithsonian Astrophysical Observatory 61-; Pres. Utsunomiya Univ. 60-64; mem. Science Council of Japan 49-59, Japan Acad. 43-; F.R.A.S. 28-; Pres. Physico-Mathematical Soc. of Japan 42; Pres. Astronomical Soc. of Japan 49-53; mem. Standing Cttee. of Int. Astronomical Union 28-, Vice-Pres. 61-68; Chair. of Comm. on Celestial Mechanics 61-68; official mem. Int. Scientific Radio Union 50-60; H.I.M. Decoration for Cultural Merit 54, Watson Medal (Nat. Acad. of Sciences of U.S.A.) 60; H. I. M. Decoration of First Rank 68; Lecturer Yale Univ. Summer Inst. on Dynamical Astronomy 60, 61, 62, 64, 65.
Leisure interests: music, Japanese ballet.
Publs. *Foundation of Celestial Mechanics I* 47, *Beyond Nebulae* 49, *General Astronomy* 55, *Astronomy* 56,

Stability in Celestial Mechanics 57, *The Stability of the Solar System* (in *The Solar System*, vol. 3, ed. Kuiper) 61, *Theories of Equilibrium Figures of a Rotating Homogeneous Fluid Mass* 70, *Celestial Mechanics* Vol. I 70, Vol. II 72, Vol. III 74, Vol. IV 75.
Himonya 6-chome, 3-7, Meguro-ku, Tokyo, Japan.
Telephone: 712-7800.

Hagman, (Erik Richard) Ragnar, LL.B.; Swedish banker; b. 14 Nov. 1908; ed. Uppsala Univ.
Began his career as a lawyer; Man. Dir. Negotiation Board of Swedish Banks 42-48, Chair. 53-57; Dir. Svenska Handelsbanken 48-57; Sec. Swedish Ironworks Commercial Asscn. 57-; Man. Dir. Swedish Iron and Steel Works' Employers' Asscn. 57-71, mem. of Board, 2nd Vice-Chair. 71-; Chair. AB Järnbruksförnödenheter; mem. Stockholm City Council; Conservative.
Järnbruksförbundet, S. Blasieholmshamnen 4A, 111 48 Stockholm C, Sweden.

Hagras, Dr. Kamal M.; Oman diplomatist; b. 15 Jan. 1927; m.; two c.; ed. Cairo, Paris and New York Univs.
Joined diplomatic service 51, served in France, then Colombia, New York, London; also in various depts. of Foreign Office; Chief of Cabinet of Under-Sec.; Amb. to France and Switzerland, Perm. Rep. to UNESCO until 75; Amb. and Perm. Rep. to UN 75-; Rockfeller Foundation Fellowship 63-65; fmr. Chair. London Diplomatic Asscn.; Oman Wissam First Class; Commdr. Légion d'Honneur.
Permanent Mission of Oman to the United Nations, 605 Third Avenue, New York, N.Y. 10016, U.S.A.
Telephone: (212) 692-0447.

Hagrup, Knut; Norwegian airline executive; b. 13 Nov. 1913, Bergen; s. of Henry Lie-Svendsen and Ebba Hagerup; m. Ester Skaugen 1945; two d.; ed. Commercial Coll. and Royal Norwegian Air Force Coll.
Chief Engineer, Norwegian Civil Aeronautics Board 45; Chief Engineer SAS 46, Vice-Pres. (Operations) 51, Vice-Pres. (Engineering) 56, Vice-Pres. (Technical and Operations) 60, Exec. Vice-Pres. (Technical and Operations) 62, Pres. 69-75; mem. IATA Exec. Cttee., Pres. IATA 74-75; mem. of Board Thai Airways Int., Linjeflyg AB; Chair. SAS Catering A/S, Scanair A/S, Transair Sweden AB, Board of Comm. on Air Transport (Int. Chamber of Commerce).
Leisure interests: golf, hunting.
Scandinavian Airlines System, P.O. Box, S-161 87 Stockholm-Bromma; Home: Slottsvägen 58, 183 52 Täby, Sweden.
Telephone: (08) 780 1000 (Office); 756-55-55 (Home).

Haguiwara, Toru; Japanese diplomatist; b. 25 May 1906, Tokyo; s. of Shuichi Haguiwara and Jun Hamao; m. Chieko Sato 1947; one s. two d.; ed. Tokyo Imperial Univ.
Entered diplomatic service 28; Chief of several sections of the Ministry of Foreign Affairs 40-46; Dir. Treaties Bureau, Ministry of Foreign Affairs 46-50; Chief of Japanese Govt. Overseas Agency Paris 50-52; Minister to France 52; Envoy and Minister to Switzerland 52, Amb. 55-57; Amb. to Canada 57-61, to France 61-67; Commr.-Gen. of Japanese Govt. for *Expo* 70 68-71; mem. OECD Group on Trade and Related Problems 71-72; Pres. XVIIth and IIIrd Extr. Conf. Gen. UNESCO 72, 73; mem. Int. Civil Service Comm. UN 74-; Adviser to Minister of Foreign Affairs 71-; consultant to several private cos. 71.
Leisure interests: literature, golf, bridge.
Publs. include two books on Diplomatic History of World War II 49, and the Peace Treaty 51.
No. 982, Hotel New Japan, Nagata-cho 2-13-8, Chiyoda-ku, Tokyo; Home: No. 502, Shinsaka 40 Apartments, Akasaka 8-10-24, Minato-Ku, Tokyo, Japan.
Telephone: 580-1387 (Office); 401-0055 (Home).

Hahn, Carl Horst, DR.RER.POL.; Austrian business executive; b. 1 July 1926, Chemnitz, Germany; m. Marisa Traina 1960; three s. one d.
Chair. of the Board, Continental Gummi-Werke AG March 73-.
Publs. *Der Schumann-Plan im besonderen Hinblick auf die deutsch-französische Stahlindustrie.*
3001 Lüdersen, Bergstrasse 6, Federal Republic of Germany.
Telephone: 05045-360.

Hahn, Erwin Louis, M.S., PH.D.; American professor of physics; b. 9 June 1921, Sharon, Pa.; s. of Israel Hahn and Mary Weiss; m. Marian Ethel Failing 1944; one s. two d.; ed. Juniata Coll. and Univ. of Illinois.
Assistant, Purdue Univ. 43-44; Research Asst., Univ. of Illinois 50; Nat. Research Council Fellow, Stanford Univ. 50-51, Instructor 51-52; Research Physicist, Watson IBM Laboratory, New York 52-55; Assoc. Columbia Univ. 52-55; Assoc. Prof. Miller Inst. for Basic Research, Berkeley 58-59, Prof. 66-67; Univ. of Calif., Berkeley 55-, Prof. of Physics 61-; mem. Nat. Acad. of Sciences, American Acad. of Arts and Sciences; Guggenheim Fellow, 61, 70; Buckley Prize 71, Int. Soc. of Magnetic Resonance Prize 71; Hon. D.Sc. Juniata Coll. 66, Purdue Univ., Indiana 75.
Leisure interests: violin, chamber music.
Publs. numerous, co-author of a book.
Department of Physics, University of California, Berkeley, Calif. 94720, U.S.A.
Telephone: 415-642-2305.

Hahnemann, Paul G.; German business executive; b. 31 Oct. 1912, Strasbourg; s. of Paul P. Hahnemann and Betty (née Orth); m. 1941; ed. Technische Hochschule, Karlsruhe and Univs. of Berlin and Heidelberg.
Former independent distributor for Opel cars, Strasbourg and Freiburg; Marketing Dir. Auto-Union 57-61; mem. Man. Board, eventually Deputy Chair., BMW (Bayerische Motorenwerke) 61-71; now independent industrial consultant; Bayerischer Verdienstorden, Grand Officer, Order of Belgian Crown, Ordine al Merito della Repubblica Italiana.
757 Baden-Baden, Brahmsstrasse 12; Home: 8000 Munich 45, Am Blütenring 76, Federal Republic of Germany.
Telephone: (089) 98-27-83.

Hahr, Henrik A. A., M.A., F.R.S.A.; Swedish broadcasting official; b. 10 Jan. 1911, Lund; s. of Prof. August Hahr and Elisabeth Larsson; m. Britt-Mari Kindahl 1938; two s. one d.; ed. Uppsala and Stockholm Univs.
Radio Reporter Swedish Broadcasting Corpn. 34-38; Foreign Corresp. (London, Brussels, Rome) *Svenska Dagbladet* 38-42; Swedish Broadcasting Corpn., Head External Relations 42-47, Programme planning 47-50, Current Affairs 50-55, Programme Dir. Sound Broadcasting 55-56, then Television 56-59, Co-ordinating Dir. Radio-TV, Dir. Int. Dept. and Asst. to Dir.-Gen. 59-64; Dir. Admin. Office and Sec.-Gen. European Broadcasting Union (E.B.U.) Geneva 64-76; mem. Swedish UNESCO Cttee. 50-64; mem. Board Swedish Inst. of Journalism 61-64; Pres. Code-of-Practice Cttee. Swedish Broadcasting Corpn. 60-64, and other Broadcasting Cttees.; Knight Nordstjärnan Order, Légion d'Honneur, Dannebrog Order, Knight Commdr. al Merito della Repubblica Italiana, and other decorations.
Leisure interest: water-colour painting.
Publs. *Vår Radio och Andras* 45, *Nordisk Radio and TV* 63.
European Broadcasting Union, 1 rue de Varembé, 1211 Geneva 20, Switzerland.
Telephone: 33-24-00.

Haidar, Mohamed Haider, LL.B.; Syrian politician; b. 1931; ed. secondary schools, Lattakia, Univ. of Damascus.

Teacher, Lattakia, Hama, Damascus 51-60; with Ministry of Agrarian Reform 60-63; Dir. Agrarian Reform Inst., Hama 63; Dir. Agrarian Reform, Damascus, Daraa, Al-Suaida 64; Dir. Legal and Admin. Affairs, Ministry of Agriculture and Agrarian Reform 65; Gov. Al-Hasakeh 66; mem. Command, Damascus Branch of Arab Socialist Ba'ath Party 67, Temporal Regional Command 70, now Regional and Nat. Commands, mem. Cen. Command Progressive Nat. Front of Syria; Deputy Prime Minister, Minister of Agriculture and Agrarian Reform, until 73; Deputy Prime Minister, Minister of Econ. Affairs Sept. 73-.
Ministry of Economic Affairs, Damascus, Syria.

Haidasz, Stanley, M.D., L.PH.; Canadian physician and politician; b. 4 March 1923, Toronto; s. of Mr. and Mrs. Peter Haidasz; m. Natalie Gugala 1950; one s. three d.; ed. St. Michael's High School, Toronto, Univ. of Ottawa and Univ. of Toronto.
Various positions in Canadian-Polish community; Pres. Toronto District Canadian Polish Congress 54-55; Nat. Chair. Canadian Polish Millenium Fund; fmr. M.P. Toronto-Trinity; M.P. Toronto-Parkdale 62-; Minister of State for Multiculturalism 72-74; Pro Merito Latvian World Fed. and other awards.
Leisure interests: reading, travel, swimming, music, theatre.
Home: 77 Sir Williams Lane, Islington, Ontario; Office: 514 Landsdowne Avenue, Toronto 5, Canada.
Telephone: 536-6604 (Office).

Haig, Gen. Alexander Meigs, Jr.; American army officer; b. 2 Dec. 1924, Phila., Pa.; s. of Alexander M. and Regina Murphy Haig; m. Patricia Fox 1950; two s. one d.; ed. U.S. Mil. Acad., Naval War Coll. and Georgetown Univ.
Joined U.S. Army 47, rising to Brig.-Gen. 69, Maj.-Gen. 72, Gen. 73; Deputy Special Asst. to Sec. and Deputy Sec. of Defence 64-65; Battalion and Brigade Commdr. 1st Infantry Div., Repub. of Viet-Nam 66-67; Regimental Commdr. and Deputy Commdt. U.S. Mil. Acad. 67-69; Senior Mil. Adviser to Asst. to Pres. for Nat. Security Affairs, the White House 69-70; Deputy Asst. to Pres. for Nat. Security Affairs 70-73; Vice-Chief of Staff, U.S. Army Jan.-July 73; special emissary to Viet-Nam Jan. 73; retd. from U.S. Army Aug. 73; Asst. to Pres. and White House Chief of Staff Aug. 73-Oct. 74; recalled to active duty, U.S. Army Oct. 74; Commdr.-in-Chief, U.S. European Command Nov. 74-; Supreme Allied Commdr. Europe, NATO Dec. 74-; numerous medals and awards.
Leisure interests: tennis, golf, squash, horse-riding.
Supreme Headquarters Allied Powers Europe, Casteau; 32 Chaussee de Binche, B.7000 Mons, Belgium.

Hailey, Arthur; Canadian author; b. 5 April 1920, Luton, Beds.; s. of George and Elsie Hailey (née Wright); m. Sheila Dunlop 1951; one s. two d. and three s. by previous marriage.
Leisure interests: reading, music, fishing, swimming, wine.
Publs. books: *Runway Zero Eight* (with John Castle) 58, *The Final Diagnosis* 59, *In High Places* 62, *Hotel* 65, *Airport* 68, *Wheels* 71, *The Moneychangers* 75; collected plays: *Close-Up* 60.
Films: *Zero Hour, Time Lock, The Young Doctors, Hotel, Airport, The Moneychangers.*
Lyford Cay, P.O. Box N.7776, Nassau, Bahamas; c/o Michael Joseph Ltd., 52 Bedford Square, London, W.C.1, England.

Hailsham of St. Marylebone, Baron (Life Peer), cr. 70, of Herstmonceux in the County of Sussex; **Quintin McGarel Hogg,** P.C., C.H., F.R.S., D.C.L., LL.D.; British politician; b. 9 Oct. 1907, London; s. of Douglas McGarel Hogg, 1st Viscount Hailsham and Elizabeth Brown; m. Mary Evelyn Martin 1944; two s. three d.; ed. Eton and Christ Church, Oxford.

Fellow, All Souls Coll., Oxford 31-38, 61-; Barrister, Lincoln's Inn 32, Bencher 56, Treas. 75; Q.C. 53; M.P. 38-50, 63-70; mem. House of Lords 50-63; served war 39-45; Parl. Under-Sec. to Air Ministry 45; First Lord of Admiralty 56-57; Minister of Educ. 57; Lord Pres. of Council 57-59, 60-64; Chair. Conservative Party 57-59; Lord Privy Seal 59-60; Minister for Science and Technology 59-64; Sec. of State for Education and Science 64; Minister responsible for dealing with unemployment in the North East 63-64; Leader of House of Lords 60-63, disclaimed title of 2nd Viscount Hailsham Nov. 63; Lord Chancellor 70-74; Rector, Glasgow Univ. 59-62.
Publs. *The Law of Arbitration* 35, *One Year's Work* 44, *The Law and Employer's Liability* 44, *The Times We Live In* 44, *Making Peace* 45, *The Left was never right* 45, *The Purpose of Parliament* 46, *The Case for Conservatism* 47, *The Law Relating to Monopolies, Restrictive Trade Practices and Resale Price Maintenance* 56, *The Conservative Case* 59, *Interdependence* 61, *Science and Politics* 63, *The Devil's Own Song* 68, *The Door Wherein I Went* 75.
The House of Lords, London, SW1A 0PW; and The Corner House, Heathview Gardens, London, S.W.15, England.
Telephone: 01-788 2256.

Hainworth, Henry Charles, C.M.G.; British diplomatist (retd.); b. 12 Sept. 1914, Tampico, Mexico; s. of Charles Samuel Hainworth and Emily Laycock; m. Mary Ady 1944; two d.; ed. Blundells School and Cambridge Univ. British Consular Service, Tokyo 39; Ministry of Information, New Delhi 42-46; service in Tokyo, London, Bucharest, Paris, Nicosia 46-57; Head of Atomic Energy and Disarmament Dept., Foreign Office 58-61; Del. Sec. for Negotiating with EEC, Brussels 61-63; Minister Counsellor and H.M. Consul-Gen., British Embassy, Vienna 63-68; Amb. to Indonesia 68-70; Amb. and Perm. U.K. Del. to Disarmament Conf., Geneva 71-74.
c/o Barclays Bank Ltd., 50 Jewry Street, Winchester, Hants., England.

Haise, Fred W. Jr.; American astronaut; b. 14 Nov. 1933, Biloxi, Miss.; m. Mary Griffin Grant; two s. one d.; ed. Univ. of Oklahoma.
Joined U.S. Navy 52, served as U.S. Marine Corps fighter pilot 54-56; fighter-interceptor pilot, Oklahoma Air Nat. Guard; Research pilot, NASA Lewis Research Center, Cleveland, Ohio 59-63; graduated from Aerospace Research Pilot School 64; Research pilot, NASA Flight Research Center, Edwards, Calif. until 66; selected as astronaut by NASA 66; mem. of crew of *Apollo XIII*, April 70; Backup Commdr. *Apollo XVI* March 72; Medal of Freedom 70.
NASA Johnson Space Center, Houston, Tex. 77058, U.S.A.

Haissinsky, Moïse; French physico-chemist; b. 4 Nov. 1898; ed. Univ. degli Studi, Rome.
Chemical Industry, Paris 28-30; with Laboratoire Curie 30-, scholar 30-35; Research Asst. Centre national de la Recherche Scientifique (C.N.R.S.) 35-45, Researcher C.N.R.S. 45-55, Research Dir. 55-58, Scientific Dir. 62-; Assoc. Prof. Sorbonne 58-59, Prof. Radio Chemistry 59-62; Hon. mem. Accad. Ligure di Scienze e Lettere, Genoa 61; Prix Hébert, Acad. des Sciences, Paris 38.
Publs. *Atomistique moderne et la chimie* 32, *La Chimie nucléaire et ses applications* 57, *Dictionnaire de radiochimie* 65, and nearly 300 papers on Radio Chemistry, Inorganic Chemistry, etc.
Laboratoire Curie, 11 rue Pierre et Marie Curie, 75 Paris 5e; Home: 31 rue de Lycée, 92 Sceaux, France.
Telephone: 633-0871.

Hait, James (Merritt), M.E.; American engineer and business executive; b. 19 April 1906, Brooklyn, N.Y.; m. Ruth Hazel Jesmier 1931; two s.; ed. Rensselaer Polytechnical Inst.

Chief Engineer, Peerless Pump Div., Los Angeles 28-42 Man. and Chief Engineer, Procurement and Engineering Div., Food Machinery Corpn., Los Angeles 42-46; Vice-Pres. and Dir. of Engineering, Food Machinery and Chemical Corpn. 46-60, Head, Ordnance Div. 51-60, Dir. 52-, Exec. Vice-Pres. 56-60, Pres. 60-66, Chair. FMC Corpn. (fmrly. Food Machinery and Chemical Corpn.) 66-71; mem. and official of many orgs.; Hon. Dr. Eng. Rensselaer Polytechnical Inst.
Leisure interests: hunting, fishing.
1105 Coleman, San José, Calif. 95106; Home: 11199 Canon Vista Drive, San José, Calif. 95127, U.S.A.
Telephone: 408-258-5743.

Haithem, Muhammad Ali; Yemeni politician; b. 1940, Dathina, Southern Arabia.
Formerly school teacher; Minister of Interior 67; mem. Presidential Council of S. Yemen 69-71; Chair. Council of Ministers 69-71; mem. Nat. Front Gen. Command.
Aden, People's Democratic Republic of Yemen.

Haitink, Bernard; Netherlands conductor; b. 4 March 1929, Amsterdam.
Originally an orchestral violinist; Conductor Netherlands Radio Philharmonic Orchestra 55-61; appeared regularly as Guest Conductor for Concertgebouw Orchestra, Amsterdam 56-61, Joint Conductor 61-64, sole Musical Dir. 64-; Principal Conductor London Philharmonic Orchestra 67-, Artistic Dir. 70-; tours with Concertgebouw in Europe, N. and S. America, Japan, with London Philharmonic in Europe, Japan, U.S.A.; Guest Conductor Los Angeles Philharmonic, Boston Symphony, Cleveland, Berlin Philharmonic, Vienna Philharmonic and other orchestras; conducted operas by Mozart and Wagner for Netherlands Opera, by Mozart for Glyndebourne Festival Opera; records for Philips; Royal Order of Orange-Nassau (Netherlands) 69, Medal of Honour, Bruckner Soc. of America 70, Hon. mem. Int. Gustav Mahler Soc., Gold Medal 71, Chevalier, Ordre des Arts et des Lettres (France) 72, Hon. mem. R.A.M. 73.
London Philharmonic Orchestra, 53 Welbeck Street, London, W1M 7HE, England.

Hájek, Jiří, D.SC.; Czechoslovak diplomatist and politician; b. 6 June 1913, Krhanice; ed. Charles Univ., Prague.
Imprisoned 39-45; Lecturer, Coll. of Political and Social Science, Prague 47-48, Prof. 48-52; Prof. of Int. Relations, Charles Univ. 52-55; Deputy to Nat. Assembly 45-54, Chair. Foreign Relations Cttee. 52-54; Ambassador to U.K. 55-58; Dep. Minister of Foreign Affairs 58-62; Perm. Rep. to UN 62-65; Minister of Educ. and Culture 65-67, Minister of Educ. 67-68, Minister of Foreign Affairs April-Sept. 68; mem. Central Cttee. C.P. of Czechoslovakia 48-69, Ideological Comm. Central Cttee. C.P. of Czechoslovakia 66-68; Corresp. mem. Czechoslovak Acad. of Sciences 65-; Dir. Inst. of Political Science, Czechoslovak Acad. of Sciences 69; scientific worker, Inst. of State and Law, Czechoslovak Acad. of Sciences 70-; Order of the Repub. 61; Klement Gottwald Order 68.
c/o Czechoslovak Academy of Sciences, Národní tř. 3, Prague 1, Czechoslovakia.

Hajri, Qadi Abdullah Ahmad al-; Yemeni politician; b. 15 Sept. 1919, Hijrat Aldhari, Yarim; s. of Ahmad and Mimonah Hajri; m. 1936; six s. five d.
Minister of Educ., Health and Communication before revolution 62; Amb. of Yemen Arab Rep. to Kuwait 70-72; mem. Pres. Council June 72-June 74; Prime Minister Dec. 72-Feb. 74.
Leisure interest: reading (world political news, scientific books).
c/o Presidential Palace, Sana'a, Yemen Arab Republic.
Telephone: 2286.

Hakim, George, M.A., L. EN D.; Lebanese diplomatist; b. 19 April 1913, Tripoli; s. of John Hakim and Victoria Antakli; m. Laura Zarbock 1951; one s. one d.; ed. American Univ., Beirut, and Univ. of St. Joseph. Appointed Adjunct Prof. of Economics, American Univ.; Beirut 43; mem. of several advisory govt. cttees. on economic and financial questions 42-46; appointed alternate del. of Lebanon to Economic and Social Council of U.N. 46; Chief Del. 49; Counsellor Lebanese Legation, Washington, D.C. 46-52; Chargé d'Affaires 48 and 51; apptd. by Pres. of Republic of Lebanon as Minister of Finance, of Nat. Economy and of Agriculture 52-53; Minister of Foreign Affairs and of Economy 53; Deputy Sec.-Gen. Ministry of Foreign Affairs Mar.-July 55; Minister to German Fed. Republic July 55-58; concurrently Minister of Nat. Economy Mar.-June 56; represented Lebanon at numerous int. confs.; Board of Govs. of the Int. Bank for Reconstruction and Development and the Int. Monetary Fund 47-50; Vice-Chair. Economic and Financial Cttee., U.N. 49; Chair. Group of Experts on economic development of under-developed countries, apptd. by Sec.-Gen. of U.N. Feb.-May 51; Ambassador to German Fed. Republic 58; Perm. Rep. to UN 59-65; Minister of Foreign Affairs 65-67; Vice-Pres. American Univ. of Beirut. 68-.
Leisure interests: reading, travelling, swimming.
American University of Beirut, Beirut, Lebanon.
Telephone: 340740, Ext. 2231/2230.

Hakim, Tewfik al-; Egyptian writer; b. 1902.
Leading playwright; mem. Acad. of the Arabic Language, Higher Council of the Arts, etc.
Publs. *The Confused Sultan* 59, *Scheherezade, Pygmalion, The Cave-Dweller, You Who are Climbing the Tree* 63, *A Magistrate's Diary, Solomon the Wise, Bird of Lebanon, Fate of a Cockroach* 72.
c/o Al-Ahram, Shalia Lal-Galaa, Cairo, Egypt.

Haksar, Ajit Narain, B.A., M.B.A.; Indian business executive; b. 11 Jan. 1925, Gwalior, Madhya Pradesh; s. of Iqbal Narain Haksar and Shyampati Mulla; m. Madhuri Sapru 1948; one s. one d.; ed. Allahabad and Harvard Univs.
Training period with J. Walter Thompson Co., N.Y. 46-48; joined India Tobacco Co. Ltd. (frmly. The Imperial Tobacco Co. of India Ltd.) as Asst. Marketing 48; on secondment to British-American Tobacco Co. Ltd., London 48-50; Marketing Dir. Board of India Tobacco 66, Deputy Chair. 68, Chair. 69-; Chair. Local Board, Indian Leaf Tobacco Devt. Co. Ltd.; Chair. Board of Govs. Indian Inst. of Technology; Gov. Indian Inst of Management; Non.-Exec. Chair. Webstar Ltd.; Dir. Reserve Bank of India and Industrial Devt. Bank of India; mem. Court of Govs., Admin. Staff Coll. of India, Hyderabad, Calcutta and Doon School, Dehra Dun; non-official mem. Special Cttee. Civil Supplies, State Advisory Cttee. for Territorial Army (W. Bengal); Past Pres. Bengal Chamber of Commerce and Industry.
Leisure interest: golf.
Office: 37 Chowringhee, Calcutta 700016; Home: 24B Raja Santosh Road, Calcutta 700027, India.
Telephone: 24-8141 (Office); 45-7696 (Home).

Halaby, Najeeb E., A.B., LL.B.; American lawyer, government official and executive; b. 19 Nov. 1915, Dallas, Tex.; s. of Najeeb E. and Laura Wilkins Halaby; m. Doris Carlquist 1946; one s. two d.; ed. Stanford Univ., Michigan Law School and Yale Univ. Law School.
Served as test pilot, U.S. Navy, Second World War; admitted to California Bar 40, law practice Los Angeles 40-42, admitted to Dist. of Columbia Bar 48; Foreign Affairs Adviser to Sec. of Defense 48-53, Deputy Asst. Sec. of Defense 52-54; with L. S. Rockefeller and Bros. 53-56; Vice-Pres. Servomechanisms Inc. 56-58, Exec.

Vice-Pres. and Dir. 59-61; Sec.-Treas. The Aerospace Corpn. 59-61; Pres. Amer. Technology Corpn.; Administrator, Fed. Aviation Agency 61-65; Senior Vice-Pres. and Dir. Pan American World Airways 65-68, Pres. 68-72, Chief Exec. Officer 69-72; Pres. Halaby Int. Co. 73-; Vice-Chair. World Banking Co. (Luxembourg); Dir. Bank America Corpn., Chrysler Corpn., Atkins & Merrill Corpn., Menlo Financial Corpn., World Banking Co. (Lux.); admitted to New York Bar 73, present practice in New York; Trustee, Stanford Univ., Aspen Inst. of Humanistic Studies, Asia Soc., Amer. Univ. of Beirut, Eisenhower Fellowships, Int. Exec. Service Corps, UN Asscn.; Vice-Chair. Business Council for Int. Understanding; Democrat.
Leisure interests: golf, tennis, flying, skiing.
1120 Fifth Avenue, New York, N.Y. 10028, U.S.A.

Halbritter, Walter; German economist and politician; b. 1928; m.; three c.
Joined Sozialistische Einheitspartei Deutschlands (SED) 46, mem. Cen. Cttee. 67-, Cand. mem. Politburo 67-; Minister and Chair. Price Office.
102 Berlin, Am Marx-Engels-Platz 2, German Democratic Republic.

Hale, John Rigby, M.A., F.S.A., F.R.HIST.S.; British historian; b. 17 Sept. 1923, Ashford, Kent; s. of Dr. E. R. S. Hale and Hilda Birks; m. 1st Rosalind Williams 1953, one s. two d.; m. 2nd Sheila Haynes 1965, one s.; ed. Jesus Coll., Oxford, Johns Hopkins and Harvard Univs.
Fellow and Tutor in Modern History, Jesus Coll., Oxford 49-64; Visiting Prof. Cornell Univ. 59; Prof. of History, Univ. of Warwick 64-69; Prof. of Italian, Univ. Coll., London 70-; Visiting Prof. Univ. of Calif., Berkeley; Chair. British Soc. for Renaissance Studies 73-, Trustees of the Nat. Gallery, London 74-; Socio Straniero, Accademia Arcadia (Rome) 72.
Leisure interest: Venice.
Publs. *England and the Italian Renaissance* 54, *The Italian Journal of Samuel Rogers* 56, *Machiavelli and Renaissance Italy* 61, *The Literary Works of Machiavelli* 61, *The Evolution of British Historiography* 64, Ed. *Certain Discourses Military by Sir John Smythe* 64, *Renaissance Europe 1480-1520* 71, Ed. *Renaissance Venice* 73.
Department of Italian, University College, Gower Street, London, W.C.1; Home: 26 Montpelier Row, Twickenham, Middlesex, England.
Telephone: 01-387-7050 (Office); 892-9636 (Home).

Halefoğlu, Vahit M., K.C.V.O., M.A.; Turkish diplomatist; b. 19 Nov. 1919, Antakya; s. of Mesrur and Samiye Halefoğlu; m. Zehra Bereket 1951; one s. one d.; ed. Antakya Coll. and Univ. of Ankara.
Turkish Foreign Service 43-, served Vienna, Moscow, Ministry of Foreign Affairs, London 46-59; Dir.-Gen., First Political Dept., Ministry of Foreign Affairs 59-62; Ambassador to Lebanon 62-65, concurrently accred. to Kuwait 64-65, Amb. to U.S.S.R. 65-66, to Netherlands 66-70; Deputy Sec.-Gen. of Political Affairs, Ministry of Foreign Affairs Dec. 70-Feb. 72; Amb. to Fed. Repub. of Germany 72-; Lebanese, Greek, Italian, German, Spanish, Finnish and British decorations.
Leisure interests: literature, music, walking, swimming.
Turkish Embassy, 53 Bonn-Bad Godesberg, Utestrasse 47, Federal Republic of Germany.

Haley, John C., B.A., M.S.; American banker; b. 24 July 1929, Akron, Ohio; s. of Arthur Reed Haley and Kathryn Moore; m. Rheba Hopkins 1951; two s. two d.; ed. Miami and Columbia Univs.
Assistant Treas., Chase Manhattan Bank N.A. 59, Second Vice-Pres. 62, Vice-Pres. 64, Senior Vice-Pres. 71; Chief Exec. Orion Banking Group 70-73; Exec. Vice-Pres. Corporate Banking Dept., Chase Manhattan Bank N.A. 73-, mem. Management Cttee. 74.

Chase Manhattan Corpn. Banking Service, I Chase Manhattan Plaza, N.Y. 10015; Home: 146 Lambert Road, New Canaan, Conn. 06840, U.S.A.
Telephone: 203 966-5904 (Home).

Haley, Sir William John, K.C.M.G., LL.D., F.R.S.L.; British journalist and administrator; b. 24 May 1901, Jersey, Channel Islands; s. of Frank Haley and Marie Sangan; m. Susan Gibbons 1921; two s. two d.; ed. Victoria Coll., Jersey.
Joint Man. Dir. *Manchester Guardian* and *Evening News* Ltd. 39-43; Dir. Reuters and Press Asscn. 39-43; Editor-in-Chief BBC 43-44; Dir.-Gen. 44-52; Editor *The Times* 52-66; Chair. Times Newspapers Ltd. 67; Editor-in-Chief *Encyclopaedia Britannica* 68-April 69; Chair. Barclay-Trust, Channel Islands 70-; Commr. of Appeal for Income Tax, Jersey; Chevalier, Légion d'Honneur; Grand Officer, Order of Orange-Nassau.
Leisure interest: reading.
Beau Site, Gorey, Jersey, Channel Islands.

Halkin, Shimon, B.A., M.A., D.H.L.; Israeli author and educationist; b. 30 Oct. 1899, Dovsk, Russia; s. of Hillel and Hannah Halkin; m. Minnie Levine 1933; one s. one d.; ed. N.Y. City Coll., Chicago, New York and Columbia Univs.
Instructor in Hebrew and Hebrew Literature, Hebrew Union Coll. School for Teachers, New York City 24-32; Teacher, Geulah High School, Tel-Aviv 32-39; Lecturer in Bible, Jewish Sociology and Modern Hebrew Literature, Chicago Coll. of Jewish Studies 40-43; Prof. of Hebrew Literature, Jewish Inst. of Religion, New York City 43-49; Prof. of Hebrew Literature, Hebrew Univ. of Jerusalem 49-70; Visiting Prof. Univ. of Calif. 54-55, Jewish Theological Seminary, New York 65-66; Prof. Emer. Hebrew Univ. of Jerusalem 69; mem. Acad. of Hebrew Language; Pres. Israel PEN Club; Tchernichovsky Prize for translation of Whitman 53, Bialik Prize for Literature 68.
Leisure interests: music, reading.
Publs. *An Ethical Philosophy of Life* 28, *Hebrew Literature in Palestine* 42, *Modern Hebrew Literature: Trends and Values* 51, *La Littérature Hébraïque Moderne* 57, *Literatura Hebrea Moderna* 68; *In Hebrew: Yehiel Ha-Hagri* 28, *Arai Va-Keva* 42, *Ad-Mashber* 45, *Yehudim ve Yahadut Be-America* 46, *Walt Whitman* 54, *Mavo La Sipporet Ha Ivrit* 53, *Collected Literary Essays and Studies* (3 vols.) 71, *Adrift, Collected Short Stories* 73; Poems: *Al Ha-Iy* (collected poems) 43, *Ma'avar Yabok* (collected poems) 65; numerous translations into Hebrew.
5 Redak Street, Jerusalem, Israel.
Telephone: Jerusalem 3-3069.

Hall, Sir Arnold Alexander, Kt., M.A., F.R.S., D.ENG., D.SC., C.ENG.; British aviation and electrical engineer and administrator; b. 23 April 1915, Liverpool; s. of Robert Alexander Hall; m. Moira Constance Dione Sykes 1946; three d.; ed. Alsop High School, Liverpool and Clare Coll., Cambridge.
Research Fellow in Aeronautics of Company of Armourers and Braziers 36-38; Royal Aircraft Establishment, Farnborough 38-45; Zaharoff Prof. of Aviation, Univ. of London 45-51; Dir. Royal Aircraft Establishment, Farnborough 51-55; Dir. Hawker Siddeley Group Ltd. 55-, Lloyds Bank Ltd. 66-; Man. Dir. Bristol Siddeley Engines Ltd. 58-63; Vice-Chair. and Man. Dir. Hawker Siddeley Group Ltd. 63-67, Chair. and Man. Dir. 67-; Pro-Chancellor, Univ. of Warwick 64-70; mem. Advisory Council on Technology (Ministry of Technology) 64; Electricity Supply Research Council 64-71; Pres. British Electrical and Allied Manufacturers' Asscn. March 67-68; Dir. Phoenix Assurance Co. Ltd. 69-, Imperial Chemical Industries Ltd. 70-; Chair. Industrial Policy Group 71-74; Vice-Pres. Soc. British Aerospace Cos. Ltd. 71-72, Pres. 72-73; Fellow, Imperial Coll. of Science and Technology,

Clare Coll., Cambridge; Hon. F.R.Ae.S., Hon. F.A.I.A.A., Hon. A.C.G.I., Hon. F.I.Mech.E., Hon. F.I.E.E.
Leisure interest: sailing.
Hawker Siddeley Group Ltd., 18 St. James's Square, London, S.W.1, England.

Hall, Colin Arthur, B.A., LL..B; South African business executive; b. 16 Nov. 1938, Pretoria; m.; one s.; ed. Univs. of Pretoria and S.A.
Official learner on gold mines 55; Articled Clerk, Pretoria law firm 56-61; joined S.A. Breweries as Management Trainee 61, and became successively Acting Estates Man., Isando Offices, Asst. to the Property Man., Estate Man. Isando, Man. SABRE Management Services (Pty.) Ltd., and Gen. Man. Beer Div., Natal; Gen. Man. Beer Div. 69-73; Group Gen. Man. S.A. Breweries 73-.
Leisure interests: squash, golf, gardening.
The South African Breweries Ltd., P.O. Box 1099, 2 Jan Smuts Avenue, Johannesburg, South Africa.

Hall, David, LL.B.; American lawyer and politician; b. 20 Oct. 1930, Oklahoma City; m. Jo Evans Hall; one s. two d.; ed. Classen High School, Univs. of Okla. and Tulsa.
Assistant County Attorney 59-62, County Attorney of Tulsa County 62-66; Prof. of Law Univ. of Tulsa 68; Gov. of Okla. 71-74; indicted and convicted by Fed. Jury March 75; Democrat.
c/o Office of the Governor, Oklahoma City, Okla., U.S.A.

Hall, Floyd D., B.S.; American airline executive; b. 4 April 1916, Lamar, Colo.; s. of Weldon H. Hall and Hattie Brown; m. 1st Mary Feild 1939, two d.; m. 2nd Kimathea Rand Griffis 1973; ed. Univs. of Colorado, Michigan and California (L.A.).
General Man. U.S. Operations, Trans-World Airlines Inc. 57-58, Gen. Man. System Flight Operations 58-59, Vice-Pres. Flight Operations 59, Vice-Pres. and Gen. Transportation Man. 59-61, Senior Vice-Pres. and System Gen. Man. 61-63; Pres. and Chief Exec. Officer, Dir. Eastern Air Lines Inc. Dec. 63-67, Chair. and Chief Exec. Officer 68-.
Eastern Air Lines Inc., 10 Rockefeller Plaza, New York, N.Y. 10020 and Miami International Airport, Miami, Fla. 33148; Home: 35 Sutton Place, New York, N.Y. 10022; and 200 Ocean Lane Drive, Island House, Key Biscayne, Fla. 331419, U.S.A.

Hall, John Goodale; American mining executive; b. 17 Jan. 1917, Omaha, Neb.; s. of the late Arthur E. and Cora Price Hall; m. Dorothy Graham Hall 1940; one s.; ed. School of Mines, Univ. of Utah.
With United States Smelting Refining & Mining Co., Utah 36-46; Gen. Supt., Chief Consolidated Mining Co., Eureka, Utah 46-52; Asst. Plant Man., later Plant Man., Nat. Lead Co., Tahawus, N.Y. 52-65; Asst. to Vice-Pres., New Mines Dept., Anaconda Co., New York 65, Asst. Vice-Pres., Mining 66, Vice-Pres. 67, Pres. 69-71, Vice-Chair. 71; mem. Amer. Inst. of Mining, Metallurgical and Petroleum Engineers, Mining and Metallurgical Soc. of America, Mining Club, New York Amer. Management Asscn.
161 East 42nd Street, New York, N.Y. 10017; Home: 14 Bonnie Heights Road, Manhasset, N.Y. 11030, U.S.A.
Telephone: 516-627-8648.

Hall, Joseph Bates, PH.B.; American business executive; b. 13 July 1899, Harvey, Ill.; m. Mildred E. Wessel; two s. one d.; ed. Univ. of Chicago.
Bookkeeper, Morris & Co., Chicago 21-22; Gordon Strong & Co., Real Estate, Chicago; Pres. Hamilton Bond & Mortgage Co., Chicago, Exec. Sec. Chicago Mortgage Bankers' Asscn., and Asst. Man. Real Estate Dept., Continental-Ill. Bank & Trust Co., Chicago 28; Gen.

Man. Real Estate Dept., The Kroger Co. 31, Man. St.
Louis Branch 35, Eastern Div. Man. 37, Vice-Pres.
Manufacturing) 42, Treas. 43, Exec. Vice-Pres. 44,
res. 46-62, Chair. 62-65; fmr. Dir. Armco Steel Corpn.,
Goodyear Tire and Rubber Co.; Dir. Emer. Cincinnati
ell Telephone Co., Tenneco; Dir. Little Miami R.R.
o., Champion Int. Inc., Access Corpn.; Chair. 4th
District Fed. Reserve Board; Pres. Cincinnati Redevt.
orpn.; mem. Business Council.
Leisure interests: golf, symphony music.
Office: Room 2620, 511 Walnut Street, Cincinnati, O.
5202; Home: 3 Grandin Terrace, Cincinnati 8, O.,
U.S.A.
Telephone: 421-1155.

Hall, Sir Noel, M.A., A.M.; British economist and
college principal; b. 23 Dec. 1902, Cramlington; s. of
Cecil Gallopine Hall and Constance Gertrude Upcher;
m. 1st Edith Evelyn Pearl Haward 1927, 2nd Elinor
Claire Marks 1946; one s. one d.; ed. Bromsgrove
School, Brasenose Coll., Oxford, Princeton Univ.
Commonwealth Fund Fellow 25-27; Lecturer in
Political Economy and Civil Service Tutor, Univ. of
London, Univ. Coll. 27-29, Senior Lecturer 29; Prof.
f Political Economy 35-38; Sec. Fellowship Advisory
Cttee. Rockefeller Foundation for Social Sciences
in Great Britain and Ireland 30-36; Dir. Nat. Inst.
o Economics and Social Research 38-43; Joint Dir.
Ministry of Economic Warfare 40-41; Minister attached
of Embassy Washington, D.C. 41-43; West African
Development Adviser 43-45; Principal Admin. Staff
Coll., Greenlands, Henley-on-Thames 46-61; Principal
Brasenose Coll. Oxford 61-73; created knight 57; New
York Univ. Medal 58; Hon. LL.D. (Lancaster) 64.
Leisure interests: golf, bridge.
Publs. *The Economist in the Witness Box* (with Stephen
King-Hall) 33, *The Exchange Equalisation Account* 35,
The Making of Executives, The Modern Challenge 58.
Homer End, Ipsden, Oxon., England.
Telephone: Checkendon 294.

Hall, Peter Reginald Frederick, C.B.E., M.A.; British
theatre, opera and film director; b. 22 Nov. 1930, Bury
St. Edmunds, Suffolk; s. of Reginald and Grace Hall; m.
1st Leslie Caron 1956 (dissolved 1965), one s. one d.;
2nd Jacqueline Taylor 1965, one s. one d.; ed. Perse
School and St. Catharine's Coll., Cambridge.
Produced and acted in over 20 plays at Cambridge; first
professional production Windsor 53; produced in
repertory at Windsor, Worthing and Oxford Playhouse; two Shakespearean productions for Arts
Council; Artistic Dir. Elizabethan Theatre Co. 53; Asst.
Dir. London Arts Theatre 54, Dir. 55-56; formed own
producing co., Int. Playwright's Theatre 57; Man. Dir.
Royal Shakespeare Theatre, Stratford-on-Avon and
Aldwych Theatre, London 60-68; mem. Arts Council
69-72; Co-Dir., Nat. Theatre with Lord Olivier (q.v.)
April-Nov. 73, Dir. Nov. 73-; Assoc. Prof. of Drama,
Warwick Univ. 66-; Chevalier Ordre des Arts et Lettres
65; London Theatre Critics' Award for Best Dir. for
The Wars of the Roses 63, *The Homecoming* and *Hamlet*
65; Antoinette Perry Award for Best Dir. for *The Home-
coming* 66; Hamburg Univ. Shakespeare Prize 67; Dr.
h.c. (Univs. of York 66, Reading 73, Liverpool 74).
Leisure interest: music.
Productions: *Blood Wedding, Immoralist, The Lesson,
South, Mourning Becomes Electra, Waiting for Godot,
The Burnt Flowerbed, Waltz of the Toreadors, Camino
Real, Gigi, Wrong Side of the Park, Love's Labours Lost,
Cymbeline, Twelfth Night, A Midsummer Night's Dream,
Coriolanus, Two Gentlemen of Verona, Troilus and
Cressida, Ondine, Romeo and Juliet, Becket, The Collec-
tion, Cat on a Hot Tin Roof, The Rope Dancers* (on
Broadway), *The Moon and Sixpence* (opera), *Henry
VI* (parts 1, 2 and 3), *Richard III, Richard II, Henry
IV* (parts 1 and 2), *Henry V, Eh?, The Homecoming,*

Moses and Aaron (opera), *Hamlet, The Government
Inspector, The Magic Flute* (opera), *Staircase, Work is a
Four Letter Word* (film), *Macbeth, Midsummer Night's
Dream* (film), *Three into Two Won't Go* (film), *A
Delicate Balance, Dutch Uncle, Landscape and Silence,
Perfect Friday* (film), *The Battle of Shrivings, La Calisto*
(opera, Glyndebourne Festival 70), *The Knot Garden*
(opera) 70, *Eugene Onegin* (opera) 71, *Old Times* 71,
Tristan and Isolde (opera) 71, *All Over* 72, *Il Ritorno di
Ulysses* (opera) 72, *Alte Zeiten* (Burgtheater, *Vienna*)
72, *Via Galactica* (musical, Broadway) 72, *The Home-
coming* 73, *Marriage of Figaro* (Glyndebourne) 73,
The Tempest 74, *Landscape* (film) 74, *Akenfield* (film)
74, *No Man's Land* 75, *Happy Days* 75, *John Gabriel
Borkman* 75, *Judgement* 75, *Hamlet* 75; acted in *The
Pedestrian* (film) 73.
The Wall House, Mongewell Park, Wallingford, Berks.,
England.

Hall, (Raymond) Steele; Australian politician; b.
30 Nov. 1928, Balaklava; s. of Sydney and Stella
Hall; m. Ann W. Fletcher 1956; one s. three d.; ed.
Owen Public School and Balaklava High School.
Member South Australia House of Assembly 59-, Oppo-
sition Whip 65, Leader Opposition 66, Premier and
Minister of Industrial Devt. 68-70; Leader Opposition
70-.
Home: 377 Seaview Road, Henley Beach, South
Australia 5022, Australia.

Hall Themido, João Manuel, L. EN D.; Portuguese
diplomat; b. 6 Jan. 1924, Coimbra; s. of António
Armando Themido and Maria dos Anjos Hall Themido;
m. Lydia Pessoa de Freitas 1954; ed. Coimbra Univ.
Joined foreign service 47; Counsellor, London 59-61;
Dir.-Gen. Political Branch 61-68; Amb. to Italy 68-71;
Amb. to U.S.A. 71-; numerous decorations from Por-
tugal, Brasil, Spain, Italy, Malta and Germany.
Publ. *Portugal e o Anticolonialismo* 59.
Embassy of Portugal, 2125 Kalorama Road, Washing-
ton, D.C. 20008, U.S.A.; Home: Av. República 28-2-A,
Lisbon, Portugal.
Telephone: 265-1643 (Office).

Halleck, Charles Abraham, A.B., LL.B.; American
lawyer and politician; b. 22 Aug. 1900; ed. Indiana
Univ.
Prosecuting Attorney, Jasper-Newton Circuit, Ind. 24;
mem. U.S. House of Reps. from 2nd Ind. District (74th-
90th Congresses) 35-68; majority leader in House, 80th
and 83rd Congresses; minority leader 86th, 87th and
88th Congresses 59-64; Republican.
Rensselaer, Ind. 47978, U.S.A.

Hallgrimsson, Geir; Icelandic politician; b. 16 Dec.
1925, Reykjavík; s. of Áslaug Geirsdóttir Zöega and
Hallgrímur Benediktsson; m. Erna Finnsdóttir 1948;
two s. two d.; ed. Univ. of Iceland and Harvard Law
School.
President Nat. Union of Icelandic Students 46-47; law
practice, Dir. of H. Benediktsson 51-59; mem. Reykja-
vík City Council 54-74; Mayor of Reykjavík 59-72; alt.
mem. Parl. (Althing) 59-70, mem. 70-; mem. Cen.
Cttee. Independence Party 65-, Vice-Chair. Indepen-
dence Party 71, Chair. 73-; Prime Minister Aug. 74-;
Grand Cross, Order of the Falcon (Iceland), Grand
Cross, Order of the Polar Star (Sweden), Commdr.,
Order of St. Olav (Norway), Commdr. 1st Class, Order
of the Lion (Finland), Grand Officier, Ordre de Mérite
(Luxembourg), Commdr., Order of Dannebrog (Den-
mark).
Forsaetisráðuneytið, Reykjavík; Home: Dyngjuvegi 6,
Reykjavík, Iceland.
Telephone: 25000 (Office); 33351 (Home).

Hallowes, Odette Marie Céline, G.C., M.B.E.; British
(b. French) wartime agent; b. 28 April 1912; ed.
Convent of Ste. Thérèse, Amiens, and privately.

Worked as British agent with Special Forces in France 42-43 when captured by the Gestapo; sentenced to death 43; endured imprisonment and torture until 45 when she left Ravensbruck Concentration Camp; Vice-Pres. Mil. Medallists' League; mem. Royal Soc. of St. George; mem. Cttee. Victoria Cross and George Cross Asscn.; Pres. 282 (East Ham) Squadron, Air Training Corps; Légion d'Honneur 50; Vice-Pres. Women's Transport Services (F.A.N.Y.).
25 St. James's Place, London, SW1A 1NH, England. Telephone: 01-493-5497.

Hallpike, Charles Skinner, C.B.E., F.R.S., F.R.C.P., F.R.C.S.; British aural physician; b. 19 July 1900, Murree, India; s. of Frank Robert Hallpike and Rosamond Helen Skinner; m. Barbara Lee Anderson 1935; two s. one d. (deceased); ed. St. Paul's School, London, and Guy's Hospital, London.
Duveen Travelling Fellow, Berlin and Hamburg; Rockefeller Travelling Fellow, Baltimore and Montreal; Foulerton Research Fellow, Royal Soc. 34; mem. Scientific Staff, Medical Research Council (M.R.C.) 40; Aural Physician and Dir. of Otological Research Unit, M.R.C., Nat. Hospital, Queen Square, London 44-65; Dir. of Research, Ferens Inst. of Otology, Middlesex Hospital, London 65-68; retd. 68; recent honours include Barany Medal, Univ. of Upsala 58, Guyot Medal, Univ. of Groningen 59, Hughlings Jackson Medal, Royal Soc. of Medicine, London 67.
Leisure interests: gardening and music.
Publs. Papers on clinical otology and otoneurology and on anatomy, physiology and pathology of the ear in *Proceedings of Royal Society*, etc.
Fern Lodge, 44 Ashurst Road, West Moors, Wimborne, Dorset, BH22 0LS, England.
Telephone: Ferndown 4418.

Hallstein, Walter, DR.IUR.; German international politician; b. 17 Nov. 1901, Mainz; ed. Univs. of Bonn, Munich and Berlin.
Assistant Faculty of Law, Berlin Univ. 25; with Inst. of Foreign and Private Int. Law, Berlin 27; Asst. Prof. of Law, Berlin Univ. 29; Prof. of Rostock Univ. 30-41; Prof. Univ. of Frankfurt 41-44, Rector 46-48; Visiting Prof. Georgetown Univ., Washington 48-49; Chair. German Comm. UNESCO 49-50; led German del. to Schuman Plan Conf. 50; Sec. of State, Foreign Office 51-58; Pres. Commission of the European Economic Community (EEC) 58-67; Pres. European Movement 68-; mem. Bundestag 69-72; Dr. h.c. Georgetown Univ., Washington; Hon Doctor of Law (Univ. of Padua, Tufts Univ., Colby Coll. Maine, Adelphi Univ. New York, Harvard Univ., Nebraska Univ., Columbia Univ., Johns Hopkins Univ., and Univs. of Liège, Bradford, Sussex, Nancy, Louvain, Oviedo, Hamburg and Tübingen); Grand Cross of Merit of the Knights of Jerusalem and Vatican, Italian, Greek, Argentine, Brazilian, Icelandic, Thai, Iranian, Austrian, Peruvian, Mexican, Swedish, Chilean, Belgian, Liberian, Bolivian, Luxembourg, German, Cuban, Venezuelan, Togolese, Niger and other African decorations; Charlemagne Prize 61, Robert Schuman Prize 69.
Leisure interests: art, travelling.
Publs. *Die Aktienrechte der Gegenwart* 31, *Die Berichtigung des Gesellschaftskapitals* 42, *Wiederherstellung des Privatrechts* 46, *Wissenschaft und Politik* 48, *United Europe: Challenge and Opportunity* 62, *Der unvollendete Bundesstaat* 69, *Europe in the Making* 72.
Europa-Büro, 53 Bonn, Oelbergstr. 3; Home: 5439 Rennerod, Oberwesterwaldkreis, Federal Republic of Germany.
Telephone: 228053 (Office).

Halperin, Tulio, D.PHIL.; Argentine historian; b. 27 Oct. 1926; ed. Univ. de Buenos Aires, Ecole Pratique des Hautes Etudes, Paris.
Professor, Univ. Nac. del Litoral (Rosario, Argentina)

55-61; Prof. Univ. de Buenos Aires 59-66, Univ. Oxford 70-71, Univ. of Calif. (Berkeley) 71-; Lecture History Dept. Harvard Univ. 67-.
Publs. *El Pensamiento de Echeverría* 51, *Un Conflic Nacional: Moriscos y Cristianos Viejos en Valencia* 5 *El Río de la Plata al Comenzar el Siglo XIX* 60, *Trad ción Política Española e Ideología Revolucionaria* Mayo 61, *Historia de la Universidad de Buenos Aires* 6 *Argentina en el Callejón* 64, *Historia contemporánea América Latina* 69, *Hispanoamérica después de Independencia* 72 (in English *The Aftermath of Revol tion in Latin America* 73), *Revolución y guerra* 72 (i English *Politics, Economics and Society in Argentina i the Revolutionary Period* 75).
History Department, University of California, Berkeley Ca. 94720 U.S.A.

Halpern, Bernard, B.SC.; French professor of experi mental medicine; b. 2 Nov. 1904, Tarnos-Rude Russia; s. of Emile and Dora Halpern; m. René Nyjenholz 1932; one s. two d.; ed. Univ. de Paris.
Lecturer in Experimental Biology, Ecole Pratique de Hautes Etudes 33-36; Dir. of Research in Pharmaco logy, Rhône-Poulenc 36-45; Master of Research French Nat. Research Council 45-48, Dir. of Research 48-60; Prof., Collège de France 60-; Dir. Inst. of Immu nobiology, Broussais Hospital Medical School 60- Pres. Biological Section, Ecole Pratique des Haute Etudes 65-; mem. French Acad. of Sciences, Acad. o Medical Sciences, Rome, Royal Acad. of Medicine Belgium, Acad. of Arts and Sciences, Belgrade.
Leisure interest: horticulture.
Publs. include studies on histamine, studies and dis covery of anti-histamines; studies on mechanism o natural immunity; studies on cancer cells.
197 Boulevard Saint-Germain, Paris 7e, France.
Telephone: 548-30-72.

Halstead, Eric Henry, E.D., M.A., B.COM., F.C.A.(N.Z.), F.C.I.S.; New Zealand diplomatist, politician and company director, chartered accountant; b. 26 May 1912, Auckland; s. of Harry B. Halstead and Alma Emma Newman; m. Millicent Joan Stewart 1940; three s. one d.; ed. Auckland Grammar School, Auckland Univ. and Teachers' Training Coll.
Major N.Z.E.F., mentioned in despatches 39-45; head of Commercial and Accountancy Dept., Seddon Memorial Technical Coll. 45-49; Member of Parliament (mem. of National Party) 49-57; Minister of Social Security and Minister-in-Charge of Tourist and Health Resorts 54-56; Minister-Asst. to the Prime Minister 54-57, concurrently Minister of Industries and Com merce and of Customs 56-57; Partner Mabee, Halstead and Co.; Pres. Auckland Savings Bank; Dir. Air New Zealand Ltd.; Vice-Pres. N.Z. Inst. of Foreign Affairs 70-; Amb. to Thailand and Laos 70-73; Deputy Chair. Asian Inst. of Technology 72-74; business consultant and company dir. 74; mem. Council Univ. of Auckland 61-70, N.Z. Medical Educ. Trust 75-.
Leisure interests: tennis, golf, swimming, reading, writing.
Publs. textbooks on accounting and commercial practice; many published articles on economic, political and foreign affairs.
5 Pere Street, Remuera, Auckland, New Zealand.
Telephone: 545-083.

Halstead, Ronald, M.A., B.SC., F.R.I.C., F.B.I.M.; British food and drug company executive; b. 17 May 1927, Lancaster; s. of Richard and Bessie Harrison Halstead; m. Yvonne Cecile de Monchaux 1968; two s.; ed. Queens' Coll., Cambridge.
Research chemist H. P. Bulmer & Co. 48-53; Mfg. Man. Macleans Ltd. 54-55; Factory Man. Beecham Products Inc. (U.S.A.) 55-60; Asst. Man. Dir. Beecham Research Laboratories Ltd. 60-62, Pres. Beecham Research Labs., Inc. (U.S.A.) 62-64; Vice-Pres. Marketing,

eecham Products, Inc. (U.S.A.) 62-64; Chair. Food
d Drink Div. Beecham Group 64-67; Chair. Beecham
roducts 67-; Man. Dir. (consumer products) Beecham
roup 73-; Vice-Chair. Proprietary Asscn. of Great
ritain 68-; Gov. Ashridge Management Coll. 70-; Pres.
c. Soc. of British Advertisers 71-73; Chair. British
utrition Foundation 71-73; Vice-Chair. Advertising
sscn. 73-; Pres. Food Mfrs. Fed. 74-; Fellow Inst. of
arketing Oct. 75-; mem. Council, British Nutrition
oundation 67, CBI 70-.
eisure interests: sailing, squash racquets, skiing.
eecham Group Ltd., Beecham House, Great West
Road, Brentford, Middx.; Home: 37 Edwardes Square,
ondon, W8 6HH, England.
elephone: 01-560-5151 (Office); 01-603-9010 (Home).

Halusa, Arno; Austrian diplomatist; b. 13 Aug. 1911,
ans, Tyrol; *m.* Constance Monro 1946; one *s.* one *d.*;
d. Ecole Libre des Sciences Politiques, Paris, and
Universität Wien.
Foreign Service 33-, served in Europe, North and South
America and South East Asia 33-54; Minister to Thai-
and, Indonesia, Philippines and Cambodia 54-58;
Amb. to India and Minister to Ceylon and Nepal
8-62; Dir.-Gen. Foreign Office, Vienna 62-64; Head of
Austrian Perm. Del. to Org. for Econ. Co-operation and
Devt. (OECD) 64-68; Deputy Sec.-Gen. Ministry of
Foreign Affairs 68-72; Amb. to U.S.A. 72-.
Austrian Embassy, 2343 Massachussetts Avenue, N.W.,
Washington, D.C., U.S.A.

Halvorsen, Tor; Norwegian politician; b. 24 Nov.
1930, Skien.
Member, Cen. Board, Nat. Insurance Scheme, Fund for
Industrial Enterprises; Chair. Herøya Labour Asscn.
5-68; Instructor, Workers' Educ. League 18-69, later
Chair. of Board; Sec. Trades Union Congress 69-73;
Minister of Environment 73-74, of Social Affairs 74-76;
Labour.
c/o Ministry of Social Affairs, Oslo, Norway.

Hamada, Shoji; Japanese potter; b. 9 Dec. 1894,
Tokyo; *s.* of Kyuzo and Ai Hamada; *m.* Kazue Kimura
1924; four *s.* two *d.*; ed. Tokyo Technical Coll., Kyoto
Ceramic Experimental Inst.
Went to St. Ives, Cornwall, England to work with
Bernard Leach (*q.v.*); constructed first *noborigama* kiln
in western world 20; first one-man exhibition Paterson
Gallery, London 23; returned to Japan 24; first one-man
exhibition Japan 25; f. Japanese Folkcraft Museum
with Soetsu Yanagi and Kanjiro Kawai 36; cultural
mission to Europe with Naoya Shiga and Soetsu
Yanagi, attended Dartington Hall Int. Craft Conf.,
England 52; succeeded Soetsu Yanagi as Dir. Japan
Folkcraft Museum 62-; Japanese del. to Japan-U.S.
Cultural and Educational Conf., Wash. 63; Dir. Japan
Folkcraft Soc. 74; mem. soc. Japanese Painters (Kokuga
Kai) 25-; mem. Council for Protection of Cultural
Properties of Japan 57-; designated Holder of Intan-
gible Cultural Property ("Living National Treasure")
of Japan 55; Medal of Honour with Purple Ribbon of
Japan 64; Hon. D.F.A. Michigan State Univ. 67;
Okinawa Times Prize 68; Order of Culture of the Em-
peror of Japan 68; Hon. Citizen of Mashiko 69, and
many other awards.
Leisure interests: travelling to all parts of the world to
experience the way of life of different people, collection
of folkcrafts.
3387 Mashiko, Mashiko Machi, Haga Gun, Tochigi Ken,
Japan.
Telephone: 028572-2036.

Hamadi, Lt.-Col. Ibrahim Muhammad al-; Yemeni
army officer; b. 1943.
Joined Army 62; attended mil. coll.; in charge of
Parachute Corps; fmr. Commdr. Western and Cen.
Regions; Deputy Prime Minister for Internal Affairs

71-72; Deputy Chief of Staff 72-74; assumed Presidency
of Governing Council after mil. coup June 74-.
Presidency Council, Sana'a, Yemen Arab Republic.

Hambro, Charles Eric Alexander; British banker;
b. 24 July 1930; *s.* of late Sir Charles Hambro and
Pamela Cobbold; *m.* Rose E. Cotterell 1954; two *s.*
one *d.*; ed. Eton Coll.
Joined Hambros Bank Ltd. 52, Man. Dir. 57-65, Deputy
Chair. 65-72, Chair. March 72-; Dir. Guardian Royal
Exchange Assurance Co., Taylor Woodrow Ltd., Union
Corpn. Ltd., Slater Walker Ltd.
Leisure interests: shooting, racing, flying.
Hambros Bank Ltd., 41 Bishopsgate, London, E.C.2;
Homes: 69 Victoria Road, London, W.8; Dixton Manor,
Gotherington, Cheltenham, Glos., England.

Hambro, Edvard; Norwegian lawyer and diplomatist;
b. 22 Aug. 1911; *s.* of Carl J. Hambro and Gudrun
Grieg; *m.* Elisabeth J. Raverat 1940; two *s.* two *d.*;
ed. Oslo Univ. and in Geneva.
Secretariat, League of Nations before World War II;
Norwegian Ministry of Foreign Affairs, London 43-45;
Head, Legal Dept., UN Secr. 45-46; Registrar, Int.
Court of Justice, The Hague 46-53; Reader, then Prof.
Norwegian School of Econs., Business Admin. 53-66;
mem. Storting 61-66; Perm. Rep. of Norway to UN
66-71; Pres. UN Gen. Assembly 70-71; mem. Int. Law
Comm. of UN 72-; Perm. Rep. to UN in Geneva 73-;
mem. Perm. Court of Arbitration; Chair. Appeals'
Board, Council of Europe 67-73, EFTA Jan.-June 76;
mem. Appeals' Board, OECD; mem. Inst. of Int. Law;
Hon. mem. American Soc. of Int. Law; Hon. LL.D.
(Brandeis Columbia, Seaton Hall, Toronto, Yale Univs.,
Luther Coll., Wagner Coll.), D.Hum.Litt. (Kent State
Univ., Ohio); Commdr. Royal Norwegian Order of St.
Olav; Grand Cross of the Finnish White Rose; Grand
Cross, Mauritanian Order of Nat. Merit; Grand Cross,
Moroccan Ouissam Alaouite Order; Peace Medal (Gold
Medal) of UN; Grand Cross Order of the Star of Yugo-
slavia.
Leisure interests: reading, walking.
Publs. include *Case Law of the International Court* Vols.
I-V (Vol. V with Prof. Arthur W. Rovine) 68, Vol. VI
72, Vol. VII 74, *The Charter of the United Nations* (with
Goodrich and Simons) 3rd edn. 69.
58 rue de Moillebeau, Geneva; Home: 149D, route de
Ferney, 1218 Grand Saconnex, Geneva, Switzerland;
and Gimle terr. 1, Oslo, Norway.
Telephone: 34-97-30 (Office); 33-76-16 (Home); 56-58-55
(Oslo).

Hambro, Jocelyn Olaf, M.C.; British banker; b.
7 March 1919; ed. Eton and Trinity Coll., Cambridge.
In Coldstream Guards 39-45; with Hambros Bank Ltd.
45-, Man. Dir. 47-72, Chair. 65-72; Chair. Hambros
Ltd. 70-, Shipping Industrial Holdings until 73; Deputy
Chair. Western American Bank (Europe) 67-76; Dir.
Phoenix Assurance Co. Ltd., Charter Consolidated Ltd.,
British Empire Investment Trust Ltd. and Diamond
Devt. Co. Ltd.
2 Halkin Place, London, S.W.1, England.

Hamburger, Christian; Danish doctor; b. 19 Feb.
1904, Copenhagen; *s.* of Dr. Ove Hamburger and
Agnete Barnekow; *m.* 1st Mary J. Frydensberg 1932,
2nd Ilse Levin 1940; two *s.* one *d.*; ed. Københavns
Universitet.
Scientific Asst., Inst. for Gen. Pathology, Univ. of
Copenhagen 32-35; Head, Hormone Dept. Statens
Seruminstitut, Copenhagen 34-74; mem. Advisory
Panel Ciba Foundation 49-73; mem. Advisory Panel on
Biological Standardisation, World Health Org. (WHO)
52-71; Pres. Danish Soc. for Endocrinology 47-72; Chief
Editor *Acta Endocrinologica* 60-73; Alfred Benzon Prize
60, Pfizer Prize 64, Thorvald Madsen Prize 66; Hon.
mem. Deutsche Gesellschaft für Endokrinologie 70,

Finnish Soc. for Endocrinology 70, Danish Soc. for Endocrinology 72, Swedish Soc. for Endocrinology 73; Hon. Fellow, Royal Coll. of Physicians, Edinburgh 74. Leisure interests: literature, painting.

Publs. *Studies on gonadotropic hormones from the hypophysis and chorionic tissues* 33, *Hypophyseal, gonadal and adrenal hormones* 50, *Hormone Research* 67.

62 Slotsvej, DK-2920 Charlottenlund, Copenhagen, Denmark.

Telephone: OR 3116.

Hamburger, Jean, M.D., PH.D.; French professor of medicine; b. 15 July 1909, Paris; s. of A. Hamburger and M. Marix; m. Catherine Deschamps 1964; two s. one d.; ed. Lycée Carnot and Faculty of Medicine, Sorbonne, Paris.

Professor of Medicine, Univ. of Paris 56-; Chief of Nephrology Dept., Hôpital Necker, Paris 58-; Dir. INSERM renal research unit and CNRS laboratory for research on graft immunology; Vice-Pres. Foundation for French Medical Research; mem. Inst. de France (Acad. des Sciences) 74, Nat. Acad. of Medicine 75; fmr. Pres. Int. Soc. of Transplantation, Int. Soc. of Nephrology; F.R.C.P. (London, Edinburgh, Canada); Commdr. Légion d'Honneur.

Publs. *Néphrologie* 66, *Nefrologia* 67, *Nephrology* 68, *La Transplantation Rénale* 70, *Renal Transplantation* 71, *Structure and Function of the Kidney* 71, *La Puissance et la Fragilité* 72 (translated into six languages).

Centre de Recherches Néphrologiques, Hôpital Necker, 161 rue de Sèvres, Paris 15e; Home: 38 rue Mazarine, Paris 6e, France.

Telephone: 273-24-42 (Hospital); 633-33-99 (Home).

Hamburger, Viktor, PH.D.; American university professor; b. 9 July 1900, Landeshut, Germany; s. of Max and Else Hamburger; m. Martha Fricke 1927 (died 1965); two d.; ed. Univs. of Heidelberg, Munich, Freiburg.

Instructor, Univ. of Chicago 32-35; Asst. Prof. of Zoology, Washington Univ., St. Louis 35-39, Assoc. Prof. 39-41, Prof. 41-; Chair. Dept. of Zoology 41-66; E. Mellinckrodt Distinguished Service Univ. Prof. 68-69; Prof. Emer. of Biology 69-; mem. Nat. Acad. of Sciences, American Acad. of Arts and Sciences.

Publs. *A Manual of Experimental Embryology* 42, 60; over 100 publications in scientific journals.

Department of Biology, Washington University, St. Louis, Mo. 63130; Home: 740 Trinity Avenue, St. Louis, Mo. 63130, U.S.A.

Telephone: 863-0100.

Hamengkubuwono IX, H.R.H. Sultan Dorodjatun; Indonesian ruler; b. 12 April 1912; ed. Univ. of Leiden. Inaugurated Sultan of Jogjakarta 40; Mil. Gov. of Special Territory (with rank of Maj.-Gen. of the Army) 45-49; Head of Special Territory 46; Gov., Head of Special Territory 59; mem. Provisional People's Consultative Assembly Aug. 59, Titular Gen. of the Army 60; Minister of State Oct. 46-49; Minister of Defence and Co-ordinator of Domestic Security Aug.-Dec. 59; Defence Minister, Cabinet of the Repub. of the United States of Indonesia Dec. 49, 53; Deputy Prime Minister 50-April 51; Curator Univ. of Gadja Mada Dec. 51; Chair. Supervisory Comm. for the Apparatus of the State Aug. 59; Minister and Head, Body for Controlling State Finance 64; First Minister for Econ. and Financial Affairs in the Presidium and Deputy Prime Minister 66-68; State Minister for Econ. Affairs, Finance and Industry 68-73; Vice-Pres. of Indonesia March 73-; Chair. Indonesian Olympic Cttee. 51, Tourist Inst. 56, Asian Games Fed. 58, Indonesian Tourist Council 62-; Chair. Session, Econ. Comm. for Asia and the Far East (ECAFE) 57, Nat. Preparatory Cttee. for New York World Fair 63; Chief del. of Indonesia, Pacific Area Travel Asscn. (PATA), U.S. 58, UN First World Conf. of Int. Travel and Tourism, Rome 63; Medal of the Guerilla, Medal ⟨ Loyalty to the Independence and the Order of th White Elephant (Thailand); Hon. titles of Maha Puty (Spes Patria) and Pramuka Agung (Supreme Scout).

Office of the Vice-President of the Republic of Ind￼ nesia, Medan Merdeka Selatan 6, Jakarta, Indonesia.

Hamer, A. W.; Australian business executive; b. 2 Nov. 1917; ed. Oxford Univ.

Joined ICI Australia, England 41, returned to Australi 42; associated with setting up of new plants; Worl Man. Yarraville plant 50-56; Controller Tech. Dep 56-59, Dir. 59-68; Chair. ICI Group of Cos. India 68-7￼ concurrently Dir. ICI Australia; Man. Dir. IC Australia Ltd. 71-; Chair. Australian Fertilizers Ltd Consolidated Fertilizers Ltd., Fibremakers Ltd.; Di ICI New Zealand; Rhodes Scholarship 37.

ICI Australia Limited, ICI House, 1 Nicholson Street Melbourne, Australia.

Hamer, Rupert James, LL.M.; Australian solicitor an￼ politician; b. 29 July 1916, Kew, Vic.; ed. Melbourn￼ and Geelong Grammar Schools, Univ. of Melbourne Joined Australian Imperial Forces 40; C.O. Vic Scottish Regt., Citizen Mil. Forces 54-58; mem. Vic Legislative Council for E. Yarra 58-71; Minister fo Immigration, Vic. 62-64, for Local Govt., Vic. 64-71 mem. Vic. Legislative Assembly for Kew 71-; Chief Sec. Deputy Premier, Vic. 71-72, Premier, Treas. an￼ Minister of the Arts Aug. 72-.

Office of the Premier of Victoria, Melbourne, Victoria Australia.

Hamid, Agha Abdul; Pakistani United Nation official; b. 2 Aug. 1912, Sialkot, W. Pakistan; m. Abid￼ Hussain 1951; one s. two d.; ed. Govt. Coll., Lahore and Emmanuel Coll., Cambridge.

Joined Indian Civil Service 35, Asst. Commr. 37; Deputy Dir.-Gen. All-India Radio 42-45; Deputy Registrar later Registrar of Co-operative Socs. 45-47; Sec. to late Liaquat Ali Khan, Prime Minister of Pakistan 48-51 Prime Minister of Kalat State 51-53, Baluchistan State Union 53-54; Joint Sec. to Central Cabinet 54-55, Join￼ Sec. in charge of Ministry of Information and Broad casting 55-56; Joint Sec. Cabinet 56-58, Cabinet Sec. 58, 66-68; Commr. in Peshawar 59-60; Administrato￼ 60-61; Dir. Civil Service Acad. 61-66; Chair. Centra￼ Public Service Comm. 66; Asst. Sec.-Gen. for Public Information, UN 68-72; UN Commr. for Namibia 72-73; Founder, later Sec. and Chair. Karachi Fine Arts Soc.; fmr. Chair. Pakistan Arts Council; Pres. Pakistan Sec tion of Int. Asscn. of Art Critics; Sitara Quaid-i-Azam. Leisure interests: study of history, literature and art.

Publs. *Majlis, Scrutiny.*

United Nations Secretariat, New York, N.Y., U.S.A.

Hamilton, Alexander Daniel, B.ENG.; Canadian engineer; b. 13 Nov. 1917, Montreal; s. of Daniel Evoy Hamilton and Isobel Stewart; m. Frances McLeod 1942; three s. two d.; ed. Westmount High School, McGill Univ.

Assistant Div. Man. Ontario Paper Co. Ltd. 60; Vice-Pres. B. C. Forest Products Ltd. 61, Pres. 64, Pres. and Chief Exec. Officer 67; Pres. Domtar Pulp and Paper Products Ltd. 68, Pres. and Chief Exec. Officer Domtar Ltd. 74-.

Leisure interests: golf, fishing, skiing, tennis.

Domtar Ltd., P.O. Box 7210, Montreal, P.Q., H3C 3M1; Home: 3 Murray Avenue, Westmount, P.Q., H3X 2X9, Canada.

Telephone: (514) 282-5255 (Office); (514) 489-1297 (Home).

Hamilton, Sir (Charles) Denis, Kt., D.S.O.; British newspaper director and editor; b. 6 Dec. 1918, South Shields, Co. Durham; s. of Charles and Helena Hamilton; m. Olive Wanless 1939; four s.; ed. Middlesbrough High School.

With *Evening Gazette*, Middlesbrough, and *Evening Chronicle and Journal*, Newcastle 37-39; served Infantry 9-46; Personal and Editorial Asst. to Viscount Kemsley 46-50; Editorial Dir. Thomson (fmrly. Kemsley) Newspapers Ltd. 50-66; Editor *The Sunday Times* 61-67; Editor-in-Chief and Chief Exec. Times Newspapers Ltd. 67-70, Chair. and Editor-in-Chief 70-; Dir. Newcastle Chronicle and Journal Ltd., Evening Gazette Ltd., Times Newspapers Ltd., The Thomson Organisation Ltd., Reuters Ltd.; Founder mem. Nat. Council for the Training of Journalists, Chair. 58-59; mem. Council NPA, Press Council, Board of the British Library 75-; Chair. British Museum Publs. Co. Ltd.; Chair. British Cttee., Int. Press Inst.; Trustee, British Museum 69-; Gov. British Inst. of Florence 74-; Hon. D.Litt. (Southampton) 75; Territorial Decoration.
Leisure interests: sailing, fruit farming.
Weston House, Nutbourne, Nr. Chichester, Sussex; and 25 Roebuck House, Palace Street, London, S.W.1; Office: Times Newspapers Ltd., P.O. Box 7, New Printing House Square, Gray's Inn Road, London, WC1X 8EZ, England.
Telephone: 01-828-0410 (Home).

Hamilton, Fowler; American lawyer; b. 7 May 1911, Kansas City; *s.* of Eugene Paul and Emily Rhodelle (Fowler); *m.* Helen Katherine Miller 1934; one *s.* two *d.*; ed. Univ. of Missouri and Oxford Univ.
Private legal practice 35-38; Special Asst. to Attorney-Gen. 38-42; Dept. of Justice 42; Econ. Warfare Div., American Embassy, London 43; Chief Enemy Branch, Foreign Econ. Admin. 42-43; U.S.A.A.F. 43-44; Chief Legal Consultant, U.S. Dept. of Justice 45; Partner, Cleary, Gottlieb, Steen and Hamilton, New York City 46-61 and 63-; Gen. Counsel Sub-Cttee. of Air Force, Senate Armed Forces Cttee. 56; mem. N.Y. County Lawyers Asscn.; mem. Council of Foreign Relations, Foreign Policy Asscn., American Coll. of Trial Lawyers; Admin. U.S. Agency for Int. Devt. 61-62; Democrat.
Office: One State Street Plaza, New York, N.Y. 1004; Home: 652 Riversville Road, Greenwich, Conn. 06830, U.S.A.

Hamilton, Hamish, M.A., LL.B.; British publisher; b. 15 Nov. 1900; ed. Rugby and Cambridge.
Called to Bar Inner Temple 26; European Rep. Harper & Bros. New York 26-31; founded Hamish Hamilton Ltd., Publishers 31, Chair. 31-, Man. Dir. 31-72; served Army 39-41; mem. staff American Div.; Ministry of Information 41-45; a Gov. British Inst. Florence; Hon. Sec. Kinsmen Trust 42-56; Chevalier de la Légion d'Honneur.
Publs. Ed. anthologies: *Decade* 41, *Majority* 52.
43 Hamilton Terrace, London, N.W.8, England.

Hamilton, Richard; British artist; b. 24 Feb. 1922; *m.* Terry O'Reilly 1947 (died 1962); ed. elementary school, evening classes, St. Martin's School of Art, Royal Academy Schools and Slade School of Art.
Jig and tool draughtsman, Design Unit 41-42, Electrical & Musical Industries (EMI) 42-45; exhbn. of *Reaper* engravings, Gimpel Fils 50; devised *Growth and Form* exhbn., Inst. of Contemporary Arts (ICA) 51; teacher of design, Central School of Arts and Crafts 52-53; mem. Independent Group, ICA 52-55; Lecturer, Fine Art Dept., King's Coll., Univ. of Durham (later Univ. of Newcastle-upon-Tyne) 53-66; teacher of Interior Design Royal Coll. of Art 57-61; exhbns. of paintings *51-55* and *56-64*, Hanover Gallery 55 and 64; organized exhbn. of works by Marcel Duchamp, Tate Gallery 66; exhbn. of *Guggenheim* reliefs and studies, London 66; exhbns. in Kassel 67, New York 67, Studio Marconi, Milan 68, Hamburg 69; exhbn. of *Swinging London* 67 and beach scene paintings, London 69; exhbn. of *Cosmetic Studies*, Milan 69, Berlin 70; retrospective exhbns., Tate Gallery 70 (seen in Switzerland and Holland also), Guggenheim Museum N.Y.C. 73,

Nationalgalerie, Berlin 74; William and Norma Copley Foundation award for painting 60; Joint First Prize, John Moores Liverpool Exhbn. 69, Talens Prize, Amsterdam 70.
c/o Tate Gallery, Millbank, London, S.W.1, England.

Hamilton, Hon. William McLean, P.C., B.SC.COM.; Canadian executive and politician; b. 23 Feb. 1919, Montreal; *m.* Ruth Isabel Seeman 1954; ed. Montreal High School and Sir George Williams Univ.
General Man. Advertising and Sales Executives' Club of Montreal 49-57; City Councillor, Montreal 50-57; mem. of Parl. 53-62; Postmaster-Gen. of Canada 57-62; Pres. Canadian Park & Tilford Distilleries Ltd. 63-66, British Columbia Int. Trade Fair 66-67; Chair. Fidelity Life Assurance Co., Century Insurance Co. of Canada 68-; Pres. Vancouver Board of Trade 70-71, Brink-Hamilton Enterprises Ltd. 70-; Pres. and Chief Exec. Officer Employers' Council of British Columbia 73-; Gov. Simon Fraser Univ.; Dir. Wasteco Disposal Ltd., Foursome Devt. Ltd., Phoenix Assurance Co. of Canada.
Leisure interest: boating.
1055 West Hastings, Vancouver, B.C., V6E 2E9; Home: 6212 Wiltshire Street, Vancouver, B.C., V6M 3M2, Canada.
Telephone: 684-3384 (Office).

Hammadi, Sadoon; Iraqi economist and politician; b. 22 June 1930, Karbala; *m.* Lamia Hammadi 1961; four *s.*; ed. in Beirut, Lebanon and U.S.A.
Professor of Econs., Univ. of Baghdad 57; Deputy Head of Econ. Research, Nat. Bank of Libya, Tripoli 61-62; Minister of Agrarian Reform 63-63; Econ. Adviser to Presidential Council, Govt. of Syria 64; Econ. Expert, UN Planning Inst., Syria 65-68; Pres. Iraq Nat. Oil Co. (INOC) 68-; Minister of Oil and Minerals 69-74, of Foreign Affairs 74-.
Leisure interests: swimming, walking, coin collection, reading novels.
Publs. *Towards a Socialistic Agrarian Reform in Iraq* 64, *Views About Arab Revolution* 69.
Ministry of Foreign Affairs, Baghdad, Iraq.
Telephone: 30091 (Office); 511733 (Home).

Hammarskjöld, Knut Olof Hjalmar Akesson, PH.M.; Swedish diplomatist; nephew of the late Dag Hammarskjöld, Sec.-Gen. of the UN; b. 16 Jan. 1922; *m.*; four *s.*; ed. Stockholm Univ.
Entered Foreign Service 46, served Paris, Vienna, Moscow, Bucharest, Kabul, Sofia 47-55; First Sec. Foreign Office 55-57; Head of Foreign Relations Dept., Royal Board of Civil Aviation, Stockholm 57-59; Deputy Head, Swedish Del. to OEEC, Paris 59-60; Deputy Sec.-Gen. European Free Trade Asscn. (EFTA) 60-66; Minister Plenipotentiary; Dir.-Gen. of Int. Air Transport Asscn. (IATA), Montreal 66-; mem. Inst. of Transport, London; Hon. Fellow, Canadian Aeronautics and Space Inst.; Commdr., Order of the Lion (Finland), Order of the Falcon (Iceland), Commdr. Orange-Nassau, Order of the Black Star (France), Grand Officer, Order Al-Istiqlal; Commdr. 1st Class, Order of the North Star.
Publs. articles on political, economic and aviation topics.
IATA, 1155 Mansfield Street, Montreal H3B 4A4, P.Q., Canada; P.O. Box 315, 1215 Geneva 15 Airport, Switzerland.
Telephone: (514) 866-1011 (Montreal); (022) 98-33-66 (Geneva).

Hammer, Armand, B.S., M.D.; American petroleum executive; b. 21 May 1898, New York; *s.* of Dr. Julius Hammer and Rose Robinson; *m.* 1st Baroness Olga von Root 1927, 2nd Frances Barrett 1956; one *s.*; ed. Columbia Univ.
Military Service, U.S. Army Medical Corps 18-19; Pres. Allied American Corpn. 23-25, A. Hammer Pencil Co. (N.Y., London, Moscow) 25-30, Hammer Galleries Inc.

30-; J. W. Dant Distilling Co. 43-54; Pres. and Chair. of Board Mutual Broadcasting System (N.Y.) 57-58; Chair. of Board and Chief Exec. Officer Occidental Petroleum Corpn. 57-; Chair. M. Knoedlers and Co., Inc. 72-; mem. Advisory Board of Inst. of Peace 50-54, Board of Govs. Eleanor Roosevelt Cancer Foundation 60-, Board of Dirs. City Nat. Bank (Beverley Hills) 62-71, Board of Trustees Eleanor Roosevelt Memorial Foundation 63-, Board of Dirs. Canadian Occidental Petroleum Ltd. 64-, Board of Dirs. Raffinerie Belge de Pétroles (RBP) 68-, Public Advisory Cttee. on U.S. Trade Policy 68-69, Nat. Petroleum Council 68-, Exec. Cttee. Econ. Devt. Board, City of L.A. 68-73, Exec. Board of Dirs. UN Asscn. of L.A. 69-, Board of Dirs. UN Asscn. of U.S.A. 70-, of the U.S.—U.S.S.R. Trade and Economic Council, Inc. 73-, of the Assocs. of Harvard Business School 75-, of the American Petroleum Inst. 75-, of the Salk Inst. for Biological Studies (mem. Board of Trustees and Chair. Exec. Cttee.) 69-; Hon. mem. Board of Dirs. Florida Nat. Bank of Jacksonville 66-; Hon. Corresponding mem. Royal Acad. of Arts 75-; Humanitarian Award, Eleanor Roosevelt Cancer Foundation 62; Commdr. Order of the Crown (Belgium) 69; Commdr. Order of Andres Bellos (Venezuela) 75.

Publ. *Quest of the Romanoff Treasure* 32.

Occidental Petroleum Corporation, 10889 Wilshire Boulevard, Suite 1500, Los Angeles, Calif. 90024, U.S.A. Telephone: 213-879-1700.

Hammerich, Louis L., PH.D., LITT.D.; Danish philologist; b. 31 July 1892, Copenhagen; s. of Kai Hammerich and Clara Bentzen; m. Clara Flensborg 1917 (died 1972); two s.; ed. Univ. of Copenhagen.
Secretary, Danish Red Cross, P.O.W. Dept. 15-17, 18-19; teacher 19-21; Sec. Schleswig Frontier Comm. 20; Prof. Germanic Philology, Univ. of Copenhagen 22-58; editor of publs., Royal Danish Acad. of Science and Letters 41-70; Pres. Int. Asscn. of Germanists 55-60, Int. Fed. for Modern Languages and Literatures 57-60, Int. Academic Union 65; Hon. degrees Utrecht, Nancy, Groningen, Kiel, Ghent, Lund, Aarhus, Helsinki; Goethe Medal, Frankfurt 58, Konrad Duden Prize, Mannheim 66, Grimm Brothers Prize, Marburg 59.
Alsvej, 4B, 2970 Hørsholm, Denmark.
Telephone: 01-86-84-16.

Hämmerling, Joachim, DR. PHIL.; German biologist; b. 9 March 1901, Berlin; s. of August and Gertrud (née Titlé) Hämmerling; m. Charlotte Klose 1931; three s. one d.; ed. Landesschule zur Pforte and Univs. of Berlin and Marburg.
Scientific Asst., Kaiser Wilhelm Inst. für Biologie, Berlin-Dahlem 24; German Dir. deutsch.-italien. Inst. für Meeresbiologie, Rovigno 40; Head of Dept., Kaiser Wilhelm Inst. für Biologie, Langenargen 45; Dir. Max Planck Inst. für Zellbiologie, Wilhelmshaven 47-70, Dir. Emer. 70-; Foreign mem. Royal Soc., London 70.
Leisure interest: music.
Publs. numerous scientific works and articles.
2940 Wilhelmshaven, Schopenhauerstrasse 27, Federal Republic of Germany.
Telephone: 04421-31214.

Hammett, Louis Plack, A.B., PH.D.; American chemist; b. 7 April 1894, Wilmington, Del.; s. of Philip Melancthon and Louise (Plack) Hammett; m. Janet Thorpe Marriner 1919; one s. one d.; ed. Harvard Coll., Columbia Univ., Technische Hochschule, Zürich.
Civilian chemist, U.S. Army 17-19; with Columbia Univ. as Instructor, Asst. Prof., Assoc. Prof., Prof. since 20; on leave 41-45 for work under direction of Office of Scientific Research and Development, U.S. Govt.; Chair. Div. of Chemistry and Chemical Technology, Nat. Research Council 46-47; Consulting Ed. Int. *Chemical Series* 40-55; Chair. Board of Directors,

American Chemical Soc. 61; Mitchill Prof. Emer. ɑ Chemistry, Columbia Univ. 61-; Visiting Senior Chemisͭ Brookhaven Nat. Laboratory 62; Distinguished Visitin Lecturer, Univ. of S. Carolina 62, Pennsylvania Stat Univ. 64, Purdue Univ. 64; mem. Emer. Nat. Acad. ͨ Sciences; Hon. Fellow Chemical Soc. (London) 65 awarded William H. Nichols Medal 57, James Flacͬ Norris Award 60, Priestly Medal, Willard Gibbs Medɑ 61, James Flack Norris Award in Physical Organi Chemistry 66, Gilbert Newton Lewis Medal 67, Natͬ Medal of Science, Charles Frederick Chandler Medɑ 68; Barnard Medal 75; D.Sc. (Hon.) Columbia Univ. 62
Leisure interest: good company.
Publs. *Solutions of Electrolytes* 29, *Physical Organi Chemistry* 40, 2nd edn. 70, *Introduction to the Study o₁ Physical Chemistry* 52.
288 Medford Leas, Medford, N.J. 08055, U.S.A.
Telephone: (609) 654-3288.

Hammond, George Simms, B.S., M.S., PH.D.; Americaͭ professor of chemistry; b. 22 May 1921, Auburn, Me.; s. of Oswald K. Hammond and Majorie Thomas; m. Marian Reese 45; three s. two d.; ed. Bates Coll. of Lewiston, Maine and Harvard Univ.
Assistant Prof. of Chem., Iowa State Univ. 48-52, Assoc. Prof. 52-56, Prof. 56-58; Prof. of Organic Chem., Calif. Inst. of Technology 58-64, Arthur Amos Noyes Prof. of Chem. 64-, Chair. Div. of Chem. and Chemical Engineering 68-71; Vice-Chancellor Sciences, Univ. of Calif., Santa Cruz 71-74, Prof. of Chemistry 71-; Foreign Sec. Nat. Acad. of Sciences 74-; mem. Nat. Acad. of Sciences, American Acad. of Arts and Sciences; Hon. D.Sc. Wittenberg Univ., Springfield, Ohio 72; Dr. h.c. (State Univ. of Ghent 73, Bates Coll., Lewiston, Maine 73); American Chemical Soc. Award in Petroleum Chem. 61, Edward Curtis Franklin Memorial Award for Outstanding Contributions to Chem. 64, James Flack Norris Award in Physical Organic Chem. 68, E. Harris Harbison Award for Gifted Teaching, Danforth Foundation 71, ACS Award in Chemical Education 74; Priestly Medallist, ACS 76, Golden Plate Award, American Acad. of Achievement 76.
Leisure interests: family, golf, Y.M.C.A., reading.
Publs. Co-author: *Quantitative Organic Analysis* 57, *Organic Chemistry* 59, 64, 70, *Advances in Photochemistry* (Co-editor) 67, 68, *Elements of Organic Chemistry* 67, *Chemical Dynamics* 68, *Annual Survey of Photochemistry* 69, *Models in Chemical Science* 70; and 250 papers and reviews.
Merrill College, University of California, Santa Cruz, Calif. 95064, U.S.A.
Telephone: 408-429-2004.

Hammond, Jay; American state governor; b. 21 July 1922, Troy, N.Y.; m. Bella Gardiner; two d.; ed. Scotia, N.Y. High School, Univ. of Alaska.
Served U.S. Navy 42-46, Marine Fighter Pilot, Capt.; Bush Pilot 46-48; Pilot for U.S. Fish and Wildlife Service 48-56; fisherman, guide and air taxi operator 56-; mem. Alaska House of Reps. 59-65, Chair. Resources Cttee., Republican Party Whip; Man. Bristol Bay Borough 65-67, Mayor 72; mem. Alaska Senate 67-72, Majority Whip, Majority Leader, Chair. Rules and Resources Cttees., Pres. of Senate; Gov. of Alaska Jan. 75-.
Publs. various poems.
State Capitol, Juneau, Alaska, U.S.A.
Telephone: (907) 465-3500.

Hammond, Dame Joan Hood, D.B.E., C.M.G.; Australian singer (retd.); b. 12 May 1912, Christchurch, New Zealand; d. of late Samuel H. and Hilda M. Blandford Hammond; ed. Presbyterian Ladies Coll., Pymble, Sydney and Sydney Conservatorium of Music (violin and singing).
Former mem. Sydney Philharmonic Orchestra and

ports writer, *Daily Telegraph*, Sydney; first public
singing) appearance, Sydney 29; London debut in
Messiah 38; operatic debut, Vienna 39; has appeared
as guest artist at Royal Opera House, Covent Garden,
Sadlers Wells, Vienna State Opera, Bolshoi Theatre,
Moscow, New York City Center, Netherlands Opera,
Barcelona Liceo, etc.; world tours have included
Europe, U.S.A., Canada, Australasia, India, S. Africa
and U.S.S.R.; repertoire includes: *Aïda, Madame
Butterfly, Tosca, Othello, Don Carlos, La Traviata, La
Bohème, Turandot, Tannhäuser, Lohengrin,* and *Die
Zauberflöte*; records for HMV (fmrly. for Columbia);
Coronation Medal 53; Sir Charles Santley Award,
Worshipful Co. of Musicians 70.
Leisure interests: golf, yachting, swimming, writing,
reading.
Publ. *A Voice, A Life.*
Private Bag 101, Geelong Mail Centre, Victoria 3221,
Australia; also c/o Bank of New South Wales, Sackville
Street, London, W.1, England.

Hammond Innes, Ralph; British author; b. 15 July
1913, Horsham, Sussex; *s.* of late William Hammond
and Dora Beatrice Innes; *m.* Dorothy Mary Lang 1937.
Financial News 34-40; Royal Artillery 40-46.
Leisure interests: cruising and ocean racing, forestry.
Publs. *Wreckers Must Breathe* 40, *The Trojan Horse* 40,
Attack Alarm 41, *Dead and Alive* 46, *The Lonely Skier* 47,
The Killer Mine 47, *Maddon's Rock* 48, *The Blue Ice* 48,
The White South 49, *The Angry Mountain* 50, *Air
Bridge* 51, *Campbell's Kingdom* 52, *The Strange Land* 54,
The Mary Deare 56, *The Land God Gave to Cain* 58,
Harvest of Journeys 60, *The Doomed Oasis* 60, *Atlantic
Fury* 62, *Scandinavia* 63, *The Strode Venturer* 65, *Sea
and Islands* 67, *The Conquistadors* 69, *Levkas Man* 71,
Hammond Innes Introduces Australia 71, *Golden Soak*
73, *North Star* 74; Films: *Snowbound, Hell Below Zero,
Campbell's Kingdom, The Wreck of the Mary Deare.*
Ayres End, Kersey, Suffolk, England.
Telephone: Hadleigh (Suffolk) 3294.

Hamouz, František; Czechoslovak politician; b. 15
Aug. 1919, Chráštany; ed. Commercial Acad., Teplice.
North Bohemian Oil Works, Ústí n/Labem; Foreign
Trade Service 48-, Oleaspol Co., later in Foreign Trade
Corpn.; Chief. Man. Foreign Trade Corpn., Motokov
51-53; Dep. Minister for Foreign Trade 53-54; Dep. Sec.
Council for Mutual Econ. Assistance, Moscow 54-58;
First Dep. Minister for Foreign Trade 59-63, Minister
for Foreign Trade 63-68; Deputy Prime Minister
April-Dec. 68; Perm. Rep. of Czechoslovakia to CMEA
68-73; Deputy to Nat. Assembly 64-69; mem. State
Planning Comm. 65-68; Deputy Prime Minister, Fed.
Govt. of Č.S.S.R. Jan. 69; Deputy to House of the
People, Fed. Assembly 69-; Minister of Foreign Trade
of Č.S.S.R. Sept. 69-Jan. 70; mem. Central Cttee. C.P.
of Czechoslovakia Sept. 69-; Chair. Council for Int.
Econ. and Scientific and Technical Cooperation at
Govt. of Č.S.S.R. 69-73; Chair. Govt. Cttee. for Tourism
72, Czechoslovak Section of Č.S.S.R.—D.D.R. Cttee.
for Econ., Scientific and Tech. Co-operation 68-; Order
of Labour 69.
Presidium of the Government of the Č.S.S.R., Prague 1,
nábř. kpt. Jaroše 4, Czechoslovakia.

Hamperl, Herwig; Austrian pathologist; b. 12 Sept.
1899, Vienna; *s.* of Dr. Franz Hamperl and Elsa Ratz;
m. Ruth Meinl 1931; ed. Univ. of Vienna.
Assistant Prof., Vienna Univ. 31-35; Assoc. Prof., Berlin
Univ. 35-40; Prof. and Dir. of Inst. Prague 40-45; Dir.
Pathological Inst. Salzburg 46-49; Prof. and Dir. of
Inst. Marburg Univ. 49-54, Bonn 54; Hon. Fellow
Royal Soc. of Medicine, Acad. nacional de Medicina de
Mexico, Soc. Española de Anatomia Patologica; mem.
Royal Soc. of Sciences (Uppsala); External mem.
Acad. of Sciences of D.D.R. (Berlin), Soc. of Physicians
of Vienna, Soc. of Physicians Duodecim (Helsinki),

American Assen. for Cancer Research; Dr. h.c. (Inns-
bruck) 69; Co-editor *Berichte der Pathologie.*
Leisure interests: piano, tennis.
Publ. *Lehrbuch der Pathologie* (trans. into Spanish and
Italian).
53 Bonn, Espenweg 4, Federal Republic of Germany.
Telephone: 28-19-12.

Hampshire, Stuart, F.B.A.; British university professor; b. 1 Oct. 1914, Healing, Lincs.; *s.* of George N.
Hampshire and Marie West; *m.* Renée Orde-Lees 1962;
ed. Repton School and Balliol Coll., Oxford.
Fellow, All Souls Coll., Oxford 36-45; service in army
and foreign office 40-46; Lecturer in Philosophy,
Univ. Coll., London 47-50; Fellow, New Coll., Oxford
50-55; Research Fellow, All Souls Coll., Oxford 55-60;
Prof. of Philosophy, Univ. Coll., London 60-63; Prof.
and Chair. Dept. of Philosophy, Princeton Univ. 63-70;
Warden of Wadham Coll., Oxford 70-; Fellow, British
Acad., American Acad. of Arts and Sciences.
Publs. *Spinoza* 51, *Thought and Action* 59, *Freedom of
the Individual* 65, *Modern Writers and Other Essays* 69,
Freedom of Mind and Other Essays 71, *Morality and
Pessimism* 72.
Wadham College, Oxford, England.
Telephone: Oxford 41638.

Hampson, H. Anthony, M.A. (ECON.); Canadian
administrator; b. 18 Aug. 1930, Montreal; *s.* of late
Harold R. Hampson and Geraldine M. Smith Hampson;
m. 2nd Pamela J. Wickett 1972; two *s.* two *d.* (by first
marriage); ed. schools in Montreal and Lennoxville and
McGill and Cambridge Univs.
Credit Analyst, Bank of Montreal 52-53; Econ. Policy
Div. Dept. of Finance, Ottawa 53-57; Dir. of Research
and Underwriting, Burns Bros. & Denton, Toronto
57-64; Sec. Royal Comm. on Banking and Finance
61-64; Vice-Pres. Power Corpn. of Canada Ltd. 64; Pres.
Capital Management Ltd. 65, Full-time Pres. 68-71;
Chair. Canada Devt. Corpn. 72-.
Leisure interests: tennis, skiing.
Canada Development Corporation, Suite 901, 130
Albert Street, Ottawa K1P 5G4, Canada.
Telephone: 613-237-6464.

Hampson, Robert J., M.B.A.; American business
executive; b. 28 May 1917, Riverside, Calif.; ed. River-
side High School, Harvard Univ.
Served in U.S. Navy; joined Ford Motor Co. 47, Man.
Facilities Analysis Dept. 49, later Man. Capital Invest-
ment Analysis Dept.; Exec. Asst. to Vice-Pres. 53,
Head of the Transmission and Chassis Div. 58-61,
Vice-Pres., Gen. Man. Ford Tractor Operations 61-69,
Exec. Vice-Pres. Non-Automotive Operations 69-72,
Dir. 70; Chair. of Board, Chief Exec. Officer, Dir.
Philco-Ford Corpn. 70-72; Exec. Vice-Pres. Ford Int.
Automotive Operations 72-73; Exec. Vice-Pres. N.
American Automotive Operations 73-.
Ford Motor Co., The American Road, Dearborn, Mich.
48121, U.S.A.

Han Hsien-ch'u; Chinese army officer; b. 1908,
Hunan.
Regimental Commdr. 38; Commdr. 40th Army, 4th
Field Army 49; Deputy Commdr. Hunan Mil. District,
People's Liberation Army 49-50; Chief of Staff Chinese
People's Volunteers in Korea 52; mem. Nat. Defence
Council 54; Alt. mem. 8th Cen. Cttee. of CCP 56; Gen.
60; Commdr. Foochow Mil. Region, PLA 60-73; Chair.
Fukien Revolutionary Cttee. 68; mem. 9th Cen. Cttee.
of CCP 69; First Sec. CCP Fukien 71-73; mem. 10th
Cen. Cttee. of CCP 73; Commdr. Lanchow Mil. Region,
PLA 74-.
People's Republic of China.

Han Suyin (Mrs. Elizabeth Comber), M.B., B.S.,
L.R.C.P., M.R.C.S.; British medical practitioner and
author; b. 12 Sept. 1917; ed. Yenching Univ., Peking,

Univ. of Brussels, Belgium, Royal Free Hospital, London Univ.

Born in China, educated in Peking and Brussels 35-38; in London 42-48; employed Queen Mary Hospital, Hong Kong 48-52, Johore Bahru Hospital, Malaya 52-55; private medical practice 55-63; Lecturer in Contemporary Asian Literature, Nanyang Univ., Singapore 60-63.

Publs. *Destination Chungking* 42, *A Many-Splendoured Thing* 52, . . . *And the Rain My Drink* 56, *The Mountain is Young* 58, *Cast but One Shadow* 62, *Winter Love* 62, *The Four Faces* 63, *The Crippled Tree* (autobiog.) 65, *A Mortal Flower* (autobiog.) 66, *China in the Year 2001* 67, *Birdless Summer* 68, *Morning Deluge—Mao Tse-tung and the Chinese Revolution* 72.

c/o Jonathan Cape, 30 Bedford Square, London, W.C.1, England.

Hancock, John Walker, Jr.; American businessman; b. 11 April 1909, Erie, Kansas; s. of John and Madge (Limbocker) Walker; m. Bernice Wedum 1933; two s. two d.; ed. Long Beach City Coll. and Southwestern Univ.

Joined Refining Dept. Hancock Oil Co. 24, Exec. Vice-Pres. 47-53, Pres. 53-58; Pres. and Dir., Walker Development Co., Newport Development Co.; Vice-Chair. and mem. Advisory Board, Long Beach State Coll.; Dir. R. M. Pyles Boys Camp, Western Oil and Gas Assen. (Pres. 56), Independent Petroleum Assen. of America, Calif. Natural Gasoline Assen.; Dir. Farmers and Merchants Bank, Long Beach.

Office: 4201 North Long Beach Boulevard, Long Beach 7, Calif.; Home: 4681 Virginia Road, Long Beach 90807, Calif., U.S.A.

Hancock, Sir Patrick Francis, G.C.M.G.; British Ambassador to Italy 69-74; see *The International Who's Who 1975-76.*

Hancock, Sir (William) Keith, K.B.E., M.A., LITT.D., F.B.A.; British university professor; b. 26 June 1898, Melbourne, Australia; s. of Rev. William Hancock; m. 1st Theaden Nancy Brocklebank 1925, 2nd Marjorie Eyre 1961; ed. Univ. of Melbourne and Balliol Coll., Oxford.

Fellow of All Souls Coll. Oxford 23; Prof. of Modern History, Univ. of Adelaide, Australia 26-33; Lecturer in Modern History, Balliol Coll., Oxford 30; Prof. of History Univ. of Birmingham 33; Chichele Prof. of Economic History, Univ. of Oxford 44-49; Supervisor of Civil Histories, War Cabinet Office 41-46; Prof. Commonwealth Affairs, Univ. of London, and Dir. Inst. of Commonwealth Studies 49-56; Dir. of Research School of Social Sciences 57-61; Prof. of History, Australian Nat. Univ., Canberra 57-65, Univ. Fellow 66-67, Emeritus Prof. 68-; Govt. expert to examine constitutional questions in Uganda 54; (Civil) Editor of British Official War Histories; Fellow, Churchill Coll. 64, St. John's, Cambridge 71-72; Hon. D.Litt. (Rhodes, Oxford, Cape Town, Birmingham); Hon. Litt.D. (Cambridge, Melbourne, A.N.U., Adelaide); Order of Merit, Italy; Foreign Hon. mem. American Acad. of Arts and Sciences.

Leisure interests: mountain walking, trout fishing.

Publs. *Ricasoli* 26, *Australia* 30, *Survey of British Commonwealth Affairs* 37-42, *Argument of Empire* 42, *Politics in Pitcairn* 47, *British War Economy* 49, *Wealth of Colonies* 50, *Country and Calling* 54, *War and Peace in This Century* 61, *Smuts: The Sanguine Years 1870-1919* Vol I 62, *Selections from the Smuts Papers* Vols. I-IV (edited with Dr. J. van der Poel), *Smuts: The Fields of Force 1919-50* Vol. II 68, *Attempting History* 69, *Discovering Monaro* 72, *Today, Yesterday and Tomorrow* 73.

49 Gellibrand Street, Canberra 2601, A.C.T., Australia. Telephone: 4-4593.

Hand, Lloyd N., B.A., LL.B.; American lawyer; b. 31 Jan. 1929, Alton, Ill.; s. of Mr. and Mrs. Nelson T. Hand; m. Lucy Ann Donoghue 1952; two s. three d.; ed. Charles M. Hilby High School, Houston and Univ. of Texas.

U.S. Naval Officer 52-55; Asst. to Senator Lyndon B. Johnson 57-61; Partner Allbritton, McGee and Hand, Houston 61-; Chief of Protocol of the U.S.A. 65; Dir. several corpns. in Los Angeles; mem. Board of Dirs. Continental Air Services; Senior Vice-Pres. TRW Inc., mem. Board of Foreign Scholarships; Dir. Continental Air Lines Inc., MTRW (Mitsubishi Electric Co.—TRW U.S.); mem. Inst. of Int. Educ. S. Calif. Regional Advisory Cttee.; Dir. L.A. World Affairs Council.

Leisure interests: golf, tennis.

Office: One Space Park, Redondo Beach, Calif.; Home: 166 Groverton Place, Los Angeles, Calif., U.S.A. Telephone: 536-1017 (Office); 476-6266 (Home).

Handler, Philip, M.S., PH.D.; American biochemist and educator; b. 13 Aug. 1917, New York City; s. of Jacob and Lena Handler; m. Lucille P. Marcus 1939; two s.; ed. City Coll., City Univ. of New York and Univ. of Illinois.

Successively Instructor, Asst. Prof., Assoc. Prof., Prof., James B. Duke Prof. of Biochemistry at Duke Univ. School of Medicine 39-, Chair. of Dept. 50-69; Full-time Pres. Nat. Acad. of Sciences 69-; Chair. Nat. Science Board 66-70; mem. Nat. Acad. of Sciences, Nat. Science Board 62-74, American Acad. of Arts and Sciences, American Philosophical Soc., New York Acad. of Sciences, American Assen. for Advancement of Science, American Chemical Soc., American Inst. of Biological Sciences, American Soc. for Cell Biology (Pres. 58-61), Biochemical Soc. (U.K.), German Acad. of Natural Sciences—Leopoldina, Woods Hole Oceanographic Inst., President's Comm. on Heart Disease, Cancer and Stroke 64-65, Nat. Advisory Health Council 58-61, Nat. Advisory Council on Research Facilities and Resources 63-67; Hon. mem. Swiss Acad. of Natural Sciences, Japanese Biochem. Soc., Nat. Acad. of Medicine of Mexico; Pres. Science Advisory Cttee. 64-73, American Soc. of Biological Chemists 62-63; Chair. Fed. of American Socs. of Experimental Biology 59-65; Council, Smithsonian Inst.; Board of Trustees, Rockefeller Univ.; Benjamin Franklin Fellow (U.K); many hon. degrees and lectureships.

Leisure interests: music, boats, reading.

Publs. Co-author: *Principles of Biochemistry* (trans. into Russian, Spanish, Japanese); Editor: *Biology and the Future of Man*; 200 technical papers on metabolism, enzymes, evolution, chemical aspects of disease; several papers on science and society.

National Academy of Sciences, 2101 Constitution Avenue, Washington, D.C. 20418, U.S.A. Telephone: 202-389-6231.

Hanes, Dalibor, LL.D.; Czechoslovak politician; b. 2 Oct. 1914, Tisovec; ed. Faculty of Law, Charles Univ., Prague.

Junior lawyer, Prešov, Banská Bystrica 40-44; Govt. Commr. Chamber of Commerce, Bratislava 45-48; Dir. Regional Admin. for purchase of agricultural products, Bratislava 48-49, Area Dir. 49-50; Lecturer, School of Econs., Bratislava 51-53, Asst. Prof. 53, Prof. 62; Chair. House of Nations and Deputy Chair. Fed. Assembly 69; Chair. Fed. Assembly 69-71, Deputy-Chair. 71; Chair. House of Nations Dec. 71-; mem. Cen. Cttee. C.P. of Czechoslovakia 69-, Alt. mem. of Presidium 70; Chair. Cen. Cttee. of Czechoslovak Soviet Friendship Union 70-72, 1st Deputy Chair. 72-; Deputy to Slovak Nat. Council 68-71, Chair. Czechoslovak Group Inter-Parl. Union 69-70, Czechoslovak-French Cttee. of Czechoslovak Soc. for Int. Relations 73-; Order of Labour, Order of Victorious February 74 and other awards.

Publs. Scientific studies and articles in economic

publication, textbooks, essays, reviews, reports and lectures.
House of Nations, Prague, Czechoslovakia.

Haniel, Klaus; German business executive; b. 14 Jan. 1916, Munich; *m.* Johanna von Lutterotti 1949; two *s.* one *d.;* ed. Wilhelm-Gymnasium, Munich and in Aachen and Berlin.
Chairman of Advisory Board Gutehoffnungshütte Aktienverein; mem. Management Board August Thyssen-Hütte AG; mem. advisory and management boards of numerous other firms.
41 Duisburg-Hamborn, Kaiser-Wilhelm-Strasse 100; 4200 Oberhausen 11, Essener Strasse 74, Federal Republic of Germany.
Telephone: 02131-540-24540 (Duisburg); 02132-67 04 90 (Oberhausen).

Hanif, Rana Muhammad; Pakistani politician; b. 1921, Garh Shanker, E. Punjab; ed. Govt. Coll., Ludhiana.
Called to the Bar, Lincoln's Inn, London 55; legal practice, Shahiwal 55-; mem. Pakistan People's Party 70-; mem. Nat. Assembly 70-; Minister of Labour, Works and Local Bodies 71-74, of Finance, Planning and Econ. Affairs Oct. 74-.
National Assembly, Rawalpindi, Pakistan.

Hanin, Charles; Belgian lawyer and politician; b. 1914, Marche-en-Famenne, Province of Luxembourg.
Former lawyer; Social-Christian Senator 65-; Minister of the Middle Classes 68-71, of French Culture Jan.-Nov. 72, of Scientific Policy 73-74, of Interior April-June 74.
c/o Ministère de l'Intérieur, Brussels, Belgium.

Hanke, Brunhilde; German social scientist and politician; b. 1930.
Leading posts in Feien Deutschen Jugend (Free German Youth), and in Sozialistische Einheitspartei Deutschlands; Mayor of Potsdam 61-; mem. Volkskammer 63-; First Deputy Chair. Cttee. for Business Regulations, Volkskammer; mem. Council of State 64-; Verdienstmedaille, and other decorations.
Staatsrat, Marx-Engels-Platz, Berlin 102, German Democratic Republic.

Hankel, Wilhelm, Dr.; German banker; b. 10 Jan. 1929, Danzig; *s.* of Oskar and Jenny (née Schoffmann) Hankel; *m.* Helga Becker; three *d.;* ed. Univs. of Mainz and Amsterdam.
Worked in Central Planning Bureau of Netherlands Govt. 51; subsequently joined Deutsche Bundesbank; served in Ministry of Econ. Co-operation and later in Foreign Ministry 54-57; with Berliner Bank, Berlin and Kreditanstalt für Wiederaufbau, Frankfurt/M. 57-68; Dir. Money and Credit Dept., Fed. Ministry of the Economy and Finance 68-72; Pres. Hessische Landesbank, Girozentrale, Frankfurt/M. 72-73; Lecturer, Univ. of Frankfurt 66-70, Hon. Prof. 70-; Vice-Pres. Board Int. Credit Bank, Geneva 72-.
Publs. *Die zweite Kapitalverteilung* 61, *Währungspolitik* 71; various articles, lectures, etc.
53 Bonn-Bad Godesberg, Wupperstrasse 3, Federal Republic of Germany.

Hankey, 2nd Baron, cr. 39, of The Chart; **Robert Maurice Alers Hankey,** K.C.M.G., K.C.V.O., B.A.; British diplomatist; b. 4 July 1905, Croydon, Surrey; *s.* of Rt. Hon. Maurice Pascal Alers, First Baron Hankey of The Chart; *m.* 1st Frances Bevyl Stuart-Menteth 1930 (died 1957), 2nd Joanna Riddall Wright 1962; two *s.* two *d.;* ed. Rugby and New Coll., Oxford.
Travelling Fellow, Queen's Coll., Oxford 26-27; entered Diplomatic Service 27; served in Berlin 27; Paris 28, Foreign Office, London 30; Private Sec. to Rt. Hon. Anthony Eden 33-36, served Warsaw 36, Bucharest 39, Cairo 41, Teheran 42, Foreign Office 43-

45; Counsellor, British Embassy, Warsaw 45-46; Head of Northern Dept., Foreign Office 46-49; British Chargé d'Affaires, Madrid 49-51; Minister to Hungary 51-53; Ambassador to Sweden 54-60; Perm. Rep. to OEEC and Official Chair. 60; Perm. Del. to OECD and Chair. of Econ. Policy Cttee. 61-65; retd. from British Diplomatic Service 65; Vice-Pres. European Inst. of Business Admin. (INSEAD), Fontainebleau 62; mem. Int. Council of United World Colls., Council of Int. Baccalaureate Foundation Geneva; Dir. Alliance Building Soc. 70.
Leisure interests: skiing, tennis, music.
Hethe House, Cowden, Edenbridge, Kent, England.
Telephone: Cowden 538.

Hanley, Edward James, B.S., M.B.A.; American steel executive; b. 27 Feb. 1903; ed. Phillips Acad., Massachusetts Inst. of Technology and Harvard Business School.
General Electric Co. 27-36; Sec. Allegheny Ludlum Steel Corpn. 36-41, Treas. 41-46, Vice-Pres. (Finance) 46-49, Dir. 47-, Exec. Vice-Pres. 49-51, Pres. 51-67, Chief Exec. Officer 51-68, Chair. 62-72; Chair. Finance Comm. 72-; Dir. of other companies.
Allegheny Ludlum Industries Inc., Oliver Building, Pittsburgh, Pa. 15222, U.S.A.

Hanley, James; British novelist; b. 1901.
Publs. *Drift* 30, *The German Prisoner* 30, *Boy* 31, *Men in Darkness* 31, *Ebb and Flood* 31, *Aria and Finale*, *Captain Bottell* 33, *The Furys* 34, *The Maelstrom* 35, *Stoker Bush* 35, *The Secret Journey* 36, *Half an Eye* 37, *Grey Children* 37, *Broken Water* (autobiography) 37, *Hollow Sea* (novel) 38, *Soldiers Wind* (essays) 38, *People are Curious* (stories) 38, *Between the Tides* 39, *Our Time is Gone* 39, *The Ocean* 41, *Sailor's Song* 44, *No Directions*, *What Farrar Saw, Emily* (novels), *Crilley* (stories), *Collected Stories* 48, *Winter Song* (novel) 50, *A Walk in the Wilderness* (stories) 50, *The Closed Harbour* (novel) 52; *Don Quixote Drowned* (essays) 53, *The Welsh Sonata* (novel) 54, *Levine* (novel) 55, *An End and a Beginning* (novel) 58, *Say Nothing* (play) 62, *Plays One* (containing *The Inner Journey* and *The Stone Flower*) 68, *The Face of Winter* (illustrated poem) 69, *John Cowper Powys: the Man in the Corner* 71, *Another World* (novel) 72, *A Woman in the Sky* (novel) 73.
c/o David Higham Associates Ltd., 5-8 Lower John Street, Golden Square, London W1R 4HA, England.

Hanley, John Weller, B.S., M.B.A.; American business executive; b. 11 Jan. 1922, Parkersburg, W. Va.; *s.* of James P. and Ida May (Ayers) Hanley; *m.* Mary Jane Reel 1948; two *s.* one *d.;* ed. Pennsylvania State Univ., Univ. of Harvard.
Engineer, Allegheny Ludlum Steel Corpn. 42-43; with Procter and Gamble 47-72, Man. Case Soap Products Div. 61-63, Vice-Pres. Household Soap Products Div. 63-67, Corpn. Vice-Pres., Group Exec. 67-70, Exec. Vice-Pres. 70-72; Pres. and Chief Exec. Officer, Monsanto Co. 72-, Chair. 75-; Hon. D.Eng. (Univ. of Mo.) 74.
Leisure interests: golf, hunting, tennis.
Monsanto Company, 800 North Lindbergh Boulevard, St. Louis, Mo. 63166. U.S.A.
Telephone: (314) 694-3003.

Hannah, H. E. Air Marshal Sir Colin Thomas, K.C.M.G., K.B.E., C.B., PH.D.; Australian state governor and fmr. air force officer; b. 22 Dec. 1914, Menzies, W.A.; *s.* of Thomas H. and Joanna Hannah; *m.* Patricia T. Gordon 1939; one *d.;* ed. Perth Boys' School, Hale School, Perth and RAAF Coll.
Cadet, RAAF Coll. 35-36; RAF Staff Coll. 46-47; RAAF Staff, London 47-49; Dir.-Gen. of Personnel 51-54; Imperial Defence Coll. 55; Senior Air Staff Officer, RAF Far East 56-59; Dir.-Gen. Plans and Policy 59-61; Deputy Chief of Air Staff 61-64; Air Officer

Commdg. Operational Command 65-68, Support Command 68-69; Chief of Air Staff 70-72; Gov. of Queensland March 72-; K. St. J.
Leisure interests: fishing, golf.
Government House, Brisbane, Queensland 4001, Australia.

Hannah, John Alfred, B.S.; American government official; b. 9 Oct. 1902, Grand Rapids, Mich.; s. of William S. and Mary E. Malone Hannah; m. Sarah M. Shaw 1938; three s. one d.; ed. Grand Rapids Junior Coll., Univ. of Michigan and Michigan State Univ.
Secretary, State Board of Agriculture 35-41; Pres. Michigan State Univ. 41-69, Nat. Asscn. of State Univs. and Land-Grant Colls. 48-49, Chair. of its Exec. Cttee. 49-51; Asst. Sec. of Defence 53-54; Chair. U.S. Section, Perm. Joint Board on Defense, Canada-U.S. 54-64, U.S. Comm. on Civil Rights 57-69, American Council on Educ. 67-68; Admin. Agency for Int. Devt. 69-73, Consultant 73-; Deputy Sec.-Gen. World Food Conf. 74; Exec. Dir. World Food Council 75-; Dir. Fed. Reserve Bank of Detroit 51-53, 56-60; mem. Int. Devt. Advisory Board 50-52, Rhodes Scholarship Selection Cttee. 61-62; numerous awards and hon. degrees.
World Food Council, Food and Agricultural Organization, Viale della Terme di Caracalla, 001000 Rome, Italy.

Hannigan, Judson; American business executive; ed. Dartmouth Coll.
Marine Corps, World War II; Asst. Chemist, Int. Paper Co. 48, Man. Hudson River Mill 61, Asst. Gen. Man. Northern Div. 62, Vice-Pres. Int. Paper Co. 64, Dir. 65, Vice-Pres. Mfg. 66, mem. Exec. Cttee. 71, Vice-Pres. Operations 71, Pres. 74-.
International Paper Co., 220 East 42nd Street, New York, N.Y. 10017, U.S.A.

Hannikainen, Antti Juhana, LL.D.; Finnish judge; b. 18 July 1910, Kerimäki; s. of Petter Albin and Ida Hannikainen (née Laamanen); m. Anna Kervinen 1939; one s. two d.; ed. Univ. of Helsinki.
Referendary at Eastern Finland Court of Appeal, Vyborg 39-49, Judge 49-; Vice-Chancellor of Justice 50-56; Justice of the Supreme Court 56-59; Minister of Justice 59-61; Chancellor of Justice 61-64; Pres. of the Supreme Court 64-; Counsellor of Legis. Body 47-50; Deputy Ombudsman 47-50; Acting Prof. of Law, Univ. of Helsinki 52-61; Chair., mem. various govt. cttees. 50-73; Hon. mem. Soc. of Finnish Jurists; Cross of Liberty with oak leaf; Grand Cross of White Rose of Finland; Commdr. of the Lion of Finland.
Publs. *About the Structure of Lien with regard to the Finnish Law* 48, and many articles in legal periodicals.
Pohjoisesplanadinkatu 3, Helsinki 10; Home: Liisankatu 3 A 17, Helsinki 17, Finland.

Hannon, John W., Jr., B.A.; American banker; b. 22 April 1922, New York; s. of John W. Hannon and Leonora King Hannon; m. Vivien Gardner 1944; one s. two d.; ed. Montclair, N.J. Public Schools and St. Lawrence Univ.
With Commercial Nat. Bank 46-51, Bankers Trust Co. after merger with Commercial Nat. Bank 51-, Dir. 73-, Chair. Exec. Cttee. 73-75, Pres. 75-; Dir. Consumers Power Co., Jackson, Private Export Funding Co., N.Y.
Leisure interests: golf, sailing.
c/o Bankers Trust Co., 16 Wall Street, New York, N.Y. 10015, U.S.A.

Hannover, Georg Wilhelm, Prinz von, DR.IUR.; German educationist; b. 25 March 1915, Brunswick; s. of the Duke and Duchess of Brunswick; m. Princess Sophie of Greece 1946; two s. one d.; ed. Hameln/Weser High School, Marlborough Coll., Schule Schloss Salem, Univs. of Vienna and Göttingen.
Head, Salemer Schulen 48-59, now mem. Board of Dirs.; Chair. Outward Bound Mountain School (Austria); King Edward VII Foundation (German

side); mem. Inst. for Town Planning; Hon. Pres. European Asscn. of Saving for Building Banks; mem. German Soc. for European Educ.; Pres. Int. Olympic Acad. 66-70; mem. IOC 66-71, Nat. Olympic Cttee. for Germany 66-, Organizing Cttee. for Munich Olympic Games 66-72; Fellow, Royal Soc. of Arts, London.
8166 Neuhaus bei Schliersee, Georgihaus, Upper Bavaria, Federal Republic of Germany.

Hansberger, R.V., A.A., B.M.E., M.B.A.; American business executive; b. 1 June 1920, Worthington, Minn.; m. Klara Katherine Kille; two d.; ed. Worthington Jr. Coll., Univ. of Minnesota, Harvard Univ. Graduate School of Business Admin.
Torpedo Devt. Officer, Chief Mechanical Design Naval Ordnance Laboratory, U.S.N.R. 42-46, Budget Dir., Asst. to Exec., Chief Engineer and Vice-Pres. Container Corpn. of America 47-54; Pres. and Dir. Western Sales Co. Inc. and Exec. Vice-Pres. and Dir. Western Kraft Corpn. 54-56; Pres., Chief Exec. and Dir. Boise Payette Lumber Co. 56-57, Boise Cascade Corpn. 57-72; Chair. and Chief Exec. Futura Industries Corpn. 72-; Dir. and fmr. Dir. of numerous companies; Visiting Prof. Boise State Univ. 75-; mem. Exec. Cttee. and Vice-Chair. The Business Council; mem. Stanford Research Inst. Advisory Board; fmr. mem. President's Comm. on Urban Housing, on the White House Fellows Program, on Population Growth and the American Future, and numerous State Comms.; fmr. Trustee Acad. for Educational Research and Devt., Calif. Inst. of Technology.
Leisure interests: hunting, fishing, skiing, golf, camping, reading.
Futura Industries Corporation, Drawer F, Suite 1010, One Capital Center, Boise, Ida., 83702, U.S.A.
Telephone: 208-336-0150.

Hansen, Bennet C. K.; Danish shipowner; b. 3 Aug. 1914.
Business experience with shipping firms in Britain and Germany; partner in shipping firm of C. K. Hansen and Copenhagen Stevedoring Co.; Chair. Steamship Co. Dantank Ltd., C. K. Hansen and Dannebrog Pension Scheme, C. K. Hansen Trust; Dir. Copenhagen Bunker Coal Depot Ltd., and Steamship Co. Dannebrog Ltd.
Amaliegade 35, Copenhagen, Denmark.

Hansen, Bent, FIL. DR.; Danish-born Swedish economist; b. 1 Aug. 1920, Ildved, Denmark; s. of Henrik Poulsen and Anna Louise (Pedersen) Hansen; m. Soad Ibrahim Refaat 1962; two s. four d.; ed. Univs. of Copenhagen and Uppsala.
Civil servant, State Dept., Copenhagen 46; Lecturer Uppsala Univ. 47-48 and 50-51, Gothenburg 48-50; Reader, Uppsala 51-55; Prof. and Head of Konjunkturinst. (National Inst. of Economic Research), Stockholm 55-64, Consultant, Inst. of Nat. Planning, Cairo 62-65; Special Consultant for OECD, Paris 65-67; Prof. of Political Economy, Stockholm Univ. 67-68; Prof. of Econs. Univ. of Calif., Berkeley 67-; Consultant ECAFE Bangkok 70-73, IMF 73, U.S. Treasury 74.
Publs. *A Study in the Theory of Inflation* 51, *The Economic Theory of Fiscal Policy* 58, *Foreign Trade Credits and Exchange Reserves* 61, *Development and Economic Policy in the UAR (Egypt)* 65, *Lectures in Economic Theory, I and II* 67, *Long and Short Term Planning* 67, *Fiscal Policy in Seven Countries,* OECD, 69, *A Survey of General Equilibrium Systems* 70, *Exchange Controls and Development: Egypt* 75.
University of California, Barrows Hall 250, Berkeley, Calif.; Home: 8336 Terrace Drive, El Cerrito, Calif. 94530, U.S.A.
Telephone: 415-525-0704 (Home).

Hansen, Charles L.; Danish mechanical engineer and businessman; b. 27 Sept. 1891, Elsinore; s. of Charles Christian Hansen; m. Edel Marie Wendelboe Jensen 1960.

Formerly with Elsinore Ship and Engine-building Yard, East Asiatic Co. A/S, Engineer Burmeister and Wain Oil Engine Co. Ltd. Glasgow 13, Vacuum Oil Co. New York 15; Chief Engineer Scandinavian Vacuum Oil Co. 20, European Technical Manager 22; Commercial Dir. Vacuum Oil Co. A/S Copenhagen 26, mem. Board 35; Asst. Manager Socony-Vacuum Oil Co. Inc. New York 37-47; Exec. Man. 47-55; Chair. of Board of Burmeister and Wain American Corpn. 49-66; Dir. Socony Bunker Oil Co. Ltd. 47-56; mem. Dansk Ingeniør Forening 46, New York Acad. of Sciences 61; Pres. Rebild Nat. Park Soc. Inc. 63-69, hon. mem. 69-; mem. Administrative Council, Celestina Foundation, Carona, Switzerland 65-69; Knight Cross 1st Class of the Order of Dannebrog.
Villa di San Zeno, 6814 Lamone, Ticino, Switzerland (all mail); and 180 Central Park South, New York City 19, N.Y., U.S.A.

Hansen, Clifford Peter, B.S.; American rancher and politician; b. 16 Oct. 1912, Zenith, Wyo.; s. of Peter and Sylvia (Wood) Hansen; m. Martha Elizabeth Close 1934; one s. one d.; ed. Univ. of Wyoming.
Vice-President, Jackson State Bank 53-74; Trustee Univ. of Wyoming 46-, Pres. Board 56-63; fmr. Chair. Advisory Cttee. on Livestock Research and Marketing to Sec. of Agriculture; Gov. of Wyoming 63-66; Senator from Wyoming 67-; mem. Wyoming Stock Growers' Asscn., Pres. 53-55; mem. American Nat. Cattlemen's Asscn., second Vice-Pres. 56-57; mem. Exec. Cttee. Nat. Govs. Conf. and Western Govs. Conf. 65-; Hon. LL.D. (Univ. Wyoming) 65; Republican.
Leisure interests: hiking, riding.
2510 Virginia Avenue, N.W., Washington, D.C. 20037, U.S.A.
Telephone: 202-337-3140; 202-224-3424.

Hansen, Guttorm; Norwegian journalist and politician; b. 3 Nov. 1920, Namsos; s. of Håkon Hansen and Agnes Selnes; m. Karin Johanne Johnsen 1947; ed. Technical School.
Journalist, Editor 45-61; Chair., mem. several municipal and public boards and cttees.; mem. Exec. Cttee. Labour Party; Deputy mem. Storting (Parl.) 58-61, mem. 61-; Vice-Chair. Labour Party Parl. Group 65-71, Chair. 71-72; Vice-Chair. Cttee. on Foreign Affairs 69-71; Pres. Storting 73-; Chair. Norwegian Atlantic Cttee. 66-; mem. Board European Movt. in Norway.
Leisure interests: reading, fishing, skiing.
Publs. *NATO, Europe and Norway, The Labour Movement in Nord-Trøndelag, Plan-Perspective-Policy.*
Stortinget, Oslo 1; Home: N. Griegs vei 26, 7800 Namsos, Norway.

Hansen, Hellmut; German mining industrialist; b. 23 Feb. 1896; ed. Univ. of Göttingen and Mining Coll., Clausthal.
Plant Man. Friedrich-Heinrich AG., Camplintfort 25-35; Dir. and Works Man. Heinitz/Saar Colliery (Saargruben AG) 35-45 (subsidiary of Frankenholz/Saar 42-); Dir. and mem. Management Bd. all Hoesch AG collieries, Essen-Altenessen 46-52; mem. Exec. Bd. Hoesch-Werke AG (Hoesch AG)., Dortmund 52-63; Chair. State Fed. of Ind. Employers Asscns. (North-Rhine Westphalia), Düsseldorf, Lippeverband, Essen; mem. Presidium, German Fed. of Employers, Cologne; Chair. Advisory Bd. Hoesch-AG Bergbau, Essen Altenessen; Fed. Labour Judge, Fed. Labour Court, Kassel 53-63; mem. Social Advisory Board, Fed. Ministry of Labour and Social Order until 63; Chair. German Inst. for Industry, Cologne; mem. Exec. Board, Econ. Asscn. for Mining, Bad Godesberg 63-64.
9 Limbecker Postweg, 46 Dortmund-Hoechsten, Federal Republic of Germany.

Hansen, Irwin Roy; American businessman; b. 16 Aug. 1913; ed. Univ. of Wisconsin.
With Haskins & Sells (C.P.A.'s) 36-44; joined Minn.

Mining & Mfg. Co., St. Paul 44, Gen. Auditor 44-50, Asst. Controller 50-54, Asst. Treas. 54-57, Treas. 57-63, Vice-Pres. (Finance) 63-; Dir. and Vice-Pres. Salisbury Cruises Ltd.; Dir. 3M Foundation; Treas. Big Rock Stone and Material Co., Prehler Electric Insulating Co.; Dir. Business Products Sales Inc., Wonework Lodge Inc., First Nat. Bank of St. Paul.
3M Center, St. Paul, Minn. 55101, U.S.A.

Hansen, Kurt, Prof. DR.ING.; German businessman; b. 11 Jan. 1910, m. Irmi Strähuber 1937; one s. one d.; ed. Technische Hochschule, Munich.
With I. G. Farbenindustrie A.G./Farbenfabriken Bayer A.G., Leverkusen 36-74; Man. Uerdingen Factory, Farbenfabriken Bayer Jan. 55, Wuppertal-Elberfeld Factory April 56-57, mem. Board of Management, Bayer AG (fmrly. Farbenfabriken Bayer) 57-61, Chair. 61-74, Chair. Supervisory Board 74-; Pres. (designate) Bundesverband der Deutschen Industrie, Cologne 77-78; mem. Supervisory Board Veba AG, Allianz Versicherungs-AG, Hapag-Lloyd AG, Kaufhof AG, Siemens AG, Otto Wolff AG.
Bayer A.G., 509 Leverkusen Bayerwerk, Federal Republic of Germany.

Hanson, Howard; American music teacher, conductor and composer; b. 28 Oct. 1896, Wahoo, Nebraska; s. of Hans and Hilma Eckstrom Hanson; m. Margaret Elisabeth Nelson 1946; ed. Luther Coll. Conservatory, Univ. of Nebraska, Inst. of Musical Art of New York and Northwestern Univ., Evanston, Illinois.
Prof. of Music and Dean of Conservatory of Fine Arts, Coll. of the Pacific 19-21; winner of Prix de Rome when Fellow of American Acad. in Rome 21-24; Dir. Eastman School of Music, Rochester, N.Y. 24-64; Dir. Inst. of American Music, Univ. of Rochester 64-; guest conductor of numerous American and foreign symphony orchestras; Fellow Swedish Royal Acad. of Music; mem. Nat. Inst. of Arts and Letters; over thirty Honorary Doctorates; Pulitzer Prize, Peabody Award, Freedom Award, Huntington Hartford Foundation Award, etc.
Works include: (orchestra) six symphonies, *Elegy in Memory of Serge Koussevitzky, Mosaics, Summer Seascape,* Concerto for Organ, Strings and Harp; (choral) *Songs from "Drum Taps"* (after Walt Whitman), *The Cherubic Hymn, Song of Democracy, Song of Human Rights;* (opera) *Merry Mount;* (chamber) Quintet for piano and strings, *Concerto da Camera* for piano and strings, String Quartet, *Bold Island Suite, Concerto for Piano and Orchestra, Four Psalms* for baritone and strings, *Summer Seascapes* Nos. 1 and 2, *150th Psalm, 121st Psalm, Dies Natalis, Streams in the Desert, Mystic Trumpeter;* piano music and songs.
Leisure interests: swimming, boating.
Publ. *Harmonic Materials of Modern Music.*
362 Oakdale Drive, Rochester, N.Y. 14618, U.S.A.
Telephone: BR1-9009.

Hanumanthaiya, Kengal; Indian politician; b. Feb. 1908, Kengeri, Mysore State; m. Mrs. B. Puttamma; two d.; ed. Maharaja Coll., Univ. of Mysore and Poona Law Coll., Bombay Univ.
Delegate to Indian Nat. Congress, Madras Session 27; practised as advocate 33-36; began work in Congress as full-time worker 36-; mem. Mysore Rep. Assembly 40-; Sec. Congress Party, Mysore Rep. Assembly 40-44, Leader 44-49; imprisoned seven times during fight for freedom of India; mem. Mysore Constituent Assembly, Constituent Assembly of India 48, Provisional Parl. of India, Cttee. of Constituent Assembly to draft Model Constitution for Indian States, Cttee. on Abolition of Caste Nomenclatures; mem. Mysore Legislative Assembly 52- and Leader, Congress Party; Chief Minister, Mysore State March 52-Aug. 56; Chair. Mysore Educ. Reforms Cttee.; fmr. Pres. Post and Telegraph Workers' Union, S. India, Pres. Mil. Eng. Staff Workers' Union,

S. Region; M.P. 62-; Deputy Leader, Congress Party 67-68; Minister of Law and Social Welfare June 70-March 71; Minister of Railways 71-73; mem. Perm. Court of Arbitration, The Hague June 70-, Indian Coffee Board, All India Council of Technical Educ.; Chair. Admin. Reforms Comm. April 67.
Kengal Krupa, Bellary Road, Bangalore-6, India.
Telephone: 22324.

Hanuszkiewicz, Adam; Polish actor and theatre director; b. 16 June 1924, Lvov, U.S.S.R.; s. of Włodzimierz Hanuszkiewcz and Stanisława Szydłowska; m. 1st Zofia Ryś, one s. one d.; m. 2nd Zofia Kucówna; ed. State High School of Drama, Łódź, and State High School of Drama, Warsaw.
Debut as actor 45, acted in Cracow, Poznań and Warsaw; debut as dir. 53, directed in Poznań and Warsaw; Artistic Dir. Theatre of Polish Television 56-63; Dir. and Producer, Teatr Powszechny (Popular Theatre), Warsaw 63-68, visited, with theatre company, Prague 64, 66, Moscow 65, London, Paris 66, Helsinki 67, Bucharest 68, Stockholm, Oslo 69; Gen. Man. and Artistic Dir. Teatr Narodowy, Warsaw 68-, visited Helsinki, Leningrad, Moscow 73; acted in 50 major roles in theatre; directed 30 plays in theatre, 100 television plays; State Prize (First Class) for TV work; City of Warsaw Award for theatre work; Theatre Critics' Prize 64; Order of Banner of Labour 74.
Principal roles include: Hamlet (*Hamlet*) 51-59, Tytus (*Berenice*, Racine) 62, Prospero (*The Tempest*, Shakespeare) 63, Raskolnikov (*Crime and Punishment*, Dostoevsky) 64, Don Juan (*Don Juan*, Molière) 65.
Plays directed include: *Wesele* (*The Wedding*, Wyspiański), *Crime and Punishment* (Dostoevsky), *Coriolanus* (Shakespeare), *Don Juan* (Molière), *Platonov* (Chekhov), *The Columbus Boys* (Bratny), *Kordian* (Słowacki), *St. Joan* (Shaw) 69, *Hamlet* 70, *Norwid* 70, *Beniowski* (Słowacki) 71, *Three Sisters* 71, *Twelfth Night* (Helsinki) 71, *Macbeth* 73, *Antigone* 73, *The Inspector General* 73, *Balladyna* (Słowacki) 74, *A Month in the Country* (Turgenev) 74.
Teatr Narodowy, Plac Teatralny 3, 00-077 Warsaw, Poland.

Hara, Shiro; Japanese journalist; b. 15 Feb. 1908, Takayama, Gifu; s. of Sanwemon and Kazuko (Sugishita) Hara; m. Masako Sasada 1938; three d.; ed. Hosei Univ.
Reporter, *Kokumin Shimbun* 34; joined *Yomiuri Shimbun* 36, Deputy Editor-in-Chief 55, Dir. 57, Exec. Dir. and Editor-in-Chief 65-; Dir. Hochi Shimbun 66-; Exec. Vice-Pres. 71-; Chair. Nihon Kisha Club (Japan Journalists Club) 69-.
Leisure interests: music, golf.
Yomiuri Shimbun, 1-7-1, Otemachi, Chiyoda-ku, Tokyo, Japan.
Telephone: 242-1111.

Hara, Sumio; Japanese banker; b. 7 March 1911, Yokosuka, Kanagawa; s. of Tokuemon and Haru Hara; m. Kazuko Mimura 1939; two s. one d.; ed. Faculty of Law, Tokyo Imperial Univ.
Joined Ministry of Finance 34; Deputy Dir. Budget Bureau 53-56; Dir.-Gen. of the Tax Bureau 56-60; Commr. Nat. Tax Admin. Agency 60-62; Deputy Pres. The Bank of Tokyo Ltd. 62-65, Pres. 65-73, Chair. 73-; Chair. Bank of Tokyo (Switzerland) Ltd., Zurich 71-; Dir. and Vice-Chair. of Board, Partnership Pacific Ltd., Sydney 69-; Chair. Private Investment Co. for Asia (PICA) S.A., Panama 75-; Commr. External Devt. Co-operation Council (Prime Minister's Office) 69-; Exec. Dir. Fed. of Econ. Orgs. 65-; Trustee Japan Cttee. for Econ. Devt. 65-; Vice-Pres. Japan Tariff Asscn. 68-; mem. Directing Cttee. Asscn. Int. pour la Promotion et la Protection des Investissements Privés en Territoires Etrangers 70-; Vice-Pres. and Dir. Japan

ECAFE Asscn. 73-; Special Adviser to the Pres. Japan Chamber of Commerce and Industry 75-; mem. Rockefeller Univ. Council, Trilateral Comm. 73-, Int. Advisory Board, Sperry Rand Corpn. N.Y. 74-, Council of American-Japan Soc. Inc. 74-76, Japan-U.S. Economic Council.
Leisure interest: Go.
Bank of Tokyo Ltd., 1-1, Nihombashi Muromachi 2-chome, Chuo-ku, Tokyo; Home: 26-14, Tsutsujigaoka, Midori-ku, Yokohama, Kanagawa, Japan.
Telephone: 03-270-8111 (Office); 045-981-7507 (Home).

Harcourt, 2nd Viscount; William Edward Harcourt, K.C.M.G., O.B.E., M.A., D.L.; British banker; b. 1908; ed. Eton Coll. and Christ Church, Oxford.
Served in Royal Artillery and on the Staff in Middle East and Mediterranean Theatres 39-45; H.M. Minister (Economic) British Embassy and Head of U.K. Treasury Del., Washington 54-57; U.K. Exec. Dir. of Int. Bank for Reconstruction and Development and of Int. Monetary Fund 54-57; Chair. Legal and Gen. Assurance Soc. Ltd., Gresham Fire Insurance Soc. Ltd., British Commonwealth Insurance Co. Ltd.; Dir. Alcan Aluminium Ltd., Econ. Forestry (Holdings) Ltd.; mem. Departmental (Radcliffe) Cttee. on Monetary and Credit Policy 57-59; mem. Plowden Cttee. on Representational Services Overseas; Chair. of Trustees, Rhodes Trust; Chair. of Board of Govs. Museum of London.
Stanton Harcourt, Oxford; and 23 Culross Street, London, W.1, England.
Telephone: 086-731-296 (Oxford); 629-6061 (London).

Harden, Donald Benjamin, C.B.E., M.A., PH.D., F.S.A., F.M.A.; British museum official (retd.); b. 8 July 1901, Dublin, Ireland; s. of Rt. Rev. John Mason Harden and Constance Caroline (née Sparrow); m. 1st Cecil Ursula Harriss 1934 (died 1963), one d.; m. 2nd Dorothy May McDonald 1965; ed. Westminster School, Trinity Coll., Cambridge, and Univ. of Michigan.
Senior Asst., Dept. of Humanity, Univ. of Aberdeen 24-26; Commonwealth Fund Fellow 26-28; Asst. Keeper, Dept. of Antiquities, Ashmolean Museum, Oxford 29-45, Keeper 45-56; Leverhulme Research Fellowship 53; Vice-Pres. Soc. of Antiquaries, London 49-53, 64-67; Pres. Council for British Archaeology 50-54; Pres. Oxford Architectural and Historical Society 52-54; Pres. Section H, British Asscn. 55; Dir. London Museum 56-70; Pres. Museums Asscn. 60-61; Pres. London and Middlesex Archaeological Soc. 59-64, Royal Archaeological Inst. 66-69, Int. Asscn. for History of Glass 67-74; Commr., Royal Comm. on Historical Monuments (England) 63-71; mem. Ancient Monuments Board for England 59-74; mem. governing body British School of Archaeology in Iraq; Pres. Soc. for Medieval Archaeology 75-; Hon. mem. German Archaeological Inst.
Leisure interests: archaeology and antiquities.
Publs. *Roman Glass from Karanis* 36, *The Anglo-Saxon Cemetery at Abingdon, Berks.* (with E. T. Leeds) 36; *The Phoenicians* 62, revised edn. 71, Editor *Dark-Age Britain* 56, and *Medieval Archaeology* (annually 57-73).
12 St. Andrew's Mansions, Dorset Street, London, W1H 3FD, England.
Telephone: 01-935-5121.

Hardenberg, Graf Hans Carl von; German diplomatist; b. 11 Dec. 1909, Hanover; s. of Graf Hans von Hardenberg and Alice (née von Campe); m. Martha Elisabeth (née Willmer) 1937; one s. one d.; ed. Univs. of Lausanne, Washington (Georgetown) and Göttingen.
Councillor to Govt., Trade Policy Dept., Ministry of Econs. of the Reich 36-42; military service and prisoner of war in the Soviet Union 43-53; Section Chief, Trade Policy Dept., Fed. Ministry of Foreign Affairs 53-57; Head of Office of State Sec. 57-61; Observer, UNO European Office, rep. at Int. Orgs., Geneva with rank

of Amb. and Consul-Gen. 61-64; Deputy Head, Trade Policy Dept., Fed. Ministry of Foreign Affairs 64; Amb. and Perm. Rep. to OECD 69-73; Order of Isabel la Católica; Order of the White Elephants; Bundesverdienstkreuz; and orders from Italy and Repub. of Peru. Leisure interests: tennis, skiing.

8 Munich, Gustav-Freytag-Strasse 11, Federal Republic of Germany.
Telephone: 984124.

Hardie, Sir Charles Edgar Mathewes, Kt., C.B.E.; British chartered accountant; b. 10 March 1910; s. of Dr. C. F. and Mrs. R. F. Hardie (née Moore); m. 1st Dorothy Jean Hobson (died 1965), one s. three d.; m. 2nd Mrs. Angela Richli 1966 (dissolved 1975); m. 3rd Rosemary Margaret Harwood 1975; ed. Aldenham School.

Qualified as Chartered Accountant 32, Partner, Dixon, Wilson & Co., London 34-; War Service (Col.) 39-44; Chair. BOAC 69-70, White Fish Authority 66-73, Metropolitan Estate & Property Corpn. Ltd. 64-71, British Printing Corpn. Ltd. 69-76, Fitch Lovell Ltd.; Dir. British American & Gen. Trust Ltd., Mann Egerton & Co. Ltd., Hill Samuel Group Ltd., Trust House Forte Ltd., Westminster Property Group Ltd., etc.; mem. Board of Dirs. Royal Bank of Canada; Legion of Merit 44.

Gillett House, 55 Basinghall Street, London, EC2V 5EA; The Old School House, Sturminster Newton, Dorset; 7 St. Paul's Court, 56 Manchester Street, London W1M 5PA, England.
Telephone: 01-628-4321 (Office); 0258-72983, 01-487-3507 (Home).

Hardin, Clifford Morris, B.S., M.S., DR. AGRIC. ECON.; American business executive; b. 1915, Knightstown, Ind.; m. Martha Love Wood; five c.; ed. Purdue Univ.

Assistant Prof. of Agricultural Econs., Univ. of Wisconsin 42-44; Assoc. Prof., Michigan State Coll. 44-46, Prof. and Chair. Agricultural Econs. Dept. 46-48, Asst. Dir. Agriculture Experimental Station 48, Dir. 49-53, Dean of Agriculture 53-54; Chancellor, Univ. of Nebraska 54-69; U.S. Sec. of Agriculture 69-71; Vice-Chair. Ralston Purina Co. 71-; mem. Exec. Cttee. Council of Higher Educ. of the American Republics 63-69; Trustee, Rockefeller Foundation 61-69, 72-, Farm Foundation 73-, Freedoms Foundation at Valley Forge 73-; mem. Board Nat. Science Foundation 66-70; mem. Nat. Industrial Energy Council; Trustee American Assembly, Int. Agriculture Devt. Service Inc., Univ. of Nebraska Foundation.

Ralston Purina Co., Checkerboard Square, St. Louis, Mo. 63188, U.S.A.

Harding, Lt.-Col. George Richardson, D.S.O., M.B.E.; British industrialist; b. 15 Sept. 1884, East Preston, Sussex; s. of Mr. and Mrs. G. S. Harding; m. Grace Henley Darby 1921; two s.; ed. Brighton.

Civil engineer, England 01-07, Canada 07-14; served First World War 14-19; Chair. Maconochie Bros. Ltd. 26-42; Dir. Aplin & Barrett 43-60, Chair. 56-; Pres. Food Manufacturers' Federation Inc. 37-43; mem. Consultative Cttee. on A.R.P., Home Office 39-43; mem. Nat. Advisory Council on Fire Prevention 41-43; mem. Council, Hon. Treas. 38, 39, Deputy Chair. 40, Chair. 41-43, Vice-Pres. 43-, London Chamber of Commerce; Chair. Food Manufacturers' Export Group 40; mem. Food Prices Control Cttee. 40; Chair. British Food Manufacturing Industries Research Asscn. 48-52; mem. Postmaster-General's Advisory Council 46-65; Vice-Pres. Asscn. of British Chambers of Commerce 49-55; mem. Council of Foreign Bondholders 44-56, and Board of Referees 53-65.

Leisure interest: gardening.
Wildwood, Abbots Drive, Virginia Water, Surrey, England.
Telephone: Wentworth 2137.

Harding of Petherton, 1st Baron, cr. 58, of Nether Compton; **Field Marshal John Harding,** G.C.B., C.B.E., D.S.O., M.C.; British army officer; b. 1896, South Petherton; m. Mary G. M. Rooke 1927; one s.; ed. Ilminster Grammar School.

Served with Territorial Army and Machine Gun Corps, First World War 14-19; Lieut. Somerset Light Infantry 20, Capt. 23; Brigade Major, British Force, Saar Plebiscite; graduated Staff Coll. 28; Brevet Major 35, Brevet Lieut.-Col. 38, Lieut.-Col. 39, Brigadier 42, Maj.-Gen. 42, Lieut.-Gen. 43, Gen. 49; served Second World War 39-45; G.O.C. Central Mediterranean Forces 46-47; G.O.C.-in-C. Southern Command 47-49; C.-in-C. Far East Land Forces 49-51; C.-in-C. British Army of the Rhine 51-52; Chief Imperial Gen. Staff 52-55, Field Marshal 53; A.D.C. to late King 50-52, to Queen 52-53; Gov. and C.-in-C. Cyprus 55-57; Dir. Nat. Provincial Bank 57-69, Standard Bank 65-71, Western Gazette Co. 58-, Sansmarez Carey and Harris Ltd. 72-; Gold Stick to H.M. The Queen 57-64; Dir. The Plessey Co. 62-64, 71-, Deputy Chair. 64-67, Chair. 67-70; Chair. Horserace Betting Levy Board 61-67, Williams (Hounslow) Ltd. 62-71, Assoc. Tees-side Stores Ltd. 62-68; Hon. D.C.L. (Durham Univ.).

Leisure interest: gardening.
Lower Farm, Nether Compton, Nr. Sherborne, Dorset, England.
Telephone: Sherborne 2576.

Hardy, Sir Alister Clavering, Kt., F.R.S., M.A., D.SC., LL.D.; British zoologist; b. 10 Feb 1896, Nottingham; s. of Richard and Elisabeth H. Hardy; m. Sylvia Lucy Garstang 1927; one s. one d.; ed. Oundle School and Exeter Coll., Oxford.

Lieutenant and Capt. First World War 15-19; Royal Engineers Asst. Camouflage Officer 18; Asst. Naturalist, Fisheries Dept., Ministry of Agriculture and Fisheries 21-24; Chief Zoologist *Discovery* Expedition 24-28; Prof. Zoology and Oceanography, Univ. Coll. of Hull 28-42; Regius Prof. Natural History, Aberdeen 42-45; Linacre Prof. Zoology and Comparative Anatomy, Oxford 45-61, now Prof. Emer.; Dir. Religious Experience Research Unit, Manchester Coll., Oxford 69-.

Leisure interest: water-colour sketching.
Publs. *The Open Sea: the World of Plankton* 56, *The Open Sea: Fish and Fisheries* 59, *The Living Stream* 65, *The Divine Flame* 66, *Great Waters* 67, *The Challenge of Chance* (with Robert Harvie and Arthur Koestler) 73, *Memoirs on Biological Oceanography*.
7 Capel Close, Oxford, England.
Telephone: Oxford 54381.

Hardy, James Daniel, PH.D.; American emeritus professor of environmental physiology; b. 11 Aug. 1904, Georgetown, Tex.; s. of James C. and Lulu Daniel Hardy; m. Augusta Ewing Haugh 1928; two s.; ed. Univ. of Mississippi, Johns Hopkins Univ.

National Research Council Fellow in Physics, Univ. of Mich. 30-32; Research Fellow, Russell Sage Inst. of Pathology, Cornell Univ. 32-41; Asst. Prof. of Physiology Medical Coll. 41-46; Assoc. Prof. 46-53, Prof. of Physiology, Univ. of Pa. 53-61; Research Dir. Aviation Medical Acceleration Lab., U.S. Navy, Johnsonville, Pa. 53-61; Prof. of Physiology, Yale Univ. School of Medicine 61-73, Prof. Emer. Epidemiology and Physiology 73-; Dir. John B. Pierce Foundation Lab. 61-Sept. 74; mem. Nat. Acad. of Sciences; Fellow, American Acad. of Arts and Sciences, Aerospace Medical Assen., American Physical Soc.; Hon. D.Sc. (Kansas City Coll. of Osteopathy and Surgery and Southwestern Univ.), Dr. h.c. (Univ. of Lyons), Hon. M.A. (Yale); Legion of Merit, Distinguished Service Cross, Purple Heart.

Leisure interests: fishing, golf, travel.
Publs. about 300 articles in professional journals; *Pain Sensations and Reactions* (with Wolff and Goodell) 52, *Physiological Problems in Space Exploration* 64;

edited *Temperature, its Measurement and Control in Science and Industry* Vol. III, Pt. 3, *Biology and Medicine* 63, *Thermal Problems in Aerospace Medicine* 68, *Physiological and Behavioral Temperature Regulation* (with Gagge and Stolwijk) 70.

John B. Pierce Foundation Laboratory, 290 Congress Avenue, New Haven, Conn. 06519; Home: 1127 Racebrook Road, Woodbridge, New Haven, Conn. 06525, U.S.A.

Telephone: (203) 562-9901 (Office); (203) 387-7986 (Home).

Hardy, Norman Edgar; Canadian business executive; b. 4 Jan. 1917, Toronto; *s.* of George and Myrtle (Dunsmore) Hardy; *m.* Dorothy Walter 1939; two *d.*; ed. Pickering Coll., Newmarket, Ont.
Joined Hardy Cartage 35; Brewers Warehousing Co. 48; Man. Labatt's Toronto Brewery 49; Gen. Man. Ont. Div. 56, Vice-Pres. 59; Exec. Vice-Pres. John Labatt Ltd. 62; Pres. Labatt Breweries of Canada Ltd. 64; Group Exec. Vice-Pres. John Labatt Ltd. 68, Pres. 69-73, Vice-Chair. of Board 73-; Dir. John Labatt Ltd., Ogilvie Flour Mills Co., Ltd., Canadian Cablesystems Ltd., Brascan Ltd.; Chair. of Board Jonlab Investments Ltd.
John Labatt Ltd., 451 Ridout Street, N., London, Ont. N6A 2P6, Canada.

Hare, Raymond Arthur, A.B.; American diplomatist; b. 3 April 1901, Martinsburg, W. Va.; *s.* of Frank Earhart Hare and Anna Marte Bowers; *m.* Julia Cygan 1932; two *s.*; ed. Grinnell Coll.
Instructor, Robert Coll., Constantinople 24-27; Exec. Sec. American Chamber of Commerce for Levant 26-27; Clerk, later Vice-Consul, U.S. Consulate-Gen., Constantinople 27-28; Language Officer, Paris, 29, 31, also Vice-Consul 31; Sec. in Diplomatic Service and Vice-Consul, Cairo 31; Vice-Consul, Beirut 32; Third Sec. and Vice-Consul, Teheran 33; Dept. of State 35; Second Sec., Cairo 39, also at Jeddah 40-44, also Consul, Cairo 40; Second Sec., later First Sec. and Consul, London 44; Dept. of State 46; Nat. War Coll. 46-47; Chief, Div. of Middle East, Indian and South Asian Affairs 47; Deputy Dir. Office of Near East and African Affairs 48; Deputy Asst. Sec. of State for Near East, S. Asian and African Affairs Oct. 49; Ambassador to Saudi Arabia and Minister to Yemen 50-53; Ambassador to the Lebanon 53-54; Dir.-Gen. U.S. Foreign Service 54-56; Ambassador to Egypt 56-58, Ambassador to U.A.R. 58-60, also Minister to Yemen 59; Deputy Under-Sec. of State (Political Affairs) 60-61; Ambassador to Turkey 61-65; Asst. Sec. of State (Near Eastern and S. Asian Affairs) 65-66; Pres. Middle East Inst. 66-69, Nat. Chair. Middle East Inst. 69-.
Leisure interests: Islamic architecture, swimming, walking, golf.
Middle East Institute, 1761 N Street, N.W., Washington, D.C. 20036; Home: 3214 39th Street, N.W., Washington, D.C. 20016, U.S.A.
Telephone: 202-244-4877.

Harewood, 7th Earl of; **George Henry Hubert Lascelles;** British musical administrator; b. 7 Feb. 1923, London; *s.* of 6th Earl of Harewood and H.R.H. The Princess Royal; *m.* 1st Maria Donata Stein 1949 (dissolved 1967), three *s.*; *m.* 2nd Patricia Tuckwell 1967; one *s.*; ed. Eton Coll. and King's Coll., Cambridge.
Captain, Grenadier Guards 42-46; prisoner of war 44-45; A.D.C. to Earl of Athlone, Gov.-Gen. of Canada 45-46; Counsellor of State during absence of the Sovereign 47, 54 and 56; mem. Board of Dirs. Royal Opera House, Covent Garden 51-53, 69-72, Admin. Exec. 53-60; Dir.-Gen. Leeds Musical Festival 58-74; Artistic Dir. Edinburgh Int. Festival 61-65; Chair. British Council Music Advisory Cttee. 56-66, Arts Council Music Panel 66-72; Artistic Adviser New Philharmonia Orchestra, London 66-; Pres. English Football Assen. 64-71, Leeds United

Football Club; Chancellor, York Univ. 63-67; Gen. Advisory Council of BBC 69-; Man. Dir. English Nat. Opera 72-; Editor *Opera* 50-53, *Kobbé's* Complete Opera Book 54, 76; Austrain Great Silver Medal of Honour 59, Lebanese Order of the Cedar 70.
Leisure interests: painting, sculpture, football.
Harewood House, Leeds, Yorks.; 3 Clifton Hill, London, N.W.8, England.

Harhoff, Preben; Danish shipowner; b. 29 Nov. 1911, Copenhagen; *s.* of late C. J. C. Harhoff and Rigmor Hansen; *m.* Else Harhoff 1937; one *s.* one *d.*; ed. Copenhagen Univ. and in Germany, England and France.
Proprietor, senior partner, C. K. Hansen Ltd. -68; Dir. Dansk Transatlantisk Rederi Ltd. 57-65, Chair. 65-; Dir. British Import Union, Copenhagen 58, Selskabet Orlogsmuseets Venner 65, Whitbread & Co. (Scandinavia) Ltd. 65, Harlang and Toksvig Reklamebureau A/S, Diversa A/S; Chair. Int. Farvefabrik A/S, Underberg Import A/S; Hon. Consul-Gen. for Tunisia in Copenhagen 62-; Council mem. Corps Consulaire; several decorations.
Leisure interests: fishing, tennis.
Office: Consulat Général de Tunisie, Strandboulevarden 130, 2100 Copenhagen Ø; Home: Olaf Poulsensvej 12, 2920 Copenhagen-Charlottenlund, Denmark.
Telephone: HE 6262.

Harkavy, Rabbi Zvi, B.A., M.A., TH.D.; Israeli author, bibliographer and librarian; b. 1 Feb. 1908, Ekaterinoslav, Russia; *s.* of Yehuda-Leib (Lev) Harkavy and Rashe-Raya (Karpas); *m.* Dina Katz 1944; one *s.*; ed. Inst. of Admin. Bibliography and Booklore in U.S.S.R., Jerusalem Teachers' Seminary, Haifa Technion, Hebrew Univ. of Jerusalem, Petach Tikva Yeshiva, C.S.R.A.
Leader in Zionist underground in U.S.S.R.; settled in Palestine 26; schoolmaster and lecturer Jerusalem Teachers' Seminaries 30-; Dir. Eretz-Yisrael Publishing House 35-; Chaplain in Israeli Army 48-49; Dir. Dept. of Refugees in Ministry of War Casualties and later Editor of Ministry of Religious Affairs *Monthly* 49-53; Dir. Cen. Rabbinical Library of Israel 53-73; Editor *Hasefer* 54-; mem. Exec. Union of Israel Librarians 55-68; Visiting Prof. Yeshiva Univ., N.Y. 59; lectured in U.S.S.R. Acad. of Sciences, Leningrad 62; Founder, Religious Writers Org., then Chair.; one of the founders of the Religious Academics Org. and fmr. Chair.; an Editor of the *General Encyclopaedia* and of numerous periodicals and books; del. to numerous congresses abroad; Komemiyut, Mishmar, Hagana and Aleh Medals.
Publs. Biographies: *Rambam, Rabbi Shmuel Strashun, Rabbi Mateth Strashun, S. Rosanes, Rabbi I. M. Pines, Professor Simcha Assaf, A. Harkavy, Rabbi Reuven Katz (Chief Rabbi of Petach Tikva), Prof. S. Klein;* research into famous families: *The Family Maskil L'eitan, The Family Harkavy; Jews of Salonica, The Jewish Community of Ekaterinoslav; Scepticism of Pascal; The Man, The Plant, The Animal, Inorganic Nature; The Secret of Happy Marriage, Sexual Hygiene from the Religious and Scientific Viewpoint; Judaica in Russian, Karaites during the Holocaust with the Nazis, The Works of A. Harkavy* (20 vols.), *Autobibliographia* 71, *Hebrew Epigraphy in Georgia* 72, *Book of Ekaterinoslav-Dnepropetrovsk* 73, *Fragment of Sefer-Hamizvot from Anan the Karaite, Efpatoria Manuscript* 75; about 1,300 books, articles and papers on bibliography, Rabbinics, theology, philosophy, philology, history and the Dead Sea Scrolls.
P.O. Box 7031, Jerusalem 91070, Israel.
Telephone: (02) 32-963.

Harker, David, B.S., PH.D.; American scientist; b. 19 Oct. 1906, San Francisco, Calif.; *s.* of George Asa and Harriette (Buttler) Harker; *m.* 1st Katherine deSavich

1930 (died 1973), two d.; m. 2nd Deborah Anne Maxwell 1974; ed. Univ. of Calif. (Berkeley), Calif. Inst. of Technology.
Research Asst., Atmospheric Nitrogen Corpn., Solvay, N.Y. 30-33; Instructor in Chemistry Johns Hopkins Univ. 36-39, Assoc. in Chemistry 39-41; Assoc., Research Laboratory, Gen. Electric Co., Schenectady, N.Y. 41-49, Head Crystallography Div. 49-50; Dir. The Protein Structure Project, Polytechnic Inst. of Brooklyn 50-59; Adjunct Prof. of Physics 53-56; Prof. of Crystallography, Polytechnic Inst. of Brooklyn 56-59; Head Biophysics Dept. Roswell Park Memorial Inst. 59-; Research Prof. of Biophysics, State Univ. of N.Y., Buffalo 60-, Professorial Lecturer 59-; Visiting Prof. of Biophysics, Univ. of Rochester 65-; Adjunct Prof. of Physics, State Univ. Coll. at Buffalo, N.Y. 66-; Research Prof., Graduate Faculty, Niagara Univ., Niagara Falls, N.Y. 68-; mem. U.S. Nat. Comm. on Crystallography, Nat. Research Council 51-56, 58-63, 64-67, 68-71, Chair. 54-55; Chief Amer. Del. to Int. Congress on X-ray Crystallography, London 46; Del. to Gen. Assembly, Int. Union of Crystallography, Stockholm 51, Paris 54, Montreal 57, Cambridge 60 and Moscow 66; fmr. mem. Electron Microscope Soc. of American (Pres. 46, 47); mem. American Soc. for X-ray and Electron Diffraction (Pres. 46), Société Française de Minéralogie et de Crystallographie, American Crystallographic Assen., Biophysical Soc., and A.A.A.S.; Fellow, New York Acad. of Sciences, American Physical Soc., American Inst. of Chemists; consultant on X-ray Diffraction to X-ray Dept. of Gen. Electric Co. 53-, to Carborundum Co. 62-; Advisory Editor, Trans. Russian Journal *Crystallography* 58-69; Dir. Center for Crystallographic Research, Roswell Park Div. of Health Research Inc., Buffalo 65-; Assoc. Prof., Faculty of Science, Univ. of Bordeaux Jan.-July 70; mem. Advisory Board Russian Trans., American Inst. Physics; Chair. Cttee. at several Int. Congresses of Crystallography 68, 69; three national awards.
Leisure interests: rifle and pistol shooting, reading detective stories.
Publs. numerous scientific papers, book reviews and contributions in journals.
Home: 23 High Street, Buffalo, N.Y. 14203; Office: Roswell Park Memorial Institute, Buffalo, N.Y. 14203, U.S.A.
Telephone: 716-845-2365.

Harkort, Peter Guenther, DR.RER.POL.; German diplomatist; b. 1 Sept. 1905, Herdecke, Ruhr; s. of Peter Hermann Harkort and Elisabeth Funcke; m. Irmgard Graeve 1935; two s.; ed. Städt. Real-Gymnasium Hagen i W., Univs. of Heidelberg, Berlin, Bonn, Kiel.
Reich Statistical Office, Reich Ministry of Nat. Econ.; Württemberg-Baden Ministry of Nat. Economy; bizonal Admin. of Nat. Economy; German Bureau for Peace Questions; Rep. to ECA, Washington 49-52; Foreign Service 52-70, Ministerial Dir., Head of Commercial Dept., Bonn 58-61; Ambassador and Perm. Rep. to the EEC and EURATOM, Brussels 61-65; Ministerial Dir., Head, Dept. Commerce and Devt., Bonn 65-69, State Sec. 69-70.
Leisure interest: books.
Mecklenburgerstr. 3, 53 Bonn-Bad Godesberg, Federal Republic of Germany.
Telephone: Bonn 37-57-33.

Harland, Sydney Cross, D.SC., F.R.S., F.R.S.E.; British agricultural consultant; b. 19 June 1891, Snainton, Scarborough, Yorks.; s. of Erasmus Harland and Eliza Harland; m. 1st Emily Cameron 1915, one s.; m. 2nd Olive Sylvia Atteck 1934, two d.; ed. King's Coll., London Univ.
Head Botanical Dept. British Cotton Industry Research Assen. Manchester 20-23; Prof. of Botany Imperial Coll. of Tropical Agriculture, Trinidad 23-26; Chief Geneticist Empire Cotton Growing Corpn. 26-35; gen. adviser Brazilian State Cotton Industry 35-39; Dir. Institute of Cotton Genetics, Nat. Agricultural Society Peru 39-50; Harrison Prof. of Botany, Univ. of Manchester 50-58, Emeritus 58-; mem. Agric. Research Council 50; Hon. Fellow Textile Inst.; Fellow, New England Inst. of Medical Research, Botanical Soc. of Edinburgh; Hon. M.Sc. (Manchester).
Leisure interests: gardening, travel, writing, music.
Cliff Grange, Snainton, Scarborough, Yorks., England; Correo Ñaña, Carretera Central, Peru.
Telephone: Snainton 549.

Harlech, 5th Baron (cr. 1876); **William David Ormsby Gore,** P.C., K.C.M.G.; British diplomatist; b. 20 May 1918; s. of 4th Baron Harlech, K.G., P.C., G.C.M.G. and Lady Beatrice Cecil; m. 1st Sylvia Lloyd Thomas 1940, 2nd Pamela Colin 1969; one s. four d.; ed. Eton and New Coll., Oxford.
War Service 39-45; Conservative M.P. 50-61; Parl. Private Sec. to Minister of State for Foreign Affairs 51-56; Parl. Under-Sec. of State for Foreign Affairs 56-57; Minister of State for Foreign Affairs 57-61; Amb. to U.S.A. Oct. 61-65; Deputy Leader Conservative Party, House of Lords 66-67; Chair. Harlech Television 67-; Pres. British Board of Film Censors 65-; Chair. Kennedy Memorial Trust; Chair. European Movt. 69-75; Pres. The Pilgrims of Great Britain; Pres. Shelter Campaign for the Homeless 69-; Trustee, Tate Gallery 71-; Deputy Chair. British Comm. on Rhodesian Opinion 72; Chair. Pilgrim Trust 74-; Dir. Morgan Crucible Co., Bank of Wales; Hon. LL.D. (New York, Farleigh Dickinson and Manchester Univ.), Hon. D.C.L. (Pittsburgh Univ.), Hon. D.Iur. (Brown Univ., Providence, and Coll. of William and Mary, Williamsburg).
Publ. *Must the West Decline?* 66.
Glyn, Talsarnau, Merioneth, N. Wales; 14A Ladbroke Road, London, W.11, England.
Telephone: Harlech 338 and 01-229-6701.

Harlem, Gudmund, M.D.; Norwegian doctor and politician; b. 24 July 1917, Oslo; s. of late Gudmund Harlem and late Olga Harlem; m. Inga Brynolf 1938; two s. two d.; ed. Medical School, Oslo Univ.
Assistant Physician Hygiene Inst., Oslo Univ. 46-48; Senior Physician State Rehabilitation Centre, Oslo 53-; studied rehabilitation in Great Britain 47, 48 and 50, in U.S.A. 49-50; as UN Technical Expert on Rehabilitation went on missions to Egypt 54, Greece and Italy 55; Deputy Chair. Oslo Labour Party 52-66, mem. Central Cttee. Labour Party 53-57; mem. Norwegian Nat. Research Council 49-57; Chair. Rehabilitation Council 55-57; Minister of Health and Social Affairs 55-61, of Defence 61-65; Resident, Oslo Univ. Hospital 65-66; Pres. Int. Soc. for Rehabilitation of the Disabled 66-69; Dir. State Rehabilitation Inst. 66-; Chair. Board of Research on Environmental Contaminations; Lasker Award 60; Labour.
Leisure interests: skiing, sailing.
State Rehabilitation Institute in Oslo, Sinsenvn. 76, Refstad, Oslo 5, Norway.
Telephone: 02-227760.

Harlow, Bryce Nathaniel; American government official; b. 11 Aug. 1916, Oklahoma City; ed. Univs. of Oklahoma and Texas.
Graduate Asst., Univ. of Texas 37; Asst. Librarian, House of Reps. 38-40; mem. Congress 40-41; Special Asst., White House Staff, Admin. Asst., Special Asst., Deputy Asst. to Pres. 53-61; Dir. Govt. Relations, Proctor and Gamble Manufacturing Co. 61-68, Vice-Pres. 71-73, 74-; Counsellor with Cabinet Rank 69-70; Pres. Counsellor without Portfolio 73-74.
Procter and Gamble Manufacturing Co. Washington, D.C. 20013, U.S.A.

Harlow, Harry Frederick, B.A., PH.D.; American professor of psychology; b. 31 Oct. 1905, Fairfield, Ia.; s. of Lon Israel and Mabel (Rock) Israel; m. 1st Clara Mears 1932 (divorced 1946), remarried 1972, 2nd Margaret Kuenne 1948 (deceased 1971); three s. one d.; ed. Stanford Univ.
Member staff, Univ. of Wisconsin 30- (two leaves of absence); Carnegie Fellow in Anthropology, Columbia Univ. 39-40; Head of Human Resources Branch, Department of Army 50-52; Prof. of Psychology, Univ. of Wisconsin 44-74, Prof. Emer. 74-; Dir. Primate Laboratory, Univ. of Wisconsin 56-74, Dir. Regional Primate Research Center, Univ. of Wisconsin 61-71; Research Prof. of Psychology, Univ. of Arizona 74-; Pres. Mid-western Psychological Association 47-48, Div. of Experimental Psychologists of American Psychological Asscn. 58-59; Editor *Journal of Comparative and Physiological Psychology* 51-63; Pres. Div. of Comparative and Physiological Psychology, American Psychological Asscn. 65; mem. Nat. Acad. of Sciences, American Philosophical Soc., Nat. Acad. of Arts and Sciences, etc.; Howard Crosby Warren Medal 56; Distinguished Psychologist Award 60; Nat. Medal of Science 67; Gold Medal Award, American Psychological Foundation 73; Annual Award of the Soc. for Scientific Study of Sex 74; Third Int. Kittay Award 75; Von Giesen Award 75.
Publs. Co-author several books 30-; more than 300 journal articles.
Office: University of Wisconsin Primate Laboratory, 22 N. Charter Street, Madison, Wis. 53706; Home: 672 Roller Coaster Road, Tucson, Ariz. 85704, U.S.A.
Telephone: (608) 263-3550 (Office); (602) 888-6548 (Home).

Harman, Avraham, B.A.; Israeli diplomatist; b. 1914; ed. Oxford Univ.
Emigrated to Israel 38; held posts in Jewish Agency 38-48; Deputy Dir. Govt. Information Bureau 48-49; Consul-Gen. Montreal 49-50, New York, and Counsellor Del. to UN 50-53; Consul-Gen. in New York 53-55; Asst. Dir.-Gen. Ministry of Foreign Affairs 55-56; Dir. Information Dept. Jewish Agency 57-59; Amb. to the U.S.A. 59-68; Pres. Hebrew Univ. of Jerusalem 68-.
Hebrew University of Jerusalem, Israel.

Harmel, Pierre Charles José Marie, D. en D.; Belgian university professor and politician; b. 16 March 1911, Uccle, Brussels.
Professor, Faculty of Law, Univ. of Liège 47-; mem. and fmr. Vice-Pres. Chamber of Reps.; Minister of Public Instruction and Fine Arts June 50-54; Minister of Justice 58; Minister of Cultural Affairs 59-60; Minister of Admin. 60-61; Prime Minister July 65-66; Minister of Foreign Affairs 66-73; co-opted Senator 71; Minister of State Feb.-Oct. 73; Pres. of Senate 73-; Croix de Guerre with palms 40.
Publs. *Principes non bis in idem et les droits d'enregistrement* 42, *La Famille et l'Impôt en Belgique* 44, *Culture et Profession* 44, *Les Sources et la Nature de la Responsabilité Civile des Notaires, en droit Belge de 1830 à 1962* 64.
30B Avenue Hamoir, 1180 Brussels, Belgium.

Harmer, Sir Frederic Evelyn, Kt., C.M.G.; British shipping executive (retd.); b. 3 Nov. 1905, Cambridge; s. of late Sidney F. Harmer and late Lady Laura Russell Harmer (née Howell); m. 1st Barbara Susan Hamilton 1931 (died 1972), one s. three d.; m. 2nd Daphne Shelton Agar 1973; ed. Eton and King's Coll., Cambridge.
Treasury 39, Temporary Asst. Sec. 43-45, served Washington 44,45; Dir. Peninsular and Orient Steam Navigation Co. 55-57, Deputy Chair. 57-70; Govt. Dir. British Petroleum Co. Ltd. 52-70; Dir. Nat. Westminster Bank Ltd.; Vice-Chair. of Govs., London

School of Econs. until Dec. 69; Chair. Int. Chamber of Shipping until 71.
Leisure interests: sailing, golf.
Tiggins Field, Kelsale, Saxmundham, Suffolk, England.
Telephone: Saxmundham 3156.

Harms, Hans, DR. ING.; German chemical executive; b. 3 Sept. 1906, Wiesbaden; s. of Johann and Lina Harms; m. Eva Pawlowski 1935; three s. one d.; ed. Technische Hochschule, Darmstadt, and Universität Freiburg/Breisgau.
Former Chair. of Management Board, E. Merck AG, Hon. mem. Presidency, Fed. of German Chemical Industry, Fed. Asscn. of Pharmaceutical Industry; mem. Commercial Political Cttee. of Asscn. of Chemical Industry; mem. U.S.S.R. Dept. of Trade Council for Foreign Trade, Chair. China Dept.; Hon. mem. Pres. Comm. Int. Group of Pharmaceutical Industries of European Common Market Countries (GIIP), Brussels; mem. Regional Advisory Cttee. for Hesse of Deutsche Bank AG, Frankfurt; mem. Admin. Board, Berliner Handelsgesellschaft/Frankfurter Bank.
Leisure interests: old oriental carpets, music, Lamaism.
61 Darmstadt, Dieburger Strasse 209, Federal Republic of Germany.
Telephone: (06151) 75660.

Harnick, Sheldon Mayer; American lyricist; b. 30 April 1924; ed. Northwestern Univ.
Wrote songs for univ. musicals; contributor to revues: *New Faces of 1952, Two's Company* 53, *John Murray Anderson's Almanac* 54, *The Shoestring Revue* 55, *The Littlest Revue* 56, *Shoestring 57* 57; with composer Jerry Bock (q.v.) wrote shows *Body Beautiful* 58, *Fiorello* 59 (Pulitzer Prize), *Tenderloin* 60, *Smiling the boy fell Dead* (with David Baker) 61, *She Loves Me* 63, *Fiddler on the Roof* 64, *The Apple Tree* 66, *The Rothschilds* 70.
c/o David J. Cogan, 350 Fifth Avenue, New York, N.Y. 10001, U.S.A.

Haroon, Mahmoud Abdullah; Pakistani diplomatist; b. 9 Sept. 1920, Karachi; s. of Sir Abdullah Haroon; m. Zubaida Abdul Ghani 1946; two d.
A.D.C. to Quaid-i-Azam Mohammad Ali Jinnah 37; mem. Pakistan Muslim League Council 42; Pres. Karachi Provincial Muslim League 44; Pres. Karachi Harbour Union 43; mem. Sind Legis. Assembly 45-50; mem. W. Pakistan Assembly 54-58; mem. Karachi Municipal Corpn. 53-58; Mayor Karachi Municipal Corpn. 53-54; mem. Nat. Assembly of Pakistan 65; Minister of Labour and Co-operation, Govt. of W. Pakistan Aug. 65; Chair. Pakistan Section, Commonwealth Press Union 65; Chair. Pakistan Herald Ltd., Pakistan Herald Publications Ltd., Haroon Industries Ltd., Eastern Film Studios Ltd., Haroon Sons Ltd.; Dir. Pakistan Services Ltd., Herbertson (Pakistan) Ltd.; High Commr. in U.K. Nov. 68-69; Minister for Agriculture and Works 69-71.
Leisure interests: educational and social work.
c/o Ministry of Agriculture, Islamabad, Pakistan.

Harper, Heather, C.B.E.; British soprano; b. 8 May 1930, Belfast; d. of Hugh and Mary Eliza Harper; m. 2nd Eduardo J. Benarroch 1973; ed. Trinity Coll. of Music, London.
Created soprano role in Britten's *War Requiem*, Coventry Cathedral 62; toured U.S.A. with BBC Symphony Orchestra 65, U.S.S.R. 67; soloist opening concerts at the Maltings, Snape 67, Queen Elizabeth Hall 67; annual concert and opera tours U.S.A. 67-; also concerts in Asia, Middle East, Australia, European Music Festivals, S. America; principal roles at Covent Garden, Bayreuth Festival, La Scala (Milan), Teatro Colón (Buenos Aires), Edinburgh Festival, Glyndebourne, Sadler's Wells, San Francisco, Frankfurt; renowned performances of *Arabella, Ariadne, Chrysothemis, Kaiserin* (Richard Strauss); TV roles include Ellen

Orford (*Peter Grimes*), Mrs. Coyle (*Owen Wingrave*); recordings include *Les Illuminations* (Britten), *Symphonies Nos.* 8 and 9 (Mahler), *Don Giovanni* (Mozart), *Requiem* and *Missa Solemnis* (Verdi), *Seven Early Songs* (Berg); Hon. mem. Royal Acad. of Music, Hon. D.Mus. (Queen's Univ.); Edison Award 71.
Leisure interests: gardening, painting, cooking, swimming, tennis.
c/o 15 Lancaster Grove, Hampstead, London, N.W.3, England.
Telephone: 01-794-4397.

Harper, John D.; American electrical engineer and business executive; b. 6 April 1910, Louisville, Tenn.; *s.* of Lafayette R. Harper and Mary A. Collier; *m.* Samma McCrary 1937; three *s.*; ed. High School and Univ. of Tennessee.
Aluminum Co. of America (ALCOA) 33-, Asst. Dist. Power Man. 43-51, Man. Rockdale Works 51-55, Asst. Gen. Man. Smelting Div., Pittsburgh 55-56, Gen. Man. Smelting Div. 56-60, Vice-Pres. (Smelting and Fabricating) 60-62, Vice-Pres. (Production) 62, Exec. Vice-Pres. 62-63, Dir. 62, Pres. 63-70, Chair. 70-75, Chief Exec. Officer 65-75, Chair. Exec. Cttee. 66-; mem. Aluminium Asscn.; Chair. The Business Round Table; Dir. U.S.-Korea Econ. Council, Communications Satellite Corpn., Mellon Nat. Corpn., Metropolitan Life Insurance Co., Goodyear Tyre and Rubber Co., Proctor & Gamble Co., Nat. Alliance of Businessmen, etc.; Sr. mem. the Conference Board, Council of the Americas; Chair. Int. Primary Aluminium Inst., Cttee. for Econ. Devt.; mem. The Business Council, Stanford Univ. Graduate School Business Advisory Council, Univ. of Tennessee Devt. Board, President's Labor-Management Cttee., Advisory Cttee., Woodrow Wilson Int. School for Scholars; Founding mem. Rockefeller Univ. Council; Nat. Exec. Cttee. Boy Scouts of America; Trustee Carnegie Mellon Univ., Council for Latin America; Fellow, American Soc. of Mechanical Engineers, American Inst. of Electrical Engineers; mem. Engineers' Soc. of Western Pennsylvania, Nat. Acad. of Engineering; distinguished life mem. Amer. Soc. for Metals; Nathan W. Dougherty Award of Univ. of Tenn., Professional Engineers' Distinguished Service Award of Pa. Soc. of Professional Engineers 66; Gold Medal, Pennsylvania Soc. 70; Knight's Cross, Royal Order of St. Olav; several hon. degrees.
Leisure interests: shooting (birds), golf.
Aluminum Company of America, 1501 Alcoa Building, Pittsburgh, Pa. 15219; Home: 880 Old Hickory Road, Pittsburgh, Pennsylvania 15243, U.S.A.

Harper, Roy W.; American judge; b. 26 July 1905, Gibson, Missouri; *s.* of Marvin and Minnie (Brooks) Harper; *m.* Ruth Butt 1941; one *s.* one *d.*; ed. Univ. of Missouri.
U.S.A. Army Air Force 42-45; admitted to Bar 29; mem. Tax Insurance Claims Dept., Shell Petroleum Corpn., St. Louis 29-30; private legal practice 31-34; mem. Ward & Reeves, Caruthersville 34-47; U.S. District Judge of Missouri, Eastern and Western Districts 47-, Chief Judge, Missouri, Eastern District 50-70; Senior Judge, Eastern and Western Districts of Missouri 71-; Chair. Missouri State Democrat Cttee. 46-47; mem. of American Missouri, St. Louis Lawyers Asscn., Pemiscot County Bar Asscn.; Order of the Coif, DeMolay Legion of Honour.
415 U.S. Court House and Custom House, St. Louis, Missouri 63101, U.S.A.
Telephone: MA 2-4220.

Harrar, J. George, A.B., M.S., PH.D.; American foundation executive; b. 2 Dec. 1906, Painesville, Ohio; *s.* of Elwood Scott and Lucetta Sterner; *m.* Georgetta Steese 1930; two *d.*; ed. Oberlin Coll., Ohio, Iowa State Univ. and Univ. of Minnesota.
Professor of Biology, Univ. of Puerto Rico 29-30, Head

of Dept. 30-33; Instructor, Plant Pathology, Univ. of Minn. 34-35; Asst. Prof. of Biology, Virginia Polytechnic Inst. 35-37, Assoc. Prof. 37-41, Prof. 41; Prof. and Head, Dept. of Plant Pathology, Washington State Univ. 41-42; Field Dir. for Agriculture, Rockefeller Foundation (Mexico) 43-52; Deputy Dir. for Agriculture, Rockefeller Foundation (N.Y.) 52-55, Dir. 55-58; Vice-Pres. Rockefeller Foundation 59-61 ,Trustee and Pres. 61-72, Pres. Emer. and Life Fellow 72-; Andrew D. White Prof.-at-Large, Cornell Univ. 71-77; mem. Board of Trustees, Oberlin Coll., Ohio 62-72, The Foundation Center 69-75; Chair. Nat. Advisory Council, Monell Chemical Senses Center, Univ. of Pennsylvania 68-, Int. Agricultural Devt. Service 75-; Chair. Exec. Cttee., The Nutrition Foundation 72-, Gov. Council, Rockefeller Archive Center 73-; Dir. Campbell Soup Co., Kimberly-Clark Corpn., Int. Flavors & Fragrances, Dreyfus Third Century Fund, Merck & Co. Inc., Viacom Int. Inc.; Fellow, American Phytopathological Soc., American Asscn. for the Advancement of Science, Royal Soc. of Arts, London 72; Trustee, Draper World Population Fund; mem. American Acad. of Arts and Sciences, American Philosophical Soc., Comm. on U.S.-Latin-American Relations 74-, Corpn. Visiting Cttee., Mass. Int. of Technology 74-; Nat. Acad. of Arts and Sciences, Italian Nat. Acad. of Agriculture, Nat. Acad. of Sciences, etc.; numerous hon. degrees; Hon. Prof. (Univ. of San Carlos, Guatemala and Catholic Univ. of Chile); Order of the Golden Heart, Philippines 64; Elvin Charles Stakman Award, Univ. of Minnesota; W. O. Atwater Medal 74, Americas Award 74; Underwood-Prescott Memorial Award 75; Hon. Chair. Population Crisis Cttee. 73-; Hon. D.Sc.(Rippon Coll.) 75; numerous other awards and honours.
Leisure interests: reading, sports.
Publs. (with E. S. Harrar) *Guide to Southern Trees* 46, (with E. C. Stakman) *Principles of Plant Pathology* 57, *Strategy for the Conquest of Hunger* 63, 67, and numerous scientific papers.
Room 907, 30 West 54th Street, New York, N.Y. 10019; and 125 Puritan Drive, Scarsdale, N.Y. 10583, U.S.A.
Telephone: (212) 582-6420; (212) 582-6476.

Harriman, E(dward) Roland; American banker; b. 24 Dec. 1895, New York; *s.* of Edward H. and Mary W. Harriman; *m.* Gladys C. C. Fries; two *d.*; ed. Yale Univ.
In banking in New York 20-; Partner Brown Brothers Harriman & Co. 31-; Chair. Board of Dirs. Union Pacific Railroad 46-69, Hon. Chair. Union Pacific Corpn. 69-.
Leisure interests: trotting horses, fishing, hunting.
59 Wall Street, New York City, N.Y. 10005, U.S.A.

Harriman, Leslie Oriseweyinmi; Nigerian diplomatist; b. 9 July 1930, Warri; ed. Govt. School, Benin, Edo Coll., Benin, Govt. Coll., Ibadan, Univ. Coll., Ibadan, Pembroke Coll., Oxford, and Imperial Defence Coll., London.
Manager, Unilever, Lagos 55-58; Second Sec. British Embassy, Spain 58-59; Counsellor and Acting High Commr. for Nigeria in Ghana 61-63; Deputy Perm. Sec. Ministry of External Affairs 65-66; High Commr. to Uganda 66-69, to Kenya 66-70; Amb. to France 70-75, also accred. to Tunisia and Perm. Del. to UNESCO 70-75; Amb. and Perm. Rep. to UN Sept. 75-.
Permanent Mission of Nigeria to the United Nations, 757 Third Avenue, 20th Floor, New York, N.Y. 10017, U.S.A.

Harriman, William Averell, HON. LL.D. (New York); American industrialist, banker, diplomatist, and government official; b. 15 Nov. 1891; *m.*; ed. Groton School and Yale Univ.
Vice-Pres. in charge of Purchases and Supplies Union Pacific R.R. Co. 15-17; Chair. of Board Merchant Shipbuilding Corpn. 17-25; Chair. of Board W. A. Harriman & Co. Inc. 20-30; partner Brown Brothers, Harriman & Co. (merger) Jan. 31-; Chair. Exec. Cttee. Illinois

Central R.R. Co. 31-42, Dir. 15-46; Dir. Union Pacific R.R. Co. 13-46, Chair. of Board 32-46; Dir. Guaranty Trust Co. of New York 15-40; at one time Dir. of Western Union Telegraph Co. and Weekly Publications Inc. (publishers of *Newsweek* Magazine); mem. N.Y. State Fair Comm. 15-17; Admin. Div. II N.R.A. Jan.-Mar. 34; Special Asst. Admin. Mar.-May 34; Admin. Officer 34-35; mem. Business Advisory Council Dept. of Commerce 33-; Chair. 37-40; served with Office of Production Management June 40-Jan. 41; special rep. of Pres. Roosevelt in Great Britain with rank of Minister Mar. 41, U.S.S.R. with rank of Ambassador Aug. 41; rep. in London of Combined Shipping Adjustment Board Feb. 42; mem. London Combined Production and Resources Board July 42; Ambassador to U.S.S.R. Oct. 43-Feb. 46; Ambassador to Great Britain April-Oct. 46; U.S. Sec. of Commerce Oct. 46-April 48; U.S. Special Rep. in Europe for E.C.A. April 48-June 50; Special Asst. to the Pres. July 50-Oct. 51; Dir. for Mutual Security Oct. 51-Jan. 53; Gov. of New York 55-59; Ambassador-at-Large Jan.-Nov. 61, 65-69; Asst. Sec. of State for Far Eastern Affairs Nov. 61-63, Under-Sec. for Political Affairs 63-65; Chief American negotiator Nuclear Test Ban Treaty, Moscow 63; took part in negotiations on war in Viet-Nam, Paris 68-69; Democrat.
Publs. *Peace with Russia?* 60, *America and Russia in a Changing World* 71, *Special Envoy to Churchill and Stalin, 1941-46* 75-.
3038 N Street, Washington, D.C. 20007, U.S.A.

Harrington, Fred Harvey, A.B., M.A., PH.D.; American historian and educational administrator; b. 24 June 1912, Watertown, N.Y.; *s.* of Arthur William and Elsie (Sutton) Harrington; *m.* Anna Howes 1935; one *s.* four *d.*; ed. Cornell and New York Univs.
Instructor in History, Washington Square Coll. of New York Univ. 36-37, Univ. of Wisconsin 37-39, Asst. Prof. 39-40; Prof. and Chair. of History and Political Science, Univ. of Arkansas 40-44; Assoc. Prof. of History, Univ. of Wisconsin 44-47, Prof. 47-, Chair. of Dept. 52-55, Special Asst. to Pres. 56-58, Vice-Pres. of Academic Affairs 58-62, Vice-Pres. 62, Pres. 62-70; Vilas Research Prof. of American Diplomatic History 70-; Program Adviser to Ford Foundation in India 71-; Visiting Prof. W. Virginia Univ. 42, Cornell Univ. 44, Univ. of Pennsylvania 49, Univ. of Colorado 51, Oxford Univ. 55, Univ. of Kyoto (Japan) 62; Frederic Courtland Penfield Fellow in Diplomacy and Int. Relations, New York Univ. 33-36; Fellow John Simon Guggenheim Memorial Foundation 43-44; Ford Foundation Faculty Fellow 55-56; Pres. Nat. Asscn. State Univs. and Land Grant Colls. 68-69; Dir. Nat. Asscn. Educational Broadcasters 65-68; Dir. American Council of Educ. 66-68; Hon. LL.D. (New York Univ., Drake Univ., Loyola Univ. and Univ. of Calif.), Hon. L.H.D. (Univ. of Maine, De Paul and Miami Univs. and Northland Coll., Wis.), Hon. Litt.D. (Univ. of Ife, Nigeria).
Publs. *God Mammon and the Japanese: Dr. Horace N. Allen and Korean-American Relations (1884-1905)* 44, *Fighting Politician: Major-General N. P. Banks* 48, *An American History* (2 vols., with Curti and Shryock, and Cochran) 50, *Hanging Judge, Isaac C. Parker and the Indian Frontier* 51, *A History of American Civilization* 53.
Van Hise Hall, University of Wisconsin, Madison, Wis. 53706; Ford Foundation, Asia and Pacific Division, 320 East 43rd Street, New York, N.Y. 10017, U.S.A. Telephone: 608-262-3682 (Madison).

Harris, Marshal of the R.A.F. Sir Arthur Travers, Bt., G.C.B., O.B.E., A.F.C.; British officer; b. 13 April 1892, Cheltenham, Glos.; *s.* of George S. T. Harris and Caroline M. (née Elliot); *m.* 1st Barbara K. Money 1916, one *s.* two *d.*; *m.* 2nd Therese Hearne 1938, one *d.*
Joined 1st Rhodesian Regt. 14, served S.W. Africa

R.F.C. 15, served First World War and with R.A.F. France, India, Iraq, Middle East; Head, R.A.F. mission to U.S. and Canada 38; Air Officer Commanding R.A.F. Palestine and Transjordan 38-39; Air Officer Commanding No. 5 Group 39-40; Deputy Chief of Air Staff 40-41; Head R.A.F. Del. U.S.A. 41, and R.A.F. mem. Joint Chiefs of Staff; Air Officer Commanding-in-Chief Bomber Command 42-45; Man. Dir. South African Marine Corpn. 46-53; awards include Order of Suvorov (U.S.S.R.) 1st Class 44, Grand Cross Polonia Restituta (Poland), Chief Commdr. Legion of Merit (U.S.A.), D.S.M. (U.S.A.), Grand Cross Order of Southern Cross (Brazil), Grand Officier Légion d'Honneur, Croix de Guerre avec Palme, Freeman of Honiton 45, Chipping Wycombe 45; Hon. LL.D. (Liverpool).
Publ. *Bomber Offensive* 46.
The Ferry House, Goring-on-Thames, Oxon., England. Telephone: Goring 2130.

Harris, Chauncy Dennison, PH.D., D.LITT.; American geographer; b. 31 Jan. 1914, Logan, Utah; *s.* of Franklin S. and Estella S. Harris; *m.* Edith Young 1940; one *d.*; ed. Brigham Young Univ., Oxford and Chicago Univs.
Professor of Geography, Univ. of Chicago 47-, Samuel N. Harper Distinguished Service Prof. 73-, Dean, Graduate Div. of Social Sciences 54-60; Dir. Centre for Int. Studies 66-; Asst. to the Pres. 73-, Vice-Pres. for Academic Resources 75-; mem. Board of Dirs., Social Science Research Council 59-70, Vice-Chair. 63-65, mem. Cttee. on Programs and Policy 59-67, Exec. Cttee. 67-70; mem. Exec. Cttee., Nat. Research Council Div. of Behavioural Sciences 67-70; mem. Int. Research and Exchanges Board 68-71; mem. Exec. Cttee. ICSU 69-72; Del. 17th Gen. Conf. UNESCO, Paris 72; mem. Int. Geog. Union, Vice-Pres. 56-64, Sec.-Gen. 68-76; mem. Asscn. of American Geographers (Pres. 57), American Asscn. for Advancement of Slavic Studies (Pres. 62), American Geog. Soc. (Vice-Pres. 69-74); Alexander Csoma de Körösi Memorial Medal, Hungarian Geographical Soc. 71; Hon. mem. Royal Geographical Soc. and geographical socs. of Paris, Berlin, Frankfurt, Rome, Florence and Warsaw; D.Econ. h.c. (Catholic Univ., Chile).
Publs. *Economic Geography of the U.S.S.R.* 49, *International List of Geographical Serials* 60 (2nd edn. 71), *Soviet Geography: Accomplishments and Tasks* 62, *Cities of the Soviet Union* 70, *Annotated World List of Selected Current Geographical Serials in English, French and German* 71; articles in professional journals.
Center for International Studies, University of Chicago, 5828 University Avenue, Chicago, Ill. 60637, U.S.A. Telephone: 312-753-3926.

Harris, Fred R., B.A., LL.B.; American lawyer and politician; b. 13 Nov. 1930; ed. Walters High School and Univ. of Oklahoma.
Private legal practice until 64; mem. Oklahoma State Senate 56-64; Senator from Oklahoma 64-73; Chair. Democratic Nat. Cttee. 69-70; Democrat.
1120 Cherry Street, Lawton, Oklahoma, U.S.A.

Harris, Michael Saul; American international official; b. 15 July 1916; *m.* Marjorie H. Kipp 1940; two *d.*; ed. public schools, Philadelphia.
Steelworkers' Organising Cttee., Congress of Industrial Orgs. (C.I.O.), Berwick, Pa. 37, Sub. Regional Dir. Philadelphia 38-41; District Dir. and mem. Int. Exec. Board United Steelworkers of America, Philadelphia 42-48; Econ. Co-operation Admin. (ECA) Special Mission to France 48, Chief ECA Special Mission to Sweden 49-51, to Germany 51-53; U.S. Minister (Econ. Affairs), Bonn 53-55; with Ford Foundation 55-63; Deputy Sec.-Gen. Organisation for Economic Co-operation and Devt. (OECD) Sept. 63-67; Dir. and fmr. Pres. Franklin Book Programs Inc., N.Y.C. 67-; Vice-Pres., Dir. John Wiley & Sons Co. 69-; Dir. and Treas. Iran

Foundation; mem. Exec. Cttee., Int. Group of Scientific, Medical and Technical Publrs.
Leisure interests: gardening, theatre, music.
605 Third Avenue, New York, N.Y.; Home: 25 Partrick Road, Westport, Conn., U.S.A.
Telephone: 867-9800 (Office); 226-0818 (Home).

Harris, Mrs. Patricia Roberts, A.B., IUR.D.; American lawyer and diplomatist; b. 31 May 1924, Mattoon, Ill.; *d.* of Bert Fitzgerald and Hildren Brodie (Johnson) Roberts; *m.* William Beasley Harris 1955; ed. George Washington Univ. Law School, Howard Univ., Univ. of Chicago and American Univ., Washington, D.C.
Program Dir. Young Women's Christian Assen. of Chicago 46-49; Asst. Dir. American Council on Human Rights 49-53; Exec. Dir. Delta Sigma Theta 53-59; Trial Attorney, U.S. Dept. of Justice 60-61; Assoc. Dean of Students and Lecturer in Law, Howard Univ. 61-63, Assoc. Prof. of Law 63-67, Prof. 67-, Dean 69-70; Amb. to Luxembourg 65-67; Alt. U.S. del. to Gen. Assembly of UN 66, 67 and Chair. Plenary Session Econ. Comm. for Europe 67; mem. U.S.-Puerto Rican Comm. on Status of Puerto Rico 64-66; mem. Comm. on Revision of Columbia District Criminal Code 68; mem. Nat. Advisory Cttee. on Reform of Fed. Penal Code 68-70, Admin. Conf. of the U.S. 68-71, Nat. Comm. Causes and Prevention of Violence 68-69, Carnegie Comm. on Future of Higher Educ. 69-73, Council on Foreign Relations; Chair. Credentials Cttee. Democratic Nat. Convention 72; Dir. IBM, Scott Paper Co., Chase Manhattan Bank, Georgetown Univ., 20th Century Fund, Greater Wash. Educ. Television 67-73; dir. Practising Law Inst. 74-; mem. Exec. Board NAACP Legal Defence Fund; mem. Board of Govs. Atlantic Inst.; Chair. District of Columbia Law Revision Comm.; Partner Fried, Frank, Harris, Shriver and Kampelman; many hon. degrees and awards.
600 New Hampshire Avenue, N.W., Washington, D.C. 20037, U.S.A.
Telephone: 202-965-9400.

Harris, Roy Ellsworth; American composer; b. **12 Feb.** 1898, Lincoln County, Okla.; *s.* of Elmer E. Harris and Laura Broddie; *m.* Beula Duffey 1936; five *c.*; ed. California Univ.
Studied under Arthur Farwell and Nadia Boulanger; Guggenheim Fellow 28-30, Pasadena Music and Art Assen. Fellow 30-33; Composer in residence, Cornell Univ. 41-42, Colorado Coll. 42-48, Utah State Univ. of Agriculture and Applied Science 48-, Univ. of Calif. 60-; Fellow, Nat. Inst. of Arts and Letters; Pres. Fellowship of American Composers 46-50; Coolidge Medal 42; Hon. Mus.D. (Rutgers and Rochester Univs.).
Compositions: twelve symphonies, fifteen compositions of chamber music, four concerti, ten vocal works and other forms of instrumental and vocal composition.
Leisure interests: sports, gardening, chess.
1200 Tellem Drive, Pacific Palisades, Calif. 90272, U.S.A.
Telephone: 213-454-7147.

Harrison, Sir Cyril Ernest, Kt., M.A.; British company director (retd.); b. 14 Dec. 1901, Leicester; *s.* of Alfred John Harrison; *m.* Ethel Wood 1927; two *s.*; ed. Burnley Grammar School.
Chairman, English Sewing Cotton Co. Ltd. 63-68, North-West Regional Council, F.B.I. 57-59, Christie Hospital and Holt Radium Inst. 59-61; Pres. Manchester Chamber of Commerce 58-60, F.B.I. 61-63; mem. Court of Govs. Manchester Univ. 58-; Pres. The Cotton Silk and Man-Made Fibres Research Assen.; mem. Nat. Econ. Devt. Council (N.E.D.C.) 62-64, mem. of Council Manchester Business School 65-72, mem. British Nat. Export Council 65-67; Joint Deputy Chair. Williams & Glyns Bank Ltd. 65-72; Chair. Board of Govs. United Manchester Hospitals 67-74; Dir. Royal Bank of Scotland 66-69; part-time mem.

North Western Electricity Board 63-72; Fellow, British Inst. of Management, Chartered Inst. of Secretaries; M.A. h.c. (Univ. of Manchester) 60, Companion Textile Inst. 61.
Leisure interests: golf, reading.
8 Harefield Drive, Wilmslow, Cheshire, England.
Telephone: WIL 22186.

Harrison, Sir Geoffrey (Wedgwood), G.C.M.G., K.C.V.O.; former British diplomatist; b. 18 July 1908, Southsea, Hants.; *s.* of Commdr. Thomas Edmund Harrison and Maud Winifred Godman; *m.* Amy Katharine Clive 1936; three *s.* one *d.*; ed. Winchester and King's Coll., Cambridge.
Entered Foreign Office 32, served Tokyo 35-37, Berlin 37-39; Private Sec. to Parl. Under-Sec., Foreign Office 39-41; First Sec., Foreign Office 41-45; Counsellor, Brussels 45-47; Minister, Moscow 47-49; Head of Northern Dept., Foreign Office 49-51; Asst. Under-Sec., Foreign Office 51-56; Amb. to Brazil 56-58, to Iran 58-63; Deputy Under-Sec. of State, Foreign Office 63-65; Amb. to U.S.S.R. 65-68.
Leisure interests: gardening, golf, reading.
Timbers, Plummersplain, nr. Horsham, Sussex; 6 Ormond Gate, London, S.W.3, England.
Telephone: Handcross 266; 01-352-9488.

Harrison, George, M.B.E.; British songwriter and performer; b. 25 Feb. 1943, Wavertree, Liverpool; *m.* Patricia (Pattie) Anne Boyd 1966; ed. Dovedale Primary School and Liverpool Inst.
Had first guitar at age of 14, now plays guitar, organ and a variety of Indian instruments; ran guitar quintet *The Rebels* 56-58; joined *The Quarrymen* 58; appeared under various titles until formation of *The Beatles* 60; appeared with *The Beatles* in the following activities: performances in Hamburg 60, 61, 62, The Cavern, Liverpool 60, 61; toured Scotland, Sweden, U.K. 63, Paris, Denmark, Hong Kong, Australia, New Zealand, U.S.A., Canada 64, France, Italy, Spain, U.S.A. 65, Germany, Spain, Philippines, U.S.A. 66; attended transcendental meditation course at Maharishi's Acad., Rishikesh, India Feb.-April 68; formed Apple Corps Ltd., parent org. of The Beatles Group of Companies 68; George Harrison composed, arranged and recorded own music for film *Wonderwall* 68; organized and performed at *The Concert for Bangladesh* 71, concert, film and record proceeds for refugees to UNICEF; founder of Material World Charitable Foundation.
Films by The Beatles: *A Hard Day's Night* 64, *Help!* 65, *Yellow Submarine* (animated colour cartoon film) 68, TV film *Magical Mystery Tour* 67, *Let it Be* 70; producer *Little Malcolm and his Struggle Against the Eunuchs* 73; *Raga* (with Ravi Shankar, *q.v.* and Yehudi Menuhin, *q.v.*) 74.
c/o EuroAtlantic, 4 Halkin Place, London, SW1X 8JG, England.

Harrison, James Merritt, C.C., PH.D ; Canadian geologist; b. 20 Sept. 1915, Regina, Saskatchewan; *s.* of Roland and Vera (Merrit) Harrison; *m.* Herta Boehmer Sliter 1944; ed. Univ. of Manitoba and Queen's Univ., Kingston, Ontario.
Geologist, Geological Survey of Canada 43-55; Lecturer Queen's Univ. 49-50; Geological Survey of Canada Chief Precambrian Div. 55-56, Dir. 56-64; Asst. Deputy Minister (Research), Dept. of Mines and Technical Surveys 64-67; Asst. Deputy Minister (Science and Technology), Dept. of Energy, Mines and Resources 67-71, Senior Asst. Deputy Minister 72; Asst. Dir.-Gen. for Science, UNESCO 73-; mem. Int. Council of Scientific Unions (ICSU) 62, Exec. and Vice-Pres. ICSU 63-65, Pres. 66-68; Pres. Int. Union Geological Sciences 61-64; Vice-Pres. Canadian Inst. of Mining and Metallurgy, Pres. 69; Pres. Royal Soc. of Canada 67-68; Companion Order of Canada 71; Kemp Memorial Medal, Columbia Univ.; Blaylock Medal, Canadian Inst. of

Mining and Metallurgy; Logan Medal, Geol. Asscn. of Canada; Outstanding Achievement Award of Public Service of Canada; several hon. degrees.

Leisure interests: colour photography, curling, golf, sailing.

UNESCO, Place Fontenoy, 75700 Paris, France. Telephone: 577-16-10.

Harrison, Reginald (Rex) Carey; British actor-director; b. 5 March 1908, Huyton, Lancs.; s. of William and Edith Harrison; m. 1st Marjorie Thomas 1934, one s.; m. 2nd Lilli Palmer 1943 (divorced 1957), one s.; m. 3rd Kay Kendall 1957 (died 1959); m. 4th Rachel Roberts 1962 (divorced 1971); m. 5th Hon. Elizabeth Rees-Williams 1971 (divorced 1975); ed. Liverpool Coll. First professional appearance Liverpool 24; first film performance 29; service in R.A.F. 41-44; Order of Merit (Italy); Hon. Ph.D. (Boston); plays include *French Without Tears, Design for Living, The Cocktail Party, Bell, Book and Candle, Venus Observed, The Love of Four Colonels, Anne of a Thousand Days, Platonov, My Fair Lady, The Lionel Touch, Henry IV, In Praise of Love,* N.Y.; films include *Night Train to Munich, Major Barbara, Blithe Spirit, The Rake's Progress, Anna and the King of Siam, Escape, Unfaithfully Yours, King Richard and the Crusaders, The Constant Husband, The Reluctant Debutante, Midnight Lace, Cleopatra, My Fair Lady, The Yellow Rolls-Royce, The Agony and The Ecstasy, The Honey Pot, Dr. Doolittle, A Flea in Her Ear, Staircase;* TV appearance in *Don Quixote.*

Leisure interests: sailing, golf, writing.

Publ. *Rex* (autobiog.) 74.

c/o Redway Associates, 5-11 Mortimer Street, London W.1; Villa San Genesio, Portofino, Italy. Telephone: Portofino 59095.

Harrison, Russell Edward, B.COMM.; Canadian banker; b. 31 May 1921, Grandview, Manitoba; s. of Edward and Annie Harrison; m. Nancy Doreen Bell 1944; one s. one d.; ed. Univ. of Manitoba.

Military Service World War II, First Canadian Parachute Bn.; with Canadian Bank of Commerce (now Canadian Imperial Bank of Commerce) 45-, Asst. Man., Hamilton 53, Toronto 56, Chief Insp. of the Bank 56; Regional Supt., Asst. Gen. Man., Montreal 59, Regional Gen. Man. 63, Exec. Vice-Pres., Chief Gen. Man. 69-73, Dir. 70-, Pres. and Chief Operating Officer Dec. 73-.

Leisure interests: golf, fishing, swimming.

Canadian Imperial Bank of Commerce, Commerce Court, Toronto, Ont. M5L 1A2; Home: 234 Dunvegan Road, Toronto, Ont. M5P 2P2, Canada. Telephone: 862-3861 (Office); 486-8025 (Home).

Harrison, Wallace Kirkman; American architect; b. 28 Sept. 1895, Worcester, Mass.; s. of James and Rachel Kirkman; m. Ellen Hunt Milton 1926; one d. Director of Office of Inter-American Affairs, Washington 45-46; fmr. Dir. of Planning, United Nations Headquarters.

Principal works include: Rockefeller Center, New York; the UN Headquarters and Lincoln Center Opera House, N.Y.; Presbyterian Church, Stamford; Theme Center, 1939 World's Fair; New York State Capitol, South Mall.

Leisure interest: architecture.

630 Fifth Avenue, New York City, N.Y. 10020, U.S.A. Telephone: 212-265-4884.

Harrod, Sir (Henry) Roy Forbes, Kt., F.B.A.; British economist; b. 13 Feb. 1900, London; s. of Henry Dawes Harrod and Frances Forbes-Robertson; m. Wilhelmine Margaret Eve Cresswell 1938; two s.; ed. Westminster School, and New Coll., Oxford.

Lecturer Christ Church 22-24; Student of Christ Church 24-67, Hon. Student 67-; Junior Censor 27-29; Senior Censor 30-31; mem. Hebdomadal Council Oxford 29-35; Bodleian Library Comm. 30-31; Pres. Section F of

British Asscn. 38; Statistical Dept. in Admiralty 40; in Prime Minister's Office 40-42 and subsequently part-time; Statistical Adviser in Admiralty 43-45; Joint Editor of *Economic Journal* 45-61; Liberal candidate for Huddersfield 45; Adviser to the Int. Monetary Fund 52; Pres. Royal Econ. Soc. 62-64; Nuffield Reader in Int. Econs., Oxford Univ. 52-67; Hon. Dr. of Law (Poitiers and Pa. Univs.); Hon. LL.D. (Aberdeen); Hon. D. Litt. (Glasgow and Warwick Univs.); Bernard Harms Prize, Kiel.

Publs. *International Economics* 33, *The Trade Cycle* 36, *A Page of British Folly* 46, *Are these Hardships Necessary?* 47, *Towards a Dynamic Economics* 48, *Life of John Maynard Keynes* 51, *And So It Goes On* 51, *Economic Essays* 52, *The Dollar* 53, *The Foundations of Inductive Logic* 56, *Policy Against Inflation* 58, *The Prof. (A Personal Memoir of Lord Cherwell)* 59, *Topical Comment* 61, (with D. C. Hague) *International Trade Theory in a Developing World* 63, *The British Economy* 63, *Reforming the World's Money* 65, *Towards a New Economic Policy* 67, *Money* 69, *Sociology, Morals and Mystery* 71.

51 Campden Hill Square, London, W.8, and The Old Rectory, Holt, Norfolk, England. Telephone: 01-727-8485 and Holt 2204.

Harroy, Jean-Paul; Belgian former colonial administrator and university professor; b. 4 May 1909, Brussels; s. of Fernand Harroy and Elina Sigel; m. Madeleine Van de Walle 1933; ed. Univ. Libre de Bruxelles. Sec. Gov. Cttee. Belgian Congo Inst. of Nat. Parks, Dir. Foundation for popularising scientific studies of Congo Nat. Parks 35-48; Guardian, Albert Nat. Park, Kivu 37-38, Garamba Nat. Park, Uélé 47-48; Sec.-Gen. Inst. for Scientific Research in Central Africa (IRSAC) 48-55; Sec.-Gen. Int. Union for Protection of Nature; Prof. of Colonial Econs., Brussels Univ. 48-; Resident-Gen. Ruanda-Urundi 55-62; Chair. Cttee. of Experts for the Conservation of Nature and Landscape of the Council of Europe 63-65; Vice-Chair. Int. Comm. on Nat. Parks 66-72; Médaille d'Or Geoffroy St. Hilaire, etc.; Commander, Ordre de Léopold.

Leisure interests: walking, travel.

Publs. *Afrique, terre qui meurt* 44, *Tropiques* (co-author). 9 avenue des Scarabées, 1050 Brussels, Belgium. Telephone: 649-87-70.

Harry, Ralph Lindsay, C.B.E.; Australian diplomatist; b. 10 March 1917, Geelong, Victoria; s. of the late A. H. Harry; m. Dorothy Sheppard 1944; one s. two d.; ed. Univ. of Tasmania and Lincoln Coll., Oxford.

Joined Dept. of External Affairs 41; Private Sec. to Minister of External Affairs; Asst. Official Sec., Ottawa 43-45; Second Sec., later First Sec., Washington, D.C. 45-49 (at UN, New York 47-48); Dept. of External Affairs, Canberra 49-53; Consul-Gen. in Geneva 53-56; Rep. in Singapore, Brunei, Sarawak and Borneo 56-57; seconded to Ministry of Defence 58-59; Asst. Sec. Ministry of External Affairs 60-66; Amb. to Belgium and the EEC 66-68, to Repub. of Viet-Nam 68-70, to Fed. Repub. of Germany 71-75, to UN May 75-; frmly. mem. UN Cttee. drafting Universal Declaration of Human Rights and Leader, Del. to UN Conf. on the Law of the Sea.

Permanent Mission of Australia to the United Nations, Dag Hammarskjöld Plaza, 885 Second Avenue, 16th Floor, New York, N.Y. 10017, U.S.A.

Harsch, Joseph Close, A.B., M.A.; American journalist; b. 25 May 1905, Toledo, Ohio; s. of Paul Arthur and Leila Katherine (Close) Harsch; m. Anne Elizabeth Wood 1932; three s.; ed. Williams Coll. Williamstown, Mass., and Cambridge Univ., England.

Correspondent *Christian Science Monitor* 29-; Asst. Dir. Inter-governmental Cttee. on Political Refugees 39, returning to *Monitor* on outbreak of war; *Monitor* corresp. Berlin Oct. 39-Jan. 41; *Monitor* war corresp. Southwest

Pacific theatre 42; Radio news analyst for Columbia Broadcasting System 43-49; Commentator for B.B.C. 43; Chief, Washington News Bureau, *Christian Science Monitor* 49-51; Radio News analyst for Liberty Broadcasting System 51-52; foreign affairs columnist *Christian Science Monitor*; News Commentator, Nat. Broadcasting Co. 53-57; Senior European Corresp. N.B.C. 57-65, Diplomatic Corresp. N.B.C., Washington 65-67; A.B.C. Commentator 67-71; Columnist, *CS Monitor*, Boston 71-; Hon. C.B.E.
Leisure interests: sailing, gardening.
Publs. *Pattern of Conquest* 43, *The Curtain Isn't Iron* 50.
Highland Drive, Jamestown, Rhode Island, U.S.A.
Telephone: 401-423-0690.

Hart, Rt. Hon. (Constance Mary) Judith, P.C., M.P.; British politician; b. September 1924, Burnley, Lancs.; d. of Harry Ridehalgh; *m.* Dr. Anthony Bernard Hart 1946; two *s.*; ed. London School of Economics.
Labour M.P. for Lanark 59-; Joint Parl. Under-Sec. of State for Scotland 64-66; Minister of State for Commonwealth Affairs 66-July 67; Minister of Social Security 67-68; Paymaster-Gen. 68-69; Minister of Overseas Devt. 69-70, 74-75; mem. Nat. Exec. Cttee. of Labour Party, and Chair. of its Industrial Policy Sub-Cttee.
Leisure interests: gardening, theatre, spending time with family.
Publ. *Aid and Liberation* 73.
House of Commons, London, S.W.1; 3 Ennerdale Road, Kew, Richmond, Surrey, England.
Telephone: 01-219-3000, Ext. 4439; 01-948-1989 (Home).

Hart, George Arnold Reeve, M.B.E.; Canadian banker; b. 2 April 1913, Toronto; *s.* of George S. and Laura M. (Harrison) Hart; *m.* 1st Jean C. Gilbert 1939 (deceased), one *d.*; 2nd Patricia I. Plant 1961; ed. Public and High Schools, Toronto, Ontario.
Bank of Montreal 31-41; Canadian Army 41-46; Bank of Montreal 46-, Asst. Gen. Man. Head Office 54-56, Deputy Gen. Man. 56-57, Gen. Man. 57-58, Vice-Pres. and Dir. 58-59, Pres. 59-67, Chief Exec. Officer 59-74, Chair. of Board 64-75, Chair. Exec. Cttee. 64-; Dir. numerous cos. and official of several commercial and other orgs.; Hon. LL.D. (Univ. of Saskatchewan, Univ. of Montreal), Hon. D.C.L. (Bishop's Univ., Acadia Univ.), Hon. D.Sc. (Univ. of Sherbrooke).
Leisure interest: golf.
Office: Bank of Montreal, 129 St. James Street West, Montreal, Quebec; Home: 1700 McGregor Street, Montreal, Quebec, Canada.

Hart, Parker T.; American business consultant and diplomatist (retd.); b. 28 Sept. 1910, Medford, Mass.; *s.* of William P. Hart and Ella L. Thompson; *m.* Jane C. Smiley 1949; two *d.*; ed. Dartmouth Coll., Harvard Univ., and Inst. Universitaire des Hautes Etudes Int., Geneva.
Translator, Dept. of State 37-38; Educator, Foreign Service 38-69, served Vienna, Pará (Brazil), Cairo, Jeddah, Dhahran 38-47; Dept. of State 47-49; Consul-Gen. Dhahran 49-51; Nat. War Coll. 51-52; Dir. Office of Near Eastern Affairs, Dept. of State 52-55; Deputy Chief of Mission Counsellor, Cairo 55-58; Consul-Gen., Damascus 58; Deputy Asst. Sec. of State, Near Eastern, S. Asian Affairs 58-61; Amb. to Saudi Arabia 61-65, concurrently accred. to Kuwait 62-63; Minister to Yemen 61-62; Amb. to Turkey 65-68; Asst. Sec. of State, Near Eastern, S. Asian Affairs 68-69; Dir. Foreign Service Inst. 69; mem. Middle East Inst., Pres. 69-73; Consultant Bechtel Corpn. 73-; Vice-Chair. Board of Trustees American Univ. of Beirut; mem. Board of Advisers, Industrial Coll. of the Armed Forces, Board of Trustees, American Univ. (Washington D.C.); mem. Visiting Cttee. on Middle East Civilizations, Harvard Univ.; mem. of Board, Inst. for Psychiatry and Foreign Affairs; mem. Royal Central Asian Soc.,

Council on Foreign Relations (New York), Washington Inst. of Foreign Affairs.
Leisure interests: bird watching, hiking, languages.
Publs. several articles in political journals.
Bechtel Corporation, 1620 I Street, N.W., Washington, D.C. 20006, U.S.A.
Telephone: (202) 393-4747.

Hart, Philip A., B.A., J.D.; American lawyer and politician; b. 10 Dec. 1912; ed. Georgetown and Michigan Univs.
Law practice in Detroit; Michigan Corpn. and Securities Commr. 49; Dir. of Price Stabilisation 51; U.S. District Attorney, Eastern Michigan 52; Legal Adviser to Gov. Williams 53; Lieut.-Gov. of Michigan 55-59; U.S. Senator from Michigan 58-; mem. Senate Judiciary Cttee.; service with U.S. Army (Lieut.-Col.) 41-46; fmr. Pres. Mich. State Bar Foundation; Croix de Guerre and other military honours; Democrat.
Senate Office Building, Washington, D.C. 20510, U.S.A.

Hartford, Huntington, B.A.; American financier and art patron; b. 18 April 1911, New York; *s.* of Edward and Henrietta (Guerard) Hartford; *m.* 1st Mary Lee Epling (dissolved 1939); 2nd Marjorie Steele 1949 (dissolved 1961), one *s.* one *d.*; 3rd Diane Brown 1962 (dissolved 1970), one *d.*; 4th Elaine Kay 1974; ed. St. Paul's School, and Harvard Univ.
Co-Chair. Oil Shale Corpn. (N.Y.C.) 49; Founder Huntington Hartford Foundation Calif. 49, Huntington Hartford Theatre Hollywood 54, Gallery of Modern Art (N.Y.C.) 64 (now called New York Cultural Center in asscn. with Fairleigh Dickinson Univ.); Developer and owner Paradise Island (Nassau, Bahamas) 59-; Publisher *Show Magazine*; Adviser Cultural Affairs to Pres. of Borough of Manhattan 67; Patron Lincoln Center for the Performing Arts; mem. Advisory Council of Columbia Univ. Dept. of Art History and Archaeology, Nat. Council of the Arts 69, U.S. People's Fund for UN Inc.; Hon. Fellow, Nat. Sculpture Soc.; Broadway Asscn. Man. of Year Award; OAS Award 66.
Publs. *Jane Eyre* (play) 58, *Art or Anarchy* 64, *You Are What You Write* 73.
420 Lexington Avenue, New York, N.Y. 10017, U.S.A.

Hartke, Vance, A.B., J.D.; American lawyer and politician; b. 31 May 1919, Stendal, Ind.; *s.* of Hugo and Ida Hartke; *m.* Martha Tiernan 1943; four *s.* three *d.*; ed. Stendal High School, Evansville Coll., Indiana Univ.
Navy and Coastguard service during World War II; Deputy Prosecutor, Vanderburgh County, Ind. 50-51; Pres. Eighth Congressional District Young Democrats, Chair. Vanderburgh County Democratic Cen. Cttee. 52-58; Mayor of Evansville, Ind. 56-58; U.S. Senator for Indiana 59-; Chair. Veterans' Affairs Cttee., Readjustment, Educ. and Employment Sub-Cttee., sub-cttees. on Foundations, Surface, Transportation and Freight, Car Shortage, Democratic Senatorial Campaign Cttee. 61-63; mem. cttees. on Finance, Commerce, Special Cttee. on Unemployment 59-61, Senate Special Cttee. on Aging, joint cttees. on Internal Revenue Taxation, Reduction of Fed. Expenditures, Budget Control, Legislative Review Cttee. of Democratic Policy Cttee.; U.S. Senate del. to interparl. meetings and confs. on trade; several hon. degrees; awards and citations especially for legislation helpful to the blind, the mentally retarded and veterans.
Publs. *Inside the New Frontier* 62, *The American Crisis in Vietnam* 68, *You and Your Senator* 70.
Suite 313, Senate Office Building, Washington, D.C. 20510; 850 Dexter Avenue, Evansville, Ind., U.S.A.
Telephone: 202-224-4814.

Hartke, Werner, D.PHIL.; German university professor; b. 1 March 1907, Eschwege; *s.* of Lic.Dr. Dr. h.c. Wilhelm Hartke and Tilly Kühne; *m.* Christa Behrendt 1936; two *s.* one *d.*; ed. Berlin Univ.

Lecturer, Königsberg and Göttingen Univs., Prof. of Classical Philology 48-55; Dean, Faculty of Philosophy, Rostock Univ. 49-51, 53-55, Prof. Latin Language and Literature, Humboldt Univ., Berlin 55-, Rector 57-59; Scientific Dir. *Goethe Wörterbuch* 67-; Dir. Berlin Inst. for Antiquity Research, Adviser for research in Ancient History and Archaeology 69-; mem. Deutsche Akad. der Wissenschaften, Pres. 58-68, Vice-Pres. 68-72; Editor: *Deutsche Literaturzeitung* 72-, *Beiträge zur Alexander von Humboldt-Forschung* 73-; mem. U.S.S.R. Acad. of Sciences, Hungarian Acad. of Sciences, Bulgarian Acad. of Sciences, Inst. d'Egypte; Academia Latinitati inter omnes gentes fovendae; Nat. Prize, gold medallist of Nat. Order of Merit, Order Kyril Methodii, etc.; Gold Medal za zásluhy o vědu a lidstvo of Czechoslovakian Acad. of Sciences, Winkelmann-Medal, etc.; D.Phil. h.c.
Leisure interests: gardening, painting, sailing, meteorology, ornithology, telecommunications, radio-television technics.
Publs. *De saeculi IV exeuntis historiarum scriptoribus* 32, *Geschichte und Politik im spätantiken Rom* 40, *Römische Kinderkaiser* 51.
Akademie der Wissenschaften der DDR, Schiffbauerdamm 19, 104 Berlin; Home: Ostendorfstrasse 26, 117 Berlin, German Democratic Republic.
Telephone: 28-25-571 (Office); 67-16-431 (Home).

Hartley, Fred L(loyd), B.SC.; American oil executive; b. 16 Jan. 1917, Vancouver, B.C., Canada; *m.* Margaret Alice Murphy 1940; one *s.* one *d.*; ed. Univ. of British Columbia.
Went to U.S.A. 39, naturalized 50; Engineering Supervisor, Union Oil Co. of Calif. 39-53, Man. Commercial Devt. 53-55, Gen. Man. Research Dept. 55-56, Vice-Pres. (Research) 56-60, Senior Vice-Pres. 60-63, Dir. 60-, Exec. Vice-Pres. 63-64, Pres. and Chief Exec. Officer 64-, Chair. Feb. 75-; Dir. American Petroleum Inst. (API), Calif. Chamber of Commerce, Petroleum Club of Los Angeles, Southern Calif. Symphony Asscn., Travel Program for Foreign Diplomats, U.S.-Korea Econ. Council, Union Bank, Rockwell Int.; mem. Nat. Petroleum Council, Stanford Research Inst. Council; Trustee Calif. Inst. of Technology, Tax Foundation, Cttee. for Econ. Devt.
Union Oil Co. of California, Box 7600, Los Angeles 90051, U.S.A.

Hartley, Col. George Holland, I.C.D., E.D., O.B.E., J.P.; Rhodesian farmer; b. 7 July 1912, Bollington, Cheshire, England; *s.* of late Charles Robert Hartley; *m.* Marion Margaret Goddard; three *s.* one *d.*; ed. Seascale, Cumberland, U.K., Univ. of Cape Town, S. Africa.
Came to Rhodesia 28; Native Affairs Dept., S. Rhodesia Govt. 30-47; served 1st Battalion, Rhodesian African Rifles in E. Africa, Ceylon, Burma 40-46; mentioned in despatches; Lt.-Col. 50, Col. 54; Dir. of Native Admin., Salisbury City Council 49-59; mem. Parl. for Victoria 62-73; Deputy Speaker, Chair. of Cttees. 67-73, Speaker 73-; Hon. Life mem. (fmr. Fellow), Inst. of Administrators of Non-European Affairs (Southern Africa); Commdr. 1st and 13th Bns., The Royal Rhodesia Regiment 50-54, Hon. Col. 10th Bn. 65-75; Independence Commemorative Decoration.
House of Assembly, Parliament of Rhodesia, P.O. Box 8055, Causeway, Salisbury; Home: Wondedzo Farm, Box 152, Fort Victoria, Rhodesia.

Hartline, Haldan Keffer, M.D.; American physiologist; b. 22 Dec. 1903, Bloomsburg, Pa.; *s.* of Daniel S. and Harriet (Keffer) Hartline; *m.* Mary Elizabeth Kraus 1936; three *s.*; ed. Lafayette Coll., Easton, Pennsylvania, and Johns Hopkins Univ., Baltimore, Maryland.
National Research Fellow in Medical Sciences, Johns Hopkins Univ. 27-29; Eldridge Johnson Traveling Research Scholar, Univs. of Leipzig and Munich 29-31;

Fellow in Medical Physics, Eldridge Johnson Research Foundation, Univ. of Pennsylvania 31-36, Asst. Prof. of Biophysics 36-40, 41-42; Assoc. Prof. of Physiology, Cornell Univ. Medical Coll. 40-41; Assoc. Prof. of Biophysics, Univ. of Pennsylvania 43-48, Prof. 48-49; Prof. of Biophysics and Chair. of Dept., Johns Hopkins Univ. 49-53; mem. and Prof. Rockefeller Univ., New York City 53-74, Emer. 74-; mem. Nat. Acad. of Sciences, Amer. Physiological Soc., Amer. Philosophical Soc., Amer. Acad. of Arts and Sciences; Foreign mem. Royal Soc. (U.K.) 66; Howard Crosby Warren Medal 48, Michelson Award 66; Nobel Prize for Medicine or Physiology 67; Lighthouse Award 69; Hon. D.Sc. (Lafayette, Univ. of Pennsylvania), Hon. LL.D. (Johns Hopkins), Hon. M.D. (Univ. of Freiburg).
Leisure interests: mountain climbing, hiking.
Rockefeller University, 66th Street and York Avenue, New York City, N.Y. 10021; Home: Patterson Road, Hydes, Md. 21082, U.S.A.
Telephone: 212-360-1215 (Office); 301-592-8162 (Home).

Härtling, Peter; German writer and journalist; b. 13 Nov. 1933, Chemnitz; *s.* of Rudolf and Erika (Häntzschel) Härtling; *m.* Mechthild Maier 1959; two *s.* two *d.*; ed. Gymnasium (Nürtingen/Neckar).
Childhood spent in Saxony, Czechoslovakia and Württemberg; journalist 53-; Literary Editor *Deutsche Zeitung und Wirtschaftszeitung*, Stuttgart and Cologne; Editor of magazine *Der Monat* 67-70, also Co-publisher; Editor and Man. Dir. S. Fischer Verlag, Frankfurt 68-74, Editor *Die Väter*; Literaturpreis des Deutschen Kritikerverbandes 64, Literaturpreis des Kulturkreises der Deutschen Industrie 65, Literarischer Förderungspreis des Landes Niedersachsen 65, Prix du meilleur livre étranger, Paris 66, Gerhart Hauptmann Preis 71; mem. PEN, Akademie der Wissenschaften und der Literatur Mainz, Akademie der Künste Berlin.
Publs. *Yamins Stationen* (poetry) 55, *In Zeilen zuhaus* (essays) 57, *Palmström grüsst Anna Blume* (essays) 61, *Spielgeist-Spiegelgeist* (poetry) 62, *Niembsch oder Der Stillstand* (novel) 64, *Janek* (novel) 66, *Das Familienfest* (novel) 69, *Gilles* (play) 70, *Ein Abend, Eine Nacht, Ein Morgen* (novel) 71, *Zwettl—Nachprüfung einer Erinnerung* (novel) 73, *Eine Frau* (novel) 74, *Hölderlin* (novel) 76.
Walldorf/Hessen, Finkenweg 1, Federal Republic of Germany.
Telephone: 06105-6109.

Hartling, Poul; Danish politician; b. 14 Aug. 1914, Copenhagen; *s.* of late M. Hartling (fmr. Minister of Education) and late Mathilde Hartling; *m.* Dr. (medical) Elsebeth Hartling (née Kirkemann) 1940; three *s.* one *d.*
Master of Divinity; Sec. to Student Christian Movement 34-35, to Denmark's Christian Movement of Senior Secondary Students 39-43, Curate of Frederiksberg Church 41-45; Chaplain of St. Luke Foundation 45-50; Principal of Zahle's Teachers' Training Coll. 50-68; mem. Folketing 57-60, 64-; Chair. Liberal Party Parl. Group 65-68; mem. Nordic Council 64-68, Pres. 66-68; Minister of Foreign Affairs 68-71; Prime Minister 73-75; Chair. Liberal Party.
Leisure interest: music.
Publs. *Sursum corda* (History of Student Christian Movement); Editor: *Church, School, Culture* 63, *The Danish Church* 64, *From 17 years in Danish politics* 74.
Emilievej 6 E, 2920 Charlottenlund, Denmark.

Hartmann, (Ernst) Franz (Johan), B.SC. (ECON.); Swedish business executive; b. 1898; *m.* Inga G. Tellander 1929; two *s.*; ed. Stockholm School of Economics and Hochschule für Landwirtschaft und Brauerei, Weihenstephan.
Assistant Man. J. W. Lyckholm & Co., Göteborg 22-25, AB J. A. Pripp & Son 26-31; Dir. for Pripps Brewery 31-50; Gen. Man. AB Pripp & Lyckholm 50-62; Chair. of Board Pripp-Bryggerierna AB 62-; Chair. of Board

Abba-Fyrtonet AB, Coronaverken AB, Skandinavska Banken, Säfveåns AB, Rederi AB Transatlantic; Vice-Chair. AB Bolinder-Munktell, Skandia-koncernen; mem. of Board, Livförsäkr AB Thule, Billeruds AB, AB Custos, Larsson, Seaton & Co. AB; Knight Commdr. Order of Vasa, Order of Dannebrog, Order of St. Olav. Pripp-Bryggerierna AB, Box 128, 401 22 Gothenburg 1; Home: Överåsgaten 22, 412 66 Gothenburg, Sweden.

Hartmann, Robert Trowbridge, A.B.; American government official; b. 8 April 1917, Rapid City, S. Dak.; s. of Miner Louis and Elizabeth (Trowbridge) Hartmann; m. Roberta Sankey 1943; one s. one d.; ed. Stanford Univ.
Reporter *Los Angeles Times* 39-41, 45-48, Editorial and Special Writer 48-54, Chief of Washington Bureau 54-63, Chief of Mediterranean and Middle East Bureau, Rome 63-64; FAO Information Adviser, Washington, D.C. 64-65; Editor Republican Conf., House of Reps. 66-69, Minority Sergeant at Arms 69-73; Chief of Staff to Vice-Pres. Gerald Ford 73-74; Counsellor to Pres. Gerald Ford, with Cabinet rank Aug. 74-; Naval Officer 41-45, now Capt. U.S.N.R. (retd.); Reid Foundation Fellow in the Middle East 51; Better Understanding Citation, English Speaking Union, U.S.A. 58; Overseas Press Club Citation 61.
Leisure interests: photography, snorkelling.
Office of the President of U.S.A., The White House, Washington, D.C. 20500; Home: 5001 Baltimore Avenue, Westgate, Md. 20016, U.S.A.
Telephone: 456-1414 (Office); 229-7616 (Home).

Hartmann, Rudolf; German opera producer and administrator; b. 11 Oct. 1900.
Producer, Altenburg (Court Theatre) 24-28, Nuremberg 28-34, Zürich and Nuremberg 46-52, Berlin State Opera 34-37; Producer, Bavarian State Opera, Munich 37-44, Admin. and Chief Producer 52-67; staged a great variety of operas and very many by Richard Strauss, including first performances of *Friedenstag, Capriccio* and *Die Liebe der Danae,* also first performances of *Die Harmonie der Welt* (Hindemith), *Der Mond* (Orff) and revised version of *Die Bernauerin* (Orff); productions throughout Germany and in London, Edinburgh, Stockholm, Paris, Milan, Rome, Venice, Zürich, Salzburg, Bayreuth and Vienna; mem. Goethe Institut; Grosses Bundesverdienstkreuz and several other awards.
8 Munich 90, Harthauserstr. 48A, Federal Republic of Germany.
Telephone: 646502.

Hartmann, Wilhelm C. B., DIPL. ING.; German civil engineer; b. 13 April 1908; ed. Belgrano School, Buenos Aires, Argentina, Wöhler-Real-Gymnasium, Frankfurt, and Technical Univs. of Darmstadt and Dresden.
Site Man. Ph. Holzmann A.G., Frankfurt 34-35; Chief Engineer, Cía. Gen. de Obras Públicas, S.A., Buenos Aires 36-46; Technical Dir. Corpn. Sudamericana de Construcciones S.A., Buenos Aires 46-55; mem. Board of Dirs. Hochtief A.G., Essen 55-; mem. Foreign Commerce Council of Fed. Ministry of Econs. 63-.
Publs. articles in technical journals.
43 Essen-Bredeney, Westerwaldstrasse 13, Federal Republic of Germany.

Hartnack, Carl Edward; American banker; b. 9 April 1916, Los Angeles, Calif.; s. of Johannes C. Hartnack and Kate Schoneman; m. Roberta DeLuce 1939; two s. one d.; ed. Belmont High School Los Angeles, Pacific Coast Banking School, Seattle, and American Inst. of Banking.
With Security First Nat. Bank (now Security Pacific Nat. Bank) Los Angeles 34-, Vice-Pres. 59, Senior Vice-Pres. 68, Pres. Jan. 69-; fmrly. Pres., now Vice-Chair. Security Pacific Corpn. 73-.
Leisure interests: boating, gardening, photography.
Security Pacific National Bank, 333 South Hope Street, Los Angeles, Calif. 90071, U.S.A.
Telephone: 613-6004.

Hartnell, Norman, M.V.O.; British dress designer; b. 12 June 1901; ed. Mill Hill School and Magdalene Coll., Cambridge.
Began dress designing 23; designed new uniform for W.R.A.C. and for Red Cross Nurses; holds Royal Warrant as Dressmaker to H.M. Queen Elizabeth II and H.M. Queen Elizabeth the Queen Mother; Neiman Marcus Award (U.S.A.) for world influence on fashion. Publs. *Silver and Gold* (autobiog.) 55, *Royal Courts of Fashion* 71.
26 Bruton Street, London, W.1; Rose Place, Sunninghill, Berks., England.
Telephone: 01-629-0992.

Hartner, Willy R., F.R.A.S.; German university professor; b. 22 Jan. 1905, Ennigerloh; s. of Friedrich Otto Hartner and Johanna Hoenig; m. Else Eckhoff 1932; one d.; ed. Johann Wolfgang Goethe-Universität, Frankfurt, Universitetet i Oslo, and Univ. de Paris (Sorbonne).
Assistant, China Inst., Frankfurt 28-31, Acting Dir. 40-41; Asst., Observatory, Frankfurt 31-35; Lecturer in Scandinavian Languages and Literatures, Univ. of Frankfurt 31-; Visiting Prof. of History of Science, Harvard Univ. 35-37; Docent, History of Science, Frankfurt Univ. 40-46, Dir. Inst. for History of Sciences 43-, Prof. of History of Science 46-, Dean of Faculty of Science 46-48, 54-55, Rector 59-60; Visiting Prof. Univ. of Chicago 49, 55, Harvard Univ. 61-62, 62-63, 64-, Cambridge Univ. 68-69; Vice-Pres. Académie Int. d'Histoire des Sciences, Paris 65-68, Pres. 71-; Assoc. Royal Astronomical Soc.; Corresp. mem. Real Academia de Buenas Letras de Barcelona; mem. Academia Nazionale dei Lincei (Rome) 75; mem. several scientific socs.; George Sarton Medal (History of Science Soc.), Rutherford Medal (U.S.S.R. Acad. of Sciences) 71.
Leisure interests: music, fine arts, tennis.
Publs. articles on history of science in numerous int. journals; *Oriens-Occidens* (selected articles 1934-1967) 68, *Die Goldhörner von Gallehus* 69.
638 Bad Homburg, Schopenhauerstrasse 5, Federal Republic of Germany.
Telephone: 06172-23684.

Hartog, Harold Samuel Arnold, K.B.E.; Netherlands business executive; b. 21 Dec. 1910, Nijmegen; s. of Jacob and Suzanne Henriette (Elias) Hartog; m. Ingeborg Luise Michael; one s.; ed. Wiedemann Coll., Geneva.
Joined Unilever 31; mem. Netherlands forces, Second World War; joined Unilever in France after Second World War, later in charge of Unilever companies in Netherlands; mem. Board Unilever N.V. 48-71; mem. Unilever Rotterdam Group Management responsible for Unilever activities in Germany, Austria and Belgium 52-60; mem. Unilever Cttee. for Overseas Interests, London 60-62; one of two World Co-ordinators, Unilever's food interests, London 62-66; Chair. Unilever N.V. 66-May 71; (retd.); Knight Order of Netherlands Lion.
Leisure interests: Chinese porcelain, golf.
40b Kösterbergstrasse 2, Hamburg 55, Federal Republic of Germany.

Hartog, Jan de; Netherlands writer; b. 22 April 1914, Haarlem; s. of Arnold and Lucretia de Hartog-Meyjes; m. Marjorie Eleanor Mein; two s. four d.
Leisure interests: travel, reading.
Publs. *Het Huis met de Handen* 34, *Ave Caesar* 36, *Oompje Owadi* 38, *Holland's Glory* 40, *God's Geuzen* Vol. I 47, Vol. II 48, Vol. III 49, *Stella* 50, *Mary* 51, *The Lost Sea* 51, *Thalassa* 52, *Captain Jan* 52, *The Little Ark* 54, *The Inspector* 61, *Waters of the New World* 61 (travel), *The Artist* 63, *The Hospital* 65, *The Captain* 67, *The Children* 69, *The Peaceable Kingdom* 72; plays: *De Ondergang van de Vrijheid* 37 (Great Nat.

Drama Prize 39), *Mist* 38, *Skipper Next to God* 46, *Death of a Rat* 46, *The Fourposter* 46; detective stories under pseudonym of F. R. Eckma: *Een Linkerbeen gezocht* 35, *Spoken te koop* 36, *Ratten op de trap* 37, *Drie Dode Dwergen* 37, *De Maagd en de Moordenaar* 38.
c/o Atheneum Publishers, New York, N.Y., U.S.A.

Hartogh, A. F. Karel, LL.M.; Netherlands diplomatist; b. 26 Jan. 1913, Amsterdam; *s.* of Dr. H. A. Hartogh and S. Fuld; *m.* C. Kans 1952 (died 1975); two *s.*; ed. Leyden Univ. Permanent Rep. to NATO Jan. 74-.
77 Avenue Franklin Roosevelt, 1050 Brussels, Belgium. Telephone: 6475777.

Hartung, Hans; German-born French painter; b. 21 Sept. 1904, Leipzig; *s.* of Curt Hartung and Margarete, née Nakonz; *m.* Anna-Eva Bergman; ed. Leipzig Univ., Leipzig and Dresden Acads. of Fine Art.
First exhibition 31; Foreign Legion in the Second World War; French nationality 46; rep. at Dunn Int. Exhibition, London 63, Tate Gallery, London 64; mem. Berlin and Munich Acads. of Fine Art; Guggenheim Prize 56, Rubens Prize 57, Grand Prize, Venice Biennale 60; Prix d'Honneur, Ljubljana Graphic Art Exhbn. 67; works rep. in numerous museums and galleries in Europe, Asia, North and South America; Retrospective exhbns. Museo Civico di Torino 66, City Museum, Birmingham 68, Musée National d'Art Moderne, Paris 69, Museum of Fine Arts, Houston 69; Commandeur de la Légion d'Honneur, Commandeur des Arts et Lettres, Médaille Militaire, Croix de Guerre.
c/o Musée National d'Art Moderne, 2 rue de la Manutention, 75-Paris 16e, France.

Hartwell, Baron (Life Peer), cr. 68, of Peterborough Court in the City of London; **(William) Michael Berry,** M.B.E., T.D.; British journalist; b. 18 May 1911; ed. Eton Coll. and Christ Church, Oxford.
Served 39-45 war; fmr. Deputy Editor-in-Chief *The Daily Telegraph*, Editor-in-Chief 54-; Editor-in-Chief *The Sunday Telegraph* 61-.
Publ. *Party Choice* 48.
18 Cowley Street, London, S.W.1; and Oving House, Whitchurch, nr. Aylesbury, Bucks., England.

Hartz, Gustav Emil; Danish civil engineer; b. 18 June 1888; ed. Royal Danish Technical Coll.
Civil engineer; Man. Industrial Asscn., Copenhagen 18; Man. Dir. Fed. Danish Industries 26-46; Man. Dir. Thomas B. Thrige's Foundation (Vice-Chair. 60-66), and Thomas B. Thrige's Works, Odense 47-60; Hon. Pres. Danish Nat. Cttee. for World Power Conf.; mem. Board of Dirs. Danish War Marine Insurance of Goods 39-67; mem. Danish Nat. Cttee. Int. Chamber of Commerce until 67; mem. Board of the Nat. Bank of Denmark 50-67; mem. Central Council Danish Conservative Party 28-67; Joint Founder and mem. Acad. of Technical Sciences; mem. Board of Fed. of Danish Industries 47-66; Chair. Foundation of Faedrelandets Vel; mem. Danish Atomic Energy Comm. 55-56; mem. Royal Electricity Council 35-67; mem. Board of Scandia Wagon Works Ltd. until 66; mem. Brandts Klaedefabrik Ltd. until 67; mem. Thomas B. Thrige, Copenhagen, Ltd. until 66; Chair. Danish Tourist Office 61-66.
Bredstedgade 25, 5100 Odense, Denmark.

Hartzog, George B., Jr., M.B.A.; American lawyer and administrator; b. 17 March 1920, Colleton County, S.C.; *s.* of George B. and Mazell (Steedly) Hartzog; *m.* Helen Carlson 1947; two *s.* one *d*; ed. The American Univ., Washington, D.C.
Attorney and Administrator, Dept. of the Interior with Bureau of Land Management and Nat. Park Service 46; principal field assignments with Nat. Park Service: Asst. Supt. Rocky Mountain Nat. Park, Colorado 55-57, Great Smoky Mountains Nat. Park,

N. Carolina-Tennessee 57-59; Supt. Jefferson Nat. Expansion Memorial, St. Louis, Mo. 59-62; Assoc. Dir. Nat. Parks Service 63-64, Dir. 64-72; Exec. Dir. Downtown St. Louis, Inc. 62-63; Prof. of Public Admin., Univ. of Southern Calif., Washington Public Affairs Center 72-; recipient of several awards for services; Hon. LL.D. (Washington Univ.).
900 17th Street, N.W., Washington, D.C. 20006; Home: 1643 Chain Bridge Road, McLean, Va. 22101, U.S.A. Telephone: 703-356-1566 (Home).

Harvey, Anthony; British film director; b. 3 June 1931; *s.* of Geoffrey Harrison and Dorothy Leon.
Entered film industry, joining Crown Film Unit 49; edited numerous films including *Private Progress, Brothers-in-Law, Carlton Brown of the Foreign Office, I'm Alright Jack, The Angry Silence, The Millionairess, Lolita, The L-Shaped Room, Dr. Strangelove, The Spy Who Came in from the Cold, The Whisperers*; directed *Dutchman* 68, *The Lion in Winter* 69, *They Might be Giants* 70, *The Abdication* 73, *The Glass Menagerie* 73.
Leisure interest: gardening.
c/o Arthur Greene, 230 Park Avenue, New York, N.Y., U.S.A.
Telephone: (212) 889-7050.

Harvie-Watt, Sir George Steven, Bt., Q.C., T.D.; British politician; b. 23 Aug. 1903, Bathgate, Scotland; *s.* of James McDougal Watt and Jessie Harvie; *m.* Jane Elizabeth Taylor 1932; two *s.* one *d.*; ed. George Watson's Coll., Glasgow and Edinburgh Univs.
Called to Bar Inner Temple Jan. 30; Brevet Major 35, Lieut.-Col. Commanding 31st Battalion R.E., T.A. 38-41; Conservative M.P. for Keighley Div. of Yorkshire 31-35 and for Richmond, Surrey, Feb. 37-59; Parl. Private Sec. to the late Rt. Hon. Euan Wallace when Parl. Sec. to Board of Trade 37-38, and to Rt. Hon. Winston Churchill 41-45; Asst. Govt. Whip 38-40; D.L. Surrey 42, Greater London Council 66; J.P. County of London 44-56; Dir. Midland Bank Ltd., Eagle Star Insurance Co. Ltd., The Clydesdale Bank; Pres. Consolidated Goldfields; fmr. Chair. Monotype Corpn. Ltd.; mem. of Queen's Bodyguard for Scotland—The Royal Company of Archers; Commdr. 63rd A.A. Brigade 48-50; A.D.C. to H.M. the King 48-52; A.D.C. to H.M. the Queen 52-59.
Earlsneuk, Elie, Fife, Scotland.
Telephone: Elie 506.

Harwood, Elizabeth Jean; British soprano; b. 27 May 1938, Barton, Seagrave; ed. Royal Manchester Coll. of Music.
Joined Glyndebourne Opera Co. 60; joined Sadlers Wells 61; toured Australia with Sutherland-Williamson Int. Opera Co. 65; has sung at Covent Garden, London, with Scottish Opera, at La Scala, Milan, Hamburg State Opera, Metropolitan Opera, N.Y., and at Salzburg and Vienna Festivals; many TV and concert appearances; roles include Constanze in *Die Entführung*, Countess in *Count Ory*, Marzellina in *Fidelio*, Norina in *Don Pasquale*, Donna Elvira in *Don Giovanni*, Fiordiligi in *Cosi fan Tutti*, Countess in *Marriage of Figaro*, Violetta in *La Traviata*, Sophie in *Der Rosenkavalier*, all four soprano roles in *The Tales of Hoffman*, title role in *Lucia di Lammermoor*; many recordings include *The Merry Widow*, *La Bohème*; Kathleen Ferrier Memorial Prize 60, Winner of Verdi Competition, Bussetto; Fellow, Royal Manchester Coll. of Music.
c/o Ibbs and Tillett, 124 Wigmore Street, London, W1H 0AX, England.

Harwood, Raymond Charles, B.C.S.; American publisher; b. 10 June 1906, Brooklyn, N.Y.; *s.* of Charles Edwin Harwood and Josephine C. Bangel; *m.* Joan Underwood 1938; two *d.*; ed. New York Univ.
Assistant Treas. Harper and Brothers 30-42, Treas. 42-58, mem. Board of Dirs. 43, mem. Exec. Cttee. 44,

Gen. Man. 45-50, Exec. Vice-Pres. 50-55, Chair. 67-68 (now Harper Row, Publishers Inc.); Sec. and Treas. Paul B. Hoeber Inc. 35-61; Chair. of Exec. Cttee., Treas., Trustee and Chair. Finance Cttee. Princeton Univ. Press (retd.); mem. Board of Dirs. Book of the Month Club.
Leisure interests: golf, arbitration, community service, travel, education.
47 Forest Road, Asheville, N.C. 28803, U.S.A.
Telephone: (704) 274-4838.

Hasan, Mubashir, PH.D.; Pakistani civil engineer and politician; b. 1922, Panipat, Punjab; ed. Govt. Coll., Lahore, Engineering Coll., Lahore, Columbia Univ. and State Univ. of Iowa, U.S.A.
Member of Staff, Civil Engineering Dept., Engineering Coll., Lahore (subsequently Univ. of Engineering and Technology) 43, later Prof. and Head of Dept. until 62; private practice, Lahore 62-67; joined Pakistan People's Party 67; arrested for political activities 68, 69; mem. Nat. Assembly 70-; Minister of Finance, Econ. Affairs and Devt. 71-74.
National Assembly, Rawalpindi, Pakistan.

Hasani, Baqir Husain, B.SC., LL.B.; Iraqi diplomatist and public administrator; b. 12 Feb. 1915, Baghdad; s. of Abdul and Bidoor Husain; ed. Columbia Univ., New York and Baghdad Univ.
Director of Commerce and Registrar of Companies, Iraq Ministry of Econs. 47-51; Dir.-Gen. of Contracts and Econ. Affairs, Development Board 51-54; Dir.-Gen. of Income Tax, Ministry of Finance 54-55; Dir.-Gen. and Chair. of Bd. of Dirs. Tobacco Monopoly Admin. 56-59; Minister, later Ambassador to Austria 59-63; Chair. Board of Govs. Int. Atomic Energy Agency (IAEA) 61-62, Special Adviser to Dir.-Gen. IAEA 63-.
Leisure interests: reading and music.
c/o International Atomic Energy Agency, Kaerntnerring 11, Vienna 1010; Home: Denisgasse 18, 1200 Vienna, Austria; and Mosbah, Karadah, Baghdad, Iraq.
Telephone: 33-11-84 (Home).

Hase, Karl-Günther von; German civil servant and diplomatist; b. 15 Dec. 1917, Wangern (Breslau); s. of Col. Günther von Hase and Ina Hicketier; m. Renate Stumpff 1945; five d.
Military service; German Foreign Service, Bonn and Ottawa; Deputy Chief, later Head of Press Dept., Foreign Office, Bonn 56-61, Head, Western Dept. 61-62; State Sec., Head, Press and Information Office of the Fed. Govt. 62-68; State Sec. Ministry of Defence 68-69; Amb. to U.K. 70-; Hon. G.C.V.O., K.C.M.G.
Leisure interests: shooting, riding, music.
Embassy of Federal Republic of Germany, 23 Belgrave Square, London, SW1X 8PZ, England.
Telephone: 01-235-5033.

Haseeb, Dr. Khair El-Din, PH.D.; Iraqi economist and statistician; b. 1 Aug. 1929, Mosul; m. 1955; one s. one d.; ed. Baghdad Univ., London School of Econs., Cambridge Univ.
Civil Service 47-54; Head of Research and Statistics Dept., Iraqi Petroleum Co. 59-60; Lecturer Baghdad Univ. 60-61, part-time lecturer 61-63; Dir.-Gen. Iraqi Fed. of Industries 60-63; Gov. Central Bank of Iraq 63-65; Act. Pres. Econ. Org. 64-65; Pres. Gen. Org. for Banks 64-65; Prof. of Econs. Baghdad Univ. 65-; Gov. of Iraq, IMF 63-65; Alt. Gov. of Iraq, IBRD 63-65; Chair. of Board Centre for Development of Industrial Management 63, Social Security Org. 63-65, Central Bank of Iraq 63-65; Dir. Iraq Nat. Oil Co. 67-68.
Leisure interests: tennis and swimming.
Publs. *The National Income of Iraq, 1953-1961,* 64, *Sources of Arab Thought in Economics in Iraq* (in Arabic) 71, *Workers' Participation in Management in*

Arab Countries (in Arabic) 71, *Sources of Arab Economic Thought in Iraq 1900-1970* (in Arabic) 73, and several articles in English and Arabic.
15/18/4, Al-Mansoor, Baghdad, Iraq.
Telephone: 514067.

Hasegawa, Norishige; Japanese chemical executive; b. 8 Aug. 1907, Kumamoto City; s. of Teiichiro and Sakae (Aoji) Hasegawa; m. Tomiko Ataka 1933; one d.; ed. Tokyo Imperial Univ.
Sumitomo Chemical Co. 31-, Dir. 51-, Man. Dir. 56, Vice-Pres. 63-65, Pres. 65-; mem. Econ. Council, Office of the Prime Minister, Industrial Structure Council and Industrial Tech. Council of Ministry of Int. Trade and Industry; Vice-Pres. Fed. of Econ. Org.; Dir. Japan Cttee. for Econ. Devt.; Exec. Councillor Osaka Chamber of Commerce and Industry; Standing Dir. Konsai Economic Fed., Japan Fed. of Employer's Asscn.; Pres. Japan Chem. Industry Asscn., Nippon Aluminium Co. Ltd.; mem. Visiting Cttee., Center for Int. Studies, M.I.T.; Pres. Japan Chemical Industry Asscn., Japan Greece Soc.; Trustee Univ. of the Sacred Heart; mem. Japan Comm. of Trilateral Comm., Advisory Cttee. Japanese Nat. Railways, Industrial Problems Research Council; Pres. Kansai Philharmonic Soc.; Dir. and Adviser Asscn. of Petrochemical Industry in Japan; Dir. numerous other cos.; mem. Exec. Cttee., Japan-U.S. Econ. Council; Deputy Chair. Japan C.I.O.S. Asscn.
Leisure interests: golf, arts.
Sumitomo Chemical Co. Ltd., 15, 5-chome Kitahama, Higashi-ku, Osaka; 12-7, Aioi-cho, Nishinomiya Hyogo Prefecture, Japan.
Telephone: 06-220-3211 (Osaka); 0798-22-2400.

Hasegawa, Takashi; Japanese politician; b. 1 April 1912; ed. Waseda Univ.
Editor *Kyushu* daily paper; Private Sec. to Minister of State; mem. House of Reps. 53-; Deputy Minister of Educ. 61-62; Vice-Chair. Public Relations Cttee., Liberal Democratic Party 63, Chair. 66; Minister of Labour Dec. 73-; Dir. Japan Athletic Asscn.
8-903, Yonban-cho, 9-chome, Chiyoda-ku, Tokyo, Japan.

Hashim, Jawad M., PH.D.; Iraqi politician; b. 10 Feb. 1938; s. of Mahmoud Hashim and Nasrat Baqer; m. Salwa Al-Rufaiee 1961; two s.; ed. London School of Econs. and Political Science, Univ. of London.
Professor of Statistics, Univ. of Baghdad 67; Dir.-Gen. Cen. Statistical Org. 68; Minister of Planning 68-71; mem. Econ. Office, Revolutionary Command Council 71-72; Minister of Planning 72-74; mem. Planning Board and Econ. Office, Revolutionary Command Council Nov. 74-; Chair. UN Econ. Comm. for Western Asia 75.
Leisure interests: sport, driving, reading.
Publs. *Capital Formation in Iraq 1957-1970, National Income—Its Methods of Estimation, The Evaluation of Economic Growth in Iraq 1950-1970, Development of Iraq's Foreign Trade Sector 1950-1970,* and eighteen articles.
Ministry of Planning, Baghdad, Iraq.

Hasior, Władysław; Polish sculptor; b. 14 May 1928, Nowy Sącz; s. of Antoni and Waleria Hassior; m. Joanna Narkiewicz; one s.; ed. Acad. of Art, Warsaw.
Teacher of sculpture, Coll. of Art Techniques, Zakopane 57-70; scenographer State Dramatic Theatre, Wrocław 64-70, Polish Theatre, Wrocław 70-71; mem. Polish Fine Arts Asscn. 58-; numerous one-man exhbns. in Poland, Stockholm, Oslo, Paris, Brussels, Copenhagen, Helsinki, Venice, New York, São Paulo, Montevideo, etc.; creator of many monuments commemorating victims of World War II; some works permanently in museums in Stockholm, Göteborg, Oslo and Amsterdam; Prize of Ministry of Culture and Art 71.
Ul. Jagielońska 3, "Borek", Zakopane, Poland.

Haskell, Arnold Lionel, C.B.E., M.A.; British ballet school governor, author and lecturer; b. 1903, London; s. of J. S. Haskell and Emmy Mesritz; m. 1st Vera Saitzoff 1926 (died 1968), two s. one d.; m. 2nd Vivienne Marks 1970; ed. Westminster and Trinity Hall, Cambridge.
Member Editorial Board of William Heinemann 29-34; joint founder Camargo Soc. 30; Ballet critic *Daily Telegraph* 34-47; lectured for Ministry of Information and other bodies on Australia 40-45; Gov. Royal Ballet School; Gov. Royal Ballet; Founder, Ballet Benevolent Fund; Vice-Pres. Varna and Moscow Ballet Competitions, Royal Acad. of Dancing; Council mem. Royal West of England Acad., Bath Univ.; Dir. Festival Ballet Trust; travelled and lectured in U.S.A., Australia, Canada, France, Germany, Italy, Spain, Portugal, U.S.S.R., Cuba, etc.; Chevalier de la Légion d'Honneur; Hon. D.Litt. (Bath).
Leisure interests: collecting sculpture and juvenilia.
Publs. *Balletomania* 34, *Diaghileff* 35, *Dancing Round the World* 37, *Ballet Panorama* 38, *Ballet: A Complete Guide to Appreciation* 38, *Balletomane's Album* 39, *Waltzing Matilda* 40, *The Australians* 42, *Australia* 42, *The National Ballet* 45, *In His True Centre* (autobiography) 51, *Saints Alive* 54, *The Russian Genius in Ballet* 63, *Ballet Retrospect* 64, *Heroes and Roses* 66, *Ballet Russe* 68, *Infantilia* 71, *Balletomane at Large* 72.
6A Cavendish Crescent, Bath, Avon, BA1 2UG, England.
Telephone: Bath 22472.

Haskell, Broderick, B.S.; American banker and industrialist; b. 22 Aug. 1899; m. 2nd Ruth Harvey Stead 1949; ed. Massachusetts Inst. of Technology.
Director Banco de Reserva del Peru 27-28; Vice-Pres. Guaranty Trust Co. of New York 30-53; Dir. Combustion Engineering Inc. 46-56 (Vice-Chair. 53-56), Lummus Co., New York 52-56, Air Preheater Corpn., New York 54-56; mem. Advisory Board, Chase Manhattan Bank 54-56; Dir. Atomic Industrial Forum 54-57; Dir. of Investments, Int. Finance Corpn. 56-61; Partner, Bache & Co. Inc. 62-65, Vice-Pres. 65-71; Dir. Foote Mineral Co., Dir. Cummings Properties Ltd. 69-71; Trustee, Cathedral of St. John The Divine; mem. Council on Foreign Relations.
Publ. (with others) *The American Individual Enterprise System.*
39 East 79th Street, New York, N.Y. 10021, U.S.A.
Telephone: BU8-7279.

Haskins, Caryl Parker, PH.D.; American scientist and educationist; b. 12 Aug. 1908, Schenectady, N.Y.; m. Edna Ferrell 1940; ed. Yale and Harvard Univs.
Member of research staff Gen. Electric Co., Schenectady 31-35; Research Assoc. Mass. Inst. of Technology 35-44; Pres., Dir. and Research Dir. Haskins Laboratories, Inc. 35-55; Research Prof. in Biophysics, Union Coll., Schenectady 37-55; Liaison Officer 40-43, Exec. Asst. to the Chair. 43-44 and Deputy Exec. Officer 44-45, Nat. Defence Research Cttee.; Scientific Adviser to the Policy Council 47 and to the Research and Devt. Board of the Nat. Mil. Establishment 48-51; Chair. Advisory Cttee. to the Sec. of Defense on special weapons 48-49; Consultant to the Sec. of Defense 48-60, to the Sec. of State 50-; mem. President's Science Advisory Cttee. 55-58, Consultant 59; Pres. Carnegie Inst. of Washington, D.C. 56-71; Presidential Certificate of Merit and King's Medal for Service in the Cause of Freedom.
Publs. *Of Ants and Men* 39, *The Amazon, The Life History of a Mighty River* 43, *Of Societies and Men* 51, *Scientific Revolution and World Politics* 64, *The Search for Understanding.*
Suite 600, 2100 M Street, N.W., Washington, D.C. 20037, U.S.A.
Telephone: (202) 833-1720.

Haskins, Sam (Samuel Joseph); South African photographer and designer; b. 11 Nov. 1926, Kroonstad; s. of Benjamin G. Haskins and Anna E. Oelofse; m. Alida Elzabe van Heerden 1952; two s.; ed. Helpmekaar School and Witwatersrand Technical Coll., Johannesburg, Bolt Court School of Photography, London.
Freelance work, Johannesburg 53-68, London 68-; one-man exhbns. in Johannesburg 53, 60, Tokyo 70, London 72, Paris 73, Amsterdam 74; Fellow, Royal Photographic Soc. 74, Soc. of Industrial Artists and Designers 74; Prix Nadar (France) for *Cowboy Kate and Other Stories* 64, Israel Museum Award, Int. Art Book Contest Award, Gold Medal Award for *Haskins Posters,* N.Y. 74.
Leisure interests: vintage car rallying, books, music.
Publs. *Five Girls* 62, *Cowboy Kate and Other Stories* 64, *African Image* 66, *November Girl* 67, *Haskins Posters* 72, and portfolios in most major international photographic magazines.
67 Glebe Place, London, S.W.3, England.
Telephone: 352-2788, 352-4923.

Hasler, Arthur Davis, PH.D.; American professor of zoology; b. 5 Jan. 1908, Lehi, Utah; m. Hanna Prusse Hasler 1932 (deceased); five s. one d.; ed. Brigham Young Univ. and Univ. of Wisconsin.
Aquatic biologist, U.S. Fish and Wildlife Service 35-37; Naturalist, U.S. Nat. Park Service 37-38; staff, Univ. of Wisconsin 37-, Chair. Dept. of Zoology 53, 55-57, Prof. of Zoology 48-, Dir. Laboratory of Limnology 63-; mem. research Cttee., Wisconsin Conservation Dept. 54-66; Chair. Lake Mendota Problems Cttee. 65-; Pres. Int. Asscn. of Ecology 67-; Dir. Inst. of Ecology 72-; mem. Nat. Acad of Sciences; Fellow, Philadelphia Acad. of Sciences 53, Amer. Inst. of Fisheries Research Biology 58, Amer. Acad. of Arts and Sciences 72; Hon. D.Sc. Univ. of Newfoundland.
Publs. *Underwater Guideposts* and over 125 research publications.
Laboratory of Limnology, University of Wisconsin, Madison, Wis. 53706, U.S.A.
Telephone: 608-262-2840.

Hasluck, Rt. Hon. Sir Paul Meernaa Caedwalla, G.C.M.G., G.C.V.O., P.C., M.A.; Australian historian, diplomatist and politician; b. 1 April 1905, Fremantle; m. 1932; two s.; ed. Perth Modern School, Western Australia Univ.
Mem. Editorial staff *The West Australian;* Hon. Sec. Western Australian Historical Soc. 30-36; Lecturer in History Western Australia Univ. 39-40; mem. staff Australian Dept. of External Affairs 41-47; Sec. Canberra Conf. Jan. 44; Adviser on Australian del. to Wellington Conf. Nov. 44; Adviser British Commonwealth meeting London April 45; Adviser San Francisco Conf. April 45; Australian del. Exec. Cttee. of United Nations Preparatory Comm. London Aug. 45; alternate del. Preparatory Comm. Nov. 45; del. General Assembly Jan. and Sept. 46; Dir. post-hostilities Div. Australian Dept. of External Affairs April 45; Counsellor-in-Charge Australian Mission UN H.Q. Mar. 46; Acting rep. of Australia on Security Council and Atomic Energy Comm. July 46; Research Reader in History, Univ. of W. Australia 48; elected to Commonwealth Parl. as Liberal M.P. Dec. 49-69; Minister for Territories, Fed. Cabinet 51-63; Minister of Defence Dec. 63-April 64, of External Affairs April 64-69; Governor-Gen. of Australia 69-74; engaged on official history of Australia in Second World War during 47, 48, 49.
Publs. *Our Southern Half-Castes* 38, *Into the Desert* 39, *Black Australians* 42, *Workshop of Security* 47, *The Government and the People, 1939-1941* (Australian Official War History) 52, 69, *Native Welfare in Australia* 53, *Collected Verse* 70, *An Open Go* 71.
95 St. George's Terrace, Perth, W. Australia.

Hassan II, King of Morocco; 17th Sovereign of the Alaouite dynasty; b. 9 July 1929; ed. Bordeaux Univ. Son of Mohammed V; invested as Crown Prince Moulay Hassan 57; C.-in-C. and Chief of Staff of Royal Moroccan Army 57; personally directed rescue operations at Agadir earthquake disaster 60; Minister of Defence May 60-June 61; Vice-Premier May 60-Feb. 61; succeeded to throne on death of his father, 26 Feb. 1961; Prime Minister Feb. 61-Nov. 63, June 65-67; Minister of Defence 72-73, Commdr.-in-Chief of the Army Aug. 72-; Chair. Org. of African Unity 72.
Royal Palace, Rabat, Morocco.

Hassan, Hon. Sir Joshua (Abraham), Kt., C.B.E., M.V.O., Q.C.; Gibraltar lawyer and politician; b. 1915, Gibraltar; s. of Abraham R. M. Hassan and Lola Hassan (née Serruya); m. 1st Daniela Salazar 1945 (dissolved 1969), two d.; m. 2nd Marcelle Bensimon 1969, one d.; ed. Line Wall Coll., Gibraltar.
Called to Bar, Middle Temple, London 39; mem. Exec. Council, Chief mem. Legislative Council, Gibraltar 50-64; Chief Minister of Gibraltar 64-69, 72-; Leader of Opposition, House of Assembly 69-72; Mayor of Gibraltar 45-50, 53-69; Deputy Coroner, Gibraltar 41-64; Chair. Cttee of Management Gibraltar Museum 52-65; Chair. Central Planning Comm. 47-70, Gibraltar Lottery Cttee. 55-69; Pres. Gibraltar Labour Party and Asscn. for the Advancement of Civil Rights.
Leisure interest: reading.
11/18 Europa Road, Gibraltar.
Telephone: 2295.

Hassel, Kai-Uwe von; German politician; b. 21 April 1913; m. 2nd Dr. Monika Weichert 1936.
Studied farming and trade in Tanganyika; Plantation trader, E. Africa 35-40, deported to Germany 40; served in Army 40-45, prisoner 45; Mayor of Glücksburg 47 and mem. of County Council; mem. of Schleswig-Holsteinischer Landtag 50-65; also elected to Bundestag, but resigned on appointment as Minister-Pres. of Schleswig-Holstein 54-63; Pres. Bundesrat 55-56; Deputy Chair. CDU 56; Minister of Defence, Federal Republic of Germany 63-66, for Refugees and Expellees 66-69; mem. of Bundestag 65-; Speaker of Bundestag 69-72, Deputy Speaker 72-; Pres. European Union of Christian Democrats.
Bundestag, Bonn, Federal Republic of Germany.

Hassel, Odd, DR. PHIL.; Norwegian chemist; b. 17 May 1897, Oslo; s. of the late Ernst Hassel and Mathilde Klaveness; ed. Univs. of Oslo, Munich and Berlin.
Reader, Univ. of Oslo 25, Lecturer 26, Prof. 34-64, Prof. Emer. 64-; Hon. Fellow, Chem. Soc. (London), Norwegian Chem. Soc.; mem. several European acads.; several hon. degrees; Knight, Order of St. Olav; Gunnerus Medal 64, Guldberg-Waage Medal 64, Nobel Prize for Chem. 69.
Publs. *Kristallchemie* (trans. in English and Russian) 34; about 250 scientific papers chiefly on molecular structures and structures of donor-acceptor complexes in European and American periodicals.
Department of Chemistry, University of Oslo, Oslo 3; Home: Holsteinveien 10, Oslo 8, Norway.
Telephone: 466800 (Office); 232062 (Home).

Hassett, Gen. Francis George, A.C., C.B., C.B.E., D.S.O., M.V.O.; Australian army officer; b. 11 April 1918, Sydney; s. of J. F. Hassett; m. Margaret Hallie Spencer 1946; two s. two d.; ed. Canterbury High School, Sydney, Royal Military Coll., Duntroon.
Member of Darwin Mobile Force 39, Australian Imperial Force 39-45 (Middle East, S.W. Pacific area); Commdr. 1 RAR and 3 RAR 51-52 (Korea), 28th Commonwealth Infantry Brigade Group 60-62 (Malaya); at Imperial Defence Coll. London 63; Deputy Chief of Gen. Staff 64-66; Head Australian Joint Services Staff, London 66-67; Extra Gentlemen Usher to H.M. The Queen 66-68; G.O.C. Northern Command 68-70; Head Army Reorg. Planning Staff 70-71; Vice Chief of Gen. Staff 71-73; Chief of Gen. Staff 73-75; Chief of Defence Force Staff 75-.
Leisure interests: boating, reading.
42 Mugga Way, Red Hill, Canberra, A.C.T. 2603, Australia.
Telephone: Canberra 95-8035.

Hassouna, Mohammed Abdel-Khalek al; Egyptian diplomatist; b. 28 Oct. 1898; ed. Cairo Univ. and Cambridge.
Began as lawyer 21; subsequently joined Egyptian Diplomatic Corps; served Berlin 26, Prague 28, Brussels 28, Rome 30, and at Ministry for Foreign Affairs, Cairo 32-39; Under-Sec. of State, Ministry for Social Affairs 39; Gov. of Alexandria 42; Under-Sec. of State, Ministry for Foreign Affairs 48; Minister of Social Affairs 49; Minister of Education 52; Minister for Foreign Affairs 52; Sec.-Gen. Arab League 52-72; Grand Cordon of the Order of the Nile; Légion d'Honneur; decorations from Belgium, Holy See, Syria, Ethiopia, Italy.
3 Rifaa Street, Manchiet El Bakri, Cairo, Egypt.

Hastings, A(lbert) Baird, B.S., PH.D.; American professor of biological chemistry; b. 20 Nov. 1895, Dayton, Ky.; s. of Otis Luther and Elisabeth (Henry) Hastings; m. Margaret Anne Johnson 1918; one s.; ed. Univ. of Michigan and Columbia Univ.
Chemist U.S. Public Health Services 17-21; Asst. Rockefeller Inst. for Medical Research 21-22; Assoc. 22-26; Prof. Physiological Chemistry Univ. of Chicago 26-28, Prof. of Biochemistry 28-35; Hamilton Kuhn Prof. of Biological Chemistry Harvard Medical School 35-58, Em. 58-; mem. Scripps Clinic and Research Foundation 59-66, mem. Emeritus 66-; Research Assoc., Dept. of Neurosciences, Univ. of Calif., San Diego 66-; Lecturer Univ. of Southern Calif. 24; mem. American Acad. of Arts and Sciences, American Philosophical Soc., Nat. Acad. of Sciences, Royal Danish Acad. of Sciences and Letters, Nat. Research Council (mem. of various cttees.); mem. cttee. on Medical Research, Office of Scientific Research and Devt., Washington 41-47; mem. Board of Review, U.S. Atomic Energy Comm. 47; Pres. Soc. for Experimental Biology and Medicine and American Soc. of Biological Chemists 45-47; Syndic, Harvard Univ. Press; Consultant, Div. of Biology and Medicine, U.S. Atomic Energy Comm. 50-62; U.S. del. Int. Conf. on Peaceful Uses of Atomic Energy, Geneva 54; U.S. Public Health Nat. Advisory Cttees. 43-; Walter Reed Army Inst. of Research 56-62, etc.; Trustee Brookhaven Nat. Laboratory, Associated Univs. Inc. 48-51, mem. Visiting Cttee. 56-; Visiting Prof. School of Medicine, Pahlavi Univ., Shiraz, Iran Nov. 67; mem. Nat. Advisory Comm. White House Conf. on Aging 71; Hon. Sc.D. (Michigan, Harvard, Columbia, Boston, Oxford and St. Louis Univ., Univ. of Indiana 72); President's Medal for Merit 48, Banting Medal of Amer. Diabetes Asscn. 62, and many other awards.
Leisure interest: fishing.
Department of Neurosciences, University of California, San Diego Campus, La Jolla, Calif.; 2130 Vallecitos, Apt. 147, La Jolla, Calif. 92037, U.S.A.
Telephone: 454-5160.

Hastrup, Aage; Danish journalist and politician; b. 22 Nov. 1919, Frederikssund, Zealand; s. of Poul and Alma Hastrup; m. Grete Hedekaer 1943; one s. two d.
Journalist for various provincial newspapers; Sec. Conservative Party's Nat. Org. 45-47, Parl. Group of Conservative Party 47-50; Reporter, newspaper *Berlingske Aftenavis* 50, Editor 56-58; Head, Conservative Party's Political Secr. 58-; Editor Conservative Information Service 59-; mem. Folketing (Parl.) 64-73;

Minister for Housing and Civil Servants 68-71; mem. Nat. Tax Exec. Cttee. 71-73; Chair. Exec. Cttee. for town devt. in Copenhagen 72-73; Council of town building in Koge Bugt 72; Admin. Dir. Dansk almennyttigt Boligselskab 72; mem. Exec. Cttee. for Danish Social Housing Org. 72; Danish Del. to UN; mem. Exec. Cttee., Nat. Educ. Soc. 46-53, Theatre Asscn. 53-68 (Chair. 57-68), Chair. Det Danske Teater 63-68; Cavling Prize for reporting 52; K.D. 71.

Publs. *Politisk Oversigt* (Political Survey) covering years 46-53, *Studiekredsen og Aftenskolen* (Study Circles and Adult Education) 47, *Skattereformen kritisk belyst* (Critical Review of the Tax Reform) 54.

Folketinget, Copenhagen; Home: Hummeltoften 10, 2830 Virum, Denmark.

Telephone: 01-377766 (Office); 851536 (Home).

Hatch, Henry Clifford; Canadian business executive; b. 30 April 1916, Toronto, Ont.; s. of Harry C. Hatch and Elizabeth Carr; m. Joan Ferriss 1940; two s. two d.; ed. St. Michael's College School, Toronto.

Salesman, T. G. Bright & Co., Ltd., Niagara Falls 33-37; Merchandising Staff, Hiram Walker Inc., Walkerville, Ont. 37, Dir. 38; Dir. Hiram Walker-Gooderham & Worts Ltd. 46, Vice-Pres. 55, Exec. Vice-Pres. 61, Pres. 64-; Dir. T. G. Bright & Co. Ltd., The Toronto-Dominion Bank, Bell Canada, Curtis Co. Ltd.

Leisure interests: sailing, curling, swimming, reading, golf.

Office: 2072 Riverside Drive East, Walkerville, Ontario, N8Y 4S5; Home: 7130 Riverside Drive East, Windsor, Ontario N8S 1C3, Canada.

Telephone: 519-254-5171 (Office); 519-944-1616 (Home).

Hatcher, Harlan Henthorne, M.A., PH.D., LIT.D., LL.D., L.H.D.; American author and university president; b. 9 Sept. 1898, Ironton, Ohio; s. of Robert E. and Linda Leslie Hatcher; m. Anne Vance 1942; one s. one d.; ed. Ohio State Univ. and Univ. of Chicago.

Instructor, Ohio State Univ. 22-28, Asst. Prof. 28-32, Prof. of English 32-51, Dean of Coll. of Arts and Sciences 44-48, Vice-Pres. 48-51; Pres. Univ. of Michigan 51-67; served U.S. Army 18, U.S. Navy 42-44; State Dir. Fed. Writers' Project in Ohio 37-39; Editorial Adviser *College English* 38-48, Pres. The Developing Great Lakes Megalopolis Research Project 68-; Commr. State of Michigan Judicial Tenure Comm. 68-.

Leisure interests: golf, travel.

Publs. *The Versification of Robert Browning* 28, *Tunnel Hill* 31, *Patterns of Wolfpen* 34, *Creating the Modern American Novel* 35, *The Buckeye Country* 40, *The Great Lakes* 44, *Lake Erie* 45, *The Western Reserve* 49, revised edn. 66, *A Century of Iron and Men* 50, *Persistent Quest for Values* 66; Editor: *The Ohio Guide* 40, *Modern Continental, British and American Dramas, with critical introductions* (3 vols.) 41, *Modern Dramas* (shorter edition) 44, *A Modern Repertory* 53, *A Pictorial History of the Great Lakes* 63, *The Persistent Quest for Values* 66.

841 Greenhills Drive, Ann Arbor, Mich. 48105, U.S.A.

Hatem, Mohammed Abdel Kader, M.SC., PH.D.; Egyptian politician; b. 1917, Alexandria; ed. Military Acad., Univs. of London and Cairo.

Member, Nat. Assembly 57; Adviser to the Presidency, subsequently Deputy Minister for Presidential Affairs 57; Minister of State responsible for broadcasting and television 59; Minister for Culture, Nat. Guidance and Tourism 62; Deputy Prime Minister for Cultural Affairs and Nat. Guidance 65; Deputy Prime Minister and Minister for Culture and Information 71-74; Chair. *Al-Ahram* 74-; Pres Adviser on Nat. Council Affairs 74-75; mem. Gen. Sec. Arab Socialist Union; two hon. doctorates from French univs.

Publ. *Information and the Arab Cause* 74.

c/o *Al-Ahram*, Gallaa Street, Cairo, Egypt.

Hatfield, Mark O.; American politician; b. 12 July 1922, Dallas, Oregon; s. of Mr. and Mrs. C. D. Hatfield; m. Antoinette Kuzmanich 1958; two s. two d.; ed Willamette Univ. and Stanford Univ.

U.S. Navy, Second World War; Instructor, Asst. Prof., Assoc. Prof. in Political Science, Willamette Univ. 49-56, Dean of Students 50-56; State Rep., Marion County 51-55, State Senator, Marion County 55-57; Sec. of State, Oregon 57-59; Gov. of Oregon 59-67; U.S. Senator from Oregon 67-, mem. Senate Appropriations Cttee., Cttee. on Interior and Insular Affairs, and Senate Rules and Admin. Cttee.; numerous awards; Republican.

Leisure interests: gardening, reading.

Publs. *Not Quite So Simple* (autobiography), *Conflict and Conscience* (religious speeches).

Room 463, Old Senate Office Building, Washington, D.C. 20510, U.S.A.

Telephone: 202-225-3753.

Hatfield, Hon. Richard Bennett, B.A., LL.B.; Canadian lawyer and politician; b. 9 April 1931, Woodstock, N.B.; s. of Heber Harold and Dora Fern (Robinson) Hatfield; unmarried; ed. Acadia Univ. and Dalhousie Univ.

Admitted to N.S. bar 56; Exec. Asst., Minister of Trade and Commerce 57-58; Sales Man. Hatfield Industries Ltd. 58-65; mem. New Brunswick Legis. Assembly 61-; Leader, New Brunswick Progressive Conservative Party 69-; Premier of New Brunswick Nov. 70-; Dir. Canadian Council of Christians and Jews, Beaverbrook Art Gallery, Fredericton; Hon. Micmac-Maliseet Chieftain 70; LL.D. (Univ. of Moncton) 71, (Univ. of New Brunswick) 72, (St. Thomas Univ.) 73.

P.O. Box 6000, Fredericton, New Brunswick, E3B 5R1, Canada.

Telephone: (506) 453-2144.

Hatfield, Robert Sherman, LL.B.; American business executive; b. 16 Jan. 1916, Utica, N.Y.; s. of Albert R. and Mary (Sherman) Hatfield; m. Roberta Sullivan 1937; one s. three d.; ed. Cornell and Fordham Univs.

Joined Continental Can Co. 36, Sales Man., Milwaukee 49-52, Area Man. North Cen. District 52-56, Gen. Man. Eastern Metal Div. 56-60, Vice-Pres., Gen. Man. Eastern Div. 60-62, Exec. Vice-Pres., Gen. Man. Metal Div. 62-69, mem. Board of Dirs. 68-, Senior Exec. Vice-Pres. and Chief Operating Officer 69-71, Pres., Chair. of Board and Chief Exec. Officer 71-; Vice-Chair. Admin. Board, Cornell Univ. Council; Dir. Nat. Center for Resource Recovery; mem. boards of industry groups.

Leisure interests: golf, tennis.

Continental Can Co., 633 Third Avenue, New York, N.Y. 10017; Home: 480 North Street, Greenwich, Conn. 06830, U.S.A.

Telephone: 212-551-7661 (Office).

Hathaway, Earl B.; American rubber executive; b. 11 Feb. 1903, Hot Springs, Ark.; m. Margaret Moinet 1932; two s. one d.; ed. Northwestern Univ.

Firestone Tire & Rubber Co. 27-; Salesman 30-32; Store Man. Alton, Springfield, St. Louis and Chicago 32-36; Asst. Man. Chicago District 36-38, District Man., Detroit 38-41; Wholesale Sales Man., Akron 41-42; Eastern Div. Man. 42-48; Trade Sales Man. 48-57; Vice-Pres. (Trade Sales) 57-59, Vice-Pres. (Sales) 59-62; Dir. 60-70; Exec. Vice-Pres. 61-64, Pres. 64-70; Dir. Automotive Old Timers, Inc.; Hon. LL.D., Univ. of Akron 65; Alumni Award Northwestern Univ. 66.

482 St. Andrews Drive, Akron, O. 44303, U.S.A.

Hathaway, Stanley K. LL.B.; American lawyer and politician; b. 19 July 1924, Osceola, Nebraska; m. Roberta Harley 1948; two d.; ed. Univ. of Nebraska.

Served Army Air Force, Second World War; practising attorney 50-; head of own law firm Hathaway, Sigler and Callahan; elected Goshen County Prosecuting

Attorney 54 and 58; Goshen County Chair. 62-64; State
Chair. Republican Party 64; Gov. Wyoming 67-74;
Sec. of the Interior June-Oct. 75; Chair. Fed. of Rocky
Mountain States 68, Interstate Oil Compact Comm. 72;
Croix de Guerre; five Air Medals.
219 Linda Vista, Torrington, Wyo., U.S.A.

Hathaway, William Dodd, LL.B.; American lawyer
and politician; b. 21 Feb. 1924, Cambridge, Mass.; *m.*
Mary Lee Bird 1945; one *s.* one *d.*; ed. Harvard Univ.
Admitted to Mass. Bar 53, Me. Bar 54; in private practice Lewiston, Me. 53-; mem. Congress 65-; Senator
from Me. 73-; Democrat.
United States Senate, Washington, D.C. 20510, U.S.A.

Hathi, Jaisukhlal; Indian politician; b. 19 Jan. 1909,
Muli, Saurashtra; *s.* of late Shri Lalshankar Hathi; *m.*
Smt. Padmaben Hathi 1927; four *s.* one *d.*
Advocate, Bombay High Court; mem. Constituent
Assembly 46-47; mem. Provisional Parl.; Chief Sec.
Saurashtra 48; mem. Rajya Sabha 52-57, 62-, Lok
Sabha 57-62; Deputy Minister of Irrigation and Power
52-62; Minister of State for Labour and Employment
April-Nov. 62; Minister of Supply 62-64; Minister of
State in Ministry of Home Affairs 64-66, also Minister
of Defence Supplies 65-66; Minister of State for Defence
Nov. 66-March 67; Minister for Labour and Rehabilita-
tion 67-69; Deputy Leader Parl. Congress Party 72-74;
Chair. Cttee. on Subordinate Legislation, Rajya Sabha;
Vice-Pres. Bharatiya Vidya Bhavan, Bar Asscn. of
India.
Leisure interest: reading.
11 Asoka Road, New Delhi, India.
Telephone: 387640.

Hatta, Mohammad; Indonesian politician; b. 1902;
ed. Rotterdam School of Economics, Holland.
Nationalist activity from schooldays; Chair. "Perhim-
punan Indonesia" (Univ. Students' Asscn.) Holland 26;
arrested by Dutch 27; tried and released 28; returned to
Indonesia 32 and founded Pendidikan Nasional
Indonesia, mass-education political party 32; arrested
34; exiled to Digul 35, later to the Moluccas; released by
Japanese 42; elected Vice-Pres. of Republic of Indonesia
45-49, 50-56; Prime Minister and Minister of Defence
48; Prime Minister and Minister of Foreign Affairs
49-50.
57 Jalan Diponegoro, Jakarta, Indonesia.

Hattersley, Rt. Hon. Roy Sydney George, P.C.,
B.SC.(ECON.); British politician; *s.* of Frederick Roy and
Enid Hattersley (née Brackenbury); *m.* Edith Mary
Loughran 1956; ed. Sheffield City Grammar School,
Univ. of Hull.
Member Sheffield City Council 56-64; Parl. Private
Sec. to Minister of Pensions and Nat. Insurance 57-65;
Dir. Campaign for European Political Community 65;
Jt. Parl. Sec. Dept. of Employment and Productivity
64-67; Minister of Defence for Admin. 67-69; Labour
Party Spokesman on Defence 70-72, on Education
72-74; Public Affairs Consultant IBM 71, 72; Visiting
Fellow, Inst. of Politics, Univ. of Harvard 72; Minister
of State for Foreign and Commonwealth Affairs March
74-.
Publs. *Nelson—A Biography* 74, *Goodbye to Yorkshire—
A Collection of Essays* 75.
Foreign and Commonwealth Office, Whitehall, London,
S.W.1, England.
Telephone: 01-233 4755.

Hattori, Motozo; Japanese shipping executive; b.
1 Jan. 1905; ed. Kyoto Imperial Univ.
Kawasaki Kisen Kaisha Ltd., Kobe 31-, Rep. New York
Branch 40-41, Sub-Man., Santiago, Chile 41-42, Man.
42-43, Sub-Man., later Man. Operating Section, Kobe
43-46; Gen. Man. Operating and Chartering Dept. 46,
Dir. 47-49, Exec. Dir. 49-50, Pres. 50-73, Chair. 73-;

Pres. Kawasaki Steamship Co., New York 55-, Kawasaki (London) Ltd. 56-70; official of other firms and
business orgs.
c/o Kawasaki Kisen Kaisha Ltd., 8 Kaigan Dori, Ikuta-
ku, Kobe, Japan.

Hattori, Seitaro; Japanese banker; b. 23 June 1920;
s. of Ichiro and Kiyoko Hattori; *m.* Tsuyako Yamakawa
1950; one *d.*; ed. Tokyo Imperial Univ.
Joined Ministry of Finance 42; Liaison Office, Ministry
of Finance 47-53; London Rep., Japan Monopoly
Corpn. 53-64, Dir. Facilities Div. 64-65, Sales Div.
65-66; Deputy Dir. Int. Finance Bureau, Ministry of
Finance 66-68; Alt. Exec. Dir. Int. Monetary Fund
68-70; Exec. Dir. for Burma, Ceylon, Japan, Laos,
Malaysia, Nepal, Singapore and Thailand, Int. Bank
for Reconstruction and Devt. (World Bank), IFC and
IDA 70-73; Adviser to Nat. Westminster Bank, Tokyo
73-; Alt. Rep., Japanese Del. to UNCTAD II, New
Delhi 67.
National Westminster Bank Ltd., Mitsubishi Building,
Marunouchi 2-chome, Chiyoda-ku, Tokyo 100, Japan.

Hauge, Gabriel; American economist and banker;
b. 7 March 1914, Hawley, Minn.; *s.* of Søren Gabrielson
Hauge and Anna B. Thompson; *m.* Helen Lansdowne
Resor 1948; two *s.* five *d.*; ed. Concordia Coll., Moorhead,
Minnesota, and Harvard Univ.
Instructor in Econs., Harvard Univ. 38-40; Senior
Statistician, Fed. Reserve Bank of New York 39;
Instructor in Econs., Princeton Univ. 40-42; U.S.
Naval Reserve 42-46; Chief, Div. of Research and
Statistics, New York State Banking Dept. 47-50;
McGraw-Hill Publishing Co. 50-52; Admin. Asst. to
Pres. of U.S. for Econ. Affairs 53-56; Special Asst. to
Pres. of U.S. (Econ. Affairs) 56-58; mem. Board of
Dirs., Chair. Finance Cttee., Manufacturers Trust Co.,
New York City 58-61; Vice-Chair. of Board, Manu-
facturers Hanover Trust Co., N.Y. City 61-, Pres. 63-71,
Chair. 71-; Commdr. Royal Order of Phoenix 64, Gran
Cruz de Isabel la Católica 67.
Leisure interests: Cathedral and church architecture,
collecting modern art.
Manufacturers Hanover Trust Co., 350 Park Avenue,
New York, N.Y. 10022, U.S.A.

Hauge, Jens Chr.; Norwegian lawyer and politician;
b. 15 May 1915; ed. Oslo Univ.
Leading member Military Organisation within Home
Front Organisation from 41; became Sec. Prime
Minister Gerhardsen 45; Minister of Defence Nov. 45-52;
practising lawyer 52-; temporary Sec. Labour Party 52;
Minister of Justice 55; Chair. of several Royal Comms.;
Chair. of Board Royal Norwegian Airlines (now Norske
Luftfartelskap A/S) 62- (concurrently S.A.S. 62),
Norwegian State Oil Co. 72-74, Nat. Theatre, Oslo.
Publs. essays and books on legal and historical subjects.
c/o Norske Luftfartelskap A/S, Fornebu Airport, Oslo,
Norway.

Haughey, Charles James; Irish politician; b. 16 Sept.
1925, Castlebar, Co. Mayo; *s.* of Commandant Sean
Haughey and Sarah McWilliams; *m.* Maureen Lemass
1951; three *s.* one *d.*; ed. Scoil Muire, Marino, Dublin,
St. Joseph's Christian Brothers School, Fairview,
Dublin, Univ. Coll. and King's Inns, Dublin.
Commissioned Officer Reserve Defence Force 47-57;
Member Dublin Corpn. 53-55; M.P. 57-; Parl. Sec. to
Minister for Justice 60-61, Minister for Justice 61-64;
Minister of Agriculture and Fisheries 64-66, Minister
for Finance 66-70; Chair. Irish Parl. Joint Cttee. on the
Secondary Legislation of the European Communities
73-; Fianna Fáil Party.
Leisure interests: reading, music, riding, swimming.
Abbeville, Kinsaley, Malahide, Co. Dublin, Ireland.
Telephone: Dublin 350111.

Haughton, Daniel Jeremiah; American aircraft executive; b. 7 Sept. 1911, Walker Co., Ala.; s. of Gayle and Mattie (Davis) Haughton; m. Martha Jean Oliver 1935; ed. Univ. of Alabama.
Cost Accountant, Consolidated Aircraft Corpn. 36-39; Lockheed Aircraft Corpn. 39-76, Gen. Man. and Vice-Pres. 52-56, Exec. Vice-Pres. 56-61, Pres. 61-67, Chair. Board of Dirs. 67-76; Dir. subsid. cos.; Chair. Nat. Multiple Sclerosis Soc.; Dir. S. Calif. Edison Co., United Calif. Bank; mem. Board of Govs. Aerospace Industries and Amer. Red Cross; mem. Nat. Defense Transportation Asscn., Aviation Hall of Fame, Navy League of the U.S.A., Air Force Asscn., Asscn. of the U.S. Army, Amer. Inst. of Aeronautics and Astronautics; Hon. degrees from Univ. of Alabama, George Washington Univ., Clarkson Coll. of Technology; numerous aerospace and management awards.
Leisure interest: fishing.
12956 Blairwood Drive, Studio City, Calif. 91604, U.S.A.

Haugland, Jens, LL.M.; Norwegian lawyer and politician; b. 16 April 1910; ed. Oslo Univ.
With firm of barristers, Stavanger 37-38; Legal Adviser City Treas., Stavanger 38-40; Junior Judge, Ryfylke District 41; established own practice Kristiansand 43; fled to Sweden where attached to Norwegian Legation 44; resumed practice Kristiansand 45; mem. Storting 54-; Minister of Justice 55-63; Minister of Municipal Affairs and Labour 63-65; Chair. Perm. Cttee. of Justice 67-, also Country Justice 68-; mem. Labour Party.
The Storting, Oslo, Norway.

Haupt, Arthur Wing, B.SC., PH.D.; American botanist; b. 9 Aug. 1894, Milwaukee, Wis.; s. of William George Haupt and Emily Wing; m. Hazel MacMillen 1921; one s. two d.; ed. Univ. of Chicago.
With U.S. Dept. of Agriculture 18; Prof. of Biology Carthage (Illinois) Coll. 19-20, St. Lawrence Univ. New York 20-23; with Univ. of California at Los Angeles 24-, Prof. of Botany 46-61, Prof. Emer. 61-; Visiting Prof. Univ. of British Columbia 36; mem. Ed. Board *Madroño* (Journal of Western Botany) 35-40; Pres. Pacific Section Botanical Society of America 37-38; botanical exploration Costa Rica 40; Pres. Haupt Botanical Lab. Inc.
Leisure interest: music.
Publs. *An Introduction to Botany, Fundamentals of Biology, Plant Morphology.*
164 Lakeshore Drive, Barrington, Illinois, 60010, U.S.A. Telephone: 312-381-7281.

Haurwitz, Bernhard, PH.D.; American (naturalized 1946) meteorologist; b. 14 Aug. 1905, Glogau, Germany; s. of Paul Haurwitz and Betty Cohn; m. 1st Eva Schick 1934 (divorced 1946), 2nd Marion B. Wood; one s.; ed. Univs. of Breslau, Göttingen, Leipzig.
Privatdozent, Leipzig 31-32; Research Assoc. Blue Hill Observatory, Harvard 33-35; Meteorological Service of Canada 35-41; Assoc. Prof., Mass. Inst. of Technology 41-47; Prof. and Chair. Dept. of Meteorology and Oceanography, N.Y. Univ. 47-59; Prof. Univ. of Colorado 59-64; Senior Scientist, Nat. Center for Atmospheric Research 64 (Dir. Advanced Study Program 67-69); Prof. (Adjoint), Univ. of Colorado 68; Prof. Univ. of Alaska 70-73; Prof. Colorado State Univ. 73-; Gauss Prof. Akad. der Wissenschaften, Göttingen 71; Rossby Award, American Meteorological Soc. 62; Bowie Medal, American Geophysical Union 70; mem. Nat. Acad. of Sciences 60, German Leopoldina Acad. 64; Hon. mem. American Meteorological Soc. 73.
Leisure interest: hiking.
Publs. *Dynamic Meteorology* 41, *Climatology* (co-author) 44, over 100 articles on dynamic meteorology and oceanography.

Department of Atmospheric Science, Colorado State University, Fort Collins, Colo. 80521, U.S.A. Telephone: 303-491-8541.

Haury, Emil W., A.B., M.A., PH.D.; American teacher b. 2 May 1904, Newton, Kans.; s. of Gustav and Clara Haury; m. Hulda Penner 1928; two s.; ed. Bethel Coll. Univ. of Ariz. and Harvard Univ.
Instructor, Univ. of Ariz. 28-29, Research Asst. in Dendrochronology 29-30, Assoc. Prof. and Head of Dept. of Anthropology 37-38, Prof. and Head of Dept. and Dir. of Ariz. State Museum 38-64, Prof. of Anthropology and Adviser to Ariz. State Museum 64-, Fred A. Riecker Distinguished Prof. of Anthropology 70-; Asst. Dir. of Gila Pueblo, Globe, Ariz. 30-37; mem. Nat. Acad. of Sciences, American Acad. of Arts and Sciences, American Philosophical Soc.; Hon. LL.D. Univ. of New Mexico; Viking Fund Medal for Anthropology 50, Univ. of Ariz. Alumni Achievement Award 57, Univ. of Ariz. Faculty Achievement Award 62, Salgo-Noren Foundation Award for Excellence in Teaching 67.
Publs. include: *The Mogollon Culture of Southwestern New Mexico* (Medallion Papers No. 20) 36, *Excavation at Snaketown, Material Culture* (with others, in *Medallion Papers* No. 25) 37, *The Excavation of Los Muertos and Neighboring Ruins in the Salt River Valley, Southern Arizona* (*Papers of the Peabody Museum of American Archaeology and Ethnology* Vol. 24, No. 1) 45, *The Stratigraphy and Archaeology of Ventana Cave, Arizona* 50, *Speculations on Prehistoric Settlement Patterns in the Southwest,* (*Prehistoric Settlement Patterns in the New World,* Edited by G. R. Willey) 56, *The Hohokam: Desert Farmers and Craftsmen, Excavations at Snaketown, 1964-65* 76.
Department of Anthropology, University of Arizona, Tucson, Ariz. 85721; and P.O. Box 4366, Tucson, Ariz. 85717, U.S.A.
Telephone: 884-1346.

Hausen, Hans Magnus, DR.PHIL.; Finnish geologist; b. 1884, Helsinki; s. of Reinhold Theodor Hausen and Anna Julia Reinholdina Böning; m. Margit Svea Grandell; two d.; ed. Helsinki Univ.
Emeritus Prof. of Geology and Mineralogy Åbo Acad.; mem. of the Finnish Society of Science, Geological Societies of Helsinki and Bonn, Finnish Geographical Soc., Inst. de Estudios Canarios, Tenerife; corresp. mem. Argentine Society of Geographical Studies, Universidad Nacional de La Plata, Inst. del Museo; journeys to Baltic Russia 10-13, Canada, Alaska 13, Argentina, Chile 14-17, Siberia 17-20, Argentina 22-23, Italy 39, Canary Islands 47, 48-50, 53-54, 57, 63, 66-67, 68-72; Order of White Rose (Finland); Hon. Medal Acad. of Åbo; Hon. mem. Geol. Soc. of Finland.
Publs. 60 books and papers, including: *Materialien zur Kenntnis der pleistozänen Bildungen in den russischen Ostseeländern* 13, *On the Lithology and Geological Structure of the Sierra de Umango Area, Province of La Rioja, Argentina* 21, *Die Apatite* 29, *Geologische Beobachtungen in den Hochgebirgen der Provinzen Salta und Jujuy, N.W. Argentinien* 30, *Zur Kenntnis der Magmengesteine der chilenischen Atacama-Wüste* 37, *Das Halditjokko-Massiv* 42, *Hidrografia de las Islas Canarias* 54; with geological maps: *Contribution to the Geology of Tenerife (Canary Islands)* 56, *On the Geology of Fuerteventura (Canary Islands)* 58, *On the Geology of Lanzarote and adjacent islands (Canarian Archipelago)* 59, *New Contribution to the Geology of Grand Canary* 62, *The History of Geology and Mineralogy in Finland 1828-1918* 68, *Some contributions to the Geology of La Palma, Canary Islands* 69, *Outlines of the Geology of Gomera* 71, *Outlines of the Geology of Hierro (Canary Islands)* 73.
Armas Lindgrensväg 7, 00570 Helsinki 57, Finland.

Hauser, Erich; German sculptor; b. 1930, Rietheim Kr. Tübingen; ed. Volksschule, Rietheim, Oberschule

Spaichingen and evening classes at Freie Kunstschule, Stuttgart.
Studied engraving in Tuttlingen and drawing and modelling under Pater Ansgar, Kloster Beuron; independent sculptor, Schramberg 52; Visiting Lecturer, Hochschule für bildende Künste, Hamburg 64-65; has held many one-man exhbns. in galleries throughout Germany and in Austria and Switzerland since 61; has participated in many group exhbns. in Europe, New Delhi, Cairo and the São Paulo Biennale 69; has executed sculptures for many public buildings in Germany including *Säulenwand* for Univ. of Konstanz, a relief for theatre foyer, Bonn and a sculpture for the Düsseldorf Stock Exchange; Kunstpreis der Stadt Wolfsburg für Plastik 65, Burdapreis für Plastik 66, Premio Itamaraty 69, Grand Prix, São Paulo Biennale 69, etc.
7210 Rottweil-Altstadt, Saline, Federal Republic of Germany.
Telephone: (0741) 6751.

Hauser, Philip M., PH.D.; American sociologist; b. 27 Sept. 1909, Chicago, Ill.; *m.* Zelda B. Hauser; one *s.* one *d.*; ed. Univ. of Chicago.
Deputy Director, U.S. Bureau of the Census 38-47, Acting Dir. 49-50; Asst. to Sec. of Commerce and Dir., Office of Program Planning, U.S. Dept. of Commerce 45-47; U.S. Rep. to Population Comm., UN 47-51; Statistical Adviser to Govt. of Union of Burma 51-52; Statistical Adviser, Thailand 55-56; Chair. Dept. of Sociology, Univ. of Chicago 56-65; Prof. of Sociology, Dir. Population Research Center and Chicago Community Inventory, Univ. of Chicago 32-37, 47-; mem. Board, UN Inst. for Research in Social Devt., Geneva 66-73, Exec. Cttee. Southeast Asia Devt. Advisory Group 68-71, Statistical Policy Cttee., U.S. Bureau of the Budget, Board of Dirs., Nat. Assembly for Social Policy and Devt. 68-, Advisory Cttee., The Population Council; mem. Council, Nat. Inst. of Child Health and Human Devt. 65-69; Chair. Technical Advisory Cttee. for Population Statistics, U.S. Bureau of the Census, Census Advisory Cttee., American Statistical Asscn.; Fellow, American Asscn. for the Advancement of Science, American Statistical Asscn.; mem. and fmr. Pres. American Sociological Asscn., Population Asscn. of America, Sociological Research Asscn.; mem. American Philosophical Soc., Int. Statistical Inst.
Publs. Several books on population, urbanization and other sociological subjects; about 450 articles in professional journals.
5729 Kimbark Avenue, Chicago, Ill. 60637, U.S.A.

Häuser, Rudolf; Austrian politician; b. 19 March 1909, Vienna; *m.;* four *c.;* ed. vocational secondary school, Vienna.
Instructor, Jugend am Werk; with Milchindustrie A.G. 37-59; Deputy Chair. Non-Governmental White-Collar Workers Union 50-60, Exec. Chair. 62-60, Chair. 62; Vice-Chair. Austrian Trade Union Fed. 63; mem. Nationalrat 62-; Vice-Chancellor and Fed. Minister for Social Welfare April 70-.
Nationalrat, Vienna, Austria.

Hausmann, Manfred, DR. PHIL.; German writer; b. 10 Sept. 1898; ed. Univs. of Göttingen, Munich and Heidelberg.
Served in Army 16-18; merchant in Bremen 22-24; on editorial staff of *Weser-Zeitung* Bremen 24-27, of *Weser-Kurier* 45-52.
Publs. *Frühlingsfeier* 25, *Marienkind* (*Legendenspiel*) 27, *Lilofee* (drama) 27, *Lampioon* 28, *Salut gen Himmel* 29, *Kleine Liebe zu Amerika* 30, *Abel mit der Mundharmonika* 32, *Abschied von der Jugend* 38, *Das Worpsweder Hirtenspiel* 42, *Das Erwachen* (translations of Greek poems) 49, *Der dunkle Reigen* (drama) 49, *Gedichte* 49, *Martin* 49, *Einer muss wachen* 50, *Liebe, Tod und Vollmondnächte* (translations of Japanese poems) 51,

Der Ueberfall 52, *Liebende leben von der Vergebung* 53, *Isabel* 53, *Hafenbar* (drama) 53, *Hinter dem Perleuvorhang* (translations of Chinese poems) 54, *Die Entscheidung* 54, *Der Fischbecker Wandteppich* (drama) 55, *Was dir nicht angehört* 56, *Andreas* 57, *Aufruhr in der Marktkirche* (drama) 57, *Das Lied der Lieder* (translations of Hebrew poems) 58, *Die Zauberin von Buxtehude* (drama) 59, *Tröstliche Zeichen* (essays) 59, *Irrsal der Liebe* (poems), 60 *Heute Noch* (short story) 62, *Kleiner Stern im dunklen Strom* 63, *Gelöstes Haar* (translations of Japanese poems) 64, *Sternsagen* 65, *Und wie Musik in der Nacht* 65, *Kassel* (*Porträt einer Stadt*) 65, *Und es geschah* (*Gedanken zur Bibel*) 65, *Brüderliche Welt* 65, *Spiegel des Lebens* 66, *Hinter den Dingen* 67, *Kreise um eine Mitte* 68, *Wort vom Wort* 68, *Gottes Ja* 68, *Keiner weiss die Stunde* 70, *Der golddurchwirkte Schleier* 70, *Das abgründige Geheimnis* 72, *Wenn dieses alles Faulheit ist* 72, *Jahre des Lebens* 73, *Kleine Begegnungen mit grossen Leuten* 73, *Im Spiegel der Errinerung* 74, *Nüchternheit* 75.
Dillener Strasse 49, 2820 Bremen 71, Federal Republic of Germany.
Telephone: 0421-603724.

Hausner, Gideon; Israeli lawyer; b. 26 Sept. 1915, Lvov, U.S.S.R.; *s.* of Dr. Bernard and Ema Hausner; *m.* Yehudit Liphshitz 1944; one *s.* one *d.*; ed. Hebrew Coll. Herzliya, Hebrew Univ.
Lecturer in Law Hebrew Univ. 54-60; del. to Zionist Congresses 54, 56, 64; Attorney-Gen. 60-63; Chief Prosecutor Eichmann Trial 61-62; mem. Knesset (Parl.) 65-; Chair. Independent Liberal Party Parl. Group 67-74; Minister without Portfolio 74-; Chair. Yad Vashem (Commemoration Authority for Martyrs of World War II) 69-.
Leisure interest: photography.
Publs. *Justice in Jerusalem* 66, and articles in law journals and general publications 41-.
Office of the Prime Minister, Jerusalem, Israel.

Havasi, Ferenc; Hungarian politician; b. 20 Feb. 1929, Piszke; *s.* of János Havasi and Ilona Trencsik; *m.* Margit Mikits 1953; one *s.*
Started as semi-skilled worker in cement factory; became mason's mate; joined Young Workers' Movement after World War II; joined Hungarian Communist Party 48 (merged to form Hungarian Socialist Workers' Party 56); Sec. local party org. in factory 49-50; Head of Dept., Tatabánya Municipal Party Cttee. 51; Head of Agitation and Propaganda Dept., Komárom County Party Cttee. 52, Second Sec. 54, First Sec. 66-75; mem. Cen. Cttee. HSWP 66-; Deputy Prime Minister 75-; Labour Order of Merit; Hungarian Freedom Order of Merit.
Council of Ministers, 1055 Budapest, Kossuth Lajos tér 1/3, Hungary.
Telephone: 126-910.

Havel, Václav; Czechoslovak playwright; b. 5 Oct. 1936, Prague; *s.* of Václav M. Havel and Božena (Vavrečková) Havel; *m.* Olga Šplíchalová; ed. Acad. of Arts, Drama Dept., Prague.
Works freelance; Austrian State Prize for European Literature 69.
Publs. *Garden Party* 63, *The Memorandum* 65, *The Increased Difficulty of Concentration* 68 (plays).
Engelsovo nábřeží 78, Prague 2, Czechoslovakia.
Telephone: 24 84 89.

Havelange, Jean Marie Faustin Godefroid (João); Brazilian lawyer; b. 8 May 1916, Rio de Janeiro; *m.*
Head of Importation and Exportation, Cia. Siderúrgica Belgo-Mineira 37-41; Dir.-Pres. Viação Cometa S.A., EMBRADATA, Orwec Química e Metalúrgica Ltda.; took part at Olympic Games as swimmer, Berlin 36, as water-polo player, Helsinki 52, Head of Brazilian Del., Sydney 56; Pres. Fed. Metropolitana de Nataçao (GB)

52-56; mem. Brazilian Olympic Cttee. 56-73; Vice-Pres. Confed. Brasiliera de Desportos 56-58, Pres. 58-73; mem. Int. Olympic Cttee. 63-; Pres. Indoor Football Int. Fed. (FIFUSA) 71; Pres. Int. Fed. of Asscn. Football (FIFA) 74-; Portuguese and Brazilian decorations.
Leisure interests: swimming on Sundays.
c/o Fédération Internationale de Football Association, Hitzigweg 11, 8032 Zurich, Switzerland.

Havelka, Jaroslav, LL.D., C.SC.; Czechoslovak politician; b. 19 Feb. 1917, Prague; ed. Law Faculty, Charles Univ.
Member Central Council of Trade Unions 45-47, Central Action Cttee. of Nat. Front 48-49; Deputy Minister, State Office for Church Affairs 49-51; Minister, Ministry of Labour Force 51-53; Chair. State Office for Church Affairs 53-56; Deputy Minister of Educ. and Culture 56-58; Amb. to Sweden 58-62; Dept. Head, State Planning Comm. 62-63; Head of Univs. and Colls. Dept., Ministry of Educ. and Culture 63-67; Dir. of Dept. for Long-term Devt., Econ. and Technical Progress, Ministry of Educ. 67-68; Deputy Minister 68, Minister and Chair. of Cttee. for Press and Information, Fed. Govt. of Czechoslovakia Jan.-Sept. 69; Deputy Minister of Labour and Social Affairs, Fed. Govt. of Czechoslovakia Dec. 69-; Alt. mem. Central Cttee. of C.P. 54-62; mem. Nat. Assembly 48-54; Sec. Govt. Population Comm. 72-; Chair. Scandinavian Cttee. of Czechoslovak Soc. for Int. Relations 72; Order of Labour 60, Order of the Repub. 68.
Ministry of Labour and Social Affairs, Prague, Czechoslovakia.

Haveman, Bastiaan Wouter, D.SC., LL.D.; Netherlands civil servant; b. 25 Nov. 1908, Opsterland; s. of Rev. Meindert Haveman and Elise A. M. Ph. van Veen; m. Louise H. van Loon 1936; one d.; ed. Technical Univ., Delft and Leiden Univ.
Secretary, High Council of Labour 35-40; Aide-de-Camp, Commdr. of Police Troops, Netherlands Army H.Q. 39-41; mem. Resistance and Editor *Je Maintiendrai* 41-45, Prisoner 45; Sec.-Gen. Employers' Asscn. 41-45; Sec. to the Prime Minister 45-46; Adviser, Del. to UN 46-47; Econ. Adviser, Ministry of Transport and Works 47-51; Govt. Commr. for Emigration 51-62; Pres. Central Court of Arbitration for Agriculture 49-62; Dir. ICEM (Intergovernmental Cttee. for European Migration), Geneva 62-69; Netherlands and foreign honours.
Leisure interests: golf and film-making.
17 Avenue de Budé, apt. 17-33, Geneva, Switzerland; and 5B Frankenslag, The Hague, Netherlands.
Telephone: 34-97-02 (Geneva); and 55-41-89 (The Hague).

Havers, Hon. Sir Cecil Robert, Kt., Q.C., LL.B., M.A.; British judge; b. 12 Nov. 1889; three s. one d.; ed. Norwich Grammar School and Corpus Christi Coll., Cambridge.
Served in First World War 14-18; called to the Bar (Inner Temple) 20; K.C. 39; Recorder of Chichester 39-51; Deputy Chair. Advisory Cttee. on Aliens 40-45; Commr. in Gold Coast 44-45; Bencher, Inner Temple 46, Treas. 71; Deputy Chair. West Kent Quarter Sessions 47-51; Commr. of Assize, Oxford and Midland Circuits 49; a Justice of the High Court 51-67; Hon. Fellow Corpus Christi Coll., Cambridge.
Leisure interests: golf, tennis.
Publ. *Landlord and Tenant Act* 27.
8 Lichfield Road, Kew Gardens, Surrey, England.
Telephone: 01-940-2658.

Haviland, Denis William Garstin Latimer, M.A., F.B.I.M., F.R.S.A., C.B.; British industrialist; b. 15 Aug. 1910, London; s. of William Alexander Haviland and Edyth Louise Latimer; ed. Rugby School and St. John's Coll., Cambridge.
London Midland and Scottish Railway 34-39; Army

service 40-46, rising to rank of Col.; Principal, Contro Office for Germany and Austria 46-47; Asst. Sec Foreign Office, German Section 47-50; Imperial Defenc Coll. 50-; Ministry of Supply 51-59, Under-Sec. 53-59 Deputy Sec. 59; Deputy Sec. Ministry of Aviatio 59-64; Chair. European Launcher Devt. Org. (ELDC Preparatory Group 62-64; Deputy Chair. Stavele Industries 64-65, Chair. and Man. Dir. 65-69; Dir Short Brothers and Harland, Organized Office Designs mem. Council British Inst. of Management 67- (Vice Chair. 73).
Leisure interests: numerous.
Home and Office: 113 Hampstead Way, London N.W.11, England.
Telephone: 01-455-2638.

Havrevold, Finn; Norwegian author and critic; b 11 Aug. 1905, Oslo; s. of Lauritz Paulsen and Marta Malene (Nielsen) Havrevold; m. Gunvor Øwre 1939; two d.; ed. Norges Tekniske Høyskole.
Qualified architect 29; book designer and illustrator; author 39; radio critic *Dagbladet* 51-; dramatic critic *Urd* 56-; Damm Prize 55 and 57, Damm-Allers Prize, Film Prize 60, Prix Italia 70, Nordic Radio Prize 70.
Leisure interests: painting, fishing, skiing.
Publs. novels: *Til de dristige* 46, *Walter den fredsommelige* 47, *Skredet* 49, *Den Ytterste Dag* 63, *De gjenstridige* 65, *Blå rytter* 68, *Pilen i lyset* 71, *Under samme tak* 72; short stories: *Det raker ikke Andersen* 39, *Tapere* 74; children's books: *Sommereventyret* 52, *Drommeveggen* 53, *Den ensomme kirger* 55, *Marens lille ugle* 57, *Viggo* 57, *Grunnbrott* 60, *Jeg flykter i natt* 63, *Putsja* 67, *Lommekniven* 69; plays: *Jubileum* 51, *Uretten* 55, *Sommerhuset* 57, *Tomannsboligen* 59, *Stakkars Anton* 61, *Regissøren* 64, *Gruppen* 64; biography: *Helge Krog* 59; radio plays: *Sensommer*, *Wilhelm og Alice*, *Eskapade*, *Katastrofe* 60, *Arabesk*, *I Kveldingen*, *Svalene Flyr*, *Lavt*, *Hjemturen* 61, *Brev til Tom* 62, *Dikterjubileum* 63, *Helens dagbok* 64, *Duellen* 65, *Situasjon* 67, *Landskapet* 67, *Leke blindebukk* 68, *En benk i parken* 70, *Credo* 70, *Avreisen*, *Brødre*, *Gisselet* 72, *Revolusjonsetyde* 74; TV play: *En Smule Kjaerlighet* 61; film scenarios: *Drapen* 60, *Farlig Kurs* 64.
Thomas Heftyes Gate 64c, Oslo 2, Norway.
Telephone: 56-39-64.

Hawari Ahmed, Mahmoud el-; Egyptian journalist; b. 12 April 1921; s. of Ahmed Farid and Hayat Ali; m. Sadia El-Kilani 1949; one d.; ed. Polytechnic School, Cairo.
Director, Arab Information Centre Press Office, New York 55-58; Man. Editor, Middle East News Agency, Cairo 58-65, fmr. Chair. of Board; Dir. Magazine Dept., Nat. Publishing House 65-67; Chair. Nat. Distributing Co. 67; Publishing Man. Al-katib Al-Arabi Publishing House 67-69; Adviser, Editing and Publishing Org. 69-71; Dir.-Gen. Egyptian Book Org. 71-72; Under-Sec. of State, Ministry of Information Feb. 76-; Gold Cross, Order of King George I of Greece 60.
Leisure interest: painting.
c/o Ministry of Information, Kornich El-Nil, Cairo, Egypt.
Telephone: 988806 (Office); 28537 (Home).

Hawke, Hon. Albert Redvers George, M.L.A.; Australian politician (retired); b. 3 Dec. 1900, Kapunda; s. of James Renfrey and Elizabeth Ann Blinman Hawke (née Pascoe); m. Mabel Evelyn Crafter 1923; one d.; ed. Kapunda Model School, South Australia.
Mem. South Australia House of Assembly for Burra Burra 24-27; Political Organiser for Labour Party in Western Australia 28; Labour Mem. for Northam 33-68; Minister for Employment, Western Australia 36-39, for Labour 36-43, for Industrial Development 39-47; Deputy Leader of the Opposition 47-52, Leader 52-53, 59-66; Premier, Treasurer and Minister for Child Welfare, Western Australia 53-59.

Leisure interests: tennis, billiards, good music, human welfare.
17 Walker Avenue, West Perth 6005, Western Australia.
Telephone: 219770.

Hawke, Robert James Lee, B.A., LL.B., B.LITT.; Australian trade union executive; b. 9 Dec. 1929, Bordertown, S. Australia; s. of A. C. Hawke; m. Hazel Masterson 1956; one s. two d.; ed. Univs. of Western Australia and Oxford.
Research Officer, Australian Council of Trade Unions 58-70, Pres. Jan. 70-; Pres. Australian Labor Party; mem. Board Reserve Bank of Australia, Gov. Body ILO.
Leisure interests: tennis, golf, cricket, reading.
Australian Council of Trade Unions, 254 Latrobe Street, Melbourne 3000, Victoria, Australia.
Telephone: 347-3966.

Hawker, Sir (Frank) Cyril, Kt.; British business executive; b. 21 July 1900, London; s. of Frank Charley and Bertha Mary (Bastow) Hawker; m. Marjorie Ann Pearce; three d.; ed. City of London School.
Bank of England 20, Deputy Chief Cashier 44-48, Chief Accountant 48-53, Adviser to Governors 53-54, Exec. Dir. 54-62; Chair. The Standard Bank Ltd. 62-74, Standard Bank of West Africa Ltd.; Deputy Chair. Midland and Int. Banks 69-74; Dir. Head Wrightson & Co. Ltd. 62-, Deputy Chair. 64-74; Dir. Midland and Int. Banks Ltd.; Hon. Treas. and Chair. Finance Cttee., Nat. Playing Fields Asscn., Standard and Chartered Banking Group Ltd. 69-74, Union Zaïroise de Banques 71-74; High Sheriff of County of London 63; Pres. MCC Oct. 70-Oct. 71.
Leisure interest: cricket.
Home: Pounsley Lodge, Blackboys, Nr. Uckfield, Sussex, England.

Hawkes, (Charles Francis) Christopher, M.A., F.B.A., F.S.A.; British archaeologist; b. 5 June 1905, London; s. of late Charles Pascoe and Eleanor Victoria Hawkes (née Cobb); m. 1st Jessie Jacquetta Hopkins (q.v. Jacquetta Hawkes) 1933 (divorced 1953), one s.; m. 2nd Sonia Elizabeth Chadwick 1959; ed. Winchester Coll., and New Coll., Oxford.
Assistant Dept. of British and Medieval Antiquities, British Museum 28, Asst. Keeper, promoted to 1st Class 38; Ministry of Aircraft Production 40-45; returned to British Museum 45, in charge of Prehistoric and Romano-British Antiquities 46; Prof. of European Archaeology, Oxford Univ. 46-72; Fellow Keble Coll., Hon. Fellow 72; Prof.-in-charge, Inst. of Archaeology 61-72; elected Nat. Sec. (U.K.) on Council Int. Congress of Prehistoric and Protohistoric Sciences 31, full mem. 48, mem. Exec. Cttee. 50, Cttee. of Honour 71; excavations on various sites in U.K. and Europe 25-64; Editor *Archaeological Journal* London 44-50; Pres. Prehistoric Society 50-54, Council for British Archaeology 61-64; Editor *Inventaria Archaeologica* for Great Britain 54-; mem. German Archaeological Inst.; Corresp. mem. Royal Irish Acad., Swiss Soc. for Prehistory; Hon. Dr. (Rennes) 71; Hon. D.Litt. (Ireland) 72.
Leisure interests: archaeology, travel, music.
Publs. *St Catharine's Hill, Winchester* (with J. N. L. Myres and C. G. Stevens) 31, *Archaeology in England and Wales, 1914-31* (with T. D. Kendrick) 32, *Winchester College* 33, *The Prehistoric Foundations of Europe* 40, *Prehistoric Britain* (with Jacquetta Hawkes) 44, *Camulodunum: The Excavations at Colchester, 1930-39* (with M. R. Hull) 47, Contrib. and Editor (with Sonia Hawkes) *Archaeology into History* Vol. I 73, Contrib and Editor (with P. M. Duval) *Celtic Art in Ancient Europe* 73.
19 Walton Street, Oxford, England.
Telephone: 56949.

Hawkes, Jacquetta, O.B.E., M.A.; British author and archaeologist; b. 1910, Cambridge; d. of Sir Frederick Gowland Hopkins, O.M. (Nobel prize winner) and Lady Hopkins (née Stephens); m. 1st Prof. (Charles Francis) Christopher Hawkes (q.v.) 1933 (divorced 1953), 2nd J. B. Priestley (q.v.) 1953; one s.; ed. Perse School and Newnham Coll., Cambridge.
Archaeological activities in Great Britain, Eire, France and Palestine 31-40; Asst. Principal, Post-War Reconstruction Secretariat 41-43; with Ministry of Education, Sec., U.K. Nat. Comm. for UNESCO 43-49 (retd.); Vice-Pres. Council for British Archaeology 49-52; Archaeological Adviser, Festival of Britain 49-51; Gov. British Film Inst. 50-55; mem. Culture Advisory Cttee., UNESCO 66-; Author Editor (with Frankfort and Woolley) *UNESCO History of Mankind* (Vol. I); Archaeological Corresp. *Sunday Times*; Kemsley Award for *A Land* 51.
Leisure interests: pictures, antiques, gardening, natural history.
Publs. *Archaeology of Jersey* 39, *Prehistoric Britain* (with Christopher Hawkes) 44, *Early Britain* 45, *Symbols and Speculations* (poems) 48, *A Land* 51, *Guide to Prehistoric and Roman Monuments in England and Wales* 51, *Dragon's Mouth* (play), *Fables* 53, *Man on Earth* 54, *Journey Down a Rainbow* (with J. B. Priestley) 55, *Providence Island* 59, *Man and the Sun* 62, *Prehistory and the Beginnings of Civilization* (with Sir Leonard Woolley) 63, *The World of the Past* 63, *King of the Two Lands* 66, *The Pharoes of Egypt* 67, *Dawn of the Gods* 68, *The First Great Civilizations* 73, Editor *Atlas of Ancient Archaeology* 74.
B 3, Albany, London, W.1; and Alveston, Stratford on Avon, Warwickshire, England.
Telephone: 01-734-6150; Stratford on Avon 3798.

Hawkes, John; American writer; b. 17 Aug. 1925, Stamford, Conn.; m. Sophie Tazewell 1947; three s. one d.; ed. Harvard Coll.
Visiting Lecturer and Instructor, Harvard Univ. 55-58; Asst. Prof. Brown Univ. 58-62, Assoc. Prof. 62-67, Prof. 67-73; Univ. Prof. 73-; Guggenheim Fellowship; Ford Foundation Fellowship; Rockefeller Foundation Fellowship; Grant in Fiction, Nat. Inst. of Arts and Letters.
Publs. novels: *The Cannibal* 49, *The Beetle Leg* 51, *The Lime Twig* 61, *Second Skin* 64, *The Blood Oranges* 71, *Death, Sleep and the Traveler* 74, *Travesty* 76; play: *The Innocent Party* 66; collected stories and short novels: *Lunar Landscapes* 69.
Department of English, Brown University, Providence, Rhode Island 02912, U.S.A.
Telephone: 401-863-2393.

Hawkins, Arthur Ernest, B.SC.(ENG.), C.ENG., F.I.MECH.E., F.I.E.E., M.INST.F., F.B.I.M.; British engineer; b. 10 June 1913, Wiltshire; s. of Rev. H. R. and Louisa Hawkins; m. Laura J. T. Draper 1939; one s. two d.; ed. The Blue School, Wells, The Grammar School, Great Yarmouth and City of Norwich Technical Coll.
District Manager, S.E. Electricity Board, Croydon 48; Chief Asst. Engineer, System Operation Branch, British Electricity Authority 51; Personal Engineering Asst. to Chief Engineer 54; System Planning Engineer, Central Electricity Generating Board (CEGB) 57; Chief Operations Engineer, CEGB 59-64; Midlands Regional Dir. CEGB 64-70; mem. Cen. Electricity Generating Board 70-, Chair. July 72-.
Leisure interests: fell walking, swimming, motoring.
Publs. articles in *Journal of Management Studies* and various papers to technical insts.
Central Electricity Generating Board, Sudbury House, Newgate Street, London, E.C.1; Home: 61 Rowan Road, Brook Green, London, W.6, England.
Telephone: 01-248-1202 (Office).

Haworth, Leland John, PH.D.; American nuclear physicist; b. 11 July 1904, Flint, Mich.; s. of Paul L. and Martha (née Ackerman) Haworth; m. 1st Barbara Mottier 1927 (died 1961), 2nd Irene Benik 1963; one s. one d.; ed. Indiana Univ. and Univ. of Wisconsin.
High school teacher, Indianapolis 26-28; Instructor in Physics, Univ. of Wisconsin 30-37; Lalor Fellow in Physical Chemistry, Mass. Inst. of Technology 37-38; Assoc. in Physics, Univ. of Illinois 38-39, Asst. Prof. 39-44, Prof. 44-47; Staff mem. Radiation Laboratory, Mass. Inst. of Technology 41-45; Asst. Dir. Brookhaven Nat. Laboratory 47-48, Dir. 48-61; Vice-Pres., Assoc. Univs. Inc. 51-60, Pres. 60-61; mem. U.S. Atomic Energy Comm. 61-63; Dir. Nat. Science Foundation 63-69; Special Asst. to Pres., Assoc. Univs., Inc. 69-; Adviser, President's Science Advisory Cttee. 63-69; Pres. Amer. Nuclear Soc. 58-59; mem. Fed. Council for Science and Technology 63-69, Nat. Acad. of Sciences, American Philosophical Soc., American Acad. of Arts and Sciences, etc.; Fellow American Nuclear Soc., American Physical Soc., New York Acad. of Sciences; numerous hon. degrees.
Leisure interests: photography, gardening.
Publs. Papers in fields of surface structure of metals, secondary electron emission, low temperature research, nuclear physics, high energy physics, especially very high energy accelerators, electronics.
15 Deer Path, Port Jefferson, N.Y. 11777, U.S.A.
Telephone: 473-4129.

Haworth, Lionel, O.B.E., F.R.S.; British aeronautical engineer; b. 4 Aug. 1912, S. Africa; s. of John B. and Anna S. (née Ackerman) Haworth; m. Joan I. Bradbury 1956; one s. one d.; ed. Rondebosch Boys' High School and Univ. of Cape Town.
Graduate apprenticeship with Associated Equipment Co. 34; Designer Rolls-Royce Ltd., Derby 36, Asst. Chief Designer 44; Dep. Chief Designer, Aero Division 51, Chief Designer (Civil Engines), Aero Div. 54, Chief Engineer (Propeller Turbines), Aero Div. 62; Chief Design Consultant, Bristol Siddeley Engines Ltd. 63, Chief Designer 64; Dir. of Design, Bristol Siddeley Engines Ltd., Bristol Engine Div. 65; Dir. of Design, Rolls-Royce Ltd., Bristol Engine Div. 68, Dir. of Design, Rolls-Royce (1971) Ltd., Bristol Engine Div. 71-; Bronze Medal, Royal Aeronautical Soc.; British Gold Medal for Aeronautics 71.
Leisure interest: sailing.
Office: Rolls-Royce (1971) Ltd., Bristol Engine Division, P.O. Box 3, Filton, Bristol BS12 7QE; Home: 10 Hazelwood Road, Sneyd Park, Bristol 9, England.
Telephone: Bristol 693871, Ext. 653 (Office); Bristol 683032 (Home).

Hawthorne, Sir William (Rede), Kt., C.B.E., M.A., SC.D., F.R.S., F.INST.MECH.E., F.R.Ae.S.; British professor of applied thermodynamics; b. 22 May 1913, Benton, Newcastle-on-Tyne; s. of William Hawthorne and Elizabeth Curle Hawthorne; m. Barbara Runkle 1939; one s. two d.; ed. Westminster School, London, Trinity Coll., Cambridge, and Mass. Inst. of Technology, U.S.A.
Development Engineer, Babcock & Wilcox Ltd. 37-39; Scientific Officer, Royal Aircraft Establishment 40-44; British Air Comm., Washington, D.C. 44-45; Deputy Dir. of Engine Research, Ministry of Supply (U.K.) 45-46; Assoc. Prof. of Mechanical Engineering, Mass. Inst. of Technology (M.I.T.) 46-48; George Westinghouse Prof. of Mechanical Engineering, M.I.T. 48-51; Prof. of Applied Thermodynamics Univ. of Cambridge 51-, Head of Engineering Dept. 68-73; Fellow, Trinity Coll., Cambridge 51-68; Master of Churchill Coll., Cambridge 68-; Hunsaker Prof. of Aeronautical Engineering, M.I.T. 55-56; Visiting Inst. Prof., M.I.T. 62-63; mem. of Corpn. of M.I.T. 69-73; Chair. Home Office Scientific Advisory Council 67-, Advisory Council on Energy Conservation

74-; Foreign Assoc. U.S. Nat. Acad. of Sciences; Vice-Pres. Royal Soc. 69-70; mem. Electricity Supply Research Council 53-; Medal of Freedom (U.S.A.) 47.
The Master's Lodge, Churchill College, Cambridge, England; 19 Chauncy Street, Cambridge, Mass. 02138, U.S.A.
Telephone: Cambridge 61200.

Haxel, Otto Philipp Leonhard, D.RER.NAT.; German physicist; b. 2 April 1909; two s.; ed. Tübingen, Munich and Berlin Univs.
Lecturer, Berlin Technical High School 37-45, Max Planck Physics Inst., Göttingen 45-50; Dir. Second Physical Inst., Heidelberg Univ. 50-69; Technical-Scientific Dir., Nuclear Research Centre, Karlsruhe 70-74; Dr. h.c.; mem. Heidelberger Akad. der Wissenschaften, Deutsche Akad. der Naturforscher Leopoldina.
Office: 69 Heidelberg, Im Neuenheimer Feld 366; Home: 69 Heidelberg, Scheffelstrasse 5, Federal Republic of Germany.
Telephone: 06221-563309 (Office); 06221-46769 (Home).

Hay, Alexandre, L. en D.; Swiss banker; b. 29 Oct. 1919, Berne; m. Hélène Morin Pons 1945 (died 1973); two s. two d.; ed. Univ. of Geneva.
Federal Political Dept. (Financial Affairs), Berne 45-48; Swiss Legation, Paris 48-53; Head of Div., Swiss Nat. Bank, Zürich 53-55; Dir. and Asst. to Head of Second Dept., Swiss Nat. Bank, Berne 55-66, Head of Second Dept. and Vice-Pres. Gen. Management 66-; mem. Cttee. on European Monetary Agreement 50-62; Pres. 62-73; Pres. Int. Cttee. of Red Cross July 76-.
Office: Swiss National Bank, Bundesplatz 1, Berne; Home: Mayweg 7, Berne, Switzerland.
Telephone: 61-42-45 (Office); 45-72-79 (Home).

Hay, David Osborne, C.B.E., D.S.O., B.A.; Australian public servant; b. 1916, Corowa, N.S.W.; s. of late H. A. Hay and Marjory Moule; m. Alison Adams 1944; two s.; ed. Geelong Grammar School, Brasenose Coll., Oxford, and Melbourne Univ.
Joined Australian Dept. of External Affairs 39 and rejoined 46, after army service 39-45; Del. to UN 49 and 50; served Ottawa 50-52; attended Imperial Defence Coll. London 54 Minister to Thailand 55-56, Ambassador 56-57, concurrently Rep. to SEATO; Asst. Sec. Department of External Affairs 57-61; High Commr. to Canada 61-64; Ambassador and Perm. Rep. of Australia to the UN 63-65; Ministry of External Affairs 65-66, Administrator, Territory of Papua and New Guinea 67-70; Sec. Dept. of External Territories 70-73; Defence Force Ombudsman 74-.
Leisure interests: skiing, sailing, gardening.
10 Hotham Crescent, Deakin, A.C.T., Australia.
Telephone: Canberra 731705.

Haya de la Torre, Victor Raúl; Peruvian politician; b. 1895; ed. Univs. of Oxford and San Marcos, Lima.
Exiled to Mexico 23-30; Founder and Leader Alianza Popular Revolucionaria Americana (A.P.R.A.) 30-; candidate for President 31; imprisoned 32-33; Political Refugee, Colombian Embassy, Lima 48-53; exile in Panama, Mexico, Belgium 54-56; Candidate for President 62, 63.
c/o Alianza Popular Revolucionaria Americana, Lima, Peru.

Hayaishi, Osamu, M.D., PH.D.; Japanese university professor; b. 8 Jan. 1920, Stockton, Calif., U.S.A.; s. of Jitsuzo and Mitsu Hayaishi; m. Takiko Satani 1946; one d.; ed. Osaka High School, Osaka Univ.
Assistant Prof., Dept. of Microbiology, Washington Univ. School of Medicine, St. Louis, Mo., U.S.A., 52-54; Chief, Toxicology, Nat. Inst. of Arthritis and Metabolic Diseases, Nat. Insts. of Health, Bethesda, Md., U.S.A. 54-58; Prof., Dept. of Medical Chemistry, Prof., Dept. of Molecular Biology, Inst. for Chemical Research, Prof., Dept. of Physiological Chemistry and Nutrition,

Kyoto Univ., 58-; Prof. Dept. of Physiological Chem. and Nutrition, Univ. of Tokyo 70-74; Prof. Inst. of Scientific and Industrial Research, Osaka Univ. 75-; Foreign Hon. mem. of American Acad. of Arts and Sciences 69, Foreign Assoc. of the U.S. Nat. Acad. of Arts and Sciences 69; mem. Japan Acad. of Sciences 74, N.Y. Acad. of Sciences 75; Hon. mem. American Soc. of Biological Chemists 74; Award of Japan Soc. of Vita-minology 64, Award of Matsunaga Science Foundation 64, Asahi Award for Science and Culture 65, Award of Japan Acad. of Science 67, Order of Culture 72, Award of Fujiwara Science Foundation 75, Médaille de Bronze de la Ville de Paris 75.
Leisure interest: golf.
Publs. *Oxygenases* 62, *Molecular Mechanisms of Oxygen Activation* 73, *Molecular Oxygen in Biology* 73, and nearly 300 scientific reviews and articles.
Department of Medical Chemistry, Kyoto University Faculty of Medicine, Sakyo-ku, Kyoto 606; Home: 23 Kitachanoki-cho, Shimogamo, Sakyo-ku, Kyoto 606, Japan.
Telephone: 075-751-2111 (Office); 075-781-1089 (Home).

Hayakawa, Samuel Ichiye, PH.D.; American university professor; b. 18 July 1906, Vancouver, B.C., Canada; s. of Ichiro Hayakawa and Tora Isono; m. Margedant Peters 1937; two s. one d.; ed. public schools in Calgary, Vancouver, and Winnipeg, Univ. of Manitoba and McGill Univ., Montreal.
Formerly taught at Univs. of Wisconsin and Chicago and Illinois Inst. of Technology, Chicago; Prof. of English, San Francisco State Coll. 55-, Pres. 69-73; Claude Bernard Prof., Inst. of Experimental Medicine and Surgery, Univ. of Montreal 59; Alfred P. Sloan Visiting Prof., Menninger School of Psychiatry, Topeka, Kan. 61; has held many other summer and visiting professorships in American univs. and colls. and lec-tured in several European countries; Hon. D.Litt. (Grinnell Coll.); Hon. LL.D. (The Citadel).
Leisure interests: African art, Chinese ceramics.
Publs. include: *Oliver Wendell Holmes* 39, *Language in Action* 41, *Language in Thought and Action* 49, *Symbol, Status and Personality* 63, *A Modern Guide to Synonyms* 68, and contributions to numerous other volumes.
P.O. Box 100, Mill Valley, Calif. 94941, U.S.A.

Haycraft, Howard; American publisher and author; b. 24 July 1905; ed. Univ. of Minnesota.
University of Minnesota Press 28; H. W. Wilson Co., New York City 29-, Vice-Pres. 40-52, Pres. 53-67, Chair. Board of Dirs. 67-; mem. Pres. Cttee. Employment of Handicapped 63-; mem. Mystery Writers of America Club, Pres. 63.
Publs. as Author, Editor or Joint Editor: *Authors Today and Yesterday* 33, *Junior Book of Authors* 34, *Boys' Sherlock Holmes* 36, *Boys' Book of Great Detective Stories* 38, *American Authors 1600-1900* 38, *Boys' Second Book of Great Detective Stories* 40, *Murder for Pleasure: The Life and Times of the Detective Story* 41, *Crime Club Encore* 42, *Twentieth Century Authors* 42, *Art of the Mystery Story* 46, *Fourteen Great Detective Stories* 49, *British Authors before 1800* 52, *Treasury of Great Mysteries* 57, *Ten Great Mysteries* 59, *Five Spy Novels* 62, *Books for the Blind: A Postscript and an Appreciation* 65.
950 University Avenue, New York, N.Y. 10452, U.S.A.

Hayden, William George, B.ECONS.; Australian poli-tician; b. 23 Jan. 1933, Brisbane, Queensland; ed. Brisbane State High School, Univ. of Queensland.
Police constable, Queensland 53-61; mem. Parl. for Oxley 61-; Parl. Spokesman on Health and Welfare 69-72; Minister of Social Security 72-75; Treasurer June 75-; Labor Party.
Parliament House, Canberra, A.C.T.; Home: 16 East Street, Ipswich, Queensland 4305, Australia.

Haydon, Walter Robert, C.M.G.; British diplomatist; b. 29 May 1920, London; s. of Walter Haydon and Evelyn Louise Thom; m. Joan Elizabeth Tewson 1943; one s. two d. (one d. deceased); ed. Dover Grammar School.
H.M. Forces 39-45; served Berne 46-47, Foreign Office 47-48, Turin 48-52; Vice-Consul 50; Vice Consul, Sofia 52-53; Second Sec. Bangkok 53-56; First Sec. and Head of Chancery, Khartoum 58-61; First Sec. U.K. Mission to UN, New York 61-65; Counsellor, Washington 65-67; Head of News Dept., Foreign and Commonwealth Office 67-71; High Commissioner in Malawi 71-73; Chief Press Sec. to Prime Minister 73-74; High Commr. in Malta 74-.
Leisure interests: walking, swimming, English water-colours.
British High Commission, St Anne Street, Floriana, Malta; Home: 74 Hyde Park Mansions, London, N.W.1, England.

Hayek, Friedrich August von, DR.JUR., DR.RER.POL. (Vienna), D.SC. (ECON.) (London), F.B.A.; British (b. Austrian) economist; b. Vienna 8 May 1899; s. of August von Hayek and Felizitas von Juraschek; m. 1st Helene B. M. von Fritsch, 2nd Helene A. E. Warhanek (née Bitterlich); one s. one d.; ed. Vienna Univ.
Austrian Civil Service 21-26; Dir. Austrian Inst. for Econ. Research 27-31; Lecturer in Econs., Vienna Univ. 29-31; Prof. of Econ. Science and Statistics, London Univ. 31-50; Prof. of Social and Moral Science, Univ. of Chicago 50-62; Prof. of Econs., Univ. of Freiburg 62-70; Nobel Prize in Econs. 74; naturalized British 38.
Publs. *Prices and Production* 31, *Monetary Theory and the Trade Cycle* 33, *Collectivist Economic Planning* 35, *Monetary Nationalism and International Stability* 37, *Profits, Interest and Investment* 39, *The Pure Theory of Capital* 41, *The Road to Serfdom* 44, *Individualism and Economic Order* 48, *J. S. Mill and Harriet Taylor* 50, *The Counter-Revolution of Science* 52, *The Sensory Order* 52, *Capitalism and the Historians* 54, *The Political Ideal of the Rule of Law* 55, *The Constitution of Liberty* 60, *Studies in Philosophy, Politics and Economics* 67, *Freiburger Studien* 69, *Law, Legislation and Liberty: Rules and Order* (Vol. I) 73, *The Mirage of Social Justice* (Vol. II) 76.
Leisure interests: music, walking.
Firmianstrasse 17A, A 5020 Salzburg, Austria.
Telephone: 44459.

Hayek, His Beatitude Ignace Antoine II, D.PHIL.; Syrian ecclesiastic; b. 14 Sept. 1910; s. of Naum Hayek and Chafica Sciamsi; ed. Séminaire Patriarcal, Charfé, Lebanon, Pontifical Coll., of Propaganda Fide, Rome, and Oriental Pontifical Inst., Rome.
Ordained priest 33; successively or concurrently Dir. of School, Curate and Vicar-Gen., Aleppo; Archbishop of Aleppo 59-68; Syrian Patriarch of Antioch 68-.
Patriarcat Syrien Catholique, B.P. 8879, Rue de Damas, Beirut, Lebanon.
Telephone: 381532.

Hayes, Alfred, B.A., B.LITT.; American banker; b. 4 July 1910, Ithaca, New York; s. of Alfred and Christine Grace Robertson Hayes; m. Vilma Chalmers 1937; one s. one d.; ed. Harvard and Yale Univs. and New Coll., Oxford.
Investment Analyst, City Bank Farmers Trust Co., New York 33-40; with Bond Dept. Nat. City Bank of New York 40-42; Asst. Sec. Investment Div., New York Trust Co. 42-47, Asst. Vice-Pres. Foreign Div. 47-49, Vice-Pres. (in charge of the Foreign Div.) 49-56; Pres. Fed. Reserve Bank of N.Y. 56-75, Vice-Chair. Fed. Open Market Cttee. 56-; mem. Foreign Exchange Cttee. of N.Y. Money Market 53-56; Dir. Bankers' Asscn. for Foreign Trade 53-56; Dir. Netherlands Chamber of Commerce in the U.S. 54-56; Pres. Trustees of Lingnan Univ., China 47-54; mem. Council on Foreign Relations,

N.Y., President's Council for New York University Schools of Business, Yale Univ. Council 61-68.
Brushy Ridge Road, New Canaan, Conn. 06840; Office: Federal Reserve Bank of New York, 33 Liberty Street, New York, N.Y., U.S.A.
Telephone: 203-966-0755 (Home).

Hayes, Helen; American actress; b. 10 Oct. 1900, Washington, D.C.; *d.* of Francis Van Arnum and Catherine Estelle (Hayes) Brown; *m.* Charles MacArthur 1928 (died 1956); one *s.*; ed. Sacred Heart Acad., Washington.
First stage appearance at the age of six; fmr. mem. Columbia Players; mem. A.P.A. Phoenix Repertory Co. 66-; Acad. Award (Oscar) 32; TV Emmy Award 54; Antoinette Perry Award (Tony) for best actress 58; Acad. Award for best supporting actress 71; Hon. Pres. Amer. Theatre Wing; Pres. Amer. Nat. Theatre; Hon. L.H.D. (Hamilton, Smith, Elmira Colls.); Hon. Litt.D. (Columbia, Denver Univs.).
Stage appearances include: *Old Dutch* 09, *Prodigal Husband* 14, *Dear Brutus* 18, *Clarence* 19, *To the Ladies* 22, *Caesar and Cleopatra* 25, *What Every Woman Knows* 26, *Coquette* 27, *Mary of Scotland* 33, *Victoria Regina* 37-38, *Ladies and Gentlemen* 39-40, *Twelfth Night* 40-41, *Candle in the Wind* 41-42, *Harriet* 43, *Happy Birthday* 46, *The Glass Menagerie* 48, *Farewell to Arms, Mrs. McThing* 52, *Mainstreet to Broadway* 53, *The Skin of our Teeth* 55, *Time Remembered* 58, *The Front Page* 69, *Harvey* 70; Films include: *The Sin of Madelon Claudet* 32 (Oscar), *A Farewell to Arms* 32, *My Son John* 51, *Anastasia* 56, *Airport* 70, *Herbie Rides Again* 74, *One of Our Dinosaurs is Missing* 75.
Publs. *A Gift of Joy* 65, *On Reflection* (autobiog.) **with** Sandford Dody 69.
25 East End Avenue, New York, N.Y. 10028, U.S.A.

Hayes, John Philip, M.A.; British economist; b. March 1924, Fleet, Hants.; ed. Corpus Christi Coll., Oxford.
With Political and Econ. Planning, London 50-53; with OEEC 53-58; Econ. Dept., IBRD 58-64; Head, Econ. Devt. Div. OECD 64-67; Dir. World Economy Div., Econ. Planning Staff, Ministry of Overseas Devt. 67-69, Deputy Dir.-Gen. of Econ. Planning 69-71; Dir. Econ. Programme and Econ. Analysis and Projections Depts., IBRD 71-73; Dir. Trade and Finance, Commonwealth Secr. 73-75; Chief Econ. Adviser FCO Sept. 75-.
Foreign and Commonwealth Office, King Charles Street, London, S.W.1; Home: 1 Elgar Avenue, London, W5 3JU, England.
Telephone: 01-567-2426.

Hayes, John S., B.A.; American communications executive and diplomatist; b. 21 Aug. 1910, Philadelphia, Pa.; *m.* Donna Gough 1957; two *s.* two *d.*; ed. Univ. of Pennsylvania.
Commanding Officer, American Forces Network, U.S. Army 42-45; Exec. Vice-Pres. The Washington Post Co. 47-66; Amb. to Switzerland 66-69; Pres. United Community Funds and Councils of America 62-64; Chair. Cttee. on Int. Broadcasting, Nat. Asscn. of Broadcasters 64; mem. Carnegie Comm. on Educational Television 66; mem. U.S. Del. to Int. Conf. on INTELSAT 69; mem. Board of Trustees Springfield Coll., Nat. Urban League 70; Chair. Meridian House Int., Washington, D.C.; Chair. United Arts Org., Washington, D.C.; Chair. Radio Liberty Cttee., N.Y.; Trustee, Fed. City Council of Washington, D.C., Int. Rescue Comm., New York; mem. Board of Dirs. Nat. Symphony Orchestra Asscn., Washington Performing Arts Board; Hon. O.B.E.; Croix de Guerre, U.S. Bronze Star.
Publ. *Both Sides of the Microphone* 38.
945 Ponte Vedra Boulevard, Ponte Vedra, Florida, U.S.A.
Telephone: 904-285-6483.

Hayes, Richard James, B.A., LL.D.; Irish librarian; b. 26 June 1902, Abbeyfeale, Co. Limerick; *s.* of R. J. Hayes and Kate Whelan; *m.* 1st Clare Keogh 1928 (died 1969), 2nd Margaret Deignan; two *s.* two *d.*; ed. Clongowes Wood Coll., Kildare, and Trinity Coll., Dublin.
Asst. Librarian Nat. Library of Ireland 24, Senior Asst. Librarian 29, Dir. 40-67; mem. Irish Manuscript Comm., Royal Irish Acad.; Librarian, Chester Beatty Library; Hon. D.Litt., Hon. Litt.D.
Leisure interests: cryptography, rugby football.
Publs. *Comparative Idiom* 27, *Clár Litridheacht na Nua-Ghaedhlige* I-III 38-40, *Foclóir Gaedhilge agus Frainncise* 54, *Manuscript Sources for the History of Irish Civilisation* I-IX 66, *Sources for the History of Irish Civilisation: Articles in Irish Periodicals* I-IX 71.
20 Shrewsbury Road, Dublin 4, Ireland.
Telephone: 692337.

Hayman, Sir Peter Telford, K.C.M.G., C.V.O., M.B.E.; British diplomatist; b. 14 June 1914, Deal, Kent; *s.* of Charles H. T. and Alys H. Hayman; *m.* Rosemary E. Blomefield 1942; one *s.* one *d.*; ed. Stowe School and Worcester Coll., Oxford.
Assistant Principal, Home Office 37-39, Ministry of Home Security 39-41; Asst. Private Sec. to Home Sec. (Herbert Morrison) 41-42; army service 42-45; Principal, Home Office 45-49; Asst. Sec. Ministry of Defence 49-52; Counsellor, U.K. Del. at NATO 52-54; Counsellor, Belgrade 55-59, Baghdad 58-61; Dir.-Gen. British Information Services, N.Y. 61-64; Minister, Berlin 64-66; Asst. Under-Sec. of State, Foreign Office 66-69, Deputy Under-Sec. of State 69-70; High Commr. to Canada 70-74; Dir. Delta Metal Overseas 74-; Chair. Estates House Investment Trust 74-; Gov. Int. Student Trust; Adviser Seatrade Publs.
Leisure interests: travel, fishing, shooting.
Uxmore House, Checkendon, Oxon., England.
Telephone: Checkendon 680-658 (Home).

Hayman, Walter Kurt, M.A., SC.D., F.R.S.; British mathematician; b. 6 Jan. 1926, Cologne, Germany; *s.* of Franz Samuel Haymann and Ruth Therese Hensel; *m.* Margaret Riley Crann 1947; three *d.*; ed. Gordonstoun School, Cambridge Univ.
Lecturer, Kings Coll., Newcastle, and Fellow, St. John's Coll., Cambridge 47; Lecturer 47-53, and Reader, Univ. of Exeter 53-56; Visiting Lecturer, Brown Univ., U.S. 49-50, Stanford Univ. Summer 50, 55, American Mathematical Soc. 61; Prof. of Pure Mathematics, Imperial Coll. of Science and Technology, London; mem. London Mathematical Soc., Cambridge Philosophical Soc., Council of the Girls' Public Day School Trust; Hon. Sec. Soc. for the Protection of Science and Learning; first organizer (64-68) British Mathematical Olympiad; 1st Smiths Prize 48; shared Adams Prize, Cambridge Univ. 49; Junior Berwick Prize 55, Senior Berwick Prize of the London Mathematical Soc. 64.
Leisure interests: music, travel, television.
Publs. *Multivalent Functions* 58, *Meromorphic Functions* 64, *Research Problems in Function Theory* 67, *Subharmonic Functions* 76, and over 80 articles in various scientific journals.
Imperial College of Science and Technology, Exhibition Road, South Kensington, London, S.W.7; Home: Morden House, 9 Westmead, London, S.W.15, England.
Telephone: 01-589-5111 (College).

Haymerle, Heinrich; Austrian diplomatist; b. 1910; ed. Univ. of Vienna.
Diplomatic Service, OEEC, Paris 48-51; Chief of Protocol, Dept. of Foreign Affairs 51-53; Austrian Observer at UN 53-55; Austrian Rep. in Madrid 55-56; Head, Political Div., Dept. of Foreign Affairs 56-60; Ambassador to U.S.S.R. 60-64; Head, Political Div., Ministry for Foreign Affairs 64-68; Deputy Sec.-Gen.

67-68; Gov. of Austria to the IAEA 65-67; Vice-Chair. Board of Govs. of IAEA 66-67; Perm. Rep. to UN 68-70; Chair. of UN-Outer Space Cttee.; Amb. to U.S.S.R., also accred. to Mongolia 71-74; Sec.-Gen. for Foreign Affairs 74-.
c/o Ministry of Foreign Affairs, Vienna, Ballhausplatz, Austria.

Haynes, Sir George Ernest, Kt., c.b.e., b.sc.; British administrator; b. 24 Jan. 1902, Middlewich, Cheshire; m. Kathleen Greenhalgh 1930; two d.; ed. Sandbach School and Liverpool Univ.
Warden, Univ. Settlement, Liverpool 28-33; Chief Advisory Officer Nat. Council of Social Service 33-37, Dir. 40-67; Chair. Temporary Int. Council of Educational Reconstruction of UNESCO 47-50, Preparatory Cttee. of World Assembly of Youth 47-49, Social Services Cttee. of National Asscn. for Mental Health 55-58, Standing Conf. on British Orgs. for aid to Refugees 53-60, Rural Industries Loan Fund Ltd. 49-68, Advisory Council of Rural Industries Bureau 63-68; Pres. Int. Conf. of Social Work 48-56, Hon. Pres. 56-68; Pres. Nat. Birthday Trust; Chair. Invalid Children's Aid Asscn. 65-69, Nat. Bureau for Co-operation in Child Care 63-68, Exec. Cttee. British Conf. on Social Welfare 48-67, British Standing Conf. on Econ. and Social Activities of UN 62-69; mem. Exec. Cttee. King George VI Foundation; U.K. Del. to Social Comm. of UN 62-67; Pres. British Asscn. of Residential Settlements 60-70, Crown Trustee City Parochial Foundation 66-75; mem. Lord Chancellor's Advisory Cttee. on Legal Aid 50-75; Chair. Conf. on Legal Aid 72-75; mem. Council of British Red Cross Society; Chair. Social Science Panel Nat. Fund for Research into Crippling Diseases 69-72; Chair. Standing Conf. for Advancement of Counselling 70-71, Pres. 72; Chair. Clinic of Psychotherapy 71-73; Deputy Chair. Joint Council of Voluntary Work for Disabled 68-72; René Sand Award 58.
103 Richmond Hill Court, Richmond, Surrey, England. Telephone: 01-940-6304.

Haynes, H. J.; American business executive; b. Forth Worth, Tex.; ed. Texas A & M Univ.
Served in U.S. Navy, Second World War; joined Standard Oil Co. of Calif. as construction engineer 47, subsequently serving in producing activities in Venezuela and East Coast marketing operations; Asst. Vice-Pres 62, producing Vice-Pres. Western Operations 63, Pres. Jan. 65; Vice-Pres. Standard Oil of Calif. 66, Dir. 66, Pres. 69, now Chair. of the Board and Chief Exec. Officer; Dir. American Petroleum Inst., First Nat. City Corpn. and First Nat. City Bank, Stanford Research Inst.; Trustee Cttee. for Econ. Devt., and Petroleum Eng. Foundation of Texas A & M; f. Ecumenical Inst. Wake Forest Univ. 68; Pres. Southern Baptist Convention 57-59.
Publ. *Hotbed of Tranquility.*
Standard Oil Company of California, 225 Bush Street, San Francisco, Calif. 94104, U.S.A.

Haynie, Roscoe G.; American business executive; b. 1910, Belgrade, Neb.; ed. Cotner Coll., Lincoln, Neb.
Joined Dold Packaging Co., Omaha, Neb. 32; Wilson and Co. Inc. 38, Pres. and Chief Admin. Officer 60, Pres. and Chief Exec. Officer 63, Chair. 67; subsequently became Dir. and Chair. Exec. Cttee. LTV Corpn. when it acquired Wilson and Co. Inc.; Pres. LTV Corpn. 72-73, LTV Aerospace Corpn. 72-73; Dir. Jones and Laughlin Steel Corpn. 68-74, Vice-Chair. 71-72, Chair., Chief Exec. Officer 74-; Dir. Wilson and Co. Inc., LTV Aerospace, Goodwill Industries; Chair. American Meat Inst. 64-67.
11766 Lake House Drive West, North Palm Beach, Fla. 33408, U.S.A.

Hays, Brooks, A.B., J.D.; American lawyer and government official; b. 9 Aug. 1898, Russellville, Ark.; s. of Adelbert Steele Hays and Sallie Butler Hays; m.

Marion Prather 1922; one s. one d.; ed. Univ. of Arkansas and George Washington Univ.
Admitted Arkansas Bar 22; held various admin. posts, Arkansas 25-35; served Farm Security Admin.; mem. 78th-85th Congress; Board of Dirs. Tennessee Valley Authority 59-61; Asst. Sec. for Congressional Relations, Dept. of State 61; Special Assistant to Pres. Kennedy 61-63; Assoc. Dir. Community Relations Service 65; A. T. Vanderbilt Prof. of Public Affairs, Rutgers Univ. 63-65; Visiting Prof. of Public Affairs, Univ. of Mass. 66-; co-founder, Former members of Congress Inc.; various hon. degrees.
314 Second Street, S.E., Washington, D.C. 20003, U.S.A.
Telephone: 202-546-6549.

Hays, Hon. Harry W., P.C.; Canadian politician; b. 25 Dec. 1909, Carstairs, Alberta; m. Muriel Alicia Bigland 1934; one s.
Rancher and livestock breeder; Mayor of Calgary 59-63; mem. of Parl. 63-66, of Senate 66-; Minister of Agriculture 63-66; Liberal.
The Senate, Ottawa, Ontario; Office: Suite 404-6707 Elbow Drive S.W., Calgary, Alberta, T2V OE5, Canada.

Hayter, Stanley William, C.B.E., B.SC.; British painter, engraver and writer; b. 27 Dec. 1901; ed. Whitgift Middle School and King's Coll., London.
Chemist, Anglo-Iranian Oil Co., Iran 22-25; founded Atelier 17, Paris 27; paintings and engravings exhibited France, England, U.S.A., Belgium, Switzerland, S. America, Japan; paintings in Tate Gallery, London, Whitney Gallery, N.Y., Musée d'Art Moderne, Paris, Nat. Gallery of Canada, Montreal, St. Louis City Museum, and Museum of Modern Art, Santiago, Chile; Int. First Prize, Tokyo 60; Légion d'Honneur, Chevalier des Arts et Lettres 66; Grand Prix des Arts de la Ville de Paris 72.
Publs. *New Ways of Gravure* 49, *About Prints* 62, *Nature and Art of Motion* 64.
12 rue Cassini, 75 Paris 14e, France.
Telephone: DAN 26-60.

Hayter, Sir William Goodenough, K.C.M.G.; British diplomatist and college principal; b. 1 Aug. 1906, Oxford; s. of late Sir William Goodenough Hayter, K.B.E. and Lady Hayter (née Slessor); m. Iris Marie Hoare 1938; one d.; ed. Winchester and New Coll., Oxford.
Entered Diplomatic Service 30; served in Foreign Office 30-31, Vienna 31, Moscow 34, Foreign Office 37, China 38, Washington 41, Foreign Office 44; Asst. Under-Sec. of State 48; Minister in Paris 49-53; Amb. to U.S.S.R. May 53-57; Deputy Under-Sec. of State 57-58; Warden of New Coll., Oxford 58-76; mem. Council G.B.-U.S.S.R. Asscn. 59-; Gold Medal for Services to Austria 67.
Publs. *The Diplomacy of the Great Powers* 60, *The Kremlin and the Embassy* 66, *Russia and the World* 70, *William of Wykeham, Patron of the Arts* 70, *A Double Life* (autobiography) 74.
New College, Oxford, England.
Telephone: Oxford 48451.

Hayward, Ronald, C.B.E.; British political administrator; b. 27 June 1917, Bloxham, Oxon.; s. of late F. Hayward; m. Phyllis O. Allen 1943; three d.; ed. Bloxham Church of England School and various R.A.F. schools and colleges.
Labour Party Agent 47-50, Asst. Regional Organizer 50-58, Regional Organizer 58-69, Nat. Agent 69-72, Gen. Sec. Oct. 72-.
Leisure interests: camping, oil painting, music.
Transport House, Smith Square, London, S.W.1; Home: Flat 21, Argyll Mansions, Kings Road, Chelsea, London, S.W.3, England.
Telephone: 01-834-9434 (Office).

Hazard, Ellison L.; American business executive; b. 6 Aug. 1911, Redlands, Calif.; *m.* Helen Hammill 1935; two *s.*; ed. Univ. of California and Harvard Univ. Business School.
Continental Can Co. 34-, in charge of aircraft and bomb parts production during Second World War, later Plant Man. and Div. Man. of Manufacturing; Vice-Pres. Central Metal Div., Continental Can Co. 58-62, Exec. Vice-Pres. (Plastics and Closures Operations Group) 62-63, Dir. 62-, Senior Exec. Vice-Pres. 63, Pres. 63, Chair. 69-71, Chair. Exec. Cttee. 71-; Dir. Kennecott Copper Corpn., Goodyear Tire and Rubber Co., Charter New York, Irving Trust Co.; mem. Nat. Industrial Conf. Board; Trustee, Cttee. for Econ. Devt.
24112 Paseo Del Campo, Laguna Niguel, Calif. 92677, U.S.A.

Házi, Vencel, D.ECON.; Hungarian diplomatist and economist; b. 3 Sept. 1925, Budapest; *m.* Judit Házi 1952; one *d.*; ed. Technical Univ. and Univ. of Economics, Budapest.
Entered diplomatic service 50; Press Attaché, London 51-53; Counsellor, Stockholm 57-58; Amb. to Iraq (also accred. to Afghanistan) 58-61; Amb. to Greece (also accred. to Cyprus) 62-64; Deputy Minister of Foreign Affairs 68-70; Head, Hungarian Del. to UN Gen. Assembly 69; Amb. to U.K. April 70-.
Leisure interests: music, opera, swimming.
Hungarian Embassy, 35 Eaton Place, London, S.W.1; Residence: Flat 25, 1 Lowndes Square, London, S.W.1, England.
Telephone: 01-235-7191 (Embassy).

Hazlitt, Henry; American journalist; b. 28 Nov. 1894, Philadelphia, Pa.; *s.* of Stuart Hazlitt and Bertha Zauner; *m.* Frances Kanes 1936; ed. Coll. of City of N.Y.
Mem. staff *Wall Street Journal* 13-16 and New York *Evening Post* 16-18; Financial Editor New York *Evening Mail* 21-23; editorial writer New York *Herald* 23-24; Literary Editor *The Sun* 25-29; Literary Editor *The Nation* 30-33; Editor *American Mercury* 34; editorial writer *New York Times* 34-46; business columnist *Newsweek* 46-66; nationally syndicated newspaper columnist Oct. 66-69; Editor *The Freeman* 50-53; Hon. Litt.D. (Grove City Coll.) 58, Hon. LL.D. (Bethany Coll.) 61.
Publs. *Thinking as a Science* 16, 69, *The Anatomy of Criticism* 33, *A New Constitution Now* 42, 74, *Economics in One Lesson* 46, *Will Dollars Save the World?* 47, *The Great Idea* 51, 66 (British title: *Time Will Run Back* 52), *The Free Man's Library* 56, *The Failure of the "New Economics": An Analysis of the Keynesian Fallacies* 59, 73, *What You Should Know about Inflation* 60, 65, *The Foundations of Morality* 64, 72, *Man Versus the Welfare State* 70, *The Conquest of Poverty* 73; ed. *A Practical Program for America* 32, *The Critics of Keynesian Economics* 60.
55 Drum Hill Road, Wilton, Conn. 06897, U.S.A.
Telephone: 203-762-7891.

Head, 1st Viscount, cr. 60, of Throope in the County of Wiltshire; **Antony Henry Head,** P.C., G.C.M.G., C.B.E., M.C.; British politician; b. 1906; ed. Eton and Royal Mil. Coll., Sandhurst.
Adjutant, Life Guards 34-37; Staff Coll. 39; Brigade Major 20th Guards' Brigade 40; Asst.-Sec. Cttee. Imperial Defence 40-41; Guards Armoured Div. 41-42 (G.S.O.2); Army Rep. with Dir. of Plans for Amphibious Operations 43-45; Conservative M.P. for Carshalton Div. Surrey 45-60; Sec. of State for War 51-56; Minister of Defence 56-57; High Commr. in Fed. of Nigeria October 60-63; High Commr. in Malaysia 63-66; Trustee the Thomson Foundation 67-; Col. Commdt. Special Air Service Regt. 68-; Pres. Royal Nat. Inst. for Blind 75-; Chair. Wessex Region of Nat. Trust.
Throope **Manor,** Bishopstone, nr. Salisbury, Wilts., England.

Healey, Rt. Hon. Denis Winston, P.C., M.B.E., M.P.; British politician; b. 30 Aug. 1917, Mottingham; *s.* of William Healey; *m.* Edna May (née Edmunds) Healey 1945; one *s.* two *d.*; ed. Bradford Grammar School and Balliol Coll., Oxford.
Major, Royal Engineers 45; Sec. Labour Party Int. Dept. 45-52; M.P. 52-; Sec. of State for Defence 64-70; Chancellor of the Exchequer March 74-; Labour.
Publs. *The Curtain Falls* 51, *New Fabian Essays* 52, *Neutralism* 55, *Fabian International Essays* 56, *A Neutral Belt in Europe* 58, *NATO and American Security* 59, *The Race Against the H Bomb* 60, *Labour Britain and the World* 63.
11 Downing Street, London, S.W.1; and House of Commons, London, S.W.1, England.

Healy, Robert Edward, B.S., D.C.S.; American advertising executive; b. 15 Aug. 1904; ed. Dwight Preparatory School and Pace Coll.
Salesman, T. J. Adikes 26, Hoover Co. 27-28; Asst. to Vice-Pres. (Sales Promotion), Johns-Manville Co. 29-33; Man. Production Section of Advertising Dept., Colgate-Palmolive Co. 34-36, Asst. Advertising Man. 36-39, Brand Advertising Man. 39-42, Gen. Advertising Man. 42-46, Vice-Pres. (Advertising) 46-52; Vice-Pres., Treas. Dir. McCann-Erickson Inc. 52-53, Vice-Pres., Gen. Man. 53-54, Gen. Man. New York Office 54, Exec. Vice-Pres. 55-58, Vice-Chair. Board of Dirs. 58-61, Chair. Board 60-62, mem. Finance Cttee. 57-61, Chair. Board McCann-Erickson Corpn. (Int.) 56-58; Pres. Interpublic S.A., Geneva, Switzerland 62-65; Exec. Vice-Pres. Interpublic Group of Companies Inc. 65-67, Pres. and Chief Exec. Officer 67-71, Chair. of Board 68-73, Hon. Chair. of Board 73.
Interpublic Group of Companies Inc., 1271 Avenue of the Americas, New York, N.Y. 10020, U.S.A.
Telephone: TN7-1122.

Hearnes, Warren Eastman, B.S. A.B., J.D.; American lawyer and politician; b. 24 July 1923, Moline, Ill.; *m.* Betty Hearnes; three *d.*; ed. U.S. Mil. Acad., West Point, and Univ. of Missouri.
U.S. Army until 49; mem. Missouri House of Representatives 51-61, Majority Floor Leader 57-61; Missouri Sec. of State 61-65; Gov. of Missouri 65-73; Chair. Midwest Governor's Conf. 67-68; mem. Advisory Comm. of Intergovernmental Relations 69-72, President's Civil Defence Advisory Council 70-72; Pres. Council of State Govts. 71; mem. Missouri Bar, American Bar Asscn.; mem. firm Hearnes, Padberg, Raack, McSweeney & Slater 73-; Democrat.
1015 Locust Street, Suite 800, St. Louis, Mo. 63101; Home: Route 3, Charleston, Mo. 63834, U.S.A.

Hearst, David Whitmire; American newspaper executive; b. 2 Dec. 1915, New York City; *s.* of William R. Hearst and Millicent V. Willson; twin brother of Randolph A. Hearst (*q.v.*) and brother of William R. Hearst (*q.v.*); ed. Princeton Univ.
Classified and Display Advt. Dept. *Los Angeles Evening Herald-Express* 38-44, Business Manager 44-45, Gen.-Man. 45-47, Exec. Publisher 47-50, Publisher 50-60; Vice-Pres. and Dir. Hearst Corpn. 60-.
Hearst Corporation, 404 North Roxbury Drive, Beverly Hills, Calif. 90210; 719 North Beverly Drive, Beverly Hills, Calif., U.S.A.

Hearst, Randolph (Apperson); American newspaper executive; b. 2 Dec. 1915, New York City; *s.* of William R. Hearst and Millicent V. Willson; twin brother of David H. Hearst (*q.v.*) and brother of William R. Hearst (*q.v.*); *m.* Catherine Campbell 1938; five *d.*; ed. Harvard Univ.
Assistant to Editor *Atlanta Georgian* 34-38; Asst. to Publisher, San Francisco *Call-Bulletin* 38-41, Exec. Editor 46-50, Publisher 50-53; Pres. and Dir. Hearst Consolidated Publications Inc., and Hearst Publishing Co. Inc. 53-64; Chair. Exec. Cttee. and Dir. The Hearst

Corpn. 65-; Trustee, William Randolph Hearst Foundation and The Hearst Foundation.
214 Hearst Building, San Francisco, Calif. 94103, U.S.A.

Hearst, William Randolph, Jr.; American newspaper executive; b. 27 Jan. 1908; s. of William R. Hearst and Millicent V. Willson; brother of David W. and Randolph A. Hearst (q.v.).
Reporter, New York 28; Publisher, *New York Journal American* 37-56, *American Weekly* 45-56; War Corresp. 43-45; Editor-in-Chief, Hearst Newspapers; Vice-Pres. and Dir. The Hearst Foundation, Inc.; Chair. Exec. Cttee. and Dir. The Hearst Corpn.; Vice-Pres. and Trustee William Randolph Hearst Foundation; Vice-Pres. and Dir. Halifax Power and Pulp Co. Ltd.; Dir. Twentieth Century-Fox Film Corpn., U.P.I.; Pulitzer Prize 56, Overseas Press Club Award 58; Hon. LL.D. (Univ. of Alaska).
959 8th Avenue, New York City 10019, N.Y., U.S.A.

Heath, Barrie, M.A., D.F.C.; British business executive; b. 11 Sept. 1916, Birmingham; s. of George and Florence Amina Heath (née Jones); m. Joy Anderson 1939; two s.; ed. Wrekin, Pembroke Coll., Cambridge.
Director, Hobourn Aero Components of Rochester 46-50; Man. Dir. Powell Duffryn Carbon Products Ltd. 50-60; Man. Dir., later Chair. Triplex Safety Glass Co. Ltd. 60-74; Dir. Triplex Holdings Ltd.; Chair. Triplex (Ireland) Ltd., Weldall & Assembly Ltd., Stern & Bell Ltd.; Dir. Pilkington Bros. Ltd., Chair. Safety Glass Div. 67-74; Chair. Glass Fibre Div., Fibreglass Ltd. 71-74; Dir. Pilkington Bros. Canada 72-74; Non-exec. Dir. Guest Keen & Nettlefolds Ltd. 72-74, Deputy Chair., Group Chair. designate April-Dec. 74, Group Chair. Jan. 75-; Chair. GKN (U.K.) Ltd. 74-, GKN (Overseas) Ltd. 74-; Dir. BHP-GKN Holdings Ltd. (Australia) 75-; Non-exec. Dir. Smiths Industries Ltd. 70-, Pilkington Bros. Ltd. 74-; Dir. Barclays Bank U.K. (Management) Ltd. 75-, Barclays Bank Ltd. 76-; Vice-Pres. Soc. of Motor Mfrs. & Traders 73-, Chair. Gen. Purposes Cttee. 73-; Vice-Pres. Engineering Employers' Fed. 75-; Freeman of City of London; Liveryman, Coachmakers and Coach Harness Makers Co.
Leisure interests: yachting, shooting.
GKN House, 22 Kingsway, London, WC2B 6LG, England.
Telephone: 01-242-1616 (Office).

Heath, Rt. Hon. Edward Richard George, P.C., M.B.E., M.P.; British politician; b. 9 July 1916; ed. Chatham House School, Ramsgate, and Balliol Coll., Oxford.
Served in Royal Artillery in Second World War, rising to rank of Lieut.-Col.; Civil Service 46-47; M.P. for Bexley 50-74, for Bexley, Sidcup 74-; Asst. Conservative Whip, Lord Commr. of the Treasury 51, Joint Deputy Govt. Chief Whip 52, Deputy Govt. Chief Whip 53-55, Parl. Sec. to the Treasury and Govt. Chief Whip 55-59; Minister of Labour 59-60; Lord Privy Seal with Foreign Office Responsibilities 60-63; Sec. of State for Industry, Trade and Regional Development, Pres. Board of Trade 63-64; Leader British delegation, Brussels Conf. for Countries seeking entry to the Common Market Oct. 61-63; Leader of Conservative Party 65-75; Leader of the Opposition 65-70; Prime Minister 70-74; Leader of the Opposition 74-75; Pres. Conservative Commonwealth and Overseas Council 75-; Hon. mem. London Symphony Orchestra 74; Visiting Chubb Fellow (Yale) 75; Charlemagne Prize 63; Freiherr von Stein Foundation Award 71; Estes Kefauver Foundation Award; Stresemann Medal 71; Hon. D.C.L. (Oxon.), Hon. D.Tech. (Bradford), Dr. h.c. (Sorbonne), Hon. LL.D. (Westminster Coll., Salt Lake City); Conservative.
Leisure interests: music, yachting (Captain, British Admiral's Cup team 71).
Publs. *One Nation: a Tory approach to social problems* (co-author) 50, *Old World, New Horizons* 70, *Sailing* 75.
House of Commons, London, S.W.1, England.

Heath, Howard Davis; American insurance executive; b. 29 March 1904; ed. Univ. of Washington.
Northwestern Mutual Insurance Co. 23-, Asst. Sec. 38, Asst. Vice-Pres. 44, Man. Eastern Claim Div. (Chicago) 45, Manager Midwestern Dept. 51, Eastern-Southern Div. 59, Vice-Pres. and Dir. 60, Pres. 61-70; Dir. Northwestern Security Insurance Co., Seattle, Washington 60-, Pres. 61-; Cream City Mutual Insurance Co., Milwaukee, Wisconsin 60-65, Pres. 61-65; Dir., mem. of Exec. Cttee., Olympic Nat. Life Insurance Co., Seattle 66; Board of Dirs. American Mutual Insurance Alliance, Chicago; mem. Governing Board Improved Risk Mutuals, New York; Trustee and Past Pres. Industrial Conf. Board (Wash. State); Gov. Board and Vice-Pres. Mutual Loss Research Bureau, Chicago 63-66.
1072 La Reina Drive, Lake San Marcos, Calif. 92069, U.S.A.

Hebb, Donald Olding, F.R.S., M.A., PH.D., D.SC., D.H.L.; Canadian psychologist; b. 22 July 1904, Chester, Nova Scotia; s. of Arthur Morrison Hebb and Mary Clara Olding; m. 1st Marion Isabel Clark 1932 (died 1933), 2nd Elizabeth Nichols Donovan 1937 (died 1962), 3rd Margaret Doreen Williamson 1966; two d.; ed. Dalhousie, McGill and Harvard Univs.
Teacher 25-34; Research, Montreal Neurological Inst. 37-39; Lecturer, Queens Univ. 39-42; Research, Yerkes Laboratories of Primate Psychology 42-47; Prof. Psychology, McGill Univ. 47-72, Chair. Dept. 48-58, Chancellor 70-74, Prof. Emer. 75; Hon. LL.D. (Dalhousie Univ.) 65, Hon. LL.D. (Queen's Univ.) 67.
Leisure interests: sailing, reading, the countryside.
Publs. *Organisation of Behaviour* 49, *Textbook of Psychology* 58, revised edns. 66, 72.
Department of Psychology, McGill University, P.O. Box 6070, Montreal 101, P.Q., Canada.
Telephone: 392-4609.

Heberlein, Dr. Georg; Swiss business executive; b. 14 Dec. 1902, Wattwil, Matura; s. of Dr. Georges Heberlein and Clara Heberlein-Staehelin; m. Elisabeth Leuenberger 1937; three d.; ed. Kantonschule St. Gallen and Univ. of Zurich.
Former mem. of the Board and Chair. Heberlein and Co. AG; Chair. Heberlein Holding AG, Gurit AG; mem. of Board Helvetia Allgemeine, Helvetia Feuer, Helvetia Unfall Versicherungsgesellschaft, Cluett, Peabody Int. AG, Piraiki Patraiki Cotton Mfg. Co., Paul Reinhart AG, Chemische Fabrik Uetikon, Varian AG, Varian Int.
Leisure interests: fishing, hunting, collecting autographs.
9630 Wattwil, Auf der Wanne, Switzerland.
Telephone: 074-6-11-11 (Office); 074-7-15-08 (Home).

Hébert, Louis; Canadian banker; b. 3 May 1908, Laprairie, Quebec; m. Simone Loiselle 1940; one d.; ed. Ecole Supérieure St.-Louis and Int. Accountants Soc.
Junior, Banque Canadienne Nationale, Mont-Laurier 25-33; Accounting Dept., Head Office 33-49; Chief Accountant 49-54; Asst. Gen. Man. 54-60; Gen. Man. 60-64; Dir. 61; mem. Exec. Cttee. 62; Vice-Pres. 63; Pres. 64-, Chair. 69-; Pres. Banque Canadienne Nationale (Europe) 69-; Dr.h.c. (Montreal).
Leisure interests: golf, fishing.
Banque Canadienne Nationale, 500 Place d'Armes, Montreal H2Y 2W3, Quebec, Canada.
Telephone: 395-6542.

Hebert, Paul Macarius, A.B., LL.B., J.S.D.; American university professor and lawyer; b. 1 Nov. 1907, Baton Rouge; s. of Paul Armand and Annie (Byrne) Hebert; m. Estelle Le Jeune 1926; one s. two d.; ed. Louisiana State Univ., Yale Univ. School of Law.
Admitted to Louisiana Bar 29; Prof. of Law Loyola Univ., New Orleans 30-31, Prof. and Dean of Law School 32-36; Asst. Prof. of Law, La. State Univ. 31-32,

Prof. and Dean of Admin. 36-37, Prof. and Dean of Law School 37-39, Acting Pres. 39-41, Dean of Law 41-49, Prof. and Dean of Univ. 49-51, Dean of Law 52-57, 59-; Attorney, La. Legislative Bureau 32, 34, 36, 38; Sec. Council of La. State Law Inst. 38-; mem. law firm of Breazeale, Sachse, Wilson and Hebert 51-52, 57-59; served in U.S. Army 42-45; Civilian Judge U.S. Mil. Tribunals, Nuremberg, Germany 47-48; mem. panel Fed. Mediation and Conciliation Service; mem. loyalty review board U.S. Civil Service Comm. 48-53; Chair. La. Labor Mediation Board 53-67; mem. La. Labor-Management Comm. of Inquiry 67-; mem. America Arbitration Asscn., Nat. Acad. of Arbitrators, La., Board of Govs. 46-47, 53; mem. Asscn. Amer. Law Schools, Chair. Cttee. on Interamerican Co-operation 45-47, Chair. Exec. Cttee. 46-47; Legion of Merit; Hon. LL.D. Loyola State Univ. 68; Democrat.

2331 Kleinert Avenue, Baton Rouge, Louisiana 70806, U.S.A.

Heck, Bruno, DR. PHIL.; German teacher and politician; b. 20 Jan. 1917; m.; three s. three d.; ed. Tübingen Univ.

Former teacher; Ministry of Education, Württemberg 50-52; Exec. Sec. Christian Democrat Party (CDU) 52-62; mem. Bundestag 57-; Minister of Family and Youth Affairs 63-69; Sec.-Gen. of CDU 67-71; Chair. Deutsche Welle.

Leisure interest: hiking.

Deutsche Welle, 5 Cologne, Bonner Strasse 211, Postfach 100444, Federal Republic of Germany.

Heckmann, Otto, DR. PHIL.; German astronomer; b. 23 June 1901, Opladen/Rhineland; s. of Max and Agnes (Grüter) Heckmann; m. Johanna Topfmeier 1925; one s. two d.; ed. Univ. of Bonn.

Asst. Bonn Univ. Observatory 25-27, Göttingen 27-35; Asst. Prof. Göttingen 35-39, Acting Dir. Göttingen Observatory 39-41; Dir. Hamburg Observatory 41-62; Dir. European Southern Observatory 62-69; Prof. of Astronomy, Univ. of Hamburg 41-69, Prof. Emer. 69-; Pres. German Astronomical Society 52-57; Pres. Int. Astronomical Union 67-70; Research Assoc. Royal Astronomical Soc. (London); Hon. mem. American Astronomical Soc.; mem. of many Acads.; several gold medals and hon. degrees.

Leisure interests: history, music, hiking.

Publs. Theorien der Kosmologie 42, (reprinted 68), numerous technical articles in scientific journals.

2b Schmiedesberg, 2057 Reinbek, Federal Republic of Germany.

Telephone: Hamburg 7221750.

Heckscher, August; American journalist and author; b. 16 Sept. 1913; ed. St. Paul's School, Concord, Yale and Harvard Univs.

Instructor in Govt., Yale Univ. 39-41; Army service 41-45; Editor Auburn (New York) Citizen-Adviser 46-48; Chief Editorial Writer New York Herald Tribune 48-56; Spl. Consultant, Pres. of U.S.A. on the Arts 62-63; Parks Commr., New York 67-; Dir. Twentieth Century Fund; Gov. Yale Univ. Press; Fellow American Acad. of Arts and Sciences.

Publs. These Are The Days 36, A Pattern of Politics 47, The Politics of Woodrow Wilson 56, Diversity of Worlds (with Raymond Aron) 57, The Public Happiness 63.

830 Fifth Avenue, New York, N.Y., U.S.A.

Heckscher, Gunnar Edvard, D.PHIL.; Swedish professor and politician; b. 8 July 1909, Djursholm; s. of Prof. Eli and Ebba (née Westberg) Heckscher; m. Anna Britta Vickhoff 1934; three s. one d.; ed. Uppsala Univ. and King's Coll., Cambridge.

Lecturer of Political Science, Uppsala Univ. 33-41, Stockholm Univ. 41-48, Prof. 48-; Dir. Stockholm School of Social Work and Local Admin. 41-54; Co-Dir. Inst. of Public Admin., Ankara 52-53; Dir. Swedish Inst. for Cultural Relations 54-57; Chair. Bd. of

Psychological Defence 54-59; mem. of Riksdag (Lower House of Parl.) 57-65; Parl. Leader and Chair. Conservative Party 61-65; Ambassador to India 65-71, to Japan 75-; mem. Consultative Assembly, Council of Europe 57-65; Chair. Econ. Cttee. 60-65.

Leisure interests: yachting, walking.

Publs. Démocratie Efficace 57, The Study of Comparative Government 57, etc.

Swedish Embassy, 10-3, Roppongi 1-chome, Minato-tu. Tokyo, Japan.

Hedayati, Hadi; Iranian educationist and politician; b. 1923; ed. Teheran Univ., Faculté de Droit, Paris Univ., and Sorbonne, Paris.

Assistant Prof. Teheran Univ. 52-62, Prof. 62-; Legal Counsellor, Iran Insurance Co. 52-57; Counsellor, High Council of Econs. 57-60; High Counsellor, Ministry of Commerce 60; Exec. Man. Bimeh (Insurance) Bank 60-62; Deputy to Majlis 63-; Advisory Minister 63; Minister of Educ. 64-68; Advisory Minister 68-73; Minister of State 73-, Exec. Asst. to Prime Minister 74-; Homayoun Medal, Palme Académique (France); Imperial Award for best book of the year 58, 59.

Publs. History of the Zand Dynasty in Iran, A Study of Iranian Handwritten Works in the 13th Hegyra Century, Cyrus the Great; translations into Persian: History of Herodotus, The Principles of Administrative Management.

Iranshahr Avenue, Kamyar Street, Teheran, Iran.

Hedberg, Hollis D., M.S., PH.D.; American petroleum geologist and stratigrapher; b. 29 May 1903, Falun, Kan.; s. of Carl A. Hedberg and Zada Mary Dow; m. Frances Murray 1932; four s. one d.; ed. Kansas, Cornell and Stanford Univs.

Petrographer, Lago Petrol Co. (Venezuela) 26-28; various posts in geology and exploration for Gulf Oil Corpn. and subsidiaries 28-; stratigrapher and asst. chief geologist (Venezuela) 28-46, exploration man., Foreign Production Div. (N.Y.) 46-52, exploration co-ordinator (Pittsburgh) 52-57, Vice-Pres. for exploration 57-64, Exploration Advisor 64-; Prof. of Geology, Princeton Univ. 59-71, Prof. Emer. 71-; American Comm. of Stratigraphic Nomenclature 46-60, Chair. 50-52; Pres. Int. Subcomm. on Stratigraphic Classification 52-; Vice-Pres. Int. Comm. on Stratigraphy 68-; Pres. Geological Soc. of America 59-60, Pres. American Geological Inst. 62-63; Chair. U.S. Nat. Cttee. on Geology 65-66, Nat. Petroleum Council Technical Subcttee. 67-73; mem. U.S. Nat. Cttee. World Petroleum Congresses 65-; Vice-Pres. Paleontological Soc. 52; Assoc. Editor American Asscn. of Petroleum Geologists 37-; Dir. Cushman Foram Foundation 57-63; Chair. JOIDES Safety and Pollution Prevention Panel 70-; Editor International Stratigraphic Guide of Int. Union of Geological Sciences 76; mem. Nat. Acad. of Sciences; mem. Corpn. Woods Hole Oceanographic Inst. 72-; Foreign mem. Geological Soc. (London), Royal Danish Acad. of Sciences; Hon. mem. Geological Soc. (Stockholm), Venezuelan Asscn. of Minerals and Geology, Medalla Honor Instrucción Pública, Venezuela 41; Sidney Powers Medal of American Asscn. of Petroleum Geology 63; Distinguished Service Award, Univ. of Kansas 63; Mary Clark Thompson Award, Nat. Acad. of Sciences 73; Human Needs Award, American Asscn. Petroleum Geologists 73, Distinguished Achievement Award, Offshore Tech. Conf. 75, Wollaston Medal, Geological Soc. of London 75.

Leisure interests: tennis, gardening, history of geology.

Publs. Gravitational compaction 26, 36, Cretaceous limestone as petroleum source rock in Venezuela 31, Stratigraphy of Rio Querecual section of northeastern Venezuela 37, Foraminifera of mid-Tertiary Carapita Formation 37, Upper Cretaceous foraminifera of Colombia 41, Oilfields of Greater Oficina area, Venezuela 47, Time-stratigraphic classification of sedimentary rocks 48,

Petroleum developments in Africa 50-61, *Geology of Eastern Venezuela* 50, *The Stratigraphic panorama* 61, *Geologic aspects of origin of petroleum* 64, *Significance of high-wax oils* 68, *Influence of Torbern Bergman on Stratigraphy* 69, *Continental margins* 70, *National-International Jurisdictional Boundary on Ocean Floor* 73, *Relation of Methane Generation to Undercompacted Shale and Mud Volcanoes* 74.
118 Library Place, Princeton, N.J. 08540, U.S.A.
Telephone: 609-921-7833.

Hedda, Ali; Tunisian diplomatist; b. 30 Oct. 1930, Sousse; *s.* of Belhassen and Nefissa Hedda; *m.* Nadra Becheur 1958; one *s.* one *d.*; ed. Inst. des Sciences Politiques, Paris.
Attaché, Tunisian Embassy, Washington, D.C. 56; Ministry of Foreign Affairs 57; seconded to Secr. of State for Planning and Nat. Econ. 58; Minister Plenipotentiary, Tunisian Embassy, Rome 66; Amb. to Senegal, concurrently accred. to Mali, Mauritania, Guinea, Liberia, Sierra Leone and The Gambia 70; Dir. of Int. Co-operation, Ministry of Foreign Affairs 72; Dir. Office of the Prime Minister 73; Amb. to U.S.A. (also accred. to Mexico) 74-; Grand Officer Order of the Repub. (Tunisia), Order of the Repub. (Italy).
Embassy of Tunisia, 2408 Massachusetts Avenue, N.W., Washington, D.C. 20008; Home: 5131 Broad Branch Road, Washington, D.C., U.S.A.

Heden, Carl-Göran, M.D.; Swedish scientist; b. 11 Sept. 1920, Stockholm; ed. Karolinska Institutet, Stockholm.
Resident Prof. of Bacteriological Bioengineering, (Medical Research Council) and Head of Dept., Karolinska Institutet; mem. Exec. Cttee. Int. Union of Biological Sciences (IUBS), Int. Council of Scientific Unions (ICSU); mem. COSPAR Consultative Group on Potentially Harmful Effects of Space Experiments, WHO Expert Advisory Panel on Immunology; mem. Special Cttee. for Int. Biological Programme; mem. Convenor Panel on Applied Microbiology of Int. Cell Research Org.; Vice-Pres. and Chair. Advisory Council Int. Asscn. of Microbiological Socs. (IAMS); Fellow New York Acad. of Sciences, World Acad. of Art and Science; mem. Royal Swedish Acad. of Engineering Sciences and Chair. Div. for Biotechnology.
Kungliga Karolinska Institutet, Stockholm 60, Sweden.

Hees, Hon. George H., P.C.; Canadian politician; b. 17 June 1910; ed. Trinity Coll. School, Royal Mil. Coll., Univ. of Toronto and Cambridge Univ.
Served overseas as Brigade Major, 5th Infantry Brigade; Dir. Woodgreen Community Centre; mem. House of Commons 50-; Minister of Transport 57-60; Minister of Trade and Commerce 60-63; Pres. Montreal and Canadian Stock Exchanges 64; Progressive Conservative.
7 Coltrin Place, Ottawa, Ont.; Rathbunwood, Cobourg, Ont., Canada.

Heeschen, David Sutphin, PH.D.; American radio astronomer; b. 12 March 1926, Davenport, Iowa; *s.* of Richard G. and Emily S. Heeschen; *m.* Eloise St. Clair 1950; two *s.* one *d.*; ed. Univ. of Illinois, Harvard Univ.
Lecturer, Wesleyan Univ. 54-55; Research Assoc. Harvard Univ. 55-56; Astronomer, Nat. Radio Astronomy Observatory 56-, Dir. 62-; mem. Nat. Acad. of Sciences, American Astron. Soc., Int. Astron. Union, Int. Scientific Radio Union, Amer. Acad. of Arts and Sciences, Amer. Philosophical Soc., Amer. Asscn. for the Advancement of Science.
National Radio Astronomy Observatory, Edgemont Road, Charlottesville, Va.; Home: 1930 Barracks Road, Charlottesville, Va., U.S.A.
Telephone: 804-296-0221 (Office); 804-296-7321 (Home).

Hefner, Hugh Marston, B.S.; American publisher and gaming promoter; b. 9 April 1926, Chicago, Ill.; *s.* of Glenn L. and Grace (née Swanson) Hefner; *m.* Mildred Williams 1949 (divorced 1975); one *s.* one *d.*; ed. Univ. of Illinois.
Editor and Publisher, *Playboy* Magazine 53-; Pres. H.M.H. Publishing Co. (now *Playboy* Enterprises) 53-.
Leisure interest: backgammon.
Playboy Enterprises Inc., 919 North Michigan Avenue, Chicago, Ill. 60611, U.S.A.
Telephone: 312-M12-1000.

Hegazy, Abdel Aziz Muhammad, D.PHIL.; Egyptian politician; b. 3 Jan. 1923; ed. Fuad Univ., Cairo, Birmingham Univ.
Dean, Faculty of Commerce, Ain Shams Univ. 66-68; mem. Nat. Assembly 69-; Minister of the Treasury 68-73; Deputy Prime Minister, Minister of Finance, Econ. and Foreign Trade 73-74; First Deputy Prime Minister April-Sept. 74, Prime Minister 74-75.
Cairo, Egypt.

Hegde, Sadanand K., M.A., B.L.; Indian judge; b. 11 June 1909, Kawdoor, Mysore; *s.* of late K. Subbaya Hegde; *m.* Meenakshi S. Hegde 1934; three *s.* three *d.*
Advocate 35; Govt. Pleader and Public Prosecutor 47-51; mem. Parl. 52-57; Judge, High Court of Mysore 57; Chief Justice, Delhi High Court 66; Judge, Supreme Court of India 67.
Leisure interest: gardening.
10 Tughlak Road, New Delhi; also 244 Palace Upper Orchards, Bangalore 6, India.
Telephone: 617715 (New Delhi); 26337 (Bangalore).

Hegen, Josef; German diplomatist; b. 24 April 1907.
Mem. Czechoslovak Communist Party 24; Sec. Czechoslovak Communist Youth League 29; joined resistance movement after invasion and occupation of Czechoslovakia; Mauthausen concentration camp; Head of People's Police, Sachsen-Anhalt 48; Chair. Magdeburg City Council 52; State Sec. Ministry of the Interior 53-57; Amb. to Poland 57-61; Deputy Minister for Foreign Affairs 61; Amb. to People's Republic of China 61-64; Deputy Foreign Minister 64-66, State Sec. and First Deputy Foreign Minister 66-.
Ministry of Foreign Affairs, Berlin, German Democratic Republic.

Héger, Charles Emile Victor, D. en D.; Belgian lawyer and politician; b. 26 May 1902, Brussels.
Member of House of Reps. 46-; Minister of Agriculture Aug. 50-54, 61-71, of the Interior 58-60; mem. Christian Social Party.
155 rue de la Loi, Brussels; and Vedrin (Province de Namur), Belgium.

Heide, Harm Ter; Netherlands trade unionist; b. 10 March 1928, Almelo; *m.* B. W. Schot 1955; ed. secondary school and Free Univ. in Amsterdam.
Railway Officer, Netherlands Railways until 57; Econ. Adviser, Nederlands Verbond Van Vakverenigingen (Netherlands Fed. of Trade Unions) 57, Sec.-Editor 65; Pres. 71-72; mem. Econ. and Social Cttee. of EEC and EURATOM 66-71; Vice-Pres. Foundation of Labour; mem. various nat. econ. and social cttees.
Publs. Many articles on social-economic problems and particularly on Common Market problems.
c/o Nederlands Verbond Van Vakverenigingen, Amsterdam-Slotermeer, P.O. Box 8110, Netherlands.
Telephone: 020-134626.

Heide-Jørgensen, Erling; Danish jurist; b. 18 Dec. 1910, Middelfart; *s.* of Henning Heide-Jørgensen and Sarita Petersen; *m.* Aase Kjærsgaard 1938; two *s.* two *d.*; ed. Københavns Universitet.
Civil Servant, Ministry of Justice 36-52, Chief of Section 50-52; Nat. Commr., Danish Police 52-; Del. Int. Criminal Police Org. 53-, mem. Exec. Cttee. 60-63; Pres. Danish Fire Protection Asscn. 59-.
Leisure interest: music.
Strandv. 223, 2920 Charlottenlund, Denmark.

Heidegger, Martin, PH.D.; German philosopher; b. 26 Sept. 1889, Messkirch, Baden; *m.* Elfriede Petri 1917; two *s.*
Professor of Philosophy Marburg Univ. 23-28; Prof. Freiburg i. Br. Univ. 28, Rector 33, Emer. 51-.
Publs. *Die Lehre vom Urteil im Psychologismus* 14, *Die Kategorien- und Bedeutungslehre des Duns Scotus* 16, *Sein und Zeit* 27, *Was ist Metaphysik?* 29, *Vom Wesen des Grundes* 29, *Kant und das Problem der Metaphysik* 29, *Die Selbstbehauptung der deutschen Universität* 33, *Vom Wesen der Wahrheit* 43, *Erläuterungen zu Hölderlins Dichtung* 44, *Platons Lehre von der Wahrheit* 47, *Der Feldweg* 49, *Holzwege* 50, *Einführung in die Metaphysik* 53, *Vorträge und Aufsätze* 54, *Aus der Erfahrung des Denkens* 54, *Was heisst Denken?* 54, *Zur Seinsfrage* 56, *Was ist das—die Philosophie?* 56, *Der Satz vom Grund* 56, *Hebel—Der Hausfreund* 57, *Identität und Differenz* 57, *Gelassenheit* 59, *Unterwegs zur Sprache* 59, *Nietzsche* (2 vols.) 61, *Die Frage nach dem Ding* 62, *Die Technik und die Kehre* 62, *Kants These über das Sein* 62, *Wegmarken* 67, *Die Kunst und der Raum* 69, *Zur Sache des Denkens* 69, *Heraklit* 70, *Phänomenologie und Theologie* 70, *Schellings Abhandlung 'Über das Wesen der menschlichen Freiheit'* 71, *Frühe Schriften* 72, *Gesamtausgabe der veröffentlichten und unveröffentlichten Schriften* 75.
78 Freiburg-Zähringen, Fillibach 25, Federal Republic of Germany.

Heidelberger, Michael, B.S., A.M., PH.D.; American chemist; b. 29 April 1888, New York; *s.* of David and Fannie (Campe) Heidelberger; *m.* 1st Nina Tachau 1916 (died 1946), 2nd Charlotte Rosen Salomonski 1956; one *s.*; ed. public and Ethical Culture schools, Columbia Univ. and Federal Polytechnic Inst., Zürich.
Assistant in Chemistry Summer Sessions Columbia Univ. 1909 and 11; Fellow, Asst., Assoc. and Assoc. Mem. of the Rockefeller Inst. for Medical Research 12-27; Chemist to Mount Sinai Hospital 27-28; and Presbyterian Hospital of N.Y. 28-56; Assoc. Prof. of Biological Chem., Columbia Univ. 29-45, Prof. of Biochemistry 45-48, Prof. of Immuno-Chem. 48-56, Emer. 56-; Visiting Prof. of Immuno-Chem., Rutgers Univ. 55-64; Adj. Prof. of Pathology (Immunology) N.Y. Univ. 64-; Chair. of the Research Council, Public Health Research Inst. of N.Y. City 51-56; Consultant to Sec. of War 42-46; mem. Nat. Acad. of Sciences, American Philosophical Soc., Amer. Chemical Soc., Amer. Soc. of Biological Chemists, Amer. Acad. of Microbiology, Amer. Soc. of Microbiologists; Past Pres. Harvey Soc., American Asscn. of Immunologists; foreign mem. Royal Danish Acad. of Sciences 57-, Accademia Nazionale dei Lincei 63-, Royal Society 75-; Hon. mem. French Soc. of Immunologists, German and British Socs. for Immunology, Mexican Soc. for Allergy and Immunology; many honorary doctorates; Ehrlich Silver Medal 33, Lasker Award 52, von Behring Prize 54, Louis Pasteur Gold Medal (Swedish Medical Soc.) 60, T. Duckett Jones Memorial Award 64; Officer Légion d'Honneur 66, Officier, Ordre de Léopold II 53; Nat. Medal for Science 67, New York Acad. of Medicine Medal 68, von Pirquet Gold Medal 71, Virchow Soc. Gold Medal 73.
Leisure interest: music.
Publs. *Advanced Laboratory Manual of Organic Chemistry* 23, *Lectures in Immuno-Chemistry* 56; numerous papers.
Home: 333 Central Park West, New York, N.Y. 10025; Laboratory: Dept. Pathology, N.Y. Univ. School of Medicine, 550 First Avenue, New York, N.Y. 10016, U.S.A.

Heidweiller, Henricus Augustinus Franciscus; Surinam diplomatist; b. 10 Feb. 1929, Paramaribo; *m.*
Lecturer in civil law, Surinam Law School 55-58; mem. Parl. 58-67; Head of Office for Foreign Relations in Paramaribo 62-68; del. to Council of Caribbean Org 60-64; Minister attached to Netherlands Mission to UI 68-75, Amb. of Surinam to UN Dec. 75-, Vice-Chair Fourth Cttee. (Trust and Non-Self Governing Territories) of Gen. Assembly 73.
Permanent Mission of Surinam to the United Nations 1 United Nations Plaza, 26th Floor, New York, N.Y 10017, U.S.A.

Heifetz, Jascha; Russian-born American violinist; b. 2 Feb. 1901; ed. Petrograd Conservatoire of Music.
First appearance at age seven; concerts Russia, Germany, Austro-Hungary, Scandinavia, U.S. 17, later England; toured Australia and New Zealand 21, Far East 23, world tour 25-27; 1st Vice-Pres. American Guild Musical Artists; hon. mem. Soc. of Concerts, Paris, Asscn. des Anciens Elèves du Conservatoire, Cercle Int. de la Jeunesse Artistique; hon. Vice-Pres. Mark Twain Society U.S.; hon. Pres. Musicians' Fund of America, Légion d'Honneur.
1520 Gilcrest Drive, Beverly Hills, Calif., U.S.A.

Heikal, Muhammed Hassanein; Egyptian journalist; b. 1923; *m.*; three *s.*
Reporter *Akher Saa* magazine 44; Editor *Al-Akhbar* daily newspaper 56-57; Editor-in-Chief *Al-Ahram* daily newspaper 57-74; mem. Central Cttee. Socialist Union 68-, Chair. *Al-Ahram* Establishment Board 60-74; Minister of Nat. Guidance April-Oct. 70.
Publs. *Nahnou wa America* 67, *Nasser: The Cairo Documents* 72, *The Road to Ramadan* 75.
Al Ahram Building, Gallaa Street, Cairo, Egypt.

Heiliger, Bernhard; German sculptor; b. 11 Nov. 1915; ed. Stettin Art School, Berlin Acad. of Fine Arts and in Paris.
Professor of Plastic Arts, High School of Applied Arts, Berlin-Weissensee 46-, High School of Pictorial Arts, Berlin-Charlottenburg 49-; numerous exhbns. in Europe and elsewhere; works in German and foreign museums and private collections; mem. Berlin Acad. of Arts; Berlin Art Prize 50, Cologne Art Prize 52, Nat. and Int. Prize, Inst. of Contemporary Arts, London and Great Art Prize, Nordrhein-Westfalen.
Notable works include *Flamme* for Ernest-Reuterplatz, Berlin, *Auftakt* for Berlin Philharmonic Orchestra, 15 reliefs in Market Place, Bremen, *Kosmos* for Reichstag, Berlin.
Käuzchensteig 12, Berlin-Dahlem, Germany.
Telephone: 8312012.

Heiller, Anton; Austrian composer and organist; b. 1923, Vienna; *s.* of Anton and Karoline Heiller; *m.* 1945; one *s.* one *d.*; ed. Akademie für Musik und darstellende Kunst, Vienna.
Professor of Music, Music Acad., Vienna 45-; concerts all over the world as organist, also as harpsichordist and conductor; Josef Marx Prize 42, Improvisation Prize, Haarlem 52, Schott prize 54, Kulturpreis der Stadt, Vienna 63, Grosser Österreichischer Staatspreis für Musik 69.
Compositions: numerous choral compositions and organ works including a Concerto for Organ and Orchestra.
Heuberggasse 26, Vienna XVII, Austria.
Telephone: 46-01-85.

Heim, Roger Jean, ING. E.C.P., D. ès sciences naturelles, F.R.S.E., F.L.S.; French scientist; b. 12 Feb. 1900; *s.* of Henri and Pauline Noémie (née Sauvion) Heim; *m.* Panca Eftimiu 1935; one *s.*
Curator, Alpine Garden (Faculty of Sciences, Grenoble) 23-25; Demonstrator, Ecole des Hautes Etudes, Paris 26; Asst. at Nat. Museum of Natural History 27-32, Deputy Dir. Cryptogamic Laboratory 32-45, Dir. Laboratory of Mycology and Phytopathology 40-72, Ultrastructural Cryptogamic 72-, Prof. and Dir. Cryptogamic Laboratory 45-73; Dir. Museum of Natural His-

tory 51-65; mem. Acad. d'Agriculture 45, Acad. des Sciences 46, Acad. des Sciences d'Outre-Mer 47, Acad. Royale de Belgique 48, Acad. Leopoldina 62-; Pres. Soc. de Pathologie végétale 37, Soc. mycologique 45, Soc. Botanique de France 48, Société française de Microscopie 48, Asscn. française pour l'avancement des Sciences 51; Union Int. pour la Conservation de la Nature 54, Société des Océanistes 54-; Pres. Fondation-Singer Polignac 58-; Pres. Académie des Sciences 63; Dr. h.c. Univ. of Uppsala; Grand Officier de la Légion d'Honneur 75, Médaille de la Résistance, Croix de Guerre, etc. Publs. *Le Genre Inocybe* 31, *Fungi iberici: Observations sur la flore mycologique catalane* 34, *Les champignons toxiques* 38, *Les Lactario—Russules de Madagascar* 38, *La reproduction chez les plantes* 38, *Etudes sur les Agarics termitophiles africains* 40-52, *La sombre route* 47, *Les champignons, tableaux d'un monde étrange* 48, *Destruction et Protection de la Nature* 52, *Les Lactaires d'Afrique Intertropicale* 55, *Un Naturaliste autour du monde* 55, *La Langue Française et la Science* 55, *Les Champignons d'Europe* 57, 69, *Les Champignons hallucinogènes du Mexique* (with R. G. Wasson) 58, *Les Champignons toxiques et hallucinogènes* 63, *Nouvelles investigations sur les Agarics hallucinogènes* 67, *L'Angoisse de l'an 2000* 73. Laboratoire de Cryptogamie du Muséum, 12 rue de Buffon, 75005 Paris, France. Telephone: 331-35-21.

Heimann, Robert Karl, B.A., M.A., PH.D.; American business executive and security analyst; b. 22 Sept. 1918, New York; s. of Charles and Elizabeth (Quinan) Heimann; m. Charlotte Temple Parker 1950; one s. one d.; ed. Princeton and New York Univs. Editor *Nation's Heritage* 48-49; Man. Editor and Exec. Editor *Forbes Magazine of Business and Finance* 49-54; Exec. Asst. The Amer. Tobacco Co. 54-60, Asst. to the Pres. 61-64, Dir. 63, Vice-Pres. for marketing and public relations 64-66, Exec. Vice-Pres. 66-69; Pres. The Amer. Tobacco Co. 69-; Pres. Amer. Brands, Inc. 69-73, Chair. and Pres. 73-. Publ. *Tobacco and Americans* 60. American Brands, Inc., 245 Park Avenue, New York, N.Y. 10017, U.S.A. Telephone: 212-557-8711.

Heimo, Marcel; Swiss diplomatist; b. 1917, Fribourg; ed. Univs. of Fribourg and Vienna and in U.S.A. Entered Swiss National Bank, Zurich 42; Federal Finance Admin. 45; joined Political Dept. 47, subsequently posted to London and Brussels; returned to Berne 52-54; mem. Swiss Del. to OEEC, Paris 54; transferred to London 61-66; Personal Adviser to Pres. of Rwanda 66-68; Amb. to India and Nepal 68-69; Head Perm. Swiss Del. to OECD 69-73; del. for Technical Co-operation, Berne 74. c/o Ministry of Foreign Affairs, Berne, Switzerland.

Heimpel, Hermann, DR. PHIL.; German historian; b. 19 Sept. 1901, Munich; s. of Hermann Martin Heimpel and Johanna Brack; m. Elisabeth Michel 1928; three s. two d. Privatdozent, Univ. of Freiburg im Breisgau 27, Prof. 31; Prof., Univ. of Leipzig 34, Strasbourg 41; Extraordinary Prof., Univ. of Göttingen 46, Prof. 47-66, Emer. 66-; fmr. Dir. of Max-Planck-Inst. for History, Göttingen; D.Iur h.c.; mem. Acads. of Science of Göttingen, Heidelberg and Leipzig, Acad. of Science and Literature, Mainz, Bavarian Acad. of Sciences, Royal Historical Soc. (U.K.), Deutsche Akademie für Sprache und Dichtung, and other historical socs. Leisure interest: music. Publs. include: *Der Mensch in seiner Gegenwart* (2nd edn.) 57, *Kapitulation vor der Geschichte* (3rd edn.) 60, *Drei Inquisitionsverfahren aus dem Jahre 1425* 69,

Studien zur Kirchen und Reichsreform 74, *Die halbe Violine* (novel)75. 34 Göttingen, Dahlmannstrasse 14, Federal Republic of Germany. Telephone: 59382, 54021.

Heindl, Gottfried, PH.D.; Austrian administrator; b. 5 Nov. 1924, Vienna; s. of Edmund Heindl and Eugenie Holzinger; m. Marianne Caliandjiev 1959; two s.; ed. Univ. of Vienna. Editor, *Österreichischer Wirtschaftsverlag* 46-50; *Neue Wiener Tageszeitung* 50-55; Press Sec. Austrian People's Party 55-66; Dir. Austrian Inst., New York 67-70; Gen. Administrator, Austrian State Opera 70; Dir. for Cultural Affairs, Austrian State Theatres 71-. Publs. *Geschichten von gestern—Geschichten von heute* 65, *Und die Grösse ist gefährlich* 69, *Wien—Brevier einer Stadt* 72. Vienna 1010, Goethegasse 1, Austria. Telephone: 52 76 36.

Heinemann, Gustav Walter, D.THEOL., DR.RER.POL., DR.IUR.; German lawyer and politician; b. 23 July 1899, Schwelm; s. of Otto and Johanna (Walter) Heinemann; m. Hilda Ordemann 1926; one s. three d.; ed. Realgymnasium, Essen, and Univs. of Münster, Marburg, Munich, Göttingen and Berlin. Solicitor, Essen 26-; Legal Counsel, Rheinische Stahlwerke, Essen 28-36, Mining Dir. 36-49; Dozent, Univ. of Cologne 33-39; Lord Mayor of Essen 46-49; Minister of Justice, North Rhine Westphalia 47-48; Fed. Minister of Interior 49-50, of Justice Dec. 66-69; Pres. of Fed. Repub. of Germany 69-74; mem. Bundestag 57-69; mem. Council Protestant Church in Germany 45-67; Christian Democrat -52, Social Democrat 57-. Leisure interests: political sciences, reading and writing political, modern historical and theological works. 43 Essen, Schinkelstrasse 34, Federal Republic of Germany.

Heinesen, Knud; Danish politician; b. 26 Sept. 1932, Kerteminde; s. of Heine S. Heinesen and Else Rasmussen; m. Aase Windfeld 1955; two s. one d. Teacher, Roskilde Folk School 59, Principal 62-67; Sec. Econ. Council, Labour Movt. 60; Gen. Sec. Fed. of Co-operative Socs. 67-68; Chair. Radio Council 67; Assoc. Prof. of Political Economy, Copenhagen Graduate School of Econs. and Business Admin. 68; mem. of Parl. 71-; Minister for Educ. 71-73, of the Budget 73-, of Finance 75-; fmr. mem. numerous educational and radio cttees. etc.; Social Democrat. Leisure interest: painting. Strandvejen 71B, 2100 Copenhagen, Denmark.

Heinesen, William; Danish (Faeroese) author; b. 15 Jan. 1900, Thorshaven, Faeroe Islands; s. of Zacharias Heinesen and Caroline Restorff; m. Elisa Johansen; three s.; ed. commercial schools, Copenhagen. Writes generally about Faeroese subjects; also draws and paints; mem. Danish Literary Acad.; Scandinavian Literature Prize 65. Publs. Novels: *Noatun* 38, *The Black Pot* 49, *The Lost Fiddlers* 50, *Mother of the Seven Stars* 52, *Windy Dawn* 61, *The Good Hope* 64; stories: *The Enchanted Light* 57, *The Bewitched Gamaliel* 60, *Cure for Evil Spirits* 67, *Don Juan from The Train Oil House* 70. Vardagöta 33, Thorshaven, Faeroe Islands. Telephone: Thorshaven 1636.

Heintze, Gerhard, DR.THEOL.; German ecclesiastic; b. 14 Nov. 1912, Wehre, Kreis Goslar; s. of late Pastor Karl and Cölestine (née Schwerdtmann) Heintze; m. Ilse Hoppe 1941; two s. three d.; ed. Humanistisches Gymnasium, Bremen and theological studies in Tübingen, Göttingen and Manchester. Ordained 38; Pastor of Hollern-Twielenfleth 42-46;

Inspector of Mission, Hermannsburg 46-50; Dir. of seminary, Hannover 50-57; Senior Minister, Hildesheim 57-61; Senior Minister of Lower Saxony, Hildesheim 61-65; Bishop of Evangelical-Lutheran Church, Brunswick 65-.
Leisure interest: music.
Publ. *Luthers Predigt von Gesetz und Evangelium* 58.
334 Wolfenbüttel, Neuer Weg 88-90, Federal Republic of Germany.
Telephone: 05331 802 229.

Heinz, Henry John, II, B.A.; American industrialist; b. 10 July 1908, Sewickley, Pa.; s. of Howard Heinz and Elizabeth Rust; m. Drue English Maher 1953; one s.; ed. Yale Univ. and Trinity Coll., Cambridge.
Salesman H. J. Heinz Co. Ltd. London 32-33, in Sales Dept. 34-37, Asst. to Pres. 37-41, Pres. 41-59, Chair. 59-; Dir. Mellon National Bank & Trust Co. Pittsburgh; Trustee, Carnegie Institute, Carnegie-Mellon Univ., Nutrition Foundation, U.S. Council of Int. Chamber of Commerce; Trustee of Cttee. for Economic Development; Chevalier, Légion d'Honneur, Commdr., Order of Merit (Italy), Cross of Commdrs. Royal Order of the Phoenix.
Leisure interest: skiing.
Home: Goodwood, Sewickley, Pennsylvania; Office: P.O. Box 57, Pittsburgh 30, Pa., U.S.A.

Heinze, Sir Bernard Thomas, Kt., M.A., F.R.C.M.; Australian university professor and conductor; b. 1 July 1894, Shepparton, Victoria; s. of Benjamin and Minnie (Greenwell) Heinze; m. Valerie Antonia Hennessy 1932; three s.; ed. Univ. of Melbourne, Royal Coll. of Music, London and Schola Cantorum, Paris.
Appointed to academic staff, Univ. of Melbourne 24, Ormond Prof. of Music, Univ. Melbourne 25-57; Dir. Gen. of Music for Australian Broadcasting Co. 29-32; Conductor, Royal Melbourne Philharmonic Society 28-; Melbourne Symphony Orchestra 33-46 and now Victorian Symphony Orchestra; Dir. State Conservatorium of N.S.W. 57-66; conductor to Australian Broadcasting Comm.; Chair. Commonwealth Assistance to Australian Composers 67-, Music Advisory Cttee. Australian Council for The Arts 69-; Officer, Order of the Crown (Belgium); Order of Polonia Restituta 72; Hon. LL.D. (Univ. of British Columbia), D.Mus. (Univ. of W. Australia).
Leisure interests: golf, philately, antique furniture.
101 Victoria Road, Bellevue Hill, Sydney, N.S.W., Australia.
Telephone: Sydney 36-3164.

Heisbourg, Georges; Luxembourg diplomatist; b. 19 April 1918, Hesperange; s. of Nicolas and Berthe (Ernsterhoff) Heisbourg; m. Hélène Pinet 1945; two s. one d.; ed. Luxembourg and Univs of Grenoble, Innsbruck and Paris.
Chief, Govt. Press and Information Service 44-45; Attaché and Sec. to Legation, London 45-51; Sec., Counsellor, Dir. Political Affairs, Ministry of Foreign Affairs 52-58; Ambassador to U.S.A. 58-64; Perm. Rep. to UN 58-61; Minister to Canada 59-60, Ambassador 60-64; Minister to Mexico 59-60, Ambassador 60-64, to Netherlands 64-67, to France 67-70; Perm. Rep. to OECD 67-70; Sec.-Gen. Western European Union 71-74; Amb. to U.S.S.R. 74-; numerous decorations from W. European countries and Mexico.
Leisure interests: tennis, swimming.
Khruschevsky Pereulok 3, Moscow, U.S.S.R.
Telephone: 2022171.

Heiskell, Andrew; American press executive; b. 13 Sept. 1915, Naples, Italy; s. of Morgan and Ann (Hubbard) Heiskell; m. 1st Cornelia Scott 1937 (dissolved), 2nd Madeleine Carroll 1950 (dissolved), 3rd Marian Sulzberger Dryfoos 1965; three c.; ed. Germany,

Switzerland, Univ. of Paris and Harvard School of Business Administration.
Science teacher, Ecole du Montcel; settled in the U.S.A. 35; Reporter, *New York Herald Tribune* 36-37; Editorial staff *Life* magazine 37-39, Asst. Gen. Man. 39-40, Paris office 40-42, Gen. Man. 42-46, Publisher 46-60; Vice-Pres. Time Inc. 49-50, Chair. of Dirs. 60-, Chief Exec. Officer 69-; mem. Board of Dirs. Inter-Amer. Press Asscn.; mem. Visiting Cttee., Joint Center for Urban Studies, M.I.T./Harvard Univ.; Board of Trustees Bennington Coll., New York Urban Coalition; Co-Chair. Nat. Urban Coalition.
Time Inc., Time & Life Building, Rockefeller Center, New York, N.Y. 10020, U.S.A.
Telephone: 556-3495.

Heisler, Philip Samuel; American newspaperman; b. 8 Sept. 1915; ed. Penn State Coll.
Reporter McKeesport (Pa.) *Daily News* 37-39; Sunpapers War Corresp. 44-45; Ed. *Sunday Sun Magazine,* Baltimore 45-46; Film Dir. Television Station WMAR-TV, Baltimore 47-49; Reporter *Evening Sun,* Baltimore 39-44, Man. Editor 49-; Owner Rabar Racing Stable.
Home: 4406 Bedford Place, Baltimore, Md. 21218; Office: The Sunpapers, Baltimore, Md., U.S.A.

Heissenbüttel, Helmut; German broadcasting official and writer; b. 21 June 1921; ed. Kaiser-Wilhelmsgymnasium, Wilhelmshaven, Realgymnasium, Papenburg, Technische Hochschule, Dresden, and Universitäten Leipzig und Hamburg.
Publishers' Reader, Claassen Verlag, Hamburg 55-57; Editor, Süddeutscher Rundfunk, Stuttgart (Chief Editor *Radio-Essay*) 57-; Hugo-Jacobipreis 60.
Publs. *Kombinationen* 54, *Topographien* 56, *Textbuch 1* 60, *Textbuch 2* 61, *Textbuch 3* 62, *Textbuch 4* 64, *Textbuch 5* 65, *Briefwechsel über Literatur* (with Heinrich Vormweg) 71, *D'Alemberts Ende* (novel) 71, *Zur Tradition der Moderne* (essays and notes) 72.
Donizettistrasse 21, 7 Stuttgart-Botnang, Federal Republic of Germany.

Heitler, Walter, PH.D., F.R.S.; Irish university professor; b. 2 Jan. 1904, Karlsruhe, Germany; s. of Prof. Adolf Heitler and Ottilie Rudolf; m. Kathleen Winifred Nicholson 1942; one s.; ed. Univs. of Berlin and Munich.
Priv. doz. Univ. of Göttingen 29-33; Research Fellow Univ. of Bristol 33-41; Prof. Dublin Inst. for Advanced Studies 41-49, Dir. 46-49; Prof. of Theoretical Physics Univ. of Zürich 49-; mem. Royal Irish Acad., Royal Soc. of Sciences of Uppsala, Acad. of Sciences, Leopoldina, Halle, Akad. der Wissenschaften, Mainz; mem. Det Kongelige Norske Videnskabers Selskab; Hon. D.Sc., Hon. Dr. rer. nat., Hon. Dr. Phil.; Max Planck Medal 68, Marcel Benoist Prize 69.
Publs. *Theory of Chemical Bond* 27, *Quantum Theory of Radiation Elementary Wave Mechanics, Der Mensch und die naturwissenschaftliche Erkenntnis* 61, 4th edn. 66, *Man and Science* 63, *Naturphilosophische Streifzüge* 70, *Naturwissenschaft ist Geisteswissenschaft* 72, *Die Natur und das Göttliche* 74, 2nd edn. 75; and papers on cosmic rays, Meson theory, Quantum-electrodynamics and philosophy of science.
Am Guggenberg 5, 8053 Zürich, Switzerland.
Telephone: 01-531266.

Hekmat, Ali Asghar: Iranian politician, educationist and writer; b. 1893, Shiraz; s. of Moazzam-e-din Hekmat; m. 1920; three d.; ed. American High School and Univ. of Paris.
Dir.-Gen. of Education 28-30; Acting Minister of Education, Religious Foundations and Fine Arts 33-34; Minister of Education 34-37; Pres. Teheran Univ. 35-38, Prof. of Literature and History of Religions 40, Prof. Emer. 63; Pres. Iranian Acad. 38; Minister of the Interior 39-40, of Public Health 41-43, of Justice 43;

head of cultural mission to India 44; Pres. Iranian Nat. Comm. for UNESCO 46-; Minister without Portfolio June 47; Vice-Pres. Iranian Red Cross 48-51; Minister of Foreign Affairs 48-50, 58-59; Amb. to India, concurrently Minister to Thailand 54-58; Pres. Soc. of Nat. Monuments 70-; Dean Coll. of Literature and Foreign Languages 64-; leader of several dels.; numerous Persian and foreign decorations; hon. mem. Arab Acad.; Hon. Ph.D.
Leisure interests: reading, writing articles for revues and magazines, studying Persian poems.
Publs. *Sarzarmin-e-Hind, Shakuntala,* translations of Shakespeare, *Djami* 43, *Majaless-ol Nafayess* 45, *From Saadi to Djami* (history of Persian literature) 48, *Parsi-el-Naghze* (anthology) 51, *Kashfol Asrar* 52, *The Proverbs of the Koran* 53, *A Short History of Persian Literature* (in English) 57, *Treatise on Navai* 58, *History of Religions* (2 vols.) 60-61, 4th edn. 70; Editor *Iranshahr* (2 vols.) 65.
Pol-é Roumi, Chémiran, Teheran, Iran.
Telephone: 870088.

Hela, Ilmo, PH.D.; Finnish oceanographer; b. 2 March 1915, Jyväskylä; *s.* of Martti and Anna Hela; *m.* Kristiina Hela 1940; two *s.*; ed. Univs. of Helsinki, Königsberg and Hamburg.
Assistant and oceanographer, Inst. of Marine Research 40-55; Assoc. Prof. Univ. of Miami 51-55; Dir. Inst. of Marine Research 55-; Dir. Int. Laboratory of Marine Radioactivity, IAEA, Monaco 61-63; mem. UNESCO Exec. Board 66-74.
Publs. Several publications in the field of marine sciences.
Tähtitorninkatu 2, P.O. Box 166, 00141 Helsinki 14; Home: Sepontie 1-x, 02130 Tapiola 3, Finland.
Telephone: 633-070 (Office); 463-789 (Home).

Helaissi, Sheikh Abdulrahman Al-: Saudi Arabian diplomatist; b. 24 July 1922; ed. Univs. of Cairo and London and in Islamic Religious Law.
Official at Ministry of Foreign Affairs; Secretary to Embassy London 47-54; Under-Sec. Ministry of Agriculture 54-57; Rep. to UN, and at conferences on Health, Agriculture, Wheat, Sugar and Locusts; Head of Del. to FAO 55-61; Amb. to Sudan 57-60; Del. to Conf. of Non-Aligned Nations, Belgrade 61; Amb. to Italy and Austria 61-66, to U.K. 66-, concurrently to Denmark 66-70.
Publ. *The Rehabilitation of the Bedouins* 59.
Embassy of Saudi Arabia, 27 Eaton Place, London, SW1X 8BW, England.

Held, Martin; German actor; b. 11 Nov. 1908, Berlin; *s.* of Max and Emma Held; *m.* Lore Hartling; two *s.*; ed. schools in Berlin, Staatliche Schauspielschule, Berlin.
Apprentice, Siemens 29; acted in theatre at Tilsit, Elbing, Bremerhaven and Darmstadt 31-41; Städtische Bühnen, Frankfurt-am-Main 41-51; mem. Staatstheater, Berlin 51-; many appearances in films and on television; mem. Acad. der Künste, Berlin; Preis der Deutschen Kritiker, 52, Filmband in Gold 55; Bundesverdienstkreuz (1st class); Staatsschauspieler.
Leisure interests: general literary interests.
1 Berlin 37, Alberlinenstrasse 15-16; Agentur Mackeben, 1 Berlin 33, Douglasstr. 2, Germany.

Helders, Gerardus Philippus, LL.D.; Netherlands civil servant and politician; b. 9 March 1905, Rotterdam; *s.* of Gerardus Philippus Helders and Jacoba Kleinbloesem; *m.* Pieternella Margaretha Meijer 1930; one *s.* four *d.*; ed. Leiden Univ.
Employed in the former Netherlands East Indies, rising to grade of Finance Inspector 30-40; at Ministry of Finance 46-48; Dir. Nationale Trust Maatschappij, Amsterdam 48-57; Minister for Overseas Affairs 57-59;

Counsellor of State 59-75; Commdr. Order of Orange Nassau; Knight Order of the Netherlands Lion, War Cross and other decorations for service in the army (Gen. Staff) and Netherlands East Indies, Grand Cross Order of Homayoun (Iran).
Leisure interests: music, literature and farming.
Storm van 's-Gravesandeweg 71, Wassenaar, Netherlands.
Telephone: 01751-17664.

Helén, Nils Gunnar, PH.D.; Swedish politician; b. 5 June 1918, Vingåker; *s.* of Gustaf Helén and Ingeborg (née Andersson); *m.* Ingrid Rying 1938; one *s.* one *d.*
With Swedish Broadcasting Corpn. 39-49; Literary Editor of *Stockholms-Tidningen* 49-55; mem. Parl. 53-66, 70-; mem. Nordic Council 54-64, 70-; Asst. Prof. Univ. of Stockholm 56-; Gov. of Province of Kronoberg 65-70; Chair. Liberal Party of Sweden 69-70; mem. Board of Govs. Swedish Nat. Debt Office 74-.
Publs. *Birger Sjöberg kriser och kransar i stilhistorisk belysning* 46, *Röst i Radion* 50, *Friheten och de två systemen* 54, *Skola, yrke, samhälle i USA* 55, *Den 9-åriga skolan* 57, *7 år av skolreformer* 57, *Rätt till utbildning* 60, *Den nya skolan* 61, *Svenska författare* 64, *Politik för ett mänskligare samhälle* 70, *Frihetigemenskap* 74.
Jacob Dubbes väg 8, Saltsjö-Duvnäs, Sweden.
Telephone: 08-7163050 and 08-142020.

Hélion, Jean; French painter; b. 21 April 1904, Couterne, Orne; *m.* Jacqueline Ventadour 1963; five *s.*
Abstract painter until 39; Prisoner-of-War 40-42 when he escaped; figurative painter 43-; first one-man exhbn. 32, later in America and Europe; designed sets and costumes for *King Lear,* Television Production 65; numerous group exhbns. and works in numerous museums.
Retrospective exhbns.: Abstracts, Galerie Louis Carré, Paris 62, General, Gallery of Modern Art, New York 64, Drawings, Galerie Yvon Lambert, Paris 64, General, Leicester Galleries, London 37-66, Galérie du Dragon, Paris 66, Galleria II Fante di Spade, Rome 68, Galleria Eunomia, Milan 69, Galerie Verrières, Lyon 69, Museum of Sables d'Olonne (Works 58-68) 70, Galeries Nationales, Grand Palais, Paris 70, Maison de la Culture d'Amiens et St. Etienne 70-71, Galerie St. Germain, Paris 73, Galerie Flinker, Paris 75.
Leisure interest: mushroom hunting.
Publ. *They Shall Not Have Me* 43.
4 rue Michelet, Paris 6e, and Bigeonnette, 28170 Chateau-neuf-en-Thymerais, France.
Telephone: 033-49-41.

Heller, John Roderick, B.S., M.D.; American medical research administrator; b. 27 Feb. 1905, S. Carolina; *s.* of John R. Heller Sr. and Elizabeth Smith Heller; *m.* Susie May Ayres 1934; three *s.*; ed. Clemson Coll. and Emory Univ.
Public Health Clinician and Admin. Georgia State Dept. of Health 30-31; Venereal Disease Clinician, U.S. Public Health Service, Ark. 31-32; V.D. Control Officer, Tenn. State Dept. of Health 32-34; entered U.S. Public Health Service 34, States Relations Admin. 34-43, Chief Dir. of Venereal Diseases 43-48; Dir. Nat. Cancer Inst. 48-60; Professional Lecturer George Washington Univ. School of Medicine 48-60; Asst. Surgeon Gen. U.S. Public Health Service 57-60 (retd.); Pres. and Chief Exec. Officer Sloan-Kettering Cancer Center 60-64; Clinical Prof. Preventive Medicine, Cornell Medical Coll., New York, N.Y. 62-65; Special Consultant on Int. Medical and Scientific Affairs, American Cancer Soc. Inc, 64-66; Special Consultant, Nat. Cancer Inst., Bethesda. Md. 65-; Hon. Sc.D. (Clemson Coll.) 58, Hon. LL.D. Hahnemann Medical Coll. 60, M.D. h.c. Perugia Univ. 61.
Leisure interests: home movies, travelling.

Publs. *The Control of Venereal Disease* (with Vonderlehr) 46, and many papers.

National Cancer Institute, Bethesda, Maryland 20014; Home: 5604 McLean Drive, Bethesda, Md. 20014, U.S.A. Telephone: 301-496-5217 (Office); 301-656-2264 (Home).

Heller, Walter Wolfgang, A.B., M.A., PH.D.; American economist and government adviser; b. 27 Aug. 1915, Buffalo, N.Y.; *s.* of Ernst Heller and Gertrude Warmburg Heller; *m.* Emily Karen Johnson 1938; two *s.* one *d.*; ed. Oberlin Coll., Ohio, and Univ. of Wisconsin.
Asst. Dir. of Tax Research, U.S. Treasury 42-46; Assoc. Prof. of Economics, Univ. of Minnesota 46-50, Prof. 50-60, 64-67, Regents' Prof. 67-; Chair. of Econs. Dept. 57-61, Chief Internal Finance, U.S. Mil. Govt., Germany 47-48; mem. E.C.A. Mission on German Fiscal Problems 51; Tax Adviser to Gov. of Minnesota 55-60; Consultant to Cttee. for Econ. Devt. 48-49, 54-57, to U.S. Census Bureau 58-61, to UN (on fiscal problems of newly-developing countries) 52-60, to Royal Comm. on Taxation, Jordan 60; Chair. President's Council of Econ. Advisers 61-64; Dir. Int. Multifoods Inc. 65-, Nat. City Bank of Minneapolis 64-, Nat. Bureau of Econ. Research 60- (Chair. 71-74), Northwestern Nat. Life Insurance Co. 66-, Fed. Nat. Mortgage Asscn. 68-71, Commercial Credit Co. 69-; mem. Oberlin Coll. Board of Trustees 66-; mem. Cttee. for Econ. Devt. Research Advisory Board 65-; Consultant to Exec. Office of the Pres. 65-69; Consultant, President's Council of Econ. Advisers 74-; Trustee, Coll. Retirement Equities Fund 69-73; Chair. OECD Group of Fiscal Experts 67-69; mem. American Econ. Asscn., Vice-Pres. 68, Pres. 74; mem. Amer. Acad. of Arts and Sciences; several hon. degrees.
Leisure interests: travel, wood-chopping, clam-digging.
Publs. *Taxes and Fiscal Policy in Under-developed Countries* (co-author) 54, *State Income Tax Administration* (co-author) 59, *New Dimensions of Political Economy* 66, *Revenue Sharing and the City* (co-author) 68, *Perspective on Economic Growth* (editor) 68, *Monetary vs. Fiscal Policy* (co-author) 69, *Economic Growth and Environmental Quality: Collision or Co-Existence?* 72, *What's Right with Economics* 74.
University of Minnesota, Minneapolis, Minnesota 55455; Home: 2203 Folwell Street, Saint Paul, Minn. 55108, U.S.A.
Telephone: 612-645-2258.

Hellesen, Gunnar; Norwegian politician; b. 23 Feb. 1913, Haugesund; *s.* of late Captain Gunnar E. Hellesen and Gina Johannessen; *m.* Marit Landrog 1946; one *s.* two *d.*; ed. commercial education.
Entered insurance business before Second World War; prisoner-of-war 40-45; mem. Haugesund City Council 46, Council Presidency 52; Mayor of Haugesund 55, 58-59; mem. Storting 61-69, Chair. Finance Cttee. 65-69; Gov. Province of Rogaland 69-73; Minister of Defence 70-71; Bank Man. 74-; Chair. Board Norwegian Oil Directorate 72-, Norwegian Industrial Fund 73-; Conservative.
Nedstrandsgt. 8, 5500 Haugesund, Norway.

Helliwell, Robert A., PH.D., American professor of radio science; b. Red Wing, Minn.; *s.* of Harold Harlowe and Grace Robson Helliwell; *m.* Jean Perham 1942; three *s.* one *d.*; ed. Stanford Univ.
Managed programme of ionospheric measurements and research aimed at improving wartime communications 42; received Ph.D. for studies of low-frequency propagation 48; continued to teach, Stanford Univ., Prof. 58-, now Dir. Stanford programme of research on whistlers and related ionospheric phenomena, including a world wide network of receiving stations and experiments in the OGO-series satellites; mem. Nat. Acad. of Sciences, Fellow Inst. of Electrical and Electronic Engineers, American Geophysics Union; mem. various Comms. of U.S. Nat. Cttee. of Int.

Scientific Radio Union (URSI); fmr. Chair. Int. Comm. IV of URSI; fmr. Consultant to Environmental Science Services Admin., Boulder Labs., Consultant to Dept. of Defense, Defense Science Board; mem. Improved IME Scientific Advisory Group, Nat. Aeronautics and Space Admin.; Chair. Panel on Upper Atmosphere Physics, Cttee. of Polar Research, Nat. Acad. Sciences 70-73; Antarctica Service Medal, Nat. Acad. Sciences 66; Appleton Prize, Royal Soc. of London 72.
Leisure interests: hiking, camping, gardening, reading, music, fencing.
Publs. 62 technical and scientific publs.; *Whistlers and Related Ionospheric Phenomena* (monograph) 65.
Radioscience Laboratory, Stanford University, Stanford, Calif. 94305, U.S.A.

Hellman, Lillian; American playwright; b. 20 June 1906, New Orleans, La.; *d.* of Max and Julia (Newhouse) Hellman; *m.* Arthur Kober 1925 (divorced 1931); ed. New York and Columbia Univs.
With Horace Liveright Inc., publishers 24-25; theatrical play reader 27-30; book reviewer *New York Herald Tribune* 25-28; scenario writer 35-; mem. Screen Writers Guild, Dramatists Guild, American Acad. of Arts and Sciences, American Acad. of Arts and Letters.
Leisure interests: boats, fishing.
Plays: *The Children's Hour* 34, *Days to Come* 36, *The Little Foxes* 39, *Watch on the Rhine* 41, *The Searching Wind* 44, *Another Part of the Forest* 46, adaptation E. Roble's *Montserrat* 49, *The Autumn Garden* 52, adaptation of Anouilh's *The Lark* 55, *Toys in the Attic* 60; *Candide*, an operetta with Leonard Bernstein and Richard Wilbur 56, *My Mother, My Father and Me* 63; memoirs: *An Unfinished Woman* 69, *Pentimento* 73; film scenarios: *The Dark Angel* 35, *These Three* 35-36, *Dead End* 37, *The Little Foxes* 40, *The North Star* 43, *The Searching Wind* 45.
630 Park Avenue, New York, N.Y. 10021, U.S.A.

Hellwig, Fritz, DR.PHIL.HABIL.; German economist and European politician; b. 3 Aug. 1912, Saarbrücken; *s.* of Friedrich H. and Albertine (Christmann) Hellwig; *m.* Dr. Margarete Werners 1939; two *s.* one *d.*; ed. Marburg, Vienna and Berlin Univs.
Staff mem. of the Saarbrücken Chamber of Industry and Commerce 33-39; Dir. of the Saarwirtschaftsarchiv 36-39; Man. of the District Organisations of the Iron and Steel Industry at Düsseldorf and Saarbrücken, 40-43; war service 43-47; Econ. Adviser and Dir. of Deutsches Industrieinstitut, Cologne 51-59; Substitute delegate, Consultative Assembly of Council of Europe 53-56; mem. of Bundestag 53-59; Chair. of the Econ. Affairs Cttee. of the Bundestag 56-59; mem. of European Parl. 59; mem. of High Authority of the European Coal and Steel Community, Luxembourg 59-67; Vice-Pres. of the Comm. of the European Communities, Brussels until 70; Exec. mem. Board of German Shipowners' Asscn. 71-73.
Leisure interests: collecting old maps, views and illustrated books.
Publs. *Westeuropas Montanwirtschaft, Kohle und Stahl beim Start der Montan-Union* 53, *Saar zwischen Ost und West, Die wirtschaftliche Verflechtung* 54, *10 Jahre Schumanplan* 60, *Gemeinsamer Markt und Nationale Wirtschaftspolitik* 61, *Montanunion zwischen Bewährung und Belastung* 63, *Politische Tragweite der europäischen Wirtschaftsintegration* 66, *Das schöne Buch und der Computer* 70, *Die Forschungs- und Technologiepolitik der Europäischen Gemeinschaften* 70, *Verkehr und Gemeinschaftsrecht: Seeschiffart und Europäische Wirtschaftgemeinschaft* 71, *Die Deutsche Seeschiffart: Strukturwandel und künftige Aussichten* 73.
53 Bonn-Bad Godesberg, Klostersbergstrasse 117C, Federal Republic of Germany.
Telephone: 02221/32-20-17.

Hellyer, Hon. Paul Theodore, P.C., B.A.; Canadian fmr. politician; b. 6 Aug. 1923, Waterford, Ont.; s. of Audrey S. Hellyer and Lulla M. Anderson; m. Ellen Jean Ralph; two s. one d.; ed. Waterford High School, Curtiss Wright Technical Inst., California, and Univ. of Toronto.
Fleet Aircraft Manufacturing Co., Fort Erie 42-44; Royal Canadian Air Force 44-45; Owner, Mari-Jane Fashions, Toronto 45-56; Treas. Curran Hall Ltd. 50, Pres. 51-62; Pres. Trepil Realty Ltd. 51-62; Pres. Hendon Estates Ltd. 59-62; mem. House of Commons 49-57, 58-74, Parl. Asst. to Minister of Nat. Defence 56-57, Assoc. Minister April-June 57, Minister of Nat. Defence 63-67, of Transport 67-69, responsible for Central Mortgage and Housing Corpn. 68-69; Chair. Task Force on Housing and Urban Devt. 68; Acting Prime Minister 68-69; joined Progressive Conservative Party July 72; Opposition spokesman on Industry, Trade and Commerce 73; Distinguished visitor, Faculty of Environmental Studies, York Univ. 69-70; Founding Chair. Action Canada 71; Syndicated Columnist, Toronto Sun 74-; mem. NATO Parliamentary Asscn., Commonwealth Parliamentary Asscn.; Fellow Royal Soc. for Encouragement of the Arts.
Leisure interests: swimming, skin and scuba diving, stamp collecting.
Publ. *Agenda: A Plan for Action* 71.
1982 Rideau River Drive, Ottawa, Ontario, Canada.
Telephone: 238-5286.

Helm, Harold Holmes, B.A., LL.D.; American banker; b. 9 Dec. 1900, Auburn, Ky; s. of T. O. Helm, M.D. and Nellie Blakey; m. Mary G. Rodes; one s. one d.; ed. Ogden Coll. and Princeton Univ.
Credit Department, Chemical Bank New York Trust Co. (fmrly. Chemical Nat. Bank) 20, Junior Officer 26, Vice-Pres. 29, Dir. 41, First Vice-Pres. 46, Pres. 47-56, Chair. 56-66, Chair. Exec. Cttee. 66-72, Dir. Advisory Cttee. 72-; Chair. Exec. Cttee. of Fed. Hall Memorial Assocs.; Dir. Associated Dry Goods Corpn., McDonnell Douglas Corpn., Reader's Digest, Lord and Taylor, etc.; Vice-Pres. Presbyterian Hospital, N.Y.; Cahir. Exec. Cttee., Columbia Presbyterian Medical Center; Emer. Trustee Princeton Univ.; Commdr. Order of St. Olav; Hon. D.C.S. (New York Univ.), Hon. LL.D. (Center Coll., Bloomfield Coll., Hampden Sydney Coll.), Hon. D.C.L. (Univ. of the South).
Chemical Bank, 277 Park Avenue, New York, N.Y., U.S.A.
Telephone: 212-922-6338 (Office).

Helms, Jesse; American senator; b. 18 Oct. 1921, Monroe, N.C.; s. of Mr. and Mrs. J. A. Helms; m. Dorothy Jane Coble 1942; one s. two d.; ed. Wingate Coll. and Wake Forest Coll. (now Wake Forest Univ. at Winston-Salem).
Served U.S. Navy 42-45; subsequently became city editor, *The Raleigh Times* and Dir. of news and programmes for Tobacco Radio Network and Radio Station WRAL; Admin. Asst. to Senators Willis Smith and Alton Lennon; Exec. Dir. North Carolina Bankers Asscn. and editor, *The Tarheel Banker* 53-60; editorial writer and presenter, WRAL-TV and Tobacco Radio Network 60; Exec. Vice-Pres., Vice-Chair. of Board and Asst. Chief Exec. Officer, Capitol Broadcasting Co. (which operates WRAL-TV and Tobacco Radio Network); Senator from North Carolina 73-; Republican.
Leisure interests: reading, community service, fishing, golf.
1513 Caswell Street, Raleigh, N.C. 27608, U.S.A.
Telephone: 919-834-0690.

Helms, Richard M.; American government official; b. 30 March 1913; ed. high schools in U.S.A., Switzerland and Germany, and Williams Coll.
Worked for United Press and *The Indianapolis Times* 35-42; joined U.S. Navy 42, in Office of Strategic Services, Second World War; Central Intelligence Group 46-47, Central Intelligence Agency 47-, Deputy Dir. for Plans 62, Deputy Dir. 65, Dir. 66-73; Amb. to Iran 73-.
United States Embassy, Takhte Jamshid Avenue, Roosevelt Avenue, Teheran, Iran.

Hélou, Charles; Lebanese lawyer, journalist and politician; b. 1911; ed. St. Joseph (Jesuit) Univ. and Ecole Française de Droit, Beirut.
Barrister, Court of Appeal and Cassation, Beirut 36; founded newspaper *L'Eclair du Nord*, Aleppo, Syria 32; founded *Le Jour*, Beirut 34; Political Dir. *Le Jour* until 47; Lebanese Minister to Vatican 47; Minister of Justice and Health, Lebanon 54-55, of Educ. Feb.-Sept. 64; Pres. of Lebanon Sept. 64-Sept. 70; Pres. Association des Parlementaires de Langue Française 73-; fmr. Sec.-Gen. Catholic Action of Lebanon.
Beirut, Lebanon.

Helpmann, Sir Robert Murray, Kt., C.B.E.; British dancer, actor and choreographer; b. 9 April 1909; ed. Prince Alfred's Coll., Adelaide.
With Sadler's Wells Ballet Company 33-50; danced in *The Sleeping Princess, Les Sylphides, Giselle, Lac des Cygnes, Coppelia, Apparitions, Comus, Hamlet, Checkmate, Miracle in the Gorbals, Don Juan, Job, Prospect Before Us, The Rake's Progress, Le Spectre de la Rose, A Wedding Bouquet, Adam Zero, Carnival*; Choreographer for: *Hamlet, Comus, The Birds, Miracle in the Gorbals, Adam Zero, The Red Shoes* (film) *and Electra*; acted in Old Vic and Stratford productions of Shakespeare's plays, and in *The Insect Play, The White Devil, He who Gets Slapped*, and *The Millionairess*; American Tour 54, Australian Tours 55, 58, Australian and South American Tours 61-62; Films: *One of our Aircraft is Missing, Caravan, Henry V, The Red Shoes, Tales of Hoffman, Iron Petticoat, Big Money, 55 Days at Peking; Chitty, Chitty, Bang, Bang, Alice in Wonderland*; Directed: *Murder in the Cathedral* (Old Vic) and *Duel of Angels* (U.S.A.), *Don Quixote* (with Nureyev); Produced operas: *Butterfly, Coq d'Or* (Covent Garden); plays: *The Tempest, As You Like It, Antony and Cleopatra* (Old Vic), *Nekrassov* (Edinburgh Festival 57 and Royal Court), *Nude with Violin* (Globe) 58, *Marriage Go Round, Aladdin* (London) 59, *Peter Pan* (London) 71; ballets: *The Sleeping Beauty* (Sydney) 73, *Perisynthyon* (Sydney) 74, *The Merry Widow* 75; Co-artistic Dir. Australian Ballet 65-74, Artistic Dir. 75-; Artistic Dir. Adelaide Artistic Festival 68-; Guest artist, Royal Ballet 58; Knight, Northern Star (Sweden), Order of the Cedar (Lebanon); Queen Elizabeth II Coronation Award, Royal Acad. of Dancing 60; Australian of the Year 65.
c/o The Royal Ballet, Covent Garden, London, W.C.2; Home: 72 Eaton Square, London, S.W.1, England.
Telephone: 01-235-2235.

Helsby, Baron (Life Peer), cr. 68; **Laurence Norman Helsby**, G.C.B., K.B.E.; British former civil servant; b. 27 April 1908, Liverpool, Lancs.; s. of Wilfred Helsby; m. Wilmett Mary Maddison; one s. one d.; ed. Sedbergh and Keble Coll., Oxford.
Lecturer in Econs., Univ. Coll. of South-West 30-31, Durham Colls. in Univ. of Durham 31-45; Asst. Sec. Treasury 46; Principal Private Sec. to Prime Minister 47-50; Dep. Sec. Ministry of Food 50-54; First Civil Service Commr. 54-59; Perm. Sec. Ministry of Labour 59-62; Jt. Perm. Sec. to Treasury and Head of Home Civil Service 63-68; Dir. Rank Org., Imperial Group, Midland Bank 68-, Industrial and Commercial Finance Corpn. 72-; Chair. Midland Bank Trust Co. 70-, Channel Islands brs. 74-.
Logmore Farm, Dorking, Surrey, England.

Heltzer, Harry, MET.ENG.; American business executive; b. 22 Aug. 1911, Cincinnati, Ohio; s. of Edward and Ann Heltzer; one s. one d.; ed. Univ. of Minnesota.

Production Man. Chemolite Plant, Minnesota Mining and Manufacturing Co. 48-52, Gen. Man. Reflective Products Div. 52-59, Div. Vice-Pres. 59-61, Corporate Vice-Pres. 61-63, Group Vice-Pres. 63-66, mem. Board of Dirs. 65-75, Chair. of Board and Chief Exec. Officer 70-May 75; Dir. Int. Road Fed. 65-, Chair. 71-73; mem. Nat. Highway Safety Advisory Cttee. 67-70; Chair. Highway Users Fed. for Safety and Mobility 70; Dir. Chamber of Commerce of U.S. 71-73; Trustee, U.S. Council of Int. Chamber of Commerce 71-; Gold Medal of Merit, Veterans of Foreign Wars 65, Outstanding Achievement Award, Univ. of Minn. 66, President's Award for Excellence, Amer. Asscn. of Motor Vehicle Administrators 72, Golden Plate Award, Amer. Acad. of Achievement 74.
Minnesota Mining and Manufacturing Company, 3M Center, St. Paul, Minn. 55101, U.S.A.

Hencken, Hugh O'Neill, PH.D., D.LITT., SC.D.; American archaeologist; b. 8 Jan. 1902, New York; s. of Albert Charles Hencken and Mary Creighton O'Neill; m. Mary Thalassa Alford Cruso 1935; three d.; ed. Princeton Univ., Cambridge Univ.
Associate, Peabody Museum, Harvard Univ. 30-31, Asst. Curator European Archaeology 31-32, Curator 32-72; Asst. Dir. American School of Prehistoric Research 40-45, Dir. 45-72, Chair. 60-72; Lecturer London and Oxford 47, Edinburgh 59; excavations in England 28, 30, 31; Dir. Harvard excavations in Ireland 32-36; Dir. American School of Prehistoric Research excavations Morocco 47, Algeria 49; mem. Hon. Cttee., Int. Council of Prehistoric and Protohistoric Sciences 48-; Hon. D.Litt. Nat. Univ. of Ireland; Pres. Archaeological Inst. of America 49-51; Fellow Amer. Acad. of Arts and Sciences, Royal Irish Acad.; Corresp. Fellow British Acad.; Hon. Fellow St. John's Coll. Cambridge 68. Leisure interest: travel.
Publs. *Archaeology of Cornwall* 32, *Ballinderry Crannog* (No. 1) 36, *Cahercommaun* 38, *Lagore Crannog* 50, *Indo-European Languages and Archaeology* 55, *Tarquinia, Villanovans and Early Etruscans* 68, *Tarquinia and Etruscan Origins* 68, *The Earliest European Helmets*.
Peabody Museum, Harvard University, Cambridge, Mass., U.S.A.
Telephone: UN8-7600, Ext. 2517.

Henderson, Douglas; American diplomatist; b. 15 Oct. 1914; ed. Boston Univ. and Fletcher School of Law and Diplomacy.
Instructor, Tufts Coll. 41-42; Diplomatic Service 42-, Vice-Consul, Nogales 42, Arica 43, Cochabamba 43; Dept. of Commerce 47; Consul 50; Second Sec. and Consul, Berne 50, First Sec. and Consul 54; Asst. Chief, Econ. Defense Div. 56; Counsellor, Econ. Affairs, Lima 60, Counsellor, Lima 61; Amb. to Bolivia 63-68; Consultant, Policy Planning Council, Dept. of State 68-69; Deputy Rep. U.S. Mission to OAS 69-; U.S. Rep. Inter-American Cttee. on Alliance for Progress 69-.
c/o Department of State, Washington, D.C. 20520, U.S.A.

Henderson, Rt. Rev. Edward Barry, D.D., D.S.C., D.LITT.; British ecclesiastic; b. 22 March 1910; ed. Radley, and Trinity Coll., Cambridge.
Ordained 34; Curate, St. Gabriel's, Pimlico 34-36; Priest, All Saints, Pimlico 36-39; Rector, Holy Trinity, Ayr 39-47; Chaplain R.N.V.R. 43-44; Vicar, St. Paul's, Knightsbridge 47-55; Rural Dean of Westminster 53-55; Bishop Suffragan of Tewkesbury 55-60; Bishop of Bath and Wells 60-Sept. 75; sub-Prelate of the Order of St. John of Jerusalem 62; Hon. Freeman of Wells.
Hill Cottage, Ryme Intrinseca, Nr. Sherbourne, Dorset, England.
Telephone: 093-587-894.

Henderson, Horace Edward; American executive; b. 30 July 1917, Henderson, N.C.; s. of Thomas Brantley Henderson M.D. and Ethel Maude Duke; m. Vera

Schubert 1966; two d.; ed. Coll. of William and Mary, Williamsburg, Virginia, and Yale Univ.
Army service, Second World War; Owner, Henderson Real Estate, Williamsburg, Virginia 47-52; Vice-Pres. Junior Chamber Int. 51-52; Nat. Pres. U.S. Junior Chamber of Commerce 52-53; Asscns. Co-ordinator, Nat. Auto Dealers Asscn., Washington 54-55; Dir. Chamber of Commerce of the U.S.A. 54; Exec. Cttee. U.S. Cttee. for the UN 54; Trustee, Freedoms Foundation 55; Vice-Chair. Operation Brotherhood 54-56; Lieut.-Gov. Va. 57; Dir. Office of Special Liaison and Special Asst., Deputy Under-Sec. of State 58; U.S. Del. to ILO 59-60, WHO 59-60, UNESCO 60, FAO 59, High Comm. for Refugees 59, ECOSOC 59, U.S. Del. to UN 60; Deputy Asst. Sec. of State, Dept. of State, Washington, D.C. 59-60; Chair. Republican Party of Virginia 62-64; mem. Republican Nat. Cttee. 62-64; Chair. of Board, Henderson Real Estate Agency, McLean, Virginia 65-; Dir. Gen. World Peace Through Law Center, Geneva 65-69; Pres. and Chair. Community Methods, Inc. 69-75; Chair. Conv. for Peaceful Settlement of Int. Disputes 74-75; Pres. Int. Domestic Devt. Corps 75; Exec. Dir. World Asscn. of Judges. Leisure interests: military, history, architecture, swimming, skiing.
508A North Birdneck Road, Virginia Beach, Va. 23451; Home: 1136 York Lane, Virginia Beach, Va. 23451, U.S.A.
Telephone: 804-425-7010 (Office); 804-428-0518 (Home).

Henderson, Sir John Nicholas, K.C.M.G., M.A.; British diplomatist; b. 1 April 1919, London; s. of Prof. Sir Hubert Henderson; m. Mary Barber 1951; one d.; ed. Stowe School and Hertford Coll., Oxford.
Assistant Private Sec. to British Foreign Sec. 44-47; served in British Embassies in Washington, Athens, Vienna, Santiago; Principal Sec. to Foreign Sec. 63-65; Minister, Madrid 65-69; Amb. to Poland 69-72, to Fed. Germany 72-75, to France 75-.
Leisure interests: tennis, gardening, dogs.
Publs. *Prince Eugen* (biography); various articles and stories in *Horizon*, *New Writing*, *History Today*.
British Embassy, rue du Faubourg-St.-Honoré 35, 75008 Paris, France; School House, Combe, Newbury, Berks.; and 6 Fairholt Street, London, S.W.7, England.

Henderson, Julia, M.A., PH.D.; American international official; b. 15 Aug. 1915, Du Quoin, Ill.; d. of Frank and Agnes Youngber Henderson; ed. Univs. of Illinois and Minnesota, and Littauer School of Public Admin., Harvard Univ.
Research Assistant, Social Science Research Council; Technical Adviser to Unemployment Compensation Div., Social Security Board; Lecturer in political science, Wellesley Coll.; worked in London with Preparatory Comm. of UN 45-46; Chief, Policy Div., UN Bureau of Finance 45-50; Dir. UN Div. of Social Welfare, Dept. of Econ. and Social Affairs 50-54, Dir. Bureau of Social Affairs 55-67; Assoc. Commr. and Dir. of Tech. Co-operation Operations for UN 67-70; Sec.-Gen. Int. Planned Parenthood Fed. (IPPF) Feb. 71-; mem. Council on Foreign Relations, U.S. Nat. Acad. of Public Admin.; mem. Comm. of the Churches on Int. Affairs, WCC; one of the founders of UN International School, New York 47, Chair. of Board of Trustees 54-71; mem. council of Soc. for Int. Devt.; Phi Beta Kappa Award, Rene Sand Award of the Int. Council of Social Welfare 72; Hon. LL.D. (Smith Coll.), Hon. D.Hum.Litt. (Rider Coll.), Hon. D.H. (Silliman Univ., Philippines).
Leisure interests: theatre, ballet, reading, golf, gardening.
International Planned Parenthood Federation, 18-20 Lower Regent Street, London, S.W.1; Home: 44 Cadogan Square, London, S.W.1, England.
Telephone: 01-839-2911 (Office); 01-584-7991 (Home).

Henderson, Loy Wesley, B.A.; American diplomatist; b. 28 June 1892, Rogers, Ark.; s. of Rev. George Milton Henderson and Mary May Davis; m. Elise Maria Heinrichson 1930; ed. Northwestern Univ., and Denver Univ. Law School.

Mem. Inter-Allied Comm. to Germany for repatriation of prisoners of war 19, mem. American Red Cross Comm. to W. Russia and Baltic States 19-20; in charge A.R.C., Germany 20-21; Vice-Consul, Dublin 22, Queenstown 23; Dept. of State 25; Third Sec. Riga, Kovno and Tallin 27; Second Sec. 29; Dept. of State 30; Moscow 34, First Sec. and intermittently Chargé d'Affaires 35-38; Asst. Chief Div. of European Affairs, Dept. of State 38; Inspector of Diplomatic Missions and Consular Offices 42-43; Counsellor and Chargé d'Affaires U.S.S.R. 42; Minister to Iraq 43-45; Dir. Near-Eastern, South Asian and African Affairs, Dept. of State 45-48; Ambassador to India, also Minister to Nepal 48-51; Ambassador to Iran 51-55; Deputy Under-Sec. of State for Admin. 55-61; Career Ambassador 56; U.S. Observer Baghdad Pact Confs. 56, 57, 59; Gov. American Red Cross 59-61; Prof. of Int. Relations and Dir. Center of Diplomacy and Foreign Policy, The American Univ. 61-68; Pres. Washington Inst. of Foreign Affairs 61-73, Chair. of Board 73-; Dept. of State Distinguished Service Award 54, Pres. Award for Distinguished Federal Civilian Service 58; Hon. LL.D. (Northwestern Univ., Bates Coll., Univ. of Ark., Wade Univ.). 2727 29th Street, N.W., Washington, D.C. 20008, U.S.A.

Telephone: 202-462-4932.

Hendricks, Sterling Brown, B.S., M.S., PH.D.; American physical and biological scientist; b. 13 April 1902, Texas; s. of James G. Hendricks and Martha Daisy Hendricks; m. Edith Ochiltree 1932; one d.; ed. Univ. of Arkansas, Kansas State Univ. and Calif. Inst. of Technology.

U.S. Dept. of Agriculture, basic research in chem., physics, mineralogy, soil science, plant nutrition, biophysics, control of flowering 28-; Chief Scientist, Mineral Nutrition Lab., U.S. Dept. of Agriculture 58-; Hillebrand Award, American Chemical Soc. 37; Day Medal, Geological Soc. of America 52; President's Civilian Service Award 60; Rockefeller Public Service Award 60; Hales Award, American Soc. of Plant Physiologists 62; Hoblitzelle Agricultural Award 64; Certificate of Merit, Botanical Soc. of America 65; Hon. LL.D. (Univ. of Arkansas) 46; Hon. Sc.D. (Univ. of N. Carolina) 62.

Leisure interest: mountaineering.
Office: Plant Industry Station, Beltsville, Md.; Home: 118 Dale Drive. Silver Spring, Md., U.S.A.

Hendy, Sir Philip, M.A.; British art historian; b. 27 Sept. 1900; ed. Westminster School and Christ Church, Oxford.

Asst. to the Keeper and Lecturer, Wallace Collection, London 23-27; studied Italian painting, Italy 27-30; Curator of Paintings Museum of Fine Arts, Boston, Mass., U.S.A. 30-33; Dir. City Art Gallery Leeds and Temple Newsam 34-45; Slade Prof. of Fine Art Oxford Univ. 36-46; Dir. Nat. Gallery 46-67; Artistic Adviser to Israel Museum, Jerusalem 68-71; now revising catalogue of paintings, Isabella Stewart Gardner Museum, Boston, Mass., U.S.A.; Pres. Int. Council of Museums 59-65; art critic *Daily Herald* 23-26, *New Statesman* 26-27, *London Mercury* 34-36, *Britain Today* 45-52.

Publs. *Hours in the Wallace Collection* 26, *Wallace Collection: Catalogue of Paintings and Drawings* 28, *Isabella Stewart Gardner Museum (Boston) Catalogue of Paintings and Drawings* 31 (revised edn. 74), *Matthew Smith* 44, *Giovanni Bellini* 45, *Spanish Painting* 46, *The National Gallery* 55, *Masaccio* 57, *Piero della Francesca and the Early Renaissance* 68.

Whistlers Barn, Great Haseley, Oxford, England.

Henize, Karl Gordon; American astronaut; b. 17 Oct. 1926, Cincinnati, Ohio; s. of Fred R. Henize and Mabel C. Redmon; m. Caroline Weber 1953; two s. two d.; ed. Univ. of Virginia and Univ. of Michigan.

United States Navy 44-46; Observer Univ. of Mich. Observatory 48-51; Carnegie Fellow, Mount Wilson Observatory 54-56; Senior Astronomer, Smithsonian Astrophysical Observatory 56-59; Assoc. Prof. of Astronomy, Northwestern Univ. 59-64, Prof. of Astronomy 64-72; Adjunct Prof., Dept. of Astronomy, Univ. of Tex., Austin 73-; Principal Investigator, Skylab Ultra-Violet Astronomy Experiment 65-76; selected as scientist-astronaut by NASA 67; mem. *Apollo XV* support crew 70-71; mem. Skylab Support Crew 72-74; mem. Amer. Astronomical Soc., Royal Astronomical Soc., Int. Astronomical Union, Astronomical Soc. of Pacific; Robert Gordon Memorial Award 68; NASA Medal for Exceptional Scientific Achievement 74.

Leisure interests: scuba diving, tennis, handball, shell collecting, stamp collecting, astronomy.
Publs. more than 50 articles on astronomical research specializing in novae, planetary nebulae, emission-line stars and ultra-violet spectroscopy.
NASA Johnson Space Center, Houston, Tex. 77058; and 18630 Point Lookout Drive, Houston, Tex. 77058, U.S.A.

Henkel, Konrad, DR. ING.; German chemist and business executive; b. 25 Oct. 1915, Düsseldorf; s. of Dr. Hugo and Gerda Henkel née Janssen; m. Gabriele Hünermann 1955; one s. three d.; ed. Technische Hochschule, Munich and Brunswick and Freiburg Univs.

Assistant to Prof. Dr. Richard Kuhn, Max-Planck Inst. for Medical Research, Heidelberg 40-46; Man. Dir. Henkel and Cie. GmbH, Düsseldorf 56-69, Chair. Supervisory Board 61-; Chair. Board of Management Henkel GmbH 61-74, Vice-Chair. Supervisory Board 61-74; Pres. and Chief Exec. Officer Henkel KGaA 75-, Vice-Chair. Cttee. of Shareholders 75-; Vice-Chair. Supervisory Board Deutche Gold- und Silberscheideanstalt, Frankfurt; Pres. Industry Club e.V., Düsseldorf, Steuben-Schurz Asscn. in Düsseldorf e.V.; mem. Board Asscn. of Chem. Industries in Germany 76-; mem. Admin. Council of Cultural Cttee. of Fed. Asscn. of German Industry 62-; Dr. rer. nat. h.c. (Univ. of Düsseldorf).

Leisure interest: golf.
Postfach 1.100, Düsseldorf 1, Federal Republic of Germany.

Henle, Günter, DR.JUR.; German businessman; b. 3 Feb. 1899, Würzburg; s. of Dr. Julius von Henle and Lida Albert; m. Anne-Liese Küpper 1933; two s. one d.; ed. Würzburg and Marburg Univs.

Diplomatic service 21-36; Partner and Gen. Man. Klöckner & Co., Duisburg 37-; Hon. Chair. Board of Dirs. Klöckner-Werke A.G., Klöckner-Humboldt-Deutz A.G., Allianz Versicherungs A.G.; founder and owner G. Henle Musikverlag; Pres. German Soc. for Foreign Policy 55-73, Hon. Pres. 73-; mem. Frankfurt Econ. Council 47-49; mem. Bundestag 49-53; mem. ECSC Common Assembly 52-53; Hon. Dr.Phil. (Cologne) 64.

Leisure interests: music, collecting old Dutch masters, golf.
Publs. *Weggenosse des Jahrhunderts* 67, *Three Spheres* (American edn.) 71.
Klöcknerhaus, 41 Duisburg, Federal Republic of Germany.
Telephone: 181.

Henle, Jörg Alexander; German business executive; b. 12 May 1934, Aachen; s. of Dr. Günter (*q.v.*) and Anne-Liese Henle; m. Eduarda Linares Reyes de Velasco 1963; two s. two d.; ed. Cologne, Munich, Princeton (N.J.), Stanford, Geneva and Berlin Univs.
Joined Klöckner-Werke AG. 62; Man. Establecimientos

Klöckner S.A., Buenos Aires 64-65; Deputy mem. directorate of Klöckner Mannstaedt-Werke, Troisdorf 65-67; mem. directorate, Klöckner-Werke AG, Hütte Bremen 67-68; mem. Man. Board Klöckner-Werke AG 68-71; Chair. and Man. Partner Klöckner & Co. 71-; mem. Board of Dirs. Deutsche Bank AG, Klöckner-Werke AG, SKF Kugellagerfabriken G.m..b.H.
Leisure interests: plastic arts, theatre, music.
Klöckner & Co., 41 Duisburg 1, Mülheimer Strasse 54, Postfach 21, Federal Republic of Germany.
Telephone: 181.

Henley, Sir Douglas Owen, K.C.B.; British civil servant; b. 5 April 1919; ed. London School of Econs. Joined H.M. Treasury 46; Financial Counsellor, Tokyo and Singapore 56-59; Asst. Under-Sec. of State, Dept. of Econ. Affairs 64-69, Deputy Under-Sec. of State 69; Deputy Sec. H.M. Treasury 69-72, Second Perm. Sec. 72-76; Comptroller and Auditor-Gen. Feb. 76-.
Exchequer and Audit Department, Audit House, Victoria Embankment, London E.C.4., England.

Henley, William Ballentine, A.M., J.D., M.S. (P.A.), LL.D., SC.D., L.H.D.; American lecturer, church administrator, educationist and lawyer; b. 19 Sept. 1905; ed. Univ. of Southern California and Yale Univ.
Attorney; Pres. United Church of Religious Science; Asst. to Co-ordination Officer, Univ. of Southern Calif. 28-29 and 30-33; Public Speaking Instructor, American Inst. of Banking 28-29; Dir. of Religious Education, First Methodist Episcopal Church, New Haven, Conn. 29-30; Exec. Sec. Women's Civic Conf. University of Southern Calif. 30-36; Asst. to Dean, School of Govt., Univ. of Southern Calif. 33-35, Acting Dean and Acting Co-ordinating Officer 35-37, Dir. Inst. of Govt. 35-37, Dir. of Co-ordination and Assoc. Prof. of Public Admin. 37-40; Pres. Calif. Coll. of Medicine 40-65; Provost, Univ. of Calif., Irvine, Calif. Coll. of Medicine 65-; Pres. Rotary Club Los Angeles 55-56; Gov. District 528 Rotary Int. 59-60; Chair. Host Club Exec. Cttee. for Rotary Int. Convention 62; mem. Los Angeles, Calif. and American Bar Asscns., Asscn. of American Medical Schools, Acad. of Political and Social Sciences, Nat. Education Asscn.; Calif. Governor's Medical Advisory Cttee. on Civil Defense 45-48, American Management Asscn., American Asscn. for History of Medicine, Western Interstate Comm. for Higher Education; Past Pres. American Asscn. Osteopathic Colls.; Educational Consultant 56-; Gen. Motors Exec. Speakers Panel 56-; on Board of Los Angeles Community Health Org. and of several charitable orgs.; mem. Defense Orientation Conf. Asscn. 65-; Vice-Pres. Los Angeles Safety Council.
Publs. *The History of the University of Southern California, Man's Great Awakening (Beautiful Mud)* 74-, and many magazine articles.
United Church of Religious Science, 3251 West Sixth Street, Los Angeles, Calif. 90020; Home: 1224 Geneva Street, Glendale, Calif. 91207, U.S.A.
Telephone: 213-388-2181 (Office); 213-245-4406 (Home).

Henneberg, Gerd Michael; German theatre director; b. 14 July 1922; ed. Acad. of Dramatic Art, Leipzig.
Actor, Civic Theatre, Aschaffenburg 40-44, Producer 43-44; Artistic Dir. Civic Theatres Ballenstadt/Harz 46; Asst. Deutsche Theater, Berlin 46; Producer and Actor, National Theatre, Weimar 47-50; Actor, Berlin 53-60; Dir. of Friedrich-Wolf Theatre, Neustrelitz; Gen. Dir. Staatstheater Dresden 62-.
Staatstheater Dresden, Julien-Grimau Allee 27, Dresden A. 1, German Democratic Republic.

Hennessy, James Patrick Ivan, C.M.G., O.B.E.; British diplomatist; b. 23 Dec. 1923; s. of late Richard George Hennessy; m. Patricia Margaret Unwin 1947; one s. (deceased) five d.; ed. Bedford School, Sidney Sussex Coll., Cambridge, London School of Econs.

H.M. Forces, Royal Artillery, Maj. 42-46; H.M. Overseas Service, Basutoland: District Officer 48, Judicial Commr. 53, Sec. of Constitutional Cttee. 57-59, Sec. to Exec. Council 60; High Commr's. Office, Cape Town and Pretoria 61-63; mem. Basutoland Legal Co. 64; Perm. Sec. for External Affairs, Internal Security and Defence and Perm. Sec. to Prime Minister of Lesotho 67, retd. 68; First Sec. U.K. Foreign Office 68; Embassy in Uruguay 70, Chargé d'Affaires 71-72; High Commr. in Uganda 73-.
Leisure interest: travel.
British High Commission, P.O. Box 7070, 10/12 Parliament Avenue, Kampala, Uganda; and Foreign and Commonwealth Office, London, S.W.1, England.
Telephone: 57054 (Kampala); 01-930 8440 (London).

Hennessy, Sir Patrick, Kt.; former British motor executive; b. 18 April 1898.
Royal Inniskilling Fusiliers 14-18; fmr. mem. Advisory Council, Ministry of Aircraft Production; fmr. Chair. and Chief Exec. Ford Motor Co. Ltd. till 68; Chair. Henry Ford and Sons Ltd., Cork, Ireland; Pres., then Deputy Pres. Soc. of Motor Manufacturers and Traders 65-68; Dir. Montego Freeport Ltd.
Larkmead, Theydon Bois, Essex, England.

Henniker-Major, Hon. Sir John Patrick Edward Chandos, K.C.M.G., C.V.O., M.C.; British diplomatist; b. 19 Feb. 1916; ed. Stowe and Trinity Coll., Cambridge. Entered Foreign Service 38; Army Service 40-45; at Embassy, Belgrade 45-46; Asst. Private Sec. to Sec. of State for Foreign Affairs 46-48; Foreign Office 48-50; at Embassy, Buenos Aires 50-52; Counsellor, Foreign Office, Head of Personnel Dept. 52-60; Amb. to Jordan 60-62, to Denmark 62-66; Civil Service Comm. 66-67; Asst. Under-Sec. for African Affairs at Foreign Office 67-68; Dir.-Gen. of the British Council 68-72; Chair. Wates Foundation 72-; Trustee, City Parochial Foundation 73.
11 Campden Hill Road, London, W.8, England.

Henning, Admiral of the Fleet Geraldo de Azevedo; Brazilian naval officer; b. 1917, Rio de Janeiro.
Joined Brazilian Navy 34; Lieut.-Commdr., World War II; fmr. Dir.-Gen. Navy Personnel; Admiral of the Fleet 73; Minister of the Navy 74-.
Ministério da Marinha, Esplanada dos Ministérios, Brasília, Brazil.

Henningsen, Eigil Juel, M.D.; Danish physician; b. 18 July 1906, Copenhagen; s. of Adolf Juel Henningsen and Helga Amalie Christensen; m. Kirsten Ottesen 1959; one s. two d.; ed. Københavns Universitet.
State Epidemiologist, State Serum Inst. 35-40; Deputy Dir.-Gen., Nat. Health Service of Denmark 40-; temporary Dir.-Gen. Danish Red Cross 45; Chair. The Mothers Aid Inst. 45-; Chair. WHO Expert Cttee. on Radiation 62; Gen. Chair. Vth Int. Poliomyelitis Conf., Copenhagen 60; Chair. European Nuclear Energy Agency (ENEA) Health and Safety Cttee. 66; Chair. Nordic Soc. for Radiation Protection; mem. other int. medical cttees.
Leisure interests: music, literature.
Office: National Health Service, St. Kongensgade 1, Copenhagen; Home: Havsgårdsvej 35, Copenhagen-Hellerup, Denmark.

Henningsen, Sven, DR. PHIL.; Danish historian; b. 2 Feb. 1910, Stubbekøbing; s. of Andreas and Christine (Jorgensen) Henningsen; m. Eugenie Henningsen 1964; ed. Københavns Universitet.
Lecturer in Modern History and Political Science, Univ. of Copenhagen 43; Asst. Prof. Univ. of Gothenburg, Sweden 44-45; Visiting Prof. Univ. of Minnesota, U.S.A. 48-49; Prof. of Contemporary History and Political Science, Univ. of Copenhagen 53-, Vice-Chancellor 67-69; Visiting Rockefeller Prof., Univ. of E. Africa 62; Chair. Danish Council for UN 59-65; mem.

Council for European Asscn. of American Studies; Chair. Nordic Asscn. for Study of Int. Relations 67-70, Council for Danish Nat. UNESCO Cttee. 61-69; Chair. Danish Political Science Asscn. 60-69; mem. Council for Danish Inst. of Foreign Policy, Chair. 67-.
Leisure interest: music.
Publs. *The Polish Corridor and Danzig* 36, *The Far East and the Great Powers* 41, *Studies in Economic Liberalism* 44, *The North Atlantic Treaty* 54, *The Foreign Policy of Denmark* 62, *The Twentieth Century* 65, *Atomic Policy 1939-1945* 71, *International Politics* 75.
Dantes Plads 4, Copenhagen V, Denmark.
Telephone: 126507.

Henrichs, Helmut; German theatre director; b. 13 April 1907; ed. Humanistisches Gymnasium and university.
Former Production Asst., Schauspielhaus, Düsseldorf; Theatre Critic, Düsseldorf and Berlin; Producer, Deutsches Theater, Berlin, Staatstheater, Stuttgart, Deutsches Theater, Göttingen; Gen. Intendant Wuppertal; Intendant Bayerisches Staatsschauspiel, Munich.
8 Munich 22, Wurzerstrasse 11, Federal Republic of Germany.

Henriksen, Rein; Norwegian business exec.; b. 17 Dec. 1915; ed. Universitetet i Oslo.
Barrister of Supreme Court of Norway; Nat. Income Tax Comm. 43-45; Norwegian Shipowners' Asscn. 45-47; Legal Dept., Aktieselskapet Borregaard (pulp for paper, oils, detergents, etc.) 47-60, Gen. Dir. 60-; Knight of St. Olav; Grand Cross (Austria); Order of Homayoun (Iran).
Borregaard Hovedgård, Sarpsborg, Norway.

Henrion, Robert; Belgian banker and university professor; b. 23 July 1915, Namur; m. Marie-Louise Ernst 1939; four c.
Barrister, Brussels 38-46; Prof. of Political Economy and Financial Affairs, Univ. Libre de Bruxelles; Vice-Pres. Inst. for European Studies; Pres. Comité de Direction and mem. Conseil Supérieur des Finances, Société Générale de Banque; Minister of Finance 66-68; Chair. Board Société Générale de Banque 71-, also Chair. Exec. Cttee.
Publs. *La structure juridique de l'entreprise et le rôle de son personnel* 57, *Financiers et banquiers* 59, *Aspects juridiques et économiques du Credit à court terme* 59 and 65, *L'abus de puissance économique* 60, *L'entreprise et le progrès social* 63, *Le secret professionel du banquier* 63, *Certains aspects récents de droit économique en Belgique* 68, *L'expérience des lois de pouvoirs exceptionnels* 68.
Société Générale de Banque, 3 Montagne du Parc, 1000 Brussels, Belgium.

Henry, David Dodds, A.M., PH.D.; American educationist; b. 21 Oct. 1905, E. McKeesport, Pa.; s. of F. W. Henry and Myrtle Byerly Henry; m. Sara Koerper 1927; one s.; ed. Pennsylvania State Univ.
Instructor, Pennsylvania State Univ. 25-29; Prof. of English and Dir. of School of Liberal Arts Battle Creek (Mich. Coll.) 29-33; Asst. State Supt. of Public Instruction Lansing (Mich.) 33-35; Prof. of English 35-52; Asst. to Exec. Vice-Pres. Wayne State Univ., Detroit 36-39; Exec. Vice-Pres. 39-45, Pres. 45-52; Exec. Vice-Chancellor, N.Y. Univ. 52-55; Pres. Univ. of Illinois 55-71; Pres. Assoc. Urban Univs. 45-46, Nat. Comm. on Accrediting 56-58; Chair. Joint Cttee. on Educational T.V. 54-55; Vice-Chair. Cttee. on Education Beyond High School 56-57; Pres. Nat. Asscn. State Univs. and Land-Grant Colls. 64-65; Dir. Council for Financial Aid to Education 58-63; Chair. American Council on Education 60-61; mem. Pres. Cttee. on Employment of Physically Handicapped 56-71, Advisory Cttee., Agency for Int. Devt.-Univ. Relations 65-66, 67-69, Advisory

Council Nat. Fund for Medical Educ. 59-71; Trustee, Carnegie Foundation for the Advancement of Teaching 60-71, Cttee. on Educational Television, Carnegie Corpn. 65-67, Inst. Int. Educ. 65-68, Carnegie Comm. on Future Structure and Financing of Higher Educ. 67-73; Pres. Asscn. of American Univs. 67-69; Distinguished Prof. of Higher Educ. 71-74; Chair. Nat. Board on Graduate Educ. 72-75; numerous hon. degrees.
College of Education, University of Illinois, Urbana, Ill. 61801, U.S.A.
Telephone: 333-1535.

Henry, William Robert; British business executive; b. 30 April 1915, Glasgow; s. of William Henry and Sarah Lindsay; m. Esther Macfadyen 1947; two s. one d.; ed. Govan High School, Univ. of London.
With J. & P. Coats Ltd. (later Coats Patons Ltd.), 34-; Head of Financial Div. 55-57, Asst. Accountant 57-63, Dir. J. & P. Coats Ltd. 63-66, Coats Patons Ltd. 66-, Deputy Chair. 70-75, Chair. Oct. 75-.
Leisure interests: sailing, gardening.
70 Monreith Road, Newlands, Glasgow, G43 2PE; Hawkstone Lodge, Ascog, Rothesay, Bute, Scotland.
Telephone: 041-649 2107; 0700-2729.

Hensel, Witold, PH.D., SC.D.; Polish archaeologist; b. 29 March 1917, Poznań; s. of Maksymilian Hensel and Maria Formanowicz; m. Maria Chmielewska 1941; three s. one d.; ed. Poznań Univ.
Lecturer and Adjunct, Lublin Univ. 44-45, Poznań Univ. 46-50, Prof. 51-56, Dean History Faculty 51-53; Prof. Warsaw Univ. 54-; Dir. Polish Acad. of Sciences Inst. for History of Material Culture 54-; Editor and Founder *Slavia Antiqua* 47-; Editor *Światowit* 65-; has led excavations at Gniezno, Kłecko, Ostrów Tumski of Poznań and Kruszwica (near Inowrocław), Czersk (near Warsaw), Styrmen and Odercy, Bulgaria, and in St.-Jean-Le-Froid, Condorcet and Montaigut, France, Cappacio Vecchia, Italy and Algiers and Tlemcen, Algeria; mem. Council Int. Congress of Prehistoric Sciences 56 and Istituto Italiano di Preistoria e Protostoria 61; Pres. Int. Cttee. of Research for Origin of Towns 62, Int. Congress Slavonic Archaeology 65-67; Vice-Pres. Int. Congress of Slavists 71-; Corresp. mem. Polish Acad. Sciences 65, mem. 73-; Foreign mem. Acad. of Sciences of G.D.R.; State Prize 55, 66; Commander's Cross of Order of Polonia Restituta 71; Medal of 30th Anniversary of People's Poland 74; Commdr. Croce al Merito della Repubblica Italiana 75; Bulgarian Order of Kirill and Methodius, 1st Class.
Leisure interest: arts.
Publs. *Studia nad osadnictwem Wielkopolski wczesnohistorycznej* (Studies of Settlement in Wielkopolska in the Early Historical Period) Vols. I-V 48-72, *Słowianszczyzna wczesnośredniowieczna—Zarys kultury materialnej* (Early Medieval Slav Culture—An outline of Material Culture) 52, 56, 65, *Sztuka społeczeństw paleolitycznych* (The Art of Palaeolithic Societies) 57, *Poznań w zaraniu dziejów* (Poznań in Protohistoric Times) 58, *Najdawniejsze stolice Polski* (Poland's Ancient Capitals) 60, *The Beginnings of the Polish State* 60, *Polska przed tysiącem lat* (Poland a Thousand Years Ago) 60, 64, 67, *Archeologia o początkach miast słowiańskich* (Origins of Slavonic Towns in Light of Archaeology) 63, *Die Slawen im frühen Mittelalter* 65, *La Naissance de la Pologne* 66, *Anfänge der Städte bei den Ost- und Westslawen* 67, *Ziemie Polskie w pradziejach* (Poland in Prehistoric Times) 69, *Archeologia i Prehistoria* (Archaeology and prehistory) 71, *Polska starożytna* (Poland in Ancient Times) 73, *Archeologia Żywa* (Alive Archaeology) 73, *Ur- und Frühgeschichte Polens* 74; Editor *Slavia Antiqua*, *Archaeologia Polona*, *Archaeologia urbium*, *Światowit* and *Polskie Badania Archeologiczne* (Polish Archaeological Researches).
Al. Świerczewskiego 105, 00-140 Warsaw; Home: Marszalkowska 84/92, Ap. 109, 00-514 Warsaw, Poland.

Henshaw, Kenneth Ralph, M.A.; British oil company exec.; b. 1 Nov. 1918, Canterbury; s. of Ralph and Elsie Henshaw; m. Patricia Helen Heath 1953; one d.; ed. King's School, Canterbury and Trinity Coll., Oxford.
Senior Vice-Pres. Sinclair and BP Explorations Inc. 59-63; Regional Man. Exploration Dept., The British Petroleum Co. Ltd. 63-65; Man. Dir. Kuwait Oil Co. Ltd. 65-73; Exec. Deputy Chair. Airwork Services Ltd. 73-; Chair. of Middle East Navigation Aids Service; Dir. Bricomin Exploration Co. Ltd.; mem. Inst. of Petroleum. Leisure interests: golf, tennis, shooting.
8 Parkside, Knightsbridge, London, S.W.1, England. Telephone: 01-235-7596.

Hensley, Stuart K.; American business executive; b. 8 July 1917, Tampa, Fla.; m.; two d.
With Pacific Mutual Life Insurance Co. 37-42; U.S. Navy 42-46; joined the Toni Co. 46, Pres. 57; Vice-Pres. and Dir. The Gillette Co. 58, Pres. June 66; Pres. Warner-Lambert Co. July 67, Chair. of Board and Chief Exec. Officer Oct. 67-73, Chair. Exec. Cttee. 73-; Dir. Jack Winter Inc., N.J. State Chamber of Commerce, Irving Trust Co.
Warner-Lambert Co., Morris Plains, N.J. 07950, U.S.A.

Henze, Hans Werner; German composer and conductor; b. 1 July 1926, Gütersloh; s. of Franz Henze and Margarete Geldmacher; ed. Staatsmusikschule, Brunswick, Kirchenmusikalisches Institut, Heidelberg.
Musical Director Heinz Hilpert's Deutsches Theater in Constance 48; Artistic Dir. Ballet of the Hessian State Theatre in Wiesbaden 50; living in Italy as an independent artist since 53; Prof. of Composition, Mozarteum, Salzburg 61; Robert Schumann Prize 52, North-Rhine-Westphalia Art Prize 56, Prix d'Italia 54, Sibelius Gold Medal, Harriet Cohen Awards, London 56, Music Critics Prize, Buenos Aires 58, Kunstpreis, Berlin, Niedersächsischer Kunstpreis 62; Dr. Mus. (Univ. of Edinburgh) 71.
Leisure interests: poetry, botany.
Composition: Operas: *Das Wundertheater, Boulevard Solitude, König Hirsch, Der Prinz von Homburg, Elegy for Young Lovers* 61, *Der Junge Lord* 64, *Die Bassariden* 65; Radio Operas: *Ein Landarzt, Das Ende einer Welt*; Ballets: *Jack Pudding, Tancred und Cantylene, Variationen, Labyrinth, The Idiot, Apoll und Hyazinth, Ondine*; Oratorio: *Novae de Infinito Laudes* 62; Cantatas: *Being Beauteous* 63, *Ariosi* 63, *Cantata della Fiaba Estrema* 63; Choral works: *Chorfantasie* 64, *Musen Siziliens* 66; Oratorio: *Medusa* 68; six Symphonies, Violin and Piano and Violoncello Concertos, Double Concerto for Oboe, Harp and Strings, two String Quartets, Wind Quintet, *Kammermusik 1958* (tenor and ensemble), *El Cimarron* 69, *The tedious way to the place of Natasha Ungeheuer* 70, *Heliogabalus Imperator* 71, *La Cubana* 72, *Voices* 73, *Tristan* 74, *Ragtime and Habanera* 75; film music for *Muriel* etc.
La Leprara, 00047 Marino, Rome, Italy.

Hepburn, Audrey; American actress; b. 4 May 1929; m. 1st Mel Ferrer 1954 (dissolved 1968), one s.; m. 2nd Dr. Andrea Dotti 1969, one s.; ed. Arnhem Conservatoire.
Studied dancing in Amsterdam and London; ballet appearances in London; played in the British films *Laughter in Paradise, The Lavender Hill Mob, Young Wives' Tale*, etc., and in American films *Roman Holiday, Sabrina Fair, War and Peace, Funny Face, Love in the Afternoon, The Nun's Story, Green Mansions, Breakfast at Tiffany's, Paris when it Sizzles, The Children's Hour, Charade, My Fair Lady, How to Steal a Million Dollars and Live Happily Ever After, Two for the Road, Wait Until Dark, Robin and Marian*; stage appearances in *Gigi* and *Ondine*; Acad. award for *Roman Holiday*.
c/o Kurt Frings, 9440 Santa Monica Boulevard, Beverly Hills, Calif. 90210, U.S.A.

Hepburn, Katharine; American actress; b. 9 Nov. 1909.
Plays in which she has appeared include *The Lake, Philadelphia Story, Without Love, As You Like It, The Millionairess, The Rainmaker, Taming of the Shrew, Measure for Measure, Anthony and Cleopatra, Coco, A Matter of Gravity*, N.Y. 76, etc.; films include *Bill of Divorcement, Christopher Strong, Sylvia Scarlett, Morning Glory, Little Women, Quality Street, Dragon Seed, Pat and Mike, Adams' Rib, Philadelphia Story, Summertime, The Rainmaker, Suddenly Last Summer, Long Day's Journey into Night, Woman of the Year, African Queen, Guess Who's Coming to Dinner, The Lion in Winter, The Madwoman of Chaillot, The Trojan Woman, The Glass Menagerie, Love Among the Ruins, Rooster Cogburn*; Gold Medal Venice 34, N.Y. Critics' Award 40 and 50, Acad. Awards for *Morning Glory, Guess Who's Coming to Dinner*.
P.O. Box 17-154, West Hartford, Conn. 06117, U.S.A.

Heppel, Leon A., PH.D., M.D.; American biochemist; b. 20 Oct. 1912, Granger, Utah; s. of Leon George Heppel and Rosa Zimmer; m. Adelaide Keller 1944; two s. ed; Univ. of Calif. at Berkeley and Univ. of Rochester, N.Y.
Commissioned Officer, U.S. Public Health Service 42; Stationed at Nat. Insts. of Health, Bethesda, Md. 42-67; Prof. of Biochemistry, Cornell Univ. 67-; mem. Nat. Acad. of Sciences; Hillebrand Award, American Chem. Soc. (Washington Section) 60.
Leisure interests: music appreciation, reading.
Publs. approximately 100 scientific papers in biochemistry since 1939.
Cornell University, Ithaca, N.Y. 14853, U.S.A.

Hepting, George Henry, PH.D.; American forest pathologist; b. 1 Sept. 1907, Brooklyn, N.Y.; s. of George Hepting and Lena Schuler; m. Anna J. Love 1934; ed. Manual Training High School, Brooklyn, N.Y., Brooklyn Technical High School and Cornell Univ.
Assistant Instructor in Pathology, Cornell Univ. 29-30; Field Asst., Div. of Forest Pathology, Bureau of Plant Industry, U.S. Dept. of Agriculture (U.S.D.A.), Mass. 31-32, Louisiana 32-33, Asst. Pathologist 33-37, Assoc. Pathologist 37-40, Pathologist 40-46, Senior Pathologist 46-53; Chief, Forest Disease Research, Southeastern Forest Experimental Station, Forest Service 53-62, Chief Research Scientist 62-71; Adjunct Prof. of Forestry and Plant Pathology, North Carolina State Univ.; Fellow, Soc. of American Foresters, American Phytopathological Soc.; mem. Nat. Acad. of Sciences; U.S.D.A. Superior Service Award 54, Barrington Moore Award of Soc. of American Foresters 63, U.S.D.A. Special Merit Award 67, Southern Forest Pathological Award 67, Int. Shade Tree Conf. Citation Award 72, Weyerhauser Award (for writings on forest history) 75.
Leisure interests: mineral collecting, gem-cutting, boating, golf.
Publs. *Plant-Disease Development and Control* 68, *Forest and Shade Tree Diseases of the United States* 71; and 150 scientific articles.
11 Maplewood Road, Asheville, N.C. 28804, U.S.A.

Herb, Raymond George, PH.D.; American emeritus professor of physics; b. 22 Jan. 1908, Navarino, Wis., s. of Joseph and Annie Herb; m. Anne Williamson 1945; two s. three d.; ed. Univ. of Wis.
Research Assoc. in Physics, Univ. of Wis. 35-39, Research Assoc. and Asst. Prof. in Physics 39-40, Assoc. Prof. 41-45, Prof. 45-61, Charles Mendenhall Prof. of Physics 61-72; Pres. and Chair. of Board Nat. Electrostatics Corpn. 65-; mem. Nat. Acad. of Sciences; Dr. h.c., Univs. of Basle and São Paulo; Tom W. Bonner Award 68.
Publ. *Van de Graaf Generators in Handbuch der Physik XLIV* 59.

National Electrostatics Corporation, Graber Road, P.O. Box 117, Middleton, Wis. 53562; Home: P.O. Box 223A, Rural Route 1, Mazomie, Wis. 53560, U.S.A.
Telephone: 608-836-6091 (Office).

Herbert, Jean Jules M. E.; French surgeon; b. 16 July 1905, St. Médard/Ille; ed. Lycée de Rennes and Univ. de Paris à la Sorbonne.
Head of clinic, Faculty of Medicine, Paris; Surgeon, Hospital Aix-les-Bains 36-; Chief Surgeon of hospitals Aix-les-Bains 41-; founder surgical centre for osteo-articular surgery and rheumatology; Pres. Centre de Recherches du Rhumatisme 48-; founder of the first French bone bank 48; Editor-in-Chief *Rhumatologie*; mem. Acad. of Surgery, and Int. Soc. of Surgery; Pres. French Soc. of Orthopaedic Surgery and Traumatology; mem. numerous socs. including Royal Soc., London, Académie Nationale de Médecine; Officier Légion d'Honneur, Croix de Guerre, Officier de la Santé publique.
Publ. *Chirurgie du rhumatisme.*
11 boulevard de la Roche du Roi, 73100 Aix-les-Bains, France.
Telephone: 35-07-01.

Herbert, Zbigniew; Polish poet, essayist and playwright; b. 29 Oct. 1924, Lvov; s. of Bolestaw Herbert and Maria Kaniak; ed. Cracow, Torun and Warsaw Univs. Co-editor *Jwórczość* 55-65, *Poezja* 65-68; mem. Polish Writers' Asscn. 55-, Gen. Board Foreign Cttee.; Prize from Polish Inst. of Sciences and Arts in America; Jurzykowski Prize, Lenau Int. Prize for European Literature, Vienna 65, Knight's Cross of Order Polonia Restituta 74.
Publs. Poetry includes: *Struna światła* (A String of Light) 56, *Hermes, pies i gwiazda* (Hermes, a Dog and a Star) 57. *Studium przedmiotu* (The Study of an Object) 61, *Napis* (The Inscription) 69, *Wiersze Zebrane* (Collected Verse) 71, *Pan Cogito* (Mr. Cogito) 74, *Selected Poems* (in English and German); radio plays and drama include: *Dramaty* (Dramas) 70, *Inny pokój* (The Other Room), *Jaskinia filozofów* (Cave of Philosophers), *Lalek*; essays: *Barbarzyńca w ogrodzie* (A Barbarian in the Garden) 63.
Krakowskie Przedmieście 87/89, Warsaw; Home: ul. Promenady 21m 4, 00-778, Warsaw, Poland.
Telephone: 41-26-77.

Herbig, George Howard, PH.D.; American astronomer; b. 2 Jan. 1920, Wheeling, W. Va.; s. of George A. Herbig and Glenna Howard; m. 1st Delia McMullin 1943, three s. one d.; m. 2nd Hannelore Tillmann 1968; ed. Univ. of Calif. (Los Angeles and Berkeley).
Martin Kellogg Fellow, Univ. of Calif. 46-48; Fellow, Nat. Research Council 48-49; Junior Astronomer, Lick Observatory, Mount Hamilton, Calif. 48-50, Asst. Astronomer 50-55, Assoc. Astronomer 55-60, Astronomer 60-; Asst. Dir. Lick Observatory 60-63, Acting Dir. 70-71; Prof. of Astronomy, Univ. of Calif. (Santa Cruz) 67-; Visiting Prof. and lecturer Chicago 59, Mexico 61, Observatoire de Paris 65, Max-Planck-Institut für Astronomie, Heidelberg 69, Stockholm 73; Sigma Xi Nat. Lecturer 72-73; Henry Norris Russell Lecturer, Amer. Astronomical Soc. 75-; lectured in U.S.S.R. and Poland under exchange agreement, U.S.-U.S.S.R. Acads. of Science 65; U.S. Nat. Science Foundation Senior Postdoctoral Fellow 65: mem. Nat. Acad. of Sciences, American Acad. of Arts and Sciences; Corresp. mem. Société scientifique Royale de Liège, Max-Planck Inst. für Astronomie, Heidelberg; mem. numerous boards, comms., consultancies, etc.; Warner Prize, American Astronomical Soc. 55; medal from Univ. of Liège 69.
Leisure interests: none.
Publs. Editor of and contributor to *Non-Stable Stars* 57, *Spectroscopic Astrophysics* 70; approximately 180 scientific papers, articles and reviews.

Lick Observatory, University of California, Santa Cruz, Calif. 95064, U.S.A.
Telephone: 408-429-2447.

Herbst, Axel, LL.D.; German diplomatist and former European Econ. Community official; b. 1918; ed. Univs. of Berlin, Cologne and Münster, Acad. of Int. Law, The Hague, and Law Society's School of Law, London.
German Foreign Service 51, German Embassy, Washington; Head, North American Desk, Fed. Ministry of Foreign Affairs 57-60; Dep. Exec. Sec. Comm. of the European Economic Community (E.E.C.) 60-63, Dir.-Gen. External Relations 63-68; Ministerial Dir. and Head of Foreign Trade and Devt. Div. Fed. Ministry of Foreign Affairs 69-73; Amb., Perm. Rep. to UN, Geneva 73-.
28D Chemin du Petit Saconnex, 1211 Geneva 19, Switzerland.
Telephone: 33-50-00.

Herdal, Harald; Danish author; b. 1900; ed. primary schools.
Publs. *Nyt Sind* 29, *Eros og Doden* 31, *Tirsdag* 32, *Bisser* 33, *Nøgene Digte* 33, *Man skal jo leve* 34, *En lidt almindelig Historie* 34, *Løg* 35, *Den første Verden* 36, *Der er noget ivejen* 36, *Mennesket* 37, *Mens vi blir voxne* 37, *En Egn af Landet* 39, *Digte gennem ti Aar* 40, *Blomstrende Tjørne* 41, *Tusmørke* 43, *Nye Digte* 44, *Barndom, Erindringer I* 44, *De unge Aar, Erindringer* II 45, *Læreaar, Erindringer III* 46, *Digte i Vinteren* 46, *Digte 1929-1949, Ukuelige Menneske* 49, *I berøring med livet* 50, *Drømmeren* 51, *Skyede Sommerdage* 52, *Guldspurven og Sølvfuglen* 53, *Jammersminde* 53, *Rast undervejs* 54, *Elise* 55, *Dagens går* 55, *Grevinde Danner* 56, *Det største* 57, *The Tin Boxes* 58; biography: *Danish Authors* 52, *Hegnets Nattergal* 60, *Moderne dansk for udlaendige* 63, *Den Danske Sommer* 63, *Traelene i Norden* 64, *Bisser* 64, *Udvalgte Fortaellinger* 67, *Bøger og pottrætter* 70, *Arbejdsdr, erindringer IV* 70, *En bibliotekslåners vandringer* 71.
Folehavej 23, 2970 Hørsholm, Denmark.
Telephone: 862457.

Héreil, Georges Jules Bernard Victor, LL.D.; French aviation and automobile executive; b. 28 Aug. 1909, Paris; s. of Charles and Henriette Héreil (née Hoïdn); m. Fernande Gilot 1939; ed. Paris Law Faculty.
Honorary Liquidator Paris Commercial Court; following merger of SNCASE and SNCASO Pres. and Dir.-Gen. Sud-Aviation 46-62, Hon. Chair. 62-; Pres. and Dir.-Gen. Papeteries de la Chapelle, Hon. Chair. 63; Hon. Pres. Union Syndicale des Industries Aéronautiques; Founder-Pres. Asscn. Int. des Constructeurs de Matériel Aéro-nautiques; Pres. Lehman Bros. Int., Hon. Chair. 63; Chair. Gen. Man. Chrysler France 63-71; Board of Dirs. Chrysler France, Chrysler España, Chrysler United Kingdom, Hewlett Packard, France; Hon. Pres. Board of Chrysler Int.; Pres. Supervisory Council Soc. Agache-Willot; Commdr. Légion d'Honneur and Italian, Finnish, Swedish, Belgian, Dutch and German orders; Médaille de l'Aéronautique.
Leisure interest: piano.
22 quai de la Mégisserie, 75001 Paris, France; Home Plateau de Frontenex 9B, 1208, Geneva, Switzerland.
Telephone: Paris 231-33-15.

Herforth, Lieselott; German physicist and politician; b. 1916.
Professor of Experimental Physics, Dresden Technical Univ.; mem. Council of State; mem. Sozialistische Einheitspartei Deutschlands.
Abteilung für experimentalische Physik, Technische Universität, Dresden, German Democratic Republic.

Hering, Gerhard F.; German theatrical director; b. 28 Oct. 1908 Rogasen; ed. Humanistisches Gymnasium, Stettin, Univs. of Berlin and Heidelberg.
Assistant, Preussisches Staatstheater Berlin; joined

Magdeburgische Zeitung 33, theatre critic and literary editor 34-37; theatre critic *Kölnische Zeitung* 37-42; forced to resign for political reasons; editor *Vision* 46-48; chief producer Deutsches Theater, Konstanz 46-50; Dir. Otto-Falckenberg-Schauspielschule der Kammerspiele, Munich 50-52; chief opera and drama producer, Württembergische Staatstheater, Stuttgart 52-54; free-lance writer and producer for radio, television and theatre in Munich, Stuttgart, Frankfurt, Göttingen 54-60; Head of W.D.R.—Studios Kultur, Düsseldorf 60-61; Dir. Landestheater, Darmstadt 61-; Hon. Prof. Theaterwissenschaft, Univ. of Giessen 67-; productions have included plays of Sophocles, Euripides, Goethe, Schiller, Grillparzer, Lessing, Gerhart Hauptmann, Georg Kaiser, Konrad Wünsche, Sartre, Genet; mem. PEN-Zentrum of German Fed. Republic, Deutsche Akad. für Sprache und Dichtung; Pres. Deutsche Akad. der Darstellenden Künste.

Publs. include *Porträts und Deutungen—Von Herder zu Hofmannsthal* 48, *Klassische Liebespaare* 48, 50, *Ein Brunnen des Lebens* 50, *Gerhart Hauptmann* 55, *Der Ruf zur Leidenschaft* 59, *Ein grosser Herr: Das Leben des Fürsten Pückler* (with Vita Huber) 69; introductions and contributions to numerous books and texts.

Landestheater Darmstadt, 61 Darmstadt, Postfach 725, Federal Republic of Germany.

Telephone: 122005.

Herlitz, Nils, DR.PHIL., DR.JUR. h.c.; Swedish jurist; b. 7 Aug. 1888, Stockholm; s. of Karl Herlitz and Gerda Fredholm; *m.* Gurli Lindström 1913 (died 1967); four *s.* one *d.*; ed. Uppsala Univ.

Prof. of Public Law Stockholm Univ. 27-55; lectured American Univs. 38; Editor *Nordisk Tidskrift* 21-46; *Förvaltningsrättslig Tidskrift* 38-55; Senator 39-55; Pres. Nordic Council 55; Conservative.

Publs. (over 200) include: *Svensk stadsförvaltning på 1830-talet* 24, *Grunddragen av svenska statsskickets historia* 28, *Om lagstiftning* 30, *Svensk självstyrelse* 33, *Riksdagens finansmakt* 34, *Föreläsningar i förvaltningsrätt* 37-49, *Sweden, A Modern Democracy* 39, *Svensk frihet* 43, *Förvaltningsrättsliga grunddrag* 43, *Förvaltningsförfarandet* 46, *Svenskt författningsliv* 47, *Svenska statsrättens grunder* 48, *Nordisk offentlig rätt* 58-63, *Swedish Administrative Law* 59, *Tidsbilder* 65, *Elements of Nordic Public Law* 69.

Eskadervägen 16, 18354 Täby, Sweden.

Telephone: Stockholm 7563248.

Hernández Acosta, Valentin; Venezuelan engineer; b. 1925, San Fernando de Apure; ed. Cen. Univ. of Venezuela, London School of Econs.

Ambassador to Libya, Tunisia and Morocco, Romania and Austria; Minister of Mines and Hydrocarbons 74-; Pres. OPEC 75.

Ministerio de Minas e Hidrocarburos, Caracas, Venezuela.

Hernández Colón, Rafael, A.B., LL.B.; Puerto Rican lawyer and politician; b. 24 Oct. 1936, Ponce; s. of Rafael Hernández Matos and Dorinda Colón Clavell; *m.* Lila Mayoral 1959; three *s.* one *d.*; ed. Valley Forge Mil. Acad., Wayne, Pa., Johns Hopkins Univ., Univ. of Puerto Rico Law School.

Private law practice 59; Assoc. Commr. of Public Service 60-62; Lecturer in Law, Catholic Univ. of Puerto Rico 61-65; Sec. of Justice 65-67; Senator at Large, Popular Democratic Party 68; Pres. of Senate 69-72; Pres. of Popular Democratic Party 69-; Gov. of Puerto Rico Nov. 72-; Trustee Carnegie Foundation for Int. Peace; mem. Inter Amer. Bar Asscn.; Dr. h.c. Johns Hopkins Univ., Catholic Univ. of Puerto Rico.

Publs. *Text on Civil Procedure* 68, and many articles on topics of law.

Office of the Governor, La Fortaleza, San Juan 00901, Puerto Rico.

Telephone: 723-0090.

Hernández Ochoa, Lic. Rafael; Mexican politician; b. 1915, Vega de la Torre, Ver; ed. Univs. of Veracruz and Mexico.

Former Agent of the Public Ministry and judge in various towns in the province of Veracruz; subsequently Pres. Nat. Cattle Confed.; Dir. of Population, Ministry of the Interior; Private Sec. to Luis Echeverria; Dir. of Political and Social Investigations; Under-Sec. for the Interior 64-70; Sec. of Labour and Social Security 70-72; mem. Chamber of Deputies 73-; State Gov., Veracruz 75-.

Oficina del Governador del Estado, Veracruz, Mexico.

Hernelius, (John) Allan, LL.B.; Swedish journalist; b. 19 March 1911, Tidaholm; s. of A. J. and Elsa (Myrsten) Hernelius; *m.* Jeanette von Heidenstam 1957; ed. Stockholm Univ.

Sec. Swedish Asscn. of Retail Grocers 39, Man. Dir. 41; Vice-Man. Dir. Swedish Retail Fed. 43; Man. Dir. Swedish Newspaper Publishers' Asscn. 45; Asst. Chief Editor *Svenska Dagbladet* 49, Chief Editor 55-70; Adviser, U.N. Conf., Geneva 48; mem. Psychological Defence Cttee. 49; Pres. Swedish Cttee., Int. Press Inst. 51-71; mem. of Board, Royal Defence Coll. 52-, Swedish Radio and Television 53-70, Stockholm Stock Exchange, *Svenska Dagbladet* 56-; Chair. Stockholm Section, Conservative Party 53-55; Chair. Int. Press Inst. Exec. Board 62-64; mem. UN Cttee. of Disarmament; mem. of Parl. 62-.

Home: Styrmansgatan 1, Stockholm Ö, Sweden.

Telephone: 62-07-05.

Heron, Patrick; British painter; b. 30 Jan. 1920, Leeds, Yorks.; s. of T. M. and Eulalie Heron (née Davies); *m.* Delia Reiss 1945; two *d.*; ed. Slade School, London.

Art Critic *New English Weekly* 45-47, *New Statesman and Nation* 47-50; London corresp. *Arts* New York 55, resigned and ceased writing 58, teacher of painting Cen. School of Arts and Crafts, London 53-55; since 47 fifty one-man exhbns. in London, New York, Zürich, Edinburgh, Oslo, Rio de Janeiro, Buenos Aires, Santiago, Lima, Caracas, Toronto, Minneapolis, Melbourne, Montreal, Perth, Sydney and Dublin, retrospective exhbns. Wakefield City Art Gallery 52, Demarco Gallery Edinburgh 67, Museum of Modern Art, Oxford 68; one-man shows at São Paulo Bienal 54, 65, Whitechapel Art Gallery, London 72 and numerous group exhbns. in Europe and America, many organized by British Council; paintings in numerous public galleries, including Tate Gallery, British Museum, Victoria and Albert Museum, Arts Council, British Council, Nat. Portrait Gallery, Stuyvesant Foundation, C. Gulbenkian Foundation, London; Nat. Museum of Wales, Cardiff; Montreal Museum of Fine Art; Musée d'Art Contemporain, Montreal; Toronto Art Gallery; Vancouver Art Gallery; Nat. Gallery of W. Australia, Perth; Power Collection, Sydney; Brooklyn Museum, N.Y.; Boymans Museum, Rotterdam; Smith Coll. Museum of Art, Mass.; Toledo Museum of Art, Ohio; Albright-Knox Art Gallery, Buffalo N.Y.; Univ. of Michigan Museum of Art, Ann Arbor, etc.; Lecture tour of Australia 73; Main Prize at John Moores Liverpool Exhbn. II 59, Silver Medal São Paulo Bienal 65.

Leisure interest: painting.

Publs. *The Changing Forms of Art* 55, *Ivon Hitchens* 55, *Braque* 58 and numerous articles on art.

Eagle's Nest, Zennor, near St. Ives, Cornwall; and 12 Editha Mansions, Edith Grove, London, S.W.10, England.

Telephone: St. Ives 6921 and 01-352-1787.

Héron de Villefosse, René; French archivist; b. 17 May 1903, Paris; s. of A. Héron de Villefosse and Lucie de Thomassin; *m.* Dauphine Delon 1965; three *c.*; ed. Ecole des Chartes.

On staff of the Petit Palais, Paris 30; Asst. Keeper 36-42; Keeper 42-47; Keeper-in-chief of Musées de la Ville

de Paris and of the Musée de l'Ile de France (Château de Sceaux) Oct. 57-; former Prof. Ecole du Louvre; Officier Légion d'Honneur, Commdr. des Arts et des Lettres and many other decorations.
Leisure interests: books, gastronomy.
Publs. *Paris vivant* 32, *Construction de Paris* 38, *Singularités de Paris* 41, *Bourgeois de Paris* 42, *Prés et Bois Parisiens* 43, *Histoire de Paris* 44, *Trésors méconnus de Paris* 46, *Aux Belles de Paris* 47, *Charles le Sage* 47, *Voyage au temps de la douceur de vivre* 47, *La Rivière Enchantée* 50, *Dames de Paris* 51, *Couronnes de Paris* 52, *A travers les Vignes* 53, *Histoire et Géographie gourmandes de Paris* 56, *Histoire et Géographie galantes de Paris* 58, *Portes maritimes de l'Europe* 61, *La Seine qui fit Paris* 61, *L'Ile de France* 65, *Segonzac et l'Ile de France* 66, *Le Coeur battant de Paris* 68, *La Nature, source de l'Art* 68, *Les graves Heures de la Commune* 70, *Les grandes Heures de la Champagne* 71, *Les Halles de Lutèce à Rungis* 73, *L'Antiversailles ou le Palais-Royal de Philippe-Egalité* 74, *Histoire des grandes routes de France* 75.
20 rue Ernest Cresson, Paris 4c, France.
Telephone: 539-59-47.

Herout, Vlastimil, DR.TECHN. ING., D.SC.; Czechoslovak natural products chemist; b. 17 March 1921, Želí; ed. Inst. of Chemical Technology, Prague.
Association of Chemical and Metallurgical Production, Pardubice-Rybitví 41-46; Inst. of Chemical Tech. 46-50; Inst. of Organic Chem. and Biochem. 50-; Prof. of Organic Chem., Inst. of Chemical Tech. 64-; Chair. of Scientific Board of Organic Chem. and Biochem., C.S.S.R. Acad. of Sciences 63-; mem. IUPAC Bureau 69-77; Chair. Czechoslovak Nat. Cttee. of Chem. 71-; Dir. Inst. of Organic Chem. and Biochem., C.S.S.R. Acad. of Sciences 70-; mem. American Chem. Soc., British Phytochemical Soc., Deutsche Gesellschaft für Arzneipflanzenforschung, American Soc. of Pharmacognosy; State Prize 51-62, several awards of C.S.S.R. Acad. of Sciences.
Leisure interests: growing orchids, tourism.
Publs. more than 250 scientific publs. including original data concerning newly discovered natural compounds from plants and their structures; monographs especially on laboratory techniques and chemical systematics; six patents in the field of organic chemistry.
Flemingovo námestí 2, 166 10 Prague 6, Czechoslovakia.
Telephone: 32-16-62.

Herrera-Báez, Lic. Porfirio; Dominican diplomatist and international lawyer; b. 8 Nov. 1915, San Pedro de Macorís; m. Silvia P. de Herrera; ed. Univ. of Santo Domingo and Columbia Univ., New York.
Joined Dominican Foreign Service and served in U.S.A. 41-45, U.K. 45-46, Italy 46-47; Amb. to Brazil 48; Under-Sec. of State for Foreign Affairs 49; mem. Advisory Comm. on State Affairs 52; Chief of Div. of UN and OAS Affairs and Int. Confs., Ministry of Foreign Affairs 53-54; Sec. of State, Office of Pres. 54-55; Sec. of State for Foreign Affairs 55-61; Amb. to Vatican 61-62; Amb. to U.K. 66-75, to Italy 75- and Portugal 72; del. to UN Gen. Assembly and other int. confs.; decorations from Dominican Repub., Peru, Spain, Panama, China, Mexico, France, Liberia, Lebanon, Germany, Paraguay and Netherlands.
Publs. included *Pedro Alejandrino Pina, El Consejo interamericano de Jurisconsultos, The Fifth Meeting of Foreign Ministers in Santiago, Chile.*
Embassy of the Dominican Republic, Via Romanga 26, Rome, Italy.
Telephone: 937-1921.

Herridge, Geoffrey Howard, C.M.G.; British oil executive; b. 22 Feb. 1904, Maisemore; s. of Edward Herridge and Mary Elizabeth Welford; m. Dorothy Elvira Tod

1935; two s. two d.; ed. Crypt School, Gloucester and St. John's Coll., Cambridge.
Joined Turkish Petroleum Co. Ltd. (later Iraq Petroleum Co. Ltd.) Iraq 26; served in Iraq, Jordan, Palestine 26-47; Gen. Man. in Middle East for Iraq Petroleum Co. and Assoc. Cos. 47-51, Exec. Dir. 53-57, Man. Dir. 57-63, Deputy Chair. 63-65, Chair. 65-70; mem. London Cttee., Ottoman Bank 64; Chair. Petroleum Industry Training Board 67-70.
Leisure interests: yachting, painting.
Flint, Sidlesham Common, Nr. Chichester, Sussex, England.
Telephone: 0243-56-357.

Herring, Lt.-Gen. the Hon. Sir Edmund Francis, K.C.M.G., K.B.E., D.S.O., M.C., E.D., Q.C., M.A.; Australian officer and lawyer; b. 2 Sept. 1892, Maryborough, Victoria; s. of late Edmund Selwyn Herring and late Gertrude Stella Fetherstonhaugh; m. Mary Ranken Lyle, D.B.E. 1922; three d.; ed. Melbourne Grammar School, Trinity Coll., Melbourne, and New Coll., Oxford.
Served first World War 14-19, King Edward's Horse and R.F.A.; called to Bar, Inner Temple 20; admitted Barrister and Solicitor, Melbourne 21; practised as Barrister 21-39; K.C. 36; served A.I.F. 39-44; commanded 6th Div. 41-42; Northern Territory Force 42; New Guinea Force 42-43; 1 Australian Corps 42-44; C.B.E. 41; Greek M.C. Class "A" 41; D.S.C. (American) 43; K.B.E. 43; Lieut.-Gov. of Victoria 45-72; Chief Justice Supreme Court of Victoria 44-64; Chancellor, Diocese of Melbourne 41-; Hon. Fellow New Coll. Oxford; Pres. Boy Scout Asscn. of Victoria 45-68, Australian Boy Scouts' Asscn. 59-, Toc H. Australia 47-; Dir.-Gen. Recruiting 50-51; Leader Australia Contingent to Coronation 53; Chair. Australian War Memorial, Canberra 59-74; Hon. Col. Melbourne Univ. Regt. 50; Hon. Bencher Inner Temple 63; Hon. D.C.L. (Oxford), Hon. LL.D. (Monash Univ.); Knight of St. John.
Leisure interest: golf.
226 Walsh St., South Yarra, Victoria 3141, Australia.
Telephone: Melbourne 261000.

Herring, James P.; American retail executive.
Founder and fmr. Pres. Sav-On Drugs Inc.; Vice-Pres. Drug Div., The Kroger Co. 60, Corporate Vice-Pres. 66, Dir. 68-, Pres. 70-75, Chief Exec. Officer 71-75, Chair. 75-; Dir. Central Trust Co. and mem. various civic orgs., etc.
The Kroger Company, 1014 Vine Street, Cincinnati, Ohio 45201, U.S.A.

Herring, (William) Conyers, PH.D.; American physicist; b. 15 Nov. 1914, Scotia, N.Y.; s. of Dr. W. Conyers Herring and Mary Joy Herring; m. Louise C. Preusch 1946; three s. one d.; ed. Univ. of Kansas and Princeton Univ.
National Research Council Fellow, Mass. Inst. of Technology 37-39; Instructor in mathematics, and Research Assoc. in Mathematical Physics, Princeton Univ. 39-40; Instructor in Physics, Univ. of Missouri 40-41; mem. Scientific Staff, Columbia Univ. Div. of War Research 41-45; Prof. of Applied Mathematics, Univ. of Texas 46; Research Physicist, Bell Telephone Laboratories 46-; mem. Inst. for Advanced Study, Princeton 52-53; mem. Nat. Acad. of Sciences; Fellow, American Acad. of Arts and Sciences; Oliver E. Buckley Solid State Physics Prize, American Physical Soc. 59, Distinguished Service Citation, Univ. of Kansas 73.
Leisure interests: tennis, church and cultural activities.
Publ. *Exchange Interactions among Itinerant Electrons* (Vol. 4 of series *Magnetism*) 66.
Bell Telephone Laboratories, Murray Hill, N.J. 07974; Home: 3 Hawthorne Place, Summit, N.J. 07901 U.S.A.
Telephone: 201-582-2308 (Office); 201-273-2338 (Home).

Herschbach, Dudley Robert, B.S., M.S., A.M., PH.D.; American professor of chemistry; b. 18 June 1932,

San José, Calif.; *s.* of Robert Dudley Herschbach and Dorothy Edith Beer; *m.* Georgene Lee Botyos 1964; two *d.*; ed. Stanford and Harvard Univs.
Asst. Prof. Univ. of Calif., Berkeley 59-61, Assoc. Prof. 61-63; Prof. of Chem., Harvard Univ. 63-; mem. Nat. Acad. of Sciences, American Acad. of Arts and Sciences; Pure Chem. Prize, American Chemical Soc. 65.
Leisure interests: photography, hiking, woodwork.
Publs. Research papers in *Journal of Chemical Physics, Proceedings of the National Academy, Review of Scientific Instruments, Advances in Chemical Physics*, etc. 55-.
Office: Department of Chemistry, Harvard University, 12 Oxford Street, Cambridge, Mass.; Home: Conant Road, Lincoln, Mass., U.S.A.
Telephone: 617-495-3218 (Office).

Hersey, John Richard, B.A.; American writer; b. 17 June 1914, Tientsin, China; *s.* of Roscoe Monroe Hersey, Sr. and Grace Baird Hersey; *m.* 1st Frances Ann Cannon 1940 (divorced 1958), 2nd Barbara Day Kaufman 1958; three *s.* two *d.*; ed. Yale Univ. and Clare Coll., Cambridge.
Secretary to Sinclair Lewis 37; Editor *Time* 37-42; War and Foreign Corresp. *Time, Life, New Yorker* 42-46; mem. Council, Author's League of America 46-70, Vice-Pres. 48-55, Pres. 75-; Fellow, Berkeley Coll., Yale Univ. 50-65; Master, Pierson Coll., Yale Univ. 65-70, Fellow 65-; Writer in Residence, American Acad. in Rome 70-71; Lecturer, Yale Univ. 71-; Visiting Prof. Mass. Inst. of Technology 75; mem. American Acad. Arts and Letters 53, Sec. 61-; mem. Nat. Inst. Arts and Letters 50; Council, Authors' Guild 46-; Hon. M.A. (Yale Univ.) 47, LL.D. (Washington, Jefferson Coll.) 46, D.H.Litt. (Dropsie Coll.) 50, L.H.D. (New School for Social Research) 50, D.Litt. (Wesleyan Univ.) 57, (Clarkson Coll. of Technology) 72; Hon. Fellow (Clare Coll., Cambridge) 67, Pulitzer Prize for fiction 45, Sidney Hillman Foundation Award 51, Howland Medal (Yale Univ.) 52.
Publs. *Men on Bataan* 42, *Into the Valley* 43, *A Bell for Adano* 44, *Hiroshima* 46, *The Wall* 50, *The Marmot Drive* 53, *A Single Pebble* 56, *The War Lover* 59, *The Child Buyer* 60, *Here to Stay* 62, *White Lotus* 65, *Too Far to Walk* 66, *Under the Eye of the Storm* 67, *The Algiers Motel Incident* 68, *Letter to the Alumni* 70, *The Conspiracy* 72, *The Writer's Craft* 74, *My Petition for More Space* 74, *The President* 75.
420 Humphrey Street, New Haven, Conn., U.S.A.

Hershey, Alfred Day, PH.D.; American research biologist; b. 4 Dec. 1908, Owosso, Mich.; *s.* of Robert D. Hershey and Alma (née Wilbur); *m.* Harriet Davidson Hershey 1946; one *s.*; ed. Mich. State Univ.
Assistant Bacteriologist, Washington Univ. School of Medicine, St. Louis, Mo. 34-36, Instructor 36-38, Asst. Prof. 38-46, Assoc. Prof. 42-50; Staff mem. Genetics Research Unit, Carnegie Inst. of Wash., Cold Spring Harbor, N.Y. 50-62, Dir. 62-74; (retd.); Fellow, American Acad. of Arts and Sciences; mem. Nat. Acad. of Sciences; Hon. D.Sc. Univ. of Chicago; Albert Lasker Award of American Public Health Assen. 58, Kimber Genetics Award of Nat. Acad. of Sciences 65; Nobel Prize for Medicine (jointly with S. Luria *q.v.*) 69
Publs. Numerous technical articles.
R.D. Box 1640, Moores Hill Road, Syosset, N.Y. 11791, U.S.A.

Hershey, Gen. Lewis Blaine; American fmr. army officer and government official; b. 12 Sept. 1893, Angola, Indiana; *s.* of Latta F. and Rosetta (Richardson) Hershey; *m.* Ellen Dygert 1917; two *s.* two *d.*; ed. Tri-State Coll., Univs. of Indiana and Hawaii and Command and General Staff School, Fort Leavenworth, and Army War Coll., Washington, D.C.
Regular Army Service 11-36; Sec. and Exec. Officer, Jt. Army-Navy Selective Service Cttee. 36; Dir. of Selective

System 41-69; Adviser on Manpower to Pres. Nixon 70-73; numerous medals.
5500 Lambeth Road, Bethesda, Md. 20014, U.S.A.

Herter, Christian Archibald, Jr.; American government official; b. 29 Jan. 1919; *s.* of Christian Herter (fmr. Sec. of State); ed. Harvard Univ.
Admitted Bar 48; Admin. Asst. to Vice-Pres. Nixon 53-54; mem. Policy Planning Staff, U.S. Dept. of State 54; Gen. Man. Govt. Relations Socony Mobil Oil Co., Inc. 61-67, Corporate Vice-Pres. for Public Affairs 67; Dir. Office of Environmental Affairs 70-; mem. American and Boston Bar Asscns.
10 Mitchell Place, New York, N.Y. 10017, U.S.A.

Hertz, Roy, PH.D., M.D., M.D.H.; American professor of obstetrics; b. 19 June 1909, Cleveland, Ohio; *s.* of Aaron D. Hertz and Bertha Lichtman; *m.* 1st Pearl Ruby Fennell 1934 (died 1962), 2nd Dorothy Oberdorfer 1962; one *s.* one *d.*; ed. Univ. of Wisconsin, Johns Hopkins Univ.
United States Public Health Service, Div. on Physiology, Nat. Insts. of Health 41-44; Nat. Cancer Inst. 44-51; Chair., Endocrinology Section Nat. Cancer Inst. 46-51; Asst. Clinical Prof. of Medicine, The George Washington Univ. Medical School 48-66; Nat. Cancer Inst., Nat. Insts. of Health, Bethesda, Md., Chief, Research Medicine, 51-53, Chief, Endocrinology, 53-65; Scientific Dir., Nat. Inst. of Child Health and Human Devt., Nat. Inst. of Health, Bethesda, Md. 65-66; Professor of Obstetrics and Gynaecology, The George Washington Univ. School of Medicine, Washington, 66-67; Chief, Reproduction Research, Nat. Inst. of Child Health and Human Devt., Nat. Insts. of Health, Bethesda, Md. 67-69; Assoc. Dir., the Population Council, The Rockefeller Univ. N.Y. 69-72; Visiting Scientist 72-; Prof. of Obstetrics and Gynaecology and of Medicine, Dir. of Clinical Research, New York Medical Coll. Valhalla, N.Y. 72-73; Research Prof. of Pharmacology and Obstetrics/Gynaecology, George Washington Univ. Medical School 73-; mem. Nat. Acad. of Sciences 72-; Fellow, American Coll. of Obstetrics and Gynaecology 70-; mem. numerous other learned societies; Lasker Foundation Medical Research Award 72, Cancer Research Award, Int. Coll. of Surgeons 69.
Leisure interests: linguistics, gardening.
Publs. Numerous articles on fertility regulation and cancer research.
22 Grafton Street, Chevy Chase, Md. 20015, U.S.A.

Hertzog, Albert, B.A., B.C.L., LL.D.; South African advocate and politician; b. 14 July 1899, Bloemfontein; *s.* of Gen. J. B. M. Hertzog; *m.* Katharine Marjorie Whiteley 1933; ed. Stellenbosch, Amsterdam, Oxford and Leyden Univs.
Member of the Council of the Univ. of S. Africa 36-39; mem. Pretoria City Council 44-51; elected M.P. for Ermelo 48, 53, 58, 61 and 66; foundation mem. of Afrikaanse Pers Beperk and Volkskas Beperk; Minister of Posts and Telegraphs, and of Health 58-68; Dir. Koopkrag, Koopkrag Bank, Afr. Boubeleggings; Leader Herstigte Nasionale Party Oct. 69-.
Leisure interest: tennis.
Publ. *Saaklike Reg en Eiendom*.
10 Edward Street, Waterkloof, Pretoria, South Africa.

Hertzog, Dirk Willem Ryk, B.A., LL.B.; South African business executive; b. 1 Dec. 1914, Jagersfontein, Orange Free State; *m.* Lorraine de la Harpe 1939; two *s.* one *d.*; ed. Jagersfontein and Univ. of Pretoria.
Practised as lawyer, Couzyn, Hertzog and Horak, Pretoria 37-53; Co-founder and Vice-Chair. Rembrandt Group Ltd.; Chair. Oude Meester Group Ltd.; Chair. S.A. Council of the Int. Chamber of Commerce; Dir. S.A. Foreign Trade Org.
Rembrandt Group Ltd., Bird Street, Stellenbosch; Home: Tuin Street, Stellenbosch, South Africa.

Hervé-Bazin, Jean-Pierre Marie, L. ÈS L. (pseudonym Hervé Bazin); French writer; b. 17 April 1911, Angers; s. of Jacques Hervé-Bazin and Paule Guilloteaux; m. Monique Serre-Gray 1967; one s.; (three s. two d. by previous marriage); ed. Faculté des Lettres de Paris.
Critic for newspaper *L'Information*; on staff of Editions Grasset, Editions Seuil; Pres. Comm. d'Aide à la Création; Vice-Pres. Asscn. of Writers; mem. Acad. Goncourt 58-; Pres. 73-, PEN Club, Soc. des Gens de Lettres, conseil Nat. des Lettres; Chevalier, Légion d'Honneur, Officier des Arts et des Lettres, des Palmes Académiques; numerous prizes.
Publs. Poetry: *Jours* 47, *A la Poursuite d'Iris* 48, *Humeurs* 53; Novels: *Vipère au Poing* 48, *La Tête contre les Murs* 49, *La Mort du Petit Cheval* 50, *Le Bureau des Mariages* 51, *Lève-toi et Marche* 52, *L'Huile sur le Feu* 54, *Qui j'ose aimer* 56, *La Fin des Asiles* 59, *Au Nom du Fils* 60, *Chapeau bas* 63, *Plumons l'oiseau* 66, *Le Matrimonie* 67, *Les Bienheureux de la Désolation* 70, *Tristan* 72, *Cri de la Chouette* 72, *Madame Ex* 75.
Leisure interest: gardening.
24 rue Leon Frot, Paris 11; Le Grand Courtoiseau, Triqueres, Loiret, France.
Telephone: 95-24-87.

Herwarth von Bittenfeld, Hans; German diplomatist; b. 14 July 1904, Berlin; m. Elisabeth, Baroness von Redwitz; one d.; ed. Univs. of Berlin, Breslau and Munich.
Entered Foreign Office 27; Attaché, Paris 30; Second Sec. and Personal Sec. to Ambassador, Moscow 31-39; mil. service 39-45; Govt. Counsellor, Dir., Bavarian State Chancellery 45-49; Ministerialdirigent and Chief of Protocol, Fed. German Govt. 50; apptd. Minister 52; Ambassador to U.K. 55-61; State Sec., Chief of Office of Fed. Pres. 61-65; Ambassador to Italy 65-Feb. 69; State Sec. Foreign Office Bonn March 69, now retd.; Chair. Comm. for Reform of Foreign Service March 69-March 71, Deutsch—Englische Gesellschaft, Düsseldorf; Pres. Goethe-Inst., Munich July 71-; Grand Cross 2nd Class, Order of Merit (Fed. Germany), G.C.V.O. (U.K.) and other decorations.
Leisure interests: antiques, shooting, skiing.
8 Munich 27, Menzelstr. 7, Federal Republic of Germany.
Telephone: 480887.

Herzberg, Gerhard, C.C., DR. ING., LL.D., D.SC.; Canadian physicist; b. 25 Dec. 1904, Hamburg, Germany; s. of Albin and Ella (Biber) Herzberg; m. 1st Luise Oettinger 1929 (died 1971), one s. one d.; m. 2nd Monika Tenthoff 1972; ed. Darmstadt Inst. of Technology and Univs. of Göttingen and Bristol.
Lecturer, Darmstadt Inst. of Technology 30-35; Research Prof. of Physics, Univ. of Saskatchewan 35-45; Prof. of Spectroscopy, Yerkes Observatory, Univ. of Chicago 45-48; Dir. of the Div. of Pure Physics, Nat. Research Council, Ottawa 49-69; Distinguished Research Scientist, Nat. Research Council 69-; Bakerian Lecturer, Royal Soc. 60; George Fisher Baker non-Resident Lecturer in Chemistry, Cornell Univ. 68; mem. Royal Soc. of Canada, Pres. Section III 51-52, Pres. 66-67; Hon. mem. Hungarian Acad. of Sciences 64, Optical Soc. of America 68; Hon. Foreign mem. Amer. Acad. of Arts and Sciences 65; Foreign Assoc. Nat. Acad. Sciences, Washington 68; Academician Pontifical Acad. of Sciences 64; Fellow, Royal Soc. of London; Hon. Fellow, Indian Acad. of Sciences, Chemical Soc. of London 68; Univ. of Liège Medal 50; Henry Marshall Tory Medal (Canadian Royal Soc.) 53; Joy Kissen Mookerjee Gold Medal (Indian Asscn. for the Cultivation of Science) 57; Frederic Ives Medal (Optical Soc. of America) 64; Willard Gibbs Medal (American Chemical Soc.) 69; Faraday Medal (Chemical Soc. of London) 70; Royal Medal (Royal Soc. of London) 71; Linus Pauling Medal (American Chemical Soc.) 71; Nobel Prize in Chemistry 71.

Leisure interest: music.
Publs. *Atomic Spectra and Atomic Structure* 37, *Molecular Spectra and Molecular Structure: I. Spectra of Diatomic Molecules* 39, *II. Infra-red and Raman Spectra of Polyatomic Molecules* 45, *III. Electronic Spectra Polyatomic Molecules* 66, *The Spectra and Structures of Simple Free Radicals: An Introduction to Molecular Spectroscopy* 71.
Home: 190 Lakeway Drive, Ottawa, Ontario, K1L 5B3; Office: National Research Council, Ottawa, Ontario, K1A 0R6, Canada.
Telephone: 746-4126 (Home); 992-2350 (Office).

Herzfeld, Karl Ferdinand, PH.D.; American physicist; b. 24 Feb. 1892, Vienna, Austria; s. of Charles August and Camilla (Herzog) Herzfeld; m. Regina Flannery 1938; ed. Schotten Gymnasium, Vienna and Univs. of Vienna, Zürich and Göttingen.
Privat-docent, Univ. of Munich 20, Prof. 23; Speyer Guest Prof. Johns Hopkins Univ. 26, Prof. of Physics 26-36; Head Dept. of Physics, Catholic Univ. of America 36-61, Prof. Emer. 67; mem. Nat. Acad. of Sciences, American Acad. of Arts and Sciences, A.A.A.S., American Physical Soc., German Physical Soc., etc.; numerous hon. degrees; Mendel Medal 31, Meritorious Public Service Award, Navy 64.
Publs. *Kinetische Theorie der Wärme* 25, *Absorption and Dispersion of Ultrasonic Waves* (with T. A. Litovitz) 59.
Department of Physics, Catholic University of America, Washington, D.C. 20017, U.S.A.

Herzog, George, PH.D.; American anthropologist, linguist, musicologist; b. 11 Dec. 1901, Budapest, Hungary; m. Elizabeth Greenbaum-Herzog 1935-1942; no c.; ed. Hungarian Music Acad., Budapest, High School of Music, Berlin, and Columbia Univ.
Assistant, Phonogram Archives, Psychological Inst., Univ. of Berlin 22-24; Research Assoc., Dept. of Anthropology, Univ. of Chicago 30-32; in charge Univ. of Chicago Dept. of Anthropology Expedition to Liberia 30-31; Research Assoc. and Asst. Prof. of Anthropology, Yale Univ. 32-35; G.S. Guggenheim Memorial Fellow 35-36 and 47; Asst. Prof. of Anthropology, Columbia Univ. 36-48; Consultant, Experimental Div. of Wartime Communications Research, Library of Congress, Washington, D.C. 42-45; in charge of Archives of Primitive Music, Dept. of Anthropology, Columbia Univ. 41-48; Fellow, N.Y. Acad. of Sciences, Vice-Pres. 46-47; Prof. of Anthropology, Indiana Univ. 48-61.
Leisure interests: collecting postal stamps for small-child-clients, drinking beer, playing the piano, talking and talking and talking.
Publs. *Jabo Proverbs from Liberia* (with Charles G. Blooah), *The Cow-Tail Switch and Other West African Stories* (with others) and over 100 other published items.
c/o Holt, Rinehart and Winston, 383 Madison Avenue, New York, N.Y. 10017, U.S.A.

Herzog, Gen. Haim, K.B.E., LL.B.; Israeli lawyer and military expert; b. 17 Sept. 1918, Belfast, N. Ireland; s. of Rabbi Dr. Isaac and Sarah Herzog; m. Aura Ambache 1947; three s. one d.; ed. Wesley Coll. Dublin, London and Cambridge Univs., Lincoln's Inn, London.
Went to Palestine 35; served in British Army, World War II; rank of Maj.; Dir. Intelligence, Israeli Defence Forces 48-50; Defence Attaché, Israeli Embassy, Washington, Ottawa 50-54; Field Commands 54-59; Dir. Mil. Intelligence 59-62; Gen. 61; Man. Dir. G.U.S. Industries 62-72; Gov. West Bank of the Jordan 67; Senior Partner, Herzog, Fox and Neeman 72-; Perm. Rep. to UN Aug. 75-; Hon. K.B.E. 70.
Leisure interests: sailing, writing, broadcasting.
Publs. *Israel's Finest Hour* (Hebrew and English) 67, *Days of Awe* (Hebrew) 73, *Judaism, Law and Ethics* 74, *The War of Atonement* 75, and numerous articles in foreign and Israeli journals.

Permanent Mission of Israel to United Nations, 800 Second Avenue, New York, N.Y. 10017, U.S.A.; Home: Zahala, Tel-Aviv, Israel.
Telephone: 500-8516 (Office); 471-415 (Home).

Herzog, Maurice; French politician and former mountaineer; b. 15 Jan. 1919, Lyon (Rhone); s. of Robert Herzog; m. Comtesse Marie Pierre de Cossé Brissac 1964; one s. one d.; ed. Collège Chaptal, Paris, Faculty of Science, Lyon and Faculty of Law, Paris. Leader, French Himalayan Expedition 50; fmr. Dir. Kléber-Colombes Soc.; High Commr. for Youth and Sport 58-63, Sec. of State 63-66; mem. UN Econ. and Social Council 66-; mem. Int. Olympic Cttee. 70-, Chief of Protocol 75; Deputy, Haute Savoie, Maire de Chamonix; Pres. Financial Comm. Rhône-Alpes Regional Council; Officier Légion d'Honneur; Croix de Guerre, and other French and foreign decorations.
Leisure interests: history, literature, science.
Publs. *Annapurna premier 8000, Regards sur L'Annapurna, L'Expédition de l'Annapurna, La Montagne.*
4 rue Jean-Richepin, Paris 16e; La Tournette, Chamonix, Haute Savoie, France.
Telephone: 260-60-00 (Nat. Ass.).

Herzog, Paul M., S.B., LL.B., M.A.; American lawyer, university professor and government officer; b. 21 Aug. 1906, New York City; s. of Paul M. and Elsie Lowenstein Herzog; m. 2nd Julie Chamberlain d'Estournelles 1959; one s. one d.; ed. Harvard Univ., Univ. of Wisconsin, Harvard Law School, Columbia Law School.
Assistant to Sec. Nat. Labor Board 33-35; practised law in New York 36-37; mem. of New York State Labor Relations Board 37; Chair. New York State Labor Relations Board 42; Lieut. U.S.N.R. 44-45; Chair. Nat. Labor Relations Board 45-53, resigned; Assoc. Dean Graduate School of Public Admin., Harvard Univ. 53-57; Exec. Vice-Pres. American Arbitration Assen. 58-, Pres. 61-63; Pres. Salzburg Seminar in American Studies 65-71; mem. Cttee. of Experts on Application of Conventions ILO (Geneva) 56-68; Vice-Pres. American Soc. for Public Admin. 56-57; mem. N.Y. D.C. and U.S. Supreme Court Bars; Great Medal of Honour (Austria) 70; Hon. LL.D. Hobart Coll. 59, Washington Univ. 71.
14 East 75th Street, New York City 21, N.Y., U.S.A.

Herzog, Raymond Harry; American business executive; b. 15 Sept. 1915, Merricourt, N.D.; s. of Harry G. and Mollie Klundt Herzog; m. Jane Cobb 1940; two s. one d.; ed. Lawrence Univ., Appleton, Wis.
Chemist, W. Virginia Coal and Coke Co. 37-38; Coach and Science Teacher, St. Croix Falls, Wis. 39-41; joined 3M Company 41, Gen. Man. Duplicating Products Div. 56-59, Div. Vice-Pres. 59-61, Corporate Vice-Pres. 61-62, Group Vice-Pres. Graphic Systems Group 63-70 Pres. 70-75, Chair. and Chief Exec. Officer May 75-; Chair. Business Equipment Mfrs. Assen. 71; Dir. Nat. Assen. of Mfrs., First Trust Co. of St. Paul, Jim Walter Co., United Way of St. Paul, U.S.-U.S.S.R. Trade and Econ. Council; Trustee, Lawrence Univ., Minn. Mutual Life Insurance Co.; mem. The Conf. Board.
Leisure interests: golf, fishing.
3M Company, 3M Center, St. Paul, Minn. 55110; Home: 23 Shady Woods Road, St. Paul, Minn. 55115, U.S.A.
Telephone: 733-1240 (Office); 426-2691 (Home).

Hesburgh, Rev. Theodore M., S.T.D.; American university president; b. 25 May 1917; ed. Univ. of Notre Dame, Gregorian Univ., Rome, and Catholic Univ. of America.
Ordained priest of Congregation of Holy Cross 43; joined Univ. of Notre Dame 45, Head of Theology Dept. 48-49, Exec. Vice-Pres. of Univ. 49-52, Pres. 52-; mem. U.S. Comm. on Civil Rights (Chair. 69-72), President's Comm. on All-Volunteer Armed Force, Carnegie Comm. on the Future Structure and Financing of

Higher Educ., Comm. on the Future of Private and Independent Higher Educ. in New York State, Adlai E. Stevenson Inst. of Int. Affairs; Perm. Rep. of Holy See to Int. Atomic Energy Agency, Vienna 57; Pres. Int. Fed. of Catholic Univs.; Trustee, Rockefeller Foundation, Carnegie Foundation for Advancement of Teaching (Pres. 63-64); Chair. Acad. Council, Ecumenical Inst. for Advanced Theological Studies in Jerusalem; fmr. Dir. American Council on Educ.; Dir. Woodrow Wilson Nat. Fellowship Corpn., Nutrition Foundation and other orgs.; Fellow American Acad. of Arts and Sciences; Distinguished Service Medal, U.S. Navy; Presidential Medal of Freedom 64; 21 hon. degrees.
Publs. *God and the World of Man* 50, *Patterns for Educational Growth* 58, *Thoughts for Our Times* 62, *More Thoughts for Our Times* 65, *Still More Thoughts for Our Times* 66, *Thoughts IV* 68, *Thoughts V* 69.
University of Notre Dame, Notre Dame, Ind. 46556, U.S.A.
Telephone: 219-283-6383.

Heseltine, Michael Ray Dibdin; British politician; b. 21 March 1933, Swansea, Wales; s. of Col. Rupert and Eileen Ray Heseltine; m. Anne Edna Harding Williams 1962; one s. two d.; ed. Shrewsbury School, Pembroke Coll., Oxford.
President Oxford Union 54; Chair. Haymarket Press 65-70; mem. Parl. for Tavistock 66-74, for Henley 74-; Parl. Sec. Ministry of Transport 70; Parl. Under-Sec. of State, Dept. of the Environment 70-72; Minister of Aerospace and Shipping 72-74; Opposition Spokesman for Industry 74-.
24 Wilton Crescent, London, S.W.1; and Soundess House, Nettlebed, Oxon., England.

Heslop-Harrison, John, D.SC., F.L.S., F.INST.BIOL., M.R.I.A., F.R.S.E., F.R.S., F.R.S.A.; British professor of plant physiology; b. 10 Feb. 1920, Middlesbrough; s. of Prof. John W. Heslop-Harrison, F.R.S. and Christian Watson Henderson; m. Yolande Massey 1950; one s.; ed. King's Coll., Durham Univ.
Military service 42-46; Lecturer King's Coll., Univ. of Durham 46; Lecturer Queen's Univ., Belfast 46-50; Lecturer and Reader, Univ. Coll. London 50-54; Prof. and Head Dept., Queen's Univ., Belfast 54-60; Mason Prof. and Head Dept., Univ. of Birmingham 60-67; Brittingham Visiting Prof., Univ. of Wisconsin 65; Visiting Scientist, Forest Genetics Research Station, U.S.D.A. Wisconsin 68; Prof. Inst. of Plant Devt. Univ. of Wisconsin, Madison 67-70, Dir. Royal Botanic Gardens, Kew 71-; Editor *Annals of Botany* 62-67; Visiting Prof. Univ. of Reading; Pres. Inst. of Biology 74-75; Foreign Fellow Indian Nat. Science Acad. 74; Corresp. mem. Royal Dutch Botanical Soc.; Trail-Crisp Medal, Linnean Soc. 67; Medallist, Univ. of Liège 67; Gunnar Erdtman Int. Medal for Palynology 71; Cooke Award, American Acad. of Allergy 74; Croonian Lecturer, Royal Soc. 74; Hon. D.Sc. (Queen's Univ., Belfast) 71.
Leisure interests: painting, hill walking, field botany.
Publs. research papers, monographic reviews in international journals.
49 Kew Green, Kew, Richmond, Surrey; Old Post, Hatfield, Leominster, Herefordshire, England.
Telephone: 01-940-1171 (Kew).

Hess, Gerhard, DR. PHIL.; German university professor; b. 13 April 1907, Loerrach/Baden; s. of Ernst and Clara Hess; m. Eva Schabert 1931; one d.; ed. Basle, Heidelberg and Berlin Univs.
Assistant Prof. Heidelberg Univ. 41, Prof. 48, Dean, Philosophical Faculty 48-49, Rector 50-51; Pres. Rectors' Conf. 50-51; Vice-Pres. Assen. of Univ. Profs. 51-55; Pres. Deutsche Forschungsgemeinschaft 55-64; Vice-Pres. Alexander von Humboldt-Stiftung 59-64; mem. Heidelberg Acad. of Sciences 51-; Chair. Aca-

demic Planning Board, Konstanz Univ. 64-66, Rector, Konstanz Univ. 66-72; Chair. Acad. Planning Board, Lucerne Univ. 73-.

Leisure interest: gardening.

Publs. *Alain in der Reihe der französischen Moralisten* 32, *Die französische Philosophie der Gegenwart* 33, *Pierre Gassend: der französische Späthumanismus und das Problem von Wissen und Glauben* 39, *Die Landschaft in Baudelaires "Fleurs du Mal"* 53, *Zur Entstehung der "Maximen" La Rochefoucaulds* 57, *Gesammelte Schriften 1938-1966* 67, *Die deutsche Universität 1930-1968* 68, *Die integrierte Gesamthochschule Konstanz* (with C. Schneider), 70 *Die Universität Konstanz 1966-1972: Ein Rechenschaftsbericht* 73; trans. of Leibniz, La Bruyère, de la Fayette.

Säntisstrasse 3, 7750 Konstanz, Federal Republic of Germany.

Telephone: 07531-62515.

Hess, Werner; German broadcasting official; b. 13 Oct. 1914, Frankfurt; s. of Wilhelm Hess; m. Marielies Elbers 1944 (died 1965); studies in evangelical theology, Germanic philology and drama, Univs. of Giessen, Marburg, Jena and Frankfurt/Main.

Church minister in Frankfurt; military service 39-45; resumed ministry in Frankfurt-Ginnheim 45-60; Film Industry Delegate of the Evangelical Church of Germany; mem. since 48 and Chair. since 59 of the Broadcasting Council of the Hessian Broadcasting Service; Founder and mem. of the Soc. for the Voluntary Control of the Film Industry; Chair. Supervisory Board of the Matthias Film Distribution Co., Stuttgart; Hessian Broadcasting and Television Service Television Programme Dir. 60-62, Gen. Dir. 62-; Chair. ARD (German Broadcasting Service) 65, 66; Vice-Pres. European Broadcasting Union 68-; Chair. European Broadcasting Union Comm. for Developing Countries.

Hessischer Rundfunk, 6 Frankfurt am Main, Bertramstrasse 8; Home: 53 Frauenlobstrasse, 6 Frankfurt am Main, Federal Republic of Germany.

Hesselbach, Walter; German banker and company director; b. 20 Jan. 1915, Frankfurt a.M.; s. of Wilhelm and Elisabeth Hesselbach (née Mayer); m. Hedwig Huth 1953; three d.; ed. Wöhler Realgymnasium.

Foreign Dept. of Deutsch-Überseeische Bank, Berlin 35-37; Merck und Co., Darmstadt 37-38; Sec. to Georg von Opel 38-40; military service and prisoner of war 40-47; Bank Deutscher Länder, Frankfurt a.M. 47-52; mem. of Board Landeszentralbank in Hessen 52-58, Bank für Gemeinwirtschaft A.G., Frankfurt a.M. 58-62, Chair. 62-; Chair. of Board Bank für Sparanlagen und Vermögensbildung A.G., Beteiligungsgesellschaft für Gemeinwirtschaft A.G., Frankfurt a.M.; Chair. of Supervisory Board Allgemeine Hypothekenbank A.G., Boswau und Knauer A.G., Deutsche Lufthansa A.G., Israel Continental Bank Ltd., Tel-Aviv, Internationale Genossenschaftsbank A.G., Basel, Bau- und Handelsbank A.G., Frankfurt/M; Deputy Chair. Braunschweig-Hannoversche Hypothekenbank, Rheinisch-Westfälische Elektrizitäts-Werke A.G.; mem. Supervisory Board August Thyssen-Hütte A.G., Bank für Arbeit und Wirtschaft A.G., Vienna, Fried. Krupp G.m.b.H., Salzgitter A.G., Ruhrkohle A.G., Volksfürsorge A.G. Insurance Group, Volkswagen A.G.; Chair. Managing Board Deutsche Bundespost, Advisory Board ATH Allgemeine Treuhandgesellschaft m.b.H; mem. Managing Board Deutsche Pfandbriefanstalt, Ges. für Wohnungs- und Siedlungswesen, Kreditanstalt für Wiederaufbau, Israel European Co. ISROP S.A., Luxembourg; mem. Advisory Board Papierwerke Waldhof-Aschaffenburg A.G., Bund deutscher Konsumgenossenschaften, Landeszentralbank in Hessen, Neue Heimat Gemeinnützige Wohnungs- und Siedlungsgesellschaft; Pres. Bank Cttee. Int. Co-operative Alliance, London, German-Israel Chamber of Commerce, Lessing

Academy; Vice-Pres. German-Israeli Soc.; mem. Econ. Cttee. of S.P.D.; mem. Board of Govs. Hebrew Univ. of Jerusalem; Dr. h.c. (Univ. of Tel-Aviv, Hebrew Univ. of Jerusalem); Grosses Verdienstkreuz (Fed. Republic of Germany).

Leisure interests: economics, politics, literature.

Publ. *Die gemeinwirtschaftlichen Unternehmungen* 66, 71.

Bank für Gemeinwirtschaft A.G., 6 Frankfurt am Main, Mainzer Landstrasse 16-24, Federal Republic of Germany.

Telephone: 71-211.

Hester, James McNaughton, M.A., D.PHIL.; American university official; b. 19 April 1924, Chester, Pa.; s. of James Montgomery Hester and Margaret (McNaughton) Hester; m. Janet Rodes 1953; three d.; ed. Princeton and Oxford Univs.

Civil Information Officer, Fukuoka Mil. Govt. Team, Japan 46-47; Capt., U.S. Marine Corps, Japan 43-46, 51-52; Rhodes Scholar, Oxford Univ. 47-50; Asst. to Rhodes Trustees, Princeton 50; Asst. to Pres., Handy Assocs. Inc. (Management Consultants) N.Y. 53-54; Account Supervisor, Gallup & Robinson Inc. 54-57; Provost, Brooklyn Center, L.I. Univ. 57-60, Vice-Pres., Trustee L.I. Univ.; Prof. of History, Exec. Dean Arts and Sciences, Dean Graduate School of Arts and Sciences, N.Y. Univ. 60-61, Trustee 62, Pres. 62-75; Rector, UN Univ., Tokyo 75-; Dir. Union Carbide Corpn. 63-, Lehman Corpn. 64-, J. Walter Thompson Co. 74-, Bowery Savings Bank 74-; Chair. Pres. Nixon's Task Force on Priorities in Higher Educ. 69; mem. Asscn. of Amer. Rhodes Scholars 62-, Japan Soc. 62-, Pilgrims, U.S. 63-, Council on Foreign Relations 62-, Council for Financial Aid to Educ. 71-75; Trustee Metropolitan Museum of Art, Inst. of Int. Educ. 63-, Phelps-Stokes Fund 62-75; Hon. LL.D. Princeton Univ. 62, Morehouse Coll., Hofstra Univ., Hahnemann Medical Coll. 67, Fordham Univ. 71, Hon. L.H.D. Lafayette and Hartwick Colls. 64, Hon. D.C.L. Alfred Univ. 65, Hon. L.H.D. Pace Univ., Univ. of Pittsburgh 71, Colgate Univ. 74; Chevalier Légion d'Honneur 64.

Home: 37 Washington Square, West, New York, N.Y. 10003, U.S.A.

Heston, Charlton; American actor; b. 4 Oct. 1924, Evanston, Ill.; s. of Russell Carter and Lilla Charlton Heston; m. Lydia Clarke 1944; one s. one d.; ed. Northwestern Univ., Evanston.

First Broadway appearance in *Antony and Cleopatra* 48; has starred in more than forty films, Hollywood 50-; Pres. Screen Actors Guild 65-71; mem. Nat. Council of Arts 67; mem. American Film Inst. 71-, Chair 73-; Acad. Award for Best Actor, *Ben Hur* 59.

Stage appearances include *Macbeth* 54, 59, 76 (London), *Mister Roberts* 54, *Detective Story* 56, *A Man for All Seasons* 65.

Films include: *Julius Caesar* 50, *Dark City* 50, *The Greatest Show on Earth* 52, *The Savage* 52, *Ruby Gentry* 52, *The President's Lady* 53, *Pony Express* 53, *Arrowhead* 53, *Bad for Each Other* 53, *The Naked Jungle* 53, *Secret of the Incas* 54, *The Far Horizons* 55, *Lucy Gallant* 55, *The Private War of Major Benson* 55, *Three Violent People* 56, *The Ten Commandments* 56, *Touch of Evil* 58, *The Big Country* 58, *The Buccaneer* 58, *Ben Hur* 59, *The Wreck of the Mary Deare* 59, *El Cid* 61, *The Pigeon that Took Rome* 62, *Diamond Head* 62, *55 Days at Peking* 62, *Major Dundee* 64, *The Greatest Story Ever Told* 65, *The Agony and the Ecstasy* 65, *The War Lord* 65, *Khartoum* 66, *Counterpoint* 67, *Will Penny* 67, *Planet of the Apes* 67, *Beneath the Planet of the Apes* 69, *The Hawaiians* 70, *Julius Caesar* 70, *The Omega Man* 71, *Antony and Cleopatra* 72, *Skyjacked* 72, *The Call of the Wild* 72, *Soylent Green* 73, *The Three Musketeers* 73, *The Four Musketeers* 74, *Earthquake* 74, *Airport 1975*, *Midway* 75.

Leisure interest: tennis.
c/o Thomas and Ford, 8574 Melrose Avenue, Los Angeles, Calif. 90069, U.S.A.
Telephone: 213-657-5838.

Hetherington, Sir Arthur Ford, Kt., D.S.C., B.A.; British engineer and business executive; b. 12 July 1911; s. of the late Sir Roger Gaskell Hetherington and Lady (Honoria) Hetherington; m. Margaret Lacey 1937; one s. one d.; ed. Highgate School, London, Trinity Coll., Cambridge.
Deputy Chair. Southern Gas Board 56-61, Chair. 61-64; Chair. East Midlands Gas Board 64-66; Deputy Chair. Gas Council 67-72, Chair. 72-73; Chair. British Gas Corpn. 73-; Hon. D.Sc. (London) 74.
Leisure interest: sailing.
32 Connaught Square, London, W.2, England.
Telephone: 01-723 3128.

Hetherington, Hector Alastair, M.A.; British journalist; b. 31 Oct. 1919, Llanishen, Glamorganshire, Wales; s. of late Sir Hector Hetherington and Lady Hetherington; m. Helen Miranda Oliver 1957; two s. two d.; ed. Gresham's School, Holt, and Corpus Christi Coll., Oxford.
Served in Royal Armoured Corps 40-46; on staff *The Glasgow Herald* 46-50; joined (*Manchester*) *Guardian* 50, Foreign Editor 53, Editor 56-75; Dir. Guardian Newspapers Ltd. 67-; with British Broadcasting Corpn. Oct. 75-, Controller BBC Scotland 75-; Fellow, Nuffield Coll., Oxford 73-.
Leisure interest: hill walking.
Broadcasting House, Queen Margaret Drive, Glasgow, G12 8DG, Scotland.
Telephone: 041-339-8844.

Hettlage, Dr. Karl Maria; German university professor; b. 28 Nov. 1902, Essen; s. of Karl Hettlage and Klara Brandenburg; m. Margarete Brenken 1929; two s. two d.; ed. Univs. of Cologne and Münster.
Government Official of Prussian Land 25-30; Financial Adviser, Cologne city admin. 30-31; Financial Dept., Berlin city admin. 31-38; senior bank official 38-51; Prof. of Public Law, Univ. of Mainz 51-73, Hon. Prof. of Financial Sciences, Univ. of Bonn 49-; State Sec. Finance Ministry, Fed. German Govt. 58-62, 67-; mem. European Coal and Steel Community (ECSC) High Authority 62-67, Sciences Council 65; Pres. IFO Inst. for Econ. Research, Munich.
Leisure interests: violin, gardening.
IFO Institut für Wirtschaftsforschung, 8000 Munich 86, Poschingerstrasse 5, Federal Republic of Germany.

Heunis, Jan Christiaan, B.A., LL.B.; South African politician; b. 20 April 1927, Uniondale; s. of J. C. Heunis and R. C. M. Lamprecht; m. Alida André van Heerden 1951; four s. one d.; ed. Outeniqua High School, George, Univ. of Stellenbosch.
Member Prov. Council, George 59, mem. Exec. Cttee. 65-70; Chair. Select Cttee. on Public Accounts for Cape Province 60-64; mem. Parl. for False Bay 70-74; mem. Select Cttee. on Public Accounts 70-72; Deputy Minister of Finance and Econ. Affairs 72-74; mem. Parl. for Helderberg 74-; Minister of Indian Affairs and of Tourism 74-75, of Econ. Affairs 75-.
Leisure interest: reading.
Private Bag X9047, Cape Town, South Africa.
Telephone: 457295.

Heusinger, Gen. Adolf Ernst; German army officer and public servant; b. 4 Aug. 1897, Holzminden; s. of Ludwig Heusinger and Charlotte Von Alten; m. Dr. phil. Gerda Krüger 1931; two d.; ed. Gymnasium in Holzminden and Helmstedt.
Commissioned 15; entered *Reichswehr* 20; posted to Gen. Staff 30; Company Commdr. 34-35, Divisional Gen. Staff 35-37; Gen. Staff Officer 37-44; arrested July 20th 44; Military Adviser of German Fed. Govt. 50; Chair.

Joint Chiefs of Staff of German Armed Forces Mar. 57-61; Chair. NATO Military Cttee. in Perm. Session 61-64; retd. 64.
Publ. *Befehl im Widerstreit* (*Schicksalstunden der deutschen Armee 1923-45*) 50.
Bayenthalgürtel, 33A, 5 Köln-Marienburg, Federal Republic of Germany.
Telephone: Cologne 38-61-16.

Heusinger, Bruno, DR.PHIL.; German lawyer; b. 2 March 1900, Holzminden/Weser; s. of Ludwig Heusinger and Charlotte von Alten; m. Sigrid Witte 1933; one s. two d.; ed. Göttingen, Berlin Univs. Served in World Wars I and II; articled 24; Assessor 27; County Court Judge 29; Provincial Court of Appeal Judge 30, Pres. 33; Senatspräsident, Provincial Court of Appeal 35; Pres. Provincial Court of Appeal, Brunswick 48, Celle 55; Pres. Federal Supreme Court, Karlsruhe 60-68; Dr. Iur. h.c.; Hon. Senator Technische Hochschule, Karlsruhe.
Leisure interests: history of law, history of art.
Publs. *Servitium Regis in der Deutschen Kaiserzeit* 22, *Vom Reichskammergericht* 72, *Rechtsfindung und Rechtsfortbildung* 75.
Wachtelweg 9, 31 Celle, Federal Republic of Germany.
Telephone: 34251.

Heusinger, Hans-Joachim; German politician; b. 7 April 1925, Leipzig; m.; three s.; ed. Akad. für Staats- und Rechtswissenschaft, Potsdam-Babelsberg.
Electrician 45-51; leading positions in Leipzig and Cottbus State Admin. and in Liberal Democratic Party; Dir. Chamber of Commerce, Cottbus; mem., Sec. Central Exec. Cttee., mem. Political Comm., Liberal Democratic Party 57, later Deputy Chair. LDP; mem. Volkskammer (People's Chamber) 61-; Deputy Chair. Council of Ministers, Minister of Justice 72-; mem. Presidium of Nat. Council of Nat. Front 74-.
Clara-Zetkin-Strasse 93, 108 Berlin, German Democratic Republic.

Hewish, Antony, M.A., PH.D., F.R.S., F.R.A.S.; British radio astronomer; b. 11 May 1924; Fowey, Cornwall; s. of Ernest W. Hewish and Grace F. L. Hewish (née Pinch); m. Marjorie E. C. Richards 1950; one s. one d.; ed. King's Coll., Taunton and Gonville and Caius Coll., Cambridge.
War service 43-46; Research Fellow, Gonville and Caius Coll., Cambridge 51-54, Super Numerary Fellow 56-61; Univ. Asst. Dir. of Research 53-61, Lecturer 61-69; Fellow, Churchill Coll. Cambridge 61-; Reader in Radio Astronomy, Univ. of Cambridge 69-71, Prof. 71-; Foreign Hon. mem. American Acad. of Arts and Sciences 70; Hamilton Prize (Univ. of Cambridge) 51, Eddington Medal, Royal Astronomical Soc. 68, Boys Prize, Inst. of Physics 70, Dellinger Medal, Int. Union of Radio Science, Hopkins Prize, Cambridge Philosophical Soc. 72, Michelson Medal, Franklin Inst. 73, Holweck Medal and Prize, Soc. Française de Physique 74, Nobel Prize for Physics 74.
Leisure interests: listening to good music, swimming, sailing.
Publs. Many papers in scientific journals; Editor: *Seeing Beyond the Invisible*.
4 Mailes Close, Barton, Cambridge, England.
Telephone: Comberton 2657.

Hewitt, William Alexander, A.B.; American manufacturing executive; b. 9 Aug. 1914; ed. Univ. of Calif.
With John Deere Plow Co., San Francisco 48-54, Vice-Pres. 50-54; Dir. Deere & Co., Moline, Ill. 51-, Exec. Vice-Pres. 54-55, Pres. 55-64, Chair. and Chief Exec. Officer 64-; Dir. Continental Illinois Nat. Bank & Trust Co. of Chicago, Conill Corpn., American Telephone & Telegraph Co., Continental Oil Co.; Chair. Nat. Council for U.S.–China Trade; Dir. U.S.–U.S.S.R. Trade and Econ. Council; mem. The Business Council, American

Soc. of Agric. Engineers, The Conf. Board, and many other orgs.; Hon. Trustee, Cttee. for Econ. Devt.; Trustee, U.S. Council Int. Chamber of Commerce; Lieut.-Commdr. U.S.N.R. 42-46.
Home: 3800 Blackhawk Road, Rock Island, Ill. 61201; Office: John Deere Road, Moline, Ill. 61265, U.S.A.
Telephone: 309-788-9200 (Home); 309-792-4114 (Office).

Hey, Donald Holroyde, D.SC., PH.D., M.SC., F.R.I.C., F.R.S.; British chemist; b. 12 Sept. 1904, Swansea, Wales; s. of Arthur Hey and Francis Hey (née Baynham); m. Jessie Jones 1931; one s. one d.; ed. Magdalen Coll. School, Oxford and Univ. Coll., Swansea.
Lecturer in Chemistry Manchester Univ. 28-38; Lecturer in Organic Chemistry Royal Coll. of Science, London Univ. 39-41; mem. Council Chemical Soc. 40, 45 and 61-66, Hon. Sec. 46-51, Vice-Pres. 51-54; mem. Council Royal Inst. Chemistry 44-46 and 54-57; mem. Chemical Council 48-50; Dir. of Research, British Schering Research Inst. 41-45; Prof. Chemistry, King's Coll., London Univ. 45-50; Daniell Prof. of Chemistry King's Coll. 50-71; Prof. Emer. Univ. of London 71-; Asst. Principal King's Coll., London 62-68; Fellow, King's Coll., London, Imperial Coll., London, Hon. Fellow, Chelsea Coll., London; Pres. Section B, British Asscn. for Advancement of Science 65; Visiting Prof. Univ. of Florida 67; Hon. Fellow, Intra-Science Research Foundation; Hon. D.Sc. (Univ. of Wales); Intra-Science Research Foundation Medallist, Santa Monica, Calif. 68.
Leisure interests: music, gardening.
Albany Lodge, The Avenue, Tadworth, Surrey, England.

Heyerdahl, Thor; Norwegian anthropologist and explorer; b. 6 Oct. 1914, Larvik; s. of Thor Heyerdahl and Alison Heyerdahl (née Lyng); m. 1st Liv Coucheron Torp 1936, 2nd Yvonne Dedekam-Simonsen 1948; two s. three d.; ed. Univ. of Oslo.
Specialized in zoology and geography at univ. but changed to anthropology during field researches among Polynesians in Marquesas Is. 37-38; research in N.W. Indian territory of Brit. Columbia (ref. theory of two separate American Indian movements into Pacific) 39-40; served free Norwegian Mil. Forces 41-45; research in Europe and U.S.A. 45-47; led Kon-Tiki expedition from Callao, Peru to Raroia, Polynesia (covering 4,300 miles in 101 days and thus proving Peruvian Indians could have settled in Polynesia) 47; founded (with Knut Haugland) Kon-Tiki Museum, Oslo 49; research and lectures in Europe and U.S.A. 48-52; led Norwegian Archæological Expedition to Galapagos (establishing evidence of pre-European visits by South American Indians) Field Research in Bolivia, Peru and Colombia 54; led Norwegian Archæological Expedition to Easter Island and the East Pacific 55-56; attempted to cross Atlantic in papyrus boat *Ra I* 69 (covering 2,800 miles in 56 days); sailed from Safi, Morocco, in papyrus boat *Ra II* May 70, in attempt to cross Atlantic and prove that ancient Mediterranean civilizations could have sailed a reed boat to America, and arrived in Barbados July 70; Vice-Pres. World Asscn. of World Federalists 66-; Vice-Pres. Int. Council United World Colls. 73-; Kiril I Metodi Order, First Class, Bulgaria 71, Commdr. of the Order of St. Olav, Officer Servicio del Mérito Distinguido of Peru 52, Grande Ufficiale dell' Ordine al Merito della Repubblica Italiana 65, Order of Merit First Class, Egypt 71, Grand Officer Royal Alaouites Order, Morocco 71, and many other awards including Acad. First Award ("Oscar") for Kon-Tiki film 51; mem. Norwegian Acad. of Science 58; Fellow, New York Acad. of Sciences 60; Hon. Ph.D. (Oslo Univ.) 61; Vega Medal (Swedish Soc. of Anthropology and Geography) 62; Patron's Gold Medal (Royal Geographical Soc., London) 64.

Leisure interest: travels.
Publs. *Pā Jakt Efter Paradiset* 38, *Kon-Tiki Ekspedisjonen* (trans. 64 languages) 48, *American Indians in the Pacific: the Theory behind the Kon-Tiki Expedition* 52, *Archaeological Evidence of Pre-Spanish Visits to the Galapagos Islands* 56, *Aku-Aku: Påskeøyas Hemmelighet* (trans. 32 languages) 57, *Reports of the Norwegian Archaeological Expedition to Easter Island and the East Pacific*, (Vol. I *Archaeology of Easter Island* 61, Vol. II *Miscellaneous Reports* 65) (with E. N. Ferdon), *Indianer und Alt-Asiaten im Pazifik* 66, *Sea Routes to Polynesia* 68, *The Ra Expeditions* 71, *Fatuhiva: Back to Nature* 74, *Zwischen den Kontinenten* 75, *The Art of Easter Island* 75, and many articles.
Colla Micheri, Laigueglia, Italy.

Hibberd, Donald James, O.B.E.; Australian business executive; b. 1916; m.; one s. one d.; ed. Fort St. Boys' High School, Sydney, Univ. of Sydney.
Formerly First Asst. Sec. Treasury Dept., Canberra; Man. Dir. Comalco Ltd. 60-69, Chair. and Chief Exec. 69-; Vice-Chair. Queensland Alumina Ltd. 64-; Chair. Munich Re-insurance Co. of Australia Ltd. 70-; mem. Board, Reserve Bank 66-; Council mem. Univ. of Melbourne 67-; Pres. Australian Mining Industry Council 72-73.
Comalco Ltd., 95 Collins Street, Melbourne; Home: Apartment 13-2, Domain Park, 193 Domain Road, South Yarra, Victoria, Australia.

Hickel, Walter Joseph; American government official; b. 18 Aug. 1919, Claflin, Kansas; s. of Robert A. Hickel and Emma Zecha (German descent); m. 1st Janice Cannon 1941 (deceased 1943), 2nd Ermalee Strutz 1945; six s.; ed. High School, Claflin, Kansas. Builder, developer, and civic leader 46-; started building homes, then built, operated and developed rental units, residential areas and hotels; operates inns, hotels and shopping centres in Alaska; Republican Nat. Ctteeman for State of Alaska 54-64; Gov. of Alaska 67-69; Sec. of U.S. Dept. of Interior 69-Nov. 70; mem. of Board Regents Gonzaga Univ., Salk Inst.; mem. World Advisory Council Int. Design Science Inst.; Dir. Western Airlines; Chair. Nat. Science Foundation panel on Geothermal Power; Kansas Golden Gloves Welterweight Championship 38; Hon. LL.D. (St. Mary of the Plains College 70, St. Martin's College 71, Univ. of Md. 71, Adelphi Univ. 71, Univ. of San Diego 72, Rensselaer Polytechnic Inst. 73); Hon. D.Eng. (Stevens Inst. of Tech. at Hoboken 70, Mich. Technological Univ. 73); Hon. Doctor of Public Admin. (Willamette Univ. 71); Alaskan of the Year 69; Horatio Alger Award, N.Y. 72; Certificate of Award for Best Non-Fiction Book, *Who Owns America*, Alaska Press Club 72.
Leisure interests: reading, boating, hiking, riding.
Publ. *Who Owns America?*
1905 Loussac Drive, Anchorage, Alaska 99503, U.S.A. Telephone: 907-279-9401.

Hicks, Brig. Sir Cedric Stanton, Kt., C.ST.J., M.SC., M.D., PH.D., F.R.I.C., F.R.S.A., F.C.S.; Australian physiologist; b. 2 June 1892, Mosgiel, Otago, N.Z.; s. of George Henry Hicks and Sarah Stanton Evans; m. 1st Florence Haggit 1925, 2nd Valerie Irene Hubbard 1948; two s.; ed. Otago Univ., N.Z., Trinity Coll., Cambridge, Freiburg, Zürich and Vienna.
Formerly Lecturer in Chemistry, Otago Univ., Lecturer in Pathology, Otago Medical School, Clinical Pathologist, Dunedin Hospital, and Govt. Analyst for Otago; mem. Cttee. on Endocrine Diseases, Medical Research Council Great Britain; studied Medical Education and Research in U.S. and Europe 24-26, 29-30 and 34-35; Emeritus Prof. Human Physiology and Pharmacology, Sheridan Research Fellow, Adelaide Univ. 26-58; Editor *Australian Journal of Experimental Biology and Medical*

Science 26-; Editorial Board *Excerpta Medica*, Amsterdam 47-66; mem. Australian Nat. Research Council; mem. Commonwealth Nutrition Advisory Cttee. 36-39; mem. Nutrition Cttee., Nat. Health and Medical Research Council 36-39; Pres. Tuberculosis Asscn.; Chair. State Nutrition Cttee. 39-64; served First World War; founder Australian Army Catering Corps, enlisted Lieut. A.I.F., Jan. 40; Col. and Dir. Army Catering, Australian Mil. Forces 40-52; Scientific Mission to Washington, D.C. and U.K. 44; Asst. Commr. St. John Ambulance Brigade (Overseas), S. Australia 40-50; mem. Scientific Advisory Cttee. (Foods), Australian Food Council 42-45; mem. Medical Advisory Cttee. Navy, Army and Air Force 40-45; mem. Nat. Red Cross Nutrition Cttee.; Chair. Commonwealth Defence Food Stuffs Research Cttee. 49-59; Scientific Food Consultant, Army, Australia 52-; Vice-Pres. Nat. Old People's Welfare Council 59-72; Editorial Board *International Journal for Vitamin Research*; mem. Australian Asscn. for Gerontology. Leisure interests: travel, archaeology, gardening. Publs. *Molecular Structure and Physiological Action, Chemistry and Pharmacology of Native Poisons, Human Ecology and Food Production, Soil Food and Life, Nutrition and Beri Beri in a Japanese P.O.W. Camp* 62, *Terrestrial Animals in the Cold: Primitive Man* 64, *Nutritional Requirements of Living Things* 68. *Land Reform in Southern Italy* 69, *Perspectives on the Environment* 73, *Just in Time* 75.
Woodley, Glen Osmond, 5064 South Australia.
Telephone: 79-1308.

Hicks, Sir Denys, Kt., O.B.E.; British solicitor; b. 2 May 1908, Bristol; *s.* of Cuthbert C. and Alice M. (née Hodder) Hicks; *m.* Irene Elizabeth Mansell (née Leach); four *d.*; ed. Clifton Coll.
Solicitor 31; mem. Council, Law Soc. 48-69, Vice-Pres. 59, Pres. 60; mem. Council Int. Bar Asscn. 60, Chair. 66-70, Pres. 70-74, Hon. Life Pres. 74-; Hon. mem. Amer. Bar Asscn., El Ilustre y Nacional Colegio de Abogados de México, Virginia State Bar Asscn. 66; mem. Royal Comm. on Assizes and Quarter Sessions 66-69; Deputy Chair. Horse Race Betting Levy Board 61-; company dir.; D.L. (County of Avon).
Leisure interest: gardening.
Damson Cottage, Hunstrete, Pensford, Bristol, BS18 4NY, England.
Telephone: Compton Dando 464.

Hicks, Sir Edwin William, Kt., C.B.E.; Australian civil servant and diplomatist; b. 9 June 1910, Melbourne, Victoria; *s.* of late William Banks Hicks and Elsie May Hicks (née Kitching); *m.* 1st Jean MacPherson 1937 (died 1959), 2nd Lois Swindon 1961; five *s.* two *d.*; ed. Haileybury Coll., Melbourne Grammar School and Canberra Univ. Coll.
Joined Commonwealth of Australia Public Service 29; Royal Australian Air Force, S.W. Pacific 42-45; Sec. Australian Dept. of Air 51-56, Dept. of Defence 56-68; Australian High Commr. in New Zealand 68-71; Dir.-Gen. Australia-Britain Soc. 72.
Leisure interests: golf, gardening, tennis.
73 Endeavour Street, Red Hill, A.C.T. 2603, Australia.
Telephone: 957378.

Hicks, Granville, A.M.; American writer; b. 9 Sept. 1901; ed. Harvard Univ.
Instr. Smith Coll. 25-28; Asst. Prof. of English, Rensselaer Polytechnic Inst. 29-35; mem. Editorial staff *New Masses* 34-39; Counsellor in American Civilization, Harvard Univ. 38-39; staff mem. radio programme "Speaking of Books" 41-43; Dir. Yaddo Corpn. 42-; Lecturer at Pacific North-west Writers' Conf. 48; Literary Editor *New Leader* 51-58; Instructor, New School for Social Research 55-58; Berg Prof. of American Literature, New York Univ. 59; Contributing Editor *Saturday Review* 58-59; Visiting Prof. Syracuse Univ.

60; McGuffey Prof. American Literature, Ohio Univ. 67-68.
Publs. *The Great Tradition—an Interpretation of American Literature since the Civil War* 33, 35, *One of Us* (with Lynd Ward) 35, *John Reed—the Making of a Revolutionary* 36, *I Like America* 38, *Figures of Transition* 39, co-editor *Proletarian Literature in the United States* 35, *The Letters of Lincoln Steffens* (with Ella Winter) 38, *The First to Awaken* (with Richard M. Bennett) 40, *Only One Storm* 42, *Behold Trouble* 44, *Small Town* 46, *There Was a Man in Our Town* 52, *Where We Came Out* 54, *The Living Novel* (editor) 57, *Part of the Truth: An Autobiography* 65, *James Gould Cozzens* 67, *Literary Horizons* 70, *Granville Hicks in the New Masses* 73.
Grafton, N.Y., U.S.A.

Hicks, Henry Davies, C.C., M.A., B.SC., B.C.L., Q.C.; Canadian barrister, politician and educator; b. 5 March 1915, Bridgetown, N.S.; *s.* of Henry Brandon Hicks and Annie May Kinney; *m.* 1st Paulene Agnes Banks (died 1964), two *s.* two *d.*; 2nd Margaret Gene MacGregor Morison 1965; ed. Mount Allison Univ., Dalhousie, and Exeter Coll., Oxford.
Admitted to Nova Scotia Bar 41; served Royal Canadian Artillery 41-45; practised law, Bridgetown 46-50; mem. Nova Scotia Legislature 45-60; first Minister of Educ. 49-55, Provincial Sec. 54-56; Premier of Province of Nova Scotia 54-56, Leader of Her Majesty's Loyal Opposition in Nova Scotia Legislature and leader, Nova Scotia Liberal Party 56-60; Pres. Canadian Nat. Comm. for UNESCO 63-67; Dean of Arts and Science, Dalhousie Univ. 60-61, Vice-Pres. 61-63, Pres. and Vice-Chancellor 63-; apptd .to Canadian Senate 72; Asscn. of Univs. and Colls. of Canada rep. on Board of Govs. Univ. of Guyana; Hon. D.Ed., Hon. D.C.L., Hon. LL.D.; Companion, Order of Canada 70.
Leisure interests: salmon fishing, philately.
6446 Coburg Road Halifax, Nova Scotia, Canada.
Telephone: 424-2511 (Office); 422-5575 (Home).

Hicks, Sir John Richard, Kt.; British economist; b. 8 April 1904, Warwick; *s.* of Edward Hicks; *m.* Ursula Kathleen Webb 1935; ed. Clifton Coll. and Balliol Coll., Oxford.
Professor of Political Economy, Univ of Manchester 38-46; Fellow of Nuffield Coll. Oxford 46-52; Prof. of Political Economy, Univ. of Oxford 52-65; Research Fellow, All Souls Coll. Oxford 65-71; Nobel Memorial Prize for Economics 72 (with K. Arrow, *q.v.*).
Publs. *Theory of Wages* 32, *Value and Capital* 39, *The Social Framework* 42, *Contribution to the Theory of the Trade Cycle* 50, *A Revision of Demand Theory* 56, *Essays in World Economics* 59, *Capital and Growth* 65, *Critical Essays in Monetary Theory* 67, *A Theory of Economic History* 69, *Capital and Time* 73, *The Crisis in Keynesian Economics* 74.
All Souls College, Oxford, England.

Hidayatullah, Mohammed, O.B.E., M.A.; Indian judge; b. 17 Dec. 1905, Betul; *s.* of H. M. Wilayatullah and Mohammadi Begum; *m.* Pushpa Shah 1948; one *s.* one *d.* (deceased); ed. Government High School, Raipur, Morris Coll., Nagpur, Trinity Coll., Cambridge, and Lincoln's Inn, London.
Advocate, Nagpur High Court 30-46; Advocate-Gen. Madhya Pradesh 43-46; Puisne Judge 46-54; Dean of Faculty of Law, Nagpur Univ. 49-53; Chief Justice, Nagpur High Court 54-56; Chief Justice, Madhya Pradesh High Court 56-58; Judge, Supreme Court of India 56-68; Chief Justice of India 68-70; Acting Pres. of India 69; Hon. Bencher, Lincoln's Inn, London; Mitchell Fellow, State Univ. of N.Y., Buffalo; Hon. LL.D. (Univ. of the Philippines, Ravishankar Univ.); Bronze Medal for Gallantry 69, Order of the Yugoslav Flag with Sash 71, Knight of Mark Twain.
Leisure interests: golf, bridge, reading.
Publs. *Democracy in India and the Judicial Process,*

The South-West Africa Case, Mulla's Mahomedan Law editor, 17th edn.), A Judge's Miscellany.
A-10 Rockside, 112 Walkeshwar Road, Bombay 400006, India.

Hiernaux, Jean-Robert-Laurent, M.D.; Belgian doctor and professor; b. 9 May 1921, Huy; m. Denyse L'Hoëst 1945; two c.; ed. Athénée Royal de Charleroi and Univ. Libre, Brussels.
Divisionary physician at the Compagnie Minière des Grands Lacs Africains 46-49; research worker of the Institut pour la Recherche Scientifique en Afrique Central 49-56; Prof. at Université Officielle du Congo Belge et du Ruanda-Urundi 56-60, and Rector 57-61, Hon. Rector 63-; Maître de recherche, Centre Nat. de la Recherche Scientifique, Paris 64-.
Leisure interest: African archaelogy.
Publs. Caractères physiques des populations du Ruanda et de L'Urundi 54, Analyse de la variation des caractères physiques humains en une région de l'Afrique Centrale: Ruanda-Urundi et Kivu 56, La Diversité Humaine en Afrique Subsaharienne, Recherches Biologiques 68, Egalité ou Inégalité des Races? 69.
156 avenue Carsoel, B-1180-Brussels, Belgium.
Telephone: 74-07-94.

Higgins, Michael Harold, M.A.; British international administrator; b. 3 Oct. 1908, London; s. of Harold and Gertrude Higgins; m. Moira Walker 1941; two s. two d.; ed. privately and at London, Edinburgh and Cambridge Univs.
Asst. Lecturer, Edinburgh and London Univs. 37-45; attached to Air Ministry 40-45; Deputy Commandant, Royal Observer Corps 41-42; Private Sec. to Vice-Chief of Air Staff 42-45; Asst. to Pres. of Council, Int. Civil Aviation Organisation 45-49; Deputy Dir. U.N. Transport and Communications Division, New York 49; mem. Mudaliar U.N. Staff Selection Cttee., New York 52, Bangkok 53, U.N. Staff Selection Board, New York 53-57, Geneva 54-55, Bangkok 56, U.N. Joint Pension Board 56-57, U.N. Appointment Review and Promotion Board 57-; Sec. Preparatory Cttee., Inter-Govt. Maritime Consultative Organisation 58-59, Exec. Sec. 1st Assembly, London 59, Dir. of Admin. and External Relations, IMCO 59-63, Admin. and Financial Services, UN Office, Geneva 63-69; Consultant, Fed. of Int. Civil Servants' Asscns. 69-74, Int. Asscn. of Conf. Interpreters 71-.
Leisure interest: archaeology.
Home: Mill Vale House, Bratton, Nr. Westbury, Wilts., England; 14 rue de l'ancien port, Geneva, Switzerland.
Telephone: Bratton 376 (Home); 32-27-54 (Office).

Higginson, John, M.D., F.R.C.P.; American professor of pathology; b. 16 Oct. 1922, Belfast, N. Ireland; s. of William Higginson and Ellen Margaret Rogers; m. Nan Russell McKee 1949; two d.; ed. Royal Belfast Academical Inst., Belfast, and Univ. of Dublin.
Pathologist, S. African Inst. for Medical Research, Baragwanath Hosp., S. Africa 50-58; Head, Geographical Pathology Unit and Cancer Registry, S. African Inst. for Medical Research 54-58; Assoc. Prof. of Pathology and Oncology, Univ. of Kansas Medical Center 58-62; American Cancer Soc. Career Professorship, Univ. of Kansas 61-66; Prof. of Pathology, Univ. of Kansas Medical Center 62-66; Dir. Int. Agency for Cancer Research, Lyons, France 66-; Hon. Fellow Royal Acad. of Medicine in Ireland, etc.
Leisure interests: golf, skiing, reading.
Publs. over 130 scientific papers in field of environmental biology and cancer research.
International Agency for Research on Cancer, 150 Cours Albert Thomas, 69008 Lyon, France.
Telephone: 78-69-81-45.

Highet, Hon. David Allan; New Zealand chartered accountant, business executive and politician; b. 27 May 1913, Dunedin; s. of David Highet and Elsie M.

Bremner; m. Margaret P. Hoyles 1938; one s. one d.; ed. Otago Boys' High School and Otago Univ.
Practised as chartered accountant, Wellington 42-60; Gen. Man. L. J. Fisher & Co. Ltd., Auckland 60-64; Senior Partner, Cox, Elliffe, Twomey, Highet & Co. (Chartered Accountants), Auckland 64-; Wellington City Councillor 54-59; mem. Parl. for Remuera 66-; Minister of Internal Affairs, Minister of Local Govt., Minister of Civil Defence and Assoc. Minister of Social Welfare Feb.-Nov. 72, of Internal Affairs Dec. 75-; Nat. Party.
Leisure interests: music, theatre, golf, tennis, bowls, travel.
28 Burwood Crescent, Remuera, Auckland, New Zealand.
Telephone: 549-507.

Highet, Gilbert, D.LITT., F.R.S.L.; American scholar and critic; b. 22 June 1906, Glasgow, Scotland; s. of Gilbert Highet and Elizabeth Gertrude Boyle; m. Helen McInnes (q.v.); one s.; ed. Hillhead High School (Glasgow), Glasgow Univ. and Balliol Coll., Oxford.
Fellow St. John's Coll., Oxford 32-38; Prof. of Greek and Latin Columbia Univ. 38-50, Anthon Prof. of Latin Language and Literature 50-72, Prof. Emer. 72; mem. Board of Judges Book-of-the-Month Club 54-; Chair. Advisory Board Horizon 58-; Guggenheim Fellowship 51; Wallace Award, Amer.-Scottish Foundation 73.
Leisure interests: two-piano duets, colour photography, gardening, golf, not going to dinner parties.
Publs. The Classical Tradition 49, The Art of Teaching 50, People, Places and Books 53, Juvenal the Satirist 54, A Clerk of Oxenford 54, Man's Unconquerable Mind 54, The Migration of Ideas 54, Poets in a Landscape 57, Talents and Geniuses 57, The Powers of Poetry 60, The Anatomy of Satire 62, Explorations 71, The Speeches in Vergil's Aeneid 72, The Immortal Profession 73.
Jefferys Lane, East Hampton, New York, N.Y. 11937, U.S.A.

Hightower, John B.; American museum director; b. 1933, Atlanta, Georgia; m. Caroline Warner; two c.; ed. Yale Univ.
Executive trainee, First Nat. City Bank 57-61; Gen. Asst. to Pres. and Publisher, American Heritage Publishing Co. 61-64; Exec. Dir. New York State Council on the Arts 64-70; Dir. Museum of Modern Art, New York 70-72; Pres. Assoc. Councils of Arts 72-; frequent adviser to arts councils throughout U.S.A.; Cultural Adviser to Presidential Latin Amer. Comm.; mem. M.I.T. Comm. to Survey the Arts.
1564 Broadway, New York, N.Y. 10036; and 321 Central Street, Auburndale 66, Mass., U.S.A.

Hilaly, Agha, M.A., S.PC.; Pakistani diplomatist; b. 20 May 1911, Bangalore; s. of late Agha Abdulla; m. Malek Taj Kazim 1938; three s.; ed. Madras and Cambridge Univs.
Entered Civil Service 36; apptd. Under-Sec. to Finance Ministry, Govt. of Bengal; transferred to pre-partition Govt. of India and served as Under-Sec. in Ministries of Agriculture, Food and Commerce 41-47; Deputy Sec. Pakistan Foreign Ministry 47-51, Joint Sec. 51-54; attended several Int. Confs. as Sec.-Gen. of Pakistan dels.; Ambassador to Sweden, Norway, Denmark and Finland 56-59, to U.S.S.R. (concurrently Minister to Czechoslovakia) 59-61; High Commr. in India and Amb. to Nepal 61-63; High Commr. in U.K. and Amb. to Repub. of Ireland 63-66; Amb. to U.S.A. (concurrently to Mexico, Venezuela and Jamaica) 66-71; mem. Board of Dirs. State Bank of Pakistan 72-; Chair. Board of Govs. Pakistan Inst. of Strategic Studies 73-.
Leisure interests: photography, hunting.
25-C Block-6, P.E.C.H. Society, Karachi 29, Pakistan.
Telephone: 411767 (Home).

Hilbe, Alfred J., DR.ECON.; Liechtenstein politician; b. 22 July 1928, Gmunden, Austria; s. of Franz and Elisabeth (née Glatz) Hilbe; m. Virginia Joseph 1951; one d.; ed. classical secondary schools in Vaduz and Zurich, Ecole Nationale des Sciences Politiques, Paris and Univ. of Innsbruck.

Several posts in private business 51-54; in foreign service 54-65, Counsellor, Liechtenstein Embassy, Berne until 65; Deputy Head of Govt. of Liechtenstein June 65-March 70, Head of the Government 70-74; Grosskreutz of Liechtenstein Order of Merit, Order of St. Gregory (Vatican); Fatherland Union Party.

Leisure interests: skiing, tennis, photography.

Garsill 762, Schaan, Principality of Liechtenstein.

Telephone: 075-22002.

Hildebrand, Joel Henry, SC.D., LL.D., PH.D.; American emeritus professor of chemistry; b. 16 Nov. 1881, Camden, N.J.; s. of Howard O. Hildebrand and Sarah S. Hildebrand; m. Emily Alexander 1908; three s. one d.; ed. Univ. of Pennsylvania and Berlin Univ.

Instructor in Chemistry Univ. of Pennsylvania 07-13; Asst. Prof. of Chemistry Univ. of Calif. 13; Assoc. Prof. 17, Prof. 18-52; Dean of Coll. of Letters and Science 39-43; Dean Coll. of Chemistry 49-51; Faculty Research Lecturer 36; Commissioned Capt. U.S. Army 17; Lieut.-Col. Chemical Warfare Service 18; awarded D.S.M. 18; Liaison Officer for Office of Scientific Research and Development, U.S. Embassy, London 43-44, King's Medal (Brit.); Pres. American Chemical Soc. for 55; Westman Lecturer, Chemistry Inst. of Canada 57; Gilbert Newton Memorial Lecture, Berkeley 71; Hildebrand 90th Birthday Symposium 71; Hon. Fellow, Royal Soc., Edinburgh, Nat. Acad. Sciences, American Philosophical Soc.; Hon. mem. American Inst. of Chemists, Calif. Acad. of Sciences; Hon. Life mem. Faraday Soc.; Nichols Medal 39; American Chemical Soc. Award in Chemical Educ. 52; Gibbs Medal 53, Jas. F. Norris Award in Chemical Educ. 61, Wm. Proctor Prize, Scientific Research Soc. of America 62, Priestly Medal 62 (American Chemical Soc.), Joseph Priestly Award 65, Hildebrand Hall Laboratory, Univ. of Calif., Berkeley dedicated in honour 66, Madison Marshall Award 67; S. C. Lind Lectures 74.

Leisure interests: Baroque music, gardening, formerly skiing, mountaineering, photography, grandchildren and great grandchildren.

Publs. *Principles of Chemistry* (with R. M. Powell) 52, 64, *Solubility of Non-Electrolytes* (with R. L. Scott) 50, *Reference Book of Inorganic Chemistry* (with W. M. Latimer) 51, *Science in the Making* 56, *Regular Solutions* (with R. L. Scott) 62, *Is Intelligence Important?* 63, *An Introduction to Molecular Kinetic Theory* 63, *Regular and Related Solutions* (with J. M. Prausnitz and R. L. Scott) 70; 250 papers.

Department of Chemistry, University of California, Berkeley, Calif. 94720; Home: 500 Coventry Road, Berkeley, Calif. 94707, U.S.A.

Telephone: 415-525-2131.

Hildesheimer, Wolfgang; German writer and artist; b. 9 Dec. 1916, Hamburg; s. of Dr. Arnold Hildesheimer and Hanna Hildesheimer (née Goldschmid); m. Silvia Dillman 1953; ed. Odenwaldschule, Heppenheim, Germany, Frensham Heights School, Surrey, England, and Central School of Arts and Crafts, London.

British Information Officer, Palestine 43-45; Lecturer, British Inst., Tel-Aviv 45-46; interpreter, War Crimes Trials, Nuremberg 47-49; now freelance writer and artist; guest lecturer in Poetry at Frankfurt Univ. 67; Radio Play Prize in aid of War Blinded 55; Literaturpreis der Freien Hansestadt Bremen 66; Georg Büchner Preis der Deutschen Akad. für Sprache und Dichtung, Darmstadt 66.

Publs. include: *Lieblose Legenden* (short stories) 52, *Die Verspätung* 62 (play), *Nachtstück* (one-act play) 63,

Tynset (novel) 65, *Rivalen* (adaptation from Sheridan) 65, *Wer war Mozart?* (essay), *Mary Stuart* (play), *Masante* (novel) 73.

7742 Poschiavo (GR), Switzerland.

Telephone: (082) 50467.

Hildred, Sir William Percival, Kt., C.B., O.B.E., M.A.; British international administrator; b. 13 July 1893, Hull, Yorks.; s. of William Kirk Hildred and Clara Varley; m. Constance Mary Chappell 1920; two s. one d.; ed. Univ. of Sheffield.

Served First World War 14-18; lectured Social History for Workers' Educational Asscn. Univ. of Sheffield 18; entered Treasury 19; Finance Officer Empire Marketing Board 26-34; Head Special Measures Branch Min. of Agriculture and Fisheries 34-36; Deputy Gen. Man. Exports Credit Guarantee Dept. 36-38; Deputy Dir.-Gen. of Civil Aviation March 38-39; Principal Asst. Sec. in Air Ministry 39-40; with Ministry of Aircraft Production 40-41; Dir.-Gen. Min. of Civil Aviation 41-46; Dir.-Gen. Int. Air Transport Asscn. (IATA) 46-66; Grand Officer Order of Orange-Nassau (Neths.) 46, Commdr. Order of the Crown of Belgium 48; Hon. LL.D. (Univ. of Sheffield and McGill Univ.).

Leisure interests: reading, writing, music, carpentry.

Spreakley House, Frensham, Surrey, England.

Telephone: Frensham 2330.

Hilgard, Ernest Ropiequet, PH.D.; American professor of psychology and education; b. 25 July 1904, Belleville, Ill.; s. of Dr. George E. Hilgard and Laura Ropiequet Hilgard; m. Josephine Rohrs 1931; one s. one d.; ed. Univ. of Illinois and Yale Univ.

Instructor in Psychology, Yale Univ. 28-33; Asst. Prof. to Prof., Psychology and Educ., Stanford Univ. 33-69, Exec. Head, Dept. of Psychology 42-51, Dean of Graduate Div. 51-55, Emer. Prof. of Psychology and Educ. 69-; Past Pres. American Psychological Asscn.; mem. Nat. Acad. of Sciences, Nat. Acad. of Educ., American Philosophical Soc., American Acad. of Arts and Sciences; Hon. Fellow, British Psychological Asscn.; Warren Medal; Distinguished Scientific Contribution Award; Hon. D.Sc. (Kenyon Coll.) 64, Hon. LL.D. (Centre Coll.) 74.

Publs. *Conditioning and Learning* 40, *Theories of Learning* 48, 56, 66, 75, *Introduction to Psychology* 53, 57 62, 67, 71, 75, *Hypnotic Susceptibility* 65, *Hypnosis in the Relief of Pain* 75; and articles in professional journals.

Office: Department of Psychology, Stanford University, Stanford, Calif. 94305; Home: 1129 Hamilton Avenue, Palo Alto, Calif. 94301, U.S.A.

Telephone: 415 497-4441 (Office).

Hill, Archibald Vivian, C.H., O.B.E., SC.D., LL.D., F.R.S.; British physiologist; b. 26 Sept. 1886, Bristol; s. of Jonathan Hill and Ada Rumney; m. Margaret Neville Keynes 1913 (died 1970); two s. (one deceased) two d.; ed. Trinity Coll., Cambridge.

Fellow of Trinity Coll. 10-16, Hon. Fellow 41; Fellow King's Coll. 16-22, Hon. Fellow 27; Foreign mem. Nat. Acad. Sciences, Washington and other Acads. and Societies; Prof. of Physiology Manchester Univ. 20-23 and Univ. Coll., London 23-25; Foulerton Research Prof. of Royal Society 26-51; Trustee British Museum 47-63, British Museum (Natural History) 63-65; Sec. Royal Soc. 35-45, Foreign Sec. 45-46; Ind. M.P. for Cambridge Univ. 40-45; Pres. British Asscn. for the Advancement of Science 52; Pres. Marine Biological Asscn. of U.K. 55-60; Sec.-Gen. Int. Council of Scientific Unions 52-56; Pres. Soc. for Visiting Scientists, London 52-66; Hon. Fellow Univ. Coll., London 48; Nobel Prize for Physiology and Medicine 22; Copley Medal, Royal Soc. 48.

Leisure interest: working.

Publs. *Living Machinery* 27, *The Ethical Dilemma of*

Science 60, *Trails and Trials in Physiology* 65, *First and Last Experiments in Muscle Mechanics* 70.
11A Chaucer Road, Cambridge CB2 2EB, England.
Telephone: Cambridge 54551.

Hill, Sir Austin Bradford, Kt., c.b.e., ph.d., d.sc., f.r.s.; British university professor; b. 8 July 1897, London; *s.* of Sir Leonard Hill and Janet Alexander; *m.* Florence Maud Salmon 1923; two *s.* one *d.*; ed. Chigwell School and London Univ.
Research worker for Industrial Health Research Board and Medical Research Council 23-32; London Univ. Reader in Epidemiology and Vital Statistics at the London School of Hygiene and Tropical Medicine 32-45, Prof. of Medical Statistics 45-61; Hon. Dir. Statistical Research Unit of Medical Research Council 45-61; Civil Consultant in Medical Statistics to the R.N and R.A.F. and mem. Flying Personnel Research Cttee., mem. Cttee. on Review of Medicines; Pres. Royal Statistical Soc. 50-52, Gold Medallist, Royal Statistical Soc. 53; Hon. Fellow, American Public Health Assen. 53, Royal Soc. of Medicine 62; Fellow, Univ. Coll., London 55; Hon. Fellow, Soc. of Occupational Medicine 57, Soc. of Social Medicine 61, Royal Coll. of Physicians 63, Faculty of Community Medicine 73, Soc. of Community Medicine 63-; Hon. mem. Inst. of Actuaries 56, Faculty of Medicine, Univ. of Chile 59, Int. Epidemiological Assen. 71; Galen Medal, Soc. of Apothecaries 59, Harben Gold Medal, Royal Inst. of Public Health and Hygiene 61, Heberden Medal 65, Jenner Medal of Royal Soc. of Medicine 65; Hon. D.Sc. (Oxford) 63, Hon. M.D. (Edinburgh) 68.
Leisure interests: gardening, travelling.
Publs. *Principles of Medical Statistics* (9th edition) 71, *Statistical Methods in Clinical and Preventive Medicine* 62.
Green Acres, Little Kingshill, Great Missenden, Bucks., England.
Telephone: Great Missenden 2380.

Hill, Christopher (*see* Hill, (John Edward) C.).

Hill, John Alexander; American business executive; b. 24 Feb. 1907, Shawnee, Okla.; *s.* of John E. Hill and Mary B. Cheek; *m.* Margaret Mikesell 1929; one *s.* two *d.*; ed. Univ. of Denver.
Aetna Life Insurance Co. 28?0, Denver 28-30, Man. Group and Pensions Depts., Detroit 30-35, District Supervisor 33-36, Gen. Agent, John A. Hill & Assocs., Toledo 36-58, Senior Vice-Pres. 58-62, Pres. 62-70, Pres. Hospital Corpn. of America 70-73, Chair. 73-; Dir. of several cos.
Leisure interests: golf, art.
Hospital Corporation of America, 1 Park Plaza, Nashville, Tenn. 37202; Home: Belle Meade Towers Apartments, 105 Leake Avenue, Nashville, Tenn., U.S.A.

Hill, (John Edward) Christopher, M.A., D.LITT.; British historian; b. 6 Feb. 1912, York; *s.* of Edward H. and Janet A. Hill; *m.* 1st Inez Waugh 1944, 2nd Bridget Irene Sutton 1956; one *s.* two *d.*; ed. St. Peter's School, York, and Balliol Coll., Oxford.
Fellow of All Souls Coll., Oxford 34-38; Asst. Lecturer, Univ. Coll., Cardiff 36-38; Fellow and Tutor in Modern History, Balliol Coll., Oxford 38-65, Master of Balliol Coll. 65-; Army and Foreign Office Service 40-45; Univ. Lecturer in 16th and 17th Century History, Oxford 59-65; mem. Editorial Board *Past and Present* 68-, Yale Edition of Milton's *Complete Prose*; Fellow of British Acad. 66; Hon. D.Litt. (Hull, Norwich and Sheffield).
Publs. *The English Revolution, 1640* 40, *Lenin and the Russian Revolution* 47, *The Good Old Cause* (documents, edited jointly with E. Dell) 49, *Economic Problems of the Church* 56, *Puritanism and Revolution* 58, *The Century*

of Revolution, 1603–1714 61, *Society and Puritanism in Pre-Revolutionary England* 64, *Intellectual Origins of The English Revolution* 65, *Reformation to Industrial Revolution* 67, *God's Englishman* 70, *Antichrist in 17th Century England* 71, *The World Turned Upside Down* 72, *The Law of Freedom and Other Selected Writings of Gerrard Winstanley* (editor) 73, *Change and Continuity in 17th Century England* 75.
Balliol College, Oxford, England.

Hill, Sir John McGregor, Kt., B.SC., PH.D., F.INST.P.; British atomic energy official; b. 21 Feb. 1921; ed. Richmond County Grammar School, King's Coll., London, and St. John's Coll., Cambridge.
Flight Lieut., R.A.F., Second World War; research at Cavendish Laboratory, Cambridge 46-48; Lecturer, London Univ. 48-50; U.K. Atomic Energy Authority 50-, mem. for Production 64-67, Chair. 67-; Chair. British Nuclear Fuels Ltd. 71-, Radiochemical Centre Ltd. 75-.
United Kingdom Atomic Energy Authority, 11 Charles II Street, London, S.W.1, England.

Hill, Robert Charles; American diplomatist and politician; b. 30 Sept. 1917, Littleton, N.H.; *s.* of late Dr. A. F. Hill and Mrs. Hill; *m.* Cecelia Gordon Bowdoin 1945; two *s.*; ed. Taft School and Dartmouth Coll.
Vice-Consul Foreign Service 43-45; Asst. Vice-Pres. W. R. Grace & Co., N.Y. 49-53; Clerk, Senate Banking and Currency Cttee. 47-48; Ambassador to Costa Rica 53-54, to El Salvador 54-55; Special Asst. to Under-Sec. of State for Mutual Security Affairs 55-56; Asst. Sec. of State for Congressional Relations 56-57; U.S. Ambassador to Mexico 57-61; mem. N.H. State Legislature 61-62; Chair. Republican Nat. Cttee. Foreign Policy Task Force 65-68; Amb. to Spain 69-72; Asst. Sec. Dept. of Defense 73; Amb. to Argentina 74-; Dir. Todd Shipyards Corpn., N.Y., New York; U.S.A.F. Exceptional Service Award, Aztec Eagle, First Class (Mexico), Grand Order of Merit (Peru), Cuerpo de Defensores de la República (Mexico), La Orden Mexicana del Derecho y La Cultura (Mexico), Gran Cruz de la Orden de Isabel la Católica and other decorations; several hon. degrees, incl. Dartmouth.
American Embassy, Sarmiento 663, Buenos Aires, Argentina; P.O. Box 350, Littleton, New Hampshire 03561, U.S.A.
Telephone: 603-444-6501.

Hill, Terrell Leslie, A.B., PH.D.; American biophysicist and chemist; b. 19 Dec. 1917, Oakland, Calif.; *s.* of George Leslie and Ollie Moreland Hill; *m.* Laura Etta Gano 1942; one *s.* two *d.*; ed. Univ. of Calif. at Berkeley and Harvard Univ.
Instructor in Chem., Western Reserve Univ. 42-44; Research Assoc., Radiation Lab., Univ. of Calif. at Berkeley 44-45; Research Assoc. in Chem., then Asst. Prof. of Chem., Univ. of Rochester 45-49; Chemist, U.S. Naval Medical Research Inst. 49-57; Prof. of Chem., Univ. of Oregon 57-67; Prof. of Chem., Univ. of Calif. at Santa Cruz 67-71, Vice-Chancellor, Sciences 68-69; Senior Research Chemist, Nat. Institutes of Health 71-; mem. Nat. Acad. of Sciences, American Chemical Soc., Biophysical Soc., American Civil Liberties Union, Nat. Assen. for Advancement of Coloured People, etc.; Guggenheim Fellow, Yale 52-53; Sloan Foundation Fellow 58-62; Arthur S. Fleming Award, U.S. Govt. 54; Dist. Civilian Service Award, U.S. Navy 55; Award of Washington Acad. of Sciences 56; Kendall Award, American Chemical Soc. 69.
Leisure interests: tennis, chess, poetry, music.
Publs. *Statistical Mechanics* 56, *Statistical Thermodynamics* 60, *Thermodynamics of Small Systems* Vol I 63, Vol II 64, *Matter and Equilibrium* 65, *Thermodynamics for Chemists and Biologists* 69; also research papers.

National Institutes of Health, Bethesda, Md. 20014; Home: 9626 Kensington Parkway, Kensington, Md. 20795, U.S.A.
Telephone: 301-496-5436 (Office); 301-946-7978 (Home).

Hill, (William) Martin, C.M.G., M.A.; British United Nations official (retd.); b. 8 April 1905, Cork, Ireland; s. of William Henry Hill and Stella A. Hill (née Harris); m. Diana Grove-Annesley 1932; one s.; ed. Malvern Coll., Oriel Coll., Oxford, London School of Economics, and Univs. of Vienna and Cambridge.
Entered League of Nations Secretariat 27; mem. Econ. and Financial Section 27-34, Political Section 34-39, Econ., Financial and Transit Dept. 39-45; Soc. to the Bruce Cttee. 39, to the Econ. and Financial Cttees. 42-45; Asst. to the Sec.-Gen. 45-46; Special Adviser to the Exec. Sec. to the San Francisco Conf. 45; Chief of Administrative and Budgetary Section, Preparatory Comm. of the U.N. 45; joined permanent secretariat of the UN 46; Special Adviser to the Sec.-Gen. 46-48; Deputy Exec. Asst. to the Sec.-Gen. and Dir. of Co-ordination for the specialized agencies and econ. and social matters 48-55; Deputy Under-Sec. for Econ. and Social Affairs and Personal Rep. of Sec.-Gen. to the Specialized Agencies 55-66; Asst. Sec.-Gen. for Inter-Agency Affairs 67-Dec. 70; Special Consultant to Sec.-Gen. 71-72; Special Fellow UNITAR 73-74; Rep. to UN of World Intellectual Property Org. 75.
Leisure interests: music, travel.
Publs. *The Economic and Financial Organisation of the League of Nations* 45, *Immunities and Privileges of International Officials* 47, *Commercial Policy in the Inter-War Period* 42, *Quantitative Trade Controls* 43, *The Administrative Committee on Co-ordination* in *The Evolution of International Organizations* (Editor Luard) 66.
260 Snowden Lane, Princeton, N.J. 08540, U.S.A.
Telephone: (609) 921-7967.

Hill of Luton, Baron (Life Peer), cr. 63; **Charles Hill,** P.C., M.A., M.D., D.P.H., LL.D.; British doctor; b. 15 Jan. 1904; ed. St. Olave's Grammar School, Trinity Coll., Cambridge, and the London Hospital.
Univ. Tutorial Lecturer in Biology 26-30; Sec. British Medical Asscn. 44-50; Pres. World Medical Asscn. 49-50; Liberal-Conservative M.P. 50-63; Parl. Sec., Ministry of Food 51-55; Postmaster-Gen. 55-57; Chancellor of the Duchy of Lancaster 57-61; Minister of Housing and Local Govt. and Minister for Welsh Affairs 61-62; Dir. Laporte Industries 62-65, Chair. 65-70; Dir. Abbey National Building Soc. 64-, Chair. Jan. 76-; Chair. Independent Television Authority 63-67; Chair. of Govs. BBC 67-72; Chair. Nat. Joint Council for Local Authorities' Administrative, Professional, Technical and Clerical Services 63-.
Publs. *What is Osteopathy?* 37, *Your Health in Wartime* 41, *Wartime Food for Growing Children* 42, *Wise Eating in Wartime* 43, *When Your Baby is Coming* 43, *Wednesday Morning Early—by the Radio Doctor* 44, *Your Body* 44, *Your Aches and Pains* 45, *The Way to Better Health* 46, *Bringing up Your Child* 50, *Dictionary of Health* 51, *Both Sides of the Hill* 64, *Behind the Screen* 74.
5 Bamville Wood, East Common, Harpenden, Herts., England.

Hill-Norton, Admiral of the Fleet Sir Peter John, G.C.B.; British naval officer; b. 8 Feb. 1915, Germiston; s. of Martin J. and Margery B. Norton; m. Margaret E. Linstow 1936; one s. one d.; ed. Royal Naval Coll., Dartmouth and Royal Naval Coll., Greenwich.
Went to sea 32; commissioned 36; served Arctic convoys, N.W. Approaches and Admiralty Naval Staff, Second World War 39-45; Commdr. 48; Captain 52; Naval Attaché, Argentine, Uruguay, Paraguay 53-55; in command H.M.S. *Decoy* 56-57, H.M.S. *Ark Royal* 59-61; Asst. Chief of Naval Staff 62-64; Flag Officer,

Second-in-Command Far East Fleet 64-66; Deputy Chief of the Defence Staff (Personnel and Logistics) 66; Second Sea Lord and Chief of Naval Personnel Jan.-Aug. 67; Vice-Chief of Naval Staff 67-68; Commander-in-Chief, Far East 69-70; Chief of Naval Staff and First Sea Lord 70-71; Chief of the Defence Staff 71-74; Chair. North Atlantic Mil. Cttee. 74-; Hon. Liveryman Worshipful Company of Shipwrights 73; Freeman of the City of London 74.
Leisure interests: golf, shooting, water-skiing.
King's Mill House, South Nutfield, Surrey, England.
Telephone: Nutfield Ridge 3309.

Hillary, Sir Edmund Percival, K.B.E.; New Zealand explorer and bee farmer; b. 20 July 1919, Auckland; s. of Percy and Gertrude Hillary; m. Louise Mary Rose 1953 (died 1975); one s. two d. (one deceased); ed. Auckland Grammar School and Univ. of Auckland.
Served R.N.Z.A.F. (on Catalinas in the Pacific) 44-45; went to Himalayas on N.Z. Garwhal expedition 51, when he and another were invited to join the British reconnaissance over Everest under Eric Shipton; took part in British expedition to Cho Oyu 52, and in British Mount Everest Expedition under Sir John Hunt 53, when he and Tenzing reached the summit on May 29th; Leader N.Z. Alpine Club Expedition to Barun Valley 54; N.Z. Antarctic Expedition 56-58, reached South Pole Dec. 57; Leader Himalayan Expeditions 61, 63, 64; Pres. Volunteer Service Abroad in New Zealand 63-64; built a hospital for Sherpa tribesmen, Nepal 66; Leader climbing expedition on Mount Herschel, Antarctica 67; Polar Medal 58; Gurkha Right Hand (1st Class), James Wattie Book of the Year Award, N.Z. 75.
Leisure interests: walking, fishing, camping.
Publs. *High Adventure* 55, *The Crossing of Antarctica* (with Sir Vivian Fuchs) 58, *No Latitude for Error* 61, *High in the Thin Cold Air* (with Desmond Doig) 63, *Schoolhouse in the Clouds* 65, *Nothing Venture, Nothing Win* (autobiog.) 75.
278A Remuera Road, Auckland, New Zealand.

Hille, (Carl) Einar, PH.D.; American professor of mathematics; b. 28 June 1894, New York; s. of Carl A. H. and Edla (née Ekman) Hille; m. Kirsti Ore 1937; two s.; ed. Palmgrenska Samskolan, Stockholm, Univ. of Stockholm, Harvard Univ. and Univs. of Göttingen and Copenhagen.
Swedish civil service 18-20; Docent, Stockholm 19; Instructor, Harvard Univ. 21-22, Princeton Univ. 22-23; Asst. Prof. Princeton Univ. 23-26, 27-30, Assoc. Prof. 30-33; Prof. Yale Univ. 33-62, Prof. Emer. 62-; Visiting Prof. Stanford Univ. 28, 41-42, Chicago 31, Univs. of Stockholm and Uppsala 49, 62, Tata Inst. Bombay 63, 64, Australian Nat. Univ. 65, 66-67, Univ. of Calif. (Irvine) 65-66, Univ. of Oregon 67-68, Univ. of New Mexico 68-72; Fulbright Lecturer, Nancy 52, Sorbonne 53, Univ. of Mainz 56; mem. Nat. Acad. of Sciences, American Acad. of Arts and Sciences, Swedish Acad. of Sciences, Lund Physiographical Soc., Connecticut Acad. of Arts and Sciences; John Ericson Medal.
Leisure interests: reading archaeology, history, linguistics, entomology, cosmology, mysteries.
Publs. *Functional Analysis and Semi-groups* 48, 57, *Analysis* (2 vols.) 64, 66, *Analytic Function Theory* (2 vols.) 59, 62, *Ordinary Differential Equations* 69, *Methods in Classical and Functional Analysis* 72 and about 150 articles in professional journals.
8862 La Jolla, Scenic Drive N., La Jolla, Calif. 92037, U.S.A.
Telephone: (714) 453-6250.

Hillebrecht, Rudolf Friedrich Heinrich, DIPL. ING.; German architect and town planner; b. 26 Feb. 1910, Hanover; s. of Ernst and Bertha (née Arning) Hillebrecht; m. 1st Ruth Frommhold 1937, 2nd Oxana

Saweljewa 1967; one *d*.; ed. Humanistisches Gymnasium, Hanover, and Technische Hochschulen, Hanover and Berlin.

Worked with Walter Gropius, Berlin 33-34; Building Inspector, Travemünde, Hamburg and Hanover 34-37; Office Manager, architectural practice of Konstanty Gutschow, Hamburg 37-45; worked in Dept. for Replanning of Hamburg 37-44; Army Service 44-45; worked with Werner Kallmorgen, Hamburg 45-46; Deputy Chief, Building Div., British Occupied Zone 46; Sec. for Building Affairs, German Advisory Council of British Zone 46-48; Municipal Town Planner and Architect, City of Hanover 48-75; Pres. German Acad. for Town and Country Planning and other orgs.; Mitglied des Ordens Pour le Mérite für Wissenschaften und Künste 64, and many other decorations.
Leisure interests: arts, literature, music.
Office: Friedrichswall 4, 3 Hanover; Home: Gneiststrasse 7, 3 Hanover, Federal Republic of Germany.

Hillel, Shlomo; Israeli politician; b. 1923, Baghdad; *m*. Tmima Rosner 1952; one *s*. one *d*.; ed. Hebrew Univ., Jerusalem.
Member, Maagan Michael 42-46; Jewish Agency for Palestine—mission to countries in Middle East 46-48, 49-51; Israel Defence Forces 48-49; Prime Minister's Office 52-53; mem. of Knesset 53-59, 74-; Amb. to Guinea 59-61, to Ivory Coast, Dahomey, Upper Volta and Niger 61-63; Dir. African Dept., Ministry of Foreign Affairs; mem. Perm. Mission to UN with rank of Minister 64-67; Asst. Dir.-Gen. Ministry of Foreign Affairs 67-69; Minister of Police 69-.
Ministry of Police, Jerusalem, Israel.

Hilleman, Maurice R., PH.D.; American virologist; b. 30 Aug. 1919, Miles City, Mont.; *s*. of Robert A. and Edith M. (Matson) Hilleman; *m*. 1st Thelma L. Mason 1943 (deceased), 2nd Lorraine Witmer 1963; two *d*.; ed. Montana State Coll. and Univ. of Chicago.
Assistant Bacteriologist, Univ. of Chicago 42-44; Research Assoc., Virus Laboratories, E. R. Squibb & Sons 44-47; Chief Virus Dept. 47-48; Medical Bacteriologist and Asst. Chief, Virus and Rickettsial Diseases, Army Medical Service Graduate School, Walter Reed Army Medical Center 48-56; Chief, Respiratory Diseases, Walter Reed Army Inst. of Research, Washington 56-58; Dir. Virus and Cell Biology Research, Merck Inst. for Therapeutic Research, Merck & Co. Inc. 58-66, Exec. Dir. 66-70; Dir. Virus and Cell Biology Research, Vice-Pres. Merck Sharp and Dohme Research Laboratories 70-; Visiting Lecturer in Bacteriology, Rutgers Univ. 47; Visiting Investigator, Hospital of Rockefeller Institute for Medical Research 51; Visiting Prof. Department of Bacteriology, Univ. of Maryland 53-57; Adjunct Prof. of Virology in Pediatrics, School of Med., Univ. of Pa. 68-; Consultant, Surgeon-Gen. U.S. Army 58-63; Children's Hosp. of Phila. 68-; Fellow, American Public Health Asscn., American Acad. of Microbiology, American Asscn. for the Advancement of Science; mem. Expert Advisory Panel on Virus Diseases, World Health Org. 52-, Cttee. on Influenza 52, Cttee. on Respiratory Diseases 58, Scientific Group on Measles Vaccine Studies 63, on Viruses and Cancer 64, on Human Viral and Rickettsial Vaccines 65, on Respiratory Diseases 67; mem. Study Section, Microbiology and Immunology Grants-in-Aid Program 53-61; mem. numerous U.S. and Int. Medical Socs.; recent awards include Distinguished Civilian Service Award given by Sec. of Defense 57; Washington Acad. of Sciences Award for Scientific Achievement in the Biological Sciences 58; Walter Reed Army Medical Center Incentive Award 60; Merck Dirs. Scientific Award 69; Dean M. McCann Award for Distinguished Service 70; Procter Award 71; American Acad. of Achievement, Golden Plate Award 75; Industrial Research Inst.

Achievement Award 75; Hon. D.Sc. (Montana) 66, (Maryland) 68.
Publs. Over 315 original publications on virology, immunology and public health.
Merck Sharp and Dohme Research Laboratories, Merck Institute for Therapeutic Research, West Point, Pennsylvania 19486, U.S.A.
Telephone: 215-699-5311.

Hillenbrand, Martin Joseph M.A. PH.D.; American diplomatist; b. 1 Aug. 1915, Youngstown, Ohio; *s*. of Joseph and Maria Hillenbrand; *m*. Faith Stewart 1941; two *s*. one *d*.; ed. Univs. of Dayton and Columbia.
Foreign Service Officer 39-; Vice-Consul, Zürich 39, Rangoon 40, Calcutta 42, Lourenço Marques 44, Bremen 44; Consul, Bremen 46; Bureau of German Affairs, State Dept. 50-52; First Sec., Paris 52-56; U.S. Political Adviser, Berlin 56-58; Dir. Office of German Affairs, State Dept. 58-62; Head of "Berlin Task Force" 62-63; Deputy Chief of Mission, Bonn 63-67; Chair. Fulbright Comm. for Germany 63-67; Amb. to Hungary 67-69; Asst. Sec. of State for European Affairs 69; Amb. to Fed. Germany 72-.
Leisure interests: reading, walking, golf.
Publs. *Power and Morals* 48, *Zwischen Politik und Ethik* (co-author) 68.
American Embassy, 532 Bad-Godesberg, Mehlemer-Aue, Federal Republic of Germany; 3313 O Street, Northwest, Washington, D.C. 20037, U.S.A.

Hiller, Dame Wendy, D.B.E.; British actress; b. 15 Aug. 1912, Stockport; *d*. of Frank Hiller and Marie Stone; *m*. Ronald Gow 1937; one *s*. one *d*.; ed. Winceby House, Bexhill.
Trained as an actress Manchester Repertory Theatre; Acad. Award for Best Actress, *Separate Tables* 59; numerous stage and film roles, plays include *Love on the Dole* (London and N.Y.) 35, *Cradle Song*, *The First Gentleman* 45, *Tess of the d'Urbervilles*, *The Heiress* (London and N.Y.) 47, *Ann Veronica*, *Waters of the Moon*, *The Night of the Ball* 55, *Moon for the Misbegotten* (N.Y.) 57, *Flowering Cherry* 58, *Toys in the Attic* 60, *Aspern Papers* (N.Y.) 62, *The Wings of the Dove* 63, *The Sacred Flame* 67, *When We Dead Awaken* (Edinburgh Festival) 68, *The Battle of Shrivings* 70, *Crown Matrimonial* 72; films include *Pygmalion* 38, *Major Barbara* 40, *I Know Where I'm Going* 45, *Separate Tables* 58, *Sons and Lovers* 60, *A Man for All Seasons* 66, *David Copperfield* 69, *Murder on the Orient Express* 75.
Leisure interest: gardening.
c/o Plunket Greene Ltd., 110 Jermyn Street, London, S.W.1., England.

Hillery, Patrick John; Irish politician; b. 2 May 1923; ed. Miltown-Malbay National School, Rockwell Coll., Cashel and Univ. Coll., Dublin.
Member of Health Council 55-57; Medical Officer, Miltown-Malbay 57-59; Coroner for West Clare 58-59; mem. Dáil 51-72; Minister for Educ. 59-65; Minister for Industry and Commerce 65-66, for Labour 66-69, of Foreign Affairs 69-72; Vice-Pres. Comm. of European Communities, Commr. for Social Affairs 73-.
Commission of the European Communities, 200 rue de la Loi, Brussels, Belgium; Spanish Point, Co. Clare, Ireland.

Hilliard, Michael; Irish politician; b. 11 March 1903, Co. Meath; *s*. of James Hilliard and Mary O'Brien; *m*. Kathleen McMahon 1925; six *s*. five *d*.
Parliamentary Sec. to Minister for Industry and Commerce 58-59; Minister for Posts and Telegraph 59-65; T. D. Meath-Westmeath 43-48, Meath 48-73; Minister for Defence 65-June 69; mem. European Parl. 73-; Fianna Fáil.
11 St. Enda's Villas, Navan, Co. Meath, Ireland.

Hills, Carla Anderson, A.B., LL.B.; American lawyer and government official; b. 3 Jan. 1934, Los Angeles; *d*. of Carl and Edith (Hume) Anderson; *m*. Roderick M.

Hills (*q.v.*) 1958; one *s.* three *d.*; ed. Stanford Univ., St. Hilda's Coll., Oxford, U.K., Yale Law School.
Assistant U.S. Attorney, Civil Div., Los Angeles 58-61; Partner, Munger, Tolles, Hills & Rickershauser, law firm 62-74; Adjunct Prof., School of Law, Univ. of Calif., Los Angeles 72; Asst. Attorney-Gen., Civil Div., U.S. Dept. of Justice 74-75; Sec. of Housing and Urban Devt. March 75-; mem. Council, Admin. Conf. of U.S. 75-; mem. at Large, Yale Law School Exec. Cttee. 73- (78); Trustee Pomona Coll. 74-; mem. Amer. Law Inst. 74-.
Leisure interest: tennis.
Publs. *Federal Civil Practice* (co-author) 61, *Antitrust Adviser* (editor and co-author) 71.
Department of Housing and Urban Development, 451 7th Street, S.W., Washington, D.C. 20410; Home: 3125 Chain Bridge Road, Washington, D.C. 20016, U.S.A.
Telephone: (202) 755-6417 (Office); (202) 966-9009 (Home).

Hills, Roderick M., LL.B.; American lawyer and government official; b. 9 March 1931, Seattle, Wash.; *s.* of Kenneth Maltman and Sarah (Love) Hills; *m.* Carla Anderson (Hills, *q.v.*) 1958; one *s.* three *d.*; ed. Stanford Univ., Calif.
Admitted to Calif. Bar 57, to Supreme Court Bar 60; Law Clerk to Justice, Supreme Court 55-57; Partner, Tolles, Hills and Rickershauser, law firm 62-71; Chair. of Board Repub. Corpn. 71-75; Counsel to Pres. of U.S.A. 75; Chair. Securities and Exchange Comm. 75-; Visiting Prof. Harvard 69-70; Lecturer, Stanford Univ. 60-; Chair. Research Cttee., American Bar Foundation, Board of Dirs., Constitutional Rights Foundation; mem. American Bar Asscn., Los Angeles County Bar Asscn., Calif. State Bar; Trustee, Claremont Univ. Centre; mem. Editorial Board, Comment Editor, *Stanford Law Review* 53-55.
Securities and Exchange Commission, 500 North Capitol Street, Washington, D.C. 20549; Home: 3125 Chain Bridge Road, N.W., Washington, D.C. 20016, U.S.A.
Telephone: (202) 755-1130 (Office); (202) 966-2065 (Home).

Hilsman, Roger, B.S., M.A., PH.D.; American diplomatist and educator; b. 23 Nov. 1919, Waco, Texas; *s.* of Colonel Roger Hilsman and Emma Prendergast Hilsman; *m.* Eleanor Hoyt 1946; two *s.* two *d.*; ed. West Point and Yale Univ.
U.S. Army 43-53; Center for Int. Studies, Princeton Univ. 53-56; Chief Foreign Affairs Div. of Legislative Reference Service, Library of Congress 56-58, Dep. Dir. (for Research) 58-61; Dir. Bureau of Intelligence and Research, Dept. of State 61-63; Asst. Sec. of State for Far Eastern Affairs 63-64; Prof. of Govt., Columbia Univ. 64-.
Leisure interest: designing toys.
Publs. *Strategic Intelligence and National Decisions* 56, *To Move a Nation* 67, *The Politics of Policy Making in Defense and Foreign Affairs* 71, *The Crouching Future, International Politics and U.S. Foreign Policy, A Forecast* 75; co-author: *Military Policy and National Security* 56, *Foreign Policy in the 60s* 65, contributor to *Alliance Policy in the Cold War* 59, *NATO and American Security* 59, *The Guerrilla—and How to Fight Him* 62, *Modern Guerrilla Warfare* 62.
448 Riverside Avenue, New York, N.Y.; and Hamburg Cove, Lyme, Conn., U.S.A.

Hilton, Conrad Nicholson; American hotel proprietor; b. 25 Dec. 1887, San Antonio, N.M.; *s.* of August Holver Hilton and Mary Laufersweiler Hilton; *m.* 1st Mary Barron 1925, 2nd Sari Gabor 1942; three *s.* (one deceased); ed. N.M. Mil. Acad., N.M. School of Mines.
Member N.M. House of Reps. 12-13; organized N.M. State Bank of San Antonio 13; officer in U.S. Army 17-19; entered hotel business 19; Founder Hilton Hotels

Corpn. 46-, Chair. of Board 60-; Chair. of Board Hilton Hotels Int. Hotel Waldorf-Astoria Corpn. 65-.
Publs. *Be My Guest* (autobiography) 57, *Inspirations of an Innkeeper* 63.
9990 Santa Monica Boulevard, Beverly Hills, Calif., U.S.A.

Hilton, Hugh Gerald, B.SC., D.ENG.; Canadian businessman; b. 31 March 1889; ed. Case School of Applied Science, Cleveland, Ohio.
Asst. Supt. of blast furnaces, Steel Co. of Canada 21, Asst. Works Man. 27, Works Man. 34, Vice-Pres. 37, Dir. 41, Exec. Vice-Pres. 43, Pres. 45-57, Chair. and Chief Exec. Officer 57-60, Chair. of the Board 60-66, Chair. Exec. Cttee. 66-; Dir. Canadian Gen. Electric Co. Ltd., Toronto, Hamilton and Buffalo Railway Co.; Hon. Vice-Pres. American Iron and Steel Inst.; mem. American Inst. of Mining and Metallurgical Engineers, British Iron and Steel Inst., Canadian Manufacturers' Asscn., American Asscn. for Advancement of Science, Newcomen Soc., Engineering Inst. of Canada.
Steel Co. of Canada, P.O. Box 205, T-D Centre, Toronto 111, Canada.

Himle, Erik; Norwegian economist and politician; b. 10 April 1924; ed. Oslo Univ.
Secretary, Ministry of Commerce 48-49; Int. Bank for Reconstruction and Devt., Washington 49-51; Ministry of Commerce 51-52; Chief of Dept., Ministry of Defence 52-55, Dir. 56-58, Under-Sec. of State 58-61, Perm. Gen. 61; Under-Sec. of State, Minister of Transport and Communications 62-63; Minister of Commerce and Shipping 63-64, of Communications 64-65; Sec. Labour group in the Storting (Parl.); Sec. financial-political cttee. under Minister of Finance 66-67; Perm. Sec. of Defence 67-; Labour.
The Storting, Oslo, Norway.

Himsworth, Sir Harold Percival, K.C.B., M.D., F.R.S., F.R.C.P.; British medical research scientist; b. 19 May 1905, Huddersfield, Yorks.; *m.* Charlotte Gray, M.B. 1932; two *s.*; ed. Univ. of London.
Formerly Prof. of Medicine Univ. of London and Dir. Medical Unit Univ. Coll. Hospital Medical School, London 39-49; Sec. Medical Research Council 49-68; Fellow Univ. Coll. London; Consulting Physician Univ. Coll. Hospital; Chair. Bd. of Management, London School of Hygiene and Tropical Medicine 69-; Prime Warden Goldsmith's Co., London; Fellow Royal Society; hon. mem. Swedish Medical Society, and Belgian Royal Acad. of Medicine; mem. Norwegian Medical Society; foreign hon. mem. Amer. Acad. of Arts and Sciences; mem. Royal Soc. Arts and Sciences, Gothenburg; hon. Fellow Royal Coll. of Radiologists; Hon. mem. Asscn. of American Physicians; Foreign mem. American Philosophical Soc.; Dr. h.c. (Toulouse); Hon. LL.D. (Glasgow, London, Wales); Hon. D.Sc. (Manchester) 56; Hon. Sc.D. (Cambridge) 64; Hon. D.Sc. (Leeds and Univ. of West Indies) 68; Hon. F.R.C.P. (Edin.) 60; Hon. F.R.S.M. 61; Hon. F.R.C.S. 65; Hon. F.R.C. Path. 69.
Publ. *The Development and Organisation of Scientific Knowledge* 70.
13 Hamilton Terrace, London, NW8 9RE, England.

Hine, Maynard Kiplinger, D.D.S., M.S.; American dentist; b. 25 Aug. 1907, Waterloo, Ind.; *s.* of Clyde L. and Delia (Kiplinger) Hine; *m.* Harriett Foulke 1932; two *s.* one *d.*; ed. Univ. of Illinois.
Instructor at Univ. of Illinois Coll. of Dentistry 30-32; Assoc. 36-38; Asst. Prof. 38-43; Assoc. Prof. and Head of the Div. of Oral Pathology at Indiana Univ. School of Dentistry 44-45; Prof. and Head of the Dept. of Periodontia and Histopathology, Indiana Univ. School of Dentistry 45-; Dean of Indiana Univ. School of Dentistry 45-68; Chancellor, Indiana Univ.-Purdue Univ. at Indianapolis Jan. 69-73; Exec. assoc. Indiana Univ. 73-; Chair. Periodontal Disease Advisory Comm. of

Nat. Inst. for Dental Research of Dept. Health Educ. and Welfare 72-; mem. Amer. Asscn. of Dental Editors, Pres. 49-50; mem. Nat. Dental Advisory Cttee. of U.S. Public Health Service 48-50; mem. Int. Asscn. Dental Research, Pres. 52; mem. Advisory Panel on Medical Sciences, Dept. of Defence; mem. Indiana State Dental Asscn., Pres. 57-58; Editor *Journal of Periodontology* 50-70; Pres. American Asscn. of Dental Schools 52; Pres. American Dental Asscn. 66; Regent Nat. Library of Medicine 60-63; mem. Advisory Council of Nat. Inst. for Dental Research; Pres. American Acad. of Periodontology 64; Hon. Fellow Royal Coll. of Surgeons (Ireland) 74.
Leisure interest: philately.
1219 W. Michigan Street, Indianapolis, Indiana, U.S.A.
Telephone: 264-8717 (Office); 255-2776 (Home).

Hines, Earl Kenneth; American jazz pianist, band leader and composer; b. 28 Dec. 1905, Duquesne, Pa.; s. of Joseph and Mary Hines; m. 1947; two d.; ed. Schenley High School, Pittsburgh.
Learned piano from Emma Young and Von Holz; formed trio and joined Lois Deppe 18; has made records 22-; joined Carroll Dickerson on tour to Calif. 26; worked with Louis Armstrong, Chicago 26, with Jimmie Noon 27; recorded first piano solos 27; formed own big band 28, leader 28-47; rejoined Louis Armstrong 48; appearances leading a small group or solo 51-; has toured Europe, Japan, Latin America, Australia 64, tour of U.S.S.R. 66; elected to *Down Beat* Hall of Fame 65.
Leisure interest: baseball, watching football, bowling.
Major compositions: *My Monday Date, Rosetta, Jelly Jelly, Deep Forest, Everything Depends on You, Stormy Monday Blues.*
815 Trestle Glen Road, Oakland, Calif. 94610, U.S.A.

Hines, Rt. Rev. John Elbridge, D.D.; American ecclesiastic; b. 3 Oct. 1910; ed. Univ. of South and Virginia Theological Seminary.
Ordained 33; Curate, St. Louis 33-35; Rector, Hannibal, Missouri 35-37, Augusta, Georgia 37-41, Houston, Texas 41-45; Bishop Coadjutor of Texas 45-55, Bishop of Texas 55-64; Presiding Bishop, Protestant Episcopal Church of U.S.A. 64-74.
Highlands, N.C., U.S.A.

Hinshaw, Horton Corwin, A.B., M.A., PH.D., M.D.; American physician; b. 1902, Iowa Falls, Ia.; s. of Milas Clark Hinshaw and Ida Bushong Hinshaw; m. Dorothy Youmans 1924; two s. two d.; ed. Coll. of Idaho, Univs. of Calif. and Pennsylvania.
Assistant Prof. of Parasitology Univ. of Calif. 27-28; Adjunct Prof. of Parasitology, School of Medicine American Univ. of Beirut, Lebanon (Chair. Dept of Parasitology and Bacteriology) 28-31; Instructor in Bacteriology, Univ. of Pennsylvania Medical School 31-33; Fellow and First Asst. in Medicine, Mayo Foundation, Rochester 33-35; fmrly. Assoc. Prof. of Medicine, Mayo Foundation, Univ. of Minnesota, and Consultant in Medicine (Head of Section), Mayo Clinic; Clinical Prof. of Medicine and Head of Div. in Diseases of the Chest, Stanford Univ. School of Medicine 49-59; Clinical Prof. of Medicine, Univ. of Calif. Medical Cen. 60-; Consultant to Letterman Army Hospital, San Francisco; Consultant, Weimar Medical Center, Calif.; Dir. Medical Services, Harkness Community Hospital and Medical Center 67-; Hon. D.Sc. (Idaho Coll.).
Leisure interests: yachting, travel.
Publs. *Streptomycin in Tuberculosis* (with H. McL. Riggins) 48, *Diseases of the Chest,* 3rd edn. 68, over 200 articles in scientific journals.
450 Sutter Street, Suite 1023, San Francisco, Calif. 94108, U.S.A.

Hinton of Bankside, Baron (Life Peer) cr. 65, of Dulwich; **Christopher Hinton,** O.M., K.B.E., F.R.S., M.A., F.I.CHEM.E., F.R.S.A.; British engineer; b. 12 May 1901,

Tisbury, Wilts.; s. of Frederick Henry Hinton and Kate Hinton (née Christopher); m. Lillian Boyer (died 1973); one d.; ed. Trinity Coll., Cambridge.
Engineering apprenticeship, Great Western Railway Co., Swindon 17-23; engineer Imperial Chemical Industries (Alkali) 26-40, and Chief Engineer 31-40; on loan from I.C.I. to Ministry of Supply 40-46; Deputy Dir.-Gen. of Filling Factories 42-46; Deputy Controller for Atomic Energy (Production), Ministry of Supply and later Man. Dir. of the Industrial Group of the United Kingdom Atomic Energy Authority 46-57; Chair. Central Electricity Generating Board 57-64, Int. Exec. Cttee. of World Power Conf. 62-66; carried out a study of transport co-ordination 65; Special Adviser to the World Bank 65-70; Deputy Chair. Electricity Supply Research Council; Chancellor Bath Univ.; Pres. Council of Engineering Insts. Feb. 76-; Hon. D.Sc. (Oxford, Southampton, Durham, Bath), Hon. LL.D. (Edinburgh), Hon. D.Sc. (Eng.) (London), Hon. D.Eng. (Liverpool), Hon. Sc.D. (Cambridge); Hon. Assoc. Manchester Inst. of Science and Technology; Hon. mem. American Soc. of Mechanical Engineers, Inst. of Gas Engineers, Inst. of Welding; Hon. Fellow, Inst. of Civil Engineers, Inst. of Mechanical Engineers (fmr. Pres.), Inst. of Electrical Engineers, Inst. of Metals; Hon. Fellow, Trinity Coll., Cambridge; Imperial Order of the Rising Sun (2nd Class).
Publs. include lectures and papers on engineering and nuclear power development.
Tiverton Lodge, Dulwich Common, London, SE21 7EW, England.
Telephone: 01-693-6447.

Hiort, Esbjörn; Danish architect; b. 2 April 1912, Copenhagen; s. of Ivar Hiort and Emma Hiort (née Lorentzen); m. Bente Andresen 1943; two s. two d.; ed. Det Kongelige Akademi for de Skønne Kunster.
Practised as Architect 37-52; Sec. Asscn. of Academic Architects 45-52; Sec.-Gen. Nat. Fed. of Danish Architects 52-59; Gen. Manager Perm. Sales Exhibition of Danish Arts and Crafts (Den Permanente) 59-67; Knight Order of Dannebrog, Officier d'Académie (France); Officer, Order of Léopold II (Belgium).
Leisure interest: heraldry and genealogy.
Publs. *Contemporary Danish Architecture* 49, *Housing in Denmark* 52, *Modern Danish Silver* 54, *Modern Danish Ceramics* 55, *Modern Danish Furniture* 56, etc.
Bel Colles Farm, Parkvej 6, 2960 Rungsted Kyst, Denmark.
Telephone: (2)868815.

Hirahara, Tsuyoshi, Japanese diplomatist; b. 25 Oct. 1920, Kagoshima; s. of Eisuke Fujita and Shizuko Hirahara; m. Kiyoko Nishi, 1946; two d.; ed. Tokyo Imperial Univ.
Military service 43-45; Attaché, Treaty Bureau, Ministry of Foreign Affairs 45-47; Sec. to Foreign Minister 47-48; Section Chief, Special Procurement Board 48-50; Sec. of Embassy, Belgium 50-52; Deputy Dir. Econ. Affairs Bureau, Ministry of Foreign Affairs 52-55, Dir. 59-61, Counsellor 61-64, Deputy Dir.-Gen. 69-70, Dir.-Gen. 70-72; Dir. Asian Section, UNESCO, Paris 55-59; Interpreter to H.I.M. the Emperor of Japan 60-64; Consul-Gen., Milan 64-66; Minister, Embassy in Belgium and Luxembourg 64-69; Amb. to Morocco 72-74, to OECD, Paris 74-; Commdr., Ordre de Couronne; Grand Officier, Ordre de Léopold II; Grand Officier, Ouissam Alaouite.
Leisure interests: golf, collecting tortoises.
54 avenue Sainte-Foy, Neuilly-sur-Seine, France.
Telephone: 722-2966, 722-2806.

Hirai, Tomisaburo, LL.B.; Japanese business executive; b. 13 Dec. 1906, Tokyo; s. of Kichibei Hirai; m. Tami Hayakawa; one s. two d.; ed. Tokyo Imperial Univ.
Joined Ministry of Commerce and Industry 31, Perm. Vice-Minister, Int. Trade and Industry 53; Exec.

Counsellor, Yawata Iron and Steel Co. Ltd. 56, Dir. Admin. Bureau, Yawata Works 56, Dir. 56, Man. Dir. 58, Senior Man. Dir. and Gen. Supt. Yawata Works 62, Exec. Vice-Pres. 67; after merger with Fuji Iron and Steel Co. Ltd., Exec. Vice-Pres. Nippon Steel Corpn. 70-73, Rep. Dir. and Pres. 73-; Chair. Japan-Brazil Econ. Cttee., Fed. of Econ. Orgs. 74; Pres. Japan Overseas Enterprise Asscn. 74; Blue Ribbon Medal 73. Leisure interest: golf.
11-4, 1-chome, Kakinokizaka, Meguro-ku, Tokyo, Japan.

Hirasawa, Kô, M.D.; Japanese university official; b. 1900, Niigata; s. of Heitaro and Chino Hirasawa; m. Matue Naganuma; two s. four d.; ed. Faculty of Medicine, Kyoto Imperial Univ.
Assistant Prof., Kyoto Imperial Univ. 25-26; Asst. Prof. Niigata Medical Coll. 26-30, Prof. 30-46; Prof. Kyoto Univ. 46-63, Dean Liberal Arts 49-51, Dean Medical Dept. 56-57, Pres. 57-63; Acad. Prize for Medical Science 51, Takeda Prize 56; mem. Japan Soc. of Neurosurgery, Japan Soc. of Neurology and Psychiatry, Japan Soc. of Anatomy, Japan Acad. 67; Pres. Kyoto Cancer Asscn. 62-.
Publs. *Der Plexus brachialis der Japaner* 32, *The cortical motor system* 51 and many articles.
141 Shinnyo-cho, Jôdoji, Sakyo-ku, Kyoto 606, Japan. Telephone: 075-771-0549.

Hirata, Kusuo; Japanese business executive; b. 7 Sept. 1909, Ooita; s. of Shuzo and Tai Hirata; m. Teruko Koinumaru 1940; two s. one d.; ed. Kwansei Gakuin Univ.
With Daicel Ltd. 33-34; joined Fuji Photo Film Co., Ltd. 34, Man. Finance Dept. 50-62, Dir. 54-64, Man. Planning Div. 62-66, Man. Dir. 64-69, Man. Sales Div. 66-71, Senior Man. Dir. 69-71, Pres. 71-; Blue Ribbon Medal 74.
Leisure interest: golf.
Fuji Photo Film Co. Ltd., 26-30 Nishiazabu 2-chome, Minato-ku, Tokyo; Home: 48-12, Utsukushigaoka 2-chome, Midori-ku, Yokohama-shi, Kanagawa, Japan. Telephone: 03-406-2111 (Office); 045-911-1771 (Home).

Hiratsuka, Masunori, M.A., LITT.D.; Japanese educationist; b. 1907, Tokyo; s. of Yunosuke and Hanako; m. Yaeko Iwai 1933; four d.; ed. Tokyo Imperial Univ.
Lecturer, Aoyama Gakuin Theological School 31-36, Ferris Seminary 32-36, St. Paul Univ. 36-39, Prof. Hiroshima Higher Normal School 39-44; Prof. Faculty of Letters, Kyushu Imperial Univ. 44-63, Faculty of Education 49-, leave of absence 60, Dean of Faculty of Educ. 54-56, Dir. Research Inst. of Educ. and Culture 56-63, Prof. Emer. 64-; Dir. Dept. of Educ., UNESCO, Paris 60, Dir.-Gen. Nat. Inst. for Educational Research 63-; mem. Cen. Advisory Council on Educ., Council on Curriculum Revision, Council on Social Educ., Japan Educ. Soc. (Gov. of Board), Japan Educ. Philosophy Soc., Japan Educ. History Soc., Gov. Board of UNESCO Inst. for Educ. in Hamburg, World Council of Comparative Educ.; Chair. Japan Comparative Educ. Soc., Nat. Asscn. of Research Inst. for Educ., Gov. Board of Nat. Educ. Hall; Pres. Japanese Nat. Comm. for UNESCO 72-; Chair. Emer. Baiko Women's Univ.; Commdr. Palmes Académiques (France) 61.
Leisure interests: music, fishing, golf.
Publs. *The Educational Thought of the Old Testament* 35 and 57, *Women's Education in Israel* 36, *History of Education in Japan* 38, *History of Modern Education in China* 44, *Future of Japan and Moral Education* 59, *Future of Japanese Education* 64.
Kokuritsu Kyoiku Kenkyusho (NIER), 6-5-22 Shimomeguro, Meguro-ku, Tokyo; Home: 1-5-44 Takanawa, Minato-ku, Tokyo, Japan.
Telephone: 714-0111 (Office); 441-7630 (Home).

Hiro, Keitaro; Japanese business executive; b. 7 Dec. 1908, Tsukaguchi, Amagasaki, Hyogo Pref.; s. of Yasukichi and Kimi Hiro; m. Sadano Kubo 1941; two s. two d.; ed. Ohkura Higher Commercial School and Ritsumeikan Univ.
Teacher, Ohkura Commercial High School 38-43; Chief, Accounting Dept., Kubota Ltd. 46, Man. Financial Dept. 50, Dir. Financing 51, Man Dir. 53, Senior Man. Dir. 60, now Pres.; Dir. Kubota Trane Ltd., Kubota Construction Co; Dir. Japan Productivity Asscn. 61, Osaka Industrialist Asscn. 61, Kansai Management Asscn. 61.
Leisure interests: reading, Chinese calligraphy.
Kubota Ltd., 22 Funadecho, 2-chome, Naniwa-ku, Osaka; 15-32 Takakuracho Nishinomiya, Hyogo Pref., Japan.

Hirohito, Emperor of Japan; b. 29 April 1901.
Son of Emperor Yoshihito; married 24 Princess Nagako Kuni; Regent 21-26; succeeded 25 Dec. 1926; heir H.I.H. Crown Prince Akihito (Tsugunomiya), b. 23 Dec. 1933, married Michiko Shoda 59; Fellow of the Royal Soc. (U.K.) 71.
Publs. Nine books on marine biology.
The Imperial Palace, Tokyo, Japan.

Hirota, Hisakazu; Japanese steel executive; b. 7 May 1899, Kyoto; two s. three d.; ed. Univ. of Kyoto.
Sumitomo Steel Works 23, Dir. Sumitomo Metal Industries Ltd. 46-, Man. Dir. 47, Senior Man. Dir. 47-49, Pres. 62, Chair. 73-, Adviser to Pres.; Pres. Kansai Productivity Center; Order of the Rising Sun.
Leisure interests: photography, oil painting and golf.
1-27-5 Tsukaguchicho, Amagasaki City, Hyogo Pref., Japan.
Telephone: 06-421-5153.

Hirota, Seiichiro; Japanese business executive; b. 25 Jan. 1905, Onga-gun, Fukuoka Pref.; m. Hideko Egawa 1928; two d.; ed. Hiroshima Univ.
Toyo Rayon Co. (now Toray Industries Inc.) 27-; Dir. 56-60, Man. Dir. 60-63, Exec. Vice-Pres. 63-66, Pres. 66-71, Senior Adviser and Dir. 71-.
Leisure interests: gardening, golf.
Toray Industries Inc., Toray Building, 2, Nihonbashi-Muromachi 2-chome, Chuo-ku, Tokyo, Japan.
Telephone: 03-270-0111.

Hirsch, Etienne; French civil engineer and administrator; b. 24 Jan. 1901; ed. Ecole des Mines, Paris.
Joined Etablissements Kuhlmann 24, attached to research laboratory 24-29, later factory man., Dir. of Research and Development and Dir. Société Marles-Kuhlmann, Société Technique pour l'Amélioration des Carburants and Société des Produits Chimiques Ethyl-Kuhlmann; joined Free French Forces 40; Asst. Dir. of Armaments, Algiers 43; Pres. French Supply Council, London, French rep. temporary Economic Cttee. for Europe 45; Head, Technical Div., Commissariat-Général au Plan 46-49, Deputy Commr. Gen. 49-52, Commr. Gen. 52-59; participated in negotiations setting up European Coal and Steel Community 50-52, NATO Cttee. of Wise Men 51-52; Pres. Euratom Comm. 59-62; Président, Inst. Technique de Prévision Economique et Sociale 62-; Prof. Free Univ. of Brussels 63-69; Président, Comité Central du Mouvement Fédéraliste Européen 64-; Commdr. Légion d'Honneur.
10 rue de la Justice, 92310 Sèvres, France.

Hirsch, Sir Peter Bernhard, Kt., M.A., PH.D., F.R.S.; British professor of metallurgy; b. 16 Jan. 1925, Berlin; s. of Ismar Hirsch and Regina Meyersohn; m. Mabel A. Kellar (née Stephens) 1959; one step s. one step d.; ed. Univ. of Cambridge.
Lecturer in Physics, Univ. of Cambridge 59-64, Reader 64-66; Fellow, Christ's Coll., Cambridge 60-66; Isaac Wolfson Prof. of Metallurgy, Univ. of Oxford and Fellow, St. Edmund Hall 66-; Chair. Metallurgy and

Materials Cttee., Science Research Council 70-73; mem. Council for Scientific Policy 71-72; mem. Council, Inst. of Physics 68-72, Inst. of Metals 68-73, Electricity Supply Research Council 69-; Rosenhain Medal, Inst. of Metals 61, Boys' Prize, Inst. of Physics and Physical Soc. 62, Clamer Medal, Franklin Inst. 70, Wihuri Int. Prize 71, Hughes Medal of the Royal Soc. 73.
Leisure interests: walking, bridge.
Publs. *Electron Microscopy of Thin Crystals* (joint author) 65, *The Physics of Metals, 2, Defects* (editor) 75 and numerous articles in learned journals.
Department of Metallurgy and Science of Materials, University of Oxford, Parks Road, Oxford, OX1 3PH, England.
Telephone: Oxford 59981.

Hirsch, Robert; French civil servant; b. 20 Nov. 1912, Paris; *m.* Jacqueline Oge 1937; ed. Lycée Janson-de-Sailly, Paris, and Ecole Polytechnique, Paris.
Sub-Lieut. French Air Force 34, Lieut. 36, Capt. 40, Commandant 44, Dir. Supply, Accommodation and Transport, Sûreté Nationale 44; Prefect, Charente Maritime 47; Dir.-Gen. Sûreté Nationale 51-54; Prefect Seine Maritime 54-59, Nord 59-63; Admin.-Gen. Atomic Energy Comm. 63-70; Admin. Electricité de France 63-70, Centre nationale d'études spatiales 68-70, Société nationale de pétroles d'Aquitaine 70-; Pres. Gaz de France 70-, Comité permanent des réformes administratives 72-; mem. of the Board of the Order of the Légion d'Honneur; Grand Officier, Légion d'Honneur, Grand Croix Ordre National du Merite, Croix de Guerre, etc.
23 rue Philibert-Delorme, 75017 Paris, France.

Hirsch, Robert Paul; French actor; b. 26 July 1925.
Member of the Comédie Française 52-74; numerous appearances include: *La Belle Aventure, Le Prince travesti, Monsieur de Pourceaugnac, Les Temps difficiles, La Double Inconstance, Le Dindon, Amphitryon, Britannicus, Crime et Chatiment, La Faim et la Soif, Monsieur Amilcar, L'Abime et la Visite.*
Films include: *Le Dindon, Votre dévoué Blake, En effeuillant la marguerite, Notre-Dame de Paris, Maigret et l'Affaire Saint-Fiacre, 125 rue Montmartre, Par question le samedi, Monnaie de singe, Martin soldat, Toute folles de lui, les Cracks, Appelez moi Mathilde, Traitement de choc, Chobizenesse;* Officier des Arts et des Lettres.
172 boulevard Berthier, 75017 Paris, France.

Hirschfelder, Joseph Oakland, B.S., PH.D.; American professor of chemistry; b. 27 May 1911, Baltimore, Md.; *s.* of Arthur Douglas Hirschfelder and May Rosalie Straus; *m.* Elizabeth Stafford Sokolnikoff 1953; ed. Univ. of Minn. and Yale and Princeton Univs.
Research Assoc., Univ. of Wis. 37-40, Instructor in Chem. and Physics 40-41, Asst. Prof. of Chem. 41-42, Prof. 46-, Dir. of Theoretical Chem. Inst. 62-; Adjunct Prof. Univ. of Calif. 74-; Consultant, Nat. Defense Research Cttee., Interior Ballistics Guns and Rockets 42-43; Group Leader, Theoretical Physics and Ordnance, Los Alamos Atomic Bomb Laboratory; Head, Theoretical Physics Div., Naval Ordnance Test Station, Inyokern and Pasadena 45-46; Chief Phenomenologist, Bikini Atomic Bomb Test 46; Fellow, American Physical Soc., Physical Soc. (London); mem. Advisory Board, Argonne Nat. Laboratory 62-66. Nat. Bureau of Standards 62-67; mem. Nat. Acad. of Sciences, American Acad. of Arts and Sciences, Int. Acad. of Quantum Molecular Science, American Chemical Soc. (Chair. of Physical Chem. Div. 59-61), Combustion Inst.; Hon. M.A.S.M.E.; Foreign mem. Royal Soc. of Norway; Debye Award of American Chemical Soc. 66, Sir Alfred Egerton Gold Medal of Combustion Inst. 66.
Leisure interests: golf, swimming, riding.
Publs. *The Effects of Atomic Weapons* (Chair. Board of

Editors) 50, *Molecular Theory of Gases and Liquids* 54, 64, *Intermolecular Forces* 67.
Theoretical Chemistry Institute, University of Wisconsin, 1101 University Avenue, Madison, Wis. 53706; Home: Thorstrand Road, Madison, Wis. 53705, U.S.A.
Telephone: 608-262-1511 (Office); 608-233-8433 (Home).

Hirzebruch, Friedrich Ernst Peter, DR. RER. NAT.; German professor of mathematics; b. 17 Oct. 1927, Hamm, Westf.; *s.* of Dr. Fritz Hirzebruch and Martha Hirzebruch (née Holtschmit); *m.* Ingeborg Spitzley 1952; one *s.* two *d.*; ed. Westfälische Wilhelms-Univ., Münster, and Technische Hochschule, Zürich.
Scientific Asst. Univ. of Erlangen 50-52; mem. Inst. for Advanced Study, Princeton, N.J., U.S.A. 52-54; Dozent, Univ. of Münster 54-55; Asst. Prof., Princeton Univ., N.J. 55-56; Full Prof., Bonn Univ. 56-, Dean, Faculty of Mathematics and Natural Sciences 62-64; Pres. German Mathematical Soc. 61-62; mem. Leopoldina, Heidelberg, Mainz, Netherlands and Nordrheinwestf. Acads.; Silver Medal, Swiss Fed. Inst. of Technology 50.
Publs. *Neue topologische Methoden in der Algebraischen Geometrie* 56; papers in mathematical journals 50-.
Mathematisches Institut der Universität, Wegelerstrasse 10, 53 Bonn; Home: Endenicher Allee 7, 53 Bonn, Federal Republic of Germany.
Telephone: 732840 (Math. Inst.); 636320 (Home).

Hitch, Charles Johnston, M.A., LL.D., D.SC.; American institution executive; b. 9 Jan. 1910, Boonville, Mo.; *s.* of Arthur Martin and Bertha Johnston Hitch; *m.* Nancy W. Squire 1942; one *d.*; ed. Oxford, Arizona and Harvard Univs.
Fellow, Tutor and Praelector, Queen's Coll. Oxford 35-48; Staff Economist, U.S. Mission for Econ. Affairs, London 41-42; Staff Economist, U.S. War Production Board 42-43; Chief of Stabilization Controls Div., U.S. Office of War Mobilization 45-46; Chief, Econs. Div. and Chair. Research Council Rand Corpn. 48-60; Asst. Sec. of Defense (Comptroller) U.S. Dept. of Defense 61-65; at Univ. of Calif., Vice-Pres. Business and Finance 65-66, Prof. of Econs. 65-75, Vice-Pres. Admin. 66-67, Pres. of Univ. 68-75; Pres. Resources for the Future, Inc. 75-; Chair. Gen. Advisory Cttee., Energy Research and Devt. Admin. 75-; Hon. LL.D. (Pittsburgh, Missouri, Arizona), Hon. D.Sc. in Commerce (Drexel Univ.), H.L.D. h.c. (Univ. of Judaism) 73; Hon. Fellow, Queen's Coll. and Worcester Coll., Oxford; Distinguished Public Service Award, U.S. Navy; Rhodes Scholar and George Webb Medley Scholar.
Publs. *America's Economic Strength* 41, *The Economics of Defense in the Nuclear Age* 60, *Decision-Making for Defense* 65.
Resources for the Future Inc., 1755 Massachusetts Avenue, N.W., Washington; D.C. 20036, Home: 5217 Westbard Avenue, Bethesda, Md. 20016, U.S.A.
Telephone: (202) 462-4400 (Office); (301) 320-5066 (Home).

Hitchcock, Alfred Joseph; American (b. British) film director; b. 13 Aug. 1899, London; *m.* Alma Reville 1926; one *d.*; ed. Univ. of London
Joined Lasky Famous Players Corpn. 20; Senior Dir. British Int. Pictures; Hon. D.F.A. (Univ. of Calif., Santa Cruz) 68, Croix, Officier des Arts et des Lettres 69.
Films produced under his direction include: *Blackmail, Juno and the Paycock, The Farmer's Wife, Hindle Wakes, Thirty-nine Steps, The Man Who Knew Too Much, Secret Agent, Sabotage, Young and Innocent, The Lady Vanishes, Jamaica Inn, Rebecca, Foreign Correspondent, Mr. and Mrs. Smith, Suspicion, Saboteur, Shadow of a Doubt, Lifeboat, Spellbound, Notorious, The Paradise Case, Rope, Under Capricorn, Stage Fright, Strangers on a Train, I Confess, Dial M for*

Murder, Rear Window, To Catch a Thief, The Trouble with Harry, The Wrong Man, Vertigo, North by Northwest, Psycho, The Birds, Marnie, Torn Curtain, Topaz, Frenzy; television series: *Alfred Hitchcock Presents* 55-61, *Alfred Hitchcock Hour* 62-65.

Publs. *Stories Not for the Nervous* 66, *Stories that Scared Even Me* 68, *Stories to Stay Awake By* 71, *Supernatural Tales of Terror and Suspense* 74; children's books: *Monster Museum* 71, *Haunted Housefull* 71.

10957 Bellagio Road, Bel Air, Los Angeles, Calif., U.S.A.

Hitchcock, Henry-Russell, M.A.; American architectural historian; b. 3 June 1903, Boston, Mass.; s. of Henry R. and Alice Davis Hitchcock; ed. Harvard Coll., Harvard Graduate School of Design.

Assistant Professor of Art, Vassar Coll. 27-28, Wesleyan Univ. 29-41, Assoc. Prof. 41-47, Prof. 47-48; Prof. of Art, Smith Coll. 48-, Sophia Smith Prof. of Art 61-68; Prof., Inst. of Fine Arts, N.Y. Univ. 69-; Dir. Smith Coll. Museum of Art 49-55; Pres. Victorian Soc. of America 70-73; American Council Learned Socs. Award 61; Hon. D.F.A. (N.Y. Univ.) 69, Hon. D.Litt (Univ. of Glasgow) 73.

Publs. *Modern Architecture* 29, 71, *The International Style* 32, 66, *Architecture of H. H. Richardson* 36, 61, 66. *In the Nature of Materials, Buildings of Frank Lloyd Wright* 42, 74, *American Architectural Books* 46, 62, *Early Victorian Architecture in Britain* 54, 74, *Architecture, 19th and 20th Centuries* 58, 63, 69, 71, *The Brothers Zimmermann* 68, *Rococo Architecture in Southern Germany* 68.

152 E. 62nd Street, New York, N.Y. 10021, U.S.A.
Telephone: 758-6554.

Hitchens, (Sydney) Ivon, C.B.E.; British painter; b. 3 March 1893, London; s. of Alfred Hitchens and Ethel Seth-Smith; m. Mary Cranford 1935; one s.; ed. Bedales, St. John's Wood Art Schools, Royal Acad. Schools.

Foundation mem. of the "Seven and Five" Group 22; first one-man exhbn. Mayor Gallery, London 25; numerous one-man exhbns. Lefevre, Leicester and Waddington Galleries, London and Poindexter Gallery, New York; retrospective shows Leeds, Sheffield, London, Venice Biennale, Vienna, Munich, Musée Nat. d'Art Moderne, Paris, Stedelijk Museum, Amsterdam, Tate Gallery, London 63; rep. in many int. exhbns. including "Masters of British Painting 1800-1950" Museum of Modern Art, New York 56, Exhbn. Universelle et Int., Brussels 58, XI Premio Lissone, Italy 59, Int. Asscn. of Art Critics 12th Exhbn., Vancouver 59, Exhbn. of British Painting 1720-1960, Pushkin Museum Moscow and Hermitage Leningrad 60, Arts Council 3 Masters of Modern British Painting 61; large mural executed for Cecil Sharpe House, London 53-54; Rural Landscape, Nuffield Coll., Oxford 59; Refectory Mural, Univ. of Sussex 62; large tapestry, Chase Manhattan Bank, London 73; works purchased by Tate Gallery, Victoria and Albert Museum, Arts Council, British Council and numerous museums and insts. in Great Britain, U.S.A., Canada, New Zealand, Australia, France and Norway.

Waddington Galleries, 2 Cork Street, London, W1X 1PA, England.
Telephone: 01-439-1866.

Hitti, Philip Khuri, B.A. PH.D.,; American orientalist; b. 24 June 1886, Shimlan, Lebanon; s. of Iskandar and Sa'da Nawful Hitti; m. Mary George 1918; one d.; ed. American Univ. Beirut, Columbia Univ.

Lecturer Oriental Dept. Columbia Univ. 15-19; Prof. American University Beirut 19-26; Asst. Prof. Semitic Literature Princeton 26-29; Assoc. Prof. 29-36; Full Prof. 36-54; Prof. Emer. 54-; Chair. Dept. of Oriental Languages 44-54; Dir. Programme in Near Eastern Studies 47-54; mem. American Oriental Soc., etc.; Hon. Litt.D., L.H.D.

Publs. *The Origins of the Islamic State* 16, 66, *The Semitic*

Languages Spoken in Syria and Lebanon 22, *The Syrians in America* 24, *Characteristics of Moslem Sects* 24, *Syria and the Syrians* 26, *An Arab-Syrian Gentleman and Warrior in the Period of the Crusades* 29, 64, *The Origins of the Druze People and Religion* 29, 65, *Kitab al I'tibar li- Usamah* 30, *History of the Arabs* 37 (revised edn. 70), *The Arabs* 43-44 (revised edn. 68), *History of Syria, including Lebanon and Palestine* 51, 57, *Lebanon in History* 57, 62, *Syria: A Short History* 59, 65, *The Near East in History* 61, *Islam and the West* 62, *A Short History of Lebanon* 65, *A Short History of the Near East* 66, *A Short History of Syria* 67, *Makers of Arab History* 68, *Islam: A Way of Life* 70, *Capital Cities of Arab Islam* 73.

Department of Near Eastern Studies, Princeton University, Princeton, N.J.; 144 Prospect Avenue, Princeton, N.J. 08540, U.S.A.
Telephone: 609-WA4-1127 (Home).

Hitzinger, Walter; German engineer and industrialist; b. 8 April 1908; ed. Technical Coll., Vienna.

Steyr-Daimler-Puch factory 35-44; Gen. Man. "Flugmotorenwerke Ostmark" 43-45; owner factories Linz and Salzburg 46-; Chair. and Gen. Man. A.G. Vöest 52-61; Chair. and Gen. Man. Daimler-Benz A.G. Stuttgart 61-66.

Hitzinger u. Co., Linz, Austria.

Hjalmarson, Harry; Swedish business executive (retd.); b. 19 May 1907, Köping; s. of Hjalmar Pettersson and Elin Danielson; m. Greta Keijser 1934; one s. one d.

Member Nat. Pension Fund 59-; mem. Board of Dirs. Commercial Banking Co. of Swedish Savings Banks, Celloplast Co., South Sweden Power Co., Sentab, Swedish Shaleoil Co. 57-; fmr. Pres. Kooperativa förbundet (Swedish Cooperative Union and Wholesale Soc.) 57-.

Home: Skinnarviksringen 10, Stockholm SV; Office: Kooperativa förbundet, Stockholm 15, Sweden.
Telephone: 69-66-22.

Hjelt, Povl; Danish railway executive; b. 29 July 1921, Asdal, Jylland; m. Anna Paula Hjelt 1946; one s.; ed. legal studies.

Danish State Railways, clerk 46, sec. 50, principal 54, chief of section 63, chief purchasing officer 68, Commercial Dir. 69, Dir.-Gen. 70-; mem. rationalising cttee. of railways 54-57; mem. numerous state cttees. on prison administration and other matters; mem. board Int. Railway Union, Presidium of Nordic Council for Railway Co-operation; Vice-Pres. Intercontainer a.s.f.

DSB, Sølvgade 40, 1349 Copenhagen K, Denmark.
Telephone: 01-140400 Ext. 2001.

Hjörne, Lars Goran; Swedish newspaper editor; b. 20 Oct. 1929, Gothenburg; s. of late Harry Hjörne; m. Anne Margaretha Gyllenhammar 1951; one s. one d. Chief Editor *Göteborgs-Posten* 69-.

Office: Polhemsplatsen 5, Gothenburg; Home: Hägnavägen 23, 430 80 Hovås, Sweden.
Telephone: 28-55-55 (Home).

Hjorth-Nielsen, Henning; Danish diplomatist; b. 22 July 1913, Copenhagen; m. Ernestine Gottfried 1947; ed. Københavns Universitet.

Ministry of Justice 38; Asst. to Gov. of Faroe Islands 39; Danish Mil. Mission, London 44; Ministry for Foreign Affairs 46-51; mem. Danish Del. to North Atlantic Treaty Org. (NATO) 51, to OEEC 54; Commercial Minister, London 59-63; Amb. to Netherlands 63-66, to NATO 66-73, to Belgium and Luxembourg 67-74, to Canada 74-75; Perm. Rep. to UN 74-; Danish and foreign awards.

Leisure interests: music, reading.

Permanent Mission of Denmark to United Nations, 235 East 42nd Street, 32nd Floor, New York, N.Y. 10017, U.S.A.

Hla Han, M.B., B.S., D.P.H.; Burmese politician; b. 26 Sept. 1918; ed. Rangoon and Liverpool Univs.
Served in Burma National Army and Resistance 42-45; joined Burma Medical Corps 49; Dir. Medical Services, Ministry of Defence 55-; promoted Col. 58; mem. Revolutionary Council and Minister for Health and Educ. 62-74; Minister for Foreign Affairs 70-72; mem. Council of State March 74-; Star of Independent Sithu (First Class).
Council of State, Rangoon, Burma.

Ho Kuang-yu; Chinese army officer.
Major-General, Deputy Commdr. Kweichow Mil. District, People's Liberation Army 58, Commdr. 66-; Vice-Chair. Kweichow Revolutionary Cttee. 67; Deputy Sec. CCP Kweichow 71.
People's Republic of China.

Ho Yu-fa; Chinese army officer.
Deputy Commdr. Kirin Mil. District, People's Liberation Army 67, Commdr. 68-; Vice-Chair. Kirin Revolutionary Cttee. 68; Sec. CCP Kirin 71.
People's Republic of China.

Hoar, William Stewart, O.C., B.A., M.A., PH.D., D.SC., F.R.S.C.; Canadian zoologist; b. 1913, Moncton, N.B.; s. of George W. Hoar and Nina B. Steeves; m. Margaret M. Hoar 1941; two s. two d.; ed. Univs. of New Brunswick, Western Ontario and Boston.
Demonstrator in Zoology, Univ. of Western Ontario 34-36; Histology asst., Boston Univ. Medical School 36-39; Asst. Prof. of Biology, Univ. New Brunswick 39-42; Physiology Research Assoc., Univ. of Toronto 42-43; Prof. of Zoology, Univ. of New Brunswick 43-45; Prof. of Zoology and Fisheries, Univ. of British Columbia 45-64, Prof. and Head, Zoology Dept. 64-71, Prof. Zoology 71-; John Simon Guggenheim Fellowship Oxford 58-59; Flavelle Medal Award 65; Hon. D.Sc.
Leisure interest: gardening.
Publs. Articles on physiology and behaviour of fish; textbook of comparative physiology.
Department of Zoology, University of British Columbia, Vancouver V6T 1W5, Canada.
Telephone: 228-4881.

Hoard, James Lynn, M.S., PH.D.; American research chemist; b. 28 Dec. 1905, Rural, Okla.; s. of Charles Ellsworth and Bertha Terpening Hoard; m. Florence Marion Fahey 1935; three s.; ed. Univ. of Washington and Calif. Inst. of Technology.
Instructor in Chemistry, Stanford Univ. 32-35; Ohio State Univ. 35-36; Cornell Univ. 36-, Prof. 46-71, Prof. Emer. 71-; Principal Investigator under contract, Cornell Univ. with Office of Scientific Research and Devt. 42-45; Columbia Univ. (Manhattan Project) 43-44; Atomic Energy Comm. 51-56; Army Research Office 59-61; Principal Investigator under research grants from Nat. Science Foundation 56-73, Nat. Inst. of Health 62-(78); mem. Nat. Acad. of Science, Amer. Asscn. for Advancement of Science, Amer. Crystallographic Asscn., Amer. Chemical Soc., Amer. Physical Soc.; Guggenheim Fellow 46, 60, 66.
Leisure interests: piano playing, omnivorous reading, gardening.
Publs. more than 100 articles in professional journals.
Department of Chemistry, Cornell University, Ithaca, N.Y. 14853; Home: 42 Cornell Street, Ithaca, N.Y. 14850, U.S.A.
Telephone: 607-256-3646 (Office); 607-273-7243 (Home).

Hobby, Oveta Culp (Mrs. William P.); American newspaper proprietor; b. 19 Jan. 1905, Killeen, Texas; d. of I. W. and Emma (Hoover) Culp; m. William P. Hobby 1931; one s. one d.; ed. public schools, private tutors and Mary Hardin Baylor Coll.
Parliamentarian, Texas House of Representatives 26-31 and 39, 41; joined *Houston Post* as Research Editor 31, became successively Literary Editor, Asst. Editor

Vice-Pres., Exec. Vice-Pres. and Editor, Editor and Publisher, resgnd. 53, returned as Pres. and Editor 55-65; Editor and Chair. of Board Houston Post Co. 65-; Dir. Station KPRC-AM-TV 45-53 and 55-65; Chair. of Board, Dir. Channel Two TV Co. 70-; Chief, Women's Interest Section, War Dept. Bureau of Public Relations 41-42; apptd. Dir. W.A.A.C. 42; Col. U.S. Army and Dir. W.A.C. 43-45; Fed. Security Admin. 53; Sec. Dept. of Health, Educ. and Welfare 53-55; Hon. LL.D. Baylor Univ. 43, Sam Houston State Teachers' Coll. 43, Univ. of Chattanooga 43, Bryant Coll. 53, Ohio Wesleyan Univ. 54, Columbia Univ. 54, Smith Coll. 54, Middlebury Coll. 54, Univ. of Pa. 55, Colby Coll. 55, Fairleigh Dickinson 56, Western Coll. 56; Hon. L.H.D. Bard Coll. 50, La Fayette Coll. 54; Hon. D.B.A. Southwestern Business Univ. 51; Hon. D.Litt. Colorado Women's Coll. 47; Hon. Dr. of Humanities Mary Hardin Baylor Coll. 56; D.S.M. 44; Philippine Mil. Merit Medal 47; Charter mem. Acad. of Texas 69.
Publs. *Mr. Chairman* (parliamentary law textbook) and syndicated column of same title
Houston Post, 4747 Southwest Freeway, Houston, Tex. 77001, U.S.A.

Hobday, Gordon Ivan, PH.D., F.R.I.C.; British business executive; b. 1 Feb. 1916, Derbyshire; s. of the late Alexander Thomas Hobday and Frances Cassandra (née Meads); m. Margaret Jean Joule 1940; one d.; ed. Long Eaton Grammar School, Univ. Coll., Notts.
Joined The Boots Co. Ltd. 39, Dir. of Research 52-68, Deputy Man. Dir. 68-70, Man. Dir. 70-73, Chair. 73-; Dir. The Metal Box Co. Ltd. 76-.
Leisure interests: lawn tennis, handicrafts, gardening.
The Boots Company Limited, Nottingham, NG2 3AA, England.
Telephone: Nottingham 56111.

Höcherl, Hermann; German politician; b. 31 March 1912, Bavaria; m. Theresia Lotter 1936; one s. three d.; ed. Univs. of Berlin, Aix-en-Provence and Munich.
Assistant Judge, Regensburg 38; served Second World War; Public Prosecutor 50, Senior Judge 51, mem. Bundestag 53-; Fed. Minister of Internal Affairs 61-65, Minister for Food, Agriculture and Forestry 65-69; Chair. Mediation Cttee. between Bundestag and Bundescrat 69-73; Deputy Chair. Christian Social Union (CSU) and Chief Financial Dept. CDU/CSU in Bundestag; Christian Social Union.
Leisure interests: literature, plastic arts.
53 Bonn, Bundeshaus; 8411 Brennberg 124, Regensburg, Federal Republic of Germany.
Telephone: 02221-163626 (Bonn); 09484-271 (Brennberg).

Hochhuth, Rolf; Swiss playwright; b.1933.
Former publisher's reader; Resident Municipal Playwright, Basle 63-.
Publs. Plays: *The Representative* 62, *The Employer* 65, *The Soldiers* 66, *Anatomy of Revolution* 69, *The Guerillas* 70, *The Midwife* 72, *Lysistrata and the NATO* 73.
Riehen Schellenberg 117, Basle, Switzerland.

Hochoy, Sir Solomon, T.C., G.C.M.G., G.C.V.O., O.B.E.; West Indian civil servant and fmr. Governor-General; b. Jamaica 20 April 1905; s. of David and Kuiyin Lue Hochoy; m. Thelma Edna Huggins 1935; one d. (adopted); ed. St. Mary's Coll., Trinidad.
Official Trinidad Port and Marine Dept. 27-39, Labour Dept. 39-46; Dep. Industrial Adviser, Labour Dept. 46-49; Commr. of Labour 49-55; Dep. Chief Sec. 55-56, Chief Sec. 56-60; Gov. Trinidad and Tobago 60-62; Gov.-Gen. of Trinidad and Tobago 62-72.
Blanchisseuse, Trinidad and Tobago.

Hochschild, Walter, B.A.; American industrialist; b. 27 Sept. 1900; ed. Phillips Acad., Andover, Mass., Yale Univ.
Began with The American Metal Co. Ltd. 20, Sec. 34-47, Dir. 28-, Vice-Pres. 42-50, Pres. 50-57, Chair. of Bd. 57-;

American Metal Co. Ltd. and Climax Molybdenum Co. merged; Chair. American Metal Climax Inc. 60-65, now Hon. Chair.; U.S. Council of Int. Chamber of Commerce; served with U.S. Army 42-45; discharged with rank of Major, Air Corps.

Home: Blue Mountain Lake, New York, N.Y. 12812; Office: 1270 Avenue of the Americas, New York, N.Y. 10020, U.S.A.

Hochwälder, Fritz; Austrian playwright; b. 28 May 1911, Vienna; s. of Leo Hochwälder and Therese König; m. Susanne Schreiner 1960; one d.; elementary education and apprenticeship as upholsterer; evening classes at Volkshochschule "Volkheim".

First performances in small Viennese theatres 32, 36; emigrated to Switzerland 38; free-lance writer in Zürich 45-; Literary Prize of City of Vienna 55; Grillparzer Prize of Austrian Acad. of Sciences 56; Anton Wildgans Prize of Austrian Industry 63; Austrian State Prize for Literature 66, Österr. Ehrenkreuz für Wissenschaft und Kunst 71; Ehrenring der Stadt Wien 72.

Publs. plays: *Esther* 40, *Das heilige Experiment* 42, *Hôtel du Commerce* 44, *Der Flüchtling* 45, *Meier Helmbrecht* 46, *Der öffentliche Ankläger* 48, *Donadieu* 53, *Die Herberge* 56, *Der Unschuldige* 58, *Donnerstag* 59, *1003* 63, *Der Himbeerpflücker* 64, *Der Befehl* 68, *Lazaretti* 74. Am Oeschbrig 27, 8053 Zürich, Switzerland. Telephone: 53-20-73.

Hocke, Gustav René; German writer and journalist; b. 1 March 1908, Brussels, Belgium; m. Traude Effenberger 1951; two s. one d.; ed. Univs. of Berlin, Paris, Bonn.

Literary editor, *Kölnische Zeitung* 34-39; Italian corresp. for several German newspapers 40-; mem. Deutsche Akad. für Sprache und Dichtung, Bayerische Akademie der Künste, Accademia del Mediterraneo, Accademia Tiberina; Commdr. Italian Republic and other awards.

Leisure interests: collection of magna graecia ceramics, violins, gardening.

Publs. *Das geistige Paris* 37, *Das verschwundene Gesicht* 39, 60, *Der tanzende Gott* (novel) 48, *Die Welt als Labyrinth* 57, *Manierismus in der Literatur* 59, *Magna Graecia* 60, *Das Europäische Tagebuch* 63, *Labyrinthe de l'Art fantastique* 67, *La funzione europea di Roma* 68, *Fabrizio Clerici* 68, *Der Mensch in Sein und Zeit* 69, *G. Usellini* 70, *Bummel durch Venedig* 73, *Leherb, Le Monde d'un Surréaliste* 73, *Verzweiflung und Zuversicht* 74, *Neomanierismus, der Weg der modernen Kunst vom Surrealismus zur Meditation* 75.

Stampa Estera, Via Mercede 54; and Genzano di Roma, Monte Fiore, Rome Italy.
Telephone: Rome 9396515.

Hocker, Alexander, DR. IUR.; German scientific administrator; b. 29 April 1913, Schweinsburg; ed. Univs. of Innsbruck, Hamburg and Leipzig.

Delegate of Fed. Germany to CERN 52-61; Adviser and Dir. in charge of Research and Devt., Ministry for Scientific Research 56-61; Admin. Man. Nuclear Research Centre of Jülich 61-69; Scientific Adviser to Volkswagenwerk Foundation 70-71; mem. Deutsche Kommission für Weltraumforschung 64-71; Pres. ESRO 65-67, Dir.-Gen. 71-74; mem. Board of Dirs. Max-Planck-Inst. für Physik und Astrophysik 68-71, Max-Planck-Inst. für Plasmaphysik 71-.

Home: 53 Bonn-Bad Godesberg, Augustastrasse 63, Federal Republic of Germany.
Telephone: (02221) 363961.

Hockney, David; British artist; b. 9 July 1937, Bradford; ed. Bradford Coll. of Art and Royal Coll. of Art.

Taught at Maidstone Coll. of Art 62, Univ. of Iowa 64, Univ. of Colo. 65, Univ. of Calif. (Los Angeles) 66, (Berkeley) 67; has travelled extensively in Europe and

U.S.A.; first one-man exhbn., Kasmin Gallery, London 63; subsequent one-man exhbns. at Museum of Modern Art, N.Y. 64, 68, Kasmin Gallery 65, 66, 68, 69, 70, 72, Stedeljik Museum, Amsterdam 66, Palais des Beaux-Arts, Brussels 66, Studio Marconi and Galleria dell'-Ariete, Milan 66, Landau-Alan Gallery, N.Y. 64, 67, Galerie Mikro, Berlin 68, Whitworth Art Gallery, Manchester 69, André Emmerich Gallery, N.Y. 69, 72, Gallery Springer, Berlin 70, Kestner-Ges., Hanover 70, Whitechapel Gallery (retrospective exhbn.), London 70, Kunsthalle, Bielefeld 71, Musée des Arts Décoratifs, Louvre, Paris 74, has participated in several group exhbns. at Inst. of Contemporary Arts (ICA) and numerous other group exhbns. throughout Europe and U.S.A., and in Japan, Australia, New Zealand and S. America 60-; group exhbns. include Second and Third Paris Biennales of Young Artists, Musée d'Art Moderne 61, 63, Third Int. Biennale of Prints, Nat. Museum of Art, Tokyo 62, London Group Jubilee Exhbn. 1914-1964, Tate Gallery 64, *Painting and Sculpture of a Decade*, Gulbenkian Foundation, Tate Gallery, London 64, *Op and Pop*, Stockholm and London 65, Fifth Int. Exhbn. of Graphic Art, Ljubljana 65, First Int. Print Biennale, Cracow 66, São Paulo Biennale 67, Venice Biennale 68, *Pop Art Redefined*, Hayward Gallery, London 69; designed sets for *Rake's Progress*, Glyndebourne 75; appeared in autobiographical documentary film *A Bigger Splash* 74; Guinness Award 61, Graphic Prize, Paris Biennale 63, First Prize 8th Int. Exhbn. of Drawings and Engravings, Lugano 64; prize at 6th Int. Exhbn. of Graphic Art, Ljubljana 65, Cracow 1st Int. Print Biennale 66; First Prize 6th John Moores Exhbn. 67.

c/o Kasmin Ltd., 10 Clifford Street, London, W.1, England.

Hoddinott, Alun, D.MUS.; British (Welsh) composer; b. 11 Aug. 1929, Bargoed, S. Wales; s. of Thomas Ivor Hoddinott and Gertrude Jones; m. Beti Rhiannon Huws 1953; one s.; ed. Gowerton Grammar School and Univ. Coll., Cardiff.

Lecturer, Cardiff Coll. of Music and Drama 51-59, Univ. Coll., Cardiff 59-65, Reader 65-67; Prof. of Music, Univ. Coll., Cardiff 67-; Artistic Dir. Cardiff Festival of Twentieth Century Music 66-; Walford Davies Prize 54, Bax Medal 57; Hon. mem. Royal Acad. of Music.

Works include: five symphonies 55-73, four sinfoniettas, eleven concertos 51-69, six piano sonatas 59-72, four violin sonatas 69-76, sonatas for harp, cello, clarinet, horn, Welsh Dances, Investiture Dances, *Black Bart*, *Dives and Lazarus* 65, *Variants* 66, *Fioriture* 68, *The Tree of Life* 71, *Ritornelli* 74, *The Beach at Falesa* (opera) 74, *The Magician* (opera), *Ancestor Worship*, *Five Landscapes* (song cycles).

Maesawelon, Mill Road, Lisuane, Cardiff, Wales.

Hodgkin, Sir Alan Lloyd, O.M., K.B.E., F.R.S., M.A., SC.D.; British physiologist; b. 5 Feb. 1914, Banbury; s. of G. L. Hodgkin and M. F. Wilson; m. Marion de Kay Rous 1944; one s. three d.; ed. Gresham's School, Holt, and Trinity Coll., Cambridge.

Scientific Officer (radar), Air Ministry and Ministry of Aircraft Production 39-45; Lecturer, later Asst. Dir. of Research, Cambridge 45-52; Foulerton Research Prof., Royal Soc. 52-69; Pres. Marine Biological Asscn. 66-76; John Humphrey Plummer Prof. of Biophysics, Univ. of Cambridge 70-; Pres. of the Royal Soc. 70-75; Chancellor, Leicester Univ. 71-; mem. Medical Research Council 59-63, Royal Danish Acad. of Sciences, Leopoldina Acad., German Democratic Repub.; Foreign mem. Amer. Acad. of Arts and Sciences; Hon. Fellow, Indian Nat. Science Acad., Royal Soc. of Edinburgh; Hon. mem. Royal Irish Acad.; numerous hon. degrees; Royal Medal, Royal Soc. 58; Copley Medal, Royal Soc. 65; shared Nobel Prize for Medicine 63.

Leisure interests: fishing, travel.

Publs. papers dealing with the nature of nervous conduction; *Conduction of the Nervous Impulse* 63. Physiological Laboratory, Cambridge, England.
Telephone: Cambridge 64131.

Hodgkin, Dorothy Crowfoot, O.M., F.R.S.; British crystallographer; b. 1910, Cairo, Egypt; d. of John Winter Crowfoot and Grace Mary Crowfoot (née Hood); *m.* Thomas Hodgkin (*q.v.*) 1937; two *s.* one *d.*; ed. Sir John Leman School, Beccles, and Somerville Coll., Oxford.
Wolfson Research Prof., Royal Soc. 60-; Fellow, Somerville Coll., Oxford; Chancellor, Bristol Univ. 70-; foreign mem. Royal Netherlands Acad. of Science and Letters, American Acad. of Arts and Sciences, Yugoslav Acad. of Sciences, Ghana Acad. of Sciences, Puerto Rico Acad. of Sciences, Australian Acad. of Sciences, Leopoldina Acad. of Sciences, Nat. Acad. of Sciences of U.S.A.; Royal Medal of Royal Soc. 57; Nobel Prize for Chem. 64; Hon. D.Sc. (Leeds, Manchester, Cambridge, Sussex, Ghana, Hull, East Anglia, London, Delhi, Harvard, Exeter, Kent).
Somerville College, Oxford; Home: 20c Bradmore Road, Oxford, England.
Telephone: 57125.

Hodgkin, Thomas Lionel; British lecturer and writer; b. 3 April 1910, Oxford; *s.* of Robert Howard Hodgkin and Dorothy Forster Smith; *m.* Dorothy Crowfoot (Hodgkin, *q.v.*) 1937; two *s.* one *d.*; ed. Winchester Coll. and Balliol Coll., Oxford.
Senior Demy, Magdalen Coll. 32-33; Asst. Sec. Palestine Civil Service 34-36; Educ. Officer, Cumberland Friends' Unemployment Cttee. 37-39; Staff Tutor in North Staffordshire, Oxford Univ. Tutorial Classes Cttee. 39-45; Sec. to Oxford Univ. Delegacy for Extra-Mural Studies, Fellow of Balliol Coll. 45-52; Visiting Lecturer, Northwestern Univ., Illinois 57, Univ. Coll. of Ghana 58; Research Assoc., Inst. of Islamic Studies, McGill Univ., Montreal 58-61; Dir. Inst. of African Studies, Univ. of Ghana 62-65; Lecturer, Govt. of New States, Univ. of Oxford, Senior Research Fellow, Balliol Coll. 65-70, Emer. Fellow 71-.
Publs. *Nationalism in Colonial Africa* 56, *Nigerian Perspectives* 60, 2nd edn. 75, *African Political Parties* 61.
Crab Mill, Ilmington, Shipston-on-Stour, Warwick; 20c Bradmore Road Oxford, England.
Telephone: Ilmington 233; Oxford 57125.

Hodgson, James; American government official and diplomatist; b. 3 Dec. 1915, Dawson, Minn.; *s.* of Fred Arthur Hodgson and Casaraha Day; *m.* Maria Denend 1943; one *s.* one *d.*; ed. Univs. of Minn. and Calif. (Los Angeles).
Former consultant to State of Calif. on manpower matters; Community Adviser to Inst. of Industrial Relations, Univ. of Calif.; joined Lockheed Aircraft Corpn. 41, Corporate Dir. for industrial relations 62-68, Vice-Pres. 68-69; Under-Sec. of Labor Feb. 69-June 70; Sec. of Labor 70-73; Senior Vice-Pres. in charge of Corporate Relations, Lockheed Aircraft Corpn. 73; Amb. to Japan 74-.
Leisure interests: golf, skiing, reading.
U.S. Embassy, Chancery, 10-5, Akasaka 1-chome, Minato-ku, Tokyo, Japan.

Hodgson, Maurice Arthur Eric, M.A., B.SC., F.I.CHEM.E., C.ENG.; British company executive; b. 21 Oct. 1919, Bradford; *s.* of Walter and Amy (née Walker) Hodgson; *m.* Norma Fawcett 1945; one *s.* one *d.*; ed. Bradford Grammar School and Merton Coll., Oxford.
Joined ICI Ltd., Fertilizer and Synthetic Products Group 42; Seconded to ICI (N.Y.) Ltd. 55-58; Head of Technical Dept., ICI Ltd. 58, Devt. Dir. Heavy Organic Chemicals Div. 60 (Deputy Chair. 64), Gen. Man. Co. Planning 66, Commercial Dir. and Planning Dir. 70, Deputy Chair. 72-; Dir. Carrington Viyella Ltd. 70-74;

Imperial Chemicals Insurance Ltd. 70- (Chair. 72); Visiting Fellow, School of Business and Organizational Studies, Univ. of Lancaster 70-; Fellow, British Inst. of Management 72-.
Leisure interests: horse-racing, swimming, fishing.
Woodsway, Eaton Park, Cobham, Surrey, England.

Hodin, Dr. Josef Paul, LL.D., PH.D., F.R.S.A.; British author, art historian and critic; b. 17 Aug. 1905, Prague, Czechoslovakia; *s.* of Eduard David Hodin and Rosa Hodin (née Klug); *m.* Doris Pamela Simms 1945; one *s.* one *d.*; ed. Kleinseitner Realschule, Neustädter Realgymnasium, Prague, Charles Univ., London Univ., Art Acadmies, Dresden and Berlin.
Press Attaché, Norwegian Govt. in London 44-45; Dir. of Studies and Librarian, Inst. of Contemporary Arts, London 49-54; Hon. mem. Editorial Council *The Journal of Aesthetics and Art Criticism*, Cleveland 55-; founder mem. British Soc. of Aesthetics; Editor *Prisme des Arts*, Paris 56-59, *Quadrum*, Brussels 59-70; Dir. foreign relations, Studio International 66-; several decorations.
Leisure interests: travelling, reading.
Publs. Monographs on *Sven Erixson* 40, *Ernst Josephson* 42, *Edvard Munch* 48, 63, 72, *Isaac Grünewald* 49, *Art and Criticism* 44, *J. A. Comenius and Our Time* 44, *The Dilemma of Being Modern* 56, *Henry Moore* 56, *Ben Nicholson* 57, *Barbara Hepworth* 61, *Lynn Chadwick* 61, *Oskar Kokoschka* 63, 66, 68, 71, 75, *Walter Kern* 66, *Ruszkowski* 67, *Bernard Leach* 67, *Giacomo Manzù* 70, *Emilio Greco* 71, *Alfred Manessier* 72, *Bernard Stern* 72, *Modern Art and the Modern Mind* 72, *Ludwig Meidner* 73, *Hilde Goldschmidt* 74, *Paul Berger-Bergner* 74, *Kokoschka and Hellas* 76.
12 Eton Avenue, London, NW3 3EH, England.
Telephone: 01-794-3609.

Hodja, Enver (see Hoxha, E.).

Hodson, Henry Vincent, M.A.; British editor, author and administrator; b. 12 May 1906, London; *s.* of Prof. Thomas C. Hodson and Kathleen (née Manly) Hodson; *m.* Margaret Elizabeth Honey 1933; four *s.*; ed. Gresham's School, Holt, and Balliol Coll., Oxford.
Fellow All Souls Coll., Oxford 28-35; Editor The Round Table 34-39; Dir. of Empire Div., Ministry of Information 39-41; Constitutional Adviser to Viceroy of India 41-42; Principal Asst. Sec., Ministry of Production 42-45; Asst. Editor *The Sunday Times* 45-50, Editor 50-61; Provost of Ditchley Foundation 61-71; Partner Hodson Consultants 71-; Consultant Editor *The International Foundation Directory* 72, *The Business Who's Who* 73; Editor *Annual Register of World Events* 73-.
Leisure interest: gardening.
Publs. *Economics of a Changing World* 33, *Slump and Recovery 1928-37* 38, *Twentieth Century Empire* 48, *The Great Divide: Britain-India-Pakistan* 69, *The Diseconomics of Growth* 72.
Office: 18 Northumberland Avenue, London, WC2N 5BJ; Home: 23 Cadogan Lane, London, SW1X 9DP, England.
Telephone: 01-930 6046 (Office); 01-235 5509 (Home).

Hoelgaard, Vagn Hoffmeyer; Danish diplomatist; b. 12 Sept. 1913, Copenhagen; *m.* Eva Tolderlund; four *c.*; ed. Copenhagen University and Inst. Universitaire de Hautes Etudes Internationales, Geneva.
Secretary, Danish Foreign Exchange Office (Valutacentralen) 38; entered Foreign Service 39; Commercial Sec., London 45-48; then in Ministry of Foreign Affairs, Copenhagen; Econ. Counsellor, Washington 52; presided over several econ. and trade dels. 56-62; Danish Del. to UN Econ. Comm. for Europe 61-62; Amb. to Peru and Bolivia 62-68; Amb. and Rep. of Denmark at Org. for Econ. Co-operation and Devt. (OECD) 68-72; Amb. to Mexico, Cuba, El Salvador, Guatemala and Honduras 73-; Commdr. Order of Dannebrog; Grand Cross Order

of Sun (Peru); Commdr. Order of Lion (Finland); Officer Order of Christ (Portugal).
Leisure interests: piano, painting, bridge and golf.
Campos Elisios 1705, Polanco, Mexico D.F.; Home: Paseo de Reforma 1825, Lomas Chapultapec, Mexico D.F., Mexico.
Telephone: 531-3060.

Hoem, Knut; Norwegian fish official and politician; b. 27 Jan. 1924.
Joined Skien police 50; Sec. Ministry of Fisheries 51-55; Sales Sec. Norwegian Unprocessed Fish Asscn., Tromsø 55, later legal adviser 55-63, Asst. Dir. 63-64; Man. Dir. Norges Råfisklag (Fishermen's Unprocessed Fish Co-operative) 64; fmr. Sec. Fish Information Board; mem. Dry Fish Export Cttee., Frozen Fish and Filleted Fish Export Cttee., mem. Board Nordfisk, Svolvaer; Minister of Fisheries March 71-Jan. 72.
c/o Ministry of Fisheries, Oslo, Norway.

Hoffa, James Riddle; American trade unionist; b. 14 Feb. 1913, Brazil, Ind.; s. of John and Veola Hoffa; m. Josephine Pozywak 1937; one s. one d.
International Brotherhood of Teamsters 32-, leader in major dispute, car hauling industry, Detroit 33-35; Pres. Teamsters Local (299) 37; Chair. Central Conf. of Teamsters Negotiating Cttee. 40; Pres. Michigan Conf. of Teamsters' 42; Pres. Joint Council (43) 46; Trustee, Int. Brotherhood of Teamsters, Vice-Pres. 52-57, Gen. Pres. 57-71, Pres. Emer. 71.
Leisure interests: fishing, hunting, gardening.
1614 Ray Court, Lake Orion, Mich. 48035, U.S.A.
Telephone: 305-8664810.

Hoffman, Grace; American mezzo-soprano singer; b. Cleveland, Ohio; d. of Dave and Hermina Hoffman; ed. Western Reserve Univ. and Manhattan School of Music, N.Y.
Completed musical studies in Italy (Fulbright Scholarship); appeared at Maggio Musicale, Florence; guest performance as Azucena (Il Trovatore) Zurich Opera and subsequently mem. of this company for two years; debut at La Scala, Milan as Fricka (Die Walküre); joined Stuttgart Opera and awarded title of Kammersängerin; has appeared at Edinburgh and Bayreuth festivals; numerous guest appearances in leading roles at Teatro Colón, Buenos Aires, San Francisco Opera, Chicago Lyric Opera, Covent Garden, Metropolitan Opera, the Vienna Opera, in Berlin, Brussels, etc.; numerous oratorio and concert appearances in the major European music centres.
Leisure interests: her house and furnishing it.
c/o Staatsoper, Postfach 982, 7 Stuttgart, Federal Republic of Germany.

Hoffman, Michael L., PH.D.; American economist and journalist; b. 13 June 1915; ed. Oberlin Coll., Ohio and Chicago Univ.
Lecturer in monetary theory and international trade at Oberlin Coll. and Trinity Coll., Connecticut; Consultant U.S. Treasury 41; Acting Dir. wartime Foreign Funds Control; U.S. Treasury Rep. Allied Force Headquarters Algiers, London and Paris; European economic correspondent The New York Times 45-56; Dir. Econ. Devt. Inst. of the Int. Bank for Reconstruction and Devt. (IBRD) 56-61, Dir. Devt. Advisory Service 62-63; Exec. Vice-Pres. and Dir. Lambert Int. Corpn. 63-65; Assoc. Dir. Devt. Services Dept., IBRD 65-73, Dir. Int. Relations Dept. 73-.
Office: 1818 H Street, N.W., Washington, D.C. 20433; Home: RFD, Vineyard Haven, Mass. 02568, U.S.A.

Hoffmann, Gene D.: American company executive; ed. Univ. of Missouri.
Marketing positions with Montgomery Ward, Chicago Tribune, Philadelphia Bulletin; served in U.S. Navy Air Force during World War II; Advertising, Sales Promotion and Public Relations Man. (St. Louis, Mo.)

The Kroger Co. 56, Marketing Man. Processed Foods Div. 61, Vice-Pres. of Processed Foods Div. 64, Vice-Pres. Mfg. Div. 66, also for private label mfg. and procurement 72, Dir. 70-, Senior Vice-Pres. 74-75, Pres. Dec. 75-; formerly Vice-Pres. and mem. Board Greater Cincinnati Chamber of Commerce, Cancer Family Care Inc.; now mem. Board Warner Nat. Corpn., Home State Savings Asscn., American Inst. of Management.
The Kroger Company, 1014 Vine Street, Cincinnati, Ohio 45201, U.S.A.
Telephone: 381-8000.

Hoffmann, Gen. Heinz; German army officer and politician; b. 28 Nov. 1910; ed. elementary school and Acad. of General Staff, U.S.S.R.
Member Kommunistische Partei Deutschlands 30; Sozialistische Einheitspartei Deutschlands (S.E.D.) 46-; apprentice fitter 25-28; official in Communist Youth Org. 26-30; emigrated to U.S.S.R. 35; fought in Spanish Civil War; Kominternschule, U.S.S.R.; fought in Second World War; teacher at Antifa-Schulen; in Germany 46; Party Functions Berlin 46-49; mem. Volkskammer 50-; Lieut.-Gen. of People's Police and Deputy Minister of Interior 52-56; mem. Central Cttee. S.E.D. 52-, mem. Politburo 73-; Lieut.-Gen. Nat. People's Army 56-59, Col.-in-Chief 59-61, Gen. 61-; Deputy Minister of Nat. Defence 56-60, Minister of Nat. Defence 60-; Rep. of D.D.R. in Supreme Command of Warsaw Pact; Karl-Marx-Orden, Vaterländischer Verdienstorden in Gold; Scharnhorst-Orden, Rotbanner-Orden, U.S.S.R.
Publs. Sozialistische Landesverteidigung 1963-1970 70, Sozialistische Landesverteidigung 1970-1974 74.
Ministerium für Nationale Verteidigung, Berlin, German Democratic Republic.

Hoffmann, Karel; Czechoslovak politician; b. 15 June 1924, Stod; ed. Coll. of Political and Social Science, Prague.
Worked on Central Cttee. of C.P. of Czechoslovakia; Gen. Dir. Czechoslovak Radio 59-67; Minister of Culture and Information 67-68; mem. Ideological Comm. of Central Cttee. of C.P. of Czechoslovakia 63-69; Dir. Central Admin. of Communications May-Sept. 68; Deputy Chair. Admin. of Fed. Material Reserves Jan.-Sept. 69; Minister Chair of Fed. Cttee. for Posts and Telecommunications Sept. 69-71; Minister of Telecommunications 71; mem. Central Cttee. of C.P. 66-, alt. mem. Presidium 71, mem. 71-; mem. Presidium of Cen. Cttee. of Nat. Front, Č.S.S.R. 71-; Chair. Cen. Council of Trade Unions 71-; Deputy to House of the People, Fed. Assembly 71-, mem. Presidium of Fed. Assembly 71-; Vice-Chair. World Fed. of Trade Unions 73-; Order of Labour 65, Order of Victorious February 73, Order of the Republic 74.
Central Committee of Communist Party of Czechoslovakia, Prague.

Hoffmann, Ladislaus von; German international finance official; b. 1927; ed. Univ. of Freiburg.
With affiliate of Fed. of German Industries 50-52; Asst. to Board, Wasag Chemie A.G. 54, Rep. in Middle East 57-59; with Int. Finance Corpn. (IFC) 60-, Dir. Dept. of Investments 65-70, Vice-Pres. IFC 70-74, Exec. Vice-Pres. 74-.
International Finance Corporation, 1818 H Street, N.W., Washington, D.C. 20433, U.S.A.
Telephone: EX3-6360.

Hoffmann, Martin R., LL.B.; American lawyer and politician; b. 20 April 1932, Stockbridge, Mass.; m. Margaret Ann McCabe; three c.; ed. Princeton Univ. and Univ. of Virginia Law School.
Served U.S. Army 54-58; Law Clerk in Alexandria, Va.; Asst. U.S. Attorney, D.C. 62-65; Minority Counsel on House Judiciary Cttee. 65-66; Legal Counsel to

Senator Charles Percy 67-69; Asst. Gen. Counsel and Asst. Sec. Univ. Computing Co. 69-71; Gen. Counsel, Atomic Energy Comm. 71-73; Special Asst. to Sec. and Deputy Sec. of Defence 73-74, Gen. Counsel of Defence Dept. 74-75, Sec. of the Army Aug. 75-.
Department of the Army, The Pentagon, Washington, D.C. 20310, U.S.A.

Hoffmann, Paul; Austrian theatre director; b. 25 March 1902, Barmen, Fed. Germany; s. of Arthur and Paula (née Hammelsbeck) Hoffmann; m. Margrit Hammelsbeck 1946; two d.; ed. Matura Humanistisches Gymnasium, Düsseldorf and Univs. of Marburg, Cologne, Würzburg, Munich and Vienna.
Former actor and producer in Würzburg, Aachen, Dresden, Stuttgart, Munich, Zürich, Berlin and Vienna; Dir. Staatstheater, Stuttgart 50-56; Dir. Burgtheater, Vienna 67-71; Grosses Bundesverdienstkreuz.
Leisure interests: history of art, chamber music.
1090 Vienna, Rooseveltplatz 13/12, Austria.
Telephone: 43-23-46.

Hoffmann, Roald, PH.D.; American professor of chemistry; b. 18 July 1937, Zloczow, Poland; s. of Paul Hoffmann and Clara Rosen; m. Eva Börjesson 1960; one s. one d.; ed. Columbia and Harvard Univs.
Junior Fellow, Soc. of Fellows, Harvard Univ. 62-65; Assoc. Prof. of Chemistry, Cornell Univ. 65-68, Prof. 68-74; John A. Newman Prof. of Physical Science 74-; mem. Amer. Acad. of Arts and Sciences, Nat. Acad. of Sciences; American Chem. Soc. Award 69, Fresenius Award 69, Harrison Howe Award 69, Annual Award of Int. Acad. of Quantum Molecular Sciences 70, Arthur C. Cope Award, Amer. Chemical Soc. 73, Linus Pauling Award 74.
Publ. *Conservation of Orbital Symmetry* 69.
Department of Chemistry, Cornell University, Ithaca, N.Y. 14850; Home: 4 Sugarbush Lane, Ithaca, N.Y. 14850, U.S.A.
Telephone: 607-256-3419 (Office); 607-273-2389 (Home).

Hoffmeyer, Erik, D.SC.; Danish banker; b. 25 Dec. 1924, Rårup; m. Eva Kemp 1949; ed. Copenhagen University.
At Danmarks Nationalbank 51-59, Econ. Counsellor 59-62, Chair. of Board of Govs. 65-; Rockefeller Fellow, U.S. 54-55; Lecturer in Econs., Univ. of Copenhagen 56, Prof. 59-64; Gov. Bikuben Savings Bank 62-64, Chair. of Board 64; Gov. for Denmark to Int. Monetary Fund (IMF) 65-; Pres. Asscn. of Political Economy 51-53; mem. Board of Management, Nat. Econ. Soc. 60-66 Presidium of Econ. Council 62-65, Board of Acad. of Technical Sciences 63, Econ. Council 65, Danish Science Advisory Council 65-72, C. L. David Collection 67-, The Housing Mortgage Fund 69-72; Dir. European Investment Bank 73-; Chair. Cttee. of Govs. of Central Banks of EEC Countries 75-76.
Publs. *Dollar Shortage and the Structure of U.S. Foreign Trade* 58, *Stabile priser og fuld beskæftigelse* 60, *Strukturændringer på penge-og kapitalmarkedet* 60, *Velfærdsteori og velfærdsstat* (edited) 62, *Industriel vækst* 63, *Dansk pengehistorie* (edited) 68.
Danmarks Nationalbank, Holmens Kanal 17, DK-1093 Copenhagen K; Hegelsvej 22, DK 2920 Charlottenlund, Denmark.
Telephone: 01-14 14 11 (Office).

Höffner, H.E. Cardinal Joseph, DR. PHIL., DR. THEOL., DR. SC. POL.; German ecclesiastic; b. 24 Dec. 1906, Horhausen/Westerwald; s. of Paul and Helene (née Schug) Höffner; ed. Gymnasiums of Montabaur and Trier, Priesterseminar Trier, Univs. of Rome and Freiburg i. Br.
Theological and philosophical studies till 43; priest in Trier 34-45; Prof. Pastoral Theology and Christian sociology, Phil.-Theologisch Fakultät Trier 45-51; Prof. Christian Sociology, Univ. of Münster 51-62;

founder and Dir. Inst. für Christliche Sozialwissenschaften, Univ. of Münster; fmr. mem. Union Int. des Etudes sociales, Brussels, Foundation Cttee. for Univ. of Bochum and many working parties and advisory councils; Bishop of Münster 62-69; Archbishop of Cologne 69-; cr. Cardinal 69; Bundesverdienstkreuz mit Stern und Schulterband.
Publs. Numerous monographs, essays and articles.
5000 Cologne, Eintrachtstrasse 164, Federal Republic of Germany.
Telephone: 20821.

Hofmeister, Paul Emil Julius; German business executive; b. 28 April 1909, Bremen; s. of Heinrich Hofmeister and Dora Meijer; m. Elisabeth Sommer 1934; one d.; ed. commercial school.
Joined Norddeutsche Affinerie 27, mem. management 47, Pres. 61-; mem. Board and presidium, Wirtschaftsvereinigung Metalle e.V., Düsseldorf; Deputy Chair. Fachvereinigung Metallhütten und Umschmelzwerke e.V., Düsseldorf; Chair. Supervisory Board, Otavi Minen- und Eisenbahn-Gesellschaft, Frankfurt; Chair. Supervisory Board, Bremer Woll-Kämmerei, Bremen; mem. Supervisory Board, H. Maihak A.G., Hamburg; Dir. Amalgamated Metal Corpn., Ltd. London; mem. Advisory Council, Deutsche Bank A.G., Frankfurt; mem. Full Assembly Chamber of Commerce, Hamburg; Orden al Mérito Bernardo O'Higgins (Chile).
Leisure interests: riding, golf.
Norddeutsche Affinerie, 2000 Hamburg 36, Alsterterrasse 2; Home: 2000 Hamburg 52, Borchlingweg 11, Federal Republic of Germany.
Telephone: 44-19-61 (Office); 880-41-34 (Home).

Hofmeyr, Murray, M.A.; South African business executive; b. 1925, Pretoria; ed. Pretoria High School, Rhodes and Oxford Univs.
Joined Anglo American Corpn., Johannesburg 61, Man. in Zambia 65-69, Chair. Anglo American Corpn. (Cen. Africa) 69-70; mem. Board, Anglo American Corpn. of S.A. Ltd. 70-72, Exec. Dir. 72-; Man. Dir. Charter Consolidated Ltd. 72-.
Charter Consolidated Ltd., 40 Holborn Viaduct, London, E.C.1, England.

Hofstadter, Robert, B.S., M.A., PH.D.; American university professor; b. 5 Feb. 1915, New York; ed. City Coll. of New York, Princeton Univ.
Instructor, Univ. of Pennsylvania, City Coll., New York 40-42; Physicist, Nat. Bureau of Standards, Washington, D.C. 42-43; Asst. Chief Physicist, Norden Laboratories Corpn., New York 43-46; Asst. Prof. of Physics, Princeton Univ. 46-50, Assoc. Prof. Stanford Univ. 50-53, Prof. 54-; Guggenheim Fellowship 58-59; Dir. High Energy Physics Lab., Stanford Univ. 67-74; Max H. Stein Prof. of Physics 71-; Assoc. Editor *Physical Review* 51-53, Review of *Scientific Instruments* 54-56, *Reviews of Modern Physics* 58-61; mem. Nat. Acad. of Sciences 58-; Fellow, Amer. Physical Soc., Physical Soc. of London; mem. Italian Physical Soc., Amer. Acad. of Arts and Sciences 70; mem. Board of Govs., Weizmann Inst. of Science, Rehovoth, Israel; Assoc. Linus Pauling Inst. of Science and Medicine 74-; Calif. Scientist of Year 59; Nobel Prize Winner in Physics 61, other prizes and awards.
Publs. *Nuclear and Nucleon Structure*, Jt. author *High-Energy Electron Scattering Tables*, over 200 scientific papers, Co-Editor *Investigations in Physics* 51-, *Nuclear Structure*, Assoc. Editor *Reviews in Modern Physics*.
Department of Physics, Stanford University, Stanford, Calif. 94305, U.S.A.
Telephone: 415-321-2300.

Hofstra, Hendrik Jan; Netherlands lawyer; b. 28 Sept. 1904, Amsterdam; s. of Jan Hofstra and Harmina Fricke; m. Wilhelmina Odilia Petri 1926; one s.

Tax inspector prior to 39, tax consultant 39-45; mem. Second Chamber of States Gen. 45-56; Dir. Central Life Insurance Bank, The Hague and Central Gen. Insurance Co., The Hague prior to 56; Minister of Finance 56-58; Gov. European Investment Bank 56-58; Vice-Pres. Verolme United Shipyards, Rotterdam 61-66; Prof. Leiden Univ. 66-; mem. Labour Party; Knight of the Netherlands Lion; Commdr. Order of Orange-Nassau.
Leisure interests: gardening, music.
Publs. *Socialistische Belastingpolitiek* 46, *Inleiding Nederlands Belastingrecht* 70.
Hoek van Hollandlaan 8, The Hague, Netherlands.
Telephone: 256172.

Hogan, Hon. Sir Michael Joseph, Kt., C.M.G., Q.C., B.A., LL.D.; British lawyer; b. 15 March 1908, Dublin; s. of Timothy and Mary Hogan; m. Patricia Galliford 1946; ed. Belvedere Coll., Stonyhurst Coll., and Trinity Coll., Dublin Univ.
Admitted solicitor, Ireland 30, Kenya Bar 31, called to Irish Bar 36; Chief Magistrate, Palestine 36; Crown Counsel 37; Attorney-Gen., Aden 45; called to Inner Temple 46; Solicitor-Gen., Palestine 47; attached to Foreign Office 49; Solicitor-Gen., Malaya 50, Attorney-Gen. 50-55; Chief Justice, Hong Kong 55-70, Chief Justice, Brunei 64-70; Pres. Brunei Court of Appeal 70-73; Judge, Court of Appeal, Gibraltar 70-; Judge, Courts of Appeal, Bahamas, Bermuda and Belize 70-75, Pres. 75-; mem. Anglo-Japanese Property Comm. (appointed under Peace Treaty).
Leisure interests: golf, bridge.
2 Carlyle Mansions, Cheyne Walk, London, S.W.3, England.
Telephone: 01-351-1360.

Hogg, Sir John Nicholson, Kt., M.A.(OXON.); British banker; b. 4 Oct. 1912, Bombay, India; s. of late Sir Malcolm Hogg and of Lorna Beaman; m. Elizabeth Garmoyle 1948; one s. one d.; ed. Eton Coll. and Balliol Coll., Oxford.
Joined Glyn Mills and Co. 34; war service with King's Royal Rifle Corps 39-45; returned to Glyn Mills and Co. 45, Man. Dir. 50, Deputy Chair. 63-68, Chair. 68-70; Deputy Chair. Williams and Glyn's Bank Ltd.; Deputy Chair. Prudential Assurance Co. Ltd., Gallaher Ltd.; Dir. Honeywell Ltd., Nat. Commercial Banking Group Ltd.; Chair. Brown Harriman and Int. Banks Ltd., Abu Dhabi Investment Board; Chair. Advisory Council of Export Credit Guarantee Dept. 62-67; Fellow Eton Coll. 51-70; mem. Commonwealth War Graves Comm. 58-64; Sherriff County of London 60; Hon. T.D.
Leisure interests: cricket, fishing, gardening.
67 Lombard Street, London, E.C.3; Home: The Red House, Shedfield, Southampton, England.
Telephone: 623-4356 (Office); Wickham 832121 (Home).

Hoggart, (Herbert) Richard; British university professor; b. 24 Sept. 1918, Leeds; s. of Tom Longfellow Hoggart and Adeline Emma Hoggart; m. Mary Holt France 1942; two s. one d.; ed. Leeds Univ.
Royal Artillery 40-46; Staff Tutor and Senior Staff Tutor, Univ. of Hull and Univ. Coll. of Hull 46-59; Senior Lecturer in English, Univ. of Leicester 59-62; Visiting Prof. Univ. of Rochester, New York 56-57; Prof. of English, Birmingham Univ. 62-73; mem. Albemarle Cttee. on Youth Services 58-60, Youth Service Development Council 60-62, Pilkington Cttee. on Broadcasting 60-62; Gov. Birmingham Repertory Theatre 63-; Dir. Centre for Contemporary Cultural Studies 64-73; mem. BBC Gen. Advisory Council 59-60, 64-70; mem. Culture Advisory Cttee. of U.K. Nat. Comm. to UNESCO 66-70; Gov. Royal Shakespeare Theatre 66-; Asst. Dir.-Gen. for Social Sciences, Humanities and Culture UNESCO 70-75; Warden of Goldsmiths' Coll. 75-; BBC Reith Lecturer 71.

Publs. *Auden* 51, *The Uses of Literacy* 57, *W. H. Auden—A Selection* 61, *Teaching Literature* 63, *The Critical Moment* 64, *How and Why Do We Learn* 65, *Essays in Literature and Culture* 69, *Speaking to each other* 70, *Only Connect* 72.
Goldsmiths' College, Lewisham Way, New Cross, London, SE14 6NW, England.

Højdahl, Odd; Norwegian trade unionist and politician; b. 5 Jan. 1921, Oslo.
Vice-Pres. Landsorganisasjonen i Norge (LO) (Norwegian Fed. of Trade Unions) 69-; Minister of Social Affairs March 71-Oct. 72; Dir. Norwegian Developing Aid Directorate, Tiden Norsk Forlag, *Arbeiderbladet* (daily newspaper), Aktietrykkeriet (printing firm) and the state-run Iron and Steel works; Del. and Adviser, ILO congresses and UN Gen. Assembly; Labour.
Landsorganisasjonen i Norge, Folkets Hus, Youngsgt. 11, Oslo, Norway.

Holan, Vladimir; Czechoslovak poet; b. 16 Sept. 1905, Prague.
Clerk Pensions Inst. 27-33; Editor *Život* periodical 33-38, *Program D40* periodical 39-40; freelance writer 40-; State Prize 48, 65, Sicilian Prize Etna Taormina 67, Nat. Artist 68, Int. Grand Prix for Poetry, Belgium 74.
Publs. *Blouznivý vějíř, Triumf smrti, Kolury, Vanutí, Torso, Oblouk, Kameni, přicházíš . . . , Zárž* 1938, *Sen, Zdhřmotí, Prvni testament, Lemuria, Chór, Terezka Planetová, Cesta mraku, Dík Sovětskému svazu, Panychida, Havranim brkem, Zpěv třikrálový, Rudoarmějci, Tobě, Prvni básně, Dokument, Prostě, Bajaja, Tři, Z dokumentu, Mozartiana, Noěni hlídka srdce, Příběhy, Na Postupu, Noc s Hamletem, Trialog, Bolest, Na Sothnách, Asklépiovi kohouta, Noc s Ofélič, Jeskyněslov, Ale je Ludba, Lamento, Babyloniaca,* and translations of Rilke, Baudelaire, Ronsard, Lermontov, Nízámí, Lenau, La Fontaine, Słowacki, Mickiewicz, Cros, Laforgue, Apollinaire, Vildrac, Supervielle, etc.
110 00 Prague 1, Staré Mèsto, Uluzického Semináře 18, Czechoslovakia.
Telephone: 532377.

Holas, B. (Théophile); French ethnologist; b. 28 Sept. 1909; ed. Univ. de Paris à la Sorbonne.
Director, Centre des Sciences humaines, Abidjan; Curator, Nat. Museum of Ivory Coast; scientific missions in Africa, North and South America, Far East and Oceania; mem. Acad. des sciences d'outre-mer, Int. African Inst., London, Soc. des Gens de Lettres, Paris; Commdr. de l'Ordre national and several other awards.
Publs. *Mission dans l'Est libérien* 52, *Les masques kono* 52, *Le Culte de Zié* 55, *Les Sénoufo* 57, *Cultures matérielles de la Côte d'Ivoire* 60, *Changements sociaux* 61, *Les Toura* 62, *La Côte d'Ivoire: passé, présent, perspectives* 64, *La Sculpture Sénoufo* 64, *Les religions de l'Afrique noire* 64, *Le Séparatisme religieux en Afrique noire* 65, *Industries et cultures en Côte d'Ivoire* 65, *Arts de la Côte d'Ivoire* 66, *Craft and Culture in the Ivory Coast* 68, *L'image du monde bété* 68, *Les dieux d'Afrique noire* 68, *La pensée africaine* 71.
B.P. 1600, Abidjan, Ivory Coast; and 12 rue Vavin, Paris 6e, France.

Holbrook, David Stearns; American steel executive; b. 17 July 1912, St. Louis, Miss.; s. of Harold Lyman and Lucy (Styring) Holbrook; m. Marguerite Somers 1931; two s. one d.; ed. Pittsburg Univ.
Steam Engineer, Carnegie Steel Co., Youngstown 33-35; Project Engineer, Carnegie-Illinois Steel Corpn. 35-40; Asst. Chief Engineer, Homestead Works, Carnegie-Illinois Steel Corpn. 40-44; Asst. Gen. Manager, Algoma Steel Corpn. Ltd., Sault Sainte Marie, Ontario, Canada 44-45, Exec. Asst. to Pres. 45-46, Vice-Pres. 46-49, Exec. Vice-Pres. 49-56 Pres. 56-, Chair. and Pres. 62-; Vice-Pres. Cannelton Industries Ltd.; Dir. Dominion Bridge Co. Ltd., The Royal Bank of Canada, American Iron

and Steel Inst., Du Pont of Canada Ltd., Int. Iron and Steel Inst.; Hon. LL.D. (Laurentian Univ.) 68.
Leisure interests: golf, boating.
The Algoma Steel Corporation Ltd., Sault Ste. Marie, Ontario, Canada.
Telephone: 945-2351.

Holden, Roberto; Angolan nationalist leader; b. 1925, São Salvador, Northern Province; ed. Belgian Congo (now Zaire).
Worked in Finance Dept., Belgian Admin., Léopoldville (now Kinshasa), Stanleyville (now Kisangani) and Bukavu; founded União das Populacões de Angola (UPA) 54; travelled widely in Africa and Europe; attended first and second All African Peoples Confs. Accra 58, Tunis 60; elected to the Steering Cttee., Tunis; founded *La Voix de la Nation Angolaise*, a fortnightly newspaper; assumed leadership of guerrilla liberation operations against the Portuguese in Angola; made several trips to U.S.A. 61; became leader of Frente Nacional de Libertação de Angola (FNLA) when UPA merged with Partido Democrático Angolano (PDA) March 62; Premier of Angolan govt. in exile, Governo Revolucionário de Angola no Exílio (GRAE) 62; leader of FNLA forces in Angolan civil war after Portuguese withdrawal Nov. 75-.
Kinshasa, Zaire.

Holder, Douglas William, M.A., PH.D., D.SC., F.R.S., D.I.C., F.C.G.I., C.ENG., F.I.C.E., F.R.AE.S.; British professor of engineering science; b. 14 April 1923, London; s. of William Arthur and Anne Holder; m. Barbara Woods 1946; two d.; ed. Imperial Coll. of Science and Technology, London.
Aircraft and Armament Experimental Establishment, Boscombe Down 43; Nat. Physical Laboratory 44-61 (in charge of work on gas dynamics 51-61); Prof. of Engineering Science and Fellow of Brasenose Coll., Univ. of Oxford 61-; Fellow of Royal Soc. 62-; mem. various Councils and Cttees. of Ministry of Defence, Dept. of Educ. and Science and Ministry of Health.
Leisure interests: lawn tennis and golf.
Publs. books, monographs and papers, mainly on fluid dynamics.
Engineering Laboratory, Parks Road, Oxford; Home: Woods End, Hamels Lane, Boar's Hill, Oxford, England.
Telephone: Oxford 56120 (Laboratory); 735171 (Home).

Hollaender, Alexander, A.B., M.A., PH.D.; American radiation biologist; b. 19 Dec. 1898, Samter, Germany; m. Henrietta Wahlert 1925; ed. Wisconsin Univ.
Asst. in Physical Chemistry, Wisconsin Univ. 29-31; Nat. Research Council Fellow in Biological Sciences 31-33; Investigator, Rockefeller Foundation 34; Investigator in charge of Nat. Research Council Wisconsin Radiation Project 34-37; Washington Biophysics Inst., Assoc. Biophysicist 37-38, Biophysicist 38-41, Senior and Principal Biophysicist 45-46, Head Biophysicist 46-50; attached to Office of Scientific Research and Development, Atomic Energy Comm. 40-45; Dir. Biology Division, Oak Ridge (Tennessee) Nat. Laboratory 46-66, Senior Research Adviser 67-74; Pres. Comité Int. de Photobiologie 54-60, Hon. Pres. 64-; Free mem. of the Exec. Cttee. 60-64; Chair. Nat. Research Council Photobiology Cttee. 55-60; mem. Radiobiology Subcttee.; mem. Genetic Effects of Atomic Radiation Panel, Nat. Acad. of Sciences 56-63; Prof. of Radiation Biology, Tennessee Univ. 57-66, Prof. of Biomedical Sciences 67-; Dir. Archives of Radiation Biology, Univ. of Tenn. 68-; mem. Cttee. on Int. Exchange of Persons, Biology Advisory Cttee. Italian Nat. Research Cttee. 57-; Pres. Int. Asscn. for Radiation Research 62-66, Hon. Pres. 66-; Pres. Environmental Mutagen Soc. 69-71; Pres. Int. Asscn. of Environmental Mutagen Socs. 74-; Fellow, Amer. Acad.; mem. Nat. Acad. of Sciences; Foreign mem. Brazilian Acad.; Sc.D. (Hon.) Univ. of Vermont, 59; Hon. D.Sc. (Leeds, Marquette,

Wisconsin); Hon. M.D. (Univ. of Chile Medical School).
Leisure interests: palaentology, modern art, hiking.
Publs. A very large number of papers in learned periodicals 29-.
Associated Universities Inc., 1717 Massachusetts Avenue, N.W., Washington, D.C. 20036, U.S.A.
Telephone: 202-462-4475 (Office); 202-332-0477 (Home).

Hollai, Imre; Hungarian diplomatist; b. 1925; m.
Entered Foreign Service 49; Counsellor Perm. Mission of Hungary to UN 56-70; Head of Int. Dept., Cen. Cttee., Hungarian Socialist Workers' Party 60-63; Amb. to Greece, concurrently accred. to Cyprus 64-70; Deputy Minister of Foreign Affairs 70-74; Perm. Rep. to UN Sept. 74-.
Permanent Mission of Hungary to the United Nations, 10 East 75th Street, New York, N.Y. 10021, U.S.A.

Holland, Eric Sidney Fostyn; New Zealand politician and business executive; b. 28 June 1921, Christchurch; s. of the late Sir Sidney Holland (former Prime Minister of New Zealand) and Lady (Florence) Holland; m. 1st 1944, 2nd 1972; one s. two d.; ed. Elmwood School, St. Andrew's Coll. and Canterbury Univ. Coll.
Member of Parl. 67-; Minister of Housing, Minister in Charge of State Advances Corpn. and Assoc. Minister of Labour Feb.-Nov. 72; Minister of Energy Resources, Electricity and Mines Dec. 75-; National Party.
Leisure interests: golf, contract bridge.
Parliament Building, Wellington; Home: 7 Moorpark Place, Christchurch, New Zealand.
Telephone: 735-435 (Parliament); 556-611 (Home).

Holland, Jerome H., PH.D., LITT.D., LL.D; American diplomatist; b. 9 Jan. 1916, Auburn, N.Y.; s. of Robert H. and Viola Bagby Holland; m. Laura Mitchell 1948; two s. two d.; ed. Cornell Univ. and Univ. of Pa.
Instructor in Sociology, Lincoln Univ., Pa. 39-42; Dir. of Personnel, Sun Shipbuilding and Drydock Co., Pa. 42-46; Dir. Div. of Political and Social Science, Tennessee A. and I. State Univ. 46-51; Social Research Consultant, Pew Memorial Foundation of Philadelphia 51-53; Pres. Delaware State Coll. 53-60; Pres. Hampton Inst., Va. 60-70; Amb. to Sweden 70-72; Dir. N.Y. Stock Exchange June 72-; serves in an official capacity on many boards and foundations dealing with current social, educational and cultural problems and interests; various honours and awards.
Leisure interests: sports (table tennis, billiards, football).
Publ. *Black Opportunity* 69.
New York Stock Exchange, 11 Wall Street, New York, N.Y. 10005, U.S.A.

Holland-Martin, Edward; British banker; b. 8 March 1900, London; s. of Robert Martin Holland-Martin and Eleanor Mary (née Bromley-Martin); m. Dagny Mary MacLean Grant 1955; one d.; ed. Eton Coll. and Christ Church, Oxford.
Martin's Bank 23-33; Dir. Bank of England 33-48; Dir. Bank of London and South America 48-71, Deputy Chair. 52-71; Dir. Racecourse Holdings Trust Ltd.
Leisure interests: racing, horse-breeding, country pursuits.
Overbury Court, Worcestershire, England.

Hollander, Franciscus Querien den; Netherlands mechanical engineer; b. 31 May 1893, Goes; ed. Technical Univ. of Delft.
Trained with Holland Railway Co. 16-17; employed by Netherlands Indies State Railways 18-37; Asst. Man. Govt. Artillery Establishments, Hembrug 38-40, Gen. Man. 40; Perm. Under-Sec., Min. of Economic Affairs 45; Man. Dir. of Traffic, Min. of Transport 45-46; Gen. Man. and Acting Pres. of Netherlands Railway 46-47, Pres. 47-59; Hon. Life Fellow Permanent Way Inst.; F.R.S.A.; Hon. mem. Inst. of Transport, Inst. of Railway Signal Engineers, Inst. of Mech. Engineers,

London, Royal Inst. of Eng., The Hague, etc.; Hon. Dr. of Technical Sciences (Delft Technological Univ.); Knight Order of Netherlands Lion; Grand Officer Order of Orange-Nassau; Officier de la Légion d'Honneur; Commdr. Order Dannebrog (Denmark), Order of North Star (Sweden), Order Grand Ducal Couronne de Chêne (Luxembourg), Kroonorde (Belgium), Order Star of Africa (Liberia), Order al merito della Repubblica Italiana, Cross Goldene Ehrenzeichen (Austria).
9A Amersfoortse Weg, Maarn, The Netherlands.
Telephone: 03432-1355.

Hollenden, Baron; **Geoffrey Hope Hope-Morley,** J.P ; British industrialist; b. 28 Jan. 1885; ed. Eton and Trinity Coll., Cambridge.
High Sheriff County of London 17; Chair. I. & R. Morley Ltd. until 65, Pres. 65-.
Ravensbourne, Stoke Fleming, Dartmouth, S. Devon, England.

Höllerer, Walter Friedrich, DR. PHIL.; German writer and critic; b. 19 Dec. 1922, Sulzbach-Rosenberg, Bavaria; s. of Hans and Christine Höllerer, née Pürkner; m. Renate von Mangoldt 1965; two s.; ed. Univs. of Erlangen, Göttingen and Heidelberg.
Dozent in German Studies, Frankfurt/Main Univ 58 Münster Univ. 59; Ord. Prof. of Literature, Berlin Technical Univ. 59-, Dir. Inst. für Sprache im technischen Zeitalter 61-; Steuben Visiting Prof. Univ. of Wisconsin 60; Dir. Literarisches Colloquium, Berlin 63-; Editor Akzente: Zeitschrift für Dichtung 54 (now co-publisher), Sprache im technischen Zeitalier 61 (now publisher); publisher Literatur als Kunst; mem. German PEN Club, Akad. für Sprache und Dichtung, Berlin Acad. of Arts, Group 47, Comunità Europea degli Scrittori, Schutzverband der Schriftsteller deutscher Sprache; Fontane Prize; Johann Heinrich Merck Prize.
Publs. Der andere Gast (poems) 52, 64, Transit: Lyrikbuch der Jahrhundertmitte (anthology) 56, Zwischen Klassik und Moderne: Lachen und Weinen in der Dichtung einer Übergangszeit (essays) 58, Junge Amerikanische Lyrik 61, Spiele in einem Akt 62, Gedichte 64, Theorie der Modernen Lyrik 65, Modernes Theater auf Kleinen Bühnen 66, Ein Gedicht und sein Autor (poems and essays) 67, Ausserhalb der Saison (poems) 67, Systeme (poems) 69, Dramaturgisches (correspondence with Max Frisch q.v.) 69, Die Elephantenuhr (novel) 73, Hier wo die Welt anfing 74.
Heerstr. 99, 1 Berlin 19, Federal Republic of Germany.
Telephone: 304-58-79.

Holley, Robert W., PH.D.; American biochemist; b. 28 Jan. 1922, Urbana, Ill.; s. of Charles E. and Viola E. Holley; m. Ann Dworkin 1945; one s.; ed. Univ. of Illinois, Cornell Univ. and State Coll. of Washington.
Assistant Prof. and Assoc. Prof. of Organic Chem., Cornell Univ., N.Y., State Agricultural Experiment Station 48-57; Research-Chemist U.S. Plant, Soil and Nutrition Lab., ARS, USDA 57-64; at Cornell Univ. Prof. of Biochemistry and Molecular Biology 64-69, Chair. of Dept. 65-66; Resident Fellow, Salk Inst. for Biological Studies 68-; Albert Lasker Award for basic medical research 65; U.S. Dept. of Agriculture, Distinguished Service Award 65; U.S. Steel Foundation Award in Molecular Biology, Nat. Acad. of Sciences 67; Nobel Prize for Medicine (with M. Nirenberg and H. G. Khorana) for work on the genetic code and its function in protein synthesis 68.
The Salk Institute for Biological Studies, P.O. Box 1809, San Diego, Calif. 92112, U.S.A.
Telephone: 714-453-4100.

Holliger, Heinz; Swiss oboeist and composer; b. 1939, Langenthal; ed. in Berne, Paris and Basle under Emile Cassagnaud (oboe) and Pierre Boulez (composition).

Has appeared at all the major European music festivals and in Japan, U.S.A., Australia, Israel, etc.; recorded over 80 works, mainly for Philips and Deutsche Grammophon; recipient of several international prizes. Compositions include: Der magische Tänzer, Trio, Siebengesang, Wind Quartett, Dona nobis pacem, Pneuma, Psalm, Cardiophonie, Kreis, String Quartett, Aternbogen.
c/o Ingpen & Williams, 14 Kensington Court, London, W.8, England.

Hollings, Ernest F., B.A., LL.B.; American lawyer and politician; b. 1 Jan. 1922; m. Rita Liddy; two s. two d.; ed. Charleston Public Schools, The Citadel and Univ. of S. Carolina.
Served U.S. Army 42-45; admitted to S. Carolina Bar 47; mem. S. Carolina House of Reps. 48-54, Speaker pro tem. 51-53; Lieut.-Gov. of S. Carolina 55-59, Gov. of S. Carolina 59-63; law practice, Charleston 63-66; Senator from S. Carolina 66-; Chair. Democratic Senatorial Campaign Cttee. 71-73; mem. Hoover Comm. on Intelligence Activities 54-55, President's Advisory Comm. on Intergovernmental Relations 59-63; mem. Senate Cttees. on Appropriations, Commerce, Post Office, Civil Service; Democrat.
U.S. Senate, Washington, D.C.; Home: Charleston, S. Carolina, U.S.A.

Hollis, Rt. Rev. Arthur Michael, M.A., B.D.; British ecclesiastic; b. 23 June 1899; ed. Trinity Coll., Oxford. Ordained Deacon 23, Priest 24; Curate St. Andrew s Huddersfield 23-24; Chaplain and Lecturer Hertford Coll. Oxford 24-31, Fellow 26-31; Examining Chaplain to Bishop of Ripon 26-31; Lecturer St. Peter's Leeds 31; S.P.G. Missionary, Bishop's Theological Seminary, Nazareth, Tinnevelly 31-37; Perpetual Curate of Charlton Kings 37-42; Bishop of Madras 42, Bishop in Madras, Church of South India 47-54, Moderator 48-54; Prof. United Theological Coll. Bangalore 55-60; Visiting Prof., Vanderbilt Divinity School, Nashville 60; Luce Prof. World Christianity, Union Theological Seminary N.Y. 61; Rector of Todwick 61-64; Asst. Bishop of Sheffield 63-66, of St. Edmundsbury and Ipswich 66-74.
Publs. Paternalism and the Church, The Significance of South India, Mission, Unity and Truth.
72 Rembrandt Way, Bury St. Edmunds, IP33 2LT, Suffolk, England.
Telephone: Bury St. Edmunds 3171.

Hollom, Sir Jasper (Quintus), K.B.E.; British banker; b. 16 Dec. 1917, Bromley, Kent; s. of Arthur Hollom and Kate Louisa Hollom; m. Patricia Elizabeth Mary Ellis 1954; ed. King's School, Bruton.
Entered Bank of England 36, Dep. Chief Cashier 56-62, Chief Cashier 62-66, Exec. Dir. 66-70; Deputy Governor 70-.
Tiryns, Forest Road, Wokingham, Berks., England.
Telephone: Wokingham 781527.

Holloway, J. E., B.A., D.SC. (ECON.), D.COM.; South African businessman and diplomatist; b. 4 July 1890, Hopetown District; s. of George J. Holloway and Hester M. Enslin; m. Christina Purchase 1913 (died 1967); one s. four d.; ed. Victoria Coll., Ghent Univ. and London School of Economics.
Lecturer Grey Univ. Coll. 19; Lecturer and later Prof. of Economics, Transvaal Univ. Coll.; Dean Commerce Faculty, Univ. of South Africa 21-25; Dir. of Census and Statistics 25-33; Chair. Native Economic Comm. 30-32 and Customs Tariff Comm. 34-35; mem. S.W. Africa Comm. 35-36, Adviser Ottawa Conf. 32, World Econ. Conf. 33, Imperial Conf. 37, Montreal Conf. 58; Econ. Adviser to Treasury 34-37; Perm. Head of Treasury 37-50; Del. Monetary Conf. Bretton Woods 44; Chair. Cttee. Gold Mining Taxation 45; Alt. Gov. Int. Monetary Fund 48-52; Leader, S. African Del., Int. Conf. on Trade and Employment, Geneva 47, Havana 48;

fmr. Dir. (now cons.) of Barclays Bank D.C.O. (South African Board); Dir. African Batignolles Construction (Pty.) Ltd., Swiss-Union Trust for S.A. (Pty.) Ltd., Anglo-Alpha Cement Ltd.; Chair. S.W. Africa Financial Comm. 51; Univs. Financial Comm. 51-53 and Comm. on univ. facilities for non-Europeans 53-54; mem. Comm. regarding Europeans in Transkei; Council Univ. of Pretoria, S.A. Foundation; Amb. to U.S.A. 54-56; High Commr. in U.K. 56-58; Leader, South African Trade Mission to Europe 61; Hutchison Research Medallist; Hon. LL.D. and D.Comm.

Leisure interests: fly fishing, golf, bowls, shooting.

Publs. *The Debacle of Money, Gold or Authoritarian Money?, Apartheid—A Challenge* (also in French and Dutch), *Value and Worth, The Worth of Gold, Money without Sweat and Tears, Inflation and Unearned Money.*
Union Corporation Buildings, 74 Marshall Street, Johannesburg; Home: 1 Rockridge Road, Parktown, Johannesburg, South Africa.
Telephone: 838-8281 (Office); 31-2882 (Home).

Holloway, Admiral James Lemuel, III; American naval officer; b. 23 Feb. 1922, Charleston, S. Carolina; s. of Admiral James L. Holloway and late Jean Hagood; m. Dabney Rawlings; one s. (died 1964) two d.; ed. U.S. Naval Acad., Md.
Commissioned Ensign in U.S. Navy 42, served on destroyers in Atlantic and Pacific Theatres, World War II; Gunnery Officer *USS Bennion*, took part in Battle of Surigao Straits; Exec. Officer of Fighter Squadron Fifty-two, *USS Boxer* (CV-21), Korea 52-54; Commdr. Attack Squadron Eighty-three, *USS Essex*, Sixth Fleet 58; Admin. Aide to Deputy Chief of Naval Operations for Air 59; Nat. War Coll. 61; Asst. to Dir. of Navy Program Planning 64; Commdg. Officer *USS Enterprise* (CVAN-65) 65-67; promoted to rank of Rear-Admiral 66; Dir. Strike Warfare Div., Program Coordinator Nuclear Attack Carrier Program, Office of Chief of Naval Operations; Commdr. Carrier Div. Six, directed operations in E. Mediterranean during Jordanian crisis 70; Deputy C.-in-C. Atlantic and U.S. Atlantic Fleet, Chief of Staff 71; Vice-Admiral 71; Commdr. Seventh Fleet 72-73; Vice-Chief of Naval Operations 73-74; Chief of Naval Operations 74-; awarded numerous medals for meritorious service including Distinguished Service Medal (three times), Legion of Merit, Distinguished Flying Cross, Bronze Star Medal with Combat "V", and several foreign decorations.
Office of the Chief of Naval Operations, Department of the Navy, Washington, D.C. 20350, U.S.A.

Holloway, John, PH.D.; British professor of modern English; b. 1 Aug. 1920; s. of George Holloway and Evelyn Astbury; m. Audrey Gooding 1946; one s. one d.; ed. New Coll., Oxford.
War service, commissioned in artillery, seconded to Intelligence; temporary lecturer in Philosophy, New Coll. 45; Fellow of All Souls Coll., Oxford, concurrently Lecturer in English, Univ. of Aberdeen 49-54; Lecturer in English, Cambridge Univ. 54-66, Reader in Modern English 66, Fellow of Queens' Coll., 55-, Prof. of Modern English 72-; Visiting Prof., Chicago 65, Johns Hopkins Univ. 72; various univ. admin. positions; D.Lit. Aberdeen 54; Fellow, Royal Soc. of Literature 58; D.Lit. Cambridge 69.
Publs. *Language and Intelligence* 51, *The Victorian Sage* 53, *The Charted Mirror* (essays) 60, (ed.) *Poems of the Mid-Century* 57, (ed.) *Selections from Shelley* 60, *Shakespeare's Tragedies* 61, *The Colours of Clarity* (essays) 64, *The Lion Hunt* 64, *Widening Horizons in English Verse* 66, *Blake, The Lyric Poetry* 68, *The Establishment of English* 72, contributions to journals; verse: *The Minute* 56, *The Fugue* 60, *The Lanet Fallers* 62, *Wood and Windfall* 65, *New Poems* 70.
Queens' College, Cambridge, England.

Hollowood, A. Bernard, M.SC.(ECON.), F.R.S.A.; British economist and journalist; b. 3 June 1910, Burslem, Staffs.; s. of late Albert Hollowood and Sarah Elizabeth Hollowood; m. Marjorie D. Lawrie 1938; one s. two d.; ed. Hanley High School, St. Paul's Coll., Cheltenham, London Univ.
Lecturer in Economics, Stoke and Loughborough Coll. 32-43; on staff of *The Economist* 44-45; Editor *Pottery and Glass* 44-50; Research Officer, Council of Industrial Design 46; Editor *Punch* 57-68; broadcaster since 39, and television appearances; Hon. M.A. (Keele).

Leisure interests: economics, cricket.

Publs. *Direct Economics* 43, *Money is No Expense* 46, *An Innocent at Large* 47, *Britain Inside-Out, Scowle and Other Papers, Poor Little Rich World* 48, *Pottery and Glass, The Hawksmoor Scandals* 49, *Cornish Engineers* 51, *The Story of Morro Velho* 54, *Tory Story* 64, *Pont, The Story of Graham Laidler* 69, *Cricket on the Brain* 70, *Tales of Tommy Barr* 70, *Funny Money* 75.
Blackmoor Paddock, Shamley Green, Surrey, England.
Telephone: Bramley 2118.

Holm, Tryggve O. A.; Swedish business executive; b. 5 Feb. 1905, Kristinehamn; s. of Hans Th. Holm and Augusta Mathiesen; m. Gunvor Bruu 1929; two d.; ed. Royal Inst. of Technology, Stockholm, and Carnegie Inst. of Technology, Pittsburgh, U.S.A.
Engineer, AB Bofors, Sweden 29-30, Hess Bright Manufacturing Co., Philadelphia 30-31; Engineer, Steel Works, AB Bofors 32-36, Chief Engineer and Man. 36-39; Pres. AB Svenska Järnvägsverkstäderna, Linköping 40-50, Saab Aktiebolag Linköping 50-67; Chair. Swedish Metal Trades Employers' Asscn. 55-67; Chair. Swedish Employers' Confederation 67-; Chair. of Board Gusums Bruk AB 64-, Hexagon AB 65-; Chair. of Board Skandinaviska Träimport AB 67-; Chair. of Board Vegete Insurance Co. 68-, Alfa-Laval AB 69-, AB Bofors 73-; mem. Board AB Svenska Järnvägsverkstäderna 40-, Saab-Scania AB 47-, AB Bofors 68, SILA 50-, Holmens Bruk AB 55-, Nat. Pension Insurance Fund 59-, ABA 57-, Skandinaviska Enskilda Banken 69-; mem. Assembly of Reps. Scandinavian Airlines System 62- (mem. Board 57-62); Danish Consul 49-; several decorations.

Leisure interest: hunting.

Office: Nygatan 54, Linköping; Home: Vasavägen 13, Linköping, Sweden.
Telephone: 013-10-08-20 (Office); 013-12-58-16 (Home).

Holmblad, Niels Erik, D.SC.(ENG.); Danish telecommunications executive; b. 24 July 1905, Århus; s. of Sophus Holmblad and Calla Tørsleff; m. Karen Clausen 1943; three s.; ed. Danmarks Tekniske Hojskole.
Joined Danish Post and Telegraphs 29, Engineer-in-Chief 37-54; Gen. Man. Great Northern Telegraph Co., Denmark 54-71; work on Int. Telecommunications Union (I.T.U.) and Int. Electrotechnical Cttee. (I.E.C.); mem. Danish Electrotechnical Cttee., Pres. 55-62, and mem. Danish Acad. of Technical Sciences, Pres. 62-68; mem. Board Dirs. several industrial undertakings; many articles on telecommunications; Commdr. of the Order of Dannebrog (Denmark), Commdr. Order of St. Olav (Norway), Commdr. of Swedish Royal Order of Vasa and Commdr. Order of the Rising Sun (Japan).

Leisure interests: literature, music.

Tranevaenget 8, DK 2900 Hellerup, Denmark.
Telephone: HE 7088 (Home).

Holmboe, Vagn; Danish composer; b. 20 Dec. 1909, Horsens, Jutland; s. of Jens Christian Gylding Holmboe and Marie Dreyer; m. Meta Josefa Elisaveta Graf 1933; one s. one d.; ed. Royal Danish Music Conservatory.
Teacher at Royal Inst. for Blind 40-49; music critic *Politiken* 47-55; Prof. of Composition and Orchestration, Royal Danish Music Conservatory 55-66; mem. Board

of Danish Composers' Asscn.; Kt. of Dannebrog; mem. Royal Swedish Acad. of Music; various prizes.
Leisure interests: philosophy, history, planting.
Compositions: 10 symphonies, 3 chamber symphonies, 4 symphonic metamorphoses, 16 concertos, 14 quartets, oratorios, chamber and orchestral music, choral works, etc.
Holmboevej 6, Ramlöse, 3200 Helsinge, Denmark.
Telephone: 03-112045.

Holmes, Dyer Brainerd; American engineer and executive; b. 24 May 1921, New York; s. of Marcellus B. and Theodora (née Pomeroy) Holmes; m. 1st Dorothy Ann Bonnet 1943 (divorced 1973), two d.; m. 2nd Roberta Donohue Plunk 1974; ed. Newark Acad., Carteret Acad., Cornell Univ., Bowdoin Coll., and Massachusetts Inst. of Technology.
Service in U.S. Naval Reserve; Bell Telephone Laboratories and Western Electric Co. 45-53; Radio Corpn. of America 53-61, engaged as Project Manager of Talos (ground-to-air-missile) and electronic count-down system for Atlas Intercontinental Ballistic Missile; Program Manager of Ballistic Missile Early Warning System (B.M.E.W.S.), Greenland, Alaska and England, Gen. Manager Defense Systems Div., Moorestown, N.J. 61; Dep. Assoc. Administrator, Manned Space Flight, NASA 61-63; Senior Vice-Pres. and Dir. Raytheon Co. 63-69, Exec. Vice-Pres. 69-75, Pres. 75-, mem. Board of Dirs.; Dir. Wyman-Gordon Co., Mass., First Nat. Boston Co., First Nat. Bank of Boston; Fellow, Inst. of Electronic and Electrical Engineers; mem. American Inst. of Aeronautics and Astronautics, Board of Govs. Aerospace Industries Asscn.; recipient of NASA Medal for Outstanding Leadership and the Arnold Air Society's Paul T. John's Award 69; Hon. D.Sc. (Univ. of New Mexico) 63.
Leisure interests: sailing, skiing, flying.
104 Westcliff Road, Weston, Mass. 02193, U.S.A.

Holmes, Admiral Ephraim Paul; American naval officer (retd.); b. 14 May 1908, Downsville, N.Y.; s. of Dr. Edward A. and Dolly M. Hathaway Holmes; m. Nancy Sellers 1933; one s. one d.; ed. Downsville High School and U.S. Naval Acad., Annapolis.
Commissioned 30, Capt. 48; Commanded destroyer U.S.S. Stockham 44; Commanding Officer U.S.S. Northampton 55-57; Special Asst. to Deputy Chief of Naval Operations (Plans and Policy), Dept. of Navy 57-58; Commdr. Cruiser Div. Four 58-60; Asst. Chief of Naval Operations (Gen. Planning) and Dir. Gen. Planning Group, Dept. of Navy 60-63; Vice-Admiral, Commdr. Amphibious Force, Pacific 63-64; Commdr. First Fleet 64; Dir. Navy Program Office, Chief of Naval Operations 64-67; Supreme Allied Commdr., Atlantic (NATO) June 67-70; C.-in-C. U.S. Atlantic Fleet 67-70; now business adviser; numerous medals and decorations.
Leisure interests: tennis, squash, golf, fishing, boating.
1600 Maritime Tower, Norfolk, Va. 23510, U.S.A.

Holmes Sellors, Sir Thomas, Kt., D.M., M.CH., F.R.C.S., F.R.C.P.; British surgeon; b. 7 April 1902, London; s. of Dr. T. B. Sellors; m. 1st Brenda Lyell (died 1928); m. 2nd Dorothy E. Chesshire 1932 (died 1953), one s. one d.; m. 3rd Marie Hobson 1955; ed. Loretto School and Oriel Coll., Oxford.
Various appointments in London hospitals; Surgeon, Harefield Hosp.; Senior Surgeon, London Chest Hosp. 34-68; Thoracic Surgeon, Middlesex Hosp. 47-69; Surgeon, Nat. Heart Hosp. 57-69; Chair. Joint Consultants Cttee.; mem. Council, Royal Coll. of Surgeons, Pres. 69-72; Pres. Thoracic Soc. 60; Pres. Soc. of Thoracic Surgeons of Great Britain and Ireland 61-62; Pres. BMA 72-73; mem. Court of Patrons, Royal Coll. of Surgeons; mem. many British and foreign medical socs.; Hon. F.A.C.S., Hon. F.R.C.S. (Edinburgh, Ireland), Hon. F.C.M. (S. Africa), Hon. F.D.S. (Royal

Coll. of Surgeons), M.S. h.c. (Southampton), Hon Fellow, Oriel Coll., Oxford; Médaille de la Reconnaissance Française, Officer, Order of Carlos Finlay (Cuba) M.D. h.c. (Groningen), D.Sc. h.c. (Liverpool).
Leisure interests: water-colour painting, gardening.
Publs. Surgery of the Thorax 33; articles in English and foreign medical publications and editor and contributor to current textbooks.
Spring Coppice Farm, Speen, Aylesbury, Bucks., England.
Telephone: Hampden Row 379.

Holmqvist, Eric Bertil; Swedish politician; b. 2 Feb. 1917, Svalöv; m. Alice Andersson 1947; two s. two d.
Member of Parl. 48-; Minister of Agriculture 61-68; Minister of Home Affairs 69-73, of Defence 73-.
Försvarsdepartementet, Fack, 103 20 Stockholm 16, Sweden.
Telephone: 08/763-25-53.

Holoubek, Gustaw; Polish actor and theatre director; b. 21 April 1923, Cracow; s. of Gustaw and Eugenia Holoubek; m. 1st Danuta Kwiatkowska, 2nd Maria Wachowiak, 3rd Magdalena Zawadzka; two d.; ed. State Higher Dramatic School, Cracow.
Actor in Cracow theatres 47-49, Wyspiański Theatre, Katowice, Artistic Man. 54-56, Polish Theatre, Warsaw 58-59, Dramatic Theatre, Warsaw 59-, Dir. and Artistic Man. 72-; Prof. State Higher Theatrical School; Vice-Chair. SPATIF (Asscn. of Polish Theatre and Film Actors) 63-70, Chair. 70-; now appears in various Warsaw theatres in leading roles which have included: Judge Caust in Leprosy at he Palace of Justice, Baron Goetze in Le diable et le Bon-Dieu (Sartre), Gustaw-Konrad in Dziady (A. Mickiewicz), Violinist in Rzeźnia (S. Mrożek), Beggar in Electra (J. Giraudoux), Oedipus, Hamlet, Richard II and Hadrian VII (Peter Luke); also appears in films and television plays; numerous decorations including State Prize 53, 66, Order of Banner of Labour 2nd Class, Chevalier's Cross of Polonia Restituta, Award Meritorius Activist of Culture 72.
Leisure interests: sports.
Ul. Wiejska 16, 00-490 Warsaw, Poland.
Telephone: 21-83-38.

Holshouser, James E., Jr.; American politician; b. 8 Oct. 1934, Watauga Co.; s. of J. E. and Virginia Holshouser; m. Pat Hollingsworth; one d.; ed. Univ. of N.C. School of Law.
Member State House of Reps. 62, re-elected 64, 68, 70; served as Republican Joint Caucus Sec. 63, House Minority Leader 65, Republican Joint Caucus Leader 69, 71, Vice-Chair. House Judiciary Cttee. 65, Vice-Chair. House Rules Cttee. 69, 71, served on various legislative study comms.; Republican State Chair. 66, re-elected 68, 70; Gov. of North Carolina Jan. 73-; mem. Cttee. on Court Study, N.C. Bar Asscn.; Board of Dirs., Davidson Coll. and Univ. of N.C. Law Alumni Asscns.; mem. Mountain Scenic Econ. Devt. Comm. and other regional orgs.
Leisure interests: golf, tennis.
State Capitol, Raleigh, North Carolina, U.S.A.
Telephone: 919-829-3615.

Holt, Homer Adams, A.B., LL.B.; American lawyer; b. 1 March 1898, Lewisburg, W.Va.; s. of Robert Byrne and Emma Louise McWhorter Holt; m. Isabel Hedges Wood 1924; one s. two d.; ed. Greenbrier Mil. School and Washington and Lee Univ.
Instructor in Mathematics Washington and Lee Univ. 20-23, Asst. Prof. of Law 23-24, Assoc. Prof. of Law 24-25; practised law, Fayetteville, W. Va. 25-33; Attorney-Gen. of W. Va. 33-37; Gov. of W. Va. 37-41; resumed law practice as mem. of firm of Brown, Jackson & Knight, Charleston 41-46; Gen. Counsel, Union Carbide & Carbon Corpn. (now Union Carbide Corpn.),

N.Y. 47-53, Vice-Pres. 49-53, Dir. 44-55, mem. **Exec.** Cttee. 50-53; mem. American Bar Asscn. 29-, W. **Va.** Bar Asscn. (Pres. 43-44) 25-, W. Va. State Bar 47-, Fayette County (W. Va.) Bar Asscn. 25-, Charleston Bar Asscn. (now Kanawha County Bar Asscn.) 41-, N.Y. State Bar Asscn. 52-53, Asscn. of the Bar of the City of N.Y. 52-, Bar Asscn. Nassau County, N.Y., Inc. 48-53, etc.; resumed law practice with Jackson, Kelly, Holt & Moxley (now Jackson, Kelly, Holt, and O'Farrell), Charleston, W. Va. 53-; Chair. W. Va. Comm. on Constitutional Revision 57-63; Dir. Kanawha Valley Bank 54-, Slab Fork Coal Co.; Trustee Emer. Washington and Lee Univ.; Hon. LL.D. (W. Va. Univ. 37 and Bethany Coll. 40).
1601 Kanawha Valley Building, Charlestown, W. Va.; Home: 1521 Bridge Road, Charleston, W. Va., U.S.A. Telephone: 304-343-4331 (Office); 346-1169 (Home).

Holte, Johan B.; Norwegian industrialist; b. 19 Feb. 1915, Notodden; s. of Peder O. Holte and Lorentze Indorff; m. Eva Bull; ed. Technical Univ. of Norway, Trondheim.
Joined Norsk Hydro 48, Dir. Research Div. 57-66, Vice-Pres. 64-66, Pres. 67-; mem. Board of Dirs. Norske Fina A/S, Dyno Industrier A/S; Board of Dirs. IBM, Oslo; mem. Cen. Council, Norwegian Confed. of Employers; mem. Exec. Board, Norwegian Industries Fed.; mem. many other industrial and social orgs.
Leisure interests: fishing, mountain walking.
Norsk Hydro, Bygdøy allé 2, Oslo 2; Home: Helmerveien 1, 1310 Blommenholm, Norway.
Telephone: 56-41-80 (Office); 54-08-29 (Home).

Holten, Cai, M.D.; Danish physician; b. 15 Nov. 1894 Frederiksberg; m. Paula Lystrup Nielsen 1928; three d.; ed. Univ. of Copenhagen.
Chief Physician, Aalborg County Hospital 31-38; Chief Physician, Aarhus Municipal Hospital 38-; Prof. of Internal Medicine, Univ. of Aarhus 39-, Vice-Chancellor 47-49, mem. of Senate 58; Head of Dept., Univ of Aarhus Medical Dept.; mem. Board of Danish Rheumatism Asscn. 43-; Advisory mem. Acad. of Human Rights 52-; hon. mem. American Rheumatism Asscn. 48; mem. N.Y. Acad. of Sciences 60; Pres. Scandinavian Congress Rheumatology, Copenhagen 62; Chair. Danish Soc for Research into Rheumatism 62; Hon. mem. Medical Soc. of Jutland 63, Danish Soc. Internal Medicine 66.
Leisure interest: music.
Publs. Various medical publications, mainly on metabolism, haematology, anti-coagulant therapy, and renal diseases.
22 Strandparken, Aarhus, Denmark.
Telephone: 121178.

Holten Eggert, Christian D., LL.M.; Danish diplomatist; b. 18 April 1912, Copenhagen; s. of C. C. D. Holten-Eggert; m. Stephanie Antoine-Feill 1942 (died 1966); no c.; ed. Metropolitanskolen and Univ. of Copenhagen.
Danish Foreign Service 37-, Asst. Chief of Section, Foreign Office 46; Dep. Perm. Rep. to UN, New York 49; Chief of Section, Foreign Office 53; Minister to Egypt and Syria 56-58, Ethiopia and Lebanon 56-61, Iraq 56-60, Jordan and Sudan 58-61; Ambassador to U.A.R. 58-61, concurrently to Iraq 60-61; Ambassador to U.S.S.R. 61-66, to Spain 66-71, to Poland 71-74, to Austria 74-; Chair. Danish Govt. dels. for negotiating trade and payment agreements abroad 46-49, 53-56.
6 Führichgasse, Vienna, Austria.

Holter, Heinz, DR. PHIL.; Danish biologist and professor; b. 5 June 1904, Leonding, Austria; s. of late M. D. A. Holter and late A. Holter (née Fischer); m. Karen Teisen 1942; one s. one d.; ed. Univ. of Vienna.
Asst. Chemical Institute Univ. of Vienna 28-30; Dept. of Chemistry Carlsberg Laboratory, Copenhagen 32-42; Chief of Dept. of Cytochemistry 42-56; Chief of Dept.

of Physiology 56-71; mem. of Danish Acad. of Sciences 42, Royal Soc. of Sciences, Uppsala 60, Royal Physiographical Soc. of Lund 62, American Acad. of Arts and Sciences 71.
Publs. Various scientific papers in the fields of organic chemistry, enzyme chemistry, cytochemistry and cell physiology.
Biological Institute of the Carlsberg Foundation, 16 Tagensvej, 2200 Copenhagen N, Denmark.

Holtfreter, Johannes F. C., PH.D.; American emeritus professor of zoology; b. 9 Jan. 1901, Richtenberg, Germany; s. of Johannes and Sabine Holtfreter; m. Hiroko Ban 1959; ed. Univs. of Rostock, Leipzig, Freiburg and Greifswald.
Assistant, Dept. of Embryology Kaiser-Wilhelm Inst. of Biology, Berlin-Dahlem 28-33; Lecturer and Assoc. Prof., Zoological Inst. Univ. of Munich 33-38; Research Worker, Zoology Dept. Univ. of Rochester, N.Y. 46-48, Prof. of Zoology 48-66, Tracy S. Harris Prof. of Zoology 66-69, Prof. Emer. 69-; mem. Editorial Board *Journal of Embryology and Experimental Morphology* London, Board of Advisers Experimental Cell Research Stockholm, Int. Board of Control Hubrecht Lab. Utrecht, Fulbright Fellowships Panel, Guggenheim Fellowships Evaluation Panel; Rockefeller Fellow 36-37, Rockefeller and Guggenheim Fellow, McGill Univ., Montreal 42-46, Fulbright Fellow, Paris 58; Jesup Lecturer, Columbia Univ. 57; numerous lectureships abroad; research in vertebrate development and cytology; Fellow, American Acad. of Arts and Sciences, A.A.A.S., John Simon Guggenheim Memorial Foundation; mem. Nat. Acad. of Sciences, American Asscn. of Anatomists and many foreign socs. and acads. including Akad. der Naturforscher Leopoldina and Swedish Acad. of Sciences; Hon. Fellow, Zoological Soc. of India.
Leisure interests: painting, gardening, travelling in exotic countries.
29 Knolltop Drive, Rochester, N.Y. 14610, U.S.A.

Holthusen, Hans Egon, D.PHIL.; German writer; b. 15 April 1913, Rendsburg, Schleswig-Holstein; m. 1st Lori Holthusen 1950, 2nd Inge Holthusen 1952; one s. one step d.; ed. Tübingen, Berlin and Munich Univs. Served in the army 39-45; writer 45-; Dir. Goethe House, New York 61-64; Del. Biennale Int. de Poésie, Knokke (Belgium) 51-52; Perm. Prof. German Literature, Northwestern Univ. Evanston, Ill. Sept. 68-; Pres. Bavarian Academy of Fine Arts 68-74; Kiel Kulturpreis 56; Bavarian Order of Merit 73.
Leisure interests: hiking, swimming, dancing, music.
Publs. *Rilkes Sonette an Orpheus—Versuch einer Interpretation* 37, *Hier in der Zeit* (poems), *Der spate Rilke* 49, *Der unbehauste Mensch* (essays) 51 and 55, *Labyrintische Jahre* (poems) 52, *Ja und Nein* (essays) 54, *Das Schiff* (novel) 56, *Das Schone und das Wahre* (essays) 58, *R. M. Rilke in Selbstzeugnissen und Bilddokumenten* (biography) 58, *Kritisches Verstehen* (essays) 61, *Avantgardismus* (essay) 64, *Plädoyer für den Einzelnen* (essays) 67, *Indiana Campus: ein amerikanisches Tagebuch* 69, *Eduard Mörike in Selbstzeugnissen und Bilddokumenten* (biography) 71.
Agnesstr. 48, Munich 40, Federal Republic of Germany; 1725 Orrington Avenue, Evanston, Ill. 60201, U.S.A. Telephone: 372161 (Germany); 864-3658 (U.S.A.).

Holton, Linwood, A. Jr., LL.B.; American awyer; b. 21 Sept. 1923, Big Stone Gap, Va.; m. Virginia Harrison Rogers; two s. two d.; ed. public schools in Big Stone Gap, Washington and Lee Univ., and Harvard Law School.
Partner, Eggleston, Holton, Butler and Glenn (law firm); served submarine force during Second World War; fmr. Chair. Roanoke City Republican Cttee.; Vice-Chair. Virginia Republican State Cen. Cttee. 60-69; del. to Republican Nat. Convention 60, 68, 72; mem.

Nat. Nixon for Pres. Cttee. March 67; Regional Co-ordinator for Nixon for Pres. Cttee.; Gov. of Virginia 70-74; Asst. Sec. of State for Congressional Relations, Dept. of State 74-Jan. 75; partner in law firm of Hogan and Hartson 75-; Republican.

Hogan and Hartson, 815 Connecticut Avenue, N.W., Washington, D.C.; Home: 6010 Claiborne Drive, McLean, Va. 22101, U.S.A.

Holtrop, Marius Wilhelm, DR.ECON.; Netherlands banker; b. 2 Nov. 1902, Amsterdam; s. of late Jan Holtrop and late Betty Holtrop-van gelder; m. 1st Josina Juchter 1926 (died 1965), 2nd Catharina Peltenburg 1966; two s. one d.; ed. Public Commercial Training School, Amsterdam, and Univ. of Amsterdam. With Royal Dutch Blast Furnaces and Steel Works 29-36, Man. Dir. 39-46; Vice-Pres. Shell Chemical Co. at San Francisco 36-39; Pres. De Nederlandsche Bank, Amsterdam 46-67; Pres. and Chair. of Board Bank for Int. Settlements, Basle until June 67; Gov. Int. Monetary Fund, Washington -67; Dir. Royal Dutch Petroleum Corpn. 67-73; Knight Order of the Nether-lands Lion, Grand Cross Order of the Crown (Belgium), Grand Cross Order of Orange-Nassau; Dr. h.c. Nether-lands School of Econs., Rotterdam, and Univ. of Basle. Home: Zomerzorgerlaan 2, Bloemendaal, Netherlands. Telephone: Haarlem 023-251503.

Holtsmark, Johan Peter, DR.PHILOS.; Norwegian phy-sicist; b. 13 Feb. 1894, Oslo; s. of Gabriel Holtsmark and Margrethe Weisse; m. 1st Elinor Rømcke 1919, 2nd Astrid Gundersen Lidemark 1954; one s. two d.; ed. Oslo, Leipzig, Würzburg and Göttingen Univs., and King's Coll., London.

Lecturer in Oslo Univ. 20; Prof. of Physics Trondheim Technical Univ. 23; Prof. of Physics Univ. of Oslo 42-64; mem. Det Norske Videnskaps Akademi i Oslo and Det Kgl. Norske Videnskabers Selskab, Trond-heim; Fellow, Acoustical Soc. of America.

Leisure interest: gardening.

Publs. *College Physics* and numerous papers in Nor-wegian and foreign scientific journals.

P.O. Box 229, N 1310 Blommenholm, Norway.
Telephone: Oslo 548677.

Holub, Miroslav, M.D., C.SC.; Czechoslovak writer and poet; b. 13 Sept. 1923, Pilsen; s. of Josef Holub and Františka Dvořáková; m. 1st Věra Koktová 1948, 2nd Marta Svikruhová 1961; one s.; ed. Charles Univ., Prague.

Scientific worker, Microbiological Inst., Czechoslovak Acad. of Sciences 53-71, Public Health Research Inst. N.Y. 65-67, Max-Planck Inst. of Immunobiology, Freiburg 68-69, Inst. of Clinical and Experimental Medicine 72-; mem. Central Cttee. Union of Czecho-slovak Writers 63-69; mem. Central Cttee. Union of Czech Scientific Workers 69-71; Editor, *Vesmír* 52-65. Leisure interests: tennis, table-tennis, fencing.

Publs. Poetry: *Denní služba* (Day Shift) 58, *Achiles a želva* (Achilles and the Tortoise) 60, 63, *Slabikář* (The Primer) 61, 65, *Jdi a otevři dveře* (Go and Open the Door) 61, *Zcela nesoustavná zoologie* (Entirely Unsystematic Zoology) 63, *Kam teče krev* (Where Blood Flows) 63, *Tak zvané srdce* (So-called Heart) 63, *Anamnesa* (Selec-ted Poems 1958-63) 64, *Selected Poems* (English) 67, *Obwohl* (German) 69, *Ačkoli* (Although) 69, *Beton* (Concrete) 70, *Model člověka* (Model of a Man, Polish) 69, *Although* (English) 71, *Aktschlüsse/Halbgedichte* (Ger-man) 74, *Een Machine Van Woorden* (Dutch) 75; Prose: *Anděl na kolečkách* (Angel on Wheels—report of trip through U.S.A.) 63, *Tři kroky po zemi* (Three Steps on the Ground) 65, *Die explodierende Metropole* (Ger-man) 67; *Žít v New Yorku* (To live in New York) 69, *Poe or the Valley of Unrest* 71; Scientific works: *Experi-mental Morphology of Antibody Formation* 58, *Mechan-isms of Antibody Formation* 60 (editor), *The Lymphocyte and The Immune Response* 67.

Institute of Clinical and Experimental Medicine Prague 4, Krč.; Home: Hrnčíře 107, Prague 4 Chodov, Czechoslovakia.
Telephone: 412 ext. 3602.

Hołuj, Tadeusz; Polish writer; b. 23 Nov. 1916, Cracow; m. Leokadia Hołuj; one s.; ed. Jagiellonian Univ., Cracow.

Studied law and philosophy at Jagiellonian Univ., Cracow; Co-Editor *Kuźnia Młodych* 36-39; soldier 39, underground 39-42; prisoner in Auschwitz, organizer of Resistance Movement 42-45; journalist 46; Pres. and Sec. Int. Auschwitz Cttee. 57-67; mem. Polish United Workers' Party; Deputy to Seym; mem. Polish Writers' Union and PEN Club, Cracow Literary Prize 46, 58; Ministry of Culture and Art Prize 62; State Prize 66; Literary Prize of Cen. Council of Trade Unions 72, 73; Order of Banner of Labour 1st Class 70. Publs. Novels and Stories: *Próba ognia* (The Test of Fire) 45, *Królestwo bez ziemi* (Kingdom without a Land) 54-56, *Koniec naszego świata* (The End of Our World) 58, *Drzewo rodzi owoce* (A Tree Bears Fruit) 63, *Róża i płonący las* (The Rose and the Forest Aflame); *Raj* (Paradise) 73, *Osoba* (Person) 73; numerous short stories and plays.

Cracow, Ul. Emaus 14/1, Poland.
Telephone: 20-981.

Holyoake, Rt. Hon. Sir Keith Jacka, G.C.M.G., C.H., M.P.; New Zealand politician and farmer; b. 11 Feb. 1904, Pahiatua; s. of Henry Victor Holyoake and Esther Holyoake; m. Norma Janet Ingram 1935; two s. three d.; ed. Tauranga, Hastings, Motueka.

Nelson Provincial Pres. Farmers' Union 30-41; Pres. N.Z. Hop Marketing Cttee. 38-41; Dominion Vice-Pres. Farmers' Union 40-50; mem. Dominion Exec. Farmers' Union 40-50; mem. N.Z. Tobacco Growers' Fed. and N.Z. Fruit Exporters' Asscn.; M.P. 32-; Deputy Leader of Opposition 47; Deputy Prime Minister and Minister of Agriculture 49-57; Prime Minister and Minister for Maori Affairs Sept.-Dec. 57; Leader of Opposition 57-60; Prime Minister 60-Feb. 72, Minister of Foreign Affairs 60-Nov. 72, of State Dec. 75-; N.Z. Rep. at Farmers' World Conf., London 46; Chair. Gen. Council FAO 55; has participated in many SEATO and ANZUS meetings and others; Hon. LL.D. (Victoria Univ.); Hon. Freeman City of London; Hon. LL.D.(Agric.) (Seoul Univ., Korea); National Party.

Leisure interest: gardening.

52 Aurora Terrace, Wellington, New Zealand.

Holzmeister, Clemens, DR.ENG.; Austrian architect; b. 27 March 1886; ed. Vienna Technical High School.

Professor, Düsseldorf Acad. of Arts 29-33; fmr. Prof. and Rector Vienna Acad. of Creative Arts, again Prof. 54-; mem. Austrian State Council 34-38; Prof. of Architecture at Technical Univ., Istanbul, Turkey, until 50; Pres. Austrian Kunstsenat 54-.

Works include designs for the Vienna Crematorium, Salzburg Festival Theatre and extensions, Govt. build-ings Ankara, Dollfuss Memorial Vienna, churches, hotels, schools, etc., in Austria, Germany and Italy; new broadcasting house, Vienna, Parl. Bldg., Ankara, Belo Horizonte Cathedral (Brazil), etc.

Association of Austrian Technical Engineers & Archi-tects, A-1010 Vienna, Eschenbachgasse 9; Home: 1060 Vienna, Esterhazygasse 11 Austria.
Telephone: 56-12-13 (Vienna).

Homann, Heinrich, DR.PHIL.; German politician; b. 6 March 1911; ed. Gymnasium and law studies.

Military service, Second World War (Prisoner-of-War); Co-Founder, Free Germany 43; mem. Nat. Democratic Party (N.D.P.D.) 48-, Political Man. 49-52. Dep. Chair. 52-; mem. Volkskammer 50-, Vice-Chair. 54-63; Deputy Chair. State Council of German Democratic Republic 60-; mem. Presidium of the Nat. Council of the Nat.

Front of Democratic Germany; mem. Presidium of German Peace Council; Order of Merit of the Fatherland in Silver; German Peace Prize; Ernst-Moritz-Arndt Medal.
National-Demokratische Partei Deutschlands, Friedrichstrasse 65, Berlin, W.8, German Democratic Republic.

Homans, George Caspar, M.A.; American sociologist; b. 11 Aug. 1910, Boston, Mass.; s. of Robert and Abigail (Adams) Homans; m. Nancy Parshall Cooper 1941; one s. two d.; ed. St. Paul's School, Concord, N.H. and Harvard Coll.
Junior Fellow, Harvard Univ. 34-39; Faculty Instructor, Harvard Univ. 39-41; U.S. Navy 41-46; Assoc. Prof. Harvard Univ. 46-53; Prof. of Sociology 53-; Chair. Dept. of Sociology 70-75; mem. Nat. Acad. of Sciences, American Philosophical Soc., American Acad. of Arts and Sciences.
Leisure interests: sailing, forestry.
Publs. *Massachusetts on the Sea* 30, *An Introduction to Pareto* 34, *Fatigue of Workers* 41, *English Villagers of the Thirteenth Century* 41, *The Human Group* 50, *Marriage, Authority and Final Causes* 55, *Social Behaviour* 61 (revised edn. 74), *Sentiments and Activities* 62, *The Nature of Social Science* 67.
Department of Sociology, 480 William James Hall, Harvard University, Cambridge, Mass. 02138; Home: 11 Francis Avenue, Cambridge, Mass., U.S.A.
Telephone: 617-495-3820 (Office); 617-547-4737 (Home).

Home of the Hirsel, Baron (Life Peer), cr. 74, of Coldstream in the County of Berwick; **Alexander Frederick Douglas-Home,** K.T., P.C.; British politician; b. 2 July 1903, London; s. of 13th Earl of Home and Lady Lilian Lambton; m. Elizabeth Alington 1936; one s. three d.; ed. Eton Coll., and Christ Church, Oxford.
Member, House of Commons 31-45, 50-51, 63-74, House of Lords 51-63; Parl. Private Sec. to Sec. of State for Scotland 31-35, to Chancellor of Exchequer 35, to Prime Minister 38-39; Joint Parl. Under-Sec. to Foreign Office 45; Minister of State, Scottish Office 51-55; Sec. of State for Commonwealth Relations 55-60, for Foreign Affairs 60-Oct. 63; Prime Minister Oct. 63-64; Leader of Conservative Party 63-65; Leader of Opposition 64-65; Lord Pres. of the Council 57, 59-60; renounced title of 14th Earl of Home Oct. 63; Chancellor Heriot-Watt Univ., Edinburgh 66-; Sec. of State for Foreign and Commonwealth Affairs 70-74; Hon. D.C.L. (Oxford); Hon. LL.D. (Harvard, Edinburgh, Aberdeen and Liverpool Univs.); Conservative.
Leisure interests: shooting, fishing, gardening.
The Hirsel, Coldstream, Berwickshire, Scotland; and Castlemains, Douglas, Lanarkshire, Scotland.
Telephone: Coldstream 2345; Douglas 241.

Hommel, Nicolas; Luxembourg diplomatist; b. 8 Oct. 1915, Wolwelange; m. Denise Ruffié 1959.
Called to the Bar 39; Foreign Service 46-; mem. Luxembourg Military Mission, Berlin 46-48; Perm. Rep. to Org. for European Econ. Co-operation (OEEC) 49-58, to North Atlantic Treaty Org. (NATO) 53-58; Amb. to Belgium 58-62, to France 62-67; Sec.-Gen. Ministry of Foreign Affairs 67-68; Amb. to Fed. Rep. of Germany April 68-73; Sec.-Gen. Council of Ministers, EEC 73-; several Luxembourg and foreign decorations.
Leisure interests: painting, tennis.
Council of Ministers of the European Communities, 170 rue de la Loi, Brussels, Belgium.

Hon Sui Sen; Singapore politician; b. 16 April 1916, Penang, Malaysia; m. Annie Voon See Chin 1942; four d.; ed. St. Xavier's Inst., Penang and Raffles Coll., Singapore.
Joined the Straits Settlements Civil Service 39; transferred to Singapore Admin. Service; Perm. Sec. Prime Minister's Office, concurrently Perm. Sec. Econ. Devt.

Div., Ministry of Finance 57-65; first Chair. Econ. Devt. Board 61-68; first Chair. and Pres. Devt. Bank of Singapore Ltd. 68-70; M.P. for Havelock April 70-; Minister of Finance Aug. 70-; Meritorious Medal 62; Malaysian Medal 64; Distinguished Service Order 67; Hon. LL.D.
Ministry of Finance, 5th Floor, Fullerton Building, Singapore 1; 35 Malcolm Road, Singapore 11.
Telephone: 76121 (Office).

Honda, Soichiro; Japanese business executive; b. 17 Nov. 1906.
Garage apprentice 23, opened own garage 28; Owner and Head, Piston Ring Production Factory 39; started producing motor cycles 48, Pres. Honda Motor Co. until 73, Dir. and Adviser 73-.
Honda Motor Co., No. 27-8, 6-chome, Jingumae, Shibuya-ku, Tokyo 150, Japan.

Hone, Major-Gen. Sir (Herbert) Ralph, K.C.M.G., K.B.E., M.C., T.D., G.C.ST.J., Q.C., LL.B.; British lawyer and colonial administrator; b. 3 May 1896, Hove, Sussex; s. of Herbert Hone and Miriam Grace Hone (née Dracott); m. 1st Elizabeth Daisy Matthews 1918, one s. one d.; m. 2nd Sybil Mary Simond 1945, one s.; ed. Varndean Grammar School, Brighton and London Univ.
Joined London Irish Rifles 15, Lieut. 16, Capt. 18, served with B.E.F. France 16, 17-18; Staff Capt. Ministry of Munitions 18-20; called to Bar, Middle Temple, practised S.E. Circuit 23-24; Registrar Zanzibar High Court 25, Resident Magistrate 28, Crown Counsel Tanganyika 30; Attorney-Gen. Gibraltar 33-36; Attorney-Gen. Uganda 37-40; Commdt. Uganda Defence Force 40; Chief Legal Adviser Political Branch G.H.Q. Middle East 41, Chief Political Officer 42-43; attached Gen. Staff War Office 43-44; Maj.-Gen. serving in E. Africa, Middle East, War Office, India, Ceylon and Malaya 43-45; Chief Civil Affairs Officer, SEAC 45-46; Sec.-Gen. to Gov.-Gen. of Malaya 46-48; Deputy Commr.-Gen. S.E. Asia 48-49; Gov. and C.-in-C. North Borneo 49-54; Head Legal Division, Commonwealth Relations Office 54-61; resumed private practice 61-; Draftsman, S. Rhodesia Constitution 61, Bahamas Constitution 63; Constitutional Adviser, Kenya 62, South Arabia 65, Bermuda 66.
Leisure interests: tennis, badminton, philately.
Office: 1 Paper Buildings, Temple, London, E.C.4.; Home: 56 Kenilworth Court, London, S.W.15, England.
Telephone: 01-788-3367.

Honecker, Erich; German politician; b. 25 Aug. 1912, Wiebelskirchen, Saarland; s. of Wilhelm Honecker; m. 1st Edith Baumann 1947 (divorced), 2nd Margot Feist (q.v. Margot Honecker) 1953; one s.
Member, German Communist Party 29-46; imprisoned for anti-fascist activity 35-45; Youth Sec., Central Cttee. of German Communist Party 45; mem. Central Cttee., German Communist Party 46; mem. Man. Cttee., Socialist Unity Party 46-; Chair. Central Cttee., Free German Youth 46-55; mem. Volkskammer 49-; mem. Cen. Cttee. of Socialist Unity Party 46-, full mem. Politburo 58-, First Sec. Cen. Cttee. May 71-; mem. State Council Nov. 71-; Order of Merit of the Fatherland in Gold; Medal for Fascist Resistance 33-45; Karl Marx Order 72; Order of Lenin of the U.S.S.R. 72.
Sozialistische Einheitspartei Deutschlands, Am Marx-Engels-Platz 2, Berlin 102, German Democratic Republic.

Honecker, Margot; German politician; b. 17 April 1927; m. Erich Honecker (q.v.) 1953.
Co-Founder Anti-Fascist Youth Cttee., Halle 45; Sec. in Freie Deutsche Jugend (F.D.J.) Cttee., Sachsen-Anhalt; Leader, Young Pioneers, later Sec. in Central Council, F.D.J. 49-54; mem. Volkskammer 50-; mem.

Central Cttee. Sozialistische Einheitspartei Deutschlands (S.E.D.) 50-; training in U.S.S.R. 53-54; Teacher Training Dept., Ministry of Educ. 55-58, Deputy Minister of Educ. 58-63, Minister of Educ. 63-.
Ministerium für Volksbildung, Berlin, German Democratic Republic.

Hongladarom, Sunthorn, M.A.; Thai politician and diplomatist; b. 23 Aug. 1912, Nakorn Sawan; m. Khunying Lamchiag Hongladarom 1937; five s. one d.; ed. Thepsirin School, Bangkok, Weymouth Coll., England and Cambridge Univ.
Chief of Foreign Div. Dept. of Information 43-46; Asst. Sec.-Gen. of Council of Ministers 48-50; Sec.-Gen. of Nat. Econ. Council 50-57; Amb. to Fed. of Malaya 57-59; Minister of Econ. Affairs 59; Minister of Finance 59-65; Deputy Minister of Nat. Devt. 63; Minister of Econ. Affairs 65-68; Amb. to the U.K. 68-69; Amb. to the U.S.A. 69-72; Sec.-Gen. SEATO 72-; Rector of Chiengmai Univ. 66; Fellow of Econ. Devt. Inst., Int. Bank of Reconstruction and Devt.; LL.D. h.c.
Leisure interests: travel, golf, bowling.
SEATO, P.O. Box 517, Bangkok, Thailand.

Honna, Takeshi; Japanese politician; b. 1912; ed. Musashi Inst. of Technology.
Member of the House of Reps.; Parliamentary Vice-Minister of Agriculture and Forestry; Deputy Sec.-Gen. of Liberal Democratic Party; Minister of State and Dir.-Gen., Office of the Prime Minister 72.
House of Representatives, Tokyo, Japan.

Hont, Ferenc, CAND. LITT., D.PHIL.; Hungarian theatrical producer; b. 1907, Szeged; m. Ilona Görög 1948; one s.; ed. Szeged.
Producer at Odeon Theatre Paris 25-28, at various Hungarian theatres 28-44; edited dramatic papers 34-38; Sec. of Histrionic Soc. 36-; escaped to Russia 44, returned 45; Dir. Acad. of Dramatic Art 45-49, Madách Theatre 46; Artistic Dir. of Hungarian Nat. Film Company 48; Dir. Youth Theatre 50, Museum of Theatrical History 52; Pres. Council of Theatrical History of the Hungarian Acad. of Sciences 67; Pres. Inst. of Theatrical and Film Science 57, Hungarian Centre Int. Theatrical Inst. 57; Dir. Inst. for Theatrical Sciences 59-69; Prof. and Pres. Universitas theatrical group; instigator of open-air Summer Festival Plays of Szeged; Kossuth Prize 49; Labour Order of Merit, golden degree (three times).
Publs. *A Színjáték, Színház és Munkásosztály, A Színészi képzelet fejlesztése, Az eltünt magyar színjáték, Költészet a dobogón, A rendező munkája, A színjátszó munkája, Valóság a színpadon, From a Director's Notebook, A cselekvés müvészete.*
Krisztina körut 71, 1016 Budapest I, Hungary.
Telephone: 368-194.

Hook, Sidney, PH.D.; American philosopher and author; b. 20 Dec. 1902, New York; s. of Isaac Hook and Jennie Halpern; m. 1st C. Katz 1924, 2nd Ann Ethel Zinken 1935; two s. one d.; ed. Coll. of City of New York and Columbia Univ.
Instructor of Philosophy, New York Univ. 27-32, Asst. Prof. of Philosophy 32-34, Assoc. Prof. and Chair. of Dept. 34-39, Prof. 39-70, Head All-Univ. Dept. of Philosophy 50-69, Emer. Prof. 70-; Dir. N.Y. Univ. Inst. of Philosophy and Editor of its *Proceedings*; Senior Research Fellow Hoover Inst. on War, Revolution and Peace; Fellow, American Acad. of Arts and Sciences, American Acad. of Educ.; Regents Prof. Univ. of Calif.; Council mem. National Endowment for the Humanities; Pres. and Treas. John Dewey Foundation; D.Hum.Litt. (Univ. of Maine) 60, (Univ. of Utah) 70; LL.D. (Univ. of Calif.) 66, (Rockford Coll.) 70, (Univ. of Florida) 71.
Leisure interests: gardening, reading.
Publs. *The Metaphysics of Pragmatism* 27, *Towards the*

Understanding of Karl Marx 33, *From Hegel to Marx* 36, *Reason, Social Myth and Democracy* 39, *The Hero in History: A Study in Limitation and Possibility* 45, *Education for Modern Man* 47, *Heresy Yes, Conspiracy No* 53, *Common Sense and the Fifth Amendment* 58, *Political Power and Personal Freedom* 59, *The Ambiguous Legacy: Marx and the Marxists* 60, *The Quest of Being* 61, *The Paradoxes of Freedom* 62, *The Fail-Safe Fallacy* 63, *Religion in a Free Society* 67, *Academic Freedom and Academic Anarchy* 70, *Education and the Taming of Power* 73, *Pragmatism and the Tragic Sense of Life.*
c/o Department of Philosophy, New York University, Washington Square, New York, N.Y. 10003; Hoover Institution, Stanford, Calif. 94305, U.S.A.
Telephone: 212-598-3903.

Hooper, Sir Robin William John, K.C.M.G., D.S.O., D.F.C.; British diplomatist; b. 26 July 1914, Shrewsbury; s. of Col. J. C. Hooper; m. Constance Mildred Ayshford Sanford 1941; three s.; ed. Charterhouse and The Queen's Coll., Oxford.
Entered Foreign Office 38; served R.A.F. 40-44; Second Sec., Paris 44-47, First Sec., Lisbon 47-49, Head of Personnel Dept., Foreign Office 50-53, Counsellor, Baghdad 53-56, Head of Perm. Under-Sec.'s Dept., Foreign Office 56-60; Asst. Sec.-Gen. (Political Affairs) NATO 60-66; Amb. to Tunisia 66-68, to People's Repub. of S. Yemen 68-Oct. 68; Deputy Sec. Cabinet Office 68-71; Amb. to Greece 71-74.
Brook House, Egerton, Ashford, Kent TN27 9AP; Flat 3, Albany, Piccadilly, London, W.1, England.

Hoopman, Harold DeWaine, B.S.; American oil executive; b. 22 July 1920, Lucas, Kan.; s. of Ira William Hoopman and Mary Dorman; m. Eleanor Gessner 1946; two s. one d.; ed. Wyoming and Harvard Univs.
Experimental Test Engineer, Wright Aeronautical Co. 42-43; joined Marathon Oil Co. 46, Resident Man., Guatemala 57-62, Vice-Pres. Int. 62-67, Asst. to Pres. 67-68, Vice-Pres. Production, U.S. and Canada 68-69, Vice-Pres. Marketing, U.S. 69-72, Dir. and Pres. 72-, Chief Exec. Officer 75-.
Leisure interests: antique autos., hunting, fishing.
Marathon Oil Company, 539 South Main Street, Findlay, O. 45840; Home: 2501 South Main Street, Findlay, O. 45840, U.S.A.
Telephone: (419) 422-2121 (Office); (419) 422-4602 (Home).

Hoover, Herbert William, Jr., A.B.; American executive; b. 23 April 1918, No. Canton, Ohio; s. of Herbert William Hoover and Grace Steele; m. Carl Good 1941; one s. one d.; ed. Rollins Coll.
Exec. Sales, The Hoover Co. 41-43; 2nd Lt. U.S. Army 43-45; Dir. of Public Relations, The Hoover Co. 45-48, Dir. 45-, Asst. Vice-Pres. 48-52, Sales Vice-Pres. 52-53, Exec. Vice-Pres. 53-54, Pres. 54-66, Chair. 59-66; Dir. Hoover Co., Canada 52-66, Pres. 54-66; Dir. Hoover (Great Britain) Ltd. 54-66, Chair. 56-66; Dir. and Pres. Hoover (America Latina) S.A., Panama 55-66, Hoover Mexicana, Mexico 55-66, Hoover Inc., Panama, Hoover Industrial y Comercial S.A., Colombia 60-67; Pres. and Chair. Hoover Worldwide Corpn. 60-66; Pres. Dir.-Gen. S.A. Hoover, France 65; fmr. Regional Vice-Chair. U.S. Cttee for UN; Dir. The Harter Bank and Trust Co. Canton, Ohio; Chair. Hoover Foundation; mem. Council on Foreign Relations, New York; Trustee, Univ. of Miami, Florida; Dir. of the Miami Heart Inst.; Hon. LL.D. Mount Union Coll.; Chevalier de la Légion d'Honneur.
70 Park Drive, Bal Harbour, Florida 33154, U.S.A.
Telephone: 305-864-8865.

Hooykaas, Reijer, D.SC.; Netherlands university professor; b. 1 Aug. 1906, Schoonhoven; m. Ilona Van Asselt 1936; one s. four d.; ed. Utrecht Univ.

Chemistry teacher, Amsterdam 30, Zeist 32; Extraordinary Prof. of History of Science, Free Univ. of Amsterdam 45-48, Prof. 48-66, Prof. of History of Science, Univ. of Utrecht 67-; Visiting Prof. Open Univ. (U.K.) 73-74; mem. Royal Netherlands Acad. of Sciences and Letters, Int. Acad. of History of Science, Hollandsche Maatschappij der Wetenschappen; assoc. mem. Comité belge d'Histoire des Sciences; foreign mem. Royal Flemish Acad. of Sciences and Acad. da Cultura Portuguesa; Vice-Pres. Int. Comm. History Geological Sciences, Moscow; Knight Order of Nederlandse Leeuw; Commdr. Order of Polonia Restituta; Grande-Oficial Order of Infante D. Henrique; Hon. D.Sc. (Coimbra).
Publs. *The Concept of Element, its historical-philosophical development* 33, *Robert Boyle: a study in Science and Christianity* 43, *The Chemical Revolution: A. L. Lavoisier* 52, *Humanisme, Science et Réforme, Pierre de la Ramée* 58, *The Principle of Uniformity in Geology, Biology and Theology* 59, 63, 70, *Physik und Mechanik in historischer Hinsicht* 63, *Introdução a História das Ciências* 65, *Nature and History* 66, *Catastrophism in Geology* 70, *History of Science, from Babel to Bohr* 71, *Religion and the Rise of Modern Science* 72, 73; numerous articles in international historical and scientific journals.
Krullelaan 35, Zeist, Netherlands.
Telephone: 03404-12488.

Hope, Alec Derwent; Australian poet; b. 21 July 1907, Cooma, N.S.W.; s. of Rev. Percival Hope and Florence Ellen Scotford; m. Penelope Robinson 1938; two s. one d.; ed. Sydney and Oxford Univs.
Former Lecturer Sydney Teachers' Coll. and Senior Lecturer Melbourne Univ.; Prof. of English, School of Gen. Studies, Australian Nat. Univ. 51-68; Library Fellow, Australian Nat. Univ. 69-72; retd. 73; Arts Council Prize 65, Britannica-Australia Award 66, Levinson Prize for Poetry (Chicago) 69, Ingram Merrill Award for Literature 69; Fellow of the Australian Acad. of the Humanities.
Leisure interests: camping, travel, reading, music.
Publs. *The Wandering Islands* 55, *Poems* 60, *The Cave and the Spring* 65, *Collected Poems* 66, *New Poems* 65-69, *Dunciad Minor* 70, *A Midsummer Eve's Dream* 70, *Collected Poems 1930-1970* 72, *Native Companions* 74, *A Late Picking* 75, verse and criticism in numerous magazines, including *Meanjin, Southerly, M.U.M., Hermes, Quadrant* and *The Southern Review*.
66 Arthur Circle, Canberra, A.C.T., Australia.
Telephone: 731342.

Hope, Bob; American (b. British) comedian; b. 26 May 1904.
First film 38; since then has appeared in numerous films and radio and television productions; American Congressional Medal of Honor 63, Award of Entertainment Hall of Fame 75; films include *College Swing* 38, *Road to Singapore* 40, *Caught in the Draft* 41, *Road to Morocco* 42, *Let's Face It* 43, *Road to Rio* 46, *Paleface* 47, *Fancy Pants* 49, *My favourite Spy* 51, *Road to Bali* 52, *Casanova* 53, *That Certain Feeling* 56, *Beau James* 57, *Paris Holiday* 58, *Alias Jesse James* 59, *The Facts of Life* 60, *The Road to Hong Kong* 61, *Call Me Bwana* 62, *A Global Affair* 64, *I'll Take Sweden* 65, *Boy, did I get a Wrong Number!* 66, *Eight on the Run* 68, *How to Commit Marriage* 69, *The Road to Ruin* 72.
Publs. *I Never Left Home, They Got Me Covered, So This Is Peace, Have Tux, Will Travel, I Owe Russia $1200* 63, *Five Women I Love* 67.
c/o Hope Enterprises Inc., 9229 Sunset Boulevard, Los Angeles, Calif. 90069, U.S.A.

Hope, Sir Charles Peter, K.C.M.G., B.SC., T.D.; British diplomatist (retd.); b. 22 May 1912, Dartmouth; s. of G. L. N. Hope; m. Hazel Mary Turner 1936; three s.; ed. Oratory School and Imperial Coll., London.
Joined War Office 38; service with Royal Artillery 39-

46; entered Foreign Service 46, served Paris 46-50; Asst. Head, U.N. Dept., Foreign Office 50-53; served as Counsellor, High Comm. Germany, later at Embassy, 53-56; Head of News Dept., Foreign Office 56-59; Minister, Madrid 59-62; Consul-Gen. Houston, U.S.A. 63-64; Alternate Rep., UN 64-68; Amb. to Mexico 68-72.
Leisure interests: shooting and fishing.
Weetwood, Mayfield, Sussex, England.

Hopkin, Sir (William Aylsham) Bryan, Kt., C.B.E.; British economist; b. 7 Dec. 1914, nr. Cardiff; s. of William Hopkin and Lilian Blanche Cottelle; m. Renée Henriette France Ricour 1938; two s.; ed. St. John's Coll., Cambridge, and Manchester Univ.
Ministry of Health 38-41; Prime Minister's Statistical Branch 41-45; Royal Comm. on Population 45-48; Cabinet Office (Econ. Section, Central Statistical Office) 48-52; Nat. Inst. of Econ. and Social Research 52-57; Council on Prices, Productivity and Incomes 57-58; Treasury (Econ. Section) 58-65; Econ. Planning Unit, Mauritius 65; Econ. Planning Staff, Ministry of Overseas Devt. 65-68; Dir.-Gen. of Econ. Planning 67-68; Dir.-Gen. Dept. of Econ. Affairs 69; Dep. Chief Econ. Adviser to H.M. Treasury 69-72, Chief Econ. Adviser Oct. 74-; Prof. of Econs., Cardiff Univ. 72-74.
Leisure interests: reading, music.
Publs. Articles on economic matters.
Aberthin House, Aberthin, Near Cowbridge, Glamorgan, South Wales.
Telephone: Cowbridge 2303.

Hopkins, Antony, C.B.E., F.R.C.M., L.R.A.M., F.R.S.A.; British musician, author and broadcaster; b. 21 March 1921, London; m. Alison Purves 1947; ed. Berkhamsted School and Royal Coll. of Music.
Composed incidental music for theatre (Old Vic, Stratford-upon-Avon), radio and cinema; composed music for winning entries, Italia Prize 52 and 57; broadcaster in series *Talking about Music*; City of Tokyo Medal 73; Chappell Gold Medal and Cobbett Prize, Royal Coll. of Music.
Compositions: *Five studies for voices, Psalm 42*, songs, recorder pieces, two ballets, *Magnificat and Nunc Dimittis* (for girls' choir), *A Time for Growing, Three's Company, Dr. Musikus, Sonatine* (for piano), *Pieces for Talented Beginners, Partita* (for solo violin), three piano sonatas and others.
Leisure interest: motoring.
Publs. *Talking about Symphonies* 61, *Talking about Concertos* 64, *Talking about Sonatas* 71, *Music Face to Face*.
Woodyard, Ashridge, Berkhamsted, Herts., England.

Hopkinson, (Henry) Thomas, C.B.E., M.A.; British journalist and author; b. 19 April 1905, Manchester; s. of the Ven. J. H. Hopkinson and Evelyn Mary Fountaine; m. Dorothy Vernon (widow) 1953; three d.; ed. St. Edward's School and Pembroke Coll., Oxford.
Asst. Editor *Weekly Illustrated* 34-38; Editor *Picture Post* 40-50, *Lilliput* 41-46; Features Editor *News Chronicle* 54-56; Editor *Drum* 58-61; Dir. for Africa, Int. Press Inst. 63-66; Senior Fellow in Press Studies Univ. of Sussex 67-69; Visiting Prof. of Journalism Univ. of Minnesota 68-69; Dir. Centre for Journalism Studies, Univ. Coll., Cardiff 70-75; contributor to *The Sunday Times, The Observer*, and British and American magazines; Hon. F.R.P.S.
Publs. *A Wise Man Foolish* 30, *A Strong Hand at the Helm* 33, *The Man Below* 39, *Mist in the Tagus* 46, *The Transitory Venus* 48, *Down the Long Slide* 49, *Love's Apprentice, George Orwell* 53, *The Lady and the Cut-Throat* 58, *In the Fiery Continent* 62, *South Africa* 64, *Picture Post 1938-50* (Editor) 70, *Much Silence, The Life and Work of Meher Baba* (with Dorothy Hopkinson) 74.
6 Marine Parade, Penarth, Glamorgan, Wales.
Telephone: Penarth 703354.

Hoppe, Iver; Danish shipping executive; b. 25 July 1920, Aarhus; s. of Arthur Hans Knudsen Hoppe and Gerda Raun Byberg; m. Ingeborg Lassen 1943; one d.; ed. Univ. of Copenhagen.

Acting Lecturer Copenhagen Univ. 46, Jurisprudential Lecturer 52-58; Advocate to the High Court and Court of Appeal 48; joined A. P. Møller Concern, Copenhagen 55, Asst. Dir. 60-64, Man. Dir. Odense Steel Shipyard Ltd., Odense and Lindø 64-71; Chair. A/S Svendborg Skibvaerft 68-71; Chair. Harland Ocean Transport Co. Ltd. 71; Man. Dir. and Chief Exec., Harland and Wolff Ltd. 71-74; mem. Board Dansk Boreselskab A/S and other cos. until 71, Den Danske Landmandsbank A/S 70-72, Danish Ship Credit Fund 65-71; mem. Council, Danish Nat. Bank 67-71; mem. Asscn. of Danish Ship-yards 64-71, Asscn. of Employers of Iron and Metal Industry in Denmark 67-71, Asscn. of Danish Industries 65-72, West of England Steam Ship Owners Protection and Indemnity Asscn. Ltd. 60-66, Danish Acad. of Technical Sciences, Shipbuilders and Repairers Nat. Asscn. Exec. Council and Man. Board, Northern Ireland Finance Corpn., British Iron and Steel Consumers' Council, Lloyd's Register of Shipping, General Cttee., Det Norske Veritas (British Cttee.), American Bureau of Shipping and other Danish and foreign orgs.; Knight of Dannebrog; Knight of Icelandic Falcon.
Leisure interests: swimming, reading, mountain walking, farming.

Hoppenot, Henri; French diplomatist and writer; b. 25 Oct. 1891, Paris; m. Hélène Delacour 1917; one d.; studied Law and Philosophy at Paris and Oxford.
Entered diplomatic service 14; Sec. and Chargé d'Affaires in Switzerland, Brazil, Iran, Chile, Germany, Syria and China; Dir. of European Affairs at Ministry of Foreign Affairs 38-40; Minister Plenipotentiary in Uruguay until resignation in 42; represented French Cttee. of Nat. Liberation in the Antilles 43; Del. of the French Provisional Govt. in Washington 43-44; Amb. to Switzerland 45-51; Permanent Del. to Security Council and UN 52-55; High Commissioner to Viet-Nam 55-56; Pres. Control Comm. for referendum and general elections in Algeria 58; Grand Officier Légion d'Honneur 55; Conseiller d'Etat 56; Pres. Cour Arbitrale de la Communauté 59-61; mem. Haut-Tribunal Militaire 61-62; Hon. Conseiller d'Etat 64.
Publs. Trois Poèmes 11, Moharem 23, Continent Perdu 27-47.
42 Quai des Orfèvres, 75001 Paris, France.
Telephone: 033-36-30.

Horecker, Bernard L., B.S., PH.D.; American bio-chemist; b. 31 Oct. 1914, Chicago, Ill.; s. of Paul Horecker and Bessie Horecker; m. Frances Goldstein 1936; three d.; ed. Univ. of Chicago.
Research Assoc., Dept. of Chem., Univ. of Chicago 39-40; Examiner U.S. Civil Service Comm., Washington, D.C. 40-41; Biochemist U.S. Public Health Service (U.S.P.H.S.) Nat. Insts. of Health (N.I.H.) Industrial Hygiene Research Laboratory 41-47, Nat. Inst. of Arthritis and Metabolic Diseases 47-53, Chief, Section on Enzymes and Cellular Biochemistry, N.I.H. Nat. Inst. of Arthritis and Metabolic Diseases 53-56; Head Laboratory of Biochemistry and Metabolism 56-59; Prof. and Chair. Dept. of Microbiology, New York Univ. School of Medicine 59-63, Dept. of Molecular Biology Albert Einstein Coll. of Medicine 62-71, Dir. Div. of Biol. Sciences 70-72, Assoc. Dean for Scientific Affairs 71-72; Vice-Chair. Div. of Biological Chem., American Chemical Soc. 75-76; mem. Roche Inst. of Molecular Biology 72-; professional Lecturer on Enzymes, George Washington Univ. 50-57; Visiting Prof., Univ. of California 54, Univ. of Illinois 57, Univ. of Paraná, Brazil 60, 63, Cornell Univ. 64, Univ. of Rotterdam 70; Visiting Investigator, Pasteur Inst. 57-58, Indian Inst. of Science, Bangalore 71; Ciba Lecturer Rutgers Univ. 62; Phillips Lecturer Haverford Coll. 65; Reilly Lecturer Notre Dame Univ. 69; Visiting Prof. Albert Einstein Coll. of Medicine 72-; Editor *Biochemical and Biophysical Research Communications* 59-; Chair. Editorial Cttee. Archives of Biochemistry and Bio-physics 68-; mem. Scientific Advisory Board, Roche Inst. of Molecular Biology 67-70, Chair. 70-72; Dir. Academic Press 68-; mem. Comm. on Personnel, American Cancer Soc. 69-73; Medical Scientist Training Program Study Section N.I.H. 70-72; mem. Scientific Advisory Comm. for Biochem. and Chemical Cardio-genesis, American Cancer Soc. 74-; Pres. American Soc. of Biological Sciences 68-69, Harvey Soc. of N.Y. 70-71; Vice-Chair. Pan American Association of Bio-chemical Societies 71, Chair. 72; mem. of numerous socs. including American Chemical Soc. (mem. Exec. Cttee. Div. Biological Chem. 70-74), American Soc. of Micro-biology, Biochemical Soc. of Great Britain, Swiss Biochemical Soc. (Hon.), Japanese Biochemical Soc. (Hon.), Spanish Biochem. Soc. (Hon.), Brazilian Acad. of Sciences (Hon.); Fellow American Acad. of Arts and Sciences, American Asscn. for the Advancement of Science; Commonwealth Fund Fellow; mem. Nat. Acad. of Sciences; Paul Lewis Laboratories Award in Enzyme Chem. 52, Fed. Security Agency's Superior Accomplishment Award 52, Hillebrand Prize, American Chemical Soc. 54, Washington Acad. of Sciences Award in Biological Sciences 54, Rockefeller Public Service Award 57, Fulbright Travel Award 63, Career Devt. Award Study Section, N.I.H. 66-70.
Leisure interests: gardening, ornithology.
Roche Institute of Molecular Biology, Nutley, New Jersey 07110, U.S.A.
Telephone: 201-235-3464.

Horgos, Dr. Gyula; Hungarian mechanical engineer and politician; b. 23 July 1920, Nagyvárad (now Oradea in Romania); s. of Pal Horgos; two s. one d.; ed. Budapest Technical Univ.
Engineer, Csepel Machine Tool Plant 43-49; post-graduate studies 49-53; Chief Engineer, Csepel Metal Works 54, later Vice-Pres. Nat. Planning Office, later Technical Dir. Csepel Metal Works; Dep. Minister of Metallurgy and Machine Industry 60-63, Minister 63-75; mem. Communist Party 45-, Cen. Cttee. 72-75; Labour Order of Merit Gold Medal 69.
Leisure interests: mathematics and chess.
c/o Ministry of Metallurgy and Machine Industry, 1525 Budapest, Mártirok utja 85, Hungary.
Telephone: 123-590.

Hori, Shigeru; Japanese politician; b. 20 Dec. 1901, Saga Prefecture; 2nd s. of Asajiro Hori; m. Toyo Hori; two s. two d.; ed. Chuo College.
Political Reporter in Hochi and Tonichi newspapers 24-28; Sec. to Minister of Agriculture; mem. House of Reps. 44; successively Parl. Vice-Minister of Commerce and Industry, mem. Exec. Board Japan Progressivist Party, Sec.-Gen. of Democratic Party; Minister of Labour 50; Sec.-Gen. of Cabinet 51; Minister of Agriculture and Forestry 53, of Construction Nov. 67; Sec.-Gen. of Cabinet 68-71; Dir. Admin. Management Agency 73-74; mem. Exec. Board Liberal Democratic Party 53.
Leisure interests: "Go" (game) and golf.
39-16, Gohongi 1-chome, Meguro-ku, Tokyo, Japan.

Hori, Taro; Japanese finance official; b. 25 Dec. 1917, Kyoto; s. of Tadashi Hori and Ayako Hayashi; m. Atsuko Ito 1949; two d.; ed. Tokyo Imperial Univ.
Entered Ministry of Finance 43; Dir. Int. Org. Div. 60-61; Dir. Foreign Capital Div. 61-65; Rep. of Ministry of Finance and Consul, New York, Financial Coun-sellor, Japanese Embassy, Washington, D.C. 65-68; Special Adviser to Minister of Econ. Planning 68-70; Exec. Dir. Honshu-Shikoku Bridge Authority 70-73;

Exec. Dir. Int. Bank for Reconstruction and Devt. (IBRD), Special Adviser to Minister of Finance, Special Asst. to Minister of Foreign Affairs.
Leisure interest: golf.
Publ. *GATT Analysis and Prospect.*
International Monetary Fund, Washington, D.C. 20431; Home: 2 Kittery Court, Bethesda, Maryland 20034, U.S.A.
Telephone: 365-0894 (Home).

Horikoshi, Teizo, LL.B.; Japanese business executive; b. 13 Dec. 1898; ed. Tokyo Imperial Univ.
Entered Bank of Japan 24, Dir. 47-; Deputy Dir. Econ. Stabilization Agency 47; Sec.-Gen. Japanese Nat. Cttee. of Int. Chamber of Commerce 50; Exec. Dir. and Sec.-Gen. Fed. of Econ. Orgs. 54-; Auditor, Toho Mutual Life Insurance Co. 59-; Pres. Securities and Exchange Council, Ministry of Finance 61-; Pres. Nippon Usiminas Co. Ltd. 65-; Hon. C.B.E. (U.K.) 66.
270 Kyodo-machi, Setagaya-ku, Tokyo, Japan.

Hornby, Robert A.; American businessman; b. 1900, Topeka, Kan.; *s.* of Alfred Joseph and Louise E. (McJilton) Hornby; *m.* Mary Louise Duffy 1925; one *d.*; ed. Univ. of Calif.
Former Pres., fmr. Dir. and mem. Exec. Cttee. Pacific Lighting Corpn.; Dir. Barclays Bank of California; Vice-Pres. Sponsors of San Francisco Performing Arts Centre, Inc.; Trustee, Univ. of S. Calif.; mem. Advisory Council and Consulting Prof. Graduate School of Business; mem. Calif. Postsecondary Educ. Comm.; Trustee, California State Univ. and Colls., Calif. Council for Econ. Educ.
810 South Flower Street, Los Angeles, Calif. 90017, U.S.A.
Telephone: 213-689-3567.

Horne, Marilyn; American mezzo-soprano singer; b. 16 Jan. 1934, Bradford, Pa.; *m.* Henry Lewis; one *d.*; ed. Univ. of Southern Calif. (under William Vennard).
Performed with several German opera companies in Europe 56; debut, San Francisco Opera 60; has since appeared at Covent Garden, London, the Chicago Lyric Opera, La Scala, Milan, Metropolitan Opera, N.Y.; repertoire includes Eboli (*Don Carlo*), Marie (*Wozzeck*), Adalgisa (*Norma*), Jane Seymour (*Anna Bolena*), Amneris (*Aida*), *Carmen*, Rosina (*Barbiere di Siviglia*), Fides (*Le Prophète*), *Mignon*.
Leisure interest: needlepoint.
c/o Metropolitan Opera, Lincoln Center, New York, N.Y. 10023, U.S.A.

Horner, Richard Elmer, B.S., M.S.E.; American business executive; b. 24 Oct. 1917, Wrenshall, Minn.; *s.* of Marion Chester and Maude Eckert Horner; *m.* Margaret Hodgson 1941; one *s.* one *d.*; ed. Univ. of Minnesota and Princeton Univ.
U.S. Air Force 40-49; civilian aeronautical development engineer, Air Force Flight Test Centre, Edwards Air Force Base, Calif. 49-53, Technical Dir. 53-55; Deputy for Requirements to Asst. Sec. of Air Force for Research and Development 55-57; Asst. Sec. to A.F. for Research and Development 57-59; Assoc. Administrator, Nat. Aeronautics and Space Admin. 59-60; Senior Vice-Pres. (Technical) Northrop Corpn. 60-70; Fellow American Inst. of Aeronautics and Astronautics, Pres. E. F. Johnson Co. 70-; American Ordnance Asscn., American Astronautical Soc., Soaring Soc. of America; Silver Star, Air Medal with 4 clusters, Presidential Unit Citation.
Leisure interests: skiing, sailing.
905 11th Street, N.E., Waseca, Minn. 56093, U.S.A.
Telephone: (507) 835-2050 (Office); (507) 835-5176 (Home).

Hornig, Donald Frederick; American chemist and university administrator; b. 17 March 1920, Milwaukee, Wis.; *s.* of Chester Arthur and Emma (Knuth) Hornig; *m.* Lilli Schwenk 1943; one *s.* three *d.*; ed. Harvard Univ.

Research Assoc. Woods Hole (Mass.) Oceanographic Inst. 43-44; Scientist, Los Alamos Lab., New Mexico 44-46; Pres. Radiation Instruments Co. 45-47; Asst. Prof. of Chemistry Brown Univ. 46-49, Assoc. Prof. 49-51, Prof. 51-57, Dir. Metcalf Research Lab. 49-57; Assoc. and Acting Dean, Graduate School, Brown Univ. 52-53; Prof. of Chemistry Princeton Univ. 57-63, Chair. Dept. 58-63, Donner Prof. of Science 59-63; Dir. W. A. Benjamin Inc. 62-64; Dir. Office of Science and Technology, Exec. Office of Pres. of U.S.A. 64-69; Vice-Pres. and Dir. Eastman Kodak Co. 69-70; Pres. Brown Univ. 70-; Dir. Upjohn Co. 71-, Westinghouse Electric Co. 72-; mem. Board of Trustees, Manpower Inst. 70-, Overseas Devt. Council 69-; mem. American Chemical Soc., American Physical Soc., etc.; Hon. mem. Nat. Acad. of Sciences (U.S.A.), American Acad. of Arts and Sciences, etc.; numerous awards and hon. degrees.
Brown University, Providence, R.I. 02912, U.S.A.
Telephone: 401-863-2234.

Horowitz, David; Israeli economist; b. 15 Feb. 1899, Drohobic; *s.* of Siegmund and Fanny Horowitz; *m.* Riva Bobkov 1922; one *s.*; ed. Vienna and Lwów.
Member Exec. Cttee. Gen. Fed. of Jewish Labour 23; journalist and writer; Economic Adviser and Sec., American Economic Cttee. for Palestine 32-35; Dir. Economic Dept. of Jewish Agency for Palestine; mem. various Govt. Cttees. under Mandatory Regime and dir. various enterprises 35-48; fmr. Dir.-Gen. Ministry of Finance (resgnd. 52), Gov.-Designate Bank of Israel 52-54, Gov. 54-71, Chair. Advisory Cttee. and Council 71-; Lecturer, High School for Law and Econs., Tel-Aviv 46-50; Liaison Officer to UN Special Cttee. on Palestine 46; mem. Jewish Del. to Lake Success 47; Head of Israel Del. to Econ. Survey Comm. of UN 48; Head of Israel Del. Financial Talks on Sterling Releases between Israel and Great Britain, London 49, and in negotiations between Israel and Great Britain on econ. and financial affairs in connection with termination of the Mandate; fmr. mem. Board of Govs. Int. Bank of Reconstruction and Devt. (World Bank); Chair. Board of Dirs. The Eliezer Kaplan School of Econ. and Soc. Sciences, Hebrew Univ.; mem. State Council for Higher Educ.; mem. Board of Govs. Hebrew Univ., Tel-Aviv Univ.; mem. Exec. Council, Weizmann Inst.; mem. Board of Trustees Truman Center for Advancement of Peace; Hon. Pres. Inst. for Int. Relations (Rome); Head, Israel Del. to UN Conf. on Trade and Devt. Geneva 64; Israel Prize of Social Sciences 67; Dr. h.c. (Hebrew Univ. and Tel-Aviv Univ.).
Publs. *Aspects of Economic Policy in Palestine* 36, *Jewish Colonisation in Palestine* 37, *Economic Survey of Palestine* (with Rita Hinden) 38, *Palestine Jewry's Economic War Effort* 42, *Postwar Reconstruction* 42, *Palestine and the Middle East, An Essay in Regional Economy* 43, *Prediction and Reality in Palestine* 45, *State in the Making* 53, *Anatomie unserer Zeit* 64, *Hemispheres North and South* 66, *The Economics of Israel* 67, *The Abolition of Poverty* 69, *The Enigma of Economic Growth, a Case Study of Israel* 72; and several publs. in Hebrew.
Home: 4 Lamed Heh Street, Jerusalem; Office: Bank of Israel, Mizpah Building, Jerusalem, Israel.
Telephone: 27026 (Office): 33182 (Home).

Horowitz, Norman Harold, PH.D.; American biologist; b. 19 March 1915, Pittsburgh, Pa.; *s.* of Joseph Horowitz and Jeanette Miller; *m.* Pearl Shykin 1939; one *s.* one *d.*; ed. Univ. of Pittsburgh and Calif. Inst. of Technology.
National Research Council Fellow 39-40; Research Fellow, Calif. Inst. of Technology, Pasadena 40-42; Research Assoc. Stanford Univ. 42-46; Assoc. Prof. of Biology, Calif. Inst. of Technology 47-53, Prof. 53-; Chief, Bioscience Section, Jet Propulsion Lab., Pasadena

65-70; Fulbright and Guggenheim Fellow, Univ. of Paris 54-55; Fellow, American Acad. of Arts and Sciences; mem. Nat. Acad. of Sciences.
Leisure interests; gardening, music.
Publs. numerous technical articles on genetics, biochemistry and space exploration.
Biology Division, California Institute of Technology, Pasadena, Calif. 91109, U.S.A.
Telephone: 213-795-6811.

Horowitz, Vladimir; American pianist; b. 1 Oct. 1904, Russia; s. of Samuel and Sophie (née Bodik) Horowitz; m. Wanda Toscanini 1933; one d.
Studied under Felix Blumenfeld and Sergei Tarnowsky; first appearance 17; U.S. début with N.Y. Philharmonic Orchestra 28; soloist N.Y. Symphony Orchestra, Philadelphia Orchestra, NBC Symphony Orchestra, Cleveland, Boston, Chicago, Detroit and St. Louis and other orchestras; Royal Philharmonic Soc. Gold Medal 72, Prix du Disque 70, 71 and winner of 12 Grammy awards for best classical performance.
Leisure interest: collecting antique American furniture and Americana.
c/o Shaw Concerts, Inc., 1995 Broadway, New York, N.Y. 10023, U.S.A.

Horrocks, Lieut.-Gen. Sir Brian Gwynne, K.C.B., K.B.E., D.S.O., M.C.; British army officer; b. 7 Sept. 1895, Ranikhet, India; s. of late Sir William H. Horrocks; m. Winifred Nancy Brook Kitchin 1928; one d.; ed. Uppingham and Royal Military Coll.
Served First World War 14-18; Commdr. 44th (H.C. Div.), 9th Armoured Div., XIII Corps, X Corps in Egypt and Africa, IX Corps in Tunis, XXX Corps in B.L.A. 39-45; G.O.C.-in-C. Western Command 46-48; G.O.C.-in-C. British Army of the Rhine 48-49; Gentleman Usher of The Black Rod, House of Lords 49-63; Dir. Bovis Ltd. 63-; Hon. LL.D. (Univ. of Belfast); Hon. Freeman City of Brussels; Commdr. Légion d'Honneur; Croix de Guerre avec Palmes (France and Belgium); Grand Officer Order of Belgian Crown; Commdr. Order of George I (Greece); Legion of Merit (U.S.A.); Knight Grand Cross, Order of Orange-Nassau (Netherlands).
Leisure interests: travel, sailing.
Publ. A Full Life 60.
Manor Farm, East Compton, Shepton Mallet, Somerset, England.

Horsfall, James Gordon, B.SC., PH.D.; American plant pathologist and science administrator; b. 9 Jan. 1905, Mountain Grove, Mo.; s. of Frank Horsfall and Margaret Vaulx Horsfall; m. Sue Belle Overton 1927; two d.; ed. Univ. of Arkansas and Cornell Univ.
Instructor, Cornell Univ. 28-29, Asst. Prof. to Prof. 29-39; Chief of Dept. of Plant Pathology, Conn. Agricultural Experiment Station 39-48, Dir. 48-71, S. W. Johnson Distinguished Scientist 72-; Editor Annual Review of Phytopathology 62-71; Lecturer in Microbiology, Yale Univ. 50-63; Fellow and Pres. American Phytopathological Soc. 51; Pres. Soc. of Industrial Microbiology 54; Consultant, President's Science Advisory Cttee. 60-70; mem. Advisory Cttee. on Biology and Medicine U.S. Atomic Energy Comm. 57-64, Nat. Advisory Comm. on Food and Fiber 65-67, Latin America Science Board, Nat. Acad. of Sciences 65-66; Chair. Agricultural Board, Nat. Acad. of Sciences 71-73; mem. American Acad. of Arts and Sciences, Nat. Acad. of Sciences; Hon. mem. Società Italiana di Fitoiatria, Pavia, Italy; mem. Accad. Nazionale di Agricoltura (Italy); Hon. Fellow, Indian Phytopathological Soc.; Hon. D.Sc. (Univ. of Vermont), D.Agr. (Univ. of Turin), LL.D. (Univ. of Arkansas); Award of Distinction, Amer. Phytopathological Soc. 69; Médaille de Mérite Agricole de France 70; Award of Distinguished Service, Amer. Inst. of Biological Science 74.
Leisure interests: woodworking, gardening.

Publs. Fungicides and Their Action 45, Principles of Fungicidal Action 56, Plant Pathology—An Advanced Treatise 3 vols. 59-60; numerous station bulletins and articles in scientific journals.
The Connecticut Agricultural Experiment Station, 123 Huntington Street, P.O. Box 1106, New Haven, Conn. 06504; Home: 49 Woodstock Road, Hamden, Conn. 06517, U.S.A.
Telephone: 203-787-7421 (Office); 203-248-3577 (Home).

Horst, Karl August, DR.PHIL.; German writer; b. 10 Aug. 1913, Darmstadt; s. of August and Blanca Horst née Meyer; m. Maria Bruckmüller 1949; ed. Univs. of Munich, Berlin, Göttingen, Bonn.
Interpreter and wireless operator in Second World War 40-45; asst. under E. R. Curtius, Univ. of Bonn 45-48; self-employed as writer 48-; literary critic Merkur.
Leisure interests: gardening, walking.
Publs. Ich und Gnade, eine Studie über Friedrich Schlegels Bekehrung 51, Zero (novel) 51, Ina Seidel, Wesen und Werk 56, Die deutsche Literatur der Gegenwart 57, Das Spektrum des modernen Romans 59, Kritischer Führer durch die deutsche Literatur der Gegenwart 62, Der Skorpion, Erzählungen 63, Das Abenteuer der deutschen Literatur im zwanzigsten Jahrhundert 64, Zwischen den Stühlen 72, Editor and translator of Erzähler der Welt (24 vols.) 66-72.
8174 Ried/Benediktbeuern, Federal Republic of Germany.
Telephone: 08857-420.

Hörstadius, Sven (Otto); Swedish zoologist; b. 18 Feb. 1898, Stockholm; s. of Wilhelm Hörstadius and Svea Hård; m. Greta Kjellström 1928; one s. one d.; ed. Univ. of Stockholm.
Reader in Zoology, Univ. of Stockholm 28-32; Assoc. Prof. 32-42; Head of Dept. of Developmental Physiology and Genetics, Wennergren Inst. of Experimental Biology 38-42; Prof. of Zoology, Uppsala Univ. 42-64; research work at several marine biological stations all over the world; received Prix Albert Brachet of Belgian Royal Acad. of Science 38; Pres. Int. Union of Biological Sciences 53-58; Pres. Sveriges Ornitologiska Forening 47-68; Pres. Int. Council Scientific Unions 62-63; Chair. European Section of Int. Council for Bird Preservation 60-72; Fellow, Royal Swedish Acad. of Science, Royal Soc. of Science, Uppsala, Royal Danish Acad. of Science, Acad. Pontificio, Rome; foreign mem. Royal Soc., London, Accad. Naz. dei Lincei, Rome, Finnish Soc. of Science, Zoological Soc., London; hon. mem. Belgian Royal Zoological Soc., Soc. Zoologique de France, British Ornithologists Union, Soc. Philomatique, Paris, Royal Inst. of Gt. Britain, etc.; Gen. Sec. Congress of Ornithology, Uppsala 50; Dr. h.c. (Univs. of Paris, Bristol and Cambridge).
Leisure interests: bird photography, ornithology, tourism.
Publs. The Neural Crest 50, Experimental Embryology of Echinoderms 73.
Zoologiska Institutionen, 751 22 Uppsala, Sweden.
Telephone: 018-111818 (Inst.); 018-302202 (Home).

Horton, Alexander Romeo; Liberian banker; b. 20 Aug. 1923, Monrovia; s. of Rev. Dr. Daniel R. Horton and Ora Milner Horton; m. Mary E. C. Horton 1956; one s. one d.; ed. B.W.I. Inst. Coll. of West Africa, Morehouse Coll., Atlanta, U.S.A. and Wharton School of Finance and Commerce, Pennsylvania Univ.
Founder and President, Bank of Liberia 54-; Asst. Econ. Adviser to Liberian Govt. 54-63; Chair. Steering Cttee. of Conf. of African Businessmen 60; Chair. ECA Cttee. of Nine African Countries on Development Bank for Africa 62; Sec. of Commerce and Industry, Liberia 64-68; Pres. Liberia Bankers Asscn.; Dean, Coll. of Business and Public Admin., Univ. of Liberia; Chair. Liberia Insurance Agency; has attended numerous int.

confs.; decorations include Knight Commdr. Order of African Redemption, Officier Nat. Order of Ivory Coast, Grand Commdr. Order of Star of Africa, Grand Band Order of Star of Africa, Grand Cross Order of Orange-Nassau.
Leisure interest: reading.
The Bank of Liberia, P.O. Box 2031, Carey and Warren Streets, Monrovia, Liberia.
Telephone: 21200, 22284 (Office); 21738 (Home).

Horton, Jack King; American businessman; b. 27 June 1916; ed. Stanford Univ. and Oakland Coll. Law School.
Admitted to Calif. Bar 41; Treasury Dept. Shell Oil Co. 37-42; private law practice 42-43; Attorney, Standard Oil Co. 43-44; Sec., Legal Counsel, Coast Counties Gas & Electric Co. 44-57, Pres. 51-54; Vice-Pres. Pacific Gas & Electric Co., San Francisco 54-; Pres. S. Calif. Edison Co. 59-, Chief Exec. Officer 65-.
Home: 315 South Windsor Boulevard, Los Angeles, Calif. 90005; Office: P.O. Box 800, Rosemead, Calif. 91220, U.S.A.
Telephone: 213-624-7111 (Office).

Horwood, Owen Pieter Faure, B.COM.; South African economist and politician; b. 6 Dec. 1916, Somerset West; s. of late Stanley Ebden Horwood and Anna Johanna Horwood; m. Helen Mary Watt 1946; one s. one d.; ed. Boys' High School, Paarl, Univ. of Cape Town.
Associate Prof. of Commerce, Univ. of Cape Town 54-56; Prof. of Econs., Univ. Coll. of Rhodesia and Nyasaland 56-57; Prof. of Econs., Univ. of Natal 57-65, Principal, Vice-Chancellor 66-70; Senator, Dir. of Cos. 70-; Minister of Indian Affairs and Tourism 72-74, of Econ. Affairs 74-75, of Finance Feb. 75-; Pres. Econ. Soc. of South Africa 64, 65; Chair., mem. several govt. comms. including Sugar Industry Comm. 67-69, Universities Comm. 68-72; Chancellor, Univ. of Durban-Westville; Gen. Editor, *Natal Regional Survey Publs.* 58-69.
Leisure interests: sport, gardening, book collecting.
Publs. *Economic Systems of the Commonwealth* (co-author) 62, and numerous articles on economics and finance in professional journals.
Private Bag X115, Pretoria, South Africa.
Telephone: Pretoria 744199.

Hossain, Kamal, M.A., B.C.L., D.PHIL.; Bangladesh Minister of Foreign Affairs 73-75; see *The International Who's Who 1975-76.*

Hotchkiss, Rollin Douglas, B.S., PH.D.; American bacterial physiologist; b. 8 Sept. 1911, S. Britain, Conn.; s. of Charles Leverett Hotchkiss and Eva Judith Platt; m. 1st Shirley Dawson 1933, 2nd Magda Gabor 1967; one s. one d.; ed. Yale Univ.
Fellow, Rockefeller Inst. (later Rockefeller Univ.) 35, Asst., Assoc., Assoc. Prof., then Prof. 55-; Rockefeller Foundation Fellow, Copenhagen, Carlsberg 37-38; Visiting Prof. of Biology, Mass. Inst. of Technology 58, Univ. of Utah 72, 73; Visiting Prof. of Genetics, Univ. of Calif. at Berkeley 68; Visiting Scientist, Hungarian Acad. Sci. Inst. of Genetics, Szeged 72, 74, 75; Visiting Prof. of Microbiology, Univ. of Paris, Orsay 75; Fogarty Scholar-in-Residence, Nat. Insts. of Health, Bethesda 71-72; Jesup Lecturer, Columbia Univ. 54, Dyer Lecturer, Nat. Insts. of Health 61; mem. Nat. Acad. of Sciences, American Asscn. Biol. Chemists, American Soc. Cell Biol., Harvey Soc. (Pres. 58), Genet Soc. of America (Pres. 72); Hon. D.Sc. (Yale Univ.) 62; Fellow-Commoner, Corpus Christi Coll., Cambridge 70; Award in Antibiotics Research, Soc. of American Bacteriologists 53.
Leisure interests: mineralogy, charcoal-drawing, boat-construction, stained glass construction.
Publs. About 100 scientific articles and monographs including: *Gramicidin, tyrocidin and tyrothricin* 44, *Bacterial action of surface active agents* 46, *Microchemical*

reaction for polysaccharides 48, *Chemical studies on transforming agent* 49, *Transfer of penicillin resistance by DNA* 51, *Double Marker transformations as evidence of linked factors in DNA* 54, *Criteria for quantitative genetic transformation* 57, *Analysis of the sulfonamide resistance locus* 58, *Fate of transforming DNA* 60, *Selective heat inactivation of DNA* 61, *Regulation of transformability* 64, *Genetic engineering* 65, *Manifestation of linear organization in DNA* 66, *Mutationally modified specific exonucleases* 71, 72, *Mechanism of Recombination* 71, 73, 74.
Laboratory of Genetics, Rockefeller University, 66th Street at York Avenue, New York, N.Y., U.S.A.
Telephone: 212-360-1323.

Hotson, Leslie, A.B., A.M., PH.D., M.A., LITT.D. (Cantab.), F.R.S.L.; American literary scholar; b. 16 Aug. 1897; ed. Harvard Univ.
Travelling Scholar and Fellow 22-25 and Instructor Harvard Univ. 24-25; Senior Research Fellow Yale Univ. 26-27; Assoc. Prof. of English New York Univ. 27-31; Prof. of English Haverford Coll. 31-42; Capt. U.S. Army Signal Corps 43-46; Fulbright Senior Research Fellow, England 49-50; Research Assoc. Yale Univ. 53-66; Fellow, King's Coll., Cambridge 54-60.
Publs. *The Death of Christopher Marlowe* 25, *The Commonwealth and Restoration Stage* 28, *Shelley's Lost Letters to Harriet* 30, *Shakespeare versus Shallow* 31, *I, William Shakespeare* 37, *Shakespeare's Sonnets Dated* 49, *Shakespeare's Motley* 52, *Queen Elizabeth's Entertainment at Mitcham* 53, *The First Night of Twelfth Night* 54, *Shakespeare's Wooden O* 59, *Mr. W. H.* 64.
White Hollow Road, Northford, Conn., U.S.A.

Hotta, Shozo; Japanese banker; b. 23 Jan. 1899, Nagoya; ed. Dept. of Econs., Kyoto Imperial Univ.
Joined Sumitomo Bank Ltd. 26, Man. Tokyo Branch 45, Chief Man. 47, Man. Dir. and Deputy Pres. 47, Pres. 52, Chair. 71-; Dir. Nippon Electric Co. Ltd. Sumitomo Real Estate Co. Ltd., Mitsui-OSK Lines Ltd.; Auditor, Kansai Oil Co. Inc., Asahi Breweries Ltd., Osaka Int. Trade Center Ltd., Meishin Kosoku Jidosha Co. Ltd.; Adviser to Kansai Electric Power Co. Inc., Sumitomo Electric Industries Ltd., Sumitomo Atomic Energy Industries Ltd.; Adviser to Ministry of Foreign Affairs; Exec. Dir. Japan Fed. of Econ. Org (Keidanren); Pres. Japan-Spanish Soc.; Roving Amb. in Europe 57; leader of govt. mission to EFTA countries 63; visited Latin America 67, Europe 68 on behalf of Minister in charge of *Expo 70*; Blue Ribbon Medal; Commdr. Orden de Isabel la Católica (Spain).
Leisure interests: reading and fine arts.
22, 5-chome, Kitahama, Higashi-tu, Osaka, Japan.

Hottel, Hoyt Clarke, A.B., S.M.; American professor of chemical engineering and engineering consultant; b. 15 Jan. 1903, Salem, Ind.; s. of Louis Weaver and Myrtle Clarke Hottel; m. Nellie Louise Rich 1929; one s. three d.; ed. Indiana Univ. and Mass. Inst. of Technology (M.I.T.).
Assistant Prof., Assoc. Prof., M.I.T. 27-41, Prof. of Fuel Engineering 41-66, Carbon Dubbs Prof. of Chemical Engineering 66-68, Prof. Emer. 68-; Dir. Fuels Research Laboratory 34-68; Section Chief on Fire Warfare, Nat. Defense Research Cttee. 42-45; Chair. Nat. Acad./Nat. Research Council Cttee. on Fire Research 55-67, Amer. Flame Research Cttee. 52-73; Vice-Pres. Combustion Inst. 52-64; mem. numerous other scientific cttees. and comms.; mem. Nat. Acad. of Sciences, Nat. Acad. of Engineering, Amer. Acad. of Arts and Sciences, Amer. Chemical Soc.; Fellow, Amer. Inst. of Chemical Engineers; Medal for Merit (U.S.), King's Medal (Great Britain), W. H. Walker Award, Amer. Inst of Chemical Engineers, Egerton Gold Medal, Combustion Inst., Melchett Medal, Inst. of Fuel (G.B.), Max Jakob Award, Amer. Soc. of Mechanical Engineers/

American Inst. of Chemical Engineers, Founders' Award American Inst. of Chemical Engineers.

Leisure interests: gardening, books, grandchildren.

Publs. *Thermodynamic Charts for Combustion Processes* (with others) 49, *Radiative Transfer* (with A. F. Sarofim) 67, *New Energy Technology—Some Facts and Assessments* 71; sections in handbooks and about 100 papers on combustion, thermodynamics, jet and flame structure, radiative transfer, solar energy utilization.

Department of Chemical Engineering, Massachusetts Institute of Technology, Cambridge, Mass. 02139; Home: 27 Cambridge Street, Winchester, Mass. 01890, U.S.A.

Telephone: 253-4578 (Office); 729-3873 (Home).

Hotter, Hans; German singer; b. 19 Jan. 1909; ed. Munich.

Concert début 29, opera début 30; mem. Vienna, Hamburg and Munich Opera companies; has appeared at concerts and in operas in major cities in Europe, Australia and the U.S., and at Festivals at Salzburg, Bayreuth and Edinburgh; renowned for Wagnerian roles; retd. 72.

Emil Dittlerstrasse 26, Munich-Solin, Federal Republic of Germany.

Hottinguer, Baron Rodolphe; French banker; b. 16 Oct. 1902, Paris; m. Odette Basset 1934; two s. two d.; ed. Ecole des Hautes Etudes Commerciales.

Associate Hottinguer & Cie., Bankers; Pres. Asscn. Professionnelle des Banques, Union pour l'épargne privée (Optima); Vice-Pres. Kléber Colombes; Pres. Banque Grindlay Ottomane; Censeur, Crédit Foncier de France; Dir. Schneider S.A., Chatillon Commentry, Tréfimétaux, Union Européenne Industrielle et Financière Mines et Fonderies de la Vieille Montagne, Grindlays Bank Ltd.; Pres. Int. Chamber of Commerce (ICC) 71-73; Commdr. Légion d'Honneur; Officier de l'Ordre Nat. du Mérite; Officier des Palmes Académiques; Croix de Guerre (39-45); Commdr. du Mérite Commercial et de l'Economie Nationale.

4 rue de la Baume, Paris 8e, France.

Hou Youn; Cambodian politician; b. 1928.

Former deputy Nat. Assembly in Prince Sihanouk's party, Sangkum Reastr Nyum (Popular Socialist Community); left Sangkum party, went underground and became active in Khmers Rouges 67; Minister of Interior, Co-operatives and Communal Reforms, Royal Govt. of Nat. Union of Cambodia (GRUNC) 70-76 (in exile 70-75, in Phnom-Penh 75-76); mem. Politburo Nat. United Front of Cambodia (FUNC) 70-, rep. in N.W. Cambodia 70-75.

c/o Ministry of the Interior, Co-operatives and Communal Reforms, Phnom-Penh, Cambodia.

Houchin, John Marvin, B.S.; American business executive; b. 11 Jan. 1909, Jackson, Miss.; s. of John Chambers Houchin and Ada Chamblin Houchin; m. Louise Dobson 1930; two s. one d.; ed. Univ. of Oklahoma.

Joined Phillips Petroleum Co. 33 working in an engineering capacity, later Asst. Gen. Supt. production dept. Bartlesville, Gen. Supt. 51, Chair. Operating Cttee. 56, Dir. and Vice-Pres. 57-62, Exec. Vice-Pres. 62-67, Chair. Exec. Cttee. 67-68, Pres. 68-71, Deputy Chair. and Deputy Chief Exec. Officer 71, Chair. 73; Trustee, Oklahoma Univ. Foundation; Dir. First Nat. Bank, Bartlesville, Trust Co., Tulsa; mem. Board of Dirs. American Petroleum Inst., Mid-Continent Oil and Gas Asscn.

Leisure interests: golf, hunting, fishing, spectator sports.

1529 Hillcrest Drive, Bartlesville, Okla. 74003, U.S.A.

Houghton, Amory, A.B.; American industrialist; b. 27 July 1899, Corning, N.Y.; s. of Alanson B. Houghton and Adelaide L. Wellington; m. Laura DeKay Richardson 1921; three s. two d.; ed. Harvard Univ.

With Corning Glass Works 21-, Exec. Vice-Pres. 28-30,

Pres. 30-41, Chair. Board 41-61, Chair. Exec. Cttee. 61-64, Hon. Chair. of Board 64-71, Chair. Emer. 71-; Dir. Pittsburgh-Corning Corpn., First Nat. City Bank 37-68, Dow Corning Corpn., Metropolitan Life Insurance Co. 38-73; Dir.-Gen. of Operations, War Production Board 42; Deputy Chief Econ. Affairs Mission, London 44; Ambassador to France 57-61; mem. Business Advisory Council Dept. of Commerce 43-; U.S. Council, Int. Chamber of Commerce 45-, Chair. 62-64, Vice-Chair. U.S. Council 62-64; mem. of Exec. Cttee. U.S. Council 64; Pres. Boy Scouts of America 46-51, Hon. Vice-Pres. 51-; Dir. Nat. Educ. Television & Radio Center 61-67, Atlantic Council of the U.S. France America Soc., Fédération des Alliances Françaises aux Etats-Unis, American Soc. of the French Legion of Honour; mem. Advisory Trust Board, First Nat. City Bank 68-71, Advisory Council, State Univ. of N.Y.; Trustee Emer. Inst. for Advanced Study, Princeton, N.J.; several hon. degrees; Order of Merit Bernardo O'Higgins (Chile); Grand Cross of the Legion of Honour (France).

2 South Road, Corning, N.Y.; Corning Glass Works, Corning, N.Y. 14830, U.S.A.

Telephone: 607-962-1234.

Houghton, Amory, Jr., M.B.A.; American executive; b. 7 Aug. 1926; ed. Harvard Univ., Business School.

Served in U.S. Marine Corps 45-46; joined Corning Glass Works 51, Dir. 55, Staff Vice-Pres. 57, Pres. 61-64, Chair. and Chief Exec. Officer 64-; Chair. of Board and Dir. Corning Glass Works of Canada Ltd.; Dir., Dow Corning Corpn., Pittsburgh Corning Corpn., B.F. Goodrich Co., Corhart Refractories Co., New York Telephone Co., Corning Fibre Box Corpn.; Trustee Corning Glass Works Foundation, The Corning Museum of Glass, Episcopal Theological School (Cambridge, Mass.), Nat. Security Industrial Asscn.; mem. Board Nat. Industrial Conf.

33 East 3rd Street, Corning, N.Y. 14830, U.S.A.

Houghton, Arthur Amory, Jr.; American executive; b. 12 Dec. 1906, Corning, N.Y.; s. of Arthur Amory and Mabel Hollister Houghton; m. Nina Rodale 1973; one s. three d. (by previous marriage); ed. St. Paul's School, Concord (N.H.) and Harvard Univ.

Corning Glass Works, Manufacturing Dept. 29, Treas. Dept. 29-30, Asst. to Pres. 30-32, Vice-Pres. 35-42; Pres. Steuben Glass 33-72, Chair. 73-; Dir. Corning Glass Works; fmr. Dir. U.S. Steel Corpn., Past Dir. Nat. Book Cttee. Inc.; Vice-Pres. Corning Museum of Glass; Curator of Rare Books, Library of Congress 40-42; Hon. Consultant in English Bibliography; Trustee and Chair. Emer. Cooper Union N.Y.; Chair. and Pres. Wye Inst. Inc.; Past Chair. and Hon. Trustee, Parsons School of Design, N.Y., Philharmonic Symphony Soc. of N.Y., Inst. of Int. Educ.; fmr. Vice-Chair. Lincoln Center for the Performing Arts, N.Y.; Trustee Emer. Pierpont Morgan Library, Metropolitan Museum of Art, fmr. Pres. and Chair.; Hon. Trustee, N.Y. Public Library; fmr. Trustee, Rockefeller Foundation, U.S. Trust Co.; fmr. Dir. N.Y. Life Insurance Co.; Dir. U.S. English-Speaking Union; mem. Council on Foreign Relations; service in U.S. Air Force (Lieut.-Col.) 42-45; Friedsam Industrial Art Medal 53; Officier, Légion d'Honneur; Commdr. de l'Ordre des Arts et des Lettres; Senior Fellow Royal Coll. of Art; Fellow Royal Soc. of Arts; Knight Most Venerable Order of the hospital of St. John of Jerusalem; Skowhegan School-Gertrude Vanderbilt Whitney Award; hon. degrees from 15 colls. and univs.

715 Fifth Avenue, New York, N.Y. 10022; Home: Wye Plantation, Queenstown, Md. 21658, U.S.A.

Telephone: 212-PL2-1441 (Office).

Houghton of Sowerby, Baron (Life Peer), cr. 74; **Arthur (Leslie Noel) Douglas Houghton,** C.H., P.C.; British trade unionist and politician; b. 11 Aug. 1898; ed. Derbyshire County Secondary School.

General Sec. Inland Revenue Staff Fed. 22-60; mem. Gen. Council, Trades Union Congress 52-60; mem. Civil Service Staff Whitley Council 23-58, Chair. 54-56; Alderman, London County Council 47-49; M.P. 49-74, Chair. Public Accounts Cttee. House of Commons 63-64; Chancellor, Duchy of Lancaster 64-66; Minister without Portfolio 66-67; Chair. Parl. Labour Party April 67-74; Chair. Party Funds Cttee. 75; Labour.

House of Lords, London, S.W.1; Home: 110 Marsham Court, London, S.W.1, England.

Telephone: 01-834-0602.

Hougron, Jean (Marcel); French writer; b. 1 July 1923; ed. Faculty of Law, Univ. of Paris.

Schoolmaster 43-46; commercial employment in export-import firm, Saigon 46-47, lorry driver 47-49, translator in American Consulate 50, news editor Radio France Asie 51; returned to France to write 52; bookseller in Nice 53-54; lived in Spain 58-60; Grand Prix du Roman, Acad. Française 53; Prix Populiste 65.

Publs. *Tu récolteras la Tempête* 50, *Rage Blanche* 51, *Soleil au ventre* 52, *Mort en Fraude* (film) 53, *Les Portes de l'Aventure* 54, *Les Asiates* 54, *Je reviendrai à Kandara* (film) 55, *La Terre du Barbare* 58, *Par qui le scandale* 60, *Le Signe du Chien* 61, *Histoire de Georges Guersant* 64, *Les Humiliés* 65, *La Geule Pleine de Dents, Les Portes de l'Aventure* 70, *L'Homme de Proie* 74.

34 rue Greneta, Paris 2e, France.

Houin, Roger; French professor of law; b. 17 Aug. 1912, Juneaux; m. Gabrielle Kostanjevic 1936; two s. one d.; ed. Univ. de Paris à la Sorbonne and Ecole des Sciences politiques.

Lecturer, Univ. of Lille 39; Prof. Univ. of Rennes 41-57, Dean of Faculty 55-57; Sec.-Gen. Comm. for Reform of Civil Law 45-65; Prof. Faculty of Law, Univ. of Paris 57-, Inst. of Political Studies 58-; Conseiller d'Etat 68-72; mem. of numerous legal orgs. and legal expert on Cttees. of European Econ. Community; Founder-Dir. quarterly *Revue de droit commercial* 48; Co-Dir.-Founder quarterly *Revue de droit européen* 65; Dir. *Bibliothèque de droit commercial* (26 vols.); Officier, Légion d'Honneur and other decorations; Dr. h.c. Univs. of Ghent (five), Brussels and Geneva.

Publs. *Précis de droit commercial* (2 vols.) 5th edn. 74; *Cours de droit commercial* 2nd edn. 69, *Les grands arrêts et la jurisprudence commerciale* 63.

6 rue Coëtlogon, Paris 6e, France.

Telephone: 222-49-61.

Houle, Cyril O., PH.D.; American educationist; b. 26 March 1913, Sarasota, Fla.; s. of John Louis Houle and Annie Hescock Houle; m. Bettie Eckhardt Totten 1947; one s.; ed. Univ. of Florida and Univ. of Chicago.

Department of Education, Univ. of Chicago 39-, Dean of Univ. Coll. 44-52, Prof. of Education 52-; mem. U.S. Nat. Comm. for UNESCO 59-64, Int. Cttee. for Advancement of Adult Education (UNESCO) 61-63, Nat. Acad. of Educ.; Visiting Senior Research Specialist, Oxford Univ. 68; Hon. LL.D. (Syracuse, Florida), D.H.L. (Rutgers, De Paul and N.Y.).

Leisure interests: travel, reading.

Publs. *Adult Education* (with F. W. Reeves and T. Fansler), *The Armed Services and Adult Education* (with others), *Libraries in Adult and Fundamental Education, The University, The Citizen and World Affairs* (with C. A. Nelson), *The Effective Board, The Inquiring Mind, Continuing Your Education, The Design of Education, The External Degree.*

Department of Education, University of Chicago, Chicago, Ill. 60637; Home: 5510 Woodlawn Avenue, Chicago, Ill. 60637, U.S.A.

Telephone: Hyde Park 3-8751 (Home).

Houmann, Borge Kruuse; Danish journalist; b. 26 March 1902, Fredericia; ed. Denmark and Derby Grammar School, England.

Sailor 20; started writing poems and short stories 23; economic dir. of Riddersalen Theatre 33; Man. Dir. of publishing firm Arbejderforlaget 35; mem. of Danish Freedom Council (underground) 43-45; mem. Danish Parliament 45-46; mem. Danish Radioraadet (Danish Broadcasting Council) 46-50; Chief Editor of Communist daily *Land og Folk* 45-54; Dir. publishing firm of Sirius 57; Dr. Phil. h.c. (Univ. of Copenhagen).

Publs. *Huset ved Havet* 23, translation of Whitman's *Leaves of Grass* 27, *Lystgas* (a novel) 32, *Forlis* (poems) 34, *Martin Andersen Nexø, Selected Speeches and Articles,* Vols. 1-3 (Editor) 54, *Drømmen om en ny verden, Martin Andersen Nexø og hans forhold til Sovjetunion* 57, *Martin Andersen Nexø Bibliography* (with notes) Vol. I-II, 61, 67, *Martin Andersen Nexø: Letters* (Editor and annotator) Vol. I 69, Vol. II 71, Vol. III 72, a number of books on Martin Andersen Nexø and many translations from English and German.

Aage Bergsvej 19, DK 8240 Risskov, Denmark.

Telephone: (06) 179549.

Houphouët-Boigny, Félix; Ivory Coast politician; b. 18 Oct. 1905, Yamoussoukro; ed. School of Medicine, Dakar.

President Syndicat Agricole Africain 44; mem. Constituent Assembly 45-46; mem. Nat. Assembly Nov. 46-, re-elected 51 and 56; successively Territorial Councillor for Korhogo, Pres. Territorial Assembly, Ivory Coast, Grand Conseiller for French West Africa; Minister attached to the Prime Minister's Office 56-57; Minister of Health 57-58; Minister of State (Pflimlin Cabinet) May 58, (de Gaulle Cabinet) June 58-Jan. 59, (Debré Cabinet) Jan.-May 59; Pres. Assembly, Ivory Coast Republic 58-59, Pres. Council May 59-Nov. 60; Pres. of the Republic Nov. 60-, concurrently Minister of Foreign Affairs 61, of Interior, Education and Agriculture 63; Pres. of Council of Ministers; Minister of Defence 63-74; Minister-Counsellor to French Govt. 59-60; Pres. Parti Démocratique de la Côte d'Ivoire.

Présidence de la République, Abidjan, Ivory Coast.

Houseman, John; American producer, director, author and actor; b. (as Jacques Haussmann) 22 Sept. 1902, Bucharest, Romania; s. of Georges Haussmann and May Davies Haussmann; m. Joan Courtney 1950; two s.; ed. France and Clifton Coll., England.

Worked on cattle ranch and later bank employee, Argentina 20-22; in grain business London and U.S.A. 22-30; Head of Negro Theatre Project and Project 891 34-37; co-founder Mercury Theatre (with Orson Welles, q.v.) 37; Producer-Dir. Lobero Theatre 41; Chief of Overseas Program Bureau, Office of War Information 42-44; Artistic Dir. American Shakespeare Festival 56-59, Theatre Group at Univ. of Calif., Los Angeles 60-64; Producing Dir. A.P.A. Repertory Co. 66-68; Head of Drama Div., Juilliard School at Lincoln Center 68-, Artistic Dir. The Acting Co. 71-; Nat. Arts Club Medal of Honor 73; Acad. Award, Best Supporting Actor (in *The Paper Chase*) 74; Nat. Book Award nomination for *Run-Through.*

Films produced include: *The Blue Dahlia* 45, *They Live by Night* 46, *Letter from an Unknown Woman* 47, *The Bad and the Beautiful* 52, *Julius Caesar* 53, *Executive Suite* 54, *The Cobweb* 55, *Lust for Life* 56, *All Fall Down* 61, *Two Weeks in Another Town* 62, *This Property is Condemned* 66, *Voyage to America, The World of the Dancer;* operas directed include: *The Devil and Daniel Webster* 39, *Otello* 63, *Tosca* 65, *The Mines of Sulphur* 68, *Antigone* 70, *The Losers* 71, *Lord Byron* 72, *Macbeth* 73; plays directed include: *Four Saints in Three Acts* 34, *Panic* 35, *Valley Forge* 35, *Hamlet* 36, *Liberty Jones* 39, *Lute Song* 47, *King Lear* 50, *Coriolanus* 53, *Murder in the Cathedral, The Three Sisters, The Iceman Cometh, Six Characters in Search of an Author, Antigone, The Seagull, Pantagleize* 67-68, *Chronicles of Hell* 68-69, *Macbeth, Measure for Measure, The Country Girl* 71,

Don Juan in Hell, Clarence Darrow; acted in films: *Seven Days in May* 65, *The Paper Chase* 74, *Rollerball* 75, *Three Days of the Condor* 75; co-author *Citizen Kane* 40, co-adaptor *Jane Eyre* 41 (film scripts); productions for TV include: *The Seven Lively Arts* 57, *Playhouse 90* 58, 59, episodes of *The Great Adventure* series, *Three By Martha Graham* (also narrator).
Publ. *Run-Through* 72.
c/o Juilliard School of the Performing Arts, Lincoln Center Plaza, New York, N.Y. 10023, U.S.A.

Housiaux, Albert, D.RER.POL.; Belgian journalist; b. 1914; ed. Athénée Royal, Ixelles, Brussels Free Univ. Joined staff of *Le Peuple* 37; news bulletin editor I.N.R.; Editorial Sec. *Socialisme*; served in the army and captured during the Second World War; Inspector-Gen. Ministry of Imports 45; Dir.-Gen. *Le Peuple* 48-54, Political Dir. (later Ed.) 54-; mem. Bureau Belgian Socialist Party (with vote); Chevalier Ordre de Léopold, Ordre de la Couronne, Officer of the Order of Merit (Italy).
Office: *Le Peuple*, 29 rue des Sables, Brussels 1; Home: 201 Avenue Rommelaere, Jette-St.-Pierre, Brussels 9, Belgium.

Houston, Clifford Granville, A.M., PH.D.; American educational psychologist; b. 5 March 1903; ed. Univs. of Colorado and Univs. of Columbia and Chicago.
Professor of Education and Psychology, State Junior Coll., Grand Junction 29-31, Pres. 31-37; Dir. Extension Div. and Dean of Summer School Univ. of Colorado 37-42; Dean Extramural Activities, Univ. of Colorado, Boulder 46-47; Dean of Students and Dir. of Student Personnel and Prof. of Education, Univ. of Colorado, Boulder 47-57, Prof. of Educ. 57-71; Pres. Board of Reps. 51-52; Chair. Academic Council Western Personnel Inst. 51-53; mem. Governor's Human Relations Comm. and Chair. of its Research Cttee. 51-53; Ford Fund for the Advancement of Education 51-53; mem. Nat. Advisory Council, Nat. Students' Asscn. 53-58; mem. Nat. Educational Advisory Council, Nat. Asscn. of Manufacturers 54-57; mem. Consulting Cttee. in Management Training, U.S. Veterans Admin., Washington, D.C. 57-60.
3840 Armer Drive, Boulder, Colo., U.S.A.

Houten, Hans Rudolf van, DR. JUR.; Netherlands diplomatist; b. 13 Aug. 1907; ed. Un,v. of Leyden.
Attaché, Neths. Legation, Copenhagen 32-33, Stockholm 33-34, Copenhagen 34-35; Sec. Berlin 35-40; Counsellor Washington 40-45, Brussels 45-48; Head of Foreign Service Dept., Ministry of Foreign Affairs (rank of Minister) 48-51; Minister to Mexico 51-54, Ambassador 54-58; Dir.-Gen. for Political Affairs, Ministry of Foreign Affairs 58-59; Under-Sec. of State for Foreign Affairs 59-63; Ambassador to Austria 64-68; Commdr. Order of Orange-Nassau; Knight Order of the Netherlands Lion; Grand Cross Léopold II of Belgium; Grand Officer of the Belgian Crown; Grand Cross Order of Merit, Austria; and numerous other decorations.
Publ. *International Status of Egypt* 30.
c/o Ministry of Foreign Affairs, The Hague, Netherlands.

Houthakker, Hendrik Samuel; American economist; b. 31 Dec. 1924, Amsterdam, Netherlands; s. of Bernard Houthakker and Marion Houthakker (née Lichtenstein); m. Anna-Teresa Tymieniecka, PH.D. 1955; two s. one d.; ed. Univ. of Amsterdam.
Research Staff mem., Dept. of Applied Econs., Univ. of Cambridge 49-51; on Research Staff, Cowles Comm. for Research in Econs., Univ. of Chicago 52-53; Prof. of Econs., Stanford Univ. 54-60, Harvard Univ. 60-; Snr. Staff Economist, Council of Econ. Advisers 67-68, mem. 69-71; Vice-Pres. Amer. Econ. Asscn. 72; Fellow, Econometric Soc. (Past Pres. and Council mem.), Amer. Statistical Asscn., Nat. Comm. on Supplies and Shortages 75-; John Bates Clark Medal of American

Econ. Asscn. 63; mem. Nat Acad. of Sciences; Corresp. mem. Royal Netherlands Acad. of Sciences; Dr. h.c. Amsterdam 72, Fribourg 74.
Leisure interests: farming, skiing.
Publs. *The Analysis of Family Budgets* (with S. J. Prais) 55, *Consumer Demand in the United States* (with L. D. Taylor) 66, *Economic Policy for the Farm Sector* 67; also articles.
Littauer Center, Harvard University, Cambridge, Mass. 02138, U.S.A.
Telephone: 617-495-2111.

Houtte, Baron Jean van, D. EN D.; Belgian emeritus university professor and politician; b. 17 March 1907, Ghent; s. of Hubert van Houtte; m. Cécile de Stella 1932; one s. three d.; ed. Univ. of Ghent.
Prof. Univ. of Liège 31, and Univ. of Ghent 37; Head of Secretariat, Ministry of the Interior 44-45; co-opted Senator 49-68; Minister of Finance 50-52; Prime Minister Jan. 52-54; Minister of Finance 58-61; Minister of State 66; Hon. Pres. Sabena Airlines; various Belgian and foreign decorations.
Publs. *Traité des sociétés de personnes à responsabilité limitée* 35, 50, 62, *La responsabilité civile dans les transports aériens* 40, *La réparation des dommages de guerre aux biens privés* 48, *Formulierboek voor notarissen* 47, *Principes du droit fiscal belge* 58, 66.
54 Boulevard St. Michel, Brussels, Belgium.
Telephone: 733-62-94.

Hovde, Frederick Lawson, B.CH.E., B.A., M.A.; American educational administrator; b. 7 Feb. 1908; s. of Martin R. and Julia (née Lawson) Hovde; m. Priscilla L. Boyd 1933; one s. two d.; ed. Minnesota and Oxford Univs.
Assistant Director, General Coll., Univ. of Minnesota 32-36; Asst. to Pres., Univ. of Rochester, New York 36-41; Head, London Mission, Office of Scientific Research and Development 41-42; Exec. Asst. to Chair. Nat. Defense Research Cttee., OSRD 42-43; Chief of Rocket Ordnance Research Div., NDRC, OSRD 43-46; Pres. Purdue Univ. 46-71, Pres. Emer. 71-; Chair. Cttee. on Guided Missiles, Research and Devt. Board 47-49; Chair. Bldg. Research Adv. Board Nat. Research Council 50-52; mem. Army Science Advisory Panel, Dept. of Army 52-60; U.S. Mil. Acad. Board of Visitors 65-67; Hon. D.Sc., Hon. D.Eng., Hon. D.H.L., Hon. D.C.L. (Oxon.), Hon. LL.D.; Rhodes Scholarship 29-32; King's Medal for Service in the Cause of Freedom (Gt. Britain) 48; President's Medal for Merit (U.S.A.) 48; Brazilian Order of Southern Cross 68.
Purdue University, Lafayette, Indiana; Home: 1701 Redwood Lane, Lafayette, Indiana 47905, U.S.A.
Telephone: 317-447-0808.

Hoveyda, Amir Abbas, E.M.A., PH.D.; Iranian diplomatist, business executive and politician; b. 18 Feb. 1919; ed. Univs. of Paris and Brussels.
Ministry of Foreign Affairs 42-58, served Paris, Fed. Germany, Teheran, UN, Geneva, Ankara; mem. Board of Dirs. and Head of Admin., Nat. Iranian Oil Co. 58-64; Minister of Finance 64-65; Prime Minister 65-; Sec.-Gen., Head of Political Office, Pres. Exec. Cttee., Nat. Political Resurrection Movt. March 75-.
Office of the Prime Minister, Teheran; Home: No. 5 Kh. Cyrus Ehteshamieh, Darrous, Teheran, Iran.
Telephone: 6161.

Hoveyda, Fereydoun, LL.D.; Iranian diplomatist; b. 21 Sept. 1924, Damascus; ed. Univ. of Paris.
Various positions, Imperial Iranian Embassy, Paris 46-51; Programme Specialist, Mass Communications Dept., UNESCO 52-64; Under-Sec. of State for Int. and Econ. Affairs, Ministry of Foreign Affairs 65-71; Perm. Rep. to UN Aug. 71-; del. to various int. confs. including UN Gen. Assembly 48, 51, 65, UNESCO Confs. 66, 68, 70 and ECOSOC sessions 66-69; Léopold Sédar Senghor Literary Prize 73.

Publs. studies: *Le Plan Septennal Iranien* 48, *La Nationalisation du Pétrole en Iran* 51, *Histoire du Roman Policier* 68; novels: *Les Quarantaines* 62, *L'Aérogare* 65, *Dans une Terre Etrange* 68, *Le Losange* 69, *Les Neiges du Sinai* 73.
Permanent Mission of Iran to United Nations, 622 Third Avenue, 34th Floor, New York, N.Y. 10017, U.S.A.

Hoving, Thomas Pearsall Field, PH.D., M.F.A.; American art gallery director; b. 15 Jan. 1931; ed. The Buckley School, New York, Eaglebrook School, Deerfield, Mass., Exeter Acad., Exeter, N.H., The Hotchkiss School, Lakeville, Conn., and Princeton Univ.
Curatorial Asst., Medieval Art and The Cloisters, Metropolitan Museum of Art 59-60, Asst. Curator 60-63, Assoc. Curator 63-65, Curator of Medieval Art and The Cloisters 65; Commr. of Parks, New York City 66; Admin. of Recreation and Cultural Affairs, New York City 67; Dir., The Metropolitan Museum of Art April 67-; Fellowship, Nat. Council of Humanities 55, Kienbusch and Haring Fellowship 57; Distinguished Citizen's Award, Citizen's Budget Cttee. 67; Hon. LL.D. (Pratt Inst.) 67.
Publs. *Guide to the Cloisters* 62, *Metropolitan Museum of Art Calendar* 66.
150 East 73rd Street, New York City, N.Y. 10021, U.S.A.

Howald, Prof. Oskar, DR. SC. TECH., DIPL. ING. AGR.; Swiss agricultural economist and professor; b. 2 March 1897, Zurich; *m.* Louise Schmid 1924; two s. two d.; ed. Fed. Technical High School, Zurich.
Deputy Dir. Swiss Farmers' Union 29-39, Dir. 39-49; scientific consultant, Tutor in Agricultural Economics, Fed. Technical High School 28-35; Prof. of Farm Management, Farm Accountancy and Agrarian Policy 36-67; Vice-Pres. European Confederation of Agriculture (CEA) 49-59; Pres. Swiss Home Works Corpn. 49-, Agricultural Information Services 44-69; Dr. h.c. Hochschule Vienna 57, Stuttgart 62; Editor *Agrarpolitische Revue* 44-69, *Wirz's Landwirtschaftlicher Taschenkalender* 46-, etc.
Leisure interests: simplification of rural work, rural sociology, viticulture.
Publs. include: *Die Dreifelderwirtschaft im Kanton Aargau* 26, *Besteuerung des ldw. Besitzes u. Einkommens u. der ldw. Organisationen* 27, *Die Organisation der Schlactviehverwertung im Ausland und in der Schweiz* 29, *Überschuldung und Entschuldung der Schweiz. Landswirtschaft* 34, *Einführung in die Agrarpolitik* 46, *Fünfzig Jahre Schweizerischer Bauernverband* 47, *ABC für Agrarpolitik und Agrarwirtschaft* 51, 65, *Schriftenfolge über Landarbeitstechnik in der Schweiz* (11 vols.) 47-67, *Entwicklung und Stand der Forschung auf dem Gebiete der Wirtschaftslehre des Landbaus* 51, *Zukunftsaussichten des bäuerlichen Familienbetriebes* 55, *Die Kleinbauernfrage in Europa* 55, *Bewertung, Buchhaltung und Kalkulation in der Landwirtschaft* 57, *Strukturwandel in der Landwirtschaft* 62, *Bauer und Landwirt in der heutigen Volkswirtschaft* 62, *Schweizerische Landwirtschaft und Schweizer Bauerntum* (Monograph) 63, *Betrachtungen zur Lehre vom bäuerlichen Familienbetrieb* 67, *Landwirtschaftliche Betriebslehre für bäuerliche Verhältnisse. 18e,* 70, etc.
Ståblistrasse 19, 5200 Brugg, Switzerland.
Telephone: 056-41-1955.

Howard, Harry Nicholas, A.B., M.A., PH.D.; American historian; b. 19 Feb. 1902, Excelsior Springs, Mo.; *s.* of Alpheus and Lois A. (Foster) Howard; *m.* Virginia Faye Brubaker 1932; two s.; ed. Univs. of Missouri and California.
Gregory Fellow in History Univ. of Missouri 26-27; Research Asst. in Modern European History Univ. of California 28-29; Asst. Prof. History, Univ. of Okla-

homa 29-30, Miami Univ. 30-37, Assoc. Prof. 37-40, Prof. 40-42; Lecturer Contemporary Problems, Univ. of Cincinnati 37-42; Head, East. European Unit Div. of Ter. Studies, Dept. of State 42-44; mem. Div. Int. Org. Aff. 44-46; Tech. Expert, U.S. Del., UNCIO 45; Adviser, Special Interrogation Comm., Germany 45; Chief N.E. Branch, Div. of Research for N.E. and Africa 46-47; Adviser, Div. of Greek, Turkish, and Iranian Affairs 47-49; Adviser U.S. Del., UNGA 47-50; UN Adviser, Dept. of State, Bureau of Near East, S. Asian and African Affairs 49-56; Acting U.S. Rep. Advisory Comm. UNRWA, Beirut 56-61; Special Asst. to Dir. of UNRWA 62-63; Adviser U.S. Del. UN Balkan Comm. 47-50; Prof. of Middle East Studies, School of Int. Service, American Univ., Washington, D.C. 63-68, Adjunct Prof. 68-; Lecturer U.S. Army War Coll. 70-72; Chair. Middle East Program, Foreign Service Inst., Dept. of State 66, 71-73; Faculty Adviser F.S.I. 66-67; Reserve Consultant, Dept. of State 67-; Assoc. Editor *Middle East Journal* 63-; Chief Consultant Middle East and North Africa, Cincinnati World, Affairs Council 68-69; mem. Middle East Inst., American Historical Asscn. Dacor, Middle East Studies Asscn.
Leisure interests: swimming, walking.
Publs. *The Partition of Turkey, A Diplomatic History 1913-1923,* 31, *Military Government in the Panama Canal Zone* 31 (with Prof. R. J. Kerner), *The Balkan Conferences and the Balkan Entente* 30-35, *A Study in the Recent History of the Balkan and Near Eastern People* 36, *The Problem of the Turkish Straits* 47, *The United Nations and the Problem of Greece* 47, *The General Assembly and the Problem of Greece* 48, *Yugoslavia* (co-author) 49, *Soviet Power and Policy* (co-author) 55, *The King-Crane Commission* 63.
Home: 6508 Greentree Road, Bradley Hills Grove, Bethesda, Md. 20034; Office: American University, Washington, D.C., U.S.A.
Telephone: 365-3693 (Home).

Howard, Jack Rohe; American newspaper and broadcasting executive; b. 31 Aug. 1910; ed. Yale Univ.
Journalist, Tokyo, Shanghai, Indianapolis, Washington 32-35; with radio companies, Knoxville, Washington and New York (now Scripps-Howard Broadcasting Co.) 36-39; Asst. Exec. Ed. Scripps-Howard Newspapers 39-42, 45-48, Gen. Ed. Man. 48-; U.S. Navy 42-45; Pres. E. W. Scripps Co. 53-; Pres., Dir. and mem. Exec. Cttee. Scripps-Howard Broadcasting Co.
200 Park Avenue, New York, N.Y. 10017, U.S.A.

Howard, Trevor Wallace; British actor; b. 29 Sept. 1916; *m.* Helen Cherry; ed. Clifton Coll., Bristol.
Service in 1st Airborne Division 40-43; plays include various Shakespeare plays at Stratford-upon-Avon and The Old Vic, London: *French Without Tears, The Recruiting Officer, Anna Christie, The Devil's General, The Cherry Orchard, Two Stars for Comfort, The Father, Table Number Seven, The Waltz of the Toreadors* 74; films include: *Brief Encounter, The Third Man, An Outcast of the Islands, The Heart of the Matter, Les Amants du Tage, Cockleshell Heroes, The Key, Roots of Heaven, Sons and Lovers, Mutiny on the Bounty, Von Ryan's Express* 66, *The Charge of the Light Brigade* 68, *Ryan's Daughter* 70, *Mary Queen of Scots* 72, *The Offence, Ludwig, A Doll's House* 73, *11 Harrowhouse* 74, *The Visitor, Hennessy* 75; TV plays include: *Hedda Gabler* 62, *The Invincible Mr. Disraeli* (Acad. Award), *Napoleon at St. Helena.*
Rowley Green, Arkley, Herts., England.

Howe, Harold, II; American educator; b. 1918, Hartford, Conn.; *s.* of Margaret Armstrong and Arthur Howe; *m.* Priscilla Foster Lamb 1940; two s. one d.; ed. Yale and Columbia Univs., Univ. of Cincinnati, and Harvard Univ.
History teacher, Darrow School, New Lebanon, New York 40-42; Lt. U.S. Naval Reserve 42-45; History

teacher, Phillips Acad., Andover, Mass. 47-50; Principal, Andover High School and Junior High School 50-53; Principal, Walnut Hills High School, Cincinnati, Ohio 53-57; Principal, Newton High School, Newton, Mass. 57-60; Supt. of Schools, Scarsdale, N.Y. 60-64; Exec. Dir. Learning Inst. of N. Carolina, Chapel Hill, N. Carolina 64-65; U.S. Commr. of Educ. Dec. 65-68; Adviser on Educ., Ford Foundation, India 68-; Vice-Pres. for Educ., Ford Foundation 71-; fmr. Trustee, Vassar Coll., Yale Univ.; Trustee and Vice-Chair. Coll. Entrance Examination Board 63-65; Hon. LL.D. (Univ. of Notre Dame, Shaw Univ., N. Carolina, Princeton Univ., Adelphi Univ., N.Y., St. Louis Univ., Missouri). Leisure interest: fishing.
Ford Foundation, 320 East 43rd Street, New York, N.Y. 10017, U.S.A.
Telephone: 212-573-4730.

Howe, Quincy, A.B.; American editor; b. 17 Aug. 1900, Boston, Mass.; s. of M. A. De-Wolfe Howe and Fanny H. Q. Howe; m. Mary L. Post 1932; one s. one d.; ed. Harvard Univ. and Christ's Coll., Cambridge. Mem. staff Atlantic Monthly Co. 22-28; Editor *Living Age* 29-35; Contributing Editor 35-36; Editor Simon and Schuster Inc., publishers; News commentator Station WQXR, New York 39-41, Columbia Broadcasting System 41-49; with C.B.S. Television 49-50; Assoc. Prof. School of Journalism, Univ. of Ill. 50-54; News Analyst American Broadcasting Co. 54-63; Radio New York World Wide 66-70; Editor of *Atlas: The Magazine of the World Press* 61-65; Pres. Nat. Board of Review of Motion Pictures.
Leisure interests: maritime, cinema, walking, swimming, gardening.
Publs. *World Diary* 29-34, *England Expects Every American To Do His Duty* 37, *Blood is Cheaper than Water* 39, *The News and How to Understand it* 40, *A World History of Our Own Times*, Vol. I 49, Vol. II 53, *Ashes of Victory* 72.
108 East 82nd Street, New York, N.Y. 10028, U.S.A.

Howe, Rt. Hon. Sir (Richard Edward) Geoffrey, Kt., P.C., Q.C., M.P.; British politician; b. 20 Dec. 1926, Port Talbot, Glam.; s. of late B. Edward Howe and of Mrs. E. F. Howe, J.P.; m. Elspeth R. M. Shand 1953; one s. two d.; ed. Winchester Coll. and Trinity Hall, Cambridge.
Called to the Bar, Middle Temple 52, Bencher 69; Deputy Chair. Glamorgan Quarter Sessions 66-70; mem. Parl. for Bebington 64-66, for Reigate 70-74, for East Surrey 74-; Solicitor-Gen. 70-72; Minister for Trade and Consumer Affairs 72-74; Opposition Spokesman for Social Services 74-75, for Treasury and Econ. Affairs Feb. 75-; fmr. Pres. British Overseas Trade Board; Conservative.
Leisure interests: cinephotography, gardening.
House of Commons, London, S.W.1, England.

Howell, Francis Clark, PH.D.; American professor of anthropology; b. 27 Nov. 1925, Kansas City, Mo.; s. of E. Ray and Myrtle M. Howell; m. Betty Ann Tomsen 1955; one s. one d.; ed. Univ. of Chicago.
Instructor in Anatomy, Washington Univ. 53-55; Asst. Prof. of Anthropology, Univ. of Chicago 55-59, Assoc. Prof. of Anthropology 59-62, Prof. of Anthropology 62-70; Prof. of Anthropology, Univ. of Calif., Berkeley 70-; mem. Nat. Acad. of Sciences, American Philosophical Soc.; Fellow American Acad. of Arts and Sciences.
Publs. *African Ecology and Early Man* (ed.) 63, *Early Man* 65, *Earliest man and environments in the Rudolf Basin* (editor) 75; numerous papers on anthropology in professional journals.
Department of Anthropology, University of California, Berkeley, Calif. 94720; Home: 1994 San Antonio, Berkeley, Calif. 94707, U.S.A.
Telephone: 415-642-1393 (Office); 415-524-6243 (Home).

Howell, John Owen, Jr.; American business executive; b. 7 Feb. 1925, Nashville, Tenn.; s. of John Owen and Margaret Lee (née Bowden) Howell; m. Margaret S. Stephens 1946; one s. two d.; ed. Middle Tennessee State Coll.
Joined GENESCO Inc. 47; Pres. Flagg Bros. Div. 58; Pres. Holiday-Wise Div. 61; Dir., mem. Exec. Cttee., mem. Finance Cttee. and Board of Govs. GENESCO Inc., Exec. Vice-Pres. 68-69, Pres. 69-73.
Leisure interests: golf, hunting, reading, sports.
4006 Brush Hill Road, Nashville, Tenn. 37216, U.S.A.

Howells, Herbert Norman, C.H., C.B.E., D.MUS. (OXON.), F.R.C.O., F.R.C.M., HON. R.A.M., HON. F.T.C.L.; British composer; b. 17 Oct. 1892, Lydney, Glos.; s. of Oliver Howells and Elizabeth Burgham; m. Dorothy Eveline Goozee 1920; one s. (deceased), one d.; ed. Royal Coll. of Music.
Prof. Royal Coll. of Music; Dir. of Music, St. Paul's Girls' School 36-62; first John Collard Fellow 31, now John Collard Life Fellow; King Edward Prof. of Music, Univ. of London 54-64, Pres. Royal Coll. of Organists 59; Fellow Royal Coll. of Music; Pres. Incorporated Soc. of Musicians 52; Pres. of Mediaeval and Plainsong Soc. 58; Master of Worshipful Company of Musicians 59; Fellow Royal School of Church Music 63; Hon. D.Mus. Cambridge 61; Hon. Fellow, St. John's Coll., Cambridge 66.
Leisure interests: history and medieval literature.
Works include *Sir Patrick Spens* (for chorus and orchestra), *Requiem* (for unaccompanied choir and soloists), *Sine Nomine, Procession, Puck's Minuet* (all for orchestra), *Pageantry* (suite for brass band), *Hymnus Paradisi* (for soprano and tenor solo, chorus and orchestra), *Missa Sabrinensis* (for four soloists, chorus and orchestra) 54, piano concerto, 'cello concerto, clarinet quintet, and many other chamber music works, songs, organ works; recent works include Concerto for strings, *Howell's Clavichord,* and a new series of church works; *Music for a Prince* (for orchestra); *A Kent Yeoman's Wooing Song* (chorus and orchestra), *An English Mass, Missa "Collegium Regale"* 56, *Missa Aedes Christi* 57, *Three Figures* (brass band) 60, *A Sequence for St. Michael* (chorus, strings and organ) 61, *Stabat Mater* (tenor solo, chorus and orchestra) 63, *The Coventry Mass* 68, *Partita for Organ* 72 (written for the Rt. Hon. Edward Heath, q.v.).
3 Beverley Close, Barnes, London S.W.13; and Royal College of Music, London, S.W.7, England.
Telephone: 01-876-5119.

Howells, William White, D.SC., PH.D.; American anthropologist; b. 27 Nov. 1908, New York; s. of John Mead Howells and Abby MacDougall White; m. Muriel Gurdon Seabury 1929; one s. one d.; ed. St. Paul's School, Concord, N.H. and Harvard Univ.
Assistant Prof. to Prof., Univ. of Wis. 39-54; Editor *American Journal of Physical Anthropology* 49-54; Prof. of Anthropology, Harvard Univ. 54-74, Emeritus 74-; Curator of Somatology, Peabody Museum 55-75, Honorary Curator 75-; Pres. Amer. Anthropological Asscn. 51; mem. Nat. Acad. of Sciences, Amer. Acad. of Arts and Sciences; Corresp. mem. Austrian Acad. of Sciences, Anthropological Socs. of Paris and Vienna, Geographical Soc. of Lisbon; Viking Fund Medal in Physical Anthropology 55.
Publs. *Mankind So Far* 44, *The Heathens* 48, *Back of History* (British edn. *Man in the Beginning*) 54, *Mankind in the Making* 59, rev. edn. 67, *The Pacific Islanders* 73, *Cranial Variation in Man* 73, *Evolution of the Genus Homo* 73.
Peabody Museum, Harvard, Cambridge, Mass. 02138; and Kittery Point, Maine 03905, U.S.A.
Telephone: 617-495-2244 (Mass.); 207-439-1302 (Maine).

Howman, John Hartley; Rhodesian lawyer and politician; b. 11 Aug. 1918, Selukwe; m. Moira W.

Maidman 1946; three *d.*; ed. Plumtree School, Bulawayo.
Partner, Coghlan, Welsh & Guest (law firm); mem. Parl. 62-74; Minister of Internal Affairs, Local Govt. and African Educ. 62-64, of Information, Immigration and Tourism 65-68, of Foreign Affairs, Defence and Public Service 68-74; Grand Officer of the Legion of Merit; Independence Decoration.
c/o Messrs. Coghlan, Welsh & Guest, P.O. Box 53, Salisbury, Rhodesia.

Howson, Hon. Peter; Australian politician and company director; b. 22 May 1919, London; *s.* of Major George Howson, M.C. and Jessie (née Gibson); *m.* Christina Synnot 1956; one *s.*; ed. Stowe School and Trinity Coll., Cambridge.
Fleet Air Arm and R.N.V.R. 40-46; Staff Man. Foy and Gibson Stores Ltd. 50, Dir. 51-55; Pres. Royal Victorian Eye and Ear Hosp. 56-64, Vice-Pres. 74-; Dir. Eagley Mills Ltd. 55, Cleckheaton (Yorkshire) Ltd. 61-64; mem. House of Reps. 55-72; Minister for Air 64-68; Minister assisting the Treas. 66-68; Minister for the Environment, Aborigines and the Arts and Minister responsible for Tourism 71-72; Pres. Australian Deafness Council 74-, Deafness Foundation (Victoria) 74-; Chair. Exec. Cttee. Commonwealth Parliamentary Asscn. 68-70; Fellow, Australian Inst. of Management; Councillor, Australian Inst. of Int. Affairs; Liberal.
Leisure interests: golf, tennis, skiing, bridge.
40 Kensington Road, South Yarra, Melbourne, Victoria 3141, Australia.
Telephone: 24-2935.

Hoxha, Enver; Albanian politician; b. 16 Oct. 1908; ed. Gjirokastra and Korça (Albania) and Faculty of Natural Sciences, Montpellier, France.
Teacher, Tirana and Korça 36-39; founder and leader, Communist Party of Albania Nov. 41, Sec.-Gen. 43-48; led national liberation struggle 39-44, achieved national independence 44; Prime Minister and Supreme Commdr. of Albanian Armed Forces 44-54; Minister of Foreign Affairs 46-53; Sec.-Gen. Party of Labour of Albania 48-54, First Sec. Central Cttee. 54-; Chair. Gen. Council of Democratic Front; mem. Presidium People's Assembly of Albania; Hero of the People (twice); Hero of Socialist Labour; Order of Suvorov (First Class).
Partija e Punes, Tirana, Albania.

Hoyle, Sir Fred, Kt., F.R.S., M.A.; British astronomer and mathematician; b. 24 June 1915, Gilstead, Bingley, Yorks.; *s.* of Ben and Mabel (née Pickard) Hoyle; *m.* Barbara Clark 1939; one *s.* one *d.*; ed. Bingley Grammar School and Emmanuel Coll. and St. John's Coll., Cambridge.
Fellow, St. John's Coll. 39-72, Hon. Fellow 73-; Univ. Lecturer in Mathematics, Cambridge 45-58; Staff mem. Mount Wilson and Palomar Observatories, Calif., U.S.A. 56-62; Plumian Prof. Astronomy and Experimental Philosophy, Cambridge Univ. 58-72, Dir. Inst. of Theoretical Astronomy 66-72; Hon. Prof. of Physics and Astronomy, Manchester Univ. 73-; Visiting Prof. at Large, Cornell Univ. 73-; Visiting Prof. of Astrophysics at Calif. Inst. of Technology, Pasadena 58-; Prof. of Astronomy Royal Institution 69-; Hon. mem. Amer. Acad. of Arts and Sciences 64, Foreign Assoc. Nat. Acad. of Sciences 69; Vice-Pres. Royal Soc. 70-; Pres. Royal Astronomical Soc. 71-73; Mayhew Prizeman 36, Smith's Prizeman 38, Goldsmith Exhibitioner 38, Sr. Exhibitioner Royal Comm. of 1851 38, Kalinga Prize 68, Royal Medal, Royal Soc. 74.
Leisure interests: music and mountaineering.
Publs. *Recent Research in Solar Physics* 49, *Nature of the Universe* 50, *Decade of Decision* 53, *Frontiers of Astronomy* 55, *The Black Cloud* 57, *Ossian's Ride* 58, *A for Andromeda* (television series with John Elliot) 62, *Astronomy* 62, *Fifth Planet* (with Geoffrey Hoyle) 63,

Of Men and Galaxies 64, *Galaxies, Nuclei and Quasars* 65, *October First is too late* 66, *Man in the Universe* 66, *Rockets in Ursa Major* (with Geoffrey Hoyle) 69, *Seven Steps to the Sun* (with Geoffrey Hoyle) 70, *The Molecule Men* (with Geoffrey Hoyle) 71, *From Stonehenge to Modern Cosmology* 72, *The Inferno* (with Geoffrey Hoyle) 72, *Nicolaus Copernicus* 73, *Into Deepest Space* (with Geoffrey Hoyle) 74, *Action at a Distance in Physics and Cosmology* 74, *Highlights in Astronomy* (U.S.)/*Astronomy Today* (U.K.) 75, *Astronomy and Cosmology* 75.
The Royal Society, 6 Carlton House Terrace, London, SW1Y 5AG, England.

Hrabal, Bohumil, LL.D.; Czechoslovak writer; b. 28 March 1914, Brno; ed. Charles Univ., Prague.
Lawyer's clerk, railway worker, insurance agent, travelling salesman, foundry worker, paper salvage worker, stage hand and stage extra 39-62; professional writer 62-; Klement Gottwald State Prize 68.
Publs. short stories: *Perlička na dně* (Pearl at the Bottom, some stories filmed) 63, *Pábitelé* 64, *Inzerát na dům, ve kterém už nechci bydlet* (An Ad. for a House in Which I Don't Want to Live Any More) 65, *Automat svět* (selected stories, some filmed) 66; short novels: *Taneční hodiny pro starší a pokročilé* (Dancing Lessons for Adults and Advanced) 64, *Ostře sledované vlaky* (Closely Observed Trains, film 66) 65, *Morytáty a legendy* (These Premises are in the Joint Care of Citizens) 68.
Na Hrázi 24, Prague 8-Libeň, Czechoslovakia.

Hřebík, Jaromir; Czechoslovak broadcasting official; b. 20 Sept. 1921, Prague; ed. School of Political Studies, Prague.
Correspondent, *Práce*, Moscow 48-53; Deputy Chair. Czechoslovak Cttee. for Radio and Television 53-58; Gen. Dir. Czechoslovak Radio 58-59; Sec. Gen. Int. Radio and Television Org. (OIRT).
OIRT, 151 13 Prague, 5 U Mrázovky 15, Czechoslovakia.

Hruškovič, Miloslav; Czechoslovak engineer and politician; b. 25 Jan. 1925, Pukanec; ed. Faculty of Electrical Engineering, Slovak Tech. Univ., Bratislava.
Deputy Dir. "Slovak Nat. Rising" Works, Žiar nad Hronom 53-62; Dir. Research Inst. of Welding, Bratislava 62-68; Minister of Technology 68; Minister Chair. of Cttee. for Technological and Investment Devt., Fed. Govt. of C.S.S.R. 69-70; Deputy Prime Minister 69-70; mem. Central Cttee. of C.P. of Slovakia 55-58, 62-68, 69-71, 72-; Alt. mem. Cen. Cttee. C.P. of Czechoslovakia 58-62; Alt. mem. Presidium, Central Cttee. of C.P. of Slovakia 62-68; Deputy, Slovak Nat. Council 64-71; mem. Presidium of Cen. Cttee., C.P. of Slovakia 68, 72-, Sec., mem. Secr. 72-, Chair. Econ. Comm. of Cen. Cttee. 72-; mem. Econ. Council 68-70; mem. Cen. Cttee. C.P. of Czechoslovakia 70-, Sec., mem. Secr. 70-72, Chair. Econ. Comm. 70-71, Alt. mem. Presidium 71-, Chair. Scientific Technical Devt. Comm. 71-; Deputy to House of Nations, Fed. Assembly 70-71, Deputy to House of the People 71-; mem. Technical Cttee., Int. Inst. of Welding 64-70; Order of Victorious February 73, Order of the Repub. 75, and several other awards.
Publs. include: *Method of Automatic Regulation of the Working Stress of Aluminium Electrolysers* 59 (patented 59).
Central Committee of the Communist Party of Czechoslovakia, nábř. Kyjevské brigády 12, Prague, Czechoslovakia.

Hryniewiecki, Jerzy; Polish architect; b. 21 April 1908, Dorpat (Tartu); *s.* of Bolesław and Janina Koźniewska; *m.* Alina Stanisławska; ed. Warsaw Polytechnic.
Senior Asst. Warsaw Polytechnic 38-39; prisoner of war 39-45; Deputy Prof., Warsaw Polytechnic 45, Prof. 59-, Dir. Inst. of Architectural Designs; Head of Section,

Warsaw Reconstruction Bureau 45; Prof. Szczecin Higher School of Engineering 48; fmr. Pres. Polish Asscn. of Architects; Chair. Industrial Projects Designing 65-; Vice-Chair. Cttee. of Architecture and Town Planning, Polish Acad. of Sciences; Hon. mem. R.I.B.A., A.I.A., Soc. of Architects of Brazil and Mexico; numerous decorations and prizes, including Gold Medal, Paris Exhbn. 37, State Prize, 1st Class 55.

Works include many industrial, sports and exhibition buildings such as Polish Printing Centre, Tenth Year Stadium (both in Warsaw) and pavilions, etc., Exhibition of Regained Territories (Wrocław).

Leisure interest: cars.

Ul. Skolimowska 6, 00-795 Warsaw, Poland.

Hsiang Chung-hua; Chinese army officer.
Deputy Political Commissar, People's Liberation Army Armoured Force 53, Political Commissar 58; Lieut.-Gen. 55; Deputy Chief of Staff PLA 71-; Alt. mem. 10th Cen. Cttee. of CCP 73.
People's Republic of China.

Hsiao Ching-kuang; Chinese army officer; b. 1904, Changsha, Hunan; ed. Hunan Provincial Normal School, Sun Yat-sen Univ. and Red Army Coll., Moscow, U.S.S.R.
Joined Communist Youth League and CCP 20; Instructor Whampoa Mil. Acad. 24; Political Commissar 5th Army Corps 31; on Long March 34-35; Commdr. Cavalry, Red Army 38; Alt. mem. 7th Cen. Cttee. of CCP 45; Commdr. Hunan Mil. District, People's Liberation Army 49; Commdr. PLA Navy 60-; Vice-Minister of Nat. Defence 54-; mem. 8th Cen. Cttee. of CCP 56, 9th Cen. Cttee. 6, 10th Cen. Cttee. 73.
People's Republic of China.

Hsieh Ch'en-hua; Chinese army officer.
Commander Shansi Mil. District, People's Liberation Army 67-; Vice-Chair. Shansi Revolutionary Cttee. 68, Chair. 69; First Sec. CCP Shansi 71; Alt. mem. 10th Cen. Cttee. of CCP 73.
People's Republic of China.

Hsieh Hsueh-kung; Chinese party official.
Shansi Provincial People's Govt. 50-52; Vice-Minister of Foreign Trade 52-58; Pres. Peking Foreign Trade Coll. 54-58; Sec. CCP Hopei 58-68; Sec. N. China Bureau 63-68; Chair. Tientsin Revolutionary Cttee. 67; mem. 9th Cen. Cttee. of CCP 69; First Sec. CCP Tientsin 71; mem. 10th Cen. Cttee. of CCP 73.
People's Republic of China.

Hsien Heng-han; Chinese party official.
Regimental Political Commissar 34; Deputy Political Commissar Tsinghai Mil. District, People's Liberation Army 49; Lieut.-Gen. 55; Political Commissar Lanchow Mil. Region, PLA 57-; Chair. Kansu Revolutionary Cttee. 68; mem. 9th Cen. Cttee. of CCP 69; First Sec. CCP Kansu 71; mem. 10th Cen. Cttee. of CCP 73.
People's Republic of China.

Hsin Chun-chieh; Chinese army officer.
Commander Hupeh Mil. District, People's Liberation Army 70-; Vice-Chair. Hupeh Revolutionary Cttee. 71.
People's Republic of China.

Hsiung Hsiang-hui; Chinese diplomatist; b. 1920; ed. Case Western Reserve Univ., Cleveland, Ohio.
Chargé d'Affaires, U.K. 62-65; now Sec. for Foreign Affairs; del. to UN Gen. Assembly 71.
Ministry of Foreign Affairs, Peking, China.

Hsiung Shih-i; Chinese author; b. 14 Oct. 1902; ed. Teachers Coll., Nat. Univ. Peking.
Assoc.-Man. Chen Kwang Theatre, Peking 22; Prof. Agricultural Coll., Nanchang 23; Editor, Commercial Press, Shanghai 26, Special Editor 28; Prof. Chung Shan Univ., Nanchang 27; Man.-Dir. Pantheon Theatres Ltd., Shanghai 29; Prof. Min Kuo Univ., Peiping 30; Sec. China Society, London 33, Hon. Sec.

35; Chinese Del. to Int. P.E.N. Congress 34, 35, 38, 39, 40, 47; to Int. Theatre Inst. Congress 48; Lecturer Cambridge Univ. 50-53; Dean, Coll. of Arts, Nanyang Univ. 54-55; Managing Dir. Pacific Films Co. Ltd., Hong Kong 55-; Chair. Board of Dirs. Standard Publishers Ltd., Hong Kong 61-; Pres. Tsing Hua Coll., Hong Kong 63-; Hon. Ph.D.
Publs. in English: *Lady Precious Stream* 34, *The Romance of Western Chamber* 35, *The Professor from Peking* 39, *The Bridge of Heaven* 43, *The Life of Chiang Kai-Shek* 48, *The Gate of Peace* 49, *The Story of Lady Precious Stream* 50, *Book of Chinese Proverbs* 53; translations into Chinese of B. Franklin's *Autobiography* 23, of Barrie's and Shaw's plays, and Hardy's novels 26-33.
41 Buckland Crescent, London, N.W.3, England; Tsing Hua College, Kowloon, Hong Kong.

Hsu Chin-ch'iang; Chinese government official.
Assistant to Minister of Petroleum Industry 56-59; Dir. of Lanchow Oil Refinery 58; Vice-Minister of Petroleum Industry 63; Acting Minister of Chemical Industry 68; Minister of the Coal Industry 75.
People's Republic of China.

Hsu Ching-chung, D.AGRIC.; Chinese politician; b. 19 July 1907, Taipei; s. of Teh An Hsu and Shyh Iuan Hung; m. Hwang Chen; two s. one d.; ed. Taipei Acad., Taipei Imperial Univ.
Professor, Nat. Taiwan Univ. 45-47; Dir. Agricultural and Forestry Admin., Taiwan Provincial Govt. 47-49; Commr. Dept. of Agriculture and Forestry, Taiwan Provincial Govt. 49-54, Commr. 54-57; mem. Cen. Planning and Evaluation Cttee., China Nationalist Party 55-61, Deputy Sec.-Gen. Cen. Cttee. 61-66; Minister of the Interior 66-72; Vice-Premier of Exec. Yuan June 72-; mem. Standing Cttee., Taiwan Land Bank 46-67, China Farmers' Bank 67-72; Medal of Clouds and Banner.
Leisure interests: horticulture, reading, painting, golf.
Publs. several studies on agricultural problems in Taiwan.
30, Lane 63, Liang Ning Street, Taipei, Taiwan.
Telephone: 772957.

Hsu Hsiang-ch'ien; Chinese politician and fmr. army officer; b. 1902, Wu-tai, Shansi; ed. Taiyuan Normal School, Whampoa Mil. Acad.
Director Political Dept., Student Army 26; joined CCP 27; Workers' Leader in Canton Uprising 27; C.-in-C. 4th Front Army 31; Deputy Commdr. 129th Div. 39; mem. 7th Cen. Cttee. of CCP 45; Commdr., Political Commissar 1st Army Corps 49; Deputy Commdr. N. China Region, People's Liberation Army 49-54; Chief of Staff PLA 49-54; Vice-Chair. Nat. Defence Council 54-; Marshal PLA 55; mem. 8th Cen. Cttee. of CCP 56; Vice-Chair. Standing Cttee., Nat. People's Congress 65-; mem. 9th Cen. Cttee. of CCP 69, 10th Cen. Cttee. 73; Vice-Chair. Mil. Affairs Cttee., CCP Central Cttee. 75-.
People's Republic of China.

Hsu Peh Yuan; Chinese international finance official; b. 1 Jan. 1903, Chekiang; m.; five c.; ed. Coll. of Commerce, Nat. Southeastern Univ. and Univs. of Chicago, Illinois and Calif.
Assistant Gen. Man. China Electric Corpn. 33-34; Deputy Dir.-Gen. Postal Remittance and Savings Bank, Shanghai 34-35; Man. Bank of Communications 35-39; mem. People's Political Council 38-40; Deputy Sec.-Gen. and Sec.-Gen. Joint Board of Four Govt. Banks 39-48; Vice-Minister of Finance 46-48; Deputy Gov. Cen. Bank of China 49-50; Chair. Bank of China 49-51; Chair. Bank of Taiwan 51-52; Commr. of Finance, Taiwan Provincial Govt. 53-54; Minister of Finance 54-58; Chair. Finance Cttee., Kuomintang 54-70; Chair. Foreign Exchange and Trade Comm. 50-51, 53-54, 55-58, 63-69; Dean Economics Dept., Nat.

War Coll. 58-70; Exec. Dir. IMF 70-72; Board Chair. CUTICO 73-.
c/o CUTICO, 150 Nanking East Road, 2nd Section, Taipei, Taiwan.

Hsu Shih-yu; Chinese army officer; b. 1906, Honan.
Commander 9th Army 33; Chief Commdr. of Cavalry 35; Brigade Commdr. 40; Commdr. Chinglo Mil. District 42, Ponai Mil. District 44; Commdr. 11th Army Corps, 3rd Field Army 48; Commdr. Shantung Mil. District, People's Liberation Army 50; Deputy Commdr. 3rd Field Army, PLA 54; mem. Nat. Defence Council 54-; Col.-Gen. 55; Alt. mem. 8th Cen. Cttee. of CCP 56; Commdr. Nanking Mil. Region, PLA 57-73; Vice-Minister of Nat. Defence 59-; Sec. E. China Bureau, CCP 66; Chair. Kiangsu Revolutionary Cttee. 68; mem. Politburo, 9th Cen. Cttee. of CCP 69; First Sec. CCP Kiangsu 71; mem. Politburo, 10th Cen. Cttee. of CCP 73; Commdr. Canton Mil. Region, PLA 74-.
People's Republic of China.

Hsueh Shao-ch'ing; Chinese army officer.
Major-General Air Force, People's Liberation Army 55; Vice-Minister of Third Ministry of Machine Building 60-65; Deputy Commdr. PLA Air Force 71-.
People's Republic of China.

Hu Nim; Cambodian politician; b. 1929.
Former deputy Nat. Assembly in Prince Sihanouk's party, Sangkum Reastr Nyum (Popular Socialist Community); left Sangkum party, went underground and became active in *Khmers Rouges* 67; Minister of Information and Propaganda Royal Govt. of Nat. Union of Cambodia (GRUNC) 70-76 (in exile 70-75, in Phnom-Penh 75-76); mem. Politburo Nat. United Front of Cambodia (FUNC) 70-, rep. in S.W. Cambodia 70-75.
c/o Ministry of Information and Propaganda, Phnom-Penh, Cambodia.

Hu Peng-fei; Chinese naval officer.
Deputy Chief of Staff of Navy, People's Liberation Army.
People's Republic of China.

Hu Wei; Chinese army officer.
Deputy Commdr., Shansi People's Liberation Army 67; Vice-Chair. Shensi Provincial Revolutionary Cttee. 68; Alt. mem. 9th Central Cttee. of CCP 69, 10th Cen. Cttee. of CCP 73; Deputy Chief of Gen. Staff, PLA 74.
People's Republic of China.

Hua Kuo-feng; Chinese politician.
Vice-Governor of Hunan 58-67; Sec. CCP Hunan 59; Vice-Chair. Hunan Revolutionary Cttee. 68, Chair. 70; mem. 9th Cen. Cttee. of CCP 69; First Sec. CCP Hunan 70; Political Commissar Canton Mil. Region, People's Liberation Army 72; First Political Commissar Hunan Mil. District, PLA 73; mem. Politburo, 10th Cen. Cttee. of CCP 73; Deputy Premier and Minister of Public Security 75-76, Acting Premier Feb.-April 76, Premier April 76-; First Vice-Chair. Cen. Cttee. of CCP April 76-.
Office of the Premier, State Council, Peking, People's Republic of China.

Huang Chen; Chinese diplomatist; b. 1907.
Deputy Dir. 18th Div., Shansi-Hopei-Shantung Border Region Army 44; after war Deputy Political Dir. in mil. admin. areas; Amb. to People's Republic of Hungary 50-54; Amb. to Republic of Indonesia 54-61; Deputy Foreign Minister 61-64; Amb. to France 64-73; Head of Mission, U.S.A. 73-; rep. at the Afro-Asian Conference 55.
Mission of the People's Republic of China, Washington, D.C., U.S.A.

Huang Chieh; Chinese civil servant; b. 2 Nov. 1903, Hunan Province; s. of Huang Tao; m. Hou Meng-liao; one d.; ed. Mil. Acad., Army War Coll. and Nat. Defence Coll.
Commandant, Cen. Training Corps 45-48; Vice-Minister

of Nat. Defence 48-49; Gov. of Hunan, concurrently Commdg. Gen. 1st Army 49; Commdg. Gen. Chinese Troops stationed in Indo-China 49-53; Taipei Garrison Command 53-54; C.-in-C. Chinese Army, concurrently C.-in-C. Taiwan Garrison Gen. H.Q. 58-62; Gov. Taiwan Province 62-69; Minister of Nat. Defence 69-72; Gen. Special Adviser to Pres. on Mil. Strategy 72-; numerous decorations from China, U.S.A., Thailand, Philippines, Spain, Iran, Iraq, Korea and Venezuela.
213 Antung Street, Taipei, Taiwan.

Huang Ching-yao; Chinese army officer.
Deputy Commdr. Heilungkiang Mil. District, People's Liberation Army 59; Commdr. Shensi Mil. District, PLA 67-; Vice-Chair. Shensi Revolutionary Cttee. 68; Sec. CCP Shensi 71.
People's Republic of China.

Huang Hua; Chinese diplomatist; b. 1913, Hopei Province; ed. in Peking.
Former Dir., Foreign Affairs Bureau of Tientsin, Nanking and Shanghai; later Dir., West European Dept., Ministry of Foreign Affairs; Amb. to Ghana 60-66, to Egypt 66-70, to Canada April-Nov. 71; Perm. Rep. to UN 71-.
Permanent Mission of the People's Republic of China to United Nations, 155 West 66th Street, New York, N.Y. 10023, U.S.A.

Huang Ou-tung; Chinese party official; b. *circa* 1907, Ping-hsiang, Kiangsi.
Regimental Commdr. 129th Div. 39, Brigade Commdr. 45; Gov. of Liaoning 49-55, 58-68; Mayor of Shenyang 52-54; Sec. CCP Liaoning 54-57, First Sec. 57-58, Second Sec. 58-68; Alt. mem. 8th Cen. Cttee. of CCP 56; Sec. N.E. Bureau, CCP 62-68; criticized and removed from office during Cultural Revolution 68; Vice-Chair. Liaoning Revolutionary Cttee. 73; Sec. CCP Liaoning 73-.
People's Republic of China.

Huang Shao-ku; Chinese politician; b. 9 June 1901; ed. National Peking Normal Univ.
Secretary-Gen. of Exec. Yuan 49-54; Vice-Premier, Exec. Yuan 54-58, 66-69; Minister of Foreign Affairs 58-60; Amb. to Spain 60-62; Sec.-Gen. Nat. Security Council 67-.
10, Lane 85, Sungkiang Road, Taipei, Taiwan.

Huant, Ernest Albin Camille; French doctor, writer, philosopher and sociologist; b. 29 Oct. 1909, Vouziers, Ardennes; s. of Alphonse Huant and Hélène Potier; m. Odette Mazoyer 1942; one s. one d.; ed. Lycée de Charleville, Louis le Grand and Faculté de Médecine, Paris.
Medical radiologist, Paris hospitals 43; Pres. Centre d'Etudes des Problèmes de l'Homme 60; mem. Soc. d'Economie Politique, Paris 58-; Scientific Adviser to Laboratoires 57-; mem. Int. Cttee. and French Del. to Int. Soc. for Cybernetic Medicine 65; Lauréat de l'Institut de France 64-65; Pres. de la Société d'études philosophiques des Sciences de la nature 67; Pres. du Centre International de Cyto-Cybernétique 67, Pres. and Founder of Centre Int. Humanae Vitae 68; Chevalier Légion d'Honneur; Carnegie Foundation Medal (U.S.A.); Sorbonne Thesis Prize 33; Prix de l'Acad. de Médecine for *Les Traitements Milotiques du Cancer* 58, and *Les Maladies de Société* 61; Prix de l'Acad. des Sciences Morales et Politiques for *Florence et Rome* and Prix Littré (Union Int. des Ecrivains Médecins) 65.
Leisure interests: Roman history, Florentine art.
Publs. *Les Radiations et la Vie* 42, *Déterminisme et Finalités* 46, *Connaissance du Temps* 51, *Biologie et Cybernétiques* 54, *Credo de Jean Rostand* 57, *L'Anti-Masse* 57, *Du Biologique au Social* 57, *Milieu et Adaptation* 59, *Les Maladies de Société* 61, *Le Péché contre la Chair* 61, *Naître ou ne pas Naître* 63, *A.D.N. Recherches*

expérimentales et Cliniques 64, *Florence et Rome* 64, *Economie et Cybernétique* 65, *Voyage en Assuro-Socyalie* 65, *Masses-Morale-Machines* 67, *Le Troisieme Trium-virat* 67, *Les Pressions du Nouveau Temporel* 68, *Les Structures Intelligibles du Réel* 68, *L'Unité Romaine de l'An 1000: Othon III* 71, *Non à l'Avortement* 72, *La Nouvelle Face de Méduse* 74, *Cybernétique des 3 "E": Economie, Environnement, Ecologie* 75, *Temporalité, Finalité, Survie, Analyse Psycho-Cybernétique* 75, *Les étranges courses du Colonel d'Hourdoff* 76.
9 avenue Niel, Paris 17e, France.
Telephone: 380-28-72.

Hubbert, Marion King, B.S., M.S., PH.D.; American geologist and geophysicist; b. 5 Oct. 1903, San Saba, Tex.; s. of William Bee Hubbert and Cora Virginia Lee; m. Miriam Graddy Berry 1938; ed. Weatherford Coll., Tex. and Univ. of Chicago.
Assistant Geologist, Amerada Petroleum Corpn. 27-28; Teaching Asst. Univ. of Chicago 28-30; Instructor in Geophysics, Columbia Univ. 31-41; Geophysicist, Ill. State, and U.S. Geological Surveys 31-37; Snr. Analyst, U.S. Board of Econ. Warfare, Washington 42-43; Research Geophysicist, Shell Oil Co., Houston 43-45, Assoc. Dir. of Research 45-51, Chief Consultant (Gen. Geology), Shell Oil Co. and Shell Devt. Co., Houston 51-64; Visiting Prof., Geology and Geophysics Stanford Univ. 62-63, Prof. 63-68; Research Geophysicist, U.S. Geological Survey 64-; Regents' Prof., Univ. of Calif., Berkeley 73; mem. Cttee. on Geoscience and Man, Int. Union of Geological Sciences 73-; mem. Nat. Acad. of Sciences, American Acad. of Arts and Sciences and others; Hon. Life mem. Soc. of Exploration Geophysicists; Hon. mem. American Asscn. of Petroleum Geologists 74, Canadian Soc. of Petroleum Geologists 74; Arthur L. Day Medal of Geological Soc. of America 54; Anthony F. Lucas Gold Medal Award, American Inst. of Mining, Metallurgical and Petroleum Engineers 71; Penrose Medal, Geological Soc. of America 73; D.Sc. h.c. (Syracuse Univ.) 72.
Leisure interests: reading, conversation, music, experimentation.
Publs. *Theory of Scale Models as Applied to the Study of Geologic Structures* 37, *The Theory of Ground-Water Motion* 40, *Exploratory Study of Faults in the Cave in Rock and Rosiclare Districts (Illinois) by the Earth-Restivity Method* 44, *Strength of the Earth* 45, *Line Integral Method of Computing Gravimetric Effects of Two-Dimensional Masses* 48, *Energy from Fossil Fuels* 49, *Mechanical Basis for Certain Familiar Geologic Structures* 51, *Entrapment of Petroleum under Hydrodynamic Conditions* 53, *Mechanics of Hydraulic Fracturing* (with David G. Willis) 57, *Role of Fluid Pressure in Mechanics of Overthrust Faulting* (with William W. Rubey) 59, *Energy Resources* 62, 69, *Are we Retrogressing in Science?* 63, *Critique of the Principle of Uniformity* 67, *Degree of Advancement of Petroleum Exploration in the United States* 67, *Application of Hydrodynamics to Oil Exploration* 67, *The Theory of Ground-Water Motion and Related Papers* 69, *Energy Resources for Power Production* 70, *The Energy Resources of the Earth* 71, *Structural Geology* 72, *Survey of World Energy Resources* 73, *U.S. Energy Resources, A Review as of 1972* 74, *World Energy Resources* 74.
U.S. Geological Survey, Reston, Va. 22092; Home: 5208 Westwood Drive, Westmoreland Hills, Washington, D.C. 20016, U.S.A.
Telephone: 703-860-6426 (Office); 301-229-7798 (Home).

Hubbs, Carl L(eavitt), A.M., PH.D.; American biologist; b. 18 Oct. 1894, Williams, Ariz.; s. of Charles L(eavitt) and Elizabeth Goss Hubbs; m. Laura C. Clark 1918; two s. one d.; ed. Stanford Univ. and Univ. of Mich.
Assistant Curator, Ichthyology and Herpetology, Field Museum of Natural History 17-20; Curator of Fishes and Instructor to Prof., Univ. of Mich. 20-44;

Prof. of Biology, Scripps Inst. of Oceanography, Univ. of Calif., San Diego 20-67, Prof. Emer. of Biology 67-; Dir. Inst. for Fisheries Research, Mich. 30-35; Field Rep., U.S. Dept. of Interior 39-40; mem. Nat. Acad. of Sciences; Hon. mem. Ichthyological Soc. of Japan; Russell Award, Univ. of Mich. 29; Joseph Leidy Award and Medal, Philadelphia Acad. of Natural Sciences 64; Fellow Award and Medal, Calif. Acad. of Sciences 66; Gold Medal for Conservation, San Diego Zoological Soc. 70; Shinkishi Hatai Award and Medal, Japan Science Asscn. 71, Award of Excellence, American Fisheries Soc. 73; Scientist of the Year, San Diego Soc. of Natural History 74; Outstanding Conservationist Award, Nat. Underwater Parks and Reserves Asscn. 74; Man-of-the-Year, Amer. Cetological Soc. 74; Special Award for 80th Birthday, Ichthyological Soc. of Japan 74.
Leisure interest: travel.
Publs. Co-author: *Methods for the Improvement of Michigan Trout Streams* 32, *Minnows of Michigan* 36, *The Small-mouthed Bass* 38, *Improvement of Lakes for Fishing,* 38, *Fishes of the Great Lakes Region* 47, 64, *Paleohydrophy and Relict Fishes of the North-Central Great Basin* 74; over 500 articles and notes.
Scripps Institution of Oceanography, University of California, La Jolla, Calif. 92037; Home: 2405 Ellentown Road, La Jolla, Calif. 92037, U.S.A.
Telephone: 452-2117 (Office); 453-0238 (Home).

Hubel, David Hunter, M.D.; American professor of neurobiology; b. 27 Feb. 1926, Windsor, Ont.; s. of Jesse H. Hubel and Elsie M. Hunter; m. Shirley R. Izzard 1953; three s.; ed. McGill Univ.
Professor of Neurophysiology, Harvard Medical School 65-67, George Packer Berry Prof. of Physiology and Chair. Dept. of Physiology 67-68, George Packer Berry Prof. of Neurobiology 68-; mem. Nat. Acad. of Sciences, Leopoldina Acad.; Ferrier Lecturer 71.
Leisure interests: music, photography, astronomy, Japanese.
Publs. articles in scientific journals.
Department of Neurobiology-B, Harvard Medical School, 25 Shattuck Street, Boston, Mass. 02115; Home: 98 Collins Road, Waban, Mass. 02168, U.S.A.
Telephone: 617-734-3300 Ext. 648 (Office); 617-527-8774 (Home).

Huber, Karl, PH.D.; Swiss government official; b. 18 Oct. 1915, Häggenschwil; s. of Carl Huber and Mathilde Haessig; m. Elizabeth Fink 1945; one s. two d.; ed. primary school and high school, St. Gall, and Univ. of Berne.
Entered Fed. Admin. 41, mem. staff of Gen. Secr. of Ministry of Political Econ.; Sec.-Gen. Ministry of Political Econ. 54; Fed. Chancellor of Swiss Confederation 67-.
Leisure interests: history, swimming, walking.
Federal Chancellery, Swiss Confederation, 3003 Berne, Switzerland.
Telephone: 031-61-37-01.

Huchel, Peter; German writer; b. 3 April 1903, Lichterfelde, Berlin; s. of Friedrich Huchel and Marie Zimmermann; m. Monica Nora Rosenthal 1953; one s. one d.; ed. Humboldt-Universität zu Berlin, Albert-Ludwigs-Universität, Freiburg-im-Breisgau and Universität Wien.
Freelance writer 25-45, 62-; lived in France 26-28; travelled in Balkans and Turkey 30-32, U.S.S.R., England, Netherlands, Belgium, Italy, Bulgaria, Czechoslovakia and Poland 52-60; Dir. and Arts Dir. Berliner Rundfunk 45-48; Chief Editor *Sinn und Form* (literary magazine) 49-62; mem. Group 47; mem. German Acad. of Arts, Berlin; Ehrenmitglied der Freien Akademie der Künste, Hamburg; Mitglied der Akademie der Künste, West Berlin; Lyrikpreis der Zeitschrift *Kolonne* 32, Nationalpreis 51, Theodor-Fontane-

Preis der Mark Brandenburg 55, Plakette der Freien Akademie der Künste, Hamburg 59, Berliner Kunstpreis für Literatur (Fontane-Preis) 63, Preis der jungen Generation, Hamburg 65, Grosser Kunstpreis des Landes Nordrhein-Westfalen 68.
Leisure interests: painting, cats.
Publs. include: *Poems* 48, *Poems* 49, *Dvanact Noci* 58, *Poems* 59, *Chausseen, Chausseen* 63, *Silnice, Silnice* 64, *Die Sternenreuse* 67, *Wiersze* 67, *Unter dem Sternbild des Hercules* 68.
c/o Suhrkamp Verlag, Postfach 4229, 6000 Frankfurt a.M., Federal Republic of Germany.

Huddleston, Rt. Rev. (Ernest Urban) Trevor, M.A.; British ecclesiastic; b. 15 June 1913; ed. Christ Church, Oxford.
Ordained Deacon 36, Priest 37; Curate, St. Mark's, Swindon 36-39; professed Community of the Resurrection, Mirfield 41; Prior and Priest-in-Charge, Sophiatown, Orlando, and Pimville, Johannesburg 43, Provincial of the Community of the Resurrection, South Africa 49-56; Novice-Master, Community of the Resurrection, England 56-58; Prior, London Community of the Resurrection 58-60; Bishop of Masasi, Tanzania 60-68; Suffragan Bishop of Stepney 68-; Vice-Pres. Anti-Apartheid Movement 69-; Trustee, Runnymede Trust 72-; Hon. D.D. (Aberdeen Univ.), Hon. D.Litt. (Lancaster Univ.).
Publs. *Naught for Your Comfort* 56, *The True and Living God* 64, *God's World* 66.
400 Commercial Road, London, E.1, England.
Telephone: 01-790 4382.

Huddleston, Walter D., B.A.; American politician; b. 15 April 1926, Cumberland County, Kentucky; s. of W. F. Huddleston; m. Jean Pearce 1947; two s.; ed. Jeffersontown High School, Ky. and Univ. of Kentucky.
State Senator, Kentucky 65, 71; Chair. Democratic Caucus, Ky. Gen. Assembly, twice Majority Leader of Ky. Senate; U.S. Senator for Ky. 72-, mem. Agriculture and Govt. Operations Cttees., 93rd Congress.
Leisure interests: tennis, golf.
3327 Dirksen Building, U.S. Senate, Washington, D.C. 20510; Home: 4139 27th Street, North Arlington, Va. 22207, U.S.A.
Telephone: (202) 224-2542 (Office); (703) 527-4148 (Home).

Hudon, L. Denis, M.A.; Canadian financial executive; b. 21 Dec. 1924; ed. Laval Univ., Quebec, and Toronto Univ.
Economic Policy Div., Dept. of Finance, Ottawa 48-51; Sec. (Financial), Perm. Canadian Mission to North Atlantic Treaty Org. (NATO) 52-54; Int. and Econ. Div. (Int. Programmes and Contributions), Dept. of Finance, Ottawa 54-60; Dir. Policy and Planning Coordination, External Aid Office 60-61; Alt. Dir. Int. Monetary Fund, Int. Bank for Reconstruction and Devt., Int. Devt. Asscn. 61-64, Exec. Dir. for Canada, Ireland and Jamaica 65-68; Deputy Dir.-Gen. External Aid Office 67-68; Vice-Pres. (Planning) Canadian Int. Devt. Agency (fmrly. External Aid Office) 68-71; Asst. Sec. to Cabinet (Econ. Policy) Privy Council Office Feb. 71-Dec. 71; Deputy Sec. to Cabinet (Operations) Privy Council Office 71-; Financial Counsellor, Canadian Embassy, Washington 61-64; Dir. Int. Programmes Div., Dept. of Finance, Ottawa 64-66.
Cabinet (Operations) Privy Council Office, Ottawa, Canada.
Telephone: 992-8427.

Hudson, Havelock Henry Trevor; British underwriter; b. 4 Jan. 1919, Hong Kong; s. of Savile E. Hudson and Dorothy Hudson (née Cheetham); m. 1st Elizabeth Home 1944 (dissolved 1956), two s.; m. 2nd Cathleen Blanch Lily 1957, one s. one d.; ed. Rugby School.
Merchant service 37-38; joined Lloyd's 38; war service

39-45, Royal Hampshire Regiment (Major) 39-42, 9th Parachute Battalion 42-44; mem. Cttee. Lloyd's Underwriters' Asscn. 63, mem. Cttee. Lloyd's 65-68, 70-73, Deputy Chair. 68, 71, 73, Chair. Jan. 75-; mem. Exec. Board Lloyd's Register of Shipping 67-; mem. Working Party under Lord Cromer on Conditions of Underwriting Membership of Lloyd's 68; Chair. Arvon Foundation 73-; Vice-Pres. Chartered Insurance Inst. 73-.
Leisure interest: shooting.
Lloyd's, Lime Street, London, EC3M 7HA; Home: The Old Rectory, Stanford Dingley, Near Reading, Berkshire, RG7 6LX, England.
Telephone: (01) 623-7100 (Office); Bradfield (073528) 346 (Home).

Hudson, Thomas Charles, C.B.E., C.A.; British business executive; b. 23 Jan. 1915, Sidcup, Kent, England; s. of Charles B. and Elsie E. (née Harris) Hudson; m. Lois A. Johnson 1944 (divorced); one s. one d.; ed. Middle High School, Nova Scotia.
Articled to Nightingale Hayman, Nova Scotia 35-40; Lieut. Royal Canadian Naval Volunteer Reserve 42-46; joined IBM 46, Man. Dir. IBM (U.K.) Ltd. 54-65; Dir. of Finance and Corporate Planning, The Plessey Co. Ltd. 66-68; Chair. and Man. Dir. T. C. Hudson Associates Ltd., Management Consultants 68-72; mem. GLC 70-73; Chair. International Computers (Holdings) Ltd. 72-.
Leisure interests: tennis, gardening, skiing.
International Computers Ltd., ICL House, Putney High Street, London, S.W.15; Home: Highgate House, Merton Lane, London, N6 6NA, England.
Telephone: 01-340-9018 (Home).

Hudson, Sir William, K.B.E., F.R.S., B.SC.(Eng).; British engineer; b. 27 April 1896, Nelson, New Zealand; s. of Dr. James Hudson Nelson and Beatrice Hudson (Andrew) Nelson; m. Ann Eileen Trotter 1926; two d.; ed. Nelson Coll., New Zealand, Univs. of London and Grenoble.
Former Engineer, Sir W. G. Armstrong-Whitworth & Co. Ltd., Public Works Dept., New Zealand, Sir Alexander Gibb & Partners, Metropolitan Water, Sewerage and Drainage Bd., Sydney; Commr. Snowy Mountains Hydro-Electric Authority, Cooma, N.S.W. 49-67; Australasian Eng. Award 57, Kernot Memorial Medal 59; Fellow, Univ. Coll. London 61-; Hon. mem. Australasian Inst. of Mining and Metallurgy 61-; Hon. mem. of the Institution of Engineers, Australia; LL.D. h.c. (Australian Nat. Univ.) 62; Hon. Fellow the Royal Australian Inst. of Architects 68, Hon. Dr. Eng. (Univ. of Melbourne) 68.
Leisure interests: yachting, trout fishing, climbing.
39 Flanagan Street, Garran, A.C.T. 2605, Australia.
Telephone: Canberra 815137.

Hüe de la Colombe, Jean; French metals executive; b. 22 March 1915; ed. Ecole Polytechnique.
Director and General Manager USINOR (Union Sidérurgique du Nord et de l'Est de la France), Chair., Chief Exec. 73-; Vice-Pres., Dir.-Gen. Denain Nord-Est Longwy 73-; Chair. Solmer 72-; Dir. Vallourec, Vice-Pres.; Chevalier, Légion d'Honneur.
USINOR S.A., 14 rue d'Athènes, 75 Paris 9e, France.
Telephone: 874-32-15.

Huebner, Robert Joseph; American virologist; b. 23 Feb. 1914, Cincinnati (Cheviot), Ohio; s. of Joseph and Philomena (Brickner) Huebner; m. Grace Berdine Hoffman 1939; three s. six d.; ed. Xavier Univ., Univ. of Cincinnati and St. Louis Univ. School of Medicine.
Intern U.S. Public Health Service Hospital (U.S.P.H.S.) (U.S. Coast Guard) 42-43; Medical Officer, Coast Guard, Alaska Command 43-44; Commissioned Officer, U.S.P.H.S. Lab. of Infectious Diseases, Nat. Microbiological Inst. 44-49, Chief Section on Virus and

Rickettsial Diseases 49-56; Chief Lab. of Viral Diseases, Nat. Inst. of Allergy and Infectious Diseases 56-68; Chief Viral Carcinogenesis Branch, Nat. Cancer Inst. 68-; mem. Nat. Acad. of Sciences; Pasteur Medal 65; Distinguished Service Medal, Public Health Service 66; Howard Taylor Ricketts Award 68; Nat. Medal of Science 69; Kimble Methodology Award 70; Rockefeller Public Service Award 70; Guido Lenghi Award, Accad. Naz. dei Lincei, Rome 71; Hon. LL.D. (Univ. of Cincinnati) 65; D.Sc. h.c. (Edgecliff Coll., Cincinnati) 70; Hon. D.Sc. (Univ. of Parma) 70; Dr. h.c. (Univ. of Leuven) 73.
Publs. Numerous articles in professional journals.
Office: National Institutes of Health, Bethesda, Md.; Home: R.F.D., Ijamsville, Md., U.S.A.
Telephone: 301-496-3301.

Huerta Diaz, Vice-Admiral Ismael; Chilean naval officer; b. 13 Oct. 1916; m. Guillermina Wallace Dunsmore Aird 1942; two s. two d.; ed. Sacred Heart School, Valparaíso, Naval Acad., Ecole Supérieure d'Electricité, Paris, Naval Polytechnic Acad., Chile.
Successive posts in Chilean Navy include, Dir. of Armaments, Dir. of Instruction, Dir. of Scientific Investigation, Dir. of Naval Polytechnic Acad., Dir. of Shipyards, Dir.-Gen. of Army Services; Prof. of Electronics, Univ. of Concepción 54, 55, 56; Prof. of Radionavigation, Catholic Univ. of Valparaíso 62-67; mem. Org. Cttee., Pacific Conf., Viña del Mar 70, Pres. Centre of Pacific Studies 70-72; Minister of Public Works 73, of Foreign Affairs 73-74; Perm. Rep. to UN 74-; Dir. Compañía de Acero del Pacífico (CAP) 70, 71, 72; Pres. Nat. Transport Cttee. 72; mem. Coll. of Chilean Engineers, Inst. of Mechanical Engineers of Chile; Decoration of Pres. of the Repub. (Chile), Grand Officer Order of Léopold II (Belgium), Gran Cruz de la Orden del Libertador San Martín (Argentina), Gran Cruz Extraordinaria de la Orden Nacional al Mérito (Paraguay), Medall Kim-Kank (Republic of Viet-Nam).
Publs. *The Role of the Armed Forces in Today's World* 68, and various technical articles.
Permanent Mission of Chile to United Nations, 809 United Nations Plaza, 4th Floor, New York, N.Y. 10017, U.S.A.

Huet, Philippe Emile Jean, D. EN D. ET SC. POL.; French economist and civil servant; b. 17 March 1920, Paris; s. of Paul Huet and Marcelle Weill; m. Antoinette Ripert 1950; five c.; ed. Ecole Saint-Louis de Gonzague, Sorbonne and Law Faculty, Paris, Ecole des Sciences Politiques, Paris.
Studied at Inspectorate-Gen. of Finance 46; Adviser to Office of the Pres. of Council 47-48, to Office of the Minister of Defence 49, to the Office of the Minister of Finance 50-51; Head of Finance and Defence Budgets Div., NATO 51-56; Dir. de Cabinet of Minister of Econ. and Financial Affairs 56-57; Financial Counsellor to French Embassy, London 57-62; Dir.-Gen. for Internal Trade and Prices, Ministry of Econ. and Finance 62-68; Auditor Bank of France 62-71; Dir.-Gen., Head of Mission for the rationalization of budget choices 68-71; Insp.-Gen. of Finance 72-; Consultant OECD Council 72-; Pres. Management Board SEITA 74-.
Leisure interests: gardening, pottering about.
Publs. *La Politique Economique de la Grande-Bretagne depuis 1945* 69, *L'Expérience Française de Rationalisation des Choix Budgétaires* 73.
SEITA, 53 quai d'Orsay, 75007 Paris; and 19 rue de Franqueville, 75016 Paris; Home: 10 avenue d'Eylau, 75116 Paris, France.
Telephone: 555-91-50 (SEITA); 524-87-26 (OECD); 553-29-84 (Home).

Huet, Pierre, D. en D.; French civil servant; b. 12 Nov. 1920, Paris; m. Catherine Viénot 1944; one s. two d.; ed. Paris Law Faculty and Ecole des Sciences Politiques.

Special Asst., French Govt. Refugee Del. 40, Asst. to Sec. of State, Ministry of Food 44; Junior mem. Conseil d'Etat, mem. Legal Cttee. of French Union 46; Asst. to Sec.-Gen., Cttee. for European Economic Co-operation 47; Legal Adviser, OEEC 48; Gen. Counsel, OEEC 56; Dir.-Gen. European Nuclear Energy Agency 58-; Sec.-Gen. Council of State 66-70; Councillor of State 70; Chair. Board, Asscn. Technique pour l'Energie Nucléaire 65, Board, Centre d'Informatique Juridique 71-; Vice-Chair. European Atomic Forum (FORATOM) 73; Commdr. Ordre de Léopold (Belgium); Grosses Goldene Ehrenzeichen für Verdienste (Austria), Chevalier, Légion d'Honneur, Officier, Ordre Nat. du Mérite.
128 boulevard Malesherbes, 75017 Paris, France.

Huggins, Charles B., B.A., M.D.; American professor of surgery and cancerologist; b. 22 Sept. 1901, Halifax, Canada; s. of Charles Edward and Bessie (Spencer) Huggins; m. Margaret Wellman 1927; one s. one d.; ed. Acadia and Harvard Univs.
Houseman in surgery, Univ. of Michigan 24-26, Instructor 26-27; Instructor in Surgery, Univ. of Chicago 27-29, Asst. Prof. 29-33, Assoc. Prof. 33-36, Prof. 36-; Dir. Ben May Laboratory for Cancer Research 51-69; mem. Nat. Acad. of Sciences 49, William B. Ogden Distinguished Service Prof. 62, American Philosophical Soc. 62; Hon. mem. Royal Soc. of Medicine 56; Hon. Fellow, Royal Coll. of Surgeons, Edinburgh 58, London 59, Amer. Coll. of Surgeons 63, Royal Coll. Surgeons, Canada 73; Chancellor, Acadia Univ. 72; Orden Pour le Mérite (Federal Republic of Germany), Orden El Sol del Perú; numerous gold medals and prizes; Charles L. Mayer Award, Nat. Acad. of Sciences 44, Francis Amory Prize 48, Ferdinand Valentine Award 62; Gold Medal Soc. Int. d'Urologie 47, Walker Prize, Royal Coll. of Surgeons, England 61, Albert Lasker Award for Clinical Research 63, Gold Medal in Therapeutics, Worshipful Soc. of Apothecaries of London 66, Gairdner Award, Toronto 66, Nobel Prize for Medicine 66.
Ben May Laboratory for Cancer Research, University of Chicago, 950 East 59th Street, Chicago, Illinois 60637, U.S.A.

Huggins, Edwin Virgil, PH.B., LL.B.; American business executive; b. 28 Sept. 1907; ed. Yale Coll., Yale Law School.
Admitted to Bar, N.Y. State 34; Assoc. Attorney, N.Y. 32-40, Attorney, Philadelphia 40-43; Joined Westinghouse Electric Corpn. as Attorney 43, Head N.Y. Office Law Dept. 45-51, Corporate Sec. 48-51, 54-57, Vice-Pres. 53-61, Chair. Exec. Cttee. 58-61, Exec. Vice-Pres. Associated Activities 61-63, Dir. 51-; Chair. and Dir. Westinghouse Broadcasting Co. Inc. and subsidiaries 54-63; Exec. Dir. Metropolitan Airlines Cttee. 66-67; Chair., Pres., Dir. Gulf States Land & Industries Inc. 68-69; Dir. and mem. Exec. Cttee. Canadian Westinghouse Co. Ltd.; Dir. Canadian Westinghouse Int. Co. Ltd.; Dir. and Vice-Chair. Industria Eléctrica de México, S.A.; Pres., Trustee and mem. Exec. Cttee., Nat. Security Industrial Asscn.
22 Canterbury Lane, Summit, N.J. 07901, U.S.A.

Hughes, Rt. Hon. Cledwyn, P.C., M.P., LL.B.; British politician; b. 14 Sept. 1916, Holyhead, Anglesey; s. of Rev. and Mrs. H. D. Hughes; m. Jean Beatrice Hughes 1949; one s. one d.; ed. Holyhead Grammar School and Univ. Coll. of Wales, Aberystwyth.
Solicitor 40; R.A.F.V.R. 40-45; mem. Anglesey County Council 46-52; M.P. Anglesey 51-, Chair. Welsh Parl. Party 53-54, Welsh Labour Group 55-56, mem. Cttee. of Public Accounts 57-64; Minister of State for Commonwealth Relations 64-66; Sec. of State for Wales 66-68; Minister of Agriculture, Fisheries and Food April 68-June 70; Vice-Chair. Parl. Labour Party March-Oct. 74, Chair. Oct. 74-; Hon. LL.D. (Wales) 70;

Hon. Freedom, Beaumaris 72, Freeman of Anglesey 76; Labour.
Leisure interests: walking, reading, writing.
House of Commons, London, S.W.1, England; and Swynol Le, Trearddur, Anglesey, Wales.
Telephone: Trearddur 860544.

Hughes, Harold Everett; American politician; b. 10 Feb. 1922, Ida Grove, Iowa; s. of Lewis C. Hughes and Etta Kelly Hughes; m. Eva M. Mercer 1941; **three** d.; ed. State Univ. of Iowa.
Engaged in transport and insurance 46-58; mem. Iowa Commerce Comm. 58-63, Chair. 59-60, 61-62; Gov. of Iowa 63-69; Senator from Iowa 69-74; mem. Exec. Cttee. Nat. Govs. Conf. 65-67; Chair. Democratic Govs. Conf. 66, 67, Midwest Democratic Conf. of Senators; mem. Senate Cttee. on Labor and Public Welfare 69-74, on Banking and Currency 69-71, on Armed Services 71-74, on Veterans' Affairs 71-74; mem. Nat. Comm. on Marihuana and Drug Abuse 70-, Select Cttee. on Equal Educational Opportunity 70-71; Pres. Int. Council on Alcohol and Addictions 72-; Vice-Chair. Democratic Comm. on Party Structure and Delegate Selection 69-72; numerous hon. degrees; Democrat.
Leisure interests: fishing, hunting, reading, music.
813 Carrie Court, McLean, Va. 22101, U.S.A.

Hughes, Howard Robard; American executive, aviator and film producer; b. 24 Dec. 1905; ed. Rice Inst., Houston and California Inst. of Technology.
Established in plane of his own design land-plane speed record 35, U.S. transcontinental record 37, world flight record 38; world's largest plane 47; Pres. Hughes Tool Co. (renamed Summa Corpn.), Hughes Aircraft Co., Air West; owns extensive property in Nevada; films produced include *Scarface, Hell's Angels, The Outlaw*; Harmon Trophy 38, Collier Trophy 39, Octave Chanute Award 40, Congressional Medal 41.
[*Died 5 April 1976.*]

Hughes, Richard, O.B.E.; British writer; b. 19 April 1900, Weybridge; s. of Arthur Hughes and Louisa Grace Hughes (née Warren); m. Frances C. R. Bazley 1932; two s. three d.; ed. Charterhouse and Oriel Coll., Oxford.
Poet, playwright, novelist and literary critic; co-founder Portmadoc Players; sometime Vice-Chair. Welsh Nat. Theatre Ltd.; sometime Gresham Prof. in Rhetoric; author world's first radio play; Admiralty 40-45; F.R.S.L.; Hon. mem. American Acad. and Inst. 63; Hon. D.Litt. (Univ. of Wales) 56.
Leisure interests: travel, sailing.
Publs. *The Sisters' Tragedy* 22, *Gipsy-Night and Other Poems* 22, *The Man Born to be Hanged* 23, *A Comedy of Good and Evil* 23, *Danger* 24, *Plays* 24, *Confessio Juvenis* (collected poems) 26, *A Moment of Time* (collected stories) 26, *A High Wind in Jamaica or The Innocent Voyage* (novel) 29, *The Spider's Palace* (children's stories) 31, *In Hazard* (novel) 38, *Don't Blame Me!* (children's stories) 41, *The Administration of War Production* (in *Official History of the War*) (with J. D. Scott) 56, *The Human Predicament* (Vol. I, *The Fox in the Attic*) (novel) 61, *Gertrude's Child* (children's story) 66, *The Human Predicament* (Vol. II, *The Wooden Shepherdess*) (novel) 73.
c/o Chatto and Windus, London, W.C.2, England.
[*Died 28 April 1976.*]

Hughes, Richard, LL.B.; American lawyer and politician; b. 9 Aug. 1909; ed. St. Charles Coll., St. Joseph's Coll. and New Jersey law school.
Private law practice, Trenton 32-39; Asst. U.S. Attorney for New Jersey 39-45; Mercer County Judge 48-53, Superior Court of N.J. 53-57, Judge, Appellate Div., New Jersey 57; private law practice 57; Gov. of New Jersey 62-70; Partner Hughes, McElroy, Connell, Foley & Geiser 70-; LL.D. h.c. (St. Joseph's Coll., Rutgers

Univ., Seton Hall Univ., St. Peter's Coll., Jersey City); Democrat.
24 Commerce Street, Newark, N.J., U.S.A.

Hughes, Ted; British poet; b. 17 Aug. 1930, Mytholmroyd, W. Yorkshire; m. 1st Sylvia Plath (died 1963), two d.; 2nd Carole Orchard 1970; ed. Cambridge Univ. Somerset Maugham Award 60, Int. Poetry Prize, City of Florence 69, Queen's Medal for Poetry 74.
Publs. *The Hawk in the Rain* 57, *Lupercal* 60, *Meet My Folks* 61, *Selected Poems: Thom Gunn and Ted Hughes* 62, *How the Whale Became* 63, *The Earth Owl and Other Moon People* 63, *Nessie the Mannerless Monster, Selected Poems of Keith Douglas* (Editor) 64, *Wodwo* 67, *Poetry in the Making* 67, *The Iron Man* 68, *Crow* 70, *A Few Crows* 70, *Crow Wakes* 70, *Shakespeare's Poem* 71, *Eat Crow* 71, *Prometheus on His Crag* 73, *Spring, Summer, Autumn, Winter* 74, *Cave Birds*.
Faber & Faber, 3 Queen Sq., London, W.C.1, England.

Hůla, Dr. Václav; Czechoslovak politician; b. 21 Sept. 1925, Skryje; ed. School of Economics, Prague.
Office of the Pres. of the Repub. 48-53; Govt. Presidium 53-65; Deputy Minister-Chair., State Comm. for Finance, Prices and Wages 65-68; Minister in charge of State Price Office 68; Sec. Bureau for directing Party work in the Czech lands, Central Cttee., C.P. of Czechoslovakia 68-69; Deputy Prime Minister 69-; Minister of Planning 69-71; Chair. Econ. Council 69-70, State Planning Comm. 71-; Chair. Czechoslovak section of Czechoslovak-Soviet Comm. for Econ., Scientific and Tech. Co-operation 74-; mem. Cen. Cttee. C.P. of Czechoslovakia 69-, Alt. mem. of Presidium of Cen. Cttee. of C.P. of Czechoslovakia 69-75; mem. of Presidium; Deputy to House of the People Fed. Assembly 71-; Order of Victorious February 73, Order of the Repub. 75.
Office: Presidium of the Czechoslovak Government, Prague 1, nábř. kpt. Jaroše 4, Czechoslovakia.

Hull, Gen. John Edwin; American army officer; b. 26 May 1895, Greenfield, Ohio; s. of Joseph M. Hull and Mary Ann Mealey Hull; m. Sara Lucile Davis 1919; ed. Miami Univ. (Ohio), Graduate Infantry School, Command & Staff School, War Coll.
Commissioned U.S. Infantry 17, served through all grades to General 51, Brigadier Gen. 45, Major Gen. 48; War Dept. Gen. Staff 42-44, Asst. Chief of Staff 44-46; Commanding Gen., Army Forces Pacific and Hawaiian Dept. 46-48 (also C.O. Task Force 7 responsible for Atomic Tests at Eniwetok 47-48); Commanding Gen. U.S. Army Pacific 48-49; Dir. Weapons System Evaluation, Defense Dept., Washington 49-51; Vice-Chief of Staff 51-53; C.-in-C. Far East Command, C.-in-C. UN Forces in the Far East and Gov. Ryukyu Islands 53-55; Pres. Manufacturing Chemists' Asscn. 55-63; decorations include D.S.M., Silver Star, Legion of Merit, Hon. C.B.E., Hon. D.Mil.Sc. (Pennsylvania), Hon. LL.D. (Miami Univ., Ohio).
Leisure interest: golf.
3133 Connecticut Avenue, Washington, D.C., U.S.A.
Telephone: NOrth 7-5325.

Hull, Field-Marshal Sir Richard Amyatt, G.C.B., D.S.O., M.A., LL.D.; British army officer; b. 7 May 1907, Cosham, Hants; s. of late Major-Gen. Sir Amyatt Hull, K.C.B.; m. Antoinette de Rougemont 1934; one s. two d.; ed. Charterhouse and Trinity Coll., Cambridge.
Joined 17th/21st Lancers 28; Commanded 17th/21st Lancers 41, 12th Infantry Brigade 43, 26th Armoured Brigade 43, 1st Armoured Div. 44, 5th Infantry Div. 45; Commdt. Staff Coll., Camberley 46-48; Dir. of Staff Duties, War Office 48-50; Chief Army Instructor, Imperial Defence Coll. 50-52; Chief of Staff, G.H.Q., Middle East Land Forces 52-54; G.O.C. British Troops in Egypt 54-56; Deputy C.I.G.S. 56-58; C.-in-C. Far East Land Forces 58-61; Chief, Imperial Gen. Staff 61-

65; A.D.C. (Gen.) to the Queen, Dec. 61-64; Chief of Defence Staff 65-67; Col. Commdt. R.A.C. 68-71; Pres. Army Benevolent Fund 68-71; Constable H.M. Tower of London 70-; Deputy Lieut., Devon 73; Dir. Whitbread and Co. Ltd.
Leisure interests: fishing, shooting.
Beacon Downe, Pinhoe, Nr. Exeter, Devon, England.

Hulme, Hon. Sir Alan Shallcross, K.B.E., F.C.A.; Australian politician; b. 14 Feb. 1907, Sydney; m. 1938; two s. one d.; ed. North Sydney Boys High School.
Honorary Treas. King's Univ. Coll. 44-49; Pres. Queensland Div. Liberal Party of Australia 46-49, 62-63; mem. House of Reps. 49-61, 63-72; mem. Commonwealth Parl. Public Accounts Cttee. 53-58; Chair. Special Commonwealth Cttee. investigating Depreciation under Income Tax Acts 55, Commonwealth Immigration Planning Council 55-58; Minister of Supply 58-61; Dir. Chandlers (Aust.) Ltd., J. B. Chandler Investment Co. Ltd. 52-58, 62-63; Postmaster-Gen. 63-72; Vice-Pres. of Exec. Council 66-72.
Highland Road, Eudlo, Queensland, Australia.

Hulst, Hendrik Christoffel van de, PH.D.; Netherlands astronomer; b. 19 Nov. 1918, Utrecht; m. Wilhelmina Mengerink 1946; two s. two d.; ed. Utrecht Univ.
Post-Doctoral Fellow Chicago Univ. 46-48; Lecturer in Astronomy Leiden Univ. 48-52, Prof. of Astronomy 52-; Pres. Comm. 34 (Interstellar Matter) Int. Astronomical Union 52-58, Nederland Astronomen Club 53-56, Cttee. on Space Research (COSPAR) 58-62; Chair. Netherlands Comm. for Geophysical and Space Research; Vice-Chair. European Space Research Org. (ESRO) 60-65, Chair. 68-70; mem. Royal Neths. Acad. of Sciences; Eddington Medal, Royal Astronomical Soc. (U.K.) 55, Draper Medal, Nat. Acad. of Sciences (U.S.A.) 56, Rumford Medal, Royal Soc. (U.K.) 64.
Publs. *A Course of Radio Astronomy* 51, *Phaenomenologie en Natuurwetenschap* (with C. A. van Peursen) 53, *Light Scattering by Small Particles* 57; numerous articles and papers, particularly on interstellar matter.
Sterrewacht Leiden, Huygens Laboratorium, Wassenaarseweg 78, Leiden 2405; Sterrewacht 8, Leiden, Netherlands.
Telephone: 071-148333 (Office).

Hulton, Sir Edward George Warris, Kt.; British periodical publisher and writer; b. 29 Nov. 1906; ed. Harrow, Brasenose Coll., Oxford.
Conservative candidate 29, 31; called to Bar Inner Temple; created Knight 57; Freeman of the City of London; Chair. and Man. Dir. Hulton Publications Ltd.
Publs. *The New Age* 43, *When I Was a Child* 52, *Conflicts* 66.
Flat 3, 22 St. James's Square, London, S.W.1, England.

Hulugalle, Herbert, M.V.O.; Ceylonese company director and journalist; b. 10 March 1899, Kurunegala, Ceylon; s. of Mr. and Mrs. W. J. Hulugalle; m. Lillian de Soysa 1926 (deceased); five s. two d.; ed. St. Thomas' Coll., Colombo, and Ceylon Law Coll.
Editor, Ceylon Daily News 31-48; Dir. of Information, Ceylon Govt. 48-54; Amb. to Italy 54-59; Chair. of Comm. on Information and Broadcasting 66; Chair. Ceylon Advisory Board, Grindlays Bank 69; Grand Officer Italian Order of Merit; Knight Grand Cross of St. Silvester (Vatican).
Leisure interests: writing, gardening, swimming.
Publs. *British Governors of Ceylon, Ceylon of the Early Travellers, Introducing Ceylon, Life and Times of D. R. Wijewardene, History of Colombo, A Guide to Ceylon, Biography of D. S. Senanayake, Sri Lanka's first Prime Minister*.
25 Anula Road, Colombo 6, Sri Lanka.
Telephone: 82072.

Humaidan, Dr. Ali; diplomatist; b. 20 Sept. 1931, Bahrain; ed. univs. of Baghdad and Paris.
Deputy Rep. of Kuwait to UNESCO 67-69; Prof. of Political Science, Univ. of Kuwait 69-70; Legal Adviser to the Abu Dhabi Govt. 71-72; Permanent Rep. of the United Arab Emirates to UN 72-.
Permanent Mission of United Arab Emirates to United Nations, 866 Second Avenue, New York, N.Y. 10017, U.S.A.

Human, Cornelis J. F.; South African businessman; b. 6 Oct. 1922, Reitz, O.F.S.; m. 1949; two s. one d.; ed. Reitz High School and Stellenbosch Univ.
Worked as clerk, Federale Volksbeleggings Beperk (The Federale Group) 47, later Sec. Johannesburg Branch, Gen. Man. 59-66, Vice-Chair. and Man. Dir. 66-; Dir.-Gen. Mining and Finance Corpn. Ltd., Trust Bank of Africa Ltd., Marine Products Ltd., Siemens S.A. Ltd.; mem. Atomic Energy Board; Councillor, Univ. of Stellenbosch.
Leisure interests: gardening, golf.
P.O. Box 2911, Johannesburg; Home: Carse O'Gowrie Road 2, Parktown, Johannesburg, South Africa.
Telephone: 838-3921 (Office); 44-4048 (Home).

Humblet, Antoine; Belgian politician; b. 28 Dec. 1922, Serinchamps; m.; nine c.; ed. Bastogne, Namur and Catholic Univ. of Louvain.
Founder of forestry and timber enterprise, Haversin; Founder Union des Exploitants Forestiers et Scieurs du Sud-Est de la Belgique, Centre Belge du Bois; Local Councillor, Alderman, Serinchamps 52-58; Councillor, Namur 61-68; Founder Econ. Office of Namur Prov. 61; mem. CERW, Vice-Pres. 71; mem. Chamber of Reps. 68-71, Senate 71-; Sec. of State for Budget 73-74; Minister of Nat. Educ., French Sector 74-; Christian Social Party.
Ministère de l'Education Nationale, 155 rue de la Loi, 1040 Brussels, Belgium.

Hume, H.E. Cardinal (George) Basil, S.T.L. (Fribourg); British teacher and ecclesiastic; b. 2 March 1923, Newcastle upon Tyne; s. of the late Sir William Hume and of Lady Hume; ed. Ampleforth Coll., York, St. Benet's Coll., Oxford, and Fribourg Univ., Switzerland.
Ordained as a Catholic priest 50; Senior Master in Modern Languages, Ampleforth Coll., York 52-63; Housemaster of St. Bede's 55-63; Prof. of Dogmatic Theology at Ampleforth Abbey 55-63; Magister Scholarum, English Benedictine Congregation 57-63; Abbot of Ampleforth 63-76; Archbishop of Westminster March 76-.
Leisure interests: squash, angling.
Archbishop's House, Westminster, London, S.W.1, England.
Telephone: 01-834 4717.

Humes, John P.; American lawyer and diplomatist; m. Jean C. Schmidlaap 1948; six s.; ed. St. Paul's School, Concord, N.H., Princeton Univ. and Fordham Law School.
Admitted to New York State Bar 48; associated with Messrs. Shearman & Sterling 48-55; Partner, Messrs. Humes, Andrews & Botzow 56-69; Amb. to Austria 69-75; Dir. Fiduciary Trust Co. of N.Y. 60-69, Barker, Carver & Morrell Inc. 60-69; Founder and Pres. The Humes Foundation Inc.; mem. American Bar Asscn., Int. Bar Asscn. etc.; trustee or mem. numerous other orgs.
708 Third Avenue, Suite 2201, New York, N.Y. 10017, U.S.A.

Humo, Avdo; Yugoslav politician; b. 1914; ed. Mostar and Belgrade Univ.
Member Fed. Exec. Council and fmr. Chair. Cttee. Nat. Development Plan of Fed. Exec. Council; Chair. Cttee. for Econ. Relations with Foreign Countries of Fed. Exec. Council 62-; mem. Parl., Central Cttee.

Yugoslav League of Communists, Fed. Cttee. for Nuclear Energy 60-; Maj.-Gen. of Reserve; Chair. of Fed. Council for Co-ordination of Scientific Activities 63-67; mem. of Presidency Yugoslav League of Communists 67-69; mem. of Council of Fed. Commission of Presidency Yugoslav League of Communists for Culture 69-; mem. of Conference Yugoslav League of Communists 69-; 1941 Partisan Commemoration Medal, Orders of Nat. Hero, Nat. Liberation, Meritorious Service to the People, 1st Class, Bravery.
Council of Federation, Bulevar Lenjina 2, Novi Beograd, Yugoslavia.
Telephone: 332-590.

Humphrey, Air Chief Marshal Sir Andrew Henry, G.C.B., O.B.E., D.F.C., A.F.C.; British air force officer; b. 10 Jan. 1921, Edinburgh; s. of late John Humphrey, C.B.E. and Agnes Beatson-Bell; m. Agnes Stevenson Wright 1952; ed. Bradfield Coll., R.A.F. Coll., Cranwell.
Has served at home and overseas, Royal Air Force 40-; Senior Instructor R.A.F. Coll., Manby 53-54; R.A.F. Staff Coll. 55; Station Commdr. R.A.F. Station Akrotiri, Cyprus 59-61; Imperial Defence Coll. 62; Air Officer Commdg. H.Q. Air Forces, Middle East 65-67 (mentioned in despatches, Aden 67); Air mem. for Personnel, Ministry of Defence 68-70; Air Officer C.-in-C. R.A.F. Strike Command 71-74; Chief of Air Staff April 74-Aug. 76.
Ministry of Defence (Air), Whitehall, London, S.W.1; Home: The Old School House, Evenlode, Moreton-in-March, Glos., England.
Telephone: Mo.-in-M. 50686 (Home).

Humphrey, Gilbert W.; American business executive; b. 4 July 1916, Saginaw, Mich.; s. of George Magoffin Humphrey and Pamela Stark Humphrey; m. Louise Ireland 1939; two s. one d.; ed. Yale Univ. and Yale Law School.
With Jones, Day, Cockley & Reavis 46-48; with M. A. Hanna Co. 48-60, Pres. 60-61, Chair. 61-65; Dir. and Chair. of Board, Hanna Mining Co. 66-; Dir. and Chair. Exec. Cttee. Nat. Steel Corpn. 68-; Dir. Sun Life Assurance Co. of Canada, Gen. Reinsurance Corpn., Gen. Electric Co., Nat. City Bank of Cleveland, Texaco Inc., and Massey-Ferguson Ltd.
Leisure interests: golf, tennis, riding, hunting, swimming, fishing.
100 Erieview Plaza, 36th Floor, Cleveland, Ohio 44114, U.S.A.
Telephone: 216-523-3030.

Humphrey, Hubert Horatio, Jr., A.M.; American politician; b. 27 May 1911; ed. Denver Coll. of Pharmacy, Univ. of Minnesota and Louisiana State Univ.
State Dir. War Production Training and Re-employment 41; State Chief of Minnesota War Service Programme 42; Asst. Dir. War Manpower Comm. 43; Prof. Political Science, Macalester Coll. 43-44; former Vice-Pres. American Political Science Asscn.; radio news commentator 44-45; Mayor, City of Minneapolis 45-49; U.S. Senator from Minnesota 49-64; American del. to UN 56; Chair. Senate Sub-Cttee. on Disarmament 55-64; Vice-Pres. of the United States 65-69; teaching posts at Univ. of Minn. and Macalester Coll. 69; mem. Board of Dirs. *Encyclopaedia Britannica* 69-; Senator from Minnesota 71-; Chair. Congressional Joint Econ. Cttee. 75-; Presidential Candidate 68; fmr. Chair. Nat. Aeronautics and Space Council; fmr. Chair. Peace Corps Advisory Council; mem. Nat. Security Council; mem. Board of Regents, Smithsonian Inst., etc.; Joseph Prize for Human Rights 75.
Publs. *The Cause is Mankind* 64, *School Desegregation: Documents and Commentaries* 64, *War on Poverty* 65, *The Political Philosophy of the New Deal*.
Senate Office Building, Washington, D.C., U.S.A.

Humphrey, John Peters, O.C., B.COM., B.A., B.C.L., PH.D.; Canadian international official and university

professor; b. 30 April 1905, Hampton, New Brunswick; s. of Frank M. Humphrey and Nellie Peters; m. Jeanne Godreau 1929; ed. Rothesay Coll., Mount Allison Univ., McGill Univ. and Univ. de Paris.
Called to Montreal Bar 29, practised law with Wainwright, Elder & McDougall 30-36; Lecturer in Roman Law, McGill Univ. 36, Sec. of Law Faculty 37-46, Gale Prof. of Roman Law and Dean of Law Faculty 46, Prof. of Law and Political Science 66-71; Visiting Prof., Law Faculty, Univ. of Toronto 71-; Carnegie Fellow in Int. Law, Paris 36-37; Dir. Div. of Human Rights, UN Secr. 46-66; Exec. Sec. UN Conf. on Freedom of Information 48, Refugees 51, Status of Stateless Persons 54, Slavery Conf. 56; Principal Sec. UN Fact-Finding Mission to S. Viet-Nam 63; Nat. Pres. UN Asscn. in Canada 68-70, Hon. Vice-Pres. 67-68, Hon. Pres. Montreal Branch 66-68, Pres. 45-46; mem. UN Sub-Comm. on Prevention of Discrimination and Protection of Minorities 66, Chair. 70; Rapporteur, Cttee. on Human Rights, Int. Law Asscn. 66-; Pres. Canadian Comm., Int. Year for Human Rights 68; mem. Int. Comm. of Jurists, Royal Comm. on Status of Women in Canada, Canadian Council of Int. Law, Int. Law Asscn., Canadian Inst. of Int. Affairs; mem. Board of Dirs. Int. League for Rights of Man; Vice-Pres. Canadian Foundation for Human Rights; Pres. Amnesty Int. (Canada); Hon. LL.D. (Carleton) 68, Hon. Dr. Soc. Sciences (Ottawa) 66, Hon. LL.D. (St. Thomas) 71, (Dalhousie) 75, Dr. h.c. (Univ. of Algiers) 44; World Jewish Congress Citation 66, World Legal Scholar award, World Peace Through Law Center 73, John Read Medal, Canadian Council of Int. Law 73, Officer, Order of Canada 74.
Publs. *The Inter-American System: A Canadian View* 42, and articles in American, British and Canadian periodicals on international, political and legal subjects.
1455 Sherbrooke Street West, Montreal, P.Q., Canada.

Humphreys, Christmas (*see* Humphreys, (Travers) C.).

Humphreys, David Colin, M.A. (CANTAB.); British civil servant; b. 23 April 1925, Sunningdale, Berks.; s. of Charles Roland L. and Joan Bethia Humphreys (née Bowie); m. Jill Allison Cranmer 1952; two s. one d.; ed. Eton Coll., King's Coll., Cambridge.
British Army 43-46; joined Air Ministry 49; Private Sec. to Sec. of State for Air 58; Counsellor U.K. Del., NATO 60; Asst. Sec. Air Force Dept., London 63; Imperial Defence Coll. 70; Civilian Dir. Defence Policy Staff 71; Asst. Sec.-Gen. Defence Planning and Policy, NATO 72-.
Leisure interests: tennis, gardening.
Defence Planning and Policy Division, North Atlantic Treaty Organization, Brussels; Home: 41 Clos des Mésanges, 1160 Brussels, Belgium.
Telephone: 672-70-75 (Home).

Humphreys, Sir Olliver William, Kt., C.B.E., B.SC., F.INST.P., C.ENG., F.I.E.E., F.R.AE.S.; British physicist; b. 4 Sept. 1902, London; s. of late Rev. J. Willis Humphreys; m. Muriel Mary Hawkins 1933; ed. Univ. Coll., London Univ.
Joined scientific staff of the G.E.C. Research Laboratories 25; Dir. G.E.C. Research Laboratories 49-61; Dir. G.E.C. 53-69; Vice-Chair. 62-68; Chair. G.E.C. (Research) Ltd. 62-68; mem. Board Assoc. Semiconductor Mfrs. Ltd. 62-69; mem. Board of Trade Cttee. on the Org. and Constitution of the British Standards Inst. 49-50; mem. Board of Inst. of Physics 51-59 and Pres. 56-58; mem. British Standards Inst. Gen. Council 53-56, and mem. of Exec. Cttee. 53-60; mem. Council Inst. Electrical Engineers 52-55, Vice-Pres. 59-64, Pres. 64-65; Chair. D.S.I.R. Radio Research Board 57-62; Chair. Int. Special Cttee. on Radio Interference 53-61; mem. British Nat. Cttee. of the Int. Electrotechnical Comm.; mem. of Board of British Nuclear Energy Conf. 55-58; Chair. Council of British Electrical and Allied Industries

Research Asscn. 58-61; Pres. Electrical Engineering Asscn. 62-64; Chair. Conf. of Electronics Industry 63-68, mem. Nat. Electronics Research Council 63-68; Fellow of Univ. Coll., London 63.

Leisure interests: reading, walking.

Publs. include lectures and papers on scientific and engineering subjects.

5 Branksome Cliff, Branksome Park, Poole, Dorset, England.

Telephone: Bournemouth 766195.

Humphreys, (Travers) Christmas, Q.C.; British lawyer; b. 15 Feb. 1901; ed. Malvern Coll., Trinity Hall, Cambridge.

Junior Counsel to Treasury 32; Junior Counsel to Treasury at Central Criminal Court 34; Recorder of Deal 42-56; Senior Prosecuting Counsel to the Crown at Central Criminal Court 50-59; Recorder of Guildford 56-68; Judge, Central Criminal Court 68-76; Founder, Pres. Buddhist Lodge, London (now Buddhist Soc.) 24; Pres. The Shakespearean Authorship Soc. 55.

Publs. *The Great Pearl Robbery of 1913* 28, *What is Buddhism?* 28, *Concentration and Meditation* 35, *The Development of Buddhism in England* 37, *Studies in The Middle Way* 40, *Poems of Peace and War* 41, *Seagulls, and other Poems* 42, *Karma and Rebirth* 43, *Shadows and other Poems* 45, *Walk On* 47, *Via Tokyo* 48, *Zen Buddhism* 49, *The Way of Action* 60, *Zen Comes West* 60, *The Wisdom of Buddhism* 60, *Poems I Remember* 60, *A Popular Dictionary of Buddhism* 62, *Zen, A Way of Life* 62, *The Buddhist Way of Life* 69, *Buddhist Poems* 71, *A Western Approach to Zen* 72, *Exploring Buddhism* 74.

58 Marlborough Place, London, N.W.8, England.

Hund, Friedrich, DR. PHIL; German physicist; b. 4 Feb. 1896, Karlsruhe; m. Dr. Ingeborg Seynsche 1931; five c.

Assistant Prof. Göttingen Univ. 25; Extra. Prof. Rostock Univ. 27 and Prof. 28; Prof. of Mathematical Physics Leipzig Univ. 29-46; Prof. of Theoretical Physics Jena Univ. 46-51; Prof. of Theoretical Physics, Frankfurt (Main) Univ. 51-56; Prof. of Theoretical Physics, Göttingen Univ. 56-64, Emer. 64-; mem. Acad. of Sciences Göttingen; Dr. phil. nat. h.c., Dr.phil. h.c. (Uppsala).

Leisure interest: history of physics.

Publs. on quantum theory of atoms, molecules and solids: *Linienspektren* 27, *Einführung in die theoretische Physik* (5 vols.) 45-50, *Materie als Feld* 54, *Theoretische Physik* (3 vols.) 56-57 and additional editions, *Theorie des Aufbaues der Materie* 61, *Geschichte der Quanten-Theorie* 67 (2nd edn. 75), *Grundbegriffe der Physik* 69, *Geschichte der physikalischen Begriffe* 72.

Tuckermannweg 5, 34 Göttingen, Federal Republic of Germany.

Telephone: (0551) 58589.

Hundertwasser, Friedensreich (Friedensreich Stowasser); Austrian artist; b. 15 Dec. 1928, Vienna; s. of Ernst and Elsa Stowasser (née Scheuer); m. 1st 1958 (dissolved 1960), 2nd Yuuko Ikewada 1962 (dissolved 1966).

First one-man exhbn. at Art Club, Vienna 53; evolved theory of "Transautomatism" and began numbering his paintings, developed this theory into a "Grammar of Vision"; exhbns. at Galerie H. Kamer, Paris 57-60, at galleries in Milan, Tokyo, at Venice Biennale, etc.; Lecturer Kunsthochschule, Hamburg; Prix du Syndicat d'Initiative, Bordeaux, Sanbra Prize, São Paulo Biennale 59, Mainichi Prize, Sixth Int. Art Exhbn., Tokyo 61.

Giudecca 43, 30100 Venice, Italy.

Telephone: 22522.

Hunlédé, Ayi Houénou, L. en D.; Togolese politician; b. 2 Feb. 1925, Anécho.

Assistant Insp. of schools, Northern Togo, then teacher at Ecole Normale d'Atakpamé 53-56; worked for French Overseas Territories Admin. 58; Asst. Admin. Mayor, Lomé; Chief, admin. subdivision of Tabligbo; Admin. Mayor of Tsévié; Amb. to France, U.K., EEC Sept. 60-July 65; High Commr. for Planning Sept. 65-April 67; Minister of Foreign Affairs April 67-.

Ministry of Foreign Affairs, Lomé, Togo.

Hunold, Albert Conrad; Swiss business and public executive; b. 4 July 1899, Zurich; s. of Albert Hunold and Elisabeth Lang; m. 1st Frieda von der Osten 1939 (divorced 1949), two s.; m. 2nd Berta Menet 1954 (died 1955), one d.; m. 3rd Maximiliane Braunschmidt 1958, one s. two d.; ed. Univs. of Zurich, Geneva and London.

Secretary, Zurich Stock Exchange Asscn. 30-45; Sec. Asscn. of Zurich Insts. of Credit 39-45; Joint Dir. Crédit Suisse 45-46; Marketing Dir. Swiss Fed. of Watch Manufacturers 47-49; Co-Founder and Sec. of the Mont Pèlerin Soc. 47-60, Vice-Pres. 60-62; Founder and exec. mem. Board Swiss Inst. of Int. Studies, Zurich 50-66; Founder and Exec. Vice-Pres. William Röpke Foundation 66-.

Publs. include *The Swiss Stock Exchanges* (in German) 49, *The Industrial Development of Switzerland* (in English, Italian and Spanish) 54, *Social Peace in Switzerland* 64; edited *Full Employment, Inflation and Planning* 51, *Economy without Miracles* 53, *Convertibility of European Currencies* 54, *The Free World in the Cold War* 55, *The Problem of the Masses in Democracy* 56, *Education for Freedom* 58, *Undeveloped Countries* 61, *Latin America—Land of Trouble and of Future* 62, *Inflation and International Monetary Order* 63, *Africa and its Problems* 65 (all in German).

9056 Gais-Zwislen AR, Switzerland.

Telephone: (071) 932188.

Hunsaker, Jerome C., D.SC., O.B.E.; American aeronautical engineer; b. 26 Aug. 1886, Creston, Iowa; s. of Walker J. and Alma Clarke Hunsaker (deceased 67); m. Alice Potter Avery 1912; four c.; ed. U.S. Naval Acad. and Massachusetts Inst. of Technology.

Officer in Navy 08-26; Asst. Vice-Pres. Bell Telephone Laboratories, New York 26-28; Vice-Pres. Goodyear Zeppelin Corpn., Akron 28-33; Head Dept. of Mechanical Engineering of Massachusetts Inst. of Technology 33-47, Head Dept. of Aeronautical Engineering 33-51; Hon. Fellow, Royal Aeronautical Society of Great Britain, Inst. of the Aeronautical Sciences, and Imperial Coll. of Science and Technology, London; hon. mem. Inst. of Mechanical Engineers and American Society of Mechanical Engineers; Guggenheim Medal, Franklin Medal, Navy Cross, Medal for Merit, Legion of Honour, Wright Trophy, Langley Medal, Gold Medal (Royal Aeronautical Soc. of Gt. Britain); Prof. Emer. Mass. Inst. of Technology.

Leisure interest: fly fishing.

10 Louisburg Square, Boston, Mass. 02108, U.S.A.

Telephone: Boston, LA3-1094.

Hunt, Baron (Life Peer, cr. 66), of Llanvair Waterdine; **John Hunt** (brother of Hugh Hunt, q.v.), Kt., C.B.E., D.S.O.; British army officer, mountaineer and administrator; b. 22 June 1910; ed. Marlborough Coll. and Royal Mil. Coll., Sandhurst.

Took part in expeditions to Karakoram 35 and to S.E. Himalayas 37 and 40; led British Expedition to Mount Everest, when Hillary and Tenzing reached the summit on May 29th 53; British Expedition to Caucasus 58, to N.E. Greenland 60; British-Soviet Expedition to the Pamirs 62; Canadian Centennial Expedition in St. Elias Mountains 67; Asst. Commdt. Staff College, Camberley 53-55; Pres. The Alpine Club 56-58; Chair. Mount Everest Foundation 56-57; Pres. British Mountaineering Council 65-68, Nat. Ski Fed. of Great Britain 69-72; Dir. The Duke of Edinburgh's Award Scheme 56-66; Rector, Aberdeen Univ. 63-66; Chair. Parole Board 68-74; Personal Rep. of British Prime

Minister in Nigeria 68, 70; Pres. Council for Volunteers Overseas 68-; mem. Comm. on the Press 74-; Hon. D.C.L. (Durham Univ.), Hon. LL.D. (Aberdeen and London Univs.); Indian Police Medal, Indian Everest Medal; Founder's Medal of Royal Geographical Soc.; Order (1st Class) of Gurkha Right Hand of Nepal.
Publs. *The Ascent of Everest* 53, *Our Everest Adventure* 54, *The Red Snows* (with Christopher Brasher) 60.
Highway Cottage, Ashton, Henley-on-Thames, England.

Hunt, Sir David Wathen Stather, K.C.M.G., O.B.E.; British diplomatist; b. 25 Sept. 1913, Durham; s. of Canon B. P. W. Stather Hunt and Elizabeth Milner; m. 1st Pamela Medawar 1948, 2nd Iro Myrianthousi 1968; two s.; ed. St. Lawrence Coll., Ramsgate and Wadham Coll., Oxford.
Served in the Middle East, Greece, N. Africa and Italy during the Second World War; Commonwealth Relations Office 47-, service in S. Africa, Pakistan, Nigeria 47-50, 52-62; Dep. High Commr., Lagos, Nigeria 60-62; Private Sec., Office of the British Prime Minister 50-52, 60; British High Commr. in Kampala, Uganda Oct. 62-65, in Nicosia, Cyprus April 65-66, in Lagos, Nigeria 67-69; Amb. to Brazil 69-73; Chair. Commonwealth Inst.
Leisure interests: golf, history, sailing.
Publs. *A Don at War* 66, *On the Spot* 75.
Old Place, Lindfield, Sussex, England.

Hunt, Gilbert Adams, C.B.E., C.ENG., M.I.BRIT.F., F.I.PROD.E., C.I.MECH.E.; British engineer and motor executive; b. 1914, Wolverhampton; s. of Harold W. Hunt; m. Diane R. Cook 1975; ed. Old Hall School, Wellington and Malvern Coll.
Director and Gen. Man. High Duty Alloys 54-60; Man. Dir. Massey-Ferguson (U.K.) Ltd. 60-67; Chair. Massey-Ferguson (Farm Services) Ltd.; Chair. and Man. Dir. Massey-Ferguson (Eire) Ltd.; Joint Man. Dir. Massey-Ferguson Holdings Ltd.; Man. Dir. and Chief Exec. Officer, Chrysler United Kingdom Ltd. 67-73, Chair. 73-; Dir. Chrysler Int. S.A., Chrysler Scotland Ltd., Chrysler Ireland Ltd., Chrysler France S.A. and Chrysler España S.A.; Dir. Reed Group Ltd. 68-75; Chair. Emerald Offshore Services Ltd. 75-; Chair. Gov. Cttee. for Industrial Technologies 72-; Pres. Soc. of Motor Mfrs. and Traders 72-73; Hon. D.Sc. (Cranfield).
Leisure interests: golf, sailing.
6 Lowndes Square, London, S.W.1, England.

Hunt, Harold Christian, A.B., M.A., ED.D.; American professor and politician; b. 9 Feb. 1902, Northville, Mich.; s. of George E. and Kate H. Hunt; m. Isabel L. Wright 1927; one s.; ed. Univs. of Michigan and Chicago and Teachers' Coll., Columbia Univ.
Teacher, Hastings High School, Michigan 23-27; Principal, St. Johns High School 27-28 and 29-31; Asst. Cashier, St. Johns Nat. Bank 28-29; Superintendent, St. Johns Public Schools 31-33, Kalamazoo Schools, Michigan 34-37, New Rochelle, N.Y. 37-40, Kansas City, Missouri 40-47, Chicago 47-53; Charles William Eliot Prof. of Education, Harvard Univ. 53-70, Prof. Emer. 70-; Under-Sec. U.S. Dept. of Health, Education and Welfare 55-57; Pres. American Asscn. of School Administrators 47-48; Chair. American Council of Education 48-49, Educational Testing Service 49-50; Hon. M.A. (Harvard Univ.), LL.D. (Park Coll., Western Michigan Coll., Univ. of Wisconsin, and St. Louis Univ.), L.H.D. (Missouri Valley Coll.); American Education Award 58.
Leisure interest: gardening.
Publs. *The Practice of School Administration* (co-author), *The School Personnel Administrator* (co-author).
5 Lantern Lane, Lexington 73, Mass., U.S.A.
Telephone: 617-862-3651.

Hunt, Hugh Sydney (brother of Lord Hunt, *q.v.*), M.A.; British theatrical director; b. 25 Sept. 1911, Camberley;

s. of Capt. C. E. Hunt, M.C. and Ethel Helen (née Crookshank); m. Janet Mary Gordon 1940; one s. one d.; ed. Marlborough Coll., Sorbonne, Heidelberg Univ. and Magdalen Coll., Oxford.
Producer, Maddermarket Theatre, Norwich 34, Croydon Repertory Theatre 34, Abbey Theatre Dublin 35-38; served Second World War 39-45; directed Bristol Old Vic Company 45-49; Dir. Old Vic Company 49-53; Dir. Elizabethan Theatre Trust, Sydney, Australia 55-60; Prof. of Drama, Univ. of Manchester 61-73; Artistic Dir., Abbey Theatre, Dublin 69-71; Vice-Pres. Int. Fed. for Theatre Research 69-74.
Leisure interest: travel.
Publs. *Old Vic Prefaces, The Director in the Theatre* 34, *The Making of Australian Theatre* 60, *The Living Theatre* 61.
Cae Terfyn, Criccieth, Caerns. LL52 0SA, Wales.
Telephone: Criccieth 2528.

Hunt, Sir John Joseph Benedict, K.C.B.; British civil servant; b. 23 Oct. 1919, Minehead; s. of Major and Mrs. A. L. Hunt; m. 1st Magdalen Mary Lister Robinson 1941 (died 1971), 2nd Madeleine Frances Charles 1973; two s. one d.; ed. Downside School and Magdalene Coll., Cambridge.
Served in R.N.V.R. 40-46; joined Home Civil Service (Dominions Office) 46; Private Sec. to Parl. Under-Sec. 47; Second Sec., Colombo 48-50; Directing Staff, Imperial Defence Coll. 51-52; First Sec., Ottawa 53-56; Private Sec. to Sec. of Cabinet and Head of Civil Service 56-58; Asst. Sec. Commonwealth Relations Office 58-60; Cabinet Office 60-62; H.M. Treasury 62-67, Under-Sec. 65; First Civil Service Commr. 68-71; Third Sec. Treasury 71-72; Second Permanent Sec., Cabinet Office 72-73; Sec. of the Cabinet 73-.
Leisure interests: reading, skiing, gardening.
Cabinet Office, Whitehall, London, S.W.1; Home: 24 Parkside, Wimbledon Common, London, S.W.19, England.

Hunt, Gen. Sir Peter Mervyn, G.C.B., D.S.O., O.B.E.; British army officer; b. 11 March 1916, London; s. of H. V. Hunt; m. Anne Stopford 1940 (died 1966); one s. one d.; ed. Wellington Coll. and Royal Military Coll., Sandhurst.
Commissioned 36; served World War II 39-45; graduated, Command and Gen. Staff School, Fort Leavenworth, U.S.A. 48; Instructor, Staff Coll., Camberley, U.K. 52-55 and Imperial Defence Coll. 56-57; Commdr., Land Forces, Borneo and Maj.-Gen. Brigade of Gurkhas 64-65; Commdt., Royal Mil. Acad., Sandhurst 66-68; Commdr., Far East Land Forces 68-70; Commdr., Northern Army Group (NATO) and C.-in-C., British Army of the Rhine Dec. 70-April 73; Chief of the Gen. Staff, U.K. 73-July 76; Order of Léopold II and Croix de Guerre (Belgium) 40.
Leisure interests: travel, photography, philately.
c/o Williams and Glyn's Bank, Holt's Branch, Whitehall, London, S.W.1; Naval and Military Club, Piccadilly, London, W.1, England.

Hunt, Reed Oliver; American business executive; b. 12 Oct. 1904, Wollochet Bay, Washington; s. of Arda Roy Hunt and Edna Elisabeth (Oliver) Hunt; m. Sarah Elizabeth Trombley 1926; one s. one d. Joined Crown Zellerbach Corpn. at Port Angeles as clerk 27, Asst. Office Man. 30, Office Man., West Linn. and Camas, Asst. to Corpn. Vice-Pres. for Manufacturing 43-47, Asst. Gen. Man. for Manufacturing 47-50, Gen. Man. 50-52, Vice-Pres. in charge of manufacturing 52-54, Vice-Pres. for operations 54-56, Exec. Vice-Pres. 56-59, Pres. and Chief Exec. Officer 59-63, Chair. of Board and Chief Exec. Officer 63-69; Hon. Dir. Crown Zellerbach Corpn. San Francisco, Canadian Imperial Bank of Commerce, Toronto, Singer Co. 75-; Dir. Peninsula State Bank and many firms and civic cttees.; Chair. Presidential Comm. on Financial Structure and

Regulation; Hon. LL.D. (Pacific Univ.), Hon. D. Hum. Litt., Northwestern Univ., Evanston, Ill.
Leisure interests: yachting, gardening.
P.O. Box 366, Gig Harbor, Washington 98335, U.S.A.
Telephone: 206-858-2171.

Hunt, William H.; American business executive; b. 23 July 1909, Madison, Wis.; *s.* of Walter H. and Henrietta Milhaupt Hunt; *m.* Mary Dolan 1932; one *s.*; ed. Wisconsin State Univ.
Teacher and athletic coach, Algoma, Wis. 29-35; Algoma Plywood and Veneer Co., Algoma 35-38; joined U.S. Plywood Corpn. 38, Vice-Pres. 53-57; Vice-Pres. Georgia-Pacific Corpn. 57-64, Exec. Vice-Pres. 64-70, Pres. 70-72, Vice-Chair. 72-73, Dir. 64-72; Chair. of Board and Chief Exec. Officer, Louisiana Pacific Corpn. 73-.
Leisure interests: golf, reading, spectator sports, travel, duck hunting.
Office: 1300 S.W. 5th Avenue, Portland, Ore. 97204; Home: 2323 S.W. Park Place, Portland, Ore. 97205, U.S.A.
Telephone: 503-221-0800 (Office); 503-222-5243 (Home).

Hunter, Sir (Ernest) John, Kt., C.B.E., D.SC., D.L.; British shipbuilder; b. 3 Nov. 1912, Newcastle upon Tyne; *s.* of George Ernest Hunter and Elsie Hunter (née Edwards); *m.* 1st Joanne Winifred Wilkinson 1937, 2nd Sybil Malfroy (née Gordon); two *s.* one stepdaughter; ed. Oundle School and Cambridge and Durham Univs.
Apprentice, Swan, Hunter & Wigham Richardson, 30-35, Drawing and Design Offices, Wallsend 35-37; Barclay, Curle & Co. Ltd. 37-39; Asst. Man., Dry Docks Dept. Swan, Hunter & Wigham Richardson, Ltd. 39-41, Asst. Gen. Man. 41-43, Gen. Man. 43-57, Dir. 45-, Chair. 57-66; Chair. Swan Hunter Group Ltd. 66-72, Exec. Chair. 72-; Chair. North East Broadcasting Co. Ltd.; Dir. Midland Bank Ltd., Newcastle & Gateshead Water Co.; Dir. many other companies; Pres. Shipbuilding Employers' Fed. 56-57; Pres. British Employers' Confederation 62-64; Chair. Cen. Training Council 64-68; Pres. S.R.N.A. 68-70.
Leisure interests: golf and gardening.
Swan Hunter Group Ltd., P.O. Box 1, Wallsend, Tyne and Wear, NE28 6EQ; Home: "The Dene", Stocksfield, Northumberland, England.
Telephone: Wallsend 628921 (Office); Stocksfield 3124.

Hunter, Evan, B.A.; American author; b. 15 Oct. 1926, New York; *s.* of Marie and Charles Lombino; *m.* 1st Anita Melnick 1949, three *s.*; *m.* 2nd Mary Vann Finley 1973, one stepdaughter; ed. Cooper Union and Hunter Coll.
Leisure interests: skiing and snorkeling.
Publs. *The Blackboard Jungle* 54, *Second Ending* 56, *Strangers When We Meet* 58 (screenplay 59), *A Matter of Conviction* 59, *Mothers and Daughters* 61, *The Birds* (screenplay) 62, *Happy New Year, Herbie* 63, *Buddwing* 64, *The Easter Man* (play) 64, *The Sentries* (as Ed McBain) 65, *The Paper Dragon* 66, *A Horse's Head* 67, *Last Summer* 68, *Sons* 69, *The Conjurer* (play) 69, *Nobody Knew They Were There* 71, *Every Little Crook and Nanny* 72, *The Easter Man* 72, *Come Winter* 73, *Streets of Gold* 74; 87th Precinct Mysteries under *pseudonym* Ed McBain: *Cop Hater* 56, *The Mugger* 56, *The Pusher* 56, *The Con Man* 57, *Killer's Choice* 57, *Killer's Payoff* 58, *Lady Killer* 58, *Killer's Wedge* 59, *'Til Death* 59, *King's Ransom* 59, *Give the Boys a Great Big Hand* 60, *The Heckler* 60, *See Them Die* 60, *Lady, Lady, I Did It* 61, *Like Love* 62, *The Empty Hours* (three novelettes) 62, *Ten plus One* 63, *Ax* 64, *He Who Hesitates* 65, *Doll* 65, *Eighty Million Eyes* 66, *Fuzz* 68 (screenplay 72), *Shotgun* 69, *Jigsaw* 70, *Hail, Hail, The Gang's All Here* 71, *Sadie When She Died* 72, *Let's Hear It for the Deaf Man* 72, *Hail to the*

Chief 73, *Bread* 74, *Where There's Smoke* 75, *Blood Relatives* 75.
c/o Scott Meredith Literary Agency Inc., 580 Fifth Avenue, New York, N.Y. 10036, U.S.A.
Telephone: Circle 5-5500.

Huong, Tran Van (*see* Tran Van Huong).

Hurd, John Gavin, A.B., LL.B.; American diplomatist; b. 2 July 1914, Sacramento, Calif.; *s.* of Dr. Eugene and Nella (née Wilson) Hurd; *m.* 1st Patricia L. Killam 1937 (deceased), 2nd Nancy L. Smith 1957; one *s.* three *d.*; ed. Harvard Univ.
Practising lawyer, Pillsbury, Madison and Sutro, San Francisco, Calif. 37-39; land and legal work, Standard Oil Co. of Calif. 39-41; U.S. Navy Intelligence and Destroyers Atlantic 41-46; cattle-ranching, oil exploration and production, finance, Killam and Hurd Ltd., Laredo, Tex. 46-; Amb. to South Africa 70-75; retd. as diplomatist 75.
Leisure interests: hunting, fishing, golf.
Killam and Hurd Ltd., Laredo, Tex.; 2 McPherson, Del Mar (P.O. Box 499), Laredo, Tex. 78040, U.S.A.

Huré, Francis, L. ès L.; French diplomatist; b. 5 Oct. 1916, Abbeville, Somme; *s.* of Louis Huré and Marthe (née Dumont); *m.* Jacqueline Félici 1947; one *d.*; ed. Faculté des lettres de Paris and Ecole libre des sciences politiques.
In Algiers 43; Attaché, French Embassy in Moscow 44-45; Foreign Office, Paris 45-46, 50; First Sec., Tokyo 47-49; Adviser French Del. to UN 53; Counsellor, London 54-58; Chargé d'Affaires, Guinea 59; Amb. to Cameroon 65-68; Amb. to Israel 68-73, to Belgium 73-; Officier Légion d'Honneur; Prix Cazes 63.
Ambassade de France, 65 rue Ducale, Brussels, Belgium; 5 boulevard Jean-Mermoz, Neuilly-sur-Seine, France; and Marine de Pino, Corsica.

Huré, Joseph Marie Paul Eugéne; French industrialist; b. 21 Jan. 1899, Abbeville; *s.* of Albert Huré and Céline Herbet; *m.* Anne-Marie Delcroix 1923; one *s.* five *d.*; ed. Abbeville Coll., Ecole Bossuet, Ecole Polytechnique and Ecole des Mines de Paris.
Army service 17-20; Engineer Corps des Mines 22-25; joined Société Française des Pétroles B.P. (then Société Générale des Huiles de Pétrole) 25, Man. 31, Dir. 36, Dir. and Asst. Gen. Manager 43-46, Vice-Pres., Gen. Man. 46-54, Pres., Gen. Man. 54-64, Chair. of Board 64-69, Hon. Chair. of Board 69-, Dir. 69-74; Dir. several other companies; Hon. C.B.E.; Commandeur de la Légion d'Honneur; Croix de Guerre.
Leisure interests: sport, tennis and golf.
Office: Société Française des Pétroles B.P., 10 quai Paul Doumer, 92400 Courveboie; Home: 11 rue Porto Riche, 92190 Meudon, France.
Telephone: ALMa 48-00 (Office); OBServatoire 12-42 (Home).

Huriaux, Charles; Belgian executive; b. 22 Sept. 1911, Arlon; ed. Univ. of Liège.
Councillor, Société Générale de Belgique 69-; Gov., Banque Nationale de Belgique 71; Admin. Dir.-Gen., S.A. Cockerill-Ougrée-Providence et Espérance-Longdoz "Cockerill"; Admin. of numerous industrial and commercial socs.; Chevalier Ordre de la Couronne; Officier Ordre de Léopold II; Officier Ordre de Léopold; Officier Ordre du Mérite de la République italienne.
S.A. "Cockerill", ave. Adolphe Greiner 1, B-4100 Seraing, Belgium.
Telephone: Liège 34-08-10 and 34-28-10.

Hürlimann, Hans, LL.D.; Swiss lawyer and politician; b. 6 April 1918, Walchwil, Zug; *m.* Marie Theres Duft 1947; two *s.* one *d.*; ed. Univs. of Fribourg and Berne.
Barrister, Zug 46; Legal Adviser, Zug 46, Town Clerk 49; mem. Legis. Chamber, Zug Canton 46, mem. Cantonal Govt. as Head of Dept. of Justice, Police and

Mil. Affairs 54-62, of Educ., Cultural and Mil. Affairs 62-73; mem. Council of States 66-73; mem. Fed. Council as Head of Dept. of Home Affairs 74-; Chair. Conf. of Heads of Cantonal Mil. Depts. 60-68, Conf. of Heads of Cantonal Educ. Depts. 68-73; mem. Council of Swiss Fed. Insts. of Tech. 70-73; fmr. mem. Exec. Board, Christian-Democratic People's Party.
Leisure interests: music, books, theatre, skiing, hiking.
Publs. *Das Recht der Stadtgemeinde Zug*, and many publs. on juridical, educational and military topics.
Department of Home Affairs, Bundeshaus, Inselgasse, 3003 Berne; and Schönbühl 3, 6300 Zug, Switzerland.
Telephone: (042) 21-24-10.

Hürlimann, Martin, D.PHIL.; Swiss publisher and writer; b. 1897; m. Bettina Kiepenheuer 1933; two s. two d.; ed. Univs. of Zürich, Leipzig and Berlin.
Founded the Atlantis Verlag 30; fmr. Dir. of Atlantis Verlag.
Leisure interest: chamber music.
Publs. consist of a series *Orbis Terrarum, France* 27, *India* 28, 66, *Indochina* 28, *Germany* 31, *Switzerland* 31, 71, *France* 37, *Paris* 51, *Spain* 51, *Italy* 51, *Athens* 56, *London* 56, *Istanbul* 57, *Europe* 58, *Moscow and Leningrad* 58, *Traveller in the Orient* 60, *Kyoto* 61, *Hongkong* 62, *Bangkok* 63, *Delhi* 64, *The World* 65, *Vienna* 68, *Japan* 71.
Witellikerstrasse 9, 8702 Zollikon, Zürich, Switzerland.

Hurwitz, Jerard, PH.D.; American research scientist; b. 20 Nov. 1928; ed. Coll. of City of New York, Indiana Univ. and Western Reserve Univ., Cleveland, Ohio.
Research Asst., Dept. of Biochemistry, Western Reserve Univ. 49-50; Instructor in Microbiology, Washington Univ., St. Louis 56-58; Asst. Prof. in Microbiology, New York Univ. School of Medicine 58-60, Assoc. Prof. of Microbiology 60-63; Prof. of Molecular Biology, Albert Einstein Coll. of Medicine, New York 63-65, Prof. Developmental Biology and Cancer 65-; mem. Biochemical Soc. of England, American Soc. of Biological Chemists; American Cancer Soc. Research Prof.; Eli Lilly Award in Biochemistry 62.
Department of Developmental Biology and Cancer, Albert Einstein College of Medicine, Yeshiva University, 1300 Morris Park Avenue, Bronx, New York, N.Y. 10461, U.S.A.

Hurwitz, Stephan; Danish academic lawyer; b. 20 June 1901; ed. Univ. of Copenhagen.
Prof. of Law, Univ. of Copenhagen 35, Vice-Chancellor 53; Parl. Commr. (State controller, Ombudsman) 55-71; Chief Danish Refugee Admin. in Sweden 43; mem. Danish Mil. Comm., London 44-45; Danish rep. on UN War Crimes Comm. 45; Pres. Danish Asscn. of Criminologists 43; Pres. Int. Cttee. of Nordic Asscns. of Criminologists 52; Pres. Royal Permanent Penal Cttee. of Denmark 60; Chief Editor *Scandinavian Journal of Criminal Science* 49; Gold Medal of Univ. of Copenhagen; D.Jur. 33; D.Jur. h.c. Stockholm 60, Oslo 61, Helsinki 63, Reykjavík 71.
Publs. *The Press Treatment of Court Proceedings* 37, various works on law of procedure in Criminal and Civil Cases, *Criminology* 48 (English, Italian and Spanish editions), *Danish Criminal Law* 50-55.
Christiansborg Ridebane 10, 1218 Copenhagen K, Denmark.
Telephone: 11-66-00 Ext. 357.

Husain, Akhter, O.B.E., H.PK.; Pakistani administrator; b. Burhanpur 1902; s. of Mian Bhaj and Zainab Husain; m. Sakina 1924; three s. one d.; ed. Hakimia High School, Burhanpur, M.A.O. Coll., Aligarh, and St. John's Coll., Cambridge.
Appointed to Indian civil service in Punjab 26; various admin. posts 30-43; Sec. Post-War Reconstruction Dept. 44; Chief Sec. Govt. Punjab 46-47; Financial

Commr. and Sec. to Govt., West Punjab 47-53; mem. Tenancy Inquiry Cttee. 51, Liaquat Ali Assassination Inquiry Cttee. 51; special duty at Karachi for reorganization of Karachi Admin. 51; Chair. Lord Boyd Orr's Expert Cttee. 53; Sec. Ministry of Defence, Govt. Pakistan 53-57; Chair. Karachi Admin. Cttee. 55; Gov. West Pakistan 57-60; Minister of Information, Nat. Reconstruction and Kashmir Affairs 60, of Kashmir Affairs 60-61, of Education and Scientific Research, Minority Affairs 61-62; Chair. Land Reforms Comm. 58, Land Comm. and Provincial Admin. Comm. 59; Chief Election Commr. (Pakistan) 62-64; Chair. Nat. Press Trust 65, Investment Corpn. of Pakistan 66; mem. Advisory Council of Islamic Ideology; Dir. Agric. Devt. Bank of Pakistan 67-70; Chair. Water Allocation and Rate Cttee. of W. Pakistan 68-70; Chair. Karachi Admin. and Metropolitan Cttee., Soc. for the Promotion of Urdu Language 62, Pakistan Paper Products Ltd., Pakistan Burmah Shell Ltd. 69-, Pakistan Diabetic Asscn. 72; Hon. LL.D. (Punjab Univ.); Hilale-Pakistan 58-71.
Leisure interests: farming and gardening.
29a Sunset Boulevard, Defence Housing Society, Karachi, Pakistan.
Telephone: 541327.

Husain, Maqbool Fida; Indian painter; b. 17 Sept. 1915.
Joined Progressive Artists Group, Bombay 48; first one-man exhbn., Bombay 50, later at Rome, Frankfurt, London, Zürich, Prague, Tokyo, New York, New Delhi, Calcutta, Kabul and Baghdad; mem. Lalit Kala Akademi, New Delhi 54; mem. Gen. Council Nat. Akademi of Art, New Delhi 55; First Nat. Award for Painting 55; Int. Award, Biennale Tokyo 59.
Major works: Murals for Air India Int. at Hong Kong, Bangkok, Zürich and Prague 57, and WHO Building, New Delhi 63; Mural in Mosaic for Lever Bros. and Aligarh Univ. 64; High Ceramic Mural for Indian Govt. Building, New Delhi; Exhibitor "Art now in India" exhbn., London 67.
Film: *Through the Eyes of the Painter* 67 (Golden Bear Award, Berlin 67).
6 Zeenat Manzil L. Jamshedji Road, Mahim, Bombay 16, India.

Husain, Mohamed Arshad, B.A.; Pakistani diplomatist; b. 9 Jan. 1910; ed. St. Catharine's Coll., Cambridge, and Middle Temple, London.
Deputy Sec. Ministry of Foreign Affairs 50-54; Counsellor and Chargé d'Affaires, Embassy of Pakistan, Brussels 54-56; Deputy High Commr. India 56; Joint Sec. Ministry of Foreign Affairs 57-59; Amb. to Sweden, Norway, Denmark and Finland 59-61, to U.S.S.R. and Czechoslovakia 61-63, to Nepal 63-65; High Commr. to India Oct. 63-68; Minister of External Affairs 68-March 69; Adviser to Gen. Yahya Khan March 69-Dec. 71; Sitara-i-Pakistan Award 67.
Home: 51/3 Lawrence Road, Lahore, Pakistan.

Husain, Mohammed Azim, M.A., BAR.-AT-LAW; Indian diplomatist; b. 5 Oct. 1913, Batala, India; s. of Sir Fazl-i-Husain, Kt., K.C.I.E., K.C.S.I.; m. Nusrat Malik 1945; one s. two d.; ed. Govt. Coll., Lahore, Christ's Coll., Cambridge, Univ. Coll., Oxford, and Lincoln's Inn, London.
Indian Civil Service in the Punjab 37-42; Under-Sec. Ministry of Defence 42-44; Deputy Sec. Ministry of Information and Broadcasting 45-48; Ministry of External Affairs 48-52; Consul-Gen., San Francisco 52-54; Joint Sec. Ministry of External Affairs 54-57; Deputy High Commr. to U.K. 57-60; Amb. to U.A.R., Yemen, Lebanon, Libya 60-64; Additional Sec. and Foreign Service Insp., Ministry of External Affairs 64-65, Sec. 65-67; Amb. to Switzerland and the Holy See, and leader Indian del. to Disarmament Conf.,

Geneva 67-70; del. to various UN, UNESCO, Afro-Asian, Commonwealth and Non-Aligned Confs.; Deputy Sec.-Gen. Commonwealth Secr. 70-.
Leisure interests: photography, history, literature.
Publs. include: *Panchayats in the Punjab* 42, *Fazli-Husain: A Political Biography* 46.
Commonwealth Secretariat, Marlborough House, Pall Mall, London, S.W.1, England.
Telephone: 01-839-3411.

Husák, Gustáv, LL.D., C.SC.; Czechoslovak politician; b. 10 Jan. 1913, Bratislava; ed. Law Faculty, Comenius Univ., Bratislava.
Junior lawyer, Bratislava 38-42; office worker 43-44; took part in Slovak Nat. Rising; Commr. of Interior 44-45; Commr. for Transport and Technology 45-46; Chair. of Board of Commrs. 46-50, concurrently Commr. for Agriculture 48; Dept. Head at Central Cttee. of C.P. of Slovakia 50-51; political imprisonment 51-60; Building Works, Bratislava 60-63; Scientific Worker, Inst. of Law, Slovak Acad. of Sciences 63-68; Deputy Premier 68; mem. 5th illegal Central Cttee. of C.P. of Slovakia; mem. Cen. Cttee., C.P. of Slovakia 43-44, 45-50, 68-71, of Presidium 43-44, 45-50, 68-69, of Secr. 68-69, First Sec. 68-69; mem. Presidium of Slovak Nat. Council 43-45, 68-69, Deputy of Slovak Nat. Council 45-50, 68-71; mem. Cen. Cttee. C.P. of Czechoslovakia 45, 49-51, 68-, of Presidium 45-50, 68-, Exec. Cttee. of Presidium 68-69, mem. Secr. 69-, First Sec. 69-71, Gen. Sec. 71-; mem. Nat. Assembly 45-51; Deputy to House of Nations, Fed. Assembly 68-71, Deputy to Slovak Fed. Assembly 71-75, Deputy to House of the People 71-73, mem. Presidium of Fed. Assembly 69-75; mem. Presidium, Cen. Cttee. Nat. Front of C.S.S.R. Jan. 71-, Chair. Cen. Cttee. 71-; C.-in-C. People's Militia of C.S.S.R. April 69, 75-; Pres. of Repub. of Czechoslovakia May 75-; Klement Gottwald Order 68, 73, Order of Lenin 69, 73, Hero of C.S.S.R. 69, 73, Order of Victorious February 73 and numerous foreign decorations.
Publs. *On the Agricultural Problem in Slovakia* 48, *The Struggle for Tomorrow* 48, *Evidence on Slovak National Rising* 64.
Secretariat of the Communist Party of Czechoslovakia, Prague, nábř. Kyjevské brigády 12; Prague-Hrad, Czechoslovakia.

Husein, Abdul-Aziz; Kuwaiti diplomatist; b. 1921, Kuwait; m. 1948; two s. one d.; ed. Teachers Higher Inst., Cairo and Univ. of London.
Former Dir. "House of Kuwait", Cairo, Dir.-Gen. Dept. of Educ., Kuwait; Amb. to the U.A.R. 61-62; Perm. Rep. to Arab League Council; appointed State Minister in Charge of Cabinet Affairs 63-64; Minister of State for Cabinet Affairs Feb. 71-.
Publ. *Lectures on Arab Society in Kuwait* 60.
c/o Ministry of State for Cabinet Affairs, Kuwait.

Husén, Torsten, M.A., PH.D.; Swedish educationist; b. 1 March 1916, Lund; s. of Johan and Betty (née Prawitz) Husén; m. Ingrid Joensson 1940; two s. one d.; ed. Univ. of Lund.
Research Asst., Inst. of Psychology, Univ. of Lund 38-43; Senior Psychologist, Swedish Armed Forces 44-51; Reader in Educational Psychology, Univ. of Stockholm 47-52, Prof. 53-56; Prof. of Educ. and Dir. Inst. of Educ. Research, Univ. of Stockholm 56-71, Prof. of Int. Educ. 71-; Chair. Int. Asscn. for the Evaluation of Educ. Achievement 62-; Fellow, Center for Advanced Study of the Behavioural Sciences, Stanford, Calif. 65-66; mem. Panel of Scientific Advisers to Swedish Govt. 62-69; Expert in Royal Comms. on Swedish School Reform 57-65; Consultant to OECD 68-; Chair. Governing Board, Int. Inst. Educ. Planning, Paris 70-; Visiting Prof., Univs. of Chicago 59, Hawaii 68, Ontario Inst. for Studies in Educ. 71; mem. Swedish Royal Acad. of Sciences 72-, U.S. Nat. Acad. of Educ.

67-; LL.D. h.c. (Chicago) 67; Medal for Distinguished Service in Int. Educ., Teachers' Coll., Columbia Univ. 70, Glasgow 74; D. Tech. (Brunel Univ.) 74; L.H.D. (Rhode Island Univ.) 75.
Leisure interest: book collecting (old books).
Publs. *Psychological Twin Research* 59, *Problems of Differentiation in Swedish Compulsory Schooling* 62, *International Study of Achievement in Mathematics I-II* 67, *Educational Research and Educational Change* 68, *Talent Opportunity and Career* 69, *Talent, Equality and Meritocracy* 74, *Social Influences on Educational Attainment* 75.
Institute for International Education, P.O. Box 5-10405, Stockholm 50; Home: Armfeltsgatan 10, 11534 Stockholm, Sweden.
Telephone: 08-15-01-60 (Office), 08-67-19-76 (Home).

Hussein, Abdirizak Haji; Somali politician; b. 1924, Galkayo District.
Joined Somali Youth League 44, Pres. 56-58; formed Greater Somali League 58, later formed Popular Movt. for Democratic Action; Minister of Interior, later of Works and Communications 60-64; Prime Minister 64-67; detained following coup 69, released April 73; Perm. Rep. to UN 74-.
Permanent Mission of Somalia to United Nations, 747 Third Avenue, 22nd Floor, New York, N.Y. 10017, U.S.A.

Hussein bin Onn, Datuk; Malaysian lawyer and politician; b. 12 Feb. 1922; ed. Cambridge School, Indian Mil. Acad., Dehra Dun, Lincoln's Inn, England.
Commissioned in Indian Army 42, served in Middle East and India; Mil. Gen. H.Q., New Delhi; with British Liberation Forces, Malaya 45; served Malay Admin. Service, Kuala Selangor and Klang 46-47; Nat. Youth Leader and Sec.-Gen. United Malays Nat. Org. (UMNO) 47; mem. Fed. Legislative Council, Jahore Council of State and State Exec. Council 48-57; called to the Bar, London 60; rejoined UMNO 68, Pres. 76-; mem. Parl. 70-; Minister of Educ. 70-73; Deputy Prime Minister 73-76, Minister of Finance and Co-ordinator of Public Corpns. 74-76; Prime Minister and Minister of Defence Jan. 76-; Seri Paduka Mahkota Johor.
Prime Minister's Office, Kuala Lumpur; Home: 3 Jalan Kenny, Kuala Lumpur, Malaysia.

Hussein ibn Talal, King of Jordan; b. 14 Nov. 1935; ed. Victoria Coll., Alexandria, Harrow School, and Royal Military Academy, Sandhurst, England.
Succeeded his father 11 Aug. 1952; came to power 2 May 1953; married 55, Princess Dina, d. of Abdel-Hamid Aoun of Saudi Arabia (marriage dissolved); married 61, Antoinette Gardiner (assumed name of Muna el Hussein), sons, Prince Abdullah b. 62, Prince Feisal b. 63, twin daughters, Princess Zein and Princess Ayeshia, b. April 68 (divorced); married 72, Alia Baha Eddin Toukan, daughter, Princess Haya b. 74.
Publs. *Uneasy Lies the Head* 62, *My War with Israel* 67.
Royal Palace, Amman, Jordan.

Husson, Jean Henri; French writer; b. 26 Feb. 1923, Paris; m. Raymonde Henry 1942; one s. two d.
Fire technician, Brigade de Sapeurs Pompiers de Paris; Palmes académiques; Grand Prix du Roman, Académie Française 65; Chevalier, Légion d'Honneur.
Leisure interest: fishing.
Publs. *La Brouillerie* 57, *Les Malles* 59, *La Bête Noire* 63, *Le Cheval d'Herbeleau* 65.
34 Avenue Franklin Roosevelt, 77 210 Avon, France.
Telephone: 422-47-26.

Hustich, Väinö Ilmari, PH.D.; Finnish professor; b. 11 Aug. 1911, Helsinki; m. Gunvor Ståhlström 1937; one s. one d.; ed. Helsinki Univ.
Professor of Econ. Geography 50-74, Rector of Swedish School of Econs., Helsinki 66-71; Chair. Comm. Archipelago Devt. 61-66; Minister of Trade and Industry

61-62; mem. State Foreign Trade Board 62-74, State Comm. for Devt. Areas 63-; Fellow, Arctic Inst. of N. America 67; Hon. mem. Geographical Soc. of Finland 71; Chair. Soc. Scientiarum Fennica 72-73, Academician 75-.
Leisure interest: nature.
Publs. on economics, political geography, Canadian and Finnish forests, etc.
Hollandarvagen 1, 00330 Helsinki, Finland.

Huston, John; Irish (b. American) film writer and director; b. 5 Aug. 1906, Nevada, Miss.; *s.* of Walter Huston and Rhea Gore Huston; *m.* Enrica Soma 1950 (died 1969), one *s.* one *d.*
Joined Warner Bros. Studio as writer 38; directed *The Maltese Falcon* 41, *In This Our Life* 42, *Key Largo* 48; writer and director Metro-Goldwyn-Mayer 49-; other films include *The Treasure of Sierra Madre* 47, *The Asphalt Jungle* 50, *The Red Badge of Courage* 51, *The African Queen* 52, *Moulin Rouge* 53, *Beat the Devil* 54, *Moby Dick* 56, *The Roots of Heaven* 58, *The Unforgiven*, *The Misfits* 60, *Freud* (or *The Secret Passion*) 62, *The Night of the Iguana* 64, *The Bible* 66, *Casino Royale* 67, *Reflections in a Golden Eye* 68, *Sinful Davey* 69, *A Walk with Love and Death* 69, *The Kremlin Letter* 70, *Fat City* 72, *The Life and Times of Judge Roy Bean* 73, *The Mackintosh Man* 73, *The Man Who Would Be King* 75; acted in *The Cardinal* 63, *The Bible* 66, *Candy* 68, *Chinatown* 74, *The Other Side of the Wind* 74; has also directed stage productions of *A Passage to Bali* 39, *No Exit* 45, *The Mines of Sulphur* 66; Screen Writers' Laurel Award 63.
Leisure interests: painting, fox hunting.
St. Clerans, Craughwell, Co. Galway, Ireland.

Huszár, István; Hungarian economist; b. 1927, Hernádkak; *s.* of István Huszár and Mária Kovács; *m.* Mária Forgó 1953; one *d.*; ed. Karl Marx Univ. of Econs., Budapest.
Joined Communist Party 48; Asst. Lecturer, Dept. of Statistics, Karl Marx Univ. of Econs. 51-53; worked in party headquarters 53-61, Deputy Head Dept. of State Admin. 61-63; mem. Cen. Cttee. Hungarian Socialist Workers' Party 70-, Political Cttee. 75-; Pres. Cen. Statistics Office, Sec. of State 69-73; First Deputy Pres. Nat. Planning Office; mem. State Planning Comm. 73; Deputy Prime Minister Nov. 73-; mem. Political Econ. Board attached to HSWP Cen. Cttee. 75-; Pres. Nat. Planning Office 75-; Vice-Pres. Hungarian Econ. Soc.; Titular Univ. Prof.
National Planning Office, 1370 Budapest, Arany János utca 6/8, Hungary.
Telephone: 111-050.

Hutasingh, Prakob, LL.B., D.JUR.; Thai judge; b. 5 Feb. 1912; ed. Vajiravuth Coll., Univ. of Jena and Thammasat Univ., Bangkok.
Joined the judiciary 37; Asst. Judge Court of Appeal 41; Sec. Supreme Court 48; Asst. Judge Supreme Court 50; Judge, Appeal Court 53; Judge, Supreme Court 60; Pres. Supreme Court 67-72; Minister of Justice 73-74; Deputy Prime Minister 74-75; Pres. Thai Bar and Inst. of Legal Educ., Thai Bar; Hon. D.C.L.
Publs. various legal textbooks.
2029/1 Banmai, Bangkok, Thailand.

Hutchins, Robert Maynard, A.B., A.M., LL.B., LL.D.; American lawyer and former university official; b. 17 Jan. 1899; ed. Oberlin Coll. and Yale Univ.
Sec. Yale Univ. 23-27, Acting Dean Yale Law School 27-28, Dean 28-29 and Prof. of Law 27-29; Pres. Univ. of Chicago 29-45, Chancellor 45-51; Dir. Encyclopaedia Britannica Inc., Encyclopaedia Britannica Ltd., and Encyclopaedia Britannica Films 43-74, and Chair. Board of Editors *Encyclopaedia Britannica* 46-74; Chair. The Great Books Foundation 47-50; Chair. Board of Editors *Measure* 49-51; Assoc. Dir. Ford

Foundation 51-54; Pres. Fund for the Republic 54-69, 75-, Chair. 69-74, Life Fellow 74-; Chief Exec. Officer Center for Study of Democratic Insts. 69-74, Life Fellow 74-, Pres. 75-; mem. American and Connecticut Bar Asscns.; Hon. mem. Chicago Bar Asscn.
Publs. *No Friendly Voice* 36, *The Higher Learning in America* 36, *Education for Freedom* 43, *St. Thomas and the World State* 49, *Morals, Religion and Higher Education* 50, *The Great Conversation* 52, *The Conflict in Education* 53, *The University of Utopia* 53, *Freedom, Education and the Fund* 56, *Some Observations on American Education* 56, *The Learning Society* 68, *Dr. Zuckerkandl* 68.
Center for the Study of Democratic Institutions, P.O. Box 4068, Santa Barbara, Calif. 93103, U.S.A.

Hutchinson, Edmond C., M.A., PH.D.; American business executive; b. 23 Nov. 1913, Rosemark, Tenn.; *s.* of Lawrence E. Hutchinson and Sue Maferrin Hutchinson; *m.* Minnie Louise Ingram 1938; two *s.*; ed. Southwestern Univ. and Univ. of Virginia.
Economist, Analyst, Railroad Retirement Board 38-42; Management Analyst, War Production Board 42-44; Provisional Dir.-Gen. of Finances, Iranian Govt. 44-46; Management Analyst, Civil Production Admin. 46, Dept. of Commerce 46-47; Budget Analyst, Dept. of Army, Japan 47-52; Budget Examiner, Dep. Divisional Chief, Bureau of Budget 53-58; Chief, Loan Operations 58-60; Asst. Deputy Man. Dir. for Operations, Development Loan Fund 60-61; Asst. Administrator for Africa, Agency for Int. Devt., Dept. of State 61-66; Chair. Exploration Devt. Group, Vice-Pres. Research Analysis Corpn. 67-72; Senior Vice-Pres. Amer. Technical Assistance Corpn. 72-.
American Technical Assistance Corpn., McLean, Va. 22101; Home: 9619 Hillridge Drive, Kensington, Maryland, U.S.A.

Hutchinson, Sir Joseph Burtt, Kt., C.M.G., F.R.S., SC.D.; British professor of agriculture; b. 21 March 1902, Burton Latimer; *s.* of Edmund and Lydia M. Hutchinson; *m.* Martha L. Johnson 1930; one *s.* one *d.*; ed. Ackworth and Bootham Schools, and St. John's Coll., Cambridge.
Formerly worked at Cotton Research Station, Trinidad, later at Inst. of Plant Industry, Indore, India; Dir. of Cotton Research Station, Namulonge, Uganda 49-57; Drapers Prof. of Agriculture, Cambridge Univ. 57-69, Prof. Emer. 69-; Chair. Council of Makerere Coll., Uganda 53-57; Fellow St. John's Coll., Cambridge, Linnean Soc.; Pres. British Asscn. for Advancement of Science 65-66; mem. Nature Conservancy 62-66; Hon. Fellow Makerere Coll.; Royal Soc. Leverhulme Visiting Prof., Indian Agric. Research Inst., Delhi, Oct. 69-Feb. 70; Royal Medal of the Royal Soc. 67; Hon. D.Sc. (Univs. of Nottingham and East Anglia); Foreign Fellow, Indian Nat. Science Acad. 74.
Leisure interest: gardening.
Publs. *The Genetics of Gossypium* 58, *Genetics and the Improvement of Tropical Crops* 58, *Application of Genetics to Cotton Improvement* 59, *Farming and Food Supply* 72; Editor *Essays on Crop Plant Evolution* 65, *Population and Food Supply* 69, *Evolutionary Studies in World Crops* 74.
St. John's College, Cambridge; Home: Huntingfield, Huntingdon Road, Cambridge CB3 0LH, England.
Telephone: Cambridge 61621 (College); Cambridge 76272 (Home).

Hutchison, Clyde A., Jr., PH.D.; American university professor; b. 5 May 1913, Alliance, Ohio; *s.* of Clyde A. Hutchison and Bessie G. Hutchison; *m.* Sarah Jane West 1937; two *s.* one *d.*; ed. Ohio State Univ.
National Research Council Fellow, Columbia Univ. 37-38; Asst. Prof. of Chemistry, Univ. of Buffalo 39-45; Research Assoc. Univ. of Virginia 42-43; Manhattan District Project, Columbia Univ. 43-45; Asst. Prof.

Enrico Fermi Inst., Univ. of Chicago 45-50, Dept. of Chem. 48-50; Assoc. Prof. Enrico Fermi Inst. and Dept. of Chem. 50-54, Prof. 54-63, Carl William Eisendrath Prof. 63-69, Carl W. Eisendrath Distinguished Service Prof. of Chem. 69-, Chair. Dept. of Chem. 59-62; Editor, *Journal of Chemical Physics*, American Inst. of Physics 53-59; mem. Nat. Acad. of Sciences, American Chem. Soc.; Fellow, American Acad. of Arts and Sciences, American Physical Soc. (mem. Council 67-71); Visiting Prof. sponsored by Japan Soc. for the Promotion of Science 75; Guggenheim Fellow, Oxford Univ. 55-56, 72-73; Ohio State Univ. Centennial Achievement Award 70; Peter Debye Award, American Chem. Soc. 72; Hon. D.Sc. (Cedarville).
Publs. 80 scientific papers, documents and contribs. to books.
Department of Chemistry, University of Chicago, Chicago, Ill. 60637, U.S.A.
Telephone: 312-753-8618.

Huvelin, Paul; French engineer; b. 22 July 1902, Chorey-les-Baune, Côte d'Or; m. Madeleine Giros 1928; eight *c.*; ed. Lycée Carnot, Dijon, and Ecole Polytechnique, Paris.
Engineer in charge of production, Société Métallurgique de Normandie 24-27; Chief Engineer, Sec. and Man. l'Electrique Lille-Roubaix-Tourcoing and Chemin de fer de l'Est de Lyon 28-36; Man. Soc. Industrielle de Gérance et d'Exploitation, later Manager Soc. Gén. d'Exploitations Industrielles (SOGEI) 36-47, Chair. of Board and Pres. 47-; Chair. and Pres. Energie Electrique du Nord de la France 40-46, Cie. Electrique de la Loire et du Centre 45-46; Chair. and Pres. Société Kleber-Colombes 59-70, Hon. Pres. 70-; Vice-Pres. Thomson-Brandt 72-; Dir. Soc. Générale d'Entreprises (SGE), Sogelerg, Cie. Financière de Suez, Cie. Péchiney Kuhlmann, Cie. Française Thomson CSF, CGE; Pres. Conseil Nat. du Patronat Français until 66 and Hon. Pres. Jan. 73-; Pres. l'Union des Industries de la Communauté Européenne (UNICE).
Leisure interests: shooting and tennis.
21 rue des Halles, 94536 Rungis, France.
Telephone: 687-22-36.

Huxley, Sir Andrew Fielding, Kt., F.R.S.; British physiologist; b. 22 Nov. 1917, London; s. of Leonard Huxley and Rosalind née Bruce; m. Jocelyn Richenda Gammell Pease 1947; one s. five d.; ed. Univ. Coll. School, Westminster School and Trinity Coll., Cambridge.
Operational Research, Anti-Aircraft Command 40-42, Admiralty 42-45; Fellow of Trinity Coll., Cambridge 41-60, Dir. of Studies 52-60, Hon. Fellow 67; Demonstrator, Dept. of Physiology, Cambridge Univ. 46-50, Asst. Dir. of Research 51-59, Reader in Experimental Biophysics 59-60; Jodrell Prof. of Physiology, Univ. Coll., London 60-69; Royal Soc. Research Prof. at Univ. Coll., London 69-; Pres. British Asscn. for the Advancement of Science 76-(77); Foreign Hon. mem. American Acad. of Arts and Sciences 61; Nobel Prize for Medicine 63; Hon. D.Sc. (Sheffield); Hon. M.D. (Saar); Hon. D.Sc. (Leicester) 67, (London) 73, (St. Andrews) 74; Copley Medal (Royal Soc.) 73.
Leisure interests: walking, design of scientific instruments.
Publs. papers chiefly in *Journal of Physiology*.
Manor Field, Grantchester, Cambridge, England.
Telephone: Trumpington 2207.

Huxley, Elspeth Josceline, C.B.E., J.P.; British author; b. 23 July 1907, London; d. of the late Josceline Grant and of Eleanor Grant; m. Gervas Huxley 1931; one s.; ed. Reading and Cornell Univs.
Assistant Press Officer, Empire Marketing Board 29-32; extensive travels in America, Africa and elsewhere with her husband Gervas Huxley; Justice of the Peace for Malmesbury; mem. Monckton Commission on Central Africa 60.
Leisure interests: reading, walking and country pursuits.
Publs. *White Man's Country, Lord Delamere and the Making of Kenya* (2 vols.) 33, *Red Strangers* (novel) 39, *The Walled City* (novel), *The Sorcerer's Apprentice* (travel) 48, *Four Guineas* (travel) 52, *A Thing to Love* (novel) 54, *The Red Rock Wilderness* (novel) 57, *The Flame Trees of Thika* (autobiography) 59, *A New Earth* 60, *The Mottled Lizard* 62, *The Merry Hippo* 63, *A Man from Nowhere* 63, *Forks and Hope* 64, *Back Street New Worlds* 64, *Brave New Victuals* 65, *Their Shining Eldorado* (travel) 67, *Love Among the Daughters* (3rd Vol. of autobiog.) 68, *The Challenge of Africa* 71, *Livingstone and his African Journeys* 74, *Florence Nightingale* 75, *Gallipot Eyes: A Wiltshire Diary* 76; also three detective novels 34-38.
Green End, Oaksey, nr. Malmesbury, Wilts., England.

Huxley, Hugh Esmor, M.B.E., F.R.S., M.A., PH.D., SC.D.; British scientist; b. 25 Feb. 1924, Birkenhead, Cheshire; s. of Thomas Hugh Huxley and Olwen Roberts; m. Frances Fripp 1966; one d.; two stepsons, one stepdaughter; ed. Park High School, Birkenhead and Christ's Coll., Cambridge.
Radar Officer, R.A.F. Bomber Command and Telecommunications Research Establishment, Malvern 43-47; Research Student, Medical Research Council Unit for Molecular Biology, Cavendish Laboratory, Cambridge 48-52; Commonwealth Fund Fellow, Biology Dept., Mass. Inst. of Technology 52-54; Research Fellow, Christ's Coll., Cambridge 53-56; mem. of External Staff of Medical Research Council and Hon. Research Assoc., Biophysics Dept., University Coll. London 56-61; mem. of Scientific Staff, Medical Research Council Laboratory of Molecular Biology, Cambridge 62-; Fellow, King's Coll., Cambridge 61-67, Churchill Coll., Cambridge 67-; Harvey Soc. Lecturer, New York 64-65; Wilson Lecturer, Univ. of Texas 68; Dunham Lecturer, Harvard Medical School 69; Croonian Lecture, Royal Soc. of London 70; Ziskind Visiting Prof. of Biology, Brandeis Univ. 71; Penn Lecturer, Univ. of Pennsylvania 71; Mayer Lecturer, Mass. Inst. of Technology 71; Miller Lecturer, State Univ. of New York 73; Carter-Wallace Lecturer, Princeton Univ. 73; Senior Visiting Lecturer, Physiology Course, Woods Hole, Mass. 66-71; mem. Advisory Board of Rosenstiel Basic Medical Sciences Center, Brandeis Univ. 71-; mem. Council of Royal Soc. of London 73-75; mem. German Acad. of Science, Leopoldina 64; Foreign Hon. mem. American Acad. of Arts and Sciences 65, Danish Acad. of Sciences 71; Feldberg Award for Experimental Medical Research 63, William Bate Hardy Prize of the Cambridge Philosophical Soc. 65; Hon. D.Sc. (Harvard) 69, (Univ. of Chicago) 74; Louisa Gross Horwitz Prize 71; Int. Feltrinelli Prize for Medicine 74; Int. Award, Gairdner Foundation 75; Baly Medal, Royal Coll. of Physicians 75.
Leisure interests: skiing, sailing.
Publs. Articles in scientific journals.
Medical Research Council Laboratory of Molecular Biology, Hills Road, Cambridge, England.
Telephone: Cambridge 48011.

Huxley, Sir Leonard George Holden, K.B.E., M.A., D.PHIL., PH.D., F.A.A.; Australian public official; b. 29 May 1902; ed. The Hutchins School, Hobart, Tasmania Univ. and New Coll., Oxford.
On scientific staff, C.S.I.R., Sydney 29-30; Lecturer, Univ. Coll., Nottingham, England 30-32; Head, Physics Dept., Univ. Coll., Leicester, England 32-40; Principal Scientific Officer, Telecommunications Research Establishment M.A.P. 40-46; Reader in Electromagnetism, Birmingham Univ., England 46-49; Elder Prof. of Physics, Adelaide Univ. 49-60; Vice-Chancellor, Australian Nat. Univ. 60-67; Pres. Australian Inst. of Physics 62-65; Fellow, Australian Acad. of Science 54-;

Chair. Radio Research Board of Australia 58-63, Radio Frequency Allocation Cttee. 60-64, Australian Nat. Standards Comm. 53-65, Gen. Council Encyclopaedia Britannica Australia 64-; mem. U.S. Education Foundation in Australia 60-64; mem. Nat. Library Council 60-, Exec. Commonwealth Scientific and Industrial Research Org. (C.S.I.R.O.) 60; mem. Australian-American Educ. Foundation 65-; Chair. Gen. Council Australia-Britannica Awards Scheme 64-; Trustee, Australian Humanities Research Council 68-70.

Publs. *Wave Guides* 47, numerous papers on gaseous electronics, electromagnetism, ionosphere and upper atmosphere.

19 Glasgow Place, Hughes, Canberra, A.C.T. 2605, Australia.

Telephone: Canberra 815560.

Huyghe, René; French art critic and historian; b. 3 May 1906, Arras, Pas de Calais; s. of Louis Huyghe and Marie Delvoye; *m.* Lydie Bouthet 1950; one s. one *d.*; ed. Ecole du Louvre and Faculty of Letters, Paris. On staff of Musée du Louvre 27; Asst. Keeper 30; Keeper of Paintings 37; Head Keeper of Paintings and Drawings 45; Prof. Ecole du Louvre; Prof. of Psychology of Plastic Arts, Coll. de France 50-; mem. French Museum Council 52, Vice-Pres. 64, Pres. 74-; Res. Prof. Nat. Gallery of Art Washington 68; Pres. UNESCO Int. Cttee. of experts to save Venice; Dir. Musée Jacquemart André 74; Dir. of art review *L'Amour de l'Art* 30-; founder and dir. of review *Quadrige* 45-; has collaborated or organized numerous exhibitions, including French Art, London 31, Van Gogh and Masterpieces of French Art, Paris 37, Modern Painting, Rio de Janeiro 45, etc.; has made three art films, including *Rubens and His Age* (Venice Festival Prize); mem. and fmr. Pres. Académie Septentrionale; Grand Officier Légion d'Honneur, Commdr. Ordre des Arts et Lettres 74, Commdr. Ordre de Léopold, Commdr. Order of Merit (Italy); mem. Acad. Française 60-; Erasmus Prize 66. Publs. *Histoire de l'Art Contemporain* 34, *Cézanne* 36, *La Peinture française: le portrait* (2 vols.) 37, *Les Dessins de Van Gogh* 37, *Les Contemporains* 39, *La Peinture actuelle* 45, *La Poétique de Vermeer* 48, *Le Dessin français au XIXe siècle* 49, *Univers de Watteau* 50, *Gauguin et Noa-Noa* 51, *Le Carnet de Gauguin* 52, *La Peinture d'Occident* 52, *Dialogue avec le Visible* 55, *L'Art et l'Homme*, Vol. I 57, Vol. II 58, Vol. III 61, *Van Gogh* 58, *Gauguin* 59, *L'Art et l'Ame* 60, *Peinture française aux XVIIe et XVIIIe Siècles*, 62, *Delacroix ou le Combat Solitaire* 63, *Les Puissances de l'Image* 65, *Sens et Destin de l'Art* 67, *L'Art et le Monde Moderne* 2 vols. 70, *Formes et Forces* 71, *La Relève du Réel* 74.

3 rue Corneille, Paris 6e, France.

Huynh Tan Phat; Vietnamese politician; b. 1913. Member Vanguard Youth 45; Editor *Thanh-nien* during anti-French struggle; remained in S. Viet-Nam after Geneva Agreement 54; mem. Democratic Party; Sec.-Gen. Nat. Liberation Front (N.L.F.) 64-; Chair. Provisional Revolutionary Govt. of Repub. of S. Viet-Nam 69- (in Saigon 75-).

Provisional Revolutionary Government, Saigon, South Viet-Nam.

Hvass, Frants, B.L.; Danish diplomatist; b. 29 Aug. 1896, Copenhagen; s. of Anders Hvass and Augusta (née Saxild); *m.* Esther Baroness Lerche; one s.; ed. Univ. of Copenhagen.

Entered foreign service 22; served Hamburg 27, Ministry of Foreign Affairs 30, London 33; Min. Foreign Affairs 36, Vice-Head of Section, Economic Div. 39, Head, Chief Admin. Div. 40, Chief Political and Judicial Div. 41; Permanent Under-Sec. of State for Foreign Affairs 45-49; Head of Military Mission, Berlin, and Head of Mission to Allied High Command Bonn 49; Amb. to Germany 51-66; Sec. Danish Del. to Disarmament Conf. Geneva 32, Danish Cttee. for Scandinavian Econ. Collaboration 37-39; mem. Del. to UN Paris 48, New York 49; mem. Scandinavian Defence Cttee. 48-49; Vice-Pres. Int. Inst. of Admin. Sciences 47, Pres. 56, Hon. Pres. 62; Grand Cross and Cross of Honour, Order of Dannebrog, Grand Cross Order of Nordstjaernan (Sweden), St. Olav (Norway), of Léopold II (Belgium); Grand Officier Légion d'Honneur; Grand Cross of Germany.

Leisure interest: reading of memoirs.

1206, Nabolös 4, Copenhagen K, Denmark.

Telephone: 141241.

Hyder, Sajjad, B.A.; Pakistani diplomatist; b. 1920; ed. Govt. High School, Jullundur, D.A.V. Coll., Jullundur, and Indian Mil. Acad., Dehradun.

Served as Commissioned Officer in Asia, Second World War; Third Sec., Indian Foreign Service, New Delhi 47, Second Sec., Washington 48; Second Sec., First Sec. and Counsellor, London 52; Dir. Pakistan Foreign Office, Karachi 55; Dep. High Commr., New Delhi 57-59, London 59-61; Ambassador to Iraq 61-65, to United Arab Repub. 65-68; High Commr. in India 68-71; Amb. to Fed. Germany 72-75, to U.S.S.R. 75-.

17 Sadova Kudrinskaya, Moscow, U.S.S.R.

Hyman, Joe; British textile executive; b. 14 Oct. 1921; *m.* 1st Corrine I. Abrahams 1950 (marriage dissolved), one s. one *d.*; *m.* 2nd Simone Duke 1963, one s. one *d.*; ed. North Manchester Grammar School.

Entered father's General Textile Merchanting Co. 37; founder Portland Woollen Co. 46; owner Melso Fabrics Ltd., now Gainsborough Cornard Ltd. (Cornard Knitting Mills Ltd., Fine Jersey Ltd., and Cooper Bros.) 57; Gainsborough Cornard and William Hollins Ltd. merged to form Viyella Int. Ltd. 61, Chair. 62-69, Dir. 61-70; Chair. John Crowther and Sons (Milnsbridge) Ltd. 71-; mem. Lloyds; Trustee, Pestalozzi Children's Village 67-; mem. Textile Council 68; Gov. Bedales School 66; Gov. London School of Econs. 68; Fellow, Royal Soc. of Arts, British Inst. of Management; Companion of Textile Inst.; Pres. Textile Benevolent Asscn.

Lukyns, Ewhurst, Surrey, England.

Hyslop, Robert, A.A.S.A.; Australian SEATO official; b. 24 Dec. 1918, N.S.W.; s. of William Hyslop and Mary Annie (Elliott); *m.* Dorothy M. Fleming 1946; two *d.*; ed. Maitland High School, Australian Admin. Staff Coll. and Joint Services Staff Coll. (U.K.).

Appointed Commonwealth Public Service 36; various posts in naval admin.; Asst. Sec. Navy Dept. 59; served U.K. Admiralty 58, in Korea and Japan 64, U.S.A. and Canada 65; Public Service Fellow Research School of Social Sciences, Australian Nat. Univ. 68-69; Dep. Sec.-Gen. South East Asia Treaty Org. (SEATO) 69-.

Leisure interests: reading, study of public administration, bowls, badminton.

Publs. Articles in journals; *Australian Naval Administration 1900-1939* 73.

Headquarters, SEATO, Sriayuthaya Road, P.O. Box 517, Bangkok, Thailand.

Hyuga, Hosai; Japanese metals executive; b. 24 Feb. 1906, Yamanashi Pref.; *m.* 1933; one s. one *d.*; ed. Univ. of Tokyo.

Head Office, Sumitomo Group 31-41; Govt. Service 41; Sumitomo Group 41-, Dir. Sumitomo Metal Industries Ltd. 49-, Man. Dir. 52-58, Senior Man. Dir. 58-60, Exec. Vice-Pres. 60-62, Pres. 62-74, Chair. 74-.

Leisure interests: short poem writing, golf.

177-2 Higashiyama-cho, Ashiya-shi, Hyogo-ken, 659 Japan.

Telephone: 0797-22-3249.

I

Iacocca, Lee A.; American automobile executive; b. 15 Oct. 1924, Allentown, Pa.; ed. Lehigh and Princeton Univs.
With Ford Motor Co. 46; District Sales Man., Washington 56; Ford Div. Truck Marketing Man. 56; Car Marketing Man. 57; Vice-Pres. and Gen. Man., Ford Div. 60-65; Vice-Pres. Car and Truck Group 65; Exec. Vice-Pres., North American Automotive Operations 67; Exec. Vice-Pres., Ford Motor Co. and Pres. Ford North American Automotive Operations 69-70, Pres. Ford Motor Co. 70-; Hon. doctorates, Muhlenberg Coll. and Babson Inst.; mem. Soc. Automotive Engineers.
571 Edgemere Court, Bloomfield Hills, Michigan, U.S.A.

Iakavos, Archbishop; American ecclesiastic; b. 29 July 1911, Island of Imbros, Turkey; s. of Maria and Athanasios Coucouzis; baptismal name Demetrios; ed. Theological School of Halki, Istanbul.
Deacon 34; ordained priest in Lowell, Mass., U.S.A. 40; Dean Cathedral of the Annunciation, Boston 42-54; Bishop of Malta 54; Rep. of Patriarch of Constantinople to World Council of Churches, Geneva 55; Archbishop, Greek Orthodox Church in North and South America 59-; Pres. World Council of Churches 59-68; 13 hon. degrees.
Orthodox Cathedral of the Holy Trinity, 10 East 79th Street, New York, N.Y. 10021, U.S.A.

Iannella, Egidio; Argentine banker; b. 16 May 1921, Buenos Aires; s. of Antonio and Carmen Bárbaro de Iannella; m. Sara Asunción Iglesias 1945; one d.; ed. Escuela Nacional de Comercio, Buenos Aires, Univ. Nacional de Buenos Aires and Centro de Estudios Monetarios Latinamericanos, Mexico.
Various positions in Banco Central de la República Argentina 39-56, Banco Argentino de Comercio 56-66; Gen. Man. Banco Central de la República Argentina 67-69, Pres. 69-70; Exec. Vice-Pres. Banco Federal Argentino 71-.
Calle Reconquista 314, Buenos Aires, Argentina.

Ibe, Kyonosuke; Japanese banker; b. 28 July 1908, Tokyo; s. of Naomitsu Ibe; m. Kimi Yokoyama 1934; two s. one d.; ed. Tokyo Imperial Univ. (now Tokyo Univ.).
Joined Sumitomo Bank 33, Dir. 57-60, Man. Dir. 60-64, Senior Man. Dir. 64-71, Deputy Pres. 71-73, Pres. 73-; Chair. Board of Trustees, Kansai Cttee. for Econ. Devt.; Trustee, Japan Cttee. for Econ. Devt. 71-72, 73-; Vice-Chair. Fed. of Bankers' Asscns. 73-74; Chair. Osaka Bankers' Asscn. 73-74, Vice-Chair. 74-; Exec. Dir. Fed. of Econ. Orgs. 73-.
Leisure interests: opera, classical music, reading, painting.
The Sumitomo Bank, 5-22 Kitahama, Higashi-ku, Osaka; Home: 31 Higashiashiya-machi, Ashiya-city, Hyogo, Japan.
Telephone: 03-227-2111 (Office); 0797-22-4153 (Home).

Ibekwe, Hon. Dan Onwura, Q.C.; Nigerian barrister-at-law; b. 1922, Onitsha, East-Central State; s. of Chief Akukalia Omedike Ibekwe and Amaliwu Nwabunie Ibekwe; m. Cecilia Nkemdilim Ibekwe 1953; two s. six d.; ed. Saint Mary's School, Onitsha, Christ the King Coll., Onitsha, Council on Legal Educ. Law School, London.
Called to the English and Nigerian Bars 51; law practice with J. I. C. Taylor 51-54, at Aba, Nigeria 54-56; Legal Adviser to the Premier, Eastern Region 56-58; Solicitor-Gen., Eastern Region 58-64; Senator and Fed. Minister in charge of Commonwealth Relations, Ministry of External Affairs 65-66; Solicitor, firm of Messrs. Irving and Bonnar 66; detained in the then Biafra 67-70;

Commr. for Works, Housing and Transport, East Cen. State 70-72; Justice of the Supreme Court Sept. 72-.
Leisure interests: gardening, music, table tennis, reading.
Publ. *Justice in Blunderland.*
The Supreme Court of Nigeria, Lagos; Residence: 11 Ikoyi Crescent, Ikoyi, Lagos, Nigeria.
Telephone: 21466 (Office).

Ibiam, Sir Francis Akanu, K.C.M.G., K.B.E.; Nigerian medical missionary and politician; b. 29 Nov. 1906; ed. Hope Waddell Training Inst., Calabar, King's Coll., Lagos and Univ. of St. Andrews (Scotland).
Medical Missionary, Church of Scotland Mission, Calabar, Nigeria 36-, built Abiriba Hospital 36-45, Medical Supt. C.S.M. Hospital, Itu 45-48, Uburu 52-57; mem. Board of Govs. Hope Waddell Training Inst. 45-57, Principal 57-60; mem. Legislative Council, Nigeria 47-52, Exec. Council 49-52, Privy Council, E. Region of Nigeria 54-59; Gov. E. Nigeria 60-66; Adviser to Mil. Gov. of Eastern Provinces, Nigeria 66-; Pres. Christian Council of Nigeria 55-58; Chair. Provisional Cttee. of All-Africa Church Council 58-62, Council of Univ. Coll., Ibadan 58-61; one of six Pres. World Council of Churches 61.
1 Mount Street, Enugu, Nigeria.

Ibingira, Grace S., LL.B.; Ugandan diplomatist; b. 23 May 1932; m. Monica Ntarumbane 1965; three c.; ed. Mbarara High School, King's Coll., Budo, Univ. of Wales and King's Coll., London.
Called to Bar, Middle Temple 59; practised law in Uganda as advocate of the High Court until 62; Minister of Justice 62; Minister of State and Sec. Gen., Uganda People's Congress 64-66; detained without trial 66-71; Perm. Rep. to UN July 71-74; Consultant, UN Fellow Programme, Carnegie Endowment for Int. Peace 74-.
Leisure interests: painting, tennis.
Publ. *The Forging of an African Nation* 73.
United Nations Plaza, 46th Street, New York, N.Y. 10017, U.S.A.

Ibrahim, Major Abu al-Qassim Mohammed; Sudanese army officer and politician; b. 1937, Omdurman; ed. Khartoum Secondary School and Military Coll.
Commissioned 61; mem. Revolutionary Council 69; Minister of Local Govt. 69-70; Asst. Prime Minister for Services 70; Minister of Interior 70-71, of Health and Social Welfare 71-73, of Agric., Food and Natural Resources 74-; mem. Political Bureau of Sudanese Socialist Union; Deputy Sec.-Gen. for Org. and Admin., SSU.
Ministry of Agriculture, Khartoum, Sudan.

Ibrahim, Sir Kashim, K.C.M.G., C.B.E.; Nigerian politician; b. 10 June 1910; ed. Bornu Provincial School, Katsina Teachers' Training Coll.
Teacher 29-32; Visiting Teacher 33-49; Education Officer 49-52; Central Minister of Social Service 52-55; Northern Regional Minister of Social Development and Surveys 55-56; Waziri of Bornu 56-62; Gov. of Northern Nigeria 62-66; Chair. Nigerian Coll. of Arts, Science and Technology 58-62, Provincial Council of Ahmadu Bello Univ. 61-62; Adviser to Mil. Gov. of Northern Nigeria 66; Chancellor, Ibadan Univ. 67-; Grand Cross Order of the Niger.
Publs. *Kanuri Reader Elementary I-IV, Kanuri Arithmetic Books I-IV for Elementary Schools.*
Government Lodge, Kaduna, Northern Nigeria, Nigeria.

Ibrahim, Mohamed Hamid; Ethiopian diplomatist; b. 21 Aug. 1931, Asbe Teferi, Harrar; ed. Univ. of Addis Ababa, McGill Univ. and Columbia Univ.
Entered Ministry of Foreign Affairs 60, Dir.-Gen. Dept.

of Int. Org. 62, Vice-Minister 72, Head of American Affairs Dept. 72-75; Perm. Rep. to UN Sept. 75-; Special Asst. to Sec.-Gen. of Founding Conf. of OAU 63; mem. Judicial Review Panel of Crown Appeal Court 65-74; Sec.-Gen. Constitutional Review Comm. 74; mem. dels. to UN Gen. Assembly 61, 65, 67, 72, 74, Vienna Conf. on Diplomatic Relations 61, Conf. of Cttee. on Disarmament 62-63, Vienna Conf. on Law of Treaties 66-67, Cttee. on Peaceful Uses of the Sea-Bed 73, Third UN Conf. on the Law of the Sea (second session) 74; mem. Sixth Cttee. (Legal) of UN Gen. Assembly.

Permanent Mission of Ethiopia to the United Nations, 866 United Nations Plaza, Room 560, New York, N.Y. 10017, U.S.A.

Ibrahim, Sid Moulay Abdullah; Moroccan politician; b. 1918; ed. Ben Youssef Univ., Marrakesh and the Sorbonne, Paris.
Member Istiqlal (Independence) Party 44-59; mem. Editorial Cttee. *Al Alam* (Istiqlal organ) 50-52; imprisoned for political reasons 52-54; Sec. of State for Information and Tourism, First Moroccan Nat. Govt. 55-56; Minister of Labour and Social Affairs 56-57; Prime Minister and Minister of Foreign Affairs Dec. 58-May 60; leader Union Nationale des Forces Populaires 59-.
Union Nationale des Forces Populaires, B.P. 747, Casablanca, Morocco.

Ibrahimov, Mirza Ajar-ogly; Soviet politician and writer; b. 5 Oct. 1911, Eva village, Sarab, Iran; ed. Inst. of Oriental History.
Member Acad. of Sciences of Azerbaizhan; mem. C.P.S.U. 30-; Minister of Educ., Azerbaizhan 42-47; Vice-Chair. Azerbaizhan S.S.R. Council of Ministers 47-52; Chair. Azerbaizhan S.S.R. Union of Writers 48-54, First Sec. 65-; Chair. of the Supreme Soviet of the Azerbaizhan S.S.R. 54-58; Deputy of the Supreme Soviet of the U.S.S.R.; mem. Comm. for Legislative Proposals Soviet of Nationalities; Red Banner of Labour; State prizewinner 51; awarded Order of Lenin 66; mem. Cen. Cttee. of Azerbaizhan C.P.
Publs. plays: *Hayat* 37, *Madrid* 38, *Mahabbeth* 42, *The Country Girl* 62, *A Good Man* 65; novels: *The Day Will Come* 51, *Beyuk Dayag* 57; scientific works: *Beyuk democrat* 39, *Hayat ve edebijyath* 47, *Halgilik ve realizm jabhesinden* 62, *According to Laws of Beauty* 64, *Collected Works* (10 vols.) 64, *Jalil Mamed—Kuli-Zade* 66, *On the Slopes of the Murovdag* 67, *Flames are blowing* 68.
Azerbaizhan S.S.R. Union of Writers, Baku, U.S.S.R.

Ibuka, Masaru; Japanese industrialist; b. 11 April 1908; ed. Waseda Senior High School and Waseda Univ.
Research Engineer, Photo-Chemical Laboratory 33-37; Man. Radio Telegraphy Dept., Japan Audio Optical Industrial Corpn. 37-40; Man. Dir. Japan Measuring Apparatus Co. Ltd. 40-45; Organizer, Tokyo Telecommunications Engineering Corpn. 45- (Sony Corpn. since 58), Pres., Man. Dir. 50-71, Chair. 71-; Chair. Japan Cttee. for Econ. Development; mem. Econ. Council; dir. several industrial asscns.; Blue Ribbon Medal 60; Founders Medal, IEEE 72; Hon. D.Sc. (Plano Univ.) 74.
7-35 Kitashinagawa 6-chome, Shinagawuku, Tokyo; and 7-1-702 Mita 2-chome, Minatoku, Tokyo, Japan.

Icaza Coronel, Jorge; Ecuadorean writer and diplomatist; b. 10 July 1906, Quito; m. Marina Moncayo 1936; two d.; ed. Colegio San Gabriel, Colegio Nacional Mejía, and Universidad Nacional, Quito.
Actor and Theatre Dir. 29-32; playwright, civil servant and businessman 33-44; Founder and Titular mem. Cultural Council, Organizer and first Sec.-Gen. Union of Writers and Artists 44-60; Dir. Nat. Library 60-73; Amb. to U.S.S.R. 73, 75- (also accred. to German Democratic Repub. and Poland); del. to various Latin

American Cultural Congresses; mem. numerous foreign literary socs.; awards include First Prize for Latin American Novel of *La Revista Americana de Buenos Aires* 36, and First Prize for Ecuadorean Novel.
Publs. Plays: *El Intruso* 29, *La Comedia sin Nombre* 30, *Por el Viejo* 31, *Cuál Es?* 31, *Como Ellos Quieren* 32, *Sin Sentido* 32, *Flagelo* 36; short stories: *Barro de la Sierra* 33, *Seis Relatos* 52, *Viejos Cuentos* 60; novels: *Huasipungo* 34, *En las Calles* 35, *Cholos* 37, *Media vida Deslumbrados* 42, *Huairapamushcas* 48, *El Chulla Romero y Flores* 58.
Ecuador Embassy, Gorokhovsky per. 12, Moscow, U.S.S.R.; Rocafuerte (Pasaje del Seguro) No. 12, Quito, Ecuador.
Telephone: 218416 (Ecuador).

Ichikawa, Kon; Japanese film director; b. 1915; ed. Ichioka Commercial School, Osaka.
Films include: *Poo-San* 53, *A Billionaire* 54, *The Heart* 54, *Punishment Room* 55, *The Burmese Harp* 56, *The Men of Tohoku* 56, *Conflagration* 58, *Fires on the Plain* 59, *The Key* 59, *Bonchi* 60, *Her Brother* 60, *The Sin* 61, *Being Two Isn't Easy* 62, *The Revenge of Yuki-No-Jo* 63, *Alone on the Pacific* 63, *Tokyo Olympiad* 64, *Seishun* 70, *To Love Again* 71, *The Wanderers* 73, *Visions of Eight* (co-dir.) 73.
c/o Ishihara International Productions, Kimuraya Building, 24 Toranomon Shiba, Minato-ku, Tokyo 105, Japan.

Ichimada, Hisato; Japanese financier and politician; b. 12 Aug. 1893; ed. Tokyo Univ.
Served with Bank of Japan 18-54, Pres. 46-54; mem. of Japanese Del. to San Francisco Peace Conf. 51; Minister of Finance 54-56, 57-58; mem. House of Reps. 55-; Chair. Overseas Economic Co-operation Special Cttee. of Liberal Democratic Party 59-; Hon. Ph.D. (Syracuse Univ.), Hon. Ph.D. (International Christian Univ.).
5-30, 3-chome, Nishi-Azabon, Minato-ku, Tokyo, Japan.

Ide, Ichitaro; Japanese politician; b. 1911; ed. Kyoto Univ.
Member, House of Reps.; Chair. House of Reps. Agriculture, Forestry and Fishery Affairs Cttee., also Budget Cttee.; fmr. Minister of Agriculture and Forestry; Vice-Chair. Liberal-Democratic Party Foriegn Affairs Research Council; Minister for Posts and Telecommunications 70-71; Chief Cabinet Sec. Dec. 74-.
House of Representatives, Tokyo, Japan.

Idemitsu, Keisuke; Japanese business executive; b. 1900; ed. Tokyo Commercial Coll.
Managing Dir. Idemitsu Kosan Co., Ltd. 47, Senior Man. Dir. 50, Pres. 66, Chair. 72-.
Idemitsu Kosan Co. Ltd., 1-1, 3-chome, Marunouchi, Chiyoda-ku, Tokyo, Japan.

Idemitsu, Sazo; Japanese business executive; b. 22 Aug. 1885, Munakata-gun, Fukuoka-ken; s. of Toroku and Chiyo Idemitsu; m. Yasuko Yamauchi 1927; one s. four d.; ed. Kobe Commercial Coll.
Founded Idemitsu Shokai 11; Pres. Moji Chamber of Commerce 33; Pres. Idemitsu Kosan Co., Ltd. (with which Idemitsu Shokai had merged) 40-66, Chair. 66-72; Blue Ribbon Medal.
Leisure interests: art collection, golfing.
Publs. *Fifty Years of Respecting Humanity* 62, *If Karl Marx Had Been Born in Japan* 66, *Capitalism and Working People* 69.
c/o Idemitsu Kosan Co. Ltd., 1-1, 3-chome, Marunouchi, Chiyoda-ku, Tokya, Japan.

Idenburg, Philippus Jacobus, DR.JUR.; Netherlands statistician and educationist; b. 26 Nov. 1901, Hillegersberg; s. of J. D. J. Idenburg and C. Th. Hoedemaker; m. 2nd S. C. Kohnstamm 1952; two s. three d. (by previous marriage); ed. Univs. of Amsterdam and Leiden.
Secretary of a Govt. Efficiency Cttee. 27-28; Chief of a

Div. of Netherlands Central Bureau of Statistics 29-38; Dir. of Bureau of Statistics 39-45; Dir.-Gen. of Educ. 46; Dir.-Gen. of Statistics 47-66; Prof. of Educ., Univ. of Amsterdam 66-71; fmr. Pres. Netherlands Arts Council, Netherlands Foundation for Statistics; Hon. D.Litt. (Durban).
Publs. Books and articles on statistics and education.
Rue de l'Eglise 129, 6925 Fays-Famenne par Wellin, Belgium.
Telephone: 084 388060.

Idris I (Sayyid Muhammad Idris as-Sanusi); Former King of Libya; b. 1890.
Son of Sayyid Muhammad al-Mahdi; succeeded his uncle, Sayyid Ahmad Asharif Idris as-Sanusi, in charge of affairs of the Senusiya Order 16; became Amir of Cyrenaica; proclaimed King of Libya 2 Dec. 50; deposed 1 Sept. 69; sentenced to death *in absentia* 71.
Now living in Egypt.

Iduarte Foucher, Andrés, LL.D., D.PHIL.; Mexican writer; b. 1 May 1907, Villahermosa, Tabasco; s. of late Chief Justice and Prof. Andrés Iduarte Alfaro y Figueroa and Adela Foucher Paullada y Molina; m. Graciela Frías-Amescua 1932; no c.; ed. Nat. Univ. of Mexico, Univ. of Paris, Central Univ. of Madrid and Columbia Univ., N.Y.
Assistant Prof. of History, Nat. Univ. of Mexico 30-32; First Sec., Ibero-American Section, Ateneo, Madrid 35; Instructor in Spanish, Columbia Univ., N.Y. 39-45, Asst. Prof. of Spanish American Literature 45-50, Acting Dir. Univ. Hispanic Inst. 49, First Cttee. for Rómulo Gallegos Int. Novel Contest 67, Assoc. Prof. 50-60, Full Prof. 60-, Asst. Dir. 55-65; mem. Cttee. for Rómulo Gallegos Int. Novel Contest 67; Dir.-Gen. Nat. Inst. of Fine Arts, Mexico 52-54; mem. Cuban Acad. of History 46, Societé Européenne de Culture 50, Mexican Acad. of Int. Law 67, Mexican Acad. of Language 69; Corresp. mem. Spanish Acad. 69; several literary prizes; Orders of Céspedes (Cuba) 46; Dr. h.c. (Univ. de San Nicolás de Hidalgo, Mexico); C.B.E. 53; Pres. Int. Inst. of Ibero-American Literature 57-59.
Leisure interests: horse riding, swimming, rowing.
Publs. *El Himno a la sangre* 28, *El Liberador Simón Bolívar* 30, *El problema moral de la juventud mexicana* 31, *El Caballero Matón* 32, *Rebeldía y disciplina en Hostas* 40, *Martí Escritor* 45, *Retrato de Rubén Romero* 46, *Sarmiento a través de sus mejores páginas* 49, *Prosas de Martí* 50, *Pláticas Hispano-americanas* 51, *Un Niño en la Revolución Mexicana* 51, *Veinte Años con Rómulo Gallegos* 54, *La Isla sin Veneno* 54, *Sarmiento, Martí y Rodó* 55, *Alfonso Reyes, el Hombre y su Mundo* 56, *Gabriela Mistral, santa a la jineta* 58, *Martín Luis Guzmán en sus libros* 60, *Don Pedro de Alba y su Tiempo* 62, *México en la nostalgia* 65, *Tres escritores mexicanos* 67, *Juárez, máximo símbolo* 67, *El Mundo Sonriente* 68, *Niño: Child of the Mexican Revolution* (Trans.) 71, *Diez estampas mexicanas* 71, *Lunes de El Nacional* 75.
Casa Hispánica, Columbia University, 612 West 116 Street, New York, N.Y. 10027, U.S.A.

Idzumbuir, Asal Bolumba; Zairian diplomatist; b. 9 Nov. 1930; ed. Lovanium-Kisantu Inst., Mayidi Seminary and Inst. of International Studies, Geneva.
Minister Plenipotentiary, Perm. Rep. to UN 63-72; Vice-Pres. UN Gen. Assembly 67; Amb. to U.K. March-Sept. 72; Dir. of Int. Orgs., Ministry of Foreign Affairs 72-73; Amb. to Brazil 73-; Nat. Order of Leopard 66.
Embassy of Zaire, Edificío Venâncio III, 2° andar, salas 201-208, Brasília, Brazil.

Ieng Sary; Cambodian politician; m. Ieng Thirith; ed. Paris.
Former teacher; active in left-wing movements and forced to flee Phnom-Penh 63; prominent in *Khmers*

Rouges insurgent movement 63-75; *Khmers Rouges* liaison officer to Royal Govt. of Nat. Union of Cambodia (GRUNC) in exile 71-75; mem. Politburo Nat. United Front of Cambodia (FUNC) 70-; Second Deputy Prime Minister with special responsibility for Foreign Affairs, GRUNC 75-76.
c/o Office of the Deputy Prime Minister, Phnom-Penh, Cambodia.

Iengar, H. V. R.; Indian banker and industrialist; b. 23 Aug. 1902, Holénarsipur, Mysore; s. of H. V. R. and Mrs. Iengar; m. Sushila Iengar 1932; one s. one d.
Held several posts in the Indian Civil Service including Sec. Ministry of Commerce and Industry; Chair. State Bank of India 56-57; Gov. Reserve Bank of India 57-62; Chair. Indian Aluminium Co. Ltd. 62-72, Herdillia Chemicals Ltd. 64-73.
Leisure interest: golf.
c/o Indian Aluminium Co. Ltd., Indal House, 50 Residency Road, Bangalore 25; Home: "Pushpanjali" 125/126 Rajamahal Vilas Extension, Bangalore 6, India.
Telephone: Bangalore 30897.

Igler, Hans, D.ECON.; Austrian business administrator; b. 29 July 1920, Vienna; s. of Robert Igler and Maria (née Seidel); m. Dorothea Monti 1948; one s. three d.; ed. Hochschule für Welthandel, Vienna.
Military service until 45, Marshall Plan consultant in Fed. Ministry of Property Control and Econ. Planning 46-50; Head ERP Office, Fed. Chancellery 50-55; Chair. Board of Man. Dirs. Österreichische Industrie-u. Bergbauverwaltungsges.m.b.H. (holding for nationalized industries) 56-59; Consultant to Govt. of Chile for UN and FAO econ. programme 59; Partner, Bankhaus Schoeller & Co. and Gebr. Schoeller, Vienna 60-; Pres. Fed. of Austrian Industrialists 72-, Elin-Union AG für Elektrische Industrie Vienna, Kabel- und Drahtwerke AG Vienna, Österr. Mineralölverwaltung AG Vienna; Chair. Nettingsdorfer Papier-u. Sulfatzellulose Fbk. AG Nettingsdorf, Wertheim-Werke AG Vienna, Austro-Olivetti-Büromaschinen-AG Vienna, Chemie Linz AG, Schmalbach-Lubeca Austria, Vienna, Siemens AG Österreich Vienna, Leipnik-Lundenburger Zuckerfabriken AG Vienna; mem. Supervisory Board Österr. Industrieverwaltungs-AG Vienna; Man. Schoeller Ges. m.b.H. Vienna, "Contex" Kontinentale Export-u. Import Grobhandelsges. m.b.H.; Board mem. Persil G.m.b.H., Vienna, Österr. Institut für Wirtschaftsforschung, Vienna; mem. Board of Man. Dirs. Deutsche Handelskammer Vienna.
1010 Wien I, Renngasse 3, Austria.
Telephone: 63-56-71.

Iglesias, Enrique V.; Uruguayan United Nations official; b. 26 March 1930; ed. Univ. of Uruguay.
Held several positions including Professor Agregado, Faculty of Political Economy, Prof. of Econ. Policy and Dir. Inst. of Econs., Univ. of Montevideo 52-67; Sec.-Gen. Sugar Comm. of Uruguay 59-60; Technical Dir. Nat. Planning Office of Uruguay 61-65; Pres. (Gov.), Central Bank of Uruguay 67-69; Pres. Gov. Council, Latin American Inst. for Econ. and Social Planning (ILPES), UN 67-71; Adviser, Inter-American Devt. Bank 68-70; Rapporteur, FAO World Food Conf. 70; Head, Advisory Mission on Planning, Govt. of Venezuela 70-71; Adviser UN Conf. on Human Environment 71-72; Exec. Sec. Econ. Comm. for Latin America (ECLA) 72-; Acting Dir.-Gen. Latin American Inst. for Econ. and Social Planning 73-.
Economic Commission for Latin America, Casilla 179D, Santiago, Chile.

Ignacio-Pinto, Louis, D. ÈS D., D. ÈS L.; Benin diplomatist and judge; b. 1903, Porto-Novo; s. of the late Ignacio Pinto and Angelia da Silva; m. Josephine Antoinette Lake 1942; one s. two d.; ed. Ecole St. Gènes, Bordeaux and Univs. of Bordeaux and Paris.

Teacher, Collège Tivoli, Bordeaux 27-28; Office-Cadet 31-32; engaged in starch manufacture 33-36; junior counsel, Paris Court of Appeal 37-39; war service in Lorraine 39-40; Counsel, Conakry 40-46; resistance worker; Rep. of Dahomey to French Senate 46-56; Vice-Pres. Comm., France d'Outre Mer 46-56; Minister of Econs., Commerce and Industry, Dahomey 57-58, Minister of Justice 58-59; returned to legal profession 59; Counsellor, French Embassy, Vatican City 60; Ambassador of Dahomey to UN, New York 60-67; Amb. of Dahomey to U.S.A. 60-67; Pres. of Supreme Court of Dahomey 67-69; Co-Pres. Cttee. of Seven for Reform of UN Secr. 68; Judge, Int. Court of Justice, The Hague 69-; Judge Admin. Tribunal of UN.
International Court of Justice, Peace Palace, The Hague 2012, Netherlands; 39 boulevard Garibaldi, Paris XVe, France; BP 216, Cotonou, Benin.
Telephone: (Paris) 734-19-99.

Ignatieff, George, C.C., LL.D., D.C.L., M.A., D.D.; Canadian diplomatist; b. 16 Dec. 1913, St. Petersburg, Russia; s. of Count Paul Ignatieff and Princess Natalie Mestchersky; m. Alison Brant 1945; two s.; ed. Jarvis Coll. Inst., Toronto, Univs. of Toronto and Oxford.
Department of External Affairs, Ottawa 40-; Third Sec., London 40-44; Dept. of External Affairs, Ottawa 44-45; Adviser, Canadian Del., UN Atomic Energy **Comm.** 46, UN Assembly 46-47; Alt. Rep. UN Security Council 45-49; Chair. Admin. and Budgetary Cttee., UN Gen. Assembly 49; Counsellor, Washington 49-53; attended Imperial Defence Coll., London 53-54; Head of Defence Liaison (First Div.) Dept. of External Affairs, Ottawa 55; Ambassador to Yugoslavia 56-58; Dep. High Commr., London 59-60; Asst. Under-Sec.; Dept. of External Affairs, Ottawa 60-62; Perm. Rep. and Amb. to NATO 62-66; Perm. Rep. to UN 66-68, Rep. of Canada to 18 Nation Disarmament Cttee., Geneva Dec. 68-72; Provost, Trinity Coll., Toronto 72-; Chair. Board of Trustees, Nat. Museums of Canada 73-; mem. Governing Council, Univ. of Toronto 74-75; hon. degrees from several Canadian and foreign univs.; Hon. Fellow, St. John's Coll., Winnipeg; Centenary Medal; Companion of the Order of Canada 74.
Leisure interest: gardening.
Trinity College, Toronto, M5S 1H8, Canada.
Telephone: 416-962-7697 (Home); 416-928-2370 (Office).

Ignatius, Paul Robert; American business executive; b. 11 Nov. 1920; m. Nancy Sharpless Wiser 1947; two s. two d.; ed. Univ. of Southern California and Harvard Business School.
Instructor in Business Admin., Harvard Business School 47-50; Vice-Pres., Dir. Harbridge House Inc. (management consultants), Boston 50-61; Asst. Sec. of Army for Installations and Logistics 61-63; Under-Sec. of Army 64; Asst. Sec. of Defence 64-67; Sec. of Navy 67-69; Pres. The Washington Post 69-71; Exec. Vice-Pres. Air Transport Asscn. of America 72, Pres. and Chief Exec. Officer Dec. 72-; U.S. Naval Reserve 43-46.
Leisure interests: tennis, swimming, skiing.
The Air Transport Association, 1709 New York Avenue, N.W., Washington, D.C. 20006; Home: 3650 Fordham Road, Washington, D.C. 20016, U.S.A.

Ihnatowicz, Zbigniew; Polish architect; b. 20 July 1906, Postawy, near Vilnius; ed. Warsaw Polytechnic.
Member of Polish Asscn. of Architects (SARP) 34-, mem. Council 61-; Assoc. Prof., Acad. of Fine Arts, Warsaw; First Prizes for urban design in Lublin, Cen. Commercial Centre in Warsaw, Stadium for 10th Anniversary of People's Poland, Church at Sochaczew; Silver Cross of Merit 53; Gold Cross 57; Officer's Cross, Order of Polonia Restituta 64; State Prize, 2nd Class 55; Hon. Prize of SARP 69; Minister of Culture and Arts Prize 74; Medal of 30th Anniversary of People's Poland 74.
Ul. Mokotowska 31 m. 15, 00-560 Warsaw, Poland.

Iida, Keizo; Japanese retail executive; b. 13 April 9100, Osaka City; m. Miyoko 1931; one s.; ed. Keio Univ.
Osaka Branch, Takashimaya Dept. Store 26, Man. 41, Dir. Takashimaya 42-, Managing Dir. 43-52, Pres. 52-60, now Chair.
1-2-18, Hibarigaoka, Takarazuka City, Hyogo Pref., Japan.

Ikebe, Ryo; Japanese actor; b. 1918.
First film appearance in *Togyo* (Fighting Fish) 41; other films include *Aoi Sanmyaku* (Blue Mountains) 49, *Akatsuki no Dasso* (Escape at Dawn) 50, *Geisha Konatsu* 54, *Byaku-fujin no Yoren* (The Legend of the White Serpent) 56, *Yukiguni* (Snow Country) 57.
c/o Toho Film Co. Ltd., 1-6 Yuraku-cho, Chiyoda-ku, Tokyo, Japan.

Ikeda, Daisaku; Japanese religious leader; b. 2 Jan. 1928, Tokyo; s. of Nenokichi and Ichi Ikeda; m. Kaneko Shiraki 1952; three s.; ed. Fuji Junior Coll.
President of Soka Gakkai 60-; Founder of Komeito (Clean Govt. Party), of Soka Junior Party, of Soka Junior and Senior High Schools, of Soka Univ., Minon Concert Asscn., Oriental Inst. of Academic Research, Fuji Art Museum 73; Pres. Nichiren Shoshu Soka Gakkai Int. 75-.
Leisure interests: music, art, travelling.
Publs. *Science and Religion* 65, *Politics and Religion* 65, *The Human Revolution* (novel) Vols. 1-8 65-73, *Family Revolution* 66, *My Thought and Opinion* 69, *New Life* (poems) 70, *Essays on Life* 70, *Essays for Women* 71, *East and West—Dialogue with Richard E. Courdenhove-Kalergi* 72, *Dialogue on Life* (Vols. 1-3) 73-74, *My Views on Buddhism* 74, *The Living Buddha* 76, *Choose Life—The Toynbee-Ikeda Dialogue* 76, other writings on Buddhism.
c/o The Soka Gakkai, 32 Shinano-machi, Shinjuku-ku, Tokyo 160, Japan.
Telephone: 353-7111.

Ikeura, Kisaburo, LL.B.; Japanese banker; b. 21 April 1916, Wakayama Prefecture; s. of Kunitaro and Sae Ikeura; m. Sumi Ueda 1944; one s. one d.; ed. Tokyo Univ.
Joined Industrial Bank of Japan Ltd. 39, Dir. 64, Man. Dir. 65, Deputy Pres. 73, Pres. 75-.
Leisure interests: travelling, reading.
3-3 Marunouchi 1-chome, Chiyoda-ku, Tokyo; Home: 22-12, 4-chome Numabukuro, Nakano-ku, Tokyo, Japan.
Telephone: 214-1111 (Office); 386-1443 (Home).

Iklé, Fred Charles, M.A., PH.D.; American social scientist and politician; b. 21 Aug. 1924, Samaden, Switzerland; m. Doris Eiseman 1953; two d.; ed. Univ. of Chicago.
Research scholar, Bureau of Applied Social Research, Columbia Univ. 50-54; Consultant to Nat. Research Council 50-54; mem. Social Science Dept., Rand Corpn. 55-61; Surprise Attack Conf. and Antartica Conf. preparations 56-58; Resident Assoc. in Int. Relations, Centre for Int. Affairs, Harvard Univ. 62-63; Assoc. Prof., then Prof. of Political Science, Mass. Inst. of Technology 63-67; Head of Social Science Dept., Rand Corpn. 68-73; Dir. U.S. Arms Control and Disarmament Agency 73-.
Publs. *The Social Impact of Bomb Destruction* 58, *Nth Countries and Disarmament* 60, *After Detection . . . What?* 61, *How Nations Negotiate* 64, *Every War Must End* 71, *Can Social Predictions be Evaluated?* 67, *Social Forecasting and the Problem of Changing Values* 71, *Can Nuclear Deterrence Last Out the Century?* 73.
U.S. Control and Disarmament Agency, Washington, D.C. 20451; Home: 4710 Woodway Lane, N.W., Washington, D.C. 20016, U.S.A.
Telephone: (202) 632-9610 (Office); (202) 244-4084 (Home).

Ikonga, Auxence; Congolese politician.
Former prefect of Sangha; fmr. Dir.-Gen. Admin.; fmr. Dir. Cabinet of Ministry of Foreign Affairs; Amb. to U.A.R. Nov. 66-June 69; Minister of Equipment, responsible for Agriculture, Water Resources and Forests June 69-Jan. 70; Minister of Foreign Affairs 70-72; Amb. to France 72-75.
c/o Ministry of Foreign Affairs, Brazzaville, Congo People's Republic.

Ilangaratne, Tikiri Bandara; Ceylonese politician, writer, playwright, novelist; b. 27 Feb. 1913, Hatarliyadda; s. of Mr. and Mrs. T. A. Ilangaratne; m. Tamara Kumari Aludeniya 1944; two s. two d.; ed. St. Anthony's Coll., Kandy.
Clerical Servant until 47; mem. of Parl. for Kandy 48, for Galaha 52; Gen. Sec. Sri Lanka Freedom Party 54-; mem. of Parl. for Hewaheta 56; Minister for Social Services and Housing 56-59, of Home Affairs 59, of Trade, Commerce, Food and Shipping 61-63, of Finance 63-64, of Trade and Supplies 64-65; Vice-Pres. Sri Lanka Freedom Party 66, mem. of Parl. for Kolonnawa 67; responsible for nationalizing foreign oil companies in Ceylon; Minister of Foreign and Internal Trade June 70-, Public Admin. and Home Affairs Sept. 75-.
Publs. (in Sinhalese). Novels: *Wilambeeta, Denuwara, Kathava, Thilaka, La Sanda, Thilaka and Thilaka, Nedeyo*; Plays: *Häramitiya, Manthri Hamuduruwo, Jataka Natyaya, Rangamandala, Handahana, Ambaryaluwo, Malsarawa, Mangala, Delova Sihina, Wivena Ginna*; short stories: *Onchillawa*.
B-20 Government Bungalow, Stanmore Crescent, Colombo 7, Sri Lanka.

Ileo Songoamba; Zairian politician; b. (as Joseph Ileo) 15 Sept. 1921, Kinshasa; m. Elisabeth Bongo; five s. five d.; ed. philosophy and sociology in Europe.
Held post in African Territories Div. of Belgian Gov.-General's Office; active in movement for independence, signatory of the "Memorandum of the Sixteen" 58; formed Congolese Nat. Movement Party with Patrice Lumumba; joined Abako Party 59; former Editor *The African Conscience*; Head of Congolese Senate July 60-Sept. 60; Premier Sept. 60-Aug. 61; Minister of Information and Cultural Affairs Aug. 61-62; Minister without Portfolio in charge Katangese Affairs 63-64; now mem. Political Bureau, Mouvement populaire de la révolution, mem. Perm. Cttee. 75-; Pres. Office Nat. de la Recherche et du Développement.
B.P. 3474, Kinshasa, Zaire.
Telephone: 2452.

Iliescu, Ion; Romanian politician; b. 3 March 1930, Oltenita, Ilfov District; m. Elena Iliescu; ed. Bucharest Polytechnic Inst. and Moscow.
Member of Union of Communist Youth (U.C.Y.) 44; mem. of Communist Party 53; mem. Cen. Cttee. of U.C.Y. 49, Sec. of Cen. Cttee. 56; Pres. of Union of Student Asscns. 57-60; Alt. mem. Cen. Cttee. of R.C.P. 65-68, mem. 68-; First Sec. Cen. Cttee. of U.C.Y. and Minister of Youth Problems 67-71; Alt. mem. of Exec. Cttee. of Cen. Cttee. of R.C.P. 69-; mem. Bureau of Nat. Council of Socialist Unity Front 68-72; Sec. C.P. Cttee., Timis County 72-; mem. Nat. Assembly 57-; mem. Acad. of Social and Political Sciences 70-; First Sec. C.P. Cttee., Lassy County 74-.
Central Committee of the Romanian Communist Party, Bucharest, Romania.

Illia, Arturo Umberto; Argentine physician and politician; b. 1901.
Former Provincial Senator; fmr. Vice-Gov. Córdoba Province; Pres. of Argentina Oct. 63-June 66; mem. People's Radical Civic Union.

Illich, Ivan, PH.D.; American educator and writer; b. 4 Sept. 1926, Vienna, Austria; ed. Gregorian Univ., Rome, Univ. of Salzburg.
Went to U.S.A. 51; Asst. Pastor in New York; Vice-Rector Catholic Univ. of Puerto Rico 56-60; Co-Founder Centre for Intercultural Documentation (CIDOC), Cuernavaca, Mexico.
Publs. *Celebration of Awareness* 69, *Deschooling Society* 71, *Tools for Conviviality* 73, *Energy and Equity* 73, *Medical Nemesis* 75, contributed to *Esprit, Temps Modernes, Kursbuch, New York Review of Books, New York Times, Le Monde.*
Apdo. 479, Cuernavaca, Mexico.
Telephone: 3-0366.

Illyés, Gyula; Hungarian author; b. 2 Nov. 1902, Rácegres; s. of János Illyés and Ida Kállay; m. Dr. Flora Kozmutza 1939; one d.; ed. Budapest, Prague, Milan, Paris, Brussels, Berlin, Warsaw, Bucharest, Zagreb, Ljubljana, Munich, London, Washington, Stockholm, Moscow, Oslo, Tokyo, etc.
Former editor of *Nyugat, Magyar Csillag* and *Válasz*; Vice-Pres. of PEN Int. 70-; awarded Kossuth Prize 48, 53 and 70, Grand Prix de Poésie, Knokke (Belgium); Herder-Preis, Hamburg-Vienna 70; Red Banner Order of Labour 72, Commdr. Ordre des Arts et Lettres 74.
Leisure interest: gardening.
Publs. *Puszták Nepe* (English, French, German, Finnish trans.), *Petöfi* (trans.), *Magyarok, Lélek és Kenyér, Kora tavasz, A tü foka, Hunok Párizsban, Lélekbúvár Osszes Versei, Az Ozorai Példa, Fáklyaláng, Dózsa, Kézfogások, Uj Versek, Ebéd a kastélyban* (French, German trans.), *Nem volt elég, Másokért egyedül, Nyitott kapu, Szives kalauz, Poèmes Choisis, Ingyen Lakoma, Dölt Vitorla, Poètes d'aujourd'hui, Poharaim, Feketefehér, Kháron ladikján* (trans.), *Hajszálgyökerek, Malom a Séden, Tiszták, Bölcsek a fán, Selected Poems, Le favori, Hommage à Gyula Illyés, Due Mani* (Italian), *Minden Lehet, Abbahagyott versek* (new books of poetry), *Poesie di Gy. Ix, Haza a magasban, Teremteni, Testvérek, Dupla vagy semmi, Orfensz a Felvilágban-Tribute to Gy. I.*
Józsefhegyi u. 9, H-1025 Budapest II, Hungary.

Ilyashenko, Kirill Fedorovich; Soviet politician; b. 15; ed. Tiraspol Pedagogical Inst.
Soviet Army 40-45; mem. Communist Party of Soviet Union 45-; Chair. State Cttee. for Co-ordination of Scientific and Research Work, Council of Ministers of Moldavian S.S.R. and Deputy Chair. of Council of Ministers of Moldavian S.S.R. 62-63; Chair. of Presidium of Supreme Soviet of Moldavian S.S.R. 63-; mem. Bureau of Central Cttee. of C.P. of Moldavian S.S.R. 63-; mem. Central Auditing Comm. C.P.S.U. 66-71; Alt. mem. C.P.S.U. Central Cttee. 71-; Deputy Chair. Presidium of Supreme Soviet of U.S.S.R. 66-.
Presidium of Supreme Soviet of Moldavian S.S.R., Kishinev, U.S.S.R.

Ilyichev, Leonid Fyodorovich; Soviet journalist and politician; b. 15 March 1906, Krasnodar; ed. North Caucasian Communist Univ. and Inst. of Red Profs., Moscow.
Worker at a factory, Krasnodar 18-24; Young Communist League work 24-27; student and assistant teacher, North Caucasian Communist Univ. 30-31; party work 31-34; Sec. *Bolshevik Journal* 38-40; mem. staff *Pravda* 40-44; Editor-in-Chief *Izvestia* 44-48; on staff C.P.S.U. Central Cttee. 48-49; Deputy Editor-in-Chief, later Editor-in-Chief *Pravda* 49-52; Dir. Press Dept., Ministry of Foreign Affairs 53-58; Dir. C.P. Agitation and Propaganda Service 58-61; Sec. Central Cttee. of C.P.S.U. 61-65, mem. Central Cttee. 61-66; Deputy Foreign Minister of U.S.S.R. 65-; mem. U.S.S.R. Acad. of Sciences 62-; Lenin Prize 60.
Ministry of Foreign Affairs, 32-34 Smolenskaya-Sennaya ploshchad, Moscow, U.S.S.R.

Ilyin, Vitaly Sergeyevich; Soviet biochemist; b. 1904, Dzambai Village, Kazakhstan; s. of Sergey Petrovich Ilyin and Eugenia Ivanovna Ilyina; m. Olga Yalmarovna Tawastsherna; one *s.* two *d.*; ed. First Leningrad Medical Inst.

Research worker, Inst. of Natural Sciences 27-40; Senior Research Worker, Leningrad Inst. of Blood Transfusion 33-39; Head of Dept., Deputy Dir. Tajik Medical Inst. 40-45; Senior Research Worker, Pavlov Inst. of Physiology 45-50; Head, Dept. of Biochemistry, Leningrad Inst. of Stomatology 45-51; Head of Dept., Inst of Experimental Medicine, U.S.S.R. Acad. of Medical Sciences, and Head of Dept., Leningrad Inst. for Postgraduate Medical Training 51-; mem. U.S.S.R. Acad. of Medical Sciences 66-; Editor of Chem. Dept. of *Great Medical Encyclopaedia* and mem. Editorial Boards of *Evolutional Biochemistry and Physiology, Biochemistry, Aspects of Medical Chemistry* and *Biochemical Medicine* U.S.A.; Order of Red Banner of Labour 51.
Leisure interest: music.
Publs. Over 160 works on cellular and molecular mechanisms of hormonal and nervous regulation of metabolism.
Institute of Experimental Medicine, 69/71 Kirovsky Prospekt, Leningrad; Home: Fontanka 26, ap. 49, Leningrad, 192028 U.S.S.R.
Telephone: 73-45-59; 32-06-41.

Ilyushin, Sergei Vladimirovich; Soviet aircraft designer; b. 31 March 1894. Diyalovo Village, Volgograd Region; ed. Air Force Engineering Acad.
Lt.-Gen. in the engineering-technical service; Prof. at the Zhukovsky Air Force Engineering Acad.; Designer-Gen. of U.S.S.R. Ministry of Aircraft Industry; Corresp. mem. U.S.S.R. Acad. of Sciences 43-68, mem. 68-; State prize winner (seven times); Hero of Socialist Labour (twice); Lenin Prize 60; Orders of Lenin (three times), Red Banner, and other decorations.
Principal designs: the TsKB-30 twin-engine plane 36, the IL-2 armoured attacker 39, the IL-12 twin-engine passenger plane 46, the IL-18 (*Moscow*) turbo-prop passenger plane 57, the IL-62 turbo-jet passenger plane 62.
Ministry of Aircraft Industry, Moscow, U.S.S.R.

Imai, Kenji; Japanese architect; b. 11 Jan. 1895, Tokyo; *s.* of Chogoro and Ine Imai; *m.* Maria Jeanne d'Arc Shizuko 1928 (died 1947); one *s.*; ed. Architectural Dept., Waseda Univ., Tokyo.
Assistant Prof. Waseda Univ. 20-37, Prof. 37-65, Hon. Prof. 65-; Prof. Kantō Gakuin Univ., Yokohama 66-; Hon. Counsellor Tama Fine Arts Univ., Tokyo 65-; studied in Europe and America 26-27; mem. Catholic Art Soc. 49-; Rep. of Japan Branch of Gaudi Friend Circle 56, participated in 10th Anniversary of Antonio Gaudi Friend Circle, Barcelona 63; Hon. mem. Rudolf Steiner Goetheanum 63; one-man exhbn. of European sketches 64; Prize of Architectural Inst. of Japan 59, 62; Marquis Ohkuma Academic Prize, Waseda Univ. 62; Japan Art Acad. Prize 66.
Leisure interests: sketching, sculpture.
Major works include: Waseda Univ. Library 25, Waseda Univ. Museum of Drama 28, sculptor Rokuzan Art Museum, Japanese Alpen Town Hotaha-machi, Nagano Pref. 38, Aeroplane Monument, Tokyo 41, Ohtakimachi Town Office, Chiba Pref. 59, Memorial Centre for Japanese 26 Martyrs, Nagasaki Pref. 62, Chapel for Sisters of the Visitation Convent (Kamakura) 65, *Toka Gakudo*—The Empress' Memorial Music Hall, Imperial Palace 66, Marquis Ohkuma Memorial Hall, Saga Pref. 66, Toyama Memorial, Fine Arts Museum, Kawagoe Prefecture 70.
Publs. *Gunnar Asplund* 30, *Das Vorbild der Katholischen Gattin—Architecture and Humanity* 54, *Ōryo Sobyō* (Sketch of Travel through Europe) 63, *Tabiji* (Voyage) 67; collection of artistic works in commemoration of 70th birthday 68.
4-12-28, Kitazawa, Setagaya-ku, Tokyo, Japan.
Telephone: 03-468-2708.

Imbert, Bertrand Sainclair Marie; French hydrographic engineer and naval officer; b. 23 Oct. 1924; ed. Collège Sait-Martin de France and Collège Sainte Geneviève.
Entered Free French Navy, Ecole Navale 43; served in Indo-China Campaign 45-47; Antarctic expeditions 51, 56 and 57; Principal Marine Nationale; Chief of French Antarctic Expeditions of the Int. Geophysical Year 56-59; mem. Atomic Energy Comm. 59-69; Asst. Man. Dir. Control-Data France 69, Man. Dir. 70-; Croix de Guerre, Chevalier Légion d'Honneur.
8 rue de l'Odéon, Paris 6e, France.

Imru Haile Selassie, Lij Mikhail; Ethiopian politician; b. 1930; ed. Oxford Univ., England.
Former Dir.-Gen. Ministry of Defence and mem. Planning Board, Ministry of Agriculture; fmr. Amb. to U.S., then to U.S.S.R.; Head Ethiopian mission to UN Office, Geneva until 74; Minister of Commerce and Industry March 74; Minister in the Prime Minister's Office in charge of Econ. and Social Affairs April-July 74, Prime Minister July-Sept. 74; Minister of Information Sept. 74-; Chief Pol. Adviser to Head of State March 75-.
Office of the Head of State, Addis Ababa, Ethiopia.

Imshenetsky, Alexander Alexandrovich; Soviet microbiologist; b. 8 Jan. 1905, Kiev; ed. Voronezh State Univ.
Teacher of Microbiology, Leningrad Chemico-Technological Inst. 32-34; Senior Scientific Worker, Inst. of Microbiology, U.S.S.R. Acad. of Sciences 32-41, Head of Dept. 41-, Dep. Dir. 45-49, Dir. 49-; Prof. of Microbiology, Piscicultural Faculty, Timiryazevsky Agricultural Acad. 35-37; mem. U.S.S.R. Acad. of Sciences 62-; First Pres. (and Founder) U.S.S.R. Microbiological Soc. 60; Editor *Microbiology*; Order of Lenin (twice), Order of Red Banner of Labour (twice), Hero of Socialist Labour.
Publs. *The Structure of Bacteria* 40, *Microbiological Processes at High Temperatures* 44, *Microbiology of Celluloses* 53, *Morphology of Bacteria* 62, *Perspectives for the Development of Exobiology* 63, *On the Multiplication of Xerophilic Micro-organisms under Simulated Martian Conditions* 73, *Detection of Extra-Terrestrial Life by Radiometric Techniques* 74, *Microbiological Research in Space Biology* 74, *On Micro-organisms of the Stratosphere* 75, *Biological Effects of Extreme Environmental Conditions* 75.
Institute of Microbiology of the U.S.S.R. Academy of Sciences, Profsoyunzaya ul. 7, Moscow, U.S.S.R.

Inaba, Osamu; Japanese politician; b. 1910; ed. Chuo Univ.
Professor of Law, Chuo Univ.; mem. House of Reps. for Niigata Pref. 47-; fmr. Parl. Vice-Minister of Educ.; Vice-Chair. Policy Affairs Research Council of Liberal Democratic Party; Minister of Educ. July-Dec. 72, of Justice Dec. 74-.
Ministry of Justice, Tokyo, Japan.

Inagaki, Hiroshi; Japanese film director; b. 1905, Tokyo; *s.* of Tomejiro Inagaki and Ei Inagaki; *m.* 1930; three *s.* two *d.*
Began career in films as actor, script-writer, etc. 14; Asst. to Teinosuke Kinugasa 27; Director 28-; at present under contract to Toho Film Co.; mem. Board Motion Picture Directors' Asscn. of Japan; Ministry of Education Awards for *Edo Saigo No Hi* 42 and *Te O Tsunagu Kora* 48; Ministry of Welfare Award for *Wasurerareta Kora* 50; American Motion Picture Acad. Award for *Samurai* (a different film from *The Seven Samurai*) 56; Venice Film Festival Grand Prix, Tokyo Gold Prize and Sankei Silver Star Prize for *Muhomatsu No Issho* 57; Ministry of Educ. Awards for *Fu Rin Ka Zan* 70.
Films include *Tenka Taiheiki, Edo Saigo No Hi* (The

Last Days of Edo), *Te O Tsunagu Kora* (Children Holding Hands Together), *Wasurerareta Kora* (Neglected Children), *Samurai, Muhomatsu No Issho* (The Rickshaw Man).

No. 7-10-5, Seijyo, Setagaya-ku, Tokyo, Japan.
Telephone: Tokyo 483-0845.

Inayama, Yoshihiro; Japanese steel executive; b. 2 Jan. 1904, Chuo-ku, Tokyo; *m.* Tsuru 1929; three *s.*; ed. Tokyo Univ.

Yawata Works, Yawata Iron and Steel Co., Ltd., Man. Dir. 50-60, Vice-Pres. 60-61, Pres. 61-70; also Pres. Japan Iron and Steel Federation; Chair. Japan Steel Exporters Asscn.; Vice-Pres. Japan Fed. of Econ. Orgs.; Chair. Int. Iron and Steel Inst. 71-73, Vice-Chair. 73-; Pres. Nippon Steel Corpn. 70-73, Chair. 73-.

Leisure interests: golf, "Tokiwazu" (Japanese classical ballad).

Nippon Steel Corpn., 6-3, Otemachi 2-chome, Chiyoda-ku, Tokyo 100; (Home) 28-8, 1-chome, Daizawa, Setagaya-ku, Tokyo, Japan.
Telephone: (Home) 421-0533.

Incer Barquero, Roberto; Nicaraguan economist and banker; b. 10 April 1933; *s.* of Armando Incer and Lucina Barquero de Incer; *m.* Marisa Pereira Deshon 1968; two *s.*; ed. Universidad Nacional Autónoma de Nicaragua, George Washington Univ. and Yale Univ., U.S.A., and London School of Economics.

Economist, Econ. Research Dept., Cen. Bank of Nicaragua 60-65; Exec. Sec. Nat. Cotton Comm. 65-67; Sec. to Presidency of Repub. of Nicaragua 67-69; Pres. Cen. Bank of Nicaragua 69-; Great Cross, Order of Merit (Fed. Germany), Order of Henry the Navigator (Portugal), Order of the Brilliant Star (China), Orden de Rubén Darío Gran Cruz Placa de Plata.

Leisure interests: baseball, photography.

Banco Central de Nicaragua, Apdos. 2252/3, Managua, Nicaragua.
Telephone: 26014.

Inchyra, 1st Baron (cr. 62), of St. Madoes in the County of Perth; **Frederick Robert Hoyer Millar,** G.C.M.G., C.V.O.; British diplomatist; b. 6 June 1900, Montrose, Scotland; *s.* of R. Hoyer Millar; *m.* Elizabeth de Marees van Swinderen 1931; two *s.* two *d.*; ed. Wellington Coll. and New Coll., Oxford.

Honorary Attaché Brussels 22; entered Diplomatic Service 23; served as Third Sec. Berlin and Paris, Second Sec. Cairo; Asst. Private Sec. to Sec. of State for Foreign Affairs 34-38; First Sec. Washington 39, Counsellor 41-42; Sec. British Civil Secr., Washington 43; Counsellor, Foreign Office 44, Asst. Under-Sec. 47; Minister, British Embassy, Washington 48; U.K. Dep. NATO 50-52; U.K. Perm. Rep. North Atlantic Council 52-53, U.K. High Commr. in Germany 53-55, Ambassador to German Fed. Repub. 55-57; Perm. Under-Sec. of State 57-61; retired 62; Dir. Gen. Accident, Fire and Life Assurance Corpn.

Leisure interest: shooting.

57 Eaton Place, London, S.W.1, England; and Inchyra House, Glencarse, Perthshire, Scotland.

Indiana, Robert, B.F.A.; American artist; b. 13 Sept. 1928, New Castle, Ind.; ed. John Herron School of Art, Indianapolis, Munson-Williams-Proctor Inst., Utica, New York, Art Inst. of Chicago, Skowhegan School of Painting and Sculpture, Univ. of Edinburgh and Edinburgh Coll. of Art.

Lived and worked in N.Y. 54-; Artist-in-Residence, Center of Contemporary Art, Aspen, Colo. 68, D.F.A. (Hon.) Franklin and Marshall Coll., Lancaster, Penn 70. One-man exhbns: Stable Gallery, N.Y. 62, 64, 66, Walker Art Center, Minneapolis 63, Inst. of Contemporary Art, Boston 63, Rolf Nelson Gallery, Los Angeles 65, Dayton's Gallery 12, Minneapolis 66, Galerie Alfred Schmela, Düsseldorf 66, Stedelijk van Abbemuseum, Eindhoven 66, Museum Hans Lange,

Krefeld (W. Germany) 66, Württembergischer Kunstverein, Stuttgart 66, Inst. of Contemporary Art, Univ. of Pennsylvania 68, Marion Koogler McNay Art Inst., San Antonio, Tex. 68, Herron Museum of Art, Indianapolis 68, Toledo Museum of Art, Ohio 68, Hunter Gallery, Aspen, Colo. 68, Creighton Univ., Omaha 69, St. Mary's Coll., Notre Dame, Ind. 69, Colby Coll. Art Museum, Waterville, Maine 69-70, Currier Gallery of Art, Manchester, N.H. 70, Hopkins Center, Dartmouth Coll. Hanover, N.H. 70, Bowdoin Coll. Museum of Art, Brunswick, Maine 70, Brandeis Univ., Waltham, Mass. 70.

Major group exhbns. include: Painting and Sculpture of a Decade, Tate Gallery, London 64, Twenty-ninth Biennial Exhbn. of American Painting, Corcoran Gallery of Art, Wash., D.C. 65, Pop Art and the American Tradition, Milwaukee 65, White House Festival of the Arts, White House, Wash. 65, American Painting Now, Expo 67, Montreal 67, Annual Exhbns of American Painting, Documenta IV, Kassel 68, Art in the Sixties, Cologne 69.

2 Spring Street, New York, N.Y. 10012; Summer Residence: Vinalhaven, Maine, U.S.A.

Indra, Alois; Czechoslovak politician; b. 17 March 1921, Medzev.

Former Head of Planning, Finance and Foreign Trade Dept., Central Cttee. of Czechoslovak C.P.; Minister-Chair. State Planning Comm. 62-63; Minister of Transport 63-68; mem. Secr. of Central Cttee. and Sec. of Cen. Cttee. of C.P. of Czechoslovakia 68-71; mem. State Planning Comm. 65-68; mem. Central Cttee. of C.P. of Czechoslovakia 62- (Econ. Comm. 63-66); Deputy to Nat. Assembly 64-69; Deputy to Czech Nat. Council 68-71; Deputy to House of the People, Fed. Assembly 69-; mem. Presidium of Fed. Assembly 69-, Chair. 71-; Alt. mem. Presidium of Central Cttee., C.P. of Czechoslovakia 70-71, mem. 71-; Presidium mem. of Cen. Cttee. of Nat. Front 71-; Medal of Govt. of Czech Socialist Repub.; Order of the Repub. 71, Order of Victorious February 73.

Federal Assembly of the Czechoslovak Socialist Republic, Vinohradská 1, Prague 1, Czechoslovakia.

Ingalls, Daniel Henry Holmes, A.B., M.A.; American orientalist; b. 4 May 1916, New York City; *s.* of late Fay Ingalls and Rachel Holmes Ingalls; *m.* Phyllis Sarah Day 1936; one *s.* two *d.*; ed. Harvard Univ. Junior Fellow, Harvard Univ. 39-42 and 46-49; Office of Strategic Services 42-44, U.S. Army 44-46; Asst. Prof. Harvard Univ. 49-54, Assoc. Prof. 54-58, Wales Prof. of Sanskrit 58-; Editor *Harvard Oriental Series*; Pres. American Oriental Soc. 59-60; Dir. Virginia Hot Springs, Inc. 46-57, Pres. 57-63, Chair. of Board 63-.

Leisure interests: reading, music, mountain climbing.

Publs. *Materials for the Study of Navya-nyaya Logic* 50, *An Anthology of Sanskrit Court Poetry* 64.

Widener Library 273, Harvard University, Cambridge, Mass. 02138, U.S.A.

Ingersoll, Ralph McAllister, B.S.; American journalist and newspaper publisher; b. 8 Dec. 1900, New Haven, Conn.; *s.* of Colin Macrae Ingersoll and Theresa McAllister; *m.* 1st Elizabeth Carden 1925, 2nd Elaine Brown Keiffer 1945, 3rd Mary Hill Doolittle 1948, 4th Thelma Saxe Bradford 1964; two *s.*; ed. Hotchkiss School, Lakeville, Conn., Yale and Columbia Univs.

Fmr. mining engineer; reporter *New York American* 23-24; freelance journalist 24-25; reporter *New Yorker* 25, Man. Editor 25-30; Associate Editor *Fortune* 30, Man. Editor 30-35; Vice-Pres. and Gen. Man. Time, Inc., publishing *Time, Life, Fortune* and *Architectural Forum* 35-40, publisher *Time* 37-40; Founder and Editor N.Y. daily newspaper *P.M.* 40-46; joined U.S. Army as private 42, rose to Col. Gen. Staff Corps; served in Africa, England, France, Italy, Belgium and Germany on staff of Gen. Devers, Field-Marshal Montgomery and

Gen. Bradley 43-45; Pres. The R.J. Co. Inc. (newspaper investments) 49-58, Capitol City Publishing Co., Inc.; Pres. Acme Newspapers Inc., Central States Publishing Inc., Mahanoy Publishing Inc., Mid-Atlantic Newspapers, Mid Hudson Publications, Milford Publishing, New England Newspapers, North Jersey Publishing, North East Publishing, Peerless Publications, Philadelphia Suburban Newspapers, Phoenix Publishing Co., Riverdale Publishing, Shenandoah Valley Publishing Corpn., Newspaper Management Inc. (N.Y.), General Publications Inc. (Conn.); Dir. Public Welfare Foundation (Wash., D.C.); awarded Legion of Merit, Assault Landing Arrowhead, Belgian Order of the Crown (Officer).
Leisure interest: travel.
Publs. *In and Under Mexico* 23, *Report on England* 40, *America's Worth Fighting For* 41, *Action on all Fronts* 42, *The Battle is the Pay Off* 43, *Top Secret* 46, *The Great Ones* 48, *Wine of Violence* 51, *Point of Departure* 61.
The Phoenix, Cornwall Bridge, Connecticut 06754, U.S.A.
Telephone: 203-672-6700.

Ingersoll, Robert Stephen; American businessman; b. 28 Jan. 1914, Galesburg, Ill.; s. of Roy Claire and Lulu (née Hinchliff) Ingersoll; m. Coralyn Eleanor Reid 1938; four d.; ed. Phillips Acad. and Sheffield Scientific School, Yale Univ.
With Armco Steel Corpn. 37-39; with Ingersoll Steel & Disc Div. (later Ingersoll Products Div.), Borg-Warner Corpn., Chicago 39-41, 42-54, Pres. Ingersoll Products Div. 50-54, Admin. Vice-Pres. Borg-Warner Corpn. 53-56, Pres. 56-61, Pres. and Chief Exec. Officer 58-61, Chair. and Chief Exec. Officer 61-72; Amb. to Japan 72-74; Asst. Sec. of State for East Asian Affairs Jan.-June 74, Deputy Sec. of State 74-; fmr. Dir. First Nat. Bank of Chicago, Atlantic Richfield, Marcor Inc., Burlington Northern Inc.; Trustee, Univ. of Chicago, Aspen Inst. of Humanistic Studies, Calif. Inst. of Technology, Smith Coll.; Dir. Amer. Nat. Red Cross; fmr. Dir., Vice-Pres. U.S. Chamber of Commerce.
Department of State, Washington, D.C. 20520, U.S.A.

Inghram, Mark Gordon, PH.D.; American professor and physicist; b. 13 Nov. 1919, Livingstone, Mont.; s. of Mark G. Inghram and Luella McNay Inghram; m. Evelyn M. Dyckman 1946; one s. one d.; ed. Olivet Coll. and Univ. of Chicago.
Physicist, Univ. of Minn. 42, Manhattan Project Columbia Univ. 43-45; Senior Physicist Argonne Nat. Lab. 45-49; Instructor in Physics, Univ. of Chicago 47-49, Asst. Prof. 49-51, Assoc. Prof. 51-57, Prof. of Physics 57-69, Chair. Dept. of Physics 59-70, Assoc. Dean Div. of Physical Sciences 64-71, Samuel K. Allison Distinguished Service Prof. of Physics 69-; mem. Nat. Acad. of Sciences; Lawrence Smith Medal of Nat. Acad. of Sciences 57.
Publs. Over 150 research papers in scientific journals.
Department of Physics, University of Chicago, Chicago, Ill. 60637, U.S.A.
Telephone: (312) 753-8303.

Ingle, Dwight Joyce, B.S., M.S., PH.D.; American professor of physiology; b. 4 Sept. 1907, Kendrick, Idaho; s. of David J. Ingle and Mattie (Self) Ingle; m. Geneva McGarvey 1930; one s. two d.; ed. Univs. of Idaho, Minnesota and Pennsylvania.
Research Scientist, The Upjohn Co., Kalamazoo, Mich. 41-53; Prof. of Physiology, Ben May Laboratory and Dept. of Physiology, Univ. of Chicago 53-73, Prof. Emer. 73-, Chair. Dept. of Physiology 59-68; Founder *Perspectives in Biology and Medicine* Editor 57-73, Advisory Editor 73-; studies on the adrenal cortex, experimental diabetes and liver regeneration; mem. Nat. Acad. of Sciences, American Acad. of Arts and Sciences, Endocrine Soc. (Pres. 59-60), Soc. for Experimental Biology and Medicine (Pres. 65-67), American Diabetes

Asscn., American Physiological Soc.; Hon. D.Sc.; Roche Organon Award 47, Upjohn Prize 48, Koch Award of Endocrine Soc. 63, Outstanding Achievement Award of Univ. of Minn. 64, Modern Medicine Award 68.
Leisure interest: sailing.
Publs. Seven books, and over 350 articles in scientific and learned journals.
Box 335, Route 1, Rapid City, Mich. 49676, U.S.A.
Telephone: 332-2045.

Inglés, José D., LL.B., LL.M., PH.B., D.C.L.; Philippine lawyer and diplomatist; b. 24 Aug. 1910, Mauban, Tayabas; m. Josefina M. Feliciano 1942; two s. two d.; ed. Univ. of the Philippines, Santo Tomás Univ., Manila, and Columbia Univ., New York.
Attorney 32-36; Private Sec. Assoc. Justice of Supreme Court; Legal Asst., Pres. of the Philippines 36-39; Asst. Solicitor-Gen. 40; Judge First Instance 41-43; Asst. Exec. Sec. to Pres. of the Philippines 44; Counsel, Senate of Philippines 45-47; Prof. Philippine Law School 45-46; Chair. Trusteeship Cttee., Paris 51; mem. Philippine Del. to UN 46-56, 62-69, Vice-Pres. Gen. Assembly 74, mem. numerous UN Cttees.; Minister to Fed. Republic. of Germany 56-58, Amb. 58-62; Amb. to Thailand 62-66; Rep. South East Asia Treaty Org. (SEATO) 62-66; mem. Standing Cttee. Asscn. of South East Asia (ASA) 63-66; Under-Sec. of Foreign Affairs 66-; Sec.-Gen. Nat. Secr. (ASEAN) 67-69; mem. Civil Aeronautics Board 69-70; Chair. Philippine Air Services Negotiating Panel 69-; Chair. Philippine Del., SEATO Council of Ministers, Wellington 68; UNESCO Gen. Conf., Paris 70; ASEAN and ASPAC Standing Cttees., Manila 70-71; Fifth ASEAN Ministerial Conf., Singapore 72; Acting Sec. of Foreign Affairs intermittently 66-76; Grosskreuz des Verdienstordens der Bundesrepublik Deutchland, Most Noble Order of the Crown of Thailand, Most Exalted Order of the White Elephant, Gran Cruz del Orden de Mayo, Grand-Croix de l'Ordre de Léopold II, Nat. Order of Viet-Nam.
Leisure interest: orchid culture.
Publs. numerous papers on economics and int. affairs.
21 Vinzons Street, Heroes' Hill, Quezon City, Philippines.

Ingram, Vernon M., F.R.S., PH.D., D.SC.; British professor of biochemistry; b. 19 May 1924, Breslau, Germany; s. of Kurt and Johanna Immerwahr; m. Margaret Young 1950; one s. one d.; ed. Birkbeck Coll., Univ. of London.
Research chemist, Thos. Morson and Son 41-45; Lecture Demonstrator, Birkbeck Coll., London 45-47, Asst. Lecturer 47-50; Rockefeller Foundation Fellow, N.Y. 50-51; Coxe Fellow, Yale Univ. 51-52; mem. staff Molecular Biology Unit, Cavendish Lab., Cambridge 52-58; Visiting Assoc. Prof. M.I.T. 58-59; Assoc. Prof. M.I.T. 59-61, Prof. of Biochem. 61-; Guggenheim Fellow, Univ. of London 67-68; mem. American Acad. of Arts and Sciences.
Leisure interest: music.
Publs. *Haemoglobin and its Abnormalities* 61, *The Haemoglobins in Genetics and Evolution* 63, *The Biosynthesis of Macromolecules* 65, 71.
Department of Biology, Massachusetts Institute of Technology, 77 Massachusetts Avenue, Cambridge, Mass. 02139, U.S.A.
Telephone: 617-253-3706.

Ingrand, Henry, M.D.; French doctor, civil servant and diplomatist; b. 18 Aug. 1908, Echire, Deux-Sèvres; ed. Univ. of Paris.
Head of a Surgical Clinic, Paris until 39; active in French Resistance Movement during 39-45 war; Commr. for Auvergne Region 44; High Commr. for Tourism 46; Chair. Tourism Cttee. O.E.E.C. 49-52; Pres. Union Internationale des Organismes officiels de Tourisme 51-52; entered Ministry of Foreign Affairs 52; Del. to UNRWA Beirut 52-55; Ambassador to

Colombia 55-59; Sec.-Gen. for Algerian Affairs Jan.-Dec. 59; Ambassador to Venezuela 61-63; Ministry of Foreign Affairs 63; Pres. Admin. Council of Houillères, Provence 64-69; Adviser on Int. Affairs, Groupe des Charbonnages de France 67-73; Adviser on Int. Affairs, Soc. Chimique des Charbonnages 73; Commdr. Légion d'Honneur, Compagnon de la Libération, Croix de Guerre, Hon. C.B.E. (U.K.).
26 rue du Tareq Sammeron, 77260 La Javotte, France.

Ingstad, Helge Marcus; Norwegian author and explorer; b. 30 Dec. 1899, Meraker; s. of Olav Ingstad and Olga Marie (née Quam); m. Anne Stine Moe 1941; one d.
Practised law as barrister, Levanger, Norway 22-25; lived as trapper N.E. of Great Slave Lake, Arctic Canada 26-30; Norwegian Gov., N.E. Greenland 32-33; Norwegian Gov. of Svalbard (Spitsbergen) 33-55; studied Apache Indians, Arizona, and made expedition to Sierra Madre Mountains, Mexico, in search of some primitive Apache Indians 36-38; studied Eskimo group *Nunamiut*, Brooks Range, N. Alaska 49-50; made expedition with wife to W. Greenland to study old Norse settlements 53; made eight archaeological expeditions to N. America, where at N. tip of Newfoundland (L'Anse aux Meadows) a Norse pre-Columbian site was discovered and excavated 60-68; made expedition to Eastern Coast of Baffin Island and located Helluland, mentioned in *Vinland Saga* 70; numerous awards including Franklin L. Burr Award (Nat. Geographic Soc., Washington) 64, Fridtjof Nansen Award, Univ. of Oslo 65, The Wahlberg Award 68; Hon. D.Sc. (Saint Olaf Coll., Minn. 65, Memorial Univ. St. John's, Newfoundland 69); Commdr. Order of St. Olav (Norway) 70.
Leisure interest: chess.
Publs. *Pelsjegerliv blant Nord-Kanadas Indianere* (Land of Feast and Famine) 31, *Øst for Den Store Bre* (East of the Great Glacier) 35, *Apache—Indianerne. Jakten pa den tapte stamme* 39, *Klondyke Bill* (Klondyke Bill) 45, *Siste Båt* (play) 46, *Landet med De Kalde Kyster* 48, *Nunamiut. Blant Alaskas Innlands-eskimoer* (Nunamiut—Among Alaska's Inland Eskimoes) 51, *Landet under Leidarstjernen* (Land under the Pole Star) 59, *Vesterveg til Vinland* (Westwards to Vinland) 65 (deals with discovery and excavation of a Norse pre-Columbian settlement in N. Newfoundland), *The Norse Discovery of America.*
Vettalivei 24, Oslo, Norway.
Telephone: 14-21-35.

Ingvaldsen, Bernt; Norwegian electrical engineer and politician; b. 12 Oct. 1902, Trondheim; s. of Ingvald Ingvaldsen and Edvarda Carstens (née Holtermann); m. Aase Matheson Brun 1928; three s.; ed. Norges Tekniske Høgskole, Trondheim.
Manager, factories of Nat. Industry Ltd., Drammen 32-49, Man. Dir. of Nat. Industry Ltd. 49-68; Vice-Chair. Conservative Party 54-62; Del. to UN Gen. Assembly 59; mem. Storting 45-, Chair. Mil. Cttee. 61-65, Pres of Storting Oct. 65-72, Vice-Pres. 72-; Deputy Chair. Nobel Peace Prize Cttee. 67-.
Stortinget, Oslo, Norway.
Telephone: 41-38-10.

Ingvarsson, Ingvi S.; Icelandic diplomatist; b. 12 Dec. 1924; m.; one d.; ed. Akureyri Coll., Glasgow Univ. and London School of Econs.
Entered diplomatic service 56; First Sec., Moscow 58-62, Washington, D.C. 62-66; Deputy Perm. Rep. to NATO 66-71, concurrently Counsellor, Paris and Brussels; Deputy Sec.-Gen. Ministry of Foreign Affairs 71-72; Perm. Rep. to UN Sept. 73-.
Permanent Mission of Iceland to United Nations, 5th Floor, 370 Lexington Avenue, New York, N.Y. 10017, U.S.A.

Inman, 1st Baron, cr. 46, of Knaresborough; **Philip Inman,** P.C., J.P.; British administrator; b. 12 June 1892; ed. Harrogate and Headingley Coll. and Leeds Univ. President Charing Cross Hosp.; Chair. Hotels Exec. of British Transport 48-51; Chair. of Publishing, Hotel and Commercial companies; Lord Privy Seal with seat in Cabinet April-Oct. 47; Chair. Board of Govs. of B.B.C. Dec. 46-April 47; underwriting mem. of Lloyds; Pres. St. Mary's School, Gerrard's Cross; mem. Council King Edward's Hospital Fund, and of Royal Albert Hall.
Publs. *The Human Touch, The Silent Loom, The Golden Cup, Oil and Wine, Straight Runs Harley Street, No Going Back* (autobiography).
Knaresborough House, Warninglid, Haywards Heath, Sussex, England.

Innes, Hammond (*see* Hammond Innes, Ralph).

Innis, Roy Emile Alfredo; American chemist and human rights organization executive; b. 6 June 1934, St. Croix, Virgin Islands; s. of Alexander and Georgianna Innis; m. Doris Funnye 1965; six c.; ed. City Coll., N.Y.
Joined U.S. Army 50, Sergeant 51, discharged 52; pharmaceutical research work, Vick Chemical Co., then medical research Montefiore Hosp. until 67; active in Harlem chapter of Congress of Racial Equality (CORE) 63, Chair. Harlem Educ. Cttee. 64, Chair. Harlem CORE 65-67, Second Nat. Vice-Chair. 67-68, Assoc. Nat. Dir. CORE Jan.-Sept. 68, Nat. Dir. Sept. 68-; Founder Harlem Commonwealth Council, First Exec. Dir. 67-68, now mem. of Board; Res. Fellow, Metropolitan Applied Research Center 67-; Co-Publisher *The Manhattan Tribune* (weekly); mem. Board and Steering Cttee. Nat. Urban Coalition; mem. of Board N.Y. Coalition, Haryou Inc., Board of Dirs. New Era Health Educ. and Welfare, Board of Advisers *Pan-African Journal*; mem. Editorial Staff *Social Policy Magazine*; Co-Chair. Econ. Devt. Task Force, N.Y. Urban Coalition.
Leisure interests: reading, sports, music.
Publs. *The Little Black Book* 71; chapters in: *The Endless Crisis, Black Economic Development* 70, *Integrating America's Heritage: A Congressional Hearing to Establish A National Commission on Negro History and Culture* 70; articles and editorials in *Manhattan Tribune, CORE Magazine, Business Weekly,* etc.
800 Riverside Drive, Apartment 6E, New York, N.Y. 10032, U.S.A.

Innocenti, Luigi; Italian industrialist; b. 19 Dec. 1923; ed. Massimo Coll., Rome and School of Engineering, Rome.
Manager, Innocenti 48-51, Gen. Vice-Dir. 51-58, Vice-Chair. 58-66, Chair. 66-.
Via Senato 19, Milan, Italy.

Inoue, Shiro; Japanese banker; b. 8 Feb. 1915, Tokyo; s. of late Junnosuke and Chiyoko Inoue; m. Utako Inoue 1939; no c.; ed. Tokyo Imperial Univ.
Joined Bank of Japan 38, Chief Rep., New York Office 60, Adviser to Gov. for Int. Finance 64, Exec. Dir. 67-; Head of Nagoya Branch 67, Rep. for Int. Affairs 68-72; Pres. Asian Devt. Bank Nov. 72-.
Leisure interests: bridge, golf.
Asian Development Bank, 2330 Roxas Boulevard, Pasay City, Philippines.
Telephone: 80-26-31 and 80-72-51.

Inoue, Yoshimi, LL.B.; Japanese business executive; b. 26 March 1908, Hiroshima Pref.; s. of Yonetaro and Ritsu Inoue; m. Motoko Nakano 1933; one s. two d.; ed. Tokyo Univ.
Manager Printing Bureau, Ministry of Finance 54-56; Dir. Kobe Steel Ltd. 58-65, Dir. and Exec. Officer 65-69, Dir. and Senior Exec. Officer 69-71, Dir. and

Vice-Pres. 71-72, Dir. and Pres. 72-74, Chair. Board of Dirs. 74-.
Leisure interests: golf, kouta, igo.
4-20-14, Miyamae, Suginami-ku, Tokyo, Japan.
Telephone: Tokyo 333-6751.

Inoue, Yuichi; Japanese artist; b. 1916, Tokyo; two c.
Co-founder "Bokujin-kai" group of calligraphers 52; rep. travelling exhbn. of Japanese Calligraphy, Europe 55, São Paulo Bienal 57, Brussels Int. Exhbn. 58, Kassel Int. Exhbn. 59, Pittsburgh Int. Exhbn. 61, São Paulo Bienal 61, one-man show at Ichibankan Gallery, Tokyo 71.
Ohkamiyashiki, 2475-2 Kurami, Samukawa, Kozagun, Kanagawa, Japan.
Telephone: 0467-74-4721.

Inouye, Daniel Ken; American lawyer and politician: b. 7 Sept. 1924, Honolulu, Hawaii; s. of Hyotaro and Kame Imanaga Inouye; m. Margaret Shinobu Awamura 1949; one s.; ed. Univ. of Hawaii and George Washington Univ. Law School.
U.S. Army 43-47; Majority Leader, Territorial House of Reps. 54-58, mem. Territorial Senate 58-59; mem. U.S. Congress 59-62; U.S. Senator from Hawaii 63-; Democrat; mem. Senate Cttee. on Appropriations, Commerce Cttee., Asst. Majority Whip 64-; mem. Democratic Senatorial Campaign Cttee.; Chair. Senate Appropriations Subcttee. on Foreign Operations; Chair. Senate Commerce Subcttee. on Foreign Commerce and Tourism 70; temp. Chair. and Keynoter 1968 Democratic Nat. Convention.
442 Old Senate Office Building, Washington, D.C. 20510; and 850 Richards Street, Suite 602, Honolulu, Hawaii 96813, U.S.A.
Telephone: 202-224-3934 and 808-538-3112.

Inouye, Kaoru; Japanese banker; b. 13 May 1906, Chiba Pref.; s. of Jiro and Masa Inouye; m. Mitsuko Shibuya 1933; three c.; ed. Tokyo Univ.
Joined The Dai-Ichi Bank, Ltd. 29, Dir. 54, Deputy Pres. 61, Pres. 62-71; Chair. The Dai-Ichi Kangyo Bank 71-; Dir. Asahi Mutual Life Insurance Co.; Auditor, Kawasaki Heavy Industries Ltd., Furukawa Electric Co. Ltd., K. Hattoril Co. Ltd.; Exec. Dir. Fed. Econ. Org.; Exec. Councillor, Tokyo Chamber of Commerce and Industry.
The Dai-Ichi Kangyo Bank, 6-2, 1-chome, Marunouchi, Chiyoda-ku, Tokyo 100, Japan.

Inozemtsev, Nikolay Nikolayevich, DR.SC.; Soviet economist; b. 4 April 1921, Moscow; ed. Inst. of Int. Relations.
Head of Dept., Deputy Dir., Dir., Inst. of World Econs. and Int. Relations, U.S.S.R. Acad. of Sciences 66-; Alt. mem. C.P.S.U. Cen. Cttee. 71-; mem. Editorial Board of Pravda 61-66; Corresp. mem. U.S.S.R. Acad. of Sciences 64-68, Academician 68-.
Publs. Works in field of world economics and international relations.
Institute of World Economics and International Relations, U.S.S.R. Academy of Sciences, 13 Yaroslavskaya ulitsa, Moscow, U.S.S.R.

Ioannides, George X.; Cyprus politician; b. 1924, Ktima, Paphos; m.; ed. Greek Gymnasium, Paphos, Middle Temple, London.
Called to Bar, London 47; law practice, Paphos 48-70; mem. House of Reps. (Patriotic Front Group) for Paphos 60-70; Minister of Justice 70-72, Jan. 75-, of the Interior and Defence 72-74; mem. of Cyprus del. to many int. meetings.
Ministry of Justice, Nicosia, Cyprus.

Ioannisiani, Bagrat Konstantinovich; Soviet designer; b. 1921.
Chief designer of the Vavilov State Inst. of Optics;

awarded Lenin Prize for designing new astronomical instruments 57.
Principal works: ASI-4 astro-photo-camera, meniscus telescope with 70 cm. aperture and 98 cm. mirror (Abastumani Observatory, Georgia), 50-metre nebular spectrograph (Crimean Observatory); BTA-6 (with 600 metre mirror).
State Institute of Optics, Leningrad, U.S.S.R.

Iofan, Boris Mikhailovich; Soviet architect; b. 28 April 1891, Odessa; ed. Odessa School of Art, Architectural Dept. of the Rome Higher Inst. of Fine Arts.
State prize winner 39, 41; awarded Order of Red Star, Order of the Red Banner of Labour (twice); mem. C.P.S.U. 26-; People's Architect of U.S.S.R. 70-.
Designs include: first draft of the Palace of Soviets in Moscow; the U.S.S.R. Pavilions at the World Fairs in Paris 37, New York 39, the Baumann underground station in Moscow, design of reconstruction of city of Novorossiysk; regional plan and supervision of re-development of Pervomaysky Borough, Moscow, also Sverdlovsky Borough, Moscow; design and construction of Inst. of Physical Culture, Moscow; Oil Scientific Research Inst., Lenin Ave., Moscow; sixteen-storey blocks of flats, Moscow; experimental block of flats with extensive use of plastics.
U.S.S.R. Union of Architects, 3 Ulitsa Shchuseva, Moscow, U.S.S.R.

Ionesco, Eugène; Romanian-born French playwright; b. 13 Nov. 1912; ed. Bucharest and Paris.
Lecturer and critic in Bucharest before finally settling in Paris 38; Chevalier Légion d'Honneur; mem. Acad. Française 70; Austrian Prize for European Literature 71; Jerusalem Prize 73; Int. Writers' Fellowship, Welsh Arts Council 73.
Publs. Plays: *The Bald Prima Donna* (first produced Paris 50, London 57), *Jacques*, *The Lesson* (Paris 51, London 55, New York 58), *The Chairs* (Paris 52, London 57, New York 58), *Amedée* (Paris 54, London 57), *Victims of Duty* (Cambridge 57), *The New Tenant* (London 56, Paris 57), *Rhinocéros* (Düsseldorf 59, Paris 60, London 60), *The Killer*, *L'Impromptu de l'Alma*, *The Picture*, *Le Piéton de l'air* (Paris 62), *Chemises de Nuit* 62, *Le roi se meurt* 63, *La Soif et la Faim* 64, *Peste* 67, *Jeu de Massacre* 70, *Ce Formidable Bordel* 73; radio play: *Le Salon de l'Automobile*; short stories: *Oriflamme* (adapted as the play *Amedée*), *La Photo du Colonel* 62 (adapted as the play *The Killer*); ballet: *Jeune Homme à Marier* (with Flemming Flindt) 65; essays: *Notes et contre notes*, *Entretiens avec Claude Bonnefoy*, *Journal en miettes* (autobiog. journal) 67, *Présent passé, passé présent* (autobiog.), *Le Solitaire* (novel) 73; film: *La Vase* 73.
14 rue de Rivoli, Paris 4e, France.

Ioniță, Gen. Ion; Romanian army officer and politician; b. 14 June 1924, Mătăsaru, Dîmbovița District; m. Cecilia Ioniță; ed. Higher Staff Acad.
Member of Romanian Communist Party 45, Alt. mem. of Cen. Cttee. 55-65; Deputy Minister of Nat. Defence 62-66; mem. Cen. Cttee. of R.C.P. 65-; Minister of Nat. Defence 66-; Alt. mem. Exec. Cttee. 69-74; Alt. mem. Exec. Political Cttee. 74-; Deputy to Grand Nat. Assembly 61-; Hero of Socialist Labour 71.
Ministry of National Defence, 2 Valter Mărăcineanu Place, Bucharest, Romania.

Iordan, Iorgu, D. ÈS L.; Romanian romance philologist; b. 29 Sept. 1888, Tecuci; s. of Toader and Elena Iordan; m. Maria N. Popescu 1914 (died 1961); ed. Liceul Internat, Jasi, and Jasi, Bonn, Berlin and Paris Univs.
Secondary school teacher 11; Prof. Jasi Univ. 26-46, Dean, Faculty of Literature 38-39; Prof. Bucharest Univ. 46-, Dean, Faculty of Philology 47-50, 56-57, Rector 57-58; Dir. Jasi Nat. Theatre 28-30; Pres.

Romanian Antifascist Asscn. 34; Amb. to U.S.S.R. 45-47; Pres. UNESCO Nat. Comm. 56-57, Vice-Pres. 58-66; Corresp. mem. Romanian Acad. 34, Titular mem. 48-, Vice-Pres. and Pres. Philological Sciences Section 58-66; Dir. Linguistic Inst., Acad. of Romanian Socialist Repub. 49-52, 58-70; Corresp. mem. Saxon Acad. of Sciences, Leipzig, German Acad. of Sciences, Berlin, Austrian Acad. of Sciences, Vienna, Bavarian Acad. of Sciences, Munich, Instituto Mexicano de Cultura; founding mem. Soc. de Linguistique Romane, Paris; mem. Soc. de Linguistique, Paris, Int. Cttee. for Onomastic Sciences (CISO); Vice-Pres. Junta Directiva Asoc. Int. de Hispanistas 71-74; mem. Conf. on Human Survival, New York 72 and of Emergency World Council, The Hague 73; Hon. Pres. Soc. Linguistic Romane 68, Comité Int. des Linguistes (CIPL); European Cultural Soc., Venice; State Prize, Order of Labour, Hero of Socialist Labour, and several other decorations, Dr. h.c. Humboldt Univ., Berlin, Univs. Montpellier, Jasi, Ghent (Belgium); mem. Romanian Communist Party 34-.
Leisure interests: walking, music, shows.
Publs. *Diftongarea lui "e" şi "o" accentuaţi în poziţiile "ă", "e"* 21, *Rumänische Toponomastik* 24-26, *Introducere în studiul limbilor romanice* 32 (English trans. 37 and 70), *Gramatica limbii române* 37 (2nd ed. 46, Russian trans. 50), *Limba română actuală. O gramatică a "greşelilor"* 43 (2nd ed. 48), *Stilistica limbii române* 44, *Nume de locuri româneşti în Republica Populară Română* (Vol. I) 52, *Limba română contemporană* 54 (2nd ed. 56), *Cronica lui Neculce* (edition of an XVIII-century chronicle, with introductory study and glossary) 55 (2nd edn. 59), *Lingvistica romanică. Evoluţie. Curente. Metode* 62 (trans. into German, Portuguese, Spanish and Russian), *Toponimia românească* 63, *Istoria limbii spaniole* 63, *Introducere în linguistică romanică* (in collaboration, trans. into Spanish and Italian) 65, *Structura morfologică a limbii române* (in collaboration) 67, *Scrieri alese* 68, *Alexandru I. Philippide* 69.
Str. Sofia 21, Bucharest, Romania.
Telephone: 33-18-86.

Iordanoglou, Ippocrates; Greek lawyer and politician; b. 1909; *m.*; two *s.*; ed. Univ. of Athens.
Admitted to Thessaloniki Bar 32; Chair. Thessaloniki School Bldg. Fund; mem. Parl. for Thessaloniki 63; Minister of Commerce April 67; Minister of Agriculture Nov. 74-.
Ministry of Agriculture, Athens, Greece.

Ipekçi, Abdi; Turkish journalist; b. 1929, Istanbul; *s.* of Cevdet and Vesime İpekçi; *m.* Sibel İpekçi 1955; one *s.* one *d.*; ed. Lycée Galatasaray and Faculty of Law, Univ. of Istanbul.
Cartoonist and reporter for various publs. 43; Staff reporter, *Yeni Istanbul* 49, Deputy Editor 50; Editor *Istanbul Express* 51; Editor-in-Chief, *Milliyet* 54-; Pres. Journalists' Union 59; Lecturer, Inst. of Journalism, Univ. of Istanbul 66; Vice-Pres. Int. Press Inst. 71-; Golden Pen Prize 56.
Leisure interest: painting.
Publs. *Africa* 59, *Ihtilâlin Içyüzü* (co-author) 60, *Inönü Atatürk'ü Anlatıyor* 68, *Liderler Diyor ki* 69, *Dünyanın Dört Bucağından* 71.
Milliyet Gazetesi, Cağaloğlu, Istanbul, Turkey.
Telephone: 22-44-10.

Ipoto Eyebu-Bakand'asi; Zairian diplomatist; b. 8 Aug. 1933, Kinshasa; *m.*; seven *c.*; ed. Institut Universitaire de Hautes Etudes Internationales, Geneva.
Director of the Cabinet, Ministry of Foreign Affairs 60-63; OAU Rapporteur, Liberation Cttee. 64, Sec. Reconciliation Cttee. on the dispute between Guinea and Ghana 65; Deputy to the Special Commr. for the Cen. Basin of the Congo 65; Technical Adviser, Foreign Ministry 66; Counsellor, Zairian Embassy, London and Rep. to the Int. Tin Council 66; Amb. to Algeria 67-69, India 70 and Ethiopia 70-72; Perm. Rep. to UN 72-74.
c/o Ministry of Foreign Affairs, Kinshasa, Zaire.

Iran, Shah of (*see* Pahlavi, Mohammad Reza).

Iredale, Randle W., M.R.A.I.C., B.ARCH.; Canadian architect; b. 1 June 1929, Calgary, Alberta; *s.* of William E. Iredale and Isobel M. Fielden; *m.* Kathryn Margaret Bahr 1953; two *s.* one *d.*; ed. Univ. of British Columbia, Univ. of Washington, D.C.
Registered Architect, British Columbia 57; established practice 58; formed Rhone & Iredale, Architects 60; Chair. of Board and Dir. of Research, Fabtec Structures 69-72; established Canadian Environmental Services 68; Dir. Cancon-Canadian Eng. Services 69-74; Guest lecturer on architectural practice and design methods (for American Inst. of Architects), Seattle 69, Sun Valley 71, Chicago 72; Guest Lecturer, Pa. State Univ. 71, Univ. of Wis. 72; Hon. Lecturer, Univ. of British Columbia School of Architecture 68-; mem. Council, Architecture Inst. of British Columbia 73-; mem. Vancouver City Design Panel 63-65; Dir. Canadian Construction Information Corpn. 72-74; Canadian Housing Design Council Awards 66, 75; American Public Power Asscn. Awards 71, 73; American Iron & Steel Inst. Citation 71; Canadian Architect Award of Excellence 70; Royal Architectural Inst. of Canada Award 74.
Leisure interests: skiing, gardening, carpentry.
Publs. Articles in specialized journals.
Rhone & Iredale, Architects, 1100 West 7th Avenue, Vancouver, B.C. V6H 1B4; Home: 1537 Westbrook Crescent, Vancouver, B.C., Canada.
Telephone: (604) 736-5581 (Office); (604) 224-7003 (Home).

Iribarrén Borges, Ignacio; Venezuelan lawyer and diplomatist; b. 1912, Valencia, Venezuela; *s.* of late Ignacio Iribarrén and Mary Borges; *m.* Carolina Terrero 1938; two *s.* one *d.*; ed. Don Bosco Coll., Valencia and Central Univ., Caracas.
District Attorney, Valencia 36; Judge, Primary Court of Claims, Valencia 36-39; Prof. of Roman Law, Miguel José Sanz School of Law, Valencia 38-39; Asst. Prof. of Civil Law, Cen. Univ., Caracas 40-44; Counsellor Cen. Univ. City Inst. 45-47; mem. Univ. Council 46-47; later Pres. Nat. Hote Corpn. (Compañía Conahotu Ltda.); Sec. Governing Junta (under Presidency of Dr. Edgard Sanabria) 58-59; Ambassador to Great Britain 59-64; Minister of Foreign Affairs 64-69; Grand Cordon, Order of the Liberator and numerous other decorations.
Leisure interests: literature, history.
Cerro Quintero, Urbanización Las Mercedes 3, Quinta Pandora, Caracas, Venezuela.
Telephone: 33-99-90.

Iriyagolle, I. M. R. A.; Ceylonese politician; b. North Western Province; *m.*; seven *c.*
Entered journalism and was Sub-Editor for two nat. newspapers, *Silumina* and *Saraswathie*, later Editor of *Sinhala Baudhaya*; Head of Publicity Section of Govt. Information Dept. during Second World War; M.P. 48-60, 65-; fmr. Minister of Home Affairs; Minister of Educ. and Cultural Affairs 65-June 70.
Publication of first novel 26.
House of Representatives, Colombo, Sri Lanka.

Irmak, Sadi; Turkish professor and politician; b. 15 May 1904, Seydişehir, Konya; *s.* of Sarbri and Saliha Irmak; *m.* Semiha Irmak 1934; one *s.* one *d.*; ed. Konya, Univs. of Istanbul and Berlin.
Teacher, Gazi Educ. Inst.; Chief Medical Officer, Ankara; Lecturer in Physiology, Istanbul Univ. 32, Prof. 40; mem. Parl. for Konya 43-50; Minister of Labour 45-47; Faculty of Medicine, Munich Univ. 50-52; Senator 74-; Prime Minister Nov. 74-March 75;

Pres. Istanbul Univ. Inst. of Research on Atatürk's Reforms; Republican People's Party.
Kazim Orbayc 14, Istanbul-Chichli, Turkey.
Telephone: 471016.

Irmler, Heinrich, D.IUR.; German banker; b. 27 Aug. 1911; ed. Realgymnasium, Leipzig, Allgemeine Deutsche Creditanstalt, Leipzig, and Univ. of Leipzig.
Deutsche Reichsbank 37-48; Army Service 39-45; Bank Deutscher Lander, Frankfurt 48-53; mem. Board of Managers and Vice-Pres. Landeszentralbank von Niedersachsen (Lower Saxony), Hanover 53-57; Vice-Pres. Landeszentralbank in Nordrhein-Westfalen (North Rhine-Westphalia), Düsseldorf 58-62; Pres. Landeszentralbank in Niedersachsen, Hanover 62-64; mem. Board Deutsche Bundesbank, Frankfurt 64-.
Frankfurt am Main, Wilhelm-Epstein-Strasse 14, Federal Republic of Germany.
Telephone: 1581.

Irobe, Yoshiaki; Japanese banker; b. 18 July 1911, Tokyo; s. of Tsuneo and Tsuneko (Hirohata) Irobe; m. Kiyoko Kodama 1939; three s. one d.; ed. Tokyo Imperial Univ.
Manager, Matsuyama Branch, The Bank of Japan 54, Deputy Chief, Personnel Dept. 56, Chief Sec. and Chief, Foreign Relations Dept. 59, Chief, Personnel Dept. 62, Man. Nagoya Branch 63; Senior Man. Dir., The Kyowa Bank Ltd. 66, Deputy Pres. 68, Pres. 71-.
Leisure interests: "Go", travel, reading.
The Kyowa Bank Ltd., 5-1, 1-chome, Marunouchi, Chiyoda-ku, Tokyo; Home: 26-6, Saginomiya 6-chome, Nakano-ku, Tokyo, Japan.
Telephone: 999-0321 (Home).

Irvine, Rt. Hon. Sir Arthur James, Kt., Q.C., M.P.; British lawyer and politician; b. 14 July 1909, Aberdeen; s. of late J. M. Irvine, K.C.; m. Eleanor Morris 1937; four s.; ed. Edinburgh Acad., Edinburgh Univ. and Oriel Coll., Oxford.
President Oxford Union 32; called to Bar 35; Sec. to Lord Chief Justice of England 35-40; Army Service 40-45; M.P. for Edgehill (Liverpool) 47-; Recorder of Colchester 65-67; Solicitor-Gen. 67-70; Labour.
20 Wellington Square, Chelsea, London, S.W.3, England.
Telephone: 01-730-3117 (Home).

Irving, K. C.; Canadian oil executive; b. 14 March 1899; ed. Dalhousie Univ. and Acadia Univ.
President Irving Oil Co. Ltd. 29-; Pres. Irving Pulp & Paper Ltd., K. C. Irving Ltd., Chair. Irving Refining Ltd.
Widdrington, Pitt's Bay Road, Pembroke, Ont., Canada.

Irwin, James B.; American fmr. astronaut; b. 17 March 1930, Pittsburgh, Pa.; m. Mary Ellen Monroe; four c.; ed. U.S. Naval Acad. and Univ. of Michigan.
Commissioned U.S. Air Force 51, flight training at Hondo Air Base, Tex., and Reese Air Force Base, Tex.; served with F-12 Test Force, Edwards Air Force Base, Calif., and AIM 47 Project Office, Wright-Patterson Air Force Base, Ohio; graduated from Air Force Experimental Flight Test Pilot School 61, Air Force Aerospace Research Pilot School 63; Chief of Advanced Requirements Branch, H.Q. Air Defense Command until 66; selected as astronaut by NASA 66; Lunar Module Pilot, *Apollo XV* 71; resigned from NASA 72.
Publ. *To Rule the Night.*
P.O. Box 479, Colorado Springs, Colorado 80901, U.S.A.

Irwin, John Nichol, II; American government official; b. 31 Dec. 1913, Keokuk, Iowa; m. Jane Watson; one s. one d.; ed. Princeton, Oxford and Fordham Univs.
Served U.S. Army, Second World War; with law firm Patterson, Belknap and Webb, New York 50-70; Deputy Asst. Sec. and Asst. Sec. of Defense for Int.

Security Affairs 57-61; Special Envoy of Pres. of U.S. to Peru in dispute over Peru's seizure of U.S.-owned oil properties; U.S. Rep. in negotiations for new draft Panama Canal Treaty 65-67; mem. Bar Asscn. of New York, American Fed. of New York, State Bar Asscns., Council on Foreign Relations, Morningside Community Center Inc.; fmr. Chair. Board of Dirs. Union Theological Seminary; Trustee numerous orgs.; Under-Sec. of State 70-73; Amb. to France 73-74.
c/o Department of State, Washington, D.C. 20520, U.S.A.

Irwin, Malcolm Robert, M.S., PH.D.; American educator and biologist; b. Artesian, S. Dak.; s. of Joseph Speer Irwin and Mary T. (McCollum) Irwin; m. Margaret C. House 1929; one s. one d.; ed. Iowa State Coll.
Teacher American Farm School, Thessaloniki, Greece 21-24; Nat. Research Council Fellow, Harvard Univ. 28-29, Rockefeller Inst. for Medical Research 29-30; Asst. Prof. of Genetics, Univ. of Wis. 30-36, Assoc. Prof. 36-39, Prof. of Genetics 39-67, Emer. Prof. of Genetics 67-; mem. Nat. Acad. of Sciences; Foreign mem. Swedish Royal Acad. of Agriculture; Daniel Giraud Elliot Medal of Nat. Acad. of Sciences 38, Alumni Award of Iowa State Univ. 60, Morrison Award of American Soc. for Animal Sciences 62, Von Nathusius Medaille of Deutsche Gesellschaft für Züchtung 65, Hon. Recognition by Wis. Agricultural Co-operatives 68.
Leisure interests: sport, especially golf and bowling, reading in science and biographical material of foreign statesmen.
Publs. About 100 biological articles and book chapters.
4720 Regent Street, Madison, Wis. 53705, U.S.A.
Telephone: 233-2809.

Irwin, Raymond, M.A., F.L.A.; British librarian and professor; b. 14 March 1902, Huddersfield; s. of John T. Irwin and Eliza Irwin; m. 1st Ivy Summerville Viggers 1929 (died 1973), 2nd Mary Elsie Allen 1974; ed. King's Coll., Taunton and Oxford Univ.
County Librarian, Northants. 24-34; County Librarian, Lancashire 34-44; Hon. Treas., Library Asscn. 47-54, Vice-Pres. 54-58, Pres. 58-, Hon. Fellow 63; Prof. Library Studies London Univ. 57-69; Dir. School of Librarianship and Archives, Univ. Coll., London 44-69, Emer. Prof. 69-.
Leisure interests: gardening, birds, wild flowers, Siamese cats, music and a hundred other things.
Publs. *The National Library Service* 47, *Librarianship: Essays on Applied Bibliography* 49, *British Bird Books: An Index to British Ornithology* 51, *British Birds and their Books: Catalogue of the Exhibition for the National Book League* 52, *The Origins of the English Library* 58, *The Heritage of the English Library* 64, *The English Library: Sources and History* 66.
24 Central Drive, Lytham St. Anne's, Lancs., England.
Telephone: 0253-736702.

Irwin, William Arthur, O.C., B.A.; Canadian journalist and diplomatist; b. 1898, Ayr, Ontario; s. of Alexander J. and Amelia J. (Hassard) Irwin; m. 1st Jean Olive Smith 1921 (died 1948), 2nd P. K. Page 1950; one s. two d.; ed. Univs. of Manitoba and Toronto.
Sometime Rodman Canadian Northern Railway Construction; later Reporter, *Toronto Mail and Empire*, and subsequently Reporter, Corresp. (Parl. Press Gallery, Ottawa) and Editorial Writer *Toronto Globe*; Assoc. Editor *Maclean's Magazine* 25-42, Man. Editor 43-45, Editor 45-50; served in France during First World War; Chair. Nat. Film Board 50-53; High Commr. in Australia 53-56; Amb. to Brazil 57-59, Mexico 60-64; Publisher *Victoria Daily Times*; Vice-Pres. Victoria Press Ltd. 64-71; Officer of Canada 73.
Publs. *The Wheat Pool* 29, *Motor Vehicle Transportation Briefs* (Royal Comm. on Railways and Transportation 32, Royal Comm. on Transportation in Ontario 37), *The Machine* 38.
3260 Exeter Road, Victoria, British Columbia, Canada.

Iryani, Sheikh Qadi Abdul Rahman; Yemeni religious and political leader.
Took part in abortive revolution 48; imprisoned 48-54; took part in uprising 55; mem. Revolutionary Council 62; Minister of Justice 62-63; Vice-Pres. Exec. Council 63-64; mem. Political Bureau Jan. 64; Chair. Peace Cttee. set up after Khamer Peace Talks May 65; Head of State of Yemen Nov. 67-March 69; Chair. Presidential Council 69-74; leader of Zaidi (Shia) sect.
c/o Military Command Council, Sana'a, Yemen Arab Republic.

Isa bin Suiman al-Khalifah, H.H. Shaikh; Ruler of the State of Bahrain; b. 3 July 1933.
Appointed heir-apparent by his father, H.H. Shaikh Sulman bin Hamad al-Khalifah 58; succeeded as Ruler on the death of his father Nov. 61; took title of Amir Aug. 71; Hon. K.C.M.G.
Rifa'a Palace, Manama, Bahrain.

Isaev, Vasily Yakovlevich; Soviet engineer and politician; b. 17; ed. Leningrad Engineering-Construction Inst.
Administrative work in construction orgs. 37-55; mem. C.P.S.U. 39-; Chief Board of Housing, Civil and Industrial Construction in Leningrad 55-61; Deputy Chair., then Chair. Exec. Cttee. Leningrad City Council of Working People's Deputies (Mayor of Leningrad) 62-64; Deputy of Supreme Soviet U.S.S.R. 62-; mem. Comm. for Youth Affairs, Soviet of Union; Deputy Chair. of Gosplan U.S.S.R. 65-; Alt. mem. Cen. Cttee. C.P.S.U. 66-.
U.S.S.R. Gosplan, 12 Prospekt Marxa, Moscow, U.S.S.R.

Isano, Masashi; Japanese business executive; b. 15 Sept. 1899; ed. Kyoto Univ.
Adviser, Kawasaki Heavy Industries Ltd.
Kawasaki Heavy Industries, Nissei-Kawasaki Bldg., 16-1 Nakamachi-Dori 2-chome, Ikuta-ku, Kobe, Japan.

Isarangkun Na Ayuthaya, Charunphan; Thai politician; b. 14 March 1914; ed. Chulalongkorn and Thammasat Univs., Bangkok, Nat. Defence Coll.
Served in Ministry of Interior 34-43; joined Ministry of Foreign Affairs 43; posted to Berne 47-51, London 56-60; Deputy Under-Sec. of State for Foreign Affairs 60; Amb. to Laos 61-65, to Spain, concurrently to Tunisia 65-70, to Austria, concurrently to Turkey 70-71; Under-Sec. of State for Foreign Affairs 71-73; Minister of Foreign Affairs 73-75.
c/o Ministry of Foreign Affairs, Bangkok, Thailand.

Isard, Walter, A.B., M.A., PH.D.; American regional scientist; b. 19 April 1919; ed. Temple, Harvard and Chicago Univs.
Instructor Wesleyan Univ. 45, Mass. Inst. of Technology 47; Visiting Lecturer Tufts Coll. 47; Assoc. Prof. of Economics, Assoc. Dir. of Teaching, Inst. of Econs., American Univ. 48-49; Research Fellow and Lecturer, Harvard Univ. 49-53; Assoc. Prof. of Regional Economics, Dir. Urban and Regional Studies, Mass. Inst. of Technology 53-56; Prof. of Economics, Chair. Dept. of Regional Science, Univ. of Pa. 56-; Visiting Prof. of Regional Science, Yale Univ. 60-61, of Landscape Architecture and Regional Science, Harvard Univ. 66-71; Chair. Graduate Group in Peace Research and Peace Science Unit 70-; Senior Research Assoc., Visiting Prof. of Econs., Regional Science and Policy Planning, Cornell Univ. 71-; Distinguished Visiting Prof., Inst. für Regionalwissenschaft, Karlsruhe 72; Consultant, Tenn. Valley Authority 51-52, Resources for the Future Inc. 54-58, Ford Foundation 55-56; Founder Regional Science Assscn. 54, Editor, Co-Editor *Papers* 54-58, Pres. 59, Hon. Chair. 60-; Ford Foundation Fellow in Econs. and Business Admin. 59-60; Editor, Co-Editor *Journal of Regional Science* 60-; Chair. OEEC Econ. Productivity Agency Conf. on Regional Econs. and Planning, Bellagio, Italy 60; Founder Peace Science Soc. (Int.) 63, Co-Editor *Papers*

63-, Exec. Sec. 64-, Pres. 68; Assoc. Editor *Quarterly Journal of Economics* 68-71; mem. Ed. Board *Journal of Conflict Resolution* 72-.
Publs. *Atomic Power: An Economic and Social Analysis* 52 (Japanese edn. 54), *Location Factors in the Petrochemical Industry* 55, *Location and Space Economy* 56, *Municipal Costs and Revenues resulting from Community Growth* 57, *Industrial Complex Analysis and Regional Development* 59, *Methods of Regional Analysis* 60, *Regional Economic Development* 61, *General Theory: Social, Political, Economic and Regional* 69, *Regional Input-Output Study* 71, *Ecologic-Economic Analysis for Regional Planning* 71.
3218 Garrett Road, Drexel Hill, Pa., U.S.A.

Isaza Calderón, Baltasar, D.PHIL., D.LITT.; Panamanian professor; b. 1904, Natá, Prov. Coclé; ed. National Inst., Panama, Pedagogical Inst., Santiago de Chile, Central Univ. of Madrid.
Secretary, Gen. Inspectorate of Primary Educ. 26-27; Prof., Nat. Inst. of Panama 34-39, Univ. of Panama 37-62; Dean, Faculty of Philosophy, Letters and Educ. Univ. of Panama 43-48; Dir. Panamanian Acad. 60-.
Publs. *El Retorno a la Naturaleza* 34, *Estudios Literarios* 57, *Estampas de Viaje* 59, *La Doctrina Gramatical de Bello* 60, *Rubén Darío* 68, etc.
Academia Panameña de la Lengua, Panama City; Calle 46, Núm. 27, Apartamento 18, Panama City, Republic of Panama.
Telephone: 25-6206.

Isbister, Claude Malcolm, PH.D.; Canadian international finance official; b. 15 Jan. 1914, Winnipeg, Manitoba; *m.*; three *c.*; ed. Univs. of Manitoba and Toronto and Harvard Univ.
Instructor in Mathematics, Univ. of Manitoba 34-35; Actuary, Sun Life Assurance Co. of Canada, Montreal 35-39; Instructor, Econs. Dept., Harvard Univ. 42-45; entered govt. service 45, served in Bureau of Statistics 45-47, Dept. of Reconstruction and Supply 47-49, Dept. of Trade and Commerce 49-58; Asst. Deputy Minister, Dept. of Finance 58-63; Dir. Canadian Nat. (West Indies) Steamships Ltd. 59-62; Deputy Minister, Dept. of Citizenship and Immigration 63-65, Dept. of Mines and Technical Surveys 65-66, Dept. of Energy, Mines and Resources 66-70; Chair. Dominion Coal Board 69-70; Exec. Dir. IBRD, IFC and IDA 70-.
International Bank for Reconstruction and Development, 1818 H Street, N.W., Washington, D.C. 20433, U.S.A.

Isherwood, Christopher; American (b. British) writer; b. 26 Aug. 1904; ed. Repton School, Corpus Christi Coll., Cambridge and King's Coll., London (Medical School).
Publs. Novels: *All the Conspirators* 28, *The Memorial* 32, *Mr. Norris Changes Trains* 35, *Good-bye to Berlin* 39, *Prater Violet* 45, *The World in the Evening* 54, *Down There on a Visit* 62, *A Single Man* 64, *A Meeting by the River* 67; Plays (with W. H. Auden): *The Dog Beneath the Skin* 35, *Ascent of F6* 36, *On the Frontier* 38; (with Don Bachardy): *A Meeting by the River* 72; Autobiography: *Lions and Shadows* 38, *Kathleen and Frank* 71; Travel: *Journey to a War* (with W. H. Auden) 39, *The Condor and the Cows* 49; Translations: *The Bhagavad-Gita* (with Swami Prabhavananda) 45, Shankara's *Crest-Jewel of Discrimination* (with Swami Prabhavananda) 47, Baudelaire's *Intimate Journals* 47, *The Yoga Aphorisms of Patanjali* (with Prabhavananda) 53; *Ramakrishna and His Disciples* (biography) 65, *Exhumations* (stories, articles, verses) 66.
145 Adelaide Drive, Santa Monica, Calif. 90402, U.S.A.

Ishibashi, Kanichiro; Japanese business executive; b. 1 March 1920, Kurume-shi, Fukuoka-ken; *s.* of Shojiro Ishibashi and Shojiro Masa; *m.* Akiko Ishibashi 1944; one *s.* two *d.*; ed. Faculty of Law, Univ. of Tokyo.
Naval service 43-45; joined Bridgestone Tire Co., Ltd. 45, Dir. 49-, Vice-Pres. 50-63, Pres. 63-73, Chair. 73-;

Dir. and Adviser Bridgestone Cycle Industry Co. Ltd.;
Dir. and Adviser Bridgestone LPG Co. Ltd.; Man. Dir.
Japan Fed. of Employers Asscns.
Leisure interests: pictures, photography, music, golf.
1 Nagasaka-cho, Azabu, Minato-ku, Tokyo, Japan.
Telephone: 03-583-0150.

Ishibashi, Shojiro; Japanese company director; b. 25
Feb. 1889; ed. Kurume Commercial School.
President Bridgestone Tyre Co. Ltd. 31, Chair. 63-73;
Chair. Prince Motors Ltd. 51; Pres. Japan Synthetic
Rubber Co. Ltd. 57, Chair. 65; Exec. Dir. Nat. Fed. of
Econ. Orgs. 49, Japan Fed. of Employers' Asscns. 52;
Dir. Kurume Univ. 51; Pres. Bridgestone Gallery 52;
Councillor, Nat. Museum of Modern Art 52, Society for
International Cultural Relations 57, Nat. Museum of
Occidental Art 59, Nat. Museum of Tokyo 59; Chair.
Ishibashi Foundation 56; Dark Blue Ribbon Medal 37,
39, 57, 59, Green Ribbon Medal 40, Blue Ribbon Medal
58; Hon. Citizen Kurume City 56; Légion d'Honneur
60; Grand Officer of Order of Merit of the Italian
Republic 61; Second Order of Sacred Treasure 64; and
other honours.
1 Nagasaka-cho, Azabu, Minato-ku, Tokyo, Japan.

Ishida, Kazuto, LL.B.; Japanese judge; b. 1903; ed.
Tokyo Imperial Univ.
Judge, Tokyo District Court 28-41; Dir. Personnel
Affairs Bureau, Gen. Sec. Supreme Court 47-50; Deputy
Sec.-Gen. Supreme Court 50-56; Chief Judge, Tokyo
District Court 56; Sec.-Gen. Supreme Court 60; Pres.
Tokyo High Court 62; Assoc. Justice, Supreme Court
63; Chief Justice, Supreme Court 69-; Vice-Pres. Int.
Legal Soc. of Japan 60-62; Dir. Japan Bar Asscn.;
Vice-Chair. World Asscn. of Judges 69; Pres. Lawyers'
Asscn. 69.
39 Wakamiya-cho, Shinjuku-ku, Tokyo, Japan.

Ishida, Taizo; Japanese automobile executive; b. 16
Nov. 1888, Kosugai, Chita-gun, Aichi-ken; s. of
Tokuzaburo Sawada and Kau Sawada; m. Masao
Kosugi 1944; one d.; ed. Shiga Prefectural Daiichi
Junior High School.
President, Toyoda Automatic Loom Works Ltd. 48-69,
Chair. 69-, Adviser 73-; Pres. Toyota Motor Co. Ltd.
50-61, Chair. 61-71, Adviser 71-; Dir. Toyota Motor
Sales U.S.A. Inc. 57-; Japan Automobile Manufacturers,
Asscn. Inc. 51-71; Chair. Textile Machinery Asscn. 51-
72; Exec. Dir. Japan Fed. of Employers' Asscns. 52-,
Fed. of Econ. Orgs. 60-; Chair. Japan Industrial
Vehicles Asscn. 68-71; Hon. Consul of Portugal 70-;
Blue Ribbon Medal 57; 2nd Order of the Sacred
Treasure 64, 1st Order of the Sacred Treasure 70.
Leisure interest: baseball.
Toyota Motor Co. Ltd., 1 Toyota-cho, Toyota-shi,
Aichi-ken 471, Japan.
Telephone: 0565-28-2121.

Ishii, Mitsujiro, B.A.; Japanese politician; b. 1889; ed.
Kobe Higher Commercial School and Tokyo Higher
Commercial School.
Entered Higher Civil Service 13; Sec. to Gov.-Gen. of
Formosa, concurrently Councillor of Govt.-Gen. of
Formosa 15; Dir. *Asahi* (Newspaper Publishing Co.) 25,
Man. Dir. 40-45; Pres. Asahi Movie Manufacturing Co.
37-41; joined Japan Liberal Party 46; elected to House
of Reps. 46; Minister of Commerce and Industry,
Yoshida Cabinet 47; Pres. Asahi Broadcasting Co.
51-52; Dir. Nishi Nippon Railroad Co. Ltd. 51-; Minister
of Transportation Nov. 52-54; Chief Sec. of Liberal
Party 54-55, Chair. Exec. Board of Liberal Democratic
Party 55-56, 60-; Dep. Prime Minister 57-58; Minister of
Trade and Industry 60, of Justice 65-66; Speaker,
House of Reps. 67-.
House of Representatives, Tokyo, Japan.

Ishikawa, Shigeru, D.ECON.; Japanese economist; b. 7
April 1918; ed. Tokyo Univ. of Commerce (now
Hitotsubashi Univ.).

Attached to Jiji Press News Agency 45-56, Hong Kong
Corresp. 51-53; Asst. Prof., Inst. of Econ. Research,
Hitotsubashi Univ. 56-63, Prof. 63-, Dir. 72-74.
Publs. *National Income and Capital Formation in
Mainland China* 65, *Economic Development in Asian
Perspective* 67, *Agricultural Development Strategies of
Asia* 70.
19-9, 4 chome Kugayama, Suginami-ku, Tokyo, Japan.
Telephone: 332-8376.

Ishkov, Alexander Akimovich; Soviet government
official; b. 29 Aug. 1905; ed. State Pedagogical Inst.,
Rostov-on-Don.
Fish industry 30-; People's Commissar for fishing
industry 40-46; U.S.S.R. Minister of Fish Industry
48-50, 54-57; Head, Fish Industry Dept., U.S.S.R.
State Planning Cttee. (Gosplan) 57-60, Chief, **Main
Admin.** of Fishing Economy (Gosplan) 60-62; Chair.
State Cttee. on the Fishing Econ. 62-65; Minister of
Fisheries 65-; Alt. mem. Cen. Cttee. of C.P.S.U. 56-,
mem. C.P.S.U. 27-; Deputy to U.S.S.R. Supreme
Soviet 46-50, 66-; mem. Cttee. of U.S.S.R. Parl. Group;
Order of Lenin (thrice), Order of Red Banner, Order of
Red Banner of Labour.
U.S.S.R. Ministry of Fisheries, 12 Rozhdestvensky
Boulevard, Moscow K-45, U.S.S.R.

Ishlinsky, Aleksandr Yulevich; Soviet applied mathe-
matician; b. 6 Aug. 1913, Moscow; s. of Yulij Eduardo-
vich Ishlinsky and Sofia Ivanovna Kirillova; m.
Natalia Vladimirovna Zaporozhets 1943; ed. Moscow
Univ.
Professor, Moscow Univ. 35-48; mem. Ukrainian Acad.
of Sciences 48; Prof. Kiev Univ. 49-55; Prof. and Head
of Dept., Moscow Univ. 55; Dir. Inst. for Problems in
Mechanics U.S.S.R. Acad. of Sciences 64-; mem.
U.S.S.R. Acad. of Sciences 60-; Deputy Chair. U.S.S.R.
Nat. Comm. of Mechanics; Chair. U.S.S.R. Scientific-
Technical Soc.; Regional mem. Int. Fed. Scientific
Workers; Deputy to Supreme Soviet U.S.S.R.; Hero of
Socialist Labour, Order of Lenin (three times), Order
of the October Revolution, Order of the Red Banner of
Labour (twice), Order of the Badge of Honour, Lenin
Prize.
Leisure interest: radiotechnique.
Publs. *The Dynamics of Ground Masses* 54, *The Theory
of the Horizon Compass* 56, *On the Equation of Problems
determining the Position of Moving Objects by using a
Gyroscope and measuring Acceleration* 57, *The Mechanics
of Gyroscopic Systems* 63, *Inertial Guidance of ballistic
rockets* 68, *Orientation, gyroscopes and inertial navigation*
75.
Institute for Problems in Mechanics, U.S.S.R. Academy
of Sciences, 117526 Moscow, prospekt Vernadskogo 101,
U.S.S.R.

Işik, Hasan Esat; Turkish diplomatist and politician;
b. 21 Oct. 1916; ed. Ankara Univ.
Ministry of Foreign Affairs 40-; Consulate-Gen., Paris
45-49; Head of Section, Dept. of Commerce and Econ.
Affairs, and Dept. of Int. Econ. Relations 49-52; staff
of Perm. Turkish Del. to European Office of UN,
Geneva 52-54; Dir.-Gen. of Dept. of Commerce and
Commercial Agreements, Ministry of Foreign Affairs
54-57; Asst. of Econ. Affairs to Sec.-Gen. of Ministry of
Foreign Affairs 57-62; Amb. to Belgium 62-64, to
U.S.S.R. 64-65, 66-68; Minister of Foreign Affairs 65;
Amb. to France 68-73; Minister of Defence Jan.-Nov. 74.
Ministry of Defence, Ankara, Turkey.

Ismagilov, Zagir Garipovich; Soviet composer; b.
8 Jan. 1917, Verkhnee Sermenevo, Byeloretsky District,
Bashkirian; ed. Moscow Conservatoire.
Executive mem., U.S.S.R. Composers' Union, Chair.
Bashkir Branch; Honoured Worker of Arts of R.S.F.S.R.
55, People's Artist of Bashkir Autonomous S.S.R. 63,
Red Banner of Labour, People's Artist of R.S.F.S.R. 68,
other decorations.

Principal compositions: Lenin Cantata 50, Symphonic Overture 51, Vocal-Choreographic Suite 53, *Salavat Yulayev* (opera) 54, *Kodasa* 59; vocal and instrumental works.
Bashkir Section, R.S.F.S.R. Composers' Union, Ufa, U.S.S.R.

Ismail, Abdul Malek; Yemeni diplomatist; b. 23 Nov. 1937, Aden; *m.*; three *c.*; ed. Tawahi and Crater, Aden, Tech. School, Maalla, Khediwi High School, Cairo and Cairo Univ. Faculty of Commerce.
Member, United Nat. Party; Editor *Al-Nour* and *Hakikah* (newspapers) 61-63; Vice-Chair. Gen. Union of Petroleum Workers 61-62, Chair. Petroleum Workers Union 62-64; Vice-Pres. Arab Fed. of Petroleum Workers 62-65; leading mem. Arab Nationalist Movement 56-63; leading mem. Nat. Front for Liberation of Occupied S. Yemen (FLOSY) 63-65; Dir. Nat. Front Office, Cairo 65-66; mem. Gen. Command of Nat. Liberation Front 66-68; Minister of Labour and Social Affairs 67-68, of Econs., Commerce and Planning April 68; Perm. Rep. to UN 70-73.
c/o Ministry of Foreign Affairs, Aden, People's Democratic Republic of Yemen.

Ismail, Ahmed Sultan, B.SC.; Egyptian mechanical engineer; b. 14 April 1923, Port Said; *m.* Rawhia Riad 1957; ed. Cairo Univ.
Worked as shift engineer, maintenance engineer at various power stations 45-64; mem. Exec. Board Electrical Projects Corpn. 64-; Nat. Defence Coll. 67; Gov. Menufia Prov. 68-71; Minister of Power 71-; Order of Repub., First Class.
Leisure interests: reading, travel.
43 Ahmed Abdel Aziz Street, Dokki, Cairo, Egypt.
Telephone: Cairo 933155.

Ismail, Mohamed Ali, M.A.; Malaysian bank official and barrister-at-law; b. 16 Sept. 1918, Port Swettenham, Selangor; *m.* Maimunah binti Abdul Latiff 1949; two *s.*; ed. Univ. of Cambridge and Middle Temple, London.
Controller, Trade Div., Ministry of Commerce and Industry 55-57; Minister Malaysian Embassy, Washington 57-58, Econ. Minister 58-60; Exec. Dir. IBRD, Int. Finance Corpn., Int. Devt. Asscn. 58-60; Deputy Gov. Central Bank of Malaysia 60-62, Gov. 62-; Chair. Capital Issues Cttee. 68-, Malaysian Industrial Devt. Finance Ltd. 69-; Pres. Malaysian Inst. of Management 66-68; mem. Nat. Devt. Planning Cttee. 62-, Council of Univ. of Malaya 62-72; Adviser, Nat. Corpn. (PERNAS) 71; mem. Urban Devt. Authority 71; Hon. LL.D. (Univ. of Malaya) 73.
Leisure interests: golf, swimming, tennis.
Central Bank of Malaysia, P.O. Box 922, Kuala Lumpur; Home: 23 Jalan Natesa, off Cangkat Tunku, Kuala Lumpur, Malaysia.
Telephone: 89931 (Office); 24185 (Home).

Ismail, Gen. Mohamed Hafez; Egyptian soldier and diplomatist.
Assistant Under-Sec. of Foreign Affairs 60-64; Amb. to U.K. 64-65, to Italy 67-69; Adviser to the Pres. on Nat. Security 71-74; Amb. to U.S.S.R. 74-.
Egyptian Embassy, Moscow, U.S.S.R.

Isong, Clement Nyong, PH.D.; Nigerian economist and banker; b. 20 April 1920, Ikot Osong, South-Eastern State; *s.* of Nathaniel Udo Isong and Maggie Udo; *m.* Nne B. Akpaete 1958; two *s.* four *d.*; ed. Univ. Coll. Ibadan, Iowa Wesleyan Coll. and Harvard Graduate School of Arts and Sciences.
Assistant economist, Fed. Reserve Bank of New York 57; Lecturer in Econs., Money and Banking, Univ. Coll. Ibadan 57-59; Sec., Central Bank of Nigeria 59-61, Dir. of Research 61-62; Adviser to African Dept. of IMF 62-67; Gov. of Cen. Bank of Nigeria 67-75, Chair. Board of Dirs.; Alt. Gov. for Nigeria, Int. Monetary Fund;

Chair. Bankers' Cttee., Asscn. of African Cen. Banks 73-.
Leisure interest: photography.
Home: 6 Queen's Drive, Ikoyi, Lagos, Nigeria.

Issigonis, Sir Alec Arnold Constantine, Kt., C.B.E., F.R.S.; British engineer and designer; b. 1906; ed. Battersea Polytechnic, London.
Draughtsman, Rootes Motors Ltd. 33-36; Suspension Engineer, British Motor Corpn. 56, Chief Engineer 57-61, Technical Dir. 61-72; Advanced Design Consultant, British Leyland (Austin-Morris) Ltd. 72-; designed the Morris Minor 48, the Mini Minor and Austin Seven 59, Morris 1100 62; Leverhulme Medal, Royal Soc. 66; Hon. D.Tech., Nat. Academic Awards Council 75.
British Leyland (Austin-Morris) Ltd., Longbridge, Birmingham, England.

Istomin, Eugène George; American pianist; b. 26 Nov. 1925, New York; *m.* Marta Montanez Casals 1975; ed. Kyriena Silote, Rudolf Serkin and at Curtis Inst., Philadelphia.
Concert pianist 43-; toured with Adolf Busch Chamber Players 44-45; first European appearance 50; charter mem. Casals Prades and Puerto Rico festivals 50-; several world tours; founded Trio with Isaac Stern and Leonard Rose 61; numerous recordings of solo, orchestral and chamber works.
Leisure interests: archaeology, history, painting, baseball.
c/o Hurok Attractions, 730 Fifth Avenue, New York, N.Y. 10019, U.S.A.

Itakura, Joji; Japanese banker; b. 3 June 1912, Kanagawa Pref.; *s.* of Takuzo and Suga Itakura; *m.* Taniko Itakura; two *s.* two *d.*; ed. Keio Univ.
Managing Dir. Mitsui Bank Ltd. 68-71, Senior Man. Dir. 71-72, Deputy Pres. 72-74, Pres. 74-.
Leisure interests: "Go", golf, reading.
The Mitsui Bank Ltd., 1-2 Yurakucho 1-chome, Chiyoda-ku, Tokyo 100; Home: 6-8 Kita 2-chome Shinoha a, Kohoko-ku, Yokohama City, Kanagawa Prefecture, Japan.
Telephone: 501-1111 (Office); 045-401-5155 (Home).

Italiaander, Rolf Bruno Maximilian; German writer and explorer; b. 20 Feb. 1913, Leipzig, Germany (Dutch citizen).
Explorer in Africa for over forty years; Visiting Prof. Inst. for European Studies, Univ. of Vienna 59, Univ. of Michigan 61, Hope Coll., Michigan 61, Kalamazoo Coll., Michigan 61, American Negro Univ. 62, Universidade de Bahia and Instituto Joaquim Nabuco, Recife, Brazil 67; Co-Founder and Hon. Sec. Free Acad. of Art, Hamburg 48-69; Founder Museum of Naive Art in Hamburg-Rade; Founder German Translators' Union 54, Hon. Pres. 60-; Co-founder Fed. Int. de Traducteurs, Paris; Hon. Consul of Senegal 64; Pres. Int. Translators Congress, Hamburg 65; mem. American Acads.; Hans Henny Jahnn Award; several decorations.
Leisure interest: collecting naive art from the whole world, gardening.
Publs. *Der ruhelose Kontinent* 58, *The New Leaders of Africa* 60, *Schwarze Haut im roten Griff* 62, *Die neuen Männer Asiens* 64, *Immer wenn ich unterwegs bin* 63, *König Leopolds Kongo* 64, *Dappers Afrika 1668* 64, *The Challenge of Islam* 64, *Im Namen des Herrn im Kongo* 65, *Die Friedensmacher* 65, *In der Palmweinschenke* 66, *Rassenkonflikte in der Welt* 66, *Frieden in der Welt* 67, *Lebensentscheidung für Israel* 67, *Heinrich Barth* 67, *Aufstieg und Sturz des Oscar Wilde* 67, *Terra Dolorosa (Indoamerika)* 69, *Weder Krankheit noch Verbrechen* 69, *Junge Kunst aus Afrika: Kongo-Bilder und Verse* 69, *Heinrich Barth: Er schloss uns einen Weltteil auf* 69, *Akzente eines Lebens* 70, *Kultur ohne Wirtschaftswunder* 70, *Albanien: Chinas Vorposten in Europa* 70, *Von der Hufe zum Museum* 70, *Naive Kunst aus*

aller Welt 70, *Die Wassermühle* 70, *Ade, Madame Muhl* 70, *Europas neue Sonntagsmaler* 71, *Profile und Perspektiven* 71, *Argumente kritischer Christen* 71, *Die neuen Herren der alten Welt* 72, *Moral—wozu?* 72, *Partisanen und Profeten* 72, *Sukagakkai, Japans neue Buddhisten* 72, *Heisses Land (New Guinea)* 72, *12 Grafiken europäischer Naiver* 72, *Sepik-Grafik* 73, *Eine Religion für den Frieden* 73, *Verantwortliche Gesellschaft (Indonesien)* 74, *Spass an der Freud (Naive Maler)* 74, *Ein Glied in der Kette* (play) 74, *Diktaturen im Nacken* 74; Biography and Bibliography: *Unterwegs mit Rolf Italiaander* 63, Paul I. Fried: *Die Welt des Rolf Italiaander* 72; Children's musicals: *Das grosse Clück des Lampenputzer, Die verrückte Oma, Sascha mit der Zieharmonika, Die Kinder von der Davidswache* 75, *Congo-Grafik* 75.

Heilwigstrasse 39, 2 Hamburg 20, Federal Republic of Germany.

Telephone: 6071110 (Museum); 473435 (Home).

Ito, Jirozaemon; Japanese business executive; b. 5 July 1902; ed. Keio Univ.

Former Pres. ceramics companies; Pres. Matsuzakaya Dept. Store Chain 47-; fmr. Pres. Nagoya Chamber of Commerce; mem. Standing Cttee. Japan Fed. of Employers' Asscn.

Matsuzakaya Department Stores, No. 16-1, Sakae-3-chome, Japan.

Ito, Shinsui; Japanese painter; b. 1898; ed. Kiyokata Art School, Tokyo.

Has exhibited many pictures of women incl. *A Mirror* (Nat. Acad. of Art Prize 46); organizer of Jitsugetsu Sha, and art league of young painters of promise; has about 100 disciples; mem. Council of the Nat. Art Exhbn.; Sec. Japan Fed. of Art Socs.

Kita-Kamakura, Kanagawa Prefecture, Japan.

Itoh, Junji; Japanese business executive; b. 10 July 1922, Tsingtao, China; s. of Hideo Itoh and Fudechiyo Itoh; m. Mizuko Takeoka 1953; two s.; ed. Keio Univ.

With Kanegafuchi Spinning Co. Ltd. (now Kanebo Ltd.) 48-60; Dir. Kanebo Ltd. 61, Man. Dir. 64, Exec. Dir. 66, Vice-Pres. 68, Pres. 68-; Pres. Kanebo Cosmetics Inc. 69-, Kanebo Acrylic Fibres Co. Ltd. 70-, Kanebo Foods Ltd. 71-, Kanebo Textiles Ltd. 72-, Kanebo Polyester Ltd. 72-, Kanebo Pharmaceutical Sales Co. Ltd. 72, Kanebo Stevens Co. Ltd. 73-; Rep. Dir. Nippon Ester Co. Ltd. 68-; Dir. Matsuyama Petrochemicals Inc. 68-, Chair. 70-; Rep. Dir. Nippon Kynol Inc. 72-; Man. Dir. Japan Fed. of Econ. Orgs. 68-, Japan Spinners' Asscn. 68- (Chair. 71-72), Japan Chemical Fibres Asscn. 68-; Vice-Chair. Japan Textile Fed. 71-72; Trustee, Keio Univ. 70; Grão Cruz Orden Academico São Francisco (Brazil) 72.

Kanebo Ltd., 3-80, Tomobuchi-cho 1-chome, Miyako-jima-ku, Osaka 534; Home: 59, Yamate-cho, Ashiya, Hyogo 659, Japan.

Telephone: (06) 921-1231 (Office); (0797) 31-3308 (Home).

Itoh, Kyoichi; Japanese textile executive; b. 27 May 1914, Kobe; s. of Chubei Itoh and Chiyo (Nagata) Itoh; m. Chikako Hongo 1941; one s. two d.; ed. Kobe Univ.

Director Kureha Spinning Co. Ltd. 56, Man. Dir. 56-63, Exec. Dir. 63-64, Pres. 64-66; Exec. Vice-Pres. Toyobo Co. Ltd. 66-73, Chair. 73-74, Gen. Adviser 74-; Chair. Nippei Industrial Co. 69; Dir. Toyo Pulp Co. 50, Chair. 50-; Hon. Consul-Gen. of Salvador, Osaka 58-.

Leisure interest: golf.

Toyobo Co. Ltd., 2-8 Dojimohama-Dori Kita-ku, Osaka 530; Home: 1845 Kuegasaka, Sumiyoshi Machi, Higashi Nadaku, Kobe 658, Japan.

Telephone: 06-344-1331 (Office); 078-851-5211 (Home).

Itokawa, Hideo; Japanese aeronautic engineer; b. 20 July 1912; ed. Tokyo Univ.

Engineer, Nakajima Aircraft Co. 35-41; Asst. Prof. of Engineering at Tokyo Univ. 41-48, Prof. 48-67; Exec.-Dir. Space Engineering Dept., Inst. of Industrial Science 55-; Pres. Japanese Rocket Soc. 56-58; Convener Nat. Cttee. on Space Research, Japan Science Council 56-; mem. Nat. Space Council 60-; Deputy Dir. Inst. of Space and Aeronautical Science 64-67; Dir. of Systems Research Inst. 67.

34-15, 4-chome, Matsubara, Setagaya-ku, Tokyo, Japan.

Iturbi, Jose; Spanish pianist, conductor and composer; b. 28 Nov. 1895, Valencia; ed. Conservatoires of Valencia and Paris.

Has given piano concerts in major cities throughout the world and has conducted most of the world's major orchestras; Musical Dir. Rochester (N.Y.) Philharmonic Orchestra 35-44; Musical and Artistic Dir. Valencia Symphony Orchestra 56-; Musical Dir. and Conductor Bridgeport Symphony Orchestra 67-72; mem. Gran Cruz Alfonso X, El Sabio, Real Academia de Bellas Artes de San Fernando (Madrid), Real Academia de Bellas Artes de San Carlos (Valencia); Légion d'Honneur (France), Medal of St. George (Greece), Gold Medal, Ministry of Labour 68, Quevedo Gold Medal 72, etc.

Compositions include *Fantasy* (for piano and orchestra), *Soliloquy* (for orchestra), *Spanish Dance* (for piano), *Cradle Song* (for piano).

915 North Bedford Drive, Beverly Hills, Calif. 90210, U.S.A.

Ivanov, Konstantin Konstantinovich; Soviet conductor; b. 21 May 1907, Efremov, Tula Region; ed. Moscow Conservatoire.

Conductor, Great Symphonic Orchestra, All-Union Cttee. for Broadcasting 41-46; Conductor, Gen. U.S.S.R. State Symphonic Orchestra 46-; performances include numerous compositions of Russian and foreign classical and modern composers; numerous tours in U.S.S.R. and abroad; U.S.S.R. State Prize 49; R.S.F.S.R. Merited Worker of Arts; People's Artist of U.S.S.R. 58. State Philharmonic Society, 21 Ulitsa Gorkogo, Moscow U.S.S.R.

Ivanov, Yuri Alexandrovich; Soviet lawyer and banking official; b. 1927, Moscow; ed. Moscow State Inst. of Int. Relations.

Legal adviser Board of U.S.S.R. State Bank (Gosbank) 51-61; mem. Board of External Trade Bank of U.S.S.R. 61-64, First Deputy Chair. 64-69, Chair. 69-.

External Trade Bank of U.S.S.R., Kopyevsky pereulok 3/5, Moscow, U.S.S.R.

Ivanov-Smolensky, Anatoly Grigorievich; Soviet pathophysiologist; b. 17 May 1895, St. Petersburg (now Leningrad); ed. Mil. Medical Acad.

Assistant in Inst. of Psychiatry and Psychiatric Clinic of Mil. Medical Acad. 18-21; worked in field of pathophysiology and psychiatry in laboratory of I. P. Pavlov 21-45; Head of Moscow Dept. of I. P. Pavlov Inst. of Physiology 45-50; Dir. Inst. of Higher Nervous Activity of Acad. of Sciences of U.S.S.R. 52-57; mem. Acad. of Medical Sciences 50-; Pavlov and State prizewinner.

Publs. *Methods of investigation of Conditional Reflexes in Man* 28, 33, *Fundamental Problems in Pathological Physiology of the Higher Nervous Activity of Man* 33, *Essays on the Patho-physiology of Higher Nervous Activity* 49, 52, *I. P. Pavlov's Teaching and Pathological Physiology* 52, *Experience of the Objective Study of the Work and Interaction of the First and Second Signal Systems of the Brain* 61, etc.

U.S.S.R. Academy of Medical Sciences, 14 Ulitsa Solyanka, Moscow, U.S.S.R.

Ivantsov, Anatoli Ivanovich; Soviet diplomatist; b. 11 Feb. 1922, Moscow; ed. Moscow Inst. of Railway Transport and High Diplomatic School, Ministry of Foreign Affairs, U.S.S.R.

Joined Diplomatic Service 44; First Sec., Soviet Embassy, Canada 61-66; ranking official, Ministry of

Foreign Affairs, U.S.S.R. 66-69; Minister to New Zealand 69-73, Amb. 73-74.

c/o Ministry of Foreign Affairs, Moscow, U.S.S.R.

Iveagh, 3rd Earl of; **Arthur Francis Benjamin Guinness;** Irish brewing executive; b. 20 May 1937; *m.* Miranda Smiley 1963; two *s.* two *d.*; ed. Eton Coll. and Trinity Coll., Cambridge.

Director Arthur Guinness Son & Co. Ltd. 58, Chair. 62-; Dir. Bank of Nova Scotia and several other Canadian companies; mem. Senate 73.

Leisure interests: antique Irish silver, 18th-century French drawings, Irish books and bookbindings.

Arthur Guinness Son & Co. Ltd., St. James's Gate, Dublin 8; Farmleigh, Castleknock, Co. Dublin, Ireland.

Iveroth, C. Axel; Swedish business executive; b. 4 Aug. 1914, Ekerö; *m.* Inger Dorthea Iveroth; two *s.* two *d.*; ed. Stockholm School of Economics.

Producer, Swedish Broadcasting Corpn. 37-41; Sec. Industrial Inst. for Econ. and Social Research 39-44; Industrial Counsellor, Swedish Embassy, Washington 44-45; Editor-in-Chief *Industria* 46; Chair. and Founder, Industrial Council for Social and Econ. Studies 48-60; Man. Dir. Cementa 47-52; Chair. and Man. Dir. Cembureau (Cement Statistical and Technical Asscn.) 52-57; Chair. Advisory Board European Productivity Agency, Paris 54-56; Dir.-Gen. Fed. of Swedish Industries 57-; mem. Exec. Board Gen. Export Asscn. of Sweden 71-; Sec.-Gen. Business and Industry Advisory Cttee., OECD 62-63, Vice-Chair. 74-; Chair. Swedish Productivity Council, Swedish-American New Exchange 52-66; Chair. Board Securitas Int. AB 50-, Integration Cttee. of European Ind. Feds. 58-, AB Folkhem 65-; mem. Board Atlas Copco 75-; Knight Commdr. of the Royal Order of Vasa (Sweden), C.B.E. (Hon.), Officier de l'Ordre de la Couronne (Belgium), Commendatore dell'Ordine al Merito della Repubblica Italiana, Order of the White Rose of Finland.

Leisure interests: angling, farming.

Publs. *Handicraft and Small Industries in Sweden* 43; many articles on politics and economics in press and professional journals.

Federation of Swedish Industries, Storgatan 19, Box 5501, S-114 85 Stockholm 5, Sweden.

Iversen, Dr. Carl; Danish economist; b. 5 March 1899, Randers; *m.* 1st 1935, 2nd 1961; one *s.* one *d.*; ed. Copenhagen and Harvard Univs.

Journalist, *Børsen* (The Exchange) 20-30; joined Staff of Copenhagen Univ. 27; Prof., Economics 39-67; Vice-Chair. Danish Nat. Bank 51; Econ. Adviser to Chile 50, Iraq 53, Ceylon 56; Visiting Prof., Univ. of Washington, Seattle 52, Johns Hopkins Univ., Baltimore 54; Rector of Copenhagen Univ. 58-66; Chair. Danish Council of Econ. Advisers 62-69; Econ. Adviser, Uganda 70; mem. Cttee. to evaluate Danish, English and Irish applicants for posts in the European Communities April-Nov. 73.

Publs. *Aspects of the Theory of International Capital Movements* 35, *Monetary Problems of Iraq* 54.

Amaliegade 40A, Copenhagen K, Denmark.

Telephone: (01) 132470.

Ives, Burl Icle Ivanhoe; American actor and singer; b. 14 June 1909, Hunt City, Ill.; *m.* Helen Ives 1946; one *s.*

Began stage career 38; has appeared in the musicals: *The Boys from Syracuse, I Married An Angel, Heavenly Express, This is the Army, Sing Out Sweet Land, Knickerbocker Holiday, Paint Your Wagon, Show Boat*; the stage plays: *The Man Who Came to Dinner, She Stoops to Conquer, Cat on a Hot Tin Roof, Joshua Beene and God*; the films *Smokey, Green Grass of Wyoming, Station West, So Dear to my Heart, Sierra, East of Eden, The Power and the Prize, Desire Under the Elms, The Big Country, The Everglades, Cat on a Hot Tin Roof, The Day of Out-

law, Our Man in Havana, The Spiral Road, Summer Magic, The Brass Bottle, Mediterranean Holiday, Ensign Pulver, Pt. Barnum's Rocket to the Moon; American Motion Picture Award for best supporting actor (*The Big Country*) 59; Hon. LL.D. (Fairleigh Dickinson Coll., Rutherford, N.J.).

Leisure interests: sailing, camping.

Publs. *The Wayfaring Stranger, The Wayfaring Stranger's Notebook, Sailing on a Very Fine Day, Burl Ives' Tales of America*; ed. *The Burl Ives Song Book, The Burl Ives Book of Sea Songs, The Burl Ives Book of Irish Songs, America's Musical Heritage* (six records with sing-along book), *Song in America—A New Song Book, Albad the Oaf.*

140 West 57th Street, New York 10019, U.S.A.

Ivory, James Francis, M.F.A.; American film director; b. 7 June 1928, Berkeley, Calif.; *s.* of the late Edward Patrick Ivory and Hallie Millicent De Loney; ed. Univs. of Oregon and Southern California.

Began to work independently as a film maker 56; dir., writer and cameraman in first films; Partner, Merchant Ivory Productions (with Indian producer Ismail Merchant) 62-; has collaborated on screenplay of numerous films with author Ruth Prawer Jhabvala; *Shakespeare Wallah* Best Foreign Film (Acad. du Cinéma, France) 68, Finland 68.

Leisure interest: collecting pictures.

Films: *Venice, Theme and Variations* 57, *The Sword and the Flute* 59, *The Delhi Way* 64, *The Householder* 63, *Shakespeare Wallah* 65, *The Guru* 69, *Bombay Talkie* 70, *Savages* 72, *The Wild Party* 75, *Autobiography of a Princess* 75 (also published as a book 75); TV film: *Adventures of a Brown Man in Search of Civilisation* 71.

400 East 52nd Street, New York, N.Y. 10022, U.S.A.

Telephone: (212) 582-8049 (Office); (212) 759-3694 (Home).

Ivy, Andrew Conway, PH.D., M.D.; American physiologist; b. 25 Feb. 1893, Farmington, Mo., *s.* of Prof. Henry McPherson Ivy and Cynthia Smith; *m.* Bmma Anna Kohman 1919; five *s.*; ed. Univ. of Chicago.

Instructor in Physiology Univ. of Chicago 17-19; Associate Prof. of Physiology Loyola Univ. 19-23; Associate Prof. of Physiology Univ. of Chicago 23-25; Chair Dept. of Physiology and Pharmacology Northwestern Univ. Medical School 25-46; Vice-Pres. Univ. Illinois in charge of Chicago Professional Schools in Clinical Science 46-53, Distinguished Prof. of Physiology, Head of Dept. of Clinical Science 46-61, Distinguished Prof. Emer. 61-; Director U.S. Naval Medical Research Institute 42-43; Consultant Nuremburg trials of war criminals; Exec. Dir. Nat. Advisory Cancer Council 47-51; Prof. Emer. Biochemistry and Dir. Medical Research Laboratory, Roosevelt Univ., Chicago 63-; Fellow, American Coll. of Physicians; mem. American Medical Asscn. (Chair. Physiology and Pathology Section 32-33); Pres. Society of Internal Medicine, Inst. of Medicine of Chicago; mem. American Asscn. of Univ. Profs., American Gastro-Enterology Asscn. (Pres.), American Physiology Society (Pres.), Society for Experimental Biology, American Inst. of Nutrition, Asscn. for Study of Internal Secretions; Hon. D.Sc. (Univ. of Nebraska, Grinnell Coll. Iowa 47, Boston Univ. 48, Hastings Coll. 51, Coe Coll. 57), LL.D. (Loyola Univ.) 50; Distinguished Service Medal of American Gastro-Enterology Asscn. 70.

Leisure interests: travel, reading philosophy.

Publs. *Peptic Ulcer, Observations on Krebiozen in Management of Cancer Patients*, numerous scientific articles.

178 W. Randolf, Chicago, Ill., 60601, U.S.A.

Telephone: 372-6005.

Iwal, Akira; Japanese railwayman and trade unionist; b. 1922; ed. Matsumoto High Elementary School, Nagano Prefecture.

Kamisuwa Engine Section, Nat. Railway 37-42; Mil. Service 42-46; Engine Driver, Kamisuwa Engine Section, Nat. Railway 46; Chief Joint Struggle Dept., Nat. Railway Workers' Union 50-51, Chief of Planning Dept. 51-55; Sec.-Gen., Gen. Council of Trade Unions of Japan (SOHYO) 55-; Lenin Prize 70.
Publs. *We, born in Taisho Era, The Workers.*
Nihon Rodo Kumiai Sohyogikai, 8-2 Shiba Park, Minato-ku, Tokyo, Japan.

Iwakoshi, Tadahiro; Japanese business executive; b. 4 July 1906, Tottori Pref.; m. Kiyoko Shimizu; two d.; ed. Univ. of Tokyo.
Joined Nissan Motor Co. Ltd. 37, Dir. 52, Man. Dir. 57-60, Exec. Man. Dir. 60-63, Exec. Vice-Pres. 63-73, Pres. 73-; Vice-Chair. Japan Automobile Mfrs. Asscn. Inc. 72-; Gov. Dir. Fed. of Econ. Orgs. (Keidanren) 74-; Blue Ribbon Medal 71.
Leisure interests: golf, reading, gardening.
Publ. *The Automobile Industry* 68.
Nissan Motor Co. Ltd., 17-1, 6-chome, Ginza, Chuo-ku, Tokyo; Home: 10-7, Shimoigusa 1-chome, Suginami-ku, Tokyo, Japan.
Telephone: 543-5523 (Office).

Iwasa, Yoshizane; Japanese banker; b. 6 Feb. 1906, Tokyo; s. of Yoshigoro Shimada, adopted into family of Teizo Iwasa; m. Michi 1928; two s. one d.; ed. Tokyo Univ.
Manager, Kanagawa Branch, Yasuda Bank 44-45, Man. Loan Dept. (Head Office) 45-46, Personnel Dept. 46-47, Chief Man. Personnel Dept. 47-48; Dir. Yasuda Bank 48; Man. Dir. Fuji Bank 48-57, Deputy Pres. 57-63, Chair. of Board and Pres. 63-71, Chair. Advisory Cttee. 71-.
Leisure interests: reading and golf.
1-5-5, Otemachi, Chiyoda-ku, Tokyo 100; (Home): 5-2-4, Minami-Aoyama, Minato-ku, Tokyo 107, Japan.
Telephone: 216-2211 (Office); 400-3814 (Home).

Iwasaki, Nobuhiko; Japanese business executive; b. 7 Nov. 1909, Tokyo; two s.; ed. Tokyo Univ.
Joined Sumitomo Shipbuilding and Machinery Co. 33, Dir. 55, Man. Dir. 59, Exec. Man. Dir. 64, Exec. Vice-Pres. 69, Pres. 70-73, Chair. 73-; Dir. Fed. of Econ. Orgs., Shipbuilders' Asscn. of Japan.
Leisure interest: stamp collection.
Sumitomo Shipbuilding and Machinery Co., 2-1, Ohtemachi 2-chome, Chiyoda-ku, Tokyo; Home: 7-13-501, Roppongi 1-chome, Minato-ku, Tokyo, Japan.
Telephone: (03) 211-1361 (Office); (03) 585-2892 (Home).

Iwaszkiewicz, Jarosław; Polish writer; b. 20 Feb. 1894, Kalnik, Ukraine; s. of Maria and Boleslaw Iwaszkiewicz; m. Anna Lilpop 1922; two d.; ed. Kijow Univ.
Sec. Polish Embassies, Copenhagen and Brussels 32-35; Editor *Życie Literackie* 45-46, *Nowiny Literackie* 47-48, *Twórczość* 55-; Pres. Union of Polish Writers 45-48, 59-; Deputy to Seym 52-; mem. Presidium of All-Polish Cttee. of Nat. Unity Front 71-; mem. World Council of Peace 50-; Foreign mem. Serbian Acad. of Science 72; L. Reynal Prize 37, Prize of Minister of Culture and Art, 1st Class 63, Italian Order of Merit 65, Lenin Prize

70, Prize of Warsaw City 74; Dr. h.c. (Warsaw) 71; Order of Banner of Labour, 1st Class 49, Order of Builders of People's Poland 64, Frédéric Joliot-Curie Gold Medal 69, Grand Cross Order of Polonia Restituta 74, Order of Friendship of Nations (U.S.S.R.) 74, Hon. Gold Medal for Fighter for Peace (U.S.S.R.) 74.
Publs. Verse: *Oktostychy* 19, *Dionizje* 22, *Powrót do Europy* (Return to Europe) 31, *Lato 1932* (Summer 1932) 33, *Ody olimpijskie* (Olympic Odes) 48, *Ciemne ścieżki* (Dark Paths) 57, *Xenie i elegie* (Xena and elegies) 70, *Śpiewnik włoski* (Italian Songbook) 74; Short Stories: *Panny z Wilka* (The Girls from Wilko) 33, *Młyn nad Utratą* (Mill on the Utrata) 36, *Nowa miłość* (New Love) 46, *Matka Joanna od Aniołów* (Mother Joan of the Angels) 46, *Nowele włoskie* (Italian Stories) 47, *Tatarak* 60, *Opowiadania muzyczne* (Music Stories) 71, *Ogrody* (Gardens) 74; Novels: *Zmowa mężczyzn* (Conspiracy of Men) 30, *Czerwone tarcze* (Red Shields) 34, *Pasje błędomierskie* (Bledomierski Passions) 38, *Sława i chwała* (Fame and Glory) Vol. I 56, Vol. II 58, Vol. III 62, *Kochankowie z Marony* (Lovers from Marona) 61; Plays: *Lato w Nohant* (Summer in Nohant) 37, *Maskarada* (Masquerade) 39, *Wesele pana Balzaka* (M. Balzac's Wedding) 59, *Kosmogonia* (Cosmogony) 67; Biographies: *Fryderyk Chopin* 38, 53, 66, *Jan Sebastian Bach* 51.
Twórczość, ul. Wiejska 16, 00-490 Warsaw, Poland.
Telephone: 58-9363 (Home).

Izmen, Mehmet; Turkish politician; b. 1909, Giresun; m. 1959; two d.; ed. Faculty of Political Science, Ankara.
Auditor 37; Dir. of Revenue and Wealth, Istanbul Treasury 40; Gen. Audit Adviser of Prime Minister 47; Asst. Chief, Board of Auditors, Ministry of Finance 48; Istanbul Treas. 50; Adviser, Ministry of Finance 51; Dir.-Gen. of Reinsurance 56; Senator for Giresun 61, 68; Minister of Agriculture 62; Minister of Communications 69; Minister of Nat. Defence 72-73.
Leisure interests: reading books in French and Turkish.
Publ. *Finance.*
c/o The Senate, Ankara, Turkey.
Telephone: Ankara 182822.

Izmerov, Nikolai Fedotovich, M.D.; Soviet doctor; b. 19 Dec. 1927, Frunze, Kirghiz; ed. Tashkent Medical School and Moscow Central Inst. for Advanced Medical Training.
Worked as doctor in Khavast rural areas, Tashkent District; Postgraduate training, Moscow 52-53; Senior Insp. U.S.S.R. Ministry of Health 53-55; Postgraduate training (Municipal Hygiene) 55-58; doctor in Moscow City Sanitary Epidemiological Station 56-59; Deputy Dir. (Int. Health), Dept. of External Relations, U.S.S.R. Ministry of Health 60-62; Vice-Minister of Health of R.S.F.S.R., Moscow, and Chief Sanitary Insp. 62-64; Asst. Dir.-Gen. World Health Org. 64-71; Dir. Inst. of Industrial Hygiene and Occupational Diseases of the U.S.S.R. Acad. of Medical Sciences 71-.
Institute of Industrial Hygiene and Occupational Diseases of the U.S.S.R. Academy of Medical Sciences.
31 prospekt Budennozo, E-275, Moscow, U.S.S.R.

J

Jabłoński, Henryk, PH.D.; Polish historian and politician; b. 27 Dec. 1909, Waliszewo; ed. Univ. of Warsaw. Professor Warsaw School of Political Sciences 46-50, Warsaw Univ. 50-; mem. Nat Council 45-47, Seym 47-; Deputy Minister of Educ. 47-53; Sec. Polish Socialist Party 46-48; mem. Cen. Cttee. Polish United Workers' Party 48-, Deputy mem. Political Bureau 70-71, mem. Dec. 71-; Minister of Higher Educ. 65-66; Minister of Educ. and Higher Educ. 66-72; Pres. Council of State (Head of State) March 72-; corresp. mem. Polish Acad. of Sciences 52-56, mem. 56-, Gen. Sec. 55-65, Vice-Pres. 66-Dec. 71; mem. Presidium of All-Polish Cttee. of Nat. Unity Front 72-; corresp. mem. Acad. of Romanian Socialist Repub. 65-; mem. Czechoslovakian Acad. of Sciences 65-; foreign mem. U.S.S.R. Acad. of Sciences 66-; mem. Mongolian Acad. of Sciences 75-; Hon. L.H.D. (Moscow), Dr. h.c. Higher School of Econs., Wrocław 72, Roland Eotvos Univ. 73, Univ. Łódź 75, Univ. Wrocław 75; State Prize 55, 64, Grand Cross, Order of Polonia Restituta 74, Order of Banner of Labour First Class 59, Order of the Builders of People's Poland 64, Order of Friendship of Nations, Grand Cross Légion d'Honneur.
Publs. *The Military Criminal Court in 1794* 35, *Aleksander Waszkowski—Warsaw's Last Military Chief in the Insurrection of 1863-64* 37, *Public Opinion, Parliament, and the Press, At the Origins of the Present Day* 47, *Polish National Autonomy in the Ukraine in 1917-18,* 48, *The Policy of the Polish Socialist Party during the First World War* 58, *The Birth of the Second Republic 1918–19* 62, *School, Teacher, Education* 72.
Belweder, Warsaw, Poland.

Jaccard, Pierre, TH.D., D. ÈS L.; Swiss university professor; b. 14 Sept. 1901, Morges; s. of Professor Henri Jaccard; m. Hélène Faillettaz 1929; one s. three d.; ed. Univs. of Lausanne, Strasbourg, Paris, and Union Theological Seminary, New York.
Professor of French, Wooster Coll., Ohio 29-34; Prof. of Systematic Theology at Neuchâtel Univ. 34-40; Prof. of Psychology, Sociology and Social Ethics, Lausanne Univ. 40-72; Pres. Lausanne Univ. Graduate School of Social and Political Sciences 54-60; Académie Française prizewinner 61, 67.
Leisure interests: literature, travel.
Publs. *Le Sens de la Direction et l'Orientation lointaine chez l'Homme* 32, *Trois Contemporains: Mauriac, Chardonne, Montherlant* 45, *Essais sur la Peinture: Breughel, Le Nain, Vermeer* 48, *La Dignité du Travail* 51, *Travail et Salaire* 51, *Politique de l'emploi et de l'éducation* 57, *Histoire sociale du travail* 60, *La Formation des Elites* 61, *Sociologie de l'Education* 62, *Investir en Hommes* 64, *Psycho-sociologie du travail* 66. *Introduction aux sciences sociales* 71, *L'Inconscient, les Rêves, les Complexes* 73.
Avenue de Chailly 31, Lausanne, Switzerland.
Telephone: 021-32-22-94.

Jack, Hon. Sir Roy Emile, Kt., LL.B.; New Zealand politician; b. 1915, New Plymouth; s. of John Bain Jack and Alice May Jack (née Hunter); m. Frances Anne Harty 1946; ed. Wanganui Collegiate School and Victoria Univ. of Wellington.
Judge's Assoc. 37-39; War Service with R.N.Z.A.F. 39-45; barrister and solicitor at Wanganui 46-; elected to Wanganui City Council 46; Deputy Mayor of Wanganui 47-56; mem. Parl. for Patea 54-63, for Waimarino 63-72, for Rangitikei 72-; Deputy Speaker of House of Reps. 61-67, Speaker 67-72, Dec. 75-; Minister of Justice and Attorney-Gen. Feb.-Nov. 72; Nat. Party.

Leisure interests: music, reading, gardening, skiing, flying.
Parliament House, Wellington; Home: 49 College Street, Wanganui, New Zealand.
Telephone: 49090, 48274, 7640 (Home).

Jackling, Sir Roger William, G.C.M.G.; British diplomatist; b. 10 May 1913, Hythe, Kent; s. of P. Jackling, O.B.E. and Lucy Jackling; m. Joan Tustin 1938; two s.; ed. Felsted School and Law Soc.
Admitted as Solicitor, Supreme Court 35; Acting Vice-Consul, New York 40-42; Commercial Sec., Quito 42-43; Second, then First Sec., Washington 43-47; Foreign Office 47; Asst. Sec. Cabinet Office 50-51; Commercial Counsellor, British Embassy, The Hague 51-53; Econ. Adviser, British High Comm., Fed. Germany 53-55; Minister (Econ.), Bonn Embassy 55-57; Counsellor, Washington 57-59; Asst. Under-Sec. of State 59-63; Deputy Perm. Rep. to UN 63-67; Deputy Under-Sec. of State 67-68; Amb. to Fed. Germany 68-72; U.K. Del. to UN Sea-bed Cttee. 72-73; Amb. and Leader U.K. Del. to UN Conf. on Law of the Sea 73-75 (retd.).
Leisure interests: reading, gardening, golf.
Publ. *Federal Republic of Germany: Economic Survey* 55.
37 Boundary Road, St. John's Wood, London, NW8 0JE, England.
Telephone: 01-624-0208.

Jackman, Oliver H.; Barbadian diplomatist; b. 10 Aug. 1929, Barbados; m.; one c.; ed. Harrison Coll., Barbados, and Magdalene Coll., Cambridge.
Broadcaster and journalist, Nigeria 54-58; Govt. Information Officer, Barbados 58-59; Deputy Fed. Information Officer, Govt. of West Indies 59-61; Information Officer and Political Affairs Officer, UN operations in Congo 61-64; Chief of Information Services, UN Econ. Comm. for Africa, Addis Ababa; Deputy Perm. Rep. to UN 67-68; Perm. Sec., Ministry of External Affairs 68-69; Perm. Rep. to UN Sept. 69-March 71; High Commr. to Canada (also accred. to Cuba) April 71-.
Barbados High Commission, 151 Slater Street, Ottawa K1P 5H3, Canada.
Telephone: 236-9517-8.

Jackson, Edwin Sydney, F.S.A., F.C.I.A., B.COM.; Canadian insurance executive; b. 17 May 1922, Regina, Saskatchewan; s. of late Edwin and Dorothy Hazel Jackson (née Bell); m. Nancy Stovel 1948; three d.; ed. Univ. of Manitoba.
Joined Mfrs. Life Insurance Co. 48, Asst. Actuary 52, Actuary 56, Actuarial Vice-Pres. 64, Senior Vice-Pres. 69, Exec. Vice-Pres., Dir. 70, Pres. 72-; Pres. Canadian Inst. of Actuaries 66-67.
Leisure interests: skiing, curling, golf.
Manufacturers Life Insurance Co., 200 Bloor Street East, Toronto, Ont. M4W 1E5; and 101 Stratford Crescent, Toronto, Ont., Canada.

Jackson, Eric Stead, C.B., M.A.; British civil servant; b. 27 Aug. 1909, Bradford; s. of E. S. Jackson; m. Yvonne Renée Doria de Bretigny 1938; one s. one d.; ed. Corpus Christi Coll., Oxford.
On Air Ministry Staff 32-40; Private Sec. to Minister of Aircraft Production 42, to Minister Resident in Washington 43; Dir.-Gen. Aircraft Branch, Control Comm., Germany 45; Deputy Pres. Econ. Sub-Comm., Berlin 47; British Head of Del. from Western Zone of Germany to OEEC, Paris 48; Under-Sec. Ministry of Supply 50; Dir.-Gen. Atomic Weapons, Ministry of Supply 56-59; Under-Sec. Ministry of Aviation 59-67; Ministry of Technology 67-70, Dept. of Trade and

Industry 70-71; mem. British Film Fund Agency 71-.
10 Ditchley Road, Charlbury, Oxon., England.
Telephone: 682.

Jackson, Sir Geoffrey (Holt Seymour), K.C.M.G., M.A.;
British diplomatist (retd.), writer and broadcaster; b.
4 March 1915, Little Hulton, Lancs.; s. of Samuel S.
Jackson and Marie-Cecile Ryder; m. Patricia M. E.
Delany 1939; one s.; ed. Bolton School and Emmanuel
Coll.. Cambridge.
Vice-Consul, Beirut, Cairo, Baghdad 37-46; First Sec.,
Bogotá 46-50, Berne 54-56; Minister, subsequently
Amb. to Honduras 56-60; Consul-Gen., Seattle 60-64;
Senior British Trade Commr., Ontario 64-69; Amb. to
Uruguay 69-71; kidnapped and held captive by
Tupamaro guerrillas Jan.-Sept. 71; Deputy Under-Sec.
of State 72.
Leisure interests: golf, swimming, skiing, music.
Publs. *The Oven-Bird* (collection of stories) 72, *Peoples,
Prison* 73, *Surviving the Long Night* 74.
63B Cadogan Square, London, S.W.1, England.
Telephone: 01-235-6870.

Jackson, Glenda; British actress; b. 9 May 1936,
Birkenhead, Cheshire; d. of Harry and Joan Jackson;
m. Roy Hodges 1958 (divorced 1976); one s.; ed. Royal
Acad. of Dramatic Art.
Former mem. Royal Shakespeare Co. where roles
included Ophelia in *Hamlet* and Charlotte Corday in
The Marat/Sade (in London and New York); played
Queen Elizabeth I in television series *Elizabeth R*;
Acad. Award ("Oscar") for *Women in Love* 71, for
A Touch of Class 74.
Leisure interests: gardening, reading, listening to music.
Plays include *The Marat/Sade*, N.Y. and Paris 65, *The
Investigation* 65, *Hamlet* 65, *US* 66, *Three Sisters* 67,
Collaborators 73, *The Maids* 74, *Hedda Gabler* 75; films
include *The Marat/Sade* 66, *Negatives* 68, *Women in
Love* 69, *The Music Lovers* 70, *Sunday, Bloody Sunday*
71, *The Boy Friend* 71, *Mary, Queen of Scots* 71, *The
Triple Echo* 72, *Bequest to the Nation* 72, *A Touch of
Class* 73, *The Romantic Englishwoman* 75, *The Tempter*
75.
Peter Crouch Ltd., 60/66 Wardour Street, London, W.1,
England.

Jackson, Gordon Noel, C.M.G., M.B.E.; British diplo-
matist; b. 25 Dec. 1913, East Langton, Leicestershire;
s. of Thomas Herbert Jackson; m. Mary April Nettlefold
1959; one s. two d.
Political Officer, Sharjah 47, Kuwait 49-50; Consular
Service, St. Louis, Basra, Lourenço Marques 53-60;
Consul-Gen. Benghazi 60-63; Ambassador to Kuwait
63-67; Amb. to Ecuador 67-70; retd.
Leisure interests: horsemanship and photography.
Publs. *Effective Horsemanship* 67, co-editor (with
William Steinkraus) *The Encyclopedia of the Horse* 73.
Lowbarrow House, The Ridings, Leafield, Oxfordshire,
England.
Telephone: Astall Leigh 443.

Jackson, Henry M., LL.B.; American lawyer and
politician; b. 31 May 1912, Everett, Wash.; of Norwegian parentage; m. Helen E. Hardin 16 Dec. 1961;
one s. one d.; ed. Everett High School, Washington and
Univ. of Washington Law School.
Practising lawyer 35-; mem. House of Reps. for Wash.
41-52; Senator (Democrat, Wash.) 53-; Chair. Democratic Nat. Cttee. July 60-Jan. 61; Chair. Senate Cttee.
on Govt. Operations (chair. sub-cttee. on Nat. Security
and Int. Operations); mem. Senate Cttee. on Atomic
Energy; Bernard M. Branch Prize (with Charles A.
Lindbergh) 68; Hon. LL.D. (Alaska).
4934 Rockwood Parkway Northwest, Washington,
D.C. 20016; 1703 Grand Avenue, Everett, Washington
98201, U.S.A.

Jackson, Laura (Riding) (*see* Riding, Laura (Jackson)).

Jackson, Rashleigh Esmond; Guyanese diplomatist;
b. 12 Jan. 1929, New Amsterdam, Berbice; m.; one s.
two d.; ed. Queen's Coll., Georgetown, Univ. Coll.,
Leicester, England, Columbia Univ. N.Y.
Entered public service 48; Master, Queen's Coll. 57;
Principal Asst. Sec., Ministry of Foreign Affairs 65,
Perm. Sec. 69-73; Perm. Rep. to UN Jan. 73-, Pres.
UN Council for Namibia 74.
Permanent Mission of Guyana to United Nations, 622
Third Avenue, New York, N.Y. 10017, U.S.A.

Jackson, Commdr. Sir Robert Gillman Allen, Kt.,
K.C.V.O., C.M.G., O.B.E.; international administrator and
consultant; b. 8 Nov. 1911, Melbourne, Australia.
Royal Australian Navy 29-37; Royal Navy 37-41;
Dir.-Gen. Middle East Supply Centre and Principal
Adviser to War Cabinet Minister 42-45; H.M. Treasury
45-; Senior Deputy Dir. UNRRA 45-47; Asst. Sec.-Gen.
for Co-ordination in UN 48; Perm. Sec. Ministry
of Nat. Devt., Australia 50-52; Adviser to Govts.
of India and Pakistan on Devt. Plans 52; Chair.
Preparatory Comm. for Volta River Project, Gold
Coast 53-56; Chair. Devt. Comm., Ghana 57-63; Adviser
to Pres. of Liberia 61-75; Senior Consultant UN Special
Fund 62-65, UN Devt. Programme 66-68; mem. of and
Consultant to Volta River Authority, Ghana 62-; mem.
Comm. on Mekong Project 61-; Adviser to Planning
Comm., Govt. of India 63; Commr. in charge, Survey of
UN Devt. Org. 68-71; Consultant to McKinsey and Co.
70-; Under Sec.-Gen. UN Relief Operation in Bangladesh 72-73; Under Sec.-Gen. in charge of UN Humanitarian Operations on Sub-Continent 73-; UN Co-ordinator for Assistance to Zambia 73-; mem. IUCN Comm.
on Govt. Policy, Law and Admin.; mem. Cttee.
Fédération Mondiale des Villes Jumelées-Cités Unies;
services recognized by various govts. in Europe, Asia
and Africa; Hon. LL.D. (Syracuse).
Leisure interests: deep sea fishing, preservation of
tigers.
United Nations, New York, N.Y. 10017, U.S.A.; Palais
des Nations, Geneva, Switzerland.

Jackson, Ronald Gordon, A.C., B.COM., F.A.S.A.; Aus-
tralian business executive; b. 5 May 1924, Brisbane; s.
of Rupert Vaughan Jackson and Mary O'Rourke; m.
Margaret Alison Pratley 1948; one s. one d.; ed. Bris-
bane Grammar School and Univ. of Queensland.
Joined CSR Ltd. 41; mil. service 42-46; Head, Sugar
Marketing Div., CSR Ltd. 58, Senior Exec. Officer 64,
Gen. Man. and Dir. 72-; Chair. Gove Alumina Ltd.;
mem. Board, Reserve Bank of Australia, Australian
Graduate School in Management, Econ. Consultative
Group, Council of Australian Admin. Staff Coll.,
Cities Comm. Advisory Cttee.; Trustee, Mitsui Educ.
Foundation; Chair. Cttee. to advise Govt. on devt. of
mfg. industry.
Leisure interests: sailing, fishing.
1-7 O'Connell Street, Sydney, N.S.W. 2000, Australia.
Telephone: 20-515.

Jackson, Roy I., B.SC.; American international civil
servant; b. 14 Nov. 1916, Juneau, Alaska; m. Priscilla
Wicks; four c.; ed. public schools, Juneau, Univ. of
Washington, Seattle and Univ. of British Columbia.
Junior biologist, Int. Pacific Salmon Fisheries Comm.,
New Westminster, B.C. 43, Asst. Dir. 51-55; Exec. Dir.
Int. North Pacific Fisheries Comm., Vancouver 55-64;
Dir. Fisheries Div., FAO 64-66; Asst. Dir.-Gen. for
Fisheries, FAO 66-71; Deputy Dir.-Gen. FAO Jan. 72-;
Fellow, American Inst. of Fishery Research Biologists;
mem. American Fisheries Soc.; rep. of FAO at numerous
int. confs. and congresses.
Food and Agriculture Organization, Via delle Terme
di Caracalla, Rome, Italy.
Telephone: 5797.

Jacob, Lieut.-Gen. Sir Edward Ian Claud, G.B.E., C.B., B.A.; British soldier and broadcasting administrator; b. 27 Sept. 1899, Quetta, India; s. of Field-Marshal Sir Claud Jacob, G.C.B., G.C.S.I., K.C.M.G.; m. Cecil Bisset Treherne 1924; two s.; ed. Wellington Coll., Royal Mil. Acad. Woolwich, and King's Coll., Cambridge.
2nd Lieut. Royal Engineers 18; Capt. 29; Maj. 38; Col. 43; T/Maj.-Gen. 44; Mil. Asst. Sec. to Cttee. of Imperial Defence 38 and to War Cabinet 39-46; attended Confs. at Atlantic Meeting, Washington, Casablanca, Quebec, Moscow, Yalta, Potsdam; retd. July 46; Controller European Services of B.B.C. 46-47; Dir. Overseas Services B.B.C. 47-52, Dir.-Gen. B.B.C. 52-59; Pres. European Broadcasting Union 50-52 and 54-60; County Council East Suffolk 60-74; County Council Suffolk 74-; Chair. Covent Garden Market Authority 60-66; Dir. E.M.I. 60-73; Trustee Imperial War Museum 66-73; Chair. Matthews Holdings Ltd.
The Red House, Woodbridge, Suffolk, England.
Telephone: Woodbridge 2001.

Jacob, François, M.D., D.SC.; French professor of genetics; b. 17 June 1920, Nancy; m. Lise Bloch 1947; three s. one d.; ed. Lycée Carnot and Univ. de Paris à la Sorbonne.
Officer Free French Forces 40-45; with Institut Pasteur 50-, Asst. 50-56, Head of Laboratory 56-60, Head of Cellular Genetics Unit 60-; Prof. of Cellular Genetics Coll. de France 64-; Foreign mem. Acad. Royale des Lettres et Sciences du Danemark 62, Amer. Acad. of Arts and Sciences 64; Foreign Assoc. Nat. Acad. of Sciences (U.S.A.) 69; Foreign mem. Royal Soc., London 73; Foreign corresp. Acad. Royal Médicale Belgique 73; Prix Charles Léopold Mayer, Acad. des Sciences 62; Nobel Prize for Medicine (jointly with A. Lwoff and J. Monod) 65; Croix de la Libération, Commdr. Légion d'Honneur.
Leisure interests: literature, painting, music.
Publ. *La Logique du Vivant* 70.
Institut Pasteur, 28 rue du Dr. Roux, Paris 15e, France.

Jacobs, Patrick William McCarthy, M.SC., PH.D., D.SC.; Canadian professor of chemistry; b. 15 Sept. 1923, Durban, South Africa; s. of Lewis Masterman Jacobs and Florence Edith Jacobs (née McCarthy); m. Elizabeth Mary Menzies 1950; two s. one d.; ed. Natal Univ. Coll. and Imperial Coll., London Univ.
Assistant Lecturer in Physical Chem., Imperial Coll., London 50-52, Lecturer 52-62, Senior Lecturer 62-64, Reader 64-65; Prof. of Chem., Univ. of W. Ontario 65-; Overseas Fellow, Churchill Coll., Cambridge 73-74.
Leisure interests: skiing, canoeing, camping.
Publs. approximately 110 papers in scientific journals.
Department of Chemistry, University of Western Ontario, London, Ont. N6A 5B7; Home: 149 Normandy Gardens, London, Ont. N6H 4B3, Canada.

Jacobs, Robert Allan, A.B.; American architect; b. 16 Sept. 1905; ed. Amherst, Columbia Architectural School.
Worked with Le Corbusier 34-35, with Harrison and Fouilhoux 35-38; in partnership with E. J. Kahn under the name of Kahn and Jacobs 40-73; Partner Kahn & Jacobs/Hellmuth, Obata & Kassabaum 73-; designed bldgs. for World's Fair, N.Y. 64; Fellow, Amer. Inst. of Architects, Associated Architects on U.S. Mission to the UN; mem. Beaux Arts Inst. Architectural League of New York and New York Building Congress; Hon. Master of Fine Arts, Amherst Coll. 57.
Home: 1065 Lexington Avenue, New York, N.Y. 10021; Office: 2 Park Avenue, New York, N.Y. 10016, U.S.A.

Jacobsen, Frithjof Halfdan, B.LL.; Norwegian diplomatist; b. 14 Jan. 1914; ed. Oslo Univ., London School of Economics and Political Science.
Entered Norwegian Foreign Service 38, served Paris, Moscow and London; Dir.-Gen. Political Affairs Dept. of the Norwegian Foreign Ministry 55-59; Ambassador

to Canada 59-61, to Soviet Union 61-66; Under-Sec. of State for Foreign Affairs 66-70; Amb. to Soviet Union 70-75, to U.K. and Ireland 75-.
Embassy of Norway, 25 Belgrave Square, London, S.W.1, England.

Jacobson, Baron (Life Peer), cr. 75, of St. Alban's, Hertfordshire; **Sydney Jacobson,** M.C.; British newspaper executive; b. 26 Oct. 1908, Zeerust, Transvaal, S. Africa; m. Phyllis June Buck 1938; two s. one d.; ed. Strand School, London, and King's Coll., Univ. of London.
Editor *The Leader* Magazine 48-49; Political Editor *Daily Mirror* 54-62; Editor *Daily Herald* 62-64, *The Sun* 64-65; Editor Dir. *The Sun* 65; Editorial Dir. Int. Publishing Corpn. Newspapers 68-73, Deputy Chair. 74-75 (retd.); mem. BBC Gen. Advisory Council; Chair. BBC Programmes for Immigrants Advisory Cttee. 74-.
Leisure interests: reading, tennis, swimming.
6 Avenue Road, St. Albans, Herts., England.

Jacobson, Herbert Laurence, B.A.; American United Nations official; b. 7 April 1915, New York; s. of Benjamin Paul and Katherine (Laurence) Jacobson; m. Baronessa Fiora Ravasini-Osti 1949; two s.; ed. Erasmus Hall and Columbia Coll.
Editor-in-Chief *World News*, N.Y. (magazine) 37-40; Head, Radio Dept., MCA, Chicago 40-41; U.S. Army Officer, Mediterranean 41-46; Dir.-Gen. Radio Network, Free Territory, Trieste 46-52; U.S. High Comm., Germany 53-55; U.S. Embassy, Rome 55-57; Foreign Business Man., Mondadori Publs., Milan 57-58; Export Man., Squibb of Italy, Rome 59-60; Dir., S. Europe, Cotton Council Int., Rome, Barcelona, St. Gall 60-64; Editor-in-Chief *International Trade Forum* (GATT) 64-67; Dir. Int. Trade Centre (UNCTAD-GATT) 64-71, Dir. (Promotion) 71-; mem. Advisory Board Waterloo Lutheran Univ., Ontario 67-; Hon. LL.D. (Waterloo) 69.
Leisure interests: book-collecting, tennis.
International Trade Centre, UNCTAD/GATT, Palais des Nations, Geneva; Home: 29D Chemin Grange Canal, Geneva, Switzerland.
Telephone: 311255 (Office); 361225 (Home).

Jacobson, Leon Orris, M.D.; American professor of medicine; b. 16 Dec. 1911, Sims, N.D.; s. of John Jacobson and Rachael Johnson Jacobson; m. Elizabeth Louise Benton 1938; one s. one d.; ed. North Dakota State Univ. and Univ. of Chicago.
At Univ. of Chicago 39-, Prof. of Medicine and Head of Haematology Sec. 51-61, Prof. and Chair. Dept. of Medicine 61-65, Joseph Regenstein Prof. of Biological and Medical Sciences 65-, Dean Div. of Biol. Sciences and Pritzker School of Medicine 66-75; mem. Advisory Cttee. on Isotope Distribution, U.S. Atomic Energy Comm. 52-56, Cttee. for Radiation Studies, U.S. Public Health Service 51-55; mem. Expert Advisory Panel on Radiation, WHO 59; U.S. Rep. to Confs. on Peaceful Uses of Atomic Energy, Geneva 55, 58; mem. Board of Scientific Counsellors, Nat. Cancer Inst. 63-67; Consultant, Inst. for Cancer Research 59-; mem. Nat. Advisory Cancer Council, Nat. Insts. of Health 68-; mem. Space Biology Advisory Sub-cttee., Space Science and Applications Steering Cttee., NASA 68-; mem. many other cttees., advisory councils, etc.; Lecturer Int. Congress of Radiology 50, 59, Fifth Int. Cancer Congress, Paris 50, Congresses of Int. Soc. of Haematology 52-64; Dir. Franklin McLean Memorial Research Inst., Univ. Chicago 74-; Janeway Lecture, American Radium Soc. 53, Jacobaeus Memorial Lecture, Helsinki 62, Malthe Foundation Lecture, Oslo 62 and many other guest and hon. lectureships; mem. Nat. Acad. of Sciences, American Acad. of Arts and Sciences, A.A.A.S., American Asscn. for Cancer Research, American Coll. of Physicians, American Medical Asscn., American Nuclear Soc., Asscn. of American Physicians,

etc.; mem. Academia Nacional de Medicina de Buenos Aires; Hon. D.Sc. (N. Dakota) 66; Janeway Medal, American Radium Soc. 53, Robert Roesler de Villiers Award, Leukemia Soc. 56, Modern Medicine Award 63, American Nuclear Soc. Award 63, Johns Phillips Memorial Award 75, and other awards.

Leisure interests: gardening, playing piano, reading historical novels.

University of Chicago, 950 East 59th Street, Chicago, Ill. 60637, U.S.A.

Jacobson, Nathan, PH.D.; American professor of mathematics; b. 8 Sept. 1910, Warsaw, Poland; s. of Charles Jacobson and Pauline Ida Rosenberg; m. Florence Dorfman 1942; one s. one d.; ed. Univ. of Alabama, Princeton Univ.

Assistant Inst. for Advanced Study Princeton 33-34, Lecturer Bryn Mawr Coll. 35-36; Nat. Research Council Postdoctoral Fellow, Chicago 36-37; Instructor Univ. of North Carolina 37-38, Asst. Prof. 38-40, Assoc. Prof. 43-47; Assoc. Ground School Instructor, Navy Pre-flight School 42-43; Assoc. Prof. Johns Hopkins Univ. 43-47; Assoc. Prof. Yale Univ. 47-49, Prof. 49-, Henry Ford II Prof. of Maths 64-; Guggenheim Fellow 51-52, Fulbright Fellow 51-52; Pres. American Mathematical Soc. 71-73; Vice-Pres. Int. Mathematical Union 72-; hon. mem. London Mathematical Soc.; mem. Nat. Acad. of Sciences, American Acad. of Arts and Sciences; Hon. D.Sc. Univ. of Chicago 72.

Leisure interests: travel, tennis, gardening.

Publs. *Theory of Rings* 43, *Lectures in Abstract Algebra* (3 vols.) 53-64, *Structure of Rings* 56, *Lie Algebras* 62, *Structure and Representations of Jordan Algebras* 68, *On Quadratic Jordan Algebras* 69, *Exceptional Lie Algebras* 71, *Basic Algebra I* 74, *PI—Algebras* 75, and numerous articles.

Department of Mathematics, Yale University, New Haven, Conn. 06520; 2 Prospect Court, Hamden, Conn., U.S.A.

Telephone: 203-624-3581.

Jacottet, Carl Maurice; Swiss industrialist; b. 7 Feb. 1904, Neuchâtel; s. of Maurice Jacottet and Jeanne (née Fitz); m. Charlotte Zeutschler 1928; two d.; ed. Gymnasium Hildesheim, and Philipps Univ., Marburg.

Behring-Werke, Marburg 22-29; Sandoz Ltd., Basle, Switzerland 29-, Sub-Man. 39-44, Deputy Man. 44-48, Man. 49-56, mem. Exec. Cttee. 56-67, Man. Dir. 60-63, Vice-Chair. 64-67, Chair. Exec. Cttee. 67-73, Chair. of Board 68-; Vice-Pres. Swiss American Soc.; Treas. Inst. Henry Dunant; Hon. mem. Acad. Suisse des Sciences Médicales 69-; Fellow, Royal Soc. for the Encourage-ment of Arts, Manufactures and Commerce (F.R.S.A.) 72-; Hon. Dr.rer.pol., Basle Univ. 69.

Leisure interests: history, music, fine arts.

Sandoz Limited, CH-4002 Basle; Home: 34 Therwiler-strasse, CH-4153 Reinach BL, Switzerland.

Telephone: (061) 24-11-11 (Office); 76-10-10 (Home).

Jacquemard, Simonne; French novelist, journalist and traveller; b. 6 May 1924; ed. "Les Oiseaux" and Univ. of Paris.

Teacher of Music, Latin and French; collaborator, Laffont-Bompiani Dictionaries; contributor to *Figaro Littéraire, La Table Ronde*; travelled in U.S.S.R.; Egypt, Greece, Italy, N. Africa and Spain; Prix Renaudot 62.

Publs. *Les Fascines* 51, *Sable* 52, *La Leçon des Ténèbres* 54, *Judith Albarès* 58, *Planant sur les Airs* 60, *Com-pagnons Insolites* 61, *Le Veilleur de Nuit* 62, *L'Oiseau* 63, *L'Orangerie* 63, *Les Derniers Rapaces* 65, *Dérive au Zénith* 65, *Exploration d'un corps* 65, *Navigation vers les îles* 67, *L'Eruption du Krakatoa* 69, *La Thessaliene* 73, *Des roses pour mes chevreuils* 74; studies on music (with Lucette Descave), and on bird life and observation of wild animals.

12 bis Val-de-Grâce, 75005 Paris, France.

Jacquet, Marc; French politician and industrialist; b. 17 Feb. 1913.

Deputy to Nat. Assembly 51-55, 58-; mem. Gen. Council of Melun-Sud 51-58; Sec. of State to the Presidency of the Council in Charge of the Associated States 53; Vice-Pres. Finance Comm., Nat. Assembly Jan.-Oct. 59, *Rapporteur général* 59-62; Minister of Public Works and Transportation 62-66; Pres. Nat. Fed. of the Fertilizer Industry 71-; Mayor of Barbizon; Pres. New Soc. for Building Industry; UDR.

26 boulevard Raspail, Paris 7e, France.

Jacquinot, Louis, D.IUR.; French lawyer and politician; b. 16 Sept. 1898; ed. Coll. de Bar-le-Duc.

Served French Army 14-19; called to Paris Bar; Dep. 32-40, 45-; Under-Sec. for Interior 39-40; served French Army 40; escaped and joined Gen. de Gaulle; Commr. for Navy 43; Minister of War 44-45; Pres. Gen. Council of the Meuse 45-; Minister of State 45, for Navy 45-47, for Overseas Territories 51-53; Presidential candidate 54; Minister of State 58-61; Minister for Overseas Territories 61-66; Pres. Nat. Comm. for Admin. of Territories 67-71; Commdr. de la Légion d'Honneur, Croix de Guerre (14-18, 39-45), Rosette de la Résistance, and other medals.

3 avenue Maréchal Maunoury, Paris 7e, France.

Jacquinot, Pierre, D.SC.; French physicist; b. 18 Jan. 1910, Frouard; m. Françoise Touchot 1937; three s. one d.; ed. Université de Nancy.

Research Scientist, Centre Nat. de la Recherche Scientifique 33-42; Faculty of Science, Université de Clermont-Ferrand 42-46; Pres. French Physical Soc. 58-59; Prof. Univ. de Paris à la Sorbonne 46-; Dir.-Gen. Centre Nat. de la Recherche Scientifique 62-69; Prof., Faculty of Science, Orsay and Dir. Lab. Aimé Cotton (C.N.R.S.) Orsay 69; mem. Académie des Sciences 66; Holweck Prize (Physical Soc. of London and French Physical Soc.) 50; Jaffé Prize (Institut de France) 62. Laboratoire Aimé Cotton CNRS II, Bat. 505 Campus, 91 Orsay, France.

Telephone: 9076050.

Jacquot, Pierre Elie; French army officer; b. 16 June 1902, Vrécourt, Vosges; m. Lucie Claire Mamet 1929; one s. (killed in action Oran 1962); one d.; ed. Ecole Spéciale Militaire de St.-Cyr, Ecole Supérieure de Guerre.

Rose from Capt. to Lt.-Gen. 39-54; G.O.C.-in-C., Indo-China 55-56; G.O.C.-in-C. French forces in Ger-many 56-59; General 57; Insp.-General French Land Forces 59-61; C.-in-C. Allied Forces Central Europe 61-63; Grand-Croix, Légion d'Honneur 61.

Publs. *Essai de Stratégie Occidentale* 53, *La Stratégie Périphérique devant la Bombe Atomique* 53.

15 avenue de Villars, Paris 7e; and Vrécourt (Vosges), 88140 Contrexéville, France.

Jaeger, John Conrad, M.A., D.SC., F.A.A., F.R.S.; Australian professor of geophysics; b. 3 July 1907, Sydney; s. of Carl Jaeger and Christina L. Sladden; ed. Sydney Church of England Grammar School, and Sydney and Cambridge Univs.

Lecturer, subsequently Prof. of Applied Mathematics, Univ. of Tasmania 35-51; Prof. of Geophysics 52-72, Emeritus Prof. 73-, and Head of Dept. of Geophysics and Geochem., Australian Nat. Univ. 65-71.

Leisure interests: farming, collecting steam engines.

Publs. *Conduction of Heat in Solids* (with H. S. Carslaw) 2nd edn. 59, *Fundamentals of Rock Mechanics* (with N. G. W. Cook) 69, and four other books; numerous scientific papers.

Private Bag 5, Post Office, Sorell, Tasmania 7172, Australia.

Jaeger, Richard, DR.IUR.; German politician; b. 16 Feb. 1913, Berlin-Schoneberg; s. of late Dr. Heinz and Elsbeth Jaeger; m. Rose Littner 1939; one s. five d.; ed.

Maximilian Gymnasium, Munich, Ludwig-Maximilians Universität, Munich, Humboldt-Universität zu Berlin and Rheinische Friedrich-Wilhelms-Universität, Bonn. Military Service, Second World War 39-45; Govt. Counsel, Bavarian Ministry of Educ., Munich 47-48; Lord Mayor, Eichstätt, Bavaria 49; mem. Bundestag 49-, Vice-Pres. Bundestag and Chair. Defence Cttee. 53-65; Fed. Minister of Justice 65-66; Vice-Pres. Bundestag 67-; Pres. German Atlantic Asscn. 57-; Vice-Pres. Atlantic Treaty Asscn. 58-66; Christian Social Union (C.S.U.); Grosskreuz des Bundesverdienstordens and other decorations.
Publs. *Soldat und Bürger—Armee und Staat* 56, 63, *Sicherheit und Rüstung* 62, *Richard Jaeger-Bundestagsreden*.
Bundeshaus, 53 Bonn, Federal Republic of Germany.
Telephone: Bonn 16-29-12.

Jaenicke, Joachim; German diplomatist; b. 2 Aug. 1915, Breslau (now in Poland); s. of Wolfgang Jaenicke; m. Jane Nicholl Jaenicke 1942; two s. one d.; ed. Univ. of Geneva, Graduate Inst. of Int. Studies, Geneva, Haverford Coll., Haverford, U.S.A., and Fletcher School of Law and Diplomacy, U.S.A.
Teacher of Modern Languages and History, Westtown School, Pennsylvania 41-46; Asst. Prof. of History and German, Earlham Coll., Richmond, Indiana 46-48; returned to Germany 48; German Foreign Service 50-; Vice-Consul, New York 51; Second Sec., Washington 51-55; Chief, American Section, Fed. Press Office, Bonn 55-56; Chief of Press Section and Spokesman of German Foreign Office, Bonn 56-58; Counsellor, Ottawa 59-62; Far East Desk, Foreign Office 62-63; Dir. in Div. of Political Affairs, North Atlantic Treaty Organization (NATO), Paris 63-65, Asst. Sec.-Gen. for Political Affairs, NATO, Brussels 66-69; Amb. to Yugoslavia 69-75.
Leisure interests: swimming, golf, photography.
c/o Ministry of Foreign Affairs, Bonn, Federal Republic of Germany.

Jaffar, Khalid Mohammad; Kuwaiti diplomatist; b. 12 June 1922; ed. Mubarakia School, Kuwait.
Schoolteacher 40-43; Chief Cashier, Kuwait Municipality 43-45; Kuwait Oil Co. 45-61; mem. of Goodwill Mission to Latin American Countries 61; Lord Chamberlain to Amir of Kuwait 61-62; Head of Cultural and Press Dept., Foreign Office, Kuwait 62; mem. del. to UN; deputized for Under-Sec. of State, Ministry of Foreign Affairs 62-63; Amb. to U.K. 63-65, to Lebanon 65-70, concurrently to France 65-67, and to Turkey 68-70, to U.S.A. July 75-; Chair. Kuwait Investment Board in London 64-65.
Embassy of the State of Kuwait, 2940 Tilden Street, Washington, D.C., U.S.A.

Jagan, Cheddi, B.SC., D.D.S.; Guyanese politician; b. 22 March 1918, Plantation Port Mourant, Berbice; m. Janet Jagan (q.v.) 1943; one s. one d.; ed. Queen's Coll., Guyana, Howard Univ., Washington, YMCA (now Roosevelt) Coll., Chicago and Northwestern Univ. Dental School, Chicago.
Member Legislative Council 47-53; Leader of People's Progressive Party, formed 50; Minister of Agriculture, Lands and Mines and Leader of House of Assembly April-Oct. 53; six months' political imprisonment 54; Minister of Trade and Industry 57-61; Leader and Chief Minister of the P.P.P. Majority Party 57-61; First Premier British Guiana (now Guyana), Minister of Devt. and Planning 61-64; Leader of Opposition 64-73; Gen. Sec. P.P.P. 70-; mem. Presidential Cttee. of World Peace Council; Hon. Pres. Guyana Agricultural Workers' Union.
Leisure interest: tennis.
Publs. *Forbidden Freedom* 54, *Anatomy of Poverty in British Guiana* 64, *The West on Trial* (autobiog.) 66,

West Indian State Pro-Imperialist or Anti-Imperialist 72.
65 Pln. Bel Air, E.C.D., Guyana.
Telephone: 72096 (Office); 62899 (Home).

Jagan, Janet; Guyanese politician; b. 20 Oct. 1920, Chicago, Ill., U.S.A.; d. of Charles and Kathryn Rosenberg; m. Cheddi Jagan (q.v.) 1943; one s. one d.
General Sec. People's Progressive Party 50-70; Editor *Thunder* 50-56; Deputy Speaker House of Assembly 53; six months' political imprisonment 54; Minister of Labour, Health and Housing 57-61; Minister of Home Affairs 63-64; Editor *Mirror* 69-72, 73-76; Int. Sec. P.P.P. 70-76; mem. Exec. Council, Int. Org. of Journalists.
Leisure interest: swimming.
Publs. *History of the People's Progressive Party* 71, *Army Intervention in the 1973 Elections in Guyana* 73.
65 Pln. Bel Air, E.C.D., Guyana.

Jagannathan, S., B.SC.(HONS.); Indian civil servant and international banking official; b. 18 May 1914; m.; two s.; ed. Univs. of Madras and London, and Imperial Defence Coll., London.
Recruited in London to Indian Civil Service 35; Sub-divisional Officer and later Under Sec. to Govt., Province of Bihar 36-42; in Defence, Supply and Civil Divs. of Ministry of Finance, Govt. of India 42-46; Deputy Sec., Cabinet Secr. of Govt. of India and also of Partition Secr. for the Partition of India into the Dominions of Pakistan and India 46-47; Deputy Sec. Ministry of Commerce 48; Chief Controller of Imports 49; Dir.-Gen. of Shipping 50-53; Joint Sec. Ministry of Production 53-56; Additional Sec. (in charge of External Finance) Ministry of Finance 58-60; Financial Commr. Indian Railways 60-66; mem. Atomic Energy Comm. of India 62-68; Perm. Sec. Ministry of Finance (Dept. of Econ. Affairs) and Alt. Gov. for India in Int. Bank for Reconstruction and Devt. (IBRD) and affiliates Nov. 66-Jan. 68, Exec. Dir. for India of IBRD and its affiliates 68-70; fmr. Gov. Reserve Bank of India, Bombay; Del. to numerous int. confs.
c/o Reserve Bank of India, Bombay 1, India.

Jagielski, Mieczysław, DR. ECON.; Polish economist and politician; b. 12 Jan. 1924, Kolomyja, Poland; ed. Main School of Planning and Statistics, Warsaw, and Scientific Cadres Educational Inst., Central Cttee. of Polish United Workers' Party.
Member Youth Fighting Union 45-46; mem. Polish Workers' Party 46-48, Polish United Workers' Party 48-, mem. Central Cttee. 59-, Deputy mem. Political Office of Central Cttee. 64-71, mem. Dec. 71-; Seym Dep. 57-; Vice Minister of Agriculture 57-59, Minister of Agriculture 59-70; Dep. Chair. Council of Ministers June 70-; Perm. Rep. of Poland to COMECON 71-; Chair. Planning Comm. attached to Council of Ministers Oct. 71-75; Order of Banner of Labour First and Second Class, Order of Builders of People's Poland and other decorations.
Urząd Rady Ministrów, Aleje Ujazdowskie 1/3, 00-583 Warsaw, Poland.

Jahanshahi, Abdol Ali, PH.D.; Iranian economist; b. 25 Sept. 1924, Teheran; s. of Shafi and Soghra Jahanshahi; m. Lili Amirkhosrovi 1954; one s. four d.; ed. Paris Univ.
With Ministry of Justice 46-57; Univ. of Teheran 57; Bank Melli Iran 57-60; Vice-Gov. Bank Markazi Iran 62-63; Minister of Educ. 64; Minister of State 64-65; Chancellor, Nat. Univ. of Iran 65-66; Alt. Exec. Dir. World Bank (IBRD) 66-71; Gov. Bank Markazi Iran (Cen. Bank of Iran) 71-73; Amb. to the European Communities 74-.
37 avenue F. D. Roosevelt, 1050 Brussels, Belgium.
Telephone: 647-64-55.

Jahn, Gerhard; German lawyer and politician; b. 10 Sept. 1927, Kassel; s. of Ernst and Lilly (née Schlüchterer) Jahn; m. Anna Waas 1950; one s. two d.; ed. Humanistisches Friedrichs Gymnasium and Universität Marburg.

Qualified as lawyer 57; Parl. Man. Sozial-Demokratische Partei (SPD) 61; Parl. State Sec. to Minister of Foreign Affairs 67; Minister of Justice 69-74.

Bundesministerium der Justiz, 53 Bonn, Rosenburg, Federal Republic of Germany.

Telephone: 20171, Ext. 300.

Jaicks, Frederick Gillies; American business executive; b. 26 July 1918, Chicago; m. Mignon Dake 1954; two s. one d.; ed. Hinsdale High School, Cornell, and Harvard Univs.

Joined Inland Steel Co. as open hearth trainee 40; served in U.S. Navy during Second World War; served in various positions in steelmaking operations at Inland Steel Co's Indiana Harbour Works, E. Chicago 45-54; Asst. Gen. Man. of Primary Production 56-59; Gen. Man. Indiana Harbour Works 59-61; Vice-Pres. Steel Manufacturing 61-62; Vice-Pres. Manufacturing and Research 62-63; Dir. Inland Steel Co. 63-, Pres. 66-71, Chair. and Chief Exec. Officer 71-; Dir. Carson Pirie Scott and Co. 69-; Dir., mem. Exec. Cttee. First Nat. Bank of Chicago 71-; Dir. R. R. Donnelley & Son 73-; mem. Asscn. of Iron and Steel Eng., American Iron and Steel Inst. (Dir., mem. Exec. Cttee. 71-), American Inst. of Mining, Metallurgical and Petroleum Eng., Conf. Board 71-, Cornell Soc. of Eng., Nat. Open Hearth Conf.; Dir. Int. Iron and Steel Inst. 71-; official of many other orgs.; Hon. LL.D. St. Joseph's Coll. 68; Benjamin F. Fairless Award 71; Management Man of the Year, Nat. Management Asscn. 72.

Leisure interest: scouting.

Inland Steel Co., 30 West Monroe Street, Chicago, Ill. 60603; 91 Graymoor Lane, Olympia Fields, Ill. 60461, U.S.A.

Jain, Shanti Prasad, B.SC.; Indian industrialist; b. 1912; ed. Banaras Hindu Univ. and Agra Univ.

Controls a chain of industries in Bihar, U.P., Rajasthan, West Bengal and Kashmir; Chair. and Dir. Sahu Jain Ltd.; Chair. Rohtas Industries Ltd., The Jaipur Udyog Ltd.; Pres. Shri Ahimsa Prachar Samity, Calcutta, Bihar Industries Asscn., Patna; formerly Pres. Federation of Indian Chambers of Commerce and Industry, New Delhi, All-India Org. of Industrial Employers, New Delhi, Indian Chamber of Commerce, Calcutta, Indian Paper Mills, Asscn., Calcutta, Indian Sugar Mills Asscn., Calcutta, Rajasthan Chamber of Commerce and Industry, Jaipur, Eastern U.P. Chamber of Commerce, Allahabad, Marwari Relief Soc., Calcutta; Founder, Baharatiya Jnanpith (Acad.), Benares.

11 Clive Row, Calcutta; and 6 Sardar Patel Marg, New Delhi 11, India.

Jain, Surendra Kumar, M.A., LL.M.; Indian international official; b. 22 Dec. 1922, India; s. of Padam Sain Jain; m. Chakresh Kumar Jain 1941; ed. High School, New Delhi, Punjab Univ. and Lucknow Univ. Lecturer, Delhi School of Law, Delhi Univ. 46-47; joined Int. Labour Office, Geneva 47, Chef de Cabinet to Dir.-Gen. 57-59, Dir. Office for Near and Middle East, Istanbul 59-62, Field Office for Asia, Colombo 62-65, Regional Dir. for Asia, Bangkok 66-75, Deputy Dir.-Gen. in charge of Technical Programmes June 75-; Gold Medal (Lucknow Univ.).

Leisure interests: photography, swimming, badminton, music.

Publs. articles on labour and social problems in *International Labour Review* and other journals.

International Labour Office, 1211 Geneva 22; Residence: 34 rue Daubin, 1203 Geneva, Switzerland.

Telephone: 98-52-11 (Office); 45-80-82 (Residence).

Jakobovits, Rabbi Immanuel, B.A., PH.D.; British Rabbi; b. 8 Feb. 1921, Königsberg, Germany; s. of Rabbi Dr. Julius Jakobovits and Paula Wreschner; m. Amélie Munk 1948; two s. four d.; ed. Jews' Coll. London, Yeshivah Etz Chaim, London, Univ. of London.

Minister of Brondesbury Synagogue, London 41-44, of South East London Synagogue 44-47, of Great Synagogue, London 47-49; Chief Rabbi of Ireland 49-58; Rabbi of Fifth Avenue Synagogue, New York 58-67; Chief Rabbi of the United Hebrew Congregations of the British Commonwealth of Nations, London 67-.

Publs. *Jewish Medical Ethics* 59, rev. edn. 67, *Journal of a Rabbi* 66, *Jewish Law Faces Modern Problems* 66.

Office of the Chief Rabbi, Adler House, Tavistock Square, London, W.C.1, England.

Jakobsen, Frode, M.A.; Danish politician; b. 21 Dec. 1906, Mors; s. of Ole Jakobsen and Ane Mette Lorentsen; m. Ruth Goldstein 1937 (died 1974); one s. one d.; ed. Univ. of Copenhagen.

Agricultural worker until 25; Lecturer in Philosophy and Literature until 40; Leader, Resistance Movement 41-45; founder-mem. Danish Freedom Council (illegal govt. during occupation) 43-45; Chief of all armed underground forces 43-45; mem. Cabinet May-Nov. 45; mem. Parl. 45-73; Civil Chief of Home Guard 48-72; mem. Consultative Assembly, Council of Europe 49-64, Vice-Pres. 53-54; mem. Govt. Cttee. for Foreign Affairs; Pres. European Movement in Denmark 49-64; Social Democratic Party; mem. Danish Defence Cttee., Govt. Cttee. on Disarmament Questions 66-; Danish Del. to UN 56-57, 61, 73, Head of Del. 62-65; Int. Council, Congress for Cultural Freedom 60-66.

Leisure interest: ornithology.

Publs. *Nietzsches Kamp med den kristelige Moral* 40, *The European Movement and the Council of Europe* 50, *Europe—and Denmark* 53, *Standpunkter* 66, *Nej, Der Skal Ikke Ties* 72, *I Danmarks Frihedsraad* 75.

Hedetoften 5, 2680 Solröd Strand, Denmark.

Telephone: 0314 1968.

Jakobson, Max; Finnish journalist and diplomatist; b. 1923, Viipuri; s. of Jonas and Helmi (née Virtanen) Jakobson; m. Marilyn S. Medney 1954; two s. one d. Journalist until 53; Press Attaché, Finnish Embassy, Washington 53-59; Chief of Press Dept., Ministry of Foreign Affairs 59-62; Asst. Dir. for Political Affairs, Ministry of Foreign Affairs 59-62, Dir. 62-65; Perm. Rep. of Finland to UN 65-72; Amb. to Sweden 72-75; Man. Dir. Council of Econ. Orgs. in Finland 75-.

Publs. include *The Diplomacy of the Winter War* and *Finnish Neutrality*.

Rahapajankatu 3B 17, 00160, Helsinki 16, Finland.

Telephone: 651884.

Jakobson, Roman, PH.D.; American philologist; b. 11 Oct. 1896, Moscow; s. of Osip Jakobson and Anna Volpert; m. Krystyna Pomorska 1962; ed. Lazarev Inst. of Oriental Languages, Moscow Univ. and Prague Univ.

Prof. of Russian Philology, Masaryk Univ. Brno 33-39; Visiting Lecturer, Univs. of Copenhagen, Oslo, Uppsala 39-41; Prof. Ecole Libre des Hautes Etudes, New York 42-46; Prof. Columbia Univ. 43-49; Samuel Hazzard Cross Prof. of Slavonic Languages, Literatures and Gen. Linguistics, Harvard Univ. 49-67, Prof. Emer. 67-; Inst. Prof. at Mass. Inst. of Technology 57-; Visiting Prof., Yale Univ. 67, Princeton 68, Brown 69-70, Brandeis 70, Collège de France 72, Louvain Univ. 72, New York Univ. 73; mem. Polish Acad. of Sciences, Norwegian Acad. of Sciences, Royal Danish Acad. of Sciences, American Acad. of Arts and Sciences, Serbian Acad. of Sciences, Netherlands Acad. of Sciences, Irish Acad. of Sciences, Italian Acad., Bologna, British Acad.; Pres. Linguistic Soc. of America 56; Vice-Pres. of Int. Cttee. of Slavicists, Int. Asscn. for Semiotic Studies; Fellow, Center for Advanced Study in the

Behavioural Sciences 58-59, 60-61, and Center for Cognitive Studies at Harvard 67-69; Consultant to UNESCO Dept. of Social Sciences 65-69; Visiting Fellow, Salk Inst. for Biological Studies 66-69; Hon. mem. Int. Phonetic Asscn., Finno-Ugrian Soc., Helsinki, American Asscn. for Armenian Studies and Research, Czechoslovak Soc. of Arts and Sciences, Royal Soc. of Letters, Lund, Philological Soc., London; Royal Anthropological Inst. of Great Britain and Ireland, Acad. of Aphasia; Hon. Pres. Tokyo Inst. for Advanced Studies of Language 67-; mem. Hon. Council Phonetic Soc. of Japan; Amer. Council of Learned Socs. award 60, Amer. Asscn. for the Advancement of Slavic Studies 70, Légion d'Honneur and other awards; Dr. h.c. (Cambridge, Oslo, Uppsala, Michigan, New Mexico, Grenoble, Nice, Prague, Rome, Yale, Chicago, Clark, Ohio State, Zagreb, Brno, Louvain, Tel-Aviv and Harvard Univs.).

Leisure interest: travelling.

Publs. *Novejshaja russkaja poezija, O cheshskom stikhe: Nejstarsi ceske pisne duchovni, Remarques sur l'évolution phonologique du russe, K kharakteristike evrazijskogo jazykovogo sojuza, Beitrag zur allgemeinen Kasuslehre, Kindersprache, Aphasie und allgem. Lautgesetze, La Geste d'Igor, Preliminaries to Speech Analysis* (with G. Fant and M. Halle), *Ivan Fedorov's Primer, Fundamentals of Language* (with M. Halle), *Selected Writings I* 62, 71, *II* 71, *IV* 66, *Essais de Linguistique générale I* 63, *II* 73, *Sofonija's Tale of the Russian-Tatar Battle* (with D. S. Worth) 63, *Studies on Child Language and Aphasia* 71, *Bibliography* 71, *Low German Manual of Spoken Russian 1607* (with L. Hammerich) *I* 61, *II* 70, *Shakespeare's Verbal Art* 70, *Questions de Poétique* 73, *Main Trends in the Science of Language* 73, *Aufsätze zur Linguistik und Poetik* 74, *Pushkin and his Sculptural Myth* 75, *N. S. Trubetzkoy's Letters and Notes* 75, etc.

Harvard University, Boylston Hall 301, Cambridge, Mass. 02138, U.S.A.

Telephone: 617-868-5619.

Jakubowski, Janusz Lech; Polish scientist; b. 9 Dec. 1905, Warsaw; s. of Wladyslaw and Wiktoria (Handzelewicz) Jakubowski; m. 1st Hanna Wiszniewska 1931; m. 2nd Zofia Wysocka-Bernadzikiewicz 1948; one d. Professor of High Voltage Technology, Warsaw Polytechnic 38-; mem. Polish Acad. of Sciences, mem. Presidium 52-69; Dir. Centre Pol. Acad. of Sciences in Paris 59-61; corresp. mem. Acad. des Sciences, Inscriptions et Belles Lettres de Toulouse 62; UNESCO Project Man., Ecole Nat. Poly., Algiers 67-71; State Prize 50, Officer's and Commdr.'s Cross, Order of Polonia Restituta 51, 54, Medal of 10th Anniversary of People's Poland 55, Order of Banner of Labour 2nd Class 65, Silver Medal Société d'Encouragement pour la Recherche et Invention (France) 68.

Leisure interest: ecology of coral reefs.

Publs. *New method of High Voltage Measurement* 35, *Measurement of Distorted High Voltages* 37, *Actual Problems of High Voltage Engineering* 39, *High Voltage Engineering* 51, *Travelling Waves in High Voltage Systems* 62, *Over Voltages in High Voltage Systems* 68, and numerous articles.

Ul. Igańska 9, 04-087 Warsaw, Poland.

Telephone: Warsaw 10-11-71.

Jalallar, Mohammed Khan; Afghan politician; b. 6 Dec. 1936, Andkhoi; ed. Commerce Vocational School, Kabul and Kabul Univ.

Member Finance Dept., Ministry of Planning 58-63, Dir. Co-ordination Dept. 63-67, Pres. Financial Section 67-71; Deputy Minister of Finance 71-72, Minister of Finance 72-73, of Commerce Jan. 74-; Golden Minapal Award.

Ministry of Commerce, Kabul; and c/o Barat Ali, Afzal Marleet, Kabul, Afghanistan.

Jalloud, Major Abdul Salam Ahmed; Libyan army officer and politician; b. 15 Dec. 1944; ed. Secondary School, Sebha, Mil. Acad., Benghazi.

Member Revolutionary Command Council 69-; Minister of Industry and the Econ., Acting Minister of the Treasury 70-72; Prime Minister July 72-.

Office of the Prime Minister, Tripoli, Libyan Arab Republic.

Jallow, Momadou Ebrima; Gambian trade unionist; b. 1928; ed. St. Augustine School and Co-operative Coll., Ibadan.

Clerk, Civil Service, later Secretariat, Income Tax Div.; founder-mem. Gambia Workers Union 57-, now Sec.; Sec.-Gen. AFRO, African Regional Organisation of International Confederation of Free Trade Unions (ICFTU) 64-.

ICFTU African Information Service, 231 Herbert Macaulay Street, Yaba, Nigeria.

Jamal, Amir Habib, B.COMM. (ECON.); Tanzanian politician; b. 26 Jan. 1922, Dar es Salaam; ed. primary school, Mwanza, secondary school, Dar es Salaam, and Univ. of Calcutta, India.

Elected mem. Tanganyika Legislative Council 58; Minister of Urban Local Govt. and Works 59, of Communication, Power and Works 60; Minister of State, President's Office, Directorate of Devt. 64; re-elected M.P. 65; Minister of Finance 65-72; Minister for Commerce and Industries 72-75, of Finance and Economic Planning Nov. 75-.

Ministry of Finance and Economic Planning, Dar es Salaam, United Republic of Tanzania.

Jamal, Jasim Yousif; Qatar diplomatist; b. 17 Sept. 1940; m.; three c.; ed. Northeast Mo. State Univ., N.Y. Univ., U.S.A.

Ministry of Education, Dir. Admin. Affairs 58-63, Cultural Adviser, U.S. 63-68, Dir. of Cultural Affairs 68-72; Perm. Rep. to UN 72-, concurrently accred. as Amb. to Canada, Brazil and Argentina.

Permanent Mission of Qatar to United Nations, 747 Third Avenue, 22nd Floor, New York, N.Y. 10017, U.S.A.

Jámbor, Ági; American pianist; b. 4 Feb. 1909, Budapest, Hungary; d. of Vilmos Jámbor and Olga Riesz; ed. Budapest Acad. of Music under Kodály and Weiner, and Musikhochschule, Berlin.

Regular concert tours throughout U.S.A.; Full Prof., Dept. of Music and Anthropology/Ethno-Musicology, Bryn Mawr Coll., Pa.; Curator of Music Instruments, Univ. Museum, Pa.; Brahms Prize, Deutsche Akad., Berlin 28; Int. Chopin Prize, Warsaw 37.

103 Pine Tree Road, Radnor, Pa., U.S.A.

Telephone: MU8-8683.

James, Harold L., B.S., PH.D.; American geologist; b. 11 June 1912, Nanaimo, B.C., Canada; of Welsh parentage; m. Ruth Graybeal 1936; four s.; ed. Washington State Univ. and Princeton Univ.

Geologist, U.S. Geological Survey 41-, Chief Geologist 65-71; Research Geologist 71-; Visiting Lecturer, Northwestern Univ. 53, 54; Prof., Univ. of Minnesota 61-65; mem. Nat. Acad. of Sciences; Pres. Soc. of Econ. Geologists 70.

Leisure interests: reading, fishing, writing.

Publs. About 40 papers in professional journals and by U.S. Geological Survey.

U.S. Geological Survey, Menlo Park, Calif. 94025; Home: Port Townsend, Washington 98368, U.S.A.

Telephone: 415-323-8111, Ext. 2650 (Office); 206-385-0878 (Home).

James, Sir John Morrice Cairns, P.C., G.C.M.G., C.V.O., M.B.E.; British diplomatist; b. 30 April 1916; s. of Lewis Cairns James; m. 1st Elizabeth Piesse (died 1966), 2nd Geneviève Sarasin 1968; one s. two d.; ed. Bradfield, Oxford Univ.

Joined Dominions Office 39; Royal Navy, Royal Marines Second World War; staff of U.K. High Comm. in S. Africa 46-47; Commonwealth Relations Office, London 47-52; Deputy U.K. High Commr., Lahore 52-53, Karachi 55-56; Deputy U.K. High Commr., India 58-61, U.K. High Commr., Pakistan 61-65; Deputy Under-Sec. of State, Commonwealth Office, London 66-68, Perm. Under-Sec. of State 68; High Commr. to India 68-71; High Commr. to Australia 71-76; King of Arms of the Most Distinguished Order of Saints Michael and George 75.
Leisure interests: travel, shooting, photography.
La Plotte, Cap Saint-Pierre, Saint-Tropez 83, Vas, France.

James of Rusholme, Baron (Life Peer), cr. 59, Kt. (cr. 56); **Eric John Francis James,** M.A., B.SC., D.PHIL. (Oxon.); British educationist; b. 13 April 1909, Derby; s. of Francis and Lilian James; m. Cordelia Wintour 1939; one s.; ed. Taunton's School, Southampton and Queen's Coll., Oxford.
Assistant Master Winchester Coll. 33-45; High Master The Manchester Grammar School 45-62; Vice-Chancellor, Univ. of York 62-73; mem. Univ. Grants Cttee. 48-58; Chair. Headmasters' Conf. 53 and 54; mem. Central Advisory Council for Educ. 57; Fellow, Winchester Coll. 63; mem. Press Council 63-67, Social Science Research Council 65-69; Chair. Cttee. on Training and Educ. of Teachers 70-71; Chair. Personal Social Services Council 73-; mem. Royal Fine Arts Comm. 73-; Hon. Fellow Queen's Coll., Oxford 60; Hon. LL.D. (McGill, York, Toronto), Hon. D.Litt. (New Brunswick), D.Univ. (York).
Publs. *Elements of Physical Chemistry* (in part) 38, *Science and Education* (in part) 42, *An Essay on the content of Education* 49, *Education and Leadership* 51.
Penhill Cottage, West Witton, Leyburn, Yorkshire, England.

Jameson, (Margaret) Storm, M.A.; British novelist; b. 1891, Whitby, Yorkshire; d. of William Storm Jameson; m. Guy Patterson Chapman 1924 (died 1972); one s.; ed. Leeds Univ. and King's Coll., London.
President English PEN Club 38-45; Hon. D.Litt.; PEN Fiction Prize 74.
Publs. *The Lovely Ship* 27, *Farewell to Youth* 28, *The Voyage Home* 29, *A Richer Dust* 31, *That Was Yesterday* 32, *A Day Off* 33, *No Time Like the Present* 33, *Company Parade* 34, *Love in Winter* 35, *In the Second Year* 36, *None Turn Back* 36, *Delicate Monster* 37, *Civil Journey* 39, *Farewell Night*, *Welcome Day* 39, *Europe to Let* 40, *Cousin Honoré* 40, *The Fort* 42, *Then We Shall Hear Singing* 42, *Cloudless May* 43, *The Journal of Mary Hervey Russell* 45, *The Other Side* 45, *Before the Crossing* 47, *The Black Laurel* 48, *The Moment of Truth* 49, *The Writer's Situation and Other Essays* 50, *The Green Man* 52, *The Hidden River* 55, *The Intruder* 56, *A Cup of Tea for Mr. Thorgill* 57, *A Ulysses Too Many* 58, *Last Score* 61, *Road from the Monument* 62, *A Month Soon Goes* 63, *The Aristide Case* 64, *The Early Life of Stephen Hind* 66, *The White Crow* 68, *Journey from the North* (autobiography) Vol. 1 69, Vol. 2 70, *Parthian Words* 70, *There Will Be a Short Interval* 73; editor Guy Chapman's *A Kind of Survivor* 75.
c/o Macmillan London Ltd., Little Essex Street, London, W.C.2, England.

Jamieson, Donald; Canadian politician; b. 1921, St. John's, Newfoundland; s. of Charles and Isabelle Jamieson; m. Barbara Oakley 1946; one s. three d.
Former broadcasting exec., from St. John's, Newfoundland; Minister of Supply and Services July 68-May 69; Minister of Transport 69-72, of Regional Economic Expansion 72-75, of Industry, Trade and Commerce Sept. 75-; Liberal.

Leisure interests: Bally Haly golf club, Rotary club, fishing, hunting, boating.
House of Commons, Ottawa, Ontario; 4 Winter Place. St. John's, Newfoundland, Canada.

Jamieson, John Kenneth, B.S.; American (b. Canadian) oil executive; b. 28 Aug. 1910; ed. Univ. of Alberta and Massachusetts Inst. of Technology.
British American Oil Co., Canada 34-48; Imperial Oil Co. Ltd., Toronto 48-58; Pres. Int. Petroleum Co. Ltd., Florida 59-61; Exxon Co. U.S.A., Houston, Texas 61-62; Exxon Corpn., New York 64-65, Pres. and Dir. 65-69, Chair. of Board 69-75 (retd.); Dir. Chase Manhattan Bank 65-, Equitable Life Assurance Soc. of the U.S. 71-; Consultant World-Wide Shipping Group 76-.
Office: 1100 Milam Building, Suite 4601, Houston, Tex. 77002, U.S.A.

Jancsó, Miklós; Hungarian film director; b. 27 Sept. 1921, Vác; s. of Sándor Jancsó and Angela Poparad; m. Márta Mészáros 1958; two s. one d.; studied legal sciences and ethnography at Kolozsvár (now Cluj), Romania, and Budapest Coll. of Cinematographic Art.
Worked at newsreel studio 53-58; Documentary film studio 62; Chief Producer, Hunnia Film Studio 63-; Grand Prix of San Francisco 61; Prize of Fédération Internationale de la Presse Cinématographique (FIPRESCI); Béla Balázs prize 65; Merited artist of the Hungarian People's Repub. 70; Best Dir. Award, Cannes Festival 72; Kossuth Prize, 2nd Degree 73.
Films: *A harangok Rómába mentek* (The Bells have gone to Rome) 59, *Oldás és Kötés* (Cantata) 63, *Szegény Legények* (The Round-Up) 66, *Így Jöttem* (My Way Home) 65, *Csillagosok—Katonák* (The Red and the White) 67, *Csend és Kiáltás* (Silence and Cry) 68, *Fényes Szelek* (The Confrontation) 69, *Sirókkó* (Winter Wind) 69, *Agnus Dei* 71, *Red Psalm* 72, *Elektreia* (Electra) 75; For Italian TV: *Il Tecnico e il Rito*, *Roma rivuole Cesare*, *La Pacifista*; Stage production: *Othello* 74.
MAFILM Studio, Lumumba utca 174, Budapest XIV; Home: Rózsa Ferenc-utca 71, H-1064, Budapest VI, Hungary.
Telephone: 831-750 (Office); 311-853 (Home).

Janeway, Eliot, B.A.; American economist, author and lecturer; b. 1913, New York City; s. of Meyer J. and Fanny Siff Janeway; m. Elizabeth Hall 1938; two s.; ed. Cornell Univ. and London School of Economics.
Business Editor and Adviser to Editor-in-Chief, *Time* and Business Trends Consultant, *Newsweek* 32-50; now Pres. Janeway Publishing & Research Corpn.; Treas. American PEN Center; Syndicated columnist, Chicago-Tribune-N.Y. News Service; econ. adviser to numerous industries, govt. officials and private companies.
Leisure interest: reading political history.
Publs. *The Struggle for Survival* 52, *The Economics of Crisis* 68, *What Shall I do with my Money* 70, *You and Your Money* 72.
15 East 80th Street, New York, N.Y. 10021, U.S.A.
Telephone: 212-249-8833.

Janiurek, Włodzimierz; Polish politician; b. 21 Sept. 1924, Chorzów.
Engaged as manual worker during occupation, then as a journalist with *Trybuna Robotnicza*, Katowice, then in Press Dept. of Cen. Cttee., Polish United Workers' Party (PZPR); Editor-in-Chief *Trybuna Robotnicza* 54-66; Amb. to Czechoslovakia 66-71; Under-Sec. of State for Information to Council of Ministers, Govt. Press Spokesman 71-; Deputy to Seym (Parl.); mem. Cttee. on Foreign Affairs; Chair. Sub-Cttee. for Poles Living Abroad; Sec. Polish-British Group of Interparl. Union 57-65; Gold Cross of Merit 54, Knight's Cross,

Order of Polonia Restituta 55, Order of Banner of Labour 2nd Class 60, Commdr.'s Cross 70.
Urząd Rady Ministrów PRL, Al. Ujazdowskie 1/3, 00-583 Warsaw, Poland.

Jankowitsch, Peter, D.D.L.; Austrian diplomatist; b. 10 July 1933, Vienna; *s.* of Karl Jankowitsch and Gertrude (née Ladstaetter) Jankowitsch; *m.* Odette Prevor 1962; ed. Vienna Univ. and The Hague Acad. of Int. Law.
Former lawyer; joined foreign service 57, worked in Int. Law Dept.; Private Sec., Cabinet of Minister of Foreign Affairs 59-62; posted to London 62-64; Chargé d'Affaires, Dakar, Senegal 64-66; Head of Office of Bruno Kreisky, Chair. Austrian Socialist Party 67; Chief of Cabinet of Fed. Chancellor (Kreisky) 70-72; Perm. Rep. to UN May 72-; Chair. UN Cttee. on Peaceful Uses of Outer Space 72-; Rep. for Austria to UN Security Council 73-75, Pres. Security Council Nov. 73, Vice-Pres. 29th Gen. Assembly; Vice-Pres. 7th Special Session of Gen. Assembly Sept. 75; mem. UN Security Council Mission to Zambia 73; mem. of Board, Vienna Inst. for Devt. 73-; Vice-Pres. Austro-African Soc. 67-; mem. Board Austrian Foreign Policy Soc. and Austrian UN League.
Leisure interests: history and baroque music.
Publs. numerous newspaper and review articles on economic development of the Third World, in particular Africa; contrib. to Wörterbuch des Völkerrechts, 60.
Permanent Mission of Austria to United Nations, 806 UN Plaza, 7th Floor, New York, N.Y. 10017, U.S.A.

Jann, Adolf Walter, DR.IUR.; Swiss business executive; b. 22 Sept. 1911, Altdorf (Uri); *s.* of Dr. med. Adolf Jann and Josefine Huber; *m.* Lydia Eicher 1940; three *s.* one *d.*; ed. Univs. of Berne, Paris and London.
Secretary, Swiss Bankers' Asscn. 37-45; joined Union Bank of Switzerland 45, Gen. Man. 49; Vice-Pres. of Board, F. Hoffmann-La Roche and Co. Ltd. 57, Pres. and Man. Dir. 65-; Dir. Union Bank of Switzerland.
Leisure interests: swimming, mountain climbing, hunting.
Publ. *Das Bankgeheimnis im Schweizerischen Recht* 37.
F. Hoffman-La Roche and Co. Ltd., Schaffhauserrheinweg 125, CH 4002 Basle; Home: Toblerstrasse 107, CH 8044 Zurich, Switzerland.
Telephone: 32-38-20 (Office); 34-68-11 (Home).

Janne, Henri, D.PHIL. ET LETTRES; Belgian university professor and sociologist; b. 20 Feb. 1908, Brussels; *s.* of Emile and Anne (née Matthys) Janne; *m.* Elisabeth Houtman 1936; one *s.*; ed. Athénée Royal d'Ixelles, Univ. of Brussels.
Directed a number of govt. economic and social services, including Dir. Office National des Vacances Ouvrières 36, Dir.-Gen. Rééquipement National 47, Dir.-Gen. Coordination Economique (Prime Minister's Office) 49; *Chef du Cabinet,* Ministries of Economic Affairs, Supplies, and Economic Co-ordination 45-49; Pres. Defence Production Board, NATO 49-51; Pres. Belgian del. to UN Economic and Social Council 54 session; Prof. of Sociology, Univ. of Brussels 51-; Dir. Institut de Sociologie Solvay 53-56; Pres. Conseil Nat. du Travail; Prof. Coll. of Europe, Bruges 52-; mem. Senate 61; Minister of Nat. Educ. and Culture 63-65; Vice-Pres. Nat. Council for Scientific Policy; mem. Int. Cttee. for Social Sciences Documentation, Int. Cttee. of UNESCO for Social Science Terminology 54, Libre Académie de Belgique, Inst. de Sociologie de France; Pres. Acad. Royale de Belgique des Sciences et des Lettres 73; Rector Brussels Univ. 56-59; Pres. d'honneur de l'Association Int. des Sociologues de Langue français; Pres. Scientific Cttee. of *Plan 2000 Education,* European Cultural Foundation 68; mem. Board Int. Council on the Future of the Univ. 73; mem. of Governing Board of Centre for Educational Research and Innovation, OECD 69-70; mem. of Board of Trustees of Int.

Council for Educational Devt. (ICED); Corresp. mem. Inst. de France 74; Croix de Guerre Française avec palme, Officier Ordre de Léopold, Officier Légion d'Honneur, Commandeur de l'Ordre de Léopold II.
Leisure interest: travelling.
Publs. *L'Antialcibade* 46, *Sociologie et Politique Sociale dans les pays occidentaux* 62, *Technique, Développement économique et Technocratie* 63, *Le Système Social, Essai de Théorie Générale* 68, *Le temps du changement* 70.
Avenue Jeanne 44, 1050 Brussels (Office); 244 Ave. Louise, 1050 Brussels, Belgium.
Telephone: 649-49-94.

Janne d'Othée, Xavier, PH.D., LL.D.; Belgian jurist; b. 31 March 1883, Liège; *m.* Gabrielle Zurstrassen 1909 (died 1967); ed. Liège Univ.
Lecturer, Liège Univ. 20, Prof. of Law 30-53 (Dean 30-31), Prof. Emer. 53-; Prof. Acad. of Int. Law, The Hague; Bâtonnier Ordre des Avocats Verviers 36; fmr. Vice-Pres. Féd. des Avocats Belges; mem. Int. Law Asscn. London, American Law Asscn., Société de Législation Comparée Paris; Vice-Pres. Henri Capitant Asscn. for Juridical Science Paris; mem. Int. Diplomatic Acad.; corresp. mem. Inst. of Comparative Law and Legislative Studies, Rio de Janeiro; mem. Acad. of Jurisprudence, Madrid; founder Janne-Zurstrassen Prize, Liège Univ.; mem. d'Honneur Asscn. Amitiés Belgo-Canadiennes; Dr. h.c. (Montpellier, Montreal, Laval); Grand Officier Ordre de la Couronne (Belgium), Ordre de la Couronne du Trône de Luxembourg; Officier Légion d'Honneur, Ordre de Léopold, Order of Polonia Restituta, Ordre de l'Instruction Publique (France); created Chevalier Dec. 66.
10 rue de la Banque, Verviers, Belgium.
Telephone: 316-83.

Jánossy, Lajos, DR.PHIL.; Hungarian physicist; b. 2 March 1912, Budapest; *s.* of Imre Jánossy and Gertrud Bortstieber; *m.* 1st Leonie Kahn 1937, three *s.* one *d.*; *m.* 2nd Alice Farkas 1965, two step *d.*; ed. Vienna and Berlin Univs.
On staff of Manchester Univ. 39-47; Senior Prof. and Dept. Head, School of Cosmic Rays, Dublin 47-50; Prof. L. Eötvös Univ., Budapest 50, Head, Dept. of Atomic Physics 57-70; Dir. Central Research Inst. for Physics, Budapest 56-70; mem. Hungarian Nat. Atomic Energy Comm.; Vice-Pres. Hungarian Acad. of Sciences 58-73; mem. Central Cttee. Hungarian Socialist Workers' Party; Vice-Chair. IAEA Board of Govs. 61-63; Pres. Hungarian Philatelic Soc. 66-; mem. Scientific Council, Joint Inst. of Nuclear Research, Dubna; mem. numerous foreign acads of science; Kossuth Award 51.
Leisure interest: philately.
Publs. *Cosmic Rays* 48 (Russian 49), *Cosmic Rays and Nuclear Physics* 48 (Italian 54), *Introduction to Cosmic Ray Research* 54 (German 55, Polish 56), *Philosophical Problems of the Theory of Relativity* (Hungarian) 63, *Theory and Practice of the Evaluation of Measurements* 65 (Russian 65, Hungarian 68), *Theory of Relativity based on Physical Reality* 71 (Hungarian 73, Japanese 74).
1016 Budapest, Czakó u. 11, Hungary.
Telephone: 151-289.

Janot, Raymond Marcel Louis, L. EN D., L. ÈS L.; French civil servant; b. 9 March 1917, Paris; *s.* of Gaston Janot and Madeleine Paumier; *m.* Catherine de Brunel de Serbonnes; two *s.* two *d.*; ed. Coll. Stanislas, Lycée Henry-IV, Paris Univ. and Ecole Libre des Sciences Politiques.
Auditeur, Conseil d'Etat 46, Maître des Requêtes 48-; Legal Counsellor, Présidence de la République 47-51; Economic Counsellor French High Comm. in Indo-China 51-52; Dir. du Cabinet, Minister for Relations with Associated States 52-53; Sec.-Gen. Conseil d'Etat 56-59; Technical Counsellor, Gen. de Gaulle June 58-Jan. 59; Sec.-Gen. French Community Feb. 59-60; Dir.-

Gen. Radiodiffusion-Télévision Française 60-62; Conseil d'Etat 62-; Pres. Devt. Cttee. of Yonne 64-; Asst. Vice-Pres. Syndicat Nat. de l'Industrie Pharmaceutique 75; Officier Légion d'Honneur, Croix de Guerre, Médaille des Evadés.
11 avenue d'Eylau, Paris 16e, France.
Telephone: 727-72-89.

Janowitz, Gundula; Austrian opera singer; b. 2 Aug. 1937, Berlin, Germany; d. of Theodor and Else Janowitz (née Neumann); m. Wolfgang Zörner 1965; one d.; ed. Acad. of Music and Performing Arts, Graz.
Debut with Vienna State Opera; has sung with Deutsche Oper, Berlin 66, Metropolitan Opera, New York 67, Teatro Colón, Buenos Aires 70, Grand Opera, Paris 73; concerts in major cities throughout the world, appearances at Bayreuth, Aix en Provence, Glyndebourne, Spoleto, Salzburg, Munich Festivals; mem. Vienna State Opera, Deutsche Oper, Berlin; recordings with Deutsche Grammophon, EMI.
Leisure interest: modern literature.
Rehetobelstrasse 81, 9000 St. Gallen, Switzerland.

Janza, Vladimir, ING.; Czechoslovak politician; b. 10 April 1929, Zilina; ed. Comenius Univ. of Bratislava, State Inst. for Econ., Moscow.
State Planning Office 53-63, Sec. State Price Cttee. 63-65; Deputy Minister-Chair. State Comm. on Finance, Prices and Wages 65-68; Deputy Minister, Fed. Price Office 68-71; Deputy Chair. State Planning Comm. 71-73, Minister Vice-Chair. 73-75, Chair. 75-; Distinction for Merit in Construction.
State Planning Commission, Prague, Czechoslovakia.

Japan, Emperor of (*see* Hirohito).

Jaq, Dr. Said Ahmed El-, M.A., PH.D.; Sudanese politician; b. 1930, Khartoum; ed. Univ. of Khartoum and in U.S.A.
Worked in Ministry of Works 54-56, later in consultative and design engineering; lecturer in Civil Eng., Univ. of Khartoum; worked on water and electricity projects for Shendi and Berber towns; founder and board mem. Sudanese Engineers Trade Union; helped to found Sudanese Teachers Asscn., Univ. of Khartoum; Minister of Works May 69-June 70; Minister of Transport and Communications June 70-Aug. 71; mem. American Eng. Soc., Sudanese Engineers Soc.
c/o Ministry of Transport and Communications, Khartoum, Sudan.

Jarman, Franklin Maxey; American business executive; b. 10 Nov. 1931, Nashville, Tenn.; s. of Walton Maxey Jarman (*q.v.*) and Sarah (Anderson) Jarman; m. Nancy M. Smith 1970; ed. Montgomery Bell Acad. and Mass. Inst. of Technology.
Joined GENESCO 57, mem. Board of Govs. 60, Advisory Board 60, Board of Dirs. 61, Treas. 62, Financial Vice-Pres. 64, Exec. Vice-Pres., mem. Finance and Exec. Cttees. 66, Pres. and Chief Exec. Officer Feb. 69, Chair. GENESCO May 69-, Chair. of Board and Chief Exec. Officer March 73-.
Leisure interests: water sports, flying.
GENESCO, 111 7th Avenue, Nashville, Tenn.; Home: 601 Bowling Avenue, Nashville, Tenn. 37215, U.S.A.
Telephone: 615-291-7748.

Jarman, Walton Maxey; American business executive; b. 10 May 1904, Nashville, Tenn.; s. of J. Franklin and Eugenia Jarman; m. Sarah Anderson 1928; one s. (Franklin M. Jarman, *q.v.*) two d.; ed. Massachusetts Inst. of Technology.
Trainee, Jarman Shoe Co. 24, Sec.-Treas. 25-32, Pres. 33-36; Pres. Gen. Shoe Corpn. 36-45; Pres. GENESCO 45-47, Chair. 47-69, Chair. Finance Cttee. 69-72; Dir. or Trustee, Mutual Life Insurance Co. of New York, Financial Fed. (Calif.), Nashville City Bank and Trust Co., Fed. Reserve Bank of Atlanta 60-66; Dir. or Trustee several religious insts.; Deacon First Baptist

Church, Nashville; Vice-Pres. American Bible Soc.; mem. Planning Cttee., Int. Congress on World Evangelization 74-, Chair. Finance Cttee. 74; Hon. LL.D. (Stetson Univ., Florida and Georgetown Coll., Ky.).
Leisure interests: reading, travel, painting.
Publs. *A Businessman Looks at the Bible* 64, *O Taste and See.*
111 7th Avenue North, Nashville, Tenn., Box 941-37202; Home: 4410 Gerald Place, Nashville, Tenn., U.S.A.
Telephone: 615-747-6356.

Jarocki, Jerzy; Polish theatre director; b. 1 May 1929, Warsaw; m.; one d.; ed. State Higher School of Acting, studies in drama production in U.S.S.R.
Directs plays mainly by Polish writers S. Witkiewicz, W. Gombrowicz, T. Różewics and S. Mrożek; productions abroad; with Old Theatre, Crakow 62-; Gold Cross of Merit; Gold Award of City of Crakow; Ministry of Culture and Arts Prize 71; State Prize, 1st Class and others.
Plays directed: *Stara kobieta wysiaduje* (Old Woman Brooding) 69, *Moja córeczka* (My Little Daughter) 68, *Ślub* (The Wedding), *Three Sisters* 69, *Pater Noster.*
Ul. Bytomska 14 m. 13, 30-075 Krakow, Poland.

Jaroszek, Henryk, M.A.; Polish diplomatist; b. 1 Oct. 1926; s. of Jan and Aniela Jaroszek; m. Anna Holendzka 1950; one s.; ed. Acad. of Pol. Sciences, Warsaw.
Ministry of Foreign Affairs, Warsaw 47-51; Second Sec. at Embassy, London 51-54, First Sec., New Delhi 54-55; Counsellor, Washington, D.C. 55-59; Amb. to Iraq. 59-62; Dir. of Asian and Middle Eastern Affairs, Ministry of Foreign Affairs 62-65; Amb. and Perm. Rep. to UN Office and Specialized Agencies, Geneva 65-69; Dir. Dept. of Int. Orgs., Ministry of Foreign Affairs 69-75; Amb., Perm. Rep. to UN 75-; Officier's Cross, Order of Polonia Restituta and other state distinctions.
Leisure interests: walking, angling.
Permanent Mission of Poland to the United Nations, 9 East 66th Street, New York, N.Y. 10021, U.S.A.
Telephone: (212) 744-2506.

Jaroszewicz, Piotr; Polish politician; b. 8 Oct. 1909, Nieśwież; ed. Free Univ., Warsaw.
Schoolmaster before, and in U.S.S.R. during Second World War; joined Polish army in U.S.S.R. 43; rose to rank of Col.; Deputy Commdr. in charge of political affairs, First Polish Army 45; Vice-Minister of Defence with rank of Lieut.-Gen. 45-50; Deputy Chair. State Comm. for Economic Planning 50-52; Vice-Premier 52-70; Minister of Coal Mining 54-56; Perm. Rep. to Council for Mutual Econ. Assistance (CMEA) 55-70; Chair. Cttee. for Econ. Co-operation with Foreign Countries 58-70; Pres. Council of Ministers 70-; mem. Central Cttee. and Deputy mem. of Political Bureau of Polish United Workers' Party until 70, mem. Political Bureau 70-; Deputy to Seym 47-; mem. Presidium of All-Polish Cttee. of Nat. Unity Front 71-; Pres. Chief Council of Union of Fighters for Freedom and Democracy May 72-; Order of Builders of People's Poland, Order of Banner of Labour First Class (twice), Grunwald Cross 2nd and 3rd Classes, Virtuti Militari, Grand Cross, Order of Polonia Restituta 74, Medal of 30th Anniversary of People's Poland 74, Order of October Revolution (U.S.S.R.) 74, Tadj Order, 1st Class (Iran) 74, and other decorations.
Urząd Rady Ministrów PRL, Aleje Ujazdowskie 3/5, 00-583 Warsaw, Poland.

Jarowinsky, Werner; German economist and politician; b. 1927; m.; one c.
Joined Communist Party 45; mem. Cen. Cttee. Sozialistische Einheitspartei Deutschlands (SED) and cand. mem. Politburo 63-; Sec. Cen. Cttee. SED.
Am Marx-Engels-Platz 2, 102 Berlin, German Democratic Republic.

Jarring, Gunnar, PH.D.; Swedish diplomatist; b. 12 Oct. 1907, Brunnby; *m.* Agnes Charlier 1932; one *d.*; ed. Lund Univ.

Associate Prof. Turkic Languages Lund Univ. 33-40; Attaché Ankara 40-41; Chief Section B Teheran 41; Chargé d'Affaires a.i. Teheran and Baghdad 45, Addis Ababa 46-48; Minister to India 48-51, concurrently to Ceylon 50-51, to Persia, Iraq and Pakistan 51-52; Dir. Political Div. Ministry of Foreign Affairs 53-56; Perm. Rep. to UN 56-58; rep. on Security Council 57-58; Amb. to U.S.A. 58-64, to U.S.S.R. 64-73, and to Mongolia 65-73; Special Envoy of UN Sec.-Gen. on Middle East situation Nov. 67-; Grand Cross Order of the North Star. Publs. *Studien zu einer osttürkischen Lautlehre* 33, *The Contest of the Fruits—An Eastern Turki Allegory* 36, *The Uzbek Dialect of Qilich, Russian Turkestan* 37, *Uzbek Texts from Afghan Turkestan* 38, *The Distribution of Turki Tribes in Afghanistan* 39, *Materials for the Knowledge of Eastern Turkestan* (Vols. I-IV) 47-51, *An Eastern Turki-English Dialect Dictionary* 64

Karlavaegen 85, 11459 Stockholm, Sweden.

Jaruzelski, Gen. Wojciech; Polish army officer and politician; b. 6 July 1923, Kurów, Poland; ed. Infantry Officers' School and Karol Świerczewski General Staff Acad.

Served with Polish Armed Forces in U.S.S.R. and Poland 43-45; various senior Army posts 45-65; Chief of Cen. Political Dept. of the Armed Forces 60-65; Deputy Minister of Nat. Defence 62-68, Minister 68-; Chief of Gen. Staff 65-68; Brig.-Gen. 56, Div.-Gen. 60, Gen. of Arms 68, Gen. of Army 73; mem. Polish United Workers' Party Cen. Cttee. 64-, mem. Political Bureau Dec. 71-; Deputy to Seym 61-; Vice-Pres. Chief Council of Union of Fighters for Freedom and Democracy 72-; decorations include Order of Builders of People's Poland, Order of Banner of Labour First Class, Cross of Order of Polonia Restituta, Silver Cross of Virtuti Militari and Cross of Valour, Medal of 30th Anniversary of People's Poland.

Ministerstwo Obrony Narodowej, ul. Klonowa 1, 61-468 Warsaw, Poland.

Järvi, Osmo Henrik, M.D.; Finnish pathologist; b. 1 Jan. 1911 Helsinki; *s.* of Prof. Toivo Henrik Järvi and Helfrid Helena (née Soderman-Siutila); *m.* Dr. Enne-Maija Kinnunen 1937; one *s.* three *d.*; ed Helsinki and Utrecht Univs. and Karolinska Inst., Stockholm.

Assistant, Anatomy Dept., Helsinki Univ. 32-38; Asst., Dept. of Pathological Anatomy 38-44; Lecturer, Microscopical Anatomy, 40-45, Prof. of Pathological Anatomy, Turku Univ. 44-; Dean, Faculty of Medicine 45-54, Rector 54-60; Chair. Finnish Medical Research Council 61-67; mem. Finnish Acad. of Science and Letters 60, Finnish Medical Soc. "Duodecim", Hon. mem. Finnish Medical Soc. "Läkaresällskapet"; mem. Swedish Medical Soc., Finnish Asscn. of Pathologists (Chair. 56-62), Swedish Asscn. of Pathologists, Scandi-navian Asscn. of Pathologists (Chair. 58-61), Patho-logical Soc. of Great Britain and Ireland, American Soc. of Clinical Pathologists, Int. Acad. of Pathology, N.Y. Acad. of Sciences, Cancer Asscn. of Finland (Chair. 67-75), Cancer Foundation of Finland (Chair. 60-66), Fellow, Int. Acad. of Cytology, etc.; Hon. Ph.D. (Åbo Acad., Finland) 68.

Leisure interest: the fine arts.

Publs. Works on secretion process and Golgi apparatus, morbid pathology of respiratory and intestinal tract, especially neoplasms, etc., exfoliated cytology; *Poh-dintaa* (Meditations) 67.

Yliopistonkatu 2K, Turku, Finland.

Telephone: 17390.

Jastrow, Robert; American physicist and writer; b. 1925.

Head Theoretical Div., Goddard Space Flight Centre, NASA 58-61, Chair. Lunar Exploration Comm. 59-60, Dir. Goddard Inst. Space Studies 61-; Prof. of Geo-physics, Columbia Univ. 61-.

Publs. *Red Giants and White Dwarfs, The Origin of the Solar System* 63, *The Evolution of Stars, Planets and Life* 67, *Astronomy: Fundamentals and Frontiers, The Venus Atmosphere* 69.

2880 Broadway, New York, N.Y. 10025, U.S.A.

Jastrun, Mieczysław, PH.D.; Polish writer; b. 29 Oct. 1903, Korolówka; ed. Cracow Univ.

Teacher secondary schools in Łódź 28-39; clandestine educ. in Lwów 39-41, Warsaw 41-44; sub-editor *Kuznica*, Łódź 45-49; returned to Warsaw 49; Gold Cross of Merit 46, Order of Banner of Labour 1st Class 49, State Prize 1st Class 50, 55, Commdr. Cross of Order of Polonia Restituta 54, Medal of 30th Anniversary of People's Poland 74, and other awards.

Publs. *Spotkanie w Czasie* (Meeting in Time), *Dzieje nieostygłe* (History Still Fresh), *Strumień i milczenie* (The Stream and Silence), *Godzina strzeżona* (The Guarded Hour), *Rzecz ludzka* (Human Affairs), *Genezy* (Genesis); biographical novel *Mickiewicz, Spotkanie z Salomeą* (Meeting with Salomea) (on J. Słowacki), *Poeta i dworzanin* (Poet and Courtier) (on J. Kochan-owski), *Między słowem a milczeniem* (Between Word and Silence; Essays) 60, *Większe od życia* (Larger than Life; Poems) 60; *Piękna Choroba* 61, *Beautiful Illness* 61, essays and translations from French, Russian and Ger-man poetry; *Mit śródziemnomorski* (Mediterranean Myth; Essays) 62, *Intonationen* 62, *Strefa owoców* (Zone of Fruits) 64, *Poezja i rzeczywistość* (Poetry and Truth; Essays) 66, *Poezje* (a selection of poems) 66; *W biały dzień* (In Broad Daylight), *Mickiewicz* (edition XI) 67, *Poezje wybrane* (a selection of poems) 68, *Godła pamieci* (Signs of Memory—poems) 69, *Wolność wyboru* (Free-dom of Choice—essays) 69, *Starry Diamond* (essays on Norwich) 71, *Eseje wybrane* (selected essays) 71, *Eseje— Mit śródziemnomorski, Wolność wyboru, Historia Fausta* (essays—Mediterranean Myth, Freedom of Choice, Faust Story) 73, *Walka o słowo* (Fighting for a Word) 73, *Wyspa* (Isle—poems) 73.

ul. Iwicka 8a m.9, Warsaw 36, Poland.

Telephone: 41-2394.

Jatoi, Ghulam Mustafa; Pakistani politician; b. 14 Aug. 1931, New Jatoi (Sind); *s.* of Khanbahadur Ghulam Rasul Khan Jatoi; ed. Karachi Grammar School.

President, District Local Board, Nawabshah 54; mem. Provincial Assembly of W. Pakistan 56; mem. Nat. Assembly 62-73; mem. Pakistan People's Party 69-; Minister for Political Affairs, Communications and Natural Resources 71-73; Chief Minister of Sind 73-; mem. Sind Provincial Assembly 73-; del. to UN Gen. Assembly 62, 65.

Chief Minister's House, Karachi, Pakistan.

Jatti, Basppa Danappa, B.A., LL.B.; Indian politician; b. 10 Sept. 1912, Savalgi, Bijapur District; ed. Bijapur Govt. High School, Rajaram Coll., Sykes Law Coll., Kolhapur.

Practised law at Jamkhandi; State Minister, Jamk-handi, later Chief Minister; mem. Legislative Assembly, Bombay, later Mysore; Deputy Minister of Health and Labour, Bombay 52; Chair. Land Reforms Cttee., Chief Minister, Mysore 58-62; Minister of Finance, Mysore 62-65, of Food, Mysore 65-67; Lieut.-Gov. of Pondicherry 68; Gov. of Orissa 72-74; Vice-Pres. of India 74-; Chair. Rajya Sabha 74-; LL.D. h.c., Karnatak Univ.

Office of the Vice-President of India, 6 Moulana Azad Road, New Delhi, India.

Jauho, Pekka Antti Olavi; Finnish scientist; b. 27 April 1923, Oulu; *s.* of Antti Arvid Jauho and Sylvi (née Pajari) Jauho; *m.* Kyllikki Hakala 1948; one *s.*; ed. Univ. of Helsinki.

Chief Mathematician, Insurance Co. Kansa 51-54; Assoc. Prof., Univ. of Helsinki 55-57 (now Technical Univ. of Helsinki), Prof. in technical physics 57-70; Dir.-Gen. The State Inst. for Tech. Research (Tech. Research Centre of Finland since 72) 70-; mem. American Nuclear Soc., European Physical Soc., RILEM: Perm. Cttee., Acad. of Technical Sciences, Finnish Acad. of Sciences, Nordisk Institut för Teoretisk Atomfysik (NORDITA) and several Finnish socs.; Hon. Prize of YDIN Power Asscn.
Leisure interest: music.
Publs. about 100 articles.
Office: Vuorimiehentie 5, 02150 Espoo 15; Home: Menninkäisentie 6L, Tapiola, Finland.
Telephone: 648931 (Office); 461437 (Home).

Javits, Jacob Koppel, LL.B.; American lawyer and politician; b. 18 May 1904, New York; s. of Morris Javits and Ida Littman; m. 1st Marjorie Ringling 1936, 2nd Marion Ann Borris 1947; one s. two d.; ed. New York Univ. Law School.
Admitted to the American Bar 27; Asst. to the Chief of Chemical Warfare Service 39-42; Asst. to the Chief of Operations, Chemical Warfare Service, Europe 43, Pacific 44; resumed law practice 45; elected to 80th Congress from N.Y. 46; re-elected 48, 50, 52; mem. of Cttee. on Foreign Affairs and Chair. Sub-Cttee. on Foreign Econ. Policy; Attorney-Gen. of N.Y. 54-56; Senator from N.Y. 57-; mem. Cttee. Foreign Relations and Ranking Minority, Labor and Public Welfare, Joint Econ. Cttee., Govt. Operations Cttee., Small Business Cttee.; partner in Javits, Trubin, Sillocks, Edelman and Purcell 58-71; U.S. Del. to UN Gen. Assembly 70; Chair. North Atlantic Assembly Cttee. of Nine 71-73; mem. Nat. Comm. on Marijuana and Drug Abuse 71-73; Legion of Merit and Army Commendation Ribbon; Republican.
Leisure interests: tennis, squash, swimming.
Publs. *A Proposal to Amend the Anti-Trust Laws* 39, *A Liberal Political Philosophy for the Republican Party* 46, *Discrimination, U.S.A.* 60, *Order of Battle, A Republican's Call to Reason* 64, *Who Makes War* 73.
110 East 45th Street, New York, N.Y. 10017, U.S.A.

Jawara, Hon. Sir Dawda (Kairaba), Kt., M.R.C.V.S., D.T.V.M.; Gambian politician; b. 16 May 1924, Barajally; s. of Almamy and Mama Jawara.
Former Principal Veterinary Officer, Gambian Civil Service; entered politics 60; Minister of Educ. 60-61; Premier 62-65; Prime Minister 65-70; Pres. of Repub. of The Gambia April 70-; Hon. G.C.M.G. 74.
Office of the President, Banjul, The Gambia.

Jaworski, Leon, LL.M.; American lawyer; b. Waco, Tex.; ed. Baylor and George Washington Univs.
Trial Judge Advocate in major World War II mil. trials in U.S.A., later Chief of War Crimes Trials Section of U.S. Army, Europe; Senior Partner Fulbright and Jaworski, law firm; Special Asst., U.S. Attorney-Gen. 62-65; Special Counsel, Attorney-Gen. of Texas 63-65, 72-73; Presidential Adviser 64-69; mem. Nat. Citizens Cttee. for Community Relations, President's Comm. on Law Enforcement and Admin. of Justice 65-67, Perm. Court of Arbitration, The Hague 65-69; fmr. Dir., Chair. Exec. Cttee. Bank of the Southwest, Houston; Special Prosecutor, Watergate Special Prosecution Force Nov. 73-Oct. 74; Pres. American Bar Asscn. 71-72; Fellow American Bar Foundation; Hon. mem. Canadian Bar Asscn.; Official many civic, educ. and charitable orgs.; Dr. h.c. (Baylor, Suffolk and Washburn Univs.); Legion of Merit; American Bar Asscn. Medal 75.
Publs. *After Fifteen Years* 61, and many articles in law journals.
Fulbright and Jaworski, 8th Floor, Bank of Southwest Building, Houston, Texas 77002, U.S.A.

Jay, Rt. Hon. Douglas Patrick Thomas, P.C., M.P.; British journalist and politician; b. 23 March 1907, Woolwich; s. of Edward Aubrey Hastings Jay and Isobel Violet Jay; m. 1st Margaret Christian Garnett 1933 (divorced 1972), two s. (Peter Jay, q.v.) two d.; m. 2nd Mary Lavina Thomas 1972; ed. Winchester Coll. and New Coll. Oxford.
Member staff *The Times* 29-33, *Economist* 33-37; City Editor *Daily Herald* 37-41; Fellow All Souls Coll. Oxford 30-37, 68-; Ministry of Supply 41-43; Principal Asst. Sec. Board of Trade 43; Personal Asst. to Prime Minister 45-46; M.P. 46-; Econ. Sec. to Treasury 47-50; Financial Sec. to the Treasury 50-51; Pres. of Board of Trade 64-67; Dir. Courtaulds 67-70, Trades Union Unit Trust 67, Chair. London Motorway Action Group 68-; Chair. Common Market Safeguards Campaign 70-; Labour.
Publs. *The Socialist Case* 37, *Who is to Pay for the War and the Peace?* 41, *Socialism in the New Society* 62, *After the Common Market* 68.
House of Commons, London, S.W.1, England.

Jay, Peter, M.A.; British economic journalist; b. 7 Feb. 1937; s. of Rt. Hon. Douglas Patrick Thomas Jay (q.v.); m. Margaret Ann, d. of Rt. Hon. James Callaghan (q.v.), 1961; one s. two d.; ed. Winchester Coll. and Christ Church, Oxford.
Midshipman and Sub-Lieut., R.N.V.R. 56-57; Asst. Principal, H.M. Treasury 61-64, Private Sec. to Joint Perm. Sec. 64, Principal 64-67; Econs. Editor *The Times* 67-, Assoc. Editor *Times Business News* 69-; Presenter, *Weekend World*, ITV 72-, *The Jay Interview* 75-; Political Broadcaster of Year 73; Royal TV Soc.'s Male Personality of Year (Pye Award) 74; Shell Int. TV Award 74; Wingate Memorial Lecture 75.
39 Castlebar Road, London, W5 2DJ, England; and Elm Bank, Glandore, West Co. Cork, Ireland.
Telephone: 01-998-3570 (London); Leap 55 (Ireland).

Jayakumar, Shunmugam, LL.B.; Singapore diplomatist; b. 12 Aug. 1939, Singapore; m. Dr. Lalitha Rajaham 1969; two s. one d.; ed. Univ. of Singapore and Yale Univ.
Dean, Law Faculty, Univ. of Singapore 64-, Assoc. Prof. of Law; Perm. Rep. of Singapore to UN 71-74; mem. Singapore del. to UN Gen. Assemblies 70, 71, 72 to Human Environment Conf., Stockholm 72, to 3rd UN Law of Sea Conf. 74.
Publs. *Constitutional Law Cases from Malaysia and Singapore* 71, *Public International Law Cases from Malaysia and Singapore*, and articles in journals.
Faculty of Law, University of Singapore, Singapore.

Jayawardena, M. D. H., DIP.ECON., BARR.-AT-LAW; Ceylonese lawyer and politician; b. 29 March 1915; ed. Trinity Coll., Kandy and Ceylon Univ. Coll., Colombo.
Advocate, Colombo and Avissawella 41; called to the Bar, Lincoln's Inn, London 49; mem. House of Reps., Ceylon 52-56, 65; Parl. Sec. to Minister of Finance 52-54; Minister of Finance 54-56; Joint Gen. Sec. United Nat. Party 58-; Minister of Health 65-June 70; fmr. Pres. Buddhist Theosophical Soc.; helped to form many cos. including Mercantile Credit Ltd., Ceylon Bulbs and Electricals Ltd. and Mahajana Credit Ltd.
House of Representatives, Colombo, Sri Lanka.

Jayawardene, Junius Richard; Ceylonese lawyer and politician; b. 17 Sept. 1906, Colombo; s. of Justice E. W. and A. H. (Wijewardene) Jayawardene; m. Elina B. Rupesinghe 1935; one s.; ed. Royal Coll., Univ. Coll., and Law Coll., Colombo.
Mem. Colombo Municipal Council 41; mem. State Council 43; mem. House of Representatives 47-; Minister of Finance 47-53; Hon. Sec. Ceylon Nat. Congress 40-47; Hon. Treasurer United Nat. Party 47-48 and Vice-Pres. 53; Leader of the House of Representatives and Minister of Agriculture and Food 53-56; Minister of Finance,

Information, Broadcasting, Local Govt. and Housing Mar. 60-July 60; Deputy Leader of Opposition July 60-65; Minister of State, and Parl. Sec. to Minister of Defence, External Affairs and Planning 65-70; Leader of Opposition 70-; Sec. United Nat. Party 72, Leader 73-June 75, July 75-; del. to numerous confs.
Publs. *Some Sermons of the Buddha, Buddhist Essays, In Council* (speeches), *Buddhism and Marxism, Selected Speeches.*
66 Ward Place, Colombo 7, Sri Lanka.
Telephone: Colombo 95028 and 92332.

Jayawickrema, Major Montague; Ceylonese politician; ed. Richmond Coll., Galle.
Commissioned in Ceylon Light Infantry 34, rose to rank of Major, commanded Colombo Airport Defences during Second World War; M.P. 48-56, 60-; fmr. Parl. Sec. to Minister of Labour and to Minister of Defence and External Affairs; fmr. Minister of Transport and Works; Minister of Public Works, Posts and Telecommunications 65-June 70; Leader of numerous Dels. to Geneva and Rome.
Leisure interests: polo, tennis, golf.
House of Representatives, Colombo, Sri Lanka.

Jean Benoît Guillaume Marie Robert Louis Antoine Adolphe Marc d'Aviano, H.R.H. Grand Duke of Luxembourg, Prince of Nassau, Prince of Bourbon-Parma; b. 5 Jan. 1921, Colmar Berg.
Married Princess Josephine-Charlotte of Belgium April 53; three *s.* two *d.*; Lieut.-Rep. of Grand Duchess 61-64; became Grand Duke of Luxembourg on abdication of Grand Duchess Charlotte Nov. 64.
Leisure interests: photography and natural history.
Grand Ducal Palace, Luxembourg.

Jeanmaire, Renée Marcelle (Zizi); French actress, dancer and singer; b. 29 April 1924; *m.* Roland Petit (*q.v.*) 1954.
Student, Paris Opera Ballet 33-40, Dancer 40-44; with Ballets de Monte-Carlo, Ballets Colonel de Basil, Ballets Roland Petit; Dir. (with Roland Petit) Casino de Paris 69-; Chevalier des Arts et des Lettres; leading roles in *Aubade, Piccoli, Carmen, La Croqueuse de Diamants, Rose des Vents, Cyrano de Bergerac, La Dame dans la Lune, La Symphonie Fantastique* 75; films: *Hans Christian Andersen, Anything Goes, Folies Bergères, Charmants Garçons, Black Tights, la Revue, Zizi je t'aime*; musical: *The Girl in Pink Tights* (Broadway); music hall appearances.
69 rue de Lille, Paris 7e, France.

Jeanneney, Jean-Marcel, L. ès. L., D. en D.; French economist and politician; b. 13 Nov. 1910, Paris; *s.* of Jules Jeanneney (fmr. Pres. of the Senate and Minister); *m.* Marie-Laure Monod 1936; seven *c.*; ed. Ecole Libre des Sciences Politiques, Paris.
Prof. of Political Economy, Grenoble Univ. 37-51, Dean of Law Faculty 47-51; Prof. of Social Economics, Paris Univ. 51-56, of Financial Economics 57-59; Dir. du Cabinet of his father, Jules Jeanneney, Minister of State, de Gaulle Provisional Govt. 44-45; mem. Admin. Council, Ecole Nat. d'Admin. 45-58; Dir. Economic Activity Study Service, Fondation Nat. des Sciences Politiques 52-58; Consultant to OEEC 53; mem. Rueff Cttee. 58; Rapporteur and del. to numerous Confs.; Minister of Industry, Debré Cabinet Jan. 59-62; Ambassador to Republic of Algeria 62-63; Chair. French Cttee. on Co-operation with Developing Countries 63; mem. and French Rep. to UN Econ. and Social Council 64-66; Prof. Political Econ., Paris Univ. 63; Minister of Social Affairs 66-May 68; Deputy June 68; Minister of State July 68-June 69, Prof. Political Econ., Paris Univ. 70.
Publs. *Essai sur les mouvements des prix en France depuis la stabilisation monétaire (1927-1935)* 36, *Economie et Droit de l'Electricité* (with C. A. Colliard) 50,

Les Commerces de détail en Europe occidentale 54, *Forces et Faiblesses de l'Economie française 1945-1956* 56, *Textes de droit économique et social français 1789-1957* (with Perrot), *Tableaux statistiques relatifs à l'économie française et l'économie mondiale* 57, *Documents économiques* (2 Vols.) 58, *Economie Politique* 59, *Essai de Comptabilité interrégionale française pour 1954,* 69, *Régions et Sénat* 69, *A Mes Amis Gaullistes* 73; seven published courses of lectures on political, social and financial economy 52-58.
102 rue d'Assas, Paris 6e and Rioz 70190, France.
Telephone: 326-39-46 (Paris) and 84-74-22-68 (Rioz).

Jędrychowski, Stefan, D.IUR.; Polish politician and economist; b. 19 May 1910, Warsaw; ed. Wilno Univ.
Active in progressive youth movement; imprisoned for political reasons 37; one of the organizers of the Polish "Kosciuszko" Division in the U.S.S.R. during the Second World War; Head Dept. of Information and Propaganda, Nat. Liberation Cttee. 44; later successively Rep. to U.S.S.R. and to France 44-45; Minister of Marine and Foreign Trade 45-47; Deputy Chair. State Economic Planning Cttee. 49-51; Vice-Premier 51-56; Chair. Planning Comm. at the Council of Ministers 57-68; mem. Seym (Parliament) 47-72; mem. Polish Workers' Party 44-48, Polish United Workers' Party 48-, mem. Political Bureau, Polish United Workers' Party 56-71; Minister of Foreign Affairs Dec. 68-71; Minister of Finance 71-74; Amb. to Hungary Jan. 75-; Order of Banner of Labour First Class, Order of Builders of People's Poland and other decorations.
Publs. *Zagadnienia terytorialnych planów finansowych w ZSRR* (Problems of territorial financial plans in U.S.S.R.), and many articles.
Polish Embassy, Gorkij fasor 16, Budapest, Hungary.

Jeffreys, Sir Harold, Kt., M.A., D.SC., F.R.S.; British astronomer; b. 22 April 1891, County Durham; *s.* of R. H. Jeffreys; *m.* Bertha Swirles 1940; ed. Rutherford Coll., Newcastle, Armstrong Coll., Newcastle, and St. John's Coll., Cambridge.
Lecturer in Mathematics, Cambridge Univ. 23-31, Reader in Geophysics 31-46, Prof. of Astronomy 46-58; Pres. Royal Astronomical Society 55-57; Pres. Int. Seismological Asscn. 57-60; Fellow St. John's Coll. Cambridge 14-; Copley and Royal Medals of the Royal Soc., Gold Medal, Royal Astronomical Soc., Vetlesen Prize 62, Guy Medal, Royal Statistical Soc., Wollaston and Murchison Medals, Geological Soc.
Leisure interests: botany, music.
Publs. *The Earth, Method of Mathematical Physics* (with Lady Jeffreys), *Scientific Inference, Theory of Probability, Asymptotic Approximations, Collected Papers.*
160 Huntingdon Road, Cambridge CB3 0LB, England.
Telephone: Cambridge (0223) 56153.

Jellicoe, 2nd Earl, (cr. 25); **George Patrick John Rushworth Jellicoe,** P.C., D.S.O., M.C.; British diplomatist and politician; b. 4 April 1918; *s.* of 1st Earl Jellicoe (Admiral of the Fleet); *m.* 1st Patricia O'Kane 1944, 2nd Philippa Ann Bridge 1966; three *s.* three *d.*; ed. Winchester and Trinity Coll., Cambridge.
Military Service 39-45; joined Foreign Office 47; First Sec. Washington, Brussels, Baghdad; Dep. Sec.-Gen. Baghdad Pact; Jt. Parl. Sec., Ministry of Housing and Local Govt. 61-62; Minister of State, Home Office 62-Oct. 63; First Lord of Admiralty Oct. 63-April 64; Minister of Defence for the Royal Navy 64; Deputy Leader of the Opposition, House of Lords 67-70; Lord Privy Seal and Leader of House of Lords 70-73; mem. Board S. G. Warburg 66-70, 73-; Dir. Smiths Industries, Tate & Lyle, Morgan Crucible, Sotheby's (Holdings); Croix de Guerre, Légion d'Honneur, Greek Mil. Cross.
Leisure interests: skiing and travel.
Tidcombe Manor, Tidcombe, Nr. Marlborough, Wilts., and 97 Onslow Square, London, S.W.7, England.
Telephone: 01-584-1551.

Jen Jung; Chinese party official.
Member Chinese People's Volunteers Korean Truce Comm., N. Korea 60; Deputy Political Commissar Tibet Mil. Region, People's Liberation Army 65, First Political Commissar 71-; Vice-Chair. Tibet Revolutionary Cttee. 68, Chair. 71; First Sec. CCP Tibet 71; Alt. mem. 10th Cen. Cttee. of CCP 73.
People's Republic of China.

Jencks, William Platt, M.D.; American biochemist; b. 15 Aug. 1927, Bar Harbor, Me.; s. of Gardner Jencks and Elinor Melcher Cheetham; m. Miriam Ehrlich Jencks 1950; one s. one d.; ed. Harvard Coll. and Harvard Medical School.
Intern, Peter Bent Brigham Hosp., Boston, Mass. 51-52; mem. staff, Dept. of Pharmacology, Army Medical Service Graduate School 53-54, Chief, Dept. of Pharmacology 54-55; Life Insurance Medical Research Fund Postdoctoral Fellow, Mass. Gen. Hosp. 55-56; U.S. Public Health Service Postdoctoral Fellow, Dept. of Chem., Harvard 56-57; Asst. Prof. of Biochem., Brandeis Univ. 57-60, Assoc. Prof. of Biochem. 60-63, Prof. of Biochem. 63-; mem. Nat. Acad. of Sciences; American Chem. Soc. Award in Pure Chem. 62.
Leisure interest: music.
Publs. *Catalysis in Chemistry and Enzymology* 69 and over 150 articles in journals.
Brandeis University, Graduate Department of Biochemistry, Waltham, Mass. 02154; Home: 11 Revere Street, Lexington, Mass. 02173, U.S.A.
Telephone: 617-647-2726 (Office); 617-862-8875 (Home).

Jenkin, Rt. Hon. (Charles) Patrick Fleeming, P.C.; British lawyer and politician; b. 7 Sept. 1926, Edinburgh; s. of late C. O. F. Jenkin and Margaret E. Jenkin (née Sillar); m. Alison Monica Graham 1952; two s. two d.; ed. Clifton Coll., Bristol, Jesus Coll., Cambridge.
Called to the Bar, Middle Temple 52; Adviser Distillers Co. Ltd. 57-70; Hornsey Borough Council 60-63; mem. Parl. for Wanstead and Woodford 64-; Opposition Spokesman on Finance, Econs. and Trade 65-66, 67-70; Financial Sec. to Treasury 70-72, Chief Sec. 72-74; Minister for Energy Jan.-March 74; Non-Exec. Dir. Tilbury Contracting Group Ltd. 74, Royal Worcs. Co. Ltd. 75; Dir. Continental and Industrial Trust Ltd. 75; Conservative.
Leisure interests: music, gardening, sailing.
House of Commons, London, S.W.1; Home: 9 Hurst Avenue, Highgate, London, N.6, England.
Telephone: 01-219-5147 (Office); 01-340-5538 (Home).

Jenkins, Alfred le Sesne, A.B., M.ED.; American foreign service officer; b. 14 Sept. 1916, Manchester, Ga.; s. of Charles Rush Jenkins and Beulah Hall; m. Martha Elisabeth Lippiatt 1945; one s. one d.; ed. Savannah High School, Emory Univ., Duke Univ., Univ. of Chicago, Chinese languages area.
Superintendent of schools, Naylor, Ga. 40-41; U.S. Army Mil. Intelligence, Pentagon 1st Lieut. 41-45; entered Foreign Service 46, served in Peking, Tientsin, Hong Kong, Taipei; Officer in Charge, Chinese Political Affairs, Dept. State 52-55; Deputy Chief of Mission, Jidda 55-57; Nat. War Coll. 58; Deputy Dir. South-east Asian Affairs 59; Far East Planning Adviser 59-61; Deputy Chief of Mission, Stockholm 61-65; Senior Insp. 66; Senior Staff Nat. Security Council 66-69; Dir. Office Asian Communist Affairs 70-73; Deputy Chief U.S. Liaison Office, Peking 73-; Superior Honour Award, Dept. of State 72; LL.D. (Emory Univ.) 73.
Leisure interests: music, philosophy, mountain house.
Rosemont Plaza 714, Bryn Mawr, Pa. 19010.

Jenkins, (David) Clive; British trade unionist; b. 2 May 1926; ed. Port Talbot Central Boys' School, Port Talbot County School and Swansea Tech. Coll.
Employed in metallurgical test house 40; mem. Port Talbot Co-operative Soc. Educ. Cttee. 45; Branch Sec. and Area Treasurer, Asscn. of Scientific Workers 46; Asst. Midlands Div. Officer, Asscn. of Supervisory Staffs, Execs. and Technicians (ASSET) 47, Transport Industrial Officer 49, Nat. Officer 54, Gen. Sec. ASSET 61-68; Joint Gen. Sec. Asscn. of Scientific, Technical and Managerial Staffs 68-70, Gen. Sec. 70-; Metropolitan Borough Councillor 54-60; Chair. Nat. Joint Council for Civil Air Transport 67-68; Editor *Trade Union Affairs* 61-63; mem. Gen. Council of Trades Union Congress 74-; mem. Nat. Research Devt. Corpn. 74-.
Publs. *Power at the Top* 59, *Power Behind the Screen* 61, *British Trade Unions Today* (with J. E. Mortimer) 65, *The Kind of Laws the Unions Ought to Want* (with J. E. Mortimer) 68; pamphlets and essays.
Office: 10/26A Jamestown Road, Camden Town, London, NW1 7DT, England.
Telephone: 01-267-4422.

Jenkins, Elizabeth; British writer; ed. Newnham Coll. Cambridge.
Publs. *Lady Caroline Lamb: a Biography* 32, *Portrait of an Actor* 33, *Harriet* (Femina Vie Heureuse Prize) 34, *The Phoenix Nest* 36, *Jane Austen—a Biography* 38, *Robert and Helen* 44, *Young Enthusiasts* 46, *Henry Fielding*, English Novelists Series 47, *Six Criminal Women* 49, *The Tortoise and the Hare* 54, *Ten Fascinating Women* 55, *Elizabeth the Great* 58, *Elizabeth and Leicester* 61, *Brightness* 63, *Honey* 68, *Dr. Gully* 72.
8 Downshire Hill, London, N.W.3, England.

Jenkins, Hugh Gater, M.P.; British politician; b. 27 July 1908; m. Marie Crosbie 1936; ed. Enfield Grammar School.
Prudential Assurance Co. 30-40; wartime service in Royal Observer Corps and R.A.F.; Dir. English Programmes, Rangoon Radio; Greater London Organizer, Nat. Union of Bank Employees, later research and publicity officer, Editor *The Bank Officer*; Asst. Sec. British Actors' Equity Asscn. 50, Asst. Gen. Sec. 57-64; mem. Parl. for Putney 64-; Opposition Spokesman on the Arts 73-74, Parl. Under-Sec. of State, Dept. of Educ. and Science, Minister responsible for the Arts 74-76; fmr. Chair. Theatres Advisory Council, Standing Advisory Cttee. on Local Authorities and the Theatre; mem. Arts Council 68-71, Drama Panel 72-74.
Publs. articles on politics, the arts, foreign affairs.
House of Commons, Westminster, London, S.W.1., England.

Jenkins, Rt. Hon. Roy Harris, P.C., M.P.; British politician and writer; b. 11 Nov. 1920; s. of Arthur Jenkins, M.P.; m. Jennifer Morris 1945; two s. one d.; ed. Abersychan Grammar School and Balliol Coll., Oxford.
Royal Artillery 39-46; mem. Staff of Industrial and Commercial Finance Corpn. 46-48; Labour M.P. 48-; Parliamentary Private Sec. to Sec. of State for Commonwealth Relations 49-50; Gov. British Film Inst. 55-58; mem. Cttee. of Management, Soc. of Authors 56-60; Chair. Fabian Soc. 57-58; mem. Council, Britain in Europe; Dep. Chair. Common Market Campaign; Dir. of Financial Operations, John Lewis Partnership Ltd. 63-64; Minister of Aviation 64-65; Sec. of State for Home Dept. 65-67, 74-; Chancellor of the Exchequer 67-70; Deputy Leader of Labour Party 70-72; Hon. Foreign mem. American Acad. of Arts and Science 73; Hon. Fellow Berkeley Coll., Yale; Hon. LL.D. Leeds 71, Harvard 72, Pennsylvania 73, Dundee 73; Hon. D.Litt. Glasgow 72; Hon. D.C.L. Oxford 73; Charlemagne Prize 72, Robert Schumann Prize 72.
Publs. *Purpose and Policy* (Editor) 47, *Mr. Attlee: An Interim Biography* 48, *New Fabian Essays* (contributor) 52, *Pursuit of Progress* 53, *Mr. Balfour's Poodle* 54, *Sir Charles Dilke: A Victorian Tragedy* 58, *The Labour Case* 59, *Asquith* 64, *Essays and Speeches* 67, *Afternoon*

on the Potomac 72, *What Matters Now* 73, *Nine Men of Power* 74.
Home Office, Whitehall, London, SW1A 2AP; and House of Commons, London, S.W.1, England.

Jenkins, William Maxwell, A.B., M.B.A.; American banker; b. 19 April 1919, Sultan, Washington; s. of Warren Maxwell Jenkins and Louise Black Jenkins; m. Elisabeth Taber 1946; three s. four d.; ed. Everett High School, Univ. of Washington and Harvard Graduate School of Business Admin.
Assistant cashier, Asst. Vice-Pres., Asst. Manager of Metropolitan Branch (Seattle), Seattle-First Nat. Bank 45-53; First Nat. Bank of Everett 53-61, Pres. 57-61; Chair. Everett Trust and Savings Bank 56-61; Exec. Vice-Pres. and Man., Everett Div., Seattle-First Nat. Bank 61-62; Chair. of Board and Chief Exec. Officer Seattle-First Nat. Bank 62-; Chair. of Board and Chief Exec. Officer, Seafirst Corpn. 74-; Dir. other companies.
Leisure interests: tennis, golf, skiing, boating and squash.
Seattle-First National Bank, Box 3586, Seattle, Washington 98124, U.S.A.
Telephone: 583-3183 (Office); 842-3368 (Home).

Jenks, Downing Bland; American railroad executive; b. 16 Aug. 1915, Portland, Oregon; s. of Charles and Della Downing Jenks; m. Louise Sweeney 1940; one s. one d.; ed. St. Paul Acad. and Yale Univ.
Assistant on Engineer Corps., Pennsylvania Railroad 37-38; Trainmaster, Div. Engineer, Roadmaster, Great Northern Railway 38-47, Div. Supt. 47; Vice-Pres. and Gen. Man., Chicago & Eastern Illinois Railroad 48, now Chair. of Board; Asst. Vice-Pres. Rock Island Lines 50, Vice-Pres. operation 51, Exec. Vice-Pres. 53, Pres. 56-60; Pres. Missouri Pacific Railroad Co. 61-72, Chair., Chief Exec. Officer 72-74, Chair. of Board 74-; Chair. of Board of Texas and Pacific Railroad and subsidiaries 68-; Dir. Chicago and Eastern Illinois Railroad 67-, First Nat. Bank in St. Louis, Bankers Life Co., Insco Corpn., River Corpn., Mississippi River Transmission Corpn.; U.S. Army service, North Africa, Italy, France, Germany, Lieut.-Col. Mil. Railway Service 42-45; Bronze Star Medal.
Leisure interests: hunting and fishing.
Missouri Pacific Building, St. Louis, Mo. 63103; and 8 Greenbriar, St. Louis, Mo. 63124, U.S.A.

Jenny, Mgr. Henri Martin; French ecclesiastic; b. 11 July 1904, Tourcoing; ed. Grand séminaire de Cambrai and Pontificia Universitas Gregoriana, Rome.
Professor of Holy Scripture, Grand Séminaire, Cambrai 29-49; Leading Curate, Saint-Géry Cambrai 50-53; Arch-Priest Douai 53-59; Auxiliary Bishop of Cambrai 59-65, Co-adjutor Bishop 65-66, Archbishop of Cambrai 66-; mem. Preparatory Comm. and mem. Comm. on Liturgy, Ecumenical Council.
Publs. *Les dimanches de l'année chrétienne, Le Mystère pascal dans l'année liturgique, La Messe, Les Actes des apôtres.*
Office of the Archbishop, B.P. 134, Cambrai 59403; and 30 rue de Noyon, Cambrai 59403, France.
Telephone: 81-34-96.

Jens, Walter, D.PHIL.; German philologist, critic and novelist; b. 8 March 1923, Hamburg; s. of Walter and Anna (Martens) Jens; m. Inge Puttfarcken 1951; two s.; ed. Hamburg and Freiburg im Breisgau Univs.
Assistant, Hamburg and Tübingen Univs. 46-50; Docent, Tübingen Univ. 50-56, Prof. of Classical Philology and Rhetoric 56-67, Dir. of Inst. für Allgemeine Rhetorik, Tübingen Univ. 67-; mem. German PEN, Berliner Akademie der Künste, Deutsche Akademie für Sprache und Dichtung; Lessingpreis der Hansestadt Hamburg 68; D.Phil., h.c.
Publs. *Nein—Die Welt der Angeklagten* (novel) 50, *Der Blinde* (novel) 51, *Vergessene Gesichter* (novel) 52, *Der Mann, der nicht alt werden wollte* (novel) 55, *Das*

Testament des Odysseus (novel) 57, *Die Götter sind sterblich* (Diary of a Journey to Greece) 59, *Statt einer Literaturgeschichte* (Essays on Modern Literature) 57, *Moderne Literatur—moderne Wirklichkeit* (essay) 58, *Die Stichomythie in der frühen griechischen Tragödie* 55, *Hofmannsthal und die Griechen* 55, *Deutsche Literatur der Gegenwart* 61, *Zueignungen* 62, *Herr Meister* (Dialogue on a Novel) 63, *Euripides-Büchner* 64, *Von deutscher Rede* 69, *Die Verschwörung* (TV play) 70, *Am Anfang der Stall, am Ende der Galgen* 73, *Fernsehen-Themen und Tabus* 73, *Der tödliche Schlag* (TV play) 74, *Der Prozess Judas* (novel) 75, *Der Ausbruch* (libretto) 75.
Sonnenstrasse 5, 74 Tübingen, Federal Republic of Germany.

Jensen, Arthur Robert, M.A., PH.D.; American educational psychologist; b. 24 Aug. 1923, San Diego; s. of Arthur Alfred Jensen and Linda Schachtmayer; m. Barbara Jane Delarme 1960; one d.; ed. Calif. (Berkeley), Columbia and London Univs.
Assistant in Medical Psychology, Univ. of Maryland 55-56; Research Fellow, Inst. of Psychiatry, London Univ. 56-58; Asst. Prof. to Prof. of Educ. Psychology, Univ. of Calif., Berkeley 58-, Research Psychologist, Inst. of Human Learning 62-; Guggenheim Fellow 64-65; Fellow, Center for Advanced Study in the Behavioral Sciences 66-67.
Publs. *Genetics and Education* 72, *Educability and Group Differences* 73, *Educational Differences* 73.
Institute of Human Learning, University of California, Berkeley, Calif. 94720; Home: 30 Canyon View Drive, Orinda, Calif. 94563, U.S.A.
Telephone: (415) 642-3909 (Office).

Jensen, Egon; Danish politician; b. 14 March 1922, Slagelse; s. of Albert Jensen and Carla Larsen; m. Henny Jørgensen 1946; three s.
Member Slagelse City Council 50-71, Deputy Mayor 66-70, Deputy Mayor of County Council 70-71; mem. Parl. 60-; Minister of Home Affairs 71-73, of the Interior 75-; Social Democrat.
Vestre Finggade 53, 4200 Slagelse, Denmark.
Telephone: 03-52-2184.

Jensen, Erling, LL.B.; Danish politician; b. 1 Nov. 1919, Frederiksberg; s. of Franciskus and Mary Jensen; m. Ria Jorgensen 1951; two s.
Clerk, later Man. Clerk, Credit Asscn. of Estate Owners 46-57; Sec.-Gen. Union of Urban Co-operative Socs. 57-60; Dir. of Labour, Folk High Schools 60-71; Minister for Commerce 71-73; mem. Folketing 73-; Minister of Trade Feb. 75-; Social Democrat.
Nørrevej 11, DK 3070 Snekkersten, Denmark.
Telephone: 03-221655.

Jensen, Kai Arne, DR. PHIL.; Danish chemist; b. 27 March 1908, Copenhagen; m. Ida Reichardt 1932; three d.; ed. Københavns Universitet.
Chemical Laboratory, Univ. of Copenhagen 33-, Assoc. Prof. of Chemistry 43-50, Prof. 50-, Head of Chemical Laboratory II; Chair. Comm. on Nomenclature of Inorganic Chemistry of Int. Union of Pure and Applied Chemistry (IUPAC) 59-72; mem. Royal Danish Acad. of Sciences and Letters, Danish Acad. of Technical Sciences, Royal Physiographical Soc. (Lund, Sweden); Knight Order of Dannebrog; Julius Thomsen Gold Medal.
Leisure interests: recreational reading.
Chemical Laboratory II of the University of Copenhagen, The H. C. Ørsted Institute, Universitetsparken 5, 2100 Copenhagen Ø; Home: Bøgehøj 64, 2900 Hellerup, Denmark.
Telephone: (01) 35-31-33 (Office); (01) 67-93-75 (Home).

Jentschke, Willibald Karl, PH.D.; Austrian physicist; b. 6 Dec. 1911, Vienna; m.; three c.; ed. Univ. of Vienna.
Docent, Univ. of Vienna 42; Research Asst. Prof.,

Univ. of Illinois, Urbana 48, Assoc. Prof. 55, Prof. 56; Prof. Univ. of Hamburg 56-70, 76-; mem. Arbeitskreis Physik (Advisory Cttee. to German Nuclear Energy Comm.) 57; Dir. DESY Lab., Hamburg 59-70; del. of Fed. Germany to CERN Council and mem. Scientific Policy Cttee. 64-67; Dir.-Gen. CERN 71-75; mem. Akad. der Wissenschaft und der Literatur, Mainz, Österreichische Akad. der Wissenschaft, Deutsches Physikalisches Gesellschaft, Soc. Italiana di Fisica; Fellow, American Physical Soc., European Physical Soc.
Institut für Experimental Physik, Universität Hamburg, Luruper Chaussee 149, 2 Hamburg 50, Federal Republic of Germany.

Jephcott, Sir Harry, Bt., M.SC., F.R.I.C., F.P.S.; British company director; b. 15 Jan. 1891, Redditch; s. of late John Josiah Jephcott; m. Doris Gregory 1919; two s.; ed. King Edward's Grammar School, Birmingham, and West Ham Technical Coll., London.
Called to Bar (Middle Temple) 25; Chair. Glaxo Laboratories Ltd. 45-63; Chair. Council of D.S.I.R. 56-61; Pres. Royal Inst of Chemistry 53-55; Chair. Asscn. of British Chemical Manufacturers 47-52, President 52-55; mem. Advisory Council Scientific Policy 53-56; Chairman Committee on Detergents 53-55; Chairman School of Pharmacy, Univ. of London 48-69; Gov. London School of Economics 52-68; Gov. N. London Collegiate School 57; Hon. D.Sc. (Birmingham); Hon. Fellow Royal Soc. Medicine 61.
Leisure interest: gardening.
Weetwood, 1 Cheney Street, Pinner, Middlesex, England.
Telephone: 01-866-0305.

Jepson, Selwyn; British novelist and screen writer; b. 1899; ed. St. Paul's School.
Served First and Second World Wars (Major; Mil. Intelligence and S.O.E.).
Leisure interests: building, music, Sunday painting.
Publs. Novels: *The Qualified Adventurer* 21, *The King's Red-Haired Girl* 23, *Rogues and Diamonds* 25, *The Death Gong* 28, *I Met Murder* 30, *Rabbit's Paw* 32, *Heads or Tails* (with Michael Joseph) 33, *Keep Murder Quiet* 40, *Man Running* 48, *The Golden Dart* 49, *The Hungry Spider* 50, *Man Dead* 51, *The Black Italian* 54, *The Assassin* 56, *Noise in the Night* 57, *The Laughing Fish* 60, *Fear in the Wind* 63, *The Third Possibility* 65, *The Angry Millionaire* 69, *Letter to a Dead Girl* 71, *The Interrogators* 73.
Play: *Dark Horizon* (with Lesley Storm); screen plays: *Going Gay, For the Love of You* 32, *Irresistible Marmaduke, Monday at Ten* 33, *The Love Nest, The Riverside Murders* 34, *White Lilac, Hyde Park Corner* 35, *The Scarab Murder, Toilers of the Sea* (adapted and directed) 36, *Sailing Along* 37, *Carnet de Bal, Double Crime on the Maginot Line* 38, *Stage Fright (Man Running)* 50; television plays incl.: *Thought to Kill, Dialogue for Two Faces* 53, *Face of the Law, The Last Moment* 54, *The Interloper* 55; radio plays: *The Hungry Spider, The Bath that Sang* 58, *Noise in the Night* 59, *Small Brother, Uncle Murderer, Art for Art's Sake, Death of a Guardian* 60, *Greymail* 62, *Dark Corners* 63.
The Far House, Liss, Hants, England.

Jerome, James Alexander, B.A.; Canadian politician; b. 4 March 1933, Kingston, Ont.; s. of Joseph Leonard Jerome and Phyllis Devlin; m. Barry Karen Hodgins 1958; three s. one d.; ed. St. Michael's Coll., Univ. of Toronto and Osgoode Hall.
Lawyer; Alderman, Sudbury 66-67; mem. Parl. 68-; Parl. Sec. to Pres. of Privy Council; Speaker House of Commons 74-; Liberal.
238 Stewart Drive, Sudbury, Ont., Canada.

Jerusalem, Patriarch of (*see* Benedictos).

Jespersen, Kaj Thomas, M.D.; Danish physician; b. 6 April 1898, Copenhagen; s. of Jens Peter Jespersen;

m. Ingrid Mørch 1924; two d.; ed. Københavns Universitet.
Assistant Supt., Mil. Hospital, Copenhagen 31; Chief Physician, Rigshospitalet, Copenhagen 39-65; Vice-Chair. Soc. of Danish Physicians 38-43; mem. Central Cttee. Danish Medical Asscn. 50-54, Vice-Chair. 52-54; Danish Del. European League against Rheumatism 47-57; Chair. Danish Org. of Physicians of Physical Medicine 38-48, Danish Soc. for Investigation of Rheumatic Diseases 51-53; Hon. mem. Danish Org. of Physicians of Physical Medicine 63; Knight Order of Dannebrog, First Degree; First prize of honour, Dansk Fysiurgisk Selskab 73.
Leisure interests: travelling and gardening.
Publ. *Forholdet mellem Febris rheumatica og rheumatoid artritis* 40 and several articles on rheumatic diseases.
Skovdraget 9, 2880 Bagsværd, Denmark.
Telephone: 02-982022.

Jessen, Borge, DR. PHIL.; Danish mathematician; b. 19 June 1907, Copenhagen; m. Ellen Pedersen 1931; ed. Univ. of Copenhagen.
Docent, Royal Veterinary and Agricultural Coll., Copenhagen 30-35; Prof. Technical Univ. of Denmark, Copenhagen 35-42; Prof. Univ. of Copenhagen 42-; mem. of the Royal Danish Acad. of Sciences and of Acad. of Technical Sciences; Dir. Carlsberg Foundation 50-63, Pres. 55-63.
Dantes Plads 3, 1556 Copenhagen V, Denmark.
Telephone: 01-145844.

Jessup, Philip C., B.A., L.C.D., LITT.D., J.D., LL.D., PH.D.; American international lawyer and professor; b. 5 Jan. 1897, New York; s. of Henry Wynans and Mary Hay Stotesbury Jessup; m. Lois Walcott Kellogg 1921; one s.; ed. Hamilton Coll. and Columbia and Yale Univs.
Served U.S. Army First World War; Lecturer, Asst. Assoc. Prof. Int. Law, Columbia Univ. 25-35, Prof. 35-46, H. Fish Prof. of Int. Law and Diplomacy 46-61; mem. Staff Office of Foreign Relief and Rehabilitation Operations, Dept. of State 43; Asst. Sec.-Gen. UNRRA 43; Asst. Tech. Sec.-Gen. UNO Bretton Woods Conf. 44; Asst. U.S. Delegation San Francisco Conf. 45; Assoc. Dir. Naval School of Military Govt. and Admin. 42-44; U.S. rep. at various sessions of UN Security Council and Gen. Assembly 48-53; apptd. Ambassador-at-Large Mar. 49, resgnd. Jan. 53; Storrs Lecturer, Yale Univ. Law School 56, Cooley Lecturer, Mich. Univ. Law School 58; Blaustein Lecturer, Columbia Univ. 70; Sibley Lecturer, Univ. of Georgia 70; Visiting Prof. Harvard Law School 38-39; Chair. Chile-Norway Perm. Conciliation Comm. 58-; Judge, Int. Court of Justice 61-70; Chair. Austria-Sweden Int. Comm. for Reconciliation and Arbitration 75-; 1st Vice-Pres. Inst. de Droit Int. 73-75; mem. American Acad. Arts and Sciences, American Philosophical Soc., Inst. de Droit Int., Governing Council Int. Inst. for Unification of Private Law 64-67; Hon. Pres. American Soc. of Int. Law 69-73, 76-, American Branch, Int. Law Asscn. 70-73; Hon. mem. Mexican Acad. of Int. Law 65-; mem. Curatorium Hague Acad. of Int. Law 57-68; Senior Research Fellow, Council on Foreign Relations 70-71; several hon. degrees and decorations.
Leisure interest: wild gardening.
Publs. *The Law of Territorial Waters and Maritime Jurisdiction* 27, *American Neutrality and International Police* 28, *The U.S. and the World Court* 29, *International Security* 35, *Neutrality, Its History, Economics and Law:* Vol. I *The Origins* (with Francis Deák) 35, Col. IV *To-day and Tomorrow* 36, *Elihu Root* (2 vols.) 38, *International Problem of Governing Mankind* 47, *A Modern Law of Nations* 48, *Transnational Law* 56, *The Use of International Law* 59, *Controls for Outer Space and the Antarctic Anology* (with Howard J.

Taubenfeld) 59, *The Price of International Justice* 71, *The Birth of Nations* 74.
Norfolk, Connecticut 06058, U.S.A.
Telephone: 203-542-5677.

Jewkes, John, C.B.E., D.SC., M.COM., M.A.; British economist; b. 29 June 1902, Barrow-in-Furness, Lancs.; *s.* of John Jewkes and Fannie (née Cope); *m.* Frances Sylvia Butterworth 1928; one *d.*; ed. Barrow Grammar School and Manchester Univ.
Assistant Sec. Manchester Chamber of Commerce 25-26; Lecturer in Econs., Manchester Univ. 26-29; Rockefeller Foundation Fellow 29-30; Prof. of Social Econs. and Dir. of Econs. Research Section 36-48; Prof. of Econ. Org., Univ. of Oxford 48-69; Dir. Industrial Policy Group 69-74; Dir. Econ. Section, War Cabinet Secr. 41; Dir.-Gen. of Statistics and Programmes, Ministry of Aircraft Production 43; Principal Asst. Sec., Office of Ministry of Reconstruction 44; Visiting Prof. Univ. of Chicago 53-54, Univ. of Princeton 61; Econ. Adviser to Arthur Guinness Ltd. 49-.
Leisure interests: gardening and music.
Publs. (With A. Winterbottom) *An Industrial Survey of Cumberland and Furness, Juvenile Unemployment*; (with E. M. Gray) *Wages and Labour in the Cotton Spinning Industry*; (with Sylvia Jewkes) *The Juvenile Labour Market; The Genesis of the British National Health Service; Value for Money in Medicine*; (with Sawers and Stillerman) *The Sources of Invention; Ordeal by Planning, Public and Private Enterprise, The New Ordeal by Planning.*
Entwood, Boars Hill, Oxford, England.
Telephone: Oxford 735104.

Jezrawi, Taha al; Iraqi politician; b. 1938, Mosul; ed. schools in Mosul and military coll.
Former army officer; mem. Regional Leadership, Arab Baath Socialist Party; Head, Arab Affairs Office, Revolutionary Command Council 69-; Minister of Industry March 70-.
Ministry of Industry, Baghdad, Iraq.

Jha, Chandra Shekhar, O.B.E., M.SC., LL.B., I.C.S.; Indian diplomatist; b. 20 Oct. 1909, Madhubani, Bihar; *s.* of Pandit Shiva Shankar Jha and Ganga Devi; *m.* Lakshmi Mishra 1931; two *s.*; ed. Patna Univ. and London School of Oriental Studies.
Joined Indian Civil Service 33; Asst. Magistrate and Collector, Bihar and Orissa 33-36; Under-Sec. Finance Department, Bihar 36-39, Deputy Commr. 39; Controller and Sec. Supply and Transport Dept., Orissa 43-46; Deputy Sec. Commonwealth Relations Dept. Govt. of India 46-47; Joint Sec. Ministry of External' Affairs 47-50; Chargé d'Affaires, Ankara 50-51; Ambassador to Turkey 51-54; Joint Sec. Ministry of External Affairs 54-57; Indian Del. and Sec.-Gen. Afro-Asian Conf., Bandung 55; Amb. to Japan 57-59; Perm. Rep. to UN 59-62, Chair. UN Cttee. on Contributions 59-62, UN Special Cttee. on Decolonization 62; Chair. Human Rights Comm. 61-62; High Commr. in Canada 62-64; Commonwealth Sec., Ministry of External Affairs 64-65, Foreign Sec. Feb. 65-67; Amb. to France 67-69; mem. Joint Inspection Unit, UN and Specialized Agencies, Geneva 69-.
Leisure interests: golf, bridge.
Palais des Nations, Geneva, Switzerland.
Telephone: 475092.

Jha, Lakshmi Kant, M.B.E., B.A., I.C.S.; Indian civil servant; b. 22 Nov. 1913, Bhagalpur; *m.* Mekhala Acharyya 1941; one *s.* two *d.*; ed. Hindu Univ., Banaras and Trinity Coll., Cambridge.
Under-Secretary, Govt. of Bihar, Local Self Govt. Dept. 41-42; Dep. Sec. Supply Dept., Govt. of India 42-46; Del. to UN Maritime Conf.; Chief Controller of Imports and Exports 47-50; Sec. Ministry of Commerce and Industry 50-56, 57-60; Sec. Ministry of Heavy

Industries 56-57; Chair. G.A.T.T. (General Agreement on Tariffs and Trade) 57-58, UN Cttee. on Int. Commodity Arrangements 59-61; Sec. Ministry of Finance, Dept. of Econ. Affairs 60-64; Dir. Reserve Bank of India and State Bank of India; Alt. Gov. Int. Bank for Reconstruction and Devt. 60-64; Sec. to Prime Minister 64-67; Gov. Reserve Bank of India 67-70; Amb. to U.S.A. 70-April 73; Gov., State of Jammu and Kashmir July 73-; Chair. UN Group of Eminent Persons on Multinational Corpns. 73-74.
Leisure interests: archaeology, sculpture, photography and broadcasting.
Publs. *India's Foreign Trade*, Parts I and II, *Price Policy in a Developing Economy, Economic Development—Ends and Means, The International Monetary Scene and the Human Factor in Economic Development.*
Raj Bhavan, Srinagar (Jammu and Kashmir), India.
Telephone: 3131.

Jiménez de Aréchaga, Eduardo, DR.JUR.; Uruguayan international lawyer; b. 8 June 1918, Montevideo; *s.* of E. Jiménez de Aréchaga and Ester Sienra; *m.* Marta Ferreira 1943; three *s.* two *d.*; ed. School of Law, Univ. of Montevideo.
Professor of International Law, Montevideo Law School 49-69; Under-Sec., Foreign Relations 50-52; Sec. Council of Govt. of Uruguay 52-55; mem. Int. Law Comm. of UN 61-69, Pres. 63; Rapporteur Cttee., Vienna Conf. on Law of Treaties 68-69; Minister of Interior 68; Judge, Int. Court of Justice 70-, Pres. Feb. 76-(79); Book award, Inter-American Bar Asscn. 61.
Leisure interest: farming.
Publs. *Reconocimiento de Gobiernos* 46, *Voting and Handling of Disputes in the Security Council* 51, *Treaty Stipulations in Favour of Third States* 56, *Derecho Constitucional de las Naciones Unidas* 58, *Curso de Derecho Internacional Público* (2 vols.) 59-61.
International Court of Justice, Peace Palace, The Hague, Netherlands; Casilla de Correo 539, Montevideo, Uruguay.
Telephone: Montevideo 501837, Maldonado 81794 (Uruguay).

Jiménez Cantú, Jorge; Mexican medical doctor; b. 27 Oct. 1914, Mexico City; *s.* of Jesús Jiménez Gallardo and Guadalupe Cantú de Jiménez; *m.* Luisa Isabel Campos Hüttich; one *s.*; ed. Escuela de Medicina, Universidad Nacional de México.
Surgeon, Hospital de Jesús; Prof. of Propadeutical Surgery, Escuela Nacional de Medicina 41-57; Prof. of Biology, Instituto México, and Centro Universitario México; Sec. Nat. Campaign for Building of Schools 48-51; Counsellor, Nat. Youth Inst.; Chief of Medical Services, Secr. of Communications and Public Works 52-57; Sec.-Gen. State of Mexico; Asst. Sec. Organizing Cttee., Olympic Games 65; Sec. for Health and Welfare 70-75.
Secretaría de Salubridad y Asistencia, Paseo de la Reforma y Lieja, México, D.F., Mexico.

Jobert, Michel; French politician; b. 11 Sept. 1921, Meknes, Morocco; *m.* Muriel Frances Green; one *s.*; ed. Meknes Lycée, Ecole Libre des Sciences Politiques, Paris and Nat. School of Admin., Paris.
Auditor Court of Accounts 49, now Counsel; attached to Departmental Staff of Sec. of State for Finance 52; Tech. Adviser, Ministry of Labour and Social Security 52-54; attached to the Office of Pierre Mendès-France 54-55 and Feb.-May 56; Principal Private Sec. to the High Commr. for French West Africa 56-59, to M. Lecourt, Minister of State 59-61; Deputy Principal Private Sec. to Prime Minister Georges Pompidou 63-66, Principal Private Sec. 66-68; Sec.-Gen. of the Presidency 69-74; Minister of Foreign Affairs 73-74; founded Movt. for Democrats March 75-; fmr. mem. Board of SOFIRAD (Radio Monte-Carlo), Havas

Agency and French Radio and Television Org.; Chair. Board of Dirs. Nat. Forestry Office 66-; Officer Légion d'Honneur; Croix de Guerre (39-45).
Publ. *Mémoires d'Avenir* 74.
21 quai Alphonse-Le Gallo, 92 Boulogne-sur-Seine, France.

Joboru, Dr. Magda; Hungarian librarian and educationist; b. 1918; *m.* Miklós Ajtai (*q.v.*); ed. High School, Budapest Univ.
Teacher, Mezotur 41-46; Dir. Ilona Zrinyi People's Coll. 46-48; Gen. Sec. Hungarian Democratic Women's Union 48-50; Dep. Minister of Education 50-58, M.P. 47-51; Dir.-Gen., Nat. Library 58-66; Chair. Hungarian Nat. Cttee. on UNESCO 55-66, and mem. Exec. Board 64-72; Vice-Pres. Exec. Board UNESCO 66-68; Amb. and Head of Perm. Del. of Hungary at UNESCO 66-68; Dir.-Gen. Nat. Library, Lecturer at Budapest Univ. (Pedagogy) 68-; Pres. 18th Session of Gen. Conf. of UNESCO 74-76; Kossuth Medal, Order of Labour.
Publs. *Life and School, The Grammar School in the Horthy Period, Education in the Capitalist Countries from 1918 until Now, Education in the Horthy period.*
Országos Széchenyi Könyvtár, Muzeum krt. 14/16, H-1088, Budapest VIII, Hungary.
Telephone: 134-400.

Jochum, Eugen; German conductor; b. 1 Nov. 1902, Babenhausen, Swabia; *m.* Marie Montz 1927; two *d.*; ed. Gymnasium St. Stephan, Augsburg, and Akad. der Tonkunst, Munich.
First Conductor, Kiel Opera House 26-29, Mannheim Nat. Theatre 29-30; Gen. Musical Dir. Duisburg 30-32, Radio Berlin 32-34, Staatsoper and Philharmonic Orchestra, Hamburg 34-49, Bayerischer Rundfunk 49-61; Chief Conductor Concertgebouw Amsterdam 61-63; Guest Conductor all over Europe 26-, U.S.A., Canada and Japan 58-; Regular Conductor Berlin Philharmonic Orchestra; tours with Berlin Philharmonic Orchestra, Concertgebouw, Bayerischer Rundfunk, Detroit Symphony Orchestra, Los Angeles Symphony Orchestra; now Perm. Guest Conductor with Concertgebouw, Amsterdam, West Berlin State Opera and Philharmonic Orchestra, Chicago Opera; Brahms and Bruckner Medals; Record Prizes, Bayerischer Verdienstorden, etc.
Leisure interests: history, architecture, archaeology, swimming, sailing.
Records (Deutsche Grammophon and Philips): include all Beethoven, Brahms, all Bruckner symphonies.
Brunhildenstrasse 2, Munich 19, Federal Republic of Germany.

Jogjakarta, Sultan of (*see* Hamengkubuwono IX).

Johannes, Herman; Indonesian engineer, professor and politician; b. 1913.
High School teacher 40; Lecturer, Medical Faculty, Jakarta Univ. 43; Lecturer, Technical Faculty, Gadjah Mada Univ., Jogjakarta 46, Prof. of Physics 48-, Dean Physics and Mathematics Faculty 49-, Rector 61-66; Minister of Public Works and Power, Repub. of Indonesia Sept. 50-April 51; mem. Exec. Board UNESCO 54-56; mem. Council for Sciences of Indonesia 56-63; mem. Planning Council 58-63; co-ordinator Higher Educ. South Central Java 66-; mem. Supreme Advisory Council 68-.
Publs. *Analysis of the Critical Depth* 39, *Flexure Factors Method* 53, *Industry and the Population Boom* 66, *Nuclear Binding Energies and the Magic Numbers* 67.
3 Sekip, Jogjakarta, Indonesia.

Jóhannesson, Ólafur; Icelandic politician; b. 1 March 1913, Skagafjördur; *m.* Dóra Gudbjartsdóttir; two *d.*; ed. Akureyn Coll. and Univ. of Iceland.
Lawyer and auditor, Fed. of Iceland Co-operative Socs. 44-47; Prof. of Law, Univ. of Iceland 47-71; mem. State Radio Council 46-53; mem. Board of Dirs. Central Bank

of Iceland 57-; mem. Althing 59-; mem. Cen. Cttee. Progressive Party 46-, Vice-Pres. 60-68, Pres. 68-, Parl. Leader 69-71; Prime Minister and Minister of Justice and Ecclesiastical Affairs 71-74; Minister of Justice and Trade Aug. 74-.
Publs. several books, mainly on constitutional law; numerous articles on law in Icelandic and foreign publications.
Ministry of Justice, Arnarhvoll, Reykjavík, Iceland.

Johansson, (Erik) Lennart Valdemar; Swedish industrialist; b. 3 Oct. 1921, Gothenburg; *s.* of Waldemar and Alma Johansson (née Nordh); *m.* Inger Hedberg 1944; two *s.* one *d.*; ed. Technical Coll.
Production Engineer AB Svenska Kullagerfabriken 43, Man. of Mfg. 61, Gen. Man. 66, Deputy Man. Dir. 69, Man. Dir., Chief Exec. Officer 71-, Group Pres. 75-; Dir. Elektriska Svetsningsaktiebolaget 68, Husqvarna AB 68, AB Volvo 72, Swedish Engineering Employers' Asscn. 63, Swedish Employers' Confed. 71; mem. Royal Swedish Acad. of Engineering Sciences 71; Commdr. Royal Order of Vasa.
Leisure interests: sailing, swimming.
AB Svenska Kullagerfabriken, 415 50 Gothenburg; Home: Götabergsgatan 34, 411 34 Gothenburg, Sweden.
Telephone: 031/840000 (Office); 031/812518 (Home).

Johansson, Rune B.; Swedish politician; b. 12 Feb. 1915, Växjö; *s.* of Axel Johansson and Hulda (née Lundkvist); *m.* Gulli Kristiansson 1941; four *s.* one *d.*; ed. Ljungby.
Worked as a baker; held positions in Ljungby Town Council; M.P. 51; Minister of the Interior 57-69; Dir. at Riksbyggen 69-71; Minister of Industry 71-; Social Democratic Labour.
Brunkebergstorg 9, 10012 Stockholm 46, Sweden.

John, Admiral of the Fleet Sir Caspar, G.C.B.; British naval officer; b. 22 March 1903, London; *s.* of late Augustus John, O.M., R.A., and Ida John; *m.* Mary Vanderpump 1944; one *s.* two *d.*; ed. Royal Naval Coll., Dartmouth.
Joined R.N. 16, Captain 41, Rear-Admiral 51, Flag Officer Commanding Third Aircraft Carrier Squadron and Heavy Squadron 51-52, Dep. Controller Aircraft 53-54, Vice-Admiral 54, Flag Officer Air 55-57, Vice-Chief of Naval Staff 57-60, First Sea Lord and Chief of Naval Staff 60-63; Chair. Housing Corpn. 64-68; Chair. Star and Garter Home 67-73; mem. Govt. Security Comm. 64-71.
Leisure interest: forestry.
25 Woodlands Road, London, S.W.13, England.
Telephone: 01-876-5596.

John, David Dilwyn, C.B.E., T.D., D.SC., LL.D.; British museum director; b. 20 Nov. 1901, Llangan, Glam., Wales; *s.* of Thomas and Julia John; *m.* Marjorie Emily Page 1929; one *s.* one *d.*; ed. Univ. Coll. of Wales.
Zoologist, engaged in oceanographical research in Antarctic seas 25; Asst. Keeper, British History (Natural History) 35, Deputy Keeper 48; Dir. Nat. Museum of Wales, Cardiff 48-68; Polar Medal.
Leisure interests: preservation of the countryside and study of coleoptera.
7 Cyncoed Avenue, Cardiff, CF2 6ST, Wales.
Telephone: 752499.

John, DeWitt, B.A., M.A., M.S.; American church director; b. 1 Aug. 1915, Safford, Arizona; *s.* of Frank H. John and Frances DeWitt John; *m.* Morley Marshall 1942; one *s.* one *d.*; ed. Principia Coll., Elsah, Ill., Univ. of Chicago, and Columbia Univ.
Editorial page writer, *St. Petersburg Times* (Florida) 38-39; mem. staff *Christian Science Monitor* 39-49, Editor 64-70; Man. Christian Science Cttees. on Publs. 62-64; U.S. Naval Reserve 42-45; Dir. First Church of Christ, Scientist 70-.

Leisure interests: skiing, classical music.
Publ. *The Christian Science Way of Life* 62.
Christian Science Center, Boston Mass. 02115; Home: Old Concord Road, Lincoln, Mass. 01773, U.S.A.
Telephone: 262-2300 (Office), 259-8390 (Home).

John, Fritz, PH.D.; American mathematician; b. 14 June, 1910, Berlin, Germany; s. of Herman Jacobsohn and Hedwig (Bürgel) Jacobsohn-John; m. Charlotte Woellmer John 1933; two s.; ed. Göttingen and Cambridge Univs.
Assistant and Assoc. Prof., Univ. of Kentucky 35-42; Mathematician, Aberdeen Proving Ground, Maryland 43-45; Assoc. Prof., New York Univ. 46-51, Prof. of Mathematics, Courant Inst. of Mathematical Sciences, New York Univ. 51-; Dir. of Research, Inst. of Numerical Analysis 50-51; mem. Nat. Acad. of Sciences; Benjamin Franklin Fellow, Royal Soc. of Arts, London; Birkhoff Prize in Applied Mathematics 73.
Leisure interests: hiking, astronomy.
Publs. *Plane Waves and Spherical Means* 55, *Lecture on partial differential equations* (Co-Author) 64, *Calculus and Analysis* 1 (Co-Author) 65, *Lecture on Advanced numerical analysis* 67, *Partial Differential Equations* 71.
Courant Institute of Mathematical Sciences, 251 Mercer Street, New York, N.Y. 10012, U.S.A.

Johns, Jasper; American painter; b. 15 May 1930; ed. Univ. of South Carolina.
Works in following collections: Tate Gallery, London, Museum of Modern Art, New York City, Albright-Knox Art Gallery, Buffalo, N.Y.; one-man exhibitions: Leo Castelli, N.Y. 58, 60, 61, 63, Galerie Rive Droite, Paris 59, 61, Galleria d'Arte del Naviglio, Milan 59, Columbia Museum of Art, Columbia, South Carolina 60, Ileana Sonnabend, Paris 62, Jewish Museum, New York City 64, Whitechapel Gallery, London 64, Pasadena Museum, Calif. 65; Prize, Pittsburgh Int. 58.
Edisto Beach, South Carolina, U.S.A.

Johnson, Alan Woodworth, F.R.S.; British professor of chemistry; b. 29 Sept. 1917, Newcastle-upon-Tyne; s. of James William and Jean Johnson; m. Lucy Ida Celia Bennett 1941; one s. one d.; ed. Morpeth Grammar School, Royal Coll. of Science, London, and Imperial Coll. of Science, London.
Chemist, Swan, Hunter and Wigham Richardson Ltd. 34; Thomas Hedley and Co. Ltd. 35-36; Royal Scholar, Imperial Coll. of Science 36-38; Research Asst. in Organic Chem., Royal Coll. of Science 40-42; Research Chemist, I.C.I. Dyestuffs Div., 42-46; I.C.I. Fellow, Univ. of Cambridge 46-48; Asst. Dir. of Research in Organic Chem., Univ. of Cambridge 48-53, Lecturer in Organic Chem. 53-55; Sir Jesse Boot Prof. of Organic Chem. and Head of Chem., Univ. of Nottingham 55-68; Prof. of Chem., Univ. of Sussex 68-; Fellow and Steward, Christ's Coll. Cambridge 51-55; Visiting Prof., Univ. of Melbourne 60, Univ. of Calif., Berkeley 62; mem. Nat. Research and Devt. Council; Hon. Dir. Agricultural Research Council Unit of Invertebrate Chem. and Physiology; Meldola Medallist, Royal Inst. of Chem. 46; Tilden Lecturer, Chemical Soc. 53; Simonsen Lecturer, Chemical Soc. 67; Chem. Soc. Award for Synthesis 72; Pedler Lecturer, Chemical Soc. 73; Hon. Fellow Imperial College of Science and Technology; Hon. D.Sc., Memorial Univ., St. Johns, Newfoundland.
Leisure interests: tennis, philately.
Publs. *Chemistry of Acetylenic Compounds,* Vol. I 46, Vol. II 50; numerous papers in chem. and biochem. journals.
The Chemical Laboratory, University of Sussex, Falmer, Brighton, BN1 9QJ, Sussex, England.
Telephone: Brighton 66755.

Johnson, Axel Ax:son; Swedish industrialist and shipowner; b. 4 Oct. 1910, Stockholm; s. of Axel and Margaret Ax:son Johnson; m. Antonia do Amaral Souza 1941; one d.
President Rederiaktiebolaget Nordstjernan (Johnson Line), A. Johnson & Co. HAB; Owner A. Johnson & Co.; Chair. Skandia Group of Insurance Cos. 74-75, Swedish Nat. Appeal for World Wildlife Fund, Avesta Jernverks AB, A. Johnson and Co. Inc., New York, A. Johnson & Co. (London) Ltd., AB Karlstads Mekaniska Werkstad, Kjellbergs Successors AB, AB Nyäs-Petroleum, Försäkrings AB Sirius, Irano-Swedish Co. AB, C. H. Sprague & Son Co., Boston, Swedish Comm. Lloyd's Register of Shipping; Vice-Chair. Adela Investment Co. 69-74, Skandinaviska Enskilda Banken, Oljeprospektering AB, Swedish American Chamber of Commerce of Western U.S.; mem. Board of Dirs. Swedish Shipowners' Asscn., Fed. of Swedish Industries, Swedish Chamber of Commerce Inc., N.Y., W. R. Grace and Co.; mem. Asscn. of Reps. of Scandinavian Airlines System (SAS), Swedish Cttee. Int. Chambers of Commerce, Board of Trustees, World Wildlife Fund; mem. Royal Swedish Acad. of Agriculture and Forestry 66-, Royal Swedish Acad. of Engineering Sciences 69-; Hon. mem. Royal Swedish Soc. of Naval Sciences 61-; Consul-Gen. of Thailand; Dr. Tech. h.c. (Royal Inst. of Technology, Stockholm); numerous national and foreign decorations.
Leisure interests: horse-riding, yachting, skiing.
Rederiaktiebolaget Nordstjernan Johnson Line, Fack, S-103 80 Stockholm 7; Home: Karlavägen 85, 3rd Floor, S-114 59 Stockholm, Sweden.

Johnson, Celia, C.B.E.; British actress; b. 18 Dec. 1908; m. Peter Fleming; ed. St. Paul's Girls' School, Royal Acad. of Dramatic Art.
First stage appearance, Huddersfield 28; first London appearance as Currita (*A Hundred Years Old*) 29; subsequent roles include Loveday Trevelyan (*Debonair*) 30, Phyl (*After All*) 31, Ophelia (*Hamlet*) (New York) 31, Anne Hargraves (*The Wind and the Rain*) 33, Elizabeth Bennet (*Pride and Prejudice*) 36, Mrs. de Winter (*Rebecca*) 40, Jennifer (*The Doctor's Dilemma*) 42, Joan (*St. Joan*) 48-49, Viola (*Twelfth Night*) 50, Olga (*The Three Sisters*) 51, Sheila Broadbent (*The Reluctant Debutante*) 55, Isobel Cherry (*Flowering Cherry*) 57-58, Aline (*The Master Builder*) 64, Mme Ranyevskaya (*The Cherry Orchard*), Chichester 66, *Relatively Speaking* London 67, *Hay Fever* 68, *Hamlet* 71, *Dame of Sark* 74; films: *In Which We Serve* 42, *Dear Octopus* 42, *This Happy Breed* 44, *Brief Encounter* 46, *The Astonished Heart* 49, *I Believe in You* 52, *The Captain's Paradise* 53, *The Holly and the Ivy* 54, *A Kid for Two Farthings* 56, *The Good Companions* 57, *The Prime of Miss Jean Brodie* 69.
Merrimoles House, Nettlebed, Oxfordshire, England.

Johnson, David Gale; American economist; b. 10 July 1916, Vinton, Iowa; s. of Albert D. Johnson and Myra Jane Reed; m. Helen Virginia Wallace 1938; one s. one d.; ed. Iowa State Coll., Univs. of Wisconsin and Chicago.
Research Assoc. Iowa State Coll. 41-42, Asst. Prof. of Econs. 42-44; Dept. of Econs., Univ. of Chicago 44-, Asst. Prof. 44-54, Prof. 54-, Assoc. Dean Div. of Social Sciences 57-60, Dean 60-70, Chair. Dept. of Economics 71-75, Vice-Pres. and Dean of Faculties 75-; Economist, Office of Price Admin. 42, Dept. of State 46, Dept. of Army 48; Office of the President's Special Rep. for Trade Negotiations 63-; Agency for Int. Development 61-62; RAND Corpn. 54-; Dir. Social Science Research Council 54-57; Pres. American Farm Econ. Asscn. 64-65, Nat. Opinion Research Center 62-; mem. President's Nat. Advisory Comm. on Food and Fibre 65-67; Adviser, Policy Planning Council, U.S.

Dept. of State 66-69; mem. Nat. Research Council, mem. Exec. Cttee. Div. of Behavioural Sciences, Nat. Research Council 69-73; mem. Nat. Comm. on Population Growth and the American Future 70-72; Acting Dir. Univ. of Chicago Library 71-72; mem. Council on Int. Economic Policy 72-.
Leisure interests: reading, travel.
Publs. *Forward Prices for Agriculture* 47, *Trade and Agriculture* 50, *Grain Yields and the American Food Supply* 63, *World Agriculture in Disarray* 73, *World Food Problems and Prospects* 75.
5617 S. Kenwood Avenue, Chicago, Illinois 60637, U.S.A.
Telephone: 312-753-3013 (Office); 312-HY3-4015 (Home).

Johnson, Donald E.; American government official; b. 5 June 1924, Cedar Falls, Iowa; *m.* Mary Jean Suchomel 1947; six *s.* four *d.*; ed. Iowa State Univ. and Eastern Oregon Coll. of Education, La Grande.
U.S. Army Service 42-46; fmr. Chair. of Board, Protein Blenders Inc., Iowa City; fmr. Vice-Pres. ME-JON Fertilizer Inc., Oxford, Iowa; fmr. Sec.-Treas. Johnson Hatcheries Inc., West Branch; Pres. West Branch Farm Supply Inc. 61-69, D.J. Services Inc. 61-69; fmr. Sec.-Treas. S. & J. Poultry Co. Inc.; Chair. Governor's Comm. on Merit in Employment 54-55; Advisory mem. U.S. Comm. on Civil Rights 58-60; Admin. of Veterans Affairs 69-74; Deputy Asst. Sec. for Domestic and Int. Business, Dept. of Commerce, Washington, D.C. 74-; Chair. Pres. Comm. on the Viet-Nam Veteran; Nat. Commdr. American Legion 64; Bronze Star; Croix de Guerre (Belgium); Purple Heart.
Department of Commerce, Washington, D.C. 20230, U.S.A.

Johnson, Donald M.; American insurance executive; b. Los Angeles; ed. Univ. of Calif., Los Angeles.
Joined Aetna Life and Casualty Co. 46, Asst. Vice-Pres. 61, Sr. Vice-Pres. Jan. 68, Exec. Vice-Pres. Oct. 68, Pres. for insurance operations 70; Pres. Aetna Fund Inc. 70; Dir. Aetna Life and Casualty Co. 70, Pres. 72-; Pres. Aetna Variable Annuity Life Insurance Co.; mem. Gen. Council Assicurazioni Generali; Chair. of Board, Aetna Business Credit, Inc.; dir. of four other companies and officer in eight insurance trade orgs.
Aetna Life and Casualty Co., 151 Farmington Avenue, Hartford, Conn. 06115, U.S.A.

Johnson, Eyvind; Swedish novelist; b. 29 July 1900; ed. primary school.
Worked in a quarry, lumber trade, brickyard 14-19; in Stockholm 19-21; began writing in Stockholm; went to Germany 21, later to France for six years; lived in Switzerland and England 47-50; mem. Swedish Acad. 57-; Nordic Council Prize for Literature, Helsinki 62; Hon. Ph.D. (Gothenburg) 53; Nobel Prize for Literature 74.
Publs. About 30 vols. of novels and stories including: *Romanen om Olof* (autobiographical) 34-37, *Grupp Krilon* 41, *Krilons resa* 42, *Krilon sjalv* 43, *Strändernas svall* 46, *Drömmar om Rosor och eld* 49, *Molnen över Metapontion* 57, *Hans nades tid* 61, *Livsdagen lang* 64, *Stunder, vagor* 65; *Sju liv* (short stories in one volume) 44.
Vitsippsvägen 8, Saltsjöbaden 2, Sweden.

Johnson, G. Griffith; American government official; b. 15 Aug. 1912; ed. Harvard Univ.
Treasury Dept. 36-37, 38-39; National Defense Admin. Comm. 40-41; Office of Price Admin. 41-46; Dir. Economic Stabilization Div., Nat. Security Resources Board 48-49; Asst. Chief, Fiscal Div., Chief Economist, Bureau of Budget 49-50; Asst. Admin. Economic Policy, Economic Stabilization Agency 50; Economist, Motion Picture Asscn. of America 52, Vice-Pres. 52-62, Exec. Vice-Pres. 71-; Consultant, Int. Economics, Dept. of State 62, Asst. Sec. of State for Econ. Affairs 62-65;

Exec. Vice-Pres. Motion Picture Export Asscn. of America 65-.
Publs. *The Treasury and Monetary Policy* 39, *Economic Effects of Federal Public Works Expenditures* (with J. K. Galbraith) 40.
5100 Dorset Avenue, Chevy Chase, Maryland 20015, U.S.A.

Johnson, Gen. Harold K.; American army officer; b. 22 Feb. 1912, Bowesmont, N.D.; *s.* of late Harold C. Johnson and Edna Thomson; *m.* Dorothy Helen Rennix 1935; two *s.* one *d.*; ed. U.S. Mil. Acad., West Point.
Second Lieut. 33; Prisoner of War 42-45; served Korea 50-51; Nat. War Coll. 53; Dept. of Army, Washington 53-56; Asst. Div. Commdr., 8th Div. 56-58; Chief of Staff, Seventh Army, Stuttgart 59; Chief of Staff, Central Army 59-60; Commdt., U.S. Army Command and Gen. Staff Coll., Fort Leavenworth, Kansas 60-63; Army Gen. Staff, Wash. 63-68, Deputy Chief of Staff (Mil. Operations) 63-64, Chief of Staff 64-68; retd. from active service July 68, subsequently Pres. Freedoms Foundations at Valley Forge, Pres. Herbert Hoover Presidential Library Asscn. 69-; Distinguished Service Cross, Distinguished Service Medal with Oak Leaf Cluster, Office Legion of Honour, and numerous foreign awards.
Leisure interests: active interest in Boy Scout movement, playing the organ.
1776 K Street N.W., Washington, D.C. 20006, U.S.A.

Johnson, Harold Lester, PH.D.; American astronomer; b. 17 April 1921, Denver, Colo.; *s.* of late Averill C. and Marie (Sallach) Johnson; *m.* Mary E. Jones 1954; one *s.* one *d.*; ed. Univ. of Denver and Univ. of Calif. (Berkeley).
Assistant Prof. of Astronomy, Univ. of Chicago 50-52, Prof. 59-61; Astronomer, Lowell Observatory, Flagstaff, Ariz. 52-59; Prof. of Astronomy, Univ. of Texas 59-61, Chair. of Dept. 61; Research Prof. Lunar and Planetary Lab., Univ. of Ariz. 62-69; research Prof. Optical Sciences Center 69-; now Research Prof. and Astronomer, Steward Observatory, Univ. of Ariz.; Investigador Titular, Instituto de Astronomía Universidad Nacional de México; Investigador Titular, Centro de Investigación Científica y Educación Superior de Ensenada, B.C., México, and Director, Laboratorio de Física Aplicada, CICESE 73; mem. Nat. Acad. of Sciences, Amer. Astronomical Soc., Int. Astronomical Union, Royal Astronomical Soc., New York Acad. of Sciences, Astronomical Soc. of the Pacific; Helen B. Warner Prize (Amer. Astronomical Soc.).
Leisure interest: construction of live steam locomotives.
Steward Observatory, University of Arizona, Tucson, Ariz. 85712; Home: 731 West Paseo Norteño, Tucson, Ariz. 85704, U.S.A.
Telephone: (602) 884-2288 (Office); (602) 297-8559 (Home).

Johnson, Harry Gordon, M.A., PH.D., LL.D., D.LITT., D.SC.; Canadian economist; b. 26 May 1923, Toronto; *s.* of Henry Herbert Johnson and Frances Lily (Muat); *m.* Elizabeth Scott Serson 1948; one *s.* one *d.*; ed. Toronto, Cambridge and Harvard Univs.
Instructor, Toronto Univ. 46-47; Asst. Lecturer, Cambridge Univ. 49, Lecturer and Fellow of King's Coll. 50-56; Prof. of Economic Theory, Manchester Univ. 56-59; Prof. of Econs., Chicago Univ. Oct. 59-, London School of Econs. and Political Science 66-74; Visiting Prof. Toronto Univ. 52, Northwestern Univ. 55, 66, Stanford Univ. 55, Indiana Univ. 63, Monash Univ. 69, Yale 72-73, Centennial Prof., Toronto Univ. 67, Wicksell Lecturer 68, Skelton-Clark Prof., Queen's Univ. 75; Asst. Editor *Review of Economic Studies* 51-59; Editor *The Manchester School* 56-59, *Journal of Political Economy* 60-66, 71-; Fellow, Amer. Acad. of Arts and Sciences 64; Fellow, British Acad. 69; Fellow, Econometric Soc. 72.

Leisure interests: travel, woodcarving.

Publs. *International Trade and Economic Growth* 58 (Japanese edn. 59), *Money, Trade and Economic Growth* 62, *Canada in a Changing World Economy* 62, *The Canadian Quandary* 63, *The World Economy at the Crossroads* 65, *Economic Policies Towards the Less Developed Countries* 67, *Essays in Monetary Economics* 67, *Comparative Cost and Commercial Policy Theory* 68, *Aspects of the Theory of Tariffs* 71, *The Two-Sector Model of General Equilibrium* 71, *Macroeconomics and Monetary Theory* 72, *Inflation and the Monetarist Controversy* 72, *Further Essays in Monetary Economics* 73, *The Theory of Income Distribution* 73, *General Equilibrium Analysis* 74, *On Economics and Society* 75, *Technology and Economic Interdependence* 75.

University of Chicago, 1126 East 59th Street, Chicago 60637; and 5825 South Dorchester Avenue, Chicago 60637, U.S.A.

Telephone: 312-753-4514 (Office); 312-643-2673 (Home).

Johnson, Sir Henry Cecil, K.B.E.; British businessman; b. 11 Sept. 1906, Lavendon, Bucks.; s. of William Longland Johnson and Alice Mary Osborn; m. Evelyn Mary Morton 1932; two d.; ed. Bedford Modern School, Bedford.

General Man., Eastern Region of British Railways 58-62, Chair. and Gen. Man., London Midland Region 62-June 67; Vice-Chair. British Railways Board June 67-Jan. 68; Chair. British Railways Board Jan. 68-Sept. 71; Metropolitan Estate and Property Corpn. (MEPC Ltd.) 71-76; Chair. Dennis Waring and Co. Ltd.; mem. Greater London Regional Board, Lloyds Bank Ltd. 71-; Dir. Imperial Life Assurance Co. of Canada 72.

Leisure interest: golf.

"Rowans", Harewood Road, Chalfont St. Giles, Bucks., England.

Telephone: Little Chalfont 2409.

Johnson, Howard C.; American financial official; b. 7 Feb. 1909; ed. Swarthmore Coll. and Harvard Business School.

Investment Banking with Lazard Frères & Co., subsequently with Morgan Stanley & Co. 33-41; U.S. Navy in Second World War, Asst. to Sec. of Joint Chiefs of Staff 43-45; Chief of Div. of Int. Security Affairs, later Adviser on Planning, Bureau of UN Affairs, State Dept. 45-52; with Ford Foundation 52-55; Asst. to Chair. of Board, U.S. Steel Corpn. 55-60, Dir. Stockholder Relations Dept. 60-63; Man. of Portfolio Sales and Participations, Marketing Dept., Int. Bank for Reconstruction and Development and Int. Finance Corpn. (IFC) 63, Dir. of New York Office, Int. Bank and IFC Nov. 63-68; Pres. and Chief Exec. World Banking Corpn., Nassau, Bahamas 68-71.

RRI Box 106, Yarmouth, Maine 04096, U.S.A.

Johnson, Howard Wesley, M.A.; American educator; b. 2 July 1922, Chicago, Ill.; s. of Albert and Laura (Hansen) Johnson; m. Elizabeth J. Weed 1950; two s. one d.; ed. Central Coll., Univ. of Chicago and Glasgow Univ.

U.S. Army 43-46; Assoc. Prof. and Dir. of Management Research, Univ. of Chicago 48-55; Assoc. Prof., Assoc. Dean, Alfred P. Sloan School of Management, Mass. Inst. of Technology, 55-59, Prof., Dean 59-66; Exec. Vice-Pres., Federated Dept. Stores 66, mem. Board of Dirs. 66-; Dir. Hitchiner Mfg. Co. 61-71, Putnam Funds 61-71, Morgan Guaranty Trust Co. 71-; mem. Council on Foreign Relations, President's Advisory Cttee. on Labor-Management Policy 66-68; Pres. Mass. Inst. of Technology 66-71, Chair. of Corpn. 71-; Dir. Fed. Reserve Bank of Boston 67-68, Chair. 68-69; Dir. John Hancock Mutual Life Insurance Co. 68-; mem. at Large, Boy Scouts of America 68-; Trustee Cttee. for Econ. Devt. 68-71; Trustee, Wellesley Coll. 68-; Trustee, Inst. for Defense Analyses 71-; Overseer Boston Symphony

Orchestra 68-72; mem. Scientific Advisory Cttee., Massachusetts Gen. Hospital 68-70, Corpn. Museum of Science (Boston) 66-, NASA ad hoc Science Advisory Cttee. 66-71, Nat. Manpower Advisory Cttee. 67-69, Nat. Comm. on Productivity 70-72; Dir. Champion Int; Corpn. 70-; Dir. E. I. Du Pont de Nemours and Co. 72-. Vice-Chair. Federated Department Stores 71-73; Trustee, Radcliffe Coll. 73-, Aspen Inst. for Humanistic Studies 73-; Pres. Boston Museum of Fine Arts 75-; Fellow, American Acad. of Arts and Sciences, American Asscn. for Advancement of Science.

Leisure interests: antique clocks, fly fishing, trap shooting.

Massachusetts Institute of Technology, Cambridge, Massachusetts 02139, U.S.A.

Telephone: 617-253-4662.

Johnson, John H.; American publisher; b. 19 Jan. 1918, Arkansas; m. Eunice Johnson; one s. one d.; ed. DuSable High School and Chicago and Northwestern Univs.

Assistant Editor 36, later Man. Editor of employees' publication, Supreme Life Insurance Co. of America; founded *Ebony* 45, *Jet* 51, *Black Stars*, *Black World*, *Ebony Jr.*; first Negro businessman to be selected as one of the "ten outstanding young men of the year" by U.S. Junior Chamber of Commerce 51; accompanied Vice-Pres. Nixon at Ghana Independence celebrations 57, appointed Special Amb. representing the U.S. at Ivory Coast Independence celebrations 61, and Kenya Independence ceremony 63; founder and Pres. Johnson Publishing Co. Inc.; Dir. and Chair. of Board Supreme Life Insurance Co.; Dir. Marina City Bank of Chicago, Service Fed. Savings and Loan Asscn., Chicago, Greyhound Corpn., Zenith, Bell & Howell, Arthur D. Little Corpn., 20th Century-Fox Corpn., United Negro Coll. Fund, etc.; Trustee, Inst. of Int. Educ., Tuskegee Inst., Howard and Fisk Univs.; Dir. Chicago Asscn. of Commerce; Hon. LL.D. of several univs. and colls.; Horatio Alger Award 66, named Publisher of the Year by Magazine Publrs.' Asscn. 72, and numerous other awards.

820 S. Michigan Avenue, Chicago, Ill. 60605, U.S.A.

Telephone: 312-786-7600.

Johnson, Joseph Esrey, PH.D.; American foundation executive (retd.); b. 30 April 1906, Longdale, Va.; s. of Joseph Esrey and Margaret Hill (Hilles) Johnson; m. Catherine D. W. Abbot 1930; one s. one d.; ed. Harvard Univ.

Instructor in History, Bowdoin Coll. 34-35, Williams Coll. 36-38, Asst. Prof. (Williams Coll.) 38-47, on leave 42-47, Prof. 47-50; Officer, Dept. of State 42-47, Acting Chief, Div. of Int. Security Affairs 44-45, Chief 45-47; Policy Planning Staff, Dept. of State 47; Deputy U.S. Rep. Interim Comm., UN Gen. Assembly 48; Pres. Carnegie Endowment for Int. Peace 50-71, Pres. Emer. 71-; Trustee 50-76, Hon. Trustee 76-; mem. Int. Inst. for Strategic Studies 59-, Vice-Pres. 65-; Special Rep. of UN Conciliation Comm. for Palestine 61-63; Alt. U.S. Rep. 24th Session, UN Gen. Assembly; Hon. LL.D. (Williams Coll.) 51, (Bowdoin Coll.) 67, (Long Island) 69.

Carnegie Endowment for International Peace, 345 East 46th Street, New York, N.Y. 10017; Home: 22 Winant Road, Princeton, N.J. 08540, U.S.A.

Telephone: 212-557-0700 (Office); 609-WA4-5836 (Home).

Johnson, Keith; Jamaican civil servant and diplomatist; b. 29 July 1921, Spanish Town, St. Catherine; s. of Septimus A. and Emily A. Johnson; m. Dr. Pamela E. B. Rodgers 1973; two d.; ed. Columbia Univ., N.Y., and Univ. of London.

Jamaican Civil Service 40-48; Research Asst., Bureau of Applied Social Research, Columbia Univ. 48; Population Div., Dept. of Econ. and Social Affairs, UN

Secr. 49-62; Consul-Gen. of Jamaica in New York 62-67; Perm. Rep. of Jamaica to UN 67-73; Chair. Preparatory Cttee. for UN Conf. on Human Environment; Chair. Fourth Cttee. of UN Gen. Assembly Session 71; non-resident Amb. to Argentina 69-Jan. 73; Amb. to Fed. Repub. of Germany, also accred. to the Netherlands and Luxembourg 73, also accred. to Israel 75-.
Leisure interests: listening to music, walking.
Embassy of Jamaica, 53 Bonn-Bad Godesberg, Am Kreuter 1, Federal Republic of Germany.

Johnson, General Leon William, M.S.; American air force officer; b. 13 Sept. 1904, Columbia, Mo.; s. of Francis Lusk Johnson and Minnie Hayward Johnson; m. Lucille Davis Taylor 1928; two d.; ed. U.S. Mil. Acad., U.S. Army Advanced Flying School, Calif. Inst. of Technology.
Army 26; Air Force 29; commdr. **Heavy Bombardment Group and Wing in Europe 42; Deputy Chief of Staff for personnel services,** H.Q., A.A.F. 45-46; **Deputy Asst. Chief of Staff for personnel H.Q., U.S.A.F.** 46-47; Commanding Gen. 15th Air Force 47-48, 3rd Air Division and 3rd Air Force (England) 48-52, and Continental Air Command 52-56; U.S.A.F. Rep. Mil. Staff Cttee. U.N. 52-56; U.S. Rep. Mil. Cttee. and **Standing Group NATO 56-58; Air Deputy SHAPE 58-61;** Dir. Net Evaluation Subcommittee, Security Council 61-65; Business Consultant 66-; awarded Congressional Medal of Honor, D.S.M., Silver Star, Distinguished Flying Cross (with oak leaf cluster), Air Medal (with 3 oak leaf clusters), Legion of Merit, D.F.C. (British), Légion d'Honneur, Croix de Guerre.
1129 Litton Lane, McLean, Va. 22101, U.S.A.
Telephone: 703-356-8511.

Johnson, Leslie Royston; Australian politician; b. 22 Nov. 1924, Sydney; s. of W. C. Johnson and M. H. English; m. Gladys Jones 1949; one s. two d.
Member Parl. for Hughes, N.S.W. 55, 58, 61, 63, 69-; Minister of Housing 72-73, for Housing and Construction 73-75, of Aboriginal Affairs June-Nov. 75.
Leisure interests: swimming, reading.
Parliament House, Canberra, A.C.T.; Home: 24 Mitchell Avenue, Jannali, N.S.W., Australia.

Johnson, Livingston Basil; Bahamian lawyer; b. 20 June, 1933, Exuma; m.; three c.; ed. Mount Allison Univ., New Brunswick, Canada, Gray's Inn, London, England.
Civil Service 41-45; Stipendiary and Circuit Magistrate 55-56; Counsel, Attorney of Supreme Court of Bahama Islands 55; Dir. Bahamas Monetary Authority 68-72; mem. Judicial and Legal Service Comm. 70-72; Perm. Rep. to UN Sept. 73-.
Permanent Mission of the Bahamas to United Nations, 1 Dag Hammarskjöld Plaza, 17th Floor, New York, N.Y. 10017, U.S.A.

Johnson, Col. Mobolaji Olufunso; Nigerian Military Governor of Lagos 67-75; see *The International Who's Who 1975-76.*

Johnson, Pamela Hansford (Lady Snow), C.B.E., F.R.S.L.; British novelist and critic; b. 29 May 1912, London; d. of Reginald Kenneth and Amy Clotilda Johnson; m. 1st G. N. Stewart 1936, 2nd C. P. Snow (Lord Snow) 1950; three c.; ed. Clapham County Secondary School.
Arts and Letters Fellow, Timothy Dwight Coll., Yale 61; Fellow, Center for Advanced Studies, Wesleyan Univ. 61; Hon. D.Litt. (Temple Univ., Philadelphia, York Univ., Toronto and Widener Coll., Chester, Pennsylvania).
Publs. Novels include: *This Bed Thy Centre* 35, *World's End* 37, *Winter Quarters* 44, *The Trojan Brothers* 45, *Too Dear for My Possessing* 40, *An Avenue of Stone* 47, *A Summer to Decide* 48, *The Philistines* 49, *Catherine Carter* 52, *An Impossible Marriage* 54, *The Last Resort* 56, *The Unspeakable Skipton, The Humbler Creation* 59, *An Error of Judgement* 62, *Night and Silence, Who is Here?* 63, *Cork Street, Next to the Hatter's* 65, *The Survival of the Fittest* 68, *The Honours Board* 70, *The Holiday Friend* 72, *The Good Listener* 75; non-fiction: *Thomas Wolfe, a Critical Study* 47, *I. Compton-Burnett, a Critical Essay* 51, *Six Proust Reconstructions* 58, *On Iniquity* (Social Criticism) 67, *Important to Me* 74; play: *Corinth House* 48; and Proustian Reconstruction broadcast 49-55.
85 Eaton Terrace, London, S.W.1; c/o Macmillan Ltd., Little Essex Street, Strand, London, W.C.2, England.

Johnson, Philip Cortelyou, A.B.; American architect; b. 8 July 1906; ed. Harvard Univ.
Director Dept. of Architecture and Design, Museum of Modern Art 32-54; works include the Annexe and Sculpture Court, Museum of Modern Art, and the Glass House, New Canaan, Connecticut, Lincoln Center Theater; assoc. with the late Mies van der Rohe in design of Seagram Building, New York City.
Publs. *The International Style, Architecture since 1922* (with H. R. Hitchcock, Jr.) 32, *Machine Art* 34, *Mies van der Rohe* 47, *Architecture 1949-1965* 66.
Home: Ponus Street, New Canaan, Conn.; Office: 375 Park Avenue, New York, N.Y. 10022, U.S.A.

Johnson, U. Alexis; American diplomatist; b. 17 Oct. 1908, Falun, Kansas; s. of Carl Theodore and Ellen Forsse Johnson; m. Patricia Ann Tillman 1932; two s. two d.; ed. Occidental Coll., Los Angeles, and George-town Univ., Washington, D.C.
Entered foreign service 35; served Tokyo 35, Seoul 37, Tientsin, China 39, Seoul 39, Manchuria 40, Rio de Janeiro 42, U.S. Army Civil Affairs Training Schools 44, Manila 45; Staff Political Adviser to SCAP, Japan 46; Consul, Yokohama 46; Deputy Dir. Office North-East Asian Affairs, Dept. of State 49-51, Dir. 51; Deputy Asst. Sec. of State for Far-Eastern Affairs 51-53; Amb. to Czechoslovakia 53-58; U.S. Rep. Geneva Conf. June-July 54, and in subsequent talks with People's Repub. of China 55-57; Amb. to Thailand 58-61; Deputy Under-Sec. of State for Political Affairs 61-64; Deputy Amb. to Republic of Viet-Nam 64-65; Deputy Under-Sec. of State for Political Affairs 65-66; Amb. to Japan 66-69; Under-Sec. of State for Political Affairs 69-73; U.S. Envoy to SALT 73-; Medal of Freedom, Career Service Award of Nat. Civil Service League, Rockefeller Public Service Award.
Leisure interest: golf.
2101 Connecticut Avenue, N.W., Washington, D.C. 20008, U.S.A.
Telephone: 234-3549.

Johnson, Uwe; German writer; b. 20 July 1934, Kamień Pomorski; s. of Erich Johnson and Erna Sträde; m. Elisabeth Schmidt 1962; one d.
Resident in German Democratic Repub. 49-59, in West Berlin 59-74, England 75-; Fontane Prize 60; Int. Publishers' Asscn. Prize 62, Büchner Prize 71, Raabe Prize 74.
Publs. *Mutmassungen über Jakob* 59, *Das dritte Buch über Achim* 61, *Karsch, und andere Prosa* 64, *Zwei Ansichten* 65, *Jahrestage* 70-76, *Eine Reise nach Klagenfurt* 74.
c/o Suhrkamp Verlag, Postfach 4229, Frankfurt/Main, Federal Republic of Germany.

Johnson, Walter, M.A., PH.D.; American university professor; b. 27 June 1915; ed. Dartmouth Coll. and Univ. of Chicago.
Instructor Univ. of Chicago 40-43, Asst. Prof. 43-49, Assoc. Prof. 49-50, Prof. and Chair. Dept. of History 50-66, Preston and Sterling Morton Prof. of History 63-66; Writing Fellow Newberry Library of Chicago 45; Dir. of Edward R. Stettinius Manuscripts 48-49; Chair. Fulbright Board of Foreign Scholarship 50-53; accom-

panied Gov. Adlai Stevenson on world tour 53; Harms-worth Prof. of American History, Oxford Univ. 58-59; Prof. of History, Univ. of Hawaii 66-.

Publs. *Battle against Isolation* 44, *William Allen White's America* 47, *Selected Letters of William Allen White* (Editor) 47, *United States' Experiment in Demo-cracy* (co-author) 47, *How We Drafted Adlai Stevenson* 55; Editor: *Roosevelt and the Russians: The Yalta Conference*, by Edward R. Stettinius 49; *Turbulent Era*, by Joseph C. Grew, *1600 Pennsylvania Avenue* 60; Editor: *The Papers of Adlai E. Stevenson* 66.

University of Hawaii, 2444 Dole Street, Honolulu, Hawaii 96822, U.S.A.

Johnson, Warren C., B.S., M.S., PH.D.; American chemist; b. 22 Sept. 1901; ed. Kalamazoo Coll., Clark and Brown Univs.

Research Instructor in Chemistry, Brown Univ. 25-27; Instructor in Chemistry, Univ. of Chicago 27-28, Asst. Prof. 28-32, Associate Prof. 32-43, Prof. 43-68, Chair. Dept. of Chemistry 45-55, Assoc. Dean, Physical Sciences Div. 46-55, Dean 55-59, Vice-Pres. 58-67; Dir. Chemistry Div., Clinton Laboratories, Oak Ridge, Tenn. 43-45; Dir. Oak Ridge Inst., Nuclear Studies 53-59, 61-67, Consultant 67-; Chair. Management Advisory Council, Oak Ridge Nat. Laboratory 62-70; Chair. Section 9-3 of Nat. Defense Research Cttee. 40-43; Consultant U.S. Atomic Energy Comm.; mem. Gen. Advisory Cttee., Atomic Energy Comm.; Fellow, American Asscn. for the Advancement of Science; Hon. D.Sc. (Kalamazoo Coll. and Brown Univ.); U.S. Atomic Energy Comm. Citation 61.

Publs. *Qualitative Analysis and Chemical Equilibrium* 37, *Ionic Equilibrium as Applied to Qualitative Analysis* 41, 46, 54, *An Introduction to Qualitative Analysis* 57.

112 East 59th Street, F. Chicago, Ill. 60637, U.S.A.

Johnson, William Summer, PH.D.; American professor of chemistry; b. 24 Feb. 1913, New Rochelle, N.Y.; s. of Roy Wilder Johnson and Josephine (Summer) Johnson; m. Barbara Allen 1940; ed. Amherst Coll. and Harvard Univ.

Research Chemist, Eastman Kodak Co. summers of 36-39; Instructor Amherst Coll. 36-37; Instructor, Univ. of Wisconsin 40-42, Asst. Prof. 42-44, Assoc. Prof. 44-46, Prof. 46-54, Homer Adkins Prof. of Chem. 54-60; Visiting Prof. Harvard Univ. 54-55, Prof. and Exec. Head of Dept. of Chem., Stanford Univ. 60-69, Prof. of Chem. 69-; mem. Nat. Acad. of Sciences; Amer. Chemical Soc. Award for Creative Work in Synthetic Organic Chem. 58, Synthetic Organic Chemical Manu-facturing Award for Creative Research in Organic Chem. 63, New York Section of Amer. Chemical Soc. Nichols Medal 68, Roussel Prize 70.

Publs. Scientific articles on synthesis and constitution of natural products, particularly steroids and related compounds.

Department of Chemistry, Stanford University, Stan-ford, Calif. 94305; Home: 191 Meadowood Drive, Portola Valley, Calif. 94025, U.S.A.

Telephone: 415-497-2784 (Office); 415-851-7886 (Home).

Johnston, Sir Charles Hepburn, G.C.M.G.; British diplo-matist, writer and company director; b. 11 March 1912; m. Princess Natasha Bagration 1944; ed. Winchester and Balliol Coll., Oxford.

Entered Diplomatic Service 36, Third Sec., Tokyo 39; First Sec., Cairo 45, Madrid 48; Counsellor, Foreign Office 51, Bonn 55; Ambassador to Jordan 56-60; Gov. and C.-in-C. Aden 60-63; High Commr. in Aden and Fed. of South Arabia 63; Deputy Under-Sec. in charge of Econ. Affairs, Foreign Office 63-65; High Commr. in Australia 65-71; Chair. Thames Estuary Devt. Corpn. 71-73, Maplin Devt. Corpn. 71-73,. Town and City Properties (Overseas) Ltd. 73, Australian Estates 74-75; Dir. British Australian Investment Trust 74-; mem. Lloyd's 62, Council of Toynbee Hall 74.

Publs. *The View from Steamer Point* 64, *Mo and other originals* 71, *The Brink of Jordan* 72, *Estuary in Scotland and other poems* 74.

32 Kingston House South, London, S.W.7, England.

Johnston, Denis (*see* Johnston, William Denis).

Johnston, Don, M.A.; American advertising executive; b. 9 March 1927; s. of George D. Johnston and Isabella Mann Johnston; m. Sarita Behar Villegas 1954; three s.; ed. Michigan State and Johns Hopkins Univs.

With J. Walter Thompson Co. 51-, Trainee 51, Asst. Account Rep., New York 52, Rep. Bogotá 53, Account Rep., Account Supervisor, N.Y. 56, Man. Dir. Amster-dam 61, Tokyo 64, Vice-Pres. Europe, Frankfurt 66, Vice-Pres. Europe, London 67, Senior Vice-Pres. Europe, London 69, Senior Vice-Pres. Latin America and Senior Vice-Pres. Admin. and Planning, N.Y. 71, Exec. Vice-Pres. Int. 72, Dir. 72, Pres. and Chief Exec. Officer Aug. 74-.

Leisure interests: tennis, guitar.

33 Woodridge Drive, New Canaan, Conn. 06840, U.S.A. Telephone: (203) 972-0309.

Johnston, Harold S., A.B., PH.D.; American professor of chemistry; b. 11 Oct. 1920, Woodstock, Ga.; s. of Smith L. Johnston and Florine Dial; m. Mary Ella Stay 1948; one s. three d.; ed. Emory Univ., Ga. and Calif. Inst. of Technology.

Instructor, Stanford Univ. 47-49, Asst. Prof. 49-53, Assoc. Prof. 53-56; Assoc. Prof. Calif. Inst. of Tech-nology 56-57; Visiting Asst. Prof., Univ. of Calif. at Berkeley 53, Prof. of Chem. 57-, Dean Coll. of Chem. 66-70; mem. Nat. Acad. of Sciences, American Acad. of Arts and Sciences; Hon. D.Sc. Emory Univ.; Gold Medal, Calif. Section of American Chemical Soc., Pollution Control Award of American Chemical Soc. 74.

Leisure interests: gardening, astronomy.

Publs. *Gas Phase Reaction Rate Theory* 66, *Gas Phase Kinetics of Neutral Oxygen Species* 68, *Catalytic Reduc-tion of Stratospheric Ozone by Nitrogen Oxides* 71.

College of Chemistry, University of California, Berkeley, Calif. 94720; Home: 132 Highland Boulevard, Berkeley, Calif. 94708, U.S.A.

Johnston, Sir John (**Baines**), K.C.M.G., K.C.V.O.; British diplomatist; b. 13 May 1918; m. Elizabeth Mary Crace 1969; one s.; ed. Banbury Grammar School and Queen's Coll., Oxford.

Army service 40-46; Asst. Principal, Colonial Office 47, Principal 48; Asst. Sec. West African Council, Accra 50-51; U.K. Liaison Officer, Comm. for Technical Co-operation in Africa South of the Sahara 52; Principal Private Sec. to Sec. of State for Colonies 53, Asst. Sec. 56, Head of Far Eastern Dept., Colonial Office 56; transferred to Commonwealth Relations Office 57, Dep. High Commr. in S. Africa 59-61; High Commr. in Sierra Leone 61-63, in Fed. of Rhodesia and Nyasaland 63, in Rhodesia 64-65; Asst. Under-Sec. of State, Common-wealth Office 66-68, Deputy Under-Sec. of State, Foreign and Commonwealth Office 68-71; High Commr. in Malaysia 71-74, in Canada 74-.

British High Commission, 80 Elgin Street, Ottawa, Ont., Canada.

Johnston, John Bennett, Jr.; American politician; b. 10 June 1932, Shreveport, La.; s. of J. Bennett Johnston; m. Mary Gunn; two s. two d.; ed. Byrd High School, Washington and Lee Univ., U.S. Mil. Acad. and Louisiana School of Law.

Military service in Judge Advocate Gen. Corps La.; State Senator 68-72; U.S. Senator from La. 72-; mem. Senate Cttee. on Interior and Insular Affairs, Cttee. on Banking, Housing and Urban Affairs, Select Cttee. on Small Business, Senate Bldg. Comm.; Democrat.

Leisure interest: tennis.

432 Russell Senate Office Building, Washington, D.C. 20510, U.S.A.

Johnston, (William) Denis, O.B.E., M.A., LL.M.; Irish barrister-at-law, broadcaster and dramatist; b. 18 June 1901, Dublin; s. of Hon. William John Johnston and Kathleen King; m. 1st Shelah Richards 1928, 2nd Betty Chancellor 1945; three s. one d.; ed. St. Andrew's Coll., Dublin, Merchiston Castle School, Edinburgh, Christ's Coll., Cambridge, and Harvard Law School, U.S.A. Barrister-at-Law, Inner Temple and King's Inns; Dir. Dublin Gate Theatre 31-35; B.B.C. Feature Programme writer and producer 36; B.B.C. War Corresp. Middle East, Italy, France and Germany 42-45; Television Programme Dir. 46-47; Prof. of English, Mount Holyoke Coll., U.S.A. 50-61; Chair., Theatre Dept., Smith Coll., U.S.A. 61-66; Visiting Prof. Amherst Coll. 66-67, Univ. of Iowa 67-68, Univ. of Calif. (Davis) 70-71, Berg Prof. New York Univ. 71-72; Arnold Prof. Whitman Coll., Wash. 72-73; Guggenheim Fellow 55.
Leisure interest: sailing.
Plays (with dates of production): *The Old Lady Says "No"* 29, *The Moon in the Yellow River* 31, *A Bride for the Unicorn* 33, *Storm Song* 34, *The Golden Cuckoo* 39, *The Dreaming Dust* 46, *A Fourth for Bridge* 49, *Strange Occurrence on Ireland's Eye* 56, *The Scythe and the Sunset* 58, *Nine Rivers from Jordan* (autobiography) 53, *In Search of Swift* 59 (biography), *John Millington Synge* 65, *The Brazen Horn* 68; Librettos for operatic versions of *Six Characters in Search of an Author* 58, and *Nine Rivers from Jordan* 68.
8 Sorrento Terrace, Dalkey, Co. Dublin, Ireland.
Telephone: 803986.

Johore, H.R.H. The Sultan of; Tunku Ismail ibni al-Marhum Sultan Ibrahim, D.K., D.M.N., S.M.N., S.P.M.J., S.P.M.K., D.K. (Brunei), K.B.E., C.M.G., D.K. (Pahang); Malaysian ruler; b. 28 Oct. 1894, Johore Bahru; s. of Sultan Ibrahim Ibni Sultan Abu Bakar and Ungku Maimunah Binte Ungku Abdul Majid; m. Ungku Tun Aminah Binte Ungku Ahmad 1920; two s. one d. Colonel Commandant, Johore Mil. and Volunteer Services; succeeded his father, Sultan Ibrahim, May 59; several foreign decorations.
Leisure interests: zoology, horses, motor cars.
Istana Bukit Serene, Johore Bahru, Johore, Malaysia.
Telephone: JB 2000.

Jolivet, Henri; French engineer and business executive; b. 8 June 1904; ed. Ecole Nationale Supérieure des Mines de Saint-Etienne.
Vice-Pres. Péchiney Ugine Kuhlmann; Pres. Soc. des Tôles Spéciales et Ugine-Guegnon; Admin. Groupement Industrie Siderurgique (GIS); Officier de la Légion d'Honneur.
10 rue du Général Foy, Paris 8e, France.

Jonathan, Chief (Joseph) Leabua; Basuto politician; b. 30 Oct. 1914; ed. Mission School, Leribe.
Worked in mines in South Africa 34-37; returned to Basutoland 37; Court Pres. 38; entered politics 52; mem. District Council 54; mem. Nat. Council 54, mem. Panel of 18 56-59; founded Basutoland Nat. Party 59, leader 59-; mem. Legislative Council 60-64; Del. at Constitutional Conf. 64; Prime Minister of Basutoland (now Lesotho) 65-, and also Minister of External Affairs 65-71, of the Civil Service 65-68, of Defence 65-, of Internal Security 68-, of Devt. and Planning 68-74, of Citizenship, Training and Statistics 69-70, and Chief of Electoral Affairs 71-.
Prime Minister's Office, P.O. Box 527, Maseru, Lesotho.

Jonckheer, Efrain; Netherlands (Antilles) politician; b. 1917; ed. in Netherlands Antilles.
Director of several companies in Curaçao; first Pres. Democratic Party 44; mem. of all Round Table Confs. leading to full autonomous status of Netherlands Antilles 47-54; mem. Staten (legislative assembly) 45-; Leader Democratic Party Group in Staten 45-54; mem. Island Council of Curaçao 51-53; Prime Minister of Netherlands Antilles and Minister of General Affairs 54-67; Minister of Transport and Communications 54-56; Minister of Social Affairs 56-57; Minister Plenipotentiary for the Netherlands Antilles at The Hague 68-70; Netherlands Amb. to Venezuela 71-; Commdr. Order Orange-Nassau.
Edif. La Estancia, 3° piso, Avenida La Estancia 10, Ciudad Comercial Tomanaco, Caracas, Venezuela.

Jones, Allen; British artist; b. 1 Sept. 1937, Southampton; two d.; ed. Hornsey School of Art, Royal Coll. of Art.
Secretary, Young Contemporaries, London 61; lived in New York 64-65; Tamarind Lithography Fellowship, Los Angeles 66; Guest Prof. Dept. of Painting, Univ. of S. Florida 69; Hochschule für Bildende Künste, Hamburg 68-70; first one-man exhbn., London 63; one-man exhbns. in U.K., U.S.A., Switzerland, Fed. Repub. of Germany, Italy, Australia, Japan 63-; many group exhbns. of paintings and graphic work; Guest Prof., Univ. of Calif., Irvine; tours in Mexico, Canada 75; designs for television and stage in Fed. Repub. of Germany and U.K.
Publs. *Allen Jones Figures* 69, *Allen Jones Projects* 71, *Waitress* 72.
c/o Leslie Waddington Gallery, 1 Cork Street, London, W.1, England.

Jones, Rt. Hon. Aubrey, B.SC.; British economist and industrialist; b. 20 Nov. 1911, Merthyr Tydfil; s. of Evan and Margaret Aubrey Jones; m. Joan Godfrey-Isaacs 1948; two s.; ed. London School of Econs.
On foreign and editorial staff *The Times* 37-39 and 47-48; served with Army Intelligence Staff, War Office and Mediterranean 40-46; joined British Iron and Steel Fed. as Special Asst. to Chair. 49, Economic Dir. 54 and Gen. Dir. 55; M.P. for Birmingham (Hall Green) 50-65; Minister of Fuel and Power 55-57; Minister of Supply 57-59; fmr. Dir. Guest, Keen & Nettlefolds Steel Co. Ltd., fmr. Chair. Staveley Industries Ltd., fmr. Dir. Courtaulds Ltd.; Chair. Nat. Board for Prices and Incomes 65-70; Chair. Laporte Industries (Holdings) Ltd. 70-72; Dir. Thomas Tilling Ltd. 70-, Inbucon Int. Ltd. 75-; Dir. Cornhill Insurance Co. Ltd. 71-, Chair. 71-73; Hon. Fellow, London School of Econs. 59, mem. Court of Govs. 64; Hon. Fellow Commoner, Churchill Coll., Cambridge 72-73; Gov. Nat. Inst. Econ. and Social Research 67; Hon. Vice-Pres. Consumers' Asscn. 67-72; Adviser to Public Service Review Comm. of Nigerian Govt. 73-74; Leading Adviser to Iranian Govt. on Agricultural Devt. Plan 74-75; UN Adviser to Iranian Govt. on Public Sector Problems 75-; Conservative.
Leisure interests: sailing, skiing.
Publs. *The Pendulum of Politics* 46, *Right and Left* 44, *Industrial Order* 50, *The New Inflation—The Politics of Prices and Incomes* 73.
4 Plane Tree House, Duchess of Bedford's Walk, London, W8 7QT, England.
Telephone: 01-937-4247.

Jones, Gen. David Charles, D.F.C.; American air force officer; b. 9 July 1921, Aberdeen, S. Dak.; s. of Maurice Jones and Helen Meade; m. Lois M. Tarbell 1942; one s. two d.; ed. Univ. of North Dakota and Minot State Coll., N. Dak., U.S.A.F. Flying School, Nat. War Coll.
Commander, 22nd Air Refueling Squadron 53-54, 33rd Bomb Squadron 54; Operations Planner, Bomber Mission Branch, HQ Strategic Air Command Sept.-Dec. 54, Aide to C.-in-C., SAC 55-57; Dir. of Material, later Deputy Commdr. for Maintenance, 93rd Bomb Wing 57-59; Chief, Manned Systems Branch, Deputy Chief and later Chief, Strategic Div., DCS/Operations, HQ U.S.A.F. 60-64; Commdr. 33rd Tactical Fighter Wing March-Oct. 65; Insp.-Gen. HQ United States Air Forces in Europe 65-67, Chief of Staff Jan.-June 67,

Deputy Chief of Staff, DCS/Plans and Operations 67-69; Deputy Chief of Staff, Operations, HQ 7th Air Force, Repub. of Viet-Nam 69, Vice-Commdr. 7th Air Force, Tan Son Nhut Airfield, Repub. of Viet-Nam 69; Commdr. 2nd Air Force 69-71; Vice-C.-in-C. U.S.A.F.E., later C.-in-C. U.S.A.F.E. and Commdr. 4th Allied Tactical Air Forces, Ramstein Air Base, Fed. Repub. of Germany 71-74; Chief of Staff, United States Air Force 74-; Hon. D. Hum. Litt. (Univ. of Nebraska) 74; Hon. D. Laws (Louisiana Tech. Univ.) 75; Distinguished Service Medal with Oak Leaf Cluster; Legion of Merit; Commdr. Légion d'Honneur 75; Grand Cross with Star and Shoulder Band, Order of Merit, Fed. Repub. of Germany, and many other decorations.
Leisure interests: jogging, sport flying, historical novels.
Headquarters United States Air Force, Pentagon, Washington, D.C. 20330; Quarters 7, Fort Myer, Va. 22211, U.S.A.
Telephone: OX 7-9225 (Pentagon); 243-4933 (Fort Myer).

Jones, Ernest Cyril Brieley; Liberian administrator and politician; b. 1896; ed. Tuskegee Institute, Tuskegee, Alabama, U.S.A.
Vocational Arts Instructor, Prairie View State Coll., Texas, U.S.A. 21-22; Dir. of Trades School, St. John A & I School, Robertsport, Liberia 22-25; Asst. Plantations Man., Firestone Plantations Co., Liberia 26-28; engaged in private enterprise 28-31; entered politics and apptd. a County District Commr. 32, First Class District Commr. 37, Provincial Commr. 44; Chief of the Bureau of Tribal Affairs 46; Asst. Sec. of Interior 48; Cabinet Minister, Sec. of Defence 49-60; Amb. to Ivory Coast Repub. 60-72; Chair. Exec. Immigration Comm., Monrovia; Knight Commdr. Star of Africa (Liberia); Commdr. Star of Benin (France); mem. National True Whig Party.
c/o President's Office, Monrovia, Liberia.

Jones, (Everett) Le Roi; American poet and dramatist; b. 7 Oct. 1934, Newark, N.J.; s. of Coyt L. Jones and Anna Lois (Russ) Jones; ed. Howard Univ., New School and Columbia Univ.
Served with U.S. Air Force; taught poetry at New School Social Research, drama at Columbia Univ., literature at Univ. of Buffalo; Visiting Prof., San Francisco State; began publishing 58; founded Black Arts Repertory Theater School, Harlem 64, Spirit House, Newark 66; Whitney Fellowship 63, Guggenheim Fellowship 65; Fellow, Yoruba Acad. 65; mem. Int. Co-ordinating Cttee. of Congress of African Peoples.
Publs. *Preface to a Twenty Volume Suicide Note* 61, *Dante* 62, *Blues People* 63, *The Dead Lecturer* 63, *Dutchman* 64, *The Moderns* 64, *The System of Dante's Hell* 65, *Home* 65, *Jello* 65, *Experimental Death Unit* 65, *The Baptism—The Toilet* 66, *Black Mass* 66, *Mad Heart* 67, *Slave Ship* 67, *Black Music* 67, *Tales* 68, *Great Goodness of Life* 68, *Black Magic, Four Black Revolutionary Plays* 69, *Black Art* 69, *In Our Terribleness* 70, *Junkies are Full of Shhh . . .* , *Bloodrites* 70, *Raise* 71, *It's Nation Time* 71, *Kawaida Studies* 72, *Spirit Reach* 72, *African Revolution* 73.
c/o Hobbs Agency, 211 East 43rd Street, New York, N.Y. 10017, U.S.A.

Jones, Sir Ewart Ray Herbert, Kt., F.R.S., F.R.I.C., D.SC., PH.D., M.A.; British professor of chemistry; b. 16 March 1911, Wrexham, Denbighs.; m. Frances Mary Copp 1937; one s. two d.; ed. Grove Park School, Univ. Coll. of North Wales, Univ. of Manchester.
Fellow, Univ. of Wales 35-37; Lecturer, Imperial Coll. of Science and Technology 38; Reader in Organic Chem. and Asst. Prof., Univ. of London 45; Sir Samuel Hall Prof. of Chem., Manchester Univ. 47-55; Arthur D. Little Visiting Prof. of Chem., Mass. Inst. of Tech-

nology 52; Waynflete Prof. of Chem., Oxford Univ. 55-; Karl Folkers Lecturer, Univs. of Illinois and Wisconsin 57; Pedler Lecturer 59; mem. Council for Scientific and Industrial Res. and Chair. Research Grants Cttee. 61-65; mem. Science Research Council and Chair. Univ. Science and Technology Board 65-69; Meldola Medal, Royal Inst. of Chem. 40; Fritzsche Award, American Chemical Soc. 62; Pres. Chemical Soc. 64-66; Fellow, Imperial Coll. 67; Pres. Royal Inst. of Chem. 70-72; mem. Council of Royal Soc. 69-71; Foreign mem. American Acad. of Arts and Sciences; Hon. D.Sc. (Birmingham, Nottingham, New South Wales, Sussex, Salford); Hon. LL.D. (Manchester).
Publs. scientific papers in *Journal of The Chemical Society*.
Dyson Perrins Laboratory, South Parks Road, Oxford, OX1 3QY; Home: 6 Sandy Lane, Yarnton, Oxford, England.
Telephone: Oxford 57809 (Office); Kidlington 2581 (Home).

Jones, Geraint Iwan; British conductor, organist and harpsichordist; b. 16 May 1917, Porth, Glamorgan; s. of Evan Jones and Caroline Davies; m. 1st M. A. Kemp 1940, 2nd Winifred Roberts 1949; one d.; ed. Caterham School and Royal Acad. of Music.
Concert organist, Nat. Gallery Concerts 40-44; Conductor, Purcell's *Dido and Aeneas*, Mermaid Theatre 50-53; Founder, Geraint Jones Singers and Orchestra 51; Musical Dir. Lake District Festival 60-, Kirckman Concert Soc. 63-; Artistic Dir. Salisbury Festival of the Arts 73-; Prof., Royal Acad. of Music; Grand Prix du Disque 59 and 66.
Frequent harpsichord recitals with violinist wife Winifred Roberts; frequent tours of Europe and America 48-; complete organ works of Bach in London 45-46 and 55; has recorded on most historic organs in Europe.
Leisure interests: photography, antiques, architecture, motoring.
The Long House, Arkley Lane, Barnet Road, Arkley, Herts., England.

Jones, Gilbert E.; American computers executive; b. 8 Jan. 1917, Convent, N.J.; m. Jean C. Morse 1942; one s. three d.; ed. Harvard Univ.
Sales Rep. Int. Business Machines Corpn. 38-42; served U.S. Navy 42-45; rejoined IBM 45, Exec. Asst. to Pres. 53-56; Sales Man. 56-59; Pres. IBM Data Processing Division 59-61, Exec. Vice-Pres., mem. Board of Dirs. and Exec. Cttee. 62; Pres. IBM World Trade Corpn., Vice-Pres. and Group Exec., Int. Business Machines Corpn. 63; Senior Vice-Pres. and mem. Management Cttee. 67; Chair. Man. Cttee. 69-70; mem. Board of Dirs. Int. Business Machines Corpn. Jan. 70-; Chair. Board and Exec. Cttee. IBM World Trade Corpn. April 70-; mem. Corp. Office IBM 72-, Vice-Chair. 74-; Dir. Continental Oil Co.; mem. Board of Trustees U.S. Trust Co.; mem. Board of Trustees and Exec. Cttee. U.S. Council, Int. Chamber of Commerce.
IBM World Trade Corporation, 821 United Nations Plaza, New York, N.Y. 10017, U.S.A.

Jones, Gwyneth, A.R.C.M.; British soprano; b. 7 Nov. 1936, Pontnewynydd, Mon., Wales; d. of Edward George Jones and Violet Webster; m. Till Haberfeld; one d.; ed. Royal Coll. of Music, London, Accad. Chigiana, Siena, Zürich Int. Opera Centre.
With Zürich Opera House 62-63; with Royal Opera House, Covent Garden 63-; Vienna State Opera House 66-; guest performances in numerous opera houses throughout the world including La Scala, Milan, Rome Opera, Berlin State Opera, Munich State Opera, Hamburg, Paris, Metropolitan Opera, New York, San Francisco, Los Angeles, Zürich, Geneva, Dallas, Teatro Colón, Buenos Aires, Tokyo, Bayreuth Festival, Edinburgh Festival and Welsh Nat. Opera; known for many opera roles including Leonora, *Il Trovatore*, Desdemona, *Otello*, Aida, *Aida* (Verdi), Leonore, *Fidelio* (Beethoven),

Senta, *Fliegender Holländer* (Wagner), Medea, *Medea* (Cherubini), Sieglinde, *Walküre* (Wagner), Lady Macbeth, *Macbeth* (Verdi), Elizabeth, *Don Carlos* (Verdi), *Madame Butterfly* (Puccini), *Tosca* (Puccini), Donna Anna, *Don Giovanni* (Mozart), *Salome* (R. Strauss), Kundry, *Parsifal* (Wagner), Aegyptische Helena, *Helena* (R. Strauss), Elizabeth/Venus *Tannhäuser* (Wagner), Marschallin *Rosenkavalier* (R. Strauss), Brünnhilde *Ring* (Wagner); TV films: *Fidelio, Aida, Flying Dutchman, Beethoven 9th Symphony*; recordings for Decca, DGG, EMI, CBS.
P.O. Box 8040, Zurich, Switzerland.

Jones, Sir Henry Frank Harding, G.B.E., M.A., F.I.CE., M.I.CHEM.E.; British engineer; b. 13 July 1906, London; *s.* of Frank Harding Jones and Gertrude Kimber; *m.* Elizabeth Langton 1934; three *s.* one *d.*; ed. Harrow School and Pembroke Coll., Cambridge.
Army Service 39-45; fmr. Deputy Chair. Watford and St. Albans Gas Co., Wandsworth and District Gas Co.; fmr. Dir. South Metropolitan, South Suburban and other gas companies; Chair. East Midlands Gas Board 49-52; Deputy Chair. Gas Council 52-60, Chair. 60-71; Vice-Chair. World Energy Conference 70-73; Hon. D.Sc. (Salford) 71; Hon. Fellow, Inst. of Gas Engineers, Pres. 56-57; Birmingham Medal, Inst. of Gas Engineers 64; Hon. LL.D. (Leeds) 67; Hon. D.Sc. (Leicester) 70.
Leisure interests: reading, gardening, fishing.
Pathacres, Weston Turville, Aylesbury, Buckinghamshire, England.

Jones, Horace C.; American business executive; b. 1916, Philadelphia, Pa.; *m.* Helen Allen; seven *c.*; ed. Hill School, Pottstown, Pa., Princeton Univ.
Served with U.S. Army Air Force World War II, with rank of Lieut.-Col.; Asst. Treasurer, Lees Carpets 38, Pres. 60-70 (became division of Burlington Industries Inc. 60); Dir. Burlington Industries Inc. 60, Exec. Vice-Pres. 67, Vice-Chair. 72, Pres. 73-75, Chief Exec. Officer 73-, Chair. April 75-.
Burlington Industries Inc., Greensboro, N.C. 27420, U.S.A.

Jones, Howard Mumford, M.A.; American university professor; b. 16 April 1892, Saginaw, Mich.; *s.* of Frank Alexander Miles Jones and Josephine Whitman; *m.* 1st Clara Edgar McLure 1918, 2nd Bessie J. Zaban 1927; one *d.*; ed. Univs. of Wisconsin and Chicago.
Adjunct Prof. of General Literature and English, Univ. of Texas 16-17; Asst. Prof. of English, State Univ. of Montana 17-19; Assoc. Prof. of Comparative Literature, Univ. of Texas 19-25; Assoc. Prof. of English, Univ. of North Carolina 25-30; Prof. of English, Univ. of Michigan 30-36; Prof. of English, Harvard Univ. 36-62, Emer. 62-; Dean Graduate School of Arts and Sciences 43-44; Abbot Lawrence Lowell Prof. of the Humanities 60; Chair. American Council of Learned Socs. 55-59; Editor-in-Chief John Harvard Library 59-62; Jusserand and Hubbell Medals; Guggenheim Fellow; Research Assoc. Henry E. Huntington Library; American Acad. of Arts and Sciences (Pres. 44-51); Fellow Center for Advanced Studies in Behavioral Sciences 57-58; Weil Lecturer 67; numerous hon. degrees; Pulitzer Prize 64; Jaffe Medal, Phi Beta Kappa (triennial award) 73.
Leisure interest: work.
Publs. *A Little Book of Local Verse* 15, *Gargoyles* (poems) 18, *The Shadow* (play) 17, *A Bibliography of Works and MSS. of Byron* (with R. H. Griffith) 24, *America and French Culture (1750-1848)* 27, *The Romanesque Lyric* (with P. S. Allen) 28, *The Life of Moses Coit Tyler* 33, *They Say the Forties* 37, *The Harp That Once* 37, *Ideas in America* 44, *Education and World Tragedy* 46, *The Theory of American Literature* 48, *The Bright Medusa* 52, *The Pursuit of Happiness* 53, *The Frontier in American Fiction, American Humanism* 57, *Reflections on Learning* 58, *One Great Society* 59,

Guide to American Literature Since 1890 59, *History and The Contemporary* 64, *O Strange New World* 64, *Jeffersonionism and the American Novel* 66, *Belief and Disbelief in American Literature* 67, *The Literature of Virginia in the Seventeenth Century* 68, *Violence and Reason* 69, *The Age of Energy* 71, *Revolution and Romanticism* 74.
14 Francis Avenue, Cambridge, Mass. 02138, U.S.A.
Telephone: TR-6-1656.

Jones, J. Wesley, A.B.; American diplomatist; b. 4 June 1907, Sioux City, Iowa; *s.* of Edward H. and Ida May (Murrison) Jones; *m.* Katharine del Valle 1938; one *s.* two *d.*; ed. Morningside Coll. and George Washington Univ.
Vice-Consul, Saltillo, Mexico 31, Calcutta 32-35; Vice-Consul and Consul, Rome 35-41; Italian Desk, State Dept. 41-43; Asst. Chief, Div. S. European Affairs, State Dept. 44-45; First Sec., Embassy, Rome 45-48; Counsellor, Embassy Nanking 48-49, Madrid 49-53; Dir. W. European Office, State Dept. 53-57; Dep. Asst. Sec. of State 57-58; Amb. to Libya 58-62, to Peru 63-69; Deputy Commandant for Int. Affairs, Nat. War Coll., Washington, D.C. 69-71; retd.; U.S. mem. Special Consultative Cttee. on Security, Org. of American States 72-.
The Commodore's Cottage, Flat Rock, N.C. 28731, U.S.A.
Telephone: 704-692-7908.

Jones, James; American writer; b. 6 Nov. 1921, Robinson, Ill.; *s.* of Ramon Jones and Ada Blessing; *m.* Gloria Mosolino 1957; one *s.* one *d.*; ed. High School, Robinson, Illinois, Hawaii and New York Univs.
Purple Heart Medal, Bronze Star Medal, National Book Award.
Leisure interests: skindiving, spearfishing, collecting antique knives.
Publs. *From Here to Eternity* 51, *Some Came Running* 58, *The Pistol* 59, *The Thin Red Line* 62, *Go to the Widow-maker* 67, *The Ice-Cream Headache* 68, *The Merry Month of May* 71, *A Touch of Danger* 73, *Viet Journal* 74.
c/o Dell Publishing Co. Inc., 1 Dag Hammarskjöld Plaza, New York, N.Y. 10017, U.S.A.

Jones, James Larkin (Jack), M.B.E.; British trade unionist; b. 29 March 1913, Liverpool; *s.* of George and Anne Sophie Jones; *m.* Evelyn Mary Taylor 1938; two *s.*; ed. Liverpool.
Worked in engineering and dock industries 27-39; served in Spanish Civil War; Midlands Official, Transport and Gen. Workers' Union 39-63, Exec. Officer 63-69; Gen. Sec. 69-; District Sec. Confed. of Shipbuilding and Engineering Unions 39-63; mem. Labour Party Nat. Exec. Cttee. 64-67; Deputy Chair. Nat. Ports Council 67-; mem. Council, Trades Union Congress 68-; Chair. Int. Cttee., TUC 72; mem. Exec. Board Int. Confed. of Free Trade Unions, European Trade Union Confed., British Overseas Trade Board; Vice-Pres. Int. Transport Workers Fed.; Fellow, Nuffield Coll., Oxford 70, Chartered Inst. of Transport 71.
Leisure interests: walking, painting.
Home: 74 Ruskin Park House, Champion Hill, London, S.E.5; Office: Transport House, Smith Square, London, S.W.1, England.
Telephone: 274-7067 (Home); 828-7788 (Office).

Jones, Le Roi (see Jones, (Everett) Le Roi).

Jones, Marvin, A.B., LL.B.; American lawyer and politician; ed. Southwestern and Texas Univs.
Admitted to Texas Bar 07, practised Amarillo; Chair. Board Legal Examiners, 7th Supreme Judicial District Texas 13; mem. Congress from Texas 17-41, Chair. House Cttee. on Agriculture 31-40; Judge U.S. Court of Claims 40-43; Agricultural Adviser to Dir. Economic

27

Stabilization Office 43; Pres. First Int. Conf. on Food and Agriculture, Hot Springs, Va. May 43; War Food Admin. June 43-July 45; Chief Justice, U.S. Court of Claims 47-64, Senior Judge 64-; Democrat.
Publs. *How War Food Saved American Lives, Should Uncle Sam Pay—When and Why?*
2807 Hughes Street, Amarillo, Tex. 79109, U.S.A.

Jones, Sir Philip Frederick, Kt., A.C.A., A.A.S.A.; Australian company director; b. 14 Aug. 1912, Napier, New Zealand; s. of J. F. Jones; m. Josephine Nancy Kirschlager 1942; ed. Barker's Coll., Hornsby, N.S.W. General Man. The Herald & Weekly Times Ltd. 53-63, Dir. 57-, Vice-Chair. 66-70, Chair. 70-; Chair. W. Australian Newspapers Ltd. 72-, Herald-Sun TV Pty. 73-; Dir. Australian Newsprint Mills Ltd. 57-, Vice-Chair. 60-; Dir. Tasman Pulp and Paper Co. Ltd. 63-74, Queensland Press Ltd. 70-.
Leisure interest: golf.
The Herald and Weekly Times Group, 44 Flinders Street, Melbourne, Vic.; Home: 99 Spring Street, Melbourne, Vic. 3000, Australia.

Jones, Reginald H.; American business executive; b. 11 July 1917, England; m. Grace B. Cole; one s. one d.; ed. Univ. of Pennsylvania.
Joined Gen. Electric Co. 39, Vice-Pres. (Finance) 68, Sr. Vice-Pres. 70, Dir. 71-, Vice-Chair. 72, Pres. 72, Chair., Chief Exec. Officer 72-; mem. American Management Asscn., Business Council of Financial Execs. Inst.; Trustee, Univ. of Pennsylvania.
General Electric Co., 570 Lexington Avenue, New York, N.Y. 10022, U.S.A.

Jones, Reginald Victor, C.B., C.B.E., M.A., D.PHIL., F.R.S.; British physicist; b. 29 Sept. 1911, London; s. of Harold V. and Alice M. Jones; m. Vera M. Cain 1940; one s. two d.; ed. Alleyn's School, Dulwich, Wadham and Balliol Colls., Oxford.
Scientific Officer, Royal Aircraft Establishment and Admiralty Research Lab. 36-39; Head Scientific Intelligence, Air. Staff 39-46, Dir. 46; Dir. Scientific Intelligence, Ministry of Defence 52-54; Chair. Research Advisory Cttee., British Transport Comm. 56-57, Safety in Mines Research Advisory Board 56-60, Electronic Research Council, Ministry of Aviation/Technology 64-70, Paul Instrument Fund, Royal Soc. 60-; Pres. Crabtree Foundation 58, Section A British Asscn. 71; Prof. of Natural Philosophy, Aberdeen Univ. 46-; British Nat. Cttee. for History of Science 70-; Hon. Fellow, Wadham Coll. Oxford 68; Vice-Pres. Royal Soc. 72; Commonwealth Prestige Fellow, New Zealand 73; Hon. D.Sc. (Strathclyde) 69; B.O.I.M.A. Prize, Inst. of Physics 34, Medal of Freedom with Silver Palm 46, Medal for Merit (U.S.A.) 47, Duddell Medal, Physical Soc. 60, Parsons Medal 67, Hartley Medal 72.
Publs. Various scientific, biographical and philosophical articles in journals; Editor *Notes and Records of the Royal Society.*
Department of Natural Philosophy, University of Aberdeen, Aberdeen, AB9 2UE; Home: 8 Queen's Terrace, Aberdeen, AB1 1XL, Scotland.
Telephone: 40241 (Office); 28184 (Home).

Jones, Roger Warren, A.B., M.A., LL.D., Hon. O.B.E.; American government official; b. 3 Feb. 1908, New Hartford, Conn.; s. of H. Roger Jones and Eleanor Drake; m. Dorothy Heyl 1930; two s. one d.; ed. Cornell and Columbia Univs.
Instructor, Coral Gables, Mil. Acad. 28-29; in commerce 29-31; Asst. Exec. Officer, Central Statistical Bd., Washington 33-39; Admin. Officer, Budget Bureau, 39-42; Col. in U.S. armed forces 42-45; Budget Examiner, and subsequently Asst. Dir. for Legislative Reference and Dep. Dir. Bureau of the Budget 45-59; Chair., Civil Service Comm. 59-61; Dep. Under-Sec. of State for Admin. 61-62; Senior Consultant, Budget Bureau

(renamed Office of Management and Budget Jan. 70) 62-69, 71-, Asst. Dir. 69-71; mem. Comm. on Political Activity of Govt. Personnel 67-68; mem. Board of Higher Educ., District of Columbia 68-73; Legion of Merit (U.S.A.); Hon. D.P.S. (George Wash. Univ.) 69.
Leisure interests: gardening, walking, military history.
Office of Management and Budget, Washington, D.C. 20503; Home: 3912 Leland Street, Chevy Chase, Md. 20015, U.S.A.
Telephone: 395-3910 (Office); 654-8135 (Home).

Jones, Thomas Victor; American aircraft executive; b. 21 July 1920, Pomona, Calif.; m. Ruth Nagel 1946; one s. one d.; ed. Pomona Junior Coll. and Stanford Univ.
Engineer, El Segundo Div., Douglas Aircraft Co. 41-47; Tech. Adviser, Brazilian Air Ministry 47-51; Prof., Head of Dept., Brazilian Inst. of Technology 47-51; Rand Corpn. 51-53; Asst. to Chief Engineer, Northrop Aircraft Inc. 53, Dep. Chief Engineer 54-56, Dir. Development Planning 56-57, Corporate Vice-Pres. 57, Senior Vice-Pres. 58-59, Pres. 59-, Chief Exec. Officer 60-, Chair. of Board 63-.
Publ. *Capabilities and Operating Costs of Possible Future Transport Airplanes* 53.
Northrop Corporation, 1800 Century Park East, Century City, Los Angeles, Calif. 90067; Home: 1050 Moraga Drive, Los Angeles, Calif. 90049, U.S.A.
Telephone: 213-553-6262 (Office).

Jones, Tom; Welsh singer; b. (as Thomas Jones Woodward) 7 June 1940, Treforest, Glamorgan; m. Malinda Trenchard 1956; one s.
Made first hit record *It's Not Unusual* 65; other records include *Once Upon A Time, Green Green Grass of Home, I'll Never Fall in Love Again, I'm Coming Home, Delilah, Help Yourself, I Who Have Nothing, Close Up, Body and Soul;* appeared in TV shows *Beat Room, Top Gear, Thank Your Lucky Stars, Sunday Night at the London Palladium* 65-; toured U.S.A. 65; appeared in *Ed Sullivan Show* at Copacabana, New York, and in variety show *This Is Tom Jones* in U.K. and U.S.A. 69; made 26 singles with Decca, 16 albums; Britain's Most Popular Male Singer in *Melody Maker* poll 67, 68.
c/o MAM Ltd., 24-25 New Bond Street, London, W.1, England.

Jong, Petrus J. S. de, D.S.C.; Netherlands naval officer and politician; b. 3 April 1915, Apeldoorn; m. Anna Geertruida Jacoba Henriette Bartels; three c.; ed. Royal Naval Coll.
Entered Netherlands Royal Navy 31, commissioned 34; submarine commander during Second World War; Adjutant to Minister for Navy 48; Capt. of frigate *De Zeeuw* 51; Staff Officer on staff Allied Commdr.-in-Chief, Channel, Portsmouth 53; Adjutant to Queen of Netherlands 55; Capt. of destroyer *Gelderland* 58; State Sec. for Defence 59-63; Minister of Defence 63-67; Prime Minister and Minister of Gen. Affairs 67-71; mem. First Chamber (Parl.); Catholic Party.
c/o Katholieke Volkspartij, The Hague, Netherlands.

Jonker, Willem, D.IUR.; Netherlands business executive; b. 2 July 1907; ed. Gymnasium, The Hague, and Univ. of Leiden.
Lawyer 31; City Councillor, The Hague 39; Man. Dir. Centraal Bureau voor de Rijn—en Binnenvaart 39-45, Pres. 45; mem. Economic and Social Cttee., European Economic Community (E.E.C.) and Euratom 58-, Vice-Chair. 62-64; mem. Comm. on Int. Affairs, Netherlands Social and Econ. Council 60-; Pres. Arbeitsgemeinschaft der Rheinschiffahrt 64-67; Man. Dir. Nederlandsche Rijnvaartvereeniging 41-67; Pres. Dutch Org. for Consultation in Transport Trade 66-; Officer Order of Orange-Nassau 63.
Hart Nibbrigkade 71 flat 22, The Hague, Netherlands.
Telephone: 246743.

Jonkman, Jan Anne, LL.D.; Netherlands politician; b. 13 Sept. 1891, Utrecht; s. of Dr. Henricus Franciscus Jonkman and Anna Margaretha Francisca van Gorkom; m. Johanna Lina Margaretha de Bruïne 1922; three s. one d.; ed. Utrecht, Toulouse and Leiden.
Joined Netherland-Indies Civil Service (Judicature) 19; mem. of Legislative Assembly Batavia 27-31; Public Prosecutor, High Court of Justice at Macassar (Celebes) 31, at Semarang (Java) 38; Speaker of Legislative Assembly 39-42; imprisoned by Japanese army of occupation in Java 42-45; Min. for the Overseas Territories of the Kingdom of the Netherlands July 46-Aug. 48; mem. Parl. 48-66; Pres. Senate 51-66; Pres. Admin. Court (on behalf of Netherlanders formerly in Indonesian service) 50-; Labour; Grand Cross Netherlands Lion and Grand Officer Orange-Nassau.
Leisure interests: history, writing memoirs as an 'amateur historian".
Publs. *The National-Indonesian foundations of education for the Indonesian population* 18, *The former Netherlands Indies* 71, *The Netherlands and Indonesia both free, seen from Netherlands Parliament* 76.
61 Schoutenstraat, The Hague, Netherlands.
Telephone: T.070-245223.

Jónsson, Emil; Icelandic engineer and politician (retd.); b. 27 Oct. 1902, Hafnarfjördur; s. of J. Jónsson and Sigurborg Sigurdardóttir; m. Gudfinna Sigurdardóttir 1925; four s. two d.; ed. Reykjavík Grammar School and Technical Univ. of Copenhagen.
Municipal Engineer, Hafnarfjördur 26-37; Mayor of Hafnarfjördur 30-37; mem. Parl. 34-71; State Dir. of Lighthouses and Harbours 37-44, 49-57; Man. Dir. Nat. Bank of Iceland 57-58; Minister of Communications 44-47, of Commerce and Communications 47-49; Minister of Foreign Affairs, a.i. 56; Speaker of the Althing 56-58; Prime Minister 58-59; Minister of Social Affairs and Fisheries 59-65; Minister of Foreign Affairs 65-71; Chair. Labour (Social Democratic) Party 57-68; fmr. Pres. North Atlantic Council.
Leisure interest: books.
Kirkjuvegur 7, Hafnarfjördur, Iceland.

Jónsson, Eysteinn; Icelandic politician; b. Djupivogur; s. of Jón Finnson and Sigridur Hansdóttir Beck; m. Sólveig Eyjóltsdóttir 1932; four s. two d.; ed. Co-operative Commercial Coll.
Director of Taxes, Reykjavík 30-34; mem. Althing (Parl.) 33-74; Minister of Finance 34-39, of Commerce 39-42; Dir. Printwork Edda 43-47; Chair. Progressive Party Althing Group 43-69; Minister of Educ. 47-49, of Finance 50-58; Leader, Progressive Party 62-68; mem. Council of Europe 67-69; mem. Nordic Council 69-71, Chair. Cultural Cttee. 69-71; Speaker United Althing 71-74; Vice-Chair. Fed. of Iceland Co-operative Socs. 46-74, Chair. 74-; Chair. Iceland Nature Conservation Council 72-.
Leisure interests: skiing, hiking, books.
Asvallagötn 67, Reykjavík, Iceland.
Telephone: 13277.

Jonsson, John Erik; American industrialist; b. 6 Sept. 1901, New York; s. of John Peter and Ellen Charlotte (Palmquist) Jonsson; m. Margaret Elizabeth Fonde 1923; two s. one d.; ed. Rensselaer Polytechnic Inst., Troy, N.Y.
Aluminium Co. of America 22-27; Dumont Motor Car Co. 27-29; Aluminium Co. of America 29-30; Texas Instruments Inc. 30-, Pres. 50-58, Chair. 58-64, Hon. Chair. 67-; Chair. Educ. Facilities Labs.; Dir. Equitable Life Assurance Soc. (U.S.) 58-73, Repub. of Texas Corpn., Dallas, Texas 58-; Chair. of Board, Dallas-Fort Worth Regional Airport; Life mem. American Man. Assen. 56-; mem. Board of Trustees, Rensselaer Polytechnic Inst., Skidmore Coll., Saratoga Sprints, N.Y., Austin Coll., Sherman; Callier Center for Communication Disorders, Dallas, American Assembly N.Y.C. 67; Mayor of Dallas 64-71; mem. Nat. Planning Council and Asscn. 58-73, Soc. of Exploration Geophysics 30-; mem. (fmr. Chair.) Board of Visitors, Tulane Univ. 68-; Chair. of Board, Lamplighter School, Inc., Dallas; mem. Board of Trustees, Univ. of Dallas; mem. Nat. Acad. of Eng., Texas Assembly, Austin Texas; Hon. D.Eng. (Rensselaer Polytechnic Inst., N.Y.), Hon. D.Sc. (Hobart, William Smith and Austin Colls.), Hon. D.C.L. (Univ. of Dallas), Hon. LL.D. (Southern Methodist Univ., Carnegie Mellon Univ., Skidmore Coll.), Hon. D.L. (Oklahoma Christian Coll.); Soc. of Industrial Realtors Industrialist of the Year Award 65, Bene Merento Medal 66, Gantt Medal 68, Hoover Medal 70, Founders Medal, Nat. Acad. of Eng. 74, Business Hall of Fame 75.
3300 Republic Bank Tower, Dallas, Tex. 75201, U.S.A.
Telephone: 214-742-7341.

Jónsson, Magnus; Icelandic politician; b. 7 Sept. 1919; ed. Univ. of Iceland.
Former attorney; Officer in Ministry of Finance 47-53; mem. Althing 51-; Gen. Sec. Independence Party 53-60; Gen. Man. Agricultural Bank of Iceland 61-65, 71-; Minister of Finance 65-71.
Búnadarbanki Islands, Austurstraeti 5, P.O. Box 1428, Reykjavík, Iceland.

Jooss, Kurt; balletmaster and choreographer of German origin; b. 12 Jan. 1901, Wasseralfingen, Württemberg; s. of Eugen and Amalie Jooss; m. Aino Siimola 1929 (deceased 1971); two d.; ed. Württemberg Music Acad., Stuttgart and Laban School of Dance, Hamburg.
Producer Münster Municipal Theatre 24; Dir. Dance Dept. Folkwang Municipal School Essen 27, 49, 56-; founded Folkwang Studio (Ballets Jooss) 32; Ballet Dir. Essen Opera House 30; Ballet School Dartington Hall, Devon 34-40; Maître de Ballet and chief choreographer Düsseldorf Opera 54-56; Dir. Folkwang Tanztheater-Studio 61-68; Dir. Ballets Jooss and Prof. of Choreography and Dir. Inst. Tanz, Folkwang Hochschule, Essen 63-; retd. 68; has since then been active with dance theatres in Stockholm, Salzburg (Festival), Munich, Cologne, New York, Łódź, Manchester, Antwerp, Wuppertal, Düsseldorf, Amsterdam, Cape Town, Tel-Aviv and Winnipeg; productions for TV in Germany, England, Sweden, U.S.A.; Order of Merit, Chile and Grosses Verdienstkreuz, Fed. Repub. of Germany.
Leisure interests: travelling, ethnological studies.
Works include libretti and choreography for ballets: *Die Brautfahrt* 25, *Tragödie* 26, *Drosselbart* 29, *Pavane for a Dead Infanta* 29, *The Green Table* 32, *Big City* 32, *The Prodigal Son* 33, *Chronica* 39, *Company at the Manor* 43, *Pandora* 44, *Juventud* (*Dithyrambus*) 48, *Journey in the Fog* 52, *Night Train* 52, Purcell's *Faerie Queene* 59, *Phasen* 67.
8185 Kreuth/Tegernsee, Upper Bavaria, Federal Republic of Germany.
Telephone: 08029-214.

Jooste, Gerhardus Petrus, M.A.; South African diplomatist; b. 5 May 1904, Winburg, O.F.S.; s. of Nicolaas Jooste and Sofie Visser; m. Anna van Zyl van der Merwe 1934; one s. one d.; ed. Univ. of Pretoria.
Entered Union Public Service 24; apptd. Private Sec. to Hon. N. C. Havenga, Minister of Finance 29; joined Dept. of External Affairs 34; Sec. of Legation and Chargé d'Affaires a.i., Brussels 37, Chargé d'Affaires to Belgian Govt.-in-Exile, London 40-41; Head of Economic Div., Dept. of External Affairs, Pretoria 41, Head of Political and Diplomatic Div. 46; Ambassador to U.S.A. and Permanent Del. to U.N. 49-54; Alternate Del. U.N. Gen. Assembly, Paris 48, Leader S. African Del., N.Y. 49, Leader and Deputy Leader, N.Y. 50, Dep. Leader, Paris 51-52, 58, Leader, N.Y. 52, 53, 54 and 63; High Commr. in Great Britain 54-56; Sec. for External Affairs, Pretoria 56; Ex-officio mem. of

Atomic Energy Board 56-66; Sec. for Foreign Affairs 61-66; Special Adv. on Foreign Affairs to the Prime Minister and Minister of Foreign Affairs July 66; mem. Comm. Water Matters 66-; Deputy Leader UN Gen. Assembly, N.Y. 66; Chair. State Procurement Board 68-71.
Leisure interests: golf and hunting.
851 Government Avenue, Arcadia, Pretoria, Republic of South Africa.
Telephone: 74-5464.

Jordan, Augustin; French diplomatist; b. 10 Dec. 1910. Ministry of Foreign Affairs 45-49; Second Sec., Athens 49-52; Political Counsellor, Bonn 52-54; Dir. of Cabinet of Ministers for Moroccan and Tunisian Affairs 54-55; Head of Gen. Affairs and Int. Transport, Dept. of Econ. Affairs, Ministry of Foreign Affairs 55-70; Amb. to Poland 70-73, to Austria 73-.
French Embassy, Techniterstr. 2, Vienna, Austria.

Jordan, Len B.; American politician; b. 15 May 1899; ed. Univ. of Oregon.
U.S. Army, First World War; Dir. Circle C Ranch and Jordan Motor Co.; mem. Idaho Legislature 47; Gov. of Idaho 51-55; mem. Int. Joint Comm. 55-57; Int. Advisory Board 58-59; U.S. Senator from Idaho Aug. 62-73; U.S. Adviser to UN Comm. on the Peaceful Uses of Outer Space; Republican.
3110 Crescent Rim Drive, Boise, Idaho 83704, U.S.A.

Jordan, Maurice; French engineer and business executive; b. 24 Aug. 1899; ed. Ecole des Roches, Verneuil-sur-Avre.
Vice-President, Dir.-Gen. Peugeot Motors, Pres. and Gen. Man. Oct. 64-72; Hon. Pres. 72-; Pres. DIN (Diffusion Industrielle Nouvelle).
Peugeot S.A., 75 avenue de la Grande-Armée, Paris 16e, France.

Jordan, Pascual, DR.PHIL.; German physicist; b. 18 Oct. 1902, Hannover; s. of Prof. E. Jordan and Eva Fischer; m. Hertha Stahn; two s.; ed. Univ. of Göttingen.
Extraordinary Prof., Univ. of Rostock 29-35, Ordinary Prof. 35-44; awarded Planck Medal of German Physical Society 42; Ordinary Prof. of Theoretical Physics and Dir. of Inst. of Theoretical Physics Berlin 44; Visiting Prof. Univ. of Hamburg 47-53, Ordinary Prof. 53-; Gauss Medal 55; mem. of Bundestag 57-61.
Leisure interests: all fields of natural sciences, mathematics.
Publs. incl. *Anregung von Quantensprüngen* (with J. Franck) 28, *Elementare Quantenmechanik* (with M. Born) 30, *Statistische Mechanik auf quantentheoretischer Grundlage* 30, *Anschauliche Quantentheorie* 36, *Die Physik des 20. Jahrhunderts* 36, *Das Bild der modernen Physik* 47, *Schwerkraft und Weltall* 52 (2nd edn. 55), *Der Naturwissenschaftler vor der religiösen Frage* 63 (6th edn. 72), *Die Expansion der Erde* 66 (English edn. 71).
Isestrasse 123, 2 Hamburg 13, Federal Republic of Germany.
Telephone: Hamburg 478026.

Jørgensen, Anker; Danish trade unionist and politician; b. 13 July 1922, Copenhagen; s. of Johannes Jørgensen; m. Ingrid Jørgensen 1948; four c.; ed. School for Orphans and evening classes.
Messenger, shipyard worker, warehouse worker 36-50; Vice-Pres. Warehouse Workers' Union 50, Pres. 58-62; Group Sec. Transport and Gen. Workers' Union 62-68, Pres. 68-72; mem. Folketing 64-; mem. Social Democratic Union 66-; mem. Board of Dirs., Workers' Bank of Denmark 69-; Prime Minister 72-73; Parl. Leader Social Democratic Group 73-75; Prime Minister Feb. 75-.
Borgbjergvej 1, 2450 S.V. Copenhagen, Denmark.

Joseph, Dov, B.A., B.C.L., PH.D.; Israeli politician; b. 1899, Montreal, Canada; s. of Roman Joseph and Sarah Fineberg; m. Goldie O. Hoffman 1922; one s. two d.; ed. McGill and London Univs.

Legal Adviser, Jewish Agency for Palestine 36-45, mem., Exec. 45-47, Treas. 57-61; mem. (for Mapai) of Knesset 49-60; Minister of Supply and Rationing 49-50, Agriculture 49-50, Transport and Communications 50-51, Trade and Industry 51-52, Justice 51-52, Development 53-55, Health 55, Justice 61-66.
Leisure interests: reading, music.
Publs. *Nationality—its Nature and Problems, British Rule in Palestine, The Faithful City (The Siege of Jerusalem)* 48.
22 Alharizi Road, Jerusalem, Israel.
Telephone: 39032.

Joseph, Rt. Hon. Sir Keith Sinjohn, Bt., M.P.; British politician; b. 17 Jan. 1918, London; s. of the late Sir Samuel George Joseph and Edna Cicely Phillips; m. Hellen Louise Guggenheimer 1951; one s. three d.; ed. Harrow School and Magdalen Coll., Oxford.
Military service 39-46; Barrister, Middle Temple 46; Councilman, City of London 46, Alderman 46-49; fmr. Underwriter, Lloyd's; Dir. Bovis Holdings Ltd. 51-59, Chair. Bovis Ltd. 58-59, Deputy Chair. 64-70; Conservative M.P. 56-; Parl. Private Sec. to Parl. Under-Sec. of State, Commonwealth Relations Office 57-59; Parl. Sec. Ministry of Housing and Local Govt. 59-61; Minister of State, Board of Trade 61-62; Minister of Housing and Local Govt. and Minister for Welsh Affairs 62-64; Sec. of State for Social Services 70-74; Founder and Chair. Management Cttee. of Centre for Policy Studies Ltd. 74-; Fellow, All Souls' Coll., Oxford 46-60, 71-; Conservative.
House of Commons, London, SW1A 0AA; and 23 Mulberry Walk, London, SW3 6DZ, England.

Joseph, Maxwell; British hotelier.
Chairman Grand Metropolitan Hotels Ltd., Giltspur Investments Ltd., Norfolk Capital Hotels Ltd., Fraser Ansbacher Ltd., Trumans Ltd., Watney Mann Ltd.; Joint Chair. Lombard Banking Ltd.; Dir. Bristol and West Hotels Ltd., Cunard Steam-Ship Co. Ltd., Express Dairy Co. Ltd.
Grand Metropolitan Hotels Ltd., 7 Stratford Place, London, W.1, England.

Josephson, Brian David, M.A., PH.D., F.INST.P., F.R.S.; British physicist; b. 4 Jan. 1904, Cardiff; ed. Cardiff High School, Cambridge Univ.
Research Fellow, Trinity Coll., Cambridge 62-; Research Asst. Prof. Univ. of Illinois 65-66; Asst. Dir. of Research, Cambridge Univ. 67-72, Reader in Physics 72-74, Prof. of Physics 74-; New Scientist Award 69, Research Corpn. Award 69, Fritz London Award 70, Nobel Prize for Physics 73.
Leisure interests: walking, ice skating, photography, astronomy.
Publs. research papers on superconductivity, critical phenomena, etc.
Cavendish Laboratory, Madingley Road, Cambridge, CB3 0HE, England.

Josephson, Erland; Swedish actor and theatre director; b. 15 June 1923.
At Municipal Theatre, Helsingborg 45-49, Gothenburg 49-56, Royal Dramatic Theatre, Stockholm 56-; Dir. of Royal Dramatic Theatre, Stockholm June 66-.
Publs. include: *Cirkel* 46, *Spegeln och en portvakt* 46, *Spel med bedrövade artister* 47, *Ensam och fri* 48, *Lyssnarpost* 49, *De vuxna barnen* 52, *Utflykt* 54, *Sällskapslek* 55, *En berättelse om herr Silberstein* 57, *Kungen ur leken* 59, *Doktor Meyers sista dagar* 64, *Kandidat Nilssons första natt* 64, *Scenes from a Marriage* 74.
Royal Dramatic Theatre, Stockholm, Sweden.
Telephone: 0223-66477.

Jost, Nestor; Brazilian politician and bank official; b. 10 Jan. 1917; ed. Anchieta High School, Pôrto Alegre.
Local govt. work 39-45; fmr. Mayor of São Lourenço do

Sul; State Deputy 47; mem. Legis. Assembly of Rio Grande do Sul 47-50; Fed. Deputy, Partido Democrático (P.S.D.) 51; Sec.-Gen. P.S.D., Rio Grande do Sul Div. 48-49; later Dir. Industrial Credit Section and Agricultural Credit Section, Bank of Brazil; Pres. Bank of Brazil 67-74; Dir. European Brazilian Bank Ltd. 72-74; Chair. Cocemtro 74-.
Brasília, Brazil.

Jouhandeau, Marcel; French novelist; b. 26 July 1888, Guéret (Creuse); s. of Paul Jouhandeau and Marie Blanchet; m. Elisabeth Toulemon 1929 (pseudonym Caryatid) (deceased).
Publs. include *La Jeunesse de Théophile* 20, *Les Pincengrain* 24, *M. Godeau intime* 25, *Les Terébinthe* 26, *Ximinès Malinjoude* 27, *Opales* 28, *Brigitte ou la Belle au bois dormant*, *Le parricide imaginaire* 29, *Le journal du coiffeur* 30, *Eloge de l'imprudence* 32, *Elise Véronicœana* 33, *M. Godeau marié* 33, *Chaminadour* (2 vols.) 34, *Images de Paris* 34, *Algèbre des valeurs morales* 35, *Le Saladier* 36, *Chroniques maritales* 38, *Le Jardin de Cordoue* 38, *De l'Abjection* 39, *L'Arbre de visages Triptyque*, *Requiem*, *Ei lux* 40, *Les miens*, *Minos et moi*, *Nouvelles chroniques maritales* 42, *L'oncle Henri* 43, *Chronique d'une passion* 44, *Petit bestiaire* 44, *Essai sur moi-même* 46, *Animaux familiers*, *Annotations en marge de la Genèse*, *Carnets de Don Juan* 47, *Don Juan, récit* 48, *Mémorial I: Le livre de mon père* 48, *II Ménagerie domestique* 48, *La Faute plutôt que le scandale* 49, *L'Imposteur* 50, *Un Monde* 50, *Mémorial III: Le Fils du Boucher* 51, *Ces Messieurs* 51, *Contes Rustiques* 51, *Elise architecte* 51, *La Paroisse du Temps Jadis* 52, *Eloge de la Volupté* 52, *De la Grandeur* 52, *Galande ou Convalescence au Village* 53, *Derniers Jours et Mort de Véronique* 53, *Endymion illustré par P. Y. Trémois* 53, *Mémorial IV: Apprentis et Garçons* 53, *Anna de Mme Apremont*, *Eléments pour une Ethique*, *Mémorial V: Le langage de la tribu* 54, *Contes de l'Enfer* 55, *Nouvelles Images de Paris* 56, *Jeunesse* 56, *Réflexions sur la Vieillesse et la Mort* 56, *Théâtre sans spectacle*, *Carnets de l'écrivain*, *St. Philippe Néri*, *Correspondance avec André Gide* 57, *Mémorial VI: les Chemins de l'Adolescence*, *Réflexions sur la Vie et le Bonheur* 58, *Les Argonautes* 59, *L'Eternel Procès* 60, *L'Ecole des Filles* 61, *Animaleries* 61, *Descente aux Enfers* (illustrated by Georges Braque); *Journaliers I-VII*, *Divertissements*, *Journaliers VIII* 66, *Journaliers IX* 67, *Journaliers X*, *Le gourdin d'Elise* 67, *Journaliers XI*, *La Vertu dépaysée* 68, *Journaliers XII*, *Nouveau Tertaines*, *Journaliers XIII*, *Magnificat*, *Journaliers XIV*, *Le Possession*, *Journaliers XV*, *Confrontation avec la poussière*, *Journaliers XVI* 71, *Six cent Actes Divers—Lettres d'une Mère à son Fils* 71, *Journaliers XVII*, *Gemonies* 71, *Memorial VII: Bon An*, *Mal An* 72, *Journaliers XVIII*, *Paulo minus ab Angelo*, *Journaliers XIX*, *Un second Soleil* 73, *Journaliers XX*, *Jeux de Miroirs* 74.
8 Av. Ducis, Parc de la Malmaison, Rueil 92, S.-et-O., France.
Telephone: 967-22-56.

Joukhdar, Mohammed Saleh, B.A., M.A.; Saudi Arabian economist; b. 1932, Jeddah; m. Malik Intabi 1957; one s. two d.; ed. Univs. of California and Southern California.
Econ. Adviser to Directorate-Gen. of Petroleum and Minerals, Saudi Arabia 58; Dir.-Gen. Min. of Petroleum and Mineral Resources 61; Dir. Arabian Oil Co.; Sec.-Gen. of OPEC 67-68; Dep. Min. of Petroleum and Mineral Resources 69; Dir. Petromin; Trustee, Coll. of Petroleum and Minerals.
Ministry of Petroleum and Mineral Resources, P.O. Box 247, Riyadh, Saudi Arabia.

Jousset, Bernard; French business executive; b. 27 May 1899, Paris; s. of André Jousset and Alice Ghesquiere-Dierickx; m. Christiane Chain 1926; two s. four d.; ed. Lycées Janson-de-Sailly and Condorcet,

Coll. Stanislas and Ecole Supérieure de la Métallurgie et des Mines, Nancy.
Served French Army 18-19; founded and became Pres., Dir.-Gen. of Société Parisienne de Cémentation; Hon. Pres. Groupement Inter-Professionnel Patronal Courbevoie Colombes; fmr. Pres. Comm. juridique, Conseil National du Patronat Français; Hon. Pres. French Catholic Employers; Chevalier, Légion d'Honneur, Commandeur de St.-Sylvestre, Chevalier de l'Ordre du Saint Sépulchre de Jérusalem.
Leisure interests: tennis, hunting.
Publs. *L'Accession des Travailleurs au Capital*, *Vers un salaire humain* (with Hyacynthe Dubreuil).
36 avenue du grand Veneur, 78110 Le Vésinet, France.
Telephone: 976-09-15.

Jouve, Géraud Henri; French journalist and diplomatist; b. 5 July 1901; ed. Univs. of Strasbourg and Paris.
Attached Lycée de Cahors 29, Institut Français, Berlin 30; corresp. for Havas Agency in Budapest, Warsaw, Berlin, Amsterdam, Bucharest 31-40; Free French Del. to Turkey and the Balkans 40-42; Dir. Radio-Brazzaville 43-44, and of Agence France-Presse (Algeria-Paris) 44-45; Consul-Gen. Ministry of Foreign Affairs 46; mem. Nat. Assembly 46-51; Permanent French Del. to Council of Europe 51-55; Amb. to Finland 55-60; French del., U.N. High Comm. for Refugees 60-66; Pres. Asscn. syndicale des Rédacteurs en chef; Officier Légion d'Honneur, Médaille de la Résistance 46.
Publs. *La Remontée de Munich à Brazzaville* 45, *Voici l'âge atomique* 46.
104, Boulevard Arago, Paris 14e, France.

Jouven, Pierre Jean Antoine; French industrialist; b. 29 March 1908, Paris; s. of Alphonse Jouven and Jeanne Bouhey; m. Madeleine Huguet 1931; three s. three d.; ed. Ecole Polytechnique and Ecole des Mines, Paris.
Engineer Corps des Mines 31-42; with Compagnie Péchiney, Paris 43-, Man. of Works 45-48, Man. Chem. Div. 48-55, Aluminium Div. 55-59, Gen. Man. 60, Chair. of Board 68-72; Chair. Péchiney-Ugine Kuhlmann 72-75, Hon. Pres. 75-; Vice-Pres. Rhône-Poulenc S.A. 75-; Dir. Seichimé, Cedegur G.P., Naphtachimie, Crédit Commercial de France; Pres. Int. Inst. of Aluminium 72-; Officier Légion d'Honneur.
23 rue Balzac, Paris 8e; 28 rue Guynomer, Paris 6e, France.

Jova, Joseph John, A.B.; American international official; b. 7 Nov. 1916, Newburgh, N.Y.; s. of Joseph Luis and Maria Josefa (Gonzalez-Cavada) Jova; m. Pamela Johnson 1949; two s. one d.; ed. Dartmouth Coll.
With Guatemala Div. United Fruit Co. 38-41; mil. service U.S. Navy 42-47; foreign service officer, Dept. of State 47-; Vice-Consul, Basra 47-49; Second Sec. and Vice-Consul, Tangier 49-52; Consul, Oporto 52-54; First Sec., Lisbon 54-57; Officer-in-Charge French-Iberian Affairs 57-58; Asst. Chief Personnel Operations Div. 59-60, Chief 60-61; Deputy Chief of Mission, Santiago 61-65; Amb. to Honduras, Tegucigalpa 65-69; Amb. to OAS, Washington 69-74; Amb. to Mexico, Mexico City 74-; Chair. Dept. of State Management Reform Task Force; Chair. U.S. dels. to Inter-American Council on Educ., Science and Culture, Panama 72, Mar del Plata 73, UN Econ. Comm. for Latin America, Santiago 71, UN Econ. Comm. for Latin American Population Conf., Mexico 74; Vice-Chair. U.S. del. to Gen. Assembly OAS 70, 71, 72, 73; mem. Mexican Acad. Int. Law, Center for Inter-American Relations; Trustee, Mt. St. Mary's Coll.; L.H.D. (Mt. St. Mary's Coll.) 73, LL.D. (Dowling Coll.) 73; Grand Cross Order Morazán (Honduras), Constantinian Order St. George; Presidential Management Improvement Award 70,

Conquistador Award, El Paso, Texas 75, New Orleans Int. House T. A. Cunningham Award 75.
American Embassy, Reforma 305, México, D.F., Mexico.

Jovanovich, William Iliya; American publisher; b. 6 Feb. 1920, Louisville, Colo.; s. of Iliya M. and Hedviga (Garbatz) Jovanovich; m. Martha Evelyn Davis 1943; ed. Univ. of Colorado and Harvard and Columbia Univs.
Harcourt Brace Jovanovich, Inc., New York City 47-, Assoc. Editor 47-53, Vice-Pres., Dir. 53-54, Pres. and Dir. 55-70, Chair. and Chief Exec. Officer 70-; Chair. Longmans Canada Ltd., 61; D.Litt. (Colo. Coll., Adelphi Univ., Alaska Univ.).
Publ. *Now, Barabbas* 64.
757 Third Avenue, New York, N.Y. 10017, U.S.A.

Joxe, Louis, L. ès L.; French diplomatist and politician; b. 16 Sept. 1901; ed. Lycée Lakanal and Faculty of Arts, Paris.
Member French del. League of Nations 32, 33, 39; Deputy Chief of Secretariat to Minister for Air and mem. French del. to Conf. for Reduction of Armaments 33-34; attached to Information Service, League of Nations 33-39; Sec.-Gen. Centre d'Etudes de Politique Etrangère, Paris Univ.; Inspector of Foreign Services, Agence d'Information 35-39; Sec.-Gen. of Cttee. for Nat. Liberation 43-44; Sec.-Gen. of Govt. 44-46, Councillor of State 44; in charge of cultural relations Ministry of Foreign Affairs, Paris 46-52; Amb. to U.S.S.R. 52-56, to Germany 56; Sec.-Gen. Ministry of Foreign Affairs 56-59; **Sec. of State, Prime Minister's Office 59-60; Minister of Nat. Education July-Nov. 60; Minister of State in charge of Algerian Affairs Nov. 60-Dec. 62, for French Admin. Reform 62-67; Minister of Justice 67-May 68;** mem. French del. to UNESCO Conf. 46, 47, 49, 50, 51; Commdr. Légion d'Honneur, Médaille de la Résistance.
39 quai de l'Horloge, Paris 1er, France.

Joyce, Eileen; Australian concert pianist; ed. Loreto Convent, Perth, Leipzig Conservatoire, studied in Germany under Teichmuller and Schnabel.
Concert debut, London, at Promenade Concerts under Sir Henry Wood; numerous concert tours, radio performances and gramophone recordings; during Second World War played in assen. with London Philharmonic Orchestra; concerts with all principal orchestras in U.K., Berlin Philharmonic Orchestra, Conservatoire and Nat. Orchestras, France, Concertgebouw Orchestra, Netherlands, La Scala Orchestra, Italy, Philadelphia Orchestra, Carnegie Hall, New York and Royal Philharmonic Society; concert tours, Australia 48, South Africa 50, Scandinavia and Netherlands 51, South America, Scandinavia and Finland 52, Yugoslavia 53, New Zealand 58, U.S.S.R. 61, India 62; contributed to sound tracks of films, including *The Seventh Veil* and *Brief Encounter*; appeared in films, including *Wherever She Goes* (autobiographical); gramophone recordings include first recording of John Ireland's Pianoforte Concerto; Hon. Mus.D. 71.
Chartwell Farm, Westerham, Kent, England.

Juan, Prince, Count of Barcelona; Pretender to the Spanish throne; b. 20 June 1913; m. H.R.H. Doña María de la Mercedes de Borbón y Orleans 1935.
Went into exile with his father King Alfonso April 31; recognized as King of Spain by his father 41.
Villa "Giralda," Estoril, Portugal.
Telephone: Lisbon 261091.

Juan Carlos I, King of Spain; b. 5 Jan. 1938, Rome; s. of H.R.H. Don Juan de Borbón y Battenberg, Count of Barcelona and H.R.H. Doña María de las Mercedes de Borbón y Orleans, and grandson of King Alfonso XIII and Queen Victoria Eugenia of Spain; m. Princess Sophia, d. of the late King Paul of the Hellenes and of Queen Frederica, 1962; one s. two d.; ed. privately in Fribourg (Switzerland), Madrid, San Sebastián, Inst. of San Isidro, Madrid, Colegio del Carmen, General Military Acad., Zaragoza and Univ. of Madrid.
Spent childhood in Rome, Lausanne, Estoril and Madrid; commissioned into the three armed forces and undertook training in each of them 57-59; has studied the organization and activities of various government ministries; named by Gen. Franco as future King of Spain 69, inaugurated as King of Spain 22 Nov. 1975, named as Captain-General of the Armed Forces Nov. 75.
Palacio de la Zarzuela, Madrid, Spain.

Jubany Arnau, H.E. Cardinal Narciso, D.CN.L.; Spanish ecclesiastic; b. 12 Aug. 1916, Sta. Coloma, Gerona. Ordained 39; Auxiliary Bishop of Barcelona 55; Bishop of Gerona 64-71; Archbishop of Barcelona 71-; cr. Cardinal 73; Pres. Episcopal Comm. on Liturgy; mem. Sacred Congregation for Divine Worship.
Calle Obispo Irurita 5, Barcelona 2, Spain.
Telephone: 218-37-34.

Judelson, David N.; American business executive; b. 22 Nov. 1928, Hackensack, N.J.; m. Maria O. Guerra; two s. one d.; ed. New York Univ.
Vice-President in charge of manufacturing, Gulf and Western Industries Inc. 58, Dir. 59-, Exec. Vice-Pres. 66, Pres. 67-; Chair. Oscar I. Judelson Inc.; Dir. Ward Foods Inc., Quebec Iron and Titanium Corpn.
Gulf and Western Industries Inc., 1 Gulf and Western Plaza, New York, N.Y. 10021, U.S.A.

Judge, Edward Thomas, M.A.; British business executive; b. 20 Nov. 1908, Leicester; s. of late Thomas Oliver and Florence (née Gravestock) Judge; m. Alice Gertrude Matthews 1934; two s.; ed. Worcester Royal Grammar School and St. John's Coll., Cambridge.
Dorman, Long & Co. Ltd. 30-67; Chair. and Gen. Man. 61-67; Pres. British Iron and Steel Fed. 65-66; Chair. Reyrolle Parsons 69-74, A. Reyrolle and Co. Ltd. and C. A. Parsons Ltd. 68-74, Anglo Great Lakes Corpn. 68-71; Dir. B.P.B. Industries, Pilkington Bros. Ltd., Fibreglass Ltd., Dorman Long Ltd., Vanderbijl Corpn., Zenith Electric Co. Ltd., E.T.J. Consultancy Services; Deputy Pres. British Electrical and Allied Manufacturers Asscn. 69-70, Pres. 70-71.
Leisure interest: fishing.
Wood Place, Aspley Guise, Milton Keynes MK17 8EP, England.
Telephone: 582029.

Judge, Thomas L.; American state governor; b. 12 Oct. 1934, Helena, Mont.; s. of Thomas P. Judge and Blanche Gulliot; m. Carol Anderson 1966; two s.; ed. Univs. of Notre Dame and Louisville.
Second Lieut. U.S. Army 58; Advertising Exec. *Louisville Courier Journal* 59-60; Pres. Judge Advertising 60-73; State Rep. Lewis and Clark County 60-66, State Senator 67-68; Lieut.-Gov. of Montana Jan. 68-72, Gov. 73-; Democrat.
Leisure interests: skiing, hunting, fishing, reading.
State Capitol, Helena, Mont.; Home: 2 Carson, Helena, Mont. 59601, U.S.A.
Telephone: 449-3111 (Office); 442-3419 (Home).

Juglas, Jean-Jacques, L. ès L.; French professor and politician; b. 10 June 1904, Bergerac, Dordogne; s. of Jean-Fernand Juglas and Marie Lacoste; m. Marie-Marguerite Lacotte 1927; one d.; ed. Collège de Bergerac and Univ. of Bordeaux.
Taught at various lycées; Prof. of Geography at Ecole Normale Supérieure d'Enseignement Technique and Ecole Nationale des Arts et Métiers, Paris; Sec.-Gen. for Information at Ministry of French Overseas Territories; served French Army 39-40; worked with Resistance during Occupation; one of founders of M.R.P. (Catholic

Party) in west of Paris; mem. of both Constituent Assemblies; Deputy for Paris 46-51, Lot et Garonne 51-56; del. to Franco-Vietnamese Conf. Fontainebleau 46, and to UN 50, 51 and 54; Pres. Comm. for Overseas Territories in the Nat. Assembly 46-55; Minister for Overseas Territories Jan.-Feb. 55; Dir. 56-60, Pres. Council of Admin. Office of Scientific and Technical Research Overseas 60-63; Prof. Econ. Geography, Conservatoire Nationale des Arts et Métiers; Pres. Cttee. for Scientific Research and Tropical Techniques; Dir. l'Institut d'Etude du Développement Economique et Social; mem. Académie des Sciences d'Outre-Mer.
Leisure interests: reading, walking, swimming.
Publ. *Traité de Géographie Economique.*
137 rue de la Tour, Paris 16e, France.
Telephone: 504-25-40 (Paris).

Julia, Gaston Maurice, D. ès s.; French university professor; b. 3 Feb. 1893, Sidi-Bel-Abbès, Algeria; s. of Joseph Julia and Dolores Bénavent; m. Marianne Chausson 1917; six s.; ed. Ecole Normale Supérieure. Lecturer, Ecole Normale Supérieure 19-28; Lecturer at the Sorbonne 20-25; Titular Prof. of Higher Analysis at the Sorbonne 25-64; Tutor at the Ecole Polytechnique 20-36; Prof. of Geometry, Ecole Polytechnique 36-64; mem. Acad. des Sciences (fmr. Pres.), Pontifical Acad. of Sciences; Grand Officier Légion d'Honneur (mil.); Croix de Guerre (14-18); Grand Invalide de Guerre (14-18).
Leisure interests: music, reading, horticulture.
Publs. Sixteen volumes and 200 monographs on analysis, geometry, and mechanics 24-47.
4 *bis* rue Traversière, 78 Versailles, France.
Telephone: 950-20-05.

Juliana Louise Emma Marie Wilhelmina, Queen of the Netherlands, Princess of Orange-Nassau, Duchess of Mecklenburgh, Princess of Lippe-Biesterfeld; b. 30 April 1909.
Daughter of Queen Wilhelmina and Prince Henry of Mecklenburg-Schwerin; married Prince Bernhard of Lippe-Biesterfeld Jan. 37; daughters Princess Beatrix Wilhelmina Armgard, b. Jan. 38, Princess Irene Emma Elisabeth, b. Aug. 39, Princess Margriet Francisca, b. Jan. 43, Princess Maria Christina, b. Feb. 47; went to Canada after German occupation 40; in England 44; returned to Netherlands 45; Princess Regent 48; Queen of Netherlands Sept. 48-.
Palace of Soestdijk, Baarn, Netherlands.

Julien, A. M. (*pseudonym* of Aman Maistre); French theatrical director and administrator; b. 24 July 1903; ed. Inst. St. Joseph, Toulon.
Founder, Compagnie des Quinze; Asst. to Cavalcanti; Artistic Dir., Radio-Cité, Editor *Vedettes* 42-44; Producer, Théâtre Sarah-Bernhardt 44, Dir. 47-59, 62-; Dir.-Gen. Paris Drama Festival 54-; Dir.-Gen. Théâtre des Nations 58-65; Admin. Paris Opéra and Opéra Comique 59-62; Vice-Pres. Syndicat des Dirs. de Théâtre; Officier Légion d'Honneur.
Les Templiers, 4 avencas, 12660 Saint-Georges de Luzençon, France.

Juma, Midhet; Jordanian diplomatist; b. 19 Aug. 1920; brother of Saad Juma (*q.v.*); ed. Cairo Univ.
Attaché to Arab League, Cairo 45-47; First Sec. and Counsellor, Cairo 47-52; Counsellor and Chargé d'Affaires, London 52-53; Minister to Pakistan 53-55; Chief of Protocol, Royal Palace Amman 56; Under-Sec. for Press and Broadcasting 56-58; Amb. to the U.S.A. 58-59, to Morocco 59-62, to Federal Republic of Germany 62-65, to Lebanon 65-67, to U.K. 67-69, to Tunisia 69-70, to Spain 71-75; numerous decorations.
c/o Ministry of Foreign Affairs, Amman, Jordan.

Juma, Saad; Jordanian diplomatist; b. 21 March 1916, Tafila; brother of Midhet Juma (*q.v.*); m. Salwa Ghanem; two s. one d.; ed. Syrian Univ., Damascus.

Civil Service for 29 years; Dir. Press and Publicity; Chief Censor; Sec. to Prime Minister; Perm. Under-Sec., Govt. of Amman; Under-Sec. for Foreign Affairs; Amb. to Iran; Amb. to Syrian Arab Republic 62, to U.S.A. 62-65; Minister for the Royal Court 65-67; Prime Minister April 67-Oct. 67; Amb. to U.K. 69-70; fmr. Personal Rep. to H.M. King Hussein; mem. Senate; honours from Jordan, Iran, Syria, Italy and China (Taiwan).
Leisure interests: reading, music, bridge.
Publs. *Conspiracy and the Battle of Destiny, Hostile Society.*
Jebel Amman, 4th Circle, Amman, Jordan.

Jumbe, (Mwinyi) Aboud; Tanzanian politician; b. 1920, Zanzibar; ed. secondary school, Zanzibar and Makerere Univ. Coll., Uganda.
Teacher 46-50; leader, Zanzibar Nat. Union 53; fmr. mem. Zanzibar Township Council; mem. Afro-Shirazi Party (ASP) 60-, later Organizing Sec., Head April 72-; mem. Nat. Assembly of Zanzibar (ASP) 61-; Opposition Whip 62-64; Minister of Home Affairs, Zanzibar Jan.-April 64; Minister of State, First Vice-President's Office, Tanzania 64-72, concurrently responsible for Ministry of Health and Social Services 64-Sept. 67; First Vice-Pres. of Tanzania April 72-; Chair. Zanzibar Revolutionary Council April 72-.
Office of the First Vice-President, Zanzibar, United Republic of Tanzania.

Jumblatt, Kamal; Lebanese politician and hereditary Druse chieftain; b. 1919.
Former Minister of National Economy; Pres. Socialist Progressive Party of Lebanon; Minister of Education and Fine Arts 60-61; Minister of State for the Interior and Planning Services 61-64; Minister of Public Works and Transport 66-67; Minister of Interior April-June 70; Order of Lenin 70; Lenin Peace Prize 72.
Chamber of Deputies, Beirut, Lebanon.

Jung, Nawab Mir Nawaz (M. Mir Khan), B.A., LL.B., M.SC.; Pakistan financier and diplomatist; b. 4 Jan. 1914, Hyderabad; s. of Nawab and Begum Ameer Nawaz Jung; one c.; ed. Nizam's Coll., Hyderabad and Univs. of London, Paris and Geneva.
In service of Hyderabad State, holding posts of Cabinet Sec., Sec. Railways and Civil Aviation, Sec. Finance, Official Dir. State Bank, Deccan Airways, Coal Mines Co., etc.; prior to partition was Hyderabad's Envoy in London; Minister of Pakistan to Sweden, Norway, Denmark and Finland 51-53; Amb. to the UN 54-57, Pres. Econ. and Social Council of the UN 57-58; Amb. to France and to the Vatican 57-59; Amb.-at-Large to African States 60; Regional Rep. of UN to N.W. Africa, Dakar 61-65; UN Rep., Tunis 65-68; Sr. Consultant to UN Devt. Programme (UNDP); Grand Officier, Légion d'Honneur (France), Ordre Nat. (Senegal, Mauritania), Grand Cordon Ordre Nat. (Tunisia).
Publs. *Federal Finance* 36, *Central Banking* 45, *Five Year Appraisals (1960-64) of UN and Agencies* (co-author).
UNDP, Palais des Nations, Geneva; and 137 rue de Lausanne, Geneva, Switzerland.
Telephone: 317082 (Home).

Jung, Richard, DR.MED.; German neurologist; b. 27 June 1911, Frankenthal; s. of Adolf and Irmgard Weitbrecht; m. Margit Reuterwall 1944; three d.; ed. Vienna, Freiburg, Paris, Berlin and Munich Univs.
Assistant, Neuro-psychiatric Clinic, Freiburg i. Br. Univ. 35-36, 38-48; Rockefeller Fellow, London and Zürich 36-37; at Hirnforschungsinst., Berlin-Buch 37-38; Dozent, Freiburg i. Br. Univ. 41, Extraordinary Prof. 47, Dir. Dept. of Clinical Neurophysiology 48, Ordinary Prof. of Neurology and Clinical Neurophysiology 51-, Dean Medical Faculty 54-55; hon. mem.,

Soc. de Neurologie (Paris), Soc. Italiana d'Elettro-encefalografia; corresp. mem., American Neurological Assen.; mem. Akademie der Wissenschaften, Mainz 60; Hon. D.Sc. 69.
Leisure interest: graphic arts.
Publs. *Eine Methodik der Ableitung lokalisierter Potentialschwankungen aus subcorticalen Hirngebieten* (with A. E. Kornmüller) 38, *Physiologische Untersuchungen über den Parkinsontremor und andere Zitterformen beim Menschen* 41, *Über rasch wiederholte Entladungen der Motoneurone und die Hemmungsphase des Beugereflexes* (with J. F. Tönnies) 48, *Mikroableitungen von einzelnen Neuronen im optischen Cortex der Katze: Die lichtaktivierten B-Neurone* (with R. von Baumgarten and G. Baumgartner) 52, *Neuronal Discharge* 53, *Allgemeine Neurophysiologie* 53, *Korrelationen von Neuronentätigkeit und Sehen* 61, *Neurophysiologie und Psychiatrie* 67, *Visual Perception and Neurophysiology* 73.
Waldhofstrasse 42, D. 78 Freiburg, Federal Republic of Germany.
Telephone: 20174215 (Office).

Jung Bahadur, Nawab Ali Yavar, B.A.; Indian diplomatist and administrator; b. 1905, Hyderabad; s. of Nawab Khedive Jung and Tyeba Begum Bilgrami; m. Zehra Begum Bilgrami 1939; three s. two d.; ed. Nizam Coll., Hyderabad, Queen's Coll., Oxford.
Professor of History and Political Science, Osmania Univ. 27-35; Dir. of Information, Hyderabad Govt. 35-37; Sec. for Constitutional Affairs, Information and Broadcasting 37-42, for Constitutional Affairs, Police, Educ., Religious Affairs and Justice 42-45; Vice-Chancellor, Osmania Univ. 45-46 and 48-52; Minister for Constitutional Affairs, Local Self-Govt., Police, Public Health and Educ. 46-47; resigned from Hyderabad Govt. 47; mem. Nat. Comm. for UNESCO; Del. to UN Gen. Assembly 46, 50, 52-55; Deputy Amb. to Argentine and Minister to Chile 52-54; Amb. to Egypt, Minister to Lebanon and Libya 54-58; Leader Indian del. to UN Econ. and Social Council 53; Chair. UN Cttee. SUNFED 56-57; Leader of Indian del. to UN 56, 57, 60; Amb. to Yugoslavia and Greece and Minister to Bulgaria 58-61, Amb. to France 61-65; Vice-Chancellor Muslim Univ. Aligarh 65-68; mem. Univ. Grants Comm. 66-68, Standing Cttee. Inter-Univ. Board, Acad. Cttee. and Gov. Board of School of Int. Studies 66-68; Chair. Study Team on Defence, Admin. Reforms Comm. 67-68; Amb. to U.S.A. 68-70; Gov. Maharashtra State 70-; mem. Cttee. on Role of Govs. 71-72; Pres. Nat. Ameer Khushrav Soc. 74-76; Hon. LL.D. (Osmania Univ.) 56; awarded Padma Bhushan 59.
Leisure interests: reading, stamp collecting, study of history and politics.
Publs. *Hyderabad in Retrospect, External Relations of Hyderabad.*
Raj Bhavan, Bombay, India.
Telephone: 36-8602.

Jungalwalla, Nowshir K., O.B.E., M.B.B.S., M.R.C.S., M.R.C.P.; Indian public health official; b. 1 Dec. 1912, Rangoon, Burma; s. of Dr. K. T. Jungalwalla and Freny Anklesaria; m. Piloo Nanavutty 1950; one s.; ed. Univ. of Rangoon and Johns Hopkins Univ., U.S.A.
Indian Army Medical Services 39-46; Deputy Public Health Commr., Ministry of Health 46-50; Regional Adviser, Regional Office for S.E. Asia, World Health Org. (WHO) 50-52, Rep. in Indonesia 52-55, Dir. Public Health Services, Geneva April 67-72; Deputy Dir.-Gen. of Health Services, India 55-57, 60-65, Additional Dir.-Gen. 65-67; Dir. All-India Inst. of Hygiene and Public Health 57-60; Dir. Health Services, Regional Office for S.E. Asia, New Delhi 72-; Hon. Fellow American Public Health Assen.; Fellow Acad.

of Medical Sciences (India); Deputy Dir.-Gen. of Health Services 63-65.
A2/2 Safdarjang Enclave, New Delhi 110016, India.
Telephone: 70591.

Jünger, Ernst; German writer; b. 29 March 1895, Heidelberg; m. 1st Gretha v. Jeinsen 1925 (died 1960), 2nd Dr. Liselotte Lohrer 1962; two s. (one deceased); ed. Hanover, Leipzig and Naples.
Served in German Army in both World Wars; awarded Pour le Mérite in First War; involved in July 20th 1944 plot while on Staff of Gen. Stülpnagel in Paris; Literary Award of City of Bremen 56, Goslar 56, Grand Cross of Merit 59, Culture Award, Fed. of German Industries 60, Immermann Award of Düsseldorf 65, Freiherr von Stein Gold Medal 70, Schiller Gedächtnispreis 74.
Leisure interest: entomology.
Publs. *In Stahlgewittern* 20, *Das Abenteuerliche Herz* 29, *Der Arbeiter* 32, *Auf den Marmorklippen* 39, *Gärten und Strassen* 42, *Der Friede* 45, *Sprache und Körperbau* 48, *Atlantische Fahrt* 48, *Heliopolis* 49, *Strahlungen* 49, *Über die Linie* 50, *Der Waldgang* 51, *Besuch auf Godenholm* 52, *Der Gordische Knoten* 53, *Das Sanduhrbuch* 54, *Am Sarazenenturm* 55, *Rivarol* 56, *Gläserne Bienen* 57, *Jahre der Okkupation, An der Zeitmauer* 59, *Der Weltstaat* 60, *Ein Vormittag in Antibes* 60, *Sgraffiti* 60, *Werke* (collected works, 10 vols.) 60-65, *Das spanische Mondhorn* 62, *Typus, Name, Gestalt* 63, *Sturm* 63, *Grenzgänge* 65, *Im Granit* 67, *Subtile Jagden* 67, *Zwei Inseln* (Formosa, Ceylon) 68, *Federbälle* 69, *Lettern und Ideogramme* (Japan), *Ad Hoc* 70, *Annäherungen, Drogen und Rausch* 70, *Bibliography* 70, *Sinn u. Bedeutung, ein Figurenspiel* 71, *Philemon u. Baucis* 72, *Die Zwille* 73, *Zahlen und Götter* 74, *Ernst Jünger-Alfred Kubin, eine Begegnung* 75, *Myrdun* (illustrated by A. Kubin, 2nd edn.) 75.
7941 Wilflingen über Riedlingen, Württemberg, Federal Republic of Germany.

Jungers, Francis; American oil executive; s. of Frank Jungers and Elizabeth Becker; m. Alison F. Morris 1947; three s. one d.; ed. Willamette Univ. and Univ. of Washington.
Joined Arabian American Oil Co. 47, various eng. and operating positions 47-62, Gen. Man. U.S. Offices 64-65, Gen. Man. Govt. Relations 69, Vice-Pres. Concession Affairs 69, Dir. 70, Senior Vice-Pres. Finance & Relations 70, Pres. 71, Chair. of Board and Chief Exec. Officer 73-; Trustee, American Univ. of Cairo 75-.
Leisure interests: golf, swimming.
Arabian American Oil Company, Dhahran, Saudi Arabia; and Arabian American Oil Company, 1345 Avenue of the Americas, New York, N.Y. 10019, U.S.A.
Telephone: (212) 977-7300 (New York).

Juniac, Baron Gontran de; French diplomatist; b. 28 July 1908, Limoges; ed. Faculté de Droit, Paris.
Has served in Munich, Berlin, Moscow, Dublin, Washington and London; Amb. to Ethiopia 60, to Turkey 65, to Belgium 70-73 (retd.).
11 boulevard du Général Koenig, 92200 Neuilly-sur-Seine, France.

Junker, Wolfgang; German building engineer and politician; b. 1929.
Member, Sozialistische Einheitspartei Deutschlands (SED); now Minister of Construction.
Ministerium für die Bauindustrie, Berlin, German Democratic Republic.

Junor, John Donald Brown, M.A.; British journalist; b. 15 Jan. 1919, Glasgow; s. of Alexander Junor; m. Pamela Welsh 1942; one s. one d.; ed. Glasgow Univ.
Served Fleet Air Arm 40-45; political columnist *Sunday Express* 48-50; Asst. Editor *Daily Express* 51-53; Deputy Editor *Evening Standard* 53-54; Editor *Sunday Express* 54-. Dir. 56-, Chair. 68-; Dir. Beaverbrook

Newspapers 60-; Hon. Dr. of Law, Univ. of New Brunswick, Canada 73.
Leisure interests: golf, tennis, sailing.
Publs. *Proletariat of Westminster* 49, *Equal Shares* 50.
Wellpools Farm, Charlwood, Surrey, England.
Telephone: Norwood Hill 862370.

Juráček, Pavel; Czechoslovak film director and scriptwriter; b. 2 Aug. 1935, Příbram; *m.* Věra Jandová 1960 (divorced 1967); one *d.*; ed. Acad. of Music and Dramatic Arts, Prague.
With Film Studio, Barrandov 62-; awards at Oberhausen and Mannheim Festivals 64, Fipresci Award at Karlovy Vary Festival 66, Special Jury Prize at Youth Film Festival, Cannes.
Directed films: *Joseph Kilian* 63, *Every Young Man* 65.
Krakovská 5, Prague 1, Czechoslovakia.
Telephone: 225725.

Jurgensen, Jean-Daniel; French diplomatist; b. 4 July 1917, Paris; *s.* of Philippe Jurgensen and Annette Boyenval; *m.* Marie-Rose Treffot 1939; two *s.* one *d.*; ed. Ecole Normale Supérieure, Paris.
Deputy to Nat. Assembly 44-46; mem. French del. to UN 47-51; Ministry of Foreign Affairs 51-59; Deputy Rep. of France to NATO 59-64; Dir. of American Affairs, Ministry of Foreign Affairs 64-69, Deputy Dir. of Political Affairs 69-72; Amb. to India 72-; Croix de Guerre, Commdr. Légion d'Honneur.
Leisure interests: music, linguistics, philology.
Publs. *Chrétien ou Marxiste?* 49, and articles in journals.
French Embassy, 2 Aurangzeb Road, New Delhi, India.

Jurinac, Sena; Yugoslav-born Austrian singer; b. 24 Oct. 1921; *m.* Dr. Josef Lederle; studied under Milka Kostrencíc.
First appearance as Mimi, Zagreb 42; mem. Vienna State Opera Co. 44-; has sung at Salzburg, Glyndebourne, etc., Festivals; sang in *Der Rosenkavalier* 66 and 71, *Tosca* 68, *Iphigénie en Tauride* 73, Covent Garden; Austrian State Kammersängerin 51; numerous tours and recordings; Ehrenkreuz für Wissenchaft und Kunst 61; Grosses Ehrenzeichen für Verdienste um die Republik Österreich 67; Ehrenring der Wiener Staatsoper 68; Ehrenmitglied der Wiener Staatsoper 71.
State Opera House, Vienna I, Austria.

Jusuf, Lieut.-Gen. Andi Mohamad; Indonesian army officer and politician; b. 23 June 1929, Sulawesi; ed. Dutch Secondary School, and Higher Secondary School.
Former Chief of Staff of Hasanuddin and Commdr. S.E. Military District; Minister of Light and Basic Industry 66, of Basic Industry and Power 66, of Trade and Commerce 67, of Industry 68-.
Ministry of Industry, Jakarta, Indonesia.

Jutikkala, Eino Kaarlo Ilmari, PH.D.; Finnish historian; b. 24 Oct. 1907, Sääksmäki; *s.* of Kaarle Fredrik Rinne and Hilma Maria Hagelberg; ed. Helsinki Univ.
Docent, Helsinki Univ. 33, Prof. of Finnish History 47-50, 54-74, Prof. of Econ. History 50-54, Dean of Faculty of Arts 66-69; Chair. State Comm. for the Humanities 67-70; mem. Culture Foundation for Finland and Sweden 60-71; mem Suomen Akatemia; Ph.D. h.c. (Stockholm), Pol.D. h.c. (Helsinki), D. h.c. (Helsinki Commercial Univ.).
Publs. include *Suomen talonpojan historia* 42, *Atlas of Finnish History* 49, *Turun kaupungin historia 1856-1917* 57, *A History of Finland* 62, *Pohjoismaisen yhteiskunnan historialliset juuret* 65; studies dealing with demographic, agrarian and parliamentary history, the history of communications, etc.; editor of several historical works and learned journals.
Merikatu 3A, Helsinki 14, Finland.
Telephone: 62-65-08.

K

Kabachnik, Martin Izrailevich; Soviet organic chemist; b. 9 Sept. 1908, Sverdlovsk; ed. Moscow Higher Chemicotechnical School.

Associate of Inst. of Organic Chemistry 39-54; Assoc. of Inst. of Elemental-Organic Compounds, U.S.S.R. Acad. of Sciences 54-; Corresp. mem. U.S.S.R. Acad. of Sciences 53-58, mem. 58-; State Prize 46.

Publs. *Investigation in the Field of Organo-Phosphorus Compounds* 46-, *Some Problems of Tautomerism* 56, *Dual Reaction Capacity and Tautomerism* 60, *Conjugation in Non-Coplanar Systems* 62.

Institute of Elemental-Organic Compounds, U.S.S.R. Academy of Sciences, 14 Ulitsa Vavilova, Moscow, U.S.S.R.

Kabalevsky, Dmitri Borisovich; Soviet composer; b. 30 Dec. 1903, Leningrad; ed. Moscow Conservatoire.

Studied under N. Y. Myaskovsky and A. B. Goldenweiser; Prof. Moscow Conservatoire 39-; Sec. Union of Soviet Composers 51-; mem. Communist Party 40-; mem. World Peace Council 55-; Deputy to U.S.S.R. Supreme Soviet 66-; mem. Acad. of Pedagogical Sciences; Deputy Chair. U.S.S.R. Supreme Soviet Parl. Group; People's Artist of the U.S.S.R.; State Prize 46, 49 and 51; R.S.F.S.R. State Prize 66; Badge of Honour 40; Order of Lenin 64, of Red Banner of Labour 66.

Works include four symphonies, two string quartets, three piano concertos 29, 35, 52; violin and 'cello concertos 48, 49, 64; cantata: *Great Motherland* 42; operas: *Colas Brugnon* 37, *Under Fire* 43, *Tara's Family* 50, *Nikita Vershinin* 54; music for films: *Petersburg Nights* 33, *Shchors* 39, *Marusya's First Year at School* 48, *Mussorgsky* 50, *Volnitsa* 56, *Sisters* 57, *18th Year* 58, *Gloomy Morning* 59; 10 Shakespeare sonnets for bass with pianoforte accompaniment 53-55; *Romeo and Juliet* (symphonic suite) 56, *Song of Morning, Spring and Peace* (children's cantata), *Spring Sings* (operetta) 57, *Lenintsy* (cantata) 59, *Sonata for 'Cello and Piano* 62, *Requiem* (oratorio) 64.

Academy of Pedagogical Sciences, Bolshaya Polyanka 58, 113095 Moscow, U.S.S.R.

Kabat, Elvin Abraham, B.S., A.M., PH.D.; American biochemist, immunochemist and professor of microbiology and human genetics and development; b. 1 Sept. 1914, New York City; s. of Harris Kabat and Doreen Otesky; m. Sally Lennick 1942; three s.; ed. Coll. of City of New York and Columbia Univ.

Laboratory Asst. in Immunochemistry, Presbyterian Hospital, N.Y. 33-37; Rockefeller Foundation Fellow at Inst. of Physical Chem., Uppsala, Sweden 37-38; Instructor in Pathology, Cornell Medical Coll. 38-41; Asst. Prof. of Bacteriology, Columbia Univ. 46-48, Assoc. Prof. of Bacteriology 48-52, Prof. of Microbiology 52-, Prof. of Human Genetics and Devt. 69-; Microbiologist, Medical Service, Presbyterian Hospital, Neurological Inst. 56-; Pres. American Asscn. of Immunologists 65-66; mem. World Health Org. (WHO) Advisory Panel on Immunology 63-(80), Editorial Board *Journal of Immunology* 61-75, Editorial Board *Immuno-chemistry*; consultant, Nat. Cancer Inst. 75; mem. Nat. Acad. of Sciences; Fellow, American Acad. of Arts and Sciences; Fogarty Scholar, Nat. Inst. of Health 74-75; Eli Lilly Award in Bacteriology and Immunology 49, Golden Hope Chest Award Nat. Multiple Sclerosis Soc. 62, Karl Landsteiner Memorial Award, American Asscn. of Blood Banks 66, Claude Bernard Medal, Univ. of Montreal 68, City of Hope Annual Research Award 74.

Publs. *Experimental Immunochemistry* (with M. Mayer) 1st edn. 48, 2nd edn. 61, *Blood Group Substances, Their*

Chemistry and Immunochemistry 56, *Structural Concepts in Immunology and Immunochemistry* 68; and numerous scientific papers.

Columbia University, College of Physicians and Surgeons, Department of Microbiology, 630 West 168th Street, New York, N.Y. 10032; Home: 70 Haven Avenue, New York, N.Y. 10032, U.S.A.

Telephone: 212-579-3519 (Office); 212-WA-7-6807 (Home).

Kac, Mark, PH.D., D.SC.; American professor of mathematics; b. 3 Aug. 1914, Krzemieniec, Poland; s. of Bencion and Chana (Rojchel) Kac; m. Katherine Elizabeth Mayberry 1942; one s. one d.; ed. Lycée of Krzemieniec and John Casimir Univ., Lwów.

Parnas Foundation Fellow, Johns Hopkins Univ. 38; mem. of Faculty, Cornell Univ. 39-61; mem. Inst. of Advanced Study, Princeton 51-52; mem., now Prof. of Maths., Rockefeller Univ. (fmrly. Rockefeller Inst.) 61-; Editor *Transactions* of the American Mathematical Soc. 55-58; Lorentz Visiting Prof. of Theoretical Physics, Leyden 63; Andrew D. White Prof.-at-Large, Cornell Univ. 65-72; Chair. Div. of Mathematical Sciences of Nat. Research Council of Nat. Acad. of Sciences 66-67; Guggenheim Fellow 46-47, Senior Visiting Fellow, Oxford Univ. 69-, Visiting Fellow, Brasenose Coll., Oxford 69-; Solvay Lecturer, Univ. of Brussels 71-; mem. Nat Acad. of Sciences, American Acad. of Arts and Sciences, American Mathematical Soc., Mathematical Asscn. of America, Inst. of Mathematics, American Philosophical Soc, Royal Norwegian Acad, Trondheim; Chauvenet Prize 50, 68.

Leisure interests: golf, bridge.

Publs. *Probability and Related Topics in Physical Science* 59, *Statistical Independence in Probability, Analysis and Number Theory* 59, *Mathematics and Logic* (with S. Ulam) 68; and numerous articles on mathematical analysis, probability theory and mathematical physics.

The Rockefeller University, New York, N.Y. 10021; Home: 6 Rectory Lane, Scarsdale, N.Y. 10583, U.S.A.

Telephone: 914-360-1905 (Univ.); 212-GR2-2654 (Home).

Kachingwe, Joe; Malawi diplomatist; b. 1931; ed. St. Francis Xavier Univ., Canada.

Served in Malawi High Comm., London; First Sec., Malawi Legation, Pretoria 67; later High Commr. in Kenya; Amb. to S. Africa 71-73; High Commr. to U.K. 73- (also accred. to Belgium, Netherlands, France and Vatican 73-75, to France and Vatican 75-).

High Commission of Malawi, 47 Great Cumberland Place, London, W1H 8DB, England.

Kaczmarek, Jan, DR.T.SC.; Polish scientist and politician; b. 2 Feb. 1920, Pabianice; s. of Władysław and Zofia Kaczmarek; m. Olga Steranka 1946; one s. one d.; ed. Cracow Technical Univ. and Acad. of Mining and Metallurgy, Cracow.

Started work at Inst. of Engineering, Cracow 49, Dir. 57-68; Head, Dept. of Metal Working, Cracow Technical Univ. 55-63, Asst. Prof. 53-62, Prof. 62, Pro-Rector for Scientific Affairs 66-68; Pres. Cttee. for Science and Technology 68-72; Chair. Chief Council, Chief Technical Org. 72-; mem. Govt. Praesidium Dec. 71-; mem. and Scientific Sec. Polish Acad. of Sciences 72-; Minister of Science, Higher Educ. and Technics 72-74; Deputy to Seym 72-; Vice-Pres. CIRP 72-73, Pres. 73-; Pres. Coll. Int. pour l'Etude Scientifique des Techniques de Production Méchanique; Foreign mem., Bulgarian Acad. of Sciences, and mem. numerous other foreign scientific socs.; mem. Cen. Cttee. PUWP and Cen. Council of Trade Unions; Dr. h.c. Technical Univ., Karl-

Marx-Stadt (German Democratic Repub.) 73, Bauman Polytechnic, Moscow 74; Knight's Cross of Polonia Restituta; Order Banner of Labour, 2nd Class; Commdr. Cross of Order of Polonia Restituta 74.

Publs. Author of numerous publs. on production engineering and theory of machining by cutting, incl. *Principles of cutting metals* 56, *Theory of machining by cutting, abrasion and erosion* 70.

Al. 1 Armii W.9, 16 m. 46, 00-582, Warsaw, Poland.
Telephone: 20-33-80 (Office).

Kadár, Ján; Czechoslovak film director; b. 1 April 1918, Budapest, Hungary; ed. Faculty of Law, Charles Univ. of Prague, and Photography and Film School under Prof. Karel Plicka, Bratislava.

Imprisoned during Second World War; Scriptwriter and Asst. Dir. at Barrandov Feature Film Studio 47-; Awards include State Prize 2nd Class 60, Gold Prize, Moscow Int. Film Festival 63, State Prize 64, Grand Prix, Karlovy Vary Int. Film Festival 64, U.S. Acad. Award Oscar 65, New York Film Critics Award 66, Selznik Prize, U.S. 66, David Di Donatello Prize 67, Honoured Artist 65, Order of Labour 68, Nat. Artist 68; Co-Dir. with Elmar Klos (*q.v.*) *Únos* (Kidnapped) 52, *Smrt si říká Engelchen* (Death is Called Engelchen) 63, *Obžalovaný* (The Accused) 64, *Obchod na korze* (The Shop on Main Street) 65 (all award-winning films), *Touha zvaná Anada* (Desire called Anada) 69, *The Angel Levine, Adrift* 70, *Lies My Father Told Me* 75.

c/o Creative Management Associates, New York; Home: 160 East 88th Street, Apartment 7-F, New York, N.Y. 10028, U.S.A.

Kadár, János; Hungarian politician; b. 22 May 1912, Fiume (now Rijeka, Yugoslavia); ed. secondary school. Member Young Communist Workers Fed. 31, illegal Communist Party 31; helped to organize resistance movement Second World War; Deputy Police Chief 45; Sec. Greater Budapest Party Cttee. 45-48; Asst. Gen. Sec. Communist Party 46-48, re-elected on merger of Communist and Social Democratic Parties to become Hungarian Working People's Party 48-51; mem. Parl. 45-51, 58-; Minister of Internal Affairs 48-50; arrested and imprisoned during Rakosi régime 51-54; Party Sec. for Budapest District, later for County of Pest 54-56; First Sec. Central Cttee. Hungarian Socialist Workers' Party 56-, mem. Politburo 56-; Prime Minister 56-58, 61-65; mem. Presidential Council 65-; Minister of State 58-61; Hero of Socialist Labour, Hero of the Soviet Union; Order of Lenin; Joliot Curie Gold Medal Award, World Peace Council 74.

Leisure interests: reading, wild game shooting, chess.

Publs. *Firm People's Power—Independent Hungary* 58, *On the Road to Socialism* 62, *Further Ahead on Lenin's Road* 64, *Patriotism and Internationalism* 68, *For a Socialist Hungary* 72, *Selected Speeches and Articles* 74, *On the Road to the Construction of the Developed Socialist Society* 75.

Magyar Szocialista Munkáspárt, Széchenyi rakpart 19, H-1387 Budapest, Hungary.

Kaddori, Fakhri Yassin, DR.RER.POL.; Iraqi economist; b. 28 Aug. 1932, Baghdad; *s.* of Yassin Kaddori Kaddori and Rafiqa (née Abdul Kadar Kalamchi); *m.* Marie-Louise Classen 1965; one *s.* two *d.*; ed. Adhamiya Inter-mediate School and Central Secondary School, Baghdad, Coll. of Commerce and Econs. (Univ. of Baghdad), State Univ. of Iowa, Cologne Univ., Int. Marketing Inst. (Harvard Univ.).

Director of Internal Trade, Ministry of the Economy 64-68; Minister of the Economy 68-71; mem. Planning Board 68-; Gen. Secr. GATT 68; Chair. Bureau of Econ. Affairs, Revolutionary Command Council; Pres. Iraqi Economist Assen.

Leisure interests: reading, music, swimming, travelling.

Publs. several articles on economic topics in profes-sional journals.

Bureau of Economic Affairs, Revolutionary Command Council, National Council Building, Baghdad, Iraq.

Kader, Yehia Abdel; Egyptian diplomatist; b. 1920, Alexandria; ed. Faculty of Law, Univ. of Cairo.

Secretary and Counsellor at the Egyptian Embassies in Belgrade, Khartoum, Milan; Amb. to Saudi Arabia 64-68, to Yugoslavia 68-71; Chair. Egyptian Radio and Television 71; Amb. to U.S.S.R. 71-74, to Greece 74-.

3 Leoforos Vassilissis Sofias, Athens, Greece.

Kadlec, Vladimír, LL.D., D.SC.; Czechoslovak econo-mist and politician; b. 4 Oct. 1912, Prague; *s.* of Bohumír and Anna Kadlec; *m.* Prof. Věra Kadlecová, M.D. 1942; two *s.* one *d.*; ed. Law Faculty, Charles Univ., Prague.

Ministry of Finance 38-42; Nat. Bank 45-46; Cen. Admin. of Banks 46-48; Office of Pres. of Repub. 48-52; Asst. Prof., Czech Technical Univ., Prague 52-62; Prof. at School of Econs., Rector 62-68; Minister of Educ. 68; mem. Econ. Comm. of Cen. Cttee. of C.P. of Czecho-slovakia 63; mem. Cen. Cttee. of C.P. of Czechoslovakia 66-69; mem. Council of Controller Gen. of Czech Socialist Repub. 69-70; mem. Dept. of Econ. Planning, School of Econs., Prague 69-70.

Publs. *Surplus of Purchasing Power* 46, *Currency Stability* 48, *Mathematical Methods in Economic Plan-ning* (trans. into German) 59, *Practical Application of Linear Planning Methods* 62, *Application of Computers in Socialist Agriculture* (trans. into German) 62, *Linear Programming in Transport* (trans. into German) 63, *Optimalization of Production Plans in Agricultural Enterprises* (trans. into Romanian) 67, *Economic Calculations on Computers in Industrial Practice* 67, etc.

Home: Čapajevovo náměstí 18, Prague 3-Vinohrady, Czechoslovakia.

Telephone: 737208.

Kadomtsev, Boris Borisovich; Soviet physicist; b. 9 Nov. 1928, Panfilov, Kazakhstan; ed. Moscow State Univ. Scientist, Physics-Energetics Inst. 52-56; Senior Research Scientist Kurchatov Inst. of Atomic Energy, U.S.S.R. Acad. of Sciences 56-73; Dir. Plasma Physics Div., Kurchatov Inst. of Atomic Energy 73-; Corresp. mem. U.S.S.R. Acad. of Sciences 62-70, Academician 70-; State Prize 70.

U.S.S.R. Academy of Sciences, 14 Leninsky Prospekt, Moscow, U.S.S.R.

Kadoorie, Horace, O.B.E., J.P.; Hong Kong business executive; b. 28 Sept. 1902, London, England; *s.* of late Sir Elly Kadoorie and Lady Kadoorie; unmarried; ed. Cathedral School, Shanghai, Ascham St. Vincents, Eastbourne, and Clifton Coll., Bristol.

Partner, Sir Elly Kadoorie and Sons, Hong Kong; Chair. and Dir. numerous public companies incl. Hong Kong & Shanghai Hotels Ltd., China Light and Power Co. Ltd., Amalgamated Rubber Estates, Hong Kong and Kowloon Wharf and Godown Co. Ltd., Hong Kong and Whampoa Dock Co. Ltd., Peak Tramways Co. Ltd., Rubber Trust Ltd., Hong Kong Carpet Manufacturers Ltd.; mem. and official numerous Hong Kong civic orgs.; Chevalier de la Légion d'Honneur; Ramon Magsaysay Award 62, Order of Leopold 66, Solomon Schechter Award 59.

Leisure interests: agriculture and gardening.

Publ. *The Art of Ivory Sculpture in Cathay* (7 vols.).

Sir Elly Kadoorie and Sons, St. George's Building, 24th Floor, Hong Kong.

Telephone: 249221.

Kadoorie, Sir Lawrence, Kt., C.B.E., LL.D., J.P., K.ST.J.(A); Hong Kong business executive; b. 2 June 1899, Hong Kong; *s.* of late Sir Elly Kadoorie and Lady Kadoorie; *m.* Muriel Gubbay 1938; one *s.* one *d.*; ed. Cathedral School, Shanghai, Ascham St. Vincents, Eastbourne, Clifton Coll., Bristol and Lincoln's Inn, London.

Partner, Sir Elly Kadoorie and Sons, Hong Kong; Chair. China Light and Power Co. Ltd., Hong Kong Engineering and Construction Co. Ltd., Franki Piling and Engineering Co. Ltd., Hong Kong Carpet Manufacturers Ltd., Major Contractors Ltd., Nanyang Cotton Mills Ltd., Schroders and Chartered Ltd., Motor Agencies Ltd.; Dir. numerous other public companies; mem. and official numerous Hong Kong civic orgs.; Solomon Schechter Award 59; Officier de la Légion d'Honneur; Officier de l'Ordre de Léopold 66; Ramon Magsaysay Award 62.
Leisure interests: travel, sports cars, photography and Chinese works of art.
Sir Elly Kadoorie and Sons, St. George's Building, Hong Kong.
Telephone: 249221.

Kadosa, Pál; Hungarian composer and pianist; b. 6 Sept. 1903, Levice, Czechoslovakia; s. of Zsigmond Weiss and Eugenia Wertheimer; ed. Budapest Acad. of Music, under Zoltán Kodály and Arnold Székely.
Teacher, Fodor Music School 27-43, Goldmark Music School 44; Prof. 45-, then mem. of Directors' Council, Budapest Acad. of Music; mem. Board, later, Acting Chair. Fed. of Hungarian Musicians; Pres. Nat. Copyright Office; Hon. mem. Royal Acad. of Music (London) 67; Corresp. mem. German Acad. of Arts 70; Prize of Liberty 46, Merited Artist 53, Kossuth Prize 50, 75, Erkel Prize 55, 62, Eminent Artist of the Hungarian People's Repub. 63, Labour Order of Merit 70, Order of Standard of Hungarian People's Republic 73. Compositions: for orchestra, symphonies, string quartets, violin and piano concertos, cantatas, choruses, songs; opera, *Huszti Kaland.*
Leisure interests: art collector/Gothic arts.
Hungarian Academy of Music, Liszt Ferenc Place 8, Budapest VI; and H-1056 Budapest V, Marcius 15 ter. 8, Hungary.
Telephone: 181-398.

Kaduma, Ibrahim Mohamed, B.SC.(ECON.), B.PHIL.; Tanzanian economist and politician; b. 1927, Mtwanga Njombe, Iringa Region; s. of the late Mohamed Maleva Kaduma and of Mwanaidza Kaduma; m. Happiness Y. Mgonja 1969; two s. one d.; ed. Makerere Univ. Coll., Uganda, and Univ. of York, England.
Accounts Clerk, the Treasury 59-61, Accounts Asst. 61, Asst. Accountant 62-65, Economist 65-66, Dir. of External Finance and Technical Co-operation 67-69, Deputy Sec. 69-70, Principal Sec. 72-73; Principal Sec. Ministry of Communications, Transport and Labour 70-72; Dir. Inst. of Devt. Studies, Univ. of Dar es Salaam 73-75; Minister for Foreign Affairs Nov. 75-; Arts Research Prize, Makerere Univ., Uganda 64-65.
Leisure interests: tennis, squash, gardening.
Ministry of Foreign Affairs, P.O. Box 9000, Dar es Salaam; Home: P.O. Box 51, Njombe, Iringa Region, Tanzania.

Kafarov, Viktor Viacheslavovich; Soviet chemist; b. 18 June 1914, Shavli, Lithuania; ed. Kirov Chemical Technology Inst., Kazan.
Engineer at designing org. in aniline industry 38-40; Postgraduate, Research Assoc. Colloid-Electrochemical Inst. U.S.S.R. Acad. of Sciences 40-44; Asst. Prof. 45-52, Prof. 53-60, Head of Chair 60-, Mendeleev Inst. of Chemical Technology; mem. C.P.S.U. 52-; Corresp. mem. U.S.S.R. Acad. of Sciences 66-.
Publs. Works on chemical technology, mathematical modelling of chemical technology processes.
U.S.S.R. Academy of Sciences, 14 Leninsky Prospekt, Moscow, U.S.S.R.

Kafka, Alexandre; Brazilian professor of economics; b. 25 Jan. 1917; s. of late Bruno and of Jana Kafka (née Bondy de Bondrop); m. Rita Petschek 1947; two d.

Prof. of Econs., Univ. of São Paulo 41-46; Adviser to Brazilian Del. to Preparatory Cttee. and Conf. of Int. Trade Org. 46-48; Asst. Div. Chief, Int. Monetary Fund (IMF) 49-51, Temp. Alt. Gov. 54-55, Exec. Dir. 66-, Vice-Chair. Deputies of Cttee. on Reform of Int. Monetary System and Related Matters 72-74; Adviser, Superintendency of Money and Credit (now Central Bank of Brazil); Dir. of Research, Brazilian Inst. of Econs. 51-54, Dir. 61-63; Chief Financial Inst. and Policies Section, UN 56-61; Prof. of Econs., Univ. of Virginia, U.S. 59-60, 63-75; Visiting Prof. of Econs., Boston Univ. 75-76; Adviser to Brazilian Minister of Finance 64.
International Monetary Fund, 19th and H Streets, Washington, D.C. 20431, U.S.A.
Telephone: 4773048 (Office); 3621737 (Home) and 804-296-0525 (Charlottesville, Va.).

Kahangi, Christopher, B.COMM.; Tanzanian international bank official; b. 20 June 1937, Tanzania; s. of Nestor K. and Magdalena K. Kabengula; m. Cecilia Bwahama 1965; two d.; ed. Univ. of Ireland, Dublin, and Mass. Inst. of Technology.
Ministry of Commerce and Industries, Tanzania, until Sept. 67, Chief Industrial Officer 65-67; training in bank credit at Union Bank of Los Angeles, U.S.A. Sept. 67-March 68; Alt. Exec. Dir. World Bank April 68-Oct. 68, Exec. Dir. World Bank Nov. 68-Oct. 70; Gen. Man. Tanzania Investment Bank 70-75.
Leisure interest: photography.
c/o Box 9373, Dar es Salaam, Tanzania.
Telephone: 28581.

Kähler, Erich Ernst, DR.PHIL.; German mathematician; b. 16 Jan. 1906, Leipzig; s. of Ernest and Elsa Kähler (née Götsch); m. 1st Luise Günther 1938 (died 1970), two s. (one deceased) one d.; m. 2nd Charlotte Schulze 1972; ed. school in Leipzig and Universität Leipzig.
Lecturer Hamburg 30; Prof. Univ. Königsberg 36; Prof. (with Chair) Univ. Leipzig 48; Prof. Technische Univ. Berlin 58; Prof. Univ. Hamburg and Hon. Prof. Technische Univ. Berlin 64-; mem. Akademie der Wissenschaften der D.D.R., Sächsische Akad. der Wissenschaften and Deutsche Akad. der Naturforscher Leopoldina; Foreign mem. Accad. Nazionale dei Lincei 61-.
Publs. *Einführung in die Theorie der Systeme von Differentialgleichungen* 34, *Geometria Aritmetica* 58, *Der innere Differentialkalkul* 63, *Wesen und Erscheinung als mathematische Prinzipen der Philosophie* 65, *Saggio di una dinamica della vita* 73, *Monadologie* 75.
Mozartstrasse 42, 2 Wedel, Holstein, Federal Republic of Germany.
Telephone: (04103) 86535.

Kähler, Otto; German bank official; b. 17 April 1905, Landkirchen; s. of Heinrich Kähler and Gertrude (née Haltermann) Kähler; m. Lotte Weisse 1938; two d.; ed. Classical High School.
Junior Bank Officer, Deutsche Reichsbank 31-38; Reichsbank, Berlin 41; mem. Berlin Stock Exchange; Dir. Deutsche Reichsbank 48-; Dir., mem. Management Board, Landeszentralbank, Kiel 51-58; Vice-Pres. Landeszentralbank Hessen, Frankfurt 58-59; Pres. Landeszentralbank, Schleswig-Holstein, mem. Federal Bank Council 60-73.
Leisure interests: hunting, yachting.
10 Luisenweg, 23 Kiel 1, Federal Republic of Germany.
Telephone: Kiel (0431) 56-27-94.

Kahn, Baron (Life-Peer), cr. 65, of Hampstead; **Richard Ferdinand Kahn,** C.B.E., M.A.; British economist; b. 10 Aug. 1905; ed. St. Paul's School and King's Coll., Cambridge.
Employed in various govt. depts. 39-46; Prof. of Econs., Cambridge Univ. 51-72; on leave of absence to work in

UN Econ. Comm. for Europe 55; Fellow of King's Coll., Cambridge, British Acad.
Publ. *Selected Essays on Employment and Growth* 73.
King's College, Cambridge, England.

Kahn, Herman, B.A., M.S.; American mathematician; b. 15 Feb. 1922; ed. Univ. of California (Los Angeles) and California Inst. of Technology.
Mathematician, Douglas Aircraft 45-46, Northrup Aviation 47; Research Analyst, RAND Corpn. 47-59; Lecturer, Center for Int. Studies, Princeton 59; Dir., Hudson Inst. 61-; Consultant to Boeing Aircraft, Office of Defense Mobilization, System Development Corpn., Planning Research Cttee., Stanford Research Inst., Scientific Advisory Board to U.S. Air Force etc.
Publs. *On Thermonuclear War* 60, *Thinking about the Unthinkable* 62, *On Escalation* 65 (with Anthony Wiener), *The Year 2000* 67, *Can We Win in Vietnam* (with others) 68, *Why ABM* (with others) 69, *The Emerging Japanese Superstate* 70, *Things to Come* (co-author) 72, *The Future of the Corporation* (editor) 74.
19 Birch Lane, Chappaqua, New York, U.S.A.

Kahn-Ackermann, Georg; German journalist, broadcaster and politician; b. 4 Jan. 1918, Berlin-Charlottenburg; *m.* Rosmarie Müller-Diefenbach 1945; one *s.* three *d.*
Member Social Democratic Party (Sozialdemokratische Partei Deutschlands—SPD) 46-; mem. Bundestag 53-57, 62-69, 70-74; Vice-Pres. Admin. Council Deutschlandfunk; Pres. Political Comm., Western European Union; Vice-Pres. Assembly, Council of Europe 73-74; Sec.-Gen. Council of Europe 74-.
Leisure interests: archaeology, horse riding.
Office of the Secretary-General, Council of Europe, Avenue de l'Europe, 67006 Strasbourg, France.
Telephone: (88) 357035.

Kahnweiler, Daniel-Henry; French art historian and art dealer; b. 25 June 1884, Mannheim, Germany; *s.* of Julius and Betty Kahnweiler (née Neumann); *m.* Lucie Godon 1904 (died 1945).
Opened gallery in Paris, helping Derain, Vlaminck, Picasso, Braque, Gris, and Léger 07; gallery seized by French authorities 14 and all pictures sold; with André Simon founded Gallery Simon 20; Gallery Simon, which was Jewish property, was bought by sister-in-law (Louise Leirus) to save it from Germans in 39-45 war; Co-Dir. Louise Leiris Gallery 45; given title of Hon. Prof. by Govt. of Baden-Württemberg 64, Dr. h.c. (Univ. of Kaiserlautern) 74.
Publs. *Der Weg zum Kubismus* 20 (English translation 49), *Juan Gris, sa vie, son oeuvre, ses écrits* 46 (new French, English, German edns. 69), *Les Sculptures de Picasso* 49 (English translation 49), *La Céramique de Picasso* 57 (English, French and German), *Mes Galeries et mes Peintres, Entretiens avec Francis Crémieux* 61 (German trans. 61, Czech trans. 64, Polish trans. 67, Swedish and Finnish trans. 68, English, New York 70), *Confessions Esthétiques* 63, *Entretiens avec Picasso* (Italian trans. 64), *Asthetische Betrachtungen* 68, *Der Gegenstand der Aesthetik* 71.
53 *bis* quai des Grands-Augustins, Paris 6e, France.
Telephone: 033-18-61.

Kahuda, František, D.NAT. SC., D.PAED., C.SC., Czechoslovak politician and scientist; b. 3 Jan. 1911, Nový Dvůr; *s.* of František and late Ružena Kahuda; *m.* Marie Crachová 1973; one *d.*; ed. Faculty of Sciences, Charles Univ., Prague.
Former Prof. of Science, Charles Univ., Prague; worked for Comenius Pedagogical Research Inst., Prague; Minister of Education 54-56, of Education and Culture 56-63, First Deputy Minister of Educ. and Culture 63-66, First Deputy Minister of Educ. 67; Prof. of Sociology, Charles Univ., Prague 68-; Dir. Inst. of Social Research of Youth and Educ. Guidance 70-; Order of Labour 61; several medals.

Leisure interests: mathematical methods in the social sciences, music.
K Měchurce 4, Prague 5, Czechoslovakia.
Telephone: 52-36-71.

Kai, Fumihiko; Japanese businessman; b. 17 May 1912; *s.* of Ryozo and Chiyo Kai; *m.* Ayako Kimura 1947; one *s.* two *d.*; ed. Tokyo Univ.
Consul-Gen., Jakarta 52-55; Deputy Rep. of Japan to 9th Session of ECAFE Conf., Bandung 53; Counsellor, The Hague 53-55; Consul-Gen., Berlin 55-57, Hamburg 57-58; Dir. Japan External Trade Org. 58-61; Counsellor, Ministry of Foreign Affairs 61, Dir. Econ. Co-operation Bureau, Ministry of Foreign Affairs 61; fmr. Amb. to Malaysia; Amb. to Australia -70; Amb. to Federal Repub. of Germany 70-73, retd. 73; Man. Dir. Nissin Sugar Mfg. Co. 73-; Panglima Mangku Negara (Malaysia); Gran Oficial Al Merito (Argentina); Grosskreuz (Fed. Republic of Germany).
Leisure interests: golf, music.
10-14 2-chome, Hatanodai, Shinagawa-ku, Tokyo, Japan.
Telephone: (03) 782-0175.

Kaim, Franciszek, B.ENG.; Polish politician; b. 13 Feb. 1919, Wola Drwińska; ed. Acad. of Mining and Metallurgy, Cracow.
Labourer, then accountant, in agriculture and forestry 39-45; worked at "Bobrek" foundry, later Chief Man. at "Małapanew" foundry 48-53; Under-Sec. of State, Ministry of Metallurgy 53-57, Ministry of Heavy Industry 57-64; Deputy Minister of Heavy Industry and Metallurgy 64-67, Minister of Heavy Industry 67-70, Vice-Pres. Council of Ministers 70-; mem. Polish United Workers' Party 51-, Alt. mem. Cen. Cttee. PUWP 68-71, mem. Cen. Cttee. 71-; Deputy to Seym 72-; Order of Banner of Labour 1st Class, Commdr's. Cross Order of Polonia Restituta.
Urząd Rady Ministrów, Aleje Ujazdowskie 1/3, 00-583 Warsaw, Poland.

Kairov, Ivan Andreyevich; Soviet educationist; b. 1893; ed. Moscow Univ.
Immediately after the Revolution of 17 he dealt with the question of agricultural education in Moscow and the Moscow region, later at the Ministry of Education, R.S.F.S.R.; Prof. of Higher Pedagogical Courses at the Timiriazev Agricultural Acad. and Dir. of the Agro-Pedagogical Inst. of the Acad.; Head, Dept. of Education at Moscow Univ. 37-49; Minister of Education R.S.F.S.R. 49-56; Pres. of the R.S.F.S.R. Acad. of Pedagogical Sciences 56-66; Pres. of the U.S.S.R. Acad. of Pedagogical Sciences 66; awarded Orders of Lenin and Orders of the Red Banner of Labour; Hero of Socialist Labour.
Academy of Pedagogical Sciences, 58 B. Polyanka, Moscow, U.S.S.R.

Kaiser, Edgar Fosburgh; American industrialist; b. 29 July 1908, Spokane, Wash.; *s.* of Henry J. and Bessie (Fosburgh) Kaiser; *m.* Sue Mead 1932 (died 1974); three *s.* three *d.*; ed. Univ. of Calif.
Construction Supt. nat. gas line Kansas to Texas 30-32; Shift Supt. Boulder Dam, Nev. 32-33; Admin. Man. Columbia Construction Co., Bonneville Dam, Bonneville, Ore. 34-38; Consolidated Builders Inc., Grand Coulee Dam, Wash. 38-41; Vice-Pres., Gen. Man. Oregon Shipbuilding Corpn. and Kaiser Co. Inc., Portland, Ore. and Vancouver, B.C. 41-45; Dir. and Pres. Kaiser Motors Corpn. 45-56; now Chair. and Dir. of affiliated Kaiser companies and subsidiaries including Kaiser Industries Corpn., Kaiser Steel Corpn., Kaiser Aluminium & Chem. Corpn., Kaiser Cement and Gypsum Corpn., Kaiser Aerospace & Electronics Corpn., Kaiser Broadcasting Corpn., Kaiser Foundation Health Plan Inc., Kaiser Foundation Hospitals, Kaiser Engineers, Kaiser Sand & Gravel; Chair., Dir. Nat. Steel & Shipbuilding Co.; Chair., mem. board of dirs. and trustee

numerous orgs., presidential cttees., schools, etc.; Fellow, American Acad. of Arts and Sciences 70; Hon. LL.D. (Univ. of Portland, Mills Coll.); Hon. L.H.D. (Univ. of Calif.); Commdr. Nat. Order Southern Cross, Brazil 65; Grand Officer Repub. of the Ivory Coast 72; Industrialist of the Year Award 66, Hoover Medal 69, and numerous other awards and honours.
Kaiser Industries Corporation, Kaiser Center, 300 Lakeside Drive, Oakland, Calif. 94604, U.S.A.
Telephone: 271-2211.

Kaiser, Khwaja Mujammad; Bangladesh diplomatist; b. 13 Sept. 1918; ed. Dacca Univ.
Indian Police Service 41-50; Second Sec. Dep. High Comm. for Pakistan, Calcutta 50; Dep. Sec. Ministry of External Affairs, Dacca 50-51; Dep. Sec. Ministry of External Affairs, Karachi 51-55; Counsellor, Peking 55-57; Consul-Gen., New York 57-60; Minister, Washington 60-62; High Commr. in Australia and New Zealand 62-65; Dir.-Gen. Ministry of Foreign Affairs, Pakistan 65-66; Amb. to Sweden, Norway, Denmark, Finland 66-68, to People's Repub. of China, also accred. to Mongolia 69-73, to Burma, also accred. to Thailand, Singapore, Democratic Repub. of Viet-Nam 73-; awarded Sitara-e-Quaid-e-Azam 62.
Embassy of Bangladesh, 106-108 Rhyu Street, Rangoon, Burma.

Kaiser, Philip M., A.B., M.A.; American diplomatist, publisher and banker; b. 12 July 1913, New York; s. of Morris and Temma Kaiser; m. Hannah Greeley 1939; three s.; ed. Univ. of Wisconsin and Balliol Coll., Oxford (Rhodes Scholar).
Federal Reserve System 39-42, Board of Econ. Warfare 42-46; joined Research Planning Div. Dept. of State 46; Exec. Asst. to Asst. Sec. of Labor (Int. Labor Affairs) 46-47; Dir. Office of Int. Labor Affairs, Dept. of Labor 47-49; Asst. Sec. of Labor 49-53; Labor Adviser, Comm. for Free Europe 53-54; Special Asst. to Gov. of New York 55-58; Prof. of Int. Labor Relations, American Univ. 58-61; Ambassador to Senegal and Mauritania 61-64; Minister, American Embassy in London 64-69; Chair. and Man. Dir. Encyclopaedia Britannica Int. Ltd., London 69-75; mem. Board, Guinness Mahon Holdings Ltd. 75-.
Leisure interests: tennis, swimming, music, ballet, theatre.
3 Lowndes Court, Lowndes Street, London, S.W.1, England.
Telephone: 01-235-2688.

Kaissouni, Abdel Moneim, B.COM., B.SC., PH.D.; Egyptian financial administrator and politician; b. 1916; ed. Univ. of Cairo and London School of Economics.
With Barclays Bank, England 42-43; Lecturer and Asst. Prof. of Economics, Univ. of Cairo 44-50; Adviser to Council of Ministers for Post-War Affairs 44-45; Deputy Dir.-Gen. of Foreign Affairs in Ministry of Nat. Economy 49-50; Dir. Middle East Dept. Int. Monetary Fund, Washington, and later Chief Technical Rep. in Middle East 46-50; with Nat. Bank of Egypt 50-54; Dep. Min. Finance and Economy 54, Min. Sept. 54-58; mem. Nat. Assembly 57; Minister of Economy and Commerce for Egypt in U.A.R. 58; Minister of Economy, U.A.R. Central Govt. 58-62, Minister of Treasury and Planning 62-64; Chair. Board of Econ. Orgs. 59; Deputy Prime Minister for Econ. Affairs and Finance and Minister of Econ. and Foreign Trade 64-65; Pres. UN Conf. on Trade and Devt., Geneva 64; Deputy Prime Minister for Financial and Econ. Affairs 65-66; Minister of Planning 67-68; Chair. Arab Int. Bank 71-; Chair. European Arab Holding, Luxembourg 72, Multilateral Trade, Luxembourg 74; mem. Higher Econ. Council, Egypt 74; Adviser, Govt. of Kuwait.
23 Sesostris Street, Heliopolis, Cairo, Egypt.
Telephone: 835835.

Kajzer, Michał, M.ECON.; Polish administrator; b. 15 Sept. 1921, Warsaw; ed. Univ. of Fribourg, Switzerland. During Second World War participated in Swiss and French resistance; after liberation returned to Poland; worked at Ministry of Shipping and Foreign Trade 45-46; Chief of Dept., Commercial Counsellor's Bureau, Prague 47-52; Dir. Dept., Ministry of Foreign Trade 52-55; Commercial Attaché, Hanoi 55-57; managerial posts at Ministry of Foreign Trade 57-65; Amb. to Sweden 65-69; Vice-Minister of Foreign Trade 69-April 71; Pres. Polish Chamber of Foreign Trade 71-74; First Vice-Pres. Int. Exhbns. Bureau 73-; mem. Polish United Workers' Party.
Polska Izba Handlu Zagranicznego, Ul. Trębacka 4, Warsaw, Poland.

Kakitsubo, Masayoshi; Japanese diplomatist; b. 8 Aug. 1907; s. of Kumataro Kakitsubo and Moto Kakitsubo; m. Noriko Kakitsubo 1947; one s. two d.; ed. Univs. of Hitotsubashi and Cambridge (England). Minister, Perm. Mission of Japan at UN 57-61, Amb. in charge of econ. and social affairs 61-62; Amb. to Pakistan 62-65, to U.A.R. 65-67, to Switzerland 67-69; Dir. UN Asian Inst. for Econ. Devt. and Planning, Bangkok 70-74.
Leisure interests: swimming, golf.
c/o UN Asian Institute for Economic Development and Planning, P.O. Box 2-136, Sri Ayudhya Road, Bangkok, Thailand.
Telephone: 815400.

Kalchenko, Stepan Vlasovich; Soviet politician; b. 31 Dec. 1908, Karashino, Ukraine; ed. Timiryazev Agricultural Acad.
Member C.P.S.U. 31-; agronomist, and successively Dir. State Grain Farm, Chief, Agricultural Admin. Board 28-48; First Dep. Chair. Exec. Cttee. Kurgun Regional Council of Workers' Deputies 48-54; Dep. Minister of State Farms, Dep. Minister of Agriculture U.S.S.R. 54-58; Chair. Exec. Cttee. Kirov Regional Council of Workers' Deputies 58-59; Minister of Agriculture R.S.F.S.R. 59-60; Chair. Exec. Cttee. Altai Rural Council of Workers' Deputies 60-64; Chair. Exec. Cttee. Altai Regional Council of Workers' Deputies 64-66; First Deputy Dir. Exhbn. of Soviet Economy Achievements 66-; Cand. mem. Cen. Cttee. C.P.S.U. 61-66; Red Banner of Labour (twice), Badge of Honour (twice), Red Star, etc.
Exhibition of Soviet Economy Achievements, Moscow, U.S.S.R.

Kalckar, Herman Moritz; Danish biochemist; b. 26 March 1908, Copenhagen, Denmark; s. of Ludvig Kalckar and Bertha Melchior; one s. two d.; ed. Univ. of Copenhagen.
Associate Prof. Inst. of Medical Physiology, Copenhagen 38-43, Research Prof. of Cytophysiology and Dir. of Research 49; Visiting Scientist, Nat. Inst. of Health 53; Prof. of Biology, Johns Hopkins Univ. 58; Prof. of Biological Chem., Harvard Medical School, and Chief, Biochemical Research, Mass. Gen. Hospital 61-; mem. Nat. Acad. of Sciences, American Acad. of Arts and Sciences; Foreign mem. Royal Danish Acad.; mem. Harvey Soc. and Harvey Lecturer 49-50; First Weigle mem. Lecturer, Calif. Inst. of Tech. 70; Prof. Emer. Harvard Univ. 74; Fogarty Scholar, Nat. Inst. of Health 75; mem. Huntington Laboratories, Mass. Gen. Hospital; Hon. D.Sc. (Washington, St. Louis, Chicago).
Publs. *Biological Phosphorylations Development of Concepts* 69, *The Role of Nucleotides for the Function and Conformation of Enzymes* 69; scientific papers.
Huntington Laboratories, Massachusetts General Hospital, Fruit Street, Boston, Mass. 02114, U.S.A.
Telephone: 617-726-8805.

Kaldor, Baron (Life Peer), cr. 74, of Newnham in the City of Cambridge; **Nicholas Kaldor,** M.A., F.B.A. B.SC.(ECON.); British economist; b. 12 May 1908; ed. Model Gymnasium, Budapest, London School of Econs. Assistant Lecturer, Lecturer and Tutor, Reader, London School of Economics 32-47; war service U.S. Strategic Bombing Survey, British Bombing Survey Unit; Dir. Research and Planning Division U.N. Econ. Comm. for Europe 47-49; Lecturer, later Reader and now Prof. of Econs. Cambridge Univ. 49-; Fellow of King's Coll., Cambridge 49-; mem. Royal Comm. in the Taxation of Profits and Income 50-55; Survey on Indian Tax Reform, Govt. of India 56; Taxation of Mexico 60; Econ. Adviser Govt. of Ghana 61; Fiscal Adviser Govt. of British Guiana 61, Govt. of Turkey 62, Reserve Bank of Australia 63; Special Adviser to Chancellor of Exchequer 64-68, 74-; Dr. h.c. (Dijon); Hon. Fellow, London School of Econs. 70.
Publs. *An Expenditure Tax* 55, and with S. Silverman *A Statistical Analysis of Advertising Expenditure* 46, *Essays in Value and Distribution* 60, *Essays in Economic Stability and Growth* 60, *Ensayos sobre Desarrollo Económico* (Mexico) 61, *Essays on Economic Policy* (2 vols.) 64, *Causes of the Slow Rate of Growth of the United Kingdom, Conflicts in Policy Objectives* 71.
King's College, Cambridge, England.

Kalesnik, Stanislav Vikentjevich, DR.SC.; Soviet geographer; b. 21 Jan. 1901, Leningrad; ed. High Military Pedagogical School and Leningrad State Univ. Teacher in military schools 22-31; Lecturer, Leningrad Inst. of Mines 29-31; Research worker, Inst. of Geological Map, Leningrad 31-32; Official, U.S.S.R. Cttee. on conducting of 2nd Int. Arctic year and Tajik-Pamirs expedition, U.S.S.R. Council of People's Commissars 32-35; scientific and teaching work Leningrad Univ. 35-, Prof. 39-, Chief of Physical Geography Faculty 50-, Dir. of Lab. of Lake Studies 55-; mem. and Head of many expeditions in Cen. Tien Shan, Arctic, Severnoe Priladozhje; Corresp. mem. U.S.S.R. Acad. of Sciences 53-68, Academician 68-; mem. C.P.S.U. 43-; Pres. Geographical Soc. of U.S.S.R. 64.
Publs. Numerous works on physical geography of various geographical zones of the U.S.S.R.
U.S.S.R. Academy of Sciences, 14 Leninsky Prospekt, Moscow, U.S.S.R.

Kalinowsky, Lothar Bruno, M.D.; American neuropsychiatrist; b. 28 Dec. 1899, Berlin, Germany; s. of Alfred Kalinowsky and Anna Schott; m. Hilda Pohl 1925; two d.; ed. Berlin, Heidelberg and Munich Univs. Assistant in Neuropsychiatry at hospitals in Berlin, Hamburg, Breslau, Vienna 22-32, Rome 33-39; Clinical Prof. of Psychiatry, N.Y. Medical Coll.; Assoc. Prof. of Neuropsychiatry, N.Y. School of Psychiatry; Consultant Psychiatrist, St. Vincent's Hospital, N.Y. 57-; Hon. Prof. of Psychiatry, Free Univ., Berlin; Hon. mem. German Soc. for Neurology and Psychiatry; Corresp. Fellow, Royal Coll. of Psychiatry.
Leisure interest: travelling.
Publs. *Somatic Treatments in Psychiatry* (with Paul H. Hoch and Brenda Grant) 61; *Pharmacological, convulsive and other somatic treatments in psychiatry* (with Hans Hippius) 69.
115 East 82nd Street, New York, N.Y. 10028, U.S.A. Telephone: RE 7-0800.

Kaliski, Div. Gen. Sylwester, D.ENG.; Polish scientist; b. 19 Dec. 1925, Toruń; s. of Wincenty and Waleria Kaliski; m. Irena Kaliski 1954; one s.; ed. Technical Univ., Gdańsk.
Scientific worker at Military Technical Acad., Warsaw 51-, Prof. 58-, Commdr./Rector 67-; Editor-in-Chief *Problemy Drgań* (Problems of Vibrations) 59-, *Bulletin Wat*; Corresp. mem. Polish Acad. of Sciences 62-69, mem. 69-, mem. Presidium Dec. 71-, Scientific Worker Inst. of Basic Technical Problems; Deputy to Seym

March 72-, Chair. Seym Comm. of Science and Technical Progress; Divisional Gen. 72-74; Minister of Science, Higher Educ. and Technics Dec. 74-; mem. Polish United Workers' Party; Order Banner of Labour 68, Knight and Commdr. Cross, Order of Polonia Restituta 61, 73; State Prize 64, 70, 74.
Publs. over 400 papers in professional journals.
Ministerstwo Nanki, Szkolnictwa Wyższego i Techniki, ul. Podwale 1/3, 00-252 Warsaw, Poland.
Telephone: 26-70-21.

Kállai, Gyula; Hungarian journalist and politician; b. 1 June 1910, Berettyóujfalu; s. of Sándor Kállai and Eszter Kiss; m. Gabriella Alnoch 1957; two d.
As a student, joined left-wing univ. movements in Budapest and Debrecen; one of leaders and organizers Hungarian Historical Mem. Cttee., helped to initiate prewar March Front Movement; mem. Editorial Board of *Nepszava*, organ of Social Democratic Party 39-44; Rep. Communist Party, Hungarian Front Exec. Cttee.; mem. Dept. of Agitation and Propaganda, H.C.P. 45-; Editor *Szabadság*; Under-Sec. Prime Minister's Office 45; Head Party Intellectual Dept. 47-49; Pres. of the Nat. Council of the Patriotic People's Front 58-; mem. Cen. Cttee., Hungarian Socialist Workers' Party 56-, mem. Politburo 56-75; Minister for Foreign Affairs 49-51; Deputy Minister of Culture 55-56; Minister of Culture 57-58; Minister of State 58-60; First Deputy Prime Minister 60-65; Prime Minister 65-67; Speaker of Nat. Assembly 67-70; Dr. h.c. Kossuth Univ., Debrecen 75.
Leisure interests: fine arts, literature, theatre.
Publs. *For Socialist Culture* 58, *Socialism and Culture* 62, *The Hungarian Movement for Independence 39-45* 65, *Socialism—People's Front—Democracy* 71.
The National Council of Patriotic People's Front, Budapest 5, Belgrád rakpart 24, Hungary.
Telephone: 182-850.

Kallós, Ödön; Hungarian commercial official; b. 6 Feb. 1917, Györ; s. of Ernö Kallós and Olga László; m. Hedvig Gárdonyi 1952; one d.
Commercial Attaché, Egypt 48, later Trade Counsellor until 55; Deputy Dir. MOGURT Hungarian Trading Co. for Motor Vehicles 55-56; Commercial Counsellor and Head of Hungarian Trade Comm. to India 56-59; Pres. Hungarian Chamber of Commerce 59-; Labour Order of Merit, golden degree 58, 69.
Leisure interests: rowing, tourism.
Hungarian Chamber of Commerce, Kossuth Lajos tér 6-8, H-1389 Budapest V, Hungary.
Telephone: 124-051.

Kalmbach, Leland J.; American insurance executive; b. 30 April 1901; ed. Univ. of Michigan.
Joined Cleveland Life Ins. Co. 23; with Lincoln Nat. Life Insurance Co., Fort Wayne, Ind. 24-47; Vice-Pres. 39-47, 1st Vice-Pres. 47, Dir. 37-47; Vice-Pres. Mass. Mutual Life Insurance Co., Springfield, Mass. 48-50, Pres. 50-62, Chair. 62-66, Hon. Chair. 66-; Dir. Sheraton Corpn. of America; Dir. N.E. Telephone and Telegraph Co.; official of several professional and civic orgs.
1295 State Street, Springfield, Mass. 01101, U.S.A.

Kamaladevi, Chattopadhyay; Indian politician and social worker; b. 3 April 1903, Mangalore; d. of Ananthayya and Girijahai Kamaladevi; m. Harindranath Chattopadhyay 1919; ed. Mangalore, Bedford Coll. London, and London School of Econs.
Joined Congress; elected to A.I.C.C. 27; Organizing Sec. and Pres. All-India Women's Conf.; imprisoned 30, 32, 34 and 42; founded Indian Co-operative Union to rehabilitate refugees through co-operatives 48; Chair. All-India Handicrafts Board 52; Vice-Chair. Sangeat Natak Akad.; Pres. Theatre Centre of India; helped to found World Crafts Council and is its Senior Vice-Pres.; Indian and foreign awards and Gold Medals; Awarded

"Deshikotlama" by Vishwa Bharati Univ. at Shantinckatan 70.

Leisure interests: designing, reading, travelling.

Publs. *In War-torn China, Japan: Its Weakness and Strength, Socialism and Society, America, the Land of Superlatives, Uncle Sam's Empire, Indian Handicrafts, Carpets and Floor Coverings of India.*

Bharatiya Natya Sangh, 34 New Central Market, New Delhi; and Flat No. 6, Chateau Marine, Subhas Road, Bombay, India.

Telephone: New Delhi 386408; Bombay 299676.

Kamana, Dunstan Weston; Zambian diplomatist; b. 19 April 1937, Choma; *m.*; four *c.*; ed. St. Mark's Coll., Mapanza.

Joined N. Rhodesian Govt. Service 59; Information Officer, Zambia Information Service 64; First Press Sec. at High Comm. in U.K. 64, to Pres. of Zambia 65; Asst. Sec. Ministry of Defence 65-66; Dir. of Zambia Information Services 66-68, of Zambia Information and Broadcasting Services 68-72; Editor-in-Chief, *Times of Zambia* 68-72; Gen. Man. Dairy Produce Board 72; Amb. to U.S.S.R. 72-74; High Commr. in Canada 74-75; Perm. Rep. to UN Aug. 75-.

Permanent Mission of Zambia to the United Nations, 150 East 58th Street, New York, N.Y. 10022, U.S.A.

Kamanda wa Kamanda, L. EN D.; Zairian lawyer and administrator; b. 10 Dec. 1940, Kikwit; ed. Coll. St. Ignace de Kiniati, Coll. Notre Dame de Mbansa Boma, Univ. Lovanium, Kinshasa.

Lawyer, Court of Appeal 64-; Legal Adviser, Féd. congolaise des travailleurs 64-65; Prof. Inst. nat. d'études politiques 65-66; Legal Adviser to Presidency of Repub. 65-66, Sec.-Gen. 66-67; Principal Adviser with responsibility for legal, administrative, political and diplomatic affairs to Presidency of Repub.; Dir. de Cabinet to Sec.-Gen. of Org. of African Unity 67-72, Asst. Sec.-Gen. Aug. 72-; Assoc. mem. Office Nat. de la Recherche Scientifique et du Développement; Vice-Pres. Zairian section, Soc. Africaine de la Culture; del. to several int. confs.

Publs. *Essai de critiques du système de la criminalité d'emprunt* 64, *Négritude face au devenir de l'Afrique* 67, *L'Université aujourd'hui en Afrique* 69, *L'Intégration juridique et le développement harmonieux des nations africaines* 69, *L'Incidence de la culture audio-visuelle sur le phénomène du pouvoir* 70, *Les Organisations africaines Vol. I: L'OUA ou la Croisade de l'Unité africaine* 70, *Vol. II* 70.

OAU General Secretariat, P.O. Box 3243, Addis Ababa, Ethiopia; B.P. 9312, Kinshasa 1, 221 Avenue de Gerbéra, Zaire.

Kamanga, Reuben Chitandika; Zambian politician; b. 26 Aug. 1929, Chitandika Village, Chipata District, Eastern Province of Zambia; *m.* Edna Mwansa 1963; three *s.* three *d.*; ed. Munali.

Imprisoned several times for political reasons 52-60; lived in Cairo 60-62; Deputy Pres. United Nat. Ind. Party; fmr. Minister of Labour and Mines; Minister of Transport and Communications 64; Vice-Pres. 64-67; Leader of House, National Assembly 64-67; Minister of Foreign Affairs 67-69, of Rural Devt. 69-73; mem. Cen. Cttee. United Nat. Independence Party (UNIP), Chair. Rural Devt. Sub-Cttee. 73-.

Leisure interests: football, dancing (traditional), music, gardening, hunting.

UNIP, Freedom House, P.O. Box 302, Lusaka, Zambia.

Telephone: 74321.

Kamara-Taylor, Christian Alusine; Sierra Leonean politician; b. 3 June 1917, Ka-Hanta, Tonko Limba Chiefdom, Kambia District; ed. School of Accountancy, London.

Served as Clerk in the Marampa Mines, Sierra Leone Devt. Co. before joining the Sierra Leone Regt.; Sergeant/Quartermaster World War II; joined the United Africa Co. Ltd. after briefly serving in the Civil Service, and later became Sec. and Public Relations Officer; M.P. 62-; Minister of Lands, Mines and Labour 68-71, of Finance 71-75, Prime Minister and Minister of the Interior July 75-; Sec.-Gen. All People's Congress; mem. Kambia District Council; Burma Star, Defence Medal.

Leisure interests: fishing, lawn tennis, walking.

Office of the Prime Minister, Freetown, Sierra Leone.

Kamaraj, K.; Indian politician; b. 1903; ed. Virudhunagar, Madras.

Entered public life during Salt Satyagraha 21, sentenced to two years; mem. Working Cttee., Tamil Nad Congress 31, Sec. 35, Pres. 39-54; sentenced to one year 32; mem. Madras Legislative Assembly 37-; detained, Satyagraha Movement 41, 42-45; mem. Constituent Assembly of India 47, All-India Congress Working Cttee., 49; Leader, Madras Legislature Congress Party 54-; Chief Minister, Madras 54-August 63; Pres. Indian Nat. Congress 63-68; mem. Parl. for Nagercoil, Madras State 69 and 71.

8 Tirumali Pillai Road, Madras 17, India.

Kamarck, Andrew Martin, B.S., M.A., PH.D.; American international bank official; b. 10 Nov. 1914, Newton Falls, N.Y.; *s.* of Martin Kamarck and Frances Earl; *m.* Margaret Goldenweiser Burgess 1941; one *s.* two *d.*; ed. Harvard Univ.

International Section, Fed. Reserve Board 39-40; Confidential Asst. to Sec. of U.S. Treasury 40-42; U.S. Army 42-44; Cen. Banking Adviser, Allied Control Comm., Italy 43-44; Chief, Financial Intelligence, Deputy Dir. Finance Div., and American Deputy on Allied Finance Directorate, Allied Control Council, Germany 45; Office of Int. Finance, U.S. Treasury, Chief of Nat. Advisory Council on Int. Monetary and Financial Problems (N.A.C.) Div., Financial Policy Cttee. preparing Marshall Plan 45-46; U.S. Treasury Rep., Chief of Finance Div. of Econ. Co-operation Admin. Mission, Financial Attaché U.S. Embassy, Rome 48-50; Chief of Africa Section, Econ. Dept., World Bank 50-52; Econ. Adviser, Dept. of Operations, Europe, Africa and Australasia, World Bank, Chief of Econ. Missions to 14 countries, Chief Economist, Uganda Survey Mission 62-64; Dir. Econ. Dept., World Bank and Int. Devt. Asscn. 65-71; Dir. Econ. Devt. Inst. 72-; mem. American Econ. Asscn., Council on Foreign Relations, Policy Board, Econ. Inst. of American Econ. Asscn. 62-65; Fellow 58, and Dir. African Studies Asscn. 61-64; Regents Prof., Univ. of Calif. 64-65; Council, Soc. for Int. Devt. 67-70.

Leisure interests: sailing, skiing.

Publs. *The Economic Development of Uganda* (co-author) 61, *The Economics of African Development* 67 (revised edn. 71).

International Bank for Reconstruction and Development, Washington, D.C. 20433; and 126 Third Street S.E., Washington, D.C. 20003, U.S.A.

Telephone: 544-8781 (Home).

Kamath, Hari Vishnu, B.SC.; Indian politician; b. 13 July 1907, Mangalore, Karnataka State; *s.* of Rama and Anandibai Kamath; ed. Mangalore and Presidency Coll., Madras.

Joined Indian civil service in London 29; served I.C.S. 30-38; resigned for political reasons; joined Congress and then the Forward Bloc as Sec.-Gen.; in prison 40-41, 42-45; mem. Constituent Assembly 46-49, and mem. Nagpur Provincial Congress Cttee.; mem. Provisional Parl. 50-52; Praja Socialist Member of Lok Sabha 55-57, 62-67; Chair. Praja Socialist Party, Madhya Pradesh 58-60; mem. Nat. Exec. Praja Socialist Party 53-71; mem. Nat. Cttee. Socialist Party 71-; Chair. Central Parl. Board, Praja Socialist Party 65-70; mem. Admin. Reforms Comm., Govt. of India 66-70; contested election to office of Vice-Pres. of India as Opposition Party candidate Aug. 69.

Leisure interests: reading (philosophy, yoga, English and Sanskrit literature), writing (occasionally for journals), hiking.
Publs. *Communist China colonises Tibet, invades India* 59, *Principles and Techniques of Administration* 71.
Western Court, New Delhi; Dhantoli, Nagpur, India.
Telephone: 386785 (New Delhi); 22359 (Nagpur).

Kamei, Masao; Japanese business executive; b. 20 April 1916, Kobe City, Hyogo Pref.; *s.* of Einosuke and Sei Kamei; *m.* Hanae Kano 1943; two *s.* one *d.*; ed. Tokyo Univ.
Director Sumitomo Electric Industries Ltd. 64-66, Man. Dir. 66-69, Senior Man. Dir. 69-71, Exec. Vice-Pres. 71-73, Pres. Nov. 73-.
Leisure interests: painting, golf.
7-25, 1-chome Kamikoshien, Nishinomiya City, Hyogo Prefecture, Japan.
Telephone: 0798-47-3948.

Kamel, Hassan, PH.D.; Egyptian diplomatist and administrator; b. 6 Sept. 1907; ed. Univs. of Montpellier, Cairo and the Sorbonne.
Member Mixed Bar 30-36; Lecturer, Admin. Law, High Coll. of Police and Admin. 36-37; joined Ministry of Foreign Affairs 37, served in several countries including Italy, Iran, France, Syria, Portugal, U.S.A., Libya and Hungary until 59; Legal Adviser, Govt. of Qatar 60; Dir.-Gen. Govt. of Qatar 61-67; Adviser to Govt. of Qatar with rank of Minister 67-; Perm. Rep. of Qatar to UN 71-72; Adviser of several dels. to UN and rep. on numerous int. confs.; Vice-Pres. Qatar Public Petroleum Corpn.; mem. Investment Board of Govt. of Qatar; mem. Int. Law Asscn., London, Amer. Soc. of Int. Law, Washington, World Peace through Law Centre, Washington; fmr. Dir. and mem. of Joint Management Cttee. of Qatar Petroleum Co. and Shell Co. of Qatar; Légion d'Honneur, Ordre National du Mérite (France), Order of the Republic (Egypt), Ordre National du Mérite (Syria) Order of Al Kawkab al Ordoni (Jordan).
Publs. numerous legal articles.
P.O. Box 636, Doha, Qatar.
Telephone: 5122.

Kamen, Martin D., B.S., PH.D.; American professor of chemistry; b. 27 Aug. 1913, Toronto, Canada; *s.* of Harry Kamen and Goldie Achber; *m.* 1st Beka Doherty (died 1963), 2nd Dr. V. L. Swanson 1967; one *s.*; ed. elementary and secondary schools, Chicago, and Univ. of Chicago.
Research Chemist (Assoc.), Radiation Lab., Univ. of Calif. (Berkeley) 37-44; Assoc. Prof. of Biochemistry and Research Assoc., Inst. of Radiology, Washington Univ. Medical School, St. Louis 45-57; Prof. of Biochemistry, Brandeis Univ., Waltham, Mass. 57-61, Univ. of Calif., La Jolla 61, Univ of Calif., Los Angeles 74; Dir. Laboratoire de Photosynthèse Centre Nationale de la Recherche Scientifique, France 67-69; mem. Nat. Acad. of Sciences, Amer. Acad. of Science and Letters, Amer. Philosophical Soc.; Fellow, Amer. Inst. of Chemists; Amer. Chemical Soc. Award for Applications of Nuclear Science to Chem. 63; Amer. Soc. of Plant Physiologists, Kettering Award 68; Dr. h.c. (Sorbonne, Paris) 69, Hon. D.Sc. (Univ. of Chicago) 69; Alumni Medal, Univ. of Chicago 73; Senior Fellow, von Humboldt Foundation, Univ. of Freiburg 74; Patten Prof., Indiana Univ. 75.
Leisure interest: music.
Publs. *Isotopic Tracers in Biology* 61, *Primary Processes in Photosynthesis* 63, *A Tracer Experiment* 64; and over 200 papers on chemical microbiology, photosynthesis and nuclear chemistry.
5698 Holly Oak Drive, Hollywood, Calif. 90068, U.S.A.
Telephone: (213) 465-0678.

Kameoka, Takao; Japanese politician; b. 27 Jan. 1920.
Served as Major in Japanese Army; Private Sec. to Minister of Health and Welfare; mem. House of Reps. 60-; Deputy Minister of Posts and Telecommunications 65; Deputy Chief Sec. of the Cabinet, Minister of State 67-68; Minister of Construction Dec. 73-Dec. 74.
13-9, Asagaya-Kita, 2-chome, Suginami-ku, Tokyo 166, Japan.

Kamimura, Eisuke, B.A.; Japanese petroleum executive; b. 11 March 1900; ed. Tokyo Imperial Univ.
Joined Nippon Oil Co. 25; with Japan Oil Transportation Co. 46-49; Dir. Nippon Oil Co. 49-50, Man. Dir. 50-58, Vice-Pres. 58-61, Pres. 61-; Dir. Nippon Petroleum Refining Co. 51-61, Pres. 61-; Chair. Japan Oil Transportation Co. 58-; Dir. Nippon Petrochemicals Co. 61-, Nisseki Real Estate Co. 59-, Nippon Petroleum Gas Co. 61-, Nippon Hodo Co. 60-, Nippon Speciality Lubricants Co. 60-; Chair. and Pres. Nippon Oil (Delaware) Ltd. 61-; Exec. Dir. Fed. of Econ. Orgs. 61, Japan Fed. of Employers' Asscns. 61.
5-2-2, Den-enchofu, Ohta-ku, Tokyo, Japan.

Kaminska, Ida; Polish actress and theatrical producer and manager; b. 1899.
First stage appearance 09; organizer and dir. of Jewish theatre companies Warsaw 18, Wilno, Lwów 33-41; since the Second World War in Łódź and Wrocław; now Dir. State Jewish Theatre, Warsaw; roles include Nora (Ibsen's *The Doll's House*), Glikl Hameln, Mother (Gergely's *The Case of Pawel Eszterag*), Ethel (Kruczkowski's *Julius and Ethel*), *Mother Courage* (Brecht), Madame Frank (Dürenmatt's *Frank V.*); appeared in Czechoslovak film *The Shop in the High Street*.
Living abroad.

Kaminsky, Horst, M.A.; German central banker; b. 1927.
Secretary of State, Ministry of Finance 63-74; Pres. Staatsbank der Deutschen Demokratischen Republik 74; Patriotic Order of Merit in Silver 64, Order of Banner of Labour 69, 74.
Staatsbank der Deutschen Demokratischen Republik, 108 Berlin, Charlottenstrasse 33, German Democratic Republic.

Kamitz, Reinhard, DR.RER.MERC.; Austrian economist; b. 18 June 1907, Halbstadt; *s.* of Dr. Wenzel Kamitz and Hermine Teuber; *m.* Margarete Schaudy 1938; one *s.* one *d.*; ed. Hochschule für Welthandel, Vienna.
Worked in paper industry and later in iron industry; on staff Austrian Inst. for Econ. Research 34-38; leading positions Austrian Chamber of Commerce 39-52; Minister of Finance 52-60; Pres. Austrian Nat. Bank 60-68; Hon. Prof. Vienna Univ.
Austrian Investment Finance Corporation, Postfach 15, 1013 Vienna, Austria.
Telephone: 0222-63-67-38.

Kammhuber, Gen. Josef; German air force officer; b. 19 Aug. 1896, Burgkirchen, Bavaria; *m.* Erika Benn 1948 (died 1962); ed. Ludwigsgymnasium, Munich.
Volunteer 14, transferred to regular army and served through all ranks to Major-Gen. 40, Lieut.-Gen. 41 and Gen. of the *Luftwaffe* 43; Chief of the German Air Force 56-62; Lieut.-Gen. 56-61; Gen. 61;, Iron Cross, I and II Class, Ritterkreuz and Grosses Bundesverdienstkreuz mit Stern und Schulterband.
Leisure interests: music, history, mountains.
Schwindstrasse 24, 8000 Munich 40, Federal Republic of Germany.
Telephone: 52-46-59.

Kamov, Nikolai Ilyich, D.SC.; Soviet aircraft designer; ed. Tomsk Inst. of Technology.
Chief Designer, U.S.S.R. Ministry of Aircraft Engineer-

ing; Co-Designer KASKR-1 Autogyro 29; Designer of helicopters: KA-8 in 45, KA-15 in 52, KA-18 in 56, KA-20, KA-22 and KA-26 in 65; Orders of Lenin, Red Banner of Labour, Hero of Socialist Labour, Hammer and Sickle Gold Medal, and other decorations.
U.S.S.R. Ministry of Aircraft Industry, Moscow, U.S.S.R.

Kampmann, Jens; Danish politician; b. 1937, Copenhagen.
Employed at Ministry of Education 62-64, Ministry of Finance 64; mem. Folketing 66-; Minister for Transport, Communications and Environmental Protection 71-73, of Public Works 73; fmr. Editor, *Verdens Gang* and *Ny Politik* (social democratic periodicals); mem. Exec. Cttee. Building Trades' Co-operative 70-; Social Democrat.
Publs. Co-author: *Ahead of the Future, People and Planning*.
Ministry of Public Works, Copenhagen, Denmark.

Kampmann, Viggo; Danish economist and politician; b. 21 July 1910, Frederiksberg; s. of late Conrad Kampmann and Ellen K. Fischer; m. 1st Eva K. Brinch 1942, three s. three d.; m. 2nd Ulla K. Rohde Knudsen 1970, three s.; ed. Univ. of Copenhagen.
Economist, Statistical Dept. 34-44; Deputy Chief, Secretariat-General, Government's Employment Cttee. 44-46; Adviser, Dept. of Taxes 46-47; Head, Government's Economic Secretariat 47-50; Pres. and Chair. Royal Mortgage Bank of Denmark 50-53; Minister of Finance 50, 53-60, Prime Minister 60-Aug. 62; Pres. State Life Insurance Co. 62-; Vice-Pres. Copenhagen Bldg. Soc. 63-.
Leisure interests: books, literary activity.
Vejbo, St. Thorøje 4640, Fakse, Denmark.
Telephone: 03-70-83-64.

Kanagaratnam, Kandiah, M.B.; Singapore international medical officer; b. 1922, Ceylon; m. Manoranjitham Arunasalam 1954; two d.; ed. Raffles Inst., Singapore, Univ. of Malaya and London School of Hygiene and Tropical Medicine.
Various posts in Ministry of Health, Singapore 53-69, including Deputy Dir. of Medical Services 64, and Chair. of Singapore Family Planning and Population Board 66; Consultant, World Health Org. (WHO), Philippines 68, Int. Bank for Reconstruction and Devt. (IBRD)—World Bank, Jamaica and Mauritius; Dir. of Population Projects Dept., World Bank Sept. 69-.
Publs. Numerous papers on public health, population and family planning.
International Bank for Reconstruction and Development, 1818 H Street, Washington, D.C. 20433, U.S.A.
Telephone: 202-477-5431.

Kanakaratne, Neville, M.A., LL.B., BARRISTER-AT-LAW; Ceylonese diplomatist; b. 19 July 1923, Colombo; s. of Mudaliar Kanakaratne and Mildrid de Silva; unmarried; ed. Royal Coll., Colombo, Univs. of Ceylon and Cambridge and Middle Temple, London.
Crown Counsel, Dept. of Attorney-Gen. 51-57; First Sec. and Legal Adviser, Perm. Mission of Ceylon at UN 57-61; Legal Adviser to Special Rep. of UN Sec.-Gen. in the Congo 61-62; Legal and Political Adviser to Commdr., UN Emergency Force, Gaza 62-64; Legal Adviser to Commdr. UN Peace Keeping Force, Cyprus and to Special Rep. of UN Sec.-Gen. 64-65; Senior Fellow, Centre for Int. Studies, New York Univ. 65-66; Minister for Econ. Affairs, Ceylon High Comm., London 67-70; Amb. to U.S.A. Sept. 70-; del to numerous int. confs. and several sessions of UN Gen. Assembly.
Leisure interests: theatre, music, reading.
Embassy of Sri Lanka, 2148 Wyoming Avenue, N.W., Washington, D.C.; Home: 2503 30th Street, N.W., Washington, D.C., U.S.A.
Telephone: 483-4025 (Office); 387-0601 (Home).

Kanayama, Masahide; Japanese diplomatist; b. 24 Jan. 1910; ed. Faculty of Law, Tokyo Univ.
Entered Ministry of Foreign Affairs 34; served France 34, Geneva 35, Ministry of Foreign Affairs, Tokyo 39-41; Third, later Second Sec. Italy 41-44; First Sec., Vatican 52; Counsellor, Philippines 52-54; Consul Gen. Honolulu 54-57; Dir.-Gen. European and Oceanic Affairs Bureau 57-61; Consul-Gen. New York 61-63; Amb. to Chile 63-67, to Poland 67-68, to Republic of Korea 68-71; Dir. Joint Research Centre of Int. Relations, Inst. of Korean Studies.
2-1, 7-chome, Minamiaoyama, Minato-ku, Tokyo 107; Home: 4-3, 1-chome, Akatsutsumimachi, Setagaya-ku, Tokyo, Japan.

Kandahl, Torolv; Norwegian journalist; b. 17 Aug. 1899, Lyngdal; s. of Tor Mathias Kandahl and Sanna Mathilde Torjesen; m. Else Margrete Cammermeyer Rød 1950; one s. one d. (deceased); ed. Oslo Univ.
Began journalistic career 28; Chief Editor *Drammens Tidende*, Drammen 45-61, *Aftenposten*, Oslo 61-70; mem. Norwegian Parl. 50-54; Chair. Norwegian Press Asscn. 38-41, Norwegian Editors' Asscn. 50-56; mem. Board, Int. Press Inst. 60-62; Pres. World League of Norsemen 63-75; Commdr., Order of St. Olav; Hon. degree, Luther Coll., Decorah, Iowa; Conservative.
Leisure interest: fishing.
Rosenborggaten 5, Oslo 3, Norway.
Telephone: Oslo 69-37-83.

Kandolo Lopepe; Zairian administrator; b. 10 Sept. 1923; m.; seven c.; ed. primary and secondary school; Univ. of Brussels.
Began his career as an administrator 40; Sec. Services Administratifs Provinciaux 52; Chef de Bureau aux Affaires Extérieures 60; Chef de Cabinet under Pres. Lumumba 60; Dept. of the Interior (with M. J. Nussbaumer) 60, 62-64; Sec.-Gen. for the Interior 61; Chef de Cabinet Aug. 61; participation in organizing Congrès Nat. 63; Sec.-Gen. Ministry for Land, Mines and Power Aug. 64; Asst. Rep. of Groupe Cominière 65; Pres. Conseil d'Administration de T.C.Za. 66; Admin. Air-Zaire 66; Admin. and Pres. of Gecamines (La Générale des Carrières et Mines du Zaïre) 68; del. to several int. confs.; Chevalier, Ordre Nat. du Léopard, Officier, Ordre du Mérite du Sénégal and various other foreign awards.
Leisure interests: cultural and sporting activities.
Gecamines, B.P. 450 Lubumbashi, Zaire.

Kane, Edward R., PH.D.; American business executive; b. 13 Sept. 1918, Schenectady, N.Y.; s. of Edward and Elva Kane; m. Doris Peterson 1948; two d.; ed. Union Coll., Mass. Inst. of Technology.
With E. I. du Pont de Nemours & Co. 43-; Textile Fibres 43-66; Asst. Gen. Man. Industrial and Biochemicals 66, Gen. Man. 67; Vice-Pres., Dir., mem. Exec. Cttee. E. I. du Pont de Nemours & Co. 69, Vice-Chair. Exec. Cttee. 71, Senior Vice-Pres. 72, Pres. 73-; Dir. Delaware Trust Co.; Trustee, Union Coll., Comm. for Econ. Devt.; Chair. American Branch of Soc. of Chemical Industry; mem. Exec. Cttee. Mfg. Chemists' Asscn.; mem. American Chemical Soc., American Inst. of Chemical Engineers, MIT Corpn. Visiting Cttee.
E. I. du Pont de Nemours & Co., Wilmington, Del. 19898, U.S.A.

Kane, Falilou; Senegalese diplomatist; b. 14 July 1938, Joal; s. of Moustapha Kane and Yacine Niang; m. Rabia Ben Zekry 1963; five s.; ed. Collège Blanchot, Saint-Louis, Lycée Van Vollenhoven, Dakar, and Faculty of Law and Econs., Univ. of Dakar.
Ministry of Foreign Affairs, Senegal 60-, successively Head of Div. of UN Affairs, Int. Orgs. and Gen. Affairs, Div. of Political Affairs, concurrently Technical Adviser to Minister of Foreign Affairs; Technical Adviser in Ministry of Justice Nov.-Dec. 62; Dir. of Political, Cultural and Social Affairs, Ministry of

Foreign Affairs; Minister at Perm. Mission of Senegal to UN 66; Minister, Embassy of Senegal, Washington until Dec. 67; Sec.-Gen. Org. Commune Africaine et Malgache (OCAM) 68-74; has taken part in numerous int. confs.; decorations from Morocco, Upper Volta, Cameroon, Chad and Repub. of Zaire.
Leisure interests: sport, reading.
c/o Ministry of Foreign Affairs, Yaoundé, Cameroon.

Kane, William J.; American business executive; b. 30 Nov. 1912, Philadelphia, Pa.; ed. St. Joseph's Coll. Joined Great Atlantic and Pacific Tea Co. Inc. 31, Pres. 68, Chair. and Chief Exec. Officer 71-75.
Great Atlantic and Pacific Tea Company Inc., 420 Lexington Avenue, New York, N.Y. 10017, U.S.A.

Kanellopoulos, Panayotis; Greek politician; b. 1902. Former Prof. of Sociology Athens Univ.; served Albanian front 41; Deputy Prime Minister and Minister of Defence 42-43; Minister, Finance and Reconstruction 44; Prime Minister Nov. 45; M.P. March 46; Minister without Portfolio April 46; Minister of Air 47; Minister of War 49-50; M.P. 50; Deputy Prime Minister and Minister of Defence in Venizelos Govt. March-April 50; in Jan. 51 formed with S. Stephanopoulos the Populist Unionist Party (LEK); at Gen. Election Sept. 51 joined forces with Marshal Papagos; Minister of Nat. Defence 52-55; Deputy Prime Minister 54-55, 59-63; Prime Minister and Minister of Foreign Affairs 3-21 April 67; co-leader of Populist Party 58, Leader Nat. Radical Union 63-67 (party suspended); Prof. of Social Sciences, Athens Acad. 59-; under house arrest April-Oct. 68.
Publs. *League of Nations* 26, *Social Progress and Social Policy* 27, *Sociology of the Imperialist Phenomena* 27, *Karl Marx* 31, *Society in our Days* 32, *Progress of Technique and Economy* 33, *Man and the Social Conflicts* 34, *Philosophical and Sociological Problems of History* 36, *Simple Sounds* (Verse) 39, *History of the European Spirit* (two vols.) 41-47, *I Shall Tell You the Truth* 45, *The Cycle of Sonnets* (Verse) 46, *The 20th Century* 50, *Christianity and Our Era* 52, *Prolegomena to Metaphysics* 55, *Athenian Dialogues* 56, *The End of Zarathustra* 56, *I Was Born in 1402* 57.
Akadima Athinon, Odos Panepistimiou, Athens, Greece.

Kanemaru, Shin; Japanese politician; b. 1915.
Member, House of Reps., re-elected six times; fmr. Chair. Liberal Dem. Party Diet Policy Cttee.; Minister of Construction 72-73; Dir. Nat. Land Agency Dec. 74-; Liberal Democratic Party.
House of Representatives, Tokyo, Japan.

Kaneshige, Kankuro; Japanese engineer; b. 5 April 1899, Osaka, Japan; m. Yasuko Sasaki 1926; one s. two d.; ed. Tokyo Imperial Univ.
Technician, Kanegafuchi Spinning Co. 23-25; Asst. Prof. of Mechanical Engineering, Tokyo Imperial Univ. 25-42; Prof. of Mechanical Engineering, Univ. of Tokyo 42-60; Dir. Inst. of Industrial Science, Univ. of Tokyo 51-54; Dir., Nat. Aeronautical Laboratory 55-57; Pres. Science Council of Japan 58-60; Full-time Commr. of Atomic Energy Comm. of Japan 60-65; Chair. Nat. Space Activities Council 60-67; mem. UN Advisory Cttee. on the Application of Science and Technology to Devt. 64-69; Full-time mem. Council for Science and Technology 65-74; Trustee, Asian Inst. of Technology 71-76.
5-46-25 Asagayakita, Suginami-ku, Tokyo 166, Japan. Telephone: 03-337-4991.

K'ang Chien-min; Chinese party official.
Divisional Commdr. 1st Field Army 49; Deputy Political Commissar Lanchow Mil. Region, People's Liberation Army 67-; Chair. Ninghsia Revolutionary Cttee. 68; Alt. mem. 9th Cen. Cttee. of CCP 69; First Sec. CCP Ninghsia 71; Alt. mem. 10th Cen. Cttee. of CCP 73.
People's Republic of China.

K'ang Shih-en; Chinese government official.
Assistant to Minister of Petroleum Industry 55-56; Vice-Minister of Petroleum Industry 56; criticized and removed from office during the Cultural Revolution 67; Minister of Petroleum and Chemical Industries 75-. People's Republic of China.

Kania, Stanisław; Polish politician; b. 8 March 1927, Wrocanka, Jasło district; ed. High School of Social Sciences of Central Cttee. of Polish United Workers' Party, Warsaw.
Member, Polish Workers' Party 45-48, Polish United Workers' Party (PUWP) 48-; Head, Agricultural Dept., Warsaw Voivodship Cttee., PUWP, then Sec. Warsaw Voivodship Cttee. 58-68; Deputy mem. Cen. Cttee., PUWP 64-68, mem. 68-, Sec. April 71-, Cand. mem. Politburo 71-75, full mem. Dec. 75-; Head, Admin. Dept., Cen. Cttee., PUWP 68-71; Deputy to Seym 72-; Order of Banner of Labour, 1st and 2nd Class; Knight's Cross and Officer's Cross, Order of Polonia Restituta. Polska Zjednoczona Partia Robotnicza, Nowy Świat 6, 00-497 Warsaw, Poland.

Kaninda Mpumbua Tshingomba, G.C.V.O., B.SC.; Zairian diplomat; b. 25 Dec. 1931, Kasai Oriental; ed. Grand Séminaire, Moba, Univs. of Montreal and Brussels.
Secretary, Mayor's Office, Rwashi-Lubumbashi 58-59; Trainee at Ministry of Foreign Affairs, Belgium 59-60; student at Montreal and Brussels Univs. 61-63; Dir. for Political Affairs, Dept. of Foreign Affairs, Kinshasa 64-65; Amb. to Tanzania 65-67, to Ghana 69-71, to Kenya 71-72, to U.K. 72-; Commdr. Ordre Nat. du Léopard.
Embassy of the Republic of Zaire, 26 Chesham Place, London, SW1 8HH, England.

Kanno, Wataro, PH.D.; Japanese politician and economist; b. 20 June 1895, Ehime; s. of Senjiro and Yone Kanno; m. Hissa Kanno 1918; one s. three d.; ed. Kyoto Univ.
Professor, Hikone Commercial Coll. 24-33, Osaka Commercial Coll. 33-35, Osaka Econ. Coll. 35-; Dir. Depts. of Educ. and Planning, Osaka 36-42; mem. House of Reps. 42-; Pres. Osaka Chamber of Commerce 43-45; Minister of State in charge of Econ. Planning Agency 59-60, Nov. 68-Jan. 70; Minister of Int. Trade and Industry 66-67; First Class Order of Rising Sun 71; Liberal Democrat.
Leisure interest: reading.
Room 732, Shugiin Daiichi Giin Kaikan, Chiyoda-ku, Home: 4-17 Tezukayama-Higashi, Sumiyoshi-ku, Osaka, Japan.
Telephone: 03-581-5111 (office).

Kante, Mamadou Boubacar; Mali diplomatist; b. Sept. 1926, Hombori; m.; two c.
Entered govt. service, Chief of Office Staff, Ministry of Labour 61-62, of Interior, Information and Tourism 62-64, of Interior 64-66; technical adviser to Office of Pres. of Mali 66-67; Perm. Rep. to UN and Amb. to Cuba 67-69; Dir.-Gen. of Political, Admin., Legal and Financial Affairs in Ministry of Foreign Affairs and Co-operation 69-71, Sec.-Gen. of Ministry 71-75; Amb. to U.S.A. and Perm. Rep. to UN Sept. 75-; Deputy Head of del. to UN Gen. Assembly 67, 68, 71-74.
Permanent Mission of Mali to the United Nations, 111 East 69th Street, New York, N.Y. 10021, U.S.A.

Kantor, Tadeusz; Polish painter and theatre organizer; b. 1915, Wielopole, near Cracow; ed. Cracow Acad. of Fine Arts.
Organized underground theatre, Cracow, during occupation; Prof. Cracow Acad. of Fine Arts 48, 69; mem. Asscn. of Polish Plastic Artists; founded Cricot 2 Theatre, Cracow 55, participated with theatre in festivals: Premio Roma 69, Mondial du Theatre, Nancy 71, Edinburgh Festival 72, 73, 8th Arts Festival,

Shiraz 74; exhibited paintings at: 30th Biennale of Art, Venice 60, L'Art Theatre exhbn., Baden-Baden 65, Happening and Fluxus exhbn., Cologne and Stuttgart 70, São Paulo Biennale 67, also at Moderna Museet, Stockholm, Museum of Modern Art, N.Y. and Solomon R. Guggenheim Museum, N.Y.; exhibits in Foksal Gallery, Warsaw: *Linia Podziatu* (The Line of Division) 65, *List* (A Letter) 67, *Lekcja anatomii wg. Rembrandta* (Rembrandt's Anatomy Lesson) 68, *Panoramiczny happening morski* (Panoramic Sea Happening) 67; Premio Marzotto, Rome 68, Prize for Painting, São Paulo 67.
Ul. Elbląska 6 m. 11, 30-054 Cracow, Poland.

Kantorovich, Leonid Vitalovich; Soviet mathematician; b. 15 Jan. 1912, Leningrad; ed. Leningrad Univ. Instructor, Leningrad Inst. of Industrial Construction Engineering 30-39; Instructor, Leningrad Univ. 32-34, Prof. 34-60; Deputy Dir. Laboratory for Use of Statistical and Mathematical Methods in Econs., Siberian Dept., U.S.S.R. Acad. of Sciences 61-; Corresp. mem. U.S.S.R. Acad. of Sciences 58-64, mem. 64-71; Head of Research Laboratory, Inst. of Nat. Economy Control, Moscow 71-; State Prize 49, Lenin Prize, Nobel Prize for Economics 75; Dr. h.c. Sorbonne 75.
Akademia nauk Leninsky prosp. 14, Moscow, U.S.S.R.

Kantorowicz, Alfred, DR.JUR.UTR.; German university professor and writer; b. 12 Aug. 1899, Berlin; *m.* Ingrid Schneider 1965; ed. Univs. of Berlin, Freiburg, Munich, Erlangen.
Army service 17-18; literary critic and foreign corresp. *Vossische Zeitung* 25-32; exile in Paris; escaped to U.S.A. 41; Dir. CBS listening station, New York; returned to Germany 46; publisher of monthly magazine *Ost und West*, Berlin 47-49; Prof. of History of German Literature, and Dir. Germanistisches Inst., Humboldt Univ. 50-57; went to Federal Republic 57; mem. German Communist Party 31-57.
Publs. *In unserem Lager ist Deutschland* (essays) 36, *Portraits* 47, *Deutsche Schicksale* 49, *Spanisches Tagebuch* 49, *Suchende Jugend* 49, *Vom moralischen Gewinn der Niederlage* 49, *Die Verbündeten* (play) 51, *Heinrich und Thomas Mann* 56, *Meine Kleider* (stories) 57, *Deutsches Tagebuch, Vol. I* 59, *Vol. II* 61, *Spanisches Kriegstagebuch* 66, *Im 2. Drittel unseres Jahrhunderts* 67; edited critical edn. of works of H. Mann 51-57.
Sierichstr. 148, 2 Hamburg 39, Federal Republic of Germany.

Kantrowitz, Adrian, M.D.; American heart surgeon; b. 4 Oct. 1918, New York City; s. of Bernard Abraham and Rose Esserman Kantrowitz; *m.* Jean Rosensaft 1947; one s. two d.; ed. New York Univ. and Long Island Coll. of Medicine.
Cleveland Teaching Fellow in Physiology, Western Reserve Univ. School of Medicine 51-52; Instructor in Surgery, New York Medical Coll. 52-55; Asst. Prof. of Surgery, New York Downstate Medical Center 55-57, Assoc. Prof. of Surgery 57-64, Prof. of Surgery 64-; Adjunct Surgeon, Montefiore Hospital, Bronx, N.Y. 51-55; Dir. (full-time) Cardiovascular Surgery, Maimonides Hospital 55-64; Attending Surgeon, Maimonides Medical Center 55-64; Dir. Surgical Services (full-time), Maimonides Medical Center and Coney Island Hospital, Brooklyn 64-70; Prof. Surgery, Wayne State Univ. School of Medicine 70-; Pres. Brooklyn Thoracic Soc. 67-68; Pres. American Soc. of Artificial Internal Organs 68-69; mem. Editorial Board *Journal of Biomedical Materials Research* 66-, mem. Scientific Review Board *Medical Research Engineering* 66-; Henry L. Moses Research Prize 49; N.Y. State Medical Soc., First Prize, Scientific Exhibit 52, First Prize Maimonides Hospital Research Soc. for work in Bladder Stimulation 63, Gold Plate Award, American Acad. of Achievement 66, Max Berg Award for Outstanding Achievement in Prolonging Human Life 66, Brooklyn

Hall of Fame Man of Year Award for Science 66, Theodor and Susan B. Cummings Humanitarian Award, American Coll. of Cardiology 67; performed first human implantation of a partial mechanical heart 66; performed first U.S. human heart transplantation 67.
Leisure interests: flying, skiing, sailing, music.
Publs. Numerous articles and films on heart surgery.
6767 West Outer Drive, Detroit, Mich. 48253, U.S.A.

Kapek, Antonin, ING., C.SC.; Czechoslovak politician; b. 6 June 1922, Roudnice nad Labem; ed. Czech Technical Univ., Prague.,
Chief Technologist, Chief Engineer, later Dir., ČKD-Sokolovo Engineering Works, Prague 53-58; Dir. ČKD-Praha Engineering Works 58-65, Gen. Dir. 65-68; mem. Cen. Cttee. C.P. of Czechoslovakia 58-, alt. mem. Presidium of Cen. Cttee. 62-68, mem. Presidium (Politburo) 70-; mem. Nat. Assembly 64-69; mem. House of People, Fed. Assembly 69-; mem. Bureau of Cen. Cttee., C.P. of Czechoslovakia, for directing party work in the Czech lands 69-70; Chief Sec. and mem. Presidium of Prague City Cttee., C.P. of Czechoslovakia 69-; Chair. Prague City Nat. Front 75-; Order for Merits in Construction, Order of Red Banner of Labour, Order of the Repub. 72, Order of Victorious February 73.
Central Committee of the Communist Party of Czechoslovakia, nábřeží Kyjevské brigády 12, Prague 1, Czechoslovakia.

Kapfer, Hans, D.JUR.; Austrian lawyer; b. 5 Sept. 1903, Sollenau, Austria; one s.; ed. Vienna Univ.
Served in Law Courts 26-46, Judge 30; entered Ministry of Justice 46, Sektionsrat 46, Ministerialrat 48, Sektionschef 53; Minister of Justice 55-56; Pres. Oberlandesgericht Vienna 58-62; Vice-Pres. Supreme Court 63-65, Pres. Supreme Court 66-68; Pres. Supreme Court of Principality of Liechtenstein 69.
Publs. (Editor) *Allgemeines bürgerliches Gesetzbuch* 48, 51, 55, 60, 61, 63, 64, 66, 67, 71, 72, 75, *Angestelltengesetz, Arbeitsgerichtsgesetz, Wechsel- und Scheckgesetz* 47, 48, 53, 57, 61, 66, 67, 73, 75, *Handkommentar Wechselgesetz* 69.
Erndtgasse 21, Vienna XVIII, Austria.
Telephone: 0222/4718854.

Kapitonov, Ivan Vasilyevich; Soviet politician; b. 1915; ed. Moscow Municipal Engineering Inst.
Managerial, Party and Govt. work 38-54; First Sec. Moscow Regional Party Cttee. 54-59, Ivanovo Regional Party Cttee. 59-64; Head of Dept. of Party Agencies, Central Cttee. of C.P.S.U. for R.S.F.S.R. 65; mem. Central Cttee., C.P.S.U. 52-, Sec. 65-; mem. Presidium of U.S.S.R. Supreme Soviet 54-62; Deputy to U.S.S.R. Supreme Soviet 50-; mem. C.P.S.U. 39-.
Central Committee of C.P.S.U., Staraya ploshchad 4, Moscow, U.S.S.R.

Kapitza, Peter Leonidovich, PH.D., F.R.S.; Soviet physicist; b. 9 July 1894, Kronstadt, Leningrad Region, s. of Leonid Petrovic and Olga Ieoronimovna Kapitza; *m.* Anna Alekseevna Krylova 1927; two s.; ed. Petrograd Polytechnic Inst.
Lecturer Leningrad Polytechnic 19-21; Asst. Dir. of Research in Magnetism, Cavendish Laboratory, Cambridge 24-32; Fellow of Trinity Coll. Cambridge 25-36; Messel Research Prof. of Royal Society and Dir. of Royal Society Mond Laboratory 30-35; Dir. Inst. for Physical Problems, Acad. of Sciences of U.S.S.R. 35-46; Editor Journal of Experimental and Theoretical Physics, U.S.S.R.; mem. Acad. of Sciences of the U.S.S.R.; Dir. Inst. for Physical Problems 55-; mem. German Acad. of Naturalists "Leopoldina" 58, Serbian Acad. of Sciences and Arts 71; Hon. mem. Inst. of Metals 43, Franklin Inst. 44, Danish Royal Acad., N.Y. Acad. of Science 46, Royal Irish Acad. 48, American Acad. of Arts and Sciences 68; Foreign Assoc. American Nat. Acad. of Sciences 46; Hon. Fellow,

Indian Acad. of Science 48, Indian Nat. Inst. of Sciences 57, Trinity Coll., Cambridge, England 66-; Foreign mem. Polish Acad. of Sciences 62-, Royal Acad. of Science, Sweden 66-, Royal Netherlands Acad. of Science 69-; Foreign mem. Finnish Acad. of Sciences and Arts 74-; State Prize 41, 43, Faraday Medal of Inst. Electrical Engineers 42, Order of Lenin 43, 44, 45, 64, 71, 74, Medal of Franklin Inst. 44, Hero of Socialist Labour 45, 74, Order of the Red Banner of Labour 54, Sir Devaprasad Sarbadhikari Gold Medal (Univ. of Calcutta) 55, Kothenius Gold Medal 59, Lomonosov Gold Medal of U.S.S.R. Acad. of Sciences 59, Great Gold Medal, Exhibition of Econ. Achievements, U.S.S.R. 62, Int. Niels Bohr Gold Medal of Dansk Ingeniør-vorening 64, Rutherford Medal of Inst. of Physics and Physical Soc. of England 66, Simon Memorial Prize of the Inst. of Physics of England 73; Rutherford Memorial Lecturer, Canada 69.
Leisure interests: chess, antiquarian horology.
Institute for Physical Problems, 2 Vorobyevskoe Chaussée, Moscow B-334, U.S.S.R.
Telephone: 137-32-47.

Kaplan, Rabbi Jacob, L. EN PHIL.; French Rabbi; b. 7 Nov. 1895, Paris; ed. Séminaire Israélite de France. Rabbi of Mulhouse 22; Rabbi in Paris 29; Auxiliary Rabbi to Chief Rabbi of France 39; Chief Rabbi of Paris 50; Chief Rabbi of France 55-; mem. Acad. des Sciences Morales et Politiques, Paris 67-; Grand Officier de la Légion d'Honneur, Croix de Guerre (twice), Grande Médaille de Vermeil de la Ville de Paris; Doctor h.c. Theological Seminary of New York; citation by Mayor of New York for distinguished service.
Publs. *Le Judaïsme et la Justice Sociale* 37, *Racisme et Judaïsme* 40, *French Jewry under the Occupation* (American Jewish Year Book) 45-46, *Le Judaïsme dans la société Française Contemporaine* 48, *Témoignages sur Israël* 49, *Les Temps d'Epreuve* 52.
1 rue Andrieux, Paris 8e, France.
Telephone: 522-33-97.

Kaplan, Joseph, B.S., A.M., PH.D.; American physicist; b. 8 Sept. 1902, Tapolcza, Hungary; s. of Heinrich and Rosa (Löwy) Kaplan; m. Katherine E. Feraud 1933; ed. Johns Hopkins Univ.
Instructor in Physics Johns Hopkins Univ. 26; Nat. Research Fellow in Physics Princeton Univ. 27-28; Asst. Prof. Univ. of California 28-35, Assoc. Prof. 35, Prof. 40-70, Prof. Emer. 70-, and Chair. Dept. of Physics 38-44, Dept. of Meteorology 40-44; Acting Dir. Inst. of Geophysics, Univ. of California, Dir. 46-47; mem. Comm. Int. Astronomical Union 22; Chief Operations Analysis Section 2nd Air Force 43-45, Air Forces Weather Service Jan.-Sept. 45; fmr. mem. Board of Dirs. Microdot Inc., New World Fund Inc.; Adviser, Axe Science Corpn.; Fellow, Physical Soc. and fmr. Local Sec. for Pacific Coast; mem. Exec. Cttee. Int. Asscn. of Terrestrial Magnetism and Electricity; Chair. Mixed Cttee. on Upper Atmosphere TMS and (IAIAM) and U.S. Cttee. for the Int. Geophysical year; Fellow, The Meteoritical Soc. (Councillor 46-50); Pres. Int. Asscn. of Geomagnetism and Aeronomy, Int. Union of Geodesy and Geophysics; Chair. U.S. Nat. Cttee. for the Int. Geophysical Year; mem. Nat. Acad. of Sciences; Fellow, Inst. of Aeronautics and Astronautics; mem. Astronomical Soc., Astronomical Soc. of the Pacific, Optical Soc. of America; Fellow, American Geophysical Union; mem. Board of Govs. Hebrew Univ. of Jerusalem, Weizmann Inst. of Science at Rehovoth, Hon. mem. and Fellow, American Meteorological Soc.; Hon. D.Sc. (Univ. of Notre Dame, Carleton Coll.); Hon. L.H.D. (Yeshiva Univ., Jewish Theological Seminary and Hebrew Union Coll.).
Leisure interests: walking, golf, writing.
Publs. *Across the Space Frontier* 50, *Physics and*

Medicine of the Upper Atmosphere 52, *Great Men of Physics* 69.
1565 Kelton Avenue, Los Angeles, Calif. 90024, U.S.A.
Telephone: 213-4738839.

Kaplan, Nathan O(ram), PH.D.; American professor of chemistry; b. 25 June 1917, New York; s. of Phillip and Rebecca (Uttef) Kaplan; m. Goldie L. Levine 1947; one s.; ed. Univ. of Calif. (Los Angeles and Berkeley).
Assistant Biochemist, Univ. of Calif. 40-42; Research Chemist, Manhattan Project 42-44; Instructor, Wayne Univ. 44-45; Assoc. Research Biochemist, Massachussetts Gen. Hosp. 45-49; Asst. Prof. of Biology, McCollum Pratt Inst., Johns Hopkins Univ. 50-52, Assoc. Prof. 52-56, Prof. 56-57; Prof. of Biochemistry and Chair. Dept. of Biochem., Brandeis Univ. 57-68; Prof. of Chem. Univ. of Calif., San Diego 68-; mem. Nat. Acad. of Sciences, A.A.A.S., American Soc. of Biochem., American Soc. of Bacteriologists, American Acad. of Arts and Sciences; Eli Lilly Award in Biochem. 53, Guggenheim Fellowship 64-65 and other awards.
Leisure interests: art collecting, boating, fishing and 'avid participant of sport activities'.
Publs. Co-author of *Methods in Enzymology* (40 vols.); author and co-author of almost 300 articles published in numerous journals.
University of California, San Diego, La Jolla, Calif. 92037, U.S.A.
Telephone: 714-452-3052.

Kaplansky, Irving, B.A., M.A., PH.D.; American mathematician; b. 22 March 1917, Toronto, Canada; s. of Samuel Kaplansky and Anna Zuckerman; m. Rachelle Brenner 1951; two s. one d.; ed. Univ. of Toronto and Harvard Univ.
Instructor, Harvard Univ. 41-44; Research Mathematician, Columbia Univ. 45; Instructor, Univ. of Chicago 45-47, Asst. Prof. 47-52, Assoc. Prof. 52-56, Prof. 56-, Chair. Dept. of Maths. 62-67; Elected to Nat. Acad. of Sciences 66; Apptd. to George Herbert Mead distinguished service Professorship 69; Hon. Dr. of Maths. (Univ. of Waterloo) 68, Hon. LL.D. (Queen's Univ.) 69.
Leisure interests: music, swimming.
Publs. Numerous research papers and books on mathematics.
5825 South Dorchester, Chicago, Ill. 60637, U.S.A.
Telephone: 667-3973.

Kapnick, Harvey Edward, Jr., B.S., C.P.A.; American accountant; b. 16 June 1925, Palmyra, Mich.; s. of Harvey E. and Beatrice Bancroft Kapnick; m. 1st Jean Bradshaw 1947 (died 1962), 2nd Mary Redus Johnson 1963; three s.; ed. Cleary Coll. and Univ. of Michigan.
Joined Arthur Andersen & Co. (Accountants) 48, Partner 56, Man. Partner, Cleveland Office 62, mem. Board of Dirs. 66-, Chair. and Chief Exec. 70-; mem. Board of Dirs. Chamber of Commerce of the U.S.A., Int. Exec. Service Corps.; Dir. Chicago 21 Corpn., Chicago Council on Foreign Relations; mem. Board of Trustees Menninger Foundation Siena Heights Coll., Orchestral Asscn., Ravinia Festival Asscn., Logistics Man. Inst. Chicago Sunday Evening Club, Museum of Science and Industry Northwestern Univ.; mem. American Inst. of Certified Public Accountants, Illinois Certified Public Accountants Soc., Iran-U.S. Business Council, U.S. Advisory Cttee. for Trade Negotiations U.S. State Dept. Advisory Cttee. on Transnational Enterprises; Hon. D.Sc. (Cleary Coll.) 71.
Arthur Andersen & Co., 69 West Washington Street, Chicago, Ill. 60602; Home: 100 Woodley Road, Winnetka, Ill. 60093, U.S.A.
Telephone: 312-F16-6262 (Office); 312-446-8047 (Home).

Kapp, Edmond X., B.A.; British artist; b. 5 Nov. 1890, London; *s.* of E. B. Kapp and Bella Wolff; *m.* 1st Yvonne Cloud 1922 (divorced 1928), 2nd Polia Chentoff 1932 (died 1933), 3rd Patricia Greene 1950; one *d.*; ed. Christ's Coll., Cambridge, London, Paris, Berlin and Rome.

First exhibition of drawings London 19, 10th retrospective and first of oil paintings, Wildenstein, London 39, 29th, Milan 54, 30th, Leicester Galleries, London 56; 50-year retrospective exhibition, Whitechapel Art Gallery, London 61; contributed drawings to *Observer, Sunday Times, Manchester Guardian, Studio, Time and Tide, New Statesman, Querschnitt,* and other publications; commissioned by British Museum and National Portrait Gallery to make 27 lithographs at L. of N., Geneva 33-35, complete lithographs exhibited and purchased by Albright Art Gallery, Buffalo, U.S.A. 39; official war artist 40-45; invited as Official Artist to UNESCO, Paris 46-47; Exhibition at UNESCO, Paris 46; represented in "British Art since Whistler", Nat. Gallery, London 45; Works acquired by many galleries and private collectors include Nat. Portrait Gallery, Victoria and Albert Museum, London Museum, Imperial War Museum, Bibliothèque National, Paris; six portraits reproduced as stained glass windows in Yale Univ. Law School; Commissioned to make seven portraits for Gonville and Caius Coll., Christ's Coll., Cambridge and Merton Coll., Oxford 65-66; retrospective exhbn. of paintings and drawings of composers, musicians and musical activities, Royal Festival Hall, London 68; 244 portrait drawings of the 'twenties and 'thirties acquired by the Barber Inst. of Fine Arts, Birmingham 69; five abstract paintings acquired by Kettle's Yard Museum of Modern Art, Cambridge Univ. 70-71.
Leisure interests: music, writing nonsense.
Publs. Collections of drawings, *Ten Great Lawyers, Minims, Personalities, Reflections, Pastiche, The Nations at Geneva,* etc.
2 Steele's Studios, Haverstock Hill, London, NW3 4RN, England.
Telephone: 01-722-3174.

Kapp, Eugen Arturovich; Soviet composer; b. 28 May 1908, Astrakhan; ed. Leningrad Conservatoire.
Professor, Tallin Conservatoire; Chair. Estonian Composers' Union, People's Artist of Estonia, People's Artist of the U.S.S.R., State Prize 46, 49, 52; Order of Lenin 50; Order of Red Banner of Labour (twice).
Principal compositions: Trio for Piano 30, *The Avenger* (Symphonic poem) 31, Concerto for Strings 35, Sonata No. 1 for Violin and Piano 36, *Kalevipoeg* (The Son of Kalev) (Overture) 38, Symphony No. 1 39, Sonata No. 2 for Violin and Piano 43, *Fires of Vengeance* (Opera) 44, *Kalevipoeg* (Ballet) 47, Sonata for 'Cello and Piano 48, *Tallin Scenes* 49, *Bard of Freedom* 50, Symphony No. 2 54, Overture on Finnish Themes 57, *Leningrad Suite* 57, *Winter's Tale* (Opera) 58, *Children's Day* (Cycle of children's songs) 58.
Estonian Composers' Union, Boulevard Estonia 4, Tallin, U.S.S.R.

Kappel, Frederick R., B.S.E.; American businessman; b. 14 Jan. 1902, Minnesota; *s.* of Fred Albert and Gertrude May Kappel (née Towle); *m.* Ruth Carolyn Ihm 1927; two *d.*; ed. Univ. of Minnesota.
Joined Bell System as groundman Northwestern Bell Telephone Co. 24, Asst. Vice-Pres. (Operations) 39, Vice-Pres. (Operations) and Dir. 42; Asst. Vice-Pres. (Operation and Engineering) American Telephone and Telegraph Co. 49, Vice-Pres. (Long Lines) 49, (Operation and Engineering) 49, Pres. Western Electric Co. 54, Pres. American Telephone and Telegraph Co. 56-67, Chair. 61-67, Chair. Exec. Cttee. 67-69; Chair. Board Int. Paper Co. 69-70, Chair. Exec. Cttee. 71-; responsible for *Telstar* communications satellite July 62; Dir. Chase Manhattan Bank 56-72, Metropolitan Life Insurance Co., Gen. Foods Corpn. 61-73, Acad. of Political Sciences; Trustee, N.Y. Presbyterian Hospital, Cttee. for Econ. Devt., Boys' Clubs of America; mem. of Advisory Board Salvation Army; mem. The Business Council, Chair. 63-64; Trustee, Columbia Univ. 62-69, Minn. Univ., Inst. of Electrical and Electronics Engineers; Outstanding Achievement Award (Minn. Univ.) 54; Chair. President's Comm. on Postal Org. 67-68; Chair. Board of Govs., U.S. Postal Service 70-74; numerous hon. degrees and awards.
Leisure interests: golf, fishing, hunting, family.
Publs. *Vitality in a Business Enterprise, Business Purpose and Performance.*
343 West Royal Flamingo Drive, Sarasota, Florida 33577, U.S.A.
Telephone: 813-365-0930.

Käppeli, Robert, DR. RER. POL.; Swiss industrialist; b. 21 July 1900; ed. Kantonsschule, Lucerne, and Universität Basel.
Institut für Weltwirtschaft und Seeverkehr, Univ. of Kiel 29-30; M. M. Warburg & Co., Hamburg 30-34; CIBA Ltd., Basle 34-70, Chair. of Board of Dirs. 56-70; Chair. Board of Dirs. CIBA-Geigy 70-72; Dr. h.c. tech. sci. (Swiss Fed. Inst. of Technology), Dr. h.c. polit. econ. (Univ. of Fribourg), Dr. phil. h.c. (Univ. of Basle); retd.
CIBA-Geigy Ltd., Basle, Switzerland.

Kaprio, Leo, M.D., M.P.H., D.P.H., F.A.P.H.A.; Finnish public health officer; b. 28 June 1918, Tuusula, Finland; *s.* of Dr. Arthur J. T. M. and Mrs. K. Molander; *m.* Aini Korhonen, M.PH.ED. 1943; two *s.* one *d.*; ed. Helsinki, Johns Hopkins and Harvard Univs.
Finnish Army Medical Corps during Second World War; Chief Medical Adviser to Finnish Pop. Asscn. (Vaestoliitto) 44-49; Chief Medical Adviser, Finnish Red Cross 51-56; Chair. of State Cttee. to reorganize Finnish Health Services 53-54; mem. of WHO Advisory Panel on Public Health Admin. 51-56; Chief, Div. of Public Health, Nat. Health Service 52-56; Regional Officer, Eastern Mediterranean and Europe, WHO 56-63; Finnish del. to WHO 53-54; Board mem. WHO of UN R.I.S.D. (Geneva) 64-67; WHO rep. at World Pop. Conf. 65; Dir. Div. of Public Health Services 63-67; Regional Dir. for Europe Feb. 67-; Hon. mem. Polish Medical Asscn., Dr. h.c. Leuven, Dr. Med. h.c. Uppsala, Prof. h.c. Govt. of Finland.
Leisure interest: history.
Publs: 50 scientific publs. in Finnish, Swedish, English and German.
European Regional Office, World Health Organization, 8 Scherfigsvej, Copenhagen Ø, Denmark.
Telephone: 290111.

Kapuściński, Ryszard, M.A.; Polish journalist; b. 4 March 1932, Pińsk, U.S.S.R.; *s.* of Józef and Maria Bobka Kapuścińska; *m.*; one *d.*; ed. Faculty of History, Warsaw Univ.
Began career with *Sztander Młodych* 51, then with *Polityka*; later Corresp. Polish Press Agency (PAP); now Deputy Editor-in-Chief *Kultura*; Gold Cross of Merit, State Prize, B. Prus Prize 75.
Publs. *Busz po polsku, Czarne gwiazdy, Kirgiz schodzi z konia, Gydby cała Afryka . . ., Dlaczego zginął Karl von Spreti, Chrystus z karabinem na ramieniu.*
Ul. Pustola 16 m. 33, 01-129 Warsaw, Poland.

Kapwepwe, Simon Mwanza; Zambian politician, b. 12 April 1922; ed. Lubwa Mission.
Former teacher; studied in India 51-55, and in U.S.A.; Co-founder African Nat. Congress, N. Rhodesia 46; Co-founder Zambian African Congress 58, Treas.; mem. United Nat. Independence Party, Deputy Leader 67-70; mem. Parl. 62-; fmr. Minister of Agriculture; Minister of Home Affairs Jan.-Oct. 64; Minister of Foreign Affairs Oct. 64-Sept. 67; Vice-Pres. of

Zambia Sept. 67-Nov. 70, also Minister of Provincial and Local Govt. Jan. 70-July 71; Leader United Progressive Party 71; mem. Nat. Assembly Dec. 71; arrested Feb. 72, released Jan. 73, given suspended sentence of two years' imprisonment Feb. 73.

Karageorghis, Vassos, PH.D., F.S.A.; Cypriot archaeologist; b. 29 April 1929, Trikomo; *m.* Jacqueline Girard 1953; one *s.* one *d.*; ed. Pancyprian Gymnasium, Nicosia, Univ. Coll., and Inst. of Archaeology, London Univ.
Assistant Curator, Cyprus Museum 52-60, Curator 60-63, Acting Dir., Dept. of Antiquities, Cyprus 63-64, Dir. 64-; Hon. mem. Council of Greek Archaeological Soc. Athens; Vice-Pres. Council of Soc. for Cypriot Studies, mem. Governing Body, Cyprus Research Centre; Fellow, Soc. of Antiquaries, London, Royal Soc. of Humanistic Studies, Lund; mem. Royal Swedish Acad.; Corresp. mem. Archaeological Soc., Athens, Acad. of Athens; Fellow, Univ. Coll., London; Corresp. Fellow, British Acad.; Ordinary mem. German Archaeological Inst., Berlin; Chevalier de la Légion d'Honneur 71; Dr. h.c. (Lyon, Göteborg, Athens, Birmingham).
Publs. *Treasures in the Cyprus Museum* 62, *Nouveaux Documents pour l'Etude du Bronze Récent à Chypre* 64, *Corpus Vasorum Antiquorum* 64, 65, *Sculptures from Salamis,* vol. I 64, vol. II 66, *Excavations in the Necropolis of Salamis,* Vol. I 67, Vol. II 70, Vol. III 74, *Mycenaean Art from Cyprus* 68, *Cyprus* (Archaeologia Mundi) 68, *Salamis in Cyprus* 69, *Altägäis und Atlkypros* (with H. G. Buchholz) 71, *Cypriot Antiquities in the Pierides Collection, Larnaca, Cyprus* 72, *Excavations at Kiton I* 74, and articles in German, American, English and French Journals.
c/o Cyprus Museum, P.O. Box 2024, Nicosia; Home: 12 Kastorias Street, Nicosia, Cyprus
Telephone: 402191 (Office); 65249 (Home).

Karajan, Herbert von; Austrian conductor; b. 5 April 1908; ed. Salzburg Gymnasium and Mozarteum, Vienna Univ. and Conservatoire.
Successively Musical Dir. Ulm, Opera and Gen. Musical Dir. Aachen, Kapellmeister, Berlin State Opera, Conductor, Berlin Philharmonic Orch.; Dir. Berlin Staatskapelle 41-45; concert tours in Europe, U.S.A. and Far East 45-; Artistic Dir. Berlin Philharmonic Orchestra 55-56, Vienna; State Opera 56-64; mem. Board of Dirs., Salzburg Festival 65-; Dir. Gesellschaft der Musikfreunde, Vienna; conducted at Salzburg and Lucerne Festivals; Mozart Ring 57; Commdr. First Class, Order of White Rose (Finland); Prix France-Allemagne 70; Hon. Citizen of Berlin 73.
c/o Festspielhaus, Salzburg, Austria.

Karakas, László; Hungarian trade unionist and politician; b. 1923, Debrecen.
Worked in bakery until 49; mem. Communist Party 45-; consecutively Sec., Chair. and Gen. Sec. Food Industry Workers' Union 49-63; Sec. Nat. Council of Trade Unions 63-66; First Sec. for County Hajdu-Bihar Party Cttee., Hungarian Socialist Workers' Party 66-70, mem. Cen. Cttee. 66-; mem. Parl. 71-; Minister of Labour 73-; mem. State Planning Cttee. 73-.
Ministry of Labour, Budapest V, Szabadság tér 15, Hungary.
Telephone: 121-770.

Karakeyev, Kurman Karakeyevich; Soviet historian. b. 7 Nov. 1913, Kurmenty Village, Kirghizia; ed; Higher Party School and Acad. of Social Sciences.
Member C.P.S.U. 38-: C.P. work 49-60; mem. and Pres. Kirghiz Acad. of Sciences 60-; Corresp. mem. U.S.S.R. Acad. of Sciences 68-; Deputy to U.S.S.R. Supreme Soviet 62-; mem. Comm. for Legislative Proposals; mem. Cen. Cttee. C.P. of Kirghizia; Orders and medals of U.S.S.R.
Presidium of Kirghiz S.S.R. Academy of Sciences, Ul. XXII Partsyezda 265-A, Frunze, U.S.S.R.

Karamanlis, Constantinos G.; Greek lawyer and politician; b. 23 Feb. 1907; ed. Univ. of Athens.
Practising lawyer since 32; Deputy 35-67, 74-; Minister of Labour 46, of Transport 47, of Social Welfare 48-50, of Nat. Defence 50-52; re-elected Deputy for Serrai 51 and 52; Minister of Public Works 52-54, of Communications and Public Works 54-55, Prime Minister 55-58, 58-61, 61-63; self-imposed exile in France 63-74; Prime Minister July 74-; Nat. Radical Union; founded New Democracy Party 74.
Office of the Prime Minister, Athens, Greece.

Karami, Rashid Abdul Hamid; Lebanese politician, b. 1921; s. of late Abdel Hamid Karami; ed. Fuad Univ., Cairo.
Minister of Nat. Economy and Social Affairs 54-55; Prime Minister and Minister of the Interior Sept. 55-Mar. 56; Prime Minister 58-60, 61-64 (also Minister of Finance), 65-66, 66-68, 69-70; Minister of Finance, Economy, Defence and Information 58-59, of Finance and Defence 59-60; Prime Minister, Minister of Finance, Defence and Information July 75-; Sunni Muslim.
Rue Karm Ellé, Beirut, Lebanon.

Karandash (*pseudonym* of Mikhail Nikolayevich Rumyantsev); Soviet circus performer; b. 22 Nov. 1906.
People's artist of the R.S.F.S.R. and of the U.S.S.R. 69; awarded the Order of the Red Banner of Labour and other decorations.
Films include *Karandash on Ice, Self-Confident Karandash, The Girl with a Temper, Old Courtyard, High Reward, Ivan Nikulin.*
All Union Association of State Circuses, 4 Pushechnaya Street, Moscow, U.S.S.R.

Karanja, Josphat Njuguna, PH.D.; Kenyan diplomatist; b. 5 Feb. 1931; ed. Alliance High School, Kikuyu, Makerere Coll., Univ. of Delhi and Princeton Univ.
Lecturer in African Studies, Fairleigh Dickinson Univ., New Jersey, U.S.A. 61-62; Lecturer in African and Modern European History, Univ. of East Africa 62-63; High Commr. for Kenya in U.K. 63-70, also accred. to Holy See 66-70; Principal, Univ. of Nairobi 70-75; Vice-Chancellor 75-.
University of Nairobi, Nairobi, Kenya.

Karasz, Arthur, LL.D.; American international finance official; b. 13 Dec. 1907, Kolozsvar, Hungary; s. of Ernest Karasz and Helen Fleischmann; *m.* Eva Waldhauser 1939; one *s.* two *d.*; ed. high school in Budapest, Univ. of Budapest and the Sorbonne, Paris.
Member Nat. Bank of Hungary 32-45, Pres. 45-46; Prof. in Central Banking Econ. Univ. of Budapest 46-48; Lecturer New School for Social Research, New York 48-49; Prof. in Monetary Policy, De Paul Univ., Chicago 49-52; UN Adviser on Monetary Matters to Bolivia 52-56; joined IBRD (World Bank) 56, Dir. European Office 68-72; Adviser to Akbank, Istanbul 73-75; Vice-Pres. Siemens S.A., St.-Denis, France 74-75, Pres. 76-.
Leisure interests: farming.
Publs. *L'Ecole des Totalitaires* 48, *Inflación, Establización* 55, *Bolivia—An Experiment in Development* 57; numerous articles in economic publs.
192 rue Lecourbe, 75015 Paris, France.
Telephone: 250 3031.

Karavaeva, Anna Alexandrovna; Soviet writer; b. 27 Dec. 1893, Perm.
Member C.P.S.U.; State Prizewinner 50, awarded Orders of Lenin, Red Banner of Labour, Red Star and Badge of Honour.
Publs. stories: *The Household* 26; *The Sawmill* 28, trilogy of novels: *Fires* 43, *On the Run* 46-48, *Native Hearth* 50, *Collected Works* in 5 vols. 57-58, *Facts of Life* 63, *World of Yesterday* (reminiscences) 64, *Facets of Life* 63, *Selected Works* 67.
U.S.S.R. Union of Writers, Ulitsa Vorovskogo 52, Moscow, U.S.S.R.

Karavayev, Georgi Arkadievich; Soviet banker and statesman; b. 1913; ed. Leningrad Water Transport Engineering Inst.

Member C.P.S.U. 40-; worker in building enterprises and ministries 35-57; Dep. Chair. Sverdlovsk Nat. Econ. Council for Construction 57-59; First Dep. Chair. State Cttee. for Construction 59-61; Chair. Stroibank (All-Union Capital Investment Bank) 61-63; First Dep. Chair. U.S.S.R. State Cttee. for Construction 63-67; Minister for Construction 67-; Cand. mem. Central Cttee. 71-; Deputy, U.S.S.R. Supreme Soviet 66-; State Prize 50.

Ministry for Construction, 8 Building 2, Pervaya ulitsa Stroitelei, Moscow, U.S.S.R.

Karayev, Kara Abulfas Ogly; Soviet composer; b. 5 Feb. 1918, Baku, Azerbaijan; ed. Moscow Conservatoire.

Member C.P.S.U. 49-; Chair. Azerbaijan Composers' Union 51-; Sec. Soviet Composers' Union, now Sec. of the Board; mem. Cen. Cttee. C.P. of Azerbaijan; Deputy U.S.S.R. Supreme Soviet; mem. Azerbaijan Acad. of Sciences; State Prize 46, 48; People's Artist of the U.S.S.R. 59; Lenin Prize 67; Order of Red Banner of Labour (twice).

Principal compositions: *Song of the Heart* (Cantata for choir, symphony orch. and dance group) 37, Azerbaijan Suite for Symphony Orch. 39, First Symphony 44, *Veten* (Opera) 45, Second Symphony 46, *Leili and Medjun* (Symphonic poem) 47, *Seven Beauties* (Ballet) 52, *Albanian Rhapsody* 52, Choreographic Sketches for Symphony Orch. 53, *Viet-Nam* (Symphonic suite) 55, Prelude for Piano 57, *Thunder Path* (Ballet) 57, Three Nocturnes for Jazz Band 58, Sonata for Violin and Piano 60; incidental music for plays: *Masquerade, The Dancing Teacher, Othello, A Winter's Tale, The Crank, An Optimistic Tragedy;* incidental music for film, *Story of Caspian Oil Workers,* and others.

Azerbaijan Composers' Union, Ulitsa Nizami 58, Baku, U.S.S.R.

Karch, George Frederick; American banker; b. 1 May 1907; ed. St. Lawrence Univ., Cleveland Law School and Rutgers Univ. Graduate School of Banking.

Cleveland Trust Co. 26-, mem. Exec. Cttee. 54-, Exec. Vice-Pres. 60-62, Pres. 62-66, Chair. and Pres. 66-69, Chair. of Board 69-73, Hon. Chair. 73-; official of many other companies.

2720 Wicklow Road, Shaker Heights, O. 44120,U.S.A.

Kardelj, Edvard; Yugoslav politician; b. 27 Jan. 1910.

Qualified as teacher; later studied econs. and political science; active mem. of Workers' Movement and illegal Communist Party of Yugoslavia since 28; imprisoned 30-32; lived abroad 34-37; mem. Cen. Cttee. of C.P. of Yugoslavia and League of Communists of Yugoslavia 37-; mem. Politbureau, Cen. Cttee. of C.P. of Yugoslavia 38-48; participated in the organization of Liberation Front of Slovenia and Yugoslavia 41; mem. G.H.Q. Nat. Army of Liberation 41; elected First Vice-Pres. of Nat. Cttee. of Liberation 43; entered Tito Govt. as Vice-Pres. 45-53; Minister for Constituent Assembly 45-46; Pres. Control Comm. 45-48; Minister for Foreign Affairs 48-53; Vice-Pres. Fed. Exec. Council and Chair. Co-ordination Cttee. 53-63; Chair. Comm. for the Drafting of New Constitution 61-63; Pres. Fed. Assembly 63-67; mem. Council of Fed. 63-; Chair. Co-ordination Comm., Constitutional Comm. of Fed. Assembly 70-74; mem. Presidency of Socialist Fed. Repub. of Yugoslavia 74-; Sec. Cen. Cttee., League of Communists of Yugoslavia 58-66, mem. Presidency of Cen. Cttee. 66-69, 74-; mem. Presidency, League of Communists of Yugoslavia 69-74, mem. Exec. Bureau of Presidency 69-72; Sec. Gen. Socialist Alliance of Working People of Yugoslavia 53-60; leader of del. to Paris Peace Conf. 46; leader of dels. to UN Gen.

Assembly 46, 48, 49, 50, 51, mem. of del. to Algiers conf. of non-aligned countries 73; mem. Serbian Acad. of Sciences and Art; Hon. mem. Slovene Acad. of Sciences and Art, Bosnian and Herzegovinian Acad. of Sciences and Art, Macedonian Acad. of Sciences and Art; Dr. h.c. (Ljubljana); Order of People's Hero of Socialist Work, Yugoslavia Grand Star, People's Liberation etc. Publs. *Development of the Slovene National Question* 39, (revised and enlarged edn. 57), *The Paris Conference* 46, *The Road of New Yugoslavia* 46, *The Problems of Our Socialist Development* (9 vols.) 54-74, *Problems of Socialist Policy in the Countryside* 59, *Socialism and War* 60, *The New Constitution of Socialist Yugoslavia* 62, *Notes on Social Criticism in Yugoslavia* 65, *The Working Class and the Bureaucracy* 69, *The Crossroads in the Development of our Socialist Society* 69, *Contradictions of Social Property in Contemporary Socialist Practice* 72, *Basic Causes and Directions of Constitutional Changes* 73.

Presidency of the Socialist Federal Republic of Yugoslavia, Belgrade, Yugoslavia.

Karefa-Smart, John Musselman, B.A., B.SC., M.D., C.M., D.T.M., M.P.H., M.R.S.H.; Sierra Leonean politician and physician; b. 17 June 1915, Rotifunk; s. of Rev. James Karefa-Smart and May Karefa-Smart (née Caulker); m. Rena Joyce Weller 1948; one s. two d.; ed. Fourah Bay and Otterbein Colls., McGill and Harvard Univs.

Lecturer, Union Coll., Bunumbu 36-38; ordained Elder of Evangelical United Brethren Church 38; Medical Officer, R.C.A.M.C. 43-45; Sierra Leone Missions Hospitals 46-48; Lecturer Ibadan Univ. Coll. (Nigeria) 49-52; Health Officer, W.H.O. 52-55, Leader Del. to W.H.O. 56 and 59; mem. House of Reps. 57-64; Minister of Lands and Survey 57-59; Africa Consultant, World Council of Churches 55-56; Minister for External Affairs 60-64; Asst. Prof. Columbia Univ. 64-65; Asst. Dir.-Gen. World Health Org., Geneva 65-70; Visiting Prof. of Int. Health, Harvard Univ. (U.S.A.) 71-; Medical Dir. Roxbur Health Centre 74-; Commdr. Order of Star of Africa (Liberia); Knight Grand Band, Order of African Redemption (Liberia); Grand Cordon, Order of the Cedar (Lebanon); Hon. LL.D. (Otterbein); Hon. LL.D. (McGill); Hon. LL.D. (Boston); Leader, United Democratic Party, Sierra Leone.

Leisure interests: private flying, photography, stamps. Publ. *The Halting Kingdom* 59.

10 Ledgewood Road, Weston, Mass. 02193, U.S.A. Telephone: 617-235-0188.

Karelskaya, Rimma Klavdievna; Soviet ballet dancer; b. 1927; ed. Moscow Ballet School of Bolshoi Theatre.

Joined Bolshoi Ballet 46; has toured with Bolshoi Ballet in Britain, Australia, Belgium, China, Netherlands, New Zealand, United Arab Republic, Poland, German Federal Republic, France, Czechoslovakia and Japan; Honoured Artist of R.S.F.S.R. 62.

Main roles include: Raymonda (*Raymonda* by Glazunov), Laurencia (*Laurencia* by Krein), Lilac Fairy (*Sleeping Beauty* by Tchaikovsky), Sovereign of the Dryads and Street Dancer (*Don Quixote* by Minkus), Mirta (*Giselle* by Adan), Odette-Odille (*Swan Lake* by Tchaikovsky), Zaremba (*Fountains of Bakhchisarai* by Asafyev), Firebird (*Firebird* by Stravinsky), the Servant Girl (*Thunder Road* by Kara Karayev), Tsar Devitsa (*Humpbacked Horse* by Pugni), the Swan (*Dying Swan* by Saint-Saëns).

State Academic Bolshoi Theatre of U.S.S.R., Ploshchad Sverdlova 1, Moscow, U.S.S.R.

Kargopolov, Mikhail Ivanovich; Soviet mathematician; b. 9 Nov. 1928, Rusakovo Village, Kurgan Region; ed. Urals Univ.

Postgraduate, Lecturer Perm Univ. 53-60; Senior

Research Assoc. Inst. of Mathematics, Siberian branch U.S.S.R. Acad. of Sciences 60-; Prof. 64-; Dr. of Sc. (Physics and Mathematics) 63; mem. C.P.S.U. 65-; Corresp. mem. U.S.S.R. Acad. of Sciences 66-.
Academgorodok, Novosibirsk, U.S.S.R.

Karhilo, Aarno, LL.M.; Finnish diplomatist; b. 22 Nov. 1927, Helsinki; *m.*; two *c.*; ed. Univ. of Helsinki. Entered diplomatic service 52, served in Helsinki, Washington and Rio de Janeiro; First Sec., Rome 61; Counsellor and Deputy Chief of Mission, UN 63-65, Moscow 66-68; Adviser to del. at UN Gen. Assembly 59-60, 63-65, 69-71, Vice-Chair. 72-76; Amb. to Japan 71-72; Perm. Rep. to UN Aug. 72-; Vice-Pres. ECOSOC 73, Pres. 74; Chair. Finnish del. for ECOSOC Sessions 72-74.
Permanent Mission of Finland to United Nations, 866 United Nations Plaza, 2nd Floor, New York, N.Y. 10017, U.S.A.

Karim, Amin Abdul; Iraqi politician; b. 1921, Baghdad; ed. Coll. of Law.
Entered Govt. service March 43; has held various govt. posts including Dir. Gen. of Finance and Revenues, and Pres. State Org. of Banks (until 68); Minister of Finance July 68-.
Ministry of Finance, Baghdad, Iraq.

Karim, Sayyid Anwarul, M.A.; Bangladesh diplomatist; *s.* of Syed and Kulsum Majid; *m.* Ayesha Karim 1961; three *s.*; ed. Calcutta and Dacca Univs., London School of Econs.
Director, Ministry of Foreign Affairs, Karachi 60; First Sec. Embassy of Pakistan, Rangoon 63, Counsellor, Baghdad 66, Counsellor, Minister, Washington, D.C. 68; Deputy Perm. Rep. Pakistan Perm. Mission to UN 70; Sec. Ministry of Foreign Affairs, Dacca Jan.-July 72; Perm. Observer of Bangladesh to UN 72-74, Perm. Rep. 74-; High Commr. to Jamaica and Barbados. Leisure interests: reading, music, bridge.
130 East 40th Street, 5th Floor, New York, N.Y. 10016, U.S.A.
Telephone: 889-4666, 686-5233.

Karim-Lamrani, Mohammed; Moroccan businessman and politician; b. 1919, Fez.
Assistant Dir. Office Chérifien des Phosphates 58-61, Dir.-Gen. 67-; Pres. Crédit du Maroc; Minister of Finance April-Aug. 71; Prime Minister 71-72; Econ. Adviser to His Majesty the King; Dir. Royal Air Maroc; Dir. or Chair. many other concerns.
Office Chérifien des Phosphates, Rabat; and 305 avenue Mohammed V, Rabat Morocco.

Karjalainen, Ahti, PH.D.; Finnish economist and politician; b. 10 Feb. 1923, Hirvensalmi; *s.* of Anshelm Karjalainen and Anna Viherlehto; *m.* Päivi Helinä Koskinen 1947; three *s.* one *d.*; ed. Helsinki Univ.
Prime Minister's Sec. 50-56; Minister of Finance 57-58, of Trade and Industry 59-61, of Foreign Affairs 61-62; Prime Minister 62-63; Minister of Foreign Affairs 64-70; Prime Minister 70-71; Minister of Foreign Affairs 72-75; mem. Board of Govs., Bank of Finland 58-; mem. Parl. 66-; Grand Cross of the Order of the White Rose of Finland, Commdr. of the Order of the Lion of Finland, Medal of Liberty, Second Class, and other decorations. Leisure interests: literature and fishing.
Home: Perustie 13, Helsinki 33, Finland.
Telephone: 48-45-48.

Karkoszka, Alojzy; Polish politician; b. 15 June 1929, Roczyny, Cracow Voivodship; ed. Tech. Univ.
Member, Fighting Youth Union 45-49, Polish Youth Union 49-51; mem. Polish United Workers' Party (PUWP) 51-, Deputy mem. Cen. Cttee. 64-71, mem. Cen. Cttee. Dec. 71-; Sec. Warsaw Cttee., PUWP 60-70; First Sec., PUWP Voivodship Cttee., Gdańsk 70-71; Minister of Construction and Construction Materials Industry 71-75; mem. Presidium of Govt. 74-,

Deputy Chair. Council of Ministers May 75-; Order of Banner of Labour, 1st and 2nd Class; Knight's Cross Order of Polonia Restituta and other decorations.
Urzan Rady Ministrów PRL, Al. Ujazdowskie 1/3, 00-583 Warsaw, Poland.
Telephone: 28-44-71.

Karlgren, Klas Bernhard Johannes, DR.PHIL.; Swedish orientalist; b. 5 Oct. 1889; ed. Uppsala and Paris.
Prof. of Far Eastern Languages Göteborg Univ. until 39; Prof. and Dir. Museum of Far Eastern Antiquities Stockholm 39-59; mem. Acad. of Sciences Stockholm, Acad. of History and Belles-Lettres Stockholm, Acad. of Sciences Copenhagen, Oslo; hon. mem. Royal Asiatic Society of Great Britain and Ireland, Société Asiatique, Paris, British Acad.; corresp. mem. Acad. des Inscriptions, Paris.
Publs. *Etudes sur la Phonologie Chinoise* 15-26, *Analytic Dictionary of Chinese, Sound and Symbol in Chinese* 23, *Philology and Ancient China* 26, *Yin and Chou in Chinese Bronzes* 36, *New Studies on Chinese Bronzes* 37, *Grammata Serica* 40, *Huai and Han* 41, *Glosses on the Odes* (1-3) 42, 44, 46, *The Book of Odes* 44, 45, *Some Weapons and Tools of the Yin Dynasty* 45, *Legends and Cults in Ancient China* 46, *Glosses on the Book of Documents I* 48, *II* 49, *The Book of Documents* 50, *Notes on the Grammar of Early Bronze Décor* 51, *Excursions in Chinese Grammar* 51, *A Catalogue of the Chinese Bronzes in the Alfred F. Pillsbury Collection* 52, *Compendium of Phonetics in Ancient and Archaic Chinese* 54, *Grammata Serica Recensa* 57, *Marginalia on some Bronze Albums I, II,* 59, 60, *Some Characteristics of the Yin Art* 62, *Loan Characters in the pre-Hans Text* I-V 63-67.
c/o Museum of Far Eastern Antiquities, Stockholm 100, Sweden.

Karlin, Dr. Samuel, PH.D.; American mathematician; b. 8 June 1924, Poland; *m.*; three *c.*; ed. Ill. Inst. of Technology and Princeton Univ.
California Inst. of Technology, Bateman Research Fellow 47-48, Asst. Prof. 49-51, Assoc. Prof. 51-55, Prof. 55-56; Visiting Asst. Prof. Princeton Univ. 50; Prof. Stanford Univ. 56-70; Guggenheim Fellow to Israel and France 60-61; Guest Mathematical Soc. of Japan 64; Head, Dept. of Pure Mathematics, Weizmann Inst. of Science, Rehovot, Israel 70-73, Dean, Faculty of Mathematics 73-; Consultant Rand Corpn., Santa Monica; Chief Editor *Theoretical Population Biology*; Editor or Assoc. Editor, *Journal of Mathematical Analysis, Logistics Journal, Journal of Applied Probability, Journal d'Analyse, Journal of Mathematics and Mechanics, Journal of Mathematical Biosciences, Journal of Approximation Theory and Advances in Mathematics*; Fellow, Inst. of Mathematical Statistics 56; fmr. mem. Int. Statistics Inst., American Acad. of Arts and Sciences and Council of American Mathematical Soc.; mem. of American Mathematical Soc., Inst. of Mathematical Statistics, Applied Mathematics, panel Nat. Research Council, U.S. Acad. of Sciences; Procter Fellow, Princeton Univ. 46; Wald Memorial Lecturer 57; Henry and Bertha Benson Chair of Mathematics 71.
Publs. over 150 articles in various journals on topics of pure and applied probability theory, game theory, decision theory and statistical methodology, mathematical analysis and mathematical biology.
Meonot Shine 13, Rehovot, Israel.

Karling, John S., M.A., PH.D., F.R.S.A.; American mycologist; b. 2 Aug. 1897, Austin, Texas; *s.* of Theodore and Marie Karling; *m.* Page Johnston 1940; one *d.*; ed. Univ. of Texas and Columbia Univ.
Dean, Texas Wesleyan Coll. 20; Instructor, Univ. of Texas 21; Columbia Univ. Fellow in Botany; Asst. Prof. 26-35; Assoc. Prof. 35-48; Prof. of Botany and Chair. Dept. of Biological Sciences, Purdue Univ. 48-59, John Wright Distinguished Prof. of Biological Sciences 59-65,

Emeritus Prof. 65-; Physiologist, Tropical Research Foundation 25-27; Dir. Chicle Research Experimental Station, British Honduras 27-32; Field Dir. Exploration Dept. U.S. Govt. Rubber Development Corpn., Brazil 42-43; Bermuda Biological Research Fellow 42; Prof. of Botany, Columbia Univ.; Consulting Botanist, American Chicle Co.; Sec. Botanical Soc. of America 45-50; Vice-Pres. 50-51; Sec. Union of American Biological Socs. 46-48; Vice-Pres. American Asscn. for Advancement of Science 50; Chair. Section G., A.A.A.S. 50; Research Fellow Int. Indian Ocean Expedition 63; Visiting Sir C. V. Raman Lecturer, Univ. of Madras 65; Fulbright Research Fellow, New Zealand 65-66; Dir. Ross Biological Reserve, Purdue Univ.
Leisure interests: fishing, flower and vegetable gardening, sports, writing.
Publs. *The Plasmodiophorales* 42, *The Simple Biflagellate Halocarpic Phycomycetes* 42, *Synchytrium* 63.
Home: 1219 Tuckahoe Lane, West Lafayette, Ind., U.S.A.
Telephone: 462-9887.

Karmen, Roman Lazarevich; Soviet film director and cameraman; b. 29 Nov. 1906, Odessa; s. of Lazar and Dina Karmen; m. Maya Ovchinnikova 1962; two s.; ed. Moscow Cinematographic Inst.
State prize winner, Lenin prize winner 60, Order of Lenin, People's Artist of R.S.F.S.R. 65, People's Artist of U.S.S.R. 66; Prof. State Inst. of Cinematography.
Principal films: *Spanish Event* 36-37, *Spain* 39, *China Struggles* 40, *The Men of Sedov* 40, *Day of the New World* 40, *War-time Leningrad* 42, *Judgment of the Nations* 46, *People's Court* 46, *Soviet Turkmenistan* 51, *Viet-Nam* 55, *India's Morning* 56, *Vast is my Land* 57, *Subjugators of the Sea* 59, *Island in Flames* 61, *Guest from Island of Freedom* 63, *Great Patriotic War* 65, *Granada, Granada, O my Granada* 68, *Continent in Flames* 72, *Chile, Time of Struggle, Time of Worry* 73, *Camaradas* 74.
Leisure interests: cars, hunting.
Publs. include: *One Year in China* 40, *Light in the Jungle* 57, *In India* 60, *No Pasaran* 72.
Studio of Documentary Films, 6 Likhov pereulok, Moscow; Kotelnicheskaya Nab. 1/15, Korp. BK. Kv, 121, Moscow, U.S.S.R.
Telephone: 227-4256 (Home).

Karnes, William George; American businessman; b. 24 March 1911, Chicago; m. Virginia Kelly 1937; ed. Univ. of Ill. and Northwestern Univ.
Admitted to Ill. bar 36; Attorney, Law Dept., Beatrice Foods Co. 36-39, Head, Employee Relations Dept. 39-43, Asst. to Pres. 43-47, Dir. 47-, Exec. Vice-Pres. 48-52, Pres. 52-72, Chair., Chief Exec. Officer 72-; Dir. Borg-Warner Corpn., Vaughan Seed Co., La Salle Nat. Bank Motta S.p.A.
120 S. La Salle Street, Chicago 3, Ill. (Office); Butterfield Lane, Flossmoor, Ill., U.S.A.

Karoli, Hermann, DR. RER. POL.; German chartered accountant; b. 27 March 1906, Hahnbach; s. of Rudolf and Emma (née Fleischer) Karoli; m. Susanne Seeberg 1943; one s. one d.; ed. Univs. of Leipzig and Innsbruck.
Member of Management Board, Deutsche Revisions-und Treuhand A.G., Berlin 38-45; independent accountant 48-; Senior Partner Karoli-Wirtschaftsprüfung G.m.b.H., Essen and Berlin; mem. various advisory boards and committees.
Leisure interests: music, golf.
Karoli-Wirtschaftsprüfung G.m.b.H, 43 Essen, Alfredstrasse 45; Home: 43 Essen-Bredeney, Am Ruhrstein 37, Federal Republic of Germany.

Karp, David, B.S.S.; American writer; b. 5 May 1922, New York City; s. of Abraham Karp and Rebecca Levin; m. Lillian Klass 1944; two s.; ed. City Coll. of the City of New York.

Continuity Dir. Station W.N.Y.C., New York 48-49; free-lance writer 49-; Guggenheim Fellowship for creative writing 56-57; mem. editorial board *Television Quarterly* 65-71, 72-; mem. Council, Writers' Guild of America, West, Inc. 67-74; Pres. Leda Productions, Inc. 68-; film and television producer (20th Century Fox, Metro-Goldwyn-Mayer, Paramount Pictures) 70-; Emmy Award by Acad. of Television Arts and Sciences 64-65; mem. PEN Club; mem. Acad. of Motion Picture Arts and Sciences; Pres. Television-Radio Branch, Writers' Guild of America, West 69-71; Trustee, Producer-Writers Guild Pension Plan 70-, Chair. Finance Cttee. 75-.
Leisure interests: reading, photography.
Publs. *One* 53, *The Day of the Monkey* 55, *All Honorable Men* 56, *Leave me Alone* 57, *The Sleepwalkers* 60, *Vice-President in Charge of Revolution* (with M. D. Lincoln) 60, *The Last Believers* 64, *Café Univers* (play) 67; also contributed many articles and reviews to magazines and has written for radio, cinema and television.
1116 Corsica Drive, Pacific Palisades, Calif. 90272, U.S.A.
Telephone: 278-1460 (Frank Cooper Agency).

Karplus, Martin, PH.D.; American professor of chemistry; b. 15 March 1930, Vienna, Austria; m. Susan Karplus 1961; two d.; ed. Harvard Univ. and Calif. Inst. of Technology.
National Science Foundation Postdoctoral Fellow, Mathematical Inst., Oxford; mem. of staff, Dept. of Chem., Univ. of Illinois 55-60; Prof. of Chem., Columbia Univ. 60-66, Harvard Univ. 66-; Visiting Prof. Univ. of Paris 72-73, Prof. 74-75; mem. Nat. Acad. of Sciences, American Acad. of Arts and Sciences, Int. Acad. of Quantum Molecular Science; Fellow, American Physical Soc.; Harrison Howe Award, American Chem. Soc. (Rochester Section), Phi Lambda Upsilon Frensenius Award.
Publ. *Atoms and Molecules* (with R.N. Porter) 70.
Department of Chemistry, Harvard University, 12 Oxford Street, Cambridge, Mass. 02138, U.S.A.
Telephone: 617-495-4018.

Karsh, Yousuf; Canadian photographer; b. 23 Dec. 1908, Mardin, Armenia-in-Turkey; s. of Bahia and Amsih Karsh; m. 1st Solange Gauthier 1939 (died 1961), 2nd Estrellita Nachbar 1962; ed. Sherbrooke, Quebec and School of Art and Design, Boston, Mass.
Photo apprenticeship to John Garo of Boston; arrived in Canada from Armenia-in-Turkey 23; specialized in portrait photography; Citizen 46; Visiting Prof. of Photography, Ohio Univ. 67-69; Photographic Adviser to *Expo 70*, Osaka, Japan 69; Visiting Prof. of Fine Arts, Emerson Coll., Boston 72-73; numerous one-man exhbns, North America 67-; touring exhbn. *Men Who Make Our World* Japan 70, U.S.A. 71-73, France, Germany, Netherlands 71-73, Belgium, Arles 74-75 (now in perm. collection Museum of Contemporary Art, Tokyo and Nat. Gallery of Australia); fmr. Nat. Vice-Pres. now corp. mem. Muscular Dystrophy Asscns. of America 70-; Trustee, Photographic Arts and Sciences Foundation 70-: LL.D. (Queen's Univ., Kingston, Ont., and Carleton Univ.), Hon. D.H.L. (Dartmouth Coll. at Hanover, New Hampshire, Emerson Coll., Boston, Mass., Mount Allison Univs.); Hon. D.C.L. (Bishop's Univ., Quebec); Canada Council Medal 65; Centennial Medal 67; Order of Canada 68.
Leisure interests: tennis, reading, archaeology, music.
Publs. *Faces of Destiny* 46, *This is the Mass* (English and French editions), *This is Rome* 59, *Portraits of Greatness* 59, *This is the Holy Land* 61, *In Search of Greatness* (autobiog.) 62, *These are the Sacraments* (co-author) 63, *The Warren Court* 64 (co-author), *Karsh Portfolio* 67, *Faces of our Time* 71.
Chateau Laurier Hotel, Suite 660, Ottawa, Ont., Canada.

Karsten, Christian Friedrich, DR.ECON.; Netherlands banker; b. 1917; s. of Rense Karsten and Anna Margaretha Graf; m. C. J. W. van Waard 1942 (divorced 1975); three s. one d.; ed. Netherlands Economic Univ. Posts in insurance and industry 40-45; Economist, Rotterdamsche Bank N.V. 45-48, Sec. to Managing Dirs. 48-52, Asst. Managing Dir. 52-55, Managing Dir. 55-65, Amsterdam-Rotterdam Bank 65-; Chair. European Banking Co. 74-; Dir. other companies; Prof. of Monetary Theory, Erasmus Univ., Rotterdam; Knight, Order of Netherlands Lion.
Publs. *Het Amerikaanse Bankwezen* 52, *Banking without Cheques* 58, *Competition between Commercial Banks and Other Financial Institutions* 60, *De rol van de banken bij de industriefinanciering* 62, *EWG-Perspektiven des Bankwesens* 63. *Transfer Systems* 64, *Should Europe Restrict U.S. Investments?* 65, *Enkele recente ontwikkelingen in het Amerikaanse Bankwezen* 72, *Analysis of a crisis* 73.
Amsterdam-Rotterdam Bank N.V., Herengracht 595, Amsterdam, Netherlands.
Telephone: 282222.

Karttunen, Osmo P., LL.LIC.; Finnish businessman and politician; b. 8 Nov. 1922, Helsinki; s. of Pekka Karttunen and Maikki Karttunen (née Pehkonen); m. Liisa Aleksandra Saastamoinen; one s. three d.; ed. Lyceum of Kuopio and Univ. of Helsinki.
Assistant Dir. H. Saastamoinen & Pojat Oy 46-51, Man. Dir. 52-67; Man. Dir. H. Saastamoinen Oy 61-67; Chair. Saastamoinen Group of Cos. 67-; Chair. Finnish Wholesalers' Assen. 60-68, Admin. Board, Tukkukauppojen Oy 62-, Admin. Board Eläkevakuutus Oy Ilmarinen 62-, Oy Uusi Suomi 63-; Minister of Finance 62-63; mem. Exec. Cttee. Féd. Int. de Football Assen. (FIFA) 72-; Finnish Liberty Cross, Commdr. of the Order of the White Rose of Finland, German Eagle Order, Stella Della Solidarietà, Gran Croce dell' Ordine al Merito (Italy); counsellor of mining h.c.
Leisure interest: philosophic literature.
Kumpusaari, Kuopio, Finland.
Telephone: 14780 and 81555.

Karunanidhi, Muthuvel; Indian politician and playwright; b. 3 June 1924, Thirukkuvalai, Thanjavur.
Started first student wing of Dravidian movement called Tamilnadu Tamil Manavar Mandram; Editor-in-Charge *Kudiarasu*; journalist and stage and screen playwright in Tamil, acting in his own plays staged to collect funds for the Party; has written over 35 filmplays including the screen version of the Tamil classic *Silappadhikaram*, stage plays and short stories; one of the founder mems. of Dravida Munnetra Kazhagam Legislative Party (D.M.K.) 49, Treas. of the Party 61-; founder-editor of the Tamil daily organ of the D.M.K. *Murasoli*; represented Kulittalai in State Assembly 57-62, Thanjavur 62-67, Saidapet 68-; Deputy Leader of D.M.K. 68; led the Kallakkudi Agitation and was imprisoned for six months; fmr. Minister of Public Works; elected Leader of D.M.K. Feb. 69; Chief Minister of Tamil Nadu (Madras) Feb. 69-; Thamizha Vell (Patron of Tamil), Assen. of Research Scholars in Tamil 71; Hon. D.Litt. (Annamalai Univ., Tamil Nadu) 71.
Office of the Chief Minister, Madras, Tamil Nadu, India.

Karunaratne, Hon. Nuwarapaksa Hewayalage Asoka Mahaname; Ceylonese politician; b. 26 Jan. 1916; ed. St. Anthony's Coll., Kandy and Nalanda Vidyalaya, Colombo.
Member of Parl. 58-; Parl. Sec. to Minister of Justice 60; Junior Minister of Justice 63, removed from office because of critical attitude to Govt.; helped to form Sri Lanka Freedom Socialist Party 64; Minister of Social Services 65-70; Sri Lanka Freedom Party.
Sri Lanka Freedom Party, Colombo, Sri Lanka.

Kasatkina, Natalia Dmitrievna; Soviet ballet dancer; b. 7 June 1934, Moscow; d. of Dmitry A. Kasatkin and Anna A. Kardasheva; m. Vladimir Vasilgov 1956; one s.; ed. Bolshoi Theatre Ballet School.
Joined Bolshoi Theatre Ballet Company 54.
Main roles include Frigia (*Spartacus*), Fate (*Carmen*), The Possessed (*Rites of Sacred Spring*).
Choreographer (with V. Vasilyov): *Vanina Vanini* 62, *Geologists* 64, *Rites of Sacred Spring* 65, *Tristan and Isolde* 67, *Preludes and Fugues* 68, *Our Yard* 70, *The Creation of the World* 71, *Romeo and Juliet* 72, *Prozrienie* 74; TV Film *Choreographic Novels*; wrote libretto and produced opera *Peter I* 75.
State Academic Bolshoi Theatre of U.S.S.R., 1 Ploshchad Sverdlova, Moscow; St. Karietryriad, h.5/10, B 37, Moscow, K-6, U.S.S.R.

Kasatonov, Admiral Vladimir Afanasievich; Soviet naval officer; b. 21 July 1910, Novy Petergof, Leningrad Region; ed. Naval Acad.
Naval service 27; Commanding and Staff posts 31-; with Gen. Staff 45-55; Commdr. Black Sea and N. Fleets 55-56; First Deputy C.-in-C. Soviet Navy 64-; Deputy to U.S.S.R. Supreme Soviet 58-; mem. Comm. for Transport and Communications, Soviet of Nationalities; Hero of Soviet Union, medal Gold Star, Orders of Lenin, Red Banner of Labour, etc.
Ministry of Defence, Naberezhnaya M. Thoreza 34, Moscow, U.S.S.R.

Käser, Helmut Alfred; Swiss lawyer and sports administrator; b. 1912; ed. Commercial High School, Neuchâtel, and Univs. of Berne and Zürich.
Lawyer, Zürich court; fmr. lawyer, Ministry of Economics; Gen. Sec. Swiss Football Assen. 42-60; Sec.-Gen. Fédération Internationale de Football Assen. (FIFA) 61-.
Publ. *Untersuchungen über den Begriff des Ersatzwertes in der Versicherung* 37.
Hitzigweg 11, 8032 Zürich, Switzerland.

Kašlik, Václav; Czechoslovak composer and conductor; b. 28 Sept. 1917, Poličná; s. of Hynek and Paula Kašlíková; m. Růžena Stučesová 1942; three s.; ed. Faculty of Philosophy, Charles Univ., Prague, Prague Conservatoire and Conductors' Master School, Prague.
Conductor, E. F. Burian Theatre, Prague 40-41; Asst. Dir. Nat. Theatre, Prague 41-43; Chief of Opera Ensemble, Opera of May 5th 45-48; Conductor, Smetana Theatre, Prague 52-62; Chief Opera Dir. Nat. Theatre, Prague 61-65, Opera Dir. 66-; tours include New York, Leningrad, Moscow, Vienna, Munich; Klement Gottwald State Prize 56; Honoured Artist 58.
Works: Operas: *Robbers' Ballad* 44, *Calvary* 50, *Krakatit* 60; ballets: *Don Juan* 39, *Jánošík* 51, *Prague Carnival* 52; Dir. of operas: *The Water Nymph* (Dvořák), Vienna 65, *Julietta* (Martinů), Hanover 66, *Albergo dei Poveri* (Testi), Milan 66, *Die Soldaten* (Zimmermann), Munich 69, *Pelléas* (Debussy), Convent Garden 69, *Don Giovanni* (Mozart), Prague 69, *Cardillac* (Hindemith), La Scala 69, *Idomeneo* (Mozart), Vienna 71, *The Greek Passions* (Martinu), Spain 72, *The Queen of Spades* (Tchaikowsky), Stockholm 73, *Katya Kabanová* (Janáček), Geneva 75; work for TV, Magic Lantern Theatre: *Hoffman's Tales* 62; *Katya Kabanová* (Janáček), TV production, Copenhagen 70.
Škrétova 10, Prague II, Czechoslovakia.
Telephone: 230083.

Kassimatis, Grigorios, D. en D., DR.RER.POL.; Greek professor and politician; b. 16 March 1906; ed. Univ. of Athens and Univ. de Paris à la Sorbonne.
Practised law 27-37; Under-Sec. for Finance (resigned) 36; in concentration camp during Second World War; Assoc. Prof. Salonica Law School, then Prof. Panteios School 37-46; Assoc. Prof. of Civil Law, Law School of Univ. of Athens 39, Prof. of Civil and Labour Law

and Social Politics 41; Prof. of Social Studies and Labour Law, Higher Industrial School, Athens 59; Assoc. Prof. Univ. of Paris; Minister of Finance and Public Welfare and Acting Minister for Labour and Justice in Govts. of P. Voularis and Archbishop Damaskinos, then Minister of Finance and Acting Minister of Agriculture in P. Kanellopoulos Govt. 45; Minister without Portfolio as Under-Sec. of Press and Information and Acting Minister of Justice and Finance, then Minister of Labour and Acting Minister for Public Works 50, Minister of Industry 51, of Labour 51-52; Minister without Portfolio and Acting Minister for Co-ordination 56-58; Minister of Educ. and Religion 61-63, of Educ. 67; Deputy of Athens 46, and as an Independent 50, for Liberal Party 51, for Nat. Radical Union 56, 58, 61, 63, 64-67 (party suspended in April 67); Head of Greek Cttee. to UN 56-57; Rep. of Greece to Int. Bank of Reconstruction and Devt.—World Bank (IBRD) 57, 58; Dr. h.c. (Univs. of Aix and Bari).
Publs. Several books and articles.
c/o Ministry of Education, Athens, Greece.

Kastl, Jörg; German international official; b. 21 June 1922, Berlin; s. of Dr. Ludwig Kastl and Gertrud Otto; m. Eva M. L. von Essen; two d.; ed. Neubeuern, Bavaria, and law studies in Lausanne and Munich.
Served in armed forces 41-45; German Foreign Service School 50-51; Vice-Consul, Paris 51-52; Second Sec. Buenos Aires 53-55, Asunción, Paraguay 55-57; First Sec. Foreign Office, Bonn 57-59, Moscow 59-61; Fellow, Center for Int. Studies, Harvard Univ. 61-62; First Sec., Washington 62-63; Counsellor, Spokesman of German Foreign Office 63-66; Head of East European Desk, Foreign Office, Bonn 67-69; Asst. Sec.-Gen. for Political Affairs, NATO 69-75; Amb. of Fed. Republic of Germany to Argentina 75-.
Maipú 942, Casilla de Correos 2979, Buenos Aires, Argentina.
Telephone: 32-9424/9.

Kastler, Alfred; French physicist; b. 3 May 1902, Guebwiller (Alsace); s. of Frédéric Kastler and Anne Frey; m. Elise Cosset 1924; two s. one d.; ed. Ecole Normale Supérieure.
Taught in lycées at Mulhouse, Colmar, Bordeaux 26-31; Asst. at the Faculty of Sciences, Univ. of Bordeaux 31-36, Prof. 38-41; Lecturer Faculty of Science, Univ. of Clermont-Ferrand 36-38; Prof. of Physics, Ecole Normale Supérieure, Paris 41-68; at Univ. of Louvain, Belgium 53-54; mem. Management Board, Centre Nat. de la Recherche Scientifique (CNRS), Dir. Atomic Clock Laboratory 58-; mem. Inst. de France; Officier Légion d'Honneur; Holweck Medal and Prize, Physical Soc., U.K. 54, Nobel Prize for Physics 66; Dr. h.c. (Univs. of Louvain, Pisa, Oxford, Edinburgh, Laval (Quebec), Hebrew Univ. Jerusalem, Belgrade, Bucharest, Pavia).
Leisure interest: German poetry.
1 Rue du Val-de-Grâce, Paris 5e, France.
Telephone: 326-17-88.

Kasuga, Ikko; Japanese politician; b. 25 March 1910, Aichi; ed. Nagoya Telecommunications Technical High School.
Worked for Nagoya Cen. Telecommunications Bureau; Pres. Kasuga Musical Instrument Mfg. Co.; elected to Aichi Prefectural Gov. 51; Japan Socialist Party mem. House of Reps. 52; visited Soviet Union 55; formed Democratic Socialist Party with Suehiro Nishio 60; fmr. Sec.-Gen., now leader Democratic Socialist Party.
Minshu-Shakaito, Shiba Sakuragawa-cho, Minato-ku, Tokyo, Japan.

Kasuri, Mian Mahmud Ali; Pakistani lawyer and politician; b. 31 Oct. 1910, Kasur; s. of late Maulana Abdul Qadir Kasuri; ed. Punjab and Bombay Univs. and King's Coll., London.

Called to the Bar, Gray's Inn, London 35; started legal practice, Lahore High Court 37; mem. All India Muslim League Council 42-49; founding mem. and Pres. Azad Pakistan Party 50-57; mem. Nat. Awami Party 57-70, Pres. W. Pakistan Nat. Awami Party 65-70; mem. Pakistan People's Party 70-, now Vice-Chair. and mem. Cen. Cttee.; mem. Nat. Assembly 71-; Minister of Law and Parl. Affairs Dec. 71-Sept. 72; founder, Pakistan Inst. of Int. Affairs.
National Assembly, Rawalpindi, Pakistan.

Kataev, Valentin Petrovich; Soviet novelist; b. 28 Jan. 1897, Odessa; ed. Odessa.
Served army 15-17, Red Army 18-20; began full-time literary work in Moscow 22, mem. Praesidium, Union of Soviet Writers 53-; Editor-in-Chief of *Yunost* (Youth) monthly magazine; State prize 46; Order of Lenin (twice), Order of Red Banner of Labour 57.
Publs. *Otets* (Father) 25, *Rastratchiki* (The Embezzlers) 26, *Vremya vperyod!* (Forward, O Time!) 32, *Beleet parus odinokii* (Lone White Sail) 36, *Ya syn trudovogo naroda* (I, Son of the Working People) 37, *Syn Polka* (Son of the Regiment) 45, *Za vlast Sovetov* (For Soviet Power) 49, 51, *The Hamlet in the Steppe* 56, *Winter Wind* 60; plays: *Kvadratura Kruga* (Squaring the Circle) 28, *Avangard* (The Vanguard) 29, *Peace to Huts, War to Palaces* 60, *Waves of the Black Sea* 61, *Time of Love* 62, *Hearths of the People* 62, *Werewolf* 63, *Small Iron Door in a Wall* 64, *Floweret of Seven Colours* 66, *Holy Well* 67.
Union of Soviet Writers, Ul. Vorovskogo 52, Moscow, U.S.S.R.

Katayama, Tetsu; Japanese lawyer and politician; b. 1887; ed. Law Coll. of Imperial Univ.
Lecturer at Tokyo Women's Coll.; helped to organize Social Democratic Party 26, and its successor, the Social Mass Party 31; elected eight times to House of Representatives before 56; protested against invasion of Manchuria and continuation of war in China; was compelled by the Govt. to retire from politics until defeat of Japan; Sec.-Gen. of Nippon Shakai To (Social Democratic Party) Nov. 45; Chair. of same Feb. 47; elected to the Diet 46; re-elected April 47; Prime Minister of Japan May 47-March 48; Chair. Nat. League for Safeguarding New Constitution 54.
Publs. *The Development of the Socialist Movement in Japan*, and *The Legal Status of Women*, etc.
2-48 Todoroki-cho, Tamagawa, Setagaya-ku, Tokyo, Japan.

Katin, Peter; British pianist; b. 14 Nov. 1930, London; s. of Jerrold and Gertrude Katin; m. 1954; two s.; ed. Royal Acad. of Music.
London debut, Wigmore Hall 48; extensive concert tours in U.K., Europe, Africa, Canada, U.S.A. and Far East; special interest in Chopin; recording for Decca, EMI, Unicorn, Everest, Phillips, CFP.
Leisure interests: writing, tape-recording, fishing, theatre, reading, photography.
c/o Tower Music, 125 Tottenham Court Road, London, W1P 9HN, England.
Telephone: 01-387-4206/2082.

Kato, Ichiro, LL.D.; Japanese lawyer, professor and university administrator; b. 28 Sept. 1922, Tokyo; s. of Shuichi and Tomi Kato; m. Teruko Aoki 1947; one s. two d.; ed. Faculty of Law, Univ. of Tokyo.
Associate Prof. of Law, Univ. of Tokyo 48-57, Prof. of Law 57-68, 74-; Dean of Law and Acting Pres., Univ. of Tokyo 68-69, Pres. 69-73; Vice-Rector UN Univ. 75-76; mem. Admin. Board, Int. Asscn. of Univs. 70-; Pres. Nat. Univ. Asscn. (Japan) 69-73; Matsunaga Foundation Prize 66.
Leisure interests: golf, Go.
Publs. Several books on civil law.
University of Tokyo, Hongo, Bunkyo-ku, Tokyo; 10-30, Seijo 3-chome, Setagaya-ku, Tokyo, Japan.
Telephone: 03-416-2769.

Kato, Tadao; Japanese diplomatist; b. 13 May 1916, Tokyo; m. Yoko Kato 1946; two s.; ed. Tokyo Univ. and Univ. of Cambridge, England.
Consul, Singapore 52; First Sec., London 53; Counsellor, Econ. Affairs Bureau, Foreign Office 56-59, Deputy Dir. of Econ. Affairs Bureau 63-66, Dir. 66-67; Counsellor, Washington, D.C. 60-63; Amb. to Org. for Econ. Co-operation and Devt. (OECD) 67-70, to Mexico 70-74, to U.K. June 75-.
Leisure interests: golf, "Go".
Japanese Embassy, 43-46 Grosvenor Street, London, W1X 0BA, England.
Telephone: 01-493 6030.

Katz, Sir Bernard, M.D., D.SC., F.R.C.P., F.R.S.; British professor of biophysics; b. 26 March 1911, Leipzig, Germany; s. of Max Katz; m. Marguerite Penly 1945; two s.; ed. Univs. of Leipzig and London.
Biophysical Research, Univ. Coll. London 35-39, Beit Memorial Fellow 38-39; Carnegie Research Fellow, Sydney Hospital, Sydney, N.S.W. 39-42; Royal Australian Air Force 42-45; Asst. Dir. of Research in Biophysics and Henry Head Research Fellow, Royal Soc. 46-50; Reader in Physiology, Univ. Coll. London 50-51; Prof. of Biophysics and Head of Dept., Univ. Coll. London 52-; Sec. Royal Soc. 68-, and Vice-Pres. 70-; mem. Agricultural Research Council 67-; Herter Lecturer, Johns Hopkins Univ. 58; Dunham Lecturer, Harvard Univ. 61; Croonian Lecturer, Royal Soc. 61; Foreign mem. Acad. Naz. Lincei, Royal Danish Acad. of Sciences 68, American Acad. Arts and Sciences 69; Baly Medal, Royal Coll. of Physicians 67; Copley Medal, Royal Soc. 67; Nobel Prize for Physiology or Medicine 70; Hon. D.Sc. Southampton, Melbourne Univs. 71.
Publs. *Electric Excitation of Nerve* 39, *Nerve, Muscle and Synapse* 66, *The Release of Neural Transmitter Substances* 69.
Department of Biophysics, University College, Gower Street, London, W.C.1, England.
Telephone: 01-387-7050.

Katz, Katriel; Israeli diplomatist; b. 16 Oct. 1908, Poland; ed. Herzliya Gymnasium and Warsaw Univ.
Came to Palestine 24; Head, Dept. of Propaganda and Education, Haganah 42-43; spokesman of the Haganah 48; spokesman, Public Relations Office, Israel Defence Army 49; on staff of Ministry of Foreign Affairs 49-; former Head, Div. of Political Research; Chargé d'Affaires, Budapest 53-56; Minister to Poland 56-58; Sec. to the Govt. 58-62; Consul-Gen., New York 62-65; Amb. to U.S.S.R. 65-67; Chair. Yad-Vashem Memorial Authority, Jerusalem 67-72; Amb. to Finland 72-73; Deputy Chair. Israeli Council of Int. Relations 74-; mem. Board of Governors, Hebrew Univ. 75-.
Publs. *Five Years of Israel's Foreign Policy 1948-53*, *A Diplomat in Lands of Estrangement* (Hebrew) 76.
4 Hamaapilim Street, Jerusalem, Israel.

Katz, Milton, A.B., J.D., LL.D.; American professor of law; b. 29 Nov. 1907, New York; s. of Morris and Clara (Schiffman) Katz; m. Vivian Greenberg 1933; three s.; ed. Harvard Univ.
Member anthropological expedition to Central Africa 27-28; various official posts U.S. Govt. 32-39; Lecturer on Law Harvard Univ. 39-40, Prof. of Law 40-50; Solicitor War Production Board 41-43; U.S. Exec. Officer, Combined Production and Resources Board 42-43; Office of Strategic Services 43-44; Lieut.-Commdr. U.S.N.R. on active duty 44-46; Ambassador of the U.S. and U.S. Special Rep. in Europe 50-51; U.S. mem. Defence Financial and Economic Cttee. under North Atlantic Treaty 50-51; U.S. Rep. Economic Comm. for Europe (UN) 50-51; Assoc. Dir. Ford Foundation 51-54; Dir. Int. Legal Studies and Henry L. Stimson Prof. of Law, Harvard Univ. 54-; Fellow and Councillor American Acad. of Arts and Sciences; Legion of Merit; Trustee Carnegie Endowment for Int. Peace (Chair. of Board),

World Peace Foundation (Exec. Cttee.), Inter-American Univ. Foundation, Citizens Research Foundation (Pres.); Dir. Int. Friendship League; Trustee Brandeis Univ.; Chair. Cttee. on Manpower, White House Conf. on Int. Co-operation 65; Trustee, Int. Legal Center, Chair. of Board; mem. Corpn. Boston Museum of Science; Trustee, Case Western Reserve Univ.; Chair. Comm. on Life Sciences and Social Policy, Nat. Acad. of Sciences—Nat. Research Council; mem. panel on Technology Assessment, Nat. Acad. of Sciences 68-69; mem. Visiting Comm., Dept. of Humanities, Mass. Inst. of Tech. 70-73; Sherman Fairchild Distinguished Scholar, Calif. Inst. of Tech. 74; Consultant and Chair. Energy Advisory Board, U.S. Office of Technology Assessment 74; mem. Advisory Board, Energy Lab., Mass. Inst. of Tech, 74-; Consultant Programme on Social Man. of Tech., Univ. of Washington 74.
Publs. *Cases and Materials on Administrative Law* 47, *Government under Law and the Individual* (with others) 56, *The Law of International Transactions and Relations: Cases and Materials* (with Kingman Brewster, Jr.) 60, *The Things that are Caesar's* 66, *The Relevance of International Ajudication* 68, *The Modern Foundation: Its Dual Nature, Public and Private* 68, *Man's Impact on the Global Environment* (with others) 70, *Assessing Biomedical Technologies* (with others) 75.
Home: 6 Berkeley Street, Cambridge, Mass.; Office: Harvard Law School, Cambridge, Mass., U.S.A.
Telephone: KIrkland 7-0057 (Home); 495-3115 (Office).

Katz, Mindru; Israeli pianist; b. 3 June 1925, Romania; ed. Bucharest Acad. of Music.
First public recital 31; first public concert with Bucharest Philharmonic Orchestra 47; tours of E. Europe 47-. U.K. 52-, South and East Africa 60, 62, Far East and Australia 61 and 66, New Zealand and S. America 61, U.S.A. 64-; has played in Belgium, France, Germany, Portugal, Denmark, Israel, Luxembourg, Spain, Sweden and Turkey; settled in Israel 59; Prof. Tel-Aviv Univ. Acad. of Music; Prizewinner, Berlin, Prague, Bucharest Int. Piano Competitions 51, 53, First Class State Prize, Romania 54.
Leisure interests: chess, films, books, excursions.
45 Hanassi Street, Herzliya, Nof-Yam, Israel.

Katzarov, Konstantin, DR.JUR.; patent attorney; b. 1898, Sofia, Bulgaria; s. of Ivan Katzarov and Zana Koishova; one s.; ed. Univs. of Berne, Paris, Berlin and London.
Professor of Commercial Law, State Univ. Sofia 31-56, of Commercial and Int. Law 36-56; Lecturer, Univ. of Geneva; mem. Supreme Lawyers' Council 40-46; founder and Pres. of Int. Law Asscn. (Bulgarian Branch) 23-49, life mem. Int. Law Asscn.; mem. Slovak Acad. of Sciences 34; Founder and mem. Admin. body, Foundation Katzarovi, Univ. of Geneva; mem. British Inst. of Int. and Comparative Law, American Soc. of Int. Law; Coop. World Copyright Encyclopaedia; Del. to several int. confs.
Publs. *Nouveaux aspects de l'immunité de l'état* 57; *Rapport sur la nationalisation* 58, *Commercial Law* (4th edn.), *La Plantification comme problème juridique* 58, *Théorie de la nationalisation* (trans. Spanish, English; Arabic), *Analyse de la Victoire* (trans. German), *Industrial property all over the World*, *Sixty Years History Lived* (memoirs) 70, and several other books in Bulgarian and other languages on various aspects of commercial and int. law, history, politics.
26 rue du Lac, 1815 Clarens, Switzerland.
Telephone: (022) 61-20-55.

Katzenbach, Nicholas deBelleville; American lawyer and government official; b. 17 Jan. 1922; Philips Exeter Acad., Princeton and Yale Univs. and Balliol Coll., Oxford.
U.S. Army Air Force 41-45; admitted to N.J. Bar 50, Conn. Bar 55, N.Y. Bar 72; with firm Katzenbach,

Gildea and Rudner, Trenton, N.J. 50; Attorney-Adviser, Office of Gen. Counsel, Air Force 50-52, part-time Consultant 52-56; Assoc. Prof. of Law, Yale Univ. 52-56; Prof. of Law, Univ. of Chicago 56-60; Asst. Attorney-Gen., U.S. Dept. of Justice 61-62, Deputy Attorney-Gen. 62-64, Attorney-Gen. 65-66; Under-Sec. of State 66-69; Dir., Vice-Pres. and Gen. Counsel, I.B.M. Corpn. 69-; mem. American Bar Asscn., American Judicature Soc., American Law Inst.; hon. degrees from Rutgers Univ., Univ. of Bridgeport (Conn.), Tufts Univ., Georgetown Univ., Princeton, Northeastern Univ., Brandeis Univ.; Democrat.
Publs. *The Political Foundations of International Law* (with Morton A. Kaplan) 61, *Legal Literature of Space* (with Prof. Leon Lipson) 61.
Home: 5225 Sycamore Avenue, Riverdale, N.Y. 10471; Office: I.B.M. Corporation, Armonk, N.Y., U.S.A.

Katzer, Hans; German politician; b. 31 Jan. 1919, Cologne; *m.* Elisabeth Kaiser 1949; one *d.*; ed. Volksschule, Realgymnasium and Höhere Fachschule für Textil.
National and Mil. Service 39-45; employed in Labour Office, Cologne 45-49; Man. Dir. Social Cttee. of Christian Democratic Employees Asscn. of Germany 50-63, Chair. 63-, publisher of political monthly *Soziale Ordnung*; Man. Chair. of Jakob Kaiser Foundation 63-65; mem. Union of Transport Workers; mem. Christian Democratic Union (C.D.U.) 45-; mem. Cologne City Council 50-57; mem. Bundestag 57-; Chair. Parl. Cttee. for Fed. Econ. Assets 61-65; Fed. Minister of Labour and Social Welfare 65-69.
Publs. *Aspekte moderner Sozialpolitik* 69, *Bundestagsreden* 72.
5000 Köln-Marienburg, Kastanienallee 7, Federal Republic of Germany.

Katzir, Ephraim, M.SC., PH.D.; Israeli Head of State and professor of biophysics; b. 16 May 1916, Russia; *s.* of Yehuda and Tsila Katchalski; *m.* Nina Gotlieb 1938; one *s.* one *d.*; ed. Hebrew Univ., Jerusalem.
Professor, Dept. of Biophysics, Weizmann Inst. of Science 51-; Chief Scientist, Ministry of Defence 66-68; Pres. of Israel 73-; mem. Israel Acad. of Sciences and Humanities, Nat. Council for Research and Devt., Council for Higher Educ., Biochemical Soc. of Israel, Israel Chemical Soc., Nat. Acad. of Sciences, U.S.A., American Acad. of Arts and Sciences (Foreign Hon. mem.), Leopoldina Acad. of Science, German Democratic Repub., American Soc. of Biological Chemists (Hon.), Ciba Foundation, Int. Union of Biochemistry and many other orgs.; mem. of the Board, *Analytical Biochemistry, Archives of Biochemistry and Biophysics, Biopolymers, Excerpta Medica* and amino acids and proteins section of *European Journal of Biochemistry*; Tchernikhovski Prize 48; Hon. Prof. New York Inst. of Tech. 75; Weizmann Prize 50; Israel Prize Natural Sciences 59; Rothschild Prize Natural Sciences 61; Linderstrøm-Lang Gold Medal 69; Hans Krebs Medal 72.
Publs. numerous papers and articles on proteins and polyamino acids.
Office of the President, Jerusalem, Israel.

Kauffmann, Johannes, D.PHIL.; German professor; b. 30 March 1896, Kiel; *s.* of Prof. Dr. Friedrich and Elli (née Brauns) Kauffmann; *m.* Ludmila Scheder-Bieschin 1924; one *s.* one *d.*; ed. Berlin, Munich and Kiel Univs.
Assistant, Staatliche Museen zu Berlin 19-20; Asst. to Dr. C. Hofstede de Groot, The Hague 20-22; Lecturer in the History of Art, Berlin Univ. 22-29, Prof. 29-36; Sen. Prof. and Dir. Inst. of History of Art, Cologne Univ. 36-57, Rector 55-56; Sen. Prof. and Dir. Inst. of History of Art, Freie Univ., Berlin 57-; mem. Rheinisch-Westfälische Akademi der Wissenschaften, Düsseldorf; Fellow Royal Soc. Arts; Commdr. Cross, Order

of Crown (Italy), Hon. Cross of Arts and Sciences (Austria).
Publs. *Rembrandts Bildgestaltung* 22, *Albrecht Dürers Rhythmische Kunst* 24, *Donatello* 35, *Über "Rinascere", "Rinascità" und einige Stilmerkmale der Quattrocento Baukunst* 41, *Die fünf Sinne in der Niederländ. Malerei des 17 Jahrhunderts* 43, *Die Kölner Domfassade* 48, *Romgedanken in der Kunst Berninis* 54, *Jacob Burckhardts "Cicerone"* 61, *Bildgedanke und Künstlerische Form* 62, *Berliner Baukunst von Schlüter bis Schinkel* 63, *Zweckbau und Monument: zu Fr. Schinkels Museum am Lustgarten* 63, *Adolph Goldschmidt* 64, *Firenze nell' Interpretazione Tedesca* 65, *Die Schützenbilder des Frans Hals* 65, *Fr. Schinkel und seine Stellung in der Architekturgeschichte* 65, *Der Werdegang der Theresagruppe von G. L. Bernini* 67, *Erwin Panofsky* 68, *G. L. Bernini, figürliche Kompositionen* 70, *Albrecht Dürer: Umwelt und Kunst* 71, *Rembrandts Potipharbilder* 72, *Albrecht Dürer: "Vier Apostel"* 72, *Wolfenbüttel* 73, *A. Dürer um 1500* 74, *Probleme griechischer Säulen* 75.
52 Bonn, Römerstrasse 118, Federal Republic of Germany.
Telephone: 801-88-52.

Kaufmann, Berwind Petersen, M.A., PH.D.; American biologist; b. 23 April 1897; *s.* of Rudolph H. T. Kaufmann and Ida Petersen Kaufmann; *m.* Jessie T. McCulloch; three *s.*; ed. Univ. of Pennsylvania.
Professor of Biology, Southwestern Coll., Memphis, Tenn. 26-28; Prof. and Head of Dept. of Botany, Univ. of Alabama 28-36; Resident Investigator, Dept. of Genetics, Carnegie Inst. of Washington 36-60, Dir. 60-62; Prof. of Zoology and Botany, Univ. of Michigan 62-67, Prof. Emer. 67-; Guest Investigator, Brookhaven Nat. Laboratory 55-62; Senior Research Scientist, Inst. of Science and Technology, Univ. of Michigan 62-67; mem. Genetics Soc. of America (Pres. 61), Nat. Research Council Fellow, Calif. Inst. of Technology 32-33; mem. Nat. Acad. of Sciences, Botanical Soc. of America, American Soc. of Zoologists, American Soc. of Naturalists, Radiation Research Soc. and others.
Publs. *Drosophila Guide* (with M. Demerec), numerous articles on cytology and genetics; Co-Editor, *Biological Abstracts*; Assoc. Editor, *The Nucleus, Caryologia, Int. Journal of Radiation Biology*.
2650 Heather Way, Ann Arbor, Mich. 48104, U.S.A.
Telephone: 313-665-5932.

Kaufmann, Johan; Netherlands diplomatist; b. 20 April 1918, Amsterdam; *m.*; one *d.*
Entered Civil Service 45; Commercial Sec. Netherlands Embassy, Washington, later Mexico; Counsellor, Perm. Mission to UN 56-61; Minister Plenipotentiary, Office of UN and Int. Orgs., Geneva; Amb. Extraordinary and Plenipotentiary 67-; Head Perm. Del. to OECD 69-73; Perm. Rep. to UN 74-
Publs. *How UN Decisions are Made* 58, *Conference Diplomacy* 68.
Permanent Mission of the Netherlands to the United Nations, 711 Third Avenue, 9th Floor, New York, N.Y. 10017, U.S.A.

Kaul, Prince Mohan, M.B., B.S., D.P.H., F.R.C.P., F.I.A.M.S., F.P.H.A.; Indian physician and health official; b. 1 March 1906, Hindaon; *s.* of late S. M. Kaul and late Mrs. R. R. Kaul; *m.* Krishna Razdon 1935; one *s.* four *d.*; ed. Punjab Univ. and Guy's Hospital, London.
Teacher, Infectious Diseases, and Medical Officer, Campbell Medical School, Calcutta 33-34; commissioned Indian Medical Service 34; army service, rose to Acting Col. 34-45; Deputy, Public Comm. Govt. of India 46; Deputy Dir.-Gen. Health Services, Ministry of Health; Dir. WHO Epidemiological Intelligence Station, Singapore 47-49; Dir. WHO Liaison Office to UN, New York 50-52; Dir. Div. External Relations and Technical Assistance 53-56; Asst. Dir.-Gen. WHO 56-67; Special

Consultant to Dir.-Gen. WHO 68-69; Consultant to WHO 70-72, short-term Consultant 73-75.
Leisure interest: philately.
17-G Maharani Bagh, New Delhi, India.
Telephone: 631481.

Kaul, Triloki Nath; Indian diplomatist; b. 8 Feb. 1913; ed. Univs. of Punjab, Allahabad, London.
Joined Indian Civil Service 37; served in United Provinces as Joint Magistrate and Collector 37-47; Sec. Indian Council of Agricultural Research, New Delhi 47; First Sec. Indian Embassy, Moscow 47-49, Washington 49-50, Counsellor 50-52, and Minister 52-53, Peking; Joint Sec. Ministry of External Affairs, New Delhi 53-57; Chair. Int. Comm. for Supervision and Control, Viet-Nam 57-58; Amb. to Iran 58-60; Deputy High Commr. U.K. 60-61, Acting High Commr. 61-62; Amb. to U.S.S.R. and Mongolia 62-66; Sec. to Govt. of India, Ministry of External Affairs, New Delhi, June 66-68; Foreign Sec. Ministry of Foreign Affairs 68-73; Amb. to U.S.A. June 73-
Embassy of India, 2107 Massachusetts Avenue, N.W., Washington, D.C. 20008, U.S.A.

Kaula, Prithvi Nath, M.A., M.LIBR.SC.; Indian professor of library science; b. 13 March 1924, Srinagar; s. of Damodar Kaula; m. Asha Kaula 1941; two s. three d.; ed. S.P. Coll., Srinagar, Punjab Univ., Delhi Univ., Bararas Hindu Univ.
Member Council, Indian Library Asscn. 49-53, 56-62; Man. Ed. *Annals, Bulletin* and *Granthalays* of Indian Library Asscn. 49-53; Sec. Ranganathan Endowment for Library Science 51-61; Gen. Sec. Delhi Library Asscn. 53-55, 58-60, Vice-Pres. 56-58; Visiting Lecturer in Library Science, Aligargh Muslim Univ. 51-58; Reader Dept. of Library Science, Univ. of Delhi 58-60; Vice-Pres. Govt. of Indian Libraries Asscn. 58-61; mem. Review Cttee. on Library Science, Univ. Grants Comm. 61-63; Visiting Lecturer Documentation, Research and Training Centre, Bangalore 62, 65; Editor *Herald of Library Science* 62-; Chair. Fed. of Indian Library Asscns. 66, Pres. 74-; mem. Governing Council, Nat. Library of India 66-69; UNESCO Expert, UNESCO Regional Centre in the Western Hemisphere, Havana 67-68; Gen. Sec. Indian Asscn. of Teachers of Library Science 69, Pres. 73-; Editor *Granthalaya Vijnana* 70-; Prof. of Library Science, Banaras Hindu Univ. 71-; Chair. Council of Literacy and Adult Educ. 71-; Expert mem. UNESCO Advisory Group on Comparability of Higher Degrees in Library Science 73-; Visiting Prof. 15 Indian Univs., 7 American Univs., Univ. of Havana, Hebrew Univ., Jerusalem, and Univs. in the G.D.R., Hungary and the U.S.S.R.; Consultant on Library Science to several int. orgs. and nat. asscns.; Organizing Sec. and Pres. of numerous confs; Honoured by Int. Festschrift Cttee. 74; Indian Library Movement Award 74; Pro Mundi Beneficio Medal 75.
Leisure interests: reading, writing, the study of library science.
Publs. 37 publications and over 600 technical papers and book reviews on library science, labour problems and student unrest.
C1, Banaras University, Varanasi 221005, India.

Kaunda, Dr. Kenneth David; Zambian politician; b. 28 April 1924, Lubwa; ed. Lubwa Training School and Munali Secondary School.
Schoolteacher at Lubwa Training School 43, Headmaster 44-47; Sec. Chinsali Young Men's Farming Asscn. 47; welfare officer, Chingola Copper Mine 48; school teaching 48-49; Founder-Sec. Lubwa branch, African Nat. Congress 50, district organizer 51, provincial organizer 52, Sec.-Gen. for N. Rhodesia 53; broke away to form Zambia African Nat. Congress 58; Pres. United Nat. Independence Party 60-; Minister of Local Govt. and Social Welfare, N. Rhodesia 62-64; Prime Minister of N. Rhodesia Jan.-Oct. 64; Pres. Pan-

African Freedom Movement for East, Central and South Africa (PAFMECSA) 63; First Pres. of Zambia Oct. 64-, and Minister of Defence 64-70, 73-; Minister of Foreign Affairs 69-70, also of Trade, Industry, Mines and State Participation 69-73; Chancellor, Univ. of Zambia 66-; Chair. Mining and Industrial Devt. Corpn. of Zambia April 70-; Chair. Org. of African Unity (OAU) 70-71, Non-Aligned Nations Conf. 70-73; Order of the Collar of the Nile; Knight of the Collar of the Order of Pius XII, Order of the Queen of Sheba; Hon. Dr. of Laws (Fordham, Dublin, Windsor (Canada), Sussex, York and Chile Univs.); Jawaharlal Nehru Award for Int. Understanding.
Publs. *Black Government* 61, *Zambia Shall be Free* 62, *A Humanist in Africa* (with Colin Morris) 66, *Humanism in Zambia and its Implementation* 67.
State House, P.O. Box 135, Lusaka, Zambia.
Telephone: 50122 (Lusaka).

Kaup, Karl; German mining engineer and executive; b. 13 May 1906; m. Hedwig Huesker 1940; one s. three d.; ed. Humanistisches Gymnasium, Wattenscheid, Munich Technical High School and Clausthal Mining Acad.
Managing Dir. Fortuna Mines, Salzgitter 35-39; Dir. of Mines for Cen. Germany, Raw Materials Section, Vereinigte Stahlwerke G.m.b.H. 39-44, Man. at Siegen 44-53; mem. Board, Barbara Erzbergbau G.m.b.H. 53-54, Pres. 54-, Chair. 69-; Pres. Rohstoffhandel G.m.b.H., Düsseldorf 59-; Chair. Board of Dirs., Exploration and Bergbau G.m.b.H., Düsseldorf, Bong Mining Co., Monrovia, Liberia; mem. Board of numerous other mining and engineering companies; Hon. Dr.rer.nat.; Grosses Bundesverdienstkreuz 71.
4 Düsseldorf-Gerresheim, Rolanderweg 70b, Federal Republic of Germany.

Kaur, Prabhjot (*see* Prabhjot Kaur).

Käutner, Helmut; German film director, theatre director and playwright; b. 25 Aug. 1908; ed. Univ. of Munich and Acad. of Arts, Cologne.
Film director 39-; films incl. *Romanze in Moll* 43, *Unter den Brücken* 44, *Nachts auf den Strassen* 52, *Die letzte Brücke* 54, *Der Hauptmann von Köpenick* 56; theatre director of plays by Anouilh, Wilder, Arthur Miller, Ustinov in Hamburg, Bochum, Berlin; opera director: *König Pausole, Der Prinz von Homburg*, Hamburg State Opera.
18c Königsallee, Berlin 33, Germany.

Kauzmann, Walter Joseph, PH.D.; American professor of chemistry; b. 18 Aug. 1916, Mount Vernon, N.Y.; s. of Albert Kauzmann and Julia Kahle; m. Elizabeth Flagler 1951; two s. one d.; ed. Cornell, Princeton Univs.
Research Fellow, Westinghouse Co.; with Nat. Defense Council Explosives Research Lab.; worked on Atomic Bomb project, Los Alamos Labs., New Mexico 44-46; Asst. Prof. Princeton Univ. 46-51, Assoc. Prof. 51-60, Prof. 60-; David B. Jones Prof. of Chem. 63-; mem. Nat. Acad. of Sciences, American Acad. of Arts and Sciences, American Chemical Soc., American Physical Soc., American Asscn. for the Advancement of Science, Federation of American Scientists, American Soc. of Biochemists; Guggenheim Fellow 57, 74-75; Visiting Lecturer Kyoto Univ. 74, Ibadan Univ. 75; first recipient Kaj Ulrik Linderstrøm-Lang Medal 66.
Publs. *Introd. to Quantrum Chemistry* 57, *Thermal Properties of Matter* (2 vols.) 66, 67, *Structure and Properties of Water* 69.
Department of Chemistry, Princeton University, Princeton, N.J. 08540, U.S.A.

Kawaguchi, Kaichi; Japanese international financial official; b. 13 April 1922, Wakayama; s. of Toshio and Saki Kawaguchi; m. Yukiko Fujii 1949; three d.; ed. Tokyo Univ.

Entered Ministry of Finance 47; First Sec. Embassy in Belgium and France 61-65; Dir. Tokyo Customs House 69-70; Insurance Comm., Ministry of Finance 71-72; Exec. Dir. Int. Monetary Fund 72-.

International Monetary Fund, 19th and H Streets, N.W., Washington, D.C. 20431; Home: 5322 Falmouth Road, Bethesda, Md. 20016, U.S.A.

Telephone: EXec. 3-6362 (Office); 229-8694 (Home).

Kawaguchi, Toshiro; Japanese business executive; b. 9 July 1909, Shizuoka Prefecture; s. of Hidesaku and Yone Kawaguchi; m. Fumie Kawaguchi 1942; two s. two d.; ed. Tokyo Univ.

Director, Honshu Paper Co. Ltd. 64-66, Man. Dir. 66-69, Exec. Dir. 69-70, Exec. Vice-Pres. 70-71, Pres. and Chief Exec. Dir. 71-74, now Chair. of Board.

Leisure interests: Noh (Japanese classical singing and dancing) and Bonsai (Japanese gardening).

Tokyo; Home: Setagayaku Okamoto 1-chome, 15-3 Tokyo, Japan.

Telephone: 03-700-8525.

Kawai, Ryoichi; Japanese business executive; b. 18 Jan. 1917; s. of Yoshinati Kawai and Chieko Kawai; m. Kiyoko Kawai 1942 (died 1973); three s.; ed. Tokyo Univ.

President, Komatsu Ltd.

Leisure interest: golf.

Komatsu Building, 3-6, 2-chome, Akasaka, Minato-ku, Tokyo, Japan.

Kawai, Takaharu; Japanese business executive; b. 1905; ed. Kyoto Univ.

President and Rep. Dir. Nippon Mining Co. Ltd.; Chair. of Board May 74-.

Nippon Mining Co. Ltd. 3 Akasaka-Aoicho, Minato-ku, Tokyo; 3-4-13 Nishiohi, Shinagawa-ku, Tokyo, Japan.

Telephone: 771-3252.

Kawakami, Kenjiro; Japanese business executive; b. 22 Dec. 1906, Ohsaka-fu; s. of Shoshiro Kawakami and Haru (Nishizaki); m. Kimiko Satani 1944; one s. one d.; ed. Tokyo Imperial Univ.

Joined Sumitomo & Co. Ltd. (later Sumitomo Head Office Ltd.) April 29; transferred to Sumitomo Copper Rolling & Steel Tubing Co. Ltd. (now Sumitomo Metal Industry Co. Ltd.) Sept. 29; Sumitomo Head Office Ltd. 44; Sieka Kogyo Co. Ltd. (now Sumitomo Coal Mining Co. Ltd.) 46, Dir. 46, Man. Dir. 48; Man. Dir. Sumitomo Metal Mining Co. Ltd. 50, Senior Man. Dir. 56, Pres. 63-; Dir. Sulawisi Nickel Devt. Corpn. Co. Ltd.; Standing Dir. Japan Fed. of Employers' Asscns., Fed. of Econ. Orgs.; mem. Japan Cttee. for Econ. Devt.; Pres. Indonesian Nickel Devt. Co. Ltd. 69-73, Chair. of Board 73-; Blue Ribbon Medal.

Leisure interests: Japanese traditional music, "Kiyo-moto" and golf.

Sumitomo Metal Mining Co. Ltd., 11-3, 5-chome, Shimbashi, Minato-ku, Tokyo; 5-26-1 Kataseyama, Fujisawa-shi, Kanagawa Pref., Japan.

Telephone: 03-434-2211 (Office); 0466-23-3018 (Home.

Kawamata, Katsuji; Japanese business executive; b. 1 March 1905; ed. Tokyo Univ. of Commerce.

Japan Industrial Bank 29-47, Branch Man. Hiroshima 46-47; Managing Dir. Nissan Motor Co. 47-57, Pres. 57-73, Chair. 73-; Chair. Nissan Diesel, Nissan Shatai Koki; Vice-Pres. Fed. of Econ. Orgs. (Keidanren).

Nissan Motor Co. Ltd., 17-1, 6-chome, Ginza, Chuo-ku, Tokyo, Japan.

Telephone: (03) 543-5523.

Kawasaki, Kunio; Japanese business executive; b. 23 Sept. 1907, Osaka; s. of Suketaro and Jiu Kawasaki; m. Haruko Yamaguchi 1935; two s.; ed. Tokyo Univ. Japan Woollen Yarn Spinning Co. Ltd. 32-42, Toyobo Co. Ltd. (after merger) 42-, Dir. 56-57, Man. Dir. 57-61, Senior Man. Dir. 61-63, Vice-Pres. 63-66, Pres. 66-74, Chair. 74-; Auditor Japan Exlan Co. Ltd. (acrylic fibres)

66-; Exec. Dir. Fed. of Econ. Orgs. 66-; Exec. Dir. Japan Fed. of Employers' Asscns. 67-; Exec. Dir. Kansai Econs. Fed. 66-68, Vice-Pres. 68-; Pres. Toyobo Petcord Co. Ltd. 69-; Pres. Osaka-São Paulo Sister City Asscn. 70-74, Dir. 74-; Gen. Counsellor, Toyo Rubber Industry Co. Ltd. 71-; Chair. Japan Spinners' Asscn. 72-73; Pres. Japan Textile Colour Design Centre 72-; Exec. Dir. Japan Textile Fed. 73-; Pres. Kansai Int. Students Inst. 74-, Osaka Int. Trade Fair Comm. 74-; Vice-Pres. Japan Overseas Enterprise Asscn. 74-; Blue Ribbon Medal 69.

Leisure interest: gardening.

Toyobo Co. Ltd., 8 Dojima Hamadori 2-chome, Kita-ku, Osaka 530; Home: 1-28, 1-chome, Hibarigaoka Yamate, Takarazuka City, Hyogo Prefecture, 665, Japan.

Telephone: 06-344-1331 (Office); 0727-59-2556 (Home).

Kawawa, Rashidi Mfaume; Tanzanian politician; b. 1929; ed. Tabora Secondary School.

Former Pres. of the Tanganyikan Fed. of Labour; Minister of Local Govt. and Housing 60-61; Minister without Portfolio 61-62; Prime Minister Jan.-Dec. 62, Vice-Pres. Dec. 62-64; Second Vice-Pres., United Republic of Tanzania 64-, also Prime Minister Feb. 72-; Vice-Pres. of T.A.N.U. (Tanganyika African Nat. Union) and mem. T.A.N.U. Cen. Cttee. and T.A.N.U. Nat. Exec. Cttee.

Office of the Prime Minister, Dar es Salaam, Tanzania.

Kawusu Conteh, Sheku Bockari; Sierra Leonean politician; b. 1928; m.; c.; ed. Koyeima Govt. Secondary School.

Secretary Koinadugu District Council 56-59; Town Clerk, Bo Municipality 62, 65-68; Exec. Officer, Cen. Govt. 64-65; mem. Parl. 67-; Deputy Minister, Prime Minister's Office 68-69; Minister of Housing and Country Planning 69-70; Resident Minister for the Southern Province 70-71; Acting Prime Minister Sept. 70; Minister of Interior May-Nov. 71, of Lands and Mines 71-73, of Mines 73-.

Leisure interests: lawn tennis, indoor games.

Ministry of Mines, Freetown, Sierra Leone.

Kaya, Seiji, D.SC.; Japanese scientist; b. 1898; ed. Tohoku Imperial Univ.

Lecturer Tohoku Imperial Univ. 24, Asst. Prof. and mem. Research Inst. for Iron, Steel and Other Metals 26-28, Prof. of Physics 30-31; studied physics in Germany, Italy and U.S.A. 28-30; Prof. Hokkaido Imperial Univ. 31-43; mem. Nat. Research Council 39; Prof. Tokyo Inst. of Technology 41-48; Prof. of Physics, Tokyo Imperial Univ. 43-58, Dean of Science Faculty 49-51; Dir. Science Educ., Ministry of Educ. 48-49; mem. Science Council of Japan 49-, Vice-Pres. 51-54, Pres. 54; mem. Japan Acad.; mem. Japanese Del. to Gen. Conf. UNESCO 54, mem. Japanese Comm. for UNESCO 56; Pres. Tokyo Univ. 58; Imperial Acad. Prize; Japanese Cultural Medal 64.

Publs. *Kyojisei-Kesshotai* (Ferro-magnetic Crystals) 35, *Kyojiseitai-ron* (Theory of Ferro-magnetism) 40, *Kyoji-sei* (Ferro-magnetism) 51.

20 Aoba-cho, Shibuya-ku, Tokyo, Japan.

Kaye, Danny; American actor; b. 18 Jan. 1913.

Stage appearances include *Straw Hat Revue* 39, *Lady in the Dark* 40, *Let's Face It* 41, *Two by Two* 70; films include *Up in Arms* 43, *Secret Life of Walter Mitty* 46, *A Song is Born* 47, *The Inspector General* 48, *Hans Christian Andersen* 52, *Knock on Wood*, *White Christmas* 54, *Court Jester* 55, *The Five Pennies* 59, *On the Double* 61, *The Man from the Diner's Club* 63, *The Madwoman of Chaillot* 69, *Peter Pan* (TV musical) 75.

Amb.-at-Large for UN Children's Fund.

Box 750, c/o J. Lefkowitz & Co., 9171 Wilshire Blvd., Beverly Hills, California, U.S.A.

Kayibanda, Grégoire; Rwandan journalist and politician; b. 1 May 1924; ed. Kabgayi and Nyakibanda, Ruanda (Rwanda since 1962).

Teacher Kigali 49-53; Information Officer Kabgayi 53-55; Editor *L'Ami* 53-55, *Kinyamateka* 55-58; Founder Ruanda Co-operative Movement 52, Hutu Social Movement 57, Democratic Republican Movement 59; Pres. TRAFIPRO Co-operative, Kabgayi; Pres. Democratic Republican Movement; President of Ruanda Oct. 60-June 62, Rwanda 62-73; sentenced to life imprisonment July 74.

Kayinga Onsi Ndai; Zairian agronomist; b. 1934; Mangai; *m.*; six *c.*; ed. Institut Vétérinaire de Dureghem, Belgium.

Formerly Counsellor at the Presidency; State Commr. for Agriculture Dec. 70-.

Office of the State Commissioner for Agriculture, Kinshasa, Zaire.

Kayla, Ziya; Turkish economist; b. 1912, Istanbul; *s.* of Col. Sevki Kayla and Zehra Vefkioglu; *m.* Sevinc Cenk 1967; ed. School of Political Sciences, Istanbul.

Ministry of Finance 34-63, Asst. Inspector, Inspector and Chief Inspector of Finance 34-60; Deputy Minister of Finance 60-63; Chair. Board of Dirs. and Dir.-Gen. Central Bank of Turkey 63-66; Alternate Gov. for Turkey, of Int. Bank for Reconstruction and Development 61-65; Pres. Banks' Asscn. of Turkey 63-66; Sec.-Gen. Comm. of Regulation of Bank Credits 63-66; Head of Foreign Investment Encouragement Cttee. 63-66; mem. Board of Controllers of the Prime Ministry 66-70; Chair. Türkiye Vakiflar Bankasi 71-.

Leisure interest: writing articles on economics for newspapers.

Publs. *Emission movements in Turkey* 67, *Treasury and Central Banks relations* 70.

Mesnevi Sokak 8/8 Çankaya, Ankara, Turkey.
Telephone: 27-10-30.

Kaysen, Carl, A.B., M.A., PH.D.; American economist; b. 5 March 1920, Philadelphia; *m.* Annette Neutra 1940; *s.* of Samuel and Elizabeth Resnick; two *d.*; ed. Overbrook High School, Philadelphia, Univ. of Pennsylvania and Harvard Univ.

National Bureau of Econ. Research 40-42; Office of Strategic Services, Washington, D.C. 42-43; U.S. Army (Intelligence) 43-45; Teaching Fellow in Econs., Harvard Univ. 47, Junior Fellow, Soc. of Fellows 47-70, Asst. Prof. in Econs. 50-55, Assoc. Prof. 55-57, Prof. 57-66, Assoc. Dean, Graduate School of Public Admin. 60-66, Lucius N. Littauer Prof. of Political Economy 64-66; Dir. Inst. of Advanced Study, Princeton July 66-; Senior Fulbright Research Scholar, London School of Econs. 55-56; Econ. Consultant to Judge Wyzanski, Fed. District Court of Mass. 50-52; Deputy Special Asst. to Pres. for Nat. Security Affairs 61-63.

Publs. *United States v. United Shoe Machinery Corporation, an Economic Analysis of an Anti-Trust Case* 56, *The American Business Creed* (with others) 56, *Anti-Trust Policy* (with D. F. Turner) 59, *The Demand for Electricity in the United States* (with Franklin M. Fisher) 62, *The Higher Learning, the Universities and the Public* 69.

Institute for Advanced Studies, Princeton, N.J. 08540; and 97 Olden Lane, Princeton, N.J. 08540, U.S.A.
Telephone: 609-924-4400 (Office); 921-7154 (Home).

Kayser, Elmer Louis, B.ED., M.A., LL.D., PH.D., L.H.D.; American historian; b. 27 Aug. 1896, Washington, D.C.; *s.* of Louis S. and Sue (Huddleston) Kayser; *m.* Margery Ludlow 1922; one *d.*; ed. George Washington Univ., Johns Hopkins Univ., and Columbia Univ.

Assistant in History, George Washington Univ. 14-17, Instructor 17-20, Asst. Prof. 20-24, Assoc. Prof. 24-32, Prof. of European History 32-67, Prof. Emeritus 67-; Asst. Librarian 14-18, Recorder 18, Sec. 18-29, Dir. of Univ. students 30-34, Dean 34-62, Dean Emeritus 67-; Univ. Marshal 32-53, Univ. Historian 62-; Sec.-Treas. 18-24, Vice-Pres. 47-50, Pres. 50-53, Gen. Alumni Asscn.; Historian Nat. Capital Sesquicentennial Comm. 50; Lay Chair. Cttee. for Improvement of Admin. of Justice in D.C.; Vice-Chair. Board of Trustees, Mount Vernon Seminary 46-66, Hon. Dir. Mount Vernon Coll. 66-; Dir. American Peace Soc.; Assoc. Chair. School of Govt., George Washington Univ. 57-58; Assoc. Editor *World Affairs*; Candidate Officer, Field Artillery, U.S. Army 18; Radio Commentator on foreign affairs 39-45; Sec. Navy's Advisory Cttee. on Naval History; Treas. American Historical Asscn. 57-73; Vice-Pres. Columbia Historical Soc. 68-; Alumni Achievement Award, George Washington Univ. 41; Commdr. Nat. Order of Merit, Ecuador.

Leisure interest: book collecting.

Publs. *The Grand Social Enterprise* 32, *A Manual of Ancient History* 37, *Contemporary Europe* 41 (co-author), *Washington's Bequest to a National University* 65, *The George Washington University 1821-1966* 66, *Luther Rice, Founder of Columbian College* 66, *Bricks without Straw* 70, *A Medical Center* 73.

Office: The George Washington University, Washington D.C. 20037; Home: 2921 34th Street, Northwest, Washington, D.C. 20008, U.S.A.
Telephone: 202-676-6535.

Kazan, Elia (Elia Kazanjoglous); American (of Greek extraction) stage and film director; b. 7 Sept. 1909, Istanbul; *m.* Barbara Loden; ed. Williams Coll. and Yale Dramatic School.

Apprentice and Stage Man. with Group Theatre; acted on stage 35-41 in *Waiting for Lefty, Golden Boy, Gentle People, Fire-Alarm Waltz, Liliom* and in two films *City for Conquest* and *Blues in the Night* 41; Stage Dir. *Skin of our Teeth* (Drama Critics Award), *One Touch of Venus, Harriet, Jacobowsky and the Colonel* (Drama Critics Award), *Streetcar Named Desire, Death of a Salesman* (Drama Critics Award), *Tea and Sympathy, Cat on a Hot Tin Roof* (Drama Critics Award), *The Dark at the Top of the Stairs, J.B., Sweet Bird of Youth,* for Lincoln Center Repertory Theater *After the Fall, But for Whom Charlie, The Changeling;* film dir. *A Tree Grows in Brooklyn* 45, *Gentlemen's Agreement* (Academy Award) 47, *Boomerang* 47, *Pinky* 49, *Panic in the Streets* 50, *Streetcar Named Desire* 51, *Viva Zapata* 52, *Man on a Tightrope* 53, *On the Waterfront* (Acad. Award) 54, *East of Eden* 55, *Baby Doll* 56, *A Face in the Crowd* 57, *Wild River* 60, *Splendor in the Grass* 61, *America, America* 63, *The Arrangement* 69, *The Visitors* 72, *The Last Tycoon* 76; Novels: *America, America, The Arrangement, The Assassins, The Understudy;* fmr. Dir. of Actors Studio.

850 7th Avenue, New York City, N.Y., U.S.A.

Kazanets, Ivan Pavlovich; Soviet politician; b. 1918; ed. Siberian Metallurgical Inst.

Electrician, Head of Workshop, Kuznetsk Metallurgical Factory 37-44; mem. C.P.S.U. 44-; Shift Foreman, Trainee Electricians Factory, Yenakievo, Rep. Sec. Factory Cttee. 44-52; First Sec. Yenakievo City Cttee. C.P. Ukraine, later First Sec. Makeyev City Cttee. C.P. Ukraine 52-53; First Sec. District Cttee. Donetsk 53-60; Sec. and mem. Central Cttee., C.P. of Ukraine 60-62, Chair. Council of Ministers of Ukraine 63-65; Minister of Ferrous Metallurgy, U.S.S.R. 65-; Alt. mem. Cen. Cttee. C.P.S.U. 56-61, mem. 61-; Deputy to U.S.S.R. Supreme Soviet 54-.

Ministry of Ferrous Metallurgy, 2/5 Ploshchad Nogina, Moscow, U.S.S.R.

Kazemi, Abdul Muttaleb al-, M.A.ECONS.; Kuwaiti politician; b. 1937, Kuwait; *m.* 1969; one *s.* one *d.*; ed. Cairo Univ., Boulder Univ., Colo., U.S.A.

Director-General State Budget Dept., Ministry of Finance and Oil 61-71; mem. Nat. Assembly 71-; Chair. Nat. Assembly Financial and Econ. Cttee.;

Dir. Arabian Oil Co. until 67; Man. Dir. Kuwait Int. Investment Co. 73-75; Minister of Oil 75-; rep. to many confs. including Afro-Asian Conf. for Econ. Co-operation.
Ministry of Oil, P.O. Box 5077, Kuwait.
Telephone: 433637.

Kazemzadeh, Hossein, LL.B.; Iranian lawyer and politician; b. 1923, Shiraz; ed. Univ. of Teheran and Princeton Univ., U.S.A.
Assistant Lecturer, Inst. of Business and Admin., Teheran Univ.; Deputy Man. Dir. Planning Org.; Deputy Prime Minister; Dir. Budget Dept.; Consulting Minister and Sec. Gen. Org. for Admin. Affairs and Employment; Minister of Science and Higher Educ. until 73.
c/o Ministry of Science and Higher Education, Teheran, Iran.

Kazin, Alfred, M.A.; American writer; b. 5 June 1915; ed. New York City Coll. and Columbia Univ.
Began his career as free-lance literary reviewer 34; Instructor in English Literature successively at New York City Coll., Queen's Coll., New School 37-41; Literary Ed. *New Republic* 42, Assoc. Ed. *Fortune*; War Corresp. in Great Britain 45; Prof. of American Studies, Amherst Coll. 55-58; Berg Prof. of Literature, New York Univ. 57; Distinguished Prof. of English, State Univ. of New York 63-; mem. Nat. Inst. of Arts and Letters; Brandeis Univ. Medal 73; Creative Award in Literature 73.
Publs. *On Native Grounds: An Interpretation of Modern American Literature* 42, *A Walker in the City* 51, *The Inmost Leaf* 55, *Contemporaries* 62, *Starting Out in the Thirties* 65, *Bright Book of Life* 73; edited: *The Portable Blake* 46, *F. Scott Fitzgerald: The Man and His Work* 51, *The Stature of Theodore Dreiser* 55, *Melville's Moby Dick* 56, *Ralph Waldo Emerson: A Modern Anthology* 58, *The Open Form: Essays for our Times* 61, *The Short Stories of Nathaniel Hawthorne* 66, *The Ambassador* 69.
440 West End Avenue, New York, N.Y. 10024, U.S.A.

Kaznin, Georgi Vladimirovich; Soviet lawyer; b. 2 March 1922, Boyarnshchiuo, Yaroslavl Region; ed. U.S.S.R. Correspondence Inst. of Law.
Chairman of Regional Court, Pskov, N.W. Russia until 61; mem. Collegium of Ministry of Justice of R.S.F.S.R. 61-63; on staff of Central Cttee. of C.P.S.U. 62-63; mem. U.S.S.R. Supreme Court 65-; Order of Badge of Honour.
U.S.S.R. Supreme Court, 15 Ulitsa Vorovskogo, Moscow, U.S.S.R.

Kearney, Richard D., LL.B.; American lawyer; b. 3 Jan. 1914, Dayton, Ky.; s. of David Richard Kearney and Mary Estelle Manouge; m. Margaret Helen Murray 1944; ed. Xavier High School and Univ., Cincinnati and Univ. of Cincinnati.
Practising lawyer, Cincinnati 38-41; Special Attorney, Anti-Trust Div., Dept. of Justice 41-42; U.S. Army 42-46; Legal Div., Mil. Govt. Headquarters, Berlin 46-48; Chief, Legal Group, Bipartite Control Office, Frankfurt 48-49; Asst. Gen. Counsel, Office of U.S. High Commr. for Germany 49; German Bureau, Dept. of State 50; Gen. Counsel, Tripartite Comm. on German External Depts. 51-53; Deputy U.S. mem., Validation Board for German Dollar Bonds 53-56; Asst. Legal Adviser for Far Eastern Affairs, Dept. of State 56-57, for European Affairs 57-62; Deputy Legal Adviser 62-67; mem. UN Int. Law Comm. (with ambassadorial rank) 67-, Pres. 72-73; Chair. Sec. of State's Advisory Cttee. on Private Int. Law; mem. Gov. Council, Int. Inst. for Unification of Private Law; mem. American Soc. of Int. Law, American Acad. of Political and Social Science; Chair. or mem. U.S. dels. to several int. confs. on legal matters.
Publs. articles on codification and unification of law in several professional journals.
Department of State, Washington, D.C. 20520, U.S.A.

Kearns, Henry, D.B.A.; American business executive; b. 30 April 1911, Salt Lake City, Utah; s. of Henry A. and Mary O. Robbins Kearns; m. Marjorie Prescott 1938; two s. two d.; ed. Univ. of Utah.
Assistant Sec. of Commerce for Int. Affairs 57-60; fmr. Vice-Pres. Pike Corpn.; Pres. Nat. Engineering Science Co., Kearns International; Dir. Firestone Tyre & Rubber Co. (Thailand) Ltd., Siam Kraft Paper Co. Ltd.; FMC Corpn. American Int. Group Inc.; Pres. and Chair. Export-Import Bank of U.S.A. 69-73; Hon. doctorates, Woodbury Coll., Los Angeles and Chungang Univ.
Leisure interest: golf.
Kearns International, 155 Sansome Street, San Francisco, Calif. 94104; Home: 4903 Rockwood Parkway, N.W., Washington, D.C. 20016, U.S.A.
Telephone: 415-986-2900 (Office).

Kearton, Baron (Life Peer), cr. 70, of Whitchurch; **Christopher Frank Kearton,** Kt., O.B.E., F.R.S.; British scientist and textiles executive; b. 17 Feb. 1911; ed. Hanley High School and St. John's Coll., Oxford.
Imperial Chemical Industries, Billingham Div. 33-40; Atomic Energy Project, U.K. and U.S.A. 40-45; Courtaulds Ltd. 46-, in charge Chemical Engineering 46, Dir. 52-, Deputy Chair. 61, Chair. 64-75; part-time mem. U.K. Atomic Energy Comm. 55-; mem. Electricity Supply Research Council 54-, Chair. 60-; mem. Govt. Advisory Council on Technology 64-70, Nat. Econ. Devt. Council 65-71; Chair. Industrial Reorganization Corpn. 66-Dec. 68; mem. Cen. Advisory Council for Science and Technology 69-70; Non-Exec. Advisory Dir. Hill Samuel 70-; Pres. Royal Soc. for the Prevention of Accidents (ROSPA) 72-, Soc. of Chemical Industry 72-73; Part-time mem. Central Electricity Generating Board 74-; Chair. East European Trade Council 75-; Chair. and Chief Exec. British Nat. Oil Corpn. 75-; Hon. LL.D. (Leeds), Hon. D.Sc. (Bath, Aston, Reading, Keele Univs., New Univ. of Ulster); Hon. Fellow, St. John's Coll., Oxford 65, Manchester Coll. of Science and Tech. 66.
The Old House, Whitchurch, nr. Aylesbury, Bucks., England.

Keating, Justin; Irish politician and veterinary surgeon; b. 1931; s. of Sean Keating; m.; three c.; ed. Veterinary Coll., Univ. Coll., Dublin and London Univ.
Lecturer in Anatomy, Veterinary Coll., Ballsbridge 55-60; Senior Lecturer, Dept. of Preclinical Studies, Trinity Coll., Dublin 60-65, 67-; Head Agricultural Programmes, Radio Teleffs Éireann 65-67; mem. Dail for North Co. Dublin 69-; Labour Party Rep. to European Parl.; Minister for Industry and Commerce March 73-.
Ministry for Industry and Commerce, Kildare Street, Dublin 2, Ireland.

Keating, Stephen Flaherty, B.S., J.D.; American business executive; b. 6 May 1918, Graceville, Minn.; s. of Luke J. and Blanche F. Keating; m. Mary Davis 1945; two s. two d.; ed. Univ. of Minnesota.
Admitted to Minn. Bar 42; Special Agent, F.B.I., Norfolk, Va., Detroit 42-43; U.S. Naval Reserve 43-46; Assoc. Otis, Faricy & Burger, St. Paul 46-48; Man. Mil. Contracts, Aero Div., Honeywell Inc. 48-54, Div. Vice-Pres. 54-56, Vice-Pres. 56-62, Dir. 60-, Exec. Vice-Pres. 61-65, Pres. 65-, Chair. of Board, Chief Exec. Officer 74-; Dir. First Bank System, Gen. Mills Inc., The Toro Co., Dayton Hudson Corpn., PPG Industries Corpn.; Trustee, Mayo Foundation, Rochester, Minn.; Dir. Minn. Metropolitan Housing Corpn; mem. Gov. Board of United Way of America, Pres. Urban Coalition of Minn.; mem. Nat. Minority Purchasing Council.
Leisure interests: golf, hunting.
c/o Honeywell Inc., 2701 Fourth Avenue South, Minneapolis, Minnesota 55408, U.S.A.
Telephone: (612) 870-2595.

Kedah, H.R.H. The Sultan of; Tuanku Abdul Halim Mu'adzan Shah ibni Al-Marhum Sultan Badishah, D.K., D.K.M., D.M.N., D.U.K., S.P.M.K., D.K. (KELANTAN), D.K. (PAHANG); Ruler of Kedah, Malaysia; b. 28 Nov. 1927, Alor Star; m. Tuanku Bahiyah binti Al-Marhum Tuanku Abdul Rahman, d. of 1st Yang di Pertuan of Malaya, 1956; three d.; ed. Sultan Abdul Hamid Coll., Alor Star and Wadham Coll., Oxford.
Raja Muda (Heir to Throne of Kedah) 49, Regent of Kedah 57, Sultan 58; Timbalan Yang di Pertuan Agung (Deputy Head of State of Malaysia) 65-70, Yang di Pertuan Agung (Head of State) 70-75; Col. Commdt. Malaysian Reconnaissance Corps 66; First Class Order of the Rising Sun, Japan 70, Bintang Maha Putera, Klas Satu, Indonesia 70, Knight Grand Cross of the Bath, U.K. 72, Knight of the Order of St. John 72, Most Auspicious Order of the Rajamitrathorn, Thailand 73.
Leisure interests: golf, billiards, photography, tennis.
Alor Star, Kedah, Malaysia.

Keddafi, Col. Moamar al- (see Gaddafi, Col. Moamar al-).

Kedrov, Bonifatiy Mikhailovich; Soviet philosopher; b. 10 Dec. 1903, Yaroslavl; ed. Kharkov Univ. and Inst. of Red Professors.
Member C.P.S.U. 18-, Cen. Cttee. of C.P.S.U. 35-37; scientific posts 38-41; Soviet Army 41-45; Prof. of Dialectical and Historical Materialism, R.S.F.S.R. Acad. of Social Sciences 46-59; at Inst. of History of Natural Sciences, U.S.S.R. Acad. of Sciences 59-, Dir. 63-; Corresp. mem. U.S.S.R. Acad. of Sciences 60-66, mem. 66-.
U.S.S.R. Academy of Sciences, 14 Leninsky Prospekt, Moscow, U.S.S.R.

Keehn, Grant; American investment banker; b. 11 Oct. 1900, Kenilworth, Ill.; s. of George Washington and Jeannette Sophronia (Shipman) Keehn; m. 1st Marjorie Elliott Burchard 1923 (died 1961), one s. two d.; 2nd Veronika M. Rona 1962, two d.; ed. Hamilton Coll., Clinton N.Y. and Harvard Graduate School of Business Admin.
With Goldman Sachs & Co. 23-31, partner 31; Vice-Pres. Kelsey-Hayes Wheel Corpn. 32-33; officer and Dir. Equity Corpn. and associated cos. 33-38; partner Grant Keehn & Co. 38-41; served U.S. Army, Maj. to Col. 41-45; Vice-Pres. First Nat. Bank of N.Y. 45-50, Exec. Vice-Pres. 50-55, Dir. 51-55; Exec. Vice-Pres. First Nat. City Bank N.Y. 55-58; Senior Vice-Pres., Dir. Equitable Life Assurance Soc. of U.S. 58-64, Pres. and Dir. 64-67, Vice-Chair. of Board, Dir. 67-69, Chair. Finance Comm. and Dir. 65-71, Financial Consultant and Dir. 69-71; Limited Partner, Goldman, Sachs & Co. 71-; Dir. of several other companies; mem. N.Y. State Comptroller's Advisory Comm., N.Y. State Common Retirement Fund; Trustee, Kirkland Coll., Hamilton Coll., N.Y. Public Library.
Goldman, Sachs & Co., 55 Broad Street, New York, N.Y. 10004; Home: 45 Sutton Place South, New York, N.Y. 10022, U.S.A.

Keeler, William Wayne; American petroleum executive; b. 5 April 1908, Dalhart, Texas; m. Ruby Hamilton; three s.; ed. Bartlesville High School and Univ. of Kansas.
Joined Phillips Petroleum Co. while at Univ. 28, employed at refineries at Kansas City, Odessa and Borger as chemist, process engineer, night supt., and Chief Process Engineer 28-41; Technical Asst. to Vice-Pres. of Refining Dept. 41-45; Man. of Refining Dept. 45-47, Vice-Pres. of Refining Dept. 47-51; Vice-Pres., Exec. Dept. 51-54, Dir. 51-; mem. Exec. Cttee. 54-56; Exec. Vice-Pres. 56-62, Chair. Exec. Cttee. 62-67, Pres. 67; Chair. and Chief Exec. Officer, Phillips Petroleum Co. 68-73; Dir. of Refining, Petroleum Admin. for Defense, Wash. D.C. 52-53; Chair. Mil. Petroleum Advisory Board 54-62; Chair. U.S. Del to Inter-American Indian Conf., Quito, Ecuador 64; mem. Nat. Advisory Cttee. on War on Poverty Program 65, President's Cttee. on Econ. Opportunity 67; official of numerous business and civic orgs.
1118 South Dewey Avenue, Bartlesville, Okla. 74003, U.S.A.

Keen, Sir Bernard A., Kt., F.R.S., D.SC.; British physicist and agriculturalist; b. 5 Sept. 1890, London; s. of Charles Bernard Keen and Sarah Jane Bagley; m. Elsie Isabel Cowley 1915 (died 1955); two s.; ed. Univ. Coll., London.
Andrews Scholar 08; Trouton Research Scholar 11; Carey Foster Research Prizeman 12; Soil Physicist, Rothamsted Experimental Station 13; served (Gallipoli and Palestine) First World War 14-17; Research Dept. Woolwich Arsenal 18; Soil Physicist, Rothamsted 19; Dir. Imperial Inst. of Agricultural Research, India 30-31; Asst. Dir. and Head Soil Physics Dept., Rothamsted Experimental Station 23-47; Scientific Adviser Middle East Supply Centre, Cairo 43-45; Adviser on rural development, Palestine 46; Chair. U.K. Govt. Mission to W. Africa 46; Adviser on agricultural policy in E. Africa 47; Dir. East African Agriculture and Forestry Research Organisation 47-55; Dir. of Research, Baird and Tatlock (London) Ltd. 56-63; Pres. Royal Meteorological Society 38, 39; Cantor Lecturer, Royal Society of Arts 42; Fellow, Univ. Coll., London 24.
Publs. The Physical Properties of the Soil 31, The Agricultural Development of the Middle East 46.
2 Crosbie Court, Troon, Ayrshire, KA10 6ES, Scotland. Telephone: Troon 312067.

Keenan, Joseph D.; American trade unionist; b. 5 Nov. 1896, Chicago, Ill.; s. of Edward and Minnie Keenan; m. 1st Myrtle Feitsch 1932, 2nd Jeffie Hennessey 1963; two s.
Representative of American Federation of Labor on Nat. Defense Council 40; Assoc. Dir. War Production Board; Labor Adviser to Gen. Lucius D. Clay 45; Labor Adviser, Nat. Production Administration and Defense Production Authority 50-53, Office of Defense Mobilisation 53-58; Int. Sec., Int. Brotherhood of Electrical Workers 54-; Special Asst. to Dir. for Labor, Consultant to Office of Emergency Planning; Vice-Pres. and mem. Exec. Council A.F.L.-C.I.O.; mem. Pres. Advisory Council on Labor Management Policy; Medal of Freedom, Award of Merit.
Leisure interest: golf.
International Brotherhood of Electrical Workers, 1125 15th Street, N.W., Washington, D.C. 20005, U.S.A.
Telephone: 202-833-7114.

Keenan, Patrick John, C.A., B.COMM., A.C.I.S.; Canadian business executive; b. 7 Jan. 1932, Montreal; s. of Thomas P. Keenan and Catherine S. Collins; m. Barbara G. Fraser 1959; one s. three d.; ed. McGill Univ.
Secretary/Treas. Iroquois Glass Ltd. 59-62; Man. of Finance, Charles Pfizer Ltd. 63-64; Controller Patiño N.V. 64-65, Treas. 66-67, Vice-Pres. (Finance) 68-70, Vice-Pres. and Dir. 71-, Pres., Chief Exec. Dec. 74-; Chief Exec. Amalgamated Metal Corpn. Ltd. until 75, British Amalgamated Metal Investment Ltd., Consolidated Tin Smelters Ltd.; Chair. Geo. L. Scott & Co. Ltd.; Vice-Pres. and Dir. Patiño Man. Services Ltd.; Dir. of many other companies.
Leisure interests: skiing, swimming, jogging.
No. 16 Whitney Avenue, Toronto M4W 2A8, Ontario, Canada.

Keener, Jefferson Ward, A.B., M.A.; American business executive; b. 6 Aug. 1908, Portersville, Ala.; s. of Joseph Ward and Mary Boston Keener; m. Marian Feudner 1931 (died 1972); three s.; ed. Birmingham Southern Coll., Ohio State Univ. and Univ. of Chicago.

Instructor, later Asst. Prof. of Econs. Ohio Wesleyan Univ. 29-37, 38-39; Dir. of business research, B. F. Goodrich Co. 39-44, asst. to financial Vice-Pres., asst. to Pres. 44-46, Vice-Pres. 46-56, Exec. Vice-Pres. 56, Pres. and Dir. 57, Pres., Chief Exec. Officer and Dir. 58, Chair. of Board 58-72, Chair. Exec. Cttee. 72-73, Dir. 73-74; fmr. Dir. other Goodrich subsidiaries and assoc. companies, B. F. Goodrich Liberia Inc., B. F. Goodrich Canada, B. F. Goodrich Australia Ltd.; Dir. Campbell Soup Co., Ohio Bell Telephone Co.; served Office of Price admin. and War Production Board in Second World War; also other public service posts; mem. advisory cttee. on civilian personnel, U.S. Army 54-56; U.S. Army Medal for Exceptional Civilian Achievement 56; mem. Business Council; Dir. Highway Users Fed. for Safety and Mobility; Hon. LL.D. (Birmingham Southern Coll., Ohio Wesleyan Univ.), Hon. D.C.S. (Millikin Univ.).
Leisure interests: golf, fishing, bridge.
Publ. *Cutting the Cost of Bank Loans* 30.
265 Hampshire Road, Akron, Ohio 44313, U.S.A.

Keenleyside, Hugh Llewellyn, C.C., PH.D., LL.D., D.SC.; Canadian diplomatist and administrator; b. 7 July 1898, Toronto; s. of Ellis William and Margaret Louise (Irvine) Keenleyside; m. Katherine Hall Pillsbury 1924; one s. three d.; ed. Univ. of British Columbia, Vancouver and Clark Univ., Worcester, Mass., U.S.A. Served with C.F.A. First World War; Lecturer in History, Univ. of B.C. 25-27; entered Dept. of External Affairs 28; opened First Canadian Mission in Japan 29, promoted to Counsellor 40; Asst. Under-Sec. of State for External Affairs 41; Canadian Amb. to Mexico 44-47; Deputy Minister of Mines and Resources 47-50; Dir.-Gen. UN Technical Assistance Admin. 50-59; UN Under-Sec. for Public Admin. 59; Chair. British Columbia Power Comm. and Adviser to Govt. of British Columbia on Resource Devt. Policies 59-62; Chair. British Columbia Hydro and Power Authority 62-69; mem. numerous wartime cttees., including Canada-U.S. Joint Board on Defence 40-45 and War Technical and Scientific Devt. Cttee. 41-45; mem. numerous govt. comms. of investigation 72-74; Dir. and one of founders of Arctic Inst. of N. America; Dir. various companies; Officer or mem. numerous welfare, educational and int. orgs.; hon. degrees from numerous Canadian and U.S.A. Univs.; Haldane Medal of Royal Inst. of Public Admin. 54, Vanier Medal of Inst. of Public Admin. of Canada 62; Companion of Canada 69; Chancellor, Notre Dame Univ. 69-, Chair. Board of Gov. 72-; Hon. Chair. Canadian Nat. Cttee. on UN Conf. on Human Settlements.
Leisure interest: gourmet cooking, reading, poker.
Publs. *Canada and the United States, History of Japanese Education* (with A. F. Thomas), *International Aid.*
Office and Home: 3470 Mayfair Drive, Victoria, B.C. V8P 1PG, Canada.
Telephone: 592-9331.

Keeton, George Williams, M.A., LL.D., F.B.A.; British lawyer and educationist; b. 22 May 1902, Sheffield; s. of John William and Mary Emma Keeton; m. 1st Gladys Edith Calthorpe 1924, 2nd Kathleen Marian Willard 1946; two s.; ed. Gonville and Caius Coll. Cambridge and Gray's Inn, London.
Reader in Law and Politics Hong Kong Univ. 24-27; Senior Law Lecturer Manchester Univ. 28-31; Reader in Law 31-37, Prof. English Law 37-, Dean Law Faculty 39-54, Univ. Coll. London; Pres. and Treasurer London Inst. of World Affairs 38-; Dean of Faculty of Laws, London Univ. 42-46; Vice-Provost, Univ. Coll., London 66-69; Prof. of Law, Brunel Univ. 69-; Editor, *Anglo-American Law Review* 70-; Leverhulme Research Fellow 71-73.
Publs. *The Development of Extra-territoriality in China* 28, *The Law of Trusts* 34, *National Sovereignty and*

International Order 39, *Russia and Her Western Neighbours* 42, *China, the Far East and the Future* 43, *Making International Law Work* (with Dr. Schwarzenberger) 46, *Extra-territoriality in International and Comparative Law* 49, *The Passing of Parliament* 52, *Social Change in the Law of Trusts* 58, *Trial for Treason* 59, *Trial by Tribunal* 60, *Guilty but Insane* 61, *The Modern Law of Charities* 62, *Lord Chancellor Jeffreys and the Stuart Cause* 65, *The Norman Conquest and the Common Law* 66, *Shakespeare's Legal and Political Background* 67, *Equity* 69, *Government in Action* 70, *The Football Revolution* 72, *English Law: The Judicial Contribution* 74, *Trusts in the Commonwealth* 76.
Picts Close, Picts Lane, Princes Risborough, Bucks., England.
Telephone: Princes Risborough 5094.

Keilis-Borok, Vladimir Isaakovich, PH.D., D.SC.; Soviet geophysicist and applied mathematician; b. 31 July 1921, Moscow; s. of Isaak Moiseevich and Kseniya Ruvimovna; m. L. N. Malinovskaja 1955; one d.: ed. S. Ordzhonikidze Inst. of Geological Prospecting, Inst. of Physics of the Earth.
Chairman Div. of Methods of Interpretation, O. Schmidt Inst. of Physics of the Earth, U.S.S.R. Acad. of Sciences 60, Chair. Dept. of Computational Geophysics 70-, Chair. Int. Cttee. on Mathematical Geophysics 75-; Chair. Comm. on Computational Geophysics, Soviet Geophysical Cttee.; mem. editorial board of several int. journals; Foreign Assoc. U.S. Nat. Acad. of Sciences; Foreign Hon. mem. Amer. Acad. of Arts and Sciences.
Leisure interests: mountaineering, literature, history of art.
Publs. *Study of Earthquake Mechanism* 57, *Interferential Surface Waves* 60, *Seismic Love Waves* 65; Ed. *Computational Seismology* series, Vols. 1-8 66-, (Selection from Vols. 1-5 published in English 72), *Theoretical and Computational Geophysics* series, vols. 1, 2, 74.
Soviet Geophysical Committee, Molodezhnaya 3, 117296 Moscow; Institute of Physics of the Earth, B. Gruzinskaja 10, 123810 Moscow, U.S.S.R.
Telephone: 252-07-26.

Keita, Modibo; Mali politician; b. 4 June 1915, Bamako; ed. William-Ponty Lycée, Dakar.
Conseiller Général, French Sudan; Co-founder, Sec.-Gen. Union Soudanaise 45; Councillor, Union Française 53-56; Deputy to French Nat. Assembly from Sudan 56-58, Vice-Pres. 56; Sec. of State for Overseas 57; Sec. of State to the Presidency; Pres. Constituent Assembly, Dakar 58-60; Président du Conseil, Sudanese Repub. Mali Fed. 59-60, Mali 60-Nov. 68; Pres. of Mali 60-Nov. 68, Minister of Nat. Defence 61-Nov. 68; in detention; Lenin Peace Prize 62.
Bamako, Mali.

Keith, Sir Kenneth Alexander, Kt.; British banker; b. 30 Aug. 1916; s. of Edward Charles Keith; m. 1st Ariel Olivia Winifred Baird 1946 (divorced 1958), one s. one d.; m. 2nd Mrs. Nancy Hayward 1962 (divorced 1972); m. 3rd Mrs. Marie Hanbury 1973; ed. Rugby and Dresden.
Trained as Chartered Accountant, London 34-39; Army Service 39-45; Asst. to Dir.-Gen. Political Intelligence Dept., Foreign Office 45-46; Asst. to Managing Dir. Philip Hill & Partners, London 46-48, Dir 47; Dir. Philip Hill Investment Trust 49, Managing Dir. 51; Managing Dir. Philip Hill, Higginson & Co. Ltd. 51-59, Philip Hill, Higginson, Erlangers Ltd. 59-62, Chair. 62-65; Deputy Chair. and Chief Exec. Hill Samuel & Co. 65-70, Group Chair. 70-; Deputy Chair. British European Airways; Chair. Rolls-Royce (1971) Ltd. 72-; Vice-Chair. Beecham Group Ltd. 75-; Dir. Times Newspapers Ltd., Eagle Star Insurance Co. Ltd., etc.; mem. Nat. Econ. Devt. Council 64-71; Chair. Econ.

Planning Council for East Anglia 65-70; Gov. Nat. Inst. of Econ. and Social Research; Council mem. Manchester Business School.
Leisure interests: shooting, farming.
80 Eaton Square, London, SW1W 9AP; The Wicken House, Castle Acre, Norfolk, England.
Telephone: 01-730-4000 (London); Castle Acre 225.

Kekkonen, Urho Kaleva; Finnish politician; b. 3 Sept. 1900; ed. Univ. of Helsinki.
Jurist, Fed. of Rural Communities 27-32; Admin. Sec. Ministry of Agriculture 33-36; M.P. (Agrarian) 36-56; Minister of Justice 36-37, 44-46; Minister of the Interior 37-39; Director, Central Bureau of Evacuees 40-43, Office of Rationalization 43-46; Speaker of the Diet 48-50; mem. Board of Managers Bank of Finland 46-56; Prime Minister and Minister of the Interior 50-51; Prime Minister 51-52, 53, 54-56; Minister of Foreign Affairs 52-53, 54; Pres. of Finland 56-; LL.D. (Helsinki); Finnish decorations: Grand Cross with Chain, Order of the White Rose, Grand Cross of the Cross of Liberty, Grand Cross Order of the Lion, Grand Cross of the Holy Lamb, Olympic Cross (First Class) of Merit, Gold Cross of Merit of Finnish Sports; numerous foreign decorations; Dr. h.c. Univs. of Moscow, Aix-en-Provence, Waterloo (Ontario), Warsaw, Delhi, Budapest and Prague.
Presidential Palace, Helsinki, Finland.

Kelani, Haissam; Syrian diplomatist; b. 6 Aug. 1926, Hamah; ed. Mil. Coll., Air Gen. Staff Coll., Paris and High Mil. Air Acad., Paris.
General Pilot 61-62; Syrian Amb. to Algeria 62-63 and Morocco 65-67; Sec.-Gen. Ministry of Foreign Affairs 67-69; Amb. to the German Democratic Repub. 69-72; Perm. Rep. to UN 72-.
Publs. eight books; many articles in Arab reviews.
Permanent Mission of Syria to United Nations, 150 East 58th Street, Room 1500, New York, N.Y. 10022, U.S.A.

Kelantan, H.R.H. the Sultan of; Tuanku Yahya Petra ibni Al Marhum Sultan Ibrahim, D.K., D.M.N., S.M.N., S.P.M.K., S.J.M.K., S.P.S.K., D.K. (Trengganu), D.K. (Selangor), D.K. (Brunei); Ruler of Kelantan, Malaysia; b. 10 Dec. 1917, Kota Bharu; one s. four d.: ed. Francis Light School, Penang, and U.K.
Tengku Temanggong 39; Private Sec. to His Late Highness Sultan Ismail 45; Asst. State Treas., District Officer of Kota Bharu until 48; Tengku Mahkota Kelantan 48; Pres. Council of Religion and Malay Custom 48-53; Regent 53, 58; installed as Sultan of Kelantan 60; Timbalan Yang di Pertuan Agung (Deputy Supreme Head of State of Malaysia) 70-75, Yang di Pertuan Agung (Supreme Head of State) Sept. 75-; Col.-in-Chief Malaysian Artillery.
Kota Bahru, Kelantan, Malaysia.

Keldysh, Mstislav Vsevolodovich; Soviet mathematician; b. 10 Nov. 1911, Riga, Latvia; ed. Moscow Univ.
Specialist in aerodynamics and the theory of functions of complex variables; Engineer, Senior Eng., Chief of Section, Chief of Dept., Cen. Inst. of Aero- and Hydrodynamics 31-46; concurrently Lecturer, Moscow Univ. Corresp. mem. U.S.S.R. Acad. of Sciences 43-46; Head of Dept., Vice-Dir. Steklov Mathematical Inst. 44-53; mem. U.S.S.R. Acad. of Sciences 46-, Pres. 61-75; Prof. Moscow Univ.; Sec. Physics and Mathematics Section, U.S.S.R. Acad. of Sciences 53-61; mem. Communist Party 48-, mem. Cen. Cttee. of C.P.S.U., Deputy to the Supreme Soviet 62-; Chair. Lenin Prize Cttee., U.S.S.R. Cttee. for Lenin and State Prizes in Science and Technology 61-; Hon. mem. American Acad. of Arts and Sciences; two State Prizes; Lenin Prize; Order of Lenin, Hero of Socialist Labour (three times).

Publs. *O razreshimosti i ustoichivosti zadachi Dirikhle* 40, *O predstavlenii funktsii kompleksnogo peremennogo ryadami polinomov v zamknutykh oblastyakh* 45, *O sobstvennykh znacheniyakh i sobstvennykh funktsiyakh nekotorykh klassov nesamosopryazhennykh upravlenii* 51, *Vibratsii v vozdushnom potoke kryla s podkosami* 38, *Prilozhenie Teorii funktsii komplexnogo peremennogo k gidrodinamike i aerodinamike* (with L. I. Sedov) 64.
U.S.S.R. Academy of Sciences, Leninsky Prospekt 14, Moscow, U.S.S.R.

Kelfa-Caulker, Richard Edmund, M.A.; Sierra Leonean diplomatist; b. 14 March 1909; ed. Sierra Leone, Otterbein Coll., Ohio, Oberlin Graduate School and Teachers' Coll., Columbia Univ.
Headmaster, Albert Acad., Sierra Leone to 59; Commr. to the United Kingdom 59, Acting High Commr. 61; Amb. to U.S.A. 61-63; Amb. and Perm. Rep. to UN 63-64; High Commr. to U.K. 64-66; Amb. to Liberia 69-73.
c/o Ministry of Foreign Affairs, Freetown, Sierra Leone.

Kellas, Arthur Roy Handasyde, C.M.G., M.A.; British diplomatist; b. 6 May 1915, Aberdeen; s. of Henry Kellas and Mary Brown; m. Katherine B. Le Rougetel 1952; two s. one d.; ed. Aberdeen Grammar School, Aberdeen Univ., Balliol Coll., Oxford and Ecole des Sciences Politiques, Paris.
Joined diplomatic service 39; served in army 39-44; Third Sec., Teheran 44-47; First Sec., Helsinki 49-51, Cairo 52-53, Baghdad 54-58; Counsellor, Teheran 58-62; Imperial Defence Coll. 63; Counsellor and Consul-Gen., Tel-Aviv 64-66; Amb. to Nepal 66-70; Amb. to People's Democratic Repub. of Yemen (Aden) 70-72; High Commr. to Tanzania 72-75; Pres. Britain-Nepal Soc. 75-.
Leisure interests: walking, reading.
Laurel Villa, Culworth, nr. Banbury, OX17 2AZ, England.
Telephone: Sulgrave 558.

Keller, George M.; American chemical engineer and business executive; b. Kansas City, Missouri; ed. Mass. Inst. of Technology.
Served U.S. Air Force, World War II; joined Engineering Dept., Standard Oil Co. of Calif. 48, Asst. Vice-Pres. of Foreign Operations 67, Asst. to Pres. 68, Vice-Pres. 69, Dir. 70, Vice-Chair. Feb. 74-.
Standard Oil Co. of California, 225 Bush Street, San Francisco, Calif. 94104, U.S.A.

Keller, Hans Gustav, PH.D., LL.D.; Swiss librarian and historian; b. 12 Nov. 1902, Thun; s. of late Gustav Keller and the late Lina Keller-Kehr; m. Margaretha Meyer 1937; two s. one d.; ed. Berne, Vienna, Clermont-Ferrand, Heidelberg, Berlin and Basle Univs.
Librarian Zürich Municipal Museum of Applied Art 34-37, Swiss Nat. Library, Berne 37-44; Dir. Cen. Fed. Library, Berne 44-67; Lecturer in Modern History, Univ. of Berne 48-63, Prof. 63-.
Leisure interests: walking, travelling.
Publs. *Die politischen Verlagsanstalten und Druckereien in der Schweiz 1840-1848* 35, *Das "Junge Europa" 1834-1836* 38, *Das historische Museum im Schloss Thun 1887-1937* 38, *Der Brudermord im Hause Kiburg* 39, *Das Leben und Leiden Jesu Christi* 40, *"La Chartreuse"* 41, *Minister Stapfer und die Künstlergesellschaft in Bern* 45, *Einigen* 46, *Vom Staatsgedanken und von der Sendung der Schweiz* 47, *Thun* 49, *Legislative und Exekutive in den Vereinigten Staaten von Amerika* 51, *Hutten und Zwingli* 52, *Chr. von Graffenried und die Gründung von Neu-Bern in Nord-Carolina* 53, *Die Wurzeln der amerikanischen Demokratie* 58, *Die Quellen der amerikanischen Verfassung* 58, *Unitarismus und Föderalismus im Werk der amerikanischen Verfassunggebenden Versammlung* 58, *Der "Virginia-Plan"* 60, *Die Idee der Unabhängigkeit* 62, *Pitt's "Provisional*

Act" 62, *Die Metaphysik Montesquieus* 65, *Montesquieu's "Esprit des Lois"* 69, *Die amerikanische Verfassunggebende Versammlung* 71.
Zumbachstr. 30, 3028 Spiegel b. Bern, Switzerland.
Telephone: 031-53-45-03.

Keller, René Jacques, D.IUR.; Swiss diplomatist; b. 19 May 1914, Paris, France; *s.* of Jacques Keller and Maria (née Geiser); *m.* Marion Werder 1942; one *s.* two *d.*; ed. Trinity Coll., Cambridge and Univ. of Geneva.
Head of News Dept., Ministry of Foreign Affairs, Berne 54-56; First Counsellor, Swiss Embassy, Paris 57-60; Amb. to Ghana, Guinea, Liberia, Mali and Togo (with residence in Accra) 60-62; Amb. to Turkey 62-65; Head of Perm. Mission to UN Office and Specialized Agencies in Geneva 66-68; Amb. to U.K. 68-71; Head of Dept. for Int. Orgs., Ministry of Foreign Affairs, Berne 71-; Amb. to Austria 76-.
Leisure interests: golf, skiing.
Swiss Embassy, Prinz Eugenstr. 7-9, 1030 Vienna, Austria.
Telephone: 725111/15.

Kellett, Brian Smith, M.A.; British industrialist; b. 8 May 1922, Romiley, Cheshire; *s.* of late Harold Lamb Kellett and Amy Elizabeth (née Smith); *m.* Janet Lesly Street 1947; three *d.*: ed. Manchester Grammar School and Trinity Coll., Cambridge.
Experimental Officer, Admiralty 42-46; Asst. Principal Ministry of Transport 46-48; with Sir Robert Watson-Watt and Partners 48-49; with Pilkington Brothers Ltd. 49-55; with Tube Investments Ltd. 55-, Dir. 66-, Man. Dir. 68-, Deputy Chair. and Chief Exec. 74-, Chair. 76-; Chair. British Aluminium Co. 72-; Dir. Unigate 74-.
Bridgewater House, St. James's, London, SW1A 1DG; Home: 10 Elm Walk, Hampstead, London, NW3 7UP, England.
Telephone: 01-839-9090 (Office); 01-458-6723 (Home).

Kelley, Clarence M., B.A., LL.B.; American government official; b. 24 Oct. 1911, Kansas City, Mo.; *s.* of Clarence Bond Kelley and Minnie (Brown) Kelley; *m.* Ruby D. Pickett 1937 (deceased); one *s.* one *d.*; ed. Univ. of Kansas, Univ. of Kansas City.
Admitted to Mo. Bar 40; with Fed. Bureau of Investigation 40-61; Special Agent in Charge, FBI Birmingham Office 57-60, FBI Memphis Office 60-61; Chief of Police, Kansas City, Mo. 61-73; Dir. FBI 73-; mem. Presidential Advisory Cttee. 71, Nat. Advisory Comm. on Criminal Justice Standards and Goals, FBI Nat. Acad. Review Cttee. 72-73; mem. Exec. Cttee. Int. Asscn. of Chiefs of Police; J Edgar Hoover Gold Medal for Outstanding Job Service 70; Hon. LL.D. Baker Univ., Kansas, Culver-Stockton Coll., Mo.
Federal Bureau of Investigation, 9th Street and Pennsylvania Avenue, N.W., Washington, D.C. 20535, U.S.A.

Kellock, Roy Lindsay, B.A., LL.D., D.C.L., C.C., Q.C.; Canadian barrister; b. 12 Nov. 1893, Perth, Ont.; *s.* of J. F. Kellock and Annie McDonald Kellock; *m.* Elinor Harris 1932; one *s.* one *d.*; ed. McMaster Univ., Osgoode Hall, Toronto.
Practised in Toronto 20-42; Judge Court of Appeal, Ontario 42; Judge Supreme Court of Canada 44-58; resumed practice in Toronto (Blake, Cassels & Graydon) 58-68; Chancellor McMaster Univ., Ontario 56-60.
c/o Waterous, Holden, Kellock and Kent, 20 Wellington Street, Brantford, Ont.; 20 Inwood Drive, Brantford, Ont., Canada.
Telephone: 759-6220 (Office); 759-2153 (Home).

Kellou, Mohamed; Algerian lawyer and diplomatist; b. 27 March 1931, Mansoura; *s.* of Arezki Kellou and Zehoua de Kellou; *m.* Anyssa Abdelkader 1965; three *d.*; ed. Univs. of Algiers and Montpellier.
Lawyer, Algiers; fmr. Vice-Pres. Union Générale des Etudiants Musulmans Algériens (U.G.E.M.A.) (in charge of Foreign Affairs); Front de Libération Nationale (F.L.N.) Rep. in U.K. 57-61; Chief of Provisional Govt. of Algeria Diplomatic Mission to Pakistan 61-62; Dir. of African, Asian and S. American Affairs, Ministry of Foreign Affairs, Repub. of Algeria 62-63; Amb. to U.K. 63-64, to Czechoslovakia 64-70, to Argentina 70-75, to People's Republic of China 75-;.
Algerian Embassy, Peking, Peoples Republic of China.

Kelly, Donald P.; American business executive; b. 24 Feb. 1922, Chicago; *m.* Byrd M. Sullivan; two *s.* one *d.*; ed. DePaul, Loyola and Harvard Univs.
Manager Data Processing Operations, then Asst. Controller, Controller, Swift & Co. 53, Dir. 70-, Vice-Pres. of Finance, of Corporate Devt.; Vice-Pres. of Finance, Esmark Inc. April-Oct. 73, Pres., Chief Operating Officer Oct. 73-; Dir. Trans-Ocean Oil, Inc., Harris Bankcorpn. Inc., Inland Steel Co.; mem. Financial Execs. Inst., Data Processing Management Asscn., Econ. Club of Chicago.
Esmark Inc., 55 East Monroe Street, Chicago, Ill. 60603, U.S.A.

Kelly, Gene Curran; American dancer and actor; b. 23 Aug. 1912; ed. Univ. of Pittsburgh.
Has appeared in *Leave it to Me* 38, *Time of Your Life* 40, *One for the Money* 39, *Pal Joey* 41; staged: *Billy Rose's Diamond Horseshoe* 40, *Best Foot Forward* 41; Dir. of dances for films: *Anchors Aweigh* 44, *The Pirate* 48, *Living in a Big Way* 47; appeared in films: *Me and My Girl* 42, *The Pirate* 48, *The Three Musketeers* 50, *An American in Paris* 50, *The Devil Makes Three* 52, *Invitation to the Dance* 53, *Brigadoon* 54, *Inherit the Wind* 60, *Gigi* 61, *The Young Girls of Rochefort* 67, *40 Carats* 73; Co-Dir. *On the Town* 49, *Singin' in the Rain* 51, *It's Always Fair Weather* 55; Dir. *Invitation to the Dance* 53, *What a Way to Go* 64, *A Guide for the Married Man* 66, *Hello Dolly!* 68, *The Cheyenne Social Club* 70; Producer, Dir. *The Happy Road* (France) 56, *Flower Drum Song* 58.
Publ. *Take Me Out to the Ball Game* 48.
725 N. Rodeo Drive, Beverly Hills, Calif., U.S.A.

Kelly, Rev. Canon John Norman Davidson, M.A., D.D.; British ecclesiastic, scholar and university official; b. 13 April 1909, Bridge of Allan, Scotland; *s.* of John Davidson and Ann (Barnes) Kelly; ed. Univs. of Glasgow and Oxford.
Ordained Deacon 34 and Priest 35; Curate, St. Lawrence's, Northampton 34-35; Chaplain and Tutor, St. Edmund Hall, Oxford 35-37, Vice-Principal, Fellow and Trustee 37-51, Principal 51-; Oxford Univ. Lecturer in Patristic Studies 48-76; Pro-Vice-Chancellor 64-66, 72-76; during World War II did part-time work for Chatham House; Canon at Chichester Cathedral 48-; Hon. D.D. (Glasgow) 58, F.B.A. 65, Hon. D.D. (Wales) 71.
Leisure interests: the cinema, travel, sightseeing.
Publs. *Early Christian Creeds* 50, *Rufinus: A Commentary on the Apostles' Creed* 55, *Early Christian Doctrines* 58, *The Pastoral Epistles* 63, *The Athanasian Creed* 64, *The Epistles of Peter and Jude* 69, *Aspects of the Passion* 70, *Jerome* 75.
Principal's Lodgings, St. Edmund Hall, Oxford, England.
Telephone: Oxford 41039.

Kelly, Sir Theo (William Theodore), Kt., O.B.E., F.A.I.M.; Australian business executive; b. 27 June 1907; *s.* of W. T. Kelly; ed. Sydney.
Served World War II, Wing Commdr. R.A.A.F. 42-44, Chair. Canteen Services Board 46-59; Man. Dir. Woolworths Ltd. Australia 45-70, Chair. 63-; Chair., Man. Dir. Woolworths (N.Z.) Ltd., Woolworths (Properties) Ltd.; mem. Board Reserve Bank of Australia 61-75; Dir. Australian Mutual Life Assurance Co.; Chair. Computer Service of Australia Pty. Ltd.;

Dir. A.M.P. Soc. 67-, A.N.T.A. 59-; mem. Board, Royal N. Shore Hosp., Sydney; Trustee, Nat. Parks and Wildlife Foundation.
Woolworths Ltd., 534 George Street, P.O. Box 4068, Sydney 2000, Australia.

Keltsch, Erhard; German business executive; b. 1 April 1912, Hamburg; ed. Technischen Universität, Braunschweig.
Overseer, Public Works of the City of Hildesheim 37-45; Preussische Elektrizitäts-AG, Hanover, Authorized Agent 45-50, mem. of the Board 70-, Chair. of the Board 71-; mem. of the Board, Nordwestdeutsche Kraftwerke AG, Hamburg 50-, and Veba AG, Düsseldorf 71-.
Preussische Elektrizitäts-AG, Papenstieg 10-12, Postfach 4849, 3000 Hanover, Federal Republic of Germany.

Kemal, Yashar; Turkish writer and journalist; b. 1923, Adana; *m.* Thilda Serrero 1952; one *s.*; self-educated; Pres. Turkish Writers' Union.
Leisure interest: folklore.
Publs. (in English) *Memed, My Hawk* 61, *The Wind from the Plain* 63, *Anatolian Tales* 68, *They Burn the Thistles* 73, *Iron Earth, Copper Sky* 74, *The Legend of Ararat* 75, *The Legend of the Thousand Bulls* 76; novels, short stories, plays and essays in Turkish.
P.K. 14, Basinköy, Istanbul, Turkey.
Telephone: 732325.

Kemball-Cook, Denis Basil; American oil executive; b. 1910, London; *s.* of Sir Basil and Lady Kemball-Cook; *m.* Mary Virginia Ricks 1935; two *s.* one *d.*; ed. Shrewsbury School and Balliol Coll., Oxford.
Director, Compañía Shell de Venezuela, Caracas 51-57; Dir. and Vice-Pres. Shell Caribbean Petroleum and Asiatic Petroleum Corpn., New York 57-58; Exec. Vice-Pres. and Dir. Shell Oil Co., New York 58, mem. Exec. Cttee. 62, Chief Operating Officer 68; Pres. and Chief Exec. Officer, Shell Oil Co. 70-71; Dir. American Petroleum Inst.; trustee Skidmore Coll. 69.
Leisure interest: yachting, mem. New York and Noroton, Conn., Yacht Clubs.
58 Andrews Drive, Darien, Conn. 06820, U.S.A.

Kemble, Edwin Crawford, D.SC., PH.D.; American physicist; b. 28 Jan. 1889, Delaware, Ohio; *s.* of Rev. Duston and Margaret Day Kemble; *m.* Harriet Tindle 1920; one *s.* one *d.*; ed. Ohio Wesleyan Univ., Case School of Applied Science, and Harvard Univ.
Assistant Instructor in Physics, Carnegie Inst. of Tech. 11-13; Engineering Physicist, Curtiss Motor Corpn. 17-18; Instructor in Physics, Williams Coll. 19; mem. Physics Faculty, Harvard Univ. 19-, Prof. 30-57, Emer. 57-, Chair. Dept. of Physics 40-45; Chair. Cttee. on Molecular Spectra in Gases, Nat. Research Council 23-27, mem. Exec. Cttee. Div. of Physical Sciences 38-40; Guggenheim Fellow 27; mem. Nat. Acad. of Sciences, Chair. Physics section 45-48; Hon. Sc.D. (Case Univ.) 31, Hon. Ed.D. (Rhode Island Coll.) 57; Oersted Medal, American Asscn. of Physics Teachers 69.
Publs. *Report on Molecular Spectra in Gases* (with others) 26, *Fundamental Principles of Quantum Mechanics* 37, *Physical Science, Its Structure and Development* 67; research on band spectra, fundamentals of quantum theory, philosophy of science.
8 Ash Street Place, Cambridge, Mass. 02138, U.S.A.

Kemeny, John G., PH.D.; American mathematician, philosopher and teacher; b. 31 May 1926, Budapest, Hungary; *s.* of Tibor and Lucy (Fried) Kemeny; *m.* Jean Alexander 1950; one *s.* one *d.*; ed. George Washington High School, New York City, and Princeton Univ.
Arrived in U.S.A. 40; U.S. Army Service in theoretical div. of Manhattan Project, Los Alamos, N.M. 45; Research Asst. to Prof. Einstein 48; Fine Instructor in

Mathematics, Princeton 49-51, Asst. Prof. Dept. of Philosophy 51-52; Prof. of Mathematics and Philosophy Dartmouth Coll. 53, Chair. of Dept. 54-66, Albert Bradley Third Century Prof. to encourage innovation in teaching 69-72, Adjunct Prof. of Maths. 72-; Pres. of Dartmouth Coll. March 70-; Chair. Dartmouth Coll. Cttee. on Equal Opportunity; mem. Board of Govs. Mathematical Asscn. of America 60-63; Chair. U.S. Comm. on Mathematical Instruction 57-60; co-inventor of computer language BASIC and co-designer of Dartmouth Time-Sharing System; Fellow, American Acad. of Arts and Sciences; mem. American Mathematical Soc., American Philosophical Asscn.; Vice-Chair. Nat. Science Foundation Advisory Cttee. on Computing; Consultant to Research Council of America; Assoc. Editor of *Journal of Mathematical Analysis and Applications*; mem. Nat. Research Council 63-66; mem. Nat. Comm. on Libraries and Information Science 71-73; Hon. D.Sc. (Middlebury Coll.) 65, Hon. LL.D. (Columbia) 71, (Princeton) 71, (N.H.) 72; Hon. D.Sc. (Boston Coll.) 73, (Penn.) 75.
Publs. Thirteen books ranging from mathematics and computing to philosophy of science and educ., including *Man and The Computer* 72.
Dartmouth College, Hanover, N.H. 03755, U.S.A.
Telephone: 603-646-2222.

Kemoularia, Claude de; French international administrator; b. 30 March 1922, Paris; *m.* Chantal Julia 1951; one *d.*; ed. Coll. Carnot, Fontainebleau, Univ. de Paris Faculty of Law and Ecole Libre des Sciences Politiques.
Early career with Ministry of Interior 45, Office of Gov.-Gen. French Zone of Occupied Germany 46-47, Ministry of Finance 48; Parl. Sec. to Paul Reynaud 48-56; Personal Asst. to Sec.-Gen. of UN, Dag Hammarskjöld 57-61, in charge of World Refugee Year 59-60; Dir. European Inf. Services of UN 61; entered private business 62; Dir. Forges de Chatillon-Commentry 62-; Special Adviser to Administrator, UN Devt. Programme 64-; Private Adviser to Prince Rainier of Monaco 65-67; Chair. Soc. Panafricaine d'Etudes et de Réalisations 65-; financial adviser for int. operations (Banque de Paris et des Pays-Bas); Chair. Soc. Néo-Calédonienne de Dévt. et Participations; Pres. French UN Asscn.
41 boulevard du Commandant Charcot, Neuilly-sur-Seine, Seine, France; 7 rue de l'Athénée, Geneva, Switzerland.

Kempe, Rudolf; German conductor; b. 14 June 1910; four *d.*; ed. Dresden Staatskapelle.
Member Leipzig Gewandhaus Orchestra 29, Conductor 36; First Conductor, Chemnitz State Theatre 42, Gen. Musical Dir. 46; Gen. Musical Dir. Nat. Theatre, Weimar 48; Sächsisches Staatstheater, Dresden 49, Bavarian State Opera, Munich 52-54; guest conductor New York, London, Vienna Operas, etc., 54-; Principal Conductor, Royal Philharmonic Orchestra London 61-75, Artistic Dir. 64-75; Principal Conductor Tonhalle Orchestra, Zürich 65-73, Artistic Dir. 65-73; Gen. Music Dir. Munich Philharmonic Orchestra 67-; Principal Conductor BBC Symphony Orchestra Sept. 75-.
[*Died* 12 May 1976.]

Kemper, Heinz Peter; German business executive; b. 1903; ed. Technische Hochschule, Berlin, and Carnegie Inst. of Washington.
Chairman, Man. Board, Vereinigte Elektrizitäts and Bergwerks AG, Düsseldorf; Chair. Supervisory Board, VEBA AG, Ruhrkohle AG, etc.; Chair. Supervisory Board Preussische Elektrizitäts-AG until 71, now mem. Supervisory Board.
4 Düsseldorf-Oberkassel, Rheinallee 142, Federal Republic of Germany.

Kempff, Wilhelm Walter Friedrich; German pianist and composer; b. 25 Nov. 1895; ed. Viktoria Gymnasium, Potsdam, Berlin Univ. and Conservatoire.
Professor and Dir. Stuttgart Staatliche Hochschule für Musik 24-29; since then concert tours as pianist throughout the world; mem. Prussian Acad. of Arts; Mendelssohn Prize, Artibus et Litteris Medal (Sweden). Compositions include two symphonies, four operas, piano concertos and chamber, vocal and choral music. Publs. *Unter dem Zimbelstern, Das Werden eines Musikers* (autobiography).
8193 Ammerland, Oberbayern, Federal Republic of Germany.

Kempný, Josef, c.sc.; Czechoslovak politician; b. 19 July 1920, Lazy-Orlová; ed. Technical Univ.
Worker, foreman, building technician in different firms 39-48; Regional Man. Asscn. of Building Works, Ostrava 48-51; various managerial posts in building enterprises 51-64; Chair. Municipal Nat. Cttee., Ostrava 64-68; Sec. Cen. Cttee. C.P. Czechoslovakia 68-69, 70-; Deputy Prime Minister of Č.S.S.R. 69-70; Prime Minister of the Czech Socialist Republic 69-70; Chair. Bureau of Cen. Cttee., C.P. of Czechoslovakia for Directing Party Work in the Czech Lands 70-71; mem. Secr. of Cen. Cttee., C.P. of Czechoslovakia 68-69, 70-, mem. Presidium 69-; mem. Cen. Cttee. of C.P. of Czechoslovakia 69-; mem. of Czech Nat. Council 68-, mem. Presidium 71-; Deputy to House of Nations, Fed. Assembly 69-; mem. Presidium of Fed. Assembly 70-; Deputy Chair. Cen. Cttee. Nat. Front of Č.S.S.R. 71-; Chair. Cen. Cttee. of Nat. Front of C.S.R. 71-; Chair. Nat. Econ. Comm. Cen. Cttee. C.P. of Czechoslovakia 71-; Order of the Repub. 70; Order of Bulgarian People's Repub. 1st Class 71; Order of Victorious February 73.
Office: Central Committee of Communist Party of Czechoslovakia, Prague 1, nábr. Kyjevské brigády 12, Czechoslovakia.

Kemula, Wiktor, DR. PHIL., DR. CHEM.; Polish university professor; b. 6 March 1902, Ismail, Russia; s. of Michał Kemula and Michalina Guzera; m. Maria Majchrowicz 1939; one s. one d.; ed. Univ. of Lwów.
Assistant, Univ. of Lwów 23-32, Lecturer 32-36, Extraordinary Prof. 36-39, Prof. 39-45; Prof. of Inorganic Chem., Univ. of Warsaw 45-68, Dean of Faculty of Science 47-50, Dir. Chemical Inst. of Faculty of Mathematics, Physics and Chem. 52-; Head of Lab. of Physico-Chem. Analytical Methods in Inst. of Physical Chem. of Polish Acad. of Sciences 52-72; Chief Editor *Roczniki Chemii* 50-, *Chemia Analityczna* 56-69; Pres. Polish Chemical Soc. 55-60, 72-74; Vice-Rector, Univ. of Warsaw 56-59; Pres. of Analytical Chem. Div. of IUPAC 69-73, Past Pres. 73-75; mem. Societas Scientarium Leopoldiensis 36-; Societas Scientarium Varsoviensis 47- (Sec. of Section III 48-51); Polish Acad. of Sciences 56-, N.Y. Acad. of Sciences 60-; Deutsche Akademie der Naturforscher Leopoldina 60; Hon. mem. Soc. de Chimie Industrielle, Paris 59; Czechoslovak Chemical Soc. 66-; Polish Chemical Soc. 70; Analytical Chem. Soc. of Japan 72; decorations include J. Sniadecki Medal of the Polish Chemical Soc. for Scientific Achievements 65; J. Hanuš Medal of Czechoslovak Chemical Soc. 66; Medal of Liège Univ. 67; Centenary Lectureship Medal of the Chemical Soc. (London) 69; Golden Hon. Badge of Merit of the Cen. Tech. Org. (NOT) 70; Medal Japanese Asscn. of Analytical Chem. 72; State Prize 55, 72; Officer's Cross of Order Polonia Restituta 56; Banner of Labour, 2nd Class 72, Medals of 10th and 30th Anniversary of People's Poland, and other awards.
Leisure interests: music, photography.
Publs. Numerous scientific works in photochemistry, chromato-polarography, polarography, and analytical chemistry.
Ul. Schillera 8, m. 7, oo-248 Warsaw, Poland.
Telephone: 32-72-69 (Office); 31-44-03 (Home).

Kendall, Donald M.; American business executive; b. 16 March 1921, Sequim, Wash.; s. of Carroll C. and Charlotte (McIntosh) Kendall; m. 1st Anne McDonnell Linkins 1945, 2nd Sigrid Ruedt von Collenberg 1965; four c.; ed. Western Kentucky State Coll.
Air Corps, U.S. Naval Reserve 42-47; Vice-Pres. Pepsi-Cola Co. 52-57; Pres. Pepsi-Cola Int. 57-63, Pepsi-Cola Co. 63-65; Pres. and Chief Exec. Officer, PepsiCo Inc. 65-71, Chair. and Chief Exec. Officer 71-; Dir. Pan American Airways, Atlantic Richfield, Investors Diversified Services Mutual Fund Group; Chair. Nat. Center for Resource Recovery, U.S.-U.S.S.R. Trade and Econ. Council, Emergency Cttee. for American Trade.
Leisure interests: tennis, golf, jogging, skiing, salmon fishing.
PepsiCo Inc., Purchase, N.Y. 10577; Home: Porchuck Road, Greenwich, Conn., U.S.A.

Kendall, James Pickering, M.A., D.SC., F.R.S.; British chemist; b. 30 July 1889, Chobham, Surrey; s. of William Kendall and Rebecca Pickering; m. 1st Alice Tyldesley 1915 (deceased), 2nd Jane Bain Steven 1955; ed. Edinburgh Univ. and Stockholm Nobel Inst.
Professor of Chem., Columbia Univ., New York 13-26, N.Y. Univ. 26-28, Edinburgh Univ. 28-59 (now Emer.), Dean of Science Faculty 53-54, and 57-59; Pres. Royal Soc. of Edinburgh 49-54; Vice-Pres. British Asscn. for Advancement of Science 51; fmr. Chair. New York Section, American Chemical Soc. and Dean of Graduate School, New York Univ.; Hon. LL.D.
Leisure interests: bridge, crossword puzzles, filling in questionnaires.
Publs. *At Home Among the Atoms, Breathe Freely, The Truth About Poison Gas, Great Discoveries by Young Chemists, Humphry Davy: Pilot of Penzance, Michael Faraday: Man of Simplicity.*
The Sheiling, Heriot Way, Heriot, Midlothian, Scotland.

Kendall, Sir Maurice George, Kt., M.A., SC.D., F.B.A.; British statistician; b. 6 Sept. 1907, Kettering; s. of John Roughton Kendall and Georgina Jessie Kendall (née Brewer); m. 1st Sheila Frances Holland Lester 1932, 2nd Kathleen Ruth Audrey Phillipson 1947, three s. one d.; ed. Central School Derby, and St. John's Coll., Cambridge.
Permanent Civil Servant with Min. of Agriculture and Fisheries 30-40; Statistician to the Chamber of Shipping of the U.K. 40-49, Joint Asst. Gen. Man. 47-49; Prof. of Statistics Univ. of London 49-61; Dir. of Scientific Services, Scientific Control Systems Ltd. 61-, Man. Dir. 62-, Chair. 67-72; Dir. World Fertility Survey 72-; Fellow, American Statistical Asscn., Inst. of Mathematical Statistics; Hon. Fellow London School of Econs. 75; mem. Int. Statistical Inst.; Silver and Gold Medallist of the Royal Statistical Soc.; Vice-Pres. Market Research Soc.; fmr. Pres. Operational Research Soc., Royal Statistical Soc.
Leisure interests: chess, music, writing.
Publs. *An Introduction to the Theory of Statistics* (with G. Udny Yule), *The Advanced Theory of Statistics* (with A. Stuart) (3 vols.) 1st edn. 66, *Contributions to the Study of Oscillatory Time-Series, Rank Correlation Methods, A Dictionary of Statistical Terms* (with W. R. Buckland), *A Course in Multivariate Analysis, The Geometry of n dimensions, Geometrical Probability* (with P. A. Moran), *Bibliography of Statistical Literature* Vols. 1-3 (with Alison Doig), *Studies in the History of Probability and Statistics* (ed. with E. S. Pearson), *Time-Series, Multivariate Analysis.*
1 Frank Dixon Close, London, S.E.21, England.
Telephone: 01-693-6076.

Kendall, William Hersey; American railway executive; b. 24 March 1910; ed. Dartmouth Coll., and Thayer School of Civil Engineering.
Maintenance Engineer, Pennsylvania Railroad 33-48; Exec. Officer, Atlantic Coast Line Railroad 48-50,

Clinchfield Railroad 50-54, now Dir. and mem. Exec. Cttee.; Exec. Officer, Louisville and Nashville Railroad 54-, Vice-Pres., Gen. Man. 57-59, Pres. 59-72; Vice-Chair. SCL Industries 72-.

1194 Starks Building, Louisville, Ky. 40202, U.S.A.

Kendrew, Maj.-Gen. Sir Douglas Anthony, K.C.M.G., C.B., C.B.E., D.S.O., K.ST.J.; British army officer and administrator; b. 22 July 1910, Barnstaple, Devon; s. of Dr. Alexander Kendrew and Eva Faviell; m. Nora Harvey 1936; one s. one d.; ed. Uppingham School.
Second Lieutenant, Royal Leicestershire Regt. 31, Major 41; Brigade Major, N. Africa 42, Cmmdr., 6th Batt., York and Lancaster Regt., North Africa and Italy 43, Brigade Cmmdr., Italy, Middle East, and Greece 43-46; Commdt. School of Infantry, Rhine Army 46-48; Commdt. Army Apprentice School, Harrogate 48-50; Chief of Staff, Northern Ireland Dist. 50-52; Commdr., 29th Infantry Brigade, Korea 52-53; Imperial Defence Coll. 54; Brigadier Admin., H.Q. Northern Command 55; Gen. Officer Commanding, Cyprus District, and Dir. of Operations 56-58; Dir. of Infantry, War Office 58-60; Head of British Defence Liaison Staff, Australia 60-63; Gov. of W. Australia 63-Oct. 73; Commr. Chelsea Hospital 74; Pres. Knights of the Round Table 75; Hon. LL.D. (Univ. of W. Australia). Leisure interests: photography, sport.
The Manor House, Islip, Northants., England.
Telephone: Thrapston 2325.

Kendrew, Sir John Cowdery, Kt., C.B.E., SC.D., F.R.S.; British molecular biophysicist; b. 24 March 1917, Oxford; s. of W. G. Kendrew; ed. Dragon School, Oxford, Clifton Coll. and Trinity Coll., Cambridge.
Ministry of Aircraft Production 40-45; Fellow of Peterhouse, Cambridge 47-75; Medical Research Council 47-74, Dep. Chair. Medical Research Council Laboratory of Molecular Biology, Cambridge 53-74; Reader, Davy-Faraday Lab., Royal Inst. 54-68; Sec.-Gen. European Molecular Biology Conf. 70-74; mem. Council for Scientific Policy 65-72, Deputy Chair. 70-72; Editor-in-Chief *Journal of Molecular Biology*; Dir. Gen. European Molecular Biol. Lab., Heidelberg 75-; Pres. British Asscn. for the Advancement of Science 74; Sec. Gen. Int. Council of Scientific Unions 74-; Trustee British Museum 74-; Nobel Prize for Chem. 62; Royal Medal, Royal Soc. 65; Foreign Assoc. U.S. Nat. Acad. of Sciences 72; Hon. Fellow, Trinity Coll., Cambridge 72, Peterhouse, Cambridge 75; Hon. D.Sc. (Keele and Reading); D. Univ. (Stirling) 74.
Publ. *The Thread of Life* 66.
4 Church Lane, Linton, Cambridge, CB1 6JX, England.
Telephone: Cambridge 891 545.

Kendrick, Sir Thomas Downing, K.C.B., D.LITT., LITT.D., F.B.A., F.S.A.; British antiquarian; b. 1895. Keeper of British Antiquities in the British Museum 38-50, Dir. and Principal Librarian 50-59.
Publs. *The Lisbon Earthquake* 56, *Saint James in Spain* 60, *Great Love for Icarus* 62, *Mary of Agreda* 67.
The Old Farm House, Organford, nr. Poole, Dorset, England.

Keng Piao; Chinese diplomatist, politician and fmr. army officer; b. 1909, Li-ling, Hunan; ed. Chinese Worker-Peasant Red Army Coll.
Major-General 46; Chief of Staff, N. China Field Army 47; Amb. to Sweden 50-56, concurrently Minister to Denmark 50-55, to Finland 51-54; Amb. to Pakistan 56-59; Vice-Minister of Foreign Affairs 60-63; Amb. to Burma 63-67, to Albania 69-71; Dir. Int. Liaison Dept., CCP 71-; mem. 9th (69), 10th (73) Cen. Cttees., CCP.
People's Republic of China.

Kennan, George Frost, A.B.; American diplomatist and scholar; b. 16 Feb. 1904, Milwaukee, Wis.; m. Annelise Sørensen 1931; one s. three d.; ed. Princeton Univ.

Vice-Consul Hamburg 27, Tallin 28; Third Sec. Riga, Kovno and Tallin 29; Language Officer Berlin 29; Third Sec. Riga 31, Moscow 34; Consul Vienna 35; Second Sec. 35; Second Sec. Moscow 35; Dept. of State 37; Second Sec. Prague 38; Consul 39; Second Sec. Berlin 39, First Sec. 40; Counsellor Lisbon 42; Counsellor to U.S. Del. European Advisory Comm. London 44; Minister-Counsellor Moscow 45; Deputy for Foreign Affairs, Nat. War Coll., Washington 46; Policy Planning Staff, Dept. of State 47; Chief, Policy Planning Staff, Dept. of State 49-50; on leave, at Inst. for Advanced Study, Princeton, N.J. 50-51, Prof. 56; Ambassador to U.S.S.R. 52-53; retd. from Foreign Service 53; Charles R. Walgreen Foundation Lecturer, Univ. of Chicago 51; Stafford Little Lecturer, Princeton 54; George Eastman Visiting Prof. Oxford Univ. 57-58; Reith Lecturer on *Russia, The Atom and the West* 57; Visiting Lecturer, History, Harvard Univ. 60, Yale Univ. 60; Amb. to Yugoslavia 61-63; Prof. Inst. for Advanced Study, Princeton 63-74, Prof. Emer. 74-; Prof. Princeton Univ. 64-66; Pres. Nat. Inst. of Arts and Letters 65-68; Pres. American Acad. of Arts and Letters 67-71; Univ. Fellow in History and Slavic Civilizations, Harvard Univ. 66-70; Fellow, All Souls Coll., Oxford 69; Fellow, Woodrow Wilson Int. Center for Scholars, Smithsonian Inst. Oct. 74-; Nat. Book Award, Bancroft Prize, Pulitzer Prize history 56, biography 68, Francis Parkman Prize; LL.D. h.c. (Yale, Dartmouth, Colgate, Notre Dame, Kenyon, New School for Social Research, Princeton, Michigan, Northwestern, Brandeis, Denison, Harvard, Rutgers, Wisconsin Univs.); Benjamin Franklin Fellow of the Royal Soc. of Arts, London 68; Hon. D.C.L. (Oxford) 69.
Publs. *American Diplomacy 1900-1950* 52, *Das Amerikanisch-Russische Verhältnis* 54, *Realities of American Foreign Policy* 54, *Soviet-American Relations 1917-1920*, Vol. I, *Russia Leaves the War* 56, Vol. II, *The Decision to Intervene* 58, *Russia, The Atom and the West* (Reith Lectures) 58, *Soviet Foreign Policy 1917-45* 60, *Russia and the West under Lenin and Stalin* 61, *On Dealing with the Communist World* 63, *Memoirs 1925-1950* 67, *Democracy and the Student Left* 68, *From Prague After Munich: Diplomatic Papers 1938-1940* 68, *The Marquis de Custine and his "Russia in 1839"* 71, *Memoirs 1950-1963* 72.
Woodrow Wilson International Center for Scholars, The Smithsonian Institution, 1000 Jefferson Drive, S.W., Washington, D.C. 20560, U.S.A.

Kennedy, David Matthew, A.B., M.A., LL.B.; American banker; b. 21 July 1905, Randolf, Utah; s. of George Kennedy and Katherine Johnson; m. Lenora Bingham 1925; four d.; ed. Weber Coll., George Washington Univ., and Stonier Graduate School of Banking, Rutgers Univ.
Special Asst. to Chair. Board, Fed. Reserve System 30-46; Vice-Pres. in charge Bond Dept. Continental Ill. Nat. Bank and Trust Co. of Chicago 46-53, Pres. 56-59, Chair. of Board and Chief Exec. Officer 59-69; Asst. to Sec. of Treasury, Wash. 53-55; Sec. of U.S. Treasury 69-Feb. 71; Amb.-at-Large dealing with int. finance 70-71; Amb. to NATO 72; U.S. Gov. IBRD, IMF, Inter-American Bank, Asian Devt. Bank 69-71; Chair. Exec. Board Comm. for Econ. and Cultural Devt. of Chicago, Chicago Clearing House Asscn.; fmr. Dir. Abbott Laboratories, Int. Harvester Co., Commonwealth Edison Co., Pullman Co., Swift and Co., Radio New York Worldwide Communications Satellite Corpn., United States Gypsum Co.; Trustee, Univ. of Chicago, Presbyterian-St. Luke's Hospital, Equitable of Iowa, Brookings Inst., George Washington Univ.; Republican.
Leisure interests: riding, hunting, fishing.
33 Meadow View Drive, Northfield, Ill. 60093, U.S.A.

Kennedy, Eamonn, M.A., B.COMM., PH.D.; Irish diplomatist; b. 13 Dec. 1921, Dublin; s. of Luke W. and Ellen (née Stafford) Kennedy; m. Barbara J. Black 1960; one s. one d.; ed. O'Connell School, Dublin, Nat. Univ. of Ireland, Dublin and the Sorbonne, Paris. Third Sec., Dept. of Foreign Affairs, Dublin 43; Second Sec., Canada 47-49; First Sec., Washington 49-50, Paris 50-54; Acting Chief of Protocol, Dept. of Foreign Affairs 54-56; Counsellor, Irish Mission to UN 56-61; Irish del. to UN Gen. Assembly 56-60; Amb. to Nigeria 61-64, to Fed. Germany 64-70, to France 70-74; Perm. Rep. to UN 74-; Grosses Bundesverdienstkreuz mit Stern, Grande Croix de Mérite de la Répub. Française. Leisure interests: golf, languages, theatre.
Permanent Mission of Ireland to United Nations, 885 Second Avenue (19th Floor), New York, N.Y. 10017; 1 East End Avenue, New York, N.Y. 10021, U.S.A.
Telephone: LE5-7738 (Home).

Kennedy, Edward Moore, A.B., LL.B.; American lawyer and politician; b. 22 Feb. 1932, Boston, Mass.; s. of late Joseph Kennedy and of Rose Kennedy; brother of late Pres. John F. Kennedy; m. Virginia Joan Bennett 1958; two s. one d.; ed. Milton Acad., Harvard Coll. and Univ. of Virginia Law School.
United States Army, Infantry, Private 1st Class 51-53; Reporter, Int. News Service, N. Africa 56; Man. Western States, John F. Kennedy Presidential Campaign 60; fmr. Asst. District Attorney, Mass.; U.S. Senator from Mass. 63-; Asst. Majority Leader, U.S. Senate 69-71; Pres. Joseph P. Kennedy Jr. Foundation; Trustee, Boston Symphony, John F. Kennedy Library, Lahey Clinic, Boston, John F. Kennedy Center for the Performing Arts; Board mem. Fletcher School of Law and Diplomacy, Mass. Gen. Hospital; numerous hon. degrees; Democrat.
Publs. *Decisions for a Decade* 68, *In Critical Condition* 72.
U.S. Senate, Washington, D.C., U.S.A.

Kennedy, Eugene Patrick, B.SC., PH.D.; American professor of biological chemistry; b. 4 Sept. 1919, Chicago; s. of Michael and Catherine Frawley Kennedy; m. Adelaide Majewski 1943; three d.; ed. De Paul Univ. and Univ. of Chicago.
Assistant Prof., Ben May Lab., Univ. of Chicago 52-55, Assoc. Prof. 55-56, Prof. of Biological Chem. 56-60; Prof. and Head, Dept. of Biological Chem., Harvard Medical School 60-65, Hamilton Kuhn Prof. of Biological Chem., Harvard Medical School 60-; mem. Nat. Acad. of Sciences, American Acad. of Arts and Sciences; Glycerine Research Award 56; Paul-Lewis Award, American Chem. Soc. 59; Assoc. Editor *Journal of Biol. Chem.* 69; Pres. American Soc. of Biol. Chemists 70-71; Lipid Chem. Award of the American Oil Chemists Soc. 70.
Publs. 102 papers.
Harvard Medical School, 25 Shattuck Street, Boston, Mass., U.S.A.
Telephone: 617-734-3300.

Kennedy, Jacqueline Lee Bouvier (*see* Onassis, Mrs. Jacqueline).

Kennet, (2nd Baron) cr. 35, of the Dene; **Wayland Young;** British writer and politician; b. 2 Aug. 1923, London; s. of Edward Hilton Young (Lord Kennet) and Kathleen Bruce; m. Elizabeth Ann Adams 1948; one s. five d.; ed. Stowe School, Trinity Coll., Cambridge, Perugia and Harvard Univs.
Royal Navy 42-45; Foreign Office 46-47, 49-51; mem. Parl. Assembly Council of Europe and Western European Union 62-65; Chair. British Cttee. for International Co-operation Year 65; Parl. Sec. Ministry of Housing and Local Govt. 66-70 Chair. Int. Parl. Confs. on the Enviroment 71-; Chair. Cttee. on Oil Pollution of the Sea 70-74; Chair. Council for the Protection of Rural England 71-72; Opposition Spokesman on Foreign Affairs, House of Lords 71-74; Dir. Europe Plus Thirty 74-.
Leisure interests: sailing, swimming, music.
Publs. *The Italian Left* 49, *The Deadweight* 52, *Now or Never* 53, *Old London Churches* (with Elizabeth Young) 56, *The Montesi Scandal* 57, *Still Alive Tomorrow* 58, *Strategy for Survival* 59, *The Socialist Imagination* (with Elizabeth Young) 60, *Disarmament: Finnegan's Choice* (with Elizabeth Young) 61, *The Profumo Affair* 63, *Eros Denied* 65, *Preservation* 72; Editor *Disarmament and Arms Control* 63-65.
House of Lords, London, S.W.1, England.

Kent, H.R.H. the Duke of; **Prince Edward George Nicholas Paul Patrick,** G.C.M.G., G.C.V.O.; b. 9 Oct. 1935; s. of the late Duke of Kent (fourth s. of King George V) and Princess Marina (d. of late Prince Nicholas of Greece); m. Katharine Worsley 1961; two s. (Earl of St. Andrews and Lord Nicholas Windsor) one d. (Lady Helen Windsor); ed. Eton Coll. and Le Rosey, Switzerland.
Second Lieut., Royal Scots Greys 55; attended Army Staff Course 66, later on staff, G.O.C. Eastern Command, Hounslow, Major 67, Lieut.-Col. 72; Col. Scots Guard 74; Ministry of Defence 72-76; Vice-Chair. Board of Trade 76-; as Queen's Special Rep. has visited Sierra Leone 61, Uganda 62, The Gambia 65, Guyana and Barbados 66, Tonga 67; A.D.C. to H.M. The Queen 67; Grand Master of the United Grand Lodge of England June 67-; tour of Australia and S. Pacific 69; Pres. All-England Lawn Tennis Club 69-; Col.-in-Chief Royal Regt. of Fusiliers 69-; decorations from Greece, Nepal, Liberia and Jordan; Hon. D.C.L. (Durham).
Leisure interests: skiing, shooting, photography, opera.
York House, St. James's Palace, London, S.W.1, England.

Kent, Sir Peter (**Percy Edward**), Kt. PH.D., D.SC., F.R.S.; British geologist; b. 18 March 1913, Nottingham; s. of Edward L. and Annie (née Woodward) Kent; m. Margaret B. Hood 1940 (died 1974); two d.; ed. W. Bridgford Grammar School and Nottingham Univ.
Joined Anglo Iranian Oil (later BP) 36; R.A.F.V.R. 41-46; geological survey work in U.K., Iran, E. Africa, Papua, Canada 46-60; Chief Geologist, Australasian Petroleum Co. 56; Adviser to Pres., BP Exploration (Canada) 57-58; Pres. BP Exploration Co. (Alaska) Inc. 59-60; Deputy Chief Geologist, BP 61-62; Regional Man., N. and S. America, BP 62-63; Technical Man. and Regional Man. (America and Western Hemisphere) BP 63-65; Chief Geologist, BP 66-71, Asst. Gen. Man. (Exploration) 71-73; Chair. Natural Environment Research Council 73-; Pres. Geological Soc. of London 74-76; Legion of Merit (U.S.A.) 46; Lyell Fund 49, Bigsby Medal 53, Murchison Medal 69 (all from Geological Soc. of London); MacRobert Award 70; Royal Soc. Royal Medal 71; Sorby Medal (Yorks. Geological Soc.) 73.
Leisure interests: walking, gardening, landscape painting, choral singing.
Publs. *Geology Lincolnshire* (co-author) 59; about 120 articles on geology and oil exploration.
43 Trinity Court, Gray's Inn Road, London, W.C.1; 38 Rodney Road, West Bridgford, Nottingham, NG2 6JH, England.
Telephone: 01-837-5275 (London); 0602-231355 (Nottingham).

Kenter, Ayşe Yıldız; Turkish actress and producer; b. 1928; ed. State Conservatoire.
Worked in State Theatre for eleven years, playing almost forty parts; Rockefeller Fellowship in Dramatic Art; teacher of Dramatic Art, State Conservatoire; now acting and producing independently; awarded Iskender Prize 60, 62, 65; Aitan Portakal Award 64, 66.
Cevdet Paşa Cad. 96/9 Bebek, Istanbul, Turkey.

Kentner, Louis Philip; British pianist; b. 19 July 1905, Karwin, Silesia; *s.* of Julius Kentner and Gisela Buchsbaum; *m.* 1st Ilona Kabos 1933 (dissolved 1945), 2nd Griselda Gould 1946; ed. Royal Acad. of Music, Budapest.
Studied with Arnold Székely, Leo Weiner and Zoltan Kodály; concert pianist at age of 14, and has since performed in many parts of the world; took up residence in England 35; gave first performance of Bartók's Second Concerto under Otto Klemperer's direction; world tour 53; gave several complete performances of Beethoven's Piano Sonatas and Violin and Piano Sonatas with Yehudi Menuhin 54-55; gave first performance of Michael Tippett's Piano Concerto in Birmingham Oct. 56; toured South America 56; five tours of U.S.A. and Canada 56-; tours of U.S.S.R. 63, 64, 67; Pres. Liszt Soc. 65-; Hon. R.A.M. 70.
Leisure interests: reading, chess.
Compositions: *3 Sonatinas for Piano.*
1 Mallord Street, London, S.W.3, England.

Kenyatta, Jomo (fmrly. Johnstone Kamau Ngengi); Kenyan politician; b. 20 Oct. 1891; ed. Dagoretti Scottish Mission and London School of Economics.
Worked for Nairobi Municipality; returned to Kenya from studies in London 46; Pres. Kenya African Union 47; convicted of managing Mau Mau movement and sentenced to imprisonment 53, released April 59, restricted to Lodwar April 59-April 61; restricted to Maralal April-Aug. 61; Pres. Kenya African Nat. Union (KANU) Aug. 61-, Leader KANU Del. to London Constitutional Conf. Feb.-March 62; mem. Legislative Council 62-; Minister of State for Constitutional Affairs and for Econ. Planning April 62-63; Prime Minister, also Minister for Internal Security and Defence and Foreign Affairs 63-64, Pres. 64-; Hon. Fellow, London School of Econs.; Knight of Grace, Order of St. John of Jerusalem 72; Order of Golden Ark, World Wildlife Fund 74; Hon. LL.D. (East Africa).
Publs. *Facing Mount Kenya, Kenya, the Land of Conflict, My People of Kikuyu, Harambee!*
Office of the President, P.O.B. 30510, Nairobi; State House, P.O.B. 530, Nairobi, Kenya; Home: Gatundu, Kenya.

Kenyon, Dame Kathleen Mary, D.B.E., D.LITT., D.LIT., L.H.D., F.B.A., F.S.A.; British archaeologist; b. 5 Jan. 1906, London; *d.* of Sir Frederic George Kenyon; ed. St. Paul's Girls' School and Somerville Coll., Oxford.
Secretary Inst. of Archaeology 35-48, Council for British Archaeology 44-49; Lecturer Univ. of London Inst. of Archaeology 48-62; Dir. British School of Archaeology in Jerusalem 51-66; Principal, St. Hugh's Coll., Oxford 62-73; has participated in and directed numerous excavations in U.K. and Middle East.
Leisure interest: gardening.
Publs. *Excavations at the Jewry Wall, Leicester* 48, *Samaria-Sebaste I* 42, *III* 57 (joint author), *Beginning in Archaeology* 54, *Digging up Jericho* 57, *Excavations at Jericho I* 60, *II* 65, *Archaeology in the Holy Land* 60, *Amorites and Canaanites* 66, *Jerusalem* 67, *Royal Cities of the Old Testament* 71, *Digging Up Jerusalem* 74.
Rose Hill, Erbistock, Wrexham, Clwyd, LL13 0DE, England.
Telephone: Overton-on-Dee 355.

Keogh, James; American journalist and government official; b. 29 Oct. 1916, Nebraska.
Joined *Omaha Herald* 38, rising to Editor 48-51; contrib. to *Time* 51, Editor 56-68; chief of research, Presidential election campaign 68; special asst. to Pres. Nixon 69-70; Dir. U.S. Information Agency 73-.
Publs. *This is Nixon* 56, *President Nixon and the Press* 72.
United States Information Agency, 1750 Pennsylvania, N.W., Washington, D.C. 20547, U.S.A.

Kępa, Józef; Polish politician; b. 18 May 1928, Rzeczyca, Rawa Mazowiecka district; *s.* of Szczepan Kępa and Rozalia Perek; *m.* Aleksandra Worwińska 1953; one *s.*; ed. Warsaw Univ.
Member, Polish United Workers' Party (PUWP) 48-, mem. Cen. Cttee. 68-, cand. mem. Politburo 70-75, full mem. Dec. 75-; Sec. PUWP District Cttee., Warsaw-Mokotów 59-60; Head, Educ. and Sciences Dept., PUWP Warsaw Cttee., 60-61; Sec. PUWP Warsaw Cttee. 61-67, First Sec. Dec. 67-; Deputy to Seym 69-; Chair. Capital Nat. Council, Warsaw Dec. 73-; Order of Banner of Labour, 1st and 2nd Class; Knight's Cross, Order of Polonia Restituta, Medal of 30th Anniversary of People's Poland and other decorations.
Leisure interests: medals, gathering mushrooms.
Polska Zjednoczona Partia Robotnicza, Nowy Świat 6, 00-497 Warsaw, Poland.

Keppel, Francis, A.B.; American educational administrator; b. 16 April 1916, New York; *s.* of Frederick and Helen T. Keppel; *m.* Edith Moulton Sawin 1941; two *d.*; ed. Harvard Coll., American Acad., Rome.
Secretary, Joint Army and Navy Cttee. on Welfare and Recreation, Washington 41-44; U.S. Army 44-46; Asst. to Provost, Harvard 46-48, Dean, Harvard Graduate School of Education 48-62; U.S. Commr. of Education, U.S. Dept. of Health, Education and Welfare Dec. 62-Oct. 65, Asst. Sec. (for Educ.) 65-66; Chair. of Board Gen. Learning Corpn. 66-74; Chair. Educ. Cttee., Lincoln Center Board of Dirs. 73-; Dir. Program in Educ. Aspen Inst. for Humanistic Studies 74-; Fellow, American Acad. of Arts and Sciences, Vice-Chair. Board of Higher Educ., City Univ. of N.Y. 67-70; mem. Board of Overseers, Harvard Univ. 67-73; Trustee, Carnegie Corpn. 70-.
Publ. *The Necessary Revolution in American Education* 66.
Office: Aspen Institute Education Program, 111 West 50th Street, New York, N.Y. 10020; Home: 984 Memorial Drive, Cambridge, Mass. 02138, U.S.A.

Kerby, William Frederick; American editor and business executive; b. 28 July 1908; ed. Univ. of Michigan.
Staff Corresp., United Press Asscn., Washington, D.C. 30-32; *Wall Street Journal*, Washington 33-35, New York 37-42, Managing Editor 43-44; Exec. Editor Dow Jones publications 45-51, Vice-Pres. Dow Jones and Co. Inc. 51-60; Exec. Vice-Pres. Dow Jones and Co. Inc. and Editorial Dir. Dow Jones publications 61-66, Pres. Dow Jones and Co. Inc. 66-72, Chair. of Board 72-.
22 Cortlandt Street, New York, N.Y. 10007, U.S.A.

Kérékou, Lt.-Col. Mathieu; Benin army officer and politician; b. 2 Sept. 1933, Natitingou; ed. Saint-Raphael Mil. School, France.
Served French Army until 61; joined Dahomey Army 61; Aide-de-camp to Pres. Maga 61-63; took part in mil. coup d'état which removed Pres. Christophe Soglo 67; Chair. Mil. Revolutionary Council 67-68; continued studies at French mil. schools 68-70; Commdr. Ouidah Paratroop Unit and Deputy Chief of Staff 70-72; leader of the military coup d'état which ousted Pres. Ahomadegbe Oct. 72; Pres. and Prime Minister, Minister of Nat. Defence 72-, fmr. Minister of Planning, of Co-ordination of Foreign Aid, Information and Nat. Orientation.
The Presidency, Cotonou, Benin.

Kerensky, Oleg Alexander, C.B.E., F.R.S., D.SC., F.I.C.E., F.I.STRUCT.E., F.INST.H.E., F.W.I.; British consulting engineer; b. 16 April 1905, St. Petersburg, Russia; *s.* of late Alexander Kerensky and Olga Kerensky; *m.* 1st Nathalie Bely 1928, one *s.*; *m.* 2nd Dorothy Harvey 1971; ed. private schools in St. Petersburg and London, and at Northampton Eng. Coll. (now the City Univ.).

Former Junior Asst. to Oxfordshire County Surveyor; Asst. Engineer, later Chief Designer in Bridge Dept. of Dorman Long & Co. Ltd. engaged on design and construction of bridges, power stations and other structures, most notable being Sydney Harbour Bridge, Storstrom Bridge, Lambeth Bridge and S. African Steelworks; Chief Engineer on construction of Wandsworth Bridge, London, and Avonmouth Jetty; in charge of fabrication and assembly in N. Wales of "Buffer Pontoons" and "Beetles" for Mulberry Harbour with Holloway Bros. (London) Ltd.; joined Freeman, Fox and Partners as principal bridge designer engaged on designs of Severn, Forth, Auckland Harbour, Ganga and other bridges; Partner, Freeman Fox & Partners 56-; responsible for Medway Bridge M2 Motorway, Grosvenor Railway Bridge, M5 Motorway (Ross Spur-East Brent), urban devts. in Bristol, Birmingham and London, Erskine Bridge over R. Clyde, motorway bridges in N. Ireland; Dir. Freeman, Fox & Assocs.; fmr. Pres. Inst. of Structural Engineers and Inst. of Highways Engineers; official of other civil engineering orgs.; Chair. Council of Construction Industry Research and Information Asscn.; numerous awards including Telford and Stephenson Gold Medals, Inst. of Civil Engineers.
Leisure interests: bridge and croquet.
Publs. several technical papers and articles.
Office: Abford House (1st floor), 15 Wilton Road, London, S.W.1; Home: 27 Pont Street, London, S.W.1, England.

Keresztury, Dezsö, PH.D.; Hungarian literary historian and writer; b. 6 Sept. 1904, Zalaegerszeg; s. of József Keresztury and Etelka Eöry; m. Mária Seiber 1934; ed. Budapest, Vienna and Berlin.
Lecturer and librarian in Hungarian Inst. of Berlin Univ. 28-36; lecturer in Hungarian Literature, Eötvös Coll. Budapest 35-45, Dir. of Coll. 45-48; Minister of Education 45-47; Chief Librarian of Hungarian Acad. 48-51; Head of Historical Collections in Nat. Széchényi Library until 71; Vice-Pres. Soc. of Hungarian Literary History, World Fed. of Hungarians, and Int. Lenau Soc.; mem. Hungarian Acad. of Sciences; edited selected speeches of Mihály Babits, Géza Laczkó, Károly Pap, the complete works of János Batsányi and János Arany; Banner Order of Hungarian People's Repub. 74; Grillparzer Ring, Vienna 74, Herder Prize 76.
Leisure interests: music, walking, water-colour painting.
Publs. Arany János, Ungarn, A német irodalom kincseskháza, Balaton, Helyünk a világban, A magyar irodalom képeskönyve, A magyar zenetörténet képeskönyve, Magyar Opera és Balett Szcenika, A német elbeszélés mesterei, A német liva kincsesháza Dunántuli hexameterek, Lassul a szél, Emberi Nyelven Festbeleuchtung auf dem Holzmarkt, S mi vagyok én, Uzenet, Orodseg, a Szépség Haszna Egri Breviarium, Égö türelem; revised and adapted two plays by Imre Madách: Mózes and Csák végnapjai and Grillparzer's Medea.
Semmelweis utcá 4, 1052 Budapest V, Hungary.
Telephone: 189-283.

Kermode, (John) Frank, M.A., F.B.A., F.R.S.L.; British university professor; b. 29 Nov. 1919, Douglas, Isle of Man; s. of John Pritchard Kermode and Doris Kennedy; m. Maureen Eccles 1947 (divorced); one s. one d.; ed. Liverpool Univ.
John Edward Taylor Prof., Manchester Univ. 58-65; Winterstoke Prof., Bristol Univ. 65-67; Lord Northcliffe Prof., Univ. Coll., London 67-74; King Edward VII Prof., Cambridge Univ. 74-; Hon. D.H.L. (Chicago); Officier de l'Ordre des Arts et des Sciences.
Publs. Romantic Image 57, The Sense of an Ending 67, Lawrence 73, The Classic 75.
King's College, Cambridge; and 17 York Mansions, Prince of Wales Drive, London, S.W.11, England.
Telephone: Cambridge 50411; 01-622-3840.

Kern, Karl-Heinz, DIPL.JUR.; German diplomatist; b. 18 Feb. 1930, Dresden; s. of Fritz and Elfriede Kern; m. Ursula Bennmann 1952; one s.: ed. Technical Coll., Dresden and Academy for Political Science and Law.
Positions in various regional authorities in German Democratic Repub. until 59; Ministry of Foreign Affairs 59-, Head African Dept. 66-71, Head of G.D.R. Mission in Ghana 62-66, Minister and Chargé d'Affaires 71-73; Amb. to U.K. Dec. 73-; Order of Merit of the Fatherland (G.D.R.) and other decorations.
Leisure interests: sports, reading, music.
Publs. various publs. on foreign affairs.
Embassy of the German Democratic Republic, 34 Belgrave Square, London, SW1X 8QB, England.
Telephone: 01-235-9941.

Kerr, Chester Brooks, B.A.; American publisher; b. 5 Aug. 1913; m. Joan Paterson Mills 1964; ed. La Villa, Lausanne (Switzerland), Univ. School, Cleveland (Ohio) and Yale Univ.
Editor Harcourt, Brace & Co. 36-40; Dir. Atlantic Monthly Press 40-42; Chief Book Div., Office of War Information and Dept. of State 42-46; Vice-Pres. Reynal & Hitchcock 46-47; Sec. Yale Univ. Press 49-59, Dir. 59-; Sec.-Treas. Asscn. of American Univ. Presses 57-59, Pres. 65-67; Consultant to Dept. of State 51, to Ford Foundation 57-65; Dir. New Haven Public Library 54-70; Dir. American Book Publishers' Council 66-69; Exec. Comm. Nat. Book Cttee. 69-; Dir. Franklin Book Program 71-.
Leisure interest: skiing.
Publs. A Report on American University Presses 49, American University Publishing 55.
Yale University Press, 149 York Street, New Haven, Conn. 06511, U.S.A.
Telephone: 203-436-0360.

Kerr, Clark, A.B., M.A., PH.D.; American educator; b. 17 May 1911, Reading, Pa.; s. of Samuel W. and Caroline Clark Kerr; m. Catherine Spaulding 1934; two s. one d.; ed. Swarthmore Coll., Stanford Univ., and Univ. of Calif. (Berkeley).
Assistant, later Assoc. Prof. of Industrial Relations, Univ. of Wash. 40; Assoc. Prof., later Prof. of Industrial Relations, Univ. of Calif. (Berkeley) 45, Chancellor 52; Pres. Univ. of Calif. 58-67; Chair. of Carnegie Comm. on Higher Educ. 67-; Godkin Lecturer, Harvard 63, Marshall Lecturer, Cambridge 67-68; has held various public posts, mainly in the field of labour relations; mem. American Acad. of Arts and Sciences; many hon. degrees.
Leisure interest: gardening.
Publs. Unions, Management, and the Public (with E. W. Bakke) 48, revised 64, 69, Industrialism and Industrial Man (with Dunlop, Harbison and Myers) 60, revised 64, 72, The Uses of University 64 (revised edn. 72), Labour and Management in Industrial Society 64, Marshall, Marx and Modern Times 69.
8300 Buckingham Drive, El Cerrito, Calif. 94530, U.S.A.

Kerr, Deborah Jane; British actress; b. 30 Sept. 1921, Helensburgh, Dunbarton, Scotland; d. of Arthur Kerr-Trimmer and Colleen Smale; m. 1st Anthony Bartley 1945 (divorced 1960), two d.; m. 2nd Peter Viertel 1960, one step-d.; ed. Rossholme Prep., Weston-super-Mare, Northumberland House, Bristol.
Began acting career at Open Air Theatre, Regent's Park 39; first film Contraband, first major role as Jenny Hill in film Major Barbara; went to Hollywood 46; film awards include four New York Drama Critics' Awards, 47 (two), 57, 60; Hollywood Foreign Press Asscn. Awards 56 (for The King and I), 58; Variety Club of G.B. Award 61; six Acad. Award nominations; awards for plays include Donaldson and Sarah Siddons Awards for Tea and Sympathy.
Films include Major Barbara 40, Love on the Dole 40,

Penn of Pennsylvania 40, *Hatter's Castle* 41, *The Day Will Dawn* 41, *The Life and Death of Colonel Blimp* 42, *Perfect Strangers* 44, *Black Narcissus* 45, *I See a Dark Stranger* 45, *The Hucksters* 46, *If Winter Comes* 47; *Edward My Son* 48, *The Prisoner of Zenda* 48, *Young Bess* 49, *King Solomon's Mines* 50, *Quo Vadis* 50, *Rage of The Vulture* 51, *Dream Wife* 52, *From Here to Eternity* 53, *The End of the Affair* 54, *The Proud and the Profane* 55, *The King and I* 56, *Heaven Knows Mr. Allison* 57, *An Affair to Remember* 57, *Separate Tables* 57/58, *The Journey* 58, *The Blessing* 58, *Beloved Infidel* 60, *The Sundowners* 60, *The Innocents* 61, *The Chalk Garden* 63, *The Night of the Iguana* 63, *Marriage on the Rocks* 65, *Gypsy Moths* 68, *The Arrangement* 68/69.

Plays: *Heartbreak House* 43, *Tea and Sympathy* 53 (U.S. tour 54/55), *The Day After the Fair* (U.S. tour 73/74), *Seascape* 74/75, *Souvenir* 75.

Leisure interests: painting, swimming.

Wyhergut, 7250 Klosters, Switzerland.

Kerr, James R.; American business executive; b. 23 Sept. 1917, Las Vegas; *s.* of Louis Alexander and Mary Louise (Lynch) Kerr; *m.* Colleen Warrick 1943; two *s.* two *d.*; ed. Pasadena City Coll.

U.S. Air Force 42-54; Dir. West Coast Office, Avco Corpn. 54-56, Vice-Pres. (Defense Planning), New York Office 56-57, Pres. Lycoming Div. 57-60, Research and Advanced Devt. Div. 58-60, Dir. 59-, Exec. Vice-Pres. 60-61, Pres. and Chief Operating Officer 61-, Chief Exec. Officer 70-; Chair. Avco Broadcasting Corpn. 64; Dir. Avco Delta, Lehman Corpn., etc.; Trustee, Nat. Safety Council; mem. Defense Advisory Council 61, Advisory Cttee. on Finances, Nat. Capital Transportation Agency.

1275 King Street, Greenwich, Conn. 06830; Home: 1175 Muirlands Drive, La Jolla, Calif. 92037, U.S.A.

Kerr, Jean; American writer; b. 1923; *m.* Walter Kerr (*q.v.*) 1943; ed. Catholic Univ. of America.

Publs. *Jenny Kissed Me* (play) 49, *Touch and Go* (play) 50, *King of Hearts* (with Eleanor Brooke) 54, *Please Don't Eat the Daisies* 57, *The Snake has all the Lines* 60, *Mary, Mary* (play) 62, *Poor Richard* (play) 63, *Penny Candy* 70, *Finishing Touches* (play) 73.

1 Beach Avenue, Larchmont, N.Y., U.S.A.

Kerr, Sir John Robert, G.C.M.G., LL.B., Q.C.; Australian lawyer and public official; b. 24 Sept. 1914, Sydney; *s.* of late H. Kerr; *m.* 1st Alison Warstead 1938 (died 1974), one *s.* two *d.*; *m.* 2nd Anne Robson 1975; ed. Fort St. Boys' High School, Sydney Univ.

Admitted to New South Wales Bar 38; war service 39-46, Col. 45-46; Principal, Australian School of Pacific Admin. 46; Organizing Sec. South Pacific Comm. 46-47; Queen's Council (N.S.W.) 53; mem. N.S.W. Bar Council 60-64; Vice-Pres. N.S.W. Bar Asscn. 62-63, Pres. 64; Vice-Pres. Law Council of Australia 62-64, Pres. 64-66; Pres. N.S.W. Marriage Guidance Council 61-62, Industrial Relations Soc. of Australia 64-66, Law Asscn. for Asia and Western Pacific 66-70; Deputy Pres. Trades Practices Tribunal 66-72, Copyright Tribunal 69-72; presided at Third Commonwealth and Empire Law Conf., Sydney, 65; mem. Medical Board of N.S.W. 63-66, Board of the Council on New Guinea Affairs 64-71; Judge of Commonwealth Industrial Court and Judge of Supreme Court of A.C.T. 66-72, Judge of Courts of Marine Inquiry 67-72; Chief Justice, Supreme Court, N.S.W. 72-74; Lieut.-Gov. N.S.W. 73-74; Gov.-Gen. of Australia 74-; Hon Life mem. Law Soc. of England and Wales 65; Hon. mem. American Bar Asscn. 67; K.St. J. 74.

Publs. papers and articles on industrial relations, New Guinea affairs, organization of legal profession, etc.

Government House, Canberra, A.C.T. 2600, Australia.

Kerr, Walter, M.A., B.S.; American drama critic; b. 8 July 1913; *m.* Jean Collins (*q.v.* Jean Kerr) 1943; ed. Northwestern Univ.

Assoc. Prof. Catholic Univ. of America 39-49; Drama Critic *The Commonweal* 49-51, *New York Herald Tribune* 51-66, *New York Times* 66-; Pres. New York Critics Circle 55-56; Hon. LL.D. (St. Mary's, Notre Dame), Hon. D.Litt. (La Salle Univ.); Campion Award 71, Laetare Medal 71, Award of Nat. Inst. of Arts and Letters 72.

Publs. Plays: *Sing Out Sweet Land* 45, *Touch and Go* (with Jean Kerr) 50, *Goldilocks* (with Jean Kerr) 58; also *How Not To Write A Play* 55, *Criticism and Censorship, Pieces at Eight* (essays) 57, *The Decline of Pleasure* 62, *The Theatre in Spite of Itself* 63, *Tragedy and Comedy* 67, *Thirty Plays Hath November* 69, *God on the Gymnasium Floor* 71, *The Silent Clowns* 75.

Office: 230 West 41st Street, New York 10018, U.S.A.

Kerschbaum, Hans, DR.PHIL., DR.-ING. E.H.; retd. German physicist and businessman; b. 19 Nov. 1902; *m.* Elsbet Trick 1927; one *d.*; ed. Stuttgart Inst. of Technology and Munich Univ.

Assistant Munich Univ.; physicist and engineer with Siemens & Halsle AG 29-, mem. Board of Management 42-, Chair. 56-67.

Almeidaweg 25, 813 Starnberg am See, Federal Republic of Germany.

Telephone: 08151-12833.

Kerst, Donald William, PH.D., D.SC.; American professor of physics; b. 1 Nov. 1911, Galena, Ill.; *s.* of Herman Samuel and Lilian (Wetz) Kerst; *m.* Dorothy Birkett 1940; one *s.* one *d.*; ed. Univ. of Wisconsin.

Instructor in Physics, Univ. of Ill. 38, Asst. Prof. 40, Assoc. Prof. 42, Prof. 43; War Work, Los Alamos 43-45; Tech. Dir. Midwestern Univs. Research Asscn. 53-57; with John Jay Hopkins Lab. for Pure and Applied Science, Atomic Div., Gen. Dynamics Corpn. 57-62; E. M. Terry Prof. of Physics, Univ. of Wisconsin 62-; mem. Nat. Acad. of Sciences; Comstock Prize, Nat. Acad. of Sciences, for devt. of betatron 45; John Scott Award 46; John Price Wetherill Medal, Franklin Inst., for devt. of betatron 50; Dr. h.c. (Univ. of São Paulo, Brazil).

Leisure interests: sailing, skiing, canoeing, swimming. Major works: devt. of betatron, devt. of spiral sector accelerator.

Department of Physics, University of Wisconsin, Physics-Astronomy Building, 1150 University Avenue, Madison, Wis. 53706; 1506 Wood Lane, Madison, Wis. 53705, U.S.A.

Telephone: 238-8142.

Kersten, Otto; German trade unionist; b. 24 Nov. 1928, Alt-Jessnitz; *m.*; one *s.* one *d.*; ed. Univs. of Rostock and Berlin.

Joined German Social Democratic Party 46; worked in foreign dept. of a bank in E. Berlin 50-52; political imprisonment 53-56; moved to Fed. Germany and worked in Cen. Fed. Bank, Frankfurt/M. 56; Trade Union Sec. European Trade Union Secr. 60, also Exec. Gen. Sec. Consumers' Cttee., EEC; Dir. Int. Dept., Deutscher Gewerkschaftsbund 65; mem. Supervisory Board, Hoesch Huttenwerk AG until April 73; has served on numerous boards, comms. and cttees., including German Foundation for Developing Countries, German Inst. for Devt. Policies, German Council of European Movement, etc.; Gen. Sec. ICFTU Jan. 72-.

International Confederation of Free Trade Unions, 37-41 rue Montagne aux Herbes Potagères, B-1000 Brussels, Belgium.

Kerwin, Commdr. Joseph P.; American astronaut; b. 19 Feb. 1932, Oak Park, Ill.; *s.* of Mr. and Mrs. Edward M. Kerwin; *m.* Shirley A. Good; three *d.*; ed. Coll. of Holy Cross, Worcester, Mass., Northwestern Univ. Medical School, Chicago, Ill. and U.S. Navy School of Aviation Medicine.

Intern, District of Columbia Gen. Hospital, Washington, D.C.; Served U.S. Navy Medical Corps since July

58; selected as NASA scientist-astronaut 65; crew mem. *Skylab* 73; Fellow, Aerospace Medical Asscn.; mem. American Medical Asscn., Aircraft Owners and Pilots Asscn.
Leisure interests: reading, classical music.
NASA Johnson Space Center, Houston, Tex. 77058, U.S.A.

Keserü, Mrs. Etelka; Hungarian economist and politician; b. 26 Aug. 1925, Gyoma; ed. Univ. of Political Economy.
Joined Communist Party 45; Deputy Minister of Light Industry 67-71, Minister 71-.
Ministry of Light Industry, Budapest II, Fő-utca 68, Hungary.
Telephone: 154-090.

Kessel, Joseph; French writer; b. 10 Feb. 1898; ed. Sorbonne, Paris.
Served French army 14-18 war; wrote for *Le Matin*, *Figaro* and *Paris Soir*; joined Free French 40; Commandeur de la Légion d'Honneur; Lauréat de l'Académie Française 27, mem. Académie Française 62-; Prix des Ambassadeurs 58.
Publs. *La Steppe Rouge, Les Captifs, Belle de Jour, L'Equipage, Vent de Sable, Les Rois Aveugles, Fortune Carrée, Les Enfants de la Chance, Le Bataillon du Ciel, Le Tour du Malheur, L'Armée des Ombres, Les Coeurs Purs, Mermoz, La Piste Fauve, La Vallée du Rubis, Témoin parmi les Hommes, Le Lion, Les Mains du Miracle* 60, *Les Alcooliques Anonymes* 63, *Tous n'étaient pas des Anges* 63, *Pour l'Honneur* 64, *Le Coup de Grâce* 65, *Terre d'Amour et de Feu* 65, *Les Cavaliers* (novel) 67, *Les Fils de l'Impossible, les Rois Aveugles* 70, *Des Hommes* 72, *Le Petit Ane blanc* 73.
18 rue Quentin-Bauchart, Paris 8e, France.

Kesten, Hermann; American (b. German) writer; b. 28 Jan. 1900; s. of Isidor Kesten and Ida Tisch; m. Toni Warowitz Kesten 1928; ed. Erlangen, Frankfurt and Rome Univs.
Chief Editor Gustav Kiepenheuer Verlag, Berlin 27-33, Allert de Lange Verlag, Amsterdam 33-40; Pres. PEN Club of Fed. Republic of Germany 72; Kleist Prize 28, Nuremberg Prize 54, Premio di Calabria 69, Büchner Prize 74.
Leisure interests: travelling, reading, writing.
Publs. *Josef Breaks Free* 27, *Happy Man* 31, *Ferdinand and Isabella* 36, *I The King, Philip II* 38, *The Children of Guernica* 39, *The Twins of Nuremberg* 46 (novels), *Copernicus and His World* 45, *Casanova* 52 (biography), *Die fremden Götter* 49, *Ein Sohn des Glücks* 56, *Abenteuer eines Moralisten* 61, *Die Zeit der Narren* 66, *Ein Mann von sechzig Jahren* 72, (novels); *Dichter im Café* 59, *Meine Freunde die Poeten* 60, *Filialen des Parnass* 61 (essays), *Die 30 Erzählungen* 62, *Deutsche Literaturim Exil* 64, *Der Gerechte* 67, *Die Lust am Leben* (essays) 68, *Ein Optimist* (essays) 70, *Revolutionäre mit Geduld* (essays) 73, *Ich bin der ich bin* (poems) 74.
c/o Gina Strauss, 3g 499 Fort Washington Avenue, New York, N.Y. 10033, U.S.A.; 00198 Rome, Via Brescia 29, Italy.
Telephone: 928-3400 (New York); 8459651 (Rome).

Keswick, Henry Neville Lindley, B.A.; British merchant; b. 29 Sept. 1938, Shanghai, China; s. of Sir William Keswick; ed. Eton and Trinity Coll., Cambridge.
Commissioned in Scots Guards; joined Jardine, Matheson & Co. Ltd. in Hong Kong 61, Dir. 67-75, Senior Man. Dir. and Chair. 72-75; Chair. Hong Kong Land Co. Ltd., Jardine Fleming & Co. Ltd., Textile Alliance Ltd., City Hotels Ltd. (all Hong Kong) until April 75; Chair. Matheson & Co. Ltd. (London) and subsidiaries July 75-; Proprietor, *The Spectator* July 75-; Dir. MacMillan Bloedel Ltd. (Canada), British Bank of Middle East, Sun Alliance & London Assurance Ltd. 75-.
Leisure interest: country pursuits.

Matheson & Co. Ltd., 3 Lombard Street, London, EC3V 9AQ; Home: 10 Egerton Place, London, SW3 2EF, England.

Keswick, Sir John, K.C.M.G.; British merchant banker; b. 1906; s. of late Henry Keswick; ed. Eton and Trinity Coll., Cambridge.
Joined Jardine, Matheson & Co. Ltd. 29, Dir. 37; served in Ministry of Econ. Warfare during Second World War, and in Embassy, Chungking, later becoming Political Liaison Officer on staff of Earl Mountbatten at SEAC; Jardine, Matheson & Co., Shanghai until 50; Chair. British and Int. Chambers of Commerce, Shanghai until 50; Man. Dir. Jardine, Matheson & Co., Hong Kong 51-56; Dir. Matheson & Co. Ltd. (U.K.) 56-, Chair. 66-70; Dir. Jardine Matheson & Co. Ltd. Hong Kong 61-, Chair. 71-72; Pres. Sino-British Trade Council 61-; Dir. Barclays Bank Ltd., Yorkshire Bank Ltd. (Deputy Chair.), Sun Alliance and London Insurance Ltd., Mercantile Credit Co. Ltd.; Chair. China Asscn.; mem. Cttee. Hong Kong Asscn.
3 Lombard Street, London, EC3V 9AQ; Home: 5 Chester Place, London, NW1 4NB, England.
Telephone: 01-626-6555.

Ketelaar, Jan Arnold Albert, PH.D.; Netherlands university professor; b. 21 April 1908, Amsterdam; s. of Albert Jans Ketelaar and L. C. M. Struycken; m. Sytske Bessem 1949; three s.; ed. Univ. of Amsterdam, and California Inst. of Technology, Pasadena.
Priv. doz. Chemical Crystallography, Univ. of Leiden 36-40, Lecturer in Physical Chemistry 40-41; Prof. of Physical Chemistry and Chemical Thermodynamics, Univ. of Amsterdam 41-60; Visiting Prof. of Chemistry, Brown Univ., Providence, R.I. 58-59; Prof. of Electrochemistry, Univ. of Amsterdam 60-; Scientific Adviser AKZO, Arnhem; mem. Royal Netherlands Acad. of Sciences, and Nat. Board of Educ.
Leisure interest: gardening.
Publs. *Monomorphe overgangen in de kristalstructuren van zilverkwikjodide, natriumnitraat en aluminium fluoride* 33, *De Chemische Binding* 47, 52 and 66, *Physische Scheikunde* 50, *Chemical Constitution* 53, 58, *Liaisons et propriétés chimiques* 60, *Chemische Konstitution* 64.
Markeloseweg 91, Ryssen, Netherlands.
Telephone: 05480-2841.

Kety, Seymour S., M.D.; American professor of psychiatric research; b. 25 Aug. 1915, Philadelphia; s. of Louis and Ethel Kety; m. Josephine Gross 1940; one s. one d.; ed. Univ. of Pennsylvania, post-doctoral Harvard Medical School and Mass. General Hospital.
Instructor, Asst. Prof., Univ. of Pa. Medical School 43-48; Prof. of Clinical Physiology, Univ. of Pennsylvania 48-51; Scientific Dir., Nat. Insts. of Mental Health and Neurological Diseases 51-56, Chief, Laboratory of Clinical Sciences 56-61, 62-67; Henry Phipps Prof. of Psychiatry, Johns Hopkins School of Medicine 61-62; Prof. of Psychiatry, Harvard Medical School 67-; Dir. Psychiatric Research Laboratories, Mass. Gen. Hospital 67-; Editor-in-Chief *Journal of Psychiatric Research* 61-; past Pres. Asscn. for Research in Nervous and Mental Disease, American Psychopathological Asscn.; mem. Nat. Acad. of Sciences, American Physiological Soc., American Soc. Pharmaceutical and Experimental Therapy; many awards including Distinguished Service Award, Dept. of Health Educ. and Welfare 58, McAlpin Medal, Nat. Asscn. for Mental Health 72, Kovalenko Award, Nat. Acad. of Sciences 73.
Leisure interests: music, art, sailing.
Publs. *Measurement of human cerebral blood flow and metabolism* 48, *Theory of exchange of diffusible substances between capillaries and tissues* 51, *Biochemical studies in schizophrenia* 59, *The heuristic aspect of psychiatry* 61, *Genetic-environmental interactions in the transmission of*

schizophrenia 68, *The biogenic amines in arousal, emotion and learning* 69.
Psychiatric Research Laboratories, Research Building, Massachusetts General Hospital, Fruit Street, Boston, Mass. 02114, U.S.A
Telephone: 617-726-8830.

Keuneman, Pieter Gerald Bartholomeus, M.A.; Ceylonese politician; b. 3 Oct. 1917, Colombo; s. of Arthur E. and Marjorie E. Keuneman; ed. Royal Coll., Colombo, Univ. Coll., Colombo, Pembroke Coll., Cambridge and Gray's Inn, London.
Worked briefly as journalist in London; Asst. Editor, *Ceylon Daily News* 40-; founder mem. and Gen. Sec. Ceylon Communist Party (now Communist Party of Sri Lanka) 42-73, Chair. 73-; mem. Parl. for Colombo Central 47-; Minister of Housing and Construction May 70-.
Leisure interests: swimming, music, reading.
Publs. several books, pamphlets and articles on socialism and political and economic problems of Sri Lanka.
Ministry of Housing and Construction, Colombo 1; Central Headquarters, Communist Party of Sri Lanka, 91 Cotta Road, Colombo 8; Home: 8/2 27th Lane, Colombo 3, Sri Lanka.
Telephone: 31466 (Ministry); 93855 (Communist Party H.Q.); 23620 (Home).

Keutcha, Jean; Cameroonian civil servant and politician; b. June 1923, Bangangté; *m.*; three *c.*; ed. Ecole Supérieure d'Agriculture de Yaoundé.
Chef de Cabinet, Minister of State with Special Responsibility 57, subsequently Chef de Cabinet, Sec. of State with responsibility for Information, Posts and Telecommunications; Asst. to Chief of Bamiléké Region 59; Sub-Prefect, Bafoussam 60; Prefect of Mifi, subsequently of Menoua 62-64; Sec. of State for Public Works 64, subsequently Sec. of State for Rural Devt. and Sec. of State for Educ.; Minister of Foreign Affairs 71-72, 75-, of Agriculture 72-75; Commdr. Ordre Camerounais de la Valeur, Grand Croix, Légion d'Honneur, Grand Officier de l'Ordre National Gabonais, etc.
Publ. *Le Guide Pratique pour la Taille du Caféier Arabica.*
Ministère des Affaires Etrangères, Yaoundé, Cameroon.

Keynes, Sir Geoffrey Langdon, M.A., LL.D., D.LITT., M.D., F.R.C.P., F.R.C.S., F.R.C.O.G.; British surgeon and bibliographer; b. 25 March 1887, Cambridge; s. of John Neville Keynes and Ada Florence Brown; *m.* Margaret Darwin 1917 (died 1974); four s. (q.v. Richard Keynes); ed. Rugby and Pembroke Coll., Cambridge.
Served in R.A.M.C. 14-18; Chief Asst. St. Bartholomew's Hospital 20; Hunterian Prof. Royal Coll. Surgeons 23, 29 and 45; mem. Council R.C.S. 44-52; Hon. Librarian, R.C.S.; Consulting Surgeon St. Bartholomew's Hospital, New End Thyroid Clinic and City of London Truss Society; Sir Arthur Sims Travelling Commonwealth Prof. 56; Acting Air Vice-Marshal and Consultant in Surgery, R.A.F. 39; Trustee Nat. Portrait Gallery 42-66, Chair. 58; Founder and Chair. William Blake Trust 49; Pres. Bibliographical Soc. of London 53-54; Harveian Orator, Royal Coll. of Physicians 58-67; Wilkins Lecturer, Royal Soc. 67; James Tait Black Memorial Prize 66, Osler Orator Royal Coll. of Physicians 68, Gold Medal for Services, Royal Coll. Surgeons 69.
Publs. *Blood Transfusion* 22 and 49, *Bibliography of John Donne* 14, 32, 58 and 73, *Bibliography of William Blake* 21, *Bibliography of Sir Thomas Browne* 24 and 68, *Bibliography of William Harvey* 28 and 53, *Bibliography of Jane Austen* 29, *Bibliography of William Hazlitt* 31, *Bibliography of John Evelyn* 37 and 68, *Bibliography of John Ray* 50; Editor of writings of William Blake 25, 27, 57 and 66, Sir Thomas Browne 28, 64, 68 and Izaak Walton 29, *Bibliography of Rupert Brooke* 54, 59,

Bibliography of Robert Hooke 60, *Bibliography of Siegfried Sassoon* 62, *Dr. Timothie Bright* 62, *Life of William Harvey* 66, *Letters of Rupert Brooke* (editor) 68, *Bibliography of Sir William Petty* 71, *Bibliography of Bishop George Berkeley* 75.
Lammas House, Brinkley, Newmarket, Suffolk, England.
Telephone: Stechworth 268.

Keynes, Richard Darwin, M.A., PH.D., SC.D., F.R.S.; British scientist; b. 14 Aug. 1919, London; s. of Sir Geoffrey Keynes (q.v.) and the late Margaret Elizabeth Darwin; *m.* Anne Pinsent Adrian; four s.; ed. Oundle School and Trinity Coll., Cambridge.
Temporary Experimental Officer, Anti-Submarine Establishment and Admiralty Signals Establishment 40-45; Demonstrator, later Lecturer in Physiology Univ. of Cambridge 49-60; Research Fellow, Trinity Coll., Cambridge 48-52; Fellow of Peterhouse, Cambridge, and Dir. of Studies in Medicine 52-60; Head of Physiology Dept., Agricultural Research Council Inst. of Animal Physiology, Babraham 60-65, Dir. of Inst. 65-73; Prof. of Physiology, Univ. of Cambridge 73-; Fellow of Churchill Coll., Cambridge 61-, Fellow of Eton 63-.
Leisure interest: sailing.
3 Herschel Road, Cambridge, England.
Telephone: Cambridge 53107.

Keys, David Arnold, S.M., PH.D., D.SC., LL.D., F.R.S.C.; Canadian physicist; b. 4 Nov. 1890, Toronto; s. of Prof. David Reid and Erskine McLean Keys; *m.* May I. Freeze 1921; one s.; ed. Upper Canada Coll., Univs. of Munich and Toronto (Trinity Coll.), Harvard Univ. and Corpus Christi Coll., Cambridge.
Fellow in Physics Univ. of Toronto 15-16; Physicist, British Admiralty 18-19; Austin Teaching Fellow, Harvard Univ 19-20; Sheldon Travelling Fellow (to Cambridge) 20-21; Asst. Cavendish Laboratory 21-22; Asst. Prof. McGill Univ. 22-26, Associate Prof. 26-29, Prof. 29-41, Macdonald Prof. of Physics 41-47; Dir. of R.C.A.F. Radio Course at McGill Univ. 41-43, ditto Army Course 43-44; mem. of Council, Nat. Research Council, Ottawa 45-55; Vice-Pres. Scientific Nat. Research Council of Canada in charge of Atomic Energy Project, Chalk River 47-55; Scientific Adviser to the Pres., Atomic Energy of Canada Ltd. 53-65; Hon. D Sc. (McMaster, McGill, Toronto and Ottawa Univs.); LL.D. (Mount Allison and Carleton Univs.); Hon. Fellow, Trinity Coll., Toronto; Doctor of Humanities, Lawrence Inst. of Technology 59; Hon. mem. Engineering Inst. of Canada 59; Hon. Fellow, Chemical Inst. of Canada 60; Canadian Asscn. of Physicists 1964 Gold Medal; Hon. mem. Royal Canadian Inst. 67; Canadian Service Medal 68; Fellow, American Physical Soc., American Asscn. for Advancement of Science.
Leisure interests: gardening, golf, writing.
Publs. *Applied Geophysics* (with A. S. Eve) 29 (revised edn. 54), *College Physics* (with others) 35 (revised edn., with Sutton 55).
P.O.B. 452, Deep River, Ont., Canada.

Khachaturov, Tigran Sergeyevich; Soviet economist; b. 6 Oct. 1906, Moscow; *m.* 1st Vera Sheremetyeva 1930 (deceased), 2nd Alexandra Demyanovich 1962; two *d.*; ed. Moscow Univ.
Department of Transport, U.S.S.R. Cen. Statistical Board 26-29; Research Inst. of Rail Transport Econs. 29-32; Asst. Prof., Prof., Inst. of Railway Engineers 31-54; Head of Dept., Dir. All Union-Research Inst. of Rail Transport 42-49; mem. C.P.S.U. 45-; Dir. Inst. of Complex Transport Problems, U.S.S.R. Acad. of Sciences 55-59; Head of Dept., Inst. of Econs., U.S.S.R. Acad. of Sciences 59-66; Chair. Scientific Council of Effectiveness of Investment Problems, Acad. of Sciences 57-; Corresp. mem. U.S.S.R. Acad. of Sciences 43-66, full mem. 66-; Chief Editor *Voprosy Ekonomiki*

(Problems of Econ.) 66-; Academician-Sec. Dept. of Econs., U.S.S.R. Acad. of Sciences 67-71; Chair. Asscn. Soviet Econ. Scientific Insts. 68-; mem. Exec. Cttee. Int. Econ. Asscn. 69-74, Adviser 75-; Hon. mem. Hungarian Acad. of Sciences 70-; Prof. Moscow Univ. 71-; Deputy Chair. Comm. for Productive Forces and Natural Resources Research, U.S.S.R. Acad. of Sciences 71-; Order of Labour Red Banner (four times), Order of Red Star, Order of October Revolution 75 and other awards.
Leisure interests: gardening, music, skiing.
Publs. include: *Allocation of Transport* 39, *Ways of Transport Development* 41, *Principles of Transport Economics* 46, *Railway Transport of U.S.S.R.* 52, *Economics of Transport* 59, *Economic Effectiveness of Investments* 64, *Soviet Economy at the Present Stage* 75; 250 other books, booklets and articles.
U.S.S.R. Academy of Sciences, 14 Leninsky prospekt, Moscow; Home: Ul. acad. Petrovskogo 3, Apt. 30, Moscow, U.S.S.R.
Telephone: 203-96-71; 139-26-75; 232-35-04.

Khachaturyan, Aram Ilych, D.SC.; Soviet composer; b. 6 June 1903, Tbilisi, Georgia; s. of Ilya and Kamash Khachaturyan; m. Nina Makarova 1940; one s. one d.; ed. Gnesin Music School (Moscow) and Moscow Conservatoire.
Studied cello and composition under M. F. Gnesin and N. Y. Myaskovsky; Sec. Union of Soviet Composers; mem. C.P.S.U. 43-; Prof. Moscow Conservatoire 51-; Hon. Academician of Acad. St. Cecilia (Rome) 60; Hon. Prof. of Conservatoire in Mexico; mem. of the Acad. of Sciences of the Armenian S.S.R.; Corresp. mem. of the Acad. of Arts of the German Democratic Repub.; mem. Presidium Union of Soviet Socs. of Friendship and Cultural Relations with Foreign Countries; Pres. Soviet Asscn. of Friendship and Cultural Relations with Latin America; Deputy to U.S.S.R. Supreme Soviet until 66; State Prizes 41, 43, 46, 50, 65, 71; People's Artist of the Georgian S.S.R., Armenian S.S.R. and U.S.S.R. 54; Merited Worker of Arts of the Uzbek S.S.R.; Lenin Prize 59; Order of Lenin (twice), Order of Red Banner of Labour (twice); Hero of Socialist Labour 73, and prizes from France, Egypt, Hungary, Romania, Bulgaria and others.
Leisure interests: theatre and books.
Works include: *Poem for Piano* 27, *Trio for Piano, Violin and Clarinet* 32, *Toccata* 32, *Violin and Piano Sonata* 32, *Dance Suite* 33, *Piano Concerto* 36, *Poem to Stalin* 38, *Violin Concerto* 40, *First Symphony* 34, *Second Symphony* 43, *Gayane* 43, *Masquerade Suite* 44, *Cello Concerto*, **Three Concert Arias for Soprano and Orchestra** 46, *Symphony Poem* 47, composed music for film *Battle of Stalingrad* 49, *Suite from the music to "Valencian Widow"* 49, *Solemn Poem* 50, *Spartacus* (ballet) 54, *Ode of Joy* (soloist, chorus and orchestra) 56, *Suite from the music to the play "Lermontov"* 57, *Sonatina for Piano* 58, *Rhapsody for Violin and Orchestra* 60, *Ballade for Bass with Orchestra* 60, *Ballad about the Homeland* 61, *Piano Sonata* 61, *Concerto and Rhapsody for Cello and Orchestra* 65.
Union of Soviet Composers, Ulitsa Nezhdanovoi 8-10, Moscow, U.S.S.R.

Khachaturyan, Karen Surenovich; Soviet composer; b. 19 Sept. 1920, Moscow; ed. Moscow Conservatoire.
Member Exec. Cttee., Soviet Composers' Union; has participated in int. festivals.
Principal compositions: Sonata for Violin and Piano 47, Sinfonietta 49, *By the Lonely Willow* (Cantata) 50, Youth Overture 51, Symphony No. 1 54, *A Simple Girl* (Operetta) 59, *Friendship* (Overture for symphony orchestra) 61, Sonata for 'Cello and Piano 62; incidental music for cartoon films.
R.S.F.S.R. Composers' Union, Ulitsa Nezhdanovoi 8-10, Moscow, U.S.S.R.

Khaddam, Abdel Halim; Syrian politician.
Minister of the Economy and Foreign Trade 69-70; Deputy Prime Minister and Minister of Foreign Affairs Nov. 70-; mem. Regional Command, Baath Party May 71-.
Ministry of Foreign Affairs, Damascus, Syria.

Khadduri, Majid, B.A., PH.D.; Iraqi educationist and writer: b. 27 Sept. 1909, Mosul, Iraq; m. Majdia Khadduri 1942; one s. one d.; ed. American Univ. of Beirut and Univ. of Chicago.
Sec.-Treas. Baghdad P.E.N. Club; mem. American Society of Int. Law; Iraqi Del. to the 14th Conf. of the P.E.N. Clubs in Buenos Aires 36; Adviser to the Iraq Del. at the San Francisco Conf. 45; Visiting Lecturer in Near Eastern History at Indiana Univ. 47-48; former Prof. Modern Middle-Eastern History at the Higher Teachers' Coll., Baghdad, Iraq 48-49; taught Middle East politics at Chicago and Harvard Univs. 49-50; Prof. Middle East Studies, Johns Hopkins Univ. 50-; Dir. of Research and Education, Middle East Inst. 50-; Visiting Middle East Prof., Columbia Univ.; mem. American Pol. Science Asscn. and Pres. Shaybani Soc. of Int. Law (Washington); Order of Rafidain (Iraq).
Publs. *The Liberation of Iraq from the Mandate* (in Arabic) 35, *The Law of War and Peace in Islam* 41, *The Government of Iraq* 44, *The System of Government in Iraq* (in Arabic) 46, *Independent Iraq* 51, *War and Peace in the Law of Islam* 55, *Islamic Jurisprudence* 61, *Modern Libya* 63, *The Islamic Law of Nations* 66, *Republican Iraq* 69, *Political Trends in the Arab World* 70, *Arab Contemporaries* 73.
4454 Tindall Street, N.W., Washington 16, D.C., U.S.A.
Telephone: 244-4454.

Khain, Viktor Yefimovich, D.SC.; b. 26 Feb. 1914, Baku; s. of Sophia and Yefim Khain; m. Valentina Kuzmina 1949; two s.; ed. Azerbaizhan Industrial Inst.
Geologist at oil fields, Azerbaizhan 35-39; Assoc. Azerbaizhan Oil Research Inst. 39-41; army service 41-45; mem. C.P.S.U. 43-; Senior Assoc. Inst. of Geology, Acad. of Sciences, Azerbaizhan S.S.R. 45-54; Prof. Azerbaizhan Industrial Inst. 49-57; Head of Dept. Museum of Earth Sciences, Moscow Univ. 54-; Senior Assoc., Vernadsky Inst. of Geochemistry and Analytical Chem., U.S.S.R. Acad. of Sciences 57-71; Prof. Geology Dept., Moscow Univ. 60-; Sec.-Gen. Subcomm. for the Tectonic Map of the World, Int. Geological Congress 72-; Senior Assoc., Geological Inst., U.S.S.R. Acad. of Sciences 72-; Corresp. mem. U.S.S.R. Acad. of Sciences 66-; mem. Moscow Soc. of Naturalists, Soc. Géologique de France; Hon. mem. Bulgarian Geological Soc.; Order of Red Labour Banner; Hon. D.Sc. Univ. P. et M. Curie, Paris, 75.
Publs. include: *Geotectonic Principles of Oil Prospecting in Baku* 54, *General Geotectonics* 64 (2nd edn. 73), *Regional Geotectonics*, Vol. I 71.
Department of Geology, Moscow State University, Moscow B-234, U.S.S.R.
Telephone: 139-11-09; 203-35-76.

Khalaf, Kadhim M., B.A.; Iraqi diplomatist; b. 20 April 1922; ed. American Univ. of Beirut and Inst. des Hautes Etudes Internationales, Paris.
Member staff Perm. Mission of Iraq to UN 48; Del. to numerous confs.; Acting Rep. for Iraq to UN 55-58; Chargé d'Affaires, Bonn 59-60; Dir.-Gen. UN Dept., Ministry of Foreign Affairs, Iraq 62-64; Under-Sec. of Ministry of Foreign Affairs 64-66, 67-68; Perm. Rep. of Iraq to UN 66-67; Amb. to U.K. 68-71.
Leisure interests: tennis, Arabic poetry.
Ministry of Foreign Affairs, Baghdad, Iraq.

Khalatbary, Abbas Ali, PH.D.; Iranian diplomatist; b. 1912, Teheran; s. of late Nasrollah Khalatbary and Iran Ghadimy Navai; m. Manzar Asfia 1942; one s. three d.; ed. Univ. of Paris.
Ministry of Foreign Affairs 42-; Second Sec., Berne 45;

First Sec., Warsaw 47; Acting Head, Dept. of Int. Orgs. 50, Dir. 51; Counsellor, Paris 53; Dir. Third Political Div. 57; Dir. Protocol Dept. 58; Amb. to Poland, Minister, Romania 59; Sec.-Gen. Cen. Treaty Org. (CENTO) 62-68; Under-Sec. for Political Affairs 68-70, Deputy Minister of Foreign Affairs 70, Minister Sept. 71-; Alt. mem. Del. to UN Gen. Assembly 51, mem. 13th Session; del. to Gen. Council of UN Relief, Rehabilitation Admin. (UNRRA) 60; Head of del. to UN Gen. Assembly 71, to Summit Islamic Conf., Lahore 74.
Leisure interests: horse-riding, reading.
Imperial Iranian Ministry of Foreign Affairs, Teheran; Home: Farmanieh, Shemiran, 26 Benafsheh Street, Teheran, Iran.

Khalid, Mansour, LL.D.; Sudanese diplomatist and lawyer; b. 17 Jan. 1931, Sudan; ed. Univs. of Khartoum, Pennsylvania and Paris.
Began his career as an attorney, Khartoum 57-59; Legal officer, UN, N.Y. 62-63; Deputy UN resident rep., Algeria 64-65; Bureau of Relations with Member States, UNESCO, Paris 65-69; Visiting Prof. of Int. Law, Univ. of Colorado 68; Minister of Youth and Social Affairs, Sudan 69-71; Chair. of Del. of Sudan to UN Gen. Assembly, Special Consultant and Personal Rep. of UNESCO Dir.-Gen. for UNWRA fund-raising mission 70; Perm. Rep. of Sudan to UN 71; Minister of Foreign Affairs 71-75, of Educ. Jan. 75-.
Ministry of Education, Khartoum, Sudan.

Khalid ibn Abdul Aziz; King of Saudi Arabia; b. 1913; brother of late King Faisal ibn Abdul Aziz; ed. religious schools.
Appointed Asst. to his brother, Prince Faisal 34; rep. of Saudi Arabia to various int. confs.; Vice-Pres. Council of Ministers 62-75; became Crown Prince 65; succeeded to the throne on death of his brother 25 March 75; Pres. Council of Ministers March 75-, Minister of Foreign Affairs March-Oct. 75.
Royal Palace, Riyadh, Saudi Arabia.

Khalidi, Ismail Raghib, B.A., M.A., PH.D.; Saudi Arabian United Nations official; b. 13 Nov. 1916; ed. St. George's School and Govt. Arab Coll., Jerusalem, American Univ. of Beirut, Michigan Univ. and Columbia Univ., U.S.A.
Assistant Script Editor, Radio Arabic Desk, U.S. Office of War Information, New York 42-44; Sec.-Gen., Inst. of Arab-American Affairs, New York 44-47; New York Corresp. for *Al Misri* (Cairo daily) 46-47; Assoc. Dir. Asia Inst. for Arabic Studies, New York 47-48; Adviser to Saudi Arabian Del., UN 49; mem. UN Secretariat 49-, UN Mission to Libya 50-52, UN Observer, British N. Cameroons 60-61; Senior Political Affairs Officer, UN Security Council Affairs Div. 55-; Principal Sec. UN Comm. for Unification and Rehabilitation of Korea (UNCURK) 62-65.
Publ. *Constitutional Development in Libya* 56.
121 Lorraine Avenue, Mount Vernon, N.Y. 10553, U.S.A.

Khalifa, Sirr el Khatim, G.C.M.G.; Sudanese educationist and politician; b. 1 Jan. 1919, Dueim; s. of Khalifa el Hassan and Nafisa el Fekki; m. Zahra el Fadil 1964; one s. three d.; ed. Gordon Coll., Khartoum.
Former teacher, Gordon Coll., Khartoum and Bakhter-Ruda Inst.; Head Khartoum Technical Inst. 60-64, 65-66; Deputy Under-Sec. Ministry of Educ. 64; Prime Minister 64-65; Amb. to Italy 66-68, to U.K. 68-69; Minister of Higher Educ. and Research 72-Jan. 75.
Ministry of Higher Education and Research, Khartoum, Sudan.
Telephone: 81267.

Khalifa bin Hamad al-Thani, Sheikh; Emir of Qatar; b. 1934.
Deputy Ruler of Qatar, Prime Minister and Minister of Finance and Petroleum Affairs Sept. 71-Feb. 72;

deposed his cousin Sheikh Ahmad and took office as Emir of Qatar Feb. 72.
The Royal Palace, Doha, Qatar.

Khalifa, Sheikh Hamed bin Isa al-; Heir Apparent to His Highness the Emir of Bahrain; b. 28 Jan. 1950; ed. Secondary School, Manama, Applegarth Coll., Godalming, Mons Officer Cadet School, Aldershot, England, and U.S. Army Command and Gen. Staff Coll., Fort Leavenworth, Kansas, U.S.A.
Founder, Commdr. Bahrain Defence Force, Head Defence Dept., Govt. of Bahrain 68-; mem. State Admin. Council 70-71; Minister of State for Defence 71-; awarded several foreign decorations.
Private Office of the Heir Apparent, Court of the Emir, Rifa'a Palace, Manama, Bahrain.

Khalifa, Sheikh Khalifa bin Sulman al-; Bahrain politician; b. 1935.
Son of the late Sheikh Sulman and brother of the ruler, Sheikh Isa; Dir. of Finance and Pres. of Electricity Board 61; Pres. Council of Admin. 66-70; Pres. State Council 70-73, Prime Minister 73-.
National Assembly, Manama, Bahrain.

Khalil, Mohamed Kamal El-Din; Egyptian diplomatist.
Formerly Dir. of Research Dept., U.A.R. Ministry of Foreign Affairs; Chargé d'Affaires, London 60-61; Dir. North American Dept., U.A.R., Ministry of Foreign Affairs 61-64; Ambassador to Jordan 64-66, to Sudan 66-71; Under-Sec. of State for Foreign Affairs 71-.
Publ. *The Arab States and the Arab League* (2 vols.) 62.
Ministry of Foreign Affairs, Cairo; and 1103 Sh. El-Nil, Garden City, Cairo, Egypt.

Khama, Sir Seretse, K.B.E., B.A., M.P.; Botswana politician and farmer; b. 1 July 1921; m. Ruth Williams 1948; four c.; ed. Fort Hare Univ., Witwatersrand Univ., South Africa, Balliol Coll., Oxford.
Legal studies, London; son of Sekgoma II (d. 25), Chief of Bamangwato Tribe, Bechuanaland Protectorate; his uncle, Tshekedi Khama, Regent of Bamangwato Tribe in Seretse Khama's minority 26-50; dispute over Chieftancy of Bamangwato Tribe resulted in Seretse Khama's banishment 50; returned to Bechuanaland and renounced all claim to Chieftancy 56; Pres. Bechuanaland Democratic Party; mem. Legislative Council and Executive Council 61-65; mem. Legislative Assembly and Prime Minister of Bechuanaland 65-66; mem. of Parl. and Pres. of the Republic of Botswana 66-; Hon. LL.D., Hon. Ph.D.
Private Bag 001, Gaborone, Botswana.

Khammao, H.R.H. Prince; Laotian diplomatist; b. 23 Sept. 1911, Luang Prabang; s. of Sisavang Vong, King of Laos; m. Princess Khamla; ed. Lycée Albert Sarraut, Hanoi and Univ. of Montpellier.
Secretary-General of the Royal Palace 41-42; Chief, Luang Prabang Province 48-51; King's Attorney, French Union, Vientiane 51-52; High Rep. of King of Laos to Pres. of Union, Paris 52-56; Amb. to Japan 56-58; Amb. to U.K. 59-62, 67-71; Sec.-Gen. Royal Palace 62-67; Perm. Rep. to UN 71-72; fmr. Pres. King's Council.

Khan, Vice-Admiral Afzal Rahman; retd. Pakistani naval officer; b. 20 March 1921, Kala Afghanan; s. of Abdur Rahman Khan and Aziz Bibi Khan; m. Hameeda Khan 1944; one s. two d.; ed. Command and Staff Coll., Quetta, and Joint Services Staff Coll., U.K.
Joined Royal Navy 38, commissioned 40; active service in Royal Navy, Second World War; later in Indian Navy, transferring to Pakistan Navy 47; C.-in-C.- Pakistan Navy 59-66; Minister of Defence, Pakistan 66-69.
The Anchorage, 27B South Central Avenue, Defence Housing Society, Karachi 4, Pakistan.
Telephone: 541550 (Home).

Khan, Akbar Ali, B.A., LL.B.; Indian lawyer and administrator; b. 20 Nov. 1899, Hyderabad; *s.* of Mahboob Ali Khan; *m.* Karamat-un-nisa Begum 1928; two *s.* two *d.*; ed. Jamia Millia, New Delhi, Aligarh Muslim Univ., Osmania (Hyderabad) and London Univs.
Called to the Bar, London; joined Congress 49; mem. Rajya Sabha 54-; Senior Advocate Supreme Court; Gov. of Uttar Pradesh 72-74, of Orissa Oct. 74-; Pres. Maulana Abul Kalam Azad Oriental Research Inst., Osmania Univ. Graduates Asscn., Econ. Soc., All India Exhbn. Soc., Hyderabad; Vice-Pres. Hyderabad Municipal Corpn., Cen. Co-operative Union, Food Relief Asscn.; mem. Exec. Cttee. All India Co-operative Unions, exec. councils of several orgs.; Padma Bhushan 65.
Leisure interests: tennis, walking, travelling and reading.
Raj Bhavan, Bhubaneswar 8, Orissa; Home: Stone House, Secretariat Road, Hyderabad, Andhra Pradesh, India.

Khan, Ali Akbar; Indian musician; b. 1922; *s.* of late Alauddin Khan.
Concert Recitals on Sarode, in India since 36, and all over the world since 55; Founder Ali Akbar Coll. of Music, Calcutta 56, and Ali Akbar Coll., San Rafael, Calif.; Musical Dir. of many films and numerous contributions on All India Radio; Lecture Recitals at Montreal and McGill Univs., Canada; first long-playing gramophone record introduced by Yehudi Menuhin; Pres. of India Award 63.
c/o Asian Music Circle, 46 Flask Walk, London, N.W.3, England.
Telephone: 01-839-6503.

Khan, Ghulam Ishaq; Pakistani civil servant; b. 1915; *m.* 1950; one *s.* five *d.*; ed. Islamia Coll., Peshawar, and Punjab Univ.
North-West Frontier Province (N.W.F.P.) Civil Service (India) 40-47, Sub-Divisional Officer, Treasury Officer and Magistrate First Class 40-44, Bursar and Sec. to Council of Management of Islamia Coll., Peshawar; Sec. to Chief Minister, N.W.P.F. 47; Home Sec. Food and Dir. Civil Supplies to Govt. N.W.F.P. 48; Devt. and Admin. Sec. for Agriculture, Animal Husbandry, Forests, Industries, Co-operatives and Village Aid 49-52; Devt. Commr. and Sec. to Devt. Dept., N.W.F.P. 53-56; Sec. for Devt. and Irrigation, Govt. of W. Pakistan 56-58; mem. W. Pakistan Water and Power Devt. Authority 58-61, Chair. 61-66; mem. Land Reforms Comm. 58-59; Sec. Finance, Govt. of Pakistan 66-70; Cabinet Sec. Govt. of Pakistan 70; Gov. State Bank of Pakistan 71-75; Sec.-Gen., Ministry of Defence 75-.
Ministry of Defence, Rawalpindi; Home: 2, 52nd Street, Shalimar 6/4, Islamabad, Pakistan.
Telephone: 68709 (Office); 26050 (Home).

Khan, Khan Abdul Qayyum; Pakistani lawyer and politician; b. 1901, Chitral; ed. Islamia Coll., Peshawar and London School of Econs.
Called to the Bar, Lincoln's Inn, London 26; practised law in Peshawar; joined All India Congress Party during Civil Disobedience Movt.; mem. Indian Cen. Legislative Assembly 37; Deputy Leader, Congress Party in Legislative Assembly; joined All-Indian Muslim League 45; mem. Frontier Legislative Assembly and Leader Muslim League Assembly Party 46; political imprisonment 47; Chief Minister, N.W. Frontier Province 47; mem. Provincial Legislative Assembly 51; Minister of Industries, Food and Agriculture, Govt. of Pakistan 53-54; Pres. Pakistan Muslim League 58; political imprisonment 60, 62; formed Quaid-i-Azam Muslim League March 69; Pres. Pakistan Muslim League Jan. 70; mem. Nat. Assembly Dec. 70-;

Minister for Interior and States and Frontier Regions April 71-.
National Assembly, Rawalpindi, Pakistan.

Khan, Air Marshal Mohammed Asghar; Pakistani air force officer and politician; b. 17 Jan. 1921; ed. Imperial Defence Coll., U.K.
Commander-in-Chief Pakistan Air Force and Mil. Adviser SEATO 57-65; Pres. Pakistan Int. Airlines 65-68; entered politics Nov. 68; head and founder of Istiqlal Party March 70.
Lahore, Pakistan.

Khan, Sultan Mohammad, B.A.; Pakistani diplomatist; b. 1919; ed. Ewing Christian Coll. and Allahabad Univ.
Commissioned Indian Army 42; Indian Political Service 46; Pakistan Diplomatic Service 47-; Pakistan High Comm., New Delhi 47, Cairo and Rome 48-50; Ministry of External Affairs, Karachi 50-53; Embassy, Peking and Ankara 53-57; Dep. High Commr. London 57-59; Ministry of External Affairs, Karachi 59-61; High Commr. in Canada 61-66, concurrently accredited as High Commr. in Jamaica 63-66, Trinidad and Tobago 63-66; Amb. to Cuba 64-66; Amb. to People's Repub. of China 66-68; Asst. Sec. for Foreign Affairs 69-72; Amb. to U.S.A. 72-73, concurrently accred. to Jamaica and Venezuela 72-73, to Mexico 73; Amb. to Japan 74-.
Embassy of Pakistan, National Azabu Appt., 4-5-2 Minami Azabu, 6-8th Floor, Koboyashi Building 1-51, Shiba, 3-chome, Minato-ku, Tokyo, Japan.

Khan, Gen. Yahya (*see* Yahya Khan, Gen. Agha Muhammad).

Khanlari, Parviz N., PH.D.; Iranian writer and politician; b. 14; ed. Teheran Univ. and Univ. of Paris.
Professor of Iranian Linguistics, Teheran Univ. 48; Editor *Sokhan* (literary monthly) 43- and *Sokhan* (scientific monthly) 62-; Deputy Minister of Interior 55; Minister of Educ. 62-64; Senator 71; Co-founder Mardom Party 47; Gen. Sec. Imperial Foundation for Iranian Cultural Studies.
Hafez Avenue, Zomorrod Passage, P.O. Box 984, Teheran, Iran.

Khanna, Charan Das, M.A., C.A.I.I.B., A.I.B.; Indian financial official; b. 22 March 1915, Kangra; *s.* of late Ram Rakha Mal; *m.* Mrs. Raj Khanna 1938; one *s.* three *d.*; ed. Punjab Univ.
Worked in various supervisory capacities in Indian and English commercial banks in India 38-48; joined Industrial Finance Corpn. of India 48, Sec. 65-66, Gen Man. 66-70, fmr. Chair.; mem. Advisory Cttee. of UNIDO for co-operation among Industrial Devt. Financial Insts. 71; Dir. Industrial Reconstruction Corpn. of India 71, Kerala Industrial and Technical Consultancy Org. 72; Trustee, Unit Trust of India 73-; Fellow, Econ. Devt. Inst. of World Bank; Pochkanwala Prize, Indian Inst. of Bankers.
Leisure interests: photography, mountaineering.
Publs. several papers on banking and industrial finance.
Industrial Finance Corporation of India, Bank of Baroda Building, 16 Parliament Street, New Delhi 1, India.
Telephone: 312440 (Office); 672832 (Home).

Kharas, Jamshed Gustadji, B.SC.; Pakistani diplomatist; b. 28 July 1919; *m.*; two *c.*
Joined Indian civil service 42; Deputy Sec. to Ministry of Interior, Govt. of Pakistan 51-54; Joint Sec. Ministry of Foreign Affairs 55-57, 59-60; attended Imperial Defence Coll., London 58; High Commr. for Pakistan in Australia and New Zealand 60-62; Dir.-Gen. Ministry of External Affairs, Karachi 62-63; Amb. to Spain 63-67 and to Holy See 66-67; Amb. to Yugoslavia and Greece 67-69, to Fed. Germany 69-72, to Italy (also accred. to Malta) 75-.
Pakistan Embassy, Lungotevere delle Armi 22, Rome, Italy.

Khariton, Yuliy Borisovich; Soviet physicist and physical chemist; b. 27 Feb. 1904, Leningrad; ed. Leningrad Polytechnical Inst.

Research worker, Leningrad Polytechnical Inst. 21-27; worked in England with Lord Rutherford 27-28; Assoc. of Inst. of Chemical Physics, U.S.S.R. Acad. of Sciences 31-; Corresp. mem U.S.S.R. Acad. of Sciences 43-53, mem. 53-; mem. C.P.S.U. 56-; Deputy to U.S.S.R. Supreme Soviet 54, 58, 62, 66, 70-; Hero of Socialist Labour (three times).

Publs. *The Problem of Chain Decay of the Basic Uranium Isotope* 39, *On the Chain Decay of Uranium under the Action of Slow Neutrons* 40, *The Problem of Impact Detonation* 40.

Institute of Chemical Physics, U.S.S.R. Academy of Sciences, 2b Vorobyevskoe Shosse, Moscow, U.S.S.R.

Kharmawan, Byanti; Indonesian international finance official; b. 1 June 1906, Tegal, Central Java; *m.*; one *c.*; ed. School of Economics, Rotterdam.

Became civil servant 49; Econ. Adviser, Ministry of Econ. Affairs and Ministry of Finance; Chief Econ. Adviser and Deputy Gov., Central Bank of Indonesia; Exec. Dir. Asian Devt. Bank 66-68; Exec. Dir. Int. Monetary Fund (IMF) 68-.

Publs. *Willem Kloos en de Dichtkunst* and articles on literary and economic topics.

International Monetary Fund, 19th and H Streets, N.W., Washington, D.C. 20431, U.S.A.

Khatib, Ahmed al-; Syrian politician; b. 1933, Al Suwaydaa; *s.* of Hassan al Khatib and Hindiya al Farra; *m.* Souraya al Khatib 1959; two *s.* one *d.*

Formerly Head, Syrian Teachers Asscn.; mem. Presidential Council Sept. 65-Feb. 66; Pres. of Syria Nov. 70-Feb. 71; Chair. People's Council Feb.-Dec. 71; Pres. Fed. Ministerial Council Fed. of Arab Repubs. Jan. 72-; mem. Baath Party, elected to Leadership Cttee. May 71.

Leisure interest: shooting.

Federation of Arab Republics, Cairo, Egypt.

Khatib, Mohammed Fathalla El-, B.COMM., PH.D.; Egyptian politician; b. 1 Jan. 1927, Gharbiyah; *m.* Amira Mohamed Khadr 1960; three *d.*; ed. Univs. of Cairo and Edinburgh.

Director of Research and UN sections, Arab States Delegations Office, New York 58-61; Lecturer in Political Science 54-58, Reader 61-67, Prof. of Comparative Govt., Univ. of Cairo 67-71, Dean of Faculty of Econs. and Political Science 68-71; Minister of Social Affairs May-Sept. 71; Adviser to the Pres. on Home, Econ. and Social Affairs Sept. 71-72; Sec.-Gen. Arab Socialist Union Governorate of Cairo 71-72; Minister of State, Chair. Council of Foreign Affairs, U.A.R. Dec. 71.

Leisure interests: reading, music.

Publs. include *Power Politics in the UN* 62, *Local Government in U.A.R.* 64, *Studies in the Government of China* 65, *Studies in Comparative Government* 67, *Introduction to Political Science* 69.

11. Sh. Ibn Zinki-Zamalek, Cairo, Egypt.

Telephone: 807240.

Khatib, Rashad al-; Jordanian politician; b. 1909, Hebron; ed. Islamic Coll., Jerusalem.

Director, Econ. Dept., Jerusalem 47; mem. House of Reps. 50-54; Senator 55-59, 63-; Minister of Nat. Economy 63; Minister of Cabinet Affairs Aug. 72-73.

The Senate, Amman, Jordan.

Khatri, Maj.-Gen. Padma Bahadur, K.C.V.O.; Nepalese diplomatist; b. Feb. 1915, Kathmandu; *s.* of late Lieut.-Col. Pahalman and Ratna Kumari; *m.* Hari Kumari; three *s.* one *d.*; ed. in Calcutta and Tri-Chandra Coll., Kathmandu.

Joined Nepal Army 35; war service 40-46; Military attaché Nepalese Embassy London 47-49; Observer, UN Gen. Assembly 48; Nepalese Liaison Officer to British Brig. of Gurkhas, Malaya 50; Nepalese rep. to Non-Aligned Conf., Bandung 55, Cairo 64; Sec. Coronation Cttee. 56; Chair. Nepal-China Boundary Cttee. 60-62; Sec. for Defence, Govt. of Nepal 62-63, Foreign Sec. 63-64, 72-; Amb. to U.S.A., Argentina, Canada and Chile 64-68; Perm. Rep. to UN 64-72; fmr. Vice-Pres. UN Gen. Ass. (twice), Pres. UN Security Council (twice); Chair. UN Special Del. to Security Council, Guinea, 70; accompanied the late H.M. King Mahendra on several State visits, etc.; Orders of Gorkha Dakshin Bahu I, Nepal Sripad II, Sainik Dirgha Sewa Patta, Nepal Tara I, Trisaktipatta I, Grand Cross (Fed. Repub. of Germany), Officier Légion d'Honneur (France).

Ministry of Foreign Affairs, Singha Durbar, Kathmandu; Gyaneswore, Kathmandu, Nepal.

Telephone: 12211, Ext. 231 (Office).

Khefacha, Mohamed El Hédi, L. ès L.; Tunisian politician; b. 11 Oct. 1916; ed. Coll. Sadiki, Lycée Carnot, Tunis and Faculté de Droit, Algiers.

Called to Bar, Tunis 42; Pres. Union of Young Lawyers of Tunisia 50-56; Gen. Inspector of Customs 56-58; Deputy 59; Sec. of State for Justice 58-66, concurrently Sec. of State for Finance 60-61; Sec. of State for Public Health 66-69, of the Interior 69-70, 71-73, of Public Works and Housing 73-74, of Defence 74-; mem. Political Bureau, Destour Socialist Party 69-; Grand Cordon, Order of the Repub. 64, Grand Cordon, Order of Independence 66.

[*Died 25 May 1976.*]

Khene, Abderrahman, M.D.; Algerian doctor, politician and administrator; b. 6 March 1931, Collo; three *s.* one *d.*; ed. Univ. of Algiers.

Secretary of State, Provisional Govt. of Algeria (G.P.R.A.) 58-60; Dir. of Political Affairs, Ministry of Interior, G.P.R.A. 60-61; Dir. of Cabinet, Ministry of Finances, G.P.R.A. 61-62; Pres. of Technical Org. for Exploiting Wealth of Saharan Sub-Soil (l'Organisme Saharien) Sept. 62-Dec. 65, Pres. Electricité et Gaz d'Algérie (E.G.A.) July-Oct. 64, Organisme Coopération Industrielle (O.C.I.) Jan. 66-Dec. 71; Minister of Public Works and Construction 66-70; Sec.-Gen. OPEC 73-74; Exec. Dir. UNIDO 75-.

United Nations Industrial Development Organization, Lerchenfelder Strasse 1, Vienna 1070, Austria; and 42 Chemin Brahimi, El-Biar, Algiers, Algeria.

Khiem, Gen. Tran Thien (see Tran Thien Khiem, Gen.).

Khieu Samphan; Cambodian politician; b. 1932; ed. Paris Univ.

Founded French-language journal, Cambodia; Deputy, Nat. Assembly in Prince Sihanouk's party, *Sangkum Reastr Nyum* (Popular Socialist Community); served as Sec. of State for Commerce; left Phnom-Penh to join *Khmers Rouges* 67; Minister of Defence in Royal Govt. of Nat. Union of Cambodia (GRUNC) May 70-76, Deputy Prime Minister Aug. 70-76 (in exile 70-75, in Phnom-Penh 75-76); mem. Politburo Nat. United Front of Cambodia (FUNC) 70-; C.-in-C. *Khmers Rouges* High Command 73-; Head of State April 76-.

Office of the Head of State, Phnom-Penh, Cambodia.

Khir Johari, Mohamed; Malaysian politician and diplomatist; b. 29 Jan. 1932, Kedah; *m.*; two *s.* five *d.*; ed. Sultan Abdul Hamid Coll., Kedah.

Secretary-General Saberkas (political body affiliated to United Malays Nat. Org.) 46; Sec.-Gen. UMNO 54-55, 66-69; played leading role in founding of UMNO-MCA-MIC Alliance; mem. Parl. for Kedah Tengah 55-; fmr. Minister of Educ., of Agriculture, and Co-operatives, of Trade and Industry; Minister without Portfolio, Amb. to U.S.A. 73-; Pres. Afro-Asian Rural Reconstruction Org. Confs., New Delhi 64, Nairobi 66, Pacific Area Travel Asscn. 71-72; leader of del. to

UNCTAD III, Santiago 72; Chair. Nat. Family Planning Board, Zoological Soc., Nat. Soc. for the Deaf and several other voluntary orgs.; has attended numerous int. econ. confs.; Hon. LL.D. (Univ. of Malaya) 66, Hon. D.Sc. & Ed. (De la Salle Coll., Manila) 67.

Embassy of Malaysia, 2401 Massachusetts Avenue, N.W., Washington, D.C. 20008; Home: 2701 Albermarle Street, N.W., Washington, D.C. 20008, U.S.A.

Khitrov, Stepan Dmitriyevich; Soviet politician; b. 1910; ed. All-Union Polytechnic Inst.

Member C.P.S.U. 32-; Soviet Army service 33-35; Deputy Chief Engineer of state farm, later construction technician, then Editor of newspaper on construction, Voronezh 35-38; Party work 38-47; Sec., then Second Sec. Voronezh Regional Cttee. of C.P., then Chair. Exec. Cttee. of Voronezh Regional Soviet of Working People's Deputies 47-59; Official, Central Cttee. C.P.S.U. 59-60; First Sec. Voronezh Regional Cttee. of C.P. 60-67; Minister of Agricultural Construction of U.S.S.R. 67-; Alt. mem. Central Cttee. C.P.S.U. 61-66, mem. 66-; Deputy to U.S.S.R. Supreme Soviet 62-.

U.S.S.R. Ministry of Agricultural Construction, 4 Building 1, Prospekt Marxa, Moscow, U.S.S.R.

Khlefawi, Gen. Abdel Rahman; Syrian army officer and engineer; b. 1930.

Representative of Syria, Joint Arab Command, Cairo 64-67; Head, Armoured Forces Admin., Damascus 67-68; Head, Officers' Board, Ministry of Defence 68-70; Minister of the Interior Nov. 70-April 71; Prime Minister April 71-Dec. 72.

Office of the Prime Minister, Damascus, Syria.

Khokhlov, Boris Ivanovich; Soviet ballet dancer; b. 22 Feb. 1932; ed. Bolshoi Theatre Ballet School.

Joined Bolshoi Theatre Ballet Company 51; Honoured Artist of R.S.F.S.R.

Chief roles include: Prince Desire (*Sleeping Beauty*), Siegfried (*Swan Lake*), the Prince (*Cinderella*), the Poet (*Chopiniana*), Basil (*Don Quixote*), Albert (*Giselle*), Vatshar (*Bakhchisarai Fountain*).

State Academic Bolshoi Theatre of U.S.S.R., 1 Ploshchad Sverdlova, Moscow, U.S.S.R.

Khokhlov, Rem Viktorovich; Soviet physicist; b. 15 July 1926, Livny, Oryol Region; s. of Viktor Khristoforovich Khokhlov and Mariya Yakovlevna Vasilyeva; m. Elena Mikailovna Dubinina 1949; two s.; ed. Moscow Univ.

Postgraduate Asst., Assoc. Prof., Prof., Rector, Moscow Univ. 49-; mem. C.P.S.U. 51-; Corresp. mem. U.S.S.R. Acad. of Sciences 66-, Academician 74-; Lenin Prize 70.

Leisure interests: mountain climbing, skiing.

Publs. Works on radiophysics, acoustics and quantum electronics.

Moscow State University, Leninskie Gory, Moscow 117234, U.S.S.R.

Kholi, Hassan Sabri el-; Egyptian diplomatist; b. 25 Feb. 1922; ed. Univ. of Cairo, Mil. and Staff Colls.

Fought in Palestine War 48; Prof., Senior Officer Studies Inst.; opened Infantry School, Syria 57; Dir. Office for Palestine at the Presidency, Office for Public Affairs; Personal Rep. of the Pres. 64-; has represented Egypt at UN, Arab League and Arab Summit Confs., numerous foreign decorations.

Publs. *The Palestine Case, Sinai, The Policy of Imperialism and Zionism towards Palestine during the First Half of the Twentieth Century,* and several research papers on Palestine.

The Presidency, Cairo, Egypt.

Khoman, Thanat; Thai diplomatist and politician; b. 9 May 1914, Bangkok; m. Khunying Molee Khoman; three c.; ed. Assumption Coll., Thailand and Univs. of Bordeaux and Paris.

Thai Foreign Office 41-, Second Sec. Thai Embassy, Tokyo, Japan 42-43; Chargé d'Affaires, Washington 46-47, Ambassador 57-59; Chargé d'Affaires, Thai Legation, New Delhi 47-49; Dir.-Gen. Dept. of Econ. Affairs, UN 50-52, Dir.-Gen. Dept. of UN Affairs 50-51; Dep. Acting Perm. Rep. of Thailand to UN 52-57; Chair. UN Int. Law Comm. 57, UN Cttee. on S.W. Africa 57 UN Gen. Assembly Trusteeship Cttee. 57; Minister of Foreign Affairs, Thailand 59-71; Thai Envoy to ASEAN 72; Knight Grand Cordon, Order of Crown, Thailand; Knight Grand Cordon, Order of White Elephant.

Publs. papers on South-East Asia affairs.

c/o Ministry of Foreign Affairs, Bangkok, Thailand.

Khorana, Har Gobind, PH.D., M.SC.; Indian-born scientist; b. 1922, Raipur; m. Esther Elizabeth Sibler 1952; one s. two d.; ed. Punjab Univ.

Began career as organic chemist; worked with Sir Alexander Todd on building nucleotides, Cambridge 50-52; later worked with Nat. Research Inst., Canada, until 60; Prof. and Co-Dir. Inst. of Enzyme Chem., Univ. of Wisconsin 60-64, Conrad A. Elvehjem Prof. in Life Sciences 64-70; Alfred P. Sloan Prof. Mass. Inst. of Technology Sept. 70-; Hon. D.Sc. (Chicago, Liverpool, Delhi); Hon. LL.D. (Simon Fraser Univ.) 69; Nobel Prize for Medicine and Physiology (with Holley and Nirenberg) for interpretation of genetic code and its function in protein synthesis 68; Louisa Gross Horwitz Prize for Biochem. 68; American Chem. Soc. Award for creative work in Synthetic Chem. 68; Lasker Foundation Award 68; American Acad. of Achievement Award 71.

Leisure interests: music, hiking.

Departments of Biology and Chemistry, Massachusetts Institute of Technology, Cambridge, Mass. 02139, U.S.A.

Khoshkish, Youssof; Iranian banker; b. 1906, Teheran; ed. Univs. of Teheran and Paris.

Bank Melli Iran 34-39, 61-, Asst. Man. Org. Dept. 36-38, Man. Supply Dept. 38-39; Govt. Rep. for Financial Affairs in Europe, Ministry of Finance, 39-40; financial del. of Indian Govt. in India 40-44; Vice-Pres. Bank Sepah 45-61; Pres. Bank Melli Iran 61-.

Bank Melli Iran, Khiaban Ferdowsi, Teheran, Iran.

Khosla, Dr. Ajudhia Nath; Indian public servant, engineer, educationist and administrator; b. 11 Dec. 1892, Jullundur City, Panjab; s. of late Shri Ralla Ram Khosla and Shrimati Karam Devi Khosla; m. Shrimati Sushilavati 1910 (died 1966); one s. six d.; ed. D.A.V. Coll., Lahore and Thomason Coll. of Engineering. Roorkee.

Chairman Cen. Water and Power Comm. 45-53; Founder Pres. Int. Comm. on Drainage and Irrigation 50, Hon. Pres. 54-; Vice-Pres. World Power Conf., Int. Comm. on Dams, Int. Asscn. for Hydraulic Research; Vice-Chancellor Roorkee Univ. 54-59; mem. Rajya Sabha (Parl.) 58-59, Planning Comm. 59-62; Gov. of Orissa 62-68; Pres. Inst. of Engineers 49-50, Cen. Board of Irrigation and Power 46-48, 51-, of Geophysics (India) 50-53, Nat. Inst. of Sciences 61-62; Chair. Boards of Consultants for Bhakra, Beas, Sabarigiri, Ramganga, Yamuna, and Bhali-Meli projects, Chair. Ramganga Board of Consultants; Vice-Pres. D.A.V. Coll. Man. Comm., New Delhi; Hon. Life mem. Inst. of Engineers (India); Fellow, Indian Nat. Science Acad.; Life mem. American Soc. of Civil Engineers, American Soc. Gen. Engineers; Hon. degrees from various Univs.

Leisure interests: social service in the field of educ. and econ. uplift of backward people of Orissa.

Publs. *Design of Weirs on Permeable Foundations, Silting of Reservoirs, Rainfall and Runoff, Pressure Observations under Dams.*

15 Jangpura-B, Mathura Road, New Delhi 14, India.

Telephone: 77168 New Delhi.

Khosrovani, Khosro, PH.D.; Iranian diplomatist; b. 16 June 1914, Mahalat; s. of Mohamad Hashem; m. Karimi Zand 1943; one s. one d.; ed. Iran and England. Former Geologist, Dept. of Mines; Foreign Service, served Ministry of Foreign Affairs, UN, Washington; later Under-Sec. Ministry of Nat. Economy; Consul-Gen. of Iran in Hamburg; Under-Sec. Ministry of Foreign Affairs for Econ. Matters 60; mem. Supreme Political Council 61; Amb. to Turkey 63-65, to U.S.A. 65-67; Del. to Gen. Assembly UN 63; Man. Dir. Foreign Transaction Co. 59; Chair. Board of Inspectorate, Nat. Iranian Oil Co. 63; Pres. of Policy Board, Foreign Ministry 70; Amb. to Egypt 71-76; Order of Homayoun. Leisure interests: reading, bridge.
c/o Imperial Iranian Ministry of Foreign Affairs, Teheran, Iran.

Khrapchenko, Mikhail Borisovich; Soviet literary critic; b. 21 Nov. 1904, Chizhooka village, Smolensk region.
Member C.P.S.U. 28-; state work 38-48; research work, Inst. of World Literature 48-63; Bureau mem. and Deputy Acad. Sec., Dept. of Literature and Language, U.S.S.R. Acad. of Sciences 57-66, Sec. 66-; Corresp. mem. U.S.S.R. Acad. of Sciences 58-66, mem. 66-; Order of Red Banner of Labour 64.
Publs. *Works of Gogol* 54, *Dead Souls by N. V. Gogol* 61, *Leo Tolstoi as Artist* 63.
U.S.S.R. Academy of Sciences, 14 Leninsky Prospekt, Moscow, U.S.S.R.

Khrennikov, Tikhon Nikolayevich; Soviet composer; b. 10 June 1913, Elets, Lipetsk region; ed. Moscow Conservatoire.
General Sec. Soviet Composers' Union 48-57, First Sec. 57-; Deputy to U.S.S.R. Supreme Soviet 62-; mem. Cttee. U.S.S.R. Parl. Group; mem. Cen. Auditing Comm., C.P.S.U. 61-; mem. C.P.S.U. 47-; State Prize 42, 46, 51, 67, People's Artist of the R.S.F.S.R. 55, of the U.S.S.R. 63; Order of Lenin 63, Red Banner of Labour 67.
Principal compositions: Five Pieces for Piano 33, Three Pieces for Piano 35, Suite for Orchestra from Music for *Much Ado About Nothing, In the Storm* (Opera) 39, Second Symphony 41, incidental music for play *Long Ago* 42, *Frol Skobeyev* (Opera) 50, *Mother* (Opera) 56, Concerto for Violin and Orchestra 59, *A Hundred Devils and One Girl* (Operetta) 61, *White Nights* (Operetta) 67. Composers' Union of the U.S.S.R., Ulitsa Nezhdanovoi 8/10, Moscow, U.S.S.R.

Khristianovich, Sergei Alexeevich; Soviet mechanical engineer; b. 27 Oct. 1908, Leningrad; ed. Leningrad Univ.
Specialist in field of hydrodynamics and gas dynamics; corresp. mem. U.S.S.R. Acad. of Sciences 39, mem. 43-; Sec. Technical Sciences Section, U.S.S.R. Acad. of Sciences 53-56; thrice State prize laureate; Zhukovsky prize of U.S.S.R. Acad. of Sciences 42; Dir. Inst. of Theoretical and Applied Mechanics, Siberian Div. 57-65; Hero of Socialist Labour 69.
Akademgorodok, Novosibirsk, U.S.S.R.

Khrunov, Col. Evgeny Vasilievich; Soviet cosmonaut; b. 10 Sept. 1933; ed. School of Military Pilots, Bataisk and Zhukovsky Air Force Engineering Acad.
Air Force Fighter Pilot 56-60; mem. C.P.S.U. 59-; joined cosmonaut training unit 60-; Engineer/Investigator of spacecraft *Soyuz-5* which formed first manned orbital station with *Soyuz-4*; carried out scientific work outside spacecraft while in orbit; Hero of Soviet Union; Gold Star Medal, Order of Lenin, Red Star; K. Tsiolkovsky Gold Medal, U.S.S.R. Acad. of Sciences.
Zvezdny Gorodok, Moscow, U.S.S.R.

Kiano, Julius Gikyono, M.A., PH.D.; Kenyan politician; b. 1926, Weithaga, Kenya; m.; several c.; ed. Makerere Univ. Coll., Antioch Coll. (U.S.), Stanford Univ. and Univ. of California.

Lecturer in Econs. and Constitutional Law at Royal Technical Coll., Kenya 56-58; African elected mem. Legis. Council for Central Province South 58-60; Minister for Commerce and Industry 60; mem. Legis. Council for Fort Hall 61; mem. Kenya Advisory Council on Technical Educ. and Vocational Training; mem. Indian Govt. Cultural Scholarships Cttee.; Chair. Nairobi Welfare Soc.; Minister for Educ. 66-69, for Local Govt. 69-73, for Commerce and Industry 73-; Chair. Kenya African Nat. Union (KANU), Muranga District.
Ministry for Commerce and Industry, Nairobi, Kenya.

Kianpour, Gholamreza, DR.ECON.; Iranian politician; b. 1929, Teheran; m.: two s. one d.; ed. Teheran Univ. Economic Counsellor, Ministry of Finance; Judge, Ministry of Justice; Head of Office of Org., Plan Org., later Dir. of Finance; Dir. Bank Etebarat Sanati; Under-Sec. Ministry of Economy; Head of Admin. High Council; Gov.-Gen. of W. Azarbaijan; Gov.-Gen. of Isfahan; Minister of Information and Tourism April 74-; Taj Second Class, Homayoun First Class, Sepass First Class and several other decorations.
Publs. *Principle of Budget Preparation, Principle of Economies, Industrial Development, Training of Human Resources for Trade and Industry, Development of Economy and Technology, Principle of Banking.*
Ministry of Information and Tourism, Teheran, Iran.

Kibaki, Mwai, B.A., B.SC.(ECON.); Kenyan politician; b. 1931, Othaya, Kenya; ed. Makerere Univ. Coll. Lecturer in Econs. at Makerere Univ. Coll. 59-60; Nat. Exec. Officer Kenya African Nat. Union 60-62; elected by Legis. Council as one of Kenya's nine reps. in Central Legis. Assembly of East African Common Services Org. 62; mem. House of Reps. for Nairobi Doonholm 63-; Parl. Sec. to Treasury 63; Asst. Minister of Econ. Planning and Devt. 64-66; Minister for Commerce and Industry 66-69; Minister of Finance Dec. 69-Nov. 70; Minister of Finance and Econ. Planning Nov. 70-.
Ministry of Finance, Nairobi, Kenya.

Kibalnikov, Aleksandr Pavlovich; Soviet sculptor; b. 22 Aug. 1912, Orekhovo village, Volgograd region; ed. Saratov Art School.
Exhibition of first works 39; designed monuments to Mayakovsky in Moscow; works in the Tretyakov Gallery, Moscow; mem. Soviet Acad. of Arts; State Prize for statue of Chernyshevsky 49, 51, Lenin Prize 59, People's Artist of U.S.S.R. 63.
U.S.S.R. Academy of Arts, 21 Kropotkin Street, Moscow, U.S.S.R.

Kibedi, Wanume, LL.B.; Ugandan lawyer and politician; b. 3 Aug. 1941, Busesa; s. of Mr. and Mrs. E. M. Kibedi; m. Elizabeth Kibedi (née Amin) 1970; one d.; ed. Busoga Coll. and Univ. of London.
Articled with Waterhouse and Co., London 61-66, admitted solicitor 66; worked in office of Attorney-Gen., Uganda 68; Partner, Binaisa and Co. (advocates) 69-70; Minister of Foreign Affairs Feb. 71-73 (resigned); del. to UN Gen. Assembly 71.
Leisure interests: chess, tennis, reading.

Kidd, Paul James Garland, Q.C.; Canadian business executive; b. 25 June 1913; s. of the late Rev. Charles and Mary (Youngson) Kidd; m. Elizabeth Dixon 1940; two d.; ed. Gananoque High School, Queen's Univ. and Osgoode Hall Law School, Toronto, Ont.
Joined Legal Dept. of Hiram Walker & Sons Ltd. (Distillers) 36; now Senior Vice-Pres. and Dir. Hiram Walker-Gooderham & Worts Ltd., and officer and Dir. of various subsidiary companies; Dir. Corby Distilleries Ltd., Liquid Carbonic Canada Ltd.
Office: 2072 Riverside Drive East, Walkerville, Ont. N8Y 4S5; Home: 7080 Riverside Drive East, Windsor, Ont. N8S 1C3, Canada.

Kieber, Walter, D.JUR.; Liechtenstein politician; b. 20 Feb. 1931, Feldkirch, Austria; s. of Alfons and Elisabeth Kieber; m. Selma Ritter 1959; one s. one d.; ed. Grammar School in Bregenz, Austria, Univ. of Innsbruck.

Lawyer in Vaduz 55-59; entered civil service as Chief of the Government Legal Office 59; Chief of Presidential Office 65-; Sec.-Gen. of Govt. 69, Deputy Head of Govt. 70-74, Head of Govt. March 74-; Grand Cross, Liechtenstein Order of Merit; Grosses Goldenes Ehrenzeichen am Bande für Verdienste um die Republik Österreich (Austria); Progressive Citizens' Party.

Regierungsgebäude, FL-9490 Vaduz; Home: Landstrasse 22, FL-9494 Schaan, Liechtenstein.

Telephone: 2-28-22 (Office); 2-25-29 (Home).

Kielmansegg, Gen. Johann Adolf, Graf von; retired German army officer; b. 30 Dec. 1906, Hofgeismar; s. of the late Adolf Graf von Kielmansegg and the late Eva Graefin von Kielmansegg (née von Werner); m. Mechthild Freiin von Dincklage 1933; two s. two d.; ed. Monastic School, Rossleben.

Army Service 26-, Officer 30; War Acad., Berlin 37-39; Gen. Staff, 1st and 6th Panzer Div. 39-42; OKH (High Command of the Army) 42-44, C.O. Infantry Regiment 111 44-45; journalistic activities 45-50; Defence Ministry 50-55; Mil. Rep. of Fed. Repub. of Germany to SHAPE, Paris 55-58; Second-in-Command, 5th Panzer Div. 59-60, later C.O. 10th Panzer Div.; Defence Ministry, Bonn until 63; promoted to rank of Gen. 63; C.-in-C. Allied Land Forces, Cen. Europe 63-66; C.-in-C. Allied Forces, Cen. Europe 66-68; now writer in politico-military matters; mem. Int. Inst. for Strategic Studies (London), and German Asscn. for Foreign Affairs; Grand Cross of the Fed. Repub. with Ribbon and Star; Commdr. Légion d'Honneur; Commdr. Legion of Merit.

Leisure interests: history, political science, horse-riding. 7812 Bad Krozingen, Batzenbergstr. 7, Federal Republic of Germany.

Telephone: 07633-3352.

Kieniewicz, Stefan, PH.D.; Polish historian; b. 20 Sept. 1907, Dereszewicze, U.S.S.R.; ed. Poznań Univ. Docent 46-49, Assoc. Prof. 49-58, Prof. 58-; Corresp. mem. Polish Acad. of Sciences (PAN) 65-69, mem. 69-; Chair. Cttee. of Historical Sciences 69-71, mem. 71-, mem. Scientific Council of PAN History Inst.; Head of Contemporary Polish History Group, Warsaw Univ.; Editor *Przegląd Historyczny* 52-; mem. Polish Historical Soc.; Knight's Cross, Order of Polonia Restituta 54, Officer's Cross 58, Commdr.'s Cross 73; State Prize 55, 64; Minister of Nat. Defence Prize 72.

Publs. *Społeczeństwo polskie w powstaniu poznańskim 1848, Ruch chłopski w Galicji 1846, Sprawa włościańska w Powstaniu Styczniowym, Między ugodą a rewolucją, Andrzej Zamoyski w latach 1861-1862, Historia Polski 1795-1864, Historia Polski 1795-1918 68, Powstanie Styczniowe 72.*

Ul. Wiktorska 83/87 m. 32, 02-582 Warsaw, Poland.

Kierans, Eric William; Canadian economist and politician; b. 2 Feb. 1914, Montreal; s. of Hugh Kierans and Lena (née Schmidt); m. Teresa Catherine Whelan 1938; one s. one d.; ed. Loyola Coll., Montreal, and McGill Univ., Montreal.

Professor of Commerce and Finance 53-60; Dir. McGill School of Commerce 53-60; Pres. Montreal and Canadian Stock Exchanges 60-63; Minister of Revenue, Quebec 63-65; Minister of Health, Quebec 65-66; Pres. Quebec Liberal Fed. 66-68; Postmaster-Gen. and Minister responsible for Dept. of Communications 68-69; Minister of Communications Oct. 69-Jan. 72; Liberal.

Publ. *Challenge of Confidence: Kierans on Canada* 67.

5631 Queen Mary Road, Hampstead, Que.; 200 Rideau Terrace, Ottawa, Ont., Canada.

Kiesinger, Kurt Georg; German lawyer and politician; b. 6 April 1904, Ebingen, Württemberg; s. of Christian Kiesinger and Dominika Grimm; m. Marie-Luise Schneider 1932; one s. one d.; ed. Tübingen and Berlin Univs.

Lawyer, Berlin 34-45, Tübingen 48; mem. Bundestag 49-58, 69-, Chair. Joint Comm. 49-57, Cttee. for Foreign Affairs 54-58; mem. Consultative Assembly, Council of Europe 50-58, Vice-Pres. 55-58, Chair. Christian Democratic Group 57-58; mem. WEU Assembly 56-58; Minister-Pres., Baden-Württemberg 58-66; Pres. Bundesrat 62-63; Fed. Chancellor 66-69; Chair. Christian Democratic Union 67-71, now Hon. Chair.; Dr.Iur. h.c. (Cologne, Coimbra, Maryland and New Delhi); Grand Cross Order of Merit of Fed. Repub. of Germany, Order of Merit of Italian Repub., Grand Officier de la Légion d'Honneur, Palmes Académiques, Bavarian Order of Merit and several other foreign decorations; Christian Democratic Union.

Bundeshaus, 53 Bonn; Home: Engelfriedshalde 48, 74 Tübingen, Federal Republic of Germany.

Telephone: Bonn 161.

Kihara, Hitoshi; Japanese scientist; b. 1893; ed. Hokkaido Univ.

Former Prof., Kyoto Univ.; has specialized in genetics and applied botany; studied cellular heredity of wheat, Germany 29; Del. Int. Congress of Genetics, Stockholm 48; Dir. Kihara Inst. for Biological Research 42; fmr. Dir. Nat. Inst. of Genetics; mem. Japanese Acad.; Foreign Assoc. American Acad. of Arts and Sciences, Nat. Acad. of Sciences (U.S.A.).

c/o National Institute of Genetics, 1-111 Yata, Mishima City, Shizuoka, Japan.

Kijima, Torazo, B.ECONS.; Japanese business executive; b. 18 Dec. 1901; ed. Tokyo Imperial Univ. (now Tokyo Univ.).

Director Japanese Nat. Railways 50-52; mem. House of Councillors 53-59; Pres. Hinomaru Ceramic Industry Co. Ltd. 53-, Aito Vehicles Industries Co. Ltd.; Chair. Board of Dirs. Nippon Express Co. Ltd. 68-; Second Grand Order of Sacred Treasure (Japan) 72, Commdr., Grand Order (Madagascar) 73.

3-12-9, Soto-Kanda, Chiyoda-ku, Tokyo; Home: 3-42-17, Wakamiya, Nakano-ku, Tokyo, Japan.

Kikhia, Mansur Rashid; Libyan lawyer and diplomatist; b. 1 Dec. 1931, Benghazi; ed. Cairo and Paris Univs.

Joined Diplomatic Service 57; Asst. in Nationality and Consular Affairs Section, Ministry of Foreign Affairs 57, Head, Treaties and Int. Confs. Section 58-60, 62-65; Second Sec. for Consular and Cultural Affairs, Paris 60-62; Chargé d'Affaires, Paris 62, Algiers 63; Consul-Gen., Geneva 65-67; mem. Perm. Mission to UN 67-69; Under-Sec. Ministry of Unity and Foreign Affairs 69-72; Perm. Rep. to UN Jan.-July 72, Aug. 75-; Minister of Foreign Affairs 72-73; private law practice in Tripoli 73-75; mem. dels. to UN Gen. Assembly 61, 66-70, Chair. of del. 70.

Permanent Mission of Libya to the United Nations, 866 United Nations Plaza, New York, N.Y. 10017, U.S.A.; Home: 72 Baghdad Street, Tripoli, Libya.

Kikoin, Isaak Konstantinovich; Soviet physicist; b. 28 March 1908, Zhagory village, Lithuania; ed. Kalinin Polytechnical Inst. Leningrad.

Instructor, Higher Technical Education establishments Leningrad, Sverdlovsk 31-44; Prof. of Physics, Engineering Inst. U.S.S.R. Acad. of Sciences 44-; Corresp. mem. U.S.S.R. Acad. of Sciences 43-53, mem. 53-; State Prize 42.

Publs. co-author *The Physics of Metals* 34, *Holl's Coefficient and Electrical Resistance of Ferrous Magnetics*

64, *Magnetic Influence on Resistance of Ferrous Magnetics* 64.
Physical and Engineering Institute, Kashirskoe chaussée 1, Moscow, U.S.S.R.

Kikutake, Kiyonori, B.A., F.A.I.A.; Japanese architect; b. 1 April 1928, Kurume; s. of Kiyoshi and Masue Kikutake; m. Norie Sasaki 1953; one s. two d.; ed. Waseda Univ.
Established Kiyonori Kikutake & Assocs. (Architects) 53, now Rep. Dir.; Prof. Dept. of Architecture, Waseda Univ. 59-; mem. Board, Architectural Inst. of Japan 62-; Visiting Prof. Univ. of Hawaii 71; del. to UNESCO Int. Conf., Zurich 70; Hon. Fellow, American Inst. of Architects 71; several awards including Ministry of Educ. Arts Award 64, Architectural Inst. of Japan Award 64, Geijutsu Sensho Prize 64, Cultural Merits of Kurume City 75; Major works include: Shimane Prefectural Museum 58, Admin. Building for Izumo Shrine, Tatebayashi City Hall 63, Hotel Tokoen, Yonago-City, Miyakonojo City Hall, Pacific Hotel, Chigasaki 66, Iwate Prefectural Library 67, Shimane Prefectural Library, Haig Civic Centre 68, Kurume Civic Centre 69, Expo Tower for *Expo 70*, Osaka 70, Pasadena Heights (Tiered mass housing) 74, Aquapolis (floating module for ocean) *Ocean Expo 75* 75, Hagi City Hall 75, Redevelopment of Yamaga city centre 75, Tsukuba Academic New Town, Pedestrian Deck Network and the Symbol Tower 76, Otsu Shopping Centre 76.
Leisure interests: swimming, photography, reading, travel.
Publs. *Metabolism 1960* 60, *Taisha Kenchi ku-ron* (Metabolic Architecture) 68, *Ningen-no-Kenchiku* (Human Architecture) 70, *Ningen-no-Toshi* (A Human City) 70, *Essence of Architecture* 73, *Floating City* 73, *Kiyonori Kikutake—Works and Methods 1956-70* 73.
1-11-15, Otsuka, Bunkyo-ku, Tokyo, Japan.

Kilbrandon, Baron (Life Peer), cr. 71, of Kilbrandon, Argyll; **Charles James Dalrymple Shaw,** P.C., LL.D., D.S.C.; British judge; b. 15 Aug. 1906, Ayrshire; s. of James E. and Gladys E. Shaw; m. Ruth C. Grant 1937; two s. three d.; ed. Charterhouse School, Balliol Coll., Oxford and Univ. of Edinburgh.
Scottish Bar 32; K.C. 49; Sheriff of Ayr and Bute 54, of Perth and Angus 57; Dean of Faculty of Advocates 57; Senator, Coll. of Justice 59-71; Chair. Scottish Law Comm. 65-71; Lord of Appeal in Ordinary 71-; Chair. Royal Comm. on Constitution 72-73; Hon. Fellow, Balliol Coll., Oxford; Hon. Bencher, Gray's Inn.
Publ. *Other People's Law* (Hamlyn Lectures) 66.
2 Raymond Buildings, Gray's Inn, London, W.C.1, England; Kilbrandon House, Balvicar, by Oban, Argyll, Scotland.
Telephone: 01-405-7587 (Office); Balvicar 239 (Home).

Killanin, 3rd Baron, cr. 1900; **Rt. Hon. Michael Morris,** M.B.E., T.D., LL.D., M.A., M.R.I.A.; Irish author, film producer and company director; b. 30 July 1914, London; s. of Lieut.-Col. Hon. George H. Morris and Dora Maryan Wesley Hall; m. Sheila M. C. Dunlop, M.B.E. 1945; three s. one d.; ed. Eton Coll., Sorbonne, Paris and Magdalene Coll., Cambridge.
Member of staff, *Daily Mail*, London 35-39; served in Second World War 39-45; Chair. Bovril (Ireland) Ltd., Chubb Group of Companies in Ireland, Ulster Investment Bank, Lombard & Ulster Banking Ltd., Dir. of Irish Shell & B.P. Ltd., Beamish and Crawford Ltd., Fitzwilton Ltd., etc.; Pres. Dublin Theatre Festival 60-70; Pres. Olympic Council of Ireland 50-72; Vice-Pres. Int. Olympic Cttee. 68-72, Pres. 72-; decorations from France, Japan, Germany, Finland, Italy, Monaco, etc.
Films include: *The Rising of the Moon, Playboy of the Western World, Gideon's Day*, etc.
Publs. *Shell Guide to Ireland, Sir Godfrey Kneller, Four Days, The Olympic Games*; contributions to British, European and American press.
30 Lansdowne Road, Dublin 4; St. Annins, Spiddal, Co. Galway, Ireland.

Killen, Denis James, LL.B.; Australian barrister and politician; b. 23 Nov. 1925, Dalby, Queensland; s. of James Walker Killen and Mabel E. Sheridan; m. Joyce Claire Buley 1949; three d.; ed. Brisbane Grammar School and Univ. of Queensland.
Member House of Reps. 55-; Minister of the Navy 69 March 71, of Defence Nov. 75-.
Leisure interests: tennis, reading.
Commonwealth Parliament Offices, Adelaide Street, Brisbane 4000; Parliament House, Canberra, A.C.T.; 22 Cook Street, Yeronga 4104, Australia.
Telephone: 2-7920 (Brisbane); 705 (Canberra); 48-3707 (Yeronga).

Killian, James Rhyne, Jr., B.S.; retd. American technologist, government official and college administrator; b. 24 July 1904, Blacksburg, S.C.; s. of James R. and Jeanette Killian; m. Elizabeth Parks; one s. one d.; ed. Duke Univ. and Massachusetts Inst. of Technology.
Assistant Managing Ed. *The Technology Review*, M.I.T. 26-27, Managing Ed. 27-30 and Ed. 30-39; Exec. Asst. to Pres. M.I.T. 39-43, Exec. Vice-Pres. 43-45, Vice-Pres. 45-48, Pres. 48-59, Chair. of Corpn. M.I.T. 59-71, Hon. Chair. 71-; Special Asst. to Pres. Eisenhower for Science and Technology 57-59; Chair. President's Foreign Intelligence Advisory, Board 61-63; Dir. Polaroid Corpn. 59-, American Telephone and Telegraph Co. 63-, Corpn. for Public Broadcasting 68-74, Ingersoll-Rand Co. 71-; Officer of the French Legion of Honour 57; Hoover Medal 63; mem. Nat. Acad. of Engineering; Trustee, A. P. Sloan Foundation 54-, Mt. Holyoke Coll. 62-72, Winston Churchill Foundation of the U.S. 60-, Boston Museum of Fine Arts 66-; numerous hon. degrees.
Leisure interests: gardening, photography, painting.
77 Massachusetts Avenue, Cambridge, Mass. 02139, U.S.A.
Telephone: (617) 253-1515.

Killick, Sir John Edward, K.C.M.G.; British diplomatist; b. 18 Nov. 1919, Isleworth; s. of late Edward W. J. Killick and Doris M. Stokes; m. Lynette de Preez 1949; no c.; ed. Latymer Upper School, Univ. Coll., London and Univ. of Bonn.
Military Service 39-46; Control Comm. for Germany 46; entered diplomatic service 46; Foreign Office 46-48, Berlin, Frankfurt and Bonn 48-51; Foreign Office 51-53; British Embassy, Addis Ababa 53-57; Nat. Defence Coll. of Canada 57-58; Foreign Office 58-61; Imperial Defence Coll. 62; British Embassy, Washington 63-68; Asst. Under-Sec. of State, FCO 68-71; Amb. to U.S.S.R. 71-73; Deputy Under-Sec. of State, FCO 73-75; U.K. Perm. Rep. to NATO 75-.
United Kingdom Delegation to NATO, Autoroute de Zaventem, 1110 Brussels, Belgium.
Telephone: 41-01-15.

Killion, George Leonard; American shipping executive; b. 15 April 1901, Steamboat Springs, Colo.; s. of James Abraham Killion and Lydia Jane Harris; m. 1st Grace Harris Killion 1922 (deceased), 2nd Margaretha Rahneberg Killion 1963; one s.; ed. Univ. of Southern California and Univ. of California.
Editorial Staff, West Coast Newspapers 25-30; Public Relations Financial Consultant, Safeway Stores, Oakland, Calif. 30-35, Public Relations and Legislative Consultant 35-39; Dir. of Finance, State of California 40-43; Asst. to Petroleum Admin. for War, Washington 43; Asst. to Treasurer, Democratic Nat. Cttee. 44, Treas. 45-47; Pres. Amer. President Lines 47-66, Consultant and Dir. 66-; Chair. Board, Metro-Goldwyn-Mayer 57-63, 63-69, 70-71, Vice-Chair. 69-70, Dir., mem. Exec.

Cttee. 63-71; Dir. Pacific Nat. Bank 60-69, Communications Satellite Corpn. 62-, First Western Bank 69-; Dir. various other companies.
555 California Street, San Francisco, Calif. 94104; Home: 1090 Chestnut Street, San Francisco, Calif. 94104, U.S.A.
Telephone: 391-3666 (Office); 771-2320 (Home).

Kim, H. E. Cardinal Stephen Sou-hwan; Korean ecclesiastic; b. 8 May 1922, Taegu; ed. Sophia Univ., Tokyo, Major Seminary, Seoul, and Sociology Dept., Univ. of Munster, Germany.
Ordained priest 51; Pastor of Andong, Archdiocese of Taegu 51-53; Sec. to Archbishop of Taegu 53-55; Pastor of Kimchon (Taegu) 55-56; Dir. Sung-Eui Schools, Kimchon 55-56; sociology studies, Univ. of Munster, Germany 56-64; Editor-in-Chief *Catholic Shibo* (weekly) 64-66; Bishop of Masan 66-68; Archbishop of Seoul 68-; cr. Cardinal 69.
Leisure interests: music, literature.
Archbishop's House, 2-ka 1, Myong-dong, Chung-ku, Seoul, Republic of Korea.
Telephone: 76-40830.

Kim Dong-Jo; Korean diplomatist; b. 14 Aug. 1918; ed. Seoul Coll. of Commerce, Kyushu Imperial Univ. Law School, Japan.
Chief Sec. to Minister of Communications 49-51, Dir. Bureau of Gen. Affairs 51; Dir. Bureau of Political Affairs, Ministry of Foreign Affairs 51-52, 54-57; Counsellor, Korean Embassy, Taiwan 52-54; Deputy Minister of Foreign Affairs 57-59; Special Envoy to Repub. of China, Malaysia, Philippines, Thailand and Repub. of Viet-Nam 59; private law practice 60-63; Head del. to Asian People's Anti-Communist League, Viet-Nam 63; Chair. Foreign Relations and Defence Cttee. 63; Pres. Korea Trade Promotion Corpn. 64; Amb. to Japan 64-65, 66-67; Amb. at large 65-66; Amb. to U.S.A. 67-73; Minister for Foreign Affairs 73-75; Hon. LL.D. (Illinois Coll.) 69.
Ministry of Foreign Affairs, Seoul; Home: San 8-35, Hannam-dong, Yongsan-ku, Seoul, Republic of Korea.

Kim Il; Korean politician.
Member, Presidium of Cen. Cttee. of Workers' Party of Korea; Vice-Premier, Democratic People's Repub. of Korea 56-57, First Vice-Premier 57-72, Prime Minister 72-76.
Office of the Prime Minister, Pyongyang, Democratic People's Republic of Korea.

Kim Il Sung, Marshal; Korean politician; b. (as Kim Song Ju) 15 April 1912, Mangyongdae, Pyongyang; s. of a peasant.
Formed Communist Youth League 27, imprisoned 29-30; joined Communist Party 31; organized and led Korean People's Revolutionary Army in struggle against the Japanese 32-45; founded Fatherland Restoration Asscn., elected Chair. 36; founded Workers' Party of Korea, elected Chair. 45; founded Korean People's Army 48, Supreme Commdr. 50-53; proclaimed the Democratic People's Republic of Korea 48, Premier 48-72, Pres. (Head of State) Dec. 72-; Marshal and Twice Hero of the Democratic People's Repub. of Korea, Order of Nat. Flag (1st Class) (three times), Order of Freedom and Independence (1st Class), Hero of Labour of the Democratic People's Repub. of Korea, Order of Lenin 72.
Publs. *Selected Works of Kim Il Sung* (6 vols.), etc.
Office of the President, Pyongyang, Democratic People's Republic of Korea.

Kim Jong Pil, Brig.-Gen.; Korean politician; b. 7 Jan. 1926, Puyo; m. Park Young Ok (niece of Pres. Park Chung Hee, *q.v.*); one s. one d.; ed. High School, Kongju, Seoul Nat. Univ. and Korean Military Acad.
Served in Korean war; Dir. Korean Central Intelligence Agency 61-63; mem. Nat. Assembly 63-68, 71-; Chair.

Democratic Republican Party 63-68; Senior Adviser to Pres. 70; Vice-Pres. Democratic Republican Party March 71; Prime Minister 71-75; mem. Spanish Nat. Acad., Korean Acad.; numerous awards from Korean and foreign govts.; Hon. LL.D. (Long Island Univ., N.Y.) 64, (Chungang Univ., Seoul) 66, (Fairleigh Dickinson Univ.) 68; Hon. D.Hum.Litt. (Westminster Coll., Fulton, Mo.) 66; Hon. Ph.D. (Hongik Univ.) 74.
Leisure interests: painting, music.
340-38, Sindang 4-dong, Sungdong-ku, Seoul, Republic of Korea.

Kim Yong Shik; Korean diplomatist; b. 11 Nov. 1913, Choongmu; s. of Kim Chai Ho and Chung Ok; m. Park Kyung Hee; ed. Chu-ou Univ., Tokyo.
Consul, Hong Kong 49; Consul-Gen., Honolulu 49; Minister, Korean Mission, Japan 51; Minister, Korean Legation, France 57; Minister, Korean Mission, Geneva 59; Perm. Vice-Minister, Ministry of Foreign Affairs 60; Amb. to U.K. (also accred. to Sweden, Denmark, and Norway) 61; Amb. to the Philippines 62; Minister of Foreign Affairs March 63; Minister without Portfolio Dec. 63; Perm. Observer of Republic of Korea at UN, concurrently accred. as Amb. to Canada 64-70; Special Asst. to Pres. for Foreign Affairs Dec. 70; Minister of Foreign Affairs 71-73, of the Board of Nat. Unification 73-74; Amb. to U.K. 74-.
Leisure interests: reading, swimming.
Embassy of Republic of Korea, 4 Palace Gate, London, W.8, England.
Telephone: 01-581-0247.

Kimura, Motoo, PH.D., D.SC.; Japanese geneticist; b. 13 Nov. 1924, Okazaki; s. of Issaku Kimura and Kana Kaneiwa; m. Hiroko Mino 1957; one s.; ed. Kyoto Univ., Univ. of Wisconsin.
Assistant, Kyoto Univ. 47-49; Researcher Nat. Inst. of Genetics 49-57, Laboratory Head 57-64, Head of Dept. of Population Genetics 64-; Visiting Prof. Univ. of Pavia 63, 65, Univ. of Wisconsin 66, Princeton Univ. 69, Stanford Univ. 73; Foreign Assoc. Nat. Acad. of Sciences, U.S.A. 73; Japanese Genetics Soc. Prize, Weldon Memorial Prize, Japan Acad. Prize, Japan Soc. of Human Genetics Prize.
Leisure interest: raising and hybridizing Lady's Slipper orchids.
Publs. *Outline of Population Genetics* (Japanese) 60, *Diffusion Models in Population Genetics* 64, *An Introduction to Population Genetics Theory* (with J. F. Crow) 70, *Theoretical Aspect of Population Genetics* (with T. Ohta) 71, *Future of Man from the Standpoint of Genetics* (Editor, Japanese) 74.
National Institute of Genetics, Yata 1, 111, Mishima 411; Home: 7-24 Kiyozumi-cho, Mishima 411, Japan.
Telephone: 0559-75-0771 (Office); 0559-75-8635 (Home).

Kimura, Toshio; Japanese politician; b. 1909; ed. Tokyo Univ.
Member, House of Reps.; fmr. Parl. Vice-Minister of Transport and Chief Cabinet Sec.; Minister of State in charge of Econ. Planning Agency 71-72; Minister of Foreign Affairs July-Dec. 74; Liberal Democrat.
Keizai Kikakucho, 3-1-1 Kasumigaseki, Chiyoda-ku, Tokyo, Japan.

Kind, Friedrich; German politician; b. 20 Dec. 1928, Leipzig; m.; ed. in Limbach.
Chairman, Potsdam District Cttee., Christlich-Demokratische Union (CDU) 52-; mem. Presidium, Cen. Cttee. CDU 60-; mem. Volkskammer (People's Chamber) 52-54, 58-; mem. Cttee. for Nat. Defence, Volkskammer 69-71; mem. State Council of German Democratic Repub. 60-; Vaterländischer Verdienstorden, Verdienstmedaille and many other decorations.
Staatsrat, Marx-Engels-Platz, 102 Berlin, German Democratic Republic.

Kindersley, 2nd Baron, cr. 41, of West Hoathly; **Hugh Kenyon Molesworth Kindersley,** C.B.E., M.C.; British company director; b. 7 May 1899, London; s. of Robert Molesworth Kindersley, 1st Baron Kindersley, G.B.E. and Gladys Margaret Kindersley; m. Nancy Farnsworth Boyd 1921; one s. two d.; ed. Eton.
Served Scots Guards 17-19 and (as Temp. Brig.) in Second World War; Vice-Pres. Officers' Asscn.; Hon. Pres. Guardian Royal Exchange Assurance; Pres. of Arthritis and Rheumatism Council for Research in Great Britain and Commonwealth 74-; fmr. Chair. Fund raising Cttee. Royal Coll. of Surgeons; mem. Court of Patrons; Hon. Fellow, Royal Coll. of Surgeons.
Leisure interest: gardening.
Ramhurst Manor, Tonbridge, Kent, England.
Telephone: Hildenborough 2174.

Kinene, Khalid Younis; Ugandan diplomatist; b. 8 Oct. 1938, Mukono; ed. Cairo, Univ. of Havana.
Foreign Service Officer 67; Ugandan Embassy, Kinshasa, subsequently Deputy Head of Mission 68-71; Senior Asst. Sec., Ministry of Foreign Affairs, Personal Asst. to Minister of Foreign Affairs until 73; Perm. Rep. to UN Jan. 74-.
Permanent Mission of Uganda to the United Nations, 801 Second Avenue, New York, N.Y. 10017, U.S.A.

King, Billie Jean; American tennis player; b. 22 Nov. 1943, Long Beach, Calif.; d. of Willard J. Moffitt; m. Larry King 1965; ed. Los Angeles State Univ.
Amateur player 58-67, professional 67-; Australian Champion 68; Italian Champion 70; French Champion 72; Wimbledon Champion 66, 67, 68, 72, 73, 75; U.S.A. Champion 67, 71, 72, 74; Fed. Repub. of Germany Champion 71; South African Champion 66, 67, 69; has won 19 Wimbledon titles (6 singles, 9 doubles, 4 mixed).
c/o United States Professional Tennis Association, P.O. Box 1115, Wakefield Station, N.Y. 10406, U.S.A.

King, Bruce; American state governor; b. 6 April 1924, Stanley, N.M.; s. of William and Molly (Schooler) King; m. Alice M. Martin 1947; two s.; ed. Stanley High School and Univ. of New Mexico.
County Commr., Santa Fé County 55-58, Chair. 57-58; mem. New Mexico House of Reps. 59-68, Speaker 63-64, 65-66, 67-68; legislative mem. State Board of Finance 61-62; Chair. Legislative Council 64, 66, 68; Democratic State Chair. 66; Gov. of New Mexico 71-Jan. 73; Dir. of various business concerns and mem. numerous civic orgs.
Office of the Governor, State Capitol, Santa Fé, New Mexico, U.S.A.

King, Cecil Harmsworth, M.A.; British company director; b. 20 Feb. 1901, London; s. of Sir Lucas White King and Geraldine Adelaide Hamilton Harmsworth; m. 1st Agnes Margaret Cooke 1923, 2nd Dame Ruth Railton 1962; three s. one d.; ed. Winchester Coll. and Christ Church, Oxford.
Director *Daily Mirror* 29; Deputy Chair. *Sunday Pictorial* 42; Dir. Anglo-Canadian Pulp and Paper Mills 44-61; Chair. Overseas Newspapers Ltd. 48-64; Chair. Daily Mirror Newspapers Ltd. and Sunday Pictorial Newspapers Ltd. 51-63; Dir. Reuters Ltd. 53-59; Chair. Scottish Daily Record and Sunday Mail Ltd. 56-58; Chair. Fleetway Publications Ltd. 59-61; Chair Newspaper Proprietors Asscn. 62-68, Int. Publishing Corpn. 63-68, Reed Paper Group 63-Dec. 68, Wall Paper Manufacturers Ltd. 65-67; Dir. Bank of England 65-68; Part-time mem. Nat. Coal Board 66-69; Chair. Iliffe-N.T.P. Inc. 66-68; mem. Nat. Parks Comm. 66-69; Chair. Butterworth & Co. Ltd. until June 68; Consultant to *The Times* 68-73; Holder of Gold Badge for Services to the City of Warsaw; Gold Medal for services to the Paper Industry; Hon. D.Litt. (Univ. Boston) 74.
Leisure interests: travel and reading.

Publs. *Strictly Personal* 69, *With Malice Towards None* 70, *Without Fear of Favour* 71, *The Cecil King Diary* Vol I 1965-70 72, Vol. II 1970-74 75, *Cecil King on Ireland* 73.
The Pavilion, 23 Greenfield Park, Dublin 4, Ireland.
Telephone: 695870.

King, Charles Glen, B.S., M.S., PH.D.; American nutritionist; b. 22 Oct. 1896, Entiat, Wash.; s. of Charles C. King and Mary Bookwalter King; m. Hilda Bainton 1919; two s. one d.; ed. public schools in Wash. and Kansas, Washington State Coll., Univ. of Pittsburgh, Columbia Univ. and Cambridge Univ.
Instructor, Univ. of Pittsburgh 20, Asst. Prof. 27, Prof. 30-42, Dir. of Buhl Foundation Research, Chair. of Faculty Council 41; Visiting Prof. Columbia Univ. 42-46, Prof. 47-62, Emer. Prof. and Special Lecturer 62-72; Scientific Dir. Nutrition Foundation 42-55, Exec. Dir. 56-60, Pres. 60-63, Trustee 63-; Past Pres. American Inst. of Nutrition, American Soc. of Biological Chemists, Fifth Int. Congress of Nutrition, American Public Health Asscn.; mem. Nat. Acad. of Sciences; Consultant, Rockefeller Foundation; mem. Int. Council of Scientific Unions; Hon. Pres. Int. Union of Nutritional Sciences; Hon. mem. Royal Soc. of Health, Soc. of Biochem., Biophysics and Microbiology of Finland; Conrad A. Elvehjem Award, Pittsburgh Bicentennial Award, John Scott Award, Nicholas Appert Award, Charles Spencer Award, Purkyne Gold medal of Acad. of Sciences of Czechoslovakia.
Leisure interests: horticulture, trout fishing, music, philosophy.
Publs. *History of the Nutrition Foundation* 76; *Second International Conference on Vitamin C* (co-editor) 75; scientific journal papers and monographs on isolation, biological synthesis and functions of vitamin C 29-69, molecular structure of fats 28-41, enzymes 30-41, nutrition and public health 41-69.
P.O. Box 192, Kendal at Longwood, Kennett Square, Pa. 19348, U.S.A.
Telephone: 215-388-1398.

King, Gen. Sir Frank Douglas, K.C.B., M.B.E.; British army officer; b. 9 March 1919, Brightwell, Berkshire; s. of Arthur King and Kate Eliza Sheard; m. Joy Emily Ellen Taylor-Lane 1947; one s. two d.; ed. Wallingford County Grammar School.
Served with 21st Royal Fusiliers 40-42, Airborne Force 43-45; Royal Mil. Coll. of Science 46; Staff Coll. 50; Command, Second Bn. Parachute Regt. 60-62, 11th Infantry Brigade Group, British Army of the Rhine (B.A.O.R.) 62-64; Div. Land-Air Warfare, Ministry of Defence 67-68; Commdt. Royal Mil. Coll. of Science 69-70; G.O.C.-in-C. Strategic Command 71-72; G.O.C.-in-C. Div. of Operations, N. Ireland 73-75; G.O.C. Northern Army Group and C.-in-C. B.A.O.R. Jan. 76-.
Leisure interests: golf, flying, gardening.
Flagstaff House, British Army of the Rhine, B.F.P.O. 40, Federal Republic of Germany; and c/o Williams & Glyns Bank, 69 Aldwych, London, W.C.2., England.
Telephone: Rhine Army, Ext. 2311.

King, Frank Lester; American banker; b. 5 Aug. 1897, Sparta, Ill.; s. of John L. King and Anna Syar; m. Lucille Alhime 1924; three s.; ed. Sparta (Ill.) High School and Northwestern Univ.
Assistant Cashier First Nat. Bank Sparta, Ill. 16-18; service in U.S. Army 19; Nat. Bank Examiner 20-25; Asst. Cashier Chicago Mutual Nat. Bank 26-27; Comptroller Continental Illinois Nat. Bank and Trust Co. 28-42; Exec. Vice-Pres. United Calif. Bank 43-44, Pres. 45-48; Chair. 59-73, Dir. March 73-; Chair. Western Bancorporation, Los Angeles 59-73, Dir. March 73-; Dir. United Calif. Bank Int., N.Y.; Dir. Cyprus Mines Corpn., U.S. Borax and Chemical Corpn., Pacific Indemnity Co., Pacific Mutual Life Insurance Co., El

Paso Natural Gas Co.; Trustee, Univ. of Southern Calif.

Leisure interests: golf, hunting.

United California Bank, P.O. Box 3666, Los Angeles, Calif. 90051; Home: 10375 Wilshire Boulevard, Los Angeles, Calif. 90024, U.S.A.

Telephone: 213-624-0111 (Office).

King, Phillip, C.B.E., M.A. (CANTAB); British sculptor; b. 1 May 1934, Tunis, Tunisia; s. of Thomas J. King and Gabrielle Liautard; m. Lilian Odelle 1957; one s.; ed. Mill Hill School, Christ's Coll., Cambridge, St. Martin's School of Art, London.

Assistant to Henry Moore (q.v.) 57-59; taught at St. Martin's School of Art 59-74; one-man exhbn., Whitechapel Gallery 68, British Pavilion at Venice Biennale with Bridget Riley (q.v.) 68, British Council touring exhbn. Krüller Muller (Netherlands), Düsseldorf, Bern, Paris and Belfast 74-75; Trustee, Tate Gallery 67-69; 1st Prize Int. Sculpture Exhbn., Piestany (Czechoslovakia) 68.

Leisure interest: holidays in Corsica close to both land and sea.

5 Parsifal Road, West Hampstead, London, N.W.6, England.

Telephone: 01-435-4283.

Kings Norton, Baron (Life Peer), cr. 65, of Wotton Underwood; **Harold Roxbee Cox,** Kt., PH.D., D.I.C., B.SC.(ENG.), F.I.MECH.E., HON. F.R.AE.S.; British engineer and scientist; b. 1902, Birmingham; s. of William John Roxbee Cox and Amelia (née Stern); m. Marjorie Withers 1927; two s.; ed. Kings Norton School, Imperial Coll. of Science and Technology.

Engineer on construction of airship R.101 24-29; Chief Technical Officer, Royal Airship Works 31; investigations in wing-flutter and stability of structures 31-35; Principal Scientific Officer, Aerodynamics Dept., R.A.E. 35-36; Head of Air Defence Dept. R.A.E. 36-38; Chief Technical Officer, Air Registration Board 38-39; Supt. of Scientific Research, R.A.E. 39-40; Deputy Dir. Scientific Research, Ministry of Aircraft Production 40-43; Dir. of Special Projects, M.A.P. 43-44; Chair. and Man. Dir. of Power Jets (Research and Devt.) Ltd. 44-46; Dir. Nat. Gas Turbine Establishment 46-48; Chair. Gas Turbine Collaboration Cttee. 41-44, 46-48; Chief Scientist, Ministry of Fuel and Power 48-54; Chair. Civil Aircraft Research Cttee. 53-58; Dir. Wilmot Breeden Ltd. 54-60; Chancellor, Cranfield Inst. of Technology; Vice-Chair. Air Registration Board 59-66, Chair. 66-72; Deputy Chair. The Metal Box Co. 59-61, Chair. 61-67; Dir. Boulton Paul Aircraft Co. Ltd. 58-68, Ricardo and Co. Engineers (1927) Ltd. 65-, Steel Co. of Wales Ltd. 65-67, Dir. Dowty Rotol Ltd. 68-75, British Printing Corpn. Ltd. 68-, Hoechst, U.K. 70-75; Chair. Berger Jenson and Nicholson Ltd. 67-75, Applied Photophysics Ltd. 72-, Landspeed Ltd. 75-; Chair. of Nat. Council for Technological Awards 60-64; Chair. of Council for Scientific and Industrial Research 61-65; Chair. Council for Nat. Academic Awards 64-71; Pres. Royal Aeronautical Soc. 47-49; Chair. Naval Educ. Advisory Cttee. 56-60; Pres. Royal Inst. of Great Britain 69-; Medal of Freedom (U.S.A.) with Silver Palm; Bronze Medal (Univ. Louvain) 46; Hon. D.Sc. (Birmingham Univ., Cranfield); Hon. D.Tech. (Brunel Univ.); Fellow of Imperial Coll., Thames Polytechnic; Hon. LL.D. (Council for Nat. Academic Awards).

Leisure interest: collecting aeronautical antiques.

3 Upper Harley Street, London, N.W.1; and Westcote House, Chipping Campden, Glos., England.

Telephone: 01-935-3167 (London); Evesham 840-440.

Kingsbury-Smith, Joseph; American journalist; b. 20 Feb. 1908, New York; m. Ruth Eileen King 1940; two d.; ed. Friends' School, Poughkeepsie, and London Univ. International News Service 24-26; United Press 26-27; I.N.S. London 27-31; Washington 31-36; Man. London

Bureau 36-38; Washington 40-44; European Gen.-Dir. 44-55; Pres. and Gen. Man. I.N.S. 55-57; Vice-Pres., Assoc. Gen. Man., United Press Int. 58-59; Trustee Hearst Estate and Fordham Univ.; Publr. N.Y. Journal-American 59-; Vice-Pres. and European Dir. Hearst Corpn. 65-; Chief Foreign Writer, the Hearst Newspapers and King Features Syndicate; various journalistic awards, and Chevalier de la Légion d'Honneur, mostly in recognition of an exchange of correspondence with Stalin (1949) during the blockade of Berlin; Pulitzer Prize 56 for Int. Reporting.

Via Boncompagni 47, Rome, Italy.

Telephone: 463-742.

Kingswell, Joseph Attard; Maltese trade unionist and diplomatist; b. 29 July 1925, Senglea; ed. Lyceum and Dockyard School.

Member Nat. Exec., Gen. Workers' Union 45-, Asst. Gen. Sec. 52-58, Gen. Sec. 58-71; Editor It-Torca 58-64; Chair. and Man. Dir. Union Press, Untours Ltd. and all other Union enterprises; Amb. to Belgium 71-, also accred. as Amb. to France, Fed. Germany, U.S.A., as High Commr. to Canada and Perm. Rep. to UN 71-, as Chief of Mission to EEC, and as Amb. to Netherlands, Luxembourg, Denmark, Sweden, Finland, Norway and Spain 72-.

Embassy of Malta, 92 chaussée de Charleroi, 1060 Brussels, Belgium.

Kinney, E. Robert, A.B.; American business executive; b. 12 April 1917, Burnham, Me.; ed. Bates Coll., Harvard Graduate School.

Joined Gorton Corpn. 54, Pres. 58-68; Vice-Pres. General Mills Inc. (following merger with Gorton Corpn.) 68, Dir. 69-, Exec. Vice-Pres. 69-70, Chief Financial Officer 70-73, Pres., Chief Operating Officer June 73-; Dir. several cos. and financing insts.; Trustee, Bates Coll., Maine Sea Coast Missionary Soc., George Putnam Fund and others; Dir., mem. Exec. Cttee. Tyrone Guthrie Theatre, Minneapolis YMCA.

General Mills Inc., P.O. Box 1113, Minneapolis, Minn. 55440, U.S.A.

Kinoshita, James Otoichi; Japanese author; b. 3 June 1889, Totori-ken; m. Fumiko Kaneko 1920; one s.; ed. Univs. of California and Southern California.

Former Correspondent, Washington Disarmament Conf.; Editor Tsingtao Leader (English daily), Staff writer of Chugai Shogyo 25, Sec.-Gen. Tokyo Press Asscn. and Dir. Liberal News Agency; Exec. Dir. Japan Trade Promotion Asscn. 30-47, Pres. 48; Founder The Friends of the UN 48 (now The Friends of the World), Man. Dir. 52-, Vice-Pres. 62-, Pres. 69-; Pres. Nippon Mutual Devt. Co. Ltd. 63; Dir. Initiating est. of Tachikawa Country Club 57.

Leisure interests: travel, archaeology, international friendship, calligraphy.

Publs. Report on International Child Welfare Week in Tsingtau 24, Analysis of American Prosperity 28, Analysis of American Prosperity 30, Educational Marketing Campaign of Silk 34, Thrice Around the World, Rationalization of American Industry, Cherry Blossom around the World: Donation of Japanese School Children 73, and several translations.

2056 Izumi, Komae-shi, Tokyo 182, Japan.

Telephone: 489-1300.

Kinoshita, Keisuke; Japanese film director; b. 1912; ed. Hamamatsu Industrial Coll.

Began his career in Shochiku Studio, Kamata; directed first film Hanasaku Minato 43; Henrietta Award for Nijushi no Hitomi 55, Golden Globe Award of Hollywood Foreign Press for Taiyo to Bara 57.

Films include Hanasaku Minato (Port of Flowers) 43, Yabure Daiko (Torn Drum), Carmen kokyo ni Kaeru (Carmen Comes Home) 49, Nippon no Higeki (The Tragedy of Japan) 53, Nijushi no Hitomi (Twenty-Four Eyes) 54, Nogiku no Gotoki Kimi Nariki (My First Love

Affair) 55, *Yuyakegumo* (Farewell to Dreams), *Taiyo to Bara* (The Rose of his Arm) 56, *Yorokobi-mo Kanashimi-mo Ikutoshitsuki* (The Lighthouse), *Fuzen no Tomoshibi* (Danger Stalks Near) 57, *Narayama-bushi Ko* (Ballad of the Narayama), *Kono ten no Niji* (The Eternal Rainbow) 58, *Kazahana* 59, *Sekishuncho*, *The River Fuefuki* 61, *Eien no Hito* (Bitter Spirit) 62.
1366 Tsujido, Fujisawa, Kanagawa Prefecture, Japan.

Kinoshita, Matasaburo; Japanese business executive; b. 13 Nov. 1889, Wakayama Pref.; s. of Kichibei Tomoyama and adopted s. of Jubei Kinoshita; m. Takako Kikuchi 1932; three s. two d.; ed. Tokyo Imperial Univ.
Joined Oji Paper Co. 16, Dir. 44, Vice-Pres. 50; Pres. Honshu Paper Co. 56-69, Chair. of Board 69-73, Adviser to Board 73-; Order of Merit.
Leisure interests: reading, travel, gardening.
Publs. *My contribution to the industry* 66, *My personal history* 69.
12-38 Kami-cho, Shibuya-ku, Tokyo 150, Japan.
Telephone: Tokyo 467-6649.

Kintner, William R., B.S., M.A., PH.D.; American professor and writer; b. 21 April 1915, Lock Haven, Pa.; s. of late S. S. Kintner and F. Kendig Kintner; m. Xandree Hyatt 1940; one s. three d.; ed. U.S. Mil. Acad., N.Y., Georgetown Univ., Washington, D.C.
Colonel in U.S. Army 40-61, European Theatre World War II, Korea 50-52; Prof. of Political Science, Univ. of Pennsylvania 61-69; Deputy Dir. Foreign Policy Research Inst. 61-69, Dir. 69-73; Amb. to Thailand 73-75.
Leisure interests: tennis, gardening.
Publs. *Atomic Weapons in Land Combat* (with George C. Reinhardt) 53, *Protracted Conflict* (co-author) 59, *The Haphazard Years* (with George C. Reinhardt) 60, *A Forward Strategy for Tomorrow* (co-author) 61, *Building the Atlantic World* (co-author) 63, *Peace and the Strategy Conflict* 67, *The Nuclear Revolution in Soviet Military Affairs* (with Harriet Fist Scott) 68, Editor, *Safeguard: Why the ABM Makes Sense* 69, *Eastern Europe and European Security* 71, *SALT: Implications for Arms Control in the 1970s* (with Robert L. Pfaltzgraff) 73, *National Strategy in a Decade of Change* (with Richard B. Foster) 73.
c/o Department of State, Washington, D.C. 20520; Home: 2470 Woodland Road, Bryn Athyn, Pa. 19009, U.S.A.

Kinzel, Augustus Braun, A.B., B.S., D.MET., D.SC.; American technical and business executive; b. 26 July 1900, New York, N.Y.; m. 2nd Mary McClymont 1945 (deceased 1973); one s. four d.; ed. Columbia Univ. Mass. Inst. of Technology and Univ. of Nancy, France.
Metallurgist, Gen. Electric Co., Pittsfield, Mass. 19-20, 22-23, Henry Disston and Sons, Inc., Phila., Pa. 23-26; Lecturer, Instructor, Extension Courses in Advanced Metallurgy, Temple Univ. 25-26; Research Metallurgist Union Carbide and Carbon Research Laboratories Inc., N.Y.C. 26-28, Group Leader 28-31, Chief Metallurgist 31-45, Vice-Pres. 45-48, Pres. 48-65, Vice-Pres. of subsidiary, Electro-Metallurgy Co. 44-54, Dir. of Research, Union Carbide Corpn. 54-55, Vice-Pres. Research 55-65; Pres. and Chief Exec. Officer Salk Inst. of Biological Studies, La Jolla, Calif. 65-67; Chair. Governing Council, Courant Inst. of Mathematical Sciences of New York Univ.; Dir. Sprague Electric Co., Gen. American Investors Co. Inc., Menasco Mfg. Co., Kalvar Corpn.; Trustee, Calif. Inst. of Technology; Adams Lecturer, American Welding Soc. 44, Campbell Lecturer, American Soc. for Metals 47, Burgess Memorial Lecturer, American Soc., for Metals 56, Howe Memorial Lecturer, American Inst. of Mining and Metallurgy Engineers 52, Sauveur Lecturer, American Soc. for Metals 52, Regent's Lecturer, Univ. of Calif., San Diego 68-69; Fellow, N.Y.

Acad. of Sciences; Benjamin Franklin Fellow, **Royal Soc. of Arts**, London; mem. Metallurgy Soc., Nat. Acad. of Sciences, Soc. for Chemical Industry; Pres. American Inst. of Mining and Metallurgy Engineers 57-58; Founding Pres. Nat. Acad. of Engineering 64, Int. Inst. of Welding (Vice-Pres.); Assoc., Linus Pauling Inst. of Science and Medicine 74-; Hon. mem. Eurospace and A.I.M.E.; Hon. D.Sc. (Univ. of Nancy, Clarkson Coll. of Technology), Hon. D.Eng. (Rensselaer and Worcester Polytechnic Insts., Univ. of Mich., Northwestern Univ., N.Y. Univ.), Hon. LL.D. (Queens Univ., Canada); Powder Metallurgy Medal, Stevens Inst. of Technology 59, Industrial Research Inst. Medal 60, James Douglas Gold Medal, Amer. Inst. of Mining, Metallurgy and Petroleum Engineers 60, Wash. Award, Soc. of Western Engineers 68; Hon. mem. Amer. Soc. for Metals (A.S.M.); Distinguished Service Award, U.S. Navy 75.
Leisure interests: sailing, flying.
Publs. *Alloys of Chromium* (snr. Author), Vols. I and II 37, 40; numerous articles on metallurgy and engineering in technical journals.
1738 Castellana Road, La Jolla, Calif. 92037, U.S.A.
Telephone: 714-454-6037.

Kipphardt, Heinar, DR.MED.; German writer; b. 8 March 1922; ed. medical studies, Düsseldorf.
Former Asst. doctor, Universitäts-Nerven-Klinik der Charité, Berlin; Chief Dramatist and Dir., Deutsches Theater, Berlin 50-59; freelance writer 59-; Deutscher Nationalpreis 53; Schiller Gedächtnispreis 62; Gerhard Hauptmann Preis 64; Adolf Grimme Preis 64; Fernsehpreis (TV Prize) der deutschen Akad. der darstellenden Künste 64.
Publs. *Shakespeare dringend gesucht* (satire) 53, *Der Aufstieg des Alois Piontek* (farce) 56, *Die Stühle des Herrn Szmil* (satire) 60, *Der Hund des Generals* (play) 62, *In der Sache J. Robert Oppenheimer* (play) 64, *Joel Brand, Die Geschichte eines Geschäfts* (play) 65, *Die Nacht, in der der Chef geschlachtet wurde* (comedy) 67, *Die Soldaten* (play) 68, *Die Ganovenfresse* (short stories) 68.
8059 Angelbruck, Oberbayern, Federal Republic of Germany.
Telephone: 8122409.

Kipping, Sir Norman Victor, G.C.M.G., K.B.E., J.P.; British industrial administrator; b. 11 May 1901, London; s. of P. P. and Rose Kipping (née Allam); m. Eileen Rose 1928; two s. one d.; ed. Univ. of London.
Transmission engineer, Int. Western Electric Co. 21-26; Standard Telephones & Cables Ltd. 27-42; Ministry of Production 42-45; Dir.-Gen. of British Industries 46-65; Hon. D.Sc. (Loughborough); Fellow, Inst. Electrical Engineers; Fellow, Inst. Production Engineers; Hon. Fellow, British Inst. Management; Chair. of Govs. Univ. Coll. School 60-72; Vice-Chair. Fulton Cttee. on the Civil Service 66-68; foreign orders.
Leisure interests: shooting, gardening.
Publs. *The Suez Contractors* 69, *Summing-up* (memoirs) 73.
Fosters, Wykeham Rise, Totteridge, London, N20 8AJ, England.
Telephone: 01-445-4054.

Kirby, Sir Arthur Frank, G.B.E., C.M.G., F.C.I.T.; British transport administrator; b. 13 July 1899, Slough, Bucks.; s. of George and Lily Kirby; m. Winifred Kate Bradley 1935; one d.; ed. Sir William Borlase's School, Marlow and London Univ.
Served in France and Belgium in First World War 17-18; with Great Western Railway 18-28; Asst. Sec. Takoradi Harbour, Gold Coast 28-35; Traffic Manager Gold Coast Railways 35-38; Asst. Supt. of the Line, Kenya and Uganda Railways 38-42; Gen. Manager Palestine Railways 42-48; Supt. of the Line, E. African

Railways and Harbours 48-51; Asst. Commr. for Transport, E. Africa High Comm. Jan. 51, Acting Commr. 52; Gen. Manager E. African Railways and Harbours 52-57; Commr. E. African Common Services Org., London 58-62; Chair. British Transport Docks Board 63-67; Pres. Shipping and Forwarding Agents 66-; Deputy Chair. Royal Commonwealth Soc. 65-68, Great Ormond Street Children's Hosp. 63-69; Gov. Nat. Hosp. for Nervous Diseases 61-69; mem. Council Royal Soc. Arts 67-72; Chair. Nat. Ports Council 67-71; Chair. Palestine Asscn.; Hon. Treas. British Inst., E. Africa.
Leisure interests: photography, social work, walking, art.
6 Baltimore Court, The Drive, Hove, Sussex, England.

Kirby, Robert E.; American business executive; b. 8 Nov. 1918, Ames, Ia.; *m.* Barbara McClintock; one *d.*; ed. Pa. State Univ.
Radar Officer, U.S. Navy, World War II; joined Westinghouse Electric Corpn. 46, Man. Industrial Electronics Eng. 52, Man. Ordnance Dept., Gen. Man. Electronics Div. 58, Vice-Pres. Eng. 63, Industrial Group Vice-Pres. 63, Exec. Vice-Pres., Dir. 66, Dir. Industry and Defence Co. 69, fmr. Vice-Chair. Operations, Chair., Chief Exec. Officer Jan. 75-; Vice-Chair. Board of Trustees Univ. of Pittsburgh; Deputy Chair. Fed. Reserve Bank of Cleveland; Dir. Pittsburgh Symphony Soc.; mem. Amer. Soc. of Naval Architects and Engs., Amer. Ordnance Asscn., Inst. of Electrical and Electronic Engs.
Leisure interests: golf, athletics, music.
Westinghouse Electric Corporation, Westinghouse Building, Gateway Center, Pittsburgh, Pa. 15222, U.S.A.

Kircheis, John Reinhardt, B.S., M.S.; American oil executive; b. 4 April 1916, N. Dakota; *s.* of J. R. Kircheis III and Ethelka Dievert; *m.* Jean Ohme 1940; two *d.*; ed. Buena Vista Coll., Drake Univ., Univ. of Iowa and Harvard Business School.
Division Man. Mobil Oil Corpn., U.S.A. 59-62; Marketing Man. Mobil Int. Div., U.S.A. 62-65; Vice-Pres. Mobil Europe, London 65-67; Man. Dir. Mobil Oil Co. Ltd., London 68, Chair. 68-75, Regional Exec. Mobil South Dec. 75-.
Leisure interests: golf, fishing.
Flat 31, 37 Grosvenor Square, London, W.1, England.
Telephone: 01-629-4762.

Kircher, Donald Peter; American businessman; b. 28 April 1915, St. Paul, Minn.; *s.* of Frank Joseph Kircher and Alma Peterson; *m.* Lois Moeller 1965; one *s.* one *d.*; ed. Univ. of Minn. and Columbia Univ.
Admitted to New York State Bar 39, private law practice 39-48, with Winthrop, Stimson, Putnam and Roberts 39-41, 46-48; Asst. to Pres. Singer Co. 48-49, Asst. Vice-Pres. 49-52, Vice-Pres. 52-58, Pres. 58-68; Pres. and Chair. Board, the Singer Co. 68-75; Dir.-Gen. Cable Corpn., Morgan Guaranty Trust Co., N.Y., Metropolitan Life Insurance Co., J. P. Morgan and Co. Inc.; Silver Star with Oak Leaf Clusters, Bronze Star, Purple Heart with Oak Leaf Cluster, Presidential Unit Citation, Chevalier, Order of Léopold, and Croix de Guerre (Belgium).
Office: 30 Rockefeller Plaza, New York City, N.Y. 10020, U.S.A.

Kirchschläger, Rudolf, DR.JUR.; Austrian politician; b. 20 March 1915, Upper Austria; *m.* Herma Sorger 1940; one *s.* one *d.*; ed. Univ. of Vienna.
Judge until 54; joined Ministry of Foreign Affairs 54, Head of Dept. of Int. Law 56, Deputy Sec.-Gen. for Foreign Affairs 62-67; Principal Private Sec. to the Minister of Foreign Affairs 63-66; Minister to Czechoslovakia until 70; Minister of Foreign Affairs 70-74; Pres. of Austria July 74-; has attended numerous int.

confs. and been mem. of Austrian del. to UN Gen. Assembly.
Leisure interests: music, walking.
Hofburg, A-1014 Vienna, Austria.
Telephone: 57-36-26.

Kirichenko, Yuri Alekseyevich; Soviet diplomatist; b. 13 Jan. 1936, Zernograd, Rostov Region; ed. Kiev Univ.
Diplomatic Service 58-; Counsellor, Egypt 64-70; on staff of Mnistry of Foreign Affairs 70-72; Minister Counsellor, Turkey 72-73; Amb. to Iceland 73-75, to Norway 75-.
Embassy of the U.S.S.R., Drammensvn. 74, Oslo 2, Norway.

Kirilenko, Andrei Pavlovich; Soviet politician; b. 8 Sept. 1906, Alexeevka, Voronezh region; ed. Higher Technical School.
Fitter 25-29; Young Communist League 29-30; mem. C.P.S.U. 31-; Engineer 36-38; Sec. District, later Regional Cttee.; Zaporozhe Regional Cttee., C.P.S.U. 38-41, 43-47; Soviet Army 41-43; First Sec. Nicolaev City and Regional Cttee., C.P.S.U. 47-50, Dnepropetrovsk Regional Cttee. 50-51, Sverdlovsk Regional Cttee. 55-62; Cand. mem. Presidium of Cen. Cttee. of the C.P. of the U.S.S.R. 57-61, mem. 62-66, Sec. 66-, mem. Politburo 66-; First Vice-Chair. Bureau for the R.S.F.S.R. 62; Deputy to U.S.S.R. Supreme Soviet 50-; Order of Lenin, Hammer and Sickle Gold Medal; Hero of Socialist Labour.
Politburo of Central Committee of the Communist Party of the U.S.S.R., 4 Staraya ploschad, Moscow, U.S.S.R.

Kirillin, Vladimir Alekseyevich; Soviet thermophysicist and politician; b. 20 Jan. 1913, Moscow; ed. Power Engineering Inst., Moscow.
Lecturer 38-41, 43-52; Prof. Moscow Power Engineering Inst. 52-53; Corresp. mem. U.S.S.R. Acad. of Sciences 53-62, mem. 62-, Vice-Pres. 63; U.S.S.R. Dep. Minister of Higher Education 54-55; Head, Dept. of Science, Higher Education Inst. and School, Central Cttee. of C.P.S.U. 55-63; mem. Central Auditing Comm. C.P.S.U. 56-61; Alt. mem. C.P.S.U. Cen. Cttee. 61-66, mem. 66-; Deputy to U.S.S.R. Supreme Soviet 62-; fmr. Chair. State Cttee. for Science and Engineering 65; Vice-Chair. U.S.S.R. Council of Ministers 65-; State Prize 51, Lenin Prize 59.
Publs. *Cycles of Turbines of Internal Combustion* 49, *Fundamentals of Experimental Thermodynamics* 50, *Steam in Power* 53, *Thermodynamics of Solutions* 56, *Thermodynamic Properties of Gases* 53, *Investigation of Thermodynamic Properties of Substances* 63.
Council of Ministers, The Kremlin, Moscow, U.S.S.R.

Kirk, Grayson, PH.D.; American university president; b. 12 Oct. 1903, Jeffersonville, Ohio; *s.* of Traine C. and Nora (Eichelberger) Kirk; *m.* Marion Sands 1925; one *s.*; ed. Miami Univ., Clark Univ., Ecole Libre des Sciences Politiques, Paris, Univ. of Wisconsin, London School of Economics.
Instructor in Political Science, Univ. of Wisconsin 29-30; Asst. Prof. 30-36, Assoc. Prof. 36-38, Prof. of Political Science 38-40; Assoc. Prof. of Govt., Columbia Univ. 40-43; Research Assoc., Yale Inst. of International Studies 43-44; Prof. of Govt., Columbia Univ. 43-47, Prof. of Int. Relations 47-49, Provost 49-50, Vice-Pres. and Provost 50-53, Acting Pres. 51, Pres. and Trustee 53-68, Pres. Emer. and Trustee Emer. 68-; Bryce Prof. Emer. of the History of Int. Relations, Columbia Univ.; Head of Security Section, Div. of Political Studies, State Dept. 42-43; mem. U.S. Del. Dumbarton Oaks 44; Exec. Officer, Third Comm. (Security Council), San Francisco Conf. 45; mem. Board of Dirs. Acad. of Political Science, International Business Machines Corpn. Inc., Nation-Wide Securities Co., Dividend

Shares Inc., The Tinker Foundation, France-America Society; Trustee, Consolidated Edison Company of N.Y., Asia Foundation, Greenwich Savings Bank, Inst. of Int. Educ., Lycée Français of N.Y.; Commdr. Order of Orange Nassau (Netherlands), Hon. K.B.E., Grand Officer Légion d'Honneur, Knight St. John, Officer, Order of Grand Cross of George I (Greece), Order of the Sacred Treasure, 1st Class (Japan), and Italian and Iranian decorations, Commdr. de l'Ordre des palmes académiques (France); Hon. LL.D. (Miami, Waynesburg, Brown, Union, Princeton, Wisconsin, Syracuse, Williams, Pennsylvania, Harvard, Tennessee, Washington, New York, Clark, Puerto Rico, Johns Hopkins, Columbia, Amherst, Dartmouth Coll., Northwestern Univ., Jewish Theol. Seminary, St. Lawrence Univ., Denver, Notre Dame, Bates Coll., Univ. of Michigan, Waseda (Japan), Sussex, Venezuelan Univs. and Univs. in India and Thailand), Hon. Ph.D. (Bologna), D.C.L. (Univ. of King's Coll., Halifax, Nova Scotia), Hon. L.H.D. (Univ. of N. Dakota).

Publs. *Philippine Independence* 36, *Contemporary International Politics* (with W. R. Sharp) 40, *War and National Policy, Syllabus* (with R. P. Stebbins) 41, *The Study of International Relations in American Colleges and Universities* 47.

Home: 28 Sunnybrook Road, Bronxville, N.Y. 10708; Office: Columbia University, 125 Maiden Lane, New York, N.Y. 10038, U.S.A.

Telephone: 943-8162.

Kirk, Sir Peter Michael, Kt., M.P.; British politician; b. 19 May 1928, Oxford; *s.* of Kenneth Escott Kirk, D.D.; *m.* Elizabeth Mary Graham 1950; three *s.*; ed. Marlborough Coll., Trinity Coll., Oxford, Univ. of Zurich. M.P. for Gravesend 55-64, for Saffron Walden 65-; mem. U.K. del., Council of Europe and Western European Union 56-63, 66-70; Chair. Gen. Affairs Cttee., Western European Union 60-63; Chair. Political Cttee., Council of Europe 69-70; Chair. Non-represented Nations Cttee., Council of Europe 59-61; Chair. Budget Cttee., Western European Union 67-69; Under-Sec. of State for War 63-64, for Defence for the Army April-Oct. 64, for Defence for the Royal Navy 70-72; Chair. Conservative group and leader of British del., European Parl. 73-.

Leisure interests: opera, walking.

Publ. *One Army Strong* 58.

Coote's Farm, Steeple Bumpstead, Haverhill, Suffolk, England.

Telephone: Steeple Bumpstead 388.

Kirkaldy, Harold Stewart, C.B.E., M.A., LL.B.; British university professor (retd.); b. 27 Dec. 1902, Titaghur, India; *s.* of late David and Anne Kirkaldy; ed. Grove Acad., Broughty Ferry, and Univ. of Edinburgh.

Assistant Sec. British Employers' Confederation 29-39; Gen. Sec. Iron and Steel Trades Employers' Asscn. 39-45; mem. British Del. Int. Lab. Conf. 29-44; Prof. of Industrial Relations, Cambridge Univ. 44-63, Fellow of Queens' Coll. 44-, Vice-Pres. 65-70; mem. of Cttee. of Experts on the Application of Int. Lab. Conventions 46-; Chair. of various Wages Councils under Wages Councils Acts 46-62; Deputy Chair. Royal Comm. on Nat. Incomes 62-65; Chair. of various Comms. of Inquiry, etc.; Perin Memorial Lecturer, Jamshedpur, India 46; mem. Admin. Board Staff Pensions Fund of ILO 46-75, Chair. 60-75; Chair. UN Joint Staff Pensions Board 60-62; mem. Industrial Disputes Tribunal 52-59; Pres. Mauritius Trade Disputes Arbitration Tribunal 59; mem. Cttee. on Remuneration of Ministers and M.P.s 63-64; Barrister-at-Law.

31A The Strand, Walmer, Deal, Kent.

Kirkconnell, Watson, M.A., PH.D., LL.D., D.LITT., D. ès L., L.H.D., D.P.EC., D.C.L.; Canadian classical scholar; b. 16 May 1895, Port Hope, Ont.; *s.* of Thomas Kirkconnell and Bertha Watson Kirkconnell; *m.* 1st

Isabel Peel 1924 (died 1925), 2nd Hope Kitchener 1930; two *s.* three *d.*; ed. Queen's Univ. (Kingston, Ont.), and Lincoln Coll., Oxford.

Lecturer in English Wesley Coll. 22, Asst. Prof. 23, Associate Prof. 24, Prof. 31; Prof. of Classics United Coll. 34-40; Prof. of English, McMaster Univ., Hamilton Ont. 40-48; Pres. Acadia Univ. 48-64, Prof. of English 64-; Knight Commdr. Order of the Falcon (Iceland), Knight Polonia Restituta, Fellow, Royal Soc., Canada, hon. mem. Petöfi Soc., Hungary; Hon. Fellow, Icelandic Soc. of Letters; Silver Laurel, Polish Acad. of Literature; foreign mem. Kisfaludy Soc., Hungary; Medal of Honour, P.E.N. Club of Hungary; mem. London School of Slavonic Studies; mem. Shevchenko Soc. of Sciences; Pres. Canadian Authors' Asscn. 42-44; 56-58; Chair. Writers' War Cttee. for Canada 42-44; Humanities Research Council of Canada 43-46; Lorne Pierce Gold Medal, Royal Society of Canada; Nova Scotia Drama League Trophy 56, Shevchenko Medal and Plaque, Gold Medal of Freedom (Magyars in Exile) 64, George Washington Medal, American Hungarian Studies Foundation 67, Centennial Medal (Canada) 67; Hon. Fellow, Univ. of Winnipeg 68, Officer, Order of Canda 68.

Publs. *International Aspects of Unemployment* 23, *European Elegies* 28, *Icelandic Verse* 30, *The European Heritage* 30, *The Magyar Muse* 33, *The Eternal Quest* 34, *Canadian Overtones* 35, *Polish Lyrics* 36, *Death of Buda* (from Magyar) 37, *Canada, Europe and Hitler* 39, *Titus the Toad* 39, *Ukrainian Canadians and the War* 40, *The Flying Bull and Other Tales* 40, *Canadians All* 41, *Twilight of Liberty* 41, *Seven Pillars of Freedom* 44, *The Quebec Tradition* (with Séraphin Marion) 46, *The Humanities in Canada* (with A. S. P. Woodhouse) 47, *Little Treasury of Hungarian Verse* 47, *Liberal Education in the Canadian Democracy* 48, *The Crisis in Education* 48, *The Celestial Cycle* 52, *Cultural Stratification in Canadian Place-Names* 54, *The Mod at Grand Pré* 55, *The Place of Slavic Studies in Canada* 58; verse translation of the Polish epic *Pan Tadeusz* 32, *The Ukrainian Poets* (with C. H. Andrusyshen) 63, *Complete Poetical Works of Taras Sherchenko* (with C. H. Andrusyshen) 64, *The Invincible Samson* 64, *Centennial Tales and Other Poems* 65, *A Slice of Canada: Memoirs* 66, *Scottish Place-names in Canada* 69, *Awake the Courteous Echo* 70, *A Georgian House on the Post Road* 71, *Climbing the Green Tree* 76.

Box 460, Wolfville, Nova Scotia, Canada.

Telephone: 902-542-3484.

Kirkley, Howard Leslie, C.B.E., A.C.I.S.; British chartered secretary; b. 13 March 1911, Manchester; *s.* of Albert and Elizabeth Kirkley; ed. Manchester Central High School.

Local govt. service, Manchester and Southall 28-41; Relief work 41-45; commercial appointments, Leeds 45-51; Gen. Sec. Oxford Cttee. for Famine Relief 51-58; Dir. Oxfam 58-74; Pres. Int. Council of Voluntary Agencies 68-71, Chair. Gov. Board 71-; Vice-Chair. Voluntary Cttee. on Overseas Aid and Devt. 73-; mem. Crown Agents Board 74-; Chair. Standing Conf. of British Org. for Aid to Refugees 74-; Kt. Commdr. Order of St. Sylvester, decorations from Tunisian and Korean govts.; Hon. M.A. (Oxford, Leeds, Bradford); Hon. Fellow (Manchester Polytechnic).

Leisure interests: walking, gardening, cricket.

Grey Barn, Stonehill Lane, Southmoor, Abingdon, Oxon., England.

Telephone: Longworth 820281.

Kirkpatrick, Miles W., LL.B.; American government official; b. 1 June 1918, Easton, Pa.; *s.* of late William H. Kirkpatrick; *m.* Anne Skerrett; one *s.* two *d.*; ed. Princeton Univ. and Univ. of Pennsylvania Law School.

Chairman Fed. Trade Comm. 70-73; Partner Morgan,

Lewis and Bockius, Washington, D.C.; mem. American Bar Asscn.

Morgan, Lewis and Bockius, 1140 Connecticut Avenue, N.W., Washington, D.C. 20036, U.S.A.

Kirkpatrick, Ralph, D.MUS.; American harpsichordist; b. 10 June 1911, Leominster, Mass.; s. of Edwin Asbury Kirkpatrick and Florence May (Clifford) Kirkpatrick; ed. Harvard Coll.

Harpsichord, clavichord and early piano exponent; tours throughout America and Europe 33-; Lecturer of Music, Yale Univ. 40, Assoc. Prof. 56-65, Prof. 65-; Ernest Bloch Prof. of Music, Berkeley, Calif. 64; recordings of much classical music including Bach's harpsichord concertos 58-60 and complete clavier works 56-67; Fellow, Amer. Acad. of Arts and Sciences; mem. Amer. Philosophical Soc.; Order of Merit Italian Republic.

Leisure interests: literature in English, French, German and Italian, visual arts, outdoor work, and the collecting of books and prints.

Publs. J. S. Bach's *Goldberg Variations* (Editor) 38, *Domenico Scarlatti* 53, Domenico Scarlatti's *Sixty Sonatas* (Editor) 53, *Complete Keyboard Works in Facsimile* (Editor) 72.

Old Quarry, Guilford, Conn. 06437, U.S.A.
Telephone: 453-3409.

Kirkup, James, B.A.; British writer; b. 23 April 1918, South Shields; s. of James Harold Kirkup and Mary Johnston; ed. Durham Univ.

Gregory Fellow in Poetry, Leeds Univ. 50-52; Visiting Poet, Bath Acad. of Art 53-56; travelling lectureship from Swedish Ministry of Education 56-57; Prof. of English Language and Literature, Salamanca (Spain) 57-58; Prof. of Eng. Lit., Tohoku Univ. 59-61; Visiting Prof. of Eng. Lit., Japan Women's Univ., Tokyo 64-; Visiting Prof. and Poet in Residence, Amherst Coll. Mass. 68-; Prof. of English Literature, Univ. of Nagoya, Japan 69-72; Literary Editor *Orient-West Magazine*, Tokyo 63-65; Atlantic Award in Literature (Rockefeller Foundation) 59, F.R.S.L. 62, First Prize, Japan P.E.N. literary contest 65, Mildred Batchelder Award, A.L.A. 68, Crowned Ollave of the Order of Bards, Ovates and Druids 74; Hon. Fellow (Inst. of Psychophysical Research, Oxford) 70; Fellow in Creative Writing (Sheffield Univ.) 74-75.

Leisure interests: macrobiotic diet, Zen Buddhist meditation, listening to good jazz (leading fan of Anita O'Day, Blossom Dearie, Lee Wylie, etc.).

Publs. *The Cosmic Shape* 47, *The Drowned Sailor* 48, *The Creation* 50, *The Submerged Village* 51, *A Correct Compassion* 52, *A Spring Journey* 54, *Upon This Rock, The Dark Child, The Triumph of Harmony* 55, *The True Mystery of the Nativity, Ancestral Voices, The Radiance of the King* 56, *The Descent into the Cave, The Only Child* (autobiography) 57; TV plays: *The Peach Garden, Two Pigeons Flying High, Sorrows, Passions and Alarms* (autobiography) 60, *The True Mystery of the Passion, The Prodigal Son* (poems) 56-60, *These Horned Islands* (travel) 62, *The Love of Others* (novel) 62, *Tropic Temper* (travel) 63, *Refusal to Conform, Last and First Poems* 63, *The Heavenly Mandate* 64, *Japan Industrial*, Vols. I and II 64-65, *Tokyo* (travel) 66, *Bangkok* (travel) 67, *Paper Windows: Poems from Japan* 67, *Michael Kohlhaas* 67, *Filipinescas* (travel) 68, *One Man's Russia* (travel) 68, *Streets of Asia* (travel) 69; *Hong Kong* (travel) 69, *White Shadows, Black Shadows: Poems of Peace and War* 69, *The Body Servant: Poems of Exile* 71, *Japan Behind the Fan* 70, *Streets of Asia* 69, *Insect Summer* (novel) 71, *A Bewick Bestiary* 71, *Transmental Vibrations* 72, *To the Ancestral North* 72, *Brand* (Ibsen) 72, *The Magic Drum* (play for children) 72, (story for children) 73, *Peer Gynt* 73, *The Winter Moon, Selected Poems of Takagi Kyozo*; Plays: *Cyrano de Bergerac* 74, *Play Strindberg* 74, *The Conformer* 75,

Don Carlos 75, *Heaven, Hell and Hara-Kiri: The Rise and Fall of the Japanese Superstate* 75, *Background to English Literature* 75, *An English Traveller in Japan* 75, and numerous trans. from French, German, Japanese and Norwegian.

BM-Box 2780, London, WC1V 6XX, England.
Telephone: 01-405-0463.

Kirloskar, Shantanu Laxman, B.SC.; Indian industrialist; b. 28 May 1903, Sholapur, Maharashtra State; m. Yamutai R. Phatak 1927; two s. one d.; ed. Massachusetts Inst. of Technology, U.S.A.

Kirloskar Brothers 26-; Chair. and Man.-Dir. Kirloskar Oil Engines Ltd., Poona; Chair. Board of Dirs. Kirloskar Pneumatic Co. Ltd., Poona, Kirloskar Consultants Ltd., Poona, Kirloskar Cummins Ltd., Poona, Swastik Rubber Products Ltd., Poona, Padamjee Pulp and Paper Mills Ltd., Poona, Kirloskar Tractors Ltd., Poona Industrial Hotel Ltd., Kirloskar Brothers Ltd., The Central Pulp Mills Ltd.; Dir. numerous other companies; fmr. Chair. Indian Inst. of Management; mem. Maharatta Chamber of Commerce and Industries, Poona; Pres. Fed. of Indian Chambers of Commerce and Industry, New Delhi 65-66; First Pres. Indo-American Chamber of Commerce; Padma Bhushan 65; Chair. Cttee. for Econ. Devt. in India; Sir Walter Puckey Prize 68; Life mem. Inst. of Engineers (India) 70, Karma Virottama 72.

Leisure interests: Western classical music, painting.

Publ. *Jet Yugateel Marathi Manus* (A Man from Maharashtra in the Jet Age).

Kirloskar Oil Engines Ltd., Corporate Office, 11 Koregaon Road, Poona 411001; Home: "Lakaki", Shivajinagar, Poona 411016, India.
Telephone: 20080 (Office); 56471 (Home).

Kironde, Apollo Kadumukasa; Ugandan diplomatist and politician; b. 1915; m. Althea Kironde; ed. King's Coll., Budo, Makerere Coll., Kampala and Adams Coll., Natal, and Univ. of S. Africa (Fort Hare).

Teacher, King's Coll., Budo 43-50; Middle Temple, London 50-52; legal practice, Uganda 52-55; Asst. Minister of Social Services 55-58; Minister of Works and Transport 58-60; Founder, United Nat. Party 60, merged with Uganda Nat. Congress (U.N.C.) 61, Leader U.N.C. 61-71; Amb. to U.S. and Perm. Rep. to UN 62-67; Special Asst. in African Problems, Dept. of Political and Security Council Affairs, UN 67; High Commr. in Canada 64-67; Dir. UN Inst. for Training and Admin. 69-70; Minister of Foreign Affairs Nov. 70-Jan. 71; Minister of Planning and Econ. Devt. 71-72; Minister of Tourism June-Dec. 72; Chair. ECA Exec. Cttee. meeting, Addis Ababa 72.

Leisure interests: carpentry, music, swimming, architecture.

c/o Ministry of Tourism, Kampala, Uganda.

Kirpal, Prem Nath, M.A., LL.B.; Indian educationist; b. 30 April 1909, Moga, Punjab; s. of Raibahadur Ishwardas and Bibi Kesari; unmarried; ed. Punjab Univ. and Balliol Coll., Oxford.

Lecturer, then Prof. of History and Political Science 34-45; Educ. Adviser, Indian High Comm., London 45-48; Deputy Sec. Ministry of Educ. and Sec.-Gen. Indian Nat. Comm. for UNESCO 48-52; Deputy Dir. then Dir. UNESCO Dept. of Cultural Activities 52-57; Joint Sec. Ministry of Educ. and Joint Educ. Adviser to Govt. of India 57-60; Sec. Ministry of Educ. 60-69; Pres. Exec. Board, UNESCO 70-72; Dir. Int. Study of Private Philanthropy 69-; Founder, Pres. Inst. of Cultural Relations and Devt. Studies, New Delhi 71-; Pres. Indian Council of Peace Research 72-; Chair. Delhi Public Library, Delhi School of Social Work; Pres. Forum of Education, India; Hon. LL.D. (Temple Univ.), Hon. D.Sc. (Leningrad Univ.), Hon. D.Litt. (Punjab Univ.).

Leisure interests: mountaineering, hiking, painting.

Publs. *East India Company and Persia 1800-1810: A Study in Diplomatic Relations, Memoirs of Wollebrant de Jong 1624, Life of Dyal Singh Majithia, Main Trends in Cultural Development of India, A Decade of Indian Education 1958-68, Indian Education—Twenty-five Years of Independence.*
Executive Board UNESCO, Place de Fontenoy, Paris 7e; Home: 63F Sujan Singh Park, New Delhi 3, India.
Telephone: 566-57-57 (UNESCO); 388-158 (New Delhi).

Kirsop, Arthur Michael Benjamin, B.A.JURIS.; British business executive; b. 28 Jan. 1931, Manchester; s. of Arthur and Sarah Kirsop (née Cauthery); m. Patricia Cooper 1957; two s.; ed. Glasgow Acad. and Oxford Univ.
Director, English Sewing Cotton Co. Ltd. 67; Dir., English Calico Ltd. (now Tootal Ltd.) 68, Joint Man. Dir. 73, Deputy Chair. 74, Chair. Feb. 75-.
Leisure interests: gardening, sport.
Tootal Ltd., 56 Oxford Street, Manchester, M60 1HJ, Lancashire; Home: Peel House, 5 Planetree Road, Hale, Cheshire, England.
Telephone: 061-228-1144 (Office); 061-980-5173 (Home).

Kirst, Hans Hellmut; German writer; b. 5 Dec. 1914, Osterode; m. Ruth Müller 1961; one d.; ed. Volksschule and Gymnasium, Osterode.
Began his career as a farmer; has been a free-lance writer since 47; mem. PEN Club, Author's Guild U.S.A.; Edgar Allan Poe Special Award, U.S.A. 65; Special Collection of Boston Univ. Library, U.S.A. 67.
Leisure interest: African sculpture.
Publs. include *Galgenstrick 51, 08/15 (trilogy) 54, Keiner kommt davon 57, Fabrik für Offiziere 60, Nacht der Generale 62, Aufstand der Soldaten 65, Die Wölfe 67, Held im Türm 70*; books translated into 28 languages.
8133 Feldafing am Starnberger See, Moorweg 3-5, Federal Republic of Germany; Caslano bei Lugano, San Michele, Casa 7, Switzerland.
Telephone: Feldafing 319 (Office); Caslano 96863 (Home).

Kirstein, Lincoln; American ballet promoter; b. 4 May 1907; ed. Harvard Univ.
Editor *Hound and Horn* (literary periodical) 27-34; Editor *The Dance Index* 41-47; established School of American Ballet, New York City, and Dir.; Dir. New York City Ballet Co.; Dir.-Gen. American Ballet.
Publs. *A Short History of Theatrical Dancing 35, Blast at Ballet 38, Low Ceiling (poems) 35, Ballet Alphabet 39, Rhymes of a P.F.C. (Private First Class) (poems) 64, Rhymes and more Rhymes of a P.F.C. 66, The Hampton Album 66, Three Pamphlets Collected 67, Movement and Metaphor: Four Centuries of Ballet 69, The New York City Ballet 73, Elie Nadelman 73, Lay this Laurel 74, Nijinsky, Dancing 74.*
State Theater, Lincoln Center, New York, N.Y. 10023, U.S.A.

Kirszenstein-Szewińska, Irena, M.ECON.; Polish sprinter; b. 24 May 1946, Leningrad, U.S.S.R.; m.; one s.; ed. Warsaw Univ.
Took part in Olympic Games, Tokyo 64 (silver medals for long jump and 200 m., gold medal for 4 x 100 m. relay), Mexico City 68 (bronze medal for 100 m., gold medal for 200 m.), Munich 72 (bronze medal for 200 m.); seven times world record holder, currently for 200 m. and 400 m.; Gold Cross of Merit 64; Officer's Cross, Order of Polonia Restituta 68, Commdr.'s Cross 72.
Ul. Bagno 5 m. 80, 00-112 Warsaw, Poland.
Telephone: 20-63-73.

Kisch, Isaak, D.IUR.; Netherlands professor; b. 1905; ed. Amsterdam and Paris Law Faculties, London School of Economics.
Called to Amsterdam Bar 32; Hon. Judge, Amsterdam Court 35; Asst. Lecturer, Law Faculty, Amsterdam Univ. 30, Lecturer 35, Asst. Prof. 38, Prof. of Comparative Law and Philosophy of Law 45-: Dir. Int. Law Inst., The Hague 49-60, Centre for Foreign Law, Amsterdam; fmr. Judge, Supreme Court of the Netherlands; mem. State Cttee. on Conflict of Law; Assoc. mem. Inst. of Int. Law; Order of the Coif, La., U.S.A.
Publs. *Rights in rem and in personam 32, Foreign Marriages 35;* various publications on civil law, comparative law, conflict of law, philosophy of law, legal history, etc.
Universiteit van Amsterdam, SPUI 21, Amsterdam, Holland.

Kishi, Nobusuke; Japanese politician; b. 1896; elder brother of the late Eisaku Sato, former Prime Minister of Japan; ed. Tokyo Imperial Univ.
Clerk of Ministry of Agriculture and Commerce 20; Chief of Industrial Administration Section, Industrial Affairs Bureau 32; concurrently Sec. to Ministry of Foreign Affairs 33; Chief of Archives Section, Ministry of Commerce and Industry 33; Sec. of Temporary Industrial Rationalization Bureau and Dir. of Industrial Affairs Bureau 35-36; served in various administrative capacities in Govt. of Manchoukuo 36-39; Vice-Minister of Commerce and Industry 39-41 and Oct.-Nov. 43; Minister of Commerce and Industry Oct. 41-April 42; elected mem. of House of Representatives 42; Minister of State without Portfolio Oct. 43-July 44; purged from public service Dec. 47; apptd. Chair. Board of Dirs. of Toyo Pulp Mfg. Co. Ltd. 49; re-elected mem. of House of Representatives 53 and 55; Chair. of Railway Construction Council 55; Minister of Foreign Affairs Dec. 56; Prime Minister 57-60; Pres. Liberal Democratic Party 57-60 (re-elected 59).
45 Nampeidai, Shibuya-ku, Tokyo, Japan.

Kishkin, Sergei Timofeyevich; Soviet metallurgist; b. 30 May 1906, Voroshilovgrad, Ukraine; ed. Moscow Higher Technical School.
Member C.P.S.U. 39-; Prof. Moscow Inst. of Aviation Technology; Corresp. mem. U.S.S.R. Acad. of Sciences 60-66, mem. 66-; Hon. Worker of Science of the R.S.F.S.R.
Publ. Numerous works on metallurgy and metal studies.
U.S.S.R. Academy of Sciences, 14 Leninsky Prospekt, Moscow, U.S.S.R.

Kisiel, Henryk, M.ECON.; Polish banker and politician; b. 1 July 1921, Łódź; ed. Faculty of Law and Econs., Łódź Univ.
Manual worker during occupation; joined Nat. Bank of Poland as trainee, Łódź 45, Dir. of Head Office 61-64; Dir. Bank Handlowy SA w Warszawie 64-66, Pres. 66-68; Under-Sec. of State, Ministry of Finance 68-71, Ministry of Foreign Trade 71; Vice-Chair. Planning Comm. of Council of Ministers 71-74; First Deputy Minister of Foreign Trade and Maritime Econ. 74; Minister of Finance Nov. 74-; Gold Cross of Merit 54, Order of Banner of Labour, 2nd Class 64, Knight's Cross, Order of Polonia Restituta 59, Officer's Cross 69, Commdr.'s, Cross 74.
Leisure interests: literature, history, sport.
Ministerstwo Finansów, ul. Swietokrzyska 12, 00-044 Warsaw, Poland.
Telephone: 26-55-95 (Office).

Kiss, Károly; Hungarian politician; b. 1903, Bicske; s. of György Kiss and Irma Gubicza; m. Ilona Kósa 1945; one s.
Leather worker; mem. Political Cttee., Hungarian Communist Party 45-53; Chair. Cen. Control Comm 46-56; Minister for Foreign Affairs 51-52; Vice-Pres. Presidential Council 49-51, 58-61, Sec. of Presidential Council 61-67; Vice-Pres. Cabinet Council 52-53; Cen. Council of Trade Unions 67-; mem. Cen. Cttee. Hungarian Socialist Workers' Party; Labour Order of Merit, golden degree 70.

Leisure interest: gardening.
Publ. *Memoirs* 74.
Central Council of Trade Unions, Dozsa György u. 84/b, 1068 Budapest VI, Hungary.
Telephone: 225-840.

Kissinger, Henry Alfred, M.A., PH.D.; American (German-born) government official and university professor; b. 27 May 1923, Fuerth, Germany; *m.* 1st Anne Fleisher 1949 (divorced 1964), one *s.* one *d.*; *m.* 2nd Nancy Maginnes 1974; ed. George Washington High School, Harvard Coll., Harvard Univ.
Went to U.S.A. 38; naturalized U.S. Citizen 43; U.S. Army Counter-Intelligence Corps 43-46, Capt. Mil. Intelligence Reserve 46-49; Consultant Operations Research Office 50, Psychological Strategic Board 52-53; Dir. Study Group on Nuclear Weapons and Foreign Policy, Council of Foreign Relations 55-56; Dir. Special Studies Project, Rockefeller Brothers Fund 56-58; Consultant, Weapons System Evaluation Group, Joint Chiefs of Staff 56-60, Nat. Security Council 61-63, U.S. Arms Control and Disarmament Agency 61-68, Dept. of State 65-68, and to various other bodies; Faculty mem. Harvard Univ. 54-71; Assoc. Dir. Harvard Univ. Center for Int. Affairs 57-60; Dir. Harvard Int. Seminar 51-71; Dir. Harvard Defense Studies Program 58-71; Assoc. Prof., Dept. of Govt., Harvard Univ. 59-62, Prof. of Govt. 62-71 (on leave of absence 69-71); Special Asst. to Pres. of U.S.A. for Nat. Security Affairs 69-75; Sec. of State Sept. 73-; prominent in Amer. negotiations for the Viet-Nam settlement of Jan. 73, and in the negotiations for a Middle East ceasefire 73, 74; Guggenheim Fellowship 65-66, Woodrow Wilson Book Prize 58, Amer. Inst. for Public Service Award 73, Nobel Peace Prize 73, Amer. Legion Distinguished Service Medal 74, Wateler Peace Prize 74, and many other awards and prizes.
Publs. *Nuclear Weapons and Foreign Policy* 56, *A World Restored: Castlereagh, Metternich and the Restoration of Peace 1812-22* 57, *The Necessity for Choice: Prospects of American Foreign Policy* 61, *The Troubled Partnership: A Reappraisal of the Atlantic Alliance* 65, *American Foreign Policy* (3 essays) 69, and over forty articles on U.S. foreign policy, international affairs and diplomatic history.
Department of State, 2201 C Street, N.W., Washington, D.C. 20520, U.S.A.

Kistiakowsky, George B(ogdan), DR. PHIL.; American chemist; b. 18 Nov. 1900, Kiev; *s.* of Bogdan and Mary Kistiakowsky; *m.* 3rd Elaine Mahoney 1962; one *d.*; ed. Univ. of Berlin.
Int. Research Fellow, Princeton 26-28; Asst. Prof. 28-30; Asst. Prof. Harvard Univ. 30-33, Assoc. Prof. 33-37; Abbott and James Lawrence Prof. of Chemistry 37-71, Emer. Prof. 71-; on leave 41-45; Chief, Explosives Div., Nat. Defence Research Cttee. 41-43; Leader, Explosives Div., Los Alamos Project of the Manhattan District, U.S.A. 44-45; Special Asst. to Pres. Eisenhower for Science and Technology 59-61; mem. American Philosophical Soc., Nat. Acad. of Sciences (Vice-Pres. 65-73); Foreign mem. Royal Soc. 60; Hon. Fellow, The Chemical Soc. (London), Medal for Merit 46; Nichols Medal of American Chemical Soc. 47; King's Medal for Service in the Cause of Freedom 47; Willard Gibbs Medal 60; Medal of Freedom 61; Nat. Medal of Science 67; C. L. Parsons Award of American Chemical Soc. 61; T. W. Richards Medal 68, Priestley Award, American Chemical Soc. 72; Hon. D.Sc. (Harvard, Pennsylvania, Rochester, Oxford and Williams Univs., Carnegie Inst. of Technology, Princeton Univ. and Case Inst. of Technology).
Publ. *Photochemical Processes* 29.
Gibbs Memorial Laboratory, Harvard University, 12 Oxford Street, Cambridge, Mass. 02138, U.S.A.
Telephone: (671) 495-4083 (Office); (617) 864-9814 (Home).

Kitagawa, Kazue, DR.ENG.; Japanese business executive; b. 26 July 1904, Nishinomiya City, Hyogo Pref.; *s.* of Eikichi and Yoi Kitagawa; *m.* Tomiko Fukunaga 1935; two *d.*; ed. Tokyo Univ.
Director of Sumitomo Electric Industries Ltd. 46-, Pres. 56-66, Chair. 66-72, Senior Adviser 72-; Fellow, I.E.E.E., U.S.A.; Order of Blue Ribbon and Purple Ribbon; First Order of the Sacred Treasure 74.
Publs. *Condenser for Electric Power* 42, *Agohige no Oshie* 58, *Creative Thinking* 66, *Computer Mind* 70, *Agriculture in the Era of Information*.
8-3, 2-chome Nikawa-kita, Takarazuka City, Hyogo, Japan.

Kitaj, R. B.; American artist; b. 1932, Ohio; ed. New York, Vienna and Royal Coll. of Arts, London.
Has lived in London since 60; Guest Prof. Univ. of Calif., Berkeley 67-68, Univ. of Calif., Los Angeles 70-71; one-man exhbns. in Marlborough New London Gallery 63, 70, Marlborough Gerson Gallery, N.Y., Los Angeles County Museum of Art 65, Stedelijk Museum, Amsterdam, Museum of Art, Cleveland and Univ. of Calif., Berkeley 67, Galerie Mikro, Berlin and tour of Fed. Germany 69-70, Kestner Gesellschaft, Hanover, Boymans-van-Beuningen Museum, Rotterdam 70, Cincinnati Art Museum, Ohio (with Jime Dine, *q.v.*) 73, Marlborough, New York 74; public collections in museums in Australia, Fed. Germany, Netherlands, Sweden, Switzerland, U.K. and U.S.A.
c/o Marlborough Fine Arts, 6 Albemarle Street, London, W.1, England.

Kittani, Ismat T.; Iraqi UN official; b. 5 April 1929, Amadiya; ed. Knox Coll., Galesburg, Ill.
High School teacher, Iraq; joined Foreign Ministry 52; Attaché, Cairo 54-57; mem. Iraqi mission to UN 57, Acting Perm. Rep. 58-59; Perm. Rep. to European Office of UN 61-64; Chief, Specialized Agencies and Admin. Cttee. of Co-ordination Affairs, Dept. of Econ. and Social Affairs, UN Secr. 64; Sec. Econ. and Social Council 65-67; Principal Officer, later Dir. Exec. Office of Sec.-Gen. of UN 67-69; Deputy to Asst. Sec.-Gen. for Inter-Agency Affairs Nov. 69-70; Asst. Sec.-Gen. for Inter-Agency Affairs 71-73; Exec. Asst. to Sec.-Gen. Sept. 73-75; Amb., Dir.-Gen. Int. Orgs. and Confs. Foreign Ministry, Baghdad 75-; fmr. del. of Iraq to various int. comms. and confs.; mem. Gov. Board ILO 59; alt. mem. Exec. Board WHO 61.
Ministry of Foreign Affairs, Baghdad, Iraq.

Kittel, Charles, PH.D.; American professor of physics and author; b. 18 July 1916, New York; *s.* of George Paul Kittel and Helen Lemler Kittel; *m.* Muriel Agnes Lister 1938; two *s.* one *d.*; ed. Massachusetts Institute of Technology and Univs. of Cambridge and Wisconsin.
Professor of Physics, Univ. of Calif. at Berkeley 51-; mem. Nat. Acad. of Sciences, American Acad. of Arts and Sciences; Buckley Prize for Solid State Physics; Berkeley Distinguished Teaching Award.
Leisure interests: friends, wine.
Publs. *Introduction to Solid State Physics* 53, 4th edn. 71, *Quantum Theory of Solids* 63, *Thermal Physics* 69.
University of Calif., Berkeley, Calif. 94720, U.S.A.

Kittikachorn, Field-Marshal Thanom; Thai officer and politician; b. 11 Aug. 1911, Tak; ed. Wat Kokplu School (Tak) and Military Acad. Bangkok.
Entered Military Survey Dept. as student officer 31, assigned to Planning Section 34; Lieut. in Mil. Education Dept. 35, Instructor 36-38, 39-41, 44-46; Capt. 38, student officer in Infantry School, active service in Shan State 41; Major 43, Lieut.-Col. 44; Instructor Mil. Acad. technical branch 46-47; Commdr. 21st Infantry Regt. 47; Colonel, Commdr. 11th Infantry Regt. 48; Deputy Commdr. 1st Infantry Division 49, Commdr. 50; Major-Gen., Dep. Commdr. 1st Army 51; Commdr. 1st Army 54; Lieut.-Gen., mem. Defence Coll. 55; Dep. Minister of Co-operatives 55; Asst. C.-in-C. of Army 57;

Dep. Minister of Defence April 57, Minister Sept. 57; Prime Minister, Minister of Defence, General 58; Dep. Prime Minister and Minister of Defence 59-63, Prime Minister 63-71, 72-73; Chair. Nat. Exec. Council Dec. 71-72; Special A.D.C. to King; Chair. United People's Party 68-73.

Kivimaa, Arvi; Finnish poet and essayist; b. 6 Sept. 1904, Hartola; *s.* of T. Kivimaa and Lyyli (née Mytkäniemi) Kivimaa; *m.* 1st Hilkka Ahti, M.A. 1931 (died 1955), 2nd Kirsti Arnold, PH.D., Asst. Prof. 1958; one *s.* one *d.*
Journalist and literary critic 22-32 and 34-37; Lecturer in Finnish, Univ. of Greifswald 32-34; Dir. Tampere Theatre 37-40; Dir. People's Theatre 40-49, and Finnish Nat. Theatre 49-50; Gen. Dir. Nat. Theatre 50-74; Chair. Finnish PEN 36 and 54-57; Vice-Chair. Asscn. Finnish Writers 41-45; Pres. Scandinavian Theatre Council 63-69, Hon. Pres. 74-; mem. Exec. Cttee. of Int. Theatre Inst. 55-65, Vice-Pres. 57-65; Pres. Finnish Centre of Int. Theatre Inst. 54-; Pres. Finnish Theatre Union 57-; mem. Scandinavian Cultural Comm. 60-71, Finnish Cttee. of UNESCO 57-71; Hon. mem. Finnish Dramatists' and Actors' Leagues; Prof. h.c. 58; Ph.D. h.c. (Helsinki) 73; Commdr. Order of the Lion of Finland, Commdr. Order of Arts and Letters (France), Officier Légion d'Honneur, Commdr. Order of Nordstjärnan (Sweden), Léopold (Belgium), Wihuri Prize 64, Henrik Steffens Prize (Hamburg) 71 and orders from Italy, Hungary and Greece.
Leisure interests: music, travel.
Publs. Selected Poems: *Airut* (Herald) 47, *Passacaglia* 50, *Sydämen levottomuus* (Restless Heart) 54; Plays: *Paula Seijes* 45, *Syntymäpäivä* (Birthday) 55; Other works: *Lähtö ja kotiinpaluu* (Farewell and Return) 38-39, *Katu nousee taivaaseen* (The Street to Heaven) 28, *Teatterivaeltaja* (Pilgrim of the Theatre) 37, *Näyttämön lumous* (Magic of the Stage) 52, *To Greece* 56, 57, *The Most Beautiful Poems* (selection) 58, *Manhattan* 59, *Joenrannan Puu* 61, *Nike of Samothrake* (poems) 64, *Prokonsuli ja Keisari* (poems) 69, *Teatterin Humanismi* (speeches) 72, *Kasvoja Valohämystä* (essays) 74, *Suomalainen Requiem* (poems) 75, and contributions to many foreign publs.
Sepänkatu 15B, Helsinki 15, Finland.
Telephone: 665648.

Kjellin, Tor Helge, PH.D.; Swedish professor of art; b. 24 April 1885; ed. Uppsala and Lund Univs.
Dozent of Art History, Lund Univ. 17-29; Prof. of Art History, Dorpat Univ. 21-24; Riga Univ. 29-31; Inspector Karlstad Art and Ethnographic Museum 28-50; expert on Church restoration, Swedish art, and Russian icons; mem. Swedish and foreign scientific societies.
Publs. *Uno Troili 1815-1875* 17, *Medeltida gravvårdsformer i Norden* 18, *Två Pietro Longhi-målningar i Sverige* 23, *Gust. Rydberg, Skånes målare* 25, *En gotl. fabeldjursfunt på Ösel* 26, *Marie gloria, en kretensisk ikon* 26, *Några romanska gravmonum, i Skåne* 27, *Ernst Norlinds konst* 27, *Die Kirche zu Karris auf Ösel und ihre Beziehungen zu Gotland* 28, *Die Hallenkirchen Estlands och Gotlands* 28, *Stilriktn. o. skolor inom det ryska ikonmåleriet* 28, *Aristoteles o. Phyllis* 28, *Vergilius i korgen o. som trollkarl* 29, *Om symboler o. emblem d gamla gravvårdar* 30, *Lettlands moderna måleri* 30, *Latviešu maksla* 32, *Icones russes* 33, *Chr. Erikssons liv och bildkonst* 34, *Två grek-byz. ikoner från Paleologtiden* 34, *Karlstads Stads 350-årsjubileum, en Minneskrönika* 34, *Lettiska bildhuggare* 35, *Glava Kyrkas Historia och Gamla Minnen* 36, *Gamla Värmländska Allmogehem och deras Möblering* 36, *Thor Fagerkvist, mästaren i Persberg* 39, *Värmlands odlingshistoria under 6,000 år* 39-41, *Wermlands Brandstods Bolag 1843-1943* 43, *Från Vänern till Västerhavet* 47, *Värmländsk konst och värmländska konstnärer* 47, *Prolog vid Hammarö köpings tillblivelse Nydrsnatten 1949* 49, *Värmlands och Dalslands kyrkor och kyrkliga konst* 52, *Christian Eriksson* 53, *Ryska ikoner i svensk och norsk ägo* 56, *Nya bidrag till Hammarö kyrkors historia (stavkyrka och blockhuskyrka)* 57, *Gravfynden i Köla kyrka* 58, *Isac Schiulström, en värmländsk bildsnidare* 58, *Nedre Ulleruds Kyrkor* 59, *Erik Jonaeus, den värmländske kyrko-målaren* 59.
Engelbrektsgatan 6, Gävle, Sweden.

Klasen, Karl Ferdinand, D.IUR.; German banker; b. 23 April 1909, Hamburg; *s.* of Heinrich and Marianne (née Treckan) Klasen; one *s.* two *d.*; ed. law studies in Freiburg, Berlin and Hamburg.
With Deutsche Bank, Hamburg 35-, Dir. 48; Pres. Landeszentralbank (Hamburg) 48-52; mem. Management Board Norddeutsche Bank 52-, Deutsche Bank 57-; Pres. Deutsche Bundesbank 70-; mem. Board of Dirs. Bank for Int. Settlements, Basle 70-; mem. of Board of Dirs. Kreditanstalt für Wiederaufbau 70-; Gov. for Germany, Int. Monetary Fund, Washington, D.C.
Deutsche Bundesbank, 6000 Frankfurt am Main, Wilhelm-Epstein Strasse 14, Federal Republic of Germany.
Telephone: 158-1.

Klassen, Elmer Theodore; American government official; b. 6 Nov. 1908, Hillsboro, Kan.; *s.* of John A. and Mary Klassen; *m.* 1st Bessie Crooks 1929, 2nd Marie Callahan 1963; one *d.* (deceased); ed. public schools in California and Harvard Univ. Graduate School of Business Admin.
With American Can Co., New York City 25-68, Pres. 65-68; Deputy Postmaster-Gen. of U.S.A. 69-Jan. 71; mem. Board of Govs., U.S. Postal Service Jan. 71-; Postmaster-Gen. of U.S.A. 72-75; Benjamin Franklin Award, U.S. Postal Service Award.
7224 Arrowood Road, Bethesda, Md. 20034, U.S.A.

Klaus, Josef, LL.D.; Austrian lawyer and politician; b. 15 Aug. 1910, Mauthen, Carinthia; *m.* Erna Seywald 1936; five *c.*; ed. Univs. of Vienna, Marburg/Lahn.
Secretary Vienna Chamber of Labour 34-38 (Deputy-Chair. of Political Economy Dept.); with timber trade firm, Vienna 38-39; war service 39-45 (prisoner of war); lawyer, Hallein, Salzburg 45-49; Gov. of Salzburg 49-61; Fed. Minister of Finance 61-63; Fed. Chancellor Feb. 64-March 70; fmr. Chair. Austrian People's Party.
Österreichische Volkspartei, 1 Kärntnerstrasse 51, Vienna, Austria.

Klauser, Theodor, DR.THEOL.; German university professor and priest; b. 25 Feb. 1894; ed. Freiburg Univ., Münster Univ., Pontificio Istituto di Archeologia Cristiana.
Vicar at Detmold 20; Rector at Brakel 27; Dozent, Bonn Univ., Catholic Theological Faculty 31; Asst. German Archaeological Inst., Rome 31; Extraordinary Prof. of Ecclesiastical History, Bonn 37; Prof., Bonn 45-, now Emer.; Rector Bonn Univ. 48-50; Chair. Deutscher Akademischer Austauschdienst 51-54; mem. Deutsches Archäologisches Inst. and Rheinisch-Westfälische Akad. der Wissenschaften; Corresp. mem. Göttingen Akad. der Wissenschaften; Dr. Phil. h.c.
Publs. *Die Kathedra im Totenkult der heidnischen und christlichen Antike* 27, 71, *Das römische Capitulare evangeliorum* 35, 72, *Doctrina duodecim apostolorum, Barnabae epistula, recensuit vertit adnotavit* 40, *Kleine abendländische Liturgiegeschichte* 43 (5th edn. 65, English trans. 69), *Der Ursprung der bischöflichen Insignien und Ehrenrechten* 49, 53, *Die römische Petrustradition im Lichte der neueren Ausgrabungen unter der Peterskirche* 56, *Frühchristliche Sarkophage in Bild und Wort* 66; Co-editor of the *Reallexikon für Antike und Christentum* 41-, *Jahrbuch für Antike und Christentum* 58-, *Theophaneia* 40-, and *Florilegium Patristicum* (with B. Geyer) 40-, *Gesammelte Arbeiten* 74.
Rheinisch Friedrich-Wilhelms-Universität, 5300 Bonn, Liebfrauenweg 3, Federal Republic of Germany.

Klaveness, A. Fredrik (Anton Fredrik); Norwegian shipowner; b. 8 Nov. 1903, Sandefjord; s. of late A. F. Klaveness and late Therese Grøn; m. Brita Zahle 1938; two s. two d.
With A. F. Klaveness and Co. A/S 23-, Chair. 47-; Chair. Overseas Shipping Co., San Francisco, A. F. Klaveness & Co. Inc., San Francisco, Forsikringsaktieselskapet Vega 58-; Chair. Board of Reps. Otto Thoresen Shipping Co. A/S; Knight, First Class, Order of St. Olav, Commdr. Order of Vasa (Sweden), Officer, Order of Orange-Nassau (Netherlands).
Drammensveien 314, 1324 Lysaker, Norway.
Telephone: 53-79-90.

Klebe, Giselher; German composer; b. 28 June 1925, Mannheim; s. of Franz Klebe and Gertrud Klebe (née Michaelis); m. Lore Schiller 1946; two d.; ed. Berlin Conservatoire and with Boris Blacher.
Composer in Berlin until 57; Prof. of Composition and Theory of Music, Nordwestdeutsche Musik-Akademie, Detmold 57-; mem. Acad. of Arts, Berlin and Hamburg; Bundesverdienstkreuz 70, and several prizes for composition.
Principal works: Operas: *Die Räuber* (Schiller 57), *Die tödlichen Wünsche* (Balzac) 59, *Die Ermordung Cäsars* (Shakespeare) 59, *Alkmene* (Kleist) 61, *Figaro lässt sich scheiden* (Ödön von Horvath) 63, *Jakobowsky und der Oberst* (Werfel) 65, *Das Märchen von der Schönen Lilie* (nach Goethe) 69, *Ein wahrer Held* (Synge/Böll) 75, *Das Mädchen aus Domremy* (Schiller) 76.
Ballets: *Signale* 55, *Menagerie* 58, *Das Testament* (nach F. Villon) 70.
Orchestral Works: *Zwitschermaschine* 50, *Deux Nocturnes* 52, *Adagio und Fuge* (with theme from Wagner's *Walküre*) 62, *Dritte Sinfonie* 67, *Herzschläge* (for Beatband and Symphony Orchestra), *Konzert für Cembalo mit elektrischen Klangveränderungen und kleines Orchester* 72; Songs: *Fünf Lieder* 62, *Vier Vocalisen für Frauenchor* 63; Church music: *Miserere Nobis* 64, *Stabat Mater* 64, *Gebet einer armen Seele* 66, *Beuge dich, du Menscher seele* (after S. Lagerlöf) for Baritone and Organ; Chamber Music: 2 String Quartets 49, 63, 2 Solo Violin Sonatas 52 and 55, 2 Sonatas for Violin and Piano 53 and 74, "*Römische Elegien*" *für Sprecher, Klavier, Cembalo und Kontrabass* 53; Piano Trio *Elegia Appassionata* 55, *Introitus, Aria et Alleluja* for Organ 64, Quintet for Piano and Strings *quasi una fantasia* 67, *Fantasie und Lobpreisung* (for organ) 70, *Variationen über ein Thema von Hector Berlioz* (for organ and three drummers) 70, *Sonate für Kontrabass und Klavier* 74, "*Nenia*" *für Solo-Violoncello* 75.
Quellenstrasse 30, 493 Detmold 18, Federal Republic of Germany.
Telephone: 05232 88954.

Klecatsky, Dr. Hans, D.IUR.; Austrian lawyer and politician; b. 6 Nov. 1920, Vienna; m.; two d.
In Air Force, Second World War; Clerk in Admin. Courts 48; Constitutional Dept. of Chancellery 51; rose to rank of Hofrat in Admin. Courts 59; Lecturer in Constitutional Law and Politics, Innsbruck Univ. 64, Prof. of Public Law, Faculty of Jurisprudence and Political Science 65; Deputy mem. Court of Constitutional Law 65; Minister of Justice 66-April 70.
Publs. *Österreichisches Staatskirchenrecht* (with H. Weiler) 58, *Das österr. Zollrecht* (with A. Kobzina) 66, *Der Rechtstaat zwischen heute und morgen* 67, *Staat und Verkehr* 68, *Das Österreichische Bundesverfassungsrecht* 73-74, and other publs.
Innsbruck, Reithmannstrasse 20, Austria.

Kleene, Stephen Cole, PH.D.; American mathematician and educator; b. 5 Jan. 1909, Hartford, Conn.; s. of Gustav Adolph Kleene and Alice Cole Kleene; m. Nancy Elliott 1942 (died 1970); three s. one d.; ed. Hartford Public High School, Amherst Coll. and Princeton Univ.

Instructor, Univ. of Wisconsin 35-37, Asst. Prof. 37-41, Assoc. Prof. 46-48, Prof. 48-64, Chair. Dept. of Mathematics 57-58, 60-62, Chair. Dept. of Numerical Analysis 62-63, Cyrus C. MacDuffee Prof. of Mathematics 64-74, of Mathematics and Computer Sciences 74-, Dean of the Coll. of Letters and Science 69-74; Assoc. Prof. Amherst Coll. 41-42; U.S.N.R. 42-46; mem. Inst. for Advanced Study 39-40, 65-66; Editor *Journal for Symbolic Logic* 50-62; Pres. Asscn. for Symbolic Logic 56-58, Int. Union of the History and Philosophy of Science 61; Chair.-Designate Div. of Mathematical Sciences, Nat. Research Council 69-72; Guggenheim Fellow, Univ. of Amsterdam 50, Visiting Prof., Princeton Univ. 56-57; Nat. Science Foundation Grantee, Univ. of Marburg 58-59; mem. Nat. Acad. of Sciences.
Leisure interests: natural history, conservation.
Publs. *Introduction to Metamathematics* 52, *The Foundations of Intuitionistic Mathematics* (with Richard E. Vesley) 65, *Mathematical Logic* 67; and articles on mathematics and mathematical logic in various journals and collections.
University of Wisconsin, Madison, Wis. 53706, U.S.A.
Telephone: 608-262-2931 (Office); 231-2118 (Home).

Kleffel, Andreas, DR.JUR.; German business executive; b. 3 July 1916, Schwerin; m.; three s.; ed. legal studies.
Chairman of the Supervisory Board, Deutsche Kreditbank für Baufinanzierung AG, Cologne, Schiess AG, Düsseldorf, Hapag-Lloyd AG, Hamburg, Horten AG, Düsseldorf; Deputy Chair. of Supervisory Board, Girmes Werke AG, Oedt, Kleinewefers G.m.b.H., Krefeld, Rheinisch-Westfälische Boden-Credit-Bank, Cologne, Hugo Stinnes AG, Mülheim/Ruhr; mem. Supervisory Board, Deutsche Continental-Gas-Gesellschaft, Düsseldorf, Neunkirchener Eisenwerk AG (fmrly. Gebr. Stumm, Neunkirchen), VEBA AG, Düsseldorf; mem. Board of Man. Dirs., Deutsche Bank AG; Adviser to Barmenia-Versicherungsgruppe, Wuppertal.
Königsallee 45/47, 4 Düsseldorf, Federal Republic of Germany.

Kleffens, Eelco Nicolaas van, LL.D.; Netherlands diplomatist; b. 17 Nov. 1894, Heerenveen; m. Margaret Helen Horstman 1935; ed. Leyden Univ.
Post-war work on shipping questions 19; mem. L.N. Secretariat 19-21; Sec. Board of Dirs. Royal Dutch Petroleum Co. 21-22; Deputy-Chief Legal Section Ministry of Foreign Affairs 22-27, Diplomatic Section 27-29; Chief of Section 29-39; Minister to Switzerland 39; Minister of Foreign Affairs 39-46; leader del. to San Francisco Conf. 45; Minister without Portfolio and Netherlands Rep. UN Security Council and Econ. and Social Council 46-47; Ambassador to U.S.A. 47-50; Minister of State 50-; Minister to Portugal 50-56; Pres. Arbitration Tribunal between France, Germany, U.K. and U.S.A. (Bonn-Paris Agreements) 57-70; Perm. Rep. on NATO Council 56-58; Pres. 9th Session UN Gen. Assembly 54; Chief Rep. in the United Kingdom of the European Coal and Steel Community 58-67.
Publs. *The Relations between the Netherlands and Japan from 1605* 19, *The Rape of the Netherlands* (also in Spanish, Dutch and German) 40, *Sovereignty in International Law* 53, *Hispanic Law* 68.
Casal de Sta. Filomena, Almoçagême, Colares, Portugal.

Kleiber, Günter; German politician and electrician; b. 1932; m.; two c.
Joined Sozialistische Einheitspartei Deutschland (SED) 49; mem. Cen. Cttee. 67-; Cand. mem. Politburo 67-; Deputy Chair. Presidium; mem. Presidium, Council of Ministers, Minister for Machine and Transport Manufactures.
Am Marx-Engels-Platz 2, 102 Berlin, German Democratic Republic.

Klein, David, A.B., A.M., M.B.A.; American diplomatist; b. 2 Sept. 1919, U.S.A.; s. of Samuel and Fannie H. Klein; m. Anne L. Cochran 1953; four s. two d.; ed. Brooklyn Coll., New York, Columbia Univ. and Harvard School of Business Admin.
Served in U.S. Army 41–46; entered foreign service 47; served in Mozambique and Burma 47–50, U.S. Embassy, Moscow 52–54, U.S. Mission, Berlin 55–58, U.S. Embassy, Bonn 58–60; Soviet Desk, Dept. of State 60–62; Asst. for European Affairs to McGeorge Bundy, White House 62–65; Nat. War Coll. 65–66; Counsellor, Moscow 66–68; U.S. Mission, Berlin 68–, U.S. Minister in Berlin 71–; Superior Honor Award, Dept. of State 64.
Leisure interests: tennis, golf, music, painting.
Publ. *Basmachi: Study in Soviet Treatment of Minority Peoples* 52.
American Mission, Berlin, Germany.

Klein, George, M.D., D.SC.; Swedish (b. Hungarian) tumour biologist; b. 28 July 1925, Budapest, Hungary; s. of Henrik Klein and Ilona Engel; m. Eva Fischer 1947; one s. two d.; ed. medical schools at Pécs, Szeged and Budapest, Hungary, and Stockholm, Sweden.
Instructor Histology, Budapest Univ. 45, Pathology 46; Research Fellow, Karolinska Inst. 47–49, Asst. Prof. of Cell Research 50–57; Prof. of Tumour Biology and Head of the Inst. for Tumour Biology, Karolinska Inst. Med. School, Stockholm; Guest Investigator, Inst. for Cancer Research, Philadelphia, Pa. 50; Visiting Prof., Stanford Univ. 61; Fogarty Scholar, NIH 72; Dunham Lecturer, Harvard Med. School 66; Visiting Prof., Hebrew Univ., Jerusalem 73–75; Harvey Lecturer 73; Head of WHO (IRAC) Int. Ref. Centre for Frozen Tumour Strains; mem. WHO Expert Advisory Council on Cancer, Board of Dirs. Swedish Cancer Soc. 61–, Cttee. on Virology and Immunology Int. Union against Cancer, Scientific Advisory Council of Swedish Govt., Scientific Advisory Board Sloan Kettering Inst., American Asscn. of Cancer Research, Int. Cttee. Int. Soc. for Cell Biology, Nobel Cttee. on Physiology and Medicine, Research Council Swedish Cancer Soc., Scientific Advisory Council of Swedish Med. Board, Council for Analysis and Projection of American Cancer Soc.; Corresp. mem. American Asscn. of Cancer Research; Foreign Assoc. Nat. Acad. of Sciences of United States; hon. mem. American Asscn. of Immunologists; hon. foreign mem. American Acad. of Arts and Sciences; Fellow, New York Acad. of Science; Editor *Advances in Cancer Research*; Bertha Goldblatt Teplitz Award (jointly) 60; Rabbi Shai Shacknai Prize in Tumour Immunology 72; Bertner Award 73; Award of American Cancer Soc. 73; Prize of Danish Pathological Soc.; Harvey Prize 75; Prize of Cancer Research Inst. 75.
Publs. 350 papers in fields of experimental cell research and cancer research.
Kottlavagen 10, 181 61 Lidingö, Sweden.

Klein, Herbert George; American journalist and government official; b. 1 April 1918, Los Angeles; s. of George J. and Amy (Cordes) Klein; m. Marjorie Galbraith 1941; two d.; ed. Univ. of Southern Calif.
Journalist 40–42; U.S. Naval Reserve 42–46; Political Reporter and News Editor, *Post Advocate* 46; Feature Writer, San Diego *Evening Tribune* 50, Editorial Writer 51; Chief Editorial Writer, San Diego *Union* 51, Editor 59; mem. office staff of Vice-Pres. Nixon 59–60; Dir. of Communications for the Exec. Branch 69–73; publicist and press sec. for many of Richard Nixon's election campaigns; Vice-Pres. Corporate Relations Metromedia Inc. 73–; Trustee, Univ. S. Calif., Los Angeles.
5746 Sunset Boulevard, Los Angeles, Calif. 90028; Home: 3248 Oakdell Lane, Studio City, Calif. 91604, U.S.A.

Kleindienst, Richard Gordon, LL.B.; American lawyer; b. 5 Aug. 1923, Winslow, Ariz.; s. of Alfred R. Klein-

dienst and the late Gladys Love; m. Margaret Dunbar 1948; two s. two d.; ed. Winslow High School, Univ. of Ariz., Harvard Coll. and Harvard Law School.
Law Clerk, Ropes, Gray, Best, Coolidge and Rugg, Boston 49–50; Partner, Jennings, Strouss, Salmon and Trask, Phoenix, Ariz. 50–57; mem. Ariz. House of Reps. 53–54; Partner, Shimmel, Hill, Kleindienst and Bishop, Phoenix 58–68; Chair. Ariz. State Republican Cttee. 56; mem. Republican Nat. Cttee. 56–60, 60–63; Nat. Dir. of Field Operations, Goldwater for Pres. 64, Nixon for Pres. 68; Deputy Attorney-Gen. of U.S.A. 69–72, Attorney-Gen. June 72–April 73; Pres. Fed. Bar Assocn. 72–73.
Leisure interests: golf, chess, classical music, art.
8464 Portland Place, McLean, Va. 22101, U.S.A.

Kleiner, Sighardus, DR. THEOL.; Austrian-born ecclesiastic; b. 7 Oct. 1904, Bregenz; s. of Viktor Kleiner and Ida Schwärzler.
Priest 28; Cistercian Monk in Abbey of Mehrerau, Austria 28; Prior of Hauterive, Switzerland 39; Gen. Procurator of Cistercian Order 50, Abbot Gen. 53–.
Piazza Tempio di Diana 14, Rome, Italy.
Telephone: 573-694.

Kleinwort, Sir Cyril Hugh, Kt.; British banker; b. 17 Aug. 1905, Haywards Heath, Sussex; s. of Sir Alexander Drake Kleinwort, Bt. and Etiennette Girard; m. Elisabeth K. Forde 1933; three d.; ed. privately.
Partner, Kleinwort Sons & Co. 27–61; Chair. North British & Mercantile Insurance Co. 57–59; Chair. Kleinwort Benson Ltd. 66–71; Chair. Kleinwort Benson Lonsdale Ltd. 68–; Vice-Chair. Commercial Union Assurance Co. Ltd. 59–75; Chair. of Board, Transatlantic Fund Inc. (of New York) 59–; Dir. Kleinwort Benson Investment Trust Ltd. 61–71; Chair. Cttee. on Invisible Exports 68–76; Deputy Chair. British Nat. Export Council 68–72; mem. Advisory Cttee. Queen's Award to Industry 70–; mem. Industrial Policy Group 71–74, British Overseas Trade Board 72–.
Leisure interests: sailing, hunting, tennis, golf.
Publs. many articles on finance.
Office: 20 Fenchurch Street, London, EC3M 3DB; Home: Eyford House, Upper Slaughter, nr. Cheltenham, Glos., GL54 2JN, England.
Telephone: 01-623 8000 (Office); 0451 30380 (Home).

Klemm, Wilhelm Karl, DR.PHIL.; German chemist; b. 5 Jan. 1896, Guhrau, near Breslau; s. of Wilhelm Klemm and Ottilie John; m. 1st Li Herrmann 1935 (died 1948), 2nd Lina Arndt 1949; ed. Real Gymnasium, Grünberg, and Univ. of Breslau.
Assistant, Wilhelm Biltz Technische Hochschule, Hanover 23, Privat Docent 27, Titular Prof. 29; Full Prof. and Dir. Inst. of Inorganic Chemistry, Technical Univ. of Danzig 33, Univ. of Kiel 47, Univ. of Münster 51, Prof. Emeritus 65; Rector, Univ. of Münster 57–58; Pres. Int. Union of Pure and Applied Chemistry 65; Vice-Pres. Int. Council of Scientific Unions 66; mem. Acads. of Halle, Munich, Göttingen, Vienna and Düsseldorf; Hon. mem. Gesellschaft Deutscher Chemiker (Pres. 52–54), Soc. Chimique de France, Verein Österreichischer Chemiker, Indian Nat. Acad. of Sciences (Allahabad), Indian Chem. Soc.; Liebig-Denkmünze 51, Moissan-Médaille 53, Carl-Duisberg-Plakette 63, Lavoisier Médaille 65; Dr. h.c. (Technische Hochschule, Darmstadt, Univs. of Bordeaux, Dijon and Lille); Fed. German Order of Merit 66.
Leisure interest: music.
Publs. *Magnetochemie* 36, *Inorganic Chemistry* (15th edn.) 71, *Experimentelle Einführung in die Anorganische Chemie* (with H. Biltz and W. Fischer) (63rd edn.) 71; also 200 published papers concerning many fields of inorganic chemistry: investigations of fused salts; chemistry of so-called rare elements (especially rare earths); application of magnetic properties on chemical prob-

lems; compounds of alkaline metals with non-metals, semi-metals and metals, chemistry of the transition metals; substances with anomalous valency (especially fluorine and oxygen compounds with high valency); transition of metals to semi-metals; preparation of compounds of alkaline metals with noble metals.
Theresiengrund 22, 44 Münster/Westf., Federal Republic of Germany.
Telephone: 81414.

Kleppe, Johan; Norwegian veterinarian and politician; b. 29 Sept. 1928, Bjornskinn, Andøya; ed. Veterinary Coll. of Norway.
Veterinarian 54-67, District Veterinarian, Andøy 63-66, Supervisory Veterinarian 66; mem. Bjørnskinn Municipal Council 56-64; Deputy Mayor of Andøy 64-66, Mayor 66-69, mem. Exec. Cttee. Andøy municipality 69-; Deputy mem. of Parl. 67; Parl. Under-Sec. of State, Ministry of Agriculture 67-69; Liberal mem. of Parl. for Nordland 69, mem. Board of Liberal Parl. faction 69-, mem. Liberal Party's Cttee. on Oil Policy and EC Cttee., now mem. Principal Planning Cttee.; Minister of Defence 72-73; mem. Liberal Nat. Exec. 66-72; fmr. Board mem. Nordland Co. Liberal Asscn.; fmr. Chair. Students Liberal Asscn., Oslo and Bjørnskinn and Andøy Liberal Asscn.; Chair. of Board, Directorate of State Forests and Chair. Nat. Council on Sheepbreeding 69-; District Veterinarian, Andøy, 73-.
c/o 9490 Risøyhamn, Norway.

Kleppe, Per; Norwegian politician; b. 13 April 1923, Oslo.
Secretary, Ministry of Finance 52-53; with Cen. Bureau of Statistics 53-54; mem. Research Councils Joint Cttee. 54-57; Asst. Sec. of State, Ministry of Finance 57-62, Chair. and Sec. Finance Policy Cttee. 62-63; Head, Econ. section, EFTA Secr., Geneva 63-67; Dir. Labour Party Research Office 67-71; Minister of Commerce and Shipping 71-72, of Finance 73-.
Ministry of Finance, Oslo Dep.; and Arbeiderpartiet, Youngstorget, Oslo, Norway.

Kleppe, Thomas S.; American politician; b. 1 July 1919, Kintyre, N.D.; m. Glendora Loew 1958; one s. three d.; ed. Valley City Teachers' Coll.
Served in U.S. Army, Warrant Officer 42-46; joined Gold Seal Co. 46, Treas. 48-58, Pres. and Treas. 58-64; Vice-Pres. J. M. Dain and Co. 64-66; Mayor of Bismarck, N.D. 50-54; mem. House of Reps. for Second Congressional District, N.D. 67-71, House Cttee. on Agriculture, House Republican Policy Cttee.; Administrator, Small Business Admin. 71-75; Sec. of the Interior Oct. 75-.
Department of the Interior, C Street between 18th and 19th Streets, N.W., Washington, D.C. 20240, U.S.A.

Klijnstra, Gerrit Dirk Ale, K.B.E.; Netherlands business executive; b. 5 Jan. 1912, Amersfoort; s. of M. J. Klijnstra and J. H. van Nieuwenhuizen; m. E. J. van Sijn 1939; three d.; ed. Gymnasium Amersfoort and Delft Univ.
Joined Unilever N.V. 38; Technical Dir. Unilever, Indonesia 46; Technical Head, Unilever, Germany 50; mem. Overseas Cttee. Unilever Ltd. 54; mem. Board of Dirs. Unilever N.V. and Ltd. 55; Head, Technical Div., Unilever Ltd. 60, Foods Co-ordinator 65; Vice-Chair. Unilever N.V. 68; Chair. Unilever N.V. and Vice-Chair. Unilever Ltd. 71-May 75; Advisory Dir. Unilever N.V. May 75-; Supervisory Dir. Amrobank 73-; Non-Exec. Dir. Imperial Chemical Industries 74-; Officer, Order of Orange-Nassau, Commdr. 75; Kt. Order of the Netherlands Lion.
Leisure interests: sailing, golf, music.
Pinetrees, The Sands, Farnham, Surrey, England.
Telephone: Runfold 2520.

Kliks, Rudolf Rigoldovich; Soviet architect; b. 25 June 1910, Moscow; ed. Kharkov Inst. of Constructional Engineers.

Assistant Chief Architect for U.S.S.R. Agricultural Exhbn. 45-56; Chief Architect and Chief Artist U.S.S.R. Econ. Achievements Exhbn. 56-60; Chief Architect for U.S.S.R. Chamber of Commerce 60-.
Principal works include: stadium to seat 10,000 in Orjonikidze 37; general plan for the reconstruction of the U.S.S.R. Agricultural Exhbn. 50-54; designs, displays and interiors of pavilions for about 40 exhbns. in the U.S.S.R. and other countries including: Czechoslovakia 48, Yugoslavia 55, Leipzig, German Democratic Republic 56, Science section of the Soviet Pavilion, Brussels World Exhbn. 58, Helsinki, Finland 59, New Delhi Int. Agricultural Exhbn. 60, Damascus Int. Fair 61, Pavilion at Trade and Industry Exhbn. in London 61, Rio de Janeiro 63, Nehru Commemorative Exhbn., Moscow 63, Izmir Int. Fair 64, Pavilion at Montreal Expo 67.
Publ. *Architecture of the U.S.S.R. Agricultural Exhibition 54.*
U.S.S.R. Chamber of Commerce, Kuibyshev Street 6, Moscow, U.S.S.R.

Klimaszewski, Mieczysław, PH.D.; Polish scientist and politician; b. 26 July 1908, Stanisławów; ed. Uniwersytet Jagielloński, Cracow.
Scientific Research Work 31-; Population and Social Welfare Office, Cracow 39-45; Prof. Extraordinary, Wroclaw Univ. 46-49; Prof. Jagiellonian Univ., Cracow 49-, Dir. Inst. of Geography, Rector of Jagiellonian Univ., Cracow 64-72; mem. Seym 65-72; mem. Council of State 65, Vice-Chair. 65-72; Chair. Cttee. for Research on Problems of Polish Emigrants, Polish Acad. of Sciences 71-73; Chair. Polish Social Cttee. for Security and Co-operation in Europe 71-73; Chair. Polonia Asscn. 67-72; Chair. Scientific Council of Tatra Nat. Park 72; Chair. Scientific Council, Inst. of Geography, Polish Acad. of Sciences, Chair. Cttee. of Geographical Sciences; mem. Polish Acad. of Sciences, Leopoldina Acad. (German Democratic Repub.), Netherlands Geographical Soc., Soviet Geographical Soc., Finnish Acad. of Sciences; Hungarian Geographical Soc.; Dr. h.c. (Univ. of Jena) 65, (Kiev Univ.) 68, (Komensky Univ., Bratislava) 70, (Alliance Coll., Cambridge) 72, (Univ. of St. Andrews) 73; Commdr. Cross with Star of Order Polonia Restituta; Grand Officier de l'Ordre du Mérite 67; Order of Banner of Labour 1st Class 73, A. Humboldt Medal, M. K. Sapper Medal.
Publs. *Geomorphological Development of W. Carpathians 34, 48, 65, 66, Problems of Geomorphological Mapping 56, 60, 63, Geomorphological Studies of Spitsbergen 60, Geomorfologia Ogólna 61, The Effect of Solifluction Processes on the Development of Mountain Slopes in the Beskidy 71.*
Ul. Wyspiańskiego 3, 30-035 Cracow, Poland.

Klimov, Alexander Petrovich; Soviet economist and co-operative worker; b. 25 Aug. 1914; ed. Higher Pedagogical Inst. of Applied Econ. and Trade.
Teacher 35-38; Principal various co-operative educ. establishments 38-42; Deputy Dept. Head, Oirot Dist. C.P.S.U. Cttee. 42-43; Chief Educ. Service, Centrosoyuz (Cen. Union of Consumer Co-ops.) 43-48, Deputy Chair. of Board 48-53, Chair. of Board 54-; Chair. Price Cttee. of U.S.S.R. 53-54; Deputy Minister of Trade 54; Deputy to U.S.S.R. Supreme Soviet 66-; mem. Board U.S.S.R. Ministry of Trade; Vice-Pres. Int. Co-operative Alliance; Vice-Pres. U.S.S.R.-G.B. Friendship Soc.; mem. Soviet Peace Cttee., Nat. Cttee. for European Security.
Centrosoyouz of U.S.S.R., Bolshoi Cherkassky 15, Moscow, U.S.S.R.

Kline, Nathan Schellenberg, B.A., M.A., M.D.; American psychiatrist; b. 22 March 1916, Philadelphia, Pa.; s. of Ignatz and Florence Kline (née Schellenberg); m. Margot Hess 1943; one d.; ed. Swarthmore Coll., Harvard Univ., New York Univ. Coll. of Medicine,

New School of Soc. Research, Princeton Univ., Rutgers Univ. and Clark Univ.

Intern and Resident St. Elizabeth's Hospital, Washington, D.C. 43-44; U.S. Public Health Service 44-46; Child Psychiatrist, Union County Mental Hygiene Soc. Clinic 46-47; Veterans Admin. Hospital, Lyons, N.J. 46-50; Assoc., Columbia Greystone 47-50; Dir. of Research, Worcester State Hosp., Worcester, Mass. 50-52; private psychiatric practice, New York 53-; Dir., Rockland Research Inst., Orangeburg, New York 52-; Dir. of Div. of Psychiatry, Bergen Pines County Hosp. Paramus, N.J. 63-75; Asst. Prof. of Clinical Psychiatry Coll. of Physicians and Surgeons, Columbia Univ. 57-69, Assoc. Prof. 69-73, Prof. 73-; Pres. Int. Cttee. against Mental Illness 61-; Contributing Editor and Int. Board of Editors *Excerpta Medica* 55-; numerous awards, including Albert Lasker Clinical Research Award 57, 64.

Leisure interests: theatre, literature, travel.

Rockland Research Institute, Orangeburg, N.Y. 10962; Home: 1155 Sussex Road, Teaneck, N.Y. 07666, U.S.A.

Klochek, Vassily Ivanovich; Soviet foreign trade official; b. 1912; ed. Moscow Economic Inst. and Acad. of Foreign Trade.

Member C.P.S.U. 40-; Chief of Section Ministry of Foreign Trade 46-47; Deputy Commercial Rep. in Hungary 47-50; Deputy Chief of Dept., Ministry of Foreign Trade 50-53; Commercial Rep. in Austria 53-58; Chief of Dept., Ministry of Foreign Trade 58-63; Commercial Rep. in German Democratic Republic 63-69; Dir. Main Board U.S.S.R. Ministry of Foreign Trade 69-; Order of Lenin, Badge of Honour, etc.

U.S.S.R. Ministry of Foreign Trade, Smolenskaya-Sennaya ploshchad 32-34, Moscow, U.S.S.R.

Klompé, Margaretha Abertina Maria, CH.D.; Netherlands politician; b. 16 Aug. 1912, Arnhem; ed. Univ. of Utrecht.

Teacher at Nijmegen 32-49; mem. of Netherlands Del. to U.N. Gen. Assembly 47, 48, 49, 50, 52, mem. of Second Chamber 48-56, of Consultative Assembly of Council of Europe 49-56, of Coal and Steel Assembly 52-56; Minister of Social Welfare 56-63; mem. Second Chamber States Gen. 63-66; Minister of Culture, Recreation and Social Welfare 66-71; Minister of State 71-, mem. Pontfical Comm. on Justice and Peace; Pres. Nat. Comm. on Justice and Peace, Nat. UNESCO Comm.; Hon. LL.D. 64; Roman Catholic People's Party.

5 Smidswater, The Hague, Netherlands.
Telephone: 070-606080.

Kloos, Andries Hein; Netherlands trade unionist; b. 12 Aug. 1922, Amsterdam; m. J. Adema 1947; ed. secondary school.

In accountant's office 39-42; Netherlands Fed. of Trade Unions 46-, in admin. depts. 46-51, Econ. Adviser 51-54, Deputy Dir. of Scientific Research Bureau 54-56, Sec. Editor of Netherlands Fed. of Trade Unions, also in charge of social-econ. activities 56-62, Vice-Pres. 62-65, Pres. 65-71; Dir. VARA (broadcasting co.), Hilversum 71-.

Leisure interest: gardening.

VARA, Heuvellaan 33, Hilversum, Netherlands.

Klos, Elmar; fmr. Czechoslovak film director; b. 26 Jan. 1910, Brno; s. of Rudolf and Marie Klos; m. Anne Vopalka 1935; one s. one d.; ed. Faculty of Law, Charles Univ., Prague.

Director, Short Film Studios 46-47; Head of Creative Art Staff, and Scriptwriter, Barrandov Feature Film Studio 48-74; Prof. of Film and TV Acad. of Prague 56-; Pres. Czechoslovak Union of Film Artists 63-66; Awards include State Prize 2nd Class 60, Gold Prize, Moscow Int. Film Festival 63, State Prize 64, Grand Prix, Karlovy Vary Int. Film Festival 64, U.S. Acad.

Award Oscar 65, New York Film Critics Award 67, Selznik Prize, U.S. 66; Honoured Artist 65, Nat. Artist 68; Co-Dir. with Ján Kadár (*q.v.*): *Únos* (Kidnapped) 52, *Smrt si říhd Engelchen* (Death is Called Engelchen) 63, *Obžalovaný* (The Accused) 64, *Obchod na korze* (The Shop on Main Street) 65 (all award-winning films), *Touha zvaná Anada* (Desire called Anada), Co-Dir. with J. Kadár 69.

Strahovská 203, Hradčany, Prague 1, Czechoslovakia.
Telephone: 536297.

Kłoskowska, Antonina, PH.D.; Polish sociologist; b. 7 Nov. 1919, Piotrków Trybunalski; ed. Łódź Univ.

Doctor 50-54, Docent 54-66, Assoc. Prof. 66-; Expert, UNESCO 67-; Head, Sociology of Culture Dept., Sociology Inst., Łódź Univ.; Chair. Cttee. of Sociological Sciences, Polish Acad. of Sciences (PAN) 72-; mem. PAN 73-, Comité Int. de Recherche sur les Aspirations, Paris, Cen. Board of Polish Sociological Soc.; Medal of 10th and 30th Anniversaries of People's Poland; Gold Cross of Merit, Knight's Cross, Order of Polonia Restituta; Scientific Prize, City of Łódź.

Publs. *Kultura masowa* 64, *Z historii i socjologii kultury* 69, *Społeczne ramy kultury* 72, *Macchiavelli jako humanista na tle włoskiego Odrodzenia.*

Instytut Socjologii Uniwersytetu Łódzkiego, ul. Rewolucji 1905 r. No. 41, 90-214 Łódź, Poland.
Telephone: 315-53.

Klosovsky, Boris Nikodimovich; Soviet physiologist and neurosurgeon; b. 16 March 1898, Stanitsa Otradnaya, Krasnodar territory; s. of Nikodim Alexandrovich Klosovsky and Ksenija Grigorevna Serebrjanaja; m. Kiseleva Zinaida Nikolaevna 1932; one d.; ed. Azerbaizhan Univ.

Postgraduate, Leningrad Brain Research Inst. 25-30; Asst. Head of Laboratory and Clinic, Inst. of Pediatrics 27-; Head of Dept., Inst. of Neurosurgery 33-48; Corresp. mem., U.S.S.R. Acad. of Medical Sciences 52-62, mem. 62-; mem. Int. Soc. for Parkinsonism Study, Int. Brain Research Org., Moscow Socs. of Morphology, Histology and Embryology, All-Union Physiological Soc., Int. Soviet Psychoneuroendocrinology Soc., Nobel Cttee. on Physiology and Medicine at Karolinska Inst., Board U.S.S.R.-Australia Friendship Soc.; Forty-six medals incl. Order of Red Banner of Labour 52, State Prize 52 and highest award of World Org. of the Int. Forum for Neurological Org.

Leisure interests: gardening, reading.

Publs. 270 works on structure and function of brain, anatomy of nerves, and physiology of vestibular apparatus and related studies; Klosovsky was first to perform *bulbotomy.*

Institute of the Brain, per. Obuha 5, 107120 Moscow; Home: Begovaja II, apt. 19, 125284 Moscow, U.S.S.R.
Telephone: 297-12-09 (Office); 256-35-18 (Home).

Kloss, Hans, LL.D.; Austrian banker and financial administrator; b. 28 Nov. 1905, Vienna; s. of Rudolf Kloss and Hermine Janda; m. Gertrude Wiedstruck 1952; ed. Univ. of Vienna.

Member of staff Österr. Luftverkehers AG, Vienna 27-38; Deutsche Lufthansa AG, Berlin 39-46; mem. staff Ministry of Finance 46, Head of Currency Dept. 51-62; Alt. Exec. Dir. Int. Bank for Reconstruction and Devt., Washington, D.C. 54-56; Austrian finance expert OEEC/OECD, Paris 47-63; Govt. Commr. Austrian Nat. Bank 56-62; Gen. Man. Genossenschaftliche Zentralbank AG 63-68; mem. Council Vienna Stock Exchange 63-69; Gen. Man., Chair. Board of Mans., Austrian Nat. Bank 69-72; Alt. Gov. for Austria, IMF 69-72; Pres. and Chair. Board of Dirs., Austrian Nat. Bank 73-; Gov. for Austria, IMF 73-; Senator of Honour Vienna School of Econs., Grand Medal of Honour in Silver.

Kupelwiesergasse 11, 1130 Vienna, Austria.

Klotz, Irving Myron, PH.D.; American professor of chemistry and biochemistry; b. 22 Jan. 1916, Chicago, Ill.; s. of Frank and Mollie (Nasatir) Klotz; m. Mary S. (Hanlon) Klotz 1966; two s. one d.; ed. Univ. of Chicago.

Research Assoc., Northwestern Univ. 40-42, Instructor in Chem. 42-46, Asst. Prof. of Chem. 46-47, Assoc. Prof. of Chem. 47-50; Prof. of Chem. and Biochemistry 50-, Morrison Prof. 63-; Fellow, Amer. Acad. of Arts and Sciences; mem. Nat. Acad. of Sciences; Eli Lilly Award 49 and Midwest Award 70 (Amer. Chem. Soc.).

Publs. *Chemical Thermodynamics* 50, 64, 72, *Energy Changes in Biochemical Reactions* 57, 67; over 200 research papers.

Department of Chemistry, Northwestern University, Evanston, Ill. 60201; Home: 2515 Pioneer Road, Evanston, Ill. 60201, U.S.A.

Klotzbach, Günter, DR.ING.; German engineer and metals executive; b. 16 Feb. 1912, Essen; s. of Dr. Arthur Klotzbach and Elisabeth Koerwer; m. Grete Holtermann 1940; three s.; ed. Goethe Gymnasium, Essen, Univ. de Lausanne and Technische Hochschule, Aachen.

With Fried. Krupp Gussstahlfabrik, Essen 37-46; Asst. to Tech. Direction Friedrich-Alfred-Hütte, then Hüttenwerk Rheinhausen AG, Rheinhausen 46-59, Technical Man. Nov. 59-62; mem. Directorate, Fried. Krupp, Essen 63-65; Chair. Management Board Fried. Krupp Hüttenwerke AG 66-73, Verein Deutscher Eisenhüttenleute, Düsseldorf 73-.

Verein Deutscher Eisenhüttenleute, 4 Düsseldorf, Breite Strasse 27; Home: 433 Mülheim-Speldorf, Tannenstrasse 27, Federal Republic of Germany.

Telephone: Düsseldorf 8894317 (Office); Mülheim 50813 (Home).

Klusák, Milan, LL.D., C.SC.; Czech diplomatist; b. 8 June 1923, Stařeč; ed. Univ. of Brno.

Diplomatic Service 48-; Czechoslovak Embassy, Moscow 50-53; Ministry of Foreign Affairs, Prague 54-60; Perm. Rep. of Czechoslovakia to European Office of UN, Geneva 60-63; Head of Dept. of Int. Orgs., Ministry of Foreign Affairs, Prague 63-65; Perm. Rep. to UN, N.Y. 65-68; External Lecturer in Int. Relations, School of Econs., Univ. of Prague 64-65; Deputy Minister of Foreign Affairs 69-73; Minister of Culture May 73-; Vice-Chair. of Czech Cen. Council of Czechoslovak-Soviet Friendship Union 74-; Order of Labour 73-.

Ministry of Culture, Valdštejnská 10, Prague 1—Malá Strana, Czechoslovakia.

Klüver, Heinrich, PH.D.; American (naturalized 1934) psychologist; b. 25 May 1897, Holstein, Germany; s. of Wilhelm and Dorothea (Wübbers) Klüver; m. Cessa Feyerabend 1927; ed. Univs. of Hamburg and Berlin, and Stanford Univ.

Went to U.S. 23; Instructor in Psychology, Univ. of Minn. 24-26; Fellow of Social Science Research Council, Columbia Univ. 26-28; Research Psychologist, Behavior Research Fund, Chicago 28-33; Research Assoc., Dept. of Pathology, Univ. of Chicago 33-35; Asst. Prof. of Experimental Psychology, Div. of Psychiatry, Dept. of Medicine, Univ. of Chicago 35-36, Assoc. Prof. 36-38, Prof. of Experimental Psychology, Div. of Biol. Sciences 38-57, Sewell L. Avery Distinguished Service Prof. of Biol. Psychology 57-62, Prof. Emer. 63-; Assoc. mem. Otho S. A. Sprague Memorial Inst., Univ. of Chicago 33-38; mem. 38-46; Principal Investigator, Nat. Inst. of Mental Health 63-; mem. Armed Forces Nat. Research Council Cttee. on Vision 60-65, Advisory Cttee. to Lab. of Perinatal Physiol., Puerto Rico 61-64, Gen. Medical Research Program-Project Cttee. of Nat. Inst. of Gen. Med. Sciences, Nat. Inst. of Health 63-66; mem. Nat. Acad. of Sciences, American Acad. of Arts and Sciences, American Philos. Soc., American Physiol. Soc.

and 24 other scientific socs., Hon. mem. Int. Brain Research Org. (IBRO) 66; American Neurological Asscn. 66; American Coll. of Neuropsychopharmacology 66; Soc. of Biological Psychiatry 75; numerous awards; Hon. M.D. (Basle) 65; Hon. Ph.D. (Hamburg) 69; Hon. M.D. (Kiel).

Publs. *An Experimental Study of the Eidetic Type* 26, *Mescal* 28, *Behavior Mechanisms in Monkeys* 33, *Visual Mechanisms* (Editor) 42, Polyak's *The Vertebrate Visual System* (Editor) 57, *Mescal and Mechanisms of Hallucinations* 66, 69.

Culver Hall, University of Chicago, Chicago, Ill. 60637, U.S.A.

Telephone: 312-753-2920.

Klychev, Anna Muchamed; Soviet politician; b. 1912; ed. Higher Party School.

Soviet Army 41-45; mem. Communist Party of Soviet Union 47-; managerial work 47-51; party and political work 53-63; Chair. Presidium of Supreme Soviet of Turkmenian S.S.R. 63-; mem. Bureau of Cen. Cttee. of C.P. Turkmenian S.S.R.; Deputy Chair. Presidium of Supreme Soviet of U.S.S.R.; mem. Cen. Auditing Comm., C.P.S.U. 66-; Deputy to Supreme Soviet of U.S.S.R. 66- and of Turkmenian S.S.R.

Presidium of Supreme Soviet of Turkmenian S.S.R., Ashkhabad, U.S.S.R.

Kłyszewski, Wacław; Polish architect; b. 7 Sept. 1910, Warsaw; ed. Warsaw Polytechnic.

Member, Polish Asscn. of Architects (SARP) 36-; Studio with J. Mokrzyński (*q.v.*) and E. Wierzbicki 36-39; Designer, Office of Rebuilding of the Capital (with Mokrzyński and Wierzbicki) 45-48; Senior Asst., Warsaw Polytechnic 45-49; now Collective Judge, SARP; Chief Designer, Warsaw Design Office of Gen. Architecture; First Prizes (with Mokrzyński and Wierzbicki) for: Polish Savings Bank in Warsaw, Polish United Workers' Party Building in Warsaw, Architect's House in Zakopane, Railway Station in Katowice, Museum of Modern Art in Skopje, Yugoslavia; Gold Cross of Merit 55, Gold Award for Rebuilding Warsaw 58, Officer's Cross, Order of Polonia Restituta 64, Order of Banner of Labour, 2nd Class 69, State Prize 3rd Class 51, 2nd Class 55, 1st Class 74; Hon. Prize, SARP 68, Prize of Katowice Branch of SARP 72; Prize of Minister of Construction, 1st Class 73.

Ul. Górnośląska 16 m. 15a, 00-432 Warsaw, Poland.

Knapp, J. Burke; American banker; b. 25 Jan. 1913, Portland, Ore.; s. of Mr. and Mrs. J. B. Knapp; m. F. A. Hilary Eaves 1939; two s. two d.; ed. Stanford Univ. and Oxford Univ.

Joined Brown Harriman and Co., Ltd. (an int. investment firm) 36-40; economist of the Federal Reserve Board, Washington 40-44; economic adviser to the American Mil. Govt. in Germany 44-45; Special Asst. on Int. matters to the Chair. of the Board 45-48; Dir. of Office of Financial and Development Policy, Dept. of State 48-49; Asst. Economic Dir. of the World Bank 49-50; economic adviser to the U.S. NATO del. in London 50-51; U.S. Chair. of the Joint Brazil-U.S. Economic Development Comm., Rio de Janeiro 51-52; Dir. of the World Bank's operations in Latin America 52-56; Vice-Pres. of the Int. Bank for Reconstruction and Devt. 56-72, Senior Vice-Pres. 72-.

Leisure interests: theatre, swimming.

Office: International Bank for Reconstruction and Development, 1818 H Street, N.W., Washington D.C.; Home: 3701 Curtis Court, Chevy Chase, Maryland, U.S.A.

Telephone: OLiver 2-3488.

Knapp, Stefan; British (born Polish) artist; b. 1921; ed. Lwów High School, Cen. School of Art, London, Slade School of Art, London Univ.

Imprisoned in Siberia 39-42; fighter pilot in R.A.F. 42-45; student 45-50; Exhibitions: One-Man Shows

London 47, 54, 55, Paris (paintings) 56, Milan 57, Pierre Matisse Gallery, New York and Caracas (painting and sculpture) 58, Middelheim (Belgium) Biennale 59, Museo de Bellas Artes, Caracas 60, Estudio Actual, Caracas 73, for British Council, Zacheta Palace, Warsaw 74; Lissone Prize, Milan 57; inventor of technique of large-scale painting on copper and steel for architectural use; murals include those at Hallfield School, Paddington (London) 55, Seagram Building, New York, St. Anne's Coll., Oxford 59, Univs. of Brunswick and Freiburg 64, New York 66, Queens Coll., New York 66, Columbia Univ., New York 66, Rowney Office Bldg., Berks., 67, Detroit Art Inst. 67, Copernicus Univ., Torun, Poland, Johnson Bldg., Amsterdam, Planetarium at Olsztyn, Poland, Lod Airport, Israel; Churchill Fellowship 72, Knight's Cross of the Order of Polonia Restituta.
Publ. *The Square Sun* (autobiography) 56.
The Studio, Sandhills, Godalming, Surrey, England.
Telephone: Wormley 2430.

Kneip, Richard F.; American state governor; b. 7 Jan. 1933, Tyler, Minn.; *m.* Nancy Pankey; eight *s.*; *ed.* Arlington High School, S. Dakota State Univ. and St. John's Univ., Collegeville, Minn.
Owner and operator, Kneip Sales (dairy equipment firm), Salem, S.D.; mem. S. Dakota State Senate 65-71; Gov. S. Dakota Jan. 71-; Democrat.
Office of the Governor, State Capitol, Pierre, S. Dak., U.S.A.

Knight, Douglas Maitland, PH.D.; American educational administrator; b. 8 June 1921, Cambridge, Mass.; *s.* of Claude Rupert and Fanny Sarah Douglas (Brown) Knight; *m.* Grace Wallace Nichols 1942; four *s.*; *ed.* Yale Univ.
Instructor of English, Yale 46-47; Asst. Prof. of English Literature, Yale 47-53; Morse Research Fellow 51-52; Pres., Lawrence Coll., Appleton, Wisconsin 54-63; Pres. Duke Univ., Durham, N. Carolina 63-69; mem. Board of Dirs. Soc. for Religion in Higher Educ.; Vice-Chair. Woodrow Wilson Nat. Fellowship Foundation; Trustee, New Coll.; Chair. Nat. Library Comm. 66-67; Div. Vice-Pres. Educational Devt., RCA, New York 69-71, Div. Vice-Pres. Educ. Services 71-72, Staff Vice-Pres. Educ. and Community Relations 72-73, Consultant 73-; Pres. RCA, Iran 71-72, Dir.; Pres. Social Econ. and Educ. Devt. Inc. 73-; numerous hon. degrees.
Publs. *Alexander Pope and the Heroic Tradition* 51, *The Dark Gate* (poems) 71; Editor and contrib.: *Medical Ventures and the University* 67; Editor: *The Federal Government and Higher Education* 60; Joint Editor Twickenham edn. of *Iliad* and *Odyssey* (trans. by Alexander Pope) 65.
Office: 30 Rockefeller Plaza, New York, N.Y. 10020; Home: R.F.D.1, Box 156, Stockton, N.J. 08559, U.S.A. Telephone: (212) 598-4985 (Office); (202) 996-2054 (Home).

Knight, George Richard Wilson, C.B.E., M.A., F.R.S.L., F.I.A.L.; British university professor and author; b. 19 Sept. 1897, Sutton, Surrey; *s.* of George and Caroline (née Jackson) Knight; unmarried; *ed.* Dulwich Coll. and St. Edmund Hall, Oxford.
English Master, Dean Close School, Cheltenham 25-31; Chancellors' Prof. of English, Trinity Coll., Univ. of Toronto 31-40; Master, Stowe School 41-46, Reader, subsequently Prof. of English Literature, Univ. of Leeds 46-62, Prof. Emer. 62-; Shakespearian productions, Hart House Theatre, Toronto 31-40; produced and acted in *This Sceptred Isle,* Westminster Theatre, London 41; Shakespearian productions and performances, Univ. of Leeds 46-60; lectured in Jamaica (for British Council) and Univ. Coll. of West Indies 51; Visiting Lecturer Univ. of Capetown 52; Lecturer at Univ. of Chicago 63, Festival Seminars, Stratford (Ont.) 63, 67; Lecture-tour, Canadian Univs. 74; Pres. Devonshire Asscn. 71; Hon.

Litt.D. (Sheffield) 67, Hon. D.Litt. (Exeter) 68; Hon. Fellow, St. Edmund Hall, Oxford 66.
Leisure interest: sun-bathing.
Publs. numerous books, articles and essays, etc., including: *The Wheel of Fire* 30, *The Imperial Theme* 31, *The Shakespearian Tempest* 32, *The Christian Renaissance* 33, *Atlantic Crossing* (autobiography) 36, *The Crown of Life* 46, *Christ and Nietzsche* 48, *Lord Byron: Christian Virtues* 52, *The Last of the Incas* (play) 54, *Lord Byron's Marriage* 57, *The Golden Labyrinth* 62, *Shakespearian Production* 64, *The Saturnian Quest* 64, *Byron and Shakespeare* 66, *Poets of Action* 67, *Shakespeare and Religion* 67, *Gold-Dust* (poetry) 68, *Neglected Powers* 71, *Jackson Knight: A Biography* 75.
Caroline House, Streatham Rise, Exeter, EX4 4PE, Devon, England.
Telephone: Exeter 59432.

Knight, Harold Murray, D.SC., M.COMM.; Australian banker; b. 13 Aug. 1919, Melbourne; *s.* of W. H. P. Knight; *m.* Gwenyth Catherine Pennington 1951; four *s.* one *d.*; *ed.* Scotch Coll., Melbourne, and Melbourne Univ.
Commonwealth Bank of Australia 36-40, 46-55; served Australian Imperial Forces and Royal Australian Navy 40-46, awarded D.S.C.; Statistics Div., Research and Statistics Dept. of IMF 55-59, Asst. Chief 57-59; Research Economist, Reserve Bank of Australia 60, Asst. Man. Investment Dept. 62-64, Man. Investment Dept. 64-68, Deputy Gov. Reserve Bank of Australia and Deputy Chair. of Bank's Board 68-75, Gov. and Chair. of Board 75-.
Publ. *Introducción al Analisis Monetario* (in Spanish) 59.
Office: Reserve Bank of Australia, 65 Martin Place, Sydney, N.S.W. 2000; Home: 20 Malton Road, Beecroft, N.S.W. 2119, Australia.

Knight, John Shively; American newspaper publisher; b. 26 Oct. 1894; *ed.* Cornell Univ.
Served in Motor Transport Corps, 113th Inf., and in Army Air Corps, A.E.F. 17-19; newspaper reporter and exec. 20-25; Man. Editor *Akron Beacon Journal* 25-33, Editor 33-71, Editorial Chair. 71-; Editorial Dir. *Springfield Sun* 25-27, *Massillon Independent* 27-33, Pres. 33-37; Chair. of Board and Publisher, *Miami Herald* 37-67, now Editorial Chair.; Pres. Beacon Journal Publishing Co., Knight Newspapers, Inc. until 66; purchased and discontinued *Miami Tribune* 37; purchased *Detroit Free Press* 40, Pres., Editor 40-67, now Editorial Chair.; fmr. owner, editor, publisher *Chicago Daily News* 44-59; Chief Liaison Officer U.S.-Brit. censorships, London 43-44; mem. and Past Pres. Amer. Soc. of Newspaper Editors, and Inter-Amer. Press Asscn.; fmr. Dir. and Officer of Assoc. Press; Hon. LL.D. (Akron, Northwestern, Ohio State and Kent State Univs.); Pulitzer Prize for editorial writing 68, Gold Medal of Achievement 72, and several other awards.
44 East Exchange Street, Akron, O. 44309; Home: 255 North Portage Path, Akron, O. 44303, U.S.A.

Knight, Reo Lindsay, B.COMM.; New Zealand economist and international finance official; b. 22 April 1931, Wellington; *m.*; two *c.*; *ed.* Hutt Valley Technical Coll. and Victoria Univ. of Wellington.
With Reserve Bank of New Zealand, Wellington 48-70, Research Officer 63-65, Asst. Chief Economist 65-66, Deputy Chief Economist 66-67, Deputy Chief Cashier 67-70; Sec. Devt. Finance Corpn. of New Zealand 64; Tutor in Econs., Victoria Univ. of Wellington 65-68; Chair. Govt. Cttee. on Foreign Investment in N.Z. 69-70; Registrar of Overseas Takeovers 67-70; Exec. Dir. IBRD, IFC and IDA 70-73.
c/o International Bank for Reconstruction and Development, 1818 H Street, N.W., Washington, D.C. 20433, U.S.A.

Knight, Ridgway Brewster, B.S., PH.B., M.B.A.; American diplomatist and banker; b. 12 June 1911; *m.* Colette Lalier 1946; four *s.*; ed. Univ. of Paris and Harvard Univ.
Assistant to Pres. Cartier Inc. 31-35; Vice-Pres. and Treas. Bellows Co. Inc. 36-41; U.S. Army 43-45; Second Sec., Paris 45-50; Dept. of State 50-53; Deputy Asst. High Commr. for Germany 54-55; Political Adviser, Supreme Allied Commdr., Europe 55-57, Minister, Karachi 57-59; Minister, Consul-Gen., Damascus 60-61; Ambassador to Syrian Arab Republic 61-65, to Belgium 65-69, to Portugal 69-73; Dir. Int. Relations, Chase Manhattan Bank 73-; numerous decorations.
Chase Manhattan Bank, 41 rue Cambon, Paris, France. Telephone: 260-33-80.

Knipling, Edward Fred, B.S., M.S., PH.D.; American agricultural research administrator and entomologist; b. 20 March 1909, Port Lavaca, Tex.; *s.* of Henry J. Knipling and Hulda Rasch Knipling; *m.* Phoebe Hall Knipling 1934; three *s.* two *d.*; ed. Texas A. and M. Univ. and Iowa State Univ.
Entomologist, U.S. Dept. of Agriculture (U.S.D.A.) 31-, various research positions in veterinary and medical problems 31-42, Dir. Research programme for devt. of control measures for diseases among U.S. and Allied Mil. Forces 42, Principal Entomologist in charge of Research on Insects Affecting Men and Animals 46, Dir. of Entomology Research Div. of Agricultural Research Services, U.S.D.A. 53-71, Science Adviser, Agricultural Research Services, U.S.D.A. 71-; mem. Nat. Acad. of Sciences; awards include President's Medal for Merit, U.S. Army Typhus Comm. Medal, U.S. Dept. of Agriculture's Distinguished Service Medal, Rockefeller Public Service Award, Nat. Medal of Science, King's Medal for Services in the Cause of Freedom (U.K.).
Leisure interests: hunting with bow and arrow, fishing, watching sporting events.
Publs. about 150 scientific articles, principally on entomology.
National Agricultural Library, Room 205, Plant Industry Station, Beltsville, Md. 20705; Home: 2623 Military Road, Arlington, Va. 22207, U.S.A.
Telephone: 344-3245 (Office); 527-5668 (Home).

Knižka, Jaroslav, ING.; Czechoslovak politician; b. 25 July 1916, Stehelčeves; *m.* Jarmila Knížková 1945; one *s.* one *d.*; ed. Czech Technical Univ., Prague.
Technician, head of building dept., Joint Steel Works Kladno, 46-51; Head of construction dept., HUKO Košice, Chief Technician 51-53; Head of Investment Dept., Ministry of the Metallurgical Industry 53-56; Deputy Dir. New Klement Gottwald Foundries, Kunčice 56-59; Dir. East Slovak Iron Works, Košice, 59-69; Minister-Chair. of Federal Cttee. for Transport 69-71; Amb. Extraordinary and Plenipotentiary, Perm. Rep. of C.S.S.R. at UN Office, Geneva 71-; mem. Central Cttee., C.P. of Slovakia 66-68; Deputy to Slovak Nat. Council 60-71; Award for Merits in Construction 58; Order of Labour 65.
Leisure interests: technical sciences, tennis, photography.
Permanent Mission of the Czechoslovak Socialist Republic to United Nations, 9 Ancienne Route, 1218 Grand-Saconnex, Geneva, Switzerland.
Telephone: 34-95-56.

Knoke, Karl Hermann; German diplomatist; b. 9 Aug. 1909; *s.* of Paul and Elisabeth Knoke; *m.* Ruth Countess Dohna, PH.D. 1941; three *s.* one *d.*; ed. Ludwig-Maximilians-Universität, Munich, Sorbonne, Paris, Friedrich-Wilhelms-Universität, Berlin, and Georg-August-Universität zu Göttingen.
Reichs Kreditgesellschaft A.G., Berlin; War Service 39-45; Land Govt., Hanover 45-47; Local Govt. Fallingbostel 47-50; Consul, First-Sec., Counsellor

Athens 50-54, Chargé d'Affaires a.i., Athens 52-53; South Eastern European Desk, German Foreign Office 54-56, Head of Eastern Dept. German Foreign Office 56-58; Minister Moscow 58-60, Paris 60-65; Amb. to Netherlands 65-68, to Israel 68-71, to Brazil 71-73; Head of Del. to Third UN Conf. on the Law of the Sea; Commandeur Légion d'Honneur; Grand Officier Ordre du Mérite; Grand Officer Order of Phoenix (Greece); Knight Commander Order of Merit (Fed. Rep. of Germany), Grand Cross of the Order of Orange-Nassau, Grand Cross Order of Cruzeiro do Sul.
Leisure interests: skiing, golf.
53 Bonn-Bad Godesberg, Mozartstrasse 28, Federal Republic of Germany.
Telephone: 352762.

Knoll, Florence Schust; American architect; b. 24 May 1917; ed. Cranbrook Acad., Architectural Asscn., London, and Illinois Inst. of Technology, Chicago.
Design Dir. Knoll Associates Inc., Knoll International Ltd.; architect, interior and furniture designer 43-65.
Home: 1801 West 27th Street, Sunset Island 2, Miami Beach, Florida, U.S.A.

Knopf, Alfred A., B.A.; American publisher; b. 12 Sept. 1892, New York; *s.* of Samuel Knopf and Ida Japhe Knopf; *m.* 1st Blanche Wolf 1916 (died 1966), 2nd Mrs. Helen Hedrick 1967; one *s.*; ed. Columbia Coll. President, Alfred A. Knopf Inc. 18-57, Chair. 57-72, Chair. of the Board Emer. 72-; publisher of Borzoi books; Hon. D.Hum.Litt. (Yale Univ.) 58, (Columbia Univ.) 59, (Bucknell Univ.) 59, (Coll. of William and Mary) 60, (Lehigh) 60, (Bates Coll.) 71; Hon. LL.D. (Brandeis Univ.) 63, (Adelphi Univ.) 66, (Univ. of Chatanooga) 66, (Long Island Univ.) 73; Hon. L.H.D. (Univ. of Michigan) 69.
201 East 50th Street, New York, N.Y. 10022, U.S.A.
Telephone: 572-2206.

Knopoff, Leon, M.S., PH.D.; American professor of physics and geophysics; b. 1 July 1925, Los Angeles, Calif.; *s.* of Max Knopoff and Ray Singer; *m.* Joanne Van Cleef 1961; one *s.* two *d.*; ed. Calif. Inst. of Tech. Assistant Prof., Assoc. Prof. of Physics, Miami Univ. 48-50; mem. staff Univ. of Calif. (Los Angeles) 50-, Prof. of Geophysics 59-, of Physics 61-, Research Musicologist 63-; Prof. of Geophysics, Calif. Inst. of Tech. 62-63; Visiting Prof. Technische Hochschule, Karlsruhe (Germany) 66; Chair. U.S. Upper Mantle Cttee. 63-70, Sec.-Gen. Int. Upper Mantle Cttee. 63-70; Assoc. Dir. Inst. of Geophysics and Planetary Physics 72-; Nat. Science Foundation Senior Postdoctoral Fellow 60-61; mem. Nat. Acad. of Sciences, American Acad. of Arts and Sciences; Int. Co-operation Year Medal (Canada) 65.
Leisure interests: mountaineering, gardening, playing piano and harpsichord.
Publs. *The Crust and Upper Mantle of the Pacific Area* (editor with others) 68, *The World Rift System* (editor with others); chapters in *Physics and Chemistry of High Pressures* (ed. R. L. Bradley) 63, *Physical Acoustics* (ed. W. P. Mason) 65, *The Earth's Mantle* (ed. T. Gaskell) 67, *The Megatectonics of Oceans and Continents* (ed. H. Johnson and B. L. Smith); papers in professional journals.
Institute of Geophysics, University of California, Los Angeles, California, U.S.A.
Telephone: 213-825-1580.

Knowles, John Hilton, A.B., M.D.; American physician; b. 23 May 1926, Chicago, Ill.; *s.* of James Knowles, Jr., and Jean L. Turnbull; *m.* Edith LaCroix 1953; four *s.* two *d.*; ed. Harvard Coll. and Washington Univ. General Dir. Massachusetts Gen. Hosp. 62-72; Prof. of Medicine, Harvard Medical School 69-72; Pres. and Trustee, The Rockefeller Foundation July 72-; Trustee Washington Univ. 73-(77), Harvard Coll. 73-(79), Duke

Univ. 74-(79), Boston Univ. 75-; many hon. doctorates in science, humane letters and law
Leisure interests: squash, golf, bibliophile.
Publs. *Respiratory Physiology and its Clinical Application* 59, *Hospitals, Doctors and the Public Interest* 65, *The Teaching Hospital: Evolution and Contemporary Issues* 66, *Views of Medical Education and Medical Care* 67.
The Rockefeller, Foundation, 1133 Avenue of the Americas, New York, N.Y. 10036; Home: 810 Fifth Avenue, New York, N.Y. 10021, U.S.A.
Telephone: 212-869-8500 (Office); 212-593-3931 (Home).

Knowles, Warren P., LL.B.; American politician; b. 19 Aug. 1908, River Falls, Wis.; s. of Warren P. Knowles and Anna D. Deneen; ed. River Falls, Carleton Coll. Minnesota and Univ. of Wisconsin Law School.
Practising attorney 33-; on county board 35-40; U.S. Navy Lieut. in Second World War; mem. State Senate 41-54 (Republican Floor Leader 43, 45, 47, 49, 51, 53); mem. Judicial Council 52-53; elected Lieut.-Gov. of Wis. 54, re-elected 56, 60; Gov. 64, re-elected 66, 68; Co-Chair. Upper Great Lakes Regional Planning Comm.; several hon. degrees and awards.
Leisure interests: hunting, outdoor sports, reading, participation in public affairs.
P.O. Box 339, Milwaukee, Wis. 53201, U.S.A.
Telephone: (414) 273-1000.

Knox, Alexander David, B.A.; British economist; b. 15 Jan. 1925, Trinidad, W. Indies; s. of James Knox and Elizabeth Maxwell Robertson; m. Beatrice Dunell 1950; one s. two d.; ed. Univ. of Toronto and London School of Econs. and Political Science.
Lecturer in Econs., London School of Econs. 51-54, Reader in Econs. (with special reference to Econs. of Underdeveloped countries) 55-63; mem. Ceylon Taxation Comm. 55, East African Comm. of Inquiry on Income Tax 56-57; Loan Officer, Int. Bank for Reconstruction and Devt. 63-65, Div. Chief, W. Hemisphere Dept. 65-66, Asst. Dir. Projects Dept. 67-68, Dir. Public Utilities Projects Dept. 68-69; Dir. Transportation Projects Dept. Oct. 69-72; Dir. Projects Dept. Latin America and the Caribbean 72-.
Leisure interests: tennis, gardening, opera, theatre.
Publs. Articles in econ. journals.
International Bank for Reconstruction and Development, 1818 H Street, N.W., Washington, D.C. 20433, U.S.A.
Telephone: 202-477-5906.

Knox, H.E. Cardinal James Robert; Australian ecclesiastic; b. 2 March 1914, Bayswater, Perth.
Ordained priest 41; Titular Archbishop of Melitene 53; Archbishop of Melbourne 67-74; created Cardinal 73; Pres. Perm. Cttee. of Int. Eucharist Congresses 73-; Prefect of Sacred Congregation for the Discipline of the Sacraments and of Sacred Congregation for Divine Worship 74; Prefect of the Sacred Congregation for the Sacraments and Divine Worship 75-.
Vatican City State, Rome, Italy.

Knox, Sir Thomas Malcolm, Kt., M.A., LL.D., D.LITT.; British university principal (retired); b. 1900, Birkenhead; s. of James Knox and Isabella Russell Marshall; m. Dorothy Ellen Jolly 1934 (died 1974); ed. Liverpool Inst. and Pembroke Coll., Oxford.
In business 23-31; Fellow and Tutor, Jesus Coll., Oxford 33-36; Prof. of Moral Philosophy, St. Andrews Univ. 36-53, Principal 53-66; Hon. Fellow, Pembroke Coll., Oxford; Gifford Lecturer, Aberdeen 65-66, 67-68.
Leisure interests: music.
19 Victoria Terrace, Crieff, Perthshire, Scotland.
Telephone: Crieff 2808.

Knudsen, Semon Emil; American automobile executive; b. 2 Oct. 1912, Buffalo, N.Y.; s. of William S. and Clara Euler Knudsen; m. Florence Anne McConnell

1938; one s. three d.; ed. Dartmouth Coll. and Mass. Inst. of Technology.
With Gen. Motors Corpn. 39-68, Vice-Pres. and Gen. Man. Pontiac Motor Div. 56-61, Chevrolet Div. 61-65, Group Vice-Pres. in charge of Overseas and Canadian Group 65-68, also responsible for domestic non-automotive divs. 66-68, Exec. Vice-Pres. (Int. Operations) 67-68; Pres. Ford Motor Co. 68-69; Founder, Chair. Rectrans Inc. 70-71; Chair. of Board White Motor Corpn. 71-.
White Motor Corporation, P.O. Box 6979, Cleveland, O. 44101; Home: 2112 Acacia Park Drive, Lyndhurst, O. 44124, U.S.A.

Knunyants, Ivan Lyudvigovich; Soviet organic chemist; b. 4 June 1906, Shusha Nagorna-Karabakh Autonomous region, Azerbayan; ed. Moscow Higher Technical School.
Research worker, Moscow Higher Technical School 28-31; Assoc. Inst. of Organic Chemistry, U.S.S.R. Acad. of Sciences 31-54, mem. C.P.S.U. 41-; Chief of Laboratory, Inst. of Elementary Organic Compounds, Acad. of Sciences 54-; Corresp. mem. U.S.S.R. Acad. of Sciences 46-53, mem 53-; State Prizes 43, 48, 50; Hero of Socialist Labour 66; Lenin Prize 72.
Publs. *Methods of Introducing Fluorine into Organic Compounds* 47, *The Interaction of Aliphatic Oxides with Hydrogen Fluoride* 47, *Modern Experimental Methods in Organic Chemistry* 60, and other works.
Institute of Elementary Organic Compounds, U.S.S.R. Academy of Sciences, 28 Ul. Vavilova, Moscow, U.S.S.R.

Knuth, Count Eggert Adam; Danish diplomatist; b. 19 April 1901, Copenhagen; m. Countess Lily Ingeborg Agnes Rantzau 1934.
Vice-Consul Sydney 29-32; Sec. Legation Reykjavík 35-36; Sec. Legation London 36-43, First Sec. 43-45; Head Div. Min. for Foreign Affairs 45-51; Counsellor, Embassy, London 51, Minister 52-56; Ambassador to Iceland 56-59, to Belgium and Luxembourg 61-67, to Italy 67-68, to Norway 69-71.
Leisure interests: golf, shooting, gardening.
Krengerup, 5620 Glamsbjerg, Denmark.

Knuth-Winterfeldt, Count Kield Gustav, LL.D.; Danish diplomatist; b. 17 Feb. 1908, Copenhagen; s. of Count Viggo Christian Knuth-Winterfeldt and Countess Clara Knuth-Winterfeldt (née Grüner); m. Gertrud Lina Baumann 1938; two s. one d.; ed. Univ. of Copenhagen.
Danish Foreign Service 31-, Vice-Consul Hamburg 35; Sec. of Legation, Tokyo 38; Sec. Ministry for Foreign Affairs 39-45, Deputy Chief of Section 45, Chief 50; Minister, Argentina 50; Chief, Commercial Information Dept., Ministry of Foreign Affairs 54, Deputy Dir. Economic Division 56; Ambassador to U.S.A. 58-65, to France 65-66, to German Federal Republic 66-72; Lord Chamberlain at the Royal Danish Court 72-; Grand Officer, Order of Dannebrog; Grand Cross, Order of Merit, G.F.R.; Officer, Order of George I (Greece), Grand Cross, Order of North Star (Sweden), Grand Officer, Order of Merit (Argentina), Grand Officer, Order of Merit (Chile), Grand Cross, Order of Falcon (Iceland), Grand Cross, Order of Victoria (U.K.), Grand Cross, Order of St. Olav (Norway), Order of the Yugoslav Flag with Ribbon, Grand Cross, Order of the House of Orange (Netherlands).
Leisure interest: farming.
9 Rosendal by Fakse, Denmark; and Christiansborg, Slots Ridebane No. 9, 1218 Copenhagen K, Denmark.

Kobayashi, Koji, D.ENG.; Japanese business executive; b. 17 Feb. 1907, Yamanashi Prefecture; s. of Tsuneo Kobayashi and Den Kobayashi; m. Kazuko Noda 1935; three d.; ed. Tokyo Imperial Univ.
Senior Vice-Pres. and Dir. Nippon Electric Co. Ltd. 56-61, Exec. Vice-Pres. and Dir. 61-62, Sen. Exec. Vice-Pres. and Dir. 62-64, Pres. 64-; Nippon Electric Tohoku

Ltd., Chair. of Board 73-; Chair. Board Nippon Avio-tronics Co. Ltd. 69-; Pres. Japan Electronic Industry Devt. Asscn. 73-; Pres. Asscn. of Communication Equipment Industries of Japan 74-; Vice-Pres. Electronic Industries Asscn. of Japan 74-; Dir. Japan Management Asscn. 53-; Chair. Space Devt. Promotion Council, Fed. of Econ. Orgs. 70-; Pres. Japan Inst. of Industrial Eng. 74-; Vice-Pres. Japan Telecommunication Industrial Fed. 74-; Prime Minister's Prize for Export Promotion 64; Blue Ribbon Medal 64.
Leisure interests: golf and gardening.
Publ. *Carrier Transmission System* 37.
Nippon Electric Co. Ltd., 33-1 Shiba Gochome, Minato-ku, Tokyo 108; and 15-7 Denenchofu 5-chome, Ohta-ku, Tokyo 145, Japan.
Telephone: 03-721-8581.

Kobayashi, Setsutaro; Japanese business executive; b. 7 Nov. 1899, Hyogo; *s.* of Daikichi and Yone Kobayashi; *m.* Chizuyo Shiose 1932; three *s.* two *d.*; ed. Kwansei Gakuin Univ.
With Iwai & Co. 23-33, Daicel Ltd. 33-34; joined Fuji Photo Film Co. Ltd. 34, Dir. 37-43, Man. Dir. 43, Senior Man. Dir. 43-58, Exec. Vice-Pres. 58-60, Pres. 60-71, Chair. of Board 71-; Pres. Fuji Xerox Co. Ltd. 62-; Blue Ribbon Medal, Order of the Sacred Treasure.
Leisure interests: golf, Igo.
Fuji Photo Film Co. Ltd., 26-30, Nishiazabu 2-chome, Minato-ku, Tokyo; Home: 34-9, Shimouma 6-chome, Setagaya-ku, Tokyo, Japan.
Telephone: 03-406-2111 (Office); 03-421-0322 (Home).

Kobzarev, Yury Borisovich, D.SC.; Soviet radiophysicist; b. 1905, Voronezh; ed. Kharkov Inst. of Educ.
Senior Research Assoc., Physical-Technical Inst., U.S.S.R. Acad. of Sciences 26-43; Head of Chair., Prof. Moscow Energy Inst. 44-55; Research Assoc., Inst. of Radiotechnics and Electrotechnics 55-, Chair. of Dept. 68-; Corresp. mem., U.S.S.R. Acad. of Sciences 53-70, Academician 70-; State Prize 41, 49.
U.S.S.R. Academy of Sciences, 14 Leninsky Prospekt, Moscow, U.S.S.R.

Koch, Alfred F., M.B.A., PH.D.; German economist; b. 5 Jan. 1926, Markersdorf, Czechoslovakia; *m.*; two *c.*; ed. Univs. of Regensburg and Munich.
Scientific Asst., German Inst. for Tourism Econs., Munich Univ. 53, later appt. Sec.-Gen. of the Inst.; Dir. Tourism Projects Dept., Int. Bank for Recon. and Devt. (IBRD)—World Bank Sept. 69-72.
Publs. numerous articles on tourism economics.
International Bank for Reconstruction and Development, 1818 H Street NW, Washington, D.C. 20433, U.S.A.

Kocheshkov, Ksenofont Alexandrovich, DR.SC.; Soviet chemist; b. 12 Dec. 1894, Moscow; ed. Moscow State Univ.
Red Army 19-21; Teacher, Sverdlov Communist Univ. 21-24; Lecturer, Moscow Univ. 24-38, Prof. 35-; Head, Chemical Dept., All-Union Inst. of Experimental Medicine 37-45; Head of Metal-organic Lab., Karpov Physico-Chemical Inst. 46-; Corresp. mem. U.S.S.R. Acad. of Sciences 46-68, Academician, 68-; State Prize 48, 67.
U.S.S.R. Academy of Sciences, 14 Leninsky prospekt, Moscow, U.S.S.R.

Kochetkov, Prof. Nikolai Konstantinovich; Soviet chemist; b. 1915, Moscow; *s.* of Konstantin Kochetkov and Marie Kochetkova; *m.* Dr. Vera Volodina 1945; one *s.* one *d.*; ed. M. V. Lomonosov Inst. of Light Chem. Technology.
Assistant, Chem. Dept. of Moscow Univ. 45-52, Dozent 52-56, Prof. 56-60; Head of Dept. of Organic Synthesis, Inst. of Pharmacology 53-60; Deputy Dir., Head of nucleic acids and carbohydrates laboratory, Inst. of Natural Products 60-66; Dir., Head of carbohydrates laboratory, Zelinsky Inst. of organic chem. 66-; Corresp. mem. U.S.S.R. Acad of Medical Sciences 57-, U.S.S.R. Acad. of Sciences 60-; mem. Soc. de Chémie 72-.
Publs. *Chemistry of Natural Products* 61, *Chemistry of Carbohydrates* 67, *Organic Chemistry of Nucleic Acids* 70.
Zelinsky Institute of Organic Chemistry, Leninsky Prospekt 47, Moscow B-334, U.S.S.R.
Telephone: 137-29-44.

Kochina, Pelageya Yakovlevna; Soviet mechanical engineer; b. 13 May 1899, Astrakhan; ed. Petrograd Univ.
In Central Geophysical Observatory 19-24, Inst. of Railway Engineers 24-30, Civil Aviation Engineers 30-35; worked in Mathematics Inst. then Inst. of Mechanics, Acad. of Sciences of the U.S.S.R. 35-59; Inst. of Hydrodynamics 59-; Corresp. mem Acad. of Sciences of the U.S.S.R. 46-56, mem. 56-; main works dedicated to theory of filtration, of dynamic meteorology, of the steadiness of plates, of floods in basins; Chair. Comm. Acad. of Sciences for Utilization and Protection of Water Resources in Siberia; State Prize U.S.S.R. 46; Hero of Socialist Labour 69.
Institute of Hydrodynamics, 90 Akademgorodok, Novosibirsk, U.S.S.R.

Kochman, Mohamed Nassim; Mauritanian lawyer, diplomatist and international civil servant; b. 25 Oct. 1932; ed. Petit Lycée, Dakar, Senegal, Van Vollenhoven Lycée, Dakar, Marcel Gambier Coll., Lisieux, France, and Faculty of Law and Economic Sciences, Grenoble, France.
Attorney at Law, Court of Appeals, Dakar, 59-61; First Sec., later First Counsellor, Embassy of Mauritania, Washington and Perm. Mission of Mauritania to UN, New York 61; Chargé d'Affaires Mauritanian Embassy, Washington, 62-64; Chief Perm. Mission of Mauritania to UN 63-64; Alt. Exec. Dir. IBRD, IDA and IFC (rep. of various African States) 63-64, Exec. Dir., Principal Resident Repub. of Mauritania to IBRD 64-74; Special Adviser to Pres. of IBRD 74-; Mauritanian del. at several world confs. and signatory to int. agreements; mem. World Peace Through Law, Washington, D.C.; decorations from Mauritania, Colombia, Senegal, Chad, Cen. African Repub., People's Repub. of Congo, Niger, Ivory Coast, Gabon, Zaire, Upper Volta, Dahomey and Madagascar.
International Bank for Reconstruction and Development, 1818 H Street, N.W., Washington, D.C., U.S.A.
Telephone: DU1-3662.

Kock, Karin, D.SC. (ECON.); Swedish economist; b. 2 July 1891, Stockholm; *d.* of Ernst Kock and Anna Aslund; *m.* Hugo Lindberg 1936 (died 1966); ed. Stockholm Univ.
Statistician and economist, Skandinaviska Banken, Stockholm 18-32; Reader (Docent) in Economics, Stockholm Univ. 33; Acting Prof. of Economics, Stockholm Univ. 38-46, now Prof. h.c.; Chief of Section, Ministry of Commerce 47; Minister without Portfolio 47-48; Minister of Supply 48-49; Dir.-in-Chief Central Bureau of Statistics 50-57; Chair. Economic Comm. for Europe 50-52, Swedish Statistical Asscn. 53-54; Research Prof. Inst. for Int. Economic Studies, Stockholm Univ. 63-69; mem. Gov. Board UNESCO Inst. for Social Sciences 51-60; Fellow, American Statistical Asscn. 56; mem. Int. Statistical Inst.; Hon. mem. Statistical Asscns. of Sweden and Finland; mem. Soc. Democratic Party.
Leisure interest: travelling.
Publs. *A Study of Interest Rates* 29, *Svenskt bankväsen i våra dagar* 30, *Skånska Privatbanken* 31, *Skånska Cement A.B.* 32, *Sveriges handelsekonomiska läge* 34, *Konjunkturuppsvingets förlopp och orsaker* 35, *Smålands Bank* 37, *National Income of Sweden 1861-1930* (together with Erik Lindahl and Einar Dahlgren) 37, *Kvinnoarbetet i Sverige* 38, *Statistiska Centralbyrån 100 år* 58,

Kreditmarknad och Räntepolitik I 61, *II* 62, *International Trade Policy and the Gatt 47-67* 69.
Jakob Westinsg. 1A, S 112 20 Stockholm, Sweden.
Telephone: 08-530868.

Kock-Henriksen, Peder, M.SC.; Danish chemical engineer and dairy executive; b. 10 July 1904, Flynder; *s.* of late Niels Henriksen and late Andrea Andersen; *m.* Asta Marie Riisberg 1931; one *s.* one *d.*; ed. Danish Technical Univ.
Director, Minsterley Creameries Ltd., Shropshire, U.K. 35-39; Managing Dir. Canned Cream and Milk Ltd., Odense 40-48; Comm., Fed. of Danish Dairy Asscns. 49-55, Deputy Dir. 55-58, Joint Man. Dir. 58-73; Sec.-Gen. 16th Int. Dairy Congress, Copenhagen 62; Pres. Econ. Comm. of Int. Dairy Fed. 70-74; del. to numerous confs.; Knight Order of Dannebrog, Officer Order of Orange-Nassau.
Publs. *Sales Possibilities of Danish Dairy Products* 50, *Denmark's Share and Possibilities in the International Trade in Dairy Products* 54, *Changes in Eating Habits over the Last Twenty-Thirty Years within the EEC, and Specification of Quantities and Development in Consumption of Different Fats in the Diet.*
59 Dalgas Avenue, 8000 Aarhus C., Denmark.
Telephone: 06-124624.

Kocsis, Zoltán; Hungarian pianist; b. 30 May 1952, Budapest; *s.* of Otto Kocsis and Maria Mátyás; ed. Budapest Music Acad. (under Pál Kadosa).
Has appeared with Dresden Philharmonic Orchestra in German Democratic Repub., and performed in Fed. Germany, U.S.S.R., Austria and Czechoslovakia 71; toured U.S.A. together with Dezsö Ranki (*q.v.*) and Budapest Symphony Orchestra (under George Lehel) 71; recitals in Netherlands, Paris, London and Ireland 72; First Prize, Beethoven Piano Competition, Hungarian Radio and Television 70, Liszt Prize 2nd Degree 73.
Leisure interests: musical records and tapes.
1157 Budapest XV, Hevesi Gyula-utca 33; Interconcert Agency, 1051 Budapest V, Vörösmarty tér 1, Hungary.
Telephone: 128-650 (Agency).

Kodama, Tadayasu; Japanese shipping executive; b. 29 July 1898; ed. Kyoto Imperial Univ.
Nippon Yusen Kaisha Ltd. (N.Y.K. Line), 22-, Dir. 47-, Man. Dir. 51-58, Vice-Pres. 58-61, Pres. 61-65, Chair. 65-71, now Board Counsellor.
Nippon Yusen Kaisha, 3-2, 2-chome, Marunouchi, Chiyoda-ku, 100, Tokyo, Japan.

Kodama, Yoshiichi; Japanese business executive; b. 1900, Okayama Pref.; ed. primary school, Tokyo.
Held various posts in agricultural orgs. in Hokkaido 34-47; mem. Hokkaido Prefectural Assembly 47-59; mem. Hokkaido Devt. Council; Dir. Snow Brand Milk Products Co. Ltd. 50, Man. Dir. 56, Senior Vice-Pres. 63, Pres. 71-73, Chair. 73-; Pres., Dir. or Adviser to many subsidiary companies; Medal of Honour with Blue Ribbon.
Snow Brand Milk Products Co. Ltd., 13 Honshio-cho, Shinjuku-ku, Tokyo, Japan.
Telephone: 357-3111.

Kodamanoğlu, Nuri, M.SC.; Turkish politician; b. 16 Aug. 1923, Ulukişla-Niğde; *s.* of Fazil and Hatice Kodamanoğlu; *m.* Ayten (Unal) Kodamanoğlu 1951; ed. Istanbul Univ.
Former civil servant, Ministry of Educ.; later Under-Sec. Ministry of Educ.; Deputy to Grand Nat. Assembly; Minister of Energy and Natural Resources 72-; mem. Business Admin. Inst., Faculty of Political Science, Univ. of Ankara.
Leisure interests: handicrafts, gardening.
Publs. *Principles of New Education* 54, *Education in Turkey* 63; various articles and reports.
Bükreş Sokak No. 6 Daire 8, Çankaya, Ankara, Turkey.
Telephone: 27-15-15.

Kodera, Shinrokuro, B.ECONS.; Japanese business executive; b. 14 Dec. 1918, Sumiyoshi, Hyogo Pref.; *s.* of Gengo and Hisa Kodera; *m.* Kimiko Sakahara 1963; ed. Keio Univ.
Joined Dainippon Spinning Co. Ltd. 41; Dir. Unitika Ltd. 70, Man. Dir. 72, Deputy Pres. 73, Pres. 74-.
Leisure interest: golf.
16, 6, 1-chome, Chigusa, Takarazuka-shi, Hyogo-ken, Japan.
Telephone: 0797-71-1601.

Koechlin, Dr. Samuel; Swiss business executive; b. 29 March 1925; ed. Univs. of Basle and Paris and London School of Econs.
Formerly with New York Agency of Swiss Credit Bank; joined Geigy Co. Inc., New York 52, J. R. Geigy, S.A., Basle 54; Chair. Exec. Cttee. J. R. Geigy, S.A. 65-68, CIBA-Geigy Ltd. 70-, Chair. Exec. Cttee. 70.
CIBA-Geigy Ltd., Basle, Switzerland.

Koelle, George Brampton, PH.D., M.D., D.SC.; American pharmacologist; b. 8 Oct. 1918, Philadelphia, Pa.; *s.* of Frederick C. Koelle and Emily M. Brampton; *m.* Winifred J. Angenent 1954; three *s.*; ed. Univ. of Pennsylvania and Johns Hopkins Univ.
Bio-Assayist, LaWall and Harrisson Labs. 39-42; Laboratory Instructor in Biological Assaying and Pharmacology, Philadelphia Coll. of Pharmacy and Science 39-42; Chalfont Fellow in Ophthalmology, Wilmer Inst., Johns Hopkins Univ. and Hospital 46-50; Asst. Prof. of Pharmacology, Coll. of Physicians and Surgeons, Columbia Univ. 50-52; Prof. of Pharmacology, Graduate School of Medicine, Univ. of Pa. 52-, Chair. Dept. of Pharmacology 59-; Visiting Prof. and Guggenheim Fellow, Univ. of Lausanne 63-64; Visiting Prof. and Acting Chair. Dept. of Pharmacology and Assoc. Dir. of Penn Team, Pahlavi Univ., Iran 69-70; mem. Nat. Acad. of Sciences, A.A.A.S. (Vice-Pres. 71), American Soc. of Pharmacology (Pres. 65), Int. Union of Pharmacology (Vice-Pres. 69-72); Hon. D.Sc. (Philadelphia Coll. of Pharmacy and Science), Hon. D.Med. (Univ. of Zurich); Borden Award 50, Univ. of Turku Memorial Medal 72, and other awards and prizes.
Leisure interest: Sherlock Holmsian.
Publs. more than 100 papers on pharmacology, histochemistry and electron microscopy.
University of Pennsylvania School of Medicine, Department of Pharmacology, Philadelphia, Pa. 19174; Home: 205 College Avenue, Swarthmore, Pa. 19081, U.S.A.
Telephone: 215-594-8416 (Office); 215-K14-4566.

Koenigswald, G. H. Ralph von, DR.PHIL.; Netherlands palaeoanthropologist; b. 13 Nov. 1902, Berlin; *s.* of Gustav Adalbert von Koenigswald and Martha Jacobi; *m.* L. S. L. Beyer; one *d.*; ed. Univs. of Berlin, Tübingen, Cologne and Munich.
Assistant, Geological Museum, Munich 28-30; Palaeontologist Geological Survey for the Dutch East Indies, Bandung, Java 30-48; Prof. of Palaeontology, State Univ., Utrecht 48-68, Prof. Emer. 68-; Research Assoc., Carnegie Inst. of Washington 39-41; Pithecanthropus and Meganthropus finds in Java 36-41, Hong Kong 35, Peking 39; discovered Gigantophithecus; with Rockefeller and Viking Fund Grant in New York's American Museum of Nat. History 46-48, fieldwork in the Philippines, East Africa and Pakistan; now Curator, Div. of Palaeoanthropology, Senckenberg-Museum, Frankfurt/M; mem. Royal Netherlands Acad. of Sciences; Foreign Assoc. Nat. Acad. of Science, U.S.A.; Life mem. New York Acad.; Huxley Medal, Anthropological Inst. (U.K.); Golden Anandale Medal, Royal Asiatic Soc., Calcutta; Darwin Medal, Academia Leopoldina, etc.
Leisure interests: ethnology, primitive art.
Publs. *Begegnungen mit dem Vormenschen* 56, *Geschichte des Menschen* 68 and about 220 scientific publications

in the fields of geology, palaeontology, Early Man, prehistory, ethnology.

Senckenberg-Museum, Senckenberganlage 25, 6 Frankfurt/M, Federal Republic of Germany.

Koestler, Arthur, C.B.E., F.R.S.L., M.INST.P.I.; British (naturalized) author; b. 5 Sept. 1905, Budapest; s. of Henrik and Adela Koestler; m. 1st Dorothy Ascher 1935, 2nd Mamaine Paget 1950; 3rd Cynthia Jefferies 1965; one d.; ed. Vienna Univ.

Foreign corresp. in Middle East, later Paris, of *Vossische Zeitung* 26-30; mem. editorial staff Ullstein's, Berlin 30-32; corresp. U.S.S.R., travelled Soviet Central Asia 32-33; freelance, Paris, London, Zürich 33-36; *News Chronicle* Special Corresp. Spanish Civil War, Egypt, Palestine, etc. 36-48; served as Private in French and British Armies; Sonning Prize, Univ. of Copenhagen 68; Hon. LL.D. (Queen's, Canada); Hon. D.Litt. (Leeds); C.Lit. 74.

Leisure interests: chess, mountaineering, boating, good wine.

Publs. *Spanish Testament* 38, *The Gladiators* 40, *Darkness at Noon* 41, *Scum of the Earth* 41, *Arrival and Departure* 43, *The Yogi and the Commissar* 45, *Twilight Bar* (play) 45, *Thieves in the Night* 46, *Insight and Outlook* 48, *Promise and Fulfilment* 49, *The God that Failed* (jointly) 50, *The Age of Longing* 50, *Arrow in the Blue* 52, *The Invisible Writing* 54, *The Trail of the Dinosaur* 55, *Reflections on Hanging* 56, *The Sleepwalkers* 59, *The Lotus and the Robot* 60, *Suicide of a Nation?* (editor) 63, *The Act of Creation* 64, *The Ghost in the Machine* 67, *Drinkers of Infinity* 68, *Beyond Reductionism—The Alpbach Symposium* (with J. R. Smythies) 69, *The Case of the Midwife Toad* 71, *The Roots of Coincidence* 72, *The Call Girls* 72, *The Challenge of Chance* (with Sir Alister Hardy and Robert Harvie) 73, *The Heel of Achilles* 74, *The Thirteenth Tribe* 76.

c/o A. D. Peters, 10 Buckingham Street, London, W.C.2, England.

Koga, Issac, PH.D.; Japanese radio engineer; b. 5 Dec. 1899; ed. Univ. of Tokyo.

Assistant Prof. Tokyo Inst. of Technology 29-39, Prof. 39-58; Prof. Univ. of Tokyo 44-60, Dean of Engineering 58-60; Vice-Pres. Int. Scientific Radio Union, Brussels 57-63, Pres. 63-66; Pres. Inst. of Elect. Communication Engineers of Japan 47-48; Pres. Inst. of Electrical Engineers of Japan 57-58; mem. Technical Advisory Cttee. Nat. Broadcasting Corpn. 51-66; mem. Advisory Cttee. for Radio Administration, Ministry of Posts and Telecommunications 63-, Chair. 70; Pres. Int. Telecommunication Union (ITU) Assen. of Japan 71-; mem. Advisory Comm. for Nat. Language, Ministry of Educ. 61-; mem. Cen. Council for Educ., Ministry of Educ. 67-71; Fellow Inst. of Electrical and Electronics Engineers, New York 57; Hon. mem. Inst. of Electrical Communication Engineers of Japan 64, Inst. of Electrical Engineers of Japan 65; Order of Cultural Merit 63; First Class Order of the Sacred Treasure 70; C. B. Sawyer Memorial Award 70.

Major works include: invention of crystal plates of zero frequency-temperature coefficient, investigation on piezoelectric oscillating crystal and quartz crystal circuit (Japan Acad. of Sciences Prize) 48, frequency demultiplier by means of a vacuum tube circuit.

17-5, 2-chome Aobadai, Meguro-ku, Tokyo 153, Japan. Telephone: (Tokyo) 461-3395.

Kogan, Leonid Borisovich; Soviet violinist; b. 14 Oct. 1924, Dnepropetrovsk, Ukraine; ed. Moscow Conservatoire under Abram Yampolsky.

Professor Moscow Conservatoire; plays music of Bach, Mozart, Vivaldi, Brahms, Tchaikovsky, Prokofiev, Shostakovich; numerous world tours; Honoured Artist of the R.S.F.S.R. 55; People's Artist of the U.S.S.R.; Lenin Prize 65.

State Concert Association of the U.S.S.R., 15 Neglinnaya, Moscow, U.S.S.R.

Koh, Tommy Thong Bee, LL.M.; Singapore law teacher and diplomatist; b. 12 Nov. 1937, Singapore; s. of Koh Han Kok and Tsai Ying; m. Siew Aing 1967; two s.; ed. Univ. of Singapore, and Harvard and Cambridge Univs.

Assistant Lecturer, Univ. of Singapore 62-64, Lecturer 64-; Sub-Dean, Faculty of Law, Univ. of Singapore 65-67, Vice-Dean 67-68; Visiting Lecturer, State Univ. of New York at Buffalo 67; fmr. Legal Adviser to trade unions in Singapore and fmr. Sec. Inst. of Int. Affairs, Singapore; Amb. and Perm. Rep. of Singapore to UN 68-71, concurrently High Commr. to Canada 69-71; Dean, Faculty of Law, Singapore Univ. 71-74; Amb. and Perm. Rep. to UN, High Commr. to Canada 74-; Adrian Clarke Memorial Medal, Leow Chia Heng Prize. Leisure interests: sport, reading, music.

Publs. law articles in *Malaya Law Review* and *Malayan Law Journal*.

Permanent Mission of Singapore to the United Nations, 711 Third Avenue, New York, N.Y. 10017, U.S.A.

Kohl, Helmut, DR.PHIL.; German politician; b. 3 April 1930, Ludwigshafen; s. of Hans and Cecilie Kohl; m. Hannelore (née Renner) 1960; two s.; ed. Univs. of Frankfurt and Heidelberg.

Member of Management of an industrial union 59; Chair. Christian Democrat Party (CDU), Rhineland-Palatinate 56, Deputy Chair. CDU Deutschlands 69-73, Chair. 73-; Minister-Pres. Rhineland-Palatinate 69-; CDU candidate for Chancellor 76.

6700 Ludwigshafen/Rhein, Tirolerstrasse 41, Federal Republic of Germany.
Telephone: 572398.

Kohler, Foy D., B.S.; American diplomatist; b. 15 Feb. 1908, Oakwood, Ohio; s. of Leander David Kohler and Myrtle McClure Kohler; m. Phyllis Penn 1935; ed. Toledo and Ohio State Univs.

Joined Foreign Service 31; Vice-Consul, Windsor (Canada) 32, Bucharest 33-35, Belgrade 35; Legation Sec. and Vice-Consul Bucharest 35-36, Athens 36-41, Cairo 41; Specialist Dept. of State 41-44, Asst. Chief Div. of Near Eastern Affairs 44-45; London Embassy and Adviser to U.S. Del. UNRRA Council 44; Political and Liaison Officer to U.S. Del. San Francisco Conf. 45; Sec.-Gen. U.S. Greek Elections Mission 45-46; studies at Cornell Univ. and Nat. War Coll. 46; 1st Sec. Moscow 47, Counsellor 48, Minister 48; Chief Int. Broadcasting Div. Dept. of State 49; Dir. Voice of America 49-52; Counsellor Ankara 53-56; seconded to Int. Co-operation Admin. (ICA) 56-58; Deputy Asst. Sec. of State 58-59, Asst. Sec. of State (European Affairs) 59-62; Amb. to U.S.S.R. 62-66; Deputy Under-Sec. of State 66-68; Prof., Univ. of Miami 68-; mem. Board Int. Broadcasting 74; D.Hum. (Ohio State Univ.), LL.D. (Univ. of Toledo, Ohio). Leisure interests: golf and swimming.

Publs. *Understanding the Russians—A Citizen's Primer* 70; Co-author *Science and Technology as an Instrument of Soviet Policy* 72, *Convergence of Communism and Capitalism* 73, *Soviet Strategy for the 70s: From Cold War to Peaceful Coexistence* 73, *The Role of Nuclear Forces in Current Soviet Strategy* 74, *The Soviet Union—Yesterday, Today, Tomorrow* 75, *Custine's Eternal Russia* 76.

University of Miami, Coral Gables, Fla. 33124; Home: 215 Golf Club Circle, Village of Tequesta, Jupiter, Florida 33458, U.S.A.

Kohli, Admiral Sourendra Nath, B.A., P.V.S.M., P.B.; Indian naval officer; b. 21 June 1916, Amritsar; s. of B. L. Kohli; m. Somitra Khanna 1946; three d.; ed. St. Stephen's Coll., Delhi.

Commissioned 38; war service, Persian Gulf and Andamans 39-42; instructor, communications officer, officer-in-charge, signal school 43-48; commanded I.N.S. *Rana* 49-50; Dir. Naval Plans 51-52, 57; Capt.

22nd Destroyer Squadron 53-55; Naval Adviser, London 55-57; Commdr. Supt. Naval Dockyard, Bombay 61-62; Chief of Material, Naval H.Q. 63-64; Rear-Adm. 65; Deputy Chief of Naval Staff 64-67; Flag Officer, Indian (Western) Fleet 67-69; Vice-Adm. 69; Commdt. Nat. Defence Coll., New Delhi 69-71; C.-in-C. Western Naval Command 71-73; Chief of Naval Staff March 73-; Param Vishisht Seva Medal 68, Padma Bhushan 72.
Leisure interests: sailing, golf.
Naval Headquarters, New Delhi 11, India.
Telephone: New Delhi 371400.

Kohn, Walter, PH.D.; American professor of physics; b. 9 March 1923, Vienna, Austria; s. of Solomon Kohn and Gusti Rappaport; m. Lois Mary Adams 1948; three d.; ed. Toronto and Harvard Univs.
Served with Canadian Infantry 44-45; Instructor Harvard Univ. 48-50; Asst. Prof., Assoc. Prof., then Prof., Carnegie Inst. of Tech. 50-59; Prof. Univ. of Calif. at San Diego 60-, Chair. Dept. of Physics 61-63; Visiting Prof., Univs. of Mich. and Pennsylvania 57-58, Imperial Coll. of Science and Tech. London 60; Nat. Research Council Fellow, Inst. of Theoretical Physics, Copenhagen 51-52; Guggenheim Fellow and Visiting Prof. Ecole Normale Supérieure Paris 63-64; Nat. Science Foundation Senior Postdoctoral Fellow Univ. of Paris 67; Councillor-at-Large, Amer. Physical Soc. 68-72; Visiting Prof. Hebrew Univ., Jerusalem 70; Fellow American Acad. of Arts and Sciences; mem. Nat. Acad. of Sciences; Hon. LL.D. (Toronto); Oliver E. Buckley Prize in Solid State Physics 60.
Leisure interests: flute, reading, sports.
Publs. Articles in *Physical Review, Reviews of Modern Physics*, etc. 45-.
Department of Physics, University of California, San Diego, La Jolla, Calif. 92093, U.S.A.
Telephone: 714-452-3267.

Kohnstamm, Max, M.A.; Netherlands educationist; b. 22 May 1914, Amsterdam; m. Kathleen Sillem 1944; two s. three d.; ed. Amsterdam Univ., American Univ. of Wash., D.C.
Prisoner of war 42-44; Private Sec. to H.M. Queen Wilhelmina 45-48; Head German Bureau, Dir. European Affairs, Ministry of Foreign Affairs 48-52; Vice-Pres. Netherlands del. during negotiations concerning Schuman Plan; Sec. to High Authority, European Coal and Steel Community 52-56; Vice-Pres. Action Cttee. for United States of Europe 56-; Pres. European Community Inst. for Univ. Studies 58-, European Univ. Inst. of Florence 73-; Hon. LL.D. (Westminster Coll., Missouri) 63.
Leisure interests: tennis, walking.
Publs. include *The European Community and its Role in the World* 63, *Weltorganisationen* 70, *Unity of the Church—Unity of Mankind* 71.
47 rue de Trèves, 1040 Brussels; Home: 12 avenue Casalta, 1180 Brussels, Belgium.
Telephone: 136710 (Office); 741672 (Home).

Kohrt, Günter; German diplomatist and politician; b. 11 March 1912.
Posts concerned with public educ., City Council of Greater Berlin 45-49; Ministry of Foreign Affairs, German Democratic Republic 49-; Ambassador to People's Republic of China 64-66; Sec. of State and First Deputy Foreign Minister 66-73; Amb. to Hungary 74-.
Embassy of German Democratic Republic, Népstadion u. 101-103, Budapest, Hungary.

Koht, Paul; Norwegian diplomatist; b. 7 Dec. 1913, Baerum; s. of the late Halvdan Koht and Karen Grude; m. Grete Sverdrup 1938; two s. one d.; ed. Oslo Univ.
Entered foreign service 38; served Bucharest 38-39, Ministry of Foreign Affairs 39-40, London 40-41, Tokyo 41-42, New York 42-46. Ministry of Foreign Affairs 46-50, 53-56, Lisbon 50-51, Paris 51-53, Denmark 56-58; Amb. to U.S.A. 58-63, to Fed. Repub. of Germany 63-68, to U.K. and Repub. of Ireland 68-75, to Denmark 75-.
Norwegian Embassy, Trondhjems Plads 4, Copenhagen Ø; Øster Allé 33, Copenhagen Ø, Denmark.

Koike, Shinzo; Japanese politician and business executive; b. 1903, Takayama City, Gifu Pref.; s. of the late Suekichi Hirose and Kinu Hirose; m. Chieko Koike 1929; one d.; ed. Yokyo Univ.
Ministry of Communications 28, later Chief, Accounting Section, Ministry of Transportation Secr., Dir. Sapporo Communications Bureau, Electric Power Bureau, Ministry of Commerce and Industry; Chief Dir. Central Japan Industrial League 50-63; mem. House of Councillors 50-54; Parl. Vice-Minister of Int. Trade and Industry 50-54; Minister of Posts and Telecommunications 63-64; Chair. Board of Dirs. Kokusai Denshin Denwa Co. Ltd. 75-; Liberal-Democratic Party.
Leisure interest: appreciation of artistic handicrafts.
Publ. *An Outline of the Electric Power Control Decree*.
No. 17-6, Jingumae 3-chome, Shibuya-ku, Tokyo, Japan.
Telephone: (402) 0088.

Koiter, Warner Tjardus; Netherlands professor of engineering; b. 16 June 1914, Amsterdam; s. of Klaas Koiter and Jacoba U. M. Greidanus; m. Louise Clara Spits 1939; two s. two d.; ed. Univ. of Technology, Delft.
With Nat. Aeronautical Research Inst., Amsterdam 36-38; Govt. Patent office 38-39; Dept. of Civil Aviation 39-49; Prof. of Engineering Mechanics, Delft Univ. of Tech. 49-; Pres. Int. Union of Theoretical and Applied Mechanics 68-72; mem. Royal Netherlands Acad. of Sciences; Foreign hon. mem. Amer. Acad. Arts and Sciences 74; Von Kármán Medal ASCE 65; Timoshenko Medal ASME 68; Hon. D.Sc. (Univ. of Leicester); Modesto Panetti Prize 71, Fairchild Distinguished Scholar Calif. Inst. of Tech. 73-74.
Leisure interests: travel, hiking, reading.
Publs. *On the Stability of Elastic Equilibrium* 45, many papers on elasticity, plasticity, elastic stability and theory of thin shells.
Laboratory of Engineering Mechanics, Mekelweg 2, Delft; Charlotte de Bourbon Straat 14, Delft, Netherlands.
Telephone: 133222, Ext. 6523 (Office); 123169 (Home).

Koivisto, Mauno Henrik, PH.D.; Finnish banker and politician; b. 25 Nov. 1923, Turku; s. of Juho Koivisto and Hymni Sofia (née Eskola) Koivisto; m. Taimi Tellervo Kankaanranta 1952; one d.; ed. Turku University.
Managing Dir. Helsinki Workers' Savings Bank 59-67; Gov. Bank of Finland 68-; Minister of Finance 66-67; Prime Minister 68-70; Minister of Finance and Deputy Prime Minister Feb.-Sept. 72; Chair. Board of Post Savings Bank 70-, Mortgage Bank of Finland Oy 68-, Board of Admin. of Co-operative Soc. ELANTO 66-; mem. Board of Admin. of Co-operative Union KK 64-; Gov. for Finland in the Int. Bank for Reconstruction and Devt. 68-69; Gov. for Finland IMF 70-.
Office: Suomen Pankki-Finlands Bank Snellmaninaukio, 00170 Helsinki 17; Home: Pitkänsillanranta 11 B 40, 00530 Helsinki 53, Finland.

Kojima, Kiyoshi, PH.D.; Japanese economist; b. 22 May 1920, Nagoya; m. Keiko Kojima 1947; ed. Tokyo Univ. of Commerce and Economics, Leeds Univ. (U.K.) and Princeton Univ. (U.S.A.).
Assistant Prof. of Int. Economics, Hitotsubashi Univ. 45-60, Prof. 60-; Secretariat (Dir.) for UN Conf. on Trade and Development 63; British Council Scholarship 52-53, Rockefeller Foundation Fellowship 53-55.
Leisure interests: golf, Noh (Utai).

Publs. (in Japanese): *Theory of Foreign Trade* 50, *Japan's Economic Development and Trade* 58, *Japan in Trade Expansion for Developing Countries* 64, *Japan and a Pacific Free Trade Area* 71, *World Trade and Multinational Corporations* 73; Editor *Papers and Proceedings of a Conference on Pacific Trade and Development* 68, 69, 73; also articles in English on int. trade.
3-24-10 Maehara-cho, Koganei-shi, Tokyo, Japan.
Telephone: 0423-81-1041.

Kokoschka, Oskar, C.B.E.; British artist and writer; b. 1 March 1886 in Austria; ed. Vienna School of Industrial Art.
Worked in Vienna from 06, where he taught at an Industrial school, then in various towns of Switzerland and in Berlin; joined the "Sturm" group in Berlin; cavalry officer on Russian and Italian fronts 15-17; Prof. Dresden Art Acad. 18-24; has travelled in Europe, Asia Minor and Northern Africa; emigré; paintings include landscapes, portraits and compositions; represented in principal European art galleries until 39, when works, as "degenerate", were sold by Nazis; paintings in U.S.A.; *Polperro, Cornwall,* presented to Tate Gallery, London, by Pres. Beneš 41, *A Woman Bathing,* presented to Nat. Gallery Edinburgh 42; Founder Int. Summer Acad. of Fine Arts, Salzburg; Teacher 53-; Retrospective Exhbn., Tate Gallery, London 62, Marlborough Gallery, London 76; rep. at Dunn Int. Exhbn., London 63; Exhbn. of portraits, Badischer Kunstverein, Karlsruhe 66; Rome Prize 60; Erasmus Prize 60; Hon. D.Litt. (Oxford); Order of Merit (Fed. Germany) 56.
Publs. Plays: *Mörder, Hoffnung der Frauen* 07, *Der brennende Dornbusch* 11, *Hiob* (music by Hindemith 21) 11, *Orpheus und Eurydice* (music by Křenek 26) 16; short stories: *A Sea Ringed with Visions* 62; *Mein Leben* (autobiography) 71, *London Views, British Landscapes* 72, *Saul and David* 73.
1844 Villeneuve, Vaud, Switzerland.

Kol, Moshe; Israeli educator and politician; b. 1911, Pinsk, Poland; *m.*; ed. Hebrew Secondary School, Pinsk and Hebrew Univ. Jerusalem.,
Co-Founder Hanoar Hazioni (Zionist Youth) movement in Poland and its Rep. on Cen. Cttee. of Zionist Org. in Poland; came to Israel and joined Hamefas pioneer group in Kfar Saba 32; Del. to all Zionist Congresses 33-; mem. Histadrut Exec. 41-46; mem. Jewish Agency Exec. and Head of its Youth Aliya Dept. 46-66; mem. Provisional State Council 48, and Chair. of its Foreign Affairs Cttee.; mem. Knesset (Parl.) 49-66; Min. of Devt. and of Tourism 66-74, of Tourism 74-; Co-Founder (in Israel), Oved Hazioni (Zionist Workers') Movement, World Confed. of Gen. Zionists; many Jewish Agency missions abroad.
Publs. *Arichim* (in Hebrew), *Youth Aliya* (in English and Hebrew).
Ministry of Tourism, Jerusalem, Israel.

Kolb, Hans Werner; German industrialist; b. 23 Aug. 1920, Mainz; ed. Univs. of Frankfurt and Giessen.
Chair. Exec. Board Buderus'sche Eisenwerke, Wetzlar.
Buderus'sche Eisenwerke, 633 Wetzlar, Sophienstrasse, Federal Republic of Germany.
Telephone: 06441-731.

Kolff, Willem Johan, M.D., PH.D.; American professor of surgery; b. 14 Feb. 1911, Leiden, Netherlands; *s.* of Jacob and Adriana Pieternella Kolff; *m.* Janke Cornelia Huidekoper 1937; four *s.* one *d.*; ed. Univs. of Leiden and Groningen.
Assistant, Pathological Anatomy, Univ. of Leiden 34-36; Asst. Medical Dept. Univ. of Groningen 38-41; Head, Medical Dept., Municipal Hosp., Kampen 41-50; Privaat Docent, Univ. of Leiden Medical School 49-51; mem. of staff, Research Div., Cleveland Clinic Foundation 50-63; Asst. Prof., later Prof. of Clinical Investigation, Educ. Foundation of Cleveland Clinic Foundation

50-67; mem. staff, Surgical Div., Cleveland Clinic Foundation 58-67, Head, Dept. of Artificial Organs 58-67, Scientific Dir. Artificial Organs Program 66-67; Prof. of Surgery, Head of Div. of Artificial Organs, Univ. of Utah Coll. of Medicine 67-, also Research Prof. of Engineering and Dir. Inst. of Biomedical Engineering; Hon. mem. Peruvian Urological Soc., Greek Soc. of Cardiology, Sociedad Medica de Santiago; Foreign mem. Hollandsch Maatschappij der Wetenschappen; Hon. D.Sc. (Tulane Univ., La.) 75; Hon. M.D. (Rostock Univ.) 75; Commdr. Order of Orange-Nassau; Orden de Mayo al Merito en el Grado de Gran Oficial (Argentina) 74; numerous medals, awards and prizes from several countries including Francis Amorny Award (American Acad. of Arts and Sciences) 48, Cameron Prize (Univ. Edinburgh) 64, Gairdner Prize (Gairdner Foundation, Toronto) 66, Gold Medal (Netherlands Surgical Soc.) 70, Benjamin Franklin Fellow (Royal Soc. of Arts, London) 72, Leo Harvey Prize (Technion Inst. of Israel) 72, Ray C. Fish Award and Medal, Texas Heart Inst. 75.
Leisure interests: bird-watching, hiking, camping.
Publs. *De Kunstmatige Nier* 46, *New Ways of Treating Uraemia* 47; over 450 articles in learned journals and chapters in books.
Division of Artificial Organs, Building 518, University of Utah, Salt Lake City, Utah 84112; Home: 2894 Crestview Drive, Salt Lake City, Utah 84108, U.S.A.
Telephone: 801-581-6296 (Office); 801-582-3056 (Home).

Kolfschoten, Henri Anthony Melchior Tieleman; Netherlands politician; b. 17 Aug. 1903, Arnhem; *m.* R. T. Ferwerda 1932; one *s.* five *d.*; ed. St. Willibrordus Coll. Katwijk, and Amsterdam Univ. (Law).
Deputy Sec., Roman Catholic State Party 27-38, Dir. 38-41; Private Sec. to Jonkheer Ruys de Beerenbrouck 28-33; representative of State Party in Politiek Convent and Vaderlandsche Comité; Min. of Justice in Schermerhorn-Drees Govt. 45-46; mem. of Eerste Kamer (First Chamber) 46-48, 49-52; Burgomaster of Eindhoven Sept. 46-Feb. 57; Burgomaster of The Hague 57-68 (retd.); Chamberlain Extraordinary to H.M. Queen Juli na; Knight Order of the Dutch Lion, Grand Officer Order of Orange-Nassau, Officier Légion d'Honneur; Hon. Knight Commdr. R.V.O.; Knight Commdr. Léopold II of Belgium and other foreign decorations.
Leisure interests: music (violin), literature, mountaineering, sport.
7 Nieuwe Duinweg, The Hague, Netherlands.
Telephone: 55-06-06.

Koliševski, Lazar; Yugoslav politician; b. 12 Feb. 1914.
Former metal worker; mem. Yugoslav Communist Party 35-; partisan, Sec. Provincial Cttee. of C.P. of Macedonia, and leader of Provincial Mil. Staff 41; imprisoned 41-44; Pres. Govt. of Macedonia 45; Sec. Central Cttee. of League of Communists of Macedonia until 63; mem. Exec. Cttee. Central Cttee. of League of Communists of Yugoslavia 52-; fmr. Pres. Macedonian Assembly and Chair. Socialist Alliance of Working People of Macedonia; Chair. Central Board of Socialist Alliance of Working People of Yugoslavia 63-67; mem. Council of Federation 67-72; mem. Presidency of Yugoslavia 72-.
Sobranie na SRM 320 no. 1, Skopje, Yugoslavia.

Kollek, Teddy (Theodore); Israeli public administrator; b. 27 May 1911, Vienna; *s.* of S. Alfred and Margaret (Fleischer) Kollek; *m.* Tamar Schwartz 1937; one *s.* one *d.*; ed. secondary school.
Founder mem. Kibbutz Ein Gev 37; Political Dept. Jewish Agency for Palestine 40; established Jewish Agency office, Istanbul, for contact with Jewish underground in Europe 42; Mission to U.S.A. for Haganah 47-48; Head of U.S. Div., Israel Foreign Ministry 50; Minister, Washington 51-52; Dir.-Gen. of Prime Minis-

ter's Office, Jerusalem 52-65; Chair. Israel Govt. Tourist Corpn. 55-65; Chair. Israel Govt. Water Desalination Joint Project with U.S. Govt. 64-; Chair. of Board Israel Museum, Jerusalem 64-, Africa-Israel Investment Co. Ltd. 64-65; Mayor of Jerusalem 65-; Rothschild Medal for Public Service 75; Bublick Prize of the Hebrew Univ. 75.

Leisure interests: archaelogy, reading, collecting ancient maps and books on the Holy Land.

Publs. *Jerusalem: A History of Forty Centuries* (Co-Author), *Pilgrims to the Holy Land* 70 (Co-Author).

City Hall, Jerusalem; Home: 6 Rashba Street, Rechavia, Jerusalem, Israel.

Telephone: 231251 (Office); 33147 (Home).

Koller, Herbert Josef, IUR.D.; Austrian business executive; b. 1911, Wösendorf; *m.* Dr. Eva Koller 1940; ed. elementary and secondary schools, Melk, and Univ. of Vienna.

Law practice and business appointments 35-44; Military Service and Prisoner-of-War 44-47; Vereinigte Österreichische Eisen und Stahlwerke (Vöest) 47-; Works Man., Hütte Krems 55-61; Gen. Man. and Chair. of Board of Dirs., Vöest 61-; Chair. Wiener Brückenbau- und Eisen-Konstruktions A.G., Vienna, Hütte Krems G.m.b.H., Binder and Co., Aktiengesellschaft Gleisdorf; Pres. of Board of Management, Vöest Italiana, Milan, Vöest Zürich, BOT Zürich; Chair. Board of Management, Importkohle Vienna, Ister Reederei, Bremen, Vöest Frankfurt, Ferrum Montage Oslo; Chair. Board of Dirs. Ferrum Copenhagen, Ferrum London; mem. Board of Dir. Int. Iron & Steel Inst.; Austrian and foreign decorations.

Muldenstr. 5, 4010 Linz/Donau, Austria.

Telephone: (07222) 5850.

Koller, Simon, LL.D.; Austrian diplomatist; b. 16 Jan. 1912, Seeboden (Carinthia); *m.* Edith (née Gheri) 1946; two *s.* two *d.*; ed. Classical High School and Univ. of Graz.

Chamber of Commerce, County Admin. of Carinthia; Austrian Foreign Service 47-, Germany, UN, Council of Europe; Deputy Dir. of Political Dept. Foreign Office 57-61; Dir. for South Tyrolian Affairs, Foreign Office 60-61; Minister to Hungary 62-64, Amb. 64-67; Vice-Pres. Danube Comm. 63-66; Deputy Dir. Political Dept. Foreign Office 67-72; Amb. to Greece and Cyprus 72-; Knight Commdr. Order of the Crown of Belgium; Commdr. German Fed. Rep.; Order of Merit; Order of Merit of the Austrian Red Cross; Grande Ufficiale (Italy); Great Insignia of Honour in Silver for services to the Republic of Austria.

Leisure interest: hunting.

Austrian Embassy, 26 Leoforos Alexandras, Athens 148, Greece.

Telephone: 8211.036.

Kollias, Konstantinos V.; Greek politician; b. 1901; ed. Athens Univ.

Prosecutor, Court of Appeal 45-46; Vice-Prosecutor, Supreme Court 46-62; Prosecutor, Supreme Court, Athens 62-68; Prime Minister April-Dec. 67.

124 Vassil. Sophias Street, Ampelokipi, Athens, Greece.

Kolman, Arnošt (Ernest), PH.D., D.SC.; Czechoslovak mathematician and philosopher; b. 6 Dec. 1892, Prague; *m.* 1934; three *s.* one *d.*; ed. Prague Univ.

Chief, Science Dept. of Moscow Cttee. of Communist Party; Prof. of Mathematics Moscow until 45; Prof. of Philosophy, Charles Univ., Prague 45-48; mem. Inst. for History of Sciences and Technology and Cybernetic Scientific Council, Acad. of Sciences, U.S.S.R.; Dir. Inst. of Philosophy, Czech. Acad. of Sciences 59-62; mem. Czech. Acad. of Sciences 60-; Order of Labour 62, Order of Red Banner of Labour 67, Medal for Valiant Labour 70.

Leisure interest: tourism.

Publs. *The Present Crisis in the Mathematical Sciences* (in *Science at the Cross-roads*) 31, *Eine neue Grundlegung der Differentialrechnung durch Karl Marx* (in *Verhandlungen des internationalen Mathematiker-Kongresses*) 32, *On the Problem of a Unified Physical Theory of Matter* (in *Phil. of Science*) 35, *Subject and Method of Modern Mathematics* 36, *Critical Account of the Symbolic Method of Modern Logic* 48, *Bernard Bolzano* 55, *The Great Russian Thinker N.I. Lobachevski* 55, *Cybernetics* 56, *Infinity in Greek Mathematics* 56, *Life and Scientific work of Rudger Boshkovich* 56, *Philosophical Problems of Modern Physics* 57, *On the Categories of Materialistic Dialectics* 57, *Critique of the Contemporary "Mathematical" Idealism* 57, *Gnosiology of Bertrand Russell* 57, *Logic* 58, *Is there a God?* 58, *Some Unsolved Problems of the History of Ancient Mathematics* 58, *Marx and the Natural Sciences* 58, *Lenin and Modern Physics* 59, *The Man of the Cosmic Age* 60, *Cybernetics Paradox and Self-Knowledge of the Brain* 61, *History of Mathematics in Antiquity, Space, Time, Matter and Motion in Cosmology* 61, *Overcoming of Infinity* 62, *An Outlook in the Future* 62, *Philosophy and Cybernetics* 62, *Expanding Mathematical Methods in New Spheres of Knowledge* 64, *Finite and Infinite in the Universe* 64, *Considerations about the Certainty of Knowledge* 65, *Philosophical and Social Problems of Cybernetics* 66, *Dialectical Development of Contemporary Physics* 67, *Recent Discovery of Plurality of Mathematics and its Philosophical Significance* 67, *K. Marx and Mathematics* 68, *Philosophical Half-Tales* 68, *A Dialogue between a Praxist and a Dialectist* 69, *The Fourth Dimension* 70, *The Concept of Simplicity in Physicomathematical Sciences* 71, *The Cosmos and the Man* 72, *The Thorny Path of Blaise Pascal* 72, *To the History of the Basing of Inductive Logic* 73, *Philosophical meditations about the Development of Modern Atomic Physics* 73.

Alabayana 10 bl. 6, fl. 151, Moscow, A80, U.S.S.R.

Kolmogorov, Andrei Nikolayevich; Soviet mathematician; b. 25 April 1903, Tambov; ed. Moscow Univ. Instructor, Moscow Univ. 25-31, Prof. 31-, Head, Chair. of Theory of Probability 37-, Dean of Faculty of Mechanics and Mathematics, Moscow Univ. 54-57; mem. U.S.S.R. Acad. of Sciences 39-, Head of Dept. of Theory of Probability and Mathematical Statistics, Inst. of Mathematics of U.S.S.R. Acad. of Sciences 39-59; Editor-in-Chief *Theory of Probability and its Application;* Chair, U.S.S.R. Acad. of Sciences Comm. on Mathematical Educ.; Hon. mem. Polish Acad. of Sciences; mem. Rumanian Acad. of Sciences, German Leopoldina Acad., American Acad. of Arts and Sciences Nat. Acad. of Sciences (U.S.A.), Royal Statistical Soc. (U.K.); mem. Presidential Board U.S.S.R.-France Friendship Soc.; Hero of Socialist Labour; State Prize 41; Lenin Prize; Order of Lenin (thrice) etc.

Publs. include *Basic Concepts of the Theory of Probability* 36; co-author *Algebra* 39 etc.

Institute of Mathematics, U.S.S.R. Academy of Sciences, 19 Leninsky Prospekt, Moscow, U.S.S.R.

Kolo, Sule Dede, B.SC.(ECON.); Nigerian diplomatist; b. 6 Aug. 1926, Nigeria; *s.* of Mohamed and Meimuna Kolo; *m.* Mrs. H. P. Kolo 1956; one *s.* three *d.*

Former Counsellor, Nigerian High Comm., London; Perm. Sec. Ministry of Defence 63, Ministry of Trade 66; Perm. Rep. to European Office of UN, Geneva; Nigerian Rep. to Disarmament Cttee. of UN; Amb. to Switzerland 66-70, also accred. to Austria and Turkey; Chair. GATT 69; Gov. IAEA 69; Vice-Chair. First Cttee. of UN; High Commr. to U.K. 70-75; Franklin Peace Medal 69.

Leisure interests: tennis, swimming.

c/o Ministry of Foreign Affairs, Lagos, Nigeria.

Kołodziej, Emil, LL.M.; Polish politician; b. 2 Jan. 1917, Futoma, Rzeszów Voivodship; *s.* of Józef and

Zofia Kolodziej; *m.* Lidia Prokopiak 1948; two *d.*; ed. Univs. of Lwów and Warsaw.
Activist of the Peasant Party 36; soldier in the Peasant Battalions during the occupation; held exec. positions, Cen. Board of Agricultural Co-operatives, Warsaw 45-57; mem. Exec. Cttee. United Peasant Party (UPP) 59, mem. Presidium 69, Sec. 69-71; Deputy to Seym; Deputy Minister of Home Trade 57-69; Minister of Food Feb. 71-; Order of Banner of Labour, 1st and 2nd Class; Commdr. and Knight's Cross, Order of Polonia Restituta; Gold Cross of Merit.
Leisure interest: hunting.
Ministry of Food, Industry and Purchases, 20 Świętokrzyska, 00-002 Warsaw, Poland.

Kolosov, Mikhail Nikolayevich; Soviet chemist; b. 11 May 1927, Kursk; ed. Lomonosov Inst. of Fine Chemical Technology.
Postgraduate Lomonosov Inst. of Fine Chemical Technology 48-51; Research Assoc. Inst. of Biological and Medical Chemistry, U.S.S.R. Acad. of Medical Sciences 51-59; Inst. of Chemistry of Natural Compounds, U.S.S.R. Acad. of Sciences 59-; Corresp. mem. U.S.S.R. Acad. of Sciences 66-; mem. C.P.S.U. 63-.
Publs. Works on chemistry of biopolymers and other natural compounds.
U.S.S.R. Academy of Sciences, 14 Leninsky Prospekt, Moscow, U.S.S.R.

Kolotyrkin, Yakov Mikhailovich; Soviet physicochemist; b. 14 Nov. 1910, Buturlinsky district, Smolensk region; ed. Moscow Univ.
Research Assoc., Dir. Karpov Physico-Chemical Inst. 38-; mem. C.P.S.U. 40-; Dr. Sc. (Chem.) Prof. 54; Corresp. mem. U.S.S.R. Acad. of Sciences 66-70; Academician 70-.
U.S.S.R. Academy of Sciences, 14 Leninsky Prospekt, Moscow, U.S.S.R.

Kolozsvári-Grandpierre, Emil, D.PHIL.; Hungarian novelist; b. 15 Jan. 1907, Kolozsvár; *s.* of the late Emil Grandpierre and Janka Krassowsky; *m.* Magda Szegö 1946; one *d.*; ed. secondary school in Transylvania, Pécs Univ.
Publisher's reader 41-44; Dir. of literature dept. of the Hungarian Radio 46-49; József Attila Literary Prize 64, 75.
Leisure interests: women, jokes, walking, swimming.
Publs. *A Rosta, Dr. Csibráky szerelmei, A Nagy Ember, Alvajárók, A sárgavirágos leány, Tegnap, Szabadság, Lófő és kora, Az értelem dicsérete, Lelkifinomságok, Mérlegen, A Csodafurulya, A Csillagszemü, A Törökfejes kopja, Elmés mulatságok, A büvös kaptafa, A tisztesség keresztje, Foltonfolt Királyfi, A boldogtalanság müvészete, Legendák nyomában, Csinnadári, Gyalogtündér, Egy szereplö visszatér, Párbeszéd a Sorssal, A lóvdtett sárkány, Csendes rév a háztetön, A Burok, Aquincumi Vénusz, Változatok hegedüre, Arcok napfényben, Utazás a valóság körül, Dráma félvállról, Nök apróban, Szellemi Galeri, Keresztben az uton, Az utolsó hullám, Harmatcseppek.*
Berkenye-u 19, 1025 Budapest, Hungary.
Telephone: 363-935.

Kolpakova, Irina Alexandrovna; Soviet ballerina; b. 22 May 1933; ed. Leningrad Choreographic School.
Prima Ballerina, Kirov Theatre of Opera and Ballet, Leningrad; People's Artist of the R.S.F.S.R. and the U.S.S.R.; Grand Prix de Ballet, Paris 66.
Principal Roles; Aurora (*Sleeping Beauty*), Juliet (*Romeo and Juliet*), Desdemona (*Othello*), Tao Khao (*The Red Poppy*), Maria (*Fountain of Bakhchisarai*), Giselle, Zolushka, Raymonda; first performer of part of Katerina (*The Stone Flower*) and Shirin (*Legends of Love*).
Kirov Theatre of Opera and Ballet, 1 ploshchad Iskusstv, Leningrad, U.S.S.R.

Kolstad, Eva; Norwegian chartered accountant and politician; b. 6 May 1918, Halden; *d.* of Chr. Hartvig and Otlu (née Lundegaard); *m.* Ragnar Kolstad 1942.
Teacher of book-keeping and other commercial subjects 38-40; Asst. Accountant 40-44; independent chartered accountant 44-; mem. Board, Int. Alliance of Women 49-58, 61-68; Pres. Norwegian Asscn. for Rights of Women 56-68; mem. Oslo City Council 60-75; mem. UN Comm. on Status of Women 69-75; deputy mem. Parl. 58-61, 65-69; Minister of Consumer Affairs 72-73; Pres. Liberal Party 74-; Co-ordinator Int. Women's Year 75.
Publs. numerous articles in newspapers, periodicals and encyclopedias.
Schivesgt. 6 B III, Oslo 2, Norway.
Telephone: 44-87-94.

Kolthoff, Izaak Maurits, PH.D.; American analytical scientist; b. 11 Feb. 1894, Almelo, Netherlands; *s.* of Moses Kolthoff and Rosetta Wijsenbeek Kolthoff; ed. Univ. of Utrecht.
Lecturer, Univ. of Utrecht 18-27; Prof. and Chief, Div. of Analytical Chem. Univ. of Minn. 27-62, Prof. Emer. 62-; mem. Nat. Acad. of Sciences; Dr.h.c. (Univs. of Chicago and Groningen); Charles Medal, Nichols Medal, Fisher Award in Analytical Chem. Anachem Award, Willard Gibbs Award Medal, Polarographic Medal, Kolthoff Gold Medal in Analytical Chem., Gold Medal Award for Scientific Achievement; mem. American Acad. Arts and Sciences; mem. of many foreign acads. and socs.; Dr. h.c. (Brandeis Univ., Hebrew Univ. of Jerusalem) 74.
Leisure interests: riding, swimming.
Publs. *Acid-Base Indicators* (with C. Rosenblum), *Konduktometrische Titrationen, Potentiometric Titrations* (with H. N. Furman), *Die Massanalyse* (2 vols.), *pH and Electrotitrations* (with H. A. Laitinen), *Volumetric Analysis* (Vols. I and II with V. Stenger, Vol. III with R. Belcher), *Textbook of Quantitative Inorganic Analysis* (1st edn. with E. B. Sandell, 4th edn. with E. B. Sandell and others.) *Polarography* (with J. J. Lingane) *Emulsion Polymerization* (with F. Bovey and others), *Treatise on Analytical Chemistry* (Co-Editor with P. J. Elving) Vols. 1-30.
School of Chemistry, University of Minnesota, Minneapolis, Minn. 55455, U.S.A.

Komai, Kenichiro; Japanese business executive; b. 17 Dec. 1900, Tokyo; ed. Coll. of Technology, Tokyo Imperial Univ.
Hitachi Ltd. 25-, Man. of Hitachi Works 46-50, Dir. 46-55, Man. Dir. 55-57, Senior Man. Dir. 57-61 Pres. 61-71, Chair. of Board 71-; fmr. Chair. Tokyo Atomic Industrial Consortium; Exec. Dir. Japan Fed. of Econ. Organizations 62-; Gov. Dir. Japan Fed. of Employers' Asscns. 62-.
Leisure interest: golf.
Hitachi Ltd., Marunouchi, Chiyoda-ku, Tokyo; and 2-3-2 Taiheidai, Tsujido, Fujisawa, Kanagawa-Ken, Japan.
Telephone: 0466-36-3956.

Komárek, Karel, LL.D.; Czechoslovak diplomatist; b. 3 Nov. 1921, Hodonín; ed. Charles Univ., Prague.
Various posts in political and State offices; mem. Scientific Council, Faculty of Law, Charles Univ., Prague 60-64; Ministry of Foreign Affairs 64-; Counsellor, Czechoslovak Embassy, Bucharest 64-69; Minister to Austria 69-74, Amb. Jan. 71-; orders for Outstanding Work and Service to the Country.
Embassy of Czechoslovakia, Penzingerstrasse 11-13, Vienna, Austria; Ministry of Foreign Affairs, Prague 1, Černínský palác, Czechoslovakia.

Komer, Robert William, S.B., M.B.A.; American diplomatist; b. 23 Feb. 1922, Chicago, Ill.; *s.* of Nathan A. Komer and Stella D. Komer; *m.* Geraldine M. Peplin

1961; two s. one d.; ed. Harvard Coll., Harvard Graduate School of Business Admin. and Nat. War Coll.
U.S. Army 43-46; Foreign Affairs Analyst, Central Intelligence Agency 48-60; Senior Staff Asst., White House 61-65; Dep. Special Asst. to Pres. for Nat. Security Affairs 65-66; Special Asst. to Pres. 66-67; Deputy to COMUSMACV for Civil Operations and Revolutionary Devt. with rank of Amb. (pacification in Viet-Nam) 67-68; Amb. to Turkey 68-69; Consultant Rand Corpn. 70-; U.S. Medal of Freedom; Sec. of State's Distinguished Honor Award; U.S. Bronze Star; Vietnamese Orders.
Leisure interests: tennis, swimming, military history.
Publs. *Civil Affairs and Military Government in the Mediterranean Theater* (2 vols.) 49, *Establishment of ACC in Italy* 50, *The Other War in Vietnam* 67, *Treating NATO's Self-Inflicted Wound* 73, and other articles.
214 Franklin Street, Alexandria, Va. 22314; and 2100 M Street, N.W., Washington, D.C. 20037, U.S.A.

Komlós, Péter; Hungarian violinist; b. 25 Oct. 1935, Budapest; s. of László Komlós and Franciska Graf; m. Edit Fehér 1960; two s.; ed. Budapest Music Acad.
Founded Komlós String Quartet 57; First Violinist, Budapest Opera Orchestra 60; Leader Bartók String Quartet 63; extensive concert tours to U.S.S.R., Scandinavia, Italy, Austria, German Democratic Repub., Czechoslovakia 58-64, U.S.A., Canada, New Zealand and Australia 70, including Day of Human Rights concert, UN H.Q. New York, Japan, Spain and Portugal 71, Far East, U.S.A. and Europe 73; performed at music festivals of Ascona, Edinburgh, Adelaide, Spoleto, Manton, Schwetzingen, Lucerne, Aix-en-Provence; recordings of Beethoven's string quartets for Hungaroton, Budapest and of Bartók's string quartets for Erato, Paris; First Prize, Int. String Quartet Competition, Liège 64; Liszt Prize 65; Gramophone Record Prize of Germany 69; Kossuth Prize 70.
Leisure interests: ship model building, watching sports.
1025 Budapest, Törökvész ut 94 Hungary.
Telephone: 365-082.

Komoto, Toshio; Japanese politician; b. 1911, Aioi City, Hyogo Prefecture; ed. Nihon Univ.
Former Parl. Vice-Minister for Econ. Planning Agency; fmr. Chair. of Justice Cttee., House of Reps.; fmr. Chair. Cabinet Cttee., House of Reps.; Minister of Posts and Telecommunications 68-70, of Int. Trade and Industry Dec. 74-; Pres. Sanko Steamship Co.; Liberal Democrat.
Ministry of International Trade and Industry, 3-1, Kasumigaseki 1-chome, Chiyoda-ku, Tokyo 100, Japan.

Konate, Tiéoulé; Mali banker and politician; b. 21 Feb. 1933, Bamako; m.; three c.; ed. Faculty of Law and Econs., Univ. of Paris, France.
Formerly Dir.-Gen. of Econ. Affairs, Mali; Gov. Bank of Mali; now Pres. and Dir.-Gen. Mali Devt. Bank; Minister of Finance 73-74.
Leisure interests: sport, reading, rural work.
c/o Ministry of Finance, Bamako, Mali.

Kondrashin, Kirill Petrovich; Soviet musician; b. 21 Feb. 1914, Moscow; ed. Moscow Conservatoire.
Assistant Conductor, Nemirovich-Danchenko Musical Theatre, Moscow 34-37; Conductor, Maly Opera Theatre, Leningrad 38-42; Bolshoi Theatre, Moscow 43-56; Conductor, All-Russia Symphony Orchestra Touring Concert Company 56-60; Chief Conductor, Moscow Philharmonic Orchestra 60-; State Prize 48, 49; Honoured Artist of R.S.F.S.R. and the U.S.S.R.; Glinka State Prize 69.
Moscow State Philharmonia, Ulitsa Gorkogo 31, Moscow, U.S.S.R.

Kondratiev, Kirill Yakovlevich, DR.SC.; Soviet physicist and meteorologist; b. 14 June 1920, Ribinsk, Yaroslavsk region; ed. Leningrad State Univ.

Lecturer, Pro-rector, Prof., Chief, Fac. of Atmosphere Physics Leningrad Univ. 46-, Rector 64-, Prof. 58-; mem. C.P.S.U. 43; Corresp. mem. U.S.S.R. Acad. of Sciences 68-.
Publs. Many works in field of physics of earth's atmosphere.
Leningrad State University, Leningrad, U.S.S.R.

Kondratiev, Viktor Nikolayevich; Soviet scientist; b. 1 Feb. 1902, Rybinsk, Yaroslavl Region; ed. Polytechnic Inst., Leningrad.
Chief, Laboratory of Elementary Processes, Inst. of Chemical Physics, Moscow 31-, Vice-Dir., Inst. of Chemical Physics 48-, Chief, Dept. of Kinetics and Combustion 56-; Prof. Polytechnic Inst. Leningrad 34-41, Moscow State Univ. 49-51, Moscow Engineering Physical Inst. 51-57; mem. C.P.S.U. 48-; Corresp. mem. U.S.S.R. Acad. of Sciences 43-53, mem. 53-, mem. Chemical Dept. Bureau, U.S.S.R. Acad. of Sciences 57-; mem. IUPAC Bureau and Exec. Cttee. 61-, Vice-Pres. 65-69, Pres. 69-; State Prize.
Publs. *Spectroscopic Studies of Chemical Gas Reactions* 44, *Structure of Atoms and Molecules* (3rd edn.) 60, *Kinetics of Chemical Gas Reactions* 58, *Rate Constants of Phase Reactions* 72, *Kinetics and Mechanisms of Gas-Phase Reactions* (with E. E. Nikitin) 74.
Institute of Chemical Physics, Moscow 2/6, Vorobyevskoe chaussée, U.S.S.R.

Kondratieva, Maria Viktorovna; Soviet ballet dancer; b. 1934; ed. Bolshoi Theatre Ballet School.
Joined Bolshoi Ballet Co. 53; People's Artist of R.S.F.S.R.
Main roles include: Cinderella (*Cinderella*), Maria (*Fountain of Bakhchisarai*), Aurora (*Sleeping Beauty*), Juliet (*Romeo and Juliet*), Katerina (*Stone Flower*), Giselle (*Giselle*), Gayane (*Gayane*), Odette-Odile (*Swan Lake*), Shirin (*Legend of Love*).
State Academic Bolshoi Theatre of U.S.S.R., 1 Ploshchad Sverdlova, Moscow, U.S.S.R.

Könecke, Fritz, D.RER.POL.; German businessman; b. 16 Jan. 1899; ed. Göttingen, Hamburg and Hanover Univs.
Joined Continental-Gummiwerke A.G., Hanover 20, Sales Man. 28, Dir. 34, Chair. and Gen. Man. 38; Dir. Hamburger Gummiwarenfabrik Phoenix A.G. 49; Asst. Chair. Daimler-Benz A.G., Stuttgart-Untertürkheim 52, Chair. 53, Gen. Man. 54-61; Grand Cross of the Fed. Republic of Germany; Hon. D.Eng.
Am Bismarckturm 54, 7 Stuttgart-N, Federal Republic of Germany.

König, H.E. Cardinal Franz; Austrian ecclesiastic; b. 3 Aug. 1905, Rabenstein, Pielach; ed. Univs. of Rome, Vienna and Lille.
Ordained 33; Dozent, Vienna Univ. 46; Prof. of Moral Theology, Salzburg 48; Titular Bishop of Livias 52; Archbishop of Vienna 56-; created Cardinal by Pope John XXIII 58; mem. Congregation; Pres. Secretariat for Non-Believers.
Publs. include *Christus und die Religionen der Erde, Religionswissenschaftliches Wörterbuch, Zarathustras Jenseitsvorstellungen und das Alte Testament* 64, *Die Stunde der Welt* 71, *Aufbruch zum Geist* 72, *Das Zeichen Gottes*.
Eb Sekretariat, Wollzeile 2, 1010 Wien, Austria.
Telephone: 529511.

König, Herbert, DR.RER.POL.; German lawyer, political and financial scientist and international consultant; b. 25 July 1925, Frankfurt; m.; ed. Univs. of Frankfurt and Graz.
Entered local govt. service, Frankfurt 45, Fed. Govt. Service 56; Fed. Acad. of Finance 57; Asst. to Pres. Fed. Audit Board 58; Budget Officer, Fed. Ministry for Econ. Affairs 62, Counsellor for Mining Affairs 66, Deputy Dir.-Gen. Cen. Dept. 68; Deputy mem. Comm.

for Reform of Foreign Service 69; Asst. Sec.-Gen. OECD 70-72; Consultant to Council of Europe and other orgs.; mem. Fed. Govt.'s Project Group on the Reform of Govt. and Admin.; part-time Prof. Univ. of Bielefeld and Cologne; attached to Ministry for Econ. Affairs, Bonn.

Publs. books and studies on organization, budget and personnel, mining and financial control.

Bundesministerium für Wirtschaft, Bonn; Home, D 5309 Meckenheim-Merl, Auf der Lehmweise 11: Federal Republic of Germany.

Telephone: (02221) 761 and 367053 (Office); (02225) 6847 (Home).

König, René, PH.D.; German sociologist; b. 5 July 1906, Magdeburg; s. of Gustav König and Marguerite née Godefroy-Leboeuf; m. Irmgard Tillmanns 1947; two s.; ed. Univs. of Vienna, Berlin and Paris.

Member Faculty Zurich Univ. 38; apptd. to Chair of Sociology Cologne Univ. 49-; Sec. First World Congress of Sociology, Zurich 50; Editor *Kölner Zeitschrift für Soziologie und Sozialpsychologie* 55; Pres. Int. Sociological Asscn. 62-66; Guest Prof. Univs. of Mich. 57, 74, Calif. 57, 59, 60, 64, 65, Columbia Univ. 59, Colo. 62; Arizona 68-69, 75; Rockefeller Fellow 52; mem. Royal Netherlands Acad. of Sciences 70; Commendatore del Ordine di Merito della Repubblica Italiana, Gold Medal, German Criminological Asscn.; Gold Medal German Asscn. of Engineers; Premio Verga 67; Medal for Education (Afghanistan) 75.

Publs. *Naturalistische Ästhetik in Frankreich* 31, *Niccolo Macchiavelli* 41, *Materialien zur Soziologie der Familie* 46 (2nd ed. 74), *Soziologie heute* 49, *Soziologie* 57, 67, *Grundformen der Gesellschaft: Soziologie der Gemeinde* 58 (English trans. *The Community* 67), *Das Buch der Mode* 58, 67, *Handbuch der empirischen Sozialforschung* (2 vols.) 62, 68 (new ed. 73), *Soziologische Orientierungen* 72, *Macht und Reiz der Mode* 71, *Soziologische Studien* 71, *Indianer Wohin? Alternativen in Arizona* 73, *Kritik der historisch-existenzialistischen Soziologie.*

5 Köln 40, Marienstrasse 9, Federal Republic of Germany.

Telephone: Cologne 50-86-13 (Home).

Konjovic, Petar; Yugoslav composer and conductor; b. 5 May 1883; ed. Prague Conservatoire.

Former Dir. Nat. Theatre, Novi Sad and Osijek; fmr. Dir. Ministry of Public Instruction and Zagreb Opera; fmr. Pres. Yugoslav Section Int. Society for Contemporary Music, Zagreb, and Society of Friends of Slavic Music, Belgrade; fmr. Dir. Inst. of Musicology and Sec. to Dept. for Arts and Music in Serbian Acad. of Sciences; fmr. Rector and Prof. Acad. of Music, Belgrade; Fellow of Serbian Acad. of Sciences and Arts.

Works include: *Vilin Veo-Ženidba Miloševa, Knezod Zete, Koštana, Majka Jugovića—La Patrie* (operas), *Seljaci* (folk opera), *Moja Zemlja,* 100 Yugoslav folk songs arranged for voice and piano; *Lyric,* 24 songs, *Makar Chudra,* symphonic poem for complete orchestra; *Koštana,* symphonic tryptichon, *Sonata* for violin and piano; *Na Selu* (In the Country) symphonic variations; *Capriccio adriatico* concerto for violin and orchestra; songs and folk songs; symphony orchestra and chamber music works (two string quartets); *Musica Divina, Liturgies, Psalms, Hymns* and 20 other works for choirs.

Publs. *Personalities in Theatre and Music, Serbian and Slav Music, Miloje Milojević, Stevan Mokranjac—a musical portrait* 56.

Prvog maja 32/III, Belgrade, Yugoslavia.

Kono, Fumihiko, B.ENG.; Japanese business executive; b. 22 Nov. 1896, Otawara City; m. 1929; one s. two d.; ed. Tokyo Univ.

Aircraft Designer, Mitsubishi Internal Combustion Engine Mfg. Co. Ltd. 21-45; Gen. Man. First Engineering Works, Mitsubishi Heavy Industries Ltd. 45,

Kawasaki Engineering Works 45-50; Dir. and Gen. Man. Kawasaki Engineering Works, Mitsubishi Nippon Heavy Industries Ltd. 50-52, Man. Dir. 52-56, Vice-Pres. 56-61, Pres. 61-64; Exec. Vice-Pres. Mitsubishi Heavy Industries Ltd. 64-65, Pres. 65-70, 70-73; Dir. Mitsubishi Shoji Kaisha Ltd., Mitsubishi Steel Co. Ltd., Mitsubishi Atomic Power Industries Inc.; Vice-Pres. Fed. of Econ. Orgs.; Blue Ribbon Medal.

Leisure interests: baseball, golf.

Mitsubishi Heavy Industries Ltd., 5-1, Marunouchi 2-chome, Chiyoda-ku, Tokyo; 33-9, 6-chome, Denenchofu, Ota-ku, Tokyo, Japan.

Telephone: 03-721-4481 (Home.)

Konophaghos, Constantine; Greek professor and politician; b. 1912; m.; one s. one d.; ed. Ecole Centrale, Paris.

With Soc. Française du Laurion; with Soc. Anonyme de Produits Chimiques et d'Engrais; Prof. at Polytechnic 63, Rector 73; mem. Parl. for Preveza 74-; Minister of Industry Nov. 74-; Gold Cross of George I, Commdr. Order of the Phoenix; Légion d'Honneur, Médaille de la Ville de Gand (Belgium).

Publs. many scientific and literary works.

Ministry of Industry, Athens, Greece.

Konotop, Vassily Ivanovich; Soviet politician; b. 1910; ed. Kharkov Machine-Building Inst.

Member Communist Party of Soviet Union 44-; worked Kolomna Engineering Works 42-52; party work, Moscow District 52-59; Chair. Exec. Cttee. Moscow District Council for Deputies of Labour 59-63; First Sec. Moscow District Cttee., C.P.S.U. 63-; Cand. mem. Central Cttee. of C.P.S.U. 61-64, mem. 64-; mem. Presidium of Supreme Soviet 66-; Deputy to U.S.S.R. Supreme Soviet 54; mem. Cttee. U.S.S.R. Parl. Group.

Moscow Regional Committee of C.P.S.U., 6 Staraya ploshchad, Moscow, U.S.S.R.

Konovalov, Sergey, M.A., B.LITT.; British Slavonic scholar; b. 31 Oct. 1899, Moscow, U.S.S.R.; s. of Alexander Konovalov and Nadejda Vtorov; m. Janina Ryzowa 1949; ed. Classical Lycée in Moscow and Exeter Coll., Oxford.

Professor Russian Language and Literature Birmingham Univ. 29-45; Lecturer Slavonic Studies Oxford Univ. 30-45; Hon. Lecturer London Univ. (School of Slavonic Studies) 31-32, 40-41; Prof. Russian Oxford Univ. 45-67, Emeritus 67-; Emeritus Fellow New Coll., Oxford 67-; mem. Int. Cttee. of Slavists 58-68.

Publs. *Anthology of Contemporary Russian Literature* 32; Editor and contrib. *Birmingham Russian Memoranda* 31-40, Co-editor *Birmingham Polish Monographs* 36-39; article on *Soviet Union, Encyclopaedia Britannica Year Book* 41; *Russo-Polish Relations—an Historical Survey* (in collaboration) 45; *Oxford and Russia* (Inaugural Lecture) 47; Editor and contributor *Blackwell's Russian Texts* 45-, *Oxford Slavonic Papers* Vols. I-XIII 50-67, and *Oxford Russian Readers* 51-; Editor (with D. J. Richards) *Russian Critical Essays* 71-72.

175 Divinity Road, Oxford, England.

Konstantinov, Fyodor Vasiliyevich; Soviet philosopher; b. 21 Feb. 1901, Novoselki, Gorky region; ed. Inst. of Red Professors.

Teacher and party worker 32-41; Soviet Army 42-45; Assoc. Inst. of Philosophy, U.S.S.R. Acad. of Sciences 45-62, Dir. 62-; Rector, Acad. of Social Sciences of Central Cttee. of C.P.S.U. 54-55; Head, Dept. of Propaganda and Agitation, Central Cttee. of C.P.S.U. 55-58; Cand. mem. Central Cttee. of C.P.S.U. 56-61; Corresp. mem. U.S.S.R. Acad. of Sciences 53-66, mem. 66-; Academic Sec. Philosophy and Law Branch, Acad. of Sciences U.S.S.R.; Chief Editor *Encyclopaedia of Philosophy;* Order of Lenin.

Institute of Philosophy of U.S.S.R. Academy of Sciences, 14 Ulitsa Volkhonka, Moscow, U.S.S.R.

Kontos, Constantine William; American United Nations official; b. 10 Aug. 1922, Chicago, Ill.; s. of William C. and Irene (Thomas) Kontos; m. Joan Fultz 1948; two s.; ed. Univ. of Chicago and London School of Economics.

Special Asst. to Dir. of Econ. Co-operation Admin., Mission to Greece 49-53; Programme Budget Officer, Foreign Operations Admin., Washington, D.C. 53-55; Senior Management Officer Int. Co-operation Admin., Washington, D.C. 55-57; Exec. Officer, Bureau of Africa and Europe 57-59; Deputy Dir. U.S. AID Mission, Ceylon 59-61; Deputy Dir. U.S. AID Mission, Nigeria 61-64; attended Nat. War Coll. 64-65; Dir. Personnel Agency for Int. Devt. 65-67; Dir. U.S. AID Mission, Pakistan 67-69; Dir. Office of Programme Educ., AID 69-72; Deputy Commr.-Gen. UN Relief and Works Agency (UNRWA) 72-74; Dept. of State Meritorious Honour Award 71.

United Nations Relief and Works Agency, Museitbeh Quarter, Beirut, Lebanon.

Konwicki, Tadeusz; Polish writer; b. 22 June 1926, Nowa Wilejka, U.S.S.R.; m. Danuta Lenica; ed. Warsaw Univ.

Partisan detachment of Home Army 44-45; mem. Polish Writers' Asscn. 49-; Editorial Staff of *Nowa Kultura* (weekly) 50-57; State Prize, 3rd Class 50, 54, First Class 66, Knight's Cross, Order of Polonia Restituta 54, Officer's Cross 64, Medal of 10th Anniversary of People's Poland 55, State Prize, 1st Class 66. Publs. novels: *Władza* 54, *Zoblężonego miasta* 54, *Rojsty* 56, *Dziura w niebie* 59, *Sennik współczesny* (A Dreambook of Our Time) 63, *Wniebowstąpienie* 67, *Zwierzoczlekoupiór* 69, *Nic albo nic* 71, *Kronika wypadków miłosnych* 74; short stories: *Ogródek z nasturcją* 47, *Przy budowie* 50, *Godzina smutku* 54, *Powrót* 54; film scripts: *Żelazna kurtyna* (Iron Curtain) 54, *Zimowy zmierzch* (Winter Twilight) 56, *Ostatni dzień lata* (Last Day of Summer) 66.

Ul. Górskiego 1 m. 68, 00-033 Warsaw, Poland.
Telephone: 27-04-81.

Koopmans, Tjalling Charles, M.A., PH.D.; American economist; b. 28 Aug. 1910, 'S Graveland, Netherlands; s. of Sjoerd and Wijtske (van der Zee) Koopmans; m. Truus Wanningen 1936; one s. two d.; ed. Univs. of Utrecht and Leiden.

Teacher, Netherlands Econ. Univ., Rotterdam 36-38; Specialist, Financial Div., League of Nations 38-40; Research Assoc. School of Public and Int. Affairs, Princeton 40-41; economist Penn Mutual Life Insurance Co. 41-42; statistician Combined Shipping Adjustment Board and British Merchant Shipping Mission 42-44; Research Assoc. Cowles Comm. Research Econs., Univ. of Chicago 44-45, Assoc. Prof. 46-48, Prof. 48-55, Dir. Research Cowles Comm. 48-54; Prof. of Econs. Yale Univ. 55-, Dir. Cowles Foundation for research econs. 61-67; mem. American Acad. of Arts and Sciences, Nat. Acad. of Sciences, Int. Statistical Inst.; Fellow, Econometric Soc., American Statistical Asscn.; Hon. D.Econ. (Netherlands School of Economics and Catholic Univ. of Louvain), Nobel Prize for Economics 75.

Publs. *Three Essays on the State of Economic Science* 57, *Scientific Papers of Tjalling C. Koopmans* 70.

Department of Economics, Yale University, New Haven, Conn. 06520, U.S.A.

Koornhof, Pieter Gerhardus Jacobus, B.A. (STELL.), D.PHIL. (OXON.); South African politician; b. 2 Aug. 1925, Leeudoringstad; ed. Cen. High School, Bloemfontein, Paul Roos Gymnasium, Stellenbosch, Stellenbosch Univ. and Oxford Univ.

Member Parl. for Primrose; Research Officer, Dept. of Bantu Admin. and Devt. 53-58; Under-Sec. Nat. Party of Transvaal 58-62; Dir. Cultural Information, FAK; Council mem. Johannesburg Gen. Hosp. Board and Staff Officer Pongola Regt., Citizens Force 62-63; mem.

S. African First Aid League, Nat. Youth Board and Vice-Chair. Management Board, Inst. for Youth Leaders 63-64; mem. Parl. for Edenvale and Liaison Officer to Immigrants 64-65; Chair. S. African Cultural Acad. and Dir. Soc. for European Immigrants 65-66; Man. Dir. Nat. Veldtrust of S. Africa 66; mem. Council for Rand Afrikaans Univ.; Deputy Minister of Bantu Admin. and Devt., Bantu Educ. and Immigration 68-72; Minister of Mines 72-76, of Immigration and of Sports and Recreation 72-76, of Nat. Educ. Jan. 76-; Grand Officer's Cross of Merit, Order of the Knights of Malta 73.

896 Government Avenue, Bryntirion, Pretoria; Home: Private Bag X433, Pretoria, South Africa.

Kopeć, Aleksander, M.SC.(ENG.); Polish politician; b. 1932, Wąsowiczówka, U.S.S.R.; ed. Wrocław Polytechnic.

Management posts, Industrial Eng. Factory, Świdnik 57-62; Chief Engineer, Van Factory, Świdnica 62-67; Dir. Dolmel Works, Wrocław 67-70; Under-Sec. of State, Ministry of the Machine (Engineering) Industry 70-73, First Deputy Minister 73-75, Minister Oct. 75-; Deputy mem. Cen. Cttee., Polish United Workers' Party (PZPR) 75-.

Ministerstwo Przemysłu Maszynowego, Ul. Krucza 36, 00-522 Warsaw, Poland.

Telephone: 28-96-05.

Köpeczi, Béla; Hungarian historian of literature; b. 16 Sept. 1921, Nagyenyed (Aiud in Romania); s. of Árpád Köpeczi and Anna Tomai; m. Edit Bölcskei 1951; ed. Budapest and Paris Univs.

Publisher 49-53; Vice-Pres., Hungarian Council of Publishing 53-55, Pres. 55-61; Chair., Hungarian Board of Publishing 55; Head, Cultural Dept., Hungarian Socialist Workers' Party 64-66; Prof. Univ. of Budapest; mem. Hungarian Acad. of Sciences, Deputy Gen. Sec. 70, 75-, Gen. Sec. 72-75; Commdr. Academic Palms, France.

Leisure interests: reading, travelling.

Il Tulipán-u. 5, 1022 Budapest, Hungary.

Koper, Danis; Turkish civil engineer and politician; b. 19 Dec. 1908, Diyadin; s. of Murat Fuat Koper and Fikriye Belbez; m. Nesime Nimetullah 1949; one s. one d.; ed. Coll. of Technology, Munich.

Engineer, Water Works Dept., Ministry of Public Works 36-48; Construction Man. Garanti İnşaat Co. 48-51; Dir. Provincial Bank 50-51; Gen. Man. Highway Dept. 51-56; Under Sec. Ministry of Public Works 56-57; Construction Man. Verdi Ltd. 57-59; Chair. Turkish Airlines 59-60; Minister of Public Works 60; mem. Constitutional Assembly 61; mem. Economic Research Foundation; Chair. Asscn. of Chambers of Turkish Engineers and Architects 58-60; Partner Bormak Co. Ltd. 60-; Chair. Board and Exec. Comm. Eregli Iron and Steel Co. 61-68; Chair. Board of Trustees, Ankara Koleji Foundation 63-68, Middle East Tech. Univ. 63-66; Gen. Sec. Turkish Atomic Energy Comm. 70-71; Trustee, Hacettepe Univ. Foundation, Ankara 70-72; Tech. Counsellor Yapi ve Kredi Bank 72-; Chair. B. Bayindirlik Construction Corpn. 72-; mem. Board Karadeniz Copper Works 72-; mem. Board and Exec. Canakkale Cement Industries Corpn. 75; Chevalier, Légion d'Honneur.

Leisure interests: reading, car driving.

378 Bagdat Cad. 8, Suadiye, Istanbul, Turkey.
Telephone: Istanbul 58-49-99 (Home), 45-80-80 (Office).

Koppel, John Patrick, F.T.I.; British company director; b. 17 Nov. 1913, London; s. of P. A. Koppel, and E. D. im Thurn; m. Hon. Jessica St. Aubyn 1939; one s. two d.; ed. Rugby School, Univ. of Freiburg-im-Breisgau, Magdalen Coll., Oxford.

Joined Courtaulds Ltd. 35, research chemist 37, 39-40; Welsh Guards (Maj.) 40-46; Geschäftsführer, Glanzstoff-Courtaulds, Cologne 46-49; Gen. Man. Courtaulds

Australia 50-53; Chief Exec. and Deputy Chair. British Cellophane 53-61; mem. board, Commercial Dir. Courtaulds Ltd. 61-69, Deputy Chair. 69-.
Leisure interests: shooting, fishing, music.
Stainforth House, Settle, North Yorks., BD24 9PH, England.
Telephone: (0792) 3579.

Kopylov, Alexander Alexandrovich; Soviet conductor; b. 1926; ed. Yerevan Conservatoire.
Toured Japan, China, Egypt, America, Canada and Europe with company of Moscow ballet dancers; Conductor, Novosibirsk Theatre of Opera and Ballet 53-63; a conductor of Bolshoi Theatre 63-; Merited Actor of R.S.F.S.R.
State Academic Bolshoi Theatre of the U.S.S.R., 1 Ploshchad Sverdlova, Moscow, U.S.S.R.

Kørbing, Johannes Alfred; Danish company director; b. 16 Nov. 1885; ed. Royal Naval Coll. in Copenhagen, and Technical High School, Charlottenburg.
Lieutenant Engineer 07; Commanding Engineer 12; Sub-Dir. Naval Dockyard 19-21; Technical Dir. The United Steamship Co. 21, Managing Dir. 34-55, Chair. 55-64; Chair. Nat. Bank of Denmark 46-67, The United Breweries Ltd., Tuborg Foundation 37-68; Vice-Chair. Harbour Board of Copenhagen 46-67; mem. Ice Breaking Council 37-55, Danish Acad. Technical Sciences; Chair. and Dir. various other companies and insts.; Chair. Danish Shipping Board 39-49, Danish Shipowners' Asscn. 39-46, Maritime Council 39-46; Knight Commdr. 1st Class Order of Dannebrog, Silver Cross of Order of Dannebrog, Knight Commdr. of Belgian Order of Leopold, of Norwegian Order of St. Olav and of Swedish Nordstjerne Order.
Vestagervej 17, Copenhagen Hellerup, Denmark.
Telephone: Rsyvang 383.

Korčák, Josef; Czechoslovak politician; b. 17 Dec. 1921, Holštejn; ed. School of Political Studies of Central Cttee. C.P. of Czechoslovakia.
Turner, Zbrojovka Brno 37-48; posts in regional cttees. of C.P. 48-60; mem. Cen. Cttee. C.P. of Czechoslovakia 58-, mem. Presidium of Cen. Cttee. 70-; mem. Bureau of Cen. Cttee., C.P. of Czechoslovakia for directing Party work in the Czech lands 69-; Minister of Construction 62-63; Minister in charge of Cen. Admin. of Power Supply 63-68; Chair. Cen. Cttee. of Czech Nat. Front 69-71; Prime Minister of Czech S.R. and Deputy Prime Minister of Č.S.S.R. 70-; Deputy to Nat. Assembly 62-69, to House of People, Fed. Assembly 69-; Deputy to Czech Nat. Council 71-; Award for Merits in Construction 58, Order of the Repub. 71, Order of Victorious February 73, etc.
Government Presidium of Czechoslovak Socialist Republic, Prague 1, nábř. kpt. Jaroše 4, Czechoslovakia.

Koren, Petter Mørch; Norwegian lawyer and politician; b. 22 Jan. 1910, Edinburgh, Scotland; s. of Dean Laurentius Stub Koren and Thordis Andrea Mørch Koren; m. Aase Dahl 1938; two s. three d.; ed. Univ. of Oslo.
Solicitor 34; Clerk 35-36; Deputy Judge, District Judge of Larvik 36-38; Sec. Ministry of Commerce 38, Ministry of Shipping 40; Head of Div. Ministry of Shipping 42, Norwegian Govt. Savings and Contribution Office 45, Ministry of Commerce 48; Judge, City Court of Oslo 56; Gov. of Oslo and Akershus 66-; Minister of Justice 63, 72-73.
H. Heyerdahls St., Oslo-Dep; Home: Østhornveien 3, Oslo, Norway.
Telephone: 33-12-80 (Office); 23-20-15 (Home).

Koren, Stephan, D.ECON.; Austrian university professor and politician; b. 14 Nov. 1919, Wiener Neustadt; m.; six c.; ed. High School and Univ. of Vienna.
Member Austrian Inst. of Econ. Research 45-65; Prof. of Econs. Univ. of Innsbruck 65-; Under-Sec. of State

for Econ. Questions, Fed. Chancellery 67-68; Minister of Finance 68-70.
Artariastrasse 6, 1170 Vienna, Austria.
Telephone: 463697.

Korhonen, Gunnar Aleksander, B.SC. (ECON); Finnish aviation executive; b. 22 April 1918, Finland; m. 1st Elli Tamminen 1943 (divorced), 2nd Seija Niemi 1969; one s.
Employed by Bank of Savo-Karjala 37-38; Office Man. and Head of Dept. of Ministry of Supply 44-47; Sec. State Price and Wage Council 47; Vice-Pres. Oy Masalin & Co. 47-50; Pres. Hoyryvarustin Oy 50-51; Head of Price Dept. Ministry of Social Affairs 51-53; Dir.-in-Chief, Trade and Supply Section of Ministry of Commerce and Industry 53-60; Chair. Board of Dirs. and Pres. of Finnair 60-; Chair. Economic Council 57-58; Delegate to the Scandinavian Council 56-59; Chair. of the Finnish Group of the Collaboration Comm. on Scandinavian Economics 57-59; Delegate at ECOSOC; Chair. of Board of Dirs. of Kar-Air Oy 68-; Minister of Social Affairs and Public Health 70; Minister of Commerce and Trade 71-72; mem. of various Boards of Admin. and Dirs.
Leisure interests: reading, boating, skiing.
Office: Finnair, Mannerheimintie 102, 00250 Helsinki 25; Home: Vanrikki Stoolinkatu 3 A 7, Helsinki 10, Finland.

Kôri, Yuichi, LL.B.; Japanese politician; b. 16 March 1902, Takanawa Kuruma-cho, Shiba-ku; s. of Atsushi and Taka-ko Kôri; m. Hisae Kameyama 1932; two s. one d.; ed. Tokyo Univ.
With Ministry of Home Affairs 29-45; Dir. Local Admin. 46; Gov. Ishikawa Prefecture 47; Deputy Chief Sec. of Cabinet 48-50; mem. House of Councillors 50-; Minister of Home Affairs 57-58; Chair. Discipline Cttee., Liberal Democratic Party 60-62; Minister of Posts and Telecommunications June 65-66; Minister of Justice July-Dec. 72; 1st Class Order of the Rising Sun 72.
Leisure interest: archery.
Publs. *Lectures on New Election System* 48, *Lectures on Secret Protection Law* 54.
19-5, Otsuka 4-chome, Bunkyo-ku, Tokyo, Japan.
Telephone: Tokyo 946-3000.

Korinek, Franz, D.IUR.; Austrian lawyer; b. 20 May 1907, Schlösselhof; s. of Wenzel and Maria Korinek; m. Viktoria Schuschu 1937; one s.; ed. Vienna Univ.
Practised law in Vienna 31-34, 38-47; Leading Sec. Provincial Union of Trades and Commerce of Carinthia 34-38; Rep. Sec.-Gen. Fed. Chamber of Commerce 47-48, Sec.-Gen. 50-66; Minister of Finance 63-64; Dir. Vienna Chamber of Commerce 48-50; Vice-Chair. Pensionsversicherungs-anstalt der Angestellten 48-63; Vice-Chair. Hauptverband der Österreichischen Sozialversicherungsträger 49-63; Man. of Security Funds for Credits 68-73; Leader, Austrian-French Comm. for Trade 68-; Chair. Board of Examiners of 2nd and 3rd State Examination, Hochschule für Welthandel, Vienna; Grand Golden Order of Merit of the Austrian Republic; Grand Cross Order of St. Silvester; Commdr. Order of the Lion (Finland), Commdr. Order of Orange-Nassau, Lion (Finland), Commdr. Order of Orange-Nassau, Grand Cross, 2nd Class, Order of Merit of German Fed. Repub. Grand Officer's Cross Order of Merit of Italian Repub., etc.; People's Party.
Leisure interests: philosophy, law and political economy, music and football.
A-1060 Vienna, Esterhazygasse 32, Austria.
Telephone: 0222-57-40-105.

Kornberg, Arthur, M.D., D.SC., LL.D., L.H.D.; American biochemist; b. 3 March 1918, New York; s. of Joseph and Lena (Katz) Kornberg; m. Sylvy R. Levy 1943; three s; ed. City Coll. of New York and Univ. of Rochester.

Commissioned Officer, U.S. Public Health Service 41-42; Nat. Insts. of Health, Bethesda, Md. 42-52; Prof. and Chair. Dept. of Microbiology, Washington Univ. School of Medicine 53-59; Prof., Dept. of Biochemistry, Stanford Univ. School of Medicine 59, Head 59-69; mem. Nat. Acad. of Sciences, American Philosophical Soc., American Acad. of Arts and Sciences; Foreign mem. Royal Soc. 70-; Nobel Prize in Medicine and Physiology (with Prof. Ochoa) 59; Hon. LL.D., City Coll. of New York 60; D.Sc. (Univs. of Notre Dame, Washington, Rochester and Pennsylvania), L.H.D. (Yeshiva Univ.) 62, D.Sc. (Princeton Univ.) 70, D.Sc. (Colby Coll.) 70, and many other awards.

Publs. Numerous original research papers and reviews on subjects in biochemstry, particularly enzymatic mechanisms of biosynthetic reactions.

Office: Department of Biochemistry, Stanford University School of Medicine, Stanford, Calif.; Home 365 Golden Oak Drive, Portola Valley, Calif., U.S.A.

Telephone: 415-851-0287.

Kornberg, Hans Leo, M.A., D.SC., SC.D., PH.D., F.R.S.; British professor of biochemistry; b. 14 Jan. 1928, Herford; s. of Max and Margarete (née Silberbach) Kornberg; m. Monica M. King 1956; twin s. two d.; ed. Queen Elizabeth Grammar School, Wakefield and Univ. of Sheffield.

John Stokes Research Fellow, Univ. of Sheffield 52-53; mem. Medical Research Council Cell Metabolism Research Unit, Univ. of Oxford 55-61; Lecturer in Biochem., Worcester Coll., Oxford 58-61; Prof. of Biochem., Univ. of Leicester 61-75; Chair. Science Board, S.R.C. 69-72, mem. 67-72; CIBA Lecturer, Rutgers N.J. 68; Life Sciences Lecturer, Univ. of Calif. (Davis) 71; Visiting Lecturer, Aust. Biochemical Soc. 73; Distinguished Visiting Prof., Univ. of Cincinnati 74; Visiting Prof., Univ. of Miami, Medical School 70-; Sir William Dunn Prof. of Biochem., Univ. Cambridge 75-; Weizmann Memorial Lecturer 75; Febs-Springer Lecturer 75; Fellow, Christ's Coll., Cambridge 75-; Commonwealth Fund Fellow (Yale and N.Y. Univs.) 53-55; Colworth Medal (Biochemical Soc.) 65; Warburg Medal (Gesellschaft für biologische Chemie der Bundesrepublik Deutschland) 73; Hon. mem. Soc. Biological Chem. (U.S.A.) 72; Fellow, Inst. of Biology 66, Vice-Pres. 69-72; Leuwenhoek Lecturer, Royal Soc. 72; Man· Trustee, Nuffield Foundation 73-; Hon. Sc.D. (Univ. Cincinatti) 74, Hon. D.Sc. (Univ. Warwick) 75.

Leisure interests: conversation, cooking.

Publs. numerous articles in scientific journals.

Department of Biochemistry, School of Biological Sciences, University of Leicester, Leicester, LE1 7RH; Home: 2 Woodland Avenue, Stoneygate, Leicester, LE2 3HG, England.

Telephone: 0533-50000 (Office); 0533-704466 (Home).

Körner, Stephan, JUR.DR., PH.D., F.B.A.; British philosopher; b. 26 Sept. 1913, Ostrava, Czechoslovakia; only s. of Emil Körner and Erna Körner (née Maier); m. Edith Laner, B.SC., J.P., 1944; one s. one d.; ed. Classical Gymnasium, Charles Univ., Prague, and Trinity Hall, Cambridge.

Army Service 36-39, 43-46; Lecturer in Philosophy, Univ. of Bristol 46-52, Prof. 52-, Dean, Faculty of Arts 65-66; Pro-Vice-Chancellor, Univ. of Bristol 68-71; Prof. Yale Univ. 71-; Visiting Prof. of Philosophy, Brown Univ. 57, Yale Univ. 60, Texas Univ. 64, Indiana Univ. 67; Editor Ratio 60-; Pres. British Soc. for Philosophy of Science 65, Aristotelian Soc. 67, Int. Union of History and Philosophy of Science (Div. of Logic, Methodology and Phil. of Science) 69-71, Mind Asscn. 73; Fellow of British Acad. 67; mem. Int. Inst. of Philosophy 71-.

Leisure interest: walking.

Publs. Kant 55, Conceptual Thinking 55, The Philosophy of Mathematics 60, Experience and Theory 66, Kant's Conception of Freedom (British Acad. Lecture) 67, What is Philosophy? 69, Categorial Frameworks 70, Abstraction in Science and Morals 71, Experience and Theory 76; Editor: Observation and Interpretation 57; contributor to philosophical periodicals.

Department of Philosophy, The University, Bristol, BS8 1RJ; Home: 10 Belgrave Road, Bristol, BS8 2AB, England.

Telephone: 24161 (Univ.); 33036 (Home).

Kornev, Pyotr Georgievich; Soviet surgeon and tuberculosis specialist; b. 27 Dec. 1883, Samara (now Kuigyshev) Region; ed. Moscow Univ.

Physician, Asst., Prof. 09-35; mem. U.S.S.R. Acad. of Medical Sciences 44-; Head of Dept., Consulting Prof., Leningrad Inst. for Postgraduate Medical Training 32-; Dir. Scientific Dir., Leningrad Inst. of Surgery for Tuberculosis 30-; mem. Editorial Boards Problems of Tuberculosis, Surgical Review, Orthopedics, Traumatology and Prosthetics; Hon. mem. Boards of All-Union and All-Russia Scientific Socs. of Phthisiologists; mem. of Board of All-Union Soc. of Surgeons; Hon. mem. of Presidium of Pirogov Surgical Soc.; Hon. Chair. of Leningrad Scientific Soc. of Traumatologists and Orthopedists; mem. Int. Union Against Tuberculosis and Int. Coll. of Surgeons; Order of Lenin 60; Red Banner of Labour 57, 64; Patriotic War, First Class, 45; Honoured Scientist of R.S.F.S.R. 40.

Publ. Over 200 works on complex treatment of bone-and-joint tuberculosis with application of surgery methods; monographs: Bone-and-Joint Tuberculosis 51, Surgery for Bone-and-Joint Tuberculosis 64.

Institute of Surgery for Tuberculosis, 5 Ulitsa Institutskaya, Leningrad, U.S.S.R.

Korom, Mihály, LL.D.; Hungarian lawyer and politician; b. 9 Oct. 1927, Mindszent; s. of Mihály Kelemen and Eszter Korom; m. Dr. Ilona Kővágó 1949; two s.; ed. Budapest Univ., Hungarian Socialist Workers' Party Univ.

Farmhand until 45; various police posts 45; mem. Hungarian Socialist Workers' Party 46-; later Dept. Head, Ministry of Interior; Maj.-Gen. and Nat. Commdr. Frontier Guard Force 60-63; Sec. Cen. Cttee. Hungarian Socialist Workers' Party 63-66; Minister of Justice 66-.

Leisure interests: sport, football.

Ministry of Justice, 1363 Budapest V, Szalay-utca 16, Hungary.

Telephone: 120-025.

Koroma, Sorie Ibrahim; Sierra Leonean politician; b. 30 Jan. 1930, Port Loko; m.; c.; ed. Govt. Model School, Freetown, Bo Govt. School and Co-operative Coll., Ibadan, Nigeria.

Worked in Co-operative Dept. 51-58; in private business 58-62; First Sec.-Gen. Sierra Leone Motor Transport Union 58; mem. Parl. 62-65, 67-; Councillor and Deputy Mayor of Freetown 64; Minister of Trade and Industry 68-69; Minister of Agriculture and Nat. Resources 69-71; Vice-Pres. of Sierra Leone 71-, Prime Minister 71-75, Minister of the Interior 71-73, of Finance 75-; Vice-Chair. FAO Conf., Rome 71; Rep. of Sierra Leone to OAU Summit Conf., Addis Ababa 71, Morocco 72; decoration from Lebanon, People's Repub. of China, Ethiopia, Liberia.

Leisure interests: reading, football, sport.

Office of the Vice-President, Tower Hill, Freetown, Sierra Leone.

Telephone: 2757.

Korry, Edward M.; American journalist and diplomatist; b. 7 Jan. 1922, New York; m. Patricia McCarthy 1950; one s. three d.; ed. Washington and Lee Univ. and Harvard Graduate School of Business Management.

National Broadcasting Company 42; United Press, New York 43-47, London 47, Chief Corresp. for U.N. 48, for Eastern Europe (Belgrade) 48-50, Man. for Germany 51, for France 52, Chief European Corresp.

54; European Editor, *Look* magazine 55-60; Asst. to Gardner Cowles and Pres. Cowles Magazine and Broadcasting Inc. 60-63; Amb. to Ethiopia 63-67, to Chile 67-71; Consultant to Pres. of Overseas Private Investment Corpn. 72; Pres. Asscn. of Amer. Publrs. 72-73, UN Asscn., U.S.A. 73-74.
351 Elm Road, Briarcliff Manor, New York, N.Y. 10510, U.S.A.

Korth, Fred, A.B., LL.B.; American banker, lawyer and government official; b. 9 Sept. 1909, Yorktown, Texas; *s.* of Fritz R. J. and Eleanor Marie (Stark) Korth; *m.* Vera Connell 1934 (divorced 1964); one *s.* two *d.*; ed. Texas and George Washington Univs.
Admitted to Bar 35; law practice Fort Worth 35-62; Dep. Counsellor, Dept. of the Army 51-52, Asst. Sec. of Army 52-53; Consultant to Sec. of Army 53-60; Exec. Vice-Pres Continental Nat. Bank, Fort Worth 53-59, Pres. 59-62; Sec. of the Navy 62-64, private law practice 64-; Co-Executor and Co-Trustee, Marjorie Merriweather Post Estate; fmr. Dir. All States Life Insurance Co., Bell Aerospace Corpn., T. & P. Railway, Panama Canal Co.; mem. American Bar Asscn., American Law Inst., Nat. Council Nat. Planning Asscn.; recipient of Exceptional Civilian Service Award, Army Dept. 53; Dir. Fischbach and Moore, Southwest Nat. Bank of El Paso, American Air Filter Co., OKC Corpn.; Hon. LL.D.
Leisure interests: hunting and fishing.
401 Barr Building, Farragut Square, Washington, D.C. 20006, U.S.A.
Telephone: 202-223-3630.

Korthals, Hendrik Albertus; Netherlands politician; b. 3 July 1911, Dordrecht; *s.* of A. H. Korthals; *m.* Marie Cécile Hamming 1940; two *s.* two *d.*; ed. Rotterdam Economic High School.
Editor *Nieuwe Rotterdamse Courant* 36-40; official, Ministry for Trade, Shipping and Industry 40-45; mem. of Parl. 45-59; mem. Cons. Assembly of Council of Europe 49-59; Parl. Coal and Steel Community and European Parl. 52-59; Deputy Premier and Minister of Transport and Waterways 59-63; mem. Council of State; Pres. Press Council; Adviser Board Netherlands Org. for Int. Development Co-operation; Vice-Pres. World Broadcasting; Liberal.
Leisure interest: history.
63 Witte Singel, Leiden, Netherlands.
Telephone: 133790.

Korüturk, Admiral Fahri S.; Turkish naval officer and politician; b. 1903, Istanbul; *m.;* two *s.* one *d.;* ed. Naval Acad. and Naval War Coll.
Joined Navy 20; Intelligence Dept. of Chief of Gen. Staff 34; Naval Attaché, Rome 35-36, Berlin and Rome 37-38, Berlin and Stockholm 42-43; Commdr. of Submarine Fleet 47-50; Rear-Adm. 50; Commdr. of Sea-Going Fleet 53-54; Chief of Intelligence, Armed Forces 54; Commdr. of the Fleet 55; C.-in-C. Straits Area 56; Adm. 57; C.-in-C. of Navy and Commdr. of Allied Forces, Black Sea 57-60; Amb. of Turkey to U.S.S.R. 60-64, to Spain 64-65; mem. Defence Cttee. of the Senate 68; Pres. of Turkey April 73-.
The Presidency, Ankara, Turkey.

Korvald, Lars; Norwegian politician; b. 29 April 1916, Nedre Eiker; *s.* of Engebret Korvald and Karen (née Wigen); *m.* Ruth Borgersen 1943; one *s.* four *d.;* ed. Coll. of Agriculture.
Teacher, Tomb School of Agric. 43-48; Chief Adviser, League of Norwegian Agricultural Clubs 48-52; Headmaster, Tomb School of Agric. 52-; mem. Storting 61-; mem. Advisory Assembly, Council of Europe 65-70; mem. Nordic Council 66-; Chair. Christian Dem. Party 67-75; Pres. Lagting (Upper House of Storting) 69-72; Prime Minister 72-73; del. to UN Gen. Assembly 63, 68.
Leisure interests: skiing, literature.
Tollef Gravs vei 147, 1342 Jar, Norway.

Korzeniewski, Bohdan, DR.PHIL.; Polish theatre and film director; b. 12 April 1905, Siedlce; *s.* of Józef and Stanisława Korzeniewski; *m.* Ewa Rostowska; one *s.* one *d.;* ed. Faculty of Humanities, Warsaw Univ.
Worked at Nat. Library, Warsaw 32; studied eighteenth-century theatre in Paris 33-34; theatre critic 34-; Lecturer in History of Theatre, State Inst. of Theatrical Art 34-39; active in resistance movt. during World War II; Literary Dir. Theatre of Polish Army, Łódź 45-46; Dean, State Higher School of Theatrical Art, Łódź 46-48, Warsaw 49-, Prof. and Dean, Dept. of Staging 56-; co-editor *Teatr* 49-52; Dir. *Teatr Polski* 49-52, *Narodowy* 54-56; Editor-in-Chief *Pamiętnik teatralny* 56-; mem. Polish Cultural Council and Science Council of State Inst. of Art; State Prize 51, 54; numerous Polish and foreign decorations.
Leisure interests: gardening, car, walking.
Publs. *Drama in Warsaw National Theatre*, a book on early 19th century melodrama, *Discussions About Theatre* (theatrical reviews), *I Want Freedom for Thunder . . . in the Theatre* (essays), and numerous translations of English, French and Russian plays.
Ul. Miączynska 11, Warsaw, Poland.
Telephone: 44-1831.

Korzhev, Gely Mikhailovich; Soviet artist; b. 7 July 1925, Moscow; ed. Surikov State Inst. of Arts, Moscow. Professional artist 50-; has participated in many Soviet and foreign exhbns. 50-; Prof. Moscow Higher Artist-Technical Inst.; mem. U.S.S.R. Acad. of Arts; Chair. of Board of Artists' Union of R.S.F.S.R.; Sec. Board of Dirs. of Artists' Union of U.S.S.R.; Merited Worker of Arts of the R.S.F.S.R.; Repin State Prize of U.S.S.R.
Artists' Union of the U.S.S.R., Gogolevsky boulevard 10, Moscow, U.S.S.R.

Korzhinsky, Dmitriy Sergeyevich; Soviet geologist; b. 13 Sept. 1899, Leningrad; ed. Leningrad Mining Inst. Geologist, All-Union Geological Inst., Leningrad 25-37; Asst. Prof., Prof. Leningrad Mining Inst. 29-40; Senior Scientific Collaborator, Inst. of the Geology of Ore Deposits, Petrography, Mineralogy and Geochemistry (I.G.E.M.), Acad. of Sciences of U.S.S.R. 37-, Head of Section of Metasomatism and Metamorphism, I.G.E.M. 56-; Dir. Inst. of Experimental Mineralogy, U.S.S.R. Acad. of Sciences 69-; Corresp. mem. U.S.S.R. Acad. of Sciences 43-53, mem. 53-; Hon. Fellow Geological Soc. of America 59; mem. Geological Soc. of London 62; hon. mem. Geological Soc. of German Democratic Repub. 63, Bulgarian Geological Soc. 68; mem. Leopoldina Acad. Natural Sciences, German Democratic Repub. 68; Vice-Pres. Int. Mineralogical Asscn. 65-70; Vice-Pres. U.S.S.R. Mineralogical Soc. 64-; U.S.S.R. State Prize for Science 46, 75, Lenin Prize 58; Hero of Socialist Labour 69; Golden V.I. Vernadskii Medal, U.S.S.R. Acad. of Sciences 72.
Publs. *Factors of Mineral Equilibria and Mineralogical Facies of Depth* 40, *Regularities of Mineral Associations in Archean Rocks of E. Siberia* 45, *Formation of Skarn Deposits* 45, *Bimetasomatic Phlogopite and Lazurite Deposits of the Archean of Baikal Region* 47, *Petrology of Turja Skarn Deposits of Copper* 48, *Outline of Metasomatic Processes* 53, 55, *Physicochemical Basis of the Analysis of the Parageneses of Minerals* 57, 59, 73, *Theory of Metasomatic Zoning* 70.
Institute of the Geology of Ore Deposits, Petrography, Mineralogy and Geochemistry (I.G.E.M.) of U.S.S.R. Academy of Sciences, 35 Pereulok Staromonetny, Moscow, U.S.S.R.

Kos-Anatolskyi, Anatoliy Yossypovych; Soviet (Ukrainian) composer; b. 1 Dec. 1909, Kolomyya, Ivano-Franko Region, Ukraine; *s.* of Yossyp Kos and Lidya Kopystianska; *m.* Nadia Opryshko 1967; two *s.* one *d.;* ed. Lviv Conservatoire, Lviv Univ.
Chairman Lviv Branch Ukrainian Composers' Union; mem. Ukrainian Composers' Union Board; mem.

U.S.S.R. Composers' Union Board; Assoc. Prof. Lviv
Conservatoire 54, Prof. 73-; mem. Soviet of National-
ities Credential Comm.; Deputy to U.S.S.R. Supreme
Soviet 70-74; People's Artist of Ukraine; Orders of Red
Banner of Labour 51, of Lenin 60, State Prize 51.
Leisure interests: archaeology, linguistics, football.
Principal compositions: opera: *Glow* 57; ballets:
Dovbush's Shawl 51, *Jay's Wing* 57, *Oryssia* 67; choral
works: *New Verkhovyna, From Moscow to the Car-*
pathians, In the Carpathian Mountains, Encounter on
the Stubble, Hutsul Waltz, Song Cycles; other works
include: *Concerto for Harp and Orchestra, Transcar-*
pathian Rhapsody for Violin and Piano, Concerto for
Piano and Orchestra, Immortal Testament (cantata),
From the Niagara to the Dnipro (oratorio), *Spring*
Storms (operetta).
Ukrainian Composers' Union, Lviv Branch, 7 Tchaikovsky Street, Lviv, U.S.S.R.

Kosaka, Tokusaburo; Japanese politician; b. 20 Jan.
1916, Nagano Pref.; ed. Tokyo Univ.
Joined Asahi Newspaper Co.; Man. Shinetsu Chemical
Industry Co. 49, Vice-Pres. 51, later Pres.; Dir. Japan
Chemical Industry Asscn., Coal Industry Asscn.,
Shinano Mainichi Newspaper Co., Shinano Broad-
casting Co.; mem. House of Reps. 69-; Dir.-Gen. Prime
Minister's Office 73-Dec. 74.
21-28, Fukazawa-cho, 7-chome, Setagaya-ku, Tokyo
158, Japan.

Kosaka, Zentaro; Japanese minister of state; b.
23 Jan. 1913; m. Masuko Ohtani 1957; two s. one d.;
ed. Tokyo Univ. of Commerce.
Mitsubishi Bank 35-39; Dir. Shinetsu Chemical Industry
Co. 40-45; Member of House of Representatives 46;
Minister of Labour 53-54; Minister of Foreign Affairs
60-62; Minister of State for Econ. Planning 72-73; Gran
Cruz de la Orden El Sol del Perú, First Class of the
Order Homayoun of Iran, and decorations from Thai-
land, Pakistan, Ethiopia, Brazil, Argentina and
Paraguay.
Leisure interests: golf, art appreciation.
Publs. *Chukyo Mitamama* (Communist China as I Saw),
Pen to Daigishi (Pen and a Diet Member), *Atarashiki*
Kuni no Ibuki (Seeking Nation's New Spirits).
Denenchofu 4-26-22, Ohtaku, Tokyo, Japan.
Telephone: 721-2838.

Koschnick, Hans Karl-Heinrich; German politician;
b. 2 April 1929; ed. Mittelschule.
Worked in Ministry of Labour concerning prisoners of
war 45; local Govt. official, Bremen 45-51 and 54-63;
Trade Union Sec. of the Union of Public Employees,
Transport and Communications 51-54; mem. Social-
Democratic Party 50-; mem. Provincial Diet (Landtag)
and City Admin. 55-63; Senator for the Interior 63-67;
Deputy of the Fed. Council (Bundesrat) 63-65; Mayor
of Bremen 65-; Pres. of the Senate, Bremen 67-.
28 Bremen, Meinkenstrasse 1, Federal Republic of
Germany.
Telephone: 320011.

Kosciusko-Morizet, Jacques; French diplomatist; b.
31 Jan. 1913, Paris; s. of Charles Kosciusko and Diane
(née Milliaud); m. Marianne Morizet 1939; two s. two d.;
ed. Lycée Rollin and Lycée Henri IV, Paris, and Ecole
Normale Supérieure.
Teacher Lycée de Grenoble, Teacher Lycée Marcelin-
Berthelot 41-42, Lycée Buffon, Paris 43-44; Asst. Prof.
of French Literature, Faculty of Letters, Paris 44-46;
Prof. Columbia Univ., U.S.A. 46; Asst. Chief of Civil
Staff of Pres. of Nat. Assembly Jan.-Dec. 46, of Pres.
of Provisional French Govt. 46-47; Chief of Civil Staff
of Pres. of France 46-53, Chief of Civil Staff of Félix
Houphouët-Boigny 56-57; French Del. to UN Trustee-
ship Council 57-63; Amb. to Congo (Kinshasa) 63-68;
Dir. of Technical and Cultural Affairs at Secr. of State

for Foreign Affairs Feb.-Dec. 68; French Perm. Rep. to
North Atlantic Council, Brussels, 69-70; Perm. Rep. to
UN 70-72; Amb. to U.S.A. 72-; Commdr. Légion
d'Honneur; Croix de Guerre (39-45); Rosette de la
Résistance; Hon. K.C.V.O.
Leisure interests: piano, tennis, skiing, golf.
Publs. *Diderot et Hagedorn* 35, *Propos sur le Ministère*
des Jeunes 55, *Pari sur la Communauté franco-africaine*
57.
Embassy of France, 2535 Belmont Road, N.W.,
Washington, D.C. 20008, U.S.A.; 20 rue de Tournon,
Paris, France.
Telephone: 033-11-70 (Paris).

Koshland, Daniel E. Jr.; B.S., PH.D.; American pro-
fessor of biochemistry; b. 30 March 1920, New York
City; s. of Daniel E. Koshland and Eleanor Haas
Koshland; m. Marian Elizabeth Elliott 1945; two s.
three d.; ed. Univs. of Calif. and Chicago.
Analytical Chemist, Shell Chemical Co. 41-42; Research
Assoc. and Group Leader, Manhattan District, Univ. of
Chicago and Oak Ridge Nat. Lab. 41-46; Post-doctoral
Fellow, Harvard Univ. 49-51; Assoc. Biochemist,
Biochemist, Senior Biochemist, Brookhaven Nat. Lab.
51-65; Affiliate, Rockefeller Univ. 58-65; Prof. of
Biochem., Univ. of Calif. 65-; Visiting Prof. Cornell
Univ. 57-58; Pres. Amer. Soc. of Biological Chemists
73-74; Chair. Dept. of Biochemistry 73-; mem. Nat.
Acad. of Sciences, Amer. Acad. of Arts and Sciences;
Guggenheim Fellow 72, Visiting Fellow, All Souls' Coll.,
Oxford, 71-72, Fellow, American Asscn. for Advance-
ment of Science; Hon. mem. Japanese Biochem. Soc.
Leisure interests: tennis, golf, sailing.
Publs. Articles on enzymes in scientific journals.
Department of Biochemistry, University of California,
Berkeley, Calif. 94720, U.S.A.
Telephone: 642-0416.

Koskimies, (Kaarlo) Rafael; Finnish literary critic;
b. 9 Feb. 1898, Savonlinna; s. of Jaakko Forsman and
Jenny Saxen; m. Airi Elli Heikinheimo 1930; three s.
two d.; ed. Helsinki State Univ.
Lecturer in Finnish Literature, Helsinki Univ. 26-38,
Prof. of Aesthetics and Modern Literature 39-61, Prof.
Emeritus 61-; mem. Board Otava Publishing Co. 43-68,
of Finnish Nat. Theatre, Chair. 48-60, of Society of Fin-
nish Literature 46-68; mem. Finnish Acad. of Science
and Letters, Pres. 63-64; Emil Aaltonen Foundation
Prize 50.
Publs. *Fredrik Cygnaeus* 23, 25, *Raunioiden romantiikka*
(The Romantic Ruins) 30, *Walter Scott* 31, *Theorie des*
Romans 35, *Saksalaisen kirjallisuuden historia* (A
History of German Literature) 36, *Yleinen runousoppi*
(General Poetics) 37, *Elävä kansalliskirjallisuus*
(Living National Literature) 44, 46, 49, *Suomen Kan-*
sallisteatteri (Finnish National Theatre) 53, 72, *Helsinki*
ja Härjänvatsa 53, *Porthanin aika* (The Times of
Porthan) 56, *Maailman kirjallisuus* (World Literature)
63-65, *Der nordische Faust* 65, *Yrjö Koskinen* 68, 74,
Der nordische Dekadent 68, *Aleksis Kivi* 74.
Leisure interest: country life.
12 Luther Str., Helsinki 10, Finland.
Telephone: 444543.

Košler, Zdeněk; Czechoslovak conductor; b. 25 March
1928, Prague; ed. Acad of Music and Dramatic Arts,
Prague.
In concentration camp during Second World War;
Guest Conductor, Prague Nat. Theatre 51-; Artistic
Dir. Olomouc Opera 58-62; Chief, Ostrava Opera 62-66;
Asst. Conductor, New York Philharmonic Orchestra
63-64; F.O.K. Orchestra, Prague 66-67; Chief Conduc-
tor Berlin Comic Opera 67-68, Opera of the Slovak Nat.
Theatre, Bratislava 71-; Guest Conductor of Czech
Philharmonic Orchestra on tour in Japan 72; Award for
Outstanding Work 58; First Prize in young conductors'
competition, Besançon 56, First Prize and Gold Medal,

D. Mitropoulos Int. Competition, New York 63, Concert tour of Japan 69, 70, Artist of Merit 74.
Prague 4, M. Pujmanové 882; and Slovak National Theatre, Bratislava, Gorkého 4, Czechoslovakia.
Telephone: Prague 435-80-32.

Kosolapov, Valery Alexeevich; Soviet journalist and literary critic; b. 10 June 1910, Ardatov, Gorky Region; ed. Gorky Teachers Training Institute.
Lecturer, Gorky Teachers Training Inst. 32-41; Soviet Army 41-48; Editor of mil. newspaper *Krasny Voin* 44-46; mem. C.P.S.U. Cen. Cttee. 48-51; Deputy Chief Editor, then Chief Editor *Literaturnaya Gazeta* 51-62; Dir. *Khudozhestvennaya literature* Publishing House 63-70; Chief Editor *Novy Mir* journal 70-74, mem. Editorial Board 74-; R.S.F.S.R. Merited Worker for Culture; Order of Red Banner of Labour, Badge of Honour.
Novy Mir, 5 Ploshchad Pushkina, Moscow, U.S.S.R.

Kostandov, Leonid Arkadyevich; Soviet chemical engineer and politician; b. 1915; ed. Moscow Inst. of Chemical Engineering.
Formerly worked at large chemical combines, Central Asia; Chair. State Cttee. for Chemical Industry until 65; Minister of Chemical Industry 65-; Deputy to U.S.S.R. Supreme Soviet 66-; Alt. mem. C.P.S.U. Cen. Cttee. 66-71, mem. 71-; State and Lenin prizes and other decorations.
Ministry of Chemical Industry, 20 ulitsa Kirova, Moscow, U.S.S.R.

Kostelanetz, André; American (Russian-born) conductor; ed. St. Peter's School, and Conservatoire, St. Petersburg.
Conductor of his own orchestra for the Columbia Broadcasting System; organised and conducted tours of army orchestras in North Africa, Persian Gulf area and Italy 44, China, Burma and India 44-45; Guest Conductor with New York Philharmonic, Boston Symphony, Philadelphia, San Francisco Symphony and numerous other leading orchestras in the U.S.A., Canada, Europe, Israel and South America; Hon. Mus.D. (Albion Coll., Michigan, Cincinnati Conservatory of Music).
c/o Columbia Broadcasting System, 485 Madison Avenue, New York 22, N.Y., U.S.A.

Kostenko, Mikhail Polievktovich; Soviet electrical engineer; b 28 Dec. 1889, Veidelevka, Byelgorod Region; s. of Polievkt Ivanovitch Kostenko and Maria Iosifovna Kuznetsova; m. Olga Vasilievna Karasiova 1919; two d.; ed. Petrograd Polytechnical Inst.
Petrograd Polytechnical Inst. 18-30; Prof. at Central Asian Industrial Inst. 41-44; Corresp. mem. U.S.S.R. Acad. of Sciences 39-53, mem. 53-; Dir. Leningrad Branch, U.S.S.R. Acad of Sciences Inst. of Automation and Telemechanics 50-55; Hon. Scientific and Technical Worker of Uzbek S.S.R. 44-; Deputy to U.S.S.R. Supreme Soviet 58; Dir. Inst. of Electromechanics, U.S.S.R. Acad. of Sciences 56-; State Prize 49, 51, Lenin Prize 58; Hero of Socialist Labour 70, Order of Lenin (twice), Red Banner of Labour (twice).
Publs. *Alternating Current Commutator Machines* 33, *Electrical Machines* 44-49, *Electrical Machine Building* 53, *Theory and Calculation of Three-Phase Commutator Machines and Cascade Systems* 64, *Electrical Machines* 74, and numerous other publications.
Institute of Electromechanics, 18 Dvorzovaya Naberezhnaya, Leningrad; Dobrolubova 21ª-28, Leningrad 197049, U.S.S.R.
Telephone: 14-67-17 (Office); 33-21-05 (Home).

Koster, Henri Johan de; Netherlands industrialist and politician; b. 5 Nov. 1914, Leiden; s. of Arie de Koster and Johanna Adriana Sythoff; m. Goverdina Burgersdyk 1958; one s. three d.; ed. Amsterdam Univ. and in London, Dublin and New York.
With Meelfabriek De Sleutels 37-, Man. Dir. 39-67;

Netherlands Commr. in New York, Food Purchasing Bureau 45; Pres. Federation of Netherlands' Employers 60-67, Union des Industries de la Communauté Européenne (UNICE) 62-67; Sec. of State for Foreign Affairs 67-71; Minister of Defence 71-73; mem. Parl. 73-; Knight, Order of Netherlands Lion, Grand Officer Order of Orange Nassau, and other decorations.
Leisure interests: reading, swimming, golf, art.
Weiduin, Prins Frederiklaen 28, Wassenaar, Netherlands.
Telephone: The Hague 468814 (Office); Wassenaar 79898 (Home).

Koster, Willem, DR. ECON.; Netherlands economist; and banker; b. 24 Sept. 1911, Utrecht; m. Henriëtte C. J. van Mastrigt 1937; three d.; ed. Neths. School of Economics, Rotterdam.
Civil servant Neths. and Neths. East Indies Govts., The Hague and Batavia 36-46; Alternate Exec. Dir., Int. Bank for Reconstruction and Development and of Int. Monetary Fund for the Netherlands, Norway and the Union of South Africa 46-49; Treasurer-Gen. of the Neths., The Hague 49-51; Int. Bank for Reconstruction and Development 51-53; Gen. Man. Netherlands Bank of South Africa Ltd. 53-65; Lecturer Econs., Univ. of Natal, Durban 66-67; Econ. Adviser The Hague; Knight Order of Netherlands Lion.
Leisure interests: reading, photography.
Publ. *Aspects of Banking and Monetary Control in South Africa* 65.
7 Sijzenlaan, The Hague, Netherlands.
Telephone: 070-394189.

Kostousov, Anatoly Ivanovich; Soviet politician; b. 1906; ed. Moscow Machine Tool and Instrument Building Inst.
Member C.P.S.U. 25-; with machine toolbuilding enterprises 33-46; Deputy Minister Machine Tool Bldg. 46-49, Minister 49-53; Deputy Minister Machine Tool Bldg. 53-54; Minister Machine Toolbuilding and Instruments Industries 54-57; Chair. Moscow Econ. Council 57-59; Chair. State Cttee. for Automation and Machinebuilding 59-65; Minister of Machine Tool Bldg. and Tool-Making Industry 65-; mem. Cen. Cttee. of C.P.S.U. 61-; Deputy to U.S.S.R. Supreme Soviet 58-.
Ministry of Machine Tool Building, 20 Gorki Street, Moscow, U.S.S.R.

Kostrzewski, Jan Karol, M.D., M.P.H.; Polish scientist and politician; b. 2 Dec. 1915, Cracow, Poland; s. of Jan Kostrzewski and Maria Sulikowska; m. Ewa Sobolewska 1948; one s. three d.; ed. Jagiellonian Univ., Cracow.
Health Service Doctor 39-51; Head of Epidemiology Dept., State Hygiene Inst., Warsaw 51-67; Prof. of Epidemiology Warsaw Higher School of Medicine 54-60; Under-Sec. of State, Min. of Health and Social Welfare and Chief Sanitary Inspector 61-68; Minister of Health and Social Welfare 68-72; Scientist State Hygiene Inst. 73-; Corresp. mem. Polish Acad. of Sciences 67-, mem. Presidium 71-, Sec. Dept. of Medical Sciences 72-; mem. Exec. Board World Health Org. 73, Chair. 75; mem. Council Int. Epidemiological Asscn. 74; Order of Banner of Labour 1st and 2nd Class, Knight's Cross, Order of Polonia Restituta, Cross of Valour, Gold Cross of Merit.
Leisure interests: sport, photography, skiing, fishing.
Publs. numerous works on epidemiology.
Państwowy Zakład Higieny, ul. Chocimska 24, Warsaw, Poland.
Telephone: 497702.

Kosygin, Aleksey Nikolayevich; Soviet politician; b. 20 Feb. 1904, St. Petersburg (now Leningrad); ed. Leningrad Textile Inst. and Leningrad Co-operative Tech. School.
Worked in Irkutsk Regional Co-operative Union and

other co-operative organisations 24-29; Shop Superintendent Zhelyabov Factory, Leningrad 35-37; Dir. October Textile Mills, Leningrad 37-38; Man. Industrial and Transport Dept., C.P.S.U. Leningrad Regional Cttee. 38; Chair. Leningrad City Soviet of Workers' Deputies 38-39; People's Commissar of Textile Industry 39-40; Vice-Chair. Council of People's Commissars 40-46; Chair. Council People's Commissars R.S.F.S.R. 43-46; Minister of Finance 48; Minister of Light Industry 48-53; Minister of Consumer Goods Production 53-54; mem. Communist Party 27-; candidate-mem. Politburo 46-48 mem. Politburo 48-52, mem. Central Cttee. 39-; Deputy Supreme Soviet 38-; mem. of Presidium of Central Cttee. Communist Party until 66, Politburo 66-; Vice-Chair. U.S.S.R. Council of Ministers 57-60, 1st Vice-Chair. 60-64, Chair. 64-; Chair. State Planning Comm. 59-60; Order of Lenin (six times), Order of Red Banner, Hero of Socialist Labour (twice). Council of Ministers, The Kremlin, Moscow, U.S.S.R.

Kosygin, Yury Alexandrovich; Soviet geologist; b. 22 Jan. 1911, Leningrad (Petersburg); s. of Alexander Ivanovich Kosygin and Zoya Alexandrovna Kosygina; m. Mariya Iosiphovna Kosygina 1945; three s.; ed. Moscow Oil Inst.
Senior Scientific Assoc., Geological Inst., U.S.S.R. Acad. of Sciences 45-58, Inst. of Geology and Geophysics, Siberian Br. 58-70, Inst. of Tectonics and Geophysics, Soviet Far East Science Centre 70-; corresp. mem. U.S.S.R. Acad. of Sciences 58-70, Academician 70-.
Leisure interest: travelling.
Institute of Tectonics and Geophysics, 22 Seryshev Street, 680028 Khabarovsk, U.S.S.R.
Telephone: 33-06-35.

Kotaite, Assad, LL.D.; Lebanese lawyer and international aviation official; b. 6 Nov. 1924, Hasbaya; s. of Adib Kotaite and Kamle Abousamra; unmarried; ed. French Univ., Beirut, Univ. of Paris and Acad. of Int. Law, The Hague.
Head of Legal and Int. Affairs, Directorate of Civil Aviation, Lebanon 53-56; Rep. of Lebanon, Council of ICAO 56-70; Sec.-Gen. ICAO, 70-76, Pres. Council 76-; Golden Merit Medal, Lebanon, Medal of Sociedad Brasileira de Direito Aeronáutica, Brazil, Gran Cruz del Merito Aeronautico, Spain.
International Civil Aviation Organisation, 1000 Sherbrooke Street West, Montreal, Quebec; Home: 1455 Sherbrooke Street West, Apartment 2207, Montreal, Canada.
Telephone: 285-8041. (Office).

Kotarbiński, Tadeusz Marian, DR. PHIL.; Polish university professor; b. 31 March 1886, Warsaw; s. of Miłosz and Ewa (née Koskowska) Kotarbiński; m. 1st Wanda Baum 1912 (died 1946), 2nd Janina Kaminska 1947; two s.; ed. Univ. of Lwów.
Lecturer in Philosophy, Univ. of Warsaw 18, Extraordinary Prof. 19-29, Ordinary Prof. 29-60, Prof. Emeritus 60-, Dean of Faculty of Letters 29; Rector Univ. of Łódź 45-49; Pres. Polish Acad. of Sciences 57-62; Pres. Polish Philosophical Soc.; Pres. Int. Inst. Philosophy 60-63; Dr. Phil. h.c., Univs. of Brussels, Łódź, Cracow, Oxford, Bratislava and Florence; Dr. h.c. Med. Acad. Łódź; mem. of Moscow, Sofia and Ulan Bator Acads. of Science, British Acad., Acad. Serbe, Soc. Scientiarum Fennica; State Prize 1st Class 72; Commdr. Légion d'Honneur; Order of Builders of People's Poland, Grand Cross, Order Polonia Restituta and other decorations.
Leisure interest: poetry.
Publs. *Szkice praktyczne* (Practical Sketches) 13, *Elementy teorii poznania, logiki formalnej i metodologii nauk* (Elements of the Theory of Cognition, Formal Logic and Methodology of Science) 29, 61, *Traktat o dobrej robocie* (Tractate on Efficiency) 55, 58, 65, 69, 73, 75;

Wykłady z dziejów logiki (Lectures on the History of Logic) 57, *Wybór pism* (Selected Works) Vol. I 57, Vol. II 58, *Kurs logiki* (Manual of Logic) 51, 53, 55, 60, 61, 63, 74, 75, *Sprawność i Błąd* (Efficiency and Error) 56, 57, 60, 66, 70, *Leçons sur l'histoire de la logique* 64, *Praxiology* 65, *Gnosiology* 66, *Medytacje o życiu godziwym* (On the Right Way of Living) 66, 67, *Hasło dobrej roboty* (A Call to Good Work) 68, *Studia z zakresa filozofii* (Philosophical papers) 70, *Abecadlo praktycznosci* (Alphabet of Practicability) 72.
Ul. Karowa 14/16 m. 18, 00-315 Warsaw, Poland.
Telephone: 26-57-33.

Kotchian, A. Carl, A.B., M.B.A.; American aircraft executive; b. 17 July 1914, Kermit, N. Dakota; s. of Adolphus C. and Mamie (Bonzer) Kotchian; m. Lucy Betty Carr 1940; one s.; ed. Stanford Univ.
Accountant, Price, Waterhouse & Co., Los Angeles 36-40; Budget Man., Vega Airplane Co., Burbank, Calif., 41-43; Budget Man., Chief Cost Accountant, Lockheed Aircraft Corpn. 43-51, successively Dir. Financial Operations, Dir. Admin., Asst. Mfg. Man., Asst. Gen. Man. Georgia Div. 51-56, Vice-Pres. and Gen. Man. Georgia Div. 56-59; Group Vice-Pres., Lockheed Aircraft Corpn. 59-65, Exec. Vice-Pres. 65-67, Pres. 67-76.
283 Bel Air Road, Los Angeles, Calif. 90024, U.S.A.

Kotelawela, Col. the Rt. Hon. Sir John Lionel, K.B.E., C.H., P.C., J.P.; Ceylonese politician; b. 4 April 1897; ed. Christ's Coll., Cambridge, and Royal Coll., Colombo.
Mem. State Council 31; helped in foundation of United National Party, Pres. until 58; Minister for Agriculture and Lands 33; Minister for Communications and Works 35; Minister for Transport and Works 47-53; Leader of the House, Parl. of Ceylon 50-56; Prime Minister and Minister of Defence 53-56; Privy Councillor 54; Grand Cross Legion of Honour and numerous other decorations; Hon. LL.D. (Univ. of Ceylon).
Publ. *An Asian Prime Minister's Story* 56.
Kandawala, Kotelawalapura, Ratmalana, Sri Lanka; Brogues Wood, Biddenden, Kent, England.

Kotelnikov, Vladimir Aleksandrovich; Soviet radio and electronics engineer; b. 6 Sept. 1908, Kazan; ed. Power Engineering Inst., Moscow.
Instructor and Dean, Radio Engineering Faculty, Moscow Power Engineering Inst. 31-47, Head, Chair. of Radio Engineering Principles, Moscow Power Engineering Inst. 47-; Deputy Dir. Inst. of Radio Engineering and Electronics, U.S.S.R. Acad. of Sciences 53-54, Dir. 54-; mem. U.S.S.R. Acad. of Sciences 53-, Vice-Pres. 70-, Acting Pres. May-Nov. 75; Deputy and Chairman, Supreme Soviet of Russian Federative Socialist Repub.; Fellow, Amer. Inst. of Electrical and Electronics Engineers; Foreign mem. German Democratic Repub. Acad. of Sciences, Polish Acad. of Sciences, Czechoslovak Acad. of Sciences; Editor-in-Chief *Radio Engineering and Electronics*; State Prize 43, 46; Lenin Prize 64; Hero of Socialist Labour 69.
Institute of Radio Engineering and Electronics, U.S.S.R. Academy of Sciences, 18 Prospekt Marxa, Moscow, U.S.S.R.

Kotoński, Włodzimierz; Polish composer; b. 23 Aug. 1925, Warsaw; ed. Warsaw State Higher School of Music.
Interested in folk music, especially of the Podhale region 50-56; worked with Experimental Music Studio of Polish Radio and Electronic Music Studio of Westdeutscher Rundfunk, Cologne 66-67; with Groupe de Recherches Musicales ORTF, Paris 70-71; Prof. of Composition and Head of Electronic Music Studio, State Higher School of Music, Warsaw 67-; Chief Music Dir. of Polish Radio and TV 74-; compositions include orchestral and chamber music, some with percussion;

also electronic and tape music, and instrumental theatre; Minister of Culture and Arts Prize 73.
Publ. *Instrumenty perkusyjne we współczesnej orkiestrze* (Percussion Instruments in the Modern Orchestra) 63.
Ul. Krasińskiego 8 m. 55, 01-601 Warsaw, Poland.

Kotsokoane, Joseph Riffat Larry; Lesotho politician; b. 19 Oct. 1922; ed. South Africa, Fort Hare Univ. Coll., Univ. of the Witwatersrand.
Teacher 45-50; Agricultural Officer, Dept. of Agriculture, Basutoland, later Principal of Agricultural Training School 51-64, Principal Agricultural Officer 64-66; with British Embassy, Bonn 66-67; High Commr. in the U.K. 67-69; Perm. Sec., Ministry of Foreign Affairs 69-70, Ministry of Educ., Health and Social Welfare 70-72; High Commr. to Kenya, also accred. to Uganda and Tanzania 72-74; Minister of Foreign Affairs 74-75.
c/o Ministry of Foreign Affairs, Maseru, Lesotho.

Kotsonis, Archbishop Ieronymos; Greek ecclesiastic; b. Ysternia, Tinos; *s.* of Ieronymos and Aneglica Kotsonis.
Former Prof. of Canon Law, Univ. of Salonica; Chaplain to Greek Royal Family 49-67; Archbishop of Athens and Primate of Greece 67-73.
Leisure interests: fishing, swimming.
Ysternia, Tinos, Greece.
Telephone: 0283-22-897.

Kott, Jan., PH.D.; Polish literary critic; b. 27 Oct. 1914.
Professor of History of Polish Literature, Univ. of Warsaw; Visiting Prof. at Yale; Visiting Prof. at Univ. of Calif. 67-68; Herder Award, Vienna 64, Hon. mem. Modern Language Asscn.
Publs. *Mitologia i realizm* (Mythology and Realism) 46, *Szkoła klasyków* (The School of the Classics) 49, *Jak wam się podoba* (As You Like It) 50, *Postęp i głupstwo* (Progress and Folly) 56, *Szkice o Szekspirze* (Essays on Shakespeare) 61, *Shakespeare, notre contemporain* (French trans.) 62, *Miarka za miarkę* (Measure for Measure) 62, *Shakespeare, Our Contemporary* (English trans.) 64, *Szekspir Współczesny* 65, *Aloes* 66, *Theatre Notebook 1947-67* 68, *The Eating of the Gods: An Interpretation of Greek Tragedy* 73.
c/o Random House Inc., 201 East 50th Street, New York, N.Y. 10022, U.S.A.

Kotzina, Vinzenz, LL.D.; Austrian lawyer and politician; b. 30 March 1908, Neunkirchen; ed. Vienna University and Université de Fribourg, Switzerland.
Lawyer's assistant 33-35; Secr. of Lower Austrian Branch, Fed. of Austrian Trade Unions 35; Leader of Upper Austrian Branch, Traders' Fed. 35; Mil. service 41-45; Man. Dir. Upper Austrian Chamber of Commerce 46-62; mem. Nationalrat 62-; State Sec., Ministry of Trade and Reconstruction 63-66; Minister without Portfolio 66, Minister of Works and Technology 66-70; People's Party.
People's Party, Kärntnerstrasse 51, Vienna 1, Austria.

Kouandété, Lieut.-Col. Maurice; Benin army officer and politician; b. 1939; ed. Ecole de guerre, Paris.
Director of Cabinet of Head of State 67-69; Head of State and Head Provisional Govt. Dec. 67; Chief of Staff of Dahomey Army July 69-June 70; leader of coup which overthrew Pres. Zinsou Dec. 69; mem. of Directory (three man body ruling Dahomey), Minister of the Economy, Finance and Co-operation 69-70; arrested 70; Dep. Sec. Gen. for Defence 70-72; arrested Feb. 72, sentenced to death May 72, granted amnesty and released Dec. 72.

Koucký, Vladimir; Czechoslovak politician and diplomatist; b. 13 Dec. 1920, Vladivostok, U.S.S.R.; ed. Secondary School, Jaroměř.
Member C.P. of Czechoslovakia 38-; with underground Party orgs. 39-45; mem. illegal Central Cttee., C.P. of Czechoslovakia 44; mem. Central Cttee., C.P. of Czechoslovakia 45-48, 53-; Deputy Editor-in-Chief *Rudé právo* 45-53, Editor-in-Chief 55-58; Sec. Central Cttee., C.P. of Czechoslovakia 58-68; Chair. Ideological Comm. of Central Cttee. 63-65, Legal Comm. of Central Cttee. 64-68; mem. Ideological Comm. of Central Cttee. 63-68; Amb. to U.S.S.R. 68-70; Amb. to Belgium and Luxembourg 70-; Deputy, Nat. Assembly 45-69; mem. Presidium, Nat. Assembly 60-68; Deputy, House of the People (Fed. Ass.) 69-71; Order of Labour 57, Czechoslovak Peace Prize 66, Order of February 25 (1st Class) and other decorations.
Ministry of Foreign Affairs, Černínský palác, Prague, Czechoslovakia.

Koulis, Ioannis, D.SC.(ECON.); Greek economist; b. Nov. 1910, Langadia, Gortynia; ed. Univs. of Athens and Munich.
Assistant Prof. of Public Finance, School of Law, Univ. of Athens 48, Assoc. Prof. of Public Finance and Fiscal Legislation 55, Prof. 59-; Dean, School of Law, Univ. of Athens; mem. Board of Dirs. Greek Soc. of Econ. Studies, Nat. Bank of Greece, Centre for Programming and Econ. Devt.; mem. Econ. Council, Univ. of Athens, Rep. Assembly of Public Power Corpn. of Greece, Supreme Advisory Council for Econ. Devt.; Chair. Scientific Council of Statistics, Public Finance Programming Cttee. of Ministry of Co-ordination; mem. many other public scientific councils; Minister of Finance 71-73.
Publs. numerous works, studies and articles on various financial questions in Greek and French.
c/o Ministry of Finance, Athens, Greece.

Koun, Karolos; Greek theatre producer, director and actor; b. 13 Sept. 1908; ed. Robert Coll., Constantinople.
Professor of English Literature, Athens Coll. 29; Founder *Laiki Skini* (popular stage) 34-36; Theatre Dir. Athens 39-41, Greek Nat. Theatre 50-53; Founder *Theatron Technis* (Art Theatre) 42, Dir. and Producer 42-; World Theatre Season, London; Produced Aristophanes' *Birds* 64-65, Aeschylus' *Persae* 65 and Aristophanes' *Frogs* 67; Dir. *Romeo and Juliet*, Stratford-upon-Avon 67; World Theatre Season, London, *Oedipus Rex, Lysistrata* 69.
Greek Art Theatre, Stadium Street, Athens, Greece.

Kountché, Lt.-Col. Seyni; Niger army officer; b. 1931, Fandou; ed. French Army School, Kati, Mali, Army School St. Louis, Senegal.
Joined French Colonial Army 49, rank of Sergeant 57, Fréjus Training School, France 57-59, promoted to Warrant Officer 60; with Niger Army 61-; Officers' Training School, Paris 65-66; Deputy Chief of Staff Armed Forces 66-73, Chief of Staff 73-74, rank of Lt.-Col.; ousted Pres. Diori in coup April 74; Head of State and Pres. Supreme Mil. Council April 74-, also Minister of Devt. April 74-, of the Interior June 74-, of Nat. Defence 74-76.
Supreme Military Council, Niamey, Niger.

Kourganoff, Vladimir, D.SC.; French astronomer; b. 1912, Moscow, U.S.S.R.; *m.* Ruth Moj 1935; one *s.* one *d.*; ed. Lycée Saint-Louis, Sorbonne, Astrophysical Insts. of Paris and Oslo.
Scholar, Centre Nat. de la Recherche Scientifique 38-42, Research Fellow 42-52; Exchange Prof. Oslo Univ. 46-48; Dir. Astronomical Laboratory, Science Faculty, Lille Univ. 52-61; Prof. Univ. of Paris XI (Orsay) 61-.
Leisure interests: piano, philosophy of research and university education.
Publs. *La part de la mécanique céleste dans la découverte de Pluton, L'ion H⁻ dans le Soleil, Basic Methods in Transfer Problems, La Recherche Scientifique* (with J. C. Kourganoff), *Astronomie Fondamentale Elémentaire, Initiation à la Théorie de la Relativité, Introduction à la Théorie générale du Transfert des Particules, Exercices d'Initiation Rapide au Russe Scientifique* (with Ruth

Kourganoff), *Introduction à la Physique des Intérieurs Stellaires, La Face Cachée de l'Université.*
20 Avenue Paul Appell, 75014 Paris, France.
Telephone: 540-50-53 (Paris).

Kouros, Andreas Kyriakou, M.A., PH.D.; Cypriot educationist; b. 6 Nov. 1918, Vasilia; s. of Kyriacos Kouros and Eleni Sava; m. Sonia Koskarian 1946; two d.; ed. London and Oxford Univs., Int. Inst. of Educ. Planning, Paris.
Teacher 44-53; Inspector of Schools, Ministry of Educ. 53-59, Senior Inspector 59-61; Head Dept. of Primary Educ. 61-68; Head of Educ. Planning 68-70; Dir. of Educ. 70-72, Minister 72-74; Educ. Specialist, Int. Bank for Reconstruction and Devt. 75-.
Leisure interests: swimming, walking
Publs. *The Construction and Validation of a Group Test of Intelligence for Greek Cypriot Children* 56, *Education in Cyprus under the British Administration* 59, *Electra* 68.
The Kenwood, 5101 River Road, Apartment 517, Chevy Chase, Md., U.S.A.
Telephone: (301) 652-2894.

Kouyoumzelis, Theodore, M.CHEM., D.SC.; Greek physicist; b. 1 Dec. 1906, Kydoniai, Ayvalik; s. of George Kouyoumzelis and Polyxeni Petridou; m. Stella Grigoriou 1940; one d.; ed. Univs. of Athens, Munich, Manchester and Heidelberg.
Assistant Prof. Physics, Athens Univ. 37-49, Prof. Extraordinary 49-58; Prof. Physics, Athens Nat. Tech. Univ. 58-72, Emer. 72, Dean Faculty of Chemical Eng. 61-69; Prof. Royal Naval Acad., Piraeus 47-72; Sec.-Gen. Greek Atomic Energy Comm. 54-60, Vice-Pres. 72-; Perm. Rep. of Greece to CERN 55-, Vice-Pres. 73-; Commdr. Orders of Phoenix and of George I.
Leisure interests: hi-fi, classical music.
Publs. *Alternating Currents* 48, 58, *Nuclear Physics* 47, *Theoretical Electricity* 48, 57, 69, *Wave Theory* 48, 63, 69, *Elements of Nuclear Physics* 60, *Elements of Physics* (4 vols. with S. Peristerakis) 60-73; articles in learned journals on research into Raman effect and structure of ions, glass and water molecular vibrations, gamma rays and their inter-action with matter, counting and electronic devices, fallout measurement.
Office: Nuclear Research Centre Democritos, Aghia Paraskevi, Athens; Home: 23 Pindou str., Filothei, Athens, Greece.
Telephone: 65-13-111 (Office); 6814-993 (Home).

Kovács, Dénes; Hungarian violinist; b. 18 April 1930, Vác; s. of József Kovács and Margit Juhász; m. Adrienne Izsóf 1955; one s. one d.; ed. Budapest Acad. of Music under Ede Zathureczky.
First Violinist, Budapest State Opera 51-60; leading Violin Prof. at Budapest Music Acad. 57-, Dir. of Budapest Music Acad. 67-; Rector Ferenc Liszt Acad. of Music 71-; concert tours all over Europe, in U.S.A., U.S.S.R., Iran, India, China and Japan; Kossuth Prize 63, awarded Eminent Artist title 70.
Music Academy, 1061 Budapest VI, Liszt Ferenc tér 8; Home: 1023 Budapest II, Frankel Leó utca 21-23, Hungary.
Telephone: 224-448 (Office).

Kovács, György; Romanian writer and politician; b. 27 April 1911, Cuşmed, Harghita County; m. Georgina Altmann 1937; two s.; ed. Bethlen-College, Aiud and Cluj Univ.
Editor-in-Chief *Igaz Szó* (literary magazine), Tîrgu Mureş 63-70; mem. Cen. Cttee. of R.C.P. 55-; Deputy Grand Nat. Assembly 52-, Vice-Pres. 65-; State Prize 52.
Publs. include *Varjak a falu felett* 34, 62, *A tüz kialszik* 34, 65, *Erdélyi tél* 38, 67, *A vörös szamár* 40, *Aranymező* 42, 55, *Boszorkány* 46, 65, *Arnyék a völgyben* 46, *Bekülo Erdély* 47, *Foggal es körömmel* 49, 50, 51, 52,

55, 60, 61 (also in German, French and Czech), *A szabadság útján* 50, *Világ fénylö reménye* 53, *A bokréta* 55, 57, 61 (also in German), *Bűnügy* 56, *Dali Jóska rózsája* 57, *Ozsdola leánya* 59, 60, *Krisztina és a halálraitélet* 59, *Katonasir* 60, *Kristófék kincse* 60, 65, *Sánta lelkek* 61, *Falusi kaland* 61, *Pletykafészek* 62, *Leányok a kertek alatt* 63, *A ki nem mondott szó* 64, *Kergetö szelek* 64, *Hinár* 64, 65 (also in Russian), *Bánat és bor* 66, *Csatangolások a világban* 68, *Kozmáné szép asszony* 69, *Döglött gránát* 70, *Pusztulás* 71.
Strada Mihai Viteazul, 6, Tîrgu Mureş, jud. Mureş, Romania.

Kovanov, Vladimir Vasilyevich; Soviet surgeon; b. 13 March 1909, Petersburg (now Leningrad); m. 1928; two s. one d.; ed. Moscow Univ.
Postgraduate, Asst., First Moscow Medical Inst. 31-41; Soviet Army Medical Officer 41-45; Instructor, Head of Section, Deputy Head of Dept., C.P.S.U. Cen. Cttee. 45-50; Head of Dept., First Moscow Medical Inst. 46-; Pro-rector, First Moscow Medical Inst. 50-56, Rector 56-66; Corresp. mem. U.S.S.R. Acad. of Medical Sciences 60-63, mem. 63-; Vice-Pres., U.S.S.R. Acad. of Medical Sciences 66-; mem. Presidium Soviet Peace Cttee.; Order of Lenin (two), Red Banner (two), Red Star 42, Patriotic War, First Class 44, Patriotic War, Second Class 44, Honoured Scientist of R.S.F.S.R. 65, Spasokukotsky Prize, Shevkunenko Prize.
Leisure interests: journalism, writing.
Publ. Over 150 works, including 10 monographs, on treatment of thoracic cage wounds, traumatic shock, surgical anatomy of extremities, cardiac surgery, and transplantation of organs.
U.S.S.R. Academy of Medical Sciences, 14 Ulitsa Solyanka, Moscow, U.S.S.R.

Kowalczyk, Edward, D.ING.; Polish politician and engineer; b. 25 May 1924, Warsaw; m. Maria Krystyna Toniakiewicz; two s.; ed. Technical Univ. of Warsaw, and Warsaw Univ.
Took part in Resistance in Warsaw during Second World War and imprisoned in Germany; mem. Democratic Party 67-, mem. Pres. Cen. Cttee. 73-; Deputy to Seym 69-72; Minister of Posts and Telecommunications 69-; Chair. Polish Cybernetic Assoc. 70-; fmr. mem. Council of Science and Technics; Vice-Chair. Scientific Society of Plock; fmr. Head of Plock Branch of Warsaw Techn. Univ.; awards include Cross of Gold for Merit.
Leisure interests: scientific and political activities.
Publs. Several books on electronics and telecommunications.
Ministerstwo Łączności, 00-066 Warsaw, Pl. Małachowskiego 2, Poland.
Telephone: 264210.

Kowalczyk, Stanisław; Polish politician; b. 12 Dec. 1924, Pabianice; ed. Acad. of Mining and Metallurgy, Cracow.
Member Polish Socialist Party 47-48, Polish United Workers' Party 48-, successively Head of Econ. Dept. of Voivodship Cttee., Katowice, Sec. Voivodship Cttee., Katowice, Head of Dept. of Heavy Industry and Transport, Cen. Cttee. PUWP 68-71; Deputy mem. Cen. Cttee., PUWP 64-68, mem. Cen. Cttee. 68-, Sec. Cen. Cttee. 71-73, Deputy mem. Political Bureau of Cen. Cttee. 73-; Deputy to Seym (Parl.) 69-; Chair. Seym Comm. for Econ. Planning, Budget and Finance 72-73; Minister of Internal Affairs 73-; Brig.-Gen. 74; Order of Banner of Labour, 1st and 2nd Class, Knight's Cross, Officer's Cross Order of Polonia Restituta, Order of Builders of People's Poland 74, Medal of 30th Anniversary of People's Poland 74, and other decorations.
Ministerstwo Spraw Wewnętrznych PRL, ul. Rakowiecka 2, 02-517 Warsaw, Poland.

Kowarski, Lew, D. ÈS SC.; French atomic physicist; b. 10 Feb. 1907, St. Petersburg (now Leningrad), U.S.S.R.; s. of N. Kowarski and Olga Vlassenko; m. 1st Dora

Heller 1929, one *d.*; *m.* 2nd Kathe A. Freundlich 1948; ed. Ecole de Chimie Industrielle de Lyon and Univ. of Paris.

Came from Russia to Belgium and then to France; technical sec. (part-time) at Aciéries et Usines à Tubes de la Sarre 29-37; did biochemical research in hospital laboratory; personal sec. to Joliot-Curie 36; worked on neutron emission in uranium fission with Joliot-Curie and Halban; with Halban brought French stocks of heavy water experimental records to England 40; in charge of construction of first Canadian atomic pile 44; returned to France after Liberation and worked for Commissariat for Atomic Energy, of which he became Scientific Dir.; adviser to French del. to UN Atomic Energy Comm. 46-48; in charge of construction of first (47-48) and second (49-52) French atomic piles; Lecturer on Nuclear Physics, Conservatoire des Arts et Métiers 51-53; Dir. Laboratory Group 52-54, Scientific and Technical Services Div. 54-60, Data Handling Div. 61-64, Senior Physicist 65-72, Consultant 72-, European Org. for Nuclear Research (CERN); Scientific adviser to European Nuclear Energy Agency, OEEC 56-61 OECD 61-71; Visiting Prof., Purdue Univ., Lafayette, Indiana 63-65; Prof. Univ. of Texas 68-71; Visiting Prof. Boston Univ. 72, Prof. 72-; Officier de la Légion d'Honneur; Fellow American Nuclear Soc.; special award by U.S. Atomic Energy Comm. 68.

Leisure interests: reading, music, friendships.

Office: CERN, Geneva 23; Home: 40 avenue William Favre, Geneva, Switzerland.

Telephone: Geneva (022) 36-59-73.

Koyama, Goro; Japanese banker; b. 25 March 1909, Gunma Prefecture; *s.* of Toichi Oshima and Han Oshima; *m.* Atsu Koyama 1934; two *s.* one *d.*; ed. Tokyo Univ.

Managing Dir. The Mitsui Bank Ltd. 63-65, Deputy Pres. 65-68, Pres. 68-74, Chair. 74-.

Leisure interests: painting, golf.

The Mitsui Bank Ltd., 1-2 Yurakucho 1-chome, Chiyo-daku, Tokyo; Home: 3-15-10 Takaido-Higashi, Sugi-namiku, Tokyo, Japan.

Telephone: 501-1111 (Office); 333-0843 (Home).

Kožešník, Jaroslav, DR.ING.; Czechoslovak scientist; b. 8 June 1907, Kněžice; *s.* of Antonín and Katerina Kožešník; *m.* Anna Kožešník 1937.

Former Dir. Combined Research Inst. of the Škoda Works; head of research and development work in heavy engineering industry; Prof. of Czech Tech. Univ., Prague; Corresp. mem. Czechoslovak Acad. of Science 53, Academician 60, and First Vice-Pres. 62, Deputy-Chair. 61-70, Acting Vice-Pres. 69-70, Pres. 70-; Polish Acad. of Sciences 66-; Dir. Inst. of the Theory of Information and Automation; State Prize 59, 67; mem. State Planning Comm. 59-64; Chair. Cttee. for Co-operation of Socialist Countries in Research and Peaceful Uses of Outer Space 68-; Deputy, House of the People, Fed. Assembly 69-; mem. Bulgarian Acad. of Sciences 69-; mem. Cen. Cttee. C.P. of Czechoslovakia 70-; Order of Labour 62, Gold Plaque "Merits for Science and Mankind" 67, Klement Gottwald State Prize 59, 67, Hero of Socialist Labour 72, Order of Victorious February 73 and other decorations.

Leisure interest: tourism.

Publs. *Physical Similarity, Mechanics of Models, Dynamics, of Machines, Mechanics of Electrical Rotating Machines, Theory of Configurations, Random Vibrations.*

Narodni Tř. 3, Prague, Czechoslovakia.

Kozhevnikov, Fyodor Ivanovich; Soviet jurist; b. 1903; ed. Moscow Univ.

Former Prof. of Int. Law and Dean of the Law Faculty, Moscow Univ.; fmr. Pres. Legal Section U.S.S.R. Soc. for Cultural Relations and mem. Legal Science Experts Cttee., Ministry of Culture; mem. Int. Law Comm. of UN 52-53; Judge, Int. Court of Justice 53-61; mem.

Editorial Board *The Soviet State and the Law* (Soviet Acad. of Sciences Inst. of Law).

Publs. *Russian State and International Law 47, Soviet State and International Law 48, Great Patriotic War of the Soviet Union and Some Problems of International Law 57.*

Institute of Law, U.S.S.R. Academy of Sciences, 10 Ulitsa Frunze, Moscow, U.S.S.R.

Kozhevnitov, Yevgeny Fyodorovich; Soviet Minister of Transport Construction 54-75; see *The International Who's Who 1975-76.*

Kozlov, Nikolai Timofeyevich; Soviet politician; b. 1925; ed. Moscow Timiryazev Acad. of Agriculture. Mem. C.P.S.U. 46; Soviet Army service 43-47; Official, Moscow Regional Cttee. of C.P.S.U. 52-58, 59-60; Head of Statistics Dept., Moscow Region 58-59; First Vice-Chair. Moscow Regional Soviet of Working People's Deputies 60; Sec. Moscow Regional Cttee., C.P.S.U. 60-63; Chair. Moscow Regional Soviet of Working People's Deputies 63-; Alt. mem. C.P.S.U. Central Cttee. 66-71; mem. 71-; Deputy to U.S.S.R. Supreme Soviet 66-; Sec. Comm. for Legislative Proposals, Soviet of Union; mem. Cttee., U.S.S.R. Parl. Group.

Moscow Regional Soviet of Working People's Deputies, 13 Ulitsa Gorkogo, Moscow, U.S.S.R.

Kozlov, Vladimir Yakovlevich; Soviet mathematician; b. 28 June 1914, Moscow; ed. Moscow Univ.

Postgraduate Moscow Univ. 37-40; Army Service 40-46; mem. C.P.S.U. 41-; Research Assoc., Asst. Prof., Prof. Inst. of Mathematics, Moscow Univ. 46-; Corresp. mem. U.S.S.R. Acad. of Sciences 66-.

U.S.S.R. Academy of Sciences, 14 Leninsky Prospekt, Moscow, U.S.S.R.

Kozłowski, Roman; Polish palaeontologist; b. 1 Feb. 1889, Wloclawek; *s.* of Zdzisław and Zofia (née Kowalewska) Kozłowski; *m.* Maria Szmidt 1912; two *s.* one *d.*; ed. Fribourg (Switzerland) and Paris Univs.

Prof. and Dir. Oruro State (Bolivia) Mining Engineering School 13-19; Dr. Sorbonne, Paris 21-23, Warsaw Free Univ. 23-27, Warsaw Univ. 27-60; Prof. Emeritus 60-; Founder and Editor *Palaeontologia Polonica* 29-, *Acta Palaeontologica Polonica* 55-; mem. Polish Acad. of Sciences 52; Chair. Scientific Council of Inst. of Palaeozoology; Corresp. mem. Acad. des Sciences and many foreign scientific socs.; Dr. h.c. Modena Univ. 75; State Prize, First Class 49; André H. Dumont Medal, Belgium 52, Order of Banner of Labour 2nd Class 54, 1st Class 59, Mary Clark Thompson Medal, Nat. Acad. of Sciences, Washington 59, Wollaston Medal, Geological Soc. London 61, Silver Medal, Czechoslovak Acad. of Sciences 66; Commdr. Cross of Order Polonia Restituta and other decorations.

Leisure interest: house-plant cultivation.

Publs. *Fossiles dévoniens de Parana 13, Les Brachiopodes du Carbonifère supérieur de Bolivie 14, Faune dévonienne de Bolivie 23, Les Brachiopodes gothlandiens de la Podolie polonaise 29, Les Graptolites et quelques nouveaux groupes d'animaux du Tremadoc de la Pologne 48-49, Les Hydroides ordoviciens à squelette chitineux 59, Crustoidea—nouveau groupe de Graptolites 62, On the Structure and relationships of Graptolites 66, Nouvelles observations sur les Convulaires 68, Early Development Stages and the Mode of Life of Graptolites 71.*

Ul. Wilcza 22 m. 4, 00-544 Warsaw, Poland.

Koźniewska, Halina, M.D.; Polish surgeon and politician; b. 28 May 1920, Komczyn, near Kutno; ed. Warsaw Univ.

Doctor 49-55, Docent 55-68, Assoc. Prof. 68-; Head of Neurosurgery Dept., Clinic of Nervous Diseases 57-64; Dir. Neurosurgery Clinic, Medical Acad. of Lublin 64-; Deputy Dean of Medical Faculty 66-69; Deputy to Seym (Parl.) 69-; mem. Council of State March 72-;

Sec. Polish Neurosurgical Soc. till 70, mem. Cen. Board and Chair. Science Comm. 70-; mem. Scandinavian and Yugoslav Neurosurgical Socs.
Kancelaria Rady Państwa, ul. Wiejska 4/6/8, 00-489 Warsaw, Poland.

Krackow, Juergen, DR.; German business executive; b. 30 May 1923.
Apprentice, Commerz-Bank; Asst. Trinkhaus-Bank; Boswall and Knauer (construction co.); Man. Sidol-Werke Siegel 57; joined management of Berliner Handelsgesellschaft (BHG) 62, Berliner Maschinenbau AG 63; mem. Man. Board, Holding AG für Industrie und Verkehrswesen 67; mem. Man. Board AG "Weser" (member of Krupp group) 69, subsequently Chair.; Chair. Man. Board Fried. Krupp GmbH Oct.-Dec. 72, Man. Dir. May 72; Chair. Man. Board Stahlwerke Röchling-Burbach Jan. 75-; mem. Supervisory Board, Berliner Maschinenbau AG; Chair. Council EEC Builders of Large Ships.
Stahlwerke Röchling-Burbach G.m.b.H., 662 Völklingen-Saar, Federal Republic of Germany.

Kraft, Christopher Columbus, Jr.; American space administrator; b. 28 Feb. 1924, Phoebus, Va.; *m.* Elizabeth Anne Turnbull; one *s.* one *d.*; ed. Virginia Polytechnic Inst.
Member, Langley Aeronautical Lab., Nat. Advisory Cttee. for Aeronautics 45; selected to join Space Task Group on Project Mercury 58; Flight Dir. all Mercury Missions; Dir. of Flight Operations, Manned Spacecraft Center 63-69; Deputy Dir. Manned Spacecraft Center 70-72; Dir. Nat. Aeronautics and Space Admin. 72-; Fellow, Amer. Inst. of Aeronautics and Astronautics 66; Fellow, Amer. Astronautical Soc., Arthur S. Fleming Award 63; NASA Outstanding Leadership Award 63; Spirit of St. Louis Medal, Amer. Soc. of Mechanical Engineers 67; NASA Distinguished Service Medal (twice) 69; Hon. D.Eng. (Indiana Inst. of Technology) 66, (St. Louis Univ., Ill.) 67.
17 Southland Drive, Hampton, Va. 23369, U.S.A.

Kraft, Robert Paul, PH.D.; American professor of astronomy and astrophysics; b. 16 June 1927, Seattle, Wash.; *s.* of Victor P. Kraft and Viola E. Ellis; *m.* Rosalie A. Reichmuth 1949; two *s.*; ed. Univ. of Washington and Univ. of Calif. at Berkeley.
Instructor in mathematics and astronomy, Whittier Coll. 49-51; Asst. Prof. of Astronomy, Indiana Univ. 56-58; Asst. Prof. of Astronomy, Univ. of Chicago 58-59; mem. staff, Mt. Wilson and Palomar Observatories 60-67; Astronomer/Prof., Lick Observatory 67-; Acting Dir. Lick Observatory 68-70, 71-73; Visiting Fellow, Joint Inst. of Laboratory Astrophysics, Univ. of Colo. 70; mem. Nat. Acad. of Sciences, Amer. Acad. of Arts and Sciences; Warner Prize, Amer. Astron. Soc. 62; Nat. Science Foundation Fellow 53-55.
Leisure interests: music (classical and rock), euology, duplicate bridge.
Publs. articles in professional journals.
Lick Observatory, University of California, Santa Cruz, Calif. 95064, U.S.A.
Telephone: 408-429-2843.

Krag, Jens Otto; Danish politician; b. 15 Sept. 1914, Randers; one *s.* one *d.*
With Directorate of Supply 40-45; Chair. of Economic Council of Labour Movement 45-47; mem. of Parl. 47-74; Minister of Commerce, Industry, and Shipping 47-50; Economic Counsellor, Danish Embassy, Wash., D.C. 50-52; Minister of Economy and Labour 53-57; Minister of External Economic Affairs 57-58; Minister of Foreign Affairs 58-62; Prime Minister 62-68, also Minister of Foreign Affairs 66-67; Prime Minister Oct. 71-Oct. 72; Lecturer Univ. of Aarhus 72-; Head Del. of Comm. of European Communities to U.S.A. 74-75; Pres. North Atlantic Council 66-67; Chair. of Social Democratic Party 62-72; Charlemagne Prize 66; Robert Schumann Prize 73; Dr. h.c. (Bradford Univ.) 73.
Leisure interest: painting.
Publs. *Kooperationen, Fremtiden og Planøkonomi* 45, *Ung mand i trediverne* 69; joint author of: *Krigsøkonomi og Efterkrigsproblemer* 44, *England Bygger op* 47, *Danmark besat og befriet* 47, *Tidehverv og Samfundsorden* 54, *Hans Hedtoft: Mandomsgerning* 55, *Wirtschaftspolitik und Socialdemokratie der skandinavischen Länder* 58, *Kamp og Fornyelse* 72, *Dagbog* 71-72, *Travl Tid God Tid* 74.
Reventlowsweg 28, 1651 Copenhagen, Denmark.

Kraigher, Sergej; Yugoslav (Slovene) politician; b. 30 May 1914, Postojna, Slovenia; *s.* of Anton Kraigher and Marija Jaške; *m.* Lidija Šentjurc 1939; two *d.*; ed. Zagreb Univ.
Frequently imprisoned for political activities until 40; active in Nat. War of Liberation 41-45; subsequently held various regional posts in Communist Party; Gov. of Nat. Bank 50-53; Dir. Fed. Inst. for Econ. Planning 53-58; Sec. Secr. for Industry and State Sec., Cttee. for Foreign Trade 58-63; Vice-Pres. Fed. Chamber of Fed. Parl. and Pres. Cttee. for Socio-Econ. Relations 63-67; Pres. Assembly of Socialist Repub. of Slovenia 67-69, 69-74; mem. Presidency of Yugoslavia 71-74; Pres. Presidency of Slovenia 74-; Partisan Medal, Hero of Socialist Labour 74; several nat. decorations and honours from Italy, Cameroon and Cen. African Repub.
Leisure interests: cultural and artistic activities, especially literature, art and theatre; mountaineering and swimming.
Publs. article on socio-political and socio-economic questions in various Yugoslav newspapers and journals.
Ljubljana, Saveljska 54, Yugoslavia.
Telephone: 65-563.

Kraijenhoff, Jonkheer Gualtherus; Netherlands business executive; b. 1922; ed. Switzerland.
Royal Air Force (U.K.) pilot 43-47; joined N.V. Organon, Oss 47, Man. Dir. 57; mem. Board of Management N.V. Kon. Zwanenberg-Organon 59, Pres. 63; mem. Board of Management, Kon. Zout-Organon N.V. 67, Pres. 69; Vice-Pres. AKZO N.V., Arnhem 69, Pres. 71-; Pres. Neths. Red Cross 66; Knight, Netherlands Lion, Order of St. John.
AKZO N.V., Arnhem, Ijssellaan 82, Postbus 186; Home: Zomerland, Louiseweg 15, Nijmegen, Netherlands.
Telephone: 085-651475 (Office).

Krajčír, František; Czechoslovak politician; b. 12 June 1913, Vienna, Austria.
Minister of Domestic Trade 48-59; Minister of Foreign Trade 59-63; Deputy Prime Minister 63-68; Amb. to German Democratic Repub. 69-; mem. Comm. of Cen. Cttee. of C.P. of Czechoslovakia for Questions of Standard of Living 63-66; mem. Cen. Cttee. of C.P. of Czechoslovakia 46-; Deputy to Nat. Assembly 46-69; Chair. State Price Cttee. 63-65; Amb. to German Democratic Repub. 69-71; Deputy, House of the People, Fed. Assembly 69-71; First Deputy Foreign Minister 71-; Order of Feb. 25, 49, Order of Labour 63, Order of Victorious Feb. 73; several decorations for Resistance heroism in Second World War; Bulgarian, Cambodian and Ethiopian decorations.
Ministry of Foreign Affairs, Prague, Czechoslovakia.

Kralj, Tone; Yugoslav painter and sculptor; b. 1900; ed. Prague.
Represented at thirty exhibitions Yugoslavia, Venice Biennial Exhibitions 26, 28, 30, 54, six exhibitions Paris, one London, two Amsterdam, two Antwerp, one Strasburg (1st Prize), one Saarbrücken, one Leipzig, three Vienna, three Prague, one Berlin, one Barcelona, four U.S.A., one Copenhagen, three Italy, etc.; works in Yugoslav galleries, Vienna, Prague; private collections U.S.A.

Works include frescoes in thirty churches in Yugoslavia and Italy.

Gerbičeva 11, Ljubljana, Yugoslavia.

Kramer, Paul Jackson, A.B., PH.D., D.SC.; American plant physiologist; b. 8 May 1904, Brookville, Ind.; s. of LeRoy Kramer and Minnie Jackson; m. Edith Sarah Vance 1931; one s. one d.; ed. Miami Univ., Ohio and Ohio State Univ.

Instructor in Botany, Duke Univ. 31, Prof. 45, James B. Duke Prof. of Botany 54-, Emer. 74; Dir. Sarah P. Duke Gardens 45-74, Consultant 74-; Program Dir. Nat. Science Foundation 60-61; Chair. Section G., Amer. Asscn. for the Advancement of Science 56; Pres., Amer. Soc. of Plant Physiologists 45, N. Carolina Acad. of Sciences 62, Amer. Inst. of Biological Sciences, and Botanical Soc. of America 64; Barnes Life mem. Amer. Soc. of Plant Physiologists; mem. Nat. Acad. of Sciences, Amer. Acad. of Arts and Sciences, and Amer. Philosophical Soc.; Certificate of Merit, Botanic Soc. of America, Outstanding Achievement Award, Soc. of Amer. Foresters.

Leisure interests: gardening, photography, birdwatching.

Publs. *Plant and Soil Water Relationships* 49, 2nd edn. 69, *Physiology of Trees* (with T. T. Kozlowski); about 130 research papers in plant science journals and chapters in several books.

Department of Botany, Duke University, Durham, N.C.; Home: 23 Stoneridge Circle, Durham, N.C. 27705, U.S.A.

Telephone: 919-684-2359 (Office).

Kramer, Stanley, B.SC.; American film producer, director; b. 29 Sept. 1913; ed. New York Univ.

M.G.M. Research Dept.; film cutter for three years and film editor; film and radio writer; served U.S. Signal Corps; formed own film production co. to produce *This Side of Innocence*; formed and is Pres. Kramer Pictures. Films incl. (assoc. producer) *So Ends Our Night, Moon and Sixpence*; (producer) *So This is New York, Home of the Brave, Cyrano de Bergerac, Death of a Salesman, High Noon, The Happy Time, Eight Iron Men, Caine Mutiny*; (producer-dir.) *Not As a Stranger, Pride and the Passion, The Defiant Ones, On The Beach, Inherit the Wind, Judgment at Nuremberg, It's a Mad, Mad, Mad, Mad World, Ship of Fools, Guess Who's Coming to Dinner, Secret of Santa Vittoria, R.P.M., Bless the Beasts and Children, Oklahoma Crude*.

c/o Samuel Goldwyn Studios, 1041 North Formosa Street, Hollywood, Calif. 90046, U.S.A.

Krämer, Werner, DR.PHIL.; German archaeologist; b. 8 March 1917, Wiesbaden; ed. Univs. of Munich, Frankfurt, Kiel, Marburg.

Curator and Departmental Dir. Bavarian State Office for Preservation of Monuments 47-56; First Dir. and Prof. Roman-German Comm. of German Archaeological Inst. Frankfurt 56-72; Pres. German Archaeological Inst. 72-.

Peter-Lenné-Strasse 28-30, 1 Berlin 33, Federal Republic of Germany.

Telephone: Berlin 832-7061.

Kranidiotis, Nicos; Cypriot scholar, journalist and diplomatist; b. 25 Nov. 1911, Kyrenia; s. of John N. Kranidiotis and Polyxeni J. Kranidiotis; m. Chryssoula Vizakas 1946; one s. one d.; ed. Pan Cyprian Gymnasium, Cyprus, Athens Univ. and Harvard Univ. Center for Int. Affairs.

Worked as schoolmaster in Cyprus; Dir. of *Hellenic Cyprus* (official political organ of Cyprus Ethnarchy) 49; Gen. Sec. Cyprus Ethnarchy 53-57, Councillor 57-60; Amb. to Greece 60-, concurrently Amb. to Yugoslavia 63-, to Italy 64-, to Bulgaria 70-, to Romania 70-; Sec. of 2nd and 3rd Cyprus Nat. Assemblies 54, 55; Founder, Dir. (with others) of *Kypriaka Grammata*

(Cyprus Literature), a literary magazine 34-, Editor 46-56.

Leisure interests: reading, writing.

Publs. *Chronicles* (short stories) 45, *The Neohellenic Theatre* (essay) 50, *Studies* (poems) 51, *Forms of Myth* (short stories) 54, *The Poet G. Seferis* (essay) 55, *The National Character of Cyprus Literature* 58, *Cyprus in her Struggle for Freedom* (history) 58, *Introduction to the Poetry of G. Seferis* (essay) 65, *Cyprus-Greece* (essay) 66, *Cypriot Poetry* (essay) 69, *Kypriaka Grammata* (essay) 70, *Epistrophi* (poems) 74, *Poesie* (poems) 74, *The Cyprus Problem* (history) 75.

Embassy of Cyprus, 16 Herodotos Street, Athens, Greece; Home: 16 Prometheus Street, Nicosia, Cyprus. Telephone: 6715780 (Athens); 2907 (Nicosia).

Krapf, Franz; German diplomatist; b. 22 July 1911, Munich; m. Helga Gerdts; one s. two d.

Diplomatic Service 38-; formerly Legation Cairo, Embassy Moscow, Tokyo and Paris; later Minister German Del. to NATO, Paris and Embassy in Washington; Head, Eastern Dept., Ministry of Foreign Affairs 61-63; Ministerial Dir. and Head of Political Dept. for East-West Affairs 63-66; Amb. to Japan 66-71; Perm. Rep. to N. Atlantic Council 71-.

North Atlantic Council, NATO, Brussels 1110, Belgium.

Krapiva (*pseudonym* of Kondrat Kondratyevich Atrakhovich, D.SC.); Soviet writer; b. 5 March 1896, Nizok, Minsk Region, Byelorussia; ed. Byelorussian Univ.

People's Writer of Byelorussia 56; mem. C.P.S.U. 41-; Academician Byelorussian S.S.R. Acad. of Sciences 50-, Vice-Pres. 56-; State prizewinner 41, 50, 71, 74; awarded Order of Lenin (three times), Order of Red Banner of Labour, Red Star, October Revolution.

Publs. fables and sketches: *Nettle* 25, *Fables* 27; plays: *Who Laughs Last* 39, *The Larks Sing* 51, *Men and Devils* 48, *Gate of Immortality* 73; satirical poem *The Bible* 26; *Collected Works* (4 vols.) 63, *Forty Fables* 66, etc.

Byelorussian S.S.R. Academy of Sciences, 66 Leninsky Prospekt, Minsk, Byelorussia, U.S.S.R.

Kraško, Wincenty, M.A.; Polish politician; b. 1 June 1916, Kotowicze, U.S.S.R.; ed. Wilno Univ.

During German occupation worked in Wilno district; Sub-Editor *Dziennik Bałtycki* 45-51; Editor-in-Chief *Kurier Szczeciński*, subsequently *Głos Wielkopolski*, *Słowo Ludu* and *Gazeta Poznańska* 51-54; mem. Polish Workers' Party 48, Polish United Workers' Party (PZPR) 48; Sec. of Propaganda, Voivodship Cttee. PZPR, Poznań 54-57, First Sec., Voivodship Cttee. PZPR, Poznań 57-60; mem. Cen. Cttee. PZPR 59-; Head, Dept. of Culture, Cen. Cttee. PZRP 60-71, Sec. Cen. Cttee. 74-; Deputy to Seym 57-; Chair. Seym Comm. of Foreign Affairs March 72-; Chair. Polish Group of Interparliamentary Union March 72-; Vice-Pres. Council of Ministers 71-72; mem. State Council March 72-; Pres. Soc. for Connection with Poles Living Abroad (Polonia) July 72-; Chair. Polish Tourist and Country-Lovers Soc. 72-74; Order of Banner of Labour, 1st and 2nd Class, Gold Cross of Merit, Medal of 30th Anniversary of People's Poland, and other decorations.

Polska Zjednoczona Partia Robotnicza, Nowy Świat 6, 00-497 Warsaw, Poland.

Krasovskaya, Vera Mikhailovna; Soviet ballet historian and critic; b. 11 Sept. 1915; d. of Michail Krasovsky and Maria Krasovskaya; m. David Zolotnitsky 1949; one s.; ed. Choreographical School, Leningrad and Inst. of Theatre, Music and Cinematography, Leningrad. Ballet Dancer, Kirov Ballet 33-41; Senior Scientific Worker Inst. of Theatre, Music and Cinematography 53-, Prof. 75; mem. Union of Soviet Writers 66; Dr. of Arts 65.

Leisure interest: reading.

Publs. *Vachtang Chabukiani* 56, 60, *Russian Ballet Theatre from the Beginning to the Middle of the XIX Century* 58, *Leningrad's Ballet* 61, *Russian Ballet Theatre of the Second Half of the XIX Century* 63, *Anna Pavlova* 64, 65, *Russian Ballet Theatre at the beginning of the XX Century*, vol. I *Choreographers* 71, vol. II *Dancers* 72, *Nijinsky* 74.
Institute of Theatre, Music and Cinematography, Leningrad; Home: Leningrad 191011, Sadovaya 14, ap. 14, U.S.S.R.
Telephone: 14-90-95 (Home).

Krasovskiy, Nikolay Nikolayevich, DR. PHYS. AND MATH. SC.; Soviet mathematician and mechanician; b. 7 Sept. 1924, Sverdlovsk; ed. Ural Polytechnic Inst.
Teaching and scientific work, Ural Polytechnic Inst. 49-55, 57-59; Research worker, Inst. of Mechanics, U.S.S.R. Acad. of Sciences 55-57, Dir. Inst. of Mathematics and Mechanics 70-; Prof. Ural Univ. 59-; Corresp. mem. U.S.S.R. Acad. of Sciences 64-68, Academician 68-.
Publs. Works in field of stability of motion theory and theory of control.
Institute of Mathematics and Mechanics, Sverdlovsk, U.S.S.R.

Kraus, Otakar, O.B.E.; British bass opera singer; b. 1909, Prague, Czechoslovakia; ed. under Konrad Wallerstein in Prague and with Fernando Carpi in Milan.
Debut as Amonasro (in *Aida*), Brno 35; sang in Bratislava 36-39; went to U.K. 39; appeared at Savoy Theatre, London in *Sorochinsky Fair* 40; joined Carl Rosa Opera 43, English Opera Group 46; subsequently mem. Netherlands Opera; debut at Covent Garden as Scarpia (in *Tosca*) 50; mem. Covent Garden Opera 51-67; has appeared at Bayreuth, Vienna, Munich, La Scala Milan, Teatro Colón Buenos Aires, etc.; created roles of Nick Shadow (*The Rake's Progress*), Venice 57, Diomede (*Troilus and Cressida*) and King Fisher (*The Midsummer Marriage*) at Covent Garden.
223 Hamlet Gardens, London, W.6, England.

Krauskopf, Konrad Bates, PH.D.; American geologist; b. 30 Nov. 1910, Madison, Wis.; s. of Francis C. Krauskopf and Maude Bates Krauskopf; m. Kathryn Isabel McCune 1936; one s. three d.; ed. Univ. of Wisconsin, Univ. of Calif. and Stanford Univ.
Instructor in Chem., Univ. of Calif. 34-35; Asst. Prof. of Geology, Stanford Univ. 39-42, Assoc. Prof. 42-50, Prof. of Geochem. 50-, Assoc. Dean, School of Earth Sciences, Stanford Univ. 63-; Chief, Geographical Section, G.2, U.S. Army, Far East Command 47-48; Geologist, U.S. Geological Survey, various times 42-; Pres. American Geological Inst. 64, Geological Soc. of America 67; mem. Nat. Acad. of Sciences; Day Medal, Geological Soc. of America 61, Pres. Geochemical Soc. 70, Hon. D.Sc. (Univ. of Wisconsin) 71.
Publs. *Fundamentals of Physical Science* 41 (6th edn. 71), *Introduction to Geochemistry* 67, *The Third Planet* 74; articles in technical scientific journals.
Office: Geology Department, Stanford University, Calif. 94305; Home: 806 La Mesa Drive, Menlo Park, Calif. 94025, U.S.A.
Telephone: 415-497-3325 (Office); 415-854-4506 (Home).

Krayer, Otto Hermann, M.D.; American pahrmacologist and educator; b. 22 Oct. 1899, Koendringen i. Br., Germany; s. of Hermann Krayer and Frieda Berta Wolfsperger; m. Erna Ruth Philipp, M.D., 1939; ed. Univs. of Freiburg, Munich and Berlin.
Lecturer (Privatdozent) on Pharmacology and Toxicology, Univ. of Berlin 29-32; Prof of Pharmacology and Toxicology, Univ. of Berlin 32-33, Acting Head, Dept. of Pharmacology, 30-32; Visiting Prof. and Head Dept. of Pharmacology American Univ. of Beirut, Lebanon 34-37; Assoc. Prof. of Pharmacology, Harvard Medical School, Boston 37-39, Head, Dept. of Pharmacology, Harvard Medical School 39-66, Assoc. Prof. of Comparative Pharmacology 39-51, Prof of Pharmacology 51-54, Charles Wilder Prof. of Pharmacology 54-64, Gustavus Adolphus Pfeiffer Prof. of Pharmacology 64-66, Emeritus 66-; mem. Nat. Acad. of Sciences, American Acad. of Arts and Sciences, German Leopoldina Acad., Swiss Acad. of Medical Sciences; Pres. American Soc. for Pharmacology and Exp. Therapeutics 57-58; Torald-Sollmann Award in Pharmacology 61; Schmiedeberg-Plakette 64; Research Achievement Award American Heart Asscn. 69.
Leisure interests: reading (philosophy, poetry, historical and biographical literature), hiking.
Publs. Scientific reports on physiology and pharmacology of autonomic system and on heart and circulation; exp. studies on pharmacology of Veratrum alkaloids and of Rauwolfia alkaloids.
Apartment 202, 3940 East Timrod Street, Tucson, Arizona 85711, U.S.A.
Telephone: 602-881-2019.

Krayevsky, Nikolai Alexandrovich; Soviet pathologist; b. 17 Sept. 1905, Pashkovo, Smolensk Region; ed. Moscow Univ.
Assistant, Moscow Univ. 28-30; Asst., Inst. of Occupational Diseases 30-32; Asst., Lecturer, Prof., Second Moscow Medical Inst. 31-54; Head of Laboratory, Cen. Inst. of Hematology and Blood Transfusion 39-51; Head of Dept., Cen. Inst. for Postgraduate Medical Training 54-60; Corresp. mem. U.S.S.R. Acad. of Medical Sciences 53-60, mem. 60-; Academician-Sec. U.S.S.R. Acad. of Medical Sciences 60-62; Head of Dept., Inst. of Experimental and Clinical Oncology, U.S.S.R. Acad. of Medical Sciences 62-; Chair. of Board of All-Union Scientific Soc. of Pathologists; mem. WHO Expert Advisory Panel; mem. Editorial Board of *Archives of Pathology*; Order of Red Star 44, Patriotic War, First Class 45, Badge of Honour, Lenin Prize 63.
Publs. Over 150 works on gastric pathology, morbid anatomy of hemotransfusional complications, and radiation complications in oncology.
Institute of Experimental and Clinical Oncology, Kashirskoye Chaussée 6, Moscow, U.S.S.R.

Krebs, Sir Hans (Adolf), M.D., M.A., F.R.S.; British biochemist; b. 25 Aug. 1900, Hildesheim (Germany); m. Margaret Fieldhouse 1938; two s. one d.; ed. Univs. of Göttingen, Freiburg, Munich, Berlin, Hamburg and Cambridge.
Priv. doz., Univ. of Freiburg 32-33; Demonstrator in Biochemistry, Cambridge Univ. 34; Lecturer in Pharmacology, Sheffield Univ. 35-45, in charge of Dept. of Biochemistry 38-45, Prof. of Biochemistry 45-54; Whitley Prof. Oxford Univ. 54-67; foreign mem. Accad. Nazionale dei Lincei, Académie de Médecine and Société de Biologie; Foreign Assoc. U.S. Nat. Acad. of Sciences; hon. degrees from Paris, Chicago, Freiburg-im-Breisgau, Glasgow, Sheffield, London, Leicester, Bristol, Jerusalem, Berlin (Humboldt), Granada, Leeds, Wales, Bordeaux, Hanover, Valencia and Pennsylvania Univs.; Lasker Award 53 and Nobel Prize (jointly) for Physiology 53; Copley Medal, Royal Soc. 61, Gold Medal, Royal Soc. of Medicine 65; Hon. mem. Deutsche Akademie der Naturforscher Leopoldina 69, Deutsche Gesellschaft für innere Medizin, Asscn. of Amer. Physicians; Hon. Fellow, Weizmann Inst. of Science.
27 Abberbury Road, Iffley, Oxford, England.

Krehbiel, V. John; American insurance executive and diplomatist; b. 29 July 1905, Castleton, Kan.; s. of John D. and Caroline Krehbiel; m. Elizabeth Findlay 1929; one d.; ed. Univ. of Kansas.
With AETNA Life Insurance Agency 29-72; Amb. to Finland 73-75; Chair. Republican Cen. Cttee. for Calif. 58-62; Vice-Chair. Republican Finance Cttee. 60-62;

mem. Trade Mission to Germany 59, to Scandinavian countries 72.
Leisure interest: golf.
c/o Department of State, 2201 C Street, N.W., Washington, D.C. 20520; Home: 132 Monarch Bay, South Laguna, Calif., U.S.A.
Telephone: (Helsinki) 11931.

Kreifels, Max; German lawyer; b. 14 July 1926, Düsseldorf; s. of Dr. Anton Kreifels and Therese Krüsemann; m. Hannelore Purucker 1954; two s. one d.; ed. Heidelberg Univ.
Executive Asst. IG Farben-Industrie i.L. 51-53; private law practice Bruckhaus, Kreifels, Winkhaus and Lieberknecht, Düsseldorf 53-; Chair., Vice-Chair. and mem. of several nat. and int. Supervisory Boards and Boards of Dirs.
Leisure interest: motor-yachting.
Publs. co-author *Frankfurter Kommentar zum Kartellgesetz*, various publs. in *Aktienrechtsreform*.
4 Düsseldorf, Berliner Allee 2, Federal Republic of Germany.
Telephone: (0211) 35-30-81.

Kreisky, Bruno, LL.D.; Austrian diplomatist and politician; b. 22 Jan. 1911, Vienna; s. of Max and Irene (née Felix) Kreisky; m. Vera Fuerth 1942; one s. one d.; ed. Univ. of Vienna.
Active mem. Austrian Social Democratic Party to 34; arrested and imprisoned 35 and again 38, when escaped to Sweden; mem. scientific staff Stockholm Co-operative Society 39-46; joined Austrian Foreign Service 46; Austrian Legation, Stockholm 46-51; Austrian Fed. President's Office 51-53; State Sec. for Foreign Affairs in Fed. Chancellery 53; elected to Parl. 56; Minister of Foreign Affairs 59-66; Chair. Socialist Party of Austria 67-; Fed. Chancellor of Austria 70-; initiator and Vice-Pres. Theodor Körner Fund for Promotion of Arts and Sciences; Vice-Chair. of Board, Inst. for Advanced Studies and Scientific Research, Vienna; Pres. Vienna Inst. for Devt.; Gold Grand Cross of Honour and twenty-three foreign awards.
Leisure interests: history, baroque art.
Publ. *The Challenge.*
Bundeskanzleramt, Ballhausplatz 2, 1010 Vienna; also Armbrustergasse 15, 1190 Vienna, Austria.
Telephone: 66-15-0.

Krejča, Otomar; Czechoslovak actor and director; b. 23 Nov. 1921, Skrýšov; ed. Charles Univ., Prague.
Member Prague Nat. Theatre 51-69, Art Chief, Nat. Theatre Drama Section 56-61; Artistic Dir. of Divadlo za branou (Theatre Beyond the Gate) 65-71, Dir. 71-72; Producer Divadlo S. K. Neumanna 73-; Chair. Union of Czechoslovak Theatre Artists 65-69; Chair. Union of Czech Theatre and Broadcasting Artists 69-70; State Prize 51, 68, Honoured Artist 58.
Plays directed include: *The Seagull* (Chekhov), *Romeo and Juliet* (Shakespeare), *Hamlet* (Shakespeare); Guest Dir. *Hamlet* and *The Seagull*, Nat. Theatre, Brussels 65, 66, *Romeo and Juliet*, Cologne, *The Seagull*, Stockholm.
Prague 8, Kubišova 26, Czechoslovakia.

Krejčí, Ing. Josef; Czechoslovak engineer and politician; b. 29 Jan. 1912, Pochválov; ed. secondary school, Rakovník, and Prague Coll. of Machine and Electrical Engineering.
Formerly in machine tool design dept., Škoda Works, Prague; later Lecturer, Czech Technical Univ., Prague; also worked in State Inst. for Testing Engines and Motors; Škoda Works, Plzeň 37-45, Pipe-Rolling Plant, Chomutov 45-49, Dir. of Production 49-52, Chief Engineer 54-56, Dir. 56-61, also Dir. of Steel Works, Most; First Deputy Minister of Metallurgy and Ore Mines 61-62, Minister 62-65; Deputy Premier and

Minister of Heavy Industry 65-68, Minister of Heavy Industry 68; Minister, Chair. of Fed. Comm. for Industry 69-70; Deputy, House of the People, Fed. Assembly 69-71; mem. Council for Int. Economic Scientific and Tech. Co-operation 69-71; Cand. mem. Cen. Cttee. of C.P. of Czechoslovakia 62-66, mem. 64-70; mem. Econ. Comm. 63-66; Deputy to Nat. Assembly 64-69; Commercial counsellor, Embassy of Č.S.S.R., Warsaw 70-; Order of Labour 52, 59.
Gottwaldovo nábř. 38, Prague 1, Czechoslovakia.

Krekeler, Heinz L., DR. PHIL.; German diplomatist; b. 20 July 1906, Bottrop; s. of Heinrich and Helene (née Lindemann) Krekeler; m. 1st Ilse Goebel 1931 (died 1963), 2nd Helga Finke 1965; one s.; ed. Univs. of Freiburg, Munich, Göttingen and Berlin.
Chemical engineer with different firms 30-46; mem. Lippe Diet 46, Diet of North Rhine-Westphalia 47-50, Fed. Assembly 49; partner and fmr. Dir. F. Eilers-Schünemann Verlag (Publishers), Bremen 48-; Consul-Gen. in N.Y. 50-51; Chargé d'Affaires, Fed. Republic of Germany, Washington, D.C. 51-53, Ambassador 53-58; mem. Euratom Comm. 58-64; Lecturer on Int. Relations and Political Science, Hochschule für Politische Wissenschaften, Munich; mem. Deutsche Gesellschaft für Auswärtige Politik, Advisory Cttee., Bologna Center, Johns Hopkins Univ.; mem. Max-Planck-Gesellschaft zur Förderung der Wissenschaften; Grand Cross of Order of Merit, 2nd Class (Germany); Grande Ufficiale dell'Ordine al Merito 59; Commendatore con Placca dell'Ordine S. Gregorio il Grande; Grand Officier Ordre de Léopold; Hon. LL.D. Xavier and Univ. of South Carolina.
Leisure interests: shooting (deer stalking), yachting, travelling.
Publs. *Die Diplomatie* 65, *Die Aussenpolitik* 67, *Wissenschaft und Politik* 75.
Gut Lindemannshof, 4902 Bad Salzuflen, Federal Republic of Germany.
Telephone: 05222 8-17-57.

Kremp, Herbert, DR.PHIL.; German journalist; b. 12 Aug. 1928, Munich; s. of Johann and Elisabeth Kremp; m. Brigitte Kremp 1956; two d.; ed. Munich Univ.
Reporter, *Frankfurter Neue Presse* 56-57; Political Editor *Rheinische Post* 57-59; Dir. Political Dept., *Der Tag*, Berlin 59-61; Bonn Corresp. *Rheinische Post* 61-63; Editor-in-Chief, *Rheinische Post* 63-68; Editor-in-Chief, *Die Welt* Jan. 69-.
Die Welt, 53 Bonn-Bad Godesberg, Kölner Strasse 99, Federal Republic of Germany.
Telephone: 304312.

Krenek, Ernst; American composer; b. 23 Aug. 1900 in Austria; ed. Univ. of Vienna and Acads. of Music in Vienna and Berlin.
Lived in Switzerland 23-25; Asst. to Dir. of Staatstheater, Kassel 25-27; lived in Vienna 27-37; emigrated to U.S.A. 37; Prof. of Music, Vassar Coll. 39-42; Prof. of Music and Dean of Fine Arts, Hamline Univ., St. Paul, Minn. 42-47; Grosses Bundesverdienstkreuz 65; Hamburg Bach Prize 66.
Compositions include: *Der Sprung über den Schatten* 23, *Orpheus und Eurydike* 23, *Jonny Spielt Auf* 25-26, *Dark Waters* 50, *Sardakai* 67-69 (operas); *Karl V* 30-33, *Pallas Athene* 52-55, *Sestina* 57, *Quaestio Temporis* 59, *Golden Ram* 62, *Horizon Circled* 67, *Perspectives* 67-68, *Kitharaulos* 71, *Statics Ecstatic* 72-73; symphonies: *No. 1* 21, *No. 2* 22, *No. 3* 22, *No. 4* 47, *No. 5* 49; piano concertos: *No. 3* 46, *No. 4* 56.
Publs. *Music Here and Now* 39, *Studies in Counterpoint* 40, *Musik im goldenen Westen* 49, *Zur Sprache gebracht* 58, *Gedanken unterwegs* 59, *Glauben und Wissen* 67.
c/o BMI, 40 West 57th Street, New York, N.Y. 10019, U.S.A.

Krenz, Jan; Polish conductor and composer; b. 14 July 1926, Włocławek; *m.* Alina Krenz; one *s.*; ed. Warsaw and Łódź.

Conductor Łódź Philharmonic Orch. 45; Conductor, Poznań Philharmonic Orch. 48-49; Dir. and First Conductor Polish Radio Symphony Orch., Katowice 53-67; Artistic Dir., First Conductor Grand Opera House (Teatr Wielki), Warsaw 67-73; tours in Hungary, Romania, Czechoslovakia, France, U.S.S.R., Germany, Italy, U.K., U.S.A., Japan, Australia etc.; State Prize 55, 72; Prize Minister of Culture and Art 55, 63; Prize of Union of Polish Composers 68; Grand Prix du Disque, France 72; numerous decorations.

Compositions include Symphony, two String Quartets, *Nocturnes for Orchestra, Rozmowa dwóch miast* (Conversation of Two Towns) (cantata), *Rhapsody for Strings, Xylophone, Tam-Tam, Timpani and Celesta* 52, *Concertino for Piano and Small Symphony Orchestra* 52; orchestral transcriptions of three fugues from *The Art of Fugue* (J. S. Bach) entitled: *Polyphonic Suite* 50, *Classical Serenade* 50; orchestral transcriptions of *Microcosm* (B. Bartók) 58, *Masses* (Szymanowski) 64. Leisure interest: painting.

Al. 1 Armii Wojska Polskiego 16/38, 00-582 Warsaw, Poland.

Kreps, Yevgeny Mikhailovich; Soviet physiologist; b. 1 May 1899, Leningrad; ed. Military Medical Acad.

Post graduate student and Junior Instructor, Mil. Med. Acad. 25-31; Head, Physiological Laboratory Murman Biological Station 23-33; worked in England 30-31; mem. Emergency Rescue Cttee., U.S.S.R. Navy 31-51; Prof. Leningrad Univ. 34-37; Head, Lab. of Comparative Physiology and Biochemistry, Pavlov Inst. of Physiology, U.S.S.R. Acad. of Sciences 36-60; Dir. Inst. of Evolutionary Physiology and Biochemistry, U.S.S.R. Acad. of Sciences 60-; Corresp. mem. U.S.S.R. Acad. of Sciences 46-66, mem. 66-; Academic Sec. Physiology Branch, U.S.S.R. Acad. of Sciences 66-, Hero of Socialist Labour 69.

Publs. Works on comparative physiology and biochemistry of nervous system, respiratory function of blood.

Institute of Evolutionary Physiology, Prospekt M. Toreza 52, Leningrad K-223, U.S.S.R.

Kreyberg, Leiv, M.D.; Norwegian pathologist; b. 22 May 1896, Bergen; *s.* of Dr. Peter Christian Kreyberg and Elizabeth (née Konow); *m.* Emmie Louise Klem 1924; two *s.* two *d.*

Professor of Pathology, Oslo Univ. 38-64, Emeritus Prof. 64-; mem. Acad. Science and Letters, Oslo; cancer research and experimental pathology; Chair. Biological Soc. Oslo 28-30, Union of Pathologists 46-47; Vice-Pres. (Europe) Int. Union against Cancer 54-58; hon. mem. Indian Asscn. Pathologists; Soc. Française d'Angiologie and Swedish Medical Asscn., Austrian Cancer Soc., Belgian Pathological Soc., Pathological Soc. of Great Britain and Ireland; Consultant in Cancer, WHO; Dr. h.c. (Perugia) 65, (Brno) 69; Commdr. of Royal Order of St. Olav.

Leisure interests: fishing and hunting.

Publs. on experimental pathology, especially problems of damage by cold, carcinogenesis and lung cancer. Books: *Histological Lung Cancer Types* 62, *Histological Typing of Lung Cancer* (WHO Geneva) 67, *Aetiology of Lung Cancer* 69, *Afghanistan* 51, *Stasis and Necrosis* 63.

Munkedams vei 79, Oslo, Norway.

Telephone: 449208.

Kripalani, Acharaya Jiwatram Bhagwandas, M.A.; Indian politician; b. 1888.

Professor in Bihar under Calcutta Univ. 12-17; worked with Gandhi 17-18, with Pandit Madan Mohan Malaviya 18; Prof. of Politics, Benares Hindu Univ. 19-20; active in Khadi and village work and Dir. Gandhi Ashram, U.P. 20-; Principal of Gujarat Vidyapith 22-27; im-

prisoned 42-45; Pres. Indian Nat. Congress 46-47; mem. Constituent Assembly 46-51; formed Congress Democratic Front 51; founded *Vigil*, political weekly 50; formed Kisan Mazdoor Praja Party 51; mem. Lok Sabha (Parl.) 52-62, 63-70.

Publs. *The Gandhian Way, The Non-Violent Revolution, The Indian National Congress, The Politics of Charkha, The Future of the Congress, The Fateful Year, Gandhi the Statesman, Basic Education, Gandhi—Life and Thought.*

A4 Sarnodaya Eudlavi, New Delhi 17; and Shri Gandhi Ashram, Lucknow, Uttar Pradesh, India.

Krishna Moorthi, C. S.; Indian civil servant; b. 1921; ed. Madras Univ.

Ordnance Officer, Indian Army 43-46; Asst. Commr. Refugees, Punjab 47-48; Sub-Collector and Joint Magistrate, Madras State 48-52; Board of Revenue, Madras 52-53; Ministry of Finance 54-58; Counsellor, Indian Comm.-Gen. for Econ. Affairs, Washington 58; Alt. Exec. Dir. Int. Bank for Reconstruction and Devt. and Int. Finance Corpn. 58; Minister (Econ.) Indian Embassy, Washington 61-63, Exec. Dir. for India, Int. Bank for Reconstruction and Development, Int. Finance Corpn. and Int. Development Asscn. 62-63; Joint Sec. Dept. of Econ. Affairs, Ministry of Finance, New Delhi 63-66; Vice-Pres. Asian Devt. Bank, Manila, Philippines 66-.

Asian Development Bank, P.O. Box 789, Manila 2800, Philippines.

Telephone: 80-72-51/143 (Office); 87-64-40 (Home).

Krishnan, Rappal Sangameswara, D.SC., PH.D., Indian physicist; b. 1911, Rappal, Kerala; *s.* of R. P. Sangameswara Iyer and C. R. Ammani Ammal; *m.* Rajammal 1934; two *s.* three *d.*; ed. Univ. of Madras, St. Joseph's Coll., Trichy, Indian Inst. of Science, and Trinity Coll., Cambridge.

Research Asst. Indian Inst. of Science 35-38; 1851 Exhibition Overseas Scholar, Univ. of Cambridge 38-41; Lecturer in Physics, Inst. of Science 42-45, Asst. Prof. 45-48, Prof. and Head of Dept. of Physics 48-72, Emer. Prof. 72-73; Vice-Chancellor Kerala Univ. 73-; Fellow of Inst. of Physics, London, of American Physical Soc., of Indian Acad. of Sciences and of Nat. Inst. of Sciences; Pres. Physics Section, Indian Science Congress 49; Nat. Science Foundation Senior Foreign Scientist, Fellow, Dept. of Physics, North Texas State Univ. Denton, Texas 71-72; Original contributions to colloid optics (Krishnan Effect), light-scattering, Raman effect, crystal physics, etc.

Leisure interests: tennis, photography.

Publs. *Progress in Crystal Physics*, Vol. I 58, *Two Chapters in Raman Effect*, Vol. I 71, and contributions to other books.

Kerala University, Trivandrum 6 95001, India.

Telephone: Trivandrum 60058 (Office); Trivandrum 60858 (Home).

Krishnaswamy, K. S., PH.D.; Indian bank official; b. 1920, Chikkamagalur; *m.* Madhura Krishnaswamy 1947; one *s.* one *d.*; ed. Univ. of Mysore and London School of Economics.

Lecturer in Econs., Univ. of Bombay 46-47; Research Officer, Planning Comm., New Delhi; Research Officer, Research Dept., Reserve Bank of India, Bombay 52-54; Deputy Dir. of Research, Research Dept. 54-56; Staff mem. Econ. Devt. Inst. (World Bank), Wash., D.C. 56-59; Deputy Chief, Industrial Finance Dept., Reserve Bank of India 59-61; Chief, Econ. Policy Section, Planning Comm. 61-64, Econ. Adviser, Planning Comm. 64-67; Dir. Econ. Devt. Inst., Int. Bank for Reconstruction and Devt. 67-71; Principal Adviser Reserve Bank of India 72, Exec. Dir. 73-, Deputy-Gov. 75-.

Leisure interests: music and letters.

Reserve Bank of India, Central Office, Bombay 400001, India.

Kriss, Anatoli Evseevich; Soviet microbiologist; b. 16 Sept. 1908; ed. Leningrad Medical Inst.
Scientific worker, Inst. of Microbiology, U.S.S.R. Acad. of Sciences 35-; Dr. of Biological Sciences 47; Head of Marine Microbiology Dept., Inst. of Microbiology 48-; Head of Electron Microscopy Laboratory, U.S.S.R. Acad. of Sciences 46-; microbiological research, Antarctic 67-; awarded title of Prof. of Microbiology 50; Lenin Prize 60.
Publs. *The Variability of Actinomycetes* 37, *Deep-Sea Microbiology* 59 (German edn. 61, English edn. 63, Japanese edn. 63), *Microbial Population of the World Ocean* 64, and over 150 scientific papers.
U.S.S.R. Academy of Sciences, 14 Leninsky Prospekt, Moscow, U.S.S.R.

Kristensen, Sven Möller, DR. PHIL.; Danish writer, literary critic and editor; b. 12 Nov. 1909, Darum, Jutland; *m.* Hanne Hahne 1937; three *d.*; ed. Copenhagen Univ.
Literary and Theatre Critic, *Land og Folk* 45-53; Editor *Athenæm* (literary magazine) 45-49, *Dialog* 50-53; Prof. of Scandinavian Literature Aarhus Univ. 53-64, Copenhagen Univ. 64-; mem. Danish Acad. 60; mem. Norwegian Acad. of Science 68.
Leisure interest: music.
Publs. *Æstetiske studier i dansk fiktionsprosa 1870-1900* 38, *Digteren og samfundet I-II* 42, 45; *Amerikansk litteratur 1920-1940* 42, *Dansk Litteratur 1918-1950* 50, *En musaik af moderne dansk litteratur* 54, *Digtningens Teori* 58, *Digtning og Livssyn* 59, *Vurderinger* 61, *Den dobbelte Eros* 66, *Frammede digterei det 20 aarhundrede* (editor) 67-68, *Litteratursociologiske* (essays) 70, *Den store generation* 74.
Copenhagen University, Vingaards allé 53, 2900 Hellerup, Denmark.
Telephone: Hellerup 1521.

Kristensen, Thorkil; Danish business economist; b. 9 Oct. 1899; ed. High School, Askov and Univ. of Copenhagen.
Teacher at Commercial Acad., Aarhus 27; Inspector of Savings-Banks 28-35; Asst. Lecturer, Univ. of Copenhagen 36-38; Prof. of Business Economics, Univ. of Aarhus 38; Copenhagen School of Economics 48; Minister of Finance 45-47, 50-53; mem. of Board of Court of Conciliation in Labour questions 40-45; mem. of Folketing 45-60; mem. Acad. of Technical Sciences 46-; Sec.-Gen. OEEC 60-61; Chair. Preparatory Cttee. Organisation for Economic Co-operation and Development (OECD) 60-61, Sec.-Gen. 61-69; Dir. Inst. for Devt. Research, Copenhagen 69-72.
Publs. *Danmarks Driftsregnskab* 30, *Undersøgelser af det kommunale Skattespørgsmaal* 35, *Faste og variable Omkostninger* 39, *Haandbog i Kredit og Hypotekforeningsforhold* 44, *The Economic World Balance* 60, *The food problem of developing countries* 68, *U-landsplanlaegning: Landrug contra industrie* 68, *Development in Rich and Poor Countries* 74.
18 Odinsvej, 3460 Birkerod, Denmark.

Kristensen, Tom; Danish writer; b. 4 Aug. 1893, London; ed. Henrik Madsens School, Copenhagen Univ.
Literary critic of *Politiken* 24-27 and 31-63; mem. Exec. Cttee. Danish Society of Authors 41-44, The Danish Acad. 60; Knight of Dannebrog 59; awarded Holberg Medal 45, Aarestrup Medal 54.
Publs. *Fribytterdrømme* (poems) 20, *Livets Arabesk* (novel) 21, *Mirakler* (poems) 22, *Paafuglefjeren* (poems) 22, *En Anden* (novel) 23, *En Kavaler i Spanien* (prose and poems) 26, *Verdslige Sange* (poems) 27, *Sophus Claussen* 29, *Haervaerk* (novel) 30, *En Fribytters Ord* (poems) 33, *Vindrosen* (short stories) 34, *Mod den yderste Rand* (poems) 36, *Digte i Døgnet* (poems) 40, *Harry Martinson* 41, *Mellem Scylla og Charybdis,* (collected poems from the twenties) 43, *Mellem Krigene* (essays) 46, *Hvad er Heta?* (short stories) 46, *En Omvej*

til Andorra (prose) 47, *Den syngende busk* (poems) 49, *Rejse i Italien* (prose) 50, *De forsvundne Ansigter* (poems) 53, *Til Dags Dato* (essays) 53, *En Bogorms Barndom* (autobiography) 53, *Den sidste Lygte* (poems) 54, *Det skabende Øje* (essays) 56, *Oplevelser med Lyrik* (essays) 57, *Den evige Uro* (essays) 58, *Hvad er Heta og andre fortaellinger* (short stories from Copenhagen) 59, *Harlekin Skelet* (detective story) 62, *I min Tid* (essays), *Udvalgte digte* (selected poems) 63, *Kriliher eller anmelder* (essays) 66, *Abenhyerlige Forliesen* (autobiog.) 66, *Bøger, bøger, bøger* (essays) 67.
Torelore, Thurø, Denmark.
Telephone: 205059.

Kristiansen, Erling (Engelbrecht); Danish diplomatist and government official; b. 31 Dec. 1912, Terndrup; *s.* of the late Kristian E. Kristiansen and Andrea Madsen; *m.* Annemarie Selinko 1938; ed. Herning Gymnasium, Univs. of Copenhagen and Geneva, Paris and London.
Danish Civil Service, Ministry of Labour 41, with Free Danish Legations Stockholm 43, Washington 44, London 45; Commercial Sec. Danish Legation, London 45-47; Head, Del. to Org. for European Economic Co-operation (OEEC) 48-50; Sec., Economic Cttee. of Cabinet 50-51; Asst. Under-Sec. of State, Ministry of Foreign Affairs 51-53, Deputy Under-Sec. 54-64; Amb. to U.K. 64-, concurrently to Ireland 64-73; Chair. Danish Dels. to major econ. confs. 54-63; Knight Commdr. Order of Dannebrog, Grand Officier Légion d'Honneur, Knight Grand Cross, The Royal Victorian Order, Order of Falcon of Iceland and other decorations.
Leisure interests: outdoor sports, languages.
Publ. *Folkeforbundet* (The League of Nations) 38.
Royal Danish Embassy, 29 Pont Street, London, SW1X 0BA; 1 Cadogan Square, London, S.W.1, England.
Telephone: 01-584-0102 (Office).

Kristiansen, Georg; Norwegian diplomatist; b. 4 March 1917; ed. Univ. of Oslo and Norwegian War Coll.
Army Service 40-45; Sec., Ministry of Foreign Affairs 46-47; Attaché, Paris 47-52; Sec. later Counsellor, Ministry of Foreign Affairs 52-57; Instructor Nat. Defence Coll., Oslo 57-59; Dir. later Dir.-Gen. Political Affairs, Ministry of Foreign Affairs 59-64; Perm. Rep. to NATO 64-70, and OECD 64-67; Dir.-Gen. Civil Defence and Emergency Planning 70-74; Amb. to OECD 74-.
109 avenue Henri-Martin, Paris 75116, France.

Krleža, Miroslav; Yugoslav writer; b. 7 July 1893. Director, Yugoslav Lexicographical Inst.
Publs. include *The Return of Phillip Latinovicz, On the Verge of Reason, A Banquet in Blithonamia, Flags* (novels); *God Mars of Croatia, 1001 Deaths* (short stories); *In Agony, Golgotha, The Glembaj Cycle, Aretaeus* (plays); *The Ballads of Petrica Kerempuh, Beisetzung in Theresienburg* 64, *Europäisches Alphabet* 64, *Essays* (6 vols.), *Collected Poems* (7 vols.), *Legends* (7 plays: *Michelangelo, Christopher Columbus,* etc.).
c/o Yugoslav Lexicographical Institute, Zagreb; Strossmayer trg. 4, Zagreb, Yugoslavia.

Krogman, Wilton, PH.D., LL.D., D.SC.; American physical anthropologist; b. 28 June 1903, Oak Park, Ill.; *s.* of Wilhelm Claus Krogman and Lydia Magdalena Wriedt; *m.* 1st Virginia M. Lane 1931 (divorced 1944), 2nd Mary Helen Winkley 1945; three *s.* one *d.*; ed. Univ. of Chicago, Western Reserve Univ. and Royal Coll. of Surgeons, London.
Instructor, Univ. of Chicago 29-30, Assoc. Prof. of Anatomy and Physical Anthropology 38-47; Assoc. Prof. of Anatomy and Physical Anthropology Western Reserve Univ. 31-38; Prof. of Physical Anthropology Graduate School of Medicine, Univ. of Pennsylvania and Dir. Philadelphia Center for Research in Child Growth 47-71; mem. Nat. Acad. of Sciences; Viking

Medal in Physical Anthropology 50, Ketcham Award of American Asscn. of Orthodontists 69.
Leisure interests: fishing, beachcombing.
Publs. *Bibliography of Human Morphology* 41, *Growth of Man* 41, *Syllabus in Roentgenographic Cephalometry* (with V. Sassouni) 57, *Human Skeleton in Forensic Medicine* 62, *Child Growth* 72.
Lancaster Cleft Palate Clinic, 24 North Lime Street, Lancaster, Pa. 17602; Home: 1127 Spring Grove Avenue, Lancaster, Pa. 17603, U.S.A.
Telephone: (717) 394-3793 (Office); (717) 299-2793 (Home).

Krohn, Hans-Broder, DR. AGRIC. SC.; German international official; b. 9 July 1915, Bredstedt; s. of Carl Krohn and Emma Amalia Nissen; m. Ilse Philipp 1941; two s. one d.; ed. Univ. of Göttingen.
Private Sec. to Minister of Food, Agriculture and Forestry; Head of Div., FAO, OECD; with EEC Comm., participated in drawing up the common agricultural policy 58; Dir. of Agricultural Econs. and Legis., Directorate-Gen. of Agric. 62, Deputy Dir.-Gen. of Agric. 68; Dir.-Gen. for Devt., Comm. of the European Communities 70-; Commdr. Order of Merit (Italy), Ordre Nat. (Senegal); Grand Officier Ordre Nat. (Madagascar), Ordre du Mono (Togo).
Leisure interests: gardening, antiques.
Publs. *Die Futtergetreidewirtschaft der Welt 1900-1955* 57, *Agrarpolitik in Europa* 62, *Das Abkommen von Lomé zwischen der Europäischen Gemeinschaft und den AKP-Staaten* 75.
Directorate-General for Development, Commission of the European Communities, 200 rue de la Loi, 1049 Brussels, Belgium.
Telephone: 735-80-40, 735-80-30.

Krol, H.E. Cardinal John Joseph, J.C.D.; American ecclesiastic; b. 26 Oct. 1910, Cleveland, O.; s. of John and Anna (Pietruszka) Krol; ed. St. Mary's Seminary, Cleveland and Pontifical Gregorian Univ., Rome, Pontifical Catholic Univ. of America.
Ordained Priest 37; Prof. of Canon Law, St. Mary's Seminary, Vice-Chancellor, Diocese of Cleveland 43-51, Chancellor 51-53; Titular Bishop of Cadi, Auxiliary Bishop to Bishop of Cleveland, also Vicar-Gen. 53-61; Archbishop of Philadelphia 61-; cr. Cardinal by Pope Paul VI 67; mem. Pontifical Comm. for Mass Media Communications 64-69; Vice-Pres. Nat. Conf. of Catholic Bishops and U.S. Catholic Conf. 66-72, Pres. 73-75; mem. Pontifical Comm. for Revision of Code of Canon Law 73-; Dr. h.c. of twelve Amer. univs.; numerous decorations.
222 North 17th Street, Philadelphia, Pa. 19103; Home: 5700 City Avenue, Philadelphia, Pa. 19131, U.S.A.

Krolikowski, Werner; German politician; b. 1928; m.; two c.
Joined Sozialistische Einheitspartei Deutschlands (SED) 46-; mem. Cen. Cttee. 63-; mem. Politburo 71-; First Sec. Dresden County Cttee. of SED.
102 Berlin, Am Marx-Engels-Platz 2, German Democratic Republic.

Krolow, Karl; German poet and essayist; b. 11 May 1915; ed. Univs. of Göttingen and Breslau.
Writer 42-; mem. Deutsche Akad. für Sprache und Dichtung (Vice-Pres. 66, Pres. 72), Mainzer Akad. der Wissenschaften und der Literatur, Acad. of Fine Arts of Bavaria, PEN Club; Georg Büchner Prize 56, Grosser Niedersächsischer Kunstpreis 65.
Publs. Poetry: *The Signs of the World* 52, *Wind and Time* 54, *Days and Nights* 56, *Foreign Bodies* 59, *Selected Poems* 62, *Invisible Hands* 62, *Collected Poems* 65, *Landscapes for Me* 65, *Everyday Poems* 68, *Nothing More than Living* 70, *Time Passing* 72; Essays: *Aspects of Contemporary German Lyric Poetry* 61, *Schattengefecht* 64, *Poetisches Tagebuch* 66; Trans.: *Contemporary French Lyric Poetry* 57, *Spanish Poems of the 20th Century* 62.
61 Darmstadt, Rosenhöhe 5, Federal Republic of Germany.

Krombholc, Jaroslav; Czech conductor; b. 30 Jan. 1918, Prague; ed. Conservatoire and Charles Univ., Prague.
Guest Conductor, Prague National Theatre and Czech Philharmonic Orchestra 40; mem. Board of Trustees, Prague Nat. Theatre Opera House 45-49, Chief Conductor 45-74, Conductor 74; Conductor Prague Nat. Theatre 49-62, First Conductor 63-68; Head of Prague Nat. Theatre Opera 68-70; Chief Conductor Czechoslovak Radio Symphony Orchestra, Prague 73-; toured U.S.S.R. with Nat. Theatre 55, visited Berlin 56, Brussels 58, staged *Její pastorkyňa* (*Jenufa*, Janáček), Vienna Opera 47, *Bartered Bride* (Smetana), Budapest 49, London 67, Warsaw 69, *Catherine Ismailovna* (Shostakovich) 65, *Katya Kabanová* (Janáček), Naples 68, *The excursions of Mr. Brouček* (Janáček), Vienna 70; Guest Conductor in Romania, Bulgaria, Rio de Janeiro, Copenhagen, Vienna, Warsaw, Poznań, France, London; State Prize 49, 55; Honoured Artist 58; Nat. Artist 66.
National Theatre, Divadelní 6, Prague, Czechoslovakia.

Kronacker, Baron Paul Georges, O.B.E., DR.SC.; Belgian Minister of State and industrialist; b. 5 Nov. 1897, Antwerp; s. of Leopold Kronacker and Marie-Laure Brunard; m. Mary Elisabeth Good 1948; two s. one d.; ed. Univ. of Brussels.
Lieut.-Col. Reserve; served army 15-19; Chair. and Dir. various industrial concerns, particularly in sugar industry; led Belgian Economic Mission in Netherlands 39; enlisted again 39; escaped to England 40; missions abroad for Belgian Govt. (London) 40-43; Mil. Attaché in London 43-44; Senator for Louvain 39-46; mem. House of Reps. 46-68; successively Minister of Imports, Minister for Supplies 44-47; Speaker, House of Reps. 58-61; member Govt. Comm. for Peaceful Atomic Energy Devt.; fmr. Chair. Int. Sugar Council; Pres. of Belgian Del. at Int. Sugar Council; Chair. Nat. Permanent Comm. for Agricultural Industries (Brussels); Honorary Chair. Int. Commission for Agricultural Industries (Paris); mem. Control Comm. of Ecole Nationale Supérieure d'architecture et des arts visuels; mem. Board Les Amis des Musées Royaux des Beaux Arts de Belgique; awards include Grand Croix de l'Ordre de la Couronne, Grand Officier de l'Ordre de Léopold, Croix de Guerre (Belgium) 14-18 and 40-45, Officer of the Legion of Merit (Mil.) (U.S.A.), Commdr. de la Légion d'Honneur (France), Officer Order of Orange Nassau (Holland), Officer Order of Merit (Hungary), Commdr. Orden Nacional de Mérito Carlos Manuel de Céspedes (Cuba), Gran Cruz, Placa de Plata Orden del Mérito Juan Pablo Duarte (Dominican Repub.), Grand Cross Order of Tadj (Iran), Gran Cruz Orden de San Martin (Argentina), Grand Cordon Order of the Trinity (Ethiopia), Grand Cross Order of the White Elephant (Thailand), Commdr. de l'Ordre National (Senegal), Grand Officier de l'Ordre du Ouissam Alaouite (Morocco).
Leisure interests: music, painting, horse riding, tennis, shooting, yachting.
54 St. Katelijnevest, B-2000 Antwerp; Home: Wolvenbosch, B-2080 Kapellen, Belgium.
Telephone: 33-59-40 (Antwerp-Office); 64-30-62 (Home).

Krone, Heinrich; German politician; b. 1 Dec. 1895.
Former Deputy Sec.-Gen. Catholic Centre Party; mem. Reichstag 25-33; Editor *Zeit im Querschnitt*, until its suppression by Nazis; travelling salesman 33-45; co-founder Caritas Notwerk (relief organization for victims of Nazism); under arrest 44; helped found Christian Democratic Union in Berlin; mem. Bundestag 49-; Chair. Bundestag CDU 55-; Minister for Special Tasks Nov. 61-64, Chancellor's Deputy in Defence

Council of German Federal Republic 63-64, Chair. Federal Defence Council 64-66; Minister for Special Affairs at the Chancellor's Office 66-Dec. 66.
53 Bonn, Erftweg 28, Federal Republic of Germany.

Kroner, Richard, PH.D.; German philosopher; b. 8 March 1884, Breslau (now Wrocław); s. of Trangott Kroner; m. Alice Mary Kauffman 1908; one d.; ed. Breslau, Berlin, Heidelberg and Freiburg i. Br. Univs. Lecturer in Philosophy Freiburg i. Br. Univ. 12; Prof. Freiburg Univ. 19, Dresden Technical Inst. 24 and Kiel Univ. 29; Research Prof. Berlin 34; Editor *Logos* 10-34; Pres. Int. Hegel League 30-35; refugee Oxford 38; Gifford Lecturer, St. Andrews 39-40; Prof. in Philosophy of Religion, Union Theological Seminary, New York 41-52, Emeritus 52-; Temple Univ., Philadelphia 44-64; Hon. Pres. Int. Asscn. for the Study of Hegel 62-.
Leisure interests: travelling, music.
Publs. *Von Kant bis Hegel* 21-24 (2nd edn. 61), *Die Selbstverwirklichung des Geistes* 28, *Kulturphilosophische Grundlegung der Politik* 31, *The Religious Function of Imagination* 41, *The Primacy of Faith* 43, *How Do We Know God?* 43, *Hegel's Early Theological Writings* 48, *Culture and Faith* 51, *Speculation in Pre-christian Philosophy* 56, *Kant's Weltanschauung* 56, *Selbstbesinnung* 58, *Speculation and Revelation in the Age of Christian Philosophy* 59, *Speculation and Revelation in Modern Philosophy* 61, *Between Faith and Thought* 66, *Freiheit und Gnade* 68.
8108 Hampden Lane, Bethesda, Maryland 20014, U.S.A.
Telephone: 022-762531.

Kroon, Ciro Dominico; Netherlands politician; b. 31 Jan. 1916, Curaçao, Netherlands Antilles; s. of Eduard Bernardus Kroon and Catrijn Zimmerman; m. Edna Huis 1936; three s. one d.; ed. Higher Grade School.
In business until 42; Admin., Social and Econ. Dept., Netherlands Antilles 42-51; mem. Legis. Council of Netherlands Antilles 49-51; Dep. for Social and Econ. Affairs and mem. Admin. Board of island territory of Curaçao 51-57; on various occasions Acting Gov. of Curaçao; Minister for Social and Econ. Affairs and Public Health, Netherlands Antilles 57-68; Prime Minister of Netherlands Antilles Feb. 68-May 69; mem. Island Council of Curaçao 71-73; fmr. Minister of Econ. Affairs, Sport, Culture and Recreation; Commdr. Order of Orange Nassau, Knight Order of Netherlands Lion, and Orders from Venezuela, Colombia and France.
Leisure interests: sailing, fishing.
Fort Amsterdam, Curaçao, Netherlands Antilles.
Telephone: 12860.

Kropotkin, Pyotr Nikolayevich; Soviet geologist; b. 24 Nov. 1910, Moscow; ed. Moscow Geology Prospecting Inst.
Geology Engineer, East Siberia 32-36; Research Assoc. Inst. of Geology U.S.S.R. Acad. of Sciences 36-; Dr. Sc. (Geology and Mineralogy); Corresp. mem. U.S.S.R. Acad. of Sciences 66.
U.S.S.R. Academy of Sciences, 14 Leninsky Prospekt, Moscow, U.S.S.R.

Krotkov, Fyodor Grigorievich; Soviet hygiene specialist; b. 28 Feb. 1896, Mosolovo, Ryazan Region; s. of Grigory and Eufimia Krotkov; m. Irina Krotkova 1942; one s. one d.; ed. Military Medical Acad.
Member C.P.S.U. 19-; Army Service 19-46; mem. U.S.S.R. Acad. of Medical Sciences 44-; U.S.S.R. Deputy Minister of Health 46-47; Academician-Sec. U.S.S.R. Acad. of Medical Sciences 47-50; Head, Dept. of Hygiene, Cen. Inst. for Postgraduate Medical Training 37-57, Prof. 31-; Vice-Pres. U.S.S.R. Acad. of Medical Sciences 53-57; Head, Dept. of Radiation Hygiene, Cen. Inst. for Postgraduate Medical Training 57-; Chair. of Board of All-Union Scientific Soc. of Hygienists; mem. WHO Expert Cttee. on Radiation Hygiene; Order of Lenin 43, 45, 66; Red Star 35; Red

Banner 45, 50; Badge of Honour 39; Patriotic War, First Class 45; Hero of Socialist Labour 66.
Publs. Over 150 works on mil. and gen. hygiene, nutritional hygiene and epidemiology.
57/65 Novoslobodskaya Street, Ap. 40, Moscow 103055, U.S.S.R.
Telephone: 251-81-88.

Kröyer, Haraldur, M.A.; Icelandic diplomatist; b. 9 Jan. 1921, Akureyri; m.; four c.; ed. Akureyri Coll. and Univ. of California (Berkeley).
Joined foreign service 45; Sec. Stockholm 47-49, Oslo 49-52, Paris 52-54; Counsellor, Paris and Perm. Rep. to Council of Europe 54-56; Sec. to Pres. of Iceland 56-62; Counsellor, Moscow 62-66; Deputy Perm. Rep. to UN 66-69; Amb. to Sweden, Finland and Austria 70-72; Perm. Rep. to UN 72-73; Amb. to U.S.A. 73-.
Embassy of Iceland, 2022 Connecticut Avenue, N.W., Washington, D.C., U.S.A.

Kruczek, Władysław; Polish politician; b. 27 April 1910, Rzeszów; s. of Tomasz and Rozalia Kruczek; m. Irena Rusiecka; one s. one d.; ed. Party School of Polish United Workers' Party (PZPR).
Member, Communist Union of Polish Youth 29, subsequently mem. C.P. of Poland; political imprisonment 34-37; active in leadership of Int. Workers' Aid Org. 39-41; army service and prisoner-of-war 42-44; Instructor, Polish Workers' Party (PPR) Cttee., Rzeszów; First Sec. PPR Town Cttee. Rzeszów 47-48; First Sec. Polish United Workers' Party (PZPR) District Cttee. Rzeszów 48-49; Sec. Voivodship Cttee. Poznań 51-52; First Sec. Voivodship Cttee. PZPR Bydgoszcz 52-56, Rzeszów 56-71; mem. PZPR Cen. Cttee. 54-, Politburo PZPR Cen. Cttee. 68-; Deputy to Seym (Parliament) 61-; Chair. Cen. Council of Trade Unions (CRZZ) 71-; Presidium mem. All-Polish Cttee. of Nat. Unity Front 71-; Vice-Chair. State Council March 72-; Chair. Cttee. Nat. Health Protection Fund 72-; Order of Builders of People's Poland, Order of Banner of Labour 2nd and 1st Class, Medal of 30th Anniversary of People's Poland, Partisan's Cross and other decorations.
Centralna Rada Związków Zawodowych, ul. Kopernika 36/40, 00-328 Warsaw, Poland.

Krug, Helfried Viktor; German business executive; b. 9 Feb. 1913, Metz; s. of Erich Walter and Erna Gielen Krug; m. Johanna Verbeek 1937; two s. one d.; ed. salesmanship studies and language studies in England.
Entered Fa. Schering AG, Berlin 35; travelled to India for Schering 37; interned in Calcutta 39-46; Head of Schering Offices in Hanover, later in Düsseldorf 47-51; joined Glaswerke Ruhr, Essen-Karnap 51, Gen. Man. of Ruhrglas 54-59; mem. Management Board, Feldmühle AG, Düsseldorf 59-64; mem. Advisory Board Dynamit Nobel AG, Troisdorf, Intercontinental Pulp Co., Vancouver (Canada), Hyltebruk Aktiebolag (Sweden), Neckermann Versand KGaA, Frankfurt/Main, VEBA-Glas AG, Essen; Deputy Chair. Advisory Board Papéteries de Belgique, Brussels; mem. Board of Dirs. Berliner Handelsgesellschaft-Frankfurter Bank, Frankfurt, and Germanisches Nationalmuseum, Nürnberg.
Leisure interest: collection of antique glass.
Publ. *Glassammlung Helfried Krug.*
c/o Feldmühle AG, 4 Düsseldorf-Oberkassel, Fritz-Vomfelde-Platz 4, Federal Republic of Germany.

Krüger, Christian Martin, D.SC.ENG. (Rand), DR.ING. E.H. (Aachen), D.ENG.H.C. (Rand); South African engineer and business executive; b. 1 May 1905, Johannesburg; s. of the late C. J. Krüger and H. C. Krüger (née Blignaut); m. Elise S. Malherbe 1937; one s. two d.; ed. Ermelo and Middelburg High Schools, Transvaal and Univ. of the Witwatersrand, Johannesburg.
With South African Iron and Steel Industrial Corpn.

Ltd. (I.S.C.O.R.) 31-69, Gen. Works Manager 53-55, Gen. Manager 55-69, Dir. 59-69, Man. Dir. 64-69; retd. 69; Director various companies; Hon. Prof. of Metallurgy and Metallurgical Engineering, Univ. of Pretoria 64-70; Gold Medal of Honour for Scientific Achievement in the Field of Engineering, Akademie vir Wetenskap en Kuns 59; Hon. Vice-Pres. Iron and Steel Inst. (England) 65-74.
Leisure interests: music, swimming, gardening, photography, walking.
210 Anderson Street, Brooklyn, Pretoria, South Africa. Telephone: 74-2086; 745030 (Office).

Kruger, James Thomas, B.A., LL.B.; South African politician; b. 20 Dec. 1917, Orange Free State; ed. Univs. of S. Africa and Witwatersrand.
Lecturer, Witwatersrand Technical Coll. 48-52; Advocate, Supreme Court 55-72; mem. Transvaal Provincial Council 62-66; mem. of Parl. 66-; Deputy Minister of Police, Interior and Social Welfare 72-74; Minister of Justice, Police and Prisons 74-; Del. to Conf. of Intellectual Property, Stockholm 66.
Union Buildings, Pretoria; Home: 11 Bryntirion, Pretoria, South Africa.

Kruijtbosch, Egbert Diederik Jan, DR. ECON.; Netherlands international civil servant; s. of Dr. D. J. Kruijtbosch and C. G. Everts; m. Johanna Grietje Thomas; one d.; ed. Municipal Univ. of Amsterdam.
Military service, ending with rank of Lieut. 48-51; Gen. Directorate for Programme of Econ. and Mil. Aid (later Gen. Directorate for European Co-operation) in Dept. of Foreign Affairs 53-59; studied at Harvard Univ. and M.I.T. 58; First Sec., later Commercial Counsellor at Netherlands Del. to OEEC (later OECD) 60-64; Chair. of Alternates of OECD Steering Board for Trade, Chair. Working Group of Trade Cttee.; Co-ordinator of Medium-Term Planning at Cen. Planning Bureau (Netherlands) 65-66; Chair. of a number of Working Cttees. for medium-term planning in several branches of industry; mem. of staff for econ. affairs and transport, Rijnmond (public authority), Rotterdam; travelled as Eisenhower Fellow in U.S.A. 70; Sec. Scientific Council for Govt. Policy, Prime Minister's Office 72-75; Sec.-Gen. Benelux Econ. Union, Brussels Sept. 75-.
Leisure interests: long distance skating, wild flowers, skiing, piano.
Publs. co-author C.P.B. report *The Netherlands Economy in 1970*; paper *Economically Feasible Physical Planning* 69; co-author *Studies in Long-Term Development of the Port of Dublin* 71, *Model of the Economic Structure of the Greater Rotterdam Region* 72, *Long-Term Planning in the Netherlands* 74.
Rue de la Régence 39, 1000 Brussels, Belgium.
Telephone: 02/513-86-80.

Krul, Wilhelmus Franciscus Johannes Maria; Netherlands engineer; b. 4 Dec. 1893, Breda; s. of J. W. Krul and Eugenie Carpreau; m. Sophia M. E. Burton 1919 (died 1957); two s.; ed. Royal Military Academy.
Lieut. on Mil. Engineering Staff 14; Engineer of State Institute for Water Supply 21 and Dir. 22-58; Prof. in Sanitary Engineering, Technological Univ., Delft 58-64; Consultant to Ministry of Public Health and Environmental Hygiene 58-; mem. Royal Inst. of Engineers (Holland), Bataafsch Genootschap Proefondervindelijke Wijsbegeerte; panel of experts of World Health Organization; Maatschappij der Nederlandsche Letterkunde; Fellow American Asscn. for the Advancement of Science; Hon. mem. New England Waterworks Asscn., British Waterworks Asscn., Int. Water Supply Asscn., Water Pollution Control Fed., Asscn. générale des Hygiénistes et Techniciens Municipaux, Netherlands Royal Inst. of Engineers, etc.; Commdr. Order of Orange-Nassau; Knight, Order of Netherlands Lion.
Leisure interest: literature.

Publs. Articles in periodicals, *Environmental Health in the Netherlands* 68.
Frankenslag 345, The Hague, Netherlands.
Telephone: 070-552470.

Krupkowski, Aleksander, ENG.D.; Polish metallurgist; b. 27 March 1894, Nadarzyn, Warsaw; s. of Hieronim Krupkowski and Paulina Nowicka; m. Dr. Maria Kuryś 1920; one d.; ed. Petersburg Polytechnic School.
Professor Acad. of Mining and Metallurgy, Cracow 30-64, Prof. Emeritus 64-; mem. Polish Acad. of Sciences 52-, Vice-Pres. 63-65; fmr. mem. Council of Science and Technology (KNiT); Chair. Cttee. of Metallurgy Polish Acad. of Sciences, Science Council Inst. of Non-Ferrous Metals; author of theory of distillation and rectification of metals; research on plastic deformation of metals; Editor-in-Chief *Archiwum Hutnictwa* 53-; mem. several foreign and Polish scientific asscns.; Hon. mem. French Metallurgical Asscn. 69; Dr. h.c. Bergakademie, Freiberg and Acad. of Mining and Metallurgy, Cracow; Gold Cross of Merit 46, Officer's Cross Order of Polonia Restituta 51, three State Prizes, Order of Banner of Labour (twice), Order of Builders of People's Poland 64 and many others.
Leisure interests: literature, history, sociology.
Publs. include *Badania nad stopami niklu z miedzią* (Investigations into nickel and copper alloys) 30, *Zasady nowoczesnej metalurgii w zarysie* (Basis of Modern Metallurgy in Outline) 51, *Zasady termodynamiki i ich zastosowanie w metalurgii i metaloznawstwie* (Principles of thermodynamics and their application in metallurgy) 58, *L'étude de la cristallisation dendritique dans les alliages fer-carbone* (XIII Nat. Congress, Milan 68), *Evolution des processus métallurgiques considérée à la lumière de la théorie des potentiels thermodynamiques* 71, *Applications des éprouvettes à dimensions réduites dans l'essai de résilience des métaux* (with Z. Poniewierski) 72, *Basic Problems of the Theory of Metallurgical Processes* 74.
Ul. Smolki 12b, 30-513 Cracow, Poland.
Telephone: 623-77.

Kruse, Hans Jakob; German shipping executive; b. 9 Oct. 1929, Hohenhorst; m. Else Henriette (Kay) Korhammer; ed. grammar school and commercial training in Hamburg.
Sales representative for a shipping agency in S. Germany 52-53; man. of a shipping agency and stevedoring co. in Spain 53-54; head of inland agency of a shipping line in Nuremberg 55-59; man. of a ship-broking co. in Hamburg 59-63; Owner's rep. in Australia of Hamburg-Amerika-Linie and North German Lloyd 64-67; Board Sec., granted proxy of Hapag 67; deputy mem. Board, responsible for world freight services, Hapag 68, mem. Board 69-73; Chair. Board, Hapag-Lloyd AG 73-.
Leisure interests: golf, bridge.
Auguststrasse 3, 2000 Hamburg 76; and Natenbergweg 20, 2105 Seevetal 1, Federal Republic of Germany.
Telephone: 22-02-310 (Hamburg); (04105) 52-330 (Seevetal).

Krutina, Vratislav; Czechoslovak politician; b. 29 June 1913, Prague.
Minister of Agric. 55, later Deputy Minister; Minister of Agriculture, Forestry and Waterways 61-63, of Food Industry Sept. 63-67; Chair. Cen. Co-operative Council 67-68; Deputy to Nat. Assembly 54-69; Deputy, House of the People, Fed. Assembly 69-71; Sec. Cen. Cttee. C.P. Czechoslovakia 53-55, 56-61, mem. 62-71; mem. Agricultural Comm., Cen. Cttee. C.P. of Czechoslovakia 63-66, Cen. Cttee. of Int. Co-operative Alliance, Exec. of I.C.A. Agricultural Cttee. 67-68; Deputy, House of the People of Fed. Assembly 69-71; Sec.-Gen. Fed. Cttee. Czechoslovak Union of Anti-fascist Fighters 70-73; mem. Presidium of Cen. Cttee. Nat. Front of

C.S.S.R. 71-; Order of the Repub. 63, Order of Feb. 25, 1948, 1st Class.
Gabčíkova 5, Prague 8, Czechoslovakia.

Krwawicz, Tadeusz Jan, M.D.; Polish ophthalmologist; b. 15 Jan. 1910, Lwów; s. of Jan and Michalina (Jasińska) Krwawicz; m. Zdzisława Hebal 1944; one s.; ed. Jan Kazimierz Univ., Lwów.
Assistant, Ophthalmology Clinic, Jan Kazimierz Univ., Lwów 39; Dir. Ophthalmology Clinic, Medical Acad. Lublin 48-, Asst. Prof. 49-51, Extraordinary Prof. 51-57, Ordinary Prof. 57-; corresp. mem. Polish Acad. of Sciences 67-; Pres. Polish Ophthalmological Socs. 67-, Soc. of Cryosurgery, Int. Coll. of Surgeons; mem. French and British Ophthalmology socs., Int. Coll. of Surgeons; originator of modern cryo-ophthalmology; Foreign mem. German Acad. of Natural Sciences (Leopoldina); Hon. mem. Polish Medical Alliance, Deutsche Ophthalmologische Gesellschaft, Scientific Ophthalmological Soc. of U.S.S.R., and others; Charter mem. Academia Internationalis Ophthalmologica 75; Dr. h.c. Medical Acad., Lublin 75; State Prize 66, Jurzykowski Foundation Award 67, Special Award of Soc. of Cryosurgery 68, Ignacio Barraquer y Barraquer Gold Medal 70, Theodor Axenfeld's Prize 72, Prix Mondial Nessim Habif (Univ. of Geneva) 74, Gold Cross of Merit, Commdr. and Knight's Cross Order of Polonia Restituta, Order of Banner of Labour 1st Class. Leisure interest: hunting.
Publs. numerous articles in professional journals.
Medical Academy, Chmielna 1, Lublin; Home: ul. Krakowskie Przedmieście 49 m. 4, 20-076 Lublin, Poland.
Telephone: 21508.

Krylov, Alexandr Petrovich, DR.TECH.SC.; Soviet mining engineer; b. 14 Aug. 1904, Tatevo village, Kalinin region; s. of Petr Lukich Krylov and Maria Alexandrovna Krylova; m. Nina Nickolaevna Krylova 1933; ed. Leningrad Mining Inst.
Engineer, oil fields in Azerbaijan 26-30; Geological oil prospecting expedition in Donbass and Sakhalin 30-32; Research worker, State Scientific Research Oil Inst. 32-35; Scientific and teaching work, Moscow Gubkin Oil Inst. 35-53; Research worker, All-Union Gas and Oil Inst. 53-; Corresp. mem. U.S.S.R. Acad. of Sciences 53-68, Academician 68-; Lenin and State prizes.
Leisure interests: reading belles-lettres, carpentry.
Publs. Scientific works in field of gas and oil deposit development.
U.S.S.R. Academy of Sciences, 14 Leninsky Prospekt, Moscow; Home: 117 334 Moscow B-334, Vorobyev High Way 11, 32, U.S.S.R.
Telephone: 137-88-23 (Home).

Krzyżanowski, Julian, PH.D.; Polish literary historian; b. 4 July 1892, Stojańce, U.S.S.R.; s. of Józef and Maria (née Dębouska) Krzyżanowski; m. 1st Emilia Roszkowska 1920, 2nd Zofia Swidninska 1948; two s. one d.; ed. Cracow Univ.
Professor Univ. of London (King's Coll.) 27-30, Riga 30-34, Warsaw 34-66, Prof. Emeritus 66-; Visiting Prof. Columbia Univ. 57-58; mem. Polish and Yugoslav Acads. of Sciences 51-; Chair. Scientific Council, Inst. of Literary Studies Polish Acad. of Sciences (IBL PAN) until 71; Vice-Chair. Polish Cttee. of Slavists; Pres. The Adam Mickiewicz Literary Asscn.; Dr. h.c. (Jagellonian Univ. Cracow); Medal of Anniversary of People's Poland 55, Order of Banner of Labour 1st Class 56, Dobrousky Medal (Czechoslovakia) 68.
Publs. *Polish Romantic Literature* (in English), *Historia literatury polskiej* (History of Polish Literature), *Od Średniowiecza do Baroku* (From the Middle Ages to the Baroque), *Polska bajka ludowa w układzie systematycznym* (Polish Folk-tales in a Systematic Arrangement), *Kalendarz życia i twórczości H. Sienkiewicza* (Journal of the Life and Works of H. Sienkiewicz), *Mądrej*

głowie dość dwie słowie (A Word to the Wise), *W wieku Reja i Stańczyka* (In the Age of Rej and Stanczyk), *Henryka Sienkiewicza żywot i sprawy* (H. Sienkiewicz, His Life and Works), *Twórczość Sienkiewicza* (Literary Production of Sienkiewicz), *Dzieje Literatury Polskiej* (Polish literature from its beginning to the present time); Editor of complete editions of Słowacki, Mickiewicz and Sienkiewicz.
c/o Polska Akademia Nauk, Pałac Kultury i Nauki, Warsaw; Home: ul. Miączyńska 23, 02-637 Warsaw.
[*Died 19 May 1976.*]

Ku Mu; Chinese politician.
Mayor of Tsinan 50-52; Deputy Sec. CCP Shanghai 53-54; Vice-Chair. State Construction Comm. 54-56, State Econ. Comm. 56-65; Chair. State Capital Construction Comm. 65-67; criticized and removed from office during Cultural Revolution 67; Minister of State Capital Construction Comm. 73-; Vice-Premier, State Council 75.
People's Republic of China.

Kubadinski, Pencho; Bulgarian politician; b. 1918; ed. High School and Higher Party School.
Young Communist League 34-40, Communist Party 40-; Local leader, later Central Cttee., Young Communist League 45-51; First Sec. Rousse District Party Cttee. 52-58; Sec. Central Cttee. of Communist Party 58, Cand. mem. Political Bureau 62, now mem.; Deputy Prime Minister 62; mem. Nat. Assembly; mem. State Council 75-.
Central Committee of the Communist Party, Sofia, Bulgaria.

Kubar, Abd al-Majid (*see* Coobar, Abdulmegid).

Kubasov, Valery Nikolaevich; Soviet cosmonaut; b. 7 Jan. 1935, Valdimir Region; ed. Moscow Aviation Inst.
Engineer 58-66; joined cosmonaut training unit 66; engineer of spacecraft *Soyuz*-6 which made group flight with *Soyuz*-7 and *Soyuz*-8 Oct. 69; mem. C.P.S.U. 68-; selected for Russian Team, Joint U.S.-Soviet Space Flight *Soyuz-19-Apollo* 75; Hero of Soviet Union (twice); Gold Star; Order of Lenin; Pilot-Cosmonaut of U.S.S.R.; K. Tsiolkovsky Gold Medal U.S.S.R. Acad. of Sciences.
Zvezdny Gorodok, Moscow, U.S.S.R.

Kubat, Ferit; Turkish politician; b. 1919, Diyarbakr; m.; two s.; ed. Univ. of Istanbul.
Held various posts in local admin. until 64; Gov. of Edirne, Hatay and Muş successively; Under-Sec. Ministry of Foreign Affairs; Minister of the Interior 71-73.
Ministry of the Interior, Ankara, Turkey.

Kubel, (Gottfried Hermann) Alfred; German politician; b. 25 May 1909, Brunswick; s. of Hermann and Anna (née Jordan) Kubel; two d.; ed. middle school, Brunswick.
Minister-President of Brunswick 46; mem. Diet of Lower Saxony 46-; Minister of Economy, Lower Saxony 46, Labour, Building and Health 48, Finance 51, Transport and Economy 57, Food, Agriculture and Forestry 59, Finance 64; Minister-Pres. of Lower Saxony 70-76; Chair. Bundesrat 74-75; Chair. Hanover Fair; Grosses Bundesverdienstkreuz mit Stern und Schulterband 61, Grosskreuz des Verdienstordens der Bundesrepublik Deutschland 71; Order of Orange-Nassau (Netherlands); Social Democrat.
Leisure interests: nature, sport.
3389 Braunlage, Am langen Bruch 6, Federal Republic of Germany.
Telephone: 05520-2346.

Kubelik, Rafael; Czechoslovak musician; b. 29 June 1914, Bychory; ed. Prague Conservatorium.
Conductor, Czech Philharmonic Society, Prague 36-39; Head of Opera, Brno 39-41; Chief Conductor, Czech

Philharmonic, Prague 41-48; Musical Dir. Chicago Symphony Orchestra 50-53; Musical Dir. **Royal Opera House**, Covent Garden 55-58; Chief Conductor Bayerischer Rundfunk, Munich 61-; Musical Dir. Metropolitan Opera, N.Y. 71-74; Guest Conductor, North and South America, Europe and Australia; tours and concerts with Vienna Philharmonic, Concertgebouw Orchestra, Amsterdam and Bavarian Radio Symphony Orchestra; Festivals at Edinburgh, Salzburg, Lucerne, Venice, Besançon, Montreux, Festival of Holland, etc. 48-.
Compositions include: 5 operas, 2 symphonies with chorus, 4 string quartets, 2 violin concertos, concerto for piano, concerto for violoncello, songs, piano, violin music, requiem *Pro Memoria Uxoris* and cantatas *Pro Memoria Patris, Libera Nos.*
Kastanienbaum, Haus im Sand, Switzerland.

Kuberski, Jerzy, M.A.; Polish politician and educator; b. 22 March 1930, Paschalin, Warsaw; *s.* of Wacław and Natalia Kuberski; *m.* Krystyna Kuberski 1951; one *d.*; ed. Pedagogical College and Warsaw Univ.
Active mem. youth organizations ZWM (Fighting Youth Union) 46-48, and ZMP (Polish Youth Union) 48-56; teacher in technical and teacher training schools, then Dir. Teachers' Coll.; School Superintendents' Office, Warsaw 64-70; School Superintendent, Warsaw District 65-70; Pres. AZS (Students' Sports and Athletics Club); Sec. Warsaw Cttee. PZPR (Polish United Workers' Party) July 70-March 72; Deputy mem. Cen. Cttee. PZPR Dec. 71-; Minister of Education March 72-; Order of Banner of Labour 2nd Class, Kt.'s Cross Order of Polonia Restituta, Gold Cross of Merit and others.
Leisure interest: aeronautics.
Ministerstwo Oświaty i Wychowania, Aleja I Armii Wojska Polskiego 25, 00-580 Warsaw, Poland.
Telephone: 28-04-61.

Kubisch, Jack B., A.B., J.D.; American diplomatist; b. 1921, Hannibal, Mo.; *s.* of Benjamin Harrison Kubisch and Beatrice Bloom; *m.* Constance Linn Rippe 1944; two *s.* two *d.*; ed. Cen. Methodist Coll., Univ. of Missouri and Harvard Graduate School of Business Admin.
Entered U.S. Foreign Service 47, served in various embassies in Europe, Latin America and Asia; served with rank of Minister in Brazil, Mexico, France; Asst. Sec. Dept. of State; Amb. to Greece Aug. 74-.
American Embassy, 91 Vass. Sofias, Athens, Greece.

Kubitschek de Oliveira, Juscelino; Brazilian politician; b. 1902; ed. Minas Gerais, Paris, Vienna and Berlin.
Qualified as doctor 27, travelled in Europe and Middle East studying surgery; on return to Minas Gerais appointed Medical Officer to various govt. services; Sec. to Gov. 33; Fed. Deputy for Minas Gerais 34-37; later Mayor of Belo Horizonte (and in charge of urban development programme) 34; Rep. for Minas Gerais to Nat. Assembly 46, Gov. 50-54; President of Brazil 56-60; established new capital of Brasília; produced study of Alliance for Progress 63; voluntary exile 64-65.

Kubota, Yutaka, DR. C. E.; Japanese engineer and company director; b. 1890, Kumamoto Pref.; *m.* Toshiko Kataoka 1916; one *s.* two *d.*; ed. Tokyo Univ.
President and Dir. Nippon Koei Co. Ltd.; Chair. Engineering Consulting Firms Asscn. of Japan, Inc.; Chair. Japan Industrial Rehabilitation Engineering Asscn.; Chair.-Dir. Yaku Island Electric Industrial Co. Ltd.; mem. Cttee. for Econ. Co-operation, Japanese Govt.; planned, designed and supervised Balu Chaung Hydro-Electric Project for Burmese Govt. 54-, Da Nhim Hydro-electric Project for Vietnamese Govt. 56, Kali Brantas Multipurpose Project for Indonesian Govt. 61, Nam Ngum Multipurpose Project for UN 58, Upper Se San Multipurpose Project in Viet-Nam for

UN 62, Karnali Hydro-electric Project in Nepal for UN 58, Phang Rang Irrigation Project, Viet-Nam 63, Sun Kosi Terai Plain Project for UNDP/FAO, Nepal 67, Sempor Irrigation Project for ADB and Indonesian Govt. 69, 72-, Tiep Nhut Irrigation Project (Mekong) for IBRD 72-, Andong Dam Project for Korean Govt. 72-; consultant to ECAFE (Econ. Comm. for Asia and the Far East) for development of Mekong River 51; Hon. mem. Japan Soc. of Civil Engineers; mem. Japan Consulting Engs. Asscn.; First Order of Sacred Treasure 74; decorations from Khmer, Laotian and Vietnamese govts.
Leisure interest: travelling.
Publs. *The Fusenko Hydroelectric Power Plant* (Tokyo World Power Conf.) 29, *Water Power Generation and Dam Building* (in *An Outline of Civil Engineering*) 40-45.
Nippon Koei Co., Ltd., 1-11 Uchisaiwaicho 2-chome, Chiyoda-ku, Tokyo, Japan.
Telephone: Tokyo 502-7571.

Kubrick, Stanley; American film writer and director; b. 26 July 1928; ed. City Coll. of New York.
Staff photographer *Look* 46-50; produced, directed and photographed documentaries for RKO (*Day of the Fight, Flying Padre*) 51, feature films *Fear and Desire* and *Killer's Kiss* for United Artists 52, 54; wrote and directed *The Killing* (U.A.) 56, wrote (with Calder Willingham) and directed *Paths of Glory* (U.A.); directed *Spartacus* (Universal Int.), *Lolita* (M.G.M.) 62, *Dr. Strangelove* (also wrote and produced) 64, *2001: A Space Odyssey* 68, *A Clockwork Orange* (also wrote screenplay) 71, *Barry Lyndon* 75; numerous awards.
c/o Louis C. Blau, 9777 Wilshire Boulevard, Beverly Hills, Calif., U.S.A.

Kučera, Bohuslav, LL.D.; Czechoslovak politician; b. 26 March 1923, Lomnice; one *d.*; ed. Law Faculty, Charles Univ., Prague.
Clerk, Velveta Nat. Enterprise, Varnsdorf 48-49; Chief of Dept., Nopako Nat. Enterprise, Nová Paka 49-50; Sec. of Club of Deputies of Czechoslovak Socialist Party 50-54; Sec. of Presidium of Czechoslovak Socialist Party 54-60, Gen. Sec. 60-68; Chair. Socialist Party 68-; Minister of Justice 68-69; Minister without Portfolio of Fed. Govt. of Czechoslovak Socialist Repub. 69-71; mem. Cen. Cttee. of Nat. Front; Deputy to Nat. Assembly 60-69; Deputy, House of the People, Fed. Assembly 69-, Vice-Chair., mem. Presidium, Fed. Assembly 71-; Chair. Govt. Cttee. for Prosecution of Nazi war criminals 68-; Deputy Chair. Legislative Council, Govt. of Č.S.S.R. 69-72; Deputy Chair. Constitutional and Legal Cttee. of Nat. Assembly 65-68; mem. Presidium of Cen. Cttee. Nat. Front of Č.S.S.R. 71-; Vice-Chair. Czechoslovak del. to Interparl. Union 71-; Chair. Benelux Cttee., Czechoslovak Soc. for Int. Relations 73-; Distinction for Merits in Construction 58, Order of Labour 65, Order of Victorious February 73, several other decorations.
Leisure interest: literature.
Prague 10, Strašnice, Gutova 26, Czechoslovakia.

Kuchel, Thomas; American lawyer and politician; b. 15 Aug. 1910; ed. Univ. of Southern California.
Practising lawyer 35-46; State Legislator, California 37-46; served U.S. Navy 42-45; State Controller 46-53; Republican Senator from California 53-69; fmr. Asst. Republican leader, U.S. Senate; partner law firm of Wyman, Bautzer, Rothman and Kuchel 69-; Del. to 29th UN Gen. Assembly 74-75; Hon. doctorates Univ. of S. Calif., Chapman Coll., Calif., Univ. of the Pacific, Calif., Tufts Univ., Boston, Univ. of Calif.; mem. of Amer. Legion, Scottish Rite Masons, etc.
600 North Hampshire Avenue, N.W., Washington, D.C. 20037; 2 Century Plaza, Los Angeles, Calif. 90067, U.S.A.; 44 Avenue des Champs Elysées, Paris, France; 2 Berkeley Square, London, England.

Küchük, Fazil, M.D.; Turkish Cypriot politician; b. 1906; ed. Istanbul and Lausanne Univs.
Owner and Editor *Halkin Sesi* (daily) 41-60; Leader, Cyprus Turkish National Union Party 43-; Chair. Evcaf High Council 56-60; Vice-Pres. Cyprus Aug. 60-Feb. 73.
P.O. Box 339, Nicosia, Cyprus.

Kuczynski, Jürgen, DR.PHIL.; German economist; b. 17 Sept. 1904, Elberfeld; *s.* of R. R. Kuczynski; *m.* Marguerite Steinfeld 1928; two *s.* one *d.*; ed. Berlin and Heidelberg Univs., and in U.S.A.
Refugee during the Nazi régime; Emeritus Prof. of Econ. History, Humboldt Univ., Berlin; mem. D.D.R. Statistical Del. to COMECON; mem. Deutsche Akad. der Wissenschaften; Fellow, Royal Statistical Soc.; Nat. Prize; Dr. h.c. rer. oec., Dr. h.c. rer. nat.
Leisure interest: low-brow detective stories.
Parkstrasse 94, 112 Berlin, German Democratic Republic.
Telephone: 5650990.

Kudriavtsev, Sergei Mikhailovich; Soviet diplomatist; b. 15 April 1915, Moscow; ed. Moscow Foreign Languages Inst.
Journalist; Tass Corresp. in Berlin 40-41; Diplomatic Service, mem. Staff Soviet Diplomatic Representations in Canada, U.K., Austria, German Federal Repub., France; Amb. to Cuba 60-62; participated in numerous int. confs. and meetings; Amb. to Khmer Repub. 68-72; mem. staff Ministry of Foreign Affairs 72-.
Ministry of Foreign Affairs, 32-34 Smolenskaya Sennaya Ploschad, Moscow, U.S.S.R.

Kudrna, Josef, D.SC.S.; Czechoslovak politician; b. 1 Sept. 1920, Ostředek; ed. Party Coll., Moscow.
First Deputy Minister of Interior 56-65; Minister of Interior 65-March 68; Cand. mem. Central Cttee. C.P. of Czechoslovakia 62-66, mem. 66-71; mem. Legal Comm. 66-68; Order of 25th February 1948 49; Order for Merits in Construction 58.
Prague, Czechoslovakia.

Kuenheim, Eberhard von; German motor executive; b. 2 Oct. 1928, Juditten, Kreis Bartenstein; ed. Höhere Schule, Salem and Technische Hochschule, Stuttgart.
Chairman of Man. Board, Bayerische Motorenwerke (BMW) A.G., Munich Jan. 70-.
Leisure interests: sciences, hockey, walking, books on politics and modern history.
Bayerische Motorenwerke A.G., 8000 Munich 81, Mauerkirchenstrasse 105, Federal Republic of Germany.
Telephone: 38952500 (Office); 480032 (Home).

Kuffler, Stephen William, M.D.; American (naturalized 1954) professor of neurobiology; b. 24 Aug. 1913, Tap, Hungary; *s.* of William and Elizabeth Kuffler; *m.* Phyllis Shewcroft 1943; two *s.* two *d.*; ed. Univ. of Vienna.
Staff mem. Kanematsu Inst., Sydney (Australia) Hospital 38-45; N.R.C. Fellow, Australia 43-45; Seymour Coman Fellow, Dept. of Physiology, Univ. of Chicago 45-47; Assoc. Prof. of Ophthalmology, Wilmer Inst., Johns Hopkins Univ. 47-56; Prof. of Ophthalmic Physiology and Biophysics 56-59; Prof. of Neurophysiology and Neuropharmacology, Harvard Medical School 59-64, Robert Winthrop Prof. of Neurophysiology 64-66, Robert Winthrop Prof. of Neurobiology and Chair. of Dept. 66-; Editor *Journal of Neurophysiology*; non-resident Fellow, Salk Inst., La Jolla, Calif. 66-; Trustee, Marine Biological Labs., Woods Hole, Mass.; Harvey Lecturer 59, Ferrier Lecturer, Royal Soc. (London) 65; Guggenheim Fellow 56; Silliman Mem. Lecturer Yale Univ. 71, Sherrington Lecturer 72; mem. Nat. Acad. of Sciences, American Acad. of Arts and Sciences, American Physiological Soc., Physiological Soc. (U.K.); Foreign mem. Royal Soc. 71, Royal Danish

Acad. of Sciences and Letters; Hon. M.A. (Harvard), Hon. M.D. (Berne), Hon. Sc.D. (Yale); many awards.
Leisure interests: skiing, tennis, walking, reading.
Publs. Articles in professional journals on nervous system studies.
Department of Neurobiology, Harvard Medical School, 25 Shattuck Street, Boston, Mass. 02115, U.S.A.
Telephone: 617-734-3300 ext. 631.

Kuhn, Ferdinand, A.B.; American journalist; b. 10 April 1905, New York; *s.* of Ferdinand and Johanna (Loeb) Kuhn; *m.* Delia E. Wolf 1931; two *s.*; ed. Columbia Univ.
Reporter *New York Times* 25-28, London staff 28-36, chief London correspondent 37-39, Editorial writer 39-40; Asst. to U.S. Sec. of Treasury 41, Head British Div. Office of War Information 43; Dir. Interim Int. Information Service (U.S. State Dept.) 45; Staff writer *Washington Post* 46-53; at present magazine writer and lecturer on international affairs.
Publs. *Commodore Perry and the Opening of Japan* 55, *The Story of the Secret Service* 57, *Borderlands* (with Delia W. Kuhn) 62, *The Philippines: Yesterday and Today* 65, *Russia On Our Minds* 70.
2915 Audubon Terrace, Washington, D.C. 20008, U.S.A.

Kühn, Heinz; German politician; b. 18 Feb. 1912; ed. Univs. of Cologne, Prague and Ghent.
Member Catholic Youth Movement "Neudeutschland", Socialist Youth Movement of Germany 28; Socialist Party (SPD) 30; Chair. of Socialist Student Group, Cologne; political emigration and studies at Univs. of Prague and Ghent 33; journalist and editor-in-chief *Rheinische Zeitung* 49-51; mem. Landtag, North Rhine-Westphalia 48-54, 62-, Chair. SPD Parl. Party 62-66; mem. Bundestag, mem. SPD Parl. Management Cttee., Bundestag Foreign Affairs Comm. and Chair. Bundestag Comm. on German Schools and Insts. Abroad 53-62; mem. Assembly, Western European Union; Chair. Bundesrat 71-72; Chair. SPD North Rhine-Westphalia 62-73; mem. Presidium SPD 66-, Deputy Chair. 73-; Minister-Pres. of North Rhine-Westphalia Dec. 66-; Deputy Chair. Council of Admin. Westdeutscher Rundfunk 54-.
Der Ministerpräsident des Landes Nordrhein-Westfalen, Düsseldorf, Haroldstrasse 2; Home: 5 Köln-Dellbrück, Roteichenweg 5, Federal Republic of Germany.

Kuhn de Chizelle, Bernard; French engineer; b. 11 Aug. 1897; ed. Lycée d'Amiens and Ecole nationale supérieure d'électro-technique et d'hydraulique, Grenoble.
Engineer, Thomson-Houston Co. 21-25; Dir. of Var and Alpes-Maritime Industrial Energy System 26-35; Dir. Heat and Light Soc., Grenoble 35-44; Dir.-Gen. *Gaz du Lyon* 44, Dir. of Mixed Distribution, *Electricité de France, Gaz de France* 54, Dir.-Gen. *Gaz de France* 59-64, Hon. Dir.-Gen. 64-; Hon. Pres. d'Etudes et de Réalisations de Cybernétique Industrielle (CERCI); mem. du Conseil économique et social 64-69; Officier, Légion d'Honneur and several other awards.
8 avenue de New York, 75116 Paris, France.

Kuhnke, Hans-Helmut, DR. JUR.; German business executive; b. 21 Sept. 1907, Heydekrug.
Chairman, Man. Board, Ruhrkohle AG until 73; Chair. Supervisory Board, Rütgerswerke AG, Frankfurt, Isola-Werke AG, Düren, Varta AG 74-; Deputy Chair. Supervisory Board, Bayerische Vereinsbank, Munich, Th. Goldschmidt AG, Essen; mem. Supervisory Board Deutsche Texaco AG, Deutsche Überseeische Bank, Bergbau AG, Ruhrgas AG; mem. Admin. Board, Stifterband für die Deutsche Wissenschaft, Wirtschaftsvereinigung Bergbau; mem. Presidium, Bundesvereinigung der Deutschen Arbeitgeberverbände, Bundesverband der Deutschen Industrie e.V.; Adviser Allianz Versicherungs AG, Allianz Lebensversicherungs

AG, Deutsche Bank AG; mem. many other business orgs. and concerns.
4321 Bredenscheid, Am Geitling 40, Hyggehof, Federal Republic of Germany.

Kuipers, J. D., M.A., D.SC.; Netherlands administrator; b. 9 July 1918, Timperley, Australia; *m.* Johanna Adriana de Roon 1940; three *s.*; ed. Univ. of Cambridge, London School of Econs. and Univ. of Amsterdam.
Professor Strathclyde Business School; Vice-Pres. Fed. of Netherlands Enterprises (V.N.O.); mem. Council of Presidents of Union of Industries, European Community (UNICE); mem. Econ. and Social Cttee. of EEC 62-70, Pres. 70-72; Officer Order of Orange Nassau, Commdr. Order Léopold II, Order of Merit (Italy).
Leisure interests: arts, history.
c/o Economic and Social Committee, European Economic Community, 3 Boulevard de l'Empereur, Brussels, Belgium.

Kukarkin, Boris Vasilievich, D.SC.; Soviet astronomer; b. 30 Oct. 1909, Nishi-Novgorod (Gorky); *m.* Nathaly Kukarkin 1949; one *s.* one *d.*
Associate State Astronomical Inst. 32-52; Prof., Moscow Univ. 51-, Head of Dept. of Stellar Astronomy, Moscow Univ. 60-; Dir. Shternberg State Astronomical Inst. 52-56; Vice-Pres. Int. Astronomical Union 55-61.
Publs. *Preliminary Catalogue of Mean Colour Equivalents of 1207 Stars* 37, *Physical Variable Stars* 39, *Visual Observations of 55 Cepheides with Long Periods* 40, *Variable Stars and Methods of their Observation* 47, *Investigation of the Structure and Development of Stellar Systems on the Basis of the Study of Variable Stars* 49, *General Catalogue of Variable Stars* (jointly) 48, 58, 69-71, *Globular Star Clusters* 74.
Moscow University, Corpus K, Apt. 122, Moscow 117234, U.S.S.R.

Kułaga, Eugeniusz, M.A.; Polish diplomatist; b. 1 Nov. 1925, Auby, France; *m.*; two *d.*; ed. Central School for Foreign Service, Warsaw.
Second, then First Sec., Perm. Del. of Poland to UN 52-55; Deputy Rep. ICSC, Vietnam 55; Act. Rep., Laos 56; Head, UN Div. Min. of Foreign Affairs, Warsaw 56-59; Deputy Rep. of Poland to UN, Geneva 59-62; Amb. of Poland to Ghana, Mali, Dahomey, Sierra Leone 62-65; Dir. of Dept. of Int. Orgs., Min. of Foreign Affairs, Warsaw 65-69; Del. of Poland to several UN Gen. Assemblies; Perm. Rep. to UN 69-75; Vice-Chair. Special Cttee. on Rationalization of Procedure and Organization of Gen. Assembly 70-71; Chair. UN Comm. on Human Rights 72-75; Vice-Chair. UN Financial Cttee. 72-75; Under Sec. of State, Ministry of Foreign Affairs 75-; Gold Cross of Merit 54, Medal of 10th Anniversary of People's Poland 54, Officer's and Kt.'s Cross, Order of Polonia Restituta 69, Medal of 30th Anniversary of People's Poland 74.
c/o Ministry of Foreign Affairs, Al. I Armii Wojska Polskiego 23, 00-580 Warsaw, Poland.

Kulakov, Fyodor Davydovich; Soviet politician; b. 1918; ed. All-Union Agricultural Inst.
Member C.P.S.U. 40-; section leader, sugar beet industry, agronomist 38-43; party, econ. and Soviet work 43-55; Deputy Minister of Agriculture, R.S.F.S.R. 55-59, Minister of Grain Products, R.S.F.S.R. 59-60; First Sec. Stavropol Area Cttee., C.P.S.U. 60-64; Head of Agricultural Dept., Central Cttee. of C.P.S.U. 64-65; mem. Central Cttee. of C.P.S.U. 61-, Sec. 65-; mem. Politburo 71-; Deputy Supreme Soviet 50-58, 62-.
Central Committee of the Communist Party of the Soviet Union, 4 Staraya ploshchad, Moscow, U.S.S.R.

Kularatnam, Karthigesapillai, M.A., PH.D., DR.SC.; Ceylonese educationist, geographer and geologist; b. 28 May 1911; *m.* Poospadevi Kularatnam.

Professor Emer. and Dean, Univ. of Sri Lanka; taught in Univs. of Edinburgh, Sheffield, Birmingham, New York, Kansas City and Sir George Williams (Montreal); Pres. Inst. of Environmental Sciences; Dir. Commonwealth Geographical Bureau, Inst. of Population Engineering; Senior Consultant, UN/ESCAP; Pres. Ceylon Geographical Soc., Gemmologists Asscn., Soil Conservation Soc.; Past Pres. of Natural Sciences, Ceylon Asscn. for the Advancement of Science; Corresp. mem. World Fed. of Scientific Workers.
Publs. several essays on geography, geology, Sri Lanka, etc.
61 Abdul Caffoor Mawatha, Colombo 3, Sri Lanka.

Kulatov, Turabay; Soviet politician; b. 1908; ed. Kzyl-Kiysk Soviet-Party School and Higher Party School.
Trade union official 34; mem. Bureau of the Central Cttee. of the C.P. of Kirghizia 38; Chair. of the Council of People's Commissars of Kirghizia 38-45; Chair. of the Presidium of the Supreme Soviet of Kirghizia 45-; Vice-Chair. of the Presidium of the Supreme Soviet of the U.S.S.R. 46-; mem. Central Auditing Comm., C.P.S.U. 39-; Deputy to U.S.S.R. (38-) and Kirghizian S.S.R. Supreme Soviets; mem. Central Cttee. C.P. of Kirghizia; awarded Order of Lenin (four times).
Supreme Soviet of Kirghizia, Frunze, U.S.S.R.

Kulichenko, Leonid Sergeyevich; Soviet politician; b. 1913; ed. Volgograd Inst. of Mechanics and C.P.S.U. Higher Party School.
Teacher 36-42; mem. C.P.S.U. 40-; party and local govt. official, Volgograd Region 42-61; Chair. Volgograd Soviet of Working People's Deputies 62-65; First Sec. Volgograd Regional Cttee. of C.P.S.U. 65-; mem. Central Cttee. of C.P.S.U. 66-; Deputy to U.S.S.R. Supreme Soviet 66-; mem. Industry Comm. Soviet of Union.
Volgograd Regional Committee of C.P.S.U., Volgograd, U.S.S.R.

Kulikov, Vasily Vasilievich; Soviet lawyer; b. 12 Jan. 1912, Ulyanovsk; ed. Kazan Inst. of Soviet Law.
Member Communist Party of Soviet Union 39-, successively Investigator, Asst. to Procurator, Dept. Procurator, Dept. Head, Deputy Chief Procurator 32-50; on staff of Central Cttee. C.P.S.U. 50-58; Deputy Gen. Procurator of U.S.S.R. 58-62; First Deputy Chair. Supreme Court of U.S.S.R. 62-; Orders of Lenin and of Red Star.
Supreme Court of U.S.S.R., 13 Ulitsa Vorovskogo, Moscow, U.S.S.R.

Kulikov, Gen. Viktor Georgievich; Soviet army officer; b. 1921.
Joined Soviet Army 38; Commdr. of Platoon 40, Chief of Staff tank battalion, regt., brigade 41-45; various command posts in tank detachments 45-48; Frunze Mil. Acad. 48-53; Commdr. tank regt., Chief of Staff tank div., Deputy Commdr. of Army, Commdr. of Army 53-66; Commdr. Kiev Mil. Area 66-69; C.-in-C. Soviet Forces in German Democratic Repub. 69-71; mem. Cen. Cttee. of U.S.S.R. Communist Party April 71-; Chief of Gen. Staff and First Deputy Minister of Defence Sept. 71-.
Ministry of Defence, 34 Naberezhnaya M. Thoreza, Moscow, U.S.S.R.

Kulpiński, Jan, M.ENG.; Polish engineer and government official; b. 27 Dec. 1922, Chełmża, Toruń District; ed. Cracow Acad. of Mining and Metallurgy.
Worked in Coal Industry since 51; Eng. in Rokitnica Coal Mine; later worked in management of five coal mines; Dir. Miechowice Mine 56-67, Siemianowice Mine 67-69; Dir.-Gen. Bytom Coal Industry Union 69-74; Minister of Mining and Energy Sept. 74-; mem. Polish

United Workers' Party; State Prize, 2nd Class; Order of Banner of Labour, 2nd Class 75.
Ministerstwo Górnictwa i Energetyki, ul. Krucza 36, 00-522 Warsaw, Poland.
Telephone: 28-99-60 (Office).

Kumarasuriar, Chelliah, B.SC.(ENG.), D.I.C., M.I.C.E., M.I.E.C.; Ceylonese chartered engineer and politician; b. 8 Aug. 1926, Taiping, Malaysia; m. Mandaleswari Kumarasuriar 1951; two s. three d.; ed. Univ. of Colombo and Imperial Coll., London.
Lecturer, Univ. of Ceylon 50; Research and Devt. Engineer, Health Dept., Ceylon until 60; Factory Dir. Glaxo-Allenbury's (Ceylon) Ltd.; Visiting Lecturer, Univ. of Ceylon; mem. Parl.; Minister of Posts and Telecommunications 70-; numerous honours and awards; Sri Lanka Freedom Party.
Leisure interests: oriental classical music, English literature, political research.
Publs. articles in specialist journals.
Ministry of Posts and Telecommunications, Colombo; Home: 4/1 Ramakrishna Road, Colombo 6, Sri Lanka.
Telephone: 29567 (Office); 83310 (Home).

Kunayev, Dinmohammed Akhmedovich; Soviet (Kazakh) politician and mining engineer; b. 12 Jan. 1912; ed. Moscow Inst. of Non-Ferrous Metals.
Former Dir. Kounrad Mine, Kazakh S.S.R.; Vice-Chair. Council of Ministers Kazakh S.S.R. 45-52, Chair. 52-60, 62-64; First Sec. Kazakh Communist Party 60-62, 64-; Alt. mem. Politburo Central Cttee. of C.P.S.U. April 66-April 71, mem. April 71-; Deputy to Supreme Soviet of the U.S.S.R. (50-) and Supreme Soviet of the Kazakh S.S.R.; mem. Presidium of Supreme Soviet of U.S.S.R. 62-; mem. C.P.S.U. Central Cttee. 56-; mem. and fmr. Pres. Acad. of Sciences of the Kazakh S.S.R.; Hero of Socialist Labour, Order of Lenin, Hammer and Sickle Gold Medal, etc.
Central Committee of Communist Party of the Kazakh S.S.R., Alma-Ata, Kazakh S.S.R., U.S.S.R.

Kuncewiczowa, Maria; Polish writer; b. 30 Oct. 1899, Samara, Russia; d. of Jozef and Adela Szczepanski; m. Jerzy Kuncewicz 1921; one s.; ed. Warsaw Univ., Jagellonian Univ., Cracow, and Univ. of Nancy.
Member Int. PEN Club; lived in France during World War II, in U.K. until 56; Founder, Centre Writers in Exile; Prof. Polish Literature, Univ. of Chicago 62-70; Literary Prize of Warsaw 37, Pietrzak Prize 66, State Prize 74.
Leisure interests: music, travel.
Publs. *Przymierze z dzieckiem* (Alliance with a Child), *Twarz mężczyzny* (Face of Man) (trans. into French, Slovak and Italian), *Miłość Panieńska* (Maiden Love), *Dwa Księżyce* (Two Moons), *Dyliżans Warszawski* (Warsaw Stage-Coach), *Cudzoziemka* (The Stranger) (trans. into Czech, French, Italian Dutch, Estonian, English, Spanish, Finnish, German, Swedish, Romanian, Slovak), *Dni Powszednie Państwa Kowalskich* (Everyday), *Miasto Heroda* (Herod's Town), *Klucze* (The Keys) (trans. into English, French, Czech), *Zmowa Nieobecnych* (The Conspiracy of the Absent) (trans. into English) 50, *Leśnik* (The Forester) (trans. into English, Italian) 54, *W Domu i w Polsce* (At Home and in Poland) 58, *Odkrycie Patusanu* (The Discovery of Patusan) 59, *Gaj oliwny* (The Olive Grove) 61, *Don Kichote i nianki* (Don Quixote and Nurses) 66, *Tristan* (trans. into English, Slovak, German, Czech, Romanian) 46, 67; *Fantomy* (Phantoms), Vol. I 71, *Natura*, Vol. II 74 (two vol. autobiography), *Dziękuję ci za różę* (Thank you for the Rose) 55 (play), *The Modern Polish Mind* (anthology).
Kazimierz Dolny, Wąwóz Małachowskiego, Poland.

Kundera, Milan; Czechoslovak writer; b. 1 April 1929, Brno; m. Věra Hrabánková 1963; ed. Film Faculty, Acad. of Music and Dramatic Arts, Prague.
Assistant, later Asst. Prof., Film Faculty, Acad. of

Music and Dramatic Arts, Prague 52-70; Prof. Slavonic Studies, Univ. of Rennes 75-; mem. Cen. Cttee. Union of Czechoslovak Writers 56-70, mem. Presidium of Cen. Cttee. 63-67; mem. Editorial Board *Literární noviny* 56-59, 63-67, 68; mem. Editorial Board *Listy* 68-69; Czechoslovak Writers' Publishing House Prize 61; Klement Gottwald State Prize 63; Union of Czechoslovak Writers' Prize 67, Czechoslovak Writers' Publishing House Prize 69, Prix Médicis (for *La Vie est ailleurs*) 73.
Leisure interests: boxing, music, dogs.
Publs. Poetry: *Man a Broad Garden* 53, *The Last May* 55, *Monologues* 57; Drama: *The Owners of the Keys* 62 (produced in Federal Germany, U.S.S.R., Hungary, Bulgaria, Uruguay, U.K., France, U.S.A., Finland, and Switzerland), *Deux oreilles deux mariages* 69; Short stories: *Ridiculous Loves* 63, *The Second Book of Ridiculous Loves* 65, *The Third Book of Ridiculous Loves* 69, *Laughable Loves* 74; Novels: *The Joke* 67, *La vie est ailleurs* 73, *La Plaisanterie* 73.
Brno, Czechoslovakia.

Kuneralp, Zeki; Turkish diplomatist; b. 5 Oct. 1914, Istanbul; m. Necla Ozdilci 1943; two s.; ed. Univ. of Berne.
Entered Diplomatic Service 40, served Bucharest 43-47, Ankara (Ministry of Foreign Affairs) 47-49, Prague 49-52, NATO (Paris) 52-57; Asst. Sec.-Gen. Ministry of Foreign Affairs 57, Sec.-Gen. 60; Ambassador to Switzerland 60, to U.K. 64-66; Sec.-Gen. Min. of Foreign Affairs 66-69; Amb. to U.K. 69-72, to Spain 72-.
Embassy of Turkey, Monte Esquinza 48, Madrid, Spain; and Fenerbahce Caddesi 85/B, Belvü Ap. D. 4, Kiziltoprak, Istanbul, Turkey.

Küng, Hans, D.THEOL.; Swiss theologian and univ. professor; b. 19 March 1928, Sursee, Lucerne; ed. Gregorian Univ., Rome, Inst. Catholique and Sorbonne, Paris.
Ordained priest 54; mem. practical ministry, Lucerne Cathedral 57-59; Scientific asst. for Dogmatic Catholic Theol., Univ. of Münster/Westfalen 59-60; Prof. Fundamental Theol., Univ. of Tübingen 63-; Prof. of Dogmatics, Dir. Inst. Ecumenical Research 63-; Hon. LL.D. (St. Louis) 57, Hon. D.D. (Pacific School of Religion, Berkeley, Univ. Glasgow), Hon. H.H.D. (Chicago).
Leisure interests: watersport, skiing, classical music.
Publs. *The Council: Reform and Reunion* 62, *That the World May Believe* 63, *The Council in Action* 63, *Justification: The Doctrine of Karl Barth and a Catholic Reflection* 64, *Structures of the Church* 64, *Freedom Today* 66, *The Church* 67, *Truthfulness* 68, *Menschwerdung Gottes* 70, *Infallible?—An Inquiry* 71, *Why Priests?* 72, *Fehlbar?—Eine Bilanz* 73, *On being a Christian* 76; ed. *Journal of Ecumenical Studies, Theologische Quartalschrift, Revue Internationale de Théologie Concilium, Theological Meditations, Ökumenische Forschungen.*
74 Tübingen, Waldhäuserstr. 23, Federal Germany.
Telephone: 62646.

Kunicki, Tadeusz; Polish politician; b. 1 June 1927, Łęki, Łódź region; ed. Univ. of Łódź.
Executive posts in Ministry of Light Industry and later in cotton industry 48-, Gen. Man. Cotton Industry Amalgamation 64-66, Under-Sec. of State Ministry of Light Industry Oct. 66-68, Minister of Light Industry April 68-; mem. Polish United Workers' Party 53-; Order of Banner of Labour 2nd Class.
Ministerstwo Przemystu Lekkiego, ul. Hoża 29, 00-521 Warsaw, Poland.

Kunihiko, Sasaki; Japanese banker; b. 20 Dec. 1908, Formosa; s. of Mikisaburo and Matsuko Sasaki; m. Shizue Shigemura 1937; three c.; ed. Tokyo Univ.
Manager, Business Devt. Dept., Yasuda Bank 47-48; Man. Business Devt. Dept., Fuji Bank 48-49, Man. Credit Dept. 49-50, Deputy Man. Osaka Branch 50-51,

Chief Man. Foreign Div. 51-54, Dir. 54-57, Man. Dir. 57-63, Deputy Pres. 63-71, Chair. of Board, Pres. 71-75, Dir. and Hon. Chair. 75-.
Leisure interest: reading.
The Fuji Bank Ltd., 1-chome, Otemachi, Chiyoda-ku, Tokyo; Home: 18-10, 6-chome, Matsubara, Setagaya-ku, Tokyo, Japan.

Kunitz, Stanley J., M.A.; American writer and educator; b. 29 July 1905, Worcester, Mass.; s. of Solomon Z. Kunitz and Yetta Helen Jasspon; m. 1st Helen Pearce 1930, 2nd Eleanor Evans 1939, 3rd Elise Asher 1958; one d.; ed. Harvard Univ.
Editor *Wilson Library Bulletin* 28-42; service with U.S. Army, rising to rank of Staff Sergeant 43-45; Prof. of Literature, Bennington Coll. (Vt.) 46-49; Dir. of Seminar, Potsdam Summer Workshop in Creative Arts 49-53; Lecturer and Dir. of Poetry Workshop, New School for Social Research, New York 50-58; Dir. Poetry Workshop, The Poetry Center, New York, 58-62; Lecturer, Columbia Univ. 63-66; Adjunct Prof. School of the Arts (Columbia) 67-; Editor, Yale Series of Younger Poets, Yale Univ. Press 69-; Poetry Consultant of the Library of Congress 74-76; mem. American Acad. of Arts and Letters, Nat. Inst. of Arts and Letters; awards include Garrison Medal for Poetry 26, Blumenthal Prize 41, Levinson Prize 56, Harriet Monroe Award 58, Pulitzer Prize for Poetry 59; Brandeis Creative Arts Poetry Medal 65; Hon. Litt. D. (Clark Univ.) 61; Fellowship Award, Acad. of Amer. Poets 68; Fellow, Yale Univ. 69; Chancellor, Acad. of Amer. Poets 70.
Leisure interests: tennis, gardening, cooking.
Publs. Verse: *Intellectual Things* 30, *Passport to the War* 44, *Selected Poems* 58; Editions: *Living Authors* 31, *Authors Today and Yesterday* 33, *Junior Book of Authors* 34, *British Authors of the XIX Century* 36, *American Authors 1600-1900* 38, *XX Century Authors* 42, *British Authors Before 1800* 52, *XX Century Authors* (First Supplement) 55, *Poems of John Keats* 64, *European Authors 1000-1900* 67, *The Testing-Tree* (verse) 71, *Poems of Akhmatova* (translations) 73, *The Terrible Threshold* (verse) 74, *Story under Full Sail* (trans. of A. Voznesensky) 74, *A Kind of Order, a Kind of Folly* 75, *The Coat Without a Seam* (verse) 75.
157 West 12th Street, New York, N.Y. 10011, U.S.A.

Kunstler, Charles; French historian, poet, essayist, lecturer and art critic; b. 22 Sept. 1887, Pissos, Landes; s. of Prof. Ignace Kunstler and Marguerite Gentès.
Vice-President of the Société des Gens de Lettres; Pres. Syndicat de la Presse Artistique, Asscn. des Ecrivains de Champagne, Dir. des Journalistes et des Nouvellistes Parisiens; Hon. Pres. Maison des Journalistes; mem. de l'Institut (Acad. des Beaux-Arts), P.E.N. Club, Conseil Supérieur des Beaux-Arts, Conseiller de la Caisse Nationale des Lettres, Asscn. des Ecrivains (anciens) Combattants; Officier de la Légion d'Honneur, decorations include La croix de guerre and la médaille militaire.
Leisure interests: a country resort in the fine season, work, lectures, drawing, visiting sick or unhappy friends.
Publs. *Paul-Emile Pissarro* 28, *Coubine* 29, *Lucien Mainssieux* 29, *La Peinture Indépendante en France* 29, *Jane Poupelet* 29, *La Gravure Originale en France* 30, *Camille Pissarro* 30, *Forain* 31, *Gauguin* 34, *Les Amours de François Villon* 34, *La Fontaine aux Trois Miracles* 35, *Watteau* 36, *Les Arts de l'Amérique Précolombienne* 38, *La Vie Privée de Marie-Antoinette* 38, *La Vie Privée de l'Impératrice Joséphine* 39, *Renoir* 41, *Gauguin* 42, *Marie-Antoinette* 43, *L'Enseigne de Gersaint* 43, *La Politique des Rois de France, par eux-mêmes* 43, *Le Testament de François Villon et Maurice L'Hoir* 45, *Pierre Prins* 45, *Fersen et son Secret* 47, *Fersen et les Femmes* 47, *Gauguin* 47, *Mondzain* 48, *La Vie Quotidienne sous Louis XVI* 50, *La Douceur d'Aimer* 51, *Précis d'Histoire Générale de l'Art* 52, *La Vie Quotidienne sous Louis XV* 53,

Paris souterrain 53, *Solitudes* 54, *L'Art au XIXe siècle* 55, *A mes Amis* 56, *Trois Peintres* 56, *Louis et le Grand-Théâtre de Bordeaux* 56, *Sur les Mémoires de Mme. de Rémusat* 57, *Hommage à Georges Duhamel* 57, *Mme. de Pompadour* 60, *Fersen et Marie-Antoinette* 61, *La Vie Quotidienne sous la Régence* 61, *Rois, Empereurs et Présidents de la France* 61, *La Sculpture en France de Rodin à nos Jours* 61, *La Verte Vieillesse de M. de Voltaire* 63, *Eugène Delacroix et la Critique* 63, *Hommage à René Maran* 65, *Elvire ou Le Songe de Don Juan* 66, *Pissarro, Villes et Campagnes* 67, *Rencontre d'un artiste parisien avec les abeilles* 68, *Les dernières années de Charles Baudelaire* 68, *Du Pavillon de Flore au Pavillon de La Boissière* 68, *Charles Chassé* 68, *Hans Ekegårdh* 68, *Marquet* 72, *Pissarro* 72, *Kiyoshi Hasegawa* 73, *Henri Busser et Darius Milhaud* 74, *Louis Hautecœur* 74, *Julien Cain* 74, *La Shahbanou Impératrice d'Iran* 74, *Lord Clark of Saltwood* 74, *Pissarro* 75.
29 rue Hippolyte-Maindron, 75014 Paris, France.
Telephone: SUF 46-95.

Kunz, Erich; Austrian opera singer; b. 20 May 1909; ed. High School for Music, Vienna
With Staatsoper, Vienna 41-; Mozart Medal, Verdienstkreuz 1st Class for Arts and Sciences; Hon. mem. Vienna State Opera; Gold Medal of Honour for services to Vienna.
Grinzingerstrasse 35, 1190 Vienna, Austria.
Telephone: 32-22-01.

Kunze, Emil, DR.PHIL.; German archaeologist; b. 18 Dec. 1901, Dresden; m. Athena Drinis 1931; two s. one d.; ed. Univs. of Vienna and Leipzig.
Studentship, German Archaeological Inst. 26-29; Asst., German Archaeological Inst., Athens 29-33; Studentship, Prussian Acad., Berlin 33-35; Asst., Museum of Casts of Classical Sculpture, Munich 35-37; Lecturer, Univ. of Marburg 36-37, Munich 37-42; Field Dir. Olympia Excavation 37-42, 52-72; Prof. of Classical Archaeology, Univ. of Strasbourg 42-45, Univ. of Munich 46-51, Hon. Prof. 71-; Dir. German Archaeological Inst., Athens 51-67; mem. German and Austrian Archaeological Insts.; mem. Bavarian Acad.; Corresp. mem. Acad. of Göttingen, Royal Acad. of Sciences, Copenhagen, Accademia Nazionale dei Lincei, Rome, British Acad., London; Hon. mem. Soc. of Hellenic Studies, London, Hellenic Archaeological Soc., Athens; Federal German Order of Merit; Dr.phil. h.c. (Univ. of Thessalonika).
Leisure interest: music.
Publs. *Kretische Bronzereliefs* 31, *Orchomenos II and III* 31, 34, *Zeus und Ganymedes* 40, *Archaische Schildbänder* 51, *Berichte über die Ausgrabungen in Olympia* (Vol. II seq.) 38-, *Drei Bronzen der Slg. H. Stathatos* 53.
8021 Grosshesselohe bei München, Immergrünstrasse 1, Federal Republic of Germany.
Telephone: Munich 796244.

Kunze, Horst, DR. PHIL.; German librarian; b. 22 Sept. 1909, Dresden; m. 1941; two s. two d.; ed. Sächsische Landesbibliothek, Dresden and Deutsche Bücherei, Leipzig.
Research Librarian, Landesbibliothek, Darmstadt 39-47; Dir. Universitäts-und Landesbibliothek Sachsen-Anhalt, Halle 47-50; Provisional Gen. Dir. Öffentliche Wissenschaftliche Bibliothek (now Deutsche Staatsbibliothek) 50-51; Gen. Dir. Deutsche Staatsbibliothek 51-; Dir. Inst. of Library Science and Scientific Information, Humboldt-Univ. Berlin 55-68; Full Prof. of Library Science, Univ. of Berlin 54-; Chair. Arbeitsgemeinschaft für das Kinder- und Jugendbuch 59-75; Pres. Deutscher Bibliotheksverband 64-68; Prof. in ord. 66.
Leisure interest: books.
Publs. *Lieblingsbücher von dazumal* 38 (reprint 65), *Wege zum wissenschaftlichen Buch* (2nd edn.) 55,

Wissenschaftliches Arbeiten (2nd edn.) 59, *Gelesen und geliebt* (2nd edn.) 63, *Über das Registermachen* 64 (3rd edn. 68), *Willst Du Bibliothekar werden?* (2nd edn.) 65, *Dunkel war's, der Mond schien helle* (7th edn.) 64, *Schatzbehalter vom Besten aus der älteren deutschen Kinderliteratur* (3rd edn.) 69, *Grundzüge der Bibliothekslehre* (3rd edn.) 66, *Werner Klemkes gesammelte Werke* 68 (2nd edn. 72), *Lexikon des Bibliothekwesens* (editor with G. Rückl) 69 (2nd edn. 2 vols.) 74-75, *Bibliophilie im Sozialismus* 69, *Spass muss sein* 72, *Geschichte der Buchillustration in Deutschland. Das 15. Jahrhundert* (2 vols.) 75.
Regatta-Strasse 246, 118 Berlin-Grünau, German Democratic Republic.
Telephone: 6714809.

Kunzru, Pandit Hriday Nath, B.A., B.SC., LL.D.; Indian politician; b. 1887, Delhi; *s.* of Pandit Ajudhiya Nath; ed. Allahabad Univ. and London School of Economics and Political Science.
Joined Servants of India Society (national missionaries pledged to devote their lives to the service of India) 09, Life Pres. 36-; Legislative Council U.P. 21-23, and mem. Indian Legislative Assembly 27-30, Council of State 37-46, Constituent Assembly 46-50, Provisional Parl. 50-52, Upper House, Indian Parl. 52-62; Leader Indian Del. Inter-Parliamentary Union 56-61; Pres. East African Nat. Congress 29; Pres. Nat. Liberal Fed. 34; mem. Defence Consultative Cttee. 42-46; Leader, Govt. of India's del. to South Africa 50; visited numerous countries to study condition of Indians settled there; mem. of Govt. of India's Del. to Malaya 46; Gen. Sec. All India Seva Samiti, Allahabad; Chair. Nat. Cadet Corps Cttee. 46-47; mem. Armed Forces Reorganization Cttee. 46-47; Nat. Commr. Bharat Scouts and Guides 50-55, 61-63, of State Re-organization Comm. 53-55, Univ. Grants Comm. 53-66; Pres. Indian Council of World Affairs 48-; Chair. Indian School of Int. Studies 55-70; mem. Exec. Council Banaras Hindu Univ. 58-65, 68-71; Trustee, India Int. Centre 60-; Chair. of Railway Accidents Inquiry Cttee. 61-63; Pres. Indian Asscn. for Advancement of Urdu 62-72; Vice-Pres. Indian Council for Cultural Relations 66-; Chair. Railways Study Team of Admin. Reform Comm. 67-69; mem. Exec. Council Delhi Univ. 68, Agra Univ. 72; Pres. Cen. Cttee., Convention on Nat. Consensus 71-74; Pres. Delhi Branch Nat. Asscn. for the Blind; mem. Gov. Body, Inst. of Econ. Growth, India Law Inst., and several other orgs.
Indian Council of World Affairs, Sapru House, Barakhamba Road, New Delhi 110001, India.
Telephone: 384943.

Kuo Mo-jo; Chinese historian and poet; b. 1891, Loshan, Szechuan; ed. Tokyo No. 1 Higher School, Okayama No. 6 Higher School, Japan, Kyushu Imperial Univ. Medical School, Japan.
Founded Creation Society (publishing house) 20; involved in Nanchang Uprising 27; lived in Japan studying history and writing 28-37; founded *Salvation Daily* 37; Vice-Chair. Standing Cttee., Nat. People's Congress 54-; Vice-Chair. State Scientific Comm. 56-58; joined CCP 58; mem. 9th Cen. Cttee. of CCP 69, 10th Cen. Cttee. 73.
Publs. include *Fallen Leaves* 24, *Research on Ancient Chinese Society, The Bronze Age, Ten Critiques* 45, *Starry Canopy*, and translations of numerous books into Chinese including Goethe, Nietzsche, Marx, Turgenev, Galsworthy.
People's Republic of China.

Kuprianov, Alexei Andreyevich; Soviet sports administrator; b. 1908; ed. Trainers' School at State Central Inst. of Physical Culture.
Textile worker and civil aviation worker 25-34; Exec. Sec. Presidium of Cen. Board of Sporting Soc. *Dynamo* 25-52, Deputy Pres. 52-; mem. Man. Cttee. Int. Union

of Cyclists; Vice-Pres. Int. Amateurs' Fed. of Cyclists; Pres. U.S.S.R. Fed. of Cycling Sport; U.S.S.R. Merited Master of Cycling Sport; mem. C.P.S.U. 39-.
State Committee for Physical Culture and Sports, 4 Skatertny pereulok, Moscow, U.S.S.R.

Kuraishi, Tadao; Japanese politician; b. 1900; ed. Hosei Univ.
Member, House of Reps.; Chair. House of Reps. Labour Affairs Cttee., Budget Cttee.; Minister of Labour 55-56, 58-59; Minister of Agric. and Forestry 67-68, 70-71, 73-74; Chair. Liberal-Democratic Party Nat. Org. Cttee.
House of Representatives, Tokyo, Japan.

Kurata, Motoharu, B.ENG.; Japanese business executive; b. 22 July 1901, Fukushima; *s.* of Tomehachiro Yokoyama and Sue Kurata; *m.* Chie Toda 1930; one *s.*; ed. Tokyo Inst. of Technology.
Joined Asahi Glass Co. Ltd. 25, Man. Dir. 50-63, Exec. Vice-Pres. 63-67, Pres. 67-73, Chair. 73-; Pres. Iwaki Glass Co. Ltd.; Chair. of Board, Asahi Fiber Glass Co. Ltd.; Dir. Nippon Kogaku K.K.; Exec. Dir. Fed. of Econ. Orgs.; Medal of Honour with Purple Ribbon and with Blue Ribbon.
Leisure interest: golf.
4-23-12, Nishigotanda, Meguro-ku, Tokyo, Japan.
Telephone: 03-218-5555 (Office); 03-491-6230 (Home).

Kuratowski, Kazimierz, PHIL.D.; Polish mathematician; b. 2 Feb. 1896, Warsaw; *s.* of Marek and Róża (Karzewska) Kuratowski; *m.* Jadwiga Kozłowska 1927; one *d.*; ed. Glasgow and Warsaw Univs.
Docent Warsaw Univ. 21; Prof. Lwów Polytechnic 27-33, Dean 29-30; Prof. Mathematics Warsaw Univ. 33-66, Prof. Emeritus 66-; Editor *Fundamenta Mathematicae* and *Monografie Matematyczne* and *Bulletin* (Polish Acad. of Sciences); fmr. Vice-Pres. Polish Acad. of Sciences, now Chair. Scientific Council Math. Inst.; fmr. Pres. and Hon. mem. Polish Mathematical Soc.; fmr. Dir. Mathematical Inst. of Polish Acad. of Science; Polish Nat. Prize 49 and 51; foreign Hon. mem. Soviet Acad. of Sciences, Hungarian Acad. of Sciences, Austrian Acad. of Sciences, Palermo Acad. of Arts and Sciences, German Acad. of Sciences, Accad. Naz. dei Lincei (Rome), Acad. of Sciences of Argentina; Hon. F.R.S. (Edinburgh), Hon. Dr. (Prague), Hon. LL.D. (Glasgow), Hon. Dr. Maths. (Wrocław), Hon. Dr. (Sorbonne), Bolzano Gold Medal (Czechoslovak Acad. of Sciences), Sierpinski Medal (Univ. of Warsaw), Jurzykowski Prize (U.S.A.) 71; Commdr. Cross of Order Polonia Restituta, Order of Banner of Labour 1st and 2nd Class, Medal of 30th Anniversary of People's Poland 74 and other awards.
Publs. *Topologie I* 33, *II* 50 (translated into English and Russian), *Calculus* 48, *Set Theory* (with Mostowski) 52, *Introduction to Set Theory and Topology* 55 (translated into French, Romanian and Spanish), *Half a Century of Polish Mathematics 1920-1970—Reminiscences and Reflections* 73, and about 170 short publications.
Ul. Kielecka 42 m. 3, 02-530 Warsaw, Poland.
Telephone: 49-15-21.

Kurbanov, Rakhmankul; Soviet teacher and politician; b. 1912; ed. Bukhara Pedagogical Inst. and Higher Party School, Moscow.
Member C.P.S.U. 40-; teacher 37-42; Party Worker 43-61; Chair. Council of Ministers Uzbek S.S.R. 61-71; mem. Central Cttee. of C.P.S.U. 61-71; Deputy to U.S.S.R. Supreme Soviet 54-; Order of Lenin (twice), Order of Red Banner of Labour, two Badges of Honour, etc.
Council of Ministers, Tashkent, U.S.S.R.

Kurdgeldiyev, Mahmed Geldiyevich; Soviet politician; b. 1912; ed. Planning and Economic Inst.
Instructor, Ashkhabad Trade and Co-operative Coll. 29-37, Dir. 38-41; mem. C.P.S.U. 41-; Vice-Chair.

Peoples' Commissars of Turkmenian S.S.R. 41-42; Business Man. Presidium of Supreme Soviet of Turkmenian S.S.R. 42-43; Attaché, New Delhi 47-50; Dir. Turkmenistan Pavilion, Exhbn. of Nat. Econ. Achievements 50-52; mem. staff Central Cttee. of C.P. of Turkmenistan 52-57; Perm. Rep. of Turkmenian S.S.R. Council of Ministers to U.S.S.R. Council of Ministers 57-; Deputy to Supreme Soviet of Turkmenistan; Badge of Honour.
Permanent Representation of Turkmenian S.S.R. Council of Ministers to U.S.S.R. Council of Ministers, Aksakov pereulok 22, Moscow, U.S.S.R.

Kurdiani, Archil Grigorevich; Soviet (Georgian) architect; b. 1903; ed. Georgian Polytechnic Inst.
Chief Architect, Tbilisi 36-44; Chief Admin. on Architecture, Georgian Council of Ministers 44-53; Chair. Union of Architects of Georgian S.S.R. 59-62, Prof. 60-; Merited Worker of Arts, Georgian S.S.R.; State Prize 41; U.S.S.R. People's Architect 70; Order of Lenin and Red Banner of Labour.
Main works: Dynamo stadium, Tbilisi 37, Pavilion of Georgian S.S.R., U.S.S.R. Econ. Achievement Exhibition 39, Didybinsky Bridge 54, Television station, Tbilisi 54, Hotels, etc.
Georgian Union of Architects, Tbilisi, U.S.S.R.

Kurdyumov, Georgy Vyacheslavovich; Soviet metallurgist; b. 14 Feb. 1902, Rylsk, Kursk; ed. Leningrad Polytechnical Inst.
Research with X-rays on quenched and tempered steel, Physical Tech. Inst., Leningrad 24-32; Head, Phase Transformation Lab., Physical Tech. Inst., Dniepropetrovsk 32-44; Prof. Metal Physics, Dniepropetrovsk Univ. 33-41; Dir. Inst. of Metallography and Metal Physics, Cen. Research Inst. of Ferrous Metallurgy, Moscow 44-; Dir. Lab. of Metal Physics, Ukraine Acad. of Sciences, Kiev 46-51, Dir. Inst. of Solid State Physics, U.S.S.R. Acad. of Sciences 62-73; Hadfield Memorial Lecturer 59; Lecturer, AJME Inst. of Metals 62; Fellow, Metallurgical Soc., AJME 65-; mem. Ukraine Acad. of Sciences 39-, Corresp. mem. U.S.S.R. Acad. of Sciences 46-53, mem. 53-; mem. Acad. of Sciences, German Dem. Repub. 69; October Revolution State Prize 49, Hero of Socialist Labour 69, Orders of Lenin (4), Red Banner of Labour (2), Grande Médaille (Chatelier) Metallurgical Soc. of France 66, Heyndenkmünze, German Soc. of Metallography 73.
Publs. *Crystal Structure of Martensite* 26-29, *Martensite-Austenite Lattice Relationships* 30, *Heat Treatment of Steels in the Light of X-Ray Investigations* 32, *Mechanism of the Phase Transformations in Eutectoid Alloys* 33, *Reversible Martensitic Transformations in the Alloys of Cu with Al, Sn and Zn* 32-41, *Theory of the Hardening and Tempering of Steel* 40, *Diffusionless (Martensitic) Transformations* 48, *Thermoelastic Equilibrium and Elastic Martensite Crystals* 48-49, *Isothermal Austenite-Martensite Transformation at Low Temperatures* 48, *Use of Radioactive Isotopes for the Study of Diffusion and the Interatomic Interactions* 55, *Strengthening of Metals and Alloys* 58-62, *Phenomena of Quenching and Tempering of Steels* 60, *Anomalies of Axial Ratio of Martensite Lattice and Mechanism of the Austenite-Martensite Transformation* 75, *Behaviour of Carbon Atoms in Martensite* 66-75.
U.S.S.R. Academy of Sciences, 14 Leninsky Prospect, Moscow, U.S.S.R.

Kurmazenko, Alexander Kirillovich; Soviet foreign trade official; b. 8 Sept. 1917; ed. Dnepropetrovsk Metallurgical Inst. and Acad. of Foreign Trade.
Member C.P.S.U. 45-; Official, Main Dept. of Soviet Property Abroad 48-56; Official, Ministry of Foreign Trade 56-58; Deputy U.S.S.R. Commercial Rep. in Italy 58-61; U.S.S.R. Commercial Rep. in Turkey 61-65; Chair. *Techmashexport* Trust 66-; Badge of Honour (three times).

Techmashexport Trust, 35 Mosfilmovskaya ulitsa, Moscow, U.S.S.R.

Kurokawa, (Noriaki) Kisho, M.TECH.; Japanese architect; b. 8 April 1934; ed. Kyoto and Tokyo Univs.
President, Kisho N. Kurokawa Architect & Assocs., Urban Design Consultants Co. Ltd.; Dir. Inst. of Social Engineering; Adviser, Japan Nat. Railways, Ministry of Public Welfare, Ministry of Educ., Japan Broadcasting Asscn.; mem. Architectural Inst. of Japan, Japan Soc. of Futurology, City Planning Inst. of Japan, etc.; awarded Takamura Kotaro Design Prize and prizes in int. competitions in Peru, France and Tanzania.
Works include: Nitto Food Co. 63, Cen. Lodge in Nat. Childrens Land 64, Hans Christian Anderson Memorial Lodge 64, Handicapped People's Town 66, Sagae City Hall 67, Odakyu Rest House 69, Sakura City Hall 69, Takara, Toshiba and Theme Pavilions, Expo 70, Sapporo Prince Hotel 71, Nakagin Business Capsule 71, Karuizawa Prince Hotel 73, Shirahama Prince Hotel 73, Bank of Fukuoka 74, Sony Building 74, Nat. Museum of Folklore 74, Hotel New Ohtani, Bulgaria 75.
Publs. include: *Concrete Prefabricated House, Metabolism* 60, *Urban Design* 64, *Action Architecture* 67, *Homo-Movens* 69, *Works of Kisho N. Kurokawa* 69, *Kisho N. Kurokawa* 69, *Creation of Contemporary Architecture* 71, *Complete Work Series of Existing Architects of Japan, Conception of Metabolism, Future of Life, Development of Post-Industrial Society, Entry into Urbanism.*
1-2-3 Kita Aoyama, Minato-ku, Tokyo, Japan.

Kurosawa, Akira; Japanese film director; b. 1910; ed. Keika Middle School.
Joined Toho Film Co. as asst. dir. 36; dir. his first film *Sugata Sanshiro* 43; First Prize, Venice Film Festival for *Rashomon*, Silver Lion for *The Seven Samurai*, American Motion Picture Acad. Award for *Rashomon*; Order of the Yugoslav Flag.
Films: *Sugata Sanshiro, Ichiban Utsukushiku, Torano Owofumu Otokotachi, Waga Seishun ni Kuinashi, Subarashiki Nichiyobi, Yoidore Tenshi, Shizukanaru Ketto, Norainu, Rashomon, Hakuchi, Ikiru, The Seven Samurai, Ikimono no Kiroku, Kumonosu Jio, Donzoko, Kakushi Toride no San Akunin, The Hidden Fortress, Throne of Blood, Yojimbo, The Bad Sleep Well, Sanjuro, High and Low, Akahige, Redbeard, Dodes'ka-den.*
1755 Nichome Matsubara-machi, Setagaya-ku, Tokyo, Japan.

Kurowski, Zdzisław; Polish politician; b. 14 April 1937, Janiec, Ciechanów Voivodship; ed. Cen. School of Agriculture, Warsaw.
Member of Peasant Youth Union (ZMW), Chair. Cen. Board 66-71; mem. of Exec. of Warsaw Voivodship Cttee., Polish United Workers' Party (PZPR) 64-66, Deputy mem. Cen. Cttee. 68-71, mem. Cen. Cttee. 71-; Deputy to Seym (Parl.) 69-; First Sec. Białystok Voivodship Cttee. of PZPR, then Chair. of Białystok People's Provincial Council 72-75; Chair. Cen. Board of Fed. of Polish Socialist Youth Unions May 75-.
Rada Główna FSZMP, ul. Nowy Swiat 18/20, 00-920 Warsaw, Poland.

Kuroyedov, Vladimir Alexeyevich; Soviet politician; b. 1906; ed. Gorky Teachers' Training Inst.
Teacher, Secondary School Dir., Deputy Head of Dept. of Educ., Gorky 28-34; Dir. Gorky Automechanical Technical Coll. 34-39; mem. C.P.S.U. 36-; Instructor, Gorky Regional Cttee. of C.P.S.U. 39-40; Dept. Head, Central Cttee. of C.P. of Lithuania 40-41; Sec. Gorky City Cttee. C.P.S.U. and Editor *Gorkovskaya Kommuna* (regional newspaper) 41-46; Dept. Head, Central Cttee. of C.P.S.U. 46-49; Sec. Sverdlovsk Regional Cttee., C.P.S.U. 49-59; Chair. of Council for Russian Orthodox Church of U.S.S.R. Council of Ministers 60-66; Chair. of

U.S.S.R. Council of Ministers' Council for Matters of Religion 66-; Order of Red Banner of Labour.
Council for Matters of Religion, U.S.S.R. Council of Ministers, 11/2 Smolensky Boulevard, Moscow, U.S.S.R.

Kursanov, Andrei Lvovich, sc.D.; Soviet plant physiologist; b. 8 Nov. 1902, Moscow; ed. Moscow Univ.
Central Inst. of Sugar Industry 29-34; A. N. Bakh Inst. of Biochemistry 34-54; Dir. K. A. Timiriazev Inst. of Plant Physiology and Head of Lab. of Translocation of Substances 52-; mem. U.S.S.R. Acad of Sciences 53-, Leopoldina German Acad. of Natural Science 58-, Acad. of Agriculture of France 64-, Polish Acad. of Science; Hon. mem. German Botanical Soc. 61-, Amer. Acad. of Arts and Sciences 62-; Hero of Socialist Labour 69; Order of Lenin (four); Red Banner of Labour; Commdr. Ordre de Léopold II (Belgium).
Publs. *The Reversible Action of Enzymes in Living Grown Cells* 40, *Synthesis and Transformation of the Tannins in Tea Leaves* 53, *The Root System as an Organ of Metabolism* 57, *The Interaction of Physiological Processes in Plants* 60, *Metabolism and the Transport of Organic Substances in the Phloem* 63, *Competition of Sugars for Penetrations into Cells* 64, *Biochemical basis of transport and accumulation of Sucrose in the Sugarbeet plant, Translocations of Assimilates in the Plant* (monograph) 76.
K. A. Timiryasev Plant Physiology Institute, Academy of Sciences, 35 Botanicheskaja, Moscow 127273, U.S.S.R.

Kurtág, György; Hungarian composer; b. 19 Feb. 1926, Lugos; ed. Budapest Music Acad. and in Paris.
Deutsche Akad. Austauschdienst (West Berlin) 71; Prof. of Composition, Music Acad. of Budapest; Erkel Prize (three times), Kossuth Prize 2nd Degree 73.
Compositions: Concerto for Viola 54, String Quartet 59, Quintet for Wind Instruments 59, Eight pieces for piano 60, *Signs* (for solo viola) 61, Eight duets for violin and dulcimer 61, *The Sayings of Peter Bornemissza* (for soprano and piano) 68, Four fragments for soprano, dulcimer and violin 69, Four capriccios for soprano and chamber ensemble 70, *Splinters* solo for cimbalom 74.
1064 Budapest VI, Rózsa Ferenc utca 46, Hungary.
Telephone: 420-819.

Kurti, Nicholas, C.B.E., M.A., DR.PHIL., F.R.S.; British physicist; b. 14 May 1908, Budapest, Hungary; s. of Charles and Margaret (née Pinter)Kurti; m. Georgiana Shipley 1946; two d.; ed. Minta Gymnasium, Budapest, Paris and Berlin Univs.
Asst. Breslau Tech. Univ. 31-33; attached to Clarendon Laboratory, Oxford 33-40, U.K. Atomic Energy Project 40-45; Demonstrator in Physics, Oxford Univ. 45-60, Reader 60-67, Prof. 67-75, Emer. Prof. 75-; Senior Research Fellow, Brasenose Coll. 47-67, Professorial Fellow 67-75, Emer. Fellow 75-; Vice-Pres. Royal Soc. 65-67; Foreign Hon. mem. American Acad. of Arts and Sciences 68; Hon. mem. Hungarian Acad. of Sciences 70, Société Française de Physique 74; Foreign mem. Finnish Acad. of Sciences and Letters 74, Acad. of Sciences of G.D.R. 75; Holweck Prize and Medal (British and French Physical Socs.) 55, Fritz London Award 57, Hughes Medal, Royal Soc. 69.
Leisure interest: cooking.
Publs. Papers on low temperature physics and magnetism.
Office: Department of Engineering, Parks Road, Oxford, OX1 3PJ; Home: 38 Blandford Avenue, Oxford, OX2 8DZ, England.
Telephone: Oxford (0865) 59988 (Office); Oxford (0865) 56176 (Home).

Kurtz, Efrem; American conductor; b. 7 Nov. 1900, St. Petersburg, Russia; m. Elaine Shaffer 1955 (died 1973); ed. St. Petersburg Conservatory and Stern Conservatory, Berlin.
Conductor, Berlin Philharmonic Orchestra 21-24;

Musical Dir. Stuttgart Philharmonic 24-33; Guest conductor N.Y. Philharmonic, N.B.C. Symphony, San Francisco, Cleveland and Chicago Symphony Orchestras 33-54; Musical Dir. Kansas City Symphony Orchestra 41-46, Houston Symphony Orchestra 48-54; during recent years has been guest conductor of major orchestras of Europe, Japan, Australia, North America, Canada, Israel, U.S.A., U.S.S.R., South Africa and at numerous festivals; Commdr. Order of Merit of Italy; Medal of Honor of Bruckner Soc. of America; awarded golden disc by Columbia Records Inc. after three millionth sale of his recordings with the N.Y. Philharmonic.
Leisure interests: drawing, collecting (paintings, stamps, historical letters), mountaineering.
c/o 19 Air Street, Regent Street, London W1R 6QL, England.
Telephone: 01-734-5459.

Kuryłowicz, Jerzy, PH.D.; Polish philologist; b. 26 Aug. 1895, Stanisławów; s. of Roman and Flora (Kleczeńska) Kuryłowicz; m. Helena Kropińska 1923; one s. one d.; ed. Lwów and French Univs.
Lecturer, Lwów Univ. 26-28, Extraordinary Prof. 28-34, Prof. 34-46; Prof. Wroclaw Univ. 46-48, Jagiellonian Univ., Cracow 48-; Prof. Emer. 65; Visiting Prof. Harvard 64-66; fmr. Chair. Linguistics Cttee. Polish Acad. of Sciences; mem. Polish Acad. of Sciences 52-, Danish Acad., Irish Acad., Norwegian Acad., Serbian Acad., American Acad. of Arts and Sciences, Austrian Acad., Italian Acad., British Acad., Académie des Inscriptions et Belles Lettres (Paris); Polish rep. Comité Int. Permanent des Linguistes; State Prize, First Class 55, 64; Prix Volney; Hon. Dr. (Sorbonne, Dublin, Vienna, Chicago, Ann Arbor, Edinburgh, Liège, Cracow); Commdr. Cross with Star of Order Polonia Restituta, Order of Banner of Labour 1st Class, Order "für Wissenschaft und Kunst" (Austria).
Publs. *Etudes indo-européennes* 35, *L'accentuation des langues indo-européennes* 52, *L'apophonie en indoeuropéen* 56, *Esquisses linguistiques* 60, *L'apophonie en sémitique* 61, *Inflectional Categories of Indo-European* 64, *Indogermanische Grammatik* 68, *Studies in Semitic Grammar and Metrics* 72, *Metrik und Sprachgeschichte* 75.
Podwale 1, 31-118 Cracow, Poland.
Telephone: 228-20.

Kusch, Polykarp, M.S., PHD..; American physicist; b. 26 Jan. 1911; ed. Case Inst. of Technology and Univ. of Illinois.
Assistant in Physics, Univ. of Illinois 31-36; Research Asst. Univ. of Minnesota 36-37; Instructor in Physics, Columbia Univ. 37-41; Vacuum Tube Engineer, Westinghouse Electric Corpn. 41-42; staff mem. Division of War Research, Columbia Univ. 42-44; mem. Tech. staff, Bell Telephone Laboratories 44-46; Assoc. Prof. of Physics, Columbia Univ. 46-49, Prof. 49-72, Vice-Pres. and Provost 69-72; Prof. of Physics, Univ. of Texas, Dallas 72-; research in atomic, molecular and nuclear physics; awarded Nobel Prize in Physics (jointly with Prof. W. E. Lamb) 55; mem. Nat. Acad. of Sciences; mem. Amer. Philosophical Soc.; Hon. D.Sc. (Case, Ohio, Ill., Colby, Gustavus Adolphus).
University of Texas at Dallas, Dallas, Tex. 75061, U.S.A.

Kuśniewicz, Andrzej, LL.M.; Polish writer and poet; b. 30 Nov. 1904, Kowenice, near Sambor; s. of the late Bolesław Kuśniewicz and Joanna Ostrawa-Tworkowska Kuśniewicz; m. Anna Kotaniec; ed. Jagiellonian Univ., Cracow.
Ministry of Foreign Affairs until 39; participated in French Resistance Movement, later held in Neue Bremm and Mauthausen concentration camps; first work published 55; worked for Polish Radio 55-; mem. Polish Writer's Asscn. 59-; mem. PEN Club 70-;

Médaille de la Guerre et Résistance 47, Minister of Culture and Arts Prize, 2nd Class 65, Gold Cross of Merit 65, Award of Meritorious Culture Worker 68, Knight's Cross, Order of Polonia Restituta 70.
Publs. poetry: *Słowa o nienawiści* 56, *Diablu ogarek* 59, *Czas prywatny* 62; novels: *Korupcja* 61, *Eroica* 63, *W drodze do Koryntu* 64, *Król obojga Sycylii* 70, *Strefy* 71, *Stan nieważkości* 73.
Ul. Juliana Bruna 28 m. 57, 02-594 Warsaw, Poland. Telephone: 25-18-71.

Kusunoki, Naomichi, B.ENG.; Japanese business executive; b. 11 May 1900; ed. Tokyo Imperial Univ. Automobile Dept., Tokyo Ishikawajima Shipbuilding and Engineering Co. Ltd. 24-29, Dept. separated, firm finally became Isuzu Motors Ltd., Exec. Dir. Isuzu Motors Ltd. 43-46, Managing Dir. 46-62, Pres. 62, now Chair.; Pres. Yamato Motor Co. Ltd. 62-; Dir. Deisel Kiki Co. Ltd. 51-, Jidosha Kiki Co. Ltd. 55-, Steel Press Works Corpn. 62-, Japan Motor Industrial Fed. 49-; Pres. Soc. of Automotive Engineers of Japan Inc. 53-56; Blue Ribbon Medal 62.
Isuzu Motors, 6-22-10 Minami-Oi, Shinagawaku, Tokyo, Japan.

Kutakhov, Chief Air Marshal Pavel Stepanovich; Soviet air force officer; b. 1914; ed. Acad. of General Staff.
Turner at factory; student at Workers' Faculty 31-35; Soviet Army 35-; graduated from pilot school 38; pilot, navigator, Commdr. of Fighter Squadron and Wing during Second World War; important posts in Ministry of Defence 46-69; C.-in-C. of Air Forces and Deputy Minister of Defence 69-; Deputy to U.S.S.R. Supreme Soviet 70-; mem. C.P.S.U. Cen. Cttee. 71-; Hero of Soviet Union, Gold Star Medal and Order of Lenin.
Ministry of Defence, 34 Naberezhnaya M. Thoreza, Moscow, U.S.S.R.

Kutakov, Leonid Nikolayevich; Soviet diplomatist; b. 1918, Moscow; m.; one s. one d.; ed. Moscow Inst. of History, Philosophy and Literature.
Soviet Army, Second World War; Chief of Historical Diplomatic Div., Ministry of Foreign Affairs 46-51; Pro-Rector Moscow State Inst. of Int. Relations 52-55; Adviser to Dir. of Peking Inst. of Diplomacy, Chinese Ministry of Foreign Affairs 55-57; Counsellor, Soviet Embassy, Japan 57-59; Deputy Dir. Inst. of History of Acad. of Sciences of U.S.S.R. 61-63; Rector, Moscow State Inst. of Int. Relations 63-65; Senior Counsellor for Political Questions, Perm. Soviet Mission to UN 65-68; Under Sec.-Gen. for Political and Security Council Affairs, UN Secr. 68-73.
Publs. *A New History of International Relations 1918-45* 58, *History of Soviet-Japanese Diplomatic Relations* 62, *The Portsmouth Peace Treaty 1905* 64, *Foreign Policy and Diplomacy of Japan* 64.
c/o Ministry of Foreign Affairs, 32-34 Smolenskaya-Sennaya Ploshchad, Moscow, U.S.S.R.

Kutscher, Hans, DR.IUR.; German judge; b. 14 Dec. 1911, Hamburg; m. Irmgard Schroeder 1946; two step-d.; ed. Univ. of Graz, Austria and Univ. of Freiburg/Br., Berlin.
Civil Servant, Ministry of Commerce and Industry, Berlin 39, Ministry of Transport, Baden-Württemberg 46-51, Ministry of Foreign Affairs, Bonn 51; Sec. Legal Cttee., Conf. Cttee., Bundesrat 51-55; Judge of Fed. Constitutional Court 55-70; Judge, Court of Justice of European Communities 70-; Grosses Bundesverdienstkreuz mit Stern und Schulterband (Fed. Germany) 70.
Leisure interests: history, literature.
Publs. *Die Enteignung* 38, *Bonner Vertrag mit Zusatzvereinbarungen* 52, and numerous contributions in professional journals.
Court of Justice of the European Communities, Kirch-

berg; Home: Luxembourg-Ville, rue Nicolas Petit 4, Luxembourg; and Viertelstrasse 10, 7506 Bad Herrenalb-Neusatz, Federal Republic of Germany.
Telephone: 4762 235 (Office); 20230 (Home); 07083-2818 (Home).

Kutyrev, Boris Mikhailovich; Soviet trade corporation official; b. 14 March 1914; ed. Bauman Mechanical Engineering Inst. and Acad. of Foreign Trade, Moscow. Engineer 38-46; Derunaft Stock Co., German Dem. Repub., Asst. Soviet Trade Rep., German Dem. Repub. 49-56; Vice-Chair. *Auto-export* (motor vehicles) 56-61; Chair. *Traktoroexport* (tractors, etc.) 61-65; Soviet Trade Rep. in People's Republic of China 65-69; Commercial Rep. to German Democratic Republic 69-; mem. Communist Party; numerous decorations.
U.S.S.R. Trade Representation, Berlin, German Democratic Republic.

Kuwabara, Takeo, B.A.; Japanese writer; b. 10 May 1904, Turuga; s. of Jitsuzo Kuwabara and Shin Uta; m. Tazu Tanaka 1933; one s. five d.; ed. Kyoto Univ.
Lecturer, Kyoto Univ. 31-42; Asst. Prof., Tohoku Univ. 43-48; Prof. Kyoto Univ. 48-68, Emer. Prof. 68-; Dir. Univ. Inst. of Humanistic Studies 59-63; mem. Science Council of Japan 50-70, Vice-Pres. 60-70; Vice-Pres. Japan PEN Club 74-75.
Leisure interest: mountaineering.
Publs. *Fiction and Reality* 43, *Reflections on Contemporary Japanese Culture* 47, *Some Aspects of Contemporary French Literature* 49, *Introduction to Literature* 50, *Conquest of Mount Chogolisa* 59, *Studies on J.-J. Rousseau* 51, *Studies on the Encyclopédie* 54, *Studies on the French Revolution* 59, *Studies on Chomin Nakae* 66, *Selected Works* (in 7 vols. and 1 supplement) 68-72, *European Civilization and Japan* 74.
421, Tonodan-Yabunosita, Kamikyo-ku, Kyoto, 602 Japan.
Telephone: 231-0261.

Kuwait, H.H. The Ruler of (*see* Sabah, Emir Sabah Al Salem Al).

Kuzmich, Anton Savvich; Soviet politician; b. 20 Dec. 1908; ed. Moscow Mining Inst.
Coal industry 31-45; Mine section superintendent, Trust manager, Chief engineer and Dir. of group of mines; Deputy Minister of Coal Industry of E. Areas of U.S.S.R., Deputy Minister of Coal Industry of U.S.S.R., Minister and Deputy Minister of Coal Industry of Ukraine 46-57; Chair. Lugansk Econ. Council 57-60; Chair. Ukrainian Econ. Council 60-63; Deputy Chair. State Cttee. of Fuel Industry attached to U.S.S.R. Gosplan 63-65; Deputy Dir. A. A. Skochinsky Mining Inst. of U.S.S.R. Acad. of Sciences 65-; Alt. mem. Central Cttee. of C.P.S.U. 62-66; Deputy to U.S.S.R. Supreme Soviet 59-66; several decorations.
A. A. Skochinsky Mining Institute, Lyubertsy 4, Moscow Region, U.S.S.R.

Kuzmin, Iosif Iosifovich; Soviet engineer, politician and diplomatist; b. 19 May 1910, Astrakhan; ed. Leningrad Electrical Engineering Inst.
Engineer, later Chief Engineer, Moscow projector factory; mem. Party Control Comm., Cen. Cttee. Communist Party of the Soviet Union (Kuibyshev Region) 40; Deputy Chair. Party Control Comm., C.P.S.U. 40-46; mem. Bureau of Agriculture and Storage 47-50, Deputy Chair. 50-52; mem. Council of Ministers of U.S.S.R. 47-57, Deputy Chair. 57-59; on staff of Cen. Cttee., C.P.S.U. 52-57; Chair. State Planning Cttee. of U.S.S.R. 57-59; Chair. Scientific Economic Council with rank of Minister 59-60; Amb. to Switzerland 60-63; Expert Consultant in Dept. of Int. Econ. Orgs., Ministry of Foreign Affairs 63-.
Ministry of Foreign Affairs, 32-34 Smolenskaya-Sennaya ploshchad, Moscow, U.S.S.R.

Kuzmin, Mikhail Romanovich; Soviet foreign trade official; b. 22 Sept. 1907; ed. Inst. of Foreign Trade.
Member C.P.S.U. 31-; in People's Commissariat for Heavy Industry 30-42; mem. Collegium, Chief of Export Dept. People's Commissariat for Foreign Trade 42-43; Deputy People's Commissar for Foreign Trade 43-46; Deputy Minister of Foreign Trade 46-65; First Deputy Minister of Foreign Trade 65-; Order of Lenin (thrice), Order of Red Banner of Labour.
Ministry of Foreign Affairs, 32-34 Smolenskaya-Sennaya ploshchad, Moscow, U.S.S.R.

Kuznets, Simon, M.A., PH.D.; American economist and statistician; b. 30 April 1901; ed. Columbia Univ.
Member staff, Nat. Bureau of Economic Research, N.Y. 27-61; Prof. of Economics and Statistics, Univ. of Pa. 36-54; Assoc. Dir. Bureau of Planning and Statistics, W.P.B., Washington, D.C. 42-44; Economic Adviser, Nat. Resources Comm. of China 46; Adviser, Nat. Income Cttee. of India 50-51; Prof. of Political Economy, Johns Hopkins Univ. 54-60, Prof. of Econs., Harvard Univ. 60-71; Fellow, Amer. Asscn. for the Advancement of Science, American Statistical Asscn.; Corresp. Fellow, British Acad.; mem. U.S. Nat. Acad. of Science, Int. Statistical Inst., American Philosophical Soc., Econometric Soc., Royal Acad. of Sciences, Sweden; Hon. Ph.D., Hebrew University of Jerusalem; Hon. Fellow, Royal Statistical Soc. (England); Hon. Sc.D. (Princeton, Pennsylvania, Harvard), D.H.L. (Columbia), LL.D. (New Hampshire); Nobel Prize for Econs. 71.
Publs. *Cyclical Fluctuations in Retail and Wholesale Trade* 26, *Secular Movements in Production and Prices* 30, *Seasonal Variations in Industry and Trade* 34, *Commodity Flow and Capital Formation* 38, *National Income and its Composition* 41, *National Product Since 1869* 46, *Upper Income Shares* 53, *Economic Change* 54, *Six Lectures on Economic Growth* 59, *Capital in the American Economy* 61, *Modern Economic Growth* 66, *Economic Growth of Nations* 71, *Population, Capital and Growth* (essays) 74.
67 Francis Avenue, Cambridge, Mass. 02138, U.S.A.

Kuznetsov, Anatoly (*see* Anatol, A.).

Kuznetsov, Vasili Vasilievich; Soviet politician and diplomatist; b. 13 Feb. 1901, Sofinovka, Gorky; ed. Leningrad Polytechnical Inst. and in U.S.A.
Worked as Engineer, Makayevka Steel Works 27-31; Engineer, Elektrostal Works, Moscow 34-37; Engineer and later Chief Engineer of Glavspetstal 37-40; Vice-Chair. State Planning Cttee. (Gosplan) 40-43; mem. State Defence Cttee. 41-45; Chair. Central Cttee. Steelworkers' Union 44; Chair. All-Union Central Council of Trade Unions 44-54; Vice-Pres. World Federation of Trade Unions 45-53; Deputy Minister of Foreign Affairs and Ambassador to China 53-55; 1st Deputy Foreign Minister 55-; Rep. of U.S.S.R. in Czechoslovakia 68-; Leader, Soviet del. to frontier talks in Peking, Oct. 69-June 70; Head Soviet Del. to UN 55; joined Communist Party 27, mem. C.P.S.U. Cen. Cttee.; Deputy to Supreme Soviet 46-; State Prize 41; four Orders of Lenin, Red Banner of Labour.
Ministry of Foreign Affairs, 32-34 Smolenskaya-Sennaya ploshchad, Moscow, U.S.S.R.

Kuznetsov, Viktor Ivanovich, DR.TECH.SC; Soviet scientist; b. 27 April 1913, Moscow; ed. Leningrad Polytechnic Inst.
Engineer at a number of enterprises of Instrument-making Industry 38-; mem. C.P.S.U. 42; Corresp. mem. U.S.S.R. Acad. of Sciences 58-68, Academician 68-; research in field of automation and technical cybernetics; State Prize 43, 46.
U.S.S.R. Academy of Sciences, 14 Leninsky Prospekt, Moscow, U.S.S.R.

Kuznetsov, Vladimir Nikolaevich; Soviet diplomatist; b. 24 July 1916, Kiven village, Kursk region; ed. Chernyshevsk Saratov State Univ.
State Service till 46; Employee, Third European Dept. 46-49; Asst. then Head of Group, Gen. Secr., Ministry of Foreign Affairs 49-56; Counsellor, Soviet Embassy, Netherlands 56-60; Counsellor, First European Dept. Ministry of Foreign Affairs 60-61; Counsellor-envoy, Soviet Embassy, Indonesia 61-67; Envoy of South East Asia Dept., Ministry of Foreign Affairs 67-68; Amb. to Malaysia 68-75; Order of Red Banner of Labour, Order of Red Star, Order of Patriotic War, 1st Class, and Medals.
c/o Ministry of Foreign Affairs, 32-34 Smolenskaya-Sennaya ploshchad, Moscow, U.S.S.R.

Kuznetsov, Yuri Alexeyevich; Soviet geologist; b. 19 April 1903, Nikolsk, Volgograd; ed. Tomsk Univ.
Postgraduate, Research Assoc. Tomsk Univ. 25-27; Research Assoc., Siberian Geology Prospecting Inst. 30-33; Asst. Prof. Tomsk Industrial Inst. 33-38; Prof. Head of Chair Tomsk Polytechnical Inst. 38-58; Head of Lab., Inst. of Geology and Geophysics, Siberian Branch U.S.S.R. Acad. of Sciences 58-; Corresp. mem. U.S.S.R. Acad. of Sciences 58-66, mem. 66-.
Publs. Works on stratigraphy, tectonics, petrology and metalogeny of Altai, Kusnetski Ala-Tau, Eastern Sayans and Yenisei Ridge.
Akademgorodok, Novosibirsk, U.S.S.R.

Kwapong, Prof. Alex. A.; Ghanaian professor; b. 1927; ed. Presbyterian junior and middle schools, Akropong, Achimota Coll. and King's Coll., Cambridge.
Visiting Prof., Princeton Univ. 62; Pro Vice-Chancellor and Head of Classics Dept., Ghana Univ.; mem. Political and Educ. Cttees., Nat. Liberation Council 66; Vice-Chancellor Univ. of Ghana 66-.
University of Ghana, P.O. Box 25, Legon, nr. Accra, Ghana.

Ky, Air Vice-Marshal Nguyen Cao (*see* Nguyen Cao Ky, Air Vice-Marshal).

Kyle, Air Chief Marshal Sir Wallace (Hart), G.C.B., C.B.E., D.S.O., D.F.C.; Australian air force officer and administrator; b. 22 Jan. 1910, Kalgoorlie, W.A.; s. of A. Kyle and Ellen Christina; m. Molly Rimington (née Wilkinson) 1941; three s. one d.; ed. Guildford Grammar School, W.A., R.A.F. Coll., Cranwell, and R.A.F. Staff Coll.
Served with 17th Squadron 30-31, Fleet Air Arm 31-34; Flying Instructor 34-39; served in war 39-45; Bomber Command 40-45; R.A.F. Staff Coll. 45-47; Middle East 48-50; ADC to King George VI 49; Asst. Commdt. R.A.F. Coll., Cranwell 50-52; Dir. of Operational Requirements, Air Ministry 52-54; Air Officer Commanding, Malaya 55-57; Asst. Chief of Air Staff, Operational Requirements 57-59; Air Officer Commanding-in-Chief, Tech. Training Command 59-62; Vice-Chief of Air Staff 62-65; ADC to the Queen 66-68; Air Officer Commanding-in-Chief, Bomber Command 65-68, Strike Command 68; retd. 68; Gov. of Western Australia Oct. 75-.
Leisure interests: golf, sailing, gardening, light music.
Government House, Perth, Western Australia; and R.A.F. Club, 128 Piccadilly, London, W.1., England.

Kyllingmark, Håkon Olai; Norwegian politician; b. 19 Jan. 1915, Honningsvåg; s. of the late Martin Kyllingmark and Sigridur Saemundsdottir; m. Ingegerd Ødegaard 1942; two s. one d.
Army Service 34-45; Commanding Officer, Home Guard, District of Nord Hålogaland 45-53; has operated own business, Svolvaer 46-; mem. Svolvaer City Council 45-47, 51-63; mem. Storting 54-; Second Deputy Chair. Nat. Cttee. of Conservative Party 58; Minister

of Defence 63; Minister of Transport and Communications 65-71.
Leisure interests: sports, fishing.
Stortinget, Oslo, Norway.
Telephone: 413810.

Kyo, Machiko, Japanese actress; b. 1924.
Began her career as a dancer with the Shochiku Girls' Opera Co., Osaka; film début in *Saigo ni Warau Otoko* (Last Laughter) 49; has appeared in over 80 films including *Rashomon* 50, *Ugetsu Monogatari* 53, *Gate of Hell* 54, *Story of Shunkin* 55, *Akasen Chitai* (Street of Shame), *Teahouse of the August Moon* 56, *Yoru no Cho* (Night Butterflies) 57, *Odd Obsession* 59, *Floating Weeds* 59, *A Woman's Testament* 60; Best Actress Award for *Rashomon* 50; Jussie (Finland) Award 57.
Uni Japan Film, 9-13 Ginza 5-chome, Chuo-ku, Tokyo 104, Japan.

Kypreos, Constantinos; Greek politician; b. 1920 Cairo, Egypt; *m.*; two *s.*; ed. Caen Univ., France.
Technical Man., Abu Zaabal Co., Egypt 46-61; mem. Board of Dirs. of Bassalia Mines, Egypt 56-61; Tech. Adviser and mem. Board of Dirs. of Arab Pharmaceutical Co., Egypt 58-61; Man.-Co-ordinator and Adviser of Lurgi Gesellschaft für Chemie und Hüttenwesen, Germany, and of Krebs of Paris, France 62-64; Gen. Man. Nitro-Fertilisers Co. 64-67, mem. Board of Dirs. and Man. Dir. Nitro-Fertilisers Co. 67; Minister of Industry 67-71.
Publs. Studies on Chemical Products, Plants and Installations.
c/o Ministry of Industry, Athens, Greece.

Kyprianou, Spyros; Cypriot lawyer and politician; b. 28 Oct. 1932, Limassol; *s.* of Achilles and Maria (née Argonzov) Kyprianou; *m.* Mimi Pagathrokliton 1956; two *s.*; ed. City of London Coll. and Gray's Inn, London.
Barrister; mem. Cyprus Ethnarchy Secr. London 54-59; Minister of Justice 60; Minister of Foreign Affairs 60-72 (resigned); Chair. of Comm. of Ministers of Council of Europe 67; legal practice 72-; mem. Cyprus del. to UN Gen. Assembly 74, *ad hoc* mem. to UN Security Council 75; numerous foreign orders and decorations.
Leisure interests: literature, music, sports.
202 Kermia Buildings, 4 Diagoras Street, Nicosia, Cyprus.
Telephone: 74400.

Kyriakopoulos, Elias; Greek politician; b. 8 Nov. 1903, Patras, Greece; *m.*; one *s.*; ed. Athens, Heidelberg and Munich Univs.
Assistant Prof. of Public Law at Econ. and Commercial School of Athens 25-26; Prof. of Public Law at Highest School of Postal Services 26-27; Asst. Prof. of Constitutional Law at Athens Univ. 27-40; Prof. of Gen. Political Sciences at Salonica Univ. 40-46, Prof. of Admin. Law 46-68; Minister of Justice 68-71; medals include Order of Phoenix, Gold Cross.
c/o Ministry of Justice, Athens, Greece.

Kyriazidis, Nicolas; Greek economist; b. 3 Sept. 1927, Athens; *m.* Ellie Kyrou; ed. Oxford, Illinois and Chicago Univs.
Head of Reports Section, Ministry of Co-ordination 49; Dir. Monetary Policy Service 50; Dir. Foreign and Trade Payments 51-54; Asst. Econ. Adviser, Bank of Greece 56-60, Alt. 60-64; Deputy Dir.-Gen. Ministry of Co-ordination 62-64; Econ. Adviser, Nat. Bank of Greece 64-67; Senior Economist Int. Monetary Fund 68-70; Adviser to Govt. of Cyprus in negotiations for association with European Community 71-73; Deputy Gov. Bank of Greece 74-; took part in negotiations for European Free Trade Area (EFTA) 57-58, for association between Greece and EEC 59-61; mem. cttee. for restoration of democratic legality 73; Commdr. George I (Greece), Kt. Commdr. Léopold II (Belgium), Knight Commdr. Order of Merit of Italian Repub., Knight Commdr. Order of Merit of Fed. Repub. of Germany.
Bank of Greece, Athens; Home: 23 Amalias Street, Kifissia, Greece.
Telephone: 80-18-954 (Home).

Kyung-Wha Chung (*see* Chung, Kyung-Wha).

L

Labidi, Abdelwahab; Tunisian financier; b. 22 April 1929, Kef; *m.*; three *c.*; ed. Collège Sidiki Tunis, Institut des Hautes Etudes, Tunis, Faculty of Law, Paris Univ.

Former Gen. Man. Banque de Tunisie; Insp. Gen. Banque Nat. Agricole de Tunisie; Man. Soc. Tunisienne de Banque; Man. Dir. Nat. Devt. Bank of Niger 64-69; Vice-Pres. African Devt. Bank 69-70, Pres. 70-; Pres. African Devt. Fund 73-; Chevalier de l'Ordre National de la République de Tunisie, Officier de l'Ordre National de la République du Niger.

African Development Bank, B.P. 1387, Abidjan, Ivory Coast.

Telephone: 22-56-60.

Labis, Attilio; French ballet dancer and choreographer; b. 5 Sept. 1936; ed. Ecole de danse académique de l'Opéra, Paris.

Member Corps de Ballet at the Paris Opera 52, Premier Danseur 59, Principal Premier Danseur 60-65, Maître de ballet adjoint 65-; Guest Dancer in London, Paris, Washington, Tokyo, Moscow, Kiev, Leningrad, Rome, Berlin, Munich, Stuttgart, and Sydney; Chief Choreographer at the Paris Opera.

36 rue du Chemin-de-fer, 78380 Bougival, France.

Labisse, Félix Louis Victor Léon; French painter and theatrical designer; b. 9 March 1905; ed. Coll. St. Jean, Douai and Lycée Michelet, Paris.

Lived in Ostend 27-32, in Paris area since 32; mem. Cttee. Salon de Mai, in charge of Surrealist and Fantastic Art Rooms; one-man exhbns. in Paris, Brussels, Liège, Antwerp, Rio de Janeiro, São Paulo, Buenos Aires, Milan, Cologne, London, New York, etc., Retrospective Exhbn. Knokke-Le-Zoute 60; mem. Institut de France, Acad. des Beaux-Arts; mem. Higher Council for Teaching of Fine Arts; mem. Comm. for Artistic Creation, Ministry of Arts and Letters; Chevalier Légion d'Honneur, Officier Ordre des Arts et Lettres, Officier Ordre de la Couronne de Belgique, Cruzeiro do Sul do Brasil, Commandeur de l'Ordre Nationale de la Côte d'Ivoire; Grand Prix Bienal of São Paulo for theatre decors 57.

Works in: Musée d'Art Moderne, Paris, Musée d'Art Moderne, Ville de Paris, Musée de Lille, and museums in Douai, Liège, Tel-Aviv, Rio de Janeiro, Ostend, and Museum of Modern Art, New York.

Major theatre decors and costumes for: *Hamlet, Les Nuits de la Colère, Le Procès* (Kafka), *Zadig, Noë, Elisabeth la Femme sans homme, L'Orestie, Le Séducteur, Fabien, Le Martyre de Saint Sébastien, Le Château* (Kafka), *Le Médium, Le Château de Barbe-Bleue, Le Marriage de Monsieur Mississippi* (Dürrenmatt), *Partage de Midi, Le Diable et le bon Dieu, Faust, Piège de lumiére, The Prisoner, Liliom, L'Amérique* (Kafka), *Padmovati, Le Roi d'Ys, La Révélation, Lazare, Iréne Innocente, Le Sabre de mon père,* etc.

21 rue Saint James, 92200 Neuilly-sur-Seine, France.

Labouchere, Sir George Peter, G.B.E., K.C.M.G.; British diplomatist; b. 2 Dec. 1905, London; *s.* of Frank Labouchere and Evelyn Stirling; *m.* Rachel Hamilton-Russell 1943; ed. Charterhouse and Univ. of Paris

Entered diplomatic service 29; served Madrid, Cairo, Rio de Janeiro, Rome, Stockholm, Nanking, Buenos Aires and Vienna; Counsellor 46; Minister to Hungary 53-55; Amb. to Belgium 55-60, to Spain 60-66; retd. 66; Fellow of the R.S.A.

Leisure interests: Oriental ceramics, contemporary art, shooting and fishing.

Dudmaston, Bridgnorth, Shropshire, England.

Telephone: 07467-351.

Labouisse, Eve Denise, B.S., PH.B. (Mrs. Henry R. Labouisse, née Curie); American writer, journalist and lecturer; b. 6 Dec. 1904, Paris, France; *d.* of Pierre and Marie (née Sklodowska) Curie; *m.* Henry R. Labouisse (*q.v.*) 1954; ed. Coll. Sévigné, Paris.

Went to London from France 40; war corresp. Libya, Russia, Burma, China 42; Lieut. Women's Aux. Forces, Free French Army 43-44; returned to Paris 45; co-publisher *Paris-Presse* 45-49; special adviser to Sec.-Gen. NATO, Paris 52-54; American citizen since 56.

Publs. *Madame Curie* 37 (trans. into 35 languages), *Journey among Warriors* 43.

1 Sutton Place South, New York, N.Y. 10022, U.S.A.

Labouisse, Henry Richardson, B.A., LL.B.; American United Nations official; b. 11 Feb. 1904, New Orleans, La.; *s.* of Henry and Frances (née Huger) Labouisse; *m.* 1st Elizabeth S. Clark 1935 (died 1945), one *d.*; *m.* 2nd Eve Curie (*q.v.* Eve Labouisse) 1954; ed. Princeton and Harvard Univs.

Attorney-at-law N.Y.C. 29-41; Asst. Chief Division of Defence Materials, Dept. of State 41-43 and Chief of Division 43; Deputy Dir. Office of Foreign Economic Co-ordination 43; Chief Eastern Hemisphere Division 44; Minister, Economic Affairs, U.S. Embassy, Paris 45; Special Asst. to Under-Sec. of State for Economic Affairs 46; Special Asst. to Dir., Office of European Affairs 46; Head U.S. del. E.E.C. 48; Co-ordinator for Foreign Aid and Assistance 48; Dir. Office of British Commonwealth and Northern European Affairs 49; Chief Special Mission to France of Economic Co-operation Admin. 51-54; Chief Mutual Security Agency Special Mission to France 52; Dir. UN Relief and Works Agency for Palestine Refugees 54-58; Consultant, Int. Bank for Reconstruction and Development 59-61; Head of IBRD Mission to Venezuela 59; Dir. Int. Co-operation Admin. 61-62; U.S. Amb. to Greece 62-65; Exec. Dir. United Nations Children's Fund (UNICEF) 65-; Hon. LL.D. (Univ. of Bridgeport) 61, (Princeton Univ.) 65, (Lafayette Coll.) 66, (Tulane Univ.) 67.

UNICEF, 6th Floor, 866 United Nations Plaza, New York, N.Y. 10017; Home: 1 Sutton Place South, New York, N.Y. 10022, U.S.A.

Telephone: PL4-1234 (Office); 751-4156 (Home).

Labuda, Gerard; Polish historian; b. 28 Dec. 1916, Nowa Huta, Kartuzy district; ed. Poznán Univ. and Lund Univ., Sweden.

Doctor 44-46, Docent 45-60, Assoc. Prof. 50-56, Prof. 56-; Rector, Poznán Univ. 62-65; Sec.-Gen. Poznán Soc. of Friends of Learning 61-70, Pres. 72-; Editor *Roczniki Historyczne* (Annals of History) 69-; Corresp. mem. Polish Acad. of Sciences 51-69, mem. 69-, mem. Praesidium 72-74; mem. European Soc. of Culture 63-; State Prizes 49, 50, 70; Knight's Cross, Order of Polonia Restituta 54, Officer's Cross 60, Commdr.'s Cross 65; Palacki Medal (Czechoslovakia) 68, Medal of 30th Anniversary of People's Poland 74.

Publs. *Pierwsze państwo słowiańskie—państwo Samona* (First Slavonic State—Samon's State) 49, *Fragmenty dziejów Słowiańszczyzny Zachodniej* (Fragments of History of the West Slavs), *Polska granica zachodnia. Tysiac lat dziejów politycznych* (The Western Frontier of Poland: A Thousand Years of Political History) 71; co-author, *Słownik Starożytności Słowiańskich* (Dictionary of Slavonic Antiquities), *Historia Pomorza* (History of Pomerania); numerous articles.

Ul. Kanclerska 8, 60-327 Poznán, Poland.

Lacarte Muró, Julio Antonio; Uruguayan diplomatist; b. 1918; ed. Inst. de Bordeaux.

Attaché and later Sec. Uruguayan Embassy, London

40-46; Deputy Dir. Div. of Int. Trade and Balance of Payments, UN and Deputy Exec. Sec. GATT 46-48; Minister-Counsellor Washington 49-51; Minister to Ecuador 51-54; Amb. to Bolivia 54-56, to U.S.A. and Rep. to Org. of American States 56-60; Amb. to German Fed. Repub. 60-67; Rep. to European Econ. Communities 63; First Vice-Pres. GATT 64, Pres. GATT; Minister of Industry and Trade 67; Amb. to Argentina 68; rep. to Intergovernmental Co-ordinating Cttee. for River Plate Basin 68-; mem. UN Cttee. for Devt. Planning; Pres. LAFTA 75; corresp. mem. Uruguayan Acad. of Economics; Ecuadorean, German and Bolivian decorations.

Publs. *New Principles in World Trade* 49, *Uruguay and the General Agreement on Tariffs and Trade* 51, *Foreign Economic Policy of Uruguay* 55.

c/o Ministerio de Relaciones Exteriores, Montevideo, Uruguay.

Lacerda, Carlos; Brazilian politician, writer, lecturer and publisher; b. 30 April 1914, State of Rio, Brazil; s. of Mauricio Paiva de Lacerda and Olga Werneck Lacerda; m. Leticia Abbruzzini 1938; two s. one d.
Writer, Students' Column *Diário de Noticias* 29; journalist on *Diário Carioca*, *O Jornal*, *Agência Meridional*, *Observador Econômico e Financeiro* and *Correio de Manhã*; founder *Tribuna da Imprensa*; fmr. Federal Deputy, Leader of the Opposition; Gov. of Guanabara State 61-65; Leader, Nat. Democratic Union; Pres. Novo Rio S.A. Credit, Novo Rio S.A. Housing Corpn., Nova Frontiera S.A. publishing house; Dir. Nova York S.A. Real Estate; Nat. Democratic Union Candidate for Pres. of Brazil; Maria Moors Cabot Prize, Columbia Univ., Mergenthaler Award, Interamerican Press Soc.
Leisure interests: fishing, gardening, travelling.
R. Carmo 27-4°, Rio de Janeiro, Guanabara, Brazil.
Telephone: 231-5830.

Lacher, Hans, LL.D.; Swiss diplomat; b. 8 Aug. 1912, Basle; m. Daisy E. Bubeck 1941; one s.; ed. Basle and Paris Univs.
Swiss Foreign Office 41-48; First Sec. Swiss Legation, Wash. 48-53; Head of Swiss Del. Berlin 54-61; Amb. to the Philippines 61-63; Consul-Gen. New York 63-69; Amb. to Fed. Germany 69-75.
Leisure interests: history, photography, art.
"Au Thovex", CH-1807 Blonay, Switzerland.

Lachs, Manfred, LL.M., LL.D., DR.JUR. (Cracow, Nancy); Polish international lawyer; b. 21 April 1914, Stanisławów; s. of Ignancy and Sophie Lachs; m. Halina Antonina; one d.; ed. Uniwersytet Jagielloński, Cracow, Univ. of Vienna and London School of Economics.
Director, Legal and Treaties Dept., Ministry for Foreign Affairs 47-60; Prof. Acad. of Political Sciences, Warsaw 49-50; Prof. of Int. Law, Univ. of Warsaw 52-66; Minister 56-60, Amb. 60-66; Judge, Int. Court of Justice, The Hague 67-, Pres. 73-76; Polish Delegate, Paris Peace Conf. 46; mem. Polish Del. to UN Gen. Assembly 46-52, 55-60, 62-64, 64-66; Rep. of Poland to UN Disarmament Cttee. 62-64; Chair. Legal Cttee., UN Gen. Assembly 49, 51, 55, Vice-Chair. 52; mem. UN Int. Law Comm. 62-, Rapporteur 62, Chair. of its sub-cttee. on Succession of States and Govts., Special Rapporteur on sub-cttee.; Chair. UN Legal Comm. for Outer Space 62-66; Trustee, UN Inst. of Training and Research; mem. Perm. Court of Arbitration, Inst. of Int. Law, Polish Acad. of Sciences, Acad. of Moral Sciences Bologna, Mexican Acad. of Int. Law, Curatorium Hague Acad. of Int. Law; involved with various other UN orgs. and cttees.; Lecturer various acads., univs. and insts. in Europe and North and South America; Distinguished Visiting Senior Fellow, New York Univ. 70; Hon. mem. Int. Acad. of Astronautics; Gold Medal for Outstanding Achievements in Law Making for Outer Space 66; Howard World Jurist Award 75; Hon.

Dr. (Univ. of Algiers); Hon. Dr. jur. et pol. sc. (Univ. of Budapest); Hon. LL.D. (Univ. of Delhi); Hon. D.Sc. (Law) (Univ. of Moscow), Hon. Dr. (Nice, Bucharest, Dalhousie, New York, Brussels, Southampton Univs.).
Leisure interests: walking, reading, science, science fiction.
Publs. Numerous essays and articles and *War Crimes, An Attempt to Define the Issues* 45, *The Geneva Agreements on Indochina* (in Polish) 55 (Russian trans. 56), *Les développements et Fonctions des Traités Multi-latéraux: Recueil des Cours* 57, *The Multilateral Treaties* (in Polish) 58 (Russian, Hungarian and Spanish trans.), *The Polish-German Frontier* (in English, French, Spanish and German), *The Law of Outer Space, A Law in-the-making, An Experience in Contemporary Law-Making* 62, *Recueil des Cours* 64.
The International Court of Justice, Peace Palace, The Hague 2012, Netherlands.
Telephone: The Hague 392344.

Laclavère, Georges; French geophysicist; b. 28 June 1906, Nice; s. of Etienne Laclavère and Marie Thérèse Huet; m. Marcelle Todd 1934; one s. one d.; ed. Ecole Polytechnique, Paris.
Service Géographique Paris 34; geodetic and astronomical operations in France and in Overseas Territories 36-40; Inst. Géographique National 40-74; Sec.-Gen. Int. Union of Geodesy and Geophysics 51-63; mem. Int. Cttee. for the Int. Geophysical Year 53-59; Chief Dept. of Cartography, Inst. Géographique National, Paris 57-63, Dir. 63-74; mem. Bureau des Longitudes 57; Pres. Scientific Cttee. for Antarctic Research 58-63, French Nat. Cttee. for Antarctic Research; Treas. Int. Council of Scientific Unions 61-69; Sec.-Gen. Comité Int. de Géophysique 59-65; mem. Centre Nat. de la Recherche Scientifique 60-; Dir. of Programme UN Conf. on Science and Technology 61-63; Pres. French Nat. Cttee. of Geodesy and Geophysics 70-; mem. Exec. Cttee. Int. Council of Scientific Unions 63-72; Officier Légion d'Honneur, Commdr. Ordre Nat. du Mérite, Croix de Guerre, Legion of Merit.
Leisure interest: stamp collecting.
Publs. *Traité de Géodésie* (with P. Tardi) 54, and numerous articles in scientific journals.
53 ave. de Breteuil, Paris 7e, France.
Telephone: 734-94-26.

Laco, Karol, LL.D., D.SC.; Czechoslovak politician; b. 28 Oct. 1921, Sobotiště; ed. Faculty of Law, Comenius Univ., Bratislava.
Member of Faculty of Law, Comenius Univ. 47-, Asst. Prof. 52, Prof. 63, Dean 53-56, 57-59, 60-61; Deputy to House of Nations, Fed. Assembly 68-71; Deputy to Slovak Nat. Council 68-71; Deputy Prime Minister of Č.S.S.R. 69-; Chair. Legislative Council of Fed. Govt. 69-; mem. Czechoslovak Pugwash Cttee. 65-; Chair. Co-ordination Cttee. of Govt. of Č.S.S.R. for Nat. Cttees. 70-; Deputy to House of the People, Fed. Assembly 71-; Order of Labour 69, 71, Gold Medal Comenius Univ. 69.
Publs. *The National Committees, the Core of the Political Basis of People's Democratic Czechoslovakia* 54, *Constitutional Law No. 33/1956 on the Slovak National Organs* 56, *The Social System of the Czechoslovak Socialist Republic* 60, *Constitution of pre-Munich Č.S.R. and Constitution of Č.S.S.R.* (Part I) 66; textbooks and study aids; contributions to specialized journals.
Presidium of the Czechoslovak Government, Prague 1, nábř. kpt. Jaroše 4, Czechoslovakia.

Lacombe, Américo Jacobina; Brazilian teacher; b. 7 July 1909; s. of Domingos Lourenço and Isabel Jacobina Lacombe; m. Gilda Masset Lacombe 1935; four s. one d.; ed. Colégio Jacobina, Rio de Janeiro, Colégio Arnaldo (Belo Horizonte), and Univ. of Rio de Janeiro.
Secretary, Nat. Council of Educ. 31-39; Pres. Casa de

Rui Barbosa 39-61; Prof. of Brazilian History at Pontifical Univ. of Rio de Janeiro; Pres. *Alliance Française* of Rio de Janeiro; mem. Comm. on Historical Texts; mem. numerous Historical Insts.; mem. Portuguese Historical Acad. and Brazilian Acad. of Letters. Leisure interest: Director of Rio de Janeiro Jockey Club Library.
Publs. *Mocidade e Exilio de Rui Barbosa* 34, *Paulo Barbosa e a Fundação de Petrópolis* 40, *Um Passeio Pela História do Brasil* 42 (trans. *Brazil: A Brief History* 54), *O Pensamento Vivo de Rui Barbosa* 44, *Brasil—Periodo Nacional* 56, *Introducão ao Estudo da História do Brasil* 74.
Rua Dezenove de Fevreiro 105 ZC 02, Botafogo, Rio de Janeiro, GB; Pontíficia Universidade Católica do Rio de Janeiro, rua Marquês de São Vicente 263, Rio de Janeiro, Brazil.
Telephone: 246-3176 (Home).

Lacombe, Henri; French oceanographer; b. 24 Dec. 1913; ed. Lycée de Nice, Lycée Saint-Louis, Paris, and Ecole Polytechnique, Paris.
Marine hydrographical engineer 35-55; Prof. of Physical Oceanography, Muséum de Paris 55-, Dir. of scientific expeditions at sea—in the Mediterranean and Strait of Gibraltar; fmr. Pres. Int. Asscn. for the Physical Sciences of the Ocean; Chair. UNESCO Intergovernmental Oceanographic Comm. 65-67; mem. French Acad. 73; Commdr. Ordre Nat. du Mérite; Officier Légion d'Honneur, Croix de Guerre, Commdr. Etoile d'Anjouan, etc.
Publs. *Etudes d'Acoustique sous-Marine* 46, *Ouvrage sur courants de Marée* 53, *Mission Hydrographique Maroc* 59; various studies on the movement of the sea 49-68: *Cours d'Océanographie Physique* 65, *Les Energies de la Mer* 68, *Les Mouvements de la Mer* 71.
Laboratoire d'Océanographie Physique du Muséum, 43 rue Cuvier, 75005 Paris; Home: 20 bis avenue de Lattre de Tassigny, 92340 Bourg-La-Reine, France.
Telephone: 707-85-44, 707-19-00, 707-01-52 (Office); 702-23-22 (Home).

Lacoste, Robert; French politician; b. 5 July 1898.
Began career in Ministry of Finance; Sec.-Gen. Féd. générale des Fonctionnaires and Editor *Tribune des Fonctionnaires* before 39; during occupation founder mem. Libération-Nord, mem. Executive Libération-Sud, co-founder Mouvements Unifiés de la Résistance; with Provisional Govt. 44; mem. both Constituent Assemblies 45-46; Socialist Deputy for the Dordogne 46-58, 62-68; Minister for Industrial Production 44-47, for Industry Oct.-Nov. 47, for Industry and Commerce 47-50; Resident Minister Algeria Feb. 56-May 58; Pres. Conseil Supérieur de l'Electricité, Gaz de France 50-66; Senator for the Dordogne 71-; Officier Légion d'Honneur, Croix de Guerre, Rosette de la Résistance.
Sénat, 75006 Paris, France.

Lacretelle, Jacques Amaury Gaston de; French writer; b. 14 July 1888, Cormatin; s. of Amaury and Juliette (née Brouzet) de Lacretelle; m. Yolande de Naurois-Turgot 1933; two s. one d.; ed. Lycée Janson-de-Sailly, Paris.
Winner Grand Prix (Novel) of Acad. Française 30, mem. Acad. Française 36-; Vice-Pres. *Le Figaro* 71-; Dir. Centre Universitaire méditerranéen 67-; Grand Croix de la Légion d'Honneur.
Publs. *Silbermann* (Fémina Prize) 22, *La Bonifas* 25, *Lettres Espagnoles* 29, *Amour nuptial* 30, *Les Hauts Ponts*, 4 vols.: *Sabine, Les Fiançailles, Années d'Espérance, La Monnaie de Plomb* 32-35, *L'Ecrivain public* 36, *Croisieres en eaux troublées* 39, *Le Demi-Dieu ou le Voyage en Grèce, Libérations* 45, *Le pour et le contre* 46, *Idées dans un chapeau* 46, *Deux Coeurs Simples* 53, *Tiroir Secret, Les Maîtres et les Amis* 59, *La Galerie des Amants, Talleyrand* 64, *Racine* 70, *Portraits d'autrefois, figures d'aujourd'hui* 73, *Journal de Bord* 74; trans.

into French: *Precious Bane* (Mary Webb), *Wuthering Heights* (Emily Brontë).
49 rue Vineuse, 75016 Paris, France.

Ladas, Ioannis; Greek retired army officer and politician; b. 9 Sept. 1920, Dyrrachion, Arcadia; s. of Elias and Chariklia Ladas; m. Ephrosyni Ladas 1949; one s. one d.; ed. Cadet Coll., Infantry School, Fort Menning Infantry School, U.S.A., Supreme War Coll. and Gen. Education School.
Commissioned 40, Col. 65; Chief of Hellenic Mil. Police 66; participated in army coup 67; retired from army with rank of Brigadier 68; Sec.-Gen. Ministry of Public Order 67-68, Ministry of Interior 68-71; Deputy Minister of Regional Admin., Thessali district 71-72; Minister of Social Services 72-73; arrested Oct. 74, sentenced to life imprisonment for high treason and 10 years' imprisonment for insurrection Aug. 75.

Ladgham, Bahi; Tunisian politician; b. 10 Jan. 1913, Tunis.
Joined Dept. of Interior 33, subsequently moved to Finance Dept.; Sec.-Gen. Socialist Desturian Party (fmrly. Neo-Destur Party) 53-73; Sec. of State for the Presidency and Sec. of State for Defence 56-Sept. 69; Prime Minister of Tunisia Nov. 69-Nov. 70; Chair. Arab Cttee. supervising the cease-fire between Jordanian Govt. and the Palestinians in Jordan Sept. 70-April 71; fmr. personal rep. of Pres. Bourguiba.
c/o The Presidency, Tunis, Tunisia.

Lafaurie, Jean; French numismatist; b. 21 Nov. 1914, Bordeaux.
Professor Ecole pratique des Hautes Etudes de la Sorbonne; Keeper, Cabinet des médailles, Nat. Library, Paris 46-; hon. mem. Int. Numismatic Comm.; Dir. *Revue Numismatique* 58-, Past Pres. Soc. Nat. Antiquaires de France, French Numismatic Soc. and Dir. Soc. for the Study of the History of Paper Money; hon. mem. Institut Grand-Ducal de Luxembourg, Swiss, Belgian and Netherlands Numismatic Socs.; Royal Numismatic Soc. Medal; Archer M. Huntington Medal of American Numismatic Soc.
Publs. *Les Monnaies des Rois de France* (2 vols.) 51, 56, *Monnaies Romaines du Bas Empire, Monnaies Merouingiennes, Monnaies Carolingiennes, Monnaies Françaises;* over 500 articles.
3 rue de l'Abbé Guilleminault, 94130 Nogent-sur-Marne, France.
Telephone: 871-15-72.

Lafay, Bernard, D. ES SC., D.M.; French physician and politician; b. 1905; ed. Lycée Buffon and Paris Univ.
Practised as a doctor 31-45; Sec.-Gen. of Radical Party 46-48; Vice-Pres. of Paris Municipal Council 48-49; Deputy 51-58; Sec. of State 52; Sec. of State for Economic Affairs 53-54; Pres. Paris Municipal Council 54-55; Minister of Public Health 54-56; Senator 59-67; Deputy for Paris 67-69, 73-; Sec. of State, Min. for Scientific and Industrial Devt. 69-July 72; Commdr. Légion d'Honneur; Croix de Guerre.
123 rue de Longchamp, 75116 Paris, France.

Lafée, Alfredo; Venezuelan civil engineer and banker; b. 21 March 1921, Caracas; m. Ines Dominici de Lafée; four c.; ed. Venezuela Central Univ.
Engineer, public drainage and water supply dept. of Min. of Public Works 41-44, in charge of works inspection 45-47; Chief of Technical Dept. Caracas Drainage Works, Nat. Inst. of Sanitary Works 47-51; mem. comm. (Ad Honorem) for widening Avenida Sucre 50-53; mem. Municipal Council 58-59; Dir. of Construction, Caracas and Maracaibo Urban Development 51-66; mem. Board of Venezuelan Chamber of Building 60-62, represented Board in numerous federal commissions 60-63, Pres. 62-64; Dir.-Gen. Banco Hipotecario de la Vivienda Popular S.A. 62-68,

First Vice-Pres. and Dir. 68-71; mem. El Conde Permanent Development Commission 63-64; mem. Council of Inter-american Federation of Building Industry 62-64; Deputy National Congress 64-69; Venezuelan Federation of Chambers of Commerce and Industry (FEDECAMARAS) mem. Board 62-64, First Vice-Pres. 64-67, Pres. 67-69, Perm. Assessor 69-, Principal mem. Board 72-; mem. Ad Honorem Commission for enquiry into the working of the Stock Market 69-71; M.P. for the State of Miranda 69-71; mem. Board Cen. Office for Co-ordination and Planning (CORDIPLAN) 70, Nat. Energy Council 71, Board of Foreign Trade Inst. 71, Nat. Banking Council 71, Nat. Council of Asociación Pro-Venezuela 71; Pres. Central Bank of Venezuela 71-; Governor, International Monetary Fund 71; Pres. Gov. Council of CEMLA 72; del. numerous int. confs.; Orden Francisco de Miranda 1st Class, Merito Industrial del Brasil 2nd Class.
Central Bank of Venezuela, Avda. Urdaneta esq. Carmelita, Caracas, Venezuela.

Lafer, Horacio; Brazilian industrialist and politician; b. 1900; ed. Univ. of São Paulo.
President, São Paulo Industry Centre; founded several industrial concerns; Brazilian del. to L. of N. before 30; mem. Federal Constituent Assembly 34, 45; Federal Rep. 34-55, 58; Minister of Finance 51-53; Chair. Joint Brazil-U.S.A. Comm. for Economic Development; Chair. Conf. of I.M.F. and I.B.R.D. 52; Chair. Int. Conf. of Economic Comm. for Latin America 53; mem. Board of Govs. I.B.R.D. 51-53; Minister of Foreign Affairs 59-61; Chair. Museum of Modern Art of São Paulo.
c/o Museu de Arte Moderna, Rua Sete de Abril 230, 2°, São Paulo, Brazil.

Lagasse, Raphael; Belgian international official; b. 20 Dec. 1927, Brussels; ed. Catholic Univ. of Louvain.
Secretary-General, Int. Org. of Employers 60-; Belgian Civic and Military Orders.
Office: 26 Chemin de Joinville, 1216 Geneva, Switzerland.

Lagercrantz, Olof, PH.D.; Swedish journalist; b. 10 March 1911, Stockholm; s. of Carl and Agnes (née Hamilton) Lagercrantz; m. Martina Ruin 1939; three s. two d.
Cultural Editor, Dagens Nyheter 51-60, Chief Editor 60-; Prize of Nordic Council (jointly) 65.
Leisure interest: writing.
Publs. Från helvetet till paradiset 64, Den pågdende skapelsen 66, Att finnas till 70, China-Report 71; biographies and collections of poems and essays.
Dagens Nyheter, 105 15 Stockholm, Sweden.

Lagerfelt, Baron Karl-Gustav; Swedish diplomatist; b. 21 Nov. 1909, Jönköping; s. of Baron G. A. Lagerfelt and Baroness G. von Essen; m. 1st Sara Champion de Crespigny 1947 (died 1967), one s. one d.; m. 2nd Monique Suetens 1974.
Foreign Service 35-, Helsinki, London, Foreign Office, London, Paris; Envoy Tokyo 51-56; Amb. to European Coal and Steel Community 57-63, to EURATOM and European Econ. Community 59-63; Amb. to Austria 64-69; Amb. to Netherlands 69-72; Amb. and Perm. Rep. to UN, Geneva, Del. to EFTA and other int. orgs. Geneva 72-75; Vice-Chair. EFTA Council Jan.-June 73.
c/o Ministry of Foreign Affairs, Box 16127, 10323 Stockholm 16, Sweden.

Laghzaoui, Mohammed; Moroccan diplomatist; b. 27 Sept. 1906, Fez; s. of Mme Laghzaoui (née Chraïbi); m. Kenza Bouayad 1940; three s. three d.; ed. Coll. Moulay Idriss, Fez.
Former Chair. Soc. marocaine des Transports Laghzaoui; mem. and Chair. Govt. Council during French Proctectorate; one of 69 principal signatories to Over Act of Independence June 44; Dir.-Gen. of Nat. Security March 56-July 60; Dir.-Gen. Office Chérifien des Phosphates; Co-ordinator, Nat. Mining and

Industrial Cos.; responsible for Ministries of Industry, Mining, Tourism and Handicrafts 65; Pres. Afro-Asiatic Asscn. for Econ. Devt. 66-69; Amb. to U.K. 69-71, to France 71-72; Cordon de l'Istiqlal (Tunisia and Jordan), other honours from Iraq, Belgium and Senegal, Ouissam El Oula (1st class), Commdr. Order of the Crown, Grand Officier, Légion d'Honneur.
Leisure interests: bridge, football.
Résidence Laghzaoui, Route de Suissi, Rabat, Morocco.

Lagrange, Maurice, L. en D.; French lawyer; b. 14 May 1900, Meudon; s. of Roger and Claire (née Gillet) Lagrange; m. Colette Ackerman 1930; one s.; ed. Lycée Charlemagne, Paris, Paris Univ., and Ecole Libre des Sciences Politiques.
Auditeur, Conseil d'Etat 24, Maître des Requêtes 34; Conseiller d'Etat 45-70, Hon. Conseiller 70-; retd.; Legal Expert, French Del. during negotiations setting up ECSC 50; Advocate-Gen., ECSC Court 52-58, 58-64; Court of the European Communities 58-64; Commdr. de la Légion d'Honneur.
Publs. La Cour de Justice de la Communauté Européenne du Charbon et de l'Acier 54, L'Ordre Juridique de la CECA vu à travers la Jurisprudence de sa Cour de Justice 58, Les Pouvoirs de la Haute Autorité 61 (all in Revue du Droit Public et de la Science Politique), The Role of the Court of Justice as seen through its Case Law 61, and articles in professional journals.
18 avenue de la Bourdonnais, 75007 Paris, France.
Telephone: 551-59-42.

Lagu, Joseph; Sudanese army officer; b. 21 Nov. 1931; s. of Yakobo Yanga and Marini Kaluma; ed. Rumbek Secondary School, Mil. Acad. Omdurman.
Served in Sudanese Army 60-63; joined South Sudan Liberation Movt. 63, Leader SSLM 69; signed peace agreement with Govt. of Sudan March 72; Order of the Two Niles 72.
Publ. The Anya-Nya—what we fight for 72.
People's Armed Forces General Headquarters, Khartoum, Sudan.

Lahr, Rolf; German diplomatist; b. 6 Nov. 1908, Marienwerder; s. of Paul and Johanna Lahr; ed. Univs. of Berlin, Giessen, and Freiburg/Br.
Foreign Trade Div., Ministry of Econs. 34-42; mil. service 42-45; Man. Fruit and Vegetable Processing Industry Asscn. for Schleswig-Holstein 45-49; Foreign Trade Div., Ministry of Econs. 49-51, Counsellor 51-53; Foreign Office 53-61; Ambassador and Del. in German-French negotiations 56, German-Soviet negotiations 57-58, German-Netherlands negotiations 58-60, German-Scandinavian air traffic 59-60; Perm. Rep. to European Econ. Community, Brussels 61; State Sec. for Foreign Affairs 61-69; Amb. to Italy 69-74; Amb. and Perm. Rep. to FAO 74-; Iron Cross (1st Class) 43; Grand Cross (2nd Class) of the Order of Merit 63, and other foreign orders.
Leisure interests: literature on history and fine arts, classical music, antique furniture and ceramics, travel.
Office of the Permanent Representative, Via Paisiello 24, 00198 Rome; Home: Via Aventina 35, Rome, Italy.
Telephone: 860-341 (Home).

Laidlaw, Christophor Charles Fraser; British oil executive; b. 9 Aug. 1922, Calcutta, India; s. of late Hugh Alexander Lyon Laidlaw and Sarah Georgina Fraser; m. Nina Mary Prichard 1952; one s. three d.; ed. Rugby School and St. John's Coll. Cambridge.
Served War of 39-45, Europe and Far East, Maj. on Gen. Staff; joined British Petroleum Co. Ltd. (BP) 48; BP rep. in Hamburg 59-61; Gen. Man. Marketing Dept. 63-67; Dir. BP Trading 67; Dir. (Operations) 71-72; Pres. BP Belgium 67-71, BP Germany 72, BP Italiana 72-73; Man. Dir. BP Co. Ltd. 72-75; Dir. BP Oil.
Leisure interest: fishing.
49 Chelsea Square, London, S.W.3, England.
Telephone: 01-352-6942.

Lain Entralgo, Pedro, M.D., CH.B., Spanish physician and educator; b. 15 Feb. 1908, Urrea de Gaén; *m.* Milagro Martínez Prieto; ed. Univs. of Zaragoza, Valencia, Madrid and Vienna.

Prof. of History of Medicine, Madrid Univ. 42-, Rector of Univ. 51; mem. of Real Acad. de Medicina 46, Real Acad. Española 54, Real Acad. de la Historia 62; Dr. h.c. Univ. San Marcos, Lima, Toulouse Univ.; Hon. Prof. Univ. of Santiago, Chile, and mem. of Akademie der Wissenschaften, Heidelberg.

Publs. *Menéndez Pelayo* 44, *La Generación del Noventa y Ocho* 45, *La Historia Clínica* 50, *Historia de la Medicina* 54, *Mind and Body* (London 55), *España como Problema* 56, *La espera de la esperanza* 56, *La curación por el palatre en la Antigüedad clásica* 58, *Teoría y Realidad del otro* 61.

c/o Real Academia Española, Calle de Felipe N 4, Madrid, Spain.

Laine, Jermu Tapani, BARR.-AT-LAW; Finnish politician; b. 17 Sept. 1931, Turku; *s.* of Johan Artturi Laine and Helmi Emilia Heinonen; *m.* Terttu Anneli Kallio 1954; three *d.*

Extraordinary Dept. Sec. Ministry of Trade and Industry 55; Extraordinary Referendary of the Govt.; Extraordinary Senior Referendary, Ministry of Trade and Industry 58; Senior Govt. Sec. 61; Commercial Counsellor, Ministry of Trade and Industry 61; Teacher of Commercial Law and Commerce, Valkeakoski Commercial Coll. 65; Headmaster of Mänttä Commercial Coll. 69; Political Sec. to Prime Minister 72; Minister for Foreign Trade 73-75.

Leisure interests: politics, cinema, theatre.

Publs. (in Finnish): *Living in Work and Equality* 71, *Basics of Economic Policy* 72, and many articles in specialized periodicals.

Haapaniemenkatu 20 D 60, 00530 Helsinki 53, Finland.

Telephone: 1601 (Office).

Laing, Hon. Arthur, P.C., M.P., B.S.A.; Canadian business executive and politician; b. 9 Sept. 1904, Eburne, B.C.; *s.* of Thomas Laing and Marion B. Mackie; *m.* E. Geraldine Hyland 1938; one *d.*; ed. Richmond High School and Univ. of British Columbia.

Manager, Fertilizers Dept., Vancouver Milling and Grain Co. Ltd. 26-33; Man. Agricultural Chemicals Div., Buckerfields Ltd. 33-51; M.P. 49-53, 63-72; Leader British Columbia Liberal Party 53-62; Minister for Northern Affairs and Nat. Resources 63-65, of Indian Affairs and Northern Devt. 66-68; Min. of Public Works 68-72; Minister of Veterans' Affairs Jan.-Nov. 72; Senator 72-; Liberal.

Leisure interests: collection of medallions, Eskimo art.

The Senate, Ottawa, Ontario; Home: 5937 Angus Drive, Vancouver 13, British Columbia, Canada.

Telephone: 613-992-1437.

Laing, Sir (John) Maurice, Kt.; British building and civil engineering contractor; b. 1 Feb. 1918, Carlisle; *s.* of Sir John (William) Laing, C.B.E., and Lady Laing; *m.* Hilda Violet Richards 1940; one *s.*; ed. St. Lawrence Coll., Ramsgate.

Laing Group of Companies, Man. Dir. 57-66, Deputy Chair. 58-, Chair. John Laing Construction Ltd. 63-; Dir. Grosvenor-Laing Holdings Ltd., Bank of England 63-; Chair. Export Group for Constr. Ind. 57-59, Fed. of Civil Engineering Contractors 59-60, Vice-Pres. 60-; Pres. British Employers' Confederation 64-65; First Pres. Confederation of British Industry 65-66; mem. Grand Council, Fed. of British Industries 56-65, Export Guarantees Advisory Council 59-63, Ministry of Labour Nat. Joint Advisory Council 60-66, Nat. Econ. Devt. Council (N.E.D.C.) 62-66.

Leisure interest: sailing.

John Laing Construction Limited, Page Street, Mill Hill, London, NW7 2ER; Home: "Reculver", 36 Totteridge Village, London, N20 8AG, England.

Telephone: 01-959-3636 (Office).

Laing, R(obert) Stanley, B.S.MECH.ENG., M.B.A.; American business executive; b. 1 Nov. 1918, Seattle; *s.* of Robert Vardy Laing and Marie (Scott) Laing; *m.* Janet Emmott Orr 1947; one *s.* four *d.*; ed. Univ. of Washington and Harvard Business School.

National Cash Register Co., Dayton, Ohio 47-72; Special Asst. in Exec. Office 47-49; Asst. to Comptroller 49; Gen. Auditor 50-53; Asst. Comptroller 53-54; Comptroller 54-60; Vice-Pres. (Finance) 60-62, Exec. Vice-Pres. 62-64, Pres. 64-72; Dir. and Chair. Business Equipment Manufacturing Asscn. 63-64; Dir. Gen. Mills Inc., Cincinnati Milacron, Inc., Armco Corpn., B. F. Goodrich Co., Sinclair Community College Foundation; Chair. Board of Trustees, Denison Univ.; mem. St. Elizabeth Medical Center Advisory Board; Trustee, Univ. of Dayton; Order of Lateran Cross (Vatican).

Office: Suite 2850, Winters Bank Tower, Dayton, Ohio 45402; Home: 245 W. Thurston Boulevard, Dayton, Ohio 45419, U.S.A.

Telephone: 513-223-8835 (Office).

Laing, Ronald David, M.B., CH.B., D.P.M.; British psychiatrist; b. 7 Oct. 1927; *s.* of D. P. M. and Amelia Laing; ed. Univ. of Glasgow.

Glasgow and West of Scotland Neurosurgical Unit 51; Cen. Army Psychiatric Unit, Netley 51-52; Psychiatric Unit, Mil. Hosp., Catterick 52-53; Dept. of Psychological Medicine, Univ. of Glasgow 53-56; Tavistock Clinic 56-60; Tavistock Inst. of Human Relations 60-, Principal Investigator, Schizophrenia and Family Research Unit 64-67; Fellow, Foundations Fund for Research in Psychiatry 60-67; Dir. Langham Clinic for Psychotherapy 62-65; Fellow, Tavistock Inst. of Medical Psychology 63-64; Chair. Philadelphia Asscn. Ltd. 64-.

Publs. *The Divided Self* 60, *The Self and Others* 61, *Reason and Violence* (introduced by J.-P. Sartre) 64, *The Politics of Experience and the Bird of Paradise* 67, *Knots* 70, *The Politics of the Family* 71; co-author *Sanity, Madness and the Family* 65.

2 Eton Road, London, N.W.3, England.

Telephone: 01-722-9448.

Laird, Melvin Robert; American government official; b. 1 Sept. 1922, Omaha, Neb.; *s.* of Melvin and Helen (Connor) Laird; *m.* Barbara Masters 1945; two *s.* one *d.*; ed. Carleton Coll., Northfield, Minn.

Served in U.S. Navy in Pacific, Second World War; mem. Wisconsin Senate 46-52; mem. U.S. House of Reps. 52-69, served on Appropriations Cttee.; U.S. Sec. of Defense 69-73; Counsellor to Pres. for Domestic Affairs 73-74; Senior Counsellor for Nat. and Int. Affairs, Readers' Digest Asscn. 74-; Republican.

Publs. include: *A House Divided: America's Strategy Gap* 62, *The Conservative Papers* (Editor) 64, *Republican Papers* 68.

P.O. Box 279, Marshfield, Wisconsin 54449, U.S.A.

Laithwaite, Sir John Gilbert, G.C.M.G., K.C.B., K.C.I.E., C.S.I., M.A.; British civil servant (retd.); b. 5 July 1894, Dublin; elder *s.* of J. G. Laithwaite; ed. Clongowes and Trinity Coll., Oxford.

Served in France 17-18 (wounded); India Office 19; Private Sec. to Parl. Under-Sec. 22-24; Asst. Private Sec. to Secs. of State 24, Principal 24; attached to Prime Minister for Second Indian Round Table Conf. 31; Sec. Indian Franchise Cttee. 32, Indian Delimitation Cttee. 35-36; Private Sec. to Viceroy of India 36-43; Sec. to Gov.-Gen. of India 37-43; Asst. Under-Sec. of State for India 43; an Under-Sec. (Civil) of the War Cabinet 44-45; Deputy Under-Sec. of State for Burma 45-47, for India 47; Deputy Under-Sec. of State for Commonwealth Relations 48-49; U.K. Rep. to Republic of Ireland 49-50, Ambassador 50-51; High Commr. for

the U.K. in Pakistan Sept. 51-54; Permanent Under-Sec. of State for Commonwealth Relations 55-59 (retd.); Chair. Council of Royal Central Asian Soc. 64-66, Vice-Pres. 67-75; Pres. Hakluyt Soc. 64-69, Royal Geographical Soc. 66-69; Dir. and Deputy Chair. Inchcape and Co. Ltd. 60-64, Dir. 64-75; mem. Standing Comm. on Museums and Galleries 59-61; Renter-Warden, Tallow-Chandlers Co. 69, Warden 70, Master 72; Hon. Fellow, Trinity Coll., Oxford 55; Hon. LL.D. (Dublin) 57; Freeman, City of London 60; Knight of Malta 60.
Publs. *The Laithwaites, Some Records of a Lancashire Family* 41, *Miscellaneous Genealogical Notes* 43, *Memories of an Infantry Officer—21st March 1918* 71.
c/o Grindlays Bank Ltd., 13 St. James's Square, London, S.W.1, England.

Lajous Martinez, Adrián, LL.B.; Mexican finance official and international negotiator; b. 25 Jan. 1920, Buenos Aires, Argentina; s. of Adrian Lajous Nelson and Evangelina Martinez de Lajous; m. Luz Vargas de Lajous 1943; four c.; ed. Univ. of Mexico and New York Univ.
Officer, private radio stations and networks 41-49, Vice-Chair. Board, Nucleo Mil. group of radio stations 49-; Gen. Counsel and Head of Credit Dept., Patronato del Ahorro Nacional 50-52; Officer Banco Nacional de Comercio Exterior 53-58; Minister-Counsellor, Mexican Embassy, Washington, D.C. 56, Commercial Counsellor 64; Dir.-Gen. Federación Interamericana del Algodón 59-63; Export Man. Unión Nacional de Productores de Azúcar 65-67; Mexican Rep. Int. Coffee negotiations 62-67; Chair. Board, Int. Sugar Org. 69, now Vice-Chair.; Exec. Dir. IBRD, IFC and IDA 70-72; Dir. Banco Nacional de Comercio Exterior 67-; Dir.-Gen. Fondo de Equipamiento Industrial 73-.
Leisure interest: bridge.
Guadalquivir 68, Mexico 5, D.F., Mexico.
Telephone: 514-98-58.

Lakas Bahas, Ing. Demetrio Basilio; Panamanian administrator and politician; b. 29 Aug. 1925, Colón; s. of Basilio Demetrio Lakas and Zaharo Bahas de Lakas; m. Elizabeth Fannia Roger de Lakas 1959; two s. one d.; ed. Texas Wesleyan Coll. and Texas Technical Coll.
Former Dir. of Social Security; Pres. of Provisional Government Council 69-72; Pres. of Panama Oct. 72-.
Leisure interests: sailing, fishing.
Palacio de las Garzas, Panama City, Panama.
Telephone: 22-8905 (Office); 23-6432 (Residence).

Laking, George Robert, C.M.G., LL.B.; New Zealand diplomatist; b. 15 Oct. 1912, Auckland; s. of Robert and Alice (née Wilding) Laking; m. Alice Hogg 1940; one s. one d.; ed. Auckland Grammar School, and Auckland and Victoria Univs.
Prime Minister's and External Affairs Depts. 40-49; Counsellor, New Zealand Embassy, Washington 49-54, Minister 54-56; Deputy Sec. of External Affairs, Wellington 56-58; Acting High Commr. for New Zealand in London 58-61; Amb. to European Economic Community (EEC) 60-61, to U.S.A. 61-67; Perm. Head of Foreign Affairs Dept. 67-72; Parl. Commr. (Ombudsman) 75-.
3 Wesley Road, Wellington, New Zealand.

Lal, Bansi, LL.B.; Indian politician; b. 10 Oct. 1927, Golagarh, Bhiwani District; s. of Ch. Mohar Singh; two s. four d.; ed. privately and Law Coll., Jullundur.
Took part in Praja Mandal Movement, Loharu State; Sec. Loharu Praja Mandal 43-44; Pres. Mandal Congress Cttee., Kural 59-60; Gen. Sec. Tosham Mandal Congress Cttee. 55; mem. Punjab PCC 59-62, Rajya Sabha 60-66, Haryana Assembly 67-; Chief Minister Haryana 68-75; Minister without portfolio, Govt. of India Nov.-Dec. 75, Minister of Defence Dec. 75-; Hon. LL.D. (Kurukshetra Univ.) 72, D.Sc. (Haryana Agric. Univ.) 72.
Ministry of Defence, New Delhi, India.

Lalbhai, Kasturbhai; Indian industrialist and banker; b. 19 Dec. 1894; m. Shardaben Chamanbhai Javeri; ed. Gujarat Coll., Ahmedabad.
President, Ahmedabad Millowners' Asscn. 33-35, Fed. Indian Chambers of Commerce 34-35, Council of Admin. of Ahmedabad Textile Industry Research Asscn. 47-; Chair. W. Coast Kandla Port Devt. Cttee. 48-; Dir. Reserve Bank of India 37-49, 57-60; Dir. numerous concerns; Leader and Pres. Jain Community in India.
Office: Pankore's Naka, Ahmedabad; Home: Lalbag, Shahibag, Ahmedabad, India.

Lall, Arthur Samuel, M.A.; Indian teacher and diplomatist; b. 14 July 1911, Lahore; s. of Parmanand and Zoe (Lewis) Lall; m. Betty Goetz 1963; one d.; ed. Punjab and Oxford Univs.
Appointed to Indian Civil Service and served in the Punjab and with central Govt.; Commercial Counsellor, High Comm., London 47-51; Consul-Gen., with rank of Minister, New York 51-54; Permanent Rep. to U.N. 54-59; Chair. U.N. Mission to Samoa 59; Ambassador to Austria 59-63; Lecturer, Cornell Univ. 63-; Prof. of International Relations, Columbia Univ., New York 65-; Consultant, UN Inst. for Training and Research, New York; Del. to UN Econ. and Social Council and Trusteeship Council; Del. to numerous econ. confs.
Leisure interest: writing novels (two novels published).
Publs. *Modern International Negotiation* 66, *How Communist China Negotiates* 68, *The UN and the Middle East Crisis* 69, *The Security Council in a Universal United Nations* 71.
230 East 81st Street, New York, N.Y. 10028, U.S.A.

Lalla Aicha, H.R.H. Princess; Moroccan diplomatist; eldest daughter of the late King Mohammed V.
Ambassador to U.K. 65-69, to Italy 69-73 (also accred. to Greece); Pres. Moroccan Red. Crescent; Grand Cordon of Order of the Throne.
c/o Ministry of Foreign Affairs, Rabat, Morocco.

Lallemand, André, D. ès sc.; French astronomer; b. 29 Sept. 1904, Cirey, Côte d'Or; m. Suzanne Ancel 1928; two s.; ed. Univ. de Strasbourg.
Astronomer, Strasbourg and Paris Observatories; Morrison Assoc., Univ. of Calif. (Berkeley); Prof., Collège de France 61-; mem. Institut de France; foreign mem. Athens Acad.; Commandeur Légion d'Honneur; Grand Officier du Mérite National; Prix de l'Académie des Sciences, Paris; Eddington Medal, Royal Astron. Soc.; Dr. h.c. (Padua, Geneva).
Publs. include: *Application de l'optique électronique à la photographie* 36, *Sur l'application à la photographie d'une méthode permettant d'amplifier l'énergie des photons* 36.
61 avenue Niel, Paris 17e, France.
Telephone: 924-76-43.

Lalonde, Marc, Q.C., P.C., M.P., LL.L., M.A.; Canadian lawyer and politician; b. 26 July 1929, Ile Perrot; s. of J. Albert and Nora (St. Aubin) Lalonde; m. Claire Tétreau 1955; two s. two d.; ed. St. Laurent Coll., Montreal and Univs. of Montreal and Oxford.
Called to the Bar, Quebec 55; Prof. of Commercial Law and Econs., Univ. of Montreal 57-59; Special Asst. to Minister of Justice 59-60; Partner, Gélinas, Bourque, Lalonde & Benoit, Montreal 60-68; Policy Adviser to Rt. Hon. Lester B. Pearson 67-68; Principal Sec. to Prime Minister 68-72; Minister of Nat. Health and Welfare Nov. 72-75; Minister Responsible for the Status of Women 74-.
Leisure interests: tennis, skiing, swimming, reading.
5440 Légaré, Montreal; also: House of Commons, Parliament Buildings, Ottawa, Ont., Canada.
Telephone: 735-0218 (Montreal); 996-5461 (Ottawa).

Lalor, Patrick Joseph; Irish politician; b. 21 July 1926, Dublin; s. of Joseph and Frances Lalor; m. Myra Murphy 1952; one s. three d.; ed. in Abbeyleix and Knockbeg Coll., Carlow.

Member Laois County Council and fmr. exec. mem. Retail Grocery, Dairy and Allied Trades Asscn. (RGDATA); mem. Dáil Eireann Oct. 61-; Parl. Sec. to Minister of Agriculture and Fisheries 65-66, to Minister for Transport, Power, Posts and Telegraphs 66-69; Minister for Posts and Telegraphs July 69-70, for Industry and Commerce 70-73; mem. Fianna Fáil, Chief Whip Parl. Party 73-.
Leisure interests: hurling, Gaelic football, golf, drama.
Dáil Eireann, Dublin; Home: Main Street, Abbeyleix, Co. Laois, Ireland.
Telephone: 0502-31206 (Home).

Lalouette, Roger, L. ÈS L., L. EN D.; French diplomatist; b. 8 Sept. 1904, Nantes; s. of René Lalouette and Thérèse Lamoureux; two d.; ed. Ecole des Sciences Politiques and Univ. of Paris.
Attaché, Berne 30; Sec. Vienna 31, Prague 35, Berlin 36; Head, Cabinet of Ministry of Foreign Affairs 39-40, at Rome 40, at French Residence, Morocco 42-44, at Dublin (French Cttee. of Nat. Liberation) 44; Rep. to Nuremberg Trials 46; Dep. Dir. of Personnel and Accountancy 48-50; Dep. High Commr. to Austria 50, Minister 51-55; Minister, Rabat 55-56; Ambassador to the Republic of Viet-Nam 58-64, to Czechoslovakia 64-69; Commdr. Légion d'Honneur; Grand Officier Mérite National; Croix de Guerre.
Leisure interest: hunting.
Ministère des Affaires Etrangères, 37 quai d'Orsay, Paris 7e; Home: 67 rue du Maréchal Foch, Versailles, France.
Telephone: 950-32-40.

Lama, Luciano, DOTT. IN SC. POL.; Italian trades union official; b. 14 Oct. 1921, Gambettola (Forlì); s. of Domenico and Paganelli Noerri; m. Lora Bosi 1947; two d.; ed. Istituto Cesare Alfieri, Florence.
Vice-Secretary, Confederazione Generale Italiana del Lavoro (CGIL) 47; Sec. Fed. of Chemical Workers 51; Sec.-Gen. Fed. of Metal Workers (FIOM) 57; Sec. CGIL 61, Sec.-Gen. 70-.
Confederazione Generale Italiana del Lavoro, Corso d' Italia 25, Rome, Italy.
Telephone: 868841.

La Malfa, Ugo, B.D.S.; Italian economist and politician; b. 16 May 1903, Palermo; m. Orsola Corrado; one s. one d.; ed. Univ. of Venice.
Member Consultative Assembly 45-46, Constituent Assembly 46-48, Chamber of Deputies 48-; Pres. Parl. Finance Board 48-50; Minister of Transport 45, of Reconstruction 46, of Foreign Trade 46; Minister without Portfolio in charge Public Corporations 50-51; Minister of Foreign Trade 51-53; Minister of the Budget 62-63; Pres. Parliamentary Budget Commission 64-66; Sec. Italian Republican Party 65-75; Minister of the Treasury 73-74; Deputy Prime Minister Nov. 74-; mem. Assembly European Coal and Steel Community; Pres. Treaties Comm.; Vice-Gov. Int. Monetary Fund.
Viale Cristoforo Colombo 179, Rome, Italy.
Telephone: 512-7386.

LaMarsh, Julia Verlyn, P.C., Q.C., LL.D.; Canadian lawyer and politician; b. 20 Dec. 1924, Chatham, Ont.; d. of Wilfrid and Rhoda (Conibear) LaMarsh; ed. Stamford, Hamilton Hormal School, Univ. of Toronto and Osgoode Hall.
Canadian Women's Army Corps 43-45; Member of Parl. 60-69; Minister of Nat. Health and Welfare 63-65; Sec. of State 65-69; mem. law firm LaMarsh, MacBeen, Slovak, Sinclair & Nicolette 69-; fmr. Vice-Pres. Ontario Asscn. of Rural-Urban Municipalities; mem. Planning Asscn. of Canada, Int. Parliamentary Union, Commonwealth Parliamentary Asscn.; Liberal.
Publ. *Memoirs of a Bird in a Gilded Cage* 69.
38 James Street, St. Catherine's, Ontario; Home: 5992 Corwin Avenue, Niagara Falls, Ontario, Canada.

Lamb, William Kaye, B.A., M.A., PH.D.; Canadian librarian and archivist; b. 11 May 1904; ed. Univs. of British Columbia, Paris and London.
Librarian and Archivist, Provincial Library and Archivist, Public Archives of Canada, Ottawa 48-Nov. 68 and also Nat. Librarian, Nat. Library of Canada, Ottawa 53-68; Fellow and Past Pres. Royal Soc. of Canada; Past Pres. Canadian Library Asscn., Canadian History Asscn., etc.; several hon. degrees; Tyrrell Medal.
7 Crescent Heights, Ottawa 1, Ont., Canada.

Lamb, Willis Eugene, Jr., PH.D., SC.D., L.H.D.; Amercian physicist; b. 12 July 1913, Los Angeles, Calif.; m. Ursula Schaefer 1939; ed. Univ. of California.
Instructor, Columbia Univ. 38, Prof. of Physics 48-52; Prof. of Physics, Stanford Univ. 51-56; Wykeham Prof. of Physics and Fellow, New Coll., Univ. of Oxford 56-62; Henry Ford II Prof. of Physics, Yale Univ. 62-72; J. Willard Gibbs Prof. of Physics, Yale Univ. 72-74; Prof. of Physics and Optical Sciences, Univ. of Arizona 74-; Loeb Lecturer, Harvard 53-54; mem. Nat. Acad. of Sciences; awarded Rumford Premium (American Acad. of Arts and Sciences) 53; Nobel Prize in Physics (shared with Prof. P. Kusch) 55; Research Corpn. Award 55; Guggenheim Fellow 60; Hon. degree Pennsylvania Univ. 53, Yeshiva Univ. 64, Hon. Sc.D., Gustavus Adolphus Coll. 75.
Department of Physics, University of Arizona, Tucson, Ariz., U.S.A.

Lambert, Allen Thomas; Canadian banker; b. 28 Dec. 1911, Regina, Sask.; s. of Willison A. and Sarah (Barber) Lambert; m. Marion G. Kotchapaw 1950; one s. one d.; Victoria Public and High Schools.
Joined Toronto Dominion Bank 27; Supervisor, Head Office, Toronto 49; Asst. Man., Montreal 50; Supt., Head Office 53, Asst. Gen. Man. 53, Gen. Man. 56, Vice-Pres. and Dir. 56, Pres. 60-72, Chair. 61-, Chief Exec. Officer Toronto Dominion Bank 72-; Chair. Board and Dir. The Toronto-Dominion Bank Trust Co., Toronto-Dominion Centre Ltd., Pacific Centre Ltd., Toronto-Dominion Centre West Ltd., Toronto-Dominion Bank Investments (U.K.) Ltd.; Pres. and Dir. Toronto-Dominion Realty Co. Ltd., Int. Monetary Conf.; Dir. of numerous cos. including Adela Investment Co. S.A., Arbuthnot Latham Holdings Ltd., Canadian World Wildlife Fund, Canadian Int. Paper Co., The Continental Corpn., Hiram Walker-Gooderham and Worts Ltd., IBM (Canada) Ltd., The Int. Nickel Co. of Canada Ltd., Dome Mines Ltd., Dominion Insurance Corpn., Edmonton Centre Ltd., Hudson Bay Mining and Smelting Co. Ltd., London Life Insurance Ltd., Midland and Int. Banks Ltd., Westinghouse Canada Ltd., Ontario Hydro; Board of Govs., York Univ.
Leisure interests: golf, curling, fishing.
The Toronto-Dominion Bank, 55 King Street W and Bay Street, Toronto M5K IA2, Ont., Canada.

Lambert, Baron Léon Jean Gustave; Belgian banker; b. 2 July 1928; ed. Canterbury School, Yale Coll., Oxford Univ., Univ. of Geneva and Inst. of International Studies, Geneva.
Président du Conseil d'Admin., Cie. Bruxelles Lambert pour la Finance et l'Industrie, Brussels; Dir. various companies in Europe, U.S.A. and Canada; Chevalier de l'Ordre de Léopold (Belgium); Commdr. de l'Ordre à la Valeur (Cameroon), Grande Ufficiale al Merito (Italy), Grosses goldenes Ehrenzeichen (Austria).
Compagnie Bruxelles Lambert, 24 avenue Marnix, 1050 Brussels, Belgium.

Lambert, Hon. Marcel Joseph Aimé, P.C., M.P.; Canadian lawyer and politician; b. 21 Aug. 1919, Edmonton, Alberta; s. of Joseph and Marie (Kiwit)

Lambert; *m.* Olive Lowles 1945; three *s.*; ed. St. Joseph's High School, Edmonton, Alberta, Univ. of Alberta, and Hertford Coll., Oxford.
Royal Canadian Army Corps 41-45; legal practice 51-; M.P. 57-; Parl. Asst. Minister of Nat. Defence 57-58; Parl. Sec. Ministry of Nat. Revenue 59-62; Speaker, House of Commons 62-63; mem. Privy Council 63-; Minister of Veterans' Affairs Feb.-April 63; Progressive Conservative.
Imperial Bank Building, Edmonton, Alberta; Home: 2249 Samuel Drive, Ottawa 8, Ontario, Canada.

Lamberz, Werner; German politician and engineer; b. 14 April 1929; *m.*; two *c.*
Joined Socialist Unity (Communist) Party 47; Cand. mem. Cen. Cttee. 63; mem. and Sec. Cen. Cttee. 67; Cand. mem. Politburo 70; mem. Politburo 71-.
102 Berlin, Am Marx-Engels-Platz 2, German Democratic Republic.

Lambetti, Ellie; Greek actress; b. 1930; ed. Athens Gymnasium.
First appeared in Marika Kotopouli's company in *Hannele* (Hauptmann) 45; subsequently played leading roles in *Blood Wedding* (Lorca) 47, *The Glass Menagerie* (Tennessee Williams), *Antigone* (Anouilh) 48, *The Heiress* 49, *Shadow and Substance* (P. V. Carroll) 50, *Peg o' My Heart* 51; formed own company with Dimitri Horn 53 and has appeared in *The Deep Blue Sea* (Rattigan) 53, *The Moon is Blue* (Herbert) 54, *Hamlet* 55, *The Rainmaker* (R. Nash), *Gigi* 57, *The Fourposter* (J. de Hartog) 58, *Two for the Seesaw, La Dame aux Camélias* 59; headed own Theatre Group 60-; has appeared in a number of films including *Windfall in Athens* 54, *A Girl in Black* 56, *A Matter of Dignity* 58 (all directed by Michael Cacoyannis).
Sina 56, Athens, Greece.

Lambo, (Thomas) Adeoye, O.B.E., M.B., CH.B., M.D., F.R.C.P., D.P.M.; Nigerian neuro-psychiatrist; b. 29 March 1923, Abeokuta; *s.* of the late Chief David Basil Lambo and Felicia Lambo; *m.* Dinah V. Adams 1945; three *s.*; ed. Baptist Boys' High School, Abeokuta, Birmingham Univ., England, London Univ. Inst. of Psychiatry.
Medical Officer, Nigerian Medical Services 50-; Govt. Specialist-in-charge, Aro Hospital for Nervous Diseases; Consultant Physician, Univ. Coll., Ibadan; Prof. and Head of Dept. of Psychiatry and Neurology, Univ. of Ibadan 63-, Dean of Medical Faculty 66-68; Vice-Chancellor, Univ. of Ibadan 68-71; Asst. Dir.-Gen. WHO 71-73, Deputy Dir.-Gen. Nov. 73-; mem. Exec. Comm. World Fed. for Mental Health 64-; Emer. mem. Scientific Advisory Panel, Ciba Foundation 66-; convened first Pan-African Conf. of Psychiatrists 61; founded Asscn. of Psychiatrists in Africa 61; Chair. Scientific Council for Africa, UN Advisory Cttee. for Prevention of Crime and Treatment of Offenders; mem. Advisory Cttee. for Mental Health, WHO, Exec. Cttee. Council for Int. Org. for Medical Sciences, UNESCO, Expert Advisory Panel on Mental Health, WHO, WHO Advisory Cttee. for Medical Research (Geneva); mem. Royal Medico-Psychological Asscn., U.K., Pontifical Acad. of Sciences 74; Hon. D.Sc. (Ahmadu Bello Univ., Nigeria, and Long Island Univ., N.Y.), Hon. LL.D. (Birmingham, Kent State Univ., Ohio), Dr. h.c. (Univ. of Dahomey, Univ. d'Aix-Marseille, France); Haile Selassie African Research Award 70.
Leisure interests: collection of ethnographic material on Africa, collection of art of traditional and tribal religions, and collection of ancient books on the history of medicine, on literature and philosophy.
Publs. *Psychiatric Disorder among the Yorubas* (co-author) 63 and numerous articles in various medical journals.
Office: World Health Organization, 1211 Geneva 27;

Home: Chemin des Châtaigniers 27, CH-1292 Chambésy, Switzerland.
Telephone: 34-60-61 (Office); 58-19-42 (Home).

Lambrakis, Christos; Greek journalist and newspaper proprietor; b. 24 Feb. 1934; ed. London School of Economics.
Publisher and Editor weekly *Tachydromos* (Courier) 55-; succeeded father as proprietor of dailies *To Vima* (Tribune), *Ta Nea* (News) and the weeklies *Economicos Tachydromos* (Economic Courier) 57, *Omada* (The Team) 58; Publisher monthly *Epoches* 63-; Pres. Greek Section, Int. Press Inst.; in prison (Folgentros Prison Island) Nov. 67.
Lambrakis Press, Christou Lada 3, Athens, Greece.
Telephone: 230-221; 237-283.

Lambrechts, Peter, PH.D., LL.D.; Belgian university professor and administrator; b. 28 June 1910; ed. Athénée Royal, Ostend, and Ghent Univ.
Asst. Univ. of Ghent 37; Prof. Liège Univ. 44; Dir. of Higher Education Ministry of Education 45-48; Prof. of Brussels Univ. 45; Prof. of Archaeology, Ghent Univ. 48 and Rector 57-61, Pro-rector 68, and Pres. of Board of Admin.; mem. Belgian Senate 65; Commdr. Ordre de Léopold; Commdr. Order of Orange-Nassau.
Publs. *La composition du Sénat romain au deuxième siècle de notre ère* 36, *La composition du Sénat romain au troisième siècle de notre ère* 37, *Contributions à l'étude des divinités celtiques* 42, *Wat Hellas en Rome ons gaven* 50, *L'exaltation de la tête dans la pensée et dans l'art des Celtes* 54.
Rijksuniversiteit te Gent, St. Pietersnieuwstraat 25, Ghent; Home: 19 Gaverland, Baarle-Drongen, Belgium.
Telephone: 09-523659 (Home).

Lamby, Werner, DR.JUR.; German business executive; b. 1 Oct. 1924, Oberwörresbach, Rheinland-Pfalz; *s.* of Peter and Anna Lamby; *m.* Gisela (née Bürfent) 1956; three *s.*; ed. Univs. of Heidelberg and Mainz.
Civil service 52-73; mem. Management Board Vereinigte Industrie-Unternehmungen AG (VIAG); Chair. and mem. of various supervisory boards.
Vereinigte Industrie-Unternehmungen AG, 53 Bonn 1, Gerichtsweg 48, Postfach 626; Home: 53 Bonn-Bad Godesberg, Lyngsbergstrasse 19, Federal Republic of Germany.
Telephone: (02221) 33-04-18 (Home).

Lamizana, Lieut.-Gen. Aboubakar Sangoulé; Upper Voltan army officer and politician; b. 1916, Dianra, Tougan; *s.* of Kafa and Diantoro Lamizana; *m.* Mouilo Kékélé Bintou 1947; six *c.*
Served in French Army in Second World War, and later in N. Africa; joined Bataillon Autonome du Soudan Nigérien, Ségou 47; with Centre d'Etudes Africaines et Asiatiques, Paris 50; served in Indo-China; Joint Chief of Mil. Cabinet, Ivory Coast 56-59; Capt. 57; served N. Africa 59-60; Chief of Staff, Army of Upper Volta 61, Lt.-Col. 64, Pres. of Upper Volta 66-; Prime Minister 66-71, 74-; Minister of Defence 66-67, of Foreign Affairs 66-67, of Information, Youth and Sports 66-67, of Justice 74-; Brig.-Gen. 67, Gen. 70, Lieut.-Gen. 73; Grand Croix, Ordre Nat. de Haute-Volta, Légion d'Honneur, Croix de Guerre, Croix de Valeur Militaire, other foreign decorations.
Leisure interest: sport.
Office of the President, Ouagadougou, Upper Volta.

Lamm, Richard D., LL.B., C.P.A.; American lawyer and state governor; b. 8 Aug. 1935, Madison, Wis.; *s.* of A. E. Lamm; *m.* Dottie Lamm; one *s.* one *d.*; ed. Univs. of Wisconsin and California.
Certified Public Accountant, Ernst & Ernst, Denver 61-62; Lawyer, Colorado Anti-Discrimination Comm. 62-63; Lawyer, Jones, Meiklejohn, Kilroy, Kehl & Lyons 63-65; private practice 65-74; mem. Colorado

House of Reps. 66-74; Assoc. Prof. of Law, Univ. of Denver 69-74; Gov. of Colo. Jan. 75-.
Leisure interests: mountain climbing, reading.
State Capitol, Denver, Colo.; Home: Governor's Mansion, 400 East 8th Avenue, Denver, Colo. 80203, U.S.A.
Telephone: 892-2471 (Office).

Lamonica, Roberto de; Brazilian artist; b. 27 Oct. 1933; ed. Escola de Belas Artes de São Paulo and Museu de Arte Moderna, Rio de Janeiro.
Professor School of Fine Arts, Lima 61-62, Univ. of Chile and Catholic Univ. of Chile 62-63, School of Fine Arts, Viña del Mar 63-64; Prof. of Printmaking, Museum of Modern Art, Rio de Janeiro 64-; has exhibited in Graphic Art Exhbns. all over the world; illustrations and covers for several books; numerous prizes.
Rua Anibal de Mendança 180, A.P. 202, Rio de Janeiro ZC-37, Brazil.

Lamontagne, Rt. Hon. Maurice, P.C., M.P., M.SC., F.R.S.C., F.R.S.A.; Canadian politician; b. 1917; ed. Rimouski Seminary, Quebec, Laval and Harvard Univs.
Professor of Econs., Dir. Dept. of Econs., Laval Univ. 49; Asst. Deputy Minister, Dept. of Northern Affairs and Nat. Resources, Ottawa 54; Econ. Adviser to Privy Council 55-57, Pres. 63-65; Prof. of Econs., Ottawa Univ. 57, Dean of Faculty of Social Sciences 58; Leader of the Opposition 58; Sec. of State and Registrar-Gen. 64-65; Senator 67-; Chair. Senate Cttee. on French Affairs 70-; Liberal.
Parliament Buildings, Ottawa; 18 Lakeview Terrace, Ottawa 1, Ontario, Canada.

Lamour, Philippe, L. EN D.; French businessman; b. 12 Feb. 1903, Landrecies; m. Geneviève Walter 1931; one s. four d.
President and Gen. Man. Compagnie Nat. d'Aménagement de la Région du Bas-Rhône-Languedoc 55-; Pres. Comm. Nat. de L'Aménagement du Territoire, Comité écon. et social de la région Languedoc-Rousillon, Conseil Supérieur du Plan, Féd. Nat. des Vins de Qualité Supérieure; Vice-Pres. Féd. des Asscns. Viticoles de France; mem. Centre national du commerce extérieur, etc.; Pres. Asscn. pour la Grande Traversée des Alpes; Mayor of Ceillac.
Leisure interest: alpinism.
Publ. *60 Millions de Français.*
Mas Saint-Louis-la-Perdrix, 30 Bellegarde du Gard (Gard), France.

Lamoureux, Hon. Lucien, P.C., Q.C., M.A.; Canadian politician and diplomatist; b. 3 Aug. 1929, Ottawa, Ontario; s. of Prime Lamoureux and Graziella Madore; m. Claire Couture 1945; two s. two d.; ed. Ottawa Univ. and Osgoode Hall Law School, Toronto.
Elected to House of Commons 62; Deputy Speaker 63-65, Speaker 66-74; Amb. to Belgium and Luxembourg July 74-; Chancellor, Univ. of Windsor; Hon. Lieut.-Col. S. D. G. Highlanders.
Canadian Embassy, 6 rue Loxum, 1000 Brussels, Belgium; Home: 505 McConnell Avenue, Cornwall, Ontario, Canada.

Lampe, William Frederick Meinhardt; Netherlands Antilles lawyer and politician; b. 5 Dec. 1896, Aruba; s. of Hendrik Meinhardt Lampe and Sophie Romalia Zeppenfeldt; m. Lena Vanterpool 1927; one d.; ed. High School, Netherlands Antilles.
Registrar, Court of Justice, St. Eustatius 17; Postmaster, St. Martin (Netherlands Antillian Part) 19; Acting Lieut.-Gov. Saba 22-27; Gov. Netherlands Windward Islands 27-30; held various posts, including Attorney for the Netherlands Antilles 30-45; Public Notary, Aruba 46; Minister of Justice and Vice-Premier, Netherlands Antilles 51-55; Minister for the Netherlands Antilles to the Netherlands 55-66; Acting Gov. of the Netherlands Antilles 67-69; mem. Windward Islands

Progressive Party; Commdr. Order of Orange-Nassau 66; Bearer Grand Cross (Peru and Argentina).
Leisure interests: swimming, reading.
Mozart Straat 7, Oranjestad, Aruba, Netherlands Antilles.
Telephone: 1547.

Lampert, Lieut.-Gen. James Benjamin; American university administrator and retd. army officer; b. 16 April 1914, Washington, D.C.; s. of the late Lt.-Col. James G. B. Lampert and the late Katharine (Barr) Lampert; m. Margery Mitchell 1937; two s. one d.; ed. U.S. Military Acad., Massachusetts Inst. of Technology, Army Engineers' School and National War Coll.
Military Service, South and South-West Pacific 42-45, Exec. Officer, Manhattan Project 46-47, Armed Forces Special Weapon Project 47-49, Army District Engineer, South Carolina and Oklahoma 49-52, Officer-in-Charge Army Atomic Energy Comm. Nuclear Power Program 52-57, Military Asst. Advisory Group, Saigon, Viet-Nam 58-60, Dir. Military Construction, Office of Chief Engineers, U.S. Army 61-63, Supt., U.S. Mil. Acad., West Point, New York 63-66; Deputy Asst. Sec. of Defence (Manpower) 66-69; U.S. High Comm. of Ryuku Islands, Comm. Gen. U.S. Army, Ryuku Islands and IX Corps, Rep. of Commdr.-in-Chief Pacific, Ryukyu Islands 69-72; retd. 72; Vice-Pres. Resource Devt. Mass. Inst. of Technology 72-; mem. Soc. Amer. Mil. Engineers, Amer. Soc. of Civil Engineers; D.S.M., Silver Star, Legion of Merit, Bronze Star Medal, Army Commendation Medal.
Leisure interests: golf, swimming, squash, fishing, reading.
77 Massachusetts Avenue, Cambridge, Mass. 02139; Home: 60 Oak Road, Concord, Mass. 01742, U.S.A.

Lamport Rodil, Lic. Jorge; Guatemalan politician; b. 3 Jan. 1928, Guatemala City; s. of Don Alfredo Lamport Bowkett and Doña Rodil Cabrera de Lamport; ed. Univ. of British Columbia, Vancouver, and Universidad de San Carlos, Guatemala.
Member of Comm. invited by Italian Govt. for improvement of Italo-Guatemalan relations 63; Sec. of Board of Guatemalan Chamber of Commerce 66; Deputy to Congress 66-70; Vice-Pres. Econ. Cttee. and Sec. Finance Cttee. of Congress 66-67; Pres. Agric. Cttee. of Congress 67-68; Minister of Finance 70-.
Ministerio de Hacienda, Guatemala City, Guatemala.

Lamptey, Jonathan Kwesi, F.R.G.S., F.R.ECON.S.; Ghanaian politician; b. 10 May 1909, Sekondi; s. of Peter Lamptey and Ambah Essilfuah; m. Adelaide Afful 1937; two s. three d.; ed. Mfantsipim School, Wesley Coll., Achimota Coll., Univ. Coll., Exeter and London Univ.
Senior Science Teacher, Mfantsipim School 33-42; Ministerial Sec. Ministry of Finance 51; mem. Legislative Assembly 51-54; Headmaster, Bobikuma Primary School 56-57; Asst. Headmaster, Fijai Secondary School 57-69; imprisoned on political grounds 61-66; mem. Ghana Constituent Assembly 69; mem. Parl. for Sekondi; Minister of Defence 69-70, of the Interior 70; Minister responsible for Parl. Affairs Jan. 71-Jan. 72.
Leisure interests: gardening, dancing, high life, listening to classical music.
c/o National Redemption Council, Accra, Ghana.

Lanc, Erwin; Austrian politician; b. 17 May 1930, Vienna; m. Melitta Fröhlich 1957; one s. one d.
With Fed. Ministry of Social Admin. 49-55; Nat. Sec. Austrian Youth Hostels Asscn. 55-59; mem. Diet and Municipal Council of Vienna 60-; mem. Special Cttee. for Examination of Vienna Public Transport Co. 61, Chair. 64; Man. Information Bureau for Communal Financing 65; mem. Parl. 66-; Minister of Transport 73-; mem. Socialist Party 48-; Pres. Viennese Workers' Asscn. for Sport and Physical Culture (ASKO) 68.

Publs. *Volksaktie ohne make-up* 60, *Gemeinden und Kapitalmarkt* 67.

Leopold Ristergasse 5, 1050 Vienna, Austria.

Lancaster, Burt(on) Stephen; American actor; b. 2 Nov. 1913; ed. New York Univ.

Acrobat 32-39; shop asst. and salesman 39-42; army service 42-45; appeared in the play *A Sound of Hunting* (New York) 45; films include *The Killers* 46, *Desert Fury* 47, *All My Sons* 48, *The Flame and the Arrow* 50, *Ten Tall Men* 51, *The Crimson Pirate* 52, *His Majesty O'Keefe, From Here to Eternity, The Rose Tattoo* 55, *Trapeze, The Rainmaker* 56, *Gunfight at O.K. Corral, Sweet Smell of Success* 57, *Separate Tables* 58, *The Devil's Disciple* 59, *The Unforgiven, Elmer Gantry* 60 (Acad. Award for Best Actor 1960), *Judgement at Nuremberg* 61, *Birdman of Alcatraz* 62, *The Leopard* 62, *A Child is Waiting* 62, *Seven Days in May* 64, *The Train* 64, *The Professionals* 66, *The Scalphunters* 68, *The Swimmer* 68, *Valdez is Coming* 70, *Lawman* 70, *Scorpio* 72, *Ulzana's Raid* 72, *Executive Action* 73, *The Midnight Man* 74, *Conversation Piece* 74, *1900* 75, *Moses* 76.

Hecht-Hill-Lancaster Productions Inc., 830 Linda Flora, Beverly Hills, Calif. 90049, U.S.A.

Lancaster, Sir Osbert, Kt., C.B.E.; British artist and writer; b. 4 Aug. 1908; ed. Charterhouse, Lincoln Coll., Oxford, and Slade School, London.

Cartoonist, *Daily Express* 39-; News Dept., Foreign Office 40; British Embassy, Athens 44-46; Sydney Jones Lecturer in Art, Liverpool Univ. 47, Hon. Litt.D. (Birmingham).

Designed sets for *Pineapple Poll*, Sadler's Wells 51, *Bonne Bouche*, Covent Garden 52, *Love in a Village*, English Opera Group 52, *High Spirits*, Hippodrome 53, *Rake's Progress*, Edinburgh (for Glyndebourne) 53, *All's Well That Ends Well*, Old Vic 53, *Don Pasquale*, Sadler's Wells 54, *Coppelia*, Covent Garden 55, Napoli Festival Ballet 54, *Falstaff*, Edinburgh (for Glyndebourne) 55, *Zuleika*, Saville 57, *L'Italiana in Algeria*, Glyndebourne 57, *Tiresias*, English Opera Group 58, *Candide*, Saville 59, *La Fille mal gardée*, Covent Garden 60, *She Stoops to Conquer*, Old Vic 60, *La Pietra del Paragone*, Glyndebourne 64, *L'Heure Espagnole*, Glyndebourne 66, *The Rising of the Moon*, Glyndebourne 70, *The Sorcerer*, D'Oyly-Carte Co. 71.

Publs. *Progress at Pelvis Bay* 36, *Our Sovereigns* 36, *Pillar to Post* 38, *Homes, Sweet Homes* 39, *Classical Landscape with Figures* 47, *The Saracen's Head* 48, *Drayneflete Revealed* 49, *Façades and Faces* 50, *Private Views* 56, *The Year of the Comet* 57, *Études* 58, *Here, of All Places* 59, *Signs of the Times* 61, *All Done from Memory* (autobiography) 64, *Graffiti* 64, *A Few Quick Tricks* 65, *With an Eye to the Future* 67, *Temporary Diversions* 68, *Sailing to Byzantium* 69, *Recorded Live* (new pocket cartoons) 70, *Meaningful Confrontations* 71, *Theatre in the Flat* 72, *The Littlehampton Bequest* 73, *Liquid Assets* 75.

12 Eaton Square, London, S.W.1, England.

Lancefield, Rebecca Craighill, A.M., PH.D.; American microbiologist and immunologist; b. 5 Jan. 1895, Fort Wadsworth, N.Y.; d. of Col. William E. Craighill and Mary W. Byram Craighill; m. Donald E. Lancefield 1918; one d.; ed. Wellesley Coll. and Columbia Univ.

Technical Asst., Rockefeller Inst. for Medical Research (now The Rockefeller Univ., New York) 18-19, 22-25, Asst. 25-29, Assoc. 29-42, Assoc. mem. 42-58, mem. and Prof. 58-65, Prof. Emer. 65-; mem. Nat. Acad. of Sciences; Pres. Soc. of American Bacteriologists 43-44, American Asscn. of Immunologists 61-62; T. Duckett Jones Memorial Award 60, American Heart Asscn.'s Achievement Award 64.

The Rockefeller University, New York, N.Y. 10021, U.S.A.

Telephone: 212-360-1347.

Land, Edwin Herbert, LL.D., L.H.D.; American scientist; b. 7 May 1909, Bridgeport, Conn.; s. of Harry M. and Matha G. Land; m. Helen Maislen 1929; two d.; ed. Norwich Acad. and Harvard Univ.

Founder, Polaroid Corpn., Cambridge, Mass. 37, later Pres., Chair., and Dir. of Research; developed first modern polarizers for light, sequence of subsequent polarizers, theories and practices for application of polarized light; during World War II developed optical systems for mil. use; created cameras, films that give instantaneous dry photographs in black and white and colour; mem. President's Science Advisory Cttee., President's Foreign Intelligence Advisory Board, Nat. Comm. on Technology, Automation and Econ. Progress; Dir. International Exec. Service Corps; Visiting Prof. M.I.T. 56; William James Lecturer on Psychology, Harvard 66-67; numerous hon. degrees; numerous medals incl. Presidential Medal of Freedom 63, Nat. Medal of Science 67; Fellow, Photographic Soc. of America; mem. American Acad. of Arts and Sciences (past-Pres.), etc.

730 Main Street, Cambridge, Mass. 02139; Home: 163 Brattle Street, Cambridge, Mass. 02138, U.S.A.

Landau, Haim; Israeli engineer and politician; b. 10 Sept. 1916, Cracow, Poland; ed. Hebrew Technical Univ.

Went to Israel 35; building engineer until 42; Chief of Staff 44-48; mem. Exec. Cttee. Herut Movement; Minister of Devt. Dec. 69-Aug. 70.

28 Semadar Street, Ramat Gan, Israel.

Landau, Moshe, LL.B.; Israeli judge; b. 29 April 1912, Danzig (now Gdańsk, Poland); s. of Dr. Isaac Landau and Betty (née Eisenstädt); m. Leah Doukhan 1937; three d.; ed. London Univ.

Went to Israel 33; called to Palestine Bar 37, Magistrate of Haifa 40, District Court Judge, Haifa 48, Justice, Supreme Court, Jerusalem 53-.

Leisure interest: piano.

The Supreme Court, Jerusalem; and 10 Alharizi Street, Jerusalem, Israel.

Telephone: 32757.

Landázuri Ricketts, H.E. Cardinal Juan, D.C.L.; Peruvian ecclesiastic; b. 19 Dec. 1913, Arequipa; ed. Univs. of Arequipa and Antonianum, Rome.

Franciscan Friar; Teacher of Canon Law; Ordained Priest 39; Titular Archbishop of Roina 52; cr. Cardinal 62; Archbishop of Lima; Kt. Commdr. of Order of Malta and many honours.

Arzobispado, Plaza de Armas, Apartado Postal 1512, Lima, Peru.

Landowski, Marcel François Paul; French composer; b. 18 Feb. 1915; ed. Lycée Janson-de-Sailly and Conservatoire nationale de musique de Paris.

Director Conservatoire, Boulogne-sur-Seine 60-65; Dir. of Music, Comédie Française, Paris 62-; Insp.-Gen. of Musical Studies 64; Dir. of Music 66-70; Dir. of Music, lyrical art and dance 70-74, Ministry of Cultural Affairs 70-; Chevalier Légion d'Honneur, Croix de guerre.

Compositions include: *Rhythmes du monde* (Oratorio), *Jean de la peur* (Symphony), *Le Rire de Nils Halérius*, *Le Fou, Le Ventriloque, Les Adieux* (Operas); two cantatas, chamber music, film music, music for *Cyrano de Bergerac* at Comédie Française.

10 rue Max-Blondat, 92 Boulogne-sur-Seine, Seine, France.

Landquist, John, PH.D.; Swedish writer; b. 3 Dec. 1881, Stockholm; m. Solveig Bohlin 1938; one d.; ed. Uppsala Univ.

Literary Critic *Dagens Nyheter* 11-17, and *Aftonbladet* 24-; Editor *Aftonbladet* 32-35; Prof. of Psychology Lund Univ. 35-46, Emeritus 47-.

Publs. *The Will* 08, *Essays* 13, *Gustav Froding* 16,

Knut Hamsun 17, *The Living Past* 19, *Knowledge of Man* 20, *Erik Gustav Geijer* 24, *Henri Bergson* 28, *Modern Swedish Literature in Finland* 29, *Humanism* 31, *The Unity of the Soul* 35, *Psychology* 40, *History of Pedagogy* 41, *As I remember them* 49, *In Youth* 57, *Charles Darwin, Life and Work* 59, *Art and Politics* 70.
Villavägen 19, Stocksund, Sweden.

Landré, Guillaume (Louis Frédéric); Netherlands composer; b. 24 Feb. 1905; ed. Univ. of Utrecht (Doctor in Law), composition under Willem Pÿper.
Teacher, Amsterdam 30-47; Gen.-Sec. Arts Council 47-57, Pres. Music Dept. 57-; Hon. Life Pres. Netherlands Composers' Guild 61; Hon. Life Pres. 2nd Fed. of Conf. Int. des Socs. d'Auteurs et Compositeurs (Cisac) 64; mem. Artistic Board Concertgebouw Orchestra; Vice-Pres. Netherlands Opera Foundation; Officer Orange-Nassau; Officer Polar Star (Sweden); Sweelinck Prize (Music Prize of the Netherlands).
Compositions: 4 Symphonies 33, 41, 51, 54, Concerto for Clarinet and Orchestra 57, *Permutazioni sinfoniche* 57, *Anagrams for Orchestra* 60, *Variazioni senza Tema per orchestra* 67-68, 4 String Quartets 29, 42, 51, 65, 2 Wind Quartets 30, 60, *Jean Lévecq* (one-act Opera) 64, *La Symphonie pastorale* (Opera) 66.
Molenweg 34, Amstelveen, Netherlands.
Telephone: 13284.

Lane, Ronald Anthony Stuart, M.C., F.I.B.; British banker; b. 8 Dec. 1917, Bushey, Herts.; s. of Wilmot Ernest Lane and Florence Blakey; m. Anne Brenda Walsh 1948; one s. one d.; ed. Lancing Coll.
Served with Chartered Bank of India, Australia and China in the Far East 39-60; 7th Light Cavalry, Indian Army 40-45; Chief Gen. Man. The Chartered Bank 72; mem. Export Guarantees Advisory Council 72; mem. Council, Inst. of Bankers 75; Man. Dir. Standard Chartered Bank Ltd. 75-.
Leisure interests: sailing, gardening.
West Hold, by the Church, West Mersea, Essex, England.
Telephone: West Mersea 2563.

Lang, André; French dramatist and journalist; b. 12 Jan. 1893, Paris; m. 1st Lise Clemenceau 1920 (died 1921); one s.; m. 2nd Sari de Megyery 1939.
Officer, Legion of Honour, Croix de Guerre 14-18; Hon. Pres. Asscn. Critique Cinéma et Television.
Leisure interest: country walks.
Publs. include Plays: *Fantaisie Amoureuse* 25, *Les trois Henry* 30 (produced at Comédie Française), *La Paix est pour demain* 37, *L'Impure* 48; novels: *Le Responsable* 21, *Fausta* 22, *Mes deux Femmes* 31; essays: *Voyage en zigzags dans la République des Lettres* 22, *Déplacements et Villégiatures Littéraires* 23, *Tiers de Siècle* 35, *L'Homme libre, ce prisonnier* (crowned by French Acad.) 46, *Le tableau blanc* (cinema) 48, *Le Voyage à Turin* (play) 56, *Le Septième Ciel* (novel) 58, *Une Vie d'orages: Germaine de Staël* (biography) 58, *Bagage à la Consigne* (autobiography) 60, *Le Sac* (play) 62, *La Dame de Coppet* (play) 64, *Pierre Brisson* (biography) 67, *La Société et l'Ecrivain* (*France, 1900-1930*) 76.
15 rue Lakanal, 75015 Paris, France.
Telephone: 828-45-46.

Lang, Anton, DR.NAT.SC.; American (naturalized 1956) plant physiologist; b. 18 Jan. 1913, St. Petersburg, Russia; s. of Dr. George Lang and Vera Davidov; m. Lydia Kamendrovsky 1946; two s. one d.; ed. High School, Berlin and Labes, Pomerania, and Univ. of Berlin.
Scientific Asst., Kaiser Wilhelm (later Max Planck) Inst. of Biology, Berlin, later Tübingen, Germany 39-49; Research Assoc., Genetics Dept., McGill Univ., Montreal 49; Visiting Prof., Agronomy and Genetics Depts., Texas Agric. and Mech. Coll. 50; Research Fellow and Senior Research Fellow, Div. of Biology, Calif. Inst. of Technology, Pasadena 50-52; Asst. and Assoc. Prof., Dept. of Botany, Univ. of Calif., Los Angeles 52-59; Prof. of Biology in charge of Earhart-Campbell Plant Research Labs., Calif. Inst of Technology 59-65; Dir. MSU/ERDA Plant Research Lab., and Prof. of Botany and Plant Pathology, Michigan State Univ., E. Lansing 65-; Lady Davis Foundation Fellowship 49; Lalor Foundation Fellowship 50-52; Senior Research Fellowship, Nat. Science Foundation 48-49; mem. Nat. Acad. of Sciences, American Acad. of Arts and Sciences, Akademie Leopoldina; Chair. Nat. Research Council Comm. on the Effects of Herbicides in Viet-Nam 71-74.
Leisure interests: gardening, reading, music.
Publs. Over 100 publs. in plant physiology (physiology of flowering, hormone physiology).
MSU/ERDA Plant Research Laboratory, Michigan State University, East Lansing, Mich. 48824; Home: 1538 Cahill Drive, East Lansing, Mich. 48824, U.S.A.
Telephone: 517-351-5431 (Home); 517-353-2270 (Office).

Lang, Fritz; American film producer, director and writer; b. 5 Dec. 1890, Austria; s. of Anton and Paula Lang.
Fmrly. artist selling picture postcards in Brussels café; joined Decla Film Co. after First World War, then UFA Berlin, Fritz Lang Film Co., later Nero Film Co.; collaborated in scenario writing with his fmr. wife, Thea von Harbou; freelance producer and director; Commdr. Cross Order of Merit (Fed. Republic of Germany) 66; Officier des Arts et des Lettres (France) 66; Golden Ribbon Motion Picture Art (Germany) 65; Order of the Yugoslav Flag 71; Hon. Prof. Univ. of Vienna 73.
Produced and directed *Dr. Mabuse, Destiny, Nibelungen Saga, The Girl in the Moon, The Spy, Metropolis, "M", The Testament of Dr. Mabuse, Lilion, Fury, You Only Live Once, You and Me, The Return of Frank James, Western Union, Manhunt, Hangmen Also Die, Ministry of Fear, The Woman in the Window, Scarlet Street, Cloak and Dagger, Secret Beyond the Door, House by the River, An American Guerila in the Philippines, Rancho Notorious, Clash by Night, Blue Gardenia, The Big Heat, Human Desire, Moonfleet, While the City Sleeps, Beyond a Reasonable Doubt, Das indische Grabmal, Der Tiger von Eschnapur, Die 1000 Augen des Dr. Mabuse;* starred as himself in *Le Mépris* by Jean-Luc Godard.
1501 Summitridge Drive, Beverly Hills, Calif. 90210, U.S.A.

Lang, Hon. Otto Emil, P.C., Q.C., M.P.; Canadian lawyer and politician; b. 14 May 1932, Handel, Sask.; s. of Otto T. Lang and Maria Theresa Wurm; m. Adrian Ann Merchant 1963; three s. four d.; ed. Univ. of Saskatchewan and Oxford Univ.
Admitted to Saskatchewan Bar 56; Asst. Prof., Univ. of Saskatchewan, Faculty of Law 56, Assoc. Prof. 57, Prof. 61, Dean of Law School 61-68; Mem. of Parl. for Saskatoon-Humboldt 68; Minister without Portfolio 68, with responsibility for Energy and Water Resources 69; Minister without Portfolio responsible for Canadian Wheat Board Oct. 69-70; Minister of Manpower & Immigration Sept. 70-Jan. 72; Minister of Justice Jan. 72-75, of Transport responsible for Canadian Wheat Board Sept. 75-; Pres. Asscn. of Canadian Law Teachers 62-63; Vice-Pres. Saskatchewan Liberal Asscn. 56-63; Fed. Campaign Chair. Liberal Party 63-64; Past Pres. Saskatoon Social Planning Council; Rhodes Scholar 55; Knight of Malta 62; Q.C. for Ontario 72; Q.C. for Saskatchewan 72.
Leisure interests: curling, bridge, golf.
Publs. *Contemporary Problems of Public Law in Canada* (Editor) 68.
House of Commons, Ottawa, Ontario K1A 0A6, Canada.
Telephone: 613-996-7501.

Lang, Paul Henry, PH.D.; American (Hungarian-born) musicologist; b. 28 Aug. 1901; ed. Budapest Royal Acad. of Music, Heidelberg, Paris and Cornell Univs. Settled in U.S.A. 28, naturalized citizen 34; Asst. Prof. of Music Vassar Coll. 30-31; Assoc. Prof. of Music Wells Coll. 31-33; Prof. of Musicology Columbia Univ. 33-; music critic for *New York Herald Tribune* 54-66; Fellow American Acad. of Arts and Sciences; Pres. Int. Musicological Soc.; mem. French, Netherlands and Belgian Musicological Socs.; Editor *The Musical Quarterly*.
Publ. *Music in Western Civilisation* 41.
33 Aldridge Road, Chappaqua, N.Y., U.S.A.

Långbacka, Ralf Runar, M.A.; Finnish theatre director; b. 20 Nov. 1932, Närpes; s. of Runar Emanuel Långbacka and Hulda Emilia Långbacka (née Backlund); m. Runa Birgitta Danielsson 1961; two s. one d.; ed. Åbo Akademi, Universität München, and Freie Univ., Berlin.
Editor of Finnish Radio literary programmes 55-56; Asst. and Dir. Lilla Teatern, Helsinki 58-60; Manager and Artistic Dir. Swedish Theatre, Turku 60-63; Dir. Finnish Nat. Theatre 63-65; Artistic Dir. Swedish Theatre, Helsinki 65-67; free-lance dir. in Finnish National Opera, Helsinki, Municipal Theatre, Gothenburg, Sweden, Royal Dramatic Theatre, Stockholm, Sweden 67-71; Artistic Dir. Municipal Theatre, Turku 71-; mem. Finnish State Comm. of Dramatic Art 67-70; The Critics Spurs 63, Pro Finlandia 73.
Leisure interests: music, politics, sports.
Rykmentintie 45 as. 20, Turku, Finland.
Telephone: 921-11788.

Langdon, Jervis, Jr.; American railroad executive; b. 28 Jan. 1905, Elmira, N.Y.; s. of Jervis and Eleanor (Sayles) Langdon; m. Irene Fortner 1949; ed. Cornell Univ. and Univ. de Dijon, France
Assistant Gen. Attorney, Chesapeake and Ohio Railway 36-38, Gen. Attorney 38-41, Asst. Vice-Pres. (Traffic) 41-42; U.S. Army Air Force 42-45; Special Counsel, Asscn. of Southeastern Railroads 47-53, Chair. 53-56; Gen. Counsel, Baltimore and Ohio Railroad 56-61, Pres. 61-64; Chair. Chicago, Rock Island and Pacific Railroad 64-65, Chair. and Pres. 65-70; Trustee, Penn Central Transport Co. 70-74, Pres., Chief Exec. Officer 74; Legion of Merit.
6 Penn Center Plaza, Philadelphia, Pennsylvania 19104; Home: Quarry Farm, Elmira, N.Y. 14902, U.S.A.

Langdon, Michael, C.B.E.; British bass singer; b. 12 Nov. 1920, Wolverhampton; s. of Mr. and Mrs. Henry Langdon; m. Vera Duffield 1947; two d.; ed. Bushbury Hill School, Wolverhampton.
Principal bass, Royal Opera House, Covent Garden 51-; sang in *Gloriana* (Britten) at Royal Command Performance 53; Promenade Concerts, Royal Albert Hall 53-; int. engagements since 61; T.V., radio, etc.; known for leading bass roles in *Fidelio, Der Rosenkavalier, Il Seraglio, Don Carlos, Wozzeck, Don Giovanni, Faust, Das Rheingold, Die Walküre, Götterdämmerung, Magic Flute, Falstaff, Tristan und Isolde, Tannhäuser, Der Fliegende Holländer, Billy Budd, Boris Godonov, Bartered Bride, Aida,* etc.; particularly well known as Baron Ochs in *Der Rosenkavalier*; Hon. Diploma (Guildhall School Music and Drama) 73.
Leisure interests: walking, swimming and association football (Wolves F.C.), plus reading science fiction and autobiographies.
34 Warnham Court, Grand Avenue, Hove, Sussex, England.
Telephone: Brighton 733120.

Lange, Gunnar, PH.D.; Swedish government official and politician; b. 9 March 1909, Stockholm; s. of Nils Lange and Magda Lovisa (née Boije) Lange; m. Marta Saul 1935; two d.; ed. Stockholm Univ.

Served on Board of Agriculture 35-38; Asst. Prof. Agriculture and Economics, Univ. of North Carolina, U.S.A. 41-43; Chief of Bureau, Swedish Food Comm. 43-46; Sec. of State Ministry of Agriculture 47-50, Ministry of Finance 50-54; Minister of Civil Service 54-55; Minister of Commerce 55-70; mem. of First Chamber of Parl. 53-70; M.P. 70-; Chair. Ministerial Council of European Free Trade Asscn. 59-60, 63, 67; Pres. of Swedish Football Asscn. 53-69, Hon. Pres. 69-; Social Democratic Labour.
Office: Riksdagen, 10012 Stockholm 46; Home: Stopvägen 84, Bromma, Stockholm, Sweden.
Telephone: 014-20-20 (Office); 08-259980 (Home).

Lange, Per; Danish writer; b. 30 Aug. 1901, Hørsholm, Denmark; s. of Sven Lange and Mimi Blad; m. Hanne Thiele 1942; one s. two d.
Free-lance translator and literary critic; former book critic of *Berlingske Tidende*; on staff of *Sind og Samfund* 32-37; Literary adviser *Gyldendals Forlag*, Copenhagen 46-.
Leisure interest: music.
Publs. Poems: *Kaos og Stjærnen* 26, *Forvandlinger* 29, *Orfeus* 32, *Relieffer* 43; *Spejlinger* (essays) 53, *Ved Musikkens Tærskel* (essays) 57, *Samtale med et Æsel* (essays) 61, *Om Krig og Krigsmænd* (essays) 66, *Dyrenes Maskerade* (essays) 69; also numerous translations of English, French and American authors.
Dr. Olgas Vej. 5, DK-2000 Copenhagen F, Denmark.
Telephone: (01) 190056.

Langemeijer, Gerard Eduard, DR. JUR.; Netherlands lawyer; b. 3 Nov. 1903, Dieren; s. of Mr. and Mrs. E. G. Langemeijer; m. 1958; ed. Univ. of Leiden.
Called to the Bar 28; District Attorney, Rotterdam 29-34; The Hague 34-39; Judge, Amsterdam 39-46; Prof. of Law, Leiden Univ. 46-58; Asst. Attorney-Gen. Supreme Court 47-57, Attorney-Gen. 57-73; Pres. Royal Netherlands Acad. of Sciences and Letters 63-68; Co-editor of *Nederlands Juristenblad* (Law Review).
Bronovolaan 20, The Hague, Netherlands.

Langenhove, Fernand Van; Belgian diplomatist; b. 30 June 1889, Mouscron; s. of Emil van Langenhove and Sarah van de Mergel; m. Nancy Willems 1920; two d.; ed. Univ. of Brussels.
Secretary, Inst. of Sociology. Brussels 10; Dir. Ministry of Econ. Affairs, Belgium 17; Prof., Univ. of Brussels 20; Dir. Ministry of Foreign Affairs 22; Chief of Cabinet, Ministry of Foreign Affairs 27; Sec.-Gen. Ministry of Foreign Affairs 29; Ambassador 36; Perm. Belgian Rep. to UN 46-57; Pres. Inst. Royal des Relations Int. 58; mem. Acad. Royale de Belgique 61, Acad. Royale des Sciences d'Outremer; Grand Cross of Order of Crown (Belgium), of Order of Netherlands Lion, of Order of Southern Cross (Brazil), of Order of Merit (Portugal), of Order of Crown (Italy); Grand Officier de la Légion d'Honneur (France), etc.
Leisure interests: reading (memoirs), classical music.
Publs. *La Nationalité Albanaise* 13, *Comment naît un cycle de légendes* 16, *Le dossier diplomatique de la question belge* 17, *L'action du Gouvernement belge en matière économique pendant la guerre* 21, *Le problème de la protection des populations aborigènes aux Nations Unies* 56, *La crise du système de sécurité collective des Nations Unies* 58, *Consciences Tribales et Nationales en Afrique Noire* 60, *Le rôle proéminent du Secrétaire Général dans l'opération des Nations Unies au Congo* 64, *La Belgique en Quête de Sécurité* 69, *La Sécurité de la Belgique* 71, *La Belgique et ses garants, L'été 1940* 72.
67 Avenue de la Floride, 1180 Brussels, Belgium.
Telephone: 74-12-87.

Langer, William Leonard, A.M., PH.D., LL.D., DR.PHIL., L.H.D., LITT.D.; American historian; b. 16 March 1896, Boston, Mass.; s. of Charles Rudolph Langer and Johanna (Rockenbach) Langer; m. 1st Susanne

Knauth 1921, 2nd Rowena Morse Nelson 1943; two *s.*; ed. Harvard and Vienna Univs.

Instructor in Modern Languages, Worcester Acad. 15-17; Asst. Prof. of History, Clark Univ. 23-25; Associate Prof. 25-27; Asst. Prof. of History, Harvard Univ. 27-31, Associate Prof. 31-36, Coolidge Prof. 36-64, Prof. Emeritus 64-; Prof. Fletcher School of Diplomacy, Medford, Mass. 33-34, 36-41; mem. American Historical Asscn., Mass. Historical Society, Council on Foreign Relations, American Acad. of Arts and Sciences, American Philosophical Society, etc.; mem. editorial board *Journal of Modern History* 29-33, *American Historical Review* 36-39, *Foreign Affairs* 55-; mem. Advisory Board *Historical Abstracts* 55-; editorial adviser to Houghton, Mifflin Co.; Chief Research and Analysis Branch, Office Strategic Services 41-45; Dir. Office of Intelligence Research and Liaison, Dept. of State 45-46, Special Asst. to Sec. of State for Research and Intelligence 46; Dir. for Nat. Estimates, Central Intelligence Agency 50-51; mem. President's Foreign Intelligence Advisory Board 61-69; mem. American Historical Asscn. (Pres. 57); Fellow, Center for Advanced Study in the Behavioral Sciences 59-60; Medal for Merit.
Leisure interests: music, golf, bowling, gardening.
Publs. *The Franco-Russian Alliance of 1890-94* 29, *European Alliances and Alignments* 31, *Foreign Affairs Bibliography* 33, *The Diplomacy of Imperialism* 35, *Our Vichy Gamble* 47, *The Challenge to Isolation* (with S. E. Gleason) 52, *The Undeclared War* (with S. E. Gleason) 53, *Gas and Flame in World War I* 65, *Political & Social Upheaval 1832-1952* 69.
1 Berkeley Street, Cambridge, Mass. 02138, U.S.A.
Telephone: 864-2557.

Langlo, Kaare, D.PHIL.; Norwegian meteorologist; b. 7 Oct. 1913, Bergen; *s.* of Einar Olsen and Borghild Langlo; *m.* Else Lökke 1943; one *s.* one *d.*
Research Asst., Observatory, Tromsö 40-43, Meteorologist 43-45, Chief of Div. 45-51; Chief Administrator, WMO 52, Chief of Technical Div. 53-67; Dir. 68-70; Deputy Sec.-Gen. WMO 71-75; WMO Rep. on SCAR and Int. Comm. on Polar Meteorology.
Leisure interests: skiing, fishing.
Publs. *Lokale Änderungen der Struktur der Ionosphäre auf hohen Breitegraden* 42, *On the amount of Atmospheric Ozone and its relation to Meteorological Conditions* 52, *The World Weather Watch* 66, *Three thousand million people—only one biosphere* 71, and numerous articles.
c/o World Meteorological Organization, 41 avenue Giuseppe Motta, Geneva, Switzerland.
Telephone: 34-64-00.

Langman, Hargert; Netherlands politician; b. 1931; *m.*; four *c.*; ed. Univ. of Amsterdam.
Former Man. Dir. Dutch Foundation for the Shipbuilding Industry; Prof. in Industrial Economy, Technological Univ., Delft and Econ. Inst. Rotterdam; Minister of Econ. Affairs 71-73; Nat. Liberal.
c/o Ministry of Economic Affairs, The Hague, Netherlands.

Langsam, Walter Consuelo, B.S., M.A., PH.D., LITT.D., SC.D. in ED., L.H.D., SC.D., LL.D.; American historian and university administrator; b. 2 Jan. 1906, Vienna, Austria; *s.* of Emery Bernhardt and Angela Virginia Bianca Langsam; *m.* Julia Elizabeth Stubblefield 1931; two *s.*; ed. City Coll. of New York and Columbia Univ.
Tutor in History, City Coll. of N.Y. 26; Instructor and Asst. Prof. of History, Columbia University 27-38; Prof. of History, Union Coll. 38-45; Visiting Prof., British Columbia, Duke, Ohio State, Columbia, N.Y. and Colorado Univs.; radio news commentator Station WGY Schenectady 41-43; Office of Strategic Services 44-45; Pres. Wagner Lutheran Coll., N.Y. 45-52; Pres. of Gettysburg Coll., Pa. 52-55, of Univ. of Cincinnati 55-71, Pres. Emer. and Distinguished Service Prof.

71-; mem. Board of Consultants, Nat. Defense Univ., Wash., D.C.; Trustee, Endicott Coll.; Chair. of Board, Cincinnati Ballet Co.; Vice-Pres. Board of Theological Educ., Lutheran Church in America 62-72; mem. Board of Dirs. Diamond Int., Southern Ohio Bank; mem.-at-large Nat. Council of Boy Scouts of America; Fellow, Int. Consular Acad.; Townsend Harris Medallist (City Coll. of New York); 125th Aniv. Alumni Medal, City Coll. of N.Y. 72; George Washington Honor Medal, Freedoms Foundation at Valley Forge 58, 73; Dept. of the Army Outstanding Civilian Service Award 68, Laurel Leaf Cluster 71, 72; Grand Cross, Order of Merit, Fed. Republ of Germany 70; Hon. Consul of Finland.
Publs. *The Napoleonic Wars and German Nationalism in Austria* 30, *The World since 1914* 33 (6th edn. 48), *Major European and Asiatic Developments since 1935* 39, *In Quest of Empire, The Problem of Colonies* 39, *Documents and Readings in the History of Europe since 1918* 39 (rev. edn. 51), *Since 1939—A Narrative of War* 41, *Francis the Good, the Education of an Emperor (1768-1792)* 49, *The World since 1919* 54 (8th edn. 71, with Otis C. Mitchell), *Franz der Gute: Die Jugend eines Kaisers* 54, *Historic Documents of World War II* 58, *World History since 1870* 63, *Where Freedom Exists* 67, *An Honor Conferred, A Title Awarded: A History of the Commercial Club of Cincinnati, 1880-1972* 73, *The Common Market: Problems and Prospects* 74; contrib. to *The American Historical Association's Guide to Historical Literature* 61, and to *Virtute Fideque: Festschrift für Otto von Habsburg zum fünfzigsten Geburtstag* (ed. Emil Franzel) 65.
University of Cincinnati, Cincinnati, Ohio 45221, U.S.A.
Telephone: 513-475-2511.

Languetin, Pierre; Swiss diplomatist; b. 1923, Lausanne; ed. Univ. de Lausanne and London School of Economics.
Diplomatic career 49-; in Div. of Exchange, OEEC, Paris; in Div. of Commerce, Fed. Dept. of Public Economy 55-57, Head of Secr. 57-61, Chief of Section IA 61-63, Chief of Subdivision 63; has been concerned with problems of European econ. co-operation; Asst. Head of Bureau of Integration, Fed. Political Dept. and Dept. of Public Economy 61; Swiss Del. to Trade Cttee., OECD, Paris 61-, Vice-Pres. 65-; mem. Swiss Del. to UNCTAD Geneva 64; Swiss Rep. at various int. orgs. 65-66; Del. of Fed. Council for Trade Negotiations, title of Minister Plenipotentiary 66-; Head of Swiss Del. to EFTA Geneva 67-, title of Amb. 68-; Head of Swiss Del. to Second UNCTAD New Delhi 68; Head of Swiss Del., Trade and Devt. Board 67-70; Deputy Head of Swiss Negotiating Team with EEC 70-.
Swiss Delegation to EFTA, 9-11 rue de Varembé, 1202 Geneva, Switzerland.

Lanocita, Arturo; Italian journalist; b. 4 June 1904; ed. Univ. degli Studi, Pavia.
Editor newspaper *L'Ambrosiano* 23-30, *La Stampa* 30; Editor *Corriere della Sera* 30-45, Vice-Editor-in-Chief 45-62. Cinema Critic 46, Editor-in-Chief 62-68; mem. Int. Jury Venice Cinema Festival 48, 50, 52, 62, Pres. 63; mem. Int. Jury San Sebastian Cinema Festival 59; Commendatore della Repubblica Italiana; Golden Pen of Cinema Critics 51, Borselli Prize 66.
Publs. *Attrici e attori in pigiama* 26, *Scrittori del tempo nostro* 28, *Quaranta milioni* 32, *Quella maledettissima sera* 39, *Salvateli dalla ghigliottina* 43, *Il Croce a sinistra* 45, *Il ragazzo che doveva mentire* 46, *Cinema, fabbrica di sogni* 50, *Gratis* 59, *Sofia Loren* 66.
Via Alessandro Volta 7, Milan, Italy.

Lanoux, Armand; French writer; b. 24 Oct. 1913, Paris; *s.* of Aimé Lanoux and Jeanne Jacoby; *m.* 2nd Catherine Tolstoi 1964; two *s.* (of 1st *m.*).
Former teacher, painter; infantry officer 39-40; profes-

sional writer 46-; Sec.-Gen., Université Radiophonique et Télévisuelle Internationale; Vice-Pres. Société des Auteurs Dramatiques; mem. Académie Goncourt 69-; Chevalier de la Légion d'Honneur, Croix de Guerre 39-40, Commdr. des Arts et Lettres; Prix Interallié 56, Prix Goncourt 63.
Leisure interests: swimming and sailing, collecting post-cards.
Publs. biographies: *Bonjour, Monsieur Zola* 54, *Maupassant, le Bel Ami* 67; novels: *Le Commandant Watrin* 56, *Le Rendez-Vous de Bruges* 58, *Quand la Mer se Retire* 63, *Margot, l'enragée* 64, *Le Violon dans le Feu* 67; poems: *Les Images d'Épinal* 69, *La Polka des Canons* 71, *Le Coq Rouge* 72; *1900, la Bourgeoisie absolute* 73, *Le Berger des Abeilles* 74, *Paris 1925* 75.
7 route de Malnoue, 77 Champs-sur-Marne, France.
Telephone: 957-21-89.

Lansdowne, 8th Marquess of; **George John Charles Mercer Nairne Petty-Fitzmaurice,** P.C.; British politician; b. 27 Nov. 1912; *s.* of the late Major Lord Charles Mercer Nairne and of Lady Violet Elliot; *m.* 1st Barbara Chase 1938 (died 1965), two *s.* two *d.* (one dec.); *m.* 2nd Mrs. Polly Carnegie (*d.* of Viscount Eccles, *q.v.*) 1969; ed. Eton Coll. and Christ Church, Oxford Univ.
Army service 39-45, Major 44, served with Free French Forces; Private Sec. to Rt. Hon. A. Duff Cooper, Ambassador to France 44-45; Lord-in-Waiting to H.M. The Queen 57-58; Joint Parl. Under-Sec. of State, Foreign Office 58-62; Chair. Intergovernmental Cttee. Malaysia Aug.-Dec. 62; Minister of State for Colonial Affairs 62-64; Pres. Franco-British Soc.; Prime Warden Fishmongers' Company 67-68; Conservative.
Meikleour House, Perthshire, Scotland.

Lantier, Raymond François; French archaeologist; b. 11 July 1886, Lisieux; *s.* of Dr. Georges Lantier and Claire Benoist-Tranchepain; *m.* Yvonne Chevalier 1918; ed. Ecole pratique des Hautes Etudes, Ecole du Louvre, and Ecole des Hautes Etudes Hispaniques, Madrid, Univ. of Caen.
With Musées Nationaux 11-14; military service 14-18; Inspector of Antiquities and Arts Tunisia 21-26; Asst. Keeper Musée des Antiquités Nationales 26-32, Keeper 33-56, Hon. Keeper 56-; Prof. of Nat. and Prehistoric Antiquities, Ecole du Louvre 27-51; mem. Acad. de la Historia, Madrid 33, Acad. des Inscriptions et Belles-Lettres, Inst. de France 46, Akad. der Wissenschaften und Literatur, Mainz 47, New York Acad. of Sciences 58; Hon. Fellow Soc. of Antiquaries, London; Officier Légion d'Honneur 52; Co-Dir. *Revue archéologique* 33-65; Chief Editor *Préhistoire* 32-67.
Leisure interest: translating Spanish literature into French.
Publs. *El santuario ibérico de Castellar de Santisteban (Jaen)* 17, *Inventaire des monuments sculptés préchrétiens de la Péninsule ibérique, 1ère partie: Lusitanie* 18, *Bronzes votifs ibériques* 35, *Recueil des bas-reliefs, sculptures et bustes de la Gaule romaine* (Vols. XII, XIII, XIV, XV, 47, 49, 54, 65), *Les origines de l'art français, Des temps préhistoriques à l'époque carolingienne* 47, *Guide illustré du Musée des Antiquités Nationales au château de Saint-Germain-en-Laye* 48, *Les Hommes de la Pierre Ancienne* (with H. Breuil) 51, 59, *La vie préhistorique* 52, 57, 65, 70, *L'Art Préhistorique* 61.
8 rue Armagis, 78100 Saint-Germain-en-Laye, Yvelines, France.
Telephone: 963-16-74.

Lantzke, Ulf, DR.IUR.; German international official; b. 9 June 1927, Reierort; *m.* Dr. Ursula Lantzke; ed. Univ. of Münster.
Legal service for North Rhine Westphalia 52-57; Energy Dept., Fed. Ministry of Economic Affairs 57-74, Head of Energy Dept. 68-74; Special Counsellor for Energy Questions to the Sec.-Gen. of OECD May 74-, Exec. Dir. Int. Energy Agency of OECD Nov. 74-.

International Energy Agency, OECD, 2 rue André-Pascal, 75775 Paris, France.
Telephone: 524-9440.

Lanusse, Gen. Alejandro Agustín; Argentine army officer; b. 28 Aug. 1918, Buenos Aires; *s.* of Gustavo Lanusse and Albertina Gelly; *m.* Ileana Bell; five *s.* four *d.*; ed. Colegio Militar de la Nación and Escuela Superior de Guerra.
Commander San Martin Regt.; Mil., Naval and Air Attaché, Mexico 58-60; Chief of Staff, 3rd Cavalry Div. 60; Deputy Dir. Escuela Superior de Guerra 60-62; Commdr. 1st Armoured Cavalry Div. 62-64; Army Command 65-66; Commdr. 3rd Army, Córdoba 67; C.-in-C. of Army 68; C.-in-C. of the Armed Forces 71-73; Pres. of Argentina 71-73.

Laos, fmr. King of (*see* Savang Vatthana).

La Paz, Lincoln, A.B., A.M., PH.D.; American mathematician; b. 12 Feb. 1897, Wichita, Kansas; *s.* of Charles Melchior and Emma Josephine (Strode) La Paz; *m.* Leota Rae Butler 1922; two *d.*; ed. Harvard and Chicago Univs.
Instructor in Mathematics, Harvard Univ. 21-22, Dartmouth Coll. 22-25; Nat. Research Fellow 28-29; Instructor, Chicago Univ. 29-30; Asst. Prof. 30-35, Assoc. Prof. 35-42, Prof. of Mathematics, Ohio State Univ. 42-45; Research Mathematician, Office of Scientific Research and Development 42-44; Technical Dir. Operations Analysis Section, H.Q. 2nd Air Force 44-45; Head, Dept. of Mathematics, and Dir. Inst. of Meteoritics, Univ. of New Mexico 45-53; Dir. Div. of Astronomy 53-62, Inst. of Meteoritics 53-66; Editor, Univ. of New Mexico *Publications in Meteoritics* 44-69; third Pres. and Fellow, Meteoritical Soc.; mem. of Int. Astronomical Union, British and Canadian Astronomical Socs., Mathematical Asscn., etc.
Leisure interest: field search for meteorites.
Publs. *Physics and Medicine of the Upper Atmosphere* 52, *Advances in Geophysics, Vol. IV* (co-author) 58, *Space Nomads* (co-author) 61, *Catalog of the Collections of the Inst. of Meteoritics* 65, *Topics in Meteoritics* 69.
3400 Wilway Drive, N.E. Albuquerque, New Mexico 87106, U.S.A.

Lapesa, Rafael; Spanish author and university professor; b. 1908, Valencia; *s.* of Prof. Rafael Lapesa and Ascensión Melgar de Lapesa; *m.* Pilar Lago Couceiro 1932; ed. Instituto Cardenal Cisneros and Madrid Univ.
Engaged in research work at Centro de Estudios Históricos, Madrid, under guidance of Ramón Menéndez Pidal 27-39; Prof. at Madrid Univ. 47-; has lectured as guest Prof. in Univs. of Princeton, Yale, Harvard, California, Pennsylvania, Wisconsin, La Plata, Puerto Rico, Colegio de México and Buenos Aires; mem. of Real Academia Española; mem. of Hispanic Soc. of America; corresp. mem. Acad. Argentina de Letras, Acad. Nac. de Letras del Uruguay, Acad. de Artes y Letras de Puerto Rico, etc.; hon. mem. Modern Language Asscn. of America and American Asscn. of Teachers of Spanish and Portuguese; Dr. h.c. Toulouse Univ.
Publs. *Historia de la Lengua Española* 42, 51, 55, etc., *Asturiano y Provenzal en el Fuero de Avilés* 48, *La trayectoria poética de Garcilaso* 48, 68, *La obra literaria del Marqués de Santillana* 57, *De la Edad Media a nuestros días* 67.
Residencia de Profesores 3, Calle de Isaac Peral, Madrid 15, Spain.

Lapham, Lewis Abbot; American banker (retd.); b. 7 March 1909, Brooklyn, N.Y.; *s.* of Roger D. and Helen Abbott Lapham; *m.* Jane A. Foster 1932; two *s.*; ed. Hotchkiss School and Yale Univ.
President, American-Hawaiian Steamship Co. 47-53; Exec. Vice-Pres. Grace Line Inc. 53-55; Chair. Exec. Cttee. Bankers Trust Co. 59-66; Dir. Bankers Trust New York Corpn. 66-, Pres. 68-74; Pres. New York

State Bankers Asscn. 70-71; Dir. Chubb Corpn., Fed. Insurance Co., Vigilant Insurance Co., Mobil Oil Corpn., Tri-Continental Corpn., H. J. Heinz Co., North American Philips Corpn. Intermodal Transportations System Inc., Crane Co.; Chair. Nat. Assocs. Board Smithsonian Inst.; mem. Governing Cttee. U.S. Philips Trust.
Leisure interests: golf, reading.
Office: 280 Park Avenue, New York, N.Y. 10017; Home: John Street, Greenwich, Conn. 06830, U.S.A. Telephone: 212-692-4790 (Office); 203-869-5522 (Home).

Lapie, Major Pierre Olivier, K.B.E., M.C.; French lawyer and administrator; b. 2 April 1901, Rennes; s. of the late Paul Lapie; m. Yolande Friedman; one d.
Barrister-at-Law; Deputy for Meurthe-and-Moselle 36, 58; Liaison Officer with B.E.F. 39; joined Gen. de Gaulle's Free French Forces June 40; Gov. of Chad Territory Nov. 40; served Libyan and Tunisian campaigns; Sec. of State for Foreign Affairs 46; Del. UN Gen. Assemblies 47, 48, 49, 51 and 54; Del. to Council of Europe 49-59; Minister of Education 50-51; Del. UNESCO Conf. 56; Vice-Pres. Nat. Assembly and mem. Foreign Affairs Cttee. 57; Chair. Franco-British Parl. Cttee. 47-59; mem. High Authority of European Coal and Steel Community 59-67; Chair. Franco-German Co-operative Cttee.; Chair. of the Asscn. "France-Grande-Bretagne"; mem. Institut (Acad. des Sciences Morales et Politiques), Franco-British Council; Croix de Guerre 40, and Commdr. Légion d'Honneur 54; Hon. K.B.E., M.C. (both U.K.); Dr. h.c. (Edinburgh Univ.).
Leisure interest: picture collecting.
Publs. Certitudes Anglaises 36, Narvik 40, Chad 42, Cromwell 48, Herriot 67, De Léon Blum à De Gaulle 69, Clés de l'Angleterre 72, etc.
11 rue de Bellechasse, 75007 Paris, France.
Telephone: 551-19-23.

Lapin, Sergei Georgievich; Soviet diplomatist and journalist; b. 1912; ed. Univ. of Leningrad.
Journalist, editor, Vice-Chair. Radio Cttee. 45-55; Diplomatic Service 55-; Head, Third European Dept. Ministry of Foreign Affairs 55-56; Ambassador to Austria 56-60; Vice-Chair. State Comm. for Cultural Relations with Foreign Countries 60; Minister of Foreign Affairs of R.S.F.S.R. 60-62; Deputy Minister of Foreign Affairs 62-65; mem. C.P.S.U. Central Cttee. 66-; Amb. to People's Republic of China 65-67; Dir. of TASS 67-70; Deputy to Supreme Soviet of U.S.S.R. 70-; mem. Cttee. U.S.S.R. Parliamentary Group; Chair. State Cttee. for Television and Broadcasting, U.S.S.R. Council of Ministers 70-; Chair. Admin. Council Int. Radio and TV Org. 73-.
State Committee for Television and Broadcasting, Pyatnitskaya ulitsa, Moscow, U.S.S.R.

Lapointe, Lt.-Col. Hugues, P.C., Q.C., B.A., LL.D.; Canadian public administrator; b. 3 March 1911; Rivière-du-Loup, Quebec; s. of Rt. Hon. Ernest Lapointe and Emma Pratte; m. Lucette Valin 1938; ed. Univ. of Ottawa and Laval Univ., Quebec.
Member of Parl. for Lotbinière 40-57; apptd. Parl. Asst. to Minister of Nat. Defence 45; Parl. Asst. to Sec. of State for External Affairs 49; Privy Councillor and Solicitor-Gen. of Canada 49; del., Gen. Assembly, UN, Paris 48, Lake Success 49, 50 (Vice-Chair. Canadian del. 50); Minister of Veterans' Affairs 50-57; concurrently Postmaster-Gen. 55-57; private legal practice 57-62; Agent Gen. for Quebec in London 61-66; Lt.-Gen. of Quebec 66-.
Leisure interests: golf, skiing, fishing.
Government House, Quebec, Que., Canada.
Telephone: 643-5385.

Laporte, William F., A.B., M.B.A.; American business executive; b. 3 Sept. 1913, New York; m. Ruth W. Hillard 1946; one s. two d.; ed. Princeton Univ., and Harvard Coll. of Business Administration.

President, Whitehall Pharmacal Co. 50-57; Vice-Pres. American Home Products Corpn. 57-60, Dir. 57-, Pres. 60-73, Chair. of Board 65-; Dir. Manufacturers Hanover Trust Co. 65-, American Standard Inc. 75-; Trustee, Dime Savings Bank of New York 66-.
American Home Products Corporation, 685 Third Avenue, New York, N.Y. 10017; Home: 435 East 52nd Street, New York, N.Y. 10022, U.S.A.

Lappas, Alfons; German trade unionist; b. 3 June 1929, Wiesbaden; s. of Peter and Therese Lappas (née Klee); m. Sigrid Albrecht 1954; one d.; ed. secondary school.
District Organizer of Horticulture, Agriculture and Forestry Union, Fulda and Darmstadt 51-57, Rheinland-Palatinate Organizer 57-59, Head of Collective Bargaining Dept., Head Office 59-61, mem. Exec. 61-, Vice-Pres. 66, Pres. 68; mem. Exec., German Trade Union Confed. (Deutscher Gewerkschaftsbund—DGB) 69; Pres. European Fed. of Agricultural Workers 68-71; Alt. mem. European Confed. of Trade Unions 69-, Finance and Gen. Purpose Cttee., Int. Confed. of Trade Unions 69; mem. Econ. and Social Cttee. of European Communities 70, Pres. 72-74.
Leisure interests: modern literature, music, cross-country running.
Deutscher Gewerkschaftsbund, 4 Düsseldorf, Hans-Boeckler-Strasse 39, Federal Republic of Germany; and Economic and Social Committee of the European Communities, 2 rue Ravenstein, 1000 Brussels, Belgium.
Telephone: 4301-386 (Fed. Germany); 12-39-20 (Belgium).

Lappas, Vice-Admiral Pirros; Greek naval officer; b. 11 Jan. 1900, Athens; s. of Dimitrios and Eleni Lappas; m. Maria Merlin 1940; ed. Naval Cadet Coll.
Commissioned in Royal Greek Navy 20; held various appointments both at sea and on shore; C.O. King George I 41, and later (after joining Free Greek Forces) Samos; participated in landing operations in Italy and Southern France; Commdr. 12th Destroyer Flotilla 44; Chief of Personnel, Admiralty 46, and later Chief of Technical Services; Commodore in charge of Light Vessels and Submarines 47; Deputy Chief of Naval Gen. Staff 49; Rear-Admiral 49; Chief of Naval Commands and Gen. Inspector of the Royal Hellenic Navy 49; C.-in-C. Royal Hellenic Fleet 50, Vice-Admiral 52; Chief of Naval Gen. Staff 52-58; Chief of military household to H.M. the King 58-60, Hon. General A.D.C. to H.M. the King 60; Hon. C.B.E.; Grand Commdr. Royal Order of George I and Grand Cross of Order of Phoenix, War Cross, D.S.M. and bars; Hon. Sec. Hellenic Olympic Cttee.; mem. Int. Olympic Cttee.
Leisure interest: sport.
26 Tsakaloff Street, Athens, Greece.
Telephone: Athens 613-221.

Laprade, Albert; French architect; b. 29 Nov. 1883; ed. Lycée de Châteauroux and Ecole nationale supérieure des beaux-arts.
French consular architect, Morocco 15-19; Hon. Insp.-Gen. of Fine Arts, mem. Académie des Beaux-Arts (Vice-Pres. 64, Pres. 65); mem. Inst. de France (Pres. 65); mem. Académie d'Architecture and des Sciences d'Outre-mer.
Major works: The French Residency, Rabat; Musée de la France d'outre-mer, Paris; French Embassy, Ankara.
Publs. include Carnets de Croquis, Lyautey urbaniste, François d'Orbay, Architecte de Louis XIV, Vies des Architectes.
27 rue Lhomond, Paris 5e, France.

Lapsley, William W., M.S.; American business executive; b. 14 Jan. 1910, Selma, Ala.; s. of Robert Kay and Ethel Baine (Pearce); m. 1st June Louise English 1935 (died 1952), 2nd Frances Vivian Lynn 1953; two d. two step s.; ed. U.S. Mil. Acad., Univ. of Calif.

Major-General U.S. Army; Programme Man. Foreign Management Dept., Kaiser Jeep Corpn., Taiwan; joined Consolidated Edison Co. of N.Y. Inc. 69, Vice-Pres. Cen. Services 69, Senior Vice-Pres. 70, Exec. Vice-Pres. Cen. Operations 71-73, Pres., mem. Board of Trustees 73-; mem. U.S. team that negotiated protocol to Columbia River Treaty with Canada.
Leisure interest: golf.
Consolidated Edison Co. of New York Inc., 4 Irving Place, New York, N.Y. 10003, U.S.A.

Laqueur, Walter; British historian and political commentator; b. 26 May 1921, Breslau, Germany; s. of Fritz Laqueur and Else (née Berliner); m. Barbara Koch 1941; two d.
Editor *Survey* 55-65; Dir. Inst. of Contemporary History and Wiener Library, London 64-; Editor *Journal of Contemporary History* 65-; Prof. of History Brandeis Univ. 67-70; Prof. of Modern History Tel-Aviv Univ. 69-; Chair. Research Board, Center for Strategic and Int. Studies, Washington, D.C. 73-; Editor *Washington Papers* 73-; Rockefeller Fellow, Guggenheim Fellow.
Leisure interests: swimming, motorboating.
Publs. *Young Germany* 62, *The Road to War 1967* 68, *Europe Since Hitler* 70, *A History of Zionism* 72, *Confrontation* 74, *Weimar* 74, *Guerrilla and Revolution* 76.
4 Devonshire Street, London, W.1, England; and Center for Strategic and International Studies, 1800 K Street, N.W., Washington, D.C., U.S.A.

Lara Bustamante, Fernando; Costa Rican lawyer and politician; b. 12 Jan. 1911, San José; s. of Ernesto Lara Iraeta and Angela Bustamante Castro; m. Ofelia Calvo; four s. four d.; ed. Liceo de Costa Rica and Escuela de Derecho.
Graduated in law 34; Police Official, San José 32-37; Official in Ministry of Educ. 37-40; Dir. *Jurisprudencia* (law magazine) 33-36; Deputy to Nat. Assembly 42, re-elected 46; mem. Editorial Comm. for Political Constitution 48; Prof. Faculty of Law 40-52; Deputy, First Sec., Legislative Assembly 49; Minister of Foreign Affairs 49-52, 66-70; Pres. Coll. of Lawyers of Costa Rica 54-55; Deputy to Legislative Assembly 58-62, 66-, Pres. 60-61; Sec.-Gen. Unión Nacional Party 58-66; decorations from Mexico, El Salvador, Panama, France, Italy, Vatican, Ecuador, Taiwan and Cuba.
Legislative Assembly, San José, Costa Rica.

Laraki, Moulay Ahmed; Moroccan physician, diplomatist and politician; b. 15 Oct. 1931, Casablanca; ed. Univ. de Paris.
With Ministry of Foreign Affairs 56-57; Perm. Rep. to UN 57-59; Head of Hosp. Services, Casablanca 56-61; Amb. to Spain 62-65, to Switzerland 65-66, to U.S.A. and concurrently accred. to Mexico, Canada and Venezuela 66-67; Minister of Foreign Affairs 67-69; Prime Minister 69-71; medical affairs 71-74; Minister of State for Foreign Affairs April 74-.
Ministry of Foreign Affairs, Rabat, Morocco.

Lardinois, Petrus Josephus; Netherlands politician; b. 13 Aug. 1924, Noorbeek; m. Maria Hubertina Gerardine Peeters; two s. three d.; ed. Wageningen Agricultural Coll.
Various agricultural posts until 60; entered Ministry of Agriculture and Fisheries Feb. 60; Agricultural Attaché, London Embassy May 60-Sept. 63; mem. Second Chamber 63-; mem. European Parl. Oct. 63-; Pres. of Brabant Farmers' Union (N.C.B.) 65; Minister of Agriculture and Fisheries 67-72; Commr. for Agriculture, Comm. of European Communities 73-(76); Catholic People's Party.
c/o Commission of the European Communities, 200 rue de la Loi, 1040 Brussels, Belgium.

Lardner-Burke, Desmond William; Rhodesian politician and lawyer; b. 17 Oct. 1909, Kimberley, South Africa; s. of Edmund Lardner-Burke and May McClelland; m. Alice May Fraser 1934; two s. two d.; ed. St. Andrew's Coll., Grahamstown, South Africa.
Attorney with Coghlan and Welsh, Bulawayo 33-41; Senior Partner, Danziger and Lardner-Burke, Gwelo 41-; Dir. of various companies; M.P. for Gwelo 48-53 and 61-74, Senator 74-; Minister of Justice, Law and Order 64-76, of Commerce and Industry Jan. 76-; Pres. of Law Soc. 55-56; Grand Officer of Legion of Merit; Independence Decoration.
Leisure interests: golf, fishing.
Publ. *Rhodesia: The Story of the Crisis* 66.
8 Richmond Road, Highlands, Salisbury, Rhodesia.
Telephone: 24199.

Lardy, Henry Arnold, B.S., M.S., PH.D.; American professor of biochemistry; b. 19 Aug. 1917, S. Dakota; s. of Nick and Elizabeth Lardy; m. Annrita Dresselhuys 1943; three s. one d.; ed. S. Dakota State Univ. and Univs. of Wis. and Toronto.
Assistant Prof., Univ. of Wis. 45-47, Assoc. Prof. 47-50, Prof. 50-66, Co-Dir. Inst. for Enzyme Research 50-, Vilas Prof. of Biological Sciences 66-; mem. Nat. Acad. of Sciences, Amer. Acad. of Arts and Sciences, Amer. Soc. Biological Chemists, Pres. 64; mem. Harvey Soc.; Paul Lewis Award in Enzyme Chem., Amer. Chemical Soc. 49, Neuberg Medal, Amer. Soc. of European Chemists 56.
Leisure interests: tennis, riding, retriever field trials.
Publs. *The Enzymes* (Co-Editor), 8 vols. 58-63; and research papers in biochemistry in scientific journals.
1702 University Avenue, Madison, Wis. 53706; Home: Thorstrand Road, Madison, Wis. 53705, U.S.A.
Telephone: 608-233-1584 (Home); 608-262-3371 (Office).

Larkin, Arthur E., Jr., B.A.; American food executive; b. 7 March 1917; ed. Blake School and Dartmouth Coll.
Served U.S. Navy 40-45; with Geo. A. Hormel & Co. 46-58, Vice-Pres. and Dir. 53-58; joined Gen. Foods Corpn. 58, Maxwell House Marketing Man. 58-59, Maxwell House Gen. Man. 59-62, Vice-Pres. Gen. Foods Corpn. 60, Exec. Vice-Pres. Operations 62-65, Dir. Gen. Foods Corpn. 63-, Exec. Vice-Pres. 65-66, Pres. and Chief Operating Officer 66-72; Pres. Keebler Co., subsidiary of United Biscuits Holding Ltd. 73-, Chair. and Chief Exec. 74-; Dir. United Biscuits Holdings Ltd.
General Foods Corporation, 250 North Street, White Plains, N.Y. 10602, U.S.A.

Larkin, Felix Edward, A.B., M.B.A., LL.B.; American business executive; b. 3 Aug. 1909, New York City; s. of John A. Larkin and Maria C. Henry; m. Evelyn M. Wallace 1937; two s. one d.; ed. Fordham Univ., New York Univ. Graduate School of Business Admin. and St. John's Univ. School of Law.
Law Sec. Court of Gen. Sessions, N.Y. County 39-47; Gen. Counsel, Dept. of Defense 47-51; joined W. R. Grace & Co. 51, Man. Industrial Relations Div., Vice-Pres. 55, Exec. Vice-Pres. in charge of Corporate Admin. 58, Dir. 63-, Pres. and Chief Operating Officer 71-74, Chair. 74-; Dir. Marine Midland Banks Inc.; mem. Exec. Reserve Office of Sec. of Defense 61-63; mem. Nat. Manpower Advisory Cttee. 62-66; mem. Advisory Cttee. Foreign Service Inst., Washington, D.C. 61-63; Chair. Board of Trustees, Fordham Univ.; Dir. American Arbitration Asscn.
Leisure interest: golf.
Publ. *Uniform Code of Military Justice.*
W. R. Grace & Co., Grace Plaza, 1114 Avenue of the Americas, New York, N.Y. 10036; 1030 Old White Plains Road, Mamaroneck, N.Y. 10543, U.S.A.
Telephone: 212-344-1200 (Office); 914-834-5886 (Home).

Larkin, Frederick George, Jr.; American banker; b. 28 Dec. 1913, Seattle; s. of Frederick George Larkin and Virginia Manny Larkin; m. Frances D. Williams 1938; one d.; ed. Univ. of Washington, Stanford Univ., and Graduate School of Banking (Rutgers Univ.).
Joined Security Pacific Nat. Bank 1936, Pres. and Dir. 61-69, Chief Exec. Officer 67-, Chair. of Board 69-; Chair., Chief Exec. Officer Security Pacific Corpn. 73-; Dir. Getty Oil Co. 62-, Western Amer. Bank (Europe) Ltd. 67- (now Chair.), Carnation Co. 69, Rockwell International Corpn. 69, Pacific Mutual Life Insurance Co. 69, Southern Calif. Edison Co. 69-, Bank of Canton (Hong Kong) 71-, Tricontinental Corpn. Ltd. (Australia) 71-, Investment and Underwriting Corpn. of the Philippines 74-, Security Pacific Interamerican Bank, S.A. (Panama) 75-; official of civic, religious and philanthropic orgs.
Office: Security Pacific National Bank, P.O. Box 2097, Terminal Annex, Los Angeles, Calif. 90051; Home: 771 South Windsor Boulevard, Los Angeles, Calif. 90005, U.S.A.

Larkin, Philip Arthur, C.B.E., M.A., F.R.S.L.; British poet and librarian; b. 9 Aug. 1922, Coventry; s. of Sydney Larkin and Eva Emily (née Day); unmarried; ed. King Henry VIII School, Coventry, and St. John's Coll., Oxford.
Posts in various libraries 43-55; Librarian of Brynmor Jones Library, Univ. of Hull 55-; Queen's Gold Medal for Poetry 65; Hon. D.Lit. (Belfast) 69, Hon. D.Litt. (Leicester) 70, (Warwick) 73, (St. Andrews, Sussex) 74; Visiting Fellow, All Souls Coll., Oxford 70-71, Hon. Fellow, St. John's Coll., Oxford 73.
Publs. *The North Ship* (poems) 45, *Jill* (novel) 46, *A Girl in Winter* (novel) 47, *The Less Deceived* (poems) 55, *The Whitsun Weddings* (poems) 64, *All What Jazz* (essays on jazz) 70, *The Oxford Book of Twentieth Century English Verse* (Ed.) 73, *High Windows* (poems) 74.
The Brynmor Jones Library, The University, Hull, Yorks., England.

Larmour, Edward Noel, C.M.G.; British diplomatist; b. 25 Dec. 1916, Belfast, N. Ireland; s. of Edward Marr Larmour and Maud Haughey; m. Agnes Margaret Bill 1946; one s. two d.; ed. Royal Academical Inst., Belfast, Trinity Coll., Dublin and Sydney Univ.
Burma Civil Service 42-48, Deputy Sec. to Gov. 48; Maj., Indian Army 42-46; Commonwealth Relations Office (C.R.O.) 48-50; First Sec., Wellington, N.Z. 50-54, Singapore 54-57; Counsellor and Head of Chancery 57; Head of Personnel, C.R.O. 59-61, Canberra 61-64; Asst. Under-Sec. of State 56; Deputy High Commr. to Nigeria 64-67; Deputy Chief of Admin., Foreign and Commonwealth Office 68-70; High Commr. to Jamaica 70-73, concurrently Amb. to Haiti; Asst. Under-Sec. of State, FCO 73-.
Leisure interests: music, cricket, golf.
68 Wood Vale, London, N.10, England.
Telephone: 444-9744.

Larock, Victor J. L.; Belgian sociologist and politician; b. 6 Oct. 1904, Ans; s. of Gustave Larock and Marie Bustin; m. Vlasta Jindrick 1952; one s.
Prof. Inst. des Hautes Etudes: Ghent 36-40; Editor of *Le Peuple* 44-54; Mem. of Parl. 49-; Minister of Foreign Trade 54-57; Minister of Foreign Affairs 57-58; Prof. State Univ. of Mons 58-; Minister of Nat. Educ. and Culture 61-63.
Publs. *Essai sur la Valeur Sociale des Personnes dans les Sociétés Inférieures* 32, *La Pensée Mythique* 45, *La Grande Cause* 53, *Hâter l'Avenir* 71.
18c rue des Champs-Elysées, 1050 Brussels, Belgium.

Larrabee, Martin Glover, PH.D.; American professor of biophysics; b. 25 Jan. 1910, Boston, Mass.; s. of Ralph Clinton Larrabee and Ada Perkins Miller; m. 1st Sylvia Kimball 1932 (divorced 1944), one s.; m. 2nd

Barbara Belcher 1944, one s.; ed. Harvard Coll. and Univ. of Pennsylvania.
Research Asst. and Fellow, Univ. of Pennsylvania 34-40, Assoc., Asst. Prof., Assoc. Prof. 41-49; Asst. Prof. of Physiology, Cornell Medical Coll., New York City 40-41; Assoc. Prof. of Biophysics, Johns Hopkins Univ. 46-63, Prof. of Biophysics 63-; mem. Nat. Acad. of Sciences, American Physiological Soc., Biophysical Soc., Int. Soc. for Neurochemistry, American Soc. for Neurochemistry, Soc. for Neuroscience; Foreign Assoc. Physiological Soc., England; Hon. M.D. (Univ. of Lausanne) 74.
Leisure interests: mountain-hiking, skiing, photography.
Publs. About 50 technical papers and 50 abstracts covering original research in the circulatory, respiratory and nervous systems of mammals, especially on synaptic and metabolic mechanisms in sympathetic ganglia.
Department of Biophysics, Johns Hopkins University, Baltimore, Md. 21218, U.S.A.
Telephone: 301-366-3300.

Larraz Lopez, José, LL.D.; Spanish economist and politician; b. 1904; ed. Madrid Univ.
Advocate 24; Advocate of State 26; Chief Counsellor Bank of Spain 30; Vice-Pres. Nat. Economic Council and Gen. Commissar for Wheat 35; Chief Nat. Banking, Monetary and Exchange Service 38; Min. of Finance Aug. 39-May 41; Academician, Real Academia de Ciencias Morales y Políticas 43-.
Publs. *La evolución económica de Bélgica* 30, *La Hacienda Pública y el Estatuto Catalán* 32, *El ordenamiento del mercado triguero en España* 35, *La época del Mercantilismo en Castilla (1500-1700)* 43, *La Meta de dos Revoluciones* 46.
Espalter 3, Madrid, Spain.

Larre, René J.; French civil servant; b. 21 Feb. 1915, Pau; m. Thérèse Allègre 1951; three d.; ed. Faculté de Droit and Ecole des Sciences Politiques, Paris.
Inspector of Finance 42-45; External Relations Dept., Ministry of Economic Affairs 46-50; Asst. Exec. Sec. Int. Materials Conf. 51; Technical Counsellor, French Embassy, Washington 52-54; Technical Adviser, Office of Minister of Finance 55; Dir. Office of Sec. of State for the Budget 56; Exec. Dir. Int. Bank for Reconstruction and Devt. 57-67; Dir. Office of Minister of Finance 57-58; Exec. Dir. European Investment Bank 58-61; Financial Minister, French Embassy in Washington, D.C. 61-67; Exec. Dir. IMF 64-67; Dir. of Treasury, Ministry of Finance, Paris 67; Gen. Man. Bank for Int. Settlements 71-.
7 Centralbahnstrasse, CH 4051 Basle, Switzerland; 31 boulevard du Commandant Charcot, 92 Neuilly-sur-Seine, France.

Larry, R. Heath, LL.D., LL.B.; American steel company executive; b. 24 Feb.1914, Huntingdon, Pa.; s. of Ralph E. and Mabel (Heath) Larry; m. Eleanor Ketler 1938; three s.; ed. Grove City Coll., Univ. of Pittsburgh.
Attorney, National Tube Co. 38-44, Sec., then Dir. 44-48; Atty., U.S. Steel Corpn. 48-52, Asst. gen. solicitor 52-58, Admin. Vice-Pres. Labour Relations 58-66; Exec. Vice-Pres., asst. to Chair. 66, Vice-Chair. Board of Dirs. 69; Board mem. Highway Users Fed. for Safety and Mobility; Dir., mem. Nat. Asscn. of Mfrs.; mem. Bituminous Coal Operators Asscn., Comm. on Int. Trade, American Iron and Steel Inst., National Comm. on Productivity and Work Quality, President's Labor-Management Cttee., The Conf. Board, Foreign Policy Asscn., Business Cttee. for the Arts; Trustee of U.S. Council of International Chamber of Commerce Inc.
Leisure interests: golfing, skiing, sailing.
600 Grant Street, Pittsburgh, Pa.15230; Home: 813 Elm Spring Road, Pittsburg, Pa. 15243, U.S.A.
Telephone: 433-1171.

Larsen, Helge, M.A.; Danish teacher and politician; b. 25 April 1915, Vester-Aaby; s. of Johs. Larsen and Kamilla Larsen; m. Tonny Lolk 1942; one s. one d.; ed. Univ. of Copenhagen.
Sec. to Chief Editor of *Politiken* (Vald. Koppel) 42-44; Sec. Social Liberal Party 43-46; teacher, Copenhagen 46-49, Nykøbing Falter 49-65; Headmaster of Gladsaxe Gymnasium 65-68; mem. Folketing 56-64, Nordic Council 57-64; mem. Board Danish State Radio and TV 59-68, 74-; Minister of Educ. 68-71.
Publs. *Kensgerninger om Sydslesvig* (Facts on Southern Schleswig) 46, *Politiske Grundtanker, liberalisme og socialisme* (Political Ideas, Liberalism and Socialism) 48; contributor to *Socialliberale Tanker* (Social-liberal Ideas) 50, *De politiske Partier* (Political Parties in Denmark) 50, 64, *Kort besked om EF* (Brief Information on the EEC).
St. Kongensgade 27, 1264 Copenhagen K, Denmark.

Larsen, Roy Edward, A.B.; American publisher; b. 20 April 1899, Boston, Mass.; s. of Robert and Stella (Belyea) Larsen; m. Margaret Zerbe 1927; three s. one d.; ed. Boston Latin School, and Harvard Univ.
With N.Y. Trust Co. 21-22; Time Inc. 22-, Circulation Man. *Time* 22, Vice-Pres. Time Inc. 27-39, *March of Time* radio 31, *March of Time* cinema 34, Dir. Time Inc. 33, Publisher *Life* 36-46, Pres. Time Inc. Sept. 39-60, Chair. Exec. Cttee. 60-69, Vice-Chair. 69-; Chair. U.S. Advisory Cttee. on the Arts; Trustee, Ford Foundation 57-69; Hon. Trustee, N.Y. Public Library; Trustee, Cttee. for Econ. Devt., etc.; Chevalier de la Légion d'Honneur (France); Hon. LL.D. (Marietta Coll., Dartmouth, Bucknell, New York, Harvard, Tufts Univs.); Hon. L.H.D. (Bard Coll., Kalamazoo Coll., Temple Univ.).
Leisure interests: conservation (Chair. Nantucket Conservation Foundation), education.
Home: 4900 Congress Street, Fairfield, Conn.; Office: Time and Life Building, Rockefeller Center, New York, N.Y. 10020, U.S.A.
Telephone: 556-4192.

Larson, Arthur, M.A., D.C.L., LL.D.; American lawyer, university professor and politician; b. 4 July 1910, Sioux Falls; s. of Judge Lewis Larson and Anna B. (Huseboe); m. Florence Faye Newcomb 1935; one s. one d.; ed. Augustana Coll., Univ. of South Dakota and Pembroke Coll., Oxford.
Practised law Milwaukee, Wisconsin 35-39; Asst. Prof. of Law, Univ. of Tennessee 39-41; Division Counsel, Office of Price Administration, Washington 41-44; Head Scandinavian Branch, Foreign Economic Administration, Washington 44-45; Prof. of Law, Cornell Law School 45-53; Dean Univ. of Pittsburgh Law School 53-54; Under Sec. of Labour, Washington 54-56; Dir. U.S. Information Agency 56-57; Special Asst. to the Pres. 57-58, Special Consultant 58-61; Dir. Rule of Law Research Centre; James B. Duke Prof. of Law, Duke Univ., Durham N.C. 59-; Consultant, U.S. Dept. of State; Consultant to Pres. on Foreign Affairs; Hon. Fellow, Pembroke Coll., Oxford.
Leisure interests: collecting and playing ancient stringed instruments, musical composition and arranging, classical guitar, folk songs, sailing.
Publs. *Towards World Prosperity* (joint author) 47, *Cases on Corporations* (with R. S. Stevens) 47, *The Law of Workmen's Compensation*, 7 vols. 52, *Know Your Social Security* 55, 59, *A Republican Looks at His Party* 56, *What We Are For* 59, *The International Rule of Law* 61, *When Nations Disagree* 61, *A Warless World* 63, *Propaganda: Towards Disarmament in the War of Words* (with J. B. Whitton) 64, *Sovereignty Within the Law* (ed. and contrib.) 65, *Vietnam and Beyond* (with D. R. Larson) 65, *Eisenhower: The President Nobody Knew* 68, *Population and Law* (with L. T. Lee) 71, *Workmen's Compensation for Occupational Injuries and Death* 72,

The Law of Employment Discrimination (2 vols.) 75.
The Law School, Duke University, Durham, N.C.; Home: No. 1 Learned Place, Durham, N.C. 27705, U.S.A.
Telephone: 919-684-3518 (Office); 919-489-4530 (Home).

Larsson, Lars-Erik; Swedish musician; b. 15 May 1908, Åkarp; s. of Lilly and Vilner Larsson; m. Brita Holm 1936; one s.; ed. Stockholm, Vienna and Leipzig.
At Royal Swedish Opera 30-31; music critic 33-37; conductor Swedish Broadcasting Co. 37-54; Prof. Kungl. Musikhögskolan 47-59; Dir. of Music, Uppsala 61-65; mem. Council Swedish Asscn. of Composers.
Compositions: three Concert Overtures, *Sinfonietta for String Orchestra, Serenade for Strings, Divertimento, Pastoral Suite, Music for the Orchestra, Orchestral Variations, Three Orchestral Pieces, Lyric Fantasy, Due Auguri, Saxophone Concerto, Violin Concerto, 12 Concertinos*, music to Shakespeare's *The Winter's Tale*; opera—*The Princess of Cyprus; Disguised God* and *The Sundial and the Urn* for solo, choir and orchestra, *Missa Brevis* and *Three Quotations* for unaccompanied choir; chamber music, songs and piano music.
Mäster Ernstgatan 6A, 25235 Helsingborg, Sweden.

Lartigue, Jacques Henri; French painter and photographer; b. 13 June 1894, Courbevoie; m. Florette Ormea 1945; ed. Acad. Jullian, Paris.
Exhibitions of painting 20-, in Paris 24-39, 46-; exhbns. of photography in various galleries 63-; Silver Medal of Paris.
Publs. include *Boyhood of J. H. Lartigue, Diary of a Century, Femmes.*
102 rue de Longchamp, 75116 Paris, France.
Telephone: 727-06-25.

Lascelles, Rt. Hon. Sir Alan Frederick, P.C., G.C.B., G.C.V.O., C.M.G., M.C., M.A.; British palace official; b. 11 April 1887; s. of Hon. F. C. Lascelles; m. Hon. Joan Thesiger 1920 (died 1971); one s. (dec.) two d.; ed. Marlborough Coll., and Trinity Coll., Oxford.
Served with Bedfordshire Yeomanry 14-18, Capt. 16; A.D.C. to Lord Lloyd when Gov. of Bombay 19-20; Asst. Private Sec. to Prince of Wales 20-29; Sec. to Gov.-Gen. of Canada 31-35; Asst. Private Sec. to the King 35-43, Private Sec. 43-52, to the Queen 52-53, Keeper of the King's Archives 45-52, Queen's Archives 52-53; Chair. Pilgrim Trust 54-60; Chair. Historic Buildings Council for England 58-63; former Dir. Midland Bank, Royal Acad. of Music; LL.D. (Hon.) Bristol and Durham; Hon. D.C.L. (Oxford) 63.
Kensington Palace, London, W.8, England.

Lasdun, Denys Louis, C.B.E., F.R.I.B.A.; British architect; b. 8 Sept. 1914, London; s. of Norman Lasdun and Julie Abrahams; m. Susan Bendit 1954; two s. one d.; ed. Rugby School and Architectural Association, London.
Architectural practice in assoc. with Wells Coates until 39; Royal Engineers 39-45; practised with Tecton & Lindsey Drake, 45-59; own architectural practice Denys Lasdun and Partners with Alexander Redhouse and Peter Softley 60-; Hoffman Wood Prof. of Architecture, Univ. of Leeds 62-63; Assessor for competition for Belgrade Opera House 70, for new Parliamentary Bldg., London 71.
Principal works: housing schemes and schools for Bethnal Green and Paddington, London; new store for Peter Robinson, London (now London headquarters of Govt. of N.S.W.); luxury flats, St. James's Place, London; Royal Coll. of Physicians, London; new coll. for Fitzwilliam, Cambridge, extension to Christ's Coll., Cambridge; Devt. Plan and bldgs., including the library, for Univ. of East Anglia; Univ. of London Redevt. (School of Oriental and African Studies, Inst. of Educ., Law Inst.); work for Univs. of Leicester and Liverpool; Nat. Theatre, South Bank, London; a new

community hosp. in the Midlands; Sotheby and Co. redevelopment; new headquarters for European Investment Bank, Luxembourg; Trustee, British Museum 75-; Hon. A.I.A.; Hon. D.Litt. (Univ. of East Anglia) 74; Hon. F.R.C.P.; sub-mem. Jerusalem Town Planning Cttee. 70, Victoria and Albert Museum Advisory Cttee. 73-; RIBA London Architecture Bronze medallist 60, 64; Civic Trust Awards: Class I 67, Group A 69; Special Award, São Paulo Biennale, Brazil 69.
25 Dawson Place, London, W.2., England.

Laskaris, Constantine; Greek trade unionist; b. 1918, Athens.
With Free Greek Armed Forces; mem. Gen. Confed. of Greek Workers; Adviser to Org. for Econ. Co-operation and Devt.; mem. Exec. Cttee. of Labour Comm., European Econ. Community; Instructor Training School for Senior Police Officers 63-67; Minister of Employment July-Oct. 74, Nov. 74-; Founding mem., mem. of Board, Greek NATO Asscn.
Ministry of Labour, Athens, Greece.

Laskey, Sir Denis Seward, K.C.M.G., C.V.O.; British diplomatist; b. 18 Jan. 1916, London; s. of F. S. and E. D. N. Laskey; m. Perronnelle M. G. Le Breton 1947; one s. three d.; ed. Marlborough Coll. and Corpus Christi Coll., Oxford.
Entered diplomatic service 39; army service 40-41; Foreign Office 41-46; served in Berlin 46-49, New York (del. to UN) 49-53; Foreign Office 53-60; Minister, Rome, 60-64; Cabinet Office 64-67; Minister, Bonn 67-69; Amb to Romania 69-72, to Austria Jan. 72-.
Leisure interests: golf, shooting, fishing.
Metternichgasse 6, 1030 Vienna, Austria.
Telephone: 73-23-46.

Laskin, Bora, P.C., M.A., D.C.L., LL.D., F.R.S.C.; Canadian judge; b. 5 Oct. 1912, Thunderbay; s. of late Max Laskin and late Bluma Singel; m. Peggy Tenenbaum 1938; one s. one d.; ed. Univ. of Toronto, Osgoodehall Law School, Harvard Univ. Law School. Lecturer in Law, Univ. of Toronto 40-43, Asst. Prof. 43-45, Prof. of Law 49-65; Lecturer in Law, Osgoodehall Law School 45-49; Judge Court of Appeal, Ont. 65-70; Judge Supreme Court of Canada 70-73; Chief Justice of Canada 73-; Hon. Bencher, Lincoln's Inn 74.
Publs. *Canadian Constitutional Law* (revised edn.) 69, *The British Tradition in Canadian Law* (Hamlyn Lectures) 69.
Supreme Court of Canada, Wellington Street, Ottawa; Home: 200 Rideau Terrace Apt. 1405, Ottawa, Canada.
Telephone: 992-5388 (Office); 746-6884 (Home).

Laskorin, Boris Nikolayevich; Soviet chemist; b. 24 June 1915, Brest; ed. Kiev Univ.
Research Assoc. Inst. of Chemical Industry 38-52; mem. C.P.S.U. 45-; U.S.S.R. Inst. of Chemical Technology 52-; Dr. Sc. (Engineering), Prof. 58; Corresp. mem. U.S.S.R. Acad. of Sciences 66-.
Publs. Works on chemistry and production technology of non-organic materials.
U.S.S.R. Academy of Sciences, 14 Leninsky Prospekt, Moscow, U.S.S.R.

Laskov, Haim; Israeli army officer and administrator; b. April 1919, Borisov, Russia; s. of Moshe and Yetta (Hirschfeld) Laskov; m. Shulamit Hen 1950; ed. Reali School, Haifa, and St. Anthony's Coll., Oxford.
Active mem. Hagana 29-40; served British Army 40-46, Major in Jewish Brigade 44; armour commdr. Israel War of Liberation 48; founder first I.D.F. Officers' School 48; Dir.-Gen. Military Training 49-50; Commdr. Israel Air Force 51-53; Dep. Chief of Staff I.D.F. 55; Armour Corps Commdr. before and during Sinai campaign 56; Commdr. Southern Command 57; Chief of Staff I.D.F. 58-61; Dir.-Gen. Israel Port Authorities 61-70; Ombudsman to I.D.F. 72-; mem. Inquiry Comm. into Yom Kippur War 73.

Publs. Military training manuals, I.D.F.; essays on military problems.
Home: 75 Einstein Street, Tel-Aviv, Israel.

Lasky, Ahmed; Moroccan civil engineer and politician; b. 30 April 1932; ed. Casablanca High School, Ecole spéciale des travaux publics and Ecole nationale des ponts et chaussées, Paris.
Public Works Engineer, Casablanca 56; Chief Engineer Agadir Region 59; Chief Engineer Casablanca Region 60-62; Dir. Casablanca Harbour 62-65; Minister of Public Works and Communications 65-67; Chair. Royal Air Maroc 67-; Minister of Higher, Secondary and Technical Educ. 71-72; Officier, Ordre du Trône (Morocco), Ordre de George I (Greece), Commdr. Ordre de l'Istiqlal (Tunisia), Ordre Egyptien, Ordre Iranien.
Publs. numerous technical pamphlets about bridges and harbours in French and foreign magazines.
c/o Royal Air Maroc, Aéroport International Casablanca, Nouassenr; and 6 Rue de Liège, Casablanca, Morocco.

Lassus Saint-Geniès, Baron Etienne de; French industrialist; b. 7 June 1887.
Honorary Pres. and fmr. Dir. Compagnie Française Thomson-Brandt; Hon. Pres. Compagnie des Lampes; Vice-Pres. Soc. Générale des Constructions Electriques et Méchaniques 51-68, Hon. Pres. 68-; fmr. Dir. Soc. Centrale de Dynamite, Compagnie Universelle d'Acétylène et Electro-métallurgie, Soc. des Grands Travaux de Marseille, Soc. Centrale pour l'Industrie; Grand Officier Légion d'Honneur, Croix de Guerre (1914-18).
63 avenue Kléber, Paris 16e, France.

Lasswell, Harold Dwight, PH.D.; American political scientist; b. 13 Feb. 1902; ed. Chicago, Geneva, Paris, London, Berlin Univs.
Political Science Asst. Chicago Univ. 22-24, Instructor 24-27, Asst. Prof. 27-32, Associate Prof. 32-38; Visiting Prof. Syracuse Univ. 26, Western Reserve Univ. 29, Univ. of California 35, Yenching (Peking) Univ., Yale Univ. 38-46; Political Scientist, Washington School of Psychiatry 38-39; Dir. War Communications Research, Library of Congress 39-45; Prof. of Law, Yale School of Law, Yale Univ. 46-70, of Political Science 52-70; Visiting Prof. Univ. of Tokyo 55; Fellow, Center for Advanced Study in the Behavioral Sciences, Stanford 54-; Visiting Prof. Mass. Inst. of Technology 60-61, Patna Univ. 69; Prof. Emer., Yale 70; Distinguished Prof. of Policy Sciences, John Jay Coll. of Criminal Justice, City Univ. of New York 70-.
Publs. *Propaganda Technique in the World War* 27, *Psychopathology and Politics* 30, *World Politics and Personal Insecurity* 35, *Politics: Who Gets What, When, How* 36, *World Revolutionary Propaganda: A Chicago Study* (with D. Blumenstock) 39, *World Politics Faces Economics* 46, *Analysis of Political Behaviour* 48, *Power and Personality* 48, *Language of Politics* (with N. Leites) 49, *National Security and Individual Freedom* 50, *Power and Society: A Framework for Inquiry* (with A. Kaplan) 50, *World Revolution of our Time* 51, *Comparative Study of Symbols* (with others) 51, *Comparative Study of Elites* (with others) 51, *The Policy Sciences* (with D. Lerner), *In Defense of Public Order* (with R. Arens) 61, *The Future of Political Science* 63, *Power, Corruption and Rectitude* (with A. Rogow) 63, *The Public Order of Space* (with others) 63, *World Handbook of Social and Economic Indicators* (with others) 64, *World Revolutionary Elites* (with others) 65, *The Sharing of Power in a Psychiatric Hospital* (with R. Rubenstein) 66, *The Interpretation of Agreements and World Public Order* (Co-Author) 67, *Political Communication* (with S. K. Arora) 69, *Propaganda Technique in World War I* 71.
John Jay College of Criminal Justice, 315 Park Avenue South, New York, N.Y. 10010, U.S.A.

Laštovička Bohuslav; Czechoslovak politician and journalist; b. 29 April 1905, Pelhřimov; ed. Mil. Acad. Editor *Rudé právo* 34-35; Commdr., Czechoslovak Volunteer Anti-aircraft Battery, Spain (civil war); in U.K. 39-45; Dir. of Czechoslovak Radio 45-48; Czechoslovak Amb. to U.S.S.R. 48-50; Deputy Minister of Nat. Defence 50-52; Editor-in-Chief *Nová mysl* 57-61; Head of Int. Dept. of Cen. Cttee. of C.P. of Czechoslovakia 61-64; Deputy to Nat. Assembly 64-69; mem. Presidium Nat. Assembly 64-68; Deputy House of the People Fed. Assembly 69-; mem. Presidium Fed. Assembly 69-71; Chair. Foreign Affairs Cttee. House of the People 69-; First Deputy Chair. of Czechoslovak Group of Inter-Parl. Union 69-70; Chair. 64-68; mem. Cen. Cttee. of C.P. of Czechoslovakia 45-52, 57-, mem. Presidium 64-68; mem. Ideological Comm. Cen. Cttee., Czechoslovak Communist Party 63-65; mem. Presidium Czechoslovak Group of Inter-Parl. Union 70-; Deputy Chair. Czechoslovak Cttee. for European Security 70-; Presidium mem. House of the People, Fed. Assembly 71-; Order of White Lion 1st Class 48, Order of the Repub. 60, Klement Gottwald Order 65, Order of the Red Star 66, Order of Victorious February 73.
Federal Assembly, Prague, Czechoslovakia.

Lászlo, Andor; Hungarian banker, university professor and economist; b. 24 Dec. 1914, Szombathely; m. 1941; one s.; ed. Budapest and Vienna Univs.
Hungarian Gen. Credit Bank, Budapest 36; Office of State Banks until 48; directed establishment of Hungarian Savings Bank System 48; Deputy Chief, Credit Dept. Nat. Bank of Hungary 48-49; Chief Banking and Credit Dept., Ministry of Finance 49-54; Prof. Karl Marx Univ., Budapest 50-; Gen. Man. Nat. Savings Bank 54-61; Pres. Nat. Bank of Hungary 61-; Sec. of State 68-; various Hungarian honours.
National Bank of Hungary, 8-9 Szabadság tér, H.1850, Budapest V, Hungary.

Latham, Sir Joseph, Kt., C.B.E., F.C.A., COMP.I.E.E. British business executive; b. 1 July 1905, Prestwich s. of John and Edith Latham (née Bown); m. Phyllis Mary Fitton 1932; one s. one d.; ed. Stand Grammar School.
Director and Sec. Manchester Collieries Ltd. 41-46; Dir.-Gen. Finance, Nat. Coal Board 46-55, Finance mem. 55-56, Deputy Chair. 56-60; Dir. Assoc. Electrical Industries Ltd. 60, Finance Dir. 61, Vice-Chair. 64, Deputy Chair. 65, Deputy Chair. and Man. Dir. 67-68; Chair. Metal Industries Ltd. 68-72; other directorships include George Wimpey & Co. Ltd., Thorn Electrical Industries Ltd., Black and Decker (Europe).
Leisure interest: golf.
Ovington, The Mount, Leatherhead, Surrey, England.
Telephone: Leatherhead 72433.

Latour-Adrien, Hon. Sir (Jean François) Maurice, Kt., LL.B.; Mauritius judge; b. 4 March 1915; s. of late Louis C. E. Adrien and Maria E. Latour; ed. Royal Coll., Mauritius, Univ. Coll., London and Middle Temple, London.
Called to the Bar, Middle Temple, and in Mauritius 40; District Magistrate 47-48; Crown Counsel 48-60; Asst. Attorney-Gen. 60-61; Solicitor-Gen. 61-64; Dir. of Public Prosecutions 64-66; Puisne Judge 66; Chief Justice of the Supreme Court of Mauritius July 70-; Editor Annual Mauritius Law Reports; Vice-Pres. I.D.E.F. (Institut de Droit d'Expression Française); Kt. Order of St. Lazarus of Jerusalem 69.
Supreme Court of Mauritius, Port-Louis, Mauritius.

La Tramerye, Raymond de, L. ÈS L., L. ÈS D., DIPL. DES SC. POLITIQUES; French industry executive; b. 6 May 1901; one s.; ed. Univ. of Paris.
Founder and Pres. Dir.-Gen. Société Tubest and Assoc. Companies 28-71, now Hon. Pres.; Chevalier de la Légion d'Honneur; Croix de Guerre (39-45); French and

Polish Resistance Medals; American Silver Star, etc. Leisure interests: riding, archaeology, photography.
6 rue Quentin-Bauchart, Paris 8e, France.
Telephone: BAL 55-68.

Latreille, André; French historian and university professor; b. 29 April 1901, Lyon; s. of Prof. Camille Latreille; m. Suzanne Ruplinger 1924; four s. six d.; ed. Lycée Ampère de Lyon, and Univ. de Lyon.
Professor, Lycées de Clermont Ferrand, Marseille and Lyon 24-37; Prof., Univ. de Poitiers 37-44; with Ministry of the Interior 44-45; Prof. of Modern History, Univ. of Lyon 45-; Prof. Institut d'Etudes Politiques (Paris, Lyon, Grenoble); mem. Comité Consultatif des Universités; historical editor *Le Monde*; Corresp. mem. L'Institut de France; hon. Dr. Laval Univ.; Officer Légion d'Honneur, Commdr. St. Grégoire le Grand.
Publs. *Napoléon et le Saint-Siège* 35, *Le Catéchisme Impérial de 1806* 35, *L'Eglise Catholique et la Révolution Française* (2 vols. 46 and 50), *Les Forces Religieuses et la Vie Politique* 51 (with A. Siegfried), *Histoire de Lyon*, Kleinclausz (Vol. III), *Cahiers d'Histoire des Universités de Lyon, Grenoble, Clermont* 56; *Histoire du Catholicisme en France* (with J. R. Palanque, E. Delaruelle and R. Rémond) (3 vols.) 57-62, *La Seconde Guerre Mondiale* 66, *Montalembert: Correspondance inédite, 1862-1870* 70, *L'Ere Napoléonienne* 74, *Histoire de Lyon et du Lyonnais* 75; complete bibliography in *Mélanges André Latreille* 72.
8 rue Dominique Perfetti, 69001 Lyon, France.

Lattimore, Owen, F.R.G.S.; American educator and writer; b. 29 July 1900, Washington, D.C.; s. of David Lattimore and Margaret Barnes Lattimore; m. late Eleanor Holgate 1926; one s.; ed. St. Bees School, Cumberland, and Harvard Univ.
Business and journalism, China 19-25; research work for Social Science Research Council in Manchuria 29-30, for Harvard-Yenching Inst. Peiping 30-31, for Guggenheim Foundation 31-33; research, China and Mongolia to 37; Editor of *Pacific Affairs* 34-41; special political adviser to Generalissimo Chiang Kai-shek 41-42; Dir. Pacific Operations, Office of War Information 43-44; mem. Vice-Pres. Wallace's mission in Siberia and China 44; Economic Adviser Amer. Reparations Mission in Japan 45-46; Chief UN Technical Aid Exploratory Mission to Afghanistan 50; ten visits to Mongolia 61-74; Prof. of Chinese Studies, Leeds Univ. 63-70; mem. American Philosophical Soc., Royal Central Asian Soc.; Foreign mem. Acad. of Sciences Mongolian People's Repub.; Hon. mem. American Geographical Soc., Körosi Csoma Soc., Hungary; Hon. Litt.D. (Glasgow), Hon. Ph.D. (Copenhagen); Cuthbert Peek Grant of Royal Geographical Soc. 30, Gold Medal Geographical Soc. of Philadelphia 33, Patron's Medal Royal Geographical Soc. 42, Gold Medal, Univ. of Ind.
Publs. *The Desert Road to Turkestan* 28, *High Tartary* 30, *Manchuria: Cradle of Conflict* 32, *The Mongols of Manchuria* 34, *Inner Asian Frontiers of China* 40, *Mongol Journeys* 41, *America and China* 43, *The Making of Modern China* (with Eleanor Lattimore) 44, *Solution in Asia* 45, *China, A Short History* (with Eleanor Lattimore) 47, *The Situation in Asia* 49, *Pivot of Asia* 50, *Ordeal by Slander* 50, *Nationalism and Revolution in Mongolia* 55, *Nomads and Commissars* 62, *Studies in Frontier History* 62, *Silks, Spices and Empire* (with Eleanor Lattimore) 68.
26 rue de Picpus, 75012 Paris, France.

Lattre, André Marie Joseph de; French banker; b. 26 April 1923, Paris; m. Colette Petit 1947; three s. two d.; ed. Univs. de Paris à la Sorbonne et Grenoble, and Ecole libre des sciences politiques.
Inspector of Finance 46; with Ministry of Finance 48-; Dept. of External Finance 49-54, Sub-Dir. 55-58; Financial Adviser to Pres. of the Republic 58-60; Perm. Sec. Ministry of Finance 60-61; Dir. of External

Finance 61; Censor, Bank of France 62, Vice-Gov. 66-; Pres. Crédit National 74; Prof. Inst. d'études politiques, Paris 58-; Alt. Extraordinary Dir. Int. Monetary Fund 54; Mission to India for Pres. of World Bank 65; Alt. Dir. BIS 73; Chevalier Légion d'Honneur and foreign awards.
Leisure interests: skiing, tennis.
9 boulevard du Château, 92 Neuilly-sur-Seine; 45 rue St. Dominique, 75007 Paris, France.
Telephone: 624-79-00 (Home).

Latymer, Baron; **Thomas Burdett Money-Coutts,** M.A. British banker; b. 6 Aug. 1901; ed. Radley Coll., and Trinity Coll., Oxford.
Entered Banking House of Messrs. Coutts & Co., London 24; fmr. Chair. London Cttee. Ottoman Bank; Chair. Investment Trust Corpn., Metropolitan Trust Co. Ltd., London Maritime Investment Trust, North Atlantic Securities Corpn., Anglo-American Securities Corpn. Ltd., London and Thames Haven Oil Wharves Ltd.; mem. of Board of Mercantile Investment Trust Ltd., U.K. Provident Inst., Messrs. Coutts & Co., Claverhouse Investment Trust Ltd., and Nat. Provincial Bank; mem. Council of Foreign Bondholders; Vice-Chair. Middlesex Hospital.
San Rebassa, Moscari, Mallorca.

Laubach, Gerald D., PH.D.; American chemical industry executive; b. 21 Jan. 1926, Bethlehem, Pa.; *m.* Winifred Isabelle Taylor; one *s.* two *d.*; ed. Newark High School, Delaware, Univ. of Pennsylvania and Massachusetts Institute of Technology.
Research fellow M.I.T. 50; joined Pfizer as research chemist 50; research supervisor 53-58, Man. Medicinal Products Research 58-61, Dir. Dept. of Medicinal Chemistry 61-63, Group Dir. Medicinal Research 63-64, Vice-Pres. Medicinal Products Research 64-69, mem. board of directors 68-; Pres. Pfizer Pharmaceuticals 69-71; Exec. Vice-Pres. Pfizer Inc. 71-72, Pres. 72-; Dir. Loctite Corpn., Conn. General Insurance Co., Pharmaceutical Mfrs. Asscn.; Trustee, Conn. Coll.; mem. American Assscn. for Advancement of Science, American Chemical Soc., American Management Asscn., New York Acad. of Sciences, Soc. of Chemical Industry and other professional and civic associations.
Pfizer Inc., 235 East 42nd Street, New York, N.Y. 10017; Home: Blood Street, Lyme, Conn., U.S.A.
Telephone: 212-573-2255.

Laufberger, Vilém, M.D., D.SC.; Czechoslovak doctor and physiologist; b. 29 Aug. 1890, Turnov.
Former Prof. of Physiology Charles Univ., Prague; Academician 52-; Vice-Pres. Czechoslovak Acad. of Sciences 52-61; Dir. Laboratory of Graphical Diagnostics 52-; experiments transforming the larva of axolotl into an adult animal 13, explanation of the mechanism of insulin effects 24, discovering ferritine and preparing it in crystalline form 37; Laureate of the State Prize 54; Order of the Repub. 55; Medal of J. E. Purkyně 56; Polonia Restituta Order 57; Gold Plaque, Czechoslovak Acad. of Sciences 62; Hon. Gold Plaque of J. E. Purkyně 70; Purkyně Prize 74.
Publs. *Hidden Facets of Life* 62, *Spatiocardiography* 64.
Vostrovská 12, Prague 6, Czechoslovakia.

Laugerud García, Gen. Kjell Eugenio; Guatemalan army officer and politician; b. 24 Jan. 1930.
Minister of Defence, Chief of Gen. Staff of Army 70-74; Presidential Candidate of Nat. Liberation Movt. and Democratic Institutional Party Coalition (Movimiento de Liberación Nacional/Partido Institucional Democrático MLN/PID) March 74; Pres. of Guatemala July 74-.
Office of the President, Guatemala City, Guatemala.

Laun, Rudolf von, LL.D.; German jurist and philosopher; b. 1 Jan. 1882; ed. Vienna and Paris Univs.

Lecturer in Public Law, Vienna Univ. 08; Ministry of Commerce, Vienna 08; Extra. Prof. Vienna Univ. 11; attached to Austro-Hungarian Ministry of War 16, to Austrian Prime Minister's Office 17, to Ministry of Foreign Affairs, Vienna 18; mem. Del. to St. Germain-en-Laye 19; Prof. of Public Law Hamburg Univ. 19, Rector 24-26; Judge, Hamburg Supreme Court of Administration 22-33; Dean of Hamburg Law School 45, Pro-Rector of Univ. 45-47, 49-51, Rector 47-49; Pres. Constitutional Court of Bremen 49-56; Dr. rer. pol. h.c.; Dr. phil. h.c.; Dr. jur. h.c.
Publs. *Das freie Ermessen und seine Grenzen* 10, *Das Recht der Meerengen und Kanäle* 18, *Recht und Sittlichkeit* 24, *Les Actes de Gouvernement* 31, *Der Wandel der Ideen Staat und Volk als Aeusserung des Weltgewissens* 33, 71, *La Démocratie* 33, *Le Pouvoir discrétionnaire* 34, *Stare Decisis* 38, *Der Satz vom Grunde* 42, 56, *Studienbehelf Allgemeine Staatslehre* 45, 50, 64, *Grundlagen der Erkenntnis* 46, *Die Haager Landkriegsordnung* 46, 50, *Der dauernde Friede* 47, *Die Menschenrechte* 48, *Allgemeine Rechtsgrundsätze* 48, *Die Lehren des Westfälischen Friedens* 49, *Zweierlei Völkerrecht* 49, *Das Recht auf die Heimat* 51, *Das Völkerrecht und die Verteidigung Deutschlands* 51, *Voraussetzungen für demokratische Wahlrechtssysteme* 53, *Freies Ermessen und Détournement de Pouvoir* 54, *Naturrecht und Völkerrecht* 54, *Nationalgefühl und Nationalismus* 54, *Mehrheitsprinzip Fraktionszwang und Zweiparteiensystem* 54, *Altösterreich als Vorbild* 55, *Zum Problem der Behandlung der nationalen Frage durch internationale Organisation* 55, *L'Autonomie du droit et le droit international* 56, *Le droit des peuples de disposer d'eux-mêmes* 58, *Das Recht der Völker auf die Heimat der Vorfahren* 58, *Grenzen von 1959 oder Demokratie?* 59, *Wozu ein Friedensvertrag?* 59, *Rechtsfragen einer Integration Europas* 60, *Freiheit und Selbstbestimmung* 61, *Allgemeine Staatslehre im Grundriss* 61, 65.
Vossberg 2, 207 Ahrensburg-Holstein, Federal Republic of Germany.

Launoit, Comte Paul de; Belgian industrialist; b. 15 Nov. 1891; ed. Ecole des Hautes Etudes Commerciales et Consulaires, Liège.
Pres. BRUFINA (Société de Bruxelles pour la Finance et l'Industrie); Vice-Pres. Société Cockerill-Ougrée; Pres. Société Minière et Métallurgique de Rodange; Pres. Société Belge de l'Azote et des Produits Chimiques du Marly; Commr.-Gen. Liège Water Exhbn. 39; Pres. Chapelle Musicale de la Reine Elisabeth; Concours Musical Int. Reine Elisabeth de Belgique; honours from Belgium, France, the Netherlands, Luxembourg, Sweden, Italy, Austria and Greece.
19 Avenue Franklin Roosevelt, Brussels 5, Belgium.

Laura, Ernesto Guido; Italian film festival director; b. 4 May 1932, Villafranca, Veronese; *s.* of the late Manuel Laura and of Pia Romei Laura; *m.* Anna Maria Vercellotti 1958; two *s.*; ed. Dept. of Law, Catholic Univ.. Milan.
Co-National Sec. Centri Universitari Cinematografici 53-54; Admin. Nat. Sec. Federazione Italiana Circoli del Cinema 54-55; Chief Editor *Bianco e Nero* 56-58, *Filmlexicon* 68; Film Critic, *Il Veltro* 58-; mem. Editorial Board *Rivista del Cinematografo* 67-; Pres. *Immagine, Centro Studi Iconografici* 68-; Dir. Venice Film Festival 69-; has directed various film documentaries including *Diario di Una Dama Veneziana* 58, *Riscoperta di un Maestro* 60, *Alla Ricera di Franz Kafka* 64, *Spielberg* 64, *Don Minzoni* (Special Award) 67.
Publs. *Il Film Cecoslovacco* 60, *La Censura Cinematografica* 61, *Ladri di Biciclette* 69.
Mostra Internazionale d'Arte Cinematografica, Venice; 285 Via Conca d'oro, 00141 Rome, Italy.
Telephone: 8103358.

Lauré, Maurice, D. EN D.; French banker; b. 24 Nov. 1917, Marrakesh, Morocco; *s.* of Prosper Lauré and

Marie-Thérèse Delpech; *m.* Marie-Claude Girard 1955; three *s.*; ed. Ecole Polytechnique and Paris Univ.
Transmissions Officer, French Army 38-41; Telecommunications Engineer 41-45; Insp. of Finances 45-49; Deputy Dir. of Taxes 49-55; Govt. Commissioner, Banque d'Etat du Maroc 55-58; Dir. of Financial Services and Programmes, Ministry of Armed Forces 58-60; Dir. Crédit National 60-67; Dir.-Gen. Société Générale S.A. 67-72, Chair. 73-; Officier Légion d'Honneur; Médaille des Evadés; Commdr. Lion of Finland; Commandeur de l'Ordre National de la Cote d'Ivoire. Leisure interest: yachting.
Publs. *L'Exposé de Concours* 52, *La Taxe sur la Valeur Ajoutée* 53, *Révolution, Dernière Chance de la France* 53, *Traité de Politique Fiscale* 56, *Au Secours de la TVA* 57. 29 Boulevard Haussmann, Paris; 26 Boulevard de la Saussaye, 92200 Neuilly-sur-Seine, France.
Telephone: 266-2999 (Office); 722-7350 (Home).

Laurent, Jacques; French author and journalist; b. 5 Jan. 1919, Paris; *s.* of Jean Laurent-Cely and Louise Deloncle; divorced; ed. Lycées Condorcet, Carnot and Charlemagne, Paris and Faculté des Lettres, Paris.
Founder of Literary review *La Parisienne* 53; Pres. Dir.-Gen. *Arts* (weekly magazine) 54-59; has written screeenplay for several films; Prix Goncourt for *Les Bêtises* 71.
Leisure interest: painting.
Publs. under pseudonym Cecil Saint-Laurent: *Caroline chérie, Le fils de Caroline chérie, Lucrèce Borgia, Prénom Clotilde, Ici Clotilde, Les Passagers pour Alger, Les Agités d'Alger, Hortense 1914-18, A Simon l'honneur, L'Histoire imprévue des dessous féminins, La Communarde, Demandezmoi n'importe quoi* 73; as Jacques Laurent: *Les Corps tranquilles, Paul et Jean-Paul, Le petit canard, Mauriac sous de Gaulle* 64, *Année* 40, *Lettre ouverte aux étudiants, Les Bêtises* 71, *Dix perles de culture* 72, *La Bourgeoise* 75.
Presses de la Cité, 8 rue Garancière, Paris 6e; c/o Gérard Lebovici, 37 rue Marbeuf, Paris 8e; also c/o Editions Grasset, 61 rue des Saints-Pères, Paris 6e, France.

Laurent, Jacques Charles Henri; French industrialist; b. 11 March 1896; ed. Ecole des Sciences Politiques, Paris.
Pres. Council Cultures Company of the Ivory Coast 27; Dir. Cie. Delmas-Vieljeux 35; mem. Gen. Council Bank of France 39, Dir.-Gen. 42-66; Dir. Union Maritime et Financière, Société de Combustibles Delmas-Vieljeux; Légion d'Honneur; Croix de Guerre 14-18 and 39-40; Polish Croix de Guerre.
7 rue de Talleyrand, Paris 7e, France.

Lauricella, Salvatore; Italian politician; b. 18 May 1922, Ravanusa; *m.*; two *s.*
Member Italian Socialist Party; fmr. Sec. Camera del Lavoro, Ravanusa; fmr. mem. of Secr. of Agrigento branch of Confederazione Generale Italiana del Lavoro (CGIL); mem. Regional Secr. of Italian Socialist Party 54, Sec. Regional Cttee. 59; mem. Central Cttee. of Italian Socialist Party; mem. Chamber of Deputies 63-; Minister without Portfolio (with responsibility for Scientific and Technical Research) 68-69; Minister of Public Works 70-72, 73-74.
Camera dei Diputati, 00100 Rome, Italy.

Laurila, Erkki Aukusti, M.SC., PH.D.; Finnish physicist; b. 20 Aug. 1913; ed. Helsinki Univ.
Assistant, Institute of Physics, Univ. of Helsinki 36-40; Head, Valmet instruments factory, Tampere 42-46; Military Service 39-40, 41-42 (Capt.); Prof. of Technical Physics, Finnish Inst. of Technology 45-63; mem. Finnish Acad. 63-; Chair. Finnish Atomic Energy Comm. 58-; Wihuri Foundation Prize 52, Kordelin Foundation Prize 60.
Publs. Two textbooks, scientific papers.
Mantytie 17 b 20, Helsinki, Finland.

Lauritzen, Ivar; Danish shipowner; b. 25 March 1900, Esbjerg; *s.* of Ditlev Lauritzen and Maren Lauritzen (née Breinholt); *m.* Lilian Lauritzen (née Kirkebye); one *s.*; ed. Coll. of Commerce and training with various firms in England, France, Spain and Germany.
Joint proprietor with Knud Lauritzen of J. Lauritzen Steamship Co. 32; Chair. Esbjerg Ropeworks Ltd., Esbjerg; Dir. Rederiet "Ocean" A/S, A/S D/S "Vesterhavet", Copenhagen, Aalborg Shipyard, Aalborg, Scandinavian Canning Co., Esbjerg, Atlas Engineering Works, Baltica Insurance Co., Baltica Life Co.; Dir. Baltic and Int. Maritime Conf.; Chair. Fanø Nautical School Jubilee Fund, Esbjerg Old Seamen's Fund; Dir. J.-L. Fund, Copenhagen.
Leisure interests: yachting, shooting, golf.
Home: Øster Allé 27, 2100 Copenhagen Ø; Office: Hammerensgade 1, 1267 Copenhagen K, Denmark.
Telephone: Øbro 6581 (Home); 11-12-22 (Office).

Lauritzen, Knud; Danish shipowner; b. 12 April 1904, Esbjerg; two *s.* four *d.*; ed. Coll. of Commerce, and training with various firms in England, France, Spain and Germany.
Became joint proprietor with Ivar Laur'tzen of J. Lauritzen Steamship Co. 32; Consul for Chile 37-50; Chair. Rederiet "Ocean" A/S, Copenhagen, Aalborg Shipyard, Aalborg, and Atlas Eng. Works, A/S D/S "Vesterhavet", United Steamship Co. Ltd., J.-L. Fund, Atlas Profit Sharing 50-56 and Hygiene Cttee. of the Danish Merchant Navy, all in Copenhagen.
Leisure interests: skiing, hiking, kayaking, corridas.
Hammerensgade 1, 1267 Copenhagen K, Denmark.
Telephone: 11-12-22.

Lauritzen, Lauritz, D.IUR.; German lawyer and politician; b. 20 Jan. 1910, Kiel; three *s.* one *d.*; ed. Albert-Ludwigs-Univ. Freiburg and Christian-Albrechts-Univ. Kiel.
Lawyer and later Head of Dept. of Commercial Org., Berlin 37; Magistrate in Berlin after Second World War; Head of Presidential Office to Pres. of Schleswig-Holstein; Provincial Dir., Ministry of Interior, Schleswig-Holstein 46-50, in partial retirement 50-51; Head of Dept., Lower Saxony Ministry of Interior 51-54; Mayor of Kassel 54-63; Minister of Justice and Fed. Affairs, Hesse 63-66; Fed. Minister of Housing and Reconstruction 66-Dec. 72; Fed. Minister of Transport 72-74; Social Democrat.
534 Bad Honnef, Dr. Konrad-Adenauer-Strasse 17, Federal Republic of Germany.
Telephone: 5552 (Home).

Lauro, Achille; Italian shipowner and politician; b. 19 June 1887.
Pres. Asscn. of Shipowners, Naples; Vice-Pres. Confed of Italian Shipowners; Mayor of Naples; Senator for Campania 54; Dep. 58-; founded Partito Monarchico Popolare 54 and leader 54-59; Joint leader Partito Democratico Italiano (merger of two former Monarchist parties) 59, fmr. Pres.
Palazzo Lauro, Via Nuova Marittima, Naples, Italy.

Laval, Jean-Baptiste; French physicist; b. 31 Jan. 1900, St. Pardoux-le-Vieux (Corrèze).
Professor, Collège de France; work on the physics of X-rays etc.; hon. Prof. Coll. de France 71-; mem. Académie des Sciences; Officier Légion d'Honneur.
82 boulevard Saint-Michel, Paris 6e, France.

Lavens, Albert, LIC.ECON.SC.; Belgian politician; b. 15 Nov. 1920, Otegem (Kortrijk); *s.* of Adolf Lavens and Madeleine Ameye; *m.* Angélique de Craene 1948;

three *s.* one *d.*; ed. Waregem High School and Catholic Univ. of Louvain.

Lecturer in Higher Technical Training 42-44; Sec. Belgian Gen. Fed. of Flax; Sec. West Flemish Asscn. of Catholic Businessmen 46; mem. Parl. for Kortrijk 58-68; Senator for Kortrijk-Ieper; Econ. Adviser, Intercommunale for Gas and Electricity; Minister of Agriculture; Christian Democrat.

Ministry of Agriculture, Brussels, Belgium.

Laver, Rod(ney) George, M.B.E.; Australian tennis player; b. 9 Aug. 1938, Rockhampton, Queensland; *s.* of R. S. Laver; *m.* Mary Benson 1966; one *s.*; ed. Rockhampton Grammar School and High School.

Professional player since 1963; Australian Champion 60, 62, 69; Wimbledon Champion 61, 62, 68, 69; U.S.A. Champion 62, 69; French Champion 62, 69; first player to win double Grand Slam 62, 69; first player to win over U.S. $1 million in total prize money 72; played Davis Cup for Australia 58, 59, 60, 61, 62 and 73 (first open Davis Cup).

Leisure interests: golf, fishing, skiing.

Publs. *How to Play Winning Tennis* 64, *Education of a Tennis Player* 71.

4501 Camden Drive, Corona del Mar, Calif. 92625; International Management Group, 1 Erieven Plaza, Cleveland, Ohio, U.S.A.

Lavergne, Bernard, LL.D.; French economist; b. 15 Dec. 1884, Nîmes; *s.* of Gérard Lavergne and Amélie Guibal; *m.* 1909; six *c.*

Prof. of Political Economy Paris Univ.; Dir. *L'Année Politique et Economique* and *Revue des Etudes Co-opératives.*

Publs. *Le principe des nationalités et les guerres* 21, *Les Coopératives de consommation en France* 23, *L'Ordre Coopératif* 26, *Le gouvernement des Démocraties modernes* 33, *Essor et décadence du Capitalisme* 38, *La crise et ses remèdes* 38, *Munich défaite des démocraties* 39, *Le problème des Nationalisations* 45, *Une révolution dans la politique coloniale de la France* 48, *Suffrage universel et autorité de l'Etat* 49, *La Révolution Coopérative ou le socialisme de l'Occident* 49, *Le Plan Schuman* 51, *La chimère de "l'Europe Unie"* 52, *L'Armée dite Euro-péenne* 52, *Les accords de Londres et de Paris* 55, *Afrique du Nord et Afrique Noire* 56, *Problèmes africains* 56, *La France trahie (Euratom et Marché Commun)* 57, *L'Hégémonie du Consommateur: Vers la rénovation de la science économique* 58, *Individualisme contre Autoritarisme* 59, *Pourquoi le Conflit Occident—Union Soviétique?* 62, *Les idées politiques en France de 1900 à nos jours—souvenirs personnels* 66, *Le problème religieux à l'heure actuelle* 67, *Le socialisme à visage humain: l'ordre coopératif, Etat consommateurs et producteurs associés* 71.

19 quai Bourbon, Paris 4e, France.

Laves, Fritz H.; German mineralogist and crystallographer; b. 27 Feb. 1906, Hanover; *s.* of Georg Laves and Margaret (Laves) Hoppe; *m.* Melitta Druckenmueller 1938; three *d.*; ed. Univs. of Innsbruck, Göttingen and Zürich.

Assistant, Univ. of Göttingen 30-43; Prof., Univ. of Halle 43-48, Univ. of Chicago 48-54, Univ. of Zürich and in Eidgenössische Technische Hochschule (E.T.H.) Zürich 54-; Dir. of Inst. for Crystallography and Petrography, E.T.H. 54-; Roebling Medal of M.S.A., U.S.A. 69, Werner Medal of Deutsche Mineralogische Gesellschaft 71; Dr. h.c. (Univ. of Bochum).

Leisure interest: music.

Publs. Work in crystal chemistry of metallic compounds 30-, and silicates 48-.

Institute of Crystallography and Petrography, Eidgenössische Technische Hochschule, Sonneggstrasse 5, Zürich, Switzerland.

Telephone: 326211.

Lavoie, Léo; Canadian banker; b. 18 March 1913, Notre-Dame-du-Lac, P.Q.; *s.* of late Phydime Lavoie and Caroline Viel; *m.* Claire Maranda 1940; one *d.*; ed. St. François Xavier Coll., Rivière du Loup and Harvard Univ.

Joined the Provincial Bank of Canada 30, Man. at Warwick, P.Q., and other branches 40-55, Asst. to Pres. 55, Asst. Gen. Man. 55, Gen. Man. 57, Dir. 60, Vice-Pres. and Gen. Man. 66, Pres. and Chief Exec. Officer 67-, Chair. Nov. 74-; dir. of several corpns., social and cultural orgs.

Leisure interests: travel, golf.

Provincial Bank of Canada, 221 James Street West, Montreal, P.Q., H2Y 1M7, Canada.

Telephone: 871-3321 (Office).

Lavrenko, Yevgeny Mikhailovich, DR.SC.; Soviet geo-botanist; b. 23 Feb. 1900, Chuguev City, Ukraine; ed. Kharkov State Univ. and Kharkov Inst. of Popular Education.

Research worker, Kharkov Inst. of Nature Protection 26-29, Ukrainian Research Inst. of Agro-Soil Science 30-33; Instructor, Kharkov Univ. 33-34, Prof. 39-; Head Dept., Komarov Botanic Inst. U.S.S.R. Acad. of Sciences 34-; Corresp. mem. U.S.S.R. Acad. of Sciences 46-48, Academician 68-; Pres. All-Union Botanical Soc.; Chief Editor *The Botanical Journal.*

Publs. Scientific works in the field of botanical geography and cartography, phytozynology, flora and vegetation history.

The Komarov Botanical Institute, Leningrad, U.S.S.R.

Lavrentiev, Mikhail Alexeyevich; Soviet mathematician; b. 19 Nov. 1900, Kazan; ed. Moscow Univ.

Professor of Mathematics, Moscow Univ. 31-41; Dir. Inst. of Mathematics, Acad. of Sciences of the Ukraine Chair. Dept. Moscow State Univ. 48-53; Dir. Inst. of Precise Mechanisms and Computing Technique, Acad. of Sciences of the U.S.S.R. 50-53; Sec. Academician Dept. of Physico-Mathematical Sciences, Acad. of Sciences of the U.S.S.R. 51-53, 55-57; Vice-Pres. and Chair. of Council of Siberian Dept. U.S.S.R. Acad. of Sciences 57-; Dir. Inst. of Hydro-dynamics, Siberian Dept. of the U.S.S.R. Acad. of Sciences 57-; mem. U.S.S.R. Acad. of Sciences 46-; Vice-Pres. Int. Mathematical Union 67-; Deputy to U.S.S.R. Supreme Soviet 58-; mem. Comm. for Public Education, Science and Culture, Soviet Nationalities; Cand. mem. C.P.S.U. Central Cttee. 61; Foreign mem. Czechoslovak Acad. of Sciences 66, Bulgarian Acad. of Sciences, Acad. of Sciences of the German Democratic Repub. 69, Polish Acad. of Sciences 70, Leopoldina Acad. of Sciences (G.D.R.) 71, French Acad. of Sciences 71; Corresp. mem. of Int. Acad. of Astronautics 68; Lenin and State Prize winner, Hero of Socialist Labour 67; Order of Lenin (twice), Red Banner of Labour (thrice), October Revolution.

Publs. include: *Fundamental Theorem of the Theory of Quasi-Conformal Depictions of Plane Areas* 48, *On Theory of Conformal Depictions* 37, *On Some Properties of Single Leaf Functions Applied to Theory of Jets* 48, *Course of Variational Calculations* 38, *Problems of Mechanics of Continuous Media* 61, *Methods of Calculations of Rail Chains by Electronic Computers* 63.

Akademgorodok, Novosibirsk, U.S.S.R.

Lavrov, Boris Alexandrovich; Soviet biologist; b. 18 Aug. 1884, Arzamas; ed. Moscow Univ.

School teacher 09-19; Lecturer, Moscow Univ. 19-32; Prof. and Head of Dept., Moscow Polytechnical Inst. 19-29; Head of Dept., All-Union Research Inst. of Vitaminology; Head, State Vitamin Control Station; Dir., Head of Dept., Consultant, All-Union Research Inst. of Vitaminology 30-; mem. U.S.S.R. Acad. of Medical Sciences 45-; Deputy Chair. Problem Comm. on Vitaminology U.S.S.R. Acad. of Medical Sciences;

Order of Lenin 53, Red Banner of Labour 44, Badge of Honour 61.
Publs. Over 110 works on physiology and role of vitamins in metabolism.
All-Union Institute of Vitaminology, Kvartal 35, Novye Cheremushki, Moscow, U.S.S.R.

Lavrov, Vladimir Sergeyevich; Soviet diplomatist; b. 4 Oct. 1919, Moscow; ed. Moscow Energy Inst.
Diplomatic Service 47-; First Sec., London 52-53; Asst. to Deputy Minister of Foreign Affairs of U.S.S.R. 53-56; Counsellor, Washington 56-59; Chargé d'Affaires *ad interim* in Yemen 59-60; Deputy Head Second European Dept. of U.S.S.R. Ministry of Foreign Affairs 60-62, Head 62-64; Amb. to Kenya 64-67, to Netherlands 67-73.
c/o Ministry of Foreign Affairs, Moscow, U.S.S.R.

Lavrushin, Vladimir, D.SC.; Soviet chemist; b. 15 May 1912; ed. Kharkov State Univ.
Worked in shoe factory 27-30; Kharkov State Univ. 30-35; postgraduate course 35; Army Service 41-45; research and educ. work, Kharkov 45-48; Prof. of Chemical Technology, later Organic Chemistry, Kharkov State Univ. 48-, Asst. Rector 56-61, Rector 61-66, Dir. Inst. of Chemistry 67-; Order of Lenin, Order of Red Star; Hon. D.Sc. (Manchester).
Publs. contributions to the study of the halocromism of organic compounds.
Kharkov A.M. Gorky State University, Ploshchad Dzerzhinskogo 4, Kharkov, U.S.S.R.

Law, Admiral Sir Horace Rochfort, G.C.B., O.B.E., D.S.C.; British naval officer; b. 23 June 1911, Dublin, Ireland; s. of Samuel Horace Law and Mary Clay; m. Heather Valerie Coryton; two s. two d.; ed. Sherborne School.
Captain, Royal Naval Coll., Dartmouth 60; Flag Officer, Sea Training, Portland 61; Flag Officer, Submarines 63; Controller of the Navy 65; C.-in-C. Naval Home Command 70-72; Chair. R. & W. Hawthorn Leslie 73; Pres. Royal Inst. of Naval Architects 75-.
Leisure interests: tennis, sailing, gardening.
West Harting, near Petersfield, Hants., England.

Law, Phillip Garth, A.O., C.B.E., M.SC., D.APP.SC., F.A.I.P., F.R.G.S.; Australian scientist, antarctic explorer and educationist; b. 21 April 1912, Tallangatta, Victoria; s. of the late Arthur James Law and Lillie Law; m. Nel Allan 1941; ed. Ballarat Teachers' Coll. and Univ. of Melbourne.
Science master in secondary schools 33-38; Tutor in Physics Newman Coll., Melbourne Univ. 40-47 and Lecturer in Physics 43-47; Research Physicist and Asst. Sec. Scientific Instrument and Optical Panel, Ministry of Munitions 40-45; Scientific Mission to New Guinea battle areas for the Australian Army 44; Senior Scientific Officer Australian Nat. Antarctic Research Expeditions 47-48, Leader 49-66; Dir. Antarctic Div., Dept. of External Affairs 49-66; Australian Observer Norwegian-British-Swedish Antarctic Expedition 50; led expeditions to establ. first permanent Australian research station at Mawson, MacRobertson Land 54 and at Davis, Princess Elizabeth Land 57; exploration of coast of Australian Antarctica 54-66; mem. gov. council Melbourne Univ. 59-, La Trobe Univ. 64-74; Vice-Pres. Victoria Inst. of Colls. 66-; Chair. Australian Nat. Cttee. on Antarctic Research 66-; mem. Council of Science Museum of Victoria 68-; Pres. Royal Soc. of Victoria 67, 68; Pres. Graduate Union, Univ. of Melbourne 72-; Award of Merit Commonwealth Professional Officers' Assoc. 57, Clive Lord Memorial Medal Royal Soc. of Tasmania 58, Founder's Medal Royal Geographical Society 60, John Lewis Gold Medal Royal Geographical Soc. of Australia 62, Vocational Service Award Melbourne Rotary Club 70.
Leisure interests: music, tennis, skiing, swimming.

Publs. *ANARE* (with Bechervaise) 57, also numerous articles on antarctic exploration and research and papers on cosmic rays, thermal conductivity, optics and education.
Victoria Institute of Colleges, 582 St. Kilda Road, Melbourne, 3004 Victoria; Home: 16 Stanley Grove, Canterbury, 3126 Victoria, Australia.

Lawrence, Arnold Walter, M.A., F.S.A.; British archaeologist; b. 2 May 1900; ed. City of Oxford School, and New Coll., Oxford.
Ur excavations 23; Craven Fellow, Oxford 24; Student of British Schools of Rome and Athens; Reader in Classical Archaeology Cambridge 30; Literary executor of T. E. Lawrence 35; Mil. Intelligence Middle East 40; Scientific Officer R.A.F. 42; with Ministry of Economic Warfare 43; Prof. of Classical Archaeology Cambridge Univ. 44-51; Fellow of Jesus Coll. Cambridge 44-51; Prof. of Archaeology, Univ. Coll. of Gold Coast and Dir. Nat. Museum of the Gold Coast 51-57; Hon. Sec. and Conservator, Monuments and Relics Comm., Gold Coast 52-57.
Publs. *Later Greek Sculpture and its Influence* 27, *Classical Sculpture* 29, *Herodotus annotated* 35, *T. E. Lawrence by his Friends* 37, *Greek Architecture* 57, 67, 74, *Letters to T. E. Lawrence* 62, *Trade Castles and Forts of West Africa* 63, *Fortified Trade Posts* 69, *Greek and Roman Sculpture* 72, *The Armenian Kingdom of Cilicia* 76 (with others), etc.
c/o Barclays Bank, 68 Lombard Street, London, E.C.3, England.

Lawrence, Henry Sherwood, M.D.; American physician and immunologist; b. 22 Sept. 1916, New York; s. of Victor J. and Agnes B. (Whalen) Lawrence; m. Dorothea H. Wetherbee 1943; two s. one d.; ed. New York Univ.
Instructor in Medicine, New York Univ. School of Medicine 49-52, Asst. Prof. 52-55, Assoc. Prof. 55-61, Prof. of Medicine 61-; Head Infectious Disease and Immunology Div. 59-; Co-Dir. New York Univ. Medical Services 64; Dir. Cancer Center 74-; Commonwealth Foundation Fellow, Univ. Coll., London 59; mem. Nat. Acad. of Sciences; Hon. Fellow, Amer. Acad. of Allergy, Soc. Française d'Allergie; Harvey Soc. Lecturer 72; Von Pirquet Award, Amer. Coll. of Physicians Award, N.Y. Acad. of Medicine Science Medal, Amer. Acad. of Allergy Scientific Achievement Award, Infectious Diseases Soc. of America Bristol Award, Chapin Medal, City of Providence, Lila Gruber Award for Cancer Research, American Acad. of Dermatology, Dowling Lectureship Award for Advancement of Immunology.
Leisure interests: landscape painting, medieval English history;
Publs. *Cellular and Humoral Aspects of Hypersensitivity* (Editor) 59, *Mediators of Cellular Immunity* 69, *Cellular Immunology* 70; articles in professional journals.
Department of Medicine, New York University School of Medicine, 550 First Avenue, New York, N.Y. 10016; Home: 343 East 30th Street, New York, N.Y. 10016, U.S.A.
Telephone: 212-679-3200 (Office); 212-684-0997 (Home).

Lawson, Frederick Henry, D.C.L., F.B.A.; British university professor; b. 14 July 1897, Leeds; s. of Frederick Henry Lawson and Mary Louisa Austerberry; m. Elspeth Webster; one s. two d.; ed. Queen's Coll., Oxford, and Göttingen Univ.
Served in Royal Artillery 16-19; called to the Bar Gray's Inn 23; Lecturer in Law, Univ. Coll., Oxford 24-25; Junior Research Fellow, Merton Coll., Oxford 25-30; Official Fellow and Tutor in Law, Merton Coll. Oxford 30-48; All Souls Reader in Roman Law 31-48; Temporary Principal Ministry of Supply 43-45; Prof. of Comparative Law Univ. of Oxford and Fellow of Brasenose 48-64; Sec.-Gen. Int. Asscn. of Legal Science 64-69;

Part-time Lecturer in Law, Univ. of Lancaster 64-72; Part-time Prof. of Law, Univ. of Lancaster 72-; Maurice Frankel Prof. of Law, Univ. of Houston 67-68; Jt. Editor *Journal of Comparative Legislation* 48-52; *Int. and Comparative Law Quarterly* 52-55; Editor *Journal of the Society of Public Teachers of Law* 55-62; Dr. h.c. (Louvain, Paris and Ghent Univs.), Dr. jur. h.c. (Frankfurt-am-Main Univ.), Hon. LL.D. (Glasgow Univ.).
Publs. *Cases in Constitutional Law* (with Sir D. L. Keir) 28, *Negligence in the Civil Law* 50, *The Rational Strength of English Law* (Hamlyn Lectures) 51; revisions of various works on Constitutional, Roman and French Law; contributions to *Law and Government in Principle and Practice* (Ed. J. L. Brierly), and 1950 edn. of *Chamber's Practice* (Ed. J. L. Brierly), and latest edn. of *Chambers's Encyclopaedia; A Common Lawyer Looks at the Civil Law* 55, *Introduction to the Law of Property* 58, *The Oxford Law School 1850-1965* 68, *The Roman Law Reader* 69, *Remedies of English Law* 72.
13 Eden Park, Lancaster, England.
Telephone: Lancaster 66598.

Lawzi, Ahmed Abdel Kareem al-; Jordanian politician; b. 1925, Jubeiha, nr. Amman; *m.*; ed. Teachers' Training Coll., Baghdad, Iraq.
Teacher, 50-53; Asst. to Chief of Royal Protocol 53-56; Head of Ceremonies, Ministry of Foreign Affairs 57; mem. Parl. 61-62, 62-63; Asst. to Chief of Royal Court 63-64; Minister of State, Prime Minister's Office 64-65; mem. Senate 65; Minister of the Interior for Municipal and Rural Affairs April-Oct. 67; mem. Senate 67; Minister of Finance Oct. 70-Nov. 71; Prime Minister 71-73; various Jordanian and foreign decorations.
The Senate, Amman, Jordan.

Laxalt, Paul; American lawyer and politician; b. 2 Aug. 1922, Reno, Nevada; *s.* of Dominique and Theresa (Alpetche) Laxalt; *m.* Jackalyn Ross 1946; four *s.* two *d.*; ed. High School, Carson City, and Univ. of Santa Clara, Calif.
Served in infantry in Second World War; graduated from Denver Univ. School of Law 49 and became attorney; joined Republican Party and was elected District Attorney of Ormsby County 50; Lieut.-Gov., Nevada 62-67; Gov. of Nevada 67-71; U.S. Senator from Nevada Jan. 75-.
Leisure interests: tennis, golf.
U.S. Senate, Washington, D.C. 20510; Home: 1600 West King Street, Carson City, Nevada 89701, U.S.A.

Laxness, Halldor; Icelandic writer; b. 23 April 1902. Many of his novels have been translated into English· Nobel Prize for Literature 55; Sonning Prize 69.
Publs. include *The Great Weaver of Cashmere* 27, *Salka Valka* 34, *Independent People* (epic) 39, *The Atom Station, Paradise Reclaimed, The Fish Can Sing, Independent People* (play) 72, etc.; translated into Icelandic Hemingway's *Farewell to Arms*, Voltaire's *Candide*, Gunna Gunnarsson's works, etc.
P.O. Box 664, Reykjavík, Iceland.

Lay, Herman Warden; American business executive; b. 3 June 1909, Charlotte, N.C.; *m.* Amelia Harper; one *s.* two *d.*; ed. Furman Univ., Greenville, S.C.
Independent food distributor 32-39; Founder, Pres. and Chair. of Board, H. W. Lay & Co. Inc., Atlantic 39-61; Pres. Frito-Lay Inc. 61-64, Chair. of Board 64-65; Chair. of Board PepsiCo. Inc. (following merger of Pepsi-Cola Co. and Frito-Lay Inc.) 65-71, Chair. Exec. Cttee. May 71-; Dir. of various banks, insurance cos. and industrial concerns, etc.; Hon. LL.D. (Drury Coll. and Furman Univ.)
PepsiCo Inc., Purchase, N.Y. 10577; Homes: 870 United Nations Plaza, East Tower, Apt. 9C, N.Y. 10017; 4935 Radbrook Place, Dallas, Tex. 75220, U.S.A.

Layton, Robert G., B.COM., F.C.A., F.C.W.A.; business executive; b. 16 May 1923; ed. Bromsgrove School, Univ. of London, Inst. of Chartered Accountants, England.
Chartered Accountant, London and Birmingham 39-47; Chief Accountant, Caracas Petroleum S.A., Caracas, Venezuela 48; Controller, Van Reekum Paper Inc., New York 48-50; Ford Motor Co., Finance Int. Division 50-54; Dir. of Finance, Ford Mexico 54-57; Dir. of Finance, Ford Germany 57-63, Gen. Man. 63-67, Vice-Pres. Sales, Ford Europe 67-68; Vice-Pres. Ford U.S., Latin America 68-69; mem. Management Board Dynamit Nobel A.G., Troisdorf 70-73; Deputy Chair. Feldmühle A.G., Düsseldorf 73-; mem. Advisory Board, Friedrich Simon Bank KG, Düsseldorf, Gerling Konzern, Cologne.
c/o Dynamit Nobel A.G., 5210 Troisdorf, Postfach 1209, Cologne, Federal Republic of Germany.

Lázár, György; Hungarian economist and politician; b. 15 Sept. 1924, Isaszeg; *s.* of Mihály Lázár and Etel Fehér; *m.* Adél Kiss; one *s.*
Began as technical draughtsman; mem. Communist Party 45-; joined Nat. Planning Office 48, Chief Dept. Head 54, Vice-Pres. 58, Pres. 73-75; Minister of Labour 70-73; Deputy Prime Minister 73-75, Prime Minister May 75-; mem. Hungarian Socialist Workers' Party Cen. Cttee., mem. Politburo 75-, mem. Political Econ. Board attached to HSWP Cen. Cttee. 75-; Co-Pres. Nat. Council for Youth Policy and Educ.
Office of the Prime Minister, Parliament Building, Kossuth Lajos tér, Budapest, Hungary.
Telephone: 123-500.

Lăzăreanu, Alexandru; Romanian diplomatist; b. 18 Feb. 1913, Bucharest; *s.* of Barbu and Sara; *m.* Ana Lăzăreanu 1946; one *s.*; ed. Bucharest Faculty of Letters and Philosophy.
Journalist 31-46; Cultural and Press Counsellor, Washington 46-48; Dir. Ministry of Foreign Affairs 49-51; First Counsellor, Chargé d'Affaires a.i., Paris 51-53; Dir., mem. Collegium, Ministry of Foreign Affairs 53-56; Deputy Minister, Ministry of Foreign Affairs 56-61; Minister to Great Britain also accred. to Iceland 61-64, Amb. 64-66; Dir. Ministry of Foreign Affairs 66-68; Amb. to Belgium and Luxembourg 68-, also accred. to Upper Volta 71-; Order of Star of Repub., Order of Labour.
Leisure interests: photography, chess.
37 rue Washington, 1050 Brussels, Belgium.

Lazareff, Helène (*see* Gordon-Lazareff).

Lazarsfeld, Paul Felix; American (b. Austrian) sociologist; b. 13 Feb. 1901; *s.* of Robert and Sofie Lazarsfeld; *m.* Patricia Lazarsfeld 1949; one *s.* one *d.*; ed. Universität Wien.
Director Radio Research, Princeton Univ. 37-40; Prof. Sociology, Columbia Univ. 40-62, Quetelet Prof. of Social Science 63-; fmr. Pres. Amer. Asscn. for Public Opinion Research; fmr. Pres. Amer. Sociological Asscn.; mem. Nat. Acad. of Science, U.S.A.; Hon. L.H.D. (Yeshiva Univ., Sorbonne); Hon. LL.D. (Chicago and Columbia Univs.); Golden Cross of Merit (Austria).
Leisure interests: music, hiking.
Publs. include: *The Unemployed of Marienthal* 32, *Radio and the Printed Page* 40, *The Peoples' Choice* 48, *Organizing Educational Research* (with Sam D. Sieber) 64, *Latent Structure Analysis* (with Neil Henry) 67.
50 West 96th Street, New York, N.Y. 10025, U.S.A.

Lazarus, Ralph; American businessman; b. 30 Jan. 1914, Columbus, Ohio; *s.* of Fred Lazarus, Jr. and Meta Marx Lazarus; *m.* Gladys Kleeman 1939; three *s.* one *d.*; ed. Dartmouth Coll.

Vice-Pres. F. & R. Lazarus & Co. 47-51; Exec. Vice-Pres. Federated Department Stores, Cincinnati 51-57, Pres. 57-67, Chair. of Board 67-; mem. Board of Dirs. Scott, Chase Manhattan, Gen. Electric Co.; mem. Board of Trustees Dartmouth Coll.; mem. Business Council, Business Roundtable.
Leisure interest: music.
Home: 1009 Catawba Valley Drive, Cincinnati, O. 45226; Office: 222 West 7th Street, Cincinnati, O. 45202, U.S.A.
Telephone: 513-852-3920 (Office).

Lazell, Henry George Leslie; British business executive; b. 23 May 1903; ed. L.C.C. Elementary School. Clerk until 30; Accountant, Macleans Ltd. 30, Sec. 30, Dir. and Sec. 36; Sec. Beecham Group Ltd. 39; Man. Dir. Macleans Ltd., and Dir. Beecham Group Ltd. 40; Man. Dir. Beecham Group Ltd. 51-58, Chair. 58-68; Pres. Beecham Group 68-70, Hon. Pres. 70-; Dir. Imperial Chemical Industries Ltd. 66-68; Chair. Govs. Ashridge Management Coll. 63; Pres. of the Appeal, British Heart Foundation.
Publ. *From Pills to Penicillin: The Beecham Story.*
Apartment A5, Fairylands Apartments, Pembroke 5-56, Bermuda.

Le Duan; Vietnamese politician; b. 1908, Quang Tri Province, Central Viet-Nam.
Secretary with local railways, Hanoi; imprisoned for political activity 31, released 36, and again 40, released 45 when Viet-Minh came to power; active mem. Communist Party of Indochina; prominent in Viet-Minh resistance 46; Commr. Mil. Headquarters, S. Viet-Nam 52; Sec. Lao Dong Cen. Cttee. for Southern Region 56, Sec.-Gen. Lao Dong Party April 59, First Sec. Sept. 59-; mem. Lao Dong Politburo, Cen. Cttee. and Secr.; accompanied Ho Chi Minh on official visits; led dels. to 23rd Soviet Party Congress 67, to Celebrations for 50th Anniversary of October Revolution 67, to Centenary of Lenin's birth 70; mem. Nat. Defence Council.
Publs. major articles in *Nhan Dan* (party organ).
Central Committee, Lao Dong Party, Hanoi, Democratic Republic of Viet-Nam.

Le Duc Tho; Vietnamese politician; b. 1910, N. Viet-Nam.
Founder mem. Communist Party of Indochina 30; imprisoned, escaped to China 40; founder mem. Viet-Minh, returned to Hanoi 45; Viet-Minh del. for S. Viet-Nam 49; Sec.-Gen. Viet-Minh Exec. Cttee., S. Viet-Nam, then mem. Cen. Cttee. Lao Dong Party; mem. Politburo, Lao Dong Party 55, Dir. Party Training School 59; mem. Lao Dong Secr. 60; Special Adviser to N. Vietnamese del. at Paris peace talks 68-72; led dels. to U.S.S.R. 61, France 65, 70, German Democratic Repub. 71, has attended several Communist Party congresses abroad; declined Nobel Peace Prize 73.
Central Committee, Lao Dong Party, Hanoi, Democratic Republic of Viet-Nam.

Leach, Bernard Howell, C.H., C.B.E.; British potter, author and artist; b. 5 Jan. 1887, Hong Kong; s. of Andrew John Leach; m. 1st Edith Muriel Hoyle 1909, 2nd Laurie Cookes, 3rd Janet Darnell; two s. one adopted s. three d.; ed. Beaumont Coll., Slade School of Art, and London School of Art.
Studied pottery in Japan and visited Korea and China 09-20; started (with Shoji Hamada) Leach Pottery at St. Ives, Cornwall 20; exhibited widely, taught, wrote and lectured 20-68; started small pottery at Dartington Hall, Devon; initiated first Int. Craft Conference of Potters and Weavers, Dartington Hall 52; exhibited, travelled and lectured, Japan 52-54, 61; U.S. lecture tours 50, 52, 60; Retrospective Exhibitions, Arts Council, London, Tokyo and Osaka 61, 69; Exhbns.: Japan 66-67, 69, Hamburg 67, 69, Tokyo 71, 73; Binns Medal, American Ceramic Soc.; Hon. Assoc., Manchester Coll.

of Art 60, Hon. D.Litt., Exeter Univ. 61; Second Order of the Sacred Treasure (Japan) 66; Freeman Borough of St. Ives, Cornwall 68, Japan Foundation Award 74.
Leisure interests: cricket, tennis, chess.
Publs. *A Potter's Book* 40, *A Potter's Portfolio* 50, *A Potter in Japan* 60, *Kenzan and his Tradition* 67, *The Unknown Craftsman, Yanagi* 72, *Drawings Verse and Belief* 73, *A Potter's Work* 73, *Hamada—A Potter* 75.
The Leach Pottery Ltd., St. Ives, Cornwall, England.
Telephone: 0736-70-6398.

Leach, Sir Edmund Ronald, Kt., M.A., PH.D., F.B.A.; British social anthropologist; b. 11 Nov. 1910, Sidmouth; s. of William Edmund and Mildred Mary Leach (née Brierley); m. Celia Joyce Buckmaster 1940; one s. one d.; ed. Marlborough Coll., Clare Coll., Cambridge, and London School of Economics.
Commercial Asst., Butterfield and Swire, Shanghai 32-37; Graduate Student, London School of Econs. 38-39, 46-47; Military Service, Burma Army 39-45; Lecturer (later Reader) in Social Anthropology, London School of Econs. 47-53; Lecturer, Cambridge Univ. 53-57, Univ. Reader in Social Anthropology 57-72, Prof. 72-; Fellow of King's Coll., Cambridge 60-66, Provost 66-; Fellow of Center for Advanced Study in Behavioral Sciences, Stanford 61; Senior Fellow, Eton Coll. 66-; Hon. Fellow, London School of Econs. 73, School of Oriental and African Studies 74; Malinowski Lecturer 59; Henry Myers Lecturer 66; BBC Reith Lecturer 67; Lewis Henry Morgan Lecturer, Univ. of Rochester 75; John Hinkley Prof. and Memorial Lecturer, Johns Hopkins Univ. 76; Sophie Davis Fellow, Brandeis Univ. 76; Radcliffe-Brown Memorial Lecturer, British Acad. 76; Field Research Formosa 37, Kurdistan 38, Burma 39-45, Borneo 47, Ceylon 54-56; Vice-Pres. Royal Anthropological Inst. 64-66, 68-70, Pres. 71-75; Chair. Asscn. of Social Anthropologists 66-70; Pres. British Humanist Asscn. 70-72; Trustee, British Museum 75-; Foreign Hon. mem. American Acad. of Arts and Sciences 68; Hon. D. H. L.(Chicago); Curl Essay Prize 51, 57; Rivers Medal 58; R.S.A. Silver Medal 73.
Leisure interest: skiing.
Publs. *Social and Economic Organization of the Rowanduz Kurds* 40, *Social Science Research in Sarawak* 50, *Political Systems of Highland Burma* 54, *Pul Eliya: A Village in Ceylon* 61, *Rethinking Anthropology* 61, *A Runaway World?* 68, *Lévi-Strauss* 70, *Genesis as Myth* 70, *Culture and Communication* 76.
Provost's Lodge, King's College, Cambridge, England.
Telephone: Cambridge 50411.

Leach, Sir Ronald George, Kt., C.B.E., F.C.A.; British chartered accountant; b. 21 Aug. 1907, London; s. of William T. Leach; m. Margaret A. Binns 1953; one s. one d.; ed. Alleyn's School, Dulwich.
Deputy Financial Sec. Ministry of Food 39-46; Senior Partner, Peat, Marwick, Mitchell and Co. (Chartered Accountants) 66-; Pres. Inst. of Chartered Accountants in England and Wales 69-70, now mem. Council; Chair. Accounting Standards Steering Cttee.; mem. Cttee. on Coastal Flooding 53, Inquiry into Shipping 67-70; Chair. Consumer Cttee. for Great Britain 58-67; Board of Trade Companies Act Accountancy Advisory Cttee. 69-; Board of Trade Insp. into the affairs of Pergamon Press 69; mem. Nat. Theatre Board 71, Council of Oxford Centre in Management Studies.
Leisure interest: farming.
Peat, Marwick, Mitchell and Co., 11 Ironmonger Lane, London, E.C.2; Home: 37-39 Lowndes Street, Carlton Lodge, London, S.W.1, also Waterlane Farm, Headcorn, Kent, England.
Telephone: 01-235-8670 and Headcorn 249 (Homes).

Leaf, Alexander, M.D.; American physician; b. 10 April 1920, Yokohama, Japan; s. of Dr. Aron L. and

Dora Hural Leaf; *m.* Barbara L. Kincaid 1943; three *d.*; ed. Univs. of Washington and Michigan.

Intern, Massachusetts General Hospital 43-44, mem. staff 49-, Physician-in-Chief 66-; Resident, Mayo Foundation, Rochester, Minn. 44-45; Research Fellow, Univ. of Mich. 47-49; mem. Faculty, Medical School, Harvard Univ. 49-, Jackson Prof. of Clinical Medicine 66-; Visiting Fellow, Balliol Coll., Oxford 71-72; mem. Nat. Acad. of Sciences, American Asscn. for Advancement of Science, American Acad. of Arts and Sciences, American Coll. of Physicians, The Biochemical Soc. (U.K.) etc.

Leisure interests: music (flautist), jogging.

Publs. 124 articles in professional journals.

Medical Services, Massachusetts General Hospital, Boston, Mass. 02114; Home: One Curtis Circle, Winchester, Mass. 01890, U.S.A.

Telephone: 617-726-2862 (Office); 617-729-5852.

Leahy, Patrick Joseph, J.D.; American lawyer; b. 31 March, 1940, Montpelier, Vt.; *s.* of Howard and Alba (Zambon) Leahy; *m.* Marcelle Pomerleau 1962; two *s.* one *d.*; ed. St. Michael's Coll., Winooski, Vt., and Georgetown Univ. Law Center, Washington, D.C.

Admitted to practise law, State of Vermont 64, U.S. Supreme Court, Second Circuit Court of Appeals, N.Y., U.S. Fed. District Court of Vt.; Senator from Vt. 75-; mem. Vt. Bar Asscn. 64-; Vice-Pres. Nat. District Attorney's Asscn.; Distinguished Service Award of Nat. District Attorneys' Asscn. 74.

Leisure interests: photography, reading, hiking, cross country skiing.

31 Green Acres Drive, Burlington, Vt., U.S.A.

Leakey, Richard Erskine Frere; Kenyan palaeontologist; b. 19 Dec. 1944, Nairobi; *s.* of the late Louis Leakey; *m.* Meave Gillian Leakey (née Epps) 1971; three *d.*; ed. The Duke of York School, Nairobi.

Leader of expeditions to West Natron, Tanzania 63, 64, Baringo, Kenya 66, Omo River, Ethiopia 67 and East Rudolf, Kenya 68-; Admin. Dir. Nat. Museums of Kenya 68-; Trustee, East African Wildlife Soc., Wildlife Clubs of Kenya.

Publs. numerous articles on finds in the field of palaeontology in scientific journals, including *Nature, Journal of World History, Science, American Journal of Physics and Anthropology,* etc.; contrib. to *General History of Africa* (vol. I), *Perspective on Human Evolution,* and *Fossil Vertebrates of Africa.*

National Museums of Kenya, P.O. Box 40658, Nairobi; Home: P.O. Box 24926, Nairobi, Kenya.

Lealofi IV, Chief Tupua Tamasese; Samoan politician and doctor; b. 8 May 1922, Apia; *m.* Lita 1953; five *c.*; ed. Fiji School of Medicine and postgraduate studies at Suva.

Medical practitioner 45-69; succeeded to Paramount Chief (Tama-a-Aiga) of Tupua Tamasese 65; mem. Council of Deputies 68-69; M.P. Feb. 70; Prime Minister of Western Samoa 70-73, 75-, Minister of Internal and External District Affairs, Labour and Audit, Police and Prisons 75-.

Leisure interests: reading, golf.

Office of the Prime Minister, Apia, Western Samoa.

Telephone: 323.

Lean, David, C.B.E.; British film director; b. 25 March 1908; ed. Leighton Park School, Reading.

Entered industry with Gaumont-British as numberboard boy 28; editor for Gaumont Sound News and British Movietone News; edited *Escape Me Never, Pygmalion, 49th Parallel*; co-directed with Noel Coward *In Which We Serve* 42; directed *This Happy Breed* 43, *Blithe Spirit* 44, *Brief Encounter* 45, *Great Expectations* 46, *Oliver Twist* 47, *The Passionate Friends* 48, *Madeleine* 49, *The Sound Barrier* 52, *Hobson's Choice* 53, *Summer Madness* (American title *Summertime*) 55,

The Bridge on the River Kwai 57, *Lawrence of Arabia* 62, *Dr. Zhivago* 65, *Ryan's Daughter* 69; Officier de l'Ordre des Arts et des Lettres.

c/o The Press Office, Columbia Pictures Corporation, 142 Wardour Street, London, W.1, England.

Lear, Evelyn; soprano; *d.* of Nina Quartin; *m.* Thomas Stewart (*q.v.*); ed. New York Univ., Hunter Coll., Juilliard Opera Workshop.

Fulbright Scholarship for study in Germany 55; joined Berlin Opera, debut in *Ariadne auf Naxos* 57; debut in U.K. in *Four Last Songs* with London Symphony Orchestra 57; debut at Metropolitan Opera in *Mourning Becomes Electra* 67; debut at La Scala, Milan in *Wozzeck* 71; regular performances with leading opera cos. and orchestras in Europe and U.S.A.; guest appearances with Berlin Opera and Vienna State Opera; soloist with the leading Amer. orchestras, has given many recitals and orchestral concerts and operatic performances with Thomas Stewart; Concert Artists Guild Award 55.

Major roles include Marie in *Wozzeck*, Marschallin in *Der Rosenkavalier*, Countess in *The Marriage of Figaro*, Fiordiligi in *Così fan Tutti*, Desdemona, Dido in *The Trojans*, Donna Elvira in *Don Giovanni*, Tatiana in *Eugene Onegin*, Lavinia in *Mourning Becomes Electra*, title role in *Lulu*.

Columbia Artists Management Inc., 165 West 57th Street, New York, N.Y. 10019, U.S.A.

Leather, Sir Edwin Hartley Cameron, K.C.M.G., K.C.V.O.; British colonial governor; b. 22 May 1919, Toronto, Canada; *s.* of Harold H. Leather, M.B.E., and Grace C. Leather; *m.* Sheila A. A. Greenlees 1940; two *d.*; ed. Trinity Coll. School, Royal Mil. Coll., Kingston, Canada.

Member Parl. for N. Somerset 50-64; mem. Exec. Cttee. British Commonwealth Producers' Asscn. 60-63, British Caribbean Asscn.; Chair. Horder Centres for Arthritics 62-65, Nat. Union of Conservative and Unionist Asscns. 70-71; Canadian Rep. Exec. Cttee., British Commonwealth Ex-servicemen's League 54-63; Chair. Bath Festivals Soc. 60-65; Deputy Chair. Yehudi Menuhin School and Orchestra 67-73; Gov. of Bermuda July 73-; Hon. Fellow, Royal Soc. of Arts 68; K.St.J. 74; Hon. D.C.L. (Univ. of Bath) 75.

Leisure interests: music, travel, reading.

Government House, Bermuda.

Leathers, 2nd Viscount; **Frederick Alan Leathers,** M.A., F.R.S.A.; British company director; b. 4 April 1908; *m.* Elspeth Stewart 1940; two *s.* two *d.*; ed. Brighton Coll., and Emmanuel Coll., Cambridge.

Member Baltic Exchange; fmr. underwriting mem. of Lloyd's, Gen. Cttee. of Lloyd's Register of Shipping; mem. Court Worshipful Co. of Shipwrights, Court Watermen's and Lightermen's Co.; Fellow. Inst. of Chartered Shipbrokers; mem. Inst. Petroleum; former Chair. Wm. Cory and Son Ltd., Cory Mann George Ltd., Hull Blyth and Co. Ltd., St. Denis Shipping Co. Ltd., Cory Ship Towage Ltd., Smit and Cory Int. Port Towage Ltd.; Nat. Westminster Bank Ltd., Outer London Regional Board; Fellow, Royal Philatelic Soc.

Hills Green, Kirdford, Sussex, England.

Telephone: Kirdford 202.

Leavis, Frank Raymond, PH.D.; British university lecturer and writer; b. 14 July 1895; ed. Perse School, Cambridge, Emmanuel Coll., Cambridge.

University teacher 24-; Editor *Scrutiny* 32-53; Univ. Lecturer in English, Cambridge 37-60, Reader 60-62; Visiting Prof. Univ. of York 65-67; Hon. Visiting Prof. Univ. of York 67-68; fmr. Fellow and Dir. of English Studies, Downing Coll., Cambridge; Hon. mem. American Acad. of Arts and Sciences; Hon. D.Litt. (Leeds and York Univs.), Hon. LL.D. (Aberdeen Univ.).

Publs. *For Continuity* 33, *New Bearings in English Poetry* 32, *Revaluation: Tradition and Development in*

English Poetry 36, *Education and the University* 43, *The Great Tradition* 48, *The Common Pursuit* 52, *D. H. Lawrence, Novelist* 55, (with Denys Thompson) *Culture and Environment* 33, *Mill on Bentham and Coleridge* 50 (editor), *Two Cultures? The Significance of C. P. Snow* 62, *Scrutiny: A Retrospect* 63, *"Anna Karenina" and Other Essays* 67, *A Selection from Scrutiny* 68 (editor), *Lectures in America* (with Q. D. Leavis) 69, *English Literature in Our Time and the University* 69, *Dickens the Novelist* (with Q. D. Leavis) 70, *Nor Shall My Sword* 72, *Letters in Criticism* 74, *The Living Principle: English as a Discipline of Thought* 75.

12 Bulstrode Gardens, Cambridge, England.
Telephone: Cambridge 52530.

Lebedev, Yevgeny Alekseyevich; Soviet actor; b. 15 Jan. 1917; s. of Alexey Mikhailovich Lebedev and Zinaida Ivanovna Lebedeva; m. Natella Alexandrovna Tovstonogova 1950; one s. one d.; ed. Moscow Theatre School.
Tbilisi Russian Theatre for Youth 40-49; Leningrad Theatre 49-56; Leningrad Academic Bolshoi Drama Theatre 56-; People's Artist of R.S.F.S.R. 62; U.S.S.R. State Prize 50, 68; People's Artist of the U.S.S.R. 68.
Main roles: Mitya (*Poverty is No Vice*), Tikhon (*Thunderstorm* by A. N. Ostrovsky), Paval Korchagin (*How the Steel Hardened* by N. Ostrovsky), Monakhov (*Barbarians* by M. Gorky), *Arturo Ui* (Brecht), Bessemenov (*Citizens* by Gorky), Rogožin (*The Idiot* by Dostoyevsky), Poprishtshin (*Madman's Diary* by Gogol), Falstaff (Shakespeare), Shtshukaz (Sholokhov), Marmeladov (*Crime and Punishment* by Dostoyevsky), etc.
Leisure interest: sculpture.
Leningrad Academic Bolshoi Drama Theatre, Petrovskaya ul. 4/2, Kv. 70, Leningrad 197046, U.S.S.R.

Lebedev, Polikarp Ivanovich; Soviet art gallery director; b. 8 March 1904, Malaya Serdoba Village, Penza Region; ed. Moscow Univ.
Member C.P.S.U. 24-; Head of Literature Dept., *Izogiz* (Fine Arts Publishing House) 34-38; Deputy Dir. State Tretyakov Art Gallery, Moscow 38-39, 53-54, Dir. 49-51, 54-; Deputy Head of Dept., Central Cttee. of C.P.S.U. 41-45, Head of Dept. 45-48; Chair. Cttee. for Arts of U.S.S.R. 48-51; Senior Scientific Editor *Great Soviet Encyclopaedia* 51-53; Corresp. mem. U.S.S.R. Acad. of Arts; Honoured Art Worker of U.S.S.R.
State Tretyakov Art Gallery, 9 Lavrushensky pereulok, Moscow, U.S.S.R.

Lebedev, Yuri Vladimirovich; Soviet diplomatist; b. 29 Sept. 1923, Orekhovo-Zuevo, Moscow Region; ed. Moscow State Inst. of Int. Relations.
Soviet Army until 46; entered diplomatic service 62; Counsellor, then Counsellor-Envoy, Soviet Embassy, Cuba 62-68; ranking official, Ministry of Foreign Affairs, U.S.S.R. 68-69; Amb. to Peru 69-.
U.S.S.R. Embassy, Avenida Salaverry 3424, Orrantia del Mar, San Isidro, Lima, Peru.

Lebègue, Raymond; French university professor and writer; b. 16 Sept. 1895, Paris; m. Yvonne Trinquet 1923; three s. one d.; ed. Lycée Louis-le-Grand and Univ. de Paris à la Sorbonne.
Teacher, Brest 19, Clermont-Ferrand 20-23; Prof. Univ. of Rennes 23-42, Univ. of Paris 42-65; mem. Institut de France 55; Pres. Société d'Histoire Littéraire de la France and Soc. des Textes Français Modernes; Officier Légion d'Honneur.
Publs. *Le Mystère des Actes des Apôtres* 29, *La Tragédie religieuse en France* 29, *Les Correspondants de Peiresc dans les anciens Pays-Bas* 43, *La Tragédie française de la Renaissance* 44, *Ronsard* 50, *La Poésie française de 1560 à 1630* 51, *Le Théâtre Comique de Pathelin à Melite* 72; Editor of Collections by Ronsard, Malherbe, R. Garnier, Chateaubriand and Stendhal.
282 rue Saint-Jacques, Paris 5e, France.
Telephone: 326-47-59.

Lebel, Claude: French diplomatist; b. 18 Feb. 1914, Paris; s. of Jaques Lebel and Marie-Germaine Delavigne; m. Claudie de Schoutheete de Tervarent; two s. two d.; ed. Lycée Pasteur, Neuilly-sur-Seine, Faculté de Droit de Paris, Ecole Libre des Science Politiques.
Entered Diplomatic service 38; served Brussels 38-39, Madrid 41-42, Athens 47-49, London 49-55, Washington 59-62; joined the Provisional French Govt. in Algiers 43-44, served in Paris 45-47, 55-59, 62-69; Amb. to Morocco 70-74, to Switzerland 75-; Officier, Légion d'Honneur, Commdr. Ordre de Mérite, Croix de Guerre.
French Embassy, 46 Schosshaldenstrasse, Berne; Residence: 44 Sulgeneckstrasse, Berne, Switzerland; Home: 11 *bis* Boulevard de Beauséjour, 75016 Paris, France.
Telephone: 43-24-24 (Office); 45-40-25 (Residence); 527-60-73 (Home).

Lebenstein, Jan; Polish painter; b. 5 Jan. 1930, Warsaw; ed. Warsaw Acad. of Fine Arts.
Works include: *Zwierzęta* (The Animals), *Pożegnanie* (Leave-Taking), *Przeciwstawienie* (Opposition), *Zwierzę zielone* (The Green Animal), *Bieg skamieniały* (The Petrified Run), *Przebudzenie* (Awakening), *Affection, Figura na przekątnych* (The Figure on the Diagonals), *Figura w błękitnej* (The Figure in a Blue Frame) (all cycles); one-man exhbns.: Musée d'Art Moderne and Galérie Lambert, Paris 61, Galérie Pauli, Lausanne 63, Galérie Lacloche, Paris 65, exhbn. of cycles *Créatures abominables, Carnet intime, Figury osiowe* (Axial Figures) Cologne 65, Galérie Desbière, Paris 70; Collections: Nat. Gallery, Warsaw, Poznań, Cracow, Musée d'Art Moderne, Paris, Municipal Museum, Amsterdam, Museum of Modern Art, New York, São Paulo, San Francisco, Nat. Gallery of Modern Art, Belgrade; S. Guggenheim Prize 58, Grand Prix, Biennale of Youth, Paris.
Living in France.

Leber, Georg; German trade unionist and politician; b. 7 Oct. 1920, Obertiefenbach; s. of Jakob Leber and Elizabeth (née Geis) Leber; m. Erna Maria Wilfing 1942; one s.; ed. primary and commercial schools in Limburg (Lahn).
Soldier 39-45; joined trade union and Social Democrat Party (SPD) 47; trade union leader, Limburg 49; Chair. of local branch of SPD 51; Editor *Der Grundstein* (trade union paper) 52; mem. Management Cttee. Bau-Steine-Erden Trade Union 53-57, Chair. 57; mem. Management Cttee. Fed. of German Trade Unions 57; mem. Management Cttee. of Int. Federation of Building and Timber Workers and Pres. Joint Cttee. of Trade Unions of Building and Timber Trade in European Common Market 57; mem. Bundestag 57-; mem. European Parl. 58-59; mem. Management Cttee. SPD Faction in Bundestag 61-, mem. Party Management 61-; Fed. Minister of Transport 66-69; Fed. Minister of Transport, Posts and Telecommunications 69-72; Fed. Minister of Defence 72-.
Bundesministerium der Verteidigung, 53 Bonn-Hardthöhe, Federal Republic of Germany.
Telephone: 20161.

Leber, Lieut-Gen. Walter Philip; American army officer and govt. official; b. 12 Sept. 1918, St. Louis, Mo.; s. of Walter P. Leber and Bonnie Vera (Blackman) Leber; m. Bernice Jean Palus 1950; two s. one d.; ed. Missouri School of Mines and George Washington Univ.
Served in Second World War, Regular Army Comm. 42; Chief, X-10 Project, Manhattan District, Oak Ridge 46, Technical Branch, Mil. Liaison Cttee. to Atomic Energy Comm., Washington 47-49; Asst. to District Engineer, Seattle District, then District Exec. Officer, Walla Walla District, North Pacific Div., Corps of Engineers 49-50; Engineer Bn. Commdr., and later, Group Commdr. Fort Sill 51; Dept. of Army Gen. Staff,

Washington 52-55; Commanding Officer, 2nd Engineer Group (Construction) Eighth Army, Korea 56-57; Exec. Officer to Chief of Engineers Washington 58-61; Lt.-Gov. Canal Zone and Vice-Pres. Panama Canal Co. 61-63; Ohio River Div. Engineer, Cincinnati 63-66; Dir. of Civil Works, Office Chief of Engineers, Washington 66; Gov. Canal Zone and Pres. Panama Canal Co. 67-71; Safeguard Anti-ballistic Missile System Manager 71-; Distinguished Service Medal and other awards.
Leisure interests: golf, water sports, travel.
Department of the Army, Commonwealth Building, Arlington, Va., U.S.A.

Le Bigot, Guillaume Charles René; French shipping executive; b. 24 Feb. 1909, Lorient, Morbihan; s. of Vice-Admiral J. Le Bigot and Louise Avenel; m. Pauline Coutret 1937; two s. three d.; ed. Ecole des Hautes Etudes Commerciales.
Chief of Budgetary and Financial Section, Ministry of Armed Forces 47-50; Chief of Liaison Mission with Allied Forces 50-51; Chief of Div. of Budget and Finance, Allied Forces in Europe 51-58; Ministerial Sec. for the Navy 58-61; Mayor of Puget-sur-Argens 59-; Chair. Compagnie des Messageries Maritimes 61-66; Admin. Union des Transports Aériens (U.T.A.) 61-66; Chair. French Cttee. of Lloyd's Register of Shipping 71-Commdr. Légion d'Honneur, Commdr. Legion of Merit.
Leisure interest: viticulture.
9 boulevard Suchet, Paris 16e, France.
Telephone: 504-65-73.

Leblanc, Félix A. E. J. G.; Belgian economist and university official; b. 26 May 1892, Brussels; m. Yvonne Bary 1915; ed. Université Libre de Bruxelles.
Served in First World War 14-18; Asst. Man. Ministry of Econ. Affairs 19, Man. 20; official of numerous industrial and financial firms 20-27; joined staff, Université Libre de Bruxelles 27, Ordinary Prof., Admin. 47-52, Vice-Pres. 52-58, Pres. 58-65, now Prof. Emer., Hon. Pres. Conseil d'Administration; Hon. Pres. Fed. des Entreprises des Fabrications métalliques (Fabrimetal) 65; Admin. Fed. of Belgian Industries; Vice-Pres. (fmr. Pres.) European Cttee. of Co-operation of Machine-Tool Industries; Croix de l'Yser (14), Grand Officier de l'Ordre de Léopold and other Belgian and foreign awards.
84 avenue Franklin Roosevelt, B-1050 Brussels, Belgium.
Telephone: 02-48-95-08.

Leblanc, Roméo A.; Canadian journalist and politician; b. 18 Dec. 1927, L'Anse-aux-Cormier, Memramcook, N.B.; s. of Philias and Lucie Leblanc; m. Joslyn Carter 1966; one s. one d.; ed. St.-Joseph and Paris Univs.
Press Sec. to Prime Minister Trudeau 67-71; mem. Parl. for Westmorland-Kent 72-; Minister of Fisheries Aug. 74-; Liberal.
P.O. Box 93, Grand Digne, N.B., Canada.

Leblond, Charles Philippe, L. ès S., M.D., PH.D., D.SC., F.R.S.C., F.R.S.; Canadian professor of anatomy; b. 5 Feb. 1910, Lille, France; s. of Oscar Leblond and Jeanne Desmarcheller; m. Gertrude Elinor Sternschuss 1936; three s. one d.; ed. Univs. of Lille, Paris, Montreal and the Sorbonne.
Assistant in Histology, Medical School, Univ. of Paris 34-35; Rockefeller Fellow, School of Medicine, Yale Univ. 36-37; Asst. Laboratoire de Synthèse Atomique, Paris 38-40; at McGill Univ. was lecturer in Histology and Embryology 42-43, Asst. Prof. of Anatomy 43-46, Assoc. Prof. 46-48, Prof. of Anatomy 48-; Chair. Dept. of Anatomy 57-75; mem. Royal Soc. of Canada, Royal Soc. (London), American Asscn. of Anatomists, Canadian Asscn. of Anatomists, American Asscn. for Cancer Research, American Soc. for Cell Biology, Int.

Soc. for Cell Biology, Histochemical Soc., Montreal Physiological Soc., Soc. for Experimental Biology and Medicine, and others; Prix Saintour, French Acad. 35; Flavelle Medal, Royal Soc. of Canada 61; Gairdner Fed. Award 65; American Coll. of Physicians Award 66; Province of Quebec Biology Prize 68.
Leisure interests: country, snowshoeing.
Publs. *The Use of Radioautography in Investigating Protein Synthesis* (with K. B. Warren) 65, and over 200 articles in scientific journals.
Department of Anatomy, McGill University, Strathcona Anatomy and Dentistry Building, 3640 University Street, P.O. Box 6070, Station A, Montreal, Quebec, H3C 3G1, Canada.
Telephone: 486-4837 (Home); 392-4931 (Office).

LeBlond, Richard Knight, II; American banker; b. 16 Nov. 1920, Cincinnati, O.; s. of Harold R. and Elizabeth (Conroy) LeBlond; m. Sally C. Chapman 1948; six s. four d.; ed. Hill School, Pottstown, Pa., Princeton Univ., Columbia Univ., Graduate School of Business Admin., Harvard Business School.
Joined New York Trust Co. (now Chemical Bank) 46, Asst. Treas. 49, Asst. Vice-Pres. 52, Vice-Pres. 58, Senior Vice-Pres. 66, Exec. Vice-Pres. 68, Dir. Chemical Bank and Chemical N.Y. Corpn. 72-, Vice-Chair. Chemical Bank and Chemical N.Y. Corpn. 73-.
Leisure interests: golf, tennis, squash, skiing, swimming.
Chemical Bank, 20 Pine Street, New York, N.Y. 10005; Home: 194 Sunset Hill Road, New Canaan, Conn. 06840, U.S.A.
Telephone: (212) 770-2175 (Office); (203) 966-4125 (Home).

Leburton, Edmond-Jules-Isidore; Belgian politician; b. 18 April 1915, Lantremange (Waremme); ed. Liège Univ.
Principal Controller of Labour 36-46; Chef de Cabinet, Ministry of Labour and Social Welfare 45-46; Commandant of Secret Army and mem. various resistance groups 39-45; mem. Chamber of Representatives 46-; mem. Socialist Party Council 47-; Burgomaster of Waremme 47-; Prof. Ecole Provinciale de Service Social, Liège, and Ecole Provinciale d'Infirmières, Herstal; Dir. of Studies at Institut d'Etudes Sociales de l'Etat, Brussels; Minister of Public Health and Family Welfare 54-58, Minister of Social Security 61-65; Minister-Vice-Pres., Co-ordinator of Infrastructure Policy 65-March 66; Minister for Economic Affairs, 69-71; Prime Minister 73-74; Nat. Pres. Socialist Party 71-73; awards include: Commdr. de l'Ordre de Léopold, Grand Cross Order of Orange-Nassau, Croix de Guerre avec palmes, Commdr. l'Ordre de la Santé Publique (France).
Publs. *Précis de Sécurité Sociale, Traité d'Economie Politique.*
c/o Parti Socialiste Belge, 17 place E. Vandervelde, Brussels; Home: Clos de Hesbaye, Waremme, Belgium.

Lecanuet, Jean Adrien François; French politician; b. 4 March 1920; ed. Lycée Corneille, Rouen, Lycée Henri IV, Paris, and Univ. of Paris.
Master of Requests, Council of State; Inspector Gen., Ministry of Information 44; Dir. of the Cabinets of Ministry of Information, Merchant Marine, Nat. Econ., Interior 46-51; Dep. to Nat. Assembly 51-55; Sec. of State, Presidency Council 55-58; Mayor of Rouen 68; Senator 59-73; Pres. Senate Cttee. of Foreign Affairs; Nat. Pres., Centre Démocratic 66-; Minister of Justice 74-; Conseiller Gen. of Rouen 58, 64, 70-; Chevalier, Légion d'Honneur, Commdr. Ordre St. Grégoire le Grand.
41 rue Thiers, 76 Rouen, France.

Le Carré, John (*see* Cornwell, David John Moore).

Lecat, Jean-Philippe; French politician; b. 29 July 1935, Dijon; s. of Jean Lecat and Madeleine Bouchard;

m. Nadine Irène Romm 1966; two *d.*; ed. Ecole Nationale d'Administration.
Member Council of State 63-66, 74-; Chargé de Mission, Prime Minister's Office 66-68; Deputy to the Nat. Ass., Beaune 68-72, 73; Nat Del. for Cultural Affairs, Union des Démocrates pour la République 70-71, Asst. Sec.-Gen. for Cultural Affairs and Information 71-72; Spokesman of the Govt. May 72-April 73; Sec. of State for Econ. 73-74; Minister of Information March-May 74; Del. to Natural Resources Conservation Conf. 75.
137 rue de Longchamp, 92 Neuilly-sur-Seine, France.

Lechín Oquendo, Juan; Bolivian politician and diplomatist; b. 1915.
Former professional footballer; fmr. Minister of Mines; President Bolivian Mine Workers' Confed.; fmr. Pres. of Senate; Vice-Pres. of Repub. 60-64; Ambassador to Italy 62-63; exiled May 65; Leader, Left Sector of Movimiento Nacionalista Revolucionario (MNR); sought asylum in Chile June 67; Exec. Sec. Cen. Obrero Boliviano 52-65, 70; re-elected Exec. Sec. Fed. Sindical de Trabajadores Mineros de Bolivia 70; now living in Argentina.

Lechín Suárez, Gen. Juan; Bolivian army officer and diplomat; b. 8 March 1921, Cochabamba; *s.* of Juan Alfredo Lechín and Julia Suárez de Lechín; *m.* Ruth Varela de Lechín 1947; one *s.* three *d.*; ed. Bolivian Military Acad., General Staff Coll. (Fort Leavenworth), U.S.A.
Chief of Operations, Bolivian Army H.Q.; Mil. and Air Attaché Bolivian Embassy Fed. Repub. of Germany; Commdr. 5th Infantry Div. (Bolivian); Pres. Bolivian Mining Corpn. and Minister of State; Commdr. 3rd Infantry Div. (Bolivian); Amb. to U.K., also accred. to Netherlands 69-74; Minister of Co-ordination to the Pres. 74-; Condór de los Andes (Bolivia), Grosses Verdienstkreuz (Fed. Germany), Guerrillero José M. Lanza, Mérito Aeronáutico, Mérito Naval (Bolivia).
Leisure interests: writing, swimming, tennis.
Publs. essays on military history and geo-politics.
Casilla 4405, La Paz, Bolivia.

Le Clézio, Jean Marie Gustave; French-British writer; b. 13 April 1940; ed. Lycée and Univ. de Nice.
Travelled in Nigeria 48, England (studied at Bristol and London Univs.), U.S.A. 65; Prix Renaudot 63.
Publs. *Le Procès-Verbal* (The Interrogation) 63, *La Fièvre* (Fever) (short stories) 65, *Le Procès* 65, *Le Déluge* 66, *L'Extase Matérielle* (essay) 67, *Terra amata* (novel) 67, *Le livre des Fuites* 69, *La Guerre* 70, *Haï* 71, *Conversations* 71, *Les Géants* 73, *Mydriase* 73, *Voyages de l'autre coté* 75.
c/o Editions Gallimard, 5 rue Sébastien-Bottin, 75007 Paris, France.

Lecourt, Robert, D. en D.; French lawyer and politician; b. 19 Sept. 1908; ed. Caen Univ.
Resistance leader, Second World War; Deputy to Constituent Assemblies 45, 46; Deputy to Nat. Assembly from Paris 46-58, from Hautes Alpes 58-60; Minister of Justice 48-49, 57-58; Pres. M.R.P. group in Nat. Assembly 46-48, 52-57; Minister of State, with special responsibility for relations between the Repub. and the French Community 59-60, for Overseas Territories, Overseas Depts. and Sahara Feb. 60-61; mem. European Community Court of Justice 62-, Pres. 67-; Officier Légion d'Honneur, Croix de Guerre, Officier de la Résistance.
Court of Justice, Centre Européen, Plateau de Kirchberg, P.O. Box 1406, Luxembourg; Home: 11 boulevard Suchet, 75016 Paris, France.

Lederberg, Joshua, B.A., PH.D.; American geneticist; b. 23 May 1925, Montclair, N.J.; *s.* of Zwi H. and Esther Goldenbaum Lederberg; *m.* Marguerite Stein Kirsch 1968; one *s.* one *d.*; ed. Columbia and Yale Univs.

Professor of Genetics and Biology, Stanford Univ. 59-; Dir. Kennedy Laboratory for Molecular Medicine, Stanford Univ.; Nobel Prize in Medicine (with Beadle and Tatum) 58.
Publs. Numerous papers and articles in various scientific and lay publications.
School of Medicine, Stanford University, Stanford, Calif. 94305, U.S.A.
Telephone: (415) 497-5801.

Lederer, Edgar, DR.PHIL., D. ÈS SC.; French biochemist; b. 5 June 1908, Vienna, Austria; *s.* of Dr. Alfred Lederer and Friederike Przibram; *m.* Hélèen Frechet 1932; three *s.* four *d.*; ed. Akademisches Gymnasium, Vienna, and Univ. of Vienna.
Postdoctoral research, Kaiser Wilhelm Inst., Heidelberg 30-33; Ella Sachs Plotz Fellow, Inst. de Biologei Physico-Chimique 33-35; Dir. Dept. of Organic Synthesis, Vitamin Inst. Leningrad 36-37; Attaché de recherches, Inst. de Biologie Physico-Chimique 38-39; served in French Army 39-40; research on natural perfumes at Laboratoire de Biochimie, Lyons 40-47; reinstated to Centre National de la Recherche Scientifique (CNRS) after liberation of France 44, Maître de recherches 45; with Inst. de Biologie Physico-Chimique 47-60, Dir. de recherches, CNRS 52, Maître de conférences 54, full Prof. 58; Prof. of Biochemistry, Centre d'Orsay, Univ. Paris-Sud 63-; Dir. Dept. de Chimie Biologique, Inst. de Chimie des Substances Naturelles, CNRS 60-; Fritzsche award and Gold Medal, American Chem. Soc. 51; August Wilhelm v. Hoffmann Gold Medal, German Chem. Soc. 64; Karrer Gold Medal, Swiss Chem. Soc. 64; CNRS Gold Medal 74; Dr. h.c. (Aberdeen) 68, (Liège) 75; foreign mem. Acads. of Austria, Fed. Repub. of Germany, Ireland, Italy, Finland; Hon. mem. London Chem. Soc., Belgian Chem. Soc., U.S. Soc. of Biological Chemists, Czechoslovak Biochemical Soc.
Publs. books on chromatography and lipid chemistry; original papers on chemistry and biochemistry of natural compounds.
Institut de Chimie des Substances Naturelles, Centre National de la Recherche Scientifique, 91190 Gif-sur-Yvette; Home: 9 blvd. Colbert, 92330 Sceaux, France.
Telephone: 907-78-28 (Office).

Lederman, Leon M., A.M., PH.D.; American professor of physics; b. 15 July 1922, New York, N.Y.; *s.* of Morris Lederman and Minna Rosenberg; *m.* Florence Gordon 1945; one *s.* two *d.*; ed. City Coll. of New York and Columbia Univ., New York.
Professor of Physics, Columbia Univ. 58-, Eugene Higgins Prof. of Physics 73-; Dir. Nevis Laboratories, Irvington, N.Y. 68-; J. S. Guggenheim Fellow 58, Nat. Science Foundation Sr. Postdoctoral Fellow 67, Sr. Scientific Visitor CERN 71; Editor *Comments on Nuclear and Particle Physics* 67-72; mem. Nat. Acad. of Sciences; Fellow, Amer. Physical Soc., Amer. Asscn. of Arts and Science; Nat. Medal of Science 67.
Publs. About 50 articles in physics journals on general problems in elementary particle physics, including *Observation of Parity Violations in Meson Decay* and *Observation of Two Neverinos.*
Department of Physics, Columbia University, New York, N.Y. 10027; and Nevis Laboratory, Irvington, N.Y., U.S.A.
Telephone: 212-280-3366 (Columbia Univ.); and 914-591-8100 (Nevis Laboratory).

Ledingham, George Aleck, M.B.E., M.SC., PH.D., F.R.S.C., F.C.I.C.; Canadian microbiologist; b. 1903; ed. Univs. of Saskatchewan and Toronto.
Research Asst. in Pathology, Univ. of Saskatchewan 27; Asst. in Botany, Univ. of Toronto 32; Research Asst., Laboratories of Cryptogamic Botany, Harvard Univ. 32; Mycologist, Nat. Research Council, Ottawa 33-47;

Dir. Prairie Regional Laboratory, Nat. Research Council, Saskatoon 47-.

Publs. include papers on soil fungi 29-36, on the Trail Smelter Question 34-39, on Production and Properties of 2, 3-Butanediol 44-49, studies on plant rusts 50-61.

936 University Drive, Saskatoon, Sask., Canada.

Ledoux, Albert Frédéric Edmond; French diplomatist; b. 5 June 1901, Sheffield; one s.; ed. Bowdon Coll., Brighton Coll., Lycée Janson de Sailly, and Ecole des Hautes Etudes Commerciales.

Attaché Constantinople 27-28; Sec., Rio de Janeiro, Madrid, Brussels, Montevideo 28-40; Gen. de Gaulle's Personal Rep. in S. America 40-41; Del. of French Nat. Cttee. for Argentina, Brazil, Chile, Paraguay and Uruguay 42-43; Dir. of Staff Accounts, Foreign Ministry 44-45; Amb. to Peru 45-49, to Uruguay 49-52, to Norway 55-57; Diplomatic Adviser to Govt. 59-62; Amb. to Denmark 62-66; Commdr., Légion d'Honneur, Médaille de la Résistance, Grand Cross of St. Olav (Norway), El Sol (Peru), Danebrog (Denmark).

Les Mimosas, 10 rue Lecerf, 06 Cannes, France.

Ledoux, Jean-Paul; French engineer; b. 23 Oct. 1904; ed. Ecole Centrale des Arts et Manufactures, Paris.

President, Dir.-Gen., Antar (Pétroles de l'Atlantique) and of Antargaz, Hon. Pres. 70-; Officier, Légion d'Honneur; Commdr. de l'Economie nationale du Mérite commercial.

137 rue de la Tour, Paris 16e, France.

Ledoux, Paul Joseph, D. ès SC.; Belgian astrophysicist; b. 8 Aug. 1914, Forrières; s. of Justin and Ida (Delperd'Ange) Ledoux; m. Aline Michaux 1939; one d.; ed. Athénée Royal, Marche-en-Famenne, Univ. de Liège, Inst. for Theoretical Astrophysics, Oslo and Yerkes Observatory, Univ. of Chicago.

Served with Belgian Forces in U.K. and R.A.F. Meteorological Service 41-46; Adviser, Service Météorologique, Régie des Voies Aériennes; mem. teaching staff, Univ. of Liège 50-, Prof. 59-; Visiting Prof., Univ. of Calif. (Berkeley) 63, Monash Univ. 67, Sussex Univ. 69, Univ. of Colorado 70; Senior Foreign Scientist Fellow, Nat. Science Foundation, Univ. of Washington 72; mem. Acad. Royale de Belgique; Assoc. Royal Astronomical Soc. 74; Prix décennal du gouvernement Belge 68; Prix Francqui 69; Eddington Medal, Royal Astronomical Soc., U.K. 72.

Leisure interests: gardening, country walks.

Publs. various articles in astrophysical journals on the problems of stellar structure, stellar stability and variable stars.

Institut d'Astrophysique, avenue de Cointe 5, 4200 Ougrée; Home: rue de la Faille 55, 4000 Liège, Belgium. Telephone: 041-52-99-80 (Office); 041-52-12-45.

Ledoux, Pierre, D. EN D., H.E.C.; French banker; b. 30 Sept. 1914, Bordeaux; s. of René Ledoux and Jeanne Dupuy; m. Renée Boissin 1949; ed. Lycée de Bordeaux and Faculté de Droit, Paris.

On special assignment with Financial Comm. in the Far East 45; Financial Attaché, China 46; Financial Attaché, French Embassy, Washington, D.C. 47-48; Office of Prime Minister on special assignment concerning the European Econ. Comm. 49-50; Gen. Sec. and Man. Banque Nationale pour le Commerce et l'Industrie (BNCI) 50-56; Pres. BNCI (Afrique) 57-72; Pres. BNCI 63-66, Banque Nationale de Paris 66-71, Chair. 71-; Chair. Banque Nationale de Paris Intercontinentale 72; Vice-Chair. BNP Canada Inc., Australian European Finance Corpn. Ltd., Cie. Arabe et Int. d'Investissement, Banque Marocaine pour le Commerce et l'Industrie, Supervisory Board Banque pour l'Expansion Industrielle, mem. Supervisory Board Banque de la Soc. Financière Européenne; Dir. Crédit National, Thomson-Brandt, Usinor, Denain Nord-Est Longwy, Soc. Française des Pétroles, Banque Nationale pour le

Commerce et l'Industrie, Banque Nationale de Paris Ltd., Banca d'America e d'Italia, French American Banking Corpn., French Bank of California, Soc. Financière Européenne, Banque Bruxelles Lambert, Private Investment Co. for Asia, S.A.; Croix de Guerre 39-45; Commdr. Légion d'Honneur.

Banque Nationale de Paris, 16 boulevard des Italiens, 75450 Paris Cedex 09; Home: 8 avenue Pierre-1er-de-Serbie, 75116 Paris, France.

Telephone: 523-55-00 (Office); 720-85-72 (Home).

Leduc, François Jacques; French diplomatist; b. 10 Nov. 1912, Paris; m. France Renaudin 1937; four s. three d.; ed. Lycée Louis-le-Grand, Univ. de Paris., and King's Coll., Cambridge.

Economic Section, Ministry of Foreign Affairs 45-47; Resident, Tunis 47-50; Ministry of Nat. Defence 51-54; Mayor of Servon 53-71; Minister-Counsellor, Bonn 55-57, 58-60, Brussels 57-58; Dir. Admin. and Consular Affairs, Ministry of Foreign Affairs 60-65; Chair. Compagnie européenne de radiodiffusion et de télévision (CERT) 63-65; Amb. to Canada 65-68, to Austria 68-73; mem. of Board, Télédiffusion de France, Institut National de l'Audiovisuel 74, Agence France Presse 75; Commdr. Légion d'Honneur, Medal of Freedom.

4 rue Oudinot, Paris 7e; and 77170 Servon, France. Telephone: 273-36-51 (Paris).

Ledwidge, Sir William Bernard John, K.C.M.G., M.A.; British diplomatist; b. 9 Nov. 1915, London; s. of Charles and Eileen (née O'Sullivan) Ledwidge; m. Anne Kingsley 1948; one s. one d.; ed. Cardinal Vaughan School, King's Coll., Cambridge and Princeton Univ. Commonwealth Fund Fellow, Princeton 37-39; Mil. Service 41-45; Principal, India and Burma Office 46-48, First Sec. Foreign Office 48-49, Counsellor 61-65; British Consul, St. Louis, U.S.A. 49-52; First Sec. British Embassy, Afghanistan 52-56; Political Adviser British Mil. Gov., Berlin 56-61; Minister, British Embassy, Paris 65-69; Amb. to Finland 69-72, to Israel 72-75.

Leisure interests: golf, bridge, chess.

c/o Foreign and Commonwealth Office, London, S.W.1, England.

Lee, Sir Henry Desmond Pritchard, Kt., M.A., D.LITT.; British university lecturer and schoolmaster; b. 30 Aug. 1908, Nottingham; s. of Canon H. B. Lee; m. Elizabeth Crookenden 1935; one s. two d.; ed. Arden House, Repton School, Cambridge Univ.

Tutor, Corpus Christi Coll., Cambridge Univ. 35-48; Lecturer, Faculty of Classics 37-48; Regional Commrs. Office (Civil Defence) 40-44; mem. Council of Senate, Cambridge Univ. 44-48; Headmaster, Clifton Coll. 48-54, Winchester Coll. 54-68; Chair. Headmasters' Conf. 59-60, 67; Research Fellow, Wolfson Coll., Cambridge 68-73; Principal Hughes Hall, Cambridge 74-; Hon. D.Litt. (Nottingham).

Leisure interests: carpentry, reading.

Publs. *Zeno of Elea* (text and trans.) 35, Aristotle's *Meteorologica* 52, Plato's *Republic* 55, Plato's *Timæus* and *Critas* 71, *Entry and Performance at Oxford and Cambridge 1966-71* 72.

8 Barton Close, Cambridge, England.

Lee, General Honkon; Korean army officer and government administrator; b. 7 Dec. 1920, Kongjoo, Choong Chung Nam-Do, Korea; s. of Kidong Lee and Jinsil Ahn; m. Haeran Lee 1946; two s. four d.; ed. Japanese Imperial Mil. Acad.

Superintendent, Korean Mil. Acad. 46-48; Mil. Attaché, Washington 49; Commdg. Gen., Eighth Republic of Korea Army Division 49-50, Third Army Corps 50-51, First Army Corps 52-54; UN Command Del. to Korean Armistice 51-52; Chair. Jt. Chiefs of Staff 54-56, Chief of Staff 56-58; Nat. Pres. Korean Veterans Asscn. 58-61;

Amb. to Philippines 61-62, to U.K. 62-67 (also to Scandinavian countries, Iceland, Malta and African countries concurrently); Amb. at large 67-69; Chair. President's Advisory Comm. on Govt. Admin. 69.
Leisure interests: horse riding, reading, music appreciation.
115-17, Taeshin-Dong, Sudaemoon-Ku, Seoul, Republic of Korea.
Telephone: 33-3333.

Lee, James E.; American oil executive; b. 13 Dec. 1921, Kiln, Mississippi; ed. Polytechnic Inst.
Gulf Oil Corpn. 42-, served in various engineering and supervisory posts 42-56; Project Adviser to Filoil Refinery Corpn., Manila 59; Area Rep. Manila, Exec. Vice-Pres., Gen. Man. Orient Gulf Oil Co. 62; Vice-Pres. of Refining, Pacific Gulf Oil Ltd., Japan 63; Area Rep. and Co-ordinator for Far East 64; Man. Dir. Kuwait, Kuwait Oil Co. 66; Pres. Gulf Oil Co. (Eastern Hemisphere) 69; Exec. Vice-Pres. Gulf Oil Corpn. 72, Pres., Dir. 73-; Trustee Carnegie-Mellon Univ. 73, Shady Side Acad. 74; mem. Board American Petroleum Inst., Western Pennsylvania Hospital, La. Tech. Eng. Foundation 73; Hon. D.S. 75.
Gulf Oil Corporation, Gulf Building, Pittsburgh, Pa. 15230, U.S.A.

Lee Kuan Yew, M.A.; Singapore politician and barrister; b. 16 Sept. 1923, Singapore; s. of Lee Chin Koon and Chua Jim Neo; m. Kwa Geok Choo 1950; two s. one d.; ed. Raffles Coll., Singapore, Fitzwilliam Coll., Cambridge, and Middle Temple, London.
One of the founders of the Socialist People's Action Party 54, Sec.-Gen. 54-; mem. Legislative Assembly 55-; (first) Prime Minister 59-; mem. Singapore Internal Security Council 59-; (first) Prime Minister Repub. of Singapore 65-; mem. Bureau of the Socialist Int. 67; Fellow, Inst. of Politics, Harvard Univ. 68; Hoyt Fellow, Berkeley Coll., Yale Univ. 70; Hon. Bencher of Middle Temple 69; Hon. Fellow, Fitzwilliam Coll., Cambridge 69, Royal Australasian Coll. of Surgeons 73, Royal Australasian Coll. of Physicians 74; Hon. LL.D. Royal Univ. of Cambodia 65, Hong Kong Univ. 70, Liverpool Univ. 71, Sheffield Univ. 71; Hon. C.H. 70; Hon. G.C.M.G. 72; First Class Order of Rising Sun (Japan), Bintang Republik Indonesia Adi Pradana 73, Order of Sikatura (Philippines) 74, numerous other awards.
Leisure interests: reading, walking and golf.
Prime Minister's Office, St. Andrew's Road, Singapore 6.
Telephone: 31155.

Lee, Laurie, M.B.E., F.R.S.L.; British author and poet; b. 26 June 1914, Stroud, Gloucestershire; m. Catherine Francesca Polge 1950; one d.; ed. Slad Village School, and Stroud Central School.
Script-writer with Crown Film Unit 40-43; editor, Ministry of Information publications 44-46; film-making in India 46-47; caption-writer-in-chief, Festival of Britain 50-51; travelling and writing 51-; Atlantic Award 47, William Foyle Poetry Prize 56, W. H. Smith and Son Award (*Cider with Rosie*) 60.
Leisure interests: music, country pleasures.
Publs. *The Sun My Monument* (poems) 44, *The Bloom of Candles* (poems) 47, *The Voyage of Magellan* (radio play) 48, *A Rose for Winter* (travel) 55, *My Many-Coated Man* (poems) 55, *Cider with Rosie* (autobiography) 59, *The Firstborn* (essay) 64, *As I Walked out one Midsummer Morning* (autobiography) 70, *I Can't Stay Long* (prose collection) 75.
49 Elm Park Gardens, London, S.W.10, England.
Telephone: 01-352 2197.

Lee, Rensselaer Wright, A.B., PH.D.; American art historian; b. 15 June 1898, Philadelphia, Pa.; s. of Francis Herbert Lee and Helen Josephine Stavers Lee; m. Stella Wentworth Garrett 1925; one s. two d.; ed. Princeton Univ.

Instructor of English, Princeton Univ. 22-23, 25-28, Chair. Dept. of Art and Archaeology 55-64, Marquand Prof. 61-66; Assoc. Prof. History of Art and Chair. of Dept., Northwestern Univ. 31-34, Prof. 34-40; Prof. Smith Coll. 41-48, Columbia Univ. 48-54, New York Univ. 54-55; Editor-in-Chief *Art Bulletin* 42-44; mem. Inst. for Advanced Study 39, 42-44, 46-47; Chair. Cttee. on Research and Publication in the Fine Arts 42-44, Protection of Cultural Treasures in War Areas 44-46; Pres. Coll. Art Asscn. of America 44-46; mem. Board of Dirs. American Council of Learned Socs. 53-61; mem. Board of Dirs. and Trustee, Renaissance Soc. of America 60-69; Harris Lecturer, Northwestern Univ. 66; Pres. American Acad. in Rome 68-71; Vice-Pres., Int. Fed. of Renaissance Socs. and Insts. 61-70; Vice-Pres. Union Académique Internationale 62-65; Vice-Pres. Int. Council for Philosophy and Humanistic Studies 65-71; Chair. Pres. Advisory Cttee. Yale Center for British Art and British Studies 72-; Fellow, American Acad. of Arts and Sciences; Hon. L.H.D. (Northwestern Univ.).
Leisure interests: travel, music, ornithology.
Publs. *Ut pictura poesis: The Humanistic Theory of Painting* 40, new edn. 67, Italian edn. 74, *Names on Trees: Ariosto into Art* 76.
120 Merser Street, Princeton, N.J. 08540, U.S.A.
Telephone: 924-2401.

Lee, General Robert Merrill; American air force officer; b. 1909, Hinsdalt, N.H.; s. of Merrill T. Lee and Maisie Townsend; m. 1st Mary Hall Van Pelt 1940 (died 1973), 2nd Mary Donnellan 1974; three s.; ed. U.S. Military Acad., West Point, Air Corps Flying Schools, Air Corps Tactical School and Nat. War Coll.
55th Pursuit Squadron 32-37, First Cavalry (Mechanized) 37-38, 12th Observation Squadron 38-40, Commdr. 40-41, Chief of Corps Aviation 41-42, Commdr. 73rd Observation Group 42-43, Chief of Staff, 1st Air Support Command 43-44, Dep. Commd. Gen. for Operations and Chief of Staff, Ninth Air Force, Western Europe 44-45, Air Section, Theater Gen. Board, Europe 45, Chief of Staff, Tactical Air Commd. Virginia 46; Nat. War Coll. 46-47; Dep. Commd. Gen., Tactical Air Comnd., Langley Field, Virginia 47-48, Commd. Gen. 48-50, Commdr. Air Task Group 3.4 for Atomic Bomb Tests *Greenhouse* 50-51, Dir. of Plans, Deputy Chief of Staff for Operations, Headquarters USAF 51-53, Commdr. Fourth Allied Tactical Air Force 53-57, of Twelfth United States Air Force in Europe 53-56, Commdr. Ninth Air Force Tactical Air Command 57-58, Chief of Staff, United Nations Command, United States Forces, Korea 58-59, Vice-Commdr. Air Defense Command 59-61, Commdr., Air Defense Command 61-63, Air Deputy to Supreme Allied Commdr. Europe, NATO 63-66; Distinguished Service Medal, Legion of Merit, Grand Officer Legion of Honour (France), Hon. C.B.E. and other decorations.
Leisure interests: shooting, hunting, fishing, golf, squash raquets, skin-diving.
318 Pine Avenue, Colorado Springs, Colo. 80906, U.S.A.
Telephone: 303-473-7546.

Lee Tsung-dao, PH.D.; Chinese physicist; b. 1926; ed. National Chekiang Univ., National Southwest Univ. (China) and Univ. of Chicago.
Research Assoc. in Astronomy, Univ. of Chicago 50, Research Assoc. and Lecturer in Physics, Univ. of California 50-51; mem. Inst. for Advanced Study, Princeton, N.J. 51-53; Asst. Prof. of Physics Columbia Univ. 53-55; Assoc. Prof. 55-56 and Prof. 56-60, 63-; Prof. Princeton Inst. for Advanced Study 60-63; mem. Nat. Acad. of Sciences; Nobel Prize in Physics 57; Albert Einstein Award in Science 57.
Publs. articles in physical journals.

Department of Physics, Columbia University, Morningside Heights, New York, N.Y. 10027; 25 Claremont Avenue, New York, N.Y. 10027, U.S.A.

Lee Yong Leng; Singapore diplomatist; b. 26 March 1930, Singapore; s. of Lee Choon Eng and Lim Swee Joo; m. Wong Loon Meng 1957; one d.; ed. Univ. of Singapore and St. Anthony's Coll., Oxford.
Lecturer and Prof. Univ. of Singapore 56-70; High Commr. to U.K. 71-75.
Leisure interests: swimming, tennis, reading, travel.
Publs. *North Borneo* 65, *Population and Settlement in Sarawak* 70.
c/o Ministry of Foreign Affairs, Singapore.

Lee of Asheridge, Baroness (Life Peeress), cr. 70, of the City of Westminster; **Jennie Lee,** P.C., M.A., LL.D.; widow of late Rt. Hon. Aneurin Bevan; British politician; b. 3 Nov. 1904; ed. Edinburgh Univ.
Member of Parliament for North Lanark 29-31, Cannock 45-70; Parl. Sec. Ministry of Public Building and Works 64-65; Minister for the Arts and Under-Sec. of State, Dept. of Educ. and Science 65-67, Minister for the Arts and Minister of State, Dept. of Educ. and Science 67-70; Dir. *Tribune*; mem. Cen. Advisory Cttee. on Housing; mem. Nat. Exec. Cttee., Labour Party 58-70, Chair. 67-68.
Publs. *Tomorrow is a New Day* 39, *Our Ally, Russia* 41, *This Great Journey* 63.
65 Chester Row, London, S.W.1, England.

Lee of Newton, Baron (Life Peer), cr. 74, of Newton in the County of Merseyside; **Frederick Lee,** P.C.; British politician; b. 3 Aug. 1906; ed. Langworthy Road School.
Former Engineer, Chair. Works Cttee. Metro-Vickers Ltd., Trafford Park, Manchester; mem. Nat. Cttee. Amalgamated Eng. Union 44-45; M.P. 45-74; fmr. Parl. Private Sec. to Chancellor of Exchequer; Parl. Sec., Ministry of Labour 50-51; Minister of Power 64-66; Sec. of State for Colonies 66-67; Chancellor of Duchy of Lancaster 67-Oct. 69, taking special responsibility for the North Oct. 67-Oct. 69; Labour.
Sunnyside, 52 Ashton Road, Newton-le-Willows, Lancs., England.

Leemans, Victor; Belgian writer and politician; b. 1901, Stekene; m. Reimonda De Rijcker 1932; three s. two d.
Member Belgian Senate 49-, European Parl. 58-69; Pres. Christian Democrat Group of Belgian Senate 64.
Leisure interests: sociology, fine arts.
Prins Albertlei 8, 2600 Berchem-Antwerp, Belgium.
Telephone: Antwerp 03-30-97-89.

Leer-Andersen, Rt. Rev. Jens Bagh; Danish ecclesiastic; b. 25 Nov. 1910, Skagen; s. of Jacob Andersen and Mette (née Sorensen); m. Inga Grethe Rasmussen; one s. one d.; ed. Stenhus Coll., Holboek, and Univ. of Copenhagen.
Minister Groendals Church, Copenhagen 36-40, Blistrup 40-47; Sec. Church Fund of Copenhagen 47-50, Exec. Sec. 50-56; Minister of St. Olaf's Church, Elsinore 56-61; Bishop of Elsinore diocese 61-.
Heslehøj Alle 4, 2900 Hellerup, Denmark.
Telephone: HE-9312.

Le Fèvre de Montigny, Gillis Johannis; Netherlands army officer; b. 1901; ed. Breda Royal Mil. Acad., General Staff Coll.
2nd Lieut. Artillery 22; until 32 with Garrison Artillery Regiment, and 1st and 2nd Field-Artillery Regiments; Staff Coll. 32-35; A.D.C. to Chief of Gen. Staff 37-38; Chief of Staff 4th Div. 39-40; prisoner of war in Germany 42-45; attached to Mil. Cabinet of Ministry of War 45-47; Asst. Chief of Staff, G.5 (Training) 47-50; Chief of Staff 1 (NL) Corps. 50-53; Deputy Chief of Staff, Allied Forces in Central Europe (N.A.T.O. H.Q.) 53; Deputy Chief of Staff (Operations and Intelligence),

Royal Netherlands Army 55; Vice-Chief of Gen. Staff Apr. 57, Chief of Gen. Staff, C.-in-C., Netherlands Land Forces 57- 62; Chair. Joint Chiefs of Staff 62-65; A.D.C. Extraordinary of H.M. Queen Juliana 62-.
Hasseltse Straat 19, The Hague, Netherlands.
Telephone: 553328.

Lefol, Lucien, D. EN D.; French industrialist; b. 21 April 1891; ed. Ecole Polytechnique, Ecole du Génie Maritime.
Naval engineer 13; joined Société des Ateliers & Chantiers de France as engineer 21, Chief Engineer 23, Dir. 25, Dir.-Gen. 29, Pres. 43, now Prés. d'Honneur; Administrateur Prés. d'Honneur Cie. des Forges et Aciéries de la Marine et de Saint-Etienne; Vice-Pres. Admin. Council Sidelor, and Chamber of Shipbuilders and Marine Engineers; mem. Admin. Council Cie. Auxiliaire de Navigation, Cie. de Construction Mécanique Sulzer, Technical Maritime and Aeronautical Asscn., Ateliers & Forges de la Loire, Soc. des Mines et Usines de Redange-Dilling, Charbonnages de Beeringen, Aciéries et Forges de Firminy, Forges & Chantiers de la Gironde; mem. Inst. of Naval Architects, Soc. of Naval Architects, Soc. of Naval Architects and Marine Engineers; corresp. mem. Acad. de la Marine; Commdr. de la Légion d'Honneur; Croix de Guerre 14-18; Commdr. du Mérite Maritime.
4 rue Mignard, Paris 16e, France.

Le Fort, Jean-Louis, L. EN D.; Swiss international civil servant; b. 26 Dec. 1917; s. of Jacques Le Fort and Cecil Roux; m. Christiane Courvoisier 1946; three s.; ed. Univ. of Geneva.
Secretary, Swiss Asscn. of Bankers, Basle 43-47; Sec. Groupement des Holdings Industriels, Vevey and Berne 47-56; Principal Administrator, OECD, Paris 56-58; Sec.-Gen. Inst. Battelle, Geneva Labs. 58-70; Sec.-Gen. Int. Red Cross 70-72.
3 route de Florissant, 1206 Geneva, Switzerland.
Telephone: 46-56-28.

Le Gallienne, Eva; American actress, director and author; b. 11 Jan. 1899, London, England; d. of Richard Le Gallienne and Julie Norregaard; ed. Coll. Sévigné, Paris.
Debut in London in *The Laughter of Fools* 15; in N.Y. starred in *Liliom* 22, *The Swan* 23; founded Civic Repertory Theatre in N.Y. City 26; played and produced there some 40 plays, including Ibsen's *Master Builder*, *Hedda Gabler*, *John Gabriel Borkman*, Chekhov's *The Cherry Orchard*, *The Seagull*, Sierra's *The Cradle Song*, Giraudoux' *Siegfried*, Dumas' *Camille*, Shakespeare's *Romeo and Juliet* and *Twelfth Night*, Barrie's *Peter Pan*, Molière's *Would-be Gentleman*, Carroll's *Alice in Wonderland*, etc.; subsequently appeared on Broadway in Rostand's *L'Aiglon*, Job's *Uncle Harry*, Shakespeare's *Henry VIII*, Ibsen's *Rosmersholm* and *Ghosts*, Williams' *The Corn is Green*; Elizabeth I in Schiller's *Mary Stuart* in New York and on tour 58-60, and in Maxwell Anderson's *Elizabeth The Queen* on tour 61-62; on tour in Chekhov's *The Seagull* and Anouilh's *Ring Round the Moon* 62-63 and in *The Trojan Women* and *The Mad Woman of Chaillot* 65-66; with A.P.A. Repertory Co., N.Y. City, in Ionesco's *Exit the King*, directed Chekhov's *The Cherry Orchard* 67-68, Ibsen's *A Doll's House*, Seattle Rep. 75; played in *All's Well That Ends Well* at the American Shakespeare Festival Theatre, Stratford, Conn. 70, Mrs. Woodfin in *The Dream Watcher* at the White Barn Theatre 75, Fanny Cavendish in *The Royal Family* at the Kennedy Center; Man. Dir. of American Rep. Theatre 46-47; Hon. M.A. (Tufts Univ.), Litt.D. (Russell Sage and Mt. Holyoke Colls.), D.H.L. (Smith Coll. and Univ. of N. Carolina), Litt.D. (Brown Univ. and Univ. of Fairfield), Gold Medal Soc. of Arts and Sciences, Gold Medal American Acad. of Arts and Letters, Cross of St. Olav (Norway).
Leisure interests: gardening, bird watching.

Publs. *At 33* (autobiography) 34, *Alice in Wonderland* (stage version, French edn.), *Flossie and Bossie* 49, *With a Quiet Heart* 53, *Six Plays by Henrik Ibsen* (translation) 58, *Seven Tales by H. C. Andersen* (trans.) 59, *The Wild Duck and other Plays by Ibsen* (trans.) 61, H. C. Andersen's *The Nightingale* (trans.) 65, *The Mystic in the Theatre: Eleonora Duse* 66.
North Hillside Road, Weston, Conn. 06880, U.S.A.

Legaz, Lacambra Luis; Spanish university professor; b. 1906; *m.* Carmen L. Niño 1937; ed. Colegio de Escolapios, Saragossa, Univs. of Saragossa, Madrid, Grenoble, Munich, Vienna, and Acad. de Droit Internat., The Hague.
Doctor of Law 32; Asst. Prof. Univ. Saragossa 32; Prof. Univ. La Laguna 35, Univ. Santiago de Compostela 35, Rector, Univ. Santiago de Compostela 42-60; Prof., Univ. of Madrid 60-; Under-Sec. Ministry of Nat. Education 62-68; award from Coimbra Univ.; Dir. Inst. de Estudios Políticos, Madrid 70-74; mem. Inst. Int. de Sociologie, Real Acad. de Ciencias Morales y Políticas, Madrid, Real Acad. de Jurisprudencia y Legislación, Fac. Int. pour l'Enseignement du Droit Comparé, Strasbourg, Int. Acad. for Comparative Law.
Leisure interest: music.
Publs. *Kelsen: Estudio Crítico* 33, *El Estado de Derecho* 35, *Introducción a la Ciencia del Derecho* 43, *Horizontes del Pensamiento Jurídico* 47, *Derecho y Libertad* 52, *Filosofía del Derecho* 53, *Justicia, Derecho y seguridad* 54, *La Obligación Política* 56, *La Función del Derecho en la Sociedad Contemporánea* 56, *Political Obligation and Natural Law* 57, *Lógica y pensamiento jurídico* 57, *Humanismo, Estado y Derecho* 59, *La Realidad del Derecho* 63, *Rechtsphilosophie* 65, *Socialización* 64, *Amor, Amistad, Justicia* 69, *Socialización, Administración, Desarrollo* 71, *Problemas y Tendencias de la Filosofía del Derecho Contemporánea* 71.
Ministro Ibáñez Martín 4, Madrid 15, Spain.
Telephone: 2432571.

Léger, Jacques; Haitian international official; b. Port-au-Prince; *s.* of Abel N. Léger and Lucie Elie; *m.* Maria Teresa Livieres Argaña 1959; five *c.*; ed. Faculty of Law, Univ. of Haiti.
Attached to Protocol Sec., Dept. of State 34-35; Sec. to Sec. of State for Foreign Affairs 35-36; service with legation in Venezuela; Dir. Haiti Service of Inter-American Affairs; Chargé d'Affaires, Venezuela 44-47; Amb. to Cuba 47-48, to Argentina and Brazil 48-50; Sec. of State for Foreign Affairs 50-51; Amb. to U.S.A. and Canada 52-56; Perm. Rep. to UN 56-57; research activities, N.Y. Public Library and Library of Congress 57-59; translator 59-63; UNDP Regional Rep., Ivory Coast 64-67, Democratic Republic of Congo (now Zaire) 67-69, N. W. Africa 69-72, Kuwait 72-; Grand Officier de la Légion d'Honneur (France) and other decorations.
Leisure interests: music (classics), reading, swimming.
c/o United Nations Development Programme, P.O. Box 2993, Kuwait City, Kuwait.

Léger, Jules, C.C., C.D. (brother of H.E. Cardinal Paul Emile Léger, *q.v.*); Canadian diplomatist and governor-general; b. 4 April 1913, Saint-Anicet, P.Q.; *s.* of Ernest and Alda Léger (née Beauvais); *m.* Gaby Carmel 1938; one *d.*; ed. Collège de Valleyfield, Univs. of Montreal and Paris.
Associate Editor *Le Droit*, Ottawa 38-39; joined Dept. of External Affairs 40; Prof. of History of Diplomacy, Univ. of Ottawa 40-42; Canadian Mission to Chile 43-47, London 47, Gen. Assembly of UN, Paris 48-49; Head European Div., Dept. of External Affairs 50-51; Asst. Under-Sec. of State for External Affairs 51-53; Amb. to Mexico 53-54; Under-Sec. of State 54-58; Amb. and Perm. Rep. to NATO, Rep. to OEEC 58-62; Amb. to Italy 62-64, to France 64-68; Under-Sec. of

State 68-73; Amb. to Belgium and Luxembourg 73; Gov.-Gen. of Canada Jan. 74-.
Government House, Ottawa, Ont., K1A 0A1, Canada.

Léger, H.E. Cardinal Paul Emile, L.TH., J.C.L. (brother of Jules Léger, *q.v.*); Canadian ecclesiastic; b. 26 April 1904, Valleyfield; ed. Grand Séminaire of Montreal and Paris.
Ordained at Montreal May 29; Prof. Issy Séminaire (near Paris) 31-32; Asst. Master of Novices, Saint-Sulpice, Paris 32-33; Founder-Superior at Fukuoka Seminary, Japan 33-39; Prof. Montreal Seminary of Philosophy 39-40; Vicar-Gen. and Cathedral Pastor Valleyfield 40-47; Rector of Canadian Coll., Rome 47-50; elected to Episcopal See 50 and enthroned as Archbishop of Montreal May 50, resigned as Archbishop of Montreal Nov. 67 to become missionary in leper colonies, W. Africa; elevated to Cardinal, with title of St. Mary of the Angels 53; papal legate to closing of the Marian Year at Lourdes 54, to crowning of statue of St. Joseph at Montreal 55, to St. Anne de Beaupré Tercentenary P.Q. 58; numerous hon. degrees; Knight Grand Cross Légion d'Honneur (France), Equestrian Order of Holy Sepulchre (Jerusalem); Sovereign Order of Malta; Order of Canada Medal; Grand Cross de Benemerencia (Portugal), etc.
1071 Cathedral Street, Montreal 3, P.Q., Canada.

Le Goy, Raymond Edgar Michel; British civil servant; b. 1919; *s.* of J. A. S. M. N. and May Le Goy; *m.* Ernestine Burnett 1960; two *s.*; ed. William Ellis School, London, Gonville and Caius Coll., Cambridge.
British Army 40-46; entered Civil Service 47, Asst. Principal, Road Transport Div., Ministry of Transport 47-48; various posts in shipping and highways divs., U.K. Shipping Adviser in Far East and S.E. Asia; Ministry of Transport and Civil Aviation 48-58; Asst. Sec. Railways and Inland Waterways Div., Ministry of Transport and Civil Aviation 58-59; Asst. Sec. Finance and Supply Ground Services and Aerodrome Management, Ministry of Aviation 59-61, Dir. of Admin. Navigational Services 61-62; Asst. Sec. Aviation Overseas Policy, Ministry of Aviation and Board of Trade 62-68; Under-Sec. of Civil Aviation 68-73; Head del. to European Civil Aviation Conf.; Dir.-Gen. of Transport, Comm. of European Communities 73-.
Leisure interests: theatre, music, race relations.
Directorate-General of Transport, Commission of the European Communities, 120 rue de la Loi, 1040 Brussels, Belgium.
Telephone: 73500-40.

Lehel, György; Hungarian conductor; b. 10 Feb. 1926, Budapest; *s.* of László Lehel and Klara Ladányi; *m.* Dr. Zsuzsa Markovits 1969; one *s.*; studied composition with Pál Kadosa and conducting with László Somogyi.
Conductor Symphonic Orchestra of Hungarian Radio 47-62, Chief Conductor and Music Dir. 62-; propagates contemporary Hungarian music; has conducted in Czechoslovakia, Poland, Switzerland, Austria, Soviet Union, Italy, Romania, France, Belgium, German Democratic Republic, German Fed. Republic, Yugoslavia, Great Britain, U.S.A. and Japan; Liszt Prize 55, 62; Merited Artist of the Hungarian Repub. 68; Kossuth Prize 2nd Degree 73; numerous recordings.
Leisure interests: literature, arts.
Symphonic Orchestra of Hungarian Radio, Bródy Sándor u. 5-7, 1800 Budapest VIII; Home: Istenhegyi-ut 48/A, H-1125 Budapest, Hungary.
Telephone: 366-993.

Lehmann, Ernst, DR.RER.POL.; Israeli banker; b. 29 April 1902, Berlin; *s.* of Eugen and Elsa Lehmann (née Bachrach); *m.* Nelly Frank 1926; one *s.*; ed. Berlin and Munich Univs.
Worked for several banks in Germany 24-35; migrated

to Palestine, apptd. Man. The Gen. Mortgage Bank of Palestine Ltd. 35; Man. Issue Dept., Anglo-Israel Bank Ltd. (now Bank Leumi le-Israel) dealt with issue of currency of Israel and admin. of Govt. Loans 48; Chair. Board of Dirs. Bank Leumi le-Israel B.M. 70-, Gen. Mortgage Bank Ltd., Bank Leumi (France) Ltd., Bank Leumi (Schweiz) Ltd.; mem. Board Bank Leumi (U.K.) Ltd.; Chair. Board of Dirs. Migdal-Binyan Insurance Co. Ltd., Africa-Israel Investment Ltd., Tel-Aviv Stock Exchange Ltd., Ihud Insurance Agencies Ltd.; mem. Advisory Council, Bank of Israel. Leisure interests: economic history, history of art, archaeology.
Publs. various articles on financial and currency problems.
23 Benjamin Street, 52 512 Ramat-Gan, Israel.
Telephone: 721904.

Lehmann, Inge; Danish seismologist; b. 13 May 1888, Copenhagen; d. of Prof. Alfred G. L. Lehmann and Ida Tørsleff; ed. Univ. of Copenhagen.
State geodesist; Chief Seismological Dept., Danish Geodetic Inst. 28-53; Hon. Sc.D. (Columbia Univ., N.Y.), Dr. Phil. h.c. (Copenhagen); Assoc. Royal Astronomical Soc. 57, Hon. F.R.S.E. 59, Foreign mem. Royal Soc. 69; Harry Oscar Wood Award in Seismology 60, Emil Wiechert Medal, Deutsche Geophysikalische Gesellschaft 64, Gold Medal, Royal Danish Acad. of Sciences and Letters 65, William Bowie Medal of American Geophysical Union 71.
Leisure interests: gardening, mountain walks.
Publs. 57 Seismological publications in various journals.
Kastelsvej 26, 2100 Copenhagen, Denmark.
Telephone: TR 408.

Lehmann, John Frederick (brother of Rosamond Lehmann, q.v.), C.B.E., F.R.S.L.; British author and editor; b. 2 June 1907, Bourne End; s. of Rudolph Chambers Lehmann and Alice Marie Davis; ed. Eton and Trinity Coll., Cambridge.
Founder and Editor of New Writing (including The Penguin New Writing and New Writing and Daylight) and of Orpheus; Partner and Gen. Man. The Hogarth Press 38-46; Man. Dir. John Lehmann Ltd. 46-53; Advisory Ed. The Geographical Magazine 40-45; Ed. New Soundings (BBC) 52-53; Ed. The London Magazine 54-61; Pres. Alliance Française in Great Britain 54-63; Pres. Royal Literary Fund 66-76; Visiting Prof. (English) Univ. of Texas at Austin 70-71, State Univ. of Calif. at San Diego 70-72, Univ. of Calif. at Berkeley 74; Grand Officier Etoile Noire, Officier Légion d'Honneur, Officier Ordre des Arts et des Lettres, Commdr. Order of George I (Greece); William Foyle Poetry Prize 64.
Leisure interests: reading, swimming, gardening.
Publs. A Garden Revisited 31, Evil was Abroad 38, Down River 39, New Writing in Europe 40, The Age of the Dragon 51, The Open Night 52, The Whispering Gallery (autobiography) 55, I Am My Brother (autobiography 2) 60, Ancestors and Friends 62, Collected Poems 63, Christ the Hunter 65, The Ample Proposition (autobiography) 66, A Nest of Tigers 68, In My Own Time (U.S.A. 69), Holborn 70, The Reader at Night (poems) 74, Virginia Woolf and Her World 75, and editor of many anthologies and symposia.
85 Cornwall Gardens, London, S.W.7, England.

Lehmann, Lotte; retd. American singer; b. 27 Feb. 1888, Perleberg, Germany; d. of Carl and Marie (Schuster) Lehmann; m. Otto Krause 1926 (died 1939); four step-children.; ed. Königliche Hochschule für Musik, Berlin.
Sang at Vienna State Opera, Metropolitan Opera, New York, Covent Garden, London and in most countries of Europe, and throughout the U.S.A. and South America and Australia; Hon. Pres. Music Acad. of the West, Santa Barbara Golden Palm of France, Officer of the Legion of Honour, Golden Medal of Sweden, Golden Medal of Austria, Cross of Honour First Class (Austria) Great Cross of Germany; four honorary degrees.
Publs. Midway in my song, More than singing, My many lives, Eternal Flight, Five Operas and Richard Strauss, Eighteen Songcycles.
4565 Via Huerto, Hope Ranch Park, Santa Barbara, Calif. 93105, U.S.A.

Lehmann, Rosamond Nina (sister of John Lehmann, q.v.); British novelist; ed. Girton Coll., Cambridge.
Publs. Dusty Answer 27, A Note in Music 30, Invitation to the Waltz 32, The Weather in the Streets 36, No More Music (play) 39, The Ballad and the Source 44, The Gypsy's Baby 46, The Echoing Grove 53, The Swan in the Evening 67.
70 Eaton Square, London, S.W.1, England.

Lehnartz, Emil Friedrich Robert, C.B.E., M.D.; Emer. German university professor; b. 29 June 1898, Remscheid; s. of Emil Lehnartz and Maria Weisenfeld; m. 1st Margarete Zimmermann 1927, 2nd Eva von Königslöw 1955; one s. three d.; ed. Cologne, Frankfurt a.M., and Freiburg i.Br.
Assistant Physiological-Chemical Inst., Frankfurt a.M. 26; Reader of Physiology 29, Extra. Prof. 35; Chief Asst. Physiological Inst., Göttingen 35; Dir. of Physiological-Chemical Inst., Münster i.W. 39-66, Prof. 46; Rector Münster Univ. 46-49; Chair. Deutsche-Englische Gesellschaft 49-69; Pres. Deutscher Akademischer Austauschdienst 59-68; mem. New York Acad. of Science, Dr. Phil. h.c. and Dr. h.c.; Grosses Bundesverdienstkreuz mit Stern, Officier Légion d'Honneur.
Publs. Die chemischen Vorgänge bei der Muskelkontraktion 33, Lehrbuch der Physiologie für Studierende der Zahnheilkunde (with E. Fischer) 34, Einfuhrung in die Chemische Physiologie (11th edition) 59; collaborated in Ernährungslehre (Editor W. Stepp) 39, Handbuch der Biologie (Editor L. v. Bertalanffy) and Die Ernährung (Editors K. Lang and R. Schön); Joint Editor: Physiologische Chemie (with B. Flaschenträger), Hoppe-Seyler/Thierfelder Handbuch der Physiologische- und Pathologisch-Chemischen Analyse (10th edn., with K. Lang and G. Siebert), Klinische Wochenschrift (co-editor), Medizinische Klinik (co-editor).
Maldmedyweg 11, 44 Münster i.W., Federal Republic of Germany.
Telephone: 81233.

Lehninger, Albert Lester, PH.D.; American professor of physiological chemistry; b. 17 Feb. 1917; s. of Albert O. and Wally S. Lehninger; m. Janet Wilson 1942; one s. one d.; ed. Wesleyan Univ. and Univ. of Wis.
Instructor, Dept. of Physiological Chem., Univ. of Wis. 42-45; Asst. Prof. Dept. of Biochem., Univ. of Chicago 45-49; Assoc. Prof. 49-52; DeLamar Prof. and Dir., Dept. of Physiological Chem., Johns Hopkins School of Medicine 52-; mem. Nat. Acad. of Sciences 56, American Phil. Soc. 72, Inst. of Medicine, Nat. Acad. of Sciences 74-(79), Presidents' Panel on Biomedial Research 75-76, Deutsche Akad. der Naturforscher Leopoldina 76-; Hon. D.Sc. (Wesleyan and Acadia Univs., Memorial Univ. of Newfoundland, Univ. of Notre Dame), Hon. M.D. (Medical Faculty, Univ. of Padua); Paul Lewis Award in Enzyme Chem. 48, Distinguished Service Award, Univ. of Chicago 65, Remsen Award, American Chem. Soc. 69, Fifth Jubilee Lecturer, Biochemical Soc. 70.
Leisure interests: golf, sailing.
Publs. The Mitochondrion 64, Bioenergetics 65 (2nd edn. 71), Biochemistry (textbook) 70 (2nd edn. 75), Short Course in Biochemistry 73, and over 250 papers on biochemistry of energy transformation in cells, particularly in the mitochondrion 42-.
Department of Physiological Chemistry, The Johns Hopkins School of Medicine, 725 North Wolfe Street, Baltimore, Md. 21205, U.S.A.
Telephone: 301-955-3110.

Lehrman, Daniel Sanford, PH.D.; American psychobiologist; b. 1 June 1919, New York City; s. of Philip Lehrman and Sophie Rubenstein; m. Dorothy Dinnerstein 1962; three d.; ed. City Coll. of New York and New York Univ.
Served, U.S.A.F. 41-45; Assoc. Psychologist, Haskins Labs., N.Y. 45-47; Lecturer in Psychology, City Coll. of N.Y. 47-50; Instructor in Psychology, N.Y. Univ. 50; Asst. Prof., Rutgers Univ. 50-56; Assoc. Prof. 56-58, Prof. of Psychology 58-, Dir. Inst. of Animal Behaviour 59-; Visiting Prof., Yale Univ. 57; mem. Nat. Acad. of Sciences, Soc. of Experimental Psychologists, American Ornithologists Union, American Soc. of Zoologists, Soc. for Experimental Biology and Medicine, Soc. for Neuroscience, Int. Brain Research Org.; Fellow, American Psychol. Asscn.; non-Res. Fellow, The Salk Inst.; Howard Crosby Warren Medal, Soc. of Experimental Psychologists.
Leisure interests: bird watching, sailing, cooking.
Publs. Numerous articles in scientific journals, contributions to encyclopedias and symposia.
Institute of Animal Behaviour, Rutgers University, Newark, N.J. 07102, U.S.A.
Telephone: 201-648-5225.

Lehto, Reino Ragnar; Finnish civil servant and politician; b. 2 May 1898; ed. Helsinki Univ.
Solicitor, Turku 22-32; Sec. to Chancellor of Justice 33-34; Solicitor to Landed Property Bank 34-36; Cabinet Counsellor and Sec.-Gen. Ministry of Commerce and Industry 36- (leave of absence 63-64); Chief Sec. Delegation for War Reparation Industries 44-48; Dir. Outokumpu Oy, Valmet Oy, Neste Oy, Oy Rego AB, Merikiito Oy, Orijärvi Oy; Prime Minister 63-64; Gov. of Uusimaa 64-; several decorations.
Nuorimichenkatu 11A, Helsinki, Finland.

Leibholz, Gerhard, DR. JURIS., DR. PHIL.; German scholar; b. 15 Nov. 1901, Berlin; s. of Councillor W. Leibholz and Régina (née Netter); m. Sabine Bonhoeffer 1926; two d.; ed. Berlin and Heidelberg.
Assistant Judge 26; Referent Inst. for Public Law, Berlin 26; Lecturer in Constitutional and Int. Law, Berlin 28; Judge 28; Prof. of Public Law and Political Science, Greifswald 29-31, Göttingen 31-35, Prof. Emer. Jan. 36-58; Fellowship World Council of Churches and Magdalen Coll., Oxford 39-48; Prof. Göttingen 58-, Coll. of Europe, Bruges 54-; Assoc. Justice Fed. Constitutional Court (Germany) 51-71; Editor Jahrbuch des öffentlichen Rechts 51-.
Publs. Fichte und der demokratische Gedanke 21, Zu den Problemen des faschistischen Verfassungsrechts 28, Die Auflösung der liberalen Demokratie und das autoritäre Staatsbild 33, Il Secolo XIX e lo Stato totalitario 38, Syndicalisme, Corporatisme et Etat Corporatif 39 (2nd edn. 58), Christianity, Politics and Power 42, Macht und Ideologie im 20. Jahrhundert 49, Staat und Gesellschaft in England 50, Der Strukturwandel der Demokratie 52, Demokratie und Rechtsstaat 57 (3rd edn. 67), Volk, Nation, Staat im 20. Jahrhundert 58 (3rd edn. 67), Strukturprobleme der modernen Demokratie 58 (4th edn. 74; Korean trans. 62), Die Gleichheit vor dem Gesetz (2nd edn. 59), Das Wesen der Repräsentation (4th edn.) 73, Verfassungsrecht und Arbeitsrecht 60, Verbot des Ermessensmissbrauches im Völkerrecht (2nd edn.) 64, Conceptos fundamentales de la Política 64, Politics and Law 65, Kommentar zum Bonner Grundgesetz 66 (4th edn. 71) (with Dr. Rinck), Stellung der Industrie-und Handels kammern 67, Demokratie und Erziehung 67, Kommentar zum Bundesverpassungs gerichts gesetz (with R. Rupprecht) 68 (appendix 71), Problemas Fundamentales de la Democracia Moderna 71, Verfassungsrecht-Verfassungsstaat 72, Korrespondenz zwischen George Bell (Bishop of Chichester) und Gerhard Leibholz (1939-51) 74; and about 200 articles in periodicals in more than 20 countries (see Bibliography by F. Schneider, 1972).

34 Göttingen, Herzberger Landstrasse 57, Federal Republic of Germany.
Telephone: Göttingen 57040.

Leiding, Rudolf Wilhelm Karl; German motor executive; b. 4 Sept. 1914, Busch, Kr. Osterburg/ Altmark; ed. engineering school.
Joined Volkswagenwerk, Wolfsburg after Second World War; Man. VW Plant, Kassel 58, also Dir. Volkswagenwerk A.G.; Man. and Chair. Man. Board, Auto Union G.m.b.H. (subsidiary of VW Group) 65-68; Head, VW do Brasil (Brazilian subsidiary) 68-71; Chair. Man. Board, AUDI NSU Auto Union A.G. April-Sept. 71; Chair. Man. Board, Volkswagenwerk A.G. 71-Dec. 74; Orden de Merito de Trabalho (Brazil) 73.
Volkswagenwerk A.G., 3180 Wolfsburg, Federal Republic of Germany.

Leigh Guzmán, Gen. Gustavo; Chilean air force officer; b. 19 Sept. 1920; m. Gabriela García Powdich; three s. one d.; ed. Liceo José Victorino Lastarria, Mil. Acad., Nat. Defence Acad.
Postgraduate studies specializing in Supply and Maintenance, Command and Staff; Academic Instructor of Operations and Logistics; Deputy Commdr. Group 11 53; Commdr. Group 10 61; Commdr. of Supply Wing 63; Air Attaché to U.S.A. 64; Sec.- Gen. Chilean Air Force 66; Dir. Aviation School 68; Chief of Gen. Staff 71; C.-in-C. of Chilean Air Force; mem. Mil. Junta 73-; many mil. decorations including Grand Mil Merit Cross, Mil. Star, and Nat. Order of Merit (Paraguay), Legion of Merit (U.S.A.), Grand Cross for Aeronautical Merit (Spain), and others.
Junta Militar de Gobierno, Santiago, Chile.

Leighton, Robert Benjamin, M.S., PH.D.; American physicist; b. 10 Sept. 1919, Detroit, Mich.; s. of George B. Leighton and Olga O. Homrig; m. Alice M. Winger 1943; two s. one d.; ed. Calif. Inst. of Technology.
Research Fellow, Calif. Inst. of Technology 47-49, Asst. Prof. 49-53, Assoc. Prof. 53-59, Prof. of Physics 59-, Chair. Physics, Mathematics and Astronomy Div. 70-75, also mem. of staff of Hale Observatories; mem. Nat. Acad. of Sciences; A.I.A.A. Award 67.
Leisure interests: astronomy, photography, optics, chamber music, reading, hiking.
Publs. Principles of Modern Physics 59, Feynman Lectures on Physics (co-author) 63; 36 articles in professional journals.
California Institute of Technology, Pasadena, Calif. 91125. U.S.A.

Leimgruber, Oscar, DR. JUR.; Swiss public servant; b. 5 July 1886, Fribourg; s. of Laurent Leimgruber and Magdalena Bieri; m. 1913; two s. one d.; ed. Fribourg, Berne and Vienna Univs.
Co-Dir. Cantonal Office of Arts and Crafts (Industrial Museum, Fribourg) 08-12; founder and Editor L'artisan et commerçant romands 09-25; Editor Liberté and Freiburger Zeitung 07-09; Cantonal advocate Uri; entered Federal State Service 12, first as mem. then Deputy Chief, Legal Dept. 12-19; Gen. Sec. Federal Post and Railways Dept. 19-25; founder and mem. Board Int. Middle Class Union 23; founder int. review La Classe Moyenne; organizer and Sec. first Int. Middle-Class Congress Berne and Interlaken 24; Gen. Commissar Congress, World Union of mems. of Parliaments 24; Founder and Deputy Pres. Int. Middle-Class Inst. 30; Founder-Pres. Int. Inst. of Admin. Sciences 30; Pres. a.i World Union of Int. Orgs.; Deputy Chancellor of Swiss Confederation 25-43, Chancellor 44-52; mem. Int. Acad. of Political Sciences, Swiss Section UNESCO, Cen. Cttee. Swiss Conservative People's Party and of Swiss Roman Catholic People's Union; Founder and Hon. Pres. Swiss Soc. for Nat. Admin.
Publs. Le problème social et la classe moyenne, Les buts et les tâches de l'Union Internationale des Classes moy-

ennes, Bericht über den ersten Internationalen Mittei-standskongress 24, Rationalisierung und Mittelstand, Gott und der Staat, Volk und Staat, Die Rationalisierung in Staat und Gemeinde, Christliche Wirtschaftsordnung und Mittelstand, Der Dienstvertrag nach schweizerischem Recht, Was Gläubiger und Schuldner von der Schuldbetreibung wissen müssen, Der Nachlassvertrag nach schweiz. Recht, Die Rationalisierung in den öffentlichen Verwaltungen, Dictionnaire populaire du droit usuel suisse, Manuel de droit civil à l'usage de l'hôtelier suisse.
Schanzeneckstrasse 17, 3000 Berne, Switzerland.
Telephone: 031-235888.

Lein, Voldemar Petrovich; Soviet politician; b. 7 July 1920, Bugrysh, Udmurtian A.S.S.R.; ed. Moscow Tech. Inst. of Food Industry and Higher Party School of C.P.S.U. Central Cttee.
Soviet Army 42-43; Section Chief, Dept. of Confectionery Industry, Food Ministry of Latvian S.S.R. 45-46; Engineer, "Laima" confectionery factory, Riga 46-49; Party work, Riga 49-; Higher Party School of C.P.S.U. Cen. Cttee. 56-58; Head, Main Dept. of Food Industry, Latvian Council of Nat. Econ. 58-60; Second Sec. Riga Town Cttee. of Latvian C.P. 60-61; Sec. Central Cttee. of Latvian C.P. 61-70; Deputy to U.S.S.R. Supreme Soviet 66-; U.S.S.R. Minister of Food Industry 70-; Alt. mem. Cen. Cttee. C.P.S.U. 71-; Orders of Lenin, Red Banner of Labour (twice), etc.
Ministry of Food Industry, 29 Building 4, Prospekt Kalinina, Moscow, U.S.S.R.

Leinsdorf, Erich; American musician; b. 4 Feb. 1912, Vienna, Austria; s. of Ludwig Julius and Charlotte (Loebl) Leinsdorf; m. 1st Anne Frohknecht 1939 (divorced 1968), 2nd Vera Graf 1968; three s. two d.; ed. Univ. of Vienna and State Acad. of Music, Vienna.
Assistant Conductor, Salzburg Festival 34-38; U.S.A. 37-; Conductor, Metropolitan Opera 37-43; Music Dir. and Conductor Cleveland Orchestra 43; Music Dir. Philharmonic Orchestra, Rochester 47-56; Dir. New York City Center Opera 56, Metropolitan Opera 57-62; Music Consultant, Metropolitan Opera Management 58-62: Music Dir. Boston Symphony Orchestra 62-69; Dir. Berkshire Music Center, Festival 63-69; former mem. Exec. Cttee. John F. Kennedy Center for the Performing Arts, Exec. Cttee. Corpn. for Public Broadcasting; mem. Mass. Council on the Arts and Humanities; Guest Conductor, Philadelphia Orchestra, New Orleans, Concertgebouw Amsterdam, San Francisco Orchestra, Vienna Opera, London Symphony, Cleveland Chicago Symphony, Boston Symphony, Metropolitan Opera and Israel Philharmonic Orchestras, etc.; Bayreuth, Holland and Prague Festivals; Fellow, American Acad. of Arts and Sciences: Hon. music degrees (Rutgers Univ. and Baldwin-Wallace, Columbia Univ. and Williams Colls.).
320 West 56th Street, New York, N.Y. 10019, U.S.A.

Leite, Antônio Dias, Jr.; Brazilian engineer and politician; b. 29 Jan. 1920, Rio de Janeiro; s. of Antônio Dias Leite and Georgeta Lahmeyer Leite; m. Manira Alcure Dias Leite 1944; two s. three d.; ed. Universidade Federal do Rio de Janeiro.
Professor of Economics, Univ. Federal do Rio de Janeiro; Under-Sec. for Econ. Affairs, Ministry of Finance 63; Pres. Companhia Vale do Rio Doce 67; Minister of Mines and Power 69-74; Economy Engineering Consultant 75.
Publs. *Caminhos do Desenvolvimento 66, Política Mineral e Energética 73.*
Universidade Federal do Rio de Janeiro, Avenida Pasteur, 250 Rio de Janeiro, RJ, Brazil.

Leito, Dr. B. M.; Netherlands Antilles economist and administrator; b. 6 Feb. 1923, Curaçao; m. 1951; two s. two d.; ed. Curaçao and Netherlands.

Junior Officer Netherlands Antilles Dept. of Social Affairs and Econ. Affairs 51; Officer Gen. Affairs Div., Curaçao 52, Finance Div. 53; mem. Curaçao Island Council 55-63; mem. Netherlands Antilles Parl. 59-62; Head of Finance Div., Curaçao 61-65; Dir. Netherlands Antilles Dept. of Finance 65-70; Pres. Supervisory Dirs. Bank of Netherlands Antilles 65-70; Chair. Socio-Econ. Council of Netherlands Antilles 67-70; Acting Lieut.-Gov. of Curaçao 68-70; Acting Gov. of Netherlands Antilles 69-70, Gov. 70-; several foreign decorations.
Governor's House, Fort Amsterdam No. 1, Willemstad, Curaçao, Netherlands Antilles.

Leivo-Larsson, Tyyne; Finnish politician; b. 3 March 1902.
Member Child Welfare Board 34-49; Chair. 45-59; Chair. Social Democratic Women's League 47-59, 65-; mem. and Deputy Chair. Helsinki City Council 47-56; mem. of several State cttees.; Minister of Social Affairs 48-50 and 54-57, 58; Dep. Prime Minister 58; Dir. Social Museum, Helsinki 40-58; Vice-Pres. Finnish Red Cross Org. 50-54; mem. Del. to UN 56-57, 66; Head Del. to Econ. and Soc. Council, UN 57-58; Amb. to Norway 58-65, and to Iceland 59-65; re-elected mem. of Parl. 66-70; mem. of Parl. Del. to the Congress of I.P.U. 66-70; mem. Nordic Councils Finnish Groups 66-70.
Temppelikatu 15, Helsinki, Finland.
Telephone: Helsinki 499353.

Lejczak, Włodzimierz; Polish politician; b. 1924, Cracow; ed. Acad. of Mining and Metallurgy, Cracow.
Worked for Zabrze Coal Industry Asscn. 48-65, Dir. Mikulczyce Colliery 52-60, Chief Engineer 61-65; Chair. Coal Mining Dept., Polish United Workers' Party Municipal Cttee. Zabrze 61-65; Vice-Pres. Supreme Mining Office 65-68; Under-Sec. of State, Ministry of Heavy Industry 68-70; Minister of Heavy Industry Dec. 70-; mem. Cen. Cttee. Polish United Workers' Party 71-; Commdr. and Officer's Cross of Order of Polonia Restituta, Order of Banner of Labour 2nd Class 74, Gold Cross of Merit 55 and other decorations.
Ministerstwo Premysłu Ciężkiego, ul. Krucza 48/52, 00-509 Warsaw, Poland.

Lejeune, Jérôme Jean Louis Marie, M.D., PH.D.; French geneticist; b. 13 June 1926, Montrouge; s. of Pierre Ulysse Lejeune and Marcelle Lermat; m. Birtke Bringsted 1959; two s. three d.; ed. Coll. Stanislas, Paris, Faculty of Medicine and Faculty of Sciences, Paris.
Centre National de la Recherche Scientifique (CNRS) 52-63, Dir. of Research 63-; Prof. of Fundamental Genetics, Univ. René Descartes 64-; mem. Pontifical Acad. of Sciences; Kennedy Prize.
Leisure interest: knowledge.
Publs. Discovery of the extra chromosome in Trisomy 21 (mongolism), research on human chromosomes, research on mental deficiency.
Institut de Progénèse, 15 rue de l'Ecole de Médecine, 75006 Paris; Home: 31 rue Galande, 75005 Paris, France.
Telephone: 326-5536, Ext. 293 (Office); 633-3182 (Home).

Lejeune, Jules Nicolas Gaston Jean-Marie, D. ès SC., D. ès SC. COM.; Belgian university professor; b. 1910; ed. Univs. of Paris and Liège and London School of Economics.
Deputy Prof. of Statistics, Univ. of Liège 36, Prof. 42; Pres. and Prof. of Statistics, Ecole Supérieure des sciences commerciales; Pres. Admin. Council of *Review of Economic Sciences*, Liège; mem. Int. Inst. of Statistics; Vice-Pres. Belgian Statistical Soc., Nat. Bookkeeping Soc.; mem. Belgian Higher Cttee. for Statistics, Comm. on Price Indices and Nat. Revenue Comm. Scientific Council of Inst. for Economic and Social

Study of the Middle Class, New York Acad. of Sciences, American Statistical Asscn. (Washington), Paris Statistical Soc.; Pres. Belgian UNA; Chevalier Légion d'Honneur, Civic Medal 1st Class, Officier Ordre de Léopold, Commdr. de l'Ordre de la Couronne; Grand Prix Scientifique de la ville de Paris 71.
Publs. *Les Méthodes de Construction des Index Numbers* 35, *Cours de Statistique professé à l'Université de Liège* 47, 61.
Institut de Mathématique, 15 avenue des Tilleuls, Liège, Belgium.

Lejeune, Michael L.; American (b. British) international finance official; b. 22 March 1918, Manchester; s. of F. Arnold and Gladys (Brown) Lejeune; m. Margaret Werden Wilson 1947; two s. one d.; ed. Cate School, Carpinteria, Calif., Yale Univ., and Yale Univ. Graduate School.
Teacher St. Paul's School, Concord, New Hampshire 41; Volunteer in King's Royal Rifle Corps in British Army 42-46; Int. Bank for Reconstruction and Devt. 46-, Personnel Officer 48-50, Asst. to Loan Dir. and Sec. Staff Loan Cttee., Loan Dept. 50-52, Chief of Div., Europe, Africa and Australasia Dept. 52-57, Asst. Dir. of Operations, Europe, Africa and Australasia 57-63, Asst. Dir. of Operations, Far East 63-64; Dir. of Admin., Int. Bank for Reconstruction and Devt., Int. Devt. Asscn. and Int. Finance Corpn. 64-67, Dir. Middle East and North Africa Dept. 67-68; Dir. Europe, Middle East and North Africa Dept. 68-69; Dir. Eastern Africa Dept. 70-74, Exec. Sec. Consultative Group on Int. Agricultural Research 74-.
International Bank for Reconstruction and Development, 1818 H Street N.W., Washington, D.C. 20433; Home: 626 Chain Bridge Road, McLean, Va. 22101, U.S.A.
Telephone: EX3-6360 (Office); JA 8-0292 (Home).

Leloir, Luis Federico; Argentine biochemical researcher; b. 6 Sept. 1906, Paris; m. Amelie Zuherbuhler de Leloir; one d.; ed. Univ. of Buenos Aires.
Early career as research worker in U.K., Argentina, and U.S.A., Research at Inst. of Biology and Experimental Medicine, Buenos Aires 46; Dir. Inst. of Biochemical Research, Campomar 47-; Head, Dept. of Biochemistry, Univ. of Buenos Aires 62-; Chair. Argentine Asscn. for Advancement of Science 58-59; mem. Directory, Nat. Research Council 58-64; mem. Nat. Acad. of Medicine 61; Foreign mem. Nat. Acad. of Sciences, U.S.A., American Acad. of Arts and Sciences, American Philosophical Soc., Royal Acad. (U.K.); many prizes and Dr. h.c. (Univ. of Paris, Univ. of Granada, Univ. of Córdoba); Nobel Prize for Chemistry 70.
Major research includes: isolation of glucose diphosphate 48, of uridine diphosphate glucose 50, of uridine diphosphate acetylglucosamine 53, mechanism of glycogen 59, of starch biosynthesis 60, isolation of adenosine nucleotides from corn grains 64.
Instituto de Investigaciones Bioquímicas, "Fundación Campomar", Obligado 2490, Buenos Aires 28, Argentina.
Telephone: 76-2871.

Lelong, Pierre Alexandre; French politician; b. 22 May 1931, Paris; s. of Prof. Marcel Lelong; m. Catherine Demargne 1958; four s. one d.; ed. Coll. Stanislas, Paris, Univ. of Paris and Ecole Nat. d'Administration.
Ministry of Finance and Econ. Affairs 58-62; Econ. Adviser to Prime Minister Pompidou 62-67; Gen. Man. Fonds d'Orientation et de Régularisation des Marchés Agricoles (FORMA) 67-68; mem. Parl. for Finistère 68-74; Sec. of State for Posts and Telecommunications 74-Jan. 75; Judge, Court of Accounts.
Leisure interests: sea fishing, hunting.
92 boulevard Raspail, 75600 Paris; 20 Grand'Rue, Morlaix, Finistère, France.
Telephone: 222-93-32 (Paris); 98-88-22-69 (Morlaix).

Lelouch, Claude; French film director; b. 30 Oct. 1937, Paris.
President and Dir.-Gen. Société Les Films 13, 66-; films directed include: *L'Amour des si. . ., La Femme-Spectacle, Vingt Quatre Heures d'amants, Une fille et des fusils, Les Grands moments, Pour un maillot jaune, Un homme et Une Femme,* (Palme d'or, Cannes 66, Acad. Award 66), *Vivre pour vivre, Treize jours en France, La Vie, l'Amour, la Mort, Un homme qui me plaît, Le Voyou, Smic, Smac, Smoc,* co-dir. *Visions of Eight* 73, *L'Aventure c'est l'aventure, La Bonne Année* 73, (producer, dir., author) *Toute une vie* 74, *Mariage* 74, *Le Chat et la Souris* 75.
15 avenue Hoche, Paris 8e, France.

Lemaignen, Robert; French businessman; b. 15 March 1893, Blois; m. Yvonne de Nervo 1919; four s.; ed. Ecole Militaire de Saint-Cyr.
War service 14-18; Pres. Soc. commerciale d'affrètements et de combustibles 40-58; fmr. Man. Compagnie de Mokta el Hadid, Tharsis Sulphur Co., Cie. Salins du Midi et de Djibouti and of other commercial and industrial enterprises in North and Central Africa; Pres. Cie. Optorg, Union Financière Internationale pour le Développement de l'Afrique, Société Marocaine Métallurgique; fmr. rep. overseas territories on the council of Air France; fmr. Pres. Cttee. of French Africa, Int. Chamber of Commerce and Hon. Pres. 58, Exec. Cttee. as Pres. of the Budget; fmr. Pres. Comm. of Economic Co-operation, fmr. Vice-Pres. of the Patronat Français; fmr. Pres. Cttee. France Actuelle; mem. EEC Comm. 58-61; Pres. Groupe d'Outre-mer; Pres. Acad. of Colonial Sciences; Commdr. of the Légion d'Honneur; Croix de Guerre; Médaille de la Résistance, and many foreign decorations.
Leisure interests: farming, shooting, tennis.
Publ. *L'Europe au berceau* 64.
Cie. Optorg, 5 Rue Bellini, Puteaux; 22 avenue Friedland, Paris 8e, France.
Telephone: CAR 2143 (Office); 722-02-50 (Home).

Lemaire, Maurice; French politician; b. 25 March 1895; ed. Ecole Polytechnique.
District Head, Northern Railways 21-37, Chief of Railway Systems, Alsace-Lorraine 37-38, Head, Fixed Installations Service 38, Dep. Dir. Eastern Railway Network 39-44, Dir. Northern Network 44; Dir.-Gen. Société Nationale des Chemins de Fer 46-49; Exec. Pres. Union Internationale des Chemins de Fer 46-51; Mayor of Colroy-la-Grande 46-; Deputy to Nat. Assembly 51-; Minister of Construction and Building 53-55, Sec. of State for Industry and Commerce 56-57, Pres. of Nat. Assembly Cttee. on Production and Trade 59-73; Commandeur, Légion d'Honneur, Officier de l'Ordre de Léopold de Belgique.
National Assembly, 75007 Paris, France; and 15 avenue de La Bourdonnais, 75007 Paris, France.

Leman, Paul H., O.C., A.B., LL.L.; Canadian business executive; b. 6 Aug. 1915, Pointe Claire, Quebec; s. of J. B. Beaudry Leman and Caroline Béique; m. Jeannine Prud'homme 1939; two s. three d.; ed. Collège Sainte-Marie, Univ. of Montreal and Harvard Graduate School of Business Admin.
Admitted to Quebec Bar 37; joined Aluminum Co. of Canada Ltd. 38; Asst. Sec. 43; Treas. Saguenay Power Co. Ltd. 45; Treas. Aluminum Co. of Canada Ltd. 49, Vice-Pres. 52, Dir. 63, Exec. Vice-Pres. 64; Dir. Alcan Aluminum Ltd. 68, Exec. Vice-Pres. 69; Pres. Aluminum Co. of Canada Ltd. 69-; Pres. Alcan Aluminum Ltd. 72-; Dir. Export Devt. Corpn. 69-74; mem. Royal Comm. on Banking and Finance 62-64.
Leisure interests: golf, bridge.
Alcan Aluminum Ltd., 1 Place Ville Marie, Montreal, P.Q.; Home: 43 Maplewood Avenue, Outremont, Montreal, P.Q. H2V 2L9, Canada.
Telephone: 514-877-3306 (Office).

LeMay, Gen. Curtis E.; American air force officer (retd.); b. 15 Nov. 1906, Columbus, Ohio; s. of Erving LeMay; m. Helen Estelle Maitland 1934; one d.; ed. Ohio State Univ.

Held various mil. posts until outbreak of Second World War; in command of 305th Bombardment Group in England 42; Commanding Gen. Third Bombardment Div. 43-44; transferred to Pacific theatre of war in command 20th Bomber Command 44-45; Commdr. of the Mariana-based 21st Bomber Command 45; Deputy Chief of Air Staff Research and Development 45-47; Commdr. U.S. Air Forces in Europe 47-48; C.-in-C. Strategic Air Command 48-57; Vice-Chief of Staff U.S. Air Force 57-61, Chief of Staff 61-64; American Independent Party candidate for Vice-Pres. of U.S.A. 68; Distinguished Service Cross, Distinguished Service Medal with three Oak Leaf Clusters, Silver Star, Distinguished Flying Cross with two Oak Leaf Clusters, Air Medal with three Oak Leaf Clusters, Medal for Humane Action and the Mackay Trophy, etc.; foreign decorations: British D.F.C., Commdr. Legion of Honour and Croix de Guerre with Palm Leaf (France), Belgian Croix de Guerre with Palm Leaf, Brazilian Order of the Southern Cross, Commdr. Moroccan Order of the Ouissam Alaouite Chérifien, Russian Order of Patriotic War, Argentine Order of Aeronautical Merit; several honorary degrees. Leisure interests: hunting, shooting.

773 Stradella Road, Los Angeles, Calif. 90024, U.S.A.

Leme, Hugo de Almeida; Brazilian agricultural specialist; b. 1917; ed. Escola Superior de Agricultura Luiz de Queiroz.

Associate Prof., Escola Superior de Agricultura Luiz de Queiroz, Piracicaba, (Univ. of São Paulo) 39-40, Prof. 40, Full Prof. 44, 46-, Vice-Dir. 58-60, Dir. 60-64; Minister of Agriculture 64-66; mem. Council for Agricultural Reform, State of São Paulo; has attended and organized numerous confs.; Ford Motor Company Prize for work on the mechanization of agriculture 61.

c/o Ministério da Agricultura, Esplanada dos Ministérios, Bloco 4, Brasília, DF, Brazil.

Lemelin, Roger; Canadian writer and publisher; b. 7 April 1919, Quebec City; s. of Joseph Lemelin and Florida Dumontier; m. Valéda Lavigueur 1945; three s. two d.

Guggenheim Fellowship 46, Rockefeller Fellowship 47; journalist Time, Life, Fortune magazines 48-52; Pres. and Publr. La Presse daily 72-; mem. Royal Soc. of Canada 49; Foreign mem. Acad. Goncourt 74; Prix David 46.

Leisure interests: golf, fishing, reading, chess, travel.

Publs. novels: Au Pied de la Pente Douce 44, Les Plouffe 48, Pierre le Magnifique 52; short stories: Fantaisie sur les Péchés Capitaux 49.

La Presse, 7 St. James Street, Montreal, Quebec H2Y 1K9; Home: 4754 St. Felix, Cap Rouge, Quebec, Canada.

Telephone: (514) 874-6802 (Office); (418) 659-1159 (Home).

Lemieux, Raymond Urgel, B.SC., PH.D., F.R.S., Canadian chemist; b. 16 June 1920; ed. Univ. of Alberta, Edmonton, and McGill Univ., Montreal.

Research Fellow, Ohio State Univ. 47; Asst. Prof., Univ. of Saskatchewan 48-49; Senior Research Officer, Nat. Research Council 49-54; Prof., Univ. of Ottawa 54-61; Prof. of Organic Chem., Univ. of Alberta 61-; Fellow, Chemical Inst. of Canada 53, Royal Society of Canada 55, Royal Society (London) 67; Chemical Inst. of Canada Medal 64; C. S. Hudson Award, American Chemical Soc. 66; Hon. D.Sc. (Univ. of New Brunswick).

Publs. over 100 research papers mostly appearing in Canadian Journal of Chemistry.

Department of Chemistry, University of Alberta, Edmonton, Alberta T69 2E1, Canada.

Lemke (von Soltenitz), Helmut, DR. IUR.; German lawyer and politician; b. 29 Sept. 1907; ed. Univs. of Kiel, Tübingen and Heidelberg.

Naval officer in Second World War; Public Prosecutor; Mayor of Eckernförde, Schleswig, Lübeck; Barrister at Law; Minister of Educ., Schleswig-Holstein 54-56, Minister of Interior 55-63; Pres. German Fed. Council 66-67 (as such for a time Acting Pres. German Federal Republic); mem. State Diet 55-, mem. Bundesrat 54-71; Minister-Pres. of Schleswig-Holstein 63-71; Pres. of State Parl., Schleswig-Holstein 71-; Grand Cross of Fed. German Order of Merit and other decorations; mem. Landesvorstand, Christian Democratic Union (C.D.U.).

Landeshaus, Kiel, Schleswig-Holstein, Federal Republic of Germany.

Telephone: 5961.

Lemmon, Jack; American actor; b. (as John Uler Lemmon III) 8 Feb. 1925, Boston; m. 1st Cynthia Boyd Stone 1950, one s.; m. 2nd Felicia Farr 1962, one d.; ed. Phillips Andover Acad., Harvard Univ.

Actor, stage, radio and television 48-; numerous Broadway appearances; Acad. Award 56, 74.

Films include: It Should Happen to You 53, Three for the Show 53, Phffft 54, My Sister Eileen 55, Mister Roberts 55, You Can't Run Away From It 56, Fire Down Below 57, Bell, Book and Candle 58, It Happened to Jane 58, Some Like it Hot 59, The Apartment 60, The Notorious Landlady 62, Days of Wine and Roses 62, Irma La Douce 63, Under the Yum Yum Tree 64, Good Neighbour Sam 64, How to Murder Your Wife 65, The Great Race 65, The Fortune Cookie 66, Luv 67, The Odd Couple 68, The April Fools 69, The Out-of-Towners 69, Dir. Kotch 71, Avanti 72, Save the Tiger 73, The Prisoner of Second Avenue 74, The Front Page 75, The War Between Men and Women.

911 Gateway West, Century City, Los Angeles, Calif. 90029, U.S.A.

Lemnitzer, Gen. Lyman L.; American army officer; b. 29 Aug. 1899, Honesdale, Pa.; s. of William L. Lemnitzer and Hannah (Blockberger) Lemnitzer; m. Katherine Mead Tryon; one s. one d.; ed. U.S. Military Acad.

Commissioned 20; pupil Coast Artillery School 20-21; served Fort Adams, R.I. 21-23; served Philippines 24-26; Instructor, U.S. Mil. Acad. 26-30; pupil, Coast Artillery School 30-31; served in Philippines 31-34; Instructor, U.S. Mil. Acad. 34-35; pupil, Commd. and Gen. Staff School 35-36; Instructor, Coast Artillery School 36-39; pupil, Army War Coll. 39-40; Bn. Commdr. 70th Coast Artillery 40; served with War Dept. Gen. Staff 41; Commdr. 34th A.A. Brigade 42; served in Europe and North Africa 42-45; with Joint Chiefs of Staff 45-47; Deputy Commdt. Nat. War Coll. 47-49; Asst. to Sec. of Defence 48 (part-time) 49-50 (full-time); pupil, Airborne Course Ft. Benning 50; Commdr. 11th Airborne Div. 51; 7th Infantry Div. (in Korea) 51-52; Deputy Chief of Staff (Plans and Research) 52-55; Commdr. U.S. Army Forces, Far East and Eighth U.S. Army April 55; C.-in-C. Far East and U.N. Commands and Gov. of the Ryukyu Islands June 55-July 57; Vice-Chief of Staff, U.S. Army 57-59, Chief of Staff 59-60; Chair. Joint Chiefs of Staff 60-62; C.-in-C. U.S. Forces in Europe 62-69; Supreme Allied Commdr. in Europe (NATO) 63-69; mem. Citizen's Comm. on C.I.A. Jan.-May 75; D.S.M., Silver Star, Legion of Merit, Legion of Merit (Officer's Degree), C.B. (Great Britain), C.B.E., Grand Croix Légion d'Honneur, Croix de Guerre (with Palm), and numerous foreign decorations.

Leisure interests: golf, photography, fishing.

3286 Worthington Street, N.W., Washington, D.C. 20015, U.S.A.

Telephone: 202-362-6611.

Le Moal, Henri Jean Alain; French university rector; b. 21 Dec. 1912, Plozevet, Finistère; s. of Jean Le Moal and Catherine Le Guellec; m. Suzanne Allée 1937; one d.; ed. Lycée La Tour d'Auvergne, Quimper and Univ. of Rennes.
Military service 38-44; Asst., Faculty of Science, Univ. of Rennes 45-47, Chef de Travaux 47-53, Asst. Prof. 53-57, Prof. of Gen. Chemistry 57, Dean 58-60, Rector, Acad. of Rennes 60-70; mem. of Admin. Council of the Association de Universités partiellement ou entièrement de langue française (AUPELF) 61-70; Pres. Rotary Club of Rennes 72-73; Vice-Pres. Commission de Développement Economique de Bretagne; Chevalier, Légion d'Honneur, Commdr. des Palmes Académiques, Commdr. de l'Ordre National de la République de la Côte d'Ivoire, Commdr. de l'Ordre du Mérite Sportif, Officier du Mérite pour la Recherche et l'Invention; Hon. LL.D. (Univ. of Exeter).
Leisure interests: sea-fishing, bridge.
Publs. (memoirs) *Bulletin de la Société chimique de France*; contributions to *La Bretagne Radicale*, *Le Rotarien*.
4 rue A. de Musset, 35000 Rennes, France.
Telephone: 36-18-22.

Lemus, Lieut.-Col. José María; Salvadorian army officer and politician; b. 1911; ed. School and Acad. of Military Staff, San Salvador, and Military Staff School, Camp Lee, U.S.A.
Under-Sec. of Defence 48-49; Minister of the Interior 49-55; Pres. of the Republic of El Salvador 56-60, deposed Oct. 60; Gran Cordón Orden del Libertador (Venezuela), Gran Cruz Orden del Mérito Civil (Spain).
Publs. many military and political works, including *Pensamiento Social de Don Bosco, Simón Bolívar, Símbolos Patrios*, etc.
Guatemala City, Guatemala.

Lenaert, Henri; Belgian banker; b. 3 Jan. 1915, Louvain; ed. Catholic Univ. of Louvain.
Department Supervision of Banking, Banking Comm. 42; Banking Auditor 46; Man. Banque Centrale du Congo Belge et du Ruanda-Urundi 51, Liquidator 61; Sec.-Gen. Man., Gen. Admin. Dept., European Investment Bank 62-; Lecturer, Catholic Univ. of Louvain 55-.
European Investment Bank, 2 Place de Metz, Luxembourg.
Telephone: 43-50-11.

Lenárt, Jozef; Czechoslovak politician; b. 3 April 1923, Lipt. Porúbka; ed. Party Coll. Moscow.
Mem. Czechoslovak underground movement, Second World War; took part in Slovak rising 44; mem. C.P. of Czechoslovakia 43-; mem. Central Cttee. C.P. of Slovakia 50-53, 57-66; Leading Sec. Bratislava Regional Cttee. C.P. of Slovakia 56-58; mem. Central Cttee. C.P. of Czechoslovakia 58-; Sec. Central Cttee. Slovak C.P. 58-62; Chair. Slovak Nat. Council 62-63; Prime Minister of Czechoslovakia 63-68; Alt. mem. Presidium of Cen. Cttee. of Czechoslovak C.P. 68-69; mem. of Cen. Cttee. Secr. 68-75; Deputy to Nat. Assembly 60-69; Sec.-Gen. Cttee. of C.P. of Czechoslovakia 68-70, mem. Presidium of Cen. Cttee. 70-; Deputy to House of the People, Fed. Assembly 69-; Chair. Econ. Comm. Cen. Cttee. C.P. of Czechoslovakia 69-70; First Sec. and mem. Presidium and Secr. Cen. Cttee. C.P. of Slovakia 70-; Deputy to Slovak Nat. Council 71-; Chair. Cen. Cttee. Nat. Front of Slovak Socialist Repub. 71-; Deputy Chair. and mem. Presidium Cen. Cttee. Nat. Front of Č.S.S.R. 71-; mem. Presidium, Fed. Assembly 71-; Commdr. of People's Militia in Slovakia 70-; Decoration for Merit in Construction 58; Order of the Nile 65; Order of the Red Banner 70; Order of Victorious February 73; Order of the Repub. 73.
Central Committee C.P. of Slovakia, Hlboká 2, Bratislava, Czechoslovakia.

Lenhartz, Rudolf, DIPL. ING.; German mining executive; b. 10 Feb. 1925, Bünde, Westphalia; ed. Bonn Univ. and Aachen Technical Coll.
Assessor des Bergfachs; Mine Supt. and Eng. Man. Rheinelbe Bergbau AG 56-63, mem. Man. Board 65-; Dir. of Mines, Carolinenglück-Graf Moltke Bergbau AG 63, mem. Man. Board 65-; Head of Production, Ruhrkohle AG 65-70, Gen. Dir. of Mining Operations 70-75; Chair. Man. Board Saarbergwerke AG 76-, also of Emschergenossenschaft, Essen; Chair. Environmental Cttee., Asscn. of German Coalmining Industry; mem. Water Advisory Council of Ministry of Food, Agriculture and Forestry, North Rhine-Westphalia; mem. Man. Board, Westfälische Bergwerkskasse.
Saarbergwerke AG, 6600 Saarbrücken, Trierer Strasse 1, Postfach 1030, Federal Republic of Germany.
Telephone: (0681) 4051.

Lenihan, Brian Joseph, B.A.; Irish politician; b. 17 Nov. 1930, Dundalk, Co. Louth; elder s. of Patrick J. Lenihan and Ann Scanlon; m. Ann Devine 1958; four s. one d.; ed. St. Mary's Coll. (Marist Brothers), Athlone, Univ. Coll., Dublin, and King's Inns, Dublin.
Called to the Bar 52; mem. Roscommon County Council and Roscommon Vocational Educ. Cttee. 55-61; mem. Consultative Assembly of Council of Europe, and of Legal, Political and Econ. Cttees. 58-61; Parl. Sec. to Minister for Lands 61-64; Minister for Justice 64-68, of Education 68-69, of Transport and Power 69-72; Pres. Eurocontrol 69-70; Minister for Foreign Affairs 72-73; mem. Seanad Éireann 57-61, 73-; mem. Dáil for Roscommon 61-73; mem. European Parl. 73-; Fianna Fáil.
24 Park View, Castleknock, Co. Dublin, Ireland.
Telephone: Dublin 383453.

Lennep, Jonkheer Emile van, DR.JUR.; Netherlands lawyer and economist; b. 20 Jan. 1915, Amsterdam; s. of Jonkheer Louis Henri van Lennep and Catharina Hillegonda Enschedé; m. Alexa Alison Labberton 1941; two s. two d.; ed. Amsterdam Univ.
Foreign Exchange Inst. 41-45; Netherlands Bank 45-48; Financial Counsellor to High Commr., Indonesia 48-49; Head of Financial Dept. of Netherlands High Commr. in Indonesia 49-50; Netherlands Bank 50-51; Treasurer-Gen. in Netherlands Ministry of Finance 51-69; Sec.-Gen. OECD, Paris 69-; Chair. Monetary Cttee. EEC 58-69; Chair. Working Party No. 3, OECD 61-69; Knight, Order of Netherlands Lion, Commdr. Order of Orange-Nassau; Grand Officier Ordre de la Couronne du Chêne (Luxembourg); Knight Commdr's. Cross (Star) of the Order of Merit of the Federal Republic of Germany; Grand Officer Order Léopold II (Belgium), Grand Officer Order of Merit (Italy); Commdr. Légion d'Honneur, France.
Leisure interests: music, sports.
44 rue de la Faisanderie, Paris 16e, France.
Telephone: 553-91-36.

Lennings, Manfred, DR.ING; German industrialist; b. 23 Feb. 1934, Oberhausen; s. of Wilhelm Lennings and Amanda Albert; m. Renate Stelbrink 1961; one s. one d.; ed. Gymnasium Geislingen/Steige, Univ. of Munich and Bergakademie Clausthal.
Chairman German Student Org. 59-60; Asst. of Management Board, Gutehoffnungshütte Aktienverein 64-67, Deputy mem. 68, Chair. 75-; mem. Management Board, Deutsche Werft AG 68-69; Chair. Management Board Howaldtswerke-Deutsche Werft AG 70-74.
Leisure interests: modern art and literature, swimming, horse riding.
Gutehoffnungshütte Aktienverein, 4200 Oberhausen 1, Essener Strasse; Home: 4307 Kettwig, Schmachtenbergstrasse 142, Federal Republic of Germany.
Telephone: 80-00-51 (Office); 45-45 (Home).

Lennon, John Ono (formerly John Winston), M.B.E.; British songwriter and performer; b. 9 Oct. 1940, Liverpool; s. of Alfred Lennon and Julia Stanley; m. 1st Cynthia Powell 1962, one s.; m. 2nd Yoko Ono 1969, one s. one step d.; ed. Dovedale Primary School, Quarrybank High School, Allerton and Liverpool Art College.

Plays guitar, organ, piano and harmonica; has written numerous songs with Paul McCartney (q.v.); formed pop group *The Quarrymen*, while at Quarrybank High School 55; appeared under various titles until formation of *The Beatles* 60; appeared with *The Beatles* in the following activities: performances in Hamburg 60, 61, 62, The Cavern, Liverpool 60, 61; toured Scotland, Sweden, U.K. 63, Paris, Denmark, Hong Kong, Australia, New Zealand, U.S.A., Canada 64, France, Italy, Spain, U.S.A. 65, Germany, Spain, Philippines, U.S.A. 66; attended Transcendental Meditation Course at Maharishi's Acad., Rishikesh, India Feb.-April 68; formed Apple Corps Ltd., parent org. of The Beatles Group of Companies 68.

John Lennon appeared in film *How I Won the War* 67. Leisure interest: working for peace.

Publs. (by John Lennon) *In His Own Write* 64 (adapted as one-act play, Nat. Theatre 68), *A Spaniard in the Works* 65, *You Are Here*, *Lennon Remembers* 72.

Films (by The Beatles): *A Hard Day's Night* 64, *Help!* 65, *Yellow Submarine* (animated colour cartoon film) 68; *Let it Be* 70; T.V. film *Magical Mystery Tour* 67.

c/o Apple Corps Ltd., 3 Savile Row, London, W.1, England; resident in U.S.A.

Lenya, Lotte (Karoline Blamauer); Austrian actress and singer; b. 18 Oct. 1900, Vienna; d. of Franz Blamauer and Johanna Blamauer (née Teuschl); m. 1st Kurt Weill 1925 (died 1950), 2nd George Davis 1951 (died 1957), 3rd Russell Detwiler (died 1969).

Member of corps de ballet, Stadttheater, Zurich, Switzerland; appeared in Shakespearean and other theatrical roles, Berlin, then in *Oedipus*, Berlin State Theatre, *The Little Mahagonny* 27, as Jenny in Brecht and Weill's *The Threepenny Opera* 28, *The Rise and Fall of the City of Mahagonny* 30, *Song of Hoboken* 32; fled to Paris and appeared in *The Seven Deadly Sins* 33; travelled to U.S.A. 35; appeared in *The Eternal Road* 37, as Cissy in *Candle in the Wind* 44, as Duchess in *The Firebrand of Florence* 45; retired from stage to assist Weill in composing; returned in *The Threepenny Opera*, Kurt Weill memorial concert 50; played Xantippe in *Barefoot in Athens* 51, Jenny in new translation of *The Threepenny Opera* 54-56, in Kurt Weill memorial concerts 58, 59, Annie in *The Seven Deadly Sins* 58-59, *Brecht on Brecht* 62, Fraulein Schneider in *Cabaret* 66; awarded "Tony" for appearance in *The Threepenny Opera* 56, "Oscar" for *The Roman Spring of Mrs. Stone*, also appeared in *From Russia with Love* 64.

c/o Columbia Records, 799 7th Avenue, New York 19, N.Y., U.S.A.

Lenz, Siegfried; German writer; b. 17 March 1926; ed. High School, Samter, and Univ. of Hamburg.

Cultural Editor *Die Welt* 49-51; freelance writer 52-; Gerhart Hauptmann Prize 61, Bremer Literaturpreis 62. Publs. novels: *Es waren Habichte in der Luft* 51, *Duell mit dem Schatten* 53, *So zartlich war Suleyken* 55, 62, *Der Mann im Strom* 57, 58, *Brot und Spiele* 59, *Stadtgespräche* 63, *Deutschstunde* 68, *Das Vorbild* 73; stories: *Jäger des Spotts* 58, *Das Feuerschiff* 60; plays: *Zeit der Schuldlosen* 61, *Das Gesicht* 63, *Haussuchung* (radio plays) 67.

Oberstrasse 72, Hamburg 13, Federal Republic of Germany.

Leodolter, Ingrid Maria Margarete, DR.MED.; Austrian physician and politician; b. 14 Aug. 1919, Vienna; d. of Dr. Leopold and Elsa Zechner; m. Dr. Josef Leodolter 1938; two s.; ed. Univ. of Vienna.

Practising doctor 44-, Intern, Head Doctor, Sophienspital Vienna 58-; Minister of Health and Environmental Protection 71-.

Leisure interests: sport, music.

Publs. about forty studies in internal medicine, particularly gastroenterology.

1140 Vienna, Hadikgasse 102, Austria.

Telephone: 823114.

León Portilla, Miguel, M.A., PH.D.; Mexican anthropologist and historian; b. 1926, Mexico City; s. of Miguel León Ortiz and Luisa Portilla Nájera; m. Ascensión Hernández Triviño 1965; one d.; ed. Loyola Univ. of Los Angeles and Nat. Univ. of Mexico.

Secretary-General, Inter-American Indian Inst. 55-59, Asst. Dir. 59-60, Dir. 60-66; Asst. Dir. Seminar for Náhuatl Culture, Nat. Univ. of Mexico 56-; Dir. *América Indígena* 60-; Dir. Inst. of History, Nat. Univ. of Mexico 63-; Adviser, Int. Inst. of Different Civilisations 60-; mem. American Anthropological Asscn. 60-, Mexican Acad. of the Language 62-, Corresp. to Royal Spanish Acad. 62-; mem. Société des Américanistes de Paris 66-; mem. Mexican Acad. of History 69-; Corresp. mem. Royal Spanish Acad. of History 69-; Guggenheim Fellow 69; mem. Nat. Coll. of Mexico 71-; Amer. Anthropological Asscn. Fifth Distinguished Lecturer 74.

Leisure interests: scouting and gardening.

Publs. *La Filosofía Náhuatl* 56, *Visión de los Vencidos* 59, *Los Antiguos Mexicanos* 61, *The Broken Spears*, *Aztec Account of the Conquest of Mexico* 62, *Rückkehr der Götter* 62, *Aztec Thought and Culture* 63, *Literaturas Precolombinas de México* 64, *Imagen del México Antiguo* 64, *Le Crépuscule des Aztèques* 65, *Trece Poetas del Mundo Azteca* 67, *Pre-Columbian Literatures of Mexico* 68, *Tiempo y Realidad en el Pensamiento Maya* 68, *Testimonios Sudcalifornianos* 70, *De Teotihuacan a los Aztecas* 71, *The Norteño Variety of Mexican Culture* 72, *The Voyages of Francisco de Ortega to California 1632-1636* 72, *Time and Reality in the Thought of the Maya* 73, *Historia Natural y Crónica de la Antiqua California* 73, *Il Rovescio della Conquista, Testimonianze Asteche, Maya e Inca* 74, *Aztecs and Navajos* 75, *Endangered Cultures: The Indian in Latin America* 75. Calle de Alberto Zamora 103, Coyoacán, México 21, D.F., Mexico.

Telephone: 548-82-05.

Leonard, Nelson Jordan, B.S., B.SC., PH.D.; American professor of chemistry; b. 1 Sept. 1916, Newark, N.J.; s. of Harvey Nelson Leonard and Olga Pauline Jordan; m. Louise Cornelie Vermey 1947; three s. one d.; ed. Lehigh, Oxford and Columbia Univs.

Research Asst., Univ. of Ill. 42-43, Instructor 43-44, Assoc. 44-45, 46-47, Asst. Prof. 47-49, Assoc. Prof. 49-52, Prof. of Chem. 52-, Head of Div. of Organic Chem. 54-63, and Prof. of Biochemistry 73-; mem. Center for Advanced Study, Univ. of Ill. 68-; Scientific Consultant and Special Investigator, Field Intelligence Agency Technical, U.S. Army and U.S. Dept. of Commerce, European Theater 45-46; Editor *Organic Syntheses* 51-58, mem. Advisory Board 58-, Board of Dirs. 71-; mem. Exec. Cttee. *Journal of Organic Chemistry* 51-54, mem. Editorial Board 57-61; mem. Editorial Board *Journal of the American Chemical Society* 60-72; mem. Advisory Board *Biochemistry* 73-; Sec., Div. of Organic Chem. of American Chemical Soc. 49-54, Chair. 56; mem. Advisory Panel for Chem. of Nat. Science Foundation 58-61, Program Cttee. in the Basic Physical Sciences of Alfred P. Sloan Foundation 61-66, Study Section in Medicinal Chem. of Nat. Insts. of Health 63-67, Educational Advisory Board of John Simon Guggenheim Memorial Foundation 69-, N.A.S. 55-; Fellow, American Acad. of Arts and Sciences 61-; Swiss American Foundation Lecturer 53, 70, Julius Stieglitz Memorial Lecturer of Chicago Section of

American Chemical Soc. 62, Backer Lecturer, Univ. of Groningen 72; American Chemical Soc. Award for Creative Work in Synthetic Organic Chem. 63; Synthetic Organic Chemical Mfrs. Asscn. Medal 70; Edgar Fahs Smith Award and Memorial Lecturer of Philadelphia Section of American Chem. Soc. and Univ. of Pa. 75; Sc.D. (Hon.).
Leisure interests: singing, skiing, swimming.
Publs. Numerous research articles in scientific journals.
Department of Chemistry, University of Illinois, Urbana, Ill. 61801; Home: 606 West Indiana Avenue, Urbana, Ill., U.S.A.
Telephone: 217-333-0363 (Office); 217-344-6266 (Home).

Leone, Giovanni; Italian professor and politician; b. 3 Nov. 1908, Naples; s. of Mauro and Maria (Gioffrida) Leone; m. Vittoria Michitto 1946; four s. (one deceased); ed. Univ. of Naples.
Professor of Law, Univ. of Naples; elected to Constituent Assembly 46, to Chamber of Deputies 48 and 53; Vice-Pres., Chamber of Deputies 48-49, Pres. 55-63; Prime Minister June-Nov. 63, June-Dec. 68; made life Senator 57; Pres. of Italian Repub. Dec. 71-; Christian Democrat.
Palazzo del Quirinale, Rome, Italy.

Leonhardt, Rudolf Walter, DR. PHIL.; German journalist; b. 9 Feb. 1921, Altenburg; s. of Rudolf Leonhardt and Paula (née Zeiger); m. Ulrike (née Zoerb); two s. one d.; ed. Berlin, Leipzig, Bonn, Cambridge and London.
Lecturer in German, Cambridge Univ. 48-50; Foreign Corresp. *Die Zeit,* London 53-55, Cultural Editor *Die Zeit,* Hamburg 57-73, Deputy Editor-in-Chief 74-.
Leisure interest: people.
Publs. *The Structure of a Novel* 50, *Notes on German Literature* 55, *77 x England* 57 (trans. into Spanish 64), *Der Sündenfall der deutschen Germanistik* 59, *Leben ohne Literatur?* 61, *x-mal Deutschland* 61 (trans. into English, Italian, Spanish 64), *Zeitnotizen* 63, *Junge Deutsche Dichter für Anfänger* 64, *Reise in ein Fernes Land* (with Marion Gräfin Dönhoff and Theo Sommer) 64 (trans. into Japanese 65); *Kästner für Erwachsene* 66, *Wer wirft den ersten Stein?* 69, *Sylt für Anfänger* 69, *Haschisch-Report* 70, *Drei Wochen und Drei Tage—Japan-Tagebuch* 70, *Deutschland* 72, *Argumente Pro und Contra* 74, *Das Weib, Das Ich Geliebet Hab—Heines Mädchen und Frauen* 75.
Elbchaussee 81, Hamburg, Federal Republic of Germany.

Leonhart, William, PH.D.; American diplomatist; b. 1 Aug. 1919, Parkersburg, W. Va.; s. of Harry Kempton Leonhart and Rae Corinne Kahn; m. Florence Lydia Sloan 1944; two d.; ed. Univ. of West Virginia, Princeton Univ. and Imperial Defence Coll., London.
In office of Co-ordinator for Inter-American Affairs 43-44; entered U.S. Foreign Service and assigned to Buenos Aires 44, in Belgrade 46-49, in Rome 49-50, in French Indo-China 50-52, in Tokyo 52-55; mem. Policy Planning Staff of Dept. of State 55-57. concurrently Alt. Dept. of State Rep. on Nat. Security Council Planning Board 56-57; in London 58; Deputy Chief of Mission, Tokyo, with personal rank of Minister 59; U.S. Amb. to Tanganyika (later Tanzania) 62-65; Deputy to Special Asst., then Special Asst. to the Pres., The White House, Washington 66-68; Special Asst. to Pres.-Elect's Personal Rep. for Foreign Policy Matters 68-69; Amb. to Yugoslavia May 69-Nov. 71; Deputy Commdt. Nat. War Coll., Fort Leslie J. McNair 71-75; Vice-Pres. Nat. Defense Univ. 75-.
National Defense University, Washington, D.C. 20319, U.S.A.
Telephone: (202) 693-1077.

Leonov, Col. Aleksey Arkhipovich; Soviet cosmonaut; b. 30 May 1934, Listvyanka; s. of Arkhip and Yevdokia Leonov; m. Svetlana Leonova; one d.; ed. Chuguevsky

Air Force School for Pilots and Zhukovsky Air Force Engineering Academy.
Pilot 56-59; cosmonaut training 60; took part in flight of space-ship *Voskhod 2,* and moved 5 metres into space outside space-ship; mem. C.P.S.U. 57-; Pilot-Cosmonaut of U.S.S.R.; first man to walk in space 65; took part in joint flight Soyuz 19–Apollo 75; Twice Hero of the Soviet Union; Chair. Council of Founders of Novosti Press Agency 69-.
Zvezdny Gorodok, Moscow, U.S.S.R.

Leonov, Leonid Maximovich; Soviet writer; b. 31 May 1899, Moscow; ed. Moscow Univ.
Deputy to Supreme Soviet-70; Dir. of Pushkin Dom (Pushkin House—U.S.S.R. Acad. of Sciences, Inst. of Russian Literature); Sec. of Board, U.S.S.R. Union of Writers; State Prize 42, Lenin Prize 57, Order of Lenin (four times), Hero of Socialist Labour, Hammer and Sickle Gold Medal, Order of Red Banner of Labour, Order of Patriotic War; Merited Worker of Arts of R.S.F.S.R.
Publs. *Barsuky* 24, *The Thief* 27, *Sotj* 30, *Skutarevsky* 32, *Road to the Ocean* 36, *The Ordinary Man* 41, *Lenushka* 43, *The Fall of Velikoshumsk* 44, *The Golden Car* 46, *Sazancha* 59, *Mr. McKinley's Flight* 61, *Evgenia Ivanovna* 63, *Plays* 64.
Union of Soviet Writers, 52 Ulitsa Vorovskogo, Moscow, U.S.S.R.

Leontief, Wassily; economist; b. 5 Aug. 1906, Leningrad; s. of Wassily and Eugenia Leontief (née Bekker); m. Estelle Helena Marks 1932; one d.; ed. Univs. of Leningrad and Berlin.
Assistant, Kiel Econ. Research Inst. 27-28, 30; Econ. Adviser to Chinese Govt., Nanking 29; Nat. Bureau of Econ. Research, N.Y. 31; Lecturer in Econs., Harvard Univ. 31, Asst. Prof. 33-38, Assoc. Prof. 39-45, Prof. 46-75; Dept. of Econs. N.Y. Univ. 75-; mem. Amer. Philosophical Soc., Amer. Acad. of Arts and Sciences, Int. Statistical Inst., Amer. Econ. Asscn., U.S. Nat. Acad. of Sciences; Legion of Honour 67; Nobel Prize for Econs. 73; Gold Medal of Paris 74.
Publs. *Structure of American Economy 1919-1920* (2nd edn.) 53, *Studies in the Structure of the American Economy* 53, *Input-Output Economics* 66, *Collected Essays* 66.
Department of Economics, Harvard University, 309 Littauer, Cambridge, Mass. 02138, U.S.A.
Telephone: (617) 495-2118.

Leontovich, Mikhail Alexandrovich; Soviet theoretical physicist; b. 7 March 1903, Moscow; ed. Moscow Univ.
Works in field of electro-dynamics, optics, statistical physics and radio-physics; worked at the Inst. of Physics of Moscow Univ. 29; the Lebedev Inst. of Physics 34-52; Inst. of Atomic Energy 52-; mem. U.S.S.R. Acad. of Sciences 46-; awarded Popov Gold Medal 52, Lenin prizewinner 58.
Publs. *Statistical Physics* 44, *Introduction to Thermodynamics* 52.
Atomic Energy Institute, U.S.S.R. Academy of Sciences, Pl. Kurchatova 46, Moscow, U.S.S.R.

Léopold III; fmr. King of the Belgians; b. 3 Nov. 1901. Son of King Albert; married Princess Astrid (died 35), niece of King Gustav V of Sweden 26; succeeded 34; Commander-in-Chief Armed Forces May 40; married Mlle. Mary Liliane Baels Sept. 41; abdicated 16 July 1951, in favour of his son, King Baudouin, b. 30.
Domaine Royal d'Argenteuil, Poste Waterloo, Belgium.

Leopold, Luna B., PH.D.; American geologist and engineer; b. 8 Oct. 1915, New Mexico; s. of Aldo Leopold and Estella Bergere; m. 1st Carolyn Clugston 1940, 2nd Barbara Beck Nelson 1973; one s. one d.; ed. Harvard Univ. and Univs. of California and Wisconsin.
United States Army 41-46; Head Meteorologist, Pineapple Research Inst. of Hawaii 46-50; Hydraulic

Engineer, U.S. Geological Survey, Washington, D.C. 50-66, Chief Hydrologist 56-66, Sr. Research Hydrologist 66-; mem. Nat. Acad. of Sciences; Kirk Bryan Award, Geological Soc. of America, Cullum Geographical Medal, American Geographical Soc., Distinguished Service Award, U.S. Dept. of Interior, Veth Medal, Royal Netherlands Geographical Soc.
Publs. Several books and over 100 scientific papers on water, hydrology and rivers.
Department of Geology, University of California, Berkeley, Calif. 94720, U.S.A.

Lepeshinskaya, Olga Vasilievna; Soviet ballerina; b. 28 Sept. 1916; ed. Bolshoi Theatre School of Ballet, Moscow.
Danced with the Bolshoi Theatre Ballet Company 33-62; ballet teacher 62-; People's Artist of U.S.S.R. 54; State prize-winner 41, 46, 47, 50.
Principal rôles: Cinderella (*Cinderella* by Prokofiev), Jeanne (*Flames of Paris* by Asafiev), Swanhilda (*Coppelia* by Delibes), Tao Tkhoa (*Red Poppy* by Glière).
State Academic Bolshoi Theatre of the U.S.S.R., 1 Ploshchad Sverdlova, Moscow, U.S.S.R.

Lépine, Pierre Raphael, M.D., L.SC.; French scientist; b. 15 Aug. 1901, Lyons; s. of Jean Lépine; m. Marie-Madeleine Dollfus 1924; two s. one d.; ed. Univ. of Lyons.
Instructor of Parasitology 24; Doctor of Medicine 25; Prof. of Pathology, American Univ., Beirut 25-26; Asst. Coll. de France 27; Chief of Lab., Institut Pasteur 28; Dir. Institut Pasteur Hellénique, Athens 30-35; Chief, Rabies Div., Institut Pasteur 36, Prof. and Chief of Virus Research 40-71, Emer. Prof. 71; Visiting Prof. Institut de Microbiologie et d'Hygiène, Univ. of Montreal 47-53; Pres. European Asscn. against Poliomyelitis 52-60; Vice-Pres. Institut Pasteur Board of Trustees 67-70; mem. WHO Experts Panel on Rabies, Influenza and Polio; Fellow, N.Y. Acad. of Sciences; mem. Nat. Acad. of Medicine, Paris; mem. Acad. of Sciences, Paris, Pontifical Acad. of Sciences, City of Paris Council 71; Hon. foreign mem. U.S.S.R. Acad. Medical Sciences, Acad. Royale de Médecine de Belgique, etc.; Commdr. de la Légion d'Honneur, Officier Santé Publique; Joseph Smadel Award 70, etc.
Leisure interests: sailing, yachting.
Publs. *Virology, Epidemiology, Elect. Microscopy, Techniques de Laboratoire en Virologie Humaine* (editor), etc.
Institut Pasteur, 25 rue du Dr. Roux, 75015 Paris; 15 rue Albéric Magnard, F.75, 75016 Paris, France.
Telephone: 734-1875 (Office); 870-61-00 (Home).

Le Portz, Yves; French financial executive; b. 30 Aug. 1920, Hennebont; m. Bernadette Champetier de Ribes 1946; five c.; ed. Univ. de Paris à la Sorbonne, Ecole des Hautes Etudes Commerciales, and Ecole Libre des Sciences Politiques.
Attached to Gen. Inspectorate of Finances 43, Ministry of Finance and Econ. Affairs 51; French Del. to Econ. and Social Council of UN 57-58; Dir.-Gen. of Finance for Algeria 58-62; Dir.-Gen. Bank for Devt. of Algeria 59-62; Vice-Chair. European Investment Bank 62-70, Chair. 70-.
European Investment Bank, 2 place de Metz, Luxembourg; Home: 127 avenue Wagram, Paris 17e, France.

Leprette, Jacques; French diplomatist; b. 22 Jan. 1920; ed. Univ. of Paris and Ecole Nationale d'Administration.
Ministry of Foreign Affairs (European Div.) 47-49, Counsellor, Council of Europe 49-52; Head, Political Div., French Military Govt., Berlin 52-55; Counsellor, French Embassy, U.S.A. 55-59; Ministry of Foreign Affairs (African Div.) 59-61; Amb. to Mauritania 61-64; Dir. Int. Liaison Service for Information 64-65;

Minister-Counsellor, Washington 66-71; Dir. of UN and international organization affairs at the Foreign Office 71-74; Asst. Dir. of Political Affairs, Cen. Admin. 75-; Chevalier de la Légion d'Honneur, Croix de Guerre, Bronze Star Medal.
37 Quai d'Orsay, 75007 Paris; 6 rue Daubigny, 75017 Paris, France (Home).

Leprince-Ringuet, Louis; French scientist; b. 27 March 1901, Alès-Gard; s. of Félix Leprince-Ringuet and Renée Stourm; m. Jeanne Motte 1939; one s. six d.; ed. Lycée Louis-le-Grand, Ecole Polytechnique and Ecole Supérieure d'Electricité et des P.T.T.
Worked as engineer and did research on cosmic rays and fundamental particles physics; Prof. at Ecole Polytechnique 36-69; Pres., Soc. française de physique 56; mem. Académie des Sciences (Physics) 49-; mem. Académie Française 66-; Dir. of Laboratory at Ecole des Hautes Etudes Pratiques; mem. Atomic Energy Comm.; Prof. of Nuclear Physics at Collège de France 59-72; Pres. CERN Scientific Council 64-66.
Leisure interests: painting, tennis, skiing.
Publs. *Rayons Cosmiques, Les Inventeurs Célèbres, Les Grandes Découvertes du XXe siècle, Des Atomes et des Hommes, La Science Contemporaine, Science et Bonheur des Hommes.*
86 rue de Grenelle, 75007 Paris, France.
Telephone: 548-75-27.

Le Quesne, Sir (Charles) Martin, K.C.M.G.; British diplomatist; b. 10 June 1917; s. of C. T. Le Quesne, Q.C.; m. 1948; three s.; ed. Shrewsbury, Exeter Coll., Oxford.
Served in Royal Artillery 40-45; joined Foreign Service 46; Second Sec., Baghdad 47-48; First Sec. Foreign Office 48-51; with Political Residency, Bahrain 51-54; at British Embassy, Rome 55-58; Foreign Office 58-60; Chargé d'Affaires, Repub. of Mali 60, Amb. 61-64; Foreign Office 64-68; Amb. to Algeria 68-71; Deputy Under-Sec. of State, Foreign and Commonwealth Office 71-74; High Commr. in Nigeria 74-76.
Leisure interests: gardening, bridge.
c/o Foreign and Commonwealth Office, London, S.W.1; Home: Beau Désert, St. Saviour's, Jersey.

Lér, Leopold; Czechoslovak politician; b. 23 Oct. 1928, Ostrava; ed. Commercial Coll., Prague.
Ministry of Finance 51-62, Deputy Minister 62, First Deputy Minister 63, Minister in Czech Govt. 69-73, Fed. Minister 73-; participated in work of Council for Mutual Econ. Assistance (CMEA) and in formation of Int. Bank for Econ. Co-operation; Deputy, Czech Nat. Council 71; Distinction for Merits in Construction 73.
Ministry of Finance, Letenská ulice, Prague 1, Czechoslovakia.

Leray, Jean, D. ès SC.; French mathematician; b. 7 Nov. 1906, Nantse; m. Marguerite Trumier 1932; two s. one d.; ed. Ecole Normale Supérieure.
Professor, Faculty of Sciences, Nancy 36-41, Paris 41-47; Prof. of Differential and Functional Equations, Collège de France 47-; mem. Inst. de France; Foreign Assoc. Nat. Acad. of Sciences (U.S.A.); Foreign mem. U.S.S.R. Acad. of Sciences, Accad. Naz. dei Quaranta, and Acad. of Sciences of Boston, Brussels, Göttingen, Milan, Palermo and Turin; Officier Légion d'Honneur; Prix Feltrinelli 71.
Publs. papers on mathematics and mechanics.
6 avenue Jean Racine, 92-Sceaux, France.
Telephone: 661-0321.

Lercaro, H.E. Cardinal Giacomo; Italian ecclesiastic; b. 28 Oct. 1891, Quinto al Mare; ed. Genoa.
Ordained priest 14; Archbishop of Ravenna and Cervia 47-52, of Bologna 52-68; created Cardinal by Pope Pius XII 53; mem. Sacred Congregations of the Council, of Religious and of Seminaries and Univs. of Study; mem. Pontifical Comm. for Biblical Studies; Moderator

Ecumenical Council 63-65; Pres. Consilium ad Ex-sequendam de Sacra Liturgia 64-68; Hon. citizen, Bologna 66.
Villa S. Giacomo, 40068 San Lazzaro di Savena, Bologna, Italy.

le Riche, William Harding, M.D., F.R.C.P.(C)., F.A.C.P.; Canadian physician and professor; b. 21 March 1916, Dewetsdorp, S. Africa; s. of Josef Daniel le Riche and Georgina Henrietta Guset le Riche (née Harding); m. Margaret Cardross Grant, 1943; two s. three d.; ed. Univ. of Witwatersrand and Harvard Univ.
Intern, Zulu McCord Hosp., Durban, S. Africa 44; Union Health Dept., Health Centre Service (Pholela, Natal and Knysna) 45-49; Epidemiologist, Union Health Dept. 50-52; Consultant, Dept. of Nat. Health and Welfare, Ottawa, 52-54; Research Medical Officer, Physicians Services Inc., Toronto 54-57; Staff, School of Hygiene, Univ. of Toronto 57, Prof. of Public Health 59, Prof. and Head of Dept. of Epidemiology and Bio-metrics 62-75, Prof. of Epidemiology and Head of Dept. of Preventive Medicine and Biostatics 75-.
Leisure interests: writing books, photography, research, public speaking, medical practice.
Publs. *Physique and Nutrition* 40, *Good Food: Good Health* 76; co-author: *The Control of Infections in Hospitals* 66, *People Look at Doctors* 71, *Epidemiology as Medical Ecology* 71.
Hygiene Fitzgerald Building, University of Toronto, 150 College Street, Toronto, Ont. M5S 1A1; Sunny-brook Medical Centre, University of Toronto, 2075 Bayview Avenue, Toronto, Ont.; Home: 30 Golfdale Road, Toronto, Ont. M4N 2B6, Canada.
Telephone: 928-2020 (Fitzgerald); 486-3447 (Sunny-brook); 489-2298 (Home).

Lerner, Alan Jay; American theatrical writer and producer; b. 31 Aug. 1918, New York City; ed. Bedales, Hampshire, England, Choate School, Wallingford, Conn., Harvard Univ.
Free-lance radio script-writer 41-; has written books and lyrics for most of his stage and film productions; mem. Dramatists' Guild of America (Pres. 58-63), President's Comm. for Nat. Cultural Centre, Washing-ton 62-.
Productions: Stage: *The Patsy* 42, *What's Up?* 43, *The Day Before Spring* 45, *Brigadoon* 47, *Love Life* 48, *Paint Your Wagon* 51, *My Fair Lady* 56, *Camelot* 60, *On a Clear Day You Can See Forever* 64, *Coco* 69, *Gigi* 73; Films: *A Royal Wedding* 51, *An American in Paris* 51, *Brigadoon* 54, *Gigi* 58, *My Fair Lady* 64, *Camelot* 68, *Paint Your Wagon* 69, *On a Clear Day You Can See Forever* 70, *The Little Prince*.
10 E. 40th Street, New York, N.Y. 10016, U.S.A.

Lerner, I. Michael, M.S.A., PH.D.; American professor of genetics; b. 15 May 1910, Harbin, China; s. of Michael and Cecilia (Sudja) Lerner; m. Ruth A. Stuart 1937; no c.; ed. private schools in China, Univs. of British Columbia and California (Berkeley).
Instructor in Poultry Husbandry, Univ. of Calif. (Berkeley) 36, Asst. Prof. 41, Assoc. Prof. 46, Prof. 51, Prof. of Genetics 58, Emer. Prof. 73-; Editor *Evolution* 59-61; Research Geneticist, Inst. Personality Assess-ment and Research 70-; mem. Nat. Acad. of Sciences, Amer. Acad. Arts and Sciences, Amer. Philosophical Soc., Accad. Economico-Agraria dei Georgofili (Flor-ence), Behavioural Genetics Asscn.; Poultry Science Research Prize, Czechoslovak Acad. of Science Medal, Weldon Memorial Prize (Oxford Univ.), Borden Award and Gold Medal, Belling Prize; three Guggenheim Fellowships; D.Sc. h.c.
Publs. *Population Genetics and Animal Improvement* 50, *Genetic Homeostasis* 54, *Genetic Basis of Selection* 58, *Modern Developments in Animal Breeding* (with H. P. Donald) 66, *Heredity, Evolution and Society* 68; Editor and translator *The Rise and Fall of T. D. Lysenko* 69.

Department of Genetics, University of California, Berkeley, Calif. 94720, U.S.A.
Telephone: 415-642-3055.

Lerner, Max, A.B., A.M., PH.D.; American writer, b. 20 Dec. 1902, Ivenitz, Russia; s. of Benjamin and Bessie (Podbereski) Lerner; m. 1st Anita Marburg 1928, 2nd Edna Albers 1941; three s. three d.; ed. Yale and Washington (St. Louis) Univs., Robert Brookings Graduate School of Economics and Govt.
Assistant Editor *Encyclopædia of the Social Sciences* 27, later Man. Editor; mem. Social Science Faculty Sarah Lawrence Coll. Bronxville (N.Y.) 32-36; Chair. Faculty Wellesley Summer Inst. 33-35; Dir. Consumers' Div. Nat. Emergency Council 34; Lecturer Dept. of Govt. Harvard Univ. 35-36; Editor *The Nation* 36-38; Prof. of Political Science Williams Coll. 38-43; Contrib. Editor *New Republic* 40-45; Editorial Dir. *PM* New York 43-48; Columnist *N.Y. Star* 48-49; radio commentator *WOR* 44-47; Columnist *New York Post* 49-; Prof. of American Civilization, Brandeis Univ. 49-73; Ford Foundation Prof. Amer. Civilization, School of Int. Studies, New Delhi, India 59-60; Internationally-syndicated news-paper columnist 59-; Ford Foundation Research and Study Grant, Paris 63-64; Visiting Prof. of Amer. Civilization, Univ. of Florida 73-75, Pomona Coll. 74-75, Graduate School of Human Behaviour, U.S. Int. Univ. (San Diego) 74-.
Publs. *It is Later Than You Think* 38, *Ideas Are Weapons* 39, *Ideas for the Ice Age* 41, *The Mind and Faith of Justice Holmes* 43, *Public Journal* 45, *The World of the Great Powers* 47, *Actions and Passions* 48, *America as a Civilisation* 57, *The Unfinished Country* 59, *Essential Works of John Stuart Mill* 61, *Education and a Radical Humanism* 62, *The Age of Overkill* 62, *Tocqueville's Democracy in America* 66, *Tocqueville and American Civilization* 69, *Values in Education* 76.
445 East 84th Street, New York, N.Y. 10028, U.S.A.
Telephone: Regent 7-3416, 349-5000.

Lernet-Holenia, Alexander; Austrian novelist and playwright; b. 21 Oct. 1897, Vienna; s. of Alexander Lernet recte de Lernet and Sidonia Baroness Boyne-burgk (née Holenia); m. Eva Vollbach 1945.
Publs. *Ollapotrida* 26, *Das Geheimnis Sankt Michaels* 27, *Die Abenteuer eines jungen Herrn in Polen* 31, *Jo und der Herr zu Pferde* 33, *Die Standarte* 34, *Die Neue Atlantis* 35, *Die Goldene Horde* 35, *Die Auferstehung des Maltravers* 36, *Der Baron Bagge* 36, *Der Mann im Hut* 37, *Strahlenheim* 38, *Ein Traum in Rot* 39, *Beide Sizilien* 41, *Die Trophae* 46, *Mars in Widder* 47, *Ger-manien* 47, *Der 20. Juli* 47, *Spanische Komödie* 48, *Der Graf von Saint-Germain* 48, *Das Feuer* 49, *Die Wege der Welt* 52, *Die Inseln unter dem Winde* 52, *Die drei Federn* 53, *Der junge Moncada* 54, *Der Graf Luna* 55, *Das Finanzamt* 55, *Das Goldkabinett* 57, *Die vertauschten Briefe* 58, *Die Schwäger des Königs* 58, *Die wahre Manon, Der wahre Werther* 59, *Prinz Eugen* 60, *Mayerling* 60, *Naundorff* 61, *Das Halsband der Königin* 62, *Das Bad an der belgischen Küste* 63, *Götter und Menschen* 64, *Drei Gesellschaftsstücke* 65, *Die weisse Dame* 65, *Pilatus* 67, *Die Hexen* 69, *Die Geheimnisse des Hauses Österreich* 71, *Drei Abenteurerromane* 72, *Die Beschwörung des Herrn* 73.
Hofburg, Vienna I, Austria; St. Wolfgang in Oberöster-reich, Austria.
Telephone: 52-40-333 and 311.

Lesage, Rt. Hon. Jean, P.C., M.P.P., Q.C., LL.D., B.A.; Canadian lawyer and politician; b. 10 June 1912; ed. Laval Univ.
Practised law, Quebec Bar; Crown Attorney 39-44; mem. Parl. for Montmagny-l'Islet 45-58; Parl. Asst. to Sec. of State for External Affairs 51, to Minister of Finance 53; Minister of Resources and Development

Sept.-Dec. 53, of Northern Affairs and National Resources Dec. 53-57; Canadian Rep. to U.N. Gen. Assembly 50 and 52; led Canadian Del. to ECOSOC, Geneva 51, New York 52; Pres. U.N. Technical Asst. Conf., Paris 52; Leader Liberal Party in Quebec 58-69; Premier of Quebec 60-66, concurrently Minister of Finance and Minister of Federal-Provincial Affairs 61-66; D.Iur. h.c. 61.
Quebec Liberal Party, Montreal, Quebec, Canada.

Lesch, George H.; American businessman; b. 10 Oct. 1909, Washburn, Illinois; m. Esther Barrett; two c.; ed. Monmouth Coll. and Univ. of Illinois.
Worked in Home Office Accounting, Colgate-Palmolive 32-36, mem. of European Auditing Staff 36-39; Office Man., Mexico 39-48; Vice-Pres. and Asst. Gen. Man. 48, Exec. Vice-Pres. and Gen. Man. 48-55; Pres. and Gen. Man. Mexican Co. (subsidiary of Colgate-Palmolive) 55-56; Vice-Pres. Colgate-Palmolive Int., responsible for sales and advertising in U.K. and Europe 56-57, Pres., Vice-Pres. and Dir. 57-60; Pres. Colgate-Palmolive Co. 60-70, Chief Exec. Officer 60-71, Chair. of Board and Chair. Exec. Cttee. April 61-; mem. Boards of Dirs. Bank of New York, American Sugar Co., F. W. Woolworth; mem. and Vice-Chair., Board of Trustees, Syracuse Univ.; Hon. LL.D. (Syracuse); Commdr. Order of Merit (Italy).
Colgate-Palmolive Company, 300 Park Avenue, New York, N.Y. 10022, U.S.A.

Lesechko, Mikhail Avksentyevich; Soviet engineer and government official; b. 1909; ed. Moscow Aviation Inst.
Former turner, technologist and factory man. 36-45; with Council of Ministers State Cttee. for Introduction of New Equipment 46-48; Dir. Moscow Counting-Analytical Equipment 48-54; First Deputy Minister of Machine Instrument Making 54-56; Minister of Instrument Making and Automation 56-57; First Vice-Chair. Ukrainian S.S.R. State Planning Cttee. 57-58; First Vice-Chair. State Planning Cttee. 58-60; Chair. of Comm. for Foreign Econ. Affairs, attached to Presidium of Council of Ministers 60-62, Deputy Chair. U.S.S.R. Council of Ministers 62-; mem. C.P.S.U. 40-, Central Cttee. C.P.S.U. 61-; Deputy to U.S.S.R. Supreme Soviet 62-; mem. Exec. Cttee. COMECON; Perm. Rep. of U.S.S.R. to COMECON; State prizewinner 54.
U.S.S.R. Council of Ministers, The Kremlin, Moscow, U.S.S.R.

Lesieur, Michel; French business executive; b. 1922; m.; seven c.
Joined French Army in N. Africa 43, posted at Ecole des Elèves Officiers de Marine, Casablanca 43-44, Lieut. of Reserve Ship 44-45; Société Georges Lesieur et ses Fils, Head Oil-cakes Dept. 46-52; charged with the creation of an org. for the purchase of groundnut seeds in Senegal 52; Admin.-Del. Société Lesieur-Afrique Dakar 55-65, Chair. 65-; responsible for the supply of oleaginous primary materials for the Lesieur Group 58-65; Dir.-Gen. Georges Lesieur et ses Fils (now Compagnie Financière Lesieur) 65-66, Chair. 66-; Chair. and Dir.-Gen. Lesieur-Cotelle et Associés; Admin. Lesieur-Sodeva, Excel-Soprodel; Vice-Pres. Institut de Recherche pour les Huiles et les Oléagineaux and Syndicat Général des Fabricants d'Huile et de Tourteaux de France; Chevalier Légion d'Honneur.
Compagnie Financière Lesieur, 122 avenue du Général Leclerc, 92100 Boulogne-Billancourt, France.
Telephone: 604-81-40.

Lesieux, Louis; French airline official; b. 16 May 1907, Liévin; s. of Louis Lesieux and Marie Lecouret; m. Claire Lefebvre 1932; two d.; ed. Ecole Polytechnique and Ecole Nationale des Ponts et Chaussées.
Engineer and Chief Engineer of Roads and Bridges, Niort, Lille and Nice; Dir.-Gen. of Paris Airport 48-55, Dir.-Gen. of Air France 55-67, Hon. Dir.-Gen. 67-;

Commdr. Légion d'Honneur; several foreign decorations.
Leisure interest: music.
180 rue de la Pompe, Paris 16e, France.
Telephone: 553-06-59 (Home).

Lesky, Albin, D.PHIL.; Austrian university professor; b. 7 July 1896, Graz; s. of Albin Lesky and Maria (née Stolz); m. Erna Klingenstein 1939; one s.; ed. Akademisches Gymnasium, Graz and Univs. of Graz and Marburg.
Privatdozent, Univ. of Graz 24-31; Prof., Vienna Univ. 32-35; Prof. Innsbruck Univ. 36-49; Prof. of Classics, Vienna Univ. 49-67, Prof. Emeritus 67-; Sec. Austrian Acad. of Sciences 59-63, Vice-Pres. 63-69, Pres. 70-71; Hon. mem. Dublin Acad., Corresp. Fellow British Acad., Corresp. mem. Bavarian Acad., Acad. des Sciences morales et politiques, Heidelberg Acad., Acad. of Athens, Acad. of Stockholm and Vlaamse Acad.; Wilhelm Hartel Prize, Austrian Acad. of Sciences 59, Österreichisches Ehrenzeichen Pro Litteris et Artibus, Purkyně Medal, Univ. of Brno, Ehrenring and Preis der Stadt Wien; Dr. Phil. h.c. (Innsbruck, Athens, Ghent, Glasgow, Salonika), Dr. Rer. Pol. h.c. (Graz); Hon. Senator (Vienna), mem. Orden pour le Mérite für Wissenschaften und Künste, Hansischer Goethepreis.
Leisure interests: reading and walking.
Publs. *Alkestis, der Mythos und das Drama* 25, *Die griechische Tragödie* 38 (4th edn. 68, English trans. 67, Spanish trans. 66, Norwegian trans., Portuguese trans. 71), *Der Kommos der Choephoren* 43, *Thalatta: Der Weg der Griechen zum Meer* 47, *Aristainetos* 50, *Die tragische Dichtung der Hellenen* 56 (3rd edn. 72), *Geschichte der griechischen Literatur* 57-58 (Italian, Greek, English and Spanish trans., 3rd edn. 71), *Göttliche und menschliche Motivation im homerischen Epos* 61, *Homeros* 66.
Alserstrasse 69/17, A-1080 Vienna VIII, Austria.
Telephone: 42-30-115.

Leslie, John Charles, B.S., M.S.; American airline executive (retd.); b. 21 July 1905; ed. Phillips Exeter Acad., Princeton Univ., and Mass. Inst. of Technology.
Fokker Aircraft Co. of U.S. 28; Asst. to Chief Engineer, Pan American World Airways 29, Asst. Div. Engineer, Miami 29-35, Div. Engineer, Pacific Div., San Francisco 35-38, Div. Operations Man. 38-41, Man. Atlantic Div., New York 41-45, Vice-Pres. System Office 46, Vice-Pres. Admin. and Dir. 50, Vice-Pres. and Asst. to Pres. 59-64, Vice-Pres. and Asst. to Chair. 64-68, Senior Vice-Pres. Int. Affairs 68-70; Senior Assoc., R. Dixon Speas Assoc. Inc. 70-.
60 East End Avenue, New York, N.Y. 10028, U.S.A.

Leśnodorski, Bogusław; Polish historian; b. 27 May 1914, Cracow; ed. Jagiellonian Univ., Cracow.
Doctor 38-47, Docent 47-51, Assoc. Prof. 51-56, Prof. 56-; Chair. Scientific Council Cttee. on History of Science and Tech., Polish Acad. of Sciences 53-; Editor-in-Chief *Kwartalnik Historyczny* 53-; Dir. History Inst., Warsaw Univ.; mem. Int. Asscn. of Historians of Law and Public Institutions, Soc. des Etudes Robespierristes, Int. Union of History and Phil. of Science, Soc. of Comparative Legislation; Dr. h.c. (Toulouse); Gold Cross of Merit, Officer's and Commdr.'s Cross, Order of Polonia Restituta, Medal of Nat. Educ. Comm., State Prize (twice).
Publs. *Dzieło Sejmu Czteroletniego, Synteza historii państwa i prawa polskiego, Studia nad myślą prawno-polityczną H. Kołłątaja, Polscy Jakobini, Historia i współczesność, Ludzie i idee, Rozmowy z przeszłością;* co-author: *A Thousand Years of Poland;* numerous articles, also in foreign languages.
Ul. Kredytowa 8 m. 20, 00-062 Warsaw, Poland.

Lesotho, King of (see Moshoeshoe II).

Lesser, Most Rev. Norman Alfred, C.M.G., M.A., TH.D., D.D.; British ecclesiastic; b. 16 March 1902; ed. Liverpool Collegiate School, Fitzwilliam House and Ridley Hall, Cambridge.
Curate, Anfield 25-26, Formby 26-29; Curate-in-Charge Norris Green 29-30; Chaplain of Cathedral, Liverpool 30-31; Vicar, Barrow-in-Furness 31-39; Hon. Canon, Rector and Sub-Dean, All Saints Cathedral, Nairobi 39-47; Provost of Nairobi 42-47; Bishop of Waiapu 47; Primate and Archbishop of New Zealand 61-71; retd. 71.
4 Sealy Road, Napier, New Zealand.
Telephone: Napier 53-509.

Lessing, Doris May; British writer; b. 22 Oct. 1919, Kermanshah, Iran; d. of Captain Alfred Cooke Tayler and Emily Maude McVeagh; m. 1st F. A. C. Wisdom 1939-43, 2nd Gottfried Anton Nicolai Lessing 1944-49; two s. one d.; ed. Roman Catholic Convent, and Girls' High School, Salisbury, Southern Rhodesia.
Somerset Maugham Award 54.
Leisure interests: friends, gardening.
Publs. include: *The Grass is Singing* 50, *Martha Quest* 52, *A Proper Marriage* 54, *Going Home* 57, *The Habit of Loving* 58, *Each His own Wilderness* (play) 58, *A Ripple from the Storm* 58, *In Pursuit of the English* (reportage) 60, *The Golden Notebook* 62, *Play With a Tiger* (play) 62, *A Man and Two Women* 63, *Landlocked* 65, *Particularly Cats* 67, *The Four Gated City* 69, *Briefing for a Descent into Hell* 71, *The Story of a Non-Marrying Man* (short stories) 72, *The Summer Before the Dark* 73, Collected Edn. African Stories (2 vols.) *This Was the Old Chief's Country* and *The Sun Between Their Feet* 73, *The Memoirs of a Survivor* 74.
Flat 3, 11 Kingscroft Road, London, NW2 3QE, England.

Lester, Richard; American film director; b. 19 Jan. 1932, Philadelphia; s. of Elliott Lester and Ella Young; m. Deirdre V. Smith 1956; one s. one d.; ed. William Penn Charter School, Univ. of Pennsylvania.
Television Dir., CBS 52-54, ITV 55-59; Composer 54-57; Film Dir. 59-; Academy Award Nomination 60; Grand Prix, Cannes Festival 65; Best Dir. Rio de Janeiro Festival 66; Gandhi Peace Prize, Berlin Festival 69; Best Dir. Teheran Festival 74.
Leisure interests: tennis, music.
Films directed: *The Running, Jumping and Standing Still Film* 59, *It's Trad, Dad* 62, *The Mouse on the Moon* 63, *A Hard Day's Night* 63, *The Knack* 65, *Help!* 65, *A Funny Thing Happened on the Way to the Forum* 66, *How I Won the War* 67, *Petulia* 69, *The Bed Sitting Room* 69, *The Three Musketeers* 73, *Juggernaut* 74, *The Four Musketeers* 74, *Royal Flash* 75, *Robin and Marian* 76.
c/o Twickenham Film Studios, St. Margarets, Middlesex, England.
Telephone: 01-892-4477.

Leszczycki, Stanisław Marian, PH.D.; Polish geographer; b. 8 May 1907, Mielec; s. of Bronislaw Leszczycki and Jadwiga Macharska; m. Jadwiga Stella-Sawicka 1950; one d.; ed. Jagiellonian Univ., Cracow.
Assistant, Jagiellonian Univ., Cracow 28-39; imprisoned in Dachau and Sachsenhausen concentration camps during Second World War; Deputy to Seym (Parliament) 45-49; Extraordinary Prof. of Anthropogeography, Jagiellonian Univ., Cracow 45-47; Prof. of Economic Geography, Warsaw Univ. 48-70; Vice-Minister of Foreign Affairs 46-50; Pres. Polish Geographical Soc. 50-53; Pres. Nat. Geographical Cttee. 56-68, 72-74; Pres. Cttee. of Space Econ. and Regional Planning Polish Acad. of Sciences 58-; Dir. Geographical Inst., Polish Acad. of Sciences 53-; mem. Presidium of Polish Acad. of Sciences 53-67; Vice-Pres. Int. Geographical Union 64-68, 72-76, Pres. 68-72; Vice-Chair. State Team of Experts for Plan of Spatial Econ. of

Poland 72-73, Chair. 73-; mem. Polish Socialist Party 45-48, Polish United Workers' Party 48-; Editor-in-Chief *Przegląd Geograficzny* (Geographical Review) and *Geographia Polonica*; Hon. mem. sixteen European Geographical Socs.; Dr. h.c. (Prague Univ.) 70; seventeen foreign and Polish decorations including Order of Banner of Labour 1st Class, Commdr. Cross with Star, Order Polonia Restituta, British K.C.M.G.
Leisure interests: photography, hiking, collecting old engravings and numismatics.
Publs. numerous works on economic geography, spatial economy and regional planning.
Krakowskie Przedmieście 30, m. 3, 00-071 Warsaw, Poland.
Telephone: 260328.

Letavet, Avgust Andreyevich; Soviet hygienist; b. 18 Feb. 1893, Senuli, Latvia; s. of Eva and Andrew Letavet; m. Alexandra Malysheva 1954; ed. Moscow Univ.
Army Physician 17-18; physician in Kursk Region 18-19; Head of Sanitary Inspectorate, Senior Asst., Head of Section, Head of Lab., Dir., Inst. of Occupational Hygiene and Occupational Diseases 48-71; Editor *Journal of Industrial Hygiene and Occupational Diseases*; Corresp. mem. U.S.S.R. Acad. of Medical Sciences 45-50, mem. 50-; Head of Dept., Cen. Inst. for Postgraduate Medical Training 31-55; Academician-Sec. Dept. of Hygiene and Microbiology, U.S.S.R. Acad. of Medical Sciences 57-60; Deputy Chair. All-Union Soc. of Hygienists; Vice-Pres. Int. Fed. for Hygiene and Preventive Medicine 60-69; Vice-Chair. Int. Comm. on Radiological Protection 65-69; Hon. mem. Purkyně Medical Soc. (Czechoslovakia), Int. Asscn. on Occupational Health 72-; Order of Lenin 51, 63, 71, Red Banner of Labour 45, 49, 54, Badge of Honour 61, State Prize 49, Lenin Prize 63.
Leisure interest: alpinism.
Publs. Over 180 works on Hygiene of Labour, particularly on microclimate at industrial enterprises, physiology of labour and radiation hygiene.
Institute of Occupational Hygiene and Occupational Diseases, 31 Meyerovsky Proyezd, Moscow; Home: Moscow 125057, Walt. Oulbrikht's Street 3 R12, U.S.S.R.
Telephone: 157-53-89 (Home).

Letelier, Orlando; Chilean diplomatist; b. 13 April 1932, Temuco; m. Isabel Margarita Morel Gumucio; four c.; ed. Instituto Nacional de Santiago, O'Higgin's Military Acad., and Univ. of Chile.
Director of Student Federation of Chile 51-52; Pres. Centre of Art and Culture, School of Law and Social Services, Univ. of Chile 53-54; Econ. Adviser Copper Dept. of Chile (now Copper Corpn.) 55-59, participating in numerous int. confs. including 20th Ass. GATT, Geneva 57, First Conf. of Copper Producing and Consuming Countries, London 57, etc.; industrial devt. consultant 59-60; Inter-American Development Bank (IBD), successively area Chief of Econ. Div., Special Assistant to Pres., Consultant to Operations Dept., Dir. of Loan Div. 60-70, also represented IDB at numerous int. confs.; one of nine experts meeting under UN auspices to establish Asian Development Bank (ADB), Bangkok, Thailand 64, also in charge of preliminary negotiations with member Govts. of ADB; Amb. to U.S.A. 71-73; Minister for Foreign Affairs May-Aug. 73, of the Interior Aug. 73, of Defence Aug.-Sept. 73; mem. Socialist Party of Chile; expelled to Venezuela Sept. 74.

Leusse, Comte Pierre de; French diplomatist; b. 24 Dec. 1905, Cannes; m. Odile Viellard 1928; two s. one d.
Attaché, French Embassy, Berne 31, Washington 33; Sec. in Vienna 35, Prague 38; Chief Sec. High Commission, Beirut 38; Aide-de-Camp to Gen. Weygand 39; Consul, Lugano 41; office revoked by Vichy Govt. 42;

rep. of French Cttee. of National Liberation in Switzerland 42; Counsellor, London 44; Dir. Dept. for German and Austrian Affairs, Paris 45; Dir. Central Europe Dept. 46; Dir. Press and Information Services 50; Amb. to Poland 54-56; Amb. to Tunisia 56; Perm. Rep. to NATO 59-62; Amb. to Morocco 62-65; Perm. Rep. to NATO 65-67; Amb. to Algeria 67-68; Pres. Admin. Council of French State TV and Radio 68-72; Special Counsellor of State 73-; Mayor of Reichshoffen 53-71; Grand Officier de la Légion d'Honneur.
Home: 4 rue de Talleyrand, Paris 7e, and La Papeterie, Reichshoffen 67, France.
Telephone: 468-2020 (Paris); and (16) (88) 090182 (Reichshoffen).

Leussink, Hans, DR.ING., DIPL.ING.; German administrator; b. 2 Feb. 1912; ed. Technische Hochschule, Dresden, and Technische Hochschule, Munich.
Manager, Soil Mechanics Inst., Technische Hochschule, Munich 39-46; Construction eng. office 46-54; Prof. and Dir. of Inst. for Soil Mechanics and Rock Mechanics, Univ. of Karlsruhe 54-69, Rector, Technische Hochschule, Karlsruhe 58-61; Pres. West German Conf. of Univ. Rectors, Bad Godesberg 60-62; at Council of Europe, Strasbourg 62-69; mem. German Scientific Council 63-69, Chair. 65-69; mem. Advisory Council for Science Policy of Fed. Govt. 67-69; Dir. Krupp Foundation 67-; Minister of Educ. and Science 69-72; Dir. Volkswagen Foundation 72-, Anglo-German Foundation 73-, Friedrich Krupp G.m.b.H. 74-; Sen. Max Planck Soc. 72-.
7500 Karlsruhe 41, Strählerweg 45, Federal Republic of Germany.
Telephone: Karlsruhe 42668.

Leutwiler, Fritz, DR.ECON.SC.; Swiss banker; b. 30 July 1924, Ennetbaden; m. Andrée Cottier 1951; one s. one d.; ed. Univ. of Zurich.
Secretary Asscn. for a Sound Currency 48-52; with Swiss Nat. Bank 52-, Dir. First Dept. 59-66, Deputy Gen. Man. Third Dept. 66-68, Head Third Dept. 68-74, Pres. Board of Gen. Management, Head First Dept. 74-; mem. Board of Dirs. Bank of Int. Settlements.
Swiss National Bank, Börsenstrasse 15, 8022 Zurich; Home: Weizenacher 4, 8126 Zumikon, Switzerland.
Telephone: 01-23-47-40 (Office); 01-89-33-36 (Home).

Levard, Georges; French trade union official; b. 24 March 1912, Paris; m. Marguerite Pardini 1939; three s. two d.; ed. Conservatoire National des Arts et Métiers.
Member of Nat. Cttee. for Productivity; mem. Econ. Council 47-, Vice-Pres. 59-69; mem. Higher Council of the Plan; mem. several other councils; mem. Federal Bureau and Vice-Pres. of French and Democratic Confederation of Labour (C.F.T.C.) 46-48, Asst. Sec.-Gen. 48-53, Sec.-Gen. 53-61, Pres. 61-67; Dir. Banque Nationale de Paris; Conseiller d'Etat 66-70.
Leisure interests: country walks, history.
Publs. L'âme du syndicalisme chrétien, Eléments d'action syndicale, Rapport sur la Réforme de l'entreprise.
60 avenue Victor-Hugo, Paris 16e, France.

Lévárdi, Dr. Ferenc, DR. TECH. SC.; Hungarian mining engineer and politician; b. 1919, Annavölgyi-bánya, Sárisáp; m. Edith Csenke 1944; one s. one d.; ed. Grammar School, Esztergom, and Sopron Technical Univ.
Assistant Lecturer in Geophysics and Mine Metrology, Sopron Technical Univ. 44-47; Mining Engineer, later Chief Engineer, Production Man., and Dir. Dorog Coal Mining Trust 47-58; First Dep. Minister of Heavy Industry 58-63, Minister 63-May 71; mem. Communist Party 47-; Pres. Hungarian Mining and Metallurgical Soc. 60-66; Pres. Mining Cttee., Hungarian Acad. of Sciences.
Leisure interest: research into the history of mining.
Bimbó ut 72, 1022 Budapest, Hungary.
Telephone: 154-607.

Levasseur, Francis; French diplomatist; b. 29 Aug. 1914; ed. Inst. Saint-Aspais, Melun, Lycée de Nice, Law Faculty, Univ. of Paris, and Ecole Libre des Sciences Politiques.
Chef de Cabinet to French Resident-Gen., Rabat 45-48; Sub-Dir., Personnel Dept. Ministry of Foreign Affairs 49-53; Counsellor, Rio de Janeiro 53; Dir. du Cabinet, French Resident-Gen., Rabat 54-55; Counsellor, Ottawa 56-61; Sub-Dir. for African and Malagasy Affairs, Ministry of Foreign Affairs 62-63, Asst. Dir. 63; Ambassador to Upper Volta 63-67, to Colombia 68-72, to Romania 72-75; Officier Légion d'Honneur, Croix de Guerre.
14 rue de Rémusat, 75016 Paris; Château du Magny, 36150 Vatan, France.

Lever, Rt. Hon. Harold, LL.B.; British politician; b. 15 Jan. 1914, Manchester; s. of the late Bernard and Bertha Lever; m. Diane Zilkha 1962; three d. (and one d. by previous marriage); ed. Manchester Grammar School and Univ. of Manchester.
Member of Parl. 45-; Joint Parl. Under-Sec., Dept. of Econ. Affairs 67; Financial Sec. to the Treasury 67-69; Paymaster-Gen. 69-70; Chair. Public Accounts Cttee. 70-73; Opposition Front Bench spokesman on European Affairs 70-72, on Trade and Industry 72-74; Chancellor of Duchy of Lancaster 74-; Labour.
House of Commons, London, S.W.1, England.

Lévesque, Very Rev. Father Georges Henri, O.C., F.R.S.C.; French-Canadian ecclesiastic; b. 1903; ed. Ecole des Frères Maristes (Roberval), Séminaire de Chicoutimi, Coll. des Dominicains (Ottawa) and Catholic Univ. of Lille.
Dominican Novitiate 23-24, ordained Priest 28; in Europe 30-33; Lecturer, Coll. des Dominicains d'Ottawa 33-38, Univ. of Montreal 35-38, Laval Univ. 36-62; Founder and first Dean, Faculty of Social Sciences, Laval Univ. 38-55; Founder-Pres. Quebec Co-operative Council 39-44; Founder, Editor Ensemble magazine 39-44, Les Cahiers de la Faculté des Sciences Sociales 41; exec. on Advisory Council to Minister of Labour 41-51; Prédicateur Général of his Order 43; mem. Royal Comm. on the devt. of art, sciences and letters in Canada 49-51; Pres. Canadian Political Science Asscn. 51; Co-Dir. in India of the Int. Seminar of the World Univ. Service 53; Rector of La Maison Montmorency 55-63; Vice-Chair. Canada Council 57-62; Fellow, Canadian Royal Soc. 49; Founder, first Pres., Univ. Nat. du Rwanda 63-71, Hon. Pres., Adviser 71-; Dr. h.c. (Univs. of B.C., Manitoba, Antigonish, Toronto, W. Ont., St.-Joseph, Saskatchewan, Ottawa, Laval, Sherbrooke and McGill); Chevalier Légion d'Honneur, Order of Canada, Molson Prize, Canada Council.
Leisure interests: music, travelling.
Publs. include: Capitalisme et Catholicisme 36, Le pluralisme démocratique, condition de l'unité canadienne 48, Culture et Civilisation 50, Humanisme et Sciences Sociales 52, Le Chevauchement des Cultures 55, Service Social, Industrialisation et Famille 56, Youth and Culture To-day 61, Les Universités 61, Mon Itinéraire Sociologique 74.
976 Rive Boisée, Pierrefonds, P.Q. H8Z 2Y7, Canada.

Levey, Michael Vincent, M.V.O., M.A.; British art historian; b. 8 June 1927, London; s. of the late O. L. H. Levey and Gladys Mary Milestone; m. Brigid Brophy (q.v.) 1954; one d.; ed. Oratory School and Exeter Coll., Oxford.
Officer, British Army 45-48; Asst. Keeper Nat. Gallery 51-66, Deputy Keeper 66-68, Keeper 68-, Deputy Dir. 70-73, Dir. 73-; Slade Prof. of Art Cambridge Univ. and Fellow of King's Coll. Cambridge 63-64; Hon. Fellow, Exeter Coll., Oxford.
Publs. Edited Nat. Gallery Catalogues: 18th Cent. Italian Schools 56, The German School 59, Painting in XVIIIth c. Venice 59; From Giotto to Cézanne 62, Later

Italian Pictures in the Royal Collection 64, *Dürer* 64, *A Room-to-room Guide to the National Gallery* (1st edn.) 64, *Rococo to Revolution* 66, *Fifty Works of English and American Literature We Could do Without* (with Brigid Brophy and Charles Osborne) 67, *Bronzino* 67, *Early Renaissance* 67 (awarded Hawthornden Prize 1968), *A History of Western Art* 68, *Holbein's Christina of Denmark, Duchess of Milan* 68, *17th and 18th Cent. Italian Schools* (Nat. Gallery Catalogue) 71, *Painting at Court* 71, *The Life and Death of Mozart* 71, *Art and Architecture in 18th Cent. France* (co-author) 72, *High Renaissance* 75, *The World of Ottoman Art* 76.

185 Old Brompton Road, London, S.W.5, England.

Levi, Doro, PH.D.; Italian archaeologist; b. 1898, Trieste; *s.* of Eduardo and Eugenia Tivoli; *m.* Anna Cosadinou 1928; ed. Florence and Rome Univs.
Member Italian Archaeological School, Athens 21-23; conducted excavations in Crete 24 and in Chiusi, Vetulonia, Volterra, Massa Marittima 26-31; Insp. of Antiquities in Florence 26, later Dir.; Organizer Italian Mission in Mesopotamia 30, first expedition to Kakzu (Assyria) 33; Lecturer Florence Univ. 31; Prof. of Archaeology and History of Classical Art in Univ. of Cagliari 35; Dir. of Art and Antiquities in Sardinia; Dir. Museums of Cagliari and Sassari 35-38; mem. Inst. for Advanced Study, Princeton, N.J.; lectureships at Princeton and Harvard Univs. 39-45; Guggenheim Fellow 41-43; Dir. Italian Archaeological School at Athens 47-; conducted excavations at Phaistos, Gortyna, Crete, Iasos in Anatolia, etc.; mem. Accad. dei Lincei, Rome, Acad. of Athens, The N.Y. Acad. of Sciences, etc.
Publs. *Arkades, Una Città Cretese all'alba della civiltà ellenica* (Annuario Scuola It. di Atene X-XII), *La necropoli etrusca del Lago dell' Accesa* (in *Monumenti Antichi Lincei XXXV*) 33, *Corpus Vasorum Antiquorum: Florence, I-II, Il Museo Civico di Chiusi* 35, *Early Hellenic Pottery of Crete* 45, *Antioch Mosaic Pavements* 47 (2nd edn. 71), *L'ipogeo di S. Salvatore di Cabras in Sardegna* 49, *L'arte romana* 50, *L'archivio di cretule a Festos*, etc. (*Annuario Scuola Atene XXXV-XXXVI* 57-58) and other papers in *Annuario, Bollettino d'Arte, La Parola del Passato, The Recent Excavations at Phaistos* 64, *Festòs e la civiltà minoica* (4 vols.).
14-16 Parthenonos Street, Athens, Greece.
Telephone: 3227675.

Levi, Edward Hirsch; American lawyer and university professor; b. 26 June 1911, Chicago; *s.* of Gerson B. and Elsa B. Hirsch; *m.* Kate Sulzberger 1946; three *s.*; ed. Univ. of Chicago and Yale.
Assistant Prof. Univ. of Chicago Law School 36-40, Prof. of Law 45-, Dean of Law Faculty 50-62, Provost 62-68, Pres. 68-75; Special Asst. to U.S. Attorney-Gen., Washington 40-45; mem. Research Advisory Board, Cttee. for Econ. Devt. 51-54, Citizens' Comm. on Graduate Medical Educ. 63-66; mem. White House Council on Domestic Affairs 64, several comms. on internal affairs 66-71; mem. Council on Legal Educ. and Professional Responsibility, Nat. Comm. on Productivity and Work Quality 70-74; Attorney-Gen. 75-; Trustee, Aspen Inst. for Humanistic Studies, Urban Inst., Nat. Council on the Humanities 74-; Fellow, Amer. Acad. of Arts and Sciences; Fellow, Amer. Bar Foundation; mem. Council of Amer. Law Inst.; Board of Dirs. Int. Legal Center; Hon. Trustee, Int. Inst. of Educ.; Trustee, Russell Sage Foundation.
Publs. *Introduction to Legal Reasoning* 49, *Four Talks on Legal Education* 52, Editor *Gilbert's Collier on Bankruptcy* (with J. W. Moore) 37, *Elements of the Law* (with R. S. Steffen) 50, *Points of View* 69, *The Crisis in the Nature of Law* 69, *The Place of Professional Education in the Life of the University* 71, *The Collective Morality of a Maturing Society* 73.
The University of Chicago, 5801 S. Ellis Avenue,

Chicago, Illinois; Home: 5855 University Avenue, Chicago, Ill. 60637, U.S.A.
Telephone: 312-753-3001.

Levi-Sandri, Lionello, LL.D.; Italian politician and government official; b. 5 Oct. 1910.
Former Prof. of Labour Law, Univ. of Rome; fmr. official in Ministry of Labour and Transport; del. to numerous int. labour confs.; Pres. of Section, State Council; mem. Comm. of the European Econ. Community Brussels 61-64, Vice-Pres. 64-67, Vice-Pres. Combined Comm. of the European Communities 67-70.
Publs. *I controlli dello Stato sulla produzione industriale* 38, *Gli infortuni sul lavoro* 52, *Linee di una teoria giuridica della previdenza sociale* 53, *La tutela dell'igiene e della sicurezza del lavoro* 54, *Lezioni di diritto del Lavoro* 62, *Istituzioni di legislazione sociale* 66.
c/o Ministry of Foreign Affairs, Rome Italy.

Lévi-Strauss, Claude; French anthropologist, university professor and writer; b. 28 Nov. 1908, Brussels, Belgium; *s.* of Raymond Lévi-Strauss and Emma Lévy; *m.* 1st Dina Dreyfus 1932; *m.* 2nd Rose Marie Ullmo 1946, one *s.*; *m.* 3rd Monique Roman 1954, one *s.*; ed. Lycée Janson de Sailly, Paris, and Univ. de Paris à la Sorbonne.
Professor Univ. of São Paulo, Brazil 35-39; Visiting Prof. New School for Social Research, New York 42-45; Cultural Counsellor, French Embassy to U.S.A. 46-47; Assoc. Dir. Musée de l'Homme, Paris 49-50; Dir. of Studies, Ecole Pratique des Hautes Etudes, Paris 50-74; Prof. Collège de France 59-; mem. Acad. Française; Foreign mem. Royal Acad. of the Netherlands, Norwegian Acad. of Sciences and Letters, American Acad. of Arts and Sciences, British Acad.; Foreign Assoc. U.S. Nat. Acad. of Sciences; Hon. mem. Royal Anthropological Inst., American Philosophical Soc., and London School of Oriental and African Studies; Dr. h.c. (Univ. of Brussels, Yale, Chicago, Columbia, Oxford, Stirling, Zaïre); Officier Légion d'Honneur; Prix Paul Pelliot 49; Huxley Memorial Medal 65, Viking Fund Gold Medal 66, Gold Medal Centre National de la Recherche Scientifique 67; Erasmus Prize 73.
Leisure interest: country life.
Publs. *La Vie familiale et sociale des Indiens Nambikwara* 48, *Les Structures élémentaires de la parenté* 49, *Tristes Tropiques* 55, *Anthropologie Structurale* 58, *Le Totémisme aujourd'hui* 62, *La Pensée Sauvage* 62, *Le Cru et le Cuit* 64, *Du miel aux cendres* 67, *L'Origine des Manières de Table* 68, *L'Homme Nu* 71, *Anthropologie structurale deux* 73, *La Voie des masques* 75.
Laboratoire d'Anthropologie Sociale, Collège de France, 11 place Marcelin-Berthelot, 75231 Paris, Cedex 05; Home: 2 rue des Marronniers, 75016 Paris, France.
Telephone: 325-62-11 (Office); 288-34-71 (Home).

Levichkin, Klement Danilovich; Soviet diplomatist; b. 27 July 1907, Moscow Region; ed. Leningrad Technological Inst.
Diplomatic Service 36-; Union Control Comm., Bulgaria 45-47; Counsellor, Sofia 47-49; Deputy Head of Dept. for Balkan Affairs, Ministry of Foreign Affairs 49-52; Envoy and later Ambassador to Bulgaria 52-55; Deputy Head of Fifth European Dept., Ministry of Foreign Affairs 55-57; Deputy Perm. Rep. to UN 57-59; Amb. to Denmark 59-66; Deputy Minister of Foreign Affairs to R.S.F.S.R. 66-68; Amb. to Greece 68-74.
c/o Ministry of Foreign Affairs, Moscow, U.S.S.R.

Levin, Harry Tuchman, A.B.; American teacher and writer; b. 18 July 1912, Minneapolis, Minn.; *s.* of I. H. Levin and Beatrice Tuchman; *m.* Elena Zarudnaya 1939; one *d.*; ed. Univs. of Harvard and Paris.
Instructor in English at Harvard Univ. 39-44; Associate Prof. 44-48, Prof. 48-55; Prof. of English and Comparative Literature 55-60; Chair. Dept. of Comparative Lit-

erature 46-51, 53-54, 60-61, 63-69, 72-73; Chair. Div. of Mod. Languages 51-52, 55-61; Irving Babbitt Prof. Comparative Literature 60-; Visiting Prof. Univ. of Paris 53, Salzburg Seminar in Amer. Studies 53, Univ. of Tokyo 55, Univ. of Calif. (Berkeley) 57, Princeton Univ. 61, Indiana Univ. 67, Cambridge Univ. 67; Visiting Fellow All Souls, Oxford 74; Chair. English Inst. 57; Vice-Pres. Int. Comparative Literature Asscn. 64-67; Pres. Amer. Comparative Literature Asscn. 65-68; mem. Amer. Inst. Arts and Letters 60, Amer. Acad. of Arts and Sciences 50-, Amer. Philosophical Soc. 61-; Award of the Amer. Inst. of Arts and Letters 47; Chevalier of the Legion of Honour 53; Award of Amer. Council of Learned Socs. 62; Hon. Litt., LL.D., L.H.D., Dr. h.c. (Univ. of Paris) 74.
Leisure interests: theatre, travel, Cape Cod.
Publs. *The Broken Column: A Study in Romantic Hellenism* 31, *James Joyce: A Critical Introduction* 41, *The Overreacher: A Study of Christopher Marlowe* 52, *Symbolism and Fiction* 56, *Contexts of Criticism* 57, *The Power of Blackness: Hawthorne, Poe, Melville* 58, *The Question of Hamlet* 59, *The Gates of Horn: A Study of Five French Realists* 63, *Refractions: Essays in Comparative Literature* 66, *The Myth of the Golden Age in the Renaissance* 69, *Grounds for Comparison* 72, *Shakespeare and the Revolution of the Times: Perspectives and Commentaries* 76.
400 Boylston Hall, Harvard University, Cambridge, Mass. 02138; Home: 14 Kirkland Place, Cambridge, Mass. 02138, U.S.A.
Telephone: 617-495-2543 (Office); 617-876-0289 (Home).

Levina, Zara Alexandrovna; Soviet composer; b. 5 Feb. 1906, Simferopol, Crimea; ed. Odessa Conservatoire and Moscow Conservatoire.
Member Bd. Moscow branch, U.S.S.R. Union of Composers; mem. editorial councils of State Music Publishing House and U.S.S.R. Radio and TV Cttees.; Merited Worker of Arts 67.
Leisure interests: crosswords, looking at the sea, cooking borsch.
Compositions include: two piano concertos, three symphonic waltzes, oratorio *Ode to a Soldier*, sonatas for piano and violin and piano, lyrical and vocal music settings for the verse of Russian, Soviet and Oriental poets, over 200 songs for children and 23 romances.
125047 Moscow A-47, Ulitsa Gotwalda 10, apt. 20, U.S.S.R.
Telephone: 253-06-45.

Levine, Jack; American artist; b. 3 Jan. 1915; m. Ruth Gikow 1946; one d.; studied with Dr. Denman W. Ross, and H. K. Zimmerman.
One-man exhibition Downtown Gallery, New York City 38; Artists 1942 Exhibition, Museum of Modern Art, New York City 43; exhibited at Jeu de Paume, Paris 38; Carnegie Int. Exhibitions 38, 39, 40; Retrospective Exhibitions Inst. of Contemporary Art, Boston 53, Whitney Museum of American Art, N.Y. 55, Palacio de Bellas Artes, Mexico 60; Dunn Int. Exhibition, Tate Gallery, London 63; pictures in Museum of Modern Art, William Hayes Fogg Museum (Harvard), Addison Gallery, Andover, Mass., Vatican Museum, etc.; mem. Nat. Acad. of Arts and Letters, American Acad. of Arts and Sciences; D.F.A. Colby Coll., Maine.
68 Morton Street, New York, N.Y., U.S.A.
Telephone: Yukon 9-5990.

Levine, Philip, M.D., M.A.; American medical scientist; b. 10 Aug. 1900, Kletsk, Russia; s. of Morris and Faye Levine; m. Hilda Lillian Perlmutter 1938; two s. one d.; ed. City Coll. of New York and Cornell Univ.
Assistant and later Assoc. Rockefeller Inst. for Medical Research and mem. of Faculty, Univ. of Wisconsin Medical School 32-35; Dir. Immunohematology Div., Ortho Research Foundation 44-65, Dir. Emer. 65-;

Consultant to St. Michael's, St. Barnabas, Nassau and Muhlenberg Hospitals; mem. A.A.A.S., N.Y. Acad. of Medicine, Soc. of Experimental Biology and Medicine, Nat. Acad. of Sciences, Harvey Soc., Int. Soc. of Hematology and Blood Transfusion, etc.; discovered genetics and racial differences of human blood M, N and P (with Landsteiner); human Rh blood factor and its role in hemolytic disease, and three blood factors; Hon. D.Sc. Michigan State Univ.; awards include Mead Johnson Award 42, Passano Award 51, Johnson Medal for Research and Devt. 60, first Franz Oehlecker Award of German Soc. of Blood Transfusion 64, Clement von Pirquet Gold Medal 66, Award of Distinction Cornell Alumni Med. Coll. 68, Distinguished Service Award American Asscn. of Blood Banks 69, F.R.C.P. London 73; Award of Merit, Netherlands Red Cross, Joseph P. Kennedy Int. Award; Editorial Board *Transfusion, Vox Sanguinis, Acta Hematologica,* Columbia Univ. Seminar, Assoc. on Genetics and Evolution of Man.
Leisure interests: travel, music, chess, biographical literature, history of medicine, history of cultural development.
Ortho Research Foundation, Raritan, N.J. 08869, U.S.A.
Telephone: 201-524-2203 (Office); 201-754-9400 (Home).

Levingston, Gen. Roberto Marcelo; Argentine army officer and politician; b. 10 Jan. 1920, San Luis; s. of Guillermo Levingston and Carmen Laborda; m. Betty Nelly Andrés 1943; two s. (one deceased) one d.; ed. Pius IX Coll., Nat. Mil. Coll., Army Intelligence School, Escuela Superior de Guerra and Center for High Mil. Studies.
Entered army as cadet, Nat. Mil. Coll. 38, Sub-Lieut. 41, Brig.-Gen. 66; Army Information Officer 47-50; mem. Gen. Staff 51-57; Prof., Escuela Superior de Guerra 58-62; Head of Army Information Services 63-64; Dir.-Gen. Lemos School of Logistics 65-66; Head of Intelligence of Joint Chiefs of Staff 67-68; Mil. Attaché Army del. to Interamerican Defense Board and Pres. Special Comm. on Acquisitions in U.S.A. 69-70; Pres. and Prime Minister of Argentina June 70-March 71; Pres. Circle of Studies of Nat. Argentine Movement.
Leisure interests: reading of all kinds, particularly on politics, economics and military subjects, music and sport.
11 de Septiembre 1735-17 A, Buenos Aires, Argentina.
Telephone: 782-4433 (Home).

Levinson, Norman, M.S., D.SC.; American mathematician; b. 11 Aug. 1912, Lynn, Mass.; s. of Max Levinson and Gussie Green; m. Zipporah A. Wallman; two d.; ed. Mass. Inst. of Technology, Cambridge Univ. and Inst. for Advanced Study, Princeton.
At Mass. Inst. of Technology 38-, Prof. of Mathematics 49-; mem. Nat. Acad. of Sciences; Guggenheim Fellow 48-49; Bocher Prize, Amer. Math. Soc. 53, Chauvenet Prize, Amer. Math. Asscn. 71.
Leisure interest: mathematics.
Publs. *Gap and Density Theorems* 40, *Theory of Ordinary Differential* (with E. A. Coddington) 55, *Complex Variables* (with R. M. Redheffer) 70; about 100 papers in complex function theory, transforms theory, differential equations, probability and number theory.
Room 2-365, Massachusetts Institute of Technology, Cambridge, Mass. 02139, U.S.A.
Telephone: 253-4387.

Levinthal, Cyrus, PH.D.; American professor of biology; b. 2 May 1922, Philadelphia, Pa.; s. of Hon. Louis E. and Lenore C. Levinthal; m. Françoise Chassaigno Levinthal 1963; five c.; ed. Swarthmore Coll. and Univ. of Calif. (Berkeley).
Instructor, Dept. of Physics, Univ. of Mich. 50-52, Asst. Prof. 52-56, Assoc. Prof. 56-57; Prof. of Biophysics, Mass. Inst. of Technology 57-68; Prof. of Biology and

Chair. Dept. of Biological Sciences, Columbia Univ. 68-; mem. Nat. Acad. of Sciences, American Acad. of Arts and Sciences.

Leisure interests: reading history, politics and biography, sailing small boats.

Publs. numerous articles in professional journals.

Department of Biological Sciences, 754 Schermerhorn Extension, Columbia University, New York, N.Y. 10027, U.S.A.

Telephone: 212-280-2439.

Lévis Mirepoix, Antoine Pierre Marie François Joseph, Duc de Lévis Mirepoix et de San Fernando Luis; French writer; b. 1 Aug. 1884; ed. Univ. of Paris. Elected mem. Acad. Française 53; Président du Cincinnati de France; Gobert History Prize; Commdr. de la Légion d'Honneur; Croix de Guerre.

Publs. Novels: *Le papillon noir, Le nouvel apôtre, Le baiser de l'Antéchrist, Le seigneur inconnu, Le voyage de Satan, La vie des poupées;* historical novel: *Montségur;* memoirs: *La Touche Tréville à Naples, La Politesse,* historical works: *François Ier, Philippe le Bel, Les Trois femmes de Philippe Auguste, Sainte Jeanne de France, La France de la Renaissance, Les guerres de Religion, Le coeur secret de Saint-Simon, Vieilles races et temps nouveaux, Aventures d'une famille française, Grandeur et Misère de l'Individualisme Français, Le Roi n'est mort qu'une fois, Saint Louis, roi de France, Henri IV, roi de France et de Navarre, La Guerre de cent ans.*

30 rue de Berri, 75008 Paris; and Léran, 09600 Laroques-d'Olmes, France.

Levitin, Yury Abramovich; Soviet composer; b. 28 Dec. 1912, Poltava, Ukraine; ed. Leningrad Conservatoire.

Member Board Moscow Branch R.S.F.S.R. Composers' Union; State Prize 52; Merited Worker of Arts 65.

Compositions include: Suite *My Ukraine* 43, eight Quartets 40, 42, 43, 46. 48, 51, 52, 58, Sonata for violin and piano 58, Sonata for flute and piano 58, Sonata for 'cello and piano 59; Concertos: for piano and string orchestra 44, for clarinet and bassoon 49, for oboe and orchestra 60, for French horn and orchestra 61; Concertino for 'cello and orchestra without strings 62, Sinfonietta 51, three ballet suites 46, two dance suites 49; Cantatas: *Lenin Lives* 60, *Happy Beggars* 63; Oratorios: *The Sacred War* 42, *Requiem for Fallen Heroes* 46, *Fatherland* 47, *Lights Over the Volga* 47; Operas: *Monna-Marianne* 39, *Moidodyr* 55, *Memorial* 63.

Moscow Branch, R.S.F.S.R. Composers' Union, 4/6 Third Miusskaya Ulitsa, Moscow, U.S.S.R.

Levy, Maurice, O.M.; French scientist and university professor; b. 1922, Tlemcen, Algeria; m.; two s.; ed. Lycée Bugeaud, Algiers and Univs. of Paris and Algiers. Physicist, Nat. Centre of Scientific Research, Paris 45-48; Research Fellow, Manchester Univ. 48-50; mem. Inst. of Advanced Study, Princeton Univ. 50-52, 54-55, 62; fmrly, Visiting Prof. Stanford and Rochester Univs., Calif. Inst. of Technology and Tata Inst. of Fundamental Research, Bombay; Prof. Bordeaux Faculty of Science and later Prof. of Theoretical Physics and High Energies, Paris Faculty of Science; served as Scientific Adviser to French Embassy, Wash.; Dir. Programming Service for Research Orgs., Ministry of Industrial and Scientific Devt.; Chair. Council of ESRO 72-75.

Publs. include studies on theoretical nuclear physics and on the theory of elementary particles.

Home: 174 rue de Rivoli, 75001 Paris, France.

Levy, Walter James, C.M.G., LL.D.; American oil consultant; b. 21 March 1911, Hamburg, Germany; s. of Moses and Bertha Levy (née Lindenberger); m. Augusta Sondheimer 1942; one s. one d.; ed. Univs. of Berlin, Freiburg, Munich, Hamburg, Heidelberg and Kiel.

Assistant to Editor, Petroleum Press Bureau, London 37-41; Special Asst. and Chief, Petroleum Section,

Office of Strategic Services; mem. of Enemy Oil Cttee. under Joint Chiefs of Staff 42-44; Special Asst. Office of Intelligence Research, Dept. of State 45-48; Consultant, Office of Dep. Admin., Chief of Oil Branch, Economic Co-operation Admin. 48-49; Economic Consultant N.Y. Sept. 49-; Consultant E.C.A. 49-50; Consultant, President's Materials Policy Comm. 51-; U.S. Oil Adviser, missions to Iran, July-Sept. 51; Consultant, Nat. Security Resources Board 52; and Policy Planning Staff 52-53; Consultant to Int. Co-operation Admin. 56-57, to Dept. of State and Office of Civil and Defense Mobilization 60, to Dept. of State, Office of Under-Sec. and Asst. Secs. 60-; Oil Adviser to the Special Emissary of Pres. Kennedy to the Pres. of Indonesia 63; Consultant to the European Econ. Community 70; mem. Advisory Council to School of Advanced Int. Studies, Johns Hopkins Univ.; mem. Council on Foreign Relations Inc.; President's Cert. of Merit, Special Plaque presented by Sec. of State; Dato Selia Laila Jasa, Brunei, Order of Taj (Iran).

30 Rockefeller Plaza, New York, N.Y. 10020, U.S.A.

Telephone: 212-JU6-5263.

Lewando, Sir Jan Alfred, Kt., C.B.E.; British business executive; b. 31 May 1909; s. of Maurice and Eugenie (née Goldsmid) Lewando; m. 1948; three d.; ed. Manchester Grammar School and Manchester Univ.

With Marks & Spencer Ltd. 29-70, Dir. 54-70; Chair. Carrington Viyella Ltd. 70-75; mem. Export Council for Europe 65-68; mem. British Nat. Export Council 68-70; mem. British Overseas Trade Board 71; Pres. British Textile Confed. 72; Dir. Heal & Son Holdings Ltd., W. A. Baxter & Sons Ltd., Bunzl Pulp & Paper Ltd. 75-; Legion of Merit (U.S.A.) 46.

Davidge House, Knotty Green, Beaconsfield, Bucks., England.

Lewandowski, Bohdan, M.A.; Polish diplomatist; b. 29 June 1926, Ostrołęka; m. Helen M. Harris 1948; two d.; ed. Acad. of Political Sciences, Warsaw and Warsaw Univ.

Ministry of Foreign Affairs, Warsaw 45-46; Polish Foreign Service in United States 46-48; Head, N. America Section, Ministry of Foreign Affairs 51-56; Deputy Dir. Dept. for U.K. and America 56-60; Polish Rep. UN Security Council 60; Perm. Rep. of Poland to UN 60-66; Dir. of Research Bureau, Ministry of Foreign Affairs 66-67; Deputy Head, Foreign Dept., Polish United Workers' Party 67-71; Dir.-Gen. Ministry of Foreign Affairs 71-72; Under Sec.-Gen. of UN 72-.

United Nations Secretariat, New York, N.Y. 10017, U.S.A.

Lewis, Sir Anthony Carey, Kt., C.B.E., M.A., MUS.B.; British professor of music; b. 2 March 1915, Bermuda; s. of Col. L. C. Lewis, O.B.E. and Mrs. K. B. Lewis; m. Lesley Lisle Smith 1959; ed. Wellington Coll. and Peterhouse, Cambridge.

On music staff, B.B.C. 35-46 (Music Supervisor, Third Programme 46); Peyton and Barber Prof. of Music, Univ. of Birmingham 47-68, Dean Faculty of Arts 61-64; Principal, Royal Acad. of Music 68-; Chair. Music Panel, Arts Council 54-65; Pres. Royal Musical Asscn. 64-69; Chair. Advisory Music Panel, British Council 66-73; Founder and Gen. Editor *Musica Britannica;* Gov. Wellington Coll.; Hon. Sec. Purcell Soc.; Hon. R.A.M.; Hon. Mus.D. (Birmingham).

Leisure interest: gardening.

Works: Compositions: *A Tribute of Praise* (for Unaccompanied Chorus), Concerto for Trumpet and Orchestra, Concerto for Horn and Strings; Editor: *Venus and Adonis* (Blow), *The Fairy Queen* (Purcell), *Apollo and Daphne* and *Athaliah* (Handel).

Royal Academy of Music, Marylebone Road, London NW1 5HT, England.

Telephone: 01-935-5461.

Lewis, Bernard, B.A., PH.D., F.B.A., F.R.HIST.S.; British university professor; b. 31 May 1916; ed. Univs. of London and Paris.
Lecturer in Islamic History, School of Oriental Studies, Univ. of London 38; served R.A.C. and Intelligence Corps 40-41; attached to Foreign Office 41-45; Prof. of History of the Near and Middle East, Univ. of London 49-74; Visiting Prof. of History, Univ. of California at Los Angeles 55-56, Columbia Univ. 60, Indiana Univ. 63, Princeton Univ. 64, Univ. of Calif. at Berkeley 65; Visiting mem. Inst. for Advanced Study, Princeton 69; Cleveland E. Dodge Prof. of Near Eastern Studies, Princeton Univ.; Long-term mem. Inst. for Advanced Study 74-.
Publs. *The Origins of Ismā'ilism* 40, *Turkey Today* 40, *British Contributions to Arabic Studies* 41, *Handbook of Diplomatic and Political Arabic* 47, 56, *Land of Enchanters* (Editor) 48, *The Arabs in History* 50, 54, 56, 58, 60, 64, 66, *Notes and Documents from the Turkish Archives* 52, *The Emergence of Modern Turkey* 61, 62, 65, 68, *The Kingly Crown* 61, *Historians of the Middle East* (co-editor with P.M. Holt) 62, *Istanbul and the Civilization of the Ottoman Empire* 63, *The Middle East and the West* 64, *The Assassins* 67, *Race and Colour in Islam* 71, *Islam in History* 73, Editor *Islamic Civilization* 74, *Islam from the Prophet Muhammad to the Capture of Constantinople* (2 vols.) 74, *History—Remembered, Recovered, Invented* 75.
Department of Near Eastern Studies, Princeton University, Princeton, N.J. 08540, U.S.A.
Telephone: (609) 452-4275.

Lewis, Dan, PH.D., D.SC., F.R.S.; British geneticist; b. 30 Dec. 1910, Stoke-on-Trent; s. of Ernest Albert and Edith Jane Lewis; m. Mary P. E. Burry 1933; one d.; ed. High School, Newcastle under Lyme, and Univs. of Reading and London.
Plant breeder, John Innes Inst. 35, Head Dept. of Genetics 47; Quain Prof. of Botany, Univ. Coll., London 57-; Visiting Prof. of Genetics, Univ. of Calif., Berkeley 61, Delhi 65, Singapore 70; Pres. Genetical Soc. 68-71; mem. Univ. Grants Cttee. 68-74.
Leisure interests: wine and music.
Publs. Articles on genetics; Editor *Science Progress.*
Department of Botany and Microbiology, University College, London, W.C.1; Home: 50 Canonbury Park North, London, N.1, England.
Telephone: 01-387-7050 (Office); 01-226-9136 (Home).

Lewis, David, B.A.; Canadian barrister and politician; b. 23 June 1909, Poland; s. of Morris Lewis and Rose (née Lazarus) Lewis; m. Sophie Carson 1935; two s. two d.; ed. McGill Univ., Canada, and Oxford Univ.
Admitted to Bar in Canada 36; Nat. Sec. Co-operative Commonwealth Fed. of Canada 37-50, Vice-Chair. 50-54, Chair. 54-58, Pres. 58-61; Counsel, law firm of Armstrong & MacLean, Toronto; helped found New Democratic Party, Nat. Vice-Pres. 61-71, Leader 71-74; mem. Parl. 62-63, 65-68, 68-74.
Publ. *Make This Your Canada* (co-author).
Home: 138 Rodney Crescent, Ottawa 5; Office: Jolliffe, Armstrong & MacLean, Suite 419, 111 Richmond Street W., Toronto 1, Ont., Canada.

Lewis, David Sloan, Jr., B.S.; American business executive; b. 6 July 1917; s. of David Sloan Lewis, Sr. and Reuben (Walton) Lewis; m. Dorothy Sharpe 1941; three s. one d.; ed. Univ. of S. Carolina and Georgia Inst. of Technology.
Aerodynamicist, Glenn L. Martin Co., Baltimore 39-46, McDonnell Aircraft Corpn., St. Louis 46-70, Chief Preliminary Design 52-55, Sales Man. 55-57, Vice-Pres. and Project Man. 57-60, Senior Vice-Pres. Operations 60-61, Exec. Vice-Pres. 61, Vice-Pres. and Gen. Man. 61-62, Pres. 62-67; Pres. McDonnell Douglas Co. and Chair. Douglas Aircraft Co. Div. 67-70; Chair., Pres.

and Chief Exec. Officer Gen. Dynamics Corpn. 70-; Dir. Bankamerica Corpn., Ralston Purina Co.; Fellow, A.I.A.A.; mem. Exec. Cttee. and Board of Govs. Aerospace Industries Asscn., Nat. Acad. of Eng.; Hon. D.Sc.
Leisure interest: golf.
General Dynamics Corporation, Pierre Laclede Center, St. Louis, Mo. 63105, U.S.A.

Lewis, David Thomas, J.D., B.A.; American judge; b. 25 April 1912, Salt Lake City, Utah; s. of Judge Thomas D. and Ettie (Ellerbeck) Lewis; m. Marie Stewart 1938; three s.; ed. Univ. of Utah.
Admitted to Utah Bar 38; in private practice 38-50; mem. Utah Legislature 47-48; state district judge 50-56; Circuit Judge, U.S. Court of Appeals, Tenth Circuit 56-; Chief Judge, U.S. Court of Appeals, Tenth Circuit 70-; Order of the Coif; Hon. LL.D. (Utah) 71.
Leisure interest: golf.
4201 Federal Building, 125 South State Street, Salt Lake City, Utah 84111; Home: 1333 Emigration Circle, Salt Lake City, Utah 84108, U.S.A.
Telephone: 801-524-5173 (Office); 801-466-0226 (Home).

Lewis, Sir Edward Roberts, Kt.; British stockbroker and businessman; b. 19 April 1900, Derby; s. of late Sir Alfred Lewis; m. 1st Mary Margaret Hutton 1923 (died 1968), two s. (one deceased); m. 2nd Jeanie Margaret Smith 1973; ed. Rugby School, and Trinity Coll., Cambridge.
Member of the London Stock Exchange 25-; Chair. Decca Ltd., The Decca Navigator Co. Ltd. 45-, Decca Radar Co. Ltd. 50-, The Decca Record Co. Ltd. 57-.
9 Albert Embankment, London, S.E.1, England.

Lewis, Hobart Durbin; American magazine executive; b. 19 Dec. 1909, New York; s. of Paul Adin and Louise (Durbin) Lewis; m. 1st Janet Brown 1933, 2nd Edith Louise Miller 1950; two s. two d.; ed. Princeton Univ.
Instructor Mercer Junior Coll., Princeton 34-38; Advertising Copy Writer N. W. Ayer and Son, Philadelphia 38-42; joined *Reader's Digest* 42, Exec. Editor, Vice-Pres. 61-64, Exec. Editor, Pres. 64-70, Editor-in-Chief, Chair., Chief Exec. 70-; Dir. Richard Nixon Foundation; Vice-Chair. American Revolution Bicentennial Comm.; Trustee, Consolidated Edison, N.Y.; Dir. Boys Clubs of America; Chair. U.S. Advisory Comm. on Information, Pilgrims, Int. Advisory Council Morgan Guaranty Trust Co.
Leisure interest: golf.
Reader's Digest, Pleasantville, N.Y. 10570, U.S.A.

Lewis, Hon. John Vernon Radcliffe, B.A.; Rhodesian judge; b. 14 Feb. 1917, London, England; ed. Prince Edward School, Salisbury, Rhodesia, Rhodes Univ., S. Africa and Balliol Coll., Oxford, England.
Admitted as advocate, High Court of S. Rhodesia 39; active service 40-45; practising lawyer, Salisbury 45-60; Queen's Counsel 56; Judge of the High Court 60; Judge of Appeal, Appellate Div. of the High Court 70-.
P.O. Box 8159, Causeway, Salisbury; Home: 5 Maasdorp Avenue, Alexandra Park, Salisbury, N.12, Rhodesia.

Lewis, Richard, C.B.E., F.R.A.M., F.R.M.C.M., L.R.A.M.; British opera singer; ed. Royal Manchester Coll. of Music, Royal Acad. of Music.
English debut in *Rape of Lucretia*, Glyndebourne; created Troilus (*Troilus and Cressida* by Walton); sang in première of Stravinsky's *Canticum Sacrum*; guest appearances at Covent Garden, Edinburgh Festival, San Francisco Opera, Glyndebourne, Vienna State Opera and Teatro Colón, Buenos Aires; appearances in oratorio and recitals in Europe, America, Australia and New Zealand; numerous broadcasts and recordings.
White Acre, Highgate Road, Forest Row, Sussex, England.

Lewis, Roger; American business executive; b. 11 Jan. 1912, Los Angeles, Calif.; s. of Clarence Vernon and Charlotte (Gibbons) Lewis; m. Elly Thummler 1938; three c.; ed. Stanford Univ.
Lockheed Aircraft Corpn. 34-37; Vice-Pres. (Sales) Canadair Ltd., Montreal 47-50; Vice-Pres. Curtiss-Wright Corpn. 50-53; Asst. Sec. of Air Force 53-55; Exec. Vice-Pres., Dir. and mem. Exec. Cttee. Pan American World Airways 55-62; Chair. of Board, Pres. and Dir. Gen. Dynamics Corpn. 62-70, Pres. and mem. of Board 70-72, Dir. Canadair Ltd. (subsid.); Pres. and Chair. Board Nat. Railroad Passenger Corpn. 71-75, Dir. 71-; Sr. Vice-Pres. and Dir. Hornblower & Weeks, Hemphill-Noger; Medal of Freedom.
955 L'Enfant Plaza, S.W., Washington, D.C. 20024, U.S.A.

Lewis, Saunders, M.A.; Welsh writer and dramatist; b. 15 Oct. 1893; ed. Liverpool Univ.
Publs. plays: *The Eve of St. John* 21, *Gwaed yr Uchelwyr* 22, *Buchedd Garmon* 37, *Amlyn ac Amig* 40, *Blodeuwedd* 48, *Eisteddfod Bodran* 52, *Gan Bwyll* 52, *Siwan a Cherddi Eraill* 56, *Gymerwch Chi Sigaret?* 56, *Brad* 58, *Esther* 60, *Serch Yw'r Doctor* (light opera libretto) 60, *Cymru Fydd* 67, *Problemau Prifysgol* 68, *Dwy Briodas Ann* 73; novels: *Monica* 30, *Merch Gwern Hywel* 64; poetry: *Mair Fadlen* 37, *Byd a Betws* 41; criticism: *A School of Welsh Augustans* 24, *Williams Pantycelyn* 27, *Ceiriog* 29, *Braslun o Hanes Llenyddiaeth Gymraeg Hyd 1535* 32, *Daniel Owen* 36, *Ysgrifau Dydd Mercher* 45, *Meistri'r Canrifoedd* 73; trans. of plays have been staged in English, German and Spanish; trans. of Molière, Beckett.
158 Westbourne Road, Penarth, South Glam., Wales.

Lewis, Thomas Lancelot; Australian politician; b. 23 Jan. 1922, Adelaide; m. Yutta Anton 1971; three s. one d.; ed. St. Peter's Coll., Adelaide.
Member N.S.W. Legislative Assembly 57-; Minister for Lands, New South Wales 65-75, for Mines 65-67, for Tourism 72-75; Premier and Treas. N.S.W. Jan. 75-Jan. 76; est. Nat. Parks and Wildlife Service.
Leisure interests: flying, skiing, swimming, water-skiing, jogging.
Redbraes, 17 Valetta Street, Moss Vale, N.S.W. 2577, Australia.
Telephone: (048) 911617.

Lewis, Wilfrid Bennett, C.C., C.B.E., M.A., PH.D., F.R.S., F.R.S.C.; British physicist; b. 24 June 1908, Castle Carrock, Cumberland; s. of Arthur Wilfrid and Isoline Maud Lewis (née Steavenson); ed. Haileybury Coll., and Gonville and Caius Coll., Cambridge Univ.
Research Fellow Gonville and Caius Coll. 34-40; Univ. Demonstrator Cambridge 35-37, University Lecturer 37-39; Senior Scientific Officer, Bawdsey Research Station, Air Ministry (later became Telecommunications Research Establishment, Malvern) 39, Chief Supt., T.R.E., Malvern 45-46; Dir. Atomic Energy Research Div. of Nat. Research Council of Canada 46-52; Vice-Pres. Research and Development, Atomic Energy of Canada Ltd. 52-63, Senior Vice-Pres. Science 63-73 (retd.); Distinguished Prof. of Science, Queen's Univ., Kingston, Ont. 73-; research in Nuclear Physics at Cavendish Laboratory, Cambridge 30-39; research and development of radar for air operations 39-46; Canadian Rep. UN Scientific Advisory Cttee.; mem. Scientific Advisory Cttee. IAEA 58-, UN Sec.-Gen.'s Cttee. of Experts on Implications of Atomic Weapons 67; Fellow and Pres. American Nuclear Soc. 61-62; Govt. of Canada Outstanding Achievement in Public Service Award 66, Atoms for Peace Award 67, U.S. Medal of Freedom (Silver Palms); C.C. (Companion of the Order of Canada) 67; Royal Medal of Royal Soc., London 72; Hon. D.Sc. Queen's Univ., Kingston 60, Saskatchewan Univ. 64, McMaster Univ., Hamilton, Ont. 65, Dartmouth Coll., New Hampshire 67, McGill

Univ., Montreal 69; Hon. LL.D. Dalhousie Univ., Halifax 60, Carleton Univ., Ottawa 62, Trent Univ., Peterborough, Ont. 68, Toronto Univ. 72; Hon. Fellow, Gonville and Caius Coll. 71; Hon. F.I.E.E. 74.
Leisure interest: walking.
Publ. *Electrical Counting* 42.
Box 189, 13 Beach Avenue, Deep River, Ontario, K0J 1P0, Canada.
Telephone: 613-584-3561.

Lewis, Sir (William) Arthur, Kt., B.COM., PH.D., LL.D.; British economist; b. 23 Jan. 1915, St. Lucia; s. of George Ferdinand and Ida Louisa Lewis; m. Gladys Jacobs 1947; two d.; ed. London School of Economics.
Lecturer, London School of Econs. 38-48; Prof. of Political Economy, Univ. of Manchester 48-58; Principal, then Vice-Chancellor, Univ. of the West Indies 59-63; Prof. of Political Economy, Princeton Univ. 63-; Pres. Caribbean Devt. Bank 70-73; mem. American Philosophical Soc., American Acad. of Arts and Sciences; Distinguished Fellow, American Econ. Asscn.; Corresp. Fellow, British Acad.
Leisure interest: music.
Publs. *Economic Survey 1918-1939* 49, *Overhead Costs* 49, *The Theory of Economic Growth* 55, *Development Planning* 66.
Woodrow Wilson School, Princeton, N.J. 08540, U.S.A.
Telephone: 452-4825.

Lewy, Hans, PH.D.; American professor of mathematics; b. 20 Oct. 1904, Breslau (now Wrocław), Poland; s. of Max and Margarete Lewy; m. Helen Crosby 1947; one s.; ed. Univ. of Göttingen.
Privatdozent, Univ. of Göttingen, Germany 27-33; Lecturer, Brown Univ. 33-35; Lecturer Mathematics, Univ. of Calif. at Berkeley 35-37, Asst. Prof. 37-39, Assoc. Prof. 39-45, Prof. 45-; mem. Nat. Acad. of Sciences.
Publs. Works in Calculus of Variations, Partial Differential Equations, Differential Geometry and Hydrodynamics.
Department of Mathematics, University of California, Berkeley, Calif. 94720, U.S.A.

Ley, Hermann Hubert, DR.SC.PHIL.; German philosopher and politician; b. 1911, Leipzig; s. of Hermann and Agnes Ley (née Dietel); m. Christine Simon 1958; ed. Helmholtz School and Leipzig Univ.
Professor of Theoretical Pedagogics, Leipzig Univ. 47-48, of Dialectics and Historical Materialism, Dresden Tech. High School 48-56; Dir.-Gen. State Cttee. for Broadcasting and Television 56-62; Prof. of Relations of Nat. Science and Philosophy, Humboldt Univ. Berlin; Silver Patriotic Order of Merit 59, National Prize 60.
Leisure interests: skiing, cats.
Publs. *Avicenna* 52, *Mittasch* 53, *Zur Entwicklungsgeschichte der europäischen Aufklärung* 55, *Bemerkungen über Kant* 54, *Bemerkungen zum Wesen echter Menschlichkeit (Auseinandersetzung mit Jakob Hommes)* 56, *Vorreformatorische Bewegung in Deutschland* 56, *Studie zur Geschichte des Materialismus im Mittelalter* 58, *Dialektischer Widerspruch zu Lakebrink* 58, *Dämon Technik* 60, *Einige erkenntnistheoretische Probleme in Naturwissenschaft und Technik* 63, *Geschichte der Aufklärung und des Atheismus I* 67, *Gesetz und Bedingung in den Technischen und Naturwissenschaften* 64, *Struktur und Prozess in Nat. und Tech.* 66, *Bildung und Erziehung* 66, *Technik, Praxis, Philosophie* 67, *Technik und Weltanschauung* 69, *Geschichte der Aufklärung und des Atheismus II* 70-71, *Kritische Vernunft und Revolution, Zur Kontroverse zwischen Hans Albert und Jürgen Habermas* 71.
Ernst-Grube-Strasse 41C, 117 Berlin, German Democratic Republic.
Telephone: 65-7-28-44.

Leydon, John; Irish business executive; b. 17 Jan.
1895, Arigna, Co. Roscommon; *s.* of the late James
Leydon and Catherine Quinn; *m.* Nan Layden 1927
(deceased); one *d.*; ed. St. Mel's Coll., Longford, and
St. Patrick's Coll., Maynooth.
Entered British Civil Service, War Office 15; transferred
to Irish Civil Service 23; mem. staff Dept. of Finance
23-32; Sec. Dept. of Industry and Commerce 32-55,
Dept. Supplies 39-45; Sec. Economic Cttee. 28; mem.
Electricity Supply Board 29; mem. Comm. of Inquiry
on Derating 30; corresp. mem. L.N. Economic Cttee.;
Chair. Aer Rianta Tta. 37-49, Aer Lingus Tta. 37-49,
and Irish Shipping Ltd. 41-49; Chair. Insurance Corpn.
of Ireland Ltd. 46-72, Pres. 72-; Chair. Wm. & P.
Thompson Ltd., Dollar Exports Advisory Cttee. 50,
Capital Investment Advisory Cttee. 56, Nat. Bank of
Ireland Ltd. 56-73, Aerlínte Éireann (Irish Airlines)
58-60; First Pres. Inst. of Public Admin. 57-60; Dir.
Cement Ltd. 55-72, Bank of Ireland 66-72, Cen. Bank
of Ireland 65-72; Pres. Inst. of Bankers in Ireland 60;
mem. Council and Exec. Cttee. of Irish Management
Inst. 57; mem. Board of Govs. Nat. Gallery of Ireland
61; Kt. Commdr. Order of St. Gregory the Great;
LL.D. h.c. (Dublin Univ.) 60.
Our Lady's Manor, Bulloch Castle, Dalkey, County
Dublin, Ireland.
Telephone: 804992.

Li Ch'eng-fang; Chinese government official; b.
Hupeh.
Army Corps Commdr., 2nd Field Army, People's
Liberation Army 49; Commdr. Kunming Mil. Region,
PLA 64-68; Sec. CCP Yunnan 66; criticized and
removed from office during the Cultural Revolution 68;
Minister of Fifth Ministry of Machine Building 75.
People's Republic of China.

Li Ch'iang; Chinese politician and telecommunica-
tions specialist.
Member 6th Exec. Cttee., Nat. Fed. of Trade Unions
48-53; Dir. Radio Bureau, Ministry of Post and
Telecommunications 50; Commercial Attaché, Embassy
in Moscow 52-54; mem. Scientific Planning Comm.,
State Council 57; Deputy Dir. Bureau for Econ.
Relations with Foreign Countries, State Council 61;
Vice-Chair. Comm. for Econ. Relations with Foreign
Countries 65-67; Vice-Minister of Foreign Trade
68-73; mem. 9th Cen. Cttee. of CCP 69; Minister of
Foreign Trade 73-; mem. 10th Cen. Cttee. of CCP 73.
People's Republic of China.

Li Chi-tai; Chinese government official.
Minister, Third Ministry of Machine Building 75.
People's Republic of China.

Li Chih-min; Chinese army officer; b. 1908, Hunan.
Political Commissar, Chinese People's Volunteers in
Korea 53; Col.-Gen. 56; Dir. Political Dept., People's
Liberation Army Mil. Acad. 63; First Political Com-
missar Foochow Mil. Region, PLA 74.
People's Republic of China.

Li Ching-ch'uan; Chinese party official; b. Huichang,
Kiangsi.
Political Commissar 1st Front Army 31; guerrilla
leader in Sikang 34; Political Commissar Suiyan-
Mongolian Mil. Region 37, Shansi-Suiyuan Mil. Region
47; Dir. W. Szechuan Admin. Office 50; Gov. of
Szechuan 52-55; Sec. CCP Szechuan 52-55, First Sec.
55-56; Political Commissar Szechuan Mil. District,
People's Liberation Army 52, Chengtu Mil. Region,
PLA 54-67; mem. 8th Cen. Cttee. of CCP 56; mem. of
Politburo, CCP 58-67; First Sec. S.W. Bureau, CCP
61-67; Vice-Chair. Nat. People's Congress 65; criticized
and removed from office during Cultural Revolution
67; mem. 10th Cen. Cttee. of CCP 73.
People's Republic of China.

Li Choh-ming, K.B.E., M.A., PH.D., LL.D., D.S.SC.;
American (b. Chinese) educator and university professor;
b. 17 Feb. 1912, Canton, China; *s.* of Kanchi and
Mewching Tsui Li; *m.* Sylvia Lu 1938; two *s.* one *d.*; ed.
Univ. of Nanking, China, and Univ. of California
(Berkeley).
Professor of Economics, Nankai, Southwest Associated
and Nat. Central Univs., China 37-43; mem. Chinese
Special Mission to U.S.A., Canada and U.K. 43-45;
Deputy Dir. Gen. Chinese Nat. Relief and Rehabilita-
tion Admin. (CNRRA) 45-47; Chief Del. of Republic
of China to UN Economic Comm. for Asia and the
Far East 47-49; Chair. Board of Trustees for Rehabilita-
tion Affairs, Nat. Govt. of China 49-50; Expert on the
UN Population Comm. and Statistical Comm. 52-57;
Lecturer, Assoc. Prof. and Prof. of Business Admin. and
sometime Dir. of Centre for Chinese Studies, Univ. of
Calif. (Berkeley) 51-73; Vice-Chancellor Chinese Univ.
of Hong Kong 63-; Pres. Asscn. of Southeast Asian
Insts. of Higher Learning 68-70; Dir. Asian Workshop
on Higher Educ. 69; mem. Editorial Boards *Asian
Economic Review, Asian Survey, Modern Asian Studies,
China Quarterly*; Life Fellow, Royal Econ. Soc., R.S.A.,
London; mem. American Econ. Asscn., Asscn. for
Asian Studies (U.S.A.) and other socs.; Dr. of Laws
h.c. (Univs. of Hong Kong, Michigan, Western Ontario
and Marquette), Hon. Dr. of Social Sciences (Univ. of
Pittsburgh); Elise and Walter A. Haas Int. Award,
Univ. of Calif. 74.
Leisure interests: Chinese calligraphy, tennis.
Publs. *Economic Development of Communist China* 59,
Statistical System of Communist China 62, *The First
Six Years 1963-69*; Editor: *Industrial Development in
Communist China* 64, *Asian Workshop on Higher
Education—Proceedings* 69.
Office of the Vice-Chancellor, The Chinese University
of Hong Kong, Shatin, New Territories, Hong Kong.
Telephone: NT-61-2581.

Li Hsien-nien; Chinese politician; b. 1905, Huang-an,
Hupeh.
Joined CCP 27; Political Commissar 30th Army, 4th
Front Red Army 35; Commdr. 5th Column, New 4th
Army 38; mem. 7th Cen. Cttee. of CCP 45; Gov. of
Hupeh 49; Commdr. Political Commissar Hupeh Mil.
District, People's Liberation Army 49; Vice-Premier,
State Council 54-; Minister of Finance 54-; mem.
Politburo, 8th Cen. Cttee. of CCP 56; Sec. Secr. of
Cen. Cttee., CCP 58-66; Vice-Chair. State Planning
Comm. 62; mem. Politburo, 9th Cen. Cttee. of CCP 69,
Politburo, 10th Cen. Cttee. 73.
People's Republic of China.

Li Jui-shan; Chinese party official.
Secretary CCP Hunan 58-68; First Sec. CCP Changsha
59; Chair. Shensi Revolutionary Cttee. 68; Political
Commissar Lanchow Mil. Region, People's Liberation
Army 68; mem. 9th Cen. Cttee. of CCP 69; First Sec.
CCP Shensi 71; mem. 10th Cen. Cttee. of CCP 73.
People's Republic of China.

Li Kuang-hsiang; Chinese army officer.
Deputy Head, Propaganda Dept., Gen. Political
Dept., People's Liberation Army 72-.
People's Republic of China.

Li Kwoh-ting, B.S.; Chinese government official; b.
28 Jan. 1910, Nanking; *s.* of Mr. and Mrs. Li Pai-Lo;
m. Pearl Soong 1938; one *s.*; ed. Nat. Central Univ.,
China, and Cambridge Univ., England.
Superintendent of Tze Yu Iron Works, Chungking
42-45; Pres. Taiwan Shipbuilding Corpn. 51-53; mem.
Industrial Devt. Comm., Econ. Stabilisation Board
53-58; Publisher of *The Industry of Free China* (monthly)
54-71; Sec.-Gen. Council for U.S. Aid 58-63; Convener
of Industrial Planning and Co-ordination Group of
Ministry of Econ. Affairs 58-63; Head of Industrial

Devt. and Investment Center 58-63; Vice-Chair. Council for Int. Econ. Cooperation and Devt. 63-73; Minister of Econ. Affairs 65-69, of Finance June 69-; mem. Nat. Security Council 67-; Vice-Chair. Nat. Reconstruction Planning Cttee. 67-72; Ramon Magsaysay Award for Govt. Service 68, and decorations from Repub. of Korea, Spain, Repub. of Viet-Nam, Jordan, Madagascar, Thailand and Gabon.

Leisure interest: golf.

Publs. *Symposium on Nuclear Physics, British Industries, Japanese Shipbuilding Industry, The Growth of Private Industry in Free China, Economic Policy and Economic Development.*

3 Lane 44, Linyi Street, Taipei, Taiwan.
Telephone: 343575.

Li Pao-hua; Chinese party official; b. 1908, Lo-t'ing, Hopei; s. of Li Ta-chao.

Alternate mem. 7th Cen. Cttee. of CCP 45; Vice-Minister of Water Conservancy 49-63 and of Electric Power 58-63; mem. 8th Cen. Cttee. of CCP 56; First Sec. CCP Anhwei 63-67; Third Sec. E. China Bureau, CCP 65; First Political Commissar Anhwei Mil. District, People's Liberation Army 66; criticized and removed from office during Cultural Revolution 67; mem. 10th Cen. Cttee. of CCP 73; Second Sec. CCP Kweichow 73-.
People's Republic of China.

Li Shui-ch'ing; Chinese politician.

Divisional Commdr., People's Liberation Army 49; Maj.-Gen. PLA 57; Chief of Staff Tsinan Mil. Region, PLA 68; mem. 9th Cen. Cttee. of CCP 69; Minister of First Ministry of Machine Building 72-; mem. 10th Cen. Cttee. of CCP 73.
People's Republic of China.

Li Ta, Gen.; Chinese army officer; b. 1905, Shensi; ed. Moscow Mil. Acad., U.S.S.R.

Staff Officer, Red 6th Army, on Long March 34-36; Staff Officer, 129th Div. 37-45; Chief of Staff, Cen. Plains Field Army 47, Chinese People's Volunteers in Korea 53-54; Vice-Minister of Nat. Defence 54-59; Gen. 55; Chair. Nat. Defence Sports Asscn. 58-67; criticized and removed from office during Cultural Revolution 67; Deputy Chief of Cen. Staff, People's Liberation Army 72-; mem. 10th Cen. Cttee. of CCP 73.
People's Republic of China.

Li Ta-chang; Chinese party official; b. 1910, Szechuan.

Director Propaganda Dept., Taihang Sub-Bureau of N. China Bureau, CCP 44; Chief of Staff Shansi-Chahar-Honan Mil. Region 46; Mayor of Mutankiang 46; Political Commissar Mongolia-Ninghsia Mil. Region 46; Dir. S. Szechuan Admin. Office 50; Gov. of Szechuan 55-68; Sec. CCP Szechuan 54-; Alt. mem. 8th Cen. Cttee. of CCP 56; Sec. S.W. Bureau, CCP 64-67; First Sec. CCP Kweichow 65; Vice-Chair. Szechuan Revolutionary Cttee. 68; mem. 9th Cen. Cttee. of CCP 69, 10th Cen. Cttee. 73.
People's Republic of China.

Li Te-sheng, Gen.; Chinese army officer.

Company Commdr., Red 4th Front Army on Long March 34-36; Div. Commdr. 2nd Field Army, People's Liberation Army 49; Gen. PLA 64; Commdr. Anhwei Mil. District, PLA 67; Chair. Anhwei Revolutionary Cttee. 68; Alt. mem. Politburo, 9th Cen. Cttee. of CCP 69; Dir., Gen. Political Dept., People's Liberation Army 69-74; First Sec. CCP Anhwei 71-73; mem. Standing Cttee. of Politburo and Vice-Chair. 10th Cen. Cttee. of CCP 73-75; Commdr. Shenyang Mil. Region, PLA 74.
People's Republic of China.

Li Ti-tsun, B.A., M.A., PH.D.; Chinese diplomatist; b. 1901; ed. Tsing Hua Coll. of Peking, Univs. of Wisconsin, Harvard and Chicago.

Prof. of Political Science, Central Political Inst. 29-30; Nat. Central Univ. 30-31; Co-founder and Editor

Current Events Monthly 29-39; Section Chief and Asst. Dir., Ministry of Foreign Affairs 29-33; Dir. Dept. of Information, Ministry of Foreign Affairs 33-39; Minister to Cuba 39-47; concurrently Minister to Venezuela, Colombia and Dominican Repub. 42-47; Expert on Nat. Resources Comm., Nanking 35-37; Foreign Relations Cttee. of Supreme Nat. Defence Council of Chungking 38-39; Ambassador on special mission to Indonesia 46-47; Ambassador to Turkey 47-57; Ambassador to Brazil May 57-63; Del. UNESCO Conf., New Delhi 56; Rep. 16th Session UN Gen. Assembly N.Y. 61; Adviser Ministry of Foreign Affairs 63-66; Chair. Dept. of English, Coll. of Chinese Culture 63-66; Lecturer, Latin American History, Nat. War Coll. 63-66; Ambassador to Chile 66-71; numerous decorations.

Publ. *Political and Economic Theories of Dr. Sun Yat-sen* 29.
Ministry of Foreign Affairs, Taipei, Taiwan.

Liang Yuen-li (Liang Yun-li), LL.B., DR.JUR.; Chinese lawyer; b. 1904, Sing-Chang; m. Siu-Ying Sheng 1936; one s. one d.; ed. Nanyang Univ. Comparative Law School, Harvard and Geneva Univs.

Editor *China Law Review* 24-26; Lecturer Comparative Law School and Legal Editor *Commercial Press* 26-27; Sec. to Minister of Foreign Affairs 27 and Minister of Justice 28; Judge Shanghai Provisional Court 28; Prof. of Law Comparative Law School 28-29; Sec. Washington Legation 29-33; Carnegie Teachers Fellow in Int. Law Harvard 30-31; Counsellor of Exec. *Yuan* 33; Senior Sec. of Ministry of Foreign Affairs 34; senior mem. Treaty Comm. of Ministry of Foreign Affairs and Prof. Central Univ. 36-37; contrib. Editor *China Critic*; First Sec. Embassy London 39-42, Counsellor 43-46; mem. Chinese del. to Dumbarton Oaks and San Francisco Conf. 44-45; Chair. Cttee. of Experts, Security Council 46; Visiting Prof., Univ. of Michigan, Summer Session 47; Prof. Hague Acad. of Int. Law 48; Lecturer, New York Univ. Law School 47-48 and 49-50, Adjunct Assoc. Prof. 51-60, Adjunct Prof. 60-; Dir. Legal Dept. United Nations 46-64; elected Assoc. Inst. of Int. Law 50; Adviser Chinese Del. to the UN Gen. Assembly 64, 65, 68; Prof. Postgraduate Inst. of Int. Law and Diplomacy, Nat. Cheng-chi Univ. Taipei 68; elected Titular mem. Inst. of Int. Law 65; Adviser to Ministry of Foreign Affairs and Dir. Treaty Dept. 69; mem. Perm. Court of Arbitration, The Hague 70-.

Leisure interest: music.

Publs. *The First Year of the Far Eastern Crisis, International Government, Sociology of Law, China* 46, *Le Développement et la Codification du Droit international* 48.
Ministry of Foreign Affairs, Taipei, Taiwan.

Liao Ch'eng-chih; Chinese party official; b. 1908, Tokyo, Japan; ed. Lingnan Univ., Canton, Waseda Univ., Japan and Berlin and Hamburg Univs., Germany.

Joined CCP 25; studied Political Econ., Germany 28; Chair. Seaman's Union 33; participated in Long March 34-36; Dir. New China News Agency 38; prisoner of Kuomintang 42-46; Alt. mem. 7th Cen. Cttee. of CCP 45; Chair. Nat. Fed. of Democratic Youth 49; Dir. Inst. of Foreign Affairs 49-54; mem. 8th Cen. Cttee. of CCP 56; Chair. Comm. for Overseas Chinese Affairs 59-67; Pres. Overseas Chinese Univ., Fukien 61-67, China-Japan Friendship Asscn. 63-; criticized and removed from office during Cultural Revolution 67; rehabilitated and returned to previous positions 72; mem. 10th Cen. Cttee. of CCP 73.
People's Republic of China.

Liao Chih-kao; Chinese party official; b. *circa* 1908 Chien-ning, Szechuan; ed. Tsinghua Univ. Peking.

Director Political Dept., N. Shensi 47; Political Commissar Sikang Mil. District, People's Liberation Army 50-55; Gov. of Sikang Provisional Govt. 50-55; Vice-Gov. of Szechuan 55-58; Sec. CCP Szechuan,

56-65, First Sec. 65-68; Alt. mem. 8th Cen. Cttee. of CCP 56; Sec. S.W. Bureau, CCP 64-68; criticized and removed from office during Cultural Revolution 68; Alt. mem. 10th Cen. Cttee. of CCP 73; First Sec. CCP Fukien 75.
People's Republic of China.

Libby, Willard Frank, B.S., PH.D.; American scientist; b. 17 Dec. 1908, Grand Valley, Colo.; s. of Ora Edward and Eva May (Rivers) Libby; m. Leonor Hickey 1940 (dissolved 1966), 2nd Leona Woods Marshall 1966; two d.; ed. Univ. of Calif., Berkeley.
Instructor of Chemistry, Univ. of Calif. 33, Asst. Prof. 38, Assoc. Prof. 45, Prof. 59-; Guggenheim Fellow, Princeton Univ. 41; mem. Columbia Univ., War Research Div. 41-45; Prof. Dept. of Chemistry, Inst. for Nuclear Studies (now Enrico Fermi Inst. for Nuclear Studies), Univ. of Chicago 45-54; mem. Atomic Energy Comm. 54-59; Research Assoc., Geophysical Laboratory, Carnegie Inst. Wash. 54-59; Prof. of Chemistry, Univ. of Calif. at L.A. 59-; Dir. Inst. of Geophysics and Planetary Physics, Univ. of Calif. 62-; Univ. of Colo. Boulder, Special Visiting Prof. of Chemistry, Physics, Astrophysics and Aero-Engineering 67-70; Special Visiting Prof. of Chemistry, Univ. of South Fla., Tampa, 72-; Guggenheim Fellow 41, 51 and 59; Atomic Energy Comm., mem. Cttee. of Senior Reviewers 45-52, Gen. Advisory Cttee. 50-54 and 60-62, mem. U.S. del. and Vice-Chair. Int. Conf. on the Peaceful Uses of Atomic Energy, Geneva 55 and 58, Plowshare Advisory Cttee. 59-72; mem. Cttee. of Selection of Guggenheim Memorial Foundation 59-, Air Resources Board, Calif. 67-72, Acad. Advisory Board, The Rand Corpn. 68-, Visiting Cttee. Jet Propulsion Laboratory 68-72, Task Force on Air Pollution 69-70, U.S. del. to U.S.-Japan Cttee. on Scientific Co-operation 70-73, Gov.'s Earthquake Council, Calif. 72-; mem. Editorial Board, *Industrial Research* 67-73, *Space Life Science* 70-, *Science of the Total Environment* 73-, *Environmental Geology* 73-; Consultant and Adviser to numerous orgs.; Pres. and Dir., The Isotope Foundation 60-; Dir. Douglas Aircraft Co. Inc. 63-67; Dir. and Chair. of the Board Scientific Research Instruments Corp. 67-; Dir. Hedge Fund of America 68-, Summit Capital Fund 68-, Nuclear Systems Inc. 69-, Research-Cottrell Inc. 71-; mem. many Amer. and foreign acads. and socs.; Research Corpn. Award for radiocarbon dating technique 51; Chandler Medal (Columbia Univ.) 54; Amer. Chemical Soc. Award for nuclear applications in chem. 56; Nobel Prize for Chem. 60; numerous medals, incl. Albert Einstein Medal 59, Gold Medal, Amer. Inst. of Chemists 70; several hon. degrees.
Leisure interest: golf.
Publs. *Radiocarbon Dating* 52, 55, 65, etc. and numerous articles.
Chemistry Department, UCLA, 405 Hilgard Avenue, Los Angeles, Calif. 90024, U.S.A.
Telephone: 213-825-1968.

Liberaki, Margarita; Greek novelist and dramatist; b. 1919, Athens; divorced; one d.; ed. Athens Univ.
Lives in Paris and Greece, writes in Greek and French.
Leisure interest: painting.
Publs. *The Trees* 47, *The Straw Hats* 50, *Trois Etés* 50, *The Other Alexander* 52; plays: *Kandaules' Wife* 55, *The Danaids* 56, *L'Autre Alexandre* 57, *Le Saint Prince* 59, *La Lune a Faim* 61, *Sparagmos* 65, *Le Bain de Mer* 67, *Erotica* 70; film scripts: *Magic City* 53, *Phaedra* 61.
7 rue de L'Eperon, Paris 6e, France; 2 Strat. Sindesmou, Athens, Greece.
Telephone: MED 05-92 (Paris).

Liberman, Yevsei Grigorievich; Soviet economist; b. 7 Oct. 1897; ed. Univ. of Kiev.
Lecturer, Kharkov Engineering and Econs. Inst., later Kharkov Univ., Prof. 57-.
Publs. include: *Structure of the Balance of an Industrial*

Undertaking 48, *Economic Accounting in a Factory* 50, *Ways of Raising the Profitability of Socialist Enterprises* 56, *Main Problems of Composite Mechanization and Automation of Production* 61, *Plan, Profit, Bonuses* 62, *The Economic Methods to Raise the Efficiency of Socialistic Enterprises* 67.
Kharkov State University, 4 Ploshchad Dzerzhinskogo, Kharkov, U.S.S.R.

Licaros, Gregario S., LL.B., B.SC.; Philippine lawyer and banker; b. 12 March 1909; ed. Far Eastern Univ.
Chairman Board of Trustees, Govt. Service Insurance System 54-61; Chair. Board of Govs., Devt. Bank of the Philippines and mem. Central Bank Monetary Board 58-61; Chair. Board of Dirs., CCP Securities Corpn. 63-65; Gov. Central Bank of the Philippines Jan. 70-, concurrently Gov. Int. Monetary Fund for the Philippines; mem. Council of Central Bank Govs. of S.E. Asia, N.Z., Australia (SEANZA) 70-, Nat. Econ. Council, Financial and Fiscal Policy Council, Foreign Trade Council, Surigao Mineral Reservation Board 70; mem. Board of Dirs., Philippine Deposit Insurance Corpn. 70-; Chair. Gold Mining Industry Assistance Board 70-; Outstanding CPA, Philippine Asscn. of Board of Examiners 58, and many other awards.
Central Bank of the Philippines, A. Mabini Street, Manila; Home: 802 Harvard Street, Mandaluyong, Rizal, Philippines.

Lichnerowicz, André, D. ès SC.; French mathematician; b. 21 Jan. 1915, Bourbon; s. of Jean Lichnerowicz and Antoinette Gressin; m. Suzanne Magdelain 1942; three s.; ed. Lycée Louis-le-Grand, Paris, Ecole Normale Supérieure, Paris, and Univ. de Paris.
Research assignments, Centre National de Recherche Scientifique 38-41; mem. staff, Univ. of Strasbourg 41-46, Full Prof. 46-49; Full Prof. Univ. of Paris 49-52, Prof. of Mathematical Physics, Collège de France 52-; mem. Acad. des Sciences, Accad. Naz. dei Lincei, Rome, Acad. Real de Ciencias, Madrid, Acad. Royale de Belgique; Officier Légion d'Honneur; Commandeur de l'Ordre du Mérite et des Palmes Académiques; Prix int. Fubini 55.
Leisure interests: philosophy, gardening, tennis.
Publs. *Algèbre et Analyse linéaire* 46, *Eléments de Calcul tensoriel* 49, *Théories relativistes de la gravitation* 54, *Théorie globale des connexions* 55, *Géométrie des groupes de transformation* 58, *Relativistic hydrodynamics and magnetohydrodynamics* 67.
6 avenue Paul Appell, Paris, France.
Telephone: 540-5166.

Licht, Frank; American lawyer and politician; b. 3 March 1916, Providence, R.I.; s. of Jacob and the late Rose (Kassed) Licht; m. Dorothy Krauss 1946; three d.; ed. Brown Univ. and Harvard Law School.
Admitted to R.I. Bar 42; partner Letts and Quinn (law firm) 43-56; Senator from Rhode Island 49-56; Assoc. Justice, R.I. Superior Court 56-68; Gov. of Rhode Island 69-73; Partner Letts, Quinn and Licht 73-; Democrat.
640 Elmgrove Avenue, Providence, R.I. 02906, U.S.A.

Lichtenberg, Paul; German banker; b. 10 Dec. 1911, Bonn.
Spokesman, Man. Board Commerzbank A.G., Frankfurt/Düsseldorf; Chair. Rheinische Hypothekenbank, Frankfurt, Berliner Commerzbank A.G., Berlin, Stern-Brauerei Carl Funke A.G., Essen, Europartners Securities Corpn., New York, Kaufhof A.G., Cologne; Deputy Chair. Hochtief A.G. für Hoch- und Tiefbauten vorm. Gebr. Helfmann, Essen; mem. Board of Dirs. Allianz Lebensversicherungs—A.G., Stuttgart, Daimler-Benz A.G., Stuttgart, Didier Werke A.G., Wiesbaden, BBC Brown, Boveri und Cie A.G., Mannheim, GHH Gutehoffnungshütte Aktienverein, Oberhausen, Hoechst A.G., Frankfurt-Hoechst; Chair. Admin. Board Allgemeine Deutsche Investmentgesellschaft

m.b.H., Munich/Düsseldorf, Commerzbank Int., Luxembourg; Adviser to Allianz-Versicherungs-A.G., and Allianz-Lebensversicherungs-A.G., Munich; mem. Advisory Cttee. Gelsenwasser A.G., Gelsenkirchen, Hermes Kreditversicherungs-A.G., Munich, Kautex-Werke Reinold Hagen, Bonn-Holzar, Robert Krups GmbH, Solingen, Rheinisch-Westfälisches Elektrizitätswerk AG, Essen; mem. Man. Board Bundesverband Deutscher Banken e.V., Cologne; mem. Zentraler Kapitalmarktausschuss Cttee. of Eleven.
Commerzbank A.G., Frankfurt am Main, Neue Mainzer Strasse 32-36, Federal Republic of Germany.
Telephone: 13621 (Frankfurt).

Lichtenstein, Roy; American painter and sculptor; b. 1923, New York City; s. of Milton and Beatrice Lichtenstein; m. Dorothy Herzka 1968; two s.; ed. Art Students League, N.Y. (under Reginald Marsh) and Ohio State Univ.
Cartographical draughtsman, U.S. Army 43-46; Instructor, Fine Arts Dept., Ohio State Univ. 46-51; first one-man show, Carlebach Gallery, N.Y. 51; product designer for various companies, Cleveland 51-57; Asst. Prof., Fine Arts Dept., New York State Univ. 57-60, Fine Arts Dept., Rutgers Univ. 60-63; one-man shows have included: Castelli Gallery, N.Y. 62, 63, 64, 65, 67, 71, 72, 73, Ferus Gallery, Los Angeles 63, Paris 65, 70, Milan 65, Pasadena Art Museum, Calif., Stedelijk Museum, Amsterdam 60, Tate Gallery, London, Kunsthalle, Berne 68, Guggenheim Museum, N.Y. 69; group exhbns. include *Six Painters and the Object*, Guggenheim Museum 63, Venice Biennale 66, U.S. Pavilion *Expo* 67, Montreal, São Paulo Biennale 68, and numerous other group exhbns. in Europe and U.S.A.
190 Bowery, New York, N.Y. 10012; Home: 36 West 26th Street, New York, N.Y. 10010, U.S.A.

Licklider, J(oseph) C(arl) R(obnett), PH.D.; American psychologist; b. 11 March 1915, St. Louis, Mo.; ed. Washington Univ., St. Louis and Univ. of Rochester.
Research Assoc. and Fellow, Psycho-Acoustic Laboratory, Harvard; Lecturer in Psychology, Harvard 46-50; with M.I.T. 56-57; joined Bolt Baranek and Newman 57, Head, Psychoacoustics Dept., Engineering Psychology Dept. and Information Systems Research Dept., Vice-Pres. 61-; Dir. Information Processing Research and Behavioural Science, Advanced Research Projects Agency, Dept. of Defense 62-64; Consultant to I.B.M., Dir. of Research 64-67; Visiting Prof., M.I.T. 65-66, Prof. of Electrical Engineering 67-; Assoc. Dir. Project MAC, Dir. 68-; fmr. Pres. Acoustical Soc. of America, Soc. of Engineering Psychologists; Fellow, American Acad. of Arts and Sciences, American Psychological Asscn.; mem. Nat. Acad. of Sciences, Soc. of Experimental Psychologists, Psychonomic Soc., Asscn. for Computing Machinery, American Asscn. for Advancement of Science.
Publs. *Libraries of the Future*, and numerous papers on psychoacoustics, communications theory, man-computer interaction, information storage and retrieval.
1200 North Nash Street, Apt. 850, Arlington, Va. 22209, U.S.A.

Liddiard, Richard England, M.A.; British commodity broker; b. 21 Sept. 1917, Nainital, India; s. of late Edgar S. and Mabel A. Liddiard; m. Constance L. Rook 1943; one s. three d.; ed. Oundle School and Worcester Coll., Oxford.
Joined C. Czarnikow Ltd. 46, Chair. 58-74, Chair. Czarnikow Group Ltd. 74-; Chair. Sugar Asscn. of London 60-; Vice-Chair. London Commodity Exchange 71, Chair. 72-; Chair. British Fed. of Commodity Asscns. 63-71, Vice-Chair. 71-.
Leisure interests: reading, golf.
Czarnikow Group Ltd., 66 Mark Lane, London, E.C.3;

Home: Oxford Lodge, 52 Parkside, Wimbledon, London, S.W.19, England.
Telephone: 01-480-6677 (Office); 01-946-3434 (Home).

Lidman, Sara; Swedish writer; b. 30 Dec. 1923; ed. Uppsala Univ.
First four books deal with life in sparsely populated N. Sweden; in S. Africa 60; in Kenya 62-64, in N. Viet-Nam 65.
Publs. include: *Tjärdalen* 53, *Hjortronlandet* 55, *Aina* 56, *Regnspiran* 58, *Bära mistel* 60, *Jag o min son* 61, *Med fem diamanter* 64.
Jungmansgrand 2, Stockholm SV, Sweden.

Lidorenko, Nikolai Stepanovich; Soviet electrochemist; b. 2 April 1916, Kursk; ed. Novocherkassk Polytechnical Inst.
Engineer 40-50; Dir. U.S.S.R. Inst. of Sources of Electric Current 50-; Prof. 63-; Corresp. mem. U.S.S.R. Acad. of Sciences 66-; Merited Scientist of R.S.F.S.R. 66.
Publs. Works on transformation of energy.
U.S.S.R. Academy of Sciences, 14 Leninsky Prospekt, Moscow, U.S.S.R.

Lieberich, Heinz, D.IUR.; German archivist and legal historian; b. 29 Jan. 1905, Kaiserslautern; s. of Heinrich and Mathilde Lieberich (née Clemens); ed. Humanistisches Gymnasium, Munich, Univ. of Munich, and School of Archives, Munich.
Bavarian State Archive Service 31-, Speyer 34-38, Central Archives, Munich 38-, Gen. Dir. Bavarian State Archives 59-70; Hon. Prof. of Legal History, Univ. of Munich 55-; Chair. of Comm. for Bavarian History, Bavarian Acad. of Sciences 60-73; mem. Exec. Cttee. Int. Council of Archives 61-68.
Publs. *Rechtsgeschichte Bayerns u. der bayerischen Schwaben* 52, *Zur Feudalisierung der Gerichtsbarkeit in Bayern* 54, *Kaiser Ludwig der Bayer als Gesetzgeber* 59, *Landherren und Landleute* 64, *Die Anfänge der Polizeigesetzgebung des Herzogtums Baiern* 69, *Deutsches Privatrecht* (with Mitteis, 6th edn.) 72, *Deutsche Rechtsgeschichte* (13th edn.) 74.
D8 Munich 40, Adalbertstr. 44/IV, Federal Republic of Germany.
Telephone: 335512.

Liebermann, Rolf; Swiss composer; b. 14 Sept. 1910; ed. Zürich Conservatoire, and Univ. of Zürich.
Mem. Musical Dept. Swiss Radio Corpn. 45-50; Head of Orchestra Dept. Swiss Radio Station Beromünster 50-57; Musical Dir. N. German Broadcasting System, Hamburg 57-59; Gen. Man. State Opera, Hamburg 59-Dec. 72; Gen. Man. Théâtre Nat. de l'Opéra, Paris Jan. 73-; Commdr. Légion d'Honneur 74.
Works, operatic: *Leonore* 52, *Penelope* 54, *School for Wives* 55; orchestral: *Polyphonic Studies* 43, *Une des Fins du Monde* 43, *Volkslieder Suite*, *Furioso* 47, *Symphony No. 1* 49, *The Song of Life and Death* 50, *Concerto for Jazzband and Symphony orchestra* 54; *Symphonie des Echanges* (for business machines) 64.
Théâtre National de l'Opéra, Place de l'Opéra, 75009 Paris, France.

Liechtenstein, Prince of (*see* Franz Josef).

Lied, Finn; Norwegian scientist, administrator and politician; b. 12 April 1916, Fana; ed. Norwegian Technological Univ., Trondheim and at Cambridge Univ.
Norwegian Armed Forces 42-45; later Research Fellow and Head of Norwegian Defence Research Establishment, Dir. 57; Minister of Industry 71-72; mem. Norwegian Acad. of Science and Letters at Oslo, Norwegian Acad. of Technical Sciences, Supreme Cttee. for Norwegian Research, Chair. Exec. Cttee. Royal Norwegian Council for Industrial Research, Board of Fund for Developing Aid and Research in Norwegian Industry,

Board of Dirs. Norwegian Telephone and Telegraph Admin.; Chair. of Board Den Norske Stats Oljeselskap A/S.

Publs. textbooks on radio technique and various papers on ionosphere physics and applied research in general.

Norwegian Defence Research Establishment, P.O. Box 25, N-2007 Kjeller, Norway.

Lieftinck, Pieter, DR. JUR.; Netherlands economist and politician; b. 30 Sept. 1902, Muiden; ed. Utrecht Univ.

Fellow, Rockefeller Foundation; economist, Dept. of Economic Affairs and Gen. Sec. Economic Council 32-34; Lecturer Neths. School of Economics at Rotterdam 34; mem. Supreme Council for Labour matters; Minister of Finance in Schermerhorn Govt. June 45-July 46; same in Beel Govt. July 46-Aug. 48, and in Drees Govt. Aug. 48-51, 51-52; Special Rep. and Chief of Missions, IBRD 52-55; Exec. Dir. IBRD, and Int. Monetary Fund 55-; Corresp. mem. Royal Netherlands Acad. of Sciences; Knight Commdr., Order of Netherlands Lion.

3751 Jocelyn Street, N.W., Washington, D.C. 20015, U.S.A.

Liepa, Maris-Rudolf Eduardovich; Soviet ballet dancer; b. 27 July 1936, Riga; s. of Eduard and Lylia Liepa; m. Margareta; one s. one d.; ed. Bolshoi Theatre Ballet School, Moscow.

Soloist with Latvian Theatre of Opera and Ballet, Riga 55-56; soloist with Moscow Stanislavsky and Nemirovich-Danchenko Theatre Ballet Co. 56-59; soloist with Bolshoi Theatre Ballet 59-; People's Artist of R.S.F.S.R.; Lenin Prize Winner 70, Nijinsky Prize 71.

Main roles include: Jean de Brien (*Raimonde*), Konrad (*Corsair*), Siegfried (*Swan Lake*), Vatslav (*Fountain of Bakhchisarai*), Phoebus (*Esmeralda*), the Poet (*Straussiana*), Basilio (*Don Quixote*), Albert (*Giselle*), Armen (*Gayane*), Spartacus, Crassus (*Spartacus*), Prince Desire (*Sleeping Beauty*), Romeo (*Romeo and Juliet*), Farkhad (*Legend of Love*), Spectre de la Rose (*Spectre de la Rose*), Vronsky (*Anna Karenina*); film roles: Prince Vseslav (*Lion's Tomb*), Jack Wheeler (*The Fourth Man*); Hamlet and Henrie (TV roles).

Leisure interest: swimming.

State Academic Bolshoi Theatre of the U.S.S.R., 1 Ploshchad Sverdlova, Moscow, U.S.S.R.

Liepmann, Hans Wolfgang, PH.D.; American professor of aeronautics and applied physics; b. 3 July 1914, Berlin, Germany; s. of Wilhelm and Emma (Leser) Liepmann; m. 1st Kate Kaschinsky 1939 (dissolved), 2nd Dietlind Wegener Goldschmidt 1954; two s.; ed. Univ of Zurich.

Research Fellow, Univ. of Zurich 38-39, Calif. Inst. of Technology 39-45; Asst. Prof. Calif. Inst. of Technology 45-46, Assoc. Prof. 46-49, Prof. of Aeronautics and Applied Physics 49-, Dir. Graduate Aeronautical Laboratories 72-; mem. Nat. Acad. of Sciences, Nat. Acad. of Engineering; First Dryden Lecturer, American Inst. of Aeronautics and Astronautics 68, Ludwig Prandtl Ring, German Soc. for Aeronautics and Astronautics 68; mem. Int. Acad. of Astronautics, A.A.A.S.; Hon. Fellow, American Inst. of Aeronautics and Astronautics 74; Warner Medal, American Soc. of Mechanical Engineers 69.

Leisure interest: tennis.

Publs. *Aerodynamics of a Compressible Fluid* (co-author) 47, *Elements of Gasdynamics* (co-author) 57, *Free Turbulent Flows* 61, and many articles in professional journals.

205-50 Firestone Flight Sciences Laboratory, California Institute of Technology, Pasadena, Calif 91125; Home: 1500 Normandy Drive, Pasadena, Calif. 91103, U.S.A. Telephone: 213-795-6811, Ext. 1535 (Office); 213-449-1172 (Home).

Lifar, Serge; Russian ballet dancer, choreographer and writer; b. 2 April 1905.

Left Russia as refugee and joined Diaghilev company, Paris 23; studied under Cecchetti; created *Apollon* (Stravinsky), *Fils Prodigue* (Prokofiev), etc.; debut as choreographer Stravinsky's *Renard* 29; produced *Prométhée*, Opera House, Paris 29; first London appearance in *Cimarosiana* and *Les Fâcheux*, Coliseum 24; Cochran's *1930 Revue*, London Pavilion 30; returned to Paris and produced and danced in *Bacchus and Ariadne*, *Le Spectre de la Rose*, and *Giselle* 31, *Icare* 35, *David Triomphant* 36, *Le Chevalier et la Demoiselle* 41, *Jean de Zarissa* 42, *Suite en Blanc* 43, *Chota Roustavelli*, *Dramma per Musica* 46, *Lucifer* 48, *Septour*, *Le Chevalier Errant*, *Phèdre* 50, *Blanche Neige* 51, *Fourberies de Scapin* 52, *Noces Fantastiques* 55, *Roméo et Juliette* (Prokofiev) 55, appeared in film *Le Testament d'Orphée* (Cocteau) 60; founder-Dir. Inst. chorégraphique at Opera House, Paris 47-; premier maître de ballet and premier danseur of Théâtre Nat. de l'Opéra, Paris 47-58, 62-63; Organizer of ballet, Coronation of Shah of Iran 67; Maître de ballet de l'Opéra, Paris 68-; Foreign mem. Acad. des Beaux-arts 70.

Publs. *Traditional to Modern* 38, *Diaghilev, a Biography* 40, *Traité de la Danse académique* 50, *Histoire du Ballet Russe* 51, *Vestris* 51, *Réflexions sur la Danse* 52, *Traité de Chorégraphie* 52, *The Three Graces* 59, *Ma Vie* (memoirs) 69.

Villa "les Lauriers", avenue du Commandant-Bret, 06-Cannes, France.

Lifshitz, Ilya Mikhailovich (brother of Yevgeny Lifshitz, q.v.); Soviet physicist; b. 13 Jan. 1917, Kharkov; ed. Kharkov State Univ.

Ukraine Physical Inst., Kharkov 39-; Corresp. mem. U.S.S.R. Acad. of Sciences 68-70, Academician 70-; Lenin Prize 67.

Publs. works on solid state theory and electronic theory of metals.

Physical and Technical Institute, Ulitsa Tchaikovskogo, Kharkov, U.S.S.R.

Lifshitz, Yevgeny Mikhailovich (brother of Ilya Lifshitz, q.v.); Soviet physicist; b. 21 Feb. 1915, Kharkov; ed. Kharkov Inst. of Mechanics and Machine-building.

Ukraine Physical Inst., Kharkov 34-38; Senior Research Scientist, Inst. of Physical Problems, U.S.S.R. Acad. of Sciences 39-; Corresp. mem. U.S.S.R. Acad. of Sciences 66-; State Prize 54, Lenin Prize 62.

Publs. *Mechanics, Theory of Fields, Quantum Mechanics, Statistical Physics, Theory of Elasticity, Electrodynamics of Continuous Media* (with L. D. Landau), etc.

Institute of Physical Problems, U.S.S.R. Academy of Sciences, 2 Vorobyevskoye Shosse, Moscow, U.S.S.R.

Lifson, Shneior, PH.D.; Israeli scientist; b. 18 March 1914, Tel Aviv; m. Hanna Stern; three c.; ed. Hebrew Univ.

Member of kibbutz 32-43; served in Science Unit, Israel Defence Forces 48-49; Weizmann Inst. of Science, attached to Polymer Dept. 49, Chair. Scientific Council 61-63, Head, Chemical Physics Dept. 63-, Science Dir. 63-67; mem. Council for Higher Education, Israel Science Teaching Centre, Comm. of Molecular Biophysics of Int. Union of Pure and Applied Biophysics, European Molecular Biology Organization, Advisory Board *Biopolymers, Current Contents* and Editorial Board *Journal of Statistical Physics* (U.S.A.); Weizmann Prize 58; Israel Prize 69.

Publs. numerous scientific papers.

c/o 15 Neve Weizmann, Rehovot, Israel. Telephone: 951721/589.

Ligachov, Egor Kuzmich; Soviet party official and politician; b. 1920; ed. Moscow Inst. of Aviation and C.P.S.U. Higher Party School.

Engineer 43-49; joined C.P.S.U. 44; Party and Local

Govt. Official Novosibirsk 49-55; Vice-Chair. Novosibirsk Regional Soviet of Working People's Deputies 55-58; Sec. Novosibirsk Regional Cttee. C.P.S.U. 59-61; with Central Cttee. C.P.S.U. 61-65; First Sec. Tomsk Regional Cttee. C.P.S.U. 65-; Alt. mem. Central Cttee. C.P.S.U. 66-; Deputy to Supreme Soviet 66-; Chair. Comm. for Youth Affairs, Soviet of the Union.
Tomsk Regional Committee, Communist Party of the Soviet Union, Tomsk, U.S.S.R.

Ligeti, Lajos, D.PHIL., D.LIT.; Hungarian orientalist; b. 28 Oct. 1902, Balassagyarmat; s. of János Ligeti and Ilona Cseh; m. Ida Tigyi 1945; ed. Budapest Univ. and Coll. Eötvös, Budapest.
Lecturer, Budapest Univ. 31, Prof. 38; Lecturer, Ecole des Langues Orientales, Paris 34-35; visits to Mongolia 28-31, Afghanistan 36-37, Japan 40; Prof., Chair of Cen. Asia, Eötvös Lóránd Univ. Budapest; mem. Hungarian Acad. 36-, Vice-Pres. 49-70; mem. Praesidium 70-73; mem. Mongolian Acad. of Sciences; Vice-Pres. Perm. Int. Cttee. of Mongolists, Ulan Bator 70; corresp. mem. Turkish Soc. of Language, Société Asiatique, Royal Asiatic Soc., American Oriental Soc., Finno-Ugrian Soc., Sächsische Akad. der Wissenschaft, Inst. de France, Acad. des Inscriptions et Belles Lettres; Kossuth Prize 49; Order of Labour 60; Indiana Univ. Prize for Altaic Studies—Gold Medal 68, Gold Medal Hungarian Acad. of Sciences 67; Order of the Flag of the Hungarian People's Repub. 70, 74; Lenin Memorial Medal 70; Nairamdal Order Mongolia 72; Diplôme d'honneur (Turkey) 74; Order of Labour, Golden Degree 75.
Publs. *Rapport préliminaire d'un voyage d'exploration fait en Mongolie Chinoise 33, Les voyelles longues en turc 38, Catalogue du Kanjur mongol imprimé 42-44, Le Subhasitaratnanidhi mongol 48, Sur le déchiffrement des "petits caractères" jou-tchen 53, L'Histoire Secrète des Mongoles 62, Un vocabulaire mongol d'Istanbul 62, Documents sino-ouigours du Bureau des Traducteurs 66-69, Monumenta Linguae Mong. 70-74, Indices Verborum 70-74.*
Belgrád-1kp. 26, 1056 Budapest, Hungary.
Telephone: 187-529.

Light, Walter Frederick, B.SC.; Canadian business executive; b. 24 June 1923, Cobalt, Ont.; s. of Herbert Light and Rosetta Elizabeth (Hoffman) Light; m. Margaret Anne Wylie Miller 1950; two d.; ed. Queen's Univ., Ont.
Joined Bell Canada 49, Vice-Pres. Engineering 67, Vice-Pres. Operations 69, Exec. Vice-Pres. Operations 70; Pres. and Chief Operating Officer Northern Electric Co. Ltd. Aug. 74-.
Leisure interests: antiques, swimming.
1600 Dorchester Boulevard West, Montreal, Quebec H3H 1R1; Home: 5 Normandy Drive, Town of Mount Royal, Quebec H3R 3H7, Canada.
Telephone: (514) 931-5711 (Office); (514) 342-1386 (Home).

Lighthill, Sir James, Kt., F.R.AE.S., F.R.S.; British professor of mathematics; b. 23 Jan. 1924, Paris, France; s. of Ernest B. and Marjorie (née Holmes) Lighthill; m. Nancy A. Dumaresq 1945; one s. four d.; ed. Trinity Coll., Cambridge.
Senior Lecturer, Manchester Univ. 46-50, Beyer Prof. of Applied Maths. 50-59; Dir. Royal Aircraft Establishment 59-64; Royal Soc. Research Prof., Imperial Coll., London 64-69; Physical Sec. Royal Soc. 65-69; Lucasian Prof. of Maths., Univ. of Cambridge 69-; Pres. Int. Comm. on Mathematical Instruction 71-74; Hon. foreign mem. American Acad. of Arts and Sciences, American Philosophical Soc., American Inst. of Aeronautics and Astronautics; Royal Medal, Royal Soc.; Gold Medal, Royal Aeronautical Soc.; Modesto Panetti Prize; Timoshenko Medal; ten hon. doctorates.
Leisure interests: music, swimming.

Publs. *Higher Approximations in Aerodynamic Theory 54, Fourier Analysis and Generalised Functions 58,* articles in collective works and learned journals.
Department of Applied Mathematics and Theoretical Physics, Silver Street, Cambridge, England.
Telephone: Cambridge 51645.

Lightner, Edwin Allan, Jr.; American diplomatist; b. 8 Dec. 1907, New York; s. of Edwin Allan and Helen Chute Lightner; m. Dorothy Boyce 1953; two s. one d.; ed. Taft School, and Princeton Univ.
Joined Foreign Service 30, served Venezuela, Chile, Brazil, Argentina 30-38; Sec. Legations Riga, Oslo, Moscow, Stockholm 38-43; Asst. Political Adviser to European Advisory Comm. 44-45; Asst. Chief, Div. of Central European Affairs, State Dept. 45-47, Assoc. Chief 47-48; Deputy Dir. Office of Political Affairs, U.S. High Comm., Frankfurt 49-51; Counsellor, Korea 51-53; Consul-Gen., Munich 53-56; Deputy Asst. Sec. of State for Public Affairs 56-59; Minister, Berlin 59-63; Amb. to Libya 63-65; State Dept. Rep., Water Resources Task Force 65-66; Deputy Commdt. Foreign Affairs, Nat. War Coll. 66-69; Amb.-in-Residence, Dayton Miami Valley Consortium 69-70; Woodrow Wilson Senior Fellow 73.
Leisure interests: hunting, gardening, painting.
Publ. *The Department of State* (co-author) 74.
4647 Kenmore Drive, N.W., Washington, D.C. 20007, U.S.A.

Likhachev, Dmitry Sergeyevich, D.SC.; Soviet professor of Russian literature; b. 28 Nov. 1906, Petersburg (Leningrad); s. of Sergei Likhachev and Vera Likhacheva; m. Zinaida Makarova 1936; two d.; ed. Leningrad State Univ.
Editor in a publishing house 32-38; Assoc. Inst. of Russian Literature (Pushkin House) of U.S.S.R. Acad. of Sciences 38-, Head of Section of Early Russian Literature 54-, Academician 70-; Lecturer, Kazan State Univ. 42-43, Leningrad State Univ. 46-53, Prof. 51-; Hon. mem. Bulgarian Acad. of Sciences, Hungarian Acad. of Sciences, Serbian Acad. of Sciences and Arts; corresp. foreign mem. Austrian Acad. of Sciences; Dr. h.c. (Oxford, Edinburgh and Torun Univs.); State Prize 52, 69.
Leisure interests: problems of town-buildings (theory) and the history of Petersburg-Leningrad.
Publs. works on the history and poetry of early Russian literature, textual criticism.
Prospekt Švernika 34, 16 Leningrad, K-21, U.S.S.R.

Likhachev, Veniamin Andreyevich; Soviet diplomatist; b. 29 Oct. 1921, Belinsky, Pensa Region; ed. Moscow Aviation Inst. and High Diplomatic School.
Second, First Sec., Soviet Embassy, Turkey 47-55; ranking official, Ministry of Foreign Affairs, 55-58; Counsellor, Soviet Embassy, Turkey 58-62; ranking official, Ministry of Foreign Affairs 62-70; Amb. to Iraq 70-74.
c/o Ministry of Foreign Affairs, Moscow, U.S.S.R.

Lilienfeld, Abraham M., A.B., M.D., M.P.H.; American epidemiologist; b. 13 Nov. 1920, New York City; s. of Eugenia Kugler and Joel Lilienfeld; m. Lorraine Zemil 1944; three c.; ed. Johns Hopkins Univ., and Univ. of Maryland.
Associate Public Health Physician, N.Y. State Dept. of Health 49-50; Dir. Southern Health District, Baltimore 50-52; Asst. Prof. of Epidemiology, Johns Hopkins Univ. 52-54, Prof. and Chair. Dept. of Chronic Diseases 58-70, Prof. and Chair. Dept. of Epidemiology 70-75; Univ. Distinguished Prof. of Epidemiology 75-; Chief Dept. of Statistics and Epidemiological Research, Roswell Park Memorial Inst., Buffalo 54-58; Assoc. Prof. Medical Statistics Univ. of Buffalo 54-58; mem. Nat. Advisory Heart Council 62-66; mem. Research Advisory Council, American Cancer Soc. 65-70; mem. Scientific Council, Int. Agency for Cancer Research

65-67; mem. Nat. Inst. Neurological Diseases and Stroke 68-71; Chair. U.S. Nat. Cttee. on Vital and Health Statistics 72-74; Fellow, American Stat. Asscn. 70, American Public Health Asscn.; Bronfman Prize of American Public Health Asscn. 68; John Snow Award, Epidemiology Section, American Public Health Asscn. 75; Hon. D.Sc. (Univ. of Md.) 75.

Publs. *Prenatal Factors in Cerebral Palsy* 51, *Prenatal Factors in Childhood Neuropsychiatric Disorders* 51-56, *Tobacco Use and Bladder Cancer* 56, *Epidemiological Methods* 57, *Epidemiology of Cancer* 54-65, *Chronic Diseases and Public Health* 66, *Cancer Epidemiology: Methods of Study* 67, *Epidemiology of Mongolism* 69, *Cancer in the United States* 72, *Epidemiological Studies on Cerebrovascular Diseases* 69-74, *Epidemiological Studies of Digestive Diseases* 74.

3203 Old Post Drive, Pikesville, Md. 21208, U.S.A. Telephone: 301-484-0652.

Lilienthal, David Eli, A.B., LL.B.; American public servant, business executive and writer; b. 8 July 1899, Morton, Ill.; *s.* of Leo Lilienthal and Minna Rosenak; *m.* Helen Lamb 1923; one *s.* one *d.*; ed. De Pauw Univ., and Harvard.

Admitted to Ill. Bar 23, Tenn. Bar 34; law practice in Chicago 23-31; mem. Wis. Public Service Comm. 31-33; Dir. Tennessee Valley Authority 33, Chair. 41-46; Chair. U.S. Atomic Energy Comm. Oct. 46-Feb. 50; Chair. U.S. State Dept. Board of Consultants on Int. Control of Atomic Energy 46; Consultant to Pres. of Colombia; Chair. Development and Resources Corpn. 55-, Iran Council of Asia Soc., N.Y.; Dir. Fund for Multinational Management Educ.; mem. Amer. Acad. of Arts and Sciences; Progressive Farmer Award for services to agriculture 45; Catholic Cttee. of the South Award 46; Public Welfare Award, Nat. Acad. of Sciences 51; Freedom House Award 49, Comendador de la Orden el Sol del Perú 64, Order of Rio Branco (Brazil) 72.

Leisure interests: gardening, small boat sailing.

Publs. *TVA: Democracy on the March* 44, *This I Do Believe* 49, *Big Business: A New Era* 53, *Change, Hope and the Bomb* 63, *The Journals of David E. Lilienthal* (Vols. I and II) 64, (Vol. III) 66, (Vol. IV) 69, (Vol. V) 71, *Management: A Humanist Art* 67.

1271 Avenue of the Americas, New York, N.Y.; and 88 Battle Road, Princeton, N.J. 08540, U.S.A.

Lilje, Johannes Ernst Richard, DR.THEOL.; German ecclesiastic; b. 20 Aug. 1899; ed. Göttingen, Leipzig and Zürich Univs.

Students' Chaplain, Technical Acad., Hanover 24-26; Gen. Sec. of German Christian Student Movement, and Vice-Pres. World Student Christian Movement 27-34; Gen. Sec. Lutheran World Convention 35-44; Pres. Cen. Cttee. for Inner Mission in Germany 45-57; Bishop of Evangelical Lutheran Church of Hanover 47-71; mem. Cen. Cttee. World Council of Churches 48, Pres. 68-75; mem. Evangelical Church Council, Germany; Pres. Lutheran World Fed. 52-57; Presiding Bishop of the United Evangelical Lutheran Church (Germany 55-69; Hon. D.Theol. (Göttingen and Helsinki Univs.), Hon. D.D. (Edinburgh Univ., Augusta and Oberlin Colls.), Hon. L.H.D. (Muhlenberg and Concordia Colls.), Hon. LL.D. (Wittenberg Coll.), L.H.D. (Pacific Lutheran Univ., Washington).

Publs. *The Technical Era* 28, *Luther's Conception of History* 32, *The Last Book of the Bible* 40, *Luther Now* 46, *The Valley of Shadow* 47, *Martin Luther* 64.

Meranerstrasse 5, 3 Hanover, Federal Republic of Germany.

Telephone: (0511) 831818.

Liljestrand, Lieut.-Gen. Bengt T:son, M.A., DIPL.C.E.I.; Swedish army officer; b. 26 Feb. 1919, Stockholm; ed. Uppsala Univ., Centre d'Etudes Industrielles, Geneva

and Inst. Univ. de Hautes Etudes Internationales, Geneva.

Instructor, Royal Nat. Defence Coll. 60-62; Co-ordination Office, Defence Dept. 62-63; Defence Staff, Org. and Total Defence Section 64-66; Commdr. Boden Artillery Regt. 68-69; Chief of Staff, Western Region 69-73; Dir., Gen. Staff Coll. of Armed Forces 73-74; Chief of Staff UN Truce Supervision Org. in Palestine 74-75; Commdr. UN Emergency Force 75-; Commdr. 1st Class Royal Swedish Order of the Sword; Kt. Finnish Order of Freedom.

Ismailia, Egypt; UNEF, P.O. Box 20, G.C.P.O., New York, N.Y. 10017, U.S.A.

Lill, John Richard, F.R.C.M.; British pianist; b. 17 March 1944, London; *s.* of George and Margery (née Young) Lill; ed. Leyton County High School and Royal Coll. of Music.

Gives recitals throughout the world and has appeared as soloist with many leading orchestras; Fellow, Trinity Coll. of Music, London, London Coll. of Music; numerous prizes include First Prize, Int. Tchaikovsky Competition, Moscow 70.

Leisure interests: chess, amateur radio, walking.

c/o Harold Holt Ltd., 122 Wigmore Street, London, W1H oDJ, England.

Telephone: 01-935 2331.

Lilley, Tom; American industrialist; b. 13 Aug. 1912, Bluefield, W. Va.; *s.* of Charles Ellis and Minnie Holland Lilley; *m.* Nancy Clegg 1936; three *d.*; ed. Harvard Univ.

Industrial Dept. Lehman Brothers, New York City 36-40; Assoc. Prof. and Asst. Dir. of Research, Harvard Business School 42-48; entered Ford Motor Co. 48, Asst. Divisional Controller 51, Asst. Gen. Man., Ford Int. Div. 54, Vice-Pres. and Gen. Man., Int. Div. 57-59; Vice-Pres. Ford Int. Staff 60-65; Dir. Export-Import Bank of the United States 65-72; Dir. Continental-Illinois Ltd., London 73-74, Population Crisis Cttee. 74-.

1522 34th Street, N.W., Washington, D.C. 20007, U.S.A.

Lillie, Beatrice (Lady Peel); British actress; b. 29 May 1898, Toronto, Canada; *d.* of John Lillie and Lucie Shaw; *m.* Sir Robert Peel 1920 (died 1934); one *s.* (dec.); ed. St. Agnes' Coll., Belleville, Ont., Canada.

Numerous appearances in revues and cabarets, London and New York 14-; first One-Woman Show, Summer Theater, New York 52, second (*Beasop's Fables*) U.S.A. 56; *An Evening with Beatrice Lillie*, London and Florida 56; appeared at Ziegfeld Follies, New York 57; played leading role in *Auntie Mame*, London 58; appeared in the films *Exit Smiling* 27, *Doctor Rhythm* 38, *On Approval* 44, *Around the World in Eighty Days* 56, *Thoroughly Modern Millie* 67; Donaldson Award 45, Antoinette Perry Award 53, etc.

Leisure interest: painting.

Publ. *Every Other Inch a Lady* (with J. Philip and J. Brough) 73.

55 Park Lane, London, W.1, England.

Lim, Manuel, A.B., LL.B., LL.M., D.C.L.; Philippine lawyer, public servant and business executive; b. 6 Aug. 1899, Bautista, Pangasinan; *s.* of the late Mariano Lim and Josefa Moran de Lim; *m.* Emilia Quintos de Lim 1923; three *s.* seven *d.*; ed. Ateneo de Manila Univ., Univ. of Philippines and Univ. of Santo Tomás.

Lawyer 21-41, 45-47, 48-57, 58-60, 62-; Dean and Prof. Coll. of Law, Ateneo de Manila 36-41, 47-59; Prof. of Law, Univ. of Santo Tomás 38-41; Assoc. Justice, Court of Appeals 46-47; Solicitor-Gen. and Under-Sec. of Justice 47-48; Pres. Realty Investments Inc. 50-; Chair. Mindanao Mother Lode Mines Inc. 49-60; Pres. Tax Service of Philippines Inc. 57-59; Sec. of Educ., Govt. of Philippines 57-59, of Commerce and Industry

60-62; Vice-Pres., Dir. and Gen. Counsel Philippine American Life Insurance Co. 62-70; Chair. Corporate Promotions Inc. 65-, Shrimp Processing Corpn. of Philippines 68-, Pentagon Mines Inc. 70-, Pacific Richfield Corpn. 75-; Chair. Comm. on Asian and Far Eastern Affairs—Int. Chamber of Commerce 67-69; Chair. Philippine Council, Int. Chamber of Commerce 63-; Pres. Philippine Motor Asscn. 73- (Dir. 65-), Philippine Constitution Asscn. 75-, Papal Awardees Asscn. of the Philippines 75-; Chair. Consumers' Union of the Philippines 73-; Vice-Chair. Energy Conservation Movement 75-; mem. Labour-Management Advisory Council 63-, and numerous legal and other associations and official of numerous industrial companies; numerous decorations.
Leisure interests: philately, photography, books, music.
103 Magallanes Avenue, Magallanes Village, Makati, Rizal, Philippines.
Telephone: 87-25-40.

Lim Kim San; Singapore politician; b. 1916, Singapore; ed. Raffles Coll., Singapore.
Director United Chinese Bank Ltd., Chair. Batu Pahat Bank Ltd., and Pacific Bank Ltd. 40-; mem. and Dep. Chair. Public Service Comm., Singapore 59-63; Chair. Housing Devt. Board; Deputy Chair. Economic Devt. Board; Minister for Nat. Devt. 63-65, for Finance 65-67, for the Interior and Defence 67-70, for Educ. 70-72, for the Environment Sept. 72-75, of Nat. Devt. and Communications June 75-; awarded Darjah Utama Temasek (Order of Temasek) 62; mem. of Dewan Ra'ayat; Ramon Magsaysay Award for community leadership 65.
Ministry for National Development and Communications, Singapore.

Lima, Francisco Negrão de; Brazilian Minister of Foreign Affairs 58-59; see *The International Who's Who 1975-76*.

Lima, Francisco Roberto, LL.D.; Salvadorian lawyer and diplomatist; b. 13 Feb. 1917; ed. Saint Michel School, Brussels, Lycée Lakanal, Paris, Quernmore School, London, and Univ. of El Salvador.
Rockefeller Foundation Fellowship, Inst. of Anthropology and Social Sciences, Univ. of Mexico 41-45; practising lawyer 45-56; Chief of Dept. of Statistics, Dept. of Labour 46; Chief of Social Security Comm., El Salvador 47-49; Alt. Rep. to UN 56-59; Rep. on Exec. Board UNICEF 57-59; Vice-Pres. Council of American States 61-62; Ambassador of El Salvador to United States and Rep. to Organization of American States (OAS) 62-64; Vice-Pres. El Salvador 62-67; Pres. OAS Cttee. on Econ. and Social Affairs 64-65.
c/o Ministry of Foreign Affairs, San Salvador, El Salvador.

Lima, Hermes; Brazilian lawyer, historian and politician; b. 1902; ed. Univ. of Bahia.
Former Lecturer, Law Faculty, Univ. of Bahia, Univ. of São Paulo; fmr. Prof., Nat. Faculty of Law, Univ. of Brazil; fmr. Dir. School of Econs. and Law, Univ. of the Fed. Dist.; fmr. Legal Dir. Soc. for Agricultural and Industrial Research; Rep. UN Gen. Assembly 51, 52; Rep. to Pan-American Conf., Caracas 54; Head of the Civilian Cabinet of Presidential Affairs 61-62; Minister of Labour 62; Prime Minister Sept. 62-Jan. 63; Minister of Foreign Affairs Jan.-June 63.
Publs. *Introdução a Ciência do Direito, Tobias Barreto—a época e o homen, Notas á vida brasileira, Lições da Crise.*
Academia Brasileira de Letras, Avenida Presidente Wilson, 203 Rio de Janeiro, Brazil.

Limerick, 6th Earl of, cr. 1803 (Ireland); **Patrick Edmund Pery,** M.A., C.A.; British merchant banker; b. 12 April 1930, London; s. of 5th Earl of Limerick (Edmund Colquhoun Pery) and Angela Olivia (née Trotter); m. Sylvia Rosalind Lush; two s. one d.; ed. Eton and New Coll., Oxford.

National Service Comm. with 2nd Dragoon Guards 48-50; Territorial Army Comm. with City of London Yeomanry 50-61; qualified as Chartered Accountant with Peat, Marwick, Mitchell & Co. 53-58; joined Kleinwort Sons & Co. 58; Dir. Kleinwort Benson Ltd. 66-72, 74-; mem. Council, London Chamber of Commerce and Industry 68; London Dir. Commercial Bank of Australia Ltd. 69-72; Parl. Under-Sec. of State for Trade 72-74; Pres. Asscn. of British Chambers of Commerce 74-; mem. British Overseas Trade Board 75-; Chair. Cttee. for Middle East Trade, British Nat. Export Council 75-; Pres. Ski Club of Great Britain 74-; Vice-Pres. Alpine Ski Club 74-.
Leisure interests: mountaineering, skiing, boating.
Publs. numerous specialist articles.
Chiddinglye, West Hoathly, East Grinstead, Sussex; 30 Victoria Road, London, W8 5RG, England.
Telephone: Sharpthorne 214 (Sussex); 01-937-0573 (London).

Lin, Chia-Chiao, B.SC., M.A., PH.D.; American applied mathematician; b. 7 July 1916, Fukien, China; s. of Kai and Y. T. Lin; m. Shou-Ying Liang 1946; one d.; ed. Nat. Tsing Hua Univ., Univ. of Toronto, Calif. Inst. of Technology.
Assistant Prof. of Applied Mathematics, Brown Univ. 45-46, Assoc. Prof. 46-47; Assoc. Prof. of Mathematics, Mass. Inst. of Technology (M.I.T.) 47-53, Prof. 53-66, Inst. Prof. of Applied Mathematics 66-; Guggenheim Fellow 54-55, 60; Pres. Soc. for Industrial and Applied Mathematics 73; mem. Nat. Acad. of Sciences; John von Neumann Lecturer, Soc. for Industrial and Applied Mathematics 73.
Leisure interest: astronomy.
Publs. *The Theory of Hydrodynamic Stability* 55, *Turbulent Flow, Theoretical Aspects* 63.
Department of Mathematics, Massachusetts Institute of Technology, Cambridge, Mass. 02139, U.S.A.
Telephone: 617-894-7997.

Lin Chin-sheng, B.L.; Chinese politician; b. 4 Aug. 1916; ed. Law Coll., Tokyo Imperial Univ.
Magistrate, Chiayi Co. Govt. 52-55; Chair. Yunlin Co. H.Q., Kuomintang 55-58; Magistrate, Yunlin Co. Govt. 58-65; Dir. Cheng-Ching Lake Industrial Waterworks 65-67; Commr. Taiwan Provincial Govt. 66-69; Sec.-Gen. Taiwan Provincial H.Q., Kuomintang 67-68, Chair. Taipei Municipal H.Q. 69-70, Deputy Sec.-Gen. Cen. Cttee. 70-72; Minister of the Interior 72-; Order of the Brilliant Star.
Ministry of the Interior, 107 Roosevelt Road, Section 4, Tapei; Home: 3 Lane 120, Hsinsheng South Road, Section 1, Taipei, Taiwan.

Lin Pin; Chinese army officer.
Commander 43rd Brigade, 15th Column, Army Corps of Hsu Hsiang-chi'ien (q.v.) 48; Maj.-Gen. 60; Deputy Chief of Staff People's Liberation Army Armoured Force 51; Deputy Commdr. PLA Armoured Forces 72-.
People's Republic of China.

Lin Yutang, M.A., PH.D., HON. D.LITT.; Chinese author and philologist; b. 10 Oct. 1895, Changchow; s. of Lin Chiseng and Yang Sunbeng; m. Liao Tsuifeng 1919; three c.; ed. St. John's Coll., Shanghai, Harvard and Leipzig Univs.
Professor of English Philology Peiping Nat. Univ. 23-26; fmr. Dean of Arts Amoy Univ.; Research Fellow in Philology and English Editor Acad. Sinica 30-35; Sec. Ministry of Foreign Affairs 27; Chancellor Nanyang Univ., Singapore 54-55; contrib. Editor *China Critic*, Shanghai 30; inventor Chinese index system and collaborator in official romanization plan; founder and Editor *Lun Yu*, Shanghai 32, *This Human World* 34, *Yuchoufeng* 36; Del. Cttee. on Intellectual Co-operation; Head, Arts and Letters Dept., UNESCO 48.
Publs. *My Country and My People* 36, *The Importance*

of Living 37, *Movement in Peking* 40, *With Love and Irony* 41, *A Leaf in the Storm* 42, *Wisdom of China and India* 42, *Between Tears and Laughter* 43, *The Vigil of a Nation* 45, *The Gay Genius* 47, *Chinatown Family* 48, *On the Wisdom of America* 50, *Peace is in the Heart* 50, *Widow, Nun and Courtesan* 51, *Famous Chinese Short Stories* 52, *Vermilion Gate* 53, *The Unexpected Island* 54, *Lady Wu* 57, *Secret Name* 59, *From Pagan to Christian* 60, *Importance of Understanding* 61, *Red Peony* 62, *The Pleasures of a Non-conformist* 63, *Juniper Loa* 64, *Flight of the Innocents* 65, *The Chinese Theory of Art* 67.
[*Died March* 1976.]

Linares Aranda, Francisco, M.S., PH.D.; Guatemalan diplomatist; b. 1921; ed. Univ. of San Carlos, Guatemala City, and School of Foreign Service, Georgetown Univ., U.S.A.
Second Sec. Washington 43-45, First Sec. 45-47, Counsellor 47-50, Chargé d'Affaires a.i. 47-48, 49; Del. to Int. Civil Aviation Conf. Chicago 44, World Fund and Bank, Savannah, Ga. 46, F.A.O. Fifth Int. Conf. Washington 49 and other Int. Confs. in U.S.A. 44-49, 57, Vienna 61, Mexico 65; Alternate Rep. on Board of Dirs. Pan American Union 47-48, on Council Organisation of American States 48-50; Minister to Great Britain 50-53; Minister to France 53-54; Chief of Protocol, Ministry of Foreign Affairs, Guatemala 54-58; Under-Sec. of State Foreign Affairs Sept. 58-59, Acting Sec. Sept.-Oct. 58; Ambassadorial rank 57; Ambassador to Federal Republic of Germany 59-62, to Chile 62-63, to Mexico 63-66, to U.S.A., Canada and OAS 66-71, to France 71-72, to Fed. Repub. of Germany (also accred. to Denmark, Norway and Sweden) 72-75. c/o Ministerio de Asuntos Exteriores, Guatemala City, Guatemala.

Lind, Nathalie, LL.B.; Danish lawyer and politician; b. 1 Oct. 1918, Copenhagen; d. of Aage Lind and Ane Johanne Lind (née Bjørndahl); m. 1st Erik Tfelt-Hansen 1943 (died 1962), 2nd Erik Langsted 1968; two s.
Secretary, Mothers' Aid Inst., Copenhagen 43-44; Asst. Chief Constable, Ålborg 45-48; barrister Ålborg 49; Asst. to Public Prosecutor, Ålborg 49; M.P. for County of Frederiksborg 64-66, for County of Ribe 68-; mem. Exec. Cttee. of Liberal Party 67-68; Minister of Social Affairs 68-71; Minister of Justice and Minister of Cultural Affairs 73-75; Judge in Court of Appeal of Social Affairs; Chair. Women's Debating Soc., Ålborg 47-55; Chair. Copenhagen Section of Danish Women's Soc. 59-62; Nat. Chair. of Danish Women's Soc. 66-68; Commdr. of Order of Dannebrog, Order of Yugoslav Flag (with ribbon).
Marielystvej 26, 2000 Copenhagen F, Denmark.

Lindberg, Stig; Swedish professor, designer and ceramic artist; b. 17 Aug. 1916, Umeå; s. of F. H. S. Lindberg and Lydia Larsson; m. Gunnel Jonsson 1939; one s. two d.; ed. Stockholm State School of Arts and Crafts.
Began work at Gustavsberg potteries 37; founded with Prof. Kage Gustavsberg Studio 43, Art Dir. 49-58, 71-; textile designer for Nordiska Kompaniet, Stockholm 47-; Chief Instructor, Stockholm State School of Arts and Crafts 57-70; now working in pottery, porcelain and textile design, posters, drawings and sculpture; invented and introduced enamel painting for murals on steel sheet 49; many exhibitions, including Stockholm 41, Zürich 47, Copenhagen 49, Berlin 52, New York 51 and 57, Tokyo 59, London 61, 66, Cologne 65, Amsterdam 68; rep. at Victoria and Albert Museum (London), Museum of Modern Art (N.Y.), Museum für angewandte Kunst (Vienna), Stockholm Nat. Museum, Kunstindustrimuseum (Copenhagen), etc.; Grand Prix Milan Triennali 51 and 54; Swedish State Art Award 67, 68; Gold Medals: Cannes 55, Prague 62, Ljubljana 65, Munich 66.

Principal Works: Terma flameware 55, ceramic wall decoration at Saltsjöbaden 49, playing-card design 48, service in bone china for Stockholm town hall 59, stoneware fountain for Stockholm Folksam Building 60; big murals: Alfa Laval Tumba 65, Nacka Hospital 66, Kabi Stockholm 67; glass design for Holmegaard Danmark 70, "Librick" tray service for hospitals 70.
Leisure interests: piano and guitar.
Gustavsberg, Sweden.
Telephone: 0766-30297.

Lindebraekke, Sjur, LL.D.; Norwegian banker and politician; b. 6 April 1909, Voss; s. of Gjert and Ida Lindebraekke (née Lie); m. Aagot Vedeler Stolz 1936; one s. two d.; ed. Univ. of Oslo.
Assistant Manager Bergens Privatbank, Bergen 40-45, Jt. Managing Dir. 45-59, Gen. Managing Dir. 59-, Chair. of the Board 68-; Pres. Governmental Reparations Directorate 45-46; Pres. Norwegian Bankers' Asscn. 54-60; mem. Parliament 45-53; Vice-Chair. Conservative Party 50-54, Chair. 62-70; Cttee. mem. The Christian Michelsen Inst. for Science and Intellectual Freedom; Hon. mem. Royal Norwegian Acad. of Sciences; mem. Int. Inst. of Banking Studies; Knight First Class St. Olav Order 60.
Leisure interests: outdoor life, literature.
Publs. *Transfer of Ownership by Voluntary Transfer of Personal Property* 40, *Negotiable Documents, Norwegian Indemnification Law, Documentary Credit Law, Ownership and Seizure in Bankruptcy Proceedings* 46, *Confidence and Political Confidence* 53, *At a New Era* 65, *Co-operative Society* 69, *The Way Onward* 73.
Bergens Privatbank, Torvalmenning 2, Bergen; Home: Blaauws vei 4, 5000 Bergen, Norway.
Telephone: 29-47-94.

Linder, Harold Francis; American banker and government official; b. 13 Sept. 1900; ed. Columbia Univ.
President, Cornell, Linder and Co. 25-33; Partner, Carl M. Loeb, Rhoades and Co. 33-38; philanthropic work and corporate directorships 38-61; U.S. Navy 41-45; Pres. Gen. American Investors Co. Inc. 48-51; Deputy Asst. Sec. of State for Econ. Affairs 51, Asst. Sec. 52-53; Pres. and Chair. Export-Import Bank 61-68; U.S. Amb. to Canada 68-69; Chair. of Board of Trustees Inst. for Advanced Study, Princeton, N.J. 69-73, Chair. Emeritus 73-; Consultant, Int. Finance Corpn.
Room 4201, 40 Wall Street, New York, N.Y. 10005, U.S.A.
Telephone: 212-944-6127.

Lindh, Sten, LL.B., B.A.; Swedish diplomatist and industrialist; b. 24 Oct. 1922; m. Maikki Birgitta Velander 1945; two s. one d.; ed. Kalmar Grammar School, Stockholm Univ. and Stockholm Business School.
Entered Swedish Foreign Service 45, served Washington, Paris, London, Geneva and Brussels; Ministry of Finance 50-51; Head of Dept., Ministry of Foreign Affairs 59, 61-63; Head of EFTA Secr., Geneva 60; Ambassador to the European Econ. Communities and Perm. Rep. to Council of Europe 64-67; Amb. en disponibilité 68; Pres. Euroc A.B. (fmrly. Skånska Cement A.B.) 68-; Dir. Gränges A.B., Skånska Cementgjuteriet A.B., A.B. Cardo, Liberian American-Swedish Minerals Co., Swedish Lamco Syndicate; mem. Royal Soc. of Letters, Lund Univ.
Euroc A.B., S 201 10 Malmö 1; Gimle, S 260 90 Båstad, Sweden.
Telephone: 040/736 60 (Office); 0431/616 20 (Home).

Lindhardt, Poul Georg, D.TH.; Danish university professor; b. 12 Dec. 1910, Nakskov; s. of G. W. Lindhardt and Caroline Christensen; m. Gerda Winding 1937; four s.; ed. Univ. of Copenhagen.
Ordained 34, Minister in various parishes 34-42; Asst. Lecturer Univ. of Copenhagen 39-41, Aarhus Univ. 41-42; Prof. of Church History, Aarhus Univ. 42-,

Dean of Faculty of Divinity 44, 48, 53, 57, 62, 69-71; Minister of Our Lady's Church, Aarhus 45.
Leisure interest: travelling.
Publs. *Konfirmationens Historie i Danmark* 36, *Danmark og Reformkoncilierne* 42, *Bibelen og det danske Folk* 42, *Den nordiske Kirkes Historie* 45, *Dines Pontoppidan* 48, *Morten Pontoppidan I* 50, *II* 53, *Grundtvig, An Introduction* 51, *Vækkelser og kirkelige retninger* 51, *Det evige Liv* 53, *En dansk Sognepræst* 54, *Fem Aalborg-Bisper* 54, *Religion og Evangelium* 54, *Kirken igaar og idag* 55, *15 Prædikener* 56, *Danmarks kirkehistorie 1849-1901*, *To Højkirkemænd*, *Repliker*, *Helvedsstrategi* 58, *Vækkelse og kirkelige retninger* (2nd edn.), *F. C. Krarups Breve til Lyder Brun* 59, *Stat og kirke* 60, *Biskop Chr. Ludwigs visitatsdagbog* 60, *Paaskud og Prædikener* 63, *Grundtvig* 64, *Det religiøse liv i senmiddelalderen* 66, *Den danske reformations historie* 66, *Den danske kirches historie 1901-65* 66, *Stat og kirke* (2nd edn.) 67, *Den nordiske kirkes historie* (2nd edn.) 67, *Nederlagets Mænd* 68, *Brudstykker af en postil* 68, *Thomas Skat Rørdam* 69, *Konfrontation* 74, *Gentagelse* 75.
The University, Aarhus; and 8541 Skødstrup, Denmark.
Telephone: 06-99-11-91.

Lindley, Sir Arnold Lewis George, D.SC., C.G.I.A., F.I.MECH.E., F.I.E.E.; British electrical manufacturing executive; b. 13 Nov. 1902, London; s. of George Dilnot Lindley and Charlotte Hooley; m. 1st Winifred May Lindley 1927 (deceased), 2nd Maud Lindley 1963; one s. one d.; ed. Woolwich Polytechnic.
Chief Engineer, British Gen. Electric Co. (B.G.E.C.), South Africa 33-45, Dir. and Man. 45-49; Dir. East Rand Eng. Co. 43-49; Gen. Man. Erith Works, Gen. Electric Co. (G.E.C.), England 49-58, Dir. G.E.C. 53-64; Asst. Man. Dir. 58-59, Man. Dir. 59-61, Chair. 61-64; Chair. Engineering Industry Training Board 64-74; Deputy Chair. Motherwell Bridge (Holdings) Ltd. 64-; Pres. British Electrical and Allied Mfg. Asscn. 61-63; Int. Electrical Asscn. 62-64, Inst. Mech. Eng. 68-69; Chair. Council of Eng. Insts. 69-72; Council of Industrial Design.
Leisure interests: golf, sailing.
The Crest, Raggleswood, Chislehurst, Kent, England.
Telephone: 01-467-2159.

Lindo, Sir (Henry) Laurence, G.C.V.O., C.M.G.; Jamaican diplomatist (retd.); b. 13 Aug. 1911, Port Maria; s. of Henry Alexander and Ethel Mary Lindo (née Gibson); m. Holly Robertson Clacken 1943; two d.; ed. Jamaica Coll., Jamaica, and Keble Coll., Oxford.
Inspector of Schools Jamaica 35; Asst. Information Officer 39-43; Asst. Sec. Colonial Secretariat 45-50, Principal Asst. Sec. 50-52; Administrator, Dominica, Windward Islands 52-59; Acting Gov. Windward Islands 57, 59; Governor's Sec., Jamaica 60-62; High Commr. for Jamaica in U.K. 62-73, concurrently Amb. to France 66-72, to Federal Republic of Germany 67-70; Order of Jamaica 75.
Leisure interests: reading, walking, watching cricket.
c/o Royal Bank of Canada, Cockspur Street, London, S.W.1, England.

Lindon, Jérôme; French publisher; b. 9 June 1925; s. of Raymond Lindon and Thérèse Baur; m. Annette Rosenfeld 1947; two s. one d.
Président-Directeur Général, Editions de Minuit 48-, has published novels of the "nouveau roman" (Beckett, Robbe-Grillet, Butor, Nathalie Sarraute, Simon, Pinget, etc.); had nine books seized in his opposition to the Algerian war.
Publ. *Jonas* 55.
Editions de Minuit 7 rue Bernard Palissy, Paris 6e, France.
Telephone: 222-37-94.

Lindsay, Jack, B.A., F.R.S.L.; British author; b. 20 Oct. 1900, Melbourne, Australia; s. of Norman Lindsay

and Catharine Parkinson; m. Meta Waterdrinker 1958; one s. one d.; ed. Queensland Univ.
Earlier work mainly verse; began series of translations of Greek and Latin poets; went to England 26; Man. and Editor Fanfrolico Press until 30; began novel-writing and direct historical work in 30's; first historical novel 34; served in Signals and in War Office 41-45; Fellow, Royal Soc. of Literature; Gold Medal Australian Soc. of Literature 60; Soviet Order Znak Pocheta 68; D.Litt. (Queensland).
Leisure interests: field archaeology, bricklaying, tree-planting.
Publs. Historical novels: *Rome for Sale, Caesar is Dead, Last Days with Cleopatra, The Barriers are Down, Thunder Underground,* and others on the ancient world; *1649, Lost Birthright, Men of Forty-eight, Fires in Smithfield,* and others on English history; biographies of Mark Antony, John Bunyan, George Meredith, Charles Dickens, J. M. W. Turner, Cézanne, Gustave Courbet and William Morris; various critical works and trans., including *I am a Roman, Medieval Latin Poets,* and *Song of a Falling World* (Latin poets A.D. 350-650); *Byzantium into Europe, Betrayed Spring, Rising Tide, Moment of Choice, Arthur and his Times, Life Rarely Tells, The Roaring Twenties* and *Fanfrolico and After* (autobiography), *Meeting with Poets;* works on Roman Britain and Roman Egypt; *Men and Gods on the Roman Nile* (third of a Nilotic trilogy) 68; art-criticism, *The Death of a Hero, A Short History of Culture, The Clashing Rocks, Ancient World, Origins of Alchemy, Cleopatra, Courbet, Origins of Astrology, The World of the Normans, Helen of Troy.*
Castle Hedingham, Halstead, Essex, England.
Telephone: Hedingham 60259.

Lindsay, John Vliet; American politician; b. 24 Nov. 1921, New York City; s. of George and Eleanor (Vliet) Lindsay; m. Mary Harrison 1949; one s. three d.; ed. The Buckley School, St. Paul's School, Concord, Yale Univ., and Yale Law School.
Admitted to New York Bar 49; mem. Webster, Sheffield, Fleischmann, Hitchcock and Christie, New York 53-60; Exec. Attorney to U.S. Attorney-Gen. 55-57; mem. U.S. House of Reps. 59-65; Mayor of New York 66-73; fmrly. Republican; joined Democratic Party Aug. 71; Commentator on ABC-TV Programmes; appearance in film *Rosebud* 75.
Publs. *Journey into Politics* 67, *The City* 70.
1 West 67th Street, New York, N.Y. 10023, U.S.A.

Lindsay, Lieut.-Gen. Richard Clark; American air force officer (retd.); b. 31 Oct. 1905, Minneapolis; s. of Edwin H. and MaBelle Clark Lindsay; m. Margaret Eloise Ball 1930 (divorced); one s. one d.; ed. Univ. of Minn.
Commissioned Second Lieut. Air Corps, U.S. Army 29, advancing through grades to Major-Gen. 48; various peacetime assignments 29-41; Asst. Chief and Chief European-African Section, Air Plans, War Dept., Washington, D.C. 41-42; Staff Asst. and Chief of Combined Subjects Section, Operations Div., War Dept. Gen. Staff 42-43; Army Air Force Mem. Joint War Plans Cttee. of Joint Chiefs of Staff 43-44; Army Air Force mem. Joint Staff Planners of Joint Chiefs of Staff Organization 44-45; Asst. Chief of Staff, Plas. (A-5), H.Q. U.S. Army Strategic Air Forces 45, at Guam and Pacific Air Commd., Manila 45; commd. 316th Bombardment Wing (VH), 8th Air Force, Okinawa 46; Asst. Chief of Staff, A-2, H.Q. F.E.A.F. 47; Chief, Policy Div., Directorate of Plans and Operations and Air Planner, H.Q. U.S.A.F., Washington, D.C. 47-48; Deputy Dir. Plans and Operations, Office of DCS/O 48-49; Deputy Dir. for Strategic Plans, The Joint Staff, Joint Chiefs of Staff 49-51; Standing Group Liaison Officer to NATO 51-52; Commdg. Gen. 3650th Air Force Indoctrination Wing, Sampson Air Force

Base, N.Y. 53-54; Dir. Plans. DCS/O 54-57; Asst. Deputy Chief of Staff, Operations Feb.-Aug. 57; Commdr. Allied Air Forces, Southern Europe 57-60; retd. from active service April 60; Res. Consultant The Rand Corpn. 61-63, Consultant 64-; Asst. to Pres. Electronic Communications Inc. 63-64; Asst. to Pres. and Dir. European Staff, Litton Systems European Div. 64-, Exec. Asst. to Pres. Econ. Devt. Div. 65; Gen. Man. Central Econ. Devt. Org., Washington 66-67; decorations include D.S.M. (U.S.), Hon. C.B.E.

Leisure interests: sound recordings (transcribing records, tapes, etc.), still and motion picture photography.

1001 East California Avenue, Apartment 12A, Glendale, Calif. 91206, U.S.A.

Telephone: 213-243-5529.

Lindskog, (Claes) Folke; Swedish business executive; b. 18 Jan. 1910, London; s. of the Rev. Jonas Lindskog and Maria (née Smit); m. Marguerite Thatcher (née Troskie) 1941; two s. one d.; ed. Royal Inst. of Technology, Stockholm.

Managing Dir. The SKF Ball Bearing Co. (Pty.) Ltd., Johannesburg S. Africa 57-60, The Skefko Ball Bearing Co. Ltd., Luton, England 60-64; Man. Dir. and mem Board Aktiebolaget Svenska Kullagerfabriken, Gothenburg, Sweden 64-71, Chair. Board 71-.

Aktiebolaget Svenska Kullagerfabriken, Hornsgatan 1, S415 50 Gothenburg, Sweden.

Telephone: 031-840000.

Lindsley, Donald Benjamin, A.B., M.A., PH.D.; American professor of psychology and physiology; b. 23 Dec. 1907, Brownhelm, Ohio; s. of Benjamin Kent Lindsley and Martha Elizabeth Jenne; m. Ellen Ford 1933; two s. two d.; ed. Wittenberg Univ. and Univ. of Iowa.

Instructor in Psychology, Univ. of Illinois 32-33; Nat. Research Council Fellow, Harvard Medical School 33-35; Research Assoc., W. Reserve Univ. Medical School 35-38; Asst. Prof. Brown Univ. and Dir. Psychology and Neurophysiology Lab., Bradley Hospital 38-46; Dir. Radar Research Project, Office of Scientific Research and Devt., Yale Univ. and Camp Murphy, Fla. 43-45; Prof. of Psychology, Northwestern Univ. 46-51; Prof. of Psychology, Physiology and Psychiatry, Univ. of Calif., Los Angeles 51-, mem. Brain Research Inst., Univ. of Calif., Los Angeles 60-, Chair. Dept. of Psychology 59-62; mem. Nat. Acad. of Sciences, Amer. Acad. of Arts and Sciences, Soc. of Experimental Psychologists; Presidential Certificate of Merit for Second World War Research Work; Distinguished Scientific Contribution Award, Amer. Psychol. Asscn.; Hon. D.Sc. (Brown Univ.) 58, (Wittenberg Univ.) 59, (Trinity Coll.) 65, (Loyola Univ.) 69.

Leisure interests: music, photography, gardening, golf, travel.

Publs. 200 publs., including scientific works in journals and 20 chapters in books; subjects: emotion, electroencephalography, neurophysiology, perception, attention, brain function, developmental neurology, autonomic function, sleep and wakefulness conditioning and learning, etc.

Department of Psychology, University of California, Los Angeles, Calif. 90024; Home: 471 23rd Street, Santa Monica, Calif. 90402, U.S.A.

Telephone: 213-825-2517 (Office); 213-394-8306 (Home).

Lindstrom, Ulla; Swedish politician; b. 15 Sept. 1909; ed. Univ. of Stockholm.

Teacher 33; Editor teachers' weekly publ. 34-46; Editor weekly publ. on housing 34-44; elected Stockholm Municipal Council 42; elected Senate 46-70; Chair. Govt. Cttees. on the Furniture Industry, the Shoe Industry, and on the Distribution of Consumer Goods 46, 48, 55; Expert, Trade Dept. 46-54; Minister without Portfolio

54-66; mem. Swedish Del. to UN 47-66; Chair. Swedish Save the Children Fed. 70-; Labour Party.

Fleminggatan 56, Stockholm, Sweden.

Lindt, Auguste Rudolph, LL.D.; Swiss diplomatist (retd.); b. 5 Aug. 1905; ed. Univs. of Geneva and Berne. Special news corresp. in Manchuria, Liberia, Palestine Jordan, the Persian Gulf, Tunisia, Rumania and Finland 27-40; served in Swiss Army 40-45; special del. of the Int. Red Cross, Berlin 45; Press Attaché and Counsellor Swiss Legation, London; Perm. Observer from Switzerland to the UN 53-56; fmr. Chair. UNICEF; Pres. UN Opium Conf. 53; UN High Commr. for Refugees 56-60; Swiss Amb. to U.S.A. 60-63; Del. Swiss Fed. Council for Technical Co-operation 63-66; Swiss Amb. to U.S.S.R. 66-69; Swiss Amb. to India and Nepal 69-70; Int. Red Cross Commr. for Nigeria-Biafra relief operation 68-June 69; Pres. Int. Union for Child Welfare 71-; Adviser to Pres. of Rwanda 73-75; Hon. Dr. Univ. of Geneva.

Leisure interests: gardening, mountaineering.

c/o Union Bank of Switzerland, Berne, Switzerland.

Lindtberg, Leopold; Swiss professor, theatre producer and film director; b. 1 June 1902, Vienna, Austria; m. Valeska Hirsch; two d.; ed. Realgymnasium Wien, and Vienna Univ.

Actor, Berlin, Vienna, Düsseldorf 24-, later producer Berliner Staatstheater, Piscator-Buehne; Artistic Dir. Zürich Schauspielhaus 33-, Dir. 65-68; Lecturer, Univ. of Zürich; more than 200 theatrical productions; stage producer Habimah Theatre, Tel Aviv 34, 35; also film director 38-; theatrical productions at Vienna Burgtheater, Hamburg Schauspielhaus, Munich Kammerspiele, Israel theatres, Salzburg Festival; opera productions Staatsoper, Vienna and Hamburg, Municipal Opera, Frankfurt and Zürich; hon. mem. Vienna Burgtheater; mem. Akad. der Künste, Berlin; numerous awards.

Principal productions: a cycle of Shakespeare's history plays, *Faust*, Salzburg Festival 60-65; first performances at Zürich of Faulkner, Wilder, Sartre, Brecht, Zuckmayer, Frisch, Dürrenmatt; films: *Marie Louise* 43, *The Last Chance* 45, *Four in a Jeep* 50, *The Village* 53, *An outpost of civilisation* 58; TV film serials *Kommissar* and *Denick*.

Leisure interest: chess.

Publs. *Shakespeare's History Plays* 62, *Reden und Aufsätze* 72.

Schuerbungert 36, Zürich, Switzerland.

Telephone: 287081.

Linen, James Alexander, III; American magazine executive; b. 20 June 1912, Waverly, Pa.; s. of Genevieve Tuthill Linen and James Alexander Linen, Jr.; m. Sara Scranton 1934; four s. two d.; ed. The Hotchkiss School and Williams Coll.

Joined *Time* magazine 34, worked New York and Detroit 34-38; on *Life* magazine, New York 38-40, Advertising Man. *Life* 40-42; Office of War Information 42-45; Publisher *Time* 45-60, Pres. Time Inc. 60-69, Chair. Exec. Cttee. Time Inc. 69-74, Dir. 74-; official of numerous civic, welfare and educational orgs.; Hon. L.H.D. (Long Island, Coll. of New Rochelle and Pace Coll.); Hon. LL.D. (Adelphi Univ.) 66; Knight Commdr. and Knight Grand Cross of Thailand; Decoration of the Crown 3rd Order, Iran 71, Nararya Meritorious Decoration of the Repub. of Indonesia 74, Grand Cordon of the Order of the Star of Jordan 75.

Time and Life Building, Rockefeller Center, New York, N.Y. 10020; Home: 200 John Street, Greenwich, Conn. 06830, U.S.A.

Telephone: (212) 556-3497.

Ling, James J.; American business executive; b. 1922; ed. St. John's College, Shreveport.

President Ling Electrics 46-58; Chair. Ling Electronics

58-60; Pres., Chair. Exec. Cttee. Ling Temco Electronics 60-61; Chair. Exec. Cttee. Ling-Temco-Vought Inc. 61-63, Chair. of Board and Chief Exec. Officer 63-70, Vice-Chair. of Board 70-; Dir. First Nat. Bank in Dallas 68, Southwest Research Inst.; Horatio Alger Award 62; mem. Hudson Inst.; Regent of Texas Technological Univ.

Ling-Temco-Vought Inc., P.O. Box 5003, Dallas, Texas 75222, U.S.A.

Link, Arthur A.; American politician; b. 24 May 1914, Alexander, N.D.; s. of John Link and Anna Mencl; m. Grace Johnson 1939; five s. one d.; ed. N.D. Agricultural Coll.

Mem. Randolph Township Board for 28 years and McKenzie Co. Welfare Board for 21 years; served on local school board for 18 years and was mem. of co. and state Farm Security Admin. Cttee.; State Rep., N.D. Legislature for 24 years; Speaker 65; served as Minority Floor Leader for seven terms, and on legislative cttees. on Education, Finance and Taxation, Business and Industry, and Labour Relations; Chair. N.D. State Advisory Council for Vocational Education 69-71; Chair. Second Interim Cttee. on Legislative Procedure and Arrangements and of the Subcttee. on Education of the Legislative Research Cttee.; U.S. House of Reps., Mem. for Second (West) District of N.D. 70, mem. Agricultural Cttee. and the Livestock and Grains, Domestic Marketing and Consumer Relations subcttees.; mem. of the House District of Columbia Cttee., serving on the Judiciary and the Business, Commerce and Fiscal Affairs subcttees.; co-sponsor of the Melcher Farm Bill; Gov. of N.D. 72-; Chair. Farmers' Union Grain Terminal Asscn. annual meeting for three years; board mem. Williston Univ. Center Foundation; fmr. board mem. McKenzie Co. Museum and Lewis and Clark Trail Museum; past pres. Alexander Lions Club and Alexander Parent-Teacher Asscn.; fmr. council pres. and Sunday School Supt. Alexander Trinity Lutheran Church.

Leisure interests: camping, fishing, horseriding, reading.
Governor's Office, State Capitol Buildings, Bismarck, N.D. 58501; Governor's Residence, Bismarck, N.D. 58501, U.S.A.
Telephone: 224-2200 (Office); 224-2190 (Residence).

Link, Karl Paul, M.S., PH.D.; American professor of biochemistry; b. 31 Jan. 1901, La Porte, Ind.; s. of Rev. George Link and Fredericka Mohr Link; m. Elisabeth Feldman 1930; three s.; ed. La Porte, Ind., High School, Univ. of Wisconsin, Univ. of St. Andrews, Scotland, Univ. of Graz, Austria and Univ. of Zürich, Switzerland.

Assistant Prof. of Biochemistry, Univ. of Wis. 27-31, Prof. 31-71, Emer. 71-; Collaborator, U.S.D.A. Northern Regional Lab. 37-45; Consultant to Clinton Corn Products Co. 33-58, to Pabst Brewery, Milwaukee 44-69; mem. Nat. Acad. of Sciences 46-; Cameron prize, Univ. of Edinburgh 52; Albert Lasker award for Medical Research 55; John Scott award 59; Albert Lasker award of American Heart Asscn. 60; Nat. Acad. of Sciences Kovalenko Medal 67; Hon. mem. Harvey Soc.
Leisure interests: gardening, loafing.
Publs. many papers on chemistry of sugars, disease resistance in plants and blood coagulation. Harvey Soc. Lecture, *The Anticoagulant from Spoiled Sweet Clover* 44, *The Discovery of Dicumarol and its Sequels* 59.
Department of Biochemistry, University of Wisconsin, Madison, Wis. 53706; 1111 Willow Lane, Madison, Wis. 53705, U.S.A.
Telephone: 608-233-4525.

Linner, Carl Sture, M.A., PH.D.; Swedish international civil servant; b. 15 June 1917, Stockholm; s. of C. W. Linner and H. Hellstedt; m. Clio Tambakopoulos 1944; two s.; ed. Stockholm and Uppsala Univs.
Associate Prof. of Greek, Uppsala Univ. 43; Del. to Int.

Red Cross, Greece 43-45; Dir. A.B. Electrolux, Stockholm 45-50; Dir. Swedish Employers' Confederation 50-51; Exec. Vice-Pres. A.B. Bahco, Stockholm 51-57; Pres. Swedish Lamco Syndicate 57; Exec. Vice-Pres. and Gen. Man. Liberian-American-Swedish Minerals Co., Monrovia 58-60; Chief UN Civilian Operations, later UN Mission, in the Congo 60-61; Special Rep. of UN Sec.-Gen. in Brussels and London 62; UN Rep. in Greece, Turkey, Israel and Cyprus 62-65, in London 65-68, in Tunis 68-71, UN Devt. Programme N.Y. 71-73; Resident Rep. UN Devt. Programme in Egypt 73-; mem. Royal Acad. of Arts and Sciences, Uppsala; Star of Africa, Order of Phoenix, Prince Carl Medal.
Leisure interests: dogs, poetry.
Publs. *Syntaktische und Lexikalische Studien zur Historia Lausiaca des Palladios* 43, *Giorgos Seferis* 63, *Roms Konungahävder* 65, *Fredrika Bremer i Grekland* 65, *W. H. Humphreys' First Journal of the Greek War of Independence* 66.
United Nations Development Programme, P.O. Box 982, Cairo, Egypt.
Telephone 817845.

Linnik, Vladimir Pavlovich; Soviet physicist; b. 6 July 1889, Kharkov; ed. Kiev Univ.
Professor, Leningrad Univ. 26-41, Prof. State Optical Inst. 26-; mem. U.S.S.R. Acad. of Sciences 39-; State Prizes 46, 50; two Orders of Lenin.
Publs. *Instrument for Interferential Investigation of Reflecting Objects under the Microscope, Instrument for Interferential Investigation of Surface Microprofile*, papers on constructing optical instruments.
State Optical Institute, Leningrad, U.S.S.R.

Linowitz, Sol Myron, LL.B.; American lawyer and diplomatist; b. 7 Dec. 1913, Trenton, N.J.; m. Evelyn Zimmerman 1939; four d.; ed. Hamilton Coll., and Cornell Univ. Law School.
Assistant Gen. Counsel, Office of Price Admin., Washington 42-44; Officer, Office of Gen. Counsel, Navy Dept. 44-46; fmr. Partner, Harris, Beach, Wilcox, Dale & Linowitz, Gen. Counsel, Chair. of Board and Chair. of Exec. Cttee. Xerox Corpn.; Chair. Nat. Urban Coalition; mem. Council on Foreign Relations, Amer. Jewish Cttee.; U.S.A. Amb. to the Org. of Amer. States and U.S. Rep. on the Inter-Amer. Cttee. of the Alliance for Progress 66-69; Senior Partner Condert Brothers (Int. Law firm) 69-; Head of Comm. for U.S.-Latin Amer. Relations; Trustee, John F. Kennedy Center for Performing Arts, Salk Inst. for Biological Studies; Fellow, Amer. Acad. of Arts and Sciences; Trustee, Cornell Univ., Hamilton Coll., Johns Hopkins Univ., Amer. Red Cross, Amer. Assembly, Inst. of Int. Educ., Educ. and World Affairs; hon. degrees (LL.D. and L.H.D.) from more than 20 colls. and univs.
Leisure interest: violin.
2325 Wyoming Ave., Washington, D.C. 20008, U.S.A.
Telephone: 483-9086.

Linthorst Homan, Johannes, LL.D.; Netherlands official; b. 17 Feb. 1903, Assen; s. of Jan Tijmen Linthorst Homan and Jeannette Madeleine Staal; m. 1st Jonkvrouwe Elisabeth Storm van 's Gravesande 1928 (died 1951), one s. three d.; m. 2nd Maria Vittoria Genni 1952; ed. Leiden Univ.
Mayor of Vledder 32; Queen's Commissioner, Province of Groningen 37-41; Pres. Nat. Office for Town and Country Planning 47; Dir. European Integration, Ministry of Economic Affairs 52; Head Netherlands del. Brussels Conf. 55-57; Pres. Netherlands Olympic Cttee. 51-59; Ambassador, Head Netherlands Mission to the European Economic Community and European Community for Atomic Energy 58; mem. High Authority, ECSC 62-67; Chief Rep. of European Community in U.K. 68-71; Nederlandse Leeuw, Grande Croix de l'Ordre de Léopold II (Belgium), Grande Croix de

l'Ordre Grand-Ducal de la Couronne de Chêne (Luxembourg), Grand Croix de l'Ordre Royal du Phénix (Greece) and other orders.
Leisure interests: history, antiques, sport.
Publs. *The Birth of Local Community in the Province of Drenthe* 34, *History of Drenthe* 46, *European Agricultural Policy* 50, *European Integration* 55, *Memoirs* 74.
56 Via Capo le Case, 00187 Rome, Italy.
Telephone: 6785677.

Lintott, Sir Henry (John Bevis), K.C.M.G.; British diplomatist; b. 23 Sept. 1908; ed. Edinburgh Acad., Edinburgh Univ., and King's Coll., Cambridge.
Customs and Excise Dept. 32-35; Board of Trade 35-48; Ministry of Econ. Warfare 39-40; Office of Minister of State, Cairo 41; Dep. Sec.-Gen. OEEC 48-56; Dep. Under-Sec. of State, Commonwealth Relations Office 56-63; High Commr. in Canada 63-68; Dir. The Metal Box Co. 68-73, Glaxo Holdings Ltd. 68-.
Rodmell Hill House, Rodmell, Lewes, Sussex, England.

Lionaes, Aase; Norwegian politician; b. 10 April 1907, Oslo; d. of Erling and Anna Lionaes; m. Kurt Jonas; one d.; ed. Univ. of Oslo and London School of Economics.
Member of Storting (Labour) 53-; Pres. of the Lagting; mem. Govt. del. to UN 46-65; mem. Nobel Peace Prize Cttee. 48-, Pres. 68-; Hon. LL.D. (Oxford Coll., Ohio).
The Storting, Oslo; Pans Vei nr. 8, Ulvøya, Oslo, Norway.
Telephone: 282408.

Liotard-Vogt, Pierre Alberto; French business executive; b. 14 Dec. 1909, London, England; s. of Alfred and Enrica (Cerasoli) Liotard-Vogt; divorced; two s.; ed. School of Higher Business Studies, Paris.
With Nestlé Co., Switzerland 33; with Société des Produits Alimentaires et Diététiques (Nestlé Products in France) 36; factory man. 38; Man. Head Office 40, Gen. Man. 42, Pres. 65; Dir. Nestlé Alimentana S.A. 67, Man. Dir. 68-75, Chair. 73-; Officier, Légion d'Honneur; Croix de Guerre.
Nestlé Alimentana S.A., 1800 Vevey; Home: Novavilla, 1807 Blonay, Switzerland.
Telephone: 021-51-01-12 (Office); 021-53-10-86 (Home).

Lipiński, Edward; Polish economist; b. 18 Oct. 1888, Nowe Miasto; s. of Jan and Teodora (née Klimkiewicz) Lipiński; m. Janina Zybert 1916; one s. one d.; ed. Leipzig and Zürich Univs.
Lecturer, Cen. School of Econ. Warsaw 23, Prof. 29; Founder Dir. Inst. for Study of Markets and Prices, Warsaw 27-39; Prof. Łódź Univ. 45; Chair. Warsaw Inst. of Economics 45-48; Prof. Warsaw Univ. 50-58, Prof. emeritus 59-; Pres. Bank Gospodarstwa Krajowego (Bank of Nat. Economy) 46-48; Deputy Chair. Economic Council 57-62, 70-; mem. Polish Acad. of Sciences 57- and several foreign scientific socs.; Hon. Pres. Polish Econ. Soc. 70; mem. Int. Inst. of Statistics, Asscn. Française de Science Economique, Int. Econometric Soc.; D. h.c. (Main School of Planning and Statistics); State Prize, First Class 53, 72, Officer and Commdr. with Star Cross of Order of Polonia Restituta 51, 56, Order of Banner of Labour 1st Class 59, Oscar Lange Scientific Prize 73, Meritorious Teacher of People's Poland 74, Medal of Nat. Educ. 74.
Leisure interests: music, art.
Publs. *Ruch robotniczy w Polsce* (The Workers' Movement in Poland), *Inspekcja Pracy* (Work Inspection) 16, *Statystyka dotycząca robotników miejskich* (Statistics Relating to Urban Workers) 18, *Poglądy ekonomiczne Mikołaja Kopernika* (Copernicus as Economist) 55, *Historia myśli ekonomicznej* (History of Economic Thought) 56, *Rewizje* (Reassessments) 57, *Studia nad historią polskiej myśli ekonomicznej* (Studies on the History of Polish Economic Thought) 55, *Teoria*

ekonomii a rzeczywistość (Economics and Economic Reality) 61, *Histoire de la pensée économique en Pologne* 61, *Historia powszechna myśli ekonomicznej do 1870 r.* (General History of Economic Thought until 1870) 68, *Karol Marks i Zagadnienia Współczesności* (Karl Marx and the Problems of our Times) 69.
Ul. Rakowiecka 6m. 26, bl. C, 02-521 Warsaw, Poland.
Telephone: 451016.

Lipkowski, Jean-Noël De, L. EN D.; French politician and diplomatist; b. 25 Dec. 1920, Paris; ed. Ecole libre des sciences politiques.
Entered diplomatic service 45-; attached to Cen. Admin. for Asia-Oceania; Third Sec. for Far East, Nanking; Attaché to French Embassy, Nanking 47-49, to Cen. Admin. 50-52; Sec. of Foreign Affairs 51; Deputy Consul, Madrid; Deputy Dir., Cabinet of the Resident-Gen. of France in Tunis and later in Rabat; Adviser for Foreign Affairs 56; Deputy to Nat. Assembly for Seine-et-Oise 56-58; Adviser to French Embassy, Beirut 58; Political Adviser, Cie. française de l'Afrique occidentale; Deputy for Charente-Maritime 62-68, 73-; Mayor of Royan 65, 71-; Sec. of State, Ministry of Foreign Affairs 68-72; Sec. of State for Foreign Affairs with rank of Minister 73-74; Minister of Co-operation Jan. 76-.
Ministère de Coopération, Paris, France.

Lipmann, Fritz (Albert), M.D., PH.D., SC.D.; American biochemist; b. 12 June 1899, Koenigsberg, Germany; m. Freda Hall 1931; one s.; ed. Univs. of Koenigsberg and Berlin.
Research Asst. Kaiser Wilhelm Inst., Berlin and Heidelberg 27-31; research Fellow Rockefeller Inst. for Medical Research, N.Y.C. 31-32; research Assoc. Biological Inst. of Carlsberg Foundation, Copenhagen 32-39; research Assoc. Dept. of Biological Chemistry, Cornell Univ. Medical School, N.Y.C. 39-41; research Fellow in Surgery, Harvard Medical School, Boston 41-43 and Assoc. in Biochemistry 43-49; Prof. of Biological Chemistry Harvard Medical School, Massachusetts Gen. Hospital, Boston 49-57; Prof. of Rockefeller Univ., New York City 57-69; has done outstanding work on energy metabolism, the metabolic function of B vitamins, and has discovered coenzyme A; Foreign mem. Royal Soc. (U.K.); Nobel Prize in Medicine and Physiology 53; Nat. Medal of Science 66; Hon. Sc.D.
Publ. *Wanderings of a Biochemist* 71.
201 East 18th Street, New York, N.Y. 10003, U.S.A.
Telephone: 212-360-1236 and 212-477-5777.

Lipscomb, William Nunn, PH.D.; American professor of chemistry; b. 9 Dec. 1919, Cleveland, Ohio; s. of Dr. William Lipscomb and Mrs. Edna Porter Lipscomb; m. Mary Adele Sargent 1944; one s. one d.; ed. Univ. of Kentucky and Calif. Inst. of Technology.
Assistant Prof. of Physical Chem., Univ. of Minn. 46-50, Assoc. Prof. 50-54, Acting Chief, Physical Chem. Div. 52-54, Prof. and Chief, Physical Chem. Div. 54-59; Prof. of Chem., Harvard Univ. 59-, Chair. Dept. of Chem. 62-65, Abbott and James Lawrence Prof. of Chem. 71-; Overseas Fellow of Churchill Coll., Cambridge 66; mem. Nat. Acad. of Sciences, Amer. Acad. of Arts and Sciences; Pres. Amer. Crystallographic Soc. 55; Hon. M.A. and Hon. D.Sc., Harrison Howe Award in Chem. 58, Award for Distinguished Service in the Advancement of Inorganic Chem. 68, Ledlie Prize, Harvard Univ. 71, Peter Debye Award in Physical Chem., Amer. Chemical Soc. 73.
Leisure interests: chamber music, tennis.
Publs. *Boron Hydrides* 63, *Nuclear Magnetic Resonance Studies of Boron and Related Compounds* (with G. R. Eaton) 69; and papers on structure and function of enzymes and natural products in inorganic chem. and theoretical chem.

Department of Chemistry, Harvard University, Cambridge, Mass. 02138; Home: 26 Woodfall Road, Belmont, Mass. 02178, U.S.A.
Telephone: 617-495-4098 (Office); 617-484-8499 (Home).

Lipton, Seymour; American sculptor; b. 6 Nov. 1903; ed. Columbia Univ.
Teacher, New School for Social Research, New York City 39-58, Cooper Union Art School, N.Y.C. 43-45, New Jersey State Teachers' Coll., Newark 44-45; One-man shows New York City 38-58, Washington 51; Visiting critic, Yale Art School 57-59; rep. Venice Biennale 58; Guggenheim Award 60, Ford Foundation Award 61 and others; represented in over 160 museums throughout the world.
302 West 98th Street, New York, N.Y., U.S.A.

Lisette, Gabriel; French international official; b. 2 April 1919, Panama; s. of Gabriel and Fiacre Lisette; m. Yeyon Darrotchetche 1945; three s. one d.; ed. Lycée Carnot (Point-à-Pitre, Guadeloupe), Lycée Henri IV (Paris) and Ecole Nat. de la France d'Outre-mer.
Admin. France d'Outre-mer 44-46; Dep. from Chad to Nat. Assembly, Paris 46-51, 56-59; Territorial Counsellor, Chad 52-59; Pres. Chad Govt. Council 57-58; Deputy Chad Legislative Assembly 59-60; Pres. Council of Ministers, Repub. of Chad 58-59, Vice-Pres. 59-60; Minister-Counsellor to French Govt. 59-60; Admin.-in-Chief of Overseas Affairs (France); Mayor of Fort-Lamy 56-60; French Govt. Perm. Rep. Econ. Comm. for Latin America (ECLA); Pres. Mutualité d'Outre-mer et de l'Extérieur 63; mem. Conseil de Direction du Comité français pour la campagne mondiale contre la faim; fmr. Vice-Pres. Rassemblement Démocratique Africain (R.D.A.); fmr. Joint leader Parti Progressiste Tchadien; First Citizen of Honour of Chad; Officier Légion d'Honneur; Commdr. Ordre Nat. de la République de Côte d'Ivoire; Grand Officier Ordre Nat. de la République du Niger; Commdr. Etoile de la Grande Couronne; Chevalier Ordre du Mérite Centrafricain.
Leisure interests: reading, the sea.
French Delegation to ECLA, Sainte-Rose, Guadeloupe, West Indies; 3 boulevard des Courcelles, Paris 8e, France.

Lissák, Kálmán; Hungarian university professor; b. 13 Jan. 1908, Budapest; s. of Kálmán Lissák and Aranka Kozák; m. 1st Janina Malachowska 1937, one s. one d.; m. 2nd Zsuzsa Frey 1975; ed. Univ. of Budapest.
Assistant, Physiological Inst., Debrecen Univ. 33-37, Reader 37-41, Prof. 41-43; Prof. of Physiology, Medical Univ. of Pécs; Dean of Medical Faculty, Univ. of Pécs 46-47, 50-51, 56-57, Rector 47-48, 48-49; mem. Hungarian Acad. of Sciences; Kossuth Prize 54; mem. Deutsche Akad. der Naturforscher Leopoldina 67; Hon. mem. Purkynje Medical Soc. of Czechoslovakia, I. P. Pavlov All Union Physiological Soc. of U.S.S.R. Acad. Sciences, North American Pavlovian Soc.
Leisure interests: horology and collecting frog-figures.
Publs. *Neurophysiology and Neuro-Endocrine Regulation of Behaviour*; numerous articles in Hungarian, English, American, German and Russian medical journals.
Physiological Institute, 7624 Pécs, Sziget-ut 12, Hungary.
Telephone: 11-122/2780.

Lissouba, Pascal, D. ÈS SC.; Congolese politician; b 15 Nov. 1931, Tsinguidi, Congo (Brazzaville); s. of Albert Lissouba and Marie Bouanga; m. 2nd Jocelyne Pierrot 1967; one s. six d.; ed. secondary education in Nice, France, and Ecole Supérieure d'Agriculture, Tunis.
Former agricultural specialist; Prime Minister of Congo (Brazzaville) Dec. 63-66, concurrently Minister of Trade

and Industry and Agriculture; Prof. of Genetics, Brazzaville 66-71, concurrently Minister of Planning 68; Minister of Agriculture, Waterways and Forests 69; Dir. Ecole Supérieure des Sciences, Brazzaville 71-.
Leisure interests: geology, music.
Ecole Supérieure des Sciences, B.P. 69, Brazzaville; and B.P. 717, Brazzaville, People's Republic of the Congo.

Lister, Sir (Charles) Percy, Kt., D.L.; British company director; b. 15 July 1897, Dursley, Glos.; s. of Charles A. Lister; m. 1953; one s.; ed. Mill Hill School, and Royal Military Coll., Sandhurst.
War service with 18th Royal (Queen Mary's Own) Hussars in France, Belgium and Germany 15-19; former Chair. and Man. Dir. R. A. Lister Co. Ltd.; Dir. Armstrong Whitworth (Engineers) Ltd. 65-69, Hawker Siddeley Group Ltd.; past mem. Capital Issues Cttee., Western Hemisphere Exports Council, Dollar Exports Council, Iron and Steel Board 53-57.
Leisure interests: sport, travel.
Stinchcombe Hill House, Dursley, Gloucestershire, England.
Telephone: Dursley 2030.

Listov, Konstantin Yakovlevich; Soviet composer; b. 19 Sept. 1900, Odessa, Ukraine; ed. Tsaritzin Musical School.
Order of Red Star 43, Honoured Worker of the Arts of R.S.F.S.R. 50.
Principal compositions: Operettas: *Coralina* 48, *Dreamers* 50, *Ira* 51, *Song of the Volgograders* 55, *Rustle of Our Forests* 57, *Sebastopol Waltz* 61; Operas: *Olesya* 57, *Daughter of Cuba* 61; Romances and songs, settings of verse by Russian and Soviet poets, many musical pieces for radio and theatre productions.
Moscow Branch, Composers' Union of the R.S.F.S.R., 4/6 3rd Miusskaya Ulitsa, Moscow, U.S.S.R.

Listowel, the 5th Earl of, cr. 1822; **William Francis Hare,** P.C., G.C.M.G., PH.D.; British philosopher and politician; b. 28 Sept. 1906; ed. Eton and Balliol Coll., Oxford, and London Univ.
Labour mem. London County Council for East Lewisham; Chief Whip Labour Party and Deputy Leader House of Lords, Parl. Under-Sec. of State India Office 44-45; Postmaster-Gen. Aug. 45-April 47; Sec. of State for India and Burma April-Aug. 47; Sec. of State for Burma, Aug. 47-Dec. 48; Minister of State for the Colonies Jan. 48-50; Joint Parl. Sec., Ministry of Agriculture and Fisheries 50-51; Gov.-Gen. of Ghana 57-60; Chair. of Cttees., House of Lords 65-.
Publs. *The Values of Life* 31, *A Critical History of Modern Aesthetics* (2nd edn. as *Modern Aesthetics: an Historical Introduction* 67).
7 Constable Close, Wildwood Road, London, N.W.11, England.

Littler, Sir Emile, Kt.; British theatrical impresario, producer, author and company director; b. 9 Sept. 1903; two d.; ed. Stratford on Avon.
Served apprenticeship working on theatre stages; Asst. Man. Theatre in Southend 22; subsequently worked as Asst. Stage Man., Birmingham Repertory Theatre; in U.S.A. 27-31; became Man. and Licensee Birmingham Repertory Theatre for Sir Barry Jackson 31; began personally in management 33; theatrical productions include *Victoria Regina, 1066 and All That, The Maid of the Mountains, The Night and the Music, Claudia, The Quaker Girl, Lilac Time, The Barretts of Wimpole Street, Song of Norway, Annie Get Your Gun, Blue for a Boy, Zip Goes a Million, Love from Judy, Book of the Month, The Lovebirds, The Happiest Millionaire, Signpost to Murder, The Right Hon. Gentleman;* for many years was a dir. of various theatres including Drury Lane, Coliseum and the Palladium; Chair. and Man. Dir. Palace Theatre, London, London Entertainments Ltd.; Dir. Theatres Mutual Insurance Co. Ltd.;

a Gov. of Royal Shakespeare Theatre, Stratford on Avon; Dir. Eagle Star Insurance.
Publs. (joint author) *Cabbages and Kings, Too Young to Marry, Love Isn't Everything*; and 15 Christmas pantomimes in London and over 200 in the provinces.
Palace Theatre, Shaftesbury Avenue, London, W1V 8AY, England.
Telephone: 01-734 -9691.

Littlewood, Joan Maud; British theatrical director; b. 1914, London; ed. Royal Acad. of Dramatic Art, London.
Began career with Manchester Repertory Theatre; founded Theatre Union 37; free-lance work for B.B.C. 39-45; founded Theatre Workshop 45, tours in Great Britain and Europe 45-53, established in Theatre Royal, Stratford (London) 53-61, 63-64, 67-; at work at Cultural Centre, Hammamet, Tunisia 66-67; productions include *Uranium 235, The Good Soldier Schweik, Lysistrata, Richard II, Volpone, The Quare Fellow, The Hostage, A Taste of Honey, Fings ain't Wot They Used T'be, Make Me an Offer, Sparrers Can't Sing* (film 63), *Oh What a Lovely War* 63, *A Kayf Up West* 64, *Macbird* 67, *Intrigues and Amours* 67, *Mrs. Wilson's Diary* 67, *The Marie Lloyd Story* 67, *Up Your End* 70, *The Projector* 70, *The Londoners* 72, *Costa Packet* 72, *Nuts* 73, *So You Want to Be in Pictures* 73, *Gentlemen Prefer Anything* 74; East Berlin Gold Medal (for *Lysistrata*) 58, Best Production Award, Théâtre des Nations (Paris) 59, Olympic Award Taormina 59, Challenge Trophy, Grand Prix Théâtre des Nations (Paris) 63.
c/o Theatre Royal, Stratford, London, E.15, England.

Littlewood, John Edensor, M.A., LL.D., D.SC., SC.D., F.R.S., F.R.A.S.; British mathematician; b. 9 June 1885; *s.* of Edward Thornton Littlewood and Silvia Maud Ackland; ed. St. Paul's School, and Trinity Coll., Cambridge.
Senior Wrangler 05; Richardson Lecturer Manchester Univ. 07-10; Lecturer Trinity Coll. 10-28 and Rouse Ball Prof. of Mathematics Cambridge Univ. 28-50; Fellow Trinity Coll. 08-; Fellow Cambridge Philosophical Society; Foreign mem. Royal Danish Acad., Royal Neths. Acad. and Royal Swedish Acad.; corresp. mem. Paris Acad., Gesellschaft der Wissenschaften zu Göttingen; Royal Medal Royal Society 29, De Morgan Medal, London Mathematical Society 39, Sylvester Medal Royal Society 43, Copley Medal, Royal Society 58. Leisure interests: music, walking.
Publs. *The Elements of the Theory of Real Functions, Lectures on the Theory of Functions, A Mathematician's Miscellany.*
Trinity College, Cambridge, England.

Littman, Mark, Q.C.; British barrister-at-law; b 4 Sept. 1920, London; *s.* of Jack and Lilian Littman; *m.* Marguerite Lamkin 1965; no *c.*; ed. Owen's School, London School of Economics and Queens Coll., Oxford.
Lieutenant R.N.V.R. 41-46; called to Bar, Middle Temple 47; practising barrister 47-67; Dir. Rio Tinto-Zinc Corpn. 68-; Pres. Bar Asscn. for Commerce, Finance and Industry; mem. Bar Council 73-75, mem. of Senate of the Inns of Court and the Bar 74-75; Deputy Chair. British Steel Corpn. Jan. 70-; Vice-Chair. Commercial Union Assurance Co. Ltd.; Dir. Rothschild Trust Co. Ltd. 70, British Enkalon Ltd., Amerada Hess Corpn., Envirotech Corpn.; Bencher of the Middle Temple 70.
79 Chester Square, London, S.W.1, England.
Telephone: 01-730-2973.

Litvak King, Jaime, M.A., PH.D.; Mexican archaeologist; b. 10 Dec. 1933, Mexico City; *s.* of Abraham Litvak and Eugenia King; *m.* 1st Elena Kaminski 1954 (divorced 1968), one *d.*; *m.* 2nd Carmen Aguilera 1972; ed. Univ. of Mexico.
Assistant Dept. of Prehistory, Inst. Nacional de Antropología e Historia 60-63, Researcher 63-66; Lecturer Escuela Nacional de Antropología e Historia 63-74; Head, Sección de Maquinas Electronicas, Museo Nacional de Antropología 66-68; Asst. Research Fellow, Anthropological Section, Univ. of Mexico 68-72, Full Research Fellow 72-74, Head of Section 73; Dir. Inst. for Anthropological Research, Univ. of Mexico 73-, Joint Chair. Archaeology, Escuela Nacional de Antropología 66-67, Chair. 69-71; Co-Editor *Antropología Matematica* 68-74; Research Editor *American Antiquity* 71-74; Advisory Editor *Mesoamerican Archaeology, Abstracts in Anthology* 73-74; Sec. Mexican Anthropological Soc. 71-; Fray Bernardino de Sahagun (Mexican Nat. Award for Anthropology) 70.
Publs. *Cihuatlán y Tepecoacuilco* 71, *El Valle de Xochicalco* 70, *Xochicalco: Un Asentamiento Urbano Prehispanico* 74, etc.
Instituto de Investigaciones Antropológicas, Universidad Nacional Autonoma de México, Torre de Humanidades, 1er piso Ciudad Universitaria, México 20, D.F., Mexico.
Telephone: 548-81-95, 548-65-60.

Liu Chieh; Chinese diplomatist; b. 16 April 1906; ed. Oxford and Columbia Univs.
Foreign Service 31-; Chinese Del. to League of Nations 32-39; Counsellor, Chinese Embassy, London 33-40, Minister, Washington 40-45; Vice-Minister for Foreign Affairs 45-47; Ambassador to Canada 47-63; mem. Chinese Del. to UN 46; Pres. UN Trusteeship Council 48; mem. Int. Law Comm. 61-66; Perm. Rep. of China to UN 62-71; Amb. to Philippines 72-.
Embassy of Taiwan, 2018-2038 Roxas Boulevard, Manila, Philippines.

Liu Chien-hsun; Chinese party official; b. 1907, Hopei. Second Sec. CCP Hupeh 52-54, Sec. 54-55; Political Commissar Hupeh Mil. District, People's Liberation Army 52; Deputy Dir. Rural Dept., CCP 56; First Sec. CCP Kwangsi 57-61; Alt. mem. 8th Cen. Cttee. of CCP 56; First Sec. CCP Honan 61-66; Political Commissar Honan Mil. District, PLA 64; Sec. Cen.-South Bureau, CCP 65-66; Sec. CCP Peking 66; Second Sec. N. China Bureau, CCP 66; Vice-Chair. Peking Revolutionary Cttee. 67; First Political Commissar Honan Mil. District, PLA 67; Deputy Political Commissar Wuhan Mil. Region, PLA 67, Political Commissar 71-; Chair. Honan Revolutionary Cttee. 68; mem. 9th Cen. Cttee. of CCP 69; First Sec. CCP Honan 71-; mem. 10th Cen. Cttee. of CCP 73.
People's Republic of China.

Liu Hai-ching; Chinese army officer.
Deputy Chief of Staff of Navy, People's Liberation Army.
People's Republic of China.

Liu Hsi-yao; Chinese party official.
Deputy Sec. CCP Hupeh 53-54; Vice-Chair. State Technological Comm. 57-59, State Scientific and Technological Comm. 59-67; Alt. mem. 9th Cen. Cttee. of CCP 69; Dir. Scientific and Educ. Group, State Council 72; Alt. mem. 10th Cen. Cttee. of CCP 73; Minister, Second Ministry of Machine Bldg. 75.
People's Republic of China.

Liu Hsiang-ping; Chinese government official.
Minister of Public Health 75.
People's Republic of China.

Liu Hsien-ch'uan; Chinese army officer; b. 1914, Chiating, Fukien.
Joined Red Army 30; Maj.-Gen. Shenyang Mil. Region, People's Liberation Army 60; Commdr. Tsinghai Mil. District, PLA 66-, Inner Mongolia Mil. District, PLA 67; Chair. Tsinghai Revolutionary Cttee. 67; Deputy Commdr. Lanchow Mil. Region, PLA 68; mem. 9th

Cen. Cttee. of CCP 69; First Sec. CCP Tsinghai 71-; mem. 10th Cen. Cttee. of CCP 73.
People's Republic of China.

Liu Hsing-yuan; Chinese party official; b. 1914, Hunan.
Deputy Political Commissar, Canton Mil. Region, People's Liberation Army 55; Second Political Commissar 63; Lieut.-Gen. 57; mem. Nat. Defence Council 65; Chair. Kwangtung Revolutionary Cttee. 69; mem. 9th Cen. Cttee. of CCP 69; First Sec. CCP Kwangtung 71; Chair. Szechuan Revolutionary Cttee. 72; First Sec. CCP Szechuan 72-; First Political Commissar Chengtu Mil. Region, PLA 73-; mem. 10th Cen. Cttee. of CCP 73.
People's Republic of China.

Liu Po-ch'eng; Chinese army officer; b. 1892, Kaihsien, Szechuan; ed. Chengtu Mil. School and Moscow Mil. Inst.
Joined CCP 26; Head Chief of Staff Nanchang Uprising 27; Chief of Gen. Staff, Red Army 32; on Long March 34-35; Pres. Red Army Univ., Kansu 36; Commdr. 129th Div., 8th Route Army 37-40; mem. 7th Cen. Cttee. of CCP 45; Commdr. 2nd Field Army 49-54; Second Sec. S.W. Bureau, CCP 50; Pres. Nanking Mil. Acad. 51-58; Vice-Chair. Nat. Defence Council 54-; Dir.-Gen. Training Dept., People's Liberation Army 54-57; Marshal PLA 55; mem. Politburo, 8th Cen. Cttee. of CCP 56; Vice-Chair. Nat. People's Congress 59-; mem. Politburo, 9th Cen. Cttee. of CCP 69, Politburo, 10th Cen. Cttee. 73.
People's Republic of China.

Liu Tao-sheng; Chinese army officer; b. 1916; ed. Red Army Coll.
Joined CCP 33; Political Commissar 22nd Div., Red Army 34; Vice-Adm. of Navy, People's Liberation Army 55, Deputy Commdr. PLA Navy 58-.
People's Republic of China.

Liu Tzu-hou; Chinese party official; b. circa 1910, Hopei.
Joined CCP 37; Deputy Gov. of Hupeh 52-54, Gov. 54-56; Second Sec. CCP Hupeh 53-56; Dir. Sanmen Gorge Construction Bureau 56-58; Gov. of Hopei 58-68; Sec. CCP Hopei 58-64; Alt. mem. 8th Cen. Cttee. of CCP 56; Sec. N. China Bureau, CCP 63-68; Second Sec. CCP Hopei Revolutionary Cttee. 64-68; First Vice-Chair. Hopei Revolutionary Cttee. 68, Chair. 70; mem. 9th Cen. Cttee. of CCP 69; First Sec. CCP Hopei 71; mem. 10th Cen. Cttee. of CCP 73.
People's Republic of China.

Liuzzi, Gen. Giorgio; Italian army officer; b. 30 Aug. 1895, Vercelli; s. of Gen. Guido Liuzzi and Elvira Pugliese; m. Gabriella Namias; two d.; ed. Turin Military Acad.
Entered army 13; Brigadier-General 43; in command of a brigade 48; Major-General 50; in command of a division 51; Lieut.-Gen. in command of army corps 53; Chief of Staff of Italian Army 54-59; columnist and and military critic, Corriere della Sera; two Bronze and one Silver military medals; Commdr. Order of the Italian Crown, Officer Order of Saints Maurice and Lazarus, Great Cross Italian Order of Merit, Commdr. Legion of Merit, Grand Officier Légion d'Honneur, Great Cross of the Order of Mil. Merit (Argentina and Spain), Gran Oficial do Ordem de Merito Militar do Brasil, Great Cross for Merit with Star and Sash of the Fed. Repub. of Germany Order of Merit, Order of Homayoun (1st Class) of Iran, Ulehi Distinguished Service Medal of South Korea, Golden Medal of the Red Cross.
Publs. include: L'Artiglieria Italiana 23-24, Compendio di Arte Militare 32, Il servizio Aereo di Artiglieria 32, Esplorazione con truppe celeri 32, L'aviazione da osservazione terrestre 33, L'aviazione per l'Esercito 33, Questioni d'impiego dell'Aviazione per l'Esercito 34,

L'osservazione aerostatica 34, Contributo dell'osservazione e della fotografia aerea alla preparazione topografica del tiro 34, Individuazione degli obiettivi e tiro con osservazione aerea 35, La brevità degli ordini d'operazioni 35, L'Esplorazione aerea strategica per l'Esercito 35, L'aviazione ed i servizi 36, La divisione celere nell'esplorazione in rapporto all'esplorazione aerea 37, Carri armati e unità corazzate 50, Panorama della guerra moderna 50, Il volo verticale, necessità dell'Escercito 51, L'Esercito di Vittorio Veneto e l'Esercito di oggi 58, L'addestramento fisico-sportivo nell'Esercito 58, Evoluzione degli ordinamenti e dei procedimenti delle forze terrestri in conseguenza delle nuove armi 59, Unificazione, integrazione delle forze e nuovo ordinamento dell'esercito 60, Caratteristiche ed esigenze di un esercito moderno 61, Italia difesa? 63, Alleanza atlantica e difesa nazionale 64, La funzione militare della NATO 67, La difesa civile 67, Difesa dell'Occidente 69.
Via Dell'Arcadia 43, Rome, Italy.
Telephone: 5120234.

Livanov, Mikhail Nikolayevich; Soviet physiologist; b. 1907; ed. Kazan Univ.
Assistant, Inst. of Horse Breeding 31-33; Head of Lab., Inst. of Brain Research, U.S.S.R. Ministry of Public Health 33-47; Head of Lab., Inst. of Intoxication, Pathology and Therapy, U.S.S.R. Acad. of Medical Sciences 47-49; Head of Lab., Inst. of Biophysics, U.S.S.R. Acad. of Sciences 49-61; Head of Lab., Inst. of Higher Nervous Activity and Neurophysiology, U.S.S.R. Acad. of Sciences 61-; corresp. mem. U.S.S.R. Acad. of Sciences 62-70, Academician 70-; mem. C.P.S.U. 40-.
U.S.S.R. Academy of Sciences, 14 Leninsky Prospekt, Moscow, U.S.S.R.

Livi, Livio, LL.D.; Italian statistician and sociologist; b. 2 Jan. 1891, Rome; s. of Ridolfo Livi and Luisa Bacci; m. Rita Olga Paladini 1924; four c.
Prof. of Statistics, Univ. of Modena 15-20, Univ. of Trieste 21-25; Prof. of Demography, Rome Univ. 26-28; Prof. of Statistics, Florence Univ. 29-48; Rome Univ. 48-, Dean Faculty of Econs. and Commerce 61-66; mem. Int. Statistical Inst.; Pres. Italian Statistical and Demographic Soc. 38-42; Pres. Inst. of Social Sciences 28-35, Vice-Pres. Int. Union for the Scientific Study of Population 49-54; mem. Higher Council of Statistics 26-56; nat. mem. Accad. Nazionale dei Lincei 61; Pres. Istituto Italiano di Antropologia 53-56; mem. Nat. Council of Economy and Labour; Pres. Soc. Ital. Antropologia e Etmologia; Dir. Centro per la Statistica Aziendale.
Leisure interest: fishing.
Publs. Gli Ebrei alla luce della statistica, 2 vols. 18, 20, Principi di Statistica 26, Il Darwinismo sociale e la Critica dei fatti 30, Lezioni di Statistica degli Affari 33, La Previsione delle Crisi e la Disciplina dell'Attività Produttiva 34, Lezioni di Demografia 35, I Fattori bio-demografici dell'ordinamento sociale 40, Le Leggi naturali della Popolazione 41, Storia Demografica di Rodi 44, La Rilevazione della Ricchezza e del Reddito Nazionale 52, Elementi di Statistica (15th edn.) 68, La vecchia e la nuova sociologia generale positiva 57, Previsioni economiche 59, Corso di Statistica Economica 59, Il Consumo del pesce nell'economia alimentare del 1 sec. d.C., 65, La durata normale della vita degli italiani 66, Sulla distribuzione della proprietà fondiaria sotto Traiano 68.
Via A. Baldesi 18, Florence, Italy.
Telephone: 51866.

Ljubičić, Gen. Nikola; Yugoslav soldier and politician; b. 1916, Karan nr. Titovo Uzice; ed. Valjevo Grammar School, Yugoslav Higher Military Coll., Operational Command School.
Ministry of Agriculture; joined Communist Party 41; fought with Nat. Liberation Army in Yugoslavia 41-45; Brig. and Second in Command Nat. Defence Corps 43;

then Commdr. Frontier Forces and 1st Army District; Sec. of State for Defence 67-; mem. Fed. Exec. Council, Presidium of League of Communists of Yugoslavia; decorations include Orders of the Nat. Hero and Partisan Star with Golden Wreath.
Kneza Miloša 33, Belgrade, Yugoslavia.

Lleras Camargo, Alberto; Colombian journalist, politician and writer; b. 3 July 1906.
Editorial staff of *El Espectador* and *El Tiempo*, Bogotá 25-30; Sec.-Gen. of Liberal Party and Editor of *La Tarde* 30; Chair. of House of Reps. 32; Sec. of Colombian Del. to Pan-American Conf. Montevideo 34; Sec.-Gen. of exec. branch of Colombian Govt. 34-35; Minister of Govt. 35; Del. to Inter-American Conf. for Maintenance of Peace Buenos Aires 36; Minister of Education 36; Minister of Govt. 36-38; Editor of *El Liberal* 38-43; elected Senator 43; Ambassador to U.S.A. and Minister of Govt. 43; Minister of Foreign Affairs 45; head of Colombian Del. to Conf. of Chapultepec Mexico and U.N. Conf., San Francisco 45; Pres. of Colombia Aug. 45-Aug. 46; Editor of *Semana* 46-47; Sec.-Gen. of Organisation of American States June 47-54; Pres. Univ. of the Andes 54-55; Pres. of Colombia 58-62; produced study of Alliance for Progress 63; Hon. Ph.D. Universidad de los Andes 57, Hon. Degree Johns Hopkins Univ. 60; Hon. LL.D. (Harvard).
Bogotá, Colombia.

Lleras Restrepo, Carlos; Colombian lawyer and politician; b. 12 April 1908, Bogotá; s. of Federico Lleras Acosta; m. Cecilia de la Fuente 1933; two s. two d.; ed. Univ. Nacional de Colombia.
Lawyer 30-; Deputy 31; Minister of Treasury 38-43; Prof. of Public Finance, Law Faculty, Univ. Nacional 39; Pres. of Nat. Liberal Party 41, 48-50, mem. Triumvirate 50, Leader 61-; Senator 42-52, 58-59, 62-; Pres. Colombian Del. to Bretton Woods Conf. 44; mem. various Colombian Dels. to UN Comms.; Vice-Pres. Econ. and Social Council, UN 46; in Europe 59-60; Pres. Colombian Del. to Geneva Conf. 64; Pres. of Colombia 66-70.
Calle 70-A, 7-37, Bogotá, Colombia.

Lleshi, Maj.-Gen. Haxhi; Albanian politician; b. 1913.
Fought with resistance against Italian and German occupations 39-45; mem. provisional Govt. 44; Minister of the Interior 44-46; Maj.-Gen. Albanian Army; Pres. Presidium of the People's Assembly (Head of State) 53-; mem. Cen. Cttee. Albanian Workers' Party 53-.
The People's Assembly, Tirana, Albania.

Llewellyn, Sir Frederick John, K.C.M.G., PH.D., D.SC., LL.D., F.R.I.C., F.N.Z.I.C., F.R.S.A. F.R.S.N.Z.; British administrator; b. 29 April 1915, Dursley, Glos.; s. of late Mr. and Mrs. R. G. Llewellyn; m. Joyce Barrett 1939; one s. one d.; ed. Dursley Grammar School, Univ. of Birmingham.
Scientific Officer, Fuel Research Station, Greenwich 38-39; Lecturer in Chemistry, Birkbeck Coll. 39-45; Dir. Ministry of Supply Research Team 41-46; I.C.I. Research Fellow, Birmingham Univ. 46-47; Prof. of Chemistry, Auckland Univ. Coll. (N.Z.) 47-55; Vice-Chancellor and Rector, Univ. of Canterbury (N.Z.) 56-61; Chair. Univ. Grants Cttee. (N.Z.) 61-66; Chair. New Zealand Broadcasting Corpn. 62-65; Chair. Nat. Council of Adult Educ. 61-66, N.Z. Commonwealth Scholarships and Fellowships Cttee. 61-66; mem. N.Z. Council for Technical Educ. 61-66, Council of Scientific and Industrial Research, N.Z. 57-61, Council of Asscn. of Commonwealth Univs. 66-; Vice-Chancellor, Exeter Univ. 66-72; Dir.-Gen. British Council Oct. 72-; mem. Inter Univ. Council for Higher Educ. Overseas 66-75, BBC S.W. Regional Advisory Cttee. 67-70, Council Ahmadu Bello Univ., Nigeria 68-72.

Leisure interests: photography, music, travel.
The British Council, 10 Spring Gardens, London, SW1A 2BN, England.
Telephone: 01-930-8466.

Llewellyn, John; American astronaut; b. 22 April 1933, Cardiff, U.K.; s. of John and Morella (Roberts) Llewellyn; m. Valerie Davies-Jones; one s. two d.; ed. Univ. Coll., Cardiff, Wales.
Research Fellow, Nat. Research Council of Canada 58-60; Assoc. Prof. School of Eng. Science, Florida State Univ. 64-72; selected by NASA as scientist-astronaut Aug. 67; Dean, School of Eng. Science, Florida State Univ. 70-72; Prof. Dept. of Energy Conversion, Coll. of Eng., Univ. of South Fla., Tampa 73-; Co-ordinator, Scientist in the Sea Project 73; Scientific consultant on marine environment and energy.
Leisure interests: sailing, underwater exploration.
3010 St. Charles Drive, Tampa, Fla. 33618, U.S.A.

Llewelyn-Davies, Baron (Life Peer), cr. 63, of Hastoe in the County of Hertford; **Richard Llewelyn-Davies,** M.A., F.R.I.B.A., M.T.P.I.; British architect; b. 24 Dec. 1912; ed. Trinity Coll., Cambridge, and Ecole des Beaux Arts, Paris.
Director of Div. for Architectural Studies, Nuffield Foundation 53-60; Prof. of Architecture, Univ. of London, and Head of Bartlett School of Architecture, Univ. Coll. 60-69; Emer. Prof. of Urban Planning, Univ. Coll., London; Head of School of Environmental Studies 71-75; Chair. Centre for Environmental Studies 67-; also senior partner Llewelyn-Davies Weeks Forestier-Walker and Bor; Hon. LL.D. (Cambridge); R.I.B.A. Bronze Medal.
Principal architectural works include: new buildings for *The Times*, London, The Stock Exchange, London, new village at Rushbrooke, Suffolk, new hospitals in U.K. and overseas; Planning work includes studies and master plans for new cities in England, at Swindon, Milton Keynes and Washington, and urban renewal redevelopment projects in U.S.A.
Publs. *Design of Research Laboratories* 57, *Children in Hospital* 58, *Psychiatric Services and Architecture, Hospital Planning and Administration* (with H. M. C. Macaulay) 66.
36 Parkhill Road, London, N.W.3, England; also 410 East 62 Street, New York, N.Y. 10021, U.S.A.
Telephone: 01-485-6576 (London).

Llorente M., Rodrigo, D.ECON.; Colombian politician, b. 25 Nov. 1928, Cali; s. of Hernando and Isabel Martinez de Llorente; m. Leonor Sardi de Llorente 1956; one s. three d.
Under-Secretary for Econ. Affairs, Ministry of Foreign Affairs 52-53; Sec.-Gen. Banco Cafetero 54-56; Man. Asecolda 56-58; Legal Consultant, Andi 58-59; Minister of Devt. 59-60; Legal Adviser, Inter-American Devt. Bank (IDB), Washington, D.C. 61-65; Rep. of IDB in Europe 66-69; Gen. Man. Banco Cafetero 69-71; Minister of Finance 71-73; Prof. of Econs., Univ. Nacional de Colombia, Colegio del Rosario and Univ. Javeriana; Pres. Interamerican Council of Trade and Production CICYP.
Interamerican Council of Trade and Production, Bogotá; Home: Carrera 8A, No. 13-82, Of. 702, Bogotá, Colombia.
Telephone: 82-22-68; 83-15-19; 83-15-39.

Lloyd, David P(ierce) C(aradoc), D.PHIL., D.SC.; American physiologist; b. 22 Sept. 1911, Auburn, Ala.; s. of Francis Ernest Lloyd, P.R.S.C. and Mary Elizabeth (Hart) Lloyd; m. 1st Kathleen M. Elliott 1937, 2nd Cynthia M. Meynell 1957; two s. one d.; ed. McGill and Oxford Univs.
Department Demonstrator, Oxford Univ. 35-36; Research Asst. and Assoc.. Rockefeller Inst. of Medical Research 39-43; Asst. Prof. Yale Univ. 43-45; Assoc. mem., Rockefeller Inst. (now Rockefeller Univ.) 46-49,

mem. of Inst., later designated Prof. at Rockefeller Univ. 49-71; Hon. Research Fellow, Univ. Coll., London 70-; mem. Nat. Acad. of Sciences 53-, mem. Emeritus 72-.

Leisure interests: music, poetry, ribaldry, literature, history.

Publs. Sections in Saunders' *Textbook of Physiology* 46, 49, 55, *James Arthur Lecture to American Museum of Natural Hist.* 59, and scientific papers in *Journal of Neurophysiology, Journal of General Physiology, Proceedings* of Nat. Acad. of Sciences, *Annotations to 'Reflex Activity of the Spinal Cord' by Creed, Denny-Brown, Eccles, Liddell and Sherrington* 72, etc.

New Cottage, Greatham, Pulborough, Sussex, RH20 2ES, England.

Telephone: Pulborough 2688.

Lloyd, Seton, C.B.E., M.A., F.B.A., F.S.A., A.R.I.B.A.; British archaeologist; b. 30 May 1902, Birmingham; s. of John Eliot Howard Lloyd; m. Ulrica Fitzwilliams-Hyde 1944; one s. one d.; ed. Uppingham and Architectural Asscn.

Assistant to Sir Edwin Lutyens, P.R.A. 27-28; excavated for Egypt Exploration Soc., Egypt 29-30, for Oriental Inst., Univ. of Chicago in Iraq 30-37, for Univ. of Liverpool in Turkey 37-39; Technical Adviser, Govt. of Iraq, Directorate-Gen. of Antiquities 39-49; Dir. British Inst. Archaeology in Ankara 49-61, Hon. Sec. 64-74, Pres. 74-; Prof. of Western Asiatic Archaeology, London Univ. 62-69, Emer. Prof. 69-.

Leisure interests: history and geography of the Near East.

Publs. *Mesopotamia* 34, *Sennacherib's Aqueduct at Jerwan* 35, *The Gimilsin Temple* 40, *Presargonid Temples* 42, *Ruined Cities of Iraq* 42, *Twin Rivers* 43, *Foundations in the Dust* 48, *Early Anatolia* 56, *Art of the Ancient Near East* 61, *Beycesultan* 62, *Mounds of the Near East* 63, *Early Highland Peoples of Anatolia* 67.

Woolstone Lodge, Faringdon, Oxon., England.

Telephone: Uffington 248.

Lloyd-Jones, Peter Hugh Jefferd, M.A., F.B.A.; British classical scholar; b. 21 Sept. 1922, St. Peter Port, Guernsey; s. of Brevet-Major W. Lloyd-Jones, D.S.O., and Norah Leila Jefferd; m. Frances Elisabeth Hedley 1953; two s. one d.; ed. Lycée Français du Royaume-Uni (London), Westminster School, and Christ Church, Oxford.

Fellow, Jesus Coll., Cambridge 48-54; Fellow and E.P. Warren Praelector in Classics, Corpus Christi Coll., Oxford 54-60; Regius Prof. of Greek and Student of Christ Church 60-; Chancellor's Prize for Latin Prose, Ireland and Craven Scholarships 47; J. H. Gray Lecturer, Cambridge 61; Visiting Prof. Yale Univ. 64-65, 67-68; Sather Prof. of Classical Literature, Univ. of Calif. at Berkeley 69-70; Alexander White Visiting Prof. Univ. of Chicago 72-; Fellow, Samuel F. B. Morse Coll., Yale Univ.; Hon. D.Hum.Litt. (Chicago) 70.

Publs. Appendix to *Aeschylus* (Loeb Classical Library) 57, *Menandri Dyscolus* (Oxford Classical Texts) 60; *Greek Studies in Modern Oxford* 61, *The Justice of Zeus* 71, (ed.) *Maurice Bowra: a Celebration* 74, *Females of the Species* 75; translated *Greek Metre* 62, Aeschylus *Agamemnon, The Liberation-Bearers* and *The Eumenides* 70; edited *The Greeks* 62, *Tacitus* 64; articles and reviews in classical periodicals.

Christ Church, Oxford; Gateways, Harberton Mead, Oxford, England.

Telephone: Oxford 48737 and 62393.

Lo Su Yin (Peter Lo), LL.B.; Malaysian lawyer and politician; b. 19 May 1923; m.; four c.; ed. St. Mary's School, Sandakan, St. Anthony's Boys School, Singapore and Victoria Univ., Wellington.

Called to New Zealand Bar 56, law practice 57-64; mem., Deputy Chair., Sandakan Town Board 59-64; mem. Public Service Comm. 61, 62; mem. Legislative Council,

North Borneo 62-63, Inter-Govt. Cttee. Sabah/Malaysia 62-63; mem. Parl. 63-; Fed. Minister without Portfolio 64; Chief Minister Sabah 65-67; Chair. Sabah Chinese Asscn. of the State Alliance Party 65-; Malaysian Medal.

P.O. Box 1475, Kota Kinabalu, Sabah, Malaysia.

Loane, Most Rev. Marcus Lawrence, M.A., D.D.; Australian ecclesiastic; b. 14 Oct. 1911, Waratah, Tasmania; s. of the late K. O. A. Loane; m. Patricia Knox 1937; two s. two d.; ed. The King's School, Parramatta, Univ. of Sydney, and Moore Theological Coll., Sydney.

Resident Tutor and Chaplain, Moore Theological Coll., Sydney 35-38, Vice-Principal 39-53, Principal 54-58; Canon, St. Andrew's Cathedral 49-58; Bishop Co-adjutor, Diocese of Sydney 58-66; Archbishop of Sydney and Metropolitan of New South Wales 66-.

Leisure interest: walking.

Publs. *Oxford and the Evangelical Succession* 51, *Cambridge and the Evangelical Succession* 52, *Masters of the English Reformation* 55, *History of Moore Theological College* 55, *Life of Archbishop Mowll* 59, *Pioneers of the Reformation in England* 63, *Sons of the Covenant* 63, *The History of the China Inland Mission in Australia and New Zealand* 65, *Makers of Our Heritage* 67, *Do You Now Believe* 67, *The Hope of Glory* 68, *This Surpassing Excellence* 69, *They Were Pilgrims* 70, *By Faith We Stand* 71, *They Overcame* 71, *Amazing Grace* 72, *The King is Here* 73.

Diocesan Church House, P.O. Box Q 190, Queen Victoria Buildings, Sydney, New South Wales, Australia.

Telephone: 26-2371.

Lobanok, Vladimir Yeliseyevich; Soviet politician; b. 1907; ed. Byelorussian Agricultural Acad. and Higher Party School, Moscow.

Member C.P.S.U. 30-; Agronomist 32-41; Soviet army service 41-44; Chair. Exec. Cttee., Polotsk Regional Council of Workers' Deputies 44-46; Deputy to U.S.S.R. Supreme Soviet 46-; Second Sec. Polessye Regional Cttee. C.P. Byelorussia 46-48, First Sec. 48-53; Chair. Gomel Regional Council of Workers' Deputies 54-56; First Sec. Vitebsk Regional Cttee. C.P. Byelorussia 56-62; First Deputy Chair. Council of Ministers of Byelorussian S.S.R. 62-; mem. C.P.S.U. Central Auditing Comm. 61-; mem. Central Cttee. of C.P. Byelorussia; Deputy to Byelorussian S.S.R. Supreme Soviet; Vice-Chair. Soviet of Nationalities, Supreme Soviet of U.S.S.R.; Hero of the Soviet Union 43, Order of Lenin, Gold Star Medal, other decorations.

Byelorussian S.S.R. Council of Ministers, Minsk, U.S.S.R.

Lobanov, Pavel Pavlovich; Soviet agriculturalist and politician; b. 1902; ed. Timiryazev Agricultural Acad., Moscow.

Director Voronezh Agricultural Inst. 37; R.S.F.S.R. People's Commissar of Agriculture 38; U.S.S.R. People's Commissar of State Farms 38-46; First Deputy U.S.S.R. People's Commissar of Agriculture 46-53; mem. U.S.S.R. Supreme Soviet 54-; Deputy Chair. U.S.S.R. Council of Ministers 55-56; Deputy Chair. State Planning Comm. 61; Chair. Union Chamber U.S.S.R. Supreme Soviet 56-62; candidate mem. Cen. Cttee. of Communist Party of Soviet Union 56-; Pres. All Union Acad. of Agricultural Sciences 56-61, 65-; mem. Comm. for Agriculture, Soviet of the Union; mem. U.S.S.R. Council for Problems of Collective Farms, Experts' Comm. U.S.S.R. State Planning Cttee., Council U.S.S.R. Ministry of Agriculture; Hero of Socialist Labour, Order of Lenin (twice), Hammer and Sickle Gold Star, other decorations.

All Union Academy of Agricultural Sciences, Bolshoi Kharitonevsky per. 21, Moscow, U.S.S.R.

Lobov, Admiral Semyon Mikhailovich; Soviet naval officer; b. 15 Feb. 1913, Smolnikovo, Moscow Region; ed. Frunze Higher Naval School in Leningrad.
Railway and factory worker 29-33; Naval Service 33-; Captain of various ships 37-; Chief of Staff, Commdr. Naval Foundation, First Deputy Commdr. Northern Fleet 55-65; Commdr. Northern Fleet 64-; Admiral of Fleet 70; mem. C.P.S.U. 40-; Alt. mem. Cen. Cttee. of C.P.S.U.; Deputy to U.S.S.R. Supreme Soviet.
Ministry of Defence, 34 Naberezhnaya M. Thoreza, Moscow, U.S.S.R.

Loc, Nguyen Van; (*see* Nguyen Van Loc).

Lochen, Einar; Norwegian lawyer and diplomatist; b. 1918; ed. Oslo Univ., London School of Economics, Chicago Univ., Calif. Univ.
Assistant judge 45-46; Lawyer 46-49; Asst. Adviser to Norwegian Ministry of Foreign Affairs 49-51; Fellow of Chr. Michelsens Institutt, Bergen 51-55; Counsellor to Norwegian Ministry of Foreign Affairs 55-58; Perm. Rep. to Council of Europe 58-63; Sec. Norwegian Del. to Nordic Council 58-72; Judge, Norwegian Court of Appeal 74.
Publs. *Norway's Views on Sovereignty* 55, *A Comparative Study of Certain European Parliamentary Assemblies* 58, *Norway in European Atlantic Co-operation* 64.
Møllebokken 1, Grini, Oslo 1, Norway.

Lochner, Louis P., B.A., LITT.D.; American journalist; b. 22 Feb. 1887, Springfield, Ill.; s. of Rev. Friedrich and Maria Lochner (née von Haugwitz); *m.* 1st Emmy Hoyer 1910 (died 1920), 2nd Hilde de Terra (née Steinberger) 1922; one s. two d. (one deceased 1969); ed. Wisconsin Univ. and Wisconsin Conservatory of Music.
Editor *The Cosmopolitan Student* 08-14, *Wisconsin Alumni Magazine* 09-14, *International Labour News Service* 18-19; free-lance journalist in Europe 21-24; mem. Berlin staff Associated Press of America 24-42; Chief of Bureau 28-42; U.S. War Corresp. in Europe 44-46; Pres. Foreign Press Assen. of Berlin 28-31 and 34-37; Pres. American Chamber of Commerce in Germany 35-42; mem. Hoover Comm. to Germany and Austria 47; Pres. Overseas Press Club of America 50 and 55; Chair. Overseas Rotary Fellowship 56-; mem. P.E.N. Club; winner Pulitzer Prize (foreign corresp.) 39; American mem. U.N. Expert Cttee. on Public Information 58; Dir. American Council on Germany 59-; Commentator, Broadcast Editorial Reports 60-63; mem. Editorial Board, *The Lutheran Witness* 51-; Chair. Eyes Right, Inc. (Eye Restoration Service) 50-67; Trustee Corresps' Fund Inc. 64-; Trustee, Overseas Press Club Foundation 66-; Life mem. Sigma Delta Chi journalistic fraternity; Commdr. Cross of the German Order of Merit 67.
Leisure interests: music, travel.
Publs. *America's Don Quixote* 23, *Das amerikanische Nachrichtenwesen* 31, *What About Germany?* 42, *The Goebbels Diaries* 48, *Fritz Kreisler* 50, *Tycoons and Tyrants* 54, *Always the Unexpected* 56, *Herbert Hoover and Germany* 60, *New York* 60 and contributions to many American magazines.
6200 Wiesbaden, Aukamm-Allee 25, Federal Republic of Germany.

Locke, Edwin Allen, Jr., A.B.; American industrialist, banker and diplomatist; b. 8 June 1910, Boston, Mass.; s. of Edwin A. and Elizabeth Ferguson Locke; *m.* 1st Dorothy Q. Clark 1934 (divorced), 2nd Karin Marsh 1952; three s. one d.; ed. Harvard Univ.
With Paris Branch, Chase Nat. Bank, N.Y. 33-35, London Branch 35-36, New York 36-40; served in Office of Co-ordinator of Purchases, Advisory Comm. to Council of Nat. Defense 40-41; Asst. Deputy Dir. Priorities Div., Office of Production Management 41; Deputy Chief Staff Officer Supply Priorities and Allocation Board 41-42; Asst. to Chair. War Production

Board 42-44; Exec. Asst. to Personal Rep. of the Pres. 44-45; Personal Rep. of the Pres., Washington and China 45-46, Special Asst. to the Pres. March-Dec. 46; Vice-Pres. of the Chase Nat. Bank, New York 47-51; apptd. Special Rep. of Sec. of State, with personal rank of Ambassador to co-ordinate economic and technical assistance programmes in the Near East Nov. 51-53; Pres. and Dir. Union Tank Car Co. 53-63; Dir. Harris Trust and Savings Bank 55-63; Dir. Federal Home Loan Bank of Chicago 56-63, Chair. 61-63; mem. special Presidential mission to Liberia and Tunisia; Pres. and Dir. Modern Homes Construction Co. 63-67, Coastal Products Corpn. 63-67; Dir. Manpower Inc. 61-, Warner Nat. Corpn. 69-; Pres. American Paper Inst. 68-.
260 Madison Avenue, New York, N.Y. 10016, U.S.A.
Telephone: 212-883-8076.

Lockspeiser, Sir Ben, K.C.B., M.A., D.SC., F.I.MECH.E., C.ENG., F.R.S.A., F.R.AE.S., F.R.S.; British scientist; b. 9 March 1891, London; s. of Leon and Rose Lockspeiser; *m.* 1st Elsie Shuttleworth 1920 (died 1964), 2nd Mrs. M. A. Heywood 1966; one s. two d.; ed. Sidney Sussex Coll., Cambridge.
Assistant Dir. Scientific Research, Ministry of Aircraft Production 39, Deputy Dir. 41, Dir. 43-; Dir.-Gen. Scientific Research (Air) Ministry of Supply 46; chief scientist to Ministry of Supply Dec. 46-49; Sec. Dept. of Scientific and Industrial Research 49-56; Pres. European Org. for Nuclear Research 55-57.
Leisure interests: gardening and music.
Birchway, 15 Waverley Road, Farnborough, Hants., England.
Telephone: Farnborough 43021.

Lockwood, Sir Joseph Flawith, Kt.; British businessman; b. 14 Nov. 1904, Southwell, Notts.; s. of Joseph Agnew and Mabel Lockwood.
Manager of flour mills in Chile 24-28; Techn. Man. Henry Simon Ltd. in Paris and Brussels 28-33; Dir. Henry Simon Ltd., Manchester 33; Dir. Henry Simon, Buenos Aires and Chair. Henry Simon (Australia) Ltd., etc. 45; Chair. EMI (fmrly. Electrical and Musical Industries) Ltd. 55-74; Dir. Smiths Industries Ltd., The Hawker-Siddeley Group Ltd., Laird Group Ltd.; Chair. Board of Govs., Royal Ballet School; Vice-Pres. Cen. School of Speech and Drama; Dir. South Bank Theatre Board 68-; Chair. Industrial Reorganization Corpn. 69-71.
Leisure interests: walking, reading.
Publs. *Provender Milling: the Manufacture of Feeding Stuffs for Livestock* 39, *Flour Milling* (in English, French, Spanish, German and Serbo-Croat) 45.
Flat 18, 33 Grosvenor Square, London, W.1, England.

Lodge, George Cabot (son of Henry Cabot Lodge, Jr., *q.v.*); American politician; b. 7 July 1927; ed. Harvard Coll.
United States Naval Reserve, Second World War; on staff of *Boston Herald* 50-54; Dir. of Information, U.S. Dept. of Labor 54-58; Asst. Sec. of Labor for Int. Affairs 58-61; Pres. Governing Body, Int. Labour Org. (ILO) 60-61; Lecturer, Harvard Business School 63-68; Dir. div. int. activities 65-66; Assoc. Prof. 68-; cand. for U.S. Senate 62; Republican.
Publs. *Spearheads of Democracy* 62, *Engines of Change* 70.
275 Hale Street, Beverly, Mass., U.S.A.

Lodge, Henry Cabot, A.B. (brother of John Davis Lodge, *q.v.*); American politician; b. 5 July 1902, Nahant, Mass.; s. of George C. Lodge and Matilda E. F. Davis; *m.* Emily Sears 1926; two s. (George Cabot Lodge, *q.v.*); ed. Harvard Coll.
With *Boston Evening Transcript* 24-25; mem. editorial staff *New York Herald Tribune* 25-31; elected Representative to Gen. Court of Mass. 32, 34; U.S. Senator from Massachusetts 36; Major U.S. Army, served with 1st American tank detachment, Libya 42; re-elected to Senate Nov. 42, resigned from Senate in order to go

on active service with Army Feb. 44; served Mediterranean and Europe until 45; Senator from Mass. 46-53; campaign manager for Republican nomination for Gen. Eisenhower 51, 52; Chair. Resolutions Cttee. Republican Nat. Convention 48; U.S. Rep. to UN; Rep. on Security Council 53-60; Republican candidate for Vice-Pres. 60; Trustee, Int. Inst. of Educ. 61; Dir.-Gen. Atlantic Inst., Paris 61-63; Amb. to Repub. of Viet-Nam 63-64, 65-67; **Amb. to German Fed. Repub. 68-69; Chief Negotiator at Viet-Nam talks in Paris 69;** Special Envoy of U.S. to the Vatican 70-; Hon. LL.D., D.C.L., D. ès L.; Legion of Merit Medal, Légion d'Honneur and Croix de Guerre avec palme, Thayer Medal, West Point, Bronze Star, six battle stars; commended by U.S. Senate for service in Viet-Nam.

Leisure interests: boating, gardening, walking in woods.
Publ. *The Storm Has Many Eyes* 73.
275 Hale Street, Beverly, Massachusetts 01915, U.S.A.
Telephone: 617-922-0404.

Lodge, John Davis, B.A., LL.B., J.D. (brother of Henry Cabot Lodge, *q.v.*); American lawyer, lecturer and diplomatist; b. Washington, D.C.; s. of George Cabot Lodge and Matilda Elizabeth Frelinghuysen Davis Lodge; *m.* Francesca Braggiotti 1929; two *d.*; ed. Middlesex School, Concord, Mass., Harvard Coll., Harvard Law School and Ecole de Droit, Paris.
Naval Officer U.S. Navy, Mediterranean Theatre 42-46; Congressman from 4th District of Connecticut 46-50; mem. Cttee. on Foreign Affairs; Gov. of Connecticut 51-55; Amb. to Spain 55-61; Chair. Cttee. Foreign Policy Research Inst., Univ. of Pennsylvania, New England Cttee. on Peaceful Uses of Atomic Energy; Pres. Junior Achievement Inc. 63-64; Amb. to Argentina 69-74; Chevalier de la Légion d'Honneur, Croix de Guerre avec palme; Grand Cross of Noble Order of Charles III (Spain), Gold Medal of Madrid; Grand Officer, Order of Merit of the Repub. of Italy; Order Polonia Restituta (Poland); numerous other foreign decorations; hon. degrees many U.S. colls. and univs.; Republican.
Leisure interests: tennis, riding, swimming, reading and writing.
Publs. articles on politics, foreign policy and Spain.
129 Easton Road, Westport, Connecticut 06880, U.S.A.
Telephone: 203-227-6192.

Loewe, Frederick; American (Austrian-born) composer; b. 10 June 1901.
Studied piano with Ferruccio Busoni and Eugène d'Albert, composition and orchestration with Nicholas Reznicek; went to U.S.A. 24; composer musical comedies: *Salute to Spring, Great Lady, Life of the Party, Day before Spring, Brigadoon, Paint Your Wagon, Camelot, The Little Prince*; collaborator (with Alan Jay Lerner, *q.v.*) music for *My Fair Lady*; composer score for film *Gigi* 59.
c/o ASCAP, 575 Madison Avenue, New York 22; Palm Springs, Calif., U.S.A.

Loewy, Raymond; American (French-born) industrial designer; b. 5 Nov. 1893, Paris; s. of Maximillian Loewy and Marie La Balme; *m.* Viola Erickson 1948; one *d.*; ed. Univ. of Paris.
Captain, Corps of Engineers 5th Army, France 14-18; Art Dir. Westinghouse Electric 29; started private org. of industrial design 29; liaison officer A.E.F., First World War; Head, Raymond Loewy Assocs. 30-61; Founder, Compagnie de l'Esthétique Industrielle, Paris 52; Chair. Raymond Loewy Int. Inc. 75-; mem. President's Cttee. on Employment of the Handicapped 65-; consultant to NASA 67-; lecturer at M.I.T., Harvard, Columbia, New York, Leningrad, Moscow Inst. of Ergonometry and Univ. of Calif.; Hon. Royal Designer to Industry; Fellow, British Royal Soc. of Arts; Past Pres. and Fellow, American Soc. of Industrial Design; Fellow, American Soc. of Interior Designers;

D.F.A. (Univ. of Cincinatti, California Art Center Coll., U.S. Acad. of Achievement); mem. French C. of C. of U.S., Board of Dirs. French Inst. of America, Soc. Automotive Engineers, Amer. Soc. Mechanical Engineers, Soc. Naval Architects and Marine Engineers, Amer. Soc. Space Medicine; Commdr. Légion d'Honneur, Croix de Guerre; hon. citizen of France by decree of the Prime Minister 60; Citizen of Honour, New York 66, Palm Springs 67.
Leisure interests: sand dune racing, yachting, painting.
Publs. *The Locomotive, Its Aesthetics* 37, *Never Leave Well Enough Alone* (transl. into six languages) 51.
110 East 59th Street, New York, N.Y. 10022; Tierra Caliente, Palm Springs, Calif., U.S.A.; Manoir de la Cense, Rochefort-en-Yvelines; also 39 avenue d'Iéna, Paris, France; U.K. Office: 25 Bruton Street, Berkeley Square, London, W.1, England.
Telephone: New York 935-3600; Paris 723-4355; London 493-0884; La Cense 484-3117; Palm Springs 714-325-0995.

Loga-Sowiński, Ignacy; Polish politician and trade union official; b. 20 Jan. 1914, Vankewitz, Germany; s. of Władysław and Howorta Loga; *m.* Wanda Długosz 1957; one *s.* one *d.*.
Active in revolutionary work from early age; imprisoned several times for his work in Łódź branch of Communist Youth Union; released from prison 39; took part in defence of Warsaw; helped organize underground group during the occupation; mem. Polish Workers' Party 42-48, Sec. Cen. Cttee. 43-44; mem. Supreme Command of People's Guard 43-44, First Govt. Plenipotentiary, First Sec. Łódź Voivodship Cttee., PWP 45-48; dismissed from the Cen. Cttee. on charge of right-wing nationalist deviation 48; mem. Polish United Workers' Party 48-, Politburo Cen. Cttee. 56-Feb. 71; Chair. Voivodship Council of Trade Unions, Wroclaw 49-53; Sec. Cen. Council of Trade Unions 54-56, Chair. 56-Jan. 71; Vice-Chair. World Federation of Trade Unions 61-69; Deputy to Seym (Parl.) 57-72; Deputy Chair. State Council 56-71; Amb. to Turkey 71-; Order of Banner of Labour 1st Class 59, Order of Builders of People's Poland 64, and other decorations.
Polish Embassy, Ankara-Çankaya Pk. 20, Atatürk Bulvari 251, Turkey.
Telephone: Ankara 184449.

Logan, Sir Douglas (William), Kt., M.A., D.PHIL., D.C.L., LL.D., D.LITT.; British barrister-at-law and university administrator; b. 27 March 1910, Liverpool; s. of Robert Logan and Euphemia Taylor Stevenson; *m.* 1st Vaire Olive Wollaston 1940, 2nd Christine Peggy Walker 1947; three *s.* one *d.*; ed. Liverpool Collegiate School, Univ. Coll., Oxford, and Harvard Law School.
Assistant Lecturer, London School of Economics 36-37; called to the Bar 37; Fellow of Trinity Coll., Cambridge 37-43; served Ministry of Supply 40-44; Clerk of Court, Univ. of London 44-47; Principal of Univ. of London 48-75; Pres. British Univs. Sports Fed. 62-75; Trustee of City Parochial Foundation 53-67; Vice-Chair. Athlone Fellowship Cttee. 59-72; mem. Commonwealth Scholarships Comm. 60-, Deputy Chair. 68-; mem. Marshall Scholarship Comm. 61-67; Vice-Chair. Asscn. of Univs. of the British Commonwealth 61-67, Chair. 62, Hon. Treas. 67-74, Deputy Hon. Treas. 74-; Deputy Chair. Nat. Theatre; mem. Nat. Theatre Board 62-68; Gov. Bristol Old Vic; Rede Lecturer 63; Hon. Bencher, Middle Temple; mem. Pharmaceutical Soc.; Hon. F.R.I.B.A.; Hon. Fellow, London School of Econs., Univ. Coll., Oxford, Univ. Coll., London, School of Pharmacy, Univ. of London; Fellow, Wye Coll., Imperial Coll. of Science and Technology; Hon. F.D.S., R.C.S. Eng.; Chevalier, Légion d'Honneur 57.
Restalrig, Mountain Street, Chilham, Kent, CT4 8DQ, England.
Telephone: 022-776-640.

Logan, Joshua; American film and stage director and author; b. 5 Oct. 1908, Texarkana, Texas; s. of Joshua Lockwood Logan and Sue Nabors Logan; m. Nedda Harrigan 1945; one s. one d.; ed. Princeton Univ.
Captain in the Air Force 42-45; theatre dir. 38-, film dir., scriptwriter and producer 36-; Pulitzer Prize for *South Pacific* 50.
Broadway productions include: *On Borrowed Time* 38, *I Married an Angel* 38, *Knickerbocker Holiday* 38, *Stars in Your Eyes* 38, *Mornings at Seven* 39, *Two for the Show* 39, *Higher and Higher* (co-author) 39, *Charlie's Aunt* 40, *By Jupiter* 42, *This is the Army* 42, *Annie Get Your Gun* 45, *Happy Birthday* 45, *John Loves Mary* 46, *Mister Roberts* (co-author) 48, *South Pacific* (co-author) 49, *The Wisteria Trees* (author) 50, *Wish You Were Here* (co-author) 52, *Picnic* 53, *Kind Sir* 53, *Fanny* 54, *Middle of the Night* 56, *Blue Denim* 58, *The World of Suzie Wong* 58, *There Was A Little Girl* 60, *All American* 61, *Mr. President* 62, *Tiger, Tiger, Burning Bright* 62, *Ready When You Are, C. B.* 64, *Look to the Lilies* 70, *Miss Moffatt* (musical) 74; films include: *Garden of Allah* 36, *I Met My Love Again* 37, *Picnic* 55, *Bus Stop* 56, *Sayonara* 57, *South Pacific* 57, *Tall Story* 59, *Fanny* 60-61, *Ensign Pulver* 63-64, *Camelot* 66-67, *Paint Your Wagon* 68-69.
Leisure interests: gardening, sculpting, painting.
435 East 52nd Street, New York, N.Y. 10022, U.S.A.

Loganathan, Chelliah, B.COM.; Ceylonese banker; b. 19 Sept. 1913, Point Pedro; m. Thilagawathy 1940; three s. three d.; ed. Hartley Coll. and Jaffna Coll., Jaffna, and Univ. Coll., Colombo.
Former mem. Nat. Planning Council; fmr. mem. Comm. of Inquiry into Employee Participation in Profits; fmr. Chair. Cttee. of Tourism; fmr. Gen. Man. and Chief Exec. Bank of Ceylon; Gen. Man. Dir. and Chief Exec. Devt. Finance Corpn. of Ceylon; Chair. Ceylonese Nat. Chamber of Int. Chamber of Commerce; Vice-Chair. Comm. on Asian and Far Eastern Affairs of Int. Chamber of Commerce; mem. Ceylon Devt. Advisory Council.
Leisure interests: reading, chess, tennis, walking, cycling.
Publs. *Development Savings Bank, Asia's Dilemma—Private Sector in Economic Development.*
42/1 Horton Place, Colombo 7, Sri Lanka.
Telephone: 92172.

Lohmann, Karl, DR.MED., DR.PHIL.; German university professor; b. 10 April 1898, Bielefeld; m. Helene Müller 1925; one d.; ed. Univs. of Münster and Göttingen (chemistry), Univ. of Heidelberg (medicine).
Rockefeller scholarship 23-24; asst. at Kaiser-Wilhelm-Institut für Biologie 24-29, later senior asst. for medical research; studied medicine at Heidelberg 31-35; Prof. Berlin Univ. and Dir. Physiological-Chemical Inst. of Berlin Univ. 37-51; mem. Deutsche Akad. der Wissenschaften 49-; Emer. Pres. of its Inst. of Nutrition and Dir. of its Inst. for Biochemistry; mem. Deutsche Akad. der Naturforscher Leopoldina, Halle; Nat. Prize 51; Vaterländischer Verdienstorden 58; Dr. Agr. h.c. Humboldt Univ. Berlin 61; Hervorragender Wissenschaftler des Volkes 63; Dr. Med. h.c. Humboldt Univ. Berlin 66.
Lindenberger Weg 78, 1115 Berlin-Buch, Germany.
Telephone: 56-98-51.

Lohse, Eduard, D.THEOL.; German ecclesiastic; b. 19 Feb. 1924, Hamburg; s. of Dr. Walther Lohse and Dr. Wilhelmine Lohse (née Barrelet); m. Roswitha Flitner 1952; two s. one d.; ed. Bethel/Bielefeld and Göttingen.
Pastor, Hamburg 52; Privatdozent, Faculty of Evangelical Theology, Mainz 53; Prof. of New Testament, Kiel, 56, Göttingen 64; Bishop of Hanover 71-; mem. Göttingen Akad. der Wissenschaften.
Leisure interest: music.
Publs. *Märtyrer und Gottesknecht* 55, *Die Offenbarung*

des Johannes 60, *Die Texte aus Qumran* 64, *Die Geschichte des Leidens und Sterbens Jesu Christi* 64, *Die Briefe an die Kolosser und an Philemon* 68, *Umwelt des Neuen Testaments* 71, *Entstehung des Neuen Testaments* 72, *Die Einheit des Neuen Testaments* 73.
3 Hannover, Haarstrasse 6, Federal Republic of Germany.
Telephone: (0511) 8001-88/89.

Loiseau, Louis Marie Jean, L. ès sc.; French museum curator (hon.); b. 9 July 1890, Bourges, Cher; s. of Louis Loiseau; m. Marie-Louise Georges 1918; two s. one d.; ed. Ecole polytechnique, Paris.
Artillery officer 13-18; naval artillery engineer 18-23; engaged as engineer in manufacture of telegraphic material 23-32; curator of the Museum of the Nat. Conservatory of Arts and Crafts, Paris 35-58, hon. curator 58-; Officer Legion of Honour; Inter-Allied Medal and Croix de Guerre 14-18.
Leisure interest: research in theoretical physics.
Publs. *Notre univers dans un espace à quatre dimensions spatiales (Théorie unitaire)* 63, *L'Univers objectif (Théorie unitaire)* 75; papers and reviews.
29 rue Madame, 75006 Paris, France.
Telephone: 222-49-37.

Lokanathan, Palamadai Samu, M.A., D.SC.; Indian economist; b. 10 Oct. 1894; ed. Univ. of Madras and London School of Economics and Political Science.
Professor of Econs., Univ. of Madras 41-42; Editor *Eastern Economist*, New Delhi 43-47; Exec. Sec. UN Econ. Comm. for Asia and the Far East (ECAFE), Bangkok 47-56; Dir.-Gen. Nat. Council of Applied Econ. Research, New Delhi 56-; Chair. Nat. Productivity Council 58-63, 64-66, Asian Productivity Org., Tokyo 63 (Dir. for India 62-66), Mettur Chemical and Industrial Corpn. Ltd., Mettur Dam, S. India and Int. Perspective Planning Team (for devt. of small industries) 63; Vice-Chair. Exec. Council of Central Inst. of Research and Training in Public Co-operation; Vice-Pres. Indian Council on World Affairs; Consultant to Inst. of Nat. Planning, Cairo 60; mem. Governing Council of Asian Inst. of Econ. Devt. and Planning, Bangkok, Nat. Savings Central Advisory Board at Ministry of Finance, Board of Trade, Export-Import Advisory Council of Industries, Panel of Economists on Planning Comm.; Visiting Prof., Dept. of Business Management and Industrial Admin., Univ. of Delhi; Hon. Fellow London School of Econs. and Political Science; Most Noble Order of the Crown of Thailand First Class.
Publs. *Industrial Welfare in India, Industrial Organization in India, Indian Industry, Indian Economic System,* and many other economic and industrial surveys and reports.
5B Pusa Road, New Delhi 5, India.

Lolli, Ettore; Italian financier; ed. Rome Univ.
Joined Società Romana di Elettrica as line repairman 30, advanced to gen. management position in 1940's; with Amer. Gas and Service Corpn. 40-45; joined Italian Embassy and helped set up Deltec, official channel for econ. relations between Italy and U.S.A. 45-50; joined Banca Nazionale del Lavoro 50, organized its N.Y. Office, Vice-Dir. Gen. 66; Chief Exec. Officer, Riunione Adriatica di Sicurtà S.p.A. 66-68, Pres. and Man. Dir. 69-; mem. of the Board of New Court European Investment Fund and of some thirty other cos.
Riunione Adriatica di Sicurtà S.p.A., Corso Italia 23, Milan, Italy.

Lollobrigida, Gina; Italian actress; b. 4 July 1927, Sibiaco; d. of Giovanni and Giuseppina Mercuri; m. Milko Skofic 1949; one s.; ed. Liceo Artistico, Rome.
First leading screen role in *Campane a Martello* 48; has since appeared in numerous films including *Cuori senza Frontiere* 49, *La Città si difende, Achtung, banditi! Enrico Caruso* 51, *Altri Tempi, Moglie per una Notte,*

Fanfan la Tulipe, La Provinciale, Les Belles de la Nuit 52, *Pane, amore e fantasia* 53, *Pane, amore e gelosia, La Romana, Il Grande Gioco* 54, *Trapeze, La Donna più Bella del Mondo* 55, *Notre Dame de Paris* 56, *Solomon and Sheba* 59, *Never So Few* 60, *Go Naked in the World* 61, *She Got What She Asked For* 63, *Woman of Straw* 64, *Le Bambole* 65, *Buona Sera Mrs. Campbell* 68, *King, Queen, Knave* 72.

Publ. *Italia Mia* (photography) 74.

120 Inglewood Drive, Toronto, Ontario, Canada.

Lomako, Pyotr Fadeyevich; Soviet metallurgist and government official; b. 1904; ed. Moscow Inst. of Non-Ferrous Metals and Gold.

Member C.P.S.U. 25-; Engineer, Dir. of Plant, Man. of Trust in Non-Ferrous Metallurgy 32-39; Deputy Minister of Non-Ferrous Metallurgy 39-40, Minister 40-48, 50-53, 57; Deputy Minister of Metallurgical Industry 48-50, 53-57; Deputy to U.S.S.R. Supreme Soviet 46-50, 54-; Chair. Krasnoyarsk Nat. Econ. Council 57-61; mem. C.P.S.U. Cen. Cttee. 61-; Deputy Chair. C.P.S.U. Cen. Cttee. Bureau for R.S.F.S.R. 61-62; Deputy Chair. U.S.S.R. Council of Ministers and Chair. State Planning Cttee. (Gosplan) 62-65; Minister of Non-Ferrous Metal Industry 65-.

U.S.S.R. Ministry of Non-Ferrous Metal Industry, 5-7 Ploshchad Nogina, Moscow, U.S.S.R.

Lomax, Alan; American collector of folk songs; b. 31 Jan. 1915, Austin, Texas; s. of John A. and Bess B. Lomax; m. 1st Elizabeth Harold 1937, 2nd Antoinette Marchand 1962; one d.; ed. Univ. of Texas, Harvard and Columbia Univs.

American Folk Music Library of Congress 37-42; C.B.S. 39-44; Decca 47-49; Research at Univ. of W. Indies 62, Columbia 63-; Dir. Cantometrics Project, Dept. of Anthropology, Columbia Univ. 63-; many lectures, radio programmes and over 100 recordings of folk and primitive music.

Leisure interests: travel, the sea.

Publs. *Harriett and her Harmonium, Mister Jelly Roll, The Rainbow Sign, Folk Songs of North America, Penguin Book of American Folk Songs, Folk Song Style, Song Structure and Social Structure*; (with J. A. Lomax): *Cowboy Songs and other Frontier Ballads, Negro Folk Songs as Sung by Lead Belly, American Ballads and Folk Songs, Folk Songs U.S.A., Our Singing Country, Folk Song Style and Culture, 3,000 Years of Black Poetry*, and many articles.

215 West 98th Street, 12-E, New York, N.Y. 10025, U.S.A.

Lombardo, Ivan Matteo; Italian politician; b. 22 May 1902, Milan; m. Maria V. Astorri 1926; one d.

Editor, Labour Section, *Avanti!* 20-22; in business 25-45; Industrial Commr. Lombardy Liberation Cttee. 45; mem. Consulta Nazionale, Under-Sec. of State for Industry and Commerce 45-46; elected to Constituent Nat. Ass. 46; Chief Italian Del. for negotiations with France 46; Sec.-Gen. Partito Socialista Italiano di Unità Proletaria (P.S.I.U.P.) 46; Chief Italian del. U.S.A. Treaty negotiations 47; mem. Nat. Ass. 48-53; Minister of Industry and Commerce 48-49, of Foreign Trade 50-51; Chief Italian del. E.D.C. Conf., Paris 51-54; Co-Pres. Italian American Council for Marketing 51-52; Pres. Nat. Productivity Council (C.N.P.) 55-67; Pres. Nat. Handicrafts Devt. Co. (C.N.A.), Florence 48-61, Milan Triennial Exhbn. 49-61, Italian Chamber of Commerce for the Americas 51-, Italian Atlantic Cttee. 55-, Atlantic Treaty Asscn. (London) 59-61, Lloyd Internazionale (Rome); Hon. Gov. Institut Atlantique; Chair. Credito Commerciale Tirreno; Knight Grand Cross, Italian Order of Merit, Officier Légion d'Honneur, Knight of Orden de Mayo (Argentina), Milan Gold Medal, Grand Cross, Portuguese Order of Infante Henrique.

Via Archimede 68, 00197 Rome, Italy.

Telephone: 87.89.58.

Łomnicki, Tadeusz; Polish actor and theatre director; b. 18 July 1927, Podhajce; m.; two c.; ed. Studio Theatrical School, Crakow, State Coll. of Theatrical Arts, Warsaw.

Old Theatre, Crakow 45-46; Wyspiański's Theatre, Katowice 46-47; Słowacki's Theatre, Crakow 47-49; Współczesny Theatre, Warsaw; Pro-Rector, State Coll. of Theatrical Arts, Warsaw 69-72, Rector 72-; acts in films and TV; Deputy mem. Cen. Cttee. Polish United Workers' Party 71-75, mem. 75-; mem. Presidium Cen. Board, Soc. for Polish-Soviet Friendship 74-; Order of Banner of Labour 2nd Class, State Prize 1st Class 68.

Roles include: title role in *The Resistible Rise of Arturo Ui*, Edgar in *Play Strindberg*, Solony in *Three Sisters*, Prisypk in *The Bed-Bug* by Majakovsky, Jester in *Twelfth Night*, Michal in *Pan Wołodyjowski* and *Potop* (films), title role in *Kordian* by Slowacki, Jan in *The First Day of Freedom* by Kruczkowski, Orestes in *Iphigenie auf Tauris*.

Ul. Piwna 21/23 m. 2, 00-265 Warsaw, Poland.

Lomonosov, Vladimir Grigorievich; Soviet politician; b. 1928; ed. Moscow Steel Inst.

Assistant Foreman, Moscow Hammer and Sickle Iron Works 53-57; mem. C.P.S.U. 50-, Party Work 58-62; Head, Central Asian Bureau, C.P.S.U. Dec. 62-64; Second Sec. Central Cttee. of C.P. of Uzbekistan 65-; mem. C.P.S.U. Central Cttee. 66-; Deputy to U.S.S.R. Supreme Soviet 66-; Vice-Chair. Planning and Budgetary Comm., Soviet of the Union.

Central Committee of the Uzbek Communist Party, Tashkent, U.S.S.R.

Lomský, Bohumir; Czechoslovak army officer and politician; b. 22 April 1914, České Budějovice; ed. Military Acads., Hranice and Moscow.

Organized Czechoslovak troops in U.S.S.R. during Second World War, Chief-of-Staff, First Czechoslovak Brigade and of Czechoslovak Corps in U.S.S.R. 43-44; various posts in Army in Czechoslovakia 45-53; First Deputy Minister of Nat. Defence 53-56, Minister 56-68; Inst. of Mil. History 68-; mem. Central Cttee., C.P. of Czechoslovakia 58-68; Deputy, Nat. Assembly 60-69; Deputy to House of the People, Fed. Assembly 69-71; Order of White Lion for Victory 48, Order of Labour 55, 64, and other Czechoslovak and foreign decorations.

Institute of Military History, Prague, Czechoslovakia.

Lon Nol, Marshal; Cambodian soldier and politician; b. 13 Nov. 1913, Kompong Leav; ed. Chasseloup Laubat High School, S. Viet-Nam, and Royal Military Acad., Cambodia.

Government official 37-52; Gov. of Kratie province 45; Chief of Nat. Police; Army Area Commdr. 52; Gov. of Battambang province 54; Minister of Nat. Defence and Chief of Gen. Staff 55-66; C.-in-C. of the Khmer Royal Armed Forces 60; Deputy Prime Minister of Cambodia 63, Prime Minister 66-67, First Vice-Pres. in Charge of Nat. Defence 67-69; Prime Minister and Minister of Nat. Defence 69-71; led coup to overthrow Prince Norodom Sihanouk (*q.v.*) March 70; Titular Prime Minister 71-72; Pres. Khmer Repub. 72-75; Supreme Commdr. of the Khmer Armed Forces 72-74; Chair. Supreme State Council 73-74, High Exec. Council 74-75; left the country April 75.

Hawaii, U.S.A.

London, Irving Myer, M.D.; American physician; b. 24 July 1918, Malden, Mass.; s. of Jacob A. London and Rose Goldstein; m. Huguette Piedzicki 1955; two s.; ed. Harvard Coll. and Harvard Medical School.

Instructor, Assoc., Asst. Prof., Assoc. Prof. of Medicine, Columbia Univ. Coll. of Physicians and Surgeons 47-55; Prof. and Chair. Dept. of Medicine, Albert Einstein Coll. of Medicine 55-70, Visiting Prof. of Medicine 70-; Prof. of Biology, Mass. Inst. of Technology (MIT) 69-; Dir. Harvard-MIT Program in Health Sciences and Technology 69-; Visiting Prof. of Medicine, Harvard

Medical School 69-72; Prof. of Medicine at Harvard Univ. and MIT 72-; mem. Nat. Acad. of Sciences; Theobald Smith Award in Medical Sciences (A.A.A.S.); Hon. D.Sc. (Univ. of Chicago).
Publs. numerous publications on the metabolism of erythrocytes and of hemoglobin 48-.
Harvard-MIT Program in Health Sciences and Technology, 77 Massachusetts Avenue, Cambridge, Mass. 02139; Home: 41 Fresh Pond Lane, Cambridge, Mass. 02138, U.S.A.
Telephone: 617-253-4030 (Office); 617-491-1272 (Home).

Long, Augustus C.; American oil executive; b. 23 Aug. 1904, Starke, Fla.; *s.* of Augustine V. and Ruby (Brownlee) Long; *m.* 1st Elizabeth Walsh 1927 (died 1963), 2nd Doris Ann Penrose 1964; four *d.* (one deceased); ed. U.S. Naval Acad.
Joined Texaco Inc. 30; Vice-Pres. in charge of E. Hemisphere operations 49-51; Dir. 50-; Exec. Vice-Pres. 51-53, Pres. 53-56, Chair. of Board of Dirs. and Chief Exec. Officer 56-65; retd. from active service 65-70; mem. Board of Dirs. and Exec. Cttee.; Chief Exec. Officer Sept. 70-Dec. 71; Chair. Exec. Cttee. Sept. 70-; Chair. Board Emer. Trustees, Presbyterian Hospital; mem. Board Miami Heart Inst.; Hon. mem. Board Amer. Petroleum Inst.; mem. The Business Council, Metropolitan Opera Asscn.; Commdr. Cross, Order of Orange-Nassau (Netherlands) 55; Commdr. Order of the Crown (Belgium) 68; Hon. LL.D. (Boston Coll. 57, St. Joseph's Coll. 61, Columbia Univ. 64), Hon. D.Sc. (Hampden-Sydney Coll.) 63.
4430 Sabal Palm Road, Miami, Fla. 33137, U.S.A.

Long, Esmond R., A.B., PH.D., M.D.; American pathologist; b. 16 June 1890, Chicago, Ill.; *s.* of John Harper Long and Catherine Belle Stoneman (Long); *m.* Marian Boak Adams 1922; one *s.* one *d.*; ed. Univ. of Chicago.
Assistant to Prof. of Pathology, Univ. of Chicago 11-32; Asst. in Pathology, Prague, Czechoslovakia 22; Dir. of Henry Phipps Inst. for the Study, Treatment and Prevention of Tuberculosis and Prof. of Pathology, Univ. of Pennsylvania 32-55; Dir. of Medical Research, Nat. Tuberculosis Asscn. (U.S.A.) 47-55; Prof. Emeritus of Pathology, Univ. of Pennsylvania 55-; Chair. Div. of Medical Sciences, Nat. Research Council (U.S.A.) 36-39; Pres. Wistar Inst. of Anatomy and Biology, Philadelphia 36-39; Col., Medical Corps, U.S. Army (service in U.S.A. and Europe) 42-46; Chief consultant on tuberculosis, U.S. Army 42-46; Editor, *Int. Journal of Leprosy* 64-69; Legion of Merit, U.S.A. 46; Hon. Sc.D., (Univ. of Pennsylvania) 48; Philadelphia Award 54; mem. Nat. Acad. of Sciences (U.S.A.), Amer. Philosophical Soc.
Publs. *Chemistry and Chemotherapy of Tuberculosis* 23, 32, 58; *History of Pathology* 28, 65; *Selected Readings in Pathology* 29, 61; *Tuberculosis in the Army of the United States in World War II* 55; *History of American Pathology* 62, *History of American Society for Experimental Pathology* 72, *History of the American Association of Pathologists and Bacteriologists* 74; journal articles on pathology, tuberculosis and history of medicine 13-72.
220 Locust Street., Apartment 23B, Philadelphia, Pa., U.S.A.
Telephone: Walnut 3-0420.

Long, Franklin Asbury; American chemist and educationist; b. 27 July 1910, Great Falls, Mont.; *s.* of Franklin A. Long and Ethel Beck; *m.* Marion Thomas 1937; one *s.* one *d.*; ed. Univs. of Montana and California (Berkeley).
Fellow in Chemistry, Univ. of California (Berkeley) 33-34; Instructor in Chemistry, Univ. of Chicago 36-37; Faculty mem. Chem. Dept., Cornell Univ. 37, Chair. 50-60; Research, Carnegie Inst. of Technology 42-45; Consultant, Nat. Defense Research Cttee. 41-45; Con-

sultant, Nat. Bureau of Standards 57, Dept. of Army 53-59, Dept. of Air Force 57-62, of Defense 59-62; Asst. Dir. U.S. Arms Control and Disarmament Agency 62-63, Consultant 63-73; Dir. Arms Control Asscn. 71; Co-Chair. Amer. Pugwash Steering Cttee. 74-; Visiting Chemical Consultant, Brookhaven Nat. Laboratory 46-; mem. President's Science Advisory Cttee. 61-66; Vice-Pres. Research and Advanced Studies, Cornell Univ. 63-69; Trustee, Assoc. Univs. Inc. 46-74; Henry R. Luce Prof. of Science and Soc., Cornell Univ. 69-; Dir. Program on Science, Technology and Soc. 69-73; Dir. Inmont Corp. 65-, Exxon Corpn. 69-; Trustee, Alfred P. Sloan Foundation 70-; mem. U.S. India Subcomm. for Educ. and Cultural Affairs 74-; mem. Amer. Chemical Soc. 39-, Amer. Physics Soc. 41-60, Nat. Acad. of Sciences 63-, Amer. Asscn. for the Advancement of Science 63-, Amer. Acad. of Arts and Science 65-, Council on Foreign Relations 64-, U.S. Continuing Comm. of Pugwash 67-71.
632 Clark Hall, Cornell University, Ithaca, N.Y.; Home: 429 Warren Road, Ithaca, N.Y., U.S.A.
Telephone: 607-256-3810.

Long, Gerald, B.A.; British journalist; b. 22 Aug. 1923, York; *s.* of Fred Harold and Sabina (Walsh) Long; *m.* Anne Hamilton Walker 1951; two *s.* three *d.*; ed. St. Peter's School, York, and Emmanuel Coll., Cambridge.
Served with British Army 43-47; Reuters 48-, Corresp. in France, Germany and Turkey 50-60, Asst. Gen. Man. 60-63, Chief Exec. 63-, Gen. Man. 63-73, Man. Dir. 73-; Chair. Visnews Ltd. 68-; Chair. Exec. Cttee. Int. Broadcast Inst. 73-; mem. Design Council 74-.
Leisure interest: cooking.
Reuters Ltd., 85 Fleet Street, London, EC4P 4AJ; and 37 Wood Lane, Highgate, London N6 5UD, England.
Telephone: 01-353-6060 (Office); 01-340-4543 (Home).

Long, Olivier, D.en D., D.ès SC.POL.; Swiss diplomatist; b. 1915, Petit-Veyrier, Geneva; *s.* of Dr. Edouard Long and Dr. Marie Landry; *m.* Francine Roels 1946; one *s.* two *d.*; ed. Faculté de Droit and Ecole des Sciences Politiques à Paris and Univ. de Genève.
With Int. Red Cross 41-46; Foreign Affairs Dept., Berne 46-49; Washington Embassy 49-53; Div. of Commerce, Berne 54-55; Govt. Del. for Commercial Agreements 55-66; Head of Swiss Del. to European Free Trade Asscn. (EFTA) 60-66; Amb. to United Kingdom and Malta 67-68; Dir.-Gen. GATT 68-; Prof. Graduate Inst. of Int. Studies Geneva 62-.
Leisure interests: music, reading, skiing, swimming.
General Agreement on Tariffs and Trade (GATT), Villa le Bocage, CH-1211, Geneva 10, Switzerland.

Long, Russell B.; American lawyer and politician; b. 3 Nov. 1918; ed. Fortier High School and Louisiana State Univ.
Served U.S. Navy 42-45; in private legal practice 45-48, Exec. Counsel to Gov. of Louisiana 48; U.S. Senator from Louisiana 48-, Senate Majority Whip 65-69; Chair. Finance Cttee. 66; Democrat.
Senate Office Building, Washington, D.C.; and 1112 Steele Boulevard, Baton Rouge, La., U.S.A.

Longacre, Robert F.; American business executive; b. 25 Feb. 1923, Johnstown, Pa.; ed. William and Mary Coll.
Joined Great Atlantic and Pacific Tea Company Inc. 48, Pres. 71-.
Great Atlantic & Pacific Tea Company Inc., 420 Lexington Avenue, New York, N.Y. 10017, U.S.A.

Longerstaey, Edouard; Belgian diplomatist; b. 14 Dec. 1919; *m.*; three *c.*
Joined diplomatic service 46; Vice-Consul, New York 47-50; Second Sec., The Hague 52-56; First Sec., Teheran 56-58; Chef de Cabinet, Ministry of Overseas

Trade, July-Nov. 58; Consul-Gen., Lille 59-61; Chief, Belgian Mission to Democratic Repub. of Congo March-Dec. 61; Chargé d'Affaires, Léopoldville (now Kinshasa) Dec. 61-Feb. 62; Amb. to Algeria 62-64; Deputy Dir.-Gen. of Foreign Econ. Affairs 64-66; Perm. Rep., UN Office, Geneva 66-68; Amb. to Italy 68-69; Perm. Rep. to UN 70-.

Permanent Mission of Belgium to the United Nations, 809 United Nations Plaza, 2nd Floor, New York, N.Y. 10017, U.S.A.

Longford, Countess of; Elizabeth Pakenham, C.B.E., F.R.S.L.; British writer; b. 30 Aug. 1906, London; d. of N. B. Harman, F.R.C.S., and Catherine Chamberlain; m. Francis A. Pakenham (now Earl of Longford, q.v.) 1931; four s. four d. (one deceased); ed. Headington School, Oxford, and Lady Margaret Hall, Oxford.

Parliamentary Candidate (Labour) Cheltenham 31, Oxford 50; Trustee, Nat. Portrait Gallery 67-; mem. Advisory Board, Victoria and Albert Museum; James Tait Black Prize for *Victoria R.I.* 64; Yorkshire Post Book of the Year Prize for *Wellington: The Years of the Sword* 69.

Leisure interests: Victoriana, gardening.

Publs. *Jameson's Raid* 59, *Victoria R.I.* 64, *Wellington: The Years of the Sword* 69, *Wellington: Pillar of State* 72, *Winston Churchill* 74, *The Royal House of Windsor* 74, *Byron's Greece* (with photographer Jorge Lewinski) 75.

18 Chesil Court, Chelsea Manor Street, London, S.W.3; Bernhurst, Hurst Green, Sussex, England.

Telephone: 01-352-7794 (London); Hurst Green 248.

Longford, 7th Earl of (cr. 1785); **Francis Aungier Pakenham** (cr. Baron 45), K.G., P.C., M.A.; British politician and writer; b. 5 Dec. 1905; s. of 5th Earl of Longford; m. Elizabeth Harman (now Countess of Longford, q.v.) 1931; four s. four d. (one deceased); ed. Eton Coll. and New Coll., Oxford.

Tutor, Univ. Tutorial Courses, Stoke-on-Trent 29-31; with Conservative Party Economic Research Dept. 30-32; Lecturer in Politics, Christ Church, Oxford 32; Student in Politics, Christ Church 34-46 and 52-; Prospective Parl. Labour Candidate for Oxford City 38; served Bucks. Light Infantry 39-40; personal asst. to Sir William Beveridge 41-44; Lord-in-Waiting 45-46; Parl. Under-Sec. to War Office 46-47; Chancellor of the Duchy of Lancaster 47-48; Minister of Civil Aviation 48-51; First Lord of the Admiralty May-Oct. 51; Lord Privy Seal and Leader of House of Lords 64-65, 66-68; Sec. of State for Colonies 65-66; Chair. Nat. Bank Ltd. 55-62; Chair. Sidgwick and Jackson Ltd. (Publishers) May 70-.

Publs. *Peace by Ordeal* (*The Anglo-Irish Treaty of 1921*), *Born to Believe* 53, *The Causes of Crime* 58, *Five Lives* 63, *Humility* 69, *De Valéra* (with T. P. O'Neill) 70, *The Grain of Wheat* 74, *The Life of Jesus Christ* 74, *Abraham Lincoln* 74.

Bernhurst, Hurst Green, Sussex; and 18 Chesil Court, Chelsea Manor Street, London, S.W.3, England.

Telephone: Hurst Green 248; 01-352 7794 (London).

Longley, James B., LL.B.; American politician; b. 22 April 1924; s. of late James B. and Catherine Wade Longley; m. Helen Longley; two s. three d.; ed. Bowdoin Coll., American Coll. of Life Underwriters, Univ. of Maine Law School.

Lecturer, Instructor Amer. Coll. of Life Underwriters 57-65; Past Pres. Board of Editors of *Query*, Soc. of Chartered Life Underwriters; Gen. Agent New England Mutual Life Insurance Co.; Pres. Longley Assocs.; Partner Longley & Buckley (on leave of absence); Gov. of Maine Jan. 75-; mem. Maine and Amer. Bar Assocns.; fmr. Chair. Maine Management and Cost Survey Study of Maine State Govt.

Office of the Governor, Augusta, Maine 04330, U.S.A.

Longo, Luigi; Italian politician; b. 15 March 1900. University student 20; Sec. of Piedmontese Communist Group which founded the Italian Communist Party 21; mem. Central Cttee. Young Communist Federation 21; del. to Fourth Congress of the Comintern 22; Editor of *L'Avanguardia* (organ of Young Communist Federation) 23; arrested and imprisoned for political activities 23-24; del. of Young Communists at Third Congress of Italian Communist Party 26; mem. Young Communists' International 26-27; responsible for youth work at Foreign Centre of Communist Party in Paris 27; del. to Sixth Congress of Comintern 28; illegal political activity in Italy; two years in Moscow 32-34; Inspector-Gen. of Int. Brigades in Spain 36-39; after end of Spanish war returned to France; imprisoned in France 39-41; in Italy 42-43; organized popular resistance to the Germans in Rome Sept. 43; Vice-Commdr. of Volunteer Liberation Corps, Commdt.-Gen. "Garibaldi" Brigades; Deputy Constituent Assembly 46, Nat. Assembly 48, 53, 58, 63, 68; Deputy Sec.-Gen. of Italian Communist Party 45-64, Sec.-Gen. 64, Chair. 72-; U.S. Bronze Star; Stella d'Oro Garibaldina.

Publs. *Un popolo alla macchia* 47, *Sulla via dell'insurrezione nazionale* 54, *Le Brigate Internazionali in Spagna* 56, *Revisionismo nuovo e antico* 57, *Il miracolo economico italiano e la critica marxista* 62.

Partito Comunista Italiano, Via delle Botteghe Oscure 4, 00186 Rome, Italy.

Telephone: 684101.

Longuet-Higgins, Hugh Christopher, F.R.S., F.R.S.E., M.A., D.PHIL.; British university professor; b. 11 April 1923; ed. Winchester Coll., and Balliol Coll., Oxford.

Research Fellow Balliol Coll. 47-48; Research Assoc. Univ. of Chicago 48-49; Lecturer and Reader in theoretical chemistry, Victoria Univ. of Manchester 49-52; Prof. of Theoretical Physics King's Coll., London Univ. 52-54; Fellow, Corpus Christi Coll. and Prof. of Theoretical Chemistry, Univ. of Cambridge 54-67; Royal Soc. Research Prof., Univ. of Edinburgh 67-74, Univ. of Sussex 74-, Harrison Memorial Prize 50; F.R.S. 58; Foreign mem. American Acad. of Arts and Sciences 61; Foreign Assoc. U.S. Nat. Acad. of Sciences 68; Life Fellow, Corpus Christi Coll., Cambridge, Hon. Fellow, Balliol Coll., Oxford 69; Dr. h.c. Univ. of York 73.

Leisure interest: music.

Publs. include about 150 papers in scientific journals.

Univ. of Sussex, Falmer, Brighton, England.

Longuet-Higgins, Michael Selwyn, M.A., PH.D., F.R.S.; British research scientist; b. 8 Dec. 1925, Lenham; s. of Henry H. L. Longuet-Higgins and A. Cecil Bazeley; m. Joan R. Tattersall 1958; two s. two d.; ed. Winchester Coll., Cambridge Univ.

Research Fellow, Cambridge Univ. 51-55; Commonwealth Fund Fellow, Scripps Inst., La Jolla, 51-52; Research Scientist, Nat. Inst. of Oceanography 54-67; Visiting Prof. Mass. Inst. of Technology 58; Visiting Prof. Inst. of Geophysics, Univ. of California 61-62; Visiting Prof. Univ. of Adelaide 63-64; Prof. of Oceanography, Oregon State Univ., Corvallis 67-69; Royal Soc. Research Prof. Cambridge Univ. (joint appointment with Inst. of Oceanographic Sci.) July 69-; Rayleigh Prize for mathematics, Cambridge Univ. 50; Fellow, Royal Soc. 63.

Leisure interests: music, gardening, mathematical toys.

Publs. Numerous contributions to scientific journals.

Department of Applied Mathematics and Theoretical Physics, Cambridge University, Silver Street, Cambridge; Institute of Oceanographic Sciences, Wormley, Godalming, Surrey; Home: 1 Long Road, Cambridge, England.

Telephone: Cambridge 47430 (Home).

Löns, Josef, D.IUR.; German diplomatist and lawyer; b. 14 Nov. 1910; ed. law studies.

Head of Legal Dept., Insurance Co.; served in Second World War; Attorney 45; Gen. Sec. C.D.U., British Zone 45-48; Deputy Mayor, Cologne 48-52; Ministerial Dir. of Foreign Office 53; Head of Personnel and Administration, Foreign Office 53-58; Amb. to the Netherlands 59-63, to Austria 63-70, to Switzerland 70-73.
4 Krautwig Strasse, Cologne/Lindenthal, Federal Republic of Germany.

Loomis, Cecil Edward; American businessman; b. 12 May 1906; ed. Ohio State Univ.
Clerk, Ohio Fuel Gas Co. 28-35; engineer, Columbia Gas System Service Corpn. 35-50, Asst. Vice-Pres. 50, Vice-Pres., Dir. 51-56, Senior Vice-Pres. 56-60, Pres. 60-61, Vice-Chair. 61-64, Chair. 64-; Asst. Vice-Pres. Columbia Gas System Inc., New York City 50-51, Vice-Pres. 51-56, Senior Vice-Pres. 56-60, Dir. 56-, Pres. 60, Vice-Chair. 61-64, Chair. 64-71; Dir. Columbia Hydrocarbon Corpn., Columbia Gas of New York Inc., United Fuel Gas Co., and numerous other companies; mem. American Soc. of Mechanical Engineers, American Gas Assoc.
Home: 1 Winfields Road, Zionsville, Pa. 18092; Office: 120 East 41st Street, New York City, N.Y. 10017, U.S.A.

Loomis, Henry, A.B.; American broadcasting executive and fmr. government official; b. 19 April 1919, Tuxedo Park, N.Y.; s. of Alfred Lee Loomis and Ellen Holman Farnsworth Loomis; m. 1st Mary Paul Macleod 1946, two s. two d.; m. 2nd Jacqueline C. Williams 1974; ed. Harvard Univ. and Univ. of Calif.
U.S. Navy 40-45; Asst. to the Pres., Mass. Inst. of Technology 47-50; Asst. to Chair. of Research and Devt. Board, Dept. of Defense, Washington, D.C. 50-51; Consultant, Psychological Strategy Board, Washington, D.C. 51-52; mem. Staff, President's Cttee. on Int. Information 53; Chief, Office of Research and Intelligence, U.S. Information Agency, Washington, D.C. 54-57; Staff Dir. to Special Asst. to Pres. for Science and Technology, White House 57-58; Dir. Broadcasting Service (Voice of America), U.S. Information Agency, Washington, D.C. 58-65; Deputy U.S. Commr. of Educ., Dept. of Health, Educ. and Welfare, Washington, D.C. 65-66; Partner, St. Vincent's Island Co., New York 66-69; Dep. Dir. U.S. Information Agency, Washington, D.C. 69-72; Pres. Corpn. for Public Broadcasting 72-; Rockefeller Public Service Award in Foreign Affairs 63; Distinguished Service Award, U.S. Inf. Agency 63.
Leisure interests: sailing, hunting, fishing, skiing, photography.
Home: Middleburg, Va. 22117, U.S.A.
Telephone: 202-293-6160 (Office); 703-687-8201 (Home).

Loos, Anita; American writer; b. 26 April 1893; ed. High School, San Diego, Calif.
Scenario writer with D. W. Griffith (five years), Douglas Fairbanks (three years), Constance Talmadge (two years).
Publs. (novels) *Gentlemen Prefer Blondes* 25, *But Gentlemen Marry Brunettes* 28, (with John Emerson) *The Whole Town's Talking, The Fall of Eve, Cherries are Ripe, The Social Register, A Mouse is Born* 50, *This Brunette Prefers Work* 56, *Gentlemen Still Prefer Blondes, No Mother to Guide Her* 61, *A Girl Like I* (autobiog.) 66, *Kiss Hollywood Goodbye* 74; (films) *Red Headed Women, Blossoms in the Dust, I Married an Angel, The Pirate;* (plays) *Happy Birthday* 46, *Gentlemen Prefer Blondes* 49, *No Mother to Guide Her* 61, *Mama Steps Out, They Met in Bombay, A Girl Like I* 66.
c/o Avon Books, 959 Eighth Avenue, New York 19, N.Y., U.S.A.

Lopes, Henri; Congolese politician; b. Sept. 1937, Léopoldville, Belgian Congo (now Kinshasa, Zaire); ed. France.
Minister of Nat. Educ. 68-71, of Foreign Affairs 71-73;

mem. Political Bureau, Congolese Labour Party 73; Pres. Revolutionary Court of Justice April 73; Prime Minister and Minister of Planning 73-75; Prix littéraire de l'Afrique noire 72.
Publs. *Tribaliques* (short stories), *La Nouvelle Romance* (novel).
c/o Office of the Prime Minister, Brazzaville, People's Republic of the Congo.

Lopes-Graça, Fernando; Portuguese composer and writer; b. 17 Dec. 1906, Tomar; s. of Silverio Lopes-Graça and Emilia da Conceição Lopes-Graça; ed. Lisbon Conservatoire, Univs. of Lisbon, Coimbra and Paris.
Professor, Instituto de Música (Coimbra) 32-36, Acad. de Amadores de Música (Lisbon) 40-54.
Compositions include: two piano concertos 40, 53, four piano sonatas 34, 39, 52, 61, *Glosas* (piano) 49-50, *Cuatro Canciones de Federico García Lorca* (for baritone and chamber instrumental ensemble) 54, *Trois Danses Portugaises pour Orchestre* 41, *Sinfonia per Orchestra* 44, *Estelas Funerárias* 48, *Suite Rústica No. 1* (for Orchestra) 50, 24 *Preludes* (piano) 52-58, *Trovas* 55, *Canções Populares Portuguesas* (for voice and piano, and for voices "a cappella") 55, *Concertino* (for piano, brass, strings and percussion) 56, *Divertimento for Wind Instruments, Percussion, Cellos and Double-basses* 57, *Melodias Rústicas Portuguesas* (piano) 57, *5 Nocturnes* (piano) 59, *História Trágico-Marítima,* for baritone, fem. chorus and orch. 43-60, Cycles for tenor and piano 59, 60, *Pequeno Cancioneiro do Menino Jesus* for fem. voices and instr. chamber ensemble 59, *Petit Triptyque* for violin and piano 60, *Gabriela, Cravo e Canela* (overture) 60, *Prelude and Fugue* (violin solo) 61, *Canto de Amor e de Morte* (orch.) 61, *Poema de Dezembro* (orch.) 61, *Para uma Criança que vai Nascer* (for strings) 61, *Mar de Setembro* (cycle for voice and piano) 62, *Concertino for Viola and Orchestra* 62, *Cosmorama* (piano) 63, *In Memoriam Bela Bartok* (7 suites for piano) 59-64, *String Quartet* 64, *9 Cantigas de Amigo* (for voice and chamber instrumental ensemble) 64, *Four Sketches* (for strings) 65, *Suite Rústica No. 2* (for string quartet) 65, *Concerto da camera col violoncello obbligato* 65, *Quatorze Anotações* (for string quartet) 66, *Sete Lembranças para Vieira da Silva* (for wind quintet) 66, *D. Duardos e Flérida* (cantata-melodrama in two parts for narrator, mezzo-soprano, alto, tenor, chorus and orchestra) 66-69, *Viagens na minha Terra* (2 suites for orchestra) 69-70, *O Túmulo de Villa-Lobos* (for wind quintet) 70, *Prelúdio e Baileto, Partita* (for guitar) 68, 71, *Six Sephardite Songs* (for voice and orchestra) 71, *Four Pieces* (for harpsichord) 71.
Publs. include *Reflexões sobre a Música* 41, *Introdução a Música Moderna* 42, *Música e Músicos Modernos* 43, *A Música Portuguesa e os seus Problemas* (Vol. I) 44, (Vol. II) 59, *Talia, Euterpe e Terpsicore* 45, *Visita aos Músicos Franceses* 48, *Viana da Mota* 49, *Bela Bartok* 53, *A Canção Popular Portuguesa* 54, *Em Louvor de Mozart* 56, *Dicionário de Música* (Vol. I) 56, (Vol. II) 58, *Igor Stravinsky and Bela Bartok* 59, *Musicália* 60, *Nossa Companheira Música* 64, *Páginas Escolhidas de Crítica e Estética Musical* 67, *Disto e Daquilo* 73, *A Música Portuguesa e os seus Problemas* (Vol. III) 74, *Um artista intervem, Cartas com alguma moral* 74, and translations of Rousseau, Mann, Keller, Mörike, Percy Buck, Alan Bush, Haskell, Romain Rolland, Balzac.
El Mio Paraiso, 2°, Ave. da República, Parede, Portugal.
Telephone: 2472824.

López, Fernando; Philippine politician; b. 13 April 1904, Jaro, Iloilo; s. of Gov. Benito López and Presentacion Hofileña; m. María Salvación Javellana y Virto 1924; two s. two d.; ed. Univ. of Santo Tomás.
Member, Philippine Bar 26; Mayor, Iloilo City 45; Senator of Philippines 47, Vice-Pres. 49, Sec. Agriculture and Natural Resources 50, Senate Pres. Pro-Tempore 58, 60; Vice-Pres. of Philippines 65-69, 69-71; Sec. Agri-

culture and Natural Resources 70-Jan. 71; Special Grand Cordon of Most Noble Order of Crown of Thailand; Officer of Nat. Order of Vietnam; Hon. LL.D., Manhattan Coll., New York City; Gran Cruz of Order of Isabel la Católica; Mil. Order of Christ, and many other awards.

Leisure interests: listening to music, swimming, movies, taking pictures.

706 Quirino Avenue, Tambo, Parañaque Rizal; 6 Flametree Place, Forbes Park, Makati Rizal, Philippines.

López, Salvador P.; Philippine journalist, diplomatist and educationist; b. 27 May 1911, Currimao, Ilocos Norte; s. of Bernabe P. López and Jegunda Sinang; m. Maria Luna 1936; two d.; ed. Univ. of the Philippines.
Columnist, Magazine Editor and Assoc. Editor *Philippines Herald* 33-41; Radio News Commentator 40-41; Philippine Army Service 42-46; Diplomatic Service 46-; Adviser on Political Affairs, Philippine Mission to UN 46-48, Senior Adviser 48-49, Chargé d'Affaires a.i. 50-52, Acting Perm. Rep. to UN 53-54; Minister to France 55-56, concurrently Minister to Belgium and Netherlands 55-59, to Switzerland 57-58, Ambassador to France 56-62, concurrently Perm. Rep. to UNESCO 58-62, Minister to Portugal 59-62; Under-Sec. of Foreign Affairs, Philippines 62-63; Sec. of Foreign Affairs 63-64; Perm. Rep. to UN 64-68, concurrently Amb. to U.S.A. 68-69; Pres., Univ. of the Philippines 69-; numerous decorations.
Leisure interests: classical music, orchids.
Publs. *Literature and Society* 51, *Freedom of Information* 53, *English for World Use* 54, *The United States—Philippines Colonial Relationship* 66, *Human Rights and the Constitution* 70.
c/o University of the Philippines, Quezon City, Philippines.
Telephone: 97-39-10.

López Arellano, Gen. Oswaldo; Honduran air force officer and politician; b. 30 June 1921; ed. School of Mil. Aviation and Flight Training, U.S.A.
Joined armed forces 39, Lieut. 47, Col. 58; Chief of Armed Forces 56-75; mem. Mil. Junta, Chief of Mil. Govt. of Honduras, Minister of Nat. Defence, Minister of Public Security 63-66; Pres. of Honduras 66-71, 72-April 75; several decorations
c/o Office of the President, Tegucigalpa, Honduras.

López Bravo, Gregorio; Spanish politician; b. 19 Dec. 1923, Madrid; s. of Sotero López and Consuelo Bravo; m. María Ángeles Velasco Schmidt; nine c.; ed. Escuela de Ingenieros Navales, Madrid.
Former Dir. Constructora Naval Co.; Dir.-Gen. of Foreign Trade 59-60; Dir.-Gen. Spanish Inst. of Foreign Currency 60-62; mem. Atomic Energy Board; Adviser, Instituto Nacional de Ingenieros; mem. Cortes; Minister of Industry 62-69; Minister of Foreign Affairs Oct. 69-June 73; Chair. Ministerial Council OECD, Paris 73; Chair. Crinavis; mem Inst. of Naval Architects (U.K.).
c/o Ministerio de Asuntos Exteriores, Madrid, Spain.

López de Letona, José María; Spanish politician; b. 26 Nov. 1922, Burgos; m.; three c.
Road Engineer until 49; Technical Engineering Dir. Vías y Construcciones S.A. 52-54, Dir.-Gen. 54-60; associated with Westinghouse Air Brake Co. and affiliated companies in Spain and Europe 60-65; Sub-Commissary to Social and Econ. Devt. Plan 66; Minister of Industry 69-74.
c/o Ministerio de la Industria, Madrid, Spain.

López-Garcia, Antonio; Spanish artist; b. 1936, Tomelloso; m. Maria Moreno; ed. Escuela de Bellas Artes de San Fernando, Madrid.
Travelled in Italy and Greece 55, 58; one-man exhbns. in Madrid 57, 61, Staempfli Gallery, N.Y. 65, 68-69, Paris, Turin 72; group exhbns. in Madrid 55, 64, World Fair Exhbn., N.Y. 64, Carnegie Int., Pittsburgh

65, 67, European tour of Contemporary Spanish Art exhbn. 68, 69; Prize of Diputación de Jaén 57, Prize of Fundación Rodriguez Acosta 58, Molino de Oro Prize of Exposición Regional de Valdepeñas 59.
c/o Marlborough Fine Art Ltd., 6 Albemarle Street, London, W.1, England.

López Michelsen, Alfonso; Colombian lawyer and politician; b. 30 June 1913, Bogotá; s. of Alfonso López Pumarejo (Pres. of Colombia 34-38) and Maria Michelsen; ed. London, Brussels, Colegio Mayor de Nuestra Señora del Rosario, Bogotá, Santiago (Chile) and Georgetown Univ., Washington, D.C., U.S.A.
Former Teacher at Nat. Univ. of Colombia, Univ. Libre de Bogotá and Colegio Mayor de Nuestra Señora del Rosario; legal practice; spent seven years as emigré in Mexico 52-58; later an Editor of *El Liberal* (weekly); mem. Chamber of Deputies 60-62, 62-66; Founder, Leader of moderate wing of Liberal Revolutionary Movement 58-67; joined Liberal Party 67; Gov. of César Dept. 67-68; Minister of Foreign Affairs 68-70; Pres. of Colombia Aug. 74-.
Publs. *Introduction to the Study of the Colombian Constitution* 42, *Benjamin Constant or the Father of Bourgeois Liberalism* 46, *Colombian Inquiries*, *The Elected* (novel).
Office of the President, Bogotá, Colombia.

López Otero, Modesto; Spanish architect; b. 1885.
Medallist of Fine Arts Exhibition, Madrid 12; First Prize winner in competition for monument of "Las Cortes de Cadiz"; Hon. Dir. Spanish School of Architecture and of Acad. of Fine Arts; Architect in charge of Madrid new Univ. City; mem. Acad. of History, Nat. Council of Architecture, Nat. Council of Educ., Int. Cttee. of Architects.
Publs. *Influence of Spanish Architecture in the Spanish Mission in California, Conservation of Monuments.*
Paseo de la Castellana 102, Madrid, Spain.

López-Portillo y Pacheco, José; Mexican lawyer and politician; b. 16 June 1920, Mexico City; s. of José López-Portillo y Weber; m. Carmen Romano; one s. two d.; ed. Law Nat. Faculty, Univ. of Mexico, Santiago Univ.
Professor of Gen. Theory on the State, Univ. of Mexico 54, Assoc. Prof. of Political Sciences 56-58; Founder Prof. in Admin. Sciences Doctorate, Comm. School of the Nat. Polytechnical Inst. 61; with Nat. Revolutionary Party (PRI) 59-64; Technical Assoc., Head Office of Ministry of Patrimony 60; Co-ordinator Border Urban Devt. Cttee. 62; mem. Intersecretarial Comm. for Nat. Devt. 66; Under-Sec. of the Presidency 68; Under-Sec. Ministry of Patrimony 70; Gen. Dir. Electricity Fed. Comm. 72-73; Sec. for Finances and Public Credit May 73-75; Presidential Candidate (PRI) in 1976 elections; Gov. for Mexico, IMF.
Leisure interests: swimming, archery and other sports.
Publs. *Valoracion de la Estatal, Génesis y Teoria del Estado Moderno, Quetzalcoatl, Don Q.*
Colegio 347, Mexico 20, D.F., Mexico.
Telephone: 5-12-10-83.

López Rodó, Laureano; Spanish lawyer and government official; b. 18 Nov. 1920, Barcelona; s. of Laureana López and Maria Teresa Rodó; ed. Univ. de Barcelona, Univ. de Madrid.
Professor of Admin. Law, Univ. de Santiago de Compostela 45-53, Univ. de Madrid 53-; Technical Sec.-Gen. Office of the Pres. 56-62; Pres. and founder Escuela Nacional de Administración Pública; Commr. for the Devt. Plan 62, also Minister without Portfolio 65-73; Minister for Foreign Affairs 73-74; Amb. to Austria 74-; Deputy Pres. Int. Inst. of Admin. Sciences; Councillor Superior Council for Scientific Investigation; M.P.; del. to numerous int. congresses; mem. Interparl. Union, Real Academia de Ciencias Morales y Políticas; Dr. h.c. (Univ. de Coimbra, Portugal); several decorations.

Embassy of Spain, Argentinierstrasse 34, 1040 Vienna, Austria; and Calle de Alcalá 73, Madrid, Spain.
Telephone: 65-85-54.

Lora Tamayo, Manuel; Spanish chemist and politician; b. 1904, Jerez de la Frontera; *m.* Amelia D'Ocon; eleven *c.*
Professor of Organic Chemistry, Seville 33-43; fmr. Prof. of Organic Chemistry, Madrid; Minister of Education 62-68; Pres. Higher Council for Scientific Research 67; Dir. Nat. Centre of Organic Chemistry; Dr. h.c. Paris; mem. Royal Acad. of Science, Acad. of Pharmacy; Corresp. mem. Nat. Acad. of Exact Sciences, Physics and Natural Science of Argentina 68-; Hon. mem. Pontificia Acad. Rome, Acad. of Science Lisbon, Heidelberg, Argentina, Puerto Rico; Hon. mem. various scientific socs.; fmr. Pres. Royal Spanish Soc. of Physics and Chem.; mem. Int. Union Pure and Applied Chem.
Universidad de Madrid, Madrid, Spain.

Lorant, Stefan; American author and editor; b. 22 Feb. 1901, Budapest, Hungary; *m.* Laurie Robertson 1963; two *s.*
Started career as film cameraman in Vienna; mem. Editorial Staff *Das Magazin* Berlin 25; Editor *Bilder Courier* Berlin 25, *Ufa Magazin* Berlin 25-26, *Münchner Illustrierte Presse* 26-33; placed in "protective custody" following Hitler's accession to "power"; upon release came to England where he founded *Weekly Illustrated, Lilliput* (Editor 37-40), *Picture Post* (Editor 38-40); now in U.S.A.; LL.D. (Knox Coll.), M.A. (Harvard).
Publs. *I Was Hitler's Prisoner* 35, *Chamberlain and the Beautiful Llama* 40, *The United States* (ed.) 40, *Lincoln: His Life in Photographs* 41, *The New World* 46, *F.D.R.: a pictorial biography* 50, *The Presidency* 51, *Lincoln, a Picture Story of Life* 52, *The Life of Abraham Lincoln* 54, *The Life and Times of Theodore Roosevelt* 59, *Pittsburgh: The Story of an American City* (revised, Bicentennial edn.) 64, *The New World: The First Pictures of America* (revised, enlarged edn.) 65, *The Glorious Burden: The American Presidency* 68, *Lincoln, the Picture Story of His Life* (revised and enlarged edn.) 69, *Sieg Heil! An illustrated history of Germany from Bismarck to Hitler* 74.
"Fairview", Lenox, Mass., U.S.A.
Telephone: 413-637-0666.

Loren, Sophia; Italian actress; b. 20 Sept. 1934; Rome; *d.* of Riccardo Scicolone and Romilda Villani; *m.* Carlo Ponti (*q.v.*) 1957; two *s.*; ed. Scuole Magistrali Superiori.
First screen appearance as an extra in *Quo Vadis*; has appeared in many Italian and other films including *E Arrivato l'Accordatore* 51, *Africa sotto i Mari* (first leading role), *La Tratta delle Bianche, La Favorita* 52, *Aida, Il Paese dei Campanelli, Miseria e Nobiltà, Tempi Nostri* 53, *Carosello Napoletano, L'Oro di Napoli* 54, *Attila, Peccato che sia una canaglia, Il Segno di Venere, La Bella Mugnaia, La Donna del Fiume* 55, *Boccaccio '70, Matrimonio All'Italiana*; and in the following American films: *The Pride and the Passion* 55, *Boy on a Dolphin, Legend of the Lost* 56, *The Key, Desire Under the Elms* 57, *Houseboat, The Black Orchid, That Kind of Woman* 58; Venice Festival Award for *The Black Orchid* 58; *It Started in Naples, Heller in Pink Tights* 60, *The Millionairess, Two Women, El Cid, Madame Sans Gêne, Yesterday, Today and Tomorrow* 63, *The Fall of the Roman Empire* 64, *Lady L* 65, *Operation Crossbow* 65, *Judith* 65, *A Countess from Hong Kong* 65, *Arabesque* 66, *More than a Miracle* 67, *The Priest's Wife* 70, *Sunflower* 70, *Hot Autumn* 71, *Man of La Mancha* 72, *Brief Encounter* (TV) 74, *The Verdict* 74, *The Voyage* 74; Cannes Film Festival Award for best actress (*Two Women*) 61.
Chalet Daniel Burgenstock, Luzern, Switzerland.

Lorente de Nó, Rapfael, M.D.; American (naturalized) physiologist; b. 8 April 1902, Zaragoza, Spain; *s.* of Francisco Lorente and Maria de Nó (de Lorente); *m.* Hede Birfield 1931; one *d.*; ed. Univ. of Madrid.
Assistant, Inst. Cajal, Madrid 21-29; Head, Dept. of Otolaryngology, Valdecilla Hospital, Santander 29-31; went to U.S. 31; neuroanatomist, Central Inst. for the Deaf, St. Louis 31-36; Assoc. physiologist, Rockefeller Inst., N.Y.C. 36-38, Assoc. mem. 38-41, mem. 41-; mem. Nat. Acad. of Sciences, American Physiological Soc., American Asscn. of Anatomists, American Neurological Soc.
Publ. *A Study of Nerve Physiology* 47 and articles in scientific journals.
32-36 Rehabilitation Center, University of California School of Medicine, Los Angeles, Calif. 90024, U.S.A.

Lorentz, Stanisław, PH.D.; Polish art historian and museum administrator; b. 28 April 1899, Radom; *s.* of Karol Lorentz and Maria Schoen; *m.* Irene Nasfeter 1927; two *d.*; ed. Warsaw Univ.
Lecturer, Vilno Univ. 29-35, Warsaw Univ. 37-39; Dir. Nat. Museum, Warsaw 35-; Dir.-in-Chief, Museums and Conservation of Monuments Dept., Ministry of Culture and Art 45-52; Extraordinary Prof. of Art History, Warsaw Univ. 47-51, Prof. 51-; mem. Parl. 65-69; Pres. Centre Int. d'Etudes pour la Conservation et la Restoration des Biens Culturales 65-70; Pres. Polish Nat. Cttees. of Int. Council of Museums and of Int. Council of Monuments and Sites, mem. Int. Exec. Cttee. of ICOM; Pres. Int. Consultative Cttee. of ICOMOS; Vice-Pres. Polish Nat. UNESCO Cttee.; Pres. Soc. of Friends of Warsaw; Corresp. mem. Polish Acad. of Sciences 52-64, mem. 64-; mem. Acad. of Fine Arts, Venice 55, Bordeaux 61; Hon. mem. Int. Union of Art Historians; Dr. h.c. (Univ. of Bordeaux) 61, (Univ. of Nancy) 66; Herder Prize 64, Polish State Prize 65, City of Kielce Cultural Prize 73; Gold Cross of Merit 36, Virtuti Militari 39, Commdr.'s Cross with Star of Order Polonia Restituta 47, Order of the Banner of Labour 1st Class 55, Order of the Builders of People's Poland 69; also has other Polish and foreign awards from Italy, France, Mexico, etc.
Publs. *Jan Krzysztof Glaubitz architekt Wileński XVIII* 37, *Natolin* 48, *Victor Louis à Varsovie* 58, *Relazioni artistiche fra l'Italia e la Polonia* 61, *Jabłonna* 61, *What remained of the Royal Palace in Warsaw* 71, *Guide to Polish Museums and Collections* 71, 74, and numerous other works in Polish, French and English.
Muzeum Narodowe, Aleje Jerozolimskie 3, 00-495 Warsaw, Poland.
Telephone: 21-10-36.

Lorentzen, Annemarie Røstvik; Norwegian politician; b. 23 Sept. 1921, Grense Jakobselv, Finnmark.
Teacher, Hammerfest Secondary School 47-49; mem. Hammerfest Municipal Council 51-63; Chair. W. Finnmark Labour Party 61-65; mem. Labour Party Nat. Exec. 61-69; mem. Norwegian Broadcasting Council 63-70, many parl. cttees.; mem. Storting (Parl.) for Finnmark 61-; mem. Standing Cttee. on Defence 69-73; Minister of Communications 73-; Labour.
Ministry of Communications, Oslo Dep., Norway.

Lorenz, Konrad, D.MED., ET. PHIL.; Austrian ethologist; b. 7 Nov. 1903, Vienna; *s.* of Adolf and Emma (née Lecher) Lorenz; *m.* Margarethe Gebhardt 1927; one *s.* two *d.*; ed. Univ. of Vienna.
Assistant Inst. of Anatomy, Vienna 28-35; Lecturer in Comparative Anatomy and Animal Psychology, Vienna 37-40; Head, Dept. of Psychology, Königsberg 40-45; Physician in the German Army 42-44; Dir. Max Planck Inst. for Physiology of Behaviour 61-73; Dir. Dept. for Animal Sociology, Inst. for Comparative Ethology, Austrian Acad. of Sciences 73-; Foreign mem. Royal Soc. (U.K.); UNESCO Kalinga Prize 70, Nobel Prize for Physiology or Medicine (jointly) 73.

Publs. *King Solomon's Ring* 52, *Man Meets Dog* 54, *Das Sogenannte Böse* 63, *Über tierisches und menschliches Verhalten* 65, *Evolution and Modification of Behaviour* 65, *On Aggression* 66, *Studies in Animal and Human Behaviour I* 69, *II* 71, *Man and Animal* 72, *Civilized Man's Eight Deadly Sins* 74.

Institut für Vergleichende Verhaltensforschung, Abt. 4 Tiersoziologie, 3422 Altenberg, Adolf-Lorenz-Gasse 2, Austria.

Loridan, Walter, DR. POL. SC.; Belgian diplomatist; b. 22 Feb. 1909; ed. Brussels Univ.

Secretary Belgian Legation, Warsaw 36; Chargé d'Affaires, Spain 37-39, Mexico 40-43; Personal Asst. to the Minister of Foreign Affairs 44-47; Prof. Brussels Univ. 45; Dir.-Gen. Political Dept., Ministry of Foreign Affairs 48-51; Minister to Mexico 51-54; Amb. to Mexico 54-55; Amb. to U.S.S.R. 55-59; Perm. Rep. to UN 59-65; Amb. to German Fed. Repub. 65-69; Amb. to U.S.A. 69-74.

12 rue des Quatre Bras, B-1000 Brussels, Belgium.

Losey, Joseph, B.A., M.A.; American film and theatre director; b. 1909, La Crosse, Wis.; s. of Joseph Walton and Ina Higbee Losey; m. four times; two s.; ed. Dartmouth Coll., New Hampshire, and Harvard Graduate School of Arts and Science.

Freelance journalist 31; stage manager, later theatre producer-dir., Broadway 32-40; dir. of radio documentaries 38-; film director 38-; settled in U.K. 55; numerous film awards; Chevalier Ordre des Arts et des Lettres 68, Hon. D. Hum. Litt., Dartmouth Coll., U.S.A. 73.

Leisure interests: teaching, work, walking.

Films include: *A Child went Forth* 41, *The Boy with Green Hair* 48, *The Lawless* (English title *The Dividing Line*) 49, *The Prowler* 50, *M* 50, *The Big Night* 51, *The Sleeping Tiger* 54, *Time Without Pity* 56, *Chance Meeting* (English title *Blind Date*) 59, *The Criminal* 60, *The Damned* 61, *The Servant* 63, *King and Country* 64, *Modesty Blaise* 65, *Accident* 66, *Boom* 67, *Secret Ceremony* 68, *The Go Between* (Grand Prix, Cannes Film Festival 71), *The Assassination of Trotsky* 72, *A Doll's House* 73, *Galileo* 73, *The Romantic Englishwoman* 75; plays include: *Galileo*, *The Wooden Dish*.

c/o Ziegler-Ross Agency, 9255 Sunset Boulevard, Los Angeles, Calif. 90069, U.S.A.; Chatto & Linnit Ltd., 113-117 Wardour Street, London, W.1, England.

Loshchenkov, Fyodor Ivanovich; Soviet politician; ed. Moscow Inst. of Aviation and C.P.S.U. Cttee. Higher Party School.

Industrial worker 32-36; Soviet Army service 36-38; Student 38-43; Engineer 43-46; mem. C.P.S.U. 43-; Party Official 46-61; First Sec. Yaroslavl Regional Cttee. C.P.S.U. and Alt. mem. C.P.S.U. Central Cttee. 61-; Deputy to U.S.S.R. Supreme Soviet 62-; mem. Comm. for Industry, Soviet of the Union.

Yaroslavl Regional Committee, Communist Party of the Soviet Union, Yaroslavl, U.S.S.R.

Losonczi, Pál; Hungarian politician; b. 18 Sept. 1919, Bolhó, County Somogy.

Agricultural labourer; mem. Communist Party 45-; set up Red Star Co-operative Farm, Barcs 48; mem. of Parliament 53-; Minister of Agriculture 60-67; Chair. Nat. Council of Co-operative Farms 65-67; Pres. of Presidential Council (Head of State) 67-; mem. Central Cttee. Hungarian Socialist Workers' Party, Political Cttee. 75-; mem. Presidium of Nat. Council of Patriotic People's Front; Kossuth Prize 56; Hero of Socialist Labour and Order of Hungarian People's Repub. 54.

The Presidential Council, H-1357 Budapest, Kossuth tér, Hungary.

Telephone: 121-754.

Lotz, Kurt; German business executive; b. 18 Sept. 1912, Lenderscheid; m. Elizabeth Lony; two s. one d.; ed. August-Vilmar-Schule, Homberg.

Joined Brown Boveri and Cie. 46, mem. of Management Board 57, Chair. of Management Board 58; mem. Board of Dirs. A. G. Brown Boveri & Cie., Baden, Switzerland (parent company) 61, Del. mem. Board of Dirs. 63; Deputy Chair. Management Board Volkswagenwerk A.G. June 67-April 68, Chair. May 68-71; mem. Volkswagen Foundation, Foundation for Furtherment of Science in Germany; Adviser, environmental protection; Hon. Senator Heidelberg Univ.; Dr. rer. pol. h.c. (Wirtschaftshochschule, Mannheim) 62, Hon. Prof. Brunswick Technical Univ. 70.

69 Heidelberg, Ludolf-Krehl-Strasse 35, Federal Republic of Germany.

Telephone: 06221-40785.

Loubatières, Auguste Louis; French professor of pharmacology and pharmacodynamics; b. 28 Dec. 1912, Agde, Hérault; s. of Felix Loubatières and Jeanne Vernière; m. 1st Suzette Vivarès 1939 (died 1957), three d.; m. 2nd Marie-Madeleine Mariani 1972; ed. Coll. d'Agde, Univs. of Montpellier and Marseilles.

Assistant Lecturer in Physiology, Univ. of Montpellier 41-44, Lecturer 44-46, Prof. 46-52, Prof. of Applied Physiology and Pharmocodynamics 52-66, Pharmacology and Pharmacodynamics 66-; mem. Institut de France, Académie des Sciences, Acad. of Sciences of New York, Nat. Acad. of Medicine of Buenos Aires, Royal Soc. of Medicine of London, Acad. Nat. de Médecine de Paris, Acad. Nat. de Pharmacie de Paris, Soc. of Biology, Soc. of Biological Chemistry, and Soc. of Therapeutics and Pharmacodynamics; Corresp. mem. Acad. Royale de Médecine de Belgique; Hon. mem. British Diabetic Asscn., Purkinje Medical Soc., Prague, European Soc. for Study of Diabetes; Vice-Pres. Foundation for French Medical Research; French rep. at Advisory Panel on the CIBA Foundation (London); numerous scientific and cultural missions overseas; Chevalier Légion d'Honneur, Officier Ordre du Mérite, Officier d'Académie, Officier des Palmes Académiques.

Major research: Discovery of the Cardiotonic and Cardio-Analeptic Actions of Heptaminol 48, Discovery of the action and mechanism of action of Hypoglycaemic and antidiabetic Sulphonamides 42-67.

Leisure interests: music and painting.

Publs. about 350 publications on physiology, pharmacology and fundamentals of applied pharmacodynamics.

Institut de Biologie, boulevard Henri IV, 34 Montpellier; and Allée des Sophoras, Résidence des Sophoras, 34 Montpellier, France.

Telephone: Montpellier 72-21-52 and 92-41-74.

Loubser, J. G. H., B.SC.ENG.; South African mechanical engineer; b. 14 Jan. 1920, Koeberg, Cape Prov.; s. of late Dr. M. M. Loubser; m. Maria Johanna Catharina Du Preez 1946; one s. two d.; ed. Univ. of the Witwatersrand.

Joined South African Railways 42; Chief Stores Superintendent 62-64, Asst. Chief Mechanical Engineer 64-66, Chief Mechanical Engineer 66-68, Head, Planning and Productivity 68, Deputy Gen. Man. 69-70, Gen. Man. 70-; mem. Prime Minister's Econ. and Planning Advisory Councils; mem. Energy Policy Cttee.; full mem. S.A. Acad. for Arts and Science; Councillor S.A. Council for Professional Engineers, S.A. Bureau of Standards; senior mem. Engineers' Asscn. of South Africa, Pres. 71; mem. American Asscn. of Mechanical Engineers; Hon. Prof. Rand Afrikaans Univ.

Leisure interests: home workshop, photography, high-fidelity records.

Room 1114, Paul Kruger Building, Johannesburg; Home: 18 Daventry Road, Bryanston, Transvaal, Republic of South Africa.

Telephone: 713-2100 (Office); 706-3720 (Home).

Louchheim, Katie S.; American government official; b. 28 Dec. 1903, New York; d. of Leonard B. and

Adele Scofield (née Joseph); *m.* Walter C. Louchheim 1926; two *d.*; ed. Rosemary Hall, and Columbia Univ. Assistant to Dir. of Public Information, UNRRA 42-46; Democratic Nat. Committeewoman D.C. 56-61; Dir. Women's Activities, Democratic Nat. Cttee. 53-60; Vice-Chair. Democratic Nat. Cttee. 56-60; Special Consultant to Promote the Role of Women in Int. Cultural Exchange Matters, State Dept. 61-62; Dep. Asst. Sec. of State for Public Affairs 62-63; mem. Defense Advisory Cttee. on Women in the Armed Services 55-62; Deputy Asst. Sec. of State for Community Advisory Services 64-66, for Educational and Cultural Affairs 66-69; American Nat. Red Cross 66-; mem. Arthur and Elizabeth Schlesinger Library on History of Women in America, Radcliffe Coll. 64-; mem. First Lady's Cttee. on Beautification 65-68; Chair. Fed. Woman's Award 62-68; U.S. mem. Exec. Board with rank of Amb., UNESCO, Paris 68-69; Hon. D.Lit. Drexel Inst. of Technology 64; Hon. D.Hum.Litt. Franklin Pierce Coll. 67.

Leisure interest: writing poetry and articles for magazines.

Publs. *With or Without Roses* (poems) 66, *By the Political Sea* 70.

2824 O Street, N.W., Washington, D.C. 20007, U.S.A. Telephone: 212-337-1096.

Loudon, Jonkheer John Hugo; Netherlands oil executive; b. 27 June 1905; ed. Univ. of Utrecht. Joined N.V. De Bataafsche Petroleum Mij., The Hague 30, served Venezuela, The Hague, U.S.A. 30-44; Gen. Man. Royal Dutch/Shell interests, Venezuela 44-47; Man. Dir. Royal Dutch Petroleum Co., N.V. De Bataafsche Petroleum Mij., Shell Petroleum Co. Ltd. 47; Pres. Royal Dutch Petroleum Co. 52-65, Chair. 65-; Chair. Board Shell Oil Co. U.S.A. 57-65; Chair. Shell Petroleum N.V. 66-, Int. Advisory Cttee., Chase Manhattan Bank 65-; Dir. other companies; Hon. K.B.E. (U.K.), Knight, Order of Netherlands Lion; Order of Liberator (Venezuela).

35 Grosvenor Square, London, W.1, England; Koekoeksduin, Aerdenhout, Netherlands.

Lougheed, (Edgar) Peter, LL.B., M.B.A., Q.C.; Canadian politician; b. 26 July 1928, Calgary, Alberta; s. of late Edgar D. and Edna (Bauld) Lougheed; *m.* Jeanne Rogers 1952; two *s.* two *d.*; ed. public and secondary schools, Calgary, Univ. of Alberta and Harvard Univ. Secretary, Mannix Co. 56, Gen. Counsel 58, Vice-Pres. 59, Dir. 60-62; private legal practice 62-; Provincial Leader, Progressive Conservative Party of Alberta 65-; mem. Provincial Parl. 67-; Leader of Opposition 67-71; Premier of Alberta Sept. 71-.

Leisure interests: skiing, golf, the symphony.

Office: 307 Legislative Building, Edmonton, Alberta T5K 2B6, Canada.

Telephone: 425-1610 (Office).

Loughran, James; British conductor; b. 30 June 1931, Glasgow; s. of James and Agnes (née Fox) Loughran; *m.* Nancy (née Coggon) 1961; two *s.*; ed. Glasgow, Bonn, Amsterdam and Milan.

Associate Conductor, Bournemouth Symphony Orchestra 61-65; début Royal Opera House, Covent Garden 64; Principal Conductor BBC Scottish Symphony Orchestra 65-70; Principal Conductor and Musical Adviser, Hallé Orchestra 70-; début New York Philharmonic with Westminster Choir 72; First Prize, Philharmonia Orchestra Conducting Competition 61.

Leisure interest: unwinding.

Hallé Concerts Society, 30 Cross Street, Manchester, England.

Telephone: 061-834-8363.

Louis, Pierre, D. ès L.; French professor and university official; b. 1 Aug. 1913; ed. Lycée Henri IV, Univ. of Paris and Fondation Thiers.

Former Dir. of Studies, Faculty of Letters, Rennes, Faculty of Letters, Lyon; fmr. Prof., Faculty of Letters, Lyon; fmr. Rector, Académie de Clermont-Ferrand; Rector, Acad. of Lyon 60-; Officier de la Légion d'Honneur, Commandeur Ordre des Palmes Académiques.

Académie de Lyon, 30 rue Cavenne, 69007 Lyon, France.

Lourie, Arthur, M.A., LL.B.; Israeli diplomatist (retd.); b. 10 March 1903, Johannesburg, South Africa; *m.* Jeannette Leibel; one *s.* one *d.*; ed. Cambridge and Harvard Univs.

Lecturer in Roman-Dutch Law, Witwatersrand Univ. 27-32; Political Sec. Jewish Agency for Palestine, London 33; Dir. UN Office, Jewish Agency 47; Consul-Gen. of Israel, New York and Deputy Head, Perm. Del. to UN 48-53; Asst. Dir.-Gen. Ministry for Foreign Affairs 53-57; Amb. on Special Mission to Emperor of Ethiopia 56; Amb. to Canada 57-59; Chair. Del. UN Gen. Assembly 59; Amb. to U.K. 60-65; Deputy Dir.-Gen. Ministry of Foreign Affairs 66-72; Political Adviser to Minister of Foreign Affairs 72-75.

Ministry of Foreign Affairs, Jerusalem, Israel.

Louw, Adriaan, B.SC.; South African mining executive; b. 26 Nov. 1920, Pretoria; s. of late Dr. and Mrs. A. H. Louw; *m.* E. Rosemarie Philcox 1947; two *s.*; ed. Univ. of Witwatersrand.

Served as pilot, S.A. Air Force, World War II; Gen. Man. West Driefontein Gold Mining Co. Ltd. 61-62; Consulting Engineer, Gold Fields of South Africa Ltd. 63-64, Man. Head Office 64-65; currently Chair. of Gold Fields of S.A. Ltd., Gold Fields Mining and Devt. Ltd. and Gold Fields S. A. Holdings Ltd., West Driefontein Gold Mining Co. Ltd.; Dir. Consolidated Gold Fields Ltd., East Driefontein Gold Mining Co. Ltd. and numerous other mining cos.; mem. S.A. Inst. of Mining and Metallurgy 63, Council of Chamber of Mines of S.A.

Leisure interests: golf, tennis, swimming.

Gold Fields of South Africa Ltd., P.O. Box 1167, Johannesburg; Home: 3 Fife Avenue, Clynton (Hurlingham), Sandton, Republic of South Africa.

Telephone: 836-0913, 838-8381 (Office); 33-8544 (Home).

Louw, Dr. Martinus Smuts (Tinie); South African businessman; b. 15 Aug. 1888, Ladismith, Karoo; ed. Stellenbosch Univ.

Teacher, Pietermaritzburg, Ladybrand, later Vice-Principal; teacher in Paarl; joined South African Nat. Life Assurance Co. Ltd. (S.A.N.L.A.M.) June 18 as asst. to actuary; attended Edinburgh Univ., Britain 18-21; appointed actuary, S.A.N.L.A.M. 21, later Manager; Man. Dir. Nov. 46-Dec. 49; ordinary Dir. Dec. 49-66; actuary and Gen. Man., African Homes Trust Assurance Co. 35-45; Hon. Vice-Pres., S.A.N.L.A.M. 66-; connected with the founding of Federale Volksbeleggings Beperk, Bonusbeleggingskorporasie van Suid-Afrika Beperk, Sentrale Nywerheidsaksepbank Beperk and Federale Mynbou Bpk; first Man. Dir. of Bonuskor; Chair., Bonuskor and Saambou 47-; Dir., Industrial Devt. Corpn.; fmr. Chair., Central Accepting Bank, Coloured Investment Corpn.; fmr. Dir., Santam; fmr. mem., Council for Scientific and Industrial Research, Board of Stellenbosch Univ., Trustee of South Africa Foundation and Nat. Cancer Soc.; Pres., Inst. for Admin. and Commerce 49; Foundation mem., later Pres., Afrikaans Chambers of Commerce; awarded Frans du Toit prize 61, Hendrik Verwoerd prize 65.

c/o Bonuskor, Sanlam Centre, Foreshore, Cape Town, South Africa.

Love, George Hutchinson; American business executive; b. Sept. 4 1900; s. of Joseph E. Love and Sara Elizabeth Jennings; *m.* 1929; one *s.* two *d.*

Chairman of Board Consolidation Coal Co., M. A. Hanna Co.; Chair. Exec. Cttee. of Chrysler Corpn. until 66; Dir. Hanna Mining Co., Bradford Computer and Systems Inc., Gen. Adjustment Bureau; Chair. Amer. European Asscn.; Hon. LL.D. (Washington and Jefferson Coll., West Virginia Univ., Bethany Coll., Carnegie Inst. of Technology, Colgate Univ.).
Leisure interests: golf, shooting, swimming, fishing.
5920 Braeburn Place, Pittsburgh, Pa., U.S.A.

Love, John A., LL.B.; American lawyer and politician; b. 29 Nov. 1916; ed. Cheyenne Mountain School and Denver Univ.
United States Naval Air Force 42-45; legal practice, Love, Cole and Mullett, Colorado Springs 45-63; Gov. of Colorado 63-73; Head Energy Policy Office June-Dec. 73; mem. Colorado State Republican Cen. Cttee., American Bar Asscn.
400 East 8th Avenue, Denver, Colo. 80203, U.S.A.

Loveday, George Arthur, M.A., T.D.; fmr. British stock exchange chairman; b. 13 May 1909, Iquique, Chile; s. of Arthur Frederic Loveday and Mary Cornelia Backus; m. 1st Sylvia Mary Gibbs 1935 (died 1967), two s.; m. 2nd Penelope Elton Dugdale Cunard 1967; ed. Winchester Coll. and Magdalen Coll., Oxford Univ.
Active in industry and commerce 32-39; served World War II, Royal Artillery, commissioned 40, Maj. 41; mem. London Stock Exchange 46, Council mem. 61-71, Deputy Chair. 71, Chair. 73-75; Partner, Read Hurst-Brown and Co. 48-.
Leisure interests: gardening, golf.
Office: c/o The Stock Exchange, London, E.C.2; Home: Bushton Manor, Bushton, Swindon, Wilts. SN4 7PX. England.
Telephone: Broad Hinton 246.

Loveday, Harold Maxwell, M.B.E.; Australian diplomatist; b. 12 Sept. 1923, Sydney; s. of R. T. Loveday; m. Cynthia Nelson 1962; one s. one d.; ed. Sydney Univ. and Canberra Univ. Coll.
Joined Dept. of Foreign Affairs as a career Foreign Service Officer 45; served in Shanghai and Nanking 46-50, Bonn and Berlin 53-54; Rep. in Korea 54-55; served in Kuala Lumpur 55-56, 64; Counsellor, Embassy in Washington, D.C. 59-62; Australian Commr., South Pacific Comm. 62-66; Asst. Sec. Dept. of Foreign Affairs 66-69; Amb. and Perm. Rep. to UN Office in Geneva 69-72; Acting Dir.-Gen. Australian Devt. Assistance Agency 73-74; High Commr. to Canada 75-.
Leisure interests: tennis, golf, skiing.
c/o Department of Foreign Affairs, Canberra, A.C.T. 2600, Australia.

Loveless, Herschel Cellel; American politician; b. 5 May 1911, Hedrick, Iowa; s. of David Helm and Ethel (Beaver) Loveless; m. Amelia Rebecca Howard 1933; one s. one d.; ed. high school.
Worked with Chicago, Milwaukee, St. Paul and Pacific Railway 27-39 and 44-47 and with John Morrell and Co.. Ottumwa, Ia. 39-44; Supt. of Streets City of Ottumwa 47-49 and Mayor 49-53; Owner-Man. Municipal Equipment Co., Ottumwa 53-56; Gov. of Iowa 57-61; mem. Renegotiation Board 61-69; Corporate Vice-Pres. Chromalloy Amer. Corpn. 69-; mem. Exec. Council of Governors' Conf. San Juan, Puerto Rico 59; Chair. Advisory Cttee. on Agriculture, Dem. Nat. Advisory Council 59; Chair. Rules Cttee. 60.
Leisure interests: sports, cabinet making, antique collecting.
7523 17th Street, N.W., Washington, D.C. 20012, U.S.A.
Telephone: 202-723-9372.

Lovell, Sir (Alfred Charles) Bernard, Kt., F.R.S., O.B.E., PH.D., M.SC.; British radio astronomer; b. 31 Aug. 1913, Oldland Common, Glos.; s. of Gilbert and Emily Laura Lovell (née Adams); m. Mary Joyce Chesterman 1937; two s. three d.; ed. Bristol Univ.
Assistant Lecturer in Physics, Univ. of Manchester 36-

39; with Telecommunications Research Est. 39-45; Lecturer in Physics, Univ. of Manchester 45-47, Senior Lecturer 47-49, Reader 49-51, Prof. of Radio Astronomy 51-; Dir. Nuffield Radio Astronomy Laboratories, Jodrell Bank 51-; Fellow, Royal Soc. 55; Hon. Foreign mem. American Acad. of Arts and Sciences 55, Hon. mem. N.Y. Acad. of Sciences 60; Pres. Royal Astronomical Soc. 69-71, British Asscn. 74-75; Royal Medal of Royal Soc. 60; mem. Aeronautical Research Council 55-58, Science Research Council 65-70; Hon. Fellow, Royal Swedish Acad. 62, Inst. of Electrical Engineers 67, Inst. of Physics 75; Daniel and Florence Guggenheim Int. Astronautics Award 61; Ordre du Mérite pour la Recherche et l'Invention 62; Polish Order of Merit 75; Maitland Silver Medal, Inst. of Structural Engineers 64; Churchill Gold Medal, Soc. of Engineers 64; LL.D. (Edinburgh, Calgary), D.Sc. (Leicester, Leeds 66, Bath 67, London 67, Bristol 70), D.Univ. (Stirling 74, Surrey 75).
Publs. *Science and Civilisation* 39, *World Power Resources and Social Development* 45, *Radio Astronomy* 52, *Meteor Astronomy* 54, *The Exploration of Space by Radio* 57, *The Individual and the Universe* (The Reith Lectures 58), *The Exploration of Outer Space* 62, *Discovering the Universe* 63, *Our Present Knowledge of the Universe* 67; Editor (with Tom Margerison) *The Explosion of Science: The Physical Universe* 67, *The Story of Jodrell Bank* 68, *The Origins and International Economics of Space Exploration* 73, *Out of the Zenith: Jodrell Bank 1957-1970* 73, *Man's Relation to the Universe* 75.
Nuffield Radio Astronomy Laboratories, Jodrell Bank, Macclesfield, Cheshire; Home: The Quinta, Swettenham, Nr. Congleton, Cheshire, England.
Telephone: Lower Withington 321.

Lovell, James A., Jr.; American astronaut; b. 25 March 1928, Cleveland, Ohio; m. Marilyn Gerlach; two s. two d.; ed. Wisconsin Univ., U.S. Naval Acad.
After graduation received flight training; served four years as test pilot at Naval Air Test Center, Patuxent River, Md.; program manager for F4H weapon system evaluation; graduated from Aviation Safety School, Univ. of S. Calif.; later flight instructor and safety officer, Fighter Squadron 101, Naval Air Station, Oceana, Va.; selected by NASA as astronaut 62; pilot of *Gemini VII* Mission 65; backup pilot *Gemini IV* Mission 65; backup command pilot *Gemini IX* Mission 66; command pilot *Gemini XII* Mission 66; navigator *Apollo VIII* Mission Dec. 68; Commdr. *Apollo XIII* Mission April 70; Deputy Dir. Science and Applications Directorate, NASA Manned Spacecraft Center 71-73; Senior Exec. Vice-Pres. Bay Houston Towing Co. 73-; NASA Exceptional Service Medal; Harmon Int. Trophy 66; American Astronautical Soc. Achievement Award; Medal of Freedom 70, Grand Medallion Award, Aero Club France 72.
Leisure interests: golf, swimming, handball, tennis.
Bay Houston Towing Co., Houston, Tex. 77058, U.S.A.

Lovell, Leopold, B.A., LL.B.; Swazi (British) advocate; b. 21 May 1907, Willowmore, S. Africa; s. of late Max and Gertrude Lovell; m. 1st Winifred Kusner 1931 (died 1974), 2nd Pondy Galgut 1975; three d.; ed. Grey Inst., Port Elizabeth, Rhodes Univ. Coll., Grahamstown, and Univ. of S. Africa.
Judge's Registrar, Grahamstown 28-29; Attorney, Benoni, Transvaal 31-61; war service, with rank of Capt. in South African Air Force 40-45; M.P. (Labour Party), Benoni 49-58; Attorney, Swaziland 61-66; Advocate of Swaziland High Court 67; M.P. and Minister for Finance, Swaziland 67-72; Chair. Swaziland Sugar Quota Board 74-.
Leisure interests: golf, reading, writing.
P.O. Box 595, Scott Street, Mbabane, Swaziland.
Telephone: 2537.

Lovering, Thomas Seward, PH.D; American economic geologist and geochemist; b. 12 May 1896, St. Paul, Minn.; s. of Thomas D. and Estelle Wilcox Lovering; m. (Alexina) Corinne Gray 1919; one s.; ed. Minnesota School of Mines and Univ. of Minn.

Instructor in Geology, Univ. of Ariz. 24-25; Geologist, U.S. Geological Survey 25-34; Prof. of Econ. Geology, Univ. of Mich. 34-47 (on leave for special investigations 42-46); geologist and geochemist, U.S. Geol. Survey 47-65; Prof. of Econ. Geology, Univ. of Ariz. 66-; Visiting Prof., Univs. of Minn., Ariz., Texas and Utah 65-70; mem. Nat. Acad. of Sciences (mem. Cttee. on Resources and Man 67-69); Pres. Geol. Soc. of America 51; U.S. del. to several int. confs.; Distinguished Service Gold Medal (U.S. Dept. of Interior) 59; Achievement Award, Gold Medal (Univ. of Minn.) 60; Jackling Award and Jackling Lecturer, American Inst. of Mining Engineers 65; Penrose Gold Medal, Soc. of Economic Geologists 65.

Leisure interests: wood and metal working, riding, birding, chess.

Publs. Over 150 publications on geochemical, geophysical and geological topics.

9560 West Ernst Avenue, Lakewood, Colo. 80226, U.S.A.

Lovett, Robert Abercrombie; American banker and railroad executive; b. 14 Sept. 1895; ed. Yale and Harvard Univs.

Clerk, Nat. Bank of Commerce, New York City 21; partner, Brown Brothers, Harriman and Co. 26-40, 46-47, 49-50; Special Asst. to Sec. of War Dec. 40-April 41; Asst. Sec. of War for Air 41-45; Under-Sec. of State 47-49; Deputy Sec. of Defense 50-51, Sec. of Defense 51-53; Gen. Partner, Brown Brothers, Harriman and Co. 53-; Special Adviser to Pres. Kennedy 61-63; dir. several financial orgs.; Navy Cross 19; Distinguished Service Medal 45; U.S. Presidential Medal of Freedom 63.

Locust Valley, Long Island, N.Y. 11560; and 59 Wall Street, New York, N.Y. 10005, U.S.A.

Lovinescu, Horia, D.ES.L.; Romanian theatre director and playwright; b. 20 Aug. 1917, Fălticeni; ed. Universitatea Bucureşti.

First Press Attaché for Cultural Relations 48-63; Dir. Nottara Theatre, Bucharest 64-; Vice-Pres. Romanian P.E.N. Club 63-, Theatre Council 63-; mem. Leading Board of Writers' Union 65-; State Prize and other Romanian awards.

Publs. *Jean Arthur Rimbaud* (critical study); Plays: *Citadela Sfărîmată* (Destroyed Citadel) 54, *Hanul de la Rascruce* (Inn at the Crossroad) 55, *Surorile Boga* (Boga Sisters) 57, *Mai Presus de Toate* (Above All) 59, *Febre* (Feber) 60, *Omul care si-a Pierdut Omenia* (The Man Who Lost his Humanity) 61, *Paradisul* (The Paradise) 62, *Moartea Unui Artist* (The Death of an Artist) 64, *Locţiitorul* (The Man Instead) 66.

C.I. Nottara Theatre, 20 Bulevardul Magheru, Bucharest, Romania.

Lovo-Cordero, Alfonso; Nicaraguan senator, businessman, lawyer and politician; b. 11 June 1927, Ocotal Nueva Segovia; s. of Alfonso Lovo-Moncada and Esperanza Cordero de Lovo; m. Teresita Blandón 1950; three s. one d.; ed. Instituto Pedagógico de Diriamba, Monroe High School, Rochester, U.S.A., Rochester Business Institute, U.S.A., Cornell Univ., Univ. Nacional de Nicaragua.

Minister of Agriculture and Livestock 67-72, mem. Nat. Gov. Council 72-74; Pres. Int. Cttee. Regional Agricultural Health (CIRSA) 67; chief of Nicaraguan del. to Panama 68; Pres. Panamanian Union Ad-Hoc Cttee. of Latin American banana producing countries, Washington, U.S.A. 67; Pres. Panamerican Meeting of Ministers of Agriculture on Foot and Mouth and Animal Disease Control, Washington, 68, 69, 70;

Vice-Pres. FAO Reg. Conf. for Latin America 68; Vice-Pres. Latin American Del. to XVth FAO Council 69; Nicaraguan Del. to Int. Coffee Council 70; Vice-Pres. Latin American Del. to 2nd FAO World Food Congress 70; Pres. Nicaraguan Del. to Int. Cotton Council 70; Vice-Pres. Latin American Del. to VIth FAO Conference; has occupied numerous senior posts in Nicaragua including Pres. Nat. Inst. Home and Foreign Trade, Pres. Nat. Cotton Comm., Vice- Pres. Agrarian Inst., Vice-Pres. Coffee Inst., mem. board Inst. Nat. Devt. (INFONAC); currently mem. Board of Dirs., Banco Nicaragüense, Booth of Nicaragua, QUINSA, INDESA, mem. exec. board Nicaraguan Devt. Inst. (INDE), Dir. exec. board Nicaraguan Devt. Foundation (FUNDE); founder and Pres. Propulsora Agrícola Industrial S.A.; Dir. Compañía Nacional de Seguros, Financiera de la Vivienda, Exportadora Agrícola S.A.; Senator 75-; Gran Cruz Placa de Plata de Rubén Darío (Nicaragua) 70, Order of the Brilliant Star 70, Order of the Propitious Cloud (China) 74, Cruz de Bocaya (Colombia) 74, and other decorations.

Leisure interests: sailing, reading, horse riding.

Managua, Nicaragua.

Telephone: 60606 (Office); 23070 (Home).

Low, Alan Roberts, M.A.; New Zealand banker; b. 11 Jan. 1916, Blenheim; s. of Benjamin and Sarah Low; m. Kathleen Mary Harrow 1940; one s. two d.; ed. Timaru Boys' High School and Canterbury Univ. Coll.

Joined Reserve Bank of New Zealand 38; Mil. Service 42-44; Econ. Adviser, Reserve Bank of New Zealand 51, Asst. Gov. 60-62, Deputy Gov. 62-67, Gov. 67-; Past Pres. New Zealand Asscn. of Economists.

Leisure interests: gardening, music.

Reserve Bank of New Zealand, P.O. Box 2498, 2 The Terrace, Wellington, New Zealand.

Telephone: Wellington 722-029.

Low, Francis Eugene, B.S., M.S., PH.D.; American physicist; b. 27 Oct. 1921, New York; s. of Bela Low and Eugenia Ingerman Low; m. Natalie Sadigur 1948; three c.; ed. Harvard Coll. and Columbia Univ.

Assistant and Assoc. Prof., Univ. of Ill. 52-57; Prof. of Physics, Mass. Inst. of Technology 57-67; Karl Taylor Compton Prof. of Physics, Mass. Inst. of Technology 68-, Dir. Center for Theoretical Physics 73-; Guggenheim and Fulbright Fellow; Loeb Lecturer, Harvard Univ.; mem. Nat. Acad. of Sciences, Amer. Acad. of Arts and Sciences.

Leisure interests: piano, composing music, skiing, tennis, flying, problems of impact of science on society.

Room 6-313, Department of Physics, Massachusetts Institute of Technology, Cambridge, Mass. 02139; 28 Adams Street, Belmont, Mass. 02178, U.S.A.

Telephone: Ivanhoe 4-1889.

Low, George Michael; American space scientist; b. 10 June 1926, Vienna, Austria; s. of Arthur and Gertrude Low; m. Mary Ruth McNamara 1949; three s. two d.; ed. Rensselaer Polytechnic Inst., Troy, New York.

National Advisory Cttee. for Aeronautics 49-58, research on Aerodynamic Heating, Boundary Layer Theory, Internal Aerodynamics, Space Technology, Chief of Special Projects Branch 56-58; Nat. Aeronautics and Space Admin. (NASA) 58-63, assisted with Mercury, Gemini and Apollo manned space flight programmes as Deputy Assoc. Administrator for Manned Space Flight; Deputy Dir. NASA Manned Spacecraft Center 64-67; Man. Apollo Spacecraft Programme, NASA 67-69; Deputy Admin. NASA 69-; Fellow, Amer. Inst. of Aeronautics and Astronautics; Dir. Nat. Aeronautics Asscn.; Hon. mem. Aerospace Medical Asscn.; Trustee, Rensselaer Polytechnic Inst.; Nat. Aeronautics and Space Agency's Outstanding Leadership Medal 62, Arthur S. Flemming Award 63; Amer. Astronautical Soc. Space Flight Award 68; NASA Distinguished Ser-

vice Medal 69; Nat. Space Club Astronautics Engineer Award 70; Nat. Space Club Robert H. Goddard Memorial Trophy 73; Nat. Civil Service League Career Service Award for Sustained Excellence 73; Hon. D. Eng. (Rensselaer Polytechnic Inst.) 69, Hon. D.Sc. (Univ. of Florida) 69; Rockefeller Public Service Award for Admin. 74.
Leisure interests: boating, water skiing, scuba diving.
National Aeronautics and Space Administration, Washington, D.C. 20546; Home: 1515 Highwood Drive, Arlington, Va. 22207, U.S.A.
Telephone: 202-755-3886.

Lowell, Ralph, A.B.; American banker; b. 23 July 1890; ed. Harvard Univ.
Joined firm of Curtis and Sanger 13; with First Nat. Bank of Boston 16-17; served in U.S. Army (Lieut.-Col.) 17-19; with Lee, Higginson and Co. 19-32; joined Clark, Dodge and Co. 32, Partner 37-43; Chair. Boston Safe Deposit and Trust Co. 43-46, Pres. 46-59, Board Chair. 59-66; trustee numerous organizations; Dir. Nat. Fund for Medical Educ.; Pres. Museum of Fine Arts; Fellow, American Acad. Arts and Sciences; Hon. LL.D. (Harvard Univ., Northeastern Univ. and Bates Coll., Boston Coll., Boston Univ., Brandeis Univ., Emerson Coll.), Hon. D.Sc. (Lowell Technicological Inst.), Hon. L.H.D. (Tufts Univ.).
1 Boston Place, Boston, Mass. 02110; Home: 214 Fox Hill Street, Westwood, Mass. 02193, U.S.A.

Lowell, Robert (Traill Spence), Jr., A.B.; American poet and playwright; b. 1 March 1917, Boston, Mass.; s. of Robert and Charlotte (Winslow) Lowell; m. 1st Jean Stafford 1940 (div. 1948); m. 2nd Elizabeth Hardwick 1949, one d.; ed. Kenyon Coll., Ohio, and Harvard Univ.
Guggenheim Fellow and Consultant in Poetry, Library of Congress 47-48; Prof. of Literature, Essex Univ., England 70-72; Pulitzer Prize and American Acad. of Arts and Letters Prize 47; Winner Nat. Book Award 59; Pulitzer Prize for *The Dolphin* 74.
Publs. *Land of Unlikeness* 44, *Lord Weary's Castle* 46, *The Mills of the Kavanaughs* 51, *Life Studies: New Poems and an Autobiographical Fragment* 59, *Imitations* 61, *The Old Glory* (play) 64, *For the Union Dead* 64, *Benito Cereno* (play) 67, *Near the Ocean* 67, *The Voyage* (poems) 68, *Prometheus Bound* 70, *Notebook* (poems) 70, *History* 73, *For Lizzie and Harriet* 73, *The Dolphin* (poems) 73.
c/o Faber & Faber Ltd., 3 Queen Square, London, W.C.1, England.

Löwenthal-Chlumecky, Max, LL.D.; Austrian diplomatist; b. 1908, Lussinpiccolo; s. of Dr. Josef and the late Alice Löwenthal-Chlumecky (née Türk von Karlovacgrad); m. Else von dem Bussche-Haddenhausent; one d.; ed. Vienna Univ.
Entered foreign service, served Prague 32-34, Paris 35, Federal Chancellery, Ministry of Foreign Affairs 35-38; with Continentale Motorschiffahrts A.G. 41-45; re-entered Fed. Chancellery, Ministry of Foreign Affairs 45-52, Head Dept. of Political Economy 47; Amb. to U.S.A. 52-54, to Argentina 54-55, to Italy 55-74, concurrently Minister to Tunisia 59-67, and Libya 61-68.
c/o Ministry of Foreign Affairs, Vienna, Austria.

Lower, Arthur R. M., C.C., M.A., PH.D., F.R.S.C.; Canadian university professor and writer; b. 1889; s. of Frederick J. Lower and Sarah A. Smith; m. Evelyn Marion Smith 1920; one d.; ed. Barrie Collegiate Inst., Barrie, Ontario, Toronto and Harvard Univs.
War Service, Navy 16-19; Head, Dept. of History, United Coll., Univ. of Manitoba 29; Douglas Prof. of Canadian History, Queen's Univ. 47-59, Prof. Emer. 59-; Visiting Prof. Univ. of Wisconsin 55-56, Univ. of Glasgow 67; Senior Fellowship Canada Council 59-60; Pres. Royal Soc. of Canada 61-62; various honorary degrees and medals.

Leisure interests: reading, writing, conversation, travelling, splitting wood, making maple syrup, cruising on Lake Ontario, swimming, enjoying autumn foliage in the woods.
Publs. *Documents in Canadian Economic History* (with others) 33, *Settlement and the Forest Frontier in Eastern Canada* 36, *The North American Assault on the Canadian Forest* 38, *Canada and the Far East* 40, *Colony to Nation: a History of Canada* 46, *Canada, Nation and Neighbour* 52, *Unconventional Voyages* 53, *This Most Famous Stream: Anglo-Saxon Liberty* 54, *Canadians in the Making* 58, *My First Seventy-Five Years* 67, *Great Britain's Woodyards* 73, *History and Myths* 75.
Horizon House, Collins Bay, Ontario, Canada.
Telephone: 613-389-2546.

Łowmiański, Henryk, PH.D.; Polish historian; b. 10 Aug. 1898, Dauguda, U.S.S.R.; ed. Stephan Batory Univ., Vilnius.
Doctor 24-32, Docent 32-34, Assoc. Prof. 34-46, Prof. 46-, Emer. 68-; Prof. Poznań Univ. 45-68; Head of Dept., Inst. of History, Polish Acad. of Sciences (PAN) 53-62, Corresp. mem. PAN 52-56, mem. 56-; Chair. Polish-Soviet Historical Comm. 65-; mem. Scientific Council Inst. of History, PAN 53-; Dr. h.c. (Poznań) 66, (Warsaw) 73; State Prize, 1st Class 55, 64; City of Poznań Prize 65; Officer's Cross, Order of Polonia Restituta 51, Commdr.'s Cross 59; Order of Banner of Labour, 2nd Class 54; Medal of 10th Anniversary of People's Poland 55; Medal of Nat. Educ. Comm. 68; Order of Builders of People's Poland 74.
Publs. *Podstawy gospodarcze formowania się państw słowiańskich* (The Economic Basis of the Formation of the Slavonic States) 53, *Zagadnienie roli Normanów w genezie państw słowiańskich* (The Problem of the Role of the Normans in the Genesis of the Slavonic States) 57; Editor *History of Poland* Vol. I; Co-Editor *Słownik starożytności słowiańskich* (Dictionary of Slavonic Antiquities).
Ul. Cześnikowska 14 m. 1, 60 330 Poznań, Poland.

Lowry, Bates, PH.B., M.A., PH.D.; American art historian; b. 21 June 1923, Cincinnati, Ohio; m. Isabel Barrett 1946; two d.; ed. Univ. of Chicago.
Assistant Prof. Univ. of Calif. 54-57; Asst. Prof. New York Univ., Inst. of Fine Arts 57-59; Chair. Art Dept. Pomona Coll. 59-63, Prof. Brown Univ. 63-68, Chair. Dept. of Art 63-68; Dir. Museum of Modern Art, New York 68-69; mem. Inst. for Advanced Study 71; Prof., Chair. Art Dept., Univ. of Mass., Boston 71-; mem. Boards of Dirs. Soc. of Architectural Historians 60-63, 64-67, College Art Asscn. 63-66; Editor-in-Chief, *Art Bulletin* 65-68; Editor College Art Asscn. Monographs Series 59-62, 65-68; Chair. Nat. Exec. Cttee., Cttee. to Rescue Italian Art (CRIA); Pres. The Dunlap Soc. 74-; Trustee, Amer. Fed. of Arts; Govs. award for Fine Arts, Rhode Island 67; Grand Officer Star of Solidarity of Italy 68, Guggenheim Fellowship 72.
Publs. *The Visual Experience* 61, *Renaissance Architecture* 62.
Art Department, University of Massachusetts, Boston, Mass. 02125, U.S.A.

Lowry, Oliver Howe, PH.D., M.D.; American professor of pharmacology; b. 18 July 1910, Chicago, Ill.; m. 1st Norma van Ness 1935 (deceased), 2nd Adrienne Kennedy 1964; three s. two d.; ed. Northwestern Univ. and Univ. of Chicago.
Instructor, Dept. of Biological Chem., Harvard Medical School 37-42; at Div. of Physiology and Nutrition, Public Health Research Inst., New York City 42-47; Prof. of Pharmacology and Head of Dept., Washington Univ. School of Medicine 47-, Dean 55-58; Commonwealth Fund Fellow, Carlsberg Laboratory, Denmark 39-40; mem. Editorial Board *Journal of Neurochemistry;* mem. Nat. Advisory Gen. Medical Sciences Council of Nat. Insts. of Health, Scientific

Advisory Cttee. of Nat. Foundation, Scientific Advisory Bd. of Scripps Clinic and Research Foundation; mem. of many socs. including Nat. Acad. of Sciences, A.A.A.S., Harvey Soc., American Chemical Soc.; Midwest Award of American Chemical Soc. 62, Merit Award of Northwestern Univ. 63, John Scott Award 63, Distinguished Service Award of Medical Alumni Asscn. of Univ. of Chicago 65, Borden Award of Asscn. of American Medical Colls. 66.
Publs. 158 papers in *Journal of Biological Chemistry*, *Journal of Neurochemistry*, other scientific journals 39-69.
Washington University School of Medicine, St. Louis, Mo. 63110, U.S.A.

Loyd, Sir Francis Alfred, K.C.M.G., O.B.E.; fmr. British overseas civil servant; b. 5 Sept. 1916, Berkhamstead; s. of Major and Mrs. A. W. K. Loyd; m. Katharine Layzell; two d.; ed. Eton Coll. and Trinity Coll., Oxford.
Cadet, Provincial Admin., Kenya 39; Military Service 40-42; Private Sec. to Gov. of Kenya 42-45; Consul, Mega, Ethiopia 45; Dist. Commr., Kenya 47-55; Commonwealth Fund Fellowship to U.S.A. 53-54; Provincial Commr., Kenya 56-62, Perm. Sec., Governor's Office and Sec. to Cabinet 62-63; Commr. for Swaziland 64-68; Dir. London House for Overseas Graduates 69-; Chair., Africa Cttee., Standing Conf. of British Orgs. for Aid to Refugees 69-75.
Leisure interests: golf, gardening.
53 Park Road, Aldeburgh, Suffolk; Office: London House, Mecklenburgh Square, London, W.C.1, England. Telephone: Aldeburgh 2478 (Home); 01-837-8888 (Office).

Loyo, Gilberto; Mexican economist and politician; b. 1901, Orizaba; m. 1929; one d.; ed. Nat. Univ. of Mexico and Univ. of Rome.
Has held various teaching posts since 23, including Prof. of Mexican and Gen. History, Political Economy, Rural Sociology and Gen. Econ. History, Nat. School of Agriculture and Prof. of Demography, Nat. Polytechnic Inst.; founded Chair of Political Demography in Nat. School of Econs.; Chief of Central Office of Census 40; organized and directed Nat. Censuses 50; fmr. statistical adviser to Mexican state govts. and to various foreign govts.; fmr. Dir. of Social Welfare, Fed. Labour Dept., Chief of Research, Secretariats of Economy and Finance and Dir.-Gen. of Credit and Statistics in these Secretariats; Minister of Economy 53-58; Dir. Consejo Técnico de los Censos Nacionales; fmr. Vice-Pres. and Pres. Mexican Soc. of Geography and Statistics; Pres. Nat. Council of Statistics 59; Nat. Comm. on Minimum Salaries 63; mem. Gov. Board of Nat. Univ. of Mexico 67; founder Mexican Cttee. for Study of Population Problems; mem. Statistical Comm. of UN; Hon. mem. Inter-Amer. Inst. of Statistics 67; Dr. h.c. (Univ. of Veracruz) 46.
Leisure interest: reading.
Publs. *La Concentración Agraria en el Mundo* 33, *La Política Demográfica de México* 35, *Evolución de la Definición de Estadística* 39, *La Concentración Agraria en 28 paises* 41, *La Presión Demográfica* 49, *Sobre Enseñanza de la Historia* 50, *La Población de México, Estado Actual y Tendencias 1960-1980* 60, *Población y Desarrollo Económico* 63, *Demasiados Hombres, Valores Humanos y Explosión Demográfica* 63, *Desarrollo Regional* 70, *Inmigración al Distrito Federal* 70, *Gobernar es Poblar* 70, etc.
Gen. León 80, Tacubaya, Mexico D.F. 18, Mexico. Telephone: 515-31-61.

Lozoya-Solis, Jésus; Mexican paediatric surgeon; b. 3 March 1910, Parral, Chihuahua; s. of late Leodegario Lozoya and late Josefa Solis; m. 1st Susana Thalmann 1937 (div. 1958); 2nd Margarito Prieto de Lozoya 1958;

five s.; ed. Military Medical School of Mexico, Western Reserve Univ. Hosp., Cleveland, Ohio, Harvard Univ. Children's Hosp.
Founder of paediatric surgery in Mexico 50-52; Hosp. Infantil of Mexico 40-52; Pres. Mexican Soc. of Paed. 48-50; Pres. Mexican branch American Acad. of Paed. 44-46; Pres. Mexican Soc. Paed. Surgery 58-60; founder and first Pres. Pan-American Paed. Surgery Asscn. 66-68, World Symposium Paed. Surgery 65-68; Asst. Prof. Paed. and Surgical Paed. 40; founder of Dept. of Paed. of Armed Forces of Mexico 40, Nat. Inst. for the Protection of Children 58; Senator of the Republic 52-55; Gov. of Chihuahua 55-56; Gen. of Mexican Army 49; Pres. Laboratorios Infan of Mexico 49-; Guest Prof. of Paed. Surgery at numerous Univs.; mem. American Acad. of Paed. 44, American Coll. of Surgeons 45, American Military Surgeons Asscn.; hon. mem. many paed. surgery asscns.; mem. organizing cttee. World Fed. of Paed. Surgery Asscns. 72-74.
Leisure interests: history, philosophy, anthropology, writing, lecturing, gardening, travelling, riding.
Publs. *Paedriatria Quirúrgica* 59, *México ayer y hoy, visto por un paedriatra mexicano* 65 and numerous articles.
Calxada Tlalpan 4515, Mexico 22, D.F., Mexico.
Telephones: 5730094, 5732200/01/02/03.

Lu Jui-lin; Chinese party official; b. 1908, Wuhsiang, Shansi.
Commander Tungchin Front Army, Shansi 46; Vice-Gov. of Sikang 50-54; Vice-Commdr. Yunnan Mil. District, People's Liberation Army 57; Deputy Commdr. Kunning Mil. Region, PLA 59-; Vice-Chair. Yunnan Revolutionary Cttee. 68; mem. 9th Cen. Cttee. of CCP 69; Sec. CCP Yunnan 71; First Sec. CCP Kweichow 73-; mem. 10th Cen. Cttee. of CCP 73.
People's Republic of China.

Lu Nan-chiao; Chinese party official.
Deputy Political Commissar, Gen. Logistics Dept., People's Liberation Army 73-.
People's Republic of China.

Lubbers, Rudolph Frans Marie; Netherlands politician; b. 7 May 1939, Rotterdam; m.; two s. one d.; ed. Erasmus Univ., Rotterdam.
Secretary to Man. Board, Lubbers Hollandia Eng. Works 63-65, Co-Dir. 65; mem. Board Netherlands Christian Employers' Fed., Fed. of Mechanical and Electrical Eng. Industries; mem. Programmes Advisory Council of Catholic Broadcasting Asscn.; Minister of Econ. Affairs May 73-; Catholic People's Party.
Ministry of Economic Affairs, Bezuidenhoutseweg 30, The Hague, Netherlands.

Lubennikov, Leonid Ignatievich; Soviet politician; b. 1910; ed. All-Union Agricultural and Pedagogical Inst. Moscow.
Member CPSU 39-; Dir. Agricultural School 39-41; Political Officer, Soviet Army 41-46; Secr. Minsk City CPSU Cttee. 46-52; First Sec. Minsk District Cttee., CPSU 53-55; First Sec. Cen. Cttee. Karelo-Finnish Rep. 55-56; mem. Cen. Cttee. CPSU 56-66; Karelia District Cttee., CPSU 56-58; First Sec. Kemerovo District Cttee. of CPSU 60-64; Deputy Chair. R.S.F.S.R. People's Control Cttee. 65-66; Vice-Chair. Centrosoyouz (Cen Union of Consumer Co-ops) 66-.
Centrosoyouz U.S.S.R., 15 Bolshoi Cherkassky pereulok, Moscow, U.S.S.R.

Lubin, Isador, A.B., PH.D.; LL.D.; American economist; b. 9 June 1896, Worcester, Mass.; s. of Harris Lubin and Hinda Francke; m. Carol Riegelman 1951; two d.; ed. Clark Coll., Univs. of Michigan and Missouri, and Brookings Institution.
Statistician U.S. Food Admin. 18; Expert U.S. War Industries Board 18-19; Asst. Prof. of Econs., Univ. of Michigan 20-22; mem. staff Brookings Inst. 22-33;

mem. teaching staff Brookings Graduate School 24-30;
Adviser to Educ. and Labour Cttee., U.S. Senate
28-29; Chair. Labour Advisory Board, Public Works
Admin. 33-36; mem. U.S. Central Statistical Board 33-
37; Commr. U.S. Bureau of Labour Statistics 33-45;
Statistical Asst. to Pres. Roosevelt 41-45; U.S. Assoc.
rep. Allied Comm. on Reparations, Moscow 45; U.S. Rep.
UN Econ. and Employment Comm. 46-50; U.S. Rep.
UN Comm. on Reconstruction of Devastated Areas
46; U.S. Rep UN Econ. and Social Council 50-53; U.S.
Rep. Advisory Cttee. to the UN Korean Recon-
struction Agency 51-53; Industrial Commr. N.Y. State
Dept. of Labor 55-59; Nat. Comm. on Money and
Credit 58-61; Pres. American Statistical Asscn. 46;
Fellow, Int. Statistical Inst. 48-; mem. Boards of
Trustees Brandeis Univ., Weizmann Inst. of Science
(Israel), New School for Social Research; Chair.
Exec. Cttee. Franklin D. Roosevelt Foundation,
Cotton Garment Industry Pension Fund; Prof.
Public Affairs. Rutgers Univ. 59-61; Chair. President's
Comm. on Railroad Labor Conditions 62; Consultant
United Israel Appeal Inc. (New York) 60-; Econ. Con-
sultant to Twentieth Century Fund 62-; Consultant,
Office of Management and Budget, Exec. Office of the
Pres. 46-73; del. UN Conf. on Application of Science and
Technology for the Benefit of Less Developed Areas 63.
Leisure interests: fishing, gardening.
Publs. *Government Control of Prices during the War* (in
collaboration) 19, *Miners' Wages and the Cost of Coal* 24,
The British Coal Dilemma (with Helen Everett) 27,
The British Attack on Unemployment 34, *Our Stake in
World Trade* 54, *U.S. Stake in the U.N.* 54.
1095 Park Avenue, New York, N.Y. 10028, U.S.A.
Telephone: LE5-4441.

Lubis, Mochtar; Indonesian journalist; b. 1922,
Padang, Sumatra; s. of Raja Pandapotan and Man-
dailing Sumatra; m. Siti Halimah 1945; two s. one d.
Joined Indonesian Antara News Agency 45; publisher
and editor daily *Indonesian Raya* 49-61, Editor 56-61,
66; arrested Feb. 75; published and edited *The Times
of Indonesia* 52, Nat. Literary Award 53; Pres. Magsaysay Award for the Press 58, Golden Pen of Freedom,
Int. Fed. of Publishers 67, Press Foundation of Asia.
Leisure interests: painting, ceramics, sculpture, orchids,
tennis, sailing, flying, gardening.
Publs. *Pers and Wartawan, Tak Ada Esok, Si Djama*
(short stories), *Djalan Ada Udjung, Korean Notebook,
Perkenalan Di Asia Tenggara, Melawat Ke Amerika,
Stories from Europe, Indonesia Dimata Dunia, Stories
from China, A Road with No End* (novel) 52, *Twilight in
Djakarta* 63, *Tiger! Tiger! Subversive Notes.*
Jalan Garah 104, Jakarta Pusat, Indonesia.

Lúčan, Matej, PAED.DR.; Czechoslovak politician;
b. 11 Jan. 1928, Gotovany; ed. Comenius Univ.,
Bratislava.
Head of Dept., Cen. Cttee., C.P. of Slovakia 51-52,
53-63; mem. Cen. Cttee., C.P. of Slovakia 58-68, 69-71;
Head of Dept. of Marxism-Leninism, Comenius Univ.,
Bratislava 52-53; Commr. for Educ. and Culture,
Slovak Nat. Council 63-67; mem. Presidium, Slovak
Nat. Council 63-68; Commr. for Educ., Slovak Nat.
Council 67-68; Minister of Education of Slovak S.R.
69-70; Perm. Rep. to Int. Office for Educ. 64-68;
Deputy Premier, Czechoslovak S.R. 70-; mem. House
of Nations, Fed. Assembly 70-; mem. Cen. Cttee.,
C.P. of Czechoslovakia 70-; Chair. State Cttee. for
Culture, Scientific and Health Relations with Foreign
Countries 71-; Order of Labour 70.
Presidium of Czechoslovak Government, nábřeží kpt.
Jaroše 4, Prague 1, Czechoslovakia.

Luce, Charles F., LL.B.; American business executive;
b. 29 Aug. 1917, Platteville, Wis.; m. Helen G. Oden;
four c.; ed. Univ. of Wis. Law School and Yale Law
School.

Admitted to Wis. Bar 41, Oregon Bar 45, Wash. Bar
46; Law clerk to late Mr. Justice Hugo Black, Supreme
Court 43-44; Attorney, Bonneville Power Admin., Port-
land, Ore. 44-46; in private law practice, Walla Walla,
Wash. 46-61; Bonneville Power Administrator 61-66;
Under-Sec. of the Interior 66-67; Chair. Board of
Trustees and Chief Exec. Officer, Consolidated Edison
Co. of New York Inc. 67-; mem. Board of Dirs. Metro-
politan Life Insurance Co., UAL Inc., United Airlines
Inc.; mem. Board of Trustees, Columbia Univ.; mem.
Board of Trustees, The Conf. Board; mem. various
advisory cttees., etc.
Consolidated Edison Co. of New York Inc., 4 Irving
Place, New York. N.Y. 10003, U.S.A.

Luce, Clare (Clare Boothe); American writer and
diplomatist.
Republican mem. 78th and 79th Congress from Fair-
field County, Conn. 43-47; fmr. Man. Editor *Vanity
Fair*; Amb. to Italy 53-57; appointed Amb. to Brazil
59; appointment approved by Senate; resigned before
taking up post; mem. Editorial Board *Encyclopaedia
Britannica* 74; Hammarskjöld Prize 66.
Publs. include: plays: *Abide with Me* 35, *The Women* 36,
Kiss the Boys Good-bye 38, *Margin for Error* 39, *Child of
the Morning* 52; novels: *Stuffed Shirts* 33, *Europe in the
Spring* 40.
New York, N.Y. 10027; also Honolulu, Hawaii 96813,
U.S.A.

Luce, Henry, III; American journalist and publisher;
b. 28 April 1925, New York; s. of Henry R. Luce and
Lila Hotz Tyng; m. 1st Patricia Potter 1947 (div. 1954),
one s. one d.; m. 2nd Claire McGill 1960 (died 1971),
three step s.; m. 3rd Nancy Bryan Cassiday 1975, two
step s.; ed. Brooks School and Yale Univ.
Commissioner's Asst., Hoover Comm. on Org. Exec.
Branch of Govt. 48-49; Reporter, Cleveland Press
49-51; Washington Corresp. Time Inc. 51-53, *Time*
writer 53-55, Head New Building Dept. 56-60, Asst. to
Publisher 60-61, Circulation Dir. *Fortune* and *Architectural Forum* 61-64, *House and Home* 62-64, Vice-Pres.
64, Chief London Bureau 66-68, Publisher *Fortune* 68-
69; Publisher *Time* 69-72; Chair. of the Board *Time
Canada* Ltd.; Pres. Asscn. of American Corresps. in
London 68; Vice-Pres. for Corporate Planning, Time
Inc. 72-; Dir. Temple-Eastex Inc., North-American
Advisory Board of Volvo; Pres. Henry Luce Founda-
tion 58-; Chair. Board, China Inst. in America; mem.
American Council for UN Univ.; Trustee, United Board
for Christian Higher Educ. in Asia, Eisenhower Ex-
change Fellowships, Nat. Asscn. of Railroad Passengers,
RAIL Foundation, Princeton Theological Seminary,
Coll. of Wooster, Skowhegan School of Painting and
Sculpture; Hon. L.H.D., St. Michael's Coll.
Time & Life Building, New York, N.Y. 10020; Home:
4 Sutton Place, New York, N.Y. 10022, U.S.A.

Luce, Robert Duncan, PH.D.; American mathematical
psychologist; b. 16 May 1925, Scranton, Pa.; s. of
Robert R. and Ruth Downer Luce; m. 1st Gay Gaer
1950, 2nd Cynthia Newby 1967; one d.; ed. Massa-
chusetts Institute of Technology.
Member of Staff, Research Laboratory of Electronics
Mass. Inst. of Technology 50-53; Asst. Prof. of Sociology
and Mathematical Statistics, Columbia Univ. 54-57;
Lecturer in Social Relations, Harvard Univ. 57-59;
Prof. of Psychology, Univ. of Pennsylvania 59-68;
Benjamin Franklin Prof., Univ. of Pa. 68-69; Visiting
Prof. Inst. for Advanced Study, Princeton, N.J. 69-72;
Prof. of Social Science, Univ. of Calif., Irvine 72-75;
Prof. of Psychology, Harvard 75-; mem. Nat. Acad. of
Sciences, American Acad. of Arts and Sciences, Soc. of
Experimental Psychologists; American Psychologists
Asscn. Distinguished Award.
Department of Psychology and Social Relations,
William James Hall, Harvard University, Cambridge,

Mass. 02138; Home: Harbor Towers II, Apartment 36B, India Street, Boston, Mass., U.S.A.

Luce, Sir William Henry Tucker, G.B.E., K.C.M.G.; British diplomatist; b. 25 Aug. 1907, Alverstoke; s. of Admiral J. Luce; m. Margaret Napier 1934; one s. one d.; ed. Clifton Coll., and Christ's Coll., Cambridge. Joined Sudan Political Service 30; Private Sec. to Gov.-Gen. 41-47, Deputy Gov. Equatoria Province 50-51, Gov. of Blue Nile Province and Dir. Sudan Gezira Board 51-53, Adviser to Gov.-Gen. on Constitutional and External Affairs 53-56; Gov. and C.-in-C. Aden 56-Aug. 60; Political Resident Persian Gulf 61-66; Dir. Eastern Bank 66-70, 72-, Tilbury Overseas Contractors and Gray Mackenzie 67-70, 72-, Inchcape 73-; Standard and Chartered Banking Group 73-; Chair. Anglo-Arab Asscn. 68-70, Oryx Investments Ltd. 74-; Special Rep. of U.K. to Persian Gulf States 70-72. Brook House, Fovant, Nr. Salisbury, Wiltshire, England. Telephone: Fovant 254.

Lucebert (*pseudonym* of L. J. Swaanswijk); Netherlands painter and poet; b. 15 Sept. 1924; ed. School of Applied Arts, Amsterdam. Member of Experimental COBRA group; has lived and worked in Berlin (with Bertolt Brecht) 54, Bulgaria 55, France 64 and Spain 65; First one-man exhbn., Galerie Espace, Haarlem 58, also Stedelijk Museum, Amsterdam 59, and Marlborough New London Gallery 63; retrospective exhbn. Stedelijk Museum, Amsterdam 69; Amsterdam Poetry Prize 54, Premio Marzotto 62, Graphic Art Prize, Biennale Carrara 62, Del Naviglio Prize, Venice Biennale 64, P.C. Hooft Prize 67. Publs. Seven books of poetry in Dutch including: *Triangel in de Jungle* 52, *Collected Poems* 65, Editor of own poems in English trans. *Lucebert, Gedichte und Zeichnungen* (German trans.), *January*, *Heads* (lithographs and poems). Boendermakerhuis, Bergen/North, Holland, Netherlands. Telephone: 02208-3551.

Lucet, Charles Ernest; French diplomatist; b. 19 April 1910; ed. Ecole libre des sciences politiques. Attaché French Embassy, Washington 35, First Sec. 42; Commissariat for Foreign Affairs, Algeria 43; Sec. to Embassy, Ankara 43; Dep. Dir. at Ministry of Foreign Affairs; First Counsellor, Beirut 46; Counsellor, Cairo 47; Head of Cultural Relations, Ministry of Foreign Affairs 50; Minister-Counsellor, Security Council, UN 53; Minister-Counsellor, French Embassy, Washington 55; Dir. of Political Affairs, Ministry of Foreign Affairs 59-65; Amb. to U.S.A. 65-72, to Italy 72-74; retd. 75; Commdr. Légion d'Honneur. 9 rue de Thann, 75017 Paris, France.

Lucey, Patrick Joseph; American politician; b. 21 March 1918, LaCrosse, Wis.; s. of Gregory and Ella (McNamara) Lucey; m. Jean Vlasis 1951; two s. one d.; ed. St. Thomas Coll., Minneapolis and Univ. of Wisconsin. Founder/owner, Lucey Realty 54-70; State legislator 48-50; State Chair. Wisconsin Democratic Party 57-63; Lieut.-Gov. State of Wisconsin 64-66; Gov. of Wisconsin 71-; Democrat. Office of the Governor, State Capitol, Madison, Wis. 53702; Home: Governor's Mansion, 99 Cambridge Road, Madison, Wis. 53704, U.S.A. Telephone: 608-266-1212 (Office); 608-262-1234 (Home).

Luchsinger, Fred W., PH.D.; Swiss journalist; b. 9 July 1921, St. Gallen; s. of Caspar and Lina Luchsinger-Schwyter; m. Dorette Walther 1950; one s. two d.; ed. Literargymnasium, Kantonschule St. Gallen, Univs. of Zurich and Basle, and Yale Univ. With *Neue Zürcher Zeitung* 49-, Foreign News Dept. 49, Bonn Corresp. 55-63, Foreign Editor 63, Editor-in-Chief 68-.

Publs. *Der Basler Buchdruck als Vermittler italienischen Geistes* 53, *Die Neue Zürcher Zeitung im Zeitalter des Zweiten Weltkrieges* 55, *Bericht über Bonn: deutsche Politik 1955-1965* 66. Neue Zürcher Zeitung, Falkenstrasse 11, 8021 Zürich, Switzerland. Telephone: 32-71-00.

Lucht, Werner; German banking official; b. 7 April 1910, Zielenzig, Neumark; m. Ruth Berger 1936; one s. one d.; ed. Handelshochschule, Berlin. Joined Reichskredit-Gesellschaft A.G. 32; joined Deutsche Reichsbank 34, posts in Halberstadt, Duisburg-Ruhrort and Northeim 34-39; adviser and English interpreter, Reichsbanknebenstelle, Lüneberg 45; Referent, Landeszentralbank von Niedersachsen, Hanover 48-59; mem. of Board, Landeszentralbank in Baden-Württemberg, Stuttgart 59-66; mem. Board of Dirs. and Central Bank Council, Deutsche Bundesbank, Frankfurt-am-Main 66-. Leisure interest: modern art. Deutsche Bundesbank, 6000 Frankfurt am Main 50, Wilhelm-Epstein-Strasse 14; Home: 624 Königstein, Im Fasanengarten 22, Federal Republic of Germany. Telephone: 0611-1581 (Office); 06174-4281 (Home).

Luciani, H.E. Cardinal Albino; Italian ecclesiastic; b. 17 Oct. 1912, Forno Di Canale, Belluno. Ordained priest 35; Bishop of Vittorio Veneto 56-59; Patriarch of Venice 69-; created Cardinal 73. Curia Patriarcale San Marco 320/A, 30124 Venice, Italy.

Lucio Paredes, Antonio José ,DR.JUR.; Ecuadorian diplomatist; b. 13 Dec. 1923; ed. Univ. Central del Ecuador and Univ. Católica de Rio de Janeiro. Joined Foreign Ministry 44; Third Sec., Rio de Janeiro 49-52; Consul-Gen., Madrid 55-56; Counsellor 56-60; Counsellor, del. of Ecuador to OAS 60-62; Prof. of Diplomatic Law, Inst. Ecuatoriano de Derecho Internacional 65-66; Prof. of Consular Law, School of Political and Admin. Sciences, Univ. Central 67-68; Under-Sec.-Gen. Foreign Ministry 67-68; Amb. to Belgium 68-71; Minister of Foreign Affairs 72-75; del. to numerous int. confs.; Gran Cruz, Orden Nacional al Mérito (Ecuador) and decorations from Brazil, Chile, Argentina and Spain. c/o Ministerio de Relaciones Exteriores, Quito, Ecuador.

Luciolli, Mario, LL.D.; Italian diplomatist; b. 17 Oct. 1910, Rome; s. of Lodovico Luciolli and Clotilde Marletta; m. Loredana Fritsch 1949; one s. one d.; ed. Univ. degli Studi, Rome. Entered Foreign Service 33; Vice-Consul Zurich 34-36, Paris 36-38; Foreign Ministry Rome 38-40, 42-43; Consul, Melbourne 40; Sec. Berlin 40-42; Consul, San Sebastian 43-44; Foreign Ministry Rome 44-48; Counsellor, then Minister Counsellor, Washington 48-55; Dip. Adviser to Pres. of the Repub., Rome 55-56; Amb. to Chile 56-61, to Turkey 61-64, to Fed. Repub. of Germany 64-. Leisure interests: photography, golf. Italian Embassy, Karl-Finkelnburg-Strasse 51, 53 Bonn-Bad Godesborg, Federal Republic of Germany. Telephone: 364015.

Lücke, Paul; German politician; b. 13 Nov. 1914, Schönenborn, Cologne; m. Rosa Fussenegger 1946; five s. one d.; ed. Higher Technical School, Berlin. Local govt. officer (head of Gummersbach Commercial Office) 45; Head of Engelskirchen local govt. 47-49; mem. of German Fed. Parl., Chair. Fed. Parl. Reconstruction and Housing Cttee. 49-57; Pres. German Local Council 54-66, Hon. Pres. 66-; Minister of Housing, Town Planning and Regional Devt. 57-65, of Interior 65-March 68. Odinweg 42, Bensberg, Bensberg/Cologne, Federal Republic of Germany.

Luckhoo, Sir Lionel Alfred, K.C.M.G., C.B.E., Q.C.; Guyanese barrister and diplomatist; b. 2 March 1914, Guyana; 3rd *s.* of Edward and Evelyn Luckhoo; two *s.* three *d.*; ed. Queen's Coll., Georgetown, Guyana, and Middle Temple, London.
Member Legis. Council, British Guiana 49, State Council 52; mem. Exec. Council and Minister without Portfolio 53; mem. Interim Govt. 53; mem. Georgetown Municipality for fifteen years; Mayor of Georgetown four times; Chair. Georgetown Sewage and Water Comms., Public Health Comm., Fire Comm., Chair. numerous other Cttees.; Pres. four Trade Unions; rep. Guyana at several confs. throughout world; High Commr. for Guyana in U.K. 66-70, for Barbados 66-70, Amb. of Guyana and Barbados to France, Fed. Repub. of Germany and Netherlands 67-70; retd. from diplomatic service 72; private law practice 72-.
Leisure interests: horse racing, cricket, magic, chess, bridge, short story writing.
Publs. *The Fitzluck Theory of Horse Breeding* 52, *I Believe, Life After Death.*
Croai Street, Georgetown, Guyana.

Ludwig, Christa; Austrian mezzo-soprano opera singer; b. 16 March 1928, Berlin, Germany; *d.* of Anton Ludwig and Eugenie Besalla-Ludwig; *m.* 1st Walter Berry (*q.v.*) 1957 (div. 1970), one *s.*; *m.* 2nd Paul-Emile Deiber 1972.
Opera debut at 18, guest appearance at the Athens Festival in Epidauros 65; joined Vienna State Opera 55; appearances at Festivals in Salzburg, Bayreuth, Lucerne, Holland, Prague, Saratoga, Stockholm; guest appearances in season in Vienna, New York, Chicago, Buenos Aires, Scala Milano, Berlin, Munich; numerous recitals and soloist in concerts; recordings of Lieder and complete operas including *Norma* (with Maria Callas), *Lohengrin, Cosi fan tutte, Der Rosenkavalier, Carmen, Götterdämmerung, Die Walküre, Herzog Blaubarts Burg, Don Giovanni, Zauberflöte, Figaros Hochzeit, Capriccio, Fidelio;* winner of Bach-Concours, record award for Fricka in *Walküre,* and *Des Knaben Wunderhorn;* awarded title of Kammersängerin by Austrian Govt. 62; Prix des Affaires Culturelles, for recording of Venus in *Tannhäuser,* Paris 72.
Leisure interests: music, archeology, reading, home movie making, cooking, sewing, fashion, shopping, weaving, rug knitting and travelling.
c/o Vienna State Opera, Vienna, Austria; Home: Rigistrasse 14, Meggen, Switzerland.

Luft, Friedrich; German journalist; b. 24 Aug. 1911, Berlin; *s.* of Prof. Fritz and Mary (née Wilson) Luft; *m.* Heide Thilo 1940; ed. Univs. of Berlin and Königsberg (Kaliningrad).
Drama and film critic *Die Neue Zeitung* 45-55, *Süddeutsche Zeitung* 55-62, *Die Welt* 55-; weekly commentator on theatre and film for Radio RIAS, Berlin 46-; mem. PEN Club; Fellow, Royal Soc. of Arts.
Publs. *Luftballons* 39, *Tagesblätter von Urbanus* 47, *Puella auf der Insel* 47, *Köpfe* (with Fritz Eschen) 57, *Altes-Neues Berlin* 59, *Kritische Jahre, Berliner Theater 1945-61* 61, *Luftsprünge* (essays) 61, *Stimme der Kritik* 65 *Zille, Mein Photo-Milieu* (editor) 67.
Maienstrasse 4, 1 Berlin 30, Federal Republic of Germany.
Telephone: 0311-245873.

Luisi, Héctor, LL.D.; Uruguayan lawyer and diplomatist; 19 Sept. 1919, Montevideo; *s.* of Rear-Adm. Héctor Luisi and Berta Rodriguez Serpa; *m.* Blanca Grosso Ledesma 1949; one *s.* one *d.*; ed. Navy School, Univ. of Uruguay and Cambridge Univ.
Corporation lawyer; Asst. Sec.-Gen. and Counsellor to Interamerican Bar Asscn.; Uruguayan Rep. at Int. Convention on Civil Aviation, Montreal 54; mem. Cttee. which drafted Uruguayan Constitution 66; Senator 66-; Minister of Foreign Affairs 67-68; Amb. to

U.S.A. 68-74; Pres. Conf. of Foreign Ministers of Org. of American States (OAS) 67; Hon. Legal Adviser, British Embassy 48-66; Hon. O.B.E. (U.K.) 65; Grand Cross Order of Merit (Chile) 67, Order of Sun (Peru) 67, Order of Isabel la Católica (Spain) 67.
Leisure interests: history, archaeology.
Br. España 2614, Montevideo, Uruguay.

Lukács, Pál; Hungarian viola player; b. 27 April 1919, Budapest.
Soloist, Nat. Opera House 47-; Prof. of Singing, Acad. of Music, Budapest 46-47, Prof. of Viola 47-; numerous concerts abroad; mem. jury Int. Geneva Competition 63; Geneva Prize 48; Kossuth Prize 65; awarded Eminent Artist title 71.
Academy of Music, Budapest; and 1066 Budapest VI, Jókai-u. 1, Hungary.
Telephone: 118-776.

Lukakamwa, Lieut.-Col. Samuel Eli; Ugandan army officer and diplomatist; b. 14 Jan. 1941, Butiti; *m.* Angela Lukakamwa; one *s.* one *d.*; ed. Mons Officer Cadet School, U.K., Nakuru Mil. Training School, Kenya, and Staff Coll., Camberley, U.K.
Commissioned, Uganda Army 63; High Commr. to U.K. 71-72; Minister of Works and Housing 74-.
Leisure interests: tennis, football, cricket.
Ministry of Works and Housing, Kampala, Uganda.

Łukaszewicz, Jerzy; Polish politician; b. 24 Sept. 1931, Warsaw; ed. High School of Social Sciences, Warsaw.
Former activist in youth orgs.; mem. Polish United Workers' Party (PUWP) 51-; Head of Propaganda Dept. PUWP Warsaw Cttee. 62-64; First Sec. PUWP District Cttee., Warszawa-Wola 64-69; Deputy mem. Central Cttee. 64-68, mem. 68-; Sec. 71-; Deputy mem. Political Bureau, Central Cttee. 75-; Sec. PUWP Warsaw Cttee. Feb. 69-Jan. 72; mem. Presidium and Sec. All-Polish Cttee. of Nat. Unity Front Jan. 72-; Deputy to Seym (Parl.) 72-; Order of Polonia Restituta, Medal of 30th Anniversary of People's Poland, and other decorations.
Komitet Centralny, Polska Zjednoczona Partia Robotnicza, Nowy Świat 6, Warsaw, Poland.

Luke, 2nd Baron, of Pavenham; Ian St. John Lawson Johnston; British business executive; b. 7 June 1905, London; *s.* of 1st Baron and Hon. Edith Laura (*d.* of 16th Baron St. John of Bletsoe); *m.* Barbara (*d.* of Sir Fitzroy Hamilton Anstruther-Gough-Calthorpe) 1932; four *s.* one *d.*; ed. Eton Coll., Trinity Coll., Cambridge.
President, Incorporated Sales Managers Asscn. 53-56, Advertising Asscn 55-58, London Chamber of Commerce 52-55; fmr. Chair. Bovril Ltd., Argentine Estates of Bovril Ltd., Virol Ltd.; Chair. Electrolux Ltd., Nat. Playing Fields Asscn.; Vice-Chair. Gateway Building Soc.; Dir. Ashanti Goldfields Corpn. Ltd., Aktiebolaget Electrolux, Lloyds Bank Ltd., Lloyds Bank Int. Ltd., Bunhill Holdings Ltd., IBM U.K. Ltd., IBM U.K. Holdings Ltd.; mem. Int. Olympic Cttee. 51-; Nat. Vice-Pres. Royal British Legion; Pres. Inst. of Export 73-.
Odell Castle, Bedfordshire, England.
Telephone: 02-308-240.

Luke, Desmond Edgar Fashole, M.A.; Sierra Leonean diplomatist and barrister; b. 6 Oct. 1935, Freetown; *m.* Florence Valerie Whitaker 1961; ed. Prince of Wales School, Freetown, King's Coll., Taunton, England, Keble Coll., Oxford.
United Nations Human Rights Fellow, research in India 64; Amb. to Fed. Repub. of Germany 69, to Italy, Netherlands, Belgium and Luxembourg 70, to France, Perm. Rep. to EEC 71-73; Minister of External Affairs 73-75; leader of del. to Int. Atomic Energy Agency Conf., Vienna 70; mem. Sierra Leone Bar Asscn., World Peace through Law Soc., Amer. Soc. of Int. Law;

Grand Order of Merit (Fed. Repub. of Germany), Grand Cordon of Order of Menelik II (Ethiopia)
Leisure interests: sports, art.
c/o Ministry of External Affairs, Freetown, Sierra Leone.

Luke, Sir Stephen Elliot Vyvyan, K.C.M.G.; b. 26 Sept. 1905, Arnside; s. of Brigadier T. M. Luke, C.B.E., D.S.O.; m. 1st Helen Margaret Reinhold 1929, 2nd Margaret Stych 1948; two s. one d.; ed. St. George's School, Harpenden, Wadham Coll., Oxford.
Assistant Clerk, House of Commons 30; Colonial Office 30; Under-Sec., Cabinet Office 47-50; Asst. Under-Sec. of State, Colonial Office 50-53; Comptroller for Development and Welfare for the West Indies and British Co-Chair. Caribbean Comm. 53-58; Senior Crown Agent Overseas Govts. and Admins. 59-68; Dir. E. D. Sassoon Banking Co. Ltd. 68-72, Pirelli Ltd. 69-76, Go-Con Concrete Ltd. 69-73, Caribbean Bank Ltd. 69-.
Leisure interests: travel, gardening, walking.
Merryfields, Breamore, Hants.
Telephone: Breamore 389.

Lulka, Arkhip Mikhailovich; Soviet aircraft jet engine designer; b. 23 March 1908, Savarka, Kiev Region; s. of Michael and Alexandra Lulka; m. Galina Lulka 1930; two s. one d.; ed. Kiev Polytechnical Inst.
Engineer researching into vapour turbines, Kharkov Turbo-Generator Works 31-33; at Kharkov Aviation Inst. 33-39, created first experimental turbo-compressor air-jet engine 37-39; worked at Leningrad Central Boiler-Turbine Inst. 39-41, other Insts. 41-45; Principal designs 45-: AL-3, AL-5 turbo-jet engines; Prof. Moscow Aviation Inst. 54-; Corresp. mem. U.S.S.R. Acad. of Sciences 60-68, mem. 68-; mem. C.P.S.U. 47-; State Prizes 48-51; Hero of Socialist Labour 57; Order of Lenin (thrice), Order of Red Banner of Labour, etc.
Leisure interests: Ukrainian literature, particularly poetry.
U.S.S.R. Academy of Sciences, 14 Leninsky Prospekt, Moscow, U.S.S.R.

Lumbard, Joseph Edward, Jr.; American judge; b. 18 Aug. 1901, New York City; s. of Joseph and Martha (Meier) Lumbard; m. Polly Poindexter 1929; one s. one d.; ed. Harvard Univ., and Harvard Law School.
Assistant U.S. Attorney, Southern District, New York 25-27; Special Asst. Attorney-Gen. New York State 28-29; mem. Fogarty, Lumbard and Quel 29-31; Asst. U.S. Attorney, Criminal Div., Southern District, New York 31-33; mem. Donovan, Leisure, Newton, Lumbard and Irvine 34-53; U.S. Attorney, Southern District, New York 53-55; U.S. Circuit Judge for Second Circuit 55-59, Chief Judge, U.S. Court of Appeals, Second Circuit 59-71; mem. Board of Overseers, Harvard 59-65; Trustee, William Nelson Cromwell Foundation; Chair. American Bar Asscn.'s Special Cttee. for the Formulation of Minimum Standards for the Administration of Criminal Justice 64-68; American Bar Asscn. Gold Medal 68; N.Y. State Bar Asscn. Gold Medal 69.
U.S. Court House, Foley Square, New York, N.Y. 10007; Home: 417 Park Avenue, New York, N.Y. 10022, U.S.A.

Lumet, Sidney; American film director; b. 25 June 1924, Philadelphia; s. of Baruch Lumet; ed. Columbia Univ.
Started as child actor, later theatrical dir. and teacher; Assoc. Dir. CBS 50, Dir. 51-.
Films include: *Twelve Angry Men* 57, *Stage Struck* 58, *That Kind of Woman* 59, *The Fugitive Kind* 60, *A View from the Bridge* 61, *Long Day's Journey into Night* 62, *The Pawnbroker* 63, *Fail Safe* 64, *The Hill* 65, *The Group* 65, *The Deadly Affair* 66, *Bye, Bye Braverman* 68, *The Seagull* 68, *The Appointment* 69, *Blood Kin* 69, *The Offence, The Anderson Tapes* 72, *Child's*

Play 73, *Serpico* 73, *Lovin' Molly* 74, *Murder on the Orient Express* 74, *Dog Day Afternoon* 75.
c/o Columbia Broadcasting Systems Inc., 6121 Sunset Boulevard, Hollywood, Calif. 90028, U.S.A.

Lumsden, James Alexander, M.B.E., LL.B.; British solicitor and company director; b. 24 Jan. 1915, Arden, Dunbartonshire; s. of the late Sir James Robert Lumsden and of Lady Lumsden (née Henrietta Macfarlane Reid); m. Sheila Cross 1947; three s.; ed. Rugby School and Corpus Christi Coll., Cambridge Univ.
Partner, Maclay Murray & Spens (Solicitors), Glasgow 47; Dir. Burmah Oil Co. Ltd. 57-, Chair. 71-75, Deputy Chair. Jan. 75-; Dir. Bank of Scotland, Scottish Provident Inst., The Weir Group Ltd., Scottish Western Investment Co. Ltd., and other companies.
Leisure interests: shooting, and other country pursuits.
Maclay Murray & Spens, 169 West George Street, Glasgow, C.2; Home: Bannachra, by Helensburgh, Dunbartonshire, Scotland.
Telephone: 041-248-5011 (Office).

Lund, Svend Aage; Danish editor; b. 18 April 1900; ed. Copenhagen Polytechnic.
Secretary Asscn. of Danish Employers 27, Fed. of Danish Industries 28; Sub-Editor *Berlingske Tidende* 29, Editor-in-Chief *Berlingske Tidende* and *Berlingske Aftenavis* 34-70; Chair. Fed. Danish newspapers 58-68; Chair. *Berlingske Tidende* 70-73.
Carl Baggers alle 8, Charlottenlund, Denmark.

Lund, Sir Thomas George, Kt., C.B.E.; British international lawyer; b. 6 Jan. 1906, London; s. of Kenneth F. Lund; m. Catherine Stirling (née Audsley) 1931; one d.; ed. Westminster School, London.
Admitted as Solicitor 29; Asst. Solicitor, Law Soc. 30, Asst. Sec. 37-38, Act. Sec. 38-39, Sec.-Gen. 39-69; Treas. Int. Bar Asscn. 50-69, Dir.-Gen. 69-; Sec.-Gen. Int. Legal Aid Asscn. 63-; Chair. Board of Management, Coll. of Law 62-69; Local Dir. Sun, Alliance and London Insurance Group.
Leisure interests: foreign travel, motoring, gardening.
Publs. *The Solicitors' Act* 41, *The International Bar Association, its Members and their Activities* 70, *Professional Ethics* 70.
International Bar Association, 93 Jermyn Street, London, SW1Y 6JE; Home: 1 Bryanston Court, George Street, London, W.1; and Brass Tacks, Biddenden, Kent, England.
Telephone: 01-930-6432 (Office).

Lundberg, Arne S.; Swedish business executive; b. 14 May 1911, Luleå; m.; one s. two d.
Journalist 29-44; specialist in Ministry of Communications 44-47, Perm. Sec., Ministry of Communications 47-51; Sec.-Gen., Ministry for Foreign Affairs 51-56; Man. Dir. Luossavaara-Kiirunawaara AB 57-76; Chair. AB Svensk Exportkredit 62-, Swedish Mine-Owners' Asscn. 63-75, Byggherreföreningen 64-, Norrbottens Järnverk AB 67-70 (mem. Board 60-70), Sveriges Investeringsbank 67-, Oljeprospektering AB (OPAB) 69-, Petroswede AB 73-, Berol Kemi AB (petrochemical) 73-, Svenska Petroleum AB 75-, Statsraff AB 75-; Vice-Chair. Post-och Kreditbanken 66-; mem. Board Swedish Ironmasters' Asscn. 62-76; mem. Swedish Acad. of Eng. Sciences (IVA) 62-, Pres. 74-76.
Leisure interests: music, hunting, sailing.
Luossavaara-Kiirunavaara Aktiebolag, Sturegatan 11, Fack, S-100 41 Stockholm, Sweden.
Telephone: 08-24-90-60.

Lundberg, Bo Klas Oskar, Dr. in Aeronautics; Swedish aircraft designer and aeronautical scientist; b. 1 Dec. 1907, Karlskoga; s. of Ehrenfried and Fanny Lundberg; m. Svea Maria Johansson 1935; two s. two d.; ed. Hudiksvalls Låroverk and Royal Inst. of Technology, Stockholm.

Designer, Test Pilot, AB Svenska Järnvägsverkstä-derna, Aeroplanavdelningen, Linköping 31-35, Spar-manns flygplanverkstad, Stockholm 35-37; Asst. Inspector at the Board of Civil Aviation, Stock-holm 37-38; Chief, Aeronautical Dept., Göta-verken, Gothenburg 39; Chief Designer, J-22 Fighter, Royal Air Board 40-44; Chief, Structures Dept., Aero-nautical Research Inst. of Sweden 44-47, Dir.-Gen. 47-67, Aviation Consultant 67-; Fellow Royal Aero-nautical Soc., Hon. Fellow American Inst. of Aero-nautics and Astronautics, Fellow Canadian Aero-nautics and Space Inst., Socio Onorario, Instituto Internazionale delle Comunicazioni; mem. American Assoc. for the Advancement of Science, Fellow Royal Swedish Acad of Engineering. Sciences; Thulin Medal, Silver 48, Gold 55, Flight Safety Foundation Air Safety Award 60, Sherman Fairchild Certificate of Merit 63, Monsanto Aviation Safety Award 63, Carl August Wicander Gold Medal 66.

Leisure interests: golf, tennis.

Publs. include *Fatigue Life of Airplane Structures* (18th Wright Brothers Lecture) 54, *Should Supersonic Air-liners be Permitted?* 61, *Some Special Problems Connected with Supersonic Transport* 61, *Speed and Safety in Civil Aviation* (3rd Daniel and Florence Guggenheim Memorial Lecture) 62, *The Allotment of Probability Shares (APS) Method, a Guidance for Flight Safety Measures* 66, *Economic and Social Aspects of Commercial Aviation at Supersonic Speeds* 72, *Why the SST Should be Stopped Once and For All* 73; numerous articles and papers mainly on the problems of aircraft safety and supersonic transport.

Gubbkärrsvägen 29/9, 16151 Bromma, Sweden.
Telephone: 08-87-75-92.

Lunde, Ivar, LL.B.; Norwegian politician and diplo-matist; b. 18 June 1908; ed. Oslo Univ.
Secretary Norwegian Consulate, Gdynia, Poland 33-35; Attaché, France 35-36; with Legation in U.S.S.R. and concurrently Chargé d'Affaires in Iran 38; diplomatic posts Turkey, then Portugal 43-45; Chief, Foreign Ministry's First Political Dept. 46-47; Adviser, Perm. Mission of Norway to UN 46-50, 55; Chargé d'Affaires, Greece and Israel 50-52; Minister to Thailand and Indonesia 52-56; Amb. to Turkey (concurrently to Iraq, Pakistan and Iran) 56-61, to Finland 61-65, to U.S.S.R. 66-70, to Austria 70-.
Norwegian Embassy, Bayerngasse 3, 1030 Vienna, Austria.

Lunding, Franklin Jerome, LL.B.; American business-man; b. 26 Feb. 1906; ed. North Dakota and George Washington Univs.
With Research Dept. U.S. Chamber of Commerce 27-28; Attorney Fed. Trade Comm. 29-31; Gen. Counsel Jewel Tea Co. Inc. (Jewel Companies, Inc. since 66) 31, later Asst. to Pres. and Exec. Vice-Pres., Pres. 42-51, Chair. Exec. Cttee. 51-61, Chair of Board 54-65, Chair. Finance Cttee. 65-71; Chair. Exec. Cttee. Lever Bros. Co. 50-57; Chair. Fed. Reserve Bank of Chicago 49-53, 65-69; Dir. Ill. Bell Telephone Co., Jewel Companies, Inc.; Hon. LL.D. Univ. of North Dakota 49, Marquette Univ. 56.
Publ. *Sharing a Business* 51.
Office: 5725 East River Road, Chicago, Ill. 60631; Home: 1630 Sheridan Road, Apt. 9M, Wilmette, Ill. 60091, U.S.A.
Telephone: 312-726-5442.

Lundquist, Evert; Swedish artist; b. 17 July 1904; ed. Royal Acad. of Fine Arts, Stockholm.
Professor, Royal Swedish Acad. of Fine Arts 60-; Exhbns. in London, Paris, New York, Chicago, Pitts-burgh, San Francisco, Milan, Venice, Brussels, São Paulo; paintings in Tate Gallery, London, Musée d'Art Moderne, Paris, Museum of Modern Art, New York, Nat. Gallery, Melbourne, Museo de Arte Moderna, São

Paulo, Moderna Museet, Stockholm; mem. Swedish Royal Acad.; Prince Eugene Medal; Fellow of the Royal Soc. of Arts, London.
Kanton, Drottningholm, Sweden.

Lundqvist, Svante; Swedish politician; b. 20 July 1919, Eskilstona; s. of Karl and Matilda Lundqvist; m. Maj- Britt Bernhardsson; one s. two d.
Member of Riksdag (Parl.) 59-; mem. Exec. Social Democratic Party 60-; Minister without Portfolio 65, Minister of Communications 67, of Physical Planning and Local Govt. 69, of Agriculture and the Environ-ment 73-.
Leisure interests: music, sport.
Jordbruksdepartementet, Fack, 103 20 Stockholm 16, Sweden.
Telephone: (68) 763 1000.

Lundvall, (Dan) Björn (Hjalmar); Swedish electrical engineer and business executive; b. 12 Aug. 1920, Stockholm; s. of Dan Lundvall and Greta Segerström; m. Patricia Luke 1951; one s. two d.; ed. Royal Inst. of Technology, Stockholm, and Management Develop-ment Inst., Lausanne, Switzerland.
Telefonaktiebolaget L. M. Ericsson 43-, Head of Dept. of Research and Devt. of Carrier Telephone Systems 54-57, Head of Marketing Activities of Long Distance Div. 57-60, Man. of Long Distance Div. 60-63, Deputy Man. Dir. 63-64, Man. Dir. 64-; Knight Commdr. Order of Vasa; Knight Commdr. of Ordem de Rio Branco.
Leisure interest: yachting.
Office: Telefonaktiebolaget L. M. Ericsson, 126 25 Stockholm; Home: Oskar Baeckströms vag 11, 126 54 Hägersten, Sweden.
Telephone: Stockholm 7190000 (Office); 465530 (Home).

Luneburg, William V., B.SC., M.B.A.; American automobile executive; b. 22 May 1912, New York; m.; one s.; ed. New York Univ. and Harvard Business School.
Director of Textile Econs., Bureau of New York 37; Financial Analyst, Ford Motor Co. 49, later Man., Cost Control and Budget Dept., then Man., Rouge Assembly Plant 56-59; Exec. Vice-Pres. Mather Spring Co., Toledo, Ohio 59-63; Vice-Pres. (Finance), American Motors Corpn. 63-65, Vice-Pres. (Automotive Manu-facturing) 65-66, Group Vice-Pres. of Automotive Operations 66-67, Pres. and Chief Operating Officer, American Motors Corpn. Jan. 67-; Dir. Motor Vehicle Mfrs. Asscn., Maccabees Mutual Life Insurance Co., etc.
American Motors Corporation, 14250 Plymouth Road, Detroit, Michigan 48232, U.S.A.
Telephone: 493-2531.

Lunenberg, Engelbartus; Netherlands administrator; b. 11 Aug. 1922; s. of Albert J. Lunenberg and Maria P. van der Woerd; m. Bella Leonie Stein Pinto 1969; ed. Netherlands School of Econs. (now Erasmus Univ.), Rotterdam.
Director UNESCO Centre, Nat. Comm. for UNESCO, Amsterdam 51-53; Dept. of Foreign Relations, Ministry of Educ., Science and Culture 53-54; Deputy Dir. Int. Statistical Inst. 54-55, Dir. 55-, Sec., Treasurer 72-; Exec. Sec. Int. Asscn. for Statistics in Physical Science, Int. Asscn. of Survey Statisticians; Sec. Int. Asscn. of Municipal Statisticians; Order of the Rising Sun, 4th Class (Japan).
International Statistical Institute, 428 Prinses Beatrix-laan, Voorburg; Home: 340 Parkweg, Voorburg, Netherlands.
Telephone: 070-694341 (Office); 070-871296 (Home).

Lunkov, Nikolay Mitrofanovich; Soviet diplomatist; b. 7 Jan. 1919, Pavlovka, Ryazan Region; ed. Lomono-sov Technical Inst., Moscow.
Diplomatic Service 43-; Asst. Minister of Foreign Affairs 51-52; Deputy Political Counsellor, Soviet Con-

trol Comm. in Germany 52-54; Counsellor, Stockholm 54-57; Deputy Head, Dept. of Int. Orgs., Ministry of Foreign Affairs 57, 3rd European Dept. 57-59; Head of Scandinavian Div., Ministry of Foreign Affairs 59-62; Amb. to Norway 62-68; Head of Dept. of Cultural Relations with Foreign Countries 68-73; Amb. to U.K. (also accred to Malta) 73-.
Embassy of the U.S.S.R., 13 Kensington Palace Gardens, London, W8 4QX, England.

Luns, Joseph Marie Antoine Hubert, G.C.M.G., C.H., D.C.L., LL.D.; Netherlands politician; b. 28 Aug. 1911, Rotterdam; m. Baroness Elisabeth Van Heemstra; one s. one d.; ed. Amsterdam and Brussels, Univs. of Leiden, Amsterdam, London and Berlin.
Ministry of Foreign Affairs 38-40; Attaché, Dutch Legation, Berne 40-41, Lisbon 41-42, Second Sec. 42-43; Second Sec. Netherlands Ministry for Foreign Affairs, London 43-44; Second, then First Sec. Dutch Embassy, London 44-49; Perm. Del. to UN 49-52; Co-Minister for Foreign Affairs 52-56; Minister of Foreign Affairs 56-71; Pres. NATO Council 58-59; Sec.-Gen. NATO 71-; Hon. Fellow, London School of Econs.; Kt. Grand Cross of the Order of the Netherlands Lion, Officer Order of Orange-Nassau, Charlemagne Prize 67, Hon. C.H. (U.K.) 71, and foreign awards.
Leisure interests: swimming, walking, reading.
Publs. Several studies on Netherlands Navy in British and Portuguese magazines and articles about current political problems in various magazines, incl. *International Affairs* and *Atlantic Review*.
Secretary-General of NATO, Boulevard Léopold III, Brussels, Belgium.

Lunt, Alfred; American actor; b. 19 Aug. 1893, Milwaukee, Wis.; m. Lynn Fontanne (*q.v.*); ed. Carroll Coll., Waukesha, Wis.
First appearance Castle Square Theater, Boston, Mass. 13; plays include *Romance and Arabella* 17, *Sweet Nell of Old Drury* 23, *The Guardsman* 25-29, *Caprice* 29, *Design for Living* 33, *The Taming of the Shrew* 35, *Idiot's Delight* 36, *Amphitryon 38* 37, *The Seagull* 38, *There Shall Be No Night* 39, *O Mistress Mine* 45, *I Know My Love* 50, *Quadrille* 52-55, *The Great Sebastians* 56, *The Visit* 58; Dir. Theatre Guild 35-; Amer. Acad. of Arts and Letters Award 47; Presidential Medal of Honour 64; Hon. D.Litt. (Milwaukee Univ.), Hon. LL.D. (Dartmouth Univ. and Carroll Coll.).
Genesee Depot, Wis. 53127, U.S.A.

Luong Bang, Nguyen (*see* Nguyen Luong Bang).

Lupis, Giuseppe; Italian lawyer, journalist and politician; b. 28 March 1896, Ragusa.
Joined Partito Socialista Italiano 19; lived in New York 26-45; contributor to *Il Nuovo Mondo, Libera Stampa,* edited *Il Mondo* while in U.S.A.; Sec. New York Branch of Italian Socialist Party; Sec. N. American Anti-Fascist League; Del. to Socialist Int. Congress, Brussels 28; mem. Consultant Assembly 45; Deputy to Constituent Assembly 46-48, mem. Chamber of Deputies 48-; Under-Sec. for Foreign Affairs 46-47, 58-59, 62-63, 63-68; Minister for Merchant Marine 68-69, 72-73, of Tourism and Entertainment 70; Minister for Italian Del. at UN 70-72, 73-74, of Culture and Environment March-Oct 74.
Camera dei Deputati, Rome; Via delle Mura Latine 38, Rome, Italy.
Telephone: 7574323.

Lupu, Petre; Romanian politician; b. 25 Oct. 1920, Iaşi; m. Nesia Lupu; one s. one d.; ed. Acad. of Social-Political Sciences.
Joined Romanian Communist Party 36; Sec. Iaşi District Cttee. of Union of Communist Youth (U.C.Y.) 40; imprisoned 40-44; Sec. of Oltenia Region Cttee. of R.C.P. 44-45; Sec. Cen. Cttee. of U.C.Y. 45, 49-50; Deputy to Grand Nat. Assembly 48-; mem. Cen. Cttee.

of R.C.P. 55-, Alt. mem. Exec. Cttee. 65-68, mem. 68-; Chair. State Cttee. of Organization and Salary Problems 66-69; Minister of Labour 69-; Hero of Socialist Labour 71.
Ministry of Labour, Str. Scaune nr. 1-3, Bucharest, Romania.
Telephone: 15-40-50.

Lupu, Radu, M.A.; Romanian pianist; b. 30 Nov. 1945, Galaţi; s. of Mayer Lupu and Ana Gabor; m. Elizabeth Wilson 1971; ed. High School, Braşov, Moscow Conservatoire, U.S.S.R.
First piano lessons 51; won scholarship to Moscow 61; entered Moscow Conservatoire 63, graduated 69; First Prize, Van Cliburn Competition 66; First Prize, Enescu Int. Competition, Bucharest 67; First Prize, Leeds Int. Competititon 69; a leading interpreter of the German classical composers; now lives in Britain and appears frequently with all the major orchestras; has toured Eastern Europe with London Symphony Orchestra; American debut 72; records for Decca.
Leisure interests: history, art, sport.
c/o Harrison Parrott Ltd., 22 Hillgate Street, London, W8 7SR, England.
Telephone: 01-229-9166.

Luraghi, Giuseppe; Italian business executive; b. 12 June 1905, Milan; ed. Univ. Commerciale Luigi Bocconi, Milan.
Started career in textile industry; with Pirelli Group 30-50; Gen. Man. Finmeccanica Group 51-56, and Dir. several subsid. and affiliated companies; Chair. and Man. Dir. Lanerossi S.p.A. 56-60; Chair. Board of Dirs. Alfa Romeo S.p.A., Milan 60-74, COGIS (Compagnia Generale Interscambi), SICA 67, Alfa Romeo Alfasud 68-74; Deputy Chair. Ente Fiera Campionaria (Trade Fair); Dir. SIP, SIT SIEMENS, Lanificio Italiano—*Il Fabbricone*.
Via Revere 2, Milan, Italy.

Luria, Aleksandr Romanovich, DR.SC., DR.MED.; Soviet psychologist; b. 16 July 1902, Kazan; s. of late Roman A. Luria; m. Lana P. Lipchina 1933; one d.; ed. Kazan Univ. and First Moscow Medical Inst.
Professor, Head of Dept. of Psycho-Physiology and Neurophysiology, Moscow State Univ. 45-; mem. U.S.S.R. Acad. of Pedagogical Sciences 47-; Foreign mem. Nat. Acad. of Sciences (U.S.A.), American Acad. of Arts and Sciences, American Acad. of Education; Hon. mem. British, Spanish, Colombian and Swiss psychological socs., French neurological soc.; mem. editorial board, *Problems of Psychology* (U.S.S.R.), *Neuropsychology* (England), *Cortex* (Italy); Hon. D.Sc. (Leicester, Nijmegen, Lublin, Brussels); Lomonosov Prize (Moscow State Univ.); Order of Lenin.
Publs. Over 300 scientific works including *Higher Cortical Functions of Man* 62 (New York 66), *Human Brain and Psychological Processes* 62 (New York 66), *Restoration of Brain Functions After War Trauma* 48 (Oxford 63), *Traumatical Afasia* 47 (The Hague 69), *Nature of Human Conflicts, The Mind of a Mnemonist* (New York) 68, *The Man With a Shattered World* (New York) 72, *The Working Brain* (London) 73, *Social History of Cognitive Processes* 74, *Neuropsychology of Memory* 74-75, *Basic Problems of Neurolinguistics* 75, etc.
13 Frunze Street, Moscow 121019, U.S.S.R.

Luria, Salvador Edward, M.D.; American professor of biology; b. 13 Aug. 1912, Turin, Italy; s. of David and Ester (Sacerdote) Luria; m. Zella Hurwitz 1945; one s.; ed. Univ. of Turin.
Research Fellow, Inst. of Radium, Paris 38-40; Research Asst., Columbia Univ. Medical School, N.Y. 40-42; Guggenheim Fellow, Vanderbilt and Princeton Univs. 42-43; Instructor in Bacteriology, Indiana Univ., Bloomington 43-45, Asst. Prof. 44-47, Assoc. Prof. 47-50; Prof. of Bacteriology, Univ. of Illinois, Urbana 50-59; Prof. and Chair. Dept. of Microbiology.

Mass. Inst. of Technology 59-, Sedgwick Prof. of Biology 64-, Inst. Prof. 70-, Dir. Center for Cancer Research 72-; Jessup Lecturer, Columbia Univ.; Nieuwland Lecturer, Univ. of Notre Dame; mem. Nat. Acad. of Sciences; Pres. American Soc. for Microbiology; Nobel Prize for Medicine (with Max Delbrück and A. D. Hershey, *qq.v.*) 69.

Research interests: bacterial genetics; bacterial viruses; structure of bacterial cell wall and membrane.

Department of Microbiology, Massachusetts Institute of Technology, Cambridge, Mass. 02139; Home: 48 Peacock Farm Road, Lexington, Mass. 02173, U.S.A.

Lurie, Richard; South African stockbroker; b. 30 March 1918, Johannesburg; *s.* of the late A. C. Lurie; *m.* Lois Harris 1949; three *s.*; ed. King Edward VII School, Johannesburg, Univ. of the Witwatersrand. Joined Johannesburg Stock Exchange 46, mem. Exchange Cttee. 60-70, Vice-Pres. 70-72, Pres. of Exchange 72-; fmr. Chair. Protea Holdings, Calan and Wit Industrials.

Johannesburg Stock Exchange, P.O. Box 1174, Johannesburg, South Africa.

Lusaka, Paul John Fermino; Zambian politician; b. 10 Jan. 1935, Broken Hill; *s.* of Firmino Lusaka and Rabecca Mutakwa; *m.* Joan Gay 1963; four *c.*; ed. Univ. of Minnesota, Univ. of Basutoland and McGill Univ.

Graduate Asst. Lecturer, Univ. of Basutoland 60; Deputy High Commr. to U.K. 66; Amb. to U.S.S.R. (also accred. to Yugoslavia, Romania, Czechoslovakia) 68-72; Perm. Rep. to UN 72-73; Minister of Rural Devt. Dec. 73-.

Ministry of Rural Development, Lusaka, Zambia.

Lush, Jay L(aurence), PH.D.; American professor of animal breeding; b. 3 Jan. 1896, Shambaugh, Iowa; *s.* of Henry Lush and Mary Eliza (Pritchard) Lush; *m.* Adaline Lincoln 1923; one *s.* one *d.*; ed. Kansas State Agricultural Coll. (now Kansas State Univ.), Univs. of Wis. and Chicago and Royal Veterinary and Agricultural Coll. of Denmark.

Animal Husbandman in Charge of Breeding Investigations, Texas Agricultural Experiment Station, Coll. Station, Tex. 21-29; Prof. of Animal Breeding, Iowa State Univ. (fmrly. Iowa State Coll.) 30-, semi-retirement 66-; Nat. Research Fellow, Denmark 34; Visiting Prof. Rural Univ. of Minas Gerais, Brazil; Lecturer Food and Agricultural Org. Training Centre, India 54, and missions for various orgs., in Britain, Australia and Argentina; mem. Nat. Acad. of Sciences; Hon. degrees (Uppsala, Giessen, Copenhagen, Michigan, Illinois, Kansas State, Wisconsin, Zurich, Norway); First Morrison Award, Borden Award in Dairy Production, Hermann von Nathusius Medal, Nat. Medal of Science 68.

Leisure interest: travel.

Publs. *Animal Breeding Plans* 37, 3rd edn. 47, *The Genetics of Populations* 48.

3226 Oakland Street, Ames, Iowa 50010, U.S.A. Telephone: 515-292-1344.

Lüst, Reimar, DR.RER.NAT.; German physicist; b. 25 March 1923, Barmen; *s.* of Hero and Grete (née Strunck) Lüst; *m.* Dr. Rhea Kulka 1953; two *s.*; ed. Univs. of Frankfurt/M and Göttingen.

Research Physicist, Max Planck Insts. Göttingen and Munich 50-60, Enrico Fermi Inst., Univ. of Chicago 55-56, Princeton Univ. 56; Head, Dept. for Extra-terrestrial Physics, Max Planck Inst. for Physics and Astrophysics 60, Dir. Inst. of Extraterrestrial Physics 63-72; Visiting Prof., Univ. of New York 59, MIT 61, Calif. Inst. of Technology 62, 66; Chair. German Research Council 69-72, Deutsche Gesellschaft für Luft-und Raumfahrt 68-72; Pres. Max-Planck-Gesellschaft June 72-; Officier Ordre des Palmes Académiques.

Publs. articles on space research, astrophysics and plasmaphysics.

Max-Planck-Gesellschaft zur Förderung der Wissenschaften e.V., 8 München 2, Residenzstrasse 1a; Home: 8000 München 45, Sondermeierstrasse 70, Federal Republic of Germany.

Lustig, Arnošt; Czech writer; b. 21 Dec. 1926, Prague; *s.* of Emil and Terezie Lustig (née Löwy); *m.* Věra Weislitz 1949; one *s.* one *d.*; ed. Coll. of Political and Social Sciences, Prague.

In concentration camps at Terezín, Auschwitz and Buchenwald, Second World War; Radio Prague war corresp. in Arab-Israeli war 48, 49; Editor *Mladý svét* (weekly) 58-59, screenplay writer for Studio Barandov 60-68, for Jadran-Film Yugoslavia 69-70; now resident writer U.S.A.; mem. Cen. Cttee. Union of Czechoslovak Writers 63-69, mem. Presidium 63-69; mem. Int. Writing Program 70-71; Visiting Lecturer Univ. of Iowa 71-72; Visiting Prof. Drake Univ., Iowa 72-73; Visiting Prof. Amer. Univ., Washington, D.C. 73-; Klement Gottwald State Prize 67; Bne'i Brit'h Prize 74. Leisure interests: sport, swimming, travelling, skiing, soccer.

Publs. *Démanty noci* (Diamonds of the Night—short stories, two of which were filmed 61, 64) 58, *Night and Hope* (short stories) filmed as *Transport z ráje* (Transport from Paradise) 62, *Modlitba za Katerinu Horowitzovou* (A Prayer for Katerina Horowitzova—novel, filmed for TV) 65, *Dita Saxova* (novel, filmed 68), *The Street of Lost Brothers* 62, *Nobody will be Humiliated* (long stories) 65, *The White Birches in Autumn* (novel) 66, *Bitter Smell of Almonds* (long stories) 68, *Darling* (novel) 69, *Darkness Casts No Shadow* (novel) 76, *Children of Holocaust* (5 vols., collected stories) 76.

4000 Tunlaw Road N.W., Apartment 825, Washington, D.C. 20007, U.S.A.

Telephone: 202-3385357.

Luterbacher, Franz; Swiss lawyer and business executive; b. 11 Jan. 1918, Burgdorf; *s.* of Dr. Otto Luterbacher and Klara Morgenthaler; *m.* Felicitas Frey; one *s.* one *d.*; ed. Gymnasium Burgdorf, and Faculty of Law, Univ. of Berne.

Head, Legal Dept., Fed. Finance Admin. 48; Financial Man. Maschinenfabrik Oerlikon, Zurich 54, Pres. Exec. Board 58, Pres. Board of Dirs. 64; Exec. Vice-Pres. Brown, Boveri and Cie. 67, Chair. Board of Dirs. 70-; mem. Board of Dirs. Swiss Bank Corpn., Heberlein Holding A.G., Wattwil.

Leisure interest: hiking.

Brown, Boveri et Cie., 5401 Baden; Home: Im Maiacher, 8126 Zumikon, Switzerland.

Telephone: 056-75-11-11 (Office); 051-89-36-93 (Home).

Lutfi, Ashraf Taufiq, B.A.; Kuwaiti civil servant (retd.); b. 1 Jan. 1919, Jaffa, Palestine; *s.* of Taufiq and Murruat Lutfi; *m.* Winfriede Knoblich 1951; ed. Scots Coll., Safad, Palestine.

Teacher in elementary and secondary schools 38-46, Welfare Officer 46-48; Sec. to State Sec. in Govt. Secr. 48-55, Asst. Sec. of State 55-61; Dir. of Office of Emir of Kuwait 61-64; Adviser on Oil Affairs, Ministry of Finance and Industry 64-65; Sec.-Gen. Org. of Petroleum Exporting Countries (OPEC) 65-Jan. 67; Adviser on Oil Affairs to Ministry of Finance and Oil 67-69; mem. Board Kuwait Nat. Petroleum Co. 61-70; Chair. Board Kuwait Aviation Fuelling Co. 62-71; Assoc. Dir., Petrologue Int., Beirut.

Leisure interests: tennis, music, travel, photography.

Publs. *Arab Oil: A Plan for the Future* 60, *OPEC Oil* 67. Gartenweg 3, 79 Ulm/Donau, Federal Republic of Germany.

Lutosławski, Witold; Polish composer and conductor; b. 25 Jan. 1913, Warsaw; *s.* of Józef and Maria Lutosławski; *m.* Maria-Danuta Dygat 1946; ed. Warsaw Conservatoire.

City of Warsaw Music Prize 48, Polish Music Festival Prize 51, State Prizes 52, 55, 64, Prime Minister's Prize for Children's Music 54, Polish Composer's Union's Prize 59 and 73, Minister of Culture's Prize 62, Koussevitzky Int. Recording Award 64; Plaque of the Freie Akad. der Künste, Hamburg 66; Gottfried-von-Herder Prize, Vienna 67; Sonning Music Prize, Copenhagen 67; Award Int. Rostrum of Composers, UNESCO 58, 64, 68; Prize ad honorem of Pres. of France 71; Maurice Ravel Prize 71, Prize Sibelius de Wihuri 73; mem. Swedish Royal Acad. of Music 63-; Hon. mem. Freie Akademie der Künste Hamburg 66-, Int. Soc. for Contemporary Music 69-, Polish Composers' Union 71-, American Acad. of Arts and Letters, Nat. Inst. of Arts and Letters 75; Extraordinary mem. Akademie der Künste Berlin 68-; Corresp. mem. Deutsche Akad. der Künste, Berlin (D.D.R.) 70-, Bayerische Akademie der schönen Künste, Munich 73; Vice-Pres. Polish Composers' Union 73-; Hon. D.Mus. (Cleveland Inst. of Music) 71, Dr. h.c. (Univ. Warsaw) 73, (Lancaster Univ.) 75, Hon. Dr. Fine Arts (Northwestern Univ. Evanston-Chicago) 74.
Works include *Symphonic Variations* 38, *Variations on a Theme of Paganini* (two pianos) 41, *Folk Melodies* (piano) 45, *Symphony* 47, *Overture* (string orch.) 49, *Little Suite for Orchestra* 51, *Silesian Triptych* (voice and orch.) 51, *Bucoliques for Piano* 52, *Dance Preludes* (clarinet) 53, *Concerto for Orchestra* 54, *Musique Funèbre* (string orch.) 58, *Five Songs* (female voice and instruments) 58, *Jeux vénitiens* 61, *Trois poèmes d'Henri Michaux* (choir and orch.) 63, *String Quartet* 64, *Paroles tissées* (tenor and chamber orch.) 65, *Second Symphony* 67, *Livre pour orchestre* 68, *Concerto for Cello and Orchestra* 70, *Preludes and Fugue for 13 Solo Strings* 72, *Les espaces du sommeil* (for tenor voice and orchestra) 75; chamber, piano, vocal and children's music; compositions for theatre, films and radio.
Leisure interests: literature. other arts, yachting.
Ul. Śmiała 39, 01523 Warsaw, Poland.
Telephone: 39 23 90.

Lutyens, Elisabeth, C.B.E.; British composer; b. 9 July 1906, London; d. of late Sir Edwin Lutyens, O.M. (architect); m. 1st Ian Glennie 1931, 2nd Edward Clark 1940; two s. two d.; ed. Ecole normale de musique, Paris, and Royal Coll. of Music, London.
First film score 44, radio score 46; sole agent The Olivan Press Universal Edn.
Major works: *O Saisons, O Châteaux* (cantata for soprano and strings) 46, *The Pit* (dramatic scene) 47, *String Quartet No. 6* 52, *Motet* (Wittgenstein) 53, *Music for Orchestra I* 54, *Valediction* (for clarinet and piano) 56, *Infidelio* (for soprano and tenor soli and seven instruments) 56, *De Amore* (cantata) 57, *Wind Quintet* 60, *Quincunx* (for large orchestra) 59-60, *Symphonies* (for piano, solo, harp and percussion) 61, *Catena* (for soprano and tenor soli and 22 instruments) 62, *Music for Orchestra II* 63, *Music for Orchestra III* 64, *String Trio No. 2* 64, *Scena* (for violin, viola and percussion) 64, *Hymn of Man* (for men's chorus) 65, *The Valley of Hatsu-se* (for soprano and four instruments) 65, *In the Temple of a Bird's Wing* (song cycle) 65, *Akapotik Rose* (for soprano and instrumental ensemble) 66, *And Suddenly it's Evening* (for Tenor and instrumental ensemble) 66, *Novenaria* (for orchestra) 67, *Essence for our Happinesses* (for tenor, chorus and orchestra) 68, *Temenos* (for organ), *Requiescat* (Igor Stravinsky) (for soprano and string trio) 71, *The Tears of Night* (for counter-tenor, six sopranos and three instrumental ensembles) 71, *The Linnet from the Leaf* (for five singers and two instrumental groups) 72, *Rape of the Moone* (for wind octet) 73, *The Numbered* (opera), *Time off? Not a Ghost of a Chance!* (a charade), *Isis and Osiris* (opera), about 100 film scores and 100 radio scores.

13 King Henry's Road, London, N.W.3, England.
Telephone: 01-722-8505.

Luvsanchültem, Nyamin; Mongolian diplomatist. Former Sec. of Presidium of People's Great Hural, now Chair. People's Great Hural; Amb. to U.S.S.R. (also accred. to Sweden and Finland) 64-75.
People's Great Hural, Ulan Bator, Mongolia.

Luxembourg, Grand Duke of (*see* Jean).

Luyt, Sir Richard Edmonds, G.C.M.G., K.C.V.O., D.C.M., M.A., LL.D.; South African (sometime British) administrator; b. 8 Nov. 1915, Cape Town, South Africa; s. of Richard Robins Luyt and Wilhelmina Roberta Frances Edmonds; m. 1st Jean Mary Wilder 1948 (died 1951), one d.; 2nd Eileen Betty Reid 1956; two s.; ed. Diocesan Coll., Rondebosch, Univ. of Cape Town and Trinity Coll., Oxford.
Colonial Service, N. Rhodesia 40; War Service 40-45; Colonial Service, N. Rhodesia 46-53; Labour Commr., Kenya 54-57; Perm. Sec. Kenya Govt. 57-60, Sec. to Cabinet 60-61; Chief Sec. Govt. of N. Rhodesia 62-64; Gov. and Commdr.-in-Chief, British Guiana 64-66; Gov.-Gen. of Guyana May-Oct. 66; Principal and Vice-Chancellor Univ. of Cape Town 68-.
Leisure interests: cricket, tennis, rugby, swimming, gardening, turtles, tortoises.
University of Cape Town, P.O.B. 594. Rondebosch, Cape Town, South Africa.
Telephone: 69-4351.

Luyten, Norbert Alfons, PH.D.; Belgian university professor; b. 8 Aug. 1909, Antwerp; s. of Louis Luyten and Hendrika van Kuyk; ed. Catholic Univ., Louvain. Professor of Philosophy, Ghent 39-45; Prof. of Philosophical Psychology, Univ. of Fribourg 45-, Dean of Philosophical Faculty 48-49, 61-63; Rector 56-58; Pres. Philosophical Soc., Fribourg; Cttee. mem. Swiss Philosophical Soc.; Vice-President Institut der Goerres Gesellschaft für interdiziplinäre Forschung.; Ed. *Grenzfragen* Freiburg, München, Consultant of Congregation of Christian Educ., Rome; Assoc. mem. Soc. Philosophique de Louvain and other learned bodies.
Publs. *La condition corporelle de l'homme* 57, *Unsterblichkeit* 57, *Universität und Weltanschauung* 58, *Teilhard de Chardin* 64, *Recherche et culture* 65, *Wetenschap en Geloof* 65, *Ordo Rerum* 69, *Problèmes actuels de la connaissance de Dieu* 69, *L'Université et l'intégration du savoir* 70, *L'Anthropologie de St. Thomas* 74.
Albertinum, CH-1700 Fribourg, Switzerland.
Telephone: 037-22-65-10.

Luyten, Willem Jacob, PH.D.; American professor of astronomy; b. 7 March 1899, Semarang, Netherlands East Indies; s. of Jacob Luyten and Marguerite C. Francken; m. Willemina Miedema 1930; one s. two d.; ed. Univs. of Amsterdam and Leiden.
Fellow, Lick Observatory, Calif. 21; Astronomer, Harvard Coll. Observatory 23-30; Prof. of Astronomy, Univ. of Minnesota 31-67, Prof. Emer. 67-; Fellow, American Acad. of Arts and Sciences; mem. Nat. Acad. of Sciences; Guggenheim Fellow 28, 37; Watson Medal, Nat. Acad. of Sciences 65; Bruce Medal, Astron. Soc. of the Pacific 68.
Leisure interest: Burgundy wines (Commdr. Confrerie des Chevaliers du Tastevin (Nuits St. Georges).
Publs. about 400 different publications in all the major astronomical periodicals 21-70.
211 Space Science Center, University of Minnesota, Minneapolis, Minn., U.S.A.

Lwin, U; Burmese diplomatist; b. 10 Dec. 1912; m.; two s. two d.
Former officer, Burma army; Mil. Adviser, Burma Del. to UN Gen. Assembly 53; Amb. to Fed. Germany 66-71, also to Netherlands 69-71; Perm. Rep. to UN 71-75.
c/o Ministry of Foreign Affairs, Rangoon, Burma.

Lwoff, André Michel; French scientist; b. 8 May 1902; ed. Lycée Voltaire, Univ. de Paris à la Sorbonne. Joined Institut Pasteur 21, Asst. 25-29, Head of Laboratory 29-38, Head Dept. of Microbial Physiology 38-68; mem. Board of Dirs. 66-; Prof. Microbiology, Univ. de Paris 59-68; Head Cancer Research Inst., Villejuif 68-72; mem. numerous French and foreign scientific societies; Foreign mem. Nat. Acad. Sciences U.S.A. 55, Foreign mem. Royal Soc. London 58, Foreign mem. U.S.S.R. Acad. of Medicine; Nobel Prize for Medicine (jointly with F. Jacob and J. Monod) 65, Einstein Award 67; Médaille de la Résistance, Commdr. Légion d'Honneur.
Publs. include: *Biological Order* 62.
Inst. Pasteur, 28 rue du Dr. Roux, 75015 Paris, France.

Lyashko, Aleksandr Pavlovich; Soviet politician; b. 1915; ed. Industrial Inst., Donetsk.
Soviet Army 41-45; mem. C.P.S.U. 42-; engineer and party worker, Donetsk Region 45-60; mem. Central Cttee. C.P.S.U. 61-; First Sec. Donetsk District Cttee., C.P. of Ukraine 60-63; Dep. to U.S.S.R. Supreme Soviet 58-; Sec Central Cttee. of C.P. of Ukraine 63-69; Chair. Bureau of Central Cttee. of Ukraine C.P. for Management, Industry and Construction 63-69; Chair. Presidium of Ukrainian S.S.R. Supreme Soviet, Vice-Chair. Presidium U.S.S.R. Supreme Soviet 69-72; Chair. Council of Ministers Ukrainian S.S.R. June 72-; mem. Politburo Central Cttee., C.P. of Ukraine; Deputy to Ukrainian S.S.R. Supreme Soviet.
Council of Ministers of the Ukrainian S.S.R., Kiev, U.S.S.R.

Lyet, J. Paul; American business executive; b. Philadelphia; *m.* Dorothy L. Storz; five *c.*; ed. Philadelphia Cen. High School and Univ. of Pennsylvania. Joined Sperry Rand's New Holland Farm Equipment Div. 43, Pres. 69-71; Vice-Pres. Sperry Rand Corpn. 70, Exec. Vice-Pres. and Dir. Oct. 70, Chair. and Chief Exec. Officer 72-.
Sperry Rand Corporation, 1290 Avenue of the Americas, New York, N.Y. 10019, U.S.A.

Lyle, Sir Ian D., Kt., D.S.C.; British businessman; b. 1907; ed. Shrewsbury School and St. John's Coll., Oxford.
Chairman Tate and Lyle Ltd. 54-64, Pres. 64-; Dir. Canada and Dominion Sugar Co. Ltd.; Pres. Aims of Industry.
Home: Barrington Court, Ilminster, Somerset; Office: Tate and Lyle Ltd., 21 Mincing Lane, London, E.C.3, England.
Telephone: 01-626-6525.

Lyle, John; British business executive; b. 26 April 1918; ed. Uppingham School, Clare Coll., Cambridge.
Tate and Lyle Ltd. 45-, Dir. 51-, Vice-Chair 62-64, Chair. 64-.
Tate and Lyle Ltd., 21 Mincing Lane, London, E.C.3, England.

Lympany, Moura, F.R.A.M.; British concert pianist; b. 18 Aug. 1916; ed. Belgium, Austria, England.
First performance, Harrogate 29; has played in U.S.A., Canada, South America, Australia, New Zealand, India and most European countries including the U.S.S.R.
c/o Ibbs & Tillet, 124 Wigmore Street, London, W.1, England.

Lynch, John Mary, B.L.; Irish lawyer and politician; b. 15 Aug. 1917, Cork; *s.* of Daniel Lynch and Norah O'Donoghue; *m.* Mairin O'Connor 1946; ed. North Monastery, Cork, Univ. Coll., Cork, and King's Inns, Dublin.
Member of Civil Service (Dept. of Justice) 36-45; called to Bar 45; mem. of Dáil Éireann (Parl.) 48-; Alderman, Cork Corpn. 50-57; Parl. Sec. to Govt. and to Minister for Lands 51-54; Minister for Educ. 57-59; Minister for Industry and Commerce 59-65, for Finance 65-66; Vice-Pres. Council of Europe 58; Pres. Int. Labour Conf. 62; Taoiseach (Prime Minister) 66-73; Leader of the Opposition March 73-; Hon. LL.D. (Dublin Univ.) 67, (Nat. Univ. of Ireland) 69; Grand Cross of Belgian Order of the Crown 68; Hon. D.C.L. Belmont Abbey, Univ. Coll., N. Carolina, U.S.A. 71.
Dáil Eireann, Dublin; Home: 21 Garville Avenue, Rathgar, Dublin 6, Ireland.

Lynch, Patrick, M.A., M.R.I.A.; Irish university professor and public administrator; b. 1918, Dublin; *s.* of Daniel and Brigid Lynch; *m.* Mrs. Mary Crotty 1965; ed. Univ. Coll., Dublin.
Joined Irish Civil Service 41; served Finance Dept. 41-48; Asst. Sec. Dept. of Prime Minister 50-52; Lecturer, Nat. Univ. of Ireland 52-66; Chair. Aer Lingus 54-75, Capital Investment Advisory Cttee.; Chair. Inst. of Public Admin., Medico-Social Research Board 66-72; Dir. Allied Irish Banks; Dir. OECD Govt. Surveys on Investment in Educ. and Research and Devt. 62-66; mem. Governing Body, Univ. Coll., Dublin 64-; mem. Senate Nat. Univ. of Ireland 72-; Fellow Commoner, Peterhouse, Cambridge; Assoc. Prof. of Political Econ. (Applied Econs.) 66-75, Prof. 75-; mem. Nat. Science Council 67, Higher Educ. Authority 68-72, Club of Rome 73.
Publs. *The Economics of Independence* 59, *Planning for Economic Development* (with C. F. Carter) 59, *Guinness's Brewery in the Irish Economy* (with J. Vaizey) 60, *The Role of Public Enterprises in Ireland* 61, essays on *The Irish Economy* in *Conor Cruise O'Brien introduces Ireland* 69, *Ireland in the War Years and after* (ed. Nowlan and Williams) 69, *Ireland in the International Labour Organization* (with B. Hillery) 70, *Economics of Educational Costing* (with J. Vaizey) 71, *Readings in Public Administration* (ed. with B. Chubb) 71, essay in *Travel and Transport in Ireland* (ed. K. B. Nowlan) 73.
68 Marlborough Road, Dublin 4, Ireland.

Lynch, Phillip Reginald, B.A., DIP.ED.; Australian politician; b. 27 July 1933, Melbourne; *s.* of Mr. and Mrs. R. T. Lynch; *m.* Leah O'Toole 1958; three *s.*; ed. Marist Bros. Coll., Hawthorn, Xavier Coll., Melbourne, Univ. of Melbourne.
Former school teacher; management consultant; fmr. co. dir.; fmr. Pres. Victorian Young Liberal Movement; mem. House of Representatives 66-; Minister for the Army 68-69; Minister for Immigration and assisting Treasurer 69-71; Minister for Labour and Nat. Service 71-72; Deputy Leader of the Opposition, House of Reps. 72-75; Treas. Nov. 75-; del. to numerous confs., incl. Ministerial Council of OECD, Paris 70; Fellow, Inst. of Dirs., Australian Inst. of Management; Liberal.
Leisure interests: tennis, swimming, reading, sailing.
House of Representatives, Canberra, A.C.T.; Home: "The Moorings", Denistoun Avenue, Mt. Eliza, Victoria 3930, Australia.
Telephone: 635967 (Office).

Lynden, Baron Carel Diederic Aernout van, LL.D.; Netherlands economist and politician; b. 23 Aug. 1915, Amsterdam; *m.* Françoise Banzet 1947; three *d.*; ed. Law Faculty, Univ. of Leiden.
Head of Dept. in Monetary Agreements of Nederlandsche Bank, Amsterdam 45-53; mem. Managing Board of European Payments Union, Paris 50-51; Alternative Head of Dutch del. at Conf. on German External Debts in London 51-52; Asst. Manager Finance Dept. of High Authority of European Community for Coal and Steel, Luxembourg 53-56; Sec.-Gen. Benelux Econ. Union, Brussels 56-75 (retd.); Officer, Order of Orange-Nassau (Netherlands), Order of Merit (Italy); Knight, Order of Netherlands Lion; Order of the Crown (Belgium); Grand Officer, Order of Merit (Luxembourg).
Leisure interest: modern art.
Rue des Adriatiques 50, 1040 Brussels, Belgium.
Telephone: 734-24-10.

Lynden, Baron Rijnhard Bernhard van, LL.M.; Netherlands diplomatist; b. 11 Aug. 1912, The Hague; *s.* of Baron W. J. van Lynden and Anna van Hangest Baroness d'Yvoy; *m.* Baroness Ada C. van Pallandt 1939; two *s.* three *d.*; ed. Univ. of Utrecht and London School of Econs.
Entered Netherlands Foreign Service 39, served in Paris, Berne, Rome, Pretoria and Brussels 39-59; Head, Dept. of European Affairs, Ministry of Foreign Affairs, 59-61, Chief of Protocol 61-64; Amb. to Greece 64-69, to U.S.A. 69-74; Knight, Order of Netherlands Lion, Officer, Order of Orange-Nassau and decorations from Greece, The Vatican, etc.
Leisure interests: golf, riding, tennis, music.
c/o Ministry of Foreign Affairs, The Hague, Netherlands.

Lynen, Feodor, DR. PHIL.; German biochemist; b. 6 April 1911; ed. Luitpold Oberrealschule and Ludwig-Maximilians-Universität, Munich.
Dozent, Univ. of Munich 42-46, Extraordinary Prof. 47-53, Prof. of Biochemistry 53-; Dir. Max Planck Inst. for Cell Chemistry, Munich 54-72; Dir. Max Planck Inst. for Biochemistry 72-; Neuberg Medal, American Soc. of European Chemists and Pharmacists 54; Liebig Award, German Chemical Soc. 55; Carus Medal, Leopoldina Acad. 61; Otto Warburg Medal, Soc. for Physiological Chemistry 63; Nobel Prize for Medicine 64; Normann Medal, Deutsche Gesellschaft für Fettwissenschaft; Dr. med. h.c. (Univ. of Freiburg); Dr. rer. nat. h.c. (Univ. of Seoul); Dr. Sc. h.c. (Univ. of Miami); Foreign mem. Royal Soc., London 75.
Publ. *Der Weg von der "Aktivierten Essigsäure" zu den Terpenen und den Fettsäuren.*
Office: Max-Planck-Institut für Biochemie, 8033 Martinsried; Home: 813 Starberg, Schiesstättstrasse 10, Federal Republic of Germany.
Telephone: 0811-8585323.

Lyng, John Daniel; Norwegian lawyer and politician; b. 22 Aug. 1905, Trondheim; ed. Oslo Univ. and legal studies in Germany and Denmark.
Legal practice 32-42; Judge 45-64; during Second World War, in the Norwegian Govt. service in Stockholm and London; mem. Trondheim Local Council 35-45, Skien Local Council 55-59; mem. Storting (Parl.) 45-53, 58-65; Leader Parl. Conservative Party 58-65; Prime Minister Aug. 63-Sept. 63; Gov. of Oslo and Akershus 64; Minister of Foreign Affairs 65-May 70.
Publs. *The Norwegian Athletic Sports* 37, *The Epoch of Treason* 48, *The Growth of State Power* 58.
Markalleen 41b, Stabekk, Oslo, Norway.

Lynn, James Thomas; American lawyer and government official; b. 27 Feb. 1927, Cleveland, Ohio; ed. Euclid Cen. High School, Adelbert Coll. of Western Reserve Univ., Harvard Law School.
Joined Cleveland law firm, Jones, Day, Cockley and Reavis 51, Partner 60-69; Gen. Counsel Dept. of Commerce 69-71, Under-Sec. 71-72; Sec. of Housing and Urban Devt. 72-75; Dir. Office of Management and Budget 75-.
Office of Management and Budget, Executive Office of the President of U.S.A., Washington, D.C. 20503, U.S.A.

Lynne, Seybourn Harris; American judge; b. 25 July 1907, Decatur, Alabama; *s.* of Seybourn Arthur Lynne and Annie Lee (Harris) Lynne; *m.* Katherine Brandau 1937; one *d.*; ed. Alabama Polytechnic Inst., and Univ. of Alabama.
Admitted to Alabama Bar 30; private legal practice, Decatur, Alabama 30-34; Judge, Morgan (Alabama) County Court 34-41; Judge, Eighth Judicial Circuit of Alabama 41-42; Staff, Judge Advocate, Central Pacific Base Command 42-46; Judge, U.S. District Court, Northern District, Alabama 46-, Chief Judge 53-73, Senior Judge Jan. 73-.

Leisure interest: trout fishing.
Federal Courthouse, Birmingham, Ala. 35203, U.S.A.
Telephone: (205) 254-1153.

Lyon, Stanley Douglas, B.SC.ENG., A.M.I.C.E., F.B.I.M.; British engineer and industrialist; b. 22 June 1917, Edinburgh; *s.* of Ernest Hutcheon Lyon and late Helen Wilson Lyon; *m.* May Alexander Jack 1941; three *s.*; ed. George Heriot's School and Edinburgh Univ.
Joined ICI Ltd. 46, Dyestuffs Div. 46, Eng. Dir. Wilton Works 57, Production Dir. Agricultural Div. 62, Deputy Chair. Agricultural Div. 64, Chair. Agricultural Div. 66, Dir. ICI Ltd. 68, Deputy Chair. 72-.
Leisure interests: golf, tennis, gardening.
Bramble Carr, Danby, Whitby, North Yorkshire; and 11 Billing Road, London, S.W.10, England.
Telephone: Castleton (Yorks.) 505; 01-325-0815.

Lyons, Dame Enid Muriel, G.B.E.; Australian politician; b. 9 July 1897, Duck River, Tasmania; *d.* of William Charles and Eliza (Tagget) Burnell; *m.* Joseph Aloysius Lyons (fmr. Prime Minister of Australia, deceased) 1915; six *s.* (one deceased) six *d.*; ed. State School, and Hobart Teachers' Training Coll.
M.P. (first woman mem. of House of Reps.) for Darwin (now Braddon), Tasmania 43-51; Int. Vice-Pres. St. Joan's Int., Social and Political Alliance 47-; Vice-Pres. of Exec. Council Dec. 49-51; newspaper columnist 51-54; mem. Australian Broadcasting Comm. 51-62; mem. Liberal Party; Hon. Fellow, Australian Coll. of Nursing.
Leisure interests: reading, gardening, needlework.
Publs. *So We Take Comfort* (autobiog.) 65, 66, *The Old Haggis* 69, *Among the Carrion Crows* 72.
Home Hill, 77 Middle Road, Devonport, Tasmania, Australia.
Telephone: Devonport 24-2250.

Lyons, Sir William, Kt., R.D.I., D.TECH., F.R.S.A.; British businessman; b. 4 Oct. 1901; *s.* of William and Mary Lyons; *m.* Greta Brown 1924; one *s.* (deceased) two *d.*; ed. Arnold School, Blackpool.
Founded, in partnership, Swallow Sidecar Co. 22, now Jaguar Cars Ltd., Chair. and Chief Exec. until 72; Pres. Soc. of Motor Manufacturers and Traders Ltd. 50-51; Pres. Motor Industry Research Assen. 54; Pres. Motor Trades Benevolent Fund 54; appointed Royal Designer for Industry by the Royal Soc. of Arts 54; Pres. Fellowship of the Motor Industry 57-58; Pres. Jaguar Cars (British Leyland U.K.) Ltd.; fmr. Deputy Chair. British Leyland Motor Corpn. Ltd.; Chair. Daimler Co. Ltd., Jaguar Cars Ltd., Coventry Climax Engines Ltd. and other subsidiaries until retirement in 72.
Leisure interest: golf.
Wappenbury Hall, Wappenbury, nr. Leamington Spa, Warwickshire, England.

Lysenko, Trofim Denisovich; Soviet scientist; b. 29 Sept. 1898, Karlovka, Ukraine; ed. Uman Agricultural School, and Kiev Agricultural Inst.
Worked at Gandze Selection Station and later at All-Union Selection and Genetics Inst., Odessa; Dir. Inst. of Genetics, U.S.S.R. Acad. of Sciences 40-65; Head of Laboratory, Inst. of Genetics, U.S.S.R. Acad. of Sciences 65-; Head of Laboratory, Experimental Research Station "Gorki Leninskyi", U.S.S.R. Acad. of Sciences 66-; mem. Ukrainian Acad. of Sciences 34-; mem. Lenin All-Union Acad. of Agricultural Sciences 35-, Pres. 38-56, 61; mem. U.S.S.R. Acad. of Sciences 39; Metchnikov Gold Medal, Acad. of Sciences 50; State Prizes, 41, 43, 49; seven Orders of Lenin; Red Banner of Labour Order; Hero of Socialist Labour 45; Silver Medal, World Peace Council 59.
Publs. *Agrobiology* 48, *Stage Development of Plants* 52, *Selected Works* 58.
c/o Academy of Sciences of the U.S.S.R., Leninsky Prospekt 14, Moscow V-71, U.S.S.R.

Lysholm, Alf James; Swedish professor; b. 14 Dec. 1893, Stockholm; *s.* of Major Rudolf Lysholm and Katty Knight; *m.* 1st Margit Ekman 1925 (died 1953); 2nd Jane Nyström 1955; one *d.*; ed. Royal Inst. of Technology, Stockholm.

Member of staff of A.B. Ljungstöms Angturbin, Stockholm 17-44, Calculating engineer 17-19, Head of turbine and calculating depts. 19-28, Chief Engineer 28-44; Consultant Engineer 44; Prof. Royal Inst. of Technology 50-60, Emer. 60-; Hon. mem. Royal Inst. Technical Research, Sweden; Fellow Inst. of Mechanical Engineers, London; Hon. mem. American Soc. of Mechanical Engineers, and Soc. of Automotive Engineers, U.S.A.; recipient of several prizes; over a hundred patented inventions of steam turbines, compressors, torque convertors, gas turbines etc.

Leisure interests: inventing, yachting, golf.

Karlaplan 11, 115 22 Stockholm, Sweden.

Lyttelton, Humphrey Richard Adeane; British bandleader and journalist; b. 23 May 1921; ed. Eton Coll.

Grenadier Guards 41-46; Camberwell Art School 47-48; formed own band 48; cartoonist for London *Daily Mail* 49-53; freelance journalist and leader of Humphrey Lytteltons' Band 53-; recorded Parlophone 50-60, Columbia 60-; contributor *Melody Maker* 54-, *Reynolds News* 55-62, *Sunday Citizen* 62-67; Compère BBC jazz programmes: *Jazz Scene, Jazz Club, Jazz 625* (TV); frequent television appearances.

Publs. *I Play as I Please, Second Chorus.*

235 Regent Street, London, W.1., England.

Lyzhin, Nikolai Mikhailovich; Soviet politician; b. 1914; ed. Higher Party School.

Consumers' co-operatives 29-36; Soviet Army 36-37; Young Communist League Official 39-41; mem. C.P.S.U. 41-; mem. Partisan Movement in Byelorussia 41-45; Student 46-50; Party Official 51-61; First Sec. Karachayevo-Cherkessy Regional Cttee., C.P.S.U. 61-70; staff of Central Cttee. C.P.S.U. 71-; Deputy to U.S.S.R. Supreme Soviet.

Central Committee, C.P.S.U., 4 Staraya ploshchad, Moscow, U.S.S.R.

M

NOTE: All names beginning Mc and Mac are treated as if they began Mac.

Ma Hui; Chinese army officer; b. 1910.
Divisional Commdr. 51; Maj.-Gen. People's Liberation Army 60; Deputy Commdr. Hopei Mil. District, PLA 64, Commdr. 65-; Vice-Chair. Hopei Revolutionary Cttee. 68; Sec. CCP Hopei 71.
People's Republic of China.

Ma Ning; Chinese air force officer; b. Chinyang, Honan.
Regimental Commdr. 46; Deputy Dir., Org. Dept., People's Liberation Army Gen. Political Dept. 56; Commdr. Air Force Unit 7311, Kirin 68; mem. 10th Cen. Cttee. of CCP 73; Commdr. of Air Force, PLA 74.
People's Republic of China.

Maaløe, Ole Urban, M.D.; Danish professor of microbiology; b. 15 Aug. 1914, Copenhagen; s. of Carl Urban Maaløe and Betsy Skårup; m. Aase Johansen 1938; two s. one d.
Director of Dept. of Biological Standards, State Serum Inst., Copenhagen 48-58; Head of Univ. Inst. of Microbiology, Copenhagen 58-; Co-Editor *Journal of Molecular Biology* 65-70; mem. council of fifteen that founded European Molecular Biology Org. (EMBO) 64; mem. Danish Pugwash Group 60-, Danish Science Advisory Council 70-72, Royal Danish Acad. of Sciences 60-, American Acad. of Arts and Sciences 68-; Anders Jahre Prize, Univ. of Oslo 68.
Leisure interests: books and paintings.
Publs. *On the Relation Between Alexin and Opsonin* 46, *Control of Macromolecular Synthesis* (with N. O. Kjeldgaard) 66.
University Institute of Microbiology, Øster Farimagsgade 2A, 1353 Copenhagen K; Home: Ahlmanns Alle 38, 2900 Hellerup, Copenhagen, Denmark.
Telephone: 01-15-8750 (Univ.); Hellerup 485 (Home).

Maazel, Lorin; American conductor and musician; b. 6 March 1930, Neuilly, France; m. Israela Margalit; one s. two d.; ed. under Vladimir Bakaleinikoff and at Univ. of Pittsburgh.
Debut as conductor 38; Conductor, American Symphony Orchestras 39-; violin recitalist; European debut 53; festivals include Bayreuth, Salzburg, Edinburgh; tours include South America, Australia, U.S.S.R. and Japan; Artistic Dir., Deutsche Oper Berlin 65-71; Musical Dir. Radio Symphony Orchestra, Berlin 65; Assoc. Principal Conductor, New Philharmonia Orchestra, London 70-72; Dir. Cleveland Orchestra 71-; Hon. D.Mus. (Pittsburgh Univ.) 68; D.Hum.Litt. (Beaver Coll.) 73.
c/o The Cleveland Orchestra, Severance Hall, 11001 Euclid Avenue, Cleveland, Ohio 44106, U.S.A.
Telephone: 216-231-7300.

Mabe, Manabu; Brazilian (b. Japanese) painter; b. 1924, Kumamoto-Ken; s. of Soichi and Haru Mabe; m. Yoshino Mabe 1951; three s.
Abstract painter; exhbn. in countries all over the world; One-man exhbn., Museum of Fine Arts, Houston, Tex. 70; Leiner Prize for Contemporary Arts 57, Braun Prize 59, Best Nat. Painter, São Paulo Bienal 59, Fiat Prize Venice Biennale 60, First Prize American Biennale, Cordoba 62.
Leisure interests: collecting pre-Columbian objects of art.
Rua das Canjeranas 321, Jabaquara, São Paulo; and c/o Yutaka Sanematsu, Praça da Sé, 28 4° andar, São Paulo, Brazil.

Mabolia Inengo Trabwato; Zairian politician; b. 1932, Kinshasa; ed. St. Joseph Coll., Kinshasa.
Teacher, St. Joseph Coll., Kinshasa 52-58, later worked

in television; fmr. Pres., Union des Enseignants Congolais and Gen. Councillor, Union Nat. des Travailleurs Congolais (UNTC); Head, Haut Commissariat au Plan et à la Réconstruction Nat. 67; Inspector of Secondary Educ.; Vice-Minister of Educ. 69-72; State Commr. (Minister) for Educ. July 72-75.
c/o Office of the State Commissioner for Education, Kinshasa, Zaire.

Mabrouk, Ezzidin Ali, LL.M.; Libyan politician; b. 28 May 1932; ed. Cairo Univ. and Univ. Coll., London.
Public Prosecutor, Tripoli 56; subsequently Judge, Summary Court, Tripoli, Pres. Tripoli Court and Counsellor of Supreme Appeal Court; Senior Legal Adviser, Org. of Petroleum Exporting Countries (OPEC); Minister of Petroleum, Libya 70-.
Ministry of Petroleum, P.O. Box 256, Tripoli, Libya.

Mabrouk, Lieut.-Col. Saleh Abdel al-; Sudanese army officer; b. 1936, Kadogli; m.; two c.; ed. Military Coll.
Commissioned 59; Sec.-Gen. Revolutionary Command Council 70; Minister of Youth, Sport and Social Affairs 71-73, of Presidential Affairs 73-74, of Egyptian Affairs in Sudan 74-.
Ministry of Egyptian Affairs, Khartoum, Sudan.

Macadam, Peter; British business executive; b. 9 Sept. 1921, Buenos Aires, Argentina; s. of Francis Macadam and Marjorie Mary Browne; m. Ann Musson 1949; three d.; ed. Buenos Aires, Stonyhurst Coll., Lancashire.
Joined British-American Tobacco (BAT) Co. Group in Argentina 46; Chair., Gen. Man. Commander S.A. (BAT subsidiary) 55-58; marketing post in Chile 58-59; Personal Asst. to BAT Dir., London 59-60; Chair., Gen. Man. BAT (Hong Kong) Ltd. 61-62; Dir. BAT Group 63-, Chairman's Policy Cttee. 70-, Chair. Tobacco Div. Board of Management 73-, Vice-Chair. BAT Co. Ltd. 75-76, Chair. April 76-.
Leisure interests: golf, shooting.
British-American Tobacco Co. Ltd., Westminster House, 7 Millbank, London, SW1P 3JE; Home: 34 Campden Hill Court, Campden Hill Road, London, W8 7HS, England.
Telephone: 01-222 1222 (Office); 01-937 1389 (Home).

Macarrón Jaime, Ricardo; Spanish painter; b. 9 April 1926, Madrid; m. Alicia Macarrón Jaime 1951; two d.; ed. Escuela Superior de Bellas Artes de San Fernando, Madrid and scholarship in Paris.
Professor of Drawing and Painting, Escuela Superior de Bellas Artes, Madrid; has painted many portraits of royalty and nobility; mem. Royal Soc. of Portrait Painters 62; numerous one-man exhbns. in Spain and abroad including two in London and one in New York; represented at Museo de Arte Contemporáneo, Madrid, Univ. of Oslo and Fundación Guell, Barcelona, portraits at the Royal Soc. of Portrait Painters; numerous awards.
Leisure interests: walking in the country, hunting, playing chess.
Agustin de Bethencourt No. 7, Madrid 3, Spain.

MacArthur II, Douglas; American foreign service officer and businessman; b. 5 July 1909, Bryn Mawr, Pa.; s. of Arthur MacArthur and Mary Hendry McCalla; m. Laura Louise Barkley 1934; one d.; ed. Milton Acad. and Yale Univ.
United States Army 33-35; Foreign Service 35-; Vancouver 35-36; Foreign Service School 36; Naples 37, Paris 38-40, Lisbon 40, Vichy 40-42; interned by Nazis 42-44; Asst. Political Adviser SHAEF 44; Paris

44-48, Brussels 48-49; Dept. of State 49-51; Counsellor in Paris and Adviser to Gen. Eisenhower at SHAPE 51-52; Counsellor of the Dept. of State 53-56; Amb. to Japan 57-61, to Belgium 61-65; Asst. Sec. of State for Congressional Relations 65-67; Amb. to Austria 67-69; Amb. to Iran 69-72; Business Consultant and dir. of several Belgian and Amer. companies 72-; mem. Board Amer. Chamber of Commerce in Belgium, Asscn. et Chambre de Commerce Belgo-Japonaise.
Leisure interests: shooting, hiking.
65 Rue Langeveld, 1180 Brussels, Belgium.
Telephone: Brussels 02-374-99-14.

Mac Arthur, Robert Helmer, PH.D.; American ecologist; b. 7 April 1930, Toronto, Canada; s. of John Wood Mac Arthur and Olive Turner (Mac Arthur); m. Elizabeth Whitemore 1952; three s. one d.; ed. Marlboro Coll., Vt., and Brown and Yale Univs.
Assistant Prof. to Prof. of Biology, Univ. of Pennsylvania 58-64; Prof. of Biology, Princeton Univ. 64-, Henry Fairfield Osborn Prof. of Biology 68-; Fellow, American Acad. of Arts and Sciences; mem. Nat. Acad. of Sciences.
Leisure interests: nature-study, mountain-climbing, music.
Publs. *Population Ecology of Some Warblers* 58, *On Bird Species Diversity* 61 (and later edns.), *Generalized Theorems of Natural Selection* 62, *The Theory of Island Biogeography* 67.
Department of Biology, Princeton University, Princeton, N.J. 08540; 106 Broadmead, Princeton, N.J. 08540, U.S.A.
Telephone: 452-3830 (Office); 924-4976 (Home).

McAuliffe, Eugene Vincent; American diplomatist; b. 25 Oct. 1918, Forest Hills, Mass.; s. of the late Thomas J. McAuliffe and Charlotte P. McAuliffe (née Metzger); m. Winifred Marie Gallivan 1946; six s. two d.; ed. Boston Public Latin School, Boston Coll., Boston Univ. Graduate Business Coll. and Nat. War Coll., Washington, D.C.
Served with U.S. Army in Europe as Captain, Infantry 42-47; Vice-Consul and Exec. Sec. High Comm. in Germany 48-54; with Exec. Secr. Dept. of State 54-58; First Sec. Embassy in Mexico City 58-62; studied Nat. War Coll. 62-63; Dir. Office of Public Services, Dept. of State 63-64, Exec. Sec. of Policy Planning Council 64-66, Dir. NATO and Atlantic Political/Mil. Affairs 66-68; Minister and Deputy Chief of Mission in Madrid 68-70; Minister Counsellor and Political Advisor to Supreme Allied Commdr. Europe 70-72, Minister Counsellor and Deputy Chief of Mission to NATO 72-75; Amb. to Hungary April 75-; Meritorious Honor Award, Dept. of State 58.
Leisure interest: bridge.
Embassy Budapest, c/o Dept. of State, Washington, D.C. 20520, U.S.A.; Residence: Zugligeti ut. 93, Budapest, Hungary.
Telephone: Budapest 329-384 and 124-224 (Office); 164-055 (Residence).

McBain, Ed (see Hunter, Evan).

MacBain, Gavin K.; American business executive; b. 9 July 1911, Closter, N.J.; m. Margaret Gristede; ed. Columbia Univ.
Sales Rep., Wood Struthers and Co., N.Y.C. 33-44; Asst. to the Treas. Bristol-Myers Co. 44, Asst. Treas. 45, Asst. Sec. 46, Treas. 47, Dir. 61-65, Pres. 65-67, Chair. of the Board Jan. 67-, Chief Exec. Officer 67-72; Chair. of the Board and Pres., Gristede Brothers, Inc. 61-65; Dir. United Mutual Savings Bank, First Fed. Savings and Loan Asscn., U.S. Trust Co. of N.Y., Simplicity Pattern Co., Kennecott Copper Corp., J. C. Penney Co. Inc.; mem. Board, Grocery Mfrs. of America; mem. Advisory Council, Nat. 4-H Club Foundation; Chair. Sponsors Cttee., Lexington School for the Deaf; fmrly. Chair. Council on Family Health

and Nat. Chair. United Community Campaigns of America 69; fmr. Pres. The Economic Club of N.Y.
Office: Bristol-Myers Co. 345 Park Avenue, New York, N.Y. 10022; Home: Bedford Village, N.Y., U.S.A.

McBride, Katharine Elizabeth, M.A., PH.D.; American college president and educator; b. 1904, Phila.; d. of Thomas Canning McBride and Sally Hulley Neals McBride; ed. Bryn Mawr Coll. and Columbia Univ.
Research in Psychology, Philadelphia 29-35 (with Dr. T. Weisenburg 29-34); Lecturer in Educ. Bryn Mawr Coll. 35-36; Asst. Prof. of Educ. and Psychology 36-38, Assoc. Prof. 38-40; Dean, Radcliffe Coll. 40-42; Pres. Bryn Mawr Coll. 42-70; Dir. Rider Coll.; mem. Amer. Psychological Asscn., Amer. Asscn. of Univ. Women, Montgomery Co., Pa., Comm. on Mental Health and Mental Retardation; Dir. of the New York Life Insurance Co., Phila. Child Guidance Clinic, Phila. Saving Fund Soc.; Hon. L.H.D., L.L.D., Ed.D.
Publs. *Aphasia* (with Theodore Weisenburg) 35; *Adult Intelligence* (with T. Weisenburg and A. Roe) 36.
c/o Bryn Mawr College, Bryn Mawr, Pa.; 704 Pennstone Road, Bryn Mawr, Pa., U.S.A.
Telephone: 215-La5-0174.

McBride, Rt. Hon. Sir Philip Albert Martin, K.C.M.G., P.C., M.P.; Australian politician; b. 18 June 1892; ed. Burra Public School and Prince Alfred Coll.
President Stockowners' Asscn. of S. Australia 30-31; mem. Federal House of Representatives 31-37, 46-; Senator 37-44; mem. War Cabinet 39-40; Asst. Minister for Commerce 39-40; Minister for Army 40, for Supply and Development and Munitions 40-41; Deputy Leader of Opposition 41-43; Minister of the Interior 49-51; Acting Minister for Defence March-Oct. 50; Minister for the Navy and for Air May-July 51; Minister for Defence Oct. 50-58; Liberal.
30 Briar Avenue, Medindi, S.A. 5082, Australia.

MacBride, Séan, S.C.; Irish barrister and politician; b. 26 Jan. 1904, Paris, France; s. of the late Maj. John MacBride and late Maude Gonne; m. Catalina Bulfin 1926; one s. one d.; ed. St. Louis de Gonzague, Paris, Mount St. Benedict, and Nat. Univ. Dublin.
Imprisoned many times for Irish nationalistic activities; Journalist for many years before being called to Bar 37; called to Inner Bar 43; founded Republican Party (Clann na Poblachta) 46; elected to Irish Parl. (Dáil Éireann) 47, re-elected 48, 51, 54 and 57; Minister for External Affairs 48-51; Pres. Council of Ministers, Council of Europe 48-51; Vice-Pres. Council of O.E.E.C. 48-51; Exec. mem. Pan European Union 50; Chair. Amnesty International; Irish Rep. to Council of Europe Assembly, and Rapporteur of Econ. Comm. 54-57; mem. Ghana Bar; Sec.-Gen. Int. Comm. of Jurists 63-70, Council of Minorities Rights Group; Chair. Exec., Int. Peace Bureau, Geneva, Int. Exec. Amnesty Int., Special N.G.O. Cttee. on Human Rights, Geneva; UN Commr. for Namibia 73-; Hon. mem. Institut des Sciences Administratives (Brussels); Hon. LL.D., Coll. of St. Thomas, Minn.; Nobel Peace Prize 74.
Leisure interest: sailing.
Publs. *Civil Liberty* 48, *Our People—Our Money* 51.
United Nations Secretariat, New York, N.Y. 10017, U.S.A.; and Roebuck House, Clonskea, Dublin 14, Ireland.
Telephone: 694225 (Dublin).

McBride, William James, M.B.E.; Irish banker and rugby football player; b. 6 June 1940, Toombridge; s. of William James McBride and Irene Patterson; m. Penny Michael 1966; one s. one d.; ed. Ballymena Acad.
First played rugby for Ireland against England 62; five Lions tours, South Africa 62, New Zealand 66, South Africa 68, New Zealand 71, South Africa 74; holder of 63 international caps (world record); 17 Test appearances for Lions (record); toured Argentina 70 and Australia 67 for Ireland; Asst. Bank Man. 74-.

Leisure interests: gardening, fishing.
Gorse Lodge, Ballyclare, Co. Antrim, Northern Ireland, United Kingdom.
Telephone: Ballyclare 2710.

McCabe, Thomas Bayard, A.B., HON. LL.D.; American industrialist and banker; b. 11 July 1893, Whaleyville; m. Jeannette Laws 1924; three s.; ed. Swarthmore Coll. Scott Paper Co., Pennsylvania, Salesman 16-17, Asst. Sales Man. 19-20, Sales Man. 20-22, Dir. 21-, Sec. and Sales Man. 22-27, Vice-Pres. 27, Pres. 27-62, Chair. and Chief Exec. 62-66, Chair. 66-68, Chair. Finance Cttee. 69-71; Dir. Fed. Reserve Bank of Philadelphia 38-48, Chair. 39-48; mem. Business Advisory Council, Dept. of Commerce 40-, Chair. 44-45; Exec. Asst. to Commr., Advisory Comm. to Council of Nat. Defense 40; Deputy Dir., Div. of Priorities, Office of Production Management 41; Deputy Lend-Lease Administrator 41-42; Army-Navy Liquidation Commr. 45; Special Asst. to Sec. of State and Foreign Liquidation Commr. 45-46; Chair., Board of Governors of Fed. Reserve System, Wash., D.C. 48-51; Chair. Board of Trustees Eisenhower Exchange Fellowships 54-68, Hon. Chair. 69-; Chair. Board of Trustees of the Marketing Science Inst. 62-70, Hon. Chair. 70; Trustee, Cttee. for Econ. Devt.; mem. U.S. Associates of the Int. Chamber of Commerce; American Del. to Congress of Int. Chamber of Commerce, Montreux 47; awarded Medal of Merit 46.
Scott Paper Company, Philadelphia, Pa. 19113; Home: 607 North Chester Road, Swarthmore, Pa. 19081, U.S.A.
Telephone: 215-SA 4-2000.

McCain, James Allen, A.B., M.A., ED.D., D.SC., LL.D.; American university official; b. 8 Dec. 1907; s. of Frank Pickering McCain and Julia Allen; one d.; ed. Wofford Coll., Duke Univ. and Stanford Univ., Calif.
Asst. Prof. of English and Journalism Colorado State Univ. 29-34; Asst. to Pres. Colo. State Univ. 34-39, Dean of Students 39-41, Dean of Vocational Educ. and Guidance, and Dir. of Summer Session 41-42; on active duty as officer-in-charge of Enlisted Classification Program, U.S. Navy, with rank of Lieut.-Commdr. 42-45; Pres. Montana State Univ. 45-50; Dir. and Chair. of the Board Helena Branch Fed. Reserve Bank of Minneapolis 48-50; Pres. Kansas State Univ. 50-; Dir. Kansas State Chamber of Commerce 54-57; mem. U.S. Nat. Comm. for UNESCO 56-58; Eisenhower Int. Exchange Fellow 57; Trustee Eisenhower Exchange Fellowships 60, Menninger Foundation 72-; mem. Advisory Council to Peace Corps 61-, Advisory Cttee. to Export-Import Bank 61-71, Advisory Board to Office of Econ. Analysis, Mid-America Governors' Transportation Cttee.; Dir. Acad. for Educational Devt. Inc., Eisenhower Library Comm., Kansas Research Foundation, Manhattan Mutual Life Insurance Co., Security Benefit Life Insurance Co., Dunlap and Assocs., Inc.; Consultant to Univs. of Iran 69; U.S. Comm. on Higher Educ. in Bogotá, Colombia 70; Awarded Dwight D. Eisenhower People-to-People Medallion for Outstanding Contributions to Int. Understanding 69; Chair. Mid-America State Univs. Asscn. 73-; Hon. LL.D. (Wofford Coll., Colorado State Univ., Univ. of Montana); Hon. D.Sc. (Andhra Pradesh Agricultural Univ.).
Leisure interests: music, golf, reading.
Publs. *Vocational Guidance for Vocational Teachers* 42, *Vocational Education* (with others) 42, *Education in the Armed Services* (with others) 42, *Universities . . . and Development Assistance Abroad* (with others) 67.
Kansas State University Campus, Manhattan, Kansas 66506, U.S.A.
Telephone: 913-532-6222.

McCall, Howard Weaver, Jr., B.A.; American banker; b. 11 Aug. 1907; ed. the McCallie School, Chattanooga, Tenn., Univ. of Virginia, and Graduate School of Banking, Rutgers Univ.

Chemical Bank New York Trust Co. 28-72, Asst. Sec. 37-41, Asst. Vice-Pres. 41-45, Vice-Pres. 45-55, Exec. Vice-Pres. 55-60, First Vice-Pres. 60-61, Vice-Chair. 61-65, Pres. 65-72, also Dir.; Dir. Chemical Int. Banking Corpn., Chemical Int. Finance Ltd., Interchemical Corpn., Liggett & Myers Tobacco Co. Inc., Lykes Bros. Steamship Co. Inc.; mem. Boards of Trustees Mutual Life Insurance Co. of New York.
68 Dorchester Road, Darien, Conn. 06820, U.S.A.

McCall, John Donald; British business executive; b. 1 Feb. 1911; s. of Gilbert Kerr McCall; m. Vere Stewart Gardner 1942; one s. one d.; ed. Clifton Coll. and Univ. of Edinburgh.
Gold mining industry, South Africa 30-39; served in Second World War 39-45; joined Consolidated Gold Fields Ltd. 46, Dir. 59, Joint Deputy Chair. 68, Chair. 69-June 76, non-exec. Dir. June 76-; Chair. Gold Fields Mining and Industrial Ltd.; Dir. Azcon Corpn., Commonwealth Mining Investments (Australia) Ltd., Consolidated Gold Fields Australia Ltd., Gold Fields American Corpn., Gold Fields of S. Africa Ltd., G.F.S.A. Holdings Ltd., Gold Fields Mining and Devt. Ltd., Newconex Canadian Exploration Ltd., Newconex Holdings Ltd., The Standard Bank Ltd., Ultramar Co. Ltd., Standard and Chartered Banking Group Ltd., U.K. S. Africa Trade Asscn. Ltd. (mem. Exec. Cttee.); Councillor African Welfare Ltd. 75-; mem. Council Australia Soc. 71.
Leisure interests: gardening, golf.
Consolidated Gold Fields Ltd., 49 Moorgate, London, EC2R 6BQ; Home: 93 Eaton Place, London, S.W.1, England.

McCall, Tom; American state governor; b. 22 March 1913, Egypt, Mass.; s. of Henry McCall and Dorothy Lawson McCall; m. Audrey Owen; two s.; ed. Univ. of Oregon.
Journalist, radio and television political analyst and documentarian; Exec. Asst. to Gov. of Oregon 49-52; Sec. of State, Oregon 63; Gov. of Oregon 66-74, re-elected 70; mem., Past Chair. Exec. Cttee. Educ. Comm., U.S.A.; mem. Citizens Advisory Cttee. on Environmental Quality; Conservationist of the Year Award, Nat. Wildlife Fed. 74; Audubon Medal 74 and several awards for film documentaries; Dr. h.c. (Linfield Coll.); Republican.
Leisure interests: hunting, fishing, golfing.
2300 S.W. Broadway Drive, Portland, Ore. 97201, U.S.A.
Telephone: 503-226-3390.

McCance, Sir Andrew, Kt., D.SC., LL.D., F.R.S., D.L.; British industrialist; b. 30 March 1889; s. of John McCance; m. Joya Harriett Gladys Burford 1936 (died 1969); two d.; ed. Morrison's Acad., Crieff, Allan Glen's School and Royal School of Mines, London.
Assistant Armour Man., W. Beardmore and Co. 10-19; Founder and Man. Dir. Clyde Alloy Steel Co. Ltd. 19-30; mem. Scientific Advisory Council Dept. Scientific and Industrial Research 41-47; fmr. Pres. Inst. Engineering and Shipbuilders, Scotland, Iron and Steel Inst. and Glasgow and West Scotland Iron and Steel Inst., Glasgow; fmr. Pres. British Iron and Steel Federation; fmr. Chair., Man. Dir. and Hon. Pres. Colvilles Ltd.; Pres. Clyde Alloy Steel Co. Ltd.; fmr. Dir. Nat. Commercial Bank of Scotland Ltd.; Chair. Colvilles-Clugston-Shaule Ltd.
27 Broom Cliff, Newton Mearns, Glasgow, Scotland.
Telephone: 041-639-5115.

McCance, Robert Alexander, C.B.E., M.A., M.D., PH.D., F.R.C.P., F.R.S.; British physician; b. 9 Dec. 1898, Belfast; s. of John Stoupe Finlay McCance and Mary Bristow; m. Mary Lindsay (MacGregor) 1922; one s. one d.; ed. Mourne Grange, Co. Down, St. Bees School, Cumberland, and Sidney Sussex Coll., Cambridge.

Royal Naval Air Service, including service with Grand Fleet 17-19; undergraduate studies 19-22; Biochemical research 22-25; qualified in medicine 27; Asst. Physician in charge of Biochemical Dept., King's Coll. Hospital 34; Reader in Medicine, Cambridge Univ. 38; Prof. of Experimental Medicine, Cambridge Univ. 45-67; Fellow of Sidney Sussex Coll., Cambridge; Dir. Dept. of Experimental Medicine, Medical Research Council, 45-67; Dir. Infant Malnutrition Unit, M.R.C., Kampala 67-69; Triennial Gold Medal, West London Medico-Chirurgical Society 49; hon. mem. American Pediatric Soc., Asscn. of American Physicians, Swiss Soc. for Research in Nutrition; Conway Evans Prize 60, James Spence Medal, British Paediatric Asscn. 61; Hon. D.Sc. (Belfast) 64; Hon. F.R.C.O.G.
Leisure interests: cycling, outdoor activities, natural observation.
4 Kent House, Sussex Street, Cambridge, England.

McCandless, Bruce, II; American astronaut; b. 8 June 1937, Boston, Mass.; s. of the late Rear-Adm. Bruce McCandless and late Mrs. Sue Worthington Bradley McCandless Inman; m. Bernice Doyle 1960; one s. one d.; ed. U.S. Naval Acad. and Stanford Univ.
Flight training, Pensacola, Fla. and Kingsville, Tex.; weapons system and carrier landing training, Key West, Fla. 60; carrier duty, Fighter Squadron 102 60-64; instrument flight instructor, Attack Squadron 43, Naval Air Station, Apollo Soucek Field, Oceana, Va.; graduate studies in electrical engineering, Stanford Univ. until 66; selected by NASA as astronaut April 66; Co-investigator Astronaut Manoeuvring Unit Experiment on Skylab 68-74; back-up crew for first Skylab Mission 73.
Leisure interests: electronics, scuba diving, sailing, photography.
NASA Johnson Space Center, Houston, Tex. 77058, U.S.A.
Telephone: 713-483-2421.

McCann, Hugh James, B.SC.(ECON.); Irish diplomatist; b. 8 Feb. 1916; s. of Hugh J. McCann and Sophie Campbell; m. Mary V. Larkin 1950; four s. one d.; ed. London School of Economics, Univ. of London, Belvedere Coll., Dublin.
Admin. Officer, Dept. of Industry and Commerce, Dublin 40-41; Private Sec. to Minister for Industry and Commerce 41-43; Superintending Officer, Dept. of Supplies 43-44; Commercial Sec. Office of the High Commr. for Ireland, London 44-46; First Sec. Dept. of External Affairs 46-48; Counsellor, Irish Embassy, Washington, D.C. 48-54; Minister to Switzerland and Austria 54-56; Asst. Sec. to the Dept. of External Affairs 56-58; Amb. to U.K. 58-63; Sec. Dept. of Foreign Affairs, Dublin 63-74; Amb. to France 74- (concurrently to Morocco 75-); Perm. Rep. of Ireland to OECD, Perm. Del. of Ireland to UNESCO.
Leisure interests: reading, photography, golf.
Ambassade d'Irlande, 12 avenue Foch, 75 Paris 16e, France; and Frankfield, Mart Lane, Foxrock, Co. Dublin, Ireland.
Telephone: 727-91-58 (Office); 893682 (Home).

McCann, Most Rev. James, M.A., PH.D., D.D.; British Protestant ecclesiastic; b. 31 Oct. 1897; ed. Royal Belfast Academical Inst., Queen's Univ., Belfast and Trinity Coll., Dublin.
Curate, Ballymena 20-22, Ballyclare 22-24, Cavan 24-28, Oldcastle 28-30; Rector, Donaghpatrick 30-36, St. Mary's, Drogheda 36-45; Canon, St. Patrick's Cathedral, Dublin 44-45; Bishop of Meath 45-59; Archbishop of Armagh and Primate of All Ireland 59-69; Ecclesiastical History Prize 17, Elrington Theological Prize 30; Hon. LL.D. (Queen's Univ. Belfast) 66.
Publ. *Asceticism: an historical study* 44.
Belgravia Hotel, Lisburn Road, Belfast, N. Ireland.

McCann, H.E. Cardinal Owen, D.D., PH.D.; South African ecclesiastic; b. 26 June 1907, Cape Town; s. of late Edward McCann and Susan Mary Plint; ed. St. Joseph's Coll., Rondebosch and Pontificium Collegium Urbanianum de Propaganda Fide.
Ordained priest 35; Titular Bishop of Stettorio 50; Archbishop of Cape Town 51-; named Asst. at the Papal Throne 60; created cardinal 65; Hon. D. Litt. (Univ. of Cape Town).
Archdiocesan Chancery, Cathedral Place, 12 Bouquet Street, Cape Town, South Africa.
Telephone: 452419.

McCardell, Archie Richard, M.B.A.; American business executive; b. 29 Aug. 1926, Hazel Park, Mich.; s. of Archie and Josephine (Gauthier) McCardell; m. Margaret Edith Martin 1950; one s. two d.; ed. Univ. of Michigan.
Finance Exec., Ford Motor Co. 49-60; Sec.-Treas. Ford of Australia 60-63; Finance Dir., Ford of Germany 63-66; Group Vice-Pres. Corporate Services, Xerox Corpn. 66-68; Exec. Vice-Pres. 68-71; Pres. and Chief Operating Officer 71-.
Xerox Corporation, Stamford, Conn. 06904; Home: 2322 Sturges Highway, Westport, Conn. 06880, U.S.A.
Telephone: 203-329-8711 (Office); 203-255-3770 (Home).

McCardle, James Joachim, B.A.; Canadian diplomatist; b. 27 April 1922, Stratford, Ont.; s. of John Patrick McCardle and Mary Keegan; m. Lannie Roth Harrison 1948; one d.; ed. Univ. of Toronto.
Canadian Army 43-46; joined Foreign Service 46; Canadian Liaison Office, Tokyo 47-49; Dept. of External Affairs 49-53; Canadian Embassy, Washington, D.C. 53-56; Dept. of External Affairs 56-59; Sec. of Canadian Section, Canada-U.S.A. Perm. Joint Board on Defence 56-59; Del. to North Atlantic Council 59-62; Dept. of External Affairs 62-69; Amb. to Ireland 69-72; High Commr. to Australia and Fiji 72-.
Leisure interests: golf, bridge.
Canadian High Commission, Commonwealth Avenue, Canberra, A.C.T. 2600; Home: 32 Mugga Way, Red Hill, Canberra, A.C.T., Australia.
Telephone: 73-3844 (Office).

McCarthy, Sir Edwin, Kt., C.B.E., B.COM.; Australian diplomatist; b. 30 March 1896; ed. Christian Brothers Coll., Melbourne and Melbourne Univ.
Australian Shipping Rep. in U.S.A. 41-44; Sec. Commonwealth Dept. of Commerce 45-50; Controller-Gen. of Food 45-48; Dep. High Commr. in London 50-58; Ambassador to Netherlands 58-62, to Belgium 59-62; Ambassador to European Economic Community 60-64; Chair. Commonwealth Economic Cttee. 64-67.
c/o University Club, Phillip Street, Sydney, N.S.W. 2000, Australia.

McCarthy, Eugene Joseph, M.A.; American politician; b. 29 March 1916, Watkins, Minn.; s. of late Michael J. McCarthy and Anna Baden McCarthy; m. Abigail Quigley 1945; one s. three d.; ed. St. John's Univ., Collegeville, Minn. and Minnesota Univ.
Successively Prof. of Economics and Education, St. John's Univ., Collegeville, Minn.; Civilian Technical Asst., War Dept. Military Intelligence Division; Acting Chair., Sociology Dept., St. Thomas Coll., St. Paul, Minn.; mem. U.S. House of Reps. (Fourth Minn. district) 48-58; Senator from Minnesota 58-71; Cardinal Newman Award 55; Hon. LL.D. St. Louis Univ. 55.
Publs. *Frontiers in American Democracy* 60, *Dictionary of American Politics* 62, *A Liberal Answer to the Conservative Challenge* 64, *The Limits of Power: America's Role in the World* 67, *The Year of the People* 69, *Other Things and the Aardvark* (poems) 70.
3053 Q Street N.W., Washington, D.C. 20007, U.S.A.

McCarthy, Mary; American writer; b. 21 June 1912, Seattle, Washington; d. of Roy Winfield McCarthy and Therese (née Preston) McCarthy; m. 1st Harold

Johnsrud 1933; *m*. 2nd Edmund Wilson 1938, one *s*.; *m*. 3rd Bowden Broadwater 1946; *m*. 4th James West 1961; ed. Vassar Coll.

Theatre critic *Partisan Review* 37-57; Instructor Bard Coll. 45-46, Sarah Lawrence Coll. 48; *Horizon* award (for *The Oasis*) 48, Guggenheim Fellowships 49 and 59, Nat. Acad. of Arts and Letters award 57.

Publs. *The Company She Keeps* (novel) 42, *The Oasis* (re-issued as *A Source of Embarrassment*) (novel) 49, *Cast a Cold Eye* (short stories) 50, *The Groves of Academe* (novel) 52, *A Charmed Life* (novel) 55, *Venice Observed* 56, *Sights and Spectacles* (theatre criticism) 56, *Memories of a Catholic Girlhood* (memoirs) 57, *The Stones of Florence* 59, *On the Contrary* 62, *The Group* 63 (film 66), *Vietnam* 67, *Hanoi* 68, *The Writing on the Wall* (literary essays) 70, *Birds of America* (novel) 71, *Medina* 72, *The Mask of State—Watergate Portraits* 74, *The Seventeenth Degree* 74; numerous essays, short stories, reviews, etc. in *The New Yorker*, *Harper's*, *Encounter*, *The New York Review of Books* and other magazines.

141 rue de Rennes, Paris 6e, France.

McCarthy, Michael W.; American financier; b. 24 May 1903.

Office Man., Mutual Stores, Oakland, Calif.; organized **Hagstrom Food Stores, Calif.** 32; Merrill Lynch, Pierce, Fenner and Beane, investment brokerage, New York City 40-68, Gen. Partner 44-48, Asst. Man. Partner 48-57, Man. Partner, Merrill Lynch, Pierce, Fenner and Smith 57-59, Pres., Merrill Lynch, Pierce, Fenner and Smith Inc. 59-61, Chair., Chief Exec. Officer 61- ,Chair. Exec. Cttee. 66-Dec. 68; fmr. Gov. New York Stock Exchange, American Stock Exchange, Asscn. Stock Exchange Firms.

1 Liberty Plaza, 165 Broadway, New York, N.Y. 10006, U.S.A.

McCartney, Paul, M.B.E.; British songwriter and performer; b. 18 June 1942, Liverpool; *m*. Linda Eastman 1969; three *d*.; ed. Stockton Wood Road Primary School, Speke, Joseph Williams Primary School, Gateacre, and Liverpool Inst.

Plays guitar, piano and organ; taught himself to play trumpet at age of 13; wrote first song 56, has since written numerous songs with John Lennon (*q.v.*); joined pop group *The Quarrymen* 56; appeared under various titles until formation of *The Beatles* 60; appeared with *The Beatles* in the following activities: performances in Hamburg 60, 61, 62, The Cavern, Liverpool 60, 61; worldwide tours 63-66; attended Transcendental Meditation Course at Maharishi's Acad., Rishikesh, India Feb. 68; formed Apple Corpn. Ltd., **parent org. of The Beatles Group of Companies** 68, left *The Beatles* after collapse of Apple Corpn. Ltd. 70; First solo album *McCartney* 70; formed own pop group *Wings* 71-; tours of Britain and Europe 72-73, U.K. and Australia 75; subsequent albums: *Ram* 71, *Wildlife* 71, *Red Rose Speedway* 73, *Band on the Run* 73, *Venus and Mars* 75; two Grammy Awards for *Band on the Run* (incl. Best Pop Vocal Performance) 75.

Paul McCartney composed soundtrack music for *The Family Way* 66, *James Paul McCartney* 73, *Live and Let Die* 73, *The Zoo Gang* (TV series) 73.

Films by The Beatles: *A Hard Day's Night* 64, *Help!* 65, *Yellow Submarine* (animated colour cartoon film) 68, *Let it Be* 70; TV film *Magical Mystery Tour* 67.

McCartney Productions Ltd., 1 Soho Square, London, W.1, England.

Telephone: 01-439 0386.

McClellan, John Little; American politician; b. 25 Feb. 1896.

Admitted to Arkansas Bar 17; practised law, Sheridan; Prosecuting Attorney 7th Judicial District of Arkansas 27-30; mem. House of Reps. 35-39; Senator from Arkansas 43- (re-elected 72); Chair. Appropriations

Cttee. 72-; George Washington Award (Freedom Foundation) 60; Democrat.

United States Senate, Washington, D.C. 20510; Union Life Building, Little Rock, Arkansas, U.S.A.

McClelland, Douglas; Australian politician; b. 5 Aug. 1926; ed. Parramatha Commercial Boys' High School, Metropolitan Business Coll.

Joined 2nd Australian Imperial Forces 44; Court Reporter 49-61; mem. N.S.W. Labor Party Exec. 57-61; mem. Senate 67-; Minister for the Media 72-75; Special Minister of State June-Nov. 75; Manager, Govt. Business in Senate 72-75; mem. Senate Select Cttee. on the Encouragement of Australian Production for Television 62-63, Joint Cttee. on Broadcasting of Parl. Proceedings 65-, Joint Select Cttee. on the New and Perm. Parl. House 67-, Senate Select Cttee. on Medical and Hospital Costs 68-, Senate Standing Cttee. on Health and Welfare 70-; Labor Party.

The Senate, Canberra, A.C.T.; Home: 1 Amy Street, Blakehurst, N.S.W. 2221, Australia.

McClelland, James Robert, B.A., LL.B.; Australian solicitor and politician; b. 3 June 1915, Melbourne, Vic.; *s*. of late R. W. McClelland; *m*. Freda McClelland; one *s*. one *d*.; St. Kevin's Coll., Melbourne, Melbourne and Sydney Univs.

Senator for N.S.W. 71-; Chair. Senate Standing Cttee. on Educ., Science and the Arts 73-75, on Constitutional and Legal Affairs 73-75; mem. Senate Standing Cttee. on Civil Rights of Migrant Australians 73-, Joint Cttee. on Pecuniary Interests of MP's 74-; Minister for Mfg. Industry Feb.-June 75, Minister for Labour and Immigration June-Nov. 75; mem. Council, Australian Nat. Univ. 74-75; Labor.

Leisure interest: tennis.

The Senate, Canberra, A.C.T., Australia.

McClintock, Barbara, M.A., PH.D.; American scientist; b. 16 June 1902; ed. Erasmus Hall High School, Brooklyn, N.Y. and Cornell Univ.

Instructor in Botany, Cornell Univ. 27-31; Fellow, Nat. Research Council 31-33; Fellow, Guggenheim Foundation 33-34; Research Assoc., Cornell Univ. 34-36; Asst. Prof. Univ. of Missouri 36-41; mem. staff, Carnegie Inst. of Washington 41-47, Distinguished Service Mem. 67-; Visiting Prof. Calif. Inst. of Technology 53-54; Andrew D. White Prof.-at-Large, Cornell Univ. 65-; Consultant, Agricultural Science Program, The Rockefeller Foundation 62-69; mem. Nat. Acad. of Sciences, American Philosophical Soc., American Acad. of Arts and Sciences, Genetics Soc. of America (Pres. 45), Botanical Soc. of America, American Asscn. for the Advancement of Science, American Inst. of Biol. Science, American Soc. of Naturalists; Hon. D.Sc. (Univs. of Rochester and Missouri, Smith Coll. and Western Coll. for Women); Achievement Award, Asscn. of Univ. Women 47; Award of Merit, Botanical Soc. of America 57; Kimber Genetics Award, Nat. Acad. of Sciences 67; Nat. Medal of Science 70; Hon. D.Sc. Williams Coll.

Carnegie Institution of Washington, Cold Spring Harbor, N.Y. 11724, U.S.A.

McCloskey, Paul N.; American politician; b. 29 Sept. 1927, San Bernadino, Calif.; *s*. of Mr. and Mrs. Paul N. McCloskey; *m*. Caroline Wadsworth 1949 (divorced 1972); two *s*. two *d*.; ed. Stanford Univ. and Calif. Inst. of Technology.

Admitted to Bar 53; Deputy District Attorney, Alameda County 53-54; practised law with Costello & Johnson, Palo Alto 55-56; founder mem. McCloskey, Wilson, Mosher & Martin 56-67; Rep. from 11th District, Calif., U.S. Congress 67-Jan. 73, 12th District Calif. Jan. 73-; U.S. del. to numerous int. maritime confs.; mem. numerous congressional cttees.; mem. many professional and community orgs.; Republican.

Leisure interest: conversation.
Publ. *Truth and Untruth*.
205 Cannon House Office Building, Washington, D.C.
20515, U.S.A.

McCloy, John Jay, B.A., LL.B.; American lawyer,
banker and administrator; b. 31 March 1895, Philadelphia, Pa.; s. of John J. McCloy and Anna Snader;
m. Ellen Zinsser 1930; one s. one d.; ed. Amherst Coll.
and Harvard Law School.
Served Field Artillery, First World War; admitted to
N.Y. Bar 21; mem. law firm Cravath, de Gersdorff,
Swaine and Wood 35-40; Asst. Sec. of War 41-45; Chair.
Civil Affairs Cttee. Combined Chiefs of Staff 43-45;
mem. law firm Milbank, Tweed, Hope, Hadley and
McCloy 45-47, partner 62-; Pres. Int. Bank for Recon-
struction and Devt. 47-49; U.S. Mil. Gov. and High
Commr. for Germany 49-52; Chair. Chase Manhattan
Bank, N.Y. 53-60; Adviser to Pres. Kennedy on Dis-
armament Matters 61; Chair. Board Ford Foundation
53-65; Chair. American Council on Germany; Hon.
Chair. Council on Foreign Relations (U.S.), Int. House,
N.Y., Atlantic Inst. (Paris); Hon. Chair. and Trustee
Emeritus Amherst Coll.; Chair. Exec. Cttee. Squibb
Corpn.; Chair. President's Gen. Advisory Cttee. on
Disarmament 61-74; mem. Co-ordinating Cttee. on
Cuban Crisis 62-63, President's Cttee. to Investigate
Assassination of Pres. Kennedy 63-64; Dir. Mercedes-
Benz of North America Inc., Olinkraft Inc., Dreyfus
Corpn.; Chair. Board, UN Devt. Corpn.; D.S.M. (U.S.);
Presidential Medal of Freedom; Grand Cross of Order
of Merit of Fed. Repub. of Germany; Grand Officer of
Legion of Honour (France); Grand Officer of Order of
Merit of Italy; numerous hon. degrees.
Leisure interests: tennis, hunting, fishing, photography.
Publ. *The Challenge to American Foreign Policy* 53.
Milbank, Tweed, Hadley and McCloy, 1 Chase Man-
hattan Plaza, New York City, N.Y. 10005; Home: 151
East 79th Street, New York, N.Y. 10021, U.S.A.
Telephone: 212-422-2660.

McClure, James A., DR. JUR.; American lawyer and
politician; b. 27 Dec. 1924; s. of W. R. and Marie
McClure; m. Louise Miller; two s. one d.; ed. Univ. of
Idaho Coll. of Law.
Private law practice; Prosecuting Attorney for Payette
County; State Senator from Payette County for three
terms; Ida. Senate Majority Leader 65-66; mem. U.S.
House of Reps. 66-72; U.S. Senator from Ida. Jan. 73-;
Chair. Senate Steering Cttee.; Chair. Task Force on
Energy and Resources of House of Reps. Republican
Conf.
U.S. Senate, Washington, D.C. 20510, U.S.A.

McCollum, Leonard Franklin, B.A.; American execu-
tive; b. 20 March 1902; ed. Univ. of Texas.
Div. Geologist Humble Oil & Refining Co. 27-34;
Exploration Manager, Carter Oil Co., Tulsa, Okla. 34-36,
Dir. 36-38, Vice-Pres. and Dir. 38-41, Pres. 41-43;
Asst. Co-ordinator of Production, Standard Oil Co.
(N.J.) and Exec. Vice-Pres., Creole Petroleum Corpn.,
N.Y. 43-44; Co-ordinator, Producing Activities, Stan-
dard Oil Co. (N.J.) 44-47; Pres. and Dir. Continental
Oil Co. of Houston, Texas , Dec. 47-64, Chair. and Chief
Exec. Officer 64-67, Chair. 67-72; Dir. Hudson's Bay Oil
and Gas Co. Ltd., Morgan Guaranty Trust Co. of N.Y.;
mem. Board of Dirs. of Chrysler Motors Corpn. 58; mem.
American Petroleum Inst., American Asscn. of Petro-
leum Geologists, Inst. of Int. Education, American
Inst. of Mining and Metallurgical Engineers; Trustee,
California Inst. of Technology.
3435 Westheimer Road, Houston, Tex. 77027, U.S.A.

McColough, Charles Peter, M.B.A.; American business
executive; b. 1 Aug. 1922, Halifax, Canada; s. of
Reginald Walker McColough and Barbara Theresa
Martin McColough; m. Mary Virginia White 1953;

four s. one d.; ed. Osgoode Hall Law School, Toronto,
Canada, Dalhousie Univ., Halifax, Canada and Har-
vard Graduate School of Business Admin.
Sales Man. Lehigh Navigation and Coal 51-54; various
exec. positions, Xerox Corpn. 54-60; Vice-Pres. for
Sales, Xerox Corpn. 60-63. Exec. Vice-Pres. of Opera-
tions 63-66, Pres. 66-71, Chief Exec. 68-, Chair. 71-;
Dir. Xerox Corpn., Rank Xerox Ltd. (London), Fuji
Xerox Co. Ltd. (Tokyo), First Nat. City Bank and
Corpn. (New York); Hon. LL.D. (Dalhousie) 70.
Leisure interests: skiing, sailing.
Xerox Corporation, Stamford, Conn. 06904, U.S.A.
Telephone: 203-329-8711 (Office).

McCombs, Terence Henderson, Kt., O.B.E., E.D.; New
Zealand diplomatist and politician; b. 5 Sept. 1905,
Christchurch; s. of James McCombs and Elizabeth
Reid (Henderson); ed. Canterbury Univ.
Member of Parl. for Lyttelton 35-51; Parl. Under-Sec.
to the Minister of Finance 45-47; Minister of Educ., in
charge of Dept. of Scientific and Industrial Research
47-49; teacher and later Headmaster of Cashmere High
School, Christchurch 56-72; mem. Council, Canterbury
Univ. 57-68, Chancellor 68-73; New Zealand High
Commr. to the U.K. 73-75; Chair. Cttee. on Secondary
Educ. 75-76; mem. Lyttelton Harbour Board, Lincoln
Coll. Board of Govs., Christchurch City Council;
Labour.
7 Freeman Street, Christchurch 8, New Zealand.

McConaughy, Walter Patrick, A.B.; American diplo-
matist and government official; b. 11 Sept. 1908; ed.
Birmingham Southern Coll. and Duke Univ.
Teacher 28-30; Dept. of State 31-, Mexico, Japan,
Bolivia, Brazil; Consul-Gen. Hong Kong 50-52; Dir.
Office Chinese Affairs, Dept. of State 52-57; Amb. to
Burma 57-60, to Republic of Korea 60-61; Asst. Sec.
for Far Eastern Affairs, Dept. of State Jan.-Nov. 61;
Amb. to Pakistan 62-66, to Taiwan 66-74.
c/o Department of State, Washington, D.C. 20520,
U.S.A.

McCone, John A.; American business executive; b.
4 Jan. 1902, San Francisco; s. of Alexander J. and
Margaret (Enright) McCone; m. 1st Rosemary Cooper
1938 (deceased), 2nd Theiline McGee Pigott 1962; ed.
Univ. of California.
Began as construction engineer, Llewellyn Iron Works;
Supt. Consolidated Steel Corpn. 29, Exec. Vice-Pres.,
Dir. 33-37; Pres. Bechtel-McCone Corpn. (engineers),
Los Angeles 37-45; Pres. Dir. Calif. Shipbuilding Corpn.
41-46; Pres., Dir. Joshua Hendy Corpn. 45-69, Chair.
58-69; Chair. Hendy Int. Co. 68-72; Dir. Int. Telephone
Corpn., New York; mem. President's Air Policy
Comm. 47-48; Deputy to Sec. of Defence 48; Under-
Sec. U.S. Air Force 50-51; Chair. U.S. Atomic Energy
Comm. 58-60; Dir. Central Intelligence Agency (C.I.A.)
61-65; Chair. Music Center Opera Asscn., Los Angeles.
Leisure interest: golf.
Office: 612 South Flower Street, Los Angeles, Calif.,
90017, U.S.A.

McConnell, Albert Joseph, M.A., SC.D.; Irish mathe-
matician and university administrator; b. 19 Nov.
1903; ed. Ballymena Acad., Trinity Coll., Dublin, and
Univ. of Rome.
Lecturer in Mathematics, Trinity Coll., Dublin 27-30,
Fellow 30-52; Prof. of Natural Philosophy, Univ. of
Dublin 30-57; Visiting Prof. Univ. of Alexandria 46-47;
Provost of Trinity Coll., Dublin 52-54; mem. Council of
State 73-; Chair. Governing Board and mem. Council,
School of Theoretical Physics, Dublin Inst. for Advanced
Studies 75-; mem. Royal Irish Acad.; Hon. D.Sc.
(Belfast, Ulster), Hon. Sc.D. (Columbia), Hon. LL.D.
(Nat. Univ. of Ireland).
Publs. *The Mathematical Papers of Sir William Rowan
Hamilton*, Vol. II (with A. W. Conway) 40, *Applications*

of the Absolute Differential Calculus 31, *Applications of Tensor Analysis* 57.

Seafield Lodge, Seafield Road, Killiney, Dublin, Ireland.

McConnell, Harden M., PH.D.; American professor of chemistry; b. 18 July 1927, Richmond, Va.; *m.* Sofia Glogovac 1956; two *s.* one *d.*; ed. George Washington Univ., Calif. Inst. of Technology and Univ. of Chicago. With Dept. of Physics, Univ. of Chicago, Nat. Research Fellow 50-52; Shell Devt. Co., Emeryville, Calif. 52-56; Asst. Prof. of Chemistry, Calif. Inst. of Technology 56-58, Assoc. Prof. of Chemistry 58-59, Prof. of Chemistry 59-63, Prof. of Chemistry and Physics 63-64; Prof. of Chemistry Stanford Univ. 64-; mem. Editorial Advisory Boards, *Chemical Physics Letters, Journal of Magnetic Resonance, Journal of Molecular Physics,* annual reviews, etc.; Fellow. American Physical Soc., Biophysical Soc., American Soc. of Biological Chemists; mem. American Chemical Soc., Biological Soc., Nat. Acad. of Sciences, Int. Acad. of Quantum Molecular Science, AAAS; Neuroscience Research Program, MIT; Calif. Section Award of American Chemical Soc. (A.S.C.) 61, Nat. A.C.S. Award in Pure Chem. 62, Harrison Howe Award 68, Irving Langmuir Award in Chemical Physics 71.

Publs. over 160 scientific publications in the field of physical chemistry/chemical physics.

Stanford University, Stanford, Calif. 94305, U.S.A.

McConnell, Joseph Howard, B.A., LL.B.; American executive; b. 13 May, 1906, Chester, S.C.; *s.* of Joseph Moore McConnell and Eliza Riggs McConnell; *m.* Elizabeth Bernard 1936; three *d.*; ed. Davidson Coll. and Univ. of Virginia.

Practised law in W. Palm Beach, Fla. 31-32, in Charlotte, N.C. 32-33; NRA, Washington, D.C. 33-35; Assoc. in law firm of Cotton, Franklin, Wright and Gordon (now Cahill, Gordon, Sonnet, Reindel and Ohl), New York City 35-41; various exec. posts with Radio Corpn. of America, including Financial Vice-Pres. and Exec. Vice-Pres. 41-49; Pres., Nat. Broadcasting Co. 49-52; Pres. Colgate-Palmolive Co. 53-55; Exec. Vice-Pres. and Gen. Counsel, Reynolds Metals Co. 55-63, Pres. 63-71 (retd.) fmr. Rector, Univ. of Virginia 70; Chair. Communications Satellite Corpn. 70-.

Leisure interests: golf, fishing.

6601 West Broad Street, Richmond, Va.; and 950 L'Enfant Plaza, S.W., Washington, D.C., U.S.A.

Telephone: 703-282-2311 (Richmond); 202-554-6020 (Washington).

McConnell, Thomas Raymond, A.M., PH.D.; American college president, dean and professor; b. 25 May 1901, Mediapolis, Iowa; *s.* of William and Nell McConnell; *m.* Ruth Kegley 1925; one *s.* one *d.*; ed. Cornell Coll., Mount Vernon, and Univ. of Iowa.

Instructor in English and Journalism Cornell Coll. 25-26, Instructor, Asst. Prof., and Prof. of Educ. and Psychology 29-36, Dean of Coll. 32-36; Prof. Educ. Psychology Univ. of Minnesota 36-50; Chair. Comm. on Educ. Research 37-47; Assoc. Dean Coll. of Science, Literature and the Arts 40-44, Act. Dean 42-44, Dean 44-50; Chancellor Univ. of Buffalo 50-54; Prof. of Higher Educ. Univ. of Calif. 54-68; Chair. Center for Study of Higher Educ. (Univ. of Calif.) 57-66; Research Educator, Center for Research and Devt. in Higher Educ. 66-; fmr. mem. Pres. Truman's Comm. on Higher Educ., and Problems and Policies, and Instruction and Evaluation, Comms. of American Council on Educ., Cttee. on Devt. of Youth of the Social Science Research Council; mem. Comm. on Plans and Objectives for Higher Educ., American Council on Educ.; mem. Research Advisory Council, U.S. Office of Educ. 62-65; Adviser to Sub Cttee. on Management and Financing of Colls. of Cttee. for Econ. Devt. 71-73; mem. Board of Editors of *Encyclopaedia of Educational Research* 57-59, Chair. 64-69; Research Cttee. of Educational Testing

Service 56-70; Founding mem. Nat. Acad. of Educ.; fmr. mem. Int. Council for Educ. Devt.; Chair. Comm. to Study Non-Public Higher Educ. in Illinois, 68-69; mem. Assembly on Univ. Goals, etc. 71; Award of American Educ. Research Asscn., Phi Delta Kappa 66; Distinguished Service Award, Univ. of Iowa 68; first annual award from Colloquium in Higher Educ. 70, Carnegie Comm. on Higher Educ. Award.

Publs. *Psychology in Everyday Living* (with others) 38, *Educational Psychology* (with others) 48, *A Restudy of the Needs of California in Higher Education* (with H. H. Semans and T. C. Holy), *A General Pattern for American Public Higher Education* 62, *Research or Development: A Reconciliation* 67, *The Redistribution of Power in Higher Education* 71, *The Faculty in University Governance* (with K. Mortimer) 71, *From Elite to Mass to Universal Higher Education: The British and American Transformations* (with R. O. Berdahl and M. A. Fay) 73. 108 Norwood Court, Calif. 94707, U.S.A.

Telephone: 415-524-6200.

MacConochie, John Angus, M.B.E., M.INST.T.; British shipping executive; b. 12 April 1908, Barnet, Herts.; *s.* of William Pitt MacConochie and Julia MacConochie; *m.* Peggy Martindale 1938; one *s.* one *d.*; ed. Royal Caledonian, Bushey.

Joined Shaw Savill Line 27; with Ministry of War Transport 42-45; on management of Shaw Savill Line 45, Man. for Australia 49, Gen. Man. for New Zealand 53, Gen. Man., London 58-; Dir. Shaw Savill & Albion Co. Ltd. 57, Man. Dir. 59, Deputy Chair. 62, Chair. 63; Deputy Chair. Furness, Withy & Co. Ltd. 67-68, Chair. April 68-Jan. 73; Pres. Chamber of Shipping of U.K. 72; mem. of Council, Fed. of Commonwealth Chambers of Commerce; mem. Inst. of Transport, British Inst. of Management, New Zealand Soc.

Leisure interests: gardening, chess, business.

The Stables, 8 Killarney Street, Takapuna, Auckland, New Zealand.

McCormack, John William; American politician; b. 21 Dec. 1891.

Admitted to Massachusetts Bar 13; practised law, Boston; mem. firm McCormack & Hardy; mem. Mass. House of Reps. 20-22, State Senate 23-26; mem. House of Reps. 27-70, House Majority Leader 55-62, Speaker 62-70, re-elected as Speaker Jan. 69-Nov. 70; Hon. LL.B. (Boston Univ.); Knight of Malta; Democrat.

111 Perkins Street, Jamaica Plain, Mass. 02130, U.S.A.

McCormick, Brooks; American business executive; b. 1917, Chicago; ed. Yale Univ.

Joined Int. Harvester Co. 40; various posts 42-50; Joint Man. Dir. Int. Harvester Co. of Great Britain Ltd. 51-54; Dir. of Manufacturing, Int. Harvester Co. 54-57, mem. of Board 58-68, Pres. 68-, Chief Exec. Officer 71-; Dir. Swift & Co., First Nat. Bank of Chicago, Esmark, Inc., Commonwealth Edison Co., Nat. Safety Council, Int. Harvester Europe 74-; Chair. Automobile Mfrs.' Asscn.; Trustee of the Ill. Inst. of Technology, etc.

International Harvester Company, 40 N. Michigan Avenue, Chicago, Ill. 60611, U.S.A.

McCowen, Alec, O.B.E.; British actor; b. 26 May 1925, Tunbridge Wells; *s.* of Duncan McCowen and Mary Walkden; ed. Skinners School, Tunbridge Wells, and Royal Acad. of Dramatic Art.

Member National Theatre; Evening Standard Best Actor 68, 73; Variety Club Stage Actor 70; Old Vic Theatre: played Touchstone, Ford, Richard II, Mercutio, Malvolio, Oberon 59-60; with Royal Shakespeare Co.: played Fool in *King Lear* 64, *Hadrian VII* 68, *The Philanthropist* 70, *The Misanthrope* 72, Dr. Dysart in *Equus* 72, Henry Higgins in *Pygmalion* 74.

Films: *Frenzy* 71, *Travels with my Aunt* 73.

Leisure interests: music and gardening.

c/o Larry Dalzell, 3 Goodwins Court, London, W.C.2, England.
Telephone: 01-240 3086.

McCoy, Charles Brelsford, M.SC.; American business executive; b. 16 April 1909, Oakland, Calif.; s. of John W. McCoy; m. Sallie L. Curtis 1934; three s.; ed. Wilmington, Delaware, Friends School, Univ. of Virginia, Mass. Inst. of Technology.
Cellophane operator, chemist, industrial engineer Du Pont de Nemours, Foreign Relations Dept., London 35, Asst. Man. 39, Dir. Chemical and Miscellaneous Sales Div. 40, Dir. Sales of Explosives Div. 43; Asst. Gen. Man. Elastomer Chemicals Dept. 58, Gen. Man. Explosives 60, Vice-Pres., mem. Board of Dirs. and Exec. Cttee. 61; Vice-Chair. Exec. Cttee. Sept. 67, Pres., Chair. Exec. Cttee. Dec. 67-73, Chair. Board of Dirs. 71-73, Chair. Finance Cttee. 74-; mem. Board of Dirs. Remington Arms Co. 63-68; Dir., Wilmington Trust Co., First Nat. City Bank, N.Y.C., Diamond State Telephone Co., Bethlehem Steel Corpn.
Du Pont de Nemours, Du Pont Buildings, Wilmington, Del. 19801, U.S.A.

McCracken, James; American tenor; b. Gary, Ind.; m. Sandra Warfield; ed. Columbia Univ.
Operatic debut with Central City (Colo.) Opera Co. 52; with Metropolitan Opera 54-57; went to Europe, debut with Bonn Opera; first performed title role in *Othello* with Washington, D.C. Opera Soc. 60, and at Met. Opera 63; has sung with San Francisco Opera Co., Zurich Opera, and at Zurich and Vienna Festivals; performed at White House celebrations for 25th Anniversary of the UN 70.
Leisure interest: fishing.
Major roles include title role in *Othello*, Manrico in *Il Trovatore*, Florestan in *Fidelio*, Samson in *Samson and Delilah*, Radames in *Aida*, Canio in *Pagliacci*, Don José in *Carmen*.
Publ. *A Star in the Family* (with Sandra Warfield) 71.
c/o S. A. Gorlinsky Ltd., 35 Dover Street, London, W1X 4NJ, England.

McCracken, Paul Winston, PH.D.; American economist; b. 29 Dec. 1915, Richland, Ia.; s. of late C. Sumner McCracken and Mary (Coffin) McCracken; m. E. Ruth Siler 1942; two d.; ed. William Penn Coll. and Harvard Univ.
Member Faculty, Foundation School, Berea Coll., Kentucky 37-40; economist, Dept. of Commerce, Washington 42-43; Financial Economist, Dir. of Research, Fed. Reserve Bank of Minneapolis 43-48; Assoc. Prof. School of Business Admin., Univ. of Mich. 48-50, Prof. 50-66, Edmund Ezra Day Univ. Prof. of Business Admin. 66- (on leave of absence 69-72); mem. Council of Econ. Advisers, Washington 56-59, Chair. 69-72.
Publs. *Hypothetical Projection of Commodity Expenditures, Northwest in Two Wars, Future of Northwest Bank Deposits, Rising Tide of Bank Lending, Balance of Payments and Domestic Prosperity, Economic Progress and the Utility Industry.*
Graduate School of Business Administration, University of Michigan, Ann Arbor, Mich. 48104, U.S.A.
Telephone: 313-764-1581.

McCrea, William Hunter, M.A., PH.D., SC.D., F.R.S.; British mathematician and astronomer; b. 13 Dec. 1904, Dublin; s. of Robert Hunter McCrea and Margaret Hutton; m. Marian Nicol Core Webster 1933; one s. two d.; ed. Chesterfield Grammar School, Cambridge and Göttingen Univs.
Lecturer in Mathematics, Edinburgh Univ. 30-32; Reader in Mathematics, Univ. of London and Asst. Prof. Imperial Coll. of Science 32-36; Prof. of Mathematics, Queen's Univ. of Belfast 36-44; Temporary Principal Experimental Officer, Admiralty 43-45; Prof. of Mathematics Univ. of London (Royal Holloway Coll.) 44-66; Comyns Berkeley Bye-Fellow, Caius Coll.,

Cambridge 52-53; Visiting Prof. of Astronomy, Univ. of Calif. 56, 67, Case Inst. of Technology 64; Research Prof. of Theoretical Astronomy, Univ. of Sussex 66-72; Emer. Prof. Univ. of Sussex 72-; Visiting Prof. of Astronomy, Univ. of British Columbia, Vancouver 75-76; Fellow of Imperial Coll. of Science and Technology, London 67-; Georges Lemaître Prof., Univ. of Louvain 69; Royal Soc. Leverhulme Visiting Prof. Cairo 73; Pres. Royal Astronomical Soc. 61-63, Mathematical Asscn. 73-74; Fellow Royal Soc.; mem. Akademie Leopoldina, Halle; Hon. D.Sc. (Nat. Univ. of Ireland, and Queen's Univ. Belfast), Sc.D. (Dublin Univ.); Dr. h.c. (Nat. Univ. of Córdoba, Argentina); Keith Prize, Royal Soc. of Edinburgh.
Leisure interests: travel and walking.
Publs. *Relativity Physics* 35, *Analytical Geometry of Three Dimensions* 42, *Physics of the Sun and Stars* 50, trans. of A. Unsöld's *The New Cosmos* 69, *Cosmology* 69, *The Royal Greenwich Observatory* 75, and numerous papers in mathematical and astronomical journals.
Astronomy Centre, University of Sussex, Falmer, Brighton BN1 9QH; 87 Houndean Rise, Lewes, Sussex BN7 1EJ, England.
Telephone: Brighton 66755, Lewes 3296 (Home).

McCready, Allan; New Zealand politician; b. 1 Sept. 1916, Kawakawa; s. of Alexander McCready; m. Grace Lorraine Maher; one s. one d.; ed. Kawakawa.
War service in army; worked in Post Office Dept.; Dir. Wellington Dairy Farmers' Co-operative; fmr. Dir. Hutt Valley Milk Treatment Corpn., Featherston Co-operative Dairy Co. Ltd.; M.P. for Otaki 60-; Postmaster-Gen., Minister of Marine and Fisheries 69-72, Minister in Charge of Govt. Printing Office -72; Minister of Defence, War Pensions and Rehabilitation Feb.-Dec. 72; Minister of Defence and Police Dec. 75-; National Party.
Parliament Buildings, Wellington; Home: South Road, Box 85, Manakau, New Zealand.

McCrum, Michael William, M.A.; British headmaster; b. 23 May 1924; s. of Capt. C. R. McCrum, R.N. (retd.) and Ivy I. H. (née Nicholson) McCrum; m. Christine M. K. fforde 1952; three s. one d.; ed. Sherborne School and Corpus Christi Coll., Cambridge.
Assistant Master, Rugby School 48-50; Fellow, Corpus Christi Coll., Cambridge 49, Second Tutor 50-51, Tutor 51-62; Headmaster of Tonbridge School 62-70; Headmaster of Eton Coll. Sept. 70-.
Eton College, Windsor, Berks., England.

McCullin, Donald; British photographer; b. 9 Oct. 1935, London; s. of Frederick and Jessica McCullin; m. Christine Dent 1959; two s. one d.; ed. Tollington Park Secondary Modern, Hammersmith Art and Crafts School.
R.A.F. Nat. Service; photographer with *Observer* for four years; photographer with *Sunday Times*, London 67-; has covered seven wars—Viet-Nam, Cambodia, Biafra, Congo, Israel, Cyprus, Chad—and many famine areas; has travelled to 64 countries; World Press Photographer 64, Warsaw Gold Medal 64, Granada TV Award 67, 69, Two Gold, One Silver Art Director Awards, U.K.
Leisure interests: walking in countries, collecting Victorian children's books, looking at things and people.
Publs. *The Destruction Business* 71, *The Concerned Photographer II* 72, *Is Anyone Taking Notice?* 73.
Redstack, 3 The Square, Braughing, Herts., England.

McCulloch, Frank Waugh, LL.B.; American lawyer, teacher and government official; b. 1905, Evanston, Ill.; s. of Frank Hathorn McCulloch and Catharine Waugh McCulloch; m. Edith F. Leverton 1937; two s.; ed. Williams Coll. and Harvard Law School.
Legal Practice 30-35; Industrial Relations Sec., Council for Social Action, Congregational-Christian

Churches, Chicago 35-46; Dir. Labor Educ. Div., Roosevelt Univ., Chicago 46-49; Admin. Asst. to U.S. Senator Paul H. Douglas 49-61; Chair. Nat. Labor Relations Board 61-70; Visiting Prof. of Law, Univ. of N. Carolina 71; mem. Center for Advanced Studies, Univ. of Virginia 71-74, Prof. of Law 71-; mem. Public Review Board, United Automobile Workers 71-; mem. Admin. Conf. of U.S. 68-70, Comm. of Experts on the Application of Conventions and Recommendations, Int. Labour Office 74-; Anglo-Amer. Admin. Law Exchange 69, Comm. on Public Employee Rights 72-; State Employee Labor Relations Council (Ill.) 73-; Hon. LL.D. (Olivet Coll., Chicago Theological Seminary, Williams Coll.).
Leisure interests: music, art, theatre, travel, tennis, mountaineering, social and community action.
Publ. *The National Labor Relations Board* (with T. Bornstein) 74.
School of Law, University of Virginia, Charlottesville, Va. 22901; Home: 104 Falcon Drive, Charlottesville, Va. 22901, U.S.A.
Telephone: 804-295-7371 (Home).

McCune, Francis Kimber; American business executive; b. 10 April 1906, Santa Barbara, Calif.; s. of Thomas H. McCune and Vernon K. McCune; m. Mary Harper Waddell 1969; two d.; ed. California Univ.
With Gen. Electric Co. 28-67, Asst. Gen. Man., Nucleonics Dept. 49, Gen. Man. Atomic Products Div. 54, Vice-Pres. 54-67, Vice-Pres. Engineering 60, Vice-Pres. Business Studies 65-67; Vice-Pres. and Dir. American Standards Assen. 65; Hon. Dir. and Past Pres. Atomic Industrial Forum Inc.; Chair. New York State Gen. Advisory Cttee. on Atomic Energy 59-62; Pres. United States of America Standards Inst. 67-69; mem. Nat. Acad. Eng.; mem. Woods Hole Oceanographic Inst.; mem. Nat. Research Council 69-71; life mem. and Fellow of I.E.E.E.; Charter mem. American Nuclear Soc.; mem. A.S.M.E.; Howard Coonley Medal 70.
Leisure interests: fishing, hunting, boating.
1564 Danny Drive, Sarasota, Florida 33580, U.S.A.
Telephone: 813-755-7177.

McCurdy, Richard Clark; American oil executive; b. 2 Jan. 1909, Newton, Ia.; s. of Ralph B. McCurdy and Florence (Clark) McCurdy; m. Harriet Sultan 1933; three s. one d.; ed. Stanford Univ.
With Shell Oil Co., Ventura, Calif. 33, Junior Engineer, later Engineer, Los Angeles, Bakersfield, Coalinga, Long Beach 35-42, Washington Office 42-43, Chief Exploitation Engineer, Pacific Coast Production Area 43-45, Acting Div. Man. San Joaquin Production Div. Bakersfield 45-47; Asst. Man., later Man., Western Div. Royal Dutch/Shell Group companies in Venezuela 47-50, Gen. Man. 50-53; Pres. Shell Chemical Co. (div. of Shell Oil Co.) 53-65, Pres. and Chief Exec. Officer Shell Oil Co. 65-69; Assoc. Administrator Org. and Management, NASA, Washington, D.C. 70; fmr. Chair. Board of Dirs. Manufacturing Chemists' Assen.; Trustee Stanford Univ., etc.; Chair. Board of Trustees, Hood Coll. 68-; mem. Soc. of Chemical Industry, Amer. Physical Soc., and Amer. Inst. of Mining and Metallurgical Engineers; Distinguished Service Medal, NASA 72.
Leisure interest: sailing.
400 Maryland Avenue, S.W., Washington, D.C. 20002, U.S.A.

McDaniel, Boyce Dawkins, PH.D.; American physicist; b. 11 June 1917, Brevard, N.C.; s. of Allen Webster McDaniel and Grace Dawkins; m. Jane Chapman Grennell 1941; one s. one d.; ed. Ohio Wesleyan Univ., Case Inst. of Technology and Cornell Univ.
Staff mem. Radiation Laboratory, Mass. Inst. of Technology 43; Los Alamos Scientific Laboratory 43-46; Asst. Prof. of Physics, Cornell Univ. 46-48, Assoc. Prof. 48-56, Prof. 56-; on sabbatic leave at Australian Nat.

Univ., Canberra 53-54, Laboratorio Nazionale di Frascati, Italy 59-60; Assoc. Dir. Laboratory of Nuclear Studies 60-67, Dir. 67-; Resident Collaborator, Brookhaven Nat. Laboratory 66-; Trustee, Associated Univs. Inc. 63-75, Univs. Research Assen. Inc. 71-; Physicist Fermi Nat. Accelerator Laboratory 72, 74; Fulbright Research Award 53, 59; Guggenheim Award 59; Fellow, American Physical Soc.
Laboratory of Nuclear Studies, Cornell University, Ithaca, N.Y. 14850, U.S.A.
Telephone: 607-256-2301.

MacDermot, Niall, O.B.E., Q.C.; British barrister-at-law; b. 10 Sept. 1916, Dublin, Ireland; s. of Henry MacDermot, K.C. and Gladys née Lowenadler; m. Ludmila Benvenuto 1966; ed. Rugby School, Balliol Coll., Oxford.
Called to the Bar 46; mem. Parl. (Labour) for Lewisham N. 57-59, for Derby N. 62-70; Deputy Chair. Bedfordshire Quarter Sessions 62; Recorder of Newark 63-64; Financial Sec. to H.M. Treasury 64-67; Minister of State for Planning and Land 67-68; Recorder of Crown Court 72-74; Bencher, the Inner Temple 70-; Trustee Tate Gallery 69-; Sec.-Gen. Int. Comm. of Jurists 70-; Chair. Special Non-Governmental Orgs.' Cttee. on Human Rights, Geneva 73-.
International Commission of Jurists, 109 route de Chêne, 1224 Chêne Bougeries, Geneva, Switzerland.
Telephone: 35-19-73.

MacDermott, Baron (Life Peer), cr. 47, of Belmont; **John Clarke MacDermott,** P.C., LL.D., M.C.; British lawyer; b. 12 April 1896, Belfast; s. of Rev. John MacDermott and Lydia Allen née Wilson; m. Louise Palmer Johnston 1926; two s. two d.; ed. Queen's Univ., Belfast.
Served with Machine Gun Corps First World War; called to Irish Bar 21; Lecturer in Jurisprudence, Queen's Univ., Belfast 31-35; M.P. for Queen's Univ., Northern Ireland Parl. 38-44; Major, Royal Artillery 39-40; Minister of Public Security Northern Ireland 40-41, Attorney-Gen. 41-44; Judge, Supreme Court Northern Ireland 44-47; Lord of Appeal in Ordinary April 47-51; Lord Chief Justice, Northern Ireland 51-71; LL.D. (h.c.) Queen's Univ., Belfast 51, Edinburgh 58, Cambridge 68.
House of Lords, London, S.W.1; and Glenburn, 8 Cairnburn Road, Strandtown, Belfast 4, Northern Ireland.
Telephone: Belfast 63361.

McDermott, Edward Aloysious, B.A., IUR.D.; American lawyer, educator and government official; b. 28 June 1920; three s. one d.; ed. Loras Coll. and State Univ. of Iowa.
Professor of Business Law, Loras Coll., Dubuque, Iowa 46-48; Prof. of Economics, Clarke Coll., Dubuque 48-50; Partner law firm O'Connor, Thomas, McDermott and Wright, Dubuque 51-61; Chief Counsel U.S. Senate Sub-cttee. on Privileges and Elections 50-51; Dep. Dir. Office of Civil and Defense Mobilisation, The White House 60-61; Dir. Office of Emergency Planning, Exec. Office of the Pres. 62-65; mem. Nat. Security Council; Chair. Emergency Planning Cttee.; U.S. Rep. Senior Civil Emergency Planning Cttee., NATO 62-65; mem. President's Cttee. on Economic Impact on Defense and Disarmament; Chair. President's Petroleum Policy Cttee. 63; Partner Law Firm Hogan and Hartson, Washington D.C.; Pres. John Carroll Soc.; mem. Board of Advisers, Industrial Coll. of Armed Forces, Washington 65-70; mem. Board of Regents, Univ. Santa Clara (Calif.), Lynchburg Coll. (Virginia), Coll. of Notre Dame (Cleveland), Loras Coll. (Dubuque) 75-; Trustee, Colgate Univ. (New York); mem. Board of Dirs. American Irish Foundation; mem. American Bar Assen., etc.; official of legal, civic and charitable orgs.
5400 Albemarle St., N.W., Washington, D.C., U.S.A.
Telephone: 301-229-8755.

MacDiarmid, Hugh (*pseudonym* of Christopher Murray Grieve); British writer; b. 11 Aug. 1892, Langholm, Dumfriesshire; s. of James Grieve and Elizabeth Graham; m. Valda Trevlyn 1931; two s. one d.; ed. Langholm Acad., Edinburgh Univ.

One of founders Scottish Nationalist Party; founder Scottish Centre PEN Club; Editor *The Voice of Scotland*; J.P. for County of Angus; Hon. LL.D. (Edin.). Leisure interest: travelling.

Publs. *Annals of the Five Senses, Contemporary Scottish Studies, Albyn, or the Future of Scotland, The Present Condition of Scottish Arts and Affairs, Scottish Scene, At the Sign of the Thistle, Scottish Eccentrics, Robert Burns: Today and Tomorrow, The Handmaid of the Lord* (translated from Spanish of Ramón Maria de Tenreiro), *The Scottish Islands*, etc.; Poetry: *Sangschaw, Penny Wheep, A Drunk Man Looks at the Thistle, To Circumjack Cencrastus, Stony Limits, and other poems, First Hymn to Lenin and other poems, Second Hymn to Lenin and other poems, Cornish Heroic Song for Valda Trevlyn, The Birlinn of Clanranald* (from Gaelic of *Scottish Poet, Lucky Poet* (autobiog.) 43, 2nd edn. 72, *Scottish Poetry, Lucky Poet* (autobiog.) 43 2nd edn. 72, *Speaking for Scotland* (publ. U.S.A.), *A Kist of Whistles, R. B. Cunninghame Graham, In memoriam James Joyce, Stony Limits and Scots Unbound, The Battle Continues, Aniara* (translated from Swedish of Harry Martinsen, with Elspeth Harley Schubert), *John Davidson: A Selection of His Poems* (with Maurice Lindsay and T. S. Eliot), *The Kind of Poetry I Want, Collected Poems, David Hume, The Company I've Kept* (autobiography), *A Lap of Honour* (poems), *A Clyack Sheaf* (poems), *Selected Essays*.

The Cottage, Brownsbank, by Biggar, Lanarkshire, Scotland.

Telephone: Skirling-Biggar 255.

McDiarmid, John, A.M., PH.D.; American international official; b. 12 Aug. 1911, Beckley, West Va.; s. of late Errett Weir McDiarmid and Allie May McCorkle McDiarmid; m. Darice Elmer 1938; two s. one d.; ed. Texas Christian Univ. and Univ. of Chicago.

Instructor in Government, Texas Christian Univ. 32-33; Research Asst. Nat. Resources Board, U.S. Govt. Washington 35; Instructor in Politics, Princeton Univ., 36-38; Asst. Prof. of Public Admin., Univ. of Southern California 38-42; various positions with U.S. Civil Service Comm. Washington 42-45; Assoc. Prof. of Political Science, Northwestern Univ., Evanston, Ill. 45-46; Official of UN Secretariat, New York 46; Deputy Dir. of Personnel, UN 54-57, Act. Dir. of Personnel 57-59, Senior Dir. Technical Assistance Board 59-64, Resident Rep. UN Devt. Programme in India 64-74, Swaziland (Act.) July-Oct. 75; Sr. Adviser to Rector, UN Univ., Tokyo 75-76.

Leisure interests: tennis (ranked 7th nationally in U.S.A., 36), reading, travel.

Publs. *Government Corporations and Federal Funds* 38, *The Administration of the American Public Library* (with E. W. McDiarmid) 43.

22 Thayer Pond Road, New Canaan, Conn. 06840, U.S.A.

Telephone: (203) 966-8574.

Macdiarmid, Niall Campbell; British business executive; b. 7 June 1919; s. of Sir Allan Campbell Macdiarmid and Grace Buchanan (née McClure); m. Patricia Isobel Mackie-Campbell 1946; three d. (one deceased); ed. Uppingham and Magdalen Coll., Oxford.

Army Service, Second World War; Stewarts and Lloyds Ltd. 46; Man. Dir. Stanton Ironworks Co. Ltd. (later Stanton and Staveley Ltd.) 57-62, Chair. 62-64; Dir. Stewarts and Lloyds 59-69; Chair. and Gen. Man. Dir. Stewarts and Lloyds Ltd. 64-69; Man. Dir. Northern and Tubes Group and mem. British Steel Corpn. 67-69; mem. Iron and Steel Board 61-67, East Midlands Gas Board 62-67; Vice-Pres. Council of Iron and Steel Inst. 66, Pres. 69; Dir. The United Steel Cos. Ltd. 64-67, Provincial Insurance Co. Ltd. 70-; Deputy Chair. Vickers Ltd. 70-71; Chair. Sanderson Kayser Ltd. 74-, CompAir Ltd. 75-, Sketchley Ltd. 75-; Chair. Trustees, Uppingham School 67-; Trustee Duke of Edinburgh's Award Scheme 63-71.

Leisure interests: shooting, golf.

Stibbington Hall, Wansford, Peterborough, PE8 6LP, England.

Telephone: Stamford 782322.

McDivitt, Brig.-Gen. James Alton; American astronaut; b. 10 June 1929, Chicago, Ill.; s. of Mr. and Mrs. James A. McDivitt, Sr.; m. Patricia Ann Haas 1956; two s. two d.; ed. Jackson Junior Coll. and Univ. of Michigan.

U.S. Air Force 51-, flew combat missions in Korean War; at U.S. Air Force Experimental Test Pilot School, Edwards Air Force Base 59-60; Experimental Test Pilot 60-62; U.S. Air Force Aerospace Research Pilot Course 61; astronaut 62-69; Command Pilot *Gemini 4* Spacecraft, making 62 orbits of the earth June 3rd-7th 65; Commdr. of *Apollo 9* Spacecraft, making 152 orbits of the earth March 3rd-13th 69; Man. lunar landing operations, *Apollo* programme 69-72; Man. Apollo Spacecraft Program 69-72; Exec. Vice-Pres. Consumer Power Co. 72-75, Pullman Inc.; Pres. Pullman Standard 75-.

Leisure interest: hunting.

Pullman Standard, 200 S. Michigan, Chicago, Ill. 60604, U.S.A.

McDonald, Sir Alexander Forbes, Kt., B.L., D.L.; British business executive; b. 14 Aug. 1911; ed. Hillhead School and Glasgow Univ.

Chartered Accountant 34; Chair. Distillers Co. Ltd. 67-; Chair. Scotch Whisky Asscn. 67-; Dir. Nat. and Commercial Banking Group.

6 Oswald Road, Edinburgh, Scotland.

Telephone: 031-667-4246.

MacDonald, Daniel Joseph, P.C., M.P.; Canadian farmer and politician; b. 23 July 1918, Bothwell, P.E.I.; s. of Daniel L. MacDonald and Elizabeth Fisher; m. Pauline Peters 1946; four s. three d.; ed. Bothwell schools.

Served Canadian Army with rank of Sergeant losing left leg and arm 40-45; entered provincial politics 62; elected constituency of 1st Kings, re-elected 66 and 70; Minister of Agriculture and Forestry for P.E.I. 66-72; M.P. for Cardigan 72-; Minister of Veterans' Affairs 72-; mem. War Amputations of Canada; Pres. local branch, Royal Canadian Legion; fmr. Pres. local branch, Co-operative Asscn. and South Lake School Board; Provincial Dir. Artificial Breeding Unit Board; mem. Fed. of Agriculture; 1939-45 Star, Italy Star, France and Germany Star, Defence Medal, Voluntary Service Medal.

Bothwell, Souris, Prince Edward Island, Canada.

Telephone: South Lake 13.

McDonald, Denis Ronald, B.A., H.DIP.ED.; Irish diplomatist; b. 22 Feb. 1910, Dublin; m. Una Sheehan 1941; one s. one d.; ed. Univ. Coll., Cork.

Minister, later Amb., to Belgium 54-60; Irish Rep. to EEC 59-60; Amb. to France 60-66, to Italy and to Turkey 66-75, to Egypt 75-; Head of Irish Del. to OEEC (now OECD) 60-66; Perm. Del. to UNESCO 61-66; Kt. Commdr. Order of St. Gregory the Great.

Irish Embassy, Room 1606, Sheraton Hotel, Cairo, Egypt.

MacDonald, Donald; Canadian trade unionist; b. 1909, Halifax; ed. Holy Redeemer School and Sydney Acad., Cape Breton and St. Francis Xavier Univ., Antigonish, N.S.

Entered coal industry and immediately became active

trade unionist 26; played prominent role in United Mine Workers of America 30-40; mem. Nova Scotia legislature 41-45, also leader of CCF Party in legislature; mem. CCF Nat. Council 41-45; Organizer, Canadian Congress of Labour 42, Regional Dir. of Org. for the Maritimes 45-51; Sec.-Treas. and Chief Exec. Officer, Canadian Congress of Labour 51-56; Sec.-Treas. Canadian Labour Congress (following merger of Canadian Congress of Labour and Trades and Labour Congress of Canada) 56-67, Acting Pres. 67-68, Pres. 68-74; Pres. ICFTU 72-75; Vice-Pres. Inter-American Regional Org. of Workers; mem. Canadian-American Cttee., British N. American Cttee., Canadian Econ. Policy Cttee., Econ. Council of Canada, Cen. Council of The Red Cross, Canadian Nat. Comm. for UNESCO; Officer Order of Canada (O.C.) 73; Hon. LL.D. (St. Francis Xavier Univ.).
Canadian Labour Congress, 2841 Riverside Drive, Ottawa, Ont., Canada.
Telephone: 521-3400.

Macdonald, Hon. Donald Stovel, P.C., LL.M., M.P.; Canadian politician and lawyer; b. 1 March 1932, Ottawa, Ont.; s. of Donald A. Macdonald and Marjorie I. Stovel; m. Ruth Hutchison 1961; four d.; ed. Ottawa public schools, Ashbury Coll., Ottawa, Univs. of Toronto and Cambridge, and Osgoode Hall and Harvard Law Schools.
With McCarthy and McCarthy, Barristers, Toronto 57-62; mem. Parl. 62-; Parl. Sec. to Minister of Justice 63-65, to Minister of Finance 65, to Sec. of State for External Affairs 66-68, to Minister of Industry 68; Minister without Portfolio 68; Pres. Privy Council and Govt. House Leader 68; Minister of Nat. Defence 70-72, of Energy, Mines and Resources 72-75, of Finance 75-; Rowell Fellowship, Canadian Inst. of Int. Affairs 56; Hon. LL.D. (St. Lawrence Univ.).
Leisure interests: fishing, cross-country skiing, tennis, squash.
House of Commons, Ottawa, Ont.; Home: 15 Westward Way, Ottawa 7, Ont. K1L 5A8, Canada.
Telephone: 992-4251 (Office); 745-7677 (Home).

Macdonald, Gordon James Fraser, A.M., Ph.D.; American professor of physics; b. 30 July 1929, Mexico, D.F.; s. of Gordon J. MacDonald and Josephine Bennett; m. Marcelline Kuglen 1960; two s. one d.; ed. Harvard Univ.
Chairman, Dept. of Planetary and Space Physics, Univ. of Calif. (Los Angeles) 65-68; Assoc. Dir. Inst. of Geophysics, Univ. of Calif., Los Angeles 60-68; Vice-Chancellor for Research and Graduate Affairs, Univ. of Calif., Santa Barbara, Prof. of Physics and Prof. of Geology Sept. 68-69; mem. Council on Environmental Quality, Wash. 69-; Staff Assoc., Geophysical Lab., Carnegie Inst., Washington 55-63; Consultant, U.S. Geological Survey 55-60; Assoc. Prof. of Geophysics, Mass. Inst. of Technology 55-58; Consultant, NASA 60-; Lecturer, France and Italy 62; mem. President's Science Advisory Cttee. 65-69, Nat. Science Foundation, Nat. Acad. of Sciences etc.; Editor *Journal of Atmospheric Sciences* 64-; *Reviews of Geophysics* 62-; Exec. Vice-Pres. Inst. for Defense Analyses 67-68; American Acad. of Arts and Sciences Monograph Prize in Physics and Biological Sciences 60; James B. Macelwane Award, American Geophysical Union 65.
Publs. *Rotation of the Earth* (with Walter Munk) 60; and articles in scientific journals.
Council of Environmental Quality, 722 Jackson Place, N.W., Washington, D.C. 20506; Home: 4823 Via Los Santos, Santa Barbara, Calif. 93105, U.S.A.

Macdonald, Hon. Hector Norman, Q.C.; Rhodesian judge; b. 3 Nov. 1915, Bulawayo; ed. Gray's Inn, London.
Called to the Bar 37; served British Army 40-43, dis-

charged with rank of Capt., Royal Artillery; practised at the Bar, Johannesburg 43-50, Bulawayo 50-58; Queen's Counsel 56; Judge, High Court of Rhodesia 58-65, Judge of Appeal 65-70, Judge Pres. of the Appellate Div. April 70-.
High Court of Justice, Salisbury; Home: 207 North Avenue, Salisbury, Rhodesia.

McDonald, John W., Jr., DR. JUR.; American lawyer, diplomatist and international official; b. 18 Feb. 1922, Koblenz, Germany; s. of John Warlick McDonald and Ethel Mae Raynor; m. Christel Meyer, 1970; one s. three d.; ed. Univ. of Illinois, Nat. War Coll., Washington, D.C.
Legal Div., U.S. Office of Mil. Govt., Berlin 47; Asst. District Attorney, U.S. Mil. Govt. Courts, Frankfurt 47-50; Sec. Law Cttee., Allied High Comm. 50-52; mem. Mission to NATO and OECD, Paris 52-54; Office of Exec. Sec. Dept. of State 54-55; Exec. Sec. to Dir. of Int. Co-operation Admin. 55-59; U.S. Econ. Co-ordinator for CENTO Affairs, Ankara 59-63; Deputy Dir. Office of Econ. and Social Affairs, Dept. of State 67-68, Dir. 68-71; Co-ordinator, UN Multilateral Devt. Programmes, Dept. of State 71-74, Acting Deputy Asst. Sec. for Econ. and Social Affairs 71, 73; Deputy Dir.-Gen. Int. Labour Org. (ILO) 74-; del. to many int. confs.; Admitted to Illinois Supreme Court Bar 46, to U.S. Supreme Court 51; Superior Honour Award, Dept. of State 72; mem. American Bar Asscn., American Foreign Service Asscn.
Leisure interests: reading, tennis, fencing, skiing.
International Labour Office, CH-1211 Geneva 22; Home: 26 chemin du Pommier, 1218 Grand-Saconnex, Geneva, Switzerland.
Telephone: 98-52-11, Ext. 2332 (Office); 98-16-91 (Home).

MacDonald, Rt. Hon. Malcolm John, O.M., P.C., M.A.; British diplomatist; b. 17 Aug. 1901, Lossiemouth, Scotland; s. of James Ramsay MacDonald (fmr. British Prime Minister) and Margaret MacDonald; m. Audrey Rowley 1946; one d.; ed. Bedales and Oxford Univ.
Labour M.P. for Bassetlaw Div. of Notts 29-31, and National Labour 31-35 and for Ross and Cromarty 36-45; Parl. Under-Sec. of State for Dominion Affairs in First and Second Nat. Govts. Aug. and Nov. 31-June 35; Sec. of State for the Colonies in reconstructed Cabinet June-Nov. 35; Sec. of State for Dominion Affairs Nov. 35-May 38; Sec. of State for the Colonies May-Oct. 38; Sec. of State for Dominion Affairs and Colonies Oct. 38-Sept. 39, for Colonies Sept. 39-May 40; Min. of Health May 40-Feb. 41; High Commr. in Canada 41-46; Gov.-Gen. of the Malayan Union and Singapore May-July 46; Gov.-Gen. of Malaya, Singapore and British Borneo 46-48; Commr.-Gen. for U.K. in S.E. Asia 48-55; High Commr. in India 55-60; Chancellor Univ. of Malaya 49-61; Co-Chair. Int. Conf. on Laos 61-62; Governor of Kenya Jan.-Dec. 63, Gov.-Gen. Dec. 63-Dec. 64; Visitor, Univ. Coll., Nairobi 63-64; High Commr. in Kenya 64-65; Special Rep. of British Govt. in a number of Commonwealth countries in East and Central Africa 65-66, in Africa 66-69; Special Envoy to Khartoum Nov. 68, Mogadishu Dec. 68; Chancellor Univ. of Durham 70-; Pres. Fed. of Commonwealth Chambers of Commerce 71-, Royal Commonwealth Soc. 71-, Pres. and Chair. 75-76; Senior Research Fellow, Univ. of Sussex 71-73; Pres. Voluntary Service Overseas 75-.
Leisure interests: bird watching, collecting works of art, writing books, water skiing, photography.
Publs. *Down North* 45, *The Birds of Brewery Creek* 47, *Borneo People* 56, *Angkor* 58, *Birds in my Indian Garden* 61, *Birds in the Sun* 62, *Treasure of Kenya* 65, *People and Places* 69, *Titans and Others* 72.
Raspit Hill, Ivy Hatch, Sevenoaks, Kent, England.
Telephone: Plaxtol 312.

Macdonald, Ray Woodward; American business executive; b. 20 Dec. 1912, Chicago, Ill.; *m.*; three *s.*; ed. Univ. of Chicago School of Business Admin.

Junior Salesman, Burroughs Corpn., Detroit 35, successively Manager Travelling Exhibit Sales Div., in Export Dept., Asst. Export Man., Export Man., Gen. Man. (Int. Activity), Vice-Pres. (Int.) 35-57, Vice-Pres. in charge Int. Div. 57-64, Exec. Vice-Pres. 64-66, Pres. 66-, Chief Exec. Officer 67-, Chair. of Board 73-, Dir. 59- and Dir. of subsidiaries: Compañía Burroughs de Máquinas, Ltd. (Argentina), Burroughs, Ltd. (Australia), Companhia Burroughs de Brasil, Inc. (Brazil), Burroughs de Colombia, S.A. (Colombia), Burroughs de Centro América S.A. (Costa Rica), Compañía Burroughs Mexicana, S.A. (Mexico), Burroughs de Perú, S.A. (Peru), Burroughs Inc. (Puerto Rico), Burroughs Machines Ltd. (South Africa), Compañía Burroughs de Venezuela, Inc. (Venezuela), Burroughs Adding Machines Ltd. (Great Britain); mem. Int. Foreign Trade Council, etc.

Office: Burroughs Place, Detroit, Mich. 48232; Home: 41 Lochmoor Boulevard, Grosse Pointe Shores, Mich. 48236, U.S.A.

McDonald, Robert E.; American business executive; b. 1915; *m.* Marion L. Wigley; two *d.*; ed. Univ. of Minnesota.

Formerly held various positions in airline industry; Pres. Sperry Univac 66; Pres. Sperry Rand Corpn. 72-. Sperry Rand Corporation, 1290 Avenue of the Americas, New York, N.Y. 10019, U.S.A.

Macdonald, Sir Thomas Lachlan, K.C.M.G.; New Zealand politician and diplomatist; b. 14 Dec. 1898; ed. Southland Boys High School, Invercargill, New Zealand. Union Steamship Co. of New Zealand 15-18; N.Z. Army, Palestine and Egypt 18-19; farming 19-37; M.P. for Mataura 38-40, 43-46, for Wallace 46-57; N.Z. Army, N. Africa 40-43; Minister of Defence 50-57, of Civil Aviation 50-54, of External Affairs 54-57, of Island Territories 54-57; High Commr. for New Zealand in U.K. 61-68; Amb. to European Econ. Community 61-67; concurrently Amb. to Ireland 66-68; New Zealand National Party.

1 Camellia Grove, Parklands, Waikanae, New Zealand.

Macdonald, Rt. Hon. William Ross, P.C., Q.C., C.D., LL.D.; Canadian barrister and politician; b. 25 Dec. 1891, Toronto, Ont.; *s.* of George Macdonald and Julie Bulley; *m.* Muriel Whitaker 1921; two *d.*; ed. Univ. of Toronto and Osgoode Hall.

Served Canadian Expeditionary Force 14-18; mem. firm Macdonald, Brown, Binkley, McIntosh & Daboll; mem. House of Commons for Brantford City 35-53; Deputy Speaker of House of Commons 45-49, Speaker 49-53; Leader of the Govt. in the Senate 53; Solicitor-Gen. 54-57; leader of the Opposition in Senate 57-63; Leader of Senate 63-Jan. 64; mem. Privy Council for Canada 53; Hon. Col. 56th Field Regiment R.C.A.; Chancellor Waterloo Lutheran Univ. 64; Lieut.-Gov. of Ontario 68-74; Liberal.

Leisure interests: golf, fishing.

Parliament Buildings, Toronto, Ontario.

40 Market Street, Brantford, Ont., Canada.

Telephone: 365-2005 (Office).

McDonnell, James Smith, B.S., M.S., in Aeronautical Engineering; American aerospace executive; b. 9 April 1899, Denver, Colo.; *s.* of James Smith McDonnell and Susan Belle Hunter McDonnell; *m.* 1st Mary Elizabeth Finney 1934 (died 1949), 2nd Priscilla Brush Forney 1956; two *s.* one stepson, two stepdaughters; ed. Princeton Univ. and Mass. Inst. of Technology.

Engineer and Pilot, Huff Daland Airplane Co., Ogdensburg, N.Y. 24; Stress analyst and draughtsman Consolidated Aircraft Co., Buffalo, N.Y. 25; Asst. Chief Engineer, Stout Metal Airplane Co., Dearborn, Mich. 25; Chief Engineer, Hamilton Aero Manufacturing

Co., Milwaukee 26-27; Engineering Consultants, McDonnell and Associates, Milwaukee 28-29, Vice-Pres. Airtransport Engineering Co. Chicago 30-31; Engineer, Test Pilot, Great Lakes Aircraft Corpn., Cleveland 32; Chief Project Engineer for Landplanes, Glenn L. Martin Co., Baltimore 33-38; Founder, Dir. and Chair. McDonnell Aircraft Corpn., St. Louis, Mo. 39-67; Chair. McDonnell Douglas Corpn. 67-; NATO Defense Coll., Ancien; Nat. Alliance of Businessmen 67-69, First Union Inc. Banking Group; mem. Advisory Council, Center for Strategic and Int. Studies, Washington D.C.; mem. Civic Progress Inc., St. Louis; mem. Board of Dirs. Atlantic Council of the U.S.A., UN Asscn. of the U.S.A., Population Crisis Cttee.; Hon. Dr. of Engineering, Missouri 57, Washington Univ. (St. Louis, Mo.) 58, Hon. LL.D. (Princeton) 60, (Univ. of Arkansas) 65; St. Louis Award 59, Daniel Guggenheim Medal Award 63; Nat. Aeronautics and Space Admin. Public Service Awards 66, 69; Meritorious Service to Aviation Award, Nat. Business Aircraft Asscn. 66, Prometheus Award of Nat. Electrical Manufacturers Asscn. 66; Nat. Acad. of Eng. Founders Medal 67, Collier Trophy 66; Forrestal Award 72; Hon. Fellow, Amer. Inst. of Aeronautics and Astronautics; mem. Board of Trustees, Nat. Space Club Scientific and Educ. Foundation.

Leisure interest: golf.

Home: 1 Glenview Road, St. Louis 24, Mo.; Office: Post Box 516, St. Louis, Mo. 63166, U.S.A.

Telephone: 314-232-0232.

McDonnell, Sanford N., M.S.; American business executive; b. 12 Oct. 1922, Little Rock, Ark.; *s.* of William A. and Carolyn C. McDonnell; nephew of James S. McDonnell (*q.v.*); *m.* Priscilla Robb; one *s.* one *d.*; ed. Princeton Univ., Univ. of Colorado and Washington Univ.

Joined McDonnell Aircraft Co. 48, Vice-Pres. (Project Management) 59, F4H Vice-Pres. and Gen. Man. 61, mem. Board of Dirs. 62-67, mem. Finance Cttee. 62, Exec. Cttee. 63; Vice-Pres. Aircraft Gen. Man. 65, Pres. 66; Dir. McDonnell Douglas Corpn. 67, Vice-Pres. March 71; Chair. McDonnell Aircraft Co. March 71; Pres. McDonnell Douglas Corpn. 71-72, Pres. and Chief Exec. Officer May 72-; Vice-Chair. Board of Govs. Aerospace Industries Asscn. Nov. 74-; Fellow, Amer. Inst. of Aeronautics and Astronautics and mem. many other professional orgs.; mem. Board of Dirs. First Nat. Bank in St. Louis; mem. Board of Trustees, Washington Univ.

McDonnell Douglas Corporation, P.O. Box 516, St. Louis, Mo. 63166; Home: 24 Oakleigh Lane, St. Louis, Mo. 63124I, U.S.A.

McDougald, John Angus; Canadian business executive; b. 14 March 1908; *s.* of late Duncan J. and Margherita E. McDougald (née Murray); *m.* Hedley Maude Eustace Smith 1934; ed. Upper Canada Coll., St. Andrew's Coll.

Chairman of Board, Pres. Argus Corpn. Ltd.; Pres. Ravelston Corpn. Ltd., Sugra Ltd., Taymac Investments Ltd., Thermax Ltd.; Vice-Pres. Taylor, McDougald Co. Ltd.; Chair. of Board and Exec. Cttee. Dominion Stores Ltd., Avco of Canada Ltd.; Chair. of Board Standard Broadcasting Corpn. Ltd., Grew Ltd., Standard Broadcast Sales (U.K.) Ltd.; Chair. Exec. Cttee. Hollinger Mines Ltd. (Vice-Pres.), Gen. Bakeries Ltd., Massey-Ferguson Ltd.; Chair. Advisory Board, Crown Trust Co.; Dir., mem. Exec. Cttee., Canadian Imperial Bank of Commerce, Domtar Ltd., St. Lawrence Corpn. Ltd.; mem. Advisory Board, First Nat. Bank in Palm Beach, Florida; Gov. Good Samaritan Hospital, Palm Beach; Dir. numerous other cos.

10 Toronto Street, Toronto, M5C 2B7; Home: Green Meadows, 5365 Leslie Street, Willowdale, Ont., Canada, M2J 2L1.

MacDougall, Sir George Donald Alastair, C.B.E., F.B.A., M.A., LL.D., LITT.D.; British economist; b. 26 Oct. 1912, Glasgow, Scotland; s. of Daniel MacDougall and Beatrice Miller; m. Bridget Bartrum 1937; one s. one d.; ed. Balliol Coll., Oxford.
Assistant Lecturer, Leeds Univ. 36-39; mem. Sir Winston Churchill's Statistical Branch 39-45 and 51-53; Fellow Wadham Coll., Oxford 45-50, Nuffield Coll. 47-64, Hon. Fellow, Wadham Coll. 64-, Nuffield Coll. 67-; Reader in Int. Econs., Oxford 51-52; Econ. Dir. OEEC Paris 48-49; Econ. Dir. Nat. Econ. Devt. Council (N.E.D.C.) 62-64; Dir.-Gen. Dept. of Econ. Affairs Oct. 64-68; Head of Govt. Econ. Service and Chief Econ. Adviser to Treasury 69-73; Chief Econ. Adviser Confed. of British Industry 73-; Pres. Royal Economic Soc. 72-74.
Leisure interests: fishing, walking.
Publ. *The World Dollar Problem* 57, *Studies in Political Economy* (2 vols.) 75, and other books and articles on economic matters.
Confederation of British Industry, 21, Tothill Street, London S.W.1, England.
Telephone: 01-930-6711.

McDowall, Robert John Stewart, D.SC., M.D., F.R.C.P. (Edin.); British physiologist; b. 1892, Auchengaillie; s. of Robert McDowall and Fanny Grace Stewart; m. 1st Jessie Mary Macbeth 1921 (died 1963); m. 2nd Jean Esther Rotherham 1964; two d.; ed. Edinburgh Univ.
Assistant Lecturer in Physiology, Edinburgh Univ. 19-21; Lecturer in Experimental Physiology and Pharmacology, Leeds Univ. 21-23; Lecturer in Applied Physiology, London School of Hygiene 27-29; served in Royal Army Medical Corps 14-18, also 40-41; Prof. of Physiology, King's Coll., London Univ.; Deputy Asst. Dir. of Medical Services, Egyptian Exp. Force; Examiner for London, Edinburgh, Bristol, Manchester, Durham, Sheffield, Aberdeen, and Leeds Univs., Royal Coll. of Physicians and Royal Coll. of Surgeons (England, Ireland, India, Australia, Egypt and Scotland); Pres. Physiology section of British Asscn. 36; Chair. and founder mem. Medical Advisory Cttee. Asthma Research Council; Pres. European Congress of Allergy 59; Parkin Prize 35, Cullen Prize 38; Arris and Gale Lecturer, Royal Coll. of Surgeons 33; Oliver Sharpey Lecturer, Royal Coll. of Physicians 41; Gold Medal, Univ. of Edinburgh 36; Medal of Honour, Univ. of Ghent 51; Hon. Fellow several Allergy Socs.
Leisure interests: golf, chess, curling (internationalist).
Publs. *The Science of Signs and Symptoms in relation to Modern Diagnosis and Treatment* (4 edns.), *Handbook of Physiology* (13 edns.), *The Control of the Circulation of the Blood* 38, *A Biological Introduction to Psychology* 41, *Sane Psychology* 43, (6 re-prints) *The Whiskies of Scotland* 67 (2nd edn. 71).
34 Park Drive, London, N.W.11, England.
Telephone: 01-455-2858.

Mace, Charles Hoyt; American United Nations official; b. 19 May 1916, Chillicote, Ohio; m.; three c.; ed. George Washington Univ., Benjamin Franklin Univ. and Industrial Coll. of the Armed Forces, Washington, D.C.
Entered govt. service 34; mil. service 44-46; joined Dept. of State 46; Chief, Dept. of Budget and Admin., Intergovernmental Cttee. for European Migration 55-57; Deputy Administrator of Security and Consular Affairs (in charge of migration and refugee questions) 62-65; Deputy Chief (with rank of Minister), U.S. Mission to European Office of UN, Geneva 65-69; Deputy UN High Commr. for Refugees July 70-.
Leisure interest: Pres. the International American Club of Geneva.
UN Deputy High Commissioner for Refugees, Palais des Nations, CH-1211 Geneva 10, Switzerland; Home: Chilicothe, O., U.S.A.

MacEachen, Rt. Hon. Allan J., P.C., M.P., M.A.; Canadian politician; b. 6 July 1921; ed. St. Francis Xavier Univ., Univs. of Toronto and Chicago, and Massachusetts Inst. of Technology.
Professor of Economics, St. Francis Xavier Univ. 46-48, later Head, Dept. of Economics and Social Sciences; mem. House of Commons 53-58, 62-; Special Asst. and Consultant on Economic Affairs to Lester Pearson 58; Minister of Labour 63-65; Minister of Nat. Health and Welfare 65-68, of Manpower and Immigration 68-70; Pres. of the Privy Council 70-74; Sec. of State for External Affairs Aug. 74-; Hon. D.Iur. (St. Francis Xavier Univ.) 64, Hon. D.C.L. (Acadia Univ.) 66, Hon. L.H.D. (Loyola Coll., Baltimore Md.) 66; Liberal.
Department of External Affairs, Ottawa; Home: Inverness, Nova Scotia, Canada.

Macedo, Air Marshal Joelmir Campos de Araripe; Brazilian air force officer; b. Rio de Janeiro.
Joined Brazilian Army 28, transferred to Air Force 41; a pioneer of the Govt. air service linking the remote areas of Brazil to provincial capitals, Correio Aereo Nacional (CAN); fmr. Minister of Aeronautics; has held posts of Dir. Galcão Air Factory, Pres. Nat. Engines Plant, Dir. of Air Routes, Pres. Co-ordinating Cttee. for Rio de Janeiro Int. Airport; Minister of Aeronautics 74-.
Ministério da Aeronática, Brazília, Brazil.

Macek, Josef, PH.D., D.SC.; Czechoslovak historian; b. 8 April 1922, Řepov; ed. Charles Univ., Prague, and State Archive School, Prague.
Professor, Coll. of Political and Econ. Sciences 49; Dir. Historical Inst., Czechoslovak Acad. of Sciences 52-69; Corresponding mem. Czechoslovak Acad. of Sciences 52-60, mem. 60, Academician 60-; Chair. Czechoslovak Soc. for Dissemination of Political and Scientific Knowledge 57-65; mem. Ideological Comm., Central Cttee. C.P. of Czechoslovakia 63-69; Deputy to Nat. Assembly 64-69; mem. Presidium World Peace Council 62-70; Chair. Czechoslovak Peace Cttee. 66-68; mem. Presidium Czechoslovak Peace Cttee. 68-70; Deputy to House of the People, Fed. Assembly Jan.-Dec. 69; Cand. mem. Central Cttee. C.P. of Czechoslovakia 62-66, mem. 66-69, Inst. of Czech Language 70-75, Inst. of Archaeology 75-; State Prize 52, Czechoslovak Peace Prize 67.
Publs. mainly on history of Hussite Movement in Bohemia, including *Husitské revoluční knuti* (Hussite Revolutionary Movement) 52 (State Prize), *Der Tiroler Bauernkrieg und M. Gaismair* 65, *Renaissance and Reformation, Il Rinascimento italiano* 72, *Jean Hus et les traditions Hussites* 73.
Institute of Archaeology, Letenská 4, Prague 1; and Kadeřákuvská 1, Prague, Czechoslovakia.
Telephone: (Home) 322013.

McElroy, William David, B.A., M.A., PH.D.; American professor and scientist; b. 22 Jan. 1917, Roger, Bell Co., Tex.; s. of William D. McElroy and Ora Shipley McElroy; m. 1st Nell Winch McElroy 1940, 2nd Marlene Anderegg DeLuca McElroy 1967; three s. two d.; ed. Reed Coll. and Stanford and Princeton Univs.
Instructor in Biology, Johns Hopkins Univ. 46, Asst. Prof. 46-48, Assoc. Prof. 48-51, Dir. McCollum-Pratt Inst. 49-64, Prof. of Biology 51-69, Chair. Dept. of Biology 56-69; Harvey Lecturer, New York Acad. of Science 57; Exec. Editor *Archives of Biochemistry and Biophysics* 58-69; Editor *Biochemical and Biophysical Research Communications* 59-; Chair. AIBS Microbiology Advisory Cttee., Office of Naval Research 52-57; mem. President's Science Advisory Cttee. 62-67, Board of Dirs. of Nat. Insts. of Health 66-; Dir. U.S. Nat. Science Foundation 69-72; Chancellor, Univ. of Calif., San Diego 72-; mem. Soc. of Biological Chemists (Pres. 63-64), American Acad. of Arts and Sciences, American Inst. of Biological Sciences (Pres. 68), Nat.

Acad. of Sciences, etc.; Hon. D.Sc. (Univ. of Buffalo); Barnett Cohen Award, American Soc. of Bacteriology 58, Rumford Prize, American Acad. of Arts and Sciences 64.
Leisure interests: golf, music.
Publs. *Cell Physiology and Biochemistry* 61, 2nd edn. 64; Editor with B. Glass: *Copper Metabolism* 50, *Phosphorus Metabolism* (2 vols.) 51-52, *Mechanism of Enzyme Action* 54, *Amino Acid Metabolism* 55, *Inorganic Nitrogen Metabolism* 56, *The Chemical Basis of Heredity* 57, *The Chemical Basis of Development* 58, *Light and Life* 61; Editor with C. P. Swanson: *Foundations of Modern Biology Series* 61.
University of California, San Diego Campus, P.O. Box 109, La Jolla, Calif. 92037, U.S.A.

McElvenny, Ralph Talbot; American lawyer and businessman; b. 20 June 1906, Tacoma, Wash.; *s.* of Alice Talbot and Robert F. McElvenny; *m.* Elisabeth Steiwer 1934; one *s.* two *d.*; ed. Stanford Univ.
Attorney, Guaranty Trust Co., New York 31-33; Nat. Bank Conservator U.S. Treasury Dept., Washington, D.C. 33-34; Asst. Dir. U.S. Securities and Exchange Comm. 34-45; Vice-Pres. and Asst. to Chair. American Natural Gas Co. 45-72; Chair. and Dir. Amer. Natural Gas Co. and Michigan Consolidated Gas Co.; Dir. of numerous other companies.
Leisure interests: tennis, golf, hunting, fishing.
Home: 225 Stephens Road, Grosse Pointe Farms, Mich. 48236; Office: 1 Woodward Avenue, Detroit, Mich. 48226, U.S.A.
Telephone: WO5-8300.

MacEntee, Sean; Irish politician; b. 22 Aug. 1889, Belfast; *s.* of James and Mary MacEntee; *m.* Mairead de Brun 1921; one *s.* two *d.*; ed. St. Malachy's Coll., Belfast and Belfast Coll. of Technology.
Consulting Elec. Engineer, Co.-Dir. and Registered Patent Agent; sentenced to death by British Court Martial June 16 for participation in Irish Insurrection in that year; sentence commuted to penal servitude for life; released under amnesty June 17; mem. Exec. Cttee. Irish Republican Army 17-21; Republican Deputy and mem. Dáil Éireann 18-22; Fianna Fáil Deputy 27-69; Minister of Finance in First De Valera Govt. 32, and subsequent Govts. 33 and 37 and in first and second Govts. of Eire 37 and 38-39; Min. of Industry and Commerce Sept. 39-Aug. 41, of Local Govt. and Public Health 41-46, of Local Govt. 46-48; Min. of Finance 51-54; Min. of Health 57-65, and Social Welfare 58-61; Tanaiste (Deputy Prime Minister) 59-65; Signatory to London Agreement 38; Nat. Treas. Sinn Fein Organisation 24-26, and Fianna Fáil 26-32; mem. Nat. Exec. Fianna Fáil 26-, Nat. Vice-Pres. 55-; mem. President's Council of State 48-; mem. Consultative Assembly, Council of Europe, Strasbourg 49-51, 67-69; retd. from active politics 69; Knight Grand Cross (1st class) of Order Pius IX; 1916 Medal with bar; Hon. LL.D. (Nat. Univ. of Ireland); Hon. Fellow in Dentistry (Royal Coll. of Surgeons, Ireland); Hon. Life Mem. Irish Dental Asscn.
Publs. *Poems* 18, *Episode at Easter* 66.
Montrose, 30 Trimleston Avenue, Booterstown, Co. Dublin, and Tignacille, Dunquin, Co. Kerry, Ireland.

Macerata, Dr. Giorgio; Italian lawyer and business executive; b. 1913, Venice; *m.* Maria Barina 1939; one *d.*; ed. Univ. of Padua.
Legal-commercial posts, Venice 35-39; Gen. Sec. Serbatoi Montani per Irrigazione ed Elettricità, SAVA Group 39-48; Sec. at President's Office, Montecatini 49-51, Vice-Central Manager 51-53, Managing Dir. Compagnie Néerlandaise de l'Azote et Ammoniaque Synthétique et dérivés, Brussels 54-59, Head, Admin. Services Dept., Montecatini 59-62; Managing Dir. and Gen. Manager Montecatini Group (now Montecatini-

Edison) 63-68, Vice-Pres. and Man. Dir. 68; Vice-Pres. and Man. Dir. Compagnie Néerlandaise de l'Azote. Leisure interests: contemporary music, jazz, modern art, reading histories and biographies.
Montecatini-Edison, Foro Bonaparte 31, Milan, Italy. Telephone: 6333 or 6334.

McEwan, Geraldine; British actress; b. 9 May 1932, Old Windsor, Berks.; *d.* of Donald and Norah McKeown; *m.* Hugh Cruttwell 1953; one *s.* one *d.*; ed. Windsor County Girls' School.
First stage appearance Theatre Royal, Windsor 49; London appearances in *Who Goes There?* 51, *Sweet Madness, For Better, For Worse, Summertime;* Shakespeare Memorial Theatre, Stratford on Avon 56, 58, 61 playing Princess of France (*Love's Labours Lost*), Olivia (*Twelfth Night*), Ophelia (*Hamlet*), Marina (*Pericles*), Beatrice (*Much Ado about Nothing*); played in *School for Scandal*, U.S.A. 62, *The Private Ear and The Public Eye*, U.S.A. 63; mem. Nat. Theatre 65-, and has played in *Armstrong's Last Goodnight, Love for Love, A Flea in her Ear, The Dance of Death, Edward II, Home and Beauty, Rites, The Way of the World, The White Devil, Amphitryon 38, Dear Love* 73, *Chez Nous* 74, *The Little Hut* 74, *Oh Coward!* (musical) 75, *On Approval* 75.
c/o Larry Dalzell, 14 Clifford Street, London W.1, England.
Telephone: 01-499-3811.

McEwen, Rt. Hon. Sir John, P.C., G.C.M.G., C.H.; Australian fmr. politician and farmer; b. 29 March 1900, Chiltern, Victoria; *s.* of David McEwen and Amy Porter; *m.* 1st Annie McLeod (died 1967), 2nd Mary Byrne 1968.
Enlisted Australian Imperial Force 18; farmer Stanhope, Victoria 19-; mem. House of Reps. for Echuca Div. 34-37, for Indi Div. 37-49, for Murray 49-71; Minister of the Interior 37-39, of External Affairs 40, and of Air and Civil Aviation Oct. 40-41; mem. War Council 41-45; Deputy Leader Country Party 43-58, Leader 58-71; led del. to GATT talks, Geneva 54; Minister of Commerce and Agriculture 49-56, of Trade 56-63, Minister for Trade and Industry 63-71; Deputy Prime Minister 58-71; interim Prime Minister Dec. 67-Jan. 68; Order of the Rising Sun (1st Class, Japan) 73.
Leisure interests: farming, reading.
Office: AMP Tower, 535 Bourke Street, Melbourne, Vic. 3000; Home: Chilgala, Stanhope, Vic. 3623, Australia.
Telephone: Melbourne 62-1734.

McFadzean, Sir Frank Scott, Kt.; British oil executive; b. 26 Nov. 1915, Troon, Ayrshire; *m.*; one *d.*; ed. Glasgow Univ. and London School of Econs.
Former civil servant, Board of Trade and the Treasury; later worked for Malayan Govt. and Colonial Devt. Corpn. in Far East; joined Shell 52, held various posts in Middle East, Far East and London; Dir. Shell Int. Petroleum Co. 62; Dir. Shell Transport and Trading Co. Ltd. 64, Man. Dir. 71-, Chair. 72-; Man. Dir. Royal Dutch/Shell Group of Companies 64-; Man. Dir. Shell Petroleum Co. Ltd. 64-72, Chair. 72-; Man. Dir. Bataafse Petroleum Maatschappij N.V. (now Shell Petroleum N.V.) 64-72; Chair. Shell Canada Ltd., Shell Int. Marine Ltd.; Dir. British Airways 75-, Chair. 76-; Visiting Prof. of Econs., Univ. of Strathclyde 67-; Chair. Trade Policy Research Centre 71-; mem. Board Beecham Group 74-; Hon. LL.D. (Strathclyde), Hon. Fellow London School of Econs. 74.
Leisure interests: reading, walking.
Shell Centre, London, SE1 7NA, England.
Telephone: 01-934-5116.

McFadzean, Baron (Life Peer), cr. 66, of Woldingham; **William (Hunter) McFadzean,** Kt., C.I.E.E., J.DIP.M.A.; British chartered accountant; b. 17 Dec. 1903; *s.* of the late Henry McFadzean; *m.* Eileen Gordon 1933; one *s.* two *d.* (one adopted); ed. Stranraer Acad. and High School, and Glasgow Univ.

Served articles with McLay, McAllister & McGibbon, Chartered Accountants, Glasgow 22-27; on staff of Chalmers Wade & Co., Chartered Accountants, Liverpool 27-32; joined British Insulated Cables Ltd. as Accountant 32, apptd. Financial Sec. 37, Exec. Manager 42; on amalgamation of British Insulated Cables Ltd. and Callender's Cable & Construction Co. Ltd. in 45 apptd. to the Board of BICC, and also Exec. Dir.; Deputy Chair. 47, Chief Exec. March 50, Man. Dir. 54-61, Chair. 54-73, Hon. Pres. 73-; Chair. British Insulated Callender's Construction Co. Ltd. 52-64, and British Insulated Callender's (Submarine Cables) Ltd. 54-73; Dir. Midland Bank Ltd. 59-, Deputy Chair. 68; Dir. Midland Bank Trust Co. Ltd. 59-67, English Electric Co. Ltd. 66-68, Steel Co. of Wales Ltd. 66-67, Canadian Imperial Bank of Commerce 67-74, Home Oil Co. Ltd. 72; Deputy Chair. RTZ/BICC Aluminium Holdings Ltd. 67-73; Dir. Anglesey Aluminium Ltd. 68-73, The Canada Life Assurance Co. 69; Deputy Chair. The Canada Life Assurance Co. (Great Britain) 71-; Chair. British Insulated Callender's Cables Finance N.V. 71-73, Canada Life Unit Trust Managers Ltd. 71-, Standard Broadcasting Corp. (U.K.) Ltd. 72, Home Oil Co. Ltd. 72; mem. Council Inst. of Dirs. 54-74, Ministry of Labour Advisory Board on Resettlement of Ex-Regulars 57-60, Board of Trade Advisory Council on Middle East Trade 58-60; Pres. Fed. British Industries 59-61; Chair. Council of Industrial Feds. of European Free Trade Asscns. 60-63, Export Council for Europe 60-64; Hon. Pres. Export Council for Europe 64-71; Pres. British Electrical Power Convention 61-62; mem. Ministry of Transport Shipping Advisory Panel 62-64; Vice-Pres. British/Swedish Chamber of Commerce 63-74; Pres. British Nuclear Forum 64-66; mem. Court of British Shippers' Council 64-74; (Pres. British Shippers' Council 68-71; Chair. British Nat. Export Council 64-66, Pres. 66-68; Chair. Commonwealth Export Council 64-66; Vice-Pres. Middle East Asscn. 65, City of London Soc. 65-72; mem. Council Anglo-Danish Soc. 65-75, Chair. 69-75, Hon. Pres. 75-; mem. Adv. Cttee. for The Queen's Award to Industry 65-67; Chair. Review Cttee. for The Queen's Award to Industry for 70-; mem. Council Confed. of British Industry 65-74; Pres. The Coal Trade Benevolent Asscn. 67-68; mem. Council Foreign Bondholders 68-74; Pres. The Electrical and Electronics Industries Benevolent Asscn. 68-69; Deputy Chair. Nuclear Corpn. Ltd. 73; Companion I.E.E. 56; Grand Officer of the Order of Infante Dom Henrique (Portugal) 72; Grand Commdr. Order of the Dannebrog (Denmark) 74.

Leisure interests: travelling, golf, gardening.

Garthland, Woldingham, Surrey; and 146 Whitehall Court, London, S.W.1, England.

Telephone: Woldingham 3222 (Surrey); 01-930-3160 (London).

McFarland, James P., M.B.A.; American business executive; b. 13 Jan. 1912, Watertown, S.D.; *m.*; two *c.*; ed. Dartmouth Coll. and Amos Tuck School of Business Admin.

Joined Gen. Mills Inc. 34; Dir. of Operations, Grocery Products Div. 54; Vice-Pres. and Gen. Man. Grocery Products Div. 57, also Gen. Man. Sperry Operations 63, Flour Div. 64, Exec. Vice-Pres. 64, Pres. and Chief Operating Officer 67, Chief Exec. Officer 68-, Chair. of Board 69-; Dir. Fed. Reserve Bank of Minneapolis, Shenandoah Oil Corpn., Northwestern Bell Telephone Co., Prudential Insurance Co. of America, Grocery Mfrs. of America, Toro Co. of America, etc.

Leisure interest: golf.

General Mills Inc., P.O. Box 1113, Minneapolis, Minn. 55440, U.S.A.

McFarlane, Alexander N., B.S.; American business executive; b. 12 Nov. 1909, Lawrence, Mass.; *s.* of Alexander and Sarah (née Nelson) McFarlane; *m.* Florence Reed Campman 1936; two *d.*; ed. Tufts Univ.

Technical Service Dept., Corn Products Co. 34-36, Technical Sales Dept. 36-39, Asst. Dir. of Research 39-44, Man. of Chemical Sales 44-47, Exec. Asst. to Gen. Sales Man. 47-56, Vice-Pres. (Sales) 56-57, Pres. Corn Products Sales Co. 57-59, Corporate Senior Vice-Pres. (Sales) 59-61, Dir. Corn Products Co. 61-, Exec. Vice-Pres. (Domestic Operations) 62-64, Pres. 64-65, Chair. and Chief Exec. Officer 65, Chair. C.P.C. Int. Inc. (formerly Corn Products Co.) 65-69, Dir. 61-70, Hon. Chair. 70-; Chair. Food and Drug Law Inst. Inc. 65-68, Nutrition Foundation 65-69, Business Council for Int. Understanding 66-69.

C.P.C. International Inc., International Plaza, Englewood Cliffs, N.J. 07632, and 28 Waldo Lane, Manhasset, N.Y. 11030, U.S.A.

MacFarquhar, Sir Alexander, K.B.E.; fmr. British United Nations official; b. 6 Nov. 1903, Inverness, Scotland; *s.* of Roderick MacFarquhar and Janet McMurtrie; *m.* Berenice Whitburn 1929; one *s.*; ed. Aberdeen Univ. and Emmanuel Coll., Cambridge.

Indian Civil Service 26-47, Deputy Commr. Ferozepore 30-33, Amritsar 33-36, Settlement Officer Amritsar 36-41, Deputy Sec. Govt. of India 41, Deputy Dir.-Gen., Directorate-Gen. of Supply 43-46, Dir.-Gen. Disposals 46-47; Commerce and Educ. Sec. Govt. of Pakistan 47-51; Resident Rep. to Pakistan of UN Technical Assistance Board (TAB) 52-55, Regional Rep. to Far East, Bangkok 55-60, Special Adviser of UN Sec.-Gen. for Civilian Affairs in the Congo 60-62; UN Under-Sec. (Dir. of Personnel) 62-Dec. 67; Chair. Pakistan Soc.

Leisure interests: investment, walking.

Ottershaw, Beverley Lane, Coombe Hill, Kingston, Surrey, England.

Telephone: 01-942-5432.

McGannon, Donald H.; American broadcasting executive; b. 9 Sept. 1920, New York; *s.* of Robert E. and Margaret (Schmidt) McGannon; *m.* Patricia H. Burke 1942; six *s.* seven *d.*; ed. Fordham Univ. and Fordham School of Law.

Network Exec., Gen. Man., owned and operated stations; DuMont Television Network 52-55; Pres., Chair. of Board, Westinghouse Broadcasting Co. Inc. (Ind.), (Md.), (Del.) 55-; Pres. Westinghouse Electric Corpn.— Broadcasting, Learning, Leisure Time Div. 68; Chair. of Board Television Advertising Representatives Inc., Radio Advertising Representatives Inc., Westinghouse Learning Corpn., WBC Program Sales Inc., WBC Production Inc., Group W Films, Broadcast Rating Council Inc., Conn. Comm. for Higher Educ.; Trustee, Nat. Urban League; Dir. of many other broadcasting asscns.; Trustee, Sacred Heart Univ., New York Univ. and others; Chair. The Advertising Council Inc.; mem. Advisory Council, Notre Dame Univ.; mem. Pontifical Comm. on Communications Media; Distinguished Service Award, Nat. Asscn. of Broadcasters 68; Hon. Degrees: Fordham, Scranton, Creighton, St. Bonaventure, Temple and Fairfield Univs., and Emerson Coll.

Westinghouse Broadcasting Co. Inc., 90 Park Avenue, New York, N.Y. 10016, U.S.A.

McGee, Gale William, A.B., M.A., PH.D.; American professor and politician; b. 17 March 1915, Lincoln, Neb.; *m.* Loraine Baker 1939; two *s.* two *d*; ed. Nebraska State Teachers' Coll., Univs. of Colorado and Chicago.

Prof. of American History Crofton High School, Neb. 36-37, Kearney High School, Neb. 37-40, Neb. Wesleyan Univ. 40-43, Iowa State Coll. 43-44, Univ. of Notre Dame 44-45, Univ. of Chicago 45-46, Univ. of Wyoming 46-58; U.S. Senator 58-; Chair. Senate Post Office and Civil Service Cttee.; mem. Senate Appropriations and Foreign Relations Cttees., Nat. Comm. on Food

Marketing; Golden Fleece Award 66; Torch of Liberty Award 66; several other awards; Hon. LL.D. (Wyoming, Eastern Kentucky, American Univ. Washington, Allegheny); Hon. L.H.D. (Seton Hall); Democrat.
Publ. *The Responsibilities of World Power.*
Senate Office Building, Washington, D.C.; and 7205 Marbury Road, Washington, D.C. 20034, U.S.A.

McGhee, George C., B.SC., D.PHIL.; American government official and business executive; b. 10 March 1912, Waco, Tex.; s. of George Summers McGhee and Magnolia Spruce; m. Cecilia DeGolyer 1938; two s. four d.; ed. Southern Methodist Univ., Dallas, Univ. of Oklahoma, Oxford Univ. and Univ. of London.
Subsurface Geologist, The Atlantic Refining Co. 30-31; Geophysicist, Continental Oil Co. 33-34; Vice-Pres. Nat. Geophysical Co., Dallas 37-39; Partner DeGolyer, Mac-Naughton and McGhee 40-41; independent explorer for and producer of oil 40-; Senior Liaison Officer OPM and WPB 41-43; U.S. Deputy Exec. Sec. Combined Raw Materials Board 42-43; Special Asst. to the Under-Sec. of State for Econ. Affairs 46-47; Co-ordinator for Aid to Greece and Turkey, Dept. of State 47-49; Special Rep. of Sec. of State to Near East on Palestine Refugee problem with personal rank of Minister 49; Special Asst. to Sec. of State 49; Asst. Sec. Near East, South Asian and African Affairs 49-51; Ambassador to Turkey 51-53; Adviser N.A.T.O. Council, Ottawa 51; Dir. Inst. of Inter-American Affairs, Inter-American Education Foundation 46-51; Director U.S. Commercial Co. 46; Dir. Foreign Service Educ. Foundation 47-; Consultant, Nat. Security Council 58-59; Counsellor, Dept. of State and Chair. Policy Planning Council Jan.-Nov. 61; Under-Sec. of State for Political Affairs Nov. 61-63; Amb. to German Federal Republic 63-68; Amb. at Large 68-69; Dir. Panama Canal Co. 62-63, Mobil Oil Co. 69-, Procter & Gamble Co. 69-, Amer. Security & Trust Co. 69-; Chair. of Board *Saturday Review/World* 73-; Chair. Smithsonian Assocs. 76-; Owner McGhee Production Co.; Dir. of Trustees, Robert Coll. Istanbul 53-61, Brookings Inst. 54-61, Cttee. for Econ. Development 57-, Aspen Inst. Humanistic Studies 58-, Vassar Coll. 59-61, Duke Univ. 62-; Chair. Business Council for Int. Understanding 69-74; Chair. English Speaking Union, U.S.A. 70-74, Deputy Chair. Int. Council of the English Speaking Union 74; Chair. Nat Trust for Historic Preservation 71-, Int. Management and Devt. Inst. 72-, Fed. City Housing Corpn. 72-, Piedmont Environmental Council; Trustee George C. Marshall Research Foundation, American Council on Germany, The Asia Foundation 74-; Pres. Fed. City Council 70-74, etc.; mem. Board Nat. Civil Service League 67-71, Salzburg Seminar 69-71; mem. Japan-U.S. Econ. Advisory Council 70-74, American Petroleum Inst., American Asscn. Petroleum Geologists, Soc. of Exploring Geophysicists, American Inst. Mining and Metallurgical Engineers, Council on Foreign Relations (N.Y.), American Foreign Service Asscn., Acad. of Political Science, Wash. Inst. of Foreign Affairs, Dept. of Conservation and Econ. Devt., Club of Rome; served in U.S.N.R. 43-46; Lieut.-Col. U.S.A.F. Reserve 49-; Hon. LL.D. (Tulane Univ. 57, Maryland Univ. 65); Hon. D.C.L. (Southern Methodist Univ. 53); Hon. Fellow, Queen's Coll., Oxford 68; Hon. D.Sc. (Univ. of Tampa 69); Legion of Merit; Asiatic Ribbon with three battle stars, mem. Order Hospital St. John of Jerusalem 72-, numerous other awards.
Home: 2808 N Street, N.W., Washington, D.C. 20007; and Farmer's Delight, Middleburg, Va. 22117, U.S.A.
Telephone: 703-687-3451.

McGill, William James, PH.D.; American university president; b. 27 Feb. 1922, New York, N.Y.; m. Ann Rowe 1948; one s. one d.; ed. Fordham Coll. and Fordham and Harvard Univs.

Instructor, Fordham Univ. and Boston Coll., then, Teaching Fellow at Harvard Univ.; at Lincoln Laboratory, Mass. Inst. of Technology 51, Asst. Prof., Mass. Inst. of Technology 54; Asst. Prof. of Psychology, Columbia Univ., N.Y. 56-58, Assoc. Prof. 58-60, Prof. 60-65, Pres. 70-; Prof. of Psychology, Univ. of Calif. at San Diego, at same time, serving as mem. and Chair. of Cttee. on Educ. Policy and as mem. of Academic Council of Academic Senate and of Chancellor's Senate Council 65-68, Chair. of state-wide Academic Senate and Chancellor of Univ. of Calif. at San Diego 68-69; Dir. American Telephone and Telegraph Co. 72-, American Council on Educ. 72-, McGraw Hill Co. 73-; Trustee Trinity School 72-, Regional Co-ordinating Council, N.Y.C. 72-; Assoc. Editor, *Journal of Mathematical Psychology* 64-, *Perception and Psychophysics* 66-70; Consulting Editor, *Psychological Bulletin* 66-70, *Psychometrika* 65-70; Fellow, A.A.A.S. 63, American Psychological Asscn. 67, mem. Soc. of Experimental Psychologists, Gov. Board Psychonomic Soc. 65-71, American Statistical Asscn., Psychometric Soc. (also on Board of Trustees 67-), Biometric Soc.; Achievement Award of Fordham Univ. 68.
Publs. Over 35 studies and reviews.
60 Morningside Drive, New York, N.Y. 10027, U.S.A. Telephone: 212-280-2825.

MacGillavry, Carolina Henriette, D.SC.; Netherlands crystallographer; b. 22 Jan. 1904, Amsterdam; d. of Donald MacGillavry and Alida Matthes; m. Dr. Jean-Henri Nieuwenhuijsen 1971; ed. Univ. of Amsterdam.
Assistant, Univs. of Leiden and Amsterdam 29-41; Conservatrix, Univ. of Amsterdam 41-47; Lecturer in Crystallography, Univ. of Amsterdam 47-50, Prof. of Chemical Crystallography 50-72; mem. Royal Acad. of Sciences, Amsterdam 50, Gen. Sec. 61-74; mem. Board of Editors of *Nederlands Tijdschrift voor Natuurkunde* 39-56; mem. Board of Editors of Int. Tables for Crystal Structure Determination 48-66; mem. Exec. Cttee. of Int. Union of Crystallography 54-60; mem. Cttee. for the Award of Fellowships, Int. Fed. of Univ. Women 52-60, Chair. 55-60; Pres. Board of Child Guidance Clinic, Amsterdam 60-72; Vice-Pres. Netherlands' Cttee., Weizman Inst. of Sciences 74; mem. Council of Netherlands Nat. UNESCO Cttee. 62-75, Deutsche Akad. der Naturforscher "Leopoldina"; Knight of Netherlands Lion.
Leisure interests: music, gardening.
Mensinge 63, Amsterdam-1011, Netherlands.
Telephone: 020-443999.

McGillicuddy, John Francis, LL.B.; American banker; b. 30 Dec. 1930, Harrison, N.Y.; s. of Michael McGillicuddy and Anna Munro; m. Constance Burtis 1954; three s. two d.; ed. Princeton Univ. and Harvard Law School.
Senior Vice-Pres. Manufacturers Hanover Trust Co. 66, Exec. Vice-Pres. and Asst. to Chair. 69, Vice-Chair. and Dir. Jan. 70-71, Pres. 71-; Dir. Cities Service Co., Kraftco Corpn., Sperry and Hutchinson Co., Reynolds Metals Co., Econ. Devt. Council of N.Y.C., Westinghouse Electric Corpn., Continental Corpn.
Manufacturers Hanover Trust Co., 350 Park Avenue, New York, N.Y. 10022; Home: Hilltop Place, Rye, New York 10580, U.S.A.
Telephone: 212-350-5381 (Office).

McGinley, Phyllis; American poet and essayist; b. 21 March 1905; ed. Public Schools, Univ. of Calif. and Univ. of Utah.
Member Inst. of Arts and Letters; Pulitzer Prize for Poetry 61, Laetare Medal, Univ. of Notre Dame 64, Campion Award 67.
Publs. *On the Contrary* 34, *One More Manhattan* 37, *Pocketful of Wry* 40, *Husbands Are Difficult* 41, *Stones From a Glass House* 46, *A Short Walk from the Station*

51, *The Love Letters of Phyllis McGinley* 54, *Merry Christmas, Happy New Year* 58, *The Province of the Heart* 59, *Times Three* 60, *Sixpence in Her Shoe* 64, *Wonderful Time* 66, *A Wreath of Christmas Legends* 67. 16 North Chatsworth Avenue, Larchmont, N.Y. 10538, U.S.A.

McGovern, George Stanley; American politician; b. 19 July 1922, Avon, S. Dakota; s. of Rev. J. C. McGovern and Frances McLean McGovern; m. Eleanor Faye Stegeberg 1943; one s. four d.; ed. Dakota Wesleyan Univ. and Northwestern Univ.
Served U.S. Air Force, Second World War; Teacher, Northwestern Univ. 48-50; Prof. of History and Government, Dakota Wesleyan Univ. 50-53; Exec. Sec. South Dakota Democratic Party 53-56; mem. U.S. House of Reps. 57-61, served Agricultural Cttee.; Dir. "Food for Peace" Programme 61-62; Senator from South Dakota 63-; Dem. cand. for U.S. Presidency 72.
Publs. *The Colorado Coal Strike 1913-14* 53, *War Against Want* 64, *Agricultural Thought in the Twentieth Century* 67, *A Time of War, a Time of Peace* 68, *The Great Coalfield War* (with Leonard Guttridge) 72, *An American Journey* 74.
U.S. Senate, Washington, D.C. 20510; and Mitchell, S. Dak., U.S.A.

McGranahan, Donald V., M.A., PH.D.; American social scientist; b. 24 June 1913, Nova Scotia, Canada; s. of Norvin G. McGranahan and Jenny MacAndrews; m. Nancy G. Ulrich 1940; two s. one d.; ed. Harvard Univ.
Instructor, Dept. of Psychology, Harvard Univ. 39-41; Govt. service 41-43; army service 43-46; Lecturer, Dept. of Social Relations, Harvard Univ. 46-48; Senior Officer, Asst. Dir. in charge of Survey, Research and Devt. Branch, Bureau of Social Affairs, UN 48-67; Dir. UN Research Inst. for Social Devt. (UNRISD) 67-; Guggenheim Fellow 46.
Leisure interests: squash, skiing, reading.
Publs. recent books include: *Contents and Measurement of Socio-economic Development* 70, *Approaches to Social Planning* 70, *Social Planning and Social Security* 70, *The Interrelations between Social and Economic Development* 70, *Analysis of Socio-Economic Development Through a System of Indicators* 71, *Methods of Estimation and Prediction in Socio-economic Development* 72, *Development Indicators and Development Models* 72.
47 Chemin Moïse Duboule, Petit Saconnex, Geneva, Switzerland.
Telephone: 33-84-62.

McGrath, Raymond, B.ARCH., R.H.A., F.R.I.B.A., F.R.I.A.I., F.S.I.A.; Australian architect; b. 7 March 1903, Sydney, N.S.W.; s. of Herbert and Edith McGrath; m. Mary Crozier 1930; one s. one d.; ed. Univs. of Sydney and Cambridge.
In private practice as architect and industrial designer London 31-39; Official War Artist 40; Principal Architect, Office of Public Works, Dublin 48-68; Appointed architect for Kennedy Memorial Concert and Congress Hall, Dublin 64; Architect for Royal Hibernian Acad. of Arts Gallery 69; in private practice in Dublin since 68; architectural work for private housing, exhibitions, restaurants, offices and industrial buildings; industrial design for furniture, glassware and carpets; Prof. of Architecture, Royal Hibernian Acad.; Fellow. Soc. of Industrial Artists; Medallion of the Board of Architects of New South Wales.
Leisure interests: drawing and painting, music, the garden.
Publs. *Twentieth Century Houses* (in Basic English) 34, *Glass in Architecture and Decoration* 37 (2nd edn. 61).
Somerton Lodge, Rochestown Avenue, Co. Dublin, Ireland.
Telephone: 853630.

MacGregor, George Lescher, B.S.; American utilities executive; b. 29 Oct. 1901, Little Rock, Ark.; s. of Arthur W. and Irene (née Lescher) MacGregor; m. Jean Edge 1929; two s.; ed. Univ. of Texas.
Joined Dallas Power & Light Co. 29, Man., Pres. 40-53, Chair. of Board 44-53, Dir. 53-68; Vice-Pres. and Dir. Texas Utilities Co. 45-53, Pres. and Dir. 53-67, Chair. 67-72; Dir. State Fair of Texas; Trustee Texas Research Foundation; Pres. and Trustee Southwestern Medical Foundation; mem. Advisory Cttee. Edison Electric Inst.; Distinguished Engineering Graduate Award, Univ. of Texas.
6322 Westchester Drive, Dallas, Tex. 75205, U.S.A.

McGregor, Oliver Ross, M.A., B.SC.(ECON.); British sociologist and social historian; b. 25 Aug. 1921, Durris, Scotland; s. of late William McGregor and Anne Olivia Ross; m. Nellie Weate 1944; three s.; ed. Worksop Coll., Univ. of Aberdeen, London School of Econs.
Simon Senior Research Fellow, Univ. of Manchester 59-60; Prof. of Social Insts., Univ. of London 64-, Head of Dept. of Sociology, Bedford Coll. 64-; Joint Dir. Rowntree Legal Research Unit 66-; Dir. of Centre for Socio-Legal Studies, Univ. of Oxford 72-75; Fellow, Wolfson Coll., Oxford 72-75; mem. Cttee. on the Enforcement of Judgment Debts 65-69, Cttee. on Statutory Maintenance Limits 66-68, Cttee. on Land Use 67, Independent TV Authority's Gen. Advisory Council 67-72, Countryside Comm. 68-, Lord Chancellor's Advisory Cttee. on Legal Aid 69-, Cttee. on One-Parent Families 69-74; mem. Royal Comm. on the Press 74, Chair. 75-.
Leisure interest: book collecting.
Publs. *Divorce in England* 57, Editor *Lord Ernle, English Farming Past and Present* (6th edn.) 60, *Separated Spouses* 70.
Royal Commission on the Press, Standard House, 27 Northumberland Avenue, London, WC2N 5AA; and Bedford College, Regent's Park, London, NW1 4NS; Home: Far End, Wyldes Close, London, NW11 7JB, England.
Telephone: 01-839-2855 (Office); 01-486-4400 (College); 01-458-2856 (Home).

McGuigan, Thomas Malcolm; New Zealand parliamentarian; b. 20 Feb. 1921; ed. Christchurch Boys' High School, Christchurch Technical Evening School.
Served in Navy 41-45; secretarial and accountancy posts in manufacturing and retailing field 46-54; admin. posts, Christchurch Hospital 55-57; Senior Admin. Officer, Princess Margaret Hospital, Christchurch 58-69; mem. Parl. 69-75; Minister of Railways, Electricity and Civil Defence 72-74, of Health and Minister in Charge of the Public Trust Office 74-75.
71 Main Road, Redcliffs, Christchurch 8, New Zealand.

McGuire, Dominic Paul, C.B.E.; Australian diplomatist and writer; b. 3 April 1903, Peterborough, South Australia; s. of James and Mary McGuire; m. Frances M. Cheadle 1927; ed. Christian Brothers' Coll., Adelaide, and Univ. of Adelaide.
Former Lecturer in History, Univ. of Adelaide, served Royal Australian Navy 39-45; Adviser, Commonwealth Prime Ministers' Conf., London 51; Del. to UN 53; Minister to Italy 53-58, Ambassador 58-59; Knight Grand Cross of St. Sylvester 59, Commendatore of Order of Merit, Italian Republic 67.
Leisure interest: living at large e.g. bushranging.
Publs. *The Two Men* 32, *The Poetry of Gerard Manley Hopkins* 35, *7.30 Victoria* 35, *Prologue to the Gallows* 35, *Cry Aloud for Murder* 36, *Born to be Hanged* 36, *Burial Service* 37, *W 1.* 37, *Restoring All Things* (with J. Fitzsimmons) 38, *Australian Journey* 39, *Spanish Steps* 40, *Westward the Course* 42, *Price of Admiralty* (with F. M. McGuire) 45, *The Three Corners of the World* 48, *Experiment in World Order* 48, *The Australian Theatre* (with

B. P. Arnott and F. M. McGuire) 48, *Freedom for the Brave* 49, *Inns of Australia* 52, etc.
136 Mills Terrace, North Adelaide 5006, South Australia.
Telephone: 67-2214.

Machado, Paulo de Almeida; Brazilian medical doctor; b. Minas Gerais.
Active in planning public health and sanitary services; Dir. Nat. Inst. for Research in the Amazon Region until 74; Minister of Health 74-.
Ministério da Saúde, Esplanada dos Ministérios, Brasília, Brazil.

Machavariani, Alexei Davidovich; Soviet composer; b. 1913, Gori, Georgia; *s.* of Maria and David Machavariani; *m.* Pachkoria Ekaterina 1946; one *s.*; ed. Tbilisi Conservatoire.
Chairman Composers' Union of Georgia 52-68; Exec. mem. U.S.S.R. Composers' Union; Sec. Composers' Union U.S.S.R. 62-74; mem. Jury Tchaikovsky Int. Competition 62, 66, U.S.S.R. Ballet Art Council 67-; Honoured Worker of the Arts of Georgian S.S.R. 50, State Prize 51, People's Artist of the U.S.S.R. 58; Badge of Honour 63, of Lenin 66, Rustaveli State Prize (Georgian S.S.R.) 71, Order of Kirill and Methodius 71, Gold Medal, Cultural Centre Braidense (Italy) 73, Order of Red Banner of Labour 73.
Principal compositions: *Khorumi* (poem for piano) 39, *Mumli Mukhasa* (symphonic suite) 39, *Elegy* (symphonic sketch) 39, *Gori Pictures* (symphony) 40, *Mother and Son* (opera) 41, *The Bridge* (symphonic suite) 42, Concerto for Piano and Orchestra 44, *Secret of Two Oceans* (symphonic suite) 44, *Solemn Overture* 47, First Symphony 47, *Death of a Hero* (symphonic poem) 49, Concerto for Violin and Orchestra 50, *Georgian Festal* 51, Ten Unaccompanied Choral Pieces 52, *Doluri* (for symphony orchestra) 52, *Doluri* (for unaccompanied violin) 52, *My Country's Day* (oratorio) 53, *Othello* (ballet) 57, Three suites (symphony orchestra)58, *Four Pieces for violin and piano* 62, Four ballades (voice, piano) 65, Twelve piano pieces for child album 65, Five monologues (voice, orchestra) 66, *Hamlet* (opera) 67, *Six pieces for violin and piano* 71, *Second symphony* 73, 25 selected ballads and songs 73, 40 pieces for piano 74, *The Knight in Tiger's Skin* (ballet) 74, incidental music for: *King Lear, Richard III, The Legend of Love*, and for films: *Cradle of the Poet, Mayakovsky*, and others.
25A Kiacheli Street, Tbilisi 8, Georgia, U.S.S.R.
Telephone: 99-03-41.

Machel, Samora Moïsés; Mozambique nationalist leader and politician; b. Oct. 1933, Lourenço Marques (now Maputo); *m.* Grace Simbine 75.
Trained as male nurse; sent to Algeria for military training 63; organized training camp programme in Tanzania; C.-in-C. army of Frente de Libertação de Moçambique (FRELIMO) in guerrilla war against the Portuguese 66-74; Sec. of Defence, FRELIMO's ruling triumvirate Feb. 66-, Pres. May 70-; Pres. of Mozambique June 75-.
Office of the President, Maputo (Lourenço Marques), Mozambique.

Machimura, Kungo; Japanese politician; b. 16 Aug. 1900, Sapporo City; ed. Tokyo Univ.
Entered Ministry of Home Affairs; Gov. Toyama and Niigata Prefs.; Dir. Police Bureau, Ministry of Home Affairs; Supt.-Gen. Metropolitan Police Bureau 45; mem. House of Reps.; affiliated to conservative group of fmr. Kaishinto (Progressive) Party, left when KP reformed to become Democratic Party, later helped to form Shinto Doshikai Party; Minister of Home Affairs 73-Dec. 74; Independent.
28-18, Higashi-ga-oka, 1-chome, Meguro-ku, Tokyo, Japan.

Machín Acosta, José María; Venezuelan diplomatist; b. 16 May 1924, Carúpana; ed. Cen. Univ. of Venezuela, Free Univ., Bogotá, Univ. of Paris.
Head, Div. of Int. Orgs. and Confs., Div. of Int. Politics, Ministry of Foreign Affairs; Deputy to Nat. Congress 61-73; Amb. to Chile 64-68; Perm. Rep. to Org. of Amer. States 74-; founding mem. Democratic Action Party; Editor *Vea y Lea*.
4201 Connecticut Avenue, N.W., Suite 609, Washington, D.C. 20008, U.S.A.

Macías Nguema, Francisco; Equatorial Guinean politician; b. 1 Jan. 1924, Msegayong, Río Muni; ed. Catholic Schools in Río Muni.
Coffee planter 44; entered Colonial Admin. 44; entered politics 63; Vice-Pres. Admin. Council 64-68; Pres. of the Repub. (Life Pres. 72) and Minister of Defence 68-, of Foreign Affairs 69-; mem. Popular Idea of Equatorial Guinea (IPGE) Party.
Office of the President, Malabo, Macías Nguema, Equatorial Guinea.

McIlraith, Rt. Hon. George James, P.C., Q.C., M.P.; Canadian lawyer and politician; b. 29 July 1908, Lanark, Ont.; *s.* of James McIlraith and Kate McLeod; *m.* Margaret Summers 1935; one *s.* three *d.*; ed. Osgoode Hall, Toronto.
Member of House of Commons 40-72; Parl. Asst. to Minister of Reconstruction 45, to Minister of Trade and Commerce 48, to Minister of Defence Production 51; Canadian rep. to UN 46; Minister of Transport 63-64; Pres. of Privy Council and Pres. of Treasury Board 64; Govt. House Leader 64-67; Minister of Public Works 65-68; Solicitor-Gen. of Canada 68-70; Senator 72-; Liberal.
Leisure interests: golf, fishing.
Room 581-F, Parliament Buildings, Ottawa; 300 Sandridge Road, Ottawa, Ontario K1L 5A3, Canada.
Telephone: 992-2044.

McIlvaine, Robinson, A.B.; American diplomatist; b. 17 July 1913; ed. Harvard Univ.
Commander, U.S. Navy 40-46; Editor-Publisher 46-53; Dep. Asst. Sec. of State and Chair. Caribbean Comm. 53-56; Consul-Gen. Lisbon 56-60, Léopoldville 60-61; Amb. to Dahomey 61-64; Dir. Interdept. Seminar, Washington 64-66; Amb. to Rep. of Guinea 66-68, to Kenya 69-73; Exec. Vice Pres. African Wildlife Leadership Foundation 73-.
1717 Mass. Avenue, N.W., Washington, D.C. 20036, U.S.A.

McIlwain, Henry, D.SC., PH.D.; British university professor; b. 20 Dec. 1912, Newcastle-on-Tyne; *s.* of John McIlwain and Louisa Widdowson; *m.* Valerie Durston 1940; two *d.*; ed. King's Coll., Durham Univ. and Queen's Coll., Oxford.
With British Medical Research Council 37-47; Senior Lecturer and Reader in Biochemistry, London Univ. 48-55, Prof. Inst. of Psychiatry 55-; Dr. h.c. (Univ. d'Aix-Marseilles) 74.
Leisure interests: contemporary arts, travel.
Publs. *Biochemistry and the Central Nervous System* 55, 4th edn. (with H. S. Bachelard) 71, *Chemotherapy and the Central Nervous System* 57, *Practical Neurochemistry* (with R. Rodnight) 62 (2nd edn. 75), *Chemical Exploration of the Brain* 63.
73 Court Lane, London, SE21 7EF, England.
Telephone: 01-693-5334.

MacInnes, Most Rev. Angus Campbell, C.M.G., M.A., D.D.; British ecclesiastic; b. 18 April 1901, Cairo, Egypt; *s.* of Rennie and Janet W. MacInnes; *m.* F. I. Joy Masterman 1928; two *s.* two *d.*; ed. Harrow School and Trinity Coll., Cambridge.
Deacon 26; Priest 27; Curate of Peckham 26-28; C.M.S. Missionary, Jerusalem 28-51; Principal, Bishop Gobat School, Jerusalem 30-44; Archdeacon in Palestine and

Transjordan 43-50; Archdeacon in Jerusalem 50-51; Examining Chaplain to Bishop n Jerusalem 43-51; Vicar of St. Michael's, St. Albans 51-54; Rural Dean of St Albans 53-57; Residential Canon, St. Albans 53-57; Lord Bishop Suffragan of Bedford 53-57; Anglican Archbishop in Jerusalem 57-68; Asst. Bishop of Salisbury 68-73; Master St. Nicholas Hospital, Salisbury 68-.
St. Nicholas Hospital, Salisbury SP1 2SW, Wilts., England.
Telephone: Salisbury 6874.

MacInnes, Helen; American (naturalized 1951) novelist; b. 7 Oct. 1907, Glasgow, Scotland; *m.* Gilbert Highet (*q.v.*) 1932; one *s.*
Went to United States 37; Wallace Award, American-Scottish Foundation 73.
Leisure interests: two piano duets, interior decoration, golf, gardening, travel, current events.
Publs. *Above Suspicion* 41, *Assignment in Brittany* 42, *While Still We Live* 44, *Horizon* 46, *Friends and Lovers* 47, *Rest and Be Thankful* 49, *Neither Five Nor Three* 51, *I and My True Love* 53, *Pray for a Brave Heart* 55, *North from Rome* 58, *Decision at Delphi* 60, *Assignment: Suspense* 61, *The Venetian Affair* 63, *Home is the Hunter* 64, *The Double Image* 66, *The Salzburg Connection* 68, *Message from Malaga* 71, *The Snare of the Hunter* 73.
Jefferys Lane, East Hampton, New York 11937, U.S.A.

Macintosh, Sir Robert Reynolds, M.A., M.D., F.R.C.S., F.F.A.R.C.S., F.R.C.O.G., D.A.; British anaesthetist; b. 17 Oct. 1897; ed. New Zealand and Guy's Hospital.
Professor of Anaesthetics Oxford Univ. 37-65; hon. consultant in Anaesthetics, R.A.F.; Hon. Fellow Pembroke Coll., Oxford, Royal Soc. of Medicine; Hon. D.Sc. (Univ. of Wales), Hon. M.D. (Buenos Aires, Aix-Marseilles and Poznań; Order of Military Merit (Spain), Order of Liberty (Norway).
Publs. *Essentials of General Anæsthesia, Physics for the Anæsthetist, Local Anæsthesia, Brachial Plexus, Lumbar Puncture and Spinal Analgesia.*
326 Woodstock Road, Oxford, England.
Telephone: Oxford 55471.

McIntosh, Sir Ronald Robert Duncan, K.C.B., B.A.; British civil servant; b. 26 Sept. 1919, Whitehaven; *s.* of late Dr. T. S. McIntosh, F.R.C.P.; *m.* Doreen MacGinnity 1951; ed. Charterhouse, Balliol Coll., Oxford.
Joined Board of Trade 47; Counsellor, British High Comm., New Delhi 57-61; Deputy Sec. Dept. of Econ. Affairs 66-68, Cabinet Office 68-70, Dept. of Employment 70-72, Treasury 72-73; Dir.-Gen. Nat. Econ. Devt. Office 73-.
Leisure interest: sailng.
National Economic Development Office, Millbank Tower, Millbank, London, S.W.1, England.
Telephone: 01-211-5386.

McIntyre, Donald Conroy; British bass opera singer; b. 22 Oct. 1934, Auckland, New Zealand; *s.* of George D. and Hermyn McIntyre; *m.* Jill Redington 1961; three *d.*; ed. Mt. Albert Grammar School, Auckland, Auckland Teachers' Training Coll. and Guildhall School of Music, London.
Principal bass, Sadlers Wells Opera 60-67; with Royal Opera House, Covent Garden 67-; regular appearances at Bayreuth Festival 67-; frequent int. guest appearances; roles include: Wotan (*Der Ring*), Dutchman (*Der Fliegende Holländer*), Telramund (*Lohengrin*), Barak (*Die Frau ohne Schatten*), Pizzaro (*Fidelio*), Golaud (*Pelleas et Mélisande*), Kurwenal (*Tristan and Isolde*), Jokanaan (*Salome*).
Leisure interests: sport (particularly golf, tennis and swimming), gardening, languages.
2 Roseneath Close, Chelsfield Hill, Orpington, Kent;

also c/o Ingpen & Williams, 14 Kensington Court, London, W.8, England.
Telephone: Farnborough 55368.

MacIntyre, Duncan, D.S.O., O.B.E., E.D.; New Zealand farmer and politician; b. 1915, Hastings; *s.* of A. MacIntyre; *m.* Diana Hunter; ed. Larchfield School, Scotland, Christ's Coll., Christchurch.
Farming 33-39, 47-; served World War II in Middle East, Italy and Japan as mem. New Zealand Cavalry Regt. 39-45; after war commanded 1st Battalion Hawke's Bay Regt.; the N.Z. Scottish Regt., 2nd Infantry Brigade and 4th Armoured Brigade in Territorial Army 49-60; Territorial mem. of N.Z. Army Board 60-; M.P. for Hastings 60-; Minister of Lands, Minister of Forests, Minister in Charge of the Valuation Dept. 66-72, of Maori and Island Affairs 69-72, of the Environment Feb.-Dec. 72, of Agriculture and Fisheries, of Maori Affairs, in Charge of the Rural Banking and Finance Corpn. Dec. 75-; National Party.
Parliament Buildings, Wellington, New Zealand.

McIntyre, H. E. Cardinal James Francis A.; American ecclesiastic; b. 25 June 1886.
Ordained priest 21; Titular Bishop of Cyrene 40; Titular Archbishop of Palto 46; Archbishop of Los Angeles 48-70; created Cardinal by Pope Pius XII 53; mem. Sacred Congregations of the Consistory, De Propaganda Fide and of Ceremonies.
637 South Kingsley Drive, Los Angeles, Calif., U.S.A.
Telephone: 381-6191.

McIntyre, Sir Laurence Rupert, Kt., C.B.E., M.A.; Australian diplomatist; b. 22 June 1912, Hobart, Tasmania; *s.* of Laurence and Hilda McIntyre; *m.* Judith Gould 1938; two *s.*; ed. Tasmania Univ. and Exeter Coll., Oxford.
Served in London 36, Canberra 40, Washington 42, Canberra (Head of Pacific Division) 47, Singapore 50, Canberra (Asst. Sec.) 51, Singapore (Commr.) 52, London (Minister) 54; Ambassador to Indonesia 57-60, to Japan 60-65; Deputy Sec. Dept. of External Affairs 65-70; Perm. Rep. of Australia to UN 70-75.
c/o Ministry of Foreign Affairs, Canberra, Australia.

MacIntyre, Malcolm Ames; American executive; b. 28 Jan. 1909, Boston; *s.* of Charles H. MacIntyre and Martha Alden; *m.* Clara Bishop 1933; one *s.* two *d.*; ed. Yale Univ. and Oxford Univ.
Admitted U.S. Bar 34; with Debevoise, Plimpton, Lyons and Gates 48-57; Pres. Chemical Div. Martin Marietta Corpn. 64-72; U.S. Air Force 42-46; Under-Sec., U.S.A.F. 57-59; Pres. Eastern Airlines Inc. 59-63; Dir. Schröder Banking Corpn.; Trustee Carnegie Corpn.; Chair. Bunker-Ramo Corpn. 68-71; mem. Airways Modernization Board 57-; Mayor, Village of Scarsdale, N.Y. 66-69; Advisory Board, N.Y. Urban Devt. Corpn. 70-.
Leisure interests: golf, tennis, swimming, painting.
60 Mamaroneck Road, Scarsdale, N.Y. 10583, U.S.A.

Macintyre, Tan Sri S. Chelvasingam; Malayan lawyer and diplomatist; b. 1903; ed. Methodist Boys' School, Kuala Lumpur and Trinity Coll., Kandy, Ceylon.
Called to the Bar 27, Advocate and Solicitor, Johore 28-, Personal Legal Adviser to H.H. Sultan of Johore 56-; mem. Batu Pahat Town Council 53-56, Batu Pahat Central Constituency 54-57, Federal Legislative Council 55-57; High Commr. for Fed. of Malaya in India 57-63, for Malaysia 63-64; concurrently in Ceylon 59-64; Amb. to Nepal 60-64; High Court Judge Sept. 64-73; Judge of Fed. Court, Malaysia 68-73; retd. 73; Panglima Mangku Negara.
Publ. *Through Memory Lane.*
Home: 63 Jalan Lee Kwee Foh, Ipoh; Office: Federal Court, Kuala Lumpur, Malaysia.
Telephone: 84414 (Office); Ipoh 2234 (Home).

McIntyre, Thomas James, B.A., LL.B.; American lawyer and politician; b. 20 Feb. 1915; ed. Dartmouth Coll. and Boston Univ. Law School.
Army Service, Second World War; Mayor of Laconia, New Hampshire 49-51; cand. for Congress 54; New Hampshire State Chair., Sen. Kefauver's campaign for Democratic Pres. nomination 56; Senator from New Hampshire 63-; Democrat.
Office: United States Senate, Washington, D.C. 20510; Home: 2923 Garfield Street, N.W. Washington, D.C. 20008, U.S.A.

MacIver, Loren; American artist; b. 2 Feb. 1909; ed. Art Students League.
One Man exhibitions, East River Gallery, New York City 38, Pierre Matisse Gallery, New York City 40-44, 49, 56, 61, 66, 70, Museum of Modern Art Travelling Exhbn. 41, Vassar Art Gallery 50, Wellesley Coll. 51, Whitney Museum 53, Dallas Museum of Fine Arts 53 etc.; rep. in numerous exhibitions including Fantastic Art, Dada, Surrealism 38, Art in Our Time 39, State Dept. Exhibition in Europe 46, Dunn Int. Exhibition, Tate Gallery, London 63, Venice Biennale 61; First Prize, Corcoran Art Gallery 57; Chicago Art Inst. 61, Univ. of Illinois 62; Ford Foundation Grant 60; mem. Nat. Inst. of Arts and Letters; Purchase Prize, Krannert Art Museum, Univ. of Illinois 63; Mark Rothko Foundation Award 72.
c/o Pierce Matisse Gallery, 57 East 57th Street, New York, N.Y. 10022, U.S.A.

Mackasey, Bryce S.; Canadian politician; b. Aug. 1921, Quebec City; m. Margaret Cecilia O'Malley; two s. two d.; ed. McGill and Sir George Williams Univs., Montreal.
Member of Parl. 62-; Parl. Sec. to Minister of Nat. Health and Welfare 65, to Minister of Labour Jan. 66-68; Cabinet Minister without Portfolio Feb.-July 68; Minister of Labour 68-72, of Man-power and Immigration Jan.-Nov. 72; Minister of State June-Aug. 74; Postmaster-Gen. Aug. 74-; Del. to UN 63, Repub. of China 65, Poland 66; Liberal.
House of Commons, Ottawa, Ont. K1A OA6, Canada.

Mackay, Ian Keith, C.M.G.; New Zealand broadcasting executive; b. 19 Oct. 1909, Nelson; s. of David and Margaret Mackay; m. Lilian Beatty 1961; one d.; ed. Nelson Coll., New Zealand.
Broadcasting Station Manager, New Zealand 39-43; Senior Exec., Commercial Div., New Zealand Broadcasting Commission 44-50; Production Man., Macquarie Network, Australia 50-61; Dir.-Gen. Nigerian Broadcasting Corpn. 61-64; Adviser, Board of Govs. 64-65; Public Relations Officer, Dept. of Information, Papua, New Guinea 66-67, Broadcasts Supervisor (Management) 68-73; Asst. to Chair. Papua New Guinea Broadcasting Comm. 73-75, Consultant 75-; mem. Royal Soc. of Literature, Soc. of Authors.
Leisure interests: reading, gardening, conchology.
Publs. *Broadcasting in New Zealand* 53, *Broadcasting in Australia* 57, *Macquarie—the Story of a Network* 60, *Broadcasting in Nigeria* 64, *Presenting Papua and New Guinea* (compiler) 67, *Directory of Papua and New Guinea* (compiler), *Broadcasting in Papua New Guinea* 76, and other articles on broadcasting.
405A Main Road, Karori, Wellington, New Zealand.

MacKay, Robert Alexander, PH.D.; Canadian university professor and diplomatist; b. 2 Jan. 1894, Victoria County, Ont.; s. of Andrew and Margaret Mackay; m. Mary Junkin 1924; one s. three d.; ed. Univ. of Toronto and Princeton Univ.
Served army 16-19; Lecturer in Politics, Princeton Univ. 24-25; Asst. Prof. of Govt. Cornell Univ. 25-27; Prof. of Govt. and Political Science, Dalhousie Univ. 27-47; mem. Royal Comm. on Dominion-Provincial Relations 37-40; Special Asst. to Under-Sec. of State for External Affairs 43-46, Asst. Under-Sec. 52-54,

Deputy Under-Sec. 54; Permanent Rep. to UN 55-58, Amb. to Norway and to Iceland 58-61; Visiting Prof. Carleton Univ. Ottawa 61-72; Pres. Canadian Political Science Asscn. 43-44; Fellow Royal Society of Canada; mem. Canada-U.S. Permanent Joint Board of Defence 50-55; Hon. LL.D. (Dalhousie and Carleton Univs.); Medal of Service, Order of Canada 70.
Publs. *The Unreformed Senate of Canada* 26 (2nd edn. 63), *Canada Looks Abroad* 38, *Newfoundland Studies* 48, *Canadian Foreign Policy 1945-54, Select Speeches and Documents* 70.
150 Argyle Avenue, Ottawa, Ontario, Canada.

McKay, Robert B., B.S., J.D.; American teacher of law; b. 11 Aug. 1919, Wichita, Kan.; s. of John B. and Ruth G. McKay; m. Kate Warmack 1954; two d.; ed. Univ. of Kansas and Yale Univ.
Assistant and Assoc. Prof. of Law, Emory Univ. 50-53; Assoc. Prof. now Prof. of Law, New York Univ. 53-, Dean, School of Law 67-.
Leisure interest: civic affairs.
Publ. *Reapportionment* 65.
Office: 40 Washington Square South, New York, N.Y. 10012; Home: 29 Washington Square West, New York, N.Y. 10011, U.S.A.
Telephone: 598-2511 (Office); 475-3076 (Home).

McKee, James W., Jr., B.COMM; American businessman; b. 19 Aug. 1922, Pittsburgh, Pa.; s. of James W. McKee and Mary Isabel Welch; m. Jayne A. Finnegan 1947; one s. two d.; ed. McGill Univ.
Cost Accountant, CPC Italian affiliate 47-50; Financial Man. CPC Brazilian affiliate 53-58; Pres. CPC Cuban affiliate 58-59; Man. CPC Brazilian affiliate 59-64; Exec. Asst. CPC Int. 64; Comptroller, CPC Int. 64-65 Vice-Pres. (Finance) 65-69, Dir. 68, Pres. and Chief Admin. Officer 69-, Chief Executive Officer 72-; Dir. Fidelity Union Trust Co. 69; Marine Midland Bank, Int. Marine Banking Co. Ltd., Grocery Mfrs. of America; Trustee U.S. Council of Int. Chamber of Commerce, Council of the Americas, New Rochelle Coll.; Cruzeiro do Sol (Brazil).
Leisure interests: golf, reading.
CPC International Inc., International Plaza, Englewood Cliffs, N.J. 07632, U.S.A.
Telephone: 201-894-2135.

McKee, John Angus; Canadian business executive; b. 31 Aug. 1935, Toronto, Ont.; s. of John W. McKee and Margaret E. Phippen; m. Susan E. Harley; one s. one d.; ed. Trinity Coll. School, Port Hope, Ont. and Univ. of Toronto.
Joined the Patiño Mining Corpn. 62, Asst. to Pres. 63, Vice-Pres. (Corporate Devt.) 66; Man. Dir. Consolidated Tin Smelters Ltd. 68-71; Pres. J. A. McKee and Assoc. Ltd. 72-75; Dir. Canadian Occidental Pete Ltd., Stone and Webster Canada Ltd., Meditest Ltd., Foodex Ltd., CVI Ltd., Major Holdings Ltd.
Leisure interests: skiing, shooting.
26 Greville House, Kinnerton Street, London S.W.1, England; 1701, 11 King Street West, Toronto, Canada. Telephone: 235-6636 (England); 416-364-0193 (Canada).

McKelway, Benjamin Mosby; American newspaperman; b. 2 Oct. 1895; ed. Va. Polytechnic Inst. and George Washington Univ.
Reporter, *Washington Times* 16; Editorial Writer and News Editor, *New Britain* (Conn.) *Herald* 19-20; successively reporter, City Editor, News Editor, Man. Editor, Assoc. Editor, *Washington Star* 21-46, Editor 46-63, Editorial Chair. 63-; Dir. Evening Star Newspaper Co.; fmr. Pres. Assoc. Press; fmr. Pres. American Soc. of Newspaper Editors; Dir. Evening Star Broadcasting Co.; Trustee, George Washington Univ. (D.C.) Public Library, Nat. Geographic Society, Library of Congress Trust Fund Board.
4920 Palisade Lane, N.W., Washington, D.C. 20016, U.S.A.

McKenna, Siobhán; Irish actress; b. 24 May 1923; d. of Owen McKenna and Margaret O'Reilly; m. Denis O'Dea; one s.; ed. St. Louis Convent, Monaghan and Galway Univ.

Semi-professional appearances at An Taibhdhearc Theatre, Galway 40-43; Abbey Theatre, Dublin 44-47; first London appearance in *The White Steed*, Embassy 47.

Plays include *Fading Mansions*, Duchess 49, *Ghosts*, Embassy, *Héloïse*, Duke of York's, Stratford-on-Avon 52; *Playboy of the Western World*, Edinburgh and Paris Festivals, *Saint Joan*, Arts 54, St. Martin's 55, *The Chalk Garden*, New York 55, *Saint Joan*, New York 56, *The Rope Dancers*, New York 57; Shakespearean seasons at Stratford, Ontario, and Cambridge Drama Festival; *Captain Brassbound's Conversion*, Philadelphia 61, *St. Joan of the Stockyards*, Dublin Festival 61, London 64, *Play with a Tiger* 62, *Laurette* 64, *The Cavern* (Anouilh) 65, *Juno and the Paycock* 66 (Toronto, London and Belfast 73-74), *Here are the Ladies* (Britain, U.S.A. and Australia 70-73), *The Morgan Yard* (Dublin Festival) 74; films include *Hungry Hill, Daughter of Darkness, The Lost People, The Adventurers, King of Kings, Playboy of the Western World, Dr. Zhivago, Philadelphia Here I Come, Here Are the Ladies*.

c/o P.L.R. Ltd., 33 Sloane Street, London S.W.1, England.

McKenzie, Sir Alexander, K.B.E.; New Zealand businessman and politician; b. 26 Oct. 1896; ed. Southland Boys' High School.

Began career as farmer; served army 14-18 war; with The Govt. Life Insurance, Invercargill; joined N.Z. Forest Products Ltd. 22, which he helped establish in N.Z., Australia and Great Britain, Business Man. for N.Z. 29; founded own business 32; a Dir. of 15 companies; mem. Auckland Stock Exchange 61-; mem. N.Z. Nat. Party, fmr. Chair. Auckland Div. of Party; Pres. N.Z. National Party 51-62.

54 Wallace Street, Herne Bay, Auckland, New Zealand.

McKenzie, Bruce Roy, E.G.H., D.S.O., D.F.C.; Kenyan politician, farmer and businessman; b. 1920, Richmond, Natal, South Africa; m. 1st Henriette Edmondson 1945 (dissolved), one s. two d.; m. 2nd Christina Bridgeman 1967, two s.; ed. Hilton Coll., Natal and Agricultural Coll.

Royal Air Force 39-46; settled in Kenya 46; mem. Legislative Council 56; Minister of Agriculture 59-61, 63-71; mem. Kenya African Nat. Union 61-; Minister of Settlement 62-63; mem. Kenyan Parl.; London Dir. Nat. & Grindlays Bank, DWA Plantations Ltd. 71, Infra Securities Ltd., Ishita Ltd.; Kenyan Chair. A. & J. Main (1968) Ltd., CMC Holdings Ltd., Ol Pejeta Ranching Ltd., Gingalili Ltd.; Dir. DCK (Kenya) Ltd., Chair. 74; Dir. Grindlays Bank Int. (Kenya) Ltd., East African Airways Corpn., Car & Gen. Ltd., East African Nat. Shipping Line, Southern Line Ltd., and other companies.

Knowle, Cranleigh, Surrey, England; Home: P.O. Box 30135, Nairobi, Kenya.
Telephone: Cranleigh 5432; (Nairobi) 65352.

Mackenzie, Chalmers Jack, C.C., C.M.G., M.C., B.E., M.C.E., D.ENG., D.SC., LL.D., D.C.L., F.R.S.C., F.R.S.; Canadian engineer; b. 10 July 1888, St. Stephen, N.B.; s. of James Mackenzie and Janet (Campbell) Mackenzie; m. 1st Claire Rees 1916, one s.; m. 2nd Geraldine Gallon, two d.; ed. Dalhousie and Harvard Univs.

Member engineering firm Maxwell & Mackenzie 12-16; served with Canadian Expeditionary Force 16-18; Prof. of Civil Engineering Saskatchewan Univ. 18-39, Dean of Engineering 21-39; Acting Pres. Nat. Research Council of Canada 39-44, Pres. 44-52; Pres. Atomic Energy of Canada Ltd. 52-53, Pres. Atomic Energy Control Board 48-61; Chancellor Carleton Univ., Ottawa 54-69; consultant numerous engineering and

scientific projects; many hon. degrees; U.S. Medal of Merit, Chevalier Légion d'Honneur, Kelvin Medal 53, R. B. Bennett Empire Prize 54, Royal Bank Award 68.
Leisure interests: golf, curling.
210 Buena Vista Road, Rockliffe Park, Ottawa, Ont., Canada.
Telephone: (613) 749-9943.

McKenzie, Lyndon L.; Australian airline executive; b. Cowell, S. Australia; m.; two d.; ed. accountancy.

Served R.A.A.F., rose to rank of Flight Lieut. 40-46; joined Trans-Australia Airlines (TAA) 46; posts in finance, admin. and airport management depts. 46-55; Man. for Victoria, subsequently for Queensland 55-57; Commercial Dir. 57-71; Asst. Gen. Man. 71-73, Acting Gen. Man. Oct. 73, Gen. Man. Oct. 73-.
Leisure interests: tennis, music.
Trans-Australia Airlines, 50 Franklin Street, Melbourne 3000, Australia.

Mackenzie, Maxwell Weir, O.C., C.M.G., LL.D., B.COM.; Canadian business executive; b. 30 June 1907, Victoria, B.C.; s. of Hugh Mackenzie and Maud Weir; m. Jean Fairbairn 1931; two s. two d.; ed. Trinity Coll. School, McGill Univ.

Joined McDonald, Currie & Co., Chartered Accountants, Montreal, and admitted to Society of Chartered Accountants of Prov. of Quebec 29; became partner in firm 35; called to Foreign Exchange Control Board and transferred to Wartime Prices and Trade Board 42, apptd. Deputy Chair. of Board 43; returned to McDonald, Currie & Co. 44; apptd. mem. of Royal Comm. on Taxation of Annuities and Family Corpns. 44; Deputy Minister of Trade and Commerce 45-51; Deputy Minister of Defence Production 51-52; Exec. Vice-Pres. Canadian Chemical & Cellulose Co. Ltd. 52-54; Pres. Canadian Chemical & Cellulose Co. Ltd. 54-59, Chemcell Ltd. 59-63; Chair. Finance Cttee., Chemcell Ltd. and Columbia Cellulose Co. Ltd. 67-68; Chair. Royal Comm. on Security 66-68; Dir. The Canadian Imperial Bank of Commerce 55-, Celanese Corpn. of America 59-67, The Royal Trust Co. 60-67, Canron Ltd. 61-, Imperial Life Assurance Co. of Canada 62-75, RCA Victor Co. Ltd. (name changed to RCA Ltd. 68) 63-, Int. Multifoods Corpn. 64; mem. Econ. Council of Canada 63-71; Pres. N.B. Multiplex Corpn. 71-; Pres. Montreal Joint Hospital Inst. 71-73; Dir. C. D. Howe Research Inst. 73-; Chair. Comm. of Inquiry into the Marketing of Beef and Veal Jan. 75; Hon. LL.D. (McGill Univ.) 73.
Leisure interests: woodworking, gardening, skiing.
383 Maple Lane, Rockcliffe Park, Ottawa, K1M 1H7, Canada.
Telephone: 613-746-0253.

MacKenzie, Norman Archibald MacRae, C.C., C.M.G., C.D., M.M. AND BAR, Q.C., B.A., LL.D., D.C.L., D.SC.SOC., D.LITT., F.R.S.C.; Canadian lawyer and public servant; b. 5 Jan. 1894, Pugwash, Nova Scotia; s. of Rev. J. A. MacKenzie and Elizabeth J. C. MacRae; m. Margaret R. Thomas 1928; one s. two d.; ed. Pictou Acad., Dalhousie Univ., Harvard, St. John's Coll., Cambridge and Gray's Inn.

Served with Canadian Infantry 14-19; called to Bar N.S. 26; Legal Adviser ILO Geneva 25-27; Assoc. Prof. of Law Univ. of Toronto 27-33, Prof. of Int. and Canadian Const. Law 33-40; Pres. Univ. of New Brunswick 40-44; Pres. Univ. of British Columbia 44-62, Pres. Emer. 62-; Chair. War-time Information Board Canada 43-45, N.B. Reconstruction Comm. 41-44, Conciliatory Boards in Labour Disputes 37-42; Trustee Carnegie Foundation for Advancement of Teaching 51-, Chair. Board of Trustees 58-59; Chair. Doukhobor Consultative Cttee. 50-; mem. Canada Council 57-63, Canadian Inst. Int. Affairs, American Soc. Int. Law, etc.; Pres. Canadian Nat. Comm. for UNESCO 57-60; Dir. Bank of Nova Scotia 60-69; Pres. Canadian Centenary Council 62-67; mem. Senate of Canada 66-69;

Hon. LL.D. (Mt. Allison, N.B., Toronto, Ottawa, Bristol, Alberta, Glasgow, Dalhousie and St. Francis Xavier, McGill, Sydney, Rochester, California, Alaska, British Columbia, Royal Mil. Coll. of Canada); Hon. D.C.L. (Whitman Coll., Saskatchewan Univ.); Hon. D.Sc.Soc. (Laval); Hon. D.Litt. (Memorial Univ. of Newfoundland); Hon. LL.D. (Cambridge); Hon. Fellow St. John's Coll. (Cambridge); John E. Read Medal, Canadian Council on Int. Law 75.
Leisure interests: hiking, flyfishing, reading.
Publs. *Legal Status of Aliens in Pacific Countries* 37, *Canada and the Law of Nations* (with L. H. Laing) 38, *Canada in World Affairs* (with others) 41, *Challenge to Education* 53, *First Principles* 54, *A Canadian View of Territorial Seas and Fisheries* (with Jacob Austin), *The Work of the Universities* (in *Canadian Education—Today*) 56.
4509 West 4th Avenue, Vancouver 8, B.C., Canada.
Telephone: 224-7800.

Mackenzie Stuart, The Hon. Lord (Alexander John), B.A., LL.B.; British judge; b. 18 Nov. 1924, Aberdeen; s. of Prof. A. Mackenzie Stuart, Q.C. and Amy Margaret Dean; m. Anne Burtholme Millar 1952; four d.; ed. Fettes Coll., Edinburgh, Cambridge and Edinburgh Univs.
Royal Engineers 42-47; admitted to Faculty of Advocates 51; Standing Junior Counsel, Scottish Home Dept. 56-57, Inland Revenue, Scotland 57-63; Queen's Counsel 63; Keeper of Advocates Library 70-72; Sheriff-Principal of Aberdeen, Kincardine and Banff 71-72; Senator, Coll. of Justice, Scotland 72; Judge, Court of Justice of European Communities Jan. 73-; Dr. h.c. (Stirling Univ.).
Court of Justice of the European Communities, P.O. Box 1406, Luxembourg; Home: 24 rue de Wormeldange, Rodenbourg, Grand Duchy of Luxembourg.
Telephone: 4762-229 (Office); 77276 (Home).

Mackerras, Charles, C.B.E.; British conductor; b. 17 Nov. 1925, U.S.A. of Australian parentage; m. Judith Wilkins 1947; two d.: ed. Sydney Grammar School, N.S.W. Conservatoire, and Prague Acad. of Music.
Principal Oboist Sydney Symphony Orchestra 43-46; Conductor Sadler's Wells 48-53, B.B.C. Concert Orchestra 54-56; guest conductor in Europe, Canada, Australia, S. Africa 57-66, guest opera conductor at Covent Garden, Sadler's Wells, Berlin State Opera, Hamburg State Opera, etc. 56-66; First Conductor, Hamburg State Opera 66-70; Musical Dir., English Nat. Opera 70-; guest conductor with U.S. Symphony Orchestras, Boston, Chicago, Cincinnati, Dallas, Los Angeles, St. Louis, San Francisco Opera, Paris Opéra; musical articles in various magazines.
Arrangements: Ballets: *Pineapple Poll* 51, *Lady and the Fool* 54, *Melbourne Cup* 65.
10 Hamilton Terrace, London, N.W.8, England.
Telephone: 01-286-4047.

Mackey, George Whitelaw, A.M., PH.D.; American mathematician; b. 1 Feb. 1916, St. Louis, Mo.; s. of William Sturges Mackey and Dorothy Frances Allison; m. Alice Willard 1960; one d.; ed. Rice and Harvard Univs.
Instructor in Mathematics, Ill. Inst. of Technology 42-43; Faculty Instructor in Mathematics, Harvard Univ. 43-46 (on leave for war work April 44-Sept. 45), Asst. Prof. of Mathematics 46-48, Assoc Prof. 48-56, Prof. 56-69, Landon T. Clay Prof. of Mathematics and Theoretical Science 69-; Walker Ames Visiting Prof., Univ. of Washington, Summer 61; George Eastman Visiting Prof. at Oxford 66-67; Visiting Prof. Tata Inst. of Fundamental Research, Bombay 70-71; mem. American Acad. of Arts and Sciences, Nat. Acad. of Sciences, American Philosophical Soc.; Guggenheim Fellow 49-50, 61-62, 70-71.
Leisure interests: conversation, reading, music.

Publs. *Mathematical Foundations of Quantum Mechanics* 63, *Lectures on the Theory of Functions of a Complex Variable* 67, *Induced Representations and Quantum Mechanics* 68, articles in mathematical journals.
c/o Mathematics Department, Harvard University, Science Center, 1 Oxford Street, Cambridge, Mass. 02138, U.S.A.
Telephone: 495-2147.

Macki, Ahmed al-Nabi; Omani diplomatist; b. 17 Dec. 1939, Muscat; m. Piedad Macki 1970; one s. one d.; ed. Cairo and Paris.
Member, Oman Del. to UNESCO 69-70; Dir. of Office of Prime Minister 70-71; Under-Sec., Ministry of Foreign Affairs 71-73; Amb. to U.S.A. 73-, also accred. to Canada and Argentina 74-.
Leisure interest: reading.
Embassy of Oman, 2342 Mass. Avenue, N.W., Washington, D.C., U.S.A.

McKie, Sir William Neil, Kt., M.V.O., M.A., D.MUS.; British musician; b. 22 May 1901, Melbourne, Australia; s. of Rev. William McKie; m. Phyllis Birks 1956; ed. Melbourne Grammar School, Royal Coll. of Music, London and Worcester Coll., Oxford.
Director of Music Clifton Coll., Bristol 26-30; City Organist Melbourne 31-38; Organist, Magdalen Coll., Oxford 38-41; Organist and Master of Choristers Westminster Abbey 41-63; war service R.A.F. 41-45; Dir. of Music, Coronation of Queen Elizabeth II 53; Hon. Sec. Royal Coll. of Organists 63-67; Hon. Fellow Worcester Coll., Oxford 54-; Hon. D.Mus. Univ. of Melbourne; Commdr. with Star Order of St. Olav.
Ten Driveway, Apartment 1401, Ottawa K2P 1C7, Ont., Canada.
Telephone: 613-234-4059.

McKinley, John K., M.S.; American business executive; b. 24 March 1920, Tuscaloosa, Ala.; s. of Virgil P. McKinley and Mary E. Key; m. Helen Heare 1946; two s.; ed. Univ. of Alabama.
Joined Texaco as chemical engineer 41; Asst. Dir. of Research, Texaco Research Lab., Beacon, N.Y. 57; Asst. to Vice-Pres. 59; Man. Commercial Devt. Processes, Research and Technical Dept., Beacon 60; Gen. Man. Petrochemical Dept., New York 60-67; Vice-Pres. in charge of Petrochemical Operations 67-70; Vice-Pres. in charge of Supply and Distribution Oct.-Dec. 70; Senior Vice-Pres. for Worldwide Refining, Petrochemicals, and Supply and Distribution Jan. 71-April 71; Pres. Texaco Inc. April 71-; Dir. American Petroleum Inst.; Fellow American Inst. of Chemical Engineers; mem. American Chem. Soc.; Hon. LL.D. (Univ. of Alabama 72, Troy State Univ. 74); George Washington Honor Medal, Freedoms Foundation 72.
Texaco Inc., 135 East 42nd Street, New York, N.Y. 10017, U.S.A.
Telephone: 212-953-6000.

McKinney, James Russell; Canadian diplomatist; b. 28 June 1925, New Brunswick; m.; three c.; ed. Dalhousie Univ.
Joined Dept. External Affairs 49, posted Belgrade 51-54; Chargé d'Affaires, Djakarta 57, First Sec., Copenhagen 59, Counsellor, Ottawa 62-66; High Commr., Trinidad and Tobago and Barbados, Canadian Commr. to West Indies Assoc. States 66-69; Head Del. to OECD 69-72; Minister, Embassy, Washington 72-.
Embassy of Canada, 1746 Massachusetts Avenue, N.W., Washington, D.C. 20036; Home: 2808 Chesterfield Pl., N.W., Washington, D.C. 20008, U.S.A.

McKinney, Robert Moody, B.A.; American newspaper publisher and diplomatist; b. 28 Aug. 1910, Shattuck, Okla.; s. of Edwin McKinney and Eva Moody; m. 1st Louise Trigg 1943; one d.; m. 2nd Marie-Louise de Montmollin 1970; ed. Univ. of Oklahoma.
Editor and Publisher, *The New Mexican*; Pres. The New

Mexican Inc.; Chair. Taos Pub. Corpn., New Mexico Econ. Devt. Comm. 49-51; Asst. Sec. U.S. Dept. of Interior 51-52; Chair. Panel to report to Congress on impact of peaceful uses of atomic energy 55-56; Perm. U.S. Rep. to Int. Atomic Energy Agency, Vienna 57-58; U.S. Rep. to 2nd Int. Conf. on Peaceful Uses of Atomic Energy 58; rapporteur, Cttee. on Scientific and Technical Co-operation, Atlantic Congress, London 59; apptd. by Joint Cttee. of U.S. Congress to review int. atomic policies and programmes of U.S.A. 59-60; Ambassador to Switzerland 61-63; Exec. Officer, Presidential Task Force on Int. Investments 63-64; Vice-Chair. Advisory Cttee. on Financial Investments 66; U.S. Rep. Int. Centre for Settlement of Investment Disputes, Washington 67-73; Chair. Presidential Industry-Gov. Special Task Force on Travel 68; war service U.S. Navy 42-45; Pres. Robert Moody Foundation; mem. Foreign Policy Asscn.; Chair. Board of Visitors and Governors, Oklahoma Univ.; Dir. Martin Marietta Corpn., Copper Range Co., Trans World Airlines Inc.; Surveyor Fund Inc.; mem. American Soc. of Newspaper Editors, Council on Foreign Relations; Distinguished Service Citation 65; Hon. LL.D. (Univ. of New Mexico); Democrat.
Leisure interests: farming, skiing.
Publs. *Hymn to Wreckage: A Picaresque Interpretation of History* 47, *The Scientific Foundation for European Integration, Reappraising the European Energy Problem, On Increasing the Effectiveness of Western Science and Technology*, all 59, *The Red Challenge to Technological Renewal* 60.
202 East Marcy Street, Santa Fé, N.M. 87501, U.S.A. Telephone: 983-3303.

McKinnon, Neil J.; Canadian banker; b. 17 Jan. 1911, Cobalt, Ont.; *s.* of Malcolm and Selina Frances McKinnon; *m.* Phyllis Adelaide Cowie 1941; one *s.* one *d.* Joined Canadian Bank of Commerce 25, Asst. Gen. Man. 45, Gen. Man. 52, Vice-Pres. and Dir. 54, Pres. 56-61, Chair. of Board 59-61; Pres. and Chief Exec. Officer Canadian Imperial Bank of Commerce 61-63, Chair. and Chief Exec. Officer 63-65, Chair. 65-73; Dir. Canada Life Assurance Co., Brascan Ltd., Allied Chemical Canada Ltd., TransCanada Pipelines Ltd., Campbell Soup Co., Honeywell Inc., Continental Oil Co., Falconbridge Nickel Mines Ltd., Ford Motor Co. of Canada Ltd., MacMillan Bloedel Ltd.
Leisure interest: golf.
116 Dunvegan Road, Toronto, Ontario, Canada.

MacKintosh, Sir Angus MacKay, K.C.V.O., C.M.G., British diplomatist (retd.); b. 23 July 1915, Inverness; *s.* of Angus MacKintosh, J.P.; *m.* Robina M. Cochrane 1947; one *s.* three *d.*; ed. Fettes Coll., Edinburgh, and Univ. Coll., Oxford.
Agricultural Econs. Research Inst., Oxford 38-41; Nuffield Colonial Research, Oxford 41-42; Army Service 42-46; Principal, Colonial Office 46-50; Principal Private Sec. to Sec. of State 50-52; Asst. Sec. 52; seconded to Foreign Office as Deputy Commr.-Gen. for U.K. in S.E. Asia 56-60; seconded to Cabinet Office 61-63; High Commr. for Brunei 63-64; Asst. Sec., Ministry of Defence 64-65; Asst. Under-Sec. of State 65-66; Senior Civilian Instructor, Imperial Defence Coll. 66-68; Asst. Under-Sec. of State, Foreign Office 68-69; High Commr. in Ceylon and Amb. to Rep. of Maldives 69-73; D.K. (Brunei) 63, N.S.A.I.V. (Maldives) 72.
The Queen's House, 36 Moray Place, Edinburgh EH3 6BX, Scotland.

McKissick, Floyd Bixler, A.B., LL.B.; American lawyer; b. 9 March 1922; ed. North Carolina Coll.
Lawyer, Durham, North Carolina; Nat. Chair. Congress of Racial Equality (CORE) 63-66, Nat. Dir. 66-68; Pres. Floyd B. McKissick Enterprises Inc. 68-.
Publ. *Three-Fifths of a Man* 68.
414 W 149th Street, New York, N.Y. 10031, U.S.A.

McKnight, Allan Douglas, C.B.E., LL.B.; Australian administrator; b. 14 Jan. 1918; ed. Fort Street High School and Univ. of Sydney.
Assistant Sec. to Cabinet 51-55; Sec. Dept. of Army 55-58; Exec. Comm. Australian Atomic Energy Comm. 58-64; Gov. for Australia, Board of Govs., Int. Atomic Energy Agency (I.A.E.A.) 59-64, Chair. I.A.E.A. Board of Govs. 61; European Rep. of Australian Atomic Energy Comm. 62-64; Inspector Gen., Int. Atomic Energy Agency, Vienna 64-68; Visiting Fellow, Science Policy Research Unit, Univ. of Sussex 68-; Lecturer U.K. Civil Service Coll. 72-
Publs. *Atomic Safeguards, I.A.E.A. and Euratom in Nuclear Non-Proliferation, Scientists Abroad*, numerous articles and research reports.
University of Sussex, Brighton, BN1 9QX, England. Telephone: Brighton 66755.

McKuen, Rod; American author and composer; b. 29 April 1933, Oakland, Calif.
Has appeared in numerous films, concerts and on television; composer of film scores and background music for television shows; composer-lyricist of many songs; Pres. of numerous record and book cos.; mem. Board of Dirs. Amer. Nat. Theatre of Ballet, Animal Concern; mem. Board of Govs. Nat. Acad. of Recording Arts and Sciences; mem. A.S.C.A.P., Writers Guild, A.F.T.R.A., M.P.A., NARAS; Grand Prix du Disque 66, Golden Globe 69, Motion Picture Daily Award 69; works include: *Symphony Number One, Concerto for Guitar and Orchestra, Concerto for Four Harpsichords, Seascapes for Piano and Orchestra, Adagio for Harp and Strings, Piano Variations, Concerto Number Three for Piano and Orchestra* 72, *The Plains of My Country* (ballet) 72, *The City* (orchestral suite) 73, *Ballad of Distances* (orchestral suite) 73, *Bicentennial Ballet* 75, *Symphony Number Three* 75; film scores: *Joanna* 68, *The Prime of Miss Jean Brodie* 69, *Me, Natalie* 69, *A Boy Named Charlie Brown* 70, *Come to Your Senses* 71, *Scandalous John* 71, *Wildflowers* 71, *The Borrowers* 73, *Lisa Bright and Dark* 73, *Awareness of Emily* 76.
Publs. *And Autumn Came* 54, *Stanyan Street and Other Sorrows* 66, *Listen to the Warm* 67, *Twelve Years of Christmas* 68, *In Someone's Shadow* 69, *With Love* 70, *Caught in the Quiet* 70, *Fields of Wonder* 71, *The Carols of Christmas* 71, *And to Each Season* 72, *Beyond the Boardwalk* 72, *Come to Me in Silence* 73, *America—An Affirmation* 74, *Seasons in the Sun* 74, *Alone, Moment to Moment* 74, *The McKuen Omnibus* 75, *Celebrations of the Heart* 75, *My Country 200* 75, *I'm Strong but I Like Roses, Sleep Warm, Beyond the Boardwalk* 76.
8440 Santa Monica Boulevard, Los Angeles, Calif. 90069, U.S.A.

MacLaine, Shirley; American film actress, writer and film director; b. 24 April 1934, Richmond, Va.; *d.* of Ira Beaty and Kathlyn MacLean; *m.* Steve Parker; one *d.*; ed. grammar school and Lee High School, Washington.
Former chorus girl and dancer; Star of the Year Award (Theatre Owners' of America) 67; Best Actress Award for role in *Desperate Characters*, Berlin Film Festival 71.
Films include: *The Trouble With Harry, Artists and Models, Around The World in 80 Days, Hot Spell, The Matchmaker, Can-Can, Career, The Apartment, Two For The Seesaw, The Children's Hour, Irma La Douce, What A Way To Go, The Yellow Rolls Royce, Gambit, Woman Times Seven, The Bliss of Mrs. Blossom, Sweet Charity, Two Mules For Sister Sara, Desperate Characters, The Possession of Joel Delaney*; revues: *If My Friends Could See Me Now* 74, *To London With Love* 76; Produced and co-directed *The Other Half of the Sky— A China Memoir* 73; producer and star of *Amelia* 75.
Publs. *Don't Fall Off The Mountain* 71, *You Can Get There From Here* 75 (Vols. 1 and 2 of autobiography).
c/o Margaret Gardner, Rogers and Cowan Inc., 31 Dover Street, London W.1, England.

MacLane, Saunders, M.A., PH.D.; American mathematician; b. 4 Aug. 1909, Norwich, Conn.; s. of Donald B. MacLane and Winifred A. Saunders; m. Dorothy M. Jones 1933; two d.; ed. Yale Coll., Univ. of Chicago, Göttingen Univ.
Benjamin Peirce Instructor in Mathematics, Harvard Univ. 34-36; Instructor Cornell Univ. 36-37, Chicago Univ. 37-38; Asst. Prof., Harvard Univ. 38-41, Assoc. Prof. 41-46, Prof. 46-47; Prof. Univ. of Chicago 47-62, Max Mason Distinguished Service Prof. in Mathematics, Univ. of Chicago 63-; mem. Nat. Acad. of Sciences, Vice-Pres. 73-(77); Vice-Pres. Amer. Philosophical Soc. 68-71; mem. Nat. Science Board 74-(80); Pres. Amer. Math. Soc. 73-74; Hon. Sc.D., Hon. LL.D.
Leisure interests; sailing, skiing, photography.
Publs. *Survey of Modern Algebra* (with G. Birkhoff) 41, 3rd edn. 66, *Homology* 63, *Algebra* (with G. Birkhoff) 67, *Categories for the Working Mathematician* 72.
Department of Mathematics, The University of Chicago, Chicago, Ill. 60637; Home: 5712 South Dorchester Avenue, Chicago, Ill. 60637, U.S.A.
Telephone: (312) 753-8073 (Office).

McLaren, Norman; Canadian (b. Scotland) film director; b. 11 April 1914; ed. Glasgow School of Art.
With G.P.O. Film Unit 37-39; moved to New York City 39, later produced independently, and for Guggenheim Museum of Non-Objective Art, several abstract colour films; Dir. of Experimental Films, Nat. Film Board of Canada 41-; assignment in China for UNESCO 49-50, in India for UNESCO 53-54; numerous awards including Royal Canadian Acad. of Arts Medal 63, Canada Council Medal 66, Molson Prize, Canada Council 72, Order of Canada 72; hon. doctorates McMaster Univ., Brock Univ., Univ. of Montreal.
Films include: *Love on the Wing, Dots, Loops, Fiddle-De-Dee, Poulette Grise, A Phantasy, Begone Dull Care, Around Is Around, Neighbours, Blinkity Blank, Rythmetic, A Chairy Tale, Le Merle, Opening Speech, Lines Vertical Horizontal, Canon, Mosaic, Pas de Deux, Spheres, Synchromy, Ballet Adagio.*
Leisure interests: music, drawing.
Publs. *Six Musical Forms* (illustrated), *"Interplay"*, 8 serigraphs.
National Film Board, Box 6100, Montreal, Quebec, H3C 3H5; Home: 3590 Ridgewood Avenue, Apt. 305, Montreal, Quebec, H3V 1C2, Canada.
Telephone: (514)-333-3329 (Office); 731-6210 (Home).

McLaughlin, Donald Hamilton, B.S., A.M., PH.D.; American mining geologist and engineer; b. 15 Dec. 1891, San Francisco, Calif.; s. of William and Katherine McLaughlin; m. 1st Eleanor Eckhart 1925 (dissolved), 2nd Sylvia Cranmer 1948; three s. one d.; ed. Calif. and Harvard Univs.
Chief Geologist, Cerro de Pasco Copper Corpn. 19-25; Prof. of Mining Geology, Harvard Univ. 25-41; Dean, Coll. of Engineering, Univ. of Calif. 41-43; Vice-Pres. and Gen. Man. Cerro de Pasco Corpn. 43-45; Pres. Homestake Mining Co. 45-61, Chair. 61-70, Hon. Chair. and Chair. of Exec. Cttee. 70-; Dir. Homestake Mining Co., San Luis Mining Co.; Dir. Int. Nickel Co. of Canada 48-73, mem. Advisory Comm. 73-; Advisory Dir. Wells Fargo Bank (of San Francisco) 60-68, Dir. Emer. 68-74; Dir. Western Air Lines Inc. 54-66, Dir. Emer. 66-; Past Pres. Amer. Inst. of Mining and Metallurgical Engineers 50 (Rand Medallist and Hon. Mem.), Soc. of Econ. Geologists, and Mining and Metallurgical Soc. of America 53; mem. Nat. Science Board, Nat. Science Foundation 50-60; Regent, Univ. of Calif. 51-66; Fellow Amer. Acad. of Art and Sciences, Geological Soc. of America; Monell Medal and Prize, Columbia Univ.; Hon. Dr. Eng. (Mich. Inst. of Mining and Technology, S. Dakota Inst. of Mining and Technology, Montana School of Mines, and Colorado School of Mines); LL.D. Univ. of California (Berkeley).
Leisure interests: gold and monetary problems, geology and exploration.
Office: Homestake Mining Co., 650 California Street, San Francisco, Calif.; Home: 1450 Hawthorne Terrace, Berkeley, Calif., U.S.A.
Telephone: 981-8150 (Office); 415-848-0699 (Home).

McLaughlin, William Earle; Canadian banker; b. 16 Sept. 1915, Oshawa, Ont.; s. of Frank McLaughlin and Frankie L. Houldon; m. Ethel Wattie 1940; one s. one d.; ed. Queen's Univ.
Joined Royal Bank of Canada 36, Asst. Man., London, Ont. 42, Head Office 45, Man. Montreal Branch 51, Asst. Gen. Man. 53, Asst. to Pres. 59, Gen. Man. 60, Pres. and Dir. 60; Chair. and Pres. The Royal Bank of Canada 62-; Dir. and Trustee of numerous companies and orgs.; Knight of Grace, Venerable Order of the Hospital of St. John of Jerusalem.
Leisure interests: golf and curling.
The Royal Bank of Canada, 1 Place Ville Marie, Montreal, Quebec; 67 Sunnyside Avenue, Westmount, Quebec, Canada.

Maclean, Baron (Life Peer), cr. 71, of Duart and Morvern in the County of Argyll; **Maj. Charles Hector Fitzroy Maclean,** Bt., K.T., P.C., G.C.V.O., K.B.E.; Scottish army officer and scout; b. 5 May 1916.
Served Scots Guards; Boy Scouts Asscn., Chief Commr. for Scotland 54-59, Chief Scout, U.K. 59-71, Commonwealth 59-75; Lord Chamberlain 71-; Lord Lieutenant for Argyllhsire 54-; Chief of Clan Maclean.
Duart Castle, Isle of Mull, Scotland.

MacLean, Alistair; British novelist; b. 1922; m. Gisela MacLean; three s.; ed. Glasgow Univ.
Has written original screenplay for *Where Eagles Dare, Deakin, Caravan to Vaccares, When Eight Bells Toll*; mem. of Lloyds.
Publs. *H.M.S. Ulysses* 56, *Ice Station Zebra, When Eight Bells Toll, Night Without End, The Guns of Navarone, Puppet on a Chain* 69, *Caravan to Vaccares* 71, *Bear Island* 71, *Captain Cook* 72, *The Way to Dusty Death* 73, *Breakheart Pass* 74, *Circus* 75, *Golden Gate*.
c/o Wm. Collins & Sons Ltd., 14 St. James Place, London, S.W.1, England.

Maclean, Sir Fitzroy, Bart., C.B.E.; British author; b. 11 March 1911, Cairo, Egypt; s. of Charles Maclean and Gladys Royle; m. Veronica Fraser (d. of 16th Baron Lovat) 1946; two s.; ed. Eton and Cambridge Univ.
Entered Diplomatic Service 33; served Paris 34-37, Moscow 37-39; enlisted in Cameron Highlanders 41; joined 1st Special Air Service Regiment 42; Captain 42, Lt.-Col. 43, Brigadier 43; Commdr. British Military Mission to Yugoslav Partisans 43-45; Conservative M.P. for Lancaster Div. 41-59, for Bute and N. Ayr 59-74; Parl. Under-Sec. of State and Financial Sec. War Office 54-57; Chair. Great Britain-U.S.S.R. Asscn. 59-; Croix de Guerre, Order of Kutuzov (U.S.S.R.), Partisan Star 1st Class.
Publs. *Eastern Approaches* 49, *Disputed Barricade* 57, *A Person from England* 58, *Back to Bokhara* 59, *Jugoslavia* 69, *A Concise History of Scotland* 70, *The Battle of the Neretva* 70, *To the Back of Beyond* 74.
Strachur House, Strachur, Argyll, Scotland.
Telephone: Strachur 242.

MacLean, Ronald Stuart, M.A.; Canadian diplomatist; b. 8 June 1928, Canada; m. Beverley Jean Cobb 1955; two s. one d.
Instructor of Int. Affairs, Mass. Inst. of Tech. 54-55; entered Dept. of External Affairs 56, posts in New Delhi, Paris, Tokyo 57-72; Dir. of Defence and External Programs, Fed. Govt. Treasury Board 72-75; Amb. and Perm. Rep. to OECD 75-.
48 avenue Georges Mandel, Paris 16, France.
Telephone: 704-9985.

McLean, William F., B.SC. (HONS.); Canadian business executive; b. 30 Oct. 1916, Toronto; ed. Univ. of Toronto Schools, Univ. of Toronto and in U.S.A. Research Chemist, Canada Packers Ltd. 39, in charge of all Plants and Equipment 49, Dir. and Vice-Pres. 50, mem. Exec. Cttee. 52, Pres. Canada Packers Ltd. 54-; served with Royal Canadian Air Force 42-46; Dir. Canadian Gen. Electric; Dir. and Vice-Pres. Canadian Imperial Bank of Commerce; Gov. Toronto Western Hospital; mem. Board of Govs., Ontario Research Foundation, Massey Hall.

Canada Packers Ltd., 95 St. Clair Avenue West, Toronto, Ont., Canada.

MacLehose, Sir (Crawford) Murray, K.C.M.G., M.B.E.; British diplomatist and administrator; b. 16 Oct. 1917, Glasgow; s. of Hamish A. and Margaret Bruce Mac-Lehose; m. Margaret N. Dunlop 1947; two d.; ed. Rugby School and Balliol Coll., Oxford.

Served with R.N.V.R. 39-45; entered diplomatic service 47; Acting Consul, Hankow 47, Acting Consul-Gen. 48; Foreign Office 50; First Sec., Prague 51; seconded to Commonwealth Relations Office for service in Wellington 54; returned to Foreign Office and transferred to Paris 56; Counsellor 59; Political Adviser, Hong Kong; Counsellor, Foreign Office 63; Principal Private Sec. to Sec. of State 65-67; Amb. to Repub. of Viet-Nam 67-69, to Denmark 69-71; Gov. of Hong Kong 71-.

Leisure interests: fishing, sailing, farming.

Government House, Hong Kong; Beoch, Maybole, Ayrshire, Scotland.

MacLeish, Archibald, B.A., LL.B., M.A., LITT.D., D.C.L., LL.D., L.H.D.; American poet; b. 7 May 1892, Glencoe, Ill.; s. of Andrew and Martha Hillard MacLeish; m. Ada Taylor Hitchcock 1916; three s. (one deceased) one d.; ed. Yale and Harvard Univs.

Pulitzer Poetry Prize 32 and 53; Librarian of Congress 39-44; Dir. Office of Facts and Figures 41-42; Asst. Dir. Office of War Information 42; Asst. Sec. of State 44-45, resgnd.; Chair. U.S. Del. to establish UNESCO 45; Deputy Chair. U.S. Del. UNESCO 46; U.S. mem. Exec. Board UNESCO 46-47; Boylston Prof. Harvard Univ. 49-62; Simpson Lecturer, Amherst Coll. 64-67; Pres. American Acad. of Arts and Letters 53-56; Pulitzer Drama Prize for *J.B.* 58; Commdr. Légion d'Honneur (France); Commdr. Order of The Sun of Peru.

Leisure interests: walking and swimming.

Publs. *The Happy Marriage* 24, *The Pot of Earth* 25, *Nobodaddy* 25, *Streets in the Moon* 26, *The Hamlet of A. MacLeish* 28, *New Found Land* 30, *Conquistador* 32, *Union Pacific* (a ballet) 34, *Panic* (a play) 35, *Public Speech* 36, *The Fall of the City* (radio verse play) 37, *The Land of the Free* 38, *Air Raid* (radio verse play) 38, *America Was Promises* (verse) 39, *The Irresponsibles* 40, *The American Cause* 40, *A Time to Speak* 41, *A Time to Act* 43, *The American Story* (broadcasts) 44, *Act Five and other Poems* 48, *Freedom is the Right to Choose* 51, *Collected Poems* 52, *This Music Crept By Me Upon the Waters* (verse play) 53, *Songs for Eve* 54, *J.B* (verse play) 58, *Poetry and Experience* (prose) 61, *The Eleanor Roosevelt Story* 65 (film 66), *Herakles* (verse play) 67, *A Continuing Journey* (prose) 67, *The Wild Old Wicked Men and other poems* 68, *Scratch* (prose play) 71, *The Human Season* (selected poems) 72, *The Great American Fourth of July Parade* (verse play for radio) 75.

Conway, Mass. 01341, U.S.A.

Telephone: 413-369-4338.

McLennan, Sir Ian Munro, K.B.E., B.E.E.; Australian engineer; b. 30 Nov. 1909, Stawell, Victoria; m. Dora Haase Robertson 1937; two s. two d.; ed. Scotch Coll., Melbourne and Melbourne Univ.

Assistant Gen. Man. Broken Hill Pty. Co. Ltd. 47-50, Gen. Man. 50-56, Dir. 53-, Senior Gen. Man. 56-59,

Chief Gen. Man. 59-67, Man. Dir. 67-71, Chair. and Dir. of Admin. 71-; Chair. Defence (Industrial) Cttee., Australian Govt.; Chair. BHP-GKN Holdings Ltd. 70-, Tubemakers of Australia Ltd. 73-; Dir. ICI Australia Ltd. 76-; Councillor, Australian Mineral Devt. Laboratories (Chair. 59-67), Australasian Inst. of Mining and Metallurgy (Pres. 51, 57, 72); mem. and Deputy Chair. Immigration Planning Council 49-67; mem. Int. Council of Morgan Guaranty Trust Co. of N.Y. 73-; Australasian Inst. of Mining and Metallurgy Medal 59, Inst. of Production Engineers' James N. Kirby Award 64, Australian Inst. of Engineers Award 68.

Leisure interests: farming, golf.

Office: 140 William Street, Melbourne, 3000; Home: Apartment 3, 112 Walsh Street, South Yarra, Vic. 3141, Australia.

Telephone: 60-0701 (Office); 263651 (Home).

Mac Liammóir, Micheál; Irish actor, designer and playwright; b. 25 Oct. 1899, Cork; s. of Alfred A. and Mary (née Lawler Lee) Mac Liammóir; ed. privately.

First stage appearance as King Goldfish in *The Goldfish* 11; studied at Slade School 15-16; painter and designer for Irish Theatre and Dublin Drama League 17-21; studied painting abroad 21-27; joined Anew McMaster's Shakespearean Company 27; opened Galway Gaelic Theatre (with Hilton Edwards) with own play *Diarmuid agus Gráinne* 28; founder (with Hilton Edwards) Dublin Gate Theatre 28; has played Hamlet, Robert Emmett in *The Old Lady Says No* 35, Romeo, Othello, Mark Antony, Faust, Raskolnikov in *Crime and Punishment*, Orin in *Mourning Becomes Electra*, Henry in *Henry IV* (Pirandello), Brack in *Hedda Gabler*, Don Pedro in *Much Ado About Nothing*, Hitler in *The Roses are Real*; compiled one-man entertainment *The Importance of Being Oscar*, Dublin and London 60, *I Must be Talking To My Friends* 63, *Talking about Yeats* 65; plays include *Ford of the Hurdles* 28, *Diarmuid Agus Gráinne* 29, *Where Stars Walk* 40, *Dancing Shadows* 41, *Ill Met By Moonlight* 46, *Portrait of Miriam* 47, *The Mountains Look Different* 48, *Home For Christmas* 50, *A Slipper For The Moon* 54, *St. Patrick* 55; other publs. include *All for Hecuba* (autobiography) 46, *Put Money in Thy Purse* (diaries) 54, *Each Actor on His Ass* (memoirs) 62, *Blath Agus Taibhse* (poems in Irish) 64, *Ireland* (travel) 66, *An Oscar of No Importance* (autobiography and study of Wilde) 68, *W. B. Yeats and His World* (with Eavan Boland) 71, *Prelude in Kazbek Street* (play) 73.

Leisure interests: travelling, balletomania.

4 Harcourt Terrace, Dublin 2, Ireland.

Telephone: Dublin 67609.

McLoughlin, Brig. Eduardo Francisco; Argentine air force officer, politician and diplomatist; b. 13 May 1918; ed. Salesians Primary and High School and Military Coll.

Air Force Cadet 37-40, promoted through ranks to Brig. (Air Vice-Marshal) 59, Aide-de-Camp to the Pres. of the Republic 55, retired from active service 61; in offices of Dir.-Gen., Air Ministry 53, mem. of Staff 55, Dir.-Gen. 56; 2nd Dir. *a.i.* Air Force Military Acad. 55; Minister Sec. of State for Air 57, 62; War Minister *a.i.* 57; Air Attaché Washington Embassy 58-61; Amb. to U.K. 66-70; Minister of Interior June-Oct. 70; mem. Aeronautical Mission to Europe 64, Argentine Del. to Interamerican Defense Board 58-61; Pres. of the Honour Tribunal for Armed Forces 65; Minister of Foreign Affairs 72-73; U.S. and Peruvian decorations.

c/o Ministry of Foreign Affairs, Buenos Aires, Argentina.

McLucas, John Luther, B.S., M.S., PH.D.; American scientist and government official; b. 22 Aug. 1920, Fayetteville, North Carolina; s. of John Luther and Viola Conley McLucas; m. Patricia Newmaker Knapp

27 July 1946; two *s.* two *d.*; ed. Davidson Coll., Tulane Univ. and Pennsylvania State Univ.
U.S. Navy 43-46; Physicist, U.S. Air Force, Cambridge Research Center 46-47; Physics Dept., Pennsylvania State Univ. 47-49; Electronics Engineer Haller, Raymond and Brown Inc. 49-50, Vice-Pres. and Technical Dir. 50-57; Pres. HRB-Singer Inc. 57-62; Chair. Pennsylvania State Univ. Industrial and Professional Advisory Council 57-62; Deputy Dir. of Research and Engineering (Tactical Warfare Programs) U.S. Dept. of Defense 62-64; Asst. Sec.-Gen. for Scientific Affairs, North Atlantic Treaty Org. (NATO) 64-66; Pres. The Mitre Corpn. 66-69; Under-Sec. Air Force 69-73, Sec. Air Force 73-75; Administrator Fed. Aviation Admin. 75-; Dept. of Defense Distinguished Civilian Service Award 64, 73 (First Bronze Palm), 75 (Silver Palm); NASA D.S.M. 75; mem. Defense Intelligence Agency Scientific Advisory Cttee. 66, New York Acad. Sciences 67, Air Force Scientific Advisory Board 67, Defense Science Board 68, Nat. Acad. Eng. 69, A.I.A.A., Ops. Research Soc., American Physics Soc.; Fellow, Inst. Electrical and Electronics Engineers; Hon. D.Sc. (Davidson Coll.) 74.
Office: Secretary of Air Force, Pentagon, Washington, D.C.; Home: 6519 Dearborn Drive, Falls Church, Virginia 22044, U.S.A.
Telephone: 202-697-7376 (Office); 703-256-1016 (Home).

McLuhan, (Herbert) Marshall, M.A., PH.D.; Canadian university professor and author; b. 21 July 1911, Edmonton, Alberta; *s.* of Herbert Ernest and Elsie Naomi (Hall) McLuhan; *m.* Corinne Lewis 1939; two *s.* four *d.*; ed. Univ. of Manitoba and Cambridge Univ.
Taught at Univ. of Wisconsin 36-37, Univ. of St. Louis 37-44, Assumption Univ. 44-46, St. Michael's Coll., Univ. of Toronto 46-, Prof. 52-; co-editor *Explorations Magazine* 54-59; Dir. Centre for Culture and Technology, Univ. of Toronto 63-; Schweitzer Prof. in Humanities, Fordham Univ. 67-68; F.R.S.C. 64, C.C. 70; Consultant Pontifical Comm. for Social Communications 73; numerous hon. degrees.
Leisure interest: boating.
Publs. *The Mechanical Bride: Folklore of Industrial Man* 51, *Selected Poetry of Tennyson* 56, *Explorations in Communications* (with E. S. Carpenter) 60, *The Gutenberg Galaxy: The Making of Typographic Man* 62, *Understanding Media* 64, *Voices of Literature* (with R. J. Schoeck) Vol. I 64, Vol. II 65, Vol. III 70, *The Medium is the Massage* 67, *War and Peace in the Global Village* 68, *Through the Vanishing Point: Space in Poetry and Painting* 68, *Counterblast* 69, *Culture is Our Business* 70, *Literary Criticism of Marshall McLuhan 1943-62* 69, *From Cliché to Archetype* (with Wilfred Watson) 70, *Take Today: The Executive As Dropout* (with Barrington Nevitt) 72.
Centre for Culture and Technology, University of Toronto, Toronto 5; Home: 3 Wychwood Park, Toronto 4, Ontario, Canada.
Telephone: (416) 654-0411.

McMahon, Rt. Hon. William, P.C., C.H., LL.B., B.EC.; Australian lawyer and politician; b. 23 Feb. 1908, Sydney, N.S.W.; *s.* of William Daniel and Mary McMahon; *m.* Sonia Rachel Hopkins 1965; one *s.* two *d.*; ed. Sydney Univ.
Practised as solicitor until 39; served 39-45 War; mem. House of Reps. 49-; Minister for Navy and Air 51-54, for Social Services 54-56, for Primary Industry 56-58, for Labour and Nat. Service 58-66, Treas. 66-69; Minister for Foreign Affairs 69-71, Prime Minister 71-72; Acting Minister of Trade 56, in charge CSIRO 56, for Labour and Nat. Service 57, Nat. Devt. 59; Acting Attorney-Gen. 60, 61; Acting Minister for Territories 62; Acting Minister for Labour and National Service Nov.-Dec. 66, Sept. 68, June-July 69, Sept.-Oct. 69; Vice-Pres. Executive Council 64-66; Acting Treas. Sept.-Oct. 71;

Deputy Leader Liberal Party 66-71, Leader 71-72; Leader Australian Del. Commonwealth Parl. Conf. New Dehli 57; Pres. ILO Regional Conf., Melbourne 62; Visiting Minister ILO Conf. Geneva 60, 64; Leader Australian Del. to IMF and World Bank Confs. Wash. 66, Rio de Janeiro 67, Wash. 68, to Commonwealth Finance Ministers Confs. Montreal 66, Trinidad 67, London 68; Gov. Asian Devt. Bank 68-69, Chair. 68-69; Leader Australian Dels. to ECAFE Bangkok, Conf. of Foreign Ministers Jakarta, SEATO Manila, Troop Contributing Countries Conf. Saigon, Devt. Assistance Cttee. Tokyo, 25th UN Gen. Assembly 70, Commonwealth Heads of Govt. Singapore 71.
Leisure interests: reading, squash, golf, swimming.
Westfield Tower, 100 William Street, Sydney, N.S.W. 2010; and Parliament House, Canberra, A.C.T., Australia.
Telephone: 358-1433 (Sydney); 731023 (Canberra).

McMichael, Sir John, Kt., F.R.S., M.D., F.R.C.P., F.A.C.P.; British emeritus professor of medicine; b. 25 July 1904; *s.* of James McMichael and Margaret Sproat; *m.* 1st Sybil E. Blake (died 1965), four *s.*; *m.* 2nd Sheila M. Howarth; ed. Kirkcudbright Acad. and Edinburgh Univ.
Beit Memorial Fellow 30-34; Johnston and Lawrence Fellow, Royal Soc. 37-39; Univ. teaching appointments, Aberdeen, Edinburgh, London; Dir. Dept. of Medicine, Postgraduate Medical School of London 46-66, British postgraduate Medical Federation 66-71; mem. Medical Research Council 49-53; Hon. mem. American Medical Asscn. 47, Medical Soc. Copenhagen 53, Norwegian Medical Soc. 54, Asscn. of American Physicians 59; Foreign mem. Finnish Acad. of Science and Letters 63, Nat. Acad. Washington 74; corresp. mem. Royal Acad. of Medicine, Belgium; numerous lectureships; Cullen Prize, Royal Coll. of Physicians (Edinburgh) 53; Jacobs Award, Dallas 58; Morgan Prof., Nashville, Tenn. 64; Moxon Medal, Royal Coll. of Physicians 60; Gairdner Award, Toronto 60; Wihuri Int. Prize, Finland 68; Trustee, Wellcome Trust 60; Vice-Pres. Royal Soc. 69-70.
Leisure interest: gardening.
Publs. *Pharmacology of the Failing Human Heart* 51; numerous papers on: splenic anaemia 31-35, cardiac output in health and disease 38-47, lung capacity in man 38-39, liver circulation and liver disease 32-43.
2 North Square, London, NW11 7AA, England.
Telephone: 01-455-8731.

McMillan, Edwin M(attison), M.S., PH.D.; American physicist; b. 18 Sept. 1907, Redondo Beach, Calif.; *m.* Elsie Blumer 1941; two *s.* one *d.*; ed. Calif. Inst. of Technology and Princeton Univ.
Nat. Research Fellow, Univ. of Calif. 33-34, Research Assoc. 35, Asst. Prof. 35-41, Assoc. Prof. 42-46, Prof. of Physics at Univ. of Calif., Berkeley 46-73, Prof. Emer. 73-; mem. Gen. Advisory Cttee. U.S. Atomic Energy Comm. 54-58; Dir. E. O. Lawrence Radiation Laboratory, Univ. of Calif. 58-71; Dir. Lawrence Berkeley Laboratory 71-73; mem. High Energy Physics Comm., Int. Union for Pure and Applied Physics 60-66; Trustee Rand Corpn. 59-69; Trustee Univ. Research Asscn. 69-74; Chair. Class I, Nat. Acad. of Sciences 68-71; Guest Prof. CERN, Geneva 74; Research Corpn. Scientific Award 51, Nobel Prize in Chemistry (with G. T. Seaborg) 51; Atoms for Peace Prize (with V. Veksler) 63; D.Sc. (h.c.), Rensselaer Polytechnic Inst. 61, Gustavus Adolphus Coll. 63; Alumni Distinguished Service Award, Calif. Inst. of Technology 66.
Univ. of California, Berkeley, Calif. 94720, U.S.A.

MacMillan, Kenneth; British ballet director; b. 11 Dec. 1929; ed. Great Yarmouth Grammar School.
Resident Choreographer, Royal Ballet until 66; Dir. of Ballet, Deutsche Oper, Berlin 66-70; Dir. The Royal Ballet 70-.

Major Choreography: *Romeo and Juliet, Song of the Earth, Rite of Spring, Las Hermanas, The Invitation, Diversions, Baiser de la Fée, Danses concertantes, Agon, Solitaire, Noctambules, House of Birds, Images of Love, The Seven Deadly Sins, Anastasia, Cain and Abel, Olympiad, Checkpoint, Triad, Pavane, Manon* 74, *Elite Syncopations* 74, *The Four Seasons* 75.
c/o Royal Opera House, Covent Garden, London, W.C.2., England.

Macmillan, Rt. Hon. (Maurice) Harold, O.M., P.C., F.R.S.; British politician and publisher; b. 10 Feb. 1894; *s.* of the late Maurice Crawford Macmillan; *m.* Lady Dorothy Cavendish 1920 (died 1966); one *s.* three *d.* (one deceased); ed. Eton Coll. and Balliol Coll., Oxford. Captain in Grenadier Guards 14-18; A.D.C. to Gov.-Gen. of Canada 19-20; Conservative M.P. for Stockton-on-Tees 24-29 and 31-July 45, Bromley Div. of Kent Nov. 45-64; Parl. Sec. Ministry of Supply May 40-Feb. 42; Parl. Under-Sec. of State for Colonies 42; Minister-Resident in N.W. Africa and Central Mediterranean 42-45; Diplomatic Rep. with French Nat. Cttee. 43-44; British mem. Advisory Council for Italy, Chair. 44-45; Sec. of State for Air May-July 45; Minister of Housing and Local Govt. 51-54, of Defence 54-55; Sec. of State for Foreign Affairs 55; Chancellor of the Exchequer 55-57; Prime Minister and First Lord of the Treasury Jan. 57-Oct. 63; Chair. Macmillan (Holdings) 63-; Chair. Macmillan Co. Ltd. 70-74, Pres. 74-; Dir. Pan Books Ltd.; Chancellor Oxford Univ. 60-; Iain McLeod Memorial Lecture 75; Hon. D.C.L. (Durham and Oxford Univs.); Hon. LL.D. (Cambridge and Sussex Univs.); Hon. D.Litt. (Leeds Univ.); Benjamin Franklin Medal 76.
Publs. *Industry and the State* (with others) 27, *Reconstruction: a plea for a National Policy* 33, *The Next Five Years* 35, *The Middle Way* 38, *Planning for Employment* 38, *Economic Aspects of Defence* 39, *Winds of Change* (autobiog. vol. I) 66, *The Blast of War* (autobiog. vol. II) 67, *Tides of Fortune* (autobiog. vol. III) 69, *Riding the Storm* (autobiog. vol. IV) 71, *Pointing the Way* (autobiog. vol. V) 72, *At the End of the Day* (autobiog. vol. VI) 73, *The Past Masters* 75.
Birch Grove House, Chelwood Gate, Hayward's Heath, Sussex, England.

Macmillan, Rt. Hon. Maurice Victor, M.P.; British politician; b. 27 Jan. 1921, London; *s.* of Rt. Hon. Harold Macmillan (*q.v.*); *m.* The Hon. Katherine M. A. Ormsby-Gore 1942; three *s.* one *d.*; ed. Eton Coll. and Balliol Coll., Oxford.
Member of Parl. for Halifax 55-64, for Farnham 66-; Chair. Macmillan & Co. Ltd. 67-70, 74-, Macmillan & Cleaver Ltd. 67-70; Deputy Chair. Macmillan (Holdings) Ltd. 66-70; fmr. Dir. Monotype Corpn. Ltd., Yorkshire Television Ltd.; Chief Sec. H.M. Treasury 70-72; Sec. of State for Employment 72-73; Paymaster-Gen. 73-74; Conservative.
Leisure interests: hunting, shooting, horse-riding.
12 Catherine Place, London, S.W.1; Highgrove, Doughton, Tetbury, Glos., England.

MacMillan, Norman John, Q.C., B.A., LL.B., LL.D.; Canadian executive; b. 8 April 1909, Bracebridge, Ontario; *s.* of John Malcolm MacMillan and Ida Alberta Brown; *m.* Doris Maude Horne 1937; one *s.* one *d.*; ed. Univ. of Manitoba and Manitoba Law School.
Law Practice, Winnipeg 35-37; Asst. Gen. Solicitor Montreal 43-; Gen. Counsel 45-; Gen. Counsel Trans-Canada Air Lines 45-56; assisted Govt. with Commonwealth Air Training Plan during Second World War; with Canadian Nat. Railways 37-, instrumental in modernization programme; Vice-Pres. and Gen. Counsel 49, Exec. Vice-Pres. 56-67, Chair. and Pres. 67-74; Chair. and Pres. of Canadian Nat. Express Co., Canadian Nat. Railway Co., Canadian Nat. Realties Ltd., Canadian Nat. Steamship Co. Ltd.,

Canadian Nat. Telegraph Co. Ltd., Canadian Nat. Transfer Co., Canadian Nat. Transportation Ltd., Canadian Northern Quebec Railway Co., Great North Western Telegraph Co. of Canada, Mount Royal Tunnel and Terminal Co. Ltd., Quebec and Lake St. John Railway Co.; Chair. Grand Trunk Corpn.; Pres. and Dir. Canadian Nat. Railways Trust Co., Central Vermont Transportation Co., Duluth, Winnipeg and Pacific Railroad Co., Northern Consolidated Holding Co. Ltd.; Dir. Air Canada, Canadian Exec. Service Overseas; mem. Canadian Bar Asscn., McGill, Sir George Williams and Univ. of Montreal Assocs., Law Soc. of Manitoba, Manitoba Bar Asscn., Delta Upsilon; Gov. Montreal Gen. Hospital, Olympic Trust of Canada and Canadian Export Asscn.
Leisure interests: photography, skiing, hunting.
Canadian National Railways, P.O. Box 8100, Montreal 101, Quebec; Home: 135 Lazard Avenue, Mount Royal, Montreal 305, Canada.

McMillen, Dale Wilmore, Jr., B.A.; American business executive; b. 6 Jan. 1914; ed. Northwestern Univ.
Production Dept., Central Soya Co. Inc., Decatur, Ind. 36-39, Vice-Pres., later Exec. Vice-Pres. 39-46, Vice-Chair. Board 46-50, Pres. 54-70, Chair. 70-, Chair. Exec. Cttee. 71-; Dir. Fort Wayne Nat. Bank 47-, Pres. Board of Aviation Commrs. Fort Wayne 59-; Dir. Central Soya-Seriom S.p.A., official of educational and church orgs.
3415 South Washington Road, Fort Wayne, Indiana, U.S.A.

McMillen, Harold Wilmore; American business executive; b. 29 Sept. 1906, Grover Hill, Ohio; *s.* of Dale and Agnes McMillen; *m.* Rachel McMillen 1947; two *s.*; ed. Oberlin Coll. and Purdue Univ.
Vice-President and Dir. of Sales, Central Soya 45-50, Exec. Vice-Pres. 50-53, Chair. of Board 53-70, Chair. Exec. Cttee. of Board 70-; Pres. Central Sugar Co. Inc. 39-45; official of several welfare and business orgs.
Leisure interests: fishing, sailing, golf.
1300 Fort Wayne National Bank, Fort Wayne, Indiana, U.S.A.

McMullin, Sir Alister Maxwell, K.C.M.G.; Australian politician; b. 14 July 1900, Scone, N.S.W.; *s.* of William G. McMullin; *m.* Thelma L. Smith 1945; one *d.*
Member the Senate 51-71, Pres. 53-71; Chair. Gen. Council of Commonwealth Parl. Asscn. 59-60, 69-; Deputy Chair. Nat. Library of Australia; Chair. Parl. Library Cttee.; Chancellor, Univ. of Newcastle, N.S.W.; Chair. Parl. Joint Select Cttee. on the New and Perm. Parl. House, Australian Advisory Council on Bibliographical Services; mem. Liberal Party.
St. Aubin's, Scone, N.S.W. 2337, Australia.
Telephone: Scone 153.

Macmurray, John, M.C., M.A., LL.D.; British philosopher; b. 16 Feb. 1891, Maxwelltown, Scotland; *s.* of James Macmurray and Mary Anna Grierson; *m.* Elizabeth Hyde Campbell 1916; ed. Glasgow and Oxford Univs.
Lecturer in Philosophy Manchester Univ. 19; Prof. Witwatersrand Univ. 21; Classical Tutor, Jowett Lecturer, and Fellow, Balliol Coll., Oxford 22; Grote Prof. Philosophy of Mind and Logic, London Univ. 28-44; Prof. of Moral Philosophy, Edinburgh Univ. 44-58; Gifford Lecturer, Univ. of Glasgow 52-54; retired 58.
Leisure interest: gardening.
Publs. *Freedom in the Modern World* 32, *Interpreting the Universe* 33, *Philosophy of Communism* 33, *Some Makers of the Modern Spirit* 33, *Marxism* 34, *Aspects of Dialectical Materialism* 34, *Creative Society* 35, *Reason and Emotion* 35, *The Structure of Religious Experience* 36, *The Clue to History* 38, *The Boundaries of Science* 40, *Challenge to the Churches* 42, *Constructive Democracy* 43, *The Conditions of Freedom* 49, *The Self as Agent* 57.

Persons in Relation 60, *Religion, Art and Science* 61, *Search for Reality in Religion* 65.
8 Mansionhouse Road, Edinburgh, EH9 1TZ, Scotland.
Telephone: 031-667-5784.

McMurray, Joseph Patrick Brendan; American economist; b. 4 March 1912, Bronx, N.Y.; *m.* Rose-Marie Barker McMurray; six *s.* three *d.;* ed. Jamaica High School, Queens, N.Y., Brooklyn Coll., and New York School for Social Research.
Economist, Gov. Agencies 40-44; Econ. Consultant, U.S. Senate Labor and Educ. Comm. 45-47; Admin. Asst. to U.S. Senator Wagner 47-48; Consultant and Staff Dir. U.S. Senate Banking and Currency Comm. 48-54; Exec. Dir. N.Y. City Housing Authority 54-55; Commr. of Housing, State of New York 55-59; Pres. Queensborough Community Coll. 59-61; Chair. Fed. Home Loan Bank Board 61-65; Pres. of Queens Coll., Flushing, N.Y. 65-71, Coll. of New Rochelle, N.Y. 71-.
Leisure interests: reading and golf.
College of New Rochelle, New Rochelle, N.Y. 10801; Home: 80 Lyncroft Road, New Rochelle, N.Y. 10804, U.S.A.
Telephone: 914-632-5300 (Office); 914-636-1842 (Home).

MacNabb, Byron Gordon; American research and development engineer; b. 14 Aug. 1910, Gary, Ind.; *s.* of Walter S. and Leila B. (née Mogle) MacNabb; *m.* Iris L. Cook 1939; one *d.;* ed. Rose Polytechnic Inst., Terre Haute, and Ill. Inst. of Technology.
Worked for Carnegie Steel Corpn., South Chicago 30-43; U.S. Navy officer 43-48; Asst. to Dir. of Research for Sandia Corpn., Albuquerque, working on A-bomb 48-50; Asst. to Dir. of Research, Pullman Standard Car Co. 50-53; Operations Man. for Cambridge Corpn. 53-55; joined Convair-Astronautics (now Gen. Dynamics/Convair) 55, Operations Man. at Air Force Missile Test Center, Cape Canaveral 55-62, Dir. of Operations 62-63; Dir. of Test Engineering, General Dynamics/Astronautics, San Diego 63-65; Operations Man. Gen. Dynamics/Convair, Cape Kennedy 65-66; responsible for Launch Operations, Atlas/Mercury Manned Orbital Project Mercury, Cape Canaveral; Man. Tests and Operations, Advanced Interplanetary Programs, Gen. Electric, Missile & Space Div. 66-68; Consulting Engineer Gen. Electric, Space and Re-entry Systems 68; Presidential Citation for devt. of first anti-kamakazi anti-aircraft weapon, and other awards.
Office: General Electric Co., 3198 Chestnut St., Philadelphia, Pa. 19101; Home: P.O. Box 402, Gwynedd Valley, Pa., U.S.A.
Telephone: 215-962-4222 (Office); 215-699-9724 (Home).

McNamara, Robert Strange, A.B., LL.D.; American businessman and government official; b. 9 June 1916; ed. Univ. of Calif. and Harvard Univ.
Asst. Prof. in Business Admin., Harvard Univ. 40-43; served Army, Air Force 43-46; Exec. Ford Motor Co. 46-61, Vice-Pres. 55-60, Pres. 60-61; U.S. Sec. of Defense 61-68; Pres. of Int. Bank for Reconstruction and Devt. (World Bank) April 68-; mem. American Acad. of Arts and Sciences; Legion of Merit; U.S. Medal of Freedom 68.
Publs. *The Essence of Security: Reflections in Office* 68, *One Hundred Countries—Two Billion People.*
International Bank for Reconstruction and Development, 1818 H Street, N.W., Washington, D.C. 20433, U.S.A.

MacNaught, Rt. Hon. J. Watson, P.C., Q.C., M.P.; Canadian lawyer and politician; b. 19 June 1904; ed. Prince of Wales Coll., Charlottetown, Prince Edward Island, and Dalhousie Univ.
Called to Nova Scotia Bar 32, Prince Edward Island Bar 32; King's Counsel 42; Law Clerk to Legis. Assembly of Prince Edward Island 35-42, Clerk 42-45; Crown Prosecutor, Prince County, Prince Edward Island 43-45; mem. House of Commons 45-; Parl. Asst. to Minister of Fisheries 48; Solicitor-Gen. of Canada April 63-65, Minister of Mines and Technical Surveys 65-68; Liberal.
Parliament Buildings, Ottawa, Canada.

Macnaughton, Hon. Alan Aylesworth, P.C., Q.C., B.A., B.C.L., LL.D.; Canadian lawyer and politician; b. 1904, Napanee, Ont.; *s.* of Donald Carmichael and Mabel Louise (Aylesworth) Macnaughton; *m.* Mary Caroline White 1942; two *s.* one *d.;* ed. McGill Univ. and London School of Economics.
Lawyer, Montreal; Crown Prosecutor Montreal 38-42; Sec. Bar of Montreal 38-39; Pres. Junior Board of Trade 39-40; Vice-Pres. Junior Chamber of Commerce Canada 40; M.P. 49-, Chair. House of Commons Public Accounts Cttee. 58-63, Speaker House of Commons 63-66; mem. Senate of Canada 66-; Liberal; Counsel, Martineau, Walker, Allison, Beaulieu, Phelan and MacKell; Chair. Pirelli Canada Ltd., Canadian Offshore Marine Ltd.; Pres. Electrofin Construction Investments Ltd.; Int. Adviser Swiss Bank Corpn.; Dir. and Sec. Aviation Electric Ltd., Hoffman-La Roche Ltd.; Dir. Brown Boveri (Canada) Ltd., Int. Trust Co., Sapac Corpn., Ont. Minn. Pulp and Paper Corpn. Ltd.; Chair. World Wildlife Fund (Canada); Hon. Life mem. Assemblée Nat. de la France.
The Stock Exchange, Tower Place, Victoria, Montreal, P.Q.; Home: Redpath Row Montreal, P.Q., Canada.
Telephone: 866-9575 (Office).

MacNaughton, Donald Sinclair, LL.B.; American business executive; b. 14 July 1917, Schenectady, N.Y.; *s.* of William MacNaughton and Marion (Colquhoun) MacNaughton; *m.* Winifred Thomas 1941; two *s.;* ed. Syracuse Univ. and Syracuse Univ. School of Law.
Teacher of History, Pulaski (N.Y.) Acad. and Central School 39-42; admitted to N.Y. Bar 48; private law practice, Pulaski 48-54; Deputy Sup. of Insurance, N.Y. State 54-55; with Prudential Insurance Co. of America 55-, Assoc. Gen. Counsel 60-61, Senior Vice-Pres. and Special Asst. to Pres. 61-65, Exec. Vice-Pres. 65-69, Pres. and Chief Exec. Officer 69-70, Chair. of Board and Chief Exec. Officer 70-; Chair. Inst. of Life Insurance; Dir. Exxon Corpn., The Conf. Board, Econ. Club of New York; Trustee S. S. Huebner Foundation for Insurance Educ., American Coll. of Life Underwriters, Syracuse Univ., Comm. for Econ. Devt., mem. New York Fed. Reserve Bank Money Market, Stanford Research Inst. Council, American Bar Asscn., UNA—U.S.A. Panel on New Approaches to Collective Security.
Leisure interests: golf, boating, reading.
Prudential Insurance Co. of America, Prudential Plaza, Newark, N.J. 07101; and 4 Park Lane, Madison N.J. 07940, U.S.A.
Telephone: 201-336 4401.

McNee, Sir John (William), Kt., D.S.O., M.D., D.SC., F.R.C.P., F.R.S.E.; British physician; b. 17 Dec. 1887, Mount Vernon, Lanarkshire, Scotland; *s.* of John McNee and Agnes Caven; *m.* Geraldine Le Bas 1923 (died 1975); ed. Glasgow, Freiburg and Johns Hopkins Univs.
Formerly Asst. Prof. of Medicine and Lecturer in Pathology Glasgow Univ., Associate Prof. of Medicine and Associate Physician Johns Hopkins Univ.; Lettsom Lecturer Medical Society of London 31; Croonian Lecturer Royal Coll. of Physicians 32; Vicary Lecturer, Royal Coll. of Surgeons 58, Examiner in Medicine Cambridge, Sheffield, St. Andrews, Edinburgh, Leeds Universities and National University of Ireland; Physician Univ. Coll. Hospital London and Holme Lecturer in Clinical Medicine Univ. Coll. Hospital Medical School; Regius Prof. of Medicine, Glasgow Univ. Sept. 36-53, Emeritus 53-; Physician to H.M. King George VI and later to H.M. Queen Elizabeth II in Scotland 37-54; Consulting Physician to R.N. 35-55; Consulting Physician to Western Infirmary, Glasgow; Consulting Physician, Univ. Coll. Hospital, London; Pres. Asscn.

of Physicians of Great Britain and Ireland 51-52; Pres. Gastro Enterological Soc. of Great Britain 50-51; Pres. British Medical Asscn. 54-55; Master, Barber-Surgeon's Co. of London 57; served with Royal Army Medical Corps 14-18, with Royal Navy 39-46; Surgeon-Rear-Admiral and Consulting Physician; Hon. M.D. (Nat. Univ. of Ireland), Hon. LL.D. (Glasgow and Toronto Univs.).
Leisure interests: country sports, reading.
Publs. *Diseases of the Liver, Gall-Bladder and Bile Ducts* (with late Sir Humphry Rolleston) 3rd edn. 29, *Textbook of Medical Treatment* (with Dunlop and David-son) 6th edn. 52, and many papers in scientific journals, especially on diseases of the liver and spleen and on war diseases.
Barton Edge, Worthy Road, Winchester, Hampshire, England.
Telephone: Winchester 65444.

McNeil, Frederick Harold; Canadian banker; b. 17 Nov. 1916, Saskatoon, Sask.; s. of Harold and Jean McNeil (née Swan); m. Marian Doreen Williams 1943; two s. one d.; ed. Univs. of Manitoba and Saskatchewan.
Journalist 45-54; Management Consultant, Brann & Co. 54-56; Dir. Management Services Powell River Co. 56-60; Dir. Org. Personnel and Admin. Planning, Ford Motor Co. of Canada 60-65; Gen. Man. Personnel Planning, Bank of Montreal 66-67, Vice-Pres. Org. and Personnel 67-68, Exec. Vice-Pres. Admin. 68-70, Exec. Vice-Pres., Gen. Man. 70-73, Pres., Chief Operating Officer 73-74, Deputy Chair. and Chief Exec. Officer Jan.-Dec. 75, Chair. and Chief Exec. Officer Dec. 75-; Air Force Cross.
Leisure interests: farming, riding.
Bank of Montreal, 129 St. James Street W., Montreal, Quebec Province H2Y 1L6; Home: 36 Surrey Gardens, Westmount, Quebec Province H3Y 1N6, Canada.
Telephone: 514-877-7044 (Office); 514-482-3861 (Home).

McNeil, Sir Hector, Kt., C.B.E., B.E., M.I.E.E., M.I.MECH.E.; British engineering executive; b. 20 July 1904, Invercargill, New Zealand; s. of Angus and Mary McNeil; m. Barbara Turner 1939; one s. one d.; ed. Univ. of New Zealand.
In Public Works Dept., New Zealand 27-29; State Electricity Comm. of Victoria 29-31; with Babcock and Wilcox Ltd. 31-74, Gen. Man. 47, Dir. 50, Man. Dir. 58; Chair. Babcock and Wilcox Ltd. 68-71, Pres. 71-73; Chair. British Nuclear Design and Construction Ltd. 71-75; Dir. Nat. Bank of New Zealand Ltd.; Pres. Inst. of Fuel 57-58; mem. Export Council for Europe 60, Chair. 66-69; mem. Export Guarantees Advisory Council 68-73; mem. ECGD Investment Insurance Advisory Cttee. 71-73.
Bramber, St. George's Hill, Weybridge, Surrey, England.
Telephone: Weybridge 48484.

McNeile, Lt.-Col. Robert Arbuthnot, M.B.E.; British brewing executive; b. 14 March 1913, Stoke Poges; m. Pamela Rachel Paton (née Pollock) 1944; three s. one d.; ed. Eton Coll. and Kings Coll. Cambridge Univ.
Taught Eton Coll. 35-36; brewer with A. Guinness Son & Co. Ltd. 36-, Man. Dir. 68-75, Joint Chair. 75-; fought in British Army (Royal Engineers) 40-46; Control Comm. in Germany—Controller of Alcohol, British Zone 46; Chair. of Brewers' Soc. 75-; Treas. Listers Inst. of Preventive Medicine.
Leisure interests: archaeology, ornithology, shooting, skiing, reading.
Broad Lane House, Brancaster, Norfolk, England.
Telephone: Brancaster 227.

McNeill, James Charles, C.B.E., F.A.S.A., F.A.I.M.; Australian accountant and business executive; b. 29 July 1916, Hamilton, N.S.W.; s. of C. A. H. McNeill; m. Audrey E. Mathieson 1942; one s.; ed. Newcastle High School, N.S.W.

Accountant, The Broken Hill Proprietary Co. Ltd. 47-54, Asst. Sec. 54-56, Asst. Gen. Man. (Commercial) 56-59, Gen. Man. (Commercial) 59-67, Exec. Gen. Man. (Finance) 67-71, Man. Dir. April 71-; Chair. Queensland Coal Mining Co. Ltd., Pres., Dir. PT BHP Indonesia; Man. Dir. Australian Iron & Steel Pty Ltd., Australian Wire Industries Pty. Ltd., BHP Nominees Pty. Ltd., Dampier Mining Co. Ltd., Groote Eylandt Mining Co. Ltd., Hematite Petroleum Pty. Ltd., Tasmanian Electro Metallurgical Co. Ltd.; Dir. BHP-GKN Holdings Ltd., Hematite Petroleum (NZ) Ltd., Private Investment Co. for Asia, Mount Newman Mining Co. Pty. Ltd.; mem. Mfg. Industries Advisory Council; Senior Vice-Pres. Australian Mining Industry Council; mem. Council, Chair. Finance Cttee., Monash Univ. The Broken Hill Proprietary Co. Ltd., B.H.P. House, 140 William Street, Melbourne, 3000; 104 Mont Albert Road, Canterbury, Victoria, Australia.

McNicol, David Williamson, C.B.E.; Australian diplomatist; b. 20 June 1913, Adelaide; s. of Donald McNicol and Elizabeth Robertson; m. Margaret Hargrave 1947; one s.; ed. Carey Grammar School, Melbourne, Kings Coll. Adelaide and Adelaide Univ.
Minister to Cambodia, Laos and Vietnam 55-56, Commr. to Singapore 58-60, High Commr. in Pakistan 62-65, in New Zealand 65-68; Amb. to Thailand and Rep. to SEATO 68-69; High Commr. to Canada 69-73; Deputy High Commr. in U.K. 73-.
Leisure interests: golf, reading, gardening.
Australian High Commission, Australia House, The Strand, London WC2B 4LA.

Macomber, William Butts, Jr., M.A., LL.B.; American government official and diplomatist; b. 28 March 1921, Rochester, N.Y.; s. of William B. and Elizabeth C. (Ranlet) Macomber; m. Phyllis Bernau 1963; ed. Phillips Andover Acad., Yale, Harvard and Chicago Univs.
Lecturer in Govt., Boston Univ. 47-49; with C.I.A., Washington 51-53; Asst. to Special Asst. to Sec. of State 53-54; Special Asst. to Under-Sec. of State 55; Special Asst. to Sec. of State 55-57; Asst. Sec. of State for Congressional Relations 57-61; Ambassador to Jordan 61-63; Asst. Admin. Agency for International Development (AID), Washington 64-67; Asst. Sec. of State for Congressional Relations 67-69; Dep. Under Sec. of State for Management 69-73; Amb. to Turkey 73-.
United States Embassy, Atatürk Bulvarı 110, Ankara, Turkey.

Macovescu, George, LL.B.; Romanian statesman and writer; b. 28 May 1913; ed. Bucharest Univ.
Secretary Gen. Information Ministry 45-47, Chargé d'affaires London 47-49, Dir.-Gen. of Cinematography 55-59; Minister, Wash. 59-61; Deputy Minister of Foreign Affairs 61-67, first Deputy Minister 67-72, Minister 72-; mem. Acad. of Social and Political Sciences 70-; mem. Writers' Union of the Socialist Repub. of Romania; Sec. Bucharest Writers' Asscn.
Publs. *Viaţa si opera lui Alexandru Sahia* (The Life and Work of Alexandru Sahia) 50, *Gheorghe Lazăr* 54, *Teoria literaturii* (Theory of Literature) 63, *Virstele Timului* (The Ages of Time) 71, *Catargele inalte* (Tall Masts) 72.
Ministry of Foreign Affairs, Bucharest, Romania.

McPherson, Harry Cummings, Jr., B.A., LL.B.; American lawyer and government official; b. 22 Aug. 1929; ed. Tyler High School, Texas, Southern Methodist Univ., Dallas, Univ. of the South, Tennessee, Columbia Univ. and Univ. of Texas Law School.
U.S. Air Force 50-53; admitted to Texas Bar 55; Asst. Gen. Counsel, Democratic Policy Cttee., U.S. Senate 56-59, Assoc. Counsel 59-61, Gen. Counsel 61-63; Deputy Under Sec. for Int. Affairs, Dept. of Army 63-64; Asst. Sec. of State for Educational and Cultural

Affairs 64-65; Special Asst. and Counsel to Pres. Johnson 65-69; Special Counsel to the President 66-69; private law practice, Washington, D.C. 69-.
Home: 30 W. Irving Street, Chevy Chase, Md. 20015, U.S.A.

McQueen, Steve; American film actor; b. 24 March 1930, Slater, Mo.; *m.* 2nd Ali MacGraw 1973; ed. Boys' Republic in Chino, Calif., Neighborhood Playhouse and Utah Hagen-Herbert Berghof Dramatic School.
Formerly held various temporary jobs and served in U.S. Marine Corps; stage appearances 52-58 included *Peg O' My Heart* (with Margaret O'Brien), *Member of the Wedding, Time Out for Ginger*, and in *The Gap* and *Hatful of Rain* on Broadway; television series include *Wanted—Dead or Alive*; since 58 has worked only on films; films include: *Never So Few* 59, *The Magnificent Seven* 60, *The Honeymoon Machine* 61, *Hell is for Heroes* 61, *The War Lover* 62, *The Great Escape* 63, *Love with the Proper Stranger* 63, *Soldier in the Rain* 63, *The Cincinnati Kid* 65, *Nevada Smith* 66, *Baby the Rain Must Fall* 66, *Bullitt* 68, *The Thomas Crown Affair* 68, *The Reivers* 70, *On Any Sunday* 71, *Le Mans* 71, *Junior Bonner* 72, *The Getaway* 72, *Papillon* 73, *The Towering Inferno* 74.
c/o Warner Bros.-Seven Arts, 666 Fifth Avenue, New York, N.Y. 10019, U.S.A.

McRuer, James Chalmers; Canadian lawyer; b. 23 Aug. 1890; ed. Osgoode Law School.
Called to Bar of Ontario 14, British Columbia 26, Alberta 40; served overseas in R.C.A. 16-19; apptd. K.C. 29; Lectured in the Law School 30-35 (Criminal Procedure); elected a Bencher of the Law Society of Upper Canada 36; mem. Royal Comm. on the Penal System of Canada 37; apptd. to the Court of Appeal of Ontario 44, Chief Justice of High Court of Justice for Ontario 45-64; Chair. Royal Comms. on insanity in criminal cases and on sexual psychopathic offenders; Chair. Ont. Law Reform Comm. 64-66, Vice Chair. 66-; Royal Commr., Enquiry into Civil Rights (Ont.) 64-; Pres. of the Canadian Bar Asscn. 46-47; Officer of the Order of Canada 68; Hon. LL.D. (Laval, Trent, Toronto and Queen's Univs., Osgoode Hall Law School), Hon. D.C.L. (Univ. of Windsor).
Publs. *The Evolution of the Judicial Process, Trial of Jesus* 64.
9 Deer Park Crescent, Apt. 1005, Toronto 7, Ont., Canada.
Telephone: 922-7098.

McShane, Edward James, PH.D., SC.D.; American mathematician; b. 10 May 1904, New Orleans, La.; *s.* of Dr. Augustus McShane and Harriet Kenner (Butler) McShane; *m.* Virginia Haun 1931; one *s.* (deceased) two *d.*; ed. Tulane Univ. and Univ. of Chicago.
Instructor, Princeton 33-34, Asst. Prof. 34-35; Prof. Univ. of Virginia 35-57, Alumni Prof. 57-74, Alumni Prof. Emer. 74-; mem. Nat. Acad. of Sciences, American Philosophical Soc.; Hon. Sc.D. (Tulane); Distinguished Service Award, Mathematical Asscn. of America 64; Chauvenet Prize 52.
Leisure interests: photography, music.
Publs. *Integration* 44, *Exterior Ballistics* (with J. L. Kelley and F. V. Reno) 53, *Order-Preserving Maps and Integration Processes* 53, *Real Analysis* (with T. A. Botts) 59, *Stochastic Calculus and Stochastic Models* 74; various research papers.
Department of Mathematics, University of Virginia, Charlottesville, Va. 22903; Home: 209 Maury Avenue, Charlottesville, Va. 22903, U.S.A.
Telephone: 804-924-7127 (Office); 804-293-8956 (Home).

McSwiney, James Wilmer; American business executive; b. 13 Nov. 1915, McEwen, Tenn.; *s.* of James S. and Delia (Conroy) McSwiney; *m.* Jewel Bellar 1940;

one *s.* one *d.*; ed. Hume Fogg High School, Nashville, Tenn.
Assistant Sec. and Treas., Brunswick Pulp & Paper Co. (subsidiary of Mead Corpn.) 44-54; Exec. Asst. to Pres. The Mead Corpn. 54-57, Vice-Pres. 57, Group Vice-Pres. and Gen. Man. 61, Exec. Vice-Pres. 63, Pres., Chief Exec. Officer and Chair. Exec. Cttee. 68-71, Chair. of Board and Chief Exec. Officer 71-.
Leisure interests: golf, swimming.
The Mead Corporation, Talbott Tower, Dayton, Ohio 45402; Home: 2300 Ridgeway Road, Dayton, Ohio 45429, U.S.A.
Telephone: 513-222-9561 (Office); 513-299-3647 (Home).

McTiernan, Rt. Hon. Sir Edward A., P.C., K.B.E., B.A., LL.B.; Australian lawyer; b. 16 Feb. 1892; ed. Sydney Univ.
Barrister 16; mem. New South Wales Legislature 20-27; Attorney-Gen. 20-22 and 25-27; mem. Federal Parliament 29-30; Justice of High Court of Australia 30-; Privy Chamberlain of Sword and Cape 28.
"Breffni", Chilton Parade, Warrawee, N.S.W., Australia.

Macy, John Williams, Jr.; American public administrator; b. 6 April 1917, Chicago, Ill.; *s.* of John Macy and Juliette Shaw; *m.* Joyce Hagen 1944; two *s.* two *d.*; ed. Wesleyan Univ., Connecticut and Nat. Inst. of Public Affairs, Washington, D.C.
Admin. Aide Social Security Board Washington 39-40; Personal Asst. Civilian Personnel Div. War Dept. 40-42; Asst. Dir. Civilian Personnel War Dept. 42-43, 46-47; Dir., Personnel and Org. Atomic Energy Comm. Los Alamos 47-51; Asst. to Under-Sec. of Army 51-53; Exec. Dir., U.S. Civil Service Comm. 53-58; Exec. Vice-Pres., Wesleyan Univ., Middletown, Conn. 58-61; Chair. U.S. Civil Service Comm. 61-69; Pres. Corpn. for Public Broadcasting 69-72; Public mem. Board of Governors, American Stock Exchange, New York 72-; Pres. Council of Better Business Bureaus Inc. 73-.
Leisure interests: sports, drama, music.
1150 17th Street, N.W., Washington, D.C.; Home: Langley Lane, McLean, Va., U.S.A.
Telephone: 467-5200 (Office); EL6-6347 (Home).

Madan, Bal Krishna, PH.D.; Indian banker and economist; b. 13 July 1911, Sahowala, Punjab; *s.* of Shivram Madan and Jamnadevi Chhabra; *m.* Savitri Pahwa 1935; four *s.*; ed. Univ. of Punjab, Lahore.
Lecturer in Economics, Univ. of Punjab 36-37; Officer for Enquiry into Resources, Punjab Govt. 37-39; Economic Adviser to Punjab Govt. 40-41; Dir. of Research, Reserve Bank of India, Bombay 41-45; Sec. of Indian del. to Bretton Woods 44; Deputy Sec. Indian Tariff Board 45; mem. Indian Legislative Assembly and Assembly Cttee. on Bretton Woods Agreement 46; Alternate Exec. Dir., Int. Monetary Fund 46-48; Int. Bank for Reconstruction and Development 47-48; Exec. Dir. Int. Monetary Fund 48-50,67-71; mem. Indian Del., First Commonwealth Finance Ministers' Conf. London 49; mem. UN Cttee. on Domestic Financing of Economic Development 49; Economic Adviser to Reserve Bank of India 50; mem. Finance Comm., Indian Govt. 52; mem. Taxation Enquiry Comm. 53-54; mem. Experts Group on UN Special Fund for Economic Development 55; Principal Adviser to Reserve Bank of India 57, Exec. Dir. 59, Deputy Gov. 64-67; mem. Governing Body Indian Investment Centre 60-67; Dir. Industrial Finance Corpn. of India 61-64, Life Insurance Corpn. of India 64-67; Chair. Steering Group on Wages, Incomes and Prices Policies 64-66; Pres. Indian Econ. Asscn. 61; Vice-Chair. Industrial Development Bank of India 64-67; Chair. Bonus Review Cttee., Indian Govt. 72-74; Chair. Management Devt. Inst. 73-; mem. Governing Body, Nat. Council of Applied Econ. Research 75-.
Leisure interests: golf, reading.

Publs. *India and Imperial Preference—A Study in Commercial Policy* 39, *Aspects of Economic Development and Policy* 64.

3/43 Shanti Niketan, New Delhi 21, India.

Madariaga, Salvador de; Spanish diplomatist and writer; b. 23 July 1886, La Coruña; s. of José de Madariaga and Ascension Rojo; *m.* 1st Constance Archibald 1912 (died 1970), two *d.*; 2nd Emilia Rauman 1970; ed. Madrid Inst. Cardenal Cisneros, Paris Ecole Polytechnique and Ecole des Mines.

Engineer Northern Spanish Railway Co. 11; Dir. Disarmament Section, LN 22-28; Prof. Spanish Studies, Oxford Univ. 28; Deputy Cortes Constituyentes 31; Ambassador, Washington 31; mem. LN Council 31-36; Del. LN Disarmament Conf. 32; Ambassador to France 32-34; Minister of Education and of Justice in Lerroux Cabinet Mar.-April 34; Chief Spanish Del. to LN 31-36; Pres. Cttee. of Five 35; Pres. Cultural Section, European Movement; Hon. Pres. Liberal Int.; Hon. Fellow Exeter Coll., Oxford; D.Litt. h.c. (Arequipa, Lima, Oxford, Poitiers, Princeton, Liège, Lille); Grand Cross Légion d'Honneur; Hanseatic Goethe Prize 67; Charlemagne Prize, Aachen 73.

Leisure interests: walking, listening to music.

Publs. *Shelley and Calderón, The Genius of Spain, The Sacred Giraffe, Englishmen, Frenchmen, Spaniards* (Ere Nouvelle Prize), *Sir Bob, Disarmament, Americans, The Price of Peace, Anarchy or Hierarchy* 37, *Theory and Practice in International Relations* 38, *The World's Design* 38, *Christopher Columbus* 39, *Hernán Cortés* 42, *Spain* 43, *The Heart of Jade* 44, *The Rise of the Spanish American Empire* 46, *Victors Beware* 46, *The Fall of the Spanish-American Empire* 47, *Bolívar* 52, *Portrait of Europe* 52, *Essays with a Purpose* 54, *A Bunch of Errors* 54, *War in the Blood* 57, *Democracy versus Liberty?* 58, *The Blowing Up of the Parthenon* 60, *Latin America Between the Eagle and the Bear* 61, *On Hamlet* 64, *Portrait of a Man Standing* 68, *Morning Without Noon* (memoirs) 74.

Hotel la Palma, CH-6600, Locarno, Switzerland.

Telephone: 093-33-67-71.

Madarikan, Hon. Charles Olusoji; Nigerian judge; b. 19 Feb. 1922, Lagos; s. of Rev. and Mrs. O. J. Madarikan; *m.* Miss T. O. Craig 1951; three s. two *d.*; ed. C.M.S. Grammar School, Lagos, Higher Coll., Yaba, Inns of Court School of Law, London.

Called to the Bar, Lincoln's Inn 48; Crown Counsel 49-56, Senior Crown Counsel 56; Legal Sec. S. Cameroons 57-58; Chief Registrar Supreme Court of Nigeria 58-59; Dir. of Public Prosecutions, W. Nigeria 59-60; Judge W. Nigeria High Court 60-67; Justice of Supreme Court of Nigeria 67-72; Pres. Western State Court of Appeal 72-.

Leisure interests: golf, gardening.

Publs. selected judgements of the Federal Supreme Court of Nigeria 57, 58, *Brett and MacLean's Criminal Law and Procedure of the Six Southern States* (2nd edn.).

Court of Appeal, Ibadan, Nigeria.

Telephone: Ibadan 24178.

Maddox, Lester Garfield; American state governor; b. 30 Sept. 1915.

Industrial supervisor 34; restaurant, then grocery shop, proprietor; Gov. of Georgia 67-71; Lieut.-Gov. 71-; Hon. mem. various Georgian asscns.; Democrat.

c/o State Capitol, Atlanta, Georgia, U.S.A.

Mader, Ing. Helmut; Austrian politician; b. 3 Dec. 1941, Innsbruck; s. of Sepp and Rosa Mader; *m.* Edeltraud Eiter 1962; three s.; ed. Höhere Technische Lehranstalt für Elektrotechnik.

Salesman and technician, Tiroler Wasserkraftwerke A.G. (TIWAG), Innsbruck 61-; mem. Bundesrat 70-, Pres. 71-72; mem. Tiroler Landtages 75-; mem. Austrian People's Party.

Leisure interests: politics, reading, education of youth. Fischnalerstrasse 24, A-6020 Innsbruck, Austria.

Telephone: 05222/31-131 (Office); 21-53-74 (Home).

Madgwick, Sir Robert Bowden, O.B.E., M.EC., D.PHIL. F.A.C.E.; Australian fmr. broadcasting executive; b. 10 May 1905 N. Sydney N.S.W.; s. of late R. C. Madgwick; *m.* 1st Ailsa M. Aspinall 1937 (died 1967), three *d.*; *m.* 2nd Mrs. Nance McGrath 1971; ed. N. Sydney Boys' High School Univ. of Sydney and Balliol Coll. Oxford.

Lecturer in Econ. History, Univ. of Sydney 36-40, Sec. of Extension Board 37; Dir. Australian Army Educ. 41-46; Warden, New England Univ. Coll. 47-54; Vice-Chancellor, Univ. of New England 54-66; Chair. Australian Broadcasting Comm. 67-73, N.S.W. Advisory Cttee. on Cultural Grants 68-, Australian Frontier 74-; Hon. D.Litt. (Sydney, Newcastle (N.S.W.), New England), Hon. LL.D. (Queensland).

Leisure interests: reading, fishing, gardening.

Publs. *Immigration into Eastern Australia 1788-1851, Outline of Australian Economics* (with E. R. Walker).

3 Collins Road, St. Ives, N.S.W. 2075, Australia.

Madia, Chunilal Kalidas; Indian writer; b. 12 Aug. 1922; ed. Bhagwatsinhji High School, Dhoraji, Gujarat, and H.L. Coll. of Commerce, Ahmedabad.

Writes mainly in Gujarati; Editorial Staff *Prabhat* and *Navsaurashtra* 42-44; Editor *Varta* (short story monthly) 43; Editorial Staff, Janmabhoomi Group of Newspapers, Bombay 45-50; Language Editor, U.S. Information Service, Bombay 50-62; now Editor *Ruchi* (literary and cultural magazine); Literary Editor *Sandesh* (Gujarati daily); Official Del. 35th P.E.N. Congress of World Writers, Ivory Coast 67; Narmad Gold Medal for Best Play Writing 51; Ranajitram Gold Medal for Outstanding Creative Writing 57; numerous other prizes. Publs. (in Gujarati): novels: *Vyajano Varas, Velavelani Chhanyadi, Liludi Dharati, Kumkum Ane Ashaka;* short stories: *Ghooghavatan Pur, Padmaja, Champo Ane Kel, Tej Ane Timir, Roop-Aroop, Antasrota;* plays: *Rangada, Vishavimochan, Raktatilak, Shoonyashesh;* poems: *Sonnet* (collected sonnets); criticism: *Granthagarima, Shahamrig, Suvarnamrig;* in Malayalam: *Gujarati Kathakal.*

B-213, Chandralok, Manav Mandir Road, Malabar Hill, Bombay 6, India.

Telephone: 36-8245.

Madigan, Russel Tullie, O.B.E., M.E., LL.B., F.S.A.S.M.; Australian business executive; b. 22 Nov. 1920; ed. Univ. of Adelaide.

Joined Zinc Corpn. 46; travelling scholarship in Canada and U.S.A. 47-49; Underground Man. Zinc Corpn. Ltd., NBHC Ltd. 56-59; Gen. Man., Gen. Mining Div., Conzinc Rio Tinto Australia Ltd. 60-64, Dir. 68-; Man. Dir. Hamersley Iron 65-71, Chair. 71-; Chair. Blair Athol Coal Pty. Ltd. 71-, Interstate Oil Ltd. 71-, Hamersley Holdings Ltd.; Dir. Rio Tinto Zinc Corpn. Ltd. 71-, Commercial Union Assurance Co. 69-, Australian Mines and Metals Asscn. 71-; mem. Australian-Japan Business Co-operation Cttee., Pacific Basin Econ. Council, Trade Devt. Council.

Hamersley Holdings Ltd., 95 Collins Street, Melbourne, Victoria; Home: 60 Broadway, East Camberwell, Victoria, Australia.

Madsen, Rt. Rev. Willy Westergaard; Danish ecclesiastic; b. 16 Jan. 1907, Copenhagen; *m.* Esther Madsen 1934; two *c.*; ed. Univ. of Copenhagen. General Sec. Social Works of the Parishes in Copenhagen 42; Bishop of Copenhagen, Primate of the Lutheran Church of Denmark 61-; editor *Fra Menighedsplejen* 42-60.

Publ. *Din Naeste* 45.

Nørregade 11, Copenhagen K, Denmark.

Telephone: P3-3508.

Maeda, Kazuo; Japanese politician; b. 1910, Waka-yama.
Former functionary, Japanese Postal Service; mem. House of Councillors 56-72; fmr. Deputy Sec.-Gen. of Liberal Democratic Party, Parl. Vice-Minister of Transport and Chair. Transport Cttee. of House of Councillors; Minister of State, Dir.-Gen. Science and Tech. Agency, Chair. Atomic Energy Comm. 72-73; Liberal Democratic Party.
c/o Liberal Democratic Party, Tokyo, Japan.

Maeda, Shichinoshim; Japanese business executive; b. 1901; ed. Tokyo Univ.
President, Fuji Electric Co., Ltd. until 74, Chair. Nov. 74-.
Fuji Electric Co., Ltd. 1-1, Tanabeshinden, Kawasaki City, Kanagawa Prefecture, Japan.

Maegraith, Brian Gilmore, C.M.G., T.D., M.B., B.S., F.R.C.P. (L. & E.), F.R.A.C.P., B.SC., M.A., D.PHIL.; Australian university professor; b. 26 Aug. 1907, Adelaide; s. of A. E. R. Maegraith; m. Lorna Langley 1934; one s.; ed. St. Peter's and St. Mark's Colls., Univ. of Adelaide, Magdalen and Exeter Colls., Univ. of Oxford.
Medical Fellow and Tutor in Physiology, Exeter Coll., Oxford 34-40; Univ. Lecturer and Demonstrator in Pathology, Oxford 37-44, Dean of Medical School 38-44; Lieut.-Col. R.A.M.C., O.C. Malaria Research Unit, War Office 39-45; mem. Medical Research Council Malaria Cttee. 43-46; Tropical Medicine Research Board (Medical Research Council) 59-69, Council Royal Society of Tropical Medicine 47-51, Vice-Pres. 49-51, 57-69, Pres. 69-71; Dean of School, Liverpool School of Tropical Medicine 44-75, Vice-Pres. 75-, Prof. Tropical Medicine 44-72, Prof. Emeritus 72-; Consulting Physician in Tropical Medicine, Royal Infirmary, Liverpool; Nuffield Consultant in Tropical Medicine, W. Africa 49-; Consultant Faculty of Tropical Medicine, Bangkok 59-, and S.E. Asian Int. Centre for Tropical Medicine 65-; Chair. Council of European Insts. of Tropical Medicine 69-72; Maurice Bloch Lecturer, Glasgow, Heath Clark Lecturer, London 70; mem. Medical Research Council Chemotherapy Cttee. 53-; hon. mem. Belgian, American and German Societies of Tropical Medicine; Chalmers Gold Medal, Royal Society of Tropical Medicine 51, Le Prince Medal, American Society of Tropical Medicine 55, Bernhard Nocht Medal (Hamburg) 57, Mary Kingsley Medal 73; Hon. D.Sc. (Bangkok), Emer. M.D. (Athens) 72; Hon. Fellow St. Mark's Coll. 56.
Leisure interests: music, painting, writing.
Publs. *Pathological Processes in Malaria* 48, *Clinical Tropical Diseases* 53 (6th Edn. 76), *Tropical Medicine for Nurses* 54 (4th Edn. 75), *Clinical Methods in Tropical Medicine* 62, *Exotic Diseases in Practice* 65.
School of Hygiene, 126 Mount Pleasant, Liverpool 2, and 23 Eaton Road, Cressington Park, Liverpool 19, England.
Telephone: 051-709-2542; and 051-427 1133.

Maekawa, Kunio, B.ENG.; Japanese architect; b. 14 May 1905, Niigata City; m. Myo Miura 1945; ed. Tokyo Imperial Univ.
Worked in Le Corbusier's office, Paris 28-30, Antonin Raymond's office, Tokyo 30-35; Pres., Kunio Maekawa Architect's Office 35-; Prof., Nihon Univ., Tokyo; Pres. Japan Architects Asscn. 59-62; mem. Japanese Del., Exec. Cttee. of Int. Union of Architects 59-69; numerous prizes.
Buildings include: Yokohama Cultural Centre 52, Kanagawa Prefectural Library 54, Japanese Pavilion, Brussels World Fair 58, Kyoto Cultural Centre 59, Gakushin Univ. 60, Tokyo Metropolitan Festival Hall 61, Saitama Cultural Centre 66, Saitama Prefectural Museum 71.
Leisure interests: music, reading.

Office: 8 Honshio-cho, Shinjuku-ku, Tokyo; Home: Kami-Oaski 3-10-59, Shinagawa-ku, Tokyo, Japan.
Telephone: Tokyo 351-7101 (Office).

Maeo, Shigesaburo; Japanese politician; b. 10 Dec. 1905, Sumiyoshi-cho, Miyazu-shi, Kyoto Prefecture; s. of Shosuke and Tomi Maeo; m. Shizuko Maeo 1939; no c.; ed. Faculty of Law, Tokyo Imperial Univ.
Former Dir. Taxation Bureau; Pres. Mint Agency of Finance Ministry; Vice-Chair. Policy Affairs Research Council of Liberal Party; Sec.-Gen. Liberal Democratic Party; Chair. Local Admin. Cttee., Foreign Affairs Cttee. House of Reps.; Minister of Int. Trade and Industry; State Minister, Dir.-Gen. Hokkaido Devt. Agency; Minister of Justice 71-72; Speaker, House of Reps. 73.
Leisure interests: go, reading and music.
Publs. include *Zei no zuihitsu shu* (Essays on Taxation), *Seijika no Saijiki* (Memoirs of a Statesman), *Seijika no Tsurezuregusa* (Gleanings from My Leisure Hours as a Statesman), *Shin keizai seichoron to shin heiwashugi* (The New Economic Growth Doctrine and the New Pacificism), *Matsurigoto no Kokoro* (The Essence of Politics).
1-10-22, Shoto, Shibuya-ki, Tokyo, Japan.
Telephone: 467-7597.

Maevsky, Viktor Vasiliyevich; Soviet journalist; b. 30 April 1921, Zhdanov; s. of Vasilii and Nadezhda Maevsky; m. Valentina Stanislavleva 1943 (died 1975); one s.; ed. Moscow Pedagogical Inst., High School of Diplomacy.
Headmaster of a Middle School 42-44; mem. *Pravda* staff 47-, mem. C.P.S.U. 47-, Correspondent in London 50-53, Editor Asia and Africa Dept. 55-61, Observer of Int. Affairs 61-; Order of Red Banner of Labour, Badge of Honour; V. Vorzovsky Prizewinner for Journalism 60.
Publs. *On the British Isles* 55, *On the Japanese Islands* 58, *Malayan Morning* 59, *First or Fifth* 60, *Skyscrapers are not Steady* 62, *Europa Without Gentlemen* 67, *Half a Million Kilometres Behind* 68, *In the Polish Lands* 68, *Battles of Peaceful Time* 71, *Devaluation of Bonifatiuses* 72, *Strong People* 74.
Pravda, Ulitsa Pravdy 24, Moscow, U.S.S.R.

Mafatlal, Arvind N.; Indian industrialist; b. 27 Oct. 1923, Ahmedabad; s. of late Navinchandra Mafatlal and of Vijayalaxmi N.; m. Sushila A. Mafatlal; two s. one d.; ed. St. Xavier's High School and Sydenham Coll. of Commerce and Econs., Bombay.
Joined Mafatlal Group of Cos. 41, Chair. 55-; Dir. Tata Iron & Steel Co. Ltd., Bombay Burmah Trading Corpn. Ltd., Nat. Machinery Mfrs. Ltd., Industrial Investment Trust Ltd.; Chair. Agricultural Services Org.; mem. Cen. Direct Taxes Advisory Cttee., Task Force on Nutrition, Governing Body, CSIR, Cen. Advisory Council of Industries; Chair. Exec. Council, Nat. Chemical Laboratory; Chair., Man. Trustee Shri Sadguru Seva Sangh Trust; del. to 43rd Session, ILO Conf.; Durga Prasad Khaitan Memorial Gold Medal 66, Business Leadership Award (Madras Management Asscn.) 71.
Leisure interest: golf.
Mafatlal House, Backbay Reclamation, Bombay 400 020; and 10 Altamount Road, Bombay 400 026, India.
Telephone: 29-11-99 (Office); 36-83-50 (Home).

Maga, Hubert Coutoucou; Benin politician; b. 10 Aug. 1916; ed. Ecole Normale de Gorée.
Headmaster of school at Nabitingou until 51; Gen. Counsellor of Dahomey 47; Grand Counsellor of Art 48-57; Deputy for Dahomey to French Nat. Assembly 51-58; Under-Sec. for Labour, Gaillard Cabinet; Minister of Labour in Dahomey 58-59, Premier 59-63, Pres. 60-63; under restriction Dec. 63-Nov. 65; Head of State

70-72, also Minister of Interior and of Defence May 70-Oct. 72; under house arrest 72; mem. Dahomeyan Democrat Group; awards incl. Mérite Social and Etoile Noire de Bénin.
Cotonou, Benin.

Magalhães, Maj.-Gen. Juracy Montenegro; Brazilian diplomatist; b. 1905; ed. Lyceu, State of Ceará, Realengo Military Acad., Gen. Staff School and Superior War Coll.
Former Army Officer; Military Attaché, Washington 53-54; Fed. Interventor, State of Bahia 31-34; Gov. of Bahia 35-37, 59-63; mem. for Bahia, Fed. Chamber of Deputies 46-50, Fed. Senator for Bahia 54, 58-; Pres. Cia. Vale do Rio Doce (iron ore exports) 51-52; Pres. Petrobrás 54; Chair. Nat. Democratic Union (UDN) 57-58; Ambassador to United States 64-65; Minister of Justice and Interior 65-66, of Foreign Affairs 66-67; numerous decorations.
Publs. *Defendendo o meu Govêrno* (In Defence of my Government), *Petróleo, Fonte de Libertação ou de Escravidão* (Petroleum, Source of Liberation or of Enslavement).
c/o Ministry of Foreign Affairs, Brasília, Brazil.

Magalhães Mota, Joaquim Jorge; Portuguese lawyer and politician; b. 17 Nov. 1935, Santarem; s. of Eloi Saraiva da Mota and Miquelina Magalhães Mota; m. Maria Manuela Almeida Martins de Silva Magalhães Mota 1962; one s. two d.; ed. Lisbon Univ.
Technical Asst., Internal Colonization Inst. 61, 64-68; Head of Office of Sec. of State for Industry 69-71; mem. Parl. (Liberal Wing) 69-73; Founder of SEDES (political asscn.) 69-; Chair. of Board Organização e Gestão de Empresas (OGE) 73-; Minister of Internal Admin. May-July 74; Minister without Portfolio July 74-75, of Internal Trade 75-; Popular Democratic Party.
Leisure interests: reading, cinema, swimming, pipe collection.
Publs. *Colonização Interna e Emparcelamento* 64 (2nd edn. 72), *A Quota de Individuo Casado em Regime de Comunhão de Bens, em Sociedade por Quotas, em que o Pacto Consagra Clausulas de Intransmissibilidade* 70, *Ser ou Não ser Deputado* 73, *Encontro de Reflexão Política.*
Rua Filipe Folque, No. 5, 1 Esq., Lisbon 1, Portugal.
Telephone: 47927.

Magalhães Pinto, José de; Brazilian banker, business executive and politician; b. 28 June 1909, Santo Antônio do Monte; m. Berenice Catão de Magalhães Pinto 1932; three s. three d.; ed. Free School of Law, Belo Horizonte.
Director, Banco da Lavoura, Minas Gerais 29-35; Pres. Assoc. Comercial, Minas Gerais 35-37; Pres. Fed. Comércio, Minas Gerais 37; Founder and Chair. of Board Banco Nacional de Minas Gerais 44; Fed. Deputy 40-60; Gov. of Minas Gerais 60-65; mem. Chamber of Deputies 45-60, Nov. 66-; Minister of Foreign Affairs March 67-Sept. 69; Pres. União Democrática Nacional (U.D.N.); mem. Senate 70-; Prof. at Econ. Univ. of Minas Gerais; Dr. h.c. Univ. Rural de Viçosa; numerous Brazilian and foreign decorations.
Avenida Atlântica 2016, Apt. 401 Copacabana ZC-07, Rio de Janeiro, GB; and SQS 309, BL C, ap. 402, DF-70,000, Brasília, Brazil.
Telephone: 236-4838 (Rio de Janeiro); 43-8460 (Brasília).

Magaloff, Nikita; Swiss pianist; b. 8 Feb. 1912, St. Petersburg (now Leningrad), Russia; s. of Dimitri and Barbara Magaloff; m. Irène Szigeti 1939; one d.; ed. Conservatoire national de musique, Paris and with Joseph Szigeti.
Professor of Virtuosity, Geneva Conservatoire 49-; numerous concerts all over the world since 39, including two tours of South America and tour round the world 60; particularly well known as Chopin interpreter;

numerous invitations to play in the major European int. music festivals; frequent mem. of jury in European Int. Piano Competitions.
Leisure interests: sightseeing, chess.
Compositions include: *Sonatina* for Violin and Piano, *Toccata* for Piano, and Songs.
1815 Baugy/Clarens (Vaud), Switzerland.
Telephone: (021)-613186.

Magariños, Gustavo; Uruguayan international civil servant; b. 31 Dec. 1922, Montevideo; s. of Mateo M. Pittaluga and Margarita M. de los Ríos; m. Ivonne Pagani 1947; one s. one d.; ed. Univ. of Montevideo.
Economic Counsellor, Uruguayan Embassy, London, and Economic Adviser, Ministry of Foreign Affairs 54-59; Dir. of Commercial and Economic Dept., Uruguayan Embassy, Buenos Aires 59-62; Dir. of Dept. of Negotiation, Latin American Free Trade Asscn. (LAFTA) 62, Asst. Exec. Sec. LAFTA Dec. 62-67, Perm. Exec. Sec. 67-73.
Leisure interests: sport, classical literature.
Juan María Pérez No. 2996, Montevideo, Uruguay.
Telephone: 79-90-56 (Home).

Magariños D., Víctor; Argentine painter; b. 10 Sept. 1924; ed. Escuela nacional de artes visuales.
Founded *Grupo Joven* 46; First one-man exhbn. Galería Juan Cristóbal 50, also at Inst. de Arte Moderno 50-51, Pres. Argentine Cttee. of Int. Asscn. for Plastic Arts, UNESCO 58; Scholarship to France 51, to U.S.A. 65; represented at Biennali: São Paulo 51-55, Venice 56; also at Concrete Art Exhbn. Museum of Modern Art 63, El Nuevo Arte Argentino, Walker Art Center, Minneapolis, A Decade of Latin-American Art, Guggenheim Museum 65-66, Museum of Modern Art, New York, Museo Nacional de Bellas Artes, Museo de Arte Moderno, Buenos Aires.
c/o Museo de Arte Moderno, Teatro General San Martín, Corrientes 1530, Buenos Aires, Argentina.

Maghrabi, Mahmoud Soliman; Libyan politician; b. 1935; ed. George Washington Univ., U.S.A.
Helped to organize strikes of port workers June 67, for which he was sentenced to four years imprisonment and deprived of Libyan nationality; released Aug. 69; following the coup of Sept. 69 became Prime Minister, Minister of Finance and Agriculture, and of Agricultural Reform until Jan. 71; Perm. Rep. to UN 71-72; Amb. to U.K. 73-.
Embassy of Libya, 58 Prince's Gate, London, SW7 2PW, England.
Telephone: 01-589-5235.

Maghur, Kamel Hassan; Libyan lawyer and diplomatist; b. 1 Jan. 1935, Tripoli; m.; five c.; ed. Univs. of Cairo, Paris and Grenoble.
Assistant Counsellor, Admin. of Legislation, Tripoli 59-60; Counsellor, Court of Cassation 60-69; Counsellor, Supreme Court of Libya 71-72; Perm. Rep. to UN Sept. 72-.
Permanent Mission of Libya to United Nations, 866 United Nations Plaza, New York, N.Y. 10017, U.S.A.

Magloire, Paul; Haitian officer and politician; b. 1907; ed. Cap Haiti High School.
Taught at Lycée National Philippe Guerrier, Cap Haiti 29-30; entered army as cadet 31; Lieut. 31; Head of Military School 34; Asst. District Commdr., Cap Haiti 35-37; Major 38; District Commdr. 38-41; Chief of Police, Port-au-Prince, and Commdr. of Palace Guard 44; mem. provisional Military Govt. and Minister of Interior 46 and 50; Pres. of Haiti 50-56; Orders of "Honneur et Mérite", "Brevet de Mérite", etc.
Port-au-Prince, Haiti.

Magnet, Alejandro; Chilean writer, journalist and diplomatist; b. 28 Oct. 1919; ed. Universidad Católica de Chile.
Founded magazine *Política y Espíritu* 45, Literary

Critic 45-52, Commentator on Int. Political Affairs 52-60; Asst. Editor *La Voz* 60-62; Commentator on Int. Affairs, Radio Chilena 54-62, TV Channel 13 62-64; Int. Political Affairs Editor *El Sur* (newspaper), Concepción 58-62, *Mensaje* (magazine) 59-64; Ambassador, Rep. of Chile to Org. of American States 64-70.
Publs. *Nuestros Vecinos Justicialistas* 53, *El Padre Hurtado* 54, *Nuestros Vecinos Argentinos* 56; children's books: *El Secreto Maravilloso* 44, *La Espada y el Canelo* 58.
Ministry of Foreign Affairs, Santiago, Chile.

Magnuson, Warren Grant; American lawyer and politician; b. 12 April 1905, Moorhead, Minnesota; *m.* Jermaine Elliot Peralta Magnuson; one *d.*; ed. Public School, Minnesota, Univ. of North Dakota, North Dakota State Univ. and Univ. of Washington.
Special Prosecuting Attorney 31; elected to Washington State Legislature 33-34; Asst. U.S. Dist. Attorney 34; Prosecuting Attorney, King County, Washington 34-36; served in House of Reps. 37-44; Senator from Washington 44-; served as Lieut.-Commdr. in U.S.N. during Second World War; awards include Metropolitan Board of Trade World Trade Award 61, American Coll. of Cardiology Distinguished Service Award 72, Albert Lasker Award for Public Service in Health 73; Hon. D.Jur., Gonzaga Univ. 66, Seattle Univ. 67, St. Martin's Coll. 67, Gallandet Coll. 72, Univ. of Alaska 73; Hon. Dr. Publ. Admin., Univ. of Puget Sound 67; Hon. Dr. rer. Pol., Univ. of the Pacific 70; Democrat.
Publs. *The Dark Side of the Marketplace* (with Jean Carper) 68, *How Much for Health?* (with Elliot A. Segal) 74.
127 Senate Office Bldg., Washington, D.C. 20510, U.S.A.

Magnussen, Einar, CAND. ECON.; Norwegian economist and politician; b. 5 June 1931, Ålesund; *s.* of Gustav Magnussen and Selma Giske; *m.* Aase Bjørg Andersen 1956; two *s.* one *d.*; ed. Oslo Univ.
Economist Norges Bank 57-60; worked on team preparing Norwegian Econ. Long Term Programme, Ministry of Finance 60-61; Economist Int. Monetary Fund 62-65; Head, Monetary Policy Div., Norges Bank 65-68; Econ. Adviser Bank of Tanzania 68-70; Dir. Monetary Policy Dept., Norges Bank 70-73; Under-Sec. of State, Ministry of Commerce and Shipping 73-74, Minister 74-75; Chair. EFTA Jan.-June 76.
Fiskekroken 31, Oslo 1, Norway.
Telephone: 28-71-80.

Magomayev, Djamal Muslimovich; Soviet politician; b. 1910; ed. Azerbaizhan Petroleum Inst.
Mechanic-engineer at oil undertakings in Azerbaizhan 32-48; mem. C.P.S.U. 40-; Vice-Chair. Azerbaizhan S.S.R. Council of Ministers 48-52, 54-57; Second Sec. Baku Regional Cttee. of C.P. of Azerbaizhan 52-53; mem. Cen. Cttee. of C.P. of Azerbaizhan; Minister of Local Industry of Azerbaizhan S.S.R. 53-54; First Vice-Chair. State Planning Cttee. of Azerbaizhan S.S.R. Council of Ministers 57-62; Perm. Rep. of Azerbaizhan S.S.R. Council of Ministers to U.S.S.R. Council of Ministers 62-; Deputy to Supreme Soviets of Azerbaizhan S.S.R. and U.S.S.R. 50-58, 66-; mem. Comm. for Industry, Soviet of Nationalities, Cttee. of U.S.S.R. Parl. Group.
Permanent Representation of Azerbaizhan S.S.R. Council of Ministers to U.S.S.R. Council of Ministers, Gogolevsky boulevard 31A, Moscow, U.S.S.R.

Magowan, Robert Anderson; American businessman; b. 19 Sept. 1903, Pennsylvania; ed. Kent School and Harvard Univ.
Merchandise Man. R. H. Macy & Co. 27-34; Vice-Pres. N. W. Ayer & Son 34-35; Vice-Pres. Safeway Stores Inc., San Francisco 35-38, Chair. 55-, Pres. 57-66, Chair. Exec. Cttee.; Chair. Canada Safeway Ltd.; Vice-Pres.

Merrill Lynch & Co. Inc. 38-40, Partner Merrill Lynch, Pierce, Fenner and Beane 40-55, Limited Partner 55-; Dir. The Bank of Calif., N.A., Caterpillar Tractor Co., Southern Pacific Co., Fibreboard Corpn., J. G. Boswell Co., Del. Monte Properties Co.; Trustee St. Andrews Dune Church of Southampton, N.Y., The Merrill Charitable Trust; mem. Advisory Council of the Stanford Graduate School of Business; official of several civic orgs.
Home: 2100 Washington Street, San Francisco, Calif.; Office: 4th and Jackson Streets, Oakland 4, Calif., U.S.A.

Magri, Salvatore; Italian accountant and business executive; b. 1897.
Qualified accountant 14; Credito Italiano 14-52; Chair. and Managing Dir. Dalmine Co. 52-60; Chair. and Managing Dir. Finanziaria Meccanica (Finmeccanica) 60-69, Hon. Chair. 69-; Chair. Manifattura Ceramica Pozzi, Mediolanum Management Co.; Hon. Degree of Economy and Commerce 54.
Manifattura Ceramica Pozzi, 20122 Milan, Via Visconti di Modrone 15; and Rome, Viale Pilsudski 92, Italy.
Telephone: 7724 (Office); 8777 (Home).

Maguire, Conor A., s.c.; Irish jurist; b. 16 Dec. 1889; ed. Univ. Coll. Dublin.
Solicitor 14; Judge of Republican Courts and Dáil Land Settlement Comm. 20-22; Called to Bar 22; Fianna Fáil Deputy for Nat. Univ. and Attorney-Gen. in De Valéra Govt. 32-36; Pres. Irish High Court 36-46; Chair. Irish Red Cross Soc. 40-46; Chief Justice 46-61; mem. European Comm. of Human Rights 62-65, European Int. Court of Human Rights 65-; Hon. LL.D. (Nat. Univ. of Ireland and Univ. of Dublin); Commdr. Légion d'Honneur, Cross St. Raimon de Penafort, Grosses Verdienstkreuz.
St. Alban's, Albany Avenue, Monkstown, Co. Dublin, Ireland.

Magyar, Dr. Imre; Hungarian liver pathologist and novelist; b. 14 Oct. 1910, Losonc (Lucenec), Slovakia; *s.* of László Magyar and Adel Deutsch; *m.* Eva Fodor 1944; one *s.* three *d.*; ed. Univ. Med. School, Budapest.
Director, Postgraduate School of Medicine 60-65; Prof. and Dir. 1st Medical Clinic of Semmelweis Univ. Medical School, Budapest 65-; board mem. Scientific Council on Public Health 65-70; mem. Expert Cttee. for Diabetics of WHO 62-; Hon. Pres. Hungarian Diabetic Asscn., Hungarian Gastroenterological Soc., Hungarian Soc. of Internal Med.; Sec. "Korányi Sándor" Scientific Asscn. 64-72; mem. Int. Asscn. for Study of Liver, European Asscn. for Study of Diabetes, Int. Soc. of Internists, European Asscn. of Internal Medicine; mem. board of *Diabetologia* (Berlin—New York) *Zeitschrift für Gastro-Enterologie* (Munich), *Zeitschrift für Stoffwechsel und Verdauungskrankheiten* (Rostock) *Orvosképzés* (Budapest), *Hungarian Archives of Medicine* (chief editor).
Leisure interests: music, reading.
Publs. *Textbook on Medicine* 9th edition 74, *Differential Diagnosis of Internal Diseases* 60, 67, 76, *Diseases of the Liver and Biliary Ducts* (also in German and Russian) 60, *Diabetes Mellitus* 64, *Cosmic Resentment* (essays) 68, 69, *Style Exercise* (essays) 71, *Korányi Sándor* (biography), *Instructive Journey* (novel) 70, *Ruth* (novel) 71, *Judith* (novel) 73, *Essentials of Internal Medicine* 75.
1137 Budapest, Radnóti Miklós-utca 21/b, Hungary.
Telephone: 295879.

Mahdavi, Fereidun, PH.D.; Iranian economist; b. 1933; ed. Hamburg Univ.
Financial and Econ. Adviser, Housing Org.; Economist Econs. Dept.; staff mem. Investment and Public Relations Dept.; Man. Econs. Dept., Asst. to Man. Dir., Industrial and Mining Devt. Bank of Iran, later Man. Dir. IMDBI; Minister of Trade April 74-.
Ministry of Trade, Teheran, Iran.

Mahdi, Saadik El; Sudanese politician; b. 1936; great grandson of Imam Abdul-Rahman El Mahdi, *s.* of late Siddik El Mahdi; ed. Comboni Coll., Khartoum and St. John's Coll., Oxford.

Leader, Umma Mahdist Party 61; Prime Minister 66-67; arrested on a charge of high treason 69; exiled April 70; returned to Sudan and arrested Feb. 72, released May 73.

Publ. *Problems of the South Sudan.*
Khartoum, Sudan.

Mahdi al Tajir, Mohamed; Dubai administrator; b. 26 Dec. 1931; ed. Bahrain Govt. School and Preston Grammar School, Lancs., England.

Department of Port and Customs, Govt. of Bahrain, Dir. 55-63; Dir. Dept. of His Highness the Ruler's Affairs and Petroleum Affairs March 63-; Dir. Nat. Bank of Dubai Ltd. 63-; Dir. Dubai Petroleum Co. April 63-; Chair. Dubai Nat. Air Travel Agency Jan. 66-; Dir. Qatar-Dubai Currency Board Oct. 66-; Chair. South Eastern Dubai Drilling Co. April 68-; Dir. Dubai Drylock Co. 73-; Amb. of the United Arab Emirates to U.K. (also accred. to France) 72-; Hon. Citizen of State of Texas, U.S.A. 63.

Embassy of the United Arab Emirates, 30 Prince's Gate, London, SW7 1PT, England; P.O. Box 207, Dubai, United Arab Emirates.

Mahgoub, Mansour; Sudanese accountant and politician; b. 1912, El Kowa; ed. Gordon Memorial Coll. Joined Dept. of Finance 35; trained with various companies in England 50-51; Inspector, Auditory Dept., Sudan Dec. 51-Jan. 54; asst. dir. of accounts, Ministry of Finance, Jan. 54-March 55; Under-Sec. for internal and monetary affairs March 55-58; Under-Sec., Ministry of Commerce, Industry and Supply 58, retd. 64; joined Sudan Commercial Bank as asst. dir. 64; Minister of the Treasury May 69-June 70; Minister of Economy, Trade and Supplies 70-72.

c/o Ministry of Economy, Trade and Supplies, Khartoum, Sudan.

Mahgoub, Mohammed Ahmed; Sudanese lawyer and politician; b. 1908; ed. Gordon Coll. and Khartoum School of Law.

Practising lawyer; fmr. mem. Legislative Assembly; accompanied Umma Party Del. to United Nations 47; mem. Constitution Amendment Comm.; non-party candidate in Gen. Election 54; Leader of the Opposition 54-56; Minister of Foreign Affairs 56-58, 64-65, Prime Minister 65-66, May 67-May 69; practising solicitor 58-64.

Publs. *Democracy on Trial* 74, and several vols. of poetry (in Arabic).

60c Prince's Gate, Exhibition Road, London, S.W.7, England.

Mahindra, Keshub, B.SC.; Indian business executive; b. 9 Oct. 1923, Simla; *s.* of late Kailash Chandra Mahindra; *m.* Sudha Y. Varde 1956; three *d.*; ed. Univ. of Pennsylvania, U.S.A.

President Asscn. of Indian Automobile Mfrs. 64-65, Bombay Chamber of Commerce and Industry 66-67, Assoc. Chamber of Commerce and Industry 69-70, Maharashtra Econ. Devt. Council 69-70; Chair. Indian Council of Trade Fairs and Exhbns. 64-69, Indian Soc. of Advertisers 68-71; Chair. Mahindra and Mahindra Ltd., Union Carbide India Ltd., Remington Rand of India Ltd., Indian Aluminium Co. Ltd., Housing and Urban Devt. Corpn. Ltd., Int. Tractor Co. of India Ltd., Otis Elevator Co. (India) Ltd., Vickers Sperry of India Ltd., Machinery Mfrs. Corpn. Ltd.; Chair. Board of Governors, Indian Inst. of Management, Ahmedabad; Dir. several cos.

Leisure interests: golf, tennis, photography, reading.
Mahindra and Mahindra Ltd., Gateway Building, Apollo Bunder, Bombay 1; Home: St. Helen's Court, Pedder Road, Bombay 26, India.

Mahler, Dr. Halfdan, M.D.; Danish health official; b. 1923, Vivild; *m.* Dr. Ebba Fischer-Simonsen; two *s.*; ed. Univ. of Copenhagen.

Planning Officer, Mass Tuberculosis Campaign, Ecuador 50-51; joined WHO 51; Senior WHO Officer attached to Nat. TB Programme, India 51-61; Visiting Prof., postgraduate medical schools, Rome and Prague 61-; Chief Medical Officer, Tuberculosis Unit, WHO Headquarters, Geneva 62-69, also Sec. to WHO Expert Panel on TB; Dir. Project Systems Analysis 69; Asst. Dir.-Gen. WHO, responsible for Div. of Family Health, Div. of Org. of Health Services, Div. of Research in Epidemiology and Communication Science 70-73, Dir.-Gen. 73-.

Publs. several publs. relating to the epidemiology and control of TB and to the utilization of operational research in health care delivery systems.
World Health Organization, Avenue Appia, 1211 Geneva, Switzerland.
Telephone: 34-60-61.

Mahmoud Aly, Abdel Halem; Egyptian ecclesiastic; b. 1910, Belbees; ed. Al-Azhar Univ. and Univ. of Paris.

Professor of Philosophy Al-Ahzar Univ. 41, Prof. of Psychology 51, Dean Coll. of Religion 64; Sec.-Gen. Islamic Research Acad. 68; Under-Sec. of Al-Ahzar Affairs 70, Minister 71; Grand Sheikh of Al-Ahzar 73-.

Publs. several books on Islamic religion.
Al-Ahzar Administration, Office of the Grand Sheikh, Cairo, Egypt.

Mahmud Husain, Abul Basher; Bangladesh judge; b. 1 Feb. 1916; *s.* of late Abdul Mutakabbir Abul Hasan; *m.* Sufia Begum 1936; three *s.* five *d.*; ed. Shaistagonj High School, M.C. Coll., Sylhet, Dacca Univ.

Pleader, Judge's Court, Dacca, 40-42; Additional Govt. Pleader, Habiganj 43-48; Advocate, Dacca High Court Bar 48-51; Attorney, Fed. Court of Pakistan 51-53 Advocate 53-58, Senior Advocate of Supreme Court of Pakistan 58-65; Asst. Govt. Pleader, High Court of East Pakistan 52-56, Senior Govt. Pleader and later acting Advocate-Gen. of East Pakistan 56-65; Judge, High Court of East Pakistan 65-72, of Bangladesh 72, of Appellate Div. of High Court 72, of Appellate Div. of Supreme Court 72-75; Chief Justice Nov. 75-; Councillor, Assam Provincial Muslim League 44-47, All-India Muslim League 45-47, All-Pakistan Muslim League 47-55; mem. Constitutent Assembly of Pakistan 49-54, Commonwealth Parl. Asscn. 50-54, Interparl. Union 50-54, Pakistan Tea Board 51-54, Exec. Council of Dacca Univ. 52-54, Bar Council of Dacca High Court 58-66.

Chief Justice's House, 19 Hare Road, Dacca 2, Bangladesh.
Telephone: 243334 and 281849.

Mahoney, David Joseph, Jr.; American advertising and business executive; b. 17 May 1923, New York City; *m.* Barbara Moore 1951; one *s.* one *d.*; ed. LaSalle Military Acad., Cathedral High School, New York, and Wharton School of Business, Univ. of Pennsylvania.

Ruthrauff and Ryan 46-51; David J. Mahoney Inc. (advertising agency) 51-56; Pres. Good Humor Corpn. 56-61; Exec. Vice-Pres. Colgate-Palmolive Co. 61-66; Pres. Canada Dry Corpn. 66-68; Pres. and Chief Exec. Officer Norton Simon Inc. 68-, Chair. 70-.

Office: 277 Park Avenue, New York, N.Y. 10017, U.S.A.
Telephone: 212-832-1000.

Mahoney, Hon. Patrick Morgan, P.C., B.A., LL.B.; Canadian politician and judge; b. 20 Jan. 1929, Winnipeg; *s.* of Paul Morgan Mahoney and Joan Ethel Tracy Patrick; *m.* Mary A. Sneath 1958; three *s.* one *d.*; ed. Univ. of Alberta.

Admitted to Alberta Bar 52; mem. Parl. 68-72; Parl. Sec. to Minister of Finance Oct. 70-Jan. 72; Minister

without Portfolio Jan.-Oct. 72; apptd. Q.C. 72; Judge of Trial Div., Fed. Court of Canada 73; Judge of Court Martial Appeal Bd. of Canada Nov. 73-; fmr. Pres. Western Football Conf., Canadian Football League.
3 Coltrin Place, Ottawa K1M 0A5, Ont., Canada.

Mahroug, Smail; Algerian economist; b. 21 Oct. 1926, Bougaa; ed. Univ. of Paris.
In Morocco 53-62, active in Front de Libération Nationale (FLN), also Dir. of Planning, Moroccan Govt.; returned to Algeria, Chef de Cabinet of Head of Econ. Affairs, Provisional Govt. 62; Econ. Counsellor to Pres. 63-70; Dir.-Gen. Caisse Algérienne de Développement 63-65; Dir.-Gen. Ministry of Finance 65-66; Minister of Finance 70-76.
c/o Ministère des Finances, Algiers, Algeria.

Mahtab, Harekrushna, D.LITT., LL.D.; Indian politician and journalist; b. Nov. 1899, Agarpada, Orissa; s. of Jorgannath Mahtab and Sm. Dhanni Bibi; m. Sm. Subhordra Mahtab 1918; ed. Ravenshaw Coll., Cuttack.
Joined non-co-operation movement 21; worker for Indian Nat. Congress 21-; mem. Bihar & Orissa Legislative Council 24; Editor, *Prajatantra* and *Jhankar*; civil disobedience movements 30, 32; Pres. Utkal Provincial Congress Cttee. 30, 37; organized Inchudi Salt Satyagraha, imprisoned 30-31, 32, 42; mem. Congress Working Cttee. 38-46; Leader, Congress Assembly Party, Orissa; Chief Minister, Orissa State 46-50, 56-61; Minister for Commerce and Industry, Govt. of India 50-52; Sec.-Gen. Congress Parl. Party 52-55, Deputy Leader 62-63; Gov. of Bombay 55-56; mem. Lok Sabha 62-67, Orissa Legislative Assembly 67-.
Leisure interests: reading, writing stories, novels and articles for magazines and newspapers.
Publs. *History of Orissa;* three novels, one play.
Ekamra Nivas, Bhuvaneshwar-2, Orissa, India.
Telephone: 51946.

Maiboroda, Georgi Illarionovich; Soviet composer; b. 1 Dec. 1913, Pelikhovshchina, Poltava region, Ukraine; s. of Illarion Ivanovitch and Davija Yeliceevna Maiboroda; m. 1946; two s.; ed. Kiev Conservatoire.
Chairman, Ukrainian S.S.R.; Honoured Worker of Arts of the Ukrainian S.S.R. 57; People's Artist of the U.S.S.R. 60; Order of Red Banner of Labour 63, Order of Lenin 70, Order of People's Friendship 73.
Leisure interest: car driving.
Principal compositions include: symphonies 40, 52, *Gutsuli Rhapsody* 51, *Friendship of the Peoples* (cantata), *Zaporozhtsy* 54, *Milana* (opera) 56, *The Arsenal* (opera) 60, *King Lear* (suite for symphonic orchestra) 59, *Taras Shevchenko* (opera) 67, *Concerto for Orchestra and Voice* 70, *Yaroslav the Wise* (opera) 73, also many romances and songs.
Composers' Union of the Ukrainian S.S.R., Shevchenko Prospekt, Kiev; Apartment 23, 9 Mikhailovski Lane, Kiev, U.S.S.R.

Maiden, Alfred Clement Borthwick, B.A., C.B.E.; Australian business executive; b. 21 Aug. 1922; ed. Taree High School, New England Univ. Coll., Univ. of Sydney.
Agricultural Attaché, Washington, D.C. 51-53; Asst. Dir. Bureau of Agricultural Econs. 53-56, Dir. 59-62; Asst. Sec. Dept. of Trade 56-57; Commercial Counsellor, Washington, D.C. 57-59; Sec. Dept. of Primary Industry 62-68; Man. Dir. Int. Wool Secr. 69-73; Chair. Australian Wool Corpn. 73-.
Australian Wool Corporation, Wool House, 578 Bourke Street, Melbourne 3000, Australia.

Maihofer, Werner; German politician; b. 20 Oct. 1918, Konstanz; m. Margrit Schiele 1942; five d.; ed. Secondary School, Konstanz and Freiburg Univ.
Professor, Univ. of the Saarland 55, Dean of Faculty of Law and Econs. 56-57, Rector 67-69; Prof. Univ. of

Bielefeld 70, Dir. Centre for Interdisciplinary Research 71; mem. Bundestag 72-; Fed. Minister without Portfolio 72; Fed. Minister of the Interior May 74-; Dr. h.c. Univ. of Nancy 68; Grand Cross, Order of Léopold II (Belgium); Freie Deutsche Partei (FDP).
Leisure interests: yachting, skiing, music.
Publs. *Der Handlungsbegriff im Verbrechenssystem* 53, *Recht und Sein* 54, *Rechtsstaat und menschliche Würde* 68, *Demokratie im Sozialismus* 68.
Bundesministerium des Innern, 5300 Bonn, Rheindorfer Strasse 198, Federal Republic of Germany.
Telephone: 02221-785253.

Mailer, Norman Kingsley, B.S.; American writer; b. 31 Jan. 1923, Long Branch, N.J.; s. of Isaac Barnett Mailer and Fanny Schneider; m. 1st Beatrice Silverman 1944 (dissolved 1951); one d.; m. 2nd Adele Morales 1954 (dissolved 1962), two d.; m. 3rd Lady Jeanne Campbell 1962 (dissolved 1963), one d.; m. 4th Beverly Rentz Bentley 1963, two s. one d.; ed. Harvard Univ.
Served in U.S. Army 44-46; Co-founder New York weekly *Village Voice* 55; mem. Editorial Board of *Dissent* magazine 53-69; Dir. films: *Wild 90* 67, *Beyond the Law* 67, *Maidstone* 68; Nat. Book Award for Arts and Letters 69; Pulitzer Prize for non-fiction 69.
Publs. *The Naked and The Dead* 48, *Barbary Shore* 51, *The Deer Park* 55 (dramatized 67), *Advertisements for Myself* 59, *Deaths for the Ladies* (poems) 62, *The Presidential Papers* 63, *An American Dream* 64, *Cannibals and Christians* 66, *Why are we in Vietnam?* (novel) 67, *The Armies of the Night* 68, *Miami and the Siege of Chicago* 68, *Moonshot* 69, *A Fire on the Moon* 70, *The Prisoner of Sex* 71, *Existential Errands* 72, *St. George and the Godfather* 72, *Marilyn* 73, *The Faith of Graffiti* 74; contributions to numerous magazines.
P.O. Box 338, Provincetown, Mass. 02657, U.S.A.

Maillard, Pierre; French diplomatist; s. of Adrien Maillard and Hélène (née Coliette); m. Evelyn George 1943; one s.; ed. Letters and Law faculties, Paris Univ.
Entered diplomatic service 42, Berne 42-43, mem. representation of French Liberation Cttee. 43; Head, French Office for Refugees in Switzerland 44; Head of Office of Sec.-Gen. for German and Austrian Affairs 45; Second Sec., London 46; Ministry of Foreign Affairs 48; participated in negotiation of Peace Treaty with Austria 49; First Sec., Vienna 50; served Secr. of Confs. 51; Deputy Head of Cen. Admin., Ministry of Foreign Affairs 53; Head of Levant Service 54; Political Dir. Council of Europe 58; Minister, Diplomatic Counsellor to Gen. Secr. of Presidency 59-64; Asst. Sec.-Gen. for Nat. Defence 64-68; mem. Board of Dirs. Nat. Centre for Space Studies 65-69; Amb. to UNESCO 70-75; Diplomatic Counsellor to the Govt. Jan. 76-; Officier, Légion d'Honneur; Commdr., Ordre Nat. du Mérite, Chevalier des Palmes Académiques, Commdr. de l'Etoile Noire.
Leisure interest: horse riding.
Ministry of Foreign Affairs, 37 Quai d'Orsay, 75007 Paris; Home: 3 square de Latour-Maubourg, 75007 Paris, France.

Maillart, Ella; Swiss traveller and writer; b. 20 Feb. 1903, Geneva; d. of Paul and Dagmar Klim; ed. Geneva.
Travelled Russia, Turkestan, Manchuria, Tibet, Iran. Afghanistan: in S. India 40; Nepal 51; Fellow Royal Geographical Society London; Hon. mem. Alpine Club, Ski Club G.B.
Leisure interests: skiing, sailing, travels, gardening in the Alps.
Publs. *Parmi la Jeunesse Russe* 32, *Des Monts Célestes aux Sables Rouges* (Turkestan Solo) 34, *Oasis Interdites* (Forbidden Journey) 37, *Gypsy Afloat* 42, *Cruises and Caravans* 42 (pub. in French, German), *The Cruel Way* 47 (publ. in Dutch, Swedish, French, Spanish and German), *Ti-Puss* (in English and German), *The Land of the Sherpas*.

10 avenue Vallette, Geneva and Chandolin Sur Sierre, Switzerland.
Telephone: 46-46-57 (Geneva).

Mailliard, William Somers, B.A.; American politician; b. 10 June 1917, Belvedere, Calif.; s. of late John Ward Mailliard, Jr. and of Kate Peterson Mailliard; m. 1st Elizabeth Whinney 1940 (divorced 1954), 2nd Millicent Fox 1957; two s. five d.; ed. The Taft School, Watertown, Conn., Yale Univ.
Naval Service 43-46, Rear-Adm. U.S. Naval Reserve 65-; Sec. to Earl Warren, Gov. of Calif. 49-51; mem. Congress 53-74; mem. Merchant Marine and Fisheries Cttee. 53-74, Foreign Affairs Cttee. 61-74, Ranking Minority mem. Foreign Affairs Cttee. 71-74; Congressional Adviser on Org. of American States 64-67, on UN Cttee. on Peaceful Uses of the Seabeds 69-74; mem. Comm. on Org. of Govt. for Conduct of Foreign Policy 73-74; Perm. Rep. to Org. of American States 74-.
Leisure interests: English and American history, swimming, bridge, hunting and fishing.
Department of State, Room 6491, Washington, D.C. 20520; Home: 3265 N Street, N.W., Washington, D.C., U.S.A.
Telephone: (202) 225-5161 (Office); (202) 965-9882 (Home).

Maina, Charles Gatere, B.A.; Kenyan civil servant; b. 1 March 1931, Nyeri; s. of Chief Gideon Gatere Wagithu and Nyamahiga Kinyugo; m. Muringo Wangari Kariuki 1959; three d.; ed. in Kianjogu, Tumutumu, Kagumo and Makerere.
Teacher, 59-61; District Educ. Officer 62; Provincial Educ. Officer 62-64; Asst. Chief Educ. Officer 64-66; Deputy Sec. for Educ. 66-68; Principal, Kenya Inst. of Admin. 68-71; mem. Council, Univ. Coll., Dar es Salaam 69-70, Univ. of Nairobi 69-; mem. Agricultural Educ. Comm. 67, Working Party on Higher Educ. in E. Africa 68; Sec.-Gen. E. African Community 71-74; Perm. Rep. to UN 74-.
Leisure interests: swimming, tennis, golf.
Permanent Mission of Kenya to United Nations, 866 UN Plaza, Room 486, New York, N.Y. 10017, U.S.A.
Telephone: (212) 421-4740.

Maingot, Rodney, F.R.C.S. ENG.; British surgeon and writer; m. 1st Rosalind Smeaton 1928 (died 1957), 2nd Evelyn Plesch 1965; ed. Ushaw Coll. and St. Bartholomew's Hospital, London.
Captain, R.A.M.C. 16-19 (mentioned in dispatches); fmr. House Surgeon, Casualty Officer, Chief Asst. to a Surgical Unit, St. Bartholomew's Hospital, London; Consulting Surgeon to Newspaper Press Fund of England, Royal Free Hospital, London, and Southend Gen. Hospital; Fellow, Asscn. of Surgeons of Great Britain; former mem. of Council and Pres. Section of Surgery, Royal Society of Medicine; Editor-in-Chief *British Journal of Clinical Practice*; Sydney Body Gold Medallist 58, Lahey Memorial Lecture Boston 63, Guest Prof. at following hospitals: Royal Prince Alfred Hospital Sydney, Mount Sinai Hospital Miami, Univ. Hospital Columbus, Anderson Memorial Hospital, South Carolina, Maadi Hospital, Cairo.
Leisure interests: writing, landscape painting, early Roman history.
Publs. *Postgraduate Surgery* 38, *Technique of Gastric Operations* 41, *War Wounds and Injuries* (part editor) 43, *The Surgical Treatment of Gastric and Duodenal Ulcer* 45, *Techniques of British Surgery* 50, *The Management of Abdominal Operations* (2nd edn.) 57, *Abdominal Operations* (6th edn.) 74, *The Relationship of Art and Medicine* 74, *The Enviable Struggle: The Autobiography of a Surgeon* 76, contrib. to *Surgery of the Gall Bladder and Bile Duct* (ed. Smith and Sherlock) 64, contrib. to *Operative Surgery* (ed. Robb & Smith) 69, 74, several lectures and papers on surgery of the stomach, gall bladder and bile ducts.

8 Ashley Court, Grand Avenue, Hove, Sussex BN3 2ND, England.
Telephone: 0271-735 339.

Maire, Edmond; French trades union official; b. 1931, Epinay sur Seine; m.; three c.; ed. Conservatoire Nat. des Arts et Métiers.
Technician, chemical industry; Perm. Sec. of Union of Chemical Industries of Parisian branch of the Confédération Française Démocratique du Travail (C.F.D.T.) 58-60; Perm. Sec. of Fed. of Chemical Industries of C.F.D.T. 60-70, Sec.-Gen. 64-70; mem. Exec. Comm. of C.F.D.T., in charge of professional and social action; Sec.-Gen. of C.F.D.T. Sept. 71-.
Confédération Française Démocratique du Travail, 26 rue de Montholon, 75439 Paris, Cédex 09, France.
Telephone: 280-62-43.

Mais, Baron, (Life Peer), cr. 67, *Alan Raymond Mais*, G.B.E., T.D., E.R.D., J.P., F.I.C.E., F.I.ARB., F.R.I.C.S.; British business executive; b. July 1911; s. of the late Capt. E. Mais; m. Lorna Aline 1936; two s. one d.; ed. Banister Court, Hants, and Coll. of Estate Man., Univ. of London.
Commissioned Royal West Kent Regt. 29; Royal Eng. 31; Maj. 39, Lieut.-Col. 41, Col. 44; served British Expeditionary Force, France 39-40 (despatches); Special Forces, Egypt, Iraq and Persia 41-43 (despatches); Normandy and N.W. Europe 44-46 (despatches); Commdr. R.E. 56; Armoured Div., Territorial Army 47-50; Command, Eng. Group, Army Emergency Reserve 51-54, Deputy Dir. Eng. Services 54-58; Civil eng. posts 31-38; private practice, A. R. Mais & Partners, Structural Eng. and Surveyors 38-39, 46-48; Dir. Trollope & Colls Ltd. (contractors) and subsidiaries 48, Asst. Man. Dir. 53, Man. Dir. 57, Deputy Chair. 61, Chair. and Man. Dir. 63, retd. 68; Dir. Nat. Commercial Bank of Scotland 66-69, Royal Bank of Scotland 69-, Slag Reduction Co. Ltd., William Sindall Ltd. 69-; Chair. City of London Insurance Co. Ltd. 70-, Hayworth MSL Consultants 71-; fmr. Pres. London Master Builders' Asscn.; mem. Land Comm. 67-69; Lord Mayor of London 72-73; Chancellor City Univ. 72-73; Pres. London Chamber of Commerce and Industry 74; mem. House of Lords Select Cttee. on EEC 74; mem. several cttees. of Corpn. of City of London, Court and Council of City Univ.; Commr. of Income Tax 72-; Gov. Birkbeck Coll., London Univ. 73-; Vice-Pres. Emer. Inst. of Quantity Surveyors; Fellow, Inst. of Structural Engineers; mem. Soc. C.E. (France); Hon. D.Sc. (City) 72; Order of Patriotic War, 1st Class (U.S.S.R.) 42; Order of the Aztec Eagle (Mexico) 73; Order of Merit (Mexico) 73; K. St. J.
Leisure interests: golf, family, Territorial Army.
Publs. Yerbury Foundation Lecture, R.I.B.A. 60, Bossom Foundation Lecture 71.
Chesham House, Wilderness Road, Chislehurst, Kent; 10 St. James' Street, London, S.W.1, England.
Telephone: 01-467 0735 (Chislehurst); 01-930 1986 (London).

Maisel, Sherman Joseph, PH.D.; American economist; b. 8 July 1918, Buffalo, N.Y.; s. of Louis Maisel and Sophia Beck Maisel; m. Lucy Cowdin 1942; one s. one d.; ed. The Nichols School, Harvard Coll. and Harvard Univ.
Economist, Fed. Reserve Board 39-41; U.S. Army 41-45; mem. staff, U.S. del. to Interallied Reparations Agency 45-46; Prof. of Business Admin. Univ. of Calif. (Berkeley) 48-65; mem. Board of Govs. Fed. Reserve System 65-72; Fellow, Inst. for Advanced Study in the Behavioral Sciences, Stanford 72-73; Prof. of Business Admin. Univ. of Calif. (Berkeley) 73-; Pres. American Finance Asscn. 73; Co-Dir. Nat. Bureau of Econ. Research-West 73-.
Publs. *Housebuilding in Transition* 53, *Fluctuations,*

Growth and Forecasting 57, *Financing Real Estate* 65, *Managing the Dollar* 73, and various pamphlets.
School of Business Administration, Barrows Hall, University of California, Berkeley, Calif. 94720; Home: 2164 Hyde Street, San Francisco, Calif. 94109, U.S.A. Telephone: (415) 771-9650 (Home).

Maisonrouge, Jacques G.; French computers executive; *m.*; five *c.*; ed. Ecole Centrale de Paris and Columbia Univ.
Joined IBM France June 48; studied electronics U.S.A. 48-49; Asst. Sales Man. IBM France 54-56; Man. of market planning and research, IBM Europe 56-58, Regional Man. 58-59, Asst. Gen. Man. for Europe 59-62, Pres. IBM Europe 64-67; Vice-Pres. IBM World Trade Corpn. 62-64, Dir. 67, Pres. 67-70, Chief Exec. 73-, Chair. 74-; Vice-Pres. IBM Corpn. 67-70, Senior Vice-Pres. 72-; Chair. IBM U.K. 71-72, Dir.; mem. American Chamber of Commerce in France and numerous other socs.; Dir. French American Banking Corpn., L'Air Liquide, Canadian Liquid Air Ltd., French Chamber of Commerce, U.S.A.; Int. Advisory Dir. Chase Int. Investment Corpn.; Treas. Int. Management Educ. Foundation.
821 UN Plaza, New York, N.Y. 10017, U.S.A.

Maiti, Abha, B.A., LL.B.; Indian social worker and politician; b. 23 May 1925; ed. Univ. Law Coll., Calcutta.
Joined Quit India Movement 42; Sec. Women's sub-cttee. of West Bengal Pradesh Congress 48-54; mem. West Bengal Pradesh Congress Cttee. 54-59; Pres. Midnapore Congress Cttee. 59; mem. West Bengal Legislative Ass. 52-57; mem. All India Congress Cttee. 52-, Congress Working Cttee. 60-, Gen. Sec. Indian Nat. Congress 60-64; fmr. mem. Rajya Sabha; Joint Sec. Paschim Banga Khadi Kendra 57-; Minister of Refugee Relief and Rehabilitation, Relief and Social Welfare and Home (Constitution and Elections) for West Bengal 62-69.
P-14 Durga Charran Mitra Street, Calcutta 6, West Bengal; and 97 South Avenue, New Delhi, India.

Maitland, Sir Donald James Dundas, Kt., C.M.G., O.B.E., M.A.; British diplomatist; b. 16 Aug. 1922, Edinburgh; *s.* of Thomas D. Maitland and Wilhelmina S. Dundas; *m.* Jean Marie Young 1950; one *s.* one *d.*; ed. George Watson's Coll. and Edinburgh Univ.
Army service 41-47; joined Diplomatic Service 47; Consul, Amara 50; British Embassy, Baghdad 50-53; Private Sec. to Minister of State, Foreign Office 54-56; Dir. Middle East Centre for Arab Studies, Lebanon 56-60; Foreign Office 60-63; Counsellor, British Embassy, Cairo 63-65; Head, News Dept., Foreign Office 65-67; Principal Private Sec. to Foreign and Commonwealth Sec. 67-69; Amb. to Libya 69-70; Chief Press Sec. to Prime Minister 70-73; Perm. Rep. to UN 73-74; Deputy Under-Sec., FCO 74-75; mem. British Overseas Trade Board 74-75; U.K. Permanent Rep. to European Communities 75-.
Leisure interests: music, hill-walking, flying.
Foreign and Commonwealth Office, London, S.W.1, England.

Majekodunmi, Chief The Hon. Moses Adekoyejo, C.M.G., M.A., M.D., F.R.C.P.I., F.M.C.O.G., M.A.O., D.C.H., L.M.; Nigerian doctor and politician; b. 17 Aug. 1916, Abeokuta; *s.* of The Hon. Chief James Bernard Majekodunmi, Otun of Egbas; *m.* Katsina S. Atta; five *s.* three *d.*; ed. Abeokuta Grammar School, St. Gregory's Coll., Lagos, Trinity Coll., Dublin.
House Physician, Nat. Children's Hospital, Dublin 41-43; Medical Officer, Nigeria 43-49; Consulting Obstetrician, Massey Street Maternity Hospital, General Hospital and Creek Hospital, Lagos 49-60; Senior Specialist Obstetrician, Nigerian Federal Gov. Medical Services 49-60; Senator and Leader of Senate 60; Minister of State for the Army 60-61, Fed. Minister

of Health 61-66; Fed. Minister of Health and Information 65; Admin. for W. Nigeria 62; Pres. 16th World Health Assembly 63; Int. Vice-Pres., 3rd World Conf. on Medical Educ., New Delhi 66, Dir. Barclays Bank (Nigeria) Ltd., Westminster Dredging Co. (Nigeria) Ltd.; mem. Board of Govs., St. Gregory's Coll., Lagos; Medical Dir. and Chair. Board of Govs., St. Nicholas Hosp., Lagos 67-; Hon. LL.D. (Trinity Coll., Dublin), Hon. D.Sc. (Lagos).
Leisure interests: riding, squash, swimming.
Publs. *Premature Infants: Management and Prognosis* 43, *Behold the Key* (play) 44, *Partial Atresia of the Cervix Complicating Pregnancy* 46, *Sub-Acute Intussusception in Adolescents* 48, *Thiopentone Sodium in Operative Obstetrics* 54, *Rupture of the Uterus involving the Bladder* 55, *Effects of Malnutrition in Pregnancy and Lactation* 57, *Medical Education and the Health Services: A Critical Review of Priorities in a Developing Country* 66.
3 Kingsway, Ikoyi, Lagos, Nigeria.
Telephone: 22450.

Majerus, Pierre, DR. IUR.; Luxembourg diplomatist; b. 29 Sept. 1909, Rosport; *s.* of Mathias Majerus and Claire Gruber; *m.* Andrée Wagner; three *s.* one *d.*; ed. Athenée and C.S. Luxembourg, and Univ. of Paris.
Barrister, Luxembourg 33; Attaché, Ministry of Foreign Affairs 36, Sec. 44, Counsellor 45; Chamberlain to Grand Duchess of Luxembourg 46, to Grand Duke 64; Chargé d'Affaires, Brussels 44-47; Chief of Political Section, Ministry of Foreign Affairs 48-51; Del. to UN Gen. Assembly 49, 50; Minister to Germany and Chief of Luxembourg Mil. Mission to Berlin 51-56; Ambassador to Fed. Germany 56-61, to Italy 61-74, concurrently to Switzerland 63-68; several decorations.
Leisure interests: history of art and civilization.
Publs. *Le Luxembourg Indépendant* 45, *L'Etat Luxembourgeois* 48 (second edn. 59), *Principes élémentaires de Droit Public Luxembourgeois* 53.
44 rue E. M. Mayiseh, Luxembourg.

Majid, Abdul, PH.D.; Afghan diplomatist; b. 14 July 1914; ed. Cornell Univ. and Univ. of California (Berkeley).
Member Afghan Inst. of Bacteriology 41, Dir. 41-42; Prof. of Biology and Physiology, Kabul Univ. 40-46, Pres. of Univ. 46-48; Minister of Public Health 48-50; Minister of Education 50-56; Amb. to Japan 56-63, to U.S.A. 63-67, to U.K. 67-70; Minister of Justice and Attorney-Gen. 73-; Leader of Afghan del. to UN 66; Order of Educ. First Class 56, Sardar-i-Ali 59, A. Haas Award (Univ. of Calif.) 66.
Ministry of Justice, Kabul, Afghanistan.

Majid, Hafiz Abdul; Pakistani international civil servant; b. 17 Oct. 1907, Kasur; *s.* of Haji Sheikh Allah Bakhsh; *m.* Husn Ara 1938; one *s.* one *d.*; ed. local schools at Kasur, Univ. of Punjab, Lahore, and Christ Church, Oxford.
Assistant Commr., Indian Civil Service 31-37; District and Sessions Judge 37-39; Deputy Commr. 39-42; Dep. Sec., Punjab Govt. 42-44; Rationing Controller, Lahore 44-46; highest Secr. jobs, Provincial Secr., Lahore 46-57; Sec. to Pakistan Govt., Dept. of Labour, later Dept. of Finance 57-62; joined Int. Labour Office, Geneva 62; Asst. Dir-Gen. Int. Labour Office 62-70; Sitara-i-Pakistan 62.
Leisure interest: bridge.
10-H Gulbarg, Lahore, Pakistan.
Telephone: 80169.

Majidi, Abdol-Majid, PH.D.; Iranian politician and lawyer; b. 11 Jan. 1928; ed. Teheran, Paris, Harvard and Illinois Univs.
Held posts in Export Devt. Bank and in Plan Org.; Head of Budget Bureau of Plan Org. 59-60; Financial and Admin. Asst. Man. Dir. of Plan Org. 62-64; Head of Budget Bureau formed in 64; Deputy Prime Minister,

Head of Cen. Budget Bureau, Plan Org. 66; Minister of Agricultural Products and Consumer Goods 67-68, of Labour and Social Affairs 68-73, of State in charge of Plan and Budget Org. 73-; mem. Arts and Culture High Council 68; Sec.-Gen. Red Lion and Sun Soc.; Hon. LL.B. (Lewis and Clark Coll., Ore.).
Plan and Budget Organization, Avenue Daneshkhadeh, Teheran, Iran.
Leisure interests: music, reading, tennis, soft-ball, swimming.
Calle Pina 34, Santo Domingo, Dominican Republic.
Telephone: 2-1178.

Major, Louis Charles; Belgian trade union leader; b. 1902, Ostend; ed. Labour Univ. of Brussels.
Secretary of the Dock Workers Trade Union in Ostend 25, and in Antwerp 36; Nat. Sec. of Gen. Fed. of Belgian Trade Unions 40-44, Asst. Gen. Sec. 44-52, Gen. Sec. 52-68; Minister of Labour June 68-Jan. 73; Deputy in the House of Representatives; mem. Exec. Cttee. of the Int. Confederation of Free Trade Unions, and of the Exec. Cttee. of the Belgian Socialist Party; fmr. Pres. Econ. and Social Cttee., European Communities; King's Medal.
42 rue Haute, Brussels, Belgium.

Major, Máté, D.TECH.SC.; Hungarian architect; b. 3 Aug. 1904, Baja; s. of Károly Major and Julia Thum; m. Elizabeth Fenyö 1928; one s.; ed. Budapest Technical Univ.
Private practice 31-36; employed by state 36-48; Prof. 49-75; mem. and Sec. Group of Socialist Artists 33-37; mem. Presidium of Union of Hungarian Architects 51-, Pres. 55-64; Corresp. mem. Hungarian Acad. of Sciences 49-60, mem. 60-; has edited several periodicals since 46; Hon. Corresp. mem. Royal Inst. of British Architects 63-; Hon. mem. Instituto de Arquitectos do Brasil and Sociedad de Arquitectos Mexicanos 64-; Foreign mem. Serbian Acad. of Arts and Sciences 65-; Kossuth Prize 49; Order of the People's Repub. 50; Golden Order of Labour 64, 70; Order for Socialist Country 67; Red Banner Order of Labour 75; Freeman of Baja City 74.
Leisure interests: letters, fine arts, music, theatre, cinema.
Publs. *History of Architecture*, Vols. I-III 54-60, (revised edn., Vol. I 74), *P.L. Nervi* 66, *Peculiarity of Architecture* 67, *Essays 49-68* 69, *Marcel Breuer* 70, *Amerigo Tot* 71, *Ernö Goldfinger* 73, *Memoirs I* 73.
Mártonhegyi Ut 31, H-1121, Budapest XII, Hungary.
Telephone: 853-807.

Major, Tamás; Hungarian actor and director; b. 1910; ed. Academy of Dramatic Art.
Budapest National Theatre Dir. 45-62, leading Stage Man. 62-; played Tartuffe, Richard III, Iago (*Othello*), etc.;mem. Central Cttee., Hungarian Socialist Workers' Party 57-66; Kossuth Prize (twice), "Red Banner" Labour Order of Merit 70, decorated Eminent Artist of the Hungarian People's Republic.
c/o National Theatre, H-1077, Budapest VII, Hevesi Sándor tér 2, Hungary.
Telephone: 413-849.

Makarevsky, Alexandr Ivanovich, DR.TECH.SC.; Soviet construction specialist; b. 16 April 1904, Mushkevich village, Smolensk region; ed. Moscow Bauman Higher Technical School.
Laboratory assistant, Engineer, Chief of Dept., Deputy Chief, Zhukovsky Central Airhydrodynamical Inst. 29-; mem. C.P.S.U. 43; Prof. Moscow Physico-technical Inst. 44; Corresp. mem., U.S.S.R. Acad. of Sciences 53-68, Academician 68-; Lenin Prize, State Prize.
U.S.S.R. Academy of Sciences, 14 Lenin Prospekt, Moscow, U.S.S.R.

Makarezos, Nikolaos; Greek politician; b. 1919, Gravia; s. of John Makarezos and Catherine N. Tsonou; m. Chariclia G. Mattheou 1941; one s. one d.; ed. graduate schools, Evelpidon Military Coll., War Coll. and British and U.S. artillery schools.
Commissioned 41; mem. Army Gen. Staff and Prof. Evelpidon Mil. Coll. and Higher War Coll.; 61; Mil. Attaché, Greek Embassy, Bonn 61-63, Chief of Operations, 1st Army Corps, 66; Minister of Co-ordination 67-71; retd. from army 67; Second Deputy Prime Minister 71-73; arrested Oct. 74; sentenced to death for high treason and insurrection Aug. 75 (sentence commuted to life imprisonment).

Makarios III, Archbishop (Mihail Christodoulou Mouskos); Cypriot ecclesiastic and politician; b. 13 Aug. 1913, Panayia, Paphos; ed. Theological Coll. of Athens Univ. and School of Theology, Boston Univ.
Ordained Deacon Greek Orthodox Church 38; studied in Greece 38-43; mem. teaching staff Kykkos Abbey 43-46; ordained Priest 46; studied in U.S.A. supported by World Council of Churches Fellowship 46-48; Bishop of Kition 48-50; Archbishop of Cyprus 50-; Cypriot national leader identified with *Enosis* (Union with Greece) movement; has travelled abroad to promote interest and support for *Enosis*; led negotiations with Sir John Harding, Gov. of Cyprus 55-56; deported to the Seychelles 56; released Mar. 57; in Athens until return to Cyprus March 59; Cyprus Transitional Cttee., March 59, President-Elect 59-60; Pres. of Cyprus 60-July 74, Dec. 74-, (re-elected 68, 73); Rep. of Cyprus to Commonwealth Prime Minister's Confs. 61, 62, 66, 69, 71; addressed UN Gen. Assembly 70; numerous official visits; Hon. Dr. of Divinity (Boston and Athens Univs.), Hon. LL.D. (Kerala, Boston, Salonica and Bogotá Univs.); numerous Greek and other decorations.
Presidential Palace, Nicosia, Cyprus.

Makarova, Natalia; ballerina; b. 1940, Leningrad, U.S.S.R.; m. Edward Karkar 1976; ed. Vagonova Ballet School, Leningrad.
Member, Kirov Ballet 59-70; sought political asylum, London 70; Principal Dancer, American Ballet Theatre Oct. 70-; Guest Artist, Royal Ballet 72; Honoured Artist of R.S.F.S.R.; best known for performance of *Giselle*.
American Ballet Theatre, 888 Seventh Avenue, New York, N.Y. 10019, U.S.A.

Makarova, Tamara Fyodorovna; Soviet film actress; b. 13 Aug. 1907, Leningrad; m.; one s.; ed. Leningrad Inst. of Scenic Arts.
Dozent at the Institute of Cinematography 44-; People's Artist of the U.S.S.R.; State prizewinner 41, 47; awarded Order Badge of Honour.
Principal roles: Dr. Okhrimenko (*Seven Brave People* 35), Natasha Solovyova (*Komsomolsk* 37), collective farmer Shumilina (*The Teacher* 39), Koshevaya (*The Young Guard* 48), Dr. Kazakova (*The Country Doctor* 52), *Memory of the Heart* 58, *Men and Beasts* 62, *The Journalist* 67, *To Love People* 73, *Mothers and Daughters* 74.
Moscow 121248, Kutesovski proezd, 2/1 k.v. 228, U.S.S.R.

Makasa, Kapasa; Zambian politician; b. 29 Jan. 1922, Musanya; ed. Lubwa Mission and Oxford Univ.
Church Elder, Church of Scotland (now United Church of Zambia), Lubwa 47; Chair. Chinsali Branch, African Nat. Congress 50-52; Pres. Northern Prov., ANC (N. Rhodesia) 53-59; Pres. Luapula Prov., Zambian ANC 60; mem. Parl. for Chinsali North 63-; Parl. Sec. Ministry of Agriculture 63; Resident Minister for Northern Prov. 64-66; Minister of State, Ministry of Foreign Affairs 67; Minister of North Western Prov. 68; Amb. to Ethiopia March-Dec. 69; Minister of

Luapula Prov. 70-72; High Commr. to Tanzania 72-75, to Kenya (also accred. to Uganda) 75-.
Zambian High Commission, International Life House, City Hall Way, P.O. Box 48741, Nairobi, Kenya.

Makhmudov, Nasyr; Soviet politician; b. 1913; ed. C.P.S.U. Higher Party School.
Teacher and journalist 31-38; Soviet Army service 36-38; Party Official 38-48; Party and Local Govt. Official, Uzbekistan 50-56; First Sec. Kara-Kalpak Regional Cttee., Communist Party, Uzbekistan 56-63; First Sec. Syr-Darya Regional Cttee. C.P. Uzbekistan 63-71; Chair. People's Control Cttee. Uzbek S.S.R. 71-; mem. C.P.S.U. 40-; mem. Central Cttee. Communist Party of Uzbekistan; Deputy to U.S.S.R. Supreme Soviet 62-70.
Uzbek S.S.R. People's Control Cttee., Tashkent, U.S.S.R.

Maki, Fumihiko, B.ARCH., M.ARCH.; Japanese architect; b. 6 Sept. 1928, Tokyo; m. Misao 1960; two d.; ed. Univ. of Tokyo, Cranbrook School of Art, Mich. and Harvard Univ.
Associate Prof. Washington Univ. 56-62, Harvard Univ. 62-66; Lecturer, Dept. of Urban Engineering, Univ. of Tokyo 64-; Principal Partner, Maki and Associates (architectural firm) 64-; Visiting Lecturer and Critic to various univs. and insts. in Canada and U.S. 60-; awards include Gold Medal of Japan Inst. of Architects 64; major works include Steinberg Hall, Washington Univ. 60, Toyoda Memorial Hall, Nagoya Univ. 60, Lecture Hall, Chiba Univ. 64, and Rissho Univ. Campus 66-; art award from Mainichi Press 69.
Leisure interests: reading, chess.
Publs. *Investigations in Collective Form* 64, *Movement Systems in the City* 65, *Metabolism* 60, *Structure in Art and Science* (contrib.) 65.
16-22, 5-chome Higashi-Gotanda, Shinagawa-ku, Tokyo, Japan.

Makita, Hisao, B.A.; Japanese industrialist; b. 13 Dec. 1909, Saga Pref.; s. of Nobuhira and Toshiko Otani; m. Hideko Ohchi 1944; three s. one d.; ed. Tokyo Univ. of Commerce.
Joined Nippon Kokan K.K. 34, Dir. 57, Man. Dir. 65, Senior Man. Dir. 67, Exec. Vice-Pres. 68, Pres. 71-; Pres. Kokan Mining Co. (subsidiary of Nippon Kokan) Nov. 61-June 66; Dir. Int. Iron and Steel Inst.; Exec. Dir. and Industrial Relations Conf. Chair., The Japan Iron and Steel Fed.; Vice-Chair. The Japan Iron and Steel Exporters Asscn.; Man. Dir. The Shipbuilders' Asscn. of Japan; Dir. Fed. of Econ. Orgs. (Keidanren); Trustee, Japan Cttee. for Econ. Devt. (Keizai Doyukai); Exec. Dir. Japan Fed. of Employers' Asscns.
Leisure interests: fishing, golf.
Nippon Kokan K.K., 1-1-Z, Marunouchi, Chiyodaku, Tokyo; Home: 2-4-1, Omiya, Suginami-ku, Tokyo 166, Japan.
Telephone: 03-311-0298.

Makki, Dr. Hassan; Yemeni politician; ed. Univs. of Bologna and Rome
Adviser, Ministry of Econ. 60-62, Deputy Minister 62, Minister 63-64; Minister of Foreign Affairs April-Sept. 66, 67-68; Amb. to Italy 68-70, to Fed. Repub. of Germany 70-72; Deputy Prime Minister 72-74; Prime Minister March-June 74; Deputy Prime Minister for Econ. Affairs June-Oct. 74; Perm. Rep. to UN Oct. 74-, Amb. to U.S.A. (also accred. to Canada) 75-.
Permanent Mission of Yemen Arab Republic to United Nations, 211 East 43rd Street, Room 2402, New York, N.Y. 10017, U.S.A.

Makowski, Zbigniew; Polish painter; b. 31 Jan. 1930, Warsaw; ed. Warsaw Acad. of Fine Arts.
Professor, State Higher School of Fine Arts, Poznań 56-57; works include: *Wnętrze* (The Interior), *Incipit mundus, Przechadzka z Wergiliuszem* (A Walk with

Virgil), *Kompozycja, Inanna w kraju ornamentów* (Inanna in the Country of Ornaments); also poetry; one-man exhbns.: Zachęta Museum, Warsaw 66; Galérie Alice Pauli, Lausanne 67; Galleria de Foscherari, Bologna 67, Marlborough Fine Arts, London, 68.
Publs. articles in *Polska, Miesięcznik Literacki, Poezja.*
Ul. Mokotowska 51/53 m. 9, 00-542 Warsaw, Poland.

Maksaryov, Yury Yevgenyevich; Soviet politician; b. 10 Aug. 1903; ed. Leningrad Inst. of Technology.
Alternative mem. Cen. Cttee. C.P.S.U. 52-61; Chair. State Cttee. for Science and Technology, Council of Ministers 57-60; Chair. State Cttee. for Inventions and Discoveries 61-; State Prize; Hero of Socialist Labour 43.
State Committee for Inventions and Discoveries, 2/6 Maly Cherkassky Pereulok, Moscow, U.S.S.R.

Maksymowicz, Stanisław; Polish diplomatist and politician; b. 12 March 1913, Tarnopol; ed. Jan Kazimierz Univ., Lwów, Handelshochschule, St. Gallen and Freiburg Univ.
Ministry of Navigation and Foreign Trade 45-46; Attaché, later Commercial Counsellor, Polish Embassy, Paris 46-50; Chief Dir. Varimex (Foreign Trade Enterprise) 50-57; Head of a Dept., Ministry of Foreign Trade 57-61; Commercial Counsellor, Polish Embassy, Vienna 61-62; Gen. Sec., Polish Chamber of Foreign Trade 62-71; Commercial Counsellor, Polish Embassy, Teheran 70-72; Commercial Attaché, Polish Embassy, Kuwait 72-.
Commercial Attaché's Office, Third Ring Road, Block No. 4, P.O. Box SAFAT 5066, Kuwait.
Telephone: 51-03-55 (Office); 51-16-66 (Home).

Maktum, H.H. Sheikh Rashid bin Said Al-; Ruler of Dubai; b. 1914; ed. privately.
Succeeded his father, Said bin Maktum, as 4th Sheikh 58; Vice-Pres. United Arab Emirates (UAE) Dec. 71-.
Royal Palace, Dubai.

Malabu, Alhaji Bello; Nigerian politician and diplomatist; b. 12 May 1913; ed. Yola Middle School and Katsina Coll.
Teacher Yola Middle School 33-48, Headmaster 48-49; Asst. Lecturer, School of Oriental and African Studies, London 49-51; Native Schools Man. 51-56; mem. Nigerian House of Reps. 51-54; mem. Nigerian Ports Authority 54-57, N. Nigerian Regional Legislature 51-60, Nigerian Senate, April-Sept. 60; Ambassador to Cameroon Repub. 60-70; Amb. to Saudi Arabia (also accred. to Jordan and Kuwait) 70-.
Embassy of Nigeria, B.P. 655, Jeddah, Saudi Arabia.

Malagodi, Giovanni Francesco, DR.IUR.; Italian politician; b. 12 Oct. 1904; ed. Rome Univ.
Joint Gen. Manager Banca Commerciale Italiana 33, Gen. Manager 47; Gen. Manager Banque Française et Italienne pour l'Amérique du Sud 37; Econ. and Financial Adviser, Ministry of Foreign Affairs 47; Chair. O.E.E.C. Manpower Cttee. 50; Deputy for Milan 53- (re-elected 58, 63, 68, 72); Sec.-Gen. Partito Liberale Italiano 54-72, Chair. July 72-; Minister of Treasury 72-73; Vice-Chair. Liberal Int. 56-58, 66, Chair. 58-66, Hon. Chair. 73-; Commdr. Ordine al Merito della Repubblica Italiana; Liberal.
Publs. *Le Ideologie Politiche* 27, *Rapporto sull'Emigrazione* 52, *Massa non Massa* 63, *Liberalismo in Commino* 65, *Sarnano-Libertà Nuova* 67.
Corso Venezia 40, Milan; Via Frattina 89, Rome, Italy.

Malamud Bernard, B.A., M.A.; American author; b. April 1914, Brooklyn, N.Y.; s. of Max and Bertha Malamud; m. Ann de Chiara 1945; one s. one d.; ed. New York City Coll. and Columbia Univ.
Evening High School teacher, Brooklyn and Harlem 40-49; English Dept., Oregon State Coll. 49-61, Assoc. Prof. 59-; mem. Literature Div. Bennington Coll. 61-; Visiting Lecturer Harvard Univ. 66-68; mem. Nat. Inst. of Arts and Letters 64; mem. American Acad. of

Arts and Sciences 67; *Partisan Review* Fiction Fellowship 56, Rosenthal Award (Nat. Inst. of Arts and Letters) and Daroff Memorial Award for *The Assistant* 58, Ford Foundation Grant in Humanities and Letters, Nat. Book Award for *The Magic Barrel* 59, Nat. Book Award for *The Fixer* 67, Pulitzer Prize for Fiction for *The Fixer* 67.

Publs. *The Natural* 52, *The Assistant* 57, *A New Life* 61, *The Fixer* 66, *Pictures of Fidelman* 69, *The Tenants* 72 (novels); *The Magic Barrel* 57, *Idiots First* 63, *Rembrandt's Hat* 73 (short stories); numerous short stories have appeared in *The Atlantic, Esquire, Partisan Review, The New Yorker, Harper's Magazine*, etc.

Leisure interests: art galleries, reading, travel.

Bennington College, Bennington, Vt. 05201, U.S.A.

Malatesta, Lamberto, PH.D.; Italian chemist; b. 20 June 1912, Milan; *s.* of Dr. Giuseppe Malatesta and Clara Tombolan Fava; *m.* Rachele Pizzotti 1947; one *s.* two *d.*; ed. Milan Univ.

Assistant to the Chair of Industrial Chem., Milan Univ. 37, Reader 40, Lecturer 42, Chair. Prof. of Analytical Chem. 48-51, of Gen. and Inorganic Chem. 51-, Dir. Istituto di Chimica Generale 51-; Dir. of a Centre of Consiglio Nazionale delle Ricerche 70-; Pres. Società Chimica Italiana 71-; Pres. of Div. of Inorganic Chem., IUPAC 75-77; Prize of the Pres. of Italian Repub. 63; Gold Medal for Educ., Culture and Art 74; Hon. Fellow, Chemical Soc. (London).

Leisure interests: skiing, playing bridge.

Publs.: *General Chemistry* (in Italian) 65, *Inorganic Chemistry* (in Italian) 68; co-author: *Isocyanide Compounds of Metals* (in English) 68, *Zerovalent Compounds of Metals* (in English) 74; about 100 original papers in scientific journals.

Via Carpaccio 2, 20133 Milano, Italy.

Telephone: 236-0350.

Malaud, Philippe, L. EN D.; French politician and diplomatist; b. 2 Oct. 1925, Paris; *s.* of Jaques Malaud and Odette (née Desruol du Tronçay); *m.* Chantal de Gorguette d'Argoeuves 1951; one *d.*; ed. Lycée Lamartine, Mâcon, Lycée Janson-de-Sailly, Paris Univ., Ecole Libre des Sciences Politiques.

Joined cen. admin. of Foreign Office 47; Embassy Attaché, Warsaw 49; 2nd Sec., Cairo 52; studied Ecole Nationale d'Administration 54-56; Personnel Dept. Foreign Office 57; Deputy Chief 58-61, then Chief of Cabinet of Foreign Ministry under Couve de Murville 61-67; Dir. Cabinet A. Bettencourt, Sec. of State for Foreign Affairs 67-68; Ind. Repub. Deputy for Saône-et-Loire 68, 73; Sec. of State for the Civil Service and Information 68-73; Minister of Information 73, of Civil Service 73-74; Mayor of Dompierre-les-Ormes 65-; Gen. Councillor for Canton of Matour Oct. 67-; Pres. of Gen. Council of Saône-et-Loire March 70-; Chevalier, Légion d'Honneur, Ordre du Mérite; Commdr. American Legion.

Leisure interests: tennis, skiing.

39 quai de Grenelle, 75015 Paris; and 71970 Dompierre-les-Ormes, France.

Malaviya, Keshava Deva, M.P., M.SC.; Indian politician; b. 11 June 1903; ed. Allahabad Univ. and Harcourt Butler Technological Inst., Kanpur.

Joined Congress Movement 21; served various sentences as political prisoner; former Gen. Sec. Uttar Pradesh Provincial Congress Cttee.; actively participated in "Quit India" Movement; Parl. Sec. to Minister for Industries and Development, U.P. Govt. 46; Minister for Industries and Development, U.P. 47-51; Parl. Sec. to Fed. Minister of Education 52; Deputy Fed. Minister of Natural Resources and Education 52-56; Fed. Minister of Natural Resources 56-57; Minister of State for Mines and Oil 57-62; Cabt. Minister Mines and Fuel 62-63; Minister of Steel and Mines Jan.-Oct. 74, of Petroleum and Chemicals 74-75, of Petroleum Dec. 75-;

Pres. Indian Asscn. for Afro-Asian Solidarity, New Delhi 65; mem. presidential Cttee. All-India Peace Council 66; mem. Exec. Cttee. Afro-Asian Peoples Solidarity Org. (Cairo); Chair. Heavy Eng. Corpn. Ranchi, Bihar 68.

Ministry of Petroleum, Shastri Bhavan, Dr. Rajendra Prasad Road, New Delhi 110001, India.

Malavolta, Euripedes, D.SC.; Brazilian agricultural biochemist; b. 13 Aug. 1926, Araraquara, São Paulo; *s.* of Antonio Malavolta and Lucia Canassa Malavolta; *m.* Leila M. B. Malavolta 1953; two *s.* three *d.*; ed. E.S.A. Luiz de Queiroz (Universidade do São Paulo) and Univ. of California (Berkeley), U.S.A.

Instructor in Agricultural Chemistry, Univ. of São Paulo 49, Private Docent 51, Prof. of Agricultural Biochemistry 58-; Research Asscn. Univ. of Calif. 52-53, Visiting Prof. 59-60; Vice-Dean, E.S.A. Luiz de Queiroz, Univ. of São Paulo 66-67, Dean 67, now Dean Inst. of Physics and Chemistry (São Carlos); mem. Brazilian Acad. of Sciences, Int. Cttee. of Plant Analysis and Fertilizer Problems.

Leisure interests: reading, playing tennis.

Publs. *Elements of Agricultural Chemistry* 54, *Manual of Agricultural Chemistry* 59, 67, *On the Mineral Nutrition of Some Tropical Crops* 62, 64, 67.

Universidade de São Paulo, Cidade Universitária, Armando de Salles Oliveira, Caixa Postal 8191, São Paulo, Brazil.

Malaysia, The Yang di Pertuan Agung of (Supreme Head of State), (*see* Kelantan, H.R.H. the Sultan of).

Malcolm, Dugald, C.M.G., C.V.O., T.D.; British diplomatist; b. 22 Dec. 1917, London; *s.* of Major-Gen. Sir Neill Malcolm, K.C.B., D.S.O.; *m.* Mrs. Peter Atkinson Clark 1957; one step *d.* one *d.*; ed. Eton and New Coll., Oxford.

Armed Forces 39-45; Foreign Service 45-; served Lima, Bonn, Seoul and London; Vice-Marshal of Diplomatic Corps 57-65; Amb. to Luxembourg 66-70, to Panama 70-74, to the Vatican 75-; mem. Queen's Bodyguard for Scotland (Royal Company of Archers).

Embassy of the United Kingdom, Via Condotti 91, 00187 Rome, Italy.

Malcolm, George (John), C.B.E., M.A., B.MUS.; British harpsichordist and conductor; b. 28 Feb. 1917, London; *s.* of George Hope Malcolm and Johanna Malcolm; ed. Wimbledon Coll., Balliol Coll., Oxford, and Royal Coll. of Music.

Originally trained as concert pianist; Master of Music, Westminster Cathedral 47-59, trained Boys' Choir for which Benjamin Britten wrote *Missa Brevis* Op. 63; harpsichordist and conductor making frequent tours especially in Europe; Artistic Dir., Philomusica of London 62-66; Cobbett Gold Medal, Worshipful Company of Musicians 60, Papal Knight, Order of St. Gregory the Great 70; Fellow Royal Coll. of Music 74; Hon. mem. Royal Acad. of Music, Hon. Fellow Balliol Coll., Oxford.

38 Cheyne Walk, London, S.W.3, England.

Telephone: 01-352-5381.

Malcolm, Wilbur George; American business executive; b. 22 June 1902; ed. Univ. of Maryland.

Instructor Univ. of Maryland 22-24; Senior Bacteriologist, Anti-Toxin and Vaccine Labs., Forest Hill, Mass. 30-34; Vice-Pres. and Gen. Man. Lederle Labs. 46-55; Chair. and Chief Exec. Officer American Cyanamid Co. until 66; mem. Int. Coll. of Surgeons, Soc. American Bacteriologists, New York Acad. of Science; Dir. Manufacturing Chemists' Asscn.

125 River Road, Grand View-on-Hudson, N.Y., U.S.A.

Małcużyński, Karol; Polish journalist; b. 20 June 1922, Warsaw; *s.* of Witold Małcużyński and Maria Małcużyńska; *m.* Irena Szymkiewicz; one *s.* one *d.*; ed. in Warsaw and Paris.

Began career as corresp. *Robotnik* daily newspaper,

Nuremberg 45; mem. editorial staff and writer, *Trybuna Ludu*, Warsaw 48-; Press Adviser, Embassy in London 57-60; Pres. ZAIKS Asscn. of Authors; mem. Admin. Council, CISAC; State Prize, 2nd Class 50, 3rd Class 53, Gold Cross of Merit 54, Medal of 10th Anniversary of People's Poland 55, Gold Award for the Rebuilding of Warsaw 55.
Publs. *Norymberga-Niemcy 1945, Oskarżeni nie przyznają się do winy* (The Accused Plead Not Guilty), *Szkice warszawskie* (Warsaw Studies) 55.
Ul. Wiejska 14 m. 9, 00-490 Warsaw, Poland.

Małcużyński, Witold; Polish pianist; b. 10 Aug. 1914, Warsaw; *m.* Colette Gaveau 1939; two *d.*; ed. Warsaw Conservatoire, Warsaw Univ.
International debut, Paris 40, American debut Carnegie Hall 42, London 45; tours since 1949 in Europe, U.S.S.R., North and South America, New Zealand, Australia, Near and Far East; mem. of jury in Int. contests; Officer's Cross, Order of Polonia Restituta 70.
Chernex sur Montreaux, Switzerland.

Maldybayev, Abdylas; Soviet composer; b. 7 July 1906, Karabulak, Kemin district, Kirghiz S.S.R.; ed. Frunze Teachers' Training Inst. and Moscow Conservatoire.
People's Artist of the U.S.S.R.; awarded Order of Lenin, three Orders of Red Banner of Labour, Badge of Honour, medal for work in Second World War, Medal for Distinguished Labour.
Works include the first Kirghiz operas: *Aichurek* 39, *On the Banks of the Issyk Kul* 50; with Vlasov and Fere he composed the music for the anthem of the Kirghiz S.S.R.; *Manas* (opera) 44; choral symphonies: *The Party—Our Happiness* 54, *Glory to the Party, Toktogul* (Opera); over 300 songs, romances and choral pieces.
Kirghiz S.S.R. Union of Composers, Frunze, U.S.S.R.

Malecela, John William Samuel; Tanzanian diplomatist and politician; b. 1934; ed. Bombay Univ. and Cambridge Univ.
Administrative Officer, Civil Service 60-61; Consul in U.S.A. and Third Sec. to the UN 62; Regional Commr., Mwanza Region 63; Perm. Rep. to the UN 64-68; Amb. to Ethiopia 68; East African Minister for Communications, Research and Social Services, East African Community 69-72; Minister of Foreign Affairs 72-75, of Agriculture Nov. 75-; Order of Merit of First Degree (Egypt); First Order of Independence (Equatorial Guinea).
Ministry of Agriculture, Dar es Salaam, Tanzania.

Malecki, Ignacy, D.ENG.; Polish physicist; b. 18 Nov. 1912, Pakiewna; *s.* of Jan and Emilia Malecki; *m.* Maria Gąssowska 1945; one *d.*
Professor, Technical Univ., Gdańsk 45-50, Warsaw 50-; mem. Polish Acad. of Sciences 53-; Dir. Inst. of Basic Technical Problems, Polish Acad. of Sciences 53-62; Chair. Council for Technical Affairs 57-60; Vice-Pres. Int. Council of Scientific Unions (ICSU) 63-70; Chair. Polish Nat. Pugwash Cttee. 64-; Vice-Chair. Polish Cttee. for UNESCO Affairs; Dir. Dept. of Science and Promotion of Basic Sciences, UNESCO 69-72; Prof. Tech. Univ. Warsaw 73-; Dir. Inst. of Fundamental Technical Research; mem. Presidium of Polish Acad. of Science 74-; mem. Acoustic Asscn. of S. America; Pres. Int. Comm. on Acoustics; mem. Polish United Workers' Party 48-; Dr. h.c. (Budapest); Gold Cross of Merit 46, 54; Officer's and Commdr.'s Cross of Polonia Restituta 57, 64; State Prize 66; Order of Banner of Labour 2nd Class 69; Cyril and Metody Order (Bulgaria) 70; Medal of French Acoustic Asscn. 71; Medal of 30th Anniversary of People's Poland 74.
Leisure interest: gardening.
Publs. *Akustyka radiowa i filmowa* (Radio and Film Acoustics) 50, *Naukowe podstawy zastosowania metod ultradźwiekowych w górnictwie i geologii* (Scientific Bases

of Applying Ultrasonic Methods in Mining and Geology) 56, *Problemy koordynacji badań naukowych* (Co-ordination of Scientific Researches) 60, *Teoria fal i układów akustycznych* (Theory of Acoustic Waves and Systems), *Podstawy teoretyczne akustyki kwantowej* Theoretical Basis of the Quantum Acoustic) 72, etc.
Polska Akademia Nauk, Pałac Kultury i Nauki, Warsaw; Home: Kaliska 17, Warsaw 02-316, Poland.
Telephone: 22-15-01 (Home).

Malek, Gustavo, PH.D.; Argentine politician and chemical engineer; b. 29 March 1929, Buenos Aires; *s.* of Agustín and Ester Szana de Malek; *m.* Esther Mercedes Perramón 1956; three *s.* one *d.*; ed. Universidad Nacional del Sur.
Lecturer in chemical and industrial engineering, Universidad Nacional del Sur 50-60; Dir. Laboratorio de la Curtiembre "La Normandie", S.A.I.C. 55-58; Head of Research Lanera San Blas, S.A.I.C. 58-68; Asst. Prof. of Industrial Engineering, Universidad Nacional del Sur 61-62, Prof. of Industrial Engineering and Head, Laboratorio de Lanas (Wool Research Laboratory) 63-69; served on numerous cttees. of Universidad Nacional del Sur; Minister of Educ. and Culture, Govt. of Argentina 71-73; mem. Argentine Chem. Soc., Argentine Asscn. of Textile Chemists and many other nat. and foreign socs. in field of textile chemistry; various prizes and decorations.
Leisure interest: rugby.
Publs. many articles on chemistry in the textile industry.
c/o Ministerio de Cultura y Educación, Buenos Aires, Argentina.

Málek, Ivan, M.D., DR.SC.; Czechoslovak microbiologist; b. 28 Sept. 1909, Zábřeh, Czechoslovakia; *s.* of Antonín Málek and Anežka Málková; *m.* 1st Jindra Málková 1935 (died 1954), 2nd Doubravka Málková 1956; two *s.* six *d.*
Professor of Medical Microbiology, Charles Univ.; Academician 52, and mem. of Presidium, Czechoslovak Acad. of Sciences 65-70, Vice-Pres. 60-65; Dir. Inst. of Microbiology, Czechoslovak Acad. of Sciences 62-70; Corresp. mem. German Acad. of Sciences, mem. Perm. Cttee. of Pugwash 64-, mem. of Bureau and Hon. Sec. World Fed. of Scientific Workers 52-; Chief Editor *Scientific World* 64-; mem. Swedish Royal Technical Acad. 65-; mem. Leopoldina-Halle/Saale German Acad. of Research in Natural Sciences 62-; Vice-Pres. World Acad. of Art and Sciences; Chair. Socialist Acad. Czechoslovakia 65-69; Vice-Pres. Int. Union of Biological Sciences 67-; mem. Central Cttee. Communist Party of Czechoslovakia 62-69; mem. Agricultural Comm. 63-66; Dep. to Nat. Assembly 60-69; Dep. to House of the People, Fed. Assembly 69-; Gold Plaque of Czechoslovak Acad. of Sciences for Services to Science and Mankind 69; mem. Bulgarian Acad. of Sciences 66-, Science Advisory Cttee. IAEA 67-, New York Acad. of Sciences, Advisory Cttee. Int. Programmes, UNESCO Int. Advisory Cttee. on Natural Resources Research 69-; Vice-Pres. IBP 69-; Laureate of the State Prize 51, 59, winner of the Medal of J. E. Purkyně 56; awarded the Order of Labour 58, Lenin Peace Prize 67; played an important role in the reform of medical studies as well as research, studies in the organization of the nationalized pharmaceutical industry, and established a number of biological insts.
Leisure interests: music, arts, gardening, sports.
Publs. *Biology in the Future* 61 (German and Russian edns. 63), *Opened Problems of Science in Czechoslovakia* 67, *Theoretical and Methodological Basis of Continuous Culture of Micro-organisms* (editor and co-author) 64 (English edn. 66, Russian edn. 68); contributed to *Conditions of World Order* 68, *Nobel Symposium 14* 70.
Na Dolinách 18, Prague 4, Czechoslovakia.
Telephone: Prague 437092.

Malek, Reda; Algerian diplomatist; b. 1931, Batna; ed. in Paris.
Editor-in-Chief *El-Moudjahid* (weekly newspaper of F.L.N.); Amb. to Yugoslavia 63-65, to France 65-70, to U.S.S.R. 70-.
Algerian Embassy, Krapivinsky per. 1-A, Moscow, U.S.S.R.

Malekou, Paul, L. EN D.; Gabonese politician; b. 17 Nov. 1938, Fougamou; five c.; ed. Univs. of Lille and Paris.
Inst. des Hautes Etudes d'Outre-Mer, and admin. course, Strasbourg.
Head, Interregional Service for Labour, Centre-Gabon, Port-Gentil 63-64; Minister of Labour and Social Affairs 64-65, of Nat. Educ., Youth and Sports, subsequently of Co-ordination in charge of Nat. Educ. 65-68; Minister Del. at the Presidency, in charge of Co-ordination and Foreign Affairs Jan.-July 68; Minister of Public Works and Transport 68-69, of Public Works and charged with Special Functions at the Presidency 69-70, of Public Works, Housing and Urbanism 70; Minister of State in charge of Public Works, Housing and Urbanism 70-74, concurrently of Land Registry 72-74; Dir.-Gen. Agence pour la Securité de la Navigation Aérienne en Afrique et a Madagascar 74-; Commdr. Etoile Equatoriale, Palmes Acad., Ordre Nat. Guinéen, Commdr. Légion d'Honneur, Grand Officier de l'Ordre Nat. du Lion (Senegal) and numerous other decorations.
Leisure interests: hunting, fishing, flying.
32 Avenue Jean-Jaurès, Libreville, Gabon.
Telephone: 205-11.

Malenkov, Georgi Maximilianovich; Soviet politician; b. 8 Jan. 1903; ed. Moscow Higher Technical Coll.
Political Commissar Eastern and Turkestan Districts during Revolution; fmr. mem. Communist Party; fmr. Sec. Bolshevik Students' Organization; worked Central Cttee. Communist Party 25-30, Organizing Sec. Moscow Section of Party 30, later Head Personnel Dept. of Central Cttee., and mem. of Secretariat; dep. of the Supreme Soviet 37-57; mem. Cttee. for State Defence 41; mem. Cttee. for Economic Rehabilitation of Liberated Districts; Deputy Chair. Council of Ministers 46-53, Chair. 53-55; Deputy Chair. Council of Ministers and Minister of Power Stations 55-57; mem. former Politburo of Communist Party 46-53; mem. Presidium of Central Cttee. 53-57; Manager of Ust-Kamenogorsk Power Station 57-63; retired 63; awarded title Hero of Socialist Labour 43, Hammer and Sickle Gold Medal, Order of Lenin (twice).
c/o Ministry of Social Security of R.S.F.S.R., 14 Shabolovka, Moscow, U.S.S.R.

Malerba, Luigi; Italian author and scriptwriter; b. 11 Nov. 1927, Berceto (Parma); s. of Pietro and Maria Olari; m. Anna Lapenna 1962; two s.; ed. Liceo Classico Romagnosi di Parma, and Faculty of Law, Univ. of Parma.
Director of review *Sequenze* 48-51; Advertising Man. of review *Discoteca* 56-60, Editor 60-65; Premio Selezione Campiello for *Il Serpente* 66; Golden Nymph Award for best television film, Int. Television Festival, Monte Carlo for *Ai poeti non si spara*; Premio Sila for *Salto Mortale* 69; Prix Médicis (France) for best non-French novel for *Salto Mortale* 70.
Leisure interests: agriculture and protection of nature.
Publs. *La scoperta dell' alfabeto* 63, *Il Serpente* 66, *Salto mortale* 68; *Millemosche senza cavallo, Millemosche mercenario, Millemosche fuoco e fiamme, Millemosche innamorato, Millemosche e il leone Millemosche e la fine del mondo, Millemosche alla ventura,* (all with Tonino Guerra, illustrations by Adriano Zannino) 69-71, *Il Protagonista* 73, *Le rose imperiali* 74.
Via Tor Millina 31, Rome, Italy.
Telephone: 6568391.

Maleta, Alfred, LL.D.; Austrian politician; b. 15 Jan. 1906, Mödling; s. of Otto Maleta and N. Pagler; m. Gerda Scheid 1946; ed. High School and Univ. of Graz.
First Sec. Austrian Chamber of Workers and Employees, and Fed. of Trade Unions of Upper Austria 34-38; arrested by Gestapo 38 and spent three years in concentration camps; Mil. service till 45; Head Fed. of Workers and Employees of Upper Austria 45; mem. Nat. Assembly 45; Sec. Gen. Austrian People's Party (Ö.V.P.) 51-60, Deputy Fed. Chair 60; Chair. Club of Ö.V.P. mems. of Nat. Assembly 53-62; Fed. Chair. Austrian Fed. of Workers and Employees 60; Deputy Chair. Nouvelles Equipes Internationales of Fed. of Christian Democratic Parties in Europe 55-60; 3rd Pres. of Nat. Assembly 61-62, Pres. 62-70.
Publs. various publications and newspaper articles.
National Assembly, Vienna I; Laudongasse 16, Vienna VIII, Austria.

Malfatti, Franco Maria; Italian politician; b. 13 June 1927, Rome.
National Del. of Youth Movt. of Christian Democratic Party until 52; worked in headquarters of Christian Democratic Party 52-64; mem. Chamber of Deputies 58-; Under-Sec. of State for Foreign Affairs June-Dec. 68; Minister of State Participations Dec. 68-Aug. 69; Minister for Posts and Telecommunications Aug. 69-June 70, of Educ. July 73-; fmr. mem. of numerous parl. cttees. on finance, educ., home and foreign affairs, etc.; Pres. of combined Comm. of European Communities July 70-March 72.
Camera dei Deputati, Rome, Italy.

Malfatti di Montetretto, Baron Francesco; Italian diplomatist; b. 13 Jan. 1920, Vienna; s. of Giuseppe M. di M. and Felicita Newickluf; m. Adonella Brenciaglia 1945; two s.; ed. Lycée Janson-de-Sailly, Paris, and Univ. of Rome.
Army Officer 39-43; Resistance Movement 43-45; on mission to London 45; Sec. to Deputy Prime Minister 46; Vice-Chef de Cabinet Ministry of Foreign Affairs 46; Sec. Italian Mission for Econ. Negotiations with U.S. 47; entered Diplomatic Service 47; Consul in Geneva 48; Consul-Gen., Munich 49, also on mission to Berlin 49; then Ministry of Foreign Affairs posts; Counsellor, Italian Embassy, Paris 56, Minister-Counsellor 58-63; later Chef de Cabinet, Ministry of Foreign Affairs; Diplomatic Counsellor to Pres. of Repub. 65-69; Amb. to France 69-; military awards for bravery in the war and in the Resistance.
Leisure interests: painting, history, tennis.
Ambassade d'Italie, 47 rue de Varenne, Paris 7e, France.
Telephone: 548-38-90.

Malherbe, Ernst G., M.A., PH.D.; South African educationist; b. 8 Nov. 1895, Luckhoff, Orange Free State; s. of E. G. Malherbe and Ella Rabie; m. Janie Nel 1922; three s. one d.; ed. Stellenbosch and Columbia Univs.
Studied Oxford, The Hague, Amsterdam, Germany; Fellow, Teachers' Coll., Columbia Univ. 23-24; South African rep. British Asscn. Centenary Meeting, London 31; fmrly. teacher Cape Town Training Coll.; Lecturer in Educational Psychology, Stellenbosch Univ.; Senior Lecturer in Education, Cape Town Univ.; Chief Investigator, Education Section, Carnegie Poor White Research Comm. 28-32; mem. Govt. Comm. to Investigate Native Education in South Africa 35; Dir. Nat. Bureau of Educational and Social Research for South Africa 29-39; Dir. of Census and Statistics for Union 39-45; Lt.-Col. Dir. Army Educ. Services 40-45; Dir Military Intelligence Union Defence Forces 42-45; Principal and Vice-Chancellor Univ. of Natal 45-65; Pres. S. African Asscn. for the Advancement of Science 50-51; Pres. South African Inst. of Race Relations 66-68; Hon. M.A. (Sydney); Hon. LL.D. (Cambridge,

Queens, Melbourne, McGill, Cape Town, Natal, Rhodes, Witwatersrand, St. Andrews).
Leisure interests: swimming, golf, gardening.
Publs. *Education in South Africa 1652 to 1922* 25, *Education and the Poor White* 31, *Education in a Changing Empire* 32, *Educational Adaptations in a Changing Society* (Editor) 37, *Entrance Age of University Students in Relation to Success* 38, *Educational and Social Research in South Africa* 39, *The Bilingual School* 43, *Race Attitudes and Education* 46, *Our Universities and the Advancement of Science* 51, *Die Outonomie van ons Universiteite en Apartheid* 57, *Education for Leadership in Africa* 60, *Problems of School Medium in a Bilingual Country* 62, *The Need for Dialogue* 67, *Education and the Development of South Africa's Human Resources* 67, *The Nemesis of Docility* 68, *Bantu Manpower and Education* 69, *Differing Values* 73, *Education in South Africa 1923 to 1975* 75.
By-die-See, Salt Rock, 4391, Natal, South Africa.
Telephone: Umhlali 103.

Malietoa Tanumafili II, H.H., C.B.E.; Samoan politician; b. 4 Jan. 1913; ed. Wesley Coll., Auckland, New Zealand.
Adviser, Samoan Govt. 40; mem. New Zealand del. to UN 58; fmr. mem. Council of State; Joint Head of State of Western Samoa 61-63, Sole Head 63-.
Government House, Vailima, Apia, Western Samoa, South Pacific.

Malik, Abdul Mutaleb, M.D.; Pakistani doctor and politician; b. 1905; ed. Calcutta Univ., Santiniketan, Bengal and Vienna Univ.
Practised medicine in Calcutta; joined All-India Muslim League 36; former mem. Executive of All-India Trades Union Congress, Secretary of All-India Seafarers' Federation, Pres. Indian Quartermasters' Union and Indian Sailors' Union Calcutta; Pres. of All-Pakistan Trades Union Federation 47; former Minister of Agriculture, Co-operation, Forests, Fisheries and Labour, East Bengal; Minister in charge of Minorities Affairs 50-51; Minister of Labour and Works and Health 49-55; Chair. of Governing Body of ILO 53-54; Amb. to Switzerland 55-58, Chinese People's Republic 58-61, Philippines 61-65, High Commr. in Australia 65-67; Minister of Health, Labour and Family Planning 69-71; Gov. of E. Pakistan (now Bangladesh) 71; arrested Dec. 71, sentenced to life imprisonment Nov. 72, released Dec. 73.

Malik, Adam; Indonesian politician and diplomatist; b. 22 July 1917, Pematang Siantar, N. Sumatra; ed. Dutch Primary school and a religious school.
Chairman, Partai Indonesia in Pematang Siantar and Medan, N. Sumatra 34; founded *Antara* Press Bureau (later *Antara* News Agency), Java 37; mem. Exec. Board Gerindo Party 40-41; later mem. Persatuan Perdjoeangan (Struggle Front) (a movt. to maintain independence); a founder of Partai Rakjat (People's Party) 46; Exec. mem. Murba Party 48-64 (when party was banned); elected to House of Reps. 56, mem. Provisional Supreme Advisory Council 59; Amb. to U.S.S.R. and Poland 59-62; mem. Exec. Board *Antara* 62; Minister of Commerce 63-65; Minister-Co-ordinator for the Implementation of Guided Economy 65; Minister of Foreign Affairs March 66-; Pres. UN Gen. Assembly 71-72; rep. of Indonesia at various int. confs. and has led Indonesian del. to sessions of UN Gen. Assembly since 66.
Ministry of Foreign Affairs, Jalan Sisinganangara 73, Kebayoran Baru, Jakarta; Jalan Diponegoro 17, Jakarta, Indonesia.

Malik, Bidhubhusan, M.A., LL.D., Barrister-at-Law; Indian lawyer; b. 11 Jan. 1895, Cuttack, Orissa State; s. of Chandra-Sekhar and Urmila Malik (née Ghosh); m. Leelabati Mitra 1916 (died 1941); two s.
Advocate, Allahabad High Court 19; called to Bar,

Lincoln's Inn 23; mem. Judicial Cttee. Benares State 41-44; Special Counsel, Income Tax Dept. 43-44; Puisne Judge, High Court Allahabad 44-47, Chief Justice High Court of Uttar Pradesh, Allahabad Dec. 47-Jan. 55 (acting Gov. U.P. Mar.-April 49); Indian Rep. to Federation of Malaya Constitutional Comm. 56-57; Commr for Linguistic Minorities 57-62; Senior Advocate, Supreme Court of India; UN Constitutional Adviser for Congo 62; Constitutional Adviser, Kenya Conference, London 62; Adviser to Mauritius Govt. at Mauritius Conf. 65; Vice-Chancellor, Calcutta Univ. 62-68, mem. Calcutta Univ. Senate, Allahabad Univ. Exec. Council; Vice-Pres. Vishwa Hindu Dharm Sammelan; Pres. Ishwar Saran Degree Coll., Allahabad, Jagat Tarau Girls' Degree Coll., Allahabad Univ.; Dir. Swadeshi Cotton Mills, Kanpur.
Leisure interests: golf, reading, writing and gardening.
23 Muir Road, Allahabad, U.P., India.
Telephone: 2589.

Malik, Charles Habib, M.A., PH.D.; Lebanese philosopher, educationist and diplomatist; b. 1906, Btirram, Al-Koura; s. of Dr. Habib K. and Zareefi K. Malik; m. Eva Badr 1941; one s.; ed. American Tripoli Boys' High School, American Univ. of Beirut and Harvard and Freiburg Univs.
Instructor Maths. and Physics, American Univ., Beirut 27-29, Instructor in Philosophy 37-39, Adjunct Prof. 39-43, Assoc. Prof. 43-45, Head of Dept. 39-45, Dean of Graduate Studies and Prof. of Philosophy 55-60; Min. of Lebanon to U.S.A. 45-53, Ambassador 53-55; Minister to Cuba 46-55; mem. and Chair. Del. of Lebanon to UN, N.Y. 45-54, Chair. 56-58; Pres. 13th Session, UN Gen. Assembly 58-59; Chair. of various UN Cttees. and Sub-Cttees.; rep. of Lebanon on Economic and Social Council, Second-Eighth sessions, and Pres. of Council 48; rep. of Lebanon on Human Rights Comm. and Rapporteur of Comm. 47-51, Chair. of Comm. 51-52; mem. UN Security Council 53-54, sometime Pres.; Gov. for Lebanon, Int. Bank and Monetary Fund 47-52, Chair. Del. of Lebanon Conf. for Conclusion and Signing Peace Treaty with Japan, San Francisco 51; Minister of Foreign Affairs 56-58, of Nat. Education and Fine Arts Nov. 56-57; M.P. for Al-Koura 57-60; Grand First Magistrate of the Holy Orthodox Church; Pres. World Council of Christian Educ. 67-71; Vice-Pres. United Bible Societies 66-72; Fellow Inst. for Advanced Religious Studies at the Univ. of Notre Dame, Indiana 69; Hon. life mem. American Bible Soc.; mem. Société européenne de Culture; Fellow American Asscn. for Advancement of Science, American Geog. Soc.; mem. American Philos. Asscn., American Philos. Soc., American Acad. of Arts and Sciences, Acad. of Human Rights, etc.; founding mem. Lebanese Acad.; Gold Medal, Nat. Institute of Social Sciences, N.Y.; Hon. Rector, Univ. Dubuque 51; numerous hon. degrees; decorated by governments of Lebanon, Italy, Jordan, Syria, Iraq, Cuba, Iran, Brazil, Dominican Repub., Austria, Greece, Repub. of China.
Leisure interests: hiking, walking, spiritual exercises, discussion with friends.
Publs. *War and Peace* 50, *Problems of Asia* 51, *Problem of Coexistence* 55, *Christ and Crisis* 62, *Man in the Struggle for Peace* 63, *God and Man in Contemporary Christian Thought* 70, *God and Man in Contemporary Islamic Thought* 72; numerous other published works and articles.
American University of Beirut, Beirut, Lebanon; and Harvard Club, 27 West 44th St., New York, U.S.A.

Malik, Gunwantsingh Jaswantsingh, B.SC., M.A.; Indian diplomatist; b. 29 May 1921, Karachi; s. of late Shri Jaswant Singh Malik and Balwant Kaur (Bhagat) Malik; m. Gurkirat Kaur 1948; two s.
Royal Air Force 43; Indian Foreign Service 47-, served Brussels, Addis Ababa 48-50; Under-Sec. Ministry of

External Affairs 50-52; served Buenos Aires, Tokyo, Singapore 52-59; Special Officer, Frontier Areas, Ministry of External Affairs 59; Ministry of Commerce 60; Counsellor (Commercial) and Asst. Commr. Singapore 60-63; Dir. Ministry of Commerce 63-64; Joint-Sec. Ministry of External Affairs 64-65; Ambassador to Philippines 65-68; Amb. to Senegal, Ivory Coast and Upper Volta 68-70, concurrently High Commissioner to The Gambia 68-70; Amb. to Chile (also accred. to Peru, Ecuador and Colombia) 70-74, to Thailand Dec. 74-.
Leisure interests: photography and literature.
Embassy of India, 139 Pan Road, Bangkok, Thailand; and 21A Nizamuddin West, New Delhi, India.
Telephone: 619785 (India).

Malik, Yakov Alexandrovich; Soviet diplomatist; b. 6 Dec. 1906, Ostroverkhovka, Zmievka district, Kharkov region, Ukraine; ed. Kharkov Inst. of Economics.
Graduated from Moscow Inst. for Diplomatic and Consular Officials 37; Asst. Chief, Press Dept., Ministry of Foreign Affairs 37-39; Counsellor, Tokyo 39-42; Amb. to Japan 42-45; Political Adviser, Allied Council for Japan 46; Deputy Minister of Foreign Affairs 46-53; Permanent Rep. of U.S.S.R. to UN, concurrently U.S.S.R. Rep. on UN Security Council 49-52; Amb. to Great Britain 53-60; Deputy Minister of Foreign Affairs 60-; Perm. Rep. to UN, New York 67-; two Orders of Lenin, two Orders of Red Banner of Labour, Order of October Revolution and Medals.
Permanent Mission of U.S.S.R. to United Nations, 136 East 67th Street, New York, N.Y. 10021, U.S.A.

Malikyar, Abdullah; Afghan diplomatist; b. 1909, Kabul; s. of Abdul Ahmad and Alamtab Malikyar; m. Anisa A. Seraj 1949; four s. four d.; ed. Isteklal Coll., Kabul, and Franco-Persian Coll., Teheran.
Secretary and Gen. Dir., Prime Minister's Office 31-35; Head, Govt. Purchasing Office, Europe 36-40; Vice-Pres. Central Bank and Deputy Minister of Commerce 41-42; Gov. of Herat 42-47, 51-52; Minister of Communications 48-50; Pres. Hillmand Valley Authority Projects 53-62; Minister of Commerce 55-57, of Finance 57-June 64, Deputy Prime Minister 63-Feb. 64; Acting Prime Minister Feb.-June 64; Amb. to U.K. 64-67, to U.S.A. 67-, concurrently to Argentina, Brazil, Canada, Chile and Mexico; Sardar Ali Reshteen Decoration.
Leisure interests: reading, fishing, gardening, photography.
Embassy of Afghanistan, 2341 Wyoming Avenue, N.W., Washington, D.C., U.S.A.

Malinga, Norman Zombodze Maguga, B.A., MASTER INT. AFFAIRS; Swazi diplomatist; b. 17 Nov. 1938, Zombodze; s. of Joel Mashesha and Dora Malinga; m.; three c.; ed. Mphumulo Teacher Training Coll., Natal, Fordham Univ. and Columbia Univ., U.S.A.
School teacher 62-65; Librarian/Warden, Staff Training Inst., Swaziland 65-68; Asst. Establishment Officer, Staff Training Inst. 68; Asst. Sec., Dept. of Foreign Affairs 68-70; Swaziland Counsellor in East Africa 70-71; Dir. of Broadcasting and Information 71-72; Perm. Rep. to UN 72-.
Leisure interests: painting, soccer.
Permanent Mission of Swaziland to United Nations, 866 United Nations Plaza, Suite 420, New York, N.Y. 10017; 261 Overlook Road, New Rochelle, New York, N.Y. 10804, U.S.A.
Telephone: (914) 235-0204 (Home).

Malinschi, Vasile, DR.ECON.; Romanian economist; b. 1 May 1912; m. Nathalie Malinschi 1944; two d.; ed. Commercial and Industrial Acad., Bucharest and Law Coll., Bucharest.
Official Nat. Bank 38; Prof. of the Econ. Acad. 49-, Chancellor 49-52; Minister for Home Trade 49-54;

Vice-Pres. State Planning Cttee. 54-56; mem. Presidium of the Romanian Acad. 55-73; Gov. Nat. Bank of the Socialist Repub. of Romania 63-; Vice-Pres. Econs. Soc.; mem. Leading Cttee., Democratic Students' Front 37-40, Central Cttee., Romanian Communist Party 55-; mem. Nat. Comms. for UNESCO and FAO 60-68; mem. Acad. of Social and Political Science 70-, Int. Asscn. of Sociology and Int. Asscn. of Agricultural Econ.; Int. Asscn. of Economists; several orders and medals.
Publs. *Socialist Economy* 39, *The Land Reform* 47, *The Agrarian Problem* 58, *Agrarian Economy and Rural Sociology* 60, *Studies of Economy* 67, *Agrarian Essays* 68, *Land Rent* 70; joint author: *Romanian Industry* 64, *Economic Development of Romania* 65, *Land Reforms in the Developing Countries* 71; several other books and articles on economics and banking.
National Bank of the Socialist Republic of Romania, 25 Lipscani Street, Bucharest; and Strada Pictor Iscovescu 32, Bucharest, Romania.
Telephone: 33-63-88 (Home).

Mallabar, Sir John, Kt., F.C.A.; British shipbuilder and chartered accountant; b. 19 July 1900, Liverpool; s. of Herbert and Gertrude Mallabar; m. 1st Henrietta Goodwin-Norris, 2nd Annie Emily (Pat) widow of Richard Howard Ford; no c.; ed. Sunbury House School and King's Coll., London.
Founder and Senior Partner J. F. Mallabar & Co., Chartered Accountants, 29-; Chair. Harland & Wolff Ltd. 66-April 70; Chair. Cttee. on Govt. Industrial Establishments 68-70.
Leisure interest: salmon fishing.
39 Arlington House, St. James's, London, S.W.1, England.

Mallaby, Sir (Howard) George, K.C.M.G., O.B.E.; British civil servant; b. 17 Feb. 1902; ed. Radley Coll. and Merton Coll., Oxford.
Asst. master at various schools 23-35; Headmaster, St. Bees School, Cumberland 35-38; District Commr. Special Area of W. Cumberland 38-39; Deputy N.W. Regional Transport Commr. 39-40; war service in army 40-45; served in mil. secretariat of War Cabinet 42-45, Col. 45; Sec. Nat. Trust 45; Asst. Sec. Ministry of Defence 46; Sec.-Gen. Brussels Treaty Defence Organisation 48-50; Under-Sec. Cabinet Office 50-54; Sec. War Council and Council of Ministers, Kenya 54; Deputy-Sec. Univ. Grants Cttee. 55-57; High Commr. for the U.K. in New Zealand 57-59; First Commissioner U.K. Civil Service 59-64; Chair. Cttee. on Staffing of Local Govt. 67, Hong Kong Govt. Salaries Comm. 71; Legion of Merit.
Publs. *Wordsworth* 32, *Wordsworth: A Tribute* 50, *From My Level* 65, *Poems by Wordsworth* (ed.) 70, *Each in his Office* 72.
Down the Lane, Chevington, W. Suffolk, England.

Mallakh, Kamal El, M.A.; Egyptian archaeologist; b. 1918; ed. Cairo Univ. and Mil. Engineering Coll.
Entered Govt. Antiquaries Dept. 44, Dir. of Giza Area and Lower Egypt 45; worked as illustrator and art critic; art critic, *Al Ahram* 45, *Akhbar el Yom* 50-; art and archaeology commentator, Egyptian Broadcasting Service 50-; Gold Cedar Decoration (Lebanon); held one-man exhibitions 39 and 49; two paintings in Cairo Museum of Modern Art.
Publs. Five books on art, archaeology and the discovery of solar boats.
173 Twenty-Sixth of July Street, Zamalek, Cairo, Egypt.

Mallart, José; Spanish educationist and psychologist; b. 10 June 1897, Espolla-Gerona; s. of Juan and Maria Mallart; m. Genoveva Palacios 1929; three c.
Professor Nat. Psychotechnic Inst. Madrid 27-; founder Spanish Cttee. for scientific organization of labour 28; Insp.-Gen. of Workers' Education 33; mem. Cttee. for Agricultural Education 34; Prof. Social School Madrid

48, Nat. Inst. for Rationalisation 49; UNESCO expert in Ecuador 57-; mem. Exec. Cttee., International Asscn. of Applied Psychology 64; Editor *Revista de Psicología General y Aplicada* 64; Gold Medal, Merito en el Trabajo 75.
Leisure interest: music, forestry, gardening.
Publs. *La educación activa* 24, *Colonias de educación* 30, *La elevación moral y material del Campesino* 33, *Organización científica del trabajo agrícola* 34, *La Organización económica internacional y el problema de la paz* 41, *Organización científica Trabajo* 42, *Orientación Funcional y Formación Profesional* 46, *El Mundo Económicosocial que nace* 47, *Obras de dignificación humana* 48, *Cuadernos de Organización Científica del Trabajo* 54-60.
San Julio 5, Madrid 2, Spain.
Telephone: 2617850.

Malle, Louis; French film director; b. 30 Oct. 1932; one s.
Assistant to Commander Cousteau on *La Calypso* 53-55, co-producer *Le Monde du Silence* 55; technical collaborator with Robert Bresson for *Un condamné à mort s'est échappé*.
Leisure interest: bicycle racing.
Films: *Ascenseur pour l'échafaud* 57 (Prix Louis-Delluc 58), *Les Amants* 58 (Special Jury Prize, Venice Film Festival 58), *Zazie dans le métro* 60, *Vie privée* 62, *Le Feu Follet* (special Jury Prize, Venice Film Festival 63), *Viva María* 65, *Le Voleur* 66, *William Wilson* 67, *Calcutta* 68, *Le Souffle au Coeur* 71, *Humain trop humain* 74, *Lacombe Lucien* (Best Film Award, Soc. of Film and TV Arts) 74, *Black Moon* 75.
c/o Nouvelles éditions de films, 16 *bis* rue Lauriston, 75016 Paris; Home: Le Couel, 46260 Limogne en Quercy, France.

Mallea, Eduardo; Argentine writer and journalist; b. 14 Aug. 1903, Bahia Blanca; s. of Narciso S. Mallea and Manuela Aztiria; m. Helena Muñoz Larreta 1944; ed. Colegio Nacional and Faculty of Law, Buenos Aires. Member Board of Dirs. of *Sur* and of *Realidad*; fmr. Pres. Argentine Soc. of Writers; literary editor on staff of *La Nación*; First Nat. Prize for Literature 46, 70; mem. Argentine Acad. of Letters; fmr. Amb. to UNESCO; Hon. D.Hum.Litt. Ann Arbor Univ. Michigan.
Publs. *Cuentos para una Inglesa Desesperada* 26, *Nocturno Europeo*, *Conocimiento y Expresión de la Argentina* 35, *La Ciudad junto al Río Inmóvil* 36, *Historia de una Pasión Argentina* 37, *Fiesta en Noviembre* 38, *Meditación en la Costa* 40, *El Sayal y la Púrpura* 41, *Todo Verdor Perecerá* 41, *La Bahía de Silencio* 40, *Las Aguilas* 41, *Rodeada está de sueño* 44, *El retorno* 46, *El Vínculo* 46, *Los Enemigos del Alma* 50, *La Torre* 51, *Chaves* 53, *La sala de espera* 53, *Notas de un novelista* 54, *Simbad* 57, *El gajo de enebro* 57, *Posesión* 59, *La razón humana* 60, *La vida blanca* 60, *Las travesías* 62, *La barca de hielo* 67, *La Penúltima Puerta* 70, *Gabriel Andaral* 71, *Triste piel del universo* 71.
c/o Editorial Sudamericana, S.A., Humberto 1° 545, Buenos Aires; Posadas 1120, Buenos Aires, Argentina. Telephone: 41-5182.

Mallet, Robert Albert Marie Georges; French university administrator; b. 15 March 1915, Paris; ed. Faculté des Lettres and Faculté de Droit, Paris.
Director, Ecole Nationale des Lettres de Tananarive 59, subsequently Dean, Faculty of Letters, Madagascar; Rector, Acad. d'Amiens 64; mem. Admin. Council O.R.T.F. 68; Rector, Université de Paris (Sorbonne) 69-71, Acad. of Paris 71-; Pres. Asscn. des universités partiellement ou entièrement de langue française 72-; Commdr. Légion d'Honneur, Commdr. des Arts et Lettres, Croix de Guerre.
25 rue Dombasle, 75015 Paris, France.

Mallon, Henry Neil, B.A.; American executive; b. 11 Jan. 1895; ed. Yale Univ.
Served in Army First World War; joined U.S. Can Co. as factory worker 20, successively Factory Man., Vice-Pres. and Gen. Man., and Dir.; Pres., later Chair. S.R. Dresser Manufacturing Co., renamed Dresser Industries Inc.; Chair. Exec. Cttee. and Dir. Dresser Industries Inc.
3800 Turtle Creek Blvd., Dallas, Tex. 75219, U.S.A.

Malloum, Brig.-Gen. Félix; Chad army officer; b. 1932, Fort-Archambault (now Sarh); ed. Military Schools, Brazzaville, Fréjus, Saint-Maixent.
Served in French Army, Indochina 53-55, Algeria; joined Chad Nat. Army; Lieut.-Col. 61, Capt. 62, Col. 68; fmr. Head of Mil. Corps at the Presidency; Chief of Staff of the Army Dec. 71-Sept. 72; C.-in-C. of the Armed Forces 72-73; under house arrest June 73, released April 1975 after coup deposed Pres. Tombalbaye; Head of State, Chair. Supreme Mil. Council, April 75-, Pres. Council of Ministers, Minister of Defence and Ex-Servicemen May 75-; Brig.-Gen. 75.
Conseil Supérieur Militaire, N'Djamena, Chad.

Mallowan, Sir Max Edgar Lucien, Kt., C.B.E., M.A., D.LIT., F.S.A., F.B.A; British archaeologist; b. 6 May 1904, London; s. of Frederick and Marguerite Mallowan (née Duvivier); m. Agatha Miller (Dame Agatha Christie) 1930 (died 1976); ed. Lancing and New Coll., Oxford.
Assistant on staff of British Museum and Museum of Univ. of Pennsylvania Expedition to Ur of the Chaldees 25-30, to Nineveh 31-32; directed excavations on behalf of British Museum and British School of Archaeology in Iraq, at Arpachiyah 33, at Chagar Bazar (Syria) 34-36, Brak (Syria) and in Balikh Valley (Syria) 37-38, at Nimrud on behalf of British School of Archaeology in Iraq 49-58; R.A.F. and seconded to British Mil. Admin., Tripolitania 39-44; Dir. British School of Archaeology in Iraq 47-61, Vice-Chair. 61-65, Chair. 65-70, Pres. 70-; Editor *Iraq* 48-71; Prof. of W. Asiatic Archaeology, Univ. of London 47-62, Emer. 62-; Fellow, All Souls Coll., Oxford 62-71; Pres. British Inst. of Persian Studies 61-; corresp. mem. Arab Acad. Baghdad, German Archaeological Inst.; Foreign mem. Académie des Inscriptions et Belles Lettres (France), Royal Danish Acad. of Sciences and Letters 74; Hon. Fellow, Metropolitan Museum of Art, New York, New Coll., Oxford 73; Trustee, British Museum; Lucy Wharton Drexel Gold Medal, Museum of Univ. of Pennsylvania, Lawrence of Arabia Memorial Medal, Royal Central Asian Soc. 69, Gertrude Bell Memorial Medal for Outstanding Services to Mesopotamian Archaeology 76.
Leisure interests: gardens, domestic architecture.
Publs. *Prehistoric Assyria*, *The Excavations at Arpachiyah* 33, *Excavations at Chagar Bazar* 36-37, *Excavations in the Balikh Valley* 38, *Excavations at Brak and Chagar Bazar* 47, *Early Mesopotamia and Iran* 65, *Nimrud and its Remains* (2 vols.) 66; *Ur Excavations*, vol. IX (with Sir Leonard Woolley) *The Neo Babylonian and Persian Periods* 62, *Ivories in Assyrian Style* (with L. G. Davies) 70, Chapters in *Cambridge Ancient History Vol I*, *Paris 1-2* 70-71, *Furniture from SW 7 Fort Shalmaneser*.
Winterbrook House, Wallingford, Oxon., England. Telephone: Wallingford 36248.

Malone, Dumas, M.A., PH.D., LL.D., LITT.D., L.H.D.; American historian; b. 10 Jan. 1892, Coldwater, Miss.; s. of John and Lillian (Kemp) Malone; m. Elisabeth Gifford 1925; one s. one d.; ed. Emory Coll., Yale Univ. Assoc. Prof. and Prof. of History Univ. of Virginia 23-29; Ed. *Dictionary of American Biography* 29-31 and Ed.-in-Chief 31-36; Dir. Harvard Univ. Press. 36-43; Prof. of History, Columbia Univ. 45-59; Editor History Book Club 48-; Guggenheim Fellow 51-52, 58-

59; Man. Editor *Political Science Quarterly* 53-58; Thomas Jefferson Prof. of History, Univ. of Virginia 59-62, Biographer in Residence 62-; Visiting Scholar Phi Beta Kappa 65-66, 67-68; Wilbur Lucius Cross Medal, Yale Univ. 72, John F. Kennedy Medal, Mass. Historical Soc. 72; Pulitzer Prize in History (for 5 vols. of *Jefferson and His Time*) 75.

Publs. *Public Life of Thomas Cooper* 26, *Edwin A. Alderman: A Biography* 40; *Jefferson and his Time: Vol. I: Jefferson the Virginian* 48, *Vol. II: Jefferson and the Rights of Man* 51, *Vol. III: Jefferson and the Ordeal of Liberty* 62, *Vol. IV: Jefferson the President: First Term* 70, *Vol. V: Jefferson the President: Second Term* 74; *Story of the Declaration of Independence* 55, *Empire for Liberty* (with Basil Rauch) (2 vols.) 60 (6 vol. edn. with individual titles 65), *Thomas Jefferson as Political Leader* 63; Editor *Correspondence between Thomas Jefferson and P. S. du Pont de Nemours* 30, *Dictionary of American Biography* (Joint Editor Vols. IV-VII, Editor Vols. VIII-XX) 29-36.

Alderman Library, University of Virginia, Charlottesville, Va.; Home: 2000 Lewis Mt. Road, Charlottesville, Va. 22903, U.S.A.

Telephone: 804-295-9735.

Malone, Thomas Francis, SC.D.; American geophysicist; b. 3 May 1917, Sioux City, Iowa; s. of John and Mary (Hourigan) Malone; m. Rosalie A. Doran 1942; six c.; ed. S. Dakota State School of Mines and Technology and Mass. Inst. of Technology (M.I.T.). Mem. of Staff M.I.T. 41-43, Asst. Prof. 43-51, Assoc. Prof. 51-54; Dir. Travelers Weather Service and Travelers Weather Research Center for Travelers Insurance Co., Hartford, Conn. 54-56, Dir. of Research Travelers Insurance Co. 56-, Second Vice-Pres. 64-66, Vice-Pres. 66-68, Senior Vice-Pres. 68-70; Dean of Graduate School, Univ. of Connecticut 70-73; Dir. Holcomb Research Inst., Butler Univ. 73-; Sec.-Gen. Scientific Cttee. on Problems of Environment; Vice-Pres. Int. Council of Scientific Unions; mem. Nat. Acad. of Sciences; Hon. D.Eng., Hon. L.H.D.; Losey Award, Inst. of Aerospace Sciences 60; Charles Franklin Brooks Award 64 and Cleveland Abbe Award 68 (American Meteorological Soc.).

Publs. Numerous articles in scientific journals.

Office: Holcomb Research Institute, Butler University, Indianapolis, Ind. 46208; Home: 6421 Sunset Lane, Indianapolis, Ind. 46260, U.S.A.

Telephone: 317-283-9421 (Office); 317-257-9986 (Home)

Malott, Deane Waldo, A.B., M.B.A., LL.D., D.C.S.; American university president; b. 10 July 1898, Abilene, Kan; s. of Michael H. and Edith G. (Johnson) Malott; m. Eleanor S. Thrum 1925; one s. two d.; ed. Kansas and Harvard Univ.

Assistant Dean, Harvard Business School 23-29, Assoc. Prof. of Business 33-39; Vice-Pres. Hawaiian Pineapple Co., Honolulu 29-33; Chancellor, Univ. of Kansas 33-51; Pres. Cornell Univ. 51-63, Pres. Emeritus 63-; Consultant, U.S. Army Air Corps. 43-45; Chair. Emer. Pacific Tropical Botanical Garden; mem. Business Council, 44-; Consultant to Asscn. of American Colls. 63-69; Dir. First Nat. Bank, Ithaca, Lane Bryant, Trustee, Teagle Foundation, William Allen White Foundation, Univ. of Kansas Endowment Asscn., Pacific Tropical Botanical Garden; Hon. LL.D. (Washburn Univ., Bryant Coll., Hamilton Coll., Univ. of Calif., Juniata Coll., Univ. of N.H., Emory Univ., Univ. of Liberia); D.C.S. (Univ. of Pittsburgh); D.H.L. Long Island Univ.).

Publs.: (with Philip Cabot) *Problems in Public Utility Management* 27, (with J. C. Baker) *Introduction to Corporate Finance* 36, (with J. C. Baker and W. D. Kennedy) *On Going into Business* 36, *Problems in*

Agricultural Marketing 38, (with B. F. Martin) *The Agricultural Industries* 39.

322 Wait Avenue, Cornell University, Ithaca, N.Y., U.S.A.

Telephone: 607-256-4010.

Malott, Robert H., A.B., M.B.A.; American business executive; b. 1926, Boston; m. Elizabeth Malott; one s. two d.; ed. Kansas Univ., Harvard Graduate School of Business Admin., N.Y. Univ. Law School.

Assistant to Dean, Harvard Graduate School of Business Admin. 50-52; joined FMC 52, Controller Niagara Chemical Div. 55, Man. Dapon Dept. of Organic Chemicals Div. 59, Div. Man. 63, Vice-Pres. Amer. Viscose Div. 65, Vice-Pres. FMC 66, Exec. Vice-Pres., Planning 67, Man. Machinery Divs., Dir. 70, mem. Exec. Cttee. 71, Pres., Chief Exec. Officer 72-, Chair. of Board 73-; Dir. Standard Oil Co. (Ind.), Bell & Howell Co., Continental Illinois Corpn., Data Documents Inc.; mem. Business Council, Mfg. Chemists Asscn., Exec. Council of Harvard Business School Asscn., Nat. Council for U.S.-China Trade, Conf. Board, Stanford Research Inst. Council.

FMC Corporation, 200 East Randolph Drive, Chicago, Ill. 60601, U.S.A.

Malraux, André; French novelist and politician; be 3 Nov. 1901, Paris; s. of Fernand Malraux and Berth. Lamy; one d.

Served with Republicans, Spanish Civil War; with Tank Div. 39-40; prisoner of war 40, but escaped to unoccupied France; active in resistance movement; Minister of Information 45-46; Minister of State for Information June-July 58, Minister responsible for youth, research and culture July 58-Jan. 59 (De Gaulle cabinet); Minister of State, responsible for Culture (Debré, Pompidou and Couve de Murville cabinets) 59-69; Pres. Asscn. for the Fifth Republic; mem. American Acad. of Arts and Sciences; Prix Goncourt (for *la Condition Humaine*) 33; Croix de la Libération, Officier Légion d'Honneur, Croix de Guerre (4 palmes), Médaille de la Résistance, D.S.O. (U.K.), Jawaharlal Nehru Award for Int. Understanding 72, and other foreign decorations.

Publs. *Lunes en papier* 21, *La Tentation de l'Occident* 26, *Royaume farfelu* 28, *Les Conquérants* 28, *La Voie royale* 30, *La Condition humaine* 33, *Le Temps du mépris* 35, *L'Espoir* (filmed) 37, *Les Noyers de l'Altenburg* 43, *Esquisse d'une psychologie du cinéma* 46, *Psychologie de l'art* (3 vols.) 47-49, *La Monnaie de l'Absolu* 49, *Les Voix du silence* 51, *Le Musée imaginaire de la sculpture mondiale* 52-55, *La Métamorphose des dieux* 57, *Antimémoires* 67, *Le Triangle Noir* 70, *Les Chênes qu'on abat* 71, *La Tête d'Obsidienne* 74, *Lazare* 74, *L'Irréel* 74, *Hôtes de Passage* 75.

2 rue d'Estienne d'Orves, 91370 Verrières-le-Buisson, France.

Malta, Eduardo; Portuguese painter and writer; b. 1900; ed. Fine Arts School, Oporto.

Mem. Nat. Acad. of Fine Arts, Lisbon; corresp. mem. Royal Acad. of Arts of San Fernando (Spain); two Prize Medals and two First Medals (Nat. Soc. of Fine Arts, Lisbon); Columbano Prize (Portuguese Govt.); Luciano Freire Prize (Nat. Acad. of Fine Arts, Lisbon); Gold Medal (Int. Exhibition, Paris 37); Dir. Museum of Contemporary Art, Lisbon.

Works include portraits of: *King Alfonso XIII, Primo de Rivera, Getulio Vargas, King Umberto of Italy, Marshal Craveiro Lopes, Oliveira Salazar, Mrs. Winston, Mrs. Guggenheim, Ricardo Espirito Santo, Barão de Saavedra.*

Publs. include: *O papagaio Azul* 25, *Montanhas Russas* 28, *Do meu oficio de pintar* 35, *No Mundo dos Homens* 36, *Retratos e Retratados* 38, *Vários Motivos de Arte.*

30 Rua Victor Cordon, Lisbon, Portugal.

Maltsev, Victor Fyodorovich; Soviet engineer and diplomatist; b. 12 June 1917, Dnepropetrovsk, Ukraine; ed. Moscow Inst. of Railway Engineers.
With Ministry of Railways 41-61; Chair. Soviet of Irkutsk Region, E. Siberia 61-67; Amb. to Sweden 67-71, to Finland 71-74; Alternating mem. C.P.S.U. Cen. Cttee. 71-.
c/o Ministry of Foreign Affairs, Moscow, U.S.S.R.

Malula, H.E. Cardinal Joseph-Albert; Zairian ecclesiastic; b. 12 Dec. 1917, Kinshasa (then Léopold-ville); ed. Petit Séminaire, Bolongo, Grand Séminaire, Kabwe.
Vicar in Parish of Christ-Roi; Auxiliary Bishop of Léopoldville 59-64; Archbishop of Kinshasa 64-; cr. Cardinal 69; Chevalier Ordre du Léopard.
B.P. 8431, Kinshasa 1, Zaire.
Telephone: 69221.

Mamanggung, Vice-Admiral Moersalin Daeng; Indonesian naval officer and politician; b. 23 Nov. 1922, Isle of Selajur, S. Sulawesi; ed. elementary school, naval acad., naval staff coll., and KKO Marine Training Coll.
Chief of Staff and Commdr. Jakarta Maritime Territory, also acting C.-in-C. of Navy 57-58; mem. House of Reps. and Provisional People's Consultative Assembly 58-60; Vice-Chair. House of Reps. 60-66, 66-68; Minister for Manpower 68-71; numerous awards and decorations.
c/o Ministry of Manpower, Jakarta, Indonesia.

Mamedov, Bakhtiyar Mamed Rza-ogly, D.SC.; Soviet politician; b. 1925; ed. Azerbaizhan Industrial Inst.
Member C.P.S.U. 50-; in oil-industry 48-51, Chief of Oil-Extracting Dept.; Chief, Main Dept., *Glavmorneft* 51-63; Minister of Oil-Extracting Industry, Azerbaizhan S.S.R. 65-; Hero of Socialist Labour; mem. Central Cttee. of C.P. of Azerbaizhan; Deputy to U.S.S.R. Supreme Soviet until 70.
Council of Ministers of Azerbaizhan S.S.R., Baku, U.S.S.R.

Mamert, Jean Albert; French public servant; b. 26 March 1928; ed. Lycée et Faculté de Droit, Montpellier, Institut d'Études Politiques, Paris, Ecole Nationale d'Administration, Paris.
Auditor 55-, later Master of Requests, Council of State; Technical Counsellor of Govt. for Constitutional Problems, 58-59, Sec.-Gen. Constitutional Consultative Cttee. 58; Chief of Prime Minister's Office Jan.-July 59; Sec.-Gen. Econ. and Social Council 59-72; mem. EEC Econ. and Social Cttee. 70-.
Place des Carme-Déchaux, 63000 Clermont-Ferrand; Home: 21 avenue de Versailles, 75016 Paris, France.
Telephone: 225-35-85 (Office).

Mamiaka, Gen. Raphaël; Gabonese politician; b. 12 Nov. 1936, Lambaréné; ed. Inst. d'Enseignement Secondaire, Paris, Ecole d'Officiers de Gendarmerie Nat., Melun, France, Univ. of Paris.
Sub-Lieutenant of Gendarmerie 64, Lieut. 66, Capt. 68, Commdt. 70; served French Army in Cen. Congo, Oubangui-Chari, Far East and Algeria; fmr. Commdr. Gendarmerie of Ndeu-N'Tem, Moanda and N'Gounie; Sec. of State for the Interior in charge of the Penitentiary Service Feb.-Dec. 69; Sec. of State at the Presidency in charge of the Interior 69-70; Minister of the Interior 70-73, of Public Health and Population 73-75, of Public Works and Buildings 75-; Commdr. Légion d'Honneur and other nat. and foreign decorations.
Ministry of Public Works and Buildings, Libreville, Gabon.

Mamo, Sir Anthony Joseph, K.ST.J., O.B.E., Q.C., LL.D.; Maltese Head of State; b. 9 Jan. 1909, Birkirkara; s. of late Joseph and Carola (née Brincat) Mamo; m. Margaret Agius 1939; one s. two d.; ed. Archbishop's Seminary, Malta and Royal Univ. of Malta.

Member, Statute Law Revision Comm. 36-42; Crown Counsel 42-51; Prof. of Criminal Law, Royal Univ. of Malta 43-57; Dep. Attorney-Gen. 52-54; Attorney-Gen. 55; Chief Justice and Pres. of H.M. Court of Appeal 57; Pres. H.M. Constitutional Court 64; Pres. H.M. Court of Criminal Appeal 67; Gov.-Gen. of Malta 71-74; Pres. of the Repub. 74-.
Leisure interest: reading.
Publs. lectures on criminal law and criminal procedure delivered at the Royal Univ. of Malta.
The Palace, Valletta, Malta.
Telephone: 21221.

Mamoudou Maidah; Niger politician; b. 1924; Tessoua, Maradi district; ed. Frederic Assumption School, Katibougou, Mali.
Deputy for Tessoua 59; former teacher; Minister of Agriculture 59-61; Minister of Educ. 61-63; Minister of Rural Economy 63-70; Minister of Foreign Affairs 70-72; Minister-Del. to the Pres. 72-74; numerous decorations.
Niamey, Niger.

Mamoulian, Rouben; American stage and film producer, director, and author; b. 8 Oct. 1897, Russia; ed. Paris Lycée Montaigne, Tiflis Gymnasium, and Moscow Univ.
Produced *Beating on the Door* in London 22; was taken to New York by George Eastman to direct American Opera Co.; Stage Dir. New York 27; Dir. in Hollywood 31-; Film festival *Tribute to Rouben Mamoulian*, New York 67; Festival of films at Nat. Film Theatre, London 68; Retrospectives and personal appearances for *Tribute to Rouben Mamoulian* at American Film Inst., Beverly Hills, Calif., Nat. Gallery of Art, Wash. D.C., Metropolitan Museum of Art N.Y., American Film Inst. Seminar for U.S.A. Educators, Sir George Williams Univ., Montreal, Canada 70; San Francisco Int. Film Festival, Science Center, Toronto, Canada, Museum of Science, Buffalo, N.Y., Univ. of Calif., Univ. of South Florida, Yale Univ. 71; *Musical Mamoulian* retrospective at the Acad. of Motion Picture Arts and Sciences, Hollywood 72; Festival of all Mamoulian films, San Sebastian, Spain, and Cinémathèque, Paris 73; Pres. Int. Jury, San Sebastian Film Festival 73; numerous appearances on radio and television.
Stage Productions include: *Porgy* 27, *Marco Millions* 28, *Wings Over Europe* 28, *R.U.R.* 29, *Month in the Country* 30, *Hand of Fate*, *Farewell to Arms* 30, *Porgy and Bess* 35, *Oklahoma!* 43, *Sadie Thompson* 44, *Carousel* 45, *St. Louis Woman* 46, *Lost in the Stars* (musical tragedy) 49, *Arms and the Girl* (musical play) 50, *Oklahoma!* for the Berlin Art Festival 51, Hollywood 53, in Paris and in various Italian cities 55; Motion Pictures include: *Applause* 29, *City Streets* 31, *Dr. Jekyll and Mr. Hyde* 31, *Love Me Tonight* 32, *Song of Songs* 32, *Queen Christina* 33, *We Live Again* 34, *Becky Sharp* 35, *The Gay Desperado* 36, *High, Wide and Handsome* 37, *Golden Boy* 39, *Mark of Zorro* 40, *Blood and Sand* 41, *Rings on her Fingers* 42, *Summer Holiday* (based on Eugene O'Neill's *Ah! Wilderness*) 47, *Carousel* 53, *Oklahoma* 55, *Silk Stockings* 57, co-author (with Maxwell Anderson) *The Devil's Hornpipe* (musical, filmed as *Never Steal Anything Small*) 59.
Publs. *Abigayil* 64, *Shakespeare's Hamlet, A New Version* 66.
1112 Schuyler Road, Beverly Hills, Calif. 90210, U.S.A.

Mamoun, Sheikh Hassan; Egyptian lawyer and religious and university official; b. 13 June 1894.
Former Judge; fmr. Supreme Judge of the Sudan; Pres. of Supreme Court of Shari'a, Grand Mufti of Egypt 55-61; mem. fmr. Nat. Assembly; mem. Arab Socialist Union; Grand Imam and Sheikh of Al-Azhar July 64-69, fmr. Chancellor of Al Azhar Univ., Cairo 64-.
Office of the Chancellor, University of Al-Azhar, Cairo, Egypt.

35

Man, Ivan Alexandrovich; Soviet sailor and polar explorer; b. 23 Sept. 1903, Mogilev Region, Byelo-Russia; ed. Leningrad Naval Polytechnic.
National navigation safety inspector; Commdr. of cargo steamers *Pravda, Transbalt* in the Arctic Ocean, and of the liners *Ukraina, Rossia* in the Black Sea; Capt. of diesel-electric ship *Ob,* flagship of the Soviet Antarctic Expedition 55; sailed to Mirny in the Antarctic 55, 56, 57; Capt. of liner *Gruzia* 61-62, *Peter Veliki* 62-64, research ship *Professor Vize,* Antarctic, 68; Chief Specialist in Navigation, Ministry of Merchant Marine 64-; Orders of Lenin, Patriotic War (1st Class), Red Banner of Labour (two), Badge of Honour and other decorations.
Ministry of Merchant Marine, Moscow, U.S.S.R.

Man, Morgan Charles Garnet, C.M.G.; British former diplomatist; b. 6 Aug. 1915; ed. Cheltenham Coll., and The Queen's Coll., Oxford.
Joined Consular service 37; Deputy Political Resident, Bahrain 59-62; Minister, Ankara 62-64; Ambassador to Saudi Arabia 64-68; Senior Civilian Instructor, Imperial Defence Coll. 68-69; Dir. Metallurgical Plantmakers Fed. 70-, British Metalworking Plantmakers Asscn. 70-, Ironmaking and Steelmaking Plant Contractors Asscn. 70-.
272 Earl's Court Road, London, S.W.5., England.
Telephone: 01-370-1860.

Manac'h, Etienne Manoël; French diplomatist; b. 3 Feb. 1910, Plouigneau; *m.* Mme Denise Lorenzet 1967; three *c.*; ed. Faculté des Lettres, Paris.
Free France Delegate to Turkey 41-42, Head of Mission to Balkans 42-43, Consul-Gen. in Istanbul 44; First Sec., French Embassy, Prague 45, Consul-Gen., Bratislava 45-51; Counsellor and Deputy Dir. Ministry of Foreign Affairs 51, Head of E. European Services 53; Technical Counsellor to Minister of Foreign Affairs 57-58; Dir. du Cabinet to Minister of State Guy Mollet 58-59; Minister plenipotentiary 60; Dir. for Asia and South Sea Islands of Central Admin. 60-69; Amb. to People's Repub. of China 69-75; Amb. de France 74.
Ministère des Affaires Etrangères, 37 quai d'Orsay, 75007 Paris, France.

Mance, Sir Henry Stenhouse, Kt., M.A.; British insurance executive; b. 5 Feb. 1913, St. Albans, Herts.; *s.* of late Brig. Sir Henry O. Mance, K.B.E., C.B., C.M.G., and of Elizabeth H. Mance; *m.* Joan E. Robertson Baker; one *s.* three *d.*; ed. Charterhouse and St. John's Coll., Cambridge.
Entered Lloyds 35, Underwriting mem. 39, mem. Cttee. 66, Deputy Chair. 67-68, Chair. 69-72; Chair. Willis Faber and Dumas (Agencies) Ltd. 73-.
Leisure interests: gardening, carpentry.
Lloyds, Lime Street, London, EC3M 7HA; Home: Gatefield Cottage, Okehurst, Billingshurst, Sussex, England.
Telephone: 01-488-3411.

Mancham, James Richard Marie, F.R.S.A.; Seychelles lawyer and politician; b. 11 Aug. 1939, Victoria, Mahé; *s.* of Richard Mancham and Evelyne Henderson; *m.* Heather Jean Evans 1963; one *s.* one *d.*; ed. Univ. of Paris and Middle Temple, London.
Called to the Bar, Middle Temple 61; mem. Legislative Council of the Seychelles 61; mem. Govt. Council 67; founder and leader, Social Democratic Party 64-; mem. Legislative Assembly 70-; Chief Minister, Council of Ministers Nov. 70-.
Publ. *Reflections and Echoes from the Seychelles.*
The White House, Bel Eau, Victoria, Mahé, Seychelles.

Manchester, William, B.A., A.M., L.H.D.; American writer; b. 1 April 1922, Attleboro, Mass.; *s.* of William Raymond Manchester and Sallie Thompson Manchester; *m.* Julia Brown Marshall 1948; one *s.* two *d.*; ed. Univ. of Mass., Dartmouth Coll., and Univ. of Missouri.
Reporter *Daily Oklahoman* 45-46; Reporter, Foreign Corresp., War Corresp., Assoc. Editor, *Baltimore Sun* 47-55; Man. Editor, Wesleyan Univ. publs. 55-63; Fellow, Wesleyan Univ. 59-60, Writer-in-Residence Wesleyan Univ. 75-; Pres. Board of Trustees, Univ. of Mass. Library 70-72; Purple Heart 45; Guggenheim Fellow 59; Fellow East Coll. Wesleyan Univ. 69-76; Dag Hammarskjöld Int. Prize in Literature 67, Overseas Press Club Award 68, Univ. of Missouri Award 69.
Leisure interest: photography.
Publs. *Disturber of the Peace* 51, *The City of Anger* 53, *Shadow of the Monsoon* 56, *Beard the Lion* 58, *A Rockefeller Family Portrait* 59, *The Long Gainer* 61, *Portrait of a President* 62, *The Death of a President* 67, *The Arms of Krupp* 68, *The Glory and the Dream* 74, *Controversy and Other Essays in Journalism* 76.
c/o Harold Matson Co., 22 East 40th Street, New York, N.Y. 10016, U.S.A.
Telephone: 212-679-4490.

Manchot, Willy, DR. ING.; German chemist and business executive; b. 10 July 1907, Würzburg; *s.* of Prof. Dr. Wilhelm Manchot and Bertha B. Haas; *m.* 1st Sigrid Henkel (died 1966), 2nd Hildegard Clauss; one *s.* two *d.*; ed. Technische Hochschulen, Munich and Darmstadt.
Chemist and Plant Man., Dr. Alexander Wacker GmbH, Mückenberg 34-39; Exec. Dir. and Production Man. Deutsche Hydrierwerke Rodleben 39-40; Exec. Dir. (Chemical and Technical Management) Henkel & Cie. GmbH 39-60, Chair. Board of Dirs. Henkel GmbH 50-59, mem. Board of Dirs. 59-; official numerous other companies; Hon. mem. Senate, Technical Univ., Munich.
Haus Langenfeld, 4021 Hubbelrath, Düsseldorf, Federal Republic of Germany.

Mancini, Giacomo; Italian politician; b. 21 April 1916; ed. Univ. of Turin.
Member Partito Socialista Italiano (P.S.I.) 43-; Dir. Socialist Federation of Cosenza 46-48; mem. Chamber of Deputies 48-; mem. Directorate P.S.I. 53-, Dir. of Party Org. 59, later Asst. Sec.; Minister of Public Health 63-64, of Public Works 64-70; Sec. Unitarian Socialist Party 70-72; Minister for Southern Devt. March-Oct. 74.
Partito Socialista Italiano, 00186 Rome, Via del Corso 476, Italy.

Mancroft, 2nd Baron, of Mancroft, Norwich; **Stormont Mancroft Samuel Mancroft,** K.B.E., T.D.; British business executive; b. 27 July 1914; ed. Winchester and Christ Church, Oxford.
Called to Bar, Inner Temple 38; Royal Artillery 39-46; mem. Bar Council 47-51; mem. St. Marylebone Borough Council 47-53; Chancellor Primrose League 52-54; a Lord-in-Waiting to the Queen 52-54; Parl. Under Sec. Home Office 54-57; Parl. Sec. Ministry of Defence 57; Minister without Portfolio 57-58; Dir. Great Universal Stores and subsidiaries 58-66; Deputy Chair. Cunard Line Ltd. 66-71, also Dir. Cunard Steamship Co. 66-71; Pres. Inst. of Marketing and Sales Management 59-63, St. Marylebone Conservative Asscn. 61-66, London Tourist Board 63-73; Chair. Cttee. for Exports to U.S.A. 67-70; Chair. Totalisator Board 71-76; Hon. Col. Commandant, Royal Artillery.
Publs. *Booking the Cooks* 69, *A Chinaman in my Bath* 74.
29 Margaretta Terrace, London SW3 5NU, England.
Telephone: 01-352 7674.

Mandel, Marvin; American state governor; b. 19 April 1920, Baltimore, Md.; *s.* of late Harry Mandel and of Rebecca Cohen; *m.* 1st Barbara Oberfeld 1941 (divorced 1974), one *s.* one *d.*; *m.* 2nd Jeanne Blackistone Dorsey 1974; ed. Baltimore City Coll. and Univ. of Maryland.

Army service 42-44; subsequently partner in law firm Mandel, Gilbert, Rocklin and Franklin until 69; mem. Maryland House of Delegates 52-69, Speaker 63-69; Gov. of Maryland Jan. 69-; mem. Baltimore, Maryland and American Bar Asscns.; Hon. LL.D. (Univ. of Md. and Towson State Coll.); Herbert Lehman Ethics Award 69, 70 and other honours; Democrat.
Leisure interests: pipe-collecting, hunting, sport.
State Capitol, Annapolis, Md., U.S.A.

Mandela, Nelson Rolihlahla; South African lawyer and politician; b. 1918, Transkei; *m.* Winnie Mandela; ed. Fort Hare, Univ. of the Witwatersrand.
Son of Chief of Tembu tribe; legal practice, Johannesburg 52; Nat. organiser African Nat. Congress (A.N.C.); on trial for treason 56-61 (acquitted 61); arrested 62, sentenced to five years imprisonment Nov. 62; on trial for further charges Nov. 63-June 64, sentenced to life imprisonment June 64.
Publ. *No Easy Walk to Freedom* 65.
Robben Island, nr. Cape Town, South Africa.

Mandele, Karel E. van der, DR.ECON.; Netherlands diplomatist (retd.); b. 13 Sept. 1907, Rotterdam; *s.* of K. P. Van der Mandele and Hermine S. M. Van Bosse; *m.* Wilhelmine Plate 1934; three *s.* one *d.*; ed. Nederlandsche Economische Hoogeschool, Rotterdam and Lausanne, Harvard and Leiden Univs.
Banking 31-38; Vice-Consul, Sydney, New South Wales 38-43; Sec. Pretoria 43-44, Washington 44-46; First Sec. Copenhagen 46; UN Division, Ministry of Foreign Affairs 47-50; Consul-Gen., Hong Kong 50-55; Minister to Ceylon 55-58; Inspector of Foreign Service 58-63; Ambassador to Denmark 63-69; mem. of Staff, Netherlands Defence Coll. 69-73; Knight Order of Netherlands Lion, Officer Order of Orange-Nassau, Commdr. Military Order of Christ, Grand Cross, Order of Dannebrog.
Leisure interests: outdoor life, history, politics.
"De Helling", Zwaluwenweg 3A, Aerdenhout, Netherlands.
Telephone: 023-242512.

Mandloi, Bhagwantrao Annabhau, B.A., LL.B.; Indian politician; b. 15 Dec. 1892, Khandwa, Madhya Pradesh; *s.* of Shri Annabhan Mandloi and Shrimati Nathu Bai Mandloi; *m.* Shrimati Durga Devi; six *s.* two *d.*; ed. Govt. Coll., Jabalpur, and Univ. School of Allahabad.
Lawyer, Khandwa; Pres. Municipal Cttee., Khandwa (15 years); mem. Legislative Assembly of Cen. Provinces and Berar 35-37, of Madhya Pradesh 37-; imprisoned for political activities 40, 42; mem. Constituent Assembly and Parl.; Chief Whip, Madhya Pradesh Assembly Party; mem. Congress Parl. Board 51-52; Minister for Revenue, Survey and Settlement, Land Records, Land Reforms and Local Self Govt., Madhya Pradesh, later for Revenue and Educ. 52-56; Minister for Revenue and Local Govt. 56-61, for Revenue and Industries 61-62; Chief Minister, Madhya Pradesh 62-August 63; Pres. Madhya Pradesh Congress Cttee. Nov. 63-; Padma-Bhushan award 70.
Leisure interests: reading and writing on politics, agriculture, industry and religious subjects.
Ramkrishna Mandloi Road, Khandwa, Madhya Pradesh, India.

Manekshaw, Field-Marshal Sam Hormuzji Framji Jamshedji, M.C.; Indian army officer; b. 3 April 1914, Amritsar; *s.* of the late Dr. H. F. J. Manekshaw and of Mrs. H. F. J. Manekshaw; *m.* Silloo Manekshaw 1939; two *d.*; ed. Sherwood Coll., Nainital, Indian Military Acad., Dehra Dun.
Commissioned 34, awarded Military Cross; graduated Staff Coll., Quetta 43; served as Brigade Maj. Razmak Brigade, Waziristan 43-44; Instructor Staff Coll., Quetta 44; active service in Burma and French Indo-China 45-46; Gen. Staff Officer Grade I, Military

Operations Directorate, Army H.Q. 46-47, Brigadier 47; Dir. Military Operations 48-52; Commdr. 167 Infantry Brigade 52-54; Col. 8th Gurkha Rifles 53-; Dir. Military Training 54-55; Commdr. Infantry School, Mhow 55; attended Imperial Defence Coll., London 57; promoted Maj.-Gen. and appointed G.O.C. 26 Infantry Div. in Jammu and Kashmir 57; Commandant Defence Services Staff Coll., Wellington 59-62; G.O.C. IV Corps. 62-63; G.O.C.-in-C. Western Command 63-64; G.O.C.-in-C. Eastern Command 64-69; awarded Padma Bhushan 68, Padma Vibhushan 72; Chief of the Army Staff 69-73; promoted Field-Marshal Jan. 73; masterminded Pakistan's defeat in Indo-Pakistan War 71; Col. 8th Gurkha Rifles.
Leisure interests: fishing, reading, music.
c/o Army Headquarters, DHQ PO New Delhi 110011, India.

Mănescu, Corneliu; Romanian politician and diplomatist; b. 8 Feb. 1916, Ploieşti, Romania; ed. Law Coll., Bucharest.
Member Democratic Students Front; mem. Romanian Workers' Party (now C.P.) 36-; Deputy Minister of Armed Forces 48-55; Dep. Chair. State Planning Cttee. 55-60; Chief of Political Dept. Ministry of Foreign Affairs 60; Amb. to Hungary 60-61; Minister of Foreign Affairs March 61-Oct. 72; mem. Central Cttee. of the Romanian C.P. 65-; Deputy to Grand Nat. Assembly 65-; Head of Romanian Del. to UN Gen. Assembly 61-72; Chair. 22nd Session of UN Gen. Assembly 67-68; Pres. of Romanian Interparl. Group 73-; Vice-Pres. of Nat. Council of Socialist Unity Front 73-; Romanian and foreign decorations.
Consiliul National al Frontului Unitătii Socialiste, Bucharest, Romania.

Mănescu, Manea; Romanian economist and politician; b. 9 Aug. 1916, Brăila; *m.* Maria Mănescu.
Gen. Dir. Cen. Statistical Office 51-55; Minister for Finance 55-57; Chair. Labour and Wages State Cttee. and First Vice-Pres. of State Planning Cttee. 57; mem. Romanian C.P. 36-; mem. Cen. Cttee. Romanian C.P. 60, Sec. 65-72, Alt. mem. Exec. Cttee. 66-68, mem. 68-, mem. Perm. Praesidium 71-74; Chair. Econ. and Financial Standing Comm. of Grand Nat. Assembly 61-69; Chair. Econ. Council 68-72; Chair. State Planning Cttee. 72-74; Vice-Pres. State Council 69-72; Vice-Chair. Council of Ministers 72-74, Chair. March 74-; Corresp. mem. Romanian Acad. of the S.R.R. 55-74, mem. 74-; mem. Acad. of Social and Political Sciences 70, Latin World Acad.; Hero of Socialist Labour 71.
Consiliul de Ministri, Bucharest, Romania.

Manessier, Alfred; French artist; b. 5 Dec. 1911; ed. Lycée d'Amiens and Paris Schools of Fine Art.
Has designed and executed stained glass for churches at Bresseux (Jura), Arles, Basle, etc.; rep. at numerous exhibitions, including the Brussels Int. Exhibition 58, Dunn Int. Exhbn., London 63; Caracas Int. Painting Prize, Carnegie Prize 55, Venice Biennale Prize 62; Chevalier Légion d'Honneur, Officier des Arts et des Lettres.
203 rue de Vaugirard, Paris 15e, France.

Mangelsdorf, Paul C., M.S., SC.D.; American scientist; b. 20 July 1899, Atchison, Kan.; *s.* of August and Mary Brune Mangelsdorf; *m.* Helen Parker 1923; two *s.*; ed. Kansas State Coll. and Harvard Univ.
Assistant Geneticist, Conn. Agricultural Experimental Station 21-26; Agronomist, Texas Agricultural Experimental Station 27-40, Asst. Dir. 36-40, Vice-Dir. 40; Asst. Dir. Botanical Museum, Harvard Univ. 40-45, Dir. 45-67, Prof. of Econ. Botany 40-67, Fisher Prof. of Natural History 62-68, Emeritus Prof. 68-; Consultant in Agriculture, Rockefeller Foundation 41-54 and periodically since; Lecturer in Botany, Univ. of N.C. 68-; mem. American Philosophical Soc., Nat.

Acad. of Sciences; Hon. D.Sc. (Park Coll.) 60, (Saint Benedict's Coll.) 65, Hon. LL.D. (Kansas State Univ.).
Leisure interests: reading, gardening.
Publs. *Genetics and Morphology of some Endosperm Characters in Maize* 26, *Origin of Indian Corn and its Relatives* (with R. G. Reeves) 39, *Races of Maize in Mexico* (with E. J. Wellhausen et al.) 51, *Races of Maize in Columbia* (with L. M. Roberts et al.) 57, *Races of Maize in Central America* (with E. J. Wellhausen et al.) 57, *Races of Maize in Peru* (with Alexander Grobman et al.) 61, *Campaigns against Hunger* (with E. C. Stakman and R. Bradfield) 67, and over 100 articles.
Room 315, Department of Botany, University of North Carolina, Chapel Hill, N.C. 27514; Home: 510 Caswell Road, Chapel Hill, N.C., U.S.A.

Mangwazu, Timon Sam, B.A.(HONS.); Malawi diplomatist; b. 12 Oct. 1933, Kasungu; *s.* of Sam Isaac Mangwazu and Malita Nyankhata; *m.* Nelly Kathewera 1958; three *s.* three *d.*; ed. Inyati Boys' Inst. (London Missionary Society) Bulawayo, Tegwani Methodist Secondary School, Plumtree, Ruskin Coll., and Brasenose Coll. Oxford.
Nyasaland Civil Service 56; Sec.-Gen. Nyasaland African Civil Servants Association 61; Asst. Registrar of Trade Unions 63; First Sec. British Embassy in Vienna 64; Amb. of Malawi to German Fed. Repub., later accred. to Norway, Sweden, Denmark, Netherlands, Belgium, Switzerland, Austria 64-67; Malawi High Commr. in U.K. 67-69, concurrently Amb. to Holy See, Portugal, Netherlands and Belgium; reading Econs. and Politics at Brasenose Coll., Oxford 69-72; Amb. to EEC, Belgium and the Netherlands 72-; Malawi Independence Medal; Malawi Repub. Medal, Knight Commdr. Cross of Order of Merit of Fed. Repub. of Germany.
Leisure interest: angling.
Malawi Embassy, 13-17 rue de la Charité, 1040 Brussels, Belgium.
Telephone: 217-43-70.

Manickavasagar, Balasegaram, M.B., F.R.C.S., F.R.C.S.E., F.R.A.C.S., F.A.C.S., F.I.C.S., F.P.C.S.; Malaysian surgeon; b. 15 April 1929, Selangor; *s.* of Manickavasagar and Navamani; *m.* Jeyaletchimy Pillai 1958; one *s.* five *d.*; ed. King Edward VII Medical Coll., Singapore and Univ. of Malaya.
Medical Officer and later Registrar, Surgical Unit, Gen. Hosp., Kuala Lumpur 57-59, Consultant Surgeon Surgical Unit II 69-, Prof. and Consultant Surgeon 72-; Consultant Surgeon, Kota Bharu, Kelantan 60-61; Consultant Surgeon and Head Dept. of Surgery, Gen. Hosp., Seremban 61-69; Examiner, Primary Fellowship Examination, Royal Coll. of Surgeons, Edinburgh 72, 74; Nat. Del. Société Internationale de Chirurgie; Editor-in-Chief Malaysian Journal of Surgery; Editorial Cttee. mem. British Journal of Surgery, Journal of Clinical Oncology, Journal of Modern Medicine, Journal of Medical Progress, Journal of the International College of Surgeons; mem. Malaysian Soc. of Parasitology and Tropical Medicine; Fellow American Asscn. of Surgery for Advancement of Trauma, Asscn. of Surgeons of Great Britain and Ireland, British Surgical Oncology; Hon. Fellow Polish Asscn. of Surgeons, Philippine Coll. of Surgeons; Hunterian Professorship, Royal Coll. of Surgeons 69; Chiene Professorship Lecture 71; Jacksonian Prize, Royal Coll. of Surgeons 70; Abraham Colles Lecturer, Royal Coll. of Surgeons of Ireland 74; many Malaysian awards.
Leisure interests: reading especially military history, philosophy, photography, athletics.
Publs. numerous papers in medical journals on hepatic, pancreatic, bileary and oesophageal surgery.
Office: Department of Surgery, General Hospital, Kuala

Lumpur; Home: 5 Jalan Liew Weng Chee, Off Jalan Yap Kwan Seng, Kuala Lumpur 04-06, Malaysia.
Telephone: 290421 Extension 686 (Office); 84053 (Home).

Maniusis, Juozas Antonovich, D.SC.; Soviet constructional engineer and politician; b. 1910.
Former constructional engineer; Army service 41-44; Party official 45-50; Minister of Construction 50-55; Sec. Cen. Cttee., C.P. of Lithuanian S.S.R. 56-67; Chair. Council of Ministers of Lithuanian S.S.R. 67-; Deputy to U.S.S.R. Supreme Soviet 62-; Alt. mem. Cen. Cttee. C.P.S.U. and mem. Cen. Cttee. of Lithuanian S.S.R.; mem. Cttee. U.S.S.R. Parl. Group.
Council of Ministers of Lithuanian S.S.R., Vilnius, U.S.S.R.

Mankiewicz, Joseph Leo, B.A.; American film writer, director and producer; b. 11 Feb. 1909, Wilkes-Barre, Pa.; *s.* of Frank and Johanna (Blumenau) Mankiewicz; *m.* 1st Rosa Stradner 1939 (died 1958) 2nd Rosemary Matthews 1962; three *s.* one *d.*; ed. Columbia Univ.
Asst. Corresp. in Berlin for *Chicago Tribune*; writer, Paramount Pictures 29-33; writer and producer, M.G.M. 33-43; writer, director and producer, Twentieth Century-Fox 43-51; Pres. Screen Directors' Guild 50; Formed own company, Figaro Inc., 1953, dissolved, 1961; Acad. of Motion Picture Arts and Sciences Award (Oscar) best screen-play and director 49 and 50; British Film Acad. Award and New York Film Critics' Award (for *All About Eve*) 51; Commdr. of the Order of Merit from Italian Republic for contribution to the Arts.
Works include: Script: *Skippy, Million Dollar Legs, If I Had a Million, Manhattan Melodrama, Forsaking All Others*; Produced: *Fury, Philadelphia Story, Woman of the Year, Keys of the Kingdom*; Script and Dir.: *Dragonwyck, Letter to Three Wives, All About Eve, People Will Talk, The Barefoot Contessa, Guys and Dolls, The Quiet American, Cleopatra, The Honey Pot, No Way Out*; Dir.: *Late George Apley, The Ghost and Mrs. Muir, House of Strangers, Five Fingers, Suddenly Last Summer, La Bohème* (at Metropolitan Opera House) 52, *There Was A Crooked Man* 69, *Sleuth* 72.
Long Ridge Road, Bedford, N.Y. 10506, U.S.A.

Mankowitz, Wolf, M.A.; British writer and theatrical producer; b. 7 Nov. 1924, East Ham, London; *s.* of Solomon Mankowitz and Rebecca Brick; *m.* Ann Seligmann 1944; four *s.*; ed. East Ham Grammar School, and Downing Coll., Cambridge.
Extensive work in journalism, radio, television and films, and as a theatrical producer; is also an expert in English Ceramics.
Leisure interests: antiquities and sleeping.
Films: *Make me an Offer, A Kid for Two Farthings* 54, *The Bespoke Overcoat* 55 (Venice Film Festival Award, British Film Acad. Award, Hollywood Oscar), *Expresso Bongo* 60, *The Long and the Short and the Tall* 61, *The Millionairess, The Day the Earth Caught Fire* 60 (British Film Acad. Award), *Waltz of the Toreadors* 62, *Where the Spies are* 65, *Casino Royale* 67, *The 25th Hour* 67, *The Assassination Bureau* 68, *Bloomfield* (screen-play and production) 69, *Black Beauty* 70. *The Hebrew Lesson* (Critics' Prize, Cork Int. Film Festival) 72, *The Hireling* (Grand Prix, Cannes) 73.
Plays: *The Boychik* 54, *The Bespoke Overcoat* 55, *The Mighty Hunter, Expresso Bongo* (musical) 58, *Make Me an Offer* (musical) 59, *Belle* (musical) 61, *Pickwick* (musical) 63, *Passion Flower Hotel* (musical) 65, *The Samson Riddle* 72.
Television includes *Conflict* series, *East End West End* series, *The Killing Stones* play-cycle 58, *A Cure for Tin Ear* 65, *The Battersea Miracle* 66, *Dickens of London* series 76.
Publs. (Fiction) *Make Me an Offer* 52, *A Kid for Two Farthings* 53, *Laugh till you Cry, Majollika and Company* 55, *My Old Man's a Dustman* 56, *The Mendelman Fire*

and Other Stories 57, *Expresso Bongo* 60, *Cockatrice* 63, *The Biggest Pig in Barbados* 65, *Penguin Wolf Manko-witz* 67, *The Blue Arabian Nights* 72, *The Day of the Women* 76; (Plays) *The Bespoke Overcoat, Five One-Act Plays* 55, *Expresso Bongo* 61, *The Samson Riddle* 72; (Ceramics) *The Portland Vase* 52, *Wedgwood* 53, *A Con-cise Encyclopedia of English Pottery and Porcelain* 57.
Simmonscourt Castle, Donnybrook, Dublin 4, Ireland.
Telephone: 01-935 1741; Dublin 685645.

Manley, Michael Norman, M.P.; Jamaican politician, journalist and trade unionist; b. 10 Dec. 1923, Kingston; *s.* of the late Norman W. Manley, Q.C., and of Edna (née Swithenbank) Manley; *m.* Beverley Anderson 1972; one *s.* three *d.*; ed. Jamaica Coll. and London School of Economics.
With B.B.C. 50-51; Assoc. Editor, *Public Opinion* 52-53; Sugar Supervisor, Nat. Workers' Union 53-54, Island Supervisor and First Vice-Pres. 55-; positions in numerous other unions and Labour cttees.; mem. of Senate 62-67; mem. House of Reps. for Central King-ston 67-; Leader of People's Nat. Party Feb. 69-; Prime Minister March 72-, also Minister of External Affairs 72-75, of Economic Affairs 72-75, of Defence 72-, of Youth and Devt. 74-75; Jamaican Rep. on Exec. Council Caribbean Congress of Labour.
Leisure interests: reading, music, gardening, boxing, tennis, cricket.
Publ. *Politics of Change* 74.
Office of the Prime Minister, P.O. Box 638, Kingston, Jamaica.

Mann, Fritz Karl, DR. JURIS., PH.D.; German-American economist; b. 10 Dec. 1883, Berlin; *s.* of Louis Mann and Johanna Behrens; *m.* Ingeborg Papendieck 1907 (died 1967); two *s.* two *d.*; ed. Freiburg, Munich, Berlin, Paris and London Univs.
Economic Expert to Military Administration of Ro-mania 17; mem. German Supreme Command; Chair. Inter-Allied Danube Comm. 17-18; Lecturer of Political Economy Kiel Univ. 14, Breslau Univ. 19; Prof. Kiel Univ. 20; Prof. Königsberg Univ. and Dir. Inst. for East German Economics 22; Prof. Cologne Univ. 26; Dir. Inst. for Int. Finance 27, Inst. for Fiscal Research 33; Prof. American Univ. Graduate School, Washington, D.C. 36, Brookings Instn. 40-41; Expert of War Dept.; Asst. Dir. and Acting Dir. of Research, Army Indus. Coll. 43-44; Fellow of Library of Congress 43-44; Dir. Institute on Federal Taxes 45-55; Chair. Dept. of Economics, American Univ. 48-54; Prof. Emeritus 56; Drs. rer. pol. h.c.
Leisure interests: riding and music.
Publs. *Marschall Vauban und die Volkswirtschaftslehre des Absolutismus* 14, *Überwälzung der Steuer* 28, *Deutsche Finanzwirtschaft* 29, *Die Staatswirtschaft unserer Zeit* 30, *Gründer der Soziologie* 32, *Steuerpolitische Ideale* 37, *The Sociology of Taxation* 43, *The Government Corporation as a Tool of Foreign Policy* 43, *The Socializa-tion of Risks* 45, *The Dual Debt System as a Method of Financing Government Corporations* 47, *The Threefold Economic Functions of Taxation* 47, *The Fiscal Com-ponent of Revolution* 47, *Re-orientation Through Fiscal Theory* 49, *Geschichte der angelsächsischen Finanz-wissenschaft* 55, *Wirtschaftsgleichgewicht und Wirt-schaftswachstum in den Vereinigten Staaten von Amerika* 57, *Die Bekämpfung der Inflationen: Amerikanische Methoden und Erfahrungen* 57, *Bemerkungen über Schumpeters Einfluss auf die amerikanische Wirtschafts-theorie* 58, *The Romantic Reaction* 58, *Die Finanzwirt-schaft als Modell und als System* 58, *Finanztheorie und Finanzsoziologie* 59, *Institutionalism and American Economic Theory: A Case of Interpenetration* 60, *Ideologie und Theorie des Haushaltsgleichgewichts* 61, *Von den Wandlungen und Widersprüchen der Steuer-ideologie* 61, *Finanzsoziologie* 61, *Vecchie e Nuove Teorie Del Pareggio Del Bilancio* 62, *Physiokratie* 62, *Die*

konjunktur- und finanzpolitische Lage der Vereinigten Staaten von Amerika; I Problemi dell'Economia Ameri-cana 63, *Economics of Fiscal Decisions in a Pluralistic Society* 64, *Festgabe für F. K. Mann* 63, *Finanzwissen-schaftliche Forschung und Lehre an der Universität zu Köln 1927-1935* 67, *Die Gesetze der Wirtschaftsmacht und die Macht der Wirtschaftsgesetzen* 68, *Die inter-mediären Finanzgewalten und der pluralistische Staat* 69, *Die Finanzwirtschaft als Privatwirtschaft, His-torische Glossen* 69, *Die Neutralisierung des Finanz-systems* 70, *J. A. Schumpeter, Das Wesen des Geldes* (editor) 70, *Perspectivas Sociológicas de la decisión politico-financiera* 71, *Zu Schumpeters Leben und Werk* 71, *Die drei Finanzwissenschaften* 71, *Die "Als-Obs" in der Finanzwirtschaftslehre* 72, *Der interpersonele und der strukturelle Ausgleich der Steuerlast* 72, *Begriff und Illusion der sozialen Marktwirtschaft* 73, *Abriss einer Geschichte der Finanzwissenschaft* 75.
3713 Williams Lane, Washington, D.C. 20015, U.S.A.
Telephone: 652-3593.

Mann, Golo, DR.PHIL.; Swiss historian of German origin; b. 27 March 1909, Munich, Germany; *s.* of Thomas Mann; ed. Schloss Salem, Univs. of Munich, Berlin and Heidelberg.
Reader in German Literature and History, Ecole Normale Supérieure, St. Cloud 33-35, Rennes Univ. 35-36; Editor *Mass und Wert*, Zurich 37-40; Prof. of Modern History Olivet Coll. (Mich.) 42-43; U.S. Army 43-46; Prof. of History Claremont Men's Coll. (Calif). 47-57; Visiting Prof. Münster Univ. 58 and 59; Prof. of History, Stuttgart Technische Hochschule 60-64; Mannheim Schillerpreis 64, Berlin Fontane Prize 62, Büchner Prize 68, Gottfried Keller-Preis 69, Pour le Mérite 74.
Leisure interests: hiking, dogs.
Publs. *Friedrich von Gentz: Geschichte eines europäischen Staatsmannes* 47, *Vom Geist Amerikas* 54, *Aussenpolitik* (with H. Pross, vol. in *Fischer-Lexikon*) 58, *Deutsche Geschichte des 19. und 20. Jahrhunderts* 58, *Politische Entwicklung Europas und der Vereinigten Staaten 1815-1871* (in *Propyläen Weltgeschichte*) 60, *Geschichte und Geschichten* 61, *Wallenstein* (biography) 71, *Gentz* 73, *Zwölf Versuche* (essays), *Wallenstein, Bilder zu seinem Leben* 73; publisher of *Propyläen Weltgeschichte* 60-64 and of *Neue Rundschau* 62-.
Alte Landstrasse 39, Kilchberg am Zürichsee, Switzer-land.
Telephone: Zürich 715-46-66.

Mann, Thaddeus Robert Rudolph, C.B.E., M.D., SC.D., PH.D., F.R.S.; British physiologist and biochemist; b. 4 Dec. 1908, Lwów, Poland; *s.* of William and Emilia (née Quest); *m.* Cecilia Lutwak, M.D., PH.D., 1934; ed. Univs. of Lwow and Cambridge.
Commenced biochemical research 33, first in field of muscle biochemistry (working with J. K. Parnas); carried out studies on various enzymes, e.g. peroxidase, polyphenoloxidase, carbonic anhydrase (with D. Keilin) 35-39; studied biochemistry of mould fungi 39-44; studied biochemistry of semen and of male reproduc-tive tract 44-; Fellow of Royal Soc. 51; Dir. Agricultural Research Council Unit of Reproductive Physiology and Biochemistry, Cambridge 54-; Fellow of Trinity Hall, Cambridge 61-; Prof. of Physiology of Reproduction, Univ. of Cambridge 67-; Corresp. mem. Belgian Royal Acad. of Medicine 71; Dr. h.c. (Univs. of Cracow and Ghent); Knight of Italian Order of Merit; Amory Prize, American Acad. of Arts and Sciences.
Publs. *Biochemistry of Semen* 54, *Biochemistry of Semen and of the Male Reproductive Tract* 64; about 200 publs. in fields of biochemistry of muscle, blood, plants, fungi, spermatozoa and reproductive organs.
Unit of Reproductive Physiology and Biochemistry, Downing Street, Cambridge, England.
Telephone: 63214, 77222.

Mann, Thomas Clifton, B.A., LL.B.; American lawyer and diplomatist; b. 11 Nov. 1912; ed. Baylor Univ.
Member, law firm Mann and Mann, Texas 34-42; Foreign Service, Uruguay, Washington, Athens, Guatemala 42-55; Amb. to El Salvador 55-57; Asst. Sec. of State for Econ. Affairs 57-60, for Inter-American Affairs 61; Amb. to Mexico 61-63; Asst. Sec. of State for Latin American Affairs 64-65; Under Sec. of State for Econ. Affairs 65-66; Pres. Automobile Manufacturers' Asscn. 67-71; Consultant May 71-; Hon. LL.D. (Notre-Dame).
8105 Middle Court, Austin, Texas 78759, U.S.A.

Mannin, Ethel; British writer and journalist; b. 11 Oct. 1900, London; d. of Robert Mannin and Edith Gray; m. 1st J. A. Porteous 1919, one d.; m. 2nd Reginald Reynolds 1938.
Associate Editor *The Pelican* 18-20.
Leisure interests: gardening, walking, reading.
Publs. include (Novels *Sounding Brass* 25, *Ragged Banners* 31, *Linda Shawn* 32, *Venetian Blinds* 33, *Men are Unwise* 34, *Cactus* 35, *The Pure Flame* (sequel to Cactus) 36, *Women also Dream* 37, *Rose and Sylvie* 38, *Darkness my Bride* 39, *Julie* 40, *Rolling in the Dew* 40, *Red Rose* 41, *Captain Moonlight* 42, *The Blossoming Bough* 43, *Proud Heaven* 44, *Lucifer and the Child* 45, *The Dark Forest* 46, *Comrade O Comrade* 47, *Late Have I Loved Thee* 48, *Every Man a Stranger* 49, *Bavarian Story* 50, *At Sundown the Tiger* 51, *The Fields at Evening* 52, *Lover Under Another Name* 53, *The Living Lotus* 56, *Pity the Innocent* 57, *Fragrance of Hyacinths* 58, *The Blue-Eyed Boy* 59, *Sabishisa* 61, *Curfew at Dawn* 62, *The Road to Beersheba* 63, *The Burning Bush* 65, *The Night and its Homing* 66, *The Lady and the Mystic* 67, *Bitter Babylon* 68, *The Midnight Street* 69, *Free Pass to Nowhere* 70, *The Curious Adventure of Major Fosdick* 72, *Mission to Beirut* 73, *Kildoon* 74, *The Late Miss Guthrie* 76; (Travel and Memoirs) *Confessions and Impressions* 30, *South to Samarkand* 36, *Privileged Spectator* (sequel to *Confessions*) 39, *Connemara Journal* 48, *German Journey* 48, *Jungle Journey* 50, *This was a Man* (memories of Robert Mannin) 52 *Moroccan Mosaic* 53, *Land of the Crested Lion* 55, *The Country of the Sea* (Brittany) 57, *Brief Voices* (autobiography) 59, *The Flowery Sword* (Japan), 60, *A Lance for the Arabs* 63, *Aspects of Egypt* 64, *The Lovely Land* (Jordan) 65, *An American Journey* 67, *England for a Change* 68, *England at Large* 70, *Young in the Twenties—a Chapter of Autobiography* 71, *My Cat Sammy* 71, *England my Adventure* 72, *Stories from my Life* 73, *An Italian Journey* 74, *Sunset over Dartmoor* (autobiography) 77; (Essays and Miscellaneous) *Common Sense and the Child* 31, *Common Sense and the Adolescent* 38, *Common Sense and Morality* 42, *Women and the Revolution* 38, *Christianity—or Chaos* 40, *Bread and Roses* (A Survey of Utopias) 44, *Two Studies in Integrity: Francis Mahony ("Father Prout") and Gerald Griffin* 54, *Rebels' Ride: the Revolt of the Individual* 64, *Loneliness: a Study of the Human Condition* 66, *Practitioners of Love: some Aspects of the Human Phenomenon* 69; (Short Stories) *Green Figs* 31, *No More Mimosa* 43, *The Wild Swans* (tales based on the ancient Irish) 52, *So Tiberias* (a novella) 54.
Overhill, Brook Lane, Shaldon, Teignmouth, Devon, England.

Manning, Rt. Hon. Ernest Charles, P.C., C.C.; Canadian politician; b. 20 Sept. 1908, Carnduff, Saskatchewan; s. of George Henry Manning and Elizabeth Mara Dickson; m. Muriel Aileen Preston 1936; two s.; ed. Rosetown, Saskatchewan.
Member Legislative Assembly (Social Credit), Alberta 35-68; Provincial Sec. and Minister of Trades and Industry Alberta Govt. 35-43; Provincial Treasurer 44-55; Minister of Mines and Minerals 52-62; Attorney-Gen. 55-68; Premier 43-68; Pres. M & M Systems Research Ltd.; Dir. Canadian Imperial Bank of

Commerce, The Steel Co. of Canada Ltd., Canadian Pacific Airlines, The Manufacturers Life Insurance Co., Melton Real Estate Ltd., McIntyre Porcupine Mines Ltd., Consolidated Graphics Ltd., Burns Foods Ltd., Haelan Industries Ltd.
P.O. Box 2317, Edmonton, Alberta, Canada.

Manning, Robert Joseph; American journalist; b. 25 Dec. 1919, Binghamton, N.Y.; s. of Joseph James Manning and Agnes Pauline Brown; m. Margaret Marinda Raymond 1944; three s.
U.S. Army service 42-43; Nieman Fellow, Harvard Univ. 45-46; State Dept. and White House Corresp. 44-46, Chief UN Corresp. 46-49; Writer, *Time* magazine 49-55, Senior Editor 55-58, Chief, London Bureau, *Time*, *Life*, *Fortune*, *Sports Illustrated* magazines 58-61; Sunday Editor, *New York Herald Tribune* 61-62; Asst. Sec. of State for Public Affairs, Dept. of State 62-64; Exec. Editor *Atlantic Monthly* 64-66, Editor-in-Chief 66-.
Office: 8 Arlington Street, Boston, Mass. 02116, U.S.A.
Telephone: 617-536-9500.

Manning, H.E. Cardinal Timothy; American (Irish born) ecclesiastic; b. 15 Nov. 1909, Balingeary, Cork, Ireland.
Ordained 34; consecrated titular Bishop of Lesvi 46, transferred to Fresno 67; consecrated titular Archbishop of Capri 69; Archbishop of Los Angeles 70-; created Cardinal by Pope Paul VI 73.
Archbishop's House, 1531 West 9th Street, Los Angeles, Calif. 90015, U.S.A.

Manojlović, Kosta P., B.A.; Yugoslav musician; b. 1890; ed. Belgrade Theological Seminary, Munich Conservatoire and Oxford Univ.
Compositions include: *Olče naš*, *Nalne Zesme*, *Mnjoga ljeta*, *Litwegija Opelo*, *By the Waters of Babylon* (for two choirs, baritone solo and orchestra), *Pesme Zemlje*, *Tužbalica*, *Pesme Zemlje Raške*, *Jugoslovenske narodne pesme;* various songs, etc.
Publs. *Zivot i rad St. Mokranjca*, *Istorijski pogled na postanak*, *rad*, *i ideje Muzičke Skole u Beogradu*, *Muzičke karakteristike našeg Juga*, *Debru i Zupi Muzičko delo našega sela*, *Istoriski pogledu na muz uki Engleskoj*, *Stevan St. Mokranjac i njegove muzičke studije u Münchena.*
Kralja Milana 84, Belgrade, Yugoslavia.

Manrique, Capt. Francisco G.; Argentine naval officer, journalist and politician; b. 1919, Mendoza; ed. Naval Acad.
Serving naval officer until 58; took part in operations in Antarctica 49; fmr. Dir. Naval Acad., Río Santiago; took part in Revolution 55; held office in the Casa Militar under Presidents Leonardi and Aramburu; journalist 58-; founded newspaper *Correo de la tarde* 58; Minister of Social Welfare June 70-Aug. 72; Presidential Candidate March 73, Sept. 73; Alianza Popular Federalista.
c/o Alianza Popular Federalista, Buenos Aires, Argentina.

Mansager, Felix Norman; American business executive; b. 30 Jan. 1911, Dell Rapids, S. Dak.; s. of Hoff and Alice (Qualseth) Mansager; m. Geraldine Larson 1931; one s. two d.; ed. Colton High School.
General Sales Manager, The Hoover Company 59, Vice-Pres. (Sales) 59-61, Exec. Vice-Pres. and Dir. The Hoover Company 61-63, Hoover Group 63-66, Pres. and Chair. 66-75; Dir. Harter Bank & Trust Co., Canton, O.; Trustee at Large and Chair. Independent Coll. Funds of America, Rotary Int. Pilgrims of the U.S.; Trustee Graduate Theological Union (Calif.), Eisenhower Exchange Fellowships; Fellow Brit. Inst. of Management; Steering Cttee. Strathclyde Univ. (Scotland); mem. and Gov. Ditchley Foundation; mem. Asscn. of Ohio Commodores, Council on Foreign Rela-

tions, The Newcomen Soc. in N. America, Ohio Foundation of Ind. Colls., Nat. Business Council for Consumer Affairs; Hon. mem. World League of Norsemen; Hon. LL.D. (Capital Univ., Columbus, Ohio and Strathclyde Univ., Scotland), Hon. L.H.D. (Malone Coll.), Medal of Honour, Vaasa Univ.; Chevalier of the Order of Léopold (Belgium), Grand Dukes of Burgundy, Knight 1st Class, Order of St. Olav (Norway) 71; British Inst. of Marketing Award 71; Canton Chamber of Commerce Award of Appreciation 71; Chevalier, Légion d'Honneur 73, Hon. C.B.E. 73.
Leisure interests: reading, golf.
The Hoover Co., North Canton, Ohio 44720, U.S.A.
Telephone: 216-499-9200.

Mansfield, Sir Alan James, K.C.M.G., K.C.V.O., K.ST.J., LL.B.; Australian judge; b. 30 Sept. 1902, Indooroopilly, Queensland; *s.* of Edward Mansfield; *m.* Beryl Susan Barnes 1933; one *s.* one *d.*; ed. Univ. of Sydney.
Admitted to Bar of N.S.W. 24, Queensland 24; Lecturer in Bankruptcy and Company Laws Univ. of Queensland 39; practised as barrister-at-law Queensland 25-40; Judge of Supreme Court of Queensland 40-; mem. Australian War Crimes Board of Enquiry 45; Australian rep. UN War Crimes Comm., London 45; Chief Australian Prosecutor Int. Mil. Tribunal for the Far East Jan. 46-Jan. 47; Chair. of Land Appeal Court, Queensland 42-45; Chair. Aliens Tribunal 42-45; Chair. Royal Comms. on Queensland Sugar Industry 42, 50; Senior Puisne Judge of Queensland 47-55; Acting Chief Justice of Queensland 50, Chief Justice 56-66; Administrator of Govt. of Queensland 57-58; Chair. Central Sugar Cane Prices Board 55; Warden, Queensland Univ. 56-66, Chancellor, Queensland Univ. 66-; Gov. of Queensland 66-72.
Leisure interests: fishing, yachting.
81 Monaco Street, Florida Gardens, Surfers Paradise, Queensland 4217, Australia.

Mansfield, J(ohn) Kenneth; American government official; b. 1921; ed. Northwestern Univ. and Yale Univ.
Instructor in Int. Relations, Yale Univ. 49-50; Chief of Staff, Mil. Applications Sub. Cttee., Joint Congressional Cttee. on Atomic Energy 50-56; combustion engine firm 56-59; Staff Dir. U.S. Senate Sub Cttee. on Nat. Policy Machinery 59-62; Insp. Gen. Foreign Assistance, Dept. of State 62-69, Deputy Dir. Operations, Office of Gen. Scientific Affairs 69-.
Department of State, Washington, D.C. 20520, U.S.A.

Mansfield, Michael Joseph, A.B., A.M.; American politician; b. 16 March 1903, New York; *s.* of Patrick and Josephine O'Brien Mansfield; *m.* Maureen Hayes 1932; one *d.*; ed. Univ. of Montana.
Former mining engineer; Prof. of History and Political Science, Univ. of Montana 33-42; mem. House of Reps. 43-52, Senator (Democrat, Montana) 52-; Majority Whip 57-61; Leader of Senate 61- (Nov. 76).
133 Senate Office Building, Washington, D.C. 20510, U.S.A.

Manshard, Walther, DR. RER. NAT.; German university professor and UNESCO official; b. 17 Nov. 1923, Hamburg; *s.* of Otto and Ida Manshard; *m.* Helga Koch 1951; one *d.*; ed. Univ. of Hamburg.
Assistant Lecturer, Univ. of Southampton, U.K. 50-52; Lecturer, Univ. of Ghana 52-60; Dozent, Univ. of Cologne 60-63; Prof. Univ. of Giessen 63-70; Principal Dir. UNESCO Dept. of Environmental Sciences 70-73; Prof., Head of Dept. Univ. of Freiburg 73-.
Leisure interest: tennis.
Publs. *Die geographische Grundlagen der Wirtschaft Ghanas* 61, *Tropisch Afrika* 63, *Agvargeographie der Tropen* 68, *Afrika—Südlich der Sahara* 70, *Tropical Agriculture* 74.
7812 Bad Krozingen, Schwarzwaldstrasse 24, Federal Republic of Germany.
Telephone: (07633) 34 88.

Mansholt, Sicco Leendert; Netherlands politician; b. 13 Sept. 1908, Ulrun, Groningen, Netherlands; *m.* H. Postel 1937; four *c.*; ed. School for Tropical Agriculture, Deventer.
Studied agriculture; worked on Dutch farms 24-34, tea plantations in Indonesia 34-36; returned to Netherlands and worked on Wieringermeer Polder from 37; during the German occupation organized important illegal work, particularly for the food supply of western provinces and worked on behalf of concentration camp victims; commanded a section of the forces of the Interior after the capitulation; became Burgomaster of Wieringermeer; Minister of Agriculture, Fisheries and Food in Schermerhorn Cabinet June 45-46; in Beel Cabinet 46-48, in Drees Cabinet 48, 51, 52 and 56-58; Head of the Netherlands Del. to UN for agriculture, and took part in negotiations for creation of Benelux Union 46; prepared *Mansholt Plan* for Agricultural Section of European Econ. Community 53; Vice-Pres. European Econ. Community Comm. 58-67; Vice-Pres. Combined Exec. of EEC, ECSC and Euratom 67-72, Pres. March 72-Jan. 73; mem. UN Eminent Persons Group to Study Multinationals 73; Dr. h.c. in Agriculture (Inst. of Agriculture, Wageningen, Gembloux); Grand Croix de l'Ordre de la Couronne de Belgique, Commdr. of the Order of the Netherlands Lion and numerous other foreign awards; Robert Schuman Prize 68.
Home: 95B Avenue Albert Lancaster, Brussels, Belgium; and Communauté Economique Européenne, 200 rue de la Loi, Brussels, Belgium.

Mansour, Ibrahim Moneim; Sudanese politician; b. 1933, Nuhud; ed. Alexandria Univ.
Formerly with Ministry of Commerce and The Agricultural Bank; Deputy Dir. Khartoum Textile Co. 64; Dir. Sudan Textile Factory; Gen. Man. Gulf Int. Corpn.; Minister of Economy and Trade 71-73, of Nat. Economy and Treasury 73-Jan. 75.
Ministry of National Economy, Khartoum, Sudan.

Manuel, Robert; French actor and producer; b. 7 Sept. 1916; ed. Lycée Carnot and National Conservatoire of Dramatic Art, Paris.
Honorary Sec. Comédie-Française; Prof., Nat. Conservatoire of Dramatic Art and Conservatoire de la rue Blanche, Lecturer and Dir. Théâtre Marigny; film actor and dir. of many TV programmes; Mayor of Roquebrune-sur-Argens 71-74; Officier, Légion d'Honneur.
Plays produced include: *Les Trois valses*, *Les Cloches de Corneville*, *Mamzelle Nitouche*, *Les Précieuses Ridicules*, *On ne saurait penser à tout*, *Mariage forcé*, *Bidule*, *Les Croulants se portent bien*, *La Grève des amoureux*, *Gigi*, *Une femme qui ne cache rien*, *La Maison de Zaza*, *la Purée*, *J'y suis, j'y reste*.
Home: Le Buisson, 78370 Plaisir, France.

Manuelli, Ernesto, M.C.S.; Italian financial executive; b. 22 Feb. 1906; ed. Rome Univ.
Banker 23-32; Gen. Sec. Sofindit (Industrial Financial Co.) 32-35; Gen. Inspector, Office of Foreign Trade and Currencies, Rome 35-40; Central Dir., Vice-Pres., Commr., Pres. Bd. of Dirs. Ansaldo S.p.A. Genoa 40-45; Gen. Man., Dir., mem. Exec. Cttee., Finsider S.p.A. Rome 45-58, Chair. Board of Dirs. 58-75; Chair. EGAM 75-; Vice-Pres. Société Financière Italo-Suisse; Dir. Alfa Romeo and other companies; Cavaliere del Lavoro.
Publs. Economic research papers.
495 Via Della Camilluccia, Rome; 122 Viale Castro Pretorio, Rome, Italy.

Manzhulo, Alexei Nikolayevich; Soviet foreign trade official; b. 15 Sept. 1913; ed. Inst. of Motor Roads, Acad. of Foreign Trade.
Member C.P.S.U. 40-; Chief of Section, later Deputy Trade Rep. of U.S.S.R. in England 46-51; Official, Ministry of Foreign Trade 51-52; Counsellor, COMECON 52-53; U.S.S.R. Commercial Rep. in Argentina 53-57; Deputy Chief of Dept., Ministry of Foreign Trade,

Cuba 60-62; Chief of Dept., Ministry of Foreign Trade 62-71; Vice-Minister, Ministry of Foreign Trade 71-; Order of Lenin and Order of Red Banner of Labour. U.S.S.R. Ministry of Foreign Trade, 32-34 Smolenskaya-Sennaya Ploshchad, Moscow, U.S.S.R.

Manzini, Raimondo, G.C.V.O.; Italian diplomatist; b. 1913, Bologna; s. of Giuseppe Manzini and Amalia Raschi; ed. Univ. of California and Univ. degli Studi, Bologna.
Diplomatic Service 40-, served San Francisco, Lisbon, Foreign Ministry, Rome, and London 40-47; Consul-Gen., Léopoldville 47-51, Stuttgart 51-53; Foreign Ministry, Rome 53-64; Italian Rep. to Org. for Econ. Co-operation and Devt. (OECD) 65-68; Amb. to U.K. 68-75; Sec.-Gen., Ministry of Foreign Affairs 75-.
Leisure interest: sailing.
Ministry of Foreign Affairs, Rome, Italy.

Manzù, Giacomo; Italian sculptor; b. 22 Dec. 1908.
Began his career working in a gilder's then a plasterer's studio; attended evening classes in plastic arts; Prof. of Sculpture Accad. Brera, Milan 40-54, Salzburg Int. Sommerakademie 54-60; Exhibition of Paintings and Drawings, Hanover Gallery, London 65; Exhibition of Sculpture at Hanover Gallery, London 69; Exhibition at Bordeaux 69; museum devoted to his work opening in Ardea, May 69; Sculpture Prize, Venice Biennale 48; major works include main door of Salzburg Cathedral, *Porta delle Morte*, San Pietro in Vaticano, Rome and *Porta della Pace e della Guerra*, St. Laurenz Church, Rotterdam; corresp. mem. Acad. des Beaux Arts (France) 69-; Hon. doctorate, Royal Coll. of Art, London 71; Lenin Peace Prize 66.
Publs. *La Porta di San Pietro* 64, *Un artista e il Papa* 68.
00040 Ardea, Rome, Italy.

Mao Tse-tung; Chinese party leader; b. 26 Dec. 1893, Shaoshan, Hunan; m. 1st Yang K'asi-hui 1920, 2nd Chiang Ch'ing (q.v.) 1939; ed. Hunan Prov. No. 1 Middle School, Hunan Prov. No. 1 Normal School.
Leader of Chinese Communist Revolution; organized New People's Soc. 17; Library Asst. Peking Univ. Library 18; edited, published *The Hsiang River Review* 19; Principal, Elementary School, Hunan 20-22; CCP activist in Hunan 22-23; mem. Politburo, 3rd Cen. Cttee. of CCP 23; Dir. Kuomintang Propaganda Dept. 25; organized Autumn Harvest Uprising, Hunan 27; Political Commissar Red Army 28; mem. 6th Cen. Cttee. of CCP 28; Chair. Cen. Chinese Soviet Repub. 31-34; led Long March to Yenan 34-36; Political Commissar, Chinese Worker-Peasant Red Army Coll. 36; Principal, Yenan Party School 42; Chair. Politburo, 7th Cen. Cttee. of CCP 45; attended Chungking Conf. between CCP and Kuomintang 45; assumed name of Li Te-sheng while heading CCP org., North Shensi 47; directed mil. operations with Chou En-Lai from Hsiaoho 47; led forces to Shensi-Chalae-Hopei Border Region 48; Chair. Standing Cttee., Preparatory Cttee. for 1st Chinese People's Political Consultative Conf. 49; Chair. Cen. People's Govt. 49-54; Chair. People's Repub. of China 54-59; Chair. 8th Cen. Cttee. of CCP 56, mem. Standing Cttee. of Politburo 56; Chair. 9th Cen. Cttee. of CCP 69, mem. Standing Cttee. of Politburo 69; Chair. 10th Cen. Cttee. of CCP 73, mem. Standing Cttee. of Politburo 73.
Publs. articles and pamphlets collected in 4 vols. of *Selected Works*.
Central Committee of the Communist Party of China, Peking, People's Republic of China.

Mara, Ratu the Rt. Hon. Sir Kamisese Kapaiwai Tuimacilai, P.C., K.B.E., M.A.; Fiji politician; b. 13 May 1920; ed. Queen Victoria School and Central Medical School, Suva, Fiji, Sacred Heart Coll., Otago Univ., Oxford Univ., and London School of Economics.
Cadet, District Officer and Commr., Overseas Colonial Service, Fiji 51-61; mem. Legis. Council, Fiji 53-; mem. Exec. Council, Fiji 59-61; mem. for Natural Resources 64-66; Leader, Fiji Del. Constitutional Conf., London 65; Chief Minister 67-70; Prime Minister 70-; Hon. Fellow Wadham Coll. 71; Hon. LL.D. (Guam, Otago, New Delhi); Grandmaster of the Order of the National Lion, Dakar 75.
The Office of the Prime Minister, Suva, Fiji.

Marai, Sándor; Hungarian-born American poet and novelist; b. 11 April 1900.
Publs. *Emlékkönyv, Versek, Panaszkönyv, A mészáros, Zendülök, Idegen emberek, Csutora, Egy Polgár vallomásai, Bébi, vagy az elsö szerelem, A szegények ishoLája, Bolhapiac, Istenek nyomdban, A féltékenyek, Válás Buddn, Kabala, Napnyugati örjdrat A négy évszak, A sziget, Müsoron kivül, Sèrbödöttek*; also many novels, plays, etc., published in Czech, German, Finnish, Danish, French, Italian, Dutch, Spanish and Swedish.
100 Park Terrace West, New York 34, N.Y., U.S.A.

Maraini, Dacia; Italian author; b. 13 Nov. 1936; d. of Fosco Maraini (q.v.); ed. Collegio S.S. Annunziata, Florence and Rome.
Prix Formentor for *L'Età del Malessere* (*The Age of Discontent*) 62.
Publs. *La Vacanza* 62, *L'Età del Malessere* 62, *Crudeltà All' Aria Aperta* (poems) 66, *A Memoria* (novel) 67, *La famiglia normale* (one-act play) 67, *Il ricatto a teatro* (play) 68, *Memoirs of a Female Thief* 73.
Lungotevere Della Vittoria 1, Rome, Italy.
Telephone: 378936.

Maraini, Fosco, D.S.C. (father of Dacia Maraini, q.v.); Italian writer; b. 15 Nov. 1912; s. of Antonio Maraini and Yoi Crosse; m. Topazia Alliata 1935 (divorced); three d.; ed. Univ. of Florence.
Asst. Prof., Univ. of Hokkaido, Japan 38-41; Reader in Italian, Univ. of Kyoto 41-43; civil internee (as anti-Fascist) in Japan 43-45; returned to Italy 46; Fellow, St. Antony's Coll., Oxford; lecturer in Japanese, Univ. of Florence; writing and research on anthropology and ethnology of Asia.
Leisure interests: music, skiing, mountaineering.
Publs. *Secret Tibet* 53, *Meeting with Japan* 59, *Karakoram* 61, *Hekura* 62, *Where Four Worlds Meet* 64, *Japan: Patterns of Continuity* 71.
Viale Magalotti 6, Florence, Italy.

Marais, Jean; French actor; b. 11 Dec. 1913; ed. Lycées Condorcet and Janson-de-Sailly, and Conservatoire Maubel.
Appeared in *L'Epervier, Le Scandale, L'Aventurier, Le Bonheur, Dans les Rues, Les Hommes Nouveaux;* also appeared in plays, including *Oedipe Roi, Les Chevaliers de la Table Ronde, Les Parents Terribles, Britannicus, La Machine à Ecrire, L'Avare, Andromaque, Pygmalion, Two For the Seesaw,* etc.; served French Army 39-40 and 44-45; later made more films, including *L'Eternal, Retour, Aux Yeux du Souvenir, Le Secret de Mayerling, Orphée, Le Château de Verre, Julietta, Elena et les Hommes, Typhon sur Nagazaky, La Vie à Deux, Amour de Poche, Les Nuits Blanches, Chaque Jour a son Secret, Versailles Le Bossu, Austerlitz, Le Testament d'Orphée, Le Capitan, La Princesse de Clèves, Les Mystères de Paris, Patate, Fantomas, Le Saint Prend l'Affut, La Provocation, Peau d'Ane;* television appearances in *Renaud et Armide* 69, *Robert Macaire* 70, *Joseph Balsam* 73, *Karatekas and Co.* 73; Pres. Union des Artistes 74-.
Artmedia, 37 rue Marbeuf, 75008 Paris, France.

Maramis, J. B. P.; Indonesian diplomatist; b. 23 Jan. 1922, Limbung, Celebes Island, Indonesia; ed. Univ. of Leyden.
Served in Directorate of Econ. Affairs, Ministry of Foreign Affairs 51-54; First Sec., Teheran 54-58; Deputy Head, Directorate of UN Affairs, Ministry of

Foreign Affairs 58-60; Counsellor, Indonesian Mission to UN 60-65; Head, Directorate of Int. Orgs., Ministry of Foreign Affairs 65-68; del. to UN Gen. Assembly 66-68; Deputy Perm. Rep. to UN 69-72, Rep. UN Econ and Social Council (ECOSOC) 68, Vice-Pres. 69, Pres. 70; Amb. to Belgium and Luxembourg and Chief Indonesian Mission to EEC 72-73; Exec. Sec. UN Econ. and Social Comm. for Asia and the Pacific (ESCAP) 73-. ESCAP, Sala Santitham, Bangkok 2, Thailand.

Marca-Relli, Corrado; American artist; b. 5 June 1913.
One man exhibition Niveau Gallery 47, 49, Rome 48, New Gallery 50, Stable Gallery 52, Kootz Gallery (all in New York City) 59; in exhibitions Whitney Museum 53, 55, Yale Univ. Gallery 54, Tate Gallery, London 63; Ford Foundation Award 59; Visiting Prof. Univ. of Calif. at Berkeley 58; Visiting Critic Yale 59-60.
411 E 57th Street, New York, N.Y., 10021, U.S.A.

Marceau, Félicien (*pseudonym* of Louis Carette); French writer; b. 16 Sept. 1913, Cortenberg, Belgium; s. of Louis Carette and Marie Lefèvre; m. Bianca Licenziati; ed. Coll. de la Sainte Trinité à Louvain and Univ. de Louvain.
Prix Interallié for *Les Elans du Coeur* 55; Prix Goncourt for *Creezy* 69; Prix Prince Pierre de Monaco 74; Grand Prix du Théâtre 75.
Leisure interest: painting.
Publs. Novels: *Chasseneuil* (By Invitation only) 48, *Bergère Légère* (The China Shepherdess) 57, *Creezy* 69, *Le Corps de mon Ennemi* 75; plays: *L'Oeuf* 56, *La Bonne Soupe* 58, *La Preuve par Quatre* 65, *Un Jour j'ai rencontré la Vérité* 67, *Le Babour* 69, *L'Ouvre-Boîte* 72, *L'Homme en Question* 73; essays: *Balzac et Son Monde* 55; memoirs: *Les Années Courtes* 68.
c/o Les Editions Gallimard, 5 rue Sébastien-Bottin, Paris 7e, France.
Telephone: 544-39-19.

Marceau, Marcel; French mime; b. 22 March 1923; ed. Strasbourg Lycée, and Ecole des Beaux-Arts, Paris.
Director Compagnie de Mime Marcel Marceau 49-; annual world tours, and numerous television appearances throughout the world; created *Don Juan* (mime drama) 64, *Candide* (ballet), Hamburg 71; creator of the character "Bip"; mimes include *Le Manteau, Exercises de Style* (both filmed), *Mort avant l'Aube, Le Joueur de Flûte, Moriana et Galvau, Pierrot de Montmartre, Les Trois Perruques, Exercices de Style,* etc.; other films: *Pantomime, Un Jardin Public, Le Fabricant de masques, Paris qui rit, Paris qui pleure, Barbarella.*
Théâtre des Champs-Elysées 15 avenue Montaigne, 75008 Paris, France.

Marcellin, Raymond, D. en D.; French politician and lawyer; b. 19 Aug. 1914; ed. Meaux Coll., Paris and Strasbourg Univs.
Under-Secretary of State of the Interior 48-49; Sec. of State of Industry 49-52, of the Pres. of the Council 52, of Information 52-57, of Public Functions 57-62; Minister of Public Health and of the Population 62-66, of Industry 66-67; Minister under Prime Minister, Responsible for Plan 67-68; Minister of Interior 68-74, of Agricultural Devt. March-May 74; Deputy 46-56, 67, 68, 73; Pres. Conseil Général du Morbihan 64; Mayor of Vannes 65-; Senator for Morbihan 74-; Croix de Guerre, Médaille des Evadés.
Publ. *L'Ordre Public et les Groupes Révolutionnaires* 69.
Le Sénat, 15 rue de Vaugirard, 75291 Paris, France.

Marchais, Georges; French politician; b. 7 June 1920, La Hoquette; m.; c.
Former metal worker; active in trade union movt.; joined French Communist Party 47, mem. Cen. Cttee. 56; mem. Political Bureau 59, Sec. Cen. Cttee. 61, Sec.-Gen. Dec. 72-; Deputy to Nat. Assembly 73-.
Publs. *Qu'est-ce que le Parti Communiste Français?* 70,

Les Communistes et les Paysans (co-author) 72, *Le Défi Démocratique* 73, *La Politique du Parti Communiste Français* 74.
Parti Communiste Français, 2 Place du Colonel Fabien, Paris 19e, France.
Telephone: 202-70-10.

Marchal, André; French professor; b. 11 Oct. 1907; ed. Lycée Henri Poincaré, Nancy and Paris Univs.
Lawyer, Nancy Court of Appeal, then at Public Prosecutor's Office 29-35; Asst. Paris Faculty of Law 33-35; Prof. Dijon Faculty of Law 35-39; served French Army 39-40; in charge of course Paris Faculty of Law 42-44; Asst. Prof. 44-45; Prof. 45; Dir. of Studies, Ecole Pratique des Hautes Etudes 54-.
Publs. *La Conception de l'Economie Nationale et des Rapports Internationaux chez les Mercantilistes Français et chez leurs Contemporains* 31, *L'Action Ouvrière et la Transformation du Régime Capitaliste* 43, *Economie Politique et Technique Statistique* 43, *Le Mouvement Syndical en France* 45, *La pensée économique en France depuis 1945* 53, *Méthode scientifique et Science économique* (2 vols.); *Systèmes et Structures économiques* 59, *L'Europe Solidaire* 64, *L'Intégration Territoriale* 65.
180 rue de Grenelle, Paris 7e, France.

Marchand, André Marius; French painter; b. 10 Feb. 1907; s. of Henri Marchand and Madeleine Cécile Michel de l'Hospital; ed. Colls. of Aix-en-Provence, Bouches du Rhône, and studied in Paris.
Has exhibited in Paris since 34; in Holland 36, Cambridge 39, Washington, Boston and Chicago 39, Rio de Janeiro 45, Brussels 45, 68, Canada 46, New York 46, Berne, 48, Geneva 48, 67, Stuttgart 48, London, Stockholm, Avignon 49, Innsbruck 50; Bienal in São Paulo 51; exhibitions in museums in Holland and Belgium 51, in London (Wildenstein Galleries) 52, in Switzerland and Germany 53; in New York (Wildenstein Gallery) 54, Venice Biennale 54, in Mexico and Guatemala 67, in Baden Baden 74; work on permanent exhibition in Musée d'Art Moderne, Galerie Maeght, Galerie Louis Carré (Paris), and in Grenoble, Arles, Algiers, Toulouse, The Hague, Liège, Eindhoven, Turin, Tokyo; a founder mem. and exhibitor in Salon de Mai (since 45); illustrated (lithographs) *Les Nourritures Terrestres* (André Gide), *Le Visionnaire* (Julien Green), etc. and designed for the works of Darius Milhaud and Jacques Audiberti; Paul Guillaume Prize 37, Arche Prize for design 52; lithographs for *Petite Cosmogonie Portative* (Raymond Queneau) 55.
31 bis rue Campagne Première, 75014 Paris, France.
Telephone: 033-10-97.

Marchand, Jean, P.C.; Canadian politician; b. 20 Dec. 1918; ed. Acad. Commerciale, Quebec and Faculty of Sciences, Laval Univ.
Organizer Confed. of Catholic Workers 45, Gen. Sec. 47-61; Pres. Confed. of Nat. Trade Unions 61; mem. Royal Comm. of Enquiry on Bilingualism and Biculturalism 63-65; Mem. of Parl. 65-; Minister of Citizenship and Immigration 65, of Manpower and Immigration 66; Minister of Forestry and Rural Devt. 68-69; Minister of Regional Econ. Expansion Oct. 69-Nov. 72; Minister of Transport Nov. 72-75; Minister without Portfolio, Sept. 75-; Liberal; Hon. doctorates, Montreal and Laval Univs.
135 Aberdeen Street, Quebec, P.Q., Canada.

Marchandise-Franquet, Jacques; French lawyer and company executive; b. 6 July 1918; Paris, s. of Paul Marchandise and Mme (née Franquet); m. Jacqueline Feuillette, 1940; three s. two d.; ed. Ecole Libre des Sciences Politiques.
Avocat stagiaire 39; sous-préfet, Dir. of office of Commissaire of the Repub. for Laon 44; auditeur, Council of State 46; head of office of Minister for War Veterans 48; legal adviser, Caisse Centrale de la France d'Outre-Mer 48; chargé de mission for Minister of

France Overseas 52, head of office 53-54; Maître des Requêtes, Council of State 54, Maître des Requêtes Honoraire 62; legal adviser, office of Pres. of Council of Ministers 54-55; Asst. Dir. to Dir.-Gen. Bureau of Mines of France Overseas 55; Sec.-Gen. Fria (int. aluminium production corpn.) 56-60, Vice-Pres. 67, Pres. 69, Vice-Pres. Friguia (part nationalised successor to Fria) 76-; Dir. Pechiney 60, Asst. Dir.-Gen. 70, Dir. délégué to Pechiney Ugine Kuhlmann 71-; Vice-Pres. Dir.-Gen. Librairie Hachette 75-; Officier, Légion d'Honneur; Officier, Ordre Nat. du Mérite; Croix de Guerre 39-45.
24 boulevard Saint-Michel, 75006 Paris; Home: 25 ter boulevard de La Saussaye, 92200 Neuilly, France.
Telephone: 325-22-11 (Office).

Marchesi, Mario; Italian business executive; b. 6 June 1904, Turin; ed. Politecnico di Torino.
Began career with Fiat, then joined Pirelli and subsequently moved to OMB; joined Finsider Group 35; directed construction of Cornigliano Works and subsequently became Gen. Man.; later became Gen. Man. Finsider and Pres. ITALSIDER; now Pres. Innocenti S. Eustacchio; also Dir. and mem. Exec. Cttee. Società Finanziaria Siderurgica Finsider, Società Italiana Impianti and Experimental Metallurgical Centre (C.S.M.); Dir. Società Dalmine and of *Assider*; Cavaliere del Lavoro.
Finsider s.p.a., Viale Castro Pretorio 122, Rome, Italy.

Marchuk, Guri Ivanovich; Soviet physicist; b. 8 June 1925, Petro-Khersonets village, Orenburg Region; ed. Leningrad State Univ.
Postgraduate student, Leningrad State Univ. 49-53; Senior Research Assoc., Head of Dept., Inst. of Physics and Energetics 53-60; Head of Central Computing Centre, Siberian Dept., U.S.S.R. Acad. of Sciences 60-; D.Sc. (Physics and Mathematics) 56, Prof. 58; Corresp. mem. U.S.S.R. Acad. of Sciences 62-68, Academician 68-.
Publs. works on problems of physics of atmosphere.
Akademgorodok, Novosibirsk, U.S.S.R.

Marchuk, Ivan Ivanovich; Soviet diplomatist; b. 14 Nov. 1922, Kozychanka, Kiev region, Ukraine; ed. Univ. of Kiev.
Diplomatic Service 47-; Counsellor, Conakry 59-62; Deputy Head of Press Dept., U.S.S.R. Ministry of Foreign Affairs 62-64; Amb. to Burundi 64-67; on staff of Ministry of Foreign Affairs 67-70; Amb. to Ecuador 70-.
U.S.S.R. Embassy, Quito, Ecuador.

Marcks, Gerhard Wilhelm Albert; German sculptor; b. 18 Feb. 1889, Berlin; m. Maria Schmidtlein 1914; two s. three d.; ed. Gymnasium in Berlin.
Teacher of sculpture Berlin 18; master at Weimar Bauhaus 19-25; teacher, then head, of studies at Halle Giebichenstein 25-33; private work 33-45; teacher at Hamburg Art School 46-50; Orden Pour le Mérite (Fed. Repub. of Germany); works include memorials in Hamburg, Cologne, Mannheim, Bochum, Hanover, Lübeck and Bourdon, France; works on view in New York Museum of Modern Art and other American museums.
Belvedere 149A, Köln-Müngersdorf, Federal Republic of Germany.
Telephone: Cologne 491488.

Marconi, Mario, DR. ECON. AND COMM. SC.; Italian industrialist; b. 14 Feb. 1896, Genoa; m. Maria Brunelli 1931; one s. one d.; ed. Univ. of Genoa.
General Man. of Vickers Terni Genoa 22-29, of Ansaldo, S p.A., Genoa 29-35, of "Aquila", Trieste 35-45; Man. Dir. Silurificio Whitehead of Fiume 35-45; Vice-Pres. Whitehead-Moto Fides, Leghorn 45-58; Man. Dir. Franco Tosi S.p.A., Milan 46-56; Chair. Compagnia Italiana Westinghouse, Freni e Segnali, Turin (1951),

Hon. Chair. 68; Chair. Rexim, Turin; Vice-Pres. Oerlikon Italiana S.p.A., Milan; mem. Board Reinach Oleoblitz S.p.A., etc.; Italian del. to Int. Materials Conf., Washington, D.C. 51-53, 54; Chair. Associazione Nazionale Industria Meccanica Varia ed Affine, ANIMA, Milan 51-54, Hon. Chair. 54-; Cavaliere del Lavoro.
Leisure interests: yachting, bibliophilism.
Via Pagana 6, 16038 Santa Margherita, Ligure (Office and Home), and S. Angelo Pauzo, 06081 Assisi, Perugia, Italy (Home).
Telephone: 0185-87137 (Office and Home); 075-812-487 (Home).

Marcos, Ferdinand Edralin; Philippine lawyer and politician; b. 11 Sept. 1917; m. Imelda Romualdez; one s. two d.; ed. Univ. of the Philippines.
Lieutenant, later Capt. in the Philippines Army and U.S. Forces in the Far East during Second World War; led own unit in anti-Japanese resistance; Special Asst. to Pres. Manuel Roxas 46-47; mem. House of Reps. 49-59, Senate 59-66; Pres. of Senate 63-65; Pres. of the Philippines 66- (re-elected 69), Prime Minister 73-; Dag Hammarskjöld Award 68; numerous war decorations.
Leisure interest: golf.
Malacañang Palace, Manila, Philippines.

Marcus, Aage; Danish writer; b. 31 Dec. 1888.
Librarian, Royal Acad. of Fine Arts, Copenhagen 28-58; editor series of works on popular science 25-34 and of several other series e.g. *Danish Classics* 48 and a series of Sacred Books of the East.
Publs. *Mester Eckehart* 17, *Bibliography of Johannes V. Jensen* 33, *Bibliography of the History of Danish Art* 35, *Leonardo da Vinci* 40, *Den blaa Drage* (Chinese Art and Philosophy) 41, *Billedkunsten* (Art History of the World) 42, *Danish Portrait Drawings* 50, *Christian Mysticism* 53, *Rejse i Sverige* 56, *Hellas* 58, *Höduft fra Havluft* (essays) 58, *Det hellige Land* (The Holy Land) 59, *Danske Levnedsböger* (Danish Memoirs) 65, *Religionernes Digtning* 67, *Den Lange Vej* (Personal Memoirs) 69.
Hørsholm, Denmark.
Telephone: 860511.

Marcus, Rudolph Arthur; American professor of chemistry; b. 21 July 1923, Montreal, Canada; s. of Myer and Esther Marcus; m. Laura Hearne 1949; three s.; ed. McGill Univ., Montreal, Canada.
Worked for Nat. Research Council of Canada 46-49; Univ. of N. Carolina 49-51; Asst. Prof. Polytechnic Inst. of Brooklyn 51-54, Assoc. Prof. 54-58, Prof. 58-64; Prof. Univ. of Illinois 64-; Visiting Prof. of Theoretical Chemistry, Oxford Univ. 75-76; temporary mem. Courant Inst. of Mathematical Sciences, New York Univ. 60-61; Chair. Board of Trustees, Gordon Research Confs. 68-69; fmr. Chair. Div. of Physical Chem., American Chemical Soc.; mem. Exec. Cttee. American Physical Soc. Div. of Chemical Physics 70-72; mem. Advisory Board American Chemical Soc. Petroleum Research Fund 70-72; mem. Review Cttee. Argonne Nat. Laboratory Chemistry Dept. 66-72 (Chair. 68-69), Brookhaven Nat. Laboratory 71-73, Radiation Lab., Univ. of Notre Dame 76-(78); mem. Nat Research Council/Nat. Acad. of Sciences Cttee. on Kinetics of Chemical Reactions 73-, Chair. 75-, Cttee. on Climatic Impact, Panel on Atmospheric Chemistry 75-; mem. editorial boards, *Journal of Chemical Physics* 64-66, *Annual Review of Physical Chemistry* 64-69; *Journal of Physical Chemistry* 68-72, *Accounts of Chemical Research* 68-73, *Int. Journal of Chemical Kinetics* 76-(78); mem. Nat. Acad. of Sciences; Fellow, American Acad. of Arts and Sciences; Prof. Fellow Univ. Coll., Oxford Univ. 75-76; Assoc. mem. Center for Advanced Studies, Univ. of Illinois 68-69; Anne Molson prize for Chem. 43; Nat. Science Foundation Senior Post-Doctoral Fellowship 60-61; Alfred P. Sloan Fellowship 60-63; Fulbright-

Hays Senior Scholar 71-72; Alexander von Humboldt Foundation Senior U.S. Scientist Award 76.
Leisure interests: music and history.
Publs. numerous articles in scientific journals, especially *Journal of Chemical Physics.*
Department of Chemistry, University of Illinois, Urbana, Ill. 61801; Home: 2207 South Anderson Street, Urbana, Ill. 61801, U.S.A.
Telephone: 217-333-0537 (Office); 217-367-8684 (Home).

Marcus, Stanley; American business executive; b. 20 April 1905; s. of late Herbert Marcus, Sr. and of Minnie Lichtenstein Marcus; m. Mary Cantrell 1932; one s. two d.; ed. Amherst Coll., Harvard Univ., and Harvard Business School.
Joined Neiman-Marcus 26, Sec., Treas. and Dir. 28, Merchandise Man. of Sports Shop 28, Merchandise Man. of all Apparel Divs. 29, Exec. Vice-Pres. 35-50, Pres. 50-72, Chair. of Board, Chief Exec. Officer 73-, Chair. Exec. Cttee. 75-; Dir. and Corporate Vice-Pres. Cartec Hawley Hale Stores Inc., Los Angeles; Dir. Republic of Dallas Corpn., New York Life Insurance Co.; Dir. Dallas Symphony Soc. (Pres. 48-49), Dallas Citizens Council (fmr. Pres.), North Texas State Comm.; Advisory Dir. Fort Worth Art Asscn.; Chair. Southern Methodist Univ. Library Advancement Programme; mem. Business Cttee. for the Arts, Bd. of Dirs. for Dallas World Trade Centre, Bd. of Publs. of Southern Methodist Univ.; Trustee, Southern Methodist Univ., Baylor Coll. of Dentistry, Eisenhower Exchange Fellowships, Cttee. for Econ. Devt., Urban Inst.; Research Fellow, Southwestern Legal Foundation; numerous awards from U.S.A., Austria, Denmark, U.K., Italy, Belgium, France; Hon. D.H. (Southern Methodist Univ.) 65.
Leisure interests: collecting primitive books, books on typography, collecting African and other primitive art.
Publ. *Minding the Store* 75.
1 Nonesuch Road, Dallas, Tex. 75214, U.S.A.

Marcuse, Herbert, PH.D.; American (naturalized 1940) professor of philosophy; b. 19 July 1898, Berlin, Germany; ed. Univs. of Berlin and Freiburg.
Went to U.S. 34; with Inst. of Social Research, Columbia Univ. 34-40, Russian Inst., Columbia and Harvard Univs. 51-53; Prof. of Politics and Philosophy, Brandeis Univ. 54-65; fmr. Prof. of Philosophy, Univ. of Calif. at San Diego; served with Office of Strategic Services and State Dept. 41-50.
Publs. *Reason and Revolution* 41, *Eros and Civilization* 54, *Soviet Marxism* 58, *One-Dimensional Man* 65, *The Ethics of Revolution* (essay) 66, *Negations* 68, *An Essay on Liberation* 69, *Counter-revolution and Revolt* 72, *Studies in Critical Philosophy* 72.
University of California, San Diego, P.O. Box 109, La Jolla, Calif. 92037, U.S.A.

Marczewski, Jan; French university professor; b. 27 May 1908, Warsaw, Poland; s. of Witold Marczewski and Rose Szymanska; m. Janine-Victoire Wroblewska 1930; one s.; ed. Lycée Henri Poincaré, Nancy, Univs. of Nancy, Strasbourg and Paris à la Sorbonne.
Early career in Polish Consular Service 26-40; War Service with Polish Army in France; Scientific Dir. Institut de Science Economique Appliquée, Paris, and mem. Higher Council for Nat. Revenue 46-50; Prof. Inst. Political Studies, Paris, Scientific Dir. East European Section of Nat. Foundation of Political Sciences, and Founder and Dir. Preparation Centre, Univ. of Caen 52-59, Hon. Prof. 59-; Prof. of Economics, Univ. of Paris I 59-; Pres. French Econ. Asscn., Soc. of Political Econ.; Scientific Dir. *Europe de l'Est et Union Soviétique* 52-59; Chevalier Légion d'Honneur, Croix de Guerre, Krzyż Walecznych (Poland).
Leisure interests: skiing, sailing, swimming.
Publs. *Politique monétaire et financière du IIIe Reich* 41, *Planification et croissance économique des démocraties*

populaires 56, *La conjoncture économique des Etats-Unis 1850-1960* 61, *L'Europe dans la conjoncture mondiale* 63, *Comptabilité Nationale* 65, *Introduction à l'Histoire Quantitative* 66, *Crise de la planification socialiste* 73 (English trans. 74, Spanish trans. 75).
53 boulevard Suchet, Paris 16e, France.
Telephone: 525-57-03.

Maree, Willem Adriaan, B.A.; South African politician; b. 7 Aug. 1920; s. of W. A. Maree and A. J. M. Marx; m. M. Jansen van Rensburg; one s. one d.; ed. High School, Brandfort (Orange Free State), and Univ. of Pretoria.
National Party Organizer 43-45; farmer 45-48; M.P. Newcastle 48-68; mem. Native Affairs Comm. 54-58; Minister of Bantu Educ. 58-66, of Indian Affairs Aug. 61-66, and of Forestry 64-66; Minister of Community Devt., Public Works, Social Welfare and Pensions 66-68, Immigration Selection Board Electricity Control Board; Gov. S.A.B.C.; dir. various private and public cos.
Leisure interests: golf, hunting.
78 Kasteel Straat, Lynnwood Glen, Pretoria, Republic of South Africa.
Telephone: 472911.

Marei, Sayed Ahmed; Egyptian politician; b. 26 Aug. 1913; m. Soad Marei 1941; two s. one d.; ed. Faculty of Agriculture, Cairo Univ.
Worked on his father's farm after graduation; subsequently with import-export, pharmaceutical, seed, and fertilizer companies; mem. Egyptian House of Commons 45-49; Del. mem. Higher Cttee. for Agrarian Reform 52-; Chair. of Board, Agricultural Co-operative Credit Bank 55-56; initiated "Supervised Credit System"; Minister of State for Agrarian Reform 56-57; Minister of Agriculture and Agrarian Reform 57-58; Central Minister for Agriculture and Agrarian Reform in the U.A.R. 58-61; later Deputy Speaker U.A.R. Nat. Assembly; Pres. Bank Misr, Cairo 63-67; Minister of Agriculture June 67-70, and of Agrarian Reform 68-70; Deputy Premier of Agriculture and Land Reform, Land Reclamation 70-72; Sec. Arab Socialist Union 72-73; Asst. to Pres. 73-75; Sec.-Gen. UN World Food Conf., Rome 74, Pres. first meeting, World Food Council, Rome June 75; Speaker People's Assembly.
Publs. *Agrarian Reform in Egypt* (in English), *Agriculture in the U.A.R. Enters a New Era* (in English); *Problems of Agrarian Reform and the Population Explosion, Food Production in Developing Countries: Possibilities and Means, Agriculture in Egypt* (in English), reports on Agricultural Missions to Syria, U.S.S.R., Italy, U.S.A. and Iraq.
People's Assembly, Cairo; and 9 Sh. Shagaret El Dorzamalek, Cairo, Egypt.
Telephone: 800166.

Marek, Bruno; Austrian politician; b. 23 Jan. 1900. Director of Vienna Int. Trade Fair 45-65; mem. Vienna District Council and Chair. of Finance Cttee. 45-; First Pres. Vienna Provincial Parl. 49-65; mem. Exec. Cttee. Austrian Socialist Party 65-; Provincial Head and Mayor of City of Vienna June 65-; mem. Bundesrat June 65-; Chair. Fed. of Austrian Cities; Austrian, German, Greek and French decorations.
Vienna VI, Capistrangasse 5/1, Austria.

Marella, H.E. Cardinal Paulo, S.T.D., J.C.D.; Italian ecclesiastic; b. 25 Jan. 1895; ed. Roman Seminary, Apollinaris, and Royal Univ., Rome.
Ordained 18; official in Sacred Congregation of Propaganda Fide 21; Counsellor, Apostolic Del. Washington 23; Titular Archbishop of Doclea 33-66, Hon. Bishop of Doclea 66-; Apostolic Del. to Japan 33, to Australia, New Zealand and Oceania 48-53, to France 53-59; Archpriest of St. Peter's Basilica; fmr. Pres. Secr. for non-Christians; cr. Cardinal 59.
Via della Conciliazione 44, 00193 Rome, Italy.

Maremont, Arnold Harold; American industrialist; b. 24 Aug. 1904, Chicago; s. of Myer D. and Kate (Wolens) Maremont; m. 1st Virginia Weisels 1928, one s.; m. 2nd Adele Heineman 1937, one s. one d.; m. 3rd Eileen Adler 1968; ed. Chicago Univ.
Admitted to Illinois Bar 26; Dir. Maremont Corpn. 48-, Pres. 52-59, Chair. Exec. Cttee. 69-71; mem. Board of Dirs. Planned Parenthood—World Population 64-68; mem. Exec. Cttee. Int. Planned Parenthood Fed. 64; First Vice-Pres. Nat. Asscn. Mental Health 63-66; Assoc. Trustee Bard Coll. 60-64; Governing Life mem. Art Inst. Chicago.
470 South Ocean Boulevard, Apt. 8, Palm Beach, Fla. 33480, U.S.A.

Maretskaya, Vera Petrovna; Soviet actress; b. 31 July 1906; ed. Vakhtangov Studio and Zavadsky Studio.
At the Rostov Drama Theatre 36-40, Mossoviet Theatre, Moscow 40-; People's Artist of the U.S.S.R.; State Prizewinner 42, 46, 48, 51.
Principal roles: Yarovaya, Marina (*Lyubov Yarovaya, On the Banks of the Neva* by K. A. Trenev), Mashenka (*Mashenka* by A. N. Afinogenov), Mirandolina (*The Innkeeper's Wife* by Goldoni), Masha (*The Seagull* by Chekhov), Mukelene (*The Revolt of Women* by Sanderbu), Lady (*Orpheus Descending* by Tennessee Williams), Moskalyova (*The Uncle's Dream* by Dostoevsky); Films: Sokolova (*The Member of the Government*), Varvara (*The Village Teacher*).
Mossoviet Drama Theatre, 16 Bolshaya Sadovaya ulitsa, Moscow, U.S.S.R.

Marette, Jacques, L. ès D., DR. SC. ECON.; French politician; b. 21 Sept. 1922; ed. Ecole Libre des Sciences Politiques.
Journalist, *France-Soir* and *Combat*; Technical Adviser to Ministry of Industry and Commerce 58-59; Dep. Sec.-Gen., Union pour la Nouvelle République 59; Municipal Councillor, Paris 59; Gen. Councillor, Seine 59; Senator 59-62; Political Dir. *Courrier de la Nouvelle République*; fmr. mem. of Supreme Council of Electricity and Gas Authority; Minister of Posts and Telecommunications 62-67; mem. Nat. Assembly Nov.-Dec. 62, 67-; Admin. Soc. Entrepose Belgium 69-73; Croix de Guerre (39-45); Médaille de la Résistance.
2 avenue du Colonel-Bonnet, 75016 Paris, France.

Margai, Sir Albert Michael, Kt.; Sierra Leonean lawyer and politician; b. 10 Oct. 1910; ed. Catholic Schools, Bonthe and Freetown, and Middle Temple, London.
Nurse and Druggist 32-44; called to the Bar 47; mem. Sierra Leone Protectorate Assembly 49, Sierra Leone Legislative Council 51; Minister of Education and Welfare, and Local Government 51-57, of Finance 62-64; Prime Minister of Sierra Leone 64-March 67; mem. Sierra Leone People's Party 51-58; founder-mem. People's Nat. Party 58; Knight of the Grand Cross of St. Gregory the Great.
8 Hornsey Rise Gardens, London, N.19, England.

Margáin, Hugo B.; Mexican lawyer and diplomatist; b. 13 Feb. 1913, Mexico City; m. Margarita Charles 1941; three s. three d.; ed. Univ. Nacional Autónoma de México.
Professor Nat. Univ. of Mexico 47-51; Dir.-Gen. Sales Tax Bureau 51, Income Tax Bureau 52-59; Asst. Sec. for Admin. Ministry of Industry and Commerce 59-61; Under-Sec. for Industry and Commerce 61-64; Pres. Nat. Comm. for Distribution of Profits 63-64; Chair. Nat. Comm. on Profit Sharing 63; Amb. to the U.S.A. 64-70; Minister of Finance 70-73; Amb. to U.K. (also accred. to Iceland) 73-.
Publs. *Importance of Fiscal Law in the Economic Development* 60, *An Adequate Public Administration* 61, World Tax Series *Taxation in Mexico* 57, and numerous financial and taxation articles.
Embassy of Mexico, 8 Halkin Street, London, SW1X 7DW, England.

Margaret Rose, H.R.H. The Princess, Countess of Snowdon, C.I., G.C.V.O., G.C.ST.J.; b. 21 Aug. 1930, Glamis Castle, Angus, Scotland.
Sister of H.M. Queen Elizabeth II; married Antony Armstrong-Jones (now 1st Earl of Snowdon, q.v.) 60; son, Viscount Linley, b. 61; daughter, Lady Sarah Frances Elizabeth, b. 64.
Chancellor, Univ. of Keele; Pres. Royal Ballet; Grand Cross Order Crown of Belgium; Hon. D.Mus. (London), Hon. LL.D. (Keele).
10 Kensington Palace, London, England.

Margerie, Christian Jacquin de; French diplomatist; b. 14 May 1911, Versailles; m. Marie-Thérèse de Laboulaye 1937; four s. two d.; ed. Collège Stanislas, Univ. de Paris à la Sorbonne, and Ecole libre des sciences politiques.
Attaché Rome 37-39; Sec. San Franciso Conf. 45; First Sec. Madrid 46-48; Counsellor, Washington 48-51, Vatican 51-53; mem. French Govt. Del., Berlin 53-55; Minister, Bonn 55-57; Dir. Econ. Affairs Cen. Admin., Paris 58-63; Amb. to Argentina 63-68, to Netherlands 68-72, to Greece 73-; Officier Légion d'Honneur, Croix de Guerre, Commdr. Ordre du Mérite.
Leisure interests: tennis, riding.
French Embassy, Boulevard Reine Sophie 7, Athens, Greece; and 37 rue de Babylone, Paris 7e, France.

Margerit, Robert; French author; b. 25 Jan. 1910, Brive; s. of Antoine Margerit and Angélique Daumard; m. Suzanne Hugon; ed. Collège de Brive, and Lycée de Limoges.
Prix Théophraste Renaudot 51, Grand Prix du Roman 63; Chevalier, Légion d'Honneur, Officier des Arts et des Lettres; Officier Ordre Nationale du Mérite.
Leisure interests: painting, sculpture.
Publs. *L'Ile des perroquets, Mont-Dragon, Le Vin des vendangeurs, Par un été torride, Le Dieu nu, La Femme forte, Le Château des bois noirs, La Malaquaise, Les Amants, La Terre aux loups, L'Amour et le temps, Les Autels de la peur, Un Vent d'acier, Les hommes perdus, Waterloo.*
46 rue Spontini, Paris 16e; and Thias, par Isle, Hte.-Vienne, France.
Telephone: 727-85-52.

Margrethe II, Queen of Denmark; b. 16 April 1940; d. of late King Frederik IX and of Queen Ingrid; m. Count Henri de Laborde de Monpezat (now Prince Henrik of Denmark) 1967; two s.; ed. Univs. of Copenhagen, Aarhus and Cambridge, The Sorbonne, Paris, and London School of Economics.
Succeeded to the throne 14 Jan. 72; previously undertook many official visits abroad with her husband, travelling extensively in Europe, the Far East, Canada and South America.
Leisure interest: archaeology.
Amalienborg Palace, Copenhagen, Denmark.

Margue, Nicolas Albert; Luxembourg politician; b. 2 Jan. 1888, Finsig; s. of Louis Margue and Catherine Brandenburger; m. Rosalie Moes 1917; three s. three d.; ed. Munich, Paris, Strasbourg and Fribourg.
Professor of History Luxembourg Athenaeum 10, Diekirch 12-17, Luxembourg Athenaeum 17-37; Municipal Councillor for City of Luxembourg 24-37; Min. of Public Instruction, Agriculture, Industry and Commerce 37-40; mem. Catholic Party; interned after German occupation 40; Minister of Nat. Educ., Agriculture, Arts and Science 45-48; mem. of Parl. 48-59; mem. Consultative Assembly of Council of Europe and Assembly of Western European Union 49-59; mem. Assembly European Coal and Steel Community 52-59; mem. Council of State 59-70.
Publs. *Biographie de J. B. Nothomb, Gegenwartsgeschichte aus der römischen Kaiserzeit, Manuel d'histoire nationale du Luxembourg, Entwicklung des Luxemburger*

Nationalgefühls, Mouvements contrerévolutionnaires dans le Luxembourg 1831-32, Jean Beck 48, Die Warte 54, Histoire Sommaire de la Ville de Luxembourg 63.
Rue Goethe 24, Luxembourg.
Telephone: Luxembourg 23227.

Margulies, Robert; German politician and administrator; b. 29 Sept. 1908, Düsseldorf; *m.* Trude Steinbacher 1934; ed. High School.
Business Man. 33-36, Agent 37-39, Man. 45-52; mem. State Constitutional Assembly, Nordwürttemberg/Nordbaden 46; mem. Baden-Württemberg Landtag 47; mem. Bundestag 49-64, European Parl. 58-64; Pres. Mannheimer Produktenbörse; mem. Presidium Gen. Asscn. of German and Wholesale Foreign Trade, Bonn; mem. Comm. of European Atomic Energy Community (EURATOM) 64-67; Vice-Pres. German Group of Liberal Int., steering board Europa Union; Bundesverdienstorden Grosses Verdienstkreuz, Grand Officer of Order of Léopold II.
Am Herzogenriedpark 22, 68 Mannheim 1, Federal Republic of Germany.
Telephone: 34147.

Maridakis, Georges; Greek lawyer; b. 1890, Sifnos; ed. Univ. of Athens.
Professor of Int. Private Law, Univ. of Athens; fmr. Minister of Justice; mem. Comm. for the drawing up of the Greek Civil Code; Counsel, Court of Cassation; mem. Permanent Court of Arbitration, The Hague; Greek Del. to 8th Private Int. Law Conf., The Hague 56; Judge European Court for Human Rights, Council of Europe; Assoc. of Inst. of Int. Law; Rector, Univ. of Athens 57-59; fmr. mem. Acad. of Athens; Corresp. mem. L'Institut de France; Dr. h.c. (Paris).
Publs. *Le droit civil dans les Novelles des Empéreurs Byzantins 22, Les tendences modernes de droit international privé 27, Le divorce selon le droit grec 38, Traité de droit international privé* (Vol. I 50, Vol. II 56), *Les principaux traits de la récente codification Hellénique touchant le droit international privé 54, Introduction au droit international privé 62, Exécution des jugements étrangers en Grece 70.*
Thiras Street 60, Athens 814, Greece.
Telephone: 871-228.

Marin, Gheorghe Gaston; Romanian politician; b. 1918; ed. Institut Polytechnique, Grenoble, France.
Assistant Prof., Institut Polytechnique, Grenoble 40-44; French resistance 40-44; mem. Communist Party of Romania 45-, Central Cttee. of Romanian Communist Party 60-; Sec.-Gen. later Deputy Minister of Industry 47-49; Minister of Electric Power 49-54; First Deputy Chair. later Chair. State Planning Cttee. 54-65; Deputy Chair. Council of Ministers 62-69, Pres. State Cttee. for Prices 69-.
Comitetul de Stat pentru Preţuri, Bucharest, Romania.

Marin, Jean (*pseudonym* of Yves Morvan); French journalist; b. 24 Feb. 1909; ed. Britanny and Paris.
Broadcast for Free French from London during World War II; Director-Gen. Agence France Presse 54, Chair., Gen. Man. 54-74; elected Pres. Dir.-Gen. 57, re-elected 60, 63, 66; Pres. European Alliance of Information Agencies 61, re-elected 63, 67; Officier Légion d'Honneur, Croix de Guerre, Hon. K.B.E. (75) and other honours.
c/o Agence France Presse, 11 Place de la Bourse, Paris 2e, France.

Marinello Vidaurreta, Juan; Cuban professor and politician; b. 2 Nov. 1898; ed. Havana and Madrid Univs.
Professor, Inst. of Modern Languages, Univ. of Havana; edited *Revista de Avance* 27-30; imprisoned for political activity; Del. to Constituent Ass. 40; Rep. to Nat. Chamber 42; mem. Nat. Council of Culture and Minister without Portfolio 43; Pres. Socialist Popular Party;

Vice-Pres. Senate 44; mem. World Peace Council 49; mem. Board for the Lenin Peace Prize 62-; Rector, Univ. of Havana 62-63, Prof. Emer. 74-; Cuban Del. to UNESCO 63; mem. Presidency World Peace Council 66.
Publs. *Poética, Ensayos 37, Literatura Hispanoamericana 37, Momento Español 39, Marti, Escritor Americano, Ocho Notas sobre Anibal Ponce 59, Meditación Americana 59, Conversación con nuestros pintores abstractos 60, Guatemala Nuestra 61, Once Ensayos Martianos 65, Contemporáneos 65, Imagen de Silvestre Resultas 66.*
Loma, Flat 684 entre Lombillo y Avenida de Colón, Nuevo Vedado, Havana, Cuba.

Marinescu, Mihai; Romanian engineer and politician; b. 22 Nov. 1917, Bîrca, Dolj County; *s.* of Nicolaie Marinescu and Maria Teodorescu; *m.* Eugenia Marinescu 1944; one *d.*; ed. Electromechanics Faculty of Polytechnic Inst. of Bucharest.
Head Engineer, Braşov Tractor Plant 54-63; Deputy Minister of Machine Construction 63-65, Minister 65-69; Deputy to Grand Nat. Assembly 67-; Vice-Chair. Council of Ministers 69-72, 75-; mem. Cen. Cttee. of R.C.P. 65-; mem. Defence Council 69-74; Minister for Technical and Material Supplies and the Control of Fixed Funds 71-72; First Vice-Pres. (with Minister rank) of Econ. Council 72-; Chair. State Planning Cttee. 75-.
Council of Ministers, Bucharest, Romania.

Marinescu, Teodor; Romanian journalist and diplomatist; b. 22 Sept. 1922; ed. Ştefan Gheorghiu Higher Party School of Romanian Communist Party.
General Dir. of Agerpres (Romanian news agency) 58-60; Editor-in-Chief *Scinteia* (C.P. organ) 60-65; Chair. State Radio and Television Cttee. 65-66; Ambassador to U.S.S.R. 66-72; Head of Section in Cen. Cttee. Romanian C.P. 72-73, Deputy Head of Section 73-; Deputy to Grand Nat. Assembly, fmr. Head Foreign Policy Cttee.; mem. Cen. Cttee. R.C.P.
Central Cttee. of Romanian Communist Party, Bucharest, Romania.

Marinho, Ilmar Penna, D.IUR.; Brazilian diplomatist; b. 29 Jan. 1913, Rio de Janeiro; *s.* of Ildefonso Aires and Ignes Penna Marinho; *m.* (2nd) Lydia Marinho 1961; one *s.* (by 1st marriage); ed. Faculty of Law, Fed. Univ. of Rio de Janeiro.
Diplomatic Service 34-; Sec., Rome, Quito, Brussels; Counsellor, Warsaw, Paris; Chargé d'Affaires, Greece 40-45; Rep. to Peace Conf. 46; Rep. to UN Gen. Ass. 48; Rep. to Inter-Governmental Cttee. for European Migration (ICEM), Geneva 58; Ministry of External Affairs, Rio de Janeiro (Head of Consular Dept., Admin. Dept., later Under-Sec. of Ministry); Perm. Rep. to the Org. of American States (OAS) 61-69; Amb. to U.S.S.R. 69-75.
c/o Ministério dos Assuntos Exteriores, Brasília, Brazil.

Marini, Marino; Italian sculptor and painter; b. 27 Feb. 1901, Pistoia; *s.* of Guido and Bianca Bonacchi; *m.* Mercedes Pedrazzini 1938; ed. Acad. of Fine Arts of Florence.
Prof. Scuola d'Arte de Villa Reale, Monza 29-40, Titular Prof. of Sculpture, Acad. of Fine Arts of Brera, Milan 40-; has exhibited works in many cities of Europe, America and Canada; Grand Prix Quadriennale Romana 35; Grand Prix de Sculpture, Venice Biennale 52; Int. Grand Prix Accademia dei Lincei, Rome 54; Médaille d'Or du Président de la République 54; Médaille d'Or de la Ville de Milano 62; Médaille d'Or, Riconoscimento della Città di Firenze 67; mem. Accademia Fiorentina delle Arti, Accademia Albertina di Bologna, Royal Flemish Acad. of Brussels, Akademisches Kollegium of Munich, Royal Acad. of Fine Arts of Stockholm, Accad. Nazionale di San Luca, Bayerische Akademie der Schonen Künste, Munich, Instituto Accademico di Roma, etc.; Hon. mem. American Acad. of Arts and

Letters, Akademie der Bildenden Künste, Nurenberg; numerous other awards and honours.
Piazza Mirabella 2, Milan 20121, Italy.
Telephone: 6591462.

Mariolopoulos, Elias, M.A., D.U.P., D. ès sc.; Greek meteorologist; b. 1900, Athens; m. Catherine Canaguini 1938; ed. Univs. of Athens, Cambridge, London and Paris.
Chief, Meteorological Dept. Nat. Observatory, Athens 25-28; Prof. of Meteorology, Univ. of Thessaloniki 28-39; Prof. of Meteorology, Univ. of Athens 39, Rector, Univ. of Athens 59-61; mem. of the Academy of Athens; Dir. Nat. Observatory, Athens 42; Pres. Nat. Cttee. of Geophysics and Geodesy; mem. Int. Climatological Comm.; several Greek and foreign decorations.
Leisure interest: philately.
Publs. *Climate of Greece* (Greek), *Atlas Climatique de la Grèce* (French), *Distribution des Eléments météorologiques en Grèce, Climate of Athens, Dodecanese, Climate of Different Regions of Greece.*
48 Aghias Lavras Street, Patissia, Athens 903, Greece.
Telephone: 280024.

Marion, Léo Edmond, C.C., M.B.E., PH.D., F.C.I.C., F.R.S.C., F.R.S.; Canadian chemist; b. 22 March 1899, Ottawa, Ontario; s. of Joseph Marion and Emma Vézina; m. Marie Paule Lefort 1933; ed. Queen's Univ. at Kingston, McGill Univ. and Univ. of Vienna, Austria.
Chemist, Nat. Research Council of Canada 29-43, Head of Organic Chem. Section 43-63, Dir. Chem. Div. 52-63, Senior Dir. 60-, Vice-Pres. (Science) 63-65; Editor-in-Chief, *Canadian Journals of Research* 47-65; Dean, Faculty of Pure and Applied Science, Univ. of Ottawa 65-69, Hon. Prof., Faculty of Science 69-; Fellow, Royal Soc. of Canada 42, Chemical Inst. of Canada, Royal Soc., London 61; Pres. Royal Soc. of Canada 64-65, Chemical Inst. of Canada 61-62; Hon. mem. Soc. Chimique de France 57, Royal Canadian Inst. 71; Asscn. Canadienne-française pour l'avancement des Sciences Medal 48, Coronation Medal 53, Chem. Inst. of Canada Medal 56, City of Paris Medal 57, Professional Inst. of Public Service Gold Medal 59, Jecker Prize, Acad. des Sciences, France 63, Centennial Medal 67, Chem. Inst. of Canada Montreal Medal 69; numerous hon. degrees.
Publs. several chapters in "*The Alkaloids*" (ed. R. H. Manske) and numerous scientific papers on the same subject.
211 Wurtemburg Street, Apt. 1413, Ottawa, Ont., K1N 8R4, Canada.

Mariotti, Luigi; Italian politician; b. 23 Nov. 1912, Florence.
Member Cen. Cttee. Italian Socialist Party 48-69; mem. Senate 53-68, Sec. Socialist Parl. Group 58, mem. Standing Cttee. for Finance and the Treasury 63, Chair. Socialist Group in Senate 63; Minister of Health 64-68, of Transport and Civil Aviation Dec. 68-69, Minister of Health March 70.
Ministry of Health, Rome, Italy.

Marjolin, Robert Ernest; French economist; b. 27 July 1911, Paris; s. of Ernest and Elise Marjolin; m. Dorothy Smith 1944; (deceased 1971) one s. one d.; ed. Univ. of Paris and Yale Univ.
Assistant to Prof. Charles Rist, Scientific Inst. of Econ. and Social Research 34-37; Chief Asst. 38-39; joined Gen. de Gaulle London 41; head of French Supply Mission to U.S.A. 44; Dir. of External Economic Relations, Min. of Nat. Economy 45; Deputy High Commr. of Modernisation and Equipment Plan 46; Sec.-Gen. O.E.E.C. 48-55; Prof. of Economics, Nancy 55-58; Vice-Pres. Comm., European Econ. Community 58-67; Prof. of Econs., Univ. of Paris 67-70; Dir. Royal Dutch, Shell Française, Robeco; mem. Int. Advisory Cttee. Chase Manhattan Bank; Econ. Consultant; Foreign

Hon. mem. American Acad. of Arts and Sciences; Dr. h.c., Yale Univ., Harvard Univ. and Univ. of East Anglia; Officier de la Légion d'Honneur; American Medal of Freedom; King's Medal, etc.; Hon. C.B.E. (U.K.).
Leisure interests: music, theatre, cinema, reading.
Publs. *L'Evolution du Syndicalisme aux Etats-Unis de Washington à Roosevelt* 36, *Prix, Monnaie, Production: Essai sur les Mouvements Economiques de Longue Durée* 45, *Europe and the United States in the World Economy* 53.
9 rue de Valois, 75001 Paris, France.
Telephone: 261-3758.

Marjoribanks, Sir James Alexander Milne, K.C.M.G., M.A.; British diplomatist; b. 29 May 1911, Edinburgh; s. of Thomas Marjoribanks and Mary Ord Logan; m. Sonya Alder 1936; one d.; ed. Edinburgh Acad., Edinburgh Univ., Strasbourg Univ., and Univ. degli Studi, Florence.
Foreign Office 34-71; Early service in Peking, Hankow, Marseille, Jacksonville, Florida, New York, Bucharest, Canberra 34-52; Deputy Head Del. to High Authority of European Coal and Steel Community 52-55; Cabinet Office, London 55-57; Econ. Minister, Bonn 57-62; Asst. Under-Sec. Foreign Office 62-65; Amb. to the European Econ. Communities and Head of Del. 65-71; Dir. Distillers Co. Ltd. 71-; Chair. Scottish Council Cttee. on EEC; Gen. Council Assessor to Edinburgh Univ. Court 75-.
Leisure interests: mountaineering, golf.
13 Regent Terrace, Edinburgh 7; Lintonrig, Kirk Yetholm, Roxburghshire, Scotland.

Mark, Herman F., PH.D.; American professor of chemistry; b. 3 May 1895, Vienna, Austria; s. of Herman C. and Lili (née Mueller) Mark; m. Mary Schramek 1922; two s.; ed. Univ. of Vienna.
Instructor, Univ. of Berlin 21; Research Fellow, later Group Leader, Kaiser Wilhelm Inst. für Faserstoff-Chemie 22-26; Research Chemist, I.G. Farben-Industrie 27-28, Group Leader 28-30, Asst. Research Dir. 30-32, concurrently Assoc. Prof. of Physical Chem., Technical Univ., Karlsruhe; Prof. of Chem. and Dir. First Chemical Inst., Univ. of Vienna 32-38; Research Man. Canadian Int. Paper Co., Canada 38-40; adjunct Prof. of Organic Chem., Polytechnic Inst. of Brooklyn 40, Prof. 42, Dir. Polymer Research Inst. 46, Dean 61-65; Dean Emer. 65-; Editor *Journal of Polymer Science* and other scientific publications; mem. American Chemical Soc., American Inst. of Chemists, American Asscn. for the Advancement of Science; Fellow, American Physical Soc., New York Acad. of Sciences, American Acad. of Arts and Sciences, Nat. Acad. of Sciences; numerous hon. degrees and other awards.
Polytechnic Institute of New York, 333 Jay Street, Brooklyn, N.Y. 11201, U.S.A.
Telephone: 212-643-2486.

Mark, Sir Robert, M.A.; British police official; b. 13 March 1917, Manchester; s. of the late John and Louisa Mark (née Hobson); m. Kathleen Mary Leahy 1941; one s. one d.; ed. William Hulme's Grammar School, Manchester.
Constable to Chief Supt., Manchester Police 37-42, 47-56; Chief Constable of Leicester 57-67; Asst. Commissioner, Metropolitan Police 67-68, Deputy Commr. 68-72, Commr. 72-; Royal Armoured Corps 42-47, Major Control Comm. for Germany 45-47; mem. Standing Advisory Council on Penal System 66; Assessor to Lord Mountbatten's Inquiry into Prison Security 66; mem. Advisory Cttee. on Police in N. Ireland 69; Visiting Fellow, Nuffield Coll., Oxford 70; Dimbleby Memorial Lecturer, BBC TV 73; Queen's Police Medal 65; Hon LL.M. (Leic.) 66.
Publs. Numerous articles in the national press and in

legal and police journals; *Edwin Stevens Lecture to the Laity at the Royal Society of Medicine* 72.

New Scotland Yard, Broadway, London, SW1H oBG, England.

Telephone: 01-230-1212.

Markall, Most Rev. Francis William, S.J., D.D.; Rhodesian (b. British) ecclesiastic; b. 24 Sept. 1905, London, England; ed. St. Ignatius Coll., London, Heythrop Coll., Oxon., England.

Entered Soc. of Jesus 24; Asst. Master, Stoneyhurst Coll. 31-34; theological studies 34-38; Missionary in Rhodesia 39-56; Titular Archbishop of Cotieo, Co-adjutor with right of succession to Archbishop of Salisbury April 56; Archbishop of Salisbury Nov. 56-.

Archbishop's House, P.O. Box 8060, Causeway, Salisbury; and 66 Fifth Street, Salisbury, Rhodesia.

Markel, Lester, LITT.D., L.H.D.; American journalist and newspaper editor; b. 9 Jan. 1894, New York; s. of Jacob L. and Lillian (Hecht) Markel; m. Meta Edman 1917; one d.; ed. Columbia School of Journalism.

Reporter 14-15, Night City Ed. and Night Ed. 15-19, Asst. Man. Ed. 19-23 *New York Tribune*: Sunday Ed. *New York Times* 23-64, Assoc Ed. 64-; Moderator and Ed. *News in Perspective* (T.V. Programme) 63-69; Distinguished Visiting Prof., Fairleigh Dickinson Univ. 69-; Assoc. in journalism, Columbia Univ.; Ed. and contributor Public Opinion and Foreign Policy; mem. Amer. Society of Newspaper Editors, Council on Foreign Relations; founder Int. Press Inst.; Hon. Litt.D., L.H.D.

Leisure interests: golf, growing flowers.

Publs. *Background and Foreground, What You Don't Know Can Hurt You—A Study in Public Opinion and Public Emotion* 72, *World Review* 72.

135 Central Park West (Home) and 10 Columbus Circle, New York City, N.Y., U.S.A. (Office).

Telephone: TR-7-4777 (Home); 581-9510 (Office).

Markelius, Sven Gottfrid, Swedish architect; b. 25 Oct. 1889, Stockholm; s. of Oscar and Hilma Jonsson; m. Karin Simon 1938; three s. two d.; ed. Stockholm, Germany, France, Italy and U.S.A.

Hon. corresp. mem. Royal Inst. of British Architects, American Inst. Architects, Town Planning Inst., London, Int. Inst. of Arts and Letters, World Acad. of Art and Science, Akad. Arkitektforening, Copenhagen, etc.; mem. Swedish Royal Acad. of Fine Arts 42; fmr. Town Planning Dir., Stockholm; mem. Advisory Cttee. for UN H.Q., Manhattan 47, UNESCO H.Q., Paris 52-58; Visiting Prof. Yale Univ. School of Architecture 49, Massachusetts Inst. of Technology 62, Univ. of California, Berkeley 62; mem. UNESCO H.Q. Art Cttee. 54-; Pres. Fed. of Swedish Architects Soc. 53-56; Howland Memorial Prize, Yale Univ. 49; Gold Medal, R.I.B.A. 62; Prof.h.c. 59; Dr. Ing. h.c. 66.

Works include: Halsingborg Concert Hall, Stockholm, Univ. of Technology Student Corps Building, Collective House, Stockholm 35, Structure for Stockholm Building Assen. 36, Swedish Pavilion, World's Fair, New York 39; interior of ECOSOC chamber of UN H.Q., N.Y. 52; Trade Union Centre, Linköping 52; Trade Union Centre, Stockholm 60; Bürgerhaus, Giessen, G.F.R. 66; Park Hotel and Sweden House, Stockholm 68; housing and town planning work.

Home: Kevinge Strand 5, 182 31 Danderyd; Office: Floragatan 11, 11431 Stockholm, Sweden.

Telephone: 755-63-85 and 755-44-66 (Home); 10-63-36.

Markert, Clement L., PH.D.; American biologist; b. 11 April 1917, Las Animas, Colo.; s. of Edwin John Markert and Sarah Esther (née Norman); m. Margaret Rempfer 1940; two s. one d.; ed. Univ. of Colorado, Univ. of Calif. at Los Angeles, Johns Hopkins Univ. and Calif. Inst. of Technology.

Assistant Prof. of Zoology, Univ. of Michigan 50-56, Assoc. Prof. 56-57; Prof. of Biology, Johns Hopkins

Univ. 57-65; Chair. Dept. of Biology, Yale Univ. 65-71; Dir. Yale Center for Research in Reproductive Biology 74-; mem. Nat. Acad. of Sciences, Nat. Inst. of Medicine 74-.

Leisure interests: skin diving, ranching.

Publs. Over seventy articles.

Department of Biology, Yale University, New Haven, Conn. 06520, U.S.A.

Telephone: 203-436-1675.

Markevitch, Igor; Italian composer and conductor; b. 27 July 1912, Kiev, Russia; s. of Boris and Zoïa (Pokitonov) Markevitch; m. 1st Kyra Nijinsky 1936, one s.; 2nd Topazia Caetani 1946, one s. two d.; ed. Coll. de Vevey, Switzerland.

Leader of Orchestra of Florence and Maggio Musicale 44-46; Int. Conductor since 46; Perm. Conductor, Stockholm Philharmonic Orchestra 52-55, Music Dir. Symphony Orchestra, Montreal 55-60, Havana Philharmonic Orchestra 57-58, Montreal Symphony Orchestra 56-60, Lamoureux Orchestra, Paris 56-61; Perm. Conductor Spanish Radio-Television Orchestra 65-70; Artistic Dir. Monte Carlo Opera and Orchestra 68-72; Perm. Conductor Santa Cecilia Orchestra, Rome 73-; Conductor Emer. Japan Philharmonic Orchestra 68-; Head of Orchestra Conducting Classes at Salzburg 47-54, Mexico Pan-american Courses 57-58, Moscow 63, Santiago de Compostela 66, Monte Carlo 68-; mem. Royal Swedish Acad.; Officier Légion d'Honneur; Commdr. des Arts et Lettres.

Compositions: *Piano Concerto* 29, *Cantata on words by Cocteau* 29, *Rebus* 31, *Icare* 32, *Psalm* 33, *Paradise Lost* 35, also chamber music.

Publs. *Made in Italy* 46, *Point d'Orgue* 61, *Introduction to Music.*

1800 Montreux, Switzerland; and 06780 Saint Cézaire, France.

Telephone: 93-36-8847 (France).

Markezinis, Spyros, LL.D.; Greek lawyer, historian and politician; b. 1909, Athens; m. Ieta Xydis 1943; one s. one d.; ed. Univ. of Athens.

Legal Adviser to late King George II of the Hellenes 36-46; served in Greek Nat. Resistance 41-44; mem. Parl. for the Cyclades 46, for Athens 52-67; founded New Party 47 (dissolved 51); Minister without Portfolio 49; Minister for Co-ordination and Econ. Planning until 54; formed Progressive Party Feb. 55; Prime Minister Oct.-Nov. 73; Knight, Gold Cross George I, D.S.M., Knight Commdr. St. Saba; Grand Cross of following: Order of Phoenix (Greece), Légion d'Honneur, Al Merito della Repubblica Italiana, Merit First Class (Germany), Order of St. Mark of the Patriarchate of Alexandria.

Leisure interests: books, chess.

Publs. *The Divorce, From War to Peace* 49, *The Supreme Ruler in Contemporary Democracies, The King, the Royal Family and their Private Lives, The King as International Representative, Political History of Modern Greece (1828-1964)* (4 vols.).

5 Lycabettus Street, Athens, Greece.

Telephone: 610-887, 610-756, 616-062.

Markiewicz, Władysław; Polish sociologist; b. 2 Jan. 1920, Ostrów Wielkopolski; ed. Poznań Univ.

Doctor 59-61, Docent 61-66, Assoc. Prof. 66-72, Prof. 72-; active mem. youth orgs. 47-50; mem. People's Council, Poznań Voivodship 49-54; Vice-Dir. Western Inst., Poznań 62-64, Dir. 65-71; Dir. Inst. of Sociology, Poznań Univ. 69-; now Head, Dept. of Sociology of Labour and Org., Warsaw Univ.; Editor-in-Chief *Studia Socjologiczne* (quarterly) and *Polish Western Affairs*; Vice-Chair. Polish Cttee. of UNESCO; Pres. Polish Sociological Soc. 68-; Corresp. mem. Polish Acad. of Sciences 71-, Sec. of Dept. of Social Sciences 71-; mem. Polish Cttee. of Pugwash confs.; Gold Cross of Merit, Knight's Cross, Order of Polonia Restituta,

Medals of 10th and 30th Anniversaries of People's Poland, Gold Award of Polish Teachers' Asscn.

Publs. *Przeobrażenia świadomości narodowej reemigrantów polskich z Francji* 60, *Społeczeństwo i socjologia w Niemieckiej Republice Federalnej* 66, *Sociology in People's Poland* 70, *Propedeutyka nauki o społeczeństwie* 71, *Socjologia a służba społeczna* 72; numerous articles.

Ul. Wiejska 18 m. 13, 00-490 Warsaw, Poland.

Marking, Henry Ernest, C.B.E., M.C.; British solicitor and airline executive; b. 11 March 1920, Saffron Walden, Essex; s. of late Isaac and Hilda J. Marking; ed. Saffron Walden Grammar School, Univ. Coll., London and Middle East Centre of Arab Studies.

Military Service 41-45; admitted solicitor 48; Asst. Solicitor, Cripps Harries Hall and Co., Tunbridge Wells 48-49; Sec. B.E.A. 50; Chief Exec. B.E.A. 64-70, Chair. and Chief Exec. Jan. 71-72; mem. Board, British Tourist Authority 69-, B.O.A.C. Jan. 71-72; Group Man. Dir. British Airways 72-74, Deputy Chair. and Man. Dir. 74-.

Airways Terminal, P.O. Box 13, Buckingham Palace Road, London, S.W.1, England.

Telephone: 01-821 4898.

Marklund, Bror Hjalmar; Swedish sculptor; b. 3 Dec. 1907, Husum; m. Gun Robertson 1947; one s.; ed. Royal Acad. of Art, Stockholm, and in France and Italy.

Professor of Drawing, Royal Acad. of Art, Stockholm; exhibitions in Norway, Denmark, Yugoslavia, Italy and U.S.A.; A. Norrland Culture Prize 60, Eugen Prize 62, Sergel Sculpture Prize 65.

Major works: bronze doors of Museum of Nat. Antiquities, Stockholm 39-50; The Sibbarp Stone 47; bronze at Govt. Offices Bldg., Stockholm 56; *Figure in a Storm* (bronze for Trelleborg town) 64; tower of Town Hall, Kiruna 65; bronze doors at main entrance to head office of Skandinaviska Banken, Stockholm Magnesite 66; main entrance to police headquarters, Stockholm.

Royal Academy of Art, Fredsgatan 12, Stockholm, Sweden.

Marko, Ján, ING.; Czechoslovak politician; b. 6 Sept. 1920, Točnica, Slovakia; ed. School of Econs., Bratislava Univ.

Office worker, Production Manager, Dir. Slovak Magnesite Works, Lovinobaňa 47-54; Finance Commr. 54-59; Deputy Chair. of Board of Commrs. 59-60; Dir. of Slovak Magnesite Works, Košice 60-62; Deputy Minister-Chair. of State Comm. for Co-ordination of Science and Technology, Prague 62-63; Slovak Comm. for Investment Building 63-65; Commr.-Chair., Minister, Slovak Comm. for Technology 65-68; Minister of Foreign Affairs, Fed. Govt. of Č.S.S.R. 69-71; mem. Slovak Nat. Council 54-71; mem. Cen. Cttee. of C.P. of Czechoslovakia 54-62, 69-, Alt. mem. 62-66; Deputy Chair. Slovak Nat. Council 65-68; mem. Cen. Cttee. of Czechoslovak-Soviet Friendship Union 66-70; mem. Cen. Cttee. C.P. of Slovakia 66-68; Deputy to House of Nations, Fed. Assembly 68-71, First Vice-Chair. Fed. Assembly 71-, Deputy to House of the People 71-; Presidium mem. Fed. Assembly, Č.S.S.R. 71; Chair. Czechoslovak Group of Inter-Parl. Union 71-; mem. Presidium Č.S.S.R. Cttee. for European Security 72-; Chair. Czechoslovak Cttee. for the Protection of the Rights of the Chilean People 74-; Order of Labour 70, and other decorations.

Federal Assembly, Prague, Czechoslovakia.

Marko, Miloš, LL.D., C.SC.; Czechoslovak journalist, broadcasting official and politician; b. 4 March 1922, Hronská Dúbrava; s. of Pavel and Alžběta Marko; m. Magda Kirchhoffová 1948; two d.; ed. Comenius Univ. Bratislava.

Journalist on various Slovak dailies; Asst. Editor-in-Chief *Pravda* 48-52, Editor-in-Chief 53-58; Editor-in-Chief *Predvoj* 58-60; Correspondent of Czechoslovak News Agency in Moscow 60-64; Asst. Prof. of Journal-

ism, Comenius Univ., Bratislava 62-; Regional Dir. Czechoslovak Radio, Bratislava 64-67; Gen. Dir. Czechoslovak Radio, Prague Feb. 67-68; mem. Ideological Comm., Central Cttee. of C.P. of Slovakia 66-69; Gen. Man. Czechoslovak Radio, Slovakia 69-73; Vice-Chair. and mem. Presidium Union of Slovak Journalists 69-72, Chair. 72-; Chair. Central Union of Journalists of Č.S.S.R. 69-72, Vice-Chair. 72-; mem. Presidium Central Cttee. Czechoslovak-Soviet Friendship Union 69-; mem. Cen. Cttee. C.P. of Slovakia 71-; Deputy to Slovak Nat. Council 71-; Gen. Man. Czechoslovak TV, Slovakia 73-; Deputy Gen. Man. Czechoslovak TV 73-; Order of Labour 70; Klement Gottwald Prize 73.

TV Bratislava, Slovakia; and Štefánikova 12, Bratislava, Czechoslovakia.

Telephone: 471-12 (Home).

Markov, Dmitry Fedorovich; Soviet philologist; b. 23 Oct. 1913, Preslav, Zaporozhye region, Ukraine; ed. Kharkov Univ.

School Teacher 36-38; Postgraduate 38-41; Army Service 41-44; Head of Chair, Pedagogical Inst. Sumy 44-56; mem. C.P.S.U. 48-; Senior Research Assoc. 56-63, Head of Sector Inst. of Slav Studies, U.S.S.R. Acad. of Sciences; Corresp. mem. U.S.S.R. Acad. of Sciences 66-.

U.S.S.R. Academy of Sciences, 14 Leninsky Prospekt, Moscow, U.S.S.R.

Markov, Konstantin Konstantinovich, D.SC.; Soviet geographer; b. 20 May 1905, Viborg; s. of Konstantin and Marie Markov; m. Anastasie Markova 1931; one d.; ed. Leningrad Univ.

Lecturer, Leningrad Univ. 26-37; Head of Section, Inst. of Geography, U.S.S.R. Acad. of Sciences 37-45; mem. staff, Moscow Univ. 37-, Prof. 40-, Head of Chair. 46, Dean, Faculty of Geography 45-55; Academician, U.S.S.R. Acad. of Sciences 70-; mem. C.P.S.U.

Leisure interests: riding, poetry.

Moscow University, Section "U", Flat 56, Moscow 117234, U.S.S.R.

Markov, Moisey Alexandrovich; Soviet theoretical physicist; b. 1908; ed. Moscow, Univ.

Assoc., Physics Inst., U.S.S.R. Acad. of Sciences 34-; Chair. of Group Joint Inst. for Nuclear Research 51-; Dir. Inst. of Semi-Conductors, U.S.S.R. Acad. of Sciences until 62; Corresp. mem. U.S.S.R. Acad. of Sciences 53-66, mem. 66-.

U.S.S.R. Academy of Sciences, 14 Leninsky Prospekt, Moscow, U.S.S.R.

Markova, Dame Alicia, D.B.E. (Lilian Alicia Marks); British prima ballerina; b. 1 Dec. 1910, London; d. of Arthur Tristman Marks and Eileen Barry; ed. privately.

First appeared in *Dick Whittington* at the Kennington Theatre 20; studied under Astafieva and appeared with Legat Ballet Group 23; taken into Russian Ballet by Serge Diaghilev 24, studied under Enrico Cecchetti and toured with the company till Diaghilev's death in 29 (*Song of a Nightingale* created for her); first Prima Ballerina of Vic-Wells (now the Royal Ballet) 33-35; formed Markova-Dolin Ballet Company 35 and toured U.K. till 38; with Ballet Russe de Monte Carlo 38-41; and Ballet Theatre 41-44; toured North and Central America with Markova-Dolin group 44-45; many guest appearances 46-47; concerts with Dolin in United States, Far East and South Africa 47-49; formed Festival Ballet company with Dolin 50-52; guest artist with Teatro Colón in Buenos Aires 52, Sadler's Wells, Ballet Theatre, Marquis de Cuevas Ballet and Metropolitan Opera 53; Royal Winnipeg Ballet 53; with de Cuevas Ballet in London 54; with Royal Danish Ballet 55; Scala Milan; Municipal Theatre Rio de Janeiro 56; Royal Ballet Covent Garden 57; Italian Opera Season, Drury Lane; Festival Ballet Tour 58, and Season 59; appearances with Royal Ballet and Festival Ballet 60; with the Metro-

politan Opera Company 54-58; Dir. Metropolitan Opera Ballet of New York 63-69; Distinguished Lecturer on Ballet at Cincinnati Univ. 70, Prof. of Ballet and Performing Arts 71-73; Vice-Pres. Royal Acad. of Dancing 58-; Gov. Royal Ballet 73-; Guest Prof. de Danse, Paris Opera Ballet 75; Guest Prof., Australian Ballet 76; Hon. Dr. Music (Leicester Univ.) 66.
Leisure interest: music.
Publ. *Giselle and I* 60.
c/o Barclay's Bank, 451 Oxford Street, London, W.1, England.

Marks, Leonard Harold, B.A., LL.B.; American lawyer and government official; b. 5 March 1916; *m.* Dorothy L. Ames 1948; two *s.,* ed. Univ. of Pittsburgh, and Univ. of Pittsburgh Law School.
Faculty Fellow, Univ. of Pittsburgh Law School 38-39, Asst. Prof. 39-42; Asst. Prof. Nat. Univ. Law School, Washington, D.C. 43-50; Asst. to Gen. Counsel, Fed. Communications Comm., Washington, D.C. 43-46; Partner, Cohn and Marks (law firm), Washington, D.C. 46-65, 69-; Dir. Communications Satellite Corpn. 63-65; Dir. U.S. Information Agency 65-69; Pres. Broadcasters' Club of Washington, Nat. Home Library Foundation, Int. Rescue Cttee. 73-; Chair. Int. Telecommunications Satellite Conference, U.S. Delegation, Washington, D.C. 69, U.S. Advisory Comm. on Int. Educational and Cultural Affairs 74-.
2833 McGill Terrace, N.W., Washington, D.C. 20008; Office: 1920 L Street, N.W., Washington, D.C. 20036, U.S.A.
Telephone: 232-7214 (Home); 293-3860 (Office).

Marland, Sidney P., Jr., M.A., PH.D.; American educationist and fmr. government official; b. 19 Aug. 1914, Danielson, Conn.; *s.* of Sidney P. Marland, Sr. and Ruth Johnson Marland; *m.* Virginia Partridge 1940; one *s.* two *d.;* ed. Univ. of Connecticut and New York Univ.
Teacher of English, William Hall High School, West Hartford, Conn. 38-41; U.S. Army Service 41-47; Supt. of Schools, Darien, Conn. 48-56, Winnetka, Ill. 56-63, Pittsburgh, Pa. 63-68; Pres. Inst. for Educational Devt., New York City 68-70; fmr. mem. Presidential Advisory Council on Educ. of Disadvantaged Children and for Office of Econ. Opportunity; U.S. Commr. of Educ. Dec. 70-72; Asst. Sec. for Educ., Health, Educ. and Welfare Dept. 72-73; Pres. Coll. Entrance Examination Board 73-; Adjunct Prof. of Educ. Admin., New York Univ. 74-; fmr. Visiting Prof. and Lecturer at Harvard, Northwestern Univ., Teachers Coll., Columbia Univ., and Nat. Coll. of Educ.; Visiting Prof. Univ. of Conn. 74-.
Leisure interests: fishing, horticulture.
Publs. *Winnetka: The History and Significance of an Educational Experiment* (with Carleton W. Washburne), *Career Education: A Proposal for Reform* 74, *The College Board and the Twentieth Century* 75, and numerous monographs, book contributions and journal articles.
College Entrance Examination Board, 888 Seventh Avenue, New York, N.Y. 10019, U.S.A.
Telephone: (212) 582-6210.

Marler, Peter Robert, PH.D.; American biologist; b. 24 Feb. 1928, London, England, *s.* of Robert A. and Gertrude Hunt Marler; *m.* Judith G. Gallen 1954; one *s.* two *d.;* ed. Univ. Coll., London and Univ. of Cambridge.
Research Fellow, Jesus Coll., Cambridge 54-56; Asst. Prof., later Prof., Univ. of Calif., Berkeley 57-66; Prof. The Rockefeller Univ. 66-; Senior Research Zoologist, N.Y. Zoological Soc. 66-72; Dir. Inst. for Research in Animal Behaviour 69-72; Dir. Rockefeller Univ. Field Research Center 72-; mem. Nat. Acad. of Sciences; Fellow, American Acad. of Arts and Sciences, American AssCn. for Advancement of Science 65, New York

Zoological Soc., American Psychological Asscn. 75; Guggenheim Fellow 64-65.
Leisure interests: gardening, natural history.
Publ. *Mechanisms of Animal Behaviour* (with W. J. Hamilton) 66.
Rockefeller University Field Research Center, Tyrrel Road, Millbrook N.Y. 12545, U.S.A.
Telephone: 914-677-5356.

Maróthy, László; Hungarian politician; b. 1942, Szeghalom; ed. Univ. of Agronomy.
Joined Communist Youth League 60, Hungarian Socialist Workers' Party 65; Sec. County Pest Communist Youth Cttee. 68-70; First Sec. Municipal Party Cttee. of Szentendre; First Sec. Nat. Communist Youth League Cen. Cttee. 73-; mem. HSWP Cen. Cttee. 73-, Politburo 75-.
Hungarian Socialist Workers' Party, 1387 Budapest, Széchenyi rakpart 19, Hungary.
Telephone: 111-400.

Marotta, Domenico; Italian chemist; b. 28 July 1886; ed. Univ. degli Studi, Palermo.
President Accad. Nazionale dei XL 62-; mem. Accad. Nazionale dei Lincei; Pres. Italian Chemical Soc.; Admin. *Gazzetta Chimica Italiana, Annali di Chimica, Rendiconti Accademia Nazionale dei XL*; Cavaliere Gran Croce Ordine al Merito della Repubblica, Commedatore Ordine Equestre de S. Agata, Officier Légion d'Honneur, Hon. C.B.E.
Publs. Numerous scientific works and translations of German scientific works into Italian; Editor of the works of *Stanislao Cannizzaro* 26, *Raffaele Piria, lavori scientifici e scritti vari* 32, *Emanuele Paterno—scritti e ricordi editi e inediti* 65; translation of Bacon's *La Nuova Atlantide* 37.
Accademia Nazionale dei Quaranta, via del Castro Laurenziano 15, 00161 Rome; Via Giusue Borsi 3, Rome, Italy.

Marples, Baron (Life Peer), cr. 74, of Wallasey in the County of Merseyside; **A. Ernest Marples,** P.C., F.C.A., F.R.S.; British politician; b. 9 Dec. 1907, Levenshulme, Manchester; *s.* of late Alfred Ernest and Mary Marples; *m.* Mrs. Ruth Dobson 1956; ed. Stretford Grammar School.
London Scottish 39; 2nd-Lt. Royal Artillery 41, Capt. 41; M.P. 45-74; Parl. Sec. Ministry of Housing and Local Govt. 51-54; Joint Parl. Sec. Ministry of Pensions and Nat. Insurance 54-55; Postmaster-Gen. 57-59; Minister of Transport 59-64, Chair. Nationalized Transport Advisory Council 63-64; Shadow Minister of Technology 64-66; Sponsor Conservative Party Public Sector Research Unit 67-70; Dir. Purolator Services Inc. (U.S.A.), Purolator Services Ltd. (U.K.) 70-; Conservative.
Leisure interests: walking, rock-climbing.
Publ. *The Road to Prosperity* 47.
33 Eccleston Street, London, S.W.1, England.

Marquadt, Klaus Max, DR.RER.POL.; German business executive; b. 8 Nov. 1926, Berlin; *s.* of Dr. Arno and Ruth Marquadt; *m.* Brigitte Weber; three *d.;* ed. Realgymnasium Berlin, Universität Berlin and Technische Universität Berlin.
Chairman, Management Board, ARAL AG.
ARAL Aktiengesellschaft, 463 Bochum, Wittenerstrasse 45; Home: 463 Bochum-Stiepel, Roggenkamp 14, Federal Republic of Germany.
Telephone: 02321-382200 (Office); 02321-791091.

Marquard, William A.; American business executive; b. 6 March 1920, Pittsburgh, Pa.; ed. Univ. of Pennsylvania.
Formerly held positions with Westinghouse Electric Corpn.; joined the Mosler Safe Co. (purchased by American Standard 67) 52, Vice-Pres. 56, Senior Vice-Pres. and Dir. 61, Pres. 67-70; Senior Exec. Vice-Pres.,

Chief Operating Officer and Dir. American Standard Oct. 70, Pres. Feb. 71-, Chief Exec. Officer Aug. 71-; mem. Conf. Board, Econ. Club of N.Y., Advisory Board, Citizens Bank; Trustee, Citizens Budget Comm. Inc.
American Standard, 40 West 40th Street, New York, N.Y. 10018, U.S.A.
Telephone: 212-484-5100.

Marquez, Vernon O.; Canadian business executive; b. 15 Sept. 1908, Trinidad, West Indies; m. Margaret Amy; two s. two d.; ed. St. Mary's Coll., Trinidad.
Joined Northern Electric Co. Ltd. 29, Gen. Man. Sales Div. 57, Vice-Pres. 60, Exec. Vice-Pres. 63, Dir. 63-, Pres. and Chief Exec. Officer 67-70, Chair. of Board and Pres. 70, Chair. of Board and Chief Exec. Officer 71-73; Dir. Bell Canada, Cleyn and Tinker Ltd., Microsystems Int. Ltd., Northern Telecom Inc., Canadian Exec. Service Overseas, Quebec Industrial Relations Inst., Quebec Soc. for Crippled Children; Chair. Bishop's Univ. Dept. of Business Admin.; Vice-Pres. Int. Chamber of Commerce, Canadian Council; Gov. Canadian Asscn. for Latin America, Canadian Export Asscn.; mem. Canadian Chamber of Commerce, Canadian Manufacturers' Asscn., Canadian Council Conf. Board, Canadian Standards Asscn. Advisory Cttee., Minister of Industry, Trade and Commerce's Advisory Cttee. and others; Life Gov. Montreal Gen. Hospital; Commdr. Brother Order of St. John of Jerusalem.
Leisure interests: riding, gardening.
2890 Ste. Angelique Road, St. Lazare, Quebec, Canada.

Marquina Barredo, Ignacio; Mexican architect and archaeologist; b. 1913; ed. Colegio Soriano, National Preparatory School, and National Acad. of Fine Arts, National Univ. of Mexico.
Professor of Composition, Nat. Acad. of Fine Arts, Nat. Univ. of Mexico; Prof. of Prehispanic Architecture, Nat. School of Anthropology and History; Dir. of Prehistoric Monuments; Adviser to Nat. Indian Inst.; Dir. numerous explorations; Dir. Nat. Inst. of Anthropology and History 47-56; Sec.-Gen. Pan-American Inst. of Geography and History 56-65; Chair. Exec. Council for building of Nat. Museum of Anthropology 63-.
Publs. *Estudio Arquitectónico de los Monumentos de Teotihuacán* 22, *Arquitectura Cristiana en el Valle de Teotihuacán* 22, *Estudio Arquitectónico Comparativo de los Monumentos Arqueológicos de México* 28, *Tenayuca, La Orientación de las Pirámides de México* 31, *Tenayuca, Estudio Arqueológico de la Pirámide* 32, *Arquitectura Prehispánica* 51.
Cádiz Sur 24, Mixcoac-Insurgentes, Mexico 20, D.F., Mexico.

Marre, Sir Alan Samuel, K.C.B., M.A.; British public servant; b. 25 Feb. 1914, London; s. of Joseph and Rebecca (née Green) Marre; m. Romola Mary Gilling 1943; one s. one d.; ed. St. Olave's Grammar School, Southwark and Trinity Hall, Cambridge.
Assistant Principal, Ministry of Health 36, Principal 41, Asst. Sec. 46, Under-Sec. 52; Under-Sec. Ministry of Labour 63; Deputy Sec. Ministry of Health 64, Ministry of Labour (later Dept. of Employment and Productivity) 66; Second Perm. Under-Sec. of State, Dept. of Health and Social Security 68-71; Parl. Commr. for Admin. (Ombudsman) 71-76, Health Service Commr. 73-; mem. Council on Tribunals April 71-, Comm. for Local Admin. 74.
Leisure interests: reading, walking.
Church House, Gt. Smith Street, London SW1P 3BW; 44 The Vale, London, NW11 8SG, England.

Marrian, Guy Frederic, C.B.E., D,SC., F.R.I.C., F.I.BIOL., F.R.S.; British biochemist; b. 3 March 1904, London; s. of Frederick Marrian and Mary Currie; m. Phyllis Lewis 1928; two d.; ed. Tollington School and Univ. Coll., London.

Lecturer Univ. Coll. London 30-33; Associate Prof. Univ. of Toronto 33-35; Prof. Univ. of Toronto 35-38; Prof. of Chemistry in Relation to Medicine, Univ. of Edinburgh 39-59; Dir. of Research, Imperial Cancer Research Fund 59-68; Meldola Medal of Royal Inst. of Chemistry 31; Francis Amory Prize of American Acad. of Arts and Sciences 47, Dale Medal of the Soc. of Endocrinology 66; Hon. M.D. (Edinburgh).
Leisure interests: gardening, bird watching.
School Cottage, Ickham, Canterbury, Kent, England.
Telephone: Littlebourne 317.

Marriner, Neville; British musician and conductor; b. 15 April 1924, Lincoln; s. of Herbert H. and Ethel M. Marriner; m. Elizabeth M. Sims 1958; one s. one d.; ed. Lincoln School, Royal Coll. of Music.
Director, Acad. of St. Martin in the Fields 59-; Conductor Los Angeles Chamber Orchestra 69-; Dir. South Bank Festival of Music 75-; Tagore Gold Medal, three Edison Awards (Netherlands), two Mozart Gemeinde Awards (Austria), Grand Prix du Disque (France).
British Artist Special Services, 54 Welbeck Street, London, W.1, England.

Marris, Stephen Nicholson, M.A., PH.D.; British economist and international civil servant; b. 7 Jan. 1930, London; s. of Eric Denyer Marris and Phyllis May Marris; m. Margaret Swindells 1955; two s. one d.; ed. Bryanston School and King's Coll., Cambridge.
Parker of Waddington Research Student, Cambridge Univ. 52-53; Nat. Inst. of Econ. and Social Research, London 53-54; with Org. for European Econ. Co-operation, later named Org. for Econ. Co-operation and Devt. (OECD) 56-, Econ. Adviser to the Sec.-Gen. 75-; Visiting Research Prof., Int. Econs., Brookings Institution, Washington, D.C. 69-70.
Leisure interest: sailing.
Publ. The Burgenstock Communique (Princeton Univ.): *A Critical Examination of the Case for Limited Exchange-Rate Flexibility* 70.
8 Sentier des Pierres Blanches, 92190 Meudon, France.
Telephone: 524-87-70 (Office); 626-34-35 (Home).

Marrou, Henri Irénée, D. ès L.; French historian; b. 12 Nov. 1904, Marseilles; s. of Louis and Alphonsine (née Brochier) Marrou; m. Jeanne Bouchet-Fouillet 1930; three c.; ed. Lycée de Marseille, Ecole Normale Supérieure, Paris, Ecole Française de Rome.
Prof. Inst. Français de Naples 32; Prof. Cairo Univ. 37; Univ. de Nancy 38; Univ. de Montpellier 40; Univ. de Lyon 41; Univ. de Paris 45-; mem. Exec. Cttee. and critic *Esprit* 34; mem. Acad. Charles Cros 47; Pres. Institut Scientifique Franco-Canadien 50; mem. Cttee. International Balzan Foundation 62; Corresp. Fellow British Acad. 65, Bavarian Acad. 68; mem. Acad. Inscriptions 67, Dutch Acad. 67, Acad. Lincei 70, Inst. Lombardo 70; Officier Légion d'Honneur, Cmmdr. Palmes Académiques.
Publs. (under pseudonym Henri Davenson) *Fondements d'une Culture Chrétienne* 34, *Traité de la Musique selon l'esprit de Saint Augustin* 42, *Le Livre des Chansons* 44, *Les Troubadours* 61; under own name *Saint Augustin et la fin de la Culture Antique* 38 (4th ed. 58), *Histoire de l'Education dans l'Antiquité* 48 (6th ed. 65), *A Diognète* 52 (2nd edn. 65), *De la Connaissance Historique* 54 (6th edn. 73), *Saint Augustin et l'Augustinisme* 56 (8th edn. 73), *Clément d'Alexandrie, Le Pédagogue* 60-70, *Nouvelle Histoire de l'Eglise*, vol. I. 63, *Théologie de l'histoire* 68.
19 rue d'Antony, 92290 Chatenay-Malabry, France.
Telephone: Paris 661-14-11.

Marschak, Jacob; American economist; b. 23 July 1898, Kiev; s. of Israel Marschak; m. Marianne Kamnitzer 1927; one s. one d.; ed. Kiev Technological Inst. and Heidelberg Univ.
Lecturer Heidelberg Univ. 30; Dir. Statistical Inst. and

Reader in Statistics, Oxford Univ. 35; mem. All Souls Coll., Oxford; fmr. Prof. New School for Social Research N.Y.; Prof. Univ. of Chicago 43-55, Dir. Cowles Comm. for Research in Econs. 43-48, Yale Univ. 55-60, Univ. of Calif. (Los Angeles) 60-; Dir. Western Management Science Inst. 65-70; Pres. Econometric Soc. 46-47; Dir. American Statistical Asscn. 45-46; Fellow Inst. of Mathematical Statistics; Joint Editor *Behavioral Science*; Fellow, Center for Advanced Behavioral Studies 55-56; Ford Research Prof. Carnegie Inst. of Technology, Pittsburgh 58-59; Senior U.S. Scholar Award A. v. Humboldt Foundation 73-74; Hon. Fellow, Royal Statistical Soc.; mem. American Acad. of Arts and Sciences, Nat. Acad. of Sciences, U.S.A., Int. Statistical Inst.; Distinguished Fellow, American Econs. Asscn.; Dr. h.c. rer. pol. (Univ. of Bonn, Univ. of Heidelberg); Hon. LL.D. (Univ. of Calif.).

Publs. *Economic Theory of Teams* (with R. Radner) 72, *Economic Information, Decision and Prediction* (selected essays, 3 vols.) 74.

968 Stonehill Lane, Los Angeles, Calif. 90049, U.S.A. Telephone: 213-472-5394.

Marsh, Dame Ngaio, D.B.E.; New Zealand novelist and theatrical producer; b. 23 April 1899, Ferdalton, Christchurch; *d.* of Henry E. and Rose Elizabeth (Seager) Marsh; ed. St. Margaret's Coll., New Zealand, and Canterbury Univ. Coll. School of Art, Christchurch, New Zealand.

Joined English theatrical company touring New Zealand; on stage for two years; Red Cross Transport Unit, Second World War; Producer, D. D. O'Connor Theatre Management, N.Z. 44; Hon. D.Litt. (Canterbury N.Z.).

Leisure interests: travel, painting, gardening.

Publs. *A Man Lay Dead* 34, *Enter a Murderer* 35, *Nursing Home Murder* (with H. Jellett) 36, *Death in Ecstasy* 37, *Vintage Murder* 37, *Artists in Crime* 38, *Death in a White Tie* 38, *Overture to Death* 39, *Death at the Bar* 40, *Surfeit of Lampreys* 41, *Death and the Dancing Footman* 42, *Colour Scheme* 43, *Died in the Wool* 45, *Final Curtain* 47, *Swing Brother Swing* 48, *Opening Night* 51, *Spinsters in Jeopardy* 53, *Scales of Justice* 55, *Off With His Head* 57, *Singing in the Shrouds* 59, *False Scent* 60, *Hand in Glove* 62, *Dead Water* 64, *Black Beech and Honey Dew* (autobiography) 66, *Death at the Dolphin* 67, *Clutch of Constables* 68, *When in Rome* 69, *Tied Up in Tinsel* 72, *Black as He's Painted* 74.

37 Valley Road, Christchurch 2, New Zealand; and 69 Great Russell Street, London, WC1B 3DH, England.

Marsh, Rt. Hon. Sir Richard William, Kt., P.C.; British politician and public servant; b. 14 March 1928; *m.* 1st Evelyn Mary Andrews 1950 (divorced 1973), two *s.*; m. 2nd Caroline Dutton 1973 (died 1975); ed. Jennings School, Swindon, Woolwich Polytechnic and Ruskin Coll., Oxford.

Health Services Officer, Nat. Union of Public Employees 51-59; mem. Clerical and Admin. Whitley Council for Health Service 53-59; M.P. for Greenwich 59-71; Parl. Sec. Ministry of Labour 64-65; Joint Parl. Sec. Ministry of Technology 65-66; Minister of Power 66-68, of Transport 68-69; Dir. Michael Saunders Management Services 70-71; Chair. British Railways Board 71-(76); mem. Nat. Econ. Devt. Council.

British Railways Board, 222 Marylebone Road, London, N.W.1, England.

Marshak, Robert E., PH.D.; American university professor; b. 1916, New York City; *s.* of Russian-born American citizens; *m.* Ruth Gup 1943; one *s.* one *d.*; ed. Columbia Coll. and Cornell Univ.

Univ. of Rochester 39-70, Chair. and Harris Prof., Dept. of Physics and Astronomy 50-64, Distinguished Univ. Prof. 64-70; mem. School of Mathematics, Inst. for Advanced Studies, Princeton 48; visiting lecturer to numerous univs. and colls. throughout the world 40-67; Avco Visiting Prof., Cornell Univ. 59, Buhl Visiting Prof., Carnegie Mellon Univ. 68, Distinguished Visitor Univ. of Texas 70; Pres. City Coll. of New York 70-; Radiation Lab., Mass. Inst. of Technology (M.I.T.), Montreal Atomic Energy Lab., Los Alamos Scientific Lab. 42-46; Chair. Fed. of American Scientists 47-48; Vice-Chair. N.Y. State Advisory Comm. on Atomic Energy 57-58; Trustee, Atoms for Peace Awards 58-70, Univs. Research Asscn. 68-70; mem. various univ. cttees. etc.; Consultant to IAEA on establishment of Int. Center for Theoretical Physics, Trieste 61-63; American mem. of Science Council, Int. Center for Theoretical Physics 67-75; Sec. Comm. of High Energy Physics, Int. Union of Pure and Applied Physics 57-63; mem. Joint Cttee. on U.S.-Japan Science Co-operative Program 68-72; mem. Amer. Acad. of Arts and Sciences (Chair. Cttee. on World Univ. and Int. Science Foundation 69-71), Nat. Acad. of Sciences (Chair. Advisory Cttee. for Soviet Union and E. Europe 63-66, Head of Del. to Poland 64, to Yugoslavia 65, mem. Report Review Cttee. 70-, Rep. on Nat. Comm. for UNESCO Exec. Cttee. 70-73, Council 71-74); mem. Interim Board for Int. Foundation of Science, Stockholm 72-75; mem. Council, American Physical Soc. 65-69, Exec. Cttee. 68-69, Vice-Chair. (and Chair. Div. of Particles and Fields) 69-70; Guggenheim Fellow 53-54, 60-61, 67-68; first Niels Bohr Visiting Prof., Inst. of Mathematical Sciences, Madras (India) 63; N.Y. Acad. of Sciences Prize in Astronomy 40.

Leisure interests: skiing, music.

Publs. *Our Atomic World* (with E. C. Nelson and L. I. Schiff) 46, *Meson Physics* 52, *Introduction to Elementary Particle Physics* (with E. C. G. Sudarshan) 61, *Perspectives in Modern Physics* (editor) 66, *Advances in Particle Physics* (joint editor, 2 vols.) 68, 69, *Theory of Weak Interactions in Particle Physics* (with Riazuddin and C. P. Ryan) 69.

City College of New York, 138th Street at Convent Avenue, New York, N.Y. 10031, U.S.A.

Marshall, David Saul, LL.B.; Singapore fmr. politician; b. 12 March 1908, Singapore; *s.* of Saul Nassim Mashaal and Flora Ezekiel; *m.* Jean Mary Gray 1961; one *s.* three *d.*; ed. Raffles Institution, Middle Temple and Univ. of London.

Worked in Singapore as sharebroker, salesman and sec. to a shipping co. 24-32; then studied law in England and began legal career in Singapore 37-; joined Singapore Volunteer Corps 38; imprisoned by Japanese 42-45; founder Sec. War Prisoners Asscn.; mem. Jewish Welfare Board; founder mem. Labour Front; Chief Minister of Singapore 55-56; mem. Singapore Legislative Assembly 61-63; Del. to XXIII Session of UN Gen. Assembly 68; Chair. Singapore Inst. of S.E. Asian Studies 70-74.

8/10 Bank of China Chambers, Singapore 1.

Marshall, Herbert, O.B.E.; Canadian statistician; b. 1887, Toronto; *s.* of John Marshall and Janet Pinkerton; *m.* Muriel I. Meek 1924; ed. Univ. of Toronto.

Served in First World War; Lecturer in Economics, Univ. of Toronto 20-22; Prices Statistician, Dominion Bureau of Statistics 22-26, Chief Internal Trade Branch 26-42, Asst. Dominion Statistician 42-45, Dominion Statistician 45-56; Statistical Adviser, West Indies Fed. 58-59; Canadian rep. International Inst. of Statistics meeting New Delhi 51; Sec. British Commonwealth Statisticians' Conf. 35; Canadian rep. (and Chair. 47) of U.N. Statistical Comm.; Pres. American Statistical Asscn. 54; Pres. Inter-American Statistical Inst. 55-62; Vice-Pres. Int. Statistical Inst. 60; Pres. Canadian Political Science Asscn. 52.

Leisure interests: skiing, golf.

6 Wick Crescent, Ottawa, Ont. K1J 7H2, Canada. Telephone: 749-2752.

Marshall, J. Howard, II, A.B., LL.B.; American business executive; b. 24 Jan. 1905, Philadelphia Pa.; s. of S. Furman and Annabelle T. Marshall; ed. George School, Haverford Coll., and Yale School of Law. Instructor and Asst. Cruise Dir. Floating Univ. **Inc.** 26-27, Cruise Dir. 28-29; Asst. Dean and Asst. Prof. of Law, Yale School of Law 31-33; Special Asst. to Attorney-Gen. and Asst. Solicitor, U.S. Dept. of Interior, and mem. Petroleum Admin. Board 33-35; Counsel, Standard Oil Co. of Calif. 35-37; Assoc., Pillsbury, Madison and Sutro (Corporate Attorneys) 37-38, Partner 38-44; Dir., Pacific City Lines, Inc. 38-41; Vice-Pres. and Dir. Long Beach Oil Development Corpn. 39-42, 59-; Chief Counsel and Asst. Deputy Administrator, **Petroleum Administration for War** 41-44; mem. Mil. Petroleum Advisory Board 44-50, 54-59; Gen. Counsel, U.S. Del., Allied Comm. on Reparations 45; Pres. Dir. Ashland Oil and Refining Co. 44-51; Exec. Vice-Pres. and Dir. Signal Oil and Gas Co. 52-60; Pres. and Dir. Union Texas Natural Gas Corpn. 61-62; Pres. Union Texas Petroleum 62-67; Exec. Vice-Pres. and Dir. Allied Chemical Corpn. 65-67; Chair. of Board The Petroleum Corpn. 68-; Dir. Nat. Industries Inc., Texas Commerce Bank (Houston); Dir. and Chair. Exec. Cttee. Coastal States Gas Corpn. 73-; Dir. MKT Railroad, etc.; Consultant to Sec. of the Interior on Petroleum Defense Program 50-52; mem. American Petroleum Inst., Nat. Petroleum Council, Independent Petroleum Asscn., fmr. Consultant.
Home: 11114 Meadowick, Houston, Tex. 77024; Office: 1320 Esperson Building, Houston, Tex. 77002, U.S.A. Telephone Home: (713) 782-6582; Office: (713) 227-7245.

Marshall, Rt. Hon. Sir John Ross, P.C., G.B.E., C.H., B.A., LL.M.; New Zealand lawyer and politician; b. 5 March 1912, Wellington; s. of Allan Marshall; m. Margaret Livingston 1944; two s. two d.; ed. Victoria Univ. Coll., Univ. of N.Z.
Admitted barrister and solicitor of Supreme Court of N.Z. 36; served with N.Z. Expeditionary Force in Pacific and Italy (Major, Infantry), Second World War 41-46; elected M.P. 46-75; Lecturer in Law, Victoria Univ. Coll. 48-51; Minister Assisting the Prime Minister and Minister for State Advances Corpn., Public Trust Office and Census and Statistics 49-54; also Minister of Health 51-54, of Information and Publicity 51-57; Minister of Justice and Attorney-Gen. 54-57; Deputy Prime Minister 57; Deputy Leader of Opposition 57-60; Deputy Prime Minister and Minister of Overseas Trade 60-72; Minister of Customs 60-61; Minister of Industries and Commerce 60-69; Attorney-Gen. 69-71; Minister of Labour and Immigration 69-72; Prime Minister Feb.-Dec. 72; Leader of the Opposition 73-74; New Zealand Rep. Colombo Plan Conf., New Delhi 53, Commonwealth Prime Ministers Conf. 62, Trade Ministers Conf. 63, 66, Parl. Conf. 65; GATT Conf., Geneva 61, 63, 66; Econ. Comm. for Asia and the Far East (ECAFE) Conf., Tokyo 62, Teheran 64, Chair. ECAFE Wellington 65, New Delhi 66, Canberra 68, Bangkok 70; UN 70; ILO Conf., Geneva 71; EEC negotiations 61-71; Chair. Nat. Devt. Conf. 68, 69; Chair. Nat. Devt. Council 69-72, New Zealand Comm. for Expo 70; Visiting Fellow Victoria Univ. of Wellington; mem. Advisory Council, World Peace through Law; Consultant Partner, Buddle Anderson Kent and Co.; Chair. Nat. Bank of N.Z. Ltd., Phillips Electrical Inds. N.Z. Ltd., Contractors Bonding and Discount Corpn. Ltd.; Dir. Philips Electrical Industries, Norwich Union Insurance Soc., Hallenstein Bros. Ltd., Fletcher Holdings Ltd., DRG (N.Z.) Ltd.; Hon. Bencher Gray's Inn 73.
Leisure interests: golf, fishing.
Publ. *Law Relating to Watercourses.*
22 Fitzroy Street, Wellington 1, New Zealand. Telephone: 736631.

Marshall, Thurgood; American lawyer and government official; b. 2 July 1908, Baltimore, Md.; s. of William and Norma Marshall; m. 1st Vivian Burey 1929 (deceased), 2nd Cecilia Suyat 1955; two s.; ed. Lincoln Univ., Pennsylvania, and Howard Univ. Law School, Washington, D.C.
Director-Gen. Nat. Asscn. for Advancement of Colored People Legal Defense and Educ. Fund 40-62; Judge, Second Circuit Court of Appeals 62-65; Solicitor-Gen. of U.S.A. 65-67; Assoc. Justice, U.S. Supreme Court 67-; Spingarn Medal 46; mem. Board of Dirs. John F. Kennedy Library; mem. American Bar Asscn., Asscn. of the Bar of the City of New York, Nat. Bar Asscn., N.Y.C. County Lawyers Asscn.; Living History Award; numerous awards, medals and citations.
U.S. Supreme Court, Washington, D.C. 20543, U.S.A.

Marshall, Walter Charles, C.B.E., PH.D., F.R.S.; British physicist; b. 5 March 1932, Wales; s. of Frank and Amy Marshall; m. Ann Vivienne Sheppard 1955; one s. one d.; ed. Birmingham Univ.
Scientific Officer, Atomic Energy Research Establishment, Harwell 54-57; Research Physicist, Univ. of Calif. and Harvard Univ. 57-59; Group Leader, Solid State Theory, Atomic Energy Research Establishment, Harwell 59-60, Head, Theoretical Physics Div. 60-66, Deputy Dir. 66-68, Dir. 68-75; Dir. Research Group, U.K. Atomic Energy Authority 69-75; mem. Nat. Research Devt. Corpn. Board 69-75; mem. U.K. Atomic Energy Authority 72-, Dep. Chair. 75-; Chief Scientist, Dept. of Energy 74-; Maxwell Medal.
Leisure interests: origami, croquet, gardening, chess.
Publ. *Thermal Neutron Scattering* 71, research papers on magnetism, neutron scattering and solid state theory.
U.K. Atomic Energy Authority London Office, 11 Charles II Street, London SW1Y 4QP; Home: Bridleway House, Goring-on-Thames, Oxon., England.
Telephone: 01-930 6262 ext. 531 (Office); Goring 2890 (Home).

Marston, Robert Quarles, B.S., M.D.; American science administrator; b. 12 Feb. 1923, Toano, Va.; s. of Warren and Helen Smith Marston; m. Ann Carter Garnett 1946; two s. one d.; ed. Virginia Military Inst., Medical Coll. of Virginia and Oxford Univ.
Intern, Johns Hopkins Univ. 49-50; Asst. Resident, Vanderbilt Univ. Hospital, Nashville, Tenn. 50-51; Asst. Resident, Medical Coll. of Virginia, Richmond 53-54, Asst. Prof. of Medicine 54-57, Dean in Charge of Student Affairs 59-61; Asst. Prof. of Bacteriology and Immunology, Univ. of Minnesota 58-59; Dir. of Univ. of Miss. Medical Center and Dean of School of Medicine, Jackson, Miss. 61-65; Vice-Chancellor, Univ. of Miss. and Dean of School of Medicine 65-66; Assoc. Dir. Nat. Insts. of Health, Bethesda, Md., and Dir. of Regional Medical Programs 66-68, Dir. Nat. Insts. of Health 68-73; Scholar-in-Residence Univ. of Virginia 73-74; Pres. Univ. of Fla. 74-; Rhodes Scholar 47-49, Markle Scholar 54-59; First Harold S. Diehl Lecturer 68; Hon. mem. Nat. Medical Asscn. 69, Amer. Hospital Asscn. 69; Distinguished Fellow Inst. of Medicine, Nat. Acad. of Sciences 73; Hon. degrees, Coll. of William and Mary and Albany Medical Coll. of Union Univ.
Leisure interests: sailing, camping, music, reading.
Publs. Numerous articles in the field of infectious diseases, medical education, and administration of health programmes.
University of Florida, Gainesville, Fla. 32601, U.S.A.

Márta, Ferenc, D.CHEM.; Hungarian chemist; b. 12 Jan. 1929, Kiskundorozsma.
Head of Dept. of Physics and Chem., József Attila Univ., Szeged 62, Rector 67-73; Corresp. mem. Hungarian Acad. of Sciences 70, Gen. Sec. 75-; mem. Szeged Municipal Exec. Cttee. of Hungarian Socialist Workers' Party 66, Cen. Cttee. 71-.

Hungarian Academy of Sciences, 1051 Budapest,
Roosevelt tér 9, Hungary.
Telephone: 113-400.

Martin, Archer John Porter, C.B.E., M.A., PH.D., F.R.S.;
British chemist; b. 1 March 1910, London; s. of Dr.
William A. P. and Lillian K. Martin; m. Judith Bagenal
1943; two s. three d.; ed. Bedford School, and Peter-
house, Cambridge.
Research, Cambridge, Physical Chemical Lab., Nutri-
tional Lab. 33-38; Wool Industries Research Asscn.,
Leeds 38-46; Boots' Pure Drug Co. Research Dept.,
Nottingham 46-48; mem. staff Medical Research Coun-
cil 48-52; Head of Physical Chemistry Div., Nat. Inst.
for Medical Research, Mill Hill, London, 52-56; Chemical
Consultant 56-59; Dir. Abbotsbury Laboratories Ltd.
59-70; Consultant to Wellcome Foundation Ltd. 70-73;
Extraordinary Prof. Eindhoven Technological Univ.,
Holland 64-74; MRC Professorial Fellowship of Chem.,
Univ. of Sussex 73; Robert A. Welch Prof. of Chem.,
Univ. of Houston, Texas 74; Berzelius Gold Medal of
Swedish Medical Society 51; shared Nobel Prize in
Chemistry 52; John Scott Award 58, John Price
Wetherill Medal 59, Franklin Inst. Medal 59, Lever-
hulme Medal 63, Kolthoff Medal 69, Callendar Medal
71; Order of the Rising Sun, 2nd Class (Japan) 72;
Achievement Award The Worshipful Co. of Scientific
Instrument Makers 72; Hon. D.Sc. (Leeds Univ.) 68,
(Glasgow Univ.) 72.
Abbotsbury, Barnet Lane, Elstree, Herts., WD6 3RD,
England.
Telephone: 01-953 1031.

Martin, Sir David Christie, Kt., C.B.E., B.SC., PH.D.,
C.CHEM., F.R.I.C., F.R.S.E.; British administrator; b. 7
Oct. 1914, Kirkcaldy, Fife; s. of David Martin and
Helen Linton; m. Jean Wilson 1943; ed. Univ. of
Edinburgh.
Assistant Sec. Royal Soc. of Arts 39-45, seconded to
Ministry of Supply for wartime duties; Gen. Sec. The
Chemical Soc. 45-47; Exec. Sec. The Royal Soc. 47-;
Man. Royal Inst. of Great Britain 51-52; Recorder
Chemistry Section British Asscn. for the Advancement
of Science 53-58; mem. Council of British Asscn. for the
Advancement of Science 59-69, 70-; mem. Exec.
Council CIBA Foundation 67-; mem. Inter-Union
Comm. On Solar Terrestial Physics of the Int. Council
of Scientific Unions 67-; mem. Council of Man. of the
Soc. for the Protection of Science and Learning 67-;
mem. Gen. Advisory Council of B.B.C. 68-; Chair.
Science Consultative Group B.B.C. 67-; mem. Council
of the Royal Soc. of Arts 72-; mem. Advisory Cttee.
Charities Aid Foundation 75-; Hon. D.Sc. (Edinburgh),
Hon. D.C.L. (Newcastle upon Tyne).
Leisure interest: fishing.
The Royal Society, 6 Carlton House Terrace, London,
S.W.1, England.
Telephone: 01-839-5561.

Martin, Edmund Fible, B.S., ENG.D.; American steel
executive; b. 1 Nov. 1902; ed. Stevens Inst. of Tech-
nology.
With Bethlehem Steel Corpn. mills, Bethlehem 22-70,
Supt. 28-39, Asst. Supt. Saucon Div. Bethlehem plant
39-46, Asst. Gen. Manager Lackawanna, N.Y., plant of
Bethlehem Steel 46-50, Gen. Manager 50-58; Vice-Pres.
Steel Div., Bethlehem Steel Corpn. 58-60; Dir. Bethle-
hem Steel Corpn. 58-70, Pres. 60-63, Vice-Chair. 63-64,
Chair. and Chief Exec. 64-70; Trustee Nat. Industrial
Conf. Board 66-70, Stevens Inst. of Technology, Lehigh
Univ., St. Luke's Hospital Bethlehem; Hon. Dir.
American Iron and Steel Inst. (Chair. and Chief Exec.
Officer 67-69), J. P. Morgan & Co. Inc., Morgan
Guaranty Trust Co., New York, The Pennsylvania
Soc., Bethlehem Area Foundation; Hon. Dr. Eng.
(Univ. of Buffalo) 61, Hon. LL.D. (Moravian Coll.) 64,
Hon. LL.D. (Lehigh Univ.) 66, Hon. Eng.D. (Stevens

Inst. of Technology) 67, Hon. LL.D. (Valparaiso Univ.)
67; Knight Commdr., Royal Order of the North Star,
Sweden; Grand Band of the Order of the Star of Africa
(Liberia); Knight Commdr. of the Southern Cross
(Brazil), numerous other awards.
Suite 310, 437 Main Street, Bethlehem, Pa. 18018, U.S.A.

Martin, Edwin McCammon; American government
official; b. 21 May 1908, Dayton, Ohio; s. of Harry
Judson and Clara McCammon; m. Margaret Milburn
1936; one s. one d.; ed. Northwestern Univ.
Economist, Central Statistical Board 35-38, Bureau of
Labor Statistics 38-40; Exec., War Production Board
40-44; Asst. Chief, and Dep. Chief of Div., Office of
Strategic Services 44-45; Chief, Japanese and Korean
Economic Affairs, Dept. of State 45-47; Chief of Div. for
Occupied Area Economic Affairs 47-48, Dep. Dir., Office
of Int. Trade Policy 48-49, Dir., Office for European
Regional Affairs 49-52; Special Asst. to Sec. of State for
Mutual Security Affairs 52-53; Alternate Perm. Rep. to
NATO 53-57; Minister for Economic Affairs, American
Embassy, London 57-59; Asst. Sec. of State for Econo-
mic Affairs 60-62, Asst. Sec. of State for Inter-American
Affairs, Dept. of State 62-64; Amb. to Argentina 64-68;
Chair. Devt. Assistance Cttee. OECD, Paris 68-74;
U.S. Co-ordinator World Food Conf. 74; Chair. Con-
sultative Cttee. on Food Production and Investment in
Developing Countries, Int. Bank for Reconstruction
and Devt.
Leisure interests: golf, wild flower photography,
history, philately, bird watching.
International Bank for Reconstruction and Develop-
ment, 1818 H Street, N.W., Washington D.C. 20433;
Home: 4101 Cathedral Avenue, Washington, D.C.
20016, U.S.A.

Martin, Graham (Anderson), A.B.; American govern-
ment official and diplomatist; b. 22 Sept. 1912, Mars
Hill, N.C.; s. of the Rev. Gustav A. Martin and Hildreth
Marshbanks; m. Dorothy Wallace 1934; one s. two d.;
ed. Wake Forest Coll.
Washington newspaper corresp. 32-33; Aide to Dep.
Admin. Nat. Recovery Admin. 33-36; Asst. to Chair.,
Social Security Board 36-37, Dist. Man. 37-41; Regional
Dir. Fed. Security Agency 41-42, Chief Field Operations
46; U.S. Army service 42-46; Chief of Bureau, War
Assets Admin. 46-47; U.S. Foreign Service 47-, Attaché,
France 47-50, Counsellor 51-55, Asst. Chief of Mission
53-55; Dept. of State Adviser, Air War Coll. 55-57;
Special Asst. to Under Sec. of State for Econ. Affairs
57-59; Special Asst., Under Sec. of State 59-60; Consul
Gen. Geneva 60-61; Amb. to UN Geneva 60-62; Deputy
Asst. Admin. Agency for Int. Development 62-63; Amb.
to Thailand 63-67; U.S. Rep. to Council of SEATO
63-67; Perm. Rep. to ECAFE 63-67; Special Asst.
to Sec. of State 67-69, 76-; Amb. to Italy 69-73, to
Repub. of Viet-Nam 73-75; mem. American Acad. of
Political and Social Science, American Foreign Service
Asscn. (Vice-Pres. 62-63); Dept. of State Distinguished
Honor Award 67, Plaque for Humanitarian Service,
Nat. Conf. on World Refugee Problems 69.
Leisure interests: golf, tennis, sailing.
Publ. *Toward A Modern Diplomacy* (report to the
American Foreign Service Asscn.) 68.
c/o Department of State, Washington, D.C. 20520, U.S.A.

Martin, John Edward; American business executive;
b. 11 Dec. 1904; ed. Bryson Coll.
Sales Engineer, Link Belt Co., Chicago 27-33, Manager,
Stoker Div. 33-41; U.S. Army Ordnance Dept. 42-43;
Gen. Manager Link Belt Ordnance Co. Chicago 44-45;
Vice-Pres. (Operations), Dir. American Type Founders
Inc. 45-47; Pres. and Dir. Firestone Steel Products Co.
48-52; Exec. Vice-Pres. Dana Corpn., Toledo 52-53,
Pres., Dir. 54-, Chair. of Board 66-72, Chair. Exec.
Cttee. 72-; Chair. of Board Hayes-Dana Ltd., Canada

62-64, Dir. 64-; Chair. of Board American Health Foundation 72-.
Dana Corporation, 4500 Dorr Street, Toledo, O. 43615, U.S.A.

Martin, Sir (John) Leslie, Kt., M.A., PH.D., F.R.I.B.A.; British architect; b. 17 Aug. 1908, *m.* Sadie Speight; one *s.* one *d.*; ed. Manchester Univ. School of Architecture.
Asst. Lecturer, Manchester Univ. 30-34; Dir. Hull School of Architecture 34-39; Principal Asst. Architect, L.M.S. Railway 39-48; Deputy Architect, London County Council 48-53, Architect 53-56; Prof. of Architecture, Cambridge Univ. 56-72; Fellow, Jesus Coll., Cambridge 56-72, Hon. Fellow 73-; Fellow, Royal Inst. of British Architects, Council mem. 52-58, Vice-Pres. 55-57; Slade Prof. Oxford 65-66; Ferens Prof. Hull 66-67; Visiting Prof. of Architecture, Yale Univ. 73-74; mem. Royal Fine Art Comm. 58-72; Hon. mem. Asscn. of Finnish Architects; Corresp. mem. Nat. Acad. S. Luca, Rome; awards include Soane Medal 30 and London Bronze Architectural Medal 54; R.I.B.A. Distinction in Town Planning; Hon. LL.D. (Leicester, Manchester and Hull); Royal Gold Medal (Arch.) 73.
The King's Mill, Great Shelford, Cambridge, England.
Telephone: Shelford 2399.

Martin, Ludwig; German lawyer; b. 25 April 1909; ed. Munich.
Assessor, Munich High Court 37-39; Scientific Assistant, Reich Court, Leipzig 39; Military Service 39-45; Chair. Sonthofen Court 46-50; Civil Rights Dept., Fed. Ministry of Justice 50-; Fed. Attorney 52-53; Fed. Judge, Fed. High Court 53-63; Fed. Solicitor-Gen. 63-74, Judge, Fed. Constitutional Court 71.
Schlossbezirk 3, Karlsruhe, Federal Republic of Germany.

Martin, Hon. Paul Joseph James, P.C., C.C., Q.C., M.A., LL.M.; Canadian lawyer and politician; b. 23 June 1903, Ottawa, Ont.; *s.* of Phillippe and Lumina Martin; *m.* Eleanor Adams 1938; one *s.* one *d.*; ed. St. Alexandre Coll., St. Michael's Coll., Osgoode Hall Law School, Toronto, Univ. of Toronto, Harvard Law School, Trinity Coll., Cambridge, and Geneva School of International Studies.
Lecturer in Political Science, Univ. of Western Ontario 31-34; senior partner firm of Martin, Laird, Easton & Cowan 34-63; mem. of Parl. for Essex East 35-68; K.C. 37; Del. to L.N. Assembly 38; Parl. Asst. to Minister of Labour 43; Chair. Canadian Govt. Del. and Chair. Employment Comm. ILO Conf. Philadelphia 44; Sec. of State of Canada 45-46; Minister of Nat. Health and Welfare 46-57; Sec. of State for External Affairs 63-68; Senior Minister and Leader of Govt. in Senate 68-74; High Commr. in U.K. 74-; Del. to 1st, 4th, 7th, 10th, 18th, 19th and 20th General Assemblies of the UN, to 1st Session of Econ. and Social Council (London) 46 and to 3rd and 5th Sessions (New York 46 and 47); Pres. North Atlantic Council 65-66; Del. Consultative Cttee., Colombo Plan, Wellington, N.Z. 56; numerous hon. degrees; Christian Culture Award 56; Liberal.
Canadian High Commission, Macdonald House, 1 Grosvenor Square, London, W.1, England; and 2021 Ontario Avenue, Windsor, Ont., Canada.
Telephone: 01-629-9492 (High Commission).

Martin, Robin Geoffrey, M.A.; British business executive; b. 9 March 1921, Wolverhampton; *s.* of Cecil Martin and late Isabel K. Martin (née Hickman); *m.* Margery Chester (née Yates) 1946; two *s.* one *d.*; ed. Cheltenham Coll. and Jesus Coll., Cambridge.
Joined Tarmac Ltd. 45, Dir. 55; Man. Dir. Tarmac Roadstone Ltd. 58; Group Man. Dir. 63; Deputy Chair. Tarmac Ltd. 67; Man. Dir. Tarmac Derby Ltd. 68; Chair. and Chief Exec. Tarmac Ltd. 71-; non-Exec. Dir. Serck Ltd. 71-74, Deputy Chair. 74-76, Chair. 76-;

Dir. Soc. de Pavage et des Asphaltes de Paris 74, Burmah Oil Co. Ltd. 75.
Leisure interests: golf, sailing, skiing.
Tarmac Ltd., Ettingshall, Wolverhampton WV4 6JP; Home: The Field, The Wergs, Tettenhall, nr. Wolverhampton, England.
Telephone: 0902-41101 (Office); 0902-751719 (Home).

Martin, Roger Léon René; French businessman; b. 8 April 1915; ed. Ecole Polytechnique and Ecole Nat. Supérieure des Mines.
Ingénieur des Mines, Nancy 41-42; Asst. to Steel Industry Dir., Dept. of Industry (French Govt.) 42-46; Lecturer Ecole Nat. des Mines 45-53; joined Compagnie de Pont-à-Mousson 48, Asst. Gen. Man. 53, Gen. Man. 59-64, Pres. and Gen. Manager 64-70; Pres. Cie. de Saint-Gobain-Pont-à-Mousson 70-; Dir. Co. Financière de Suez, Crédit Industriel et Commercial, Electricité de France, Pricel, Rhône-Poulenc, Agence Havas, Int. Saint-Gobain; Commdr. Légion d'Honneur.
54 avenue Hoche, 75365 Paris, Cédex 08; Home: 86 rue d'Assas, Paris 6e, France.

Martin, William Frederick, B.S.; American petroleum executive; b. 31 March 1917, Blackwell, Okla.; *s.* of Fred and Emma Buchholz Martin; *m.* Betty J. Randall 1941; one *s.* one *d.*; ed. Blackwell High School and Univ. of Okla.
Joined Phillips Petroleum Co. 39, Treas. 60, Treas. and Sec. 62, mem. Board of Dirs. 64, Senior Vice-Pres. 65, Exec. Vice-Pres. 68, Pres. Oct. 71-73, Pres. and Chief Exec. Officer 73-74, Chair. and Chief Exec. Officer 74-.
Office: 18 Phillips Building, Bartlesville, Okla. 74004; Home: 615 East 16th Place, Bartlesville, Okla. 74003, U.S.A.
Telephone: 661-3817 (Office); 336-8159 (Home).

Martin, William McChesney, Jr., B.A.; American financier; b. 17 Dec. 1906; ed. Yale and Columbia Univs., Benton College of Law, St. Louis.
Federal Reserve Bank of St. Louis 28-29; Head, Statistical Dept. A. G. Edwards and Sons, St. Louis 29-31, Partner 31-38; mem. N.Y. Stock Exchange 31-38, Gov. 35-38, Chair. Comm. on Constitution 37-38, Sec. Conway Comm. to reorganise the Exchange 37-38; Chair. of Board and Pres. *pro tem.* May-June 38, Pres. 38-41; published and edited *Economic Forum* 32-34; drafted as private, U.S. Army 41; attained rank of Col. 45; Asst. to Exec., President's Soviet Protocol Cttee. and Munitions Assignments Board 42; Dir. Export-Import Bank of Washington 45, Chair. and Pres. 46; Asst. Sec. of the Treasury 49-51; Chair. Federal Reserve Board 51-70; Dir. U.S. Steel 70-, Caterpillar Tractor; Chair. Comm. to reorganize N.Y. Stock Exchange 71; U.S. Exec. Dir., Int. Bank 49-52; Trustee Berry Schools, Rome, Georgia and The Johns Hopkins Univ.; Fellow Nat. Geographic Soc.; LL.D. (Temple, Tulane, Washington, Trinity, Pennsylvania, Yale, Tufts, Columbia, Washington and Lee, Hamilton, Rutgers, Harvard, Princeton, New York, Bishop's (Canada), Delaware, Michigan and Georgetown Univs., Amherst, Bowdoin, Marietta, Middlebury and Williams Colls.); Legion of Merit.
800 17th Street, N.W., Washington D.C. (Office); 2861 Woodland Drive, N.W., Washington D.C. 20008, U.S.A.

Martin-Artajo, Alberto; Spanish politician; b. 1905; ed. Univ. of Madrid.
Pres. Catholic student del. to Paris 32, to Washington 39; chief editorial writer of *El Debate* and *Ya*; Foreign Minister 45-57; Gen. Sec. Council of State 57-; mem. Cortes, Royal Acad. of Politics.
Publs. *Doctrina Social-Católica, Como organizar el régimen corporativo en España, La misión social de la familia, según la doctrina pontificia, Hacia una Comunidad Hispánica de Naciones, Doctrina Política de los Papas, La Conciencia Social de los Españoles.*
Calle General Sanjurjo 34, piso 5°, Madrid 3, Spain.

Martin Villa, Rodolfo; Spanish engineer, trade union official and politician; b. 3 Oct. 1934, Santa María del Páramo, León; ed. Escuela de Ingeniería Industrial, Madrid.
Leader of Madrid Section, Sindicato Español Universitario, Nat. Leader 62-64; Sec.-Gen. Syndical Org. 69-74; mem. Council of the Realm; Nat. Econ. Adviser, Nat. Inst. of Industry; Nat. Econ. Adviser, Banco de Crédito Industrial, later Pres.; Civil Gov. of Barcelona and Provincial Head of Falangist Movement 74-75; Minister for Relations with Trade Unions Dec. 75-; fmr. mem. special group of industrial engineers assisting Treasury.
Ministerio de Relaciones Sindicales, Madrid, Spain.

Martineau, Rt. Hon. Paul, P.C., Q.C.; Canadian lawyer and politician; b. 10 April 1921, Bryson, Quebec; s. of Alphonse Martineau and Lucienne Lemieux; m. Hélène Neclaw 1946; two d.
Former Crown Attorney for District of Pontiac, Quebec; M.P. 58-65; Parl. Asst. to Prime Minister 59-61; Deputy Speaker of House of Commons 62-63; Minister of Mines and Technical Surveys 62-63; mem. Royal Comm. on Admin. of Justice 67; Progressive Conservative.
Leisure interests: painting, writing, travelling, hiking.
102 Main Street, Hull, Quebec; Home: Mountain Road, Lucerne, Quebec, Canada.
Telephone: 827-2065 (Home).

Martinelli, Mario; Italian politician; b. 12 May 1906, Como; m. Francesca Vergottini 1929; three s. four d.; ed. commercial coll.
Commercial adviser; sometime Pres. Youth Fed., Diocese of Como; mem. P.P.I. (People's Party) 22-26; active resistance movement 43-45; Sec. Como Christian Democrat Party 45-46; Deputy (for Como-Sondrio-Varese) to Constituent Assembly, later Chamber of Deputies 46-62; Senator 63-; mem. Nat. Council of the Christian Democratic Party 49-51, 58-60, 62-, of Cen. Cttee. 50-51, 65-; Under-Sec., Treasury 51, Ministry of Foreign Trade 53; Minister of Foreign Trade (Scelba Govt.) 54-55; Pres. Transport Section of European Assembly 58-, Finance and Treasury Cttee., Chamber of Deputies 58-60; Minister of Foreign Trade 60-62, of Finance 63; Vice-Pres. Finance and Treasury Cttee., Senate 64-68, Pres. 68-72; Pres. Fiscal Reform Cttee. 72; Chair. Senate Transport Comm. 72-75; Minister of Transport Nov. 74-; Knight Grand Cross (Somalia), Elephant (1st Class, Afghanistan), Order Economie, Nat. Medal of Honor (France), Al Merito (Argentina), El Sol del Peru, San Gregorius Magnus (Vatican).
Via Dante 100, Como 22100, Italy.

Martinez Esteruelas, Cruz; Spanish politician and lawyer; b. 1932; m.; three c.; ed. Univs. of Barcelona and Deusto.
Called to the Bar 57; Dir.-Gen. Patrimonio del Estado, Ministry of Finance 62-65; Chief Exec. Legal Advisory Board, Secr.-Gen. of the Movt. 65-68; mem. Parl. 68-; Minister of Devt. Planning July-Dec. 73, of Educ. and Science Dec. 73-75; Grand Cross of Civil Merit, Order of Cisneros.
Publs. *La Enemistad Política* 71, *Estudios de Sociología Política.*
c/o Ministerio de Educación y Ciencia, Madrid, Spain.

Martinez Ordóñez, Roberto, B.S.; Honduran diplomatist; b. 18 Sept. 1922, Tegucigalpa; m.; three s. one d.; ed. Escuela José Trinidad Cabañas, Tegucigalpa, Instituto Nacional, Tegucigalpa, Escuela Militar, San Salvador and Univ. of Alabama.
General Staff Officer, 41-43; Engineer, Inter-American Public Health Co-operative Service 46-47; Chief Surface Engineer, Nueva York Honduras Rosario Mining Co. 47-49; with Ministry of Communications and Public Works 58-59; del. to Org. of Cen. American States 59-60; Amb. to El Salvador 59-60; Pres. Nat. Election Board of Honduras 60-63; Rep. Nat. Constitutional Assembly 65, Nat. Congress 65-68; mem. Cen. Exec. Cttee. of Liberal Party 65-67; Perm. Rep. to UN Oct. 71-; fmr. Pres. Nat. Electric Power Corpn.; Pres. Nat. Housing Inst.; mem. Board of Dirs., Nat. Devt. Bank; mem. Nat. Council; Pres. Nat. Railways.
Permanent Mission of Honduras to United Nations, 415 Lexington Avenue, Room 1310, New York, N.Y. 10017, U.S.A.

Martínez Zuviría, Gen. Gustavo; Argentine army officer, diplomatist and historian; b. 28 Dec. 1915, Santa Fé; s. of Dr. Gustavo Martínez Zuviría and Matilde de Iriondo; m. Maria Eugenia Ferrer Deheza 1940; four s. four d.; ed. Colegio del Salvador, Buenos Aires, Mount St. Mary's Coll., England and Colegio Militar de San Martin.
Teacher, Colegio Militar de la Nación; took part in unsuccessful coup d'état Sept. 51; imprisoned 51-53; Mil. Attaché, Peru 55-57; Head, Cavalry Regt. 3 57-58; Dir. Colegio Militar de la Nación, Escuela Superior de Guerra; Chief of Staff, Cavalry Corps.; Insp. of Cavalry; Commdr. 2nd Div. of Cavalry 64-65; Chief of Staff, 3rd Army 66-70; Commdr. First Army Corps; Sec. for Information 70; Amb. to U.K. 70-73; mem. Acad. Nacional, Sanmartiniana, Instituto Nacional, Ciencias Genealógicas; numerous awards from Argentine, Peru, Brazil, Chile and Federal Republic of Germany.
Leisure interests: reading, riding, writing.
Publs. numerous historical and military works.
Avenida del Libertador 15249, Acassuso Buenos Aires, Province, Argentina.
Telephone: 743-5379/3960.

Martini, Fritz, DR. PHIL. HABIL; German university professor; b. 5 Sept. 1909; ed. Univs. of Zürich, Graz, Heidelberg, Grenoble, Berlin.
Extraordinary Prof. of Literary Science and Aesthetics, Technical Univ., Stuttgart 43-49, Ordinary Prof. 49-; mem. Presidium Deutsche Akad. für Sprache und Dichtung, Darmstadt.
Publs. incl. *Heinrich von Kleist und die geschichtliche Welt* 39, *Deutsche Literaturgeschichte, Das Wagnis der Sprache, Das Zeitalter des Realismus* 60.
Universität Stuttgart, 7000 Stuttgart, Huberstrasse 16; Grüneisenstrasse 5, Stuttgart, Federal Republic of Germany.

Martini, Herbert, D.IUR.; German banker; b. 4 July 1903, Reichenbach.
Member Supervisory Board Hoffmans Stärkefabriken, Salzuflen, Reichs-Kredit-Gesellsch., Berlin; mem. Advisory Board Colonia Versicherung, Cologne.
Parkstrasse 40, 6242 Kronberg-Schönberg, Federal Republic of Germany.
Telephone: 06173-2373.

Martinka, Karol, ING.; Czechoslovak economist and politician; b. 5 July 1923, Púchov; ed. Univ. of Econs., Bratislava.
Deputy Chair. Slovak Planning Office, Bratislava 56-63; Chair., Plan Co-ordination Group, Council of Mutual Econ. Assistance (CMEA) 63-68; Minister of Finance, Slovak S.R. Jan.-Oct. 69; State Sec. Ministry of Planning of C.S.S.R. 69-70; Minister without Portfolio, Fed. Govt. of C.S.S.R. 70-71; Minister and Dep. Chair. State Planning Comm. 71-72; Vice-Premier of Slovak Socialist Repub., Chair. Slovak Planning Comm. 72-; mem. Slovak C.P. Cen. Cttee. 72-; Deputy to House of the People, Fed. Assembly 73-; Order of Labour 73.
Slovak Planning Commission, Kýčerského 1, 881 22 Bratislava, Czechoslovakia.

Martino, Francesco de; Italian politician and university professor; b. 1907.
Professor of History, Univ. of Naples; fmr. Sec.-Gen.

Partito Socialista Italiano (PSI); Deputy Prime Minister 70-72; Presidential candidate Dec. 71. Council of Ministers, Rome, Italy.

Martins, Rudolf, LL.D.; Austrian diplomatist; b. 9 Feb. 1915, Zürich; s. of Martin and Carola (née Dobolschek) Martins; ed. Humanistisches Gymnasium (Vienna XIII), and Universität Wien.
With Federal Chamber of Commerce, Vienna 46-47; Austrian Trade Commr. for Switzerland and Liechtenstein and Sec. of Austrian Chamber of Commerce for Switzerland, Zürich 47-49; with Fed. Chamber of Commerce, Vienna 49-59; Counsellor, Adviser on Multilateral Trade and Commerce, Ministry of Foreign Affairs 59-63; Counsellor, Head of Dept. for Multilateral Trade and Commerce Questions, Ministry of Trade and Reconstruction 63-65; Amb. and Perm. Austrian Rep. to Office of UN and UN Specialized Agencies, Geneva, and Leader of Austrian Del. to European Free Trade Asscn. (EFTA) 65-68, 72-; Envoy Extraordinary and Minister Plenipotentiary, Head of Dept. for Multi-lateral trade and Commerce Questions, Ministry of Foreign Affairs 68-72; Goldenes Ehrenzeichen für Verdienste um die Republik Österreich.
Leisure interests: music, linguistics.
9 rue de Varembé, CH-1211 Geneva 20; Home: Schloss Schönbrunn 39, A-1130 Vienna, Austria.
Telephone: 33-77-50 (Geneva).

Martinuzzi, Napoleone; Italian sculptor; b. 5 May 1892, Murano, Venice; s. of Giovanni Martinuzzi and Amalia Fuga.
Works include *War Memorial* (exhibited Venice Biennial Exhibition), *Vittoria*, in honour of D'Annunzio, *Vittoria* (Vidor War Memorial Church), *Grande lampadario a fontana* (Venice Biennial Exhibition), Plans for the tomb of D'Annunzio and his mother, Equestrian statue in Gov.'s Palace, Grosseto, Decorations for Post and Telegraph Buildings in Ferrara and Palermo; sculptures in Rome and Venice galleries; a group of Mermaids in bronze for the town of Ostia, a bust of Tintoretto for the church of the Madonna dell' Orto, Venice, a Monumental Gate for the Palace of the I.N.A., Rome; War Memorial 1940-45, Univ. of Ca' Foscari, Venice; marble statue *L'Eroismo* (Palazzo della Civiltà Italiana, Rome); bronze statue of Pope Pius X, St. Mark's, Venice; bronze statue *Il Vetraio*, Murano, marble *Ospitalità*, Hotel Danieli, Venice; bronze bust of Count Volpi di Misurata, Palazzo Gambara, Venice; bronze bust of Claudio Monteverdi, Basilica dei Frari, Venice; three bas-reliefs in stone for Venice Cemetery; large figure of Christ in bronze for City of Milan; architecture and sculpture of the Lepanto Chapel in the Basilica di S. Antonio, Padua, etc.; mem. Insigne Accademia di S. Luca, Rome, Coll. Accademico artistico di Venezia, Accademico Tiberino, Rome; Prize for sculpture in glass, Venice Biennale 52.
Leisure interests: antiquities, reading, particularly books on history of Venice.
Campo Santa Ternita, Castello 3059, 30122 Venice, Italy.
Telephone: 80118.

Martodihardjo, Lieut.-Gen. Sarbini; Indonesian army officer and politician; b. 10 June 1914; s. of M. Martoredjo; m. Sockinah 44; one s.; ed. Kebumen, Cen. Java; ed. elementary and secondary schools and various military schools and courses.
Former public health service employee; subsequently served as commissioned officer in Indonesian army; Minister of Veteran Affairs and Demobilization 64-66, 66-68; Minister of Defence Feb.-March 66, of Transmigration and Co-operatives 68-71; mem. of Supreme Advisory Council of Indonesia 71-; Chair. Nat. H.Q. of Indonesian Scout Movt., Central Council H.Q. of Veterans Legion of Indonesia; Chair. Univ. of Islamic Devt.; Vice-Chair. Supreme Advisory Council.

Leisure interests: hunting, bridge, table-tennis.
Graha Purna Yudha, Jalan Jenderal Soedirman, Semanggi, Jakarta; Home: Jalan Imam Bonjol 48, Jakarta, Indonesia.
Telephone: 52924 (Office); 45534 (Home).

Martola, Lieut.-Gen. Armas Eino Iimari; Finnish army officer and former United Nations official; b. 12 May 1896, Raahe; s. of Johan Martola and Anni Simelius; m. Anne Ignatius 1923; three d.
Attended Nat. War Coll., Paris 19-21; Officer in Finnish Army; mem. Defence Revision Cttee. 23-24; mem. Disarmament Comm., Geneva 26-34; Finnish Military Attaché, Paris 28-31; Army Commdr. 44; Deputy Foreign Minister 44; later Gov. of Uusimaa Province until 46; later Man.-Dir. Paper Office, Finnish Paper Mills Asscn.; Personal Adviser to UN Sec.-Gen. on Military Matters Relating to UN Emergency Force 56-57; Commdr. UN Forces in Cyprus (UNFICYP) 66-70; Pres. Finnish Red Cross 51-71.
Leisure interests: languages, history.
Merikatu 5, Helsinki 14, Finland.
Telephone: 639921.

Marty, H.E. Cardinal François, D.THEOL.; French ecclesiastic; b. 18 May 1904; ed. Collège de Graves et de Villefranche de Rouergue (Aveyron), Grand Séminaire de Rodez (Aveyron) and Inst. Catholique de Toulouse.
Ordained 30; Priest, Villefranche and Rodez 32-40, Curé, Bournazel, Rieupeyroux and Millau 40-51; Vicar-Gen., Rodez 51-52; Bishop of Saint-Flour 52; Archbishop of Rheims 60-68; Archbishop of Paris 68-; cr. Cardinal March 69; Président de la Conférence épiscopale de France May 69-75; mem. of Conseil Permanent; Chevalier Légion d'Honneur.
Maison diocésaine, 8 rue de la Ville l'Evêque, 75008 Paris, France.
Telephone: 266-21-20.

Martynenko, Vladimir Nikiphorovich; Soviet (Ukrainian) diplomatist; b. 1923; m.; one d.; ed. Kiev Univ.
Soviet Army 41-46; Ukrainian Soc. for Friendship and Cultural Relations with Foreign Countries 51-56; Ukraine Diplomatic Service 56-; Embassy of U.S.S.R. to Canada 65-68; Deputy Minister of Foreign Affairs of Ukraine 68-73; Perm. Rep. to UN 73-.
Permanent Mission of Ukrainian S.S.R. to United Nations, 136 East 67th Street, New York, N.Y. 10021, U.S.A.

Martynov, Nikolai Vasilievich; Soviet politician; b. 1910; ed. Moscow Energy Inst.
Member C.P.S.U. 32-; Engineer 34-41; Deputy Commissar for Munitions U.S.S.R. 41-46; Deputy Minister then First Deputy Minister of Agricultural Machine Building, U.S.S.R. 46-53; Dept. Head, Ministry of Automobile, Tractors, and Agricultural Machine Building 54-55, Deputy Minister 55-57; First Deputy Chair. Tashkent Nat. Econ. Council 57-59, Chair. 59-60; Chair. Uzbekistan Nat. Econ. Council 60-63; Sec. Central Cttee. of C.P. of Uzbekistan 63-65; First Deputy Chair. U.S.S.R. Council of Ministers State Cttee. for Material and Equipment Supplies 65-; Deputy to Supreme Soviet 62-; mem. Comm. for Industry.
U.S.S.R. Council of Ministers State Committee for Material and Equipment Supplies, 4 Dyakovsky Pereulok, Moscow, U.S.S.R.

Marusi, Augustine Raymond; American food processing executive; b. 30 Nov. 1913, New York, N.Y.; s. of Dante K. and Victoria (Sacchi) Marusi; m. Ruth Sinclair Travis 1940; two s. one d.; ed. Rensselaer Polytechnic Inst.
Sales Engineer, Chemical Div. of Borden Co., N.Y.C. 39-42, S. Regional Man. 45-47, Dir., Gen. Man. Alba S.A., São Paulo, Brazil 47-52, Vice-Pres. (Chem. Div.) 52-54, Pres. Chem. Div. 54-64, Vice-Pres. Borden Co. 55-64, Exec. Vice-Pres. 64-67, Pres. 67-73, Chief Exec. Officer 67- (name changed from The Borden Co. to

Borden Inc. April 68), Dir. 59-, now also Chair.; official of other orgs.

Borden Inc., 277 Park Avenue, New York, N.Y. 10017, U.S.A.

Marvel, Carl Shipp, M.S., M.A., D.SC., PH.D.; American professor of organic chemistry; b. 11 Sept. 1894, Waynesville, Ill.; s. of John Marvel and Lucy Wasson; m. Alberta Hughes 1933; one s. one d.; ed. Illinois Wesleyan Univ., and Univ. of Illinois.

Instructor Univ. of Illinois 20, Assoc. 21-23, Asst. Prof. 23-27, Assoc. Prof. 27-30, Prof. of Organic Chemistry 30-53, Research Prof. 53-61, Emeritus 61-; Prof. of Chemistry, Arizona Univ. 61-; Pres. American Chemical Society 45; mem. of Board for the Co-ordination of Malarial Studies 44-46, Nat. Advisory Health Council U.S. Public Health Service 45-57, Nat. Acad. of Sciences 38-; American Philosophical Society 45-; American Academy of Arts and Sciences; mem. Materials Advisory Cttee. Nat. Research Council 54-64, Chair. 62-64, Advisory Board Macromolecules 67-72; Chair. of the Comm. of Int. Union in dealing with *Encyclopaedia Compendia* 47-50; Assoc. Editor *Journal of the American Chemical Society* 43-52; mem. of Editorial Board *Journal of Organic Chemistry* 36-56; Editor Vols. V and XI *Organic Syntheses* 25 and 31; Advisory Board *Journal of Polymer Science* 51-; Hon. D.Sc. Illinois Wesleyan Univ. 46, Univ. of Illinois 63; awarded Nichols Medal N.Y. Section American Chemical Society 44; Willard Gibbs Medal, Chicago Section, American Chemical Society 50; Gold Medal American Inst. of Chemists 55; Priestley Medal, American Chemical Soc. 56, Int. Award, Soc. of Plastic Engineers 64, ACS Award in Polymer Chem. sponsored by WITCO Co. 64, Perkin Medal, American Section, Soc. of the Chemical Industry 65, Madison Marshall Award, N. Ala. Sec. of ACS 66, American Inst. of Chemists Inc. Chemical Pioneer Award 67, and numerous other awards; Hon. Dr. (Univ. of Louvain, Belgium) 70, John R. Kuebler Award, Alpha Chi Sigma Fraternity 70, ACS Award in the Chem. of Plastics and Coatings, sponsored by Borden Foundation Inc. 73.

Leisure interest: bird watching.

Department of Chemistry, University of Arizona, Tucson, Arizona 85721; 2332 East 9th Street, Tucson, Arizona 85719, U.S.A.

Telephone: 884-1915 (Office); 622-0762 (Home).

Marx, Groucho (Julius Henry); American comedian; b. 2 Oct. 1890, New York; s. of Samuel and Minna (Schoenberg) Marx; one s. two d.

Appeared with his brothers, Harpo, Chico, Gummo and Zeppo, in vaudeville, musical plays and films; radio show with *Chico Flywheel, Shyster and Flywheel* 34, own radio programme, later TV programme *You Bet Your Life*; Peabody Award 48, Nat. Acad. Television Arts and Sciences Award 51, Commdr. des Arts et Lettres 72, Acad. Award 74.

Broadway shows include *I'll Say She Is* 24, *The Cocoanuts* 25, *Animal Crackers* 28; films include *The Cocoanuts* 29, *Animal Crackers* 30, *Monkey Business* 31, *Horsefeathers* 32, *Duck Soup* 33, *A Night at the Opera* 35, *A Day at the Races* 37, *Room Service* 38, *A Night in Casablanca* 46, *Love Happy* 49; Solo film appearances in *Copacabana* 47, *Double Dynamite* 51, *Behave Yourself* 51, *A Girl in Every Port* 52, *The Story of Mankind* 57, *Skidoo* 68.

Publs. *Beds* 30, *Many Happy Returns* 42, *Time for Elizabeth* (play, with Norman Krasna) 48, *Groucho and Me* 59, *Memoirs of a Mangy Lover* 63, *The Groucho Letters* 67, *The Secret Word is Groucho* 76.

c/o Tom Wilhite, Rogers & Cowan, 9665 Wilshire, Beverley Hills, Calif. 90212; Home: 1083 Hillcrest Road, Beverly Hills, Calif., U.S.A.

Telephone: (213) 275-4581 (agent); (213) 271-7769 (Home).

Masamune, Isao, B.ECON., Japanese banker; b. 30 March 1912, Tokyo; s. of Tokusaburo and Chiyoko Masamune; m. Yorie Ogimoto 1943; two s. two d.; ed. Tokyo Univ.

Joined Industrial Bank of Japan Ltd. 33, Dir. 57, Man. Dir. 59, Deputy Pres. 64, Pres. 68-75, Chair. 75-.

Leisure interests: golf, go.

3-3, Marunouchi 1-chome, Chiyoda-ku, Tokyo; Home: 2-21-5 Uehara, Shibuya-ku, Tokyo, Japan.

Telephone: 214-1111 (Office); 467-1843 (Home).

Masani, Minoo; Indian politician, writer and business consultant; b. 20 Nov. 1905, Bombay; m. Shakuntala Srivastava 1946; one s.; ed. Elphinstone Coll., Bombay, and London School of Economics.

Barrister of Lincoln's Inn; one of the founders of Congress Socialist Party and Sec. till 39; Mayor of Bombay 43-44; mem. Constituent Assembly and Provisional Parl. of India 47-52; Ambassador of India in Brazil 48-49; mem. UN Sub-Comm. on Discrimination and Minorities 47-52; mem. Lok Sabha (Parl.) 63-70; Chair. Public Accounts Cttee. 67-69; Pres. Swatantra Party 70-71; Editor *Freedom First*; Patron Liberal Int.

Leisure interest: reading.

Publs. *Our India, Socialism Reconsidered, Your Food, Picture of a Plan, Plea for the Mixed Economy, Our Growing Human Family, Communist Party of India—a Short History, Congress Misrule and the Swatantra Alternative, Is J.P. the Alternative?*.

Personnel and Productivity Services, 148 Mahatma Gandhi Road, Bombay 1, India.

Telephone: 254171.

Mascherini, Marcello; Italian artist; b. 1906; ed. Trieste Industrial Inst.

Sculptor in stone, wood and bronze; designer of theatrical décors and costumes, Teatro del l'Opera, Rome (*Tantologos* 69, *Don Giovanni* 70); has also executed lithographs and decorative works for the Milan Triennale and Italian liners, decorations of Padua and Trieste Univs.; first exhibited 25, since exhibited in Italy and abroad; teacher of bronze sculpture at Int. Sommerakademie für bildende Kunst, Salzburg 70, 71; mem. Accademia Nazionale di San Luca, Rome, Académie Royale, Brussels; Second Prize for Sculpture, Biennale of São Paulo do Brazil 54; First Prize, Int. Exhbn. of Carrara 57; Gold Medal for Sculpture, Exposition Universelle de Bruxelles 58; Prize for Sculpture, Venice Biennale 60.

Trieste, Italy.

Masefield, Sir Peter Gordon, Kt., M.A., C.ENG., F.R.Ae.S., F.C.INST.T.; British engineer and administrator; b. 19 March 1914, Trentham, Staffordshire; s. of late Dr. W. Gordon Masefield, C.B.E., M.R.C.S., L.R.C.P. and Marian Ada (née Lloyd-Owen); m. Patricia Doreen Rooney 1936; three s. one d.; ed. Westminster School, Chillon Coll., Switzerland and Jesus Coll., Cambridge.

On Design Staff, Fairey Aviation Co. Ltd. 35-37; Asst. Technical Editor *The Aeroplane* 37-39, Technical Editor 39-43; war corresp. and air corresp. *The Sunday Times* 40-43; Personal Adviser on Civil Air Transport to Lord Privy Seal and Sec. of Civil Aviation Cttee. of War Cabinet 43-45; British Civil Air Attaché, British Embassy, Washington, D.C. 45-46; Dir.-Gen. of Long-Term Planning and Projects, Ministry of Civil Aviation 47-48; Chief Exec. and mem. of Board British European Airways 49-56; Man. Dir. Bristol Aircraft Ltd. 56-60, British Executive and General Aviation Ltd., Beagle Aircraft Ltd. 60-67 (Chair. 68-); Dir. Pressed Steel Co. Ltd. 60-67; Pres. Inst. of Transport 55-56; mem. Aeronautical Research Council 56-60, Pres. Royal Aeronautical Soc. 59-60; Chair. Air Transport Section, London Chamber of Commerce 62-65; Chair. British Airports Authority 65-71; Chair. Royal Aero Club of the U.K. 68-70; Vice-Chair. United Service and Royal

Aero Club, Imperial War Museum; Chair. Project Management Ltd.; Dir. Worldwide Estates Ltd., Worldwide Properties Ltd.; mem. CAA Flight Time Limitations Board, Board of London Transport Exec.; Dir. Nationwide Building Soc.; Council mem. Royal Soc. of Arts; Hon. Fellow Inst. Aeronautics and Astronautics (U.S.A.).
Leisure interests: reading, writing, gardening, photography, flying.
Rosehill, Doods Way, Reigate, Surrey, England.
Telephone: Reigate 42396.

'Maseribane, Chief Sekhonyana Nehemia; Lesotho Chief; b. 4 May 1918; ed. Eagles Park Coll., Basutoland. Prominent Trader in Quthing District; descendant of First Paramount Chief of Basutoland, Chief Moshoeshoe I, Chief of Mount Moorosi; mem. Econ. Planning Council of Basutoland; Pres. Basuto Courts 47, and Assessor to Basutoland High Court; mem. Econ. Mission to U.S.A. 62; Prime Minister of Basutoland May-July 65, Deputy Prime Minister and Minister of Internal and External Affairs, and Leader of the House July 65-Jan. 66; Minister of Internal Security and Home Affairs 66-70; Deputy Prime Minister 68-; Minister of Agriculture 70-74, of Posts and Telecommunications 74-75, of Works 74-; Vice-Pres. Nat. Party.
Ministry of Works, Posts and Telecommunications, Maseru, Lesotho.

Masevitch, Alla Genrikhovna, D.SC.; Soviet astronomer; b. 9 Oct. 1918, Tbilisi; d. of Henrik Masevitch and Natalie Zhgendi; m. Joseph Friedlander 1942; one d.; ed. Moscow *Industrial* Pedagogical Inst.
Assistant Prof. of Astrophysics Moscow Univ. 46-48, Prof. 48-; Vice-Pres. Astronomical Council, Soviet Acad. of Sciences 52-; in charge of visual tracking of Soviet space vehicles; Chair. Working Group I, Cttee. for Space Research (COSPAR) 61-66; Vice-Pres. Comm. 44 YUA (Extraterrestrial Astronomy) 61-67; Pres. Comm. 35 YaU (Internal Structure of Stars) 67-70; Vice-Pres. Inst. for Soviet-Amer. Relations 67; mem. of Board, Soviet Peace Cttee. 67; Foreign mem. Royal Astronomical Soc. 63; mem. Int. Acad. of Astronautics 64.
Publs. 88 papers on internal structure of stars, stellar evolution and optical tracking of satellites, mainly in *Astronomical Journal of the U.S.S.R., Publications of the Sternberg Astronomical Institute and Scientific Information of the Astronomical Council* 45-.
Astronomical Council of the U.S.S.R. Acad. of Sciences, 48 Pjatnitskaja Street, Moscow; 1 Vosstania Square 403, Moscow, U.S.S.R.
Telephone: 231-5461.

Mashayekh Faridani, Mohammed Hossein, M.A., PH.D.; Iranian diplomatist and educationist; b. 1914; s. of Mohammad Baghar and Omme Kulsoum; m. Ezzat 1953; two s. one d.; ed. Pahlavi Coll., Darolfonoon Coll. an Teheran Univ.
Lecturer in Literature and Philosophy, Teheran 40-44; Technical Inspector, Teheran Secondary Schools 44-46; Dir. of Cultural Dept., Ministry of Education 46; Editor, Education and Instruction Magazine 46; Cultural Counsellor, Karachi 48-52, New Delhi 52-55; Cultural Adviser, Ministry of Foreign Affairs 55-56; Dir. of Cultural Relations, Ministry of Foreign Affairs 57, Dir. of Public Relations and Editor of Magazine 57; Dir. Asian Countries Dept. 58, Dir.-Gen. Political Affairs 64; Minister-Counsellor, Baghdad 59-63, Amb. to Iraq 63-64, to Saudi Arabia 64-68, to Pakistan 69-73.
Leisure interests: collection of Persian manuscripts.
Zafranieh, Teheran, Iran.
Telephone: 872242 (Home).

Masherov, Pyotr Mironovich; Soviet politician; b. 13 Feb. 1918; ed. Vityebsk Pedagogical Institute.
Member C.P.S.U. 43-; Partisan Movement, Byelorussia. Second World War; Komsomol work 44-54; Second

Sec., Minsk Regional Cttee., C.P. Byelorussia 54-55; First Sec., Brest Regional Cttee., C.P. Byelorussia 55-59; Sec., Second Sec., Central Cttee. C.P. Byelorussia 59-65; First Sec., Central Cttee. C.P. Byelorussia 65-; mem. Central Cttee. C.P.S.U. 64-, mem. Presidium of Supreme Soviet 66-; Alt. mem. Politburo 66-; Deputy to the Supreme Soviet of the U.S.S.R. 50-62, 66-; Hero of the Soviet Union; Order of Lenin (six), Gold Star Medal and other decorations.
Central Committee of the Communist Party of Byelorussia, Minsk, U.S.S.R.

Mashologu, Mothusi Thamsanga; Lesotho diplomatist; b. 7 March 1939, Morija; s. of Bennie and Sarah Mashologu; m. Debrah Mashologu (née Mokhitli) 1968; one s. two d.; ed. Univ. Coll. of Fort Hare, S. Africa, Univ. of Rhodesia and Nyasaland, Queens Univ., Belfast, and London School of Economics.
Teacher at Basutoland Training Coll. and at Basutoland High School 60-64; Asst. Sec., Ministry of External Affairs and Asst. Sec. in Cabinet Office 65-66; Counsellor, Perm. Mission of Lesotho to UN 66-68; Principal Asst. Sec. and Acting Perm. Sec., Ministry of Foreign Affairs 68-69; Amb. to U.S.A. 69-73, also Perm. Rep. to UN 69-71; Sec. to Cabinet 74-75; Pro-Vice Chancellor, Nat. Univ. of Lesotho Oct. 75-.
National University of Lesotho, Roma, Lesotho.

Mashologu, Teboho J.; Lesotho diplomatist; b. 9 Nov. 1942; m.; four c.; ed. Lehigh Univ.
Assistant Sec., Ministry of Foreign Affairs 66; Counsellor, London 68; Principal Asst. Sec., Ministry of Foreign Affairs 70, Perm. Sec. 73; Perm. Rep. to UN 74-75, Amb. to U.S.A. Sept. 75-; del. to numerous int. confs.
Lesotho Embassy, 1601 Connecticut Ave., N.W., Washington D.C., U.S.A.

Mashour, Ahmed Mashour; Egyptian engineer; b. April 1918; ed. Cairo Univ., Staff Officers' Coll., U.K., and Fort Belvoir, U.S.A.
With Min. of Transport 41; Army Engineer 42; Lecturer, Egyptian Acad. of War 48-52; Staff Officer, Egyptian Corps of Engineers; Dir. of Transit, Suez Canal Authority 56; mem. Board of Dirs. Timsah Shipbuilding Co., Ismailia; Chair. and Man. Dir. Suez Canal Authority 65-; various decorations.
Suez Canal Authority, Ismailia, Egypt.

Mashuri Saleh, Dr.; Indonesian politician; b. 19 July 1925, Pati, Central Java; ed. Faculty of Law, Gadjah Mada Univ., Jogjakarta.
Teacher in schools in Jogjakarta and Dir. Army Secondary School 53-56; Chair. Team of Experts attached to Cen. War Admin. 57-60; mem. Advisory Board of Nat. Front for Liberation of W. Irian; in private employment 60-65; Deputy Minister of Higher Learning 66; Dir.-Gen. of Higher Learning 67; Minister of Educ. and Culture 68-73, of Information 73.
c/o Ministry of Information, Jakarta, Indonesia.

Masina, Giulietta; Italian actress; b. 22 Feb. 1921; m. Federico Fellini (q.v.); ed. Univ. of Rome.
Began acting career in radio plays; in films since 41.
Films: *Senza Pietà* 47, *Luci del Varietà* 48, *Persiane Chiuse, Cameriera Bella Presenza Offresi . . ., Europa 51, Wanda la Peccatrice, Lo Sceicco Bianco* 52, *Sette Ore di Guai, Il Romanzo della mia Vita, Ai Margini della Metropolil Donne Proibite, Via Padova 46, Cento Anni d'Amore, La Strada* 54, *Il Bidone* 55, *Buonanotte Avvocato!, Le Notte, di Cabiria* 57, *Fortunella* 58, *Nella Citta l'Inferno* 59, *Giulietta degli spiriti* 65, *The Madwoman of Chaillot* 69.
Via Archimede 141a, Rome, Italy.

Masire, Dr. Quet Ketumile Jonny; Botswana politician; b. 23 July 1925; ed. Kanye and Tiger Kloof.
Founded Seepapitso Secondary School 50; reporter, later dir., *African Echo* 58; mem. Bangwaketse Tribal

Council, Legislative Council; fmr. mem. Exec. Council; founder mem. Botswana Democratic Party (BDP), Sec.-Gen. and Editor of party newspaper *Therisanyo*; mem. Legislative (now Nat.) Assembly March 65; Deputy Prime Minister March 65-April 66; attended Ind. Conf., London Feb. 66; Vice-Pres. and Minister of Finance 66-, and of Devt. Planning 67-.
Office of the Vice-President, Gaborone, Botswana.

Masmoudi, Mohamed; Tunisian politician; b. 29 May 1925, Mahdia; s. of Mohamed and Amna (née Bennour) Masmoudi; m. Alya Boulakbèche 1956; seven c.; ed. Tunis and Univ. of Paris.
Member of Tunisian Nationalist Movement 34; Minister of State in Govt. negotiating Tunisian independence 53-55; Minister of the Economy 55-56; Amb. to France 56-58, 65-68; Minister of Information 58-61; Sec.-Gen. Destour Socialist Party 69-74; Minister of Foreign Affairs 70-74; assoc. with *Action*, later renamed *Afrique Action*.
Leisure interests: literature, antiques, chess.
La Manouba, Tunis, Tunisia.

Mason, Arthur Malcolm; British business executive; b. 19 Dec. 1915; s. of Mr. and Mrs. Charles Mason; m. Mary Hall 1938; one s. one d. (deceased); ed. Blundells School, Tiverton.
Director, Chiswick Products Ltd. (name now altered to Reckitt and Colman Products Ltd.), Chair. 58-67; Dir. Reckitt and Colman Ltd. 58, Chair. 70-.
Leisure interests: motoring, sailing.
Reckitt and Colman Ltd., P.O. Box 26, Burlington Lane, London, W4; 7 Pinecroft, St. George's Road, Weybridge, Surrey, KT13 0EN, England.
Telephone: 01-994-6464; Weybridge 48690.

Mason, Basil John, C.B., D.SC., F.R.S.; British meteorologist; b. 18 Aug. 1923, Docking, Norfolk; s. of late John Robert and Olive Mason; m. Doreen Sheila Jones 1948; two s.; ed. Fakenham Grammar School and Univ. Coll., Nottingham.
Commissioned, Radar Branch, R.A.F. 44-46; Shirley Research Fellow, Univ. of Nottingham 47; Asst. Lecturer in Meteorology, Imperial Coll., London 48-49, Lecturer 49; Warren Research Fellow, Royal Soc. 57; Visiting Prof. of Meteorology, Univ. of Calif. 59-60; Prof. of Cloud Physics, Imperial Coll. of Science and Technology, Univ. of London 61-65; Dir.-Gen. Meteorological Office 65-, Pres. Royal Meteorological Soc. 68-70; mem. Exec. Cttee. World Meteorological Org. 65-75; Chair. Council, Univ. of Surrey 71-75; Hon. D.Sc. (Nottingham 66, Durham 70); Hon. Fellow Imperial Coll. of Science and Technology 74; Hon. D.Sc., Strathclyde Univ. 75; Hugh Robert Mill Medal, Royal Meteorological Soc. 59; Charles Chree Medal and Prize, Physical Soc. 65; Bakerian Lectures, Royal Soc. 71; Rumford Medal, Royal Soc. 72; Glazebrook Medal and Prize, Inst. of Physics 74; Symons Memorial Gold Medal, Royal Meteorological Soc. 75.
Leisure interests: music, foreign travel.
Publs. *The Physics of Clouds* 57, 2nd edition 71, *Clouds, Rain and Rain-making* 62 (2nd edn. 75).
The Meteorological Office, London Road, Bracknell, Berks.; and 64 Christchurch Road, East Sheen, London, S.W.14, England.
Telephone: 876-2557 (Home); Bracknell 20242 (Office).

Mason, Birny, Jr., B.CHEM.; American chemical engineer and executive; b. 27 Feb. 1909, Brownsville, Pa.; s. of Birny Mason and Mary Carmack Mason; m. Elisabeth Brownson Smith 1935; one s.; ed. Cornell Univ.
Joined Union Carbide Corpn. 32, Man. Industrial Relations staff 52-55, Sec. 55, Pres. Union Carbide Development Co. 56; Vice-Pres. Union Carbide Corpn. and mem. Appropriations Cttee. 57-58, Exec. Vice-Pres. 58-60, Dir. 58-, Pres. 60-66, Chair. 66-71, Chair. Exec.

Cttee. 71-74; Dir. Metropolitan Life Insurance Co., New York, North American Philips Corpn.
Leisure interests: golf, sailing.
Union Carbide Corporation, 270 Park Avenue, New York, N.Y. 10017, U.S.A.

Mason, Sir Frederick Cecil, K.C.V.O., C.M.G.; British diplomatist; b. 15 May 1913, London; s. of late Ernest Mason and late Sophia Charlotte Mason (née Dodson); m. Karen Rørholm 1941; two s. one d.; ed. City of London School and St. Catharine's Coll., Cambridge.
British Vice-Consul, Antwerp 35-36, Paris 36-37, Léopoldville 37-39; Consul Faroe Islands 40-42, Colon, Panama 42-45; First Sec., British Embassy, Santiago, Chile 46-48; Press Attaché, Oslo 48-50; Asst. Labour Adviser, Foreign Office 50-53; First Sec., U.K. High Comm., Bonn 53-55; Commercial Counsellor, Athens 55-57; Econ. Counsellor, Teheran 57-60; Head, Econ. Relations Dept., Foreign Office 60-64; Under-Sec. Ministry of Overseas Devt. 64-65, Commonwealth Office 66; Amb. to Chile 66-70; Under-Sec. Foreign and Commonwealth Office 70-71; Amb. and Perm. Rep. UN, Geneva 71-73; U.K. mem. Int. Narcotics Control Board, Geneva 74-; Dir. New Court Natural Resources Ltd.; Grand Cross, Chilean Order of Merit "Bernardo O'Higgins".
Leisure interests: painting, ball games.
The Forge, Ropley, Hampshire, England.

Mason, James Neville, M.A.; British actor; b. 15 May 1909, Huddersfield, Yorks.; s. of John Mason and Mabel (née Gaunt); m. 1st Pamela Kellino 1941 (dissolved 1964), one s. one d.; m. 2nd Clarissa Kaye 1971; ed. Marlborough Coll., and Peterhouse, Cambridge.
Acted in plays and films in England 31-46; resident in U.S.A. 46-62; notable films include *I Met a Murderer* 39, *The Man in Grey* 43, *The Seventh Veil* 45, *Odd Man Out* 46, *Rommel—Desert Fox* 51, *Five Fingers* 52, *Julius Caesar* 53, *A Star is Born* 54, *Bigger than Life* 56, *A Touch of Larceny* 60, *Lolita* 62, *Tiara Tahiti* 62, *The Pumpkin Eater* 64, *Lord Jim* 65, *Les Pianos Mécaniques* 65, *Georgy Girl* 66, *The Deadly Affair* 67, *The Seagull* 69, *Age of Consent* 69, *Spring and Port Wine* 70, *Child's Play* 72, *The Last of Sheila* 73, *Dr. Frankenstein* 73, *Mackintosh Man* 73, *11 Harrow house* 74, *Marseille Contract* 74, *Mandingo* 75, *Autobiography of a Princess* 75, *The Voyage* 76.
Publ. (with Pamela Kellino) *The Cats in Our Lives* 49.
c/o Al Parker, 50 Mount Street, London, W.1, England.
Telephone: 01-499-3080.

Mason, L. Ralph; American motor executive; b. 31 Oct. 1910, Lynchburg, Va.; ed. Virginia Polytechnical Inst., Blacksburg.
Associated with Gen. Motors 35-; with Chevrolet Div. of Gen. Motors 35-66; Man. Dir. Adam Opel A.G., Fed. Repub. of Germany 66-70; Gen. Dir. European Operations, Gen. Motors Overseas Corpn. 70-74; Special Asst. to Gen. Man., N.Y. Div. Feb. 74-.
c/o General Motors Overseas Corporation, 767 Fifth Avenue, New York, N.Y. 10022, U.S.A.
Telephone: 212-486-5000.

Mason, Philip, C.I.E., O.B.E.; British writer and administrator; b. 19 March 1906, London; s. of Dr. H. A. Mason; m. Eileen Mary Hayes 1935; two s. two d.; ed. Sedbergh, Oxford Univ.
Member Indian Civil Service 28-47; Under-Sec., War Dept. 33-36; Dep. Commr., Garhwal 36-39; Dep. Sec., Defence Co-ordination and War Depts. 39-42; Sec., Chiefs of Staff Cttee., India, and Head of Conf. Secretariat, S.E. Asia Command 42-44; represented War Dept., Central Assembly 46; Jt. Sec., War Dept. 44-47; Dir. of Studies in Race Relations, Chatham House, London 52-58, Dir. Inst. of Race Relations, London 58-69; Chair. Nat. Cttee. for Commonwealth

Immigrants 64-65, B.B.C. Advisory Council for Immi-
grants 65; Exec. U.K. Council for Overseas Student
Affairs 69; Hon. Fellow, School of Oriental and African
Studies, Univ. of London 70; Hon. D.Sc.(Soc.) (Bristol)
71, D.Litt. (Oxon.) 72.
Leisure interests: reading, sailing, gardening.
Publs. (as Philip Woodruff): *Call the Next Witness* 45,
The Wild Sweet Witch 47, *Whatever Dies* 48, *The
Sword of Northumbria* 48, *The Island of Chamba* 50,
Hernshaw Castle 50, *Colonel of Dragoons* 51, *The Men
Who Ruled India: Vol. I The Founders* 53, *Vol. II The
Guardians* 54; (as Philip Mason): *An Essay on Racial
Tension* 54, *Christianity and Race* 56, *The Birth of a
Dilemma* 58, *Year of Decision* 60, *Common Sense about
Race* 61, *Prospero's Magic* 63, *Patterns of Dominance*
70, *Race Relations* 70, *How People Differ* 71, *A Matter of
Honour* 74, *Kipling—The Glass, The Shadow and The
Fire* 75.
Hither Daggons, Cripplestyle, Alderholt, Nr. Fording-
bridge, Hants., England.
Telephone: Cranborne 318.

Mason, Rt. Hon. Roy, P.C., M.P.; British politician;
b. 18 April 1924, Barnsley, Yorks.; s. of Joseph and
Mary Mason; m. Marjorie Sowden 1945; two d.; ed.
Carlton Junior School, Royston Senior School, and
London School of Economics (T.U.C. Course).
Branch official, Nat. Union of Mineworkers 47-53; mem.
Yorkshire Miners' Council 49-53; M.P. for Barnsley 53-;
Minister of State (Shipping), Board of Trade 64-67;
Minister of Defence (Equipment) 67-68; Postmaster-Gen.
April-June 68; Minister of Power 68-69; Pres. Board of
Trade 69-70; Sec. of State for Defence 74-; Labour.
Ministry of Defence, Main Building, Whitehall,
SW1A 2HB; and House of Commons, London, S.W.1,
England.

Massad, A. Carlos; Chilean international finance
official; b. 29 Aug. 1932, Santiago; m.; five c.; ed. Univs.
of Chile and Chicago.
Research Asst. Inst. of Econs., Univ. of Chile 43-53,
Head of Research 54-55, Asst. Dir. 56, Dir. a.i. 61, Dir.
62-64: Prof. of Monetary and Banking Theory and
Policy, Univ. of Chile 63-; Chair. Comm. for Reform of
Federico Santa María Technical Univ. 68; mem. Nat.
Scientific Comm. 68; Chair. Board of Govs., Centre for
Latin American Monetary Studies 68-70; mem. Exec.
Board, Latin American Social Sciences Council 67-70;
Vice-Chair. Chilean Planning and Devt. Asscn. 68-70;
Gov. IMF and IBRD 65-70; Vice-Pres. Cen. Bank of
Chile 64-67, Pres. 67-70; Exec. Dir. IMF 70-75.
c/o Ministerio de Finanzas, Santiago, Chile.

Massamba-Débat, Alphonse; Congolese politician;
b. 1921; ed. Teacher Training Coll., Brazzaville.
Teacher, primary school, Fort-Lamy, Chad 40; Sec.-Gen.
Asscn. des Evolués du Tchad 45-47; Headmaster,
primary schools, Mossendjo and Brazzaville; mem.
Congo Progressive Party 47; mem. Democratic Union
for Defence of Interests of Africa (UDDIA) 56; Asst.
to Minister of Educ.; mem. Legislative Assembly
59-61, Pres. 59-61; Minister of State 61; Minister of
Planning and Equipment 61-63; Head of Provisional
Govt. and Minister of Defence Aug.-Dec. 63; Pres.
63-68; Prime Minister Jan.-Aug. 68, assumed full
powers Aug.-Sept. 68; arrested Oct. 69.

Massart, Edward Marie Lucien; Belgian biochemist
and university professor; b. 1908; ed. Royal Athenaum,
Antwerp, and Univ. of Brussels.
Asst. and first Asst. Prof. of Biochemistry, State Univ.
of Ghent, and Prof. 34-; Vice-Pres. Ghent Univ. 61-62;
Dir. Biochemical Laboratory of the Faculty of Sciences
and of the Veterinary Coll., Ghent Univ. 58; Pres. Nat.
Council on Scientific Politics 59; mem. Royal Flemish
Acad. of Medicine of Belgium; Francqui Award in
Natural Sciences 57, etc.
Rysschenbergstraat 46B, Ghent, Belgium.

Massé, Pierre, DR. ÈS SC.; French engineer; b. 13 Jan.
1898; ed. Ecole Polytechnique.
Began career as electrical engineer 28; Dir. (Electrical
Equipment) Electricité de France 46, Dep. Dir. Gen.
48; Commr. Gen. du Plan d'Equipement et de la
Productivité 59-65; Pres. Electricité de France 65-69,
Hon. Pres. 69-; Assoc. Prof., Univ. of Paris; Pres.
Admin. Council, Fondation de France 69-73; Foreign
Hon. mem. American Acad. of Arts and Sciences 68;
Grand Officier Légion d'Honneur; Croix de Guerre.
Publs. *Les Réserves et la Régulation de l'Avenir* 46, *Le
Choix des Investissements* 59 (English edn. 62), *Le Plan
ou l'Anti-hasard* 65, *Les Dividendes du progrès* (co-
author) 69, *La Crise de développement* 73.
33 avenue du Maréchal-Lyautey, Paris 16e, France.

Massey, Sir Harrie Stewart Wilson, Kt., M.SC., PH.D.,
F.R.S.; British physicist; b. 1908; ed. Melbourne Univ.
Aitchison Travelling Scholar Melbourne Univ. 29-31;
research in atomic physics, Cavendish Laboratory,
Cambridge 29-33; Independent Lecturer in Mathe-
matical Physics, Queen's Univ., Belfast 33-38; Goldsmid
Prof. of Mathematics, Univ. Coll., Univ. of London 39-
50; Quain Prof. of Physics, Univ. Coll. 50-75, Emer.
Prof. of Physics, Univ. of London 75-; Vice-Dean
of Faculty of Science Oct. 47-50; Fellow, Royal Soc. 40;
Chair. Atomic Scientists' Asscn. 46, Vice-Pres. 47-53,
Pres. 53-57; mem. Radio Research Board 46-50, 56-60;
Scientific Adv. Panel, British Council 47-57; mem. Mete-
orological Research Cttee. 55-60; Vice-Pres. Royal
Astronomical Soc. 50-52; Council Royal Soc. 50-52, 59-
60; Council Physical Soc. (London) 49-54, Pres. 54-56;
Hughes Medallist, Royal Soc. 55, Royal Medallist 58;
Pres. European Space Research Org. 59-64; Chair.
British Nat. Cttee. for Space Research, Council for
Scientific Policy 65-70; mem. Gov. Body, Rugby
School 54-59, Chelsea Polytechnic 56-59, Nat. Inst. for
Research in Nuclear Science 57-65, Advisory Council
of Science Museum 59-61, Steering Group for Space
Research 59-63, Bureau of Int. Cttee. on Space Re-
search 59-, Central Advisory Council for Science and
Technology 67-70, Physical Sec. and Vice-Pres. 69-;
Vice-Pres. Royal Soc. 69; Vice-Provost Univ. Coll.,
London 69-73; Chair. Prov. Space Science Advisory
Board for Europe 74-; mem. Royal Comm. for Exhbn. of
1851 72-, Anglo-Australian Telescope Board 75-,
American Philosophical Soc. 75-; corresp. mem. Acad.
of Sciences Liège 74-; Assessor Science Research
Council 74-; Hon. D.Sc. (Belfast and Leicester) 64,
(Hull) 68, (Melbourne, Adelaide, Heriot-Watt, Liver-
pool) 75; Hon. LL.D. (Glasgow) 62.
Publs. *The Theory of Atomic Collisions* (with N. F.
Mott) 33 (3rd edn. 65), *Negative Ions* 38 (2nd edn. 49),
Electronic and Ionic Impact Phenomena (with E. H. S.
Burhop) 51, *Atoms and Energy* 52, *The Upper Atmo-
sphere* (with R. L. F. Boyd) 58, *Ancillary Mathematics*
(with H. Kestleman) 58 (2nd edn. 64), *The New Age in
Physics* 60 (2nd edn. 66), *Space Physics* 64.
Department of Physics, University College, London,
W.C.1; Kalamunda, Pelhams Walk, Esher, Surrey,
England.
Telephone: 551-01-71.

Massigli, René; French diplomatist (retd.); b. 22
March 1888; ed. Ecole Normale Supérieure.
Mem. Ecole Française de Rome 10-13; Lecturer, Lille
Univ. 13-14; Sec. Conf. of Ambassadors 20; Asst. Sec.
French Delegation to Washington 21; Sec. of Delegation
to Genoa 21; Sec. Lausanne Conf. 22-23; mem. Council
of State 24-28; Chief of L.N. Section, Ministry of Foreign
Affairs 28-33; mem. French Delegation to Naval
Conf., London 30; fmr. Deputy-Del. to Disarmament
Conf. 32; Asst. Dir. of Political Section at Ministry of
Foreign Affairs 33-37, Dir. 37-38; Ambassador to
Turkey 38-40; arrived London, joined de Gaulle 43,
Nat. Commr. for Foreign Affairs 43; Commr. for

Foreign Affairs, French Cttee. for Nat. Liberation 43-44, mem. Advisory Council on Italy 43-44; Ambassador to Great Britain 44-55; Sec.-Gen. Ministry of Foreign Affairs 55-56; Pres. French Channel Tunnel Study Groups 57-70; Grand Cross, Légion d'Honneur; Hon. G.C.V.O., C.H., K.B.E.

Publs. *Sur quelques maladies de l'Etat* 58, *La Turquie devant la Guerre* 64.
3 Avenue Robert-Schuman, Paris 7e, France.

Massine, Léonide; American choreographer; b. 9 Aug. 1896; ed. Imperial School of Opera, Moscow; studied under Domashoff, Enrico Cecchetti and Nicolas Legat. Choreographer and principal dancer, Diaghilev Ballet, in Europe and America 14-20; first London appearance Drury Lane 14, New York Century Theatre 16; formed company to tour S. America 21; founded ballet school London 21-23; appeared Cochran's revues, London Pavilion, and produced ballets for Diaghilev 25-27; produced ballets Roxy Theatre, N.Y. 28-29, Opera House, Paris, and La Scala, Milan; produced dances and appeared in Cochran-Reinhardt production of *The Miracle*, Lyceum 32; producer and dancer, *Ballets Russes de Monte Carlo* 32-41, National Ballet Theatre, N.Y. 41-44; organised *Ballet Russe Highlights*, N.Y. 45-46; guest artiste and choreographer Sadler's Wells Ballet, Covent Garden 47-48; Royal Opera House, Copenhagen, La Scala, Milan, Opéra-Comique, Paris 49-52, Teatro dell'Opera, Rome, Rome Accad. di Danza 53-54. Ballets include: *Good-Humoured Ladies, Parade, Boutique Fantasque, Tricorne, Beau Danube, Choreartium, The School of Ballet, The Miracle, Gaîté Parisienne, Seventh Symphony, Noble Vision, Sacre du Printemps, Rouge et Noir, Bacchanal, Labyrinth, Aleko, Les Saisons (Symphonie Allégorique), Clock Symphony, Donald of the Burthens, Laudes Evangelii* 52, *Resurrection and Life* 53, *Hymne à la Beauté* 56, etc.; Films (composed and danced his part): *Red Shoes* 48, *Tales of Hoffman* 51, *Carosello Napoletano* 53.
Publ. *My Life in Ballet* 68.

Massip, Roger; French journalist; b. 6 Nov. 1904, Montauban; s. of Jean Massip; m. Renée Massip 1930; ed. Univ. of Paris.
Correspondent *Agence Havas* Bucharest 31-34, *Le Petit Parisien* Warsaw 34-37, Asst. Foreign Editor of latter 37-40; Editor underground newspaper *Libération* 42-44, Asst. Editor *Libération* 44-47; Foreign Editor *Le Figaro* 47-; Officier Légion d'Honneur, Officier de la Résistance, Hon. C.B.E.
Publs. *Que sera la nouvelle société des Nations?* 45, *Voici l'Europe* 58, *De Gaulle et l'Europe* 63, *La Chine est un miracle* 73.
c/o *Figaro*, 14 Rond Point des Champs Elysées, Paris 8e, France.

Masson, André; French artist; b. 4 Jan. 1896; ed. Académie Royale des Beaux-Arts, Brussels, and Ecole des Beaux-Arts, Paris.
Former mem. Cubist and Surrealist groups, Paris; illustrated many books; ballet sets *Les Présages* 33; U.S.A. 41-45; settled Aix-en-Provence 47; retrospective exhibitions Paris, London, New York, Hanover, Zurich, etc.; rep. at Dunn Int. Exhbn., London 63; commissioned to paint ceiling of Théâtre de France 65; took part in Surrealist exhbn., New York 68; represented in principal galleries of contemporary art in Europe and America; Officier Légion d'Honneur, Commdr. des Arts et des Lettres; Grand Prix nat. des Arts 54, São Paulo Biennale Prize 63.
Publs. *Anatomie de mon Univers* 42, *La Pieuvre* 44, *La Rencontre de la Chimère* 44, *Mémorandum* 36-45, *Bestiaire* 45, *Métamorphoses* 46, etc.
26, rue de Sévigné, Paris 4e, France.

Masson, Marcel; French painter; b. 25 June 1911, Nangis, Seine et Marne; m. 1933; one c.; ed. privately.
Began painting in cinemas and theatres, afterwards set up studio in Montmartre; one-man exhibitions in Paris, Canada, South America, Morocco, Tunisia, etc.; Médaille Ville de Paris, etc.
Leisure interest: pétanque (French bowls).
3 rue Alfred Stevens, Paris 9e, France.
Telephone: 878-42-39.

Masson, Paul Jean-Marie, L. en D.; French civil servant and diplomatist; b. 21 July 1920, Ussel (Corrèze); m. Simone Ageron 1943; one s. one d.; ed. Ecole Nat. de la France d'Outre-Mer.
Career in West Africa 45-60; fmr. Sec.-Gen. Guinea; High Commr. to Upper Volta 58-60; Dir.-Gen. Bureau pour le développement de la production agricole 61-67; mem. French dels. to FAO Confs. 61, 63, 65; Préfet du Lot 67-71; Dir. de Cabinet of Minister of Defence 71-73; Préfet de la Région Centre, Préfet du Loiret 73-; Officier Légion d'Honneur, Commdr. Etoile Noire; Officier du Mérite Agricole, Officier Ordre Nat. du Mérite, Officier Palmes Académiques.
Publ. *Bilateral assistance—help, trade or strategy*.
4 avenue Emile-Pouvillon, Paris 7e, France.

Massot, Henri Victor Joseph; French journalist; b. 25 April 1903; ed. Lycée Thiers, Marseille, and Faculté de Droit, Aix.
Journalist; with *Radical de Marseille* 22, *Petit Marseillais* 24; Editor *Marseille Matin* 32; Gen. Admin. *Paris Presse* 44, Dir.-Gen. 49-65, *France Soir* 65-74; Man. Dir. France Editions et Publications Group; Pres. Syndicat de la Presse Parisienne and Conseil Supérieur des Messageries; Vice-Pres. Fédération Nationale de la Presse Française; mem. Conseil Supérieur Agence France Presse; Commdr. Légion d'Honneur.
2 bis rue Deleau, 92 Neuilly-sur-Seine, France.
Telephone: 637-32-83.

Massu, Gen. Jacques; French retired army officer; b. 5 May 1908, Châlons/Marne; m. Suzanne Rosambert 1948; one s. two d.; ed. Ecole Spéciale Militaire de St. Cyr.
Joined Free French Forces Aug. 40; took part in all the campaigns of Gen. Leclerc's 2nd Armoured Div.; Cmmdr., Hanoi, Indochina 45-47, 1st Demibrigade, Colonial Parachute Commandos, 4th A.O.F. Brigade 51-54; Gen. of Brigade 55; as Commdr. 10th Parachute Div., directed airborne operation and landing at Port Said, Nov. 56; Mil. Commdr., Department of Algiers Jan. 57-60; headed the first Cttee. of Public Safety set up in Algiers and called upon Gen. de Gaulle to assume power May 58; Commdr. Algiers Army Corps 58-60; retd. 60; recalled to be Mil. Gov. of Metz Nov. 61-66; C.-in-C. French Troops in Germany 66-69; Grand Croix de la Légion d'Honneur, Compagnon de la Libération, Croix de Guerre, D.S.O., etc.
Leisure interests: riding, tennis, fishing, hunting, gardening.
23 boulevard d'Argenson, 92200 Neuilly-sur-Seine, France.

Masterman, Sir John Cecil, Kt., O.B.E., M.A.; British educationist; b. 12 Jan. 1891, Kingston Hill, Surrey; s. of Capt. John Masterman, R.N., J.P. and Edith Margaret (née Hughes); ed. Royal Naval Colls. Osborne and Dartmouth, Worcester Coll., Oxford and Freiburg Univ.
Midshipman 08; Student of Christ Church Oxford 19-46; Censor 20-26; Lieut. Intelligence Corps 40; Major (specially employed) 41-45; Provost of Worcester Coll. Oxford Jan. 46-61; Fellow of Eton Coll. 42-64; Governor Wellington Coll. 44-65; Vice-Chancellor, Univ. of Oxford 57-58; Hon. Student of Christ Church; Hon. Fellow St. Catharine's Coll., Cambridge, Hon. LL.D. Toronto Univ., Hon. D.C.L. King's Coll. Halifax, Nova Scotia, Hon. D.Litt. Heriot-Watt Univ.; Order of Crown of Yugoslavia (3rd Class).
Publs. *An Oxford Tragedy* 33, *Fate Cannot Harm Me* 35, *Marshal Ney* 37, *To Teach the Senators Wisdom* 52, *The*

Case of the Four Friends 57, *Bits and Pieces* 61, *The Double-Cross System in the War of 1939-1945* 72, *On the Chariot Wheel* (autobiography) 75.
6 Beaumont Street, Oxford, OX1 2LR, England.
Telephone: 42133.

Mastroianni, Marcello; Italian film actor; b. 28 Sept. 1924; ed. Univ. of Rome.
Films include *Una Domenica d'Agosto* 49, *Le Notti Bianche* 57, *I Soliti Ignoti* 58, *Bell'Antonio* 60, *La Dolce Vita* 60, *La Notte* 61, *A Very Private Affair* 61, *Divorce —Italian Style* 61, *8½* 63, *Family Diary* 63, *Yesterday, Today and Tomorrow* 64, *Fantasmi a Roma* 64, *Casanova 70* 65, *Marriage—Italian Style* 65, *The Organizer* 65, *The 10th Victim* 65, *Ciao Rudy* 66, *Lo Straniero* 67, *Viaggio di G. Mastorna* 67, *Shout Louder, I Don't Understand, L'Etranger* 67, *The Man with the Balloons* 68, *Diamonds for Breakfast* 68, *Leo the Last* 70, *The Priest's Wife* 70, *Drama of Jealousy* 70 (Prize for Best Actor, Cannes 70), *Sunflower* 70, *The Pizza Triangle* 70, *What?* 72, *La Grande Bouffe* 73, *Salut L'Artiste* 73, *Massacre in Rome* 73, *Touche Pas la Femme Blanche* 74, *Allonsanfan* 75, *Gangster Doll* (*Per le Antiche Scale*) 75.
c/o Avv. Cav Via Maria Adelaide 8, Rome, Italy.

Maswanya, Saidi Ali; Tanzanian politician; b. 1923, Usungu, Tabora District; ed. Govt. Secondary School, Tabora.
Served with Uganda and Tanganyika Police; District Sec. of Tanganyika African Nat. Union (T.A.N.U.) at Shinyanga 56-58; Chair. T.A.N.U., Western Province 58-59; Deputy Organizing Sec.-Gen. of T.A.N.U. 59-60, and to T.A.N.U. Exec. Cttee. 61; Deputy Mayor, Dar es Salaam 60; Minister without Portfolio 62; Minister of Health; Minister of Agriculture, Forests and Wildlife until Sept. 65; Minister of Lands, Settlement and Water Devt. Sept. 65-June 67; rep. for Tabora West, Tanzania Nat. Assembly; Minister for Home Affairs 67-73.
National Assembly, Dar es Salaam, Tanzania.

Matane, Paulias Nguna; Papua New Guinea diplomatist; b. 5 July 1932; m.; four c.
Senior positions in Dept. of Educ. 57-59; mem. Public Service Board 69; Head, Dept. of Lands, Surveys and Mines 69, of Business Devt. 70-75; Amb. to U.S.A. Sept. 75-, Perm. Rep. to UN Oct. 75-.
Permanent Mission of Papua New Guinea to the United Nations, 801 Second Avenue, 12th Floor, New York, N.Y. 10017, U.S.A.

Matano, Kensuke, M.A., B.A.; Japanese business executive; b. 8 Jan. 1894; ed. Chuo, Columbia and Berlin Univs.
Former Pres., Iino Kaiun Kaisha, Ltd., Iino Sangyo Kaisha, Ltd.; Adviser, Japan Air Lines 57-; Chair. Iino Air Service Co. Ltd. 62; mem. Nippon Ship Owners' Asscn., Fed. of Econ. Orgs., Japan Fed. of Employers' Asscns., Japan ECAFE Asscn., Int. Chamber of Commerce; Medal of Honour with Blue Ribbon 59, with Dark Ribbon 60.
1-1, 1-chome, Ychisaiwai-cho, Chiyodaku, Tokyo, Japan.

Matano, Robert Stanley; Kenyan politician; b. 28 April 1925, Mazeras; m.; eight c.; ed. Alliance High School, Kikuyu, Makarere Univ. Coll.
Assistant Educ. Officer in Naivasha, Rift Valley 54-55, in Mombasa 55-56; studies in admin. of educ. at Cardiff, U.K. 56; Asst. Minister for Coast Province 57-60; Asst. Minister Foreign Health and Home Affairs 61; election to Legislative Council (KADU) for Kwale West; Parl. Sec. Ministry of Educ. 61-62; election to House of Representatives 63; Vice-Pres. Coast Regional Assembly 63-65; Asst. Minister Foreign Affairs 64, Health 65, Home Affairs 66; Asst. Sec.-Gen. KANU 66; Asst. Minister Home Affairs 69-73; Minister of Information and Broadcasting 73-74, of Co-operative Devt. Nov.

74-; mem. KADU 60-64; mem. KANU 64-, acting Sec.-Gen. 72; Chair. Child Welfare Soc. 63; Pres. Miji Tribal Union.
Leisure interests: fishing, scouting.
Ministry for Co-operative Development, Nairobi, Kenya.

Matanzima, Chief Kaiser; South African (Transkei) lawyer and politician; b. 1915; ed. Lovedale Missionary Institution and Fort Hare Univ. Coll.
Chief, Amahale Clan of Tembus, St. Marks' District 40; mem. United Transkeian Gen. Council 42-56; Perm. Head Emigrant Tembuland Regional Authority and mem. Exec. Cttee. Transkeian Territorial Authority 56-58; Regional Chief of Emigrant Tembuland 58-61; Presiding Chief Transkeian Territorial Authority 61-63; Chief Minister of Transkei 63-.
Office of the Chief Minister, Umtata, Transkei, South Africa.

Matchanov, Nazar Matcarimovich, D.VET.SC.; Soviet politician; b. 1923; ed. Samarkand Agricultural Inst.
Member C.P.S.U. 49-; Chief Veterinary Surgeon, District Agricultural Dept., Chief of Vet. Dept., Regional Agric. Board, Chief of Vet. Dept., Ministry of Agric., Deputy Minister of Agric., Uzbek S.S.R. 49-60; Sec. Agric. Dept., Bukhara Regional Cttee., C.P. of Uzbekistan 60-61; Vice-Chair. Council of Ministers, Uzbek S.S.R. 61-62; First Sec. Bukhara Regional Cttee. of Uzbek C.P. 62-65; Sec. Cen. Cttee. of C.P. of Uzbekistan 65-70; Chair. Presidium of Supreme Soviet of Uzbek S.S.R., Vice-Chair. Presidium of Supreme Soviet of U.S.S.R. 70-; mem. Cen. Cttee. of C.P.S.U. 71-; mem. Bureau of Cen. Cttee. of C.P. of Uzbekistan 65-; Order of Lenin (three times), Order of Red Banner of Labour, Badge of Honour, and several medals.
Presidium of Supreme Soviet of Uzbek S.S.R., Tashkent, U.S.S.R.

Matenje, Dick Tennyson, B.A.; Malawian politician; b. 29 Jan. 1929, Blantyre; six s. one d.; ed. Blantyre Secondary School, Univs. of Bristol, U.K. and Ottawa, Canada, and in Australia.
Formerly Headmaster Namadzi School, Henry Henderson Inst., Soche Hill Secondary School; District Educ. Officer 69; Principal Domasi Teachers Coll. 71; mem. Parl. 71-; Educ. Officer in charge of staffing secondary schools; Parl. Sec. for Trade and Industry Jan.-Feb. 72; Minister of Trade and Industry Feb.-April 72, of Finance April 72-, and of Trade, Industry and Tourism 73-75.
Leisure interests: listening to music, dancing, writing poetry, shooting.
Ministry of Finance, P.O. Box 53, Zomba, Malawi.
Telephone: Zomba 611, Ext. 263.

Mates, Leo; Yugoslav diplomatist; b. 1911; ed. Univ. of Zagreb.
Chief Editor Tanjug Agency of Yugoslavia 45; entered Foreign Service 45; Counsellor for Information, Yugoslav Embassy, London, and later Dir. U.N. Dept. Ministry of Foreign Affairs 47-48, Asst. Minister of Foreign Affairs 48-; Del. to U.N. Gen. Assembly 46-48 and 51-55. Permanent Rep. 53; Ambassador to U.S.A. 54-58; Sec.-Gen. to Pres. 58-61; Asst. to Sec. of State for Foreign Affairs 61-62; Dir. Inst. for Int. Politics and Economics, Belgrade 62-.
Institute for International Politics, Makedonska 25, 11000 Belgrade, Yugoslavia.

Mathé, Georges, M.D.; French professor of medicine; b. 9 July 1922; ed. Lycée Banville, Moulins, and Univ. de Paris.
Head of Clinic, Medical Faculty, Paris Univ. 52-53, Prof. of Cancer Research Fac. Medicine, Paris 56-67; Head, Service of Haematology, Inst. Gustave-Roussy 61-; Technical Counsellor, Ministry of Health 64-66; Dir. Inst. de Cancérologie et d'Immunogénétique 65-;

Prof. of Experimental Cancerology, Faculté de Médecine de l'Université de Paris-Sud, Villejuif; Editor-in-Chief *European Journal of Clinical and Biological Research*; since Jan. 73 *Biomedicine*; mem. Cen. Cttee. Union des Démocrates pour la République; Prés. Comité Consultatif de la Recherche Scientifique et Technique 72-; Médaille d'or des Hôpitaux, Chevalier Légion d'Honneur.
Publs. *Le Métabolisme de l'Eau* (with J. Hamburger) 52, *La Greffe* (with J. L. Amiel) 62, *Aspects Histologiques et Cytologiques des Leucémies et Hématosarcomes* (with G. Sémar) 63, *L'Aplasie Myélo-Lymphoide de l'Irradiation Totale* (with J. L. Amiel) 65, *Sémiologie Médicale* (with G. Richet) 65 (2nd edn. 73), *La Chimiothérapie des Cancers* 66 (3rd edn. 74), *Le Cancer* 67, *Bone Marrow Transplantation and White Cells Transfusions* (with J. L. Amiel and L. Schwarzenberg) 70, *La Santé—est-elle au dessus de nos moyens* (with Catherine Mathé) 70, *Natural History and Modern Treatment of Hodgkin's Disease* (with M. Tubianan) 73, *Histocytological typing of the neoplastic diseases of the haematopoietic and lymphoid tissues* (with H. Rappaport) 73, *Cancérologie générale et clinique a l'usage du practicien et de l'étudiant* with (A. Cattan) 74, *Le temps d'y penser* 74.
Institut de Cancérologie et d'Immunogénétique, Hôpital Paul-Brousse, 14 Avenue Paul-Vaillant-Couturier, 94 Villejuif; Home: Le Fonbois, Rue du Bon Puits, 91 La Norville, France.
Telephone: 726-4510 (Office); 490-03-58 (Home).

Mather, Kenneth, C.B.E., D.SC., LL.D., F.R.S.; British geneticist and former university vice-chancellor; b. 22 June 1911, Nantwich; s. of R. W. Mather; m. Mona Rhodes 1937; one s.; ed. Nantwich and Acton Grammar School and Univs. of Manchester and London.
Lecturer in Galton Laboratory, Univ. Coll. London 34-37; Rockefeller Research Fellow, California Inst. of Technology and Harvard Univ. 37-38; Head of Genetics Dept., John Innes Horticultural Inst. 38-48; Prof. of Genetics Univ. of Birmingham 48-65; Vice-Chancellor Univ. of Southampton 65-71; Hon. Prof. of Genetics Univ. of Birmingham 71-; mem. Agricultural Research Council 49-54, 55-60, 69-, Science Research Council 65-69, Govt. Advisory Cttee. on Irradiation of Food 67-74; Weldon Medal, Univ. of Oxford 62; Darwin Medal, Royal Soc. 64.
Publs. *The Measurement of Linkage in Heredity* 38, *Statistical Analysis in Biology* 43, *Biometrical Genetics* 49, *The Elements of Genetics* (with C. D. Darlington) 49, *Genes, Plants and People* (with C. D. Darlington) 50, *Human Diversity* 64, *Elements of Biometry* 67, *Biometrical Genetics* (2nd edn. with J. L. Links) 71, *Genetical Structure of Populations* 73.
Department of Genetics, University of Birmingham, P.O. Box 363, Birmingham, B15 2TT; Home: 296 Bristol Road, Birmingham, B5 7SN, England.
Telephone: 021-472-1301 (Office); 021-472-2093 (Home).

Mather, Kirtley F., B.SC., PH.D.; American geologist; b. 13 Feb. 1888, Chicago, Ill.; s. of William Green and Julia King Mather; m. Marie Porter 1912 (died 1971); three d.; ed. Denison and Chicago Univs.
Instructor Univ. of Arkansas 12-14; Fellow in Geology Univ. of Chicago 14-15; Associate Prof. of Geology Queen's Univ. Kingston, Canada 15-17 and Prof. of Palæontology 17-18; Prof. of Geology Denison Univ. 18-24; Associate Prof. of Physiography Harvard Univ. 24-27, Prof. of Geology 27-54 and Dir. Summer School of Arts and Sciences 34-43, Prof. Emeritus 54-; Geologist U.S. Geological Survey 17-45; Fellow Royal Geographical Soc.; Pres. American Asscn. Scientific Workers 42-46; Chair. editorial Cttee. Scientific Book Club 29-46; Pres. National Council Y.M.C.A. 46-48; Pres. American Asscn. for Advancement of Science 51, Foundation for Integrative Education 49-, Educational Research Corpn. 48-53; Pres. American Acad. of Arts

and Sciences 57-61; Pres. Oliver Wendell Holmes Asscn. 63-73; Hon. Sc.D., Litt.D., L.H.D., LL.D.; Washburn Medal, Boston Museum of Science 64, Cullum Medal, American Geographical Soc. 65.
Leisure interests: photography, travel.
Publs. *Old Mother Earth* 28, *Science in Search of God* 28, *Sons of the Earth* 30, *Adult Education: A Dynamic for Democracy* (with Dorothy Hewitt) 37, *A Source Book of Geology* (with S. P. Mason) 39, *Enough and to Spare* 44, *Crusade for Life* 49, *The World in Which we Live* 61, *The Earth Beneath Us* 64 (revised edn. 75); Editor *Source Book in Geology 1900-1950* 67.
1044 Stanford Drive, N.E., Albuquerque, New Mexico 87106, U.S.A.

Mather, Leonard Charles, B.COM., F.I.B., F.C.I.S.; British banker; b. 10 Oct. 1909, Cheshire; s. of Richard and Elizabeth Mather; m. Muriel Armor Morris 1937; ed. Oldershaw School, Wallasey.
Joint Gen. Man. Midland Bank Ltd. 58-63, Asst. Chief Gen. Man. 64-66, Deputy Chief Gen. Man. 66-68, Dir. 68-, Chief Gen. Man. 68-72, Vice-Chair. 72-74; Chair. United Dominions Trust Ltd. 68-74; Dir. Midland Bank Trust Co. 68-74, Midland and Int. Banks Ltd. 69-74, Montagu Trust Ltd. 69-74, European Banks Int. Co. S.A. 70-72, Clydesdale Bank Ltd. 72-74, Northern Bank Ltd. 72-74, Northern Bank Devt. Corpn. Ltd. 72-74, European Banking Co. Ltd. 73-74; Chair. European Banks Int. Co. S.A. 72-74; Deputy Chair. Euro-Pacific Finance Corpn. Ltd. 71-74; Deputy Chair. Inst. of Bankers 67-69, Pres. 69-70, Life Vice-Pres. 70-, Hon. Fellow 74; Inst. of Bankers' Prize.
Leisure interests: golf, bridge, theatre.
Publs. *The Lending Banker* 55, *Banker and Customer Relationship and the Accounts of Personal Customers* 56, *The Accounts of Limited Company Customers* 58, *Securities Acceptable to the Lending Banker* 60.
United Dominions Trust Ltd., 51 Eastcheap, London, EC3P 3BU; Home: Rochester House, Parkfield, Seal, Sevenoaks, Kent, England.
Telephone: 01-623-3020 (Office); 0732-61007 (Home).

Mathers, Fred Desbrisay, B.A.; Canadian businessman; b. 11 Jan. 1896, Neepawa, Manitoba; m. Gladys Catherine Robinson 1920; one s. one d.; ed. Univ. of Edinburgh and McGill Univ.
Chair. Board of Dirs. Delnor Frozen Foods Ltd. 35-, Royal City Foods Ltd. 39-; Admin., Processed Fruits and Vegetables, Wartime Prices and Trade Board, Ottawa 42-45; Commr., Int. Pacific Salmon Fisheries Comm. 56-60; Pres. Canadian Manufacturers' Asscn. 61-62, Dir. British Columbia Hydro and Power Authority 62-; mem. Advisory Cttee. Guaranty Trust 57-; Pres. Fraser Canadian Club 68-69; Canadian Govt. Medal of Merit.
Leisure interests: hunting, fishing, piloting single-engine plane.
3676 Bainbridge Avenue, Burnaby 2, B.C., Canada.
Telephone: 604-291-9421.

Matheson, James Adam Louis, C.M.G., M.B.E., PH.D., F.I.C.E., F.I.STRUCT.E., F.I.E.AUST.; fmr. Australian university vice-chancellor; b. 11 Feb. 1912, Huddersfield, Yorks.; s. of William and Lily Edith Matheson; m. Audrey Elizabeth Wood 1937; three s.; ed. Bootham School, York and Manchester Univ.
Lecturer, Birmingham Univ. 38-46; Prof. Civil Eng., Univ. of Melbourne 46-50; Beyer Prof. of Eng., Manchester Univ. 50-59; Vice-Chancellor, Monash Univ., Victoria, Australia 59-76; mem. Mission on Technical Educ. to the W. Indies 57, Ramsay Cttee. on Devt. of Tertiary Educ. in Victoria 61-63, Commonwealth Scientific and Industrial Research Org. Advisory Council 62-67; Royal Comm. into Failure of Kings Bridge 62-63; Trustee Inst. of Applied Science of Victoria, now Science Museum of Victoria 64-; mem.

Council Inst. of Engineers, Australia 65-, Senior Vice-Pres. 74-; Council Inst. of Civil Engineers 66-68, Interim Council Univ. of Papua New Guinea 65-73; Chair. Papua New Guinea Inst. of Technology 66-73, now Papua New Guinea Univ. of Technology, Chancellor 73-75; Australian Vice-Chancellors Cttee. 67-68, Asscn. of Commonwealth Univs. 67-69; Vice-Pres. Inst. of Structural Engineers 67-68; Kernot Medal 70; Hon. D.Sc. (Hong Kong), Hon. LL.D. (Manchester, Melbourne and Monash Univs.).
Leisure interest: music.
Publs. Papers on technical and educational subjects.
3 Koornalla Crescent, Mt. Eliza, 3930 Victoria, Australia.
Telephone: 787-1931.

Mathews, Elbert George, A.B.; American diplomatist; b. 24 Nov. 1910, Troy, N.Y.; *m.* Naomi P. Meffert 1934; ed. Kidder Acad. and Jr. Coll. and Univ. of California. Research Asst., Institute of Child Welfare, Univ. of Calif. 30-33; Accountant Golden State Co. Ltd. 33-35; joined Foreign Service, served Vancouver, Sydney, Managua, Washington, Kabul, Calcutta, Washington, Istanbul, Oslo 35-55; mem. Policy Planning Staff, State Dept. 55-59, Dep. Asst. Sec. Policy Planning 57-59; Ambassador to Liberia 59-62; Dir., Office of Eastern and Southern African Affairs, Dept. of State 62-64; Amb. to Nigeria 64-69; Co-ordinator, Senior Seminar in Foreign Policy, Dept. of State 69-72.
Department of State, Washington, D.C. 20520, U.S.A.

Mathews, (Forrest) David, PH.D.; American politician; b. 6 Dec. 1935, Grove Hill, Ala.; *m.* Mary Chapman; two *d.*; ed. Univ. of Alabama and Columbia Univ.
Infantry Officer, U.S. Army 59-60; Asst. Dean of Men, Univ. of Alabama 60-65, Interim Dean of Men 65-66, Exec. Asst. in Office of Pres. 66-68, Exec. Vice-Pres. 68-69, Pres. 69-75, Lecturer in History 65-75; Sec. of Health, Educ. and Welfare Aug. 75-; mem. Board, Charles F. Kettering Foundation, Acad. for Educ. Devt.; mem. Advisory Council, American Revolution Bicentennial Admin.; co-founder Alabama Consortium for Devt. of Higher Educ.; Trustee, Judson Coll.; Algernon Sidney Sullivan Award, Univ. of Alabama.
Publs. several works on history of Southern U.S.A. and higher educ. in America.
Department of Health, Education and Welfare, Washington, D.C., U.S.A.

Mathias, Charles McC., Jr.; American lawyer and politician; b. 24 July 1922, Frederick, Md.; *s.* of Charles McC. Mathias, Sr., and Theresa Trail Mathias; *m.* Ann Hickling Bradford 1958; two *s.*; ed. public schools, Frederick, Md., Haverford Coll., Yale Univ. and Univ. of Maryland.
Apprentice seaman 42, Commissioned Ensign 44, sea duty, Pacific 44-46; Captain U.S. Naval Reserve retd.; admitted to Maryland Bar 49, to U.S. Supreme Court Bar 54; Asst. Attorney-Gen. of Maryland 53, 54; City Attorney, Frederick, Md. 54-59; mem. Md. House of Dels. 58; mem. U.S. House of Reps. 60-68; U.S. Senator from Maryland 69-; Republican.
United States Senate, Washington, D.C. 20510; R.2., Frederick, Md., 21701, U.S.A.

Mathiesen, Matthías (Árnason), CAND. JURIS; Icelandic lawyer and politician; b. 6 Aug. 1931, Hafnarfjörður; *s.* of Árni M. Mathiesen and Svava E. Mathiesen; *m.* Sigrún Thorgilsdóttir 1956; two *s.* one *d.*; ed. Univ. of Iceland.
Chief Exec. Hafnarfjörður Saving Bank 58-67, Chair. 67; Advocate, Supreme Court 67-74; mem. Althing (Parl.) 59-, Speaker Lower Chamber 70-71; Rep. of Althing to Nordic Council 65-74, mem. Presidium 70-71, 73-74, Pres. 70-71; Del. North Atlantic Assembly, NATO 63-69, 72, Chair. Icelandic Del. 64-69, Pres. of Ass. 67-68; Dir. Nat. Bank of Iceland 61-, Vice-Chair. 66-72; Deputy Rep. to World Bank Group (IBRD,

IDA, IFC) 74; Minister of Finance Aug. 74-; mem. Central Cttee., Independence Party 65-.
Ministry of Finance, Arnarhvoll, Reykjavik; Home: Hringbraut 59, Hafnarfjörður, Iceland.
Telephone: (91) 5-02-76 (Home).

Mathieu, Georges Victor Adolphe; French painter; b. 27 Jan. 1921, Boulogne; *s.* of Adolphe Mathieu d'Escaudoeuvres and Madeleine Dupré d'Ausque.
Teacher of English; Public Relations Man., United States Lines; exhibited at Paris 50, New York 52, Japan 57, Scandinavia 58, England, Spain, Italy, Switzerland, Germany, Austria and South America 59, Middle East 61-62, Canada 63; special exhbn. of work held at Musée Municipal d'Art Moderne, Paris 63; exhbn. of one hundred paintings, Galerie Charpentier, Paris 65; posters for Air France exhibited at Musée Nat. d'Art Moderne, Paris 67; presented architectural works, ceramics, tapestries and medals to Musée de la Manufacture Nat. des Gobelins 69; creator of "Tachism".
Publ. *Au-delà du Tachisme, Le privilège d'Etre.* Principal works: *Hommage à la Mort* 50, *Hommage au Maréchal de Turenne* 52, *Les Capétiens Partout* 54, *La Bataille de La Victoire de Denain* 63, *Hommage à Jean Cocteau* 63, *Paris, Capitale des Arts* 65, *Hommages aux Frères Boisserée* 67, *Hommage à Condillac* 68, *La prise de Berg op Zoom* 69, *Election de Charles Quint* 71.
11 *bis*, avenue Léopold II, Paris 16e, France.

Mathrani, Kewalram Pribhdas; Indian civil servant; b. 21 Aug. 1911, Shikarpur, Sind; *s.* of Pribhdas and Satyabhama Mathrani; *m.* Kalavati Batheja 1939; two *s.* two *d.*; ed. Univ. of Edinburgh, Univ. Coll., London and School of Oriental Studies, London.
Indian Civil Service 36-; Sec. Finance Dept., Govt. of Saurashtra and Govt. of Bombay 48-51; Joint Sec. Ministry of Rehabilitation, Govt. of India 52-56; Sec. Ministry of Rehabilitation 64-65; Sec. Political and Services Dept., Bombay State 56-57; Sec. Industries and Co-operation Dept., Govt. of Bombay 58; Joint Sec. to Cen. Cabinet and Dir. Org. and Methods Div., Govt. of India 58-59, Additional Sec. Ministry of Finance 59-61, Sec. Ministry of Rehabilitation 64-65, Sec. Ministry of Irrigation and Power 65-69, Ministry of Agriculture (Dept. of Food) 69-; Chair. Industrial Finance Corpn. of India and Nat. Industries Devt. Corpn. Ltd. 61-64, Gen. Insurance Services Integration Cttee., Ministry of Finance 72-.
Leisure interests: bird-watching, flowering trees.
25 Tughlak Road, New Delhi 11, India.
Telephone: 372123 (Office); 617919 (Home).

Mathys, Sir Herbert Reginald, Kt., B.SC.; British industrialist; b. 28 March 1908, London; *s.* of Albert William Mathys and Minnie (née Bullen); *m.* Marjorie Kay 1939; one *s.* one *d.*; ed. Cranleigh School, Surrey, and Birkbeck Coll., London Univ.
Chartered Patent Agent in general practice 26-39; joined Courtaulds Ltd. (man-made fibres and textiles) as Head of Patent Dept. 46; Dir. Courtaulds Ltd. 54-73, Deputy Chair. 62-73; mem. Council Fed. of British Industries 59-65, Confed. of British Industry 65-; mem. British Nat. Export Council 64-; mem. Cttee. to Examine the Patent System and Patent Law; Chair. Cttee. to Examine Law and Practice of Trade Mark Registration; Vice-Pres. Trade Marks, Patents and Designs Fed. 54-.
Leisure interests: gardening, sailing small boats.
Publs. A number of articles in journals, primarily on matters relating to Letters Patent.
Catherine's Cottage, Lymore Valley, Milford-on-Sea, Lymington, Hants., SO4 0TW, England.
Telephone: Milford-on-Sea 2634 (Hants.).

Matoka, Peter Wilfred; Zambian politician and diplomatist; b. 8 April 1930, Mwinilunga, North-Western Province; *m.* Grace J. Mukahlera 1957; two *s.*

one *d.*; ed. primary and secondary schools, Fort Hare Univ. Coll. and American Univ., Washington, D.C. Civil Servant 55-63; Minister of Information and Postal Services 64-65, of Health 65-66, of Works 67, of Power, Transport and Works 68; Minister for Luapula Province 69; High Commr. of Zambia in U.K. 69-70, concurrently accredited to the Vatican; Minister for the Southern Province 70-71, of Health 71-72, of Local Govt. and Housing 72-75, of Devt. and Planning 75-; Knight of St. Gregory (Vatican) 64; Knight, Egypt and Ethiopia.
Leisure interests: fishing, bird shooting, group discussion and photography.
Ministry of Development and Planning, Lusaka, Zambia.

Mátrai, László, PH.D.; Hungarian librarian and writer; b. 17 Jan. 1909, Budapest; *s.* of Zoltán Miles-Mátrai and Malvina Grimm; *m.* Jolán Zemplén 1933; Edith Schweitzer 1957; one *s.* two *d.*; ed. Budapest Univ.
Assistant 33, Librarian 35, Director-in-Chief of University Library, Budapest 45-; mem. I.I.P. (Inst. Int. Philosophy) 37-, Docent, Budapest Univ. 40-; Corresp. mem. Hungarian Acad. of Sciences 47-, regular mem. 62-; Prof. Univ. Budapest 64-.
Leisure interest: music.
Publs. *A jelenkori esztétika föirányai* (Principal Trends in Present Day Aesthetics) 31, *Modern gondolkodás* (Modern Thinking) 38, *Élmény és mü* (Experience and Oeuvre) 40, *Karakterológia* (Characterology) 43, *Haladás és fejlödés* (Progress and Development) 47, *Gondolat és szabadság* (Thought and Liberty) 61, *Régi magyar filozófusok XV-XVII* (Old Hungarian Philosophers) 61, Introduction to a Hungarian bilingual edition of J. Locke's *Epistolae de Tolerantia* 73.
University Library, Károlyi Mihály u. 10, P.O. Box 483, 1372 Budapest, Hungary.
Telephone: 185-865.

Matsebula, Mhlangano Stephen; Swazi business executive and politician; b. 16 July 1925, Maphalaleni, Mbabane; *s.* of Khwane and Simpompoza Matsebula, *m.* Fihliwe Zwane 1952; one *s.* six *d.*; ed. High School.
Regional Sec., Swazi Commercial Amadoda; Exec. mem. Imbokodvo Nat. Movt.; mem. House of Assembly 67-; Minister of State for Foreign Affairs May 72-.
Leisure interests: handicrafts, reading, football.
Department of Foreign Affairs, P.O. Box 518, Mbabane, Swaziland.

Matskevich, Vladimir Vladimirovich; Soviet agriculturist and politician; b. 1909; ed. Kharkov Inst. of Veterinary Science.
Dir. Kharkov Inst. of Veterinary Science 39; First Deputy Minister of Animal Husbandry of the Ukraine 46-47, Minister 49-53; First Dep. Minister of Agric. of U.S.S.R. 53-55, Minister 55-56, 58-60, 65-; Chair. Exec. Cttee. of Workers' Deputies, Tselinograd, Kazakh S.S.R. 60-65; mem. C.P.S.U. 39-, Central Cttee. C.P. 56-61, 66-; Vice-Chair. State Econ. Comm. 57-60; Leader, Soviet Agric. Del. to U.S.A. and Canada; Chair. U.S.S.R. Council of Collective Farms 70-73; Deputy to U.S.S.R. Supreme Soviet 50-; Amb. to Czechoslovakia 73-.
U.S.S.R. Embassy, Pod Kaštany 1, 125 41 Prague, Czechoslovakia.

Matsuda, Kohei; Japanese business executive; b. 28 Jan. 1922, Osaka; *s.* of Tsunjei and Misako Matsuda; *m.* Setsuko Tsutsui 1950; two *s.* one *d.*; ed. Law Dept., Keio Univ.
Director, Hiroshima Mazda Co. Ltd. 46, Pres. 56; Pres. Mazda Auto Hiroshima Co. Ltd. 59; Exec. Vice-Pres. Toyo Kogyo Co. Ltd. 61, Pres. 70-; Chair. Japan Automatic Transmission Co. Ltd.
Leisure interests: photography, driving.
10-31, Kaminobori-cho, Hiroshima, Japan.
Telephone: 0822-(21)-1438.

Matsukata, Masanobu; Japanese business executive; b. 13 Aug. 1907; ed. Keio Univ.
With Tokyo Gas, Electric and Engineering Co. Ltd. 32; Head of Gen. Affairs Dept., Tokyo Automobile Industry Co. Ltd., Hino Plant 40; Head of Sales Dept., Hino Heavy Industry Co. Ltd. 42, Head of Supply Div. 43, Dir. and Gen. Man. 45; Man. Dir. Hino Industry Co. Ltd. 46; Senior Man. Dir. Hino Diesel Industry Co. Inc. 50, Vice-Pres. 54; Pres. Hino Motors Ltd. 61-74, Chair. 74-; now also Chair. Hino Motor Sales Ltd., Sitsui Seiki Kogyo Co. Ltd., Teikoku Auto Industry Co. Ltd.; Dir. Sawafuji Electrical Co. Ltd., Auto Industry Employers' Asscn., Japan Automobile Mfrs. Asscn. Inc., Japan Ordinance Asscn., Japan Automobile Chamber of Commerce; Financial Dir. Japan Fed. of Employers' Asscns.; Blue Ribbon Medal.
Leisure interests: golf, floriculture.
Hino Motors Ltd., Hinodai 3-1-1, Hino City, Tokyo, Japan.
Telephone: 03-272-4811 (Office).

Matsumoto, Shigeharu, B.A.; Japanese writer and executive; b. 2 Oct. 1899, Osaka; *s.* of Matsuzo Matsumoto; *m.* M. Hanako 1929; two *s.* one *d.*; ed. Faculty of Law, Univ. of Tokyo, Yale Univ., Univs. of Wisconsin, Geneva and Vienna.
Assistant, Faculty of Law, Univ. of Tokyo 28-30; Lecturer Chuo Univ., Hosei Univ., Japan Women's Univ. 29-33; Rep. Shanghai Branch Rengo News Service 33-34, Domei (now Kyodo) News Service 35-39; Editor-in-Chief Domei News Service 40-44, and Man. Dir. 44-45; mem. U.S. Educ. Comm. (Fulbright), Tokyo 54-57; Columnist Asahi Newspaper 56; Gen. Partner Matsumoto, Kojima and Matsukata (law office) 47-; Man. Dir. Int. House of Japan, Inc. 52-65, Chair. Board of Dirs. Int. House of Japan, Inc. 65-; Pres. Japanese Asscn. for American Studies 52-67, Man. Dir. 68-; Pres. Inst. of Nat. Econ. (Kokumin Keizai Kenkyu Kyokai) 51-61; Dir. Nippon Light Metal Co. 57-, Dentsu Advertising Ltd. 61-; Vice-Pres. Nat. Comm. of Japan for UNESCO 57-63; Counsellor, Inst. of Asian Econ. Affairs 60-; mem. Board of Govs. Japan Broadcasting Corpn. 61-65; Chair. Grew Foundation 71-, Bancroft Educational Aid Fund 71-; Hon. Dr. of Laws (Rutgers Univ.) 66; First Class Order of the Sacred Treasure 69.
Leisure interest: golf.
Publs. edited *Memoirs of Aisuke Kabayama* (in Japanese) 56; co-edited *A Documentary History of American People* 6 vols. (in Japanese) 50-58; translated: Albert Thomas's *Histoire Anecdotique du Travail* 28, Dr. S. Johnson's *Beikoku San-ijin no Shogai to sono Shiteki Haikei* (with Y. Takagi) 29, C. A. Beard's *The Republic* 2 vols. 48-49, *A Basic History of the United States* 2 vols. (with K. Kishimura) 54-56, *American Spirit* (with Y. Takagi) 54; edited: Arnold Toynbee's *Lessons of History* (lectures in Japan) 57, *A History of the World* 45-61 (in Japanese) 62, *The Mind of India* (lectures in Japan by J. Nehru and others) 61, *Lectures on Aspects of American Culture* (lectures in Japan by David Riesman) 62, *Basic Problems of U.S. Foreign Policy* (lectures in Japan by George Kennan) 65.
The International House of Japan, Inc., 11-16, 5-chome, Roppongi, Minato-ku, Tokyo, Japan.
Telephone: 401-9151.

Matsuno, Raiszo; Japanese politician; b. 12 Feb. 1917; ed. Keio Univ.
Formerly with Hitachi Ltd.; Japanese Navy, Second World War; fmr. Pres. Johoku Brewing Co.; fmr. Private Sec. to Prime Minister (Mr. Yoshida); mem. House of Reps.; fmr. Parl. Vice-Minister, Ministry of Welfare; Dir.-Gen. Prime Minister's Office; Minister of Labour 59-60; Minister of State in charge of Defence Agency June 65-66; Minister of Agriculture 66-67;

Chair. Policy Affairs Research Council, Liberal-Democratic Party Dec. 74-; Liberal-Democrat.
84 Imazato Shirogane, Shiba, Minato-ku, Tokyo, Japan.

Matsushita, Konusuke; Japanese businessman; b. 27 Nov. 1894, Wasa Village, Wakayama Prefecture; *s.* of Masakusa Matsushita and Tokue Matsushita; *m.* Mumeno Iue 1915; one *d.*
Founded Matsushita Electric Housewares Mfg. Works 18, incorporated into Matsushita Electric Industrial Co. Ltd. 35, fmr. Pres., Chair. 61-73, Adviser, mem. of Board 73-; Pres. Matsushita Communication Industrial Co. Ltd. 58-66, Chair. 66-70; Pres. Matsushita Real Estate Co. Ltd. 52-; Pres. Matsushita Electronics Corpn. 52-66, Chair. 66-71, Dir. 71-; Chair. Kyushu Matsushita Electric Co. Ltd. 55-74, Adviser 74-; Chair. Matsushita Reiki Co. Ltd. (fmrly. Nakagawa Electric Co. Ltd.) 53-74, Matsushita Electric Works Ltd. 51-; Adviser Matsushita Electric Trading Co. Ltd.; Chair. Matsushita Electric Corpn. of America 59-74; Chair. Victor Co. of Japan Ltd. 62-70; Vice-Pres. Electronic Industries Asscn. of Japan 58-68; Man. Dir. Fed. of Econ. Orgs. of Japan 56-73; mem. Int. Chamber of Commerce 61-, Advisory Cttee. Japan Nat. Railway 62-71; Blue Ribbon Medal 56; Commdr., Order of Orange-Nassau (Netherlands) 58, Rising Sun 65, Commdr. Ordre de la Couronne (Belgium); Hon. LL.D. (Waseda, Keio and Doshisha Univs.).
Leisure interest: performance of tea ceremony.
Publs. *What I do, and What I think*, *The Dream of My Work and the Dream of Our Life*, *The Words of Peace and Happiness through Prosperity*, *My View Towards Prosperity*, *My Thoughts on Man*, *Looking Back on the Past and Forward to Tomorrow*, *Reflections on Business*, *Reflections on Management*, *A Way to Look at and Think About Things, Why?*.
571 1006 Kadoma, Kadoma City, Osaka, Japan.
Telephone: Osaka 908-1121.

Matsushita, Masaharu, B.IUR.; Japanese businessman; b. 17 Sept. 1912, Tokyo; ed. Tokyo Imperial Univ.
Mitsui Bank 35-40; Matsushita Electric Industrial Co. Ltd. 40-, Auditor 44-47, Dir. 47-49, Vice-Pres. 49-61, Pres. 61-; Dir. Matsushita Electronics Corpn. 52-72, Chair. 72-; Auditor, Matsushita Real Estate Co. Ltd. 52-68, Dir. 68-; Dir. Matsushita Communication Industrial Co. Ltd. 58-70, Chair. 70-; Dir. Matsushita Seiko Co. Ltd. 58-, Kyushu Matsushita Electric Co. Ltd. 55-, Matsushita Reiki Co. Ltd. (fmrly. Nakagawa Electric Inc.) 61-, Matsushita Electric Corpn. of America 59-74 (Chair. 74-); Pres. Electronics Industries Asscn. of Japan 68-70.
Matsushita Electric Industrial Co. Ltd., 571 1006 Kadoma, Kadoma City, Osaka, Japan.
Telephone: Osaka 908-1121.

Matsushita, Masatoshi, PH.D.; Japanese lawyer and university administrator; b. 1901; ed. Rikkyo (St. Paul's) Univ., Tokyo, Carleton Coll. and Columbo Univ.
Professor, Rikkyo (St. Paul's) Univ. 29; Attorney for Gen. Tojo, Int. Mil. Court of the Far East; Pres. Rikkyo (St. Paul's) Univ. 55-67; personal envoy of Prime Minister of Japan to Great Britain, requesting a suspension of nuclear tests 57; mem. House of Councillors 68-.
Publs. *War Power of the United States*, *Fundamental Principles of American International Law*.
3B Roppongi Fortress Apts., 12-2, 3-chome, Roppongi Azabu, Minato-ku, Tokyo, Japan

Matsuzawa, Takuji; Japanese banker; b. 17 July 1913, Tokyo; *s.* of Takanori and Tameko Matsuzawa; *m.* Toshiko Yoshioka 1942; one *s.* one *d.*; ed. Tokyo Imperial Univ.
Joined The Yasuda Bank Ltd. 38 (name changed to The Fuji Bank Ltd. 48), Chief Man. Planning and Co-ordination Div. 59-61, Dir. and Chief Man. Planning and Co-ordination Div. 61-63, Man. Dir. 63-71, Deputy Pres. 71-75, Chair. of Board and Pres. The Fuji Bank

Ltd. 75-; Chair. of Research and Policy Cttee., Japan Cttee. for Econ. Devt. (Keizai Doyukai) 73-; Man. Dir. Japan Fed. of Econ. Orgs. (Keidanren) 75-.
Leisure interests: playing golf, reading, theatre-going.
The Fuji Bank Ltd., 5-5, 1-chome Otemachi, Chiyoda-ku, Tokyo; Home: 8-7, 2-chome Shoto, Shibuya-ku, Tokyo, Japan.
Telephone: 467-8838.

Matsuzawa, Yuzo; Japanese politician.
Member of House of Reps. (seven times); Chair. Lower House Social and Labour Cttee.; fmr. Deputy Sec.-Gen. Liberal Democratic Party; Dir.-Gen. Admin. Management Agency Dec. 74-.
Administrative Management Agency, Prime Minister's Office, Tokyo, Japan.

Matta (R. A. S. Matta-Echaurren); Chilean artist; b. 11 Nov. 1911; ed. Catholic Univ., Santiago, Ecole d'Urbanisme et Architecture, Paris and Atelier Le Corbusier.
U.S.A. 39-; exhbns. at Julien Levy Gallery 40, Pierre Matisse Gallery 41, 43, 45, 47, Sidney Janis Gallery 49, 51, 54, Allen Frumkin Gallery (all in New York City) 54, Alexandre Idlas Gallery, N.Y. 64-, and other galleries in Paris 64-, Geneva 64-, Stockholm 59, Bologna 63, Amsterdam 64, Cuba 64, Lucerne 65; works permanently displayed at Museum of Modern Art, New York City, Harvard Athenaeum, St. Louis Museum, etc.
Boissy Sans Avoir, S.-et-O., France.

Matteoli, Jean, LIC. EN DROIT; French business executive; b. 20 Dec. 1922, Montchanin; *s.* of Joseph and Jeanne Matteoli (née Pernot); *m.* Christine Gibassier 1946; four *s.* two *d.*
Assistant with Special Functions to Cabinet of Commr. of the Repub. of Bourgogne-Franche Comté 45-46, to Cabinet of Administrator of French Occupied Zone in Germany 46-48, to Collieries of Nord and Pas-de-Calais 48-68; Dir. External Relations, Comm. for the Industrialization of Nord and Pas-de-Calais 53-68, Sec. of Exec. Council 57-72; Pres. Ardennes Industrialization Bureau 68-72; Pres. Dir.-Gen. SICCA (Société Industrielle et commerciale des charbonnages) 72; Pres. Exec. Council, Charbonnages de France 73-; Croix de Guerre, Médaille de la Résistance, Commdr. Légion d'Honneur.
Leisure interest: painting.
Charbonnages de France, 9 avenue Percier, 75008, Paris; Home: 11 rue Magellan, 75008 Paris, France.
Telephone: 359-63-36 (Office); 720-03-36 (Home).

Matteotti, Gianmatteo; Italian journalist and politician; b. 17 Feb. 1921, Rome; *s.* of Giacomo and Titta Velia Matteotti; *m.* Giuliana Candiani 1954; two *d.*; ed. Ginnasio-Liceo "Terenzio Mamiani", Rome, and Univ. of Rome.
Secretary, Fed. of Socialist Youth 44-46; Deputy to Constituent Assembly 46-48; Deputy to Parl. 48-68; Nat. Sec. Partito Socialista Democratico Italiano 54-57, mem. Directorate 63-66, mem. Secr. 70-; Minister of Tourism and Culture 70-72; Minister of Foreign Trade 72-Oct. 74.
Leisure interests: archaeology, music, numismatics.
Publs. *La classe operaia sotto il fascismo* 44.
00197 Rome, Via Luciani 45, Italy.
Telephone: 804478.

Matthau, Walter; American actor; b. 1 Oct. 1920; ed. New York.
New York Drama Critics Award 51, 58; Antoinette Perry Award 61, 64; Acad. Award for *The Fortune Cookie*; British Soc. of Film and TV Arts Award for *Pete 'n' Tillie* and *Charlie Varrick*.
Stage appearances in *Anne of a Thousand Days* 48, *The Liar* 49, *Season in the Sun* 50, *Fancy Meeting You Again* 51, *Twilight Walk* 51, *One Bright Day* 51, *In Any Language* 52, *The Grey-Eyed People* 52, *The*

Ladies of the Corridor 53, *Will Success Spoil Rock Hunter* 55, *Once More with Feeling* 58, *Once There Was a Russian* 60, *A Shot in the Dark* 61, *My Mother, My Father and Me* 63, *The Odd Couple* 64.
Films include *The Fortune Cookie*, *A Guide for the Married Man*, *Lonely Are the Brave*, *Secret Life of An American Wife*, *Cactus Flower*, *Mirage*, *Charade*, *The Kentuckian*, *Slaughter on Tenth Avenue*, *Ride a Crooked Trail*, *Hello Dolly*, *A Face in the Crowd*, *Bigger Than Life*, *Fail Safe*, *Odd Couple*, *A New Leaf*, *Plaza Suite*, *Kotch*, *Pete 'n' Tillie*, *Charlie Varrick*, *An Investigation of Murder* 73, *Earthquake* 74, *The Front Page* 74, *The Taking of Pelham 1, 2, 3* 75, *The Sunshine Boys* 75.
9777 Wilshire Boulevard, Beverly Hills, Calif. 90212, U.S.A.

Matthes, Heinz; German engineer and politician; b. 1927.
Member, Cen. Cttee. Sozialistische Einheitspartei Deutschlands; Minister and Chair. Workers' and Farmers' Inspectorate.
Ministerrat, Berlin, German Democratic Republic.

Matthews, Sir Bryan Harold Cabot, Kt., C.B.E., F.R.S., SC.D.; British physiologist; b. 14 June 1906, Bristol; m. 1st Rachel Eckhard 1926, 2nd Audrey Wentworth Stewart (née Tynedale) 1970; one s. two d.; one stepson three stepdaughters; ed. Clifton Coll. and King's Coll., Cambridge.
Beit Memorial Fellow for Medical Research 28-32; Fellow, King's Coll., Cambridge 29-73, Life Fellow 73; Asst. Dir. Physiological Research, Cambridge 32-48; Reader in Experimental Physiology, Cambridge Univ. 48-52, Prof. of Physiology 52-73, Prof. Emer. 73-; Consultant in Physiology to R.A.F. 41-; Head of R.A.F. Physiological Laboratory 40-44 and of the Inst. of Aviation Medicine from its foundation 44-46; Vice-Pres. Royal Soc. 57 and 58; Pres. Section I British Asscn. 61; Chair. Flying Personnel Research Cttee. R.A.F. 67-.
Leisure interests: sailing, ocean racing.
King's College, Cambridge, England.
Telephone: Cambridge 811227.

Matthews, Denis, C.B.E., F.R.A.M.; British pianist; b. 27 Feb. 1919; Coventry, Warwicks.; s. of Arthur Matthews and Elsie (née Culver); m. 1st Mira Howe 1941, one s. three d.; m. 2nd Brenda McDermott 1963, one s. one d.; ed. Warwick School and Royal Acad. of Music, London.
First concerts, London 39; since then numerous recitals and tours in Great Britain, U.S.A., Canada, World Tour 64, Latin America 68, 70; teaching, lecturing; numerous recordings; Prof. of Music, Univ. of Newcastle upon Tyne 71-; Hon. F.T.C.L. 72; Hon. M.A. (Newcastle) 71, Hon. D.Mus. (St. Andrews) 73; Cobbett Medal 73.
Leisure interests: astronomy, 18th Century English furniture, reading.
Publs. *In Pursuit of Music* 66, *Beethoven's Piano Sonatas* 67, *Keyboard Music* 72.
Department of Music, University of Newcastle upon Tyne, England.

Matthews, Herbert Lionel; American newspaperman; b. 10 Jan. 1900; ed. Columbia Univ.
U.S. Army Service, First World War; *New York Times* 22-, successively Reporter, Foreign Editor and War Corresp., Paris Bureau 31-34, Abyssinian War 35-36, Spanish Civil War 36-39, Rome 39-42, India 42-43, Italian Campaign 43-45; Chief, London Bureau, *New York Times* 45-49, Editorial Staff, *New York Times*, New York 49-67; numerous decorations.
Publs. *Eyewitness in Abyssinia* 37, *Two Wars and More to Come* 38, *The Fruits of Fascism* 43, *The Education of a Correspondent* 46, *Assignment to Austerity* (with Edith Matthews) 50, *The Yoke and the Arrows* 56, *The Cuban Story* 61, *Cuba* 64, *Castro—A Political*

Biography 69, *A World in Revolution* 72, *Half of Spain Died* 73.
New York Times, 229 West 43rd Street, New York 36, N.Y., U.S.A.
Telephone: 556-1234.

Matthews, Horatio Keith, C.M.G., M.B.E.; retd. British diplomatist; b. 4 April 1917; m.; two d.; ed. Epsom Coll. and Gonville and Caius Coll., Cambridge.
Served in Indian Civil Service in Madras Presidency 40-47; joined foreign service 48; First Sec., Lisbon 49-51, Bucharest 53-54; Imperial Defence Coll. 55; Political Officer with Middle East Forces, Cyprus 56-59; Counsellor, Canberra 59-61; Political Adviser to Gen. Officer Commanding, Berlin 61-64; Insp. Foreign Office 64, Diplomatic Service 65; Minister, Moscow 66-67; High Commr. to Ghana 68-70; Under-Sec.-Gen. for Admin. and Management, UN Secr. 70-72; Asst. Under-Sec. of State, Ministry of Defence 73-74; J.P., Isle of Wight 75-.
Elm House, Bembridge, Isle of Wight, England.
Telephone: Bembridge 2327.

Matthews, Sir Peter Alec, Kt.; British business exec.; b. 21 Sept. 1922, Duncan, Vancouver Island, B.C., Canada; s. of Major Alec B. Matthews and Elsie Lazarus Barlow; m. Sheila D. Bunting 1946; four s. one d.; ed. Shawnigan Lake School, Vancouver Island, and Oundle School.
Army service 40-46; joined Stewarts and Lloyds Ltd. 46, Dir. of Research and Tech. Devt. 62-68; mem. Research and Devt., British Steel Corpn. 68-70; Man. Dir. Vickers Ltd. 70-; Dir. British Aircraft Corpn. (Holdings) 71-; Vice-Pres. Engineering Employers' Foundation 71-; Council mem. Confederation of British Industry 71-; Deputy Chair. British Steel Corpn. 73-; mem. British Overseas Trade Board 73-; mem. Export Guarantees Advisory Council 73-; Dir. Lloyds Bank Ltd. 74-; mem. Nat. Research Devt. Corpn. 74-; Fellow, British Inst. of Management.
Leisure interests: sailing, gardening, tennis.
Vickers Ltd., Vickers House, Millbank Tower, Millbank, London, S.W.1; Home: Ladycross House, Dormansland, Surrey, England.
Telephone: 01-828-7777 (Office); Dormans Park 314 (Home).

Matthias, Bernd T., PH.D.; American physicist; b. 8 June 1918, Frankfurt am Main, Germany; s. of late Ludwig Matthias and late Marta Lipman Matthias; m. Joan Trapp 1950; ed. Eidgenössische Technische Hochschule, Zürich.
Scientific collaborator, Eidgenössische Technische Hochschule, Zürich 42-47, Mass. Inst. of Technology 47-48; Asst. Prof. Univ. of Chicago 49-51; Prof. of Physics, Univ. of Calif., San Diego 61-; Asst. Dir. Inst. for Pure and Applied Physical Sciences (U.C.S.D.) 67-71, Dir. 71-; Staff mem. Bell Telephone Labs. Inc., Murray Hill, N.J. 48-; mem. Nat. Acad. of Sciences 65-; Fellow, American Asscn. for Advancement of Science 65-, American Physical Soc., American Acad. of Arts and Sciences; Research Corpn. Award 62; John Price Wetherill Medal 63; Industrial Research Man of the Year Oct. 68; Oliver E. Buckley Solid State Physics Prize 70.
Leisure interest: telepathy.
Publs. 287 papers in int. and nat. scientific journals.
Department of Physics, University of California, San Diego, La Jolla, Calif. 92093, U.S.A.
Telephone: 714-452-4024.

Matthiasen, Niels; Danish politician; b. 1924, Copenhagen.
Served apprenticeship in clerical work; employee, Denmark Publishing House 39-57; Sec. Social Democratic Union 57, Gen. Sec. 61-70; mem. Folketing 60-73, 75-; Minister for Cultural Affairs 71-73, for Culture and Public Affairs Feb. 75-; mem. Exec. Cttee., Fed.

of Trade Unions 62-67; mem. Bureau, Socialist Int. 63-66; Co-founder and Sec. Danish Atlantic Asscn. 50-57; mem. many other cttees.; Editor *Verden's Gang* (Social-Democratic periodical) 58-61, *Ny Politik* 70-71.
Leisure interests: gardening, tennis.
Publs. *A Pioneer* 48; Co-editor: *Ideas and Everyday Life* 68, *Ends and Means* 69; political and literary articles in the press.
Home: Holbergsgade 30, 1057 Copenhagen, Denmark.
Telephone: (0113) 3007.

Matthiensen, Ernst; German banker; b. 17 May 1900, Oldenburg, Holstein.
Vice-Chairman Supervisory and Admin. Boards of Dresdner Bank A.G.; Chair. Supervisory Board, Deutscher Investment-Trust Gesellschaft für Wertpapieranlagen m.b.H.; Vice-Chair. Supervisory Board, Münchener Rückversicherungs Gesellschaft; mem. Supervisory Board Esso A.G., August Thyssen-Hütte A.G.
6000 Frankfurt a.M., 7-8 Gallusanlage, Federal Republic of Germany.
Telephone: 2633342.

Matthöfer, Hans; German politician; b. 25 Sept. 1925, Bochum; *m.* Traute Mecklenburg 1951; ed. Univs. of Frankfurt/Main and Madison, Wis., U.S.A.
Member of Social Democratic Party (SPD) 50-; mem. Econ. Dept. IG Metall 53, Head of Educ. and Training Dept. 61; mem. OEEC Mission to Washington and Paris 57-61; mem. Bundestag (Parl.); mem. Bundestag Cttees. for Econ., Econ. Co-operation, Law, Foreign Affairs; Parl. Sec. of State, Ministry of Econ. Co-operation 72; Minister for Research and Technology May 74-; Vice-Pres. Latin Amer. Parliamentarians' Group; mem. hon. Presidium of German Section, Amnesty Int.; Pres. Deutsche Stiftung für Entwicklungsländer (Foundation for Overseas Devt.) 71-73.
Leisure interests: chess, reading.
Publs. *Der Unterschied zwischen den Tariflöhnen und den Effektivverdiensten in der Metallindustrie der Bundesrepublik* 56, *Technological Change in the Metal Industries* 61/62, *Der Beitrag politischer Bildung zur Emanzipation der Arbeitnehmer—Materialien zur Frage des Bildungsurlaubs* 70, *Streiks und Streikähnliche Formen des Kampfes der Arbeitnehmer im Kapitalismus* 71, numerous articles on trade union and development politics.
Bundesministerium für Forschung und Technologie, 53 Bonn-Bad Godesberg, Stresemannstrasse 2, Federal Republic of Germany.
Telephone: 59-30-00, 59-30-01.

Mattila, Olavi Johannes; Finnish engineer, diplomatist and politician; b. 24 Oct. 1918, Hyvinkää; *s.* of Juho Fredrik Mattila and Aino Sylvia Sihvonen; *m.* Ebba Sylvia Annikki Vestinen 1956; three *c.*; ed. Inst. of Technology and Helsinki School of Economics and Economic Sciences.
Commercial Rep., Finnish Embassy, Peking 52-56, Commercial Attaché, Buenos Aires 57-60; Chief of Bureau, Ministry of Foreign Affairs 60; Head of Commercial Div., Ministry of Trade and Industry 60-62; Head of Commercial Div., Ministry of Foreign Affairs 62-64; Second Minister for Foreign Affairs 63-64; Minister of Trade and Industry Dec. 63-64; Pres. and Chair. Valmet Org. 65-73, Chair. 73-; Minister of Trade and Industry May-July 70; Minister of Foreign Trade July 70-Oct. 71; Minister of Foreign Affairs Oct. 71-Feb. 72; Chair. Enso-Gutzeit Osakeyhtio 73-; Commdr., Order of Lion of Finland, and other decorations.
Leisure interests: tennis, fishing, trade politics.
Puistokatu 3.A.12, Helsinki, 626734, Finland.

Mattingly, Thomas K., II; American astronaut; b. 17 March 1936, Chicago, Ill.; ed. Auburn Univ.

Entered U.S. Navy 57, completed flight training 60; assigned to Attack Squadron 35 60-63; served in A3 B aircraft on carriers 63; student at Air Force Aerospace Research Pilot School until 66; selected by NASA as astronaut April 66; Command Module Pilot, *Apollo XVI* April 72.
NASA Johnson Space Center, Houston, Texas 77058, U.S.A.

Matulis, Juozas Juozo; Soviet chemist; b. 19 March 1899, Tatkonis, Kupishkis District, Lithuania; *s.* of Juozas Kazimero Matulis and Urshule Nikodemo (Tatoryte) Matuliene; *m.* Adele Antano (Malelaite) Matuliene; one *s.* one *d.*; ed. Kaunus State Univ.
Teacher, Kaunus State Univ. 28-40, Vilnius State Univ. 40-44; Pro-rector Vilnius State Univ. 44-; mem. Lithuanian Acad. of Sciences 41-, Pres. 46-; Corresp. mem. U.S.S.R. Acad. of Sciences 46-; mem. C.P.S.U. 50-, Central Cttee. C.P. of Lithuania, Mandat Comm. Union of Soviets U.S.S.R. Supreme Soviet; Hero of Socialist Labour, Order of Lenin (3), Red Banner of Labour (2), Merited Worker of Science of Lithuanian S.S.R.
Leisure interests: fishing and hunting.
Lithuanian S.S.R. Academy of Sciences, 3 Leninsky Prospekt, Vilnius 232600, Lithuania, U.S.S.R.

Matuschka-Greiffenclau, Graf Richard; German winegrower; b. 11 May 1893, Wiesbaden; *s.* of Guido and Klara Matuschka-Greiffenclau; *m.* Eleonore Gräfin Neipperg 1936; three *s.*; ed. Bonn and Berlin Univs.
Civil servant until 34; political and business activity 46-; mem. Hesse Landtag 48-50; Hon. Pres. Deutscher Weinbauverband 48; Vice-Pres. Central Cttee. for German Agriculture 54-; Hon. Pres. Asscn. of Wine-Growers in European Econ. Community; Grosses Verdienstkreuz.
Leisure interests: historical examinations, archaeology.
Schloss Vollrads, 6227 Winkel im Rheingau, Federal Republic of Germany.
Telephone: 06723-3377.

Matute Ausejo, Ana María; Spanish writer; b. 26 July 1925, Barcelona; *d.* of Facundo Matute and Mary Ausejo; *m.* 1952 (dissolved 1963); one *s.*; ed. "Damas Negras" French Nuns Coll.
Collaborated on literary magazine *Destino*; Visiting Lecturer, Indiana Univ. 65-66, Oklahoma Univ. 69-; mem. Hispanic Soc. of America; "Highly Commended Author", Hans Christian Andersen Jury, Lisbon 72.
Leisure interests: painting, drawing, the cinema.
Publs. *Los Abel* 47, *Fiesta Al Noroeste* (Café Gijon Prize) 52, *Pequeño Teatro* (Planeta Prize) 54, *Los niños tontos* 56, *Los Hijos Muertos* (Nat. Literary Prize and Critics Prize) 59, *Primera Memoria* (Nadal Prize) 59, *Tres y un sueño* 61, *Historias de la Artamila* 61, *El Rio* 63, *El Tiempo* 63, *Los Soldados lloran de noche* 64 (Fastenrath Prize 69), *El Arrepentido y otras Narraciones* 67, *Algunos Muchachos* 68, *La Trampa* 69, *La Torre Vigia* 71, *Olvidado Rey Gudu* 74; Children's books: *El Pais de la Pizarra* 56, *Paulina* 61, *El Sal Tamontes Verde* 61, *Caballito Loco* 61, *El Aprendiz* 61, *Carnavalito* 61, *El Polizon del "Ulises"* (Lazarillo Prize) 65.
Urgel, 55, S/a. 2a, Barcelona 11, Spain.
Telephone: 254-98-31.

Matveyev, Alexei Nikolayevich; Soviet scientist; b. 22 March 1922, Moscow; *s.* of Nikolai Matveyev and Metlova Nadezda; *m.* M. Zamtchalova 1951; two *d.*; ed. Moscow State Univ.
Senior Scientific Worker, Moscow State Univ. 54-60; Prof. of Theoretical Physics, Moscow State Univ. 60-64, 69-; Head of Dept. of Univs., Ministry of Higher Educ., R.S.F.S.R. 60-62; Asst. Dir.-Gen. for Science, UNESCO 64-69; Order of Red Banner (twice), Order of the Patriotic War, Order of Alexander Nevski, Order of Red Banner of Labour, Order of Honour.

Publs. *Electrodynamics and Theory of Relativity* 64, *Quantum Mechanics and Structure of Atoms* 65, *Mechanics* 76.
Moscow State University, Moscow, U.S.S.R.

Matz, Friedrich; German archaeologist; b. 15 Aug. 1890; ed. Univs. of Tübingen and Göttingen.
Teacher, Berlin 21; bibliographical work, German Archaeological Inst., Rome 25-29; Dozent, Berlin Univ. 28; Asst. Dir. Archaeological Inst., Berlin 29-34; Prof. Univ. of Muenster 34, Marburg Lahn Univ. 41; Prof. and Rector Philipps Univ. Marburg 46-47, Emeritus 58.
Publs. *Die Frühkretischen Siegel* 28, *Katalog der Bibliothek des Deutschen Archäologischen Instituts in Rom* 30-32, *Ein Zeuskopf in Villa Borghese* 31, *Kretisch-Mykenische Kunst, Antike* 36, *Wesen und Wirkung der Augusteischen Kunst* 38, *Geschichte der griechischen Kunst*, Vol. I 50, *Die Aegaeis* 50, *Der Gott auf dem Elefantenwagen* 52, *Kreta, Mykene, Troia* 56, *Götter-erscheinung und Kultbild im minoischen Kreta* 58, *Ein römisches Meisterwerk* 58, *Kreta und frühes Griechenland* 62, *Das Problem der Orans und ein Sarkophag in Cordoba* 68, *Die Dionysischen Sarkophage I-III* 68/69, *Der Sarkophag eines Centurio der I. Cohors Praetoria* 70.
Biegenstrasse 11, Marburg/Lahn; Home: Georg-Voigtstrasse 25, Marburg/Lahn, Federal Republic of Germany.
Telephone: 2349.

Maude, Angus Edmund Upton, T.D., M.A., M.P.; British politician and author; b. 8 Sept. 1912, London; s. of Col. Alan H. and Dorothy M. Maude; m. Barbara E. E. Sutcliffe; two s. two d.; ed. Rugby School and Oriel Coll., Oxford.
Financial journalist 33-39; war service (prisoner of war 3½ years) 39-45; Deputy Dir. Political and Economic Planning 49-50; Conservative Mem. of Parl. 50-58, 63-; Dir. Conservative Political Centre 51-55; Editor *The Sydney Morning Herald* 58-61; Deputy Chair. Conservative Party 75-; Chair. Conservative Party Research Dept. 75-.
Publs. *The English Middle Classes* (with Roy Lewis) 49, *Professional People* (with Roy Lewis) 52, *Biography of a Nation* (with Enoch Powell) 56, and editor of *One Nation* 50 and *Change is our Ally* 54 (booklets on social policy by nine M.P.s), *Good Learning* 64, *South Asia* 66, *The Common Problem* 69.
South Newington House, nr. Banbury, Oxon., England.
Telephone: 01-219-4467 (Office).

Maude, Evan Walter, C.B.; British civil servant; b. 11 Feb. 1919, London; s. of late Sir E. John Maude, K.C.B., K.B.E.; m. Jennifer Bulmer (née Robinson) 1949; three d.; ed. Rugby School, and New Coll., Oxford.
R.N.V.R. (Fleet Air Arm) 40-45; H M. Treasury 46; Asst. Private Sec. to Chancellor of Exchequer and Econ. Sec. 47-48; Private Sec. to Sec. of State for Co-ordination of Transport, Fuel and Power 51-53; Principal Private Sec. to Chancellor of Exchequer 56-58; Asst., then Deputy Under-Sec. of State, Dept. of Econ. Affairs 64-67; Econ. Minister British Embassy, Wash. 67-69; Third Sec. Treasury 69-70; Deputy Sec. Ministry of Agric., Fisheries and Food Oct. 70-; Exec. Dir. IBRD, IFC, IDA Aug. 67-69; Exec. Dir. IMF 67-69.
Leisure interests: sailing, music.
5 Downshire Hill, London, N.W.3, England.

Maudling, Rt. Hon. Reginald, P.C., M.P.; British politician; b. 7 March 1917; ed. Merton Coll., Oxford.
Called to Middle Temple Bar 40; served Royal Air Force and Air Ministry during 39-45 war; Conservative M.P. for Barnet Div. of Hertfordshire 50-74, for Chipping Barnet Div. of Barnet 74-; Parl. Sec. to Minister of Civil Aviation 52; Minister of Supply 55-57; Paymaster-General with seat in Cabinet 57-59; Pres. of Bd. of Trade 59-61; Sec. of State for the Colonies 61-62; Chancellor of the Exchequer 62-64;

Exec. Dir. Kleinwort Benson Ltd. 64-70; Dir. Dunlop Rubber Co. 64-70, Associated Electrical Industries 64-70; Vice-Chair. and Dir. Shipping and Industrial Trust 65-70; Pres. Nat. Union of Conservative and Unionist Asscns. 67; Sec. of State for the Home Dept. 70-72; Opposition Spokesman for Foreign and Commonwealth Affairs Feb. 75-.
Bedwell Lodge, Essendon, Herts., England.

Maulnier, Thierry (*pseudonym* of Jacques Louis André Talagrand); French writer; b. 1 Oct. 1909; ed. Lycée Louis-le-Grand, Paris, and Ecole Normale Supérieure.
Journalist on *l'Action Française*, later *Figaro* 30-; playwright 42-; dramatic critic *Combat* and *La Revue de Paris*; founded (with François Mauriac) *La Table Ronde*; mem. Académie Française 64-; Officier, Légion d'Honneur, Grand Prix de Littérature de l'Académie Française 59, Prix Pelman de la presse 59.
Plays: *Antigone* 44, *La Course des rois* 47, *Jeanne et les Juges* 49, *Le Profanateur* 52, *Oedipe-Roi* (adaptation) 52, *La Maison de la Nuit* 53, *La Condition humaine* (adaptation) 54, *Procès à Jésus* (adaptation) 58, *Le Sexe et le Néant* 60, *Signe du feu* (adaptation) 60.
Prose works inc. *La crise est dans l'Homme* 32, *Nietzsche* 33, *Racine* 34, *Introduction à la poésie française* 39, *Violence et Conscience* 45, *La Face de méduse du communisme* 52, *Cette Grèce où nous sommes nés* 65, *La Défaite d'Hannibal, la Ville au fond de la mer* 67, *Lettre aux Américains* 68, *l'Honneur d'être juif* 70 (with G. Prouteau).
3 rue Yves-Carriou, 92 Marnes-la-Coquette, France.

Maurer, Friedrich, DR.PHIL.; German university professor; b. 5 Jan. 1898; ed. Univs. of Frankfurt, Heidelberg and Giessen.
Lecturer Univ. of Giessen 25, Extra. Prof. 29, Prof. of Germanic Philology Erlangen 31, Freiburg 37.
Publs. *Untersuchungen über die deutsche Verbstellung* 26, *Studien zur mitteldeutschen Bibelübersetzung* 29, *Die Sprache Goethes* 32, *Volkssprache* 33, 64, *Die Erlösung* (editor) 34, 64, *Das Rolandslied* (editor) 40, 64, *Nordgermanen und Alemannen* 42, 52, *Deutsche Wortgeschichte* Vols. I-III (with Stroh) 43, 59, *Leid* 51, 52, 64, 69, *Die politischen Lieder Walthers von der Vogelweide* 54, 64, *Dichtung und Sprache des Mittelalters* 63, 71, *Die religiösen Dichtungen des 11. und 12. Jahrhunderts* Vols. I and II 65, Vol. III 70, *Die Pseudoreimare* 66, etc.
Schlossweg 18, 7802 Merzhausen bei Freiburg i. Br., Federal Republic of Germany.
Telephone: Freiburg 404340.

Maurer, Georg, HON. C.B.E., M.D.; German surgeon; b. 29 May 1909, Munich; m.; two s. two d.; ed. Univ. of Munich.
Surgical Asst., later Chief Asst., Univ. Clinic of Surgery, Munich 33-45; Surgeon-in-Chief Hospital, Munich-Perlach 46-53; Surgeon-in-Chief Hospital Rechts der Isar, Munich 53-67, Medical Dir. 59-; Prof. Extraordinary, Univ. of Munich 48; Prof., Technical Univ., Munich 67-. Dean, Medical Faculty 67; City Councillor, Munich; Congress Sec. German Soc. of Surgery; Regional Pres. German Asscn. of Medical Dirs.; Bayer, Verdienstorden 69.
Publs. *Morbus Fraenkel* 44, *Problem of salt-water balance in surgery* 58, *Tetanus prophylaxis* 59, *History of Surgery in Bavaria* 60, *Pancreatitis* 60, *Modern Shock Treatment* 65, *Weather Conditions and Surgery* 66, *Indications for Conservative and Operative Fracture Treatment* 68, *Neurotraumatology* 69.
8000 Munich-Geiselgasteig, Gabriel-von-Seidl-Strasse 32, Federal Republic of Germany.

Maurer, Ion Gheorghe, LL.D., D.IUR.; Romanian jurist and politician; b. 23 Sept. 1902, Bucharest; ed. Craiova Military School and Bucharest Univ.
Joined Romanian Communist Party 36; imprisoned in

concentration camp for political activities; Under Sec. of State for Transport 44-46, Ministry of Nat. Economy 46-47; mem. Cen. Cttee. Romanian Workers' Party (now Romanian Communist Party) 45-, Grand Nat. Assembly 48-, Political Bureau 60-65, Exec. Cttee. of Cen. Cttee. of Romanian C.P. 65-, and Perm. Presidium 65-74; Deputy Minister of Industry and Trade 48; Minister for Foreign Affairs 57-58; Chair. Presidium Grand Nat. Assembly (Head of State) 58-61, Chair. Council of Ministers 61-74; mem. Defence Council of Romania 69-74; mem. Acad. of Romanian People's Repub. 55-, Acad. of Social and Political Sciences 70-; fmr. Dir. Inst. of Juridical Research 54-58; Hero of Socialist Labour 62, Order "Victoria Socialismului" 71, Hero of Socialist Republic of Romania 72, etc.
c/o Council of Ministers, Bucharest, Romania.

Mauriac, Claude, D.IUR.; French writer; b. 25 April 1914; s. of late François Mauriac; ed. Lycée Janson-de-Sailly.
Secretary to Gen. de Gaulle 44-49; Film Critic *Figaro Littéraire*; weekly literary column "La Vie des Lettres" in *Le Figaro*; Contrib. to *L'Express* 72-; Admin. Soc. Figaro-Edition 72-; Prix Sainte-Beuve for *André Breton* 49, Prix Médicis for *Le Dîner en Ville* 59.
Publs. Non-fiction: *Aimer Balzac, Malraux ou le Mal du Héros, André Breton, Marcel Proust par Lui-Même, Conversation avec André Gide, Hommes et Idées d'Aujourd'hui, La Littérature Contemporaine, Un autre de Gaulle 1944-54* 71; Novels: *Toutes Les Femmes Sont Fatales* 57, *Le Dîner en Ville* 59, *La Marquise Sortit à Cinq Heures* 51, *L'Agrandissement* 63, *Femmes Fatales* 66, *l'Oubli* 66; Plays: *La Conversation* 64, *Ici, maintenant* 71.
24 Quai de Béthune, Paris 4e, France.

Maurice-Bokanowski, Michel; French politician; b. 6 Nov. 1912; ed. Lycée Condorcet, Paris.
Former Sec.-Gen., Paris Region Rassemblement du Peuple Français (R.P.F.); Dep. from Seine (5th Div.) 51-58, elected U.N.R. Dep. from Bois-Colombes (Asnières) 58; Sec. of State for the Interior Jan. 59-Feb. 60; Minister of Posts and Telecommunications Feb. 60-April 62; Minister of Industry April 62-66; Senator for Hauts-de-Seine Oct. 68-; Mayor of Asnières 59-; Dir. of several companies; Commdr. Légion d'Honneur, Compagnon de la Libération, Croix de Guerre.
40 quai des Célestins, Paris 4e, France.

Maurstad, Toralv; Norwegian actor and theatre director; b. 24 Nov. 1926, Oslo; s. of Alfred and Tordis Maurstad; m. Eva Henning 1956; one s.; ed. Universitet i Uppsala and Royal Acad. of Dramatic Art, London.
Début in Trondheim 47; Oslo Nye Teater 51; Oslo National Theatre 54; Managing Dir. Oslo Nye Teater (Oslo Municipal Theatre) 67-; Oslo Critics Award.
Leisure interests: skiing, hunting, fishing.
Plays acted in or directed include: *Young Woodley* 49, *Pal Joey* 52, *Peer Gynt* 54, *Long Day's Journey* 62, *Teenage Love* 63, *Hamlet* 64, *Arturo Ui* (in Bremen, Germany) 65, *Brand* (Ibsen) 66, *Of Love Remembered* (New York) 67, *Cabaret* 68; films: *Line* 60, *Kalde Spor* 62, *Song of Norway* 70.
Thorleif Haugsvei 18, Voksenkollen, Oslo, Norway.

Mavromihalis, Stylianos; Greek judge; b. 1900; ed. Univs. of Athens, Munich and Zurich.
Judge 23-, Pres. of the Areopagus (Supreme Court) 63-68; Prime Minister Sept.-Nov. 63.
Athens, Greece.

Mavros, George, LL.D.; Greek lawyer and politician; b. 1909, Castellorizon; m. 1953; one s.; ed. Athens and Berlin Univs.
Lawyer, Athens 32-; Asst. Prof. of Int. Law, Univ. of Athens 37-; M.P. 46-; Under-Sec. of State for Justice 45-46, Minister of Justice 46; Minister of National

Econ. (Trade and Industry) 49-50, of Finance 51, of Defence 52; Gov. for Greece to IBRD 49-52; Minister of Co-ordination 63-64; Gov. Nat. Bank of Greece 64-66; under house arrest April-Oct. 68; fmr. Pres. Centre Union Party, Pres. Centre Union-New Forces Party 74-; arrested and deported to Yiaros island March 74, released May 74; Deputy Prime Minister, Minister of Foreign Affairs July -Oct. 74.
Leisure interests: classical music, golf, swimming.
Publs. *Walker's Private International Law* 29, *Problems in the Differentiation of Real Property and Chattels in the International Law on Wills* 36, *Naval Privileges in International Law* 37.
8 Akadimias Street, Athens 134, Greece.

Mawby, Sir Maurice, Kt., C.B.E.; Australian mining executive; b. Broken Hill; ed. Broken Hill High School and Tech. Coll.
Joined The Zinc Corpn. Ltd. 28; mem. Commonwealth Minerals Cttee. 41-44; Chief Metallurgist, The Zinc Corpn. Ltd. 44, later Dir. of Exploration and Research; Dir. of Research and Devt., The Broken Hill Associated Smelters Pty. Ltd.; Gen. Man. Enterprise Exploration Pty. Ltd., subsequently, Chair.; Vice-Chair. Consolidated Zinc Pty. 53, Chair 61; Dir. The Consolidated Zinc Corpn. Ltd. (U.K.), The Zinc Corpn. and New Broken Hill Consolidated Ltd. 55; Chair. Conzinc Riotinto of Australia Ltd. 62-74; Dir. Hamersley Iron Pty. Ltd., Bougainville Mining Ltd., Atlas Steels (Australia) Pty. Ltd., Guardian Royal Exchange Assurance, Tioxide Australia Pty. Ltd.; Coun. Australasian Inst. of Mining and Metallurgy; Hon. mem. American Inst. of Mining and Metallurgical Engineers, Inst. of Mining and Metallurgy (London); mem. Canadian Inst. of Mining and Metallurgy, Inst. of Chemical Engineers (London); Kernot Medallist (Univ. of Melbourne), Bronze Medal, Australasian Inst. of Mining and Metallurgy 56, Gold Medal, Inst. of Mining and Metallurgy (London); Fellow, Australian Acad. of Science and Sydney Technical Coll.; Hon. D.Sc. (Univ. of N.S.W.).
102 Mont Albert Road, Canterbury, Victoria 3126, Australia.

Maximos V Hakim (fmrly. **Archbishop George S. Hakim**), D.D.; Lebanese ecclesiastic; b. 18 May 1908; ed. St. Louis School, Tanta, Holy Family Jesuit School, Cairo and St. Anne Seminary, Jerusalem.
Teacher Patriarchal School, Beirut 30-31; Rector and Principal Patriarchal School, Cairo 31-43; Archbishop of Acre, Haifa, Nazareth and all Galilee 43-67; elected Greek Catholic Patriarch of Antioch and all the East, Alexandria and Jerusalem Nov. 67; founded *Le Lien* (French) Cairo 36, *Ar-Rabita* (Arabic) Haifa 43; Commdr. Légion d'Honneur; Dr. h.c. (Laval Univ., Canada and many U.S. univs.).
Publ. *Pages d'Evangile lues en Galilée* (trans. into English, Dutch and Spanish) 54.
Greek Catholic Patriarchate, P.O. Box 50076, Beirut, Lebanon.

Maximova, Yekaterina Sergeyevna; Soviet ballet dancer; b. 1 Feb. 1939; ed. Bolshoi Theatre Ballet School.
Joined Bolshoi Theatre Ballet Co. 58; Honoured Artist of R.S.F.S.R.
Main roles: Masha (*Nutcracker*), Katerina (*Stone Flower*), Seventh Waltz, Prelude (*Chopiniana*), Maria (*Fountain of Bakhchisarai*), Giselle (*Giselle*), Mavka (*Song of the Forest* by Zhukovsky), Jeanne (*Flames of Paris*), the Muse (*Paganini* by Rachmaninov), Lizzie (*Thunder Road* by Karayev), Cinderella (*Cinderella*), Aurora (*Sleeping Beauty*), Kitri (*Don Quixote*), Frigina (*Spartacus* by Khachaturyan).
State Academic Bolshoi Theatre of U.S.S.R., 1 Ploshchad Sverdlova, Moscow, U.S.S.R.

Maxwell, (Ian) Robert, M.C.; British publisher and politician; b. 10 June 1923; s. of Michael and Ann Hoch; m. Elisabeth Meynard 1945; three s. four d.; self-educated.
Served Second World War 40-45; German Section of Foreign Office (Head of Press Section, Berlin) 45-47; Chair. Robert Maxwell & Co. Ltd., 48-; Publisher and Chair. Board Pergamon Press, Oxford and London 49-69, 74-, New York 49-; Dir. Gauthier-Villars (Publishers) Paris 61-69; Chair. Labour Nat. Fund Raising Foundation 60-69; Chair. Labour Working Party on Science, Govt. and Industry 63-64; M.P. for Buckingham 64-70; mem. Council of Europe, Vice-Chair. Cttee. on Science and Technology 68; Treasurer Centre 42, 65-70; Kennedy Fellow, J. F. Kennedy School of Govt., Harvard Univ. 71; Hon. mem. Int. Acad. of Astronautics 74-; Co-produced films *Don Giovanni* (Mozart), Salzburg Festival 54, *Bolshoi Ballet* 57, *Swan Lake* 68; Editor *Information U.S.S.R.* 63, *The Economics of Nuclear Power* 65, Author *Public Sector Purchasing* (Report) 67, Joint Author *Man Alive* 68.
Leisure interests: chess, mountain-climbing.
Headington Hill Hall, Oxford, England.
Telephone: Oxford 64881.

Maxwell Davies, Peter (*see* Davies, Peter Maxwell).

May, Henry Leonard James; New Zealand politician; b. 13 April 1912, Petone; s. of James May; m. 1st Mary Anne McNeill 1940 (deceased), two s. two d.; m. 2nd Doreen E. Langton 1970; ed. Petone Convent, Petone and Wellington Technical Schools.
Member Parl. for Onslow 54-57, for Porirua 57-69, for Western Hutt 69-75; Minister of Local Govt., of Internal Affairs, of Civil Defence, Minister in charge of Valuation Dept. 72-75; Chair. Hutt Valley Electric Power Board 50-54.
Leisure interest: photography.
16 Dowse Drive, Lower Hutt, New Zealand.

May, William Frederick, B.S., DR.ENG.; American business executive; b. 25 Oct. 1915, Chicago; s. of Arthur W. and Florence Hartwick May; m. Kathleen Thompson 1947; two d.; ed. Oak Park and River Forest High School, Oak Park, Illinois, Univ. of Rochester, N.Y., and Harvard Business School.
Executive Dept., American Can Co. 59, Corpn. Vice-Pres. and General Man. Canco Div. 59-62, Corpn. Vice-Pres. and Gen. Manager (Planning and Development) 62-64, Corpn. Exec. Vice-Pres. (Admin.) 64-65, Vice-Chair. 65, Chair. and Chief Exec. Officer 65-75; Dir. Lincoln Center, Johns-Manville Corpn., Bankers Trust, C.E.D., American Paper Inst., Nat Council on Crime and Delinquency, *The New York Times*; Trustee Univ. of Rochester, Polytechnic Inst. of New York, Presbyterian Hospital in City of New York; Overseer, Dartmouth Coll.
Office: American Lane, Greenwich, Conn. 06830, U.S.A.
Telephone: 203-552-2011.

Mayall, Nicholas Ulrich, PH.D.; American astronomer; b. 9 May 1906, Moline, Ill.; s. of Edwin L. Mayall, Sr. and Olive Ulrich; m. Kathleen Czarina Boxall 1934; one s. one d.; ed. Univ. of Calif. at Berkeley.
Teaching Fellow in Astronomy, Univ. of Calif. at Berkeley 28-29, Martin Kellog Fellow in Astronomy 31-33; Asst. (Computer) Mount Wilson Observatory, Pasadena, Calif. 29-31; Observing Asst. Lick Observatory 33-35, Asst. Astronomer 35-42, Assoc. Astronomer 45-49, Astronomer 49-60; Staff mem. at Radiation Laboratory, Mass. Inst. of Technology 42-43; Resident Assoc., Calif. Inst. of Technology, Pasadena 43-45; Observatory Dir. Kitt Peak Nat. Observatory, Tucson, Ariz. 60-71; mem. American Astronomical Soc., American Acad. of Arts and Sciences, American Philosophical Soc., Astronomical Soc. of the Pacific

(Pres. 42, 58-59, Dir. 56-62), Nat. Acad. of Sciences (Chair. Astronomy Section 58-61, Draper Fund Cttee. 59-62, and on Space Science Board 64-70), Int. Astronomical Union (Pres. Comm. 28-, Extragalactic Nebulae 58-61), Royal Astronomical Soc., London; corresp. mem. Acad. des Sciences, Institut de France, Paris.
Leisure interests: music, reading, photography.
Publs. Numerous scientific papers including *The Radial Velocities of Fifty Globular Star Clusters* (*Astrophysical Journal*, Vol. 104) 46, *Redshifts and Magnitudes of Extragalactic Nebulae* (with M. L. Humason and A. R. Sandage, in *Astronomical Journal*, Vol. 61) 56, *Photoelectric Photometry of Galactic and Extragalactic Star Clusters* (with G. E. Kron, in *Astronomical Journal*, Vol. 65) 60, *The Expansion of Clusters of Galaxies* (with J. L. Lovasich and others, in *Proceedings of the 4th Berkeley Symposium on Mathematical Statistics*, Vol. 3) 62.
Kitt Peak National Observatory, 950 North Cherry Avenue, P.O. Box 26732, Tucson, Ariz. 85726, U.S.A.
Telephone: 602-327-5511.

Maybray-King, Baron (Life Peer), cr. 71, of the City of Southampton; **Rt. Hon. Horace Maybray King,** PH.D., LL.D., D.C.L., F.K.C.; British politician; b. 25 May 1901, Grangetown; s. of John William King and Margaret Ann King; m. 1st Victoria Harris 1924 (died 1966), 2nd Una Porter 1967; one d.; ed. Stockton Secondary School and King's Coll., Univ. of London.
Head of English Dept., Taunton's School, Southampton 25-46; Headmaster Regents Park School, Southampton 47-50; M.P. 50-71; Speaker's Panel, Chair. 53-64; Chair. of Ways and Means 64-65; Speaker of House of Commons 65-71; Deputy Speaker of House of Lords 71-; several hon. degrees.
Leisure interests: music and the entertainment of children.
Publs. *Selections from Macaulay* 33, *Selections from Homer* 40, *Selections from Sherlock Holmes* 48, *Parliament and Freedom,* 51 *State Crimes* 67, *Before Hansard* 68, *Songs in the Night* 68, *The Speaker and Parliament* 73.
37 Manor Farm Road, Southampton, Hants., England.
Telephone: Southampton 55884.

Mayer, Albert, A.B., B.S. in C.E.; American architect and town planner; b. 29 Dec. 1897, N.Y.C.; s. of Bernhard and Sophia Mayer; m. Marion Mayer 1960; one s. one d.; ed. Columbia Univ. and Mass. Inst. of Technology.
Superintendent, Gen. Sup., Gen. Man. and Pres. J. H. Taylor Construction Co. Inc. 22-34; architectural and planning practice 34-, mem. of Mayer and Whittlesey and of Mayer, Whittlesey and Glass 37-59; Consultant U.S. Housing Admin., N.Y. State Housing Div. 35-38, United Provinces (Govt. of India) 46-60, U.S. Public Housing Admin. 62-; Fellow American Inst. of Architects, Soc. for Applied Anthropology 67; Visiting Prof. Columbia Univ. 69-70; mem. American Soc. of Civil Engineers, American Inst. of Town Planning, American Inst. of Architects Cttee. on Urban Design; numerous awards and medals; designs incl. New City of Kitimat (B.C.), New City of Ashdod, Israel (consultant), New York City New School for Social Research, New Delhi Regional Plan, New City of Maumelle, Arkansas.
Publs. *Pilot Project India* 59, papers and lectures, incl. *Israel Plans* 59, *Some Implications of the Delhi Plan* 60, *Social Analysis and National Economic Planning in India* 61, *The Urgent Future* 66, *Greenbelt Towns Revisited, Town Planning in the United States* 70; *It's Not Just the Cities* (articles) 69-70; contributor to *Encyclopaedia of Urban Planning* 73.
31 Union Square West, New York, N.Y. 10003; Home: 240 Central Park South, New York, N.Y. 10019, U.S.A.
Telephone: 212-Algonquin-5-8700 (Office); 212-489-0014 (Home).

Mayer, Hans; German university professor; b. 19 March 1907; ed. Univs. of Cologne, Bonn, Berlin, and Graduate Inst. of Int. Studies, Geneva.

Emigrated from Germany 33-45; research at Int. Inst. of Social Research, New York, and Graduate Inst. of Int. Studies, Geneva 33-40; literary and dramatic critic in Switzerland 39-45; Chief Editor Frankfurt Radio 45-47; Lecturer in Sociology and the History of Culture, Akad. der Arbeit, Frankfurt 47-48; Prof. of History of Culture, Univ. of Leipzig 48-50, Prof. of the History of German Literature 50-64; Prof. History of German Literature, Technical University, Hanover 65-; Prof. and Dir. of Inst. for the History of German Literature 55; mem. Exec. Deutsche Goethe-Gesellschaft, Deutsche Schillergesellschaft, Deutsche Schiller-Stiftung, P.E.N. Club; German National Prize for Science 55; Literaturpreis der deutschen Kritiker 65, D.Phil. h.c. (Brussels) 69.

Publs. *Von der dritten zur vierten Republik: Geistige Strömungen in Frankreich 1939-1945* 45, *Georg Büchner und seine Zeit* 46, *Thomas Mann, Werk und Entwicklung* 50, *Studien zur deutschen Literaturgeschichte* 54, *Schiller und die Nation* 54, *Deutsche Literatur und Weltliteratur: Reden und Aufsätze* 57, *Richard Wagner* 59, *Von Lessing bis Thomas Mann* 59, *Meisterwerke deutscher Literaturkritik*, Vol. I 54, Vol. II 56 (editor), *Bertolt Brecht und die Tradition* 61, *Aragon, Die Karwoche* (translation from the French), *Heinrich von Kleist, Der geschichtliche Augenblick* 62, *Ansichten zur Literatur der Zeit* 62, *Dürrenmatt und Frisch, Anmerkungen* 63, *Zur deutschen Klassik und Romantik* 63, *Anmerkungen zu Brecht* 65, *Anmerkungen zu Richard Wagner* 66, *Grosse deutsche Verrisse* (editor) 67, *Zur deutschen Literatur der Zeit: Zusammenhänge, Schriftsteller, Bücher* 67, *Das Geschehen und das Schweigen, Aspekte der Literatur* 69, *Der Repräsentant und der Märtyrer, Konstellationen der Literatur* 71, *Brecht in der Geschichte* 71.

Technische Universität, 3000 Hanover; 3000 Hanover, Vinnhorsterweg 101, Federal Republic of Germany. Telephone: 71 73 88.

Mayer, John Anton, B.S., M.B.A.; American banker; b. 30 July 1909, Terre Haute, Ind.; m. Effie Fleming Disston 1937; three s.; ed. Univ. of Pennsylvania.

Joined Penn Mutual Life Insurance Co. 33, Asst. to Vice-Pres. and Comptroller 34-35, Asst. Sec. 36-39, Asst. to Pres. 39-47, Sec. 47-49; Pres. and Dir. Reliance Life Insurance Co. 49-51; Vice-Pres. Mellon Nat. Bank and Trust Co. (now Mellon Bank, N.A.) 51-57, Exec. Vice-Pres. 57-59, Pres. 59-67, Dir. 59-, Chief Exec. Officer 63-, Chair. of Board 67-; Chair. of Board and Chief Exec. Officer, Mellon Nat. Corpn. 72-; Dir. Aluminum Co. of America, H. J. Heinz Co., PPG Industries Inc., First Boston (Europe) Ltd., Gen. Motors Corpn.; official of other companies and orgs.

3955 Bigelow Boulevard, Pittsburgh, Pa. 15213, U.S.A.

Mayer, Joseph E., B.S., PH.D.; American chemical physicist; b. 5 Feb. 1904, New York City; s. of Joseph Mayer and Catherine Proescher; m. Maria Goeppert (deceased) 1930, 2nd Margaret Gannon Griffin 1972; one s. one d.; ed. Calif. Inst. of Technology and Univ. of Calif.

Asst. Dept. of Chemistry Univ. of Calif. 27-28; Int. Educ. Board Fellow, Göttingen Germany 29-30; Assoc. Chemistry Johns Hopkins Univ. 30-34, Assoc. Prof. 34-39; Assoc. Prof. Chemistry, Columbia Univ. 39-45; Prof. of Chemistry, Inst. of Nuclear Studies, Univ. of Chicago 45-55; Carl William Eisendraht Prof. of Chemistry, Enrico Fermi Inst. of Nuclear Studies, Univ. of Chicago 55-60; Prof. Chemistry, Univ. of Calif. at La Jolla 60-, Chair. Dept. of Chemistry 64-67; Consultant, Aberdeen Proving Ground, Ordnance Dept. U.S. Army 42-, Los Alamos Scientific Laboratory; Editor *Journal of Chemical Physics* 41-52; mem. Nat. Acad. of Sciences and New York Acad. of Sciences; Corresp. mem. Heidelberg Akad. der Wissenschaften; mem. American Chemical Soc., American Physical Soc. (Pres. 73), Faraday Soc., American Philosophical Soc., American Acad. of Arts and Sciences; Chair. Comm. on Thermodynamic and Statistical Mechanics; Vice-Pres. Cttee. of Constants, Int. Union of Pure and Applied Physics, Scientific Cttee. Solvay Inst., Brussels; Dr. h.c. (Univ. Libre de Bruxelles); Fellow, American Inst. of Chemists; G. N. Lewis Medal and Peter Debye Prize (Amer. Chem. Soc.); Chandler Medal (Columbia Univ.); Kirkwood Medal (Yale Univ.); James Flack Norris Award of American Chemical Soc.

Leisure interests: gardening, travel, archaeology.

Publs. *Statistical Mechanics* (with M. G. Mayer) 40, *Theory of Real Gases* (*Handbuch der Physik*) 58, *Phase Transformations in Solids* (with others) 51, *Equilibrium Statistical Mechanics* 68; scientific articles.

2345 Via Siena, La Jolla, Calif. 92037, U.S.A. Telephone: 714-459-3030.

Mayer-Gunthof, Franz Josef, DR.JUR.; Austrian industrialist; b. 18 Aug. 1894; ed. Vienna and Oxford Univs.

War Service 14-18; took over firm V. Mayer & Söhne 20; Gen. Man. A. G. der Vöslauer Kammgarn-Fabrik Bad Vöslau 45-71; Pres. Fed. of Austrian Industrialists 60-72, Textile Section, Fed. Chamber of Commerce 48; Vice-Pres. Wiener Börsekammer 49; Dir. Creditanstalt-bankverein 48, Gesellschaft der Musikfreunde und Konzerthausgesellschaft 47; Pres. Austrian U.N. Asscn. 56; mem. of Board, German Chamber of Commerce; Censor Oesterreichische Nationalbank; Hon. Citizen, Technical Univ., Vienna.

Mozartgasse 4, Vienna IV, Austria. Telephone: 65-32-25.

Mayer-Kuckuk, Theo, DR.RER.NAT.; German nuclear physicist; b. 10 May 1927, Rastatt; m. Marianne Meyer 1965; two s.; ed. Univ. of Heidelberg.

Research Fellow, Max Planck Institut für Kernphysik, Heidelberg 53-59, Scientific mem. 64; Research Fellow, California Inst. of Tech., Pasadena 60-61; Dozent, Univ. of Heidelberg 62, Tech. Univ. Munich 63; Prof. of Physics, Univ. of Bonn 65-, Dir. Inst. of Nuclear and Radiation Physics 65-; Röntgenpreis, Univ. of Giessen 64.

Leisure interest: sailing.

Publs. *Physik der Atomkerne* (2nd edn.) 74, research papers and review articles in physics journals.

Institut für Strahlen- und Kernphysik der Universität Bonn, Nussallee 14, 5300 Bonn; Home: Böckingstrasse 9, 534 Bad Honnef, Federal Republic of Germany. Telephone: (02221) 651015 (Office); (02224) 5140 (Home).

Mayhew, Christopher Paget, M.A.; British politician, writer and broadcaster; b. 12 June 1915, London; s. of Sir Basil Mayhew, K.B.E. and Dorothea Mary (née Paget); m. Cicely Elizabeth Ludlam 1949; two s. two d.; ed. Haileybury Coll. and Christ Church, Oxford.

M.P. for South Norfolk 45-50; Parl. Private Sec. to Lord Pres. of Council 45-46; Under-Sec. of State for Foreign Affairs Oct. 46-50; M.P. for Woolwich East 51-74; Minister of Defence for the Navy 64-66; Chair. ANAF Foundation, Nat. Asscn. for Mental Health (MIND), Middle East Int. Publrs. Cttee.; Labour until 74, joined Liberal Party 74.

Leisure interests: music, golf.

Publs. *Planned Investment* 39, *Those in Favour* 51, *Men Seeking God* 55, *Commercial Television: What is to be Done?* 59, *Co-existence Plus* 62, *Britain's Role Tomorrow* 67, *Party Games* 69, *Europe—The Case for Going In* (jointly) 71, *Publish It Not . . .* (with Michael Adams) 75.

39 Wool Road, Wimbledon, London, S.W.20, England. Telephone: 01-946-3460 (Home).

Mayneord, William Valentine, C.B.E., F.R.S.; British medical physicist; b. 14 Feb. 1902; s. of the late Walter Mayneord; m. Audrey Morrell 1963; ed. Prince Henry's Grammar School, Evesham and Birmingham Univ. Chairman Int. Comm. on Radiological Units. 50-53, Medical Research Council Cttee. on Protection against Ionizing Radiations 51-58; mem. Int. Comm. on Radiological Protection 50-58, U.K. Del. to UN Scientific Cttee. on Effects of Atomic Radiation 56-57; Hon. Adviser, Scientific Cttee. of Nat. Gallery 52-, Trustee, Nat. Gallery 66-71; Pres. Int. Org. for Medical Physics 65-69; Consultant to WHO; Prof. Emer. of Physics as Applied to Medicine, Univ. of London; formerly Dir. of Physics Dept., Inst. of Cancer Research, Royal Cancer Hosp.; many awards and hon. memberships of British and foreign institutions.
Publs. *Physics of X-Ray Therapy* 29, *Some Applications of Nuclear Physics to Medicine* 50, *Radiation and Health* 64; articles on application of physics to medicine and radiation hazards.
7 Downs Way Close, Tadworth, Surrey, England.
Telephone: Tadworth 2297.

Mayo, Robert Porter, A.B., M.B.A.; American government official and banker; b. 15 March 1916, Seattle, Wash.; s. of Carl A. and Edna A. Mayo; m. Marian A. Nicholson; two s. two d.; ed. Univ. of Washington.
Director of Research and tax auditor, Wash. State Tax Comm., Olympia, Wash. 38-41; Econ. Analyst and Asst. Dir. of Tech. Staff, Office of Sec. of Treasury, Wash., D.C. 41-52; Chief, Debt Analysis Staff, Treasury 53-58; Asst. for Debt Management to Sec. of Treasury 59-60; Trust Investments Vice-Pres. Continental Illinois Nat. Bank & Trust Co. of Chicago 60-67; Staff Dir. Presidents' Comm. on Budget Concepts 67; special public affairs assignments for senior management, Continental Bank 68; Dir. Bureau of the Budget and Counsellor to Pres. of U.S.A. Jan. 69-July 70; Pres. Federal Reserve Bank of Chicago July 70-.
Leisure interests: camping and travelling with family, carpentry, music.
Federal Reserve Bank, Chicago, Ill. 60690, U.S.A.
Telephone: 312-HA7-2320.

Mayobre, José A., LL.D.; Venezuelan economist and diplomatist; b. 21 Aug. 1913, Cumaná; s. of Ramón B. Mayobre and Eva Cova; m. Esperanza Machado 1941; two s.; ed. Central Univ., Caracas, London School of Economics.
Chief, Dept. of Economic Research, Central Bank of Venezuela; Alternate Gov. for Venezuela, Int. Monetary Fund; Asst. Dir. Mexican Bureau, E.C.L.A.; Resident Rep. of TAB in Central America; Dir. Venezuelan Development Corpn.; Prof. of Economic Analysis 46-60; Minister of Finance 58-61; Ambassador to U.S.A., concurrently Rep. to OAS 60-62; Commr. for Industrial Development, UN Dept. of Econ. and Social Affairs 62-63; Exec. Sec. UN Economic Comm. for Latin America (ECLA) 63-67; Minister of Mines and Petroleum, Venezuela 67-68; Rep. Sec.-Gen. of UN in Dominican Republic 65; Dir. H. L. Boulton & Cia S.A. Caracas 69-70.
Leisure interests: music, swimming.
Publs. *The Parity of the Bolivar, Philosophy and Economic Science, The Economic Situation of Venezuela; Las Inversiones Extranjeras en Venezuela;* numerous UN publications.
1a Avenida Montecristo 9, Caracas, Venezuela.
Telephone: 34-17-13.

Mayr, Ernst, PH.D.; American professor of zoology; b. 5 July 1904, Kempten, Germany; s. of Otto Mayr and Helene Pusinelli; m. Margarete Simon 1935; two d.; ed. Univs. of Greifswald and Berlin.
Assistant Curator, Univ. of Berlin 26-32; Assoc. Curator, Whitney-Rothschild Collection of American Museum of Natural History 32-44, Curator 44-53; Alexander Agassiz Prof. of Zoology, Harvard Univ. 53-, Dir. Museum of Comparative Zoology 61-70; Visiting Prof., Univ. of Minn. 49, 74, Univs. of Pavia and Wash. 51-52; Lecturer, Columbia Univ. 41, 50, Philadelphia Acad. of Sciences 47, Univ. of Calif. at Davis 67; Expeditions to Dutch New Guinea, Mandated Territory of New Guinea and Solomon Islands 28-30; six U.S. and foreign Hon. doctorates; Fellow, American Acad. of Arts and Sciences; mem. Nat. Acad. of Sciences, American Philosophical Soc.; Corresp. Fellow, Zoological Soc. of India; Hon., Foreign and Corresp. mem. of 19 foreign socs.; numerous awards including Leidy Medal of Acad. of Natural Sciences, Philadelphia 46, Wallace Darwin Medal of Linnean Soc., London 58, Daniel Giraud Eliot Medal of Nat. Acad. of Sciences 67, Centennial Medal of American Museum of Natural History 69, Nat. Medal of Science 70.
Leisure interests: natural history, history of biology.
Publs. *List of New Guinea Birds* 41, *Systematics and the Origin of Species* 42, *Birds of the Southwest Pacific* 45, *Birds of the Philippines* 46, *Methods and Principles of Systematic Zoology* 53, *The Species Problem* (Editor, American Asscn. for the Advancement of Science Publication No. 50) 57, *Animal Species and Evolution* 63, *Principles of Systematic Zoology* 69, *Populations, Species and Evolution* 70, *Evolution and the Diversity of Life* 76, and 390 articles in journals.
Museum of Comparative Zoology, Harvard University, Cambridge, Mass. 02138; Home: 11 Chauncy Street, Cambridge, Mass. 02138, U.S.A.
Telephone: 495-2476 (Office); 354-6769 (Home).

Maytag, Lewis B.; American airline executive; b. 1926; ed. Colorado College.
Chairman of Board and Pres. Nat. Airlines, Inc.; Dir. Maytag Co.
Office: P.O. Box 592055 AMF, Miami, Fla. 33159, U.S.A.

Mazar, Benjamin, D.PHIL.; Russian-born Israeli archaeologist; b. 28 June 1906; ed. Berlin and Giessen Univs.
Settled in Palestine 29; joined staff of Hebrew Univ. Jerusalem 43, Prof. of Biblical History and Archaeology of Palestine 51-, Rector 52-61, Pres. 53-61; Chair. Israel Exploration Soc.; Dir. excavations Ramat Rahel 32, Beth Shearim 36-40, 56, Beth Yerah 42-43, Tell Qasile 48-50, 59, Ein Gedi 60, 62, 64, 65, Old City of Jerusalem 68-73; Hon. mem. British Soc. for Old Testament Study, American Soc. of Biblical Literature and Exegesis; mem. Admin. Council, Int. Asscn. of Univs.; Hon. D.H.L. Hebrew Union Coll. (Jewish Inst. of Religion, U.S.A.), Jewish Theological Seminary of America.
Publs. *Untersuchungen zur alten Geschichte Syriens und Palästinas* 30, *History of Archaeological Research in Palestine* 36, *History of Palestine from the early days to the Israelite Kingdom* 38, *Beth Shearim Excavations 1936-40* 40 (2nd edn. 58), *Historical Atlas of Palestine: Israel in Biblical Times* 41, *Excavations at Tell Qasile* 51, *Ein Gedi* 64, *The World History of the Jewish People* Vol. II 67, *The Western Wall and the Ophel Hill* 74; Chair. Editorial Board *Encyclopaedia Biblica* 50.
Hebrew University of Jerusalem, Jerusalem; 9 Abarbanel Street, Jerusalem, Israel.
Telephone: 39857.

Mazeaud, Pierre; French politician; b. 24 Aug. 1929, Lyon.
Judge of Tribunal of Instance, Lamentin, Martinique 61; Sec. of State to Prime Minister 61; Judge of Tribunal of Great Instance, Versailles 62; Sec. of State to Minister of Justice 62; Sec. of State to Minister of Youth and Sports 67-68; Deputy for Hauts-de-Seine 68-73; Vice-Pres. Groupe des deputés sportifs 68; Sec. of

State to Prime Minister responsible for Youth and Sport 73-.

3 rue Palatine, 75006 Paris, France.

Mazia, Daniel, PH.D.; American biologist; b. 18 Dec. 1912, Scranton, Pa.; *s.* of Aaron Mazia and Bertha Kurtz; *m.* Gertrude Greenblatt 1938; two *d.*; ed. Univ. of Pennsylvania.

National Research Council Fellow 37-38; Asst. Prof., Assoc. Prof., Univ. of Missouri 38-42; Capt. U.S. Army Air Force 42-45; Assoc. Prof., Prof., Univ. of Missouri 45-50; Prof. of Zoology, Univ. of Calif., Berkeley 51-53; Prof. Marine Biology Laboratory, Woods Hole; mem. Nat. Acad. of Sciences; Exec. Editor *Experimental Cell Research.*

Publs. *Mitosis and the Physiology of Cell Division* 61, Editor *General Physiology of Cell Specialization* 63, 160 articles in field of cell biology.

900 Shattuck Avenue, Berkeley, Calif. 94720, U.S.A. Telephone: 525-2448.

Mazio, Aldo Maria; Italian diplomatist; b. 1907, Rome; *s.* of Alberto and Iseult Mazio; *m.* Augusta Cantu 1944; one *s.* two *d.*; ed. Università degli Studi, Rome, and Yale Univ.

Research fellow, Yale Univ. 29-30, Asst. Prof. 30-31; joined Italian Foreign Service 32, early service Cairo, Ottawa, Washington, and Holy See; Consul-Gen., New York 49-52; Asst. Perm. Sec. Ministry of Foreign Affairs 52-55; Minister Dublin 55-58; Ambassador to Tunisia 58-62; Ambassador to the Netherlands 63-65; Amb. to Belgium 65-71; Head, Del. of Comm. of European Communities in U.S.A. 71-73; retd.

Leisure interests: reading, travelling.

c/o Ministry of Foreign Affairs, Rome, Italy.

Mazrui, Ali A., M.A., D.PHIL.; Kenyan educationist; b. 24 Feb. 1933, Mombasa; ed. Univs. of Manchester, Columbia (N.Y.) and Oxford.

Lecturer in Political Science, Makerere Univ., Uganda 63-65, Prof. of Political Science 65-73, Dean of Social Sciences 67-69; Assoc. Editor *Transition* Magazine 64-73, Co-Editor *Mawazo* Journal 67-73; Visiting Prof. Univ. of Chicago 65; Research Assoc. Harvard Univ. 65-66; Dir. African Section, World Order Models Project 68-73; Visiting Prof. Northwestern Univ., U.S.A. 69, McGill and Denver Univs. 69, London and Manchester Univs. 71, Dyason Lecture Tour of Australia 72; Vice-Pres. Int. Political Science Asscn. 70-73, Int. Congress of Africanists 67-73; Fellow, Center for Advanced Study in the Behavioural Sciences, Stanford 72-73; Prof. of Political Science, Univ. of Michigan 73-; Senior Visiting Fellow, Hoover Inst. on War, Peace and Revolution, Stanford 73-; Int. Org. Essay Prize 64, Northwestern Univ. Book Prize 69.

Publs. *Towards a Pax Africana* 67, *On Heroes and Uhuru-Worship* 67, *The Anglo-African Commonwealth* 67, *Violence and Thought* 69, Co-Editor *Protest and Power in Black Africa* 70, *The Trial of Christopher Okigbo* 71, *Cultural Engineering and Nation Building in East Africa* 72, Co-Editor *Africa in World Affairs: The Next Thirty Years* 73.

Department of Political Science, University of Michigan, Haven Hall, Ann Arbor, Mich. 48104, U.S.A.

Mazurov, Kiril Trofimovich; Soviet politician; b. 1914; ed. Gomel Highway Technicum and Higher Party School.

Technician, road and bridge-building 33-36; served Soviet Army 36-39; engaged in Communist Youth League activities Gomel and Brest Oblasts 39-40; mem. C.P.S.U. 40-; served Army 41; resistance work 42; Sec. Byelorussian Communist Youth League 42-47; 1st Sec. Minsk City Party Cttee. 49-50, Regional Cttee. 50-53; Deputy to U.S.S.R. Supreme Soviet 50-; Chair. Byelorussian Council of Ministers 53-56; mem. C.P.S.U. Central Cttee. 56-; First Sec. Byelorussian C.P. 56-65; First Vice-Chair. U.S.S.R. Council of Ministers 65-;

Alt. mem. Presidium of Cen. Cttee. of C.P.S.U. 56-65, mem. 65-66, mem. Politburo 66-.

U.S.S.R. Council of Ministers, The Kremlin, Moscow, U.S.S.R.

Mbaya, Robert Bernard; Malawi civil servant and diplomatist; b. 30 June 1933, Nkhota Kota; *m.*; five *c.*; ed. Univ. of Ghana, and public admin. studies, Mpemba. Laboratory Asst., Chitedze 57; Accounts Asst., Account-ant-Gen.'s Dept. 58-62, study leave 62-66, Admin. Officer 66; Asst. District Commr., Kasupe 66; Admin. Officer, Ministry of Devt. and Planning 67, of Econ. Affairs 67-68, of Labour and Supplies 68; Principal Admin. Officer, Ministry of Labour and Supplies 68-69; Exec. Sec. Repub. Anniversary Celebrations 69; Principal Admin. Officer, Ministry of Information and Tourism 69-70; Under-Sec. Ministry of Transport and Communications 70-71; Deputy Sec. Ministry of Agriculture and Natural Resources 71-72; Perm. Sec. Ministries of Natural Resources and Transport and Communications March-June 72; Amb., Malawi Mission to UN 72-73; Amb. to U.S.A. and Perm. Rep. of Malawi to UN 73-75; High Commissioner to U.K. 75-.

Malawi High Commission, 47 Great Cumberland Place, London, W1H 8DB, England.

Mbita, Lieut.-Col. Hashim Iddi; Tanzanian journalist and army officer; b. 2 Nov. 1933, Tabora; ed. Govt. Town School, Tabora Govt. Senior Secondary School, East African School of Co-operatives, Kabete, Kenya, American Press Inst. (Columbia Univ., New York), Mons Officer Cadet School, Aldershot, England.

Assistant Co-operative Inspector 58-60; Public Relations Officer 60-62; Press Officer 62-64; Senior Press Officer 64-65; Press Sec. to the Pres. 66-67; Publicity Sec. Tanganyika African Nat. Union 67-68, Nat. Exec. Sec. 70-72; Army Officer 69; Exec. Sec., OAU Liberation Cttee. Aug. 72-.

Liberation Committee, P.O. Box 1767, Dar es Salaam, Tanzania.

M'bow, Amadou-Mahtar, L. ès L.; Senegalese educationist; b. 20 March 1921, Dakar; *m.* Raymonde Sylvain 1951; one *s.* two *d.*; ed. Faculté des Lettres, Univ. de Paris.

Professor, Coll. de Rosso, Mauritania 51-52; Dir. Service of Fundamental Educ. 53-57; Minister of Education and Culture 57-58; Prof. Lycée Faidherbe, St. Louis 58-64; Ecole Normale Supérieure, Dakar 64-66; Minister of Educ. 66-68; Minister of Culture, Youth and Sport 68-70; Asst. Dir.-Gen. for Educ., UNESCO Nov. 70-Nov. 74; Dir.-Gen. UNESCO Nov. 74-; Dr. h.c. Univs. of Buenos Aires, Granada (Spain), Sherbrooke (Canada), West Indies (Jamaica); Commdr. Ordre National (Ivory Coast), Commdr. des Palmes académiques (France), Officier, Ordre du Mérite (Senegal), Commdr. de l'Ordre national de Côte d'Ivoire, de Haute Volta.

Publs. numerous monographs, articles in educational journals, textbooks, etc.

UNESCO, Place de Fontenoy, 75700 Paris, France. Telephone: 577-16-10.

Mead, Sir Cecil, Kt.; British business executive; b. 24 Dec. 1900.

With Guest, Keen & Nettlefolds Ltd. before First World War; R.N.V.R. in First World War; after First World War joined Technical Service org. of British Tabulating Machine Co. Ltd. (now Int. Computers and Tabulators Ltd.), later District Man., Birmingham, then Asst. Sales Man., Sales Man. 39, and Dir. Hollerith Machines (South Africa) (Pty.) Ltd. (now Int. Computers and Tabulators S.A. (Pty.) Ltd.) 39; Deputy Man. Dir. British Tabulating Machine Co. Ltd. 49-55, Man. Dir. 55-59; Man. Dir. Int. Computers and Tabulators Ltd. (merger of British Tabulating Machine Co. and Powers-Samas Accounting Machines Ltd.)

59-64, Deputy Chair. 60-65, Chair. and Chief Exec. 65-67; Chair. British Inst. of Management 63-64; Dir. Int. Tutor Machines; Chair. Software Sciences Ltd. 70-; Gov. Ashridge Management Coll.; mem. Council Foundation for Management Educ.

20 Wolsey Road, East Molesey, Surrey, England.

Mead, Margaret, M.A., PH.D., D.SC., LL.D.; American anthropologist; b. 16 Dec. 1901, Philadelphia, Pa.; *d.* of Edward Sherwood and Emily Fogg Mead; one *d.*; ed. Barnard Coll. and Columbia Univ.

National Research Council Fellow (Study of Adolescent Girl in Samoa) 25-26; Asst. Curator of Ethnology, American Museum of Natural History 26-42; Assoc. Curator of Ethnology, American Museum of Natural History 42-64; Social Science Research Fellow (Study of Young Children in Admiralty Islands) 28-29; expeditions to New Guinea 31-33, 67, 73, to Bali 36-38, to Admiralty Islands 53, 64, 65, Bali 57-58; Visiting Lecturer in Child Study, Vassar Coll. 39-40, 40-41; Exec. Sec. Cttee. on Food Habits, Nat. Research Council 42-45; Dir. Columbia Univ. Research in Contemporary Cultures 48-50; adjunct. Prof. of Anthropology Columbia Univ. 54-73, Special Lecturer in Anthropology, Columbia Univ. 73-; Visiting Prof. Univ. of Cincinnati 57-, Sloan Prof. Menninger Foundation 59-63; Fogarty Scholar-in-Residence Nat. Insts. of Health 73; Pres. World Fed. for Mental Health 56-57; Pres. American Anthrop. Asscn. 60, Scientists Inst. for Public Information 70-73, Soc. for Gen. Systems Research 72-73; Curator of Ethnology, American Museum of Nat. History 64-69, Curator Emer. 69-; Consultant, Div. Social Sciences, Fordham Univ. 68-69, Chair. Div. Social Sciences and Prof. of Anthropology 68-71; mem. Nat. Acad. of Sciences 75; Pres. American Asscn. for the Advancement of Science 75; Arches of Science Award 71; Kalinga Prize 71; Wilder Penfield Award 72, Lehmann Award New York Acad. of Sciences 73.

Publs. *Coming of Age in Samoa* 28, *Growing Up in New Guinea* 30, *The Changing Culture of an Indian Tribe* 32, *Sex and Temperament in three Primitive Societies* 35, *Balinese Character: A Photographic Analysis* (with Gregory Bateson) 42, *And Keep Your Powder Dry* 42, *Male and Female* 49, *Soviet Attitudes towards Authority* 51, *Growth and Culture* (with Frances Cooke Macgregor) 51, *The Study of Culture at a distance* (ed. with Rhoda Metraux) 53, *Primitive Heritage* (ed. with Nicolas Calas) 53, *Themes in French Culture* (with Rhoda Metraux) 54, *Childhood in Contemporary Cultures* (ed. with Martha Wolfenstein) 55, *New Lives for Old* 56, *An Anthropologist at Work: The Writings of Ruth Benedict* 59, *People and Places* 59, *Continuities in Cultural Evolution* 64, *Family* (with Ken Heyman) 65, *Anthropologists and What They Do* 65, *American Women* (ed. with Frances B. Kaplan) 65, *Culture and Commitment: A Study of the Generation Gap* 70, *A Way of Seeing* (with R. Metraux) 70, *Rap on Race* (with James Baldwin *q.v.*) 71, *Blackberry Winter: My Earlier Years*, *Twentieth Century Faith* 72, *Ruth Benedict* 74, *World Enough: Rethinking the Future* (with Ken Heyman).

American Museum of Natural History, Central Park West, at 79th Street, New York, N.Y. 10024; Home: 211 Central Park West, New York, N.Y. 10024, U.S.A.

Meade, James Edward, C.B., F.B.A., M.A.; British economist; b. 23 June 1907, Swanage, Dorset; *s.* of Charles Hippisley Meade and Kathleen (née Cotton-Stapleton); *m.* Elizabeth Margaret Wilson 1933; one *s.* three *d.*; ed. Malvern Coll., Oriel Coll., Oxford, and Trinity Coll., Cambridge.

Fellow and Lecturer in Economics, Hertford Coll., Oxford 30-37, Bursar 34-37; mem. Financial Section and Economic Intelligence Service, LN; Editor LN *World Economic Survey* 38-40; mem. Economic Section Cabinet Office 40-45, Dir. 46-47; Prof. of Commerce with special reference to Int. Trade, London School of Economics 47-57; Prof. of Political Economy, Univ. of Cambridge 57-69; Nuffield Senior Research Fellow, Christ's Coll. Cambridge 69-74; Visiting Prof. of Economics and Finance in Australian Nat. Univ. 56; Pres. Section F of British Asscn. for the Advancement of Science 57; Chair. Econ. Survey Mission to Mauritius 60; Pres. Royal Econ. Soc. 64-66; Chair. Inst. for Fiscal Studies Cttee. on U.K. Tax Structure 75-.

Publs. *Public Works in their International Aspect* 33, *The Rate of Interest in a Progressive State* 33, *Economic Analysis and Policy* 36, *Consumers' Credits and Unemployment* 37, *The Economic Basis of a Durable Peace* 40, *Planning and the Price Mechanism* 48, *The Theory of International Economic Policy*, Vol. I 51, Vol. II 55, *A Geometry of International Trade* 52, *Problems of Economic Union* 53, *The Theory of Customs Unions* 55, *The Control of Inflation* 58, *A Neo-Classical Theory of Economic Growth* 61, *Efficiency, Equality, and the Ownership of Property* 64, *The Stationary Economy* 65, *The Growing Economy* 68, *The Theory of Indicative Planning* 70, *The Controlled Economy*, *The Theory of Economic Externalities* 73, *The Intelligent Radical's Guide to Economic Policy* 75.

40 High Street, Little Shelford, Cambridge CB2 5ES, England.

Meadows, Bernard William; British sculptor; b. 19 Feb. 1915; ed. City of Norwich School, Norwich School of Art and Royal Coll. of Art.

Exhibited Venice Biennale 52, 64, British Council Exhbns., N. and S. America, Germany, Canada, New Zealand, Australia, Scandinavia, Finland and France; open-air exhbns. of Sculpture, Battersea Park, London 52, 60, 63, 66, Holland Park 57, Antwerp 53, 59, Arnhem 58, British Pavilion, Brussels 58, São Paulo Bienal 58, Carnegie Inst., Pittsburgh 59-61; one-man exhibitions London and New York 57-; works in Tate Gallery, Victoria and Albert Museum and collections in Europe, America and Australia; Prof. of Sculpture, Royal Coll. of Art, London 60-.

34 Belsize Grove, London, N.W.3, England.

Meagher, Blanche Margaret, O.C., B.A., M.A.; Canadian diplomatist, retd.; b. 27 Jan. 1911; ed. St. Patrick's High School, Mount St. Vincent Coll., and Dalhousie Univ., Halifax, Nova Scotia.

Teacher, Halifax Public Schools 32-42; Dept. of External Affairs 42-, served Ottawa, Mexico, London, Tel Aviv, Vienna, Kenya, Uganda; Ambassador to Israel 58-61, concurrently High Commr. in Cyprus 61; Ambassador to Austria 62-66; Gov. from Canada, Int. Atomic Energy Agency 62-66; Chair. Board of Govs., Int. Atomic Energy Agency Sept. 64-65; High Commr. to Kenya Feb. 67-Aug. 69, to Uganda April 67-Aug. 69; Amb. to Sweden 69-73; Diplomat-in-Residence, Dalhousie Univ., Halifax, Nova Scotia Sept. 73-; mem. Board of Trustees, Nat. Museums Corpn.; D.C.L. h.c. 6899 Armview Avenue, Halifax, Nova Scotia, Canada. Telephone: 423-0895.

Meany, George; American trade unionist; b. 16 Aug. 1894, N.Y.C.; *m.* Eugenia McMahon 1919; three *d.*

Plumber's apprentice 10, journeyman plumber 15; business rep. Plumbers' Local Union 463 N.Y.C. 22-34; Pres. N.Y. State Fed. of Labor 34-39; Sec.-Treas. American Fed. of Labor 40-52, Pres. 52-55; Pres. American Fed. of Labor and Congress of Industrial Organisations (AFL-CIO) (combined org.) 55-; mem. Nat. Defense Mediation Board 41-42; War Labor Board 42-45, U.S. Del. UN 57, 59; Hon. Dr. Iur. (Seton Hall, Long Island Univ., Univ. of Pennsylvania, DePaul Univ., St. John's Univ., Boston Coll., Univ. of Mass., Fordham Univ., Catholic Univ., Georgetown Univ., Iona Coll.); Laetare Medallist 55; Americanism Gold Medal VFW 49; Presidential Medal of Freedom Award

64; Grand Official of Order of Merit of the Republic of Italy, and other honours; Democrat.
Leisure interests: golf, painting.
Home: 7535 Cayuga Avenue, Bethesda, Md.; Office: AFL-CIO Building, 815 16th Street, N.W., Washington, D.C. 20006, U.S.A.

Mébiame, Léon; Gabonese politician; b. 1 Sept. 1934, Libreville; ed. Coll. Moderne, Libreville, Centre de Préparation aux Carrières Administratives, Brazzaville, Ecole Fédérale de Police, Ecole Nat. de Police, Lyon, France.
Posted in Chad 57-59; Police Supt. 60; further studies at Sûreté Nat. Française, Paris; Deputy Dir. Sûreté Nat., Gabon 62-63, Dir. 63-67; successively Under-Sec. of State for the Interior, Minister Del. for the Interior and Minister of State in charge of Labour, Social Affairs and the Nat. Org. of Gabonese Women 67; Vice-Pres. of the Govt., Keeper of the Seals and Minister of Justice Jan.-July 68; Vice-Pres. of the Govt. in charge of Co-ordination 68-75, Pres. Nat. Consultative Council 72; Prime Minister, Minister of Co-ordination, Housing and Town Planning April 75-; Commdr. Etoile Equatoriale; Grand Officier, Ordre Nat. de Côte d'Ivoire, du Mérite Centrafricain; Chevalier, Etoile Noire du Bénin.
Office du Premier Ministre, B.P. 546, Libreville, Gabon.

Mechelen, Frans van; Belgian politician; b. 26 April 1923, Turnhout (Antwerp); s. of Peter August van Mechelen and Eugenia van Noppem; m. Maria-Jozefa van de Velde 1950; two s. one d.; ed. Université Catholique de Louvain.
Former civil servant, Ministry of Labour and Social Welfare; Prof. of Sociology, Catholic Univ., Louvain; Deputy (Social Christian Party) 65-; Pres. Bond van Grote en van Jonge Gezinnen, Mens en Riumte; Minister of Dutch Culture 68-73.
Leisure interest: reading.
c/o Christelijke Volkspartij, Tweekerkenstraat 41, B-1040 Brussels; Waversebaan 180, B 3030 Heverlee, Belgium.
Telephone: 02/2-19-10-70 (Office); 016/22-47-01 (Home).

Mecklinger, Ludwig; German lawyer, doctor and politician; b. 1919.
Minister of Health 71-.
Ministerium für Gesundheitswesen, Rathausstrasse 3, 102 Berlin, German Democratic Republic.

Medani, Mustafa, M.A.; Sudanese diplomatist; b. 1930; m.; four c.; ed. Cambridge Univ.
Joined Ministry of Foreign Affairs 58; Consul-Gen. Damascus 58-60; Asst. Head of Confs. and Treaties Section, Ministry of Foreign Affairs 60-61; First Sec., London 61-63; Amb. to Lebanon, concurrently accred. to Syria and Jordan 65-69, to Czechoslovakia, concurrently accred. to Hungary 69-71; Deputy Under-Sec. for Political Affairs and Acting Under-Sec. 71-72; Amb. to Ethiopia 72-74; Perm. Rep. to UN Oct. 74-; Head of del. to UN Conf. on Human Rights, Teheran 67, to Foreign Ministers' Conf., OAU 74, del. to several int. confs.
Permanent Mission of Sudan to the United Nations, 757 Third Avenue, 24th Floor, New York, N.Y. 10017, U.S.A.

Medaris, Maj.-Gen. John; American army officer (retd.) and clergyman; b. 12 May 1902, Milford, Ohio; s. of William R. Medaris and Jessie LeSourd (both deceased); m. Virginia Smith 1931; one s. two d.; ed. Ohio State Univ.
U.S. Marine Corps in First World War 18-19; army service 21-27; management and business in S. America and U.S.A. 28-39; recalled to U.S. Army 39; served in France, Germany and Central Europe; Chief U.S. Army Mission to Argentina 48-52; Commdg. Gen., Army Ballistic Missile Agency, Redstone Arsenal 56-58; Commdg. Gen., U.S. Army Ordnance Missile Command

58-60; Pres. Lionel Corpn. 60-62, Vice-Chair. 62-63; Chair. Board Electronic Teaching Labs., Washington 60-61; Chair. Exec. Cttee. All-State Devt. Corpn., Miami 62-63; Pres. Medaris Management Inc. 63-70, Chair. of Board 70-; Chair. Radio Free Europe; Board of Dirs. Pan Amer. Funds 73-; ordained Deacon, Episcopal Church 69, Priest 70; Assoc. Rector, Episcopal Church of the Good Shepherd 73-; Chair. Board, World Center for Liturgical Studies 73-; D.S.M. (one Oak Leaf Cluster), Soldiers Medal, Legion of Merit (Oak Leaf Cluster), Croix de Guerre with Palm.
Leisure interests: golf, fishing.
Publ. *Count Down for Decision* 60.
Episcopal Church of the Good Shepherd, Maitland, Fla. 32751; Home: 1050 Cottontail Lane, Maitland, Fla. 32751, U.S.A.

Medawar, Sir Peter Brian, C.H., Kt., C.B.E., M.A., D.SC., F.R.S.; British biological scientist; b. 28 Feb. 1915, Rio de Janeiro, Brazil; s. of Nicholas Medawar and Edith Muriel (Dowling); m. Jean Shinglewood Taylor 1937; two s. two d.; ed. Marlborough Coll. and Magdalen Coll., Oxford.
Lecturer in Zoology, Oxford Univ. 38-47; Mason Prof. of Zoology, Birmingham Univ. 47-51; Jodrell Prof. of Zoology, Univ. Coll., London Univ. 51-62; Dir. Nat. Inst. for Medical Research 62-71; currently Head, Div. of Surgical Sciences, Clinical Research Centre; Pres. British Asscn. for Advancement of Science 68-69; Hon. Foreign Assoc. Nat. Acad. of Sciences, U.S.A., American Philosophical Soc., American Acad. Arts and Sciences, New York Acad. of Sciences; Royal Medallist, Royal Soc. 59, Nobel Prize in Medicine and Physiology 60; Copley Medal, Royal Soc. 69, Hamilton Fairley Medal, Royal Coll. of Physicians 71.
Publs. *The Uniqueness of the Individual* 58, *The Future of Man* 60, *The Art of the Soluble* 67, *Induction and Intuition in Scientific Thought* 69, *The Hope of Progress* 72, *Introduction to Biological Ideas* 76; scientific papers on growth, ageing, wound healing and transplantation.
25 Downshire Hill, London NW3 1NT, England.
Telephone: 01-435-0822.

Medeiros, H. E. Cardinal Humberto S.; American ecclesiastic; b. 6 Oct. 1915, Arrifes, Island of São Miguel, Portuguese Azores; ed. Catholic Univ., Washington, D.C.
Ordained 46; Asst. Priest, St. John of God, Somerset 46, St. Michael's, Fall River 46-47, Our Lady of Health, Fall River 47, Mount Carmel Parish Church, New Bedford 49; Chaplain, St. Vincent de Paul Health Camp 48-49; research 49-50; Asst. Priest, Holy Name parish, Fall River 50; Asst. Chancellor, Fall River diocese 51-53, Vice-Chancellor and subsequently Chancellor 53-56; Pastor, St. Michael's, Fall River 60-66; Bishop of Brownsville, Tex. 66-70; Archbishop of Boston 70-73; created Cardinal by Pope Paul VI 73.
2101 Commonwealth Avenue, Brighton, Mass. 02135, U.S.A.

Médici, Gen. Emilio Garrastazú; Brazilian army officer and politician; b. 4 Dec. 1905, Bagé, Rio Grande do Sul; ed. Military Acad., Rio Grande do Sul.
Head, Secret Service of 2nd Mil. Region, subsequently Chief of Staff; Head, Brazilian Mil. Acad., Agulhas Negras 64; Mil. Attaché, Washington, D.C. 64-66; Commdr. 3rd Mil. Region 66; Head, Nat. Intelligence Service 67; Head, Third Army Command April-Oct. 69; Pres. of Brazil 69-74.
c/o Office of the President, Brasília, Brazil.

Medici, Giuseppe; Italian agricultural economist and politician; b. 24 Oct. 1907; ed. Univs. of Milan and Bologna.
Professor of Agricultural Econs., Univ. of Perugia 35, of Turin 36-47; Pres. Istituto Nazionale di Economia

Agraria, Rome 47-62; mem. Italian dels. to ECA international confs.; Pres. Ente Maremma (Land Reform Agency) 51-53; Prof. Univ. of Naples 52, Univ. of Rome 60; mem. of the Senate (Christian Democrat); Minister of Agriculture 54-55, of the Treasury 56-June 58, of the Budget July 58-Jan. 59, of Education Feb. 59-July 60; Minister without Portfolio (with responsibilities for Administrative Reform) 62-63, Minister of the Budget June-Nov. 63, Minister of Industry and Commerce Dec. 63-March 65; Minister of Foreign Affairs June-Dec. 68, 72-73; Gov. European Investment Bank 58; Pres. Senate Comm. for Foreign Affairs 60-62; Pres. World Food Conf., Rome 74.

Publs. include *Principii di Estimo* 48 (abridged edn. in English *Principles of Appraisal* 53); *Italy: Agricultural Aspects* 49, *I Tipi d'Impresa dell'Agricoltura* 51, *Agricoltura e Disoccupazione* Vol. I 52, *Land Property and Land Tenure in Italy* 52, *Lezioni di Politica Economica* 67.
The Senate, Rome, Italy.

Medvedev, Roy Alexandrovich, PH.D.; Soviet historian and sociologist; b. 14 Nov. 1925, Tbilisi; s. of Alexander Medvedev and Yulia Medvedeva; twin brother of Zhores Medvedev (*q.v.*); m. Galina A. Gaidina 1956; one s.; ed. Leningrad State Univ., Acad. of Pedagogical Sciences of U.S.S.R.
Teacher of History, Ural Secondary School 51-53; Dir. of Secondary School in Leningrad region 54-56; Deputy to Editor-in-Chief of Publ. House of Pedagogical Literature, Moscow 57-59; Head of Dept., Research Inst. of Professional Educ., Acad. of Pedagogical Sciences of U.S.S.R. 60-70, Senior Scientist 70-71.
Publs. *Professional Education in Secondary School* 60, *A Question of Madness* (with Zhores Medvedev) 71, *Let History Judge* 72, *On Socialist Democracy* 75, *Qui a écrit le "Don Paisible"?* 75, *Khrushchev—The Years in Power* (with Zhores Medvedev) 76.
Abonement Post Box 45, Moscow G-19, U.S.S.R.

Medvedev, Zhores Alexandrovich, PH.D.; Soviet biologist; b. 14 Nov. 1925, Tbilisi; s. of Alexander Romanovich Medvedev and Yulia Medvedeva; twin brother of Roy Medvedev (*q.v.*); m. Margarita Nikolaevna Buzina 1951; two s.; ed. Timiriasev Acad. of Agricultural Sciences, Moscow, Inst. of Plant Physiology, U.S.S.R. Acad. of Sciences.
Scientist, later Senior Scientist, Dept. of Agrochemistry and Biochemistry, Timiriasev Acad. 51-62; Head of Laboratory of Molecular Radiobiology, Inst. of Medical Radiology, Obninsk 63-69; Senior Scientist All-Union Scientific Research Inst. of Physiology and Biochemistry of Farm Animals, Borovsk 70-72; with Nat. Inst. for Medical Research, London 73-.
Leisure interests: social research and writing, travel.
Publs. *Protein Biosynthesis and Problems of Heredity, Development and Aging* 63, *Molecular-Genetic Mechanisms of Development* 68, *The Rise and Fall of T. D. Lysenko* 69, *The Medvedev Papers* 70, *A Question of Madness* (with Roy Medvedev) 71, *Ten Years After* 73, *Khrushchev—The Years in Power* (with Roy Medvedev) 76.
c/o National Institute for Medical Research, Mill Hill, London NW7, England.
Telephone: 01-959-3666.

Meeker, Leonard C., A.B., LL.B.; American lawyer and diplomatist; b. 4 April 1916, Montclair, N.J.; s. of Irving Avard Meeker and Elizabeth Louise Carpenter; m. 2nd Beverly Joan Meeker 1969; two s. two d. (by previous m.); ed. Amherst Coll. and Harvard Univ.
Attorney, Treasury Dept. 40-41, Dept. of Justice 41-42; U.S. Army Lieut. 42-46; Asst. to the Legal Adviser, Dept. of State 46-51, Asst. Legal Adviser for UN Affairs 51-61, Dep. Legal Adviser 61-64, Acting Legal Adviser 64-65, Legal Adviser 65-69; U.S. Amb. to Romania 69-73; Trustee, Potomac School 59-67,

Chair. of Board 60-63; mem. American Bar Asscn., Fed. Bar Asscn., American Soc. of Int. Law; Hon. LL.D. Amherst Coll.; Rockefeller Public Service Award 68.
3000 Chain Bridge Road, N.W., Washington, D.C. 20016, U.S.A.

Meer, Khurshid Hasan; Pakistani lawyer and politician; b. 14 July 1925, Srinagar; ed. Aligarh Muslim Univ. and Law Coll., Lahore.
Practising lawyer, Rawalpindi 52-; joined Azad Pakistan Party 52; Sec. Combined Opposition Parties, Rawalpindi 64; founding mem. Pakistan People's Party; mem. Nat. Assembly 70-; Minister of Presidential Cabinet 72-74, of Labour, Health, Social Welfare and Population Planning Oct.-Dec. 74.
National Assembly, Rawalpindi, Pakistan.

Meester, Eibert; Netherlands politician; b. 1919; ed. Technical Evening School.
Draughtsman and Asst. Managing Dir. Electrical Apparatus Works 35-43; Resistance Movement, Second World War; Second Sec. and District Official, Labour Party 46; Gen. Sec. Youth Section, Labour Party, Co-founder and Sec. Politieke Jongeren Contactraad 46-52; Sec. Zuid-Holland District, Labour Party 52-59; Nat. Sec. and Treas., Labour Party 58-67; M.P. 63-.
Tesselschadestraat 31, Amsterdam-West, Netherlands.

Megson, Claude Walter, M.ARCH.; New Zealand architect; b. 29 July 1936, Whangarei; s. of Cecil Wallace Megson and Anne Storey; m. Cherie Elizabeth Willson 1968; ed. Whangarei Boys High School, Auckland Univ.
Began architectural practice 63; Senior Lecturer Auckland Univ. School of Architecture 69-; Nat. Award of Merit (Jopling House), N.Z. Inst. of Architects 67, Bronze Medal (Wong House), N.Z. Inst. of Architects 69, Architectural Design Awards of Architectural Asscn. for Shopping Complex 69, Town Houses 71, Architect's Own House 72.
Major works: Wade House 63, Jopling House 65, Wong House 67, Mrkusich Town Houses 68, Good House 69, Todd House 70, Barr House 73, Cocker Town Houses 74.
Leisure interests: classical music, photography, modern art, gardening.
27 Dingle Road, St. Heliers, Auckland 5, New Zealand. Telephone: 556-822.

Mehedebi, Bahsir; Tunisian politician; b. 1912.
Ambassador to Lebanon, Kuwait, Libya 65-70; Sec.-Gen. Ministry of Foreign Affairs 70-71; Minister of Defence 71-72; Amb. to U.K. 72-74, to Morocco 74-; mem. Political Bureau, Socialist Destour Party Oct. 71-.
Embassy of Tunisia, 6 avenue de Fez, Rabat, Morocco.

Mehl, Robert Franklin, PH.D., D.SC., D.ENG.; American university professor and consultant; b. 30 March 1898, Lancaster, Pa.; s. of George H. Mehl and Sarah W. Mehl; one s. two d.; ed. Franklin and Marshall Coll., Lancaster, Princeton and Harvard Univs.
Superintendent, Div. of Physical Metallurgy, Naval Research Lab., Wash. 27-31; Asst. Dir. of Research Armco Steel Co., Middletown, Ohio 31-32; Prof. Dept. Chair. Metallurgy 35-60; Dean of Graduate Studies Carnegie-Mellon Univ., Pittsburgh 57-60; Consultant U.S. Steel Corpn., Zurich 60-65; Distinguished Visiting Prof. Univ. of Del. 65-67, Syracuse Univ., N.Y. 67-69; Emer. Dean of Graduate Studies, Carnegie-Mellon Univ. 66-; mem. Nat. Acad. of Sciences; Hon. mem. several foreign scientific socs.; twelve medals; seven hon. doctorates.
Leisure interests: painting, literature, travel and history of science.
Publs. *Iron and Steel* (in Portuguese) 44, *Brief History*

of the Science of Metals 48, and two hundred scientific papers, relating chiefly to reactions in the solid state. Royal Windsor Apartments, No. 701, 222 Melwood Avenue, Pittsburgh, Pa. 15213, U.S.A.

Mehlhouse, Harvey G., B.A.; American business executive; b. Olivia, Minn.; *m.* Ellen Larsen 1932; one *s.* one *d.*; ed. North Cen. Coll., Naperville, Ill.
With Western Electric Co. 29-, Supt. of Mfg. Engineering 51-, mem. Staff of subsid., Sandia Corpn. 52-55, Gen. Man. Merrimack Valley works of Western Electric Co., N. Andover, Mass. 55, Vice-Pres. Western's Mfg. Area Operations 57, Vice-Pres. in Charge of Mfg. Div. Staff Functions 60, Vice-Pres. Personnel and Public Rels. 62, Dir. and Exec. Vice-Pres. in Charge of Corporate Staff Activities 65, mem. Exec. Cttee. and Exec. Vice-Pres. in Charge of Mfg. Operations and related Engineering Activities 67, Senior Exec. Vice-Pres. Oct. 69, Pres., Chief Exec. Officer 69-71, Chair. of Board 71-72; Dir. Bell Telephone Laboratories, Sandia Corpn., Teletype Corpn., MFB Mutual Insurance Co., Uniroyal Inc.; Hon. D.Sc. (North Cen. Coll., Naperville, Ill.).
Leisure interests: golf, photography, bridge.
875 Camino Real, Boca Raton, Fla. 33432, U.S.A.

Mehnert, Klaus, PH.D.; German professor and journalist; b. 10 Oct. 1906, Moscow, Russia; *s.* of Hermann Mehnert and Louise (née Heuss); *m.* Enid Keyes 1933 (died 1955); ed. Univs. of Tübingen, Munich, Berlin and California (Berkeley).
Secretary German Academic Exchange Service, Berlin 29-31, German Soc. for Study of Eastern Europe (also Editor *Osteuropa*) 31-33; newspaper corresp. in Moscow 34-36; Visiting Prof. Univ. of Calif. 36-37; Asst. Prof. of Modern History and Political Science, Univ. of Hawaii 37-41; Prof. German Medical Acad. and St. John's Univ.; Editor *The XXth Century*, Shanghai 41-45; in charge of Russian section, German Office for Peace Questions, Stuttgart 47-48; Editor-in-Chief *Christ und Welt* 49-54, *Osteuropa* 51-75; Radio and TV Commentator 50-; Prof. of Political Science, Aachen Inst. of Technology 61-72; Senior Fellow Columbia Univ., New York 72-73, 75; mem. Deutsche Akademie für Wissenschaft und Literatur, Mainz, PEN Club; Grand Cross of the Order of Merit.
Leisure interest: hiking.
Publs. *Youth in Soviet Russia* 32, *The Russians in Hawaii 1804-19* 39, *Stalin versus Marx* 51, *Asien, Moskau und Wir* 56, *Soviet Man and His World* 60, *Peking and Moscow* 63, *Maos Zweite Revolution* 66, *Der Deutsche Standort* 67, *Peking and The New Left* 69, *China Today* 72, *Moscow and the New Left* 75.
7298 Lossburg 2, Schömberg-Blumenhof, Federal Republic of Germany.

Mehr, Farhang, LL.M., PH.D.; Iranian lawyer and economist; b. 1924; ed. Univs. of Teheran, Southampton and London.
Professor of Law and Public Finance; Legal Adviser, Head of Industrial Relations Dept., Nat. Iranian Oil Co. 57; Adviser to High Council of Econs. and to Minister of Commerce 58; Dir.-Gen. Petroleum and Int. Affairs 59; Gov. for Iran, Org. of Petroleum Exporting Countries 63-68; Dir.-Gen. of Econ. Affairs 63-; Deputy Minister of Finance 64-; Asst. Prime Minister 66-; Chair. of Board, Man. Dir. Iran Insurance Co. 67-; Chair. Ancient Iranian Cultural Soc. 63, Zoroastrian Anjuman 65; mem. Boards of Trustees, Teheran Coll. of Insurance, Kerman Univ., Computer Coll., Inst. for Int. Political and Economic Studies; Chancellor Pahlavi Univ. 72-; Order of Homayoun Third and Second Class, Order of Taj Second Class, Order of Sepah First Class, Order of Kah First Class, Order of Abadani va Pishraft First Class.
Publs. *Labour Law and Social Insurance* 60, *Government Corporation* 64, *Public Finance* 67.
Chancellor's Office, Pahlavi University, Shiraz, Iran.

Mehra, Air Chief Marshal Om Parkash, M.A., P.V.S.M.; Indian air force officer; b. 19 Jan. 1919, Lahore (now in Pakistan); *s.* of Jagat Ram Mehra and Rani Amma; *m.* Satya Mehra 1946; three *s.* one *d.*; ed. Govt. Coll. Lahore and Punjab Univ.
Joined Air Force 40; graduated Staff Coll., Quetta 43; commanded air force training insts. 47-53; Dir. Training Air H.Q. 53-54; Dean Inst. of Armament Technology 60-63; Air Officer in charge of Maintenance Command 63-67, in charge Maintenance at Air H.Q. 67-69; Deputy Chief Air Staff 69-71; Chair. Hindustan Aeronautics Ltd. 71-73; Chief of Air Staff 73-; Param Vishisht Seva Medal 68.
Leisure interest: golf, gardening, reading.
Air Headquarters, Vayu Bhavan, New Delhi 110011, India.
Telephone: New Delhi 372517.

Mehta, Asoka, B.A.; Indian politician; b. 24 Oct. 1911; ed. Wilson Coll., Bombay, and Bombay Univ. School of Economics.
Founder-mem. of former Socialist Party; imprisoned five times; Editor of official organ of former Socialist party 35-39; mem. Nat. Exec. of Socialist Party for 25 years; fmr. Chair. Praja Socialist Party; mem. Lok Sabha 54-57, 58-61, 67-; Deputy Chair. Indian Planning Comm. 63-66; Minister of Planning 66-67, of Petroleum, Chemicals and Social Welfare 67-Aug. 68.
Publs. *The Communal Triangle in India, Who Owns India, Political Mind of India, Democratic Socialism, Politics of Planned Economy, Socialism and Peasantry, Indian Shipping and The Plan: Perspective and Problems.*
5 Dadysett Road, Bombay, India.
Telephone: 35-77-36.

Mehta, Hansa; Indian educationist and social reformer; b. 3 July 1897, Surat (Gujerat); *d.* of Sir Manubhat Mehta; *m.* Dr. Jivraj Mehta (*q.v.*); one *s.* one *d.*; ed. Baroda Coll. and Bombay Univ.
President Gujerat Women's Co-operative Society, Bombay 28-48, The Bhagini Samej, Bombay 44-52; Parl. Sec. (Educ. and Health) Govt. of Bombay 37-39; mem. Bombay Legislative Council 37-39, 41-52; Vice-Chancellor Indian Women's Univ. 46-48; Pres. All Indian Women's Conf. 45-46; Mem. Human Rights Comm. 47-52, Vice-Chair. 50-52; mem. Bombay Legislative Council 37-40, Constituent Assembly 47-50, Secondary Educ. Comm. Govt. of India 52; Vice-Chancellor, Maharaja Sayajirao Univ. of Baroda 49-58; mem. Gen. Advisory Board of Education, Govt. of India; mem. Exec. Board UNESCO 58-60; Padma Bhushan 59; Hon. LL.D. (Leeds 64), Hon. D.Litt. (Allahabad 58, Baroda 59).
Leisure interests: reading, writing, weaving.
Publs. (Gujerati) *Balwartavali* 26, *Kishorvatavali* 28, *Tran Natako* 28, *Rukmini* 32, *Bavalana Parakrano* 34, *Golibarni Musafri* 34, *Arun nu Adbhut Swapnu* 34, *Himalaya Swarup ne Bija Natako* 41, Gujerati trans. *Hamlet* and *Merchant of Venice* 42, 44; (English) *Women under the Hindu Law of Marriage and Succession* 44, *Tract on Post-War Educational Reconstruction* 45, *Civil Liberties* 45, *Adventures of King Vikram* 48.
Everest House, 14 Carmichael Road, Bombay 26, India.
Telephone: 364159.

Mehta, Jivraj Narayan, L.M.S., F.C.P.S. (Bombay), M.D., M.R.C.P. (London); Indian politician, physician and diplomatist; b. 29 Aug. 1887, Amreli, Gujarat; *s.* of Narayan Mulji and Jamakbai Mehta; *m.* Kumari Hansaben Manubhai 1924; one *s.* one *d.*; ed. Amreli High School, Grant Medical Coll., Bombay and The London Hospital, London.
Chief Medical Officer State of Baroda 23-25; Dean, Seth G.S. Medical Coll. and K.E.M. Hospital 25-42; Pres. India Medical Conf. 30-44, 47; Imprisoned for activities in "Quit India" Movement 32-34, 42-44; mem. Board of

Scientific and Industrial Research India 44-63; Sec. and Dir.-Gen. Health Services Govt. of India 47-48; Dewan State of Baroda 48-49; Minister for Public Works, Govt. of Bombay 49-51, Minister for Finance 52-60; Pres. Indian Conf. of Social Work 50, 52-54; mem. Atomic Research Cttee. 51-60; Vice-Chair. Gandhi Memorial Leprosy Foundation 52-; mem. Governing Body All India Inst. of Medical Sciences 57-63, 71-; Chair. Exec. Council Central Drug Research Inst., Lucknow 48-60; Chief Minister Gujarat 60-63; Indian High Commr. in U.K. 63-66; Chair. Amreli Jilla Vidya Sabha (Educ. Soc.) 59-; Chair. Bombay Gandhi Memorial Trust 67-70; Vice-Chair. All-India Prohibition Council 68-73; mem. Lok Sabha 71-.

Leisure interest: social work.

Publs. *Presence of Glycogen in Suprarenal Bodies*, *The Height, Weight & Chest measurements enquiry relating to some School Children in Bombay*.

Everest House, 14 Carmichael Road, Bombay 26, India.

Mehta, Zubin (son of violinist Mehli Mehta); Indian conductor; b. 1936, Bombay; ed. Vienna Acad. of Music, studied under Hans Swarowsky.

First professional conducting in Belgium and Yugoslavia; Chief Conductor of Montreal Symphony; Musical Dir. Los Angeles Philharmonic Orchestra 61-; conductor at festivals of Holland, Prague, Vienna, Salzburg and Spoleto; debut at La Scala Milan 66; conducts regularly with the Vienna, Berlin and Israel Philharmonic Orchestras; Musical Adviser, Israel Philharmonic 68-; winner of Liverpool Int. Conductors' Competition 58; Music Dir. Maggio Musicale, Florence 69.

Office: 135 North Grand Avenue, Los Angeles, Calif. 90012, U.S.A.

Meinwald, Jerrold, M.A., PH.D.; American professor of chemistry; b. 16 Jan. 1927, New York, N.Y.; s. of Dr. Herman Meinwald and Sophie Baskind; m. Dr. Yvonne Chu 1955; two d.; ed. Brooklyn and Queen's Colls., Univ. of Chicago and Harvard Univ.

Instructor in Chem. Cornell Univ. 52-54, Asst. Prof. 54-58, Assoc. Prof. 58-61, Prof. 61-72, Act. Chair. of Chem. 68; Prof. of Chem. Univ. of Calif., San Diego 72-73; Prof. of Chem. Cornell Univ. 73-; Chemical Consultant, Schering Corpn. 57-, Norwich Pharmacal Co. 58-; mem. of Visiting Cttee. for Chem., Brookhaven Nat. Lab. 69-73; numerous lectureships incl. Louderman Lecturer Washington Univ. 64, Venable Lecturer Univ. of N. Carolina 70; Stieglitz Lecturer Univ. of Chicago 72; Reilly Lecturer, Notre Dame Univ. 72; Priestly Lecturer, Pa. State Univ. 73; Sigma Xi, National Lecturer 75; mem. Medicinal Chem. Study Section "A" of Nat. Insts. of Health 64-66, Chair. 66-68; Editorial Board of *Organic Reactions* 67-, *Journal of Chemical Ecology* 74-; Chair. Div. of Organic Chem., American Chemical Soc. 68; Alfred P. Sloan Foundation Fellow 58-62, Guggenheim Fellow 60-61, Nat. Insts. of Health Special Postdoctoral Fellow 67-68; Research Dir. Int. Centre of Insect Physiology and Ecology, Nairobi 70-; Advisory Board, Petroleum Research Fund 70-73; Visiting Prof. Rockefeller Univ. 70; Visiting Prof. Univ. of Calif., San Diego 70; mem. Nat. Acad. of Sciences, Fellow, American Acad. of Arts and Sciences.

Leisure interests: playing flute and recorder.

Publs. Over 160 research articles in major chem. journals; *Advances in Alicyclic Chemistry* Vol. I (Co-Author) 66.

Department of Chemistry, Cornell Univ., Ithaca, New York 14853, U.S.A.

Telephone: 607-256-3301.

Meir, Golda; Israeli politician; b. Goldie Mabovitch 3 May 1898, Kiev, Ukraine (now U.S.S.R.); m. Morris Myerson (deceased); hebraized name to Meir 56; one s. one d.; ed. Teachers' Seminary, Milwaukee, U.S.A.

Teacher and leading mem. Zionist Labour Party, Milwaukee; Del. U.S. section World Jewish Congress until 21; immigrated Palestine 21; joined Merhavia collective farm village; with Solel Boneh, Histadruth Contracting and Public Works Enterprise 24-26; Sec. Women's Labour Council of Histadruth 28; mem. Exec. and Secretariat Fed. of Labour 29-46; Chair. Board of Dirs., Workers' Sick Fund 36; Head Political Dept., Fed. of Labour; Mapai Del., Actions Cttee., World Zionist Organization; mem. War Economic Advisory Council of Palestine Govt. 39; Head Political Dept., Jewish Agency for Palestine, Jerusalem 46-48; Israel Minister to U.S.S.R. Aug. 48-April 49; mem. Knesset until 74; Minister of Labour and Social Insurance 49-56; Minister of Foreign Affairs June 56-Jan. 66; Sec.-Gen. Mapai Feb. 66-68; Prime Minister 69-74; Hon. doctorate (Tel-Aviv Univ.) 71.

Publ. *My Life* (autobiog.) 75.

8 Habaron Hirsch Street, Ramat Aviv, Israel.

Meister, Alton, B.S., M.D.; American professor of biochemistry; b. 1 June 1922, New York, N.Y.; s. of Morris and Florence G. Meister; m. Leonora Garten Meister 1943; two s.; ed. Harvard Coll. and Cornell Univ. Medical Coll.

Intern and Asst. Resident, New York Hospital, N.Y. 46; Commissioned Officer (Biochemical research), Nat. Insts. of Health, Bethesda, Md. 47-55; Prof. and Chair. Dept. of Biochem., Tufts Univ. School of Medicine, Boston, Mass. 55-67; Prof. and Chair. Dept. of Biochem., Cornell Univ. Medical Coll. 67-; Visiting Prof. of Biochem., Univ. of Washington, Seattle 59, Univ. of Calif. (Berkeley) 61; mem. Nat. Acad. of Sciences; Fellow, American Acad. of Arts and Sciences; Paul Lewis Award, American Chem. Soc. 54.

Publs. *Biochemistry of the Amino Acids* 65; various papers and scientific reviews.

Department of Biochemistry, Cornell University Medical College, 1300 York Avenue, New York, N.Y. 10021, U.S.A.

Telephone: 212-879-9000.

Meitus, Yuli Sergeyevich; Soviet composer; b. 28 Jan. 1903, Kirovograd, Ukraine; s. of late Sergei Meitus and Keznes Meitus; m. Alexandra Vasilyeva 1936; one s.; ed. Kharkov Inst. of Music and Drama.

Member Board, U.S.S.R. Composers' Union; Honoured Worker of the Arts of the Turkmen S.S.R. 44, and of the Ukrainian S.S.R. 48; State Prize 51, Order of Red Banner of Labour 60.

Principal compositions: First Symphonic Suite, on Ukrainian Themes 28, Second Symphonic Suite, *Dneprostroi* 28, Third Symphonic Suite, on the Liberation of West Ukraine 39, Fourth Symphonic Suite, for 25th Anniversary of October Revolution 42, Fifth Symphonic Suite, on Ukrainian Themes 44; Operas: *Perekop* 38, *Haidamaki* 41, *Abadan* 42, *Leili and Mezhnun* 45, *Young Guards* 46, *Dawn Over the River Dvina* 54, *Stolen Happiness* 57-58, *Makhtumkuli* 61, *The Wind's Daughter* 63-64, *The Ulyanov Brothers* 65-66, *Anna Karenina* 69, *Yaroslav Sage* 71-72, *Richard Sorge* 74-75; and other symphonic and choral works.

Leisure interest: philately.

Composers' Union of the Ukrainian S.S.R., 32 Pushkinskaya ul., Kiev 4, U.S.S.R.

Mejia-Palacio, Jorge; Colombian financial officer; b. 1912; ed. Universidad del Cauca, Colombia.

Director La Patria, Manizales 41-46; mem. Municipal Council, Manizales 41-45; Dep. to Ass., Dept. of Caldas 43-45; Colombian Chargé d'Affaires, Sweden 47-48; Minister Counsellor, Colombian Embassy, Wash. 48-52; Rep. at Interamerican Economic and Social Council 49-52, Pres. 51; Exec. Dir. Banco Francés e Italiano of Latin America, Bogotá 53-54; Exec. Dir. La Nacional Insurance Co., Bogotá 53-54; Exec. Dir. for Brazil,

Philippines, Colombia, Ecuador and Dominican Republic of Int. Bank for Reconstruction and Development 54-68, Colombian Alternate Gov. 68; Dir. Int. Finance Corpn. 56, Dir. Int. Devt. Asscn. 60-68; Minister of Finance, Colombia 62-63; Dir. Cen. Bank of Colombia 62-, Nat. Coffee Fed. of Colombia 62, Bogotá Electric Power Co. 69, Colombia Nat. Railroads 70; Pres. Latin American Bankers Fed. 68; Pres. Colombian Bankers Asscn. 68; del. to several Int. Confs.
Calle 13, No. 8-39, Apartado 13994, Bogotá, Colombia. Telephone: 416263.

Melchior, Mogens Gustav Ivar; Danish diplomatist; b. 14 July 1904, Espergaerde; s. of Prof. Dr. med. M. Melchior and Mrs. Melchior (née de Asker-Kilde); m. Karen Westenholz 1935; one s. two d.; ed. Gl. Hellerup Gymnasium and Univ. of Copenhagen.
Entered Danish Diplomatic Service 30-; in China, Belgium, Switzerland, Finland, U.S.S.R., Norway, New Zealand and Ministry of Foreign Affairs, Copenhagen; Deputy Under-Sec. of State (Dir.-Gen. of Political Affairs) 57; Amb. to Turkey 59-60, to Yugoslavia 60-68, to Switzerland 68-74; Knight Commdr. Order of Dannebrog with Cross of Honour; Medal for Merit and foreign decorations.
Leisure interests: history, riding.
3115 Gerzensee, Switzerland.
Telephone: 031/928316.

Melen, Ferit; Turkish politician; b. 1906, Van; m.; two c.; ed. School of Political Science, Univ. of Ankara.
District Officer, Local Admin. 31-33; Auditor, Ministry of Finance 33-43, Dir-.Gen. of Incomes 43-50; Deputy for Van (Repub. People's Party) 50-64; Minister of Finance 62-65; Senator for Van 64-67; mem. Council of Europe 66-67; participated in formation of Nat. Reliance Party 67, now Deputy Leader; Minister of Nat. Defence 71-72, April 75-; Prime Minister 72-73.
c/o Milli Guven Partisi, Ankara, Turkey.

Melentiev, Lev Alexandrovich; Soviet energy specialist; b. 9 Dec. 1908, Leningrad; ed. Leningrad Polytechnical Inst.
Engineer, Leningrad Power System 29-33; Chief Designing Bureau, Leningrad Energy Cttee. 33-35; Senior Lecturer, Prof. Leningrad Engineering-Econ. Inst. 36-42; Senior Scientific Worker, U.S.S.R. Acad. of Sciences Inst. of Energy 42-60; Dept. Chief, Prof. Leningrad Engineering-Econ. Inst. 45-60; Pres. Board U.S.S.R. Acad. of Sciences Eastern Siberian Branch 60-65; Dir. U.S.S.R. Acad. of Sciences Siberian Dept. Inst. of Energetics 60-73; Chief of Dept., U.S.S.R. Acad. of Sciences Inst. of High Temperatures 73-; Deputy Academician and Sec. of Dept. of Physics— Technical Problems of Energetics 73-; mem. C.P.S.U. 47-; Corresp. mem. U.S.S.R. Acad. of Sciences 60-66, mem. 66-; Hero of Socialist Labour 69, several decorations.
Publs. Works on general problems of energy development, energy systems and industrial heating, systems analysis in energetics.
Academy of Sciences of the U.S.S.R., 14 Leninsky Prospect, Moscow B-71, U.S.S.R.

Melikishvili, Georgy Alexandrovich; Soviet (Georgian) historian; b. 30 Dec. 1918, Tbilisi; s. of Alexandr and Yekaterina; m. Yelena Iosifovna Dochanashivili 1942; one s. two d.; ed. Tbilisi Univ.
Works deal with the ancient history of the Near East and Transcaucasia; Prof. Tbilisi Univ.; Dir. of Historical Inst. of Georgian Acad. of Sciences; mem. Acad. of Sciences of Georgian S.S.R. 60-; Lenin Prize 57.
Publs. Nairi-Urartu 54, Urartian Inscriptions in Cuneiform Characters 60, History of Ancient Georgia 59.
Academy of Sciences, Rizhskaya ulitsa 3, kv. 37, Tbilisi 30, U.S.S.R. 380030.
Telephone: 22-10-06.

Mellanby, Kenneth, C.B.E., B.A., PH.D., SC.D.; British entomologist and research worker; b. 26 March 1908, Barrhead, Scotland; s. of Prof. A. L. Mellanby; m. 1st Helen Nielson Dow 1933 (dissolved), 2nd Jean Louie Copeland 1949; one s. one d.; ed. Barnard Castle School, King's Coll., Cambridge, and London Univ.
Research work London School of Hygiene and Tropical Medicine 30-36, Wandsworth Fellowship 34; Sorby Research Fellow of the Royal Soc. 36; Univ. Lecturer Sheffield 36; Army Service (Major, R.A.M.C.) 42-45; Dep. Field Dir. M.R.C. Scrub Typhus Comm. in S.E. Asia; Univ. Reader in Medical Entomology, London School of Hygiene and Tropical Medicine 45-47; research worker 53-55; Principal Univ. Coll. Ibadan, Nigeria 47-53; Head of Dept. of Entomology, Rothamsted Experimental Station 55-61; Dir. Monks Wood Experimental Station, Huntingdon 61-74; Pres. Inst. of Biology, British Asscn. Section D; Editor Environmental Pollution; Hon. D.Sc. (Univs. of Ibadan, Bradford, Leicester); Hon. Prof. of Biology (Univ. of Leicester); Hon. Professorial Fellow (Univ. Coll., Cardiff).
Leisure interests: gardening, wine and food.
Publs. Scabies 43, Human Guinea Pigs 45, The Birth of Nigeria's University 58, Pesticides and Pollution (New Naturalist) 67, The Mole (New Naturalist) 71, The Biology of Pollution 72, The Lonely Mole 74, Britain Can Feed Itself.
Hill Farm, Wennington, Huntingdon PE17 2LU, England.
Telephone: Abbots Ripton 392.

Melles, Carl; Austrian conductor; b. 15 July 1926, Budapest; m. Gertrud Dertnig 1963; one s. one d.; ed. gymnasium and Acad. of Music, Budapest.
Conducts all the major orchestras of Europe; Vienna and Berlin Philharmonic, New Philharmonia London; guest appearances at Salzburg and Bayreuth Festivals and Vienna State Opera; concert tours in Europe, Japan, S. Africa; Franz Liszt Prize, Budapest 54.
Grünbergstrasse 4, 1130, Vienna, Austria.

Mellink, Machteld Johanna, PH.D.; Netherlands archaeologist; b. 26 Oct. 1917, Amsterdam; d. of Johan Mellink and Machteld Kruyff; ed. Amsterdam and Utrecht Univs.
Field Asst. Tarsus excavations 47-49; Asst. Prof. of Classical Archaeology Bryn Mawr Coll. 49-53, Assoc. Prof., Chair. Dept. of Classical and Near Eastern Archaeology 53-62, Prof. 62-; staff mem. Gordion excavations organized by Pennsylvania Univ. Museum 50-, during which the putative tomb of King Midas was discovered 57; Field Dir. excavations at Karataş-Semayük in Lycia 63-; excavator, archaic and Graeco-Persian painted tombs near Elmali 69-.
Publs. Hyakinthos 43, A Hittite Cemetery at Gordion 56; Archaeology in Asia Minor (reports in American Journal of Archaeology) 55-; Co-author Frühe Stufen der Kunst 74; Editor Dark Ages and Nomads 64.
Bryn Mawr College, Bryn Mawr, Pa. 19010, U.S.A.
Telephone: 215-LA5-1000.

Mellish, Rt. Hon. Robert Joseph, P.C., M.P.; British politician; b. 3 March 1913; ed. elementary schools.
Army Service 39-45; Labour M.P. Rotherhithe Div. of Bermondsey 46-50; Parl. Private Sec. and Financial Sec. to Admiralty 46-49; M.P. for Bermondsey 50-74, for Southwark, Bermondsey 74-; Parl. Private Sec. to Minister of Supply 50-51, to Minister of Pensions 51; Joint Parl. Sec. Minister of Housing and Local Govt. Oct. 64-Aug. 67; Minister of Public Building and Works Aug. 67-April 69; Parl. Chief Whip, Labour Party April 69-May 70; Minister of Housing May-June 70; Opposition Chief Whip 70-74; Govt. Chief Whip 74-76; Knight Commdr. of St. Gregory.
House of Commons, London, S.W.1, England.
Telephone: 01-219 3000.

Mellon, Paul, B.A., M.A.; American business and foundation executive; b. 11 June 1907; ed. Choate School, Yale Univ. and Cambridge Univ.
Pres. and Trustee Nat. Gallery of Art, Washington; Trustee The Andrew W. Mellon Foundation (successor to merged Old Dominion Foundation and Avalon Foundation), N.Y.C.; Dir. Mellon Nat. Bank and Trust Co., Pittsburgh; Trustee, A. W. Mellon Educational and Charitable Trust, Pittsburgh, Hon. K.B.E. 74.
1729 H Street, Washington, D.C. 20006, U.S.A.

Mellor, Sir John Serocold Paget, Bart.; British business executive; b. 6 July 1893, London; s. of Sir John Mellor, Bt., K.C.B.; one s.; ed. Eton and New Coll., Oxford.
Barrister, Inner Temple; Army Service, First World War; Conservative M.P. 35-55; Dir. Prudential Assurance Co. Ltd. 46-72, Deputy Chair. 59-65, Chair. 65-70, Pres. 72-; Dir. City and Int. Trust Ltd., C.L.R.P. Investment Trust Ltd.
Binley House, nr. Andover, Hants., England.

Melnikov, Ivan Ivanovich; retd. Soviet trade union official; b. 17 Dec. 1914; ed. forestry technical school.
Forestry worker, becoming Dir. of Forestry 43-45; mem. Communist Party of Soviet Union 41-; Sec. Central Cttee. Trade Union of Agricultural Workers and State Purchases 62-75; Cand. mem. All-Union Council of Trade Unions.
c/o Central Committee Trade Union of Agricultural Workers, 42 Leninsky Prospekt, Moscow, U.S.S.R.

Melnikov, Nikolai Vasilievich; Soviet scientist; b. 28 Feb. 1909, Sarapul, Udmurtian U.S.S.R.; ed. Sverdlovsk Mining Inst.
Engineer and Administrator in mining and coal industries 34-45; Deputy Minister of Coal Industry in East Areas of U.S.S.R. 44-48; mem. U.S.S.R. Council of Ministers Bureau for Fuel and Coal Industries 44-54 Deputy Dir. Inst. of Mining U.S.S.R. Acad. of Sciences 55-60, Dir. 60-61; Corresp. mem. Acad. of Sciences of the U.S.S.R. 53-62, mem. 62-, now mem. Presidium; Chair. State Cttee. for Fuel Industry, U.S.S.R. Gosplan 61-65; Head A. A. Skochinsky Laboratory of Open-Cast Mining, U.S.S.R. Acad. of Sciences 65-; Chair. of Council for Physical and Engineering Problems of Exploitation of Mineral Resources, U.S.S.R. Acad. of Sciences; joint State prizewinner for fundamental improvement in open-cast coalmining 46.
Publs. *Open-Cast Mineral Mining* 48, *Drilling Wells and Blast Holes at Open-Cast Workings* 53, *Mechanization of Works in Open-Cast Mining* 54, *Development of Science in the Field of Open-Cast Mining in the U.S.S.R.* 57, 61, *Reference Book for Engineers and Technicians on Open-Cast Mining Works* 50-62, *Fundamentals of Line Technology in Open-Cast Mining* 62, etc.
A. A. Skochinsky Mining Institute, U.S.S.R. Academy of Sciences, 4 Luybertsy, Moscow Region, U.S.S.R.

Melville, Sir Eugene, K.C.M.G.; British diplomatist (retd.); b. 15 Dec. 1911, Dundee, Scotland; s. of George E. Melville; m. Elizabeth Strachan 1937; two s. one d.; ed. Queen's Park School, Glasgow, and St. Andrews Univ.
Colonial Office 36; Colonies Supply Mission, Washington 41-45; Private Sec. to Sec. of State for Colonies 45-46; Financial Adviser, Control Comm. for Germany 49-52; Asst. Under-Sec. of State, Colonial Office 52-61; Asst. Under-Sec. of State, Foreign Office 61-62; Minister (Econ.), British Embassy, Bonn 62-65; Perm. U.K. Del. to Council of European Free Trade Asscn. (EFTA) and to Gen. Agreement on Tariffs and Trade (GATT) 65-66; Head of U.K. Mission to Office of UN and other Int. Orgs. in Geneva 66-71; Special Adviser to Dept. of the Environment on Channel Tunnel 71-73; Dir.-Gen. British Property Asscn. 74-.
35 Catherine Place, London, S.W.1; Home: 51 West-

minster Mansions, Little Smith Street, London, S.W.1, England.
Telephone: 01-222-4540 (Home).

Melville, Sir Harry (Work), K.C.B., PH.D., D.SC., LL.D., D.CL., D.TECH., F.R.I.C., F.R.S.; British chemist; b. 27 April 1908, Edinburgh; s. of Thomas Melville; m. Janet Marian Cameron 1942; two d.; ed. George Heriot's School, Edinburgh, Edinburgh Univ. and Trinity Coll., Cambridge.
Fellow Trinity Coll., Cambridge 33-43; Asst. Dir. Colloid Science Laboratory, Cambridge Univ. 38-40; Prof. of Chemistry, Aberdeen Univ. 40-48; Scientific Adviser to Chief Superintendent Chemical Defence, Min. of Supply 40-43; Superintendent Radar Research Station 43-45; Mason Prof. and Dir. of Chemistry Dept., Birmingham Univ. 48-56; mem. Advisory Council for Scientific and Industrial Research 46-51; mem. Scientific Advisory Council, Ministry of Supply 49-51, 53-56; Advisory Council on Scientific Research and Development 53-56; mem. Scientific Advisory Council, British Electricity Authority 49-56; mem. Scientific Advisory Council, Ministry of Power 54-60; mem. Advisory Council on Research and Development, Ministry of Power (now Dept. of Trade and Industry) 60-, Chair. 70-; Sec. Dept. of Scientific and Industrial Research 56-65; Chair. Science Research Council 65-67; Principal Queen Mary Coll., London 67-(76).
Publ. *Experimental Methods in Gas Reactions* 38.
Norwood, Dodds Lane, Chalfont St. Giles, Bucks., England.
Telephone: Chalfont St. Giles 2222.

Melville, Sir Leslie Galfreid, K.B.E., B.EC.; Australian economist; b. 26 March 1902, Marsfield; m. Mary Maud Seales 1925; two s.; ed. Church of England Grammar School, Sydney, and Univ. of Sydney.
Public Actuary of South Australia 24-28; Prof. of Economics, Univ. of Adelaide 29-31; mem. of Cttees. on S. Australian Finances 27-30; mem. of Cttees. on Australian Finances and Unemployment 31 and 32; Financial Adviser to Australian Dels. at Imperial Economic Conf. 32, and to Australian Del. at World Economic Conf. 33; mem. Australian Financial and Economic Advisory Cttee. 39; Chair. Australian Del. to UN Monetary Conf., Bretton Woods 44; mem. Advisory Council of Commonwealth Bank 45-50; Chair. UN Sub-Comm. on Employment and Econ. Stability 47-50; Asst. Gov. (Central Banking) Commonwealth Bank of Australia; Exec. Dir. Int. Monetary Fund and Int. Bank for Reconstruction and Devt. Nov. 50-53; Vice-Chancellor, Australian Nat. Univ. Canberra 53-60; mem. Board, Reserve Bank 59-63, 65-75; Chair. Commonwealth Grants Comm. 66-74; Chair. Tariff Board 60-63; Devt. Advisory Service, Int. Bank for Reconstruction and Devt. 63-65.
71 Stonehaven Crescent, Canberra, Australia.
Telephone: 811838.

Memmi, Albert; Tunisian writer; b. 15 Dec. 1920, Tunis; s. of François Memmi and Marguerite née Sarfati; m. Germaine Dubach 1946; two s. one d.; ed. Lycée Carnot, Tunis, Univ. of Algiers and Univ. de Paris à la Sorbonne.
Teacher of Philosophy in Tunis 55; Dir. Psychological Centre, Tunis 56; Researcher, Centre national de la recherche scientifique, Paris 59-; Asst. Prof. Ecole pratique des hautes études 59-66, Prof. 66-70; Prof. Univ. of Paris 70-, Dir. Social Sciences Dept.; mem. Acad. des Sciences d'Outre-mer; Commdr. Ordre de Nichan Iftikhar; Palmes académiques, Prix de Carthage, Prix Fénéon.
Leisure interest: literature.
Publs. include: *The Pillar of Salt* 53, *Strangers* 55, *Anthologie des écrivains nord-africains* 55, *Colonizer, Colonized* 57, *Portrait of a Jew* 62, *Le français et le*

racisme 65, *The Liberation of the Jew* 66, *Dominated Man* 68, *The Scorpion* 70, *Juifs et Arabes* 74.
5 rue Saint Merri, Paris 4e, France.
Telephone: 278-02-63.

Menard, Henry William, PH.D.; American teacher and researcher; b. 10 Dec. 1920, Fresno, Calif.; *s.* of Henry William Menard and Blanche Hodges; *m.* Gifford Merrill 1946; one *s.* two *d.*; ed. Calif. Inst. of Technology and Harvard Univ.
Oceanographer, Navy Electronics Lab., San Diego 49-55; Assoc. Prof. of Marine Geology, Inst. of Marine Resources, Univ. of Calif., San Diego 55-61; Prof. 61-; with Office of Science and Technology, Exec. Office of the Pres. 65-66; Leader or mem. of numerous Deep-Sea Oceanographic Expeditions; U.S.N.R. service 42-46; Consultant, American Telephone and Telegraph Co., Rand-McNally, Time-Life; mem. Nat. Acad. of Sciences; Guggenheim Fellow 62-63; Churchill Fellow 70-71.
Leisure interests: surfing, diving.
Publs. *Marine Geology of the Pacific* 64, *Anatomy of an Expedition* 69, *Science: Growth and Change* 71, *Geology, Resources and Society* 74.
Scripps Institution of Oceanography, University of California, San Diego, P.O. Box 109, La Jolla, Calif. 92307, U.S.A.
Telephone: 714-452-2168.

Mende, Erich, DR. IUR.; German politician; b. 28 Oct. 1916; ed. Gross-Strehlitz Coll. and Univs. of Cologne and Bonn.
Army service 36-45; studied law, Univs. of Cologne and Bonn 45-48, studied political science, Univ. of Cologne 48-49; co-founder of the Free Democratic Party (F.D.P.), British Occupied Zone 45, mem. Exec. Cttee. Fed. Org. of F.D.P. 49-70; mem. Bundestag 49-; Whip, Parl. Group of F.D.P. and mem. Exec. Cttee. 50-53; Deputy Chair. Parl. Group of F.D.P. 53-57, Chair. 57-63; Chair. F.D.P. 60-68; Federal Minister for All-German Affairs and Deputy Federal Chancellor 63-Oct. 66; left F.D.P. to join Christian Democratic Union (C.D.U.) Oct. 70; Knight of the Iron Cross.
Publ. *Die Freie Demokratische Partei—Daten, Fakten, Hintergründe* 72.
5300 Bonn-Bad Godesberg, Am-Stadwald 62, Federal Republic of Germany.
Telephone: Bad Godesberg 35-67-00.

Mendels, Morton M., O.B.E., M.A., B.C.L.; Canadian lawyer and administrator; b. 1 March 1908, Montreal; *s.* of Louis Mendels; *m.* 1st 1931 (dissolved 1954), one *s.* one *d.*; *m.* 2nd Constance Ladue 1970; ed. McGill Univ., Montreal.
Entered law practice 32 serving as legal Counsel to the Canadian Inst. of Plumbing and Heating and as Consultant Economist, served with Canadian Army 40-45 with final rank of Lt.-Col., Chief of Army Estimates, Finance, and Parl. liaison, Canadian Gen. Staff; Sec. Int. Bank for Reconstruction and Devt. 46-73.
Leisure interests: bridge, walking, reading, music.
3400 Garrison Street, N.W., Washington, D.C., U.S.A.
Telephone: 202-363-0081.

Mendelssohn, Kurt Alfred Georg, D.PHIL., M.A., F.R.S.; British physicist; b. 7 Jan. 1906, Berlin, Germany; *s.* of Ernst M. Mendelssohn and Eliza Ruprecht; *m.* Jutta Lina Charlotte Zarniko 1932; one *s.* four *d.*; ed. Goethe School, Berlin, and Berlin Univ.
Research and teaching posts, Berlin Univ. 29-31, Breslau Univ. '31-32, Univ. of Oxford 33-73; Emer. Professorial Fellow of Wolfson Coll.; Emer. Reader in Physics, Univ of Oxford; Chair. Int. Cryogenic Engineering Cttee.; Pres. Comm. A2 of Int. Inst. of Refrigeration; Consultant U.K.A.E.A.; Editor *Cryogenics*; Visiting Prof. Rice Univ., Tex. 52, Purdue Univ. 56, Tokyo Univ. 60, Kumasi Univ., Ghana 64, Tata Inst., Bombay 69-70; Hughes Medal, Royal Soc.

67; Simon Memorial Prize, Inst. of Physics and Physical Soc. 68.
Leisure interests: oriental art, photography, Egyptology.
Publs. *What is Atomic Energy?* 46, *Cryophysics* 60, *The Quest for Absolute Zero* 66, *In China Now* 69, *The World of Walther Nernst* 73, *The Riddle of the Pyramids* 74, *Science and Western Domination* 76, *The Basis of White Domination* 76; numerous papers and articles on low temperature physics, medical physics, Egyptology and science in various countries.
Wolfson College, Oxford; Home: 235 Iffley Road, Oxford, England.
Telephone: 56711, 58991 (Office); 43747 (Home).

Mendes, Murilo; Brazilian poet; b. 1901; ed. Rio de Janeiro; studied music, art and literature.
Civil servant; journalist; part of "Mouvement Moderniste" 22-; Prof. of Brazilian Literature, Rome Univ. 57; Graça Aranha Prize (Brazil) 31; mem. Int. Asscn. of Art Critics, European Soc. of Culture, European Community of Writers.
Publs. *Poemas* 30, *Tempo e Eternidade* 35, *A Poesia em Panico* 38, *O Visiondrio* 41, *As Metamorfoses* 44, *Mundo Enigma* 45, *O Discipulo de Emaús* 44, *Poesia Liberdade* 47, *Contemplação de Ouro Preto* 54, *Poesias Completas* 59, *Tempo Espanhol* 59, *Siciliana* 59, *Janela do Caos* 61, *Poesie* 61, *A Idade do Serrote* 68.
Via del Consolato 6, Rome, Italy.
Telephone: 651836.

Mendès-France, Pierre, LL.D.; French lawyer, economist and politician; b. 11 Jan. 1907, Paris; two *s.*
Deputy 32-40, 45-58, 67-68; Professor Ecole Nationale d'Administration; Under-Sec. for the Treasury 38; tried by Vichy administration 40; escaped to serve with Fighting French Air Force; Finance Minister French Provisional Govt. 43-44; Head French Financial Missions Washington and Bretton Woods 44; Min. of Nat. Economy 44-45; Prime Minister and Minister of Foreign Affairs June 54-Feb. 55; Minister of State without Portfolio Feb.-May 56; Dir. *Courrier de la République* (monthly journal); Officier de la Légion d'Honneur, Croix de Guerre, Rosette de la Résistance, Médaille des Evadés, Grand Officier de l'Ordre de Léopold (Belgium).
Publs. *L'oeuvre financiere du gouvernement Poincaré, Histoire de la Stabilisation du Franc* 28, *Liberté, Liberté Chérie* 43 (trans. into English as *The Pursuit of Freedom* 55), *La Science Economique et l'Action* 54 (trans. into English), *Gouverner c'est Choisir* 53, *7 mois et 7 jours* 55, *La Politique et la Vérité* 58, *Rencontres* 58 (with A. Bevan and P. Nenni), *La République Moderne* 62 (trans. into English), *Dialogues avec l'Asie d'aujourdhui* 72, *Science économique et lucidité politique* (co-author) 73, *Choisir* 74, *La Vérité guidait leurs Pas.*
Les Monts, 27-Louviers, France.

Méndez Docurro, Ing. Eugenio; Mexican engineer and politician; b. 17 April 1923, Veracruz; ed. Instituto Politécnico Nacional, Harvard Univ. and Univ. de Paris.
Director-General of Telecommunications 53-60; Dir. Instituto Politécnico Nacional 49-62; mem. Mexican Del. to UNESCO Assembly 60; Under-Sec. of Communications and Transport 65-70, Sec. 70-.
Secretaría de Communicaciones y Transportes, Avenida Universidad y Xola, Mexico D.F., Mexico.

Méndez Montenegro, Dr. Julio César; Guatemalan law professor and politician; b. 23 Nov. 1915, Guatemala City; *s.* of Marcial Méndez Mendoza and Mélida Montenegro de Méndez; *m.* Sara de la Hoz de León 1950; two *s.* one *d.*
Professor of law, Dean of Faculty of Law, Universidad de San Carlos; Pres. Colegio de Abogados; fmr. Under-Sec. of Admin. and of Foreign Affairs; fmr. Gen. Sec. to the Presidency of the Repub.; Pres. of Guatemala

66-70; Partido Revolucionario; author of numerous works on law.

c/o Partido Revolucionario, 4A Calle 6-09, Zona 1, Guatemala City, Guatemala.

Mendoza, Eugenio; Venezuelan business executive; b. 13 Nov. 1907.

Began career as office boy in hardware store 24; Head, Eugenio Mendoza y Cía. Sucrs. C.A. (cement, paper and paint); Head Mendoza Foundation 55, Poliomyelitis Foundation (philanthropic orgs.).

Eugenio Mendoza y Cía. Sucrs. C.A., Avenida Sucre, Catia, Caracas; P.O.B. 332, Caracas, Venezuela.

Menemencioğlu, Turgut; Turkish diplomatist; b. 1914, Istanbul; s. of Muvatfak and Kadriye Menemencioğlu; m. Nermin Moran 1944; two s.; ed. Robert Coll., Istanbul and Geneva Univ.

Turkish Ministry of Foreign Affairs 39-; Perm. Del., European Office UN, Geneva 50-52; Counsellor, Turkish Embassy, Washington 52; Dir. Gen. Econ. Affairs, Ministry of Foreign Affairs 52-54; Dep. Perm. Rep. to UN 54-60; Ambassador to Canada 60; Perm. Rep. to UN 60-62; Ambassador to U.S.A. 62-67; Sec.-Gen. of CENTO (Central Treaty Org.) 67-72; Adviser to Minister of Foreign Affairs 71-72; Amb. to U.K. (also accred. to Malta) Nov. 72-.

Embassy of Turkey, 43 Belgrave Square, London, SW1X 8PA; and 69 Portland Place, London, W.1, England; Home: Kuloğlu Sokak 11, Çankaya, Ankara, Turkey.

Menen, (Salvator) Aubrey Clarence; British author; b. 22 April 1912, London; s. of Kali Narain Menen and Alice Violet Everett; ed. Univ. Coll., London.

Dramatic Critic *The Bookman* 34; Dir. The Experimental Theatre, London 35-36; Dir. Personalities Press Service, London 37-39; Script Editor, Information Films, Govt. of India 43-45; Educ. Officer, Backward Tribes, Political Dept. of Govt. of India 46; fmr. Chief of Motion Picture Dept., J. Walter Thompson (Eastern) Ltd.

Leisure interests: archaeology, architecture, travel.

Publs. *The Prevalence of Witches* 49, *The Stumbling Stone* 49, *The Backward Bride* 40, *The Duke of Gallodoro* 52, *Dead Man in the Silver Market* 53, *The Ramayana* 54, *The Abode of Love* 56, *The Fig Tree* 59, *Rome for Ourselves* 60, *Speaking the Language Like a Native* 62, *Shela* 62, *A Conspiracy of Women* 65, *India* 69, *The Space within the Heart* 70, *Upon this Rock, Cities in the Sand* 72, *Fonthill* 75.

c/o Lois Wallace, William Morris Agency Inc., 1350 Avenue of the Americas, New York, N.Y. 10019, U.S.A.

Menezes, Djacir Lima; Brazilian university rector; b. 16 Nov. 1907, Maranguape, Ceará; s. of Dr. Paulo Elpídio de Menezes and Oda Freire de Lima Menezes; m. Stela Pontes Menezes; three s. one d.; ed. Liceu do Ceará, Faculdade de Direito do Ceará and Univ. do Brasil.

Dr., Faculdade de Direito do Ceará 31-32; Regional Insp. of Educ. 31; Prof. of Psychology, Escola Normal Justiniano de Serpa 32-38; Prof. of Law, Faculdade de Direito do Ceará 38; Teacher, Ceará Military Coll. 39; Founder and First Dir. Faculdade de Ciencias Economicas do Ceará 40; also Prof. of Political Science; mem. Nat. Council of Labour 41-42; Prof. of Political Science and Econ. Theory, Univ. do Brasil; Dir. Teaching Dept., Argentine-Brazilian Cultural Inst., Buenos Aires 53; Dir. and Founder, Bolivian-Brazilian Cultural Centre, La Paz 58; Prof. of Brazilian Literature, Univ. Nacional Autónoma de México 59; Dir. Faculty of Econs., Univ. Federal do Rio de Janeiro 60-64, Dir. Inst. of Philosophy and Social Sciences 65; mem. Fed. Council of Culture; Prof. Emer., Univ. Federal do Rio de Janeiro, Rector 70-72, Pres. 72-.

Publs. include: *O Problema da Realidade* 32, *Preparação*

do Método Científico 38, *As Elites Agressivas* 53, *Proudhon, Hegel e a Dialética* 66, *Textos Dialéticas de Hegel* 68, *O Outro Nordeste* 70, *Ideias contra Ideologias* 72, *Teses quase Legelianas* 72.

Universidade Federal do Rio de Janeiro, Cidade Universitária, Ilha do Fundão, Rio de Janeiro; Home: Bulhões de Carbalho, 272-apt. 1001, Rio de Janeiro, Brazil.

Telephone: 2303882 (Office); 2272998 (Home).

Menge, Walter Otto; American insurance executive; b. 11 Sept. 1904, Buffalo, N.Y.; s. of Jacob H. Menge and Elizabeth C. Hamelman; m. Elsie C. Cramer 1927; one s. one d.; ed. Wayne Univ. and Univ. of Mich.

Actuary, Grange Life Insurance Co., Lansing, Mich. 26-28; Assoc. Prof. Mathematics, Univ. of Mich. 28-37; Assoc. Actuary, Lincoln Nat. Life Insurance Co., Fort Wayne, Ind. 37-43, 2nd Vice-Pres. 43-45, Vice-Pres. 45-51, First Vice-Pres. 51-54, Pres. 54-64, Chair. 64-69, Hon. Chair. 69-; Chair. of Board Lincoln Nat. Life Ins. Co. of N.Y. 61-65; Pres. Reliance Life Insurance Co., Pittsburgh 51-53; Dir. of several other companies and official of various professional and civic orgs. Leisure interests: golf, fishing, gardening.

200 Beach Road, Tequesta, Fla. 33458, U.S.A.

Telephone: 305-746-4671.

Menges, Dietrich Wilhelm von, D.IUR.; German business executive; b. 26 Oct. 1909; ed. Wilhelm Gymnasium, Königsberg, and Georg-August-Universität zu Göttingen.

In Export Dept., Ferrostaal AG, Essen 38; mem. Management Board, Ferrostaal AG 47-49, Chair. of Management Board 49-66; mem. Management Board Gutehoffnungshütte Aktienverein 61-66, Chair. Management Board 66-75, mem. Board of Dirs. 75-; Chair. Management Board Gutehoffnungshütte Sterkrade AG 66-71; Pres. German Chamber of Industry and Commerce 74-; Chair. and mem. numerous Advisory Boards.

43 Essen-Bredeney, Am Wiesental 16, Federal Republic of Germany.

Mengesha, Lieut.-Gen. Iyassu; Ethiopian army officer and diplomatist; b. 16 Oct. 1915, Keren; ed. Lycée Teferi Makonnen, Addis Ababa, St. Cyr French Mil. Acad. and Army Command and Gen. Staff Coll., Fort Leavenworth, U.S.A.

Training Officer, Ethiopian Army 35; Chief Sec. Ministry of Defence, Addis Ababa 49-52; Gov. Madji Province 52-56; Dir. of Budget and Installations, Ministry of Defence 56-60; Commdr. of the Ethiopian Contingent in the Congo 60; Chief of Staff, UN Forces in the Congo 60; Deputy C.-in-C. 61; UN Chief Mil. Adviser to the Repub. of the Congo and Chief UN Mil. Advisory Programme, Congo 62-64; Minister of State for Nat. Defence 64; Chief of Staff, Imperial Ethiopian Armed Forces and Commdr. Ground Forces 64-69; Amb. to U.K. 70-74; Grand Cordon of the Order of the Star of Hon., Ethiopia, Grand Officer, Mil. Order of Menelik the Second and other foreign decorations.

Menichella, Donato; Italian banker; b. 1890; ed. Inst. Cesare Alfieri, Florence (Dr. of Social Science).

Employee of Bank of Italy 22-23, Banca Italiana di Sconto 23-28; Dir. of National Credit Bank 29-30; Dir.-Gen. of the Inst. for Industrial Reconstruction 33-43, of the Bank of Italy 46-48; Gov. of the Bank of Italy 48-60, Hon. Gov. 60-; Pres. of the Italian Foreign Exchange 48-60; fmr. Dir. Bank for Int. Settlements; Gov. for Italy, Int. Bank for Reconstruction and Development 48-60, alternate Gov. 61.

c/o Bank of Italy, Via Nazionale 91, Rome; Home: Via Merulana 247, Rome, Italy.

Menk, Louis W.; American railroad executive; b. 8 April 1918, Englewood, Colo.; s. of Louis Albert Menk and Daisy Deane (Frantz); m. Martha Jane

Swan 1942; one s. one d.; ed. S. Denver High School, Denver and Harvard.

Messenger, telegrapher, Union Pacific Railroad 37-40; from telegrapher to Chair. and Pres. St. Louis-San Francisco Railroad 40-65; Pres. and Dir. Burlington Lines 65-66; Pres. and Dir. Northern Pacific Railway Co. 66-70; Chair. and Dir. Burlington Inc. March 70-71, Chair. of Board, Chief Exec. Officer and Dir. 71-; Dir. numerous other companies; mem. Board of Trustees, Univ. of Denver, Business Roundtable, New York, Nat. Exec. Board, Boy Scouts of America; Seley Award 70; Hon. LL.D. Drury Coll. 65, Univ. Denver 66, Monmouth Coll. 67.

BN Building, 176 East 5th Street, St. Paul, Minn. 55101; Home: 5904 S. Robert Trail, RR10, South St. Paul, Minn. 55075, U.S.A.

Menne, W. Alexander Dr.; German company director; b. 20 June 1904, Dortmund; m. Marianne Müller 1945; one d.

Member of Bundestag, Free Democratic Party (F.D.P.) 61-69, May-Dec. 72; Chair. Econ. Cttee. of Bundestag 65-69; Man. Dir. Glasso Paint Products, London 29-39; Dir. Glasruit-Werke AG, Hamburg 39-51, Farbwerke Hoechst AG, Frankfurt 52-69; mem. board of various companies and banks; Vice-Pres. Fed. of German Industry, Cologne 49-68, mem. Board 68-, Chair. of its EEC and Atomic Industry Cttees.; Pres. Asscn. of Chemical Industry, Frankfurt 46-56, mem. Board 56-; Chair. German Cttee. for Trade Fairs, Cologne 61-; mem. Foreign Trade Advisory Board at Ministry of Economics; Pres. German-American Steuben-Schurz Soc. 54-; Grand Cross Order of Merit with Star (Germany).

Leisure interests: golfing, hunting, fishing.

Farbwerke Hoechst AG, Carl Bosch-Haus, Hamburger Allee 26-28, 6000 Frankfurt (Main) 90; Home: 6242 Kronberg/Ts., Im Brühl 37, Federal Republic of Germany.

Telephone: (0611) 778279.

Menner, Vladimir Vasilievich; Soviet geologist and paleontologist; b. 24 Nov. 1905, Shatsk, Ryazan Region; ed. Moscow State Univ.

At staff Moscow section Geological Cttee. 27-29; Asst. Prof. Moscow Mining Acad. 29-30; Lecturer, Moscow Geology Investigating Inst. 30-65; scientific research work Petroleum Prospecting Inst. 32-34; U.S.S.R. Acad. of Sciences Paleontological Inst. 35-36; Senior Scientific Worker, Dept. Chief, Asst. Dir. U.S.S.R. Acad. of Sciences Geological Inst. 34-; Corresp. mem. U.S.S.R. Acad. of Sciences 63-66, mem. 66-.

U.S.S.R. Academy of Sciences, 14 Leninsky Prospekt, Moscow, U.S.S.R.

Mennin, Peter, M.MUS., PH.D.; American composer; b. 17 May 1923; ed. Eastman School of Music and Rochester Univ.

Mem. Composition Faculty, Juilliard School of Music, New York City 47; Dir. Peabody Conservatory of Music, Baltimore 58-; Pres. Juilliard School of Music 62-; Nat. Music Council, Naumberg Music Foundation; Officer of Nat. Inst. of Arts and Letters; Board of Dirs. A.S.C.A.P., American Music Center; Pres. Nat. Music Council; Pres. Naumberg Music Foundation; works commissioned by Koussevitsky Foundation, Coolidge Foundation, Library of Congress, Juilliard Music Foundation, etc.; works have been performed throughout U.S.A., and in Europe, South America and the Far East; American Acad. of Arts and Letters Award, first George Gershwin Memorial Award, two Guggenheim Awards, Columbia Records Chamber Music Award, Naumburg American Music Recording Award, Bearns Prize (Columbia Univ.).

Compositions include: eight symphonies, cello concerto, **piano concerto** and other orchestral works, *Sonato*

Concertante for violin and piano, and other chamber and piano works, choral music, *Cantata de Virtute* for mixed chorus, children's chorus, soloists, narrator and orchestra.

Juilliard School, Lincoln Center, New York, N.Y. 10023, U.S.A.

Telephone: 799-5000.

Menninger, Karl Augustus; American psychiatrist; b. 22 July 1893, Topeka, Kan.; s. of Charles Frederick and Flora (Knisely) Menninger; m. 1st Grace Gaines 1916 (dissolved 1941), one s. two d.; 2nd Jeanetta Lyle 1941, one d.; ed. Washburn Coll., Indiana Univ., Univ. of Wisconsin and Harvard Univ. Medical School.

Chief of Staff, Menninger Clinic 25-, Dir. Dept. of Education, Menninger Foundation 46-62, Dean, Menninger School of Psychiatry 46-, Chair. Menninger Foundation 54-; Pres. American Psychoanalytic Asscn. 41-43; Chair. Cttee. on Reorganisation, American Psychiatric Asscn. 44-49; Dir., Nat. Citizens Comm. for Public Schools 53-55; mem. Editorial Board, *Journal of American Psychoanalytic Asscn.* 54-56; Vice Pres. American Soc. of Criminology 60-62; Consultant, Bureau of Prisons, Dept. of Justice 56-, Forbes Air Force Base 60-73; Chair. Educ. Cttee., Topeka Inst. for Psychoanalysis 60-70; Senior Consultant Topeka State Hospital, Topeka Veterans Admin. Hospital; Prof. Univ. of Health Sciences, Chicago Medical School; Consultant for Illinois State Psychiatric Inst.; mem. Chicago Council on Foreign Relations, Presidential Task Force, Prisoner Rehabilitation 69; Hon. mem. Royal Medico-Psychological Asscn., Environmental Research Foundation; mem. Board of Dirs. Katharine Wright Psychiatric Clinic, Chicago, Int. Cttee. Against Mental Illness; mem. Board of Trustees Fund for Advancement of Camping; Hon. D.Sc. Washburn Univ., Univ. of Wisconsin 65, Hon. L.H.D. Park Coll., Hon. LL.D. Jefferson Medical Coll., Parsons Coll., Kansas State Univ. 62, Saint Benedict's Coll., Baker Univ., Kansas 65, Okla. Univ. 66, Pepperdine Univ. 73; numerous awards.

Leisure interests: horticulture, soil conservation, wildlife preservation, chess, recorded music, American Indians, wines.

Publs. *Man Against Himself* 38, *Love Against Hate* 42, *The Human Mind* 45, *A Guide to Psychiatric Books* 56 (3rd edn. 72), *A Manual for Psychiatric Case Study* 62, *Theory of Psychoanalytic Technique* 58 (revised 73), *A Psychiatrist's World* 59, *The Vital Balance* 63, *The Crime of Punishment* 68, *Whatever Became of Sin* 73, *Sparks* (with Lucy Freeman) 73.

The Menninger Foundation, Box 829, Topeka, Kansas 66601; Home: 1819 Westwood Circle, Topeka, Kansas 66604, U.S.A.

Menon, Chelat Achutha, B.A., B.L.; Indian politician; b. 27 Jan. 1913, Trichur; s. of M. Achutha Menon; m. Lakshmykutty Amma 1943; one s. two d.

District Court Pleader, Trichur; took part in congress and trade union activities; restricted for one year for anti-war speech 40; joined Communist Party and detained for communist activities 42; Sec. District Cttee. of Communist Party 43-47; underground 48-52; elected to Travancore-Cochin Legislative Assembly 52; mem. Kerala Legislative Assembly 57, later Finance Minister; mem. Rajya Sabha 68-; Chief Minister of Kerala Nov. 69-.

Leisure interest: literature.

Publs. Translation of *Short History of the World* by H. G. Wells, *Soviet Nadu, A Kissan Text Book, Kerala State—Possibilities and Problems*, translation of *Man Makes Himself* by Gordon Child, *Sheafs from Memory*. Office of the Chief Minister of Kerala, Trivandrum, Kerala State, India.

Telephone: 4259 (Office); 62801 (Residence).

Menon, K. P. S.; Indian diplomatist; b. 18 Oct. 1898; ed. Madras Christian Coll. and Oxford Univ.

Joined I.C.S. 21; Deputy Sec. to Govt. of India in Foreign and Political Dept.; Agent to Govt. of India in Ceylon 29-33; fmr. Minister of Bharatpur State; Agent-Gen. in China 43; Alternate Rep. U.N. Gen. Assembly, N.Y. 46; Ambassador to China 47-48; Chair. U.N. Temporary Comm. on Korea 47; Sec. Ministry of Foreign Affairs 48-52; Ambassador to U.S.S.R. 52-61. Publs. *The Flying Troika* 63, *Many Worlds* (autobiog.) 66, *China Past and Present* 69, *The Indo-Soviet Treaty—Setting and Sequel* 73.

Palat House, Ottapalam, Kerala State, India.

Menon, Lakshmi N., M.A., L.T., T.DIP., LL.B.; Indian politician; b. 1899, Trivandrum; d. of Rama Varma Thampan; m. Prof. V. K. N. Menon 1930; ed. H.H. Maharaja's School and Coll. for Women, H.H. Maharaja's Arts Coll., Trivandrum, Lady Willingdon Training Coll., New Delhi, and Maria Grey Training Coll., London, Lucknow Univ.

Lecturer, Queen Mary's Coll., Madras 22-25, Gokhale Girls Schools, Calcutta 28-30, Isabella Theburn Coll., Lucknow 30-33; Alt. Del. to UN Gen. Ass. 48, 50, 53, 54, to UN Comm. on Status of Women, Beirut 49; Chief, Section on Status of Women, Human Rights Div., UN Secr., Lake Success 49-50; Principal, Women's Training Coll., Patna 51-53; Rep. Cttee. on Information from Non-Self Governing Territories 53; Parl. Sec. to the Prime Minister 52-57; Dep. Minister of External Affairs 57-62; Minister of State, Ministry of External Affairs 62-66; State Commr. for Guides, Bihar 52-; Pres. All India Women's Conf. 55-59, Indian Fed. of Univ. Women 61-67; mem. Rajya Sabha 52-66; Chair. Kasturba Gandhi Nat. Memorial Trust 72-; Life mem. Cochin Univ. Senate 73-.

Leisure interests: reading, writing, work among women and children.

Publs. *The Position of Women* and articles on women's status, education and participation in public affairs.

Plain View, Trivandrum, India.

Menon, Mambillikalathil Govind Kumar, M.SC., PH.D., F.R.S.; Indian physicist; b. 28 Aug. 1928, Mangalore; s. of Kizhekepat Sankara Menon and Mambillikalathil Narayaniamma; m. Indumati Patel 1955; one s. one d.; ed. Jaswant Coll., Jodhpur, Royal Inst. of Science, Bombay, and H. H. Wills Physics Laboratory, Univ. of Bristol.

Research Assoc., Univ. of Bristol 52-53; Senior Award of Royal Comm. for Exhbn. of 1851, Univ. of Bristol 53-55; Reader Tata Inst. of Fundamental Research, Bombay 55-58; Assoc. Prof. 58-60, Prof. and Dean of Physics Faculty 60-64, Senior Prof. and Deputy Dir. (Physics) 64-66, Dir. Tata Inst. of Fundamental Research 66-75; Pres. Indian Acad. of Sciences 74-76; Fellow, Indian Nat. Sci. Acad.; Chair. Cosmic Ray Comm. of Int. Union of Pure and Applied Physics (IUPAP) 73-75; Pres. Asia Electronics Union; Shanti Swarup Bhatnagar Award for Physical Sciences. Council of Scientific and Industrial Research 60; Repub. Day (Nat.) Awards, Govt. of India; Padma Shri 61, Padma Bhushan 68; Sec. to Govt. of India, Dept. of Electronics; Chair. Electronics Comm.; Scientific Adviser to Minister for Defence, Dir.-Gen. Defence Research and Devt. Org. and Sec. to Govt. of India for Defence Research and Devt.; Hon. D.Sc. (Jodhpur, Delhi and Sardar Patel Univs.); Foreign Hon. mem. American Acad. of Arts and Sciences.

Leisure interests: bird-watching, photography.

Publs. 60 papers on cosmic ray and elementary particle physics.

Department of Electronics, Vigyan Bhavan Annexe, Maulana Azad Road, New Delhi 110011; Home: 81 Lodi Estate, New Delhi 11003, India.

Telephone: 381310 (Office); 611533 (Home).

Menon, Nedyam Balachandra, B.A.; Indian diplomatist; b. 18 March 1921, South India; s. of K. M. R. Menon; m. Anect Menon 1947; three s. one d.; ed. Allahabad Univ.

Indian Navy 43-46; Indian Embassy, The Hague 49; Indian Mil. Mission, Berlin 51; Indian Embassy, Katmandu 54; High Comm. of India, Ottawa 57; Indian Embassy, Washington 59; Ministry of External Affairs Dir. (China Div.) 61; Nat. Defence Coll. 64; Indian Embassy, Bangkok and Perm. Del. to ECAFE 65; Deputy High Commr., Kuala Lumpur 66; Political Officer for Sikkim and Bhutan 67-70; Indian Amb. to Indonesia 70-73; Joint Sec. Ministry of External Affairs 73-75; Amb. to Turkey Aug. 75-.

Embassy of India, 24 Kibris Sokak, Cankaya, Ankara, Turkey.

Telephone: 272420.

Menon, Parakat Achutha, B.A.; Indian diplomatist; b. 2 Jan. 1905, Palghat; s. of the late Sir Mannath Krishnan Nair; m. Palat Padmini Menon 1930; one s. one d.; ed. Presidency Coll., Madras, and New Coll., Oxford.

Joined Indian Civil Service 29, and held various posts in Madras Provincial Govt. and Cen. Govt., including Under-Sec., Public Works Dept., Govt. of Madras 34-37; Under-Sec., Home Dept., Govt. of India 38-41; Collector and District Magistrate, Guntur, Madras 41-43; mem. Indian Legislative Assembly 38-39; Deputy Sec. and Sec., India Supply Mission, Washington, D.C. 44-47; adviser, Indian Del. to UN, San Francisco 45, N.Y. 46; served on Far East Comm., Washington, D.C. 46-47; Del. UNRRA Conf., Atlantic City 46; Jt. Sec. Ministry of External Affairs, Govt. of India 47-49; Minister to Portugal 49-51; Ambassador to Belgium and concurrently Minister to Luxembourg 51-54; Amb. to Thailand 54-56; High Commr. in Australia and New Zealand 56-59; Amb. to Argentina 59-60, to Fed. Germany 61-64; Chair. Fertilizers and Chemicals Travancore Ltd. (FACT), Kerala 65-70; Dir. State Bank of India 65-73, Cochin Refineries Ltd., Mysore Tools Ltd., Premier Breweries Ltd.; Pres. Madras Musical Asscn., Fed. of Indo-German Socs. in India; Chair. Madras Industrial Linings Ltd., Indo-German Chamber of Commerce Southern Region Council, Madras Literacy Soc., Madras Kerala Samaj Educ. Soc., Indian Council of World Affairs (Madras Branch); Pres. Madras Musical Asscn., Fed. of Indo-German Socs. in India, New Delhi; Vice-Pres. Indian Council of World Affairs, New Delhi, Indian Inst. of Public Admin. (Madras Branch); mem. Exec. Council Indian Inst. of Public Admin., New Delhi.

Leisure interests: reading, music.

"Padmaja", 4A Tank Bund Road, Madras 34, India.

Telephone: 82832 (Home).

Menon, Vatakke Kurupath Narayana, M.A PH.D.; Indian radio official; b. 27 June 1911, Trichur, Kerala; s. of Parameswaran Nambudiripad; m. Rekha Devi Mukherji 1945; one d.; ed. Univ. of Madras and Edinburgh Univ.

Script Writer, Producer and Adviser for E. Services of B.B.C. during Second World War; returned to India 47; Dir. of Broadcasting, Baroda State 47-48; joined All-India Radio as Dir. of Staff Training 48, became Dir. of Delhi, Madras and Calcutta Stations, Dir. of External Services and Deputy Dir.-Gen.; Sec. Nat. Acad. of Music, Dance and Drama, India 63-65; Dir.-Gen. All-India Radio 65-68; Pres. Int. Music Council (UNESCO) 66-68, mem. Exec. Board 71-; mem. Faculty of Music, Delhi Univ.; Exec. Dir. Nat. Centre for the Performing Arts, Bombay 68-; Vice-Chair. Int. Inst. for Comparative Music Studies, Berlin; Hon. Exec. Dir. Homi Bhabha Fellowship Council 68-; Trustee Int. Broadcasting Inst.; Scholar-in-Residence, Aspen Inst. for Humanistic Studies 73; Padma Bhushan 69.

Leisure interest: mass communication media.
Publs. *Development of William Butler Yeats* 42, 60, *Kerala, a Profile* 61, *Balasaraswathi* 63.
National Centre for the Performing Arts, Nariman Point, Bombay 400021, India.
Telephone: 310011.

Menotti, Gian Carlo; Italian composer; b. 7 July 1911; ed. Curtis Inst. of Music, Philadelphia, Pa.
Went to U.S.A. 28; mem. teaching staff Curtis Inst. of Music 41-55; Guggenheim Award 46, 47; Pulitzer Prize 50, 55; Hon. Assoc. Nat. Inst. of Arts and Letters 53; Pres. Festival of Two Worlds, Spoleto, Italy; Hon. B.M. (Curtis Inst. of Music).
Compositions include: Operas: *Amelia Goes to the Ball, The Old Maid and the Thief, The Island God, The Telephone, The Medium, The Consul, Amahl and the Night Visitors, The Labyrinth* (own libretti), *The Saint of Bleecker Street* 54, *The Last Savage* 63, *Martin's Lie* 64, *Help, Help, The Glotolinks* (space opera for children) 68, *The Most Important Man in the World* 71, *Tamu Tamu*; Ballet: *Sebastian*; Film: *The Medium* (producer); *Vanessa* (libretto) 58, *The Unicorn, The Gorgon and The Manticore—a Madrigal Fable, Maria Golovin* 59, *The Last Superman* 61, *The Death of a Bishop of Brindisi* (cantata) 63; chamber music, songs, etc.
27 East 62nd Street, New York, N.Y. 10021, U.S.A.

Mensah, Joseph Henry, M.SC.; Ghanaian politician; b. 31 Oct. 1928; ed. Achimota Coll., Univ. Coll. of Gold Coast (now Univ. of Ghana), London School of Econs. and Stanford Univ.
Assistant Insp. of Taxes 53; Research Fellow, Univ. Coll. of Gold Coast 53-57; Lecturer in Economics Univ. of Ghana 57-58; Economist, UN H.Q., New York 58-61; Chief Economist, Principal Sec. and Exec. Sec. of Nat. Planning Comm. Ghana 61-65; Economist, UN Dir. Div. of Trade and Econ. Co-operation, and Econ. Comm. for Africa (ECA) 65-May 69; Commr. of Finance April 69-July 69; M.P. for Sunyani (Progress Party) 69-72; Minister of Finance 69-72, and of Econ. Planning 69-71; arrested Jan. 72, released July 73.
c/o Ministry of Finance, Accra, Ghana.

Menuhin, Yehudi; American violinist; b. 22 April 1916, New York; s. of Moshe and Marutha Menuhin; m. 1st Nola Ruby Nicholas 1938, one s. one d.; m. 2nd Diana Rosamund Gould 1947, two s.; ed. privately in America and Europe.
Studied with Sigmund Anker, Louis Persinger, Georges Enesco (in Romania) and with Adolph Busch in Basle; New York debut 25, Paris 27 and Berlin 29 (with Bruno Walter and the Berlin Philharmonic); first world tour 35, in retirement 35-37, subsequently appeared as soloist in orchestras under Toscanini, Furtwängler, Stokowski, Koussevitsky, Beecham, Paul Paray, Walter, Mitropoulos, etc., etc.; has undertaken much research and restoration of neglected compositions; gave numerous benefit concerts during and after World War II; since 45 has toured extensively all over the world and has made documentary musical films in Europe and America; Pres. Trinity Coll. of Music, London; f. the Yehudi Menuhin School, Surrey 63; yearly festival at Gstaad 57-, Bath 59-68, Windsor 69; records for His Master's Voice; appeared in film, *Raga* (with George Harrison and Ravi Shankar) 74; Hon. D.Mus. (Oxford, Belfast, Leicester, London, Cambridge, Ottawa, Paris, Surrey), Hon. LL.D. (St. Andrews, Liverpool, Sussex, Bath), Hon. D.Lit. (Warwick, Leicester), Hon. Doctorate (California), Hon. Swiss Citizen 70, Freedom of Cities of Edinburgh and Bath; Medaille d'Or de la Ville de Paris, Royal Order of Phoenix, Greece, Legion of Honour, France, Order of Leopold, Order of Crown, Belgium, Order of Merit, Germany, Hon. K.B.E. (U.K.), Mozart Medal 65, Nehru Award for Peace and Int. Understanding (India) 70, Sonning Music Prize, Denmark 72, 30th Anniversary

Medal of Israel Philharmonic Orchestra, Canadian Music Council Gold Medal, Rosenberger Medal of Univ. Chicago.
Publs. *The Violin—Six Lessons with Yehudi Menuhin* 71, *Theme and Variations* 72, *The Violin* 76.
c/o Harold Holt, 122 Wigmore Street, London, W.1, England.

Menzel, Donald H., PH.D.; American astronomer; b. 11 April 1901, Florence, Colo.; s. of Charles Theodore Menzel and Ina Grace Zint; m. Florence Kreager 1926; two d.; ed. Univ. of Denver and Princeton Univ.
Instructor, Univ. of Iowa 24-25; Asst. Prof. Ohio State Univ. 25-26; Asst. Astronomer, Lick Observatory, Univ. of Calif. 26-32; Asst. Prof. Harvard Univ. 32-35, Assoc. Prof. 35-38, Prof. 38-, Chair. Dept. of Astronomy 46-49; Assoc. Dir. for Solar Research, Harvard Observatory 46-54; Dir. Sacramento Peak Station of Harvard Coll. Observatory 51-52; Acting Dir. Harvard Coll. Observatory 52-54, Dir. 54-66; Paine Prof. of Practical Astronomy 56-71, Emer. 71-; Research Scientist, Smithsonian Astrophysical Observatory 66-71, Emer. 71-; Scientific Dir. Electronic Space Systems Corpn.; U.S. Navy Service 42-45; Pres. American Astronomical Society 54-56; Pres. Comm. 13 on Solar Eclipses, Int. Astronomical Union 48-55; Pres. Comm. 17 on Moon, Int. Astronomical Union 64-67; Chair. Working Group on Lunar Nomenclature, Int. Astronomical Union 67-75; mem. Nat. Acad. of Sciences, American Acad. of Arts and Sciences; mem. American Philosophical Soc., Vice-Pres. 65-68; Hon. D.Sc. Univ. of Denver 54.
Leisure interests: writing, music, ballroom dancing.
Publs. *Stars and Planets* 31, 35, 38, *Elementary Manual of Radio Propagation* 48, *Our Sun* 49, 59, *Mathematical Physics* 53 (revised edn. 61), *Flying Saucers* 53, *The Story of the Starry Universe* 54, *Fundamental Formulas of Physics* 55, 60, *Writing a Technical Paper* 61, *Selected Papers on Physical Processes in Ionized Plasmas* 62, *The World of Flying Saucers* 63, *Stellar Interiors* 63, *Field Guide to the Stars and Planets* 64, *The Friendly Stars* 64, *Selected Papers on the Transfer of Radiation* 66, *Principles of Atomic Structure* 68, *Astronomy* 70, *Survey of the Universe* 71, *Flying Saucers Down to Earth* 76, *Astrology and the Sky Above* 76.
Center for Astrophysics, Harvard College Observatory—Smithsonian Astrophysical Observatory, 60 Garden Street, Cambridge, Mass. 02138; Home: 1010 Memorial Drive, Cambridge, Mass. 02138; 2566 Lantern Lane, Naples, Fla. 33940, U.S.A.

Menzies, Arthur Redpath, B.A., M.A.; Canadian diplomatist; b. 29 Nov. 1916; ed. Canadian Acad., Kobe, Japan, Univ. of Toronto and Harvard Univ.
Department of External Affairs 40-, Second Sec., Havana 45-46; Head of American and Far East Div., Dept. of External Affairs, Ottawa 48-50; Head of Canadian Liaison Mission, Tokyo 50, later Chargé d'Affaires, Tokyo; Head, Far Eastern Div., Dept. of External Affairs 53-58; High Commr. in Malaya 58-61, concurrently Ambassador to Burma 58-61; Head of Defence Liaison (I) Div., Dept. of External Affairs 62-65; High Commr. in Australia 65-72, concurrently High Commr. to Fiji 70-72; Perm. Rep. to N. Atlantic Council 72-.
North Atlantic Council, Brussels 1110, Belgium.

Menzies, Sir Peter (Thomson), M.A., F.INST.P., C.I.E.E., F.R.S.A.; British business executive; b. 15 April 1912, Chichester, Sussex; s. of John C. Menzies and Helen S. Aikman; m. Mary McPherson Alexander Menzies 1938; one s. one d.; ed. Musselburgh Grammar School and Univ. of Edinburgh.
Inland Revenue Department 33-39; Treasurer's Dept., Imperial Chemical Industries (I.C.I.) Ltd. 39-47, Asst. Treasurer 47-52, Deputy Treasurer 52-56, Finance Dir. 56-67, Deputy Chair. 67-72; Chair. Imperial Metal Industries Ltd. 64-72, Electricity Council 72-; Dir.

Commercial Union Assurance Co. 62-; Part-time mem. Central Electricity Generating Board 60-72; Dir. Nat. Westminster Bank Ltd. 68-; Pres. Int. Union of Producers and Distributors of Electrical Energy (UNIPEDE) 73; Fellow Inst. of Directors 74.
The Electricity Council, 30 Millbank, London, SW1P 4RD, England.

Menzies, Rt. Hon. Sir Robert Gordon, K.T., C.H., F.R.S., P.C., Q.C., LL.M.; Australian politician; b. 20 Dec. 1894, Jeparit, Victoria; s. of James Menzies and Kate Sampson; m. Pattie Maie Leckie 1920; two s. (one deceased) one d.; ed. Melbourne Univ.
Mem. Victoria Legislative Council 28-29; mem. Victoria Legislative Assembly 29-34; Hon. Minister Victorian Govt. 28-29, Attorney-Gen. and Minister for Railways 32 and Deputy Premier 32-34; mem. Federal House of Representatives for Kooyong 34-66; Commonwealth Attorney-Gen. and Minister for Industry 34-39; Prime Minister 39-41; Treas. 39-40; Minister for Defence Co-ordination Nov. 39-41, for Trade and Customs Feb.-Mar. 40, for Information Mar.-Dec. 40, for Munitions June-Nov. 40; mem. United Australia Party, Deputy Leader 36-39, Leader 39-41 and 43; Opposition mem. Advisory War Council 41-44; Leader Fed. Opposition 43-49; Prime Minister 49-66; Lord Warden of Cinque Ports 65-; Chancellor, Univ. of Melbourne 67-72; Leader of Mission to Pres. Nasser in Cairo on Suez Canal Aug./Sept. 56; numerous honorary degrees.
Leisure interest: watching first-class cricket.
Publs. *The Rule of Law During War* 17, *Studies in the Australian Constitution* (joint author) 33, *To the People of Britain at War* (speeches) 41, *The Forgotten People* 43, *Speech is of Time* 58, *The Changing Commonwealth* 60, *Afternoon Light* (memoirs, vol. I) 67, *Central Power in the Australian Commonwealth* 67, *The Measure of the Years* (memoirs, vol. II) 70.
Office: 95 Collins Street, Melbourne, 3000 Victoria; Home: 2 Haverbrack Avenue, Malvern, 3144 Victoria, Australia.
Telephone: 639463 (Office); 205111 (Home).

Meo, Jean Alfred Emile Edouard; French company director; b. 26 April 1927, Vosne Romanée, Côte d'Or; s. of Gaston Meo and Marcelle Lamarche; m. Nicole Odelin 1955; one s. two d.; ed. Lycée Henri IV, Ecole Polytechnique, Ecole Nat. Supérieure des Mines, Inst. d'Etudes Politques.
Operations engineer, Lorraine Basin coalfields 52-53; Head of sub-regional mineralogical admin., Lille, teacher at Inst. Industriel du Nord 54-56; technical adviser to Minister of Finance 57; worked in office of Gen. de Gaulle 58, in Secr. of Presidency 59-60; Chief Eng. corps. des mines 66-; Asst. Man. Dir., later Man. Dir. Union Générale des Pétroles 64-72 (name changed to Elf Union 67); Asst. Man. Dir. div. of refining and distribution, ERAP 66-72 (name changed to Elf-Enterprise Pétrolière 67); mem. Board of Dirs. and Man. Dir. SOCANTAR 70-72; Deputy Man. Dir. France-Editions et Publications 72-74; Deputy Man. Dir. attached to Chair., Agence Havas 74, Chair. and Man. Dir. June 74-; Chair. and Man. Dir. Avenir Publicité 74-; Chevalier, Légion d'Honneur.
136 Avenue Charles de Gaulle, 92200 Neuilly-sur-Seine; Home: 9 Villa Saïd, 75116 Paris, France.

Mercado Jarrín, Gen. Luis Edgardo; Peruvian army officer and politician; b. 19 Sept. 1919, Barranco, Lima; s. of Dr. Alejandro Mercado Ballon and Florinda Jarrin de Mercado; m. Gladys Neumann Teran de Mercado 1951; one s. four d.; ed. primary and secondary school, Colegio la Libertad de Moquegua, Escuela Militar de Chorrillos.
Commissioned 40, Gen. of Div. Jan. 70-; Prof. Escuela Militar, Escuela de Artillería, Escuela Superior de Guerra, Centro de Altos Estudios Militares, etc.; Dir. of Army Intelligence; Del. of Peruvian Army to several inter-American army confs.; guest lecturer to U.S. Army, Fort Holabird and Fort Bragg; Commdt.-Gen. Centro de Instrucción Militar del Perú 68; Minister of Foreign Affairs 68-71; Army Chief of Staff Jan.-Dec. 72; Prime Minister and Minister of War 73-75; awards include Grand Cross of Orden Militar de Ayacucho and Orden al Mérito Militar, Orden del Sol and orders from Colombia, Portugal, Argentina, Bolivia, Brazil and Venezuela.
Leisure interests: tennis, riding, classical music, reading (contemporary), military philosophy, sociology and economics.
Publs. *La Política y la Estrategia Militar en la Guerra Contrasubversiba en América Latina, El Ejército de Hoy en Nuestra Sociedad en Período de Transición y en el Campo Internacional, El Ejército y la Empresa;* contributor to magazine of Interamerican Defence Coll., U.S.A., *Revista Militar del Perú,* Brazilian *Military Journal.*
Avda. Velasco Astete 1140, Chacarrilla del Estanque, Lima, Peru.
Telephone: 256823.

Merchant, Livingston Tallmadge, B.A.; American diplomatist; b. 23 Nov. 1903, New York; s. of Huntington Wolcott and Mary Tallmadge Merchant; m. Elizabeth Stiles 1927; one s. two d. (one deceased); ed. Princeton Univ.
Assistant in investment firm 26-30, partner 30-42; Asst. Chief Div. of Defense Materials, Dept. of State 42, Chief Blockade and Supply Div. 43, Chief, War Areas Econ. Div. 44; U.S. Rep. Central Rhine Comm., Strasbourg 45; Econ. Counsellor, Paris 45; Chief, Aviation Div. Dept. of State 46; Foreign Service Officer 47; Counsellor, Nanking 47; Deputy Asst. Sec. of State for Far Eastern Affairs 49; Deputy to U.S. Special Rep. in Europe and Alt. Perm. Rep. NATO 52; Asst. Sec. of State 53-56, 58-59; Ambassador to Canada 56-58,61-62; Under-Sec. of State (Political Affairs) 59-61; Special Rep. for Multilateral Force Negotiations 63-64; U.S. Exec. Dir. World Bank 65-68; Trustee Emeritus Princeton Univ., Dir. Nat. Life Assurance Co. of Canada 63-72; Dir. Glens Falls Insurance Co. 63-72; Dir. Research Analysis Corpn. 64-75; Hon. D.C.L.; Hon. LL.D.
Leisure interests: reading, bridge, golf.
[*Died* 15 *May* 1976.]

Mercier, Pierre; French doctor of medicine; b. 6 Aug. 1910, Auxerre, Yonne; m. Yvonne Magniat 1936; one s. one d.; ed. Lycée Auxerre and Faculté de Médecine, Univ. de Paris.
Assistant at Hôpital Raymond-Poincaré 38-51; successively research worker, laboratory head and section head, Institut Pasteur, Paris 38-51; Dir. Institut Pasteur, Athens 51-62; Attaché French Embassy, Athens 51-62; Asst. Sec.-Gen. Inst. Pasteur 63-66, Sec.-Gen. Jan.-June 66, Dir. 66-71, Hon. Dir. 71-; Technical Adviser to Minister of Health 71-; mem. Acad. de Médecine; Officier Légion d'Honneur, Officer Order of George I and Commdr. Order of Phoenix (Greece), Chevalier Ordre de Léopold.
Publs. over 140 works from 34-62.
11 *bis* avenue Emile-Deschanel, 75 Paris 7e, France.

Mercouri, Melina; Greek film actress; b. 18 Oct. 1925; m. Jules Dassin (q.v.).
Films include: *Stella* 55, *He Who Must Die* 56, *Gipsy and the Gentleman, Never on Sunday* 59, *Phaedra* 61, *The Victors* 63, *Light of Day* 63, *Les Pianos Mécaniques* 64, *A Man Could Get Killed* 66, *10.30 p.m. Summer* 66, *Gaily, Gaily* 70, *Promise at Dawn* 70, *Once Is Not Enough* 75; song and dance version of *Never on Sunday* called

Illya Darling, Broadway 67, *Lysistrata* (musical) 72. Publ. *I was born Greek* (autobiography) 71.
c/o Alain Bernheim, 16 avenue Hoche, Paris 8e, France.

Mercure, Jean; French actor and theatrical director; b. 27 March 1909; ed. Lycée Rollin, Paris.
Director Théâtre de la Ville, Paris; has directed and played leading roles in *The Flashing Stream, Skipper Next to God, Miss Mabel, Living Room, La Volupté de l'Honneur, Tea and Sympathy, Sur la Terre comme au Ciel, Sud, Cardinal d'Espagne, Vol de Nuit, Six Personnages en Quête d'Auteur* 68, *L'Engrenage* 69. *La Guerre de Troie n'Aura Pas Lieu* 71, *Les Possédés* 72, *The National Health*; Grand Prix de la Mise en Scène 53, Prix de la meilleure réalisation lyrique for *Vol de Nuit* 60; Chevalier, Légion d'Honneur; Officier des Arts et Lettres.
Publs. French adaptations of *Skipper Next to God* (J. de Hartog), *Sur la Terre comme au Ciel* (with R. Thieberger) (Hochwälder), *Le Silence de la Mer* (Vercors), *Thunder Rock* (Ardrey), *The Living Room, The Potting Shed* (Greene) and *The Royal Hunt of the Sun* (Shaffer).
12 Villa Leandre, Paris 18e, France.

Merikoski, Veli Kaarlo, DR. IUR.; Finnish politician and university professor; b. 2 Jan. 1905, Pyhtaa; s. of Kaarlo Merikoski and Salli Nevalainen; m. Wava Margit Winge 1941 (died 1968); two s. one d.; ed. Helsinki Univ.
Assistant teacher of Public Law, Helsinki Univ. 36, Prof. of Admin. Law 41-69, Dean, Faculty of Law 47-51; mem. High Court of Impeachment 50-71; Chair. Union of Finnish Lawyers 46-51, 56-58; Chair. Finnish People's Party 58-61; Minister of Foreign Affairs 62-63; mem. Hague Int. Court of Arbitration 66-; mem. Finnish Acad. of Science and Letters; Pres. Int. Asscn. of Univs. 70-75, Hon. Pres. 75-; Chancellor of Turku School of Economics 74; numerous awards and decorations.
Leisure interest: riding.
Publs. *Freedom of Association* 35, *The Concept of Dispensation* 36, *The System of Government Grants* 38, *Textbook of Finnish Public Law,* Vol. I 44, Vol. II 46, *Lectures on the Legal Aspect of Social Welfare* 48, *The Rule of Law* 53, *Juridical Position of Universities and Student Organisations* 54, *Précis du Droit Public de la Finlande* 54, *The Citizen's ABC-book* 55, *Finnish Public Law,* Vol. I 52, Vol. II 62, *Le Pouvoir Discrétionnaire de l'Administration* 58, *The System of Legal Protection in Administration* 59, *University Autonomy* 66, *The Politicization of Public Administration* 69, *The Question of University Administration in Finland 1969-1970* 70.
Urheilutie 15 A 2, 02700 Kauniainen, Finland.
Telephone: 50-25-15.

Merino Castro, Admiral José Toribio; Chilean naval officer; b. 14 Dec. 1915; m. Gabriela Margarita Riofrío Busto 1952; three d.; ed. Naval Acad.
Specialized as Gunnery Officer, Naval Acad.; naval service on *Maipo* 36, *Rancagua* 40, Instructor *Blanco Encalada*; Div. Officer *Almirante Latorre* 43; Artillery Officer *Serrano* 45; Commdr. of Corvette *Papudo* 52; Technical Adviser of Armaments 55; Commdr. of Destroyer *Williams* 62, *Riveros* 63; Chief of Staff of the Fleet 64; Chief of Gen. Staff 64; Staff Coll. Course 65, 66-69; C.-in-C. of the Fleet 71, 72; C.-in-C. of First Naval Zone 72, 73; C.-in-C. of Navy 73-; mem. Gov. Council 73-; Armed Forces Medal III, II, Grand Star of Merit, Cross for Naval Merit, Decoration of Pres. of Repub. (Chile).
Naval Headquarters, Santiago, Chile.

Meritt, Benjamin Dean, A.B., A.M., LL.D., PH.D., D.LITT., L.H.D.; American philologist; b. 31 March 1899, Durham, N.C.; s. of Arthur H. and Cornelia (Dean)

Meritt; m. 1st Elizabeth Kirkland 1923, 2nd Lucy T. Shoe 1964; two s.; ed. Hamilton Coll., American School of Classical Studies Athens, and Princeton Univ.
Instructor in Greek, Univ. of Vermont 23-24, Brown Univ. 24-25; Asst. Prof. of Greek Princeton Univ. 25-26; Asst. Dir. American School of Classical Studies Athens 26-28; Associate Prof. of Greek and Latin Univ. of Michigan 28-29, Prof. 29-33; Visiting Prof. American School of Classical Studies Athens 32-33, 69-70, Annual Prof. 36 and 54-55; Dir. Athens Coll. 32-33; Francis White Prof. of Greek Johns Hopkins Univ. 33-35; Prof. Inst. for Advanced Study, Princeton 35-69; Visiting Prof. Univ. of Texas 71-72, Visiting Scholar 73-; Fellow American Acad. of Arts and Sciences; hon. councillor, Greek Archaeological Society; mem. American Philological Asscn. 22-, Pres. 53; Eastman Prof. Oxford 45-46; Sather Prof. Univ. of Calif. 59; corresp. mem. Royal Flemish Acad.; mem. American Philosophical Soc.; corresp. mem. British Acad.; hon. mem. Soc. for the promotion of Hellenic Studies; mem. German Archaeological Inst.; Commdr. Royal Order of Phoenix (Greece) and Commdr. Royal Order of George I (Greece).
Publs. *The Athenian Calendar in the Fifth Century* 28, *Supplementum Epigraphicum Græcum,* Vol. V (with Allen B. West) 31, *Corinth,* Vol. VIII, Part I, *Greek Inscriptions* 31, *Athenian Financial Documents* 32, *The Athenian Assessment of 425 B.C.* (with Allen B. West) 34, *Documents on Athenian Tribute* 37, *The Athenian Tribute Lists* (with H. T. Wade-Gery and M. F. McGregor), Vol. I 39, Vol. II 49, Vol. III 50, Vol. IV 53, *The Chronology of Hellenistic Athens* (with W. K. Pritchett) 40, *Epigraphica Attica* 40, *The Athenian Year* 61, *Agara XV: The Athenian Councillors* (with John S. Traill) 74.
716 West 16th Street, Austin, Tex. 78701, U.S.A.
Telephone: Austin 476-3103.

Merkatz, Hans-Joachim von, DR.JUR.; German lawyer and politician; b. 7 July 1905, Stargard, Pommern; s. of late Benno von Merkatz and Amély née Schneider; m. Margarete Müller-Wusterwitz 1937; two d.; ed. Univs. of Jena and Munich.
On research staff Kaiser-Wilhelm-Inst. für Ausländisches Öffentliches Recht und Völkerrecht (now Max-Planck-Inst.) 35-38, Ibero-Amerika Inst. 38-45; legal adviser to Deutsche Partei 46; mem. Bundestag 49-69; Dep. Chair. Deutsche Partei 53-55; Minister for Justice 56-57; Minister for Bundesrat and Länder Affairs 55-62; Minister for Refugees 60-61; mem. Christian Democratic Union 60-; mem. of Exec. Board of UNESCO 64; Prof. 66-; Hon. Knight Order of St. John; Commdr. Légion d'Honneur; Grand Cross Order of Merit.
Leisure interests: literature, handicrafts, history, political analysis.
Publs. *Politische Entwicklung und rechtliche Gestaltung der Ministerverantwortlichkeit* 35, *Germany To-day* (co-Editor) 54, *Politik im Widerstreit* 57, *Die konservative Funktion* 57, *In der Mitte des Jahrhunderts* 63, *Besinnung auf Preussen* (Co-Editor) 64.
Waldstrasse 74, 53 Bonn-Bad Godesberg, Federal Republic of Germany.
Telephone: 363332.

Merkulov, Vassily Yefimovich; Soviet foreign trade official; b. 1917; ed. Moscow Petroleum Inst. and Academy of Foreign Trade.
Member C.P.S.U. 44-; Dir. of Office, *Soyuznefteksport* Trust 50-51; Man. Dir., later Gen. Dir. Joint-Stock Soc., Finland 51-56; Vice-Chair. *Soyuznefteksport* Trust 57-64; U.S.S.R. Commercial Rep. in U.A.R. 64-68; Chair. All-Union Asscn. *Soyuznefteksport* 68-; Order of Lenin, Order of Patriotic War, Second Degree.
All-Union Association Soyuznefteksport, U.S.S.R. Ministry of Foreign Trade, 32-34 Smolenskaya-Sennaya ploshchad, Moscow, U.S.S.R.

Merle d'Aubigné, Robert Aimé; French surgeon; b. 23 July 1900, Neuilly; s. of Charles Merle d'Aubigné and Lucy Maury; m. Anna de Gunzburg 1932; one s. one d.; ed. Lycée Pasteur, Univ. of Paris.

Hospital surgeon 36-39; Capt. in medical corps 39-41; active in Resistance; Prof. of Orthopaedic and Reconstructural Surgery, Univ. of Paris 48-70; Surgeon, Cochin Hospital 48-60; Dean of Faculty, Cochin 68-69; mem. Acad. des Sciences, Institut de France; mem. Acad. of Surgery, Nat. Acad. of Medicine and many French and Int. learned socs.; Commdr. Légion d'Honneur; Officier, Ordre de la Résistance; Croix de Guerre; Officier Ordre de la Santé publique.
Leisure interest: mountaineering.
Achères-la-Forêt, 77760 La Chapelle-la-Reine, France.

Merlin, Jacques Joseph Alfred; French banker and insurance executive; b. 27 Aug. 1901; ed. Ecole Sainte-Croix, Neuilly.

Chairman Crédit Commercial de France 60-75, Hon. Chair. 75-; Chair. Union des Sociétés par Actions de Capitalisation du Secteur Privé; Chair. and Pres. Soc. Française d'Assurances pour Favoriser le Crédit; Vice-Chair. S.A. Française de Réassurances, Fédération Française des Sociétés d'Assurances; Dir. la Prévoyance R.D. & la Prévoyance Vie, Crédit Mobilier Industriel (SOVAC), Ciments Lafarge, Soc. de Produits Alimentaires et Diététiques (SOPAD), Lafarge Cement of N. America; mem. Office and Econ. Comm. of Conseil Nat. du Patronat Français; fmr. Vice-Chair. Chambre de Commerce de Paris; Officier Légion d'Honneur.
Office: 1 rue Euler, 75008 Paris; Home: 6 boulevard Suchet, 75016 Paris, France.

Merrick, David; American theatrical producer; ed. St. Louis Univ.

Producer of numerous plays on Broadway, including *Fanny* 54, *The Matchmaker* 55, *Look Back in Anger*, *Romanoff and Juliet*, *Jamaica* 57, *The Entertainer*, *The World of Suzie Wong*, *La Plume de ma Tante*, *Epitaph for George Dillon*, *Maria Golovin* 58, *Destry Rides Again*, *Gypsy*, *Take Me Along* 59, *The Good Soup*, *Vintage '60'*, *Irma la Douce*, *A Taste of Honey*, *Becket*, *Do Re Me* 60, *Carnival* 61, *Sunday in New York* 61, *Ross* 61, *I Can Get it for You Wholesale* 62, *Stop the World, I Want to Get Off* 62, *Tchin Tchin* 62, *Oliver!* 62, *Rehearsal* 63, *Hello Dolly* 64, *Pickwick* 65, *Inadmissible Evidence* 65, *Cactus Flower* 65, *Marat/Sade* 65, *Don't Drink the Water* 66, *I do! I do!* 66, *Philadelphia, Here I Come* 66, *Rosencrantz and Guildenstern Are Dead* 67, *How Now, Dow Jones* 67, *The Happy Time* 67, *Promises Promises* 68, *40 Carats* 68, *Play it Again Sam* 69, *Private Lives* 69, *Child's Play* 70, *A Midsummer Night's Dream*, *Four on a Garden*, *The Philanthropist* 71, *There's One in Every Marriage*, *Vivat, Vivat Regina!*, *Moonchildren*, *Sugar* 72, *Child's Play* 72, *Out Cry* 73, *The Great Gatsby* (film) 73.
246 West 44th Street, New York City, N.Y., U.S.A.
Telephone: 212-LO-3-7520.

Merrifield, (Robert) Bruce; American biochemist; b. 15 July 1921, Texas; s. of George and Lorene Merrifield; m. Elizabeth Furlong 1949; six c.; ed. Univ. of California, Los Angeles (U.C.L.A.).

Chemist, Park Research Foundation 43-44; Teaching Asst., Chemistry Dept. UCLA 44-47, Research Asst., Medical School 48-49; Asst. to Assoc. Prof. Rockefeller Inst. 49-66, Prof. of Biochemistry 66-; developed solid phase peptide synthesis; mem. Nat. Acad. of Sciences; Nobel Guest Prof. 68; Lasker Award 69, Gairdner Award 70, Intra-Science Award 70, American Chem. Soc. Award 72, Nichols Award 73.
Leisure interests: tennis, camping, hiking.
Publs. 75 articles in various scientific journals.
Rockefeller University, New York, N.Y. 10021; 43 Mezzine Drive, Cresskill, N.J. 07626, U.S.A. (Home). Telephone: 212-360-1461 (Office); 201-567-0329 (Home).

Merrill, John Ogden; American architect; b. 10 Aug. 1896; ed. Wisconsin Univ., Mass. Inst. of Technology.

Chief Architect, Mid-Western States Fed. Housing Admin. 39; in partnership with Skidmore and Owings 39-58, 59-, with whom he designed numerous govt. projects and private buildings including Oak Ridge, Tennessee, U.S. base at Okinawa, Lever House, New York, Terrace Plaza Hotel, Cincinnati, etc.; Fellow, American Inst. of Architects; Vice-Pres. San Francisco Planning and Urban Renewal Asscn. 69-.
101 Gardner Place, Colorado Springs, Colo. 80906, U.S.A.

Merrill, Maurice Hitchcock, A.B., LL.B., S.J.D.; American lawyer and university teacher; b. 3 Oct. 1897, Washington, D.C.; s. of George Waite and Mary Lavinia (Hitchcock) Merrill; m. Orpha Roberts 1922 (died 1971); one d.; ed. Univ. of Oklahoma and Harvard Univ.

Served in U.S. Army 18; taught in Univ. of Okla. 19-22; practised law in Tulsa Okla. 22-26; Assoc. Prof. of Law Univ. of Idaho 25-26; Asst. Prof. of Law Univ. of Nebraska 26-28; Prof. of Law 28-36; Prof. of Law Univ. of Okla. 36-50, Research Prof. of Law 50-68, Research Prof. Emeritus 68, Act. Dean 45-46; Law practice Norman, Okla. 68-; Gen. Counsel, Oklahoma Asscn. of Municipal Attorneys 71-; mem. Judicial Council of Okla. 45-46, 47-65; Commr. from Okla. to Nat. Conf. of Commrs. on Uniform State Laws 44-, mem. Exec. Cttee. 61-68, Vice-Pres. 63-67, Chair. Okla. del. 49-; mem. Panel of Labor Arbitrators U.S. Conciliation Service 46-; mem. Nat. Acad. of Arbitrators, Permanent Editorial Board for Uniform Commercial Code 63-; Board of Advisers S.W. Inst. of Local Govt. Law 68-; mem. Special Comm. on Constitutional Revision (Okla.) 69-70; Fellow, American Bar Foundation 56-; Hatton W. Sumners Award 64; Distinguished Service Citation, Univ. of Okla. 68; Oklahoma Hall of Fame 70, President's Award, Oklahoma Bar Asscn. 72; Hon. D. Hum. Litt., Oklahoma Christian Coll. 74.
Leisure interests: writing, gardening.
Publs. *Law of Covenants Implied in Gas and Oil Leases* 26, *Nebraska Annotations to Restatement of Contracts* (with William Sternberg and Lester B. Orfield) 32, *Nebraska Annotations to Restatement of Agency* 33, *Oklahoma Annotations to Restatement of Agency* 40; mem. of Board of Eds. and Ed. for Volume III (*The Nation and the States*), *Selected Essays on Constitutional Law* 38, *Cases and Materials on Administrative Law* 50, *Law of Notice* 52, *Administrative Law* (American Casebook Series) 54, *The Public's Concern with the Fuel Minerals* 60.
Home: 800 Elm Avenue, Norman, Oklahoma, U.S.A.; Office: 556 Monnet Hall, 630 Parrington Oval, University of Oklahoma, Norman, Oklahoma, U.S.A.
Telephone: 321-6585 (Home); 325-5091 and 325-4373 (Office).

Merrill, Robert; American baritone; b. 4 June 1919, Brooklyn, New York; s. of Abraham Miller and Lillian (née Balaban) Merrill; m. Marion Machno 1954; one s. one d.

Debut at Metropolitan Opera as Germont (*La Traviata*) 45; has since appeared throughout U.S.A. and Europe in most of the baritone repertoire including: Gerard (*Andrea Chenier*), Renato (*Un Ballo in Maschera*), Figaro (*Il Barbiere di Siviglia*), Rodrigo (*Don Carlo*), Scarpia (*Tosca*), Amonasro (*Aida*) and Rigoletto; many concert and television appearances; frequent recordings.
Leisure interests: art and golf.
c/o Metropolitan Opera Association, Lincoln Center, New York, N.Y. 10023, U.S.A.

Merrison, Sir Alexander Walter, Kt., D.L., PH.D., F.R.S.; British nuclear physicist and university vice-chancellor; b. 20 March 1924, London; s. of Violet Henrietta Merrison and the late Henry Walter Merrison;

m. 1st Beryl Glencora Le Marquand 1948 (died 1968), 2nd Maureen Michele Barry 1970; three *s.* one *d.*; ed. Enfield Grammar School and King's Coll., London.

Experimental Officer, Signals Research and Devt. Establishment, Christchurch, Hants. 44-46; Senior Scientific Officer, Atomic Energy Research Establishment, Harwell 46-51; Leverhulme Fellow and Lecturer, Univ. of Liverpool 51-57, Prof. of Experimental Physics 60-69; Physicist European Org. for Nuclear Research (CERN), Geneva 57-60; Dir. Daresbury Nuclear Physics Laboratory, Science Research Council 62-69; Vice-Chancellor, Univ. of Bristol 69-; Fellow, Inst. of Physics; Charles Vernon Boys Prize of Inst. of Physics and Physical Soc. 61.

Publs. Contributions to scientific journals on nuclear and elementary particle physics.

Senate House, Tyndall Avenue, Bristol, England. Telephone: 0272-24161.

Merritt, H. Houston, M.D.; American neurologist and administrator; b. 12 Jan. 1902, Wilmington, N.C.; *s.* of Hiram Houston Merritt and Dessie Cline Merritt; *m.* Mabel Carmichael 1930; no *c.*; ed. Vanderbilt and Johns Hopkins Univs.

Assistant, Harvard Medical School 31, Assoc. Prof. till 44; Prof. of Clinical Neurology, Columbia Univ. and Chief., Div. of Neuropsychiatry, Montefiore Hospital, N.Y. 44-48; Prof. of Neurology and Chair., Dept. of Neurology, Columbia Univ. and Dir. of Service of Neurology, Neurological Inst., Presbyterian Hosp., N.Y. 48-68; Dean, Faculty of Medicine and Vice-Pres. in charge of Medical Affairs, Columbia Univ. Coll. of Physicians and Surgeons 59-70; Dean. Emer 70-; Vice-Pres. Emer. 70-; Henry L. and Lucy Moses Prof. of Neurology, Columbia Univ. 59-70; Prof. Emer. 70-; Max Weinstein Award, United Cerebral Palsy Asscns. Inc. 62; Bronze Hope Chest Award, Nat. Multiple Sclerosis Soc. 66; Lennox Award, American Epilepsy Soc. 67; The North Carolina Soc. Award, Modern Medicine Award; Grand Officer, Portuguese Order of Santiago; Golden Anniversary Medal of Asscn. for Research in Nervous and Mental Diseases; Thomas W. Salmon Distinguished Service Award in Psychiatry and Mental Hygiene 73.

Leisure interests: reading, bridge, swimming.

Publs. *A Textbook of Neurology* 5th edn. 73; in collaboration: *The Cerebrospinal Fluid* 37, *Neurosyphilis* 46, *Fundamentals of Clinical Neurology* 47; approximately 220 articles in professional journals.

710 West 168 Street, New York, N.Y., 10032, U.S.A. Telephone: 579 5240.

Merry del Val y Alzola, Alfonso (Marqués de Merry del Val); Spanish diplomatist; b. 1903; ed. Stonyhurst College and Deusto and Valladolid Univs.

Diplomatic Service 29-; Ambassador to the United States 64-71.

Ministry of Foreign Affairs, Madrid, Spain.

Mertens de Wilmars, Jonkheer (Ecuyer) Jacques E.M.J., DR. JUR., DR. POL. AND SOC. ECON., LIC. PHIL.; Belgian economist, univ. prof. and banker; b. 1 Feb. 1917, Oxford, England; *m.* Anne-Marie de Meester de Heyndonck 1947; one *s.* three *d.*; ed. Univ. Leuven.

Barrister 39-45; Asst. Faculty of Economic and Social Sciences, Univ. Leuven 39-43, Lecturer 44, Asst. Prof. 45, Prof. 49, Dean 62-63; Chair. Inst. of Econ. Science 61-64; Econ. Adviser to Minister of Finance 45-46 and 47-48; Attaché, Nat. Bank Belgium 43, Sec. Gov. 46, Adviser 48, Chief Econ. Studies 53-58, Deputy Dir. 61-65, Adviser to the Board 65-68, Econ. Adviser 68-; Chief of Cabinet to Prime Minister 58-61, Hon. Chief of Cabinet to Prime Minister 61; mem. UN Population Comm. 51-64, Vice-Chair. 55-58, Chair. 59-63; mem. Pontifical Comm. on Problems of Population, Family and Birth 64-66; mem. Belgian Del. ECOSOC (UN) 52,

Special Financial Mission, UN Technical Assistance, Iran 52, Arbitration Comm. to Indonesia 53-56; Deputy mem. Monetary Cttee. EEC 58-, Chair. Deputies 68-74; Vice-Chair. Comité de Politique Conjoncturelle EEC 60-71; Officer Order of Léopold, Commdr. Order Crown, Commdr. Order of Orange-Nassau, Commdr. Order Merit (Austria), Commdr. Order Crown of Oak (Luxembourg), Commdr. Order St. Gregorius the Great (Holy See).

Leisure interests: golf, swimming.

Publs. *La naissance et le développement de l'étalon-or 1696-1922* 44, *La politique du plein emploi et ses limites* 52, *Les objectifs de la politique économique sont-ils compatibles entre-eux?* 62, *The Economics of Aid to Less-Developed Countries* 63, *De Recente Hervormingen van het I.M.F. en de Toekomst van het Internationale Geldstelsel* 68, *Vaste of Fluctuerende Wisselkoersen* 70, *The Relaunching and Pursuit of Economic and Monetary Union* 72.

228 Winston Churchill Avenue, 1180 Brussels, Belgium. Telephone: 02/343-73-85.

Mertens de Wilmars, Joseph H. C., D.L., D.POL.SC.; Belgian judge; b. 22 June 1912, St. Niklaas; *s.* of Albert Mertens de Wilmars and Jeanne Meert; *m.* Betty van Ormelingen 1939; eight *c.*; ed. Abbey School St. Andries, Bruges, Univ. of Louvain.

Member of Bar 35-67; Assessor, Conseil d'Etat 48-51; mem. Parl. 51-61; Prof. of Law, Univ. of Louvain 67-; Judge, Court of Justice of European Communities 67-, now a Pres. of the Chamber; Knight Order of Léopold.

Court of Justice of the European Communities, Centre Européen, Plateau de Kirchberg, P.O. Box 1406, Luxembourg; and Jan Van Ryswycklaan 192, Antwerp, Belgium.

Telephone: 352-47-621 (Office); (03) 38-07-68 (Home).

Merton, Robert K., PH.D.; American professor of sociology; b. 5 July 1910, Philadelphia, Pa.; *m.* Suzanne C. Merton 1934; one *s.* two *d.*; ed. Temple Univ. and Harvard Univ.

Tutor and Instructor in Sociology, Harvard Univ. 36-39; Assoc. Prof. and Prof. Tulane Univ. 39-41; Asst. Prof. to Prof., Columbia Univ. 41-63, Giddings Prof. of Sociology 63-74, Univ. Prof. 74-; Assoc. Dir., Bureau of Applied Social Research, Columbia Univ. 42-70; mem. Nat. Acad. of Sciences, American Philosophical Soc., American Acad. of Arts and Sciences, Nat. Acad. of Educ., World Acad. of Arts and Sciences; Pres. American Sociological Asscn. 57, Sociological Research Asscn. 68, Eastern Sociological Soc. 69; Pres. Soc. for Social Studies of Science 75-76; mem. John Simon Guggenheim Memorial Foundation Educ. Advisory Board 64-, Chair. 71-; Prize for Dist. Scholarship in Humanities, American Council of Learned Socs.; Lectureship in Recognition of Outstanding Scientific Achievement, Nat. Insts. of Health; many hon. degrees.

Publs. *Science, Technology and Society in 17th-Century England* 38, 71, *Mass Persuasion* 46, *Social Theory & Social Structure* 49, 68, *Continuities in Social Research* 50, *Reader in Bureaucracy* 52, *Focused Interview* 56, *Student-Physician* 57, *Freedom to Read* 57, *Sociology Today* 59, *Contemporary Social Problems* 61, 71, *On the Shoulders of Giants* 65, *On Theoretical Sociology* 68, *Social Theory and Functional Analysis* 69, *Sociology of Science* 73, *Sociological Ambivalence* 76, *The Metric of Science* 76.

Department of Sociology, Fayerweather 415, Columbia University, New York, N.Y. 10027, U.S.A. Telephone: 212-280-3696.

Merz, Charles; American journalist; b. 23 Feb. 1893, Sandusky, Ohio; *m.* Evelyn Scott 1924; ed. Yale Univ. Manager Editor *Harper's Weekly* 15-16; Associate Editor *New Republic* 16-20; staff correspondent and Assoc. Editor *New York World* 21-30; mem. Editorial

staff *New York Times* 31-38, Editor 38-61, Editor Emeritus 61-; Hon. Litt.D. (Yale, Columbia, Colgate, Wooster).
Publs. *The Great American Bandwagon* 28, *The Dry Decade* 31, *Days of Decision* 39.
10 Gracie Square, New York, N.Y., U.S.A.
Telephone: RE-7-4118.

Merzagora, Cesare; Italian industrialist and politician; b. 9 Nov. 1898, Milan; *s.* of Luigi and Fenini Elisa Merzagora; *m.* Giuliana Benucci 1933; four *d.*
Served in First World War 15-18; Dir. Banca Commerciale Italiana in Bulgaria 20-27; also Italian Consul at Philippopolis; founder of anti-fascist newspaper *La Voce d'Italia*, suppressed in 24; Dir. of banking institutes in foreign countries 27-38; Dir. of Pirelli and associated firms 38; mem. of Liberation Movement in Northern Italy; Pres. of its Central Economic Comm.; Minister of Foreign Trade in fourth and fifth De Gasperi Cabinets 47-49; Senator (Independent, Milan) 48-; Pres. of the Senate 53-Nov. 67, Life Senator 63-; Acting Pres. of Italy Aug.-Dec. 64; Chair. Assicurazioni Generali April 68-; Chair. Montedison 70.
1 Via di Villa Grazioli, Rome, Italy.
Telephone: 856-267.

Merzban, Mohammed Abdullah, M.A.; Egyptian politician; b. 20 Jan. 1918, Fayoum; *m.*; ed. Fouad Univ. and Harvard Univ.
Lecturer, Faculty of Commerce, Cairo Univ. until 56; Sec.-Gen. Ministry of Industry 56-58; Gen. Man. Industrialization Authority 58-60; Chair. Al-Nasr Org. 60-61; Chair. Spinning & Weaving Org. 61-66; Chair. Bank of Cairo 66-68; Minister of Supply and Home Trade 68-70, of Economy and Foreign Trade 70-73; Acting Minister of Supply and Home Trade 71-73; Deputy Prime Minister 72-73.
Publs. *Financial Management, Sales Management, Mathematics of Marketing.*
c/o Ministry of Economy and Foreign Trade, Cairo, Egypt.

Meselson, Matthew Stanley, PH.B., PH.D., F.A.A.A.S.; American professor of biology; b. 24 May 1930, Denver, Col.; *s.* of Hymen Avram and Ann Swedlow Meselson; *m.* Sarah Leah Page 1969; two *d.*; ed. Univ. of Chicago and Calif. Inst. of Technology.
Research Fellow, Calif. Inst. of Technology 57-58, Asst. Prof. of Physical Chemistry 58-59, Senior Research Fellow in Chemical Biology 59-60; Assoc. Prof. of Biology, Harvard Univ. 60-64, Prof. of Biology 64-; Prize for Molecular Biology, Nat. Acad. of Sciences 63, Eli Lilly Award in Microbiology and Immunology 64; mem. U.S. Nat. Acad. of Sciences, Inst. of Medicine; Hon. D.Sc. (Columbia Univ.) 71, (Univ. Chicago) 75; Public Service Award, Fed. of American Scientists 72; Alumni Medal, Univ. of Chicago Alumni Asscn. 71; Alumni Distinguished Service Award, Calif. Inst. of Technology 75.
Publs. numerous papers on the biochemistry and molecular biology of nucleic acids in various numbers of *Proceedings* of Nat. Acad. of Sciences and of *Journal of Molecular Biology*, etc.
The Biological Laboratories, 16 Divinity Avenue, Harvard University, Cambridge, Mass. 02138, U.S.A.
Telephone: 617-495-2264.

Meshel, Yeruham; Israeli trade unionist; b. 24 Nov. 1912, Pinsk, Russia; *m.* Rachel Frank 1939; one *s.* one *d.*
Immigrated to Palestine 33; Sec. Metal Workers' Union, Tel-Aviv, mem. Tel-Aviv Labour Council Exec. 45; mem. Trade Union Centre of Histadrut Exec. Cttee., Chair. Industrial Workers' Div. 50-60, mem. Central Exec. Bureau 60-, Chair. Trade Union Centre 61, Deputy Sec.-Gen. Histadrut 64-74, Head of Histadrut Social Security Centre and Arab Workers'

Dept., Acting Sec.-Gen. 73, Sec.-Gen. 74-; mem. Central Cttee. of Mapai 61, mem. Secr. Mifleget Ha'avoda 64; rep. to numerous int. labour confs.
Histadrut, 93 Arlosorof Street, Tel-Aviv, Israel.
Telephone: (03) 261111.

Meskill, Thomas Joseph, B.S.; American state governor; b. 30 Jan. 1928, New Britain, Conn.; *s.* of late Thomas Joseph Meskill and of Laura Ryan Meskill; three *s.* two *d.*; ed. New Britain Senior High School, Trinity Coll., Hartford, Univ. of Conn. Law School and N.Y. Univ. School of Law.
Assistant Corpn. Counsel, New Britain 60-62; Mayor of New Britain 62-64; Corpn. Counsel 65-66; elected to Congress 66, 68; Gov. of Conn. 70-74; mem. American Bar Asscn.; Republican.
990 Prospect Avenue, Hartford, Conn. 06105, U.S.A.
Telephone: 203-523-7014.

Mesnil du Buisson, Robert Du, Count, D. ès L., D. en D.; French archaeologist; b. 19 April 1895, Bourges; *s.* of late Léon Count du Mesnil du Buisson and Berthe Roussel de Courcy; *m.* 1st Jeanne Le Clerc de Pulligny 1923 (died 1964), four *s.* two *d.*; 2nd Pauline Husson de Sampigny 1965.
Dir. French Archaeological Missions in Syria, Egypt and France; Dir. Excavation at Palmyra 65-; Pres. Société Nat. des Antiquaires de France 46-47; Pres. Société Historique et Archéologique de l'Orne 47-55; Hon. Pres. 56-; Pres. Soc. du Manoir d'Argentelles 57-; Dir. du Centre Culturel et Touristique de l'Orne 57-; Vice-Pres. Soc. d'Ethnographie de Paris 60-69, Pres. 69-; Commdr. Légion d'Honneur 66; Lauréat de l'Institut de France 40, 58, 63; Médaille d'Or de la Société d'Encouragement au Progrès 73, Croix du Combattant de l'Europe 74.
Leisure interest: Preservation of buildings and art objects in the Orne region of France.
Publs. *Les ruines d'El-Mishrifé au Nord-Est de Homs* 27, *La technique des fouilles archéologiques* 33, *Le site archéologique de Mishrifé-Qatna* 35, *Les noms et signes égyptiens désignant des vases* 35, *Souran et Tell Masin* 35, *Le site de Qadesh* 36, *Inscriptions juives de Doura-Europos* 37, *Inventaire des inscriptions palmyréniennes de Doura-Europos* 39, *Les peintures de la Synagogue de Doura* 245-246 *ap. J.-C.* 39, *Les tessères et monnaies de Palmyre* 44, *Les ouvrages du siège à Doura-Europos* 45, *Le site archéologique d'Exmes (Uxoma)* 46, *Le sautoir d'Atargatis et la chaîne d'amulettes* 47, *Baghouz, l'ancienne Corsôté* 48, *Une voie commerciale de haute antiquité dans l'Orne* 51, *Les dieux et les déesses en forme de vase dans L'Antiquité Orientale, La palissade gauloise d'Alençon* 52, *L'alcôve royale dite "Lit de Justice d'Argentelles"* 53, *Un constructeur du Château de La Celle-Saint-Cloud, Jacques Jérémie Roussel* 54, *Saint-Germain-en-Laye* 54, *Poissy* 55, *Chantilly* 57, *Une famille de Chevaliers de Malte, les Costart* 60, *Plaques de cheminées de l'Orne* 47-67, *Les tessères et les monnaies de Palmyre de la Bibliothèque Nationale* 62, *Inscriptions sur jarres de Doura-Europos* 59, *Origine et évolution du panthéon de Tyr, Les Chausson de la Salle* 63, *Le dieu-Griffon à Palmyre et chez les Hittites* 63, *Les origines du panthéon Palmyrénien* 64, *Le dieu Ousô sur des monnaies de Tyr* 65, *Le drame des deux étoiles du matin et du soir dans l'antiquité orientale* 67, *Le décor des deux cuves de Tell Mardikh* 67, *Le Manoir d'Argentelles, Guide du visiteur, Origines phéniciennes des Dioscures, Le décor asiatique du couteau de Gebel el-Arak* 69, *Etudes sur les dieux phéniciens hérités par l'Empire Romain* 70, *Nouvelles études sur les dieux et les mythes de Canaan* 73, *Géographie et astronomie mythiques, Les voyages de Gilgamesh* 74.
63 rue de Varenne, Paris 7e, France, and Château de Champobert, par 61310 Exmes (Orne), France.
Telephone: (Paris) 551-00-06; (Orne) 34-67-93-61.

Messer, Thomas M., B.A., M.A.; American museum director; b. 9 Feb. 1920, Bratislava, Czechoslovakia; s. of Richard and Agatha (Albrecht) Messer; m. Remedios Garcia Villa 1948; ed. Thiel Coll. (Greenville, Pa.), Boston, Paris and Harvard Univs.
Dir., Roswell Museum, New Mexico 49-52; Asst. Dir. in charge of Nat. Exhibitions Programme, American Fed. of Arts 52-53, Dir. of Exhibitions 53-55, Dir. 55-56; Dir., Boston Inst. of Contemporary Art 57-61, Solomon R. Guggenheim Museum, New York 61-; First Vice-Pres. American Fed. of Arts 73-75; Pres. Asscn. of Art Museum Directors 74-75; Chair. Int. Cttee. for Museums and Collections of Modern Art, Int. Council of Museums 74-(77); Adjunct Prof., Harvard Univ. 60; Adjunct Prof. of Art History, Barnard Coll. 66, 71; Senior Fellow, Center for Advanced Studies, Wesleyan Univ. 66; Trustee Center for Inter-American Relations 74-(76); Trustee U.S. Int. Council of Museums 70-; Trustee and Chair. Arts Admission Comm. of MacDowell Colony Corpn.; Trustee, Czechoslovak Asscn. of Arts and Sciences, Wooster School; mem. Museum Advisory Panel of Nat. Endowment for the Arts, Art Advisory Panel to Commr. of Internal Revenue Service 74-(77), Comm. on U.S.-Latin American Relations, Museum Advisory Group to Office of Attorney-General of N.Y. State Admissions Cttee. Century Asscn. 73-(76); Dr. Fine Arts h.c., Univ. of Mass.; Knight, Royal Order of St. Olav (Norway).
Leisure interests: the theatre, literature, music.
Publs. *Edvard Munch* 73; Museum Catalogues on: Vasily Kandinsky, Paul Klee, Edvard Munch, Egon Schiele, etc.; articles and contributions to art journals, *Art in America, Art International, American Scholar, Arts, Art News, Saturday Review/World, Studio International, The Art Gallery.*
The Solomon R. Guggenheim Museum, 1071 Fifth Avenue, New York, N.Y. 10028; Home: 1105 Park Avenue, New York, N.Y., U.S.A.
Telephone: (212) 860-1309.

Messerer, Asaf Mikhailovich; Soviet choreographer and dancer; b. 19 Nov. 1903; ed. Moscow School of Choreography.
Joined the Bolshoi Theatre Co. 21, *Premier Danseur* to 54; People's Artist of the R.S.F.S.R.; State prizewinner 41, 47.
Principal roles in: *Swan Lake, The Nutcracker* by Tchaikovsky, *Don Quixote* by Minkus, *Flames of Paris, Fountain of Bakhchisarai* by Asafiev, *Red Poppy* by Gliere, *Petrushka* by Stravinsky, etc.
State Academic Bolshoi Theatre, 1 Ploshchad Sverdlova, Moscow, U.S.S.R.

Messerschmitt, Willy, DR. ING.; German aviation engineer and businessman; b. 26 June 1898; ed. Technical Coll., Munich.
Designed gliders and sailplanes with engineer Harth 12-23; designed sporting and transport airplanes (single-spar wing), Bamberg, Germany 23-37; chief designer and Dir. Bayer. Flugzeugwerke, later called Messerschmitt A.G., Augsburg 27-45; Me 109 speed record for land planes 37; world speed record 38; jet-propelled airplane Me 262; worked on reconstruction of industrial works, designing work in various engineering fields 45-54; Pres. Messerschmitt and Co. K.G. and Hon. Chair. of the Board, Messerschmitt-Bölkow-Blohm G.m.b.H. Ottobrunn; Nat. Prize for Art and Science; Knight's Cross; War Service Cross; Bavarian Service Cross; Great Service Cross of Fed. Repub. of Germany with Star.
Mauerkircherstrasse 46, 8 Munich 86, Federal Republic of Germany; El Velerin, Estepona/Málaga, Spain.
Telephone: 48-15-16.

Messiaen, Olivier; French composer and organist; b. 10 Dec. 1908, Avignon, Vaucluse; s. of Pierre Messiaen and Cécile Sauvage; m. 1st Claire Delbos (died 1959), one s.; m. 2nd Yvonne Loriod 1961.
Organist, Trinité, Paris 31-; Co-founder *Jeune-France* movement 36; Prof. Ecole Normale and Schola Cantorum 36-39; Prof. of Harmony, Paris Conservatoire 41-47, of Analysis, Aesthetics and Rhythm 47-, of Composition 66-; Grand Officier de la Légion d'Honneur, Grand Officier de l'Ordre national du Mérite, Commdr. des Arts et des Lettres; mem. Institut de France, Akad. der Künste, Berlin, Bayerische Akad. der Wissenschaften, Munich, Royal Acads. of Sweden, London and Madrid, American Acad. of Arts and Letters; Erasmus Prize 71; Sibelius Prize 71.
Compositions include: *Le Banquet Céleste* for organ 28, *Préludes* for piano 29, *Le Diptyque* for organ 29, *L'Ascension* for organ 33, *La Nativité du Seigneur* for organ 35, *Poèmes pour Mi* for voice and piano 36, *Chants de Terre et de Ciel* for voice and piano 38, *Les Corps Glorieux* for organ 39, *Quatuor pour la Fin du Temps* for violin, cello, clarinet and piano 41, *Visions de l'Amen* for two pianos 43, *Vingt Regards sur l'Enfant Jésus* for piano 44, *Trois Petites Liturgies de la Présence Divine* for choir and orchestra 44, *Harawi* song cycle 45, *Turangalila Symphonie* for piano, onde and orchestra 46-48, *Cinq Rechants* for choir a capella 49, *Etudes de Rythme* for piano 49, *Messe de la Pentecôte* for organ 49, *Livre d'Orgue* 51, *Réveil des Oiseaux* 53, *Oiseaux Exotiques* 55, *Catalogue d'Oiseaux* for piano 56-58, *Chronochromie* for large orchestra 59, *Sept Haïkaï* for piano and small orchestra 63, *Couleurs de la Cité céleste* for orchestra 64, *Et Exspecto Resurrectionem Mortuorum* for orchestra 65, *La Transfiguration de notre Seigneur Jésus-Christ* for choir, orchestra and seven instrumental soloists 69, *Des Canyons aux Etoiles* for piano and orchestra 70-74.
230 rue Marcadet, 75018 Paris, France.

Messmer, Pierre Auguste Joseph, LL.D.; French politician and overseas administrator; b. 20 March 1916, Vincennes; s. of Joseph and Marthe (née Farcy) Messmer; m. Gilberte Duprez 1947; ed. Faculté de droit de Paris.
Military service with "Free French" forces 40-45; Sec.-Gen. Interministerial Cttee. for Indochina 46; Dir. of Cabinet High Comm. in Indochina 47-48; Gov. Mauritania 52, Ivory Coast 54-56; High Commr. Cameroon 56-58; High Commr.-Gen. French Equatorial Africa 58, French West Africa July 58-60; Minister for the Armed Forces 60-69; Minister of State for Overseas Depts. and Territories Feb.-July 72; Prime Minister 72-74; Deputy to Nat. Assembly 74-; Commdr. Légion d'Honneur, Compagnon de la Libération, Croix de Guerre.
1 rue du Général-Delanne, 92200 Neuilly-sur-Seine, France.

Messmer, Thomas M.; American art expert and gallery director; b. 1920, Bratislava, Czechoslovakia; m. Remedios García Villa 1948; ed. Thiel Coll., Pa., Boston Univ., Sorbonne, Harvard Univ.
Director, Roswell Museum, N.M. 49-52; Asst. Dir. American Fed. of Arts 52-53, Dir. of Exhbns. 53-55, Dir. 55-56, 1st Vice-Pres. 73-75; Dir. Inst. of Contemporary Art, Boston 57-61, Solomon R. Guggenheim Museum 61-; Adjunct Prof. Harvard Univ. 60, Barnard Coll. 66, 71; Senior Fellow, Centre for Advanced Study, Wesleyan Univ. 66; Chair. Int. Cttee. for Museums and Collections of Modern Art, ICOM 74-(77); Chair. Admission Cttee. on Visual Arts, McDowell Colony Inc. 69-; Pres. Asscn. of Art Museum Dirs. 74-75, Chair. Future Directions Cttee. 75-; Kt. First Class Royal Order St. Olav (Norway); Officer's Cross, Order of Merit (Fed. Repub. of Germany).
Publs. *Edvard Munch* 73, museum catalogues including Kandinsky, Klee, Munch, Schiele, Julius Bissier; articles in many art journals.

The Solomon R. Guggenheim Museum, 1071 Fifth Avenue, New York, N.Y. 10028; Home: 1105 Park Avenue, New York, N.Y. 10028, U.S.A.
Telephone: (212) 860-1309 (Office).

Mestiri, Mahmoud; Tunisian diplomatist; b. 25 Dec. 1929, Tunis; *s.* of Mohamed Mestiri and Zohra Lasram; divorced; one *s.* one *d.*; ed. Inst. d'Etudes Politiques, Univ. de Lyons.
Served in several Tunisian Dels. to UN; Alt. Rep. to UN 58, 59; Head of Tunisian special Diplomatic Mission to Congo (Leopoldville) 60; Asst. to Personal Rep. of UN Sec.-Gen. to Govt. of Belgium 61; Deputy Perm. Rep. of Tunisia to UN 62-65; Sec.-Gen. for Foreign Affairs, Tunis 65-67; Perm. Rep. to UN 67-69; Chair. UN Special Cttee. on the Situation with Regard to Implementation of Declaration on the Granting of Independence to Colonial Countries and Peoples 68-69; Amb. to Fed. Germany 71-73, to U.S.S.R., also accred. to Poland Dec. 73-.
Leisure interests: ping-pong, swimming, watching football.
Embassy of Tunisia, 28/1 ul. Katchalova, Moscow, U.S.S.R.

Mesyats, Valentin; Soviet politician; ed. Moscow Agricultural Acad.
Formerly Second Sec. of C.P.S.U., Kazakstan; mem. C.P.S.U. Cen. Cttee.; Deputy Minister of Agriculture, R.S.F.S.R. 65-71; Minister of Agriculture March 76-.
Council of Ministers, The Kremlin, Moscow, U.S.S.R.

Metcalf, George C.; Canadian business executive.
President and Man. Dir. George Weston Ltd.; Chair. of numerous companies including Eddy Paper Co. Ltd., E. B. Eddy Co., Mawen's Ltd., G. J. Hamilton & Sons Ltd., Howardsgate Holdings Ltd., Loblaw Inc., Nat. Tea Co., Westfair Foods Ltd., Somerville Industries; Pres. Loblaw Companies Ltd., Loblaw Grocetarias Co. Ltd., Paulin Chambers Co. Ltd., Perrin Investments Ltd.; Dir. Weston Biscuit Co. Inc., etc.
George Weston Ltd., 25 King Street, West, Toronto, Ontario; Home: 22 Rosemary Lane, Toronto 10, Ontario, Canada.

Metcalf, Gordon M.; American business executive; ed. Morningside Coll., Iowa, and Northwestern Univ. School of Commerce.
Joined Sears, Roebuck and Co. 33, Gen. Man. Kansas City zone 45, Asst. to Pres. in charge of retail admin. 46, Gen. Man. Chicago area 48-57, Vice-Pres. Midwest Territory 57-67, Chair. of Board and Chief Exec. Officer 67-73; Chair. U.S. Industrial Payroll Savings Cttee. 70; Dir. Allstate Insurance Co., First Nat. Bank of Chicago, First Nat. City Bank of New York, Simpson-Sears Ltd., U.S. Steel Corpn., Radio Free Europe; Trustee, Nat. Industrial Conf. Board; mem. Business Council.
Savings and Profit Sharing Fund of Sears Employees, Sears Tower, Chicago, Ill. 60684, U.S.A.

Metcalf, Keyes DeWitt, A.B., LITT.D., L.H.D., LL.D.; American librarian; b. 13 April 1889, Elyria, Ohio; *s.* of Isaac Stevens and Harriet Howes Metcalf; *m.* 1st Martha A. Gerrish 1914 (died 1938), 2nd Elinor Gregory 1941; one *s.* one *d.*; ed. Oberlin Coll.
Exec. Asst. Oberlin Coll. Library 12, Acting Librarian 16-17; Chief of Stacks New York Public Library 13-16 and 17-18, Exec. Asst. 19-27, Chief of Reference Dept. 28-37; Librarian Harvard Coll., Dir. Harvard Univ. Library 37-55, Emeritus 55-; Pres. American Library Asscn. 42-43; Prof. of Bibliography Harvard Univ. 45-55; Prof. of Library Admin., Rutgers Univ. 55-58; library consultant 55-; Fulbright Lecturer, Nat. Commonwealth Library, Canberra, Australia 58-59; Consultant in over 400 libraries in 45 states and assignments in Australia, New Zealand, India, Africa, Middle East, Thailand, The Philippines, Ireland, England,

Western Europe, Japan, Latin America, Costa Rica and Canada 55-72; Fulbright Distinguished Scholar, Queens' Univ. Belfast 66; Lecturer, York, England 66; mem. Bibliographical Socs., America and Great Britain; New York Public Library 50th Anniversary Award for services to research libraries; thirteen hon. doctorates including Harvard, Yale, Oberlin, Notre Dame and Toronto Univs.
Leisure interest: gardening.
Publs. *Planning Academic and Research Library Buildings* 65, *Study of Library Lighting* 70, and articles in professional periodicals.
68 Fairmont Street, Belmont, Mass. 02178, U.S.A.
Telephone: 484-3699.

Metcalf, Lee; American lawyer and politician; b. 28 Jan. 1911; ed. Montana State Univ.
Associate Justice Montana Supreme Court 46-52; mem. U.S. House of Representatives 52-60; Senator from Montana 61-; Democrat.
U.S. Senate, Washington, D.C. 20510, U.S.A.

Metcalf, Robert Lee, M.A., PH.D.; American entomologist; b. 13 Nov. 1916, Columbus, Ohio; ed. Univ. of Illinois and Cornell Univ.
Assistant Entomologist, Tenn. Valley Authority, Wilson Dam 43-44, Assoc. Entomologist 44-46; Asst. Entomologist Univ. of Calif., Riverside 46-49, Assoc. Entomologist 49-53, Prof. of Entomology and Entomologist 53-68, Chair. Entomology Dept. 51-63, Vice-Chancellor 63-66; Prof. of Entomology, Univ. of Illinois 68-; mem. Nat. Acad. of Sciences, N.A.S. Nat. Research Council Exec. Cttee. of Div. of Biology and Agric., N.A.S. Agric. Board, Entomol. Soc. of America (Pres. 58), American Chemical Soc., American Asscn. for Advancement of Science, American Mosquito Control Asscn., WHO Expert Cttee. on Insecticides; Chair. Panel on Pesticides, U.S.—Japan Co-op. Science Program, Nat. Science Foundation; mem. Subpanel on Pesticides, President's Science Advisory Cttee.; Consultant to WHO, AID, U.S. Dept. of Agric., U.S. Tenn. Valley Authority; Faculty Research Lecturer, Univ. of Calif., Riverside, Calif. 59; Order of Cherubini, Univ. of Pisa, Italy 66; Int. Award Pesticide Chem. 72; Charles F. Spencer Award, American Chemical Soc. 66; Chancellor's Award for Excellence in Research, Univ. of Calif., Riverside 67; Editor *Advances Pest Control Research* 56-.
Publs. *Destructive and Useful Insects, Organic Insecticides—Their Chemistry and Mode of Action*; Co-editor *Advances Environmental Sciences Technology*; approx. 250 scientific publs. mainly on chemistry and toxicology of insecticides, insect physiology and toicology, medical entomology, insect control.
Department of Entomology, University of Illinois, Urbana, Ill. 61801, U.S.A.

Methven, Donald James, M.A. (OXON); British lawyer and business executive; b. 24 Aug. 1914, London; *s.* of late Sir Harry Methven, K.B.E. and Lady Methven; *m.* Pamela Joan Sidebottom 1941; one *s.* two *d.*; ed. Wellington Coll. and Magdalen Coll., Oxford.
Qualified as barrister 37, as solicitor on leaving the Bar 46; military service, finishing in Mil. Operations Branch of War Office with rank of Maj. 39-45; Partner, Stephenson, Harwood and Tatham, Solicitors 46-73; Chair. Cadbury Schweppes Europe Ltd. 73; Deputy Chair. Cadbury Schweppes Ltd. Jan. 75-.
Leisure interests: shooting, walking, golf.
Cadbury Schweppes Ltd., 1/10 Connaught Place, London, W.2; Home: Thatchers, Russells Water, Henley-on-Thames, Oxon., England.

Methven, (Malcolm) John, M.A., LL.B.; British lawyer; b. 14 Feb. 1926, Southampton; *s.* of Col. M. D. Methven and Mrs. H. M. Methven; *m.* Margaret Field Nicholas 1952; three *d.*; ed. Mill Hill School, Gonville and Caius Coll., Cambridge.

Assistant Solicitor, Birmingham Corpn. 52-57; Legal Dept., ICI Ltd. 57-68, Head of Cen. Purchasing Dept. 68-70, Deputy Chair. Mond Div. 70-73; Dir.-Gen. of Fair Trading 73-76; Dir.-Gen. Confed. of British Industry June 76-; part-time mem. Monopolies Comm. 72-73.
Leisure interests: music, sailing, reading.
Confederation of British Industry, 21 Tothill Street, London, SW1H 9LP, England.
Telephone: 01-930 6711.

Mettler, Ruben Frederick, B.S., M.S., PH.D.; American electrical engineer and business executive; b. 23 Feb. 1924, Shafter, Calif.; s. of Henry F. and Lydia Mettler; m. Donna Jean Smith 1955; two s.; ed. California Inst. of Technology.
Associate Dir. of Radar Div., Hughes Aircraft Co. 49-54; Asst. to Asst. Sec. of Defense for Research and Devt. 54-55; Assoc. Dir. of Guided Missile Research Div. and Thor Program Dir., The Ramo-Woolridge Corpn. 55-57; Vice-Pres. The Ramo-Woolridge Corpn. 57-58; Exec. Vice-Pres. Space Technology Laboratories 58-62; Pres. TRW Systems Group (formerly Space Technology Laboratories) 62-68; Exec. Vice-Pres. TRW Inc. 65-68, Exec. Vice-Pres. and Asst. Pres. 68-69, Pres. 69-, also mem. Board of Dirs.; mem. Nat. Acad. of Engineering; Fellow, Inst. of Electrical and Electronics Engineers, American Inst. of Aeronautics and Astronautics, American Astronautical Soc.; mem. Advisory Board, Bank of America 70-; Outstanding Young Electrical Engineer 54; S. Calif. "Engineer of the Year" 64; Distinguished Service Award, Caltech 65; Distinguished Civilian Meritorious Award, Dept. of Defense 69.
Publs. several book length classified reports on airborne electronic systems; holds joint patent for major interceptor fire control system.
Office: 23555 Euclid Avenue, Cleveland, Ohio 44117; Home: 12846 Highwood Street, Los Angeles, Calif. 90049, U.S.A.
Telephone: (216) 383-3070.

Metz, Charles William, B.A., PH.D., D.SC.; American zoologist (cytology and genetics); b. 17 Feb. 1889, Sundance, Wyo.; m. Blanch Stafford 1913; three s. one d.; ed. Pomona Coll. Calif., Stanford Univ. and Columbia Univ.
Staff mem., Carnegie Inst. of Wash., Dept. of Experimental Evolution 14-30, Dept. of Embryology 30-40; Visiting Prof. Johns Hopkins Univ. 30-37; Prof. of Zoology, Univ. of Pa., Philadelphia 30-59, Chair. of Dept. 30-55, Prof. Emer. 59-; Emer. mem. Nat. Acad. of Sciences; Hon. D.Sc.
Leisure interests: birds, photography, camping, American Indian affairs.
Publs. *Paired association of chromosomes in Diptera and its significance* 16, *Comparative interspecific chromosome studies on Drosophila* (with Moses and Mason) 23, *Genetic evidence of selective segregation of chromosomes in Sciara* 26, *Cytology of the male germ cells* 28, *Factors influencing chromosome movements in mitosis* 36, *Chromosome behaviour, inheritance and sex determination in Sciaridae* 38, *Chromosome structure* 41, *Species hybrids, chromosome changes and mechanism of chromosome rearrangements in Sciaridae* 41, *Structure of giant salivary gland chromosomes* 41, *Duplication of chromosome parts as a factor in evolution* 47, *Chromosome behaviour and cell lineage in triploid and mosaic salivary glands of species hybrids in Sciara.*
28 Hyatt Road, P.O. Box 714, Woods Hole, Mass. 02543, U.S.A.
Telephone: 617-548-2724.

Metz, Victor Raoul de; French industrialist; b. 28 April 1902; ed. Ecole Polytechnique, Ecole des Mines.
President and Dir.-Gen. Compagnie Française des Pétroles to 71, Hon. Pres. 71-; Pres. Compagnie Navale des Pétroles 45-72, Hon. Pres. 72-; Vice-Pres. Compagnie Française de Raffinage 45-71, Soc. Algérienne des Pétroles Mory 40-71, Compagnie Industrielle et Financière des Chantiers et Ateliers de Saint-Nazaire, Crédit National, Pechelbronn; Dir. Desmarais Frères; mem. Conseil d'Escompte, Banque de France; Officier Légion d'Honneur.
5 rue Michel-Ange, 75016 Paris, France.

Meulemeester, Pierre M. V. de; Belgian, fmr. United Nations official; b. 22 July 1908, Bruges; s. of Alphonse de Meulemeester and Marie Bouylant; ed. Lycée Français, London, Athénée Royal, Bruges, Univ. of Brussels and Catholic Univ., Louvain.
Private Sec. to Minister, Belgian Legation, Ottawa 37-38; Ministry of Econ. Affairs, N.Y. World Fair 38-39; Resistance Movement, Belgium 40-45; Belgian Ministry of Econ. Affairs 45-46; Dep. Chief of Protocol, Exec. Office of Sec.-Gen. of UN 46-62, Chief of Protocol 62-68; Dir. World Resorts Ltd. 68-; Dir. External Relations, Architects Collaborative Int., Cambridge, Mass. 70-; several decorations.
37 Beekman Place, New York, N.Y. 10022, U.S.A.
Telephone: MU8-2985.

Mey, Luis B., D.ECON., M.B.A.; Argentine fmr. international finance official and consultant; b. 24 Dec. 1919, Buenos Aires; s. of Bernhard J. Mey and Malvina P. De Meyer; m. Ana Maria R. Schmid 1961; one s. two d.; ed. Univ. of Buenos Aires and Columbia Univ., New York.
Management and econ. consultant 45-; trustee of several Corpns.; Assoc. Prof., Business School, Faculty of Econ. Sciences, Univ. of Buenos Aires 62-68, Dir. Graduate Dept. 66-67, Dean, Faculty of Econ. Sciences 67-68; Prof. of Econs., Colegio Nacional, Buenos Aires; Under Sec. of Finance, Province of Buenos Aires 66-67; Adviser to Minister of Defence 68-69; Sec. of State for Finance, Argentina 69-70; Exec. Dir. IBRD, IFC and IDA Nov. 70-72; currently dir. of reorg. of Banco de Desarrollo Agropecuario, Panama.
Leisure interests: golf, reading, music.
Avenida Roque Sáenz Peña 760, Buenos Aires, Argentina.
Telephone: 49-2269 and 49-2448 (Office); 743-5729 (Home).

Meyer, André Benoit Mathieu; banker; b. 3 Sept. 1898, Paris.
Senior Partner, Lazard Frères & Co., N.Y.C., Lazard Frères & Cie., Paris; Dir. Lazard Bros. & Co., Ltd., London, Chase Int. Investment Corpn., Newmont Mining Corpn.; mem. Board Mount Sinai Hospital; Grand Officier, Légion d'Honneur.
Lazard Frères & Co., One Rockefeller Plaza, New York, N.Y. 10020, U.S.A.

Meyer, Armin Henry; American diplomatist; b. 19 Jan. 1914, Fort Wayne, Ind.; s. of Rev. Armin Paul Meyer and Leona Buss; m. Helen Alice James 1949; one d.; ed. Lincoln Junior Coll., Capital Univ., Columbus, Ohio, Capital Univ. Theological Seminary and Ohio State Univ., Columbus, Ohio.
Asst. Prof. and Dean of Men, Capital Univ. 35-41; Radio Technician, Douglas Aircraft Co., Eritrea 42-43; News Editor, Office of War Information, Cairo 43-44; Public Affairs Officer, American Embassy, Baghdad 44-48; Public Affairs Adviser, Dept. of State 48-52; First Sec., Beirut 52-55, Counsellor, Kabul 55-57; Dep. Dir. Office of South Asian Affairs, Dept. of State 57-58, Office of Near Eastern Affairs 59-61, Dep. Asst. Sec. of State for Near Eastern and South Asian Affairs 61; Ambassador to Lebanon Oct. 61-April 65, to Iran April 65-July 69, to Japan 69-72; Special Asst. to Sec. of State 72-73; Visiting Prof. American Univ. 74-75; Professorial Lecturer in Diplomacy, Dir. of Ferdows' Project, Woodrow Wilson Visiting Fellow, private Middle East

Consultant, Georgetown Univ., Washington, D.C. 75-.
Leisure interest: amateur radio.
Publ. *Assignment Tokyo* 74.
4610 Reno Road, N.W., Washington, D.C. 20008, U.S.A.
Telephone: (202) 244-7737.

Meyer, Charles Appleton, B.A.; American businessman
and fmr. government official; b. 27 June 1918, Boston,
Mass.; *m.* Suzanne Seyburn; two *d.*; ed. Harvard Univ.
Served as Capt. U.S. Army, Second World War; Asst.
to Chair. of Board of Sears, Roebuck and Co. for Latin
American Affairs 47; Pres. of a Sears Latin American
subsid., Bogotá 53-55; Vice-Pres. in charge of Latin
American Operations, Sears, for five years; Dir.
Eastern Operations, Sears, Roebuck and Co. 66-69;
Asst. Sec. of State for Inter-American Affairs and U.S.
Co-ordinator, Alliance for Progress 69-72; Vice-Pres.
Corporate Planning, Sears, Roebuck & Co. 73-; Adviser
to U.S. Del. to Econ. Conf. of OAS 57; fmr. mem. Nat.
Advisory Comm. on Inter-American Affairs; fmr. Chair.
Latin American Cttee., Business Advisory Council; fmr.
Chair. Advisory Board Export-Import Bank; fmr. Dir.
numerous companies.
925 Homan Avenue, Chicago, Ill. 60607, U.S.A.

Meyer, Emmanuel R.; Swiss business executive; b.
6 April 1918; ed. Zurich State Commercial Coll.
Practical training at Swiss Nat. Bank; joined Swiss
Aluminium Ltd. (Alusuisse) 42, exec. positions in
subsidiaries in Hungary, Fed. Germany, Italy and
U.S.A. 42-56; transferred to head office 56, Chief Exec.
60, Deputy Chair. and Man. Dir. 64, Chair. and Man.
Dir. Dec. 66-.
Alusuisse, Feldeggstrasse 4, P.O. Box 8034, Zurich,
Switzerland.

Meyer, Ernest, D.IUR.; French press official; b. 3
April 1908, Fraulautern; *s.* of J. Meyer and F. Meyer-
Haas; *m.* Paule Falconetti 1949; one *s.* two step-
children; ed. Univs.
French Army and Free French Armed Forces 39-45;
Head of French Press Service, French High Comm.
and French Embassy, Austria 45-51; Head of Publica-
tion Service, French Embassy, Saar 51-56; Dir. Int.
Fed. of Periodical Press 57-69; Dir. French Asscn. of
Tech. and Professional Press 57-69; Dir. Int. Press
Inst. 69-75; Croix de Guerre, Bronze Star, etc.
International Press Institute, Münstergasse 9, 8001
Zürich, Switzerland.
Telephone: 01-34 48 38.

Meyer, Frank; Luxembourg steelworks executive;
b. 5 Sept. 1911, Dudelange; *s.* of Aloyse and Marie
Barbe Eugénie (née Heintz) Meyer; *m.* Lucie-Catherine
Margue 1937; two *s.* two *d.*; ed. London School of Econs.
and Technische Hochschule, Aachen.
ARBED (Aciéries Réunies de Burbach-Eich-Dude-
lange): Blast Furnace Engineer, Belval 35, Dept. Man.
Head Office, Luxembourg 42, Holder of Power of
Attorney 43, Man. Head Office 47, Man. Dudelange-
plant 48, Man. Belval-plant 57, Man. for the exploitation of the ARBED plants located in Luxembourg 61,
Asst. Gen.-Man. 72, Gen.-Man. 73-; Chair. S.A. Trefil-
arbed, Luxembourg; Deputy Chair. Board and Chair.
Exec. Cttee. SIDMAR S.A., Ghent, Belgium; mem.
Board of Columeta (Comptoir Métallurgique Luxem-
bourgeois), ARBED Finance S.A., S.A. Métallurgique
de Bissen, Luxembourg, BRASILUX S.A., Manu-
facture de Tabacs Heintz van Landewyck S.A.R.L.,
Luxbg., SIDMAR S.A., Ghent, Belgium; mem. Exec.
Cttee. Groupement des Industries Sidérurgiques Luxem-
bourgeoises; mem. Supervisory Board of Stahlwerke
Röchling-Burbach G.m.b.H., Völklingen, Germany, and
Eschweiler Bergwerks-Verein, Herzogenrath, Germany;
mem. Consultative Board Companhia Siderurgica
Belgo—Mineira, Sabara, Brazil.
Leisure interests: shooting, fishing, literature.
ARBED S.A., 19 avenue de la Liberté; Home: 156 rue

de Luxembourg, Bofferdange, Grand Duchy of Luxembourg.
Telephone: 47921 (Office); 339-735 (Home).

Meyer, Jean; French actor and theatrical director;
b. 19 June 1914; ed. Conservatoire Nat. d'Art Drama-
tique.
Sociétaire, Comédie Française 42-59, Hon. Sociétaire
59-; Prof. Conservatoire Nat. d'Art Dramatique; Dir.
Théâtre du Palais Royal 60, Centre d'Apprentissage
d'Art Dramatique, Théâtre Michel 64; directed and
acted in the films *Le Bourgeois Gentilhomme* 58, *Le
Mariage de Figaro* 59; produced *Trois Mariages de
Mélanie* 65; Chevalier Légion d'Honneur.
Publs. *L'Age idiot* (play) 63, *Gilles Shakespeare ou les
Aventures de Jean Perrin, Molière-Micmac* (play), *Le
Vice dans La Peau* (play).
5 rue Jacques Dulud, 92 Neuilly-sur-Seine, France.

Meyer, John M. Jr.; American business executive; b.
16 July 1906, Oak Park, Ill.; ed. Univ. of Chicago.
With Guaranty Co. 28-33; joined J. P. Morgan & Co.
33, Vice-Pres. 40; served in Navy during Second
World War, Senior Vice-Pres. Morgan Bank 55, mem.
Board of Dirs. 57-59 when firm merged with Guaranty
Trust to form Morgan Guaranty; Exec. Vice-Pres.
Morgan Guaranty 62, Dir. and mem. Exec. Cttee. 63,
Pres. 65, Chair. of Board and Chief Exec. Officer 69-71;
Chair. J. P. Morgan & Co. Inc. April 69-71; Dir. Aetna
Life and Casualty Co., Eastman Kodak Co., Gillette
Co., Burlington Northern Inc., Texas Gulf Sulphur Co.,
U.S. Steel Corpn., Saudi Int. Bank 75-.
Morgan Guaranty Trust Co. of New York, 23 Wall
Street, New York, N.Y. 10015, U.S.A.

Meyer, Karl, M.D., PH.D.; American professor of
biochemistry; b. 4 Sept. 1899, Kerpen, Cologne,
Germany; *s.* of Louis Meyer and Ida Aaron; *m.* Marthe
M. Ehrlich 1930; one *s.* one *d.*; ed. Univs. of Cologne
and Berlin.
Assistant, Kaiser Wilhelm Inst., Berlin 27-28; Fellow,
Int. Educ. Board, Dept. of Organic Chem., Eidgenös-
sische Technische Hochschule, Zürich 28-29; Fellow,
Deutsche Notgemeinschaft, K.W. Inst. für Physikal-
ische Chimie, Berlin 30; Asst. Prof. of Experimental
Biology, Univ. of Calif., Berkeley 30-32; Asst. Prof. of
Biochem., and Chemist to Inst. of Ophthalmology,
Columbia Univ., N.Y. 30-42, Assoc. Prof. of Biochem.
42-52, Prof. of Biochem., 52-66, Emer. 66-; Consultant
and Special Lecturer, Dept. of Medicine, Columbia
Univ. 67-; Prof. of Biochem., Dept. of Chem., Yeshiva
Univ. 67-; Visiting Prof. Albert Einstein Coll. of
Medicine 71-72; mem. Nat. Acad. of Sciences; Fellow
American Acad. of Arts and Sciences; Lasker Award
56; T. Duckett Jones Award 59; Gairdner Award
(Canada) 60; Award of N.Y. Medical Coll. 61.
Leisure interest: history.
Publs. Articles in scientific journals.
Belfer Graduate School of Science, Yeshiva University,
2469 Amsterdam Avenue, New York, N.Y. 10033;
Home: 642 Wyndham Road, Teaneck, N.J. 07666,
U.S.A.
Telephone: 568-8400 (Office); TE6-2407 (Home).

Meyer, Pieter Johannes, D.PHIL., D.LITT.; South
African journalist and teacher; b. 22 Jan. 1909,
Ladybrand, O.F.S.; *m.* Isabella Jacobs; one *s.* one *d.*;
ed. Univ. of South Africa, and in Amsterdam.
Teacher in a primary school 31, high school 32; Lecturer
in Psychology in a training school, Chair. Board of
secondary school, Chair. District Board, Afrikaans
Training Coll., Johannesburg, Chair. Rand Cttee. for
establishment of an Afrikaans Univ. for Witwatersrand
33-68; mem. Editorial Cttee., journalist *Die Volksblad*
34-35; Political Corresp. *Dagbreek en Sondagnuus* 34-51;
first Editor *Volkshandel*; Head of Liaison Dept.,
Rembrandt Group 51-59; mem. Exec. Cttee. Afrikaanse
Handelsinstituut; Dir. various cos.; Chair. South

African Broadcasting Corpn.; mem. S.A. Acad. for Science and Art; several hon. degrees.

Publs. *The Afrikaner, Moedertaal en Tweetaligheid, Nog nie die Einde nie, Inleiding tot die Eksistensialisme, Trek Verder.*

South African Broadcasting Corpn., P.O. Box 8606, Johannesburg 2000; Home: 16 Kafue Road, Emmarentia, Johannesburg, South Africa.

Meyer-Cording, Dr. Ulrich; German economist; b. 22 May 1911, Dresden; *m.* Dr. Gisela Cording 1950; one *s.*; ed. high school, Dresden, and Univs. of Grenoble, Berlin, Kiel, Exeter and Leipzig.

Lawyer, Stuttgart 48-50; Ministerial Adviser, Ministry of Justice, Bonn 50-57; Ministerial Man. in Ministry of Atomic Affairs 57-58; Ministerial Dir. and Head of European Dept., Ministry of Commerce 58-64; Prof. of Commercial and Business Law, Univ. of Cologne 58-64; Vice-Chair. European Investment Bank, Brussels 64-72; with Rheinische Hypothekenbank, Cologne 72-.

Leisure interests: literature, sport.

Publs. *Das Recht der Banküberweisung* 51, *Monopol und Marktbeherrschung als Rechtsbegriffe* 54, *Die Vereinsstrafe* 57.

Gregor-Mendel-Strasse 27, 53 Bonn, Federal Republic of Germany.

Meyers, Franz, DR.JUR.; German lawyer and politician; b. 31 July, 1908, Mönchengladbach; *s.* of Franz and Emma (née Havenstein) Meyers; *m.* 1937; no *c.*; ed. Univs. of Freiburg and Cologne.

Lawyer 34-; mem. Diet of North-Rhine-Westphalia 50-70; Mayor of Mönchengladbach 52; Minister of Interior of North-Rhine-Westphalia 52-56; mem. Bundesrat 52-56, Bundestag 57-58; Minister-Pres., North-Rhine-Westphalia 58-66; Pres. Bundesrat 61-62; now Chair. Supervisory Board, Klöckner-Werke AG; Pres. German Leisure Asscn.; Grosskreuz des Verdienstordens der Bundesrepublik Deutschland, Bayerischer Verdienstorden and numerous foreign decorations.

405 Mönchengladbach, Bergstrasse 137, Federal Republic of Germany.

Meyerson, Martin, SC.D.; American university president; b. 14 Nov. 1922, New York City; *m.* Margy Ellin Lazarus; two *s.* one *d.*; ed. Columbia Univ., Harvard Univ.

Assistant Prof. of Social Sciences, Univ. of Chicago 48; successively Research Dir., Exec. Dir., Vice-Pres., Vice-Chair., American Council to Improve Our Neighbourhoods; Assoc. Prof., Prof., Univ. of Pennsylvania Inst. for Urban Studies and Dept. of City and Regional Planning 52-57; Adviser on urban problems for UN in Indonesia, Japan and Yugoslavia 58-66; Frank Backus Williams Prof. of City Planning and Urban Research, Harvard Univ. 57-63; Dir. Joint Center for Urban Studies of M.I.T. and Harvard Univ. 57-63; Dean, Coll. of Environmental Design, Univ. of Calif. (Berkeley), Acting Chancellor 63-66; Pres. State Univ. of New York at Buffalo, Prof. of Policy Sciences 66-70; Pres. Univ. of Pennsylvania Sept. 70-; Gov. Centre for Environmental Studies, London; fmr. Gov. American Inst. of Planners; Fellow American Asscn. for the Advancement of Science; American Acad. of Arts and Sciences; Hon. LL.D. (Queens Univ., Canada, D'Youville Coll., Alfred Univ., Rutgers Univ., Univ. of Pennsylvania, Stonehill Coll.); Hon. D.Sc. (Univ. of Chattanooga); Hon. Prof. Nat. Univ. of Paraguay.

Publs. Co-Author *Politics Planning and the Public Interest* 55, *Housing, People and Cities* 62, *Face of the Metropolis* 63, *Boston* 66, *Conscience of the City* 70.

University of Pennsylvania, Philadelphia, Pa. 19174, U.S.A.

Meynell, Laurence W.; British writer; b. 9 Aug. 1899, Wolverhampton; *s.* of Herbert and Agnes Meynell; *m.* 1st Shirley Darbyshire 1932 (deceased),

one *d.*; *m.* 2nd Joan Henley 1966; ed. St. Edmund's Coll., Ware.

Former schoolmaster, land agent; served with R.A.F.; Literary Editor *Time and Tide* 58-60; Past Pres. Johnson Soc.

Leisure interests: walking, gardening.

Publs. *Blue Feather* 28, *On the Night of the 18th* 36, *The Door in the Wall* 36, *The Dandy* 38, *The Hut* 38, *Dark Square* 40, *Strange Landing* 46, *The Evil Hour* 47, *The Bright Face of Danger* 48, *The Echo in the Cave* 49, *Party of Eight* 50, *Famous Cricket Grounds* 51, *The Man No One Knew* 51, *The Frightened Man* 52, *Too Clever by Half* 53, *Builder and Dreamer* (life of I. K. Brunel) 53, *Man of Speed* (life of C. S. Rolls) 53, *Give me the Knife* 54, *Under the Hollies* 54, *Policeman in the Family* 54, *Bridge under the water* 55, *Where is she now?* 55, *Great Men of Staffordshire* 55, *Life of James Brindley* 56, *Life of T. Telford, The Breaking Point* 57, *One Step from Murder* 58, *The Abandoned Doll* 60, *The House in Marsh Road* 60, *The Pit in the Garden* 61, *Virgin Luck* 62, *Sleep of the Just* 63, *More Deadly than the Male* 64, *Scoop* 65, *The Suspect Scientist* 65, *Die by the Book* 66, *The Mauve Front Door* 67, *Week End in the Scampi Belt* 67, *Death of a Philanderer* 68. *The Curious Crime of Miss Julia Blossom* 70, *The Fatal Flaw* 71, *A Little Matter of Arson* 71, *Death by Arrangement* 72, *The End of the Long Hot Summer* 72, *A View from the Terrace, The Fortunate Miss East* 73, *Hooky and the Crock of Gold* 74; and under the pseudonym of Robert Eton: *The Pattern* 34, *The Bus Leaves for the Village* 36, *Palace Pier* 38, *The Legacy* 39, *The Faithful Years, The Corner of Paradise Place, St. Lynn's Advertiser* 46, *The Dragon at the Gate* 48; as Stephen Tring (for children): *The Old Gang* 51, *Barry Gets His Wish* 52, *Barry's Exciting Year* 52, *Penny Dreadful* 52, *Penny Penitent* 53, *Penny Triumphant* 54, *Penny Dramatic* 55, *Penny in Italy* 57, *Penny and the Pageant, Nurse Ross Takes Over* 58, *Nurse Ross Saves the Day* 60.

9 Clifton Terrace, Brighton, Sussex BN1 3HA, England. Telephone: Brighton 28523.

Meynen, Johannes, IUR.D.; Netherlands business exec.; b. 13 April 1901, Baarderadeel Frisia; *m.* Nelia Laura Wetserhuis; two *s.* three *d.*; ed. Free Univ. of Amsterdam.

Assistant Sec., Arnhem Chamber of Commerce 25-26; Sales Man. European Office Hercules Powder Co. (U.S.A.), The Hague 27-40; N.V. Philips, Eindhoven 40-45; Major, Netherlands Army 44-45; Sec.-Gen. Netherlands War Office 45; Minister of War 45-46; Exec. Vice-Pres. Algemeene Kunstzijde Unie N.V. (A.K.U.) 47-62, Pres. 62-67, Deputy Chair. 67-71; Vice-Chair. Nat. Bank of the Netherlands; Dir. Amsterdam-Rotterdam Bank, Overseas Gas and Electricity Works, and numerous other companies; Peter Stuyvesant Award; Knight, Netherlands Lion; Order of British Empire; Medal of Freedom (U.S.A.).

Leisure interests: walking, swimming, travelling, reading, gardening.

Pinkenbergseweg 33, Velp (Gld), Netherlands.

Meyner, Robert Baumle, A.B., LL.B.; American politician; b. 3 July 1908, Easton, Pa.; *s.* of late Gustave Herman Meyner and late Mary Sophia Baumle Meyner; *m.* Helen Day Stevenson 1957; no *c.*; ed. Lafayette Coll. and Columbia Univ. Law School.

State Senator (Dem.) from Warren Co., N.J. 48-52; Senate Minority Leader 50; Gov. of New Jersey 54-58, 58-62; Partner Meyner, Landis and Verdon (law firm) 62-; Admin., Cigarette Advertising Code, Inc.

Gateway 1, Newark, N.J. 07102; and 16 Olden Lane, Princeton N.J. 08540, U.S.A.

Telephone: 201-624-2800.

Michalowski, Jerzy, LL.B.; Polish diplomatist; b. 26 May 1909; *m.* Mira Zandel; two *s.*; ed. Univ. of Warsaw.

Asst. in Polish Inst. of Social Affairs 33-36; Asst. Dir. of Polish Workers' Housing Organisation 36-39; Chief of Housing Dept. of Warsaw City Council 45; Counsellor of Polish Embassy in London Oct. 45-March 46; Deputy Del. of Poland to UN March to Nov. 46; Amb. to Great Britain 46-53; Under-Sec. of State for Education 54-56; Polish rep. to Comm. of Supervision and Control in Vietnam 55-56; Permanent Rep. to the UN 56-60; Dir.-Gen. Ministry of Foreign Affairs, Warsaw 60-67; Amb. to U.S.A. 67-71; retd.; fmr. First Vice-Pres. ECOSOC 59, Pres. 62; mem. United Polish Workers' Party.
Publs. *Unemployment of Polish Peasants* 34, *Housing Problems in Poland* (published by L.N.) 35, *The Big Game for the White House* 72.
Al. I Armii Wojska Polskiego 16, Warsaw, Poland.

Michałowski, Kazimierz, DR. PHIL.; Polish archaeologist; b. 14 Dec. 1901, Tarnopol; *s.* of Marian and Kazimiera Michałowski; *m.* Krystyna Baniewicz 1945; one *s.* one *d.*; ed. Lwów Univ.
Vice-Director Warsaw Nat. Museum, in charge of Franco-Polish excavations Egypt 37-39, Polish excavations, Crimea 56-58, Egypt (Tell Atrib 57-, Alexandria 60-, Deir el Bahari 61-), Sudan (Faras 61-64, Dongola 65-, Kadero 73-, Kasr Ibrim with Anglo-American expedition 73-), Syria (Palmyra 59-), Cyprus (Nea Paphos 65-); Prof. of Mediterranean Archaeology, Warsaw Univ. to 72, Prof. Emer. 72-; Head Inst. of Mediterranean Archaeology, Polish Acad. of Sciences; Chair. Int. Working Group of Archaeologists and Landscape Architects, Abu Simbel; Chair. Soc. for Nubian Studies; Dir. of Polish Centre of Archaeology, Cairo; mem. Polish Acad. of Sciences 52-, (mem. Presidium 52-54), Acad. Naz. dei Lincei, British Acad., Heidelberg Acad., German Acad. (Berlin), Saxon Acad. and others; Prix, Acad. des Inscriptions et Belles-Lettres 33, 69, State Prize 55, 66, Herder Prize 71, Prize of Minister of Culture and Art, 1st Class 73; Commdr. and Commdr. with Star, Crosses of Orders of Polonia Restituta 47, 52; Gold Cross of Merit 51; Knight's and Officer's Crosses Légion d'Honneur 38, 47; Commdr. Cross Corona d'Italia 47; and numerous other Polish and foreign awards and decorations; Dr. h.c. (Strasbourg) 62, (Cambridge) 71.
Leisure interest: detective stories.
Publs. *Les portraits hellénistiques et romains* 32, *Fouilles Franco-Polonaises à Tell Edfou* 37-50, *Mirmeki* 56, *Palmyre-Fouilles Polonaises, Vols. I-V* 60-66, *Faras/Fouilles Polonaises, Vols. I-II* 62-65, *Die Kathedrale aus dem Wüstensand* 67, *L'Art de l'Ancienne Egypte* 68, (English version 69), *Faras—the Mural Paintings in the Collection of National Museum in Warsaw* 74.
Ul. Sewerynów 6 m. 19, 00-331 Warsaw, Poland.
Telephone: 26-39-79.

Michalski, Jan, SC.D.; Polish chemist; b. 7 June 1920, Łódź; ed. Warsaw Polytechnic, Jagiellonian Univ. Cracow, Cambridge Univ.
Scientific worker, Łódź Polytechnic 45-; Corresp. mem. Polish Acad. of Sciences 62-69, mem. 69-, Sec. of Third Dept. 72-; Dir. Centre of Molecular and Macromolecular Research, Łódź, Assoc. Prof. 58-64, Prof. 64-; Foreign mem. Churchill Coll., Cambridge Univ. 64-; mem. Polish Cttee. of Pugwash Confs., Polish Chemical Soc., American Chemical Soc., Chemical Soc. of London and others; Knight's Cross, Order of Polonia Restituta 58, Commdr.'s Cross 74, Medal of City of Paris 69, Medal of 30th Anniversary of People's Poland 74.
Ul. Brzeźna 6 m. 3, 90-303 Łódź, Poland.

Michel, Joseph; Belgian lawyer; b. 25 Oct. 1925, Saint-Mard; *m.*; three *s.* two *d.*; ed. Catholic Univ. of Louvain.
President of Young Christian Democrats of Virton 49; Councillor of Virton 58; Mayor of Virton 70; mem. House of Reps. 61-; Minister of Interior June 74-; political columnist *Avenir du Luxembourg.*

Publ. *Economic History of the Province of Luxembourg during the Nineteenth Century* 54.
76 avenue Bouvier, 6760 Virton, Belgium.
Telephone: (063) 577404.

Michelangeli (Arturo Benedetti Michelangeli); Italian concert pianist; b. 5 Jan. 1920; ed. privately and Conservatorio G. Verdi in Milan.
Taught by Paolo Chiuieri in Brescia, then by Giovanni Anfassi of Milan; studied violin, organ and composition at the Conservatoire in Milan; winner of Grand Prix of Geneva 39; given concerts throughout world; Academician of Accad. Sta. Cecilia, Rome, and Accad. Cherubini, Florence; Gold Medal of Italian Republic.
c/o Harold Holt Ltd., 122 Wigmore Street, London, W.I, England.

Micheli, Pierre; Swiss diplomatist; b. 4 Dec. 1905; ed. Univs. of Oxford, Berlin and Geneva.
Former Sec. to Pres. of Port and Waterways of Danzig; Swiss Fed. Political Dept. 33-, Paris, The Hague, Rio de Janeiro, Batavia, Tokyo 33-45; Chief of Div. of Int. Orgs. Berne 46; Minister Plenipotentiary 52; Minister to France 56-57, Ambassador to France 57-61; Sec.-Gen. Fed. Political Dept. of Switzerland 61; mem. Assembly of Int. Red Cross.
Junkerngasse 21, 3000 Berne, Switzerland.
Telephone: 031-22-16-65.

Michelin, François; French industrialist; b. 3 July 1926.
Manager Compagnie Générale des Etablissements Michelin, "Michelin & Cie." 59-.
Usines Michelin (Tyres), place des Carmes-Déchaux, 63 Clermont-Ferrand; 12 cours Sablon, 63 Clermont-Ferrand, France.

Michelmore, Laurence, PH.D.; American United Nations official; b. 1909, Philadelphia, Pa.; *s.* of John and Lily Elwert Michelmore; *m.* Janet Brownlee Hunter 1937; two *d.*; ed. Univ. of California and Harvard Univ.
Administrative Officer, Los Angeles Country Relief Admin. 34-35, Idaho Works Progress Admin. 35-36; Asst. Prof., Wayne Univ. 36-42; Research Dept. Detroit Bureau of Governmental Research 36-42; Staff, U.S. Budget Bureau 42-46; United Nations Secretariat 46-71, Deputy Controller 52-55, Senior Dir. Technical Assistance Board 55-59, Dep. Dir. of Personnel 59-63, Personal Rep. of Sec.-Gen. on Malaysia 63; Commr. Gen. of UN Relief and Works Agency (UNRWA) 64-71.
5610 Marengo Road, Washington, D.C. 20016, U.S.A.
Telephone: 320-4441.

Michelsen, Hans Günter; German playwright; b. 1920, Hamburg.
Military Service and Prisoner-of-War 39-49; began to write 49; now freelance writer in Frankfurt/Main; Förderpreis des Niedersächsischen Kunstpreises, Hanover 63; Förderpreis des Gerhart-Hauptmann-Preises, Berlin 63; Gerhart-Hauptmann-Preis, Berlin 65; Literaturpreis der Freien Hansestadt Bremen 67.
Publs. plays: *Stienz* 63, *Feierabend 1* and *2* 63, *Lappschiess* 64, *Drei Akte* 65, *Helm* 65, *Frau L* 66, *Planspiel* 69, *Drei Hörspiele* 71; radio play: *Episode* 64.
Frankfurt am Main, Lindenstrasse 35, Federal Republic of Germany.
Telephone: 746292.

Michener, Charles Duncan, B.S., PH.D.; American biologist (entomology); b. 22 Sept. 1918, Pasadena, Calif.; *s.* of Harold and Josephine Rigden Michener; *m.* Mary Hastings 1941; three *s.* one *d.*; ed. Univ. of Calif., Berkeley.
Technical asst. in Entomology, Univ. of Calif. 39-42; Asst. Curator, Lepidoptera and Hymenoptera, American Museum of Natural History, N.Y.C. 42-46, Assoc. Curator 46-48, Research Assoc. 49-; Curator, Snow

Entomological Museum, Univ. of Kansas 49-; Assoc. Prof. of Entomology, Univ. of Kansas 48-50, Prof. 50-; Chair. Dept. of Entomology 49-61, 72-75, Watkins Dist. Prof. of Entomology 59-, of Systematics and Ecology 69-; State Entomologist, S. Div. of Kansas 49-61; mem. American Acad. of Arts and Sciences, Nat. Acad. of Sciences; Guggenheim Fellow to Brazil 55-56, Africa 66-67; Fulbright Scholar, Australia 57-58; Morrison Prize, N.Y. Acad. of Sciences.
Leisure interests: travel, field work.
Publs. *Comparative external morphology, phylogeny, and a classification of the bees (Hymenoptera)* 44, *American social insects* (with M. H. Michener) 51, *The nest architecture of the sweat bees* (with S. F. Sakagami) 62, *A classification of the bees of the Australian and S. Pacific regions* 65, *The social behaviour of the bees* 75.
Office: Departments of Entomology and of Systematics and Ecology, University of Kansas, Lawrence, Kansas 66045; Home: 1706 West 2nd Street, Lawrence, Kansas 66044, U.S.A.
Telephone: 913-864-4610 (Office); 913-843-4598 (Home).

Michener, Rt. Hon. (Daniel) Roland, P.C., C.C., C.M.M., C.D., Q.C., B.C.L., M.A.; Canadian lawyer, business executive and fmr. Governor-General; b. 19 April 1900, Lacombe, Alberta; s. of late Edward and Mary Edith (Roland) Michener; m. Norah Evangeline Willis; three d.; ed. Univ. of Alberta and Oxford Univ.
Barrister, Middle Temple (England) 23, Ontario 24; Practising lawyer, Lang, Michener and Cranston, Toronto 24-57; mem. Ontario Legislature for St. David, Toronto 45-48, Provincial Sec. and Registrar for Toronto 46-48; Progressive Conservative mem. of House of Commons 53-62; Speaker of House of Commons 57-58, 58-62; High Commr. in India 64-67; Gov.-Gen. and Commdr.-in-Chief of Canada April 67-Jan. 74; Chancellor and Principal Companion of the Order of Canada 67; Chancellor and Commdr. Order of Military Merit 72; Prior for Canada, and Knight of Justice, of Most Venerable Order of the Hospital of St. John of Jerusalem 67; Gen. Sec. for Canada for Rhodes Scholarships 36-64; mem. of Council, Commonwealth Parliamentary Asscn. 59-61; Chair. Manitoba Royal Comm. on Local Govt. and Finance 62-64; Chancellor Queen's Univ., Kingston 74-; Pres. Canadian Inst. of Int. Affairs; Chair. of Board, Metropolitan Trust Co., Teck Corpn. Ltd.; public gov. Toronto Stock Exchange; Dir. E.L. Financial Corpn., Pamour Porcupine Mines Ltd., assoc. counsel Lang, Michener, Cranston, Farquharson and Wright; fmr. Gov. Toronto Western Hospital, Univ. of Toronto; fmr. Pres. Lawyers Club, Empire Club, Board of Trade Club, Toronto; fmrly. Hon. Counsel and Chair. of Exec. Cttee., Canadian Inst. of Int. Affairs; fmr. Hon. Counsel Red Cross Ontario Div.; fmr. Chair. of Exec. Canadian Asscn. for Adult Educ.; Hon. Fellow Hertford Coll. Oxford 61, Acad. of Medicine 67, Royal Coll. of Physicians and Surgeons of Canada 68, Royal Architectural Inst. of Canada 68, Trinity Coll. Toronto 68, Frontier Coll. Toronto 72, Royal Soc. of Canada 75; Hon. mem. Canadian Medical Asscn. 68; Hon. Bencher Law Soc. of Canada 68; numerous hon. degrees.
First Canadian Place, Toronto, Ont. M5X 1A2; Home: 24 Thornwood Road, Toronto, Ont., M4W 2S1, Canada.

Michener, James Albert, A.B., A.M.; American writer; b. 3 Feb. 1907; ed. Swarthmore Coll., Colorado State Coll. of Education, Ohio State Univ., Univs. of Pennsylvania, Virginia, Harvard and St. Andrews (Scotland). Teacher 29-36; Prof. Colorado State Coll. of Educ. 36-41; Assoc. Ed., Macmillan Co. 41-49; U.S. Naval Reserve 44-45; mem. Advisory Cttee. on the Arts, U.S. State Dept. 57; Chair. Pres. Kennedy's Food for Peace Program 61; mem. U.S. Advisory Comm. on Information 71; Pulitzer Prize for *Tales of the South Pacific* 47; Einstein Award 67.

Publs. *Unit in the Social Studies* 40, *Tales of the South Pacific* 47, *The Fires of Spring* 49, *Return to Paradise* 51, *The Voice of Asia* 51, *The Bridges at Toko-ri* 53, *Sayonara* 54, *Floating World* 55, *The Bridge at Andau* 57, *Rascals in Paradise* (with A. Grove Day) 57, *Selected Writings* 57, *The Hokusai Sketchbook* 58, *Japanese Prints* 59, *Hawaii* 59, *Report of the County Chairman* 61, *Caravans* 63, *The Source* 65, *Iberia* 68, *The Drifters* 71, *The Fires of Spring* 72, *Centennial* 74.
Box 125, Pipersville, Pa. 18947, U.S.A.

Micklem, Nathaniel, C.H., M.A., D.D., LL.D.; British minister of religion, politician and professor; b. 10 April 1888, Brondesbury, London; s. of Nathaniel Micklem, Q.C. and Ellen Ruth Curwen; m. Agatha Frances Silcock 1916; three s.; ed. Rugby School and Univ. of Oxford. Prof. Old Testament, Selly Oak Colleges, Birmingham 21-27; Prof. New Testament, Queen's Theological Coll., Queen's Univ., Ontario 27-31; Principal Mansfield Coll., Oxford 32-53; Wilde Lecturer in Natural Theology and Comparative Religion, Oxford 49-50, Visiting Prof. and Cole Lecturer, Vanderbilt Univ., Tennessee 54; Pres. of the Liberal Party 57-58; Patron Liberal Int. 73; Univ. of Oxford Select Preacher 60.
Leisure interest: grandchildren.
Publs. *National Socialism and the Roman Catholic Church* 39, *Religion* 48, *Law and the Laws* 52, *Faith and Reason: a Question from Duns Scotus* 53, *Ultimate Questions* 55, *The Abyss of Truth* 56, *The Idea of a Liberal Democracy* 57, *The Labyrinth Revisited* 60, *The Doctrine of Our Redemption* 61, *The Place of Understanding* 63, *A Religion for Agnostics* 65, *Christian Thinking Today* 67, *Behold the Man* 69, *The Religion of a Sceptic* 75.
Sheepstead House, Abingdon, Oxon., England.
Telephone: Frilford Heath 252.

Micombero, Lieut.-Gen. Michel; Burundian army officer and politician; b. 1940; ed. Catholic Colls. of St. Esprit, Bujumbura, and Military Acad., Brussels. Recalled from Brussels Mil. Acad. when Burundi became independent 62; became Minister of Nat. Defence; Chief of Secs. of State 65-66; Prime Minister 66-72, June 73-, Pres. Nov. 66-; Minister of Foreign Affairs 67-68, of the Interior June-Aug. 73.
Office of the President, Bujumbura, Burundi.

Mićunović, Veljko; Yugoslav diplomatist; b. 16 Jan. 1916, Cetgne, Montenegro; s. of Jovan and Marica Mićunović; m. Budislava Dapčević 1950; one s. one d.; ed. Belgrade Univ.
One of the organizers of National uprising in Montenegro and Belgrade; political leader in Montenegro and Belgrade; mem. Yugoslav Govt. 49-51; Asst. Minister of the Interior; Asst. Minister of Foreign Affairs 52; Ambassador to U.S.S.R. 56-58; Under-Sec. of State for Foreign Affairs 58-61, Deputy Sec. of State 61-62; Amb. to U.S.A. 62-67, to U.S.S.R. 69-71; mem. Cen. Cttee. of Yugoslav League of Communists; mem. Presidium of Yugoslavia 71-74, Council Fed. of Yugoslavia 74-; Order of Nat. Hero, Meritorious Services to the People, 1st Class, etc.
Leisure interest: fishing.
Council of the Federation of Yugoslavia, Belgrade, Yugoslavia.
Telephone: 334-873.

Middelburg, Duco G. E.; Netherlands diplomatist; b. 15 Sept. 1907, The Hague; s. of Gerrit Middelburg and Gerardina H. W. van Rooy; m. Stephanie E. Sprajc 1931; one s. one d.; ed. Rotterdam Inst. of Economics. Netherlands Foreign Service 31-72, served London, Hong Kong, Kobe, Paris 31-39; with Netherlands Govt. in exile in London during Second World War; Consul-Gen., Montreal, Shanghai, Antwerp and Singapore after Second World War; Amb. to Poland 59-62, to Chile

63-67; Perm. Rep. to UN 67-70; Amb. to Portugal 70-72.
Leisure interests: genealogy, photography.
Apartado 22, Estoril, Portugal.
Telephone: Lisbon 261238.

Middelmann, Werner G.; German United Nations official (retd.); b. 10 Oct. 1909, Offenbach, Main; s. of Wilhelm Middelmann and Annie Hoffmann-Steinhaeuser; m. Vera L. Holtermann 1935; three s. one d.
Electrical appliance and chemical industry, Germany 26-45, Exec. Dir. 35-45; in charge of Refugees and Expellees, Baden-Württemberg 45-46, U.S. Zone of Occupation 47, U.S. and British Zones of Occupation 47-49; Perm. Sec. Fed. Ministry for Expellees, Refugees, and War Victims, Bonn 49-61; Dir., E. Mediterranean Region, United Nations Children's Fund (UNICEF) 61-65; Comptroller, UNICEF New York 66-74.
Leisure interests: swimming, history, geography, economic literature, travel.
Neue Schanze 2, Bregenz, 6900 Austria.
Telephone: 238265.

Middendorf, J. William, II, B.S., M.B.A.; American diplomatist; b. 22 Sept. 1924, Baltimore, Md.; s. of Henry Stump and late Sarah Boone Middendorf; m. Isabella J. Paine 1953; two s. three d.; ed. Holy Cross Coll., Harvard Univ. and New York Graduate School of Business Administration.
United States Navy service during Second World War; in Credit Dept. of Bank of Manhattan Co. (now Chase Manhattan Bank) 47-52; Analyst, brokerage firm of Wood Struthers and Co. Inc., New York 52-58, Partner 58-62; Senior Partner investment firm of Middendorf, Colgate and Co., New York City 62-69; U.S. Amb. to the Netherlands 69-73; Under-Sec. of the Navy 73-74, Sec. 74-.
Compositions: has composed five symphonies.
Publ. *Investment Policies of Fire and Casualty Insurance Companies.*
Department of the Navy, The Pentagon, Washington, D.C. 20350, U.S.A.

Middleton, Drew, B.S.; American journalist; b. 14 Oct. 1914; ed. Syracuse Univ.
Sports editor Poughkeepsie (N.Y.) *Eagle News* 36; reporter Poughkeepsie *Evening Star* 36-37; sports writer N.Y. office Assoc. Press 39; war corresp. attached to B.E.F. France and Belgium 39-40, to R.A.F. 40-41, to U.S. Army and Navy, Iceland 41-42, Allied Forces, London 42; staff of *New York Times*, London 42; corresp. North Africa and Mediterranean area and Allied H.Q. Algiers 42-43; with U.S. Eighth Air Force and R.A.F. Bomber Commd. 43-44; U.S. First Army and SHAEF 44-45; Frankfurt, Berlin and Int. Mil. Trials, Nuremberg 45-46; Chief Corresp. *New York Times* in U.S.S.R. 46-47, Germany 47-53, London 53-62, Paris 62-65, UN (New York) 65-69, European Affairs Corresp. 69-70; U.S. Medal of Freedom 48; O.B.E. (Mil. Div.) 47; Hon. D.Litt. (Syracuse Univ.) 63.
Publs. *Our Share of Night* 46, *The Struggle for Germany* 49, *The Defence of Western Europe* 52, *The British* 57, *The Sky Suspended* 60, *The Supreme Choice: Britain and the European Community* 63, *The Crisis in the West* 65.
c/o The New York Times, 229 West 43rd Street, New York, N.Y. 10036, U.S.A.

Middleton, Sir George Humphrey, K.C.M.G.; British diplomatist; b. 21 Jan. 1910; s. of George Close Middleton and Susan Sophie (née Harley); m. Françoise Sarthou; one s.; ed. St. Lawrence Coll., Ramsgate, and Magdalen Coll., Oxford.
Entered Consular Service 33; Vice-Consul, Buenos Aires; Third Sec., Asunción 34, in charge of Legation 35, New York 36; Consul at Lemberg (Lwów) 39; in charge of Vice-Consulate, Cluj 39-40, Genoa 40, Madeira 40, Foreign Office 43; Second Sec., Washington 44; First Sec. 45; Foreign Office 47; Counsellor 49; Counsellor,

British Embassy, Teheran 51; Chargé d'Affaires 51 and 52; Deputy High Commr. for U.K., Delhi 53-56; Amb. to the Lebanon 56-58; Political Resident in Persian Gulf 58-61; Amb. to Argentina 61-64, to United Arab Republic 64-65; mem. *ad hoc* Cttee. for UN Finances 66; Consultant Ind. Reorganisation 66-68; Chief Exec. Br. Industry Road Campaign; Chair. Michael Rice (Overseas) Ltd.; Dir. Liberty Life Assurance Co. Ltd., Neuwirth Investment Fund Ltd., Britarge Ltd., Decor France Ltd., H. P. Brauner Ltd., Johnson and Blox Holdings Ltd., Meer Bros. Holdings; Fellow, Royal Soc. of Arts; Chair. Bahrain Soc., Anglo-Peruvian Soc.
53 Albert Hall Mansions, London, S.W.7, England.
Telephone: 01-589-8406.

Mieghem, Jacques Van; Belgian meteorologist; b. 26 Oct. 1905, Malines; s. of Louis Van Mieghem and Jeanne Misson; m. Elvyre Allaeys 1930; ed. Univ. of Brussels.
Head of Royal Meteorological Institute of Belgium 62-70; Prof. Free University of Brussels 47-; mem. Royal Flemish Acad. of Belgium 47-75; Pres. of Aerological Comm. 51-57; mem. Special Cttee. Int. Geophysical Year 53-59, Int. Geophysical Cttee. 59-; Vice-Pres. Int. Asscn. of Meteorology 54-57; Pres. Int. Asscn. of Meteorology and Atmospheric Physics 57-60, Belgian Polar Inst. 58; Sec.-Gen. Int. Council of Scientific Unions 61-63; mem. WMO Exec. Cttee. 63-71; Pres. *Ad Hoc* Advisory Group on Meteorology (NATO Scientific Div.) 64, of Panel of Experts on Meteorological Educ. and Training (WMO) 65-70; Chevalier Ordre de Léopold 43, Commdr. 57, Grand Officier 73; Officier de l'Ordre de la Couronne 47, Grand Officier 67.
Leisure interest: history.
Publs. *Etude sur la théorie des ondes* 34, *Prévision du temps par l'analyse des cartes météorologiques* 36, *Propagation des ondes électromagnétiques en milieu homogène* 44, *Thermodynamique de l'atmosphère* (with L. Dufour) 49, *Atmospheric Energetics* 73.
34 Avenue des Armures, Forest 1190, Brussels, Belgium.
Telephone: (02) 3455085.

Mielke, Erich; German shipping clerk and politician; b. 1908; m.; two c.
Joined Communist Youth League 21, Communist Party 25; mem. Cen. Cttee. Sozialistische Einheitspartei Deutschlands 63-, Cand. mem. Politburo 71-; Minister of State Security 57-.
102 Berlin, Am Marx-Engels-Platz 2, German Democratic Republic.

Mięsowicz, Marian, PH.D.; Polish physicist; b. 21 Nov. 1907, Lvov, U.S.S.R.; ed. Jagiellonian Univ. Cracow.
Doctor 32-39, Docent 39-46, Assoc. Prof. 46-48, Prof. 48-; Corresp. mem. Polish Acad. of Sciences 59-64, mem. 64-, Vice-Pres. 69-, Chair. Cracow Branch; Deputy to Seym (Parl.); Dir. Inst. of Nuclear Eng. of Mining Acad., Cracow; Head, Dept. of High Energy Physics, Inst. of Nuclear Physics, Cracow; mem. European Physical Soc., Società Italiana di Fisica, American Physical Soc.; Dr. h.c. (Jagiellonian Univ.) 75; Gold Cross of Merit 46; State Prize, 3rd Class 52, 1st Class 64; Knight's Cross, Order of Polonia Restituta 54, Commdr.'s Cross 58, with Star 74; Order of Banner of Labour, 1st Class 62; Order of Builders of People's Poland 74; Medal of 30th Anniversary of People's Poland 74.
Ul. Mikołajska 6 m. 7, 31-027 Cracow, Poland.

Miettunen, Martti; Finnish politician; b. 17 April 1907, Simo; m. Henna Salovaara; ed. Agricultural Inst.
Member of Parl. 45-58; Sec. Agrarian Party 46-50; Minister of Agriculture 51-53, 56-57, 58, 68-70, of Communications 50-51, 54-56, of Finance 57; Prime Minister 61-62, Nov. 75-; Dir. Central Union of Agric. Producers 47-58; Chair. Admin. Council Kemijoki Oy 56-; Pres. Provincial Asscn. Municipalities of Province

of Lapland 59-72; Chair. Board of Admin. Central Bank of Co-operative Banks of Finland Ltd. 71-75; Grand Cross, Order of White Rose of Finland, Cross of Merit, in Gold, of Finnish Sport, Grand Cross, Order of North Star.
Office of the Prime Minister, Helsinki, Finland.

Mifune, Toshiro; Japanese actor and film producer; b. 1 April 1920, Chintago, China; *m.* Takeshi Shiro, 1950; two *s.*
First screen appearance in *Shin Baka Jidai* (These Foolish Times) 47; played leading role in *Rashomon* 50; other films in which he has played important roles include *Yoidore Tenshi* (Drunken Angel) 48, *Shichinin no Samurai* (The Seven Samurai), *Miyamoto Musashi* (The Legend of Musashi) 54, *Kumonosu-Jo, Muhomatsu No Issho* (The Rickshawman) 58, *Kakushitoride No San Akunin* (The Hidden Fortress) 58, *Nippon Tanjo* (The Three Treasures) 59, *Taiheiyo No Arashi* (The Storm of the Pacific), *Yosimbo, Tsubaki Sanjuro, Rebellion, Akahige* 65, *Grand Prix* 66, *Admiral Yamamoto* 68, *Hell in the Pacific* 68, *Furinkazan* 69, *Red Sun* 71, *Paper Tiger* 74.
Leisure interests: hunting, yachting, flying, riding.
Mifune Productions Co. Ltd., 9-30-7, Seijyo, Setagaya-ku, Tokyo, Japan.
Telephone: 484 1111.

Migdal, Arkadiy Baynusovich; Soviet theoretical physicist; b. 11 March 1911, Lida, Byelorussia; *s.* of Beinus K. Migdal and Rashel' A. Pupko; *m.* Tat'yana Soboleva 1944; one *s.* one *d.*; ed. Leningrad Univ.
Professor Moscow Engineering and Physics Inst. 44-; Corresp. mem. U.S.S.R. Acad. of Sciences 53-66, mem. 66-; Order of Lenin; Order of Red Banner of Labour.
Leisure interests: sculpture, skin-diving.
Publs. *Theory of Finite Fermi Systems* 65, *Approximation Methods in Quantum Mechanics* 66, *Nuclear Methods: The Quasiparticle Theory* 68, *The Qualitative Methods of Quantum Theory* 75.
U.S.S.R. Academy of Sciences, 14 Leninsky Prospekt, Moscow, U.S.S.R.

Migone, Bartolomeo; Italian executive and retd. diplomatist; b. 2 June 1901, Genoa; *s.* of the late Giovanni Maria Migone and the late Maria Anna de'Amicis; *m.* Jacquette Hamilton 1937; one *s.* one stepdaughter; ed. Inst. of Social Sciences, Florence.
Entered Foreign Office 23; Sec. Italian Del. to League of Nations Assembly 28; Sec. Italian Legation Berne 30, Cairo 31; First Sec. Washington 33, Moscow 36; Counsellor of Embassy Santiago 40; Head of Press Bureau Foreign Office Rome 44; Counsellor Office of Italian Rep. London 44, Minister Counsellor, Chargé d'Affaires London 47; Minister Counsellor, Italian Embassy London 47-48; Minister to Sweden 48-51; Dir.-Gen. for Cultural Relations, Ministry of Foreign Affairs, Rome 52-55; Del. 7th Gen. Conf., UNESCO Paris 52, 8th Gen. Conf. Montevideo 54; mem. Cttee. of Cultural Experts, Council of Europe, Strasbourg 52-55; Chief of Foreign Minister's Cabinet, Ministry of Foreign Affairs 55-57; mem. dels. to UN, NATO, ECSC, WEU, EURATOM 55-57; Amb. to Holy See 58-64; mem. Town Council, Genoa 65-66; now Pres. Altas Copco Italia S.p.A., Milan, EMAC S.p.A., Turin; Chair. Italian Nat. Freedom From Hunger Campaign Comm.; Hon. Sec. Italian Comm., mem. Board Dir. Int. Council and U.K. Comm. United World Colleges; mem. Council "Contensioso Dipl.", Min. Foreign Affairs; mem. Gen. Council Int. Fair, Genoa.
Leisure interests: music, mountains.
Via Valdagno 8, 00191 Rome, Italy.
Telephone: 322735.

Migulin, Vladimir Vasilyevich, D.P.M.SC.; Soviet physicist; b. 10 July 1911, Furmanov, Ivanovskaya Region; *s.* of Vasiliy Alekseyevich and Polina Migulin; *m.* Marianna Nikolayevna Sokolova 1922; two *s.* one *d.*;

ed. Faculty of Physics and Mechanics of Polytechnical Inst. of Leningrad.
Engineer in Research Inst. of Leningrad 32-34; Senior Research Fellow, Chief of Div. Physical Inst. of the Acad. of Sciences of U.S.S.R., Moscow, 34-51; Asst. Lecturer 35-38, Lecturer 39-46, Prof. 47-54, 57-, Deputy Dean of the Faculty of Physics 54-57, Moscow Univ.; Dir. Inst. of Physical Research at Suchumi 51-54; Deputy Dir.-Gen. Int. Atomic Energy Agency for the Div. of Training and Technical Information 58-59; Editor *Moscow Univ. Bulletin*, Physics and Astronomy section 60-69; Chief, Div. of Inst. of Radio-engineering and Electronics, Acad. of Sciences of U.S.S.R. 62-69; Dir. Inst. of Terrestrial Magnetism, the Ionosphere and Radio Wave Propagation (IZMIRAN), Acad. of Sciences of U.S.S.R. 69-; Vice-Pres. URSI 72-; mem. Popov Soc. on Radio Technology and Electrocommunications 49-; Corresp. mem. U.S.S.R. Acad. of Sciences 70-; mem. CPSU 45-; State prizewinner (twice) for scientific works; several Orders of the Soviet Union and French-Soviet and U.S.-Soviet medals.
Publs. include numerous books, papers and articles in scientific journals on investigations on electrical oscillations in non-linear and parametric systems, investigations on the propagation of radio waves by interference methods and circuit theory and investigations on new methods of receiving of mm and sub-mm e-m waves.
Izmiran, P/O Academgorodok, Moscow Region, 142092, U.S.S.R.

Mihálik, Vojtech; Czechoslovak (Slovak) poet and politician; b. 30 March 1926, Dolná Streda; ed. Comenius Univ., Bratislava.
Slovak Writers' Publishing House, Bratislava 49-51; mem. editorial staff *Československý vojдk* 52-54; Sec. Union of Slovak Writers 54-60; Editor-in-Chief, Slovak Writers' Publishing House 60-64; Slovak Centre of Publishing and Book Trade 64; Deputy to Slovak Nat. Council 64-, mem. Presidium 68-69; First Sec. Union of Slovak Writers 65-67, Chair. 69-; mem. Central Cttee. of C.P. of Slovakia 66-68, 69-71, alt. mem. 71-; mem. Presidium Fed. Assembly 69-71, Deputy Chair. of Fed. Assembly and Chair. of House of Nations 69-71, Deputy to House of Nations 71-; mem. Communita Europea degli Scrittori (COMES) 62-; Chair. Cttee. for Education and Culture, Slovak Nat. Council 69-70; Chair. Cultural Cttee., House of Nations, Fed. Assembly 71-; Artist of Merit 66.
Publs. Sixteen vols. of poetry including: *The Plebeian Shirt* 50, *The Singing Heart* 52 (State Prize), *Archimedes Circles* 60, *The Rebel Job* 60 (Prize of Czechoslovak Union of Writers 61), *Appassionata* 65 (Prize of the Slovak Writers' Publishing House); translations of Greek, Latin, Polish, French, Spanish and American poetry.
Bratislava, Hollého 15, Czechoslovakia.

Mihály, András; Hungarian composer and professor of chamber music; b. 6 Nov. 1917, Budapest; *s.* of Dezsö Mauthner and Erzsébet Grosz; *m.* 2nd Klára Pfeifer 1951, 3rd Csilla Varga; two *s.*; ed. Berzsenyi Gymnasium and F. Liszt Conservatoire of Music, Budapest.
First violoncello solo in orchestra of Budapest Opera House 46-47; Gen. Sec. of Budapest Opera 48-49; Prof. of Chamber Music, F. Liszt Conservatoire, Budapest 50-; Reader of Contemporary Music, Musical Dept., Hungarian Broadcasting Corpn. 59-; Leader New Hungarian Chamber Ensemble; Kossuth Prize 55; Erkel Prize 50, 65; Liszt Prize 72; Labour Order of Merit golden degree 70; Eminent Artist of Hungary.
Leisure interest: reading.
Works include: Concerto for Violoncello and Orchestra 53, Concerto for Pianoforte and Orchestra 54, Fantasy for Wind Quintet and String Orchestra 55, Songs on

the Poems of James Joyce 58, Concerto for Violin and Orchestra 59, String Quartet 60, Symphony 62, *Together and Alone* (opera in two acts) 65.
Vérhalom tér 9b, 1025 Budapest II, Hungary.
Telephone: 352-295.

Mikhailov, Alexander Alexandrovich; Soviet astronomer; b. 26 April 1888, Morshansk, Tambov Region; ed. Moscow Univ.
Professor Moscow Univ. 18-48; Dir. Main Astronomical Observatory, U.S.S.R. Academy of Sciences, Pulkovo 47-64; Corresp. mem. U.S.S.R. Acad. of Sciences 43-64, mem. 64-; Chair. Astronomical Council, U.S.S.R. Acad. of Sciences 39-60; mem. C.P.S.U. 56-; Vice-Pres. Int. Astronomical Union 46-48, 67; mem. Deutsche Akademie der Naturforscher Leopoldina 59; Assoc. Royal Astronomical Soc. 60; Corresp. mem. Bureau des Longitudes, Paris 46; Order of October Revolution, Polish Order of Merit; Order of Lenin (three times).
Pulkovo Observatory, 196140 Leningrad, U.S.S.R.

Mikhalkov, Sergei Vladimirovich; Soviet poet, playwright and children's writer; b. 12 March 1913, Moscow.
Began writing 28, verses for children 35; joint author (with El-Registan) Soviet Anthem 43; mem. C.P.S.U. 50-; First Sec. Moscow Branch, R.S.F.S.R. Union of Writers 65-70, Chair. of Union 70-; Deputy to Supreme Soviet of R.S.F.S.R. 67-70, to U.S.S.R. Supreme Soviet 70-; mem. Comm. for Youth Affairs, Soviet of Nationalities; fmr. Corresp. mem. Acad. of Pedagogical Sciences, Academician 70-; three Orders of Lenin, Hero of Socialist Labour 73, Red Banner, Red Banner of Labour, Red Star, Lenin Prize 70, three State Prizes, Merited Worker of Arts of R.S.F.S.R. 67.
Publs. *Dyadya Styopa* (Uncle Steve) 36 and *Collected Works* (poems, stories, plays) in two vols.; Film script: *Frontovye podrugi* (Frontline Friends) 41; Plays: *Tom Kenti* (after Mark Twain) 38, *Krasnyi galstuk* (Red Neckerchief) 47, *Ilya Golovin, Ya khochu domoi* (I Want to Go Home) 49, *Raki* (Lobsters) 52, *Zaiha-Zaznaika* 55, *Basni Mikhalkova* 57, *Sombrero* 58, *Pamyatnik Sebe* (A Monument to Oneself) 58, *Dikari* (Campers) 59, *Collected Works* (4 Vols.) 64, *Green Grasshopper* 64, *We are Together, My Friend and I* 67, *In the Museum of Lenin* 68.
U.S.S.R. Union Writers, ulitsa Vorovskogo 52, Moscow, U.S.S.R.

Miki, Takeo, LL.M.; Japanese politician; b. 17 March 1907, Tokushima-ken; s. of Hisakichi Ino and Takano Miki; m. Mutsuko Mori 1940; two s. one d.; ed. Meiji Univ., Tokyo.
Member House of Reps. 37-; Minister of Communications 47-48, of Transport 54-55; Sec.-Gen. Liberal-Democratic Party 56, 64; State Min., Dir. of Economic Planning Agency 58-59; Dir. of Economic Planning 58-59; State Minister, Dir. of Science and Technology Agency, Chair. of Atomic Energy Comm. 61-62; Minister of International Trade and Industry 65-66; Minister of Foreign Affairs 66-68; Deputy Prime Minister, Minister of State and Dir. Environmental Agency 72-74; Pres. Liberal-Democratic Party 74-75; Prime Minister Dec. 74-; Hon. LL.D. (Univ. of Southern Calif.); mem. Japanese Liberal Democratic Party.
Leisure interest: gardening.
18-20 Nampeidai-machi, Shibuya-ku, Tokyo 150, Japan.
Telephone: (03) 463-8000.

Miko, Benjamin Ecua; Equatorial Guinea diplomatist; b. 23 June 1949, Ebebiyun, Rio Muni; m.; two c.; ed. Bata and Malabo.
Administrative official, Ministry of External Relations 70-72; Second Sec., Embassy in Ethiopia 72-74; Perm. Rep. to UN Sept. 74-; mem. del. to OAU and UN confs.
Permanent Mission of Equatorial Guinea to the United Nations, 440 East 62nd Street, Apt. 6D, New York, N.Y. 10022, U.S.A.

Mikoyan, Anastas Ivanovich (brother of the late Artem Mikoyan); Soviet politician; b. 25 Nov. 1895.
Member Communist Party 15-; a leading Party organizer in Baku Oct. 17; on Soviet defeat in 18 he was imprisoned, but freed 19; organized general strike in Baku; was jailed, escaped; was rearrested and deported to Georgia; escaped again and returned to Baku; after Soviet victory held various positions in the Caucasus; mem. Cen. Cttee. of Communist Party 23-; Candidate for Politburo 26-35, mem. 35-52; People's Commissar for Supplies 30-34 and for the Food Industry 34-Jan. 38; mem. Council of Labour and Defence; Vice-Chair. Council of People's Commissars 37-46; Minister for Foreign Trade until 49; participated British and American Missions, Moscow; mem. Cttee. of State Defence 42-45; former mem. Cttee. for Economic Rehabilitation of Liberated Areas; Vice-Chair. Council of Ministers and Minister of Home and Foreign Trade 53-55; First Deputy Chair. Council of Ministers 55-64; mem. Presidium Cen. Cttee., Communist Party 52-66; Chair. of Presidium of Supreme Soviet of U.S.S.R. July 64-Dec. 65, mem. 65-75; awarded five Orders of Lenin, title Hero of Socialist Labour, and Hammer and Sickle Gold Medal 43, Order of October Revolution, Red Banner, etc.
Publ. autobiography 68.
Presidium of Supreme Soviet of U.S.S.R., Kremlin, Moscow, U.S.S.R.

Mikulin, Alexandr Alexandrovich; Soviet aircraft engine designer; b. 1893.
Constructor at the Scientific Inst. for Auto-Motors 23; Major-Gen. in the Engineering-Technical Service; Dip. of Dr. of Technological Science 38; mem. Acad. of Sciences of U.S.S.R. 54-; Hero of Socialist Labour; State Prizewinner (four times); Order of Lenin (three times), Order of Suvorov 1st and 2nd Class; many other decorations.
Principal designs: the AM-34 engine (first Polar Flight) 29, the AM-35, used in MiG planes 37, the AM-38f, for the IL-2 fighter 41-45; the AM-42; the first Soviet turbo-compressor and variable-pitch airscrew; also a number of jet engines.
Ministry of Aircraft Industry, Moscow, U.S.S.R.

Milbank, Samuel Robbins, A.B.; American banker; b. 16 March 1906; ed. Princeton Univ.
With Brown Bros. & Co., New York 29-31; joined Wood, Struthers and Winthrop 31, Gen. Partner 36-69, Chair. of Board 69-71, Consultant 72-; Pres. Milbank Memorial Fund; Pres. Pine Street Fund 49-72, Dir. 72-; Pres. Memton Fund; Dir. many corpns.; Chair. Board of Trustees, Barnard Coll., N.Y.; Pres. American Numismatic Soc.; Fellow Royal Numismatic Soc. (Great Britain).
20 Exchange Place, New York, N.Y. 10005; Home: 100 North Arlington Street, Reno, Nev. 89501, U.S.A.

Mileikowsky, Curt, DR.TECH.; Swedish business executive; b. 1 May 1923, Stockholm; s. of Gregor Mileikowsky and Margit Wallis; m. Ulla B. Varenius 1947; two s.; ed. Royal Inst. of Technology.
Research engineer, ASEA, Ludvika 46; Research Asst. to Prof. Lise Meitner 46-47, Nobel Inst. of Physics 48-54, ASEA, Västerås 54; Man. Nuclear Power Dept. ASEA 58, Exec. Vice-Pres. for Sales 62; Pres. SAAB (SAAB-Scania AB) 69-, Linköping 68-.
Publs. Scientific and technical publications in Sweden and U.S.A.
SAAB-Scania AB, 581 88 Linköping; Home: Kungsgatan 43, 582 22 Linköping, Sweden.

Miles, Sir Bernard, Kt., C.B.E.; British actor and director; b. 27 Sept. 1907; ed. Uxbridge County School and Pembroke Coll., Oxford.
First stage appearance 30; written for, directed, and acted in films 37-; West End stage appearances 38-; music-hall stage appearances 50-; founded Mermaid

Theatre, North London 50, formed Mermaid Theatre Trust, opened Mermaid Theatre, City of London (Puddle Dock) 59.
Mill Cottage, Little Bardfield, nr. Dunmow, Essex, England.

Miles, Frank Stephen, C.M.G., M.A., M.P.A.; British diplomatist; b. 7 Jan. 1920, Edinburgh; s. of late Harry and Mary Miles; m. Joy Theaker 1953; three d.; ed. Daniel Stewart's Coll. Edinburgh, St. Andrews Univ., Harvard Univ.
Served with Fleet Air Arm, Lt. RNVR 42-46; Scottish Home Dept. 48; Foreign and Commonwealth Office 48-; has held diplomatic posts in New Zealand 49-52, Pakistan 54-57, Ghana 59-62, Uganda 62-63; Deputy High Commr. in Tanzania 63-65; Acting High Commr. in Ghana March-April 66; Consul-Gen. St. Louis 67-70; Deputy High Commr. in Calcutta 70-74; High Commr. in Zambia Oct. 74-.
Leisure interests: cricket, tennis, golf.
British High Commission, P.O. Box RW 50, Lusaka; Home: 347 Independence Avenue, Lusaka, Zambia. Telephone: 51122 (Office).

Miles, Josephine, M.A., PH.D.; American poet; b. 11 June 1911; ed. Univ. of California (Los Angeles and Berkeley).
Instructor in English, Univ. of California (Berkeley) 40, Prof. of English 52-, Univ. Prof. 73-; mem. American Acad. of Arts and Sciences 64; Shelley Award for Poetry 35, Nat. Inst. of Arts and Letters Award for Poetry 56; Nat. Endowment for the Arts Award 68.
Publs. Poetry: *Lines of Intersection* 39, *Poems on Several Occasions* 41, *Local Measures* 46, *Prefabrications* 55, *Poems 1930-60* 60, *Civil Poems* 66, *Kinds of Affection* 67, *Fields of Learning Poems* 68, *To All Appearances: Poems New and Selected* 74; Prose: *Vocabulary of Poetry* 46, *Continuity of Poetic Language* 51, *Eras and Modes in English Poetry* 57 (revised edn. 64), *Renaissance, Eighteenth Century and Modern Language in Poetry* 60, *Emerson* 64, *Style and Proportion in the Language of Prose and Poetry* 67, *Poetry and Change* 74.
2275 Virginia Street, Berkeley, California 94709, U.S.A.

Mili, Mohamed Ezzedine; Tunisian telecommunications engineer and international official; b. 4 Dec. 1917, Djemmal; m. Mlle. Zouhir 1950; three s. two d.; ed. Teacher's Training Coll. Tunis, Ecole Normale Supérieure, Paris, Sorbonne and Ecole Nat. Supérieure des Télécommunications, Paris.
Joined Posts, Telegraphs and Communications (P.T.T.) Admin. 48; Chief Engineer and Dir.-Gen. of Telecommunications, Ministry of P.T.T. 57; Tunisian del. to ITU confs. 56-, mem. ITU Admin. Council 60-65, Chair. of 19th session 64; Deputy Sec.-Gen. ITU 65-67, Sec.-Gen. 67-; Officer, Order of Independence of Tunisia, Commdr. Order of the Tunisian Repub., Commdr. Swedish Order of Vasa, Grand Cross Order of Duarte, Sanchez y Mella with silver star (Dominican Repub.), Honour Merit Medal (Paraguay).
Leisure interests: reading scientific publications, youth movements.
International Telecommunications Union, Place des Nations, 1211 Geneva 20; Home: 17 route de Mon Idée, 1226 Moillesulaz, Geneva, Switzerland.
Telephone: 022-48-79-19. (Home).

Millan, Rt. Hon. Bruce, P.C.; British politician; b. 5 Oct. 1927; m. Gwendoline Fairey 1953; one s. one d.; ed. Harris Acad., Dundee.
Worked as Chartered Accountant 50-59; M.P. for Craigton Div. of Glasgow 59-; Parl. Under-Sec. of State for Defence (R.A.F.) 64-66, for Scotland 66-70; Minister of State, Scottish Office 74-76, Sec. of State for Scotland April 76-; Labour.

House of Commons, Westminster, London, S.W.1
Home: 46 Hardy Road, London, S.E.3, England.
Telephone: 01-858-5634 (Home).

Millard, Sir Guy Elwin, K.C.M.G., C.V.O.; British diplomatist; b. 22 Jan. 1917; m. 1st Anne Mackenzie 1946; one s. one d.; 2nd Judy Dugdale 1964; two s.
Joined Foreign Office 39; navy service 40-41; Foreign Office 41-45; Paris 45-49; Ankara 49-52; Imperial Defence Coll. 53; Foreign Office 54-55; Private Sec. to Prime Minister 55-57; Office of Paymaster-Gen. 57-59; Counsellor, Teheran 59; Foreign Office 62-64; Deputy Perm. Rep. NATO 64-67; Amb. to Hungary 67-69; Minister, Washington, D.C. 70-71; Amb. to Sweden 71-74, to Italy 74-.
British Embassy, Via XX Settembre 80A, Rome, Italy.

Millas Correa, Orlando; Chilean journalist and politician; b. 14 Dec. 1918, Santiago; m. Adriana Perez Ibáñez; one s. two d.; ed. Instituto Nacional and Univ. of Chile.
General Sec. Círculo de Periodistas (journalists' union) 35-53; mem. Council Nat. Society of Journalists; mem. Soc. of Authors of Chile; Dir. *El Siglo* (Santiago newspaper); mem. Political Bureau, Communist Party of Chile; mem. Chamber of Deputies 61-73, Vice-Pres. 63; Minister of Finance 72-73, of Economy March-Sept. 73.
Leisure interests: politics, reading economic and marxist works.
Publs. *El fracaso del Gobierno de los Gerentes, Los comunistas, los católicos y la libertad* 63, *Prontuario de la Ley Mordaza* 64.
c/o Embassy of Netherlands, Santiago, Chile.

Mille, Hervé; French journalist; b. 23 Sept. 1909.
Editor *Eclaireur de Nice* and *Paris Soir* 28-32; London correspondent of *Paris Soir* 33-35; Editorial Dir. *Paris Soir, Paris Midi, Marie Claire, Match* 36-42; Dir. *Paris Match* 49-69, *Marie Claire* 54-69, *Télé-sept-jours* 60-; Co-Dir. Société d'étude des média 67-68.
51 rue Pierre-Charron, Paris 8e, France.

Miller, Arjay Ray, B.S.; American business executive; b. 4 March 1916, Shelby, Neb.; s. of Rawley John Miller and Mary Gertrude Schade; m. Frances M. Fearing 1940; one s. one d.; ed. Univ. of California.
Teaching Asst. Univ. of Calif. Berkeley 37-40; Research Technician, Calif. State Planning Board 41; Economist, Fed. Reserve Bank of San Francisco 41-43; U.S.A.F. 43-46; Asst. Treas. Ford Motor Co. 47-53, Controller 53-57, Vice-Pres. and Controller 57-61, Vice-Pres. (Finance) 61-62, Vice-Pres. (Staff-Group) 62-63, Dir. 62-, Pres. 63-68, Vice-Chair. Feb. 68-July 69; Dean Graduate School of Business Admin., Stanford Univ. 69-; Trustee of several insts. and mem. of various cttees.; Hon. D.Jur. (Calif., Nebraska Univs., Whitman Coll.); Dir. Wells Fargo Bank 68; Dir. Wells Fargo, Utah Int. Inc., Washington Post Co., Levi Strauss & Co., Ford Motor Co.
Leisure interests: archaeology, golf, hunting, forestry.
Publ. *An Economic and Industrial Survey of the Los Angeles and San Diego Areas* (with Arthur G. Coons) 41.
Graduate School of Business, Stanford University, Stanford, Calif. 94305, U.S.A.

Miller, Arthur, A.B.; American playwright; b. 17 Oct. 1915; m. 1st Mary Grace Slattery 1940, one s. one d.; 2nd Marilyn Monroe 1956 (divorced); 3rd Ingeborg Morath 1962, one d.; ed. Univ. of Michigan.
Received Hopwood Award for play-writing, Univ. of Michigan 36 and 37, Theatre Guild Nat. Award 38; N.Y. Drama Critics Circle Award 47 and 49; Pulitzer Prize for Drama 49; Antoinette Perry Award 53; American Acad. of Arts and Letters Gold Medal for Drama 59; Pres. Int. PEN Clubs Org. 65-69.
Publs. *The Man Who Had All the Luck* 43, *Situation Normal* 44, *Focus* 45, *All My Sons* 47, *Death of a Salesman* 49, *The Crucible* 53, *A View From The Bridge*

55, *A Memory of Two Mondays* 55, *Collected Plays* 58, *The Misfits* (screenplay) 59, *After the Fall* 64, *Incident at Vichy* 64, *I Don't Need You Any More* (short stories) 67, *The Price* (play) 68, *In Russia* (with Inge Morath) 69, *The Creation of the World and Other Business* (play) 72, *Up From Paradise* 74.

c/o ICM, 40 W. 57th Street, New York, N.Y. 10019, U.S.A.

Miller, George A., M.A., A.M., PH.D.; American professor of psychology; b. 3 Feb. 1920, Charleston, W. Va.; ed. Univ. of Alabama and Harvard Univ.
Associate Prof. of Psychology, Mass. Inst. of Technology 51-55, Harvard Univ. 55-58; Co-Dir. Center for Cognitive Studies, Harvard Univ. 60-67; Chair. Dept. of Psychology, Harvard 64-67, Prof. of Psychology, Harvard 58-68; Visiting Prof., The Rockefeller Univ. 67-68, Prof. of Psychology 68-; Pres. American Psychol. Asscn. 68-69; Fellow, Nat. Acad. of Sciences; Pres. Eastern Psychol. Asscn. 61-62; Distinguished Scientific Contribution Award, American Psychol. Asscn. 63.
Institute for Advanced Study, Princeton, N.J. 08540, U.S.A.

Miller, George William, B.S., J.D.; American business executive; b. 9 March 1925, Sapulpa, Okla.; ed. U.S. Coast Guard Acad., New London, Univ. of Calif. School of Law, Berkeley.
Served as line officer in Pacific area, stationed in China for a year; lawyer with Cravath, Swaine and Moore, N.Y.C. 52-56; joined Textron Inc. as Asst. Sec. 56, Vice-Pres. 57-60, Pres. 60-74, Chief Exec. Officer 68-, Chair. 74-; Dir. Allied Chem. Corpn., Fed. Reserve Bank of Boston, Nat. Alliance of Business, UN Asscn. of U.S.; Trustee, Conf. Board; mem. Business Council, Nat. Council on the Humanities 66-67, State Bar of Calif., Asscn. Bar City of N.Y.; nat. fund-raising chair. for Brown Univ.'s medical educ. programme 66-69.
Textron Inc., 10 Dorraine Street, Providence, R.I. 02903, U.S.A.

Miller, Henry; American writer; b. 26 Dec. 1891; ed. City Coll., New York, and Cornell Univ.
Lived in Paris 30-38, ed. and contributed to *Phoenix*, *Booster*, and other literary magazines; Athens 38-39; returned to U.S.A. 40; mem. Nat. Inst. Arts and Letters.
Publs. Novels include: *Tropic of Cancer* 32, *Tropic of Capricorn* 35, *Black Spring* 36, *Max and the White Phagocytes* 38, *The Cosmological Eye* 39, *The Wisdom of the Heart* 41, *The Colossus of Maroussi* 41, *Sunday after the War* 44, *The Air-Conditioned Nightmare* (two vols.) 45-47, *Maurizius Forever* 46, *The Smile at the Foot of the Ladder* 48, *The Books in My Life* 52, *Big Sur and the Oranges of Hieronymus Bosch* 58, *A Letter* 62, *World of Sex* 65, *Nexus* 65, *Plexus* 65, *Sexus* 65, *Quiet Days in Clichy* 65; play: *Just Wild About Harry* 63; autobiography: *My Life and Times* 72.
c/o Grove Press, 80 University Place, New York, N.Y. 10013, U.S.A.

Miller, Jack Richard, A.B., M.A., LL.B.; American lawyer, judge and politician; b. 6 June 1916, Chicago, Ill.; s. of Forest W. and Blanche M. Miller; m. Isabelle Margaret Browning 1942; one s. three d.; ed. Creighton Univ., Catholic Univ., Washington, D.C., Columbia Univ.
Attorney, Office of Chief Counsel, Internal Revenue Service (Fed. Govt.) 47-48; Lecturer in Taxation, George Washington Univ. 48; Asst. Prof. of Law, Notre Dame Univ. Coll. of Law 48-49; mem. Iowa House of Reps. 55-56, Iowa State Senate 57-60, U.S. Senator from Iowa 61-73; Judge, U.S. Court of Customs and Patent Appeals 73-; U.S.A.F. in Second World War; Brig.-Gen. U.S.A.F. Reserve; Republican.
Leisure interests: golf, fishing, hunting.
Publ. *Prentice-Hall Tax Ideas Service* (in co-operation).
717 Madison Place, N.W., Washington, D.C. 20439, U.S.A.

Home: 5417 Kirkwood Drive, Washington, D.C. 20016, U.S.A.
Telephone: (202) 347-4261 (Office); (301) 320-4392 (Home).

Miller, James Roscoe, LL.D., M.D., M.S., D.SC.; American fmr. university chancellor; b. 26 Oct. 1905, Murray, Utah; s. of Leroy Cromwell and Marjorie (née Sidley); m. Berenice Johannesen 1928; one s. two d.; ed. Univ. of Utah and Northwestern Univ.
Assistant Prof. of Medicine Northwestern Univ. Med. School 38-41, Assoc. Prof. 41-49, Prof. 49-, Asst. Dean 33-41, Dean 41-49; Pres. Northwestern Univ. 49-69, Chancellor 69-74, Emeritus Chancellor 74-; Dir. First Nat. Bank and Trust Co., Evanston, Ill., Fidelity Life Asscn., Fed. Kemper Life Assurance Co., Northwestern Memorial Hosp., American Hosp. Supply Corpn., Prentice Women's Hosp. and Maternity Center of Chicago, Evanston Hosp.; Trustee, Evanston Hosp., Museum of Science and Industry, Field Museum of Natural History, Savings and Profit Sharing Fund of Sears Employees; mem. Board of Overseers Hoover Inst.; fmr. mem. Hoover Comm. Medical Task Force; Hon. L.H.D. and Litt.D.
Publs. on internal medicine and medical education.
633 Clark Street, Evanston, Illinois 60201, U.S.A.

Miller, Dr. Jonathan Wolfe, M.B., B.CH.; British stage and film director and physician; b. 21 July 1934, London; m. Helen Rachel Collet 1956; two s. one d.; ed. St. Paul's School, St. John's Coll., Cambridge and Univ. Coll. Hosp. Medical School, London.
Co-authored and appeared in *Beyond the Fringe* 61-64; directed John Osborne's *Under Plain Cover*, Royal Court Theatre 62, Robert Lowell's *The Old Glory*, New York 64 and *Prometheus Bound*, Yale Drama School 67; directed at Nottingham Playhouse 68-69; directed Oxford and Cambridge Shakespeare Co. production of *Twelfth Night* on tour in U.S.A. 69; Research Fellow in the History of Medicine, Univ. Coll., London 70-; Assoc. Dir. Nat. Theatre 73-; mem. Arts Council 75-.
Productions for Nat. Theatre, London: *The Merchant of Venice* 70, *Danton's Death* 71, *The School for Scandal* 72, *The Marriage of Figaro* 74; other productions *The Tempest*, London 70, *Prometheus Bound*, London 71, *The Taming of the Shrew*, Chichester 72, *The Seagull*, Chichester 73, *The Malcontent*, Nottingham 73, *The Family in Love*, Greenwich Season 74, *Arden Must Die* (opera) 74, *The Importance of Being Earnest* 75, *The Cunning Little Vixen* 75, *All's Well That Ends Well*, *Measure For Measure*, Greenwich Season 75; films: *Take a Girl like you* 69 and several films for television including *Whistle and I'll come to you* 67, *Alice in Wonderland* 67.
c/o The National Theatre, The Archway, 10A Aquinas Street, London, S.W.1, England.

Miller, Keith Harvey; American fmr. state governor; b. 1 March 1925, Seattle, Wash.; s. of H. Keith Miller and Sarah Margaret Harvey Miller; m. Diana Doyle 1953; ed. Univs. of Idaho and Washington.
Member House of Reps. 63-64; Sec. of State, Alaska 66-69; Gov. of Alaska 69-71; Republican.

Miller, Otto Neil, PH.D.; American business executive; b. 9 Jan. 1909; m. Alberta Maeder Hogue 1935 (deceased 1973); ed. Univ. of Michigan.
Researcher, Standard Oil Co. of Calif. 34, Arabian operations 41-43, Gen. Man. Mfg. Dept. 46-53, Vice-Pres. nat. gas utilization, crude pricing, East coast operations 57-58, Dir. and Vice-Pres. foreign operations 59-60, Pres. 61-65, Chair. and Chief Exec. Officer 66-74; Chair. of Board American Petroleum Inst., Nat. Ind. Conf. Board; Dir. Calif. State Chamber of Commerce, San Francisco Opera Asscn., Crocker Nat. Bank, Weyerhaeuser Co. 73, Equitable Life Assurance Soc. of U.S.; mem. Business Council, Nat. Acad. of Engineering,

Nat. Petroleum Council, Conf. Board Inc., U.S. Nat. Cttee. of the World Energy Conf., American Inst. of Chemical Engineers, Nat. Review Board of East-West Center, Honolulu; Trustee, Cttee. for Econ. Devt.
555 Market Street, San Francisco, Calif. 94105, U.S.A.

Miller, Paul A.; American business executive; *m.*; one *s.*; ed. Western Reserve Univ.
Joined Leece-Neville Co. 34, Vice-Pres. until 54; joined Ford Motor Co., Gen. Mfg. Man., Gen. Man.; Gen. Man. Fasteners Div., Eaton Corpn. 59, Gen. Man. Axle Div. 69, Vice-Pres. Truck Components 70, Exec. Vice-Pres. Operations 71-73, Dir. 72-, Pres. Aug. 73-; Dir. Nat. City Bank of Cleveland; mem. Hon. Advisory Cttee. Soc. of Automotive Engineers, American Management Asscn., Newcomen Soc. and other professional, civic and philanthropic orgs.
Eaton Corporation, 100 Erieview Plaza, Cleveland, Ohio 44114, U.S.A.

Miller, Paul Lukens, A.B.; American investment banker; b. 6 Dec. 1919, Philadelphia, Pa.; *s.* of Henry C. L. and Elsie (Groff) Miller; *m.* Adele Olyphant 1950; one *s.* three *d.*; ed. William Penn Charter School, Philadelphia, and Princeton Univ.
First Boston Corpn. 46-, Vice-Pres. 55-64, Dir. 59-, mem. Exec. Cttee. 63-, Pres. 64-; Dir. Aluminum Co. of America, Cummins Engine Co., Inc., Trustee Seamen's Bank, Celanese Corpn., Ogilvy and Mather Int., Inc.
First Boston Corporation, 20 Exchange Place, New York, N.Y. 10005, U.S.A.
Telephone: 212-344-1515.

Miller, Terence George, M.A., F.G.S.; British geologist; b. 16 Jan. 1918, Cambridge; *s.* of George Frederick Miller and Marion Johnston; *m.* Inga Catriona Priestman 1944; one *s.* three *d.*; ed. Perse School and Jesus Coll., Cambridge.
Army Service 39-46; Univ. Demonstrator in Geology, Univ. of Cambridge 48-53; Lecturer and Senior Lecturer in Geology, Univ. of Keele 53-65; Prof. of Geography, Univ. of Reading 65-67; Principal, Univ. Coll. of Rhodesia 67-69; Dir. Polytechnic of N. London 71-; Harkness Scholarship 48; Territorial Decoration 64.
Leisure interests: walking, sailing, beachcombing.
Publs. *Geology & Scenery in Britain* 53; papers in *Journal of Palaeontology, Palaeontology, Geological Magazine, Nature,* etc. 47-66.
5 Bittacy Rise, Mill Hill, London NW7 2HH, England.
Telephone: 01-346-4788.

Miller, William E., LL.B.; American lawyer and politician; b. 22 March 1914; ed. Notre Dame Univ., Albany Law School.
Private law practice Lockport; U.S. Commr. for W. New York; U.S. Army 42-46; Asst. Prosecutor, Nürnberg War Crimes Trials; District Attorney, Niagara County 48; mem. U.S. House of Reps. 50-64; Chair. Republican Nat. Cttee. 61-64; nominated Republican candidate for Vice-Presidency of the U.S. July 64.
[*Died* 13 *April* 1976.]

Millet, Pierre Georges Louis, D. en D.; French industrial officer; b. 11 April 1922, St. Maurice, Seine; ed. Ecole Nationale d'Administration.
Ministry of Finance 48-51; Deputy Dir. Int. Inst. of Patents 52-54; Ministry of Finance 55-57; Dir. of Contingency Fund and mem. Monetary Cttee., EEC 58-60, Dir. of Econ. Policy and Devt. 60-61; mem. Admin. Board, European Investment Bank 60-61; Dir.-Gen. of Home Market, EEC 61-65; Asst. Dir. of Foreign Econ. Relations, Ministry of Finance 65-66; Deputy Vice-Pres. Union des industries chimiques 66-; Dir.-Gen. Service d'Exploitation Industrielle des Tabacs et des Allumettes (SEITA) 72-; Chevalier, Légion d'Honneur.
SEITA, 53 quai d'Orsay, 75007 Paris, France.

Millet, René Philippe Yves; French diplomatist; b. 15 Aug. 1910; ed. Ecole Fénelon, Lycées Condorcet et Janson-de-Sailly, Paris, Ecole Libre des Sciences Politiques, Paris.
Second Sec. French Embassy, Ankara 45, First Sec. 46; Consul, Johannesburg 47-49, to Cen. Admin. 49-50; Perm. Rep. to Econ. Comm. for Asia and Far East, Second Counsellor, Bangkok 50-52; Second Counsellor, Manila, and Chargé d'Affaires 52-54; Counsellor, High Comm., Saigon 54-56; Consul Gen. Bizerta 56-60, Los Angeles 60-62; Amb. to Chad 62-65, to Burma 65-69, to Kenya Dec. 69-72; Consul-Gen., Monaco 73-; Commdr. Légion d'Honneur; Compagnon de la Libération; Croix de Guerre.
Villa Trotty, Chemin du Tenao, Monte Carlo, Monaco; and 37 quai d'Orsay, Paris 7e, France.

Millhiser, Ross Randolph; American business executive; *m.* Eleanor McGue; three *s.* one *d.*; ed. Yale Univ.
Served U.S. Army 42-45, with rank of Maj.; Asst. Foreman Philip Morris Inc. 45, Marlboro Brand Man. 54-57, Asst. Dir. of Marketing 57, Vice-Pres. 58, Asst. Chief of Operations 59, Dir. of Marketing 60, Dir. 63, Exec. Vice-Pres. Marketing 65, Pres. Philip Morris U.S.A. 66-73, Pres. Philip Morris Inc. 73-; Dir. First & Merchants Corpn.; Trustee, Virginia Foundation for Independent Colls., Independent Coll. Funds of America Inc.; mem. Exec. Cttee. Tobacco Inst.
Philip Morris Inc., 100 Park Avenue, New York, N.Y. 10017, U.S.A.

Milligan, Robert Lee; American oil executive; b. 11 Oct. 1900; ed. Ohio Wesleyan Univ.
Superintendent The Fairbanks Co., Springfield, Ohio 22-24, Vice-Pres., Gen. Man. 24-29; Treas. Indianopolis Switch & Frog Co. 26-29; Asst. to Treas. The Pure Oil Co. Chicago 29-33, Asst. Sec.-Treas. 33-47, Treas. 47-49, Vice-Pres., Treas. 49-51, Exec. Vice-Pres. 51-54, Pres. 54-65, Chair. 65-71.
2440 Lincolnwood Drive, Evanston, Ill. 60201, U.S.A.

Milliken, Frank Roscoe; American mining executive; b. 25 Jan. 1914; ed. Massachusetts Inst. of Technology.
Chief Metallurgist, Gen. Eng. Co., Salt Lake City 36-41; Asst. Manager Titanium Div. Nat. Lead Co. 41-52; Vice-Pres. (Mining Operations), Kennecott Copper Corpn. 52-58, Exec. Vice-Pres. 58-61, Dir. 58-, Pres., Chief Exec. Officer 61-; Pres. and Dir. Braden Copper Co.
Kennecott Copper Corporation, 161 East 42nd St., New York, N.Y. 10017, U.S.A.

Milliken, William Grawn; American state governor; b. 26 March 1922, Traverse City, Mich.; *s.* of James T. Milliken and Hildegarde Grawn Milliken; *m.* Helen Wallbank Milliken 1945; one *s.* one *d.*; ed. Yale Univ.
Senator from Mich. 61-64; Lieut.-Gov. of Mich. 65-69; Gov. of Mich. 69-; Chair. Republican Governors' Asscn. 71-72; several hon. degrees; Republican.
Leisure interests: reading, tennis, swimming, skiing, hiking.
Office of the Governor, The Capitol, Lansing, Mich.; 2520 Oxford Road, Lansing, Mich., U.S.A.

Millot, Jacques, D. EN MED., D. ES SC.; French museum director; b. 9 July 1897; *m.* Henrietta Alvin 1919; one *d.*; ed. Univ. de Paris à la Sorbonne and Muséum nat. d'Histoire naturelle.
Professor, Faculty of Medicine, Univ. of Paris 29-31; Prof. Inst. of Ethnology 31-; Prof. Sorbonne 33-; Prof. Muséum nat. d'Histoire naturelle 43-67; Dir. Scientific Research, Madagascar 47-60; Pres. Acad. Malgache 48-58; Pres. Scientific Asscn. of Countries of Indian Ocean 57; Dir. Musée de l'Homme, Paris 60-67; Pres. Acad. des Sciences d'Outre-Mer 63; mem. Acad. des Sciences (France) 63-; Hon. Dr. (Witwatersrand and Perth).
Leisure interest: rare books.
Publs. *Cicatrisation* 31, *Les races humaines* 36, *Traité*

de Zoologie—Classe des Arachnides 49, *Biologie des races humaines* 51, *Le troisieme coelacanthe* 54, *Les crossoptérygiens actuels* 58, *Anatomie de Latimeria Chalumnae I* 58, *II* 65, *Archéologie Malgache*.
Musée de l'Homme, Palais de Chaillot, Paris 16e, France.

Mills, Donald Owen; Jamaican diplomatist; b. 23 July 1921, Mandeville; *m.*; four *c.*; ed. Jamaica, and London School of Econs.
Entered civil service 39; with the Treasury 41-50; Cen. Bureau of Statistics 50-55, Deputy Dir. 55; with Jamaica Cen. Planning Unit 57-68, Dir. 62; Registrar Univ. of West Indies 65-66; Perm. Sec. Ministry of Devt. of the Bahamas 68-70; Alt. Exec. Dir. for Jamaica, Canada, Ireland, Barbados, IMF 71-72; Perm. Rep. to UN Jan. 73-.
Permanent Mission of Jamaica to United Nations, 747 Third Avenue, 30th Floor, New York, N.Y. 10017, U.S.A.

Mills, John, C.B.E.; British actor; b. 22 Feb. 1908, North Elmham, Suffolk; *s.* of Lewis Mills; *m.* Mary Hayley Bell; one *s.* two *d.*; ed. Norwich High School.
Debut in chorus of *The Five O'Clock Girl* 29; appeared in repertory 29-30; appeared as The Aunt in *Charley's Aunt*, London, 30; has since appeared in numerous West End productions including the following plays by his wife Mary Hayley Bell: *Men in Shadow* 42, *Duet for Two Hands* 45, *Angel* 47, *The Uninvited Guest* 52; numerous theatre and film awards include Best Actor of the Year (for *Of Mice and Men*) 39, Best Actor (for *Great Expectations*) 47, Venice Film Festival Best Actor Award (for *Tunes of Glory*) 60, San Sebastian Film Festival Best Actor Award (for *The Family Way*) 68; mem. Council Royal Acad. of Dramatic Art (RADA); mem. Board of Govs. of British Film Inst.; Acad. Award (Oscar) for role in *Ryan's Daughter* 71.
Other stage appearances include: Noel Coward's *Cavalcade* 31 and *Words and Music* 32, *Give me a Ring* 33, *Jill Darling* 34, *Red Night* 36, *A Midsummer Night's Dream, She Stoops to Conquer, The Damascus Blade* 50, *Figure of Fun* 51, *The Uninvited Guest* 52, *Ross* (Broadway production) 61, *Powers of Persuasion* 63, *Veterans* 72, *At the End of the Day* 73, *Good Companions* (musical) 74, *Great Expectations* (musical) 75.
Film appearances include: *The Midshipmaid, Those Were the Days, Doctor's Orders, Royal Cavalcade, Tudor Rose, O.H.M.S., Goodbye Mr. Chips* (37), *Four Dark Hours, Black Sheep of Whitehall, The Young Mr. Pitt, In Which We Serve, Waterloo Road, This Happy Breed, The Way to the Stars, Scott of the Antarctic, The History of Mr. Polly, The Rocking Horse Winner, Morning Departure, Hobson's Choice, The Colditz Story, Above Us The Waves, Escapade, War and Peace, The Baby and the Battleship, Round the World in 80 Days, Dunkirk, Ice Cold in Alex, Monty's Double, Summer of the Seventeenth Doll, Tiger Bay, Swiss Family Robinson, Tunes of Glory, The Singer Not the Song, Flame in the Streets, Tiara Tahiti, King Rat, The Chalk Garden, Operation Crossbow, The Wrong Box, The Family Way, Chuka, Cowboy in Africa, Adam's Woman, Lady Hamilton, Oh, What a Lovely War, Run Wild, Run Free, A Black Veil for Lisa, Ryan's Daughter, Dulcima, Young Winston, Oklahoma Crude, The Human Factor, Trial by Combat.*
Leisure interests: skiing, golf, painting.
c/o International Famous Agency Ltd., 11-12 Hanover Street, London, W.1, England.

Mills, Wilbur Daigh; American politician; b. 24 May 1909, Kensett; *s.* of A. P. Mills and Abbie Lois Daigh Mills; *m.* Clarine Billingsley 1934; two *d.*; ed. Hendrix Coll. and Harvard Law School.
Admitted to Ark. Bar 33, private legal practice, Searcy; County and Probate Judge, White County 34-38; Cashier, Bank of Kensett 34-35; mem. U.S. House of

Reps. for Arkansas 39-, Chair. Ways and Means Cttee. 58-74; Democrat.
1600 South Eads Street, Arlington, Va., U.S.A.
Telephone: 920-8669.

Millsaps, Knox, B.S., PH.D.; American mathematician; b. 10 Sept. 1921, Birmingham, Ala.; *s.* of Knox Taylor Millsaps and Millie May Joyce; *m.* Lorraine Marie Hartle 1956; one *s.* three *d.*; ed. Auburn Univ. and Calif. Inst. of Technology.
Associate Prof. Ohio State Univ. 47-48; Physicist Wright Air Devt. Center 48-49, Mathematician 50-51, Chief Mathematician 52-55; Prof. of Physics, Auburn Univ. 49-50, 51-52; Prof. of Mechanical Engineering, Mass. Inst. of Technology 55-56; Chief Scientist, Air Force Missile Devt. Center, U.S.A.F. 56-60; Exec. Dir. Air Force Office of Scientific Research, U.S.A.F. 61-62; Research Prof. of Aerospace Eng., Univ. of Florida 63-68; Head Prof. Mechanical Eng., Colorado State Univ. 68-73; Chair. Engineering Science, Mechanics and Aerospace Engineering, Univ. of Florida 73-.
Leisure interests: gardening, crinums, camellias.
P.O. Box 13857, Gainesville, Fla. 32604, U.S.A.
Telephone: 904-372-3018.

Milne-Watson, Sir Michael, Kt., C.B.E.; British company executive; b. 16 Feb. 1910, London; *s.* of Sir David Milne-Watson, 1st Bart., and Lady Olga (Herbert) Milne-Watson (died 1952); *m.* Mary Lisette Bagnall 1940; one *s.*; ed. Eton and Balliol Coll., Oxford.
Gas Light and Coke Co. 33-49, Gov. 46-49; Chair. North Thames Gas Board 49-64; Chair. Richard Thomas & Baldwins Ltd. 64-67; mem. Org. Cttee. Nat. Steel Corpn. 66-67; Deputy Chair. (Admin.) Nat. (now British) Steel Corpn. 67-69; Chair. William Press Group of Companies Dec. 69-74; R.N.V.R. 43-45; Dir. Industrial and Commercial Finance Corpn. Ltd., Commercial Union Assurance Co. Ltd., Finance for Industry Ltd.; mem. Court of Governors, Admin. Staff Coll., Henley-on-Thames; Pres. of Council, Reading Univ.; Gov. British United Provident Asscn.
Office: Finance for Industry Limited, 91 Waterloo Road, London, SE1 8XP; Home: 39 Cadogan Place, London, SW1X 9RX, England.
Telephone: 928-7822 (Office); 235-3467 (Home).

Milner, Aaron Michael; Zambian politician; b. 31 May 1932; ed. Embakwe Mission, Plumtree, Rhodesia.
Minister of State for the Cabinet and Civil Service; Minister of State for Presidential Affairs Sept. 67-Jan. 70; Minister of Transport, Power and Works Jan. 70-Nov. 70; Sec.-Gen. to Govt. 70-73, also Minister of Provincial and Local Govt. and Culture 71-73; Minister of Defence Aug.-Dec. 73, of Home Affairs Dec. 73-.
Ministry of Home Affairs, Lusaka, Zambia.

Milnes, Sherrill, B.MUS.; American opera singer; b. 10 Jan. 1935, Hinsdale, Ill.; *s.* of James Knowlton and Thelma Roe Milnes; *m.* Nancy Stokes 1969; two *s.* one *d.*; ed. Drake Univ., Northwestern Univ.
Studies with Boris Goldovsky, Rosa Ponselle, Andrew White, Hermanes Baer; with Goldovsky Opera Co. 60-65, N.Y.C. Opera Co. 64-67, debut with Metropolitan Opera, N.Y. 65, leading baritone, Met. Opera 65-; has performed with all American city opera cos. 62-73; performed in *Don Giovanni, Vesperi Siciliani* and most standard Italian repertory baritone roles, Met. Opera and at San Francisco Opera, Hamburg Opera, Covent Garden, London, Teatro Colón, Buenos Aires, Vienna State Opera, Paris Opera and Chicago Lyric Opera 73-75; recordings for RCA Victor, London Decca, EMI Angel, Phillips, 27 albums 67-; Chair. of Board Affiliate Artists Inc.; two hon. degrees.
Leisure interests: table tennis, swimming, horse riding.
c/o Herbert Barrett, 1860 Broadway, New York, N.Y. 10023, U.S.A.

Milward, Sir Anthony (Horace), Kt., C.B.E., O.B.E., B.A.; British airline executive; b. 2 March 1905, Redditch; s. of Henry T. Milward and Elsie T. Newton; m. Frieda von der Becke 1931; one s. one d.; ed. Rugby School and Clare Coll., Cambridge.
Employed in the textile industry 26-40; with Fleet Air Arm 40-45; with British Overseas Airways Corpn. Jan.-April 46; with British European Airways April 46-70, Chief Exec. 56-, Chair. 64-70; mem. Air Registration Board 64-70, Board of British Overseas Airways Corpn. 64-70; Chair. London Tourist Board 71-.
Leisure interests: walking, fishing, shooting, swimming.
Dene House, Lower Slaughter, Glos., England.

Mima, Yasuichi, B.COM.; Japanese mining executive; b. 3 Aug. 1903; ed. Tokyo Commercial Univ.
Kuhara Mining Co. (now Nippon Mining Co.) 28-, Dir. Nippon Mining Co. Ltd. 46-, Man. Dir. 47-57, Pres. 57, Chair. of Board until 74; Pres. Toho Titanium Co. 59, now Chair.; Dir. Teikoku Oil Co. Ltd. 57-, Japan Petroleum Fed. 57-; Governing Dir., Japan Fed. of Employers' Asscns. 59-, Exec. Dir., Japan Fed. of Econ. Orgs. 59-, Dir. Japan Management Asscn. 59-, Pres. Japan Mining Industry Asscn. 62-; Order of Merit, Chile 62.
108 Sekinecho, Suginamiku, Tokyo, Japan.

Minah, Francis Misheck, LL.M.; Sierra Leonean lawyer and politician; b. 19 Aug. 1929, Pujehun; m. Gladys Emuchay; four c.; ed. Methodist Boys' High School, Freetown, King's Coll. (London Univ.).
President Sierra Leone Students' Union of Great Britain and Ireland 60-62; mem. House of Reps. 67-; Minister of Trade and Industry 73-75, of Foreign Affairs 75-; UNESCO Fellowship to study community devt. in India and Liberia.
Ministry of Foreign Affairs, 13 Gloucester Street, Freetown; Home: Juba Hill, Juba, Sierra Leone.

Minai, Ahmad, M.A., PH.D.; Iranian economist; b. 10 Sept. 1921; s. of Abdolhossein and Gohartaj Minai; ed. Teheran Univ., Univs. of Glasgow and Oxford, American Univ., Washington, D.C.
Lecturer London Univ. 49-50; joined Foreign Service 50; Third Sec., Washington, D.C. 53; First Sec. Ankara 60; Special Aide to Prime Minister with rank of Dir.-Gen., mem. High Econ. Council 61-62; Economic Counsellor, Washington, D.C. 63; Vice-Gov. Agricultural Bank of Iran 65-66; Dir. Dept. of Econ. Affairs, Ministry of Foreign Affairs 66-67; Minister-Counsellor Islamabad 67; Consul-Gen., Karachi 69; Minister-Counsellor, London 70; Dir. Fourth Political Dept., Ministry of Foreign Affairs 73; Amb. 74; Sec.-Gen. Regional Co-operation for Devt. May 74-.
Leisure interests: mountaineering, photography, music.
Publs. several articles on economic topics.
The Secretariat, Regional Co-operation for Development, 5 Los Angeles Avenue, Teheran, Iran.

Minh, Lt.-Gen. Duong Van (see Duong Van Minh, Lt.-Gen.).

Minić, Miloš; Yugoslav lawyer and politician; b. 1914, Čačak, Serbia; s. of Dragomir and Jovanka Minić; m. Milka 1936; two d.
Member, League of Communist Youth 35, League of Communists of Yugoslavia 36; organizer Communist activities Serbia 41-; Public Prosecutor Serbia 45-50; Minister in Govt. of Serbia 50-53; Pres. People's Cttee. of Belgrade 55-57; Pres. Exec. Council of Serbia 57-62; Vice-Pres. Federal Exec. Council 63-65; Pres. Assembly of Serbia 57-69; Vice-Pres. Federal Exec. Council and Federal Sec. for Foreign Affairs Dec. 72-; mem. Council of the Federation; mem. Central Cttee. of League of Communists of Yugoslavia 52-; mem. Standing Conference of League of Communists of Yugoslavia; 1941 Partisan Memorial Medal and other decorations.

Publs. Several legal and political studies and articles.
Federal Executive Council, 2 Bulevar Lenjina, Belgrade, Yugoslavia.
Telephone: 342-427.

Minin, Viktor Ivanovich; Soviet diplomatist; b. 4 Jan. 1926, Moscow; ed. Moscow State Inst. of Int. Relations.
Diplomatic Service 48-; with Balkan Countries Dept., Ministry of Foreign Affairs 48-52; Second Sec. Soviet Embassy, Albania 52-55; Ministry of Foreign Affairs 55-57; Sec., First Sec. Soviet Embassy, Canada 57-61; Counsellor, S.E. Asia Dept. Ministry of Foreign Affairs 63-65; Counsellor, Soviet Embassy, Turkey 65-68; Amb. to Kingdom of Laos 68-72; Order of Badge of Honour.
Ministry of Foreign Affairs, 32-34 Smolenskaya-Sennaya Ploshchad, Moscow, U.S.S.R.

Minkowski, Rudolph Leo, PH.D.; American astronomer; b. 28 May 1895, Strasbourg, France; s. of Oscar Minkowski and Marie Siegel; m. Luise Amalie David; one s. one d.; ed. Univs. of Breslau and Berlin.
Assistant, Physikalisches Staatsinstitut, Hamburg 22; Privatdozent, Hamburg 26-31, Prof. 31-35; mem. staff, Mount Wilson Observatory, Carnegie Inst. 35-48, Mount Wilson and Palomar Observatories, Pasadena, Calif. 48-60, Univ. of Calif., Berkeley 61-65; Visiting Prof., Univ. of Wisconsin 60-61; mem. Nat. Acad. of Sciences, American Astron. Soc., Royal Astron. Soc., Astron. Soc. of the Pacific; LL.D. h.c. (Univ. of Calif.); Catherine Wolfe Bruce Gold Medal, Astron. Soc. of the Pacific 61.
Radio Astronomy Laboratory, University of California, Berkeley, Calif. 94720; Home: 1011 Siler Place, Berkeley, Calif. 94705, U.S.A.
Telephone: 415-642-3792.

Minnelli, Liza; American actress and singer; b. 12 March 1946; d. of Vincente Minnelli (q.v.) and Judy Garland (deceased); m. 1st Peter Allen 1967 (divorced 1970), 2nd Jack Haley, Jr., 1974.
Early appearances off-Broadway New York, London Palladium 64, Broadway musical *Flora, the Red Menace* 65; films include: *Charlie Bubbles* 68, *The Sterile Cuckoo* 69, *Tell Me That You Love Me Junie Moon* 70, *Cabaret* (Acad. Award for Best Actress) 72, *Lucky Lady* 75.
c/o Creative Management Associates, 600 Madison Avenue, New York 10022, U.S.A.

Minnelli, Vincente; American film director; b. 28 Feb. 1913, Chicago, Ill.
Child Actor, Minnelli Brothers Dramatic Tent Show; Asst. stage presentations, Balban & Katz, then N.Y.C. Paramount Theatre; stage DuBarry, N.Y.; Art Dir., Radio City Music Hall; screen debut 43; Acad. Award for best direction in *Gigi*.
Stage productions: *At Home Abroad, Ziegfeld Follies, The Show is On—Hooray for What!, Very Warm for May*; films: *Cabin in the Sky, Meet Me in St. Louis, Madame Bovary, Father of the Bride, An American in Paris, Bad and the Beautiful, The Bandwagon, Long Long Trailer, Brigadoon, Kismet, Lust for Life, Tea and Sympathy, Gigi, Reluctant Debutante, Some Came Running, Home From the Hills, Bells are Ringing, Four Horsemen of the Apocalypse, The Courtship of Eddie's Father, 1963, Goodbye Charlie, Sandpiper, On a Clear Day You Can See Forever*.
Publ. *I Remember It Well* (autobiog.).
812 North Crescent Drive, Beverly Hills, Calif. 90210, U.S.A.

Minnis, C. M., D.SC., C.ENG., M.I.E.E., F.INST.P.; British physicist; b. 13 Sept. 1912, Saintfield, Co. Down; s. of Frank Ward Minnis and Mary Rea; ed. Methodist Coll. Belfast and Queen's Univ., Belfast.
Worked on devt. of radar at Air Ministry establishments 36-42; commissioned in R.A.F. 42-44; Scientific

Officer, Air Ministry Experimental Establishment, Amesbury 45-46; Principal Scientific Officer, Radio and Space Research Station, Slough 47-62; Scientific Sec. Special Cttee. for Int. Years of the Quiet Sun 62-67; Sec. Comité Int. de Géophysique 63-67; Sec.-Gen. Int. Union of Radio Science 68-.
Leisure interest: music.
Publs. Numerous papers on ionospheric physics and related subjects in *Journal of Atmospheric and Terrestrial Physics.*
International Union of Radio Science, 81 rue de Nieuwenhove, B-1180 Brussels, Belgium.
Telephone: 343-76-78.

Minobe, Ryokichi, DR.POL.ECON.; Japanese district governor; b. 5 Feb. 1904; ed. Dept. of Econs., Tokyo Imperial Univ.
Professor, Hosei Univ. 35-38, Tokyo Univ. of Educ. 49-67; on Editorial Staff, *Mainichi Shimbun* 45-46; First Grade Official of the Cabinet 46; Chief of Statistic Datum Div., Administrative Control Agency 52, Dir. of Statistic Datum Bureau 57-59; Governor of Tokyo 67-.

Minotis, Alexis; American theatre producer and actor; b. 1906, Canea, Crete; m. Katina Paxinou (deceased).
Acting on Greek stage since 25; mem. Nat. Theatre of Greece 30-; Artistic Dir. of Nat. Theatre to 67, Gen. Dir. 74-; has played principal roles in and produced most classical plays from Aeschylus to Pirandello; has made many tours outside Greece with Nat. Theatre; produced Cherubini's opera *Medea*, with Callas in leading role, for Dallas (Texas) Civic Opera, at Covent Garden, London and at La Scala, Milan; Ancient Greek Drama Festivals at Epidaurus and Athens 55-; produced *Oedipus Rex, Hecuba Medea* 55-58, *Oedipus at Colonus, Antigone* 62 at Théâtre des Nations, Paris; produced Friedrich Dürrenmatt's *Visit of the Elderly Woman*, Royal Theatre, Greece 61; played Oedipus in *Oedipus Rex*, London 66; formed own theatre company in Athens with Katina Paxinou 67, and since produced works by O'Neil, O'Casey, Strindberg, Lorca, Brecht, Ibsen, Büchner and Shakespeare, playing Shylock in *The Merchant of Venice* 71-72; several Greek and foreign decorations.
Leisure interest: writing articles, books, etc.
Lykiou 13, Athens, Greece.
Telephone: 715687.

Minow, Newton N.; American lawyer; b. 17 Jan. 1926, Milwaukee, Wis.; s. of Jay A. and Doris (Stein) Minow; m. Josephine Baskin 1949; three d.; ed. Northwestern Law School.
Law Clerk to Supreme Court Chief Justice Vinson 51; Admin. Asst. to Governor of Illinois (Adlai Stevenson) 52-53; served Stevenson's law firm 55-57, Partner 57-61; Chair. Fed. Communications Commission 61-63; Exec. Vice-Pres. General Counsel Encyclopaedia Britannica, Chicago 63-65; mem. Board of Trustees, Rand Corpn. 65-75, Chair. 70-72; Partner, Sidley and Austin (fmrly. Leibman, Williams, Bennet, Baird & Minow) 65-; Hon. Chair. and Dir. Chicago Educational Television Asscn.; Dir. Aetna Casualty and Surety Co. of Ill., Aetna Life Insurance Co. of Ill.; Professorial Lecturer, Northwestern Univ., Medill School of Journalism; mem. Board of Lay Trustees, Notre Dame Univ.; Dir. Adler Planetarium; Trustee Northwestern Univ., Chicago Orchestral Asscn., MAYO Foundation; Chair. Board of Overseers, Jewish Theological Seminary of America; Gov., Public Broadcasting Service; Democrat.
Publs. *Presidential Television* (co-author), *Equal Time.*
Sidley and Austin, 1 First National Plaza, Chicago, Ill.; Home: 375 Palos Road, Glencoe, Ill., U.S.A.
Telephone: 312-329-5555 (Office); 312-VE5-3118 (Home).

Mintaredja, Hadji Mohamad Sjafa'at, LL.D.; Indonesian lawyer; b. 17 Feb. 1921, Bogor, Java; s. of Mohamad Sjafe'i Mintaredja and Halimah Emon; m.

Siti Romlah Abdulkadir 1945; three s. three d.; ed. Gadjahmada Univ., Leiden Univ., Netherlands, and Univ. of Indonesia, Jakarta.
Member of Board of many nat. youth movements 36-44; founder Himpunan Mahasiswa Islam; Judge, Court in Bandung 44-46; Chief, Legal Dept., Foreign Exchange Control 50-55; in private business (import, export, banking and industry) 57-65; Pres. and Dir. of two state construction companies 66-68; mem. of Board Muhammadiyah 65-71; Chair. Partai Muslimin Indonesia 70; Minister of State 68-71; Minister of Social Affairs Sept. 71-; Gen. Exec. Chair. Partai Persatuan Pembangunan 73-.
Leisure interests: driving cars, golf.
Publs. *Moslem Society and Politics in Indonesia* 71; many articles in Indonesian magazines and journals.
Jalan K. H. A. Dahlan 21, Kebajoran Baru, Jakarta, Indonesia.
Telephone: 46717 (Office); 71216 (Home).

Mintoff, Dominic, B.SC., M.A.; Maltese politician; b. 6 Aug. 1916, Cospicua; s. of Lawrence Mintoff; m. Moyra de Vere Bentinck 1947; two d.; ed. Univs. of Malta and Oxford.
Civil engineer in Great Britian 41-43; practised in Malta as architect 43-; rejoined and helped reorganize Maltese Labour Party 44; Elected to Council of Govt. and Executive Council 45; Mem. Legislative Assembly 47-; Deputy Leader of Labour Party, Deputy Prime Minister and Minister for Works and Reconstruction 47-49; resigned Ministry, Leader of Labour Party 49-; Prime Minister and Minister of Finance 55-58; Leader of the Opposition 62-71; Prime Minister June 71-.
Leisure interests: tennis, swimming, water skiing, bocci, horse riding.
"The Olives", Tarxien, Malta.
Telephone: 22404 (Home).

Mints, Isaak Israilevich; Soviet historian; b. 3 Feb. 1896, Krinichki, Ukraine; ed. Inst. of Red Professors, Moscow.
Member U.S.S.R. Acad. of Sciences 46-; Chair. Scientific Council of U.S.S.R. Acad. of Sciences for Solution of problems in *History of Great October Socialist Revolution;* mem. C.P.S.U. 17-; State Prizes 43, 46.
Publs. Works on history of October Revolution, Civil War and foreign military intervention.
Institute of History, U.S.S.R. Academy of Sciences, Ulitsa D. Ulyanova 19, Moscow, U.S.S.R.

Miranda y Gomez, H.E. Cardinal Miguel Dario; Mexican ecclesiastic; b. 19 Dec. 1895, León.
Ordained 18; Bishop of Tulancingo 37; Titular Archbishop of Selimbria 55; Archbishop of Mexico 56-; cr. Cardinal 69.
Apartado postal 8877, México 1 D.F., Mexico.
Telephone: 533-61-65.

Mirfenderesky, Ahmad, LL.B.; Iranian diplomatist; b. 1918; ed. French Univ., Beirut.
Career with Ministry of Foreign Affairs 42-, served U.S.S.R., Netherlands, India, Turkey; Dir. Dept. of Econ. Affairs, Second Political Dept., Political Dir.-Gen. 62-64; Deputy Minister, Political and Parl. Depts. 64-65; Amb. to U.S.S.R. Oct. 65-71; now Deputy Minister for Foreign Affairs.
Ministry of Foreign Affairs, Teheran, Iran.

Mirghani, Abdel Karim; Sudanese Minister of Planning 69-70; see *The International Who's Who 1975-76.*

Miró, Joan; Spanish artist; b. 20 April 1893, Barcelona; s. of Michel Miró Adzirias and Dolores Ferra; m. Pilar Juncosa 1929; one d.; ed. Barcelona Acad. of Fine Art.
Apart from painting, has executed ceramics, sculptures, engravings and lithographs; divides his time between Paris and Palma; Guggenheim Award for ceramic

mural "Night and Day", UNESCO Building, Paris 58; Fondation Maeght Building, St.-Paul-de-Vence, France; exhbns. in New York, Paris, Zürich, London (Tate Gallery) 64, Tokyo and Kyoto 66; retrospective exhbn. Barcelona 68; Commdr. Légion d'Honneur 74.
c/o Galerie Maeght, 13 rue de Téhéran, Paris 8e, France.

Mironova, Zoya Vassilievna; Soviet chemical engineer and diplomatist; b. 26 Feb. 1912, Yadrin, Chuvash; ed. Moscow Inst. of Chemical Technology.
Deputy Mayor of Moscow 51-59; then Deputy Perm. Soviet Rep. to UN and Soviet Rep. on UN Cttee. on Women's Rights; then at Ministry of Foreign Affairs, Moscow; Perm. Rep. of U.S.S.R. at UN European Office and other int. orgs. in Geneva 66-; rank of Amb.; State Prize (for work on producing a rare metal and its compounds) 50; Red Banner of Labour (twice), Badge of Honour, Order of the October Revolution, etc.
15 avenue de la Paix, 1202 Geneva, Switzerland.

Miroshnichenko, Boris Panteleimonovich, DR.ECON.SC.; Soviet scientist and diplomatist; b. 30 May 1911, Kharkov; ed. Kharkov Planning Inst.
Scientific work in Higher educational Insts. and work in State Offices until 54; Counsellor, Soviet Embassy, German Democratic Repub. 54-57; Counsellor, Ministry of Foreign Affairs, 57-65; Rector, Moscow Inst. of Int. Relations; mem. of Coll. Ministry of Foreign Affairs, Amb. to Canada 68-73, to Kenya 73-; Order of Red Banner of Labour, Order of Red Star, Order of Badge of Honour and medals.
U.S.S.R. Embassy, Lenana Road, P.O. Box 30049, Nairobi, Kenya.

Misasi, Riccardo; Italian lawyer and politician; b. 1932, Cosenza.
Former mem. Italian Catholic Action, Nat. Council of Christian Democrat Youth Movement; fmr. acting Chair. Comm. for S. Italy; Dir. Christian Democratic Central Research Office; elected 58, 63, 68 to Chamber of Deputies for Catanzaro constituency; mem. Parl. Comm. to investigate Mafia; Under-Sec. of Justice in 1st, 2nd and 3rd Moro govts.; Under-Sec. for State Participation, 1st Rumor govt.; Minister of Foreign Trade; Minister of Education March 70-72.

Mischnick, Wolfgang; German politician; b. 29 Sept. 1921; ed. High School, Dresden.
Co-founder, Liberal Democratic Party, Dresden 45; town official, Dresden 46-48; mem. Central Cttee. of Liberal Democratic Party, Soviet Zone 46-48; fled to Fed. Germany 48; mem. Provincial Ass., Hesse, 54-57, Parl. Leader of F.D.P.; Fed. Chair. F.D.P. Youth Movement and Ed. *Stimmen der jungen Generation* 54-57; mem. Bundestag 57-; Dep. Chair. F.D.P., Hesse 57-; Fed. Minister for Refugees 61-63; Deputy Chair. F.D.P. 64-, F.D.P. Chair. in Bundestag 68-.
Kullmanstrasse 16, Frankfurt am Main, Federal Republic of Germany.

Mishin, Vasily Pavlovich; Soviet engineer; b. 18 Jan. 1917, Moscow; ed. Moscow Aviation Inst.
Specialist in applied mechanics; mem. C.P.S.U. 43-; Corresp. mem. U.S.S.R. Acad. of Sciences 58-66, mem. 66-.
U.S.S.R. Academy of Sciences, 14 Leninsky Prospekt, Moscow, U.S.S.R.

Mišković, Vojislav, D.SC.; Yugoslav university professor; b. 1892.
Assistant, Marseilles Observatory 19-22; Astronomer, Nice Observatory 22-25; Founder and Dir. Belgrade Observatory 25-46; later Prof. Univ. of Belgrade; mem. Serbian Acad. of Sciences 39-, Gen. Sec. 45-48; Vice-Dir. Mathematical Inst. of Acad. 48, Dir. Astronomical Inst. 48-54; Editor of bulletins of Belgrade Observatory.

Publs. *Etudes de Statistique stellaire* 24, *Nouvelles tables de précession* 35.
Serbian Academy of Sciences, Knez Mihailova 35/1, Belgrade, Yugoslavia.

Misra, Sirdar Iswary Raj, M.A., B.L.; Nepalese diplomatist; b. 29 Oct. 1917, Kathmandu; s. of Pandit Delli Raj Misra and Nara Kumari Debi; m. Indira Devi 1933; one s. one d.; ed. St. Xavier's Coll., The Scottish Church Coll. and Univ. Law Coll., Calcutta, and Calcutta Univ.
Sectional Head, Dept. of Law, Katmandu 42; Head of Buying Agency to Govt. of Nepal, Calcutta 43-45; Dept. of Law, Katmandu 45-47; First Sec. Nepalese Embassy, London 47, later Counsellor; Deputy Sec. Ministry of Foreign Affairs 56-59; Registrar of Supreme Court, Katmandu 59-60; Judge of Western High Court 60-61; Judge of Supreme Court 61-65; Ambassador to France 65-67, to U.K. 65-69, and concurrently to Italy and Greece 68-69; Amb. to Pakistan 69-, concurrently to Iran and Turkey 70-; Suprasidha Prabala Gorakha Dakshina Bahu (Nepal); Knight Commdr. Order of Orange Nassau (Netherlands), Grand Officier of Merit (France), Officier Légion d'Honneur.
Leisure interests: golf, shooting.
Royal Nepalese Embassy, No. 10, 88th Street, Ramna 6/3, Islamabad, Pakistan.
Telephone: 23522.

Missoffe, François; French industrialist and politician; b. 13 Oct. 1919; ed. Prytanée militaire de La Flèche.
Army service 40-46; U.N.R. (Union for the New Republic); Deputy to Nat. Ass. 58-61, 62, 67, 68-; Gen. Treas. U.N.R. 59; Sec. of State for Domestic Trade April-Oct. 62, Minister of Repatriation 62-64; Amb. to Japan 64-66; Minister for Youth and Sports 66-May 68; Special Envoy of the French Govt. in Asiatic Countries 73; Chevalier, Légion d'Honneur; Croix de Guerre; Médaille de la Résistance.
Home: 38 rue Boileau, Paris 16e, France.

Mistler, Jean; French writer; b. 1 Sept. 1897; ed. Lycées de Carcassonne and Henri IV, Paris and Ecole normale supérieure.
Cultural Attaché, Budapest, and Priv. Dozent Univ. of Budapest; Head of Section, Ministry of Foreign Affairs 26; mem. Chamber of Deputies 28; Under-Sec. of State for Fine Arts 32; Minister of Posts, Telecommunications and Commerce 34; Pres. of Comm. for Foreign Affairs 36-40; Dir.-Gen. Maison du livre française 47-60; Dir. Dept. of Gen. Literature, Librarie Hachette 64-68; mem. Acad. Française 66-, Perm. Sec. 73-; Dir. Accumulateur Fulmen and Cie. Industrielles des Téléphones.
Publs. include *Châteaux en Bavière, La Symphonie inachevée, Hoffmann le Fantastique, A Bayreuth avec Richard Wagner, Epinal et l'imagerie populaire, Le 14 Juillet, Le Bout du monde, Les Orgues de Saint Sauveur, Gaspard Hauser, La Route des étangs, Le Naufrage du Monte-Christo,* and numerous articles for *L'Aurore* 54-, and *Revue de Paris* 28-40.
11 rue de l'Université, Paris 7e, France.

Mitchell, Broadus, B.A., PH.D., L.H.D.; American economist; b. 27 Dec. 1892, Georgetown, Ky.; s. of Samuel Chiles Mitchell and Alice Virginia Broadus; m. Louise Pearson Blodget 1936; two s. two d.; ed. Johns Hopkins Univ.
Reporter 13-18; successively Instructor, Assoc. and Assoc.Prof. of Political Economy Johns Hopkins Univ. 19-39; Visiting Prof. Occidental Coll. 39-41; Candidate of Socialist Party for Governorship of Maryland 34; Consultant to Dir. N.R.A. Div. of Review Nov. 35-March 36; twice mem. Exec. Cttee. American Economic Asscn.; Act. Dir. of Research Int. Ladies' Garment Workers' Union 43-47; Lecturer in Economics Rutgers

Univ. 47-49, Prof. 49-; Visiting Prof. Hofstra Univ. 58-67; Pres. Metropolitan Econ. Asscn. 50-51.
Leisure interests: carpentry, poultry raising.
Publs. *The Rise of Cotton Mills in the South* 21, *General Economics* 37, *Depression Decade* 47, *American Adventure* 49, *Alexander Hamilton* (2 vols.) 57, 62, *Great Economists in their Times* 66, *Postscripts to Economic History* 67, *Alexander Hamilton, the Revolutionary Years* 70, *The Road to Yorktown* 71, *The Price of Independence* 74; in co-operation: *The Industrial Revolution in the South* 30, *Practical Problems in Economics* 38, *American Economic History* 47, *Economics, Experience and Analysis* 50, *A Biography of the Constitution of the U.S.* 64 (2nd edn. 74).
49 Barrow Street, New York, N.Y. 10014, U.S.A.
Telephone: CHelsea 2-8436.

Mitchell, Sir Derek, K.C.B., C.V.O.; British civil servant; b. 5 March 1922, Wimbledon, Surrey; s. of the late Sidney Mitchell and Gladys Mitchell; m. Miriam Jackson 1944; one s. two d.; ed. St. Paul's School, London and Christ Church, Oxford.
Served, Royal Armoured Corps and H.Q. London District 42-45; served in H.M. Treasury 47-63, Principal Private Sec. to Chancellor of the Exchequer 62-63; Principal Private Sec. to Prime Minister 64-66; Deputy Under-Sec. of State, Dept. of Econ. Affairs 66-67, Ministry of Agric., Fisheries and Food 67-69; Econ. Minister, British Embassy, Washington and Exec. Dir. IBRD, IMF, etc. 69-72; Second Perm. Sec. H.M. Treasury 73-.
Leisure interests: opera, concerts, theatre, travelling.
9 Holmbush Road, Putney, London, S.W.15, England.

Mitchell, Donald George; American industrialist; b. 26 April 1905; ed. Univ. of Cincinnati and Univ. of Florida.
Chief, Marketing Div. American Can Co. 33-37; Gen. Sales Man., Marshall Field and Co. 37-39; Vice-Pres. Pepsi-Cola Co. 39-42; Vice-Pres. (Sales) Sylvania Electric Products Inc. 42-46, Exec. Vice-Pres. 46, Pres. 46-53, Chair. 53-62; Pres. Gen. Telephone and Electronics Corpn. 59-61, Vice-Chair. 61-62; Chair. General Time Corpn. 64-; Chair. American Management Asscn.; Outstanding Civilian Service Award, U.S. Dept. of the Army 61; official of welfare orgs.
206 Oakridge Avenue, Summit, New Jersey, U.S.A.

Mitchell, Capt. Edgar D., B.S., SC.D.; American astronaut; b. 17 Sept. 1930, Hereford, Tex.; s. of the late Joseph T. Mitchell and of Ollidean M. (Arnold) Mitchell; m. 1st Louise Elizabeth Randall 1951 (divorced 1972), two d.; m. 2nd Anita Kaye Rettig 1973; ed. Carnegie Inst. of Technology, U.S. Naval Postgraduate School and Mass. Inst. of Technology.
Entered U.S. Navy 52, commissioned 53, completed flight training 54; assigned to Patrol Squadron 29, Okinawa; flew A3 aircraft on carrier duty, Heavy Attack Squadron 2 57-58; research project officer, Air Devt. Squadron 5 58-59; earned doctorate in aeronautics/astronautics, Mass. Inst. of Tech. until 64; Chief, Project Management Div., Navy Field Office for Manned Orbiting Lab. 64; later attended Air Force Aerospace Research Pilot School; selected by NASA as astronaut April 66; Lunar Module Pilot *Apollo XIV*, landed on Moon 5 Feb. 71; Back-up Pilot for *Apollo XVI* mission April 72; resigned from NASA Oct. 72; Hon. D.Sc. (New Mexico State Univ.), Hon. D.E. (Carnegie Mellon Univ.).
Publ. *Psychic Exploration: A Challenge For Science* 74.
The Institute of Noetic Science, 575 Middlefield Road, Palo Alto, Calif. 94301, U.S.A.
Telephone: 415-328-2340.

Mitchell, George Wilder, B.A.; American economist; b. 23 Feb. 1904, Richland Center, Wis.; s. of George Ray and Minnie (German) Mitchell; m. 1st Grace

Marion Muir 1927, 2nd Mary Toft Petty 1964; one s. three d.; ed. Wisconsin, Iowa and Chicago Univs.
Research Asst. Univs. of Wisconsin, Iowa and Chicago 25-33; Dir. of Research, Illinois Tax Comm. 33-39, 41-43, mem. of Comm. 39-40; Asst. to Dir., Dept. of Revenue, State of Illinois 43; Dir. Dept. of Finance, State of Illinois 49-51; Tax Economist, Federal Reserve Bank of Chicago 44-48, Vice-Pres. 51-61; mem. Board of Govs. of the Fed. Reserve System 61-73, Vice-Chair. Board of Govs. 73-76; mem. Nat. Cttee. on Govt. Finance 61-65.
Publs. *Survey of Local Finance in Illinois* 39-40, *Assessment of Real Estate in Iowa and other Midwestern States* 31.
c/o Federal Reserve System, Washington, D.C. 20551, U.S.A.

Mitchell, Sir Godfrey Way, Kt.; British company director; b. 31 Oct. 1891, London; s. of Christopher and Margaret (Way) Mitchell; m. late Doreen Lilian Mitchell 1929; two d.; ed. Aske's (Haberdashers' School).
With Rowe & Mitchell 08-14; served in Royal Engineers France, First World War 14-18; Man. Dir. George Wimpey & Co. Ltd. 19, Chair. 30-73, now Exec. Dir.; Chair. Mono Containers Ltd. 47-61; mem. Restrictive Practices Court 57-63.
Office: George Wimpey & Co. Ltd., Hammersmith Grove, London, W.6; Home: Wilton Place, Ledborough Lane, Beaconsfield, England.
Telephone: 01-748-2000 (Office); 0494-6-3128 (Home).

Mitchell, John Newton; American government official; b. 15 Sept. 1913, Detroit, Mich.; m. Martha Beall; three c.; ed. Fordham Univ. and Columbia Univ. Law School.
Admitted to Bar 38; served in U.S. Navy in Pacific, Second World War; partner in law firm Nixon, Mudge, Rose, Guthrie, Alexander and Mitchell; Attorney-Gen. of U.S.A. 69-72; Election Campaign Man. for Richard Nixon Feb.-July 72; indicted by Supreme Court May 73; sentenced to 2½-8 years imprisonment Feb. 75.
Watergate East, Washington, D.C. 20037, U.S.A.

Mitchell, Joseph Stanley, C.B.E., M.D., PH.D., F.R.S., F.R.C.P., F.R.C.R.; British radiotherapist; b. 22 July 1909, Birmingham; s. of Joseph Brown Mitchell and Ethel Maud Mary Arnold; m. Dr. Lilian Mary Buxton 1934; one s. one d.; ed. Univ. of Birmingham, and St. John's Coll., Cambridge.
House Physician, Gen. Hospital, Birmingham 34; Fellow St. John's Coll., Cambridge 36-; Radiotherapist, Emergency Medical Service 39; Medical Officer in charge, later Dir., Radiotherapeutic Centre, Addenbrooke's Hospital, Cambridge 43; in charge of medical investigations, Montreal Laboratory, Nat. Research Council of Canada 44; Prof. of Radiotherapeutics, Univ. of Cambridge 46-57, 75-76; Regius Prof. of Physics in the Univ. of Cambridge 57-75, Emeritus Regius Prof. 75-; Pres. English Section Anglo-German Medical Soc. 59-68; Hon. Consultant, Atomic Energy Authority; Hon. mem. German Roentgen Soc. 67; Foreign Fellow Indian Nat. Science Acad. 74; Hon. D.Sc.; Pirogoff Medal 67.
Leisure interests: modern languages, walking.
Publs. *Studies in Radiotherapeutics* 60, *The Cell Nucleus* 60, *Treatment of Cancer* 65, *Some Aspects of the Effects of Radiations on the Metabolism of Tissues and Tumours* 66, *Cancer: If curable why not cured?* 71.
Thorndyke, Huntingdon Road, Cambridge, England.
Telephone: Cambridge 76102.

Mitchell, William S., C.P.A.; American business executive; b. 19 Sept. 1914, Alameda; m.; ed. Univ. of Calif. (Berkeley) and Stanford Univ. Graduate School of Business.
Joined Safeway Stores Inc. 36, Dir. 53-, Vice-Pres. in charge of procurement and manufacturing operations

56, Senior Vice-Pres. 60, Exec. Vice-Pres. 66, now Pres., Chief Exec. Officer 73-.
Leisure interests: sailing, gardening.
Safeway Stores Inc., P.O. Box 660, Oakland, Calif. 94604, U.S.A.

Mitchison, Naomi; British novelist and farmer; b. 1 Nov. 1897, Edinburgh; d. of John Scott Haldane and Louisa Kathleen Trotter; m. Gilbert Richard Mitchison 1916; three s. two d.; ed. Dragon School, Oxford.
Editor *Outline for Boys and Girls* 32; Labour candidate for Scottish Univs. 35; mem. Bakgatla tribe (S.E. Botswana).
Publs. *The Conquered* 23, *When the Bough Breaks* 24, *Cloud Cuckoo Land* 25, *Black Sparta* 28, *Anna Comnena* 28, *Nix-Nought-Nothing* 28, *Barbarian Stories* 29, *The Corn King and the Spring Queen* 31, *The Delicate Fire* 32, *We Have Been Warned* 35, *The Fourth Pig* 36, *Socrates* (with R. H. S. Crossman) 37, *Moral Basis of Politics* 38, *The Kingdom of Heaven* 39, *As it Was in the Beginning* (with L. E. Gielgud) 39, *The Blood of the Martyrs* 39, *Re-Educating Scotland* 45, *The Bull Calves* 47, *Men and Herring* (with D. Macintosh) 49, *The Big House* 50, *Lobsters on the Agenda* 52, *Travel Light* 52, *Swan's Road* 54, *Graeme and the Dragon* 54, *Land the Ravens Found* 55, *Chapel Perilous* 55, *Little Boxes* 56, *Behold Your King, The Far Harbour* 57, *Other People's Worlds, Five Men and a Swan* 58, *Judy and Lakshmi* 59, *Rib of the Green Umbrella* 60, *The Young Alexander* 60, *Karensgaard* 61, *Memoirs of a Spacewoman* 62, *The Fairy Who Couldn't Tell a Lie* 63, *When We Become Men* 64, *Return to the Fairy Hill* 66, *Friends and Enemies* 66, *African Heroes* 68, *The Family at Ditlabeng* 69, *The Africans: A History* 70, *Sun and Moon* 70, *Cleopatra's People* 72, *A Danish Teapot* 73, *A Life for Africa* 73, *Sunrise Tomorrow* 73, *Small Talk* 73, *All Change Here* 75, *Solution Three* 75, *Snake!* 76.
Carradale House, Carradale, Argyll, Scotland.

Mitchum, Robert Charles Duran; American actor; b. 6 Aug. 1917, Bridgeport, Conn.; s. of James and Anne Mitchum; m. Dorothy Spence 1940; two s. one d.
Films include: *River of no Return, Not as a Stranger, Night of the Hunter, The Longest Day, Man with a Gun, Wonderful Country, Sundowners, Cape Fear, Man in the Middle, El Dorado, The Way West, Five Card Stud, Anzio, Secret Ceremony, Good Guys Bad Guys, Ryan's Daughter, The Friends of Eddie Coyle, The Yakuza, Midway* 75, *Farewell My Lovely* 75.
c/o William Morris Agency Inc., 151 El Camino Drive, Beverly Hills, California 90212, U.S.A.

Mitford, Jessica (sister of late Hon. Nancy Mitford); American (b. British) writer; b. 11 Sept. 1917.
Went to U.S.A. 39; Distinguished Prof. San José State Univ. Sept. 73-.
Publs. *Hons and Rebels* (autobiography) 60, *The American Way of Death* 63, *The Trial of Dr. Spock* 70, *Kind and Unusual Punishment* 73.
6411 Regent Street, Oakland, Calif., U.S.A.

Mitin, Mark Borisovich; Soviet philosopher; b. 5 July 1901, Zhitomir, Ukraine; ed. Inst. of Red Professors, Moscow.
Party work 29-36; Scientific worker, Inst. of Philosophy 36-44; Lecturer, Higher Party School 45-50; mem. Central Cttee. of C.P.S.U. 39-56; mem. U.S.S.R. Acad. of Sciences 39-; Chief Editor *For a Lasting Peace, For a People's Democracy*, Prague 50-56; mem. staff All-Union Soc. *Znania* (Knowledge) 56-60; Chief Editor *Questions of Philosophy* 60-; State Prize 43; Order of Lenin (twice); Order of Red Banner of Labour (twice).
14 Ulitsa Volkhonka, Moscow, U.S.S.R.

Mitra, Sombhu; Indian actor and stage director; b. 22 Aug. 1915; ed. Ballygunge Govt. High School and St. Xavier's Coll., Calcutta.
Joined Stage, Calcutta 39; Producer-Dir.-Actor, Indian

People's Theatre Asscn. 43-46; Producer-Dir.-Actor Bohurupee (non-commercial theatre) 48-; Fellow Sangect Natak Akademie, New Delhi; Head Dept. of Drama, Rabindra Bharati Univ.; Grand Prix Karlovy Vary Film Festival 57; Nat. Honour Padma Bhusan 70.
Productions include: *Four Chapters* (Tagore) 51, *An Enemy of the People* (Ibsen) 52, *Red Oleanders* (Tagore) 54, *The Doll's House* (Ibsen) 58, *Sacrifice* (Tagore) 61, *The King of the Dark Chamber* (Tagore) 64, *Oedipus Rex* (Sophocles) 64, *Baki Itihas* 67, *Pagla Ghora* 71.
Publs. *Abhinay-Natak-Mancha* 57, *Putul Khela* 58, *Kanchanranga* 61, *Ghurnee* 67, *Raja Oidipous* 69.
Bohurupee, 11a Nasiruddin Road, Calcutta 17, India.

Mitry, Emmanuel Comte de, French industrialist; b. 21 June 1892.
President, Gen. Man. Soc. des Forges de Gueugnon 40-74, Pres. De Wendel et Cie, 52-72; Hon. Pres. De Wendel-Sidelor 68-; Vice-Pres. Etablissements Nozal; Dir. Anciens Etablissements Chavanne-Brun Frères, Distilleries de la Suze, Soc. Lorraine de Laminage Continu (SOLLAC); Officier Légion d'Honneur, Croix de Guerre.
10 rue de Clichy, Paris 9e; Château de Betange, 57 Florange (Moselle), France.

Mitscherlich, Alexander, DR. MED.; German professor of medicine; b. 20 Sept. 1908; ed. Gymnasium, Hof, Bavaria, and Univs. of Munich, Prague, Berlin, Freiburg, Zürich and Heidelberg.
Director of Psychosomatic Clinic, Univ. of Heidelberg Medical School 48-67, Extraordinary Prof. of Psychosomatic Medicine 52-58, Prof. 58-; Prof. of Psychology, Univ. of Frankfurt; Dir. Sigmund Freud Inst. for Psychoanalysis and Psychosomatic Medicine, Frankfurt/Main 59-; Hon. mem. American Psychosomatic Soc. 52; Peace Prize of West German Book Trade 69.
Publs. *Vom Ursprung der Sucht* 47, *Freiheit und Unfreiheit in der Krankheit* 48, *Medizin ohne Menschlichkeit* 60, *Auf dem Weg zur vaterlosen Gesellschaft* 63, *Die Unwirtlichkeit unserer Städte* 65, *Krankheit als Konflikt-Studien zur psychosomatischen Medizin I, II* 66-67, *Die Unfähigkeit zu trauern* (with M. Mitscherlich-Nielsen) 67, *Der Kranke in der modernen Gesellschaft* (editor, inter al.) 67, *Die Idee des Friedens und die menschliche Aggressivität* 69, *Versuch, die Welt besser zu bestehen* 70, *Thesen zur Stadt der Zukunft* 71, *Massenpsychologie ohne Ressentiment* 73.
Myliusstr. 20, Frankfurt, Federal Republic of Germany.
Telephone: 729245.

Mitsotakis, Constantine; Greek politician; b. 18 Oct. 1918; ed. Univ. of Athens.
Lawyer, Athens 41-, Crete 42-44; Publisher *Kiryx* 45; mem. Chamber of Deputies 46-67, for Liberal Party 46-61, for Centre Union 61-67; Minister of Finance, Transport and Public Works 51, of Finance 63-65; Minister of Co-ordination and *ad interim* of Mercantile Marine July 65-66; returned to Greece 73.
1 Paravantinou Street, Athens 138, Greece.
Telephone: 724-997.

Mitsui, Shingo, DR.AGR.SC.; Japanese agricultural scientist; b. 1 Jan. 1910, Tokyo; m. Kikuko Mitsui 1935; one s. one d.; ed. Univ. of Tokyo.
Senior Chemist, Dept. of Agricultural Chem. Nat. Agricultural Experiment Station of Ministry of Agriculture and Forestry 32-45, Dir. of Dept. of Soil and Fertilizer 45-48; Asst. Prof. (Fertilizer and Plant Nutrition) Faculty of Agriculture, Univ. of Tokyo 48-52, Prof. (Fertilizer and Plant Nutrition) 52-63, Dean of Dept. of Chemical Sciences of Graduate School 63-65, Prof. Emer. 70-; mem. Scientific Advisory Cttee. of Int. Atomic Energy Agency (IAEA) 65-; Lecturer, FAO Int. Training Centre on Fertilizer and Soil for Rice, India 52; Councillor Japan Radio Isotope Asscn. and Scientific Expert to Atomic Energy Comm. Japan 55-; Dir. Fertilizer Research Inst. 69-; Del. to

numerous int. confs. on rice cultivation and peaceful uses of atomic energy; Prize of Japan Acad. and others.
Leisure interests: golf, violin.
Publs. *Dynamic Studies on the Nutrients Uptake by Crop Plants* (with others) Parts 1-45 51-64, *Inorganic Nutrition Fertilization and Soil Amelioration for Lowland Rice* 54, *Efficient Use of Urea Fertilizer in Japan* 65.
Higashi Fushimi 2-2-25, Hoya-shi, Tokyo, Japan.
Telephone: 0424-63-1453.

Mittag, Günter; German politician; b. 8 Oct. 1926; ed. Stettin, and Transport Coll., Dresden.
Former Railway Inspector; mem. Socialist Unity Party (S.E.D.) 46-; Cand. mem. Central Cttee. 58-62, mem. 62-, Cand. mem. Politburo 63-66, mem. 66-; Sec. Econ. Comm. of Politburo (S.E.D.) 58-62, Sec. for Econs. 62-73, Head of Bureau for Industry and Building 63; mem. Volkskammer; mem. State Council 63-71; First Deputy Chair. Council of Ministers Oct. 73-; Vaterländischer Verdienstorden in Silber 59, Gold 64; Order of Banner of Labour.
Sozialistische Einheitspartei Deutschlands, 102 Berlin, 2 Werderscher Markt, German Democratic Republic.

Mitterer, Otto; Austrian politician; b. 22 Oct. 1911, Vienna; *m.* Ilse Pichler; one *d.*; ed. grammar school and business college.
Family wholesale clock firm 32-40, 40-; mil. service 40-45; entered politics, mem. Austrian Econ. Union 47, Chair. Trade Section 55; Minister of Trade and Industry, 68-70; Pres. Vienna Chamber of Commerce; mem. of the Nat. Council 68-; Kommerzialrat 56; Grosse Silberne Ehrenmedaille Vienna Chamber of Commerce 59; Grosses Silbernes Ehrenzeichen for Services to the Repub. of Austria 63.
Leisure interests: riding, skiing, skating, film making, theatre, cinema.
Vienna 1, Goldschmiedgasse 10, Austria.

Mitterrand, François Maurice Marie; French politician; b. 26 Oct. 1916; ed. Univ. of Paris.
Served 39-40; taken prisoner, escaped back to France where active in prisoner-of-war and resistance movements; missions to London and Algiers 43; Sec.-Gen. Organisation for Prisoners of War, War Victims and Refugees 44-46; Deputy 46-58, 62-; Minister for Ex-Service men 47-48; Sec. of State for Information attached Prime Minister's Office 48-49; Minister for Overseas Territories 50-51; Chair. U.D.S.R. 51-52; Minister of State Jan.-Feb. 52, Mar. 52-July 53; Del. to Council of Europe July-Sept. 53; Minister of the Interior June 54-Feb. 55; Minister of State 56-57; Senator 59-62; Candidate for Pres. of France 65, 74; Pres. of Federation of Democratic and Socialist Left 65-Nov. 68; First Sec. Socialist Party 71-; Pol. Dir. *Le Courrier de la Nièvre*; Officier Légion d'Honneur, Croix de Guerre, Rosette de la Résistance.
Publs. *Aux frontières de l'Union française, La Chine au défi* 61, *Le Coup d'Etat permanent* 64, *Technique économique française* 68, *Ma part de vérité* 69, *Un socialisme du possible* 71, *La rose au poing* 73, *La Paille et le Grain* 75.
22 rue de Bièvre, 75005 Paris, France.

Miyake, Shigemitsu; Japanese banker; b. 27 Feb. 1911, Osaka; *s.* of Shigetaka and Fumi (Ito) Miyake; *m.* Hina Inoue 1935; one *s.* two *d.*; ed. Tokyo Imperial Univ.
With Bank of Japan 33-67, Dir. 62-67; Deputy Pres. Tokai Bank Ltd. 67-68, Pres. 68-69, Chair. and Pres. 69-75; Chair. 75-; Exec. Dir. Japan Man. Orgs. 70; Exec. Dir. Fed. of Japan Econ. Orgs. 71; Pres. Nagoya Chamber of Commerce and Ind. 74; Vice-Pres. Japan Chamber of Commerce and Ind. 74; Blue Ribbon Medal 74.
Tokai Bank Ltd., 3-21-24 Nishiki, Naka-ku, Nagoya;

Home: 2-24-3, Shimoyama-cho, Mizuho-ku, Nagoya, Japan.
Telephone: 052-211-1111 (Office), 052-831-6792 (Home).

Miyamori, Kazuo; Japanese oil executive; b. 17 Sept. 1902; ed. Meiji Univ.
With Yamaguchi Bank Ltd. 25-33, joined Sanwa Bank Ltd. 33, Dir. 56, Deputy Pres. 64-66; Pres. and Chief Exec. Officer Maruzen Oil Co., Ltd. 64-; Pres. Maruzen Tanker Co., Ltd. and Maruzen Real Estate Co. 65-; Dir. Maruzen Petro Chemical Co., Ltd. 64-, Kansai Oil Co. and Kansai and Osaka Petro Chemical Cos., Ltd. 65-, Kanegabuchi Gosei Kagaku Kogyo Co., Ltd. 67-; Auditor, Palace Side Bldg. Co. 63-, Ohbayashi Road Construction Co. Ltd. and Japan Industrial Land Devt. Co. 64-.
261, Chofu, Unokicho, Otaku, Tokyo, Japan.

Miyamoto, Kenji; Japanese writer and politician; b. 17 Oct. 1908; ed. Tokyo Imperial Univ.
Member C.P. of Japan 31-, mem. Cen. Cttee. 33-, Gen. Sec. of Cen. Cttee. 58-, Chair. Presidium Cen. Cttee. 70-; imprisoned 33-45.
Publs. *Problems of Democratic Revolution* 47, *Advance Towards Freedom and Independence* 49, *Twelve Years' Letters* 52, *World of Yuriko Miyamoto* 54, *Prospects of Japanese Revolution* 61, *The Path of Our Party's Struggle* 61, *Actual Tasks and the Communist Party of Japan* 66, *Selections from Literary Critiques of Kenji Miyamoto* 68, *The Road towards a New Japan* 70, *Standpoint of the Communist Party of Japan* 72, *Dialogues with Kenji Miyamoto* 72, *Kenji Miyamoto with Pressmen* 73, *Abashiri Note* 75.
Central Committee of the Communist Party of Japan, Sendagaya 4-chome 26, Shibuya-ku, Tokyo, Japan.

Miyazaki, Kagayaki; Japanese chemical executive; b. 19 April 1909, Nagasaki Prefecture; *s.* of Matsunosuke and Sue Miyasaki; *m.* Sumito Miyasaki 1937; one *s.* one *d.*; ed. Tokyo Univ.
Governing Dir. Japan Fed. of Employers' Asscns. 49-; mem. Employers' Cttee. of Cen. Labour Relations Board 53-62; Asahi-Dow Ltd. 52; Pres. Asahi Chemical Industry Co. Ltd. 61-; Dir. Fed. of Econ. Org. 61-; mem. Export and Import Trading Council, Ministry of Int. Trade and Industry 69-; Vice-Pres. Japan Textile Fed. 69-; mem. Tariff Council of Ministry of Finance 70-; Counsel, Japan Chemical Fibres Asscn. 71-; mem. Japan External Trade Operational Council 71-.
Leisure interest: walking.
Asahi Chemical Industry Co. Ltd., 12, 1-chome, Yurakucho, Chiyoda-ku, Tokyo; 144 Funabashi-cho, Setagaya-ku, Tokyo, Japan.
Telephone: 429-2027.

Miyazaki, Kazuo; Japanese banker; b. 17 Feb. 1904, Tokyo; *m.* Teiko Nakano 1941; one *s.* four *d.*; ed. Tokyo Univ. of Commerce.
Managing Dir., The Long-Term Credit Bank of Japan Ltd. 52-58, Senior Man. Dir. 58-63, Deputy Pres. 63-66, Pres. 66-71, Chair. of Board 71-; Medal with Blue Ribbon.
Leisure interest: golf.
The Long-Term Credit Bank of Japan Ltd., 2-4 Otemachi 1-chome, Chiyoda-ku, Tokyo 100; Home: 10, Nakamura 1-chome, Nerima-ku, Tokyo 176, Japan.
Telephone: Tokyo 211-5111 (Office); Tokyo 990-0854 (Home).

Miyazawa, Kiichi; Japanese politician; b. 1919; ed. Tokyo Univ.
Member House of Reps. (three times) and House of Councillors (twice); fmr. Sec. to Minister of Finance; fmr. Chair. House of Councillors Steering Cttee.; Parl. Vice-Minister for Educ.; Dir.-Gen. Econ. Planning Agency; Minister for Int. Trade and Industry (in charge of *Expo 70*) 70-71; Minister of Foreign Affairs 74-.
House of Representatives, Tokyo, Japan.

Mizener, Arthur, M.A., PH.D.; American university professor; b. 3 Sept. 1907, Erie, Pa.; s. of Mason P. and Mabel (Moore) Mizener; m. Rosemary Paris 1935; one d.; ed. Princeton and Harvard Univs.
Instructor in English, Yale Univ. 34-40; Asst. Prof. Wells Coll. 40-43, Assoc. Prof. 43-45; Prof. Carleton Coll. 45-51; Prof. Cornell Univ. 51-; Fulbright Lecturer in American Studies, Univ. of London 55-56; Guggenheim Fellow 65-66; Senior Fellow, Nat. Endowment for the Humanities 68.
Publs. *The Far Side of Paradise: A Biography of F. Scott Fitzgerald* 51, *Afternoon of an Author,* 57 *The Sense of Life* 64, *Twelve Great American Novels* 67, *The Saddest Story: A Biography of Ford Madox Ford* 71, *Scott Fitzgerald and His World* 73.
105 Miller Street, Ithaca, N.Y. 14850, U.S.A.

Mizukami, Tatsuzo, M.A.; Japanese business executive; b. 15 Oct. 1903, Kitakoma-gun; s. of Kanzaburo and Chizu Mizukami; m. Tsune Inoue 1929; two d.; ed. Tokyo Commercial Coll.
Mitsui Bussan Kaisha 28-47; Exec. Man. Dir. Daiichi Bussan Kaisha Ltd. 47-57, Exec. Vice-Pres. 57-59; Exec. Vice-Pres. Mitsui and Co. 59-61, Pres. 61-69, Chair. 69-71, Senior Adviser and Dir. 71-; mem. Foreign Exchange Control Council 56-, Inquiry Comm. on Tax System 59-, Overseas Immigration Council 60-, Foreign Trade Transaction Control Council 61-; Dir. Japan Foreign Trade Council 60-68, Vice-Pres. 68-; Exec. Dir. Fed. of Econ. Orgs. 62-; Co-Chair. Japan Cttee. for Econ. Devt. 61-; Chair. Foreign Trade Div., Superior Export Council 62-, Exec. Dir. Fed. of Econ. Orgs. 64; Chair. of Overseas Immigration Council 68-; Medal of Honour with Blue Ribbon and various awards.
Leisure interests: golf, "bonsai".
Office: 2-9 Nishi Shimbashi Itchome, Minato-ku, Tokyo; Home: 2-30-2 Chome, Kakinokizaka, Meguro-ku, Tokyo, Japan.

Mizuno, Seiichi, B.LITT., D.LITT.; Japanese university professor; b. 24 March 1905, Kobe, Japan; s. of Torata and Fuji Mizuno; m. Takayo Mizuno 1931; one s.; ed. Kyoto Univ.
Studied Chinese archaeology in Peking 29-31; Research mem. of Research Inst. of Oriental Culture 31-48; Prof. of Research Inst. for Humanities, Kyoto Univ. 48-68, Prof. Emer. 68-; mem. Specialist Cttee. of Protection for Nat. Properties 59-; awards include Asahi-Sho and Onshi-Sho.
Publs. *Inner Mongolia and the Region of the Great Wall* (with N. Egami) 35, *Study of Cave-Temples at Lung-men, Honan* (with T. Nagahiro) 41, *Tsushima* (with others) 52, *Yun-kang* (with T. Nagahiro) (16 vols.) 50-55, *Bronze and Jades of Ancient China* 59, *Bronze and Stone Sculpture of China* 60, *Horyuji Monastery* 65.
91 Jodoji-Kamibambacho, Sakyo-ku, Kyoto 606, Japan.
Telephone: 771-6564.

Mizushima, Sanichiro, D.SC.; Japanese physical chemist; b. 21 March 1899, Tokyo; s. of Sanemon Mizushima and Kiku Yamamoto; m. Tokiko Shoda 1927; three s. three d.; ed. Univ. of Tokyo.
Professor of Physical Chem., Univ. of Tokyo 38-59, Prof. Emer. 59-; mem. Japan Science Council 50-62; Dir. Tokyo Research Inst. of Yawata 59-69, Hon. Dir. 69-73; mem. Japan Acad.; Bureau mem. Int. Union of Pure and Applied Chem. 55-67; Hon. mem. Chemical Soc. of Japan (Pres. 61-62), Royal Spanish Soc. of Physics and Chem., Higher Science Council of Spain, Indian Acad. of Science, American Acad. of Arts and Sciences; mem. Pontifical Acad. of Sciences, Nat. Acad. of Sciences, U.S.A.; Chemical Soc. Prize 29, Imperial Acad. Prize 38; Decoration of Emperor for Cultural Merits 61, First Class 70.
Leisure interest: writing essays.
Publs. *Quantum Chemistry* 40, *Electric Waves and Matter* 46, *Structure of Molecules and Internal Rotation*

54, *Raman Effect* 58, *Collection of Scientific Papers* 59, *A History of Physical Chemistry in Japan* 72, *Ancient Tokaido Roads* 73.
2-10-6, Tamagawa-Denenchofu, Setagayaku, Tokyo 158, Japan.
Telephone: Tokyo 721-4045.

Mizuta, Mikio; Japanese politician; b. 1905; ed. Kyoto Univ.
Elected eight times as member of House of Reps. 46-; Parliamentary Vice-Minister of Finance 49-50; Dir. Economic Deliberation Board 53; Minister of International Trade and Industry 56-57; Minister of Finance 60-62, 66-68, 71-72; fmr. teacher, Senshu Univ.; fmr. Dir. Tokyo Kohan Kogyo Co.; Liberal-Democratic Party.
2027, Hojo, Tateyama City, Chiba Prefecture, Japan.

Mjartan, Jozef; Czechoslovak politician; b. 22 Feb. 1900, Cigel, Prievidza; m. Anna Snircova 1927; two s. one d.
Farmer 25-52; mem. Unified Agricultural Co-operative 52-; Deputy to Nat. Assembly 45-54, 60-69 (retd.); Dep. Chair., Board Commrs. 48-53; Deputy and Deputy Chair. Slovak Nat. Council 53-60; mem. Presidium Cen. Cttee. Nat. Front, Č.S.S.R. 66-, mem. Presidium Slovak Cen. Cttee. Nat. Front 66-; mem. Presidium Slovak Reconstruction Party 48-, Deputy Chair. 50-66, Chair. 66-; Deputy to House of the People, Fed. Assembly 69-71; mem. Presidium of Fed. Assembly 69-71; Deputy to Slovak Nat. Council 71-; Order of Slovak Nat. Rising First Class 46; Order of 25th February 1948 First Class 48; Order of Labour 60; Order of the Red Star 69; Order of the Republic 70.
Leisure interest: hunting.
Slovak Reconstruction Party, Sedlárska 7, Bratislava, Czechoslovakia.
Telephone: 305-65.

Mládek, Jan Victor, D.IUR. ET RER.POL.; American (b. Czech) economist; b. 7 Dec. 1911; ed. Charles Univ., Prague, Paris Univ., Masaryk Univ., Brno.
Worked in Central Office, Brno 38-39; served with Czechoslovak Army in Exile, France, U.K. 39-42; Head of Monetary Dept., Ministry of Finance, Czechoslovak Govt. in Exile, London 42-45; Head of Currency and Banking Dept., Prague 45-46; Dir. Nat. Bank of Czechoslovakia 45-47; Gov. and Exec. Dir. Int. Monetary Fund (IMF) 46-48, Dep. Dir. of Operations 48-50, Dep. and Acting Dir. European and N. American Dept. 50-53, Dir. European Office (Paris) 53-61, work in underdeveloped countries 55-61, Dir. in charge of org. of African Dept. 61-64, now Dir. Central Banking Service.
Publ. *International Economic Institutions* 46.
International Monetary Fund, 19th and H Streets, N.W., Washington, D.C. 20431, U.S.A.

Mladenov, Peter Toshev; Bulgarian politician; b. 22 Aug. 1936, Toshevtsi, Vidin; ed. Moscow State Inst. of Int. Relations.
Secretary, subsequently First Sec., Vidin District Cttee., League of Young Communists 63-66; Sec. Cen. Cttee. League of Young Communists Oct. 66-69; First Sec. Vidin District Cttee., Bulgarian C.P. March 69-Dec. 71; mem. Cen. Cttee. Bulgarian C.P. April 71-; Deputy to Nat. Assembly; Minister of Foreign Affairs Dec. 71-.
Ministry of Foreign Affairs, Sofia, Bulgaria.

Moalla, Mansour, L. EN D., L. ÈS L., LL.D.; Tunisian economist; b. 1 May 1930, Sfax; ed. Inst. des Etudes Politiques, Ecole Nat. d'Administration, Paris.
Inspecteur des Finances 56; Technical Adviser, Ministry of Finance 57-58; Dir.-Gen. Banque Centrale de Tunisie 58-61; Dir. of Admin., Office of the Pres. 61-63, 68-69; Dir. Ecole Nat. d'Administration (ENA) 63-67; Under-Sec. of State, Ministry of Commerce and Industry 67-68; Sec. of State (then Minister) for Posts,

Telegraphs and Telecommunications (PTT) 69-70; Deputy Minister in charge of the Nat. Plan 70-71, Minister 71-74; mem. Cen. Cttee., Political Bureau, Destour Socialist Party 71-; Grand Cordon, Order of the Repub.; Grand Cordon Order of Independence.
32 avenue de la République, Carthage, Tunisia.

Moberg, Sven Torsten, PH.D.; Swedish civil servant and politician; b. 19 Nov. 1919, Gothenburg; s. of Simon Moberg and Olivia Nylander; m. Cecilia Brilioth 1946; two s. two d.
Assistant Prof. in Statistics Univ. of Lund 52-53; Head of Div., Nat. Social Welfare Board, Stockholm 53-55; Chief Sec. of Govt. Comm. on Planning of Univ. Educ. 55-60; Head of Dept., Ministry of Educ. 60-63, Under-Sec. of State, Ministry of Educ. 63-67, Minister without Portfolio in Charge of Educational and Cultural Affairs 67-73; Gen. Dir. Ministry of Finance 73-.
Publ. *Vem blev student och vad blev studenten?* (Sociological studies of five-year group Swedish students 1910-1943).
Burträskgatan 10, S-162 21 Vällingby, Sweden.
Telephone: 08/874770.

Moberly, John Campbell, C.M.G.; British diplomatist; b. 27 May 1925, Exmouth, Devon; s. of the late Sir Walter Moberly and Lady Moberly (née Gwendolen Gardner); m. Patience Proby 1959; two s. one d.; ed. Winchester Coll. and Magdalen Coll., Oxford.
War service in Royal Navy 43-47; entered Foreign (later Diplomatic) Service 50; service at Foreign Office and in Bahrain and Kuwait 50-59; British Political Agent in Doha, Qatar 59-62; First Sec., Athens 62-66; with FCO 66-68; Canadian Nat. Defence Coll., Kingston, Ont. 68-69; Counsellor, Washington, D.C. 69-73; Dir. Middle East Centre for Arab Studies, Shemlan, Lebanon 73-75; Amb. to Jordan Oct. 75-.
Leisure interests: skiing, mountains, swimming.
British Embassy, Jebel Amman, 3rd Circle, Amman, Jordan; Home: The Cedars, Temple Sowerby, Penrith, Cumbria, England.
Telephone: 41261-7 (Amman); Kirkby Thore 437 (Home).

Mobutu Sese Seko, Lieut.-Gen. (Joseph-Désiré Mobutu); Zairian politician; b. 14 Oct. 1930; ed. Léopoldville (now Kinshasa) and Coquilhatville (now Mbandaka).
Sergeant-Major, Accountancy Dept., Force Publique, Belgian Congo 49-56; course at Institute of Social Studies, Brussels; journalist, Léopoldville; mem. Mouvement National Congolaise; del. Brussels Round Table Conf. on Congo independence 59-60; Sec. of State for Nat. Defence, Lumumba cabinet, June 60; Chief of Staff, Congo Army, July 60; took over supreme power in name of army and suspended all political activity for three months Sept. 60; appointed a College of High Commrs. to take over govt.; Maj.-Gen. and C.-in-C. of Congolese Forces Jan. 61-65, Lt.-Gen. and Pres. of Congo (now Zaire) Nov. 65-, also Pres. of Cabinet Oct. 66-, concurrently Minister of Foreign Affairs 66-72, also Minister of Nat. Defence. Ex-Servicemen and Planning; adopted present name Jan. 72; Hon. LL.D. (Duquesne Univ., U.S.A.) 70, Order of the Source of the Nile (Uganda) 72.
Office of the President, Kinshasa, Zaire.

Moc, Miroslav; Czechoslovak journalist; b. 12 Feb. 1928, Předlice; ed. School of Political Studies of Central Cttee. of C.P. of Czechoslovakia.
Member of editorial staff of N. Bohemian regional weekly of C.P. of Czechoslovakia, Ústí nad Labem 46-47; mem. editorial staff *Mladá fronta*, Prague 47-63; mem. editorial staff, later Deputy Chief Editor *Rudé právo* 63-69, Chief Editor April 69-75; mem. Cen. Cttee. C.P. of Czechoslovakia Sept. 69-, mem. Secr. Jan. 70-75; Deputy to House of the People, Fed. Assembly 71-;

Amb. to Switzerland 75-; Order of Labour 70, Order of Victorious February 73.
Embassy of the Czechoslovak Socialist Republic, Muristrasse 53, Berne, Switzerland.

Moch, Jules; French politician; b. 15 March 1893, Paris; s. of Gaston Moch and Alice Pontremoli; m. 1st Germaine Picard 1917, two s. (one deceased); m. 2nd Eliane Bickert 1963; ed. Ecole Polytechnique.
Served Army 14-18 War; Dir. of Services for industries and agric. restitution in Germany and ex-enemy countries 18-20; engineer 20-27; Deputy for Hérault 28-40; Sec.-Gen. in Prime Min. Blum's Office 36; Under-Sec. of State 37; Min. of Public Works 38; served in French Navy 39-40; imprisoned for anti-Pétain vote 40-41; active in resistance movement; later joined Gen. de Gaulle in London, rejoined Free French Naval Forces and Gen. Staff of Free French Armed Forces 43; sat in Consultative Assembly, Algiers; took part in Mediterranean operations; Deputy to Nat. Constituent Assembly, Algiers; took part in Mediterranean operations; Deputy to Nat. Constituent Assembly, Nat. Ass. 46-58, 62-67; Minister of Public Works and Transport in four cabinets; Minister of Nat. Economy and Reconstruction Oct.-Nov. 47; Minister of the Interior and Vice Prime Minister 47-50, of Defence 50-51; Ministry of Interior 58; Perm. Del. to UN Disarmament Comm. 53-60; mem. Dir. Cttee., Socialist Party (S.F.I.O.); Croix de Guerre for both World Wars, Commdr. Légion d'Honneur, Médaille de la Résistance.
Leisure interests: painting, piloting a 'plane.
Publs. *Restitutions et Réparations* 21, *La Russie des Soviets* 25, *Socialisme et rationalisation* 27, *Jean Jaurès et les problèmes du temps présent* 27, *Le Parti Socialiste et la politique financière* 28, *Le rail et la Nation* 31, *Capitalisme et transports* 32, *Socialisme, crises, nationalisations* 32, *L'Espagne républicaine* (co-author) 33, *Pour marcher au pouvoir* 35, *Arguments et documents* 36, *Guerre aux trusts* 45, *Arguments socialistes* 45, *Confrontations* 52, *Yougoslavie, terre d'expériences* 53, *Alerte* 54, *La Folie des hommes* 54, *U.S.S.R., les yeux ouverts* 56, *Washington D. Smith, banquier de Wall Street* 57, *En retard d'une paix* 58, *Socialisme Vivant* 60, *Paix en Algérie* 61, *Le Pont sur la Manche* 62, *Non à la Force de Frappe* 64, *Histoire du réarmement allemand depuis 1950* 65, *Rencontres avec Darlin et Eisenhower* 68, *Destin de la Paix* 69, *Rencontres avec Léon Blum* 70, *Le Front Populaire, Grande Espérance* 71, *Rencontres avec de Gaulle* 71, *Socialisme de l'Ere Atomique* 73.
97 boulevard Murat, Paris 16e, France.

Moch, Paul Albert; French mining executive; b. 8 Feb. 1908, Neuilly-sur-Seine; s. of Samuel and Alice (née Bernard) Moch; ed. Collège Chaptal and Ecole nationale supérieure des mines de Paris, Grad. Ecole Polytechnique.
Pres. Elf Union, Socantar, Elf Mineraloel; Vice-Pres. Enterprise de Recherches et d'Activités Pétrolières (ERAP); Admin., Soc. nationale des pétroles d'Aquitaine (SNPA), Soc. Elf pour la recherche et l'Exploitation des Hydrocarbures (ELF R.E.), ELF France, ELF Gabon, Institut Français des Combustibles et de l'Energie (IFCE), AMREP; mem. Econ. and Soc. Council 59-; Commdr. Légion d'Honneur, Officier du Mérite S aharien; Commdr. Mérite Industriel et Commercial.
Office: 12 rue Jean Nicot, 75007 Paris; Home: 2 avenue Emile-Bergerat, 75016 Paris, France.

Moczar, Gen. Mieczysław; Polish politician; b. 25 Dec. 1913, Łódź.
Polish communist guerilla activities, East and South-East Poland, Second World War; Head of Public Security Office, Łódź 45-48; Voivodship Gov., then Chair. Voivodship People's Council, Olsztyn 48-52, Białystok 52-54, Warsaw 54-56; Minister of State Farms 56; Deputy Minister of Home Affairs 56-64,

Minister 64-68; Chair. of Presidium, Union of Fighters for Freedom and Democracy 64-72, Vice-Chair. Chief Council 72-; Deputy to Seym 57-; mem. State Council 69-; Chair. Supreme Board of Control 71-; mem. Polish Workers' Party 42-48, Polish United Workers' Party 48-, Cen. Cttee. 56-, Sec. of Cen. Cttee. 68-71, mem. Politburo 70-71; Grunwald Cross 3rd Class, Order of Banner of Labour 1st Class 59, Order of the Builder of the Polish People's Repub. 64, and other decorations.
Publ. *Barwy walki* (novel).
Najwyższa Izba Kontroli, ul. Marszałkowska 82, 00-517 Warsaw, Poland.

Mod, Péter; Hungarian politician and diplomatist; b. 21 May 1911; *m.*; three *c.*; ed. Univ. of Budapest, Univ. of Paris.
Volunteer, French Army 39-40; French Resistance 40-45; entered Hungarian diplomatic service 47; Counsellor, Paris 49; Dir. Municipal Library "Ervin Szabó", Budapest; Head, Near and Middle East Dept., Ministry of Foreign Affairs 56; Head, Perm. Mission to the UN 56-62; First Deputy Foreign Minister 61-68; Amb. to France 68-74; Chair. Hungarian UN Soc. 75-; Red Banner Order of Labour 74 and many other Hungarian and foreign decorations.
Zichy Géza-u. 5, 1146 Budapest XIV, Hungary.
Telephone: 428-391.

Modiano, Patrick Jean; French novelist; b. 30 July 1945, Boulogne-Billancourt; *s.* of Albert Modiano and Luisa Colpyn; *m.* Dominique Zehrfuss 1970; one *d.*; ed. schools in Biarritz, Chamonix, Deauville, Thône, Barbizon; Coll. in Paris.
Prix Roger Nimier 68, Prix Felix Fénéon 69, Grand Prix de l'Académie Française 72.
Publs. *La Place de l'Etoile* 68, *La Ronde de Nuit* 69, *Les Boulevards de Ceinture* 72, *Lacombe Lucien* (screenplay) 73, *Villa Triste* (novel) 75.
29 rue Daubigny, Paris XVIIe, France.

Mödl, Martha; German singer; ed. Munich and Nuremberg Conservatoires.
Numerous appearances at German and foreign opera houses, and at Bayreuth Festivals 51-; mem. Staatsoper Stuttgart 53-.
Steindorfstrasse 6, Munich 22, Fed. Rep. of Germany.

Moe, George Cecil Rawle, Q.C., M.A., LL.M.; Barbadian barrister-at-law and politician; b. 12 March 1932, Barbados; *s.* of Cecil S. and Odessa M. (née Marshall) Moe; *m.* Olga Louise Atkinson 1957; two *s.* one *d.*; ed. Harrison Coll., Oxford Univ. and Columbia Univ., New York.
Called to the Bar, Middle Temple, London; Magistrate 60-62; Acting Asst. Legal Draftsman 62-63; Acting Crown Counsel 63-66; Senior Crown Counsel 67-71; Acting Perm. Rep. to UN 70-71; Attorney-Gen. and Minister of Legal Affairs 71-, also Minister of External Affairs 72-; Leader of Senate 72-.
Leisure interests: music, cricket, gardening, swimming.
The Attorney-General's Chambers, Government Headquarters, St. Michael; Home: Torwood, Erdiston Hill, St. Michael, Barbados.
Telephone: 62436 (Office); 93341 (Home).

Moell Hans, DR. RER. NAT.; German business executive; b. 1920, Freiburg/Br.; ed. Humanistisches Gymnasium, Freiburg and Univs. of Freiburg and Erlangen.
Joined BASF 53, Dir. 65, Deputy mem. Man. Board 66 mem. Man. Board 68-74, Deputy Chair. Man. Board 74-, Deputy Chair. Supervisory Board 76-; mem. Exec. Cttee. and Board of Organic Chem. Section of Union of Chem. Industry, Frankfurt, Cttee. for Agrarian Science, Bundesverband der Deutschen Ind., Cologne, Presidency and Board of Union of Nitrogen

Ind., Düsseldorf, Max-Planck-Gesellschaft for the Advancement of Science, Munich.
BASF Aktiengesellschaft, 6700 Ludwigshafen/Rhein, Federal Republic of Germany.

Moeneclaey, Etienne, B.LITT., B.SC.; French civil servant; b. 14 Feb. 1897, Paris; *s.* of Frédéric Moeneclaey and Marie-Paule Deledicque; *m.* 1st Denise Masson 1925 (died 1961), 2nd Jacqueline Vignal 1962; one *s.* one *d.*
Served in Army in First World War; Asst. to Insp. of Finances 20; Insp. of Finances 23; Asst. Sec. in Office of M. Tardieu, Min. of Public Works 26-28, Min. of the Interior 28-29, and Prime Min. 29-30; various other secretarial and financial posts 30-36; Directeur des Monnaies 34-46; Insp.-Gen. of Finances 46-67, Hon. Insp.-Gen. 67-; Commissaire de Gouvernement à l'Immobilière-construction de Paris 47 and of C.O.F.I.M.E.G. 66-; served in French Army 39-40; Commdr. de la Légion d'Honneur; Croix de Guerre 14-18 and 39-45.
50 avenue Duquesne, Paris 7e, France.
Telephone: Segur 51-50.

Moens de Fernig, Count George; Belgian businessman; b. 1899.
Chairman of Industrial Cos.; President Chamber of Commerce, Brussels 46-47; Minister of Food and Imports 47-48; Minister of Foreign Trade 49; Gen. Commr. for Int. Exhibition in Brussels 58; Grand Cross Orange Nassau (Neths.); Grand Cross, Crown of Luxembourg; Grand Cross, Légion d'Honneur (France); Commdr. of the Order of Léopold; Grand Cross of the Belgian Crown; Grand Cross, Order of Merit (Italy), etc.
66 rue Veydt, Brussels 5, and "Bleuterveld", Zelem (Limbourg), Belgium.

Moffatt, Sir John; Zambian farmer and politician; b. April 1905; ed. Grey High School, Port Elizabeth, South Africa and Glasgow Univ.
Cadet, Colonial Service, Northern Rhodesia 27, District Officer 29; Commissioner for Nat. Development 45; retired from civil service 51; mem. Legislative Council N. Rhodesia 51-64; mem. Fed. Parl., Salisbury 54-62; Chair. Fed. African Affairs Board; leader Liberal Party, N. Rhodesia (disbanded Nov. 62).
Mkushi, Zambia.

Moffo, Anna; Italian soprano; b. 27 July, Wayne, Pa.; *m.* Robert Sarnoff (*q.v.*) 1974.
Debut on Italian TV in *Madame Butterfly* 57; sang at opera houses in Paris, London, Salzburg and in Italy; debut in U.S.A. with Chicago Lyric Opera Co. 57, debut at Metropolitan Opera 59; major roles include *La Bohème, Mignon, Rigoletto, Falstaff, Madame Butterfly, Barber of Seville, Marriage of Figaro, La Traviata, La Juive, Turandot*; Fulbright Scholarship 56; Philadelphia Orchestra Young Artists Award 55; Verdi Medal, Parma 63; First Prize for *La Sonnambula*, Int. TV Festival, Cannes 58; Golden Rose, Int. TV Festival, Montreux 64; Commdr. Order of Merit (Italy); Dr. h.c. 65.
Leisure interests: hockey, cooking, silver collection.
c/o Edgar Vincent Associates, 156 East 52nd Street, New York, N.Y. 10022, U.S.A.
Telephone: (212) 752-3020.

Mogami, Thebe David; Botswana diplomatist; b. 16 June 1942, Lerala; *s.* of Tsimane Rodgers Mogami and Tetang Mogami; *m.* Hermetina Thebe 1969; one *s.* one *d.*; ed. Univ. of Botswana, Lesotho and Swaziland, and Columbia Univ., New York.
Assistant Sec., Office of the Pres. 68-71, Under-Sec. for External Affairs 71-72; Perm. Rep. to UN July 72-; del. to several OAU and non-aligned Summit confs.
Permanent Mission of Botswana to United Nations, 2 Dag Hammarskjöld Plaza, 866 Second Avenue, 15th Floor, New York, N.Y. 10017, U.S.A.

Mohale, Albert Steerforth, M.A.; Lesotho diplomatist; b. 26 April 1928, Mohale's Hoek; s. of Solomon and Alice Mohale; three d.; ed. Pius XII Univ. Coll., South Africa, and Univ. of St. Francis Xavier, Canada.
Former teacher, Basutoland and South Africa; Lecturer and Deputy Dir. Extension Dept., Pius XII Univ. Coll. 60-61; Co-operative Training Officer, Basutoland 61, later Asst. Registrar of Co-operative Socs.; Supernumerary Head of Govt. Training Section 65; Amb. to U.S.A., High Commr. to Canada and Perm. Rep. to UN 66-69; High Commr. to Kenya 69; Perm. Sec. Public Service Dept. 69-70, Ministry of Agriculture 70-71, Ministry of Interior 71; Minister of Transport and Communications 75-; Gen. Man. Lesotho Nat. Devt. Corpn., Special Adviser 75-; Man. Dir. Lesotho Nat. Bus Service 75-.
Lesotho National Development Corporation, P.O. Box 666, Maseru, Lesotho.
Telephone: 2901 (Office); 3040 (Home).

Mohammed, Kamaluddin, M.P.; Trinidadian politician; b. 1927; ed. San Juan Church Missionary School and privately.
Member Legislative Council 56; Minister of Agriculture, Lands and Fisheries 56-61, of Public Utilities 61-67, of West Indian Affairs 67-73, of External Affairs 70-73, of Health and Local Govt. Feb. 73-; founder mem. People's Nat. Movt., Deputy Political Leader 71-; Leader, House of Reps.; Gen. Sec. Trinidad Islamic Asscn.
Ministry of Health and Local Government, Port of Spain, Trinidad.

Mohammed Zahir Shah; fmr. King of Afghanistan; b. 15 Oct. 1914; ed. Habibia High School, Istiqlal Coll. (both in Kabul), Lycée Janson-de-Sailly and Lycée of Montpellier, France.
Graduated with highest honours; attended Infantry Officers' School, Kabul 32; married Lady Homira, 4 November 1931; children, Princess Bilqis, Prince Ahmad Shah, Princess Maryam, Prince Mohammed Nadir, Prince Shah Mahmoud, Prince Mohammed Daoud, Prince Mirvis; Asst. Minister in Ministry of National Defence 32-33; acting Minister of Education 33; crowned King 8 Nov. 33; deposed July 73, abdicated Aug. 73.

Mohn, Reinhard; German publisher; b. 29 June 1921; ed. high school.
Army Service 39-43; Prisoner of War in N. Africa and U.S.A. 43-46; Chair. of Board, Bertelsmann A.G. 47-.
Bertelsmann A.G., 4830 Gütersloh 1, Eickhoffstrasse 14/16, Federal Republic of Germany.
Telephone: (05241) 1811.

Mohrt, Michel, L. en D.; French editor and writer; b. 28 April 1914; ed. Law School, Rennes.
Lawyer, Marseilles Bar until 52; Editor at Les Editions Gallimard 52-; Croix de Guerre; Grand Prix du roman de l'Académie française for La Prison Maritime 62; Grand Prix de la Critique Littéraire 70.
Publs. Novels: Mon Royaume pour un Cheval 49, La Prison Maritime 61, La Campagne d'Italie 67, L'Ours des Adirondacks 69, Deux Indiennes à Paris 74; essays: Le nouveau roman Américain 56, L'air du large 69; play: Un jeu d'enfer 70.
4 bis rue du Cherche-Midi, Paris 6e, France.
Telephone: 222-42-12 (Paris).

Moi, Daniel Arap; Kenyan politician; b. 1924, Sacho, Baringo district; ed. African Mission School, Kabartonjo, A.I.M. School and Govt. African School, Kapsabet.
Teacher 45-57; Head. Teacher, Govt. African School, Kabarnet 46-48, 55-57, Teacher Tambach Teacher Training School, Kabarnet 48-54; African Rep. mem., Legislative Council 57-63; Chair. Kenya African Democratic Union (KADU) 60-61; mem. House of Reps. 61-; Parl. Sec., Ministry of Educ. April-Dec. 61;

Minister of Educ. Dec. 61-62, Local Govt. 62-64, Home Affairs 64-67; Pres. Kenya African Nat. Union (KANU) for Rift Valley Province 66-67; Vice-Pres. of Kenya Jan. 67-, concurrently Minister of Home Affairs; mem. Rift Valley Educ. Board, Kalenjin Language Cttee.; Chair. Rift Valley Provincial Court.
Ministry of Home Affairs, P.O. Box 30520, Nairobi, Kenya.

Moini, Amir-Ghassem; Iranian mechanical engineer and politician; b. June 1925, Teheran; s. of Mahmoud and Fatemeh Moini; m. Fakhereh Sadigh 1949; three s.; ed. Teheran Univ.
Ministry of Labour and Social Affairs 47-; Teheran Labour Dept.; Deputy Head Inspection Office; Acting Head of Fars Prov. Labour Dept., later Head; Deputy Head Teheran Branch of Workers' Social Insurance Org.; Deputy Dir.-Gen.; Sec.-Gen. Graduate Guidance Org.; Technical Under-Sec. Ministry of Labour and Social Affairs; mem. Parl.; Acting Sec.-Gen. Iran Novin Party 71; Minister of Labour and Social Affairs 73-; Homayoun Orders of Third and First Grade.
Leisure interests: sports, reading.
Ministry of Labour and Social Affairs, 457 Avenue Eisenhower, Teheran, Iran.
Telephone: 931050.

Moinot, Pierre, L. ès L.; French civil servant; b. 29 March 1920, Deux-Sèvres; m. Madeleine Sarrailh 1947; one s. four d.; ed. Univs. de Paris, Caen and Grenoble.
Senior Civil Servant 46-; Technical Adviser, Private Office of André Malraux 59; Dir. Theatres and Cultural Action 60-62; French Del. to UNESCO 66; Dir.-Gen. of Arts and Letters 66-; Chief Adviser, Audit Office 67-; Prix du Roman de l'Académie Française, Prix Sainte-Beuve, Prix des libraires de France.
Leisure interests: hunting, carpentry.
Publs. Armes et Bagages 51, La Chasse Royale 54, La Blessure 56, Le Sable Vif 63, Héliogable 71.
44 Rue du Cherche-Midi, Paris 6e, France.
Telephone: 260-3739.

Moir, John Chassar, C.B.E., M.A., M.D., F.R.C.S.(E.), F.R.C.O.G.; British gynaecologist; b. 21 March 1900, Montrose, Scotland; s. of John Moir and Isobella Pirie Moir; m. Grace Hilda Bailey 1933; two s. two d.; ed. Montrose Acad. and Edinburgh Univ.
Assistant, Univ. Coll. Hosp., London 30-35; Reader in Obstetrics, British (later Royal) Postgraduate Medical School 35-37, Visiting Prof. 68-; Nuffield Prof. of Obstetrics and Gynaecology and Fellow, Oriel Coll., Univ. of Oxford 37-67; Gold Medal Thesis (Edinburgh Univ.) 30; Hon. LL.D. (Queen's Univ., Ont.) 55, Hon. D.Sc. (Edinburgh Univ.) 70, (Manchester Univ.) 72; Hon. Fellow (Oriel Coll. Oxford) 74.
Leisure interest: handiwork.
Publs. Operative Obstetrics (8th edn.) 71, The Vesico-Vaginal Fistula (2nd edn.) 67.
Farnmore, Woodstock Road, Charlbury, Oxon., England.

Moiseyev, Igor Aleksandrovich; Soviet choreographer; b. 21 Jan. 1906; ed. Bolshoi Theatre School of Choreography.
Artist and ballet master at the Bolshoi Theatre 24-39; Dir. of the Choreographic Dept. of the Theatre of People's Art 36; was one of the organisers of the U.S.S.R. Festival of Folk Dancing; Art Dir. of the Folk Dance Ensemble of the U.S.S.R. 37-; People's Artist of the U.S.S.R.; State Prizewinner 42, 47, 52; Lenin Prizewinner 67; two Orders of Red Banner of Labour; Order of Lenin; Hero of Socialist Labour 76.
State Folk Dance Company of the U.S.S.R., 20 Ploshchad Mayakovskogo, Moscow, U.S.S.R.

Mojsov, Lazar, D.IUR.; Yugoslav journalist, politician and diplomatist; b. 19 Dec. 1920, Negotino, Macedonia; s. of Dono and Efka Mojsov; m. Liljana Jankov 1945; two d.; ed. Belgrade Univ.
Former mem. Anti-Fascist Assembly for the Nat. Liberation of Macedonia; fmr. Public Prosecutor, Macedonia; Dir. *New Macedonia*; fmr. Head of Press Department, Fed. Govt. of Macedonia; mem. Yugoslav Fed. Parliament and Parliament of Macedonia; mem. Exec. Board, Socialist League of Working People of Yugoslavia; mem. Exec. Cttee. of Cen. Cttee., Macedonian League of Communists; mem. Central Cttee. League of Communists of Yugoslavia; Ambassador to U.S.S.R. 58-61; Dir. Inst. for Study of Workers' Movements 61-62; Dir. and Chief Editor *Borba* 62-64; Amb. to Austria 67-69; Perm. Rep. to UN 69-74; Deputy Fed. Sec. for Foreign Affairs 74-; Order of Merit for Exceptional Achievements First Class, Order of Merit for Services to the Nation, First and Third Class, Order of Brotherhood and Unity.
Leisure interest: philately.
Publs. *The Bulgarian Working Party (Communist) and the Macedonian National Question* 48, *Vasil Glavinov: First Propagator of Socialism in Macedonia* 49, *Concerning the Question of the Macedonian National Minority in Greece* 54.
Ministry for Foreign Affairs, Kn. Miloša 24, Belgrade, 11000, Yugoslavia.

Mokaddem, Sadok; Tunisian diplomatist; b. 1914; ed. Lycée Carnot, Tunis, Faculty of Sciences, Montpellier and Faculty of Medicine, Paris.
Physician, Tunis; mem. Neo-Destour 34-, mem. Political Bureau 52-; Sec. of State for Justice 54-55, for Public Health 55; Dep. to Constituent Ass. 56-59; Amb. to Egypt 56-57; Sec. of State for Foreign Affairs 57-62; Amb. to France 62-64; Pres., Nat. Assembly 64-69, 69-; Grand Cordon of Nat. Order of Independence and of the Republic; several foreign decorations.
National Assembly, Tunis, Tunisia.

Mokrzyński, Jerzy; Polish architect; b. 22 Sept. 1909, Rzeszów; ed. Warsaw Polytechnic.
Senior Designer in Warsaw Design Office of Gen. Architecture 48-; mem. Polish Asscn. of Architects (SARP) 36-, Vice-Pres. Cen. Board 52-56, Chair. Cen. Board of Control 57, mem. Co-ordination Cttee. of Competition Judges 73, Collective Judge and mem. SARP Council for many years; mem. ZAIKS Asscn. of Authors 47-; First Prizes (with W. Kłyszewski (*q.v.*) and E. Wierzbicki (*q.v.*)) for: Bank Gospodarstwa Krajowego in Poznań, Community Centre in Krynica, Puppet Show in Białystok, Recreation Centre in Romanowo and many others; Officer's Cross, Order of Polonia Restituta 57; Gold Award for the Rebuilding of Warsaw 58; Hon. Award, ZAIKS; Order of Banner of Labour, 2nd Class 69; State Prize, 3rd Class 51, 2nd Class 55, 1st Class 74; Hon. Prize, SARP 68, of Katowice Branch of SARP 72.
Ul. Marszałkowska 140 m. 18, 00-061 Warsaw, Poland.

Molapo, Mooki Vitus; Lesotho diplomatist; b. 2 June 1937; m.; three c.; ed. Inkamana High School, Natal, Pius XII Coll., Univ. of South Africa, Univ. of Dar es Salaam, and Univ. of West Indies, Trinidad and Tobago.
Teacher, Maseru secondary school 65; Information Officer, Dept. of Information, Maseru 66; Chief announcer, Radio Lesotho 66-67; First Sec. Lesotho Embassy, Washington 67-70; Chief of Protocol, Ministry of Foreign Affairs 70-71; Perm. Rep. to UN 71-74; del. to UN Gen. Assembly 67-75, and rep. at many other int. confs.; Amb. to Iran 74-, also accred. to Romania, Yugoslavia, the Holy See, United Arab Emirates.

Embassy of the Kingdom of Lesotho, P.O. Box 12-1346, Teheran, Iran.
Telephone: 681396.

Molchanov, Kirill Vladimirovich; Soviet composer; b. 7 Sept. 1922, Moscow; ed. Moscow Conservatoire.
Director Bolshoi Ballet 73-75; Honoured Worker of the R.S.F.S.R. 63.
Principal compositions: Concerto No. 1 for Piano and Orchestra 45, Concerto No. 2 for Piano and Orchestra 47, Concerto No. 3 for Piano and Orchestra 53; Operas: *Stone Flower* 50, *Dawn* 56, *Del Carno Street* 60, *Romeo, Juliet and Gloom* 62, Incidental music for films: *It Happened in Penkovo* 50, *Vast is My Land* 58, *Stars of May* 59, *To the Seven Winds* 62, *Shore Leave* 62, Music for plays: *Griboyedov* 51, *Mary Stuart* 56, *Three Fat Men* 56, *Last Stop* 57, *Attacking the Storm* 65; music for radio and television.
Composers' Union of the R.S.F.S.R., 8-10 Ulitsa Nezhdanovoi, Moscow, U.S.S.R.

Moldovan, Roman; Romanian politician and economist; b. 14 Dec. 1911, Daia, Mures, County; s. of Elisei and Ana Moldovan; m. Elena Moldovan 1938; two d.
University Prof.; Corresp. mem. Acad. of Socialist Repub. of Romania 63-; Deputy to Grand Nat. Assembly; mem. Cen. Cttee. of Romanian Communist Party 65-; Chair. State Planning Cttee. 65; Chair. Nat. Council of Scientific Research and Deputy Chair. Council of Ministers 65-67; Chair. State Cttee. for Price Fixing 67-69; Vice-Pres. Econ. Council 69-71; Vice-Pres. Acad. of Social and Political Sciences 72-; Chair. Romanian Chamber of Commerce and Ind. 72-.
Leisure interests: mountains, tourism.
Publs. include: *Formation and Movement of Capital in Romania* 40, *Planned Management of National Economy in Romanian People's Republic* 59, *Logic, Methodology and Philosophy of Science* 73, *Les changements structuraux économiques et sociaux dans le processus d'édification du socialisme* 74; Co-author: *Romania's Economic Development 1944-1974, Romania's Industry 1944-1964.*
Romanian Chamber of Commerce and Industry, Bd. Nicolae Bălcescu 22, Bucharest, Romania.
Telephone: 15-24-29.

Moldt, Ewald; German diplomatist; b. 1927; ed. Deutsche Akademie für Staats- und Rechtswissenschaften.
Former Counsellor, Poland; Amb. of German Democratic Repub. to Romania 65-71; Vaterländischer Verdienstorden in Silber und Bronze.
Ministry of Foreign Affairs, Berlin, German Democratic Republic.

Molefhe, Topo James, B.A., U.E.D.; Botswana diplomatist; b. 1927, Mafeking, S. Africa; m.; five c.; ed. Fort Hare Univ. Coll. and Univ. of London.
Teacher, S. Africa and Botswana 50-63; taught at Teacher Training Coll., Serowe, Botswana 63; Vice-Principal Teacher Training Coll., Lobatse, Botswana 66; Asst. Sec. Dept. of External Affairs 66; Private Sec. to Pres. of Botswana 67; Perm. Rep. to UN 68-72.
Leisure interests: art, music, model railways.
c/o Ministry for Foreign Affairs, Gaborone, Botswana.

Molina Barraza, Col. Arturo Armando; Salvadorian army officer and politician; b. 6 Aug. 1927, San Salvador; s. of Mariano Molina and Matilde Barraza de Molina; m. María Elena Contreras de Molina; four s. one d.; ed. Escuela Militar, El Salvador, Escuela Superior de Guerra, Mexico, Escuela de Infantería, Spain.
Section and Co. Commdr., Escuela Militar; Artillery Garrison, Asst. Dir. Escuela de Armas, Section and Dept. Chief, Staff HQ; Del. 6th Conf. of American Armed Forces, Peru 65, 7th Conf. Buenos Aires; Gen.

Co-ordinator, 2nd and 3rd Confs. of Defence Council of Cen. American States; Dir. Exec. Comm. for Shipping; Dir. Nat. Cttee. of Caritas, El Salvador; Pres. of El Salvador July 72-.
Palacio Presidencial, San Salvador, El Salvador.

Molina Quesada, José Luis, LIC. EN DER.; Costa Rican lawyer and diplomatist; b. 23 July 1926, San José; ed. Univ. of Costa Rica.
One of the founders of Social Democratic Party; mem. Nat. Political Cttee. of Nat. Liberation Party; Legal Adviser, Ministry of Public Educ. 48-49; Deputy Legislative Assembly of Costa Rica 53-57, 66-70, Pres. 69-70; Dir. Social Security Fund of Costa Rica 57, 62; Prof. of Constitutional Law and of History of Costa Rican Public Admin., Univ. of Costa Rica 64-; Perm. Rep. to UN 70-73.
c/o Ministerio de Asuntos Exteriores, San José, Costa Rica.

Molina Silva, Sergio; Chilean economist and politician; b. Dec. 1928, Santiago; s. of Sergio Molina Borgoño and Violeta Silva de Molina; m. Paulina Barros Holman 1957; three d.
Former Dir.-Gen. of Budget and Finances, Ministry of Finance; Del. several int. confs.; Minister of Finance Nov. 64-67; Exec. Vice-Pres. Corpn. de Fomento de la Producción; Prof., Faculty of Economics, Univ. de Chile, Dean of Faculty of Economic Sciences 63-64; fmr. Pres. Banco Central de Chile; Gov. Banco Interamericano (BID) 64-68; mem. Consejo Latinoamericano de Planificación, Inter-American Cttee. on the Alliance for Progress; Ind.
Moneda 921 Of. 810, Santiago, Chile.

Molinari, Ricardo E.; Argentine writer; b. 20 March 1898; ed. secondary school.
Has received every poetry prize in Argentina.
Publs. include: *El Huésped y la Melancolía* 46, *Días donde la Tarde es un Pájaro* 54, *Unida Noche* 57, *El Cielo de las Alondras y las Gaviotas* 63, *Una sombra antigua Canta* 66, *La Hoguera Transparente* 70, *La Escudilla* 73, *Las Sombras del Pájaro Tostado* (complete works) 74.
Julián Alvarez 2092, Buenos Aires 25, Argentina.

Möller, Alex; German politician, businessman and journalist; b. 26 April 1903, Dortmund; s. of Alexander and Charlotte Möller; widower.
Member S.P.D. 22-; mem. Landesparlament, Stuttgart 46-61; mem. Bundestag 61-; Deputy Chair. Parliamentary Party, S.P.D. 64-69, 72-; Minister of Finance 69-71; mem. Admin. Board, Süddeutscher Rundfunk, Stuttgart; Chair. Advisory Board, Bavaria Atelier G.m.b.H. -69, 71-, Rundfunkwerbung G.m.b.H., Stuttgart; Prof. Dr. h.c., Dr. Ing. e.h. (Univ. Freiburg and Technische Hochschule, Karlsruhe); Grosses Bundesverdienstkreuz mit Stern und Schulterband; First Class Award, German Red Cross.
Leisure interests: sport and music.
Publs. *Unruhige Zeiten, Währung und Aussenpolitik* (in German and English), *Kommentar zum Gesetz zur Förderung der Stabilität und des Wachstums der Wirtschaft.*
75 Karlsruhe 51, Märchenring 50, Federal Republic of Germany.
Telephone: 0721/883658.

Møller, Christian, D.PHIL.; Danish physicist; b. 22 Dec. 1904, Notmark; s. of Jørgen Hansen Moller and Marie Terkelsen; m. Kirsten Pedersen 1931; one s. one d.; ed. Univs. of Copenhagen, Rome and Cambridge.
Lecturer, Copenhagen Univ. 33-40, Dozent 40-43, Prof. of Mathematical Physics 43-, Dean of Faculty 47-48; Dir. Theoretical Study Group, CERN (European Centre for Nuclear Research) 54-57, mem. Scientific Policy Cttee. 59-; Dir. Nordita (Nordic Inst. for Theoretical Atomic Physics) 57-71; mem. Royal Danish Acad. of Sciences, Royal Norwegian Acad. of Science, Kungl.

Fys. Selsk, Swedish Acad. of Science; Hon. D.Phil. (Åbo Academi) 68; awarded Ole Romer Medal 66, H. C. Ørsted Medal 70.
Leisure interest: music.
Publs. *The Theory of Relativity* 52 (new edn. 72); papers on atomic theory and relativity.
Frølichsvej 42a, Copenhagen, Denmark.
Telephone: Ordrup 4690.

Møller, Knud Ove, PH.D., M.D.; Danish pharmacologist; b. 21 June 1896; ed. Københavns Universitet.
Professor of Pharmacology 37-66; Chair. Danish Pharmacopœia Comm. 38-67; Chair. Danish Cttee. of Foreign Scientists in Danish Laboratories 46-51; mem. Nordic Pharmacopœia Council 48-67; Co-founder and Editor *Acta Pharmacologica et Toxicologica* 45-64; Co-founder and Chair. Nordic Soc. for Pharmacology; Co-founder and mem. Int. Council for Pharmacologists 53-62; mem. WHO Expert Advisory Panel of Int. Pharmacopoeia 51-71, WHO Sub-Cttee. on Int. Non-Proprietary Drug Names 59-71; Danish, Norwegian and Swedish decorations.
Publs. *Pharmakologie für Zahnärzte* 34, *Stimulants* 45, *Manual in Pharmacology* (6th Danish edn.) (5th Swiss edn.) 66.
Marienlyst Allé 30, 3000 Helsingør, Denmark.
Telephone: (03) 217605.

Møller, Maersk Mc-Kinney; Danish shipowner; b. 13 July 1913, Copenhagen; s. of Arnold Peter and Chastine Estelle Mc-Kinney Møller; m. Emma Marie Neergaard Rasmussen 1940; three d.
Partner A. P. Møller 40-; Chair. Steamship Co. of 1912 Ltd., Steamship Co. Svendborg Ltd., Steamship Co. of 1960 Ltd., Maersk Line A/S, Odense Steel Shipyard Ltd., Maersk Kemi A/S, Roulunds Fabriker Ltd., The Tanganyika Planting Co. Ltd., Dansk Borelskab A/S, Dansk Industri Syndikat A/S; mem. Int. Business Machines Corpn. Inc., Det Danske Staalvalsevaerk A/S; Chair. Danish Shipping Board.
Kongens Nytorv 8, DK-1098 Copenhagen K, Denmark.
Telephone: 01-14 15 14.

Møller, Poul; Danish barrister and politician; b. 13 Oct. 1919, Frederiksberg, Copenhagen; s. of Hugo Møller; m. Lis Møller; two s.; ed. Københavns Univ.
Civil Servant 39-52; Barrister 52-; Chief Editor *Dagens Nyheder* (Daily News) 53-58; leader writer 58-61; Auditor of Public Accounts 61-68; Minister of Finance 68-71; Chair. Nat. Youth Org. of Conservative People's Party 43-48; mem. Folketing 50-, Finance Cttee. of Folketing 57-58, Nordic Council 58-68, Foreign Affairs Cttee. of Folketing 60-68, Youth Comm. 45-50, Council of Europe 64-68, Nat. Insurance Comm. 50-55, Tariff Comm. 53-59.
Leisure interest: history.
Publs. *Our Idea* 42, *Denmark—Socially* 46, *Parliamentary Government in Danish Humour* 49, *Political Reference Book* 50, *The Icelandic Manuscripts* 65, *Men and Opinion* 70, numerous articles.
Grønningen 23, 1270 Copenhagen K, Denmark.

Møller-Christenson, Peter Vilhelm, M.D.; Danish professor of medical history, osteo-archaeologist and writer; b. 28 June 1903, Haslev, Sealand; s. of N. Chr. Christensen and Marie Møller; m. 1st Emmy Stamer 1930, 2nd Martha Nielsen 1966; one s. two d.; ed. Haslev Gymnasium and Københavns Universitet.
Medical practice 32-56; School Medical Officer 56-64; Fellow of Univ. of Copenhagen 63-, Prof. of Medical History and Dir. of Medical-Historical Museum 64-73; mem. Royal Nord. Oldskriftass. 36-, Int. Asscn. of Leprology 53-, Danish Odontological Soc. 54-, Danish Medical History Soc. 35-, Pres. 65-; editor of Centaurus 64; Berliner Gesellschaft f. Geschichte der Medizin E.V. 65; Corr. mem. Int. Acad. History of Medicine 70, Danish Otolaryngological Soc. 71, Aachener Geschichtsverein 72; M.D. h.c. (Univ. of Bergen) 70; Münchener

Vereinigung für Geschichte der Medizin 73; numerous decorations.

Leisure interests: archaeology, travelling.

Publs. *The History of the Forceps* (thesis) 38, *Ten Lepers from Naevsted in Denmark* 53, *Bone Changes in Leprosy* 61, *Encyclopedia of Bible Creatures* 65, *Osteo-archaeological Excavations in Medieval Danish Abbeys and Leprosy Hospital Cemeteries* 35-75.

Office: 42 Østervang, 4000 Roskilde, Denmark.

Telephone: (03)-35-57-22 (Home).

Molnár, Antal; Hungarian musician; b. 7 Jan. 1890, Budapest; s. of Dr. Moritz (Maurice) Molnár and Malvina Frankel; m. Marguerite Zechmeister 1927; ed. Budapest High School of Music.

Mem. Waldbauer-Kerpely String Quartet 10-13; Teacher in Budapest 13-19; winner Francis Joseph Prize for composition 14; mem. Dohnányi-Hubay-Kerpely-Molnár Piano Quartet 16-18; Sec. Music Section of Art and Science Fed. 18; Prof. High School of Music Budapest 19-59; Dir. Pedagogic Society of Music 31-34; Leader-Dir. Syndicate of Musicians 46; Kossuth Prize 57; composer and critic; Labour Order of Merit 70; "Eminent Artist" 71.

Leisure interests: concerts, books, theatre, travel.

Publs. *A zeneművészet könyve* 22, *Az új zene* 25, *A zenetörténet szociológiája* 23, *Bevezetés a zenekultúrába*, *Jazzband* 28, *Fizika és muzsika* 30, *Liszt esztétikája* 36, *A Ma zenéje* 37, *Zeneesztétika* 38, *Azene és az élet* 46, *Az új muzsika szelleme* 48, *Examples for Romantic Harmony* 53, *Schubert Emlékezete* 54, essays on Hungarian music 55-57, *Repertory of Baroque music* 58, *Brahms* 59, *Collection of Essays* 61, 63, *The World of the Composer* 69, *Practical Aesthetics of Music* 71, *Memoirs* 74.

Karinthy-ut 14, Budapest XI, Hungary.

Telephone: 260-665.

Molnar-C. Pál; Hungarian painter and engraver; b. 28 April 1894, Battonya; s. of József Molnár and Jeanne Contat; m. Alice Gstettner 1931; two d.; ed. Ecole des Beaux Arts, Budapest.

Exhibited Lausanne 19, Budapest 27, Venice Biennale 30, 32, 34, etc.; awarded Prix de Rome 28, Gold Medal, Milan 32 and 35, Grand Prix and Gold Medal, Paris Int. Exhbn. 37, and many other prizes; represented in Nuremberg Municipal Museum, Rome, Venice, Chicago, New York, Edinburgh, Laing Art Gallery, Newcastle, Budapest, etc.; has illustrated many books, including *Angyali Udvözlet*, *The Little Flowers of St. Francis*, *Corialanus*, *Cyrano de Bergerac*, *Coriolan*, *Autobiography of Benvenuto Cellini* 57; executed decorative panels for Paris Universal Exposition, and monumental frescoes in various churches and buildings; hon. mem. Accademia Adriatica d'Italia, Österreichischer Künstler Bund; Labour Order of Merit, Golden Degree 74.

Leisure interests: reading, handiwork, inventing.

Ménesi ut. 63, 1118 Budapest XI, Hungary.

Telephone: 657-983.

Molotov, Vyacheslav Mikhailovich (*pseudonym* of V. M. Skryabin); retd. Soviet politician and diplomatist; b. 9 March 1890; ed. St. Petersburg (now Leningrad) Polytechnic.

Organized Bolshevik student groups and worked on *Zvezda* and *Pravda*; mem. Petrograd Soviet Exec. Cttee. Feb. 17; mem. Petrograd Military-Revolutionary Cttee. Oct. 17; held Party posts in Petrograd, Nijni Novgorod, Donbass 18-20; Sec. Central Cttee. of Communist Party of the Ukraine 20; mem. Political Bureau of Party 21-53; mem. Presidium of Exec. Cttee. of the Communist Int. 28-34; Chair. Council of People's Commissars 30-41, Deputy Chair. Council of Ministers of U.S.S.R. 41-57; mem. Cttee. for drafting reforms to Constitution 35; Commissar, later Minister, for Foreign Affairs 39-49; mem. State Cttee. of Defence

41; Pres. Moscow Del. Anglo-Soviet Talks Sept. 41; First Vice-Chair. Council of Ministers and Minister for Foreign Affairs 49-56; Minister of State Control 56-57; mem. Presidium of Central Cttee. of Communist Party until 57; Ambassador to Mongolian People's Republic 57-60; Perm. Rep. U.S.S.R. Int. Atomic Energy Agency, Vienna Aug. 60-61; removed from C.P.S.U. 62; now retd.; awarded Order of Lenin, Hammer and Sickle Gold Medal and title Hero of Socialist Labour; Hon. mem. U.S.S.R. Acad. of Sciences.

Publs. (in Russian) *The Party's Policy in the Villages*, *Elections to the Soviets*, *Problems of the Working Class*, *On the Lessons of Trotskyism*, etc.

c/o Ministry of Social Security, 14 Shabolovka, Moscow, U.S.S.R.

Molstad, Melvin Carl, B.A., B.S., PH.D.; American university professor; b. 18 Nov. 1898; ed. Carleton Coll., Mass. Inst. of Technology and Yale Univ.

Junior Chemist, Dept. of Agriculture, Fixed Nitrogen Laboratory 20-21, Chemical Engineer 23-26; Instructor Yale Univ. 26-29; with Du Pont Co. 29-31; Asst. Prof. Yale Univ. 31-39; Assoc. Prof. Univ. of Pennsylvania 39-42, Prof. of Chemical Engineering 42-51, Dept. Chair. 51-61, Prof. Emer. 69-; Consultant, Atlantic Refining Co. 41, Davison Chemical Co. Baltimore 42-; Fulbright Prof., Trondheim Technical Univ. 54-55, Univ. of Tokyo 61-62; Ford Foundation Prof. Dartmouth Coll. 67; Fulbright Prof. Technical Univ. of Helsinki 69; mem. American Soc. of Engineering Educ.; Hon. A.I.Ch.E., A.C.S. (American Inst. of Chemists).

University of Pennsylvania, Towne Building, Philadelphia 4, Pa. 19104; Home: 19 Shady Hill Road, Moylan, Pa. 19063, U.S.A.

Telephone: 215-594-7953 (Office); 215-565-0864 (Home).

Molyakov, Nikolai Ivanovich; Soviet diplomatist; b. 16 Dec. 1910, Pokrov, Moscow Region; ed. Leningrad Herzen Pedagogic Inst.

Member C.P. of Soviet Union 39-; First Sec., Soviet Embassy, Washington 44-46; First Sec., Soviet Mission to UN 46-48; First Sec., Asst., Deputy Head of U.S. Dept. of Min. of Foreign Affairs, Moscow 48-53; Counsellor, Embassy at Oslo 54-57; Deputy Head, Dept. for Int. Orgs. of Ministry of Foreign Affairs 57-61, Head of South East Asia Dept. 61-62; Perm. Soviet Rep. to UN and other Int. Orgs. in Geneva 62-66; Head, Consular Dept., Ministry of Foreign Affairs 66-; Order of Red Banner of Labour, etc.

Ministry of Foreign Affairs of the U.S.S.R., 32-34 Smolenskaya-Sennaya Ploshchad, Moscow, U.S.S.R.

Momigliano, Arnaldo Dante, D.LITT., LITT.D., D.H.L., D.PHIL., F.B.A.; Italian historian; b. 5 Sept. 1908, Caraglio, Cuneo; s. of Riccardo Momigliano and Ilda Levi; m. Gemma Segre 1932; one d.; ed. Univs. of Turin and Rome.

Professor Extraordinary Univ. of Rome 32-36; Prof. Univ. of Turin 36-39; research work, Univ. of Oxford 39-46; Supernumerary Prof. Univ. of Turin 45-64, Scuola Normale Superiore, Pisa 64-; Reader Univ. of Bristol 47-51; Prof. of Ancient History Univ. Coll., London 51-75; Alexander White Visiting Prof. Univ. of Chicago 59; Sather Prof. in Classics, Univ. of Calif. 62, Gray Lecturer, Cambridge Univ. 63; Lauro de Bosis Lecturer and Visiting Prof., Harvard Univ. 65, Jackson Lecturer 68; Jerome Lecturer, Univ. of Michigan 71-72; Trevelyan Lecturer, Cambridge Univ. 73; Flexner Lecturer, Bryn Mawr 74; Fellow, Dumbarton Oaks, Harvard Univ. 72; Assoc. mem. All Souls Coll., Oxford 75-; Alexander White Prof., Univ. Chicago 75-(78); Feltrinelli Prize Accad. Lincei 60; Co-Editor *Rivista Storica Italiana* 48-; Socio Nazionale Accad. dei Lincei, Arcadia, Accad. Scienze Torino; Corresp. mem. German Archaeological Inst.; Foreign mem. Royal Dutch Acad., and Sciences, American Acad. of Arts and Sciences,

American Philosophical Soc. etc.; Hon. mem. American Historical Asscn.; Hon. K.B.E.; several hon. degrees; Kaplun Prize, Univ. of Jerusalem 75.
Leisure interests: travelling, music, walking.
Publs. *La composizione della storia di Tucidide* 29, *Prime linee di storia della tradizione maccabaica* 31, 68, *L'opera dell'imperatore Claudio* 32, 61, *Filippo il Macedone* 34, chapters in *Cambridge Ancient History X* 34, *Contributo alla Storia degli Studi Classici* 55, *Secondo Contributo alla Storia degli Studi Classici* 60, *The Conflict Between Paganism and Christianity in the Fourth century* (editor) 63, *Terzo Contributo alla Storia degli Studi Classici* 66, *Studies in Historiography* 66, *Quarto Contributo alla Storia degli Studi Classici* 69, *The Development of Greek Biography* 71, *Quinto Contributo alla Storia degli Studi Classici* 75, *Alien Wisdom* 75, *Essays on Historiography* 76.
All Souls College, Oxford, England.

Mommsen, Ernst Wolf; German business executive; b. 12 May 1910, Berlin; s. of Dr. Ernst Mommsen and Clara Weber; m. Eva Connor; one s.; ed. Ruprecht-Karl-Universität, Heidelberg, Christian-Albrechts-Universität, Kiel and Humboldt-Universität zu Berlin.
Management post, German Reich Industrial Asscn. 39; Ministry of Armament and War Production 40-45, finally Head of Central Div.; in Electrical Industry 46-48; mem. Board of Management Iron and Steel Fed. 48-52; Man. Klöckner-Drahtindustrie 52; mem. Management Board Klöckner-Werke A.G., Duisburg 52; mem. Management Board Rheinische Röhrenwerke A.G. 54, and Phoenix-Rheinrohr A.G. Vereinigte Hütten-und Röhrenwerke, Düsseldorf after merger of Hüttenwerke Phoenix A.G. with Rheinische Röhrenwerke A.G. 54-65; Pres. Phoenix-Rheinrohr Vereinigte Hütten- und Röhrenwerke 65-, now Thyssen Röhrenwerke A.G.; Chair. of Board of Dirs. Thyssen Rohrleitungsbau G.m.b.H., Düsseldorf, Thyssenrohr Int. G.m.b.H., Düsseldorf, Deutsche Fina G.m.b.H., Frankfurt, Stahlform Berlin G.m.b.H., Berlin; Vice-Chair. Board of Dirs. Thyssen Steel and Pipe (Great Britain) Ltd., London, Blohm & Voss A.G., Hamburg, Handelsunion A.G., Düsseldorf; Chair. Man. Board Friedrich Krupp G.m.b.H. 73-75, mem. Supervisory Board 75; Dr. rer. pol. h.c. (Univ. of Munich); mem. Science Council, Advisory Board for Foreign Trade of the Federal Minister of Econs. 69-72; Pres. Productivity Centre of German Economy; Pres. or mem. various industrial orgs.
Leisure interests: literature, classical music, history.
Publs. *The Problem of Competition in the Steel Industry* (with von Grosse and Wessels) 54, *Creation of an Elite in the Economy* 55, *Planning without Planification* 62, *Structural Changes in the Raw Material Supply of the European Iron and Steel Industry* 62, *The Policy of Internal Management Development* 62, *Future of Capitalism* 67, *Germany in the Upheaval of World Economy* 68.
Thyssen Röhrenwerke A.G., Düsseldorf, August-Thyssen-Strasse 1; Home: Düsseldorf, Orsoyer Strasse 58, Federal Republic of Germany.
Telephone: 8241 (Office); 434215 (Home).

Mondadori, Alberto; Italian publisher; b. 8 Dec. 1914; ed. Verona, Milan and Univ. of Pavia.
At an early age Asst. Producer and Producer of motion pictures; founded *Tempo* magazine and directed it for four years; joined Mondadori Editore 45, Vice-Pres. until April 68; founded and directed *Epoca*, the first Italian magazine in colour 50; founded own publishing house Il Saggiatore di Alberto Mondadori Editore 58, Pres. 68-; Viareggio Prize for volume of poetry.
Sa Ilggiatore, Via Guastalla 3, 20122 Milan, Italy.

Mondale, Walter Frederick, LL.B.; American lawyer and politician; b. 5 Jan. 1928, Ceylon, Minn.; s. of Rev. and Mrs. Theodore Sigvaard Mondale; m. Joan Adams

1955; two s. one d.; ed. Minnesota public schools, Macalester Coll., Univ. of Minnesota and Univ. of Minnesota Law School.
Attorney-General, Minnesota 60-64; Senator from Minnesota 64-; fmr. mem. President's Consumer Advisory Council; fmr. mem. Exec. Board Nat. Asscn. of Attorneys General, and other legal orgs.; Democrat-Farmer-Labor.
Russell Senate Office Building, Washington, D.C. 20510, U.S.A.

Monday, Horace Reginald, C.B.E.; Gambian diplomatist; b. 26 Nov. 1907, Bathurst (now Banjul); s. of late James Thomas Monday and late Rachel Davies; m. Wilhelmina Roberta Juanita 1932; one s.; ed. Methodist Mission Schools, Bathurst and correspondence course (London School of Accountancy).
Clerk 25-48; Asst. Accountant, Treasury 48-52; Accountant and Storekeeper, Marine Dept. 53-54; Accountant-Gen. to the Gambia Govt. 54-65; Chair. Gambia Public Service Comm. 65-68; Dir. Gambia Currency Board 64-68; Pres. Gambia Red Cross Soc. 67-68; High Commr. to U.K. 68-71; Chair. Banjul City Council 71-, Gambia Utilities Corpn. 72-; Commdr. Nat. Order of Repub. of Senegal.
Leisure interest: reading.
Rachelville, 24 Clarkson Street, Banjul, The Gambia.

Mondjo, Nicolas; Congolese diplomatist; b. 24 June 1933, Fort Rousset, French Equatorial Africa; ed. Inst. des Hautes-Etudes d'Outre Mer, Paris.
Former Dir. of Admin., Ministry of the Interior; Amb. to France; Perm. Rep. to EEC; Minister of Foreign Affairs 68-69; Dir. of Cabinet of Pres. of Repub. 69-70; Perm. Rep. to UN June 70-; del. to XXII and XXIII sessions of UN Gen. Assembly; del. to various int. confs.
Permanent Mission of the People's Republic of the Congo to United Nations, 801 Second Avenue, 4th floor, New York, N.Y. 10017, U.S.A.

Monelli, Paolo, D.IUR.; Italian journalist and novelist; b. 15 July 1894; ed. Bologna Univ.
Officer of "Alpini" 15-21; prisoner of war 17-18; mem. of mil. missions 19-21; Vienna corresp. *Gazzetta del Popolo* 21-22; Berlin corresp. *La Stampa*, with special missions to the Near East, Spitzbergen, etc. 22-26; Special corresp. *Corriere della Sera* 26-29, *La Stampa* 29-35; war corresp. Ethiopia 35-36; Dir. Paris office *Corriere della Sera* 36-39, war corresp. 40-43; imprisoned by Fascist govt. 43; Lieut.-Col. Corpo Italiano di Liberazione 44-45; special corresp. *La Stampa* 46-67; Editor and special corresp. *Corriere della Sera* 67; contributor to *Il Mondo, Tempo, Espresso, France Soir*; Saint Vincent Great Prize for Journalism 60, Great Prize for Journalism, Accademia della Crusca, Florence 65; Gold Medal of Italia Nostra for defence of ancient monuments and landscape; four Medaglie al valore, Croix de Guerre Belge, etc.
Publs. *Le Scarpe al sole* 21, 55, 65 (English and American trans. *Toes Up*, French trans. *Les pieds devant*, also film), *Questo mestieraccio* 28, *La guerra è bella ma è scomoda* 29, 51, *Io e i tedeschi* 29, *Barbaro dominio* 33, *Il ghiottone errante* 35, 47, *Roma 1943* 45 (new edn. 63), *Naja parla* 47, *Mussolini piccolo borghese* 50 (English and American trans. *Mussolini: Intimate Life of a Dictator.* also Dutch trans.; new edn. 64), *Nessuna nuvola in cielo* 57, *Avventura nel primo secolo* 58, 64, *Il vero bevitore* 63, *Ombre Cinesi* 65, etc.
Via Venti Settembre 3, 00187 Rome, Italy.

Mongo Beti (*pseudonym* of Alexandre Biyidi-Awala); Cameroonian writer and teacher; b. 1932, Mbalmayo; ed. Lycée de Yaoundé, Université d'Aix-en-Provence and Sorbonne, Paris.
Exiled from Cameroon, became teacher and writer in Paris; undertook research in sociology, Paris Univ.

57-59; currently Prof. Lycée Corneille, Rouen; Prix Sainte-Beuve for *Mission Terminée* 58.
Publs. *Le Pauvre Christ de Bomba* 56 (trans. in English), *Mission Terminée* 57 (trans. in English), *Le Roi Miraculé* 58 (trans. in English), *Main Basse sur le Cameroun, autopsie d'une décolonisation* (political essay) 72 (banned in France), *Remember Ruben* 74, *Perpétue et l'Habitude du Malheur* 74.
6 rue d'Harcourt, 76000 Rouen, France.
Telephone: (35) 70 14 56.

Monguno, Alhaji Shettima Ali; Nigerian educationist and politician; b. 1926, Borno; s. of Rahma and Janna Monguno; m. Ashe Meta 1948; two s. five d.; ed. Bornu Monguno elementary school, Bornu Middle School, Bauchi Teacher Training Coll., Katshina Higher Coll., Nigerian Coll. of Arts, Science and Technology, Zaria and Univ. of Edinburgh.
Native Authority Educ. Sec., Northern Nigeria 59; Councillor for Educ., Borno Native Authority Council; mem. Fed. Assembly 59-; Fed. Minister of Int. Affairs 65-66; Fed. Commr. for Industries 67-71, for Mines and Power 71-75; del. from XVI to the XXV sessions of UN Gen. Assembly and other int. confs.; Pres. of OPEC 72; Councillor for Natural Resources and Co-operatives, Borno Local Authority 75-; active in many voluntary orgs.; various int. awards.
Leisure interests: reading, cycling.
Borno Local Authority, Maiduguri, Nigeria.
Telephone: 2060 (Office); 2089 (Home).

Monicelli, Mario; Italian film director; b. 16 May 1915; ed. Università degli Studi, Pisa.
Former Asst. to Pietro Germi; writer of film *Riso Amaro*; film dir. 49-; Golden Lion, Venice Film Festival; Silver Medal, Berlin Film Festival; Silver Laurel Medal, San Francisco Film Festival.
Films include: *Guardie e Ladri* 48, *The Big Deal of Madonna Street* 55, *The Great War* 58, *The Organiser* 60, *Casanova '70* 63, *L'Armata Brancaleone* 65.
Piazza Teatro Pompeo 19, Rome, Italy.

Mönkemeyer, Karl, DR.RER.NAT.; German business executive; b. 24 July 1916, Osterwieck/Harz; s. of Carl and Johanna (née Träger) Mönkemeyer; m. Ursula Kümpel 1943; two s.; ed. Humanistisches Gymnasium, Wernigerode, Bergakademie Clausthal and Univ. of Munich.
Joined Chemische Werke Hüls A.G. 52, Deputy mem. Man. Board 64-66, mem. Man. Board 66-70, Deputy Chair. 70-72, Chair. Management Board June 72-.
Leisure interests: archaeology, photography, travel.
4370 Marl, Flämingstrasse 11, Federal Republic of Germany.

Monnerville, Gaston Charles François, L. ès L., D. en D.; French public servant; b. 2 Jan. 1897, French Guiana; s. of Saint-Yves Monnerville and Françoise Orville; m. Marie-Thérèse Lapeyre 1923; ed. Faculty of Law, Toulouse.
Admitted to Bar of Toulouse 18, Paris 21; Pres. of Union of Young Lawyers at the Paris Court 27; Deputy for Guiana 32-; Mayor of Cayenne 35; mem. of Radical and Radical-Socialist Party; Vice-Pres. of Party 38; Under-Sec. of State for Colonies 37, 38; served in Navy in Second World War; after Armistice was active in resistance movement 40-44; mem. of Consultative Assembly 44; Pres. of Comm. of Overseas France; re-elected for Guiana to Constituent Assembly Oct. 45 and June 46; Del. of France to U.N. Assembly; Councillor of the Republic Dec. 46; Senator for Lot 48, 55, 58, 65; Pres. of Council of the Republic 47-58; Pres. Senate of the Republic and Senate of the Community 58-68; mem. Constitutional Council 74-; Pres. Gen. Council of the Lot Dept. 51-70, Hon. Pres. 70-; mem. Council of Paris Univ. 59-69; mem. Société des Gens de Lettres 68; Croix de Guerre 40; Medal of the Resistance with

Rosette; Chevalier de la Légion d'Honneur; Maire de Saint-Céré (Lot) 64-71.
Leisure interests: swimming, walking, skiing, golf, music.
Publs. *l'Enrichissement sans cause* 21, *Le Sénat* 65, *Clemenceau* 68, *Histoire générale de l'Afrique* (with others) 72, *Témoignage*, Vol. I 75.
27 avenue Raymond-Poincaré, 75116 Paris, France.

Monnet, Jean; French politician; b. 9 Nov. 1888, Cognac; m. Silvia de Bondini.
French rep. on Inter-Allied Maritime Comm. First World War, awarded Hon. G.B.E.; fmr. 1st Deputy Sec.-Gen. L.N.; Chair. Franco-British Economic Co-ordination Cttee. 39; mem. British Supply Council in Washington 40-43, Algiers 43-44; Commr. for Armament Supplies and Reconstruction, French Cttee. Nat. Liberation 43-44; Gen. Commr. for Modernization Plan 47; Pres. ECSC High Authority 52-55; Chair. Action Cttee. for a United States of Europe 56-75; Hon. mem. Royal Geographical Soc. 72; Wateler Peace Prize 51, Charlemagne Prize 53, U.S. Freedom Award 62; Freedom Medal 63; Family of Man Award for Peace; Robert Schuman Prize, Univ. of Bonn 66; Aspen Inst. for Humanistic Studies Prize 71; Hon. Companion of Honour (U.K.) 72; Dr. h.c. (Columbia, Glasgow and Princeton Univs.), Hon. LL.D. (Cambridge, Yale, Oxford, Cologne, Lausanne).
Publ. *Les Etats Unis d'Europe ont commencé* (extracts from speeches).
Houjarray, 78 Montfort-l'Amaury (Seine-et-Oise); 83 avenue Foch, Paris 16e, France.

Monnier, Claude Michel, PH.D.; Swiss journalist; b. 23 March 1938, Rwankéri, Rwanda; s. of Henri Monnier and Olga Pavlov; m. Estela Troncoso Balandrán 1958; two s.; ed. Univs. of Geneva and Mexico, Graduate Inst. of Int. Studies, Geneva.
Educational tour in Asia and America 56-58; Research Fellow, Swiss Nat. Fund for Scientific Research, Tokyo 63-66; Tokyo Corresp. *Journal de Genève* 63-66, Foreign Editor 66-70, Ed. in Chief 70-.
Leisure interests: walking, light aircraft flying.
Publs. *Les Americains et sa Majesté l'Empereur*: *Etude du Conflict culturel d'où naquit la Constitution japonaise de 1946* 67.
Journal de Genève, 5-7 rue de General Dufour, 1211 Geneva 11; Home: Chemin de Saussac 41, 1256 Troinex, Geneva, Switzerland.
Telephone: (022) 28-03-50 (Office); (022) 43-59-96 (Home).

Monod, André Théodore, D. ès sc.; French zoologist; b. 9 April 1902, Rouen; s. of Rev. Prof. Wilfred Monod and Dorina Monod; m. Olga Pickova 1930; two s. one d.; ed. Ecole Alsacienne and Paris Univ.
Former Prof. Muséum Nat. d'Histoire Naturelle, Paris; fmr. Dir. Inst. Français d'Afrique Noire, Dakar; fmr. Dean, Faculty of Sciences, Dakar Univ.; mem. Inst. de France (Acad. des Sciences), Acad. des Sciences d'Outremer, Acad. de Marine; Dr. h.c. (Univs. of Cologne and Neuchâtel); Officer Légion d'Honneur, Ordre Palmes Académiques, Ordre of Golden Ark; Commdr. Order of Christ, Mérite Saharien, Mérite Nat. Mauritanie, Ordre Nat. Sénégal; Gold Medal, Royal Geographical Soc. and American Geographical Soc.; Haile Selassie Prize for African Research.
Leisure interest: field natural history.
Home: 14 quai d'Orléans, Paris 4e; Office: Muséum National d'Histoire Naturelle, 57 rue Cuvier, Paris 5e, France.
Telephone: 331-40-10 (Office); 326-79-50 (Home).

Monod, Jacques L.; French molecular biologist; b. 1910.
Head of Dept. of Cellular Biochemistry, Pasteur Inst., Paris; Dir. Inst. Pasteur April 71-; Prof. Collège de France, Paris 67; Hon. Prof. Coll. de France, Paris

73; mem. Deutsche Akademie der Naturforscher Leopoldina 66-; Foreign mem. Royal Soc. (U.K.), Czechoslovak Acad. of Sciences, Nat. Acad. of Sciences (U.S.A.), American Philosophical Soc.; Nobel Prize for Medicine 65; works include: research into physiology, kinetics and metabolism of growth of bacteria, the mechanism of the biosynthesis of enzymes and the regulation of cellular metabolism.
Publs. *Le Hasard et la Nécessité* 70, *Chance and Necessity* 71.
Institut Pasteur, 25-28 rue du Dr. Roux, Paris 15e. [*Died* 31 *May* 1976.]

Monrad, Carl Corydon, M.S.E., PH.D.; American chemical engineer; b. 15 Jan. 1905, Buffalo, N.Y.; s. of Chas O. Monrad and Wilhelmina Lagergren Monrad; m. Christine Clark 1930; one s. one d.; ed. Univ. of Michigan.
Chemical engineer, Standard Oil Co. (Ind.) 30-37; Assoc. Prof. Carnegie Inst. of Technology 37-42, Prof. of Chemical Engineering 42-, Head of Dept. of Chemical Engineering 47-65; adviser and consultant to many govt. depts. 40-45; Assoc. Dean Coll. of Engineering and Science 65-73; retd. 73; mem. American Chemical Soc., American Inst. of Chemical Engineers, American Soc. for Engineering Educ.
Publs. Various publications on different aspects of chemical engineering.
55 Daley Terrace, Orleans, Mass. 02653, U.S.A.
Telephone: 617-255-5811.

Monreal Luque, Alberto, DR.ECON.SC.; Spanish politician and economist; b. 18 Nov. 1926, Madrid; m.; three c.; ed. Univ. of Madrid.
Member of Cuerpo de estadísticos facultativos 56-; Prof. Faculty of Econ. Sciences, Univ. of Madrid 57-; Perm. Spokesman, Comisión Superior de Personal 63; Adviser to Council for Land, Sea and Air Transport; Gen. Tech. Sec. Ministry of Public Works until 65; fmr. Chief, Econ. Advisory Board to Ministry of Commerce; Under-Sec. Ministry of Educ. and Science 68-69; mem. Cortes; Minister of Finance Oct. 69-June 73.
c/o Ministry of Finance, Madrid, Spain.

Mons, Jean; French civil servant; b. 25 Feb. 1906; s. of Antonie and Mme. Mons (née Martinie); m. Françoise Delval (deceased); one d.
Teacher and engineer for agricultural industries; Chief Controller of Indirect Contributions 24-26; served French Army 39-40; Prefect (First Class) 44; Sec.-Gen. of the Seine; Dir. Office of Prés. du Conseil 46; placed at disposal of Ministry of Foreign Affairs; Resident Gen. in Tunis 47-50; Perm. Sec.-Gen. for Nat. Defence 50-56; Conseiller Maître à la Cour des Comptes 56; mem. Cttee. of Enquiry into Public Costs 60-, Nat. Conciliation Cttee. for Nat. Educ. 61-; Prés de Chambre à la Cour des Comptes 70-; Commdr. Légion d'Honneur, Croix de Guerre, Rosette de la Résistance, etc.
63 rue de Prony, Paris 17, France.
Telephone: WAG 31-57.

Monsarrat, Nicholas John Turney, F.R.S.L.; British writer; b. 22 March 1910, Liverpool; s. of late K. W. Monsarrat; m. 1st Eileen Rowland 1939 (dissolved 1952), one s.; m. 2nd Philippa Crosby 1952 (dissolved 1961), two s.; m. 3rd Ann Griffiths 1961; ed. Winchester Coll. and Trinity Coll., Cambridge.
Writer and broadcaster 34-; Dir. U.K. Information Office, Johannesburg 46-53, Ottawa 53-56; Chair. Nat. War Memorial Health Foundation (S. Africa) 51-53; Board of Govs. Stratford Shakespeare Festival of Canada 56; Board of Dirs. Ottawa Philharmonic Orchestra 56; Heinemann Foundation Prize for Literature 51, Coronation Medal 53, Chevalier, Sovereign Order of St. John of Jerusalem 73.
Leisure interests: sailing, music.

Publs. include: *Think of Tomorrow* 34, *At First Sight* 35, *The Whipping Boy* 36, *This is the Schoolroom* 39, *Three Corvettes* 45, *Depends What You Mean by Love* 47, *My Brother Denys* 48, *The Cruel Sea* 51, *H.M.S. Marlborough Will Enter Harbour* 52, *The Story of Esther Costello* 53, *The Tribe That Lost Its Head* 56, *The Ship that Died of Shame* 59, *The Nylon Pirates* 60, *The White Rajah* 61, *The Time Before This* 62, *Smith and Jones* 63, *To Stratford with Love* 63, *A Fair Day's Work* 64, *The Pillow Fight* 65, *Something to Hide* 65, *Richer than All His Tribe* 68, *The Kappillan of Malta* 73, *Monsarrat at Sea* 75; *Life is a Four-Letter Word* (autobiography), Vol. I 66, Vol. II 70; also films *The Cruel Sea* 53, *The Ship that Died of Shame* 55, *The Story of Esther Costello* 57, *Something to Hide* 73.
15 Triq Il-Wileg, San Lawrenz, Gozo, Malta; c/o Campbell Thomson and McLaughlin Ltd., 31 Newington Green, London, N.16, England.
Telephone: 76977 (Malta).

Monsen, Per; Norwegian newspaper editor; b. 4 May 1913, Hamar; s. of Christian Fredrik and Aasta Monsen; m. 1st Beret Scheflo 1941 (divorced); 2nd Ursula Krogvig 1952; one s. one d.; ed. Hamar Kathedralskole.
Newspaper *Sörlandet* 32-37, *Bergens Arbeiderblad* 37-39, *Arbeiderbladet*, Oslo 39-, Editor 52-64; Norwegian Govt. Information Service, Stockholm 41-43, London 43-45; Press Attaché, Norwegian Military Mission, Berlin 48, 49; Dir. Int. Press Inst., Zürich 64-68; Chair. Norwegian Press Federation 54-58; editor Arbeiderbladet 68-70; Gen. Man. and Chief Editor Norwegian News Agency 70-.
Leisure interests: skiing, motoring, reading.
Skjerstadveien 4b, Oslo 1, Norway.
A/S Norsk Telegrambyrå, Pressens Hus, Rosenkrantzgt. 3, Oslo 1, Norway.

Monson, Sir William Bonnar Leslie, K.C.M.G., C.B.; British diplomatist, retd.; b. 28 May 1912, Edinburgh; s. of John William and Selina Leslie Monson; m. Helen Isobel Browne 1948; ed. Edinburgh Acad. and Hertford Coll., Oxford.
Dominions Office 35-39; Colonial Office 39-64; Chief Sec., West African Council 47-51; Asst. Under-Sec. of State Colonial Office 52-64; High Commr. in Zambia 64-66; Asst. Under-Sec. of State, Commonwealth Office 66-67; Deputy Under-Sec. of State Commonwealth Office 67-68; Deputy Under-Sec. of State, Foreign and Commonwealth Office 68-72.
Leisure interest: oriental ceramics.
Golf House, Goffers Road, London, S.E.3, England.
Telephone: 01-852-7257.

Montagne, Adhemar; Peruvian diplomatist; b. 1911, Peru; m.; one d.; ed. Peru and Italy.
Entered Diplomatic Service 32; Vice-Consul, Milan 32-37; Consul 37-42; Consul-Gen., Havana 42-44; First Sec., Washington 44-47; Consul-Gen., Genoa 47-57; Minister Plenipotentiary, Lebanon 57-62; Chief of Protocol, Ministry of Foreign Affairs 62-64; Amb. to Morocco 64-67; Uruguay 67-69, U.K. (also accred. to Malta) 69-; decorations from Peru, Germany, Italy, Lebanon and Malta.
Peruvian Embassy, 52 Sloane Street, London, SW1X 9SP, England.
Telephone: 01-235-1917.

Montagne Sánchez, Gen. Ernesto; Peruvian army officer and politician; b. 18 Aug. 1916, Barranco, Lima; s. of Gen. Ernesto Montagne Markholtz and Raquel de Montagne; m. Isabel Landázuri de Montagne; one s. one d.; ed. Military School of Chorrillos.
Captain 44, Lieut.-Col. 53, Col. 58, Brig.-Gen. 63, Gen. of Div. 68; taught at various mil. schools; several posts as Divisional Chief of Staff; Dir. Chorrillos Mil. School; Dir. Escuela Superior de Guerra; Prefect of Lima;

Gen. Commdr. 3rd Mil. Zone; Minister of State for Educ.; Dir. of Personnel; Deputy Chief of Staff of Army; Gen. Commdr. 1st Mil. Zone and Gen. Inspector of Army; Gen. Commdr. of Army, Pres. of Council of Ministers and Minister of War 68-72; Orden Militar de Ayacucho, Cruz Peruana al Mérito Militar, Orden del Sol, Orden de San Gregorio Magno, and numerous other foreign awards.
Leisure interest: sailing.
Lima, Peru.

Montagu, Hon. David Charles Samuel; British banker; b. 6 Aug. 1928, London; s. of Rt. Hon. Lord Swaythling and Mary Levy; m. Christiane F. Dreyfus; one s. two d.; ed. Eton Coll. and Trinity Coll., Cambridge.
Joined Samuel Montagu & Co. Ltd. 48, Dir. 54, Chair. 70-73; Rep. of U.K., United Nations Investment Cttee. 72-; Dir. Trades Union Unit Trust, United British Securities Trust, Carreras, Derby Trust, London Week-end Television, Drayton Commercial Investment Trust; Chair. and Chief Exec. Orion Bank Ltd. March 74-.
Leisure interests: racing, shooting, theatre.
Orion Bank Ltd., 1 London Wall, London, E.C.2; Home: 25 Kingston House South, Ennismore Gardens, London, S.W.7; also The Kremlin, The Severals, New-market, Suffolk, England.
Telephone: 01-600-6222 (Office); 01-581-2549 (Home); Newmarket 2467.

Montagu, Hon. Ivor, M.A.; British film producer and writer; b. 23 April 1904, London; s. of 2nd Baron Swaythling; m. Eileen Hellstern 1923; ed. Westminster School, Royal Coll. of Science and Technology and King's Coll., Cambridge.
Research in Mammalian systematics 18-25; founded Film Society London 25; produced films 25-; directed *Bluebottles*, co-directed *Wings Over Everest*, *Man—One Family*; associate producer *The Man Who Knew Too Much*, *39 Steps*; produced Spanish War films and *Peace and Plenty*; Technical Dir. Soviet Film Agency 41-42; leader-writer London *Daily Worker* 43-47; Pres. Soc. of Cultural Relations G.B./U.S.S.R.; mem. World Peace Council; Order of Liberation First Class (Bulgaria) 52, Lenin Peace Prize 59, Order of the Pole Star of Mongolia 63.
Publs. *On the Burrow of the Rodent Spalax* 24, *The Political Censorship of Films* 29, *The Traitor Class* 40, *The Red Army* 41, *Stalin* 42, *Soviet Soldier in Europe* 46, *Negotiation or War* 51, *Plot Against Peace* 52, *Land of Blue Sky* 56, *Film World* 64, *Germany's New Nazis* 67, *With Eisenstein in Hollywood* 69, *The Youngest Son* 70; Co-Author *Scott of the Antarctic* (screen play).
Old Timbers, Verdure Close, Watford, WD2 7NJ, England.

Montale, Eugenio; Italian poet; b. 12 Oct. 1896, Genoa; s. of Domenico and Giuseppina (Ricci) Montale; m. Drusilla Tanzi (died 1963).
Helped found literary journal *Primo Tempo* 22; on editorial staff, Bemporad (publishers) 27-28; Dir. Gabinetto Vieusseux Library, Florence 28-38; journalist, contributor to several literary journals and poetry critic for *La Fiera Letteraria* 38-48; literary editor, later music critic, *Corriere della Sera* 48-; Antico Fattore Poetry Prize (for *Casa dei doganieri*) 32; Premio Manzotto (for *La bufera e altro*) 56; Feltrinelli prize 63-64; Calouste Gulbenkian Prize, Acad. du Monde Latin, Paris 71; Nobel Prize for Literature 75; hon. degrees from Univs. of Milan, Rome and Cambridge.
Leisure interests: music, drawing and etching.
Publs. Principal works include: poetry: *Ossi di Seppia* 25, *La casa dei doganieri e altre poesie* 32, *La bufera e altro* 56, *Satura* 62, *Xenia* 66; prose: *La farfalla di Dinard* 56, *Auto da fé* 66, *Fuori di casa* 69.
c/o Corriere della Sera, Milan; Home: Via Bigli 11, Milan, Italy.

Montand, Yves (*pseudonym* of Yves Livi); French actor and singer; b. 13 Oct. 1921; m. Simone Signoret (q.v.) 1951; ed. primary school, Marseilles.
Interpreter of numerous famous songs; stage performances in straight plays and variety; films include *Les Portes de la Nuit, Le Salaire de la Peur, Les Héros sont Fatigués, Marguerite de la Nuit, Hommes et Loups, Les Sorcières de Salem, Premier Mai, La Loi, Temps d'Aujourd'hui, Napoléon, Un Dénommé Squarcio, Aimez-vous Brahms, Ma Geisha, La Guerre est finie, Vivre pour vivre, Un soir un train, Z, Le Diable par la queue, L'Aveu, On a Clear Day You Can See Forever, Le Cercle Rouge, Tout Va Bien, Etat de Siège, Le Hasard et la Violence, Vincent, François, Paul et les Autres*.
Publ. *Du Soleil plein la tête* (memoirs) 55.
15 place Dauphine, 75001 Paris, France.

Montanelli, Indro; Italian journalist and writer; b. 22 April 1909; ed. Univ. degli Studi, Florence and Univ. de Paris à la Sorbonne.
Special Corresp. *Corriere della Sera* 39-73; War Corresp. in Finland, Norway, Spain, Albania and Greece; Founder, Man. Editor *Il Giornale* 74-; has won Bagutta and Marzotto Prizes.
Publs. *Storia di Roma* 57, *Storia dei Greci* 58, *Incontri* 61, *Garibaldi* 62, *Gente qualunque* 63, *Dante e il suo secolo* 64, *Italia dei secoli bui* 65; Plays: *I sogni muoiono all'alba* (also film), *Il Generale della Rovere* (also film), *Kibbutz*.
Piazza Navona 93, Rome, Italy.

Montgomery, Arthur, PH.D.; Swedish economic historian; b. 2 Sept. 1889; m. Eva Mörner 1939; ed. Univs. of Uppsala and Stockholm.
Lecturer in Economic History, Univ. of Uppsala 21-24; Prof. of Economics, Swedish Univ. of Åbo, Finland 24-39; Prof. of Economic and Social History Univ. Coll of Commerce, Stockholm 40-58; Hon. D. Pol. Sc. Univ. of Åbo 48.
Publs. In English: *How Sweden Overcame the Depression of 1930-33* 38, *The Rise of Modern Industry in Sweden* 39, *From a Northern Customs Union to EFTA* (Scandinavian Economic History Review) 60; in Swedish: *Swedish Social Policy in the Nineteenth Century* 34, *Swedish Economic History 1913-39* 46, *Russia and Our Foreign Policy* 49, *Stalinism* 53.
Karlavägen 72A, Stockholm Ö, Sweden.
Telephone: Stockholm 349560 (Office); Stockholm 606320 (Home).

Montgomery, David (b. Phillip Meckenberg); American photographer; b. 8 Feb. 1937, Brooklyn, N.Y.; s. of Arthur Montgomery Meckenberg and Lucille Ruth Phillips; m. Caroline Blanche Maidlow 1962; two d.; ed. Midwood High School.
Toured U.S.A. as musician; freelance photographer 60-; photographed H.M. Queen Elizabeth II for *Observer* magazine; contrib. to *Sunday Times, Vogue*, fmr. *Queen* magazines; Joint exhbn., Inst. of Contemporary Arts, London 73.
Leisure interests: gardening, photography, day-dreaming.
c/o Robert Montgomery, 5-6 Portland Mews, D'Arblay Street, London W.1, England.
Telephone: 01-439-1877.

Montgomery, Deane, PH.D.; American mathematician; b. 2 Sept. 1909, Weaver, Minn.; s. of Richard and Florence (Hitchcock) Montgomery; m. Katherine Fulton 1933; one s. one d.; ed. Hamline Univ. and Univ. of Iowa.
Assistant Prof. of Mathematics, Smith Coll. 35-38, Assoc. Prof. 38-42, Prof. 42-46; Assoc. Prof. Yale Univ. 46-48; Perm. mem. Inst. of Advanced Study, Princeton 48-51, Prof. of Mathematics 51-; Vice-Pres. Int. Mathematical Union 67-72, Pres. 75-(78); Hon. Dr. (Hamline, Yeshiva and Tulane Univs.).

Publ. (with Leo Zippin) *Topological Transformation Groups* 55.
Institute for Advanced Study, Princeton, N.J. 08540; Home: 55 Rollingmead, Princeton, N.J. 08540, U.S.A.

Montjoie, René; French administrator; b. 29 Sept. 1926, Lille; *s.* of Marcel and Adrienne (Polliart) Montjoie; *m.* Noëlle Kirchner 1953; one *d.*; ed. Ecole Polytechnique and Univ. of Chicago.
Assistant to Chief of Iron Metallurgy, Ministry of Industry 52-53; mineralogical work in the Metz region 54-57; Prof. of Economy, Ecole nat. supérieure des mines, Nancy 55-58; Asst. to Dir. of Mines, Ministry of Industry 57-62; Technical Adviser to Office of Prime Minister (Georges Pompidou) 62-67; Admin. of Electricité de France 64-, now Vice-Pres. of Man. Board; Commr.-Gen. of the Plan d'Equipement et de la Productivité 67-74.
Leisure interest: tennis.
32, rue de Monceau, 75008 Paris, France.
Telephone: 755-94-10.

Montoya, Joseph M.; American lawyer and politician; b. 24 Sept. 1915; ed. Regis Coll., Denver, and Georgetown Univ.
Admitted to New Mexico Bar 39; mem. New Mexico State Legislature 37-40, Democratic Floor Leader 39-40; State Senator 40-46, 54-55; Lieut-Gov. of New Mexico 47-51, 55-57; mem. U.S. Congress 56-64; Senator from New Mexico 65-.
209 Callecita Place, Santa Fe, New Mexico; and U.S. Senate, Washington, D.C. 20510, U.S.A.

Montrémy, Philipe Marie Waldruche de, L. en D., L. ès L.; French business executive; b. 25 July 1913, Paris; ed. Ecole Libre des Sciences Politiques.
Inspecteur des Finances 42; Deputy Dir. Direction des Prix 47; Deputy Dir. Office of Minister of Finance and Econs. 49; Dir. of Finance, Morocco 55; Econ. and Financial Counsellor, French Embassy, Morocco 56; Dir.-Gen. of Customs and Excise 58-71; Insp. Gen. of Finance 64-; Admin. Cie. Générale Transatlantique 62-74, Cie. des Messageries Maritimes 64-74, Aéroport de Paris 74-; mem. Conseil d'Admin. Service d'Exploitation Industrielle des Tabacs et des Allumettes (SEITA) 71, Pres. Dec. 71-74; Commdr. Légion d'Honneur, Croix de Guerre, Officier, Ordre National de Mérite.
28 avenue de New-York, 75116 Paris, France.

Mookerjee, Sir Birendra Nath, Kt., M.A., M.I.E.; Indian businessman; b. 14 Feb. 1899; ed. Hastings House and Sibpur Engineering Coll., Calcutta, and Trinity Coll., Cambridge.
Asst. Martin & Co. 24; Partner, Burn & Co. 31- and Martin & Co. 34-, Governing Dir. Martin Burn Ltd. 58-; mem. Munitions Board and Defence Council, Second World War; Sheriff, Calcutta 40; Chair. Board of Governors, Indian Inst. of Technology, Kharagpur; Chair. Calcutta Board, fmr. Imperial Bank of India; Pres. Governing Body, Sibpur Engineering Coll., fmr. Fellow Faculty of Engineering, Calcutta Univ.; Chair. Steel Corpn. of Bengal Ltd., Indian Iron and Steel Co. Ltd., Calcutta -72; Dir. Darjeeling Himalayan Railway Co., Indian Copper Corpn. Ltd., Alkali and Chemical Corpn. of India Ltd., The Statesman Ltd., Jardine Henderson Ltd., and many others; trustee and mem., Exec. Cttee. Victoria Memorial Hall, Calcutta.
7 Harrington Street, Calcutta 16, India.

Moore, Arch Alfred, Jr., LL.B.; American politician and lawyer; b. 16 April 1923, Moundsville, W. Va.; *s.* of Mr. and Mrs. Arch A. Moore; *m.* Shelley Riley 1949; one *s.* two *d.*; ed. Moundsville High School, West Virginia Univ.
Served in Army, Second World War, as Combat Sergeant until severely injured and discharged; entered Law School 48; admitted to W. Va. State Bar 51, joining family law partnership in the same year;

elected Vice-Pres. W. Va. Bar Asscn.; elected to W. Va. House of Dels. 52; elected to Congress 56; Gov. of W. Va. Jan. 69-, re-elected 72; Chair. Nat. Governors' Conf. 71; Co-Chair. Appalachian Regional Comm. 71; elected to Steering Cttee. of Educ. Comm. of U.S. 73; Republican; Purple Heart Medal; Commdr. and Grand Officer, Order of Merit (Italy).
Office of the Governor, Executive Department, State Capitol, Charleston, W. Va. 25305, U.S.A.
Telephone: 304-348-2000.

Moore, Brian; British novelist; b. 25 Aug. 1921, Belfast, N. Ireland; *s.* of James Bernard Moore and Eileen McFadden; *m.* Jean Denney 1967; one *s.*
Authors Club of Great Britain Novel Award 56; Quebec Literary Prize 1958; Guggenheim Fellowship 59; Canada Council Senior Fellowships 61, 75; Gov.-Gen. of Canada Fiction Award 61; U.S. Nat. Inst. of Arts and Letters Award 61; W. H. Smith Award (U.K.) 72.
Publs. novels: *The Lonely Passion of Judith Hearne* 56, *The Feast of Lupercal* 58, *The Luck of Ginger Coffey* 60, *An Answer from Limbo* 63, *The Emperor of Ice Cream* 65, *I Am Mary Dunne* 68, *Fergus* 71, *Catholics* 72, *The Great Victorian Collection* 75; non-fiction: *The Revolution Script* 71, *Canada* (with the Editors of *Life*) 63, 67.
c/o Curtis Brown, 60 East 56th Street, New York, N.Y. 10022, U.S.A.
Telephone: (212) PL 54200.

Moore, George Stevens, B.S.; American banker; b. 1 April 1905, Hannibal, Missouri; *s.* of George Victor and Etha (née Stevens) Moore; *m.* 1st Beatriz Braniff Bermejillo 1938 (divorced 1967), one *s.*; *m.* 2nd Charon Crosson 1967, one *s.* two *d.*; ed. Washington Univ., St. Louis, and Yale Univ.
Joined The Farmers Loan and Trust Co. (now First Nat. City Trust Co.), Asst. Sec. 31; Asst. Vice-Pres. First Nat. City Bank of New York 34-39, Vice-Pres. 39-52, Exec. Vice-Pres. (Domestic Div.) 52-57, Exec. Vice-Pres. (Overseas Div.) 57-59, Pres. 59-67, Chair. 67-70; Dir. U.S. Steel Corpn., W. R. Grace & Co., Olympic Airways, White, Weld & Co. Inc., White, Weld & Co. Ltd., Mercantile Stores Co. Inc., Union Pacific Corpn., Lincoln Center for the Performing Arts, Center for Inter-American Relations; Pres. and Dir. The Spanish Inst., Metropolitan Opera Asscn. Inc.; Trustee The Hispanic Soc. of America, Lahey Clinic Foundation, Soc. of New York Hosp.
Leisure interests: family, opera, golf.
399 Park Avenue, New York, N.Y. 10022, U.S.A.
Telephone: 212/559-4755 (Office).

Moore, Gerald, C.B.E.; British pianist; b. 30 July 1899, Watford, Herts.; *m.* Enid Kathleen Richard 1936; ed. Watford Grammar School, and Univ. of Toronto, Canada.
Studied piano with Prof. Michael Hambourg in Toronto 16; toured Canada as a boy pianist; returned to England 20; was accompanist and played chamber music; has accompanied most leading singers and instrumentalists and played at Festivals of Edinburgh, Salzburg, Holland, Granada, Seville, Besançon, Berlin, Vienna, etc., retd. from concert platform 67; also lectures and gives broadcast and television talks on music and the art of accompanying; lectured annually in U.S.A.; Master Classes in Song Interpretation in U.S.A., Japan, Sweden, Salzburg, Helsinki, England 49-67; records; Pres. Inc. Soc. of Musicians 62; Cobbett Gold Medal for services to chamber music 51; Grand Prix du Disque for the recording of his farewell recital 67 and for *Homage to Gerald Moore* 69; Edison Award, Amsterdam 67-69; Granados Medal, Barcelona 71; D.Litt. h.c. (Univ. of Sussex) 68; Mus. Doc. h.c. Cambridge 73; Hon. R.A.M.
Leisure interests: reading, gardening, bridge.
Publs. *The Unashamed Accompanist* 43, *Singer and*

Accompanist 53, *Am I Too Loud?* (memoirs) 62, *The Schubert Song Cycles* 75.
Beechwood Cottage, Penn Bottom, Penn, Bucks., England.

Moore, Henry, O.M., C.H., F.B.A.; British sculptor; b. 30 July 1898; ed. Leeds School of Art and Royal Coll. of Art.
Trustee Tate Gallery 41-48, 49-56, Nat. Gallery 55-63, 64-; mem. Royal Fine Art Comm. 47-71, Swedish Royal Acad. of Fine Arts; exhibited in London (Warren Gallery) 28, subsequently in Italy, Germany, Sweden, Switzerland, France, U.S.A. and Australia; retrospective exhibitions in Brussels, Paris 49, in Germany and Switzerland 50, London (Tate Gallery), Athens, New York 51, in South Africa and Sweden 52, Denmark, Norway, Netherlands, Fed. Germany, Brazil 53, Madrid 59, Hamburg, Essen, Zürich, London and Munich 60, Tate Gallery, London 68, Netherlands, Fed. Germany 68, Munich, Harlow 71, Florence 72, London (graphic work) 73; works in Victoria and Albert Museum and Tate Gallery (London), Whitworth Inst. and Corpn. Gallery (Manchester), City Art Gallery (Wakefield and Leeds) Allbright Art Gallery (Buffalo), Museum of Modern Art (New York), Washington Univ. and museums in Tel-Aviv and St. Louis; foreign hon. mem. American Acad. of Arts and Sciences 55, Acad. des Lettres et des Beaux Arts de Belgique; Foreign mem. Swedish Royal Acad. of Fine Arts; foreign corresp. mem. Acad. Flamande des Sciences; Hon. mem. Vienna Secession 71-; Trustee, Nat. Gallery 71-; Assoc. mem. French Acad. of Fine Arts 73, awarded first prize for sculpture, Venice 48, São Paulo 53, Antonio Feltrinelli Prize for Sculpture, Rome; Hon. D.Lit. (London, Oxford, Reading, Hull and Leeds), Dr. h.c. (Cambridge, Harvard, Berlin, and Royal Coll. of Art, London); Grand Cross with Star of West German Order of Merit 68, Erasmus Prize 68, Order pour le Mérite der Wissenschaft und Kunst (Fed. Germany) 73.
Works include: *Mother and Child, Reclining Figure, Madonna and Child, Three Standing Figures, Family Group, King and Queen, Reclining Figure* (for Lincoln Center, New York), Sundial for *The Times* building, London.
Publs. *Heads, Figures and Ideas* 58, *Henry Moore on Sculpture* 66.
Hoglands, Perry Green, Much Hadham, Herts., England.

Moore, J. H., F.C.A.; Canadian business executive; b. 27 Dec. 1915, London, Ont.; s. of J. McClay Moore and Phyllis Henderson Moore; m. S. Elizabeth Wood 1939; ed. Ridley Coll., St. Catherine's, Ont. and Royal Mil. Coll., Kingston, Ont.
Chartered Accountant, Gordon & Co., Toronto 45, Resident Partner, London, Ont. 50; Dir. of Finance and Treas., John Labatt Ltd. 53, Vice-Pres. and Gen. Man. 56, Exec. Vice-Pres. and Man.-Dir. 57, Pres. 58-69, Chair. of Board 67-; Pres. Brascan Ltd. 69; Dir. Allied Breweries Ltd., U.K., B.P. Canada Ltd., Bell Canada, Cadillac Devt. Corpn., Canada Devt. Corpn., Canadian Imperial Bank of Commerce, Canadian Pacific, Hudson's Bay Company; mem. Int. Council, The Morgan Guaranty Trust Co. of New York.
John Labatt Ltd., P.O. Box 5050, London, Ont., Canada.

Moore, John A(lexander), M.A., PH.D.; American biologist; b. 27 June 1915, Charles Town, W. Va.; s. of George Douglas Moore and Louise Hammond Blume Moore; m. Anna Betty Clark 1938; one d.; ed. Columbia Coll. and Columbia Univ.
Tutor of biology Brooklyn Coll. 39-41; instructor at Queens Coll. 41-43; Asst. Prof. Zoology Barnard Coll. 43-47, Assoc. Prof. 47-50, Prof. 50-68; Chair. Zoology Dept. 48-52, 53-54, 60-66; Res. Assoc. American Museum of Natural History 42-; Asst. Zoology Dept., Columbia 36-39, Chair. 49-52, Prof. 54-68; Prof. Biology Dept. Univ. of Calif. 69-; Fulbright Research

Scholar, Australia 52-53; Walker Ames Prof. Univ. of Washington 66; Guggenheim Fellowship Award 59; Biological Sciences Curriculum Study 59-; Commission on Science Education 67-73, Chair. 71-73; mem. Marine Biology Lab., American Asscn. for Advancement of Science, Int. Soc. of Developmental Biologists, Genetics Soc. of America, American Soc. of Zoologists, Pres. 74, Harvey Soc., American Soc. of Naturalists, Pres. 72, Soc. for Study Evolution, Pres. 63, American Acad. Arts and Sciences, Nat. Acad. of Sciences.
Leisure interests: photography, history of American science.
Publs. *Principles of Zoology* 57, *Heredity and Development* 63, 72, *A Guide Book to Washington* 63, *Biological Science: An Inquiry into Life* 63, 68, 73 (Supervisor), *Physiology of the Amphibia* (Editor) 64, *Ideas in Modern Biology* (Editor) 65, *Interaction of Man and the Biosphere* (Co-author) 70, 75, *Ideas in Evolution and Behavior* (Editor) 70, *Science for Society: A Bibliography* 70, 71, *Readings in Heredity and Development* 72.
Department of Biology, University of California, Riverside, Calif. 92502; Home: 11522 Tulane Avenue, Riverside, Calif. 92507, U.S.A.
Telephone: 714-684-0412 (Home).

Moore, Robert F. (Bobby), O.B.E.; British professional footballer; b. 12 April 1941, Barking, Essex; s. of Robert E. Moore and Doris Moore; m. Christina E. Moore 1962; one s. one d.; ed. Thomas Hood Technical Coll., Leyton.
Played for West Ham Football Club 58-74, Fulham F.C. March 74-; 18 England Youth Caps (record); many Under-23 Caps; 108 Full Int. Caps (record), 90 times as Captain; Winner's Medals in F.A. Cup Final 64 (West Ham), European Cup Winners Cup Final 65 (West Ham), World Cup Final 66 (England); Runners-up Medal in F.A. Cup Final 75 (Fulham); Footballer of the Year 64; Player of Players in World Cup 66.
Leisure interests: music, golf, different sports to relax.
Morlands, Stradbroke Drive, Chigwell, Essex, England.

Moore, Stanford, B.A., PH.D.; American biochemist; b. 4 Sept. 1913, Chicago, Ill.; s. of John Howard and Ruth Fowler Moore; ed. Vanderbilt Univ. and Univ. of Wisconsin.
Asst., Rockefeller Inst. for Medical Research, N.Y.C. 39-42, Associate 42-49, Assoc. mem. 49-52, mem. 52-, Prof. of Biochem. 52-; Technical Aide, Office of Scientific Research and Devt., Wash. D.C. 42-45; Visiting Prof. (Francqui Chair.), Univ. of Brussels 50-51; Visiting Investigator, Univ. of Cambridge 51; mem. Editorial Board *Journal of Biological Chem.* 50-60; mem. American Soc. of Biological Chemists, Treasurer 56-59, Pres. 66; mem. American Chem. Soc. (Richards Medal 72), Biochem. Soc. (Great Britain), Harvey Soc., U.S. Nat. Acad. of Sciences; Trustee, Vanderbilt Univ. 74; Hon. mem. Belgian Biochem. Soc., Belgian Royal Acad. of Medicine; Founder's Medal, Vanderbilt Univ. 35; Hon. M.D. (Univ. of Brussels) 54; Dr. h.c. (Univ. of Paris) 64; Linderstrøm-Lang Medal 72, Nobel Prize for Chemistry (with C. B. Anfinsen and W. H. Stein) 72.
Publs. Technical articles on the characterization of carbohydrates, chromatographic determination of amino acids, and the determination of the structures of protein molecules.
The Rockefeller University, 66th Street and York Avenue, New York, N.Y. 10021, U.S.A.
Telephone: 212-360-1220.

Moore, William H.; American Chairman of Bankers Trust Co. 57-74; see *The International Who's Who 1975-76*.

Moore, William Harreld; American railway executive; b. 8 May 1916, Hazard, Ky.; s. of William Ray and Mary Roberts Moore; m. Virginia P. Smith 1941; two s.; ed. Danville Military Acad. and Virginia Military Inst.

Electrical engineer, Sperry Products Inc. 37-41; joined Southern Railway System 41, Vice-Pres. in charge of Operations 65-70, Exec. Vice-Pres. (Operations) 70-; Pres. Terminal Railroad Asscn. of St. Louis 63-65; Pres. and Chief Exec. Officer, Penn Central Transportation Co. 70-74; Dir. American Security and Trust Co., Griffith-Consumers Co., Acacia Mutual Life Insurance Co., Nat. Railroad Passenger Corpn., Asscn. of American Railroads.

Penn Central Transportation Co., 1846 Six Penn Center Plaza, Philadelphia, Pa. 19104, U.S.A.
Telephone: 215-594-2214.

Moorehead, Alan, C.B.E.; Australian writer; b. 22 July 1910, Melbourne; s. of Richard Moorehead; m. Lucy Milner 1939; two s. one d.; ed. Scotch Coll. and Melbourne Univ.
Sunday Times Gold Medal 56; Duff Cooper Award 56. Publs. *Mediterranean Front* 41, *A Year of Battle* 43, *The End in Africa* 43, *African Trilogy* 44, *Eclipse* 45, *Montgomery* 46, *The Rage of the Vulture* 48, *The Villa Diana* 51, *The Traitors* 52, *Rum Jungle* 53, *A Summer Night* 54, *Gallipoli* 56, *The Russian Revolution* 58, *No Room in the Ark* 59, *The White Nile* 60, *The Blue Nile* 62, *Coopers Creek* (Royal Soc. of Literature Award) 63, *The Desert War* 65, *The Fatal Impact* 66, *Darwin and the Beagle* 69, *A Late Education* 70.
c/o National Bank of Australasia, Australia House, Strand, London, W.C.2, England.

Moorer, Admiral Thomas Hinman, D.S.M., D.F.C.; American naval officer; b. 9 Feb. 1912, Mount Willing, Ala.; s. of the late Richard Randolph Moorer and Hulda Hinson; m. Carrie Foy 1935; three s. one d.; ed. U.S. Naval Acad.
Service in U.S. warships 33-35, aviation squadrons 36-43; Commdr. of bombing squadron 43; Gunnery and Tactical Officer, Staff of Commdr., Naval Air Force, Atlantic 44-45; Strategic Bombing Survey, Japan 45-56; Naval Aviation Ordnance Test Station 46-48; Exec. Officer aircraft carrier *Midway* 48-49; Operations Officer on Staff of Commdr. Carrier Div. Four, Atlantic Fleet 49-50; Naval Ordnance Test Station, Inyokern 50-52; Capt. 52; Staff of Commdr., Naval Air Force, Atlantic Fleet 53-55; Aide to Asst. Sec. of Navy for Air 55-56; Commdr. U.S.S. *Salisbury Sound* 56-57; Special Asst., Strategic Plans Div., Office of Chief of Naval Operations, Navy Dept. 57-58; Rear Adm. 58; Asst. Chief of Naval Operations (War Gaming Matters) 58-59; Commdr. Carrier Div. Six 59-60; Dir. Long Range Plans 60-62; Vice-Adm. 62; Commdr. U.S. Seventh Fleet, W. Pacific 62-64; Adm. 64; C.-in-C. U.S. Pacific Fleet 64-65; C.-in-C. U.S. Atlantic Fleet, C.-in-C. Atlantic and Supreme Allied Commdr. Atlantic (NATO Forces) 65-67; Chief of Naval Operations, U.S. 67-70; Chair. U.S. Joint Chiefs of Staff 70-74; Silver Star Medal 42, Legion of Merit 45, Gray Eagle of U.S. Navy Award 72, Defense Distinguished Service Medal 73, and many U.S. and foreign decorations.
6901 Lupine Lane, McLean, Va. 22101, U.S.A.

Moores, Hon. Frank Duff; Canadian politician; b. 18 Feb. 1933, Carbonear, Newfoundland; s. of Dorothy Duff and Silas Wilmot Moores; m. Janis Johnson 1973; one s. six d. (by previous marriage).
Member of Parl. 68-; fmr. Minister of Fisheries; Premier of Newfoundland 72-.
Leisure interests: golf, fishing, hunting.
Mount Scio House, St. John's, Newfoundland, Canada.

Moos, Malcolm, M.A., PH.D.; American educationist; b. 19 April 1916, St. Paul, Minn.; s. of Charles John Moos and Katherine (née Grant) Moos; m. Margaret Tracy Gager 1945; two s. three d.; ed. Univs. of Minnesota and California.
Teaching Fellow, Political Science Dept., Univ. of Minnesota 38-39, Univ. of California 39-41; Research Asst. Bureau of Public Admin., Univ. of Alabama

41-42; Asst. Prof. of Political Science, Univ. of Wyoming 42, Johns Hopkins Univ. 42-46; Assoc. Prof. Johns Hopkins Univ. 46-52, Prof. 52-61, 63; Assoc. Editor, Baltimore Evening Sun 45-48; Visiting Prof., Univ. of Michigan 55; Consultant, White House Office 57-58; Admin. Asst. to Pres. of U.S.A. 58-60; White House Special Asst. 60-61; Prof. of Public Law and Govt., Columbia Univ. 63-65; Dir. of Policy and Planning, Ford Foundation 64-66, of Office of Govt. and Law Dec. 66-Aug. 67; Pres. Univ. of Minnesota 67-74, Center for the Study of Democratic Insts. 74-75; mem. numerous social service and educ. comms. and cttees., Boards of Dirs. and Trustees; Chair. and Vice-Chair. of various comms.; Hon. LL.D., Ohio Northern Univ., Univ. of North Dakota, Georgetown Univ., Johns Hopkins Univ., Litt.D. (Hon.) Coll. of Saint Thomas.
Publs. *State Penal Administration in Alabama* 42, *Politics, Presidents and Coattails* 52, *The Republicans: A History of Their Party* 56; co-author of several publications.
Center for the Study of Democratic Institutions, Santa Barbara, Calif.; Home: 176 N. Mississippi River Boulevard, St. Paul, Minn. 55104, U.S.A.

Moraes, Dominic; Indian writer and poet; b. 19 July 1938; s. of late Frank Moraes; ed. St. Mary's High School, Bombay, and Jesus Coll., Oxford.
Consultant UN Fund for Population Activities 73; Man. Editor *The Asia Magazine* Hong Kong 72-; Hawthornden Prize for *A Beginning* 57.
Publs. include: *A Beginning* 57, *Gone Away* 60, *My Son's Father* (autobiog.) 68, *The Tempest Within* 72-73, *The People Time Forgot* 72, *A Matter of People* 74; books of poems and travel books on India.
c/o 31 Queen's Road Central, Hong Kong.

Moraes, Vinicius de, LL.B.; Brazilian writer and diplomatist; b. 1913; ed. Nat. Faculty of Law, Colégio Santo Ignácio and Magdalen Coll., Oxford.
Ministry of Educ. 36-38; Ministry of Foreign Affairs 43; Film Critic 40-45; Sec. Embassy 44-47; Vice-Consul, Los Angeles 47-50; Consul, Montevideo 58-60.
Publs. Poetry: *O Caminho para a Distância* 33, *Forma e Exegese* 40, *Ariana a Mulher* 36, *Novos Poemas* 38, 59, *Cinco Elegias* 43, *Poemas, Sonetos e Baladas* 46, *Patria Minha* 48, *Livro de Sonetos* 57, *Antologia Poética* 54, *Orfeu da Conceição* 56; Prose: *Procura-se uma Rosa* 61, *Para Viver um Grande Amor* 62; numerous translations.
Editora do Autor, Avenida Nilo Peçanha 155, G.R. 207, Rio de Janeiro, Brazil.

Morales, Armando; Nicaraguan artist; b. 15 Jan. 1927; ed. Instituto Pedagógico de Varones, Managua, Escuela de Bellas Artes, Managua and Pratt Graphic Art Center, New York.
First one-man exhbn. Lima 59, subsequently at Toronto, New York, Washington, D.C., Panama, Bogotá, Detroit, Caracas, Mexico City; Group exhbns. all over N. and S. America and in Europe; numerous awards for painting in the Americas including Carnegie Int. 64, and award at Arte de América y España Exhbn., Madrid.
32 West 82nd St. (3B), New York, N.Y. 10024, U.S.A.
Telephone: 799-2539.

Morales, Bermúdez, Gen. Francisco; Peruvian army officer and politician; b. 4 Oct. 1921, Lima; grandson of the late Col. Remiro Morales (President of Peru, 1890-94); m. Rosa Pedraglio de Morales Bermúdez; four s. one d.; ed. Chorillos Mil. School.
Founder mem. Dept. of Research and Devt., Army Gen. Staff; taught at School of Eng. and at Army Acad. of War; Chief of Staff of First Light Div., Tumbes; Asst. Dir. of Logistics, Dir. of Econ., War Ministry; advanced courses at Superior Acad. of War, Argentina, and Centre for Higher Mil. Studies, Peru; appointed to reorganize electoral registration system 62; Minister of Econ. and Finance 68-74; Chief of Army

Gen. Staff 74-75; Prime Minister, Minister of War and Commdr.-Gen. of Army Feb.-Aug. 75; Pres. of Peru Aug. 75-.
Oficina del Presidente, Lima, Peru.

Moran, 1st Baron, cr. 43, of Manton; **Charles McMoran Wilson**, Kt., M.C., M.D., F.R.C.P.; British physician; b. Skipton, Yorkshire; s. of W. John Forsythe Wilson; m. Dorothy Dufton 1919; two s.
Medical Officer 1st Battn. Royal Fusiliers 14-17; Medical Officer in charge Medical Side 7th Stationary Hospital Boulogne 17-18; Dean St. Mary's Hospital Medical School 20-45; Pres. Royal Coll. of Physicians 41-50; Consulting Physician St. Mary's Hospital; Hon. Fellow, Australasian Coll. of Physicians; Fellow, American Coll. of Physicians; Chair. Advisory Cttee. on Distinction Awards for Consultants; mem. Senate and Hon. Sec. Faculty of Medicine, Univ. of London.
Publs. *The Anatomy of Courage* 45, *Winston Churchill* 66.
Newton Valence Manor, nr. Alton, Hants., England.

Moran, Michael; Irish lawyer and politician; b. 25 Dec. 1912, Castlebar, Co. Mayo; s. of Brian Moran and Helen Rowland; m. Máiréad Ní Suibhne 1949; two s. one d.; ed. St. Gerald's Coll., Castlebar, and Univ. Coll., Dublin.
Admitted Solicitor 33; mem. Mayo County Council 38-57; Chair. County Mayo Cttee. of Agriculture for number of years; T.D. South Mayo 38-; Minister for the Gaeltacht 57-59, 61-68; Minister for Lands 59-68; Minister of Justice 68-May 70; Fianna Fáil.
Leisure interests: shooting, hunting, fishing.
Ellison Street, Castlebar, Co. Mayo, Ireland.
Telephone: Castlebar 42.

Morand, Paul; French diplomat and novelist; b. 13 March 1889, Paris; m. 1927; one stepson; ed. Univs. of Paris and Oxford.
Former Sec. of French Embassies in London 13, Rome 17 and Madrid 18; Chargé d'Affaires in Siam 25; fmr. Dir. of French Works Abroad at Ministry of Foreign Affairs; Liaison Officer British Ministry of Economic Warfare and French Ministry of Blockade 39-40; Minister Plen. in London July 40, Bucharest 43; Amb. at Berne 44; Officier, Légion d'Honneur; mem. Académie Française.
Publs. Novels: *Lewis et Irène* 24, *Bouddha vivant* 27, *L'Homme pressé* 41, *Le Flagellant de Séville* 51, *Hécale et ses chiens* 55, *Tais-toi* 65; Short stories: *Tendres Stocks* 21, *Ouvert la nuit* 22, *Fermé la nuit* 23, *L'Europe galante* 25, *Magie noire* 28, *La Folle amoureuse* 56, *Fin de siècle* 57; Essays: *New York* 30, *London* 33, *Le nouvel Londres* 63; Memoirs: *Journal d'un attaché d'ambassade* 47, *Bains de mer, bains de rêve* 60, *Venises* 71; History: *Fouquet ou le soleil offusqué* 61, *La Dame Blanche des Habsbourg* 63, *Ci-gît Sophie-Dorothée de Celle*; Literary essays: *Mon plaisir . . . en littérature* 68, *Mon plaisir . . . en histoire* 69, *Venises* 73, *Les écarts amoureux* 74.
Château de l'Aile, Vevey, Switzerland.

Morandi, Luigi, B.SC.; Italian chemical executive; b. 15 May 1898, Milan.
Technical Manager Montecatini Co., Milan 39-43; Gen. Manager 45-46, Man. Dir. 46-49, Vice-Pres. 49- (now Montecatini-Edison); Pres. Lombard Section, Italian Chemical Soc. 48; Pres. Board of Dirs. State Technical Inst. for Industrial Chemical Experts "Ettore Molinari", Milan 48-64; Pres. Fed. of Scientific and Technical Socs. of Milan 50; Vice-Pres. Gen. Council Società Chimica Italiana (Pres. Lombard Section) 48; OECD Expert for Examination of Science Policy in France 64; mem. Lombard Inst., Acad. of Sciences and Arts 50; Nat. mem. Accademia Pugliese delle Scienze 64; Officier, Légion d'Honneur.
Publs. *I Funghi* (Mushrooms) 54, *Viaggio di un*

tecnico curioso nella civiltà sovietica (Journey of an Interested Technologist to the Soviet Union) 61.
Montecatini-Edison S.p.a., Largo Donegani 1/2, Milan, Italy.

Moravia, Alberto; Italian writer and journalist; b. 28 Nov. 1907.
Pres. Int. PEN 59.
Publs. novels: *Gli indifferenti* 29, *Le Ambizioni Sbagliate* 35, *La Mascherata* 41, *Agostino* 44, *La Romana* 47, *La Disubbidienza* 48, *L'Amore Coniugale* 49, *Il Conformista* 51, *Il disprezzo* 54, *La Ciociara* 57, *La noia* 61, *L'Attenzione* 65; plays: *Teatro* 58, *Beatrice Cenci* 65, *Il mondo è quello che è* 66, *Il dio Kurt* 67, *La Vita è Gioco* 70; short stories: *La bella vita* 35, *L'Imbroglio* 37, *I Sogni del Pigro* 40, *L'Amante infelice* 43, *L'Epidemia* 45, *Due Cortigiane* 45, *Racconti Romani* 45, *I Racconti* 54, *Nuovi Racconti Romani* 59, *L'Automa* 63, *Una cosa è una cosa* 66, *Il Paradiso* 70, *Io e lui* 71, *Un' altra Vita* 73; essays: *La speranza, L'Uomo, Come fine* 65, *A quale tribù appartieni* 74; travel: *La rivoluzione culturale in Cina* 67.
Lungotevere della Vittoria 1, Rome, Italy.
Telephone: 378836.

More, Kenneth (Gilbert), C.B.E.; British actor; b. 20 Sept. 1914, Gerrards Cross, Bucks.; s. of Charles Gilbert More and Edith Winifred (née Watkins); m. 1st Beryl Johnstone 1940 (dissolved); m. 2nd Mabel E. Barkby 1952 (dissolved), one d.; m. 3rd Angela J. Douglas 1968; ed. Victoria Coll., Jersey.
First stage appearance at Windmill Theatre 36; R.N.V.R. during Second World War; returned to stage in *And no Birds Sing* 46; other stage appearances include *Power Without Glory* 47, *Peace in Our Time* 48, *Out of the Crocodile* 63, *Our Man Crichton* 64, *The Secretary Bird* 68, *The Winslow Boy* 70, *Getting On* 72, *Signs of the Times* 73.
British Film Acad., Best Actor Award 54, Venice Volpi Cup, Best Actor 55, Picturegoer Award.
Films include: *Scott of The Antarctic, Chance of a Lifetime, Genevieve, Doctor in the House, Raising a Riot, The Deep Blue Sea, Reach for the Sky, The Admirable Crichton, Next to no Time, A Night to Remember, The Sheriff of Fractured Jaw, The Thirty Nine Steps, North West Frontier, Sink the Bismarck!, Man in the Moon, The Greengage Summer, The Longest Day, Some People, We Joined the Navy, The Comedy Man, Dark of the Sun, Battle of Britain, Cinderella, Oh! What a Lovely War, Scrooge, The Slipper and the Rose.*
Television appearances include Eurovision Production *Heart to Heart, The Forsyte Saga* 66-67, *Father Brown* 74-75.
Leisure interests: golf, underwater swimming.
Publs. *Happy go Lucky* (autobiog.) 59, *Kindly Leave the Stage* 65.
Bute House, 9 Ladbroke Terrace, London W.11, England.

Moreau, Jeanne; French actress; b. 23 Jan. 1928; ed. Paris.
Stage actress with Comédie Française 48-52; Théâtre National Populaire 53; Pres. Cannes Film Festival July 75; since 54 has appeared in *L'Heure élbouissante, La Machine Infernale, Pygmalion, La Chatte sur un toit brûlant, La Bonne Soupe, La Chevauchée sur le Lac de Constance,* etc.; since 48 acted in numerous films incl.: *Touchez pas au grisbi, Le salaire du péché, Ascenseur pour l'Echafaud, Les Amants, Moderato Cantabile, Les Liaisons dangereuses, Dialogue des Carmélites, Jules et Jim, Eve, The Victors, La Baie des Anges, Peau de Banane, Le Train, Le Journal d'une Femme de Chambre, Mata Hari—H21, The Yellow Rolls-Royce* 64, *Viva Maria* 65, *Mademoiselle* 65, *Chimes at Midnight* 66, *L'Amour à travers les âges* 67, *The Sailor from Gibraltar* 67, *The Bride wore Black* 67, *The Great Catherine* 68, *Le Corps de Diane* 70, *Une*

histoire immortelle, Monte Walsh, Le Petit Théâtre de Jean Renoir, L'Humeur Vagabonde, Comptes a rebours 71, *Chère Louise* 72, *Jeanne, la Française* 72, *Nathalie Granger* 72, *Je t'aime* 73, *Les valseuses* 73, *La Race des Seigneurs* 73, *Pleurs* 74, *Le jardin qui bascule* 74, *Souvenirs d'en France* 74, *Lumière* (also dir.) 76.
9 rue de Cirque, 75008 Paris, France.

Moreau-Néret, Olivier, L. en D., L. ès L.; French banker; b. 29 Jan. 1892.
Inspector of Finances 19; Deputy Dir. Treasury, Ministry of Finance, Head of Mission to London and Washington for discussion of Inter-allied debts 23-26; Hon. Dir. at Ministry of Finance 26; Sec.-Gen. then Dir. of Crédit Lyonnais 26-39; Sec.-Gen. Ministry of Finance 40; Dir.-Gen., later Pres., of Crédit Lyonnais 42-62; Prof. Inst. d'Etudes politiques; mem. of Acad. des Sciences morales et politiques; Grand Officier de la Légion d'Honneur 49; Commdr. Order of Léopold; Croix de Guerre.
Publs. *La Balance des Comptes* 36, *La Bourse* 38, *Les Valeurs Mobilières* 39, *Les Contrôle des Prix* 42, *Les Valeurs Etrangères* 56, *Les Valeurs Françaises depuis 1940* 57.
11 rue Dupont des Loges, 75007 Paris, France.

Moreira, Adriano José Alves, LL.D.; Portuguese university professor and politician; b. 1922, Grijó; s. of António and Leopoldina Moreira; m. Isabel Mónica de Lima Mayer 1968; one s.; ed. Univ. of Lisbon.
Associate Prof., Higher Inst. for Social Sciences (ISOPO) 50-54, Prof. 54-58, Dir. 58-61; Under-Sec. of State for Overseas Affairs 60-61; Minister for Overseas Affairs 61-62; fmr. Head of Lisbon Geographical Soc.; Hon. Pres. Int. Acad. Portuguese Culture, Lisbon; mem. Nat. Educ. Board; mem. Portuguese del. to UN Gen. Assembly 56-59; Plenipotentiary to Geneva Slavery Conf.; Consultative Cttee. of the Overseas Council 57-60; Military Order of Christ; Grand Officer, Order of Prince Henry; Grand Cross, Order of Saint Sylvester; Grand Cross of Catholic Queen; Grand Cross of Southern Cross of Brazil; Grand Cross of Order of Africa; Grand Cross of Order of Christ.
Publs. *The Prison Problem of the Overseas Provinces, Overseas Policy* 56, *Portugal and Article 73 of the United Nations Charter* 57, *International Jurisdiction and the Vote Problem in the United Nations* 58, *Juridical Studies* 60, *The Battle of Hope* 62, *Portuguese Party* 62, *Political Ideologies* 64.
Rua Vieira Lusitano 29, Lisbon, Portugal.
Telephone: 68-47-05.

Morelli, Gaetano, LL.D.; Italian judge and university professor; b. 23 May 1900; ed. Univ. of Rome.
Lecturer in International Law, University of Urbino 27-32; Prof. Univ. of Modena 32-33, Univ. of Padua 33-35, Naples 35-51, Rome 51-; Judge, Int. Court of Justice 61-70; mem. Institut de droit international 50-, First Vice-Pres. 61-63, Pres. 71-73; mem. Perm. Conciliation Comm. between Luxembourg and Switzerland 50-, Higher Council of Public Educ. 51-58, Perm. Court of Arbitration 55-, Italian Nat. Comm. for UNESCO 56-61.
Publs. *La sentenza internazionale* 31, *Diritto processuale civile internazionale* (2nd edn.) 54, *La théorie générale du procès international* 37, *Lezioni di diritto internazionale privato* (2nd edn.) 43, *Nozioni di diritto internazionale* (7th edn.) 67, *Elementi di diritto internazionale privato italiano* (10th edn.) 71, *Studi di diritto processuale civile internazionale* 61, *Studi sul processo internazionale* 63, etc.
Faculty of Law, University of Rome, Rome; and Via Lucrezio Caro 67, Rome, Italy.

Moreno Martínez, Alfonso, LL.D.; Dominican Republic professor and diplomatist; b. 8 Dec. 1922, San Francisco de Macorís; m.; five c.; ed. Univ. of Santo Domingo.
Founder and first Pres. Social Christian Revolutionary Party 61; Pres. Fifth Congress of Christian Dem. Org. of America (ODCA) 69; Prof. of Sociology, Rural Sociology and Introduction to Social Sciences, Autonomous Univ. of Santo Domingo 63-69; Prof. of Sociology and the History of Culture, Pedro Henríquez Ureña Univ. 74-75; Perm. Rep. to UN Feb. 75-.
Permanent Mission of the Dominican Republic to the United Nations, 144 East 44th Street, 4th Floor, New York, N.Y. 10017, U.S.A.

Moreno Valle, Dr. Rafael; Mexican medical officer and politician; b. 23 Aug. 1917; ed. Escuela Médico Militar.
Postgraduate work in various North American hospitals; Prof. of Traumatology and Orthopaedics, Escuela Médico Militar 44-; Rep. for Military Health at national surgeons' assemblies 44-60; Brigadier-Gen. 52; Senator for Puebla State 58-64; Pres. of Senate twice; Pres. of Foreign Affairs Comm., Health Comm., and Perm. Comm., of Congress 62; Political Action Sec. of Nat. Exec. Cttee. of Partido Revolucionario Institucional 62-64; Sec. of State for Health and Public Assistance until 70; mem. Mexican Del., Mexico-N. America Inter-Parl. meetings; mem. Legislators' Comm. which travelled throughout world seeking disarmament and ban on nuclear weapons' tests; Founder-mem. Mexican Orthopaedics Soc.; mem. Latin American Orthopaedics and Traumotology Soc. and various North American acads. and asscns.
c/o Secretaría de Salubridad y Asistencia, Mexico City, Mexico.

Moretti, Marino; Italian writer; b. 18 July 1885.
Novelist, short-story writer, poet; for many years connected with *Corriere della Sera.*
Publs. include *Poesie scritte col lapis* 10, *I Pesci fuor d'acqua* 14, *Il Sole del Sabato* 16, *Poesie scelte* 19, *La voce di Dio* 20, *I puri di cuore* 24, *Il segno della croce* 26, *L'Andreana* 35, *Scrivere non è necessario* 37, *La vedova Fioravanti* 40, *I coniugi Allori* 46, *Il fiocco verde* 48, *Il Pudore* 50, *I grilli di Pazzo Pazzi* 51, *Il Tempo Migliore* 52, *Uomini soli* 54, *1945* 56, *La camera degli Sposi* 58, *Tutte le Novelle* 59, *Il Libro dei Miei Amici* 60, *Romanzi della mia Terra* 61, *Tutti i ricordi* 62, *Anna degli Elefanti* 63, *Romanzi dal primo all'ultimo* 65, *Tutte le poesie* 66, *Romanzi dell 'Amorino* 67, *L'Ultima Estate* 69, *Tre Anni e un Giorno* 71.
Cesenatico (Forlì), Italy.

Morf, Rudolf, PH.D.; Swiss chemist; b. 10 Nov. 1908, Kyburg, Canton Zürich; m. Irène Keller 1932; one s. three d.; ed. Univ. of Zürich and Oxford Univ.
Research chemist, Nestlé Co., later Production Man. of a factory 34-40; Pharmaceutical Dept., Sandoz Ltd., Basle 41-59; with F. Hoffmann-La Roche & Co. Ltd. 59-; Sec.-Gen. XIVth Int. Congress of Pure and Applied Chem. 53-55; Sec.- Gen. of Int. Union of Pure and Applied Chem. (IUPAC) 56; Sec.-Gen. Swiss Acad. of Sciences 65-70.
Office: P.O.B. 165, 8058 Zürich Airport; Home: Kyburg (Canton Zürich), Switzerland.

Morgan, Graham James; American chemical and industrial executive; b. 19 Sept. 1917; ed. Carleton Coll.
U.S. Gypsum Co. 39-, Sales 39-45, management posts 45-49, Gen. Merchandise Dir. 51-53, Vice-Pres. (Merchandising) 53-54, Vice-Pres. and Asst. to Chair. of Board 54-59, Exec. Vice-Pres. 59, Pres. and mem. Exec. Cttee. 60-71, Dir. 58-, Chief Exec. Officer 65-71, Chair. and Chief Exec. Officer 71-; Dir. of numerous other companies.
Home: 1500 North Lake Shore Drive, Chicago, Ill. 60610; Office: United States Gypsum Company, 101 South Wacker Drive, Chicago, Ill. 60606, U.S.A.

Morgan, Lee Laverne, B.S.; American business executive; b. 4 Jan. 1920, Aledo, Ill.; s. of Laverne Morgan and Gladys Hamilton Morgan; m. Mary Harrington 1942; ed. Univ. of Illinois.

Joined Caterpillar Tractor Co., various training, sales and advertising 46-56, Man. Sales Promotion Dept. 56-61, Vice-Pres. 61-65, Dir. 65, Exec. Vice-Pres. 65-72, Pres. 72-; Dir. Commerical Nat. Bank, Cen. Illinois Light Co., First Chicago Corpn. and subsidiary First Nat. Bank of Chicago, Minnesota Mining and Mfg. Co., U.S. Chamber of Commerce, Proctor Community Hosp. of Peoria; Trustee, Monmouth Coll., Ill.
Leisure interests: golf, tennis, travel.
100 NE Adams Street, Peoria, Ill. 61629; Home: 7510 North Edgewild Drive, Peoria, Ill. 61614, U.S.A. Telephone: 309-675-5311 (Office); 309-691-7744 (Home).

Morgan, Michèle (Simone Roussel); French actress; b. 29 Feb. 1920.
Studied with R. Simon (Paris); acted in a large number of films including *Quai des Brumes, Symphonie Pastorale, Fabiola, Les Sepls Péchés Capitaux, Les Orgueilleux, Obsession, Les Grandes Manoeuvres, Marguerite de la Nuit, Marie Antoinette, Si Paris Nous Etait Conté, Le Miroir à Deux Faces, Femmes d'un Eté, Pourquoi Viens-tu si Tard? Les Scélérats, Fortunat, Le Puits aux Trois Vérités, Les Lions sont Lâches, Rencontres, Le Crime Ne Paie Pas, Landru, Constance aux Enfers, Les Yeux cernés, Dis-moi qui tuer, Les Centurions, Benjamin*; Cannes Festival Prize for Best Actress 46; French "Victoire" for Best Actress 46, 48, 50, 52, 55. Publ. *Mes Yeux ont vu* 65.
2 rue Saint Louis en l'Isle, 75004 Paris, France.

Morgan, Sir Morien Bedford, Kt., C.B., M.A., F.R.S., C.ENG., F.R.AE.S.; British aeronautical engineer; b. 20 Dec. 1912, Bridgend, Glam.; s. of late John B. and Edith M. (née Thomas) Morgan; m. Sylvia Axford 1941; three d.; ed. Rutlish School and St. Catharine's Coll., Cambridge.
Apprenticed, Mather & Platt Ltd. 34-35; engaged in aerodynamic research in flight, specializing in stability and control, Royal Aircraft Establishment, Farnborough 35-46, Head of Aero Flight 46-48, Head of Guided Weapons Dept. 48-53, Deputy Dir. 54-59; Scientific Adviser, Air Ministry 59-60; Deputy Controller of Aircraft (Research and Devt.), Ministry of Aviation 60-63; Controller of Aircraft 63-66; Controller of Guided Weapons and Electronics 66-69; Dir. Royal Aircraft Establishment 69-72; Master, Downing Coll., Cambridge 72-; Pres. Royal Aeronautical Soc. 67-68; Silver Medal 57, Gold Medal 71, Busk Prize 72, J. B. Seeley Prize in Aeronautics, Hon. Fellow of St. Catharine's Coll., Cambridge 73.
Leisure interests: music, hill-walking.
The Master's Lodge, Downing College, Cambridge, England.
Telephone: Cambridge 56338.

Morgan, Robert Burren, B.J., LL.B; American lawyer and senator; b. 5 Oct. 1925, Lillington, N.C.; s. of James H. and Alice Morgan; m. Katie Owen; one foster s. two d.; ed. E. Carolina Univ. and Wake Forest Law School.
Member of N.C. State Senate for five terms; Attorney-Gen. N.C. 69-74; U.S. Senator for North Carolina Jan. 75-; Wyman Award 74; Democrat.
Leisure interests: reading, jogging.
Senate Office Building, Washington, D.C. 20510, U.S.A. Telephone: (202) 224-3154.

Morgan, Thomas Ellsworth; American legislator and physician; b. 13 Oct. 1906; ed. Waynesburg Coll., Detroit Coll. of Medicine and Surgery and Wayne Univ., Detroit.
Intern, Grace Hospital, Detroit 33-34; Medical and surgical practice, Fredericktown, Pennsylvania 34-73; mem. U.S. House of Reps. 45-, Chair. Advisory Cttee. on Improving Govt. Org. 49, Chair. Cttee. on Foreign Affairs 59-; Democrat.
U.S. House of Representatives, Washington, D.C., U.S.A.

Morgan, Walter Thomas James, C.B.E., PH.D., D.SC., D.SC.TECH., F.R.I.C., F.R.S.; British biochemist; b. 5 Oct. 1900, London; s. of Walter Morgan and Annie E. James; m. Irene Price 1930; one s. two d.; ed. Univs. of London, Graz, and Zürich.
Grocers' Company Research Student 25-26; Beit Medical Research Fellow 26-28; Biochemist and First Asst. to Serum Dept., Lister Inst., Elstree 29-36; Rockefeller Research Fellow 36-37; mem. of staff of Lister Inst., London 28-, Emer. Prof. of Biochemistry 68-, Dir. 72-; Hon. Sec. Biochemical Soc. 40-45, Biological Council 44-47; mem. Govt. Scientific Advisory Council 55-59; Croonian Lecturer Royal Soc. 59; Vice-Pres. Royal Soc. 61-64; Conway Evans Prize (Royal Soc. and Royal Coll. Physicians) 64, Karl Lansteiner Prize American Asscn. of Blood Banks 67, Paul Ehrlich Prize 68, Royal Medal (Royal Soc.) 68; M.D. h.c. (Basle), D.Sc. h.c. (Mich.); mem. Medical Research Council 66-70.
57 Woodbury Drive, Sutton, Surrey, England.

Morgan, William Wilson, PH.D.; American astronomer; b. 3 Jan. 1906, Bethesda, Tenn.; s. of William T. and Mary W. Morgan; m. 1st Helen M. Barrett 1928 (deceased), 2nd Jean D. Eliot 1966; one s. one d.; ed. Washington and Lee Univ. and Univ. of Chicago.
Managing Editor *The Astrophysical Journal* 47-52; Dir. of Yerkes and McDonald Observatories 60-63; Chair. Dept. of Astronomy, Univ. of Chicago 60-66, Bernard E. and Ellen C. Sunny Distinguished Prof. of Astronomy 66-; mem. Nat. Acad. of Sciences, American Acad. of Arts and Sciences, Pontifical Acad. of Sciences, Royal Danish Acad. of Sciences and Letters, Soc. Royale des Sciences de Liège; Corresp. mem. Nat. Acad. of Sciences of Argentina; Bruce Gold Medal of Astronomical Soc. of the Pacific 58; Ph.D. h.c. (Univ. of Cordoba).
Publs. *An Atlas of Stellar Spectra* (with P. C. Keenan and Edith Kellman) 43; numerous research articles in professional journals.
Yerkes Observatory, Williams Bay, Wis. 53191; Home: Parkhurst Place, Williams Bay, Wis. 53191, U.S.A. Telephone: 414-245-5555 (Office); 414-245-5839 (Home).

Morgens, Howard J(oseph), A.B., M.B.A.; American businessman; b. 16 Oct. 1910; ed. Washington Univ. and Harvard Business School.
With Procter and Gamble Co. 33-, Advertising Man. 46, Vice-Pres. (Advertising) 48, Dir. 50-, Exec. Vice-Pres. 54, Pres. 57-71, Chair. of Board 71-74; Dir. Owens-Corning Fibreglass Corpn., Gen. Motors Corpn., Morgan Guaranty Trust Co. of N.Y., J. P. Morgan Co.; Dir. and fmr. Chair. Advertising Council; Trustee, Washington Univ.; Hon. LL.D. (Washington and Miami Univs. and Univ. of Cincinnati).
c/o Procter and Gamble, Cincinnati, O. 45202, U.S.A.

Morghen, Raffaello; Italian university professor and writer; b. 19 Sept. 1896, Rome; m. Gemma Calisti 1923 (died 1968); two d.; ed. Univ. degli Studi, Rome.
Teacher of History 23-30; Prof. Modern History, Univ. of Rome 30-33; Editor Modern History Section *Enciclopedia Italiana* 32-37; Prof. Medieval History Univ. of Palermo 38-41; Prof. Modern History Univ. of Perugia 42-48; fmr. Prof. Medieval History Univ. of Rome 48-; Chancellor Accad. dei Lincei 27-59; Pres. Italian Medieval Historical Inst. 53-; Foreign Assoc. Institut de France; mem. various academies including Accad. dei Lincei; several honours.
Publs. *Il Tramonto della potenza sveva in Italia* 36, *L'Età degli Svevi in Italia* 74, *Gregorio VII* 39, *Gregorio VII e la Riforma della Chiesa nel secolo XI* 74, *Medioevo cristiano* 51 and 58, *La formazione degli Stati Europei* 59, *L'Idea d'Europa* 60, *Profilo storico della Civiltà Europea* 66, *Repertorium Fontium Medii Aevi* (ed.), Vol. I 62, Vol. II 67, Vol. III 70, Vol. IV 74, *Civiltà medievale al tramonto* 74.
Istituto Storico Italiano per il Medio Evo, Piazza dell 'Orologio 4, 00186 Rome, Italy.

Mori, Haruki; Japanese diplomatist; b. 1911; m. Tsutako Masaki 1940; ed. Univ. of Tokyo.
Ministry of Foreign Affairs, served U.S.A. and Philippines 35-41; Head of Econ. Section, Dept. of Political Affairs 50-53; Counsellor Rome 53-55; Counsellor Asian Affairs Bureau, Tokyo 55-56; Private Sec. to Prime Minister 56-57; Deputy Dir.-Gen. Econ. Affairs Bureau 57; Dir.-Gen. of American Affairs Bureau 57-60; Minister to U.K. 60-63, to France 63-64; Amb. to OECD 64-67; Deputy Vice-Minister for Foreign Affairs 67-70, Vice-Minister 70-72; Amb. to U.K. 72-75.
Ministry of Foreign Affairs, Tokyo, Japan.

Morice, André; French politician; b. 11 Oct. 1900; ed. Nantes Lycée and Univ. of Paris.
In business 31-39; served army 39-44; Town Councillor for Nantes 45-, Asst. to Mayor 45-47; Deputy for Loire Inférieure 45-58; Under-Sec. for Technical Education, Schuman Govt. 47-48, Marie Govt. 48; Sec. of State for Technical Education and Sports in Queuille Govt. 49, Bidault Govt. 49-50, Pleven Govt. 50-51, Queuille Govt. 51; Minister of Nat. Education, Queuille Govt. July 51; Minister of the Merchant Marine, Pleven Govt. 51-52, Faure Govt. 52; Minister of Public Works, Travel and Tourism, Pinay Govt. 52 and Mayer Govt. 53; Dir. *Eclair de l'Ouest* 54; Minister of Industry and Commerce, Faure Govt. 55-56; Minister of Nat. Defence 57-58; Mayor of Nantes 65-; Senator for Loire-Atlantique 65-; Pres. Asscn. Française pour la Promotion du Travail, Mouvement Libéral pour l'Europe Unie; Croix de Guerre; Chevalier Légion d'Honneur.
Le Sénat, 75006 Paris; Home: 13 boulevard Raspail, 75007 Paris, France.

Morimoto, Kanzaburo; Japanese business executive; b. 13 Dec. 1892; ed. Kyoto Univ.
Takeda Chemical Industries Ltd. 19-, Statutory Auditor 25-33, Dir. 33-38, Man. Dir. 38-47, Senior Man. Dir. 47-60, Vice-Pres. 60-63, Chair. of Board of Dirs. 63-73, Advisory Councillor 73-; Pres. Daiwa Real Estate Co. Ltd. 57-; Yellow Ribbon Medal 63.
Takeda Chemical Industries, 2-27 Doshomachi, Higashi-ku, Osaka, Japan.

Morin, Jean, L. EN DR.; French civil servant; b. 23 June 1916, Melun; m. Janine Lamourouy 1942; one s. two d.; ed. Ecole Libre des Sciences Politiques.
Secretary General Inst. Scientifique des Recherches Economiques et Sociales 39; Auditeur, Cour des Comptes 41; Dir. of Personnel, Ministry of the Interior 44; Prefect, Manche 46; Dep. Dir. du Cabinet to Pres. of Provisional Govt. 46, to Minister of Foreign Affairs 47-48; Technical Adviser, Minister of the Interior 48-49; Prefect, Maine-et-Loire 49; Conseiller Référendaire, Cour des Comptes 49; Prefect, Haute-Garonne and Extraordinary Insp. Gen. of Admin. (5th Region) 58-60; Del.-Gen. in Algeria 60-62; Sec.-Gen. of Merchant Navy 62-68; Pres. Société auxiliaire minière du Pacifique (Saumipac) 68-72; Pres. Compagnie française industrielle et minière du Pacifique 69-72; Admin. Publicis S.A. 70-, Vice-Pres. 72-, Admin. Publicis Conseil 70-; Pres. Communication et Publicité 72-, Intermarco 74-; Pres., Dir.-Gen. Régie-Presse 74-; Commdr. Légion d'Honneur, Croix de Guerre, Médaille de la Résistance.
Leisure interest: bridge.
133 avenue des Champs-Elysées, 75008 Paris; 107 avenue Henri-Martin, 75016 Paris, France.

Morinaga, Teiichiro; Japanese financier; b. 9 Sept. 1910, Miyazaki Prefecture; s. of Sadauemon Morinaga and Nobu Kishita; m. Takako Tawara 1936; one s. one d.; ed. Tokyo Imperial Univ.
Ministry of Finance 32-59, Deputy Vice-Minister of Finance 49-53, Dir. Budget Bureau 53-57, Admin. Vice-Minister of Finance 57-59; Pres. Small Business Finance Corpn. 61-62; Gov. The Export-Import Bank of Japan 62-67; Pres. Tokyo Stock Exchange 67-74; Gov. The Bank of Japan 74-.

The Bank of Japan, 2-2-1 Hongokucho, Nihonbashi, Chuo-ku, Tokyo; Home: 6-23-18 Honkomagome, Bunkyo-ku, Tokyo, Japan.

Morinigo, Gen. Higinio; Paraguayan officer and politician; b. 1897, Paraguari; ed. Nat. Coll. Asunción and Military School.
2nd Lieut. 19, served Northern Operational Dept. and 2nd and 3rd Infantry Regts. to 28; Capt. 27; War Coll., apptd. Staff Major; Battn. Commdt. Military School 32; Dir. Reserve School; served Chaco War; fmr. Chief of Staff to Commdr.-in-Chief, Ministry of War and Marine and Ministry of Interior; General 43; Pres. of Republic 40-June 48; exiled in Argentina 48-51, Brazil 51-56; returned to Paraguay 56, now living in Argentina; Cruz del Chaco, Cruz del Defensor and many other decorations; Dr. h.c. Fordham and Brazil Univs.
Calle General Urguiza 625-Acassuso, Buenos Aires, Argentina.
Telephone: 792-4823.

Morison, Samuel Eliot, D.LITT.; American Rear-Admiral (retd.) and historian; b. 9 July 1887, Boston, Mass.; m. Priscilla Barton 1949; ed. Harvard Univ. and Ecole Libre des Sciences Politiques, Paris.
Harmsworth Prof. of American History, Oxford 22-25; Trumbull Prof. of American History, Harvard 25-55; served with U.S.N.R. during World War II; Fellow American Philosophical Society, British Academy; Pulitzer Prizes for *Admiral of the Ocean Sea* and *John Paul Jones*; Legion of Merit with Combat Clasp, Balzan Award in History 63, Medal of Freedom 64.
Publs. *Life of Harrison Gray Otis* 13, *Maritime History of Massachusetts* 21, *Oxford History of the U.S.* 27, *Builders of Bay Colony* 30, *Tercentennial History of Harvard Univ.* (5 vols.) 30-36, *Puritan Pronaos* 36, *Growth of the American Republic* (with Henry Steele Commager) 42, *Admiral of the Ocean Sea* 42, *History of U.S. Naval Operations in World War II* (15 vols.) 46-62, *By Land and Sea* 53, *Christopher Columbus, Mariner* 55, *Freedom in Contemporary Society* 56, *The Story of the "Old Colony" of New Plymouth* 56, *Strategy and Compromise* 58, *John Paul Jones: a Sailor's Biography* 59, *One Boy's Boston* 62, *Journals and Other Documents of Columbus* 63, *The Two-Ocean War* 63, *Vistas of History* 64, *The Caribbean as Columbus Saw It* 64, *The Oxford History of the American People* 65, *Spring Tides* 65, *Old Bruin: the life of Commodore Matthew C. Perry, U.S.N.* 67, *Harrison Gray Otis 1765-1848, Urbane Federalist* 69, *European Discovery of America I: The Northern Voyages A.D. 500-1600* 71, *Samuel de Champlain, Father of New France* 72, *European Discovery of America II: The Southern Voyages 1492-1616* 74.
[*Died 15 May 1976*].

Morita, Akio; Japanese business executive; b. 26 Jan. 1921, Nagoya; s. of S. Kyuzaemon and Shuko (Toda) Morita; m. Yoshiko Kamei 1950; two s. one d.; ed. Osaka Imperial Univ.
Co-Founder, SONY Corpn., Tokyo 46, Exec. Man. Dir. 58-59, Exec. Vice-Pres. 59-71, Pres. 71-; Pres. SONY Corpn., America 60-66, Chair. of Board 66-74, also Pres. 68-71; Chair. Exec. Cttee. SONY Corpn. of America; Dir. IBM World Trade Americas (Far East Corpn.); mem. Int. Council, Morgan Guaranty Trust Co., Rockefeller Univ. Council; Edwardo Rihan Award for Int. Marketing 69.
Leisure interests: listening to music, playing golf.
Publs. *Gakureki Muyouron* 66, *Shin Zitsuryoku Shugi* 69.
SONY Corporation, 7-35, Kitashinagawa 6-chome, Shinagawa-ku, Tokyo, Japan.
Telephone: 03-448-2002.

Moriyama, Kinji; Japanese politician; b. 10 Jan. 1917, Tochigi Pref.; s. of Kunio and Hatsue Moriyama; m. Mayumi Furukawa 1949; two d.; ed. Tokyo Univ.
Served in Ministry of Foreign Affairs; mem. House of

Reps. 49-; Pres. Japan Camera Inspection Inst. 54-;
Parl. Vice-Minister of Posts and Telecommunications
60-; Chair. of Labour and Welfare Cttee. 58-, 71-;
Chair. Construction Cttee. of House of Reps. 65-;
Minister of State in charge of Science and Technology
73-74.
Leisure interests: golf, philately.
13-2, Hanegi-cho, 1-chome, Setagaya-ku, Tokyo 156,
Japan.

Morley, Grace L. McCann, M.A., D. DE L'UNIV.
DE PARIS; American art historian and museum director;
b. 3 Nov. 1900; ed. Calif., Paris, Grenoble and Harvard
Univs.
Instr. in French, later in History of Art, Goucher Coll.,
Baltimore 27-30; Curator, Cincinnati Art Museum 30-33;
Dir. San Francisco Museum of Art 35-60; Asst. Dir.
Soloman R. Guggenheim Museum 59-60; Dir. Nat. Mus.
of India 60-66; Head ICOM Regional Agency in Asia
67-; Pacific House Golden Gate Int. Exposition, San
Francisco 40; Advisory Cttee. on Art, State Dept. Div.
of Cultural Relations 41-44; Pres. Western Asscn. of
Art Museum Dirs. 39-40; mem. American Asscn. Art
Museum Dirs., Vice-Pres. 52-53, Pres. 54-55; mem.
American Fed. of Arts, Vice-Pres. 39-51; Pres.
Western Museums Conf. 46-48; mem. American
Asscn. of Museums, College Art Asscn., Int. Council
Museums of G.B.; Fellow, Royal Soc. of Arts, Museum
Asscn. of India; mem. U.S. Nat. Comm. for UNESCO
50-55; Editorial Board *UNESCO Museum*; Museums
Consultant to UNESCO 46 and 52; Head of Museums
UNESCO, Paris 47-49; Dir. UNESCO Int. Seminar on
Museums and Education, Athens 54; Pres. Museums
Asscn. of India 62-66; Vice-Chair. Govt. of India Central
Advisory Board of Museums, Adviser on Museums,
Ministry of Educ. (India) 66-; Watumull Award, India
62; Chevalier de la Légion d'Honneur 49; Hon. D.F.A.,
Hon. LL.D., Hon. D.Hum.Litt.
ICOM Agency, 3/4 Sapru House Annexe, New Delhi 1,
India.

Morley, Robert, C.B.E.; British actor and dramatist;
b. 26 May 1908; ed. Wellington Coll.
First London appearance in *Treasure Island*, Strand
Theatre 29; first appearance in N.Y. 38; appeared in
provinces and established repertory company with
Peter Bull at Perranporth, Cornwall; has appeared in
the plays *The Great Romancer, Pygmalion, The Man
Who Came to Dinner, The First Gentleman, Edward My
Son, The Little Hut, Hippo Dancing, A Likely Tale,
Fanny, Halfway Up the Tree, How the Other Half Loves*
70, *A Ghost on Tiptoe* (also co-author with Rosemary
Anne Sisson) 74, etc.; dir. *The Tunnel of Love* 57, *Once
More with Feeling* 59; films since 37 include *Marie Antoi-
nette, Major Barbara, Young Mr. Pitt, The Outcast of the
Islands, The African Queen, Beat the Devil, Loser Takes
All, Law and Disorder, The Journey, The Doctor's
Dilemma, Libel, The Battle of the Sexes, Oscar Wilde,
Those Magnificent Men in their Flying Machines, The
Loved One, The Alphabet Murders, Sinful Davey, Hot
Millions, Song of Norway, Cromwell, When Eight Bells
Toll, Theatre of Blood, Murder at the Gallop, Great
Expectations.*
Publs. *Goodness How Sad* 37, *Staff Dance* 44, *Edward
My Son* (with Noel Langley) 48, *The Full Treatment*
(with Ronald Gow) 52, *Hippo Dancing* 54, *Six Months
Grace* (with D. Hamilton) 57, *Robert Morley: Respon-
sible Gentleman* (with Sewell Stokes) 66, *A Musing
Morley* 74.
Fairmans, Wargrave, Berkshire, England.

Moro, Aldo; Italian lawyer and politician; b. 23 Sept.
1916; ed. Bari Univ.
Former Pres. of Federazione Universitaria Cattolica
Italiana and of Movement of Catholic Graduates; mem.
Constituent Assembly and of Co-ordination Cttee. of 18
for drafting of new Constitution; re-elected 48 and 53;

Under-Sec. of State Foreign Affairs 49; Pres. Christian
Democrat Parl. Group in the Chamber of Deputies 53-
55; Minister of Justice 55-57, of Education 57-59;
Political Sec. Christian Democrat Party 59-63; Prime
Minister 63-68, concurrently Minister of Foreign
Affairs Dec. 65-Feb. 66; Minister of Foreign Affairs
69-72, 73-74; Prime Minister Nov. 74-.
Publs. *La capacità giuridica penale* 39, *Lo Stato* 43,
L'Antigiuridicità 47, *Unità e pluralità di reati* 51.
Office of the Prime Minister, Rome; Piazza del Gesu 46,
Rome, Italy.

Moro, Vincenzo; Italian industrial executive; b. 26
Jan. 1922, Sartirana Lomellina, Pavia; s. of Paolo Moro
and Carmelita Gei; m. Gianna Tagliabue 1948; one s.
one d.
With Naclon Farmaceutici 37; joined Filotecnica
Salmoiraghi 39, Sales Dir. 54-59; Deputy Dir. Alfa
Romeo S.p.A. 59, Special Affairs Dir. 60, Sales Dir. 62,
Deputy Gen. Man. 69, Man. Dir. and Gen. Man. 74-;
Chair. Autodelta S.p.A.
Alfa Romeo S.p.A., Via Gattamelata 45, Milan, Italy.
Telephone: (02) 93391.

Moross, Manfred David, B.SC., M.B.A.; South African
business executive; b. 30 Aug. 1931; m. Edna Jacobson
1956; three s. one d.; ed. Witwatersrand and Harvard
Univs.
Chair. Schlesinger Ltd., Schlesinger European Invest-
ments Ltd., Trident Gen. Insurance Co. Ltd., Trident
Life Assurance Co. Ltd., U.K. Property Co. Ltd.,
Portman Estates Ltd.; Dir. Rand Selection Corpn. Ltd.,
S.A. Eagle Insurance Co. Ltd.
Leisure interests: tennis, reading.
P.O. Box 1182, Johannesburg, South Africa.

Morozov, Platon Dmitrievich, D.IUR.; Soviet lawyer
and diplomatist; b. 1906, Leningrad; ed. Leningrad
Law Inst.
Practised as Barrister and held high posts in office of
Procurator of the U.S.S.R. until 49; Diplomatic Service
49-70, Deputy Chief, Treaty and Legal Dept. of Min. of
Foreign Affairs 49-60; U.S.S.R. Rep. on UN Comm. for
Human Rights and Del. to numerous Sessions of UN
Gen. Assembly 51-68; Deputy Rep. of U.S.S.R. on
Security Council of UN and Deputy Perm. Rep. to UN
60-68; Judge, Int. Court of Justice, The Hague 70-;
mem. of U.S.S.R. Del. at Int. War Tribunal, Tokyo 46;
Rep. of U.S.S.R. on UN Special Cttee. for the Prepara-
tion of the Convention on Prevention and Punishment
of the Crime of Genocide; numerous other UN missions.
Publs. Works and articles on legal questions.
International Court of Justice, Peace Palace, The
Hague 2012, Netherlands.

Morrey, Charles Bradfield, Jr., PH.D.; American
mathematician; b. 23 July 1907, Columbus, Ohio; s. of
Charles Bradfield and Grace (Jones) Morrey; m.
Frances E(leanor) Moss 1937; three s. one d.; ed. Ohio
State Univ.
Member of Faculty, Univ. of Calif. at Berkeley 33,
Prof. of Mathematics 45-73, Chair. of Dept. 49-54, 57-58;
Mathematician Aberdeen Proving Ground 42-45; Nat.
Research Council Fellow 31-33; mem. Nat. Acad. of
Sciences, American Mathematical Soc. (Pres. 67-68),
American Acad. of Arts and Sciences.
Publs. *University Calculus* 62, *First Course in Calculus*
(with Murray H. Protter) 64, *Modern Mathematical
Analysis* (with Murray H. Protter) 64, *Multiple Inte-
grals in the Calculus of Variations* 66, *Analytic Geometry*
66, *Calculus for College Students* 67; also research articles.
210 Yale Avenue, Berkeley, Calif. 94708, U.S.A.

Morrill, James Lewis, A.B.; American educator; b.
24 Sept. 1891, Marion, Ohio; s. of Harrison Delmont
and Mary Lewis Morrill; m. Freda Rhodes 1915; one
s. two d.; ed. Ohio State Univ.
Newspaperman 13-19; Exec. Sec. U.S. Food Admin. in

Ohio and Ohio Branch, Council of Nat. Defence 17-19; Alumni Sec. and Ed. Ohio State Univ. 19-28; Instructor in Journalism and Educ. 25-29; Junior Dean Coll. of Educ. 28-32 and Vice-Pres. 32-41; Pres. Univ. of Wyoming 42-45, Univ. of Minnesota 45-60; Pres. Asscn. Land Grant Coll. and State Univs. 47-48, Chair. Nat. Defence Cttee. 52-54, mem. 55-57, mem. Cttee. on Govt. Controls of Higher Education 57-58, Chair. 59; Chair. American Council on Education 50-51, Chair., Cttee. on Relationships of Higher Education to Fed. Govt. 51-56; mem. Comm. on Education and Int. Affairs 57-59; Consultant Co-ordination of Exchange of Persons Programmes of Int. Educational Exchange Service and Int. Co-operation Administration, Dept. of State 55-56; Vice-Pres. Asscn. of American Univs. 52-54, Pres. 54-56; Pres. Nat. Asscn. of State Univs. 57-58; mem. Board of Trustees Inst. of Int. Education 57-60; mem. Board of Dirs. Educational Facilities Laboratory (Ford Foundation) 57-; Chair. Ford Foundation Cttee. on the Univ. and World Affairs 59-60; Hon. LL.D. (Miami, Ohio State, Wyoming, Cincinnati and North-western Univs., Univs. of Exeter (England) and Calif. at Los Angeles, Carleton and Macalester Colls., Iowa State Coll., Michigan State Univ., Wisconsin, Minnesota and Hamline Univs.), L.H.D. (Muhlenburg Coll.); Commdr. Royal Order of North Star (Sweden) 56.
1752 Ardleigh Road, Columbus, Ohio 43221, U.S.A.
Telephone: 451-6749.

Morris, Benjamin Stephen, B.SC., M.ED.; British edu-cationist and psychologist; b. 25 May 1910, Sherborne, Dorset; s. of Rev. Benjamin Stephen and Annie (McNicol) Morris; m. Margaret Lamont 1938; two s. one d.; ed. Rothesay Acad., Isle of Bute, and Univ. of Glasgow.
Asst. Master Glasgow schools 36-38; Lecturer in Psy-chology, Logic and Ethics, Jordanhill Training Coll., Glasgow 39-40, in Education, Univ. of Glasgow 40-46; Statistical and Intelligence Officer, Ministry of Food 41-42; Research Psychologist, War Office Selection Boards 42-45, Senior Psychologist (Lt.-Col.) 45; Senior Staff, Tavistock Inst. of Human Relations 46-50 and Chair. Management Cttee. 47-48; Dir. Nat. Foundation for Educational Research in England and Wales 50-56; Prof. of Education, Univ. of Bristol 56-75, Emer. Prof. 75-, Dir. Inst. of Educ. 56-68, Dir. Div. of Advanced Studies and Higher Degrees, Univ. of Bristol, School of Education 68-75.
Leisure interests: music, theatre, living in the country.
Bracken Hill, Wrington, Bristol, BS18 7PN, England.
Telephone: Wrington 862261.

Morris, Brewster Hillard, B.S., B.A., B.LITT.; American diplomatist; b. 7 Feb. 1909, Bryn Mawr, Pa.; s. of George L. and Fanny S. (Hilliard) Morris; m. Ellen Downes 1948; ed. Haverford Coll. and Oxford Univ.
Vice-Consul Montreal 36, Vienna 38, Dresden 39, Berlin 40-41; Third Sec. Berlin 40-42; Third Sec. and Vice-Consul Stockholm 42-43, Second Sec. 44; Sec. Office of U.S. Political Adviser on German Affairs, Supreme H.Q., A.E.F. 44-48; First Sec. and Consul Moscow 48, Counsellor 49; attached to Nat. War Coll. 51; Dir. Office of German Political Affairs, State Dept. 52; in charge of political affairs, Office of German Affairs 53; Foreign Service Insp. 54-56, Senior Insp. 56; Political Counsellor London 57, Consul Gen. 58; Counsellor Bonn 60, Minister and Consul Gen. 61-63; Ambassador to Chad 63-67; Minister to Berlin 67-71; retd.
Leisure interests: tennis, sailing, music.
430 Ridge Road, Tiburon, Calif. 94920, U.S.A.

Morris, Desmond John, B.SC., D.PHIL.; British zoologist; b. 24 Jan. 1928, Purton, Wilts.; s. of Capt. Harry Howe Morris and Marjorie (née Hunt); m. Ramona Joy Baulch 1952; one s.; ed. Dauntsey's School, Wilts., Birmingham Univ. and Oxford Univ.
Head of Granada TV and Film Unit at Zoological Soc.

of London 56-59; Curator of Mammals at Zoological Soc. of London 59-67; Dir. Inst. of Contemporary Arts, London 67-68; now Research Fellow at Wolfson Coll., Oxford and privately engaged in writing books on animal and human behaviour.
Publs. *The Ten-spined Stickleback* 58, *The Biology of Art* 62, *The Mammals: A Guide to the Living Species* 65, *Men and Snakes* (with Ramona Morris) 65, *Men and Apes* (with Ramona Morris) 66, *Men and Pandas* (with Ramona Morris) 66, *Primate Ethology* (Editor) 67, *The Naked Ape* 67, *The Human Zoo* 69, *Patterns of Reproductive Behaviour* 70, *Intimate Behaviour* 71.
Leisure interests: painting and archaeology.
Wolfson College, Oxford, England.
Telephone: (0865) 53085.

Morris, James (Humphrey) (see Morris, Jan).

Morris, Jan, F.R.S.L.; British writer; b. 2 Oct. 1926. Editorial staff *The Times* 51-56, Editorial staff *The Guardian* 57-62; Commonwealth Fellowship, U.S.A. 54; George Polk Memorial Award for Journalism (U.S.A.) 61; Heinemann Award for Literature 61.
Publs. as James Morris, *Coast to Coast* 56, *Sultan in Oman* 57, *The Market of Seleukia* 57, *Coronation Everest* 58, *South African Winter* 58, *The Hashemite Kings* 59, *Venice* 60, *The Upstairs Donkey* (for children) 62, *The Road to Huddersfield* 63, *Cities* 63, *The Presence of Spain* 64, *Oxford* 65, *Pax Britannica* 68, *The Great Port* 70, *Places* 72, *Heaven's Command* 73; as Jan Morris, *Conundrum* 74, *Travels* 76.
Trefan Bach, Fforest, Abergavenny, Gwent, Wales; 9 Marlborough Buildings, Bath, Somerset, England.

Morris, John, C.B.E., M.A., M.SC.; British author and broadcaster; b. 27 Aug. 1895, Gravesend, Kent; s. of late Frank and Julia Morris; ed. King's Coll., Cam-bridge.
Served in Regular Army (3rd Q.A.O. Gurkha Rifles) 15-33; William Wyse Student, Univ. of Cambridge 34-37; Prof. of English, Keio Univ., Tokyo 38-42; Talks Producer, B.B.C. Eastern Service 43, Head of B.B.C. Far Eastern Service 44-52; Controller, B.B.C. Third Programme Dec. 52-58; mem. Mount Everest Expedi-tions 22 and 36; Murchison Memorial Award, Royal Geo-graphical Society, for explorations in Central Asia 29.
Leisure interests: music, reading.
Publs. *Living with Lepchas* 38, *Traveller from Tokyo* 43, *The Phoenix Cup* 47, *From the Third Programme* (Editor) 56, *Hired to Kill* 60, *A Winter in Nepal* 63, *Eating the Indian Air* 68.
21 Friday Street, Henley-on-Thames, Oxon., England.
Telephone: 049-12-4369.

Morris, Rt. Hon. John, P.C., Q.C., M.P.; British barris-ter and politician; b. 5 Nov. 1931, Aberystwyth; s. of the late D. W. Morris; m. Margaret M. Morris 1959; three d.; ed. Ardwyn, Aberystwyth, Univ. Coll. of Wales, Aberystwyth, Gonville and Caius Coll., Cam-bridge, and Acad. of Int. Law, The Hague.
Commissioned Royal Welch Fusiliers and Welch Regt.; Called to Bar, Gray's Inn 54; Labour M.P. for Aberavon Oct. 59-; Parl. Sec. Ministry of Power 64-66; Joint Parl. Sec. Ministry of Transport 66-68; Minister of Defence for Equipment 68-70; Sec. of State for Wales 74-; fmr. Deputy Gen. Sec. and Legal Adviser, Farmers' Union of Wales; mem. U.K. Del., Consultative Assem-bly, Council of Europe and Western European Union 63-64; Chair. Nat. Pneumoconiosis Joint Cttee. 64-66, Nat. Road Safety Advisory Council 67-68, Joint Review of Finances and Management, British Railways 66-67; mem. North Atlantic Ass. 70-74; mem. Courts of Univ. Colls., Aberystwyth, Swansea and Cardiff.
Leisure interest: agriculture.
Welsh Office, Gwydyr House, Whitehall, London, SW1A 2ER; and House of Commons, London, S.W.1 England.

Morris, Sir Philip Robert, K.C.M.G., C.B.E., M.A., LL.D.; British educationist; b. 6 July 1901, Hildenborough, Kent; s. of M. Charles and Jane Morris (née Brazier); m. Florence Redvers Davis (née Green) 1926; two s. one d.; ed. Tonbridge School, St. Peter's, York, and Trinity Coll., Oxford.
Lecturer in History and Classics Westminster Training Coll. 23-25; Admin. officer Kent Education Cttee., Asst. Dir. 32, Dir. 38-44; Educational Adviser H.M. Prisons 38-44; Dir.-Gen. of Army Education 44-46; Vice-Chancellor Univ. of Bristol 46-66; Vice-Chair. British Council 46-59; Chair. Secondary School Exams. Council 48-51; National Advisory Council on Training and Supply of Teachers 47-59; Life Trustees Carnegie U.K. Trust; Chair. B.B.C. West Regional Advisory Council 47-52, Vice-Chair. 61-68; Gov. of B.B.C. 52-60 (Vice-Chair. 54-60); Chair. Management Cttee. Theatre Royal Bristol 46-63, Cttee. of Vice-Chancellors and Principals of the Univs. of the United Kingdom 55-58; Chair. Bristol Old Vic Trust Ltd. 63-71, Pres. 71-; mem. Exec. Council Asscn. of Commonwealth Univs., Vice-Chair. 51-55; Pres. Library Asscn. 55; Vice-Chair. United Bristol Hospital Board 48-66; Chair. Commonwealth Educ. Conf. 59, Commonwealth Educ. Liaison Cttee. 59-62; Hon. F.R.C.S., Hon. A.R.C.V.S.
Bryncoedifor Vicarage, Rhydymain, Gwynedd, LL40 2AN, Wales.
Telephone: Rhyd 237.

Morris, Willie, B.A., M.A.; American editor and writer; b. 29 Nov. 1934, Jackson, Miss.; s. of Henry Rae and Marian Weaks Morris; m. Celia Buchan 1958; one s.; ed. Yazoo City High School, Mississippi, Univ. of Texas and New College, Oxford.
Editor-in-Chief *The Texas Observer* 60-62; Executive Editor *Harper's Magazine* 65-67, Editor-in-Chief 67-71; Rhodes Scholarship 56; Houghton-Miflin Literary Fellowship Award 67; several hon. degrees.
Publs. *The South Today, 100 Years After Appomatox* (Editor) 66, *North Toward Home* 67, *Yazoo: Integration in a Deep Southern Town* 71, *The Last of the Southern Girls* 73, *Good Old Boy* 73.
Box 702, Bridgehampton, N.Y., U.S.A.

Morris of Borth-y-Gest, Baron, cr. 60 (Life Peer); **John William Morris,** P.C., C.H., C.B.E., M.C., D.L., LL.D.; British judge; b. 11 Sept. 1896, Liverpool; s. of Daniel and Ellen (née Edwards) Morris; unmarried; ed. Liverpool Inst., Trinity Hall, Cambridge and Harvard Law School, U.S.A.
Called to the Bar 21; K.C. 35; Judge of Appeal, Isle of Man 38-45; Chair. Caernarvonshire Quarter Sessions 43-69; Judge of the High Court, King's Bench Div. 45-51; a Lord Justice of Appeal 51-60; Lord of Appeal in Ordinary 60-Jan. 75; hon. mem. Canadian and American Bar Asscns.; Pro-Chancellor, Univ. of Wales 56-74.
House of Lords, London, S.W.1, England; Bryn Gauallt, Portmadoc, North Wales.

Morrison, William Lawrence, B.ECONS.; Australian politician; b. 3 Nov. 1928; ed. North Sydney Technical High School, Univ. of Sydney, London School of Slavonic and East European Studies.
Joined Australian Diplomatic Service 50; Australian Embassy, Moscow 52-54; Econ. Relations Branch, Dept. of External Affairs 54-57; Australian Embassy, Bangkok, concurrently Liaison Officer UN Econ. Comm. for Asia, Chair. SEATO Cttee. on Soviet Econ. Penetration in Asia and Far East 57-61; Australian Embassy, Washington 59-61, Moscow 61-63; Head, Information and Cultural Relations Branch, Dept. of External Affairs 63-66; Deputy High Commr. to Malaysia 67-68; mem. Parl. for St. George, N.S.W. 69-75; Deputy Chair. Joint Parl. Foreign Affairs Cttee. 69-72; Minister for Science 72-75; and External Territories 72-73; Asst. Minister for Foreign Affairs 73; Asst. Defence Minister 74-75, Defence Minister June-Nov. 75; Labor Party.
20A Gipps Street, Arncliffe, N.S.W. 2205, Australia.

Morrison-Scott, Sir Terence Charles Stuart, Kt., D.S.C., D.SC.; British museum director; b. 24 Oct. 1908, Paris; s. of the late R. C. S. Morrison-Scott, D.S.O. and Douairière Jhr. R. F. H. Quarles van Ufford; m. Rita Layton 1935; ed. Eton Coll., Christ Church, Oxford, and Royal Coll. of Science.
Assistant Master, Eton Coll. 35; joined staff British Museum (Natural History) 36; served World War II; Dir. Science Museum 56-60, British Museum (Natural History) 60-68; Chair. Nat. Conservation Panel 70-, Architectural Panel 73-; mem. Council, Nat. Trust 68-74; mem. Standing Comm. and Museums and Galleries 73-; Treas. Zoological Society of London 50-; Fellow, Linnean Soc.
Publs. *Checklist of Palaearctic and Indian Mammals* (with J. R. Ellerman) 51, *Southern African Mammals: A Reclassification* (with J. R. Ellerman and R. W. Hayman) 53.
Upperfold House, Fernhurst, Sussex GU27 3JH, England.

Morrow, Sir Ian Thomas, C.A., F.C.M.A., J.DIP., M.A., F.B.I.M.; British chartered accountant; b. 8 June 1912, Manchester; s. of George Morrow and the late Jamesina Hunter; m. 1st Elizabeth Mary Thackray 1940 (dissolved 1967), 2nd Sylvia Jane Taylor 1967; one s. two d.; ed. Dollar Acad., Scotland.
Chartered Accountant 36; Asst. Accountant Brocklehurst-Whiston Amalgamated Ltd. 37-40; Partner, Robson, Morrow & Co. Ltd. 42-51; Financial Dir. The Brush Electrical Eng. Co. Ltd. (now The Brush Group Ltd.) 51-52, Deputy Man. Dir. 52-56, Joint Man. Dir. 56-57, Man. Dir. 57-58; Joint Man. Dir. H. Clarkson & Co. Ltd. 61-72; Chair. Associated Fire Alarms Ltd. 65-70, Rowe Bros. & Co. (Holdings) Ltd. 60-70, Crane Fruehauf Trailers Ltd. 69-71; now Deputy Chair. Siebe Gorman Holdings Ltd.; Dir. Hambros Ltd., Hambros Industrial Man. Ltd., U.K. Wiseman Pty. Ltd., Ian Prince Ltd., Vision Screening Ltd., James North (Africa) Ltd., James North (Japan) Ltd., Int. Harvester Co. of Great Britain Ltd., Waddington & Duval (Holdings) Ltd., Lindustries Ltd.; Deputy Chair. and Man. Dir. U.K. Optical & Industrial Holdings Ltd.; Chair. U.K. Optical Co. Ltd., U.K. Optical Ltd., Emerson Optical Ltd., U.K. Optical (Export) Ltd., Salvoc Ltd., J. H. Vavasseur Group Ltd., E. B. Meyer Brokers Ltd., W. M. Still & Sons Ltd., Mills & Allen Int. Ltd., etc.; mem. The Press Council, Performing Rights Tribunal; Freeman, City of London; Liveryman, Worshipful Co. of Spectaclemakers.
Leisure interests: reading, music, golf, skiing.
23 Chester Terrace, Regent's Park, London, NW1 4ND, England.
Telephone: 01-486-4250.

Mors, Dr. Walter B.; Brazilian chemist; b. 23 Nov. 1920, São Paulo; s. of Oscar G. and Ingeborg Flora Mors; m. Haydée Machado 1944; two s. one d.; ed. Universidade de São Paulo.
Research Chemist, Northern Agricultural Inst., Belém 43-46; Research Chemist, Inst. of Agricultural Chemistry, Rio de Janeiro 47-62; Research Chemist, Inst. of Agricultural and Food Technology, Ministry of Agriculture 63-74, Dir. 66-73; Prof. of Phytochemistry, Natural Products Research Center, Inst. of Biomedical Sciences, Fed. Univ. of Rio de Janeiro; mem. Brazilian Acad. of Sciences, Sec.-Gen. 65-69; Sec. Brazilian Chemical Soc. 52-54.
Leisure interest: botany.

Publs. include *Useful Plants of Brazil* (with Carlos Toledo Rizzini) 66.
Estrada de Jacarepaguá 6784, Rio de Janeiro ZC-89, Brazil.
Telephone: 392-0925.

Mörsch, Karl; German journalist and politician; b. 11 March 1926, Calw/Württ.; *s.* of Karl F. Mörsch; *m.* Waltraut Schweikle 1947; one *s.*; ed. Univ. of Tübingen.
Journalist in Ludwigshafen, Bad Godesberg (*Deutscher Forschungsdienst*) and Frankfurt (Editor of *Die Gegenwart*) 56-58; Head of Press Dept., Freie Demokratische Partei (FDP) 61-64; free-lance journalist 64-; mem. Bundestag; Parl. Sec. of State, Ministry of Foreign Affairs July 70-.
Publs. numerous newspaper articles etc.
Auswärtiges Amt, 53 Bonn, Adenauerallee; Home: Ludwigsburg-Ossweil, Aalener Strasse 10, Federal Republic of Germany.
Telephone: 171 (Office); 8-15-98 (Home).

Morse, Sir (Christopher) Jeremy, K.C.M.G.; British banker; b. 10 Dec. 1928, London; *s.* of late Francis J. and Kinbarra (née Armfield-Marrow) Morse; *m.* Belinda M. Mills 1955; three *s.* one *d.*; ed. Winchester and New Coll., Oxford.
Formerly with Glyn, Mills & Co., Dir. 64; Dir. Legal and General Assurance Society Ltd. 63-64, 75-; Exec. Dir. Bank of England 65-72; Alt. Gov. IMF 66-72; Chair. of Deputies of "Committee of Twenty", IMF 72-74; Deputy Chair. Lloyds Bank Ltd., May 75-; Fellow, All Souls Coll., Oxford 53-68; Fellow, Winchester Coll. 66-.
c/o Lloyds Bank Ltd., 71 Lombard Street, London E.C.3; Home: 102a Drayton Gardens, London SW10 9RJ, England.
Telephone: 01-370-2265.

Morse, David A., LITT.B., LL.B.; American lawyer; b. 31 May 1907; ed. Rutgers Univ. and Harvard Law School.
Admitted to N.J. Bar (also mem. of Bar of N.Y. and D.C.) 32; U.S. Dept. of Interior, Solicitor's Staff 33-34; Chief Counsel, Petroleum Labour Policy Board 34-35; Special Asst. to U.S. Attorney-Gen. 34-35; Regional Attorney, Nat. Labour Relations Board 35-38; Partner, Law Firm of Coult, Satz, Tomlinson & Morse, Newark, N.J. 38-47; Lecturer on Labour Relations, Labour Law and Administrative Law, various colls. and law schools 38-47; Dir. Labour Div., Allied Mil. Govt., Sicily and Italy 43-44; Dir. Manpower Div., U.S. Group Control Council (Germany) 44-45; Gen. Counsel Nat. Labour Relations Board, Washington 45-46; Asst. Sec. of Labour 46-47; Under-Sec. of Labour 47-48; Acting Sec. of Labour June-Aug. 48; fmr. U.S. Govt. mem. on the Governing Body of the ILO, and Govt. Del. to Int. Labour Confs.; Dir.-Gen. ILO Sept. 48-70; now Partner Surrey, Karasik and Morse, New York, Washington, Paris, Beirut; Chair. Advisory Panel on Planning and Policy, UN Devt. Program; Dir. Franklin D. Roosevelt Foundation, Gustav Pollak Lecturer on Research in Govt., Harvard Univ. 55-56; mem. Board of Dirs. World Rehabilitation Fund; Charter Trustee, Rutgers Univ., New Brunswick 72-(78); Board of Trustees, American Arbitration Asscn.; Hon. LL.D. (Rutgers, Geneva, Strasbourg, Laval, Brandeis); numerous awards.
14 East 75th Street, N.Y. 10021, U.S.A.
Telephone: 212-988-4319.

Morse, F. Bradford, B.S., LL.B.; American politician and United Nations official; b. 7 Aug. 1921, Lowell, Mass.; *s.* of Frank Young and Inez Rice (née Turnbull) Morse; *m.* Vera Francesca Cassilly 1955; one *s.* one *d.*; ed. Lowell Public School and Boston Univ.
Service with U.S. Army 42-46; admitted to Mass. Bar 48; Law Clerk, Supreme Judicial Court, Mass. 49; law practice, Lowell 49-53; lecturer, Instructor School of

Law, Boston Univ. 49-53; City Councillor, Lowell, Mass. 52-53; Special Counsel, U.S. Senate Cttee. on Armed Services 53-54; Chief Asst. to Senator Leverett Saltonstall 55-58; Deputy Admin. of Veterans Admin., Washington 58-60; mem. U.S. House of Reps. 60-72, mem. Foreign Affairs Cttee.; Administrator of UNDP Dec. 75-; Under-Sec.-Gen. for Political and Gen. Assembly Affairs, UN 72-; Congressional Adviser U.S. Del. to 18 Nation's Disarmament Cttee., Geneva; U.S. Observer Council of Europe, Latin American Parl.; Chair. Mems. of Congress for Peace Through Law 68-70; mem. American Bar Asscn., Council on Foreign Relations; mem. Board of Trustees, Boston Univ.; Board of Visitors, School of Foreign Service, Georgetown Univ.; Board Dirs., Boxton World Affairs Council, Pan-American Devt. Foundation.
c/o United Nations, First Avenue, New York, N.Y. 10017, U.S.A.
Telephone: 754-1234.

Morse, Marston, A.B., PH.D.; American professor of mathematics; b. 24 March 1892, Waterville, Me.; *s.* of Ella Phoebe and Howard Calvin Morse; *m.* 1st Celeste Phelps 1922, two *c.*; 2nd Louise Jefferys 1940, two *s.* three *d.*; ed. Coburn Classical Inst., Colby Coll. and Harvard Univ.
Served France, First World War, Croix de Guerre; Prof. of Mathematics, Harvard Univ. 26-35, Inst. for Advanced Study, Princeton 35-62; Research under U.S. Govt. contract, Inst. for Advanced Study 62-; mem. Nat. Acad. of Sciences; Assoc. French Acad. of Science; Pres. American Math. Soc. 40-42; Corresp. mem. Heidelberg Acad. of Sciences and other Acads. and Socs.; Bôcher Prize 32; Nat. Medal of Science 64; Chevalier Légion d'Honneur; numerous hon. degrees. Leisure interests: music, arts, philosophy, religion (Catholic).
Publs. *Calculus of Variations in the Large* 32, *Functional topology and abstract variational theory* (France) 38, *Topological methods in the theory of functions of a complex variable* 47, *Critical point theory in global analysis and differential topology* (with S. S. Cairns) 69, *Variational Analysis: Critical Extremals and Sturmian Extensions* 73; about 300 papers on mathematics.
Office: Institute for Advanced Study, Princeton, N.J. 08540; Home: 40 Battle Road, Princeton, N.J. 08540, U.S.A.
Telephone: 609-924-4400 (Office); 609-924-0757 (Home).

Morse, Philip McCord, B.S., M.A., PH.D.; American professor of physics; b. 6 Aug. 1903, Shreveport, La.; *s.* of Allen Crafts Morse and Edith McCord; *m.* Annabelle Hopkins 1929; one *s.* one *d.*; ed. Case Inst. of Technology, Univ. of Munich and Princeton and Cambridge Univs.
Physicist Bell Telephone Laboratories 29; Instructor Princeton Univ. 29-30; Rockefeller Fellow 30-31; Asst. Prof. of Physics, Mass. Inst. of Technology 31-33, Assoc. Prof. 33-36, Full Prof. 36-69, Emeritus Prof. 69-; Dir. U.S. Navy Operations Evaluation Group 42-46, Brookhaven Nat. Laboratory 46-48, U.S. Dept. Defense Weapons Evaluation Group 49-50, M.I.T. Computation Center 55-66, M.I.T. Operations Research Center 53-69; Editor *Annals of Physics* 57-; Exec. Sec. Int. Fed. of Operations Research Socs. 60-63; Chair. Governing Board, American Inst. of Physics 75-; mem. Board of Dirs. Control Data Corpn. 65-; Trustee, Rand Corpn. 48-58, Analytical Services Corpn. 62-73, and other orgs.; Consultant, NATO 57-63, OECD 62-71; Fellow, Nat. Acad. of Sciences, American Acad. of Arts and Sciences, American Physical Soc. (Pres. 72-73, Chair. Panel on Public Affairs 75), Acoustical Soc. of America (Pres. 50-51), Operations Research Soc. of America (1st Pres. 51-52); Hon. Sc.D. (Case Inst. of Technology) 40; U.S. Presidential Medal for Merit 46, Silver Medal of Operations Research Soc., London 65, Gold Medal,

Acoustical Soc. of America 73, Kimball Prize of Operations Research Soc. of America 74.
Leisure interests: hiking, mountain-climbing, photography, music.
Publs. *Quantum Mechanics* (with E. U. Condon) 29, *Vibration and Sound* 36, *Methods of Operations Research* (with G. E. Kimball) 50, *Methods of Theoretical Physics* (with H. Feshbach) 53, *Queues, Inventories and Maintenance* 58, *Linear Acoustic Theory* (with K. U. Ingard, in *Handbuch der Physik*, Vol. XI/1 61), *Thermal Physics* 65, *Operations Research for Public Systems* (Ed. with Laura W. Bacon) 67, *Theoretical Acoustics* (with K. U. Ingard) 68, *Library Effectiveness* 68, and numerous technical articles.
Room 24-215, Department of Physics, Massachusetts Institute of Technology, Cambridge, Mass. 02139; Home: 126 Wildwood Street, Winchester, Mass. 01890, U.S.A.
Telephone: 617-253-3602 (Office); 617-729-1440 (Home).

Mortimer, Charles G.; American business executive; b. 26 July 1900, Brooklyn; *s.* of Charles Greenough Mortimer and Cecilia Clara Dessoir; *m.* Elizabeth Kempley Atterbury 1927; four *c.*; ed. East Orange High School and Stevens Inst. of Technology.
Nat. Aniline & Chemical Co. 19-21, R. B. Davis Co. 21-24, Geo. Batten Co. 24-28; with Gen. Foods Corpn. 28-65, various marketing and operating positions 28-43; Vice-Pres. 43-52, Dir. 50-, Exec. Vice-Pres. 52-54, Pres. and Chief Exec. Officer 54-59, Chair. 59-65, Chief Exec. 65, Chair. Exec. Cttee. of the Board of Dirs. 65-71; active in several areas of public service; Dir. UN Asscn. of U.S.A., Fed. Street Fund Inc., Boston; mem. of Corporation The Presbyterian Hospital of N.Y.C.; Chair. Westchester Medical Center Devt. Board; Trustee, N.Y. Medical Coll., Stevens Inst. of Technology; mem. of Board World Rehabilitation Fund; hon. degrees Stevens Inst. of Technology, Hamilton Coll., Long Island and Jacksonville Univs.; Parlin Memorial Award 59.
Leisure interest: breeding Morgan horses.
17 Platt Place, White Plains, N.Y., U.S.A.

Mortimer, Raymond, C.B.E.; British writer; b. 25 April 1895; ed. Malvern and Balliol Coll., Oxford.
Literary critic on the *Sunday Times*; Chevalier Légion d'Honneur.
Publs. *Channel Packet* 42, *Manet's Bar aux Folies-Bergères* 44, *Duncan Grant* 44.
5 Canonbury Place, London, N.1, England.

Mortimer, Rt. Rev. Robert Cecil, D.D.; British ecclesiastic; b. 6 Dec. 1902, Bristol; *s.* of late Edward and Ellen Snell (Merrick) Mortimer; *m.* Mary Hope Walker 1933; two *s.* two *d.*; ed. Keble Coll., Oxford.
Curate, St. Mary Redcliffe Bristol 26-29; Student and Tutor Christ Church Oxford 30-44; Regius Prof. of Moral and Pastoral Theology and Canon of Christ Church 44-49; Chancellor of Diocese of Blackburn 48-49; Bishop of Exeter 49-73.
Publs. *Gambling* 33, *Origins of Private Penance* 39, *The Elements of Moral Theology* 47, *Marriage in Church and State* 47, *Christian Ethics* 50, *The Duties of a Churchman* 51, *Western Canon Law* 53.
The Old Rectory, Newton Reigny, Penrith, Cumberland, England.
Telephone: Penrith 4119.

Morton, Sir Brian, Kt., F.R.I.C.S.; British chartered surveyor (retd.) and company executive; b. 24 Jan. 1912, Belfast; *s.* of Alfred Oscar Morton and Margaret Osborne Hennessy; *m.* Hilda Evelyn Elsie Hillis 1937; two *s.* (one deceased); ed. Campbell Coll., Belfast.
Principal, Brian Morton & Co. (estate agents) 36-64; Councillor (Ulster Unionist), Belfast Corpn. 67-69; mem. Craigavon Devt. Comm. 67-69; Chair. Londonderry Devt. Comm. 69-73; Chair. Harland & Wolff Ltd. 75-.

Leisure interests: golf, boating, gardening, landscape painting.
Rolly Island, Comber, Co. Down, BT23 6EL, Northern Ireland.
Telephone: Killinchy 472.

Morton, Henry Vollam, F.R.S.L.; British author and journalist.
Assistant Editor *Birmingham Express* 12; Sub-Editor *Daily Mail* 13-14; mem. staff *Evening Standard* 19-21 and *Daily Express* 21-31; Special writer *Daily Herald* 31-40; Kt. Commdr. Order of Phoenix (Greece), Cavaliere Ufficiale, Ordine al Merito (Italy).
Publs. include: *The Heart of London* 25, *In Search of England* 27, *In Search of Scotland* 29, *Blue Days at Sea* 32, *Scotland Again* 33, *In the Steps of the Master* 34, *In the Steps of St. Paul* 36, *Guide to London* 37, *Through the Lands of the Bible* 38, *Ghosts of London* 39, *Middle East* 41, *I Saw Two Englands* 42, *Atlantic Meeting* 43, *In Search of South Africa* 48, *In Search of London* 51, *In the Steps of Jesus* 54, *A Stranger in Spain* 55, *A Traveller in Rome* 57, *This is Rome* 60, *This is the Holy Land* 61, *A Traveller in Italy* 64, *The Waters of Rome* 66 (entitled *The Fountains of Rome* in America), *A Traveller in Southern Italy* 69, *H. V. Morton's England* 75.
Box 67, Somerset West, 7136 Cape Province, Republic of South Africa.
Telephone: Somerset West 21203.

Morton, John C. A. B. M., C.B.E.; British journalist; b. 7 June 1893; ed. Harrow and Oxford.
"Beachcomber" of the *Daily Express* 24-76.
Publs. include: *The Barber of Putney* 19, *Tally-Ho!* 22, *Mr. Thake* 29, *By the Way* 31, *Maladetta* 32, *Sobieski: King of Poland* 32, *St. Martin of Tours* 32, *Hag's Harvest* 33, *Morton's Folly* 33, *The Death of the Dragon* 34, *Skylighters* 34, *Vagabond* 35, *Stuff and Nonsense* 35, *The Bastille Falls* (Studies of French Revolution) 36, *The Dauphin* 37, *A Diet of Thistles* 38, *A Bonfire of Weeds* 39, *Saint-Just* 39, *I Do Not Think So* 40, *Fool's Paradise* 41, *Captain Foulenough and Company* 44, *The Gascon* 46, *The Tibetan Venus* 51, *Camille Desmoulins* 51, *Hilaire Belloc: A Memoir* 55, *Springtime: Tales of the Café Rieu* 56, *Marshal Ney* 58, *Merry-go-Round* 58, *The Best of Beachcomber* 63.
Melleray, Sea Lane, Ferring, Sussex, England.

Morton, Richard Alan, PH.D., D.SC., F.R.I.C., F.R.S.; British biochemist; b. 22 Sept. 1899, Liverpool; *s.* of John and Ann Morton; *m.* Myfanwy Heulwen Roberts 1926; one *d.*; ed. Univ. of Liverpool.
Lecturer in Chemistry 24, in Spectroscopy 31; Visiting Prof., Ohio State Univ. 30; Prof. of Biochem., Univ. of Liverpool 44-67, Prof. Emer. 67-; Leverhulme Visiting Prof., Royal Univ., Malta 69; mem. Council of Royal Soc. 59-61, 70-72; Chair. Biochem. Soc. 59-61, now Hon. mem.; mem. Scientific Advisory Cttee., British Egg Marketing Board 61-69; mem. Council, Royal Inst. of Chem. 58-60, Vice-Pres. 60-62; Chair. Food Additives and Contaminants Cttee. 64-69; hon. mem. American Inst. of Nutrition; Emer. Fellow Leverhulme Trust 70-72; Hon. D.Sc. (Univs. of Coimbra, Portugal, and Wales); Hon. Sc.D. (Trinity Coll., Dublin); Meldola Medal 30.
Leisure interests: history of science.
Publs. *Biochemistry of Quinones, Fat Soluble Vitamins, Absorption Spectra of Vitamins and Hormones, History of Biochemical Society, Biochemical Spectroscopy.*
39 Greenhill Road, Liverpool L18 6JJ, England.
Telephone: 051-724-1331.

Morton, Rogers Clark Ballard; American government official; b. 19 Sept. 1914, Louisville, Ky.; *s.* of David C. and Anne Morton; brother of Thruston B. Morton, *q.v.*; *m.* Anne Jones; two *c.*; ed. Yale Univ.
Joined U.S. Army 43, attaining rank of Captain; Congressman from Maryland 62-71; Chair. Republican

Nat. Cttee. April 69-71; served on various cttees. in House of Representatives and was a mem. of its Cttee. on Ways and Means; mem. Advisory Board of Air Training Command, U.S. Air Force 56-63, Public Land Law Review Comm. and Puerto Rican Status Comm. 65; Sec. of the Interior 71-75; Chair. Energy Resources Council 74-; Sec. of Commerce 75-76; Counsellor at the White House 76-.
c/o Department of Commerce, Washington, D.C., U.S.A.

Morton, Thruston Ballard, A.B.; American politician; b. 19 Aug. 1907, Louisville, Ky.; s. of David C. and Anne Morton; brother of Rogers Morton, q.v.; ed. Yale Univ.
Entered Ballard and Ballard Co. 29, and Pres. 46; fmr. Pres. of the Goodwill Industries of Kentucky, Inc.; served with U.S. Navy 41-45; mem. of U.S. Congress (Repub.) 46-52; managed the campaign of John Sherman Cooper 52; Asst. Sec. of State for Congressional Relations 53-56; U.S. Senator from Kentucky 57-68; Chair. Republican Nat. Cttee. 59-61; Chair. Republican Senatorial Campaign 63; Vice-Chair. Liberty Nat. Bank & Trust Co., Louisville 68-.
1415 Willow Avenue, Louisville, Kentucky, U.S.A.

Morton, William H., B.A.(ECONS.); American banking and travel agency executive; b. 17 Sept. 1909, New Rochelle, N.Y.; m. Margaret S. Dobbin; one s. one d.; ed. Dartmouth Coll.
Vice-President Investment Dept., Chase Nat. Bank of N.Y. 42-46; Founder, W. H.Morton & Co. Inc. (later changed to Equitable Securities, Morton & Co. Inc.) 46, Chair. Equitable Securities, Morton & Co. Inc. 68-71; Dir. American Express Co. 65, Vice-Chair. of Board 66-68, Pres. 68-75; Pres. American Bond Club of N.Y. 49-50; mem. Board of Dirs. Louisville and Nashville Railroad; mem. of Board American Express Securities, S.A., France, Dir. Fireman's Fund Insurance Co.; mem. Investment Bankers' Asscn. (Chair. Municipal Securities Cttee. 48-49 and fmr. Gov. and Vice-Pres.).
American Express Company, 65 Broadway, New York, N.Y. 10006, U.S.A.
Telephone: 212-944-2000.

Moruzzi, Giuseppe, M.D.; Italian physiologist; b. 30 July 1910, Campagnola Emilia; s. of Giovanni Moruzzi and Bianca Carbonieri; m. Maria Vittoria Venturini 1941; two s.; ed. Univ. of Parma.
Assistant Prof., Dept. of Physiology, Univ. of Parma 33-36, Univ. of Bologna 36-42; Acting Prof. of Physiology, Univ. of Siena 42-43, Univ. of Parma 45-47; Prof. of Physiology, Univ. of Ferrara 47-48; Prof. of Physiology and Head of Inst. of Physiology, Univ. of Pisa 48-; Fellow, Rockefeller Foundation, Brussels 37-38, Cambridge Univ. 38-39; Visiting Prof., Northwestern Univ. 48-49; Hon. mem. American Physiological Soc., American Acad. of Arts and Sciences, American Neurological Asscn., E.E.G. Soc.; Foreign mem. American Philosophical Soc., Norske Videnskaps Akademi (Oslo), Kungl. Svenska Vetenskapsakademien (Stockholm); mem. Accad. Naz. dei Lincei; many hon. degrees.
Publs. *L'epilessia sperimentale* 46 (French 50), *Problems in Cerebellar Physiology* 50, *The Physiology and Pathology of the Cerebellum* (with R. S. Dow) 58, *Fisiologia della vita di relazione* 75.
Via S. Zeno 31, 56.100 Pisa, Italy.
Telephone: 22218 (Home).

Mosbacher, Emil, Jr.; American government official; b. 1 April 1922, Mt. Vernon, N.Y.; s. of Emil and Gertrude Mosbacher; m. Patricia Ryan 1950; three s.; ed. The Choate School and Dartmouth Coll.
Trustee, Dollar Savings Bank 64-69; Dir. Lily Tulip Corpn. 62-68, Nat. Life Insurance Co, 68, Abercrombie & Fitch Co. 68, United Merchants & Mfg. Inc. 68; mem. Advisory Board First Nat. City Bank, Westchester 68;

Trustee, Lenox Hill Hospital, N.Y.C. 57-, The Choate School 62; Chief of Protocol of the U.S. 69-72; Chair. N.Y. State Racing and Wagering Board 73 ; Hon. M.A. (Dartmouth), Hon. LL.D. (Long Island).
Leisure interest: yachting (successful defense of America's Cup 1962 and 1967).
515 Madison Avenue, New York, N.Y. 10022, U.S.A.

Mosby, Hakon, DR.PHIL.; Norwegian university professor; b. 10 July 1903, Kristiansand S; s. of Salve Mosby and Mette Catharina Nodeland; m. Alfhild Heiberg Mowinckel 1930; two d.; ed. Univ. of Oslo.
Assistant to Prof. Nansen, Univ. of Oslo 23; Amanuensis, Geofysisk Institutt, Bergen 27; Prof. of Physical Oceanography, Bergen Museum 47, Univ. of Bergen 48-73; Dir. of Geophysical Inst. 48-58, 63-70; Dean of Faculty of Sciences, Univ. of Bergen 54-59, Rector 66-71; Pres. Int. Asscn. of Physical Oceanography of the Int. Union of Geodesy and Geophysics 54-60; Chair. Norwegian Geophysical Comm. 48-58, 66-; Pres.NATO sub-cttee. on Oceanographic Research 60-65; mem. NATO Science Cttee. 65-70; mem. Acad. of Sciences Oslo, Bergen, Gothenburg, Helsinki.
Leisure interest: string quartet.
Publs. about 60 papers in Physical Oceanography and Meteorology partly concerning polar regions.
c/o Geofysisk Institutt, Universitetet i Bergen, Allégaten 70, N-5014, Bergen, Norway

Mosca, Ugo, D. EN D.; Italian diplomatist; b. 30 April 1914, Rome; ed. Univs. of Milan and Florence.
Entered Diplomatic Service 39; successively Vice-Consul, Tien-Tsin, Second Sec., Bangkok; Third Sec. Belgrade 47, Second Sec. 49; Consul, La Plata 50; various posts in Econ. Affairs Dept., Ministry of Foreign Affairs 55, 56, 60; Minister-Counsellor, Deputy Perm. Rep. to EEC 61; Dir.-Gen. of Finance and Econ. Affairs, Comm. of EEC May-Oct. 67, Comm. of European Communities Oct. 67-; mem. several econ. cttees. of Communities; Admin. European Investment Bank.
Directorate-General of Economic and Financial Affairs, Commission of the European Communities, 200 rue de la Loi, 1040 Brussels, Belgium.

Moser, Sir Claus Adolf, K.C.B., C.B.E., F.B.A.; British statistician; b. 24 Nov. 1922, Berlin; s. of Dr. Ernest Moser and Lotte Moser; m. Mary Oxlin 1949; one s. two d.; ed. Frensham Heights School, London School of Econs.
Royal Air Force 43-46; Asst. Lecturer in Statistics, London School of Econs. 46-49, Lecturer 49-55, Reader in Social Statistics 55-61, Prof. of Social Statistics 61-70; Statistical Adviser Cttee. on Higher Educ. 61-64; Dir. LSE Higher Educ. Research Unit 64-; Dir. Central Statistical Office, Head of Govt. Statistical Service 67-; Visiting Fellow, Nuffield Coll. 72-; Dir. Royal Opera House Covent Garden 65-, Chair. 74-; Chair. Conf. of European Statisticians; mem. Gov. Body, Royal Acad. of Music 67- (Hon. Fellow 70); mem. Council, British Acad. 72-, Gov. Body, Royal Ballet School 74-; Hon. D.Sc. S., Southampton Univ. 75; Silver Rose Award 75.
Leisure interest: music.
Publs. *Measurement of Levels of Living* 57, *Survey Methods in Social Investigation* 58, *Social Conditions in England and Wales* (co-author) 58, *British Towns* (co-author) 61, and papers in statistical journals.
Central Statistical Office, South Block, Great George Street, London, SW1P 3AQ; Home: 3 Regents Park Terrace, London, NW1 7EE, England.
Telephone: 01-233 6117 (Office); 01-485 1619 (Home).

Moser, Josef; Austrian politician; b. 2 Jan. 1919, St. Lambrecht, Styria; m.; one c.; ed. secondary school, Graz.
Employed by Austrian Tenants' Asscn. 46-61; subsequently Man. Graz Regional Office, Workers' Pension Inst.; mem. Graz Municipal Council 53-59; mem.

Nationalrat 59-; Minister of Building and Technology April 70-; Socialist Party.

Federal Ministry of Building and Technology, Vienna, Austria.

Moser, Jürgen K.; American professor of mathematics; b. 4 July 1928, Königsberg, Germany; *s.* of Kurt Moser; *m.* Gertrude Moser 1955; two *d.*; ed. Univ. of Göttingen.

Assistant Prof. New York Univ. 56, Mass. Inst. of Technology 57-60; Prof. of Mathematics, New York Univ. 60-, Dir. Courant Inst. of Mathematical Sciences 67-70; mem. Nat. Acad. of Sciences; Sloan Fellow 61, Guggenheim Fellow 70-71; G. D. Birkhoff Prize; J. C. Watson Medal 70.

Publs. *Lectures on Celestial Mechanics* (with C. L. Siegel) 71, *Stable and Random Motions in Dynamical Systems* 73.

Courant Institute of Mathematical Sciences, New York University, 251 Mercer Street, New York, N.Y. 10012, U.S.A.

Telephone: 212-460-7442.

Moser, Stephen B.; American business executive; b. 2 Nov. 1908, Seattle, Wash.; *m.* Ruth Moser; three *d.*; ed. Seattle Public Schools, Univ. of Wash.

Served in U.S. Navy 41-45; with Lewis-Bean Co. 28-41; Sec.-Treas., Dir. Cascade Lumber Co. 46-52, Vice-Pres., Treas., Dir. 53-59; Dir. Boise Cascade Corpn. 58-, Vice-Pres. 59-67, Exec. Vice-Pres. 67-72, Vice-Chair. June-Oct. 72, Chair. of Board Oct. 72-; Pres. Nat. Forest Products Asscn. 72-73, Chair. 73-74; Chair. Econ. Council Forest Products Industry; Dir. American Plywood Asscn.

Leisure interests: golf, hunting.

Boise Cascade Corpn., P.O. Box 51, Yakima, Wash. 98907; Home: 5910 Scenic Drive, Yakima, Wash. 98902, U.S.A.

Telephone: (509) GL3-3131 (Office); (509) 966-1827 (Home).

Moses, Sir Charles Joseph Alfred, Kt., C.B.E.; Australian broadcasting official; b. 21 Jan. 1900, Little Hulton, Lancs., England; *s.* of Joseph and Lily (Henderson) Moses; *m.* Kathleen O'Sullivan 1922; one *s.* one *d.*; ed. Oswestry Grammar School, and Royal Mil. Coll., Sandhurst.

Lieut. in 2nd Border Regt. (British Regular Army) 18-22; fruit-grower, Bendigo, Australia 23-24; motor salesman and sales manager 24-30; announcer, Nat. Broadcasting Service 30-32; N.S.W. Sporting and Talks Ed., Australian Broadcasting Comm. 33-34; Fed. Talks Controller, A.B.C. 35; Gen. Man. A.B.C. 35-65; Sec.-Gen. Asian Broadcasting Union 65-; joined A.I.F. 40; rose to rank of Lt.-Col. 42; served in Malaya Feb. 41-Feb. 42, New Guinea Sept. 42-Feb. 43; mentioned in despatches Sept. 43; Commdr., Order of Merit (Austria); Dir. Australian Elizabethan Theatre Trust; Vice-Pres. Royal Agricultural Soc.; Pres. Austrian-Australian Cultural Soc.; Trustee, Int. Broadcast Inst. (London); Councillor, Asian Mass Communications and Information Centre (Singapore); mem. Council Royal Inst. for Deaf/Blind Children, Australian-American Asscn., Int. Advisory Cttee. of Prix Jeunesse Foundation (Munich); Hon. Dir. Postgraduate Medical Foundation.

Leisure interests: walking, tree-felling, music.

Home: 78 New Beach Road, Darling Point 2027; Office: c/o Asian Broadcasting Union, 203 Castlereagh Street, Sydney, N.S.W., Australia.

Telephone: 617406 (Office); 324224 (Home).

Moses, David Gnanapragasam, M.A., PH.D.; Indian philosopher; b. 22 Jan. 1902; ed. Madras Christian Coll. Madras Univ., Union Theological Seminary, Columbia Univ.

Philosophy Lecturer Noble Coll., Madras Univ. 24-26; Prof. Hislop Coll., Nagpur 26-40, Principal 40-61, Dean,

Faculty of Arts 58-61; Vice-Pres., Int. Missionary Council 47-61; Pres. Nat. Christian Council of India 59-63; mem. Presidium, World Council of Churches 61-69.

Publ. *Religious Truth and the Relation Between Religions.*

Hislop College, Nagpur, India.

Moses, Robert, B.A., M.A., PH.D.; American public official; b. 18 Dec. 1888, New Haven, Conn.; *s.* of Emanuel and Bella Moses; *m.* 1st Mary Louise Sims 1915, two *d.*; 2nd Mary A. Grady 1966; ed. Yale, Oxford and Columbia Univs.

Municipal Investigator, New York City 13; Chief of Staff, N.Y. State Reconstruction Comm. 19-21; Sec. N.Y. State Asscn. 21-26; Pres. L.I. State Park Comm. and Chair. State Council of Parks 24-63; Sec. of State, New York 27-28; Chair. Jones Beach State Parkway Authority and Bethpage Park Authority 33-63; Republican Candidate for Gov. of New York 34; New York City Park Commr. to consolidate City Park and Parkway system 34-60; sole mem. Henry Hudson Parkway Authority and Marine Parkway Authority 34-38, absorbed by New York City Parkway Authority 38; mem. Triborough Bridge Authority 34, Chair. 36; mem. New York City Planning Comm. 42-60; Chief Exec. Officer, New York City Tunnel Authority 45-46; Chair. Consolidated Triborough Bridge and New York City Tunnel Authority 46-68; New York City Construction Co-ordinator 46-60; Chair. Mayor's Slum Clearance Cttee. 48-60; Chair. Power Authority, State of N.Y. 54-63; Co-ordinator of Arterial Projects, New York City 60-66; Pres. New York World's Fair 1964-1965 Corpn. 60-67; Dir. Lincoln Center for Performing Arts 60-69; mem. Nat. Cttee. for Immigration Reform 65; mem. New York City Transportation Council 66-67; Lifetime mem. of New York Building Congress 66; Special Adviser to Gov. on Housing 74-75; mem. Temporary New York State Comm. to commemorate 200th Anniversary of American Revolution and 200th Anniversary of Creation of State of New York 74-; Consultant and official on numerous urban reconstruction schemes; Benjamin Franklin Fellow R.S.A. 68; numerous awards, lectureships and honorary degrees.

Leisure interests: fishing, swimming, writing.

Publs. *La Guardia, A Salute and a Memoir* 57, *A Tribute to Governor Smith* 62, *Public Works: A Dangerous Trade* 70.

Randall's Island, New York, N.Y. 10035; Homes: One Gracie Terrace, New York 10028; and Gilgo Beach, Long Island, N.Y. 11702, U.S.A.

Mosevics, Mark; Israeli industrialist; b. 22 Aug. 1920; *m.* Blanka Griffin; one *s.*; ed. Dulwich Coll., London, Jesus Coll., Cambridge, England, Hebrew Univ., Jerusalem.

Chairman Board of Dirs., Israel Export Inst. 66-68; Chair. Board of Dirs., Israel Industrial Bank 68-72, mem. Board of Dirs. 72-; Chair. Board of Dirs., Elite Chocolate and Sweets Mfg. Co. Ltd., Co-ordinating Bureau of Econ. Orgs. 68-; Pres. Mfrs. Asscn. of Israel 69-; mem. Board of Dirs., Israel Corpn. Ltd. 70-; Chair. Board, First Int. Bank of Israel 73-; mem. Presidium, Prime Minister's 3rd Econ. Conf.; Hon. Pres. A'KIM (Appeal for Retarded Children) 72-.

Elite Chocolate and Sweets Manufacturing Co. Ltd., P.O. Box 19, Tel-Aviv; and 7 Wisotsky Street, Tel-Aviv, Israel.

Moshoeshoe II, King, (Constantine Bereng Seeiso); King of Lesotho (Basutoland); b. 2 May 1938; *s.* of Seeiso Griffith, late Paramount Chief of Basutoland and 'Ma-Bereng; *m.* Princess Tabitha 'Masentle, *d.* of Chief Lerotholi Mojela, 1962; ed. Roma Coll., Lesotho, Ampleforth Coll. and Corpus Christi Coll., Oxford.

Paramount Chief of Basutoland 60; King (since restoration of Lesotho's independence) 66-; children:

Prince Letsie David, Principal Chief-designate of Matsieng and heir apparent to the throne, b. 17 July 1963; Prince Seeiso Simeone, b. 16 April 1966; Princess Constance Christina Sebueng; b. 24 Dec. 1969; exiled from Lesotho April-Dec. 70; Chancellor, Nat. Univ. of Lesotho, fmrly. Univ. of Botswana, Lesotho and Swaziland 71.
Maseru, Lesotho.

Moskalenko, Marshal Kiril Semyonovich; Soviet army officer; b. 11 May 1902, Grishino, Donetsk District, Ukraine; ed. Dzerzhinski Artillery Academy.
Joined Soviet Army 20; Commdr. Rifle Corps, Voronezh Front 43; Commdr. 38th Army Group Kursk-Orel, commanded Dnieper battle 43-44; captured Vinnitsa and Zhmerinka 44; served Carpathia and Czechoslovakia 44-45; Commdr. Moscow Mil. District Anti-Aircraft Defence 45-53; Mil. Commdr., Moscow Mil. Region 53-60; Deputy Minister of Defence and C.-in-C. of Rocket Forces 60-62; Chief Insp., Ministry of Defence, Deputy Minister of Defence 62-; mem. Central Cttee. of C.P.S.U. 56-; Deputy to U.S.S.R. Supreme Soviet 46-; Hero of Soviet Union, Hero of Czechoslovakia, Orders of Lenin (five times), Gold Star Medal (Czechoslovakia), October Revolution, Red Banner (five times), Suvorov (twice), Kutuzov (twice), Sword of Honour with Gold Coat-of-Arms, and other awards.
Publ. *At the South-Western Direction.*
Ministry of Defence, Naberezhnaya M. Thoreza 34, Moscow, U.S.S.R.

Moskalev, Vasily Nikitovich; Soviet trade union official; b. 13 Jan. 1909, Odessa; ed. Higher Party School.
Worker in plant and Govt. Orgs. 24-41; Red Army 41-46; C.P.S.U. work 46-60, Instructor of Dept., Cen. Cttee. of C.P.S.U. 55-60; Chair. Cen. Cttee. of Trade Union of Local Industry and Public Services Workers 60-73; mem. C.P.S.U. 32-; Order of Red Banner of Labour etc.
c/o Central Committee of the Trade Union of Local Industry and Public Services Workers, 42 Leninsky Prospekt, Moscow, U.S.S.R.

Mosler, Hermann, LL.D.; German international lawyer; b. 26 Dec. 1912, Hennef; s. of Karl and Marga Mosler (née Loenartz); m. Anne Pipberger; five c.; ed. Bonn Univ.
Assistant, later Research Fellow, Kaiser Wilhelm Inst. for Foreign Public Law and Public Int. Law 37; Barrister-at-Law, Bonn 46; Privat Dozent in Public Int. Law, Constitutional Law and Admin. Law, Univ. of Bonn 46; Ord. Prof. of Public Law, Univ. of Frankfurt 49; Visiting Prof. of Int. Law, Georgetown Univ. 50; Head of Legal Dept., Fed. Ministry of Foreign Affairs 51-53; Ord. Prof. Univ. of Heidelberg 54-; Dir. Max-Planck Inst. for Foreign Public Law and Public Int. Law, Heidelberg 54-; mem. Perm. Court of Arbitration 54-; Judge of European Court of Human Rights 59-, Vice-Pres. 74-; Lecturer, Hague Acad. of Int. Law 57, 74; *ad hoc* Judge, Int. Court of Justice 68-69, Judge 76-; mem. Council, German Soc. of Int. Law and German Branch, Int. Law Asscn.; mem. Heidelberg Acad. of Sciences 75; Corresp. mem. Austrian Acad. of Sciences 72; Dr. Iur. h.c. (Brussels) 69.
6900 Heidelberg, Berliner Strasse 48, Federal Republic of Germany.
Telephone: 06221-42133.

Mosley, Sir Oswald Ernald, Bt.; British politician; b. 16 Nov. 1896; s. of Sir Oswald Mosley, 5th Bt., and Maude Heathcote; m. 1st Lady Cynthia Curzon, d. of Marquis Curzon of Kedleston, 1920 (died 1933), two s. one d.; 2nd Hon. Diana Mitford, d. of Lord Redesdale 1936, two s.; ed. Winchester and Sandhurst.
Officer 16th Lancers, attached Royal Flying Corps. 1914-18; Conservative M.P. for Harrow 18-22; Independent M.P. 22-24; joined Labour Party 24; Labour M.P. for Smethwick 26-31; Chancellor of Duchy of Lancaster in Second Labour Govt. 29-30, when he resigned on question of unemployment policy; formed New Party 31; New Party Candidate for Stoke at General Election and was defeated; leader of British Fascist movement 32-40, when it was dissolved; detained under Defence Regulations 40, released 43; entered publishing business 46; founded Union Movement to promote union of Europe 48-.
Leisure interests: reading, walking, swimming, fencing, listening to music.
Publs. *The Greater Britain* 32, *My Answer* 46, *The Alternative* 47, *Europe: Faith and Plan* 58, *Right or Wrong* 61, *My Life* 68.
1 rue des Lacs, Orsay 91400, Essonne, France; White's Club, St. James's, London, S.W.1, England.
Telephone: 590 4211 (Orsay).

Moss, Frank Edward, A.B., D.IUR.; American lawyer and politician; b. 23 Sept. 1911; ed. Utah and George Washington Univs.
Member legal staff, Securities and Exchange Comm., Washington 37-39; Law Clerk to Justice James H. Wolfe of Utah State Supreme Court 39; Judge, Salt Lake City Court 40-50; attached to U.S. Army Air Force Judge Advocate's Department during Second World War; Salt Lake County Attorney 50-58; Senator from Utah 58-; Chair. Senate Cttee. on Aeronautical and Space Sciences; mem. Policy Cttee., Steering Cttee., Senate Cttees. on Commerce, Post Office and Civil Service, and Special Cttee. on Ageing; fmr. Pres. Utah State Asscn. of County Officials, Nat. Asscn. of County and Prosecuting Attorneys; fmr. Dir. Utah UN Asscn.; Democrat.
Senate Office Building, Washington, D.C. 20510, U.S.A.

Mössbauer, Rudolf, PH.D.; German physicist; b. 31 Jan. 1929, Munich; s. of Ludwig and Erna Mössbauer; m. Elisabeth Pritz 1957; one s. two d.; ed. Technische Hochschule, Munich.
Research Asst. Max-Planck Inst., Heidelberg 55-57; Research Fellow, Technische Hochschule, Munich 58-60; Research Fellow, California Inst. of Technology 60, Senior Research Fellow 61, Prof. of Physics Dec. 61; Prof. of Experimental Physics, Tech. Univ. of Munich 64-; Research Corpn. Award 60, Röntgen Prize, Univ. of Giessen 61, Elliot Cresson Medal of Franklin Inst., Philadelphia 61, Nobel Prize for Physics 61; mem. American Physical Soc., German Physical Soc., European Physical Soc., various Acads. of Sciences; Hon. D.Sc. (Oxford) 73.
Leisure interests: piano, hiking, photography, languages.
Publs. Papers on Recoilless Nuclear Resonance Absorption.
Arcisstrasse 21, 8 Munich 2, Federal Republic of Germany.
Telephone: 0811 3898602.

Mostel, Zero (Sam Mostel), B.A.; American actor and painter; b. 28 Feb. 1915; ed. Coll. of the City of New York.
Artist W.P.A. Project 37-39; taught painting at Progressive Art Center; lecturer Museum of Modern Art, Frick Museum, Metropolitan Museum; started acting 42; appeared in several films, incl. *Dubarry was a Lady, Panic in the Streets, The Enforcer, Monsieur Lecoq, Great Catherine, Hot Rock,* etc.; theatre appearances on and off Broadway and also in Europe: *Beggar's Holiday* 46, *Good as Gold, Flight into Egypt, Ulysses in Nighttown, A Funny Thing Happened on the Way to the Forum* 61, *Fiddler on the Roof* 65; award for best male actor, Paris Festival 59; Antoinette Perry (Tony) Award Best Actor 61, 62, 64.
c/o David W. Katz Co., 10 East 40th Street, New York, N.Y. 10016, U.S.A.

Motherwell, Robert, A.B.; American painter; b. 24 Jan. 1915, Aberdeen, Wash.; s. of Robert Burns Motherwell and Margaret Hogan; m. Helen Frankenthaler (q.v.) 1958; two d. by previous marriage; ed. Stanford, Harvard, Grenoble and Columbia Univs.

A founder in New York of Abstract Expressionism (Tachisme); One-Man Shows Guggenheim Gallery 44, Kootz Gallery 46, 48, 49, 52, Janis Gallery 57, 59, 61, 62, Museum of Modern Art 65 (all New York), San Francisco Museum 46, 67, Chicago Arts Club 46, Oberlin Coll. 53, Bennington Coll. 59, Berggruen Gallery, Paris 61, Odyssia Gallery, Rome 62, Der Spiegel Gallery, Cologne 62, The Phillips Collection, Washington 65; Minnesota Museum 65, Witte Memorial Museum, Tex. 66, Utah Museum 66, Southern Florida Museum 66, Contemporary Arts Museum, Houston 66, Baltimore Museum 66, Indiana Museum 66, Virginia Museum of Art, Richmond 69, Toledo Museum 69, Museum of Fine Arts, Houston 72, Boston Museum of Fine Arts 73; work has been exhibited at Tate Gallery (London), New York, Paris, and Madrid Museums of Modern Art and at Brussels, Moscow, Venice, São Paulo, Amsterdam, West Berlin, Kassel, Rome and elsewhere; works in U.S. Pavilion, Venice 50, São Paulo 53, Brussels 58, Moscow 59, São Paulo 61; Gen. Editor *Documents of Modern Art* 44-52; Asscn. Prof. Hunter Coll. 51-58; Dir. Coll. Art Asscn. 65-68; Art Adviser *Partisan Review* 63-65; Educ. Adviser Guggenheim Foundation 65-; Counsellor Smithsonian Inst. 66-68; Adviser Washington Univ. 68-; Gen. Editor *Documents of XX Century Art* 68-; Advisory Editor *The American Scholar* 69-.

Lawrence Rubin Gallery, 49 West 57th Street, New York, N.Y. 10019; 909 North Street, Greenwich, Conn. 06830, U.S.A.

Mothes, Kurt, D.PHIL.; German plant biochemist; b. 3 Nov. 1900, Plauen; s. of Albin Hermann and Anna (Gemeinhardt) Mothes; m. Dr. Hilda Eilts 1929; three s. one d.; ed. Univ. of Leipzig and Martin-Luther-Universität, Halle-Wittenberg.

Dozent in Botany and Pharmacognosy, Univ. of Halle 25-35; Prof. of Botany and Pharmacognosy, and Dir. of Botanical Inst., Univ. of Königsberg 35-45; Head, Dept. of Chemical Physiology, Inst. für Kulturpflanzenforschung, Gatersleben 49-57; Dir. Botanical Inst., Univ. of Halle 58-; Dir. of Botanical Studies, Univ. of Halle; Dir. of Plant Biochemistry Inst. of Acad. of Sciences, Berlin, at Halle 58-67; Prof. of Plant Biochemistry, Hon. senator Univ. of Halle; Pres. Deutsche Akademie der Naturforscher Leopoldina; Foreign mem. Royal Soc. (U.K.) 71; Nat. Prize 53; Honoured People's Scientist; mem. numerous Acads.; Dr. med. h.c. (Halle), Dr.agr. h.c. (Kiel), Dr.phil. h.c. (Vienna), Dr.rer.nat. h.c. (Halle), Dr. pharm. h.c. (Szeged), Dr.rer.nat. h.c. (Greifswald); Cothenius Medal (Leopoldina Acad.), Pazmany Medal (Univ. of Budapest); Humboldt Medal (D.A.W., Berlin), Gregor-Mendel Medal (Czech Acad. of Sciences), Otto Warburg Medal (Soc. for Physiological Chemistry), Carl-Mannich Medal (German Pharmaceutical Soc.), Hoest-Madsen Medal (Fed. Int. Pharm.), Paul Karrer Medal (Zürich), Kekule Medal, Döbereiner Medal (G.D.R.), Österreichisches Ehrenzeichen für Wissenschaft und Kunst 75, Pour le Mérite (Fed. Repub. of Germany).

Publs. *Stickstoff-Stoffwechsel, Physiologie und Biochemie der Alkaloide, Stoffwechselregulation (Kinin).*

402 Halle/Saale, Hoher Weg 23, German Democratic Republic.

Telephone: 21717.

Mott, Sir Nevill Francis, Kt., M.A., D.SC., F.R.S.; British physicist; b. 30 Sept. 1905, Leeds; s. of C. F. Mott and Lilian Reynolds; m. Ruth Horder 1930; two d.; ed. Clifton Coll. and St. John's Coll., Cambridge.

Lecturer, Manchester Univ. 29-30; Fellow and Lecturer, Gonville and Caius Coll., Cambridge 30-33; Melville Wills Prof. of Theoretical Physics, Bristol Univ. 33-48; Dir. H. H. Wills Physics Laboratory and H. O. Wills Prof. of Physics, Bristol Univ. 48-54; Cavendish Prof. of Experimental Physics, Univ. of Cambridge 54-71; Chair. Board of Dirs., Taylor and Francis Ltd. 69-; Chair. and Trustee Nat. Extension Coll. 71-; Pres. Int. Union of Physics 51-57; mem. Inst. for Strategic Studies; Master, Gonville and Caius Coll., Cambridge 59-66; Hon. D.Sc. (London, Paris, Oxford and others). Leisure interests: photography, numismatics.

Publs. *An Outline of Wave Mechanics* 30, *The Theory of Atomic Collisions* (with H. S. W. Massey) 33, *The Theory of the Properties of Metals and Alloys* (with H. Jones) 36, *Electronic Processes in Ionic Crystals* (with R. W. Gurney) 40, *Wave Mechanics and its Applications* (with I. N. Sneddon) 48, *Elements of Wave Mechanics* 52, *Atomic Structure and the Strength of Metals* 56, *Electronic Processes in Non-Crystalline Materials* (with E. A. Davis) 71, *Elementary Quantum Mechanics* 72, *Metal-Insulator Transitions* 74.

31 Sedley Taylor Road, Cambridge, England.

Telephone: Cambridge 45380.

Moukambi, Paul; Gabonese politician; b. 20 March 1938, Moupoupa; ed. Coll. de Mitzic, Lycée Savorgnan de Brazza, Lycée de Libreville, Univs. of Poitiers and Paris, France.

Secretary, then Principal Sec. of Admin., Ministry of the Civil Service 61-62; studies in France 62-66; Drafter of Deeds, Legal Dept., Caisse Primaire Centrale d'Assurance Maladie de la Région Parisienne, Paris 66-68; Trainee, Direction de la Prévision, Ministry of Econ. and Finance, France 68; Sec.-Gen., Ministry of Nat. Econ., Gabon, subsequently Deputy Sec.-Gen. at the Presidency 68-69; Personal Adviser to the Pres., in charge of Co-ordination, Planning, Devt. and Statistics 69-72; Minister of Finance and the Budget Feb.-Sept. 72, of Econ. and Finance 72-75; Commdr. Ordre Nat. de l'Etoile Equatoriale.

c/o Ministère de l'Economie et des Finances, Libreville, Gabon.

Mouknass, Hamdi Ould; Mauritanian lawyer and diplomatist; b. 1935, Port-Etienne.

Member, political office of Parti du peuple mauritanien (P.P.M.) June 66-; Govt. Commr. Court of State Security 66-; High Commr. for Youth and Sport Feb. 66-Jan. 68; social Chargé d'Affaires Oct. 66-Jan. 68; Minister for Youth, Cultural Affairs and Information Jan.-July 68; Minister for Foreign Affairs July 68-April 70, 71-; Minister of Nat. Defence April 70-Aug. 71.

Ministry of Foreign Affairs, Nouakchott, Mauritania.

Moulay Hassan Ben el Mehdi, H.R.H. Prince (cousin of King Hassan II); Moroccan diplomatist; b. 1912.

Caliph Northern Zone of Morocco 25; Ambassador to Great Britain 57-64, to Italy 64-67; now Gov. Banque du Maroc; decorations include Ouissam Alaoui, Charles I Medal, Great Military Ouissam, Great Medal of Portugal, Great Dominican Medal, Great Naval Medal, Great Mahdaoui Medal, Great Houssni Medal.

Banque du Maroc, 277 avenue Mohammed V, Rabat, Morocco.

Moulins, Max; French government official; b. 2 Jan. 1914, Saint-Brieuc; s. of Georges and Marguerite (Roques) Moulins; m. Lucie Coute 1937; two s. two d.; ed. Lycée de Lyon, Faculty of Arts, Lyon, Faculty of Law, Paris.

Successively Sec.-Gen. of Hérault, Dep. Prefect of Aix-en-Provence, later of Cherbourg, Prefect of Rennes, Albi and Niort; Dir. of La Sûreté Nationale; Prefect of Haut-Rhin 55-58; Prefect, Regional Insp.-Gen. Algeria 59-60, Sec.-Gen. of Algeria 60-61; Sec.-Gen. Overseas Dept. 61-; Prefect Rhône-Alpes Region 66-72, Prefect 72-; Pres. Cie. Nat. du Rhône; Commdr. de la Légion d'Honneur, Grand Officier, Ordre Nat. du Mérite, Croix de Guerre.

2 rue André Bonin, 69004 Lyon; and 28 rue Jacob, 75006 Paris, France.
Telephone: 633-46-65.

Moulton, Alexander Eric, C.B.E., R.D.I., M.A., C.ENG., F.I.MECH.E., F.I.R.I.; British engineer; b. 9 April 1920, Stratford-on-Avon, Warwicks.; s. of John Coney and Beryl Latimer Moulton; ed. Marlborough Coll., King's Coll., Cambridge.
Worked in Engine Research Dept., Bristol Aeroplane Co. 39-44, Personal Asst. to Sir Roy Fedden 40-42; established Research Dept. of George Spencer, Moulton & Co. Ltd., originating work on rubber suspensions for vehicles and designing Flexitor, Works Man. then Tech. Dir. 45-56; formed Moulton Developments Ltd., development work on own designs of rubber suspensions for British Leyland including Hydrolastic and Hydragas 56, Chair. and Man. Dir. 56-67, Man. Dir. 67-; formed Moulton Bicycles Ltd. to produce own design Moulton Bicycle 62, Chair. and Man. Dir. 62-67, Dir. 67-; Dir. Moulton Consultants Ltd., Bicycle Consultants Ltd.; Fellow, Royal Soc. of Arts; Design Centre Award 64, Amb. Award 64, Bidlake Memorial Plaque 64, Gold Medal Milan Triennale 64, Queens Award to Industry for Tech. Innovation (Moulton Developments Ltd)., Hon. Dr. Royal Coll. of Art, Hon. D.Sc. (Bath Univ.). Leisure interests: power boating, canoeing, cycling, motor cycling.
Publs. Various papers on vehicle suspension.
The Hall, Bradford on Avon, Wiltshire, England.
Telephone: Bradford on Avon 2991.

Mountain, Sir Brian (Edward Stanley), Bt.; British business executive; b. 22 Aug. 1899; ed. Charterhouse and Royal Military Coll., Sandhurst.
Army Service, First World War and Second World War; fmr. Gen. Man. Eagle Star Insurance Co. Ltd., Chair. until 74, Pres. 74-; Dir. Eagle Star Insurance Co. Ltd. 26, United Dominions Trust Ltd. 29-75, Air Holdings 62, South African Eagle Insurance Co. Ltd. 65, United Racecourses Ltd. 66, British Air Transport (Holdings) Ltd. 68, Australian Eagle Insurance Co. Ltd. 69, African Eagle Life Assurance Soc. Ltd. 73-, and many others.
Eagle Star Insurance Co. Ltd., 1 Threadneedle Street, London, E.C.2, England.

Mountbatten of Burma, 1st Earl, cr. 47; **Admiral of the Fleet Louis (Francis Albert Victor Nicholas) Mountbatten,** K.G., P.C., O.M., G.C.B., G.C.S.I., G.C.I.E., G.C.V.O., D.S.O., F.R.S.; b. 25 June 1900; British naval officer and public servant; ed. Locker's Park, Osborne, Dartmouth, Christ's Coll., Cambridge.
Naval Cadet 13, Midshipman 16, Sub-Lieut. 18, Lieut. 20, Lieut.-Commdr. 28, Commdr. 32, Capt. 37, Commodore 41, Acting Vice-Admiral 41, Acting Admiral 43, substantive Rear-Admiral 46, Vice-Admiral 49, Admiral 53, Admiral of the Fleet 56; Col. of the Life Guards 65, Col.-Commdt. Royal Marines 65; served H.M.S. *Lion* 16, *Queen Elizabeth* 17, H.M. Submarine K6 18, H.M.S. P31 18, *Renown* 20, 21 (Prince of Wales tour to Australia and New Zealand 20, and India, Japan and the Far East 21), *Repulse* 21, *Revenge* 23; Signal School, Portsmouth 24, R.N. Coll. Greenwich 25; Asst. Fleet Wireless Signal Officer, Mediterranean Fleet 27-28, Senior Wireless Instr. 29-31; Fleet Wireless Officer 31-33; 2nd Destroyer Flotilla Signal and Wireless Officer 28-29; commanded H.M.S. *Daring* 34, *Wishart* 35; Personal Naval A.D.C. to King Edward VIII 36, to King George VI 37-52; Capt. of *Kelly* and 5th Destroyer Flotilla 39-41; in command aircraft carrier *Illustrious* to Oct. 41; Adviser on Combined Operations 41-42, Chief of Combined Operations and mem. of Chiefs of Staff Cttee. 42-43; Supreme Allied Commdr. S.E. Asia 43-46; Viceroy of

India March-Aug. 47; Gov.-Gen. of Dominion of India Aug. 47-June 48; Flag Officer Commanding First Cruiser Squadron, Mediterranean Fleet Oct. 48-50; 4th Sea Lord, and Chief of Supplies and Transport June 50-52; C.-in-C. Mediterranean 52-54; C.-in-C. Allied Forces, Mediterranean 53-54; First Sea Lord and Chief of Naval Staff 55-59; Chief of Defence Staff and Chair. Chiefs of Staff Cttee. 59-65; Gov. of Isle of Wight 65, Lord Lieut. 74-; Chair. of Nat. Electronics Council; Personal A.D.C. to H.M. the Queen 53-; Legion of Merit and D.S.M. (U.S.A.); Grand Croix de la Légion d'Honneur and Croix de Guerre (France); Grand Cross of the Lion (Neths.), Grand Cross of Order of George I (Greece), Special Grand Cordon of the Cloud and Banner (China), Agga Maha Thiri Thudhamma (Burma), etc.; Hon. LL.D. (Cambridge, Leeds, Edinburgh, Southampton, London, Sussex), Hon. D.C.L. (Oxford), Hon. D.Sc. (Delhi and Patna); Hon. Lieut.-Gen., Hon. Air Marshal.
Broadlands, Romsey, Hants.; 2 Kinnerton Street, London, S.W.1; and Classiebawn Castle, Cliffoney, Co. Sligo, Ireland.
Telephone: Romsey 3333, 01-235-0081 (London) and Cliffoney 6.

Mountcastle, Vernon Benjamin, Jr.; American neurophysiologist and educator; b. 15 July 1918, Shelbyville, Ky.; s. of Vernon B. Mountcastle and Anna-Francis Marguerite Waugh; m. Nancy Clayton Pierpont 1945; two s. one d.; ed. Roanoke Coll., Salem, Va., and Johns Hopkins Univ. School of Medicine.
House Officer, Surgery, The Johns Hopkins Hospital, Baltimore, Md. 43; with U.S. Navy Amphibious Forces 43-46; through junior ranks, The Johns Hopkins Univ. School of Medicine 48-59, Prof. of Physiology 59-, Dir. of Dept. of Physiology 64-; Visiting Lecturer University Coll., London, and Collège de France, Paris 59; Penfield Lecturer, American Univ., Beirut 71; Sherrington Lecturer, Liverpool Univ. 74; Nat. Pres. Soc. for Neuroscience 71-72; mem. Nat. Acad. of Sciences, American Acad. of Arts and Sciences; Lashley Prize, American Phil. Soc. 74.
Leisure interests: sailing, horsemanship.
Publs. *Medical Physiology* (two vols.) (Editor and major contributor) 68 (2nd edn. 73); and more than 50 articles in scientific journals on the physiology of the central nervous system especially on the neuronal mechanisms in sensation and perception.
Department of Physiology, The Johns Hopkins University School of Medicine, 725 North Wolfe Street, Baltimore, Md. 21205, U.S.A.
Telephone: 703-955-3881.

Mountford, Charles Pearcy, O.B.E., M.A., DIP.ANTHROP. (Cantab.); British ethnologist and student of Australian primitive art; b. 9 May 1890, Hallett, S. Australia; s. of Charles and Arabella Mountford; m. 1st Florence J. Purnell 1914 (died 1925), one s. one d.; 2nd Bessie I. Johnstone 1932; ed. Univs. of Adelaide and Cambridge.
Accompanied Univ. of Adelaide Expeditions as Ethnologist to Warburton Ranges, Western Australia 35, Granites, Central Australia 36, Nepabunna, South Australia 37, Yuendumu, Central Australia 51; and as Leader to Nepabunna, South Australia 38 and 39, Mann and Musgrave Ranges, Central Australia 40, Haaste Bluff, Central Australia 42, Western Arnhem Land 49, North-Eastern Arnhem Land 51, Ayers Rock, Central Australia 52, Central Mount Wedge, Central Australia 56, North-Western Central Australia 60, Ayers Rock 60, North-Western Australia 63, North-Eastern Australia 64; leader of Nat. Geographic Society of America Expeditions to Arnhem Land, Northern Australia 48, Melville Island, Northern Australia 54, North-western Australia 63, Cape York, N.E. Australia; Hon. Life Fellow Nat. Geographic Soc. of America, John Lewis Gold Medal, Royal

Geographic Soc. (South Australian Branch), Founder's Gold Medal, Royal Geographic Soc. of Australia (Queensland Branch), Franklin Burr Award, Nat. Geographic Soc. of America; Nuffield Research Scholar 57-59; Natural History Medallion of Australia 49; Sir Joseph Verco Medal, Royal Soc. of S. Australia 71; Hon. D.Litt. (Melbourne).
Leisure interest: photography.
Publs. *The Art of Albert Namatjira* 44, *Brown Men and Red Sand* 48, *The Art, Myth and Symbolism of Arnhem Land* 56, *Australian Tree Portraits* 56, *The Tiwi, Their Art, Myth and Ceremony* 58, *Australian Aboriginal Art* 61, *Aboriginal Paintings from Australia* 65, *Ayers Rock—its People, their Beliefs and their Art* 65, *The Dreamtime: Aboriginal Mythology in the Art of Ainslie Roberts* 66, *Australian Aboriginal Portraits* 67, *Winbaraku and the Myth of Jarapiri* 67, *The Dawn of Time: Aboriginal Mythology in the Art of Ainslie Roberts* 69, *The Aborigines and Their Country* 69, *The First Sunrise, Nomads of the Australian Deserts: their Beliefs and their Art* 72, *The Rainbow Serpent Myth of Australia* 72, *The Dreamtime Book* 73, *Aboriginal Spirit Children, the Mystical Beliefs* 73, *Sacred Engraved Objects of the Australian Aborigines* 76, *Cave Paintings of Northern Queensland* 76.
148 Beulah Road, Norwood, S.A. 5067, Australia.
Telephone: 31-1806.

Mountford, Sir James Frederick, Kt., M.A., D.LITT., D.C.L., LL.D.; British Latinist and educationalist; b. 15 Sept. 1897, West Bromwich, Staffs.; s. of Alfred Mountford; m. Doris May Edwards 1922; three d.; ed. West Bromwich Grammar School, Birmingham Univ., and Oriel Coll., Oxford.
Lecturer in Classics, King's Coll., Newcastle 18-19; Latin Lecturer, Edinburgh Univ. 19-24; Prof. of Classics, Cornell Univ. 24-27; Fereday Fellow, St. John's Coll., Oxford 24-27; Latin Prof. Univ. of Wales 28-32; Latin Prof. Liverpool Univ. 32-45; Chair. Joint Matriculation Board 47-49; Chair. of Cttee. of Vice-Chancellors 48; Pres. Classical Asscn. 63; Vice-Chancellor Liverpool Univ. 45-63; Pres. Virgil Soc. 66-69.
Leisure interests: music, photography.
Publs. *Quotations from Classical Authors in Medieval Latin Glossaries* 25, *Abavus Glossarium* 26, *Greek Music in Papyri and Inscriptions* (in New Chaps. in Greek Lit.) 29, edition of *Kennedy's Revised Latin Primer* 30, *The Scholia Bembina* 34, edition of *Arnold's Latin Prose Composition* (and Latin Versions) 38-40, *Outline of Latin Prose Composition* 42; Edition of *Sidgwick's Greek Prose Composition* 51, *Greek Verse Composition* 55, *British Universities* 66, *Keele: An Historical Critique* 72.
11 The Serpentine, Liverpool 19, England.
Telephone: 051-427-3199.

Mourant, Arthur Ernest, M.A., D.PHIL., F.R.C.P., F.R.C.PATH., D.M., F.R.S.; British doctor of medicine; b. 11 April 1904, Jersey, C.I.; s. of Ernest Charles Mourant and Emily Gertrude Bray; ed. Victoria Coll., Jersey, Oxford Univ., St. Bartholomew's Hospital Medical Coll.
Engaged in geological survey of Great Britain 29-31; chemical pathologist, Jersey 35-38; Nat. Blood Transfusion Service 44-45; Galton Laboratory Serum Unit, Cambridge 45-46; Dir. Bloodgroup Reference Laboratory (Ministry of Health and Medical Research Council) 46-65 (incorporating World Health Org. Int. Blood Group Reference Laboratory); Dir. Serological Population-Genetics Laboratory (Medical Research Council) 65-72; Visiting Prof. of Serology, Colombia Univ. 53; Hon. Senior Lecturer in Haematology, Medical Coll., St. Bartholomew's Hosp. 65-; Pres. Section H (Anthropology) British Asscn. for the Advancement of Science 56; Foreign Corresp. mem. Acad. des Sciences, Inscriptions et Belles Lettres de Toulouse 70; Hon. mem. Int. Soc. of Blood Transfusion 75; Huxley

Memorial Medal of the Royal Anthropological Inst. 61, Landsteiner Memorial Award (American Asscn. of Blood Banks) 73.
Leisure interests: geology, archaeology, photography, alpine gardening, reading in sciences other than his own, travel.
Publs. *The Distribution of the Human Blood Groups* 54 (2nd edn. 76), *The ABO Blood Groups* (with others) 58, *Man and Cattle* (joint editor) 63, *Blood Groups and Diseases* (with others) 76.
c/o St. Bartholomew's Hospital, West Smithfield, London, E.C.1; 5 Mercier Road, Putney, London, S W.15, England; Maison de Haut, Longueville, St. Saviour, Jersey, Channel Islands.
Telephone: 01-788-1496 (London).

Moureu, Henri Bertrand Vincent; French engineer and research scientist; b. 2 Aug. 1899, Paris; s. of Charles Moureu; ed. Ecole Supérieure de Physique et de Chimie, Paris, and Collège de France.
Assistant, then Deputy Dir., Collège de France 21-41; Dir. Municipal Laboratory of Paris 41-64; Dir. Ecole Pratique des Hautes Etudes 41-72; Scientific Dir. Centre d'Etudes des Projectiles Autopropulsés, Ministry of Armed Forces 45-64; Admin. Soc. l'Air Liquide 64-70, Pres. Scientific Cttee. 71; Pres. Soc. Française d'Astronautique 64, 65; mem. Int. Acad. of Astronautics 65-; Pres. Soc. Chimique de France 65, 66; Pres. Asscn. pour la Prévention de la Pollution atmosphérique 64-; mem. Acad. des Sciences 61-; Scientific Adviser to Paris Prefect of Police 64-; Admin. Maison de la Chimie, Inst. Pasteur 67-70, and Inst. océanographique de France 67-; Co-editor *Annales de Chimie* 67; Pres. Asscn. Etude Problèmes Avancés 64-; Officier Légion d'Honneur, and other decorations.
Leisure interests: sport and music.
Publs. include: *Notions fondamentales de Chimie organique* 46, *Astronautique et Recherche spatiale* 64.
18 rue Pierre et Marie Curie, Paris 5e, France.
Telephone: 033-12-59.

Mousa, Omar al-Hajj; Sudanese politician; b. 1924, El Kowa; ed. Gordon Memorial Coll. and Mil. Coll.
Former army officer, Dir. of Gen. Staff until 69; Minister of Nat. Guidance 69-71, of Information and Culture 71-75; Asst. Sec.-Gen. Sudanese Socialist Union Jan. 75-.
Sudanese Socialist Union, Khartoum, Sudan.

Moussa, Pierre L.; French civil servant; b. 5 March 1922, Lyon, Rhône; m. Anne-Marie Trousseau 1957; ed. Ecole Normale Supérieure.
Inspector of Finances 46-50; Technical Adviser to Sec. of State for Finance 50-51, Dept. of External Econ. Relations 51-54, Dir. Ministry for Overseas Territories 54-59; Dir. of Civil Aviation, Ministry of Public Works and Transport 59-62; Dir. Dept. of Operations for Africa, Int. Bank for Reconstruction and Development 62-64; Pres. French Fed. of Assurance Companies 65-69; Pres. Banque de Paris et des Pays-Bas 69-; Chevalier, Légion d'Honneur.
Publs. *L'économie de la zone franc, Les Chances Economiques de la Communauté Franco-Africaine, Les nations prolétaires, Les Etats-Unis et Les Nations Prolétaires.*
87 Quai d'Orsay, Paris 7e, France.
Telephone: 260-35-00.

Moussatché, Haity; Brazilian physiologist and pharmacologist; b. 21 Feb. 1910, Smyrna (now Izmir), Turkey; s. of Isidor and Sarina Moussatché; m. Cadem Soriano Moussatché; one s. one d.; ed. Instituto Universario Fluminense and Universidade do Brazil.
Instructor in Physiology, Univ. de Rio de Janeiro (now Univ. do Brasil) 31-33, Asst. Prof. of Physiology 35; mem. staff Laboratory of Physiology, Instituto Oswaldo Cruz 34-35; Yellow Fever Lab., Rockefeller

Foundation, Rio de Janeiro 35-37; mem. Div. of Physiology and Pharmacodynamics, Instituto Oswaldo Cruz 37-, Head of Dept. of Pharmacodynamics 54-, Dept. of Physiology 58-64; Prof. of Physiology, Rio de Janeiro 46-47; Private Docent, Univ. do Brasil 48-; Head of Investigation Unit in Physiological Sciences, Univ. Centro Occidental; mem. Brazilian Acad. of Sciences 52-; Vice-Pres. Brazilian Soc. for Advancement of Science 60-62; mem. N.Y. Acad. of Science, Amer. Asscn. for Advancement of Science, Int. Soc. of Toxicology, Venezuelan Asscn. for Advancement of Science. Publs. include studies in experimental convulsions and studies on histamine release and cell metabolism in anaphylaxis pharmacology of natural products (animal venoms, plant products), pharmacology of snake venoms and their fractions, the brown rat.
Unidad de Investigación en Ciencias Fisiológicas, Universidad Centro Occidental, Barquisimeto, Lara, Venezuela.

Moustiers, Pierre Jean, L. en D.; French author; b. 13 Aug. 1924, La Seyne (Var.); unmarried; ed. Univs. of Aix-Marseilles and Neuchâtel.
Attaché at the Office des Changes, French zone in Germany 47-49; Chief, Information Services, Nat. Information and Protection Centre for Construction (C.N.I.P.) 50-60; medical delegate, pharmaceutical laboratory MERCK, Darmstadt 61-, later regional inspector; literary critic *Nice-Matin*, Radio-Marseille; Médaille des Combattants de la Résistance; Hommes et Lectures prize 62; Grand Prix de littérature sportive; Grand Prix du Roman, Acad. Française 69, Prix des Maisons de la Presse for *L'Hiver d'un Gentilhomme* 72, Grand Prix littéraire de Provence for *Une place forte* 75.
Leisure interests: mountaineering, reading, painting and drawing, taxidermy.
Publs. *Le journal d'un geôlier* 57, *La Mort du Pantin* 61, *Le Pharisien* 62, *La Paroi* 69, *L'Hiver d'un Gentilhomme* 71, *Une place forte* 74; Plays: *Les Epreuves de Rembrandt* 57, *L'Argent de Poche* 63; essay: *Hervé Bazin ou le romancier en mouvement* 73; TV adaptation of *L'Hiver d'un Gentilhomme* in eight episodes 73, of *La Mort du Pantin* 75.
Campagne Sainte Anne, Boulevard des Acacias, 83 Toulon, France.
Telephone: 41-09-36.

Moutia, Sydney, D. PHIL., B.SC.; Mauritius agriculturist and administrator; b. 22 June 1932, Port Louis; s. of Raoul Moutia and Odette Haoust; m. Suzie L'Aimable 1961; one s. three d.; ed. Royal Coll., Curepipe, Coll. of Agriculture, Mauritius, Wye Coll., Univ. of London, St. John's Coll., Oxford, Univ. of Gauhati, India.
Agricultural Officer, Mauritius 59-61, Agronomist 61; Lecturer Coll. of Agriculture 61-67; Senior Agricultural Officer, Mauritius 68-70, Principal Agricultural Officer 70-74; Sec.-Gen. Org. Commune Africaine et Mauricienne (OCAM) 74-.
Leisure interests: gardening, walking.
Publs. *The Effect of Gibberellic Acid and Growth Substances on Tea* 65, *Outline of Mauritian Agriculture* 74.
OCAM, B.P. 965, Bangui, Central African Republic.
Telephone: 33-46, 37-77.

Mowat, Farley McGill, B.A.; Canadian author; b. 12 May 1921, Belleville, Ont.; s. of Angus and Helen (née Thomson) Mowat; m. 1st Frances Mowat 1949, 2nd Claire Mowat 1961; two s.; ed. Toronto Univ.
Served in the Canadian Army 39-45; Arctic exploration 47-49; full-time writer 50-; Gov. General's Award (twice), Canadian Centennial Medal, Leacock Medal for Humour, Hans Christian Anderson Award, Anisfield Wolf Award, Mark Twain Award, etc.; Hon.D.Lit. (Laurentian Univ.), Hon. D.Laws (Univs. of Lethbridge and Toronto).
Leisure interests: travel, sailing.

Publs. *People Of The Deer* 52, *The Regiment* 55, *Lost In The Barrens* 56, *The Dog Who Wouldn't Be* 57, *Coppermine Journey* 58, *The Grey Seas Under* 59, *The Desperate People* 59, *Ordeal By Ice* 60, *Owls in the Family* 61, *The Serpent's Coil* 61, *The Black Joke* 62, *Never Cry Wolf* 63, *West Viking* 65, *Curse of the Viking Grave* 66, *Canada North* 67, *Polar Passion* 67, *This Rock Within The Sea* 68, *The Boat That Wouldn't Float* 69, *Sibir* 70, *A Whale For The Killing* 72, *Tundra* 73, *Wake of the Great Sealers* (with David Blackwood) 73.
25 St. John Street, Port Hope, Ont., Canada.

Mowrer, Edgar A.; American journalist; b. 8 March 1892, Bloomington, Ill.; s. of Rufus and Nell (Scott) Mowrer; m. Lilian Thomson 1916; one d.; ed. Chicago Univ., Univ. of Michigan and the Sorbonne.
War Correspondent *Chicago Daily News* in France and Belgium 14-15 and afterwards on Italian front; Chief Berlin Bureau of *Chicago Daily News* until 33, of Paris Bureau 34, later in Washington Bureau; with Office of Facts and Figures and Office of War Information 42-43; awarded Pulitzer Journalism Prize 33; syndicated columnist on world affairs 43-69; also American Editor *Western World* 56-60.
Leisure interests: walking, reading, talking, chess.
Publs. *Immortal Italy* 22, *This American World* 28, *The Future of Politics* 30, *Germany Puts the Clock Back* 32, *Mowrer in China* 38, *Global Warfare* (with Marthe Rajchman) 42, *The Nightmare of American Foreign Policy* 48, *Challenge and Decision* 50, *A Good Time to be Alive* 59, *An End to Make-Believe* 61, *Triumph and Turmoil—a Personal History of our Time* 68, *Umano and the Price of Lasting Peace* (with Lilian T. Mowrer) 73.
Wonalancet, N.H., U.S.A.
Telephone: 323-7357.

Moxnes, Einar Hole; Norwegian politician; b. 11 June 1921, Alstahaug; s. of Einar Moxnes and Agnes (née Hole) Moxnes; m. Dagny Kluken 1951; two s. one d.; ed. Folk High School, Agricultural School and State Training Coll. for Teachers.
Manager of farms 42-45; management adviser in local farmers' asscns.; County Consultant in counties Åfjord and Stoksund 51; Mayor 56-66; mem. Storting 58-; Minister of Fisheries 68-71, of Agriculture 72-73; mem. Centre Party.
Storting, Oslo, Norway.

Moya, (John) Hidalgo, C.B.E., F.R.I.B.A.; British architect; b. 5 May 1920, Los Gatos, Calif., U.S.A.; s. of Hidalgo Moya and Lilian Chattaway; m. Janiffer Innes Mary Hall 1947; one s. two d.; ed. Oundle School, Royal West of England Coll. of Art and Architectural Asscn. School of Architecture.
Qualified 44; in private practice with Michael Powell and Philip Powell (q.v.) 46-50, with Philip Powell 50-61, with Philip Powell, Robert Henley and Peter Skinner 61-; Pimlico Housing Scheme, Winning Design in Open Competition 46; Vertical Feature Festival of Britain Winning Design 50; R.I.B.A. London Architecture Bronze Medal 50; Festival of Britain Award 51; Mohlg Good Design in Housing Award 53, 54; R.I.B.A. (Bucks., Berks. and Oxon.) Bronze Medal 58, 61; Civic Trust Awards (Class I and II) 61; Architectural Design Project Award 65; R.I.B.A. Architectural Award 67 (London and S.E. Regions).
Major works include: Churchill Gardens flats, Westminster 48-62; "Skylon" for Festival of Britain 51; Mayfield School, Putney 55; Brasenose Coll., Oxford, extensions 61; Christ Church Oxford Picture Gallery and undergraduate rooms 67; St. John's Coll., Cambridge, new buildings 67; Chichester Festival Theatre 62; Public Swimming Baths, Putney 67; Mental Hospital extensions at Fairmile 57 and Borocourt 64; Gen. Hospitals at Swindon, Slough, High Wycombe

and Wythenshawe; British Pavilion, Expo 70, Osaka, Japan.

Powell and Moya, Architects, 30 Percy Street, London, W1P 0BA; Home: Day's Farm, Lippitt's Hill, High Beech, Loughton, Essex, England.

Telephone: 01-636-7292 (Office); 01-508-5272 (Home).

Moya Palencia, Lic. Mario; Mexican politician; b. 1933; Mexico City; s. of Mario Moya Iturriaga and Concepción Palencia de Moya; m. Lic. Marcela Ibañez de Moya 1959; one s. one d.; ed. Univ. Nacional Autónoma de México.

Public Relations Dept., Nat. Railways of Mexico 55-58; in Dept. of Nat. Property 59-64; Dir. Gen. of Cinematography, Dept. of Interior 64-68; Pres. of Board of Dirs. of Productora e Importadora de Papel, S.A. (PIPSA) 68-69; Under-Sec., Dept. of Interior 69; Sec. of Interior 70-.

Leisure interests: reading, horseback riding.

Secretaría de Gobernación, Bucareli 99, Mexico City; and Rio Tigris 121, Dept. 1, Mexico D.F., Mexico.

Telephone: 514-34-89.

Moyano Llerena, Carlos, DR.ECON.; Argentine lawyer, economist and politician; b. 1914, Córdoba; ed. Univs. of Buenos Aires and Oxford.

Civil servant until 52; Dir. Gen. of Credit, Ministry of Finance 50-52; Prof., School of Law, Univ. of Buenos Aires 40-56; Prof. Univ. Católica Argentina 58-; Prof. Army Staff Coll. 52-; Dir. Banco Industrial 58-62; f. magazine *Panorama de la Economía Argentina*; Econ. Adviser to Govt. of Argentina 67-70; Minister of Economy and Labour June-Oct. 70; mem. Academia Nacional de Ciencias Económicas.

Pontificia Universidad Católica Argentina, Rio Bamba 1227, Buenos Aires, Argentina.

Moyers, Bill D.; American journalist; b. 5 June 1934; s. of Henry Moyers and Ruby Johnson; m. Judith Davidson 1954; two s. one d.; ed. Univ. of Texas, Edinburgh Univ. and Southwestern Baptist Theological Seminary.

Executive Asst. to Senator Lyndon Johnson 59-60; Assoc. Dir. U.S. Peace Corps 61-63, Deputy Dir. 63; Special Asst. to Pres. Johnson 63-66, Press Sec. to Pres. July 65-66; Publisher of *Newsday*, Long Island, N.Y. 66-70; host of *This Week*, weekly current affairs TV programme 70-; Editor-in-Chief *Bill Moyers Journal*, Public Broadcasting Service; Contrib. *Newsweek* 74-75.

Publ. *Listening to America* 71.

76 4th Street, Garden City, N.Y. 11530, U.S.A.

Moyersoen, Ludovic Marie Odilon; Belgian lawyer and politician; b. 1 Aug. 1904; m. Teresa Thuysbaert; five s. six d.; ed. Collège Saint Joseph, Alost, Collège Notre Dame de la Paix, Namur and Université de Louvain.

Secretary of Union Catholique Belge 35-38; Asst. Chef de Cabinet to Prime Minister 44-45; Co-founder Social Christian Party 45, mem. Nat. Cttee. 45-47; Deputy for Alost 46-; Minister of Justice 50-52, of Interior 52-54; Vice-Pres. Chamber of Deputies 58-64, First Vice-Pres. 64; Sec. Comm. for Revision of Constitution 65; Minister of Nat. Defence 65-66; mem. Belgian Del. to UN 48; Alt. mem. Council of Europe 49-50, mem. 60; mem. Western European Union 60-63, Vice-Pres. 63-65; Pres. ITECO (Int. Technical Co-operation) and Nat. Cttee. for Voluntary Service Overseas 58-68; Pres. Cttee. for Economic Devt., District of Alost 59-; numerous decorations.

Publ. *Prosper Poullet en de politiek van zijn tijd.*

Chamber of Deputies, Brussels; and Hof Villa "Ten Berg", Aelbrechtlaan, Aalst (Alost), Belgium.

Telephone: 053-21454.

Moyle, Colin James; New Zealand politician; b. 18 July 1929; ed. Auckland Grammar School, Auckland Teachers' Training Coll., Auckland Univ.

Schoolteacher and dairy farmer 50-60; Dominion Organizer, N.Z. Labour Party 60-63; mem. Parl. 63-; Minister of Agriculture, Fisheries, Forests and Science 72-75.

Parliament Buildings, Wellington; Home: 125 Coronation Road, Papatoetor, Auckland, New Zealand.

Moyne, 2nd Baron, cr. 32, of Bury St. Edmunds; **Bryan Walter Guinness,** M.A., BAR. AT LAW, F.R.S.L.; British and Irish brewer and writer; b. 27 Oct. 1905, London; s. of Walter Guinness, 1st Lord Moyne, and Lady Evelyn Erskine; m. 1st Diana Mitford 1929 (dissolved 1934), two s.; 2nd Elisabeth Nelson 1936, four s. five d.; ed. Eton and Christ Church, Oxford.

Former Major, Royal Sussex Regiment; Vice-Chair. Arthur Guinness, Son and Co.; Trustee Iveagh (Housing) Trust, Dublin, Guinness (Housing) Trust, London; a Gov., Nat. Gallery of Ireland 55; Pro-Chancellor Trinity Coll., Dublin; Hon. LL.D. (Trinity Coll., Dublin) 58, (Nat. Univ. of Ireland) 61; mem. Irish Acad. of Letters.

Leisure interest: travelling.

Publs. *23 Poems* 31, *Singing out of Tune* 33, *Landscape with Figures* 34, *Under the Eyelid* 35, *Johnny and Jemima* 36, *A Week by the Sea* 36, *Lady Crushwell's Companion* 38, *The Children in the Desert* 47, *Reflexions* 47, *The Animal's Breakfast* 50, *Story of a Nutcracker* 53, *Collected Poems* 56, *A Fugue of Cinderellas* 56, *Catriona and the Grasshopper* 57, *Priscilla and the Prawn* 60, *Leo and Rosabelle* 61, *The Giant's Eye* 64, *The Rose in the Tree* (verse) 64, *The Girl with the Flower* (short stories) 66, *The Engagement* 69, *The Clock* 73, *Dairy Not Kept* 75

Biddesden House, Andover, Hants., England; Knockmaroon, Castleknock, Dublin, Ireland.

Moynet, André; French politician and businessman; b. 19 July 1921; m. Madeleine de Fabre de Latude 1954; one s. two d.; ed. Collège Saint-Michel, Lycée Voltaire, Paris.

With Free French Air Force, Cameroun, Gabon, Chad; with R.A.F., U.K.; with U.S.S.R. Air Force in Normandy; Commdr. Ecole des Moniteurs, Tours 45-46; Dep. to Nat. Ass. 46-, Sec. of State to President's Council 54-55; Pres. Nat. Ass. Cttee. of Nat. Defence and Armed Forces 62-67; Test Pilot, Hurel-Dubois 32-01 and Caravelle 66-70; builder of Moynet Jupiter aircraft, Moynet 860 motor boats, Moynet Sport Prototype racing cars; Dir.-Gen. Aérospatiale; Pres. Saint Chamond Granat; Commandeur, Légion d'Honneur, Médaille de l'Aéronautique, Compagnon de la Libération and several foreign decorations; Ind. Republican.

Leisure interests: golf, flying, yachting.

Publ. *Pilote de Combat.*

32 boulevard de la Saussaye, 92200 Neuilly-sur-Seine, France.

Telephone: 722-1520 (Home); 747-0712 (Office).

Moynihan, Daniel Patrick, PH.D.; American university professor; b. 16 March 1927, Tulsa, Oklahoma; s. of John Henry and Margaret A. Phipps Moynihan; m. Elizabeth T. Brennan 1955; two s. one d.; ed. City Coll. of New York, Tufts Univ. and Fletcher School of Law and Diplomacy.

Director of Public Relations, International Rescue Comm. 54; successively Asst. to Sec., Asst. Sec., Acting Sec. to Gov. of N.Y. State 55-58; mem. N.Y. Tenure Comm. 59-60; Dir. N.Y. State Govt. Research Project, Syracuse Univ. 59-61; Special Asst. to Sec. of Labor 61-62, Exec. Asst. to Sec. 62-63, Asst. Sec. of Labor 63-65; Dir. Joint Center Urban Studies, Mass. Inst. of Technology and Harvard Univ. 66-69; Prof. of Educ. and Urban Politics, Senior mem., Kennedy School of Govt., Harvard 66-69, 71-; Asst. to Pres. of U.S.A. for Urban Affairs 69, Counsellor to Pres. (with Cabinet rank) 69-70; Amb. to India 73-74; Perm. Rep. to UN 75-76; Chair. Board of Trustees Hirshhorn Museum;

mem. American Philosophical Soc., American Acad. of Arts and Sciences; Hon. Fellow, London School of Economics; numerous honorary degrees.
Publs. *Maximum Feasible Misunderstanding*, *Beyond the Melting Pot* (co-author), Editor: *On Understanding Poverty*, *Toward A National Urban Policy*.
57 Francis Avenue, Cambridge, Mass. 02138, U.S.A.

Moynihan, Maurice Gerard, B.COMM.; Irish banker; b. 19 Dec. 1902, Tralee, County Kerry; *s.* of Maurice and Mary (née Power) Moynihan; *m.* Mae Conley 1932; two *s.* three *d.*; ed. Univ. Coll., Cork.
Secretary Executive Council, Irish Free State 37; Sec., Govt. of Ireland 37-60; Civil Service Commr. 37-53; Dir. Central Bank of Ireland 53-60; Gov. 61-69; Dir. Trinity Bank Ltd., Dublin; mem. Commrs. of Charitable Donations and Bequests for Ireland 61-; D.Econ. Sc. h.c. (Nat. Univ. of Ireland) 55; Knight Commdr. of St. Gregory 59.
Publ. *Currency and Central Banking in Ireland 1922-60* 75.
48 Castle Avenue, Clontarf, Dublin 3, Ireland.
Telephone: 333936.

Moynihan, Rodrigo, C.B.E., R.A.; British artist; b. 17 Oct. 1910; *s.* of Herbert James Moynihan and Maria de la Puerta; *m.* 1st Elina Smith 1931, one *s.*; 2nd Anne Dunn 1960, one *s.*; ed. University Coll. School, various schools in U.S.A. and Slade School of Art.
Member London Group 33; War Artist 43-44; shows include: Redfern Gallery 40, 58, 61, Hanover Gallery 63, 67, Egan Gallery, New York 66, Tibor de Nagy 68; pictures owned by Chantrey Bequest, Tate Gallery, Contemporary Art Soc., and numerous private collectors; Fellow, Univ. Coll. London 70.
Publs. *Goya* 51, *Art and Literature* (a magazine, ed. with Anne Dunn) 60-.
70 Avenue de Léman, Lausanne, Switzerland.

Moyola, Baron (Life Peer), cr. 71, of Castledawson in the County of Londonderry; **Rt. Hon. Major James Dawson Chichester-Clark**; British politician and farmer; b. 12 Feb. 1923, Castledawson; *s.* of James Jackson Chichester-Clark and Marion Caroline Chichester; *m.* Moyra Maud Haughton 1959; one step *s.* two *d.*; ed. Eton Coll.
Entered Army 42, Second Lieut. Irish Guards Dec. 42; wounded Italy 44; A.D.C. to Gov.-Gen. of Canada (Field-Marshal Earl Alexander of Tunis) 47-49; attended Staff Coll., Camberley 56; retd. from Army as Major 60; M.P. for South Derry, Parl. of N. Ireland 60-72, Asst. Whip March 63, Chief Whip 63-67; Minister of Agriculture, N. Ireland 67-April 69; Leader of Unionist Party and Prime Minister of N. Ireland May 69-March 71; Privy Councillor Northern Ireland 66, Deputy Lieutenant 54; Vice-Lieut. Co. Derry 72-.
Leisure interests: fishing, shooting and skiing.
Home: Moyola Park, Castledawson, Co. Derry, N. Ireland.

Moyzes, Alexander; Czechoslovak composer; b. 4 Sept. 1906, Kláštor pod Znievom; ed. State Conservatoire, Prague.
Professor of Theory of Music and Composition, Acad. of Music and Dramatic Arts, Bratislava 28-48; Chief of Music Section, Czechoslovak Radio, Bratislava 37-48; Prof. Coll. of Music and Dramatic Arts, Bratislava 49-, Rector 67, 69; mem. Central Cttee. Union of Czechoslovak Composers 50; Chair. Union of Slovak Composers 69-70; Chair. Fed. Union of Czech and Slovak Composers 69-70; one of the founders of contemporary Slovak music; numerous prizes; Honoured Artist 61, Nat. Artist 66, Order of Labour 69.
Compositions include: chamber: Sonata in E minor 25, *String Quartet* 39, *Wind Quartet* 33; vocal: *Colours on the Palette* 28, twelve folk songs from Šariš 29, *They are Singing in the Mountains* 33, *They are Singing, Playing,*

Dancing 38, *Whose Organs are Playing* 47, Ballad Cantata 60, *In the Autumn* 61; orchestral: seven symphonies 29-55, *Jánošík, Nikola Suhaj* 34, *Down the River Váh* 35, *Concerto for Violin and Orchestra* 58, *Sonatina Giocosa* 62, *Concerto for Flute and Orchestra* 67; opera: *The Brave King* 62; music for theatre, radio plays and films.
College of Music and Dramatic Arts, Bratislava, Štúrova 7, Czechoslovakia.

Mozzoni, H. E. Cardinal Umberto; Argentine ecclesiastic; b. 29 June 1904, Buenos Aires.
Ordained priest 27; consecrated titular bishop of Side 54; Papal Nuncio to Brazil 69; created cardinal by Pope Paul VI 73.
Palazzo Altemps, 8 via di S. Apollinare, 00186 Rome, Italy.
Telephone: 56-22-72.

Mphahlele, Ezekiel; South African author; b. 17 Dec. 1919, Marabastad; ed. teacher training and private study.
Teacher of English and Afrikaans, Orlando, Johannesburg till 57; Fiction Editor *Drum* magazine 55; Lecturer in English Literature, Dept. of Extra-Mural Studies, Univ. Coll., Ibadan, Nigeria 57; Dir. African Programme for the Congress for Cultural Freedom, Paris; has lectured at Cultural Centre, Nairobi, and Univ. of Zambia; later at Univ. of Denver.
Publs. include *Man Must Live, The Living and the Dead* (short stories), *Down Second Avenue* (autobiography), *The Wanderers* 72, *In Corner B, The African Image* (essays), *Voices in the Whirlwind* (essays).
Department of English, University of Denver, Denver, Colorado 80210, U.S.A.

Mrani Zentar, Mehdi, L. en D.; Moroccan diplomatist; b. 6 Sept. 1929, Meknes; *s.* of Mhamed Mrani Zentar and Cherifa Ali; *m.* Milouda Abbes 1959; one *d.*; ed. univ. in France.
Former Dir. of African Affairs, Ministry of Foreign Affairs, later Dir. of American Affairs and Int. Orgs., Dir. of Political Affairs; Amb. to Yugoslavia; Amb. to Egypt; Perm. Rep. to UN 71-75.
Leisure interests: reading, music, swimming, travelling and driving.
c/o Ministère des Affaires Etrangères, Rabat, Morocco.

Mravinsky, Yevgeni Aleksandrovich; Soviet conductor; b. 4 June 1903, Leningrad; ed. Leningrad Conservatoire.
Conductor Kirov State Acad. Opera and Ballet Theatre, Leningrad 32-38; Winner, All Union Conductors' Competition 38, Conductor Leningrad State Philharmonic Orchestra 38-; has toured England, Austria, German Fed. Republic, German Democratic Republic, Finland, Czechoslovakia, Switzerland, U.S.A., etc.; People's Artist of the U.S.S.R. 54-, Badge of Honour, State Prize, Lenin Prize 61.
Leningrad State Philharmonic Orchestra, 1 Ploshchad Iskusstv, Leningrad, U.S.S.R.

Mrozek, Sławomir; Polish writer; b. 1930.
Former cartoonist and journalist.
Publs. include *The Elephant* 57, *The Rain* 62 (short stories), *The Ugupu Bird* (short stories) 68; Plays: *The Police* 58, *What a lovely Dream, Let's Have Fun, The Death of the Lieutenant* 63, *Striptease* 64, *Tango* 64, *On the High Seas, Vatzlac* 70, *Blessed Event*.
Living abroad.

Msuya, Cleopa David, B.A.; Tanzanian civil servant; b. 4 Jan. 1931, Usangi Pare District; *s.* of David Kilenga and Maria Ngido; *m.* Rhoda Chritopher 1959; four *s.* two *d.*; ed. Makerere Univ. Coll.
Civil Service. Community Devt. Officer 56-61, Commr. for Community Devt. 61-64, Principal Sec. to Ministry of Community Devt. and Nat. Culture 64, to Ministries of Land Settlement and Water Devt. 64-67, to Ministry

of Econ. Affairs and Devt. Planning 67-70 and to Treas. 70-72; Minister of Finance 72-75; Minister for Industries 75-; Gov. IMF; mem. Board of Dirs. of several public corpns.

Ministry of Industries, Dar es Salaam, Tanzania.

Mtei, Edwin Isaac Mbiliewi; Tanzanian public servant; b. 1932, Moshi; ed. Makerere Univ. Coll., Uganda.

Management trainee, East African Tobacco Co. 57-59; entered govt. service 59; responsible for Africanization and training in the Civil Service; worked with East African Common Services Org. until 65; Principal Sec. to Treasury 64; Gov. Bank of Tanzania 66-74.

P.O. Box 2939, Mirambo Street, Dar es Salaam, Tanzania.

Mubarak, Musa al-, M.A.; Sudanese politician; b. 1932, Abu Si'id, Omdurman; *m.*; three *s.*; ed. Univs. of London and Khartoum.

Former school teacher; Lecturer in History, Univ. of Khartoum; mem. Parl. (Nat. Unionist Party) 65-68, (Democratic Unionist Party) 68-69; Minister of Industry and Mineral Resources 69-70; Man., Chief Editor Al-Ayam Printing and Publishing House 70-71; Minister of Labour Aug.-Oct. 71; Minister of State for Cabinet Affairs 71-72; Minister for Treasury April-Oct. 72.

P.O. Box 1701, Khartoum, Sudan.

Mubiru, Joseph M., M.A., F.I.B., F.I.B.A.; Governor, Bank of Uganda 66-71; see *The International Who's Who 1975-76.*

Much, Walter; German lawyer and professor of law; b. 3 June 1913, Breslau; *m.* Hannelore Siegelmann 1950; one *s.* one *d.*

Rapporteur, Ministry of Justice, Bavaria 49; Rapporteur for Constitutional and Int. Law, Fed. Ministry of Justice 49-51; Legal Adviser to German Del. at Schuman Conf. on a European Coal and Steel Community 50-52; entered Diplomatic Service 51; Legal Adviser to High Authority of ECSC 52, Dir.-Gen. Legal Service 66; Asst. Dir.-Gen., Legal Service, Comm. of European Communities 68-70, Dir.-Gen. 70-.

Legal Service, Commission of the European Communities, 200 rue de la Loi, 1049 Brussels, Belgium.

Mückenberger, Erich; German politician; b. 8 June 1910.

Former locksmith, Chemnitz; mem. Socialist Unity Party (S.E.D.) 46-, Sec. Cen. Cttee. 53-, mem. Politbüro of Cen. Cttee. 54-; mem. Volkskammer 50-; several decorations.

Volkskammer, Berlin, German Democratic Republic.

Mudenda, Elijah Haatukali Kaiba; Zambian agriculturist and politician; b. 6 June 1927; ed. Makerere Univ. Coll., Uganda, and Cambridge Univ.

Agricultural expert until 62; mem. Legislative Assembly 62-64; Parl. Sec. for Agriculture 62-64; mem. Zambian Parl. 64-; Minister of Agriculture 64-67, of Finance 67-68, of Foreign Affairs Dec. 68-69, 70-73, of Devt. and Finance 69-70; Prime Minister May 75-; Minister of Nat. Guidance and Culture 75-.

Office of the Prime Minister, Lusaka, Zambia.

Mueller, George E.; American electrical engineer and missile scientist; b. 16 July 1918, St. Louis, Mo.; *s.* of Edwin and Ella F. (Bosch) Mueller; *m.* Maude Rosenbaum 1941; two *d.*; ed. Missouri School of Mines, Purdue Univ., Ohio State Univ.

Vice-Pres. for Research and Devt., Space Technology Laboratories, Los Angeles until Aug. 63; Assoc. Admin. for Manned Space Flight, Nat. Aeronautics and Space Admin. (N.A.S.A.) Sept. 63-Dec. 69; Sen. Vice-Pres. Gen. Dynamics 70-71; Chair., Pres. System Devt. Corpn. 71-; Fellow A.I.A.A., I.E.E.E., Royal Aeronautical Soc., Vice-Pres. Int. Astronautical Fed.; American Physical Soc.; mem. Nat. Acad. of Engineering, N.Y. Acad. of Sciences, American Geophysical Union; Hon. Fellow British Interplanetary Soc.; NASA Distinguished Service Medal 66, 68, 69; Eugen Sanger Medal 70; Nat. Medal of Science 71.

Publ. *Communications Satellites* (with E. Spangler), etc.

System Development Corporation, P.O. Box 3356, Santa Monica, Calif. 90403, U.S.A.

Mueller, Rt. Rev. Reuben Herbert; American ecclesiastic; b. 2 June 1897; ed. North Central Coll., and Evangelical Theological Seminary, Naperville, Illinois.

Minister of Evangelical United Brethren Church 20-; High School Teacher Wisconsin and Minnesota 19-24; Instructor North Cen. Coll. 24-26; Pastor at Minneapolis, South Bend and Indianapolis 21-37; District Supt. Indiana Conf. of Evangelical Church 37-42; Exec. Sec., Christian Educ. 42-56, Vice-Pres. of Board 57; also on Board of World Council of Christian Educ.; Assoc. Sec. of Evangelism 46-54; Bishop 54-68; Bishop, Indiana area United Methodist Church 68-; Chair. Joint Comm. on Church Union (with Methodists) 54-; mem. Cen. Cttee. World Council of Churches 61-; Pres. Nat. Council of Churches of Christ 63-66; mem. numerous Church Cttees.; many honorary degrees.

Publs. *Becoming a Christian, One Body, One Spirit, Motive in Christian Teaching, Renew My Church, The Living Word, His Church* 66.

133 West Franklin Avenue, Apt. 1, Naperville, Ill. 60540, U.S.A.

Muetterties, Earl Leonard, A.M., PH.D.; American chemist; b. 23 June 1927, Elgin, Ill.; *s.* of Earl C. and Muriel G. (Carpenter) Muetterties; *m.* JoAnn M. Wood 1956; three *s.* three *d.*; ed. Northwestern and Harvard Univs.

Research Chemist, E. I. du Pont de Nemours & Co. 52-57, Research Supervisor 57-65, Assoc. Dir. of Research 65; Visiting Prof. of Chem., Princeton Univ. 67-69; Adjunct Prof., Chem. Dept., Univ. of Pa. 69; Assoc. mem. Monell Chem. Senses Center, Univ. of Pa. 69-; Prof. of Chem., Cornell Univ. 73-; mem. Nat. Acad. of Sciences, American Acad. of Arts and Sciences; American Chem. Soc. Award in Inorganic Chem. 65.

Leisure interests: skiing, fishing, surfing.

Publs. *Chemistry of Boron and its Compounds* (Editor) 67, *Polyhedral Boranes* 68, *Chemist's Guide* 69, *General Structural-Stereochemical Principles and Topological Analysis* 70, *Transition Metal Hydrides* (Editor) 71.

Department of Chemistry, Cornell University, Ithaca, N.Y. 14850, U.S.A.

Telephone: (607) 256-7220.

Muetzelfeldt, Rev. Bruno, D.D.; Australian ecclesiastic; b. 7 Feb. 1918, Düsseldorf, Germany; *s.* of Carl and Gertrude Muetzelfeldt; *m.* Frieda Stolz 1942; two *s.*; ed. Immanuel Coll., Adelaide, and Lutheran Theological Seminary, Adelaide, S. Australia.

Minister of Lutheran Church, Albury, New South Wales 39-46; Exec. Sec. Lutheran Youth Dept. 46-51; Chaplain, Commonwealth Immigration Centre, Australia 47-51; Dir. Lutheran World Fed., Dept. of World Service in Australia and Exec. Sec. Board of Immigration, United Evangelical Lutheran Church in Australia 51-60; N.S.W. Pres. United Evangelical Lutheran Church in Australia 54-60; Sec. for Resettlement and Relief, Lutheran World Fed., Dept. of World Service, H.Q., Geneva 60-61; Dir. Lutheran World Fed., Dept. of World Service, Geneva 61-; mem. Int. World Refugee Year Cttee. 60-61; Chair. Int. Council of Voluntary Agencies 63-65; Consultant, Div. of Inter-Church Aid, Refugees and World Service, World Council of Churches 61-71; Star of Jordan 64.

Leisure interests: swimming, cabinet making.

Lutheran World Federation, Ecumenical Centre, 150 Route de Ferney, 1211 Geneva 20, Switzerland.

Telephone: 33-34-00.

Müezzinoğlu, Ziya; Turkish civil servant and diplomatist; b. 1919; ed. Ankara Univ. and Germany and Switzerland.
Inspector of Finance, Turkish Ministry of Finance 42-53; Adviser to Treasury, Ministry of Finance 53-59; Dir.-Gen. of Treasury 59-60; Dir. Gen. of Treasury and Sec.-Gen. Org. for Int. Econ. Co-operation in Turkey 60; mem. Constituent Assembly 60; Chair. Interministerial Cttee. for Foreign Econ. Relations 62; Sec. of State of State Planning Org. 62-64; Amb. to Fed. Repub. of Germany 64-67; Amb., Perm. Delegate of Turkey to the European Communities 67-72; Minister of Finance 72-73.
c/o Ministry of Finance, Ankara, Turkey.

Müftüoğlu, Sadik Tekin; Turkish politician; b. 1927, Çaycuma, Zonguldak.
Member of Parl. for Zonguldak 65-; Minister of Commerce 66-67, of State 67-69, of Finance 73-74; Justice Party.
National Assembly, Ankara, Turkey.

Muggeridge, Malcolm; British journalist; b. 24 March 1903; ed. Selhurst Grammar School and Selwyn Coll., Cambridge.
Lecturer, Egyptian Univ., Cairo 27-30; editorial staff, *Manchester Guardian* 30-32; *Manchester Guardian* corresp. in Moscow 32-33; Asst. Editor, *Calcutta Statesman* 34-35; editorial staff, *Evening Standard* 35-36; served in East and North Africa, Italy and France, Major, Intelligence Corps, in Second World War 39-45; *Daily Telegraph* Washington corresp. 46-47; Deputy Managing Editor, *Daily Telegraph* 50-52; Editor of *Punch* 53-57; Rector of Edinburgh Univ. 66-68; Légion d'Honneur, Croix de Guerre (with Palm), Médaille de la Résistance Française.
Publs. *Three Flats* (produced by Stage Society 31), *Autumnal Face* 31, *Winter in Moscow* 33, *The Earnest Atheist: a life of Samuel Butler* 36, *In a Valley of this Restless Mind* 38, *The Thirties* 40; edited English edition of *Ciano's Diary* 47, *Ciano's Papers* 48; *Affairs of the Heart* 49, *Tread Softly for you Tread on my Jokes* 66, *London à la Mode* (with Paul Hogarth) 66, *Muggeridge Through the Microphone* 68, *Jesus Rediscovered* 69, *Something Beautiful for God* 71, *Paul—Envoy Extraordinary* (with Alec Vidler) 72, *Chronicles of Wasted Time: Vol. I The Green Stick* 72, *Vol. II The Infernal Grove* 73.
Park Cottage, Robertsbridge, Sussex, England.

Muhammad, Ali Nasser; Yemeni politician; b. 1944, Dathina Rural District.
Active mem. of Nat. Liberation Front (NLF) 63-67; Gov. Second Province 67; mem. Nat. Front Gen. Command March 68; Minister of Local Govt. April 69, of Defence Dec. 69; mem. Front Exec. Cttee. 70; mem. Presidential Council of People's Democratic Repub. of Yemen 71-; Chair. Council of Ministers 71-; mem. Political Bureau of Nat. Front 72-; Minister of Educ. 74-75.
Ministry of Education, Aden, People's Democratic Republic of Yemen.

Muhammadullah; Bangladesh lawyer and politician; b. 21 Nov. 1921, Saicha; m. Serajun Nahar Muhammadullah; three s. two d.; ed. Dacca and Calcutta Univs.
Joined Dacca Bar 50; Lawyer, High Court 64; mem. Awami League 50-; Sec. E. Pakistan Awami League 52-72; mem. E. Pakistan Provincial Assembly 70; Politicial Adviser to Acting Pres. Syed Nazrul Islam 71; Deputy Speaker Bangladesh Constituent Assembly April-Nov. 72, Speaker 72-73; Speaker Bangladesh Parl. 73-74; Acting Pres. of Bangladesh Dec. 73-Jan. 74, Pres. 74-75; Minister of Land Admin. and Land Reforms Jan.-Aug. 75; Vice-Pres. of Bangladesh Aug.-Nov. 75.

Muhieddin, Zakaria; Egyptian politician; b. 7 May 1918; ed. Military Coll., and Staff Officers' Coll., Cairo.
Former lecturer Mil. Coll. and Staff Officers' Coll., and Dir.-Gen. Intelligence; Minister of the Interior 53-58; Minister of Interior, United Arab Republic April 58-61; Vice-Pres. U.A.R. 61; mem. Presidency Council 62-64; Deputy Pres. 64-65; Prime Minister 65-66; First Deputy Prime Minister June 67-March 68.

Mühlbock, Otto, PH.D., M.D.; Netherlands oncologist; b. 4 Jan. 1906; ed. Humboldt-Universität zu Berlin.
Endocrinologist, Pharmacological Inst., Amsterdam 34-40; Head, Dept. of Biology, Netherlands Cancer Inst. 46-; Asst. Prof. of Oncology, Univ. of Amsterdam 54-58, Prof. 58; Chair. Research Comm., Int. Union against Cancer 58-66, mem. Council 66-70; mem. Royal Acad. of Science of Netherlands; Pres. European Asscn. for Cancer Research; De Snoo-Van't Hoogerhuis Award 58.
Publs. scientific work on carcinogenesis.
Sarphatistraat 108, Amsterdam, Netherlands.

Muir, Sir David John, Kt., C.M.G., F.C.I.S., F.A.S.A., F.A.I.M., A.A.U.Q., J.P.; Australian civil servant; b. 20 June 1916, Brisbane; s. of John Arthur Muir and late Grace Elizabeth Muir; m. Joan Haworth 1942; one s. one d.; ed. Commercial High School, Brisbane.
Clerk, Lands Dept. 33; Private Sec. to Queensland Premier 39; Investigations Officer, Sugar Cane Prices Board 43; Official Sec. to Premier 46; Permanent Under-Sec., Premier and Chief Sec.'s Dept., and Clerk, Exec. Council of Queensland 48; Agent-Gen. for Queensland in London 51-64; Dir. of Industrial Development, Queensland 64-; Australian rep. on Int. Sugar Council 51-64 (Chair. 58); Pres. Chartered Inst. of Secs. 64, Chair. Queensland Theatre Co. 69-.
Leisure interests: golf, gardening.
Home: 28 Buena Vista Avenue, Coorparoo, Brisbane; Office: M.I.M. Building, Ann Street, Brisbane, Queensland, Australia.
Telephone: 398-3012 (Home); 221-7765 (Office).

Muir, Malcolm; American publisher; b. 1885; ed. public and private schools.
With McGraw-Hill Publishing Co. 05-37, Vice-Pres. 16-28, Pres. 28-37; Pres. and Publisher *Newsweek* 37-Feb. 59, Chair. Editorial Board 49-56, Chair. Board and Editor-in-Chief 59-61, Hon. Chair. Board *Newsweek* Inc.; Dep. Administrator N.R.A. 33; Dir. Nat. Asscn. of Manufacturers 35-43, Chair. War Cttee. 42-43; Past-Dir. American Arbitration Asscn.; Nat. Industrial Conf. Board; Labor-Management Council of War Production Board 43; N.Y. Chamber of Commerce; Citizens' Cttee. for Control of Crime in N.Y. City 40-43; Econ. Club of N.Y., Council on Foreign Relations; Past-Dir. Nat. Publishers' Asscn.; Board of Trustees of Cttee. for Econ. Development, Int. Press Institute, Foreign Policy Asscn., U.S. Council Int. Chamber of Commerce; Chair. American Advisory Council, Ditchley Foundation 67-73; Chair. U.S. Comm. for the United World Colls. 67-73; Republican.
435 East 52nd Street, New York, N.Y. 10022; and *Newsweek* Building, 444 Madison Avenue, New York, N.Y. 10022, U.S.A.

Muirshiel, 1st Viscount (cr. 64), of Kilmacolm; **John Scott Maclay,** K.T., P.C., C.H., C.M.G.; British ship owner and politician; b. 26 Oct. 1905; ed. Winchester and Trinity Coll., Cambridge.
M.P. for Montrose Burghs 40-50, for Renfrewshire West 50-64; Head British Merchant Shipping Mission to U.S.A. 44; Parl. Sec. Ministry of Production 45; Minister of Transport and Civil Aviation 51-52; Minister of State for Colonial Affairs 56-57; Sec. of State for Scotland 57-62; Pres. Assembly Western European Union 55-56; Pres. Nat. Liberal Council 57-65; Lord Lieutenant of the County of Renfrew.
Knapps, Kilmacolm, Renfrewshire, Scotland.

Mujeeb, Muhammad, B.A.; Indian educationist; b. 1902; ed. Oxford Univ.

Joined Jamia Millia 26; fmr. Vice-Chancellor Jamia Millia.

Publs. *History of Russian Literature, History of European Political Thought, Story of the World* (in Urdu), *A Glimpse of New China, World History—Our Heritage, Kimiyagar* (Urdu short stories), *Ordeal, The Indian Muslims, Education and Traditional Values, Ghalib, Akbar (The Great), Islamic Influence on Indian Society, Dr. Zakir Husain—A Biography.*

Naseem Bagh, Jamianagar, New Delhi 110025, India. Telephone: 631434.

Mujica Lainez, Manuel; Argentine writer and journalist; b. 11 Sept. 1910, Buenos Aires; s. of Manuel Mujica Farías and Lucía Lainez; m. Ana María de Alvear 1936; two s. one d.; ed. Colegio Lacordaire, Buenos Aires, Colegio Nacional de San Isidro, Ecole Descartes, Paris, and Faculty of Law, Univ. of Buenos Aires.

On staff of *La Nación* 32-, Art Critic; Sec. Nat. Museum of Decorative Arts 36-46; Gen. Dir. of Cultural Relations, Foreign Office 55-58; mem. Argentine Acad. of Letters, Nat. Acad. of Fine Arts; Nat. Prize for Letters; Grand Prix, Argentine Soc. of Writers; John F. Kennedy Prize; Forti Glori Prize, and other awards. Leisure interest: drawing.

Publs. *Glosas Castellanas* 36, *Don Galaz de Buenos Aires* 38, *Miguel Cane, padre* 42, *Vida de Aniceto el Gallo* 43, *Canto a Buenos Aires* 43, *Vida de Anastasio el Pollo* 47, *Aquí Vivieron* 49, *Misteriosa Buenos Aires* 51, *Los Idolos* 53, *La Casa* 54, *Los Viajeros* 55, *Héctor Basaldua* 56, *Invitados en el Paraíso* 57, *Bomarzo* 62, *El Unicornio* 65, *Crónicas Reales* 67, *De Milagros y de Melancolías* 68, *Cécil* 73.

O'Higgins 2150, Buenos Aires, Argentina. Telephone: 781-1662.

Mukherjee, J. N., C.B.E., D.SC., F.N.I.; Indian research scientist; b. 1893, Mahadebpur, Rajshahi; s. of Durga Das Mukherjee and Saratsasi Banerjee; m. Ajita Chaudhuri 1922; one s.; ed. Univs. of Calcutta and London.

Assistant to Palit Prof. of Chemistry, Calcutta Univ. 15-19; Guruprasad Prof. of Chemistry 21-37, Ghose Prof. of Chemistry 37-45; fmr. Dir. Indian Agricultural Research Inst., New Delhi and Central Building Research Inst., Roorkee; fmr. Chair. Sub-Cttee. Nat. Planning Cttee. of Indian Nat. Congress; Leader, Indian Del. 3rd Int. Congress of Soil Science 35; Convener and Pres. Indian Society of Soil Science 35; mem. India Scientific Mission to U.K. and U.S.A. 45; mem. Royal Society Empire Scientific Conf. and British Commonwealth Official Scientific Conf. 46; Leader, Indian Del. to Conf. on Tropical and Sub-Tropical Soil, U.K. 48; mem. U.N. Scientific Conf. on Conservation and Utilisation of Resources and Pres. of its Land Section Meeting U.S.A. 49; mem. Gen. Assembly Int. Council of Scientific Unions, London 46, Copenhagen 49; mem. Exec. Cttee. and Board Int. Council of Scientific Unions 47-52; Vice-Pres. Int. Soil Science Congress, Netherlands 50, Foreign Sec. Nat. Inst. of Sciences of India 52; Pres. Indian Science Congress Asscn. 52; Pres. Trustees Surendraneth Teaching Insts. 52-; mem. Central Tea Board 54; Scientific Adviser, Dept. of Agriculture and Forests, West Bengal 52-56; Administrator, Board of Secondary Educ., West Bengal 55-56; mem. Union Public Service Comm. 56-58; Chair. Land Utilization Board, West Bengal 59-66; Padma Bhusan 64. Leisure interests: scientific studies, agricultural trials, educational institutions.

Publs. Over 250 papers on Physical Chemistry, Electro-Chemistry, Colloids, Soil Science, etc.

10 Puran Chand Nahar Avenue, Calcutta 13, India. Telephone: 24-3845.

Mukhitdinov, Nuritdin Akhramovich; Soviet government official and diplomatist; b. 19 Nov. 1917, Tashkent, Uzbek S.S.R.; ed. All-Union Extra-Mural Co-operative Inst.

Party and State activity, Uzbekistan 47-55; mem. Central Cttee. of the C.P.S.U. 52-61; First Sec. Central Cttee. of the Uzbek C.P. 55-57; alternative mem. Presidium of the Central Cttee. of the C.P.S.U. 56-57, mem. 57-61; mem. Cen. Cttee. of the C.P.S.U. 52-66; Deputy Chair. *Tsentrosoyuz* (Cen. Co-operative Alliance) 61-66; First Vice-Pres. Cttee. for Cultural Relations with Foreign Countries, U.S.S.R. Council of Ministers July 66-68; Amb. to Syrian Arab Repub. 68-; awarded Order of Lenin (twice).

U.S.S.R. Embassy, Boustan el-kouzbari, rue d'Alep, Damascus, Syrian Arab Republic.

Mukke, Mikhail Ivanovich; Soviet politician; b. 16 Nov. 1907, Irbit, Sverdlovsk Region; ed. Plekhanov Inst. of National Economy.

With consumer co-operative orgs. and state reading system 27-41, 46-62; mem. C.P.S.U. 44-; with the Soviet Army 41-46; Perm. Rep. of Latvian S.S.R. Council of Ministers to U.S.S.R. Council of Ministers 62-; mem. Central Cttee. Latvian C.P.; Deputy to Latvian Supreme Soviet; Orders of the Red Banner of Labour, Red Star (twice), Badge of Honour (twice).

Permanent Representation of the Latvian S.S.R. Council of Ministers to the U.S.S.R. Council of Ministers, ulitsa Chaplygina 3, Moscow, U.S.S.R.

Mulaisho, Dominic Chola, B.A.; Zambian business executive; b. 15 Aug. 1933, Feira; ed. Canisius Coll., Munali Training Centre, Chalimbana Teachers' Coll., Univ. Coll. of Rhodesia and Nyasaland.

Permanent Sec. Office of the Pres. 65-66, Ministry of Lands and Natural Resources 66-67, of Mines 67-68, of Educ. 68-70; Exec. Chair. Mindeco Ltd. 70-72, Man. Dir. July 72-; Chair. Roan Consolidated Mines and Nchanga Consolidated Copper Mines 70-73.

Publ. *The Tongue of the Dumb* (novel).

P.O. Box 90, Lusaka, Zambia.

Mulamba Nyunyi Wa Kadima, Gen. (Léonard); Zairian army officer and politician; b. 1928, Kawanga, Luluabourg; s. of Kadima and Ngalula Mulamba; m. Adolphine N'galula 1956; six s. two d.; ed. Military School, Luluabourg.

Commissioned 54; Maj. and Deputy Dir. of Cabinet, Ministry of Defence 61-64; Lieut.-Col. 62; Col., Chief of Staff and Commr. of Eastern Province (now Haut Zaire) after re-occupation of Kivu Province 64-65; Prime Minister 65-Oct. 66; Pres. Société Nationale d'Assurances (SONAS) 66; Amb. to India 67-69; Amb. to Japan 69-, also accred. to Repub. of Korea 71-; Mil. Medal, Cross of Bravery, Commdr., Ordre de la Couronne (Belgium), Grand Officier, Ordre Nat. du Léopard (Zaire), Ordre du Mérite (Central African Repub.).

Leisure interests: hunting, reading.

Embassy of Zaire, 5th Floor, Odakyn Minani Aoyami Building, 8-1 Minami Aoyama 7-chome, Minato-ku, Tokyo, Japan.

Mulatier, Léon Frédéric; French telecommunications official; b. 26 May 1887, Eurre, Drôme; s. of Hippolyte Frédéric Mulatier and Nathalie Savert; m. Germaine Lavielle 1912; one s. one d.; ed. Coll. classique, Montélimar, Ecole spéciale des Travaux publics and Ecole nat. supérieure des Postes et Télégraphes, Paris.

Joined Postal and Telegraph Service 06; Clerk, Ministry of Posts, Telegraphs and Telephones 19, Deputy Chief of Dept. 24, Chief of Dept. 33, Deputy Dir. of Personnel 34, Dir. of Personnel a.i. 34-35, Dir. of Telegraph and Radiocommunications Development 35; Vice-Dir. Int. Telecommunications Office, Berne 40, Dep. Sec.-Gen. 48, Sec.-Gen. 50-63 (now retd.); Prof. Ecole nat. supérieure des PTT 26-40; served in First World War

14-18; Dep. Chief, Posts and Telegraphs Service, Upper Silesia, Inter-Allied Govt. and Plebiscite Comm. 20; responsible for first radio-telephone link with U.S.A. 35, etc.; Head of French Del. at numerous int. telecommunications confs.; Sec.-Gen. of Telecommunications Confs., Atlantic City 47, Buenos Aires 52, Telegraph and Telephone Conf., Paris 49, Radiodiffusion Conf., Florence-Rapallo 50; Commdr. de la Légion d'Honneur (France), Grand Officer, Order of the Crown (Italy), Grand Officer Order of St. Sava (Yugoslavia), Commdr. Order of St. Charles (Monaco), Commdr. Order of White Lion (Czechoslovakia), and other decorations.
55 Route de Chêne, Geneva, Switzerland.
Telephone: 36-33-92.

Mulder, Cornelius Petrus, B.A., PH.D.; South African politician; b. 5 June 1925, Warmbaths, Transvaal; s. of Commdt. P. W. A. Mulder; m. Suzanne de Wet; three s. one d.; ed. Univs. of Potchefstroom and Witwatersrand.
Teacher Randgate Afrikaans Medium and Secondary Schools 46-52; at Riebeeck Secondary School, Randfontein 52-58; M.P. April 58-; Asst. Information Officer of Nat. Party 66-67, Chief Information Officer July 67-68; Minister of Information 68-, of Immigration 68-72, of Social Welfare and Pensions 68-74, and of Interior July 72-; Mayor of Randfontein 53, 57; Chair. Divisional Cttee. of Nat. Party at Randfontein and Pres. of Transvaal Municipal Asscn. 55; Leader Nat. Party in Transvaal Sept. 72-; mem. of numerous parl. select cttees.
Leisure interests: tennis, reading.
Ministry of Information, Pretoria, Transvaal, South Africa.

Muldoon, Rt. Hon. Robert, P.C., M.P., F.C.A.N.Z., C.M.A.N.Z., F.C.W.A., F.C.I.S., A.I.A.N.Z.; New Zealand politician and public accountant; b. 21 Sept. 1921, Auckland; s. of James H. and Amie R. Muldoon; m. Thea Dale Flyger 1951; one s. two d.; ed. Mount Albert Grammar School.
Senior Partner, Kendon Mills Muldoon and Browne, Auckland; Lecturer in Auditing 48-54; Pres. New Zealand Inst. of Cost Accountants 56, Auckland Horticultural Council 59-60; M.P. for Tamaki 60-; Parl. Under-Sec. to Minister of Finance 64-66; Minister of Tourism and Publicity 67, of Finance 67-72, 75-; Deputy Prime Minister Feb.-Dec. 72; Deputy Leader of the Opposition 73-74, Leader 74-75; Prime Minister Dec. 75-; mem. Select Cttee. on Fishing Industry 63, Road Safety 65, Parl. Procedure 67; mem. Public Expenditure Cttee. 61-66, Chair. 63-66; Dominion Councillor, New Zealand Nat. Party 60-; Fellow, New Zealand Inst. of Cost Accountants, New Zealand Soc. of Accountants, Inst. of Cost and Management Accountants, Inst. of Cost and Management Accountants, London, Royal Horticultural Soc.; Leverhulme Prize, Inst. of Cost and Works Accountants 46, Maxwell Award, New Zealand Inst. of Cost Accountants 56.
Home: 290 Kohimarama Road, Auckland 5, New Zealand.
Telephone: 583-788.

Mulholland, William David, M.B.A., LL.D.; American banker; b. 16 June 1926, Albany, N.Y.; s. of William David and Helen Flack Mulholland; m. Nancy Louise Booth 1957; five s. four d.; ed. Christian Brothers Acad., Albany, Harvard Coll. and Harvard Graduate School of Business Admin.
Served with U.S. Army, with service in Philippines as Co. Commdr. 44-46; joined Morgan Stanley & Co. (investment bankers) New York 52, Partner 62-69, resigned; Pres. and Chief Exec. Officer, Churchill Falls (Labrador) Corpn. Ltd. 69-74, Brinco Ltd. 69-75; Pres. Bank of Montreal Jan. 75-.

Leisure interests: fishing, shooting, hunting.
1296 Redpath Crescent, Montreal, Quebec H3G 2KI, Canada.
Telephone: 845-1600.

Mulikita, Fwanyanga Matale, M.A.; Zambian politician; b. 24 Nov. 1928, Mongu; ed. Fort Hare Univ. Coll., Rhodes Univ., S. Africa and Stanford Univ., U.S.A.
Headmaster, Chalimbana Secondary School 61-64; Perm. Rep. of Zambia to UN 64-66; Perm. Sec., Ministry of Educ., Lusaka 66-68, Ministry of Foreign Affairs 68; Cabinet Minister, Luapula Province 69; Minister of Labour and Social Services, also of Health 69-71, of Power, Transport and Works 71-73, of Educ. 73-.
Publs. *Batili Ki Mwanaka* 58, *A Point of No Return* 67, *Shaka Zulu* 67, and many poems.
Ministry of Education, Lusaka; Home: P.O. Box 76, Chilanga, Zambia.

Muliro, Masinde, B.A.; Kenyan politician; b. 1922, Matili, Mimilili, Bungoma District, Western Province; ed. Tororo Coll., Uganda and Univ. of Cape Town.
Teacher, African Girls' High School, Kikuyu, subsequently at Siriba Teachers' Training Coll.; mem. Legislative Council 57; Minister for Commerce, Industry and Communications 61-63, for Co-operatives and Social Services 69-74, of Works Nov. 74-June 75.
Ministry of Works, Nairobi, Kenya.

Müller, Charles; Swiss diplomatist and international official; b. 4 July 1922, Zürich; s. of Hans Martin Müller and Clara (née Meyer); m. Marlise Brügger 1950; ed. Univs. of Zürich and Geneva and Graduate Inst. of Int. Studies, Geneva.
Ministry of Foreign Affairs 46-50; Embassy, Cairo 50-55, Moscow 55-58; Ministry of Foreign Affairs 58-60; Head of Gen. and Legal Dept., European Free Trade Asscn. (EFTA) 60-61, Asst. Sec.-Gen. 61-65, Deputy Sec.-Gen. 65-66; Deputy Head of Mission, Washington, D.C. 67-70; Amb. to Indonesia, Khmer Repub. and Repub. of Viet-Nam 70-73; Head, Europe-North America Div., Ministry of Foreign Affairs 73-75; Sec.-Gen. EFTA Jan. 76-.
Leisure interests: skiing, golf, painting.
EFTA Secretariat, 9-11 rue de Varembé, 1211 Geneva 20; Home: 2 rue des Granges, 1204 Geneva, Switzerland.
Telephone: 34-90-00 (Office); 21-92-56 (Home).

Müller, Gebhard; German lawyer; b. 17 April 1900, Füramoos, Biberach; s. of Johannes and Josefa Müller; m. Marianne Lutz 1940; three s.; ed. Univs. of Tübingen and Berlin.
Lawyer by profession; held several legal positions in Württemberg Courts 29-45; engaged in reconstruction of judicial system in Württemberg-Hohenzollern 45; Ministerial Dir. in Provincial Ministry of Justice Dec. 46; Provincial Pres. of C.D.U. March 47-57; Pres. of State, Minister of Finance and of Justice of Württemberg-Hohenzollern 48-52, Prime Minister of Baden-Württemberg 53-58; Pres. Constitutional Court, Karlsruhe 59-71.
Leisure interests: modern history, 18th and 19th century French literature.
Friedrich Ebertstrasse 112, 7000 Stuttgart, Federal Republic of Germany.
Telephone: 25-15-83.

Muller, Hilgard, D.LITT., LL.B., F.R.S.A., M.P.; South African politician and diplomatist; b. 4 May 1914, Potchefstroom, Transvaal; s. of C. J. Muller; m. Anita Dyason 1943; one s.; ed. Pretoria Univ., Oxford Univ., Univ. of South Africa.
University lecturer 41-46; Partner, Dyason, Douglas, Muller and Meyer, Pretoria 47-; elected mem. Pretoria City Council 51; Mayor 53-55; Nat. Party M.P. for Pretoria East 58-60; Amb. to the U.K. 61-64; Minister of Foreign Affairs 64-; Chancellor, Univ. of Pretoria 64;

Dir. of various companies; mem. Acad. of Science and Arts; D.Phil. (h.c.); Grand Cross, Order of Merit of Paraguay 66, of the Order of Christ of Portugal 69, of the Order of Infante Dom Henrique of Portugal 73; Grand Chancellor of Order of Good Hope of S. Africa.
Publs. *Christians and Pagans from Constantine to Augustus, Merkwaadige figure uit die Oudheid*, other books on history and biography; numerous literary articles.
Ministry of Foreign Affairs, Pretoria, South Africa.

Müller, Margarete; German politician; b. 1930.
Chairman of an agricultural production co-operative; joined Sozialistische Einheitspartei Deutschlands 51, mem. Cen. Cttee. and cand. mem. Politburo 63-; mem. Council of State 71-.
102 Berlin, Am-Marx-Engels Platz 2, German Democratic Republic.

Müller, Dr. Paul H.; Swiss business executive; b. 19 Jan. 1918; ed. Univ. of Basle.
Joined Swiss Aluminium Ltd. (Alusuisse) 43, mem. Man. Board 63-, Gen. Man. Dec. 66-75, Exec. Vice-Pres. 75.
Alusuisse, 8034 Zurich, Feldeggstrasse 4, Switzerland.
Telephone: 01-34-90-90.

Muller, Stephanus Louwrens, LL.B.; South African politician; b. 27 Sept. 1917, Cape Province; *m.* Ruby Olive Oxborrow; two *d.*; ed. Cape Tech. Coll.
Practised law 49-56; mem. Cape Provincial Council 56-59; Chair. Cape Provincial Council 59-60; M.P. for Ceres, Cape Province 61-; Deputy Minister of Justice, Police and Prisons 66, of Police, Finance and Econ. Affairs 66-68; Minister of Police and of the Interior 68-70, of Police and Econ. Affairs 70-74, of Transport 74-; Nat. Party.
Leisure interest: golf.
Ministry of Transport, Pretoria, South Africa.

Muller, Steven, PH.D.; American university president; b. 22 Nov. 1927, Hamburg, Germany; *s.* of Werner A. and Marianne (Hartstein) Muller; *m.* Margie Hellman 1951; two *d.*; ed. Hollywood High School, Los Angeles, Univ. of Calif., Los Angeles, Oxford Univ. (U.K.) and Cornell Univ., Ithaca, N.Y.
Instructor in Political Science, Wells Coll. 53; U.S. Army 54-55; Research Fellow in Social Science, Cornell Univ. 55-56; Asst. Prof. of Political Science, Haverford Coll. 56-58; Asst. Prof. of Govt., Cornell Univ. 58-61, Assoc. Prof. and Dir. Center for Int. Studies 61-66, Vice-Pres. for Public Affairs 66-71; Provost, Johns Hopkins Univ. 71-72, Pres. 72-; Pres. Johns Hopkins Hosp. 72-; Trustee, Baltimore Museum of Art, Whitney Museum of American Art, N.Y., Maryland Acad. of Science; Hon. D.Litt. (Alfred Univ.) 66, (Coll. of Charleston) 74, Hon. D.Litt. (Univ. of Maryland) 72, Hon. S.Sc.D. (Washington Coll.) 74.
Publs. articles in learned journals.
The Johns Hopkins University, Garland Hall, 34th and Charles Streets, Baltimore, Md. 21218; Home: 222 Gateswood Road, Lutherville-Timonium, Md. 21093, U.S.A.
Telephone: 366-3300, Ext. 211-212 (Office); 301-252-7318 (Home).

Müller, Theodor; German business executive (retd.); b. 24 April 1911.
Representative for machine tools in Spain 32-36; joined Ferrostaal A.G., Essen 37; Army service 42-45; returned to Ferrostaal A.G. 45; Deputy Gen. Man. Cia. Ferro e Aco, Vitoria, Brazil 59; Rep. for Ferrostaal in Spain 63; mem. Management Board Maschinenfabrik Esslingen, Esslingen 64; mem. Management Board Gutehoffnungshütte Sterkrade A.G. 66-74; retd.
43 Essen, Kantorie 43a, Federal Republic of Germany.

Muller, Thomas Frederik; South African businessman; b. 12 Dec. 1916; *s.* of late Cornelius Johannes Muller and Martha Aletta Muller (née Dreyer); *m.* 1st Susanna

Elizabeth Jordaan 1942 (died 1968), two *d.*; *m.* 2nd Nicolette van Schalkwyk 1970, one *s.*; ed. Ermelo High School, Univ. of the Witwatersrand and Birmingham Univ., England.
Employed by Rand Leases Mine of Anglo-Transvaal group of companies 37-49; Mine Man., Virginia Mine 49-55; Asst. Consulting Engineer, Head Office 55-57; Technical Man., Federale Mynbou Beperk Feb. 57-58, Gen. Man. 58-61, Man. Dir. 61-71; Man. Dir. Gen. Mining and Finance Corpn. Ltd. Oct. 63-71; Chair. South African Iron and Steel Industrial Corpn. Ltd. (ISCOR) 71-; Chair. Amcor, Metkor, Int. Pipe and Steel Investments and other companies in the ISCOR group; fmr. Pres. Chamber of Mines of S. Africa, Afrikaanse Handelsinstituut; mem. Prime Minister's Econ. Advisory Council; Hon. D.Comm. (Potchefstroom).
Leisure interests: golf and angling.
Publs. Several papers on mining matters, especially on shaft-sinking at Virginia and Merriespruit Mines.
Office: ISCOR, P.O. Box 450, Pretoria 0001; Home: 17 Molesey Avenue, Auckland Park, Johannesburg 2001, South Africa.
Telephone: 3-9151 (Office); 31-2182 (Home).

Müller-Armack, Alfred, DR.RER.POL.; German economist; b. 28 June 1901; ed. Goethe-Gymnasium, Essen, Giessen, Freiburg, Munich and Cologne Univs.
Lecturer, Cologne Univ. 26; Extraordinary Prof. Cologne Univ. 34; Münster 38; Prof. Münster Univ. 40, Cologne 50-; Dir. Dept. of Econ. Policy, Fed. Ministry of Econ. Affairs 52-57, Sec. of State 57-63; Dr.Iur. h.c. (Vienna).
Publs. *Ökonomische Theorie der Konjunkturpolitik* 28, *Entwicklungsgesetze des Kapitalismus* 32, *Genealogie der Wirtschaftsstile* 44, *Wirtschaftslenkung und Marktwirtschaft* 47, *Das Jahrhundert ohne Gott* 48, *Diagnose unserer Gegenwart* 49, *Religion und Wirtschaft* 59, *Wirtschaftsordnung und Wirtschaftspolitik* 66, *Auf dem Weg nach Europa* 71.
Office: Institut für Wirtschaftspolitik, Universität zu Köln, Lindenburger Allee 32, 5000 Köln-Lindenthal; Home: Auf der Ruhr 11, 5039 Weiss (Kreis Köln), Federal Republic of Germany.
Telephone: 4704272 (Office).

Mulley, Rt. Hon. Frederick William, P.C., M.P.; British barrister, economist and politician; b. 3 July 1918, Leamington Spa, Warwicks.; *m.* Joan Phillips 1948; two *d.*; ed. Warwick School and Christ Church, Oxford.
Former clerk, Nat. Health Insurance Cttee., Warwickshire; Army Service 39-45, Prisoner-of-War 40-45; Adult Scholar, Christ Church, Oxford 45-47; Research Studentship, Nuffield Coll., Oxford 47-48; Fellow of St. Catharine's Coll., Cambridge 48-50; M.P. 50-; Parl. Private Sec. to Minister of Works 51; Called to Bar, Inner Temple 54; mem. Nat. Exec. Cttee. Labour Party 57-58, 60-; Deputy Sec. of State for Defence and Minister of Defence for the Army 64-65; Minister of Aviation 65-67; Minister of State for Foreign Affairs 67-69; Minister of Transport 69-70, 74-75; Chair. Labour Party 74-75; Sec. of State for Educ. and Science 75-.
Leisure interests: gardening, sport, reading.
Publ. *The Politics of Western Defence* 62.
House of Commons, London, S.W.1, England.

Mulli, Henry Nzioka, B.SC., DIP.ED.; Kenyan educationist, politician and diplomatist; b. 24 Sept. 1925; *m.* Annah I. Mulli 1957; four *s.* two *d.*; ed. Alliance High School, Kikuyu, Makerere Univ. Coll., Fort Hare Univ. Coll. and Oxford Univ.
Analytical Chemist, Govt. of Tanganyika 51-53; Head of Science Dept., Machakos High School 57-60; Parl. Sec. for Defence 62-63; Amb. to People's Republic of China 64-65, to U.A.R. 65-68, to Somali Democratic Repub. 68-70, to Fed. Repub. of Germany 70-74, to France 74-75.

Leisure interests: photography, golf.
c/o Ministry of Foreign Affairs, Nairobi, Kenya.

Mulliken, Robert Sanderson, B.S., PH.D.; American professor of physics and chemistry; b. 7 June 1896, Newburyport, Mass.; s. of Prof. Samuel Parsons Mulliken and Katherine Wilmarth Mulliken; m. Mary Helen von Noé 1929 (died 1975); two d.; ed. Mass. Inst. of Technology and Univ. of Chicago.
Organic Chemical Research (mainly Chemical Warfare) 17-19; research on separation of isotopes 19-23; on isotope effect in diatomic spectra 23-26; on electronic spectra and electronic structure of diatomic and poly-atomic molecules, and valence theory 25-; Nat. Research Fellow 21-25; Asst. Prof. of Physics, Washington Square Coll., New York Univ. 26-28; Assoc. Prof. of Physics, Univ. of Chicago 28-31, Prof. 31-61, Distinguished Service Prof. 61-; work on Plutonium Project at Chicago 42-45; Scientific Attaché, American Embassy, London 55; Ernest de Witt Burton Distinguished Service Prof. 56-61; Distinguished Research Prof. of Chemical Physics, Florida State Univ. 64-71; mem. American Nat. Acad. of Sciences, American Philosophical Soc., American Acad. of Arts and Sciences, Int. Acad. of Quantum Molecular Science; Baker Lecturer, Cornell Univ. 60; Silliman Lecturer, Yale Univ. 65; Visiting Prof. Bombay and Kanpur 62, Amsterdam 65, Santa Barbara 68, Paris 68, Austin, Texas 70; Gilbert N. Lewis Gold Medal 60, Theodore W. Richards Gold Medal 60, Peter Debye Award 63, J. G. Kirkwood Medal 65, J. Willard Gibbs Medal 65, C.C.N.Y. Gold Medal 65, Chicagoan of the Year Press Club Award 66, Nobel Prize in Chemistry 66; Hon. Fellow, Chemical Soc. (London); Foreign mem. Royal Soc. (U.K.) 67; Hon. mem. Société de Chimie Physique; Hon. Fellow, Indian Nat. Acad. of Sciences; Corresp. mem. Société Royale des Sciences, Liège; Hon. Sc.D. (Columbia, Gustavus Adolphus Coll.), Hon. Ph.D. (Stockholm); Hon. Sc.D. (Cambridge) 67.
Leisure interests: Japanese prints, oriental rugs, botany.
Chemistry Department, University of Chicago, Chicago, Ill. 60637; and 5825 South Dorchester Avenue, Chicago, Ill. 60637, U.S.A.
Telephone: 753-8313-4 (Office); 493-0322 (Home).

Mumcuoğlu, Hayri; Turkish lawyer; b. 1914, Istanbul; ed. secondary schools, Istanbul.
Assistant Judge, Bartin 37; Judge for Penal Affairs, Akçaabat, Saframbolu; Asst. Prosecutor, Ankara; Judge, Chief Prosecutor of the Repub.; Chief Prosecu-tor, Ministry of Justice; mem. Court of Cassation; mem. Parl. for Tekirdağ (New Turkey Party) 61; Minister of Housing and Reconstruction 63; joined Repub. People's Party 67, resigned 72; Minister of Justice 73, 74-75; Independent.
National Assembly, Ankara, Turkey.

Mumford, Lewis; American writer; b. 19 Oct. 1895, Flushing, N.Y.; s. of Lewis Mumford and Elvina Baron; m. Sophia Wittenberg 1921; one s. (killed 1944) one d.; ed. New York City Coll., New York Univ., Columbia Univ.
Assoc. Editor The Dial 19; Acting Editor Sociological Review London 20; Lecturer, Geneva School of Int. Studies 25 and 29; Guernsey Centre Moore Foundation Lecturer, Dartmouth Coll. 29; Earle Lecturer, Pacific School of Religion 47; Bampton Lecturer, Columbia Univ. 51; co-Editor The American Caravan 26-36; mem. Board of Higher Education, City of New York 35-37; mem. Comm. on Teacher Education, American Council on Education 38-44; Consultant on Planning, City and County Park Board, Honolulu 38; Prof. of Humanities, Stanford Univ. 42-44; Prof. Univ. Pennsylvania 52-60, Hon. Fellow Royal Inst. British Architects 42; Hon. mem. Town Planning Inst. (Gt. Britain) 46; Hon. Vice-Pres. Int. Housing and Town Planning Fed. 47; Bemis Prof. Massachusetts Inst. of Technology 57-60,

Visiting Abrams Prof. 75; Hon. Fellow Stanford Univ. 41; Fellow American Acad. of Arts and Sciences; mem. American Philosophical Soc.; mem. Nat. Inst. of Arts and Letters, Pres. American Acad. of Arts and Letters 63-65; Consultant on Planning, Christ Church, Oxford, England; hon. mem. American Inst. of Architects, American Inst. of Planners; Vice-Pres. Société Europé-enne de Culture; Co-Chair. Wenner-Gren Conf. on Man's Role in shaping the Face of the Earth 55; Gold Medal, Town Planning Inst. 57; Guggenheim Fellow 32, 38, 56; Ford Research Prof. Univ. of Pa. 59-61, Univ. of Calif. 61-62; Saposnekow lecturer, City Coll. of N.Y. 62; Gold Medal, Town Planning Inst. 57; Royal Gold Medal, R.I.B.A. 61, Presidential Medal of Freedom 64, Emerson-Thoreau Medal American Acad. of Arts and Sciences 65; Brandeis Award in Creative Arts 69; Gold Medal (Belles-Lettres) Nat. Inst. of Arts and Letters 70; Award of Merit, Philadelphia Aer Alliance 71; Leonardo da Vinci Medal, Soc. for History of Technology 69; Hodgkins Medal, Smith-sonian Inst. 71, Thomas Jefferson Memorial Medal 72, Nat. Medal for Literature 72; Hon. LL.D., Edinburgh, Hon. D.Arch., Rome.
Leisure interest: gardening.
Publs. Story of Utopias 22, Sticks and Stones 24, The Golden Day 26, Herman Melville 29 (revised edn. 60), The Brown Decades 31, Technics and Civilisation 34, The Culture of Cities 38, Whither Honolulu? 38, Men Must Act 39, Faith for Living 40, The South in Archi-tecture 41, The Condition of Man 44, City Development 45 Values for Survival 46, Green Memories—The Story of Geddes Mumford 47, The Conduct of Life 51, Art and Technics 52, In the Name of Sanity 54, The Transfor-mations of Man 56, The City in History 61, The Highway and the City 63, Technics and Human Development 67, The Urban Prospect 68, The Pentagon of Power 70, Interpretations and Forecasts 1922-1972 72, Findings and Keepings 1914-1936—Analects for an Autobiography 75.
Amenia, N.Y. 12501, U.S.A.
Telephone: 914-373-8579.

Mumford, L. Quincy, M.A.; American library adminis-trator (retd.); b. 11 Dec. 1903; s. of Jacob Edward and Emma Luvenia (née Stocks) Mumford; m. 1st Permelia C. Stevens 1930 (died 1961), 2nd Betsy Perrin Fox 1969; one d.; ed. Duke and Columbia Univs.
Duke Univ. Library 22-28; Columbia Univ. Library 28-29; New York Public Library 29-45; Asst. Dir. Cleveland Public Library 45-50, Dir. 50-54; Librarian of Congress 54-74; retd. 74; Benjamin Franklin Fellow of the Royal Soc. for the Encouragement of Arts, Manu-facturers and Commerce (London); Del. to Int. Fed. of Library Assocns; mem. British Museums Soc.
3721 49th Street, N.W., Washington, D.C. 20016, U.S.A.

Mumford, Milton Christopher, A.B.; American busi-nessman; b. 14 April 1913, Marissa, Ill.; s. of Manly J. Mumford and Emily Stearns; m. Dorothea Louise Greene 1942; three c.; ed. Univ. of Illinois.
Joined Marshall Field and Co., Chicago 35, Vice-Pres. 48-54, Gen. Man. Fieldcrest Mills Div. 50-53; Pres. Fieldcrest Mills Inc. 53-54; Vice-Pres. Lever Bros. Co. 54-55, Exec. Vice-Pres. 55-59, Pres. and Chief Exec. Officer 59-65, Chair. of Board 64-72; Dir. Equitable Life Assurance Society of U.S. 62-; Chair. Educational Facilities Laboratories Inc. (Ford Foundation) 59-72; Trustee, Consolidated Edison Co. of New York 64-; Dir. Stamford Hospital, Stamford, Conn. 64-, Crown Zellerbach Corpn. 65-, Nat. Educational Television 65-69, Unilever subsidiaries 65-, Fed. Reserve Bank of New York 66-72; Nat. Volunteer Chair., United Com-munity Campaigns of America 66; mem. Nat. Industrial Conf. Board 59-72; Dir. Nat. Merit Scholar Scholarship Corpn. 65-71; Trustee, Presbyterian Hospital (N.Y.)

67-; mem. Nat. Council Foreign Policy Asscn. 67-, Emergency Cttee. for American Trade 68-72, Nat. Ind. Pollution Control Council 70-72, Nat. Advisory Cttee. of "Jobs for Veterans" 70; Dir. Int. Executives Service Corps. 68-72; Legion of Merit, U.S. Navy 45; Alumni Achievement Award (Univ. of Illinois) 71; Hon. LL.D. (Long Island Univ.).
Lever Brothers Co., 390 Park Avenue, New York, N.Y. 10022, U.S.A.
Telephone: 212-688-6000.

Muna, Solomon Tandeng; Cameroonian politician; b. 1912, Ngen-Mbo, Momo Division; s. of Muna Tayim and Ama Keng Muna; m. Elizabeth Fri Muna 1937; seven s. one d.; ed. Teacher Training Coll., Kumba and Univ. of London Inst. of Education.
Member of Parliament for Bamenda District 51; Eastern Nigeria Minister for Public Works 52; Minister of Works, subsequently Minister of Commerce and Industries, Minister of Finance, Southern Cameroon Region; Minister of Transport, Mines, Posts and Telecommunications of Cameroon 61-68; Prime Minister of West Cameroon 68-72, also Vice-Pres. Fed. Repub. of Cameroon 70-72; Minister of State at the Presidency 72-74; Pres. Nat. Assembly 74-; fmrly. Chair. Board of Dirs. Cameroon Railways, Chair. Higher Cttee. on Cameroon Ports; has represented Cameroon at various int. confs.; Commdr., Ordre de la Valeur du Cameroun; Ordre du Sénégal; Grand Cordon, Ordre de L'Etoile d'Afrique (Liberia); Officer, Légion d'Honneur; Grand Officer de l'Ordre de la République Tunisienne, African Redemption Medal (Liberia), Grand Officier, Ordre de la République Gabonaise, Distinguished Public Service Medal (Nigeria).
Leisure interests: horseback riding, stamp collecting, scouting.
National Assembly, Yaoundé, United Republic of Cameroon.
Telephone: Buea 328256 (Home).

Münch, Guido, PH.D., M.SC.; American astronomer; b. 9 June 1921, Mexico; s. of August Münch and Maria Paniagua; three s. one d.; ed. Univs. of Mexico and Chicago.
Instructor Univ. of Chicago 47-51; with Calif. Inst. of Tech. 51-, Prof. 59-; Fellow, American Acad. of Arts and Sciences, Nat. Acad. of Sciences.
Publs. Many articles in various scientific journals and chapters in monographs and books.
Hale Observatories, 1201 E. California Street, Pasadena, Calif. 91109; 1999 Rose Villa, Pasadena, Calif. 91107, U.S.A.
Telephone: 213-795-6841 (Office); 213-681-8829 (Home).

Münchinger, Karl; German musician; b. 29 May 1915, Stuttgart; s. of Karl and Emilie Münchinger; m. Olga Rockenhäuser; ed. Staatliche Musikhochschule, Stuttgart and Konservatorium Leipzig.
Church organist in Stuttgart 37-41; Conductor Niedersachsenorchester Hanover 41-43; founded Stuttgart Chamber Orchestra 45 and its Conductor 45-, Klassische Philharmonie Stuttgart 66 and its Conductor 66-; guest conductor of various symphony orchestras; Grosses Verdienstkreuz mit Stern; Commdr. des Arts et des Lettres, Officier des Arts et des Lettres; Hon. Prof. Kulturministerium Baden-Württemberg.
Leisure interests: collecting antiques and books.
Haus am Rebenhang, 7 Stuttgart-Rotenberg, Federal Republic of Germany.
Telephone: Stuttgart 29-45-26.

Münchmeyer, Alwin; German banker; b. 19 March 1908, Hamburg; s. of Hermann and Elisabeth Münchmeyer; m. Gertrud Nolte 1934; one s. four d.; ed. High School.
Chairman Advisory Board, Schröder, Münchmeyer, Hengst and Co., Hamburg, Frankfurt, Offenbach; mem. Exec. Cttee. German Section, Int. Chamber of Com-

merce; mem. Council Int. Chamber of Commerce; Chair. Foreign Trade Advisory Board, Ministry of Econ., Bonn; Chair. Allgemeine Kreditversicherung AG, Mainz, Philips GmbH, Hamburg, Nord-Deutsche Versicherungs-AG, Hamburg, Nord-Deutsche Lebensversicherungs-AG, Hamburg, Vereins-und Westbank AG, Hamburg; mem. Boards and Advisory Boards of other companies.
Leisure interests: riding, tennis, hiking, icons.
Schröder, Münchmeyer, Hengst and Co., 2 Hamburg 1, Ballindamm 33, Federal Republic of Germany.
Telephone: 32 951.

Munekata, Eiji, DR.ENG.SC.; Japanese engineer; b. 24 Jan. 1908, Tokyo; s. of late Nagaharu and Haruko Nagaike; m. Miyoko Kitaoka 1938; two s. one d.; ed. Tokyo Imperial Univ.
Section Chief, Nippon Bemberg Silk Co. 31; Chief Engineer, Chosen Artificial Petroleum Mfg. Co. 39; Head of Dept., Nippon Chisso Fertilizer Co. 44; Dir., subsequently Man. Dir. Asahi Chemical Industry Co. 47; Dir. Japan Atomic Energy Research Inst. 62, Pres. 68-.
Leisure interests: sports (golf, swimming), gardening.
Publs. Separation 50, Man-made Fibre 55, Researches on Chemistry and Industrialization 65.
31 1-chome, Zenpukuji-machi, Suginami-ku, Tokyo, Japan.
Telephone: 03-390-6364.

Mungai, Joseph James; Tanzanian politician; b. 24 Oct. 1943; m. Mary Chawe 1967; two s. one d.
Joined Singer Sewing Machine Co. as internal auditor 65, later Training and Devt. Man.; Commercial Man. Tanzania Elimu Supplies Ltd. Dec. 69, Gen. Man. July 70; mem. for Mufindi in Nat. Assembly, Tanganyika African Nat. Union (TANU); Minister for Agriculture 72-75; fmr. Chair. TANU Elimu Supplies Party Branch; mem. TANU Youth League, Nat. Union of Tanganyika Workers; Vice-Chair. Tanzania Inst. of Management.
Leisure interests: squash, soccer, tennis.
P.O. Box 9192, Dar es Salaam, Tanzania.

Mungai, Njoroge, M.D.; Kenyan politician and doctor; b. 1926 Dagoretti, Kikuyu; ed. Presbyterian Church Elementary School, Kikuyu, Alliance High School, Fort Hare Univ. (S. Africa), Stanford Univ., Calif., and Columbia Univ. Presbyterian Medical Center, N.Y.
East African Airways Ground Officer 46-47; bus driver 47-48; Intern King's County Hospital, New York 58; returned to Kenya and practised medicine at private clinics in Thika, Riruta and Embu and ran mobile clinic; mem. Nat. Exec. KANU, Chair. Thika branch of KANU; mem. House of Reps. 63-74; Minister for Health and Housing 63-65; Minister of Defence 65-69; Minister of Foreign Affairs 69-74; mem. Kenya Educ. Fund Cttee., Nat. Nutritional Council; fmr. Pres. Kenya Medical Asscn.; personal physician to Pres. Jomo Kenyatta.
Leisure interest: golf.
Ministry of Foreign Affairs, P.O. Box. 30551, Nairobi, Kenya.

Munir, Muhammad, N.Q.A., M.A., LL.B., LL.D. (Hon.); Pakistani lawyer; b. 3 May 1892, Khanpur, Hoshiarpur District, India; s. of Dr. Muhammad and Amirunnissa Bakhsh; one s.
Practising lawyer in Amritsar 21, in Lahore 22-36; Pres. Income Tax Appellate Tribunal 40; High Court Judge 49-54; Chief Justice of Pakistan 54-60; Minister of Law and Parl. Affairs 62; Acting Gov.-Gen. 54; represented Pakistan at conf. of Int. Comm. of Jurists, Athens 55; Vice-Chair. Int. Criminal Jurisdiction Cttee., UN.
Leisure interests: Shikar and writing.
Publs. Principles and Digest of Law of Evidence, Constitution of the Islamic Republic of Pakistan, Islam in

History—Commentary on 1973—Constitution of the Islamic Republic of Pakistan.
39 Gulberg V, Lahore, Pakistan.
Telephone: 81673.

Muñiz, Carlos Manuel, LL.D.; Argentine diplomatist; b. 2 Feb. 1922, Buenos Aires; unmarried; ed. Univ. of Buenos Aires.
Under-Secretary of Interior and Justice 55, of Interior 55-56; Amb. to Bolivia 56-59, to Brazil 59-62; Minister of Foreign Affairs and Worship 62-63; Prof. of Int. Public Law, Univ. of La Plata 63-, also Dir. Int. Law Inst.; Prof. of Constitutional Law, Univ. of Buenos Aires; Special Prof. of Int. Law and Int. Relations, Catholic Univ. of La Plata; Amb. to U.S.A. 71-73; decorations from govts. of Bolivia, Brazil, Japan, Peru, Paraguay.
Publs. many books and articles on legal, sociological and literary themes.
Parera 117, Buenos Aires, Argentina.
Telephone: 42-3227.

Munk, Frank; American (fmr. Czechoslovak) economist and political scientist; b. 26 May 1901, Kutna Hora, Czechoslovakia; s. of Alfred and Marie (Mautnerová) Munk; m. Nadežda Prasilová 1925; one s. one d.; ed. Prague, Columbia and Harvard Univs.
Student and youth leader Czechoslovakia; Fellow Rockefeller Foundation U.S. 31-33; Chair. Prague Univ. L.N. Fed. 34-36; Masaryk Acad. 31-38; with Social Inst. Min. of Welfare Prague 31-39; Lecturer Reed Coll. Portland, Oregon 39-41; Lecturer in Economics Univ. Calif. Berkeley, to 44; Dir. UNRRA Training Centre, Univ. Maryland 44-45; Chief Economic Adviser UNRRA 46; Prof. Reed Coll., Portland, Oregon 46-65; Dean Northwest Inst. Int. Relations 47-56; Visiting Prof. Univ. of Wash. 52; Public mem. Regional Wage Stabilisation Board 51-52; mem. Exec. Council, Pacific North-west Political Science Asscn. 52-55, Pres. 68-69; Adviser on Intellectual Co-operation to the European Dir. Radio Free Europe, Munich 58-60; Research Fellow, Atlantic Inst. (Paris) 61-62; Visiting Prof. Political Science, Coll. of Europe (Brussels) 61-62; Research Consultant, Foreign Policy Research Inst., Univ. of Pennsylvania 63-65; Prof. of Political Science and Assoc. Dir. Central European Studies Center, Portland State Coll. 65-; Exec. Council Western Slavic Asscn. 70-72; Pres. World Affairs Council of Oregon 72-73; World Affairs Commentator, Public T.V. Oregon 75-.
Leisure interests: hiking, swimming, photography.
Publs. include *The Legacy of Nazism* 43, *Atlantic Dilemma* 63.
3808 S.W., Mt. Adams Drive, Portland, Oregon 97201, U.S.A.
Telephone: 503-227-3334.

Munk, Walter Heinrich, PH.D.; American professor of geophysics; b. 19 Oct. 1917, Vienna, Austria; s. of Hans and Rega (Brunner) Munk; m. Judith Horton 1953; two d.; ed. Calif. Inst. of Technology and Scripps Inst. of Oceanography.
Assistant Prof. of Geophysics, Univ. of Calif. at San Diego 47-49, Assoc. Prof. 49-54, Prof. Inst. of Geophysics and Scripps Inst. 54-; Assoc. Dir. Inst. of Geophysics and Planetary Physics, Univ. of Calif. and Dir. La Jolla unit 59-; Guggenheim Fellow, Oslo Univ. 48, Cambridge Univ. 55, 62; Josiah Willard Gibbs Lecturer, American Mathematical Soc. 70; Fellow, American Meteorological Soc., A.A.A.S., Explorers Club; mem. American Geological Soc., National Acad. of Sciences (Chair. Geophysics Section 75-78), American Acad. of Arts and Sciences, American Philosophical Soc., Deutsche Akademie der Naturforscher Leopoldina, American Geophysical Union (Vice-Pres. Oceanography Section 54-56, Pres. 60-61), Acoustical Soc. of America; D.Phil. h.c., Univ. of Bergen (Norway); Arthur L.

Day Medal of Geological Soc. of America 65, Sverdrup Gold Medal of American Meteorological Soc. 66, Alumni Distinguished Service Award of Calif. Inst. of Technology 66, Gold Medal of Royal Astronomical Soc. 68, Calif. Scientist of the Year Award of Calif. Museum of Science and Industry 69, Award for Ocean Science and Engineering (co-recipient), Marine Tech. Soc. 69.
Leisure interests: skiing, swimming.
Publs. Co-author *The Rotation of the Earth: A Geophysical Discussion* 60, and numerous scientific articles 45-.
Institute of Geophysics and Planetary Physics, A-025 University of California, San Diego, La Jolla, Calif. 92093; Home: 9530 La Jolla Shores Drive, La Jolla, Calif. 92037, U.S.A.
Telephone: 714-452-2877 (Office); 714-453-2452 (Home).

Muñoz Duque, H. E. Cardinal Anibal; Colombian ecclesiastic; b. 3 Oct. 1908, Santa Rosa de Osos-Antioquia-Col.; s. of Jesús Muñoz and Rosa Duque de Muñoz.
Ordained 33; consecrated Bishop of Socorro y San Gil 51; transferred to Bucaramanga 52; Archbishop of Nueva Pamplona 59-68; Apostolic Administrator Bogotá 67; Pres. Colombian Episcopal Conf. 64-72; titular Archbishop of Cariana 68; Archbishop of Bogotá 72-; mem. Sagrada Congregación para los Sacramentos; created Cardinal by Pope Paul VI 73.
Arzobispado, Carrera 7 no. 10-20, Bogotá 1, D.E., Colombia.

Muñoz Ledo, Porfirio; Mexican politician and university professor; b. 1933; ed. Univ. Nacional de México.
Professor of Political Science, Univ. Nacional de México and El Colegio de México 58-69; Gen. Sec. Instituto Mexicano del Seguro Social 66-70; worked for election campaign of Pres. Echeverría (q.v.) 69; Private Sec. to Pres. Echeverría 70-72; Sec. for Labour and Social Security 72-75; Pres. Partido Revolucionario Institucional, Oct. 75-.
CEN, Partido Revolucionario Institucional, Insurgentes Norte 59, México, D.F., Mexico.

Muñoz Vega, H.E. Cardinal Paolo, S.J., D.PHIL., D.THEOL.; Ecuadorian ecclesiastic; b. 23 May 1903, Mira; s. of Antonio Muñoz and Josefa Vega.
Ordained 33; Prof. of Phil., Gregorian Univ. 38-45, Prof. Theol. 45-50; Rector, Pontificio Colegio Pio-Latino-Americano 55-57; Rector, Pontifical Gregorian Univ., Rome 57-64; Titular Bishop of Ceramo 64-67; Archbishop of Quito 67-; cr. Cardinal 69; mem. Sacred Congregation of Catholic Educ.; mem. Sacred Congregation of Religious Life.
Publs. *Introducción a la síntesis de San Agustín* 45, *Causalidad filosófica y determinismo científico* 46, *El estudio del hombre como introducción al problema de lo sobrenatural* 48, *Los Problemas de la experiencia mística a la luz del pensamiento agustiniano en Augustinus Magister* 54, *Fe e inteligencia en los origines de la ciencia moderna* 65.
Palacio Arzobispal, Apartado 106, Quito, Ecuador.
Telephone: 210-703.

Munro, Dana G.; American diplomatist and historian; b. 18 July 1892, Providence, R.I.; s. of Dana Carlton and Alice (Beecher) Munro; m. Margaret Bennett Wiley 1920; three c.; ed. Wisconsin, Pennsylvania and Brown Univs.
Regional Economist Dept. of State 19-20; Economist Consul at Valparaiso 20-21; mem. Latin-American Div. of State Dept. 21-25; 1st Sec. Panama 25-27 and Nicaragua 27-29; Chief Latin-American Affairs Div. of State Dept. 29-30; Minister to Haiti 30-32; Prof. of Latin-American History and Affairs Princeton Univ. 32-61; Vice-Pres. Foreign Bondholders' Protective Council N.Y. 38-58, Pres. 58-67, Chair. Exec. Cttee. 67-69; Dir. Woodrow Wilson School of Public and Int.

Affairs, Princeton Univ. 39-58; mem. Nat. Advisory Cttee. on Inter-American Affairs 59-61.

Leisure interests: sailing, gardening.

Publs. *The Five Republics of Central America* 18, *The United States and the Caribbean Area* 34, *The Latin American Republics: A History* 42, *Intervention and Dollar Diplomacy in The Caribbean 1900-21* 64, *The United States and the Caribbean Republics 1921-33* 74.

345 Harrison Street, Princeton, N.J. 08540, U.S.A.

Telephone: 609-924-1238.

Munro, Hon. John Carr; Canadian lawyer and politician; b. 16 March 1931; Hamilton, Ont.; s. of John Anderson Munro, Q.C. and Katherine Alexander Carr; m. Marguerite Harriet Clay 1956; two d.; ed. Central Public School, Westdale Composite School, Univ. of Western Ontario, and Osgoode Hall Law School, Toronto.

Member Hamilton City Council 55; Liberal mem. for Hamilton, East; Parl. Sec. to Minister of Citizenship and Immigration 63, later Parl. Sec. to Ministers of Nat. Health and Welfare, Trade and Commerce, and Manpower and Immigration; Minister without Portfolio April-June 68; Minister of Nat. Health and Welfare 68-72, of Labour Nov. 72-; mem. Canadian Inst. of Int. Affairs.

Department of Labour, 340 Laurier West, Ottawa, Ont., Canada.

Telephone: 613-996-6451.

Munshi, Lilavati Kanaiyalal; Indian politician; b. 1899.

Joined Satyagraha movement 30; mem. All-India Congress Cttee. 31-34; arrested and sentenced to one year's imprisonment 32; mem. Bombay Municipal Corpn. 35-46; Chair. 39-40; Vice-Pres. Nat. Council of Women in India 53-58; Pres. Bombay Presidency Women's Council 50-51; Pres. All-India Women's Food Cen. Council 50-64; Chair. Delhi Conf. of Social Work; mem. Film Advisory Board and Cen. Board of Film Censors; mem. Indian Council of Agricultural Research 50-59; founder-mem. Gujarat Research Soc.; fmr. Editor *Pushpa* and *New Outlook;* Congress mem. Bombay Legislative Council 36-46; Chair. Rajkamal Publications Ltd.; Dir. Bombay Life Insurance Co., Oudh Sugar Mills and Lallubhai Shamaldas Co-operative Bank.

Publs. *Rekhachitro ane Bija Lekho, Jeevanmathi Judeli, Kumavdevi, Rekha Chitro June ane Nava.*

Bharatiya Vidya Bhavan, Chowpatty Road, Bombay 7, India.

Munson, Charles Sherwood, B.A.; American industrialist; b. 14 Sept. 1888; s. of John Newton Munson and Florence Averill Seeley; m. Marjorie Jean Oatman 1922; one s.; ed. Yale Univ.

Joined Amoskeag Manufacturing Co. 12; Treas. Cuban Air Products 17, Pres. 19-42, Chair. 42-; Pres. Nat. Carbide Corpn. 19-41; Vice-Pres. AIRCO Inc. (Air Reduction Co.) 24-37, Pres. 37-48, 49-64, Chair. Exec. Cttee. 64-, Hon. Chair. of Board 69-; Pres. U.S. Industrial Chemicals 31-43, Chair. Exec. Cttee. 43-49; Dir. and mem. Advisory Council Morgan Guaranty Trust Co. of N.Y.; Dir. Nat. Distillers and Chemical Corpn.; Dir. and mem. Exec. Cttee. Greyhound Corpn., Gen. Fire and Casualty Co.; Dir. Baxter Laboratories, WARNCO Inc. (Warner Bros. Co.), Michigan, Gas Utilities Co., and numerous other companies.

Home: Sasco Hill, Southport, Conn. 06490; Office: 840 Madison Avenue, New York 10021, N.Y., U.S.A.

Telephone: 212-535-2000 (Office); 203-259-0111 (Home).

Murakami, Isamu; Japanese politician.

Member House of Reps. (twelve times) for Oita Pref.; Minister of Posts and Telecommunications 55, of Construction 59, of Posts and Telecommunications Dec. 74-; Liberal Democratic Party.

Ministry of Posts and Telecommunications, Tokyo, Japan.

Muralt, Alexander von, M.D., PH.D.; Swiss physiologist; b. 19 Aug. 1903.

Research Fellow (Rockefeller Foundation) Harvard Univ. 29, Research Assoc. Harvard Univ. 30, Kaiser Wilhelm Inst. 30-35; Prof. of Physiology, Univ. of Berne 35-69; Dir. Scientific Station, Jungfraujoch 37; Pres. Swiss Acad. of Sciences 46-52; Pres. Th. Kocher Foundation 44, Foundation for Fellowships in Medicine and Biology 42-48, Pres. I.C.S.U. 49-52, Swiss Nat. Science Foundation 52; Rector Berne Univ. 55-56; hon. degrees from Berne, Lausanne, Manchester, Geneva, Basle, Zürich, Cologne, Brussels and Rio de Janeiro Univs.

Publs. *Signalübermittlung im Nerven* 46, *Praktische Physiologie* 48, *Neue Ergebnisse der Nervenphysiologie* 58.

Ostring 90, Berne, Switzerland.

Muralt, Leonhard von; Swiss historian; b. 17 May 1900; ed. Univs. of Geneva and Zürich.

Lecturer in History, Univ. of Zürich 30-40; Ordinary Prof. for Modern General and Swiss History, Univ. of Zürich 40-72; Hon. Dr. Theol. (Univ. of Berne).

Publs. *Die Badener Disputation 1526* 26, *Reformation und Gegenreformation* (in *Geschichte der Schweiz*) 32, *Huldrych Zwingli, Von göttlicher und menschlicher Gerechtigkeit* 34, *Das Zeitalter der Renaissance* (in *Die Neue Propyläen-Weltgeschichte*) 41, *Machiavellis Staatsgedanke* 45, *Der Friede von Versailles und die Gegenwart* (trans. into English as *From Versailles to Potsdam* 48) 47, *Bismarcks Reichsgründung* 47, *Zürich im Schweizerbund* 51, *Quellen zur Geschichte der Täufer in der Schweiz I: Zürich* 52, *Bismarcks Verantwortlichkeit* 55, *Die Reformation* (in *Historia Mundi VII*) 57, *Der Historiker und die Geschichte, Ausgewählte Aufsätze und Vorträge* 60, Editor *Huldreich Zwinglis Sämtliche Werke* (*Corpus Reformatorum*) VI (I) 61, VI (II) 64-68, *Renaissance und Reformation* (in *Handbuch der Schweizergeschichte*) 69, *Die diplomatisch-politische Vorgeschichte* (in *Entscheidung 1870*) 70.

Wybüelstrasse 20, Zollikon bei Zürich, Switzerland.

Telephone: 051-658761.

Muramaya, Nagataka; Japanese newspaper proprietor; b. 1894; ed. Kyoto Imperial Univ.

Director *Asahi Shimbun* 20-; Man. Dir. Asahi Welfare and Cultural Asscn. 52; Chair. of Board *Asahi Evening News* 53-; Dir. Asahi Broadcasting Corpn., Osaka 55; Pres. Japan Newspaper Publishers and Editors Asscn. 55; Vice-Pres. Fed. Int. des Editeurs de Journaux et Publications 58-; Pres. *Asahi Shimbun* 60-64; numerous decorations.

16 1-chome, Ichibeicho, Azabu, Minato-ku, Tokyo, Japan.

Murano, Tatsuo, B.A.; Japanese banker; b. 18 May 1907, Gase City, Nara Pref.; m. Wakako 1936; one s. two d.; ed. Faculty of Econs., Tokyo Univ.

Joined Yamaguchi Bank 32, Dir. 57, Man. Dir. 59, Senior Man. Dir. 61, Deputy Pres. 64; Pres. Sanwa Bank Ltd. 71-; Vice-Chair. Fed. of Bankers' Asscns. of Japan.

Leisure interests: music, photography.

601, 5-12-24 Minamiaoyama Minato-ku, Tokyo 107; and 5-3-24 Nigawa-cho Nishinomiya, Hyogo 662, Japan.

Telephone: (03) 406-3366 (Tokyo); (0798) 52-8226 (Osaka).

Muraoka, Sadakatsu, B.ENG.; Japanese business executive; b. 2 Jan. 1910, Kyoto; s. of Yukichi and Masu Muraoka; m. Fuji Hirose 1937; two s. one d.; ed. Kyoto Imperial Univ.

Director Nippon Mining Co. Ltd. 60, Senior Man. Dir. 69, Exec. Vice-Pres., Gen. Man. Research and Devt. Div., Corporate Co-ordination add Control Div., Environmental Measures Promotion Centre 71-; Dir. Koyo Iron Works and Construction Co. Ltd. 65-, Nissho Shipping Co. Ltd. 67-; Pres. Bio Research Center

Co. Ltd. 72-; Chair. Orient Catalyst Co. Ltd. 73-, Toho Titanium Co. Ltd. 73-; Medal with Blue Ribbon 70.
Leisure interest: golf.
Nippon Mining Co. Ltd., 3 Akasaka Aoi cho, Maitno-ku, Tokyo; Home: 1163-2, Ichigao-cho, Midori-ku, Yoko-hama, Kanagawa Prefecture, Japan.
Telephone: 03-582-2111 (Office); 045-971-2469 (Home).

Murata, Masachika; Japanese architect; b. 6 Sept. 1906, Yokkaichi Mie Pref.; s. of Masaichi and Hisa Murata; m. Yuri Kagitomi 1935; two s.; ed. Tokyo Acad. of Fine Arts.
Designer, Shinichiro Okada Architect Office, Tokyo 29-30, Building Dept. of Ministry of Imperial House-hold, Tokyo 31-36; Researcher of facilities of Museums of Europe and America at request of Ministry of Educ. 37-39; Architect, Kameki Tuchiura Architect Office 40-46; Vice-Chief of Architectural Div., Conf. of Devt. of Kainan-tow (Hainan Island, China) 43; Pres. Masachika Murata Architect Office 46-; Dir. Board, Japan Architects Asscn. 54-; Dir. Sports and Recrea-tion Facilities, Union of Int. Architects 59-.
Works include: Yokohama building of Yokohama Trading Building Co. Ltd. (Kanagawa Prefecture Architectural Prize) 51; Tokyo Metropolitan Indoor Pool, Tokyo 57; Exhbn. Halls of Tokyo Int. Trading Center, Tokyo 59; Miyazaki Kanko Hotel, Miyazaki Pref. 61; Ochiai Sewage Treatment Plant, Tokyo, 61; Tokyo Olympic Komazawa Stadium (Special Prize of Architectural Inst. of Japan and Building Contractors' Soc. of Japan) 62; Morigasaki Sewage Treatment Plant, Tokyo, 62; Italian Embassy, Tokyo 63; Kyodo News Service Building, Tokyo 64; Y.M.C.A. Int. Youth Cen-ter, Shizuoka Pref. 64; Hotel Matsukura, Nagasaki Pref. 64; Hotel Hodaka, Nagano Pref. 64; Residence of Consul Gen. of South Africa, Tokyo 65; Education Center I.B.M. Japan 66; Police Headquarters, Aichi Pref. 68; Mt. Tateyama Int. Hotel and Bus Terminal, Toyama Pref. 68; Dentsu Advertising Office, Kyoto 69; Netherlands Pavilion, Expo 70; Matsuzakaya Dept. Store, Shizuoka 70, new Exhbn. Hall of Tokyo Int. Trading Centre, Tokyo 71; Yamagata Civic Centre, Yamagata 71; Itabashi Central Library, Tokyo 71; Yotsuya Civic Centre, Tokyo 72; Ryoyu Club, Tokyo 72; Yokkaichi Central Library Architectural Prize of Middle Part of Japan 72; Tamagawa Sewage Treat-ment Plant, Tokyo 73; Recreational facilities for Shinjuku-ku people, Hakone National Park 74; Nagano Municipal Stadium 75.
Leisure interests: golf, skiing, painting.
Office: Jingugaien Building, 2-7-25 Kita Aoyama, Minato-ku, Tokyo 107; Home: 2-14-4 Moto-Azabu, Minato-ku, Tokyo 106, Japan.
Telephone: 403-1451 (Office); 451-1672 (Home).

Muravyev, Nikolai Ivanovich; Soviet trade corpora-tion official; b. 6 Dec. 1907; ed. Inst. of Foreign Trade.
Worked in trade orgs. 24-39; trade missions to Germany 39-41, U.K. 42; Asst. Dir. (Fur Dept.) Amtorg Stock Co., U.S. 42-48, Chair. 52-58; Dir. Karakul and Fur Office Soyuzpushnina (furs, etc.) 48-52, Vice-Chair. 58-62, Chair. 62-72; mem. Communist Party; Order of Badge of Honour (twice), etc.
V/O Soyuzpushnina, ul. Kuibysheva 6, Moscow, U.S.S.R.

Murdoch, (Jean) Iris, C.B.E.; British writer and philosopher; b. 15 July 1919; m. John O. Bayley; ed. Froebel Educational Inst. (London), Badminton School (Bristol) and Somerville Coll., Oxford.
Worked at the Treasury 42-44, with UNRRA 44-46; Philosophy Studentship Newnham Coll., Cambridge 47-48; Fellow, St. Anne's Coll., Oxford 48-63, Hon. Fellow 63-; mem. Irish Acad. of Letters; Hon. mem. American Acad. of Arts and Letters 75, Nat. Inst. of Arts and Letters 75; James Tait Black Prize for Fiction (for The Black Prince) 74, Whitbread Literary Award

for Fiction (for The Sacred and Profane Love Machine) 74.
Publs. Sartre: Romantic Rationalist 53, Under the Net 54, The Flight from the Enchanter 55, The Sandcastle 57, The Bell 58, A Severed Head 61 (play 63), An Unofficial Rose 62, The Unicorn 63, The Italian Girl 64 (play 67), The Red and the Green 65, The Time of the Angels 66, The Nice and the Good 68, Bruno's Dream 69, A Fairly Honourable Defeat 70, The Sovereignty of Good 70, The Servants and the Snow (play) 70, An Accidental Man 71, The Three Arrows (play) 72, The Black Prince 73, The Sacred and Profane Love Machine 74, A Word Child 75.
Cedar Lodge, Steeple Aston, Oxfordshire, England.

Murdoch, (Keith) Rupert; Australian newspaper publisher; b. 11 March 1931, Melbourne, Victoria; s. of the late Sir Keith Murdoch and of Dame Elisabeth Murdoch; m. Anna Maria Torv 1967; two s. two d.
Managing Dir., News Ltd., and assoc. companies, publishers of The Australian, The News (Adelaide), The Daily Mirror (Sydney), Sunday Mirror (Sydney), Sunday Truth (Brisbane), Sunday Mail (Adelaide), Sunday Times (Perth), The News (Darwin), The New Idea, etc.; Chair. Southern Television Corpn. Adelaide; Chair. and Joint Man. Dir. News International Ltd. and assoc. cos., U.K., publishers of News of the World, The Sun 69-; Propr. San Antonio Express, San Antonio News; founded National Star weekly 74.
News of the World, 30 Bouverie Street, London, E.C.4, England.

Murdock, George Peter, PH.D.; American anthro-pologist; b. 11 May 1897, Meriden, Conn.; s. of George Bronson and Harriet (Graves) Murdock; m. Carmen Swanson 1925; one s.; ed. Yale Univ.
Instructor in Sociology, Univ. of Maryland 25-27; Asst. Prof., Assoc. Prof., Prof., Yale Univ. 28-60; Mellon Prof. of Anthropology, Univ. of Pittsburgh 60-73, Emer. Prof. 73-; Chair. Div. of Behavioural Sciences, Nat. Research Council 64-66; mem. Nat. Acad. of Sciences; Pres. American Anthropological Asscn. 55, American Ethnological Soc. 52-53; Viking Fund Medal 49, Herbert E. Gregory Medal, Tokyo 66, Huxley Medal London 71.
Leisure interest: tennis.
Publs. Our Primitive Contemporaries 34, Social Structure 49, Africa 59.
Wynnewood Plaza, Apt. 107, Wynnewood, Pa. 19096, U.S.A.
Telephone: M19-6273

Murena, H. A.; Argentine writer; b. 14 Feb. 1923, Buenos Aires.
Lecturer in Philosophy, Univ. of Buenos Aires 68-.
Publs. Primer testamento (story) 46, La vida nueva (poetry) 51, El juez (play) 53, El pecado original de América (essay) 54, La fatalidad de los cuerpos (novel) 55, El centro del infierno (short stories) 56, El círculo de los paraísos (poetry) 58, Las leyes de la noche (novel) 58, El escándalo y el fuego 59, Homo atomicus 61, Relámpago de la duración 62, Ensayos sobre subversión 62, El demonio de la armonía 64, Los herederos de la promesa 65, El nombre secreto (essays) 69, Epitalámica (novel) 69, Nimas Nimenos (novel) 69, La cárcel de la mente (essays) 70, El coronel de caballería (short stories) 70, Caina muerte (novel) 71, F.G. un bárbaro entre la belleza (poetry) 72.
San José 910, Buenos Aires, Argentina.

Murgulescu, Ilie, D.SC.; Romanian chemist and politi-cian; b. 27 Jan. 1902, Cornu, Dolj County; s. of G. D. and Floarea Murgulescu; m. Elena Salageanu 1934; ed. Charles 1 High School, Craiova, and Univs. of Cluj and Leipzig.
Director of Studies and Prof. of Analytical and Physical Chemistry, Timişoara Polytechnical Inst. 34-49; Prof. of Physical Chemistry, Univ. of Bucharest 49-72, Consulting Prof. 72-; mem. Grand Nat. Assembly 48-;

Deputy Minister of Educ. 50-51, Minister 51-56, 60-63; mem. Romanian Acad. of Sciences 48-, Pres. 63-66; Dir. Centre of Physical Chemistry 63-; Vice-Pres. Romanian Council of State 65-67; Vice-Pres. Grand Nat. Assembly 67-; Foreign mem. U.S.S.R. Acad. of Sciences, Czechoslovak, Hungarian and Bulgarian Acads. of Sciences; Laureate, State Prize of Romania 64; Gold Medal of 39th Int. Congress of Ind. Chemistry 70; Hero of Socialist Labour 71.
Leisure interest: philosophy.
Publs. Over 200 papers in analytical and physical chemistry in Romanian and foreign scientific journals.
Şoseaua Kiseleff 22, Bucharest, Romania.

Murnaghan, Francis Dominic, M.A., D.SC., PH.D.; American professor; b. 4 Aug. 1893, Omagh, Co. Tyrone, Ireland; s. of George Murnaghan and Angela Mooney; m. Ada M. Kimbell 1919; one s. one a.; ed. Nat. Univ. of Ireland and Johns Hopkins Univ.
Instructor Rice Inst. 16; Assoc. Johns Hopkins Univ. 18, Assoc. Prof. 21, Prof. and Head of Dept. of Maths. 28-48; Prof. Instituto Técnico de Aeronáutica, Brazil 49-59; Consultant U.S. Navy, David Taylor Model Basin 55-63.
Leisure interests: walking, gardening.
Publs. *Vector Analysis and the Theory of Relativity* 22, *Theoretical Mechanics* (with J. S. Ames) 29, *Hydrodynamics* (with H. Bateman and H. L. Dryden) 32, *The Theory of Group Representations* 38, *Analytic Geometry* 46, *Differential and Integral Calculus* 47, *Introduction to Applied Mathematics* 48, *Finite Deformation of an Elastic Solid* 51, *Cálculo Avançado* 54, *Algebra Elementar e Trigonometria* 54, *Equações Diferenciais* 55, *The Laplace Transformation* 62, *The Calculus of Variations* 62, *The Unitary and Rotation Groups* 62.
6202 Sycamore Road, Baltimore 12, Md., U.S.A.

Murphy, Charles S.; American government official; b. 20 Aug. 1909, Wallace, N.C.; s. of William F. and Kate W. Murphy; m. Kate C. Graham 1931; one s. two d.; ed. Duke Univ., Durham, North Carolina.
Admitted to N. Carolina Bar 34; Office of Legislative Counsel, U.S. Senate 34-46; Admin. Asst. to Pres. of U.S. 47-50, Special Counsel 50-53; Partner, Morison, Murphy, Clapp and Abrams 53-61; Counsel to Dem. Nat. Advisory Council 57-60; Under-Sec. Dept. of Agriculture 60-65; Chair. Civil Aeronautics Board 65-68; Counsellor to Pres. of U.S. 68-69; Partner Morison, Murphy, Abrams and Haddock 69-; mem. Board of Dirs., Harry S. Truman Library 68-; Trustee, Duke Univ. 70-; Chair. Board of Visitors Duke Univ. Law School 73-.
Leisure interest: boating.
1776 K Street, N.W., Washington, D.C. 20006, U.S.A.
Telephone: 202-293-6260.

Murphy, Franklin David, A.B., M.D.; American educator and publisher; b. 29 Jan. 1916, Kansas City, Miss.; s. of Franklin E. Murphy and Cordelia Brown Murphy; m. Judith Harris Murphy 1940; one s. three d.; ed. Univs. of Kansas and Göttingen and Univ. of Pennsylvania School of Medicine.
Dean of School of Medicine and Assoc. Prof. of Internal Medicine, Univ. of Kansas 48-51; Chancellor, Univ. of Kansas 51-60; Chancellor, Univ. of Calif. at Los Angeles 60-68; Chair. Times Mirror Co. 68-; Dir. Ford Motor Co., Norton Simon Inc., Bank of America, Hallmark Cards; Pres. Kress Foundation; Hon. LL.D., Hon. L.H.D., Hon. D.Sc.
Publs. in field of chemotherapy, cardiovascular diseases, medical education and general education.
Times-Mirror Co., Times Mirror Square, Los Angeles, Calif. 90053; 419 Robert Lane, Beverly Hills, Calif. 90210, U.S.A.

Murphy, George Arthur; American banker; b. 13 Dec. 1905; ed. Oglethorpe Univ., New York Univ. and Harvard Univ.

Joined Irving Trust Co., New York City 31, Vice-Pres. (Personal Trust Div.) 47-53, Senior Vice-Pres. (Loan Admin. Div.) and Senior Loaning Officer 54-57, Pres. 57-60, Chair. 60-70, Dir. 56-; Chair. Charter New York Corpn. 66-70, Dir. 66-, Chair. Exec. Cttee. 71-.
Home: Washington, Conn. 06793; Office: 1 Wall Street, New York, N.Y. 10005, U.S.A.

Murphy, George Lloyd; American actor and politician; b. 4 July 1902, New Haven, Conn.; s. of Mike Murphy and Nora Long; m. Juliette Henkel 1926; one s. one d.; ed. Peddie Inst., Highstown, N.J., Pawling School, N.Y., and Yale Univ.
Former actor and executive in motion picture industry; Chair. Republican State Cen. Cttee. of Calif. 53; fmr. Pres. Screen Actors Guild; Vice-Pres. Desilu Productions and Technicolor Corpn.; Senator from Calif. 65-71; Republican.
807 North Rodeo Drive, Beverly Hills, Calif. 90210, U.S.A.

Murphy, Lionel Keith, LL.B., B.SC.; Australian politician; b. 31 Aug. 1922, Sydney; s. of William and Lily Murphy (née Murphy); m. Ingrid Gee 1969; two s. one d. by previous marriage; ed. Sydney High School and Univ. of Sydney.
Admitted to N.S.W. Bar 47, Victoria 58; Q.C., N.S.W. 60-, Victoria 61-; mem. Senate 62-75, Leader of the Opposition 67-72; Attorney-Gen., Minister of State for Customs and Excise and Leader of Govt. in Senate 72-75; Judge, Australian High Court 75-; mem. Exec. Int. Comm. of Jurists Australian Section 63-; del. to UN Conf. on Human Rights, Teheran 68; mem. Exec. Council of Australian Nat. Univ.
Leisure interests: water skiing, scientific and other literature.
High Court of Australia, Taylor Square, Darlinghurst, N.S.W. 2010, Australia.
Telephone: 25-2304 (Sydney).

Murphy, Richard William, B.A., A.B.; American diplomatist; b. 29 July 1929, Boston, Mass.; s. of John D. Murphy and Jane K. Diehl; m. Anne Herrick Cook 1955; one s. two d.; ed. Harvard Univ. and Emmanuel Coll., Cambridge.
United States Consul, Aleppo, Syria 60-63; Political Officer, U.S. Embassy, Jeddah 63-68, Amman 66-68; Country Dir. for Arabian Peninsula Affairs, U.S. Dept. of State 70-71; Amb. to Mauritania 71-74, to Syria 74-; Dept. of State Superior Service Award 69.
Leisure interests: music, tennis.
American Embassy, Damascus, Syria.
Telephone: 332315.

Murphy, Robert Daniel, LL.M.; American diplomatist and businessman; b. 28 Oct. 1894; ed. Marquette Acad. and George Washington Univ.
Clerk Post Office Dept. 16-17, Legation Berne 17-19; Asst. to Chief, Treasury Dept. 19-20; Vice-Consul Zürich 21, Munich 21-24; Consul Seville 25-29; Consul Paris 30-41, Counsellor Embassy 39-41; American rep. Algiers 43-44; U.S. mem. Advisory Council for Italy 43-44; Political Adviser, with rank of Ambassador, to Gen. Eisenhower 44-45; Ambassador to Belgium 49-52, to Japan 52-53; Asst. Sec. of State 53-54; Deputy Under-Sec. of State 54-59; Under-Sec. of State (Political Affairs) June-Nov. 59; Hon. Chair. Corning Glass Works Int.; responsible for liaison with outgoing Admin. (U.S. Govt.) 69.
Publ. *Diplomat Among Warriors* 64.
717 5th Avenue, New York, N.Y. 10022; Home: 1701 Kalmia Road, N.W., Washington, D.C. 20012, U.S.A.

Murphy, Thomas A.; American motor executive; b. 10 Dec. 1915, Hornell, N.Y.; ed. Leo High School, Chicago and Univ. of Illinois.
Joined Gen. Motors Corpn. 38, Asst. Treas. 59, Comp-

troller 67, Treas. 68-70, Vice-Pres. 70-72, Vice-Chair. 72-74, Chair. 74-.
General Motors Corporation, General Motors Building, Detroit, Mich. 48202, U.S.A.

Murphy, William Beverly, B.S.; American business executive; b. 17 June 1907, Appleton, Wis.; s. of S. W. and Hilma (née Anderson) Murphy; m. Helen Brennan 1930; three s. one d.; ed. Univ. of Wisconsin.
Executive Vice-Pres. A. C. Nielsen Co. 28-38; Campbell Soup Co. 38-42; War Production Board, Washington 42-45; rejoined Campbell Soup Co. 45, Dir. 49-, Pres. 53-72; Dir. American Telephone and Telegraph Co., Merck & Co. Inc., Int. Paper Co.; Life mem. and Trustee, Wisconsin Alumni Research Foundation, The Nutrition Foundation; Life mem. Mass. Inst. of Technology; Chair. Business Council 65-66.
110 Maple Hill Road, Gladwyne, Pa., U.S.A.

Murphy, William Parry, A.B., M.D.; American physician; b. 6 Feb. 1892; ed. Univ. of Oregon and Harvard Univ. Medical School.
Intern, Rhode Island Hospital, Providence 20-22; Asst. Resident Physician Peter Bent Brigham Hospital, Boston 22-23, Junior Associate in Medicine 23-28, Associate in Medicine 28-35, Senior Associate in Medicine and Consultant in Haematology 35-58, Emer. 58-; Asst. in Medicine Harvard Univ. Medical School 23-28, Instructor 28-35, Associate in Medicine 35-48; Lecturer on Medicine 48-58, Emer. 58-; discoverer (with Dr. George R. Minot) of liver treatment for pernicious anaemia; mem. Board, Cordis Corpn.; awarded Cameron Prize of Edinburgh Univ. 30, bronze medal American Medical Asscn. 34, Nobel Prize in Physiology and Medicine 34, Gold Medal Mass. Humane Society, Dip. in Internal Medicine 37, etc.; mem. Kaiserl. Leopold. Carolin. Deutsche Akad. der Naturforscher, American Society for Clinical Investigation, Asscn. of American Physicians, Society of Arts and Sciences, American Asscn. for the Advancement of Science, Fellow American Medical Asscn., Nat. Inst. of Social Sciences, Robert Kennedy Duncan Society of Mellon Inst.; Hon. mem. Society of Finnish Physicians for Internal Diseases, Int. Soc. for Research on Civilisation Diseases and Vital Substances 69, New York Acad. of Sciences, Univ. of Oregon Medical Alumni Asscn. 64; Commdr. Order of White Rose (Finland), Nat. Order of Merit, Carlos J. Finlay (Cuba); Hon. D.Sc. Gustavus Adolphus Coll., Distinguished Achievement Award, Boston 65, Int. Bicentennial Symposium Award.
Publ. *Anæmia in Practice: Pernicious Anæmia* 39.
Office: 1101 Beacon Street, Brookline, Mass.; 97 Sewall Avenue, Brookline 46, Mass., U.S.A

Murray, A. Rosemary, M.A., D.PHIL., J.P.; British chemist and university administrator; b. 28 July 1913, Havant; d. of late Admiral A. J. L. Murray and Ellen Maxwell Spooner; ed. Downe House School and Lady Margaret Hall, Oxford.
Lecturer in Chem., Royal Holloway Coll. 38-41, Univ. of Sheffield 41-42; W.R.N.S. 42-46; Fellow and Tutor, Girton Coll., Cambridge 46-54; Pres. New Hall, Cambridge 54-; Univ. Demonstrator in Chem. 47-52, Vice-Chancellor Cambridge Univ. Oct. 75-; Chair., mem. many cttees. and councils in univ., colls. of educ., schools, wages councils, Armed Forces Pay Review Body and others.
Leisure interests: sailing, gardening, bookbinding and restoring.
New Hall, Cambridge, CB3 0DF, England.
Telephone: 0223-51731.

Murray, Sir (Francis) Ralph (Hay), K.C.M.G.; British diplomatist; b. 3 March 1908; ed. Brentwood School and St. Edmund Hall, Oxford.
British Broadcasting Corpn. 34-39; Foreign Office 39-45; Allied Comm. for Austria 45-46; Special Commr.'s Staff, S.E. Asia 46-47; Foreign Office 47-51; Counsellor,

Madrid 51-54; Minister, Cairo 54-56; Asst. Under-Sec. of State Foreign Office 57-61; Dep. Under-Sec. of State, Foreign Office 61-62; Amb. to Greece 62-67; Gov. of BBC 67-73; Chair. C.G.E. Int. (U.K.) Ltd; Chair. CSM Parl. Consultants 74-, and Dir. other companies.
The Old Rectory, Stoke Hammond, Bletchley, Bucks., England.

Murray, James Dalton, C.M.G.; British diplomatist; b. 6 March 1911, Edinburgh, Scotland; s. of Dr. James Murray and Eleanor Mortimer; m. 1st Dora M. Carter 1949 (died 1958), 2nd M. Rose Eden; three s. two d.; ed. Stowe School and Magdalene Coll., Cambridge.
Joined Consular Service 33, Vice-Consul, San Francisco 33-36, Mexico City 36-39; Second Sec. Washington 39-43; First Sec. and Consul La Paz 43-45; First Sec. Prague 45; Foreign Office 45-48; Office Commr.-Gen. for S.E. Asia 48-50; Counsellor, Foreign Office 50-52; Deputy High Commr. in Pakistan 52-55; Foreign Office 55-59; Counsellor Lisbon 59-61; Minister Romania 61-63, Amb. 63-65; High Commr. in Jamaica 65-70; non-res. Amb. to Haiti 66-70; retd. 70, then First Sec. and Consul (Chargé d'Affaires), Port-au-Prince, Haiti.
c/o British Embassy, P.O. Box 1302, Port-au-Prince, Haiti.

Murray, Lionel (Len), O.B.E.; British trade unionist; b. 2 Aug. 1922; ed. Wellington Grammar School, Univ. of London, New Coll., Oxford.
With Econ. Dept., Trades Union Congress 47, Head of Dept. 54-69; Asst. Gen. Sec. TUC 69-73, Gen. Sec. 73-; mem. Social Science Research Council 65-70; Vice-Pres. European Trade Union Confed. 74; Vice-Chair. Nat. Savings Cttee. for England and Wales.
Trades Union Congress, 23-28 Great Russell Street, London, W.C.1, England.

Murray of Newhaven, Baron (Life Peer) cr. 64, of Newhaven; **Keith (Anderson Hope)** Murray, K.C.B., PH.D., B.LITT., M.A.; British university administrator; b. 28 July 1903, Edinburgh; s. of Rt. Hon. Lord Murray, C.M.G., K.C., LL.D.; ed. Edinburgh Acad., Edinburgh Univ., Cornell Univ., N.Y. and Oxford Univ. Ministry of Agriculture 25-26; Commonwealth Fund Fellow 26-29; Agricultural Econs. Research Inst., Oxford 29-32, Research Officer 32-39; Ministry of Food 39-40; R.A.F.V.R. 41-42; Dir. of Food and Agriculture, Middle East Supply Centre 42-45; Fellow and Bursar, Lincoln Coll., Oxford 37-53, Rector 44-53; Chair. Univ. Grants Cttee. 53-63; Chancellor, Southampton Univ. 64-74; Visitor, Loughborough Tech. Univ. 68-; Dir. Leverhulme Trust 65-72; Trustee, Wellcome Trust 65-73; Hon. Fellow, Oriel and Lincoln Colls., Oxford, Downing Coll., Cambridge, Birkbeck Coll., London; Hon. LL.D., Hon. D.C.L., Hon. D.Litt., Hon. D.U.
224 Ashley Gardens, London, SW1P 1PA, England.
Telephone: 01-828-4113.

Murthy, B. S., B.A., B.ED.; Indian politician; b. 1907; ed. Government Arts Coll. Rajahmundry, Training Coll., Rajahmundry, Madras Christian Coll. and Madras Law Coll.
Parliamentary Sec. for Labour and Industry, Madras 37-39, 46-47; Chief Whip, Madras Legislative Congress Party 46-47; Pres. Andhra Pradesh Agricultural Labour Congress 46-, Andhra Provincial Harijan Sewak Sangh 40-49; fmr. Editor *Navjiwan* (Teluga weekly); mem. Lok Sabha 52-; Dep. Minister of Community Devt. and Co-operation April 62-67; Deputy Minister of Health and Family Planning 67, of Health, Family Planning and Urban Devt. Nov. 67-69; Minister of State for Health, Family Planning, Works, Housing and Urban Devt. 69; mem. Exec. Cttee. Gandhi Smarak Nidhi.
Publs. *Revolt of Six Cross, Agony, Andhra Virakumar, The Glimmer in Darkness, Depressed and Oppressed.*
5 Ashoka Road, New Delhi, India.

Murumbi, Joseph A.; Kenyan politician; b. 18 June 1911; s. of Peter Nicholas Zuzarte and Njambiak Ole Murumbi; m. 1966; one s.; ed. Bangalore and Bellary, S. India.
Staff of Admin. of Somalia 41-51; Asst. Sec. Movement for Colonial Freedom 51-57; Press and Tourist Officer, Moroccan Embassy, London 57-62; Treas. Kenyan African Nat. Union (KANU) 62; mem. Kenya House of Reps. 63-; Minister of State in Prime Minister's Office 63-64; Minister of External Affairs 64-66; Vice-Pres. of Kenya May-Dec. 66; Chair. and Dir. several Kenya companies.
Leisure interests: gardening and collecting stamps, art and Africana.
Office: P.O. Box 41730, Nairobi; Home: 72 Muthaiga Road, Nairobi, Kenya.
Telephone: Nairobi 65096 (Home).

Musafir, Giani Gurmukh Singh; Indian writer and politician; b. 15 Jan. 1899, Udhwal, Pakistan; s. of Sujan Singh and Mathra Devi; m. Ranjit Kaur 1912; five s. one d.; ed. Rawalpindi and Training Coll., Lahore.
Joined Congress 23; mem. All-India Congress Cttee. 30-; mem. Constituent Assembly 47-52; mem. Parl. 52-66; mem. Exec. Congress Party in Parl. 52-66; mem. Working Cttee. of All-India Congress Cttee. 52-57; Pres. Punjab Pradesh Congress Cttee. 47-59; Chief Minister of Punjab 66-67; mem. Legislative Council, Punjab 66-; mem. Rajya Sabha 68-; Chair. Jallianwala Bag Memorial Trust Man. Cttee.; took active part in Akali movement; Gen. Sec. Shri Gurudwara Prabandhak Cttee. and Shiromani Akali Dal; Leader and Del. to numerous int. confs.
Leisure interests: travelling, writing.
Publs. Short Stories: *Vakhri Duniya, Sasta Tamasha, Alne de Bot, Kandhan Bol Pahiyan, 27 January, Sab Achha, Gutar, Allah Wale, Urwar Par*; Poetry: *Sabar de Ban, Prem Ban, Jivan Pandh, Toote Khamb, Musafirian, Kav Saneh, Sahaj Seti, Vakhra Vakhra, Katra Katra*; General: *Gandhi Gita, Anand Marg, Bagi Jernel, Vinvi Sadi de Shahid, Vekhia Suniya Gandhi, Vekhia Suniya Jawaharlal.*
Leisure interests: travelling, writing.
21 Feroze Shah Road, New Delhi, India.
Telephone: 387591.

Musgrave, Sir Cyril, K.C.B.; British administrator (retd.); b. 21 June 1900, Ealing, Middlesex; s. of Frank Musgrave and Edith Clarkson; m. 2nd Jean Soulsby 1945; two s. (also one s. one d. by 1st marriage); ed. St. George's Coll., London.
With Inland Revenue 20-37, Air Ministry 37-40, Ministry of Aircraft Production 40-46; Under-Sec. (Air), Ministry of Supply 46-51, Deputy Sec. 51-53, Second Permanent Sec. 53-56, Permanent Sec. 56-59; Chair. Iron and Steel Board 59-67; Dir. various companies 61-76; mem. Organizing Cttee. for Steel Nationalization 66-67, part-time mem. British Steel Corpn. 67-70.
Leisure interests: gardening, the gramophone.
Willows House, Walsham-le-Willows, Bury St. Edmunds, Suffolk, England.
Telephone: Walsham-le-Willows 486.

Musgrave, Thea, MUS.B.; British composer; b. Edinburgh; d. of James and Joan Musgrave; m. Peter Mark 1971; ed. Edinburgh Univ. and Paris Conservatoire (under Nadia Boulanger).
Lecturer, Extra-Mural Dept., London Univ. 58-65; Visiting Prof. Univ. of California, Santa Barbara 70; Koussevitzky Award 72; Guggenheim Fellow 74-75.
Leisure interests: cooking, cinema, reading.
Works includes: *Chamber Concerto for 2 & 3* 66, *Concerto for Orchestra* 67, *Clarinet Concerto* 68, *Beauty and the Beast* (ballet) 69, *Night Music* 69, *Horn Concerto* 71, *The Voice of Ariadne* (chamber opera) 72-73, *Viola*

Concerto 73, *Space Play* 74; chamber music, songs, choral music, orchestral music.
c/o Novello and Co. Ltd., 1-3 Upper James Street, London, W1R 4BR, England.
Telephone: 01-734-8080.

Muskhelishvili, Nikolai Ivanovich; Soviet mathematician; b. 16 Feb. 1891, Tbilisi; ed. St. Petersburg Univ. Professor at the Tbilisi Polytechnical Inst. and Univ. 22-; his main research concerns the theory of elasticity, integral equations, problems of the theory of functions; Pres. of Acad. of Sciences of Georgian S.S.R. and Dir. of Maths. 41-; mem. U.S.S.R. Acad. of Sciences; Chair. U.S.S.R. Nat. Cttee. of Pure and Applied Mechanics; mem. Exec. Board, Int. Union of Pure and Applied Mechanics; Deputy to U.S.S.R. Supreme Soviet 38-; mem. Comm. for Foreign Affairs; mem. Central Cttee., C.P. of Georgian S.S.R.; State Prize 41, 47, Hero of Socialist Labour 45, awarded Order of Lenin (four times), Order of the Red Banner of Labour, Order of October Revolution, "Hammer and Sickle" Gold Medal.
Publs. *Singular Integral Equations* 46, *Analytical Geometry Course* 47, *Certain Fundamental Problems of the Mathematical Theory of Elasticity* 49.
Academy of Sciences of Georgian S.S.R., Tbilisi, U.S.S.R.

Muskie, Edmund Sixtus, A.B., LL.B.; American lawyer and politician; b. 28 March 1914, Rumford, Maine; m. Jane Gray 1948; two s. three d.; ed. Bates Coll., Maine and Cornell Law School, Ithaca, New York.
Admitted to Massachusetts Bar 39, Maine Bar 40, Federal District Court 41; practised as lawyer, Waterville Maine 40-; served U.S. Navy 42-45; mem. Maine House of Reps. 47-51; Democratic Floor leader 49-51; District Dir. for Maine, Office of Price Stabilisation 51-52; City Solicitor Waterville, Maine 54-55; Gov. of the State of Maine 55-59; Senator from Maine 59-; Senate Asst. Majority Whip 66-; Chair. Senate Sub-Cttees. on Environmental Pollution, Intergovt. Relations, Arms Control and Int. Orgs., Surveillance, and Health of the Elderly; Chair. Dem. Senatorial Campaign Cttee. 67-69; Candidate for Vice-presidency of U.S.A. 68; Chair. Senate Budget Cttee. 74-; Exec. Cttee. Nat. Govs. Conf.; mem. American Acad. of Arts and Sciences, Roosevelt Campobello Int. Park Comm.; Hon. LL.D. (Bates, Lafayette, Bowdoin and Colby Colls., Maine, Portland and Suffolk Univs.); Democrat.
Leisure interests: photography, golf, gardening.
Publ. *Journeys* 72.
Senate Office Building, Washington, D.C. 20510, U.S.A.
Telephone: 202-225-5344.

Mustafa, Zaki, LL.M., PH.D., Sudanese lawyer; b. 17 Oct. 1934, Dongola; s. of Mustafa Abdel Mageed and Amna Mohamed Ibrahim; m. Mahasin Abdel Monheim 1957; one s. three d.; ed. Univs. of Khartoum and London.
Tutor, Faculty of Law, Univ. of Khartoum 59-71, Lecturer 61-66, Senior Lecturer 66-69, Dean 65-69; Prof., Dean of Law Ahmadu Bello Univ., Nigeria 69-72; Prof. of Law, Haile Sellassie I Univ., Ethiopia 72-73; Attorney-Gen. May 73-; several academic prizes.
Publs. *The Civil Law of the Sudan—Its History and Characteristics* (Arabic) 68, *Common Law in the Sudan* 71, *The Legal System of the Sudan* 74, and several articles.
Leisure interests: music, walking.
Attorney-General's Chambers, Khartoum, Sudan.
Telephone: 77513; 74231.

Mustapha bin Datu Harun, Tun Datu, S.M.N., S.P.D.K., S.I.M.P., P.N.B.S., S.P.M.J., S.P.M.P., S.P.C.M., K.R.C.L., K.V.O., O.B.E.; Sabah (Malaysian) administrator; b. 31 Aug. 1918; m. Helen Moore 1974.
Member Legislative Council of North Borneo 56-63; Chair. Sabah (North Borneo) Nat. Council; Chair. and

Leader United Sabah Nat. Org.; Yang di-Pertua Negara (Head of State) of Sabah 63-67, Chief Minister 67-75; Minister of Defence, Malaysia 74-75.
c/o Office of the Chief Minister, State Secretariat, Kota Kinabalu, Sabah, Malaysia.

Muttukumaru, Maj.-Gen. Anton Marian, O.B.E., E.D., B.A., Barrister-at-Law (Gray's Inn); Ceylonese army officer; b. 1908, Colombo; m. Margaret Vasanthi Ratnarajah 1944; three s.; ed. St. Joseph's Coll., Colombo, and Jesus Coll., Oxford.
Advocate of Supreme Court in Ceylon 34-39 and 46-48; served in Ceylon Defence Force 34-49, Regular Force 49-59; Military A.D.C. to the Queen 54-59; Commdr. of the Army 55-59; High Commr. in Pakistan 60-62, Minister to Afghanistan 60-61, Ambassador to Iraq 61-62, Ambassador to Iran 62, High Commr. Australia and New Zealand 63-66; Amb. to U.A.R. 66-69, concurrently accred. to Yugoslavia, Lebanon, Sudan, Jordan; Pres. Ceylon Inst. of World Affairs.
Leisure interests: music, collection of walking sticks.
Ceylon Institute of World Affairs, 82B Ward Place, Colombo 7, Sri Lanka.

Mutuale Tshikanie; Zairian lawyer and diplomatist; b. 22 June 1938, Kabinda; m.; five c.; ed. Lovanium Univ.
Head of UN and OAU Affairs Div., Ministry of Foreign Affairs 64-65; with Perm. Mission of Zaire to UN 65-71; Dir.-Gen. for Political Affairs, Ministry of Foreign Affairs 71, later Chef de Cabinet; Amb. to Cen. African Repub., to Algeria 72; Perm. Rep. to UN Aug. 74-; mem. American Soc. of Int. Law; Judge UN Admin. Tribunal 69-.
Permanent Mission of Zaire to the United Nations, 866 Second Avenue, 7th Floor, New York, N.Y. 10017, U.S.A.

Muwanba, Jake Thomson X.; Malawi diplomatist; b. 14 Oct. 1925, Ndola, Zambia; m.; four c.; ed. High School in S. Africa, Swansea Univ. Coll., S. Wales.
Welfare Officer, later Asst. Personnel Officer, Anglo-American Group of Mines 54-62; Head of Dept. of Social Welfare, Govt. of Malawi 62-69; formed Dept. of Tourism 69, Dir. of Tourism 71-75; Perm. Rep. to UN Dec. 75-; also served as first interim Dir. of Sports and Culture, served on a number of school boards.
Permanent Mission of Malawi to the United Nations, 777 Third Avenue, 24th Floor, New York, N.Y. 10017, U.S.A.

Muzorewa, Abel Tendekayi, M.A.; Rhodesian ecclesiastic; b. 14 April 1925, Old Umtali; ed. Old Umtali Secondary School, Nyadiri United Methodist Mission, Central Methodist Coll., Fayette, Missouri, Scarritt Coll., Nashville, Tenn., U.S.A.
Pastor, Chiduku North Circuit 55-57; studied in U.S.A. 58-63; Pastor, Old Umtali Mission 63; Dir. of Youth Work, Rhodesia Annual Conf. 65; Jt. Dir. of Youth Work, Rhodesia Christian Council 65; Travelling Sec. Student Christian Movt. 65; Resident Bishop, United Methodist Church (Rhodesia Area) 68-; Pres. African Nat. Council 71-, All-Africa Conf. of Churches; Hon. D.D. (Central Methodist Coll., Missouri) 60; UN Prize for Outstanding Achievement in Human Rights 73.
Publ. *Manifesto for African National Council* 72.

Mwaanga, Vernon Johnson; Zambian diplomatist; b. 1939; ed. Hodgson Technical Coll., Lusaka, Stanford Univ., U.S.A. and Oxford Univ., U.K.
Joined Zambian independence movement 60; mem. United Nat. Independence Party 61-, later Regional Party Sec., Monze and Come Areas; Deputy High Commr. for Zambia in U.K. 64-65; Ambassador to U.S.S.R. 65-68; Perm. Rep. to UN 68-72; Editor-in-Chief *Times of Zambia* 72-73; Minister of Foreign Affairs 73-75; mem. UNIP Cen. Cttee. 75-.
Ministry of Foreign Affairs, Lusaka; and P.O. Box 394, Lusaka, Zambia.

Mwakawago, Daudi Ngelautwa; Tanzanian politician; b. Sept. 1939; ed. Makerere Univ., Manchester Univ.
Tutor at Kivukoni Coll., Dar es Salaam 65-72, Vice-Principal 70, Principal 71; mem. Tanganyika African Nat. Union (TANU); Minister for Information and Broadcasting Feb. 72-; fmr. mem. Historical Asscn. of Tanzania, Nat. Adult Educ. Asscn. of Tanzania, African Adult Educ. Asscn., Income Tax Local Cttee., Board of Inst. of Adult Educ., Nat. Advisory Council on Educ.; fmr. dir. Nat. Devt. Corpn., Nat. Museum.
National Assembly, Dar es Salaam, Tanzania.

Mwanakatwe, John; Zambian politician.
Minister of Educ. until Sept. 67; Minister of Lands and Mines Sept. 67-Jan. 69; Sec.-Gen. to the Govt. Jan. 69-Nov. 70; Minister of Finance 70-73.
Publ. *The Growth of Education in Zambia since Independence.*
c/o Ministry of Finance, Lusaka, Zambia.

Mwemba, Joseph Ben; Zambian teacher and diplomatist; b. 28 July 1917, Monze; s. of Benjamin Mwemba and Martha Miyanda (née Shikabasa); m. Norah Nompumelelo Solontsi 1952; two s. three d.; ed. Univ. Coll., Fort Hare, South Africa, Ball State Univ., Muncie, Ind., U.S.A., and American Univ., Washington, D.C.
Primary school teacher 47-48, Secondary school teacher 52-60; mem. African Nat. Congress 50-60, United Nat. Independence Party (UNIP) 60-; Man. of Schools 61-62; Educ. Officer 63; Admin. Officer, Ministry of Finance 64-65; Perm. Sec., Ministry of Educ. 65-66; Amb. and Perm. Rep. to UN 66-68; Commr. for Technical Educ. and Vocational Training 68-69; Deputy Dir. Nat. Provident Fund 69-74; mem. Parl. 73-; Minister of State 74-; Pres. Northern Rhodesia Teachers' Asscn. 53-60; mem. Lockwood Cttee. for establishment of Univ. of Zambia 61-64, Univ. of Zambia Prov. Council 65-66.
Leisure interests: photography, writing.
Publs. *Mubekwabekwa, Mukandeke.*
P.O. Box 2144, Lusaka, Zambia.
Telephone: 62621.

Mwendwa, Eliud Ngala; Kenyan politician; b. 1925, Kitui; ed. Kagumo Teacher Training Coll.
Teacher at Govt. African School, Kitui 47-52; head teacher Matinyani D.E.B. Intermediate School 53-57; teacher at Mutene Teacher Training Coll. 59-61; mem. Legislative Council for Kitui 61-; Minister for Health and Housing 63; Minister for Labour and Social Services 63-65; Minister for Commerce, Industry and Co-operative Dev. 65-66; Minister for Power and Communications 66-69; Minister of Labour 69-74; Chair. Kenya African Nat. Union (K.A.N.U.) in Kitui.
Ministry of Labour, Nairobi, Kenya.

Myers, Charles Franklin, Jr.; American industrial executive; b. 17 July 1911; m. Rebecca Wright; four d.; ed. Davidson Coll. and Harvard Univ.
Bank of New York 35-39; Lt.-Commdr. U.S. Navy, World War II; Vice-Pres. Wachovia Bank and Trust Co. 39-47; Head Financial Services Dept., Burlington Industries Inc. 47, Treas. 53, Dir. 55, Vice-Pres. 61, Pres. 62, Chief Exec. Officer 62-73, Chair. 68-74; Chair. Finance Cttee. 74-75, mem. Exec. Cttee.; Dir. Chase Manhattan Bank, U.S. Steel Corpn., R. J. Reynolds Industries Inc., Wachovia Bank and Trust Co., Jefferson-Pilot Corpn.; mem. Business Council, Business Cttee. for the Arts, Advisory Council on Japan-U.S. Econ. Relations; fmr. mem. Pres. Nixon's Comm. on Int. Trade and Investment Policy; fmr. Pres. American Textile Mfrs. Inst.; mem. Board of Trustees, Davidson Coll., Union Theological Seminary, Chatham Hall School, North Carolina Foundation of Church Related Coll., Univ. of Virginia Graduate Business School.
Burlington Industries Inc., Greensboro, N.C. 27420, U.S.A.
Telephone: (919) 379-2188.

Myers, Dale D., B.S.A.E.; American engineer; b. 8 Jan. 1922, Kansas City, Mo.; s. of Wilson A. and Ruth Hall Myers; m. Marjorie Williams 1943; two d.; ed. Univ. of Washington, Seattle.
Aerophysics Dept., North American 46, Chief Engineer Missile Div. 54, Vice-Pres. and Program Man. Hound Dog Program 60; Vice-Pres. and Program Man., *Apollo CSM*, North American 64, Vice-Pres. and Gen. Man. Space Shuttle Program 69; Assoc. Admin. for Manned Space Flight, NASA Headquarters Jan. 70-; Fellow, American Astronautical Soc., American Inst. of Aeronautics and Astronautics; NASA Certificate of Appreciation 69, NASA Public Service Award for contributions to success of *Apollo XI* 69, NASA District Service Medal for contributions to continuing success of Apollo program 71; Hon. Ph.D. (Whitworth Coll.).
National Aeronautics and Space Administration, Washington, D.C. 20546, U.S.A.
Telephone: 202-962-0224.

Myers, George Vincent, B.A.; American business executive; b. 21 May 1916, Townsend, Montana; s. of Arthur E. Myers and Mabel Etnoyer; m. Christine MacDougal MacGregor 1949; three d.; ed. Univ. of Chicago.
Controller Westinghouse Brake Co.; Financial Vice-Pres. Amoco Productions Co. 53; Gen. Man. of Production, Standard Oil Co. (Indiana) 56, Dir. 56-, Vice-Pres. 58, Exec. Vice-Pres. 59, Pres. Feb. 74-; Dir. Walter E. Heller Int. Corpn., American Nat. Bank and Trust Co. of Chicago, American Petroleum Inst.
Standard Oil Co. (Indiana), 200 East Randolph Drive, Chicago, Illinois 60601, U.S.A.

Myers, William Irving, B.S., PH.D.; American agriculturalist (retd.); b. 18 Dec. 1891, Lowman, N.Y.; s. of George B. and Florence (née Lowman) Myers; m. Marguerite Troyell 1915; one s. four d.; ed. Cornwell Univ.
Instructor in Farm Management, Cornell Univ. 14-18; Asst. Prof. of Farm Management 18-20; Prof. of **Farm Finance** 20-59, Emer. 59-; Head Dept. of Agricultural Econs. 38-43; Dean N.Y. State Coll. of Agriculture 43-59; Asst. to Chair. Federal Farm Board 33; Dep. Gov. Farm Credit Admin. 33, Gov. 33-38; Pres. Federal Farm Mortgage Corpn. 34-38; Dir. Federal Surplus Relief Corpn. and Commodity Credit Corpn. 34-38; Chair. Land Cttee. of Nat. Resources Planning Board 38-43; mem. N.Y. State War Council 43-46, Research Advisory Board of Cttee. for Econ. Development 42-45; Dep. Chair. and Dir. Federal Reserve Bank N.Y. 42-54; Dir. several companies; mem. President's Famine Cttee. 46; N.Y. State Comm. on Agriculture; President's Cttee. on Foreign Aid 47; Agricultural Cttee. U.S. Chamber of Commerce 51-54; Trustee, Twentieth Century Fund 41-47; Rockefeller Foundation, Gen. Educ. Board 41-57; Mutual Life Insur. Co. N.Y. 43-; Trustee of American Inst. of Co-operation 44-59, Chair. of Board 44-48; Trustee Carnegie Inst. of Washington.; Chair. Nat. Agricultural Advisory Comm. 52-60; Consultant for Agricultural Sciences Rockefeller Foundation 59-66; Trustee, Agricultural Devt. Council; mem. Int. Devt. Advisory Board, Int. Co-operation Admin. 53-57; Trustee, Vassar Coll. 55-63; Dir. N.Y. State Science and Technology Foundation 64-; Dir. and Chair. Exec. Cttee. Marine Midland Trust Co. of Southern N.Y. 65-70; mem. N.Y. State Council of Economic Advisers; Dir. N.Y. State Electric & Gas Corpn., American Agriculturalist Inc.
1483 East Shore Drive, R.D.1, Ithaca, N.Y., U.S.A.
Telephone: 607-273-7425.

Myint Maung, U; Burmese diplomatist; b. 10 March 1921, Magwe; m.; three c.; ed. Univ. of Rangoon.
Joined Army 42; has held the following positions: Head of Co-operative Dept.; Chief of Admin. Div. of Burma Socialist Programme Party, also mem. Party Inspection

Cttee.; mem. Pyithu Hluttaw (People's Congress) for Magwe Constituency; mem. Board of Dirs. of People's Bank of the Union of Burma, Exec. Cttee. of Burma Sports and Physical Fitness Cttee., Cen. Cttee. of Burma Red Cross Soc.; Chair. Resettlement Cttee. of Cen. Security and Admin. Cttee., Independence Award Cttee.; Perm. Rep. to UN Aug. 75-.
Permanent Mission of Burma to the United Nations, 10 East 77th Street, New York, N.Y. 10021, U.S.A.

Mykle, Agnar; Norwegian writer; b. 8 Aug. 1915; ed. Univ. of Economical and Political Sciences, Bergen. Sec. A.O.F. Oslo (Workers' Educational Asscn.), head of Drama Dept.; worked for newspaper and founded Norwegian Puppet Theatre; writes novels and short stories.
Publs. *Taustigen* (The Rope Ladder) 47, *Tyven, tyven skal du hete* (The Hotel Room in U.K. and U.S.A.) 51, *Jeg er like glad, sa gutten* (It's all the same to me, said the boy) 53, *Lasso rundt fru Luna* (Lasso round the Moon) 55, *Puppet theatre* (a manual), *Sangen om den røde rubin* (The Song of the Red Ruby) 56, *Kors på halsen* (Cross my Heart) 58, *Rubicon* 65, *Largo* 67 (the Book of the Century), *A Man and his Sink* (stories) 68.
Asker, Norway.

Mynors, Sir Humphrey (Charles Baskerville), Bt.; British banker; b. 28 July 1903, Langley Burrell, Wiltshire; s. of Rev. A. B. Mynors; m. Lydia M. Minns 1939; one s. four d.; ed. Marlborough and Corpus Christi Coll., Cambridge.
Fellow Corpus Christi Coll. Cambridge 26-33; with Bank of England 33-64, Dir. 49-54, Deputy Gov. 54-64; Chair. Finance Corpn. for Industry Ltd. 64-73, (retd.).
Treago, St. Weonards, Hereford, England.

Mynors, Sir Roger (Aubrey Baskerville), Kt., M.A.; British university professor; b. 28 July 1903, Langley Burrell, Wiltshire; s. of Rev. A. B. Mynors; m. Lavinia Alington; ed. Eton Coll. and Balliol Coll., Oxford.
Fellow Balliol Coll., Oxford 26-44 (now Hon. Fellow); Prof. of Latin and Fellow of Pembroke Coll., Cambridge 44-53; Prof. of Latin and Fellow of Corpus Christi Coll., Oxford 53-70; Longman Fellow, Inst. of Bibliography and Textual Criticism, Leeds 74-75; Fellow British Acad. 44; Hon. D.Litt. Cambridge, Edinburgh, Sheffield and Durham; Hon. mem. American Acad. of Arts and Sciences; fmr. Pres. Union Académique Internationale.
Publs. *Cassiodorus* 37, *Durham MSS* 39, *Catullus* 60. *Pliny's Letters* 63, *Balliol MSS* 63, *Panegyrici* 64, *Virgil* 69.
Treago, St. Weonards, Hereford, England.

Myrberg, Pekka Juhana, PH.D.; Finnish mathematician; b. 30 Dec. 1892; ed. Univ. of Helsinki.
University Lecturer 19-26; Prof. of Mathematics, Finland Inst. of Technology 26-38; Univ. of Helsinki 38-59; Chancellor Univ. of Helsinki 52-62; Pres. State Cttee. for Scientific Research 49-64.
Publs. Several works on mathematical subjects, especially the theory of functions.
Mannerheimintie 75A, Helsinki 27, Finland.

Myrdal, Alva; Swedish cabinet minister, diplomatist, sociologist and writer; b. 31 Jan. 1902, Uppsala; m. Karl Gunnar Myrdal (*q.v.*) 1924; one s. two d.; ed. Stockholm and Uppsala Univs., U.S.A. and Geneva.
Director, Training Coll. Stockholm 36-48; Principal Dir. UN Dept. of Social Affairs 49-50; Dir. UNESCO Dept. of Social Sciences 51-55; Minister to India, Burma and Ceylon 55-56, Amb. 56-61; Swedish Foreign Office 61; Senator 62, Minister for Disarmament 66-72, for Church Affairs 69-72, without portfolio 72-73; Sec. Govt. Comm. on Women's Work 35-38; mem. Royal Comm. on the Handicapped 43-47, on Educ. Reform 46-50, etc.; Del. to ILO Conf., Paris 45, Geneva 47, and to UNESCO Confs., Paris 46, New Delhi 56;

Leader, Swedish Del. to 18-Nation Disarmament Cttee., Geneva 62-; Deputy Leader del. to UN 67-; mem. UN Cttee. to examine methods of resolving situation in S. Africa 64; Chair. Swedish Fed. of Business and Professional Women 35-38 and 40-42; Vice-Chair. Int. Fed. Business and Professional Women 38-47, Swedish Inst. 61-64; Chair. World Council on Pre-School Educ. 47-49, Cttee. Int. Peace Research Inst. 64-66, etc.; exec. mem. World Fed. of UN Asscns. 48-50; Hon. LL.D. (Mount Holyoke Coll., Leeds, Edinburgh, Columbia and Temple Univs.); Peace Prize of West Germany (with K. Gunnar Myrdal, *q.v.*) 70.

Leisure interests: reading, cooking, travel and theatre.

Publs. *Crisis in the Population Question, City Children, Nation and Family, Comments on World Affairs, Post War Planning, Are we too many?, Women's Two Roles* (with Viola Klein); Editor *Via Suecia* (multilingual refugee magazine) 45-47 and *Round Table on Social Problems* (for the Co-op Movement) 46-48; and numerous contributions to Swedish, English and German publs.

Ministry of Foreign Affairs, Stockholm, Sweden.

Myrdal, Jan; Swedish writer; b. 19 July 1927, Stockholm; one *s.* one *d.*

Sunday Columnist (politics, culture) *Stockholms-Tidningen* 63-66, *Aftonbladet* 66-72; Chair. and Publr. *Folket i Bild/Kulturfront* 71-72, columnist 72-.

Works include: films *Myglaren* (feature) 66, *Hjalparen* (feature) 68, *Balzac or the triumphs of realism* 75; books in Swedish: *Folkets Hus* (drama) 53, *Hemkomst* (novel) 54, *Jubelvår* (novel) 55, *Att bli och vara* (novel) 56, *Badrumskranen* (novel) 57, *Resa i Afghanistan* (travel) 60, *Bortom berg och öknar* (travel) 62, *Rescontra* (autobiog.) 62, *Samtida bekännelser* (autobiog.) 64, *Söndagsmorgon* (essays) 65, *Turkmenistan* (travel) 66, *Moraliteter* (drama) 67, *Skriftställning* (essays) 68, *Ansikte av sten, Angkor* (art) 68, *Garderingar* (drama) 69, *Skriftställning II* (essays) 69, *Kina: Revolutionen gar vidare* (political) 70, *Albansk utmaning* (political) 70, *Skriftställning III* (essays) 70, *B. Olsen* (drama) 72, *Ett 50-tal* (political history) 72, *Skriftställning IV* (essays) 73, *V* 75, *Lag utan ordning, Kinesiska frågor* (politics), *Karriär* (novel) 75, *Ondskan tar form* (art) 76; books in English: *Report from a Chinese Village* 65, *Chinese Journey* 65, *Confessions of a Disloyal European* 68, *Angkor: an essay on art and imperialism* 70, *China: the revolution continued* 71, *Gates to Asia* 71, *Albania defiant* 76.

Fagervik, S-150 30 Mariefred, Sweden.

Telephone: Mariefred 108-38.

Myrdal, Karl Gunnar, LL.D.; Swedish economist and politician; b. 6 Dec. 1898, Gustafs, Dalecarlia; *s.* of Carl A. Pettersson and Anna Sofia Carlsdotter; *m.* Alva Reimer (*q.v.* Alva Myrdal) 1924; one *s.* two *d.*; ed. Stockholm Univ.

Lecturer in Political Economy, Stockholm Univ. 27; Asst. Prof. Geneva Institut Universitaire de Hautes Etudes Internationales 30; Prof. Political Economy and Financial Science, Stockholm Univ. 33-50; Govt. Adviser on financial, economic and social questions 33; conducted investigation on American Negroes for Carnegie Corpn. 38-43; Minister of Trade and Commerce 45-47; Exec. Sec. UN Economic Comm. for Europe, Geneva April 47-57; Prof. of Int. Economy, Stockholm Univ. 60-; mem. Board UNRISD; Senator; Hon. LL.D. (Harvard, Yale, Brandeis, Leeds, Edinburgh, Swarthmore, Sir George Williams, Michigan, Lehigh, Howard and Atlanta Univs.); Hon. Dr.Litt. (Fisk, Uppsala Coll.),

Hon. L.H.D. (Columbia, New School of Social Research, Wayne State Univ.); Hon. D.D. (Lincoln), Hon. Jur.dr., Fil dr. (Stockholm); Hon. J.D. (Nancy); Dr. Phil. h.c. (Oslo), Hon. Dr. of Soc. Sc. (Birmingham, Louisville, Jyväskylä, Dartmouth Coll., N.H.); Hon. D.C.L. (Temple Univ., Pa.); Hon. D.Hum.Litt. (Uppsala Coll.); Peace Prize of West Germany (with Alva Myrdal, *q.v.*) 70; Nobel Prize for Econs. 74.

Leisure interests: travelling, reading.

Publs. *Prisbildningsproblemet och föränderligheten* 27, *Sveriges väg genom penningkrisen* 31, *Das politische Element in der nationalökonomischen Doktrinbildung* 32, *The Cost of Living in Sweden 1830-1930* 33, *Kris i befolkningsfrågan* 34, *Finanspolitikens ekonomiska verkningar* 34, *Monetary Equilibrium* 39, *Population, A Problem for Democracy* 40, *An American Dilemma: The Negro Problem and Modern Democracy* 44, *Warnung gegen Friedensoptimismus* 45, *The Political Element in the Development of Economic Theory* 53, *An International Economy, Problems and Prospects* 56, *Economic Theory and Under-developed Regions* 57, *Value in Social Theory* 58, *Beyond the Welfare State* 60, *Challenge to Affluence* 63, *Asian Drama* 68, *Objectivity in Social Research* 69, *The Challenge of World Poverty: A World Anti-Poverty Program in Outline* 70, *Critical Essays on Economics* 73, *Against the Stream* (essays) 74.

Västerlånggatan 31, Stockholm C; and Stockholm University, Inst. for Int. Econ. Studies, Sveav. 166, S-113 46 Stockholm, Sweden.

Telephone: 30-99-52 (Office); 21-36-41 (Home).

Myres, John Nowell Linton, C.B.E., M.A., F.B.A., F.S.A.; British librarian; b. 27 Dec. 1902, Oxford; *s.* of Prof. Sir John L. Myres; *m.* Joan Stevens 1929; two *s.*; ed. Winchester Coll., New Coll., Oxford.

Lecturer, Tutor, Christ Church, Oxford 28-48, Librarian 38-48; Ministry of Food 40-45; Librarian, Bodleian Library, Oxford Univ. 48-65; Pres. Council for British Archaeology 58-61; Vice-Pres. Soc. of Antiquaries 59-63, Dir. 66-70, Pres. 70-75; Chair. Standing Conf. of Nat. and Univ. Libraries 59-61; Ford's Lecturer, Oxford 58-59; Pres. Library Asscn. 63; Pres. Soc. for Medieval Archaeology 63-66; mem. Royal Comm. on Historical Monuments, England 69-75; Fellow, Winchester Coll. 51-; Hon. Student Christ Church, Oxford 71-; Hon. Fellow, New College, Oxford 73; Hon. LL.D. (Toronto), Hon. D.Litt. (Reading), Hon. D.Lit. (Belfast).

Leisure interest: British archaeology.

Publs. *St. Catharine's Hill, Winchester* (with others) 30, *Roman Britain and the English Settlements* 36, *Anglo-Saxon Pottery and the Settlement of England* 69.

Manor House, Kennington, Oxford, England.

Telephone: Oxford 735353.

Myrvoll, Ole; Norwegian economist and politician; b. 18 May 1911, Kragerø; *s.* of Kristian and Marie Jensen; *m.* Ebba Tangen 1938; three *d.*; ed. Univ. of Oslo, School of Banking, and Univ. of Virginia, U.S.A.

Teacher, Norwegian School of Econs. and Business Admin., Bergen 42-, Prof. of Theoretical Social Econs. 57-; Visiting Prof. Colgate Univ., U.S.A. 58-59; Visiting Tallman Prof., Bowdoin Coll., Maine 62; mem. State Banks Comm. 55, Monetary and Credit Political Comm. 60-63; mem. Council Bergens Privatbank 60; mem. Bergen City Council 48-55, 72-; Alt. mem. Storting 55; Minister of Wages and Prices 63; Minister of Finance 65-71; Mayor of Bergen 72-; Liberal.

Statefossveien 40, Bergen, Norway.

Telephone: 21-82-85.

N

Na Champassak, Sisouk; Laotian government official and diplomatist; b. 1928; ed. Univ. of Paris and Acad. of Int. Law, The Hague.
Former Head, Political Dept., Board of Council of Ministers, later Head, Perm. Secr. of Political Affairs, Board of Council of Ministers; Dir., Secr.-Gen. of Council of Ministers 55-56; Dep. Perm. Rep. to UN 56-58; Sec. of State for Information and Youth 58-61; Perm. Rep. to UN 61-63; Ambassador to India 63-64; Minister of Finance 64-74, of Defence and War Veterans 74-75.

Nabokov, Vladimir; American author and lepidopterist; b. 23 April 1899, St. Petersburg, Russia; s. of Vladimir D. Nabokov and Hélène Rukavishnikov; m. Véra Slonim 1925; one s.; ed. St. Petersburg and Cambridge Univ., England.
Left Russia 19, studied England, lived Germany and France, in U.S.A. 40-; Lecturer, Wellesley Coll. 40-41, 42-48; Research Fellow in Lepidoptera, Harvard Univ. Museum of Comparative Zoology 42-48; Prof. of Russian Literature, Cornell Univ. 48-59; Guggenheim Awards 43 and 53, American Acad. of Arts and Letters Award, Brandeis Univ. Award 64, Medal of Merit of American Acad. of Arts and Letters 69, Nat. Medal for Literature 73.
Publs. include verse and novels in Russian and in English. Biography: *Nikolai Gogol*; Treatise on butterflies: *The Nearctic Members of the Genus Lycaeides*; Translations: *Three Russian Poets* 45, *The Song of Prince Igor's Campaign* 60, *Eugene Onegin* (with commentary) 64; Short stories: *Nine Stories, Nabokov's Dozen, Nabokov's Quartet, A Russian Beauty and Other Stories* 73, *Tyrants Destroyed* 75; Play: *The Waltz Invention*; Memoirs: *Conclusive Evidence* 51, *Speak, Memory* 66; Novels: *The Real Life of Sebastian Knight* 41, *Bend Sinister* 47, *Lolita* 55, *Pnin* 57, *Invitation to a Beheading* 59, *Pale Fire* 62, *The Gift* 63, *The Defence* 64, *The Eye* 65, *Despair* 65, *King, Queen, Knave* 68, *Nabokov's Congeries* (anthology) 68, *Ada* 69, *Mary* 70, *Glory* 71, *Transparent Thing* 72, *Look at the Harlequins* 75; Poetry: *Poems and Problems* 71, *Strong Opinions* (collection of public prose) 74.
c/o McGraw-Hill Book Co., Trade Division, 1221 Avenue of The Americas, New York, N.Y. 10020, U.S.A.

Nabrit, Samuel Milton, M.S., PH.D.; American foundation executive; b. 21 Feb. 1905, Macon, Georgia; s. of James M. and Augusta G. West Nabrit; m. Constance Crocker 1927; ed. Morehouse Coll. and Brown Univ.
Prof. of Biology, Morehouse Coll. 25-31; Prof., Chair. of Dept. of Biology, Atlanta Univ. 32-55, Dean, Graduate School 47-55; Pres., Texas Southern Univ., Houston 55-66; Commr. U.S. Atomic Energy Comm. 66-67; Co-ordinator, Carnegie Grants-in-Aid Program 48-55; mem. Nat. Cttee. on Research Science Education 36-, mem. Nat. Scientific Board 56-59, etc.; Exec. Dir. The Southern Fellowships Fund 67-; Hon. D.Sc. (Brown, Howard, Atlanta Univs. and Bishop Coll.), Hon. LL.D. (Morgan, Morehouse and Bethune-Cookman Colls., Kentucky Univ.); mem. Pi Delta Phi, Phi Beta Kappa, Beta Kappa Chi, Sigma XI.
Leisure interests: bridge, reading, travel, sports.
The Southern Fellowships Fund, 795 Peachtree Street, N.E., Suite 484, Atlanta, Georgia 30308, U.S.A.
Telephone: 404-874-4891.

Nabulsi, Omar, L. EN D., M.A.; Jordanian politician; b. 1 April 1936, Nablus; s. of Hajj Nimre Nabulsi and Safia Ali; m. Haifa Hatough 1966; two s.; ed. Cairo and Ain Shams Univs.
Legal Adviser, Sasco Petroleum Co., Libya 59-61;

Political Attaché, League of Arab States 61-70; Asst. Dir. Dept. of Admin., Royal Hashemite Court Jan.-Sept. 70; Minister of Nat. Economy 70-72; Amb. at the Foreign Ministry, Amman 72; Amb. to the U.K. 72-73; Minister of Agriculture June-Nov. 73, of Nat. Economy 73-Jan. 75; Order of Al-Kawkab of Jordan.
Leisure interests: reading, cricket, squash, music, theatre.
c/o Ministry of National Economy, Amman, Jordan.
Telephone: Amman 39310/39361.

Nachmansohn, David, M.D.; American biochemist; b. 17 March 1899, Ekaterinoslav, Russia; s. of Moses Nachmansohn and Regina Nachmansohn (née Klinkowstein); m. Edith Berger 1929; one d.; ed. Univ. of Berlin and Kaiser-Wilhelm Inst., Berlin-Dahlem.
Independent Investigator, Faculty of Science, Univ. of Paris 33-39; Instructor, School of Medicine, Yale Univ. 39-42; at Coll. of Physicians and Surgeons, Columbia Univ., New York 42-, Prof. of Biochemistry 55-, Prof. Emeritus of Biochemistry and Special Lecturer in Biochemistry 67, Dir. Neurochemistry Research Unit 58-; mem. Advisory Board of Hadassah 50-55, Board of Govs. Weizmann Inst. of Science, Israel 72- (Hon. Fellow 72), Editorial Cttee. *Annual Review of Biochemistry* 73-; mem. Nat. Acad. of Sciences, American Acad. of Arts and Sciences, German Acad. of Sciences (Leopoldina); Counsellor Harvard Soc. 66-69; Fellow and mem. about 20 professional socs.; Pasteur Medal 52; Neuberg Medal 53; Nicloux Medal 62; Gold Medal of Spanish Superior Council for Scientific Investigations, Madrid 75; Hon. M.D. (Free Univ. of Berlin) 64.
Leisure interests: art, opera, history of arts and sciences, history, archaeology, int. scientific relations.
Main research contributions: analysis of proteins and enzymes of excitable membranes and their role in generating bio-electricity, the basic problem of nerve impulse conduction, since 1937 has used for this work electrical organs of fish. This work has contributed to elucidation of mechanism of action of nerve gas and insecticides and to devt. of an efficient antidote against insecticide poisoning; work described in over 400 original articles and monograph *Chemical and Molecular Basis of Nerve Activity* 59 (2nd edn. 75).
Office: College of Physicians and Surgeons, Columbia Univ., 630 West 168 Street, New York, N.Y. 10032; Home: 560 Riverside Drive, New York, N.Y. 10027, U.S.A.
Telephone: 212-579-3697 (Office); 212-749-5142 (Home).

Naço, Rako; Albanian diplomatist; b. 15 July 1923, Pogradec; ed. Univ. of Tirana.
Joined Ministry of Foreign Affairs 50; First Sec., Warsaw 53-56, Belgrade 56-59, Perm. Mission to UN 63-66; Counsellor, Paris 66-68; Perm. Rep. to UN May 72-; del. to UN Gen. Assembly 63-65, 68, 71.
Permanent Mission of Albania to United Nations, 250 East 87th Street, 21st Floor, N.Y. 10028, U.S.A.

Nadao, Hirokichi; Japanese politician; b. 1899; ed. Tokyo Univ.
Entered Home Ministry 24; Gov. Oita Prefecture 41; Chief, Livelihood Bureau and Sanitation Bureau, Home Ministry 44; Vice-Minister of Home Affairs 45; mem. House of Reps. 45-; Minister of Education 56-57, 58-59, 63-64, 67-68; fmr. mem. House of Reps. Standing Cttees. for the Budget and Local Education; fmr. Vice-Chair. Political Affairs Investigation Cttee. of Liberal Democratic Party, Chair. Exec. Council Dec. 74-; mem. Local Admin. System Research Council; Dir. Paper Bag Mfg. Co.; Liberal Democratic Party.
Liberal Democratic Party, Tokyo, Japan.

Nader, Ralph; American lawyer and author; b. 27 Feb. 1934; ed. Princeton and Harvard Univs.
Admitted to Conn. Bar 58, Mass. Bar 59, also U.S. Supreme Court; U.S. Army 59; law practice in Hartford, Conn. 59-; Lecturer in History and Govt., Univ. of Hartford 61-63; Lecturer, Princeton Univ. 67-68; mem. American Bar Asscn.; has advanced cause of consumer protection, particularly with regard to car safety, in U.S.A.; Woodrow Wilson Award (Princeton Univ.) 72.
Publs. *Unsafe at Any Speed* 65, *Who Runs Congress?* 72, Editor *The Consumer and Corporate Accountability* 74.
53 Hillside Avenue, Winsted, Conn., U.S.A.

Nadezhdina, Nadezhda Sergeyevna; Soviet ballet master; b. 3 July 1908, Leningrad; ed. Second Petrograd Ballet School.
Ballerina at Bolshoi Theatre 25-34; Ballet Master, Moscow Variety Soc. 35-48; Organizer, Leader and Ballet Master Beriozka Dance Ensemble; People's Artist of U.S.S.R. 66; State Prize; Gold Medal of World Peace Council.
Moscow Philharmonic Society, 19 Ul. Gorkogo, Moscow, U.S.S.R.

Nadjakov, Georgi; Bulgarian scientist; b. 8 Jan. 1897, Stanke Dimitrov; s. of Stephan D. Nadjakov and Vasilka G. Nadjakova; m. Vera Todorova Postompirova 1928; one s. one d.; ed. Univ. of Sofia.
Research worker in Paris 25-26; Prof. Experimental Physics, Sofia 32; Vice-Pres. Bulgarian Acad. of Sciences 45-58; Foreign mem. Acad. of Sciences of U.S.S.R. 58-; Rector of Univ. of Sofia 47-52; Vice-Pres. Cttee. for the Peaceful use of Atomic Energy at the Council of Ministers; Dir. Inst. of Physics and Atomic Research Centre, Sofia since its foundation 46-71; corresp. mem. Göttingen Acad. of Sciences 40-.
Leisure interest: gardening.
Bulgarian Academy of Sciences, Sofia; and 1 T. Strashimirov Str., Sofia, Bulgaria.
Telephone: 72-08-54, 73-41/640 (Office); 44-25-14 (Home).

Naffah, Fouad Georges, LIC. EN DROIT; Lebanese lawyer; b. 1 March 1925, Zouk Mikhaël; s. of Georges Naffah and Malvina Takla; m. Zbeide Sfeir; three s. one d.; ed. Coll. des Frères Maristes, Coll. d'Antoura, Univ. St. Joseph, Beirut.
Elected Deputy for Kesrouan 60, 72; Lecturer in Constitutional Law and Lebanese Constitution, Coll. de la Sagesse and Univ. Libanaise; Minister of Agriculture March-May 72, of Finance 72-73, of Foreign Affairs 73-74.
Home: Raouché, Beirut, Lebanon.
Telephone: 314333.

Nagai, Michio; Japanese politician; ed. Kyoto Univ., Ohio State Univ.
Assistant Prof. Kyoto Univ.; later taught at Tokyo Inst. of Technology; Editorial Writer *Asahi Shimbun* 70; Dir. Communications Inst. of East-West Center, Hawaii 72-73; Minister of Educ. Dec. 74-.
Ministry of Education, Tokyo, Japan.

Nagano, Shigeo; Japanese business executive; b. 15 July 1900, Matsue-shi, Shimane; s. of Hoojo and Yae Nagano; m. Setsu Ohtsuka 1927; three s. one d.; ed. Tokyo Imperial Univ.
General Man. Fuji Steel Works, Japan Iron and Steel Co. Ltd. 34-40; Gen. Man. Japan Iron and Steel Co. Ltd. 40-46, Man. Dir. 46-47, 48-50; Deputy Dir.-Gen. Govt. Econ. Stabilization Board 47-48; Pres. Fuji Iron and Steel Co. Ltd. 50-70; Chair. Nippon Steel Corpn. 70-73, Dir., Hon. Chair. 73-; Hon. Pres. Japan Iron and Steel Fed. 65-; Vice-Pres. Pacific Basin Econ. Council 70-; Pres. Japan Chamber of Commerce and Industry, Tokyo Chamber of Commerce and Industry 69-;

Adviser, Fed. of Employers' Asscns. 70-, Fed. of Econ. Orgs. 70-; Counsellor, Bank of Japan 70-; Chair. Prime Minister's Council for Foreign Econ. Co-operation 69-; Order of Sacred Treasure 70.
Leisure interests: Go, golf.
Office: Nippon Steel Corporation, 6-3, Otemachi 2-chome, Chiyoda-ku, Tokyo; Home: 34-4, Matsubara 4-chome, Setagaya-ku, Tokyo, Japan.
Telephone: 242-4111 (Office); 321-0141 (Home).

Nagata, Takao; Japanese business executive; b. 1 Sept. 1911; ed. Nagasaki Commercial High School.
With Hitachi Shipbuilding and Engineering Co. 34-, Dir. 51-60, Vice-Pres. 60-62, Pres. 62-; Chair. Japan Shipbuilders Asscn.
Hitachi Shipbuilding and Engineering Co., Ltd., 47, Edobori, 1-chome, Nishi-ku, Osaka, Japan.

Nagata, Takesi; Japanese geophysicist; b. 24 June 1913, Tokyo.
Director Nat. Inst. of Polar Research; Prof. Emer. Tokyo Univ.; recipient of lunar samples from U.S. *Apollo* missions; Foreign mem. Nat. Acad. of Sciences (U.S.A.).
National Institute of Polar Research, 9-10, Kaga-1, Itabashi-ku, Tokyo, 173, Japan.

Nagel, Louis; French publisher; b. 1908, Iglo, Hungary; m. Josiane Champart 1942; ed. Univs. of Vienna, Prague and Geneva.
Founder of Nagel Publications; publisher of Nagel Travel Guides; Pres. of Int. Acad. of Tourism and mem. of P.E.N. Club; Vice-Pres. Robert Schumann Asscn. for Europe; Gold Medal of City of Rome, Silver Medal of City of Rome, Silver Medal of Paris, Officer of Order of the Phoenix (Greece), Hon. G.C.M.G., Grand Officer of Order of Malta, Commdr. Ordine al Merito della Repubblica Italiana, Diploma "Prestige de la France", Ordre de la Couronne (Iran), Meridue Culturii of Romania (1st class); Consul-Gen. of Cyprus in Switzerland.
Leisure interests: skiing, riding, swimming.
Publs. Works on philosophy, including *La Paix éternelle, est-elle une utopie?* 46.
7 rue de Savoie, Paris 6e, France; and 5 rue de l'Orangerie, Geneva, Switzerland.

Naggar, Abd El Moneim El; Egyptian army officer and diplomatist; b. 7 July 1920, Alexandria; s. of Ibrahim El Naggar and Amina El Said Abdou; m. Bouchra Ahmed El Naggar 1942; one s. two d.; ed. Cairo Mil. Acad., Cairo Staff Acad., Cairo Univ. and Inst. des Hautes Etudes, Univ. of Paris.
Egyptian Army 39-57; Mil. Attaché, Paris 53-54, Madrid 55-57; Head of East European Dept., Ministry of Foreign Affairs, Cairo 58; U.A.R. Consul-Gen., Bombay 59-62, Hong Kong 62; Amb. to Greece 63, to France 64-68; Head, Western, Culture and Technical Depts.; Ministry of Foreign Affairs 68-71; Amb. to Iraq 72-; numerous decorations.
Leisure interests: tennis, shooting.
Embassy of Egypt, Karradat Mariam, Baghdad, Iraq.
Telephone: 34127/28.

Nagy, János; Hungarian diplomatist; b. 23 Sept. 1928, Ujcsalános; s. of István Nagy and Julianna Pankucsi; m. Éva Peredi 1950; one d.; ed. Budapest Univ. and Acad. of Diplomacy.
Entered Diplomatic Service 48; Asst. Attaché, Hungarian Legation, London 49-51; Officer, Ministry of Foreign Affairs 51-53, Senior Officer 60, Chief of Dept. 67; posts in Washington 55-56, Jakarta 57-60; Amb. to India 63-67, to U.S.A. 68-71; Deputy Foreign Minister 71-.
Leisure interests: reading and listening to music.
Ministry of Foreign Affairs, H-1394, Budapest, Hungary.
Telephone: 350-100.

Nagy, Mrs. József; Hungarian politician; b. 1921, Nagysimonyi, Vas; *d.* of Gyula Szarka and Eleonóra Varju; *m.* József Nagy 1939; one *s.*
Textile worker; Dir. textile factory 48-; Deputy Minister of Light Industry 51; Deputy Pres. Nat. Planning Office 52-55; Minister of Light Industry 55-May 71; mem. Central Cttee. Hungarian Socialist Workers' Party, Labour Order of Merit, golden degree 69.
c/o Ministry of Light Industry, H-1251, Budapest; Budapest, II. Fö u. 68, Hungary.
Telephone: 155-257.

Nahavandi, Houshang, L. EN D., DR.ECON.SC.;Iranian economist, educationist and politician; b. 1930; ed. Univ. of Paris.
Adviser to High Council of Econs. 58-61, to Ministry of Labour 59-61; Econ. Attaché, Iranian Embassy, Brussels 61-63; Deputy Head, Del. to European Econ. Community 62-63; Man. Dir. Foreign Trade Co. 63-64; Minister of Housing and Devt. 64-68; Chancellor, Pahlavi Univ. 68-71, Univ. of Teheran 71-; Civil Aide-de-Camp to H.I.M. The Shahanshah Aryamehr; mem. Board of Trustees, Mashad Univ., Charity Foundation of H.I.H. Princess Shams, High Council of Nat. Soc. for the Protection of Animals, High Council for Nat. Educ.; Chevalier Légion d'Honneur (France); Commdr. Ordre de la Couronne (Belgium); Homayoun Decoration 1st Class, 4th Class; Sepasse Decoration and several other awards.
Publs. numerous books and articles.
University of Teheran, Teheran, Iran.

Nahmias, Joseph Jacques; French petroleum executive; b. 14 May 1901, Comotini, Greece; *m.* Mathilde Modiano 1923; one *d.*
Founded Société France-Pétrole (later called Pétrofrance) 34, founded Société Pétrotankers 37, Pres./Dir.-Gen. Pétrofrance; Pres. Pétrofrance Inc., New York; Dir., Pétrotransport, Pétrorep, Pétrosarep, Propétrol, Cofimap, Banque Louis-Dreyfus et Cie., Selected Risk Investments S.A., Energy Int. N.V.; Hon. Pres. A.I.P.
42 avenue Raymond-Poincaré, Paris 16e, France.
Telephone: 553-50-00.

Naicker, Gangathura Mohambry; South African doctor; b. 1910, Durban, Natal; *s.* of P. G. and Dhanamal Naicker; *m.* Mariemoothamal Appavoo 1936; one *s.* one *d.*; ed. Edinburgh Univ.
President, Natal Indian Congress 45-63; Pres. South African Indian Congress 54-63; arrested five times 46-60 for opposing measures discriminating against Indian community and non-European Community; arrested and charged with treason 58; released, having been found not guilty 60; arrested during 1961 emergency and placed under banning order 61-73.
Leisure interests: reading, golf, billiards, table tennis.
Publ. *Historical Synopsis of Anti-Indian Legislation in South Africa* 45.
26 Short Street, Durban, Natal, South Africa.
Telephone: 23408.

Naik, Vasantrao Phulsing; Indian politician; b. 1 July 1913; ed. Neil City High School, Nagpur, Morris Coll., and Univ. Coll. of Law, Nagpur.
Director Madhya Pradesh Co-operative Central Bank 51-52; mem. Legislative Assembly, Madhya Pradesh 52; Dep. Minister for Revenue, Madhya Pradesh; Minister for Co-operation, Bombay 56-57, for Agriculture and Aarey Milk Colony, Bombay 57-60; Minister for Revenue, Maharashtra 60-63, Chief Minister, Gen. Admin., Home Planning and Information 63-.
Office of the Chief Minister, Bombay, Maharashtra, India.

Naipaul, V. S., B.A.; Trinidadian writer; b. 17 Aug. 1932; *m.* 1955; ed. Queen's Royal Coll., Port-of-Spain and Univ. Coll. Oxford.

For two years freelance broadcaster with the B.B.C., producing programmes for the Caribbean area; fiction reviewer on *New Statesman* 58-61; grant from Trinidad Govt. to travel in Caribbean 61; in India 62-63, in Uganda 65-66, in U.S. 69; John Llewelyn Rhys Memorial Prize 58; Somerset Maugham Award 61; Phoenix Trust Award 62; Hawthornden Prize 64; W. H. Smith Award 68; Booker Prize 71.
Publs. *The Mystic Masseur* 57, *The Suffrage of Elvira* 58, *Miguel Street* 59, *A House for Mr. Biswas* 61, *The Middle Passage* 62, *Mr. Stone and the Knights Companion* 63, *An Area of Darkness* 64, *The Mimic Men* 67, *A Flag on the Island* 67 (collection of short stories), *The Loss of El Dorado* 69, *In a Free State* 71, *The Overcrowded Barracoon* 72, *Guerrillas* 75.
c/o André Deutsch Ltd., 105 Great Russell Street, London, W.C.1, England.

Nair, Vallillath Madhathil Madhavan, M.A., BAR.-AT-LAW; Indian diplomatist; b. 8 Oct. 1919, Mangalore; *s.* of C. K. Nair and Padmavathy Amma; *m.* Krishnakumari 1945; one *s.* one *d.*; ed Presidency Coll., Madras, Brasenose Coll., Oxford, Gonville and Caius Coll., Cambridge, and Inner Temple, London.
Entered Indian Civil Service 42. Sub-Divisional Officer, Sitamarhi (Bihar) 44-46; Under Sec. Ministry of External Affairs, New Delhi 46-49; First Sec., Cairo 50-53; Deputy Sec. Ministry of External Affairs 53-55; Deputy High Commr. for India, Ceylon 55-56, Acting High Commr. Ceylon 56-57; Commr. for India in Malaya and Singapore 57, High Commr. for India in Malaya 57-58; Ambassador to Cambodia 58-60, to Norway 60-63; Joint Sec. Ministry of External Affairs 64-67; Amb. to Poland 67-70, to Morocco and Tunisia 70-74, to Spain 74-.
Leisure interests: reading, photography.
Embassy of India, Velázquez 93, Madrid 6, Spain.
Telephone: 276-7643.

Najar, Amiel Emile, LIC. en DR.; Israeli diplomatist; b. 6 Sept. 1912; *m.* Aviva Weisman; ed. Univ. of Paris.
Pres. of Exec., Zionist Fed. of Egypt 43-47; Dir Western European Div., Ministry of Foreign Affairs 52-57, Asst. Dir.-Gen. Ministry of Foreign Affairs 57-58; Minister to Japan 58-60; Ambassador to Belgium and Luxembourg, Head of Mission to the European Econ. Community, the European Atomic Energy Community and the European Coal and Steel Community 61-68; Amb. to Malta 68-71; mem. Israeli Del to UN 48, 51-57, 64, 67; Amb. to Italy 71-73.
c/o Ministry of Foreign Affairs, Jerusalem, Israel.

Najmabadi, Farrokh; Iranian civil servant; b. 1922; ed. U.K.
Consultant Engineer, Central Exploration and Extraction Dept., Nat. Iranian Oil Co., Head of Dept. of Statistics, Deputy to Head of Exploration and Production; Head of Production Dept., Org. of Petroleum Exporting Countries; Deputy and Alt. Man. Dir. NIOC, Head of Oil Affairs Office NIOC Exploration and Production Dept.; Dir.-Gen. for Oil, Ministry of Finance; Pres. of Board, Man. Dir. Iran Telephone Joint Stock Co.; Industry and Mines Under-Sec., Ministry of Econ.; Minister of Mines and Industries April 74-.
Ministry of Mines and Industries, Teheran, Iran.

Nakabe, Kenkichi; Japanese business executive; b. 25 March 1896, Akashi, Hyogo; *s.* of Ikujiro and Koma Nakabe; *m.* 1st Yoshiko Kinashi 1919, 2nd Haruko Morishita 1960; four *s.* four *d.*
Hayashikane Store 10-, Exec. Dir. 24-42; Dir. Taiyo Fisheries Co. Ltd. 35-, Pres. 53-; Pres. Japan Fisheries Asscn. 64-69, Dir. 70-; Exec. Dir. Japan Fed. of Employers' Asscns., Fed. of Econ. Orgs; Councillor, Tokyo Chamber of Commerce and Industry; Medal of Honour with Blue Ribbon, 2nd Class Order of Rising Sun.
Leisure interest: painting.

Taiyo Fishery Co. Ltd., 5-1 1-chome, Marunouchi, Chiyoda-ku, Tokyo; Home: 2-14 1-chome, Ichigaya, Sadohara-cho, Shinjuku-ku, Tokyo, Japan.
Telephone: (03) 216-0811 (Office); (03) 269-2209 (Home).

Nakagawa, Toru; Japanese diplomatist; b. 30 March 1911, Tokyo; s. of Kenzo Nakagawa; m. Sachiko Yano 1939; two s. one d.; ed. Tokyo Univ.
Foreign Service 33-, served New York, and Ministry of Foreign Affairs 33-39; Sec. to Premier 39; Sec. China, concurrently Consul, Shanghai 42; Dir. Japanese Overseas Office, Philippines 52-53; Head, Asia Bureau, Ministry of Foreign Affairs 53-57; Minister, U.K. 57-60; Head, Treaty Dept., Ministry of Foreign Affairs 60-64; Ambassador to Italy 64-65, to U.S.S.R. 65-71; Perm. Rep. to UN 71-73.
Leisure interests: golf, skating.
c/o Ministry of Foreign Affairs, 2-1 Kasumigaseki 2-chome, Chiyoda-ku, Tokyo 100; and 1-14 Nishiogi-minami, Suginamiku, Tokyo, Japan.

Nakai, Haruo; Japanese business executive; b. 18 May 1911, Mie-ken; s. of late Ichitaro and Saki Nakai; m. Tatsuko Yamazawa 36; one s. three d.; ed. Nagoya Univ.
Joined Nippon Suisan Kaisha Ltd. 33, Man. Accounting Dept. 51-57, Dir. 52-55, Man. Dir. 55-58, Senior Man. Dir. 58-61, Exec. Vice-Pres. 61-63, Exec. Pres. 63-, Exec. Chair. 73-75, Dir. and Adviser Dec. 75-; Dir. Japan Fed. of Econ. Orgs.; mem. Nat. Fisheries Co-ordination Council, Nat. Marine Devt. Council; Blue Ribbon Medal.
Leisure interest: Go.
Nippon Suisan Kaisha Ltd., 6-2 Otemachi 2-chome, Chiyoda-ku, Tokyo; Home: 3-6, 1-chome, Hikari-cho, Kokubunji-shi, Tokyo, Japan.
Telephone: 244-7012 (Office); 0425-72-0333 (Home).

Nakamura, Toshio; Japanese banker; b. 7 Jan. 1910, Ibaraki Pref.; s. of Sataro Nakamura and Kiku Saito; m. Yachiko Tsukasaki 1940; one s. one d.; ed. Law Dept., Tokyo Univ.
Joined the Mitsubishi Bank Ltd. 32, Dir. 60-, Man. Dir. 63, Deputy Pres. 65, Pres. 70-, Chair. 75-; Dir. Mitsubishi Warehouse Co. Ltd.; Auditor Mitsubishi Petroleum Devt. Co. Ltd. and Mitsubishi Petrochemical Co. Ltd.; Counsellor, Japan Fed. of Employers' Asscn.; Trustee, Japan Cttee. for Econ. Devt.
Leisure interests: golf and reading.
Office: 7-1, Marunouchi 2-chome, Chiyoda-ku, Tokyo; Home: 17-8, Mejirodai 1-chome, Bunkyo-ku, Tokyo, Japan.

Nakamura, Umekichi; Japanese lawyer and politician; b. 1902, Tokyo; ed. Hosei Univ.
Entered law practice 40; mem. House of Reps. 36-; joined Japan Liberal Party; Minister of Justice 56, 73-74.
5-26, Meijiro, 2-chome, Toshima-ku, Tokyo 171, Japan.

Nakasone, Yasuhiro; Japanese politician; b. 27 May 1918; ed. Tokyo Imperial Univ.
Member House of Reps.; fmr. Minister of State, Dir.-Gen. of Science & Technology Agency; Chair. Nat. Org. Liberal-Democratic Party, Joint Cttee. on Atomic Energy, Special Cttee. on Scientific Technology; Pres. Takushoku Univ.; Minister of Transport 67-68; Minister of State and Dir.-Gen. Defence Agency Jan. 70-71; Chair. Exec. Council, Liberal-Democratic Party 71-72; Minister of International Trade and Industry 72-74; Sec.-Gen. Liberal-Democratic Party Dec. 74-.
Leisure interests: golf, swimming and painting.
Publs. *Ideal of Youth, South Pole–Human & Science, Frontier in Japan.*
Liberal-Democratic Party, Tokyo; Home: 2-18-6, Takada, Toshima-ku, Tokyo, Japan.
Telephone: 982-7896 (Home).

Nakayama, Komei; Japanese surgeon; b. 25 Sept. 1910, Tokyo; m. Yoshiye Nakayama; one s. one d.; ed. Chiba Univ.
Assistant Prof. of Surgery, Chiba Univ. 41-47, Prof. of Surgery 47-63; Prof. of Surgery, Tokyo Women's Medical Coll. 64-, Pres. of Inst. of Gastroenterology; Visiting Prof. St. Vincent Hospital, Sydney, Australia 61; Vice-Pres. Medical Div., Japanese Science Council; fmr. Pres. Int. Coll. of Surgeons; numerous Japanese and foreign awards.
Leisure interest: fishing.
2-3-18-704 Hirakawa-cho, Chiyoda-ku, Tokyo, Japan.
Telephone: 261-0661.

Nakayama, Sohei, M.COM.; Japanese banker; b. 5 March 1906, Tokyo; s. of Kinzaburo Nakayama and Tei Takami; m. Hisako Kadowaki 1935; two s.; ed. Tokyo Coll. of Commerce.
Nippon Kogyo Ginko (Industrial Bank of Japan Ltd.) 29-, Dir. 47-50, Man. Dir. 50-51; Dir. Japan Devt. Bank 51-54; Deputy Pres. Industrial Bank of Japan 54-61, Pres. 61-68, Chair. 68-70, Counsellor 70-; mem. Exec. Cttee. Japan Cttee. for Econ. Devt. 59-; Exec. Dir. Fed. of Econ. Orgs. 62-; Pres. Overseas Technical Co-operation Agency 68-; Dir. Matsushita Electric Industrial Co. Ltd. 71-; Chair. Cttee. for Energy Policy Promotion 73-.
Leisure interests: reading, sports.
3-3, Marunouchi 1-chome, Chiyoda-ku, Tokyo 100; Home: No. 10, 10, 6-chome, Zushi, Zushi-City, Kanagawa Prefecture, Japan.

Nakayama, Yoshihiro; Japanese diplomatist; b. 30 Jan. 1914, Onomichi, Hiroshima-Ken; s. of Ikutaro Nakayama; m. Chieko Ohmura 1942; two s. one d.; ed. Faculty of Law, Tokyo Imperial Univ.
Entered Japanese Diplomatic Service 38; served in France, N. Vietnam, U.K., Belgium and Ministry of Foreign Affairs 38-63; Dir.-Gen. Economic Affairs Bureau 63-66; Amb. to Republic of Vietnam 66-67; Amb. to Int. Orgs., Geneva 67; Amb. to France 70-75; Vice-Chair. GATT.
Leisure interests: skiing, literature.
4-8-29, Takanawa, Minato-ku, Tokyo, Japan.
Telephone: 441-2852.

Nakib, Ahmed Abdul Wahab al-; Kuwaiti diplomatist; b. 30 July 1933, Kuwait; m. Hannan Mohamed al-Bahar 1971; one s.; ed. Adam State Coll., Colorado, U.S.A.
First Sec. Kuwait Embassy, London 62-63; Counsellor first Perm. Mission of Kuwait to UN 63-66; Consul-Gen., Kenya 66-67; Amb. to Pakistan 67-70, to U.K. 71-75.
c/o Ministry of Foreign Affairs, Kuwait City, Kuwait.

Nałęcz, Maciej, DR.; Polish scientist; b. 27 April 1922, Warsaw; ed. Warsaw Technical Univ.
Doctor 49; scholarship to Case Inst. of Tech., Cleveland, U.S.A. 61-62; Assoc. Prof. 62-72, Prof. 72-; Corresp. mem. Polish Acad. of Sciences 67-73, mem. 73-; Dir. Inst. of Automatic Control 62-72, Sec. of Tech. Sciences and Chair. Biomedical Eng. Cttee. of Section IV 72-, mem. Presidium 72-; Chair. Nat. Cttee. for Pugwash Confs. 72-, Pugwash Council 74-; mem. Int. Measurement Confed. (IMEKO), Cttee. on Data for Science and Technology (CODATA) of ICSU; mem. Int. Fed. of Automatic Control, Chair. Exec. Cttee. 72-; Knight's Cross, Order of Polonia Restituta 59, Officer's Cross 64, Order of Banner of Labour, 2nd Class 72; State Prize, 2nd Class 72, Medal of 30th Anniversary of People's Poland 74; Award med tack för värdefull insats (Sweden) 57.
Publs. *Trends in Control Components* (monograph), *The Technology of Hall Generators and Their Use in Measurement and Conversion* 72.
Ul. Hoza 5/7 m. 70, 00-528 Warsaw, Poland.

Nalivkin, Dmitry Vasilievich; Soviet geologist and palaeontologist; b. 25 Aug. 1889, Leningrad; ed. Petrograd (now Leningrad) Mining Inst.

Professor at the Petrograd Mining Inst. 20; on the Geological Cttee. Trust 17-49; Pres. Stratigraphy Cttee. of U.S.S.R.; principal work devoted to the stratigraphy and palaeontology of the Palaeozoic in U.S.S.R.; in Institute of Pre-Cambrian Geology, U.S.S.R. Acad. of Sciences 56-; State prizewinner 46; awarded Karpinsky Gold Medal of the Acad. of Sciences of the U.S.S.R. 49, Lenin Prize for directing the compilation of the geological map of the U.S.S.R. 57; mem. U.S.S.R. Acad. of Sciences 46; Hero of Socialist Labour; Orders of Lenin (3); Red Banner of Labour (3); etc.

Leisure interests: books, philately.

Publs. *Outline of Geology of Turkestan* 26, *Brakhiopods of Late and Middle Devon in Turkestan* 30, *Semiluk and Voronezh Layers* 30, *Geological Structure of the Pamirs* 32, *Don and Elets Layer* 34, *Brakhiopods of Late and Middle Devon and Early Carbon in North Eastern Kazakhstan* 38, *Second Baku Oil Deposits Between the Volga and the Urals* 39, *Brakhiopods of the Main Devon Field* 41, *Geological History of the Urals* 43, *Devon Sedimentations in the U.S.S.R.* 47, *Atlas of Main Forms of Fossils in the U.S.S.R.* 47, *Treaties on Facies: Geographical Conditions of Sedimentation Formation* 55-56, *Short History of Geology in the U.S.S.R.* 57, *Geology in the U.S.S.R.* 62, *Problems of Global Geology: Some General Causes of Tectogenesis and Regularities of Location of Mineral Resources* 63.

Laboratory of Pre-Cambrian Geology, U.S.S.R. Academy of Sciences, Naberezhnaya Makarova 2, Leningrad; Home: Apt. 65, Glinki Str. 3, 190000 Leningrad, U.S.S.R.

Nam Duk Woo, PH.D.; Korean economist and politician; b. 10 Oct. 1924; s. of Sang Bom Nam and Cha Soon Yoo; m. Hye Sook Choi 1953; two s. one d.; ed. Kook Min Coll., Seoul, Seoul Nat. Univ., Okla. and Stanford Univs.

With Bank of Korea 52-54; Asst. Prof., Assoc. Prof., Prof., Dean of Econ. Dept., Kook Min Coll. 54-64; Prof. Sogang Univ. and Dir. Research Inst. for Econ. and Business 64-69; Minister of Finance 69; Gov. for Korea, IMF, IBRD, ADB 69-72, Chair. Board of Govs. Asian Devt. Bank 69-72; Deputy Prime Minister and Minister of Econ. Planning Board 74-75; mem. Advisory Cttee. on Evaluation of Econ. Devt. Plan, Nat. Mobilization Board 64-69; Adviser to Korea Devt. Bank 64-69; Assoc. mem. Econ. and Scientific Council 67-69.

Leisure interests: reading, music appreciation.

Publs. *History of Economic Theory* 58, *Price Theory* 65, *History of Economic Theory* (co-author) 62, *The Determinants of Money Supply and Monetary Policy: in the case of Korea 1954-64* 66.

Home: 395-101 Seokyo-Dong, Mapo-Ku, Seoul, Republic of Korea.

Namboodiripad, E. M. Sankaran; Indian politician; b. 14 June 1909, Elamkulam Village, Malappuram District; s. of E. M. Parameswaran Namboodiripad and E. M. Vishnudatha Antherjanam; m. E. M. Arya Antherjanam 1937; two s. two d.; ed. Board High School, Perintalmanna, Victoria Coll., Palghat, St. Thomas Coll., Trichur.

Chief Minister, Kerala 57-59, 67-Oct. 69; Acting Gen. Sec., Indian C.P. 62-63, now Leader Communist (Marxist) Party of India; detained July 75.

Publs. *The Peasant Question in Kerala* 50, *The National Question in Kerala* 52, *Mahathma and the Ism* 58, *Economics and Politics of India's Socialist Pattern* 66, *India under Congress Rule* 67, *Kerala-Yesterday, Today, Tomorrow* 67, *Indian Planning in Crisis* 74, *Conflicts and Crisis: Political India 1974* 74.

10, Shanthi Nagar, Press Road, Trivandrum, Kerala State, India.

Namèche, Louis Hubert Ghislain; Belgian politician; b. 8 Dec. 1915, Jemeppe sur Sambre; s. of Aimé Namèche and Emilie Lien; m. 1st Marie Marin 1938 (deceased), 2nd Louisa Kinet 1967; two d.; ed. Ecole Communale, Jemeppe sur Sambre, and Univ. du Travail, Charleroi.

Prisoner of War 40-45; career with Fédération Générale du Travail de Belgique; Socialist Deputy 49-; mem. Parl. Comms. on Employment and Labour, Social Welfare and Nat. Defence; Minister of Public Health 68-72, of Social Affairs 72-73.

Parti Socialiste Belge, Maison du P.S.B., 13 boulevard de l'Empereur, Brussels, Belgium.

Namgyal, Miwang Chogyal Chenpo Palden Thondup, O.B.E.; fmr. Ruler of Sikkim; b. 22 May 1923; m. 1st Sangay Deki, d. of Theiji Tsewang Rinzing Namgyal of Lhasa, 1950 (died 1957), two s. one d.; m. 2nd Hope Cooke 1963, one s. one d.; ed. St. Joseph's Coll., Darjeeling and Bishop Cotton School, Simla.

President Sikkim State Council 44-49; Pres. Maha Bodhi Soc. of India 53; Founder-Pres. Namgyal Inst. of Tibetology, Gangtok, Sikkim; succeeded his father as Chogyal of Sikkim 63-75, deposed after annexation of Sikkim to India April 75; Padma Vibhushan 54; Commdr. Ordre de l'Etoile Noire 56, Order of Druk Jung Thusay, First Class 74; Hon. Maj.-Gen. of Indian Army 65, fmr. Col.-in-Chief Sikkim Guards.

Gangtok, Sikkim, India.

Namwisi, Ma Nkoyi; Zairian politician.

Minister of Economy March 69-Aug. 69; Minister of Finance Aug. 69-Sept. 70; Minister of Finance 70-72; Minister of Trade 72-74.

Ministry of Trade, Kinshasa, Zaire.

Namy, Louis Lucien; French painter and politician; b. 14 June 1908.

Senator from Seine-et-Oise 51-58; Senator from Essonne 68-; Conseiller-Gen. from Arpajon 45-51, 58-; Judge, High Court 68-; Chevalier des Palmes Académiques; Communist.

Palais du Luxembourg, Paris 6e; 18 rue de 22 Août 1944. Arpajon (S. et O.), France.

Nana Opoku Ware II, Matthew; Ghanaian ruler (The Asantehene); b. 1919; successor and nephew of Sir Osei Agyeman Prempeh II; ed. England.

Former barrister; fmr. Commr. for Communications; named Amb. to Rome 70; King of the Ashantis July 70; mem. Council of State 71-72; Pres., Nat. House of Chiefs, Ghana.

Asantehene's Palace, Manhyia, Kumasi, Ashanti, Ghana.

Nanda, Guizarilal, B.A., M.A., LL.B.; Indian politician; b. 4 July 1898; ed. Forman Christian Coll., Lahore, Agra Coll. and Allahabad Univ.

Professor of Economics, Bombay Nat. Coll. and Sec., Textile Labour Asscn. 22-46; imprisoned 32 and 42-44; Parl. Sec. Govt. of Bombay 37-39; Chair. Standing Cttee. of Ahmedabad Municipality 40-42; Del. to I.L.O. Conf. 47, Asian Regional Conf. 47; organiser of Indian T.U. Conf. 47; Minister for Labour, Govt. of Bombay 48-50; Deputy Chair. Nat. Planning Comm. 50-51; Minister for Planning 51-52; Minister for Planning, Irrigation and Power 52-57; Minister for Labour, Employment and Planning 57-63; Minister for Home Affairs 63-Nov. 66; Acting Prime Minister May-June 64, 66, Minister of Railways 70-March 71.

Publs. *Some Aspects of Khadi, Approach to the Second Five-Year-Plan,* etc.

5 Tughlaq Road, New Delhi, India.

Nannen, Henri; German editor; b. 25 Dec. 1913, Emden, s. of Klaas Nannen and Elise Buitenduif; m. Martha Kimm 1947; one s.; ed. Ludwig-Maximilians-Univ., Munich (art history).

Art Editor for Bruckmann Verlag, Munich 37-39; served in Second World War; Publisher and Editor *Han-*

noversche Neueste Nachrichten 46-47, *Abendpost* Hanover 47-48; Publisher and Editor-in-Chief *Der Stern* (magazine), Hamburg 48-; Hon. Citizen of Volkach 62.
Leisure interest: yachting.
Publs. *Glanz von Innen* 43, *Kleines Musikbrevier* 43.
Hamburg-Wellingsbüttel, Wellingsbütteler Weg 92, Federal Republic of Germany.

Napoli, Jacopo; Italian composer; b. 26 Aug. 1911; ed. S. Pietro a Majella Conservatoire of Music, Naples. Obtained diplomas in Composition, Organ and Piano; held Chair of Counterpoint and Fugue at Cagliari Conservatoire, and at Naples Conservatoire; Dir. S. Pietro a Majella Conservatoire of Music, Naples 55, 62; Dir. Giuseppe Verdi Conservatoire of Music, Milan; Dir. Scarlatti Arts Soc. 55-; works performed in Germany, Spain and on Italian radio.
Works: (operas) *Il Malato Immaginario* 39, *Miseria e Nobiltà* 46, *Un curioso accidente* 50, *Masaniello* 53, *I Pescatori* 54, *Il Tesoro* 58, (oratorio) *The Passion of Christ, Il Rosario* 62, *Il Povero Diavolo* 63, *Piccola Cantata del Venerdì Santo* 64, (orchestral works) *Overture to Love's Labours Lost* 35, *Preludio di Caccia* 35, *La Festa di Anacapri* 40.
55 Via Andrea da Isernia, Naples, Italy.

Nara, Yasuhiko; Japanese diplomatist; b. 28 April 1917, Tokyo; s. of Mr. and Mrs. Shizuma Nara; m. Michi Hayashi 1954; one d.; ed. Hitotsubashi Univ., Tokyo.
Attaché, Embassy in Thailand 42; Ministry of Foreign Affairs 43; Second Sec. and Consul, London 51-52; Dir. No. 3 Div., Ministry of Trade and Commerce 53, No. 3 Div., European and American Bureau, Ministry of Foreign Affairs 54; served in Royal Courts 56; Dir. N. America Div., Econ. Bureau, Ministry of Foreign Affairs 61; Counsellor, Embassy in United Arab Repub. 62; Consul-Gen., Chicago 65, New York 66; Amb. to Singapore 69, to Repub. of Viet-Nam 72-75, to Canada April 75-.
Leisure interest: golf.
Embassy of Japan, Suite 1005, 75 Albert Street, Ottawa, Ont. K1P 5E7; Home: 725 Acacia Avenue, Rockcliffe, Ottawa, Ont. K1M 0M8, Canada.

Narain, Govind, B.SC., M.SC.; Indian civil servant and business administrator; b. 5 May 1917, Mainpuri, Uttar Pradesh; s. of late Ram and Rajrani Narain; m. Chandra Lall 1939; three d.; ed. Allahabad Univ. and Balliol Coll., Oxford.
District Magistrate 45-47; Home Sec. Uttar Pradesh 48-51; Adviser-Sec. to King of Nepal 51-54; Sec. to Uttar Pradesh Public Works Dept., Power and Information Depts. 54-55; Development Commr. to Uttar Pradesh Govt.; Sec. Depts. of Planning, Econs., Statistics and Information 55-58, Chief Sec. Uttar Pradesh Govt. 58-61; Managing Dir. The State Trading Corpn. of India Ltd. 61-63, Chair. May-Sept. 63; Chair. Minerals and Metals Trading Corpn. of India Ltd. Oct. 63-66; Adviser to Govt. of Kerala 65; Sec. Dept. of Family Planning, Govt. of India March-Dec. 66; Sec. Ministry of Health and Family Planning, Govt. of India Jan. 67-Nov. 68; Sec. Defence Production, Ministry of Defence, Govt. of India 68-Dec. 70; Sec. Ministry of Home Affairs 71-73, Ministry of Defence May 73-.
Leisure interests: photography, gardening.
The Secretary, Ministry of Defence, New Delhi 110011; Residence: 11 Thyagaraja Marj, New Delhi 110011, India.
Telephone: 372380 (Office); 372781 (Residence).

Narasimhan, Chakravarthi Vijayaraghava, M.B.E., M.A.; Indian civil servant; b. 21 May 1915, Srirangam, Madras; m. Janaki 1938; two d.; ed. Madras and Oxford Univs.
Entered Indian Civil Service 36, appointed to Madras Cadre 37, District Officer Madras 37-42, Madras Govt. Secretariat (successively Under Sec., Deputy Sec. and

Sec., Food Department and Board of Revenue) 42-50; successively Deputy Sec. and Joint Sec. Ministry of Food and Agriculture, Ministry of Finance, Govt. of India 50-56; Exec. Sec. UN Economic Comm. for Asia and the Far East 56-59; Under-Sec. for Special Political Affairs, UN 59-61, Chef de Cabinet 61-72; Under-Sec.-Gen. for Gen. Assembly Affairs 62-69, Deputy Admin. UN Devt. Programme 69-72; Under-Sec.-Gen. for Inter-Agency Affairs and Co-ordination 72-; two hon. degrees.
Leisure interests: Sanskrit literature, south Indian classical music, tennis.
300 East 33rd Street, Apt. 11-M, New York, N.Y. 10016, U.S.A.
Telephone: 212-686-2398.

Narayan, Jayaprakash; Indian politician; b. 11 Oct. 1902; ed. Bihar and U.S.A.
Member Working Cttee. Indian Nat. Congress 31, Act. Sec.-Gen. 31-32; founded Congress Socialist Party 34, Sec.-Gen. 34-50; founded Socialist Party 48; merged with Kisan Mazdoor Sabha Praja Party to form Praja Socialist Party, leader 52-57; a leader of Quit India Movement 42-43; imprisoned several times; Pres. Indian Railwaymen's Fed., All India Post and Telegraph Employees Union and Defence Employees Fed 46-52; engaged in Bhoodan (Land Gift Movement) 57-; detained June 75, released on parole Nov. 75; Pres. All India Panchayat Parishad, All India Asscn. of Voluntary Agencies for Rural Development 59-63; Chair. All-India Peace Brigade, Afro-Asian Council, India-Pakistan Reconciliation Group, Co-Chair. World Peace Brigade.
Kadam Kuan, Patna 3, Bihar, India.

Narayan, Rasipuram Krishnaswamy; Indian writer; b. 10 Oct. 1906.
Publs. (all in English), novels: *Swami and Friends* 35, *The Bachelor of Arts, The Dark Room, The English Teacher, Mr. Sampath, The Financial Expert, Waiting for the Mahatma, The Guide* 58, *The Man-Eater of Malgudi* 61, *Gods, Demons and Others* 64, *The Sweet-Vendor* 67, *Ramayana* 72; short stories: *An Astrologer's Day, The Lawley Road, A Horse and Two Goats; My Days* (autobiog.) 74.
Yadavagiri, Mysore 2, India; c/o David Higham Associates, 5-8 Lower John Street, Golden Square, London, W1R 4HA, England.

Narayan, Shriman; Indian administrator and diplomatist; b. 13 July 1912; ed. Allahabad Univ. and Calcutta Univ.
Principal, Seksaria Coll., Wardha, 40-52; Dean, Faculty of Commerce, Nagpur Univ. 42-48; Gen. Sec. Indian Nat. Congress and Chief Editor, A.I.C.C. *Economic Review* 52-58; mem. Parl. 52-57; mem. Planning Comm. 58-64; Amb. to Nepal 64-67; Pres. All India Nature Cure Fed.; Chair. All India Nai Talim (Basic Educ.) Samiti and Sevagram Ashram Foundation; Chair. Gandhi Nat. Memorial Trust 74-; Editor *Gandhi Marg* (Hindi); Governor of Gujarat 67-73; Hon. D.Litt. (Karnataka Univ.) 73, (Kashi Vidyapith) 74, (Kanpur Univ.) 75.
Publs. include *Gandhian Plan for Economic Development, Gandhian Constitution for Free India, Fountain of Life, Socialism in Indian Planning, The Two Worlds, Towards a Socialist Economy, The Tragedy of a Wall, Trends in Indian Planning, Medium of Instruction, One Week with Vinoba, Principles of Gandhian Planning, Letters from Gandhi Nehru Vinoba, Gandhi: The Man and His Thought, Towards Better Education, India and Nepal, Vinoba: His Life and Work, Relevance of Gandhian Economics, Mahatma Ghandi: The Atomic Man, Memoirs: Window on Ghandi and Nehru, Education of the Future, Jamnalal Bajaj.*
Jivan Kutir, Wardha, Maharashtra State, India.
Telephone: Wardha 196.

Narita, Tomomi; Japanese politician; b. 21 April 1912; s. of Takaji and Sei Narita; m. Toshiko Narita 1935; ed. Tokyo Univ.
Former Pres. Kagawa Prefectural Fed. of Socialist Party; mem. House of Reps.; successively, mem. Cen. Exec. Cttee. of Socialist Party, Chair. Control Cttee., Left Wing Socialist Party, Chair. Policy Board, Socialist Party 61-62, Sec.-Gen. 62-67, Chair. of Party 68-.
Leisure interest: reading.
2-1-12, Bancho, Takamatsu City, Kagawa Prefecture, Japan.
Telephone: 0878-21-4615.

Narlikar, Jayant Vishnu, F.R.A.S., M.A., PH.D., SC.D.; Indian scientist; b. 19 July 1938, Kolhapur; s. of Prof. and Mrs. V. V. Narlikar; m. Mangala S. Rajwade 1966; two d.; ed. Banaras Hindu Univ. and King's Coll., Cambridge.
Berry Ramsey Fellow, King's Coll. Cambridge 63-69; Graduate Staff Mem., Inst. of Theoretical Astronomy, Cambridge 66-72; Senior Research Fellow, King's Coll. 69-72; Jawaharlal Nehru Fellow 73-75; Prof., Tata Inst. of Fundamental Research; Fellow, Indian Acad. of Sciences; awarded Padmabhushan by the Indian Govt. Jan. 65.
Leisure interests: walking, photography.
Publs. Articles on cosmology, general relativity and gravitation, quantum theory, astrophysics etc. in the *Proceedings of the Royal Society*, London, *The Monthly Notices of the Royal Astronomical Society*, London, *The Astrophysical Journal, Nature, Observatory,* and scientific articles in various magazines; *Action at a distance in physics and cosmology* (with Sir F. Hoyle) 74.
Tata Institute of Fundamental Research, Bombay, India; and Flat 701, Colaba Housing Colony, Homi Bhabha Road, Bombay, India.
Telephone: Bombay 214677.

Narovchatov, Sergei; Soviet poet; b. 3 Oct. 1919, Khvalynsk, Saratov, R.S.F.S.R.; m. Galina Nikolaevna Narovchatova; one d.; ed. Inst. of History, Philosophy and Literature, Maxim Gorky Literary Inst.
Served in World War II; First Sec. Moscow Writers' Org. 70-74; Chief Editor *Novy Mir* 74-; Gorky State Prize R.S.F.S.R. 74.
Leisure interest: reading.
Publs. poetry: *Bonfire* 48, *Bitter Love* 55, *A Quarter of a Century* 65, *Noon* 67, *Selected Poetry* (2 vols.) 71; criticism: *Lermontov's Lyrics* 64, *Poetry in Motion* 66, *Unusual Literary Criticisms* 70, *Atlantida Rows from You* 72, and many others.
Ul. Stroitelei 4, Korp 1, Moscow B-311, U.S.S.R.
Telephone: 130-34-58.

Nasalli Rocca di Corneliano, H.E. Cardinal Mario; Vatican ecclesiastic; b. 12 Aug. 1903, Piacenza.
Ordained 27; Archbishop of Anzio 69; created Cardinal 69; mem. Sacred Congregation of Sacramental Discipline, Secr. for Non-Believers.
00193 Rome, Piazza della Città Leonina 9, Italy.

Nash, John Northcote, C.B.E., R.A.; British artist; b. 11 April 1893, Kensington; s. of William H. Nash; m. Dorothy Christine Kühlenthal 1918; ed. Wellington Coll.
Artists Rifles 16, served France until 18 when commissioned paint war pictures for Imperial War Museum; mem. Society of Wood Engravers and of London Group; Asst. Teacher of Design, Royal Coll. of Art 34; represented in Tate Gallery, Victoria and Albert Museum, Manchester, Leeds, Sheffield, Bath, Dublin, Brighton, Rochdale, Newport, Aberdeen, Durban (S.A.); A.R.A. 40; Official War Artist to Admiralty 40-41; Capt. Royal Marines 41; Acting Major 43-44; R.A. 51; Hon. Fellow Royal Coll. of Art; Dr. h.c. Univ. of Essex.
Leisure interests: gardening, music and country pursuits.

Bottengom's Farm, Wormingford, nr. Colchester, Essex, England.
Telephone: Great Horkesley 308.

Nash, Kenneth Twigg; British defence official; b. 15 Sept. 1918, Rotherham; s. of Albert Nash and Marjorie Nora Twigg; m.; two s.; ed. Rotherham Grammar School and Gonville and Caius Coll., Cambridge.
Joined the Admiralty 48; called to the Bar, Inner Temple 55; Defence Counsellor, British Embassy, Washington 65; Asst. Under-Sec. (Policy), Ministry of Defence 68; Asst. Sec.-Gen. for Defence Planning and Policy, NATO 69-71; Asst. Under-Sec. (Defence Staff), Ministry of Defence 72-74; Deputy Under-Sec. of State 74-.
104 Wise Lane, Mill Hill, London, N.W.7, England.

Nash, Philleo; American anthropologist; b. 25 Oct. 1909, Wisconsin Rapids, Wis.; s. of Guy Nash and Florence B. Philleo; m. Edith Rosenfels 1935; two d.; ed. Univs. of Wisconsin and Chicago.
Lecturer in Anthropology, Univ. of Toronto 37-41; Man. Biron Cranberry Co. 41-42, Pres. 46-; Special Asst. to Dir., White House liaison, Office of War Information 42-46; Special Asst., The White House 46-52; Admin. Asst. to Pres. of U.S. 52-53; Lieut.-Gov. of Wis. 59-61; Asst. to Asst. Sec. for Public Land Management, Dept. of Interior 61-62, U.S. Commr. of Indian Affairs 61-66; Consulting Anthropologist 66-; Asst. Prof. Amer. Univ., Wash. 71-73, Prof. 73-; Dir. Asscn. American Indian Affairs 43-.
Leisure interest: music.
1028 Connecticut Avenue, N.W., Washington, D.C. 20036; and 540 N. Street, S.W., Washington, D.C. 20024, U.S.A.
Telephone: 202-296-3960; 202-554-3775.

Nashashibi, Nasser Eddin; Arab journalist and politician; b. 1924; ed. American Univ. of Beirut.
Chief Adviser, King Abdullah of Jordan 50, Acting Chief Chamberlain 51; fmr. Chief Controller and Dir. Hashemite Broadcasting; fmr. Head Press Dept., Foreign Office, Amman; Roving Editor *Akhbar El Yom*, Cairo; Chief Editor of daily *Al-Goumhouria*, Cairo 59-64; Special Diplomatic Envoy of daily *Al-Ahram* in Europe; Roving Amb. of the Arab League 65-67.
Publs. sixteen books.
38 Rue Athenée, Geneva, Switzerland.
Telephone: Geneva 463763.

Nasi, Giovanni, D.ING.; Italian industrialist; b. 24 Aug. 1918, Villarperosa, Turin; s. of Carlo Nasi and Aniceta Agnelli; m. 1944; one s. one d.; ed. Politecnico di Torino.
Grandson of Giovanni Agnelli (founder of FIAT); Vice-Chair. of FIAT (manufacturers of land, sea and air vehicles and engines) until 72; Chair. Società Assicuratrice Industriale (SAI) 72-; Pres. Turin Agency for Int. Exhbns., Centre for Winter Road Transit; Chair. Società Italiana Assicurazione Trasporti (SIAT); Mayor of Sestriere; Commendatore della Repubblica Italiana.
Leisure interests: golf, skiing.
12 Corso Galileo Galilei, Turin, Italy.

Nasir, Ibrahim, K.C.M.G.; Maldivian politician; b. 2 Sept. 1926, Malé; s. of Ahmed Didi and Aishath Didi; m. 1st Aishath Zubair 1950, 2nd Mariyam Saeed 1953, 3rd Naseema Mohamed Kalegefaan 1969; four s.; ed. Ceylon (now Sri Lanka).
Under-Sec. of State to Minister of Finance and to Minister of Public Safety, Republic of Maldives 54; Minister of Public Safety 56, of Home Affairs Aug. 57; Prime Minister (1st term) Dec. 57, Prime Minister (2nd term) and Min. of Home Affairs, Finance, Educ., Trade, External Affairs and Public Safety Aug. 59, Prime Minister (3rd term) and Minister of Finance, Educ., External Affairs and Public Safety 64; Pres. of the

Repub. of Maldives 68- (re-elected 73); Award of Nishan Ghazee ge Izzaten Veriya, Ranna Bandeiri Kilegefaan.

Leisure interests: fishing, yachting, gardening.

Office of the President, Malé; Home: Velaanaage, Henvaru, Malé, Republic of Maldives.

Telephone: 822, 270 (Office); 546, 594 (Home).

Nasir, Sharif Husain bin; Jordanian politician.

Former Minister of Royal Court; Prime Minister April 63-July 64; Chief of the Royal Cabinet 67; mem. Consultative Council 67-; Great Uncle of King Hussein. Amman, Jordan.

Nason, John William, A.M.; American educator; b. 9 Feb. 1905, St. Paul, Minn.; s. of Albert J. Nason and Mary E. Eaton; m. 1st Bertha D. White 1935 (died 1955), 2nd Elizabeth M. Knapp 1957; two s. one step s. two step d.; ed. Chicago Latin School, Phillips Exeter Acad., Carleton Coll., Yale Divinity School, Harvard Graduate School, Oxford Univ.

Instructor in Philosophy Swarthmore Coll. 31-34, Asst. Prof. 34-40, Pres. 40-53; Pres. Foreign Policy Asscn. 53-62; Pres. Carleton Coll. 62-70; Asst. to American Sec. Rhodes Trust 34-40; Pres. United Nations Council Philadelphia 42-45, Vice-Pres. 45-47; Pres. World Affairs Council of Philadelphia 49-51, 52-53; Fellow and mem. Board of Dirs. Soc. for Religion in Higher Educ.; Trustee, Edward W. Hazen Foundation, Vassar Coll. 54-62, Eisenhower Exchange Fellowships 53-65, Danforth Foundation 61-68; Educator's Advisory Comm. Esso Educ. Foundation 64-68, Foreign Policy Asscn. 71-; Advisory Council to Inst. for Educational Management (Harvard) 75-; Dir. of Studies, Asscn. of Governing Boards of Univs. and Colls. 73-75; Dir. of Study of Foundation Trustees for Council on Foundation 75-; Hon. LL.D. (Pennsylvania, Carleton, Swarthmore, Hamilton, Brandeis, Johns Hopkins); Litt.D. (Mühlenberg Coll., Hahnemann Medical School and Coll.); L.H.D. (Dropsie Coll., St. Olaf Coll. and Coll. of Wooster).

Leisure interests: tennis, skiing, mountain climbing, woodworking, mystery stories.

Publs. *American Higher Education in 1980—Some Basic Issues* 66, *Crises of the University* 70, *The Future of Trusteeship: The Role and Responsibilities of College and University Boards* 75.

Rocky Point, Keene, N.Y. 12942, U.S.A.

Telephone: 518-576-4506.

Nasriddinova, Yadgar Sadikovna; Soviet civil engineer and politician; b. 1920; ed. Inst. of Railway Transport Engineering, Tashkent.

Works Supt. Great Ferghana Canal, and the Construction of the Railway Line at "Angrenugol" Coalmines; later Sec. for School affairs Cen. Cttee. Young Communist League of Uzbekistan 42-50; mem. C.P.S.U. 42-; Party work 50-52; Minister of Building Materials, Uzbek S.S.R. 52-55, Vice-Chair. Council of Ministers 55-59; Dep. to U.S.S.R. Supreme Soviet 58-74; Chair. Presidium, Supreme Soviet of the Uzbek S.S.R. 59-70; Vice-Chair. Presidium of Supreme Soviet of U.S.S.R. 59-70; mem. Central Cttee. of C.P.S.U. 56-; mem. Central Cttee. of C.P. of Uzbekistan 52-; Chair. Soviet of Nationalities, U.S.S.R. Supreme Soviet 70-74; First Vice-Chair. Committee U.S.S.R Parl. Group.

Presidium of U.S.S.R. Supreme Soviet, Moscow, U.S.S.R.

Nasution, Gen. Abdul Haris; Indonesian army officer; b. 3 Dec. 1918, Kotanopan (Tapanuli), N. Sumatra; s. of Hadji Abdul Halim Nasution and Hadji Sahara Lubis; m. Johana Sunarti Gondokusmo 1947; two d. (one deceased); ed. Netherlands Military Acad., Bandung.

Sub-Lieut. Netherlands Indies Army 41; Col. 45; Commdr. Siliwangi Division 46-48; Deputy C.-in-C. Armed Forces 48; Commander of Java, planned and led

guerrillas against Dutch 48-49; Army Chief of Staff 50-52, reappointed 55-62; Chair. of Joint Chiefs of Staff and mem. Nat. Council 57; Lieut.-Gen. 58; planned campaign against rebellion in Sumatra and Sulawesi 58; Minister of Defence and People's Security 59-66; Chair. People's Consultative Congress 66-72 (retd.); apptd. Gen. 60; Deputy C.-in-C. West Irian (W. New Guinea) Liberation Command 62; numerous awards from Indonesia and foreign countries.

Publs. *Principles of Guerrilla Warfare, The Indonesian National Army, Notes on the Army Policy of the Republic of Indonesia, Truth and Justice, The Fight for Freedom.*

40 Teuku Umar, Jakarta, Indonesia.

Nasyrova, Halima; Soviet singer; b. 1913; ed. the Uzbek Opera Studio of the Moscow Conservatoire.

Soloist (soprano), Uzbek Navoi State Theatre of Opera and Ballet 39-; Deputy, Uzbek Supreme Soviet 37-58, to Supreme Soviet of the U.S.S.R. 58; People's Artist of U.S.S.R. 37; State prizewinner 42, 51; awarded Order of Lenin (twice), Order of Honour (twice), Red Banner of Labour (twice).

Principal roles: Carmen, Leili (*Leili and Mejnun*), Gyulsara (*Gyulsara*), Zukhra (*Takhiz and Zukhra*), Zainab (*Zainab and Omon*), Akjunus, (*Yertargin*), Anorgul (*Buron*), Nodira (*The Great Canal*), Maisara (*Maisara's Pranks*), Nagriz (*Nagriz*), Perikolla (*Perikolla*), etc.

Uzbek Navoi State Theatre of Opera and Ballet, Tashkent, Uzbek S.S.R., U.S.S.R.

Naszkowski, Marian, M.A.; Polish politician; b. 15 Aug. 1912, Lwów; s. of Michał and Jadwiga Naszkowski; m.; two s. one d.; ed. Lwów Univ.

Active in revolutionary youth movement and later in Communist Party before World War; imprisoned for political activities 38-39; during the war took part in formation of Polish army in U.S.S.R.; Chief Polish Mil. mission, Paris 45-47; Amb. to U.S.S.R. 47-50; Vice-Minister of Defence and Chief Gen. Political Board of Polish Army 50-52; Vice-Minister of Foreign Affairs 52-68; Deputy to Seym 52-56; mem. Cen. Cttee. Polish United Workers' Party 50-68, mem. Cen. Comm. of Party Control 68-; Chair. Polish Del. to Eighteen Nations Cttee. on Disarmament, Geneva 62; Editor-in-Chief *Nowe Drogi* 68-72; Rep. of Poland to I.L.O., Geneva 72-; numerous decorations; Commdr. Cross of Polonia Restituta, Order of the Banner of Labour (1st Class), Legion d'Honneur.

Publs. *Niespokojne dni* (Unrestful Days) and *Lata próby* (The Years of Test) memoirs.

45 avenue de Champel, 1206 Geneva, Switzerland.

Telephone: 47-24-70.

Natali, Lorenzo; Italian lawyer and politician; b. 2 Oct. 1922; ed. Collegio d'Abruzzo dei Padri Gesuiti and Univ. di Firenze.

Deputy to Parl.; Under-sec. of State for the Press and Information 55-57; Under-sec. of State in Ministry of Finance 57-59, in Ministry of Treasury 60-64; Minister for the Merchant Marine Feb. 66-68, of Public Works 68, of Tourism and Entertainments 68-69; Minister of Agriculture 70-73; Christian Democrat.

Leisure interests: education, sport.

Camera dei Deputati, Rome; Home: Via Nibby 18, Rome, Italy.

Natel, Laudo; Brazilian banker and public official; b. 14 Sept. 1920, São Manuel, São Paulo; s. of Bento Alves Natel and Albertina Barone Natel; m. Maria Zilda Gamba Natel; two s.; ed. Mirassol, Araquaria Coll., São Paulo.

Former Vice-Governor of São Paulo, now Governor; Exec. Dir. Banco Brasilero Tedesconto S.A.; Pres. Bank Consultative Cttee. of the Nat. Monetary Council; mem. Brazilian Olympic Cttee.; Pres. or mem. of several institutions and clubs in São Paulo; Orden do

Mérito Militar; Commendador Soverano Orden São Paulo; numerous foreign decorations.

Office of the Governor of São Paulo, São Paulo, Brazil.

Nathan, Otto, PH.D.; American economist; b. 15 July 1893, Bingen, Germany; s. of Jacob and Sara Nathan; ed. Würzburg, Freiburg and Munich Univs.

Statistical and Econ. Adviser to German Dept. of Econs. 20-33; Dir. Dept. for Research on Int. Econ. Problems, German Inst. for Business Cycle Research; Co-Editor *Vierteljahrshefte für Konjunkturforschung* 26-30; mem. German Del. to World Econ. Conf., Geneva 27; Lecturer Hochschule für Politik Berlin 28-33; Economic Adviser to Pres. Hoover's Emergency Cttee. on Employment 31; Visiting Lecturer Princeton Univ. 33-35; Associate Prof. of Economics N.Y. Univ. 35-58; Prof. of Economics Vassar Coll. 42-44; Chief Economic Analyst U.S. Treasury Dept. 44-45; Visiting Prof. of Econs., Howard Univ. 46-52; Consultant on Econ. Literature, Library of Congress 46-52.

Publs. *Some Considerations of Unemployment Insurance in the Light of German Experience, The N.I.R.A. and Stabilisation, Cartels and the State in the Light of German Experience, International Economic Action and Peace, Consumption in Germany during the Period of Rearmament, The Nazi Economic System* 44, *Nazi War Finance and Banking* 44, *Private Enterprise and Full Employment, Development of Underdeveloped Countries and the Development of Poland since 1945;* edited *Die Wirtschaft des Auslandes, 1900-07* 27, 28, co-ed. *Einstein on Peace* 60, *Economics of Permanent Peace* 63.

24 Fifth Avenue, New York, N.Y. 10011, U.S.A. Telephone: 212-477-2948.

Nathan, Robert; American novelist; b. 2 Jan. 1894, New York; s. of Harold and Sallie Nathan; m. Joan Boniface Winnifrith 1970; one d.; ed. Exeter Acad. and Harvard Univ.

Lecturer in Poetry, New York Univ. 24-25; mem. Exec. Cttee. U.S. P.E.N. Club (Pres. 40-42); mem. and Vice-Pres. Nat. Inst. of Arts and Letters; Chancellor and Hon. Fellow, Acad. of American Poets; mem. Acad. Motion Picture Arts and Sciences.

Leisure interest: music.

Publs. *Peter Kindred* 19, *Autumn* 21, *Youth Grows Old* 22, *The Puppet Master* 23, *Jonah* 25, *Fiddler in Barly* 26, *The Woodcutter's House* 27, *The Bishop's Wife* 28, *A Cedar Box* 29, *There is Another Heaven* 29, *The Orchid* 30, *One More Spring* 33, *Road of Ages* 35, *Selected Poems* 35, *The Enchanted Voyage* 36, *Winter in April* 37, *The Barly Field* 38, *Music at Evening* (play) 38, *A Winter Tide* 39, *Portrait of Jennie* 39, *Dunkirk* 40, *They Went on Together* 41, *Tapiola's Brave Regiment* 41, *The Sea Gull Cry* 41, *Journal for Josephine* 42, *But Gently Day* 43, *Morning in Iowa* 44, *The Darkening Meadows* 45, *Mr. Whittle and the Morning Star* 47, *Long After Summer* 49, *The River Journey* 49, *The Green Leaf* 50, *Married Look* 50, *The Sleeping Beauty* (play) 50, *The Innocent Eve* 51, *Jezebel's Husband* (play) 51, *Sir Henry* 55, *The Rancho of the Little Loves* 56, *So Love Returns* 58, *The Snowflake and the Starfish* 59, *The Weans* 60, *The Color of Evening* 60, *The Wilderness Stone* 61, *A Star in the Wind* 62, *The Married Man* 62, *The Devil with Love* 63, *The Fair* 64, *The Mallot Diaries* 65, *Juliet in Mantua* (play) 66, *Stonecliff* 67, *Mia* 70, *The Elixir* 71, *Summer Meadows* 73, *Evening Song* 73, *Heaven and Hell and the Megas Factor* 75.

1240 North Doheny Drive, Hollywood, Calif. 90069, U.S.A.

Natta, Giulio, DR. ING.; Italian chemist; b. 26 Feb. 1903, Imperia; s. of Francesco and Elena Natta; m. Rosilie Beati 1936; one s. one d.; ed. Polytechnic Inst. of Milan.

Former Prof., Univs. of Pavia, Rome and Turin; Prof. and Dir., Dept of Industrial Chemistry, Polytechnic

Inst. of Milan 38-; Nobel Prize for Chemistry 63; Dr. h.c. (Turin, Mainz, Genoa, Brooklyn Polytechnic, Catholic Univ. of Louvain); numerous Italian and foreign awards including Gold Medal of Pres. of Italian Republic, Gold Medal District of Milan, Lomonosov Gold Medal of Moscow Acad. of Sciences 69, etc.

Leisure interest: natural sciences.

Publs. About 450 scientific articles.

Via S. Sebastiano 11, S. Vigilio, Bergamo, Italy. Telephone: 221100.

Naudé, Stefan Meiring, M.SC., PH.D.; South African physicist; b. 31 Dec. 1904, De Doorns; s. of Charl F. Naudé and Annie Lötter; m. Josephine L. Ziervogel; two s. four d.; ed. Univs. of Stellenbosch, Berlin and Chicago.

Instructor Univ. of Chicago 29-30, Research Fellow 31; Senior Lecturer in Physics, Univ. of Cape Town 31-33; Prof. of Experimental Physics, Univ. of Stellenbosch 34-45; Dir. Nat. Physical Laboratory, Pretoria 46-50; Vice-Pres. Council of Scientific and Industrial Research 50-52, Pres. 52-71; Scientific Adviser to Prime Minister 71-; Chair. Scientific Advisory Council, Water Research Comm., Advisory Planning Comm.; mem. American Physical Soc., Deutsche Physikalische Gesellschaft, South African Asscn. for the Advancement of Science, Int. Rotary, Associated Scientific and Technical Socs.; Chair. Council Univ. of Pretoria; Nat. Chair. Simon van der Stel Foundation; Chair. Foundation for Educ., Science and Technology; Trustee, South Africa Foundation; Hon. D.Sc., Hon. LL.D.

Leisure interest: farming.

Home: 420 Friesland Avenue, Lynnwood, Pretoria; Office: Council for Scientific and Industrial Research, P.O. Box 395, Pretoria, Republic of South Africa. Telephone: 74-6011.

Naudé, Willem Christiaan, D.COMM.; South African diplomatist; b. 5 May 1909; ed. Boys' High School, Stellenbosch and Stellenbosch and London Univs.

Served London 29-36, 46-49; Washington 37-46; Consul-Gen. Lourenço Marques 51-54; Del. Food and Agriculture Conf., Hot Springs, Va., 43, Bretton Woods Conf. 44, UNGA 53, 59, 63, 65, GATT Ministers Conf., Tokyo 73; Leader, South African Dels. to GATT, Geneva 54-57, 66, 68, 70, to ICEM 56-57, to UNCTAD II, New Delhi 68; Minister, Switzerland 56-57; Under-Sec. for External Affairs 57-59, Deputy Sec. 59-60; Amb. to United States 60-65; Principal Deputy Sec. for Foreign Affairs 65-66; Amb., Perm. Rep. Geneva 66-71; Amb., Head of South African Mission to European Communities 71-.

28 rue de la Loi, Brussels 1040, Belgium.

Naumann, William L.; American business executive. Joined Caterpillar 29, Man. Joliet Ill. Plant 52, East Peoria Plant Man. 56, Vice-Pres. 60, Admin. Dir. of Mfg., Purchasing, Quality and Traffic Gen. Offices 63, Exec. Vice-Pres. 66, Dir. 67-, Vice-Chair. 72-75, Chair. Feb. 75-; Dir. Abex Corpn., Jefferson Trust & Savings Bank of Peoria, Pekin Nat. Bank, IC Industries Inc. and Int. Exec. Service Corps.

Caterpillar Tractor Co., Peoria, Ill. 61629, U.S.A.

Nauta, Walle Jetze Harinx, M.D., D.SC.; American anatomist; b. 8 June 1916; ed. Univ. of Leiden.

Lecturer, Univ. of Utrecht 41-46; Assoc. Prof. Univ. of Leiden 46-47; Assoc. Prof. Univ. of Zürich 47-51; Neurophysiologist, Walter Reed Army Inst. of Research 51-64; Prof. of Anatomy, Univ. of Maryland 55-64, Mass. Inst. of Technology 64-; mem. Nat. Acad. of Sciences, American Acad. of Arts and Sciences, American Philosophical Soc.; Pres. Soc. for Neuroscience 73.

Publs. *Hypothalamic Regulation of Sleep in Rats* 46, *Silver Impregnation of Degenerating Axons* 54, *Ascending Pathways in the Brain Stem Reticular Formation* 58,

Hippocampal Projections 58, *Fiber Connections of the Hypothalamus* 69, *The Problem of the Frontal Lobe* 71.
Department of Psychology, Massachusetts Institute of Technology, Cambridge, Mass. 02139, U.S.A.

Navarre, Général Henri; French army officer; b. 31 July 1898, Villefranche de Rouergne; s. of Octave Navarre and Clémence Navarre (née Dupuy); m. Suzanne Boulard 1922; one s.; ed. Ecole Spéciale Militaire, St. Cyr.
Joined 2nd Régiment de Hussards 17, served through all ranks to Brigadier 45, Divisional Gen. 50 and Gén. de Corps d'Armée 52; served in the Levant (Spahis) 20-22, in Germany 22-26; Cours des Hautes Etudes Germaniques 25; Cours d'Auto-mitrailleuses 26; Ecole de Guerre 28-30; in Morocco 31-34; Chief of German Section, General Staff of Army 36-40; Chief of Staff to Gen. Weygand and to Gen. Juin in Algiers 40-42, recalled to France by Admiral Darlan 42; Resistance leader 43-45; brigade command during advance into Germany; Dir. of the Council of the Gen. C.-in-C. Germany 45-48; Commdr. Constantine Div. 48-49; Inst. des Hautes Etudes de la Défense Nationale 49-50; in command 5th Armoured Division 50-52; Dep. C.-in-C. French Forces in Germany 52, Chief of Staff of the C.-in-C. Central Europe 52-53; C.-in-C. (Combined Forces) Indo-China 53-54; mem. Conseil Supérieur de Guerre 56; retd. 56; awards include Grand-Officier Légion d'Honneur.
Leisure interest: history.
Publ. *Agonie de l'Indo-chine* 56.
Bastide du Malvan, "L'Ara", Vence (A.-M.), France.
Telephone: 58-11-15.

Navarro Rubio, Mariano; Spanish lawyer and politician; b. 14 Nov. 1913; ed. Univ. of Zaragoza.
Colonel in legal dept. of the army; Under-Sec. of Public Works April 55-Feb. 57; Minister of Finance Feb. 57-65; Governor, Bank of Spain 65-July 70; Cruz de guerra con palmas, Great Cross of Carlos III, Légion d'Honneur, and several other decorations.
Plaza de Cristo Rey 4, Madrid, Spain.

Navasqués y Ruiz de Velasco, Emilio de, Conde de Navasqués, D. EN D., LIC. EN FIL.; Spanish diplomatist; b. 23 March 1904, Madrid; s. of Emilio and Angela Ruiz de Velasco; m. María Elisa Bertran 1935; one s. five d.; ed. Univ. de Madrid and Ecole Libre des Sciences Politiques, Paris.
Secretary of Spanish Comm. of League of Nations 33-34; First Sec., Lisbon 43; Dir.-Gen. (Political and Econ.), Ministry of Foreign Affairs 44-47; Under-Sec. for Foreign Econs. and Trade 47; Minister, The Hague 48-50; Amb. to Argentina 50-51; Under-Sec. for Foreign Affairs 51-55; Insp.-Gen., Ministry of Foreign Affairs 55-56; Amb. to Italy 56-59; Dir. of Escuela Diplomática 59-; Pres. Council of Admin. of IBERIA (Spanish Airlines) 65; Pres. Calatrava (oil firm) 65-; Vice-Pres. Empresa Nacional Siderúrgica 65-; later Amb. to Portugal; Gran Cruz de Isabel la Católica, and orders from Portugal, Argentina, Peru, Egypt, Lebanon, etc.
Leisure interests: walking, hunting.
Avenida de Miraflores 31, Madrid (20), Spain
Telephone: 2161299.

Naville, Marcel A.; Swiss International Red Cross official; b. 12 Aug. 1919, Geneva; s. of Frédéric Naville and Dora Amphoux; m. Béatrice Vernet 1943; one s. two d.; ed. Coll. and Univ. de Genève.
Attached to Foreign Interests Dept. of Swiss Fed. Political Dept. 42-43; mem. Juridical Div. of Int. Cttee. of Red Cross 43-46; studies in Rome and Paris 47-51; Capt. in Swiss Army 48; banking career 52-69, Dir. Banque Populaire Suisse, Geneva 65-69; Pres. Cercle de la Presse et des Amitiés étrangères, Geneva 64-69; mem. Int. Cttee. of Red Cross 67, Pres. 69-73.

Leisure interests: reading, walking, swimming.
33 chemin du Velours, 1211 Conches-Genève, Switzerland.
Telephone: 022-470564.

Navrátil, Jan, M.D., D.SC.; Austrian surgeon; b. 26 Jan. 1909, Neu Spielberg, Melk, Austria; ed. Medical Faculty, Masaryk Univ., Brno.
Assistant Prof. of Surgery Purkyně Univ., Brno 46-53, Head of Second Surgical Clinic, Medical Faculty 53-67, Prof. of Surgery 54-; Corresp. mem. Czechoslovak Acad. of Sciences 65-; Head of Second Surgical Clinic, Vienna 67-; mem. Czechoslovak Surgical Soc., Deutsche Akad. der Naturforscher Leopoldina, Halle, Soc. Int. Cardio-Vasculaire, Soc. Int. de Chirurgie, Brussels, American Heart Asscn., New York, American Coll. of Chest Physicians, Chicago, Int. Coll. of Surgeons, Chicago, Austrian Acad. of Science; Czechoslovak Peace Prize 59, J. E. Purkyně Medal 60, 69, Order of Repub. 62.
Publs. *Repair of Heart defects by Open Chest Surgery* 63, *Cardiosurgery* 70; and papers in Czechoslovak and foreign medical journals.
Spitalgasse 23, 1090 Vienna 19, Austria.
Telephone: 4289/4100.

Navrotsky, Vasily Korneyevich; Soviet hygiene specialist; b. 11 Feb. 1897, Dedno, Bobruisk District, Byelorussia; ed. Kharkov Medical Inst.
Physician in Byelorussia and Ukraine 21-27; Head of Dept., Dir., Ukrainian Inst. of Occupational Hygiene and Occupational Diseases 27-49; Corresp. mem. U.S.S.R. Acad. of Medical Sciences 48-60, mem. U.S.S.R. Acad. of Medical Sciences 60-; Head of Dept. Kharkov Inst. for Postgraduate Medical Training 49-; mem. Board All-Union and Ukrainian Socs. of Hygienists; Badge of Honour 45, and other decorations.
Publs. Over 100 works on occupational hygiene in chemical, coal and iron ore industries, and industrial toxicology.
Kharkov Institute for Postgraduate Medical Training, Prospekt Pravdy 15, Kharkov, U.S.S.R.

Nawwar, Maj.-Gen. Ali Abu; Jordanian army officer and diplomatist.
Chief of Staff, Jordanian army 56; in exile in Egypt 57-64; Personal Rep. of King Hussein Oct. 70-Feb. 71; Amb. at Ministry of Foreign Affairs May 70; Amb. to France 71-74.
c/o Ministry of Foreign Affairs, Amman, Jordan.

Nayar, Sushila, M.B., B.S., M.D., M.P.H., DR.P.H.; Indian doctor; b. 26 Dec. 1914, Kunjah District, Gujrat, Pakistan; d. of Brindaban and Taradevi Nayar; unmarried; ed. Lahore Coll. for Women, Lady Hardinge Medical Coll., Delhi, Johns Hopkins Univ., U.S.A.
Medical attendant to Mahatma Gandhi and his Ashram; work for communal harmony in West Punjab, Noakhali; Chair. Kasturba Health Soc.; Dir. Mahatma Gandhi Inst. of Medical Sciences; Pres. All-India Prohibition Council; mem. Lok Sabha 57-71; fmr. Minister of Health, Rehabilitation and Transport, Delhi State; Speaker Delhi Legislative Assembly 52-56; Minister of Health, Govt. of India 62-67; freedom fighter, imprisoned 42-44.
Leisure interests: writing, painting, reading, bridge.
Publs. *Kasturba, Karavas ki Kahani*, etc.
Kasturba Health Society, Sevragram, Wardha; A.2 Soami Nagar, New Delhi 17, India.
Telephone: 022-R33; 74147 (New Delhi).

Nazarkin, Konstantin Ivanovich; Soviet banker and politician; b. 06; ed. Tashkent Finance and Econs. Inst.
Began work in Gosbank system 25; Manager Uzbek Repub. Board of U.S.S.R. Gosbank 44-49; mem. Board of U.S.S.R. Gosbank 49-57; Deputy Chair. Board of Foreign Trade Bank of U.S.S.R. 61-63; Chair. Board of Int. Bank for Econ. Co-operation Oct. 63-.
International Bank for Economic Co-operation, Kuznetsky Most 15, Moscow, U.S.S.R.

Ndabaniwe, Joseph; Burundian diplomatist; b. 6 May 1940, Nyarubenga; *m.*; four *c.*; ed. Univs. of Bujumbura and Libre, Brussels.

Assistant Dir., later Dir., Ministry of Foreign Affairs and Co-operation; Ministry of Finance 67; Asst. Dir. Burundi Soc. of Textile Industries (BURTEX) 68; entered diplomatic service 70; Amb. to Ethiopia 70-73; Perm. Rep. to UN and Amb. to U.S.A. April 73-; rep. to several UN, UNCTAD and OAU confs.

Permanent Mission of Burundi to United Nations, 305 East 45th St., 21st Floor, New York, N.Y. 10017, U.S.A.

Ndegwa, Duncan Nderitu, M.A.; Kenyan civil servant; b. 11 March 1925, Nyeri District; ed. Alliance High School, Kikuyu, Makerere Univ. Coll., Uganda and Univ. of St. Andrews, Scotland.

Statistician, E. African High Comm. 56-59; Asst. Sec. Kenya Treasury 59-63, Deputy Perm. Sec. 63; Perm. Sec. and Head of Civil Service 63-66; Sec. to Cabinet 63-67; Gov. Cen. Bank of Kenya and Alt. Gov. IMF 67-; Chair. Comm. of Enquiry (Public Service Structure and Remuneration Comm.) 70; Chief of the Burning Spear. P.O. Box 20423, Nairobi, Kenya.

Ndongala, Tadi Lewa, D.ECON.; Zairian economist; b. 1933, Kumbi, Bas-Zaire; ed. Univ. of Lovanium, Kinshasa and Brussels Nat. Inst. of Statistics.

Research Asst. in rural econ., Inst. de Recherches Economiques et Sociales, Univ. of Lovanium 63; attended Congress of African Research Insts., Bellagio, Italy 64; research work at the Inst. Malassis, Rennes 65; mem. Vice-Rectorate, Univ. Officielle du Congo 67-68; Deputy Del. in charge of econ. and financial research, Office Nat. de Recherche et de Développement 68-69, concurrently Personal Adviser to Pres. Mobutu; Vice-Minister of Nat. Econ. 69-70, of Foreign Trade Sept.-Oct. 70, of Agriculture Oct. 70-71, of Finance 71-72; State Commr. (Minister) of Nat. Econ. Feb. 72-74.

c/o Office of the State Commissioner for National Economy, Kinshasa, Zaire.

Ne Win, U (Maung Shu Maung); Burmese politician and fmr. army officer; b. 24 May 1911; ed. Govt. High School, Prome and Rangoon Univ.

Joined Allied Forces 45; Vice-Chief of Gen. Staff and Major-Gen. 48; Deputy Prime Minister 49-50; Gen. 56; Prime Minister and Minister of Defence Oct. 58-60; Chief of Gen. Staff 62-72; Prime Minister, Minister of Defence, Finance, and Revenue, Nat. Planning and Justice 62-63; Prime Minister, Minister of Nat. Planning and Defence 63; Prime Minister and Minister of Defence, also Chair. of Revolutionary Council 65-74; Chair. Exec. Cttee. Burma Socialist Programme Party 73-; Pres. of Burma 74-; Legion of Merit (U.S.A.). Office of the President, Rangoon, Burma.

Neagle, Dame Anna (Florence Marjorie Wilcox), D.B.E.; British actress and producer; b. 20 Oct. 1904, London; *d.* of Capt. H. W. Robertson and Florence Neagle Robertson; *m.* Herbert Wilcox, C.B.E., 1943; ed. St. Albans High School, Wordsworths Physical Training Coll.

Began theatrical career with Andre Charlot 25; C. B. Cochran Revues 26-30; juvenile lead as Jack Buchanan in *Stand Up and Sing,* London 31; many film awards. Leisure interests: reading, swimming, walking, theatre, cinema, cats, music.

Theatre appearances in *Rosalind and Olivia* 34, *Peter Pan* 37, *Emma* 44, *The Glorious Days* 52-53, *The More the Merrier* 60, *Charlie Girl* 65-71, *No, No, Nanette, The Dame of Sark* 75. Films include, *Goodnight Vienna* 32, *The Little Damozel* 33, *Bitter Sweet, Nell Gwynn* 34, *Peg of Old Drury* 35, *Victoria the Great* 37, *Sixty Glorious Years* 38, *Nurse Edith Cavell* 39, *Irene* 39, *Sunny* 40, *They Flew Alone* 41, *I Live in Grosvenor Square* 44, *Piccadilly Incident* 46, *The Courtneys of Curzon Street* 47,

Spring in Park Lane 48, *Maytime in Mayfair* 49, *Odette* 50, *The Lady with the Lamp* 51, *Lilacs in the Spring* 54, *My Teenage Daughter* 56, *The Man Who Wouldn't Talk* 57, *The Lady is a Square* 59; TV Plays: *A Letter from the General, Shadow in the Sun;* produced films *These Dangerous Years* 56, *Wonderful Things* 58, *The Heart of a Man* 59.

Publ. *There's Always Tomorrow* (autobiog.) 74.

c/o Herbert de Leon, 13 Bruton Street, London, W.1; Home: 117 Hamilton Terrace, London, N.W.8, England.

Neal, Sir Leonard Francis, Kt., M.A., C.B.E.; British industrial relations official; b. 27 Aug. 1913, London; *s.* of Arthur Henry Neal and Mary Cahill; *m.* Mary L. Puttock 1939; one *s.* one *d.*; ed. London School of Econs. and Trinity Coll., Cambridge.

Deputy Employee Relations Adviser, Esso Petroleum Co. 62-66; Labour Adviser, Esso Europe Inc. 66; mem. for Personnel, British Railways Board 67-71; Chair. Comm. on Industrial Relations 71-74; Pres. Asscn. of Supervisory and Exec. Engineers 74-; Adviser Marks and Spencers 74-, Ranks, Hovis McDougall 74-; Visiting Prof. of Industrial Relations, Manchester Univ. 69-72. Leisure interests: gardening, reading.

Publ. *A Manager's Guide to Industrial Relations* (with A. Robertson).

Brightling, nr. Robertsbridge, Sussex, England. Telephone: 01-828 9528.

Neal, Patricia; actress; b. 1926, Packard, Ky., U.S.A.; *d.* of William Burdette Neal and Eura Mildred Petrey; *m.* Roald Dahl 1953; one *s.* four *d.*

Stage appearances include: *Another Part of the Forest* 46, *The Children's Hour* 53, *A Roomful of Roses* 54, *Suddenly Last Summer* 58, *The Miracle Worker* 59; Antoinette Perry Award (Tony) 46; Academy Award (Oscar) for film *Hud* 63.

Leisure interests: playing bridge, cooking.

Films: *John loves Mary* 49, *The Hasty Heart* 49, *The Fountainhead* 49, *The Breaking Point* 50, *Three Secrets* 50, *Raton Pass* 51, *The Day the Earth Stood Still* 51, *Diplomatic Courier* 52, *Something for the Birds* 53, *A Face in the Crowd* 57, *Breakfast at Tiffanys* 61, *Hud* 63, *The Third Secret* 64, *In Harms Way* 65, *The Subject was Roses* 68, *The Road Builder* 70, *The Boy* 72.

Gipsy House, Great Missenden, Bucks., England.

Neame, Ronald; British film director; b. 23 April 1911, London; *s.* of Elwin Neame and Ivy Close; *m.* Beryl Heanly; one *s.*

Messenger and tea boy, British Int. Film Studios 25; became Dir. of Photography 32; films photographed include: *The Gaunt Stranger, The Ware Case, Four Just Men, Major Barbara, One of Our Aircraft is Missing;* with David Lean (*q.v.*) and Anthony Have-lock-Allen, formed Cineguild and produced *Great Expectations, Oliver Twist* and *The Passionate Friends,* and photographed *In Which We Serve, This Happy Breed, Blithe Spirit;* film director 50-; films directed include: *The Golden Salamander, The Magic Box, The Card, The Million Pound Note, The Man Who Never Was, Windom's Way, The Horse's Mouth, Escape from Zahrain, I Could Go On Singing, The Chalk Garden, Mr. Moses, A Man Could Get Killed, Gambit, The Prime of Miss Jean Brodie, Scrooge, The Poseidon Adventure, The Odessa File.*

Leisure interests: photography, stereo and hi-fi equipment.

c/o Rogers, Cowan and Brenner, Inc., International Division, 52 Mount Street, London, W1Y 5RE, England.

Telephone: 01-499-0691.

Neckermann, Josef; German businessman; b. 5 June 1912, Würzburg; *m.* Annemarie Brückner 1934; two *s.* one *d.*; ed. grammar school, Würzburg.

Joined his father's business 33; in charge of a Würzburg

store 34-38; Head of mail order house Berlin 38; State Commr. for Clothing 39-45; Head, Zentrallagergemeinschaft m.b.H., Berlin 39-45; Founder textile wholesale business Frankfurt am Main 48; Owner and Manager Neckermann Versand KGaA 50, Mail Order Houses, Frankfurt am Main; founded Neckermann Eigenheim G.m.b.H. 63, Neckura Neckermann Versicherungs A.G. 65, N.U.R. Neckermann und Reisen G.m.b.H. 64; Hon. Consul of Kingdom of Denmark; Pres. Stiftung Deutsche Sporthilfe; Bronze Medal, Olympic Games 60; Gold Medal, Olympic Games 64; World Championship of dressage 66; Silver and Gold Medal, Olympic Games 68; Bronze Medal, Olympic Games 72; Dr. med. vet. h.c.; Grand Cross of Merit.

6000 Frankfurt/Main, Hanauer Landstr. 360, German Federal Republic.

Telephone: 404-201.

Needham, James J.; American securities official and accountant; b. 1926, Woodhaven N.Y.; *m.*; three *s.* two *d.*; ed. Cornell and St John's (Brooklyn) Univs.

Partner, Price Waterhouse & Co., then Raymond T. Hyer & Co.; joined A. M. Pullen & Co. 57, subsequently partner, in charge of N.Y. office and mem. Exec. Cttee.; Commr. Securities and Exchange Commission 69-72; Chair. New York Stock Exchange 72-76; Vice-Pres. Int. Fed. of Stock Exchanges 73-75, Pres. 76-; mem. American Inst. Certified Public Accountants, N.Y. State Soc. of Certified Public Accountants, N.Y. Chamber of Commerce and Industry, U.S. Council of Int. Chamber of Commerce; fmr. mem. N.Y. Credit and Financial Management Asscn., Bishop's Cttee. of the Laity; Hon. DLL. St. John's Univ. Oct. 72; N.Y. State Soc. of Certified Public Accountants Award.

New York Stock Exchange Inc., 11 Wall Street, New York, N.Y. 10005, U.S.A.

Needham, Joseph, PH.D., SC.D., F.R.S., F.B.A.; British biochemist, historian of science and orientalist; b. 1900, London; *s.* of Joseph and Alicia Needham; *m.* Dorothy Moyle 1924; ed. Oundle School and Cambridge Univ.

Fellow Caius Coll. 24-, Pres. 59-66, Master 66-; Univ. Demonstrator in Biochemistry, Cambridge 28-33; Visiting Prof. of Biochemistry, Stanford Univ., Calif. 29; Dunn Reader in Biochemistry, Cambridge 33-66; Lecturer Yale Univ., Cornell Univ., Oberlin Coll. 35; Oliver Sharpey Lecturer, Royal Coll. Physicians 35-36, Herbert Spencer Lecturer, Oxford 36-37; lectured Warsaw, Lwów, Cracow and Wilno Univs. 37; Head of Sino-British Science Co-operation Office and Counsellor British Embassy, Chungking 42-46; Head of Div. of Natural Sciences UNESCO 46-48; now Honorary Counsellor to UNESCO; Chair. Ceylon Govt. Comm. on Univ. Education 58; Hitchcock Prof. Univ. of Calif., Noguchi Lecturer, Johns Hopkins Univ. 50; Hobhouse Lecturer, London Univ. 50; Visiting Prof. Univ. of Lyon 51; Dickinson Lecturer, Newcomen Soc., London 56; Wilkins Lecturer, Royal Soc. London 58; lectured Colombo, Singapore, Peking, Jaipur Univs. 58; Grey Lecturer, Newcastle 61; lectured Bucharest, Iaşi, Cluj, Timişoara Univs. 62, Peking, Kyoto, Osaka Univs. 64; Myers Lecturer Royal Anthropological Inst. 64; Rapkine Lecturer, Paris 70; Harveian Lecturer, London 70; Fremantle Lecturer, Balliol Coll., Oxford; Bernal Lecturer, Birkbeck Coll., London; Ballard Matthews Lecturer, Bangor Univ. 71; Irvine Lecturer, St. Andrews; Dresser Lecturer, Leeds 73; Visiting Prof. Coll. de France, Paris 73; Carr-Saunders Lecturer, London; Walters Lecturer, Bath; First John Caius Lecturer, Padua 74; Visiting Prof. Univ. of British Columbia 75; foreign mem. Nat. Acad. of China (Academia Sinica); Pres. Int. Union of the History of Science 72-75; mem. Int. Acads. of the Philosophy of Science and the History of Medicine; Order of Brilliant Star (China); Hon. D.Sc. (Brussels, E. Anglia); Hon. LL.D. (Toronto); Hon. D.Litt. (Hong Kong,

Salford); Sir Wm. Jones Medallist, Asiatic Soc. of Bengal; George Sarton Medallist, History of Science Soc.; Leonardo da Vinci Medallist, History of Technology Soc.

Leisure interests: theology, philosophy, archaeology, railway engineering.

Publs. *Man a Machine* 27, *The Sceptical Biologist* 29, *Chemical Embryology* (3 vols.) 31, *The Great Amphibium* 32, *A History of Embryology* 35, *Order and Life* 35, *Adventures before Birth* (trans.) 35, *Biochemistry and Morphogenesis* 42, *Time, the Refreshing River* 42, *History is on Our Side* 44, *Chinese Science* 45, *Science Outpost* 48, *Science and Civilisation in China* (7 vols.) 54-, *The Development of Iron and Steel Technology in China* 58, *Heavenly Clockwork* 60, *Time and Eastern Man* 65, *Clerks and Craftsmen in China and the West* 70, *The Grand Titration, Science and Society in East and West* 70, *Within the Four Seas, the Dialogue of East and West* 70, *Moulds of Experience, a Pattern of Natural Philosophy* 76; Editor: *Science, Religion and Reality* 25, *Christianity and the Social Revolution* 35, *Perpectives in Biochemistry* 36, *Background to Modern Science* 38, *Science in the Soviet Union* 42, *The Teacher of Nations* 42, *Hopkins and Biochemistry* 49, *The Chemistry of Life* 70.

The Master's Lodge, Gonville and Caius College, Cambridge, England.

Telephone: Cambridge 52183 and 53275, extension 301.

Neel, James Van Gundia, PH.D., M.D.; American geneticist; b. 22 March 1915, Hamilton, Ohio; *s.* of Hiram A. Neel and Elizabeth Van Gundia; *m.* Priscilla Baxter 1943; one *d.* two *s.*; ed. Coll. of Wooster, Ohio, and Univ. of Rochester, N.Y.

Inst. of Zoology, Dartmouth 39-41; Fellow in Zoology, Nat. Research Council 41-42; Strong Memorial Hospital 44-46; Acting Dir. Field Studies, Atomic Bomb Casualty Comm., Nat. Research Council 47-48; Assoc. Geneticist, Lab. of Vertebrate Biology, Asst. Prof. of Internal Medicine, Univ. of Mich. 48-51; Geneticist, Inst. of Human Biology 51-56; Chair. and Lee R. Dice Univ. Prof., Dept. of Human Genetics, Univ. of Mich. Medical School 56-; Cutter Lecturer, Harvard Univ. 56; mem. Nat. Acad. of Sciences, American Phil. Soc., Asscn. of American Physicians, American Soc. of Human Genetics (Vice-Pres. 52-53, Pres. 53-54, Board Dir. 68-70), American Acad. of Arts and Sciences, Inst. of Medicine (Nat. Acad. of Sciences); Dir. Centre Royaumont pour une Science de l'Homme; Consultant Nat. Research Council, WHO, Pan American Health Org., etc.; Lasker Award 50; Modern Medicine Award 60; Allan Award, American Soc. of Human Genetics 65; Russell Award, Univ. of Mich. 66; Nat. Medal of Science 74.

Publs. *Human Heredity* (with W. J. Schull) 54, *A Clinical, Pathological and Genetic Study of Multiple Neurofibromatoses* (with F. W. Crowe and W. J. Schull) 56, *Changing Perspectives on the Genetic Effects of Radiation* 63, *Effects on Inbreeding on Japanese Children* (with W. J. Schull) 65; Editor (with Crow) *Proc. III Int. Congress Human Genetics.*

University of Michigan, Department of Human Genetics, 1137 E. Catherine, Ann Arbor, Mich. 48104; Home: 2235 Belmont, Ann Arbor, Mich. 48104, U.S.A. Telephone: 764-5490 (Office); 761-0224 (Home).

Neel, Louis Boyd, O.C., C.B.E., M.A., M.R.C.S., L.R.C.P., HON. R.A.M.; British musician; b. 19 July 1905, London; *s.* of Louis Neel and Ruby le Couteur; ed. R.N. Coll., Dartmouth, and Caius Coll., Cambridge.

Qualified and practised as doctor; forsook medicine for music and founded the Boyd Neel Orchestra (of which he is Conductor) 33; the orchestra appeared at the Salzburg Festival 37; toured Portugal 39; during Second World War returned to medical work; the orchestra

toured France, Australia and N.Z. 47, Germany, Holland, Portugal 48-49; France, Denmark, Norway, Sweden and Finland 50; Italy, Germany, France 51; Canada, America 52; conducted first performance Glyndebourne 34; conductor, Sadler's Wells Opera 45; D'Oyly Carte London Seasons 48-49; Edinburgh Festival 48, 51; Mayer Children's Concerts, London; Dean, Royal Conservatory of Music, Toronto 53-71; formed Hart House Orchestra 54, performed at Stratford, Ontario, Festival 55, Brussels World Fair with Hart House Orchestra 58, toured Canada with Hart House Orchestra 58-60, conducted orchestras in New Zealand and Australia for ABC 64; toured Sweden, Finland, Norway (Bergen Festival), Belgium and England with Hart House Orchestra, playing at Aldeburgh Festival 66, and at *expo* 67, Montreal 67; Dir. Blue Mountain Summer School of Music, Collingwood, Ont.; records for Deutsche Grammophon and Decca-London.
Leisure interests: tennis, sailing.
Publ. *The Story of an Orchestra* 50.
44 Charles Street West, Apt. 2619, Toronto M4Y 1R7, Ont., Canada.
Telephone: 964-2628.

Néel, Louis Eugène Félix; French scientist; b. 22 Nov. 1904, Lyon, Rhône; *m.* Hélène Hourticq 1931; one *s.* two *d.*; ed. Lycée du Parc, Lyon, Lycée Saint-Louis, Paris, and Ecole Normale Supérieure, Paris.
Professor, Univ. of Strasbourg 37-45, Grenoble 45-76; Scientific Adviser to Navy 52-; French Rep. to Scientific Cttee. of NATO; Pres. French Physical Soc. 57; Pres. Int. Union of Pure and Applied Physics 63-65; Pres. Inst. Nat. Polytechnique, Grenoble 71-76; mem. Acad. of Sciences (Paris); Foreign mem. U.S.S.R. Acad. of Sciences, Royal Netherlands Acad., German Leopoldina Acad., Romanian Acad. of Sciences, Royal Soc. (U.K.), American Acad. of Arts and Sciences, Polish Acad. of Sciences; Croix de Guerre 40; Commandeur des Palmes Académiques; Grand Croix Légion d'Honneur; Prix Holweck 52, Gold Medal (Centre Nat. de la Recherche Scientifique) 65; Nobel Prize for Physics 70; many hon. degrees.
Publs. over 200 works on various aspects of magnetism.
15 rue Marcel Allégot, 92190 Meudon, France.
Telephone: (1) 027-36-51.

Ne'eman, Yuval, DIP.ING., D.E.M., D.I.C., PH.D.; Israeli professor of physics; b. 14 May 1925, Tel-Aviv; *s.* of Gedalia and Zipora Ne'eman; *m.* Dvora Rubinstein 1951; one *d.* one *s.*; ed. Herzliya High School, Tel-Aviv, Israel Inst. of Technology, Haifa, and London Univ.
Hagana volunteer, taking part in activities against British rule in Palestine 46-47; Hydrodynamical Design Engineer 46-47; Capt., Israeli Defense Forces (Infantry) 48, Major 49, Lieut.-Col. 50; Dir. Defense Planning Branch 52-54; Col. 55; Deputy Dir. Defense Intelligence Div. 55-57; Defense Attaché, London 58-60; resigned from Israeli Defense Forces active service May 60; took part in six day war June 67; Scientific Dir. Israel Atomic Energy Establishment 61-63; Research Assoc. Calif. Inst. of Technology, Pasadena 63-64, Visiting Prof. of Theoretical Physics 64-65; Prof. of Physics and Head of Dept. Tel-Aviv Univ. 65-, Vice-Pres. 65-66; Prof. of Physics and Dir. Center for Particle Theory, Univ. of Texas 68-; Pollak Prof. of Theoretical Physics, Tel-Aviv Univ. 68-; Pres. Tel-Aviv Univ. 71-; Adviser to Head of Mil. Intelligence 73-74; Special Adviser to Israel Defence Ministry 75-76; mem. Israel Atomic Energy Cttee. 66-, Israel Nat. Acad. of Sciences 66-; co-discoverer of Unitary Symmetry Theory; conceived basic field explaining compositeness of nuclear particles; Hon. D.Sc. (Israel Inst. of Technology) 66, (Yeshiva Univ., N.Y.) 72; Weizmann Prize for Sciences 66; Rothschild Prize 68; Israel Prize for Sciences 69; Albert Einstein Medal and Prize for Physics 70; Foreign Hon.

mem. American Acad. Arts and Sciences; Hon. Life mem. N.Y. Acad. of Sciences 73; Foreign Assoc. Nat. Acad. of Sciences 72-.
Leisure interests: music, history, linguistics.
Publs. *The Eightfold Way* (with M. Gell-Mann) 64, *Algebraic Theory of Particle Physics* 67, *One Way to Unitary Symmetry, The Past Decade in Particle Theory* (with E. C. G. Sudarshan).
Tel-Aviv University, Tel-Aviv, Israel.
Telephone: Tel-Aviv 416111.

Nef, John Ulric, S.B., PH.D., F.R.S.A.; American historian; b. 13 July 1899, Chicago, Ill.; *s.* of John Ulric and Louise B. Comstock Nef; *m.* 1st Elinor Castle 1921, 2nd Evelyn Stefansson 1964; ed. Harvard Univ. and Brookings Grad. School.
Assistant Prof. of Econs., Swarthmore Coll. 27-28, Asst. Prof. of Econs., Chicago Univ. 29-31, Assoc. Prof. 31-35, Assoc. Prof. of Econ. History 35-36, Prof. 36-50; Chair. Cttee. Social Thought 45-64; Visiting Prof. Inst. d'Etudes Politiques, Paris 49; temporary Prof. Coll. de France, Paris 53; Wiles Lecturer, Univ. of Belfast 56; Smith Lecturer, Univ. of St. Thomas 61; Vice-Chair. American Council of Learned Socs. 52-53; Chair. Center for Human Understanding 58-68; Pres. John and Evelyn Nef Foundation 66-; f. Cttee. on Social Thought, Univ. of Chicago; Fellow, World Acad. of Art and Science, World-Wide Acad. of Scholars; Dr. h.c. (Paris, Strasbourg); Officier Légion d'Honneur; Order of the Phoenix (Greece).
Leisure interests: swimming, walking, travelling with wife.
Publs. *The Rise of the British Coal Industry* (2 vols.) 32, *Industry and Government in France and England, 1540-1640* 40, *The United States and Civilization* 42 (2nd edn. 67), *The Universities Look for Unity* 43, *La route de la guerre totale* 49, *War and Human Progress* 50, *Letters and Notes of Elinor Castle Nef,* Vol. I 53, *La Naissance de la Civilisation industrielle et le Monde contemporain* 54, *Cultural Foundations of Industrial Civilisation* 58, *Religion and the Study of Man* 61, *A la Recherche de la Civilisation* 62, *Bridges of Human Understanding* 64, *Conquest of the Material World* 64, *Towards World Community* 68, *Search for Meaning* (*Autobiography of a Non-conformist*) 73.
2726 N Street, N.W., Washington, D.C. 20007, U.S.A.
Telephone: 333-2983.

Neff, William Duwayne, PH.D.; American research scientist and teacher; b. 27 Oct. 1912, Lomax, Ill.; *s.* of Lyman Melvin Neff and Emma Mary (Jacobson) Neff; *m.* 1st Ernestine Anderson Neff 1937 (divorced 1960), 2nd Palmer Anderson Neff 1961; one *s.* one *d.*; ed. Univ. of Illinois and Univ. of Rochester.
Research Assoc., Swarthmore Coll. 40-42, Columbia Univ. and Univ. of Calif. Divs. of War Research 42-46; Asst., Assoc. and Full Prof. of Psychology, Univ. of Chicago 46-61, Prof. of Psychology and Physiology 59-61; Scientific Liaison Officer, London Branch Office, Office of Naval Research 53-54; Dir. of Psychophysiology Lab., Bolt, Beranek and Newman Inc. 61-63; Prof. of Psychology, Indiana Univ. 63-64, Research Prof. Indiana Univ. 64-, Dir. Center for Neural Sciences 65-; mem. Nat. Acad. of Sciences; Award of Beltone Inst. for Hearing Research 69.
Leisure interest: golf.
Publs. Articles in scientific journals.
Center for Neural Sciences, Indiana University, Bloomington, Indiana 47401; Home: 3505 Bradley Street, Bloomington, Indiana 47401, U.S.A.
Telephone: 812-337-6063 (Office); 812-336-3489 (Home).

Negahban, Ezatollah, M.A., PH.D.; b. 1 March 1925; *s.* of Abdol Amir Negahban and Roghieh Dideban; *m.* Miriam Lois Miller 1955; five *s.*; ed. Teheran and Chicago Univs.
Associate Prof. Univ. of Teheran 56-62, Prof. 62-, Dir.

Univ. Inst. of Archaeology 58-, Head, Dept. of Archaeology 68-, Dean, Faculty of Letters and Humanities 75-; Technical Dir. Iranian Archaeological Service 60-65; Technical Adviser to Ministry of Culture 65-; Dir. Museum Iran Bastan 66-68; Gen. Sec. Int. Congress of Iranian Art and Archaeology 68-; excavated at Marlik 61-62, Haft Tepe 66-, Dir. Gazvin Plain Expedition (Zaghe, Qabrestan and Sagzabad) 70-; mem. German Archaeological Inst., Exec. Cttee., Congress of Pre- and Proto-History.
Leisure interests: building and development.
Publs. *The Gold Treasures of Marlik* 62, *Preliminary Report On Marlik Excavation* 64.
Faculty of Letters, University of Teheran, Teheran; 63 Bagh-Negahban, Darband, Tajrish, Teheran, Iran. Telephone: 6112582 (Office); 873856.

Nègre, Louis-Pascal, L. EN D.; Mali banker and politician; b. 16 April 1928; ed. Univ. of Paris, Ecole Nat. d'Administration d'Outre-Mer.
Technical Counsellor at the Presidency 61-63; Gov. Bank of Mali 64-68; Minister of Finance 66-69, of Finance and Commerce 69-70; Pres. Council of Ministers UDEAO 68-70; Pres. African Group, World Bank and IMF 68-70; Vice-Pres. African Development Bank 70-. African Development Bank, B.P. 1387, Abidjan, Ivory Coast.

Nègre, Maurice; French journalist; b. 20 April 1901. On editorial staff of *Eclair, Journal, Matin, Ami du Peuple*, successively 21-31; Dir. Warsaw Office of Havas Agency 31-34; Budapest Office 34-38; Bucharest Office 38-39; Dir. Information Service, French Embassy, Bucharest 40; worked for Allies in Balkans 40-42; played prominent part in French Resistance, founding clandestine news service "Supernap" 42-44; arrested and sent to Buchenwald 44, liberated 45; Dir.-Gen. Agence France-Presse 45-47 and 49-54; foreign affairs commentator, Radiodiffusion Française 47-49; Public Relations Consultant 55-; Technical Adviser, Société Ediradio 64; Commdr. de la Légion d'Honneur, Médaille de la Résistance, Croix de Guerre (Belgium), Officier de la Couronne de Belgique and other awards.
14 avenue du Général-Claverie, 75016 Paris, France.

Neguib, Gen. Mohamed; Egyptian army officer; b. 1901, Khartoum, Sudan; ed. Sudan Schools, Gordon Coll., Khartoum, Royal Mil. Acad. and Egyptian Univ., Cairo.
Commissioned in Infantry 17; served in Gen. Staff, Adjutant-Gen. and Q.M.-Gens'. Depts. during Second World War; Sub-Gov. of Sinai and Gov. of Red Sea Provinces in Frontier Corps; Col. Commdg. 2nd Machine Gun Battalion; Brig., 2nd in commd. of Egyptian troops in Palestine and commdg. successively 1st, 2nd, 3rd, 4th and 10th Infantry Brigades during hostilities with Israel 48; Dir.-Gen. Frontier Corps 50, Dir.-Gen. Infantry 51, C.-in-C. Egyptian Army July 52; Prime Minister, Minister for War and Marine, C.-in-C. of the Army and Mil. Gov. of Egypt Sept. 52-53; Pres. of the Repub. of Egypt June 53-Dec. 54.
Cairo, Egypt.

Nehru, Braj Kumar, B.SC., B.SC.(ECON.); Indian civil servant and Barrister-at-Law; b. 4 Sept. 1909, Allahabad; s. of Brijlal and Rameshawri Nehru; m. Magdalena Friedman 1935; three s.; ed. Allahabad Univ., London School of Economics, Balliol Coll., Oxford, Inner Temple, London.
Joined Indian Civil Service 34; Asst. Commr. 34-39; Under-Sec. Dept. of Educ., Health and Lands, Govt. of India 39; mem. Indian Legis. Ass. 39; Officer on special duty, Reserve Bank of India, Under-Sec. Finance Dept., Govt. of India 40, Joint Sec. 47; Exec. Dir. Int. Bank for Reconstruction and Devt. 49-54, 58-62; Minister, Indian Embassy, Washington 49-54; Sec. Dept. of Econ. Affairs, Ministry of Finance 57-58, Commr.-Gen. for Econ. Affairs 58-61; Amb. to U.S.A.

61-68; Gov. of Assam and Nagaland 68-73, of Manipur, Meghalaya and Tripura 72-73; Chair. North-Eastern Council 72-73; High Commr. to U.K. June 73-; rep. Reparations Conf. 45, Commonwealth Finance Ministers Conf., UN Gen. Assembly 49-52, 60, FAO Confs. 49-50, Sterling Balances Confs. 47-49, Bandung Conf. 55; deputed to enquire into Australian Fed. Finance 46; mem. UN Advisory Cttee. on Admin. and Budgetary Questions 51-53; Adviser to Sudan Govt. 55; mem. UN Investments Cttee. 62-; Fellow, London School of Econs.; Hon. LL.D. (Mo. Valley Coll.), Hon. Litt.D. (Jacksonville Univ.).
Leisure interests: bridge, reading, conversation.
Publs. *Speaking of India, Australian Federal Finance*.
India House, Aldwych, London, WC2 4NA; Home: 9 Kensington Palace Gardens, London, W.8, England. Telephone: 836-8484 (Office); 229-7241 (Home).

Nehru, Ratan Kumar; Indian civil servant and diplomatist; b. 10 Oct. 1902; ed. Allahabad and Oxford Univs.
Joined Indian Civil Service 25; served Madhya Pradesh 25-33; joined Central Govt. Admin., successively held posts of Collector of Customs, Bombay and later Madras, Commr. of Northern India Salt Revenue, Deputy and Joint Sec. in various Govt. depts. and Chair. Central Board of Revenue; Sec. to Ministry of Communications 47; Minister in Washington 48; Minister to Sweden, Denmark and Finland 49-51; Special Sec. for U.N. Affairs and later Commonwealth Sec. in Ministry of External Affairs 51-52; Foreign Sec. in Ministry of External Affairs 52-55; Ambassador to China 55-58; Ambassador to U.A.R. concurrently accred. to Lebanon and Libya 58-60; Sec.-Gen. Ministry of External Affairs 60-65, Chair. Preparatory Cttees. of Govt. of India for Conf. on Disarmament, and the UN Trade and Development Conf. 63-65; mem. Board of Trade and Nat. Defence Council; Vice-Chancellor, Allahabad Univ. 65-70.
c/o Senate House, Allahabad, India.

Neidlinger, Gustav; German baritone singer; b. 21 March 1912; ed. Humanistisches Gymnasium, Mainz, and Opernschule, Frankfurt/Main.
Has performed at Stadttheater, Mainz, Stadttheater, Plauen, Staatsoper, Hamburg, Staatsoper, Stuttgart, Bayreuth Festival, Deutsche Oper, Berlin, La Scala, Milan, Covent Garden, London, Grand Opera, Paris, Teatro La Fenice, Venice, Rome Opera and Opera S. Carlo, Naples; currently with Staatsoper, Stuttgart.
7 Stuttgart, Traubergstr. 3, Federal Republic of Germany.

Neilan, Edwin Peter; American banker; b. 24 Oct. 1905, Mason County, Mich.; s. Peter A. and Goldie (née Comstock) Neilan; m. Julia E. Motheral 1929; ed. Omaha Univ., Rice Univ., Texas Univ., Rutgers Graduate School of Banking, South Texas School of Law.
Securities Analyst, Houston Bank & Trust Co. 28-33; Chief Trust Examiner Federal Reserve Bank of Dallas 33-36, New York 36-37, Philadelphia 37-40; Assoc. Trust Officer, Bank of Delaware 40-42; U.S. Naval Reserve 42-46; Vice-Pres. and Sec. Bank of Delaware 46-52, Exec. Vice-Pres. 52-56, Pres. 56-69, Chair. of Board 59-71; Pres. Delaware Bankers 52; Chair. Board, Greater Wilmington Development Council 61-63; Pres. United Fund Northern Delaware 61-63; Vice-Pres. Chamber of Commerce of U.S. 62-63, Pres. 63-64, Chair. of Board 64-65; Vice-Pres. State Bank Div., American Bankers Asscn. 62-64, Pres. 64-65; American Employer Del. ILO; mem. Governing Body, ILO and Vice-Chair., Finance and Admin. Committee 66-; Vice-Pres. 50th Anniversary Conf. ILO 69; Vice-Chair. 65-69, Pres. 70-71, mem. Exec. Committee 70-, Int. Org. of Employers; mem. BIAC (U.S.A.) to OECD 67-70.
Leisure interests: swimming, travel.
62 Town House Lane, Corpus Christi, Tex. 78412, U.S.A.

Neild, Robert Ralph; British economist; b. 10 Sept. 1924, Peterborough; s. of Ralph and Josephine Neild; m. Elizabeth W. Griffiths; one s. four d.; ed. Charterhouse, and Trinity Coll., Cambridge.
Royal Air Force 43-44, Operational Research, R.A.F., 44-45; Secr., UN Econ. Comm. for Europe, Geneva 47-51; Econ. Section, Cabinet Office (later Treasury) 51-56; Lecturer in Econs. and Fellow of Trinity Coll., Cambridge 56-58; Nat. Inst. of Econ. and Social Research 58-64; Econ. Adviser to Treasury 64-67; mem. Fulton Cttee. on the Civil Service 66-68; Dir. Stockholm Int. Peace Research Inst. May 67-71; Prof. of Economics, Trinity Coll., Cambridge 71-.
Publ. *Pricing and Employment in the Trade Cycle* 64.
5 Cranmer Road, Cambridge, England.
Telephone: Cambridge 56902.

Neill, Rt. Rev. Stephen Charles, M.A., F.B.A.; British ecclesiastic; b. 31 Dec. 1900, Edinburgh, Scotland; s. of Rev. Charles Neill and Dr. Margaret P. Monro; ed. Dean Close School, and Trinity Coll., Cambridge.
Fellow, Trinity Coll., Cambridge 24-28; Missionary in Diocese of Tinnevelly 24-27 and 28-30; Warden, Bishop's Theological Coll., Nazareth, S. India 30-39; Examining Chaplain to Bishop of Tinnevelly 29-39; Bishop of Tinnevelly 39-45; Chaplain, Trinity Coll. Cambridge, and Lecturer in Theology 45-47; Select Preacher, Univ. of Oxford 45, Univ. of Cambridge 48, 73; Hulsean Lecturer, Cambridge 46-47; Asst. Bishop to the Archbishop of Canterbury 47-50; Co-Dir. Study Dept. World Council of Churches 46-48, Assoc. Gen. Sec. 48-51; Gen. Editor, World Christian Books 52-62, Dir. 62-72; Visiting Prof. of Missions, Univ. of Hamburg 56-57, Prof. 62-67; Visiting Prof. of Religions, Univ. of Nairobi, Kenya 68, Prof. of Philosophy and Religious Studies 69-73; Visiting Prof. of Religion, Univ. of Durban Westville 75; Bampton Lecturer, Univ. of Oxford 64; Hon. D.D. (Trinity Coll., Toronto, Culver-Stockton, Acadia Univ., Nova Scotia and Glasgow); Hon. Th.D. (Hamburg and Uppsala); Hon. Litt.D. (St. Paul's Univ., Tokyo).
Leisure interests: mountain-walking, listening to the young.
Publs. *How Readest Thou?* 25, *Out of Bondage* 28, *Builders of the Indian Church* 34, *Beliefs* 38, *Foundation Beliefs* 42, *The Challenge of Jesus Christ* 44, *Christ, His Church and His World* 48, *The Cross over Asia* 48, *Fulfil Thy Ministry* 52, *The Christian Society* 53, *Christian Partnership* 53, *Towards Church Union* 37-52, 53, *Under Three Flags* 54, *The Christian's God* 54, *Christian Faith Today* 55, *The Christian Character* 55, *Who is Jesus Christ?* 56, *The Unfinished Task* 57, *Anglicanism* 58, *Paul to the Galatians* 58, *A Genuinely Human Existence* 59, *Christian Holiness* 60, *Brothers of the Faith: the Ecumenical Movement 1919-1960* 60, *What is Man?* 60, *Christian Faith and Other Faiths* 61, *The Eternal Dimension* 63, *Christian Missions* 64, *The Interpretation of the New Testament* 64, *Colonialism and Christian Missions* 66, *The Church and Christian Union* 68, *The Story of Christianity in India and Pakistan* 70, *Call to Mission* 70, *Bible Words and Christian Meanings* 71, *Bhakti Hindu and Christian* 74.
Wycliffe Hall, Oxford, England.
Telephone: Oxford 53213.

Neilson, Hon. William Arthur; Australian politician; b. 27 Aug. 1925, Hobart; ed. Ogilvie Commercial High School.
Member of Tasmanian House of Assembly 46-; Labor Party Whip 46-55; Minister for Tourists and Immigration and for Forests 56-58; Attorney-Gen. and Minister of Educ. 58; Treas. and Minister of Educ. 59; Minister of Educ. 59-69, 72-74; Attorney-Gen. 74-75; Deputy Premier, Minister for the Environment, Minister administering Police Dept. and the Licensing Act 74-75; Premier and Treas. March 75-; Pres. Tasmanian Section of Australian Labor Party 68-69.
Parliament House, Hobart, Tasmania 7000; Home: 40 Cornwall Street, Rose Bay, Tasmania 7015, Australia.

Neirinck, José D., DR. SC.S.; Belgian international civil servant; b. 1920; m. H. de Meulemeester; ed. Univ. of Ghent.
Executive Asst. to Deputy Prime Minister, Minister of Econ., Minister of Social Affairs and several posts as Govt. Official 54-63; Dir.-Gen. at EEC 63-68, Hon. Dir.-Gen. 68-; Dir.-Gen. of Fed. of Belgian Cement Industry; rep. of Liaison Cttee. of Cement Industry in EEC; mem. of various nat. and int. orgs. for cement research and industrialization of building industry; Officer Order of Crown, Order of Léopold, commemoration medals Armed Resistance and World War II.
Publs. on social-economic matters; English works incl. *The Rome Treaty Social Policy and EEC Applied Labour Economics* 69, *Social Policy of the European Economic Community* 70.
Fédération de l'Industrie Cimentière, Rue de Trèves 96, 1040 Brussels; Home: Maarschalklaan 16, Ukkel, 1180 Brussels, Belgium.
Telephone: (02) 511-65-40.

Neizvestny, Ernst Iosifovich; Soviet artist and sculptor; b. 9 April 1925, Sverdlovsk; ed. V. I. Surikov State Inst. of Arts (M. G. Manizer's studio).
Soviet Army 42-45; sculptor at studios of U.S.S.R. Agricultural Exhbn. (now Econ. Achievements of U.S.S.R. Exhbn.) 53-54; mem. Artists' Union of U.S.S.R. 55-57; granted permission to emigrate to Israel 76.
Main works: *Kremlin Builder, First Wings, The Youth, Mother,* series: *War—is . . .; Robots and Semi-robots, Great Mistakes,* etc.

Nekrasov, Viktor Platonovich; Soviet writer; b. 17 June 1911, Kiev; ed. Inst. of Engineering and Architecture, Kiev.
Former architectural student; Actor and Set Designer, Kiev, Vladivostok, Kirov, Rostov-on-Don 37-41; Army Officer (Engineers) 41-44; journalist; writer 47-; expelled to Kiev March 74; Stalin Prize for Literature 47; Badge of Honour, Red Star.
Publs. *In the Trenches of Stalingrad* (novel) 46, *The Native Town* (novel) 54, *First Journey* (essays on a visit to Italy) 58, *Vassia Konakoff* (short stories) 60, *Kira Georgievna* (novel) 62, *Both Sides of the Ocean* (essays on a visit to Italy and U.S.A.) 62, *A Month in France* 65, *Distance of 12,000 Kilometres* (Stories about Kamchatka) 65, *Travels in Different Measurements* 67.
Ukrainian S.S.R. Branch, U.S.S.R. Union of Writers, Kiev, U.S.S.R.

Nelissen, Roelof J.; Netherlands banker; b. 4 April 1931, Hoofdplaat, Zeeland province; m.; three s. one d.; ed. grammar school at Dongen and Faculty of Law, Catholic Univ. of Nijmegen.
Various posts in employers' asscns., Amsterdam and The Hague 56-; Sec.-Gen. Netherlands Catholic Employers' Asscn. June 62, Fed. of Catholic and Protestant Employers' Asscns. Sept. 68; mem. Second Chamber, Netherlands Parl. June 63-; Vice-Chair. Parliamentary Catholic People's Party; deputy mem. Council of Europe, Council of WEU; Minister of Econ. Affairs 70-71; First Deputy Prime Minister, Minister of Finance 71-73; mem. Board Man. Dirs. Amsterdam-Rotterdam Bank N.V. 74-.
Amro Bank, Herengracht 595, Amsterdam, Netherlands.

Nellemose, Knud; Danish sculptor; b. 12 March 1908; ed. Royal Acad. of Art, Copenhagen.
First exhbn. of sculpture 31; mem. State Art Foundation 58-64; awarded Eckersberg Medal 44, Kai Nielsen

Bequest 47, Carlsberg Travelling Scholarship 47-48, Thorvaldsen Medal 68; Knight of the Order Dannebrog; busts of Their Majesties King Frederik, Queen Ingrid and Queen Margrethe II of Denmark; Statue of Søren Kierkegaard; works represented in the State Gallery of Copenhagen and in other Danish Museums, Nat. Museums of Stockholm and Oslo, Auschwitz, Poland and include *Group of Wrestlers* and *Young Man with Discus* and a marble bust of Hans Andersen for his 150th anniversary celebrations; represented at Venice Biennale 50, and other int. exhbns.
Mathilde Fibigersvej 3, Copenhagen F, Denmark.

Nelson, Gaylord Anton, LL.B.; American lawyer and politician; b. 4 June 1916; ed. Clear Lake High School (Polk County, Wis.), San José State Coll., Calif., and Wisconsin Univ. Law School.
Practising Attorney, Madison, Wis. 46-58; Wisconsin State Senator 48-58; Gov. of Wisconsin 58-62; U.S. Senator from Wisconsin 63-; army service 42-46; Democrat.
c/o Senate Office Building, Washington, D.C. 20510; Home: 618 Bordner Drive, Madison, Wisconsin 53705, U.S.A.

Nelson of Stafford, Baron, succeeded to title 62; **Henry George Nelson,** M.A., C.ENG., F.I.C.E., HON. F.I.MECH.E., F.I.E.E., F.R.AE.S.; British industrialist; b. 2 Jan. 1917, Manchester; s. of 1st Baron Nelson of Stafford and Florence M. Howe; m. Pamela R. Bird 1940; two s. two d.; ed. Oundle and King's Coll., Cambridge.
With English Electric Co. Ltd. 39-42; Man. Dir. D. Napier & Son Ltd. 42-49; Exec. Dir. Marconi's Wireless Telegraph Co. Ltd. 46-58; Dep. Man. Dir. English Electric Co. Ltd. 49-56, Man. Dir. 56-62, Chair. and Chief Executive 62-68; Chair. The General Electric Co. Ltd. 68-; Dir. Nickel of Canada, London Board of Advice, Nat. Bank of Australasia; Joint Chair. Babcock & Wilcox & Taylor Woodrow Atomic Power Construction Co. Ltd.; Dir. Bank of England 61-; Joint Deputy Chair. British Aircraft Corpn.; Minister of Technology's Advisory Council 64-70; Pres. ORGALIME (Organisme des Liaison des Industries Métallique Européennes) 66-70; Pres. Inst.E.E. 70-71, Sino-British Trade Council 73-; mem. many other councils and cttees.; Hon. D.Sc. (Aston, Cranfield and Keele), Hon. LL.D. (Strathclyde).
Leisure interests: shooting, tennis, riding, skiing.
19 Acacia Road, St. John's Wood, London, NW8 6AN; 1 Stanhope Gate, London, W1A 1EH, England.
Telephone: 01-493-8484 (Office).

Nemerov, Howard; American writer and teacher; b. 1 March 1920; ed. Fieldston School and Harvard Coll.
Royal Canadian Air Force, U.S. Army Air Force, attached R.A.F. Coastal Command 41-45; Instructor in English, Hamilton Coll., Clinton, N.Y. 46-48; mem. Faculty of Literature, Bennington Coll. 48-66, at Brandeis Univ. 66-; mem. Nat. Inst. of Arts and Letters; Visiting lecturer, Univ. of Minnesota 58-59; Writer in residence, Hollins Coll. 62-63; Consultant in Poetry, Library of Congress, Washington, D.C. 63-64; Fannie Hurst Prof. Creative Literature, Wash. Univ., St. Louis 69-, now Prof. of English, Edward Mallinckrodt Dist. Univ. Prof. 76-; Fellow, American Acad. of Arts and Sciences; Hon. degree Lawrence Univ. 64; several awards.
Publs. *The Image and the Law* 47, *The Melodramatists* 49, *Guide to the Ruins* 50, *Federigo* 54, *The Salt Garden* 55, *The Homecoming Game* 57, *Mirrors and Windows* 58, *A Commodity of Dreams and Other Stories* 59, *New and Selected Poems* 60, *The Next Room of the Dream* 62, *Essays on Poetry and Fiction* 63, *Journal of the Fictive Life* 65, *The Blue Swallows* (poems) 67, *Stories, Fables and Other Diversions* 71, *Reflexions on Poetry and Poetics* 72, *Gnomes and Occasions* (poems) 73, *The*

Western Approaches, Poems 1973-75, Figures of Thought 76 (essays).
Washington University, St. Louis, Mo.; Home: 6970 Cornell Avenue, St. Louis, Mo. 63130, U.S.A.

Nemery, Maj.-Gen. Jaafar Mohammed al-; Sudanese army officer and political leader; b. 1 Jan. 1930, Omdurman; ed. Sudan Military Coll.
Former Commdr. Khartoum garrison; campaigns against rebels in Southern Sudan; placed under arrest on suspicion of plotting to overthrow the government; led successful mil. coup May 69; promoted from Col. to Maj.-Gen. May 69; Chair. Revolutionary Command Council (RCC) 69-71, C.-in-C. of Armed Forces 69-73; Prime Minister Oct. 69-, Minister of Foreign Affairs 69-70, of Econ. and Planning 70-71, of Planning Aug. 71-72; Pres. of Sudan Oct. 71-.
Office of the President, Khartoum, Sudan.

Nemes, Dezsö; Hungarian politician and historian; b. 6 Sept. 1908, Löcse (now Levoca in Czechoslovakia); s. of Ádolf Nemes and Teréz Neufeld; m. Piroska Szabó; one s.; ed. University.
Joined the Communist Party 26; imprisoned 28-31; Sec. Hungarian Trades Union Council 45-48; Dept. Head, Ministry of Culture 50-53; Dir. *Szikra* (publishers) 53-56; Ed.-in-Chief *Népszabadság* (daily newspaper) 57-61; mem. Central Cttee., Hungarian Socialist Workers' Party, Alt. mem., Political Cttee. 57-59, mem. Political Cttee. 59-, Sec. Central Cttee. 61-65; Head of Directorate, Inst. for the Research of Party History, Hungarian Acad. of Sciences 65-66; Head of Directorate, Party Acad. 67-75, Rector 75-; Kossuth Prize; State Prize 75; Decoration of Liberty (silver); People's Econ. Decoration (4th degree); Order of Labour Medal.
Leisure interests: history, reading
Publs. *International Labour Movement* 49, *History of the General Worker Society 1868-1873* 52, *Documents of the History of the Counter-Revolution 1-3,* 53-59, *Liberation of Hungary* 55, *History of the Counter-Revolution in Hungary in 1920-1921* 62, *The Foreign Policy of the Bethlen Government* 64, *History of the Hungarian Revolutionary Working Class* (3 vols.) 70, *Lenin With Us* 70, *About the History of the Hungarian Labour Movement* 74.
Hungarian Socialist Workers' Party, Széchenyi rakpart 19, H-1387, Budapest V, Hungary.
Telephone: 228-830.

Nemeslaki, Tivadar; Hungarian politician; b. 1923, Tatabánya.
Began career as a fitter, Tatabánya; joined Hungarian Communist Party 45, various posts in County and Cen. Admin. 45-56, also in factory trade union org.; Sec. Komárom County Cttee., Hungarian Socialist Workers' Party 58, First Sec. 59, mem. Cen. Cttee. 61-; mem. Nat. Assembly 62-; Gen. Sec. Iron Workers' Union 66; Sec. Nat. Council of Trade Unions 70, Deputy Gen. Sec. 73; Minister of Foundry and Machine Eng. 75-; Gold Award, Labour Order of Merit.
Ministry of Foundry and Machine Engineering, 1024 Budapest, Mártirok utja 85, Hungary.
Telephone: 122-690.

Németh, Julius; Hungarian professor emeritus; b. 2 Nov. 1890, Karcag; m. Irene Sebestyén 1917; two d.; ed. József Eötvös Coll., Budapest, Leipzig and Kiel.
Studied Turkish Languages in Turkey, U.S.S.R., Bulgaria, Albania, Yugoslavia 07-66; reader in Turkish Philology, Univ. of Budapest 15, Prof. 16-65, Prof. Emer. 65-; Dean of Faculty of Arts 32-33, 35, Rector of Univ. 47-49; Dir. of Inst. of Linguistics of the Hungarian Acad. 51-65; mem. Hungarian, Bulgarian, German, Saxon Acads. of Sciences; Hon. mem. Societas Uralo-Altaica, Göttingen, Finno-Ugrian Soc. Helsinki, Royal Asiatic Soc. London, Turkish Linguistic Soc. Ankara, Turkish History Soc. Ankara, Polish Oriental Soc. Warsaw; Kossuth Prize, Gold Medal of Labour;

Red Banner of Labour 70; Banner Order of Hungarian People's Repub. 75; Indiana Univ. prize for Altaic Studies 67; Körösi Csoma Medal; Kiril I Metod Medal; Dipl. Türk. Cumh. 23-73; Dr. h.c. (Budapest) 70.
Leisure interests: novels, poems, paintings.
Publs. *Türkische Grammatik* 16, *A honfoglaló magyarság kialakulása* 30, *Die Inschriften des Schatzes von Nagy-Szent-Miklós* 32 (re-edited 64), *Zur Einteilung der türkischen Mundarten Bulgariens* 56, *Eine Wörterliste der Jassen, der ungarländischen Alanen* 59, *Turkish Grammar* 62, *Die Türken von Vidin—Sprache, Folklore, Religion* 65, *Turkish Reader for Beginners* 66, *Die Türkische Sprache in Ungarn im siebzehnten Jahrhundert* 70, *Gombocz Zoltán* 72.
Karinthy ut 24. III. 1, H-1111, Budapest XI, Hungary.

Németh, Károly; Hungarian politician; b. 14 Dec. 1922, Páka, County Zala; s. of József Németh and Anna Bek; m. Ilona Balázs 49; one s. one d.; ed. Party Acad. Former meat industry worker; joined Communist Party 45; First Sec. County Csongrád Party Cttee. 54-59; Head Party Cen. Cttee. Dept. of Agriculture 60-61; First Sec., Budapest Party Cttee., Hungarian Socialist Workers' Party 65-74, Sec. Cen. Cttee., HSWP 74-; alt. mem. Political Cttee., HSWP, mem. 70-, Head of Political Econ. Board attached to HSWP Cen. Cttee. 75-; mem. of Pres. Council; mem. Parl. 67-.
Leisure interests: music, reading, watching sports, football, cinema, angling, wild-game shooting.
Hungarian Socialist Workers' Party, H-1387 Budapest, Széchenyi rakpart 19, Hungary.

Nemoto, Ryutaro; Japanese politician; b. 1907; ed. Kyoto Univ.
Member, House of Reps.; fmr. Minister of Agriculture and Forestry; Chief Cabinet Sec.; Minister of Construction; Chair. Liberal-Democratic Party Policy (LDP) Board; Chair. LDP Org. Research Council; Minister of Construction 70-71.
House of Representatives, Tokyo, Japan.

Nenni, Pietro; Italian journalist and politician; b. 9 Feb. 1891.
Socialist; imprisoned (with Mussolini) 11 for participating in riots against Italo-Turkish war; Co-editor with Carlo Rosselli *Il quarto stato*; Paris Corresp., later Editor *Avanti* until its suppression 26; emigrated to France 26; with Randolfo Pacciardi, Political Commissar of Garibaldi Brigade in Spain; arrested in Vichy France and sent to Italy, where imprisoned; released Aug. 43; Sec.-Gen. Italian Socialist Party Aug. 44-63; Vice-Pres. Council of Ministers in Parri Cabt. 45; Vice-Premier and Minister of Constituent Assembly in De Gasperi Cabt. 45-46; Minister of Foreign Affairs 46-Jan. 47, Dec. 68-69; Deputy Prime Minister Dec. 63-68; Pres. Partito Socialista Italiano, now Pres. Econ. Cttee., PSI.
Partito Socialista Italiano, 476 Via del Corso, 00186 Rome, Italy.

Neporozhny, Pyotr Stepanovich, D.SC.(ENG.); Soviet engineer and politician; b. 1910; ed. Leningrad Water Transport Engineering Inst.
Power engineer 35-; mem. C.P.S.U. 40-; fmr. engineer on hydro-technical projects, Northern U.S.S.R., construction of hydro-electric stations, Ukraine; fmr. Vice-Chair. Council of Ministers of Ukrainian S.S.R., Chair. Ukraine Building Cttee.; First Deputy Minister of Electric Power Station Construction (U.S.S.R.) 59-62, Minister of Power Eng. and Electrification 63-65; Minister of Electric Power Development and Electrification 65-; Alt. mem. Cen. Cttee. of C.P.S.U. 66-71, mem. 71-; Deputy to U.S.S.R. Supreme Soviet; Lenin prizewinner 66.
Ministry of Electric Power Development and Electrification of the U.S.S.R., 7 Kitaisky proezd, Moscow, U.S.S.R.

Nepote, Jean; French police official; b. 24 Jan. 1915; ed. Lycée Corneille, Rouen, and Univ. de Lyon.
Public service 35-; Commr. of Police, Sûreté Nationale 41; Asst. to Sec.-Gen., INTERPOL (Int. Police Org.) 46-63, Sec.-Gen. of INTERPOL 63-; Officier Légion d'Honneur, Croix de Guerre.
26 rue Armengaud, 92 Saint-Cloud, Hauts de Seine, France.

Nerée tot Babberich, Marie Frederik Frans Antoon de, DR.IUR.; Netherlands and international civil servant; b. 8 Jan. 1915; m. Johanna Baroness de Vos van Steenvijk; three s. three d.; ed. Klein Coll., Groot Coll. (Roermond), Leiden Univ.
Official at Cour des Comptes 38, Ministry of Econ. Affairs 40; Joint Sec.-Gen., States Gen. (Second Chamber), The Hague 45; Sec.-Gen. E.C.S.C. Common Assembly 52-58, European Parliament 58-61; political prisoner 42-44; military service (major of reserve) 44-45; lecturer at Saarbrücken Univ. 54; Deputy Commr.-Gen. Int. Exhbn., Montreal; Dir. several companies; mem. provincial states Gelderland; Commdr. Order of Merit of Italian Republic, Ordre de Léopold II, Ordre de la Couronne de Chene, Officer Order of Orange-Nassau.
Leisure interests: literature, bible study (apocryphal texts), shooting, travel.
Publs. On Netherlands public law, and political subjects. "Camphuysen", Babberich, Netherlands.

Nerman, Einar; Swedish artist; b. 6 Oct. 1888; ed. Norrköping, Stockholm, and under Matisse, Paris.
Cartoonist various European and American journals, including *The Tatler*, *The Sketch*, *Die Dame*, *Strix*, *Thalia*, *The New Yorker*, *Vogue*, *La Vie Parisienne*; portrait painter and decorative artist; composer music for Swedish nursery rhymes, children's musicals and songs and Swedish songs; exhibited London 25 and 27, New York 28; went to New York 39; working there as a portrait painter, cartoonist, illustrator of children's papers; illustrated *The Goose Girl*, New York 29, Selma Lagerlöf's *Jerusalem* 30, *En saga om en saga* 35, *A Child's First Book* 45, *Let's Play* 46, *Fairy Tales from the North* 46, *Carikature* for *The Studio*, New York 46, *Celibriteter och lackerheter* 53, *100 gubbar* 58, *Darling of the Gods* (autobiography) 63; *Middagena pa Traneholm* (novel) 68, *Livet en dröm* (autobiog.); composed music for children's musical *Pang-Pang* 71.
Hersbyholms Gård, Lidingö, Sweden.

Nerva, Marquis de, Francisco Javier Elorza; Spanish Ambassador and Permanent Representative to OECD 70-73; see *The International Who's Who 1975-76*.

Nervi, Pier Luigi; Italian architect; b. 21 June 1891; ed. Bologna Univ.
Pioneer in the use of reinforced concrete in architecture; has designed and constructed numerous stadiums, dockyards, aerodromes, oil storage plants, etc.; Partner Nervi and Nebbiosi 23-32, Nervi and Bartoli 32-; Prof. Rome Univ. 47-61, Harvard 61-62; mem. Int. Conf. of Modern Architecture 47, Accad. S. Luca 60-, Bayerische Akad. 60-; Hon. mem. American Acad. of Arts and Letters, American Acad. Arts and Sciences; Foreign mem. Swedish Royal Acad. of Fine Arts; Corresp. mem. Acad. des Beaux Arts, Paris 71; Grand Cross, Italian Order of Merit, Pubblica Istruzione Gold Medal, "Frank P. Brown Medal" (Franklin Inst. Philadelphia) 57, Österreichischer Gewerbeverein "Exner Medal" 58, R.I.B.A., Royal Gold Medal 60, Premio A.I.T.E.C., Rome 62, American Concrete Industry Board Award 63, Deutscher Beton Verein E.V. "Emil Mörsch" Medal 63; hon. degrees Edinburgh Univ., Technische Hochschule Munich, Warsaw Univ., Harvard Univ., Dartmouth Coll. N.H., Cavaliere del Lavoro, Rome; Gold Medal of the American Inst. of Architects 64; Gold Medal, Inst. of Structural Engineers, U.K. 68; Grand Cross of St. Gregory the Great (Vatican) 71.

Publs. *New Structures* 63, *Aesthetics and Technology in Building* 65.
Lungotevere A. da Brescia 9, Rome, Italy.

Nesmeyanov, Alexander Nikolayevich, DR. CHEM. SCI.; Soviet organic chemist; b. 9 Sept. 1899, Moscow; ed. Moscow Univ.
Research Asst. 22, Professor 35, Rector of Moscow Univ. 48-51; elected corresp. mem. U.S.S.R. Acad. of Sciences 39, Academician 43-, Pres. 51-61, mem. of Presidium; Dir. Inst. of Organic Chem. 39-54, and Inst. of Elementary Organic Compounds 54-; Deputy to the Supreme Soviet of the U.S.S.R. 51-61, Supreme Soviet of the R.S.F.S.R. 47-50; fmr. Chair. Lenin Prize Cttee. (Science and Inventions); Hon. mem. Acads. of Science of Germany, New York, Bulgaria, Rumania, Hungary, Czechoslovakia, Poland; Scottish Royal Soc.; Foreign mem. Royal Soc. 61, New York Acad. of Arts and Sciences; Dr. h.c., Univs. of Paris, Jena, Calcutta; awarded State Prize, First Class, Hero of Socialist Labour, five Orders of Lenin and the Order of the Red Banner of Labour.
Institute of Elementary Organic Compounds, Academy of Sciences of U.S.S.R., 14 Ulitsa Vavilova, Moscow, U.S.S.R.

Nesterov, Anatoly Innokentievich; Soviet internist and rheumatologist; b. 8 Nov. 1895, Chistoostrovskoe, Siberia; ed. Tomsk Univ.
Intern, Asst., Lecturer, Prof., Tomsk Univ. 20-35; Dir., Sochi Inst. of Clinical Medicine 35-39; Dir., Moscow Inst. of Health Resort Treatment 39-41; Prof., Novosibirsk Medical Inst. 41-43; Deputy Dir. Moscow Inst. of Physiotherapy 43-44; Dir. Moscow Inst. of Physiotherapy 44-51; mem. C.P.S.U. 46-; Corresp. mem. U.S.S.R. Acad. of Medical Sciences 45-50, mem. 50-; Head of Dept., Second Moscow Medical Inst. 47-; Academician-Sec., U.S.S.R. Acad. of Medical Sciences 53-57; Dir. Inst. of Rheumatism, U.S.S.R. Acad. of Medical Sciences 58-; Chair. All-Union Soc. of Internists; mem. Board All-Russian and Moscow Socs. of Internists; Deputy Chair. Medical Comm. and mem. Lenin Prizes Cttee.; Chair. Problem Comm. on Rheumatism, U.S.S.R. Acad. of Medical Sciences; Editor *Problems of Rheumatism;* Vice-Pres. League Against Rheumatism; Hon. mem. Rheumatological Socs. of Poland, U.S.A., Italy, Sweden, Netherlands and Turkey, and Purkyně Medical Soc. (Czechoslovakia); Hero of Socialist Labour.
Publs. Over 120 works on rheumatism and joint troubles, complex treatment of war trauma and diseases, etc.
Academy of Medical Sciences, Ulitsa Solyanka 14, Moscow 109801, U.S.S.R.

Nestingen, Ivan Arnold, PH.B., LL.B.; American lawyer and former government official; b. 23 Sept. 1921, Sparta, Wis.; s. of Eddie A. Nestingen and Lena G. Espeseth; m. Geraldine A. Krawczak 1952; three d.; ed. Univ. of Wisconsin.
Admitted to Wis. Bar 49, practice in Madison 49-56; mem. Common Council, Madison, Wis. 51-55, Wisconsin Legislature 55-56; Mayor of Madison 56-61; Under-Sec. U.S. Dept. of Health, Educ. and Welfare 61-65; lawyer, Washington, D.C. 65-.
Leisure interests: bridge, spectator sports, reading, swimming, fishing.
Suite 700, 1010 16th Street, N.W., Washington, D.C. 20036, U.S.A.
Telephone: 202-296-5374.

Netherlands, H.R.H. the Prince of the (Bernhard Leopold Frederik Everhard Julius Coert Karel Godfried Pieter), Prince zur Lippe-Biesterfeld, G.C.B., G.C.V.O., G.B.E.; b. 29 June 1911, Germany; s. of H.S.H. the late Prince Bernhard zur Lippe and Princess Armgard, Baroness von Seirstorpff-Cramm; m. Juliana Louise

Emma Marie Wilhelmina, *q.v.*, Queen of the Netherlands 1937; four d.; ed. Gymnasiums at Zuellichau and Berlin and Univs. of Lausanne, Munich and Berlin.
Assumed Netherlands nationality 36; studied at Netherlands Staff Coll.; appointed mem. State Council; after German invasion of Holland, May 40, evacuated family to England and returned to Continent with army until fall of France; returned to England and qualified as pilot 41; appointed Hon. Air Commodore R.A.F.V.R. 41; subsequently Chief Netherlands Liaison Officer with British Forces, Col. later Major-Gen. and Chief of Netherlands Mission to War Office; visited war fronts in North Africa and Normandy; maintained liaison throughout the war between Netherlands Underground and the Allied Govts.; appointed Supreme Commdr. (Lieut.-Gen.) Netherlands Armed Forces 44, and played important part in liberation of Netherlands; decorated for his services in this operation by H.M. Queen Wilhelmina (M.W.O.) and H.M. King George VI (G.B.E.); subsequently resigned from office of Supreme Commdr. 45; appointed Chair. Joint Chiefs of Staff, mem. Council for Mil. Affairs of the Realm, and mem. Joint Defence, Army, Admiralty and Air Force Councils; also Inspector-Gen. of Armed Forces; Admiral, General R. Neth. A.F., General (Army) 54; Hon. Air Marshal R.A.F. 64; mem. Board of the Netherlands Trade and Industries Fair, Royal Netherlands Blast Furnaces and Steelworks (Ijmuiden), Royal Dutch Airlines (K.L.M.), Royal Netherlands Aircraft Factories Fokker; has greatly contributed to post-war expansion of Netherlands trade; founder and regent Prince Bernhard Fund for the Advancement of Arts and Sciences in the Netherlands; Chairman European Cultural Foundation and Bilderberg Conferences; Regent Praemuim Erasmianum Foundation; President World Wildlife Fund; Hon. mem. Royal Aeronautical Soc., Royal Inst. Naval Architects, Aeromedical Soc., Royal Spanish Academy; Hon. degrees Univs. of Utrecht, Delft, Montreal, British Columbia, Amsterdam and Basle, Michigan; many decorations.
Leisure interests: golf, skiing, filming, hunting.
Soestdijk Palace, Baarn, Netherlands.

Netherthorpe, Baron, cr. 59, of Anston; **James Turner,** Kt., B.SC.(AGRIC.); British agriculturist; b. 6 Jan. 1908; s. of the late Albert E. M. Turner and Lucy Helliwell; m. Margaret L. Mattock 1935; three s.; ed. Leeds Univ. Engaged in farming since 28; Chair. Notts. County Branch Nat. Farmers' Union 39, 40 and 41; Notts. del. to Nat. Farmers' Union Council 42-44; Pres. Nat. Farmers' Union 45-60; leader U.K. del. to Dominions and U.S.A. 44 and 45; Dir. Abbey Nat. Building Soc., J. H. Fenner and Co. (Holdings) Ltd., Fisons Ltd. (Chair. 61-73), Lloyds Bank Ltd., Lloyds Bank Unit Trust Managers Ltd., Rank Foundation, Rank Group Holdings Ltd., F. D. & R. Holdings Ltd., Steetley Co. Ltd., Unigate Ltd. (Vice-Chair. Jan. 76-); Pres. Int. Fed. of Agricultural Producers 46-48; mem. Council of Royal Agricultural Soc. of England; Pres. Royal Agricultural Soc. 65; mem. British Productivity Council.
Leisure interests: shooting, golf.
Hadley Hurst, Hadley Common, Barnet, Herts., England.

Neto, Antônio Agostinho, M.D.; Angolan physician, poet and politician; b. 1922, Icolo-e-Bengo; s. of Agostinho Pedro Neto and Maria de Silva Neto; m. Maria Eugenia da Silva 1958; one s. two d.; ed. Protestant School, Luanda, and Univs. of Coimbra and Lisbon.
Colonial Health Service, imprisoned three times 52-60; mem. Movimento Popular de Libertação de Angola (MPLA) 57-, Pres. 62-; qualified as Doctor 59; imprisoned Cape Verde Islands, later Portugal 60-62, escaped July 62; led MPLA guerrilla campaign against Portuguese rule 62-74, also campaign against rival

nationalist movements 74-; Pres. People's Repub. of Angola Nov. 75-.
Office of the President, Luanda, Angola.

Netto, Carlos Monteiro do Amaral; Portuguese politician and civil engineer, b. 31 Dec. 1908, Lisbon; s. of Carlos Pereira do Amaral Netto and D. Ana Vaz Monteiro do Amaral Netto; m. D. Maria Raquel Almeida Brandão Abecassis; two s.; ed. Instituto Superior Técnico, Lisbon.
President, Town Council of Chamusca 36-59; Pres. Gen. Assembly, Casa do Povo, Chamusca 41-; Chief, Dept. of Works, Ministry of Public Works 43-46; Pres. District Council of Santarém 60-69; Deputy to Nat. Assembly 49-74; Pres. Nat. Assembly 69-74; Grã-Cruz da Ordem de Cristo.
Leisure interests: reading, travel.
Rua da Estrela 31, Lisbon 2; Rua Direita de S. Pedro 45, Chamusca, Portugal.
Telephone: 66-66-19/66-93-64; 76396 (Chamusca).

Neubauer, Joseph Allen; American chemical engineer and business executive, b. 24 July 1911, Cleveland, Ohio; s. of Ferdinand and Mary Neubauer; m. Marian A. Donges 1935; one s. two d.; ed. Lincoln High School and Case Inst. of Technology, Cleveland.
Joined Chemical Div. of Pittsburgh Plate Glass Co. 33, Devt. Dept. 34-36, Asst. Production Superintendent 36-41; Construction Engineer, Defense Plant Corps Chlorine Plant (operated by Pittsburgh Plate Glass Co.), New Martinsville 41-43, Superintendent 43-45; Tech. Adviser, Columbia Chemical Div. 45, Tech. Dir. 49; Vice-Pres. and Tech. Dir. Columbia Southern Chemical Corp. (subsidiary) 55, Pres. 57; Vice-Pres. and Gen. Man. Chemical Div., Pittsburgh Plate Glass Co.; Dir. Pittsburgh Plate Glass Co. 62, Exec. Vice-Pres. 66, Pres. 67- (name changed to PPG Industries Inc. 68); also Dir. of numerous subsidiary cos.; Dir. Pittsburgh Nat. Bank, Dravo Corpn., Brockway Glass Co. Inc., Wean United Inc.
Leisure interests: swimming, sailing, fishing, ice-skating, photography.
PPG Industries Inc., One Gateway Center, Pittsburgh, Pa. 15222; Home: 1355 Terrace Drive, Pittsburgh, Pa. 15228, U.S.A.

Neuberger, Albert, C.B.E., M.D., PH.D., F.R.C.P., F.C. PATH., F.R.S.; British professor of chemical pathology; b. 15 April 1908, Würzburg, Germany; s. of late Max Neuberger and of Bertha Neuberger; m. Lilian Ida Dreyfus; four s. one d.; ed. Gymnasium, Würzburg, Univs. of Würzburg and London.
Beit Memorial Research Fellow 36-40; research at Biochemistry Dept., Cambridge 39-42; mem. Scientific staff, Medical Research Council 43; Adviser to G.H.Q., Delhi (Medical Directorate) 45; Head of Biochemistry Dept., Nat. Inst. for Medical Research 50-55; Emer. Prof., Chemical Pathology, Univ. of London 55-73; Visiting Lecturer in Medicine, Harvard Univ. 60; mem. Editorial Board, *Biochemical Journal* 47-55, Chair. 52-55; mem. Medical Research Council 62-66; Chair. Biochemical Soc. 67-69; mem. Agricultural Research Council 70-; Chair. Governing Body, Lister Inst. 70-; Chair. Joint ARC/MRC Comm. on Food and Nutrition Research; William Julius Mickle Fellowship, Univ. of London 46-47; Heberden Medal 59; Frederick Gowland Hopkins Medal 60; Kaplun Prize 73; Hon. LL.D. (Aberdeen), Hon. Ph.D. (Jerusalem).
Publs. Papers in *Biochemical Journal, Proceedings of Royal Society* and other learned journals.
22 West Heath Avenue, London, N.W.11, England.

Neuberger, Maurine Brown; American politician; b. 9 Jan. 1907; ed. Univ. of Oregon.
Former teacher Milton-Freewater, Newberg, Portland (Oregon); mem. Oregon House of Reps. 51-55; Senator from Oregon 60-67; Chair. President's Advisory Council on Status of Women; mem. Gen. Advisory Cttee. of U.S.

Arms Control and Disarmament Agency; Lecturer in American Govt., Boston Univ. and Radcliffe Inst.; Democrat.
Department of Labor Building, Washington, D.C. 20211, U.S.A.
Telephone: 202-961-3777.

Neubert, Karel; Czechoslovak politician; b. 27 April 1915, Třebíč.
Locksmith 29-33; worker, mechanic, foreman Bata firm, later G. Kliment Works, Třebíč 34-64, Gen. Dir. 51-64; Chair. S. Moravian Regional Nat. Cttee. 64-69, Chief Sec., Brno Regional Cttee. C.P. of Czechoslovakia 69-; Alt. mem. Central Cttee. of C.P. of Czechoslovakia 62-68; mem. Presidium 68-69 and Central Cttee. of C.P. of Czechoslovakia 68-; mem. Bureau of Central Cttee. for direction of Party work in Czech lands 68-71; Deputy to House of Nations, Fed. Assembly of Č.S.S.R. 69-71; Deputy, Czech Nat. Council 68-71; Deputy Chair. Fed. Assembly 69, mem. Presidium Fed. Assembly 69-71; Deputy to House of the People, Fed. Assembly 71-; Chair. Regional Cttee. Nat. Front, S. Moravia 71; Leading Sec. S. Moravian Regional Cttee., C.P. of Czechoslovakia; Order of Labour 56, 75, Order of Victorious February 73.
Office: Regional Committee, Communist Party of Czechoslovakia, Brno; Central Committee of C.P. of Czechoslovakia, nábř. Kyjevské brigády 12, Prague 1, Czechoslovakia.

Neuman, Alois, LL.D.; Czechoslovak politician; b. 12 March 1901, Smidary; ed. Charles Univ., Prague.
Member Nat. Assembly 35; Burgomaster of České Budějovice 37-39; mem. Int. Illegal Cttee. of Political Prisoners, Buchenwald Concentration Camp 43; mem. Provisional Nat. Assembly 45, Constituent Nat. Assembly 46; Vice-Chair. Central Cttee. Czechoslovak Socialist Party 48; Vice-Chair. Central Action Cttee. of Nat. Front 48; Minister of Posts 48-60; Deputy Chair. Czechoslovak Socialist Party 48-60, Chair. 60-68, Hon. Chair. 68-, Govt. Comm. for Legislature 66-68; Minister of Justice 60-68; Deputy to Nat. Assembly 45-69; Deputy to House of People, Fed. Assembly 69-; mem. Presidium, Czechoslovak Socialist Party 73-; Order of February 25th, 1948 (1st Class) 49; numerous decorations.
Publs. *Sickness, Invalidity and Old Age Insurance* 28, *Communities and Social Insurance* 34, *Workers Social Insurance* 34, *Soviet Man and his Country* 51, *German People on New Roads* 52, *In the Great Chinese Country* 53, *People's Democratic Legal Order in the Service of the Working People* 55, *German Democratic Republic—New State, New People, New Life* 56.
Prague, Czechoslovakia.

Neumann, Alfred; German politician; b. 15 Dec. 1909; ed. elementary school.
Carpenter by trade; active mem. labour movement since 28; mem. Int. Brigade in Spain; 1st Sec. Greater Berlin District of Socialist Unity Party (S.E.D.) until 57; mem. Politburo S.E.D. 57-; Pres. Econ. Council until 65; Minister of Materials 65-69, First Deputy Chair. Council of Ministers 65-; mem. Volkskammer; Hans Beimler Medal; Vaterländischer Verdienstorden (gold).
Staatsrat, Berlin, German Democratic Republic.

Neumann, Bernhard Hermann, DR.PHIL., PH.D., D.SC., F.A.C.E., F.A.A., F.R.S.; British mathematician; b. 15 Oct. 1909, Berlin-Charlottenburg, Germany; s. of Richard Neumann and Else Aronstein; m. 1st Hanna von Caemmerer 1938 (died 1971), three s. two d.; m. 2nd Dorothea F. A. Zeim 1973; ed. Berlin-Charlottenburg, Univs. of Freiburg, Berlin, Cambridge.
Temporary Asst. Lecturer Univ. Coll. Cardiff 37-40; Army Service 40-45; Lecturer Univ. Coll. Hull 46-48; Lecturer, Senior Lecturer, Reader, Univ. of Manchester

48-61; Prof., Head of Dept., Australian Nat. Univ. 62-74, Emer. Prof., Hon. Fellow 75-(79); Senior Research Fellow, Div. of Mathematics and Statistics, Commonwealth Scientific and Industrial Research Org. 75-; Visiting Lecturer Australian Univs. 59, Visiting Prof. Tata Inst. Fundamental Research, Bombay 59, Courant Inst. Mathematical Sciences, N.Y. Univ. 61-62, Univ. Wisconsin 66-67, Vanderbilt Univ. 69-70, Univ. of Cambridge 70, Univ. Illinois Urbana-Champaign 75; Visiting Fellow, Fitzwilliam Coll., Cambridge 70; Editor *Proceedings of London Mathematical Soc.* 59-61; Assoc. Editor *Pacific Journal of Mathematics* 64-; Foundation Editor *Bulletin of Australian Mathematical Soc.* 69-; mem. Editorial Board *Zentralblatt Didaktik Math.* 69-, *Communications in Algebra* 72-, *Houston Journal of Mathematics* 74-, *Math. Student* 74-, *Math. Scientist* 75-, *Indian J. Math. Educ.* 75-; Council London Math. Soc. 54-61 (Vice-Pres. 57-59); Council Aust. Math. Soc. 63-(Vice-Pres. 63-64, 66-68, 71-73, Pres. 64-66); Council Aust. Acad. Science 68-71, Vice-Pres. 69-71; Foundation Pres. Aust. Asscn. Maths. Teachers 66-68, Vice-Pres. 68-69; Foundation Pres. Canberra Math. Asscn. 63-65, Vice-Pres. 65-66; Chair. Aust. Nat. Cttee. Maths. 66-75; Chair. Aust. Sub-Cttee., Int. Comm. Math. Instruction 68-75; Prize of Wiskundig Genootschap te Amsterdam 49; Adams Prize (Cambridge Univ.) 51-52; Fellow, Royal Soc. 59; Fellow, Aust. Acad. of Science 64; Fellow, Aust. Coll. Educ. 70; Hon. D.Sc., Univ. of Newcastle N.S.W. 74.

Leisure interests: chamber music, orchestral music (cello), chess, cycling.

Publs. Over 100 papers in mathematical journals.

Department of Mathematics, Institute of Advanced Studies, Australian National University, P.O. Box 4, Canberra, A.C.T. 2600; CSIRO-DMS, P.O. Box 1965, Canberra, A.C.T. 2601; Home: 20 Talbot Street, Forrest, A.C.T. 2603, Australia.

Telephone: 494504 (Office); 732270 (Home).

Neumann, Robert Gerhard, PH.D., M.A.; American diplomatist; b. 2 Jan. 1916, Vienna, Austria; s. of Hugo and Stephanie Taussky; m. Marlen Eldredge 1941; two s.; ed. High School and Consular Acad., Vienna, Univ. of Rennes, Geneva School of Int. Studies, Amherst Coll., Mass., Univ. of Minnesota.

Teacher of Political Science and Econs., State Teachers' Coll., Oshkosh, Wis. 41-42; Lecturer in Political Science, Univ. of Wisconsin 46-47; Asst. Prof., Univ. of Calif., Los Angeles 47-52, Assoc. Prof 52-58, Prof. of Political Science 58-67, Dir. Inst. of Int. and Foreign Studies 58-65; Chair. Atlantic and West European Program 65-66; Amb. to Afghanistan 66-73, to Morocco 73-75; Editorial Writer *Los Angeles Times* 52-59; Chevalier Légion d'Honneur 57; Order of the Star, 1st Class (Afghanistan) 73; Commdr. Order of Merit (Fed. Repub. of Germany) 74; Hon. Medal Univ. of Brussels 55.

Leisure interests: skiing, hiking.

Publs. *European and Comparative Government, The Government of Germany* 66, and numerous articles in professional journals.

Home: 4312 Inglewood Boulevard, Los Angeles, Calif. 90066, U.S.A.

Telephone: 303-61 (Office); (213) 397-3212 (Home).

Neumann, Václav; Czechoslovak conductor; b. 29 Sept. 1920, Prague; ed. Prague Conservatoire.

Former viola player, Smetana Quartet; mem. Czech Philharmonic Orchestra; deputised for Rafael Kubelík 48; later conducted orchestras in Karlovy Vary and Brno; Conductor Prague Symphony Orchestra 56-63, Prague Philharmonic 63-64; Chief Conductor Komische Oper, Berlin 57-60, conducted first performance of *The Cunning Little Vixen* (Janáček); Conductor Leipzig Gewandhaus Orchestra and Gen. Music Dir. Leipzig Opera House 64-67; conductor Czech Philharmonic Orchestra 67-68, Chief Conductor 68-; Conductor Munich Opera Ensemble 69; has toured Austria, England, France, Switzerland and Fed. Repub. of Germany 64-; has also toured numerous countries with Czech Philharmonic Orchestra including U.S.A., Japan, Yugoslavia 69, Bulgaria 70, Hungary, U.S.S.R. 71, German Democratic Repub. 72, Japan, Yugoslavia 74, Finland 75; Nat. Prize of German Democratic Repub. 66; Honoured Artist 67.

Prague 1-Staré Město, Široká 10, Czechoslovakia.

Neumeyer, Fritz; German professor of music, harpsichordist and composer; b. 2 July 1900; studied under F. Bölsche, A. von Fielitz, J. Kwast and W. Klatte, and at Univs. of Cologne and Berlin.

Orchestra Conductor, Saarbrücken Municipal Theatre 24-27; Leader Saarbrücken Asscn. for Early Music, and harpsichordist 27; Chamber Trio for Early Music (with Scheck and Wenzinger) 35-62; Lecturer, Hochschule für Musik, Berlin 39-44; Prof. of Historical Keyboard instruments, Hochschule für Musik, Freiburg/Breisgau 46-69; concert harpsichordist with *Capella Coloniensis* and Wiener Solisten and duo on historical keyboard instruments with Rolf Junghanns 68-; has considerable collection of old keyboard instruments; Johann-Stamitz Prize, Bundesverdienstkreuz.

Works include: ballads, songs, choral works, Four Meditations for String Trio.

78 Freiburg/Breisgau, Silberbachstrasse 21, Federal Republic of Germany.

Neunylov, Boris Alexandrovich; Soviet agrochemist; b. 1908; ed. Far Eastern Agricultural Inst.

Agronomist 27-30; Senior Research Assoc. Head of Dept., Deputy Dir. Far Eastern Rice Experimental Station 40-63; Chief Agronomist of Rice Farm 40-46; Postgraduate Dokuchayev Soil Inst. U.S.S.R. Acad. of Sciences 53-55; Chair. Presidium Far Eastern Section, Siberian Branch U.S.S.R. Acad. of Sciences 64-71; mem. U.S.S.R. Acad. of Agricultural Science 66-; Corresp. mem. U.S.S.R. Acad. of Sciences 70-; Hero of Socialist Labour, Order of Lenin, "Hammer and Sickle" Gold Medal, etc.

Publs. Works on selection of high-yield rice varieties in Soviet Far East.

Academy of Agricultural Sciences, Bolshoi Kharitonevsky Per. 21, Moscow, U.S.S.R.

Neurath, Hans, PH.D.; American biochemist; b. 29 Oct. 1909, Vienna, Austria; s. of Rudolf and Hedda Samek Neurath; m. Hilde Neurath 1936, Susi Neurath 1960; one s.; ed. Elementary and High School, Vienna, and Univ. of Vienna.

Research Fellow, Univ. of London 34-35; Instructor and George Fischer-Baker Fellow, Cornell Univ., N.Y. 36-38; Asst. Prof., Assoc. Prof., Prof. of Physical Biochemistry, Duke Univ. 38-50; Chair. and Prof. of Biochemistry, Univ. of Washington, Seattle 50-; mem. U.S. Nat. Acad. of Sciences; Fellow American Acad. of Arts and Sciences; specializes in biochemistry of proteins and enzymes, relation of their structure and function; D.Sc. (Univ. of Geneva) 70.

Leisure interests: music (piano), mountaineering, skiing.

Publs. Over 200 original publs. in biochemistry; Editor *Biochemistry, The Proteins.*

Office: University of Washington, J-405 Health Sciences Building, Seattle, Wash. 98105; Home: 5752 60th N.E. Seattle, Wash. 98105, U.S.A.

Telephone: 206-543-1660 (Office); LA2-0814 (Home).

Neustadt, Richard Elliott; American political scientist; b. 27 June 1919; ed. Univ. of California (Berkeley) and Harvard Univ.

Economist, Office of Price Admin. 42; Staff mem. Bureau of Budget 46-50; White House 50-53; Prof. of Public Admin. Cornell Univ. 53-54. of Govt., Columbia Univ. 54-65, Harvard Univ. 65-; Assoc. Dean, Kennedy

School of Govt. 65-, Dir. Inst. of Politics, Harvard 65-71; mem. Inst. for Strategic Studies 63-; Fellow, American Acad. of Arts and Sciences 64-; Visitor, Nuffield Coll., Oxford 61-62, Assoc. mem. 65-; Special Consultant, Sub-Cttee. on Nat. Policy Machinery, U.S. Senate 59-61; mem. Advisory Board on Comm. on Money and Credit 60-61; Special Consultant to Pres.-Elect Kennedy 60-61, to Pres. Kennedy 61-63, to Bureau of Budget 61, to Dept. of State 63; mem. Council on Foreign Relations 63; Consultant to Pres. Johnson 64, to Rand Corpn. 64-; Democrat.

Publs. *Presidential Power* 60, *Alliance Politics* 70. Office: Littauer Center 127, Harvard University, Cambridge, Mass. 02135; Home: 10 Traill Street, Cambridge, Mass. 02138, U.S.A.

Telephone: 617-491-6127 (Home).

Neústupný, Jiři, PH.D., D.SC.; Czechoslovak archaeologist and museologist; b. 22 Sept. 1905, Pilsen, Bohemia; s. of František and Antonie Neústupný; m. Anna Neústupný 1931; two s. one d.; ed. Charles Univ., Prague. Keeper, Nat. Museum Prague 25-; Lecturer, Charles Univ. 50, Prof. of Prehistory and Museology 69; mem. Council Int. Congress of Prehistoric Sciences 48-, Vice-Chair. 66; rep. Czechoslovak museums, UNESCO Confs. Mexico City 47, Paris 48, Great Britain 56 and 64, U.S.A. 65, Japan, Australia, New Zealand 68, Leningrad, Moscow 70; Head of Centre for Museological Education 67; Dir. many excavations in Czechoslovakia; mem. German Archaeological Inst.; Scientific Prize of Bohemia 48, Distinction for Outstanding Labour 66.

Leisure interests: problems I have not yet solved.

Publs. *Prehistory of Mankind* 47, *Questions de muséologie moderne* 50, *Vorgeschichte der Lausitz* 51, *Studies on the Eneolithic Plastic Arts* 56, *Czechoslovakia before the Slavs* 61, *Museum and Research* 68, *Some Problems of the Settlement of Czechoslovak Territory in Prehistory* 68; Editor *Fontes Archaeologici Pragenses* 58.

Národní Museum, Václavské nám. 68, Prague I, Czechoslovakia.

Telephone: 26-94-51.

Nevanlinna, Rolf Herman, D.PHIL.; Finnish mathematician; b. 22 Oct. 1895, Joensuu; s. of Dr. Otto Nevanlinna and Margaretha Romberg; m. Sinikka Kallio 1958; three s. two d.; ed. Helsinki Univ. Dozent of Mathematics, Helsinki Univ. 22-26, Prof. 26-47, Dean of the Faculty of Sciences 33-36, 38-39, Rector 41-45; Prof. of Mathematics, Zürich Univ. 47-48; Chancellor Univ. Turku 65-70; mem. Acad. of Finland 48-; Pres. Int. Mathematical Union 59-62, Board of Sibelius Academy; Hon. Prof. Zürich Univ.; Hon. Fellow Georg-August-Univ., Göttingen; Dr. h.c. Heidelberg, Bucharest, Giessen, Jyväskylä, Glasgow, Uppsala Univs., Freie Univ. Berlin; Hon. mem., Foreign mem., Corresp. mem. several acads.; Wihuri Int. Mathematical Prize 58, Henrik Steffens Int. Prize 66.

Leisure interest: music.

Publs. *Le théorème de Picard-Borel et la théorie des fonctions méromorphes* 29, *Eindeutige analytische Funktionen* 36, 53, *Uniformisierung* 53, *Absolute Analysis* (with F. Nevanlinna) 59; *Raum, Zeit und Relativität* 64; *Einführung in die Funktionentheorie* (with V. Paatero) 65, *Analytic Functions* 70; numerous mathematical papers and articles on philosophy, pedagogy, the arts, etc.

Ads. Bulevardi 9A, Helsinki 12, Finland.

Nevelson, Louise; American sculptor; b. 1900, Kiev, Russia; d. of Isaac Berliawsky and Minna Sadie Smolerank; m. Charles Nevelson 1920.

Studied with Hans Hoffman, Germany 31; one-man exhbns. in U.S.A. and Europe 63-; retrospective exhbn. Whitney Museum of American Art; perm. exhbns. at Whitney Museum of American Art, Brooklyn Museum, Newark Museum, Carnegie Inst., Museum of Modern Art, N.Y., and others; First Award United Soc. of Artists 59, Award of Chicago Inst. 59, Gold Medal MacDowell Colony, Brandeis Univ. Creative Arts Award for Sculpture, Skowhagen Medal for Sculpture.

29 Spring Street, New York, N.Y. 10012, U.S.A.

Neville, John, O.B.E.; British actor and theatre director; b. 2 May 1925, Willesden, London; s. of Reginald D. Neville and Mabel L. Fry; m. Caroline Hooper 1948; two s. three d.; ed. Chiswick County Grammar School and Royal Acad. of Dramatic Art, London.

With Bristol Old Vic Co., Old Vic Co. London 53, played Othello, Iago, Hamlet, Aguecheek and Richard II; mem. Chichester Theatre Co. 62; created part of Alfie (*Alfie* by Bill Naughton), London 63; Dir. Nottingham Playhouse 63-68, Newcastle Playhouse 67; Hon. Prof. in Drama, Nottingham Univ. 67-; Drama Adviser to Howard and Wyndham Ltd.; in musical *Mr. & Mrs.* 68; series of television plays 68; presented four plays at Fortune Theatre, London with the Park Theatre Co.; appeared in *The Apple Cart*, Mermaid Theatre, London 70; went to Canada 73; staged *The Rivals*, Nat. Arts Theatre, Ottawa; Dir. opera *Don Giovanni*, Festival Canada, Ottawa; played Prospero (*The Tempest*), Judge Brack (*Hedda Gabler*), Sir George Croft (*Mrs. Warren's Profession*), in *Sherlock Holmes*, N.Y. 75; Artistic Dir. of Citadel Theatre, Edmonton, Alberta June 73-.

Leisure interests: watching football, listening to music (all kinds), thinking about gardening.

Films acted in include: *Mr. Topaz, Oscar Wilde, Billy Budd, A Study in Terror, Adventures of Gervard.*

Larry Dalzell Associates Ltd., Bond Street House, 14 Clifford Street, London, W.1., England.

Newbigin, Rt. Rev. Lesslie, C.B.E., M.A., D.D.; British missionary; b. 8 Dec. 1909, Newcastle upon Tyne; s. of Edward R. Newbigin and Annie E. Affleck; m. Helen S. Henderson 1936; one s. three d.; ed. Leighton Park School, Queens' Coll., Cambridge, and Westminster Coll., Cambridge.

Secretary, Student Christian Movement, Glasgow 31-33; ordained to Ministry, Church of Scotland 36; with Mission, Madras, S. India 36-39; Missionary in charge, Kancheepuram 39-46; Bishop in Madura, Church of South India 47-59; Gen. Sec. Int. Missionary Council 59-61; Assoc. Gen. Sec. World Council of Churches, and Dir. Div. of World Mission and Evangelism 61-65; Bishop in Madras 65-74; Lecturer, Selly Oak Colls. 74-.

Leisure interests: music, climbing mountains.

Publs. *Christian Freedom in the Modern World* 37, *The Reunion of the Church* 48, *South India Diary* 51, *The Household of God* 53, *Sin and Salvation* 55, *One Body, One Gospel, One World* 58, *A Faith for this One World?* 61, *Trinitarian Faith for Today's Mission* 64, *Honest Religion for Secular Man* 66, *The Finality of Christ* 69.

Central Office, Selly Oak Colleges, Birmingham, B29 6LE, England.

Newby, Percy Howard, C.B.E.; British author; b. 25 June 1918, Crowborough, Sussex; s. of Percy Newby and Isabel Clutsam (Bryant); m. Joan Thompson 1945; two d.; ed. St. Paul's Coll., Cheltenham.

Served in Army (R.A.M.C.) 39-42; Lecturer in English Literature Fouad I Univ., Cairo 42-46; mem. B.B.C. Talks Dept. 49-58, Controller Third Programme 58-70, Controller Radio Three 70-71; Dir. of Programmes, Radio 71-75, Man. Dir. Radio 76-; Atlantic Award for Literature 46; Somerset Maugham Prize 48, *Yorkshire Post* Fiction Award 68, Booker Prize for *Something to Answer For* 69.

Leisure interests: music and gardening.

Publs. *A Journey to the Interior* 45, *Agents and Witnesses* 47, *Mariner Dances* 48, *The Snow Pasture* 49, *Maria Edgeworth* 50, *The Young May Moon* 50, *The Novel 45-50, A Season in England* 51, *The Retreat* 53, *The*

Picnic at Sakkara 55, *Revolution and Roses* 57, *Ten Miles from Anywhere* 58, *A Guest and his Going* 59, *The Barbary Light* 62, *One of the Founders* 65, *Something to Answer For* 68, *A Lot to Ask* 73.
Upton House, Cokes Lane, Chalfont St. Giles, Bucks., England.
Telephone: Little Chalfont 2079.

Newell, Homer Edward; American physicist; b. 11 March 1915, Holyoke, Mass.; *s.* of Homer E. Newell and Nan Davis; *m.* Janice M. Hurd 1938; one *s.* three *d.*; ed. Harvard Univ. and Univ. of Wisconsin.
Graduate Asst. Mathematics Dept. Univ. of Wisconsin 37-40; Instructor, Asst. Prof., Mathematics Dept. Univ. of Maryland 40-44; Theoretical Physicist, Naval Research Laboratory, Head, Rocket-Sonde Research Branch; Act. Supt. Atmosphere and Astrophysics Div., Naval Research Lab. 55-58; also Science Program Co-ordinator for Project Vanguard; Asst. Dir. for Space Sciences, Nat. Aeronautics and Space Admin. (N.A.S.A.) 58-60, Deputy Dir. Space Flight Programs 60-61, Dir. Office of Space Sciences 61-63, Assoc. Admin. for Space Science and Applications 63-67, Assoc. Admin. N.A.S.A. 67-73, retd.; mem. American Geophysical Union (Fellow, Pres. 70-72), American Asscn. for the Advancement of Science (Fellow), American Inst. of Aeronautics and Astronautics (Fellow), Research Soc. of America; Hon. D.Sc. (Central Methodist College); awarded American Rocket Soc. Pendray Award 58, American Astronautical Asscn. Space Flight Award 60, AMVETS Civil Servant of the Year Award 61, President's Award for Distinguished Fed. Civil Service for 65; Career Service Award of Nat. Civil Service League 65; N.A.S.A. Distinguished Service 67, Cleveland Abbe Award, American Meteorological Soc. 71.
Leisure interests: swimming, hiking, the piano, reading.
Publs. *High Altitude Rocket Research* 53, *Vector Analysis* 55, *Space Book for Young People* 58, *Guide to Rockets, Missiles and Satellites* 58, *Sounding Rockets* 59, *Window in the Sky* 59, *Express to the Stars* 61.
3704 33rd Place, N.W., Washington, D.C. 20008, U.S.A.
Telephone: 202-966-3234.

Newhouse, Samuel Irving; American newspaperman; b. 1896.
President numerous newspapers, including *Long Island Daily Press, Syracuse Herald-Journal, Syracuse Post-Standard, Harrisburg Patriot-News, Portland-Oregonian, St. Louis Globe-Democrat, Birmingham News, Times Picayune, States-Item.*
Star Ledger Plaza, Newark, N.J. 07101, U.S.A.

Newman, Maxwell Herman Alexander, M.A., F.R.S.; British mathematician; b. 7 Feb. 1897, London; *s.* of Herman Newman and Sarah Pike; *m.* 1st Lyn Irvine 1934 (died 1973), two *s.*; *m.* 2nd Margaret Penrose 1974; ed. City of London School, St. John's Coll., Cambridge, and Princeton Univ.
University Lecturer, Cambridge Univ. 27-45; Fellow, St. John's Coll., Cambridge 24-25; Prof. of Mathematics, Univ. of Manchester 45-64, now Emer. Prof.; Visiting Prof. Australian Nat. Univ., Univ. of Wisconsin, Univ. of Utah, Rice Univ., Univ. of Warwick, Michigan State Univ. 64-69, George A. Miller Visiting Prof. Univ. of Illinois 69-70; Pres. London Math. Soc. 50-52, Math. Asscn. 60; Sylvester Medal, Royal Soc. 58; De Morgan Medal, London Math. Soc. 62; Hon. D.Sc. (Hull).
Publs. *Topology of Plane Sets of Points* 39; numerous papers on mathematics in scientific journals.
Cross Farm, Comberton, Cambridge, England.
Telephone: Comberton 2276.

Newman, Melvin Spencer, PH.D.; American professor of organic chemistry; *s.* of Jacob K. Newman and Mae Polack; *m.* Beatrice Crystal 1933; two *s.* two *d.*; ed. Yale Univ.
Instructor, Ohio State Univ. 36-40, Asst. Prof. of Organic Chem. 40-44, Prof. 44-65, Regents Prof. 65-; mem. Nat. Acad. of Sciences; American Chem. Soc. Award for Creative Work in Synthetic Organic Chem. 61; Morley Medal, Cleveland Section American Chem. Soc. 69; Wilbur Cross Medal, Yale Univ. 70.
Leisure interests: music, golf, billiards and pool, gardening.
Publs. Editor: *Steric Effects in Organic Chemistry* 56, *An Advanced Organic Laboratory Course* 72; over 300 publs. in scientific journals.
Chemistry Department, Ohio State University, Columbus, Ohio 43210; Home: 2239 Onandaga Drive, Columbus, Ohio 43221, U.S.A.
Telephone: 614-422-2420 (Office); 614-488-6441 (Home).

Newman, Paul; American actor; b. 26 Jan. 1925; *m.* Joanne Woodward (*q.v.*) 1958; ed. Kenyon Coll. and Yale Univ. School of Drama.
Military service 43-46; Best Actor, Acad. of Motion Pictures, Arts and Sciences 59, 62, 64.
Stage appearances include: *Picnic* 53-54, *Desperate Hours* 55, *Sweet Bird of Youth* 59, *Baby Want a Kiss* 64.
Films include: *The Rack* 55, *Somebody Up There Likes Me* 56, *Cat on a Hot Tin Roof* 58, *Rally Round the Flag, Boys* 58, *The Young Philadelphians* 58, *From the Terrace* 60, *Exodus* 60, *The Hustler* 62, *Hud* 63, *The Prize* 63, *The Outrage* 64, *What a Way to Go* 64, *Lady L* 65, *Torn Curtain* 66, *Hombre* 67, *Cool Hand Luke* 67, *The Secret War of Harry Frigg* 68, *Butch Cassidy and the Sundance Kid* 69, *WUSA* 70, *Pocket Money* 72, *The Life and Times of Judge Roy Bean* 73, *The Mackintosh Man* 73, *The Sting* 73, *The Towering Inferno* 74, *The Drowning Pool* 75; Dir. *Rachel, Rachel* 68, *The Effect of Gamma Rays on Man in the Moon Marigolds* 73; actor and Dir. *Never Give an Inch* 71.
c/o Charles H. Renthal, 1501 Broadway, New York City 36, N.Y., U.S.A.

Newmark, Nathan Mortimore, B.S., M.S., PH.D.; American consulting engineer and university professor; b. 22 Sept. 1910, Plainfield, N.J.; *s.* of Abraham S. Newmark and Mollie Nathanson Newmark; *m.* Anne M. Cohen 1932; one *s.* two *d.*; ed. Rutgers Univ. and Univ. of Illinois.
Univ. of Illinois 34-, Research Asst. 34-36, Research Assoc. 36-37, Research Asst. Prof. 37-43, Research Prof. 43-56, Head of Dept. and Prof. of Civil Engineering 56-73; Prof. Civil Engineering and Center for Advanced Study 73-; mem. Nat. Acad. of Sciences, Nat. Acad. of Engineering; Fellow, American Acad. of Arts and Sciences; Washington Award; von Karman Medal, Norman Medal, Howard Award, Moisseff Award, Croes Medal, American Soc. of Civil Engineers; Bendix Award, American Soc. of Civil Engineers; Bendix Award, American Soc. for Engineering Educ.; Nat. Medal of Science 68; Outstanding Civilian Service Medal, Dept. of the Army 71; Hon. Sc.D. (Rutgers Univ.) 55; Dr. h.c. (Univ. of Liège) 67; LL.D. (Univ. of Notre Dame) 69.
Leisure interest: photography.
Publs. *Fundamentals of Earthquake Engineering* 71, and over 180 papers in structural analysis and design, applied mechanics, numerical methods of stress analysis, effects of impact, shock, vibration, wave action, blast and earthquakes on structures.
Department of Civil Engineering, University of Illinois, Urbana, Ill. 61801; Home: 1705 South Pleasant Street, Urbana, Ill. 61801, U.S.A.
Telephone: 217-333-3813 (Office); 217-344-4795 (Home).

Newsom, David Dunlop, A.B., M.S.; American diplomatist; b. 6 Jan. 1918; ed. Richmond Union High School and Calif. and Columbia Univs.
Reporter, *San Francisco Chronicle* 40-41; U.S. Navy 41-45; Newspaper publisher 45-47; Information Officer, U.S. Embassy, Karachi 47-50; Consul, Oslo 50-51; Public Affairs Officer, U.S. Embassy, Baghdad 51-55;

Dept. of State 55-59; U.S. Nat. War Coll. 59-60; First Sec. U.S. Embassy, London 60-62; Dir. Office of Northern African Affairs, State Dept. 62-65; Amb. to Libya 65-69; Asst. Sec. of State for African Affairs 69-73; Amb. to Indonesia Jan. 74-; Dept. of State Meritorious Service Award 58, Nat. Civil Service League Career Service Award 71, Rockefeller Public Service Award 73.

American Embassy, 5 Jalan Merdeka Selatan, Jakarta, Indonesia.

Newton, Ivor, C.B.E., F.R.C.M.; British pianoforte accompanist; b. 15 Dec. 1892, London; s. of William and Gertrude Newton.

Accompanist with Kirsten Flagstad, John McCormack, Melba, Tetrazzini, Chaliapine, Gigli, Tito Schipa, Jussi Björling, Lotte Lehmann, Elisabeth Schumann, Maria Callas, Tito Gobbi, Clara Butt, Ysaye, Piatigorsky, Pablo Casals, Yehudi Menuhin, Victoria de los Angeles; has toured extensively in Europe, U.S.A., Canada, Africa, Australia and New Zealand.

Publ. *At the Piano—Ivor Newton* (autobiog.) 66.

Kirsten House, 24 Kinnerton Street, London, S.W.1, England.

Telephone: 01-235-2882.

Newton, Sir (Leslie) Gordon, Kt., B.A. (CANTAB.); British journalist; b. 16 Sept. 1907; ed. Blundell's School and Sidney Sussex Coll., Cambridge.

Entered journalism 35; Army Service 39-45; joined *Financial Times* 46, Features Editor, Leader Writer and Columnist 46-50, Editor 50-72; Chair. J. H. Vavasseur & Co. 73-74; Chair. Lion Int. 73, Deputy Chair. 74-; Chair. London Broadcasting Co.; Dir. Pearson-Longman 72-76, Industrial and Trade Fairs Holdings 68-, Throgmorton Publs. 68-, Trust Houses Forte 73-; Int. Publ. Corpn. Hannen Swaffer Award as Journalist of the Year 66-67.

Little Basing, Vicarage Walk, Bray-on-Thames, Berks., England.

Ney, Edward, PH.D.; American professor of physics; b. 28 Oct. 1910, Minneapolis, Minn.; s. of Otto F. and Jessamine Purdy Ney; m. June V. Felsing 1942; three s. one d.; ed. Univ. of Minnesota and Virginia.

Research Asst., Univ. of Va. 40-42, Research Assoc. 43-46, Asst. Prof. 46-47; Consultant Naval Research Lab. 43-44; Asst. Prof. Univ. of Minn. 47-50, Assoc. Prof. 50-55, Prof. of Astrophysics 55-, Regents' Prof. 74; mem. Nat. Acad. of Sciences.

Publs. over 100 articles in professional journals.

School of Physics and Astronomy, University of Minnesota, Minneapolis, Minn. 55455, U.S.A.

Telephone: 612-373-4687.

Ney, Edward Noonan, B.A.; American advertising executive; b. 26 May 1925, St. Paul, Minn.; s. of John and Marie Noonan Ney; m. 2nd Judith Ney 1974; one s. two d. (by previous marriage); ed. Amherst Coll.

Account exec., Young and Rubicam Inc. 51, Pres. Int. Div. 68-70; Pres., Chief Exec. Officer, Young and Rubicam Int. Inc. 70-; Vice-Pres. Nat. Games Inc. 55-56; Dir. Amer. Asscn. of Advertising Agencies 73-, The Advertising Council 73-, U.S. Council of Int. Chamber of Commerce 72-, Radio Free Europe 75-; Trustee, Hampshire Coll. 70-, Cttee. for Econ. Devt. 73-, Nat. Urban League 74-.

Leisure interests: tennis, paddle tennis, reading.

285 Madison Avenue, New York 17, N.Y., U.S.A.

Telephone: (212) 953-2022 (Office).

Neyman, Jerzy, PH.D.; American university professor; b. 16 April 1894, Bendery, Russia; s. of Polish parents; m. Olga Solodovnikov 1920; one s.; ed. Univs. of Kharkov, Russia and Warsaw, Poland.

Lecturer, Inst. of Technology, Kharkov 17; Statistician, Agricultural Inst., Bydgoszcz, Poland 21; Head, Bio-metric Laboratory, Nencki Inst., Warsaw; Docent,

Univ. of Warsaw and Univ. of Cracow 28-34; Reader in statistics, Univ. Coll., London 34-38; Prof. of Mathe-matics, Univ. of Calif. (Berkeley) 38-55, Dir. Statistical Laboratory 38-, Chair. Dept. of Statistics 55-57; Messenger Lecturer, Cornell Univ. 71; Chair. Editorial Board, the Copernican Volume, Nat. Acad. of Sciences; mem. Nat. Acad. of Sciences, Royal Swedish Acad. of Sciences, Nat. Acad. of Science of Poland; Pres. Int. Asscn. for Statistics in Physical Sciences 69-71; Hon. Pres. Int. Statistical Inst. 72; Hon. mem. London Mathematical Soc. 74; Guy Medal in Gold, Royal Statistical Soc. (U.K.) 66-67; Nat. Medal of Science 69, Alfred Jurzykowski Foundation Award in Science 71; Hon. D.Sc. (Univ. of Chicago 59, Univ. of Warsaw 74, Indian Statistical Inst. 74); Hon. LL.D. (Univ. of Calif., Berkeley 63); Hon. Ph.D. (Univ. of Stockholm 64).

Leisure interests: literature, music.

Publs. Numerous papers in scientific journals; *Nicholas Coperniais (Mikołaj Kopernik): An intellectual revolu-tionary* 74, *The Heritage of Copernicus: Theories Pleasing to the Mind* (editor).

Statistical Laboratory, Department of Statistics, University of California, Berkeley, Calif. 94720; Home: 212 Amherst Avenue, Berkeley, Calif. 94708, U.S.A.

Telephone: 415-642-3357 (Office); 415-525-1801 (Home).

Neyman, Leonid Robertovich, D.SC. (ENG.); Soviet electrical engineer; b. 1902; ed. Leningrad Poly-technical Inst.

Lecturer 30-52, Head of Chair., Leningrad Poly-technical Inst. 52-; Head of Section, Leningrad Electrophysical Inst. 31-35, 40-; Senior Research Assoc. 46-53, Head of Lab., Energy Inst., U.S.S.R. Acad. of Sciences 53-; corresp. mem. U.S.S.R. Acad. of Sciences 53-70, Academician 70-.

Polytechnical Institute, 29 Politkhnicheskaya ulitsa, Leningrad, U.S.S.R.

Nezeritis, Andreas; Greek composer; b. 1897, Patras; m. Irena Skoufou 1939; ed. Conservatoire of Athens, and studies under Denis Lavrangas.

President League of Greek Composers 57; awarded First Prize, Acad. of Athens 52; Gold Cross, Order of King George 65; Silver Medal and Prize, Acad. of Athens 71; works performed in Greece, Germany, Netherlands, France, Italy, U.S.S.R., Czechoslovakia and U.S.A.; Fellow, Int. Inst. of Arts and Letters 58-.

Leisure interest: gardening.

Works include: two operas *The King Aniliagos* and *Hero and Leander*; three symphonies, No. 1 in G minor, No. 2 in C minor and No. 3 in D minor; Concerto for Violin and Orchestra; Concerto for Violoncello and Orchestra; Concertino for Piano and Orchestra; Five Psalms of David for four Soloists, Mixed Chorus and Full Orchestra; Concerto for String Orchestra; two Greek Rhapsodies; five Symphonic dances; Greek Dance Suite on Cypriot Themes; also ballet and vocal music and piano music.

54 Eptanissou Street, Athens (807), Greece.

Telephone: 873-239.

Nezu, Kaichiro; Japanese business executive; b. 29 Sept. 1913; ed. Economics Department, Tokyo Univ.

Director, Fukotu Life Insurance Co. 40-, Tokyo Gas Co. Ltd., Yokohama Warehouse Co. 40-; Pres. Tobu Railway Co. 41-; Vice-Pres. All-Japan Private Railways Asscn.; Dir. Fed. of Econ. Orgs. 41-; Councillor, Japan Central Cultural League, Chamber of Commerce and Industry, Tokyo.

Tobu Railway Co. Ltd., 2, 1-chome, Oshiage, Sumida-ku, Tokyo, Japan.

Ngapo Ngawang-jigme; Tibetan leader; b. 1909, Tibet.

Leader Tibetan Army resisting Chinese Invasion 50; First Deputy Commdr. Tibet Mil. Region, People's

Liberation Army 52; Vice-Chair. Preparatory Cttee. for Tibet Autonomous Region 59-65; Vice-Chair. Standing Cttee., Nat. People's Congress 65; Chair. Tibet Autonomous Region People's Govt. 65-68; Vice-Chair. Tibet Revolutionary Cttee. 68.

Ngei, Paul, B.SC.(ECON.); Kenyan politician; b. 1923, Machakos; grandson of Akamba Paramount Chief Masaku; ed. Makerere Coll., Kampala.
Army service, Second World War; founded *Wasya wa Mukamba* newspaper and Swahili magazine *Uhuru wa Mwafrika* 50; Deputy Gen. Sec. Kenya African Union 51-52; imprisoned and under restriction for connection with Mau-Mau 53-61; Pres. Kenya African Farmers' and Traders' Union 61; founded African Peoples' Party 62; Chair. Maize Marketing Board 63-64; Minister for Co-operatives and Marketing 64-65; Minister for Housing and Social Services 65-66; Minister for Housing 66-74, of Local Govt. 74-75, unseated by High Court ruling; M.P. for Kagunda Jan. 76-; Minister of Co-operative Devt. March 76-; Man. Dir. Akamba Carving and Industrial Co.
Ministry of Co-operative Development, Nairobi, Kenya.

Nghaky, Nzo Ekhan (*see* Ekangaki, Nzo).

Ngo Dinh Nhu, Madame; Vietnamese politician.
Widow of Ngo Dinh Nhu, brother and Adviser to the late President Ngo Dinh Diem; arrested by Viet Minh, later escaped 46; organized first popular demonstration in support of Govt. of Prime Minister Ngo Dinh Diem 54; Official Hostess for Pres. Ngo Dinh Diem 55-63; fmr. Dep., Nat. Ass., author of "Family Bill"; founder of programme of paramilitary service for women Oct. 61; Founder-Pres. Vietnamese Women's Solidarity Movement.

Ngom Jua, Augustine; Cameroonian politician; b. Nov. 1924; ed. St. Anthony's School, Njinikom, Elementary Training Centre, Kake-Kumba, and Govt. Teacher Training Coll., Kumba.
Teacher, Bafut Catholic School 40-42; Headmaster, Muyuka Catholic School 46-47, Catholic School, Dikome 49-50, Catholic School, Njinikom 51; Sec. Kom Improvement Asscn. 52; Chair. Regional Consultative Cttee., Enugu 53; mem. House of Assembly 54-57; Minister of Educ. and Social Services 59; Sec. of State for Finance and Deputy Minister of Health 61-62; Prime Minister of West Cameroon May 65-67; Grand Order of Valour (Cameroon), Knight Commdr. Humane Order of African Redemption (Liberia), Great Cross Second Class of the Order of Merit of the Fed. Repub. of Germany, Order of Commdr. (Tunisia), Grand Officer of the Nat. Order of Senegal.
Buea, United Republic of Cameroon.

Ngonda, Putteho Muketoi, B.SC.ECON.; Zambian diplomatist; b. 16 Aug. 1936, Mongu; ed. Mongu and Mundi Secondary Schools, Univ. Coll. of Rhodesia and Nyasaland, Salisbury.
District Officer 63-64; Second Sec. Zambia Perm. Mission to U.S.A. 64-65; First Sec. Zambian Embassy, Washington 67-68; Asst. Sec. (Political), Ministry of Foreign Affairs 68-70, Under-Sec. 70-72; Amb. to Ethiopia 72-74; High Commr. in U.K. 74-75; Perm. Sec., Ministry of Foreign Affairs 75-.
Ministry of Foreign Affairs, P.O. Box RW69, Lusaka, Zambia.

Ngouabi, Major Marien; Congolese army officer and politician; b. 31 Dec. 1938, Ombele; *m.*; four *s.* three *d.*; ed. Leclers Military School, Brazzaville, Military Training School, Strasbourg, France, and Joint Services Military School, Coëtquidam (Saint-Cyr), France.
Returned to Congo from St. Cyr 62, successively Adjutant, Infantry Co. Commdr., Capt.; then attached to Bureau of Studies of GHQ; led insurrectional movement of Nat. Popular Army, Civil Defence and Nat.

Progressist Forces July 68; Pres. of Nat. Council of Revolution and Head of State 68-; Pres. Cen. Cttee. of Congolese Workers' Party, Pres. of Repub., Pres. of State Council 69-; Pres. UDEAC 76-.
Leisure interests: football, table tennis, swimming.
Publ. *Soldier of the People.*
Présidence du Conseil d'Etat, Brazzaville, People's Republic of the Congo.

Ngoyi, Lilian; African politician; b. 24 Sept. 1911, Transvaal; *m.* John Ngoyi 1936 (died 1946); one *s.* two *d.*; ed. in Transvaal.
Machinist in clothing factory; mem. African Nat. Congress 52-, Nat. Exec. 54, Head of A.N.C. Women's League; mem. Nat. Exec. Fed. of South African Women 54-, Nat. Pres. 56-; on trial for treason 56-61 (acquitted 61); detained without trial for five months 60; banned from attending gatherings 62-; detained 71 days without trial 63; confined to Orlando for five years 63; arrested 64, banned and confined in Johannesburg for further five years 68-Oct. 72.
Leisure interest: was tennis.
9870B Nkungu Street, Orlando West 2, P.O. Phirima, South Africa.

Ngugi, Wa Thiong'o (James); Kenyan novelist; b. 1938, Limuru; ed. Makerere Univ. Coll., Uganda and Leeds Univ., England.
Acting Head, Dept. of Literature, Univ. of Nairobi.
Publs. *The Black Hermit* (play) 62, *Weep Not Child* 64, *The River Between* 65, *A Grain of Wheat* 67, *Homecoming* 72, *Secret Lives* 74.
c/o Heinemann Educational Books (African Writers Series), 48 Charles Street, London, W1X 8AH, England.

Nguyen Cao Ky, Air Vice-Marshal; Vietnamese air force officer and politician; b. 8 Sept. 1930; ed. High School, Hanoi, and Officers' Training School, Hanoi.
Flight Training, Marrakech until 54; commanded Transport Squadron 54, later commander Tan Son Nhât Air Force Base, Republic of Viet-Nam; spent six months at U.S. Air Command and Staff Coll., Maxwell Field, Alabama, U.S.A.; later, Commdr. Air Force, Repub. of Viet-Nam; Prime Minister 65-67; Vice-Pres. Repub. of Viet-Nam 67-71; went to U.S.A. April 75.

Nguyen Huu Tho; Vietnamese politician; b. 10 July 1910, Cholon.
Participated in liberation war against French colonialists; organized mass demonstration, Saigon-Cholon area March 50 against U.S. interference; imprisoned 50-52; opposed 1954 Geneva agreements on Indo-China; founded Saigon-Cholon Peace Movement; subsequently arrested, escaped 61; Chair. Nat. Liberation Front Central Cttee. 62-; Chair. Presidium of N.L.F. Central Cttee. 64-; Chair. Consultative Council, Provisional Revolutionary Govt. of Republic of South Viet-Nam June 70- (in Saigon 75-).
Provisional Revolutionary Government, Saigon, South Viet-Nam.

Nguyen Khanh, Lieut.-Gen.; Vietnamese army officer and politician; b. 1927; ed. Viet-Nam Military Acad., Dalat, Army Staff Schools, Hanoi and France, and U.S. Command and General Staff Coll., Fort Leavenworth.
French Colonial Army 54, Vietnamese Army 54-; Chief of Staff to Gen. Duong Van Minh 55; took part in coup against Pres. Diem Nov. 63; Prime Minister Jan.-Oct. 64; Chair. Armed Forces Council Dec. 64-Feb. 65; led coup Jan. 65; Roving Amb. 65.

Nguyen Luong Bang; Vietnamese politician; b. 1904, Hai Duong.
Frequently arrested for political activities; sentenced to twenty years imprisonment 31, escaped 32, recaptured 33, escaped again 43; mem. Central Cttee. Working People's Party, Democratic Repub. of Viet-Nam 45; fmr. Dir. of State Bank and Govt. Gen. Inspector; fmr. Head Party Control Cttee.; Amb. to

U.S.S.R. 52-57; Vice-Pres. of Democratic Repub. of Viet-Nam Sept. 69-.
Office of the Vice-President, Hanoi, Democratic Republic of Viet-Nam.

Nguyen Phu Duc, LL.D., DR.JUR.; Vietnamese diplomatist; b. 13 Nov. 1924, Son-Tay; m.; two s.; ed. Univ. of Hanoi, Harvard Law School.
Permanent Observer to UN 64-65; Special Asst. for Foreign Affairs to Pres. Thieu 68; Envoy to Thailand, Khmer Repub., Laos, Indonesia, U.S.A. 72; Minister of Foreign Affairs 73; Amb. to Belgium 74-75; has attended confs. on Viet-Nam 66, 67, 68, 69, 73, active in negotiations leading to Paris Conf. 68, and to Paris Agreement 73.

Nguyen Thi Binh, Madame; Vietnamese politician; b. 1927; ed. Saigon.
Student political leader in Saigon; organized (with Nguyen Huu Tho) first anti-American demonstration 50; imprisoned by French authorities 51-54; Vice-Pres. South Vietnamese Cttee. for Solidarity with the American People; Council mem. Union of Women for the Liberation of South Viet-Nam; mem. Cen. Cttee. Nat. Liberation Front (NLF); appointed NLF spokesman to four-party peace talks, Paris Nov. 68; Minister for Foreign Affairs, Provisional Revolutionary Govt. of South Viet-Nam June 69- (in Saigon 75-).
Ministry of Foreign Affairs, Saigon, South Viet-Nam.

Nguyen Van Loc, LL.M.; Vietnamese lawyer, writer and politician; b. 24 Aug. 1922, Vinh-Long; s. of Nguyen Van Hanh and Tran Thi Ngo; m. Nguyen Thi Mong Hoa; two s.; ed. Univs. of Montpellier and Paris.
Lawyer, Saigon Court of Appeal 55; Lecturer, Nat. Inst. of Admin. 65; Chair. People and Armed Forces Council 66, People and Armed Forces Council Political Cttee. 66; Vice-Chair. Constituent Assembly Electoral Law Preparation Cttee.; mem. Barristers Fraternity 61-67; Del. in charge of campaigning, Cttee. for Aid to War Victims (Viet-Nam Red Cross); Counsellor, Viet-Nam Asscn. for Protection of Human and People's Rights; Sec.-Gen., Inter-Schools Asscn. 65-67; Prime Minister of Repub. of Viet-Nam Nov. 67-May 68; Prof. Univ. of Hoa Hao 70; Founder and Rector, Cao-Dai Univ. 71-75.
Leisure interests: fishing, water skiing.
Publs. *Uprising* (novel) 46, *Rank* 48, *New Recruits* (novel) 48, *Poems on Liberation* (collection) 49, *Recollections of the Green Years* 60, *Free Tribune* (collection) 66, *Poisonous Water* (novel) 71.
162 Gia Long, Saigon, South Viet-Nam.

Nguyen Van Thieu, Lt.-Gen.; Vietnamese army officer and politician; b. 5 April 1923, Ninh Tvuan; m. Nguyen Thi Mai Anh 1951; one s. one d.; ed. Catholic Pellerin School, Hué, and Nat. Military Acad., Hué.
Viet-Nam Nat. Army 48-54; Republic of Viet-Nam Army 54-; Commdr. First Infantry Div. 60-62, Fifth Infantry Div. 62-64; Deputy Premier and Minister of Defence 64-65; Chair. Nat. Leadership Cttee. and Head of State 65-67; Pres. of Repub. of Viet-Nam 67-April 75; f. Dan Chu Party 73; went to Taiwan April 75.

Nguyen Van Vy, Lt.-Gen.; Vietnamese politician; b. 16 Jan, 1916, Hanoi; ed. Univ., Tong Officers' School and School of Command and Staff, Paris.
Chief Military Cabinet of Chief of State 52; Commdr. Coastal Interzone 54; Acting Chief, Gen. Staff, Vietnamese Army Oct. 54; Inspector Gen. Dec. 54; Asst. Chief of Staff for Training, R.V.N.A.F. Jan. 64; Asst. to C.-in-C. Nov. 64; Commdt. Quang Trung Training Centre Feb. 65; Commdr. Training Command, R.V.N.A.F. June 65; C.-of-S. Joint Gen. Staff R.V.N.A.F. 66-67; Minister of Defence 68-Aug. 72; Grand Officer Nat. Order of Viet-Nam; Army and Air Force Distinguished Service Orders; Officier Légion d'Honneur.
285 Phan Thanh Gian Street, Saigon, South Viet-Nam.
Telephone: 23140.

Nguza Karl-i-Bond; Zairian diplomatist and politician; b. 1938, Musumba; ed. Catholic schools, Elisabethville (now Lubumbashi), and Univ. of Louvain, Belgium.
Announcer, Radio Lubumbashi 57-60, Radio Kinshasa 64; mem. of Prime Minister Tshombe's private cabinet 64; Counsellor, Congolese Embassy, Brussels 64-66; Govt. Commr. Union Minière 65-66; Counsellor, Congolese Del. to UN, New York 66-68; Deputy Perm. Rep. to UN 68; Minister, later Amb., and Perm. Rep. at UN Office, Geneva 70-72; State Commr. for Foreign Affairs 72-74, 75-, mem. Political Bureau 72-.
Office of the State Commissioner for Foreign Affairs, Kinshasa, Zaire.

Nhu, Madame (*see* Ngo Dinh Nhu, Madame).

Ni Chih-fu; Chinese engineer.
Started work at the age of twelve in Japanese-owned factory; invented "Ni Chih-fu drill-head" 53; Engineer Peking No. 1 Machine Tool Plant 64; mem. 9th Cen. Cttee. of CCP 69; active in Labour Union activities 70-; Alt. mem. Politburo, 10th Cen. Cttee. of CCP 73.
People's Republic of China.

Niarchos, Stavros Spyros, LL.D.; Greek shipowner; b. 3 July 1909; m. 1st Eugenie Livanos 1947 (died 1970), four c.; m. 2nd Tina Livanos 1970 (died 1974); ed. Athens Univ.
Joined family grain and shipping business; started independent shipping concern 39; served in R.H.N.V.R. 41-45; Hon. Naval Attaché, Greek Legation, Washington 44-48; returned to shipping business; pioneered supertankers; head of Niarchos group of companies; Grand Cross, Order of the Phoenix, Commdr. of Order of George I, Commdr. Order of St. George and St. Constantine.
c/o Niarchos (London) Ltd., 41-43 Park Street, London, W.1, England.

Niazi, Maulana Kausar; Pakistani journalist and politician; b. 21 April 1934; ed. Punjab Univ.
Former editor *Tasneem* (daily), Lahore and later *Kausar*, Lahore; founded *Shahab* (weekly) 60; Information Sec. Pakistan People's Party 70-; political imprisonment 70; elected mem. Nat. Ass. while in prison 70; Adviser to Pres. for Information and Religious Affairs 71-; Minister of Information and Broadcasting, Auqaf and Haj 72-74, of Religious Affairs Oct. 74-.
Publs. several books on religious, historical and literary topics.
Ministry of Religious Affairs, Islamabad, Pakistan.

Nicholas, Sir Herbert Richard (Harry), Kt., O.B.E.; British political party executive; b. 13 March 1905, Bristol; s. of Richard Henry and Rosina Nicholas; m. Rosina Grace Brown 1932; ed. elementary school, Avonmouth, Bristol, and evening classes and correspondence courses.
Clerk, Port of Bristol Authority 19-36; District Officer, Transport and General Workers' Union, Gloucester 36-38, Regional Officer, Bristol 38-40, Nat. Officer, London (Commercial Road Transport Group) 40-42; Chemical Section, Transport & Gen. Workers' Union 42-44, Metal and Engineering Group 44-56, Asst. Gen. Sec. 56-68 (Acting Gen. Sec. Oct. 64-July 66); mem. Nat. Exec. Cttee., Labour Party 56-64, 67-68; mem. T.U.C. Gen. Council 64-66; Treasurer, Labour Party 60-64; Gen. Sec. Labour Party 68-72.
Leisure interests: rugby football, fishing, reading, gardening.
33 Madeira Road, Streatham, London, S.W.16, England.
Telephone: 01-769-7989.

Nichols, Beverley; British writer; s. of John and Pauline Nichols; ed. Marlborough and Balliol Coll., Oxford.
Editor *The American Sketch*, New York 28-29; contrib. feature *Sunday Chronicle*.

Publs. *Prelude, Patchwork, Self, Crazy Pavements, Are They the Same at Home? Twenty-Five, The Star-Spangled Manner, Women and Children Last, Evensong, Down the Garden Path, For Adults Only, A Thatched Roof, Failures, Cry Havoc!, A Village in a Valley, The Fool Hath Said . . . , No Place Like Home, News of England, Revue, Green Grows the City, Men do not Weep, Verdict in India, The Tree That Sat Down, The Stream That Stood Still* 47, *All I Could Never Be* 49, *Uncle Samson* 50, *The Magic Mountain* 50, *Merry Hell* 51, *A Pilgrim's Progress* 52, *Laughter on the Stairs* 53, *No Man's Street* 54, *The Moonflower* 55, *Sunlight on the Lawn* 56, *Death to Slow Music* 57, *The Rich Die Hard, The Sweet and Twenties* 58, *Murder by Request* 60, *Cats A.B.C., X.Y.Z., A Case of Human Bondage* 66, *The Art of Flower Arrangement* 67, *Garden Open Tomorrow* 69, *The Wickedest Witch in the World* 71, *Father Figure* (autobiog.) 72, *Down the Kitchen Sink* 74; plays: *The Stag, Cochran's 1930 Revue, Avalanche, Evensong* (with Edward Knoblock), *When the Crash Comes, Dr. Mesmer, Floodlight, Song on the Wind* (operetta), *Shadow of the Vine, The Sun in My Eyes* 69, *Lady's Guide.*
Leisure interests: gardening, music.
Sudbrook Cottage, Ham Common, Surrey, England.

Nichols, Mike; American entertainer, stage and film director; b. Michael Igor Peschkowsky 6 Nov. 1931, Berlin, Germany (family name changed 1939); *m.* twice; one *d.*; ed. private schools and Univ. of Chicago. Started Playwrights Theatre Club, Chicago which became the Compass Players and later Second City; formed improvised nightclub double-act with Elaine May, touring for two years and recording television programmes and record albums; appeared in *An Evening with Mike Nichols and Elaine May* New York 61-62; acted in Shaw's *St. Joan* and directed *The Importance of being Earnest*, Vancouver; directed shows *Barefoot in the Park* New York 63, *The Knack* 64, *Luv* 64, *The Odd Couple* 65, *The Apple Tree* 66, *The Little Foxes* 67, *Plaza Suite* 68; directed films *Who's Afraid of Virginia Woolf?* 66, *The Graduate* 67, *Catch-22* 69, *Carnal Knowledge* 71, *Prisoner of Second Avenue* 71, *Day of the Dolphin* 73, *The Fortune* 75; Antoinette Perry (Tony) awards for direction *Barefoot in the Park, Luv, The Odd Couple, Plaza Suite*; Oscar for *The Graduate*; Emmy award for television programme *Julie and Carol at Carnegie Hall*; Nat. Asscn. Theatre Owner's Achievement Award for direction for *Who's Afraid of Virginia Woolf?*
Leisure interest: Arabian horse breeding.
c/o Marvin Meyer, Rosenfeld, Meyer and Susman, 9601 Wilshire Boulevard, Beverly Hills, Calif. 90210, U.S.A.

Nichols, Thomas S.; American businessman; b. 8 May 1909, Cambridge, Md.; *s.* of John P. and Emma M. Nichols; *m.* Tatiana McKenna 1971; one *s.* one *d.*; ed. Univ. of Pennsylvania.
With E. I. du Pont de Nemours & Co. 26-37; Vice-Pres. and Dir. Prior Chemical Corpn. 37-48; Pres. Chair. and Dir. Mathieson Chemical Corpn., N.Y. 48-54, merged with Olin Industries Inc., forming Olin Corpn., Pres. 54-57, Chair. of Board 57-63, Chair. of Exec. Cttee. 63-74; Dir. of Olin, other companies and official of numerous educational and business orgs.
Leisure interests: hunting, fishing, golf.
Home: P.O. Box 253, Owings Mills, Maryland 21117; Office: 460 Park Avenue, New York City, N.Y. 10022, U.S.A.
Telephone: 301-833-3140 (Home).

Nicholson, Ben, O.M.; British artist; b. 10 April 1894, Denham; *s.* of Sir William Nicholson and Mabel Pryde; *m.* 1st Winifred Roberts (divorced), two *s.* one *d.*; *m.* 2nd Barbara Hepworth 1931 (dissolved), one *s.* two *d.*; *m.* 3rd Dr. Felicitas Vogler 1957; ed. Heddon Court, Cockfosters, Gresham School (one term), Slade School of Art (one term).

Works in Tate Gallery, Victoria and Albert Museum, Kettle's Yard, Univ. of Cambridge, Arts and British Council collections, galleries in Europe, U.S.A. Canada, Australia, S. America, Japan, etc.; retrospective exhibitions at Temple, Newsam, Leeds 44, Venice Biennale 54, Stedelijk Museum, Amsterdam 54, Musée d'Art Moderne, Paris 55, Palais des Beaux Arts, Brussels 55, Kunsthalle, Zürich 55, Tate Gallery, London 55, 56, 69, 70, São Paulo 57, Rio de Janeiro 58, Buenos Aires 58, Kunsthaus, Berne 59, Marlborough Gallery, London 67, 71, Galerie Beyeler, Basle 68; First Prize 39th Carnegie Int. Exhbn. 52, Ulissi Prize XXVII Venice Biennale 54, Gov. of Tokyo Award, 3rd Int. Exhbn., Tokyo 55, Grand Prix, 4th Int. Exhbn., Lugano 56, U.S.A. Guggenheim Int. Award 56, Int. Prize for painting, IVth Bienal, São Paulo, Brazil 57, Rembrandt Prize, Goethe Foundation 74.
Publs. *Lund Humphries* (Monograph Ben Nicholson), *Paintings, Reliefs and Drawings,* Vol. 1, 48, Vol. 2, 56 (introduction by Sir Herbert Read); *Monograph BN— The meaning of his art* (introduction by Dr. J. P. Hodin) 57; *Monograph BN* (introduction by Sir John Summerson) 48, *Monograph BN* (introduction by David Baxandall) 62, *Monograph BN* (introduction by Sir Herbert Read) 62, *Monograph BN* (introduction by Ronald Alley) 63, *Drawings, Paintings and Relief 1911-1968,* 69, *Monograph BN 1911-1969* (introduction by John Russell), *Monograph BN* (ed. M. de Sausmarez) 69.
c/o Banca della Svizzera, Locarno, Ticino, Switzerland.

Nicholson, Jack; American actor and film maker; b. 22 April 1937; *s.* of John and Ethel May Nicholson. Films include *Cry-Baby Killer* 58, *Studs Lonigan* 60, *The Shooting* (produced and acted), *Ride the Whirlwind* (wrote, prod. and acted), *Hell's Angels on Wheels* 67, *The Trip* (wrote screenplay) 67, *Head* (co-scripted, co-prod.) 68, *Psych-Out* 68, *Easy Rider* 69, *On a Clear Day You Can See Forever* 70, *Five Easy Pieces* 71, *Drive, He Said* (directed) 71, *Carnal Knowledge* 71, *The King of Marvin Gardens* 72, *The Last Detail* 73, *Chinatown* 74, *The Passenger* 74, *Tommy* 74, *The Fortune* 75, *The Missouri Breaks* 75; *One Flew over the Cuckoo's Nest* 75.
c/o Sandy Bresler & Assocs., Suite 206, 360 North Bedford Drive, Beverly Hills, Calif. 90210, U.S.A.

Nicholson, Sir John (Norris), Bt., K.B.E., C.I.E., J.P.; British shipping executive; b. 19 Feb. 1911; ed. Winchester Coll. and Trinity Coll., Cambridge.
Captain 4th Cheshires (T.A.) 39-41; Ministry of War Translator, India and South East Asia 42-46; Chair. Liverpool Port Employers' Asscn. 57-61, Martins Bank Ltd. 62-64 (Deputy Chair. 59-62), Cttee. of European Nat. Shipowners' Asscns., Management Cttee. *H.M.S. Conway* 58-65, Ocean Steam Ship Co. Ltd. 65-71; Dir. Ocean Steam Ship Co. Ltd., Barclays Bank Ltd., Royal Insurance Co. Ltd., Martins Bank Ltd.; mem. Shipping Advisory Panel 62-64; Pres. U.K. Chamber of Shipping 70-71; Vice-Lord-Lieutenant and Keeper of the Rolls, Isle of Wight 74-; mem. Econ. and Social Cttee., EEC 73-74.
Mottistone Manor, Isle of Wight, England.

Nicholson, Rt. Hon. John Robert, P.C., O.B.E., Q.C., LL.D.; Canadian businessman and politician; b. 1 Dec. 1901, Newcastle, N.B.; *s.* of Dr. Robert and Margaret Russell Nicholson; *m.* Charlotte Jean Annand 1924; one *s.*; ed. Harkins Acad. and Dalhousie Univ., Halifax.
Called to the Bar 23, fmr. partner Locke, Lane, Nicholson and Shepherd, Vancouver; Dep. Controller of Supplies, Dept. of Munitions and Supply, Ottawa 41-42; Gen. Man. Polymer Corpn. Ltd., Ontario 42-43, Man. Dir. 43-47, Exec. Vice-Pres. 47-51; Chief in Brazil of Brazilian Traction Light and Power Co. Ltd. 51-57; Pres. Council of Forest Industries of British Columbia 60-61; M.P. 62-65; Minister of Forestry 63-64; Postmaster Gen. 64-65; Minister of Citizenship and Immigra-

tion 65; Minister of Labour Dec. 65-April 68; Lieut.-Gov. of B.C. 68-73.

2090 Comox Street, Vancouver 5, B.C., Canada.

Nickerson, Albert Lindsay, B.SC.; American business executive; b. 17 Jan. 1911; ed. Harvard Univ.

Began as service station attendant, Socony Mobil Oil Co. Inc. 33; elected to Board of Dirs. Mobil Oil Co. Ltd., London 45, Chair. 46; Dir. Socony Mobil Oil Co. Inc. (now called Mobil Oil Corpn.) 46, Vice-Pres., Dir. 51, Pres. 55, Chair. Exec. Cttee. and Chief Exec. Officer 58-69, Chair. of the Board 61-69; Dir. and Treas. American Petroleum Inst. 65-66, Treas. 66-68; Dir. Fed. Reserve Bank of N.Y. 64-67; Trustee, Rockefeller Univ.; Fellow of Harvard Coll.; Chair. Balance of Payments Advisory Cttee. of U.S. Dept. of Commerce; Chair. the Business Council 66-68; Dir. Metropolitan Life Insurance Co., Transportation Asscn. of America; mem. Exec. Board of Nat. Alliance of Businessmen.

Lexington Road, Lincoln, Mass. 01773, U.S.A.

Nicodim (*see* Rotov, Most Rev. Boris Georgievich).

Nicol, Davidson Sylvester Hector Willoughby, M.A., M.D., PH.D., F.R.C.PATH.; Sierra Leonean diplomatist, scientist and educationist; b. 14 Sept. 1924, Freetown; *m.* Dr. Marjorie Nicol, M.B., CH.B. 1950; three *s.* two *d.*; ed. Prince of Wales School, Freetown, Cambridge Univ., London Hospital.

Medical and scientific research and teaching, London, Nigeria and Cambridge 50-59; Fellow, Christ's Coll., Cambridge; Senior Pathologist, Sierra Leone Govt. 58-60, Hon. Consultant Pathologist 60-; guest lecturer numerous Amer. univs.; Principal, Fourah Bay Coll., The Univ. Coll. of Sierra Leone, Freetown 60-67; Vice-Chancellor, Univ. Sierra Leone 66-68; Chair. Conf. of Inter-Univ. Co-op. in W. Africa 61, Needs and Priorities Cttee., Univ. of E. Africa 63, Sierra Leone Nat. Library Board; attended WHO Annual Meetings 59, 60, UNESCO Conf. on Higher Educ. 63, OAU Defence Comm. 65, Commonwealth Prime Ministers Conf. 65, 68, 71; Pres. Sierra Leone Nat. Red Cross Soc. 63-65, W. African Science Asscn. 63-65; Vice-Pres. African Univs. Asscn. 65-68; Dir. Cen. Bank Sierra Leone 63-; Perm. Rep. to UN 69-71, mem. Econ. and Social Council 69-70, Security Council 70-71, Chair. Special Cttee. on Decolonization 70; High Commr. to U.K. and Amb. to Denmark, Sweden, Finland, and Norway 71-72; Under-Sec.-Gen. UN and Exec. Dir. UNITAR Sept. 72-; Commonwealth Lecturer (Cambridge) 75; Hon. D.Sc. (Newcastle upon Tyne, and Kalamazoo Coll. Michigan, U.S.A.); Hon. LL.D. (Leeds); Hon. D.Litt. (Davies and Elkins Coll.); Grand Commdr. Order of Rokel (Sierra Leone); Grand Commdr. Star of Africa (Liberia); Companion of Order of St. Michael and St. George; Margaret Wrong Prize for Literature 52.

Leisure interests: creative writing, numismatics, travel.

Publs. *The Structure of Human Insulin* 60, *Africa, A Subjective View* 64, *African Self-Government 1865: The Dawn of Nationalism, The Truly Married Woman and Other Stories* 65, *New and Modern Role for the Commonwealth.*

United Nations Institute for Training and Research, 801 United Nations Plaza, New York, N.Y. 10017, U.S.A.

Telephone: 212-PL-41234.

Nicol-Cole, Silvanus B., C.M.G., O.B.E.; Sierra Leonean banking executive; b. 8 Aug. 1920, Nigeria; *s.* of Joseph B. and Evelyn M. Cole (née Nicol); *m.* Rebecca Benjamin 1948; three *d.*; ed. Durham and Oxford Univs.

Part-time Lecturer in Applied Econs., Fourah Bay Coll.; Asst. Sec., Deputy Perm. Sec. Ministry of Trade 49-60; Devt. Sec. Ministry of Devt. 60-62; Deputy Gov. Bank of Sierra Leone 62-66, Gov. 66-70; Alt. Gov. IMF 66-70, Alt. Exec. Dir. 70-72, Exec. Dir. 72-74;

Deputy Man. Dir. Barclays Bank of Sierra Leone Ltd. 74-.

Leisure interests: swimming, hunting, gardening, fishing.

Barclays Bank of Sierra Leone Ltd., 25-27 Siaka Stevens Street, P.O. Box 12, Freetown, Sierra Leone. Telephone: 2501.

Nicolin, Curt René; Swedish executive; b. 10 March 1921; ed. Royal Inst. of Technology, Stockholm.

President, Svenska Turbin AB Ljungström, Finspong 55-59, Turbin AB de Laval Ljungström, Finspong 59-61; Interim Pres. Scandinavian Airlines System (S.A.S.) 61-62; Pres. ASEA, Västerås 61-.

Villa Asea, Villagatan 1, Västerås, Sweden.

Nicoll, (John Ramsay) Allardyce; British literary historian; b. 28 June 1894; *s.* of David Binny Nicoll and Elsie Allardyce; *m.* 1st Josephine Calina 1920, 2nd Maria Dubno 1963; ed. Glasgow Univ.

Professor English Language and Literature London Univ. 24-34; Prof. of History of Drama and Dramatic Criticism and Chair. Drama Dept. Yale Univ. 34-45; Prof. English Language and Literature Univ. of Birmingham 45-61, Emeritus Prof.; Dir. Shakespeare Inst. Stratford-upon-Avon 51-61; Visiting Prof., Univ. of Pittsburgh, U.S.A. 63-64, 65, 67 and 69; Editor *Shakespeare Survey* 48-68; Hon. degrees, Univs. of Toulouse, Montpellier, Durham, Glasgow, Brandeis; Pres. Soc. for Theatre Research.

Publs. *The Development of the Theatre, Masks, Mimes and Miracles, British Drama, History of English Drama 1660-1900, Theory of Drama, Film and Theatre, The English Stage, Stuart Masques and the Renaissance Stage, World Drama, The Elizabethans, The World of Harlequin, The Theatre and Dramatic Theory, English Drama 1900-1930: The Beginnings of the Modern Period* 73.

Wind's Acre, Colwall, nr. Malvern, Worcs., England.

[*Died* 17 *April* 1976.]

Niculescu-Mizil, Paul; Romanian politician; b. 25 Nov. 1923, Bucharest; ed. Acad. of Higher Commercial and Industrial Sciences, Bucharest.

Professor at Bucharest Univ., later at "Ştefan Gheorghiu" Acad. of Social and Political Sciences, Bucharest; mem. Romanian C.P. 45-, mem. Cen. Cttee. 55-, mem. Exec. Cttee. 65- and Sec. of Cen. Cttee. 65-72; mem. Perm. Presidium of Cen. Cttee. 66-74; Deputy to Grand Nat. Assembly 57-; Chair. Standing Comm. for Culture and Educ. of Grand Nat. Assembly 65-; mem. Nat. Council of Socialist Unity Front 68-; mem. Defence Council 69-74; Deputy Premier and Minister of Educ. 72-; mem. Acad. of Social and Political Sciences 70; Hero of Socialist Labour 71.

Grand National Assembly of Socialist Republic of Romania, Bucharest, Romania.

Nieh Jung-chen; Chinese politician and fmr. army officer; b. 1899, Chiang-tsin, Szechuan; ed. Univ de Travail, France, Far Eastern and Red Army Univs., Moscow.

Joined CCP 23; Political Instructor, Whampoa Mil. Acad. 25; participated in Nanchang and Canton Uprisings 27; Political Commissar 10th Army Corps 31-36; Commdr. Shansi-Chaha-Hopei Field Army 37-48; mem. 7th Cen. Cttee. of CCP 45; Mayor of Peking 49-51; Vice-Chair. Nat. Defence Council 54-; Marshall 55; mem. 8th Cen. Cttee. of CCP 56; Vice-Premier, State Council 56-74; Chair. Scientific and Technological Comm. 58-; mem. 9th Cen. Cttee. of CCP 69, 10th Cen. Cttee. 73.

People's Republic of China.

Nielsen, (Hans Karl) Helge; Danish politician; b. 12 Oct. 1918, Copenhagen; *s.* of late Johan G. and Sofie P. (née Poulson) Nielsen; *m.* Alice Larsen 1972; two *s.*; ed. primary school, Borups folk high school and workers' coll.

Member of board, Glovers Asscn. 42-; Chair. Nordic Glovers' Union 50-60; teacher, workers' coll. 56-70; mem. Parl. 60-: Sec. to Parliamentary Group of Social Democratic Party 65-71; mem. Nordic Council 66-68; mem. Finance Cttee. 68-70; Minister of Housing 71-73, of the Environment 73-75, of Housing and Environmental Protection Feb. 75-.
Leisure interest: gardening.
Publs. Contributions to political magazines.
Askeengen 40, 2740 Skovlunde, Denmark.
Telephone: 94-10-66.

Nielsen, K(nud) Axel; Danish lawyer and politician; b. 10 Feb. 1904, Hvorup; s. of Christen and Else Nielsen; m. Helga K. Behrens 1933; two s. two d.; ed. Univ. of Copenhagen.
Lawyer 32-; mem. Parl. 53-73; Minister of Justice 64-68, 71-73; mem. Nordic Council 68-73; Chair. Danish Traffic-safety Council 69-71; Town Councillor 74-; Social Democrat.
Leisure interest: literature.
Munksvej 4, Hadsund, Denmark.
Telephone: Hadsund (08) 57-20-04.

Nielsen, Morris; American businessman; b. 4 Aug. 1904, Belden, Neb.; m. Terese Roan 1935; ed. schools in Nebraska.
Joined The Babcock and Wilcox Co., New York City 24, rose to Vice-Pres. Boiler Div. 54-55, Exec. Vice-Pres. 55-57, Pres. 57-65, Dir. 54-, Chair. and Chief Exec. Officer 65-68, Chair. 68-73; Dir. and Trustee of several companies and orgs.
Leisure interest: boating.
Home: 50 East Road, Delray Beach, Fla. 33444; Office: 161 E. 42nd Street, New York, N.Y. 10017, U.S.A.
Telephone: 305-278-5976 (Home); 212-687-6700 (Office).

Nielsen, Niels, DR.PHIL.; Danish geographer; b. 3 Oct. 1893; ed. Copenhagen Univ. and Sorbonne, Paris.
Geographical investigations Iceland 23, 24, and 27; expeditions to Vatnajökull Iceland 34 and 36; Head Skalling Laboratory (Inst. for research on tides, dunes and salt marshes) 30; Vice-Pres. Royal Danish Geographical Soc. 31; Danish Sec. Union Int. de Géographie 34; Prof. Geography Univ. of Copenhagen 39-64; Editor *Geografisk Tidsskrift, Meddelelser fra Skalling Laboratoriet, Folia Geographica Danica, Kulturgeografiske Skrifter*; Chief Editor *Meddelelser om Grønland.*
Publs. *La production du fer en Jutland* 26, *Evidence of the Extraction of Iron in Greenland by the Norsemen* 29, *Contributions to the Physiography of Iceland* 32, *Eine Methode zur exakten Sedimentationsmessung* 35, *Vatnajökull* 37, *Atlas of Denmark*, Vol. I 49.
Strandboulevarden 32, Copenhagen Ø, Denmark.

Nielsen, Sivert Andreas; Norwegian diplomatist; b. 24 Nov. 1916, Copenhagen; s. of Konrad Nielsen; m. Harriet Nielsen (née Eyde) 1945; one s. one d.; ed. Oslo Univ.
Worked Bank of Norway 40-41; political prisoner 41-45; Deputy Attorney Oslo Police 45-46; UN Secr. 46-48; Sec. Norwegian Embassy, Washington 48-50; Section Chief, Ministry of Defence 50-51; Dir. NATO Int. staff 50-51; Div. Chief, Ministry of Defence 52-55; Under-Sec. for Defence 55-58; Permanent Del. to UN 58-66; participated in preparatory work NATO and ministerial confs. NATO 49-58; rep. Advisory Cttee. to Sec.-Gen. UNEF 58; Norwegian Rep. on UN Security Council 63-64, Chair. or Vice-Chair. Norwegian Del. to 13th-21st Sessions of Gen. Assembly of UN; Gen. Man. Bergens Privatbank, Oslo; Chair. Board of Dirs. Norwegian Agency for Int. Devt.; Dir. Finanzierungsgesellschaft Viking, Zürich, Deutsche Schiffahrtsbank, Bremen, Banque Scandinave en Suisse, Geneva.
c/o Bergens Bank, Kirkegaten 23, Oslo, Norway.
Telephone: 20-70-90 (Oslo).

Nielsen, Sven Aage; Danish diplomatist; b. 23 June 1921, Herning; s. of Carl Nielsen; m. Aase Espersen 1953; two d.; ed. Aarhus Univ.
Danish Foreign Service 47-, served Bucharest, Belgrade, Athens, Buenos Aires 47-62; Deputy Head of Secr. for Technical Co-operation with the Developing Countries, Copenhagen 62-63; Deputy Head Danish Del. to Org. for Econ. Co-operation and Development (OECD) 63-65, Head 65-68; Minister (Economic, Commercial and Consular), Danish Embassy, London 68-73; Amb. to Iceland 73-.
Leisure interests: painting, reading.
Royal Danish Embassy, Hverfisgata 29, Reykjavík, Iceland.

Niemeyer, Gerhart, DR.JUR.; American political scientist; b. 1907; ed. Cambridge, Munich and Kiel Univs.
Lecturer, Law Faculty, Madrid Univ. 33; Research Associate, Inst. of Int. and Economic Studies, Madrid 34; Prof. Fed. Spanish Asscns. Int. Studies 34; Lecturer in Politics, Princeton Univ. 37, Asst. Prof. 40-44; Visiting Lecturer, Yale Univ. 42; Prof. of Political Science, Oglethorpe Univ. 44-50; Assoc. Prof. Yale Univ. Summer 46; Visiting Prof. Columbia Univ. Summer 52; U.S. Dept. of State 50-53; Council on Foreign Relations 53-55; Yale Univ. 54-55, Univ. of Notre-Dame 55-, The Nat. War Coll. 58-59; Fulbright Prof. Univ. of Munich 62-63, Co-Dir. Inst. of Communism and Constitutional Democracy, Vanderbilt Univ. 62-66, Foreign Policy Task Force, Republican Party 65-68; Special Consultant, U.S. Information Agency 73; ordained Deacon, Episcopal Church 73.
Publs. *Einstweilige Verfügungen des Weltgerichtshofs* 32, *Vom Wesen der gesellschaftlichen Sicherheit* 35, *The Significance of Function in Legal Theory* 40, *Law Without Force* 41, *An Inquiry into Soviet Mentality* 56, *Facts on Communism: 1, The Communist Ideology* 59; co-author *The Second Chance* 44; Editor *Hermann Heller: Staatslehre* 34; co-editor *Handbuch des Weltkommunismus* 58, *Handbook on Communism* 62 (English Edition), *Hermann Heller: Gesammelte Schriften* 71, *Communists in Coalition Governments* 63, *Outline of Communism* 66, *Deceitful Peace* 71, *Between Nothingness and Paradise* 71.
806 East Angela Boulevard, South Bend, Ind. 46617, U.S.A.
Telephone: 219-234-9949.

Niemeyer, Oscar; Brazilian architect; b. 15 Dec. 1907, Rio de Janeiro; ed. Escola Nacional de Belas Artes, Rio de Janeiro.
Designed Ministry of Education and Health Building, Rio de Janeiro 37-43, Brazilian Pavilion, New York World Fair 39, with others designed U.N. building New York City 47; Dir. of Architecture for new capital of Brasília and given a free hand in design of public and other buildings 57-; Designer of Bienal Exhbn. Hall, São Paulo, urban area of Grasse (near Nice) 66, French C.P. bldg., Paris 66, Palace of Arches (for Foreign Ministry) Brasília; Lenin Peace Prize 63, Prix Int. de *l'Architecture d'aujourd'hui* 66.
Rua Carvalho Azevedo 96, Rio de Janeiro, Brazil.

Niemöller, (Friedrich Gustav Emil) Martin; German theologian; b. 14 Jan. 1892, Lipstadt, Westphalia; s. of Pastor Heinrich Niemöller and Paula Müller; m. Else Bremer 1919; four s. three d.; ed. Elberfeld Gymnasium and Univ. of Münster.
Served in German Navy 10-18, becoming submarine commdr.; ordained 24; Man. Provinzialverband der Inneren Mission, Westfalen 24-31; Pastor Berlin-Dahlem 31-37; founder and Pres. Pfarrer-Notbund (Pastors' Union) and Die Bekennende Kirche (Confessing Church); imprisoned Sachsenhausen and Dachau concentration camps 37-45; Pres. Kirchliches Aussenamt (Office for External Relations of Evangelical Church in Germany) 45-56; Pres. Evangelical Church in Hesse and

Nassau 47-64; Pres. World Council of Churches 61-68; Lenin Peace Prize 67; Grosskreuz des Bundesverdienstordens 70; Hon. D.D. (Göttingen, St. Louis, Halifax, Prague, Puerto Rico, Chicago, Bethany Biblical Seminary, Budapest, Bratislava, London, Ontario), Hon. D.Litt. (New Delhi).

Publs. *Vom U-Boot zur Kanzel* 34; sermons: *... dass wir an Ihm bleiben* 38, *Alles und in allen Christus!* 35, *Dennoch getrost* 39, *Ach Gott vom Himmel sieh darein* 46, *... zu verkündigen ein gnädiges Jahr des Herrn!* 46, *Herr ist Jesus Christus* 46, *Herr, wohin sollen wir gehen?* 57, *Reden (1945-54)* 58, *Reden (1955-57)* 58, *Reden (1958-61)* 61, *Reden (1961-63)*.

Brentanostrasse 3, Wiesbaden, Federal Republic of Germany.

Telephone: 85097.

Nier, Alfred O(tto) C(arl), M.S.E.E., PH.D.; American physicist; b. 28 May 1911; s. of August L. Nier and Anna J. Stoll; m. 1st Ruth E. Andersen 1937, 2nd Ardis L. Hovland 1969; one s. one d.; ed. Univ. of Minnesota.

National Research Fellow, Harvard Univ. 36-38; Asst. Prof. Univ. of Minnesota 38-40, Assoc. Prof. 40-44, Prof. of Physics 44-66 (on leave for war work 43-45), Regents' Prof. of Physics 66-; first to separate rare isotope of uranium U-235, 40; mem. Nat. Acad. of Sciences, American Philosophical Soc., Max Planck Inst. für Chemie and others.

University of Minnesota, Minneapolis, Minn. 55455, U.S.A.

Telephone: 612-373-3325.

Nierenberg, William Aaron, M.A., PH.D.; American physicist; b. 13 Feb. 1919, New York City; s. of late Joseph Nierenberg and of Minnie Nierenberg (née Drucker); m. Edith Meyerson 1941; one s. one d.; ed. Townsend Harris Hall, N.Y.C., City Coll. of N.Y., Univ. of Paris and Columbia Univ.

Tutor, City Coll. of N.Y. 42; Physicist, Manhattan Project 45; Instructor, Dept. of Physics, Columbia Univ. 48; Asst. Prof. Dept. of Physics, Univ. of Mich. 50; Asst. Prof. Univ. of Calif., Berkeley 51, 53; Hudson Labs., Dobbs Ferry, N.Y. 51, Project Dir. 54; Prof., Miller Inst. for Basic Research, Univ. of Calif., Berkeley 57-59; Dept. of Physics 60-65; Asst. Sec.-Gen. of NATO 60-62; Prof. Dept. of Physics, Univ. of Calif., San Diego 65-, Vice-Chancellor, Marine Sciences 69-; Dir. Scripps Inst. of Oceanography, La Jolla, Calif. 65-; Consultant, Office of Science and Technology 73-; Adviser-at-Large, Dept. of State; mem. White House Task Force on Oceanography 70; Chair. Nat. Advisory Cttee. on Oceans and Atmosphere 72-; sometime consultant or adviser to various industrial corpns., govt. agencies, etc.; mem. Nat. Acad. of Sciences, Nat. Science Board, American Acad. of Arts and Sciences, American Philosophical Soc., Joint U.S.-U.S.S.R. Cttee. for the U.S.S.R. Agreement for Co-operative Studies of the World Ocean; Nat. Research Council Fellowship, Guggenheim Fellowship, Sloan Foundations Grant, NATO Senior Science Fellowship, etc.; Officier Ordre National du Mérite (France), Golden Dolphin Award (Asscn. Artistico Letteraria Internationale).

Leisure interests: flying, hunting.

Publs. About 130 articles in professional journals.

Scripps Institution of Oceanography, University of California at San Diego; Home: 9581 La Jolla Farms Road, La Jolla, Calif. 92037, U.S.A.

Telephone: 714-452-2826.

Nieto Caballero, Agustín, LL.B.; Colombian educationist; b. 1889; ed. Colombia and U.S. Univs., Univ. of Paris, and Coll. de France.

Studied in U.S.A. and Europe 04-14; co-founder and Rector Gimnasio Moderno, Bogotá, principal modern school of S. America 14-; initiator of many educational reforms and founder of students' organizations and institutions; Dir.-Gen. of Primary and Secondary Education in Ministry of Education and responsible for reform of primary and secondary schools 32-36; Del. to L.N. 31 and 34; guest of honour World Education Congress, Cheltenham 36; Pres. 5th Int. Conf. of Public Instruction, Geneva 36; Rector Nat. Univ. of Colombia 38-41; Pres. Colombian Del. to 8th American Scientific Congress 40; Amb. to Chile 41-43; mem. Nat. Council of Education; Head of Colombian Del. to World UNESCO Conf. Nov. 47 and del. to many other Int. Confs. on Education to date; Pres. World Education Conf., Geneva 58; Pres. Int. Cttee. of ten for curriculum studies UNESCO; corresp. mem. Colombian Acad., Inst. de France; Gran Oficial Cruz de Boyacá, Order of the Alliance for Progress (Pan American Union), Medalla de Oro (Spain) 64, and other decorations.

Publs. *Rumbos de la Cultura, Los Maestros, La Segunda Enseñanza y Reformas de la Educación, Crónicas de Viaje, Crónicas Ligeras, Una Escuela.*

Gimnasio Moderno, Cra. 9 No. 74-99, Bogotá, Colombia.

Telephone: 494526.

Nieto Gallo, Dr. Gratiniano; Spanish art official; b. 6 March 1917, La Aguilera, Burgos; s. of Francisco and Genoveva Nieto Gallo; m. María de Mergelina Cano-Manuel; one s. one d.; ed. Institución Teresiana, Instituto Ramiro de Maeztu and Univ. de Madrid.

Professor, Univ. de Valladolid 40-52; Dir. Colegio Mayor Santa Cruz de Valladolid 43-52; Sec. School of Art and Archaeology, Univ. de Valladolid 40-52; Dir. Colegio Mayor Nebrija, Univ. de Madrid 52-56; Tech. Sec.-Gen. Directorate of Archives and Libraries 56-61; attached to Univ. de Murcia 59-61; Dir.-Gen. of Fine Arts 61-68; Dir. Central Inst. for Conservation and Restoration of Works of Art 68-; Prof. Univ. Madrid 68-; Rector, Univ. Autónoma de Madrid 73-; decorations from Spain, Portugal, Malta, Federal Republic of Germany, Italy, France and Peru.

Leisure interests: swimming, rowing, mountaineering.

Publs. *La Necrópolis Ibérica del Cabecico del Tesoro* 40, 44, 47, *Las tablas flamencas de la Igl. del Salvador de Valladolid* 41, *Criterio de Reconstrucción de Objetos Arqueológicos* 41, *El Oppidum de Iruña* 49, *Guía Artística de Valladolid* 54, *Historia de los Monumentos de Lerma* 59, *La cueva artificial del Bronco I de Alguazas* 59, *Tendencias Actuales de la Arqueología* 59, *Guía de la Exposición Conmemorativa de la Paz de los Pirineos* 63, *Las Bellas Artes en España* 63, *Conservación del Patrimonio Artístico* 68, *Museos de Artes y Costumbres Populares* 68, *Conservación de Objetos Arqueológicos* 69, *Panorama de los Museos Españoles y cuestiones museológicas* 71, *Reflexiones sobre la Universidad* 73.

Universidad Autónoma de Madrid, Km. 15 Carretera de Colmenar Viejo, Canto Blanco, Madrid, Spain.

Nigrelli, Ross F., B.S., M.S., PH.D.; American pathologist; b. 12 Dec. 1903, Pittston, Pa.; s. of Emanuelo Franco and Castrenza Nigrelli; m. Margaret Carrozza 1927; one d.; ed. Pennsylvania State Univ. and New York Univ.

U.S. Dept. of Agric. 27; Teaching Fellow Biology N.Y. Univ. 27-29, Inst. 29-31; Research Fellow N.Y. Zoological Soc. (N.Y. Aquarium) 31-32, Parasitologist 32-34; Instr. Biology Coll. City of N.Y. (Evening and Summer session) 36-43; Instr. Biology N.Y. Univ. 43-45; Pathologist, Aquarium, N.Y. Zoological Society 34-; Adjunct Assoc. Prof. New York Univ. 49-58; Consultant U.S. Dept. Interior 43-48; Consultant Bingham Oceanographic Lab. Yale Univ. 43-60; Fed. Security Agency Food and Drug Admin. 45-; Tech. Advis. Cttee. Atlantic States Marine Fisheries' Comm. 46-56; Dept. Marine and Aviation N.Y.C. 46-; Vice-Pres. of N.Y. Acad. Sciences and Chair. Biology Section 45-47, Record Sec. 54; Adjunct Prof. of N.Y. Univ. Grad. School Arts and Sciences 58-; Dir. Laboratory of Marine Biochemistry

and Ecology, N.Y. Zoological Soc. 58-63, Dir. of Research 63-65; Dir. Osborn Laboratories of Marine Sciences 64-73, Sr. Scientist and Pathologist 73-; mem. American Socs. of Zoologists, Parasitologists, Tropical Medicine, Protozoologists (Pres. 48-49), President's Advisory Cttee., Sub-panel on Biological Oceanography 65-66, Mayor's Oceanographic Advisory Comm., N.Y. City 68-73, Board of Govs., N.Y. Acad. of Sciences 70-74; Fellow, American Asscn. for Advancement of Science, N.Y. Zoological Soc., N.Y. Acad. of Sciences (Vice-Pres. 55-57, Pres. 57), American Acad. of Microbiology 57-; Hon. Fellow, Consular Law Soc., Affiliate Royal Soc. of Medicine; Trustee, N.Y. Acad. of Sciences 59; Founding mem. New York Inst. of Ocean Resources Board 70-72; Dir. Hudson River Environmental Soc. 70-74; Dir. New York Aquarium 66-70; Order of Merit, Soc. d'Encouragement pour la Recherche et l'Invention (France) 64.
Leisure interests: travelling, painting, gardening, golf.
Office: New York Aquarium, West 8th Street, Brooklyn, N.Y. 11224; Home: 27 Barracuda Road, East Quogue, Long Island, N.Y. 11942, U.S.A.
Telephone: 212-266-8500.

Niilus, Leopoldo Juan; Argentine lawyer; b. 19 Jan. 1930, Tallinn, Estonia; s. of Jaan Eduard Niilus and the late Meta Kiris; m. Malle Reet Veerus de Niilus 1961; one d.; ed. primary and secondary schools in Estonia, Buenos Aires Law School (Nat. Univ.), Southern Methodist Univ., Dallas, Tex.
Formerly practising lawyer, Buenos Aires; founding mem. Argentine Inst. of Science and Admin. and Inst. de Sociología Económica, Buenos Aires; fmr. mem. Exec. Cttee. and legal adviser, Iglesia Evangélica Luterana Unida (IELU) Buenos Aires; fmr. Chair. Argentine Student Christian Movt.; mem. World Student Christian Fed. (WSCF) political comm.; mem. Christian Peace Conf. (CPC) working party and other orgs. dealing with socio-religious literature and research; has participated in numerous major ecumenical consultations; Dir. Argentine Dept. River Plate Centre of Christian Studies 66-67; Gen. Sec. ISAL (Comm. for Church and Society in Latin America) 68-69; Dir. Comm. of the Churches on Int. Affairs of World Council of Churches (WCC) Geneva 69-; participated in mediation for Sudan peace negotiations 72; Order of Two Niles, 1st grade (Sudan).
Leisure interests: theatre, literature.
Publs. *On Penal Law* (essays); articles and essays in several ecumenical publications, in *Cahiers Protestants* (Geneva), *Christianisme Social* (Paris), etc.
Office: Commission of the Churches on International Affairs, World Council of Churches, 150 route de Ferney, 1211 Geneva 20; Home: 7 Chemin Champ d'Anier, Apt. 012, Petit Saconnex, 1209 Geneva, Switzerland.
Telephone: 33-34-00 (Office); 98-32-59 (Home).

Niitamo, Olavi Ensio, D.ECON.; Finnish economist; b. 11 Nov. 1926, Kotka; s. of Tenho Armas Niitamo and Alja Elisabet Väliaho; m. Helka Narinen 1953; three s. one d.; ed. Lyceum of Kotka and Univ. of Helsinki.
Chief, Econ. Statistics Div., Central Statistical Office of Finland 59-63, Chief, Nat. Income Statistics Div. 63-71, Chief, Planning Div. 71-; Docent of Economics, Univ. of Helsinki 62-; Acting Prof. of Econs. 64-65; Acting Prof. of Econometrics 70-; Acting Prof. of Econs., Univ. of Tampere 65-66; Visiting Fellow, Univ. of Calif. (Berkeley) and Harvard Univ. 67-68; mem. Finnish Acad., mem. Cen. Research Board 71-; Knight, First Class of White Rose of Finland.
Leisure interests: family life, car racing, cybernetics of human life.
Publs. various articles in learned journals.
Central Statistical Office of Finland, Annankatu 44,

00100 Helsinki 10; Home: Haukisalo C 47, Matinkylä, Finland.
Telephone: 645-121 (Office); 426209 (Home).

Nijalingappa, Siddavanahalli; Indian lawyer and politician; b. 10 Dec. 1902, Haluvagalu, Bellary District; s. of Adivappa and Neelamma Nijalingappa, m. Smt. Murigamma 1927; three s. six d.; ed. Bangalore and Poona Univ.
Advocate in Mysore High Court 26-39; convicted for political reasons 39, disbarred 40, imprisoned 39-40, 42-44, 47; mem. Mysore Congress Working Cttee. 39-51; Pres. State Congress 45-46, Karnataka Provincial Congress Cttee. 46-54; mem. Indian Constituent Ass. 46-49, of Lok Sabha 52-56; Chief Minister of Mysore and leader Mysore Congress Legislative Party 56-58, 62-68; Pres. Indian Nat. Congress 67-71, Treas. 71-72; Chair. Indian Oil Co. 60-62.
Leisure interests: gardening, trees and forests; interested in afforestation.
Venkateshpur, Chitraduga, Karnataka, India.

Nikaido, Susumu; Japanese politician; b. 1910; ed. Univ. of Southern Calif.
Member, House of Reps.; Deputy Sec.-Gen. Liberal Democratic Party; fmr. Dir.-Gen. Science and Technology Agency; Dir.-Gen. Hokkaido Devt. Agency; Chief Cabinet Sec. 72-74; Sec.-Gen. Liberal Democratic Party Nov.-Dec. 74.
House of Representatives, Tokyo, Japan.

Nikoi, Amon, PH.D.; Ghanaian banker; b. 19 Jan. 1930, Labadi, Accra; m. Gloria née Addae (Principal Sec. Minister of Foreign Affairs); three c.; ed.Achimota Coll., Amherst Coll., U.S.A., Harvard Coll., U.S.A.
Trade and Economic Section, Embassy of Ghana, Washington 57-59; Perm. Mission of Ghana to the UN 59-60; Alt. Exec. Dir., IMF 61-65, Exec. Dir. 65-68; Principal Sec. Minister of Finance and Planning 69-73; Gov., Bank of Ghana 73-.
Leisure interests: farming, gardening, walking.
Bank of Ghana, P.O. Box 2674, Accra, Ghana.

Nikolayenko, Boris Zinovyevich; Soviet foreign trade official; b. 5 March 1914, ed. Moscow Power Inst.
Academy of Foreign Trade 48-; Senior Engineer for Soviet Trade Representation in Hungary 48-55; Vice-Chair. *Soyuzpromexport* 57-64, Chair. 64-; mem. C.P.S.U.; Red Banner of Labour.
Soyuzpromexport, Ministry of Foreign Trade, Smolenskaya-Sennaya ploshchad 32-34, Moscow, U.S.S.R.

Nikolayev, Anatoly Vasiliyevich; Soviet chemist; b. 27 Nov. 1902, Orenburg; ed. Leningrad Univ.
Head, Pavlodar Salt Expedition, U.S.S.R. Acad. of Sciences 27-31, Head, Combined Kulunda Expedition 31-35; at Inst. of Gen. and Inorganic Chemistry, U.S.S.R. Acad. of Sciences 34-57; Instructor, Moscow, Polygraphic Inst. 36-41; Instructor, later Prof., Moscow Inst. of Non-Ferrous Metals and Gold 46-57; Dir. Inst. of Inorganic Chemistry, Siberian Dept., U.S.S.R. Acad. of Sciences 57; Chair. Novosibirsk State Univ. 59; Corresp. mem. and Presidium mem. Siberian Dept., U.S.S.R. Acad. of Sciences 58-66, mem. 66-.
Academy of Sciences, 14 Leninsky Prospekt, Moscow, U.S.S.R.

Nikolayev, Maj.-Gen Andriyan Grigorievich; Soviet cosmonaut; b. 5 Sept. 1929; m. Valentina Vladimirovna Tereshkova (q.v.); ed. Forestry Coll. and Zhukovsky Air Force Engineering Acad.
Former lumberjack; Army 50-; Air Force Fighter Pilot, later Test Pilot; cosmonaut training 60-, stand-in for Maj. Herman Titov 61; launched into orbit around Earth August 11th 62, returned Aug. 15th after completing 64 orbits; Commdr Soviet Astronauts' Detachment 64-; mem. Communist Party 57-; Deputy Supreme Soviet R.S.F.S.R., Pilot *Soyuz 9*, 1-19 June 70; Order of the Red Star, Order of Lenin, Hero of Soviet

Union (twice), Gold Star Medal (twice); Daniel and Florence Guggenheim Int. Astronautics Award 70.
Zvezdny Gorodok, Moscow, U.S.S.R.

Nikolayeva, Tatyana Nikolayevna; Soviet trade union official; b. 25 Dec. 1919, Baskaki; ed. Ivanovo Pedagogical Inst.
Assistant Head, later Head, Propaganda and Agitation Dept. of Ivanovo City Cttee. of Communist Party 48-50; Sec., later First Sec. Ivanovo City Cttee. of C.P.S.U. 50-59; Sec. All-Union Cen. Council of Trade Unions 59-; mem. Central Cttee. of C.P.S.U.; Dep. to U.S.S.R. Supreme Soviet 62-; mem. Comm. for Public Educ., Science and Culture; mem. Committee, U.S.S.R. Parliamentary Group; Perm. Rep. of U.S.S.R. in UN Comm. on the Status of Women; mem. Cttee. of World Fed. of Trade Unions, Presidium of Soviet Peace Cttee.; Vice-Pres. Soviet-Polish Friendship Soc.; Order of Lenin and other decorations.
All-Union Central Council of Trade Unions, 42 Leninsky Prospekt, Moscow, U.S.S.R.

Nikolsky, Boris Petrovich, D.SC.; Soviet physicist and chemist; b. 14 Oct. 1900, Menselinsk, Tatar S.S.R.; ed. Leningrad State Univ.
Lecturer, Dozent, Prof.. Chief of Faculty, Leningrad Univ. 25-, Head of Dept. and Laboratory, Chlopin Radium Inst. 49-; Academician, U.S.S.R. Acad. of Sciences 68-; Lenin Prize, State Prize, Hero of Socialist Labour, Order of Lenin, "Hammer and Sickle" Gold Medal, etc.
Leningrad State University, Leningrad, U.S.S.R.

Nikula, Karl Oscar, DR. PHIL.; Finnish historian; b. 31 May 1907, Vasa; s. of Karl Nikula and Emilia Glasberg; m. Sigrid M. Rinne 1933; four s.
Schoolteacher in Jakobstad and Helsinki 32-45; Dir. of Historical Museum of Turku/Åbo 45-52; Lecturer, Åbo Acad. 45-51; Prof. Åbo Acad. 51-77, Rector 62-66. Publs. Åbo sjöfarts historia 30, Svenska skärgårdsflottan 1756-91 33, Tenala och Bromarf socknars historia 1-11 38; Boktryckarna Frenckell och deras föregångare vid Åbo akademi 42, Malmska handelshuset i Jakobstad 48, Jakobstad 1652-1952 52, W. Rosenlew & Co., Aktiebolag 1853-1953 53, La Flotte suédoise de l'archipel au XVIIIième siècle (Revue int. d'histoire militaire) 55, The Castle of Turku 55, Augustin Ehrensvard 1701-1772 60, Les troupes légères de l'armée suède 61, The Story of the Tobacco Factory in Jakobstad 62, Finnlands Ostgrenze 63, Turun kaupungin historia 1721-1809 71, Turun kaupungin historia 1809-56 72.
Slottsgatan 28A, 20100 Åbo 10, Finland.
Telephone: 17-494.

Nilsson, Birgit (Fru Bertil Niklasson); Swedish opera singer (soprano); b. 17 May 1918; ed. Stockholm Royal Acad. of Music.
With Stockholm Opera 47-51; sang at Glyndebourne (England) 51, Bayreuth 54, Munich 55, Hollywood Bowl, Buenos Aires and Florence 56, Bayreuth 57-, London (Covent Garden) 57, 62, 63, 73, Milan (La Scala), Naples, Vienna, Chicago and San Francisco 58, New York (Metropolitan) 59, Moscow 64; sang in Turandot Paris 68, Josen New York 68, Elektra London 69; Royal Court singer 54; Austrian Kammersängerin, Bavarian Kammersängerin and Hon. mem. of the Vienna State Opera 68; Commdr. Order of Vasa 68; Medal Litteris et Artibus 60; particularly well known for her Wagnerian roles; Medal for Promotion of Art of Music, Royal Acad. of Music, Stockholm 68.
Box 522, Stockholm C, Sweden.

Nilsson, Gösta; Swedish engineer and business executive; b. 18 Feb. 1912, Jonstorp in Skåne; s. of Jöns and Hilda (Hansson) Nilsson; m. Ingeborg Nilsson 1939; one s. and three d.
High Tension and Lighting Research Inst., Uppsala 36-37; Admin. Investigator, Swedish State Power

Board 37-44, Head of Operations and Planning Dept. 44-46, Head of Älvkarleby Power Station 46-48, Dir.-Gen. and Vice-Chief, Swedish State Power Board 48-53; Man. Dir. AB Scania-Vabis (manufacturers of trucks, buses, diesel engines) 53-69; Deputy Chair. Linjeflyg AB 59-65, Swedish Metal Trades Employers Asscn. 58-63, SAAB-Scania 69-; Dir. AB Statsgruvor (State Mines Co.) 50-65, Swedish Asscn. of Automotive Industries and Wholesale Merchants 53-69, Stockholm Chamber of Commerce 56-70, German-Swedish Chamber of Commerce 61-, Gen. Asscn. of Swedish Exporters 63-, Finnish-Swedish Chamber of Commerce 64, Swedish Road Asscn. 64-; Chair. AB Svenska Volkswagen 69-, Science Museum in Stockholm 70-; Dir. Swedish Wine Monopoly 64-, Svenska Dagblad et 65-, Svenska BP 69-, GKN Stenman 70-, Bygg-Platzer 70-, Swedish Tobacco Co. 70-.
Leisure interests: golf, beef-cattle breeding.
Uddeboö Gård, 76100 Norrtälje, Sweden.
Telephone: 0176-36064.

Nilsson, Karl N. A.; Swedish business executive; b. 28 Aug. 1907, Malmö; s. of Per and Matilda Nilsson; m. Maj E. Ljung 1938; one s. two d.; ed. Royal Inst. of Technology, Stockholm.
With Svenska Fläktfabriken 32-33, 43-59, Sales Man. 49, Exec. Vice-Pres. 53; A.S.E.A. Rep. in India 33-43, Exec. Vice-Pres. 59, Acting Pres. 61; Pres. Scandinavian Airlines System 62-69; Chair. Svenska Fläktfabriken 70-, Zander and Ingeström 72-, Swedish Standards Inst. (SIS) 74-, Wasabröd AB 75-; Vice-Chair. Alfa-Laval 70-, Nife Jungner AB 71-; mem. of Boards of Electro-Invest 60-, Nordiska Ackumulatorfabriker Noack AB 73-, Gadelius AB 74-, Wasa G.m.b.H. (Germany) 75-, The Sweden-America Foundation 69-; Commdr. Royal Order of Vasa (Sweden), Royal Order of Dannebrog (Denmark), Order of St. Olav (Norway), Commdr. with Star Order St. Gregorius Magnus (Vatican), Grosses Verdienstkreuz (Federal Germany), Officier Légion d'Honneur (France).
Leisure interests: tennis, table tennis, gardening.
Styrmansgaten 39, S-11454 Stockholm, Sweden.
Telephone: 676700.

Nilsson, Torsten; Swedish politician; b. 1 April 1905; ed. in Sweden and Germany.
Began career as bricklayer 22-29; Sec. Social Dem. Youth Organization, Skåne 27-30, Chair. 30-34, Chair. Soc. Dem. Youth Org. of Sweden 34-40, Sec., Social Dem. Party 40-48; mem. of Parl. 41-; Minister of Communications 45-51, of Defence 51-57; Minister of Social Welfare 57-62; Minister for Foreign Affairs 62-71.
Parliament Buildings, Stockholm, Sweden.

Nimmanhaemin, Bisudhi, B.COM.; Thai banker; b. 23 May 1915, Chiangmai; s. of Kee and Kimhaw (née Chutima) Nimmanhaemin; m. M. R. Bhanchompunoot Tongtaem 1943; two s. one d.; ed. Suan Kularb Coll., Bangkok, Henry Thornton School, London and London School of Econs.
Ministry of Finance 40; Thai Nat. Banking Bureau 41-42; Chief, Public Debt Div., Bank of Thailand 43-47, Chief, Exchequer Dept. 48-53, Dir., Asst. to Gov. 54-64, Deputy Gov. 65-71, fmr. Gov.; Man. Exchange Equilization Fund of Thailand 59-64; Alt. Gov. IMF 59-64; Alt. Gov. IBRD 65-71; fmr. Gov. IMF; Assoc. mem. Cttee. of Twenty; Knight Grand Cross, Order of the Crown of Thailand.
Leisure interests: photography, golf.
Bank of Thailand, P.O. Box 154, Bangkok; Home: 19, Soi Intamra 3, Sudhisarn Road, Bangkok 4, Thailand.
Telephone: 818-890 (Office); 74-800 (Home).

Nin-Culmell, Joaquín María; American musician; b. 5 Sept. 1908, Berlin, Germany; s. of Joaquín Nin and Rosa Culmell; ed. Schola Cantorum and Nat. Conservatoire, Paris.

Studied privately with Manuel de Falla; Instructor, Middlebury Coll., Vermont 38, 39, 40, Williams Coll. 40-50; Prof. of Music, Univ. of Calif. 49-74, Emer. Prof. 74-, Inst. of Creative Arts 65-66; has appeared as pianist and conductor with the San Francisco Symphony and other orchestras in the United States and Europe; Corresp. mem. Royal Acad. of Fine Arts of San Fernando (Madrid 1962); mem. Int. Jury Maria Canals Int. Competition, Barcelona, Marguerite Long Int. Competition, Paris.
Compositions: Piano Concerto, *El burlador de Sevilla* (ballet), Piano Quintet, *Sonata Breve*, *Tonadas* (piano), *Three Old Spanish Pieces* (orchestra), *Diferencias* (orchestra), Concerto for cello and orchestra (after Padre Anselmo Viola), *Mass in English* (for mixed chorus and organ), *La Celestina* (opera), Cantata for voice and harpsichord or piano and strings (after Padre José Pradas), songs, choral pieces, etc.
Leisure interests: philosophy, detective stories, swimming.
165 Hillcrest Road, Berkeley, Calif. 94705, U.S.A.

Nininger, Harvey Harlow, A.M., SC.D.; American meteorite expert; b. 17 Jan. 1887, Conway Springs, Kansas; *s.* of J. B. and M. A. B. Nininger; *m.* Addie Delp 1914; one *s.* two *d.*; ed. Northwestern State Normal School, Okla., McPherson Coll., Kansas, Pomona Coll., Calif., and Univ. of California.
Substitute Prof. of Biology, State Teachers Coll., Alva, Okla. 12-13, Prof. of Biology, La Verne Coll., Calif. 14-18; Instr. Pomona Coll. 16; Laboratory Asst. Univ. of California 18; Special Field Agent, U.S. Bureau Entomology 18-19; Extension Entomologist, Kansas State Agricultural Coll. 19; Prof. of Biology, Southwestern Coll. 19-20, McPherson Coll. 20-30; Pres. Kansas Acad. of Science 24-25; organized Nininger Laboratory 30 (became American Meteorite Laboratory 37); Curator of Meteorites Colorado Museum of Natural History 30-46; Dir. American Meteorite Laboratory Denver; Instr. in Meteoritics Denver Univ.; Pres. Society for Research on Meteorites 37-41; Fellow, American Asscn. for Advancement of Science, Arizona Acad. of Science; began study of meteorites 23; has discovered more than 255 different meteorite falls; possesses the largest private collection of meteorites in the world; Founder and Dir. American Meteorite Museum 46-60; mem. and fmr. Pres. Kansas Acad. Sciences; expeditions to tektite fields, Philippines, Vietnam, Thailand, Australia, Czechoslovakia, Germany, Australian meteorite craters, European meteorite collections 58-60; meteorite consultant, Arizona State Univ. 60-; endowed with Addie Nininger the annual Nininger Award; Leonard Memorial Medal 67; Oct. 67 issue of *Journal of the Geochemical Society* dedicated to him.
Publs. *A Field Guide, Birds of Central Kansas* 27, *Our Stone-Pelted Planet* 33, *A Comet Strikes the Earth* 42, *Chips from the Moon* 47, *The Nininger Collection of Meteorites* 50, *Out of the Sky* 52, *Arizona's Meteorite Crater—Present, Past and Future* 56, *Ask a Question about Meteorites* 62, *The Published Papers of H. H. Nininger* 71, *Find a Falling Star* 72.
P.O. Box 420, Sedona, Arizona 86336, U.S.A.
Telephone: 282-3613.

Ninn-Hansen, Erik; Danish lawyer and politician; b. 1922, Skørpinge; *m.* Astrid Ninn-Hansen 1947; one *s.* one *d.*
Sec. to E. Div. of High Court 48-55; called to Bar 52, practising advocate 55-; Chair. Conservative students 44-48, mem. Managing Cttee. Nat. Students' Asscn. 45-47; Chair. Nat. Asscn. of Young Conservatives 48-50; mem. Folketing (Parliament) 53-, mem. Cttee. Conservative Parl Group 64-; mem. Greenland Cttee. 57, Chair. 57-58, 61-62; mem. Board of Dirs. Royal Greenland Trade Dept. 57, 58, 61 62; mem. Greenland Council 64-; Editor *Vor Tid* (Our Time) 55-60; mem.

Comm. for Greenland's Industrial and Political Dept. 60-; mem. Board of Dirs. Øresund Cryolite Co. Ltd. 61-; mem. Gen. Council of the Investor (investment company) 62-; Minister of Defence Feb. 68-71, of Finance 71.
Publ. *Seven Years for VKR* 74.
Folketing, Copenhagen, Denmark.

Nirenberg, Louis, M.S., PH.D.; American professor of mathematics; b. 28 Feb. 1925, Hamilton, Ont., Canada; *s.* of Zuzie Nirenberg and Bina Katz; *m.* Susan Blank 1948; one *s.* one *d.*; ed. McGill and New York Univs.
Instructor, New York Univ 49-51, Asst. Prof. 51-54, Assoc. Prof. 54-57, Prof. 57-; Dir. Courant Inst. of Mathematical Sciences 70-72; mem. Nat. Acad of Sciences, American Acad. of Arts and Sciences; Bôcher Prize of American Mathematical Soc.
Leisure interests: classical music, reading fiction, cinema, walking.
Publs. Various papers in mathematical journals.
Courant Institute of Mathematical Sciences, New York University, 251 Mercer Street, New York, N.Y. 10012, U.S.A.
Telephone: 212-460-7451.

Nirenberg, Marshall Warren, PH.D.; American biochemist; b. 10 April 1927; *m.* Perola Zaltzman; ed. Univ. of Florida and Univ. of Michigan.
Postdoctoral Fellow, Amer. Cancer Soc., Nat. Insts. of Health (N.I.H.) 57-59, U.S. Public Health Service, N.I.H. 59-60; mem. staff, N.I.H. 60-, research biochemist 61-62; research biochemist, Head of Section for Biochem. Genetics, Nat. Heart Inst. 62-66; Chief, Laboratory of Biochem. Genetics, Nat. Heart and Lung Inst. 66-; has researched on mechanism of protein synthesis, genetic code, nucleic acids, regulatory mechanism in synthetic macromolecules; mem. Nat. Acad. of Sciences, Pontifical Acad. of Sciences 74; Molecular Biology Award, Nat. Acad. of Sciences 62; Medal from Dept. of Health, Educ. and Welfare 63; Modern Medicine Award 64; Nat. Medal for Science, Pres. Johnson 65; Nobel Prize for Medicine (with Holley and Khorana) for interpreting the genetic code and its function in protein synthesis 68; Louisa Gross Horwitz Prize for Biochemistry 68.
Laboratory of Biochemical Genetics, National Heart and Lung Institute, National Institutes of Health, Bethesda, Md. 20014, U.S.A.

Nishimura, Eiichi; Japanese politician; b. 1898; ed. Tohoku Univ.
Member, House of Reps.; fmr. Parliamentary Vice-Minister of Transport; fmr. Minister of Health and Welfare; fmr. Minister of Posts and Telecommunications; Minister of Construction July 71-July 72; fmr. Leader of the Democratic Socialist Party.
c/o Democratic Socialist Party, Shiba Sakuragawa-cho, Minato-ku, Tokyo, Japan.

Nishimura, Naomi; Japanese politician; b. 1905; ed. Tokyo Univ.
Chief Sec. to Prime Minister 48; Parliamentary Vice-Minister (Ministry of Finance) 51, Minister of State and Dir.-Gen. of Defence Agency 60-61; Chair. Liberal-Democrat Party Policy Board Dec. 66-68; Minister of Agriculture and Forestry Feb.-Dec. 68; Minister of Defence Aug. 71-July 72.
Publ. *Stranger in Moscow.*
8-5-28-604 Akasaka, Minato-ku, Tokyo, Japan.

Nishio, Suehiro; Japanese politician; b. 1891; ed. Primary School.
Factory apprentice 05; mem. Yuaikai (Workers' Friendship Soc., first Japanese trade union) 15, Sec. 19; founded Preparatory Cttee. for Trade Unions 16; arrested 20, 21, 22; del. to ILO Confs. 24, 32; Sec.-Gen. Sodomei (Gen. Fed. of Trade Unions) 25-40 (suppressed); founder mem. Exec. Shakai Minshu (Socialist People's)

Party 25; mem. House of Reps. 28-38 (expelled) 39-; formed Kinro Kokumin To (Nat. Workers' Party) of expelled mems. of Shakai Taishu (Socialist Mass) Party 40, party banned; founded Social Democratic Party of Japan 45; re-established Sodomei 46; Dep. Prime Minister May 47-Feb. 48; resigned from Social Democratic Party 59; Founder Japan Democratic Socialist Party and Chair. 61-67.

Publs. *With People* (autobiography) 50, *Road to the New Party* 59.

1 Shiba Sakuragawa-cho, Minato-ku, Tokyo, Japan.

Nissim, Isaac; Israeli Rabbi; b. 1896, Baghdad, Iraq. In Israel 25-; Chief Rabbi of Israel and Pres. Rabbinical High Court 55-72; Pres. Rabbinical Seminary, Jerusalem 57-; Chair. Gt. Rabbinical Court; fmr. Head of Sephardic Community.

Publs. *Yen Hatov, Canogah Zidkah.*

c/o Office of The Chief Rabbi of Israel, Balfour Street 7, Jerusalem, Israel.

Nitisastro, Widjojo, PH.D.; Indonesian politician; b. 23 Sept. 1927, Malang; ed. Univ. of Indonesia and Univ. of Calif., Berkeley, U.S.A.

Dean, Faculty of Econs., Univ. of Indonesia 65-67; seconded to UN as expert engaged in drawing up plan for 2nd UN Econ. Devt. Decade and mem. Gov. Council, UN Asian Inst. of Devt. and Planning 67-71; Minister of State for National Planning and Construction Sept. 71-.

Publs. include: *Population Trends in Indonesia, The Relevance of Growth Models for Less Developed Economics, The Role of Research in a University, Public Policies, Land Tenure and Population Movements, Population Problems and Indonesia's Economic Development.*

Ministry for National Planning and Construction, Jakarta, Indonesia.

Nitze, Paul Henry; American administrator; b. 16 Jan. 1907, Amherst, Mass.; s. of William A. and Anina (Hilken) Nitze; m. Phyllis Pratt 1932; two s. two d.; ed. Harvard Univ.

New York Investment Banker 29-40; financial Dir. Office of Co-ordinator of Inter-American Affairs 41-42; Chief, Metals and Minerals Branch, Board of Econ. Welfare, Dir. Foreign Procurement and Devt. 42-43; Vice-Chair. Strategic Bombing Survey 44-46; Deputy Dir. Office of Int. Trade Policy 46-48; Deputy to Asst. Sec. of State for Econ. Affairs 48-49; Dir. Policy Planning Staff, Dept. of State 50-53; Pres. Foreign Service Educ. Foundation 53-61; Asst. Sec. of Defense for Int. Security Affairs 61-63; Deputy Sec. of Defense 67-69; mem. Board Schroders Ltd., and Schroders Inc. 69-; Sec. of the Navy Oct. 63-67; Chair. Advisory Council, School of Advanced Int. Studies, Johns Hopkins Univ.; Chair. Board, Aspen Skiing Corpn.; Dir. American Security and Trust Co., Northwestern Mutual Life, Mortgage and Realty Investors; Trustee, Johns Hopkins Univ.; Consultant, System Planning Corpn.; mem. U.S. Del. to Strategic Arms Limitation Talks 69-74.

Leisure interests: skiing, tennis.

Publ. *U.S. Foreign Policy 1945-1954.*

1500 Wilson Boulevard, Suite 1500, Arlington, Va. 22209 (Office); 3120 Woodley Road, Washington, D.C. 20008, U.S.A.

Niven, (James) David Graham; British actor; b. 1 March 1910; ed. Stowe and Royal Mil. Coll., Sandhurst.

Officer in British Army 29-32, 39-46; various occupations 32-35; film extra, Hollywood 35-38; starring roles since 38 in the films *Bachelor Mother, Wuthering Heights, Raffles, The First of the Few, The Way Ahead, A Matter of Life and Death, The Elusive Pimpernel, The Moon is Blue, Carrington V.C., Around the World in Eighty Days, The Little Hut, Bonjour Tristesse, My Man Godfrey,*

Separate Tables, Ask Any Girl, Happy Anniversary, Please Don't Eat the Daisies, The Guns of Navarone, The Best of Enemies, The Pink Panther, 55 Days at Peking, Bedtime Story, Lady L, Where the Spies Are, Eye of the Devil, Casino Royale, Extraordinary Seaman, Prudence and the Pill, The Important Years, Before Winter Comes, The Brain, King, Queen, Knave, Paper Tiger, Vampira, and many others; American Motion Picture Acad. Award, Best Actor of the Year for *Separate Tables;* American Legion of Merit and British medals.

Publs. *Round the Rugged Rocks, The Moon's a Balloon* (reminiscences) 71, *Bring On the Empty Horses* 75.

Château D'Oex, Vaud, Switzerland; c/o Coutts & Co., 440 Strand, London, W.C.2, England.

Niwa, Kyoshiro; Japanese politician; b. 1904; ed. Tokyo Univ.

Member, House of Reps.; fmr. Parliamentary Vice-Minister of Home Affairs; Dep. Sec.-Gen. Liberal Democratic Party; Minister of Transport 71-72.

c/o Liberal Democratic Party, 7 2-chome, Hirakawacho, Chiyoda-ku, Tokyo, Japan.

Nixon, Peter James; Australian politician and farmer; b. 28 March 1928, Orbost, Victoria; s. of Percival C. and Grace Hunter Nixon; m. Sally J. Dahlsen 1954; two s. one d.; ed. Wesley Coll. Melbourne.

Elected to House of Representatives 61; mem. Joint Cttee. Public Accounts 64; mem. Joint Cttee. Foreign Affairs 67; Minister for the Interior Oct. 67-Feb. 71, for Shipping and Transport 71-72; Minister of Transport Nov. 75-; Postmaster-Gen. Nov.-Dec. 75; Country Party.

Leisure interests: golf, shooting, fishing, chess, theatre.

Parliament House, Canberra, A.C.T., Australia.

Telephone: Canberra 721211.

Nixon, Richard Milhous, A.B., LL.B.; American lawyer and politician; b. 9 Jan. 1913, Yorba Linda, Calif.; s. of Francis A. and Hannah (Milhous) Nixon; m. Thelma Catherine ("Pat") Ryan 1940; daughters: Patricia (Mrs. Edward Finch Cox) and Julie (Mrs. Dwight D. Eisenhower II); ed. Whittier Coll. and Duke Univ. Law School.

Practised law in Whittier 37-42; Attorney with Office of Emergency Management, Washington, D.C. 42; served with U.S. Navy 42-46; attained rank of Lieut.-Commdr.; mem. Congress for 12th Calif. District 47-50; Senator from Calif. 50-53; Vice-Pres. of U.S.A. Jan. 53-61; Republican candidate for Presidency (ran against John F. Kennedy) 60; affiliated with law firm Adams, Duque and Hazeltine 61-63; Republican Candidate for Governor, Calif. 62; mem. Mudge, Stern, Baldwin and Todd 63-64; partner, Nixon, Mudge, Rose, Guthrie, Alexander & Mitchell 64-68; 37th Pres. of U.S.A. 69-74, resigned Aug. 74; responsible for Viet-Nam Peace Settlement Jan. 73; first U.S. Pres. to make official visit to People's Repub. of China Feb. 72, U.S.S.R. May 72; revisited China Feb. 76.

Publ. *Six Crises* 62.

La Casa Pacifica, San Clemente, Calif., U.S.A.

Niyazbekov, Sabir Bilyalovich; Soviet politician; b. Dec. 1912, Tselinograd District; s. of Bilyal Niyazbekov and Zhibek Suleymenova; m. Rauza Sabirovna Akhmetova 1940; four d.; ed. Higher Party School of C.P.S.U. Central Cttee.

Secretary Village Soviet, District Soviet 28-31; Komsomol work 31-35; Army Service 35-38; State work 38-41; Party work 41-65; First Sec., West Kazakhstan, Tselinograd, South Kazakhstan, Alma-Ata, Regional Cttees. Communist Party of Kazakhstan; Chair. Presidium, Supreme Soviet, Kazakh S.S.R.; Vice-Chair. Presidium, U.S.S.R. Supreme Soviet 65-; Candidate mem. C.P.S.U. Central Cttee. 66-71, mem. 71-; mem. Cen. Cttee. C.P. of Kazakhstan; Deputy to U.S.S.R. Supreme Soviet 62-.

Leisure interests: reading, films, plays, walking.
Presidium, Supreme Soviet of the Kazakh S.S.R., Alma-Ata, U.S.S.R.

Nizsalovszky, Endre, LL.D.; Hungarian jurist; b. 25 Sept. 1894, Békéscsaba, Békés; s. of Endre Nizsalovszky and Maria Medvigy; m. Gabriella Kun 1922; two d.; ed. Debrecen and Berlin Univs.
Mem. Law Court 16-20; mem. Codification Section of Ministry of Justice 20-30; Prof. of Commercial Law, Debrecen Univ. 30-34 and of Civil and Commercial Law, Royal Hungarian Palatine-Joseph Univ. of Technical and Economic Sciences 34-38; Prof. of Juridical Procedure, Péter Pázmány Univ. Budapest 38-43; Prof. of Civil Law, Lorand Eötvös (fmrly. Péter Pázmány) Univ., Budapest 43-57; corresp. mem. Hungarian Acad. of Sciences 39-54, full mem. 54-; mem. St. Stephen Acad. 41-51; mem. Permanent Court of Arbitration, The Hague 55-61; mem. Court of Arbitration, Hungarian Chamber of Commerce 63-; Hungarian Order of Working, golden degree 54, 74.
Leisure interests: philately, long-playing records, photography.
Recent publs. incl.: *Eötvös József levelei Szalay Lászlóhoz* 67, *Eötvös József és a notaperek* (József Eötvös et les procès d'infidélité) 67, *Order of the Family: Legal Analysis of Basic Concepts* 68, *Az állami vállalatok forgalmi viszonyainak alakulásához* (Sur l'établissement des rapports d'échanges de marchandises des entreprises d'état) 69, *Gesetz und Wirklichkeit im sozialistischen ehelichen Güterrecht* 70, *Právne otázky transplantácie orgánov* 70, *L'incidence de la biologie et de la médecine moderne sur le droit civil* 70, *A szuletésszabályozás egyes változatainak jogi vonatkozásai* (Legal aspects of some methods of birth control) 70, *Fruchtbarkeit und Stabilität der Ehen* 71, *A családtervezés joga és korlátai* (Right and the Limits of Family Planning) 71, *Frank Ignác emlékezete 1788-1850* (In commemoration of Ignac Frank 1788-1850) 72, *Eötvös József és a—jövö zeneje* (Joseph Eötvös and the dreams of the future) 73, *Gesetzgebungsmittel der Familenpolitik* 74, *Legal Approach to Organ Transplantation and Some Other Medical Actions* 74, *La situation juridique des enfants nés hors mariage* (with Tibor Pap) 74, *Déak Ferenc és a Magyar polgári magánjog kialakulása* (Francis Deák and the development of Hungarian Civil Law), *Társadalmi, gazdasági fejlödéünk és az öröklési jog* (The social and economic evolution of Hungary and the Inheritance Law).
Borbolya utca 5, H-1023 Budapest, Hungary.
Telephone: Budapest 154-985.

N'Jie, Alhaji Alieu Badara, M.B.E., J.P.; Gambian politician; b. 1904; ed. Wesleyan Boy's High School, Bathurst, Gambia.
Gambian Civil Service 25-59, ultimately first Registrar Supreme Court; mem. Banjul City Council 47-, Chair. Gen. Purposes Cttee. 59-61; Minister of Works and Services 62, of Works and Communications 62-65; Minister of External Affairs and High Commr. in Senegal 65-67; Chair. Gambia Tourist Board 67; Minister for Local Govt., Lands and Mines 68; Minister of State at the President's Office 70-72; Minister of Agriculture 72-74, of External Affairs 74-.
Ministry of External Affairs, Banjul, The Gambia.

Njine, Michel; Cameroonian diplomatist; b. 1 Jan. 1918.
Cameroon Admin. Service 37; Counsellor of Territorial Assembly of Cameroon 52; Deputy of Legis. Assembly 56; Minister of Public Works, Transportation and Mines 57-58; Deputy Prime Minister in Charge of Nat. Educ., Youth and Sports 58-59; Dir. Cameroon Nat. Office of Tourism 60-62; Amb. to Ivory Coast 62-65, to German Fed. Repub. 65-67; Perm. Rep. to UN 67-75.
c/o Ministry of Foreign Affairs, Yaoundé, Cameroon.

Njoku, Eni, M.SC., PH.D.; Nigerian university teacher and administrator; b. 6 Nov. 1917, Ebem Ohafia; s. of Njoku Eni and Obo Uche; m. Winifred Olive Beardsall; one s. three d.; ed. Ebem Ohafia primary school, Hope Waddell Coll., Calabar, Yaba Higher Coll. and Univ. of Manchester, England.
Teacher, Hope-Waddell Secondary School 40-42, Clerk (Army) Training School 42-44; studied in Manchester 44-48; Lecturer, Univ. of Ibadan 48-52; Minister for Mines and Power, Govt. of Nigeria 52-53; Senior Lecturer, Prof. of Botany, Univ. of Ibadan 53-62; Vice-Chancellor and Prof. of Botany, Univ. of Lagos 62-65; Visiting Prof. of Botany, Michigan State Univ. 65-66; Vice-Chancellor, Univ. of Nigeria 66-70; Prof. of Botany, Univ. of Nigeria 66-; mem. House of Reps. 52-53, Senate 60-62; Chair. Electricity Corpn. of Nigeria 56-62; Pres. Science Asscn. of Nigeria 59-60; mem. Commonwealth Scientific Cttee. 61-66; mem. UN Cttee. on Application of Science and Technology to Devt. 64-69; mem. Provisional Council of Univ. of Zambia 64-65; mem. Superior Academic Council of Univ. of Lovanium (Kinshasa) 63-66; Hon. D.Sc. (Univs. of Nigeria and Lagos), Hon. LL.D. (Michigan State Univ.).
Publs. *Plant Life in a Tropical Environment* 54 and numerous research articles in botanical journals.
University of Nigeria, Nsukka, East Central State; Home: Ebem Ohafia, East Central State, Nigeria.

Njoku, Raymond Amanze, LL.B.(LOND.), G.C.G.G., C.F.R.; Nigerian barrister and solicitor, company director and former politician; b. Aug. 1916, Emekuku Owerri; s. of Njoku Ndudu Dike and Adamma Ejeka; m. Magdalen Opara; five s. three d.; ed. St. Charles Coll. Onitsha, Kings Coll., Univ. of London, and Inns of Court (Middle Temple), London.
Teacher 33-43; Law practice 47-54; mem. Eastern House of Assembly 53-54; mem. House of Reps. 53-66; Fed. Minister of Trade and Industry 54-57; Minister of Transport 57-59, of Transport and Aviation 59-64, of Communications 65-66; mem. Gov. Privy Council 54-55, Gov.-Gen. Privy Council 55-60; Pres. Eastern Region Cttee. Nat. Convention of Nigerian Citizens 51-53, Second Nat. Vice-Pres. 57-64; Chair. Gen. Council Commonwealth Parl. Asscn. 61-62; Knight Grand Cross of Equestrian Order of St. Gregory the Great (Vatican) 64; Commander of the Federal Republic (Nigeria) 64.
Leisure interests: reading, gardening, music, lawn tennis.
Providence Villa, 14-16 Mere Street, P.O. Box 150, Owerri, Nigeria.
Telephone: 59.

Njonjo, Charles, B.A., LL.B.; Kenyan lawyer; b. 1920; s. of ex-Senior Chief Josiah Njonjo of Kiambu; m. Margaret Bryson 1972; ed. Fort Hare Univ. (South Africa), Univ. Coll. Exeter (U.K.), London School of Economics, Gray's Inn.
Assistant Registrar-General, Kenya 55-60; Crown Counsel 60-61; Senior Crown Counsel 61-62; Deputy Public Prosecutor 62-63; Attorney-Gen. 63-; mem. of Parl. (ex-officio).
Attorney-General's Office, Nairobi, Kenya.

Njoroge, Ng'ethe, B.SC.; Kenyan diplomatist; ed. Alliance High School, and at Busoga, Central State Coll., Wilberforce, Ohio, and Boston Univ.
Assistant Sec. Ministry of Lands and Settlement 63-64; Senior Asst. Sec. Ministry of Foreign Affairs 64, later Head, Africa and Middle East Desk, Ministry of Foreign Affairs; then Counsellor, Bonn; High Commr. in U.K. 70-; mem. Kenya Del. to UN Gen. Assembly 64, 65, 66.
Kenya High Commission, London W1N 4AS, London.

Nkama, Moto; Zambian politician and diplomatist; b. 1937, Mufulira; ed. Mufulira Mine Upper Primary School, Kasama School, Eagle's Peak Coll. and Roma

Coll., Lesotho and Inst. for Commonwealth Studies, Oxford.

Worked in Mufulira Mine Welfare Dept. 61; election Supervisor, United Nat. Independence Party (UNIP) 62; Dep. Dir. of elections Aug. 62; Regional Sec. UNIP 62-63; First Sec. and Counsellor, United Nations 64-68; mem. UN Council for Namibia (South West Africa) 68; Private Sec. to Pres. Kaunda 68; mem. Parl. 68-; Asst. Minister for the Copperbelt and Minister of State for Foreign Affairs 68-69; Minister of State in charge of Cen. Province 69, for Foreign Affairs 69-70; Amb. to Fed. Repub. of Germany 70-74; Perm. Rep. to UN June 74-; concurrently accredited to France and to Italy; Minister for Cen. Province 71.
Permanent Mission of Zambia to United Nations, 150 East 58th Street, New York, N.Y. 10022, U.S.A.

Nkambo Mugerwa, Peter James; Ugandan lawyer; b. 10 Jan. 1933; ed. King's Coll., Budo, Makerere Univ., Trinity Coll., Cambridge and Gray's Inn, London.
Lecturer in Law, Univ. Coll., Dar-es-Salaam 62-64; Solicitor-Gen., Uganda 64-71; Attorney-Gen. and mem. Council of Ministers 71-73; private practice 73-; mem. African Inst. of Int. Law, American Soc. of Int. Law.
Mpanga and Mugerwa, Advocates, Diamond Trust Building, Box 7166, Kampala, Uganda.

Nkomo, Joshua; Rhodesian politician; b. 1917; ed. Adam's Coll., Natal, Univ. of S. Africa, Johannesburg.
Welfare Officer, Rhodesia Railways, Bulawayo, then Organizing Sec., Rhodesian African Railway Workers' Union 45-50; Pres. African Congress; employed in insurance and real estate; Pres.-Gen. African National Congress 57; lived abroad when African National Congress banned 59; elected Pres. Nat. Dem. Party Aug. 60; returned to S. Rhodesia; Pres. Zimbabwe African People's Union (ZAPU) 61-, amalgamated in African Nat. Council (ANC) 74; imprisoned 63-64; banished to Nuanetsi area April 64, to Gonakudzingula Restriction Camp, near Mozambique border Nov. 64 and for a further five years Dec. 68, released Dec. 74; involved in constitutional negotiations with Prime Minister Ian Smith; Leader, Branch of ANC in Rhodesia.
c/o African National Council, Salisbury, Rhodesia.

Nkundabagenzi, Fidèle; Rwandan diplomatist; b. 1 Jan. 1932, Rubayi-lez-Shangi; m.; four c.; ed. Univ. of Louvain.
Worked in Secretariat of UN Econ. Comm. for Africa 63-65; Sec.-Gen. Ministry of Planning June-Nov. 65; Sec.-Gen. Ministry of Int. Co-operation; fmr. Alt. Gov. IBRD; fmr. Pres. of Board, Bank of Rwanda; Perm. Rep. to UN 69-74; Amb. to U.S.A. and Canada 69-74.
Publs. *Rwanda Politique 1958-60, Evolution de la Structure Politique du Rwanda.*
c/o Ministry of Foreign Affairs, Kigali, Rwanda.

Nkweta, Lucas Zaa; Cameroonian agronomist and diplomatist; b. 17 Jan. 1929; ed. Umuahia Coll., E. Nigeria, School of Agriculture, Ibadan, and Univ. Coll., Ibadan.
Former agronomist, Cameroon Devt. Corpn., and fmr. Principal Agricultural Officer, W. Cameroon Govt.; First Sec., Cameroon Embassy, London 63; Consul-Gen., Lagos 64-65; Amb. to U.K. 65-73; Chevalier de l'Ordre de la Valeur.
c/o Ministry of Foreign Affairs, Yaoundé, Cameroon.

Noaman, Ismail Saeed, B.SC., M.A.; Yemeni diplomatist; b. 16 Aug. 1941, Aden; m. 1970; one d.; ed. Aden Coll., Dickinson Coll., Pennsylvania, and in Boston, Mass.
Teacher, Aden College Jan.-Aug. 67; Asst. Sec. to Aden Electricity Corpn. Aug. 67-April 68; Amb. and Perm. Rep. of S. Yemen to UN May 68-70; Sales Man. Nat. Co. of Home Trade 70-72; Technical Man. Yemen Nat. Oil Co. 72-.
Leisure interests: reading, travelling.

Khalifa Street, Block 31/127, Almansoura, Aden, People's Democratic Republic of Yemen.
Telephone: 82366.

Noble, Sir Peter (Scott), Kt., M.A., LL.D.; British classical scholar; b. 17 Oct. 1899, Fraserburgh; s. of Andrew Noble and Margaret Trail; m. 1928; two s. one d.; ed. Aberdeen and Cambridge Univs.
Lecturer in Latin, Liverpool Univ. 26-30; Fellow, St. John's Coll., Cambridge 28-31; Prof. of Latin Language and Literature, Leeds Univ. 30-38; Regius Prof. of Humanity, Univ. of Aberdeen 38-52; mem. Univ. Grants Cttee. 43-53; Principal King's Coll. London 52-67; mem. Gen. Dental Council 56-66; Vice-Chancellor, Univ. of London 61-64.
17 Glenorchy Terrace, Edinburgh, EH9 2DG, Scotland.
Telephone: 031-667-6287.

Noble, Robert Laing, M.D., PH.D., D.SC., F.R.S.C.; Canadian university professor; b. 3 Feb. 1910, Toronto; s. of late Dr. Robert Thomas Noble and Susannah Harriett (née Hodgetts) Noble; m. Eileen A. Dillon 1934; four s.; ed. Univs. of Toronto and Aberdeen.
Assistant Editor *Journal of Endocrinology,* London 38; Sec. of Canadian Physiological Soc. 45-49; fmr. Prof. and Assoc. Dir. The Collip Medical Research Laboratory, Univ. of Western Ontario; Ellen Mickle Fellowship 34; Leverhulme Fellowship of Coll. of Physicians 35-37; Pres. Canadian Physiological Soc. 59; Dir. Brit. Columbia Cancer Research Centre, Univ. of B.C., and Prof. of Physiology 60-75.
Leisure interests: fishing, hunting.
Publs. over 150 written works, especially on endocrinology, cancer and vinca alkaloids.
4746 West 2nd Avenue, Vancouver, B.C., Canada.
Telephone: 224-0818.

Noel, Emile; French civil servant; b. 17 Nov. 1922, Constantinople; ed. Ecole normale supérieure, Paris.
With Int. Secr., European Movt., Paris 49; Sec. of Gen. Affairs Comm., Consultative Assembly, Council of Europe 49-52; Dir. of Constitutional Comm. of Assembly, to look at the possibilities of a European Political Community 52-54; Chef de Cabinet to Pres. Consultative Assembly, Council of Europe 54-55; Chef de Cabinet, then Asst. Dir. de Cabinet of Pres. of the Council of Ministers, Paris 56-57; Exec. Sec. Comm. of EEC, Brussels 58-67; Sec.-Gen. Comm. of European Communities 68-.
Office of the Secretary-General, Commission of the European Communities, 200 rue de la Loi, 1040 Brussels, Belgium.
Telephone: 35-00-40/35-80-40.

Noel, Philip W.; American lawyer and politician; b. 6 June 1931, Warwick, R.I.; s. of S. Joseph Noel and Emma Crudeli; m. Joyce Sandberg 1956; three d. two s.; ed. Brown Univ. and Georgetown Univ. Law School.
Admitted to R.I. Bar, U.S. District Court Bar 57; Practising Attorney 57-66; mem. City Council, Warwick 60-66, Mayor of Warwick 66; Gov. of R.I. 72-; Democrat.
Leisure interests: fishing, boating, reading, sports, crafts.
Office of the Governor, State Capitol, Providence, R.I.; Home: 21 Kirby Avenue, Warwick, R.I., U.S.A.

Noel-Baker, Rt. Hon. Philip J., P.C.; British politician; b. Nov. 1889; ed. Bootham School, York, Haverford Coll., Pennsylvania, Cambridge and Munich Univs., and the Sorbonne.
Hon. Fellow of King's Coll., Cambridge 61-; Cassell Prof. of Int. Relations, London Univ. 24-29; Labour M.P. for Coventry 29-31, for Derby South 36-70; Parl. Private Sec. to Sec. of State for Foreign Affairs 29-31; Dodge Lecturer, Yale Univ. 34; mem. Foreign Office Advisory Council on Aliens 40-42; Parl. Sec. to Ministry of War Transport 42-45; Minister of State 45-Oct. 46; Sec. of

State for Air Oct. 46-47; Sec. of State for Commonwealth Relations Oct. 47-50; Minister of Fuel and Power 50-51; Pres. Int. Council of Sport and Physical Educ. (UNESCO) 60-; Chair. Parl. Labour Party Foreign Affairs Group 64-70; Nobel Peace Prize 59, Albert Schweitzer Book Prize 60.
Publs. *Disarmament, The League of Nations at Work, The Juridical Status of the British Dominions in International Law, The Private Manufacture of Armaments, The Arms Race: a Programme for World Disarmament* 58, *World Disarmament Now* 64, etc.
16 South Eaton Place, London, S.W.1, England.

Nofal, Sayed, DR. ARTS; Egyptian international civil servant; b. 16 March 1910, Al Mansoura; s. of Mohamed Ali Nofal and Fatima Al Sayed Amer; m. 1940; three s.; ed. Cairo Univ.
Head of Literary Dept. *Al Siyassa* 35-38; Teacher, Cairo Univ. 38; later Dir. of Technical Secr., Ministry of Educ. and Ministry of Social Affairs; later Dir. of Legislative Dept., Upper House of Egyptian Parl.; later Dir. Political Dept., Arab League; Asst. Sec.-Gen. Arab League 60-.
Publs. include *History of Arabic Rhetoric* 40, *Poetry of Nature in Arabic and Western Literature* 44, *Egypt in the United Nations* 47, *The Egyptian Parliament in a Quarter of a Century* 51, *The Political Status of the Emirates of the Arab Gulf and Southern Arabia* 59, *Joint Arab Action* Book I 68, Book II 71.
9 Khan younis Street, Madinat Al-Mohandiseen, Dokki, Cairo, Egypt.
Telephone: 807999.

Noguchi, Isamu; American sculptor and landscape designer; b. 7 Nov. 1904; ed. High Schools, Rolling Prairie and La Port, and Columbia and New York Univs. Apprentice to Onorio Ruotolo 23, to Brancusi, Paris 27; First Exhbn., N.Y. 28; works include sculpture and gardens for Connecticut Gen. Life Insurance Co., The First Nat. Bank of Fort Worth, Chase Manhattan Bank, Yale Library of Precious Books, UNESCO Building, Paris and The John Hancock Building; Billy Rose Art Garden at Israel Museum, Jerusalem; ballet and stage sets; exhibits in many perm. collections; exhbn. at Gimpel Fils, London 68, 72.
Publ. *A Sculptor's World* 67.
33-38 10th Street, Long Island City, N.Y. 11106, U.S.A.

Nogueira, Albano Pires Fernandes; Portuguese diplomatist; b. 1911; ed. Coimbra Univ.
Entered Diplomatic Service 41; posts in embassy in Washington, and legations in Pretoria and Tokyo 44-49; Chargé d'Affaires and Rep. to Allied High Comm. in Japan 50-52, Rep. of Portuguese Govt. to Japanese Govt. 52; Counsellor, London 52; Consul-Gen., Bombay 55, New York 55; mem. Perm. Mission of Portugal at UN 55-68; Amb. to EEC 68; Perm. Rep. to North Atlantic Council 70-74; Amb. to U.K. 74-.
Embassy of Portugal, 11 Belgrave Square, London, SW1X 8PP, England.

Nogueira, Alberto Franco; Portuguese diplomatist and politician; b. 1918; ed. Lisbon Univ.
Third Sec., Ministry of Foreign Affairs 43-45, Second Sec. 45-51; Second Sec. and Chargé d'Affaires, Portuguese Embassy, Tokyo 46-50; First Sec., Ministry of Foreign Affairs 51-54; Head of Political Affairs 54; Consul-Gen., London 55-58; Portuguese Rep., C.C.T.A. 55-60; Dir.-Gen. Political Affairs 60-61; Minister of Foreign Affairs 61-Oct. 69.
Publs. *Journal of Literary Critic* 53, *Struggle for the East* 57, *United Nations and Portugal* 63, *The Third World* 67.
c/o Ministry of Foreign Affairs, Lisbon, Portugal.

Nogueira, Dênio Chagas; Brazilian economist; b. 12 Dec. 1920, Rio de Janeiro; s. of Outubrino Nogueira and Anna Candida Nogueira; m. Orsina de Fonseca

1956; one s. one d.; ed. Universidade do Brazil and Univ. of Michigan.
Head, Finance Dept. Nat. Econ. Council 51-64; Editor-in-Chief *Conjuntura Econômica* 53-; Econ. Consultant to Econ. Comm. for Latin America and OAS on Foreign Investments in Latin American Free Trade Asscn. 60, to OAS on the Treaty of Montevideo (LAFTA) 61; Exec. Dir. Superintendency of Money and Credit, Brazil (SUMOC) 64-65; fmr. Pres. Central Bank of Brazil; Pres. Banco Geral do Brasil.
Leisure interests: tennis, yachting.
Publs. *Joint International Business Ventures in Brazil* 59, *Foreign Private Investments in LAFTA* 60, *Reforma Agraria Problemas e Soluções* 64.
Banco Geral do Brasil, S.A., Belém, Brazil.

Nogueira, Gen. Dirceu de Araujo; Brazilian army officer; b. 1912, Rio Grande do Sul.
Joined army 31; promoted to rank of Gen. 71; Head of Army Engineering and Communications Dept., Brasília; Minister of Transport March 74-.
Ministério dos Transportes, Brasília, Brazil.

Nokin, Max; Belgian businessman; b. 10 Dec. 1907; m. Denise Malfeson; two s. three d.; ed. Liège Univ.
Société Générale de Belgique 49-61, Gov. 62-; Chair. Usines de la Vieille Montagne, S.I.D.M.A.R.; Chair. and Man. Dir. Cimenteries C.B.R. Cementbedrijven; Vice-Chair. A.R.B.E.D., Métallurgie Hoboken, Cockerill; Dir. Westinghouse Electric Corpn., Genstar Ltd. (Montreal); Croix de Guerre avec palme, Grand Officier Ordre Léopold II, Commdr. Ordre de Léopold, Officier Ordre de la Couronne, Hon. K.B.E., Commdr. Ordre du Chêne (Luxembourg).
Leisure interests: golf, astronomy.
Rue Royale 30, 1000 Brussels, Belgium.

Nolan, Sidney Robert, C.B.E.; Australian artist; b. 22 April 1917; m. Cynthia Hansen; ed. Melbourne State and Technical schools, Melbourne Nat. Gallery.
One-Man Shows Paris, London, New York, Rome, Venice and capital cities of Australia; Arts Council Travelling Exhibition, Great Britain; also exhibited at Pittsburgh Int. Exhibition 53, 54, 55, 64, 67, 70, 71, New Delhi Int. Exhibition 53, Pacific Loan Exhibition, Australia and U.S.A. 56, Brussels Int. Exhibition 58, Documenta II, Kassel 59, Dunn Int. Exhibition, London 63, Edinburgh Festival 64, Aldeburgh Festival 64, 68, 71; Retrospective Exhibition New South Wales 67, Darmstadt, Edinburgh 71, Dublin 73; set designs for *Icare*, Colonel de Basil's Ballet Russe 40, the *Rite of Spring*, Covent Garden 62, *The Display*, Canberra 65; Commr. for Australia and Del. for Australian Documentary Films, Venice Biennale 54; Italian Govt. Scholarship 56; Commonwealth Fund Fellowship for travel in U.S.A. 59-61; Nat. Univ., Canberra Fellowship 65; Britannica Award (Australia) 69; Hon. LL.D., Nat. Univ. Australia 68, Hon. Fellow York Univ. 71, Hon. D.Litt. London Univ. 71, Fellow Bavarian Acad. 71.
Principal works in Tate Gallery (London), Museum of Modern Art (New York), Nat. Galleries of Australia, Tom Collins Memorial (Perth Univ.), Contemporary Art Soc. and Arts Council of Great Britain (London).
Publs. *Ned Kelly* 63, *Sidney Nolan: Myth and Imagery* 67, *Open Negative* 67, *Paradise Gardens* 71.
c/o Bank of New South Wales, 9 Sackville Street, London, W.1, England.

Nolan, Thomas Brennan, PH.B., PH.D.; American geologist; b. 21 May 1901, Greenfield, Mass.; s. of Frank Wesley and Anna (née Brennan); m. Mabelle Orleman 1927; one s.; ed. Yale Univ.
Geologist, U.S. Geol. Survey 24-44, Asst. Dir. 44-56, Dir. 56-65, Research Geologist 65-; mem. Nat. Acad. of Sciences, American Philosophical Soc., American Acad. of Arts and Sciences; Pres. Soc. of Economic Geologists 50, Geological Soc. of America 61; Vice-Pres. Int. Union

of Geological Sciences 64; Hon. Fellow, Royal Soc. of Edinburgh; Foreign mem. Geological Soc. of London; Spendiaroff Prize, Int. Geol. Congress 33; K.C. Li Medal and Prize, Columbia Univ. 54; Rockefeller Public Service Award, Princeton Univ. 61; Silver Medal, Tokyo Geog. Soc. 65; Hon. LL.D. (St. Andrews) 62.
Publs. Geological articles in scientific journals.
U.S. Geological Survey, Reston, Virginia 22092; Home: 2219 California Street, N.W., Washington, D.C. 20008, U.S.A.
Telephone: 703-860-7270 (Office); 202-462-2040 (Home).

Noland, Kenneth Clifton; American artist; b. 10 April 1927, Asheville, N.C.; s. of Harry C. and Bessie (Elkins) Noland; m. 1st Cornelia Langel (divorced), 2nd Stephanie Gordon 1967; three c.; ed. Black Mountain Coll., North Carolina and Paris.
Teacher Inst. of Contemporary Arts 50-52, Catholic Univ. 51-60, Bennington Coll. 68; one man shows: Galerie Creuze, Paris 49, Tibor de Nagy, New York City 57, 58, French and Co., New York City 59, André Emmerich Gallery 67, Nicholas Wilder Gallery, Los Angeles 67; work in permanent collections in Museum of Modern Art, Guggenheim Museum, Whitney Museum, Tate Gallery, Stedelijk Museum (Amsterdam), Zurich Kunsthaus and others.
c/o Lawrence Rubin Gallery, 49 West 57th Street, New York, N.Y. 10019; and Shaftsbury, Vermont, U.S.A.

Nolting, Frederick Ernest, Jr., M.A., PH.D.; American diplomatist and banker; b. 24 Aug. 1911, Richmond, Va.; s. of Frederick E. Nolting and Mary Buford; m. Olivia Lindsay Crumpler 1940; four d.; ed. St. Christopher's School, Richmond, Virginia, Univ. of Virginia and Harvard Univ.
Investment Firm, Richmond 34-39; Lecturing Fellowship in Philosophy, Univ. of Va. 41-42; U.S. Navy 42-46; Dept. of State 46-64, Asst. to Deputy Under-Sec. of State 50-53, Special Asst. to Sec. of State for Mutual Security Affairs 53-55; Dir. Office of Political Affairs, U.S. Del. to NATO 55-57; Dep. Chief of Mission, U.S. Del. to NATO and European Regional Orgs. (USRO), Alt. U.S. Rep. on North Atlantic Council 57-61; Ambassador to Viet-Nam 61-63; Vice-Pres. European Offices Morgan Guaranty Trust Co. of New York 64-69, Asst. Chair. 69-73, Consultant 73-; Diplomat-in-Residence, Univ. of Virginia 71-73; Olsson Prof. of Business Admin., Grad. School of Business, Univ. of Virginia 73; Dir. Miller Center of Public Affairs, Univ. of Virginia 75-.
Leisure interests: sport, music.
Stony Point Road, Charlottesville, Virginia, U.S.A.
Telephone: 804-295-3869.

Nono, Luigi; Italian composer; b. 29 Jan. 1924; s. of Mario and Maria Manetti Nono; m. Nuria Schoenberg 1955; two d.
Studied with Bruno Maderna and Hermann Scherchen; teacher New Music Summer School, Kranichsteiner Musikinstitut, Darmstadt 57-, Dartington Hall Music Summer School, Devon (England) 59, 60.
Compositions. Variazioni canoniche sulla serie dell' op. 41 di A. Schoenberg 50, Polifonica-Monodia-Ritmica 51, Composizione per Orchestra, I Epitafio per F. García-Lorca, II Epitafio per F. García-Lorca 52, III Epitafio per F. García-Lorca, Due Espressioni per Orchestra 53, La Victoire de Guernica (poem by P. Eluard), Liebeslied, Der Rote Mantel (ballet) 54, Canti per 13, Incontri 55, Il Canto Sospeso 56, Varianti 57, La Terra e la Campagna (words by C. Pavese), Cori di Didone (words by G. Ungaretti) 58, Composizione per Orchestra N. 2—Diario Polacco '58 59, Ha Venido (words by A. Machado) 60, Sarà dolce tacere (words by C. Pavese) 60, Omaggio a Emilio Vedova (electronic music) 60, Intolleranza 1960 61 (words by A. M. Ripellino, V. Mayakovsky, P. Eluard, H. Alleg, J.-P. Sartre, B. Brecht, I. Fucik), Sul Ponte di Hiroshima 62 (words by G. Anders, J. L. Pacheco and C. Pavese), Canciones A Guiomar 63 (words by A. Machado), Dal Diario Italiano 64, A Floresta è Jovem e Cheia de vida 66, La Fabrica illuminata (words by G. Scabia) 66, Ricorda Cosa ti Hanno Fatto in Auschwitz 66, Per bastiana tai-yangcheng 67, Contrappunto dialettico alla mente (words by S. Sanchez, N. Balestrini; for tape) 68, Musica manifesto N.1: Un volto, del mare (words by C. Pavese; for voice and tape) 68-69, Y entonces comprendió (words by C. Franqui; for tape, 6 women's voices and chorus) 69-70, Ein Gespenst geht um in der Welt (words by K. Marx, C. Sanchez, H. Santamaria; for solo soprano, chorus and orchestra) 71, Como una ola de fuerza y luz (words by J. Huasi; for soprano, piano, orchestra, tape) 71-72, Al gran sole carico d'amore (words by E. Guevara, A. Rimbaud, Louise Michel, T. Bunke, B. Brecht, K. Marx, Lenin, C. Pavese, C. Sanchez, H. Santamaria, etc.; scenic action in two acts) 72-75, Canto per il Vietnam (mixed chorus) 73, Für Paul Dessau (for tape) 74.
Giudecca 882, 30123 Venice, Italy.
Telephone: Venice 28368.

Norberg, Dag, D.PH.; Swedish classical scholar; b. 31 July 1909, Strängnäs; s. of Otto Norberg and Gunhild Rappe; m. Brita von Otter 1939; four s.; ed. Uppsala Univ.
Docent, Uppsala Univ. 37-48; Prof. of Latin Language and Literature, Stockholm Univ. 48-75, Dean, Faculty of Humanities, 60-63; President (Rector), Stockholm Univ. 66-74; mem. Human Vetenskapssamfundet i Uppsala 46, Vitterhetsakademien 55, Danske Videnskabernes Selskab 64, Vetenskapsakademien 65; Pres. Int. Fed. of Socs. of Classical Studies 64-69.
Publs. In Registrum Gregorii Magni studia I-II, 37-39, Syntaktische Forschungen 43, Beiträge zur spätl. Syntax 44, Horatius sista lyriska diktning 45, La poésie latine rythmique du haut moyen âge 53, Introduction à l'étude de la versification latine médiévale 58, Den romerska litteraturen in Bonniers allmänna litteraturhistoria 59, Epistulae s. Desiderii Cadurcensis 61, Processen mot Caelius och Ciceros försvarstal 65, Manuel pratique de latin médiéval 68, Au seuil du Moyen Age 74.
University of Stockholm, Drottninggatan 116, Stockholm, Sweden.
Telephone: 34-08-60.

Norbom, Jon Ola; Norwegian economist and politician; b. 15 Dec. 1923, Baerum; m. Ellen Ann Hook 1954; two d.; ed. Oslo Univ.
Secretary, Ministry of Industry 50-54; Asst. Research Economist, Nat. Bureau of Econ. Research, N.Y. 54; Statistician UN Office, N.Y. 55; Research Econ. and later Expert on Commercial Policy, GATT, Geneva 59-67; Parl. Under-Sec. of State, Ministry of Finance 67-69; Dir. Int. Trade Centre, UNCTAD/GATT, Geneva 71-72, 73-; Minister of Finance and Customs Oct. 72-73; Chair. Norwegian Young Liberals 50-52; mem. Nat. Exec. Liberal Party.
International Trade Centre UNCTAD/GATT, Geneva; Home: 1299 Commugny, Vaud, Switzerland.

Nord, Hans Robert, D.IUR.; Netherlands lawyer and international civil servant; b. 11 Oct. 1919, The Hague; s. of Charles F. L. Nord and Philippina C. Elshout; m. Margaret Ena Bevan 1951; two s.; ed. Gymnasium, The Hague, and Leiden Univ.
Barrister, The Hague 43-45; Legal Adviser 45-61; Pres. European Movement in the Netherlands 58-61; Chair. Netherlands Atlantic Cttee. 54-61; Sec.-Gen. European Parl. 61-; Officer, Order of Orange-Nassau, Commdr. Order of Merit of Italy, Commdr. Order of San Carlos, Columbia, Commdr. Nat. Order, Ivory Coast.
Leisure interests: music, literature, travel.
Publs. The Idea of Representation in Constitutional Law 45, Problems of International Government 48, International and Supra-National Co-operation 52, In Search

of a Political Framework for a United Europe 56, *NATO* 61.

15 Rue Conrad I, Luxembourg-ville, Luxembourg.
Telephone: 22703.

Nordal, Jóhannes, B.SC. (ECON.), PH.D.; Icelandic economist and central banker; b. 11 May 1924, Reykjavík; s. of Prof. Sigurdur Nordal and Ólöf Jónsdóttir; m. Dóra Gudjónsdóttir 1953; one s. five d.; ed. Reykjavík Grammar School and London School of Economics.
Chief Economist, Nat. Bank of Iceland 54-59, Gen. Man. 59-61; Governor, Central Bank of Iceland (Sedlabanki Íslands) 61-, Chair. Board of Governors 64-; Chair. of Board Nat. Power Co. (Landsvirkjun) 65-; Gov. Int. Monetary Fund for Iceland 65-; Chair. Humanities Div. of Science Fund for Iceland 58-; mem. Soc. Scientiarum Islandica 59-; Grand Knight Order of Falcon 66.
Publs. *Iceland* 66; Editor *Fjármálatíðindi* (Financial Review) 54-; Co. Editor *Nýtt Helgafell* (literary periodical) 55-59.
Laugarásvegur 11, Reykjavík, Iceland.
Telephone: 33350(Home); 20500 (Office).

Norden, Albert; German politician and professor; b. 4 Dec. 1904; ed. Wuppertal-Elberfeld.
Joined German Communist Party 20; wood-work instructor, Elberfeld 21-23; imprisoned for anti-fascist activity 23-24, 27, 39-40; Ed. *Deutschlands Stimme* 45; Man. Press Dep., Ministry of Information 46; Prof. Humboldt Univ., Berlin 46; mem. Social Dem. Party 46 ; mem. Cen. Cttee., Social Dem. Party 55-, Politburo of the Cen. Cttee. 58-; mem. Presidium of Nat. Council, Nat. Front of Dem. Germany 54-68; mem. Presidium, German Peace Council 58-; mem. Bureau, World Council for Peace 58-; fmr. mem. of Board German Press Asscn.; Nat Prize for Art and Literature (2nd Class) 51; Order of Merit of the Fatherland (Silver) 58, etc.
Central Committee of the Social Democratic Party, 102 Berlin, 2 Werderscher Markt, German Democratic Republic.

Nordenfalk, Carl (Adam Johan), M.A., FIL.DR.; Swedish museum official; b. 13 Dec. 1907; ed. Univs. of Uppsala, Stockholm, Gothenburg.
Assistant Curator, Gothenburg Art Museum 35-44; Curator, Nat. Museum of Arts, Stockholm 44-58, Dir.-Gen. 58-69; Mellon Prof., Univ. of Pittsburgh 71-72, 73-; Slade Prof. Univ. of Cambridge 72-73; Kress Prof. Nat. Gallery, Washington 73-; mem. Royal Soc. of Sciences (Uppsala), Royal Swedish Acad. of Letters; Visiting mem. Inst. for Advanced Study, Princeton 49-50, 57, 67-70; Prof. h.c.; Corresp. Fellow British Acad. 67-, Bavarian Acad. of Sciences (Munich), German Archaeological Inst. etc.; Hon. mem. Swedish Royal Acad. of Fine Arts, Real Acad. de Bellas Artes de San Fernando (Madrid), American Philosophical Soc.
Publs. *Die spätantiken Kanontafeln* 38, *Vincent van Gogh* 43, *Kung Praktiks och Drottning Teoris jaktbok* 55, *Die spätantiken Zierbuchstaben* 70, *Codex Caesareus Upsaliensis* 71; also co-author of several books: (with A. Grabar) *Le Haut Moyen-Age* 57, *La peinture romaine* 58, *Treasures of Swedish Art* 65, *Medieval and Renaissance Miniatures from the Lessing J. Rosenwald collection* 75, *Vergilius Augusteus* 76.
Department of Fine Arts, University of Pittsburgh, Pa. 15260, U.S.A.

Nordenson, Harald, PH.D.; Swedish industrialist; b. 10 Aug. 1886, Göttingen; s. of Dr. med. Erik Nordenson and Bertha Kleman; m. Clare Lagercrantz 1914; three s. one d.; ed. Uppsala Univ.
Lecturer physical chemistry, Uppsala Univ. 14-19; Technical Dir. Liljeholmens Stearin A.B., Stockholm 17-29, Man. Dir. 29-50, Chair. 50-63; Chair. *Svenska Dagbladet*, Stockholm, 40-62, Stockholms Superfosfat Fabriks AB 31-60, Nitroglycerin A.B. 38-60, A.B. Stockholms Bryggerier 50-63, The Royal Dramatic Theatre 33-38; Pres. Chamber of Commerce, Stockholm 39-57; Cons. mem. of First Chamber of the Riksdag 38-53; mem. Swedish Acad. of Sciences, Soc. of Sciences Uppsala, Swedish Acad. of Eng. Sciences.
Leisure interests: physics, philosophy, philately.
Publ. *Relativity, Time and Reality.*
15022 Nykvarn, Sweden.
Telephone: 0755-40018.

Nordli, Odvar; Norwegian politician; b. 3 Nov. 1927, Stange, Hedmark; ed. in business administration.
Assistant, Baerum Municipal Auditor's Office 48-49; Chief Clerk, Hedmark County Auditor's Office 49-57; District Auditor, Vang and Löten 57-61; mem. Storting 61-; mem. and Deputy Chair. Stange Municipal Council 52; Chair. Municipal Cttee. of Hedmark Labour Party 60-; Deputy mem. Central Cttee. of Labour Party 65, Chair. Hedmark Labour Party 68; Chair. Trade Union and Labour Party Tax Cttee. 67-68; Leader Parl. Labour Party 73-76; Vice-Chair. Parl. Municipal Cttee. 65-69; Chair. Parl. Social Welfare Cttee. 69-71; Minister of Labour and Municipal Affairs March 71-Oct. 72; Chair. Comm. of Defence 74-75; Prime Minister Jan. 76-.
Akersgt. 42, Oslo dep., Oslo 1, Norway.
Telephone: 11-90-90.

Nordoff, Paul; American musician; b. 6 June 1909; ed. Philadelphia Musical Acad., Juilliard School, New York City.
Teacher Philadelphia Conservatoire; Asst. Prof. Mich. State Coll.; won two Guggenheim Fellowships, Ford Foundation Faculty Fellowship 54-55; Pulitzer award 40; Prof. Bard Coll. 49-59; music therapy for handicapped children, England 59, autistic children, U.S.A. 61-65, Inst. of Logopedics, Kansas 62, Teacher Consultant, Board of Public Educ., Philadelphia, Pennsylvania 62-67; Chief Music Therapist, Univ. of Pennsylvania, Dept. of Child Psychiatry 62-67; travelled on a Music Therapy Demonstration and Training Project for Handicapped Children in Scandinavia 67-69; Dr. Mus. h.c. (Combs Coll. of Music).
Compositions include two piano concertos, opera, *Secular Mass*, music for Katherine Cornell's production *Romeo and Juliet*, *The Masterpiece* (opera) 41, *Tallyho* (ballet, with Agnes de Mille), *Salem Shore*, *Every Soul is a Circus* (dances for Martha Graham), *The Sea Change*, *Mr. Fortune* (operas with Ralph Knight); *Robert Burns: Poems and Songs*; *Music Therapy for Handicapped Children: Investigations and Experiences*, *Pif-Paf-Poltrie*, *Children's Play-Songs* Vol. I and II, *The Story of Artaban*, *The Three Bears*, *The Children's Christmas Play*, *Fun for Four Drums* (all with Clive Robbins).
c/o RFD 1 Chester Springs, Pa. 19425, U.S.A.

Nørgaard, Ivar, M.A. (ECON.); Danish politician; b. 26 July 1922, Kongens Lyngby; s. of Ingvar and of the late Olga Nørgaard; m. 1st Inge Gothenborg 1947 (died 1972), two d.; m. 2nd Sonja Nørgaard 1974; ed. Copenhagen Univ.
Secretary, Customs Dept., Ministry of Finance 47; Sec., Econ. Council, Labour Movement 48-55; Dir. Workers' High School, Esbjerg 55; Political Editor-in-Chief *Aktuelt* 61-64, Man. Editor 64-65; Minister of Econ. Affairs 65-68, also Minister for European Market Relations 67-68; mem. Parl. 66-; taught at Danish High School of Admin. 69; Minister for Foreign Econ. Affairs 71-72, for Foreign Affairs 72-73, for Foreign Econ. Affairs and Nordic Relations Feb. 75-; Dir. Workers' Educ. Asscn. 64-65; mem. Board of Danish Nat. Bank 68, Lyngby-Taarbaek Municipality 54-55, Atomic Energy Comm. 56-65, Nat. Wage Board 68-71; co-founder and fmr. Vice-Pres. of Social Democratic students org. Free Forum; mem. EC Council, Nordic Ministerial Council; mem. and Vice-Pres. European Parl. 74-75.

Publs. *Lærebog i Nationaløkonomi* (Textbook on National Economy) 49, *Focus på Nationaløkonomien* (Focus on the National Economy), *Din løn og Samfundets økonomi* (Your Wage and the National Economy); Editor and Co-author *Din økonomi og Samfundets* (Your Own and the Community's Economy) 60; Co-editor and Co-author *Arbejderhåndbog for Samarbejdsudvalg* (Workers' Manual on Industrial Council Work) 54.
Nydamsvej 15, 2880 Bagsvoerd, Denmark.
Telephone: 01-12 48 25.

Norindr, Phagna Pheng; Laotian diplomatist; b. 17 May 1919, Luang Prabang; *m.*; twelve *c.*; ed. in France.
Professor, Pavie School, Vientiane 41-46; Personal Sec. to Prime Minister Xieng Mao 46; Dir. Savannakhet School 47-51; Dir. of Customs 54-58; Dir. of Cabinets of Prime Ministers Phoui Sananikone and Kon Abhay 58-60; Deputy to Nat. Assembly 60-65; Sec. Gen. Govt. of Laos 65-72; Amb. to U.S.A. and Perm. Rep. to UN 72-74.
c/o Ministry of Foreign Affairs, Vientiane, Laos.

Norling, Bengt Olov; Swedish politician; b. 12 Jan. 1925, Malmö; *s.* of David Norling and Margareta Thorsén; *m.* Elisabeth Stöfling 1946; one *s.*; ed. privately.
Railway worker -56; Ombudsman, Swedish Railwaymen's Union 56-65; Ombudsman, Swedish Confed. of Trade Unions 65-68, Sec. 69; Minister of Transport and Communication 69-; mem. of Parl. (Social Democratic Party) 71-.
Leisure interest: music.
Kommunikationsdepartementet, Fack, 103 20 Stockholm, Sweden.

Norlund, Niels Erik, PH.D.; Danish mathematician; b. 26 Oct. 1885, Slagelse; *s.* of Alfred Christian and Sophie (Holm) Norlund; *m.* Agnete Weaver 1912; two *d.*; ed. Copenhagen, Paris and Göttingen Univs.
Former Prof. of Mathematics Copenhagen Univ.; former Dir. Danish Geodetic Inst.; Pres. Rask-Örsted Foundation 28-64; Pres. Royal Danish Acad. of Science 27-33; Vice-Pres. Int. Council of Scientific Unions 31, Pres. 34; Foreign mem. Royal Society and Royal Astronomical Society; mem. Acads. of Science in Paris, Rome, Stockholm, Oslo, Uppsala, Naples and Helsinki; Editor *Acta mathematica*; Hon. D.Sc. (London and Dijon); Hon. D.Eng. (Darmstadt); Hon. Ph.D. (Lund and Oslo).
Publs. *Vorlesungen über Differenzenrechnung* 24, *Leçons sur les séries d'interpolation* 26, *Leçons sur les équations aux différences finies* 29, *The Map of Denmark* 42, *The Map of Iceland* 44.
Malmøgade 6, Copenhagen, Denmark.
Telephone: Øbro 3046.

Norman, Sir Arthur Gordon, K.B.E., D.F.C.; British business executive; b. 18 Feb. 1917, North Pertherton, Somerset; *s.* of Christopher William Norman and Mary Christine Milton; *m.* Margaret Doreen Harrington 1944; three *s.* two *d.*; ed. Blundell's School.
Thomas De La Rue and Co. 34-, Asst. Gen. Man. 47, Dir. 51, Man. Dir. 53; Chair. The De La Rue Co. Ltd. 64-; R.A.F. 41-46; Pres. Confederation of British Industry 68-70, Vice-Pres. 70-74; Dir. Sun Life Assurance Soc., S.K.F. (U.K.) Ltd.; Trustee, R.A.F. Museum, World Wildlife Fund; Gov. Sherborne School.
Leisure interests: tennis, golf, country life.
Office: 84-86 Regent Street, London, W1A 1DL; Home: Sturminster Newton, Dorset, England.
Telephone: 01-734-8020.

Norman, Willoughby Rollo; British business executive; b. 12 Oct. 1909, Hindhead; *s.* of Sir Henry Norman and The Hon. Lady Florence Priscilla McLaren; *m.* The Hon. Barbara Jacqueline Boot 1934; one *s.* two *d.*; ed. Eton Coll. and Magdalen Coll., Oxford.
Army Service 39-45; Vice-Chair. Boots Pure Drug Co.

Ltd. 54-61, Chair. 61-72, Hon. Pres. 72-; Dir. Nat. Westminster Bank Ltd. and Chair. Eastern Region; Underwriting mem. of Lloyds; Dir. Guardian Royal Exchange Assurance, Sheepbridge Engineering Ltd.; Deputy Chair. English China Clays Ltd.
Leisure interests: shooting, fishing, gardening.
Pickwell Manor, Melton Mowbray, Leics.; and 31 Hurst Mill, Petersfield, Hants; 28 Ranelagh House, Elystan Place, London, S.W.3, England.
Telephone: Somerby 215; and 01-589-0467.

Normann, A. Christian; Danish merchant and politician; b. 23 March 1904, Hjerm; *s.* of P. C. Normann Hjerm and Caroline (née Kristensen); *m.* Inge Haustrup 1934; one *s.* two *d.*; ed. agricultural school.
Journalist 23-33; Purchasing and Sales Man. Haustrup Fabriker Ltd., Odense 34-46, Dir. 34-; mem. Odense Town Council 43-46; f. Normann Publishing Office, Odense; Chair. *Helsinger Dagblad* 58-, Chief Editor 72-; M.P. 50-72; Minister of Fisheries 60-64; Dir. The Danish Nat. Bank 57-60, Danish Milk Co. Ltd. 67-68; mem. Nordic Council 57-60, 64-68, European Council 66-68, Danish Defence Cttee.; Minister of Fisheries and for Greenland 68-71; Liberal.
Leisure interest: literature.
Bergmannsdal, Sdr. Strandvej 54, Elsinore, Denmark.
Telephone: 01-630016 (Office); Elsinore 214063 (Home).

Normann, Leif Otto; Danish shipowner; b. 1 Oct. 1890, Copenhagen; *s.* of Capt. C. O. E. Normann, R.N. and Camilla Hoppe; *m.* Lili Koefoed-Nielsen 1924; two *d.*; ed. Public High School and Naval Coll., Copenhagen.
Royal Danish Navy 06-10; joined shipping firm 10; N.Y. 12-15, South America 21-22; Man. United Steamship Co. Ltd. 23, Managing Dir. 34-64; Chair. Danish Shipowners' Asscn. 53-59, Maritime Council 53-59, Titan Motor Works, Hotel Codan and Baltica Insurance Co. 47-64; Vice-Chair. Elsinore Shipbuilding & Engineering Co. Ltd., Frederikshavns Shipbuilding Yard Ltd., Aarhus Shipbuilding and Engineering Co. Ltd. 36-65; Private Insurers Ltd., etc.; Dir. War Risk Insurance Inst. for Danish Ships, Copenhagen Free Port Co. Ltd. 48-56, etc.; mem. Council of Tourist Asscn., Int. Chamber of Commerce (Danish Cttee.), Ice-Breaking Council, Danish Shipping Board 39-49 and 52-61; Vice-Pres. Int. Chamber of Shipping 54-56; Judge, Maritime and Mercantile Court 37-41; Knight Commdr. 1st Class and Silver Cross of Order of Dannebrog; Knight Commdr. of Norwegian Order of St. Olav, Knight Commdr. Swedish Order of Vasa, Greek Order of George I.
Leisure interest: history.
5 Kvaesthusgade, Copenhagen, Denmark.
Telephone; Copenhagen 01-151597.

Normant, Henri, D.ès SC.; French scientist; b. 25 June 1907, Plozévet; *s.* of Jean Normant and Anne Gentric; *m.* Madeleine Sosson 1932; two *s.* three *d.*; ed. Collège Saint Louis, Brest, and Univ. de Caen.
Prof. of Organic Synthesis, Faculty of Sciences, Paris 52-; Pres. Second Section, Ecole Pratique des Hautes Etudes 69-; mem. Centre Nat. de la Recherche Scientifique; mem. Conseil Nat. de l'Enseignement Supérieur et de la Recherche; mem. Acad. des Sciences 66, Deutsche Akademie Leopoldina; Lauréat de la Soc. Chimique de France et l'Acad. des Sciences; Pres. Soc. Chimique de France 71; Fellow, Royal Soc. of Arts; Chevalier Légion d'Honneur; Officier de l'Instruction Publique.
Leisure interests: hunting and fishing.
Publs. *Chimie Organique* (2nd edition) 68, *Recherches sur les Hétérocycles Oxygénés, sur les Organo-Métalliques (Magnésiens Vinyliques) et sur les Solvants*.
40 bis rue Violet, Paris 15e, France.
Telephone: SUF 9999.

Norodom Sihanouk, Prince Samdech Preah; former King of Cambodia; b. 31 Oct. 1922; s. of late King Norodom Suramarit and Queen Kossamak Nearireath; ed. in Saigon and Paris.
Elected King April 41, abdicated March 55; Prime Minister and Minister of Foreign Affairs Oct. 55, March 56, Sept. 56, April 57; Perm. Rep. to UN Feb.-Sept. 56; elected Head of State after death of his father 60, took oath of fidelity to vacant throne 60, deposed March 70; resided in Peking, China; established Royal Govt. of Nat. Union of Cambodia (GRUNC) May 70; restored as Head of State when GRUNC forces overthrew Khmer Repub. April 75, resigned April 76; Head of the Popular Socialist Community 55-70; musician and composer; producer of film *Le Petit Prince*.
Publ. *My War With the C.I.A.* (with Wilfred Burchett) 73.

Norris, Sir Eric George, K.C.M.G.; British diplomatist; b. 14 March 1918, Hertford; s. of late Henry F. Norris and of Ruth Norris; m. Pamela Crane 1941; three d.; ed. Hertford Grammar School and St. Catharine's Coll., Cambridge.
Military service 40-46; Dominions Office 46; First Sec., Dublin 48-50, Pakistan 52-55; Counsellor, Delhi 55-57; Deputy High Commr., Bombay 57-60, Calcutta 62-65; Asst. Under Sec. of State, Commonwealth Office 66-68; High Commr. to Kenya 68-72; Deputy Under Sec. of State, Foreign and Commonwealth Office 72-73; High Commr. to Malaysia Jan. 74-.
British High Commission, Wisma Damansara, Jalan Samantan, Kuala Lumpur, Malaysia.

Norrish, Ronald George Wreyford, PH.D., SC.D., F.R.I.G., F.R.S.; British chemist; b. 9 Nov. 1897, Cambridge; s. of Herbert Norrish and Amy Norrish; m. Annie Smith 1926; two d.; ed. Perse School, Cambridge, and Emmanuel Coll., Cambridge.
Served in France, First World War 16-19; Fellow of Emmanuel Coll., Cambridge 25-; Lecturer 30-36, Prof. of Physical Chemistry, Univ. of Cambridge 37-65, Prof. Emer. 65-; Pres. Faraday Soc. 53-55; Vice-Pres. Royal Inst. of Chem. 57-59; Liversidge and Faraday Lecturer, Chemical Soc. 58, 65; Pres. British Asscn., Section B 60-61; Bakerian Lecturer, Royal Soc. 66; Hon. mem. Polish Chemical Soc., Corresp. mem. Acad. of Sciences, Göttingen, Royal Soc. of Sciences, Liège 60; Hon. mem. Faraday Soc. 66, Société de Chimie Physique, Paris; Foreign mem. Polish Acad. of Sciences 62; Hon. mem. Royal Soc. of Science, Uppsala 64, N.Y. Acad. of Sciences 68; Foreign mem. Bulgarian Acad. of Sciences 69; Hon. Fellow Royal Soc. of Edinburgh 72; Meldola Medal, Royal Inst. of Chemistry 26, Davy Medal, Royal Soc., London 65; Lewis (Combustion Inst.) Medal 64, Faraday Medal, Chemical Soc. 65; Longstaff Medal, Chemical Soc. 69; Nobel Prize for Chemistry 67; Hon. D. de l'Univ. (Paris) 58; Hon. D.Sc. (Sheffield, Leeds 65, Liverpool, Lancaster 65; Hon. D.Sc. (Univ. of British Columbia) 69, Commdr. de l'Ordre des Chevaliers du Tastevin, Burgogne 71, Knight's Cross Order of Polonia Restituta 74, Bulgarian Order of Cyril and Methodius (1st Degree) 74.
Leisure interests: discussion, travel.
Publs. Scientific Papers in the *Proceedings of the Royal Society, The Transactions of the Faraday Society, Journal of Chemical Society,* and in various journals, etc.
Department of Physical Chemistry, and Emmanuel College, Univ. of Cambridge; Home: 7 Park Terrace, Cambridge, England.
Telephone: Cambridge 66499 and 65411 (Office); Cambridge 55147 (Home).

Norstad, Gen. Lauris; American air force officer; b. 24 March 1907; ed. U.S. Military Acad.
Commissioned Cavalry 30; attended Air Corps Flying Schools 30-31; Air Corps Service 31-36; Adjutant 61st School Squadron, G.H.Q., Long Island 36, 9th Bombardment Group; entered Air Corps Tactical School, Alabama 39; Officer-in-Charge 9th Bombardment Group Navigation School 40; Asst. Chief of Staff in Intelligence, G.H.Q., Virginia 40-42; Asst. Chief of Staff (Operations) Twelfth Air Force, in England and N. Africa 42; Dir. of Operations, Mediterranean Allied Air Forces 43-44; Chief of Staff Twentieth Air Force, Washington 44-45; Asst. Chief of Air Staff (Plans) 45; Dir. of Plans and Operations, War Dept. 46-47; Lieut.-Gen. 47; Deputy Chief of Staff (Operations) 47-50; Acting Vice-Chief of Staff 50; C.-in-C. U.S. Air Forces in Europe 51-56; Supreme Allied Commdr. in Europe 56-62; Chair. Owens-Corning Fiberglas Corpn. 67-72, now Dir.; Dir. United Air Lines, English-Speaking Union of U.S.A. 64, Continental Oil Co., Abitibi Paper Co.; mem. Gen. Advisory Cttee., U.S. Arms Control and Disarmament Agency; Trustee Rand Corpn., Toledo Hospital, Toledo Museum of Art, Asscn. of Graduates of U.S. Mil. Acad.; Chair. Trustees, Eisenhower Coll., Seneca Falls; D.S.M. with two Oak Leaf Clusters, Silver Star, Legion of Merit with Cluster, Air Medal; Hon. O.B.E., Légion d'Honneur, Croix de Guerre, Ordre du Ouissam Alaouit Cherifien (Morocco), Dr. of Mil. Science (Maryland), Diploma for the Royal Order of King George I (Greece), Grand Cross Order of Avis (Portugal).
Office: 717 Fifth Avenue, New York, N.Y. 10022, U.S.A.
Telephone: 419-259-3100.

Northrop, John Howard, B.S., A.M., PH.D.; American chemist; b. 5 July 1891, Yonkers, N.Y.; s. of Dr. John I. Northrop and Alice Belle Rich; m. Louise Walker 1917; one s. one d.; ed. Columbia Univ.
W. B. Cutting Travelling Fellow, Columbia Univ.; working in Jacques Loeb's Laboratory, Rockefeller Inst. 15; apptd. to staff of Rockefeller Inst. 16, mem. 24-61, Emer. 61-; Visiting Prof. Univ. of Calif. 49-58, Emer. 62-; Stevens Prize, Coll. of Physicians and Surgeons Columbia Univ. 31; Capt. Chemical Warfare Service 17-18; discovered and worked on fermentation process for manufacturing acetone; Sc.D. Harvard Univ. 36, Columbia Univ. 37, Yale Univ. 37, Princeton Univ. 40, Rutgers 41; LL.D. Calif. 39; De Lamar Lecturer, School of Hygiene and Public Health, Johns Hopkins Univ. 37; Jessup Lecturer Columbia Univ. 38; Hitchcock Lecturer Calif. 39; Thayer Lecturer Johns Hopkins Univ. 40; Chandler Medal, Columbia Univ. 37; Daniel Giraud Elliot Medal for 1939, Nat. Acad. of Sciences; shared Nobel Prize in Chem. 46; Alex. Hamilton Award, Columbia Univ. 61; mem. Nat. Acad. of Sciences, Halle Akademie der Naturforscher, etc.; Cert. of Merit U.S.A. 48; Hon. mem. Chemical Soc., London, Benjamin Franklin Fellow, Royal Soc. for the Encouragement of Arts; Fellow, World Acad. Arts Soc.
Leisure interests: hunting, fishing.
Publ. *Crystalline Enzymes* 39.
P.O. Box 1387, Wickenburg, Ariz. 85358, U.S.A.

Norvik, Erling; Norwegian politician; b. 9 April 1928, Vadsø; s. of Mosse and Erling Norvik; m. Mardon Norvik 1950; one s. one d.; ed. Higher School of Commerce.
Editor of local newspapers in Finnmark 49-56; Sec. Finnmark Conservative Party 56-61; mem. Parl. 61-73; First Vice-Chair. of Conservative Party 70-72, Sec.-Gen. 72-74, Chair. 74-.
Høyres Hovedorganisasjon, Stortingsgt. 20, Oslo 1, Norway.
Telephone: 336970 (Office); 130711 (Home).

Nosaka, Sanzo; Japanese politician; b. 1892, Hagi, Yamaguchi Prefecture; m. Nosaka Ryo 1919 (died 1971); ed. Keio Univ.
Secretary Brotherhood Asscn. (later called Japanese

Fed. of Labour) 17; visited U.K., Europe and Russia 19-22 and joined Communist Party of Great Britain during stay in U.K.; mem. Communist Party of Japan 22; arrested for first time 23; mem. Cen. Cttee. Communist Party of Japan 31; in Moscow as mem. Presidium Exec. Cttee. Communist International 35-43; anti-war activities in U.S.A. 34-38, and in China 40-45; returned to Japan and elected mem. Cen. Cttee. and Politburo Communist Party of Japan 46; mem. House of Reps. 46-50; underground activity 50-55; mem. House of Councillors 56-; Chair. Cen. Cttee. Communist Party of Japan 58-.
Publs. *Selected Works*, 2 vols., *My Stormy Path* (autobiography).
26, 4-chome, Sendagaya, Shibuya-ku, Tokyo, Japan.
Telephone: 03-403-6111.

Nosavan, General Phoumi; Laotian army officer and politician.
Secretary of State for Defence 59; promoted to Gen. 60; Minister of Defence 60, and Sports, Youth and Ex-Servicemen 60; Dep. Premier, Minister of the Interior, Culture and Social Welfare (Prince Souvanna Phouma Cabinet) 60; Dep. Premier and Minister of Defence (Prince Boun Oum Cabinet) 61; Vice-Premier and Minister of Finance (Provisional Nat. Union Govt. Cabinet) July 62-65; exiled 65; Leader of Social Democratic Party.

Nosek, Jiří; Czechoslovak international administrator; b. 29 Aug. 1911, Čerčany; ed. School of Economic Science, Prague.
Acting Perm. Rep. of Czechoslovakia to UN 50-53; First Vice-Pres. ECOSOC 51, 52, Second Vice-Pres. 54; Perm. Rep./Ambassador to UN 53-55; Vice-Minister of Foreign Affairs 55-56; Ambassador to India and Ceylon 56-59; Vice-Minister of Foreign Affairs 59-62; Under-Sec., Office of Conf. Services, UN 62-72; Chair. Econ. and Financial Cttee. UN 52, 57, of Social, Humanitarian and Cultural Cttee. 54, of Admin. and Budgetary Cttee. 59; Order of Labour 58.
c/o Ministry of Foreign Affairs, Prague, Czechoslovakia.

Nossack, Hans Erich; German writer; b. 30 Jan. 1901, Hamburg; s. of Eugen Nossack and Elita Kröhnke; m. Gabriele Knierer 1925; ed. Jena Univ.
Factory worker 19-22; employed by commercial firms 25-33; in business of his own 33-56; full-time writer 56-; Guest Prof. of Poetry, Frankfurt Univ. 68, mem. Akademie der Wissenschaften und der Literatur, Mainz, Deutsche Akademie für Sprache und Dichtung, Darmstadt; Georg Büchner-Preis 61, Wilhelm Raabe-Preis 63, Pour le Mérite 73, Alexander Zinn Preis 74.
Publs *Gedichte* (poems) 47, *Nekyia* (novel) 47, *Interview mit dem Tode* 48, *Die Rotte Kain* (play) 49, *Der Neugierige* (story) 55, *Die Begnadigung* (story) 55, *Spätestens im November* (novel), *Die Hauptprobe* (play) 56, *Spirale* (novel) 56, *Über den Einsatz* (essay) 56, *Begegnung im Vorraum* (stories) 58, *Der Juengere Bruder* (novel) 58, *Unmögliche Beweisaufnahme* (novel) 59, *Freizeitliteratur* (essay) 59, *Nach dem letzten Aufstand* (novel) 61, *Ein Sonderfall* (play) 63, *Sechs Etüden* (stories) 64, *Das kennt man* (novel) 64, *Das Testament des Lucius Eurinus* (story) 65, *Die schwache Position der Literatur* (essays) 66, *Der Fall d'Arthez* (novel) 68, *Dem unbekannten Sieger* 69, *Pseudoautobiographische Glossen* (essays) 71, *Die gestohlene Melodie* (novel) 72, *Bereitschaftsdienst* (novel) 73, *Ein glücklicher Mensch* (novel) 75, *Der Angeklagte hat das Wort* (letters) 76.
Hansastrasse 20, 2 Hamburg 13, Federal Republic of Germany.
Telephone: 45-19-06.

'Noto, David Ketso; Lesotho civil servant and diplomatist; b. 21 July 1934, Quthing; m.; two s.; ed. Morija Training Coll.
Executive Officer, Ministry of Works 53-61; with Ministry of Finance 61-74, Accountant-Gen. 69-74;

Perm. Sec. Cabinet Personnel 74-75; Perm. Rep. to UN Aug. 75-; attended financial talks, U.K. 69, OAU meeting of Heads of State and Govt., Kampala 75.
Permanent Mission of Lesotho to the United Nations, 866 United Nations Plaza, Suite 580, New York, N.Y. 10017, U.S.A.

Nouira, Hedi; Tunisian politician; b. 6 April 1911, Monastir.
Secretary of Gen. Confed. of Tunisian Workers 38; in detention 38-43; Sec.-Gen. of Neo-Destour Party 42-54, 69-; Minister of Commerce 54-55, of Finance 55-58; Dir. of Central Bank of Tunisia 58-70; Minister of State in Charge of the Economy June-Oct. 70; Prime Minister Nov. 70-.
Office of the Prime Minister, Tunis, Tunisia.

Nourissier, François; French writer and journalist. b. 18 May 1927, Paris; s. of Paul E. E. Nourissier; m. Cécile Muhlstein 1962; three c.; ed. Lycée Saint Louis, Lycée Louis-le-Grand, Paris, Ecole libre des Sciences politiques, Paris, and Faculté de Droit, Paris.
On staff of Secours Catholique Int., and work with Int. Refugee Org. 49-51; Dir. Chalet Int. des Etudiants, Combloux (World Univ. Service) 51-52; Sec.-Gen. Editions Denoël 52-56; Editor-in-Chief *La Parisienne* (review) 56-58; Literary Adviser to Editions Grasset 58-; Literary Dir. *Vogue* (French) 64-66, Contributing Editor *Vogue* (American) 64-; Literary Critic *Les Nouvelles littéraires* 63-; Cinema Critic *L'Express* 70-72; Literary Critic *Le Point* 72-; Prix Félix Fénéon 52, Grand Prix de la Guilde du Livre 65 (Swiss), Grand Prix du Roman de l'Académie française 66, Prix Fémina 70, Prix Prince Pierre de Monaco 75, Chevalier Légion d'Honneur, Officier des Arts et Lettres.
Publs. *L'Eau grise* (novel) 51, *Lorca* (essay) 55, *Les Orphelins d'Auteuil* (novel) 56, *Le Corps de Diane* (novel) 57, *Portrait d'un indifférent* 57, *Bleu comme la nuit* 58, *Un petit bourgeois* 64, *Une Histoire française* 66, *Les Français* (essay) 67, *Le Maître de Maison* 68, *The French* (trans. of *Les Français*) 70, *Cartier-Bresson's France* 71, *La Crève* (novel) 70, *Allemande* (novel) 73, *Lettre à mon chien* (essay) 75.
23 rue Henri Heine, 75016 Paris; and "Le Presbytère", Englesqueville-en-Auge, 14800 Calvados, France; 1824 Caux (Vaud), Switzerland.
Telephone: 647 54-80 (Paris).

Novak, Grga, D.SC.; Yugoslav university professor; b. 2 April 1888, Hvar; m. Lina Kargotic 1920; one d.; ed. Zagreb Univ., Charles Univ., Prague and Univ. of Vienna.
Schoolteacher and Asst., Split Museum of Archaeology 12-20; Lecturer in Gen. History of the Middle Ages, Faculty of Philosophy, Skopje 20, Reader 22, Prof. Univ. of Zagreb 24-59, Rector 46-47; mem. Yugoslav Acad. 47-, Pres. 58-; mem. numerous nat. and foreign insts., socs. and acads.; Gold Medal, Graz Univ. 61; Hon. Ph.D. (Vienna) 65; Order of Merit with Gold Star, Order of Labour and decorations from Italy.
Publs. over 500 books and articles.
Kršnjavova ul. 25, Zagreb, Yugoslavia.
Telephone: 441-237.

Novák, Josef, DR.RER.NAT., DR.SC.; Czechoslovak mathematician; b. 19 April 1905, Třebětín, Letovice; m. Vladimíra Plocek 1936; one s. one d.
Assistant, Univ. of Brno 35-45, Prof. Mathematics, Univ. of Brno 45-48; Czech Technical Univ., Prague 48-51; Charles Univ. Prague 52-; Mathematics Inst. of the Czechoslovak Acad. of Sciences 52-; Academician, Czechoslovak Acad. of Sciences 52-; Chair. of Mathematics and Physics Section of the Czechoslovak Acad. of Sciences 55-61; Chair. Board of Mathematics, Czechoslovak Acad. of Sciences 66-; Chair. Asscn. of Czechoslovak Mathematicians and Physicists; mem. Advisory Cttee. for Science and Technology, UN Econ. and Social

Council 72-75; Order of Labour 65; Gold Medal of Bernard Bolzano 70.
Leisure interests: genetics, music, gardening.
Žitná 25, Prague I, Czechoslovakia.
Telephone: 226601-03.

Novikov, Anatoly Grigorievich; Soviet composer; b. 30 Oct. 1896, Skopin; ed. Moscow Conservatoire.
Has composed many popular songs and choral songs to words by Pushkin; won first prize at the Prague International Festival of Democratic Youth for his *Hymn of the Democratic Youth* 47; Chair. Organizing Cttee., Union of Composers of R.S.F.S.R. 57-, Sec. of Union 60-; he won two prizes at the Berlin Festival 51, and Budapest Festival 49; Art Worker of Merit of the R.S.F.S.R.; State prizewinner 46, 48; Order of Red Banner of Labour 56, of Lenin 66; People's Artist of R.S.F.S.R.; People's Artist of the U.S.S.R. 70.
Work: *When You are with Me* 62.
Union of U.S.S.R. Composers, 8/10 Ulitsa Nezhdanovoi, Moscow, U.S.S.R.

Novikov, Ignaty Trofimovich; Soviet administrator; b. 1906; ed. Dneprodzerzhinsk Metallurgical Inst.
Director of power station 33-37; mem. C.P.S.U. 26-; Chief Engineer and subsequently Dir. of factory Saratov 37-41; Sec. Saratov District Cttee. C.P. 41-43, Chief *Glavenergozapchast* (Soviet area electricity authority) 43-50; Deputy Head of Construction Gorky Power Station 50-54; Head of Construction Kremenchug Power Station 54-58; Minister of Power Station Construction 58-62; Vice-Chair. Council of Ministers 60-; Chair. State Cttee. for Construction 62-; mem. Central Cttee. C.P.S.U. 61-; Deputy to U.S.S.R. Supreme Soviet 62-; Hero of Socialist Labour, Order of Lenin, "Hammer and Sickle" Gold Medal, etc.
State Committee for Construction, U.S.S.R. Council of Ministers, 4 Prospekt Marxa, Moscow, U.S.S.R.

Novikov, Ilya Alexandrovich; Soviet trade union official; b. 1 Aug. 1911, Kaluga; ed. secondary school.
Young Communist League 30-37, Party work 38-50; Vice-Chair. Moscow City Trade Union Council 50-54; Chair. Cen. Cttee. of Trade Union of the Workers of the Timber, Paper and Woodworking Industries 54-63; mem. All-Union Central Council of Trade Unions 64-68; Chair. Auditing Comm., All-Union Central Council of Trade Unions 63-; mem. C.P.S.U.; Order of Lenin; Order of Red Banner of Labour (twice), etc.
All-Union Central Council of Trade Unions, 42 Leninsky Prospekt, Moscow, U.S.S.R.

Novikov, Vladimir Nikolayevich; Soviet politician; b. 1907; ed. Technical Inst., Leningrad.
Technician, Designer, Engineer and Dir. Izhevsk Armaments Plant; mem. C.P.S.U. 36-; Deputy Commissar for Armaments 41-48; mem. staff Ministry of Defence Industry 48-54, Deputy Minister of Defence Industry 54-55; First Deputy Minister of Machine Building 55-57; Chair. Leningrad Regional Econ. Council 57-58; Chair. R.S.F.S.R. Planning Cttee. and First Deputy Chair. R.S.F.S.R. Council of Ministers 58-60; Chair. U.S.S.R. Planning Cttee. (GOSPLAN) 60-62; Perm. Soviet Rep. to Exec. Cttee. of Council for Mutual Econ. Aid (COMECON) 62-70; Chair. U.S.S.R. Council of Ministers Comm. for Foreign Econ. Affairs 62-; Vice-Chair. U.S.S.R. Council of Ministers 65-; mem. C.P.S.U. Central Cttee. 61-; Deputy to U.S.S.R. and R.S.F.S.R. Supreme Soviets 38-46, 58-; Hero of Socialist Labour, Order of Lenin, "Hammer and Sickle" Gold Medal, etc.
U.S.S.R. Council of Ministers, The Kremlin, Moscow, U.S.S.R.

Novomeský, Ladislav; Czechoslovak writer; b. 27 Dec. 1904, Budapest, Hungary; ed. Teachers Coll., Modra.
Teacher in Bratislava 23-25; Editor of dailies *Pravda chudoby, Rudé právo, Haló-noviny, Ludový denník,*

Slovenské zvesti, periodicals *Tvorba, DAV, Budovatel* 25-44; Deputy Chair. Slovak Nat. Council 44; Commr. of Slovak Nat. Council for Educ. and Culture 45-50; political imprisonment 51-56; Museum of Nat. Literature, Prague 56-63; professional writer 63-; mem. Cen. Cttee. of C.P. of Slovakia 44-50, 68-; mem. Slovak Nat. Council 44-45; Deputy to Nat. Assembly and Slovak Nat. Council 45-50; Chair. Asscn. of Slovak Writers 46, Matica Slovenská 68-74, Hon. Chair. 74-; mem. Cen. Cttee. of C.P. of Czechoslovakia 49-50, 68-71; mem. Ideological Comm. Cen. Cttee. C.P. of Czechoslovakia 63-66; mem. Presidium of Cen. Cttee. C.P. of Czechoslovakia 68-71; Deputy and mem. Presidium of Slovak Nat. Council 68-71; mem. Presidium Slovak Writers Union 67-68, 69-, Nat. Editorial Council of Slovak Socialist Rep. 70-; State Prize of Slovak Socialist Repub. 69; Lenin Order/Soviet Decoration 69; Hero of Č.S.S.R. 69; Hero of Socialist Labour 69; Order of Slovak Nat. Rising First Class, Klement Gottwald State Prize 64, Nat. Artist 64, L. Štúr Prize 67, Klement Gottwald Order 68, Czechoslovak Peace Prize 69, Order of Victorious February 73, Klement Gottwald State Prize 74, Order of the Repub. 74, Gold Medal, Slovak Acad. of Sciences 74; Dr. h.c. Comenius Univ., Bratislava 69.
Publs. Collections of poems: *Sunday* 27, *Rhomboid* 32, *The Open Window* 35, *Saints Behind the Village* 39, *Villa Theresa* (poem) 63, *30 Minutes to Town* (poem) 63, *The Unexplored World* 64, *From there and Others* (poems) 70.
Bratislava, Martinčekova 32, Czechoslovakia.

Novoselova, Alexandra Vasilyevna, D.SC.; Soviet chemist; b. 1900; ed. Moscow State Univ.
Lecturer, Moscow State Univ. 26-41, 43-46, Prof. 46-, Dean of Faculty of Chemistry 49-55; Senior Research Assoc., U.S.S.R. Inst. of Experimental Medicine 41-43; corresp. mem. U.S.S.R. Acad. of Sciences 53-70, Academician 70-; U.S.S.R. State Prize 48.
Moscow State University, Leninskie Gory, Moscow, U.S.S.R.

Novosyolov, Efim Stepanovich; Soviet politician; b. 1906; ed. Kharkov Engineering Inst.
Worker, later engineer, Staro Kramatorsk Engineering Factory (Donets Basin) 22-29, 33-38; mem. C.P.S.U. 25-; engineer, People's Commissariat of Heavy Engineering 38-39; Chief Engineer, Dir. of Central Research Inst. for Engineering Technology 39-42; Dir. of Novo-Kramatorsk Engineering Factory, Elektostal (Moscow Region) 42-49; Deputy Minister for Building and Road Building Engineering 49-53; Head of Central Heavy Engineering Div. of Ministry for Heavy and Transport Engineering 53-54; Minister for Engineering for the Building and Road Building Industries 54-57; Head of Dept., State Planning Cttee. of U.S.S.R. 57-60; Vice-Chair. State Econ. Council of U.S.S.R. 60-62; Chair. State Cttee. for Engineering for Building, Road Building and Municipal Industries (U.S.S.R. State Cttee. for Construction) 62-65; Minister of Machine Building for Construction, Road Building and Municipal Services 65-; mem. Cen. Auditing Cttee. C.P.S.U. 66-, Deputy to U.S.S.R. Supreme Soviet 66-.
Ministry of Machine Building for Construction, Road Building and Municipal Services, Prospekt Kalinina 23, Moscow, U.S.S.R.

Novozhilov, Valentin Valentinovich; Soviet mechanical engineer; b. 18 May 1910, Lublin, Poland; ed. Leningrad Physico-mechanical Inst.
Leningrad Research Insts. 31-46; Instructor, Leningrad Univ. 46-49, Prof. 49-; Assoc. Laboratory of Mathematical and Econ. Problems, Eng. Econ. Inst. 62-; Corresp. mem. U.S.S.R. Acad. of Sciences 58-66, mem. 66-, Hero of Socialist Labour 69, Order of Lenin etc.
Leningrad University, Leningrad, U.S.S.R.

Nowacki, Paweł Jan, D.SC., M.I.E.E.; Polish university professor and nuclear physicist; b. 25 June 1905, Berlin; *s.* of Jan and Katarzyna (née Misiek) Nowacki; *m.* 1st Stefania Barbara Leszczyńska 1937 (died 1962), 2nd Irena Natalia Sztark 1963 (died 1969); one *s.* one *d.*; ed. Jahn Realschule, Berlin, High School, Poznań, Technical Univ., Lwów.
Lecturer, Technical Univ., Lwów 29, 31-36; Design Engineer, Siemens Co., Germany and Poland 30-37; Senior Scientific Officer, Royal Aircraft Establishment, Farnborough 42-46; Chief Engineer, Study Office, Polish Central Electricity Board 47-52; Prof. Chair. of Electrical Machinery, Technical Univ., Wroclaw 47-53, Electrical Instruments 53-59, Nuclear Engineering 59-, Technical Univ. of Warsaw 51-70; Dir.-Gen. Inst. of Nuclear Research, Warsaw 58-70; Corresp. mem. Polish Acad. of Sciences 56-61, mem. 61-; Corresp. mem. Royal Swedish Acad. of Technical Sciences 58-, Schweizerische Gesellschaft für Automatik 59, mem. Polish State Council for the Utilization of Atomic Energy 56-; mem. Exec. Council, Int. Fed. of Automatic Control (IFAC) 57-61, Vice-Pres. 61-66, Pres. 66-69; Chair. Scientific Station Polish Acad. of Sciences, Paris 71-; mem. Inst. of Electrical Engineers, London; Officer's Cross, Order of Polonia Restituta 58, Silver Cross of Merit, Royal Swedish Acad. of Tech. Sciences 58, Order of Banner of Labour 2nd Class 59, 1st Class 66.
Leisure interests: painting, motor sport, sailing.
Publs. *Long Transmission Lines* 53, *The Calculation of Short-Circuit Currents in Electrical Networks* 55, *Symmetric Components* 54, *Theory of Automatic Control*, Vol. I 58, Vol. II 62, *The Polish Power Programme* 47, (with other) *The Polish Nuclear Power Programme* (Second Geneva Conference) 58, *Theory of the Magnetohydrodynamic Generator* 61, *The Programming and Utilisation of Research Reactors* (IAEA Symposium, Vienna) 61, *Théorie et Applications de la Physique des Plasmas à Basses Températures* 65, *The Importance of Automatic Control* 69.
Ulica Wałowa 4 m. 34, 00-211 Warsaw, Poland; and Centre Scientifique de l'Académie Polonaise des Sciences, 74 rue Lauriston, Paris 16e, France.
Telephone: 314373 (Warsaw).

Nowacki, Witold, DR. ING.; Polish university professor; b. 20 July 1911, Zakrzewo; *s.* of Ludwik Nowacki and Bronisława Czyzewska; *m.* Janina Sztaba 1936; two *s.* one *d.*; ed. Gdańsk Polytechnic.
Dozent Warsaw Polytechnic 45; Prof. Gdańsk Polytechnic 46-52; Prof. Warsaw Polytechnic 52-54; Prof. Warsaw Univ. 55-, Dir. Inst. of Mechanics; Head of Cttee. for Research and Prognosis "Poland 2,000", Polish Acad. of Sciences; Chair. Scientific Council, Inst. of Basic Technical Problems; mem. Polish Acad. of Sciences 52, Deputy Gen. Sec. 57-65, Gen. Sec. 65-68, Vice-Pres. 69-; mem. Asscn. Int. des Ponts et Charpents, Int. Union of Theoretical and Applied Mechanics; Foreign mem. Czechoslovak Acad. of Sciences, Bulgarian Acad. of Sciences, Austrian Acad. of Sciences; mem. Polish United Workers' Party; Polish State Prize 49, 55 and 65; Dr. h.c. Univ. of Glasgow and Gdańsk Polytechnic; numerous decorations including Order of the Banner of Labour (1st Class), Commdr. Cross with Star of Polonia Restituta, State Prize 1st Class 55, 64, Medal of 30th Anniversary of People's Poland 74.
Publs. *Mechanics of Structural Analysis, Thermoelasticity, Dynamics of Elastic Systems, Theory of Elasticity,* papers on applied mechanics, especially theories of structure and elasticity.
Polska Akademia Nauk, Pałac Kultury i Nauki, Warsaw, Poland; Home: Ul. Wiejska 18, m. 8, 00-490 Warsaw, Poland.
Telephone: 20-41-68 (Office); 29-13-31 (Home).

Nowak, Tadeusz; Polish writer and poet; b. 11 Nov. 1930, Sikorzyce, near Dąbrowa Tarnowska; ed. Jagiellonian Univ., Cracow.
Work first published 48; mem. Polish Writers' Asscn. 52-; Editor poetry section in *Tygodnik Kulturalny*, Warsaw 65-; Prize of City of Cracow 66; Gold Cross of Merit 67; St. Piętak Prize 69; Prize of Minister of Culture and Arts, 1st Class 71.
Publs. poetry: *Uczę się mówić* 53, *Porównania* 54, *Prorocy już odchodzą* 56, *Ślepe koła wyobrźani* 58, *Kolędy stręczyciela* 62, *Psalmy* 71, *Bielsze nad śnieg* 73, *Wybór wierszy* (selected poems) 73; novels: *Obcoplemienna ballada* 63, *A jak królem, a jak katem będziesz* 68, *Diabły* 71, *Takie większe wesele* 73, *Dwunastu* 74; short stories: *Przebudzenia* 62, *Wybór opowiadań* (selected short stories) 69.
Ul. Słomiana 5 m. 39, 30-316 Cracow, Poland.
Telephone: 655-98.

Nowak, Zenon; Polish politician and diplomatist; b. 27 Jan. 1905, Pabianice.
Former miner in Westphalia and Silesia and weaver in Pabianice; mem. Union of Communist Youth; frequently arrested and imprisoned for political activities; prisoner-of-war 40-45; Sec. Voivodship Cttee., Polish Workers' Party, Poznań 47-48, then 1st Sec. Katowice; mem. Cen. Cttee. Polish United Workers' Party 48-; Sec. Cen. Cttee. Polish United Workers' Party 48-56; mem. Political Bureau 48-56; Vice-Chair. Council of Ministers 52-68; Deputy to Seym 53-56, 61-72; Chair. Party Control Cen. Comm. 68-71; Chair. Supreme Chamber of Control 69-71; Amb. to U.S.S.R. June 71-; Order of Builder of People's Poland, Order of Banner of Labour, Order of Polonia Restituta, 2nd Class 75, Order of October Revolution (U.S.S.R.) 75.
Polish Embassy, Ul. A. Mitskevicha 1, Moscow, U.S.S.R.

Nowar, Ma'an Abu; Jordanian diplomatist; b. 26 July 1928, Salt; *m.* Vivian Ann Richards (died 1974); two *s.* seven *d.*; ed. London Univ.
Joined Jordanian Arab Army 43, Commdr. Infantry Brigade 57-63; Counsellor, Jordanian Embassy, London 63; Dir. Jordan Civil Defence 64-67, Jordan Public Security 67-69; Asst. Chief of Staff for Gen. Affairs 69-72; Minister of Culture and Information 72; Amb. to U.K. 73-; Jordanian Star 1st Class.
Leisure interests: reading, music, theatre, sports, television, cinema, museums.
Royal Jordan Embassy, 6 Upper Phillimore Gardens, London, W8 7HB, England.

Noyes, Albert (*see* Noyes, (William) Albert).

Noyes, Eliot Fette, B.A., M.ARCH.; American architect and industrial designer; b. 12 Aug. 1910, Boston, Mass.; *s.* of Atherton Noyes and Margaret D. Noyes; *m.* Mary Duncan Weed 1938; two *s.* two *d.*; ed. Phillips Acad., Andover, Harvard Coll. and Harvard Graduate School of Architecture.
Worked in office of Gropius and Breuer, Cambridge, Mass.; fmr. Dir. of Dept. of Industrial Design, Museum of Modern Art, New York; U.S. Air Force, Second World War; Design Dir., Norman Bel Geddes & Co. 46-47; Eliot Noyes and Assocs. (architecture and industrial design) 48-; Assoc. Prof. (critic in architectural design) Yale Univ. 48-51; Pres. Int. Design Conf. in Aspen 65-70; Consultant Dir. of Design for Int. Business Machines (IBM), Mobil Oil Co. and Westinghouse; Fellow, American Inst. of Architects, Industrial Designers Soc. of America, Royal Soc. of Arts; D.F.A. (Hon.) 69.
Leisure interests: skiing, flying.
Principal works: Bubble Houses of Concrete, Florida, own house, New Canaan, IBM Typewriter, IBM Executary Dictating Machine, office buildings, schools, exhbns. at World's Fairs, etc.
Eliot Noyes and Associates, 96 Main Street, New

Canaan, Connecticut 06840; and 210 Country Club Road, New Canaan, Connecticut, U.S.A.
Telephone: 203-966-9561 (Office); 203-966-0752 (Home).

Noyes, W(illiam) Albert, Jr., B.A., D. ÈS S.; American chemist; b. 18 April 1898, Terre Haute, Indiana; s. of William Albert Noyes and Flora Collier Noyes; m. Sabine Onillon 1921; one s.; ed. Grinnell Coll., Univ. of Paris, Univs. of Geneva, Illinois and Calif.
Instructor, Univ. of Calif. 21-22, Univ. of Chicago 22-23, Asst. Prof. 23-29; Assoc. Prof. Brown Univ. 29-35, Prof. 35-38; Prof. Univ. of Rochester 38-63, Emer. 63-; Chair. Chem. Dept. 39-55, Dean, Graduate School 52-56; Act. Dean and Dean Coll. of Arts and Science 56-58, Univ. Distinguished Prof. 61-63; Ashbel Smith Prof. of Chem., Univ. of Texas 63-73, Emer. 73-; Prof. Univ. of Nancy 69; Section Chair. Nat. Defence Research Cttee. 40-42, Div. Chief 42-46; Staff, Chief Chemical Warfare Service, U.S. Army 42-46; Adviser, Dept. Army and Dept. of State; Chair. Div. of Chem. and Chemical Technology, Nat. Research Council 47-53; mem. Board of Trustees, Sloan-Kettering Inst. for Cancer Research 50-63; mem. Executive Cttee. Int. Union of Pure and Applied Chemistry 55-59, Pres. 59-63; Pres. American Chemical Society 47; mem. Nat. Acad. of Sciences, American Philosophical Society; Hon. mem. Société Chimique de France; Royal Soc. of Physics and Chemistry (Spain), Soc. of Chemistry (Belgium); foreign hon. mem. Acad. of Sciences, Lisbon, Chemical Soc., London; King's Medal for Service in Cause of Freedom (British), Medal of Merit (U.S.A.), Officier, Légion d'Honneur, Priestley Medal, Willard Gibbs Medal, Charles L. Parsons Award; Hon. D.Sc. (Grinnell Coll., Rhode Island, Paris, Indiana Univs., Univ. of Ottawa, Univ. of Montreal, Univ. of Illinois, Univ. of Rochester, Carleton Univ. (Ottawa), Laval Univ.); Editor *Chemical Reviews* 39-49, *Journal of American Chemical Society* 50-62, *Journal of Physical Chemistry* 52-64.
Leisure interests: history, international affairs, music.
Publs. *Photochemistry of Gases* (with P. A. Leighton) 41, *Modern Alchemy* (with W. A. Noyes) 32, *Traité de Chimie Physique* (with H. Weiss); translation into French of book by E. W. Washburn 25; (Ed.) *Chemistry in World War II* 48, *Photochimie et Spectroscopie* 37, *Advances in Photochemistry* Vols. 1-7 (with G. S. Hammond, J. N. Pitts).
5109 Lucas Lane, Austin, Texas 78731, U.S.A.
Telephone: 512-472-5571.

Nsanze, Terence; Burundi Ambassador and Permanent Representative at the UN 65-73; see *The International Who's Who 1975-76.*

Nsekela, Amon James, M.A., DIP.ED.; Tanzanian diplomatist; b. 4 Jan. 1930, Lupepo, Rungwe; s. of Ngonile Reuben Nsekela and Anyambilile Nsekela (née Kalinga); m. Matilda Kyusa 1957; two s.; ed. Rungwe District School, Malangali Secondary School, Tabora Govt. Sr. Secondary School, Makerere Univ. Coll., and Univ. of the Pacific, Calif., U.S.A.
With Regional Admin. 60-63; Perm. Sec. Ministry of External Affairs and Defence 63-64; Principal Sec. Ministry of Commerce and Industries 64-66; Principal Sec. to Treasury 66-67; mem. E. African Legis. Assembly 67-70; mem. and Sec. of Presidential Comm. on the Establishment of a Democratic One-Party State, mem. Pratt Cttee. on Decentralization of Govt.; mem. Parl. 73-74; High Commr. to U.K. 74-; Chair. and Man. Dir. Bank of Commerce 67-74; Chair. Nat. Insurance Corpn. of Tanzania 67-72, Univ. Council 71-, Council of the Inst. of Finance Management 71-; fmr. Chair. Nat. Provident Fund Investment Cttee., Ralli Estates Ltd., Int. Trading and Credit Co. of Tanganyika, Tanganyika Devt. Corpn. (now Nat. Devt. Corpn.), Tanganyika Electric Supply Co. Ltd., Instant Coffee Co. Ltd., Nyanza Salt Mines Ltd., TANITA Co. Ltd.; Dir. Board of Internal Trade, Coastal Hotels

Ltd., Dar es Salaam Motor Transport, Nat. Devt. Corpn.; fmr. Dir. Williamson Diamonds Ltd., E. African Airways, Tanzania Investment Bank; Pres. Econ. Soc. of Tanzania until 72.
Publs. *Minara ya Historia ya Tanganyika: Tanganyika hadi Tanzania, Demokrasi Tanzania, Socialism and Social Accountability in a Developing Nation, The Development of Health Services in Mainland Tanzania: Tumetoka Mbali* (with Dr. A. L. Nhonoli).
Tanzania High Commission, 43 Hertford Street, London, W.1; Home: Lupa Way, P.O. Box 722, Mbeya, Tanzania.

Ntlhakana, Thabo Ephraim; Lesotho diplomatist and civil servant; b. 23 June 1935, Leribe; s. of Seth S. E. and Adelaide Ntlhakana; m. Maselometsi Regina 1961; one s. four d.
Secondary school teacher 57-62; Information Officer, newspaper editor and broadcaster in Govt. Dept. of Broadcasting and Information 65-70; Counsellor, Lesotho High Comm., U.K. 70-74; Chief U.K. Protocol, Maseru Oct. 74-May 75; Dir. Information and Broadcasting June-Sept. 75; High Commr. in U.K. Oct. 75-.
Leisure interests: singing, gardening, football, tennis, athletics.
Office: Lesotho High Commission, 16A St. James's Street, London, S.W.1; Home: 30 Milverton Road, London, N.W.6, England.
Telephone: 459-4469 (Office); 839-1154 (Home).

Nu, U (formerly **Thakin Nu**), B.A.; Burmese politician and writer; b. 1907; ed. Rangoon Univ.
For some years headmaster Nat. High School, Pantanaw; joined Dobhama Asiayone (Our Burma) Organization; sentenced to term of imprisonment at outbreak of Second World War; released after Japanese occupation; organized Dobhama Asiayone and later joined wartime Govt. as Minister of Foreign Affairs in Dr. Ba Maw's Cabinet 43-44; Minister for Publicity and Propaganda 44-45; elected Vice-Pres. Anti-Fascist People's Freedom League (Nationalist Coalition) after Allied re-occupation; elected Speaker Constituent Assembly 47; Deputy Chair. Gov.'s Exec. Council July 47; signatory Anglo-Burmese Treaty, London, preliminary to Burmese Independence and first Prime Minister of Burmese Republic 48-56; resigned to devote himself to the reorganization of Anti-Fascist People's Freedom League; Prime Minister 57-58; Prime Minister, Minister of Home Affairs, Relief and Resettlement, Democratization of Local Administration, Information, Transport, Posts and Telegraphs, Shipping and Aviation, Housing and Rehabilitation 60-62; in custody 62-Oct. 66; left Burma 69 to organize opposition movement to Burmese regime; living in Thailand Nov. 69-Oct. 70; returned to Burma to lead revolutionary movement opposing Government of Gen. Ne Win Oct. 70.
Publs. Plays and stories.

Nujoma, Sam; South West African nationalist leader; b. 12 May 1929, Ongandjera; ed. Finnish Protestant Mission School, St. Barnabas School, Windhoek.
With State Railways until 57; Municipal Clerk, Windhoek 57; Clerk in wholesale store 57-59; Founder, with Herman Toivo ja Toivo, and Pres. SWAPO (S.W. Africa People's Org.) April 59-; arrested Dec. 59; went into exile 60; appeared before UN Cttee. on S.W. Africa June 60; set up SWAPO provisional HQ in Dar es Salaam, Tanzania March 61; arrested on return to Windhoek and formally ordered out of the country March 60; turned to armed struggle after rejection by Int. Court of Justice of SWAPO complaint against S. Africa Aug. 66; gave evidence at UN Security Council Oct. 71.
c/o Mr. Peter H. Katjavivi, 21/25 Tabernacle Street, London, E.C.2, England.

Nunes, Admiral Adalberto de Barros; Brazilian naval officer and politician; b. 20 Oct. 1905, Rio de Janeiro; *s.* of Admiral Adalberto Nunes and D. Maria Cândida de Barros Nunes; *m.* Maria Carolina de Souza Nunes 1931; no *c.*; ed. Colégio Militar do Rio de Janeiro, Escola Naval and Escola de Guerra Naval.
Head of Naval Information Services 56-57; Chief of Cabinet of Minister of the Navy 57-58; Dir. Escola Naval 58-60; Dir.-Gen. of Hydrographics and Navigation 60-62, of Naval Electronics 62-63; C.-in-C. of Fleet 63-64; Dir.-Gen. of Ports and Coastlines 64-66; Sec.-Gen. of the Navy 66-68; Chief of Staff of Navy 68-69; Minister of the Navy 69-74; orders from Brazil, Argentina, Chile, Peru, Belgium, Portugal, Spain, Italy and Bolivia.
Leisure interests: sport (especially football), country life.
Avenida Atlantica, 514 Apto. 407-Leme, Rio de Janeiro, Brazil.

Nunes, H.E. Cardinal José da Costa; Portuguese ecclesiastic; b. 15 March 1880.
Ordained 03; appointed Priest at Macão 20, consecrated 21; Archbishop of Goa and Damão 40-53; Titular Patriarch of Odessa 53-62; created Cardinal by Pope John XXIII 62; mem. of the Council, Propaganda Fide, Rites; Vice-Chamberlain of the Holy Roman Church.
00186 Rome, Via dei Portoghesi 2, Italy.
Telephone: 65-24-96.

Núñez-Jiménez, Capt. Antonio; Cuban scientist and politician; b. 1923; ed. Havana Univ.
Professor at Central Univ., Las Villas 55; fought under Major Che Guevara with Castro's guerrillas; Exec. Dir. Agrarian Reform Inst. (INRA) 60-62; Pres. Academia de Ciencias de la República de Cuba 62-72; Amb. to Peru 72-.
Publs. *Geography of Cuba*, etc.
Embassy of Cuba, Coronel Portillo 110, San Isidro, Lima, Peru; Calle 7A, No. 6614 e/66 and 70, Miramar, Marianao, Havana; Capitolio Nacional, Havana, Cuba.

Nungesser, Roland; French politician; b. 9 Oct. 1925, Nogent-sur-Marne; *m.* Michèle Jeanne Elizabeth Selignac 1957; three *d.*; ed. Ecole Libre des Sciences Politiques.
Commissaire-général du Salon Nautique International; Vice-Pres. Chambre Syndicale des Industries Nautiques; Pres. Conseil National de la Navigation de Plaisance; Mayor of Nogent-sur-Marne 59; mem. Chamber of Deputies 58-, Sec. of State for Housing 66-67; Sec. of State at Ministry of Economy and Finance 67-68; Minister of Youth and Sports May-July 68; Union pour la nouvelle République; Pres. Franco-Soviet Chamber of Commerce 69-; Vice-Pres. Nat. Assembly; Pres. Conseil Général du Val de Marne 70; Vice-Pres. Comité Parlementaire d'amitié France-U.S.A.
Leisure interests: motor yachting, athletics, tennis, golf.
Assemblée Nationale, Paris 7e; 18 avenue Duvelleroy, 94 Nogent-sur-Marne, France.
Telephone: 871-16-53.

Nunn, Louie B.; American state governor and attorney; b. 8 March 1924, Park, Barren Co., Ky.; *m.* Beula C. Aspley; one *s.* one *d.*; ed. Bowling Green Univ., Univs. of Cincinnati and Louisville.
Barren County Judge 54-58; fmr. Republican State Campaign Chair.; unsuccessful candidate for governorship of Kentucky 63, Gov. of Kentucky 68-72; Republican.
Office of the Governor, Frankfort, Kentucky 40601, U.S.A.

Nunn, Sam; American politician and lawyer; b. 8 Sept. 1938, Perry, Ga.; *s.* of Samuel Augustus Nunn and Elizabeth Canon Nunn; *m.* Colleen O'Brien 1964; one *d.* one *s.*; ed. Emory Univ. and Emory Univ. Law School, Atlanta.

State Representative to Ga. Gen. Assembly 68-72; U.S. Senator from Georgia 73-; Democrat.
Leisure interest: golf.
110 Russell Office Building, Washington, D.C. 20510, U.S.A.
Telephone: (202) 225-3521.

Nuorvala, Aarne Johannes; Finnish judge; b. 18 April 1912, Viipuri; *s.* of Karl Elias Nylenius and Aino Tyyne Ranta; *m.* Hellin Helena Hintikka 1945; one *s.* three *d.*; ed. Helsinki Secondary School and Univ. of Helsinki.
Civil Servant, Ministry of Finance 44; Junior Cabinet Sec. 45, Senior 46-50; Junior mem. Comm. for Drafting Legislation 50-55, Senior mem. 55; Extra Justice of Supreme Admin. Court 55-57, Justice 57-63; Sec.-Gen., Deputy Prime Minister and mem. Cabinet 63-64; Chancellor of Justice 64, Pres. Supreme Admin. Court 65; mem. High Court of Impeachment 65-; Chair. Supreme Court of Office 66-.
Korkeavuorenkatu 13A 2, 00130 Helsinki 13, Finland.
Telephone: 62-66-38.

Nur Elmi, Hussein; Somali diplomatist; b. 1 April 1926, Obbia; ed. Somalia and Italy.
Deputy Sec.-Gen. Territorial Council of Somalia 54-58; Regional Gov. of Hiran 59-60, of Mogadiscio, Benadir 60-62; Consul-Gen. in East Africa 62-63; Amb. to Tanzania 63-65, to Belgium, Netherlands and Luxembourg, Perm. Rep. to EEC 65-68; Amb.-at-Large 69-70; Alt. Perm. Rep. to UN 70-72, Perm. Rep. 72-74; Amb. to Italy 74-.
Embassy of Somalia, Via dei Gracchi 305, Rome, Italy.

Nur Khan, Air Marshal M.; Pakistani air force officer and airline executive; b. 1923, Tamman, Punjab; *m.*; one *s.* three *d.*; ed. Col. Brown's Cambridge School and Prince of Wales Royal Indian Mil. Coll., Dehra Dun.
Commissioned Royal Indian Air Force 41; Man. Dir. Pakistan Int. Airlines 59-65; C.-in-C. Pakistan Air Force 65-69; Gov. W. Pakistan 69; Chair. PIA Nov. 73-; Pres. Pakistan Hockey Fed. 67-69; Hilal-e-Jurat 65.
Leisure interests: boxing, football, hockey, swimming, squash.
Pakistan International Airlines Corporation, PIA Building, Karachi Airport, Pakistan.
Telephone: 412011, Ext. 2666.

Nureyev, Rudolf Hametovich; Ballet dancer (b. U.S.S.R.); b. 17 March 1938, Ufa; ed. Kirov Ballet School, Leningrad.
Formerly with Kirov Ballet; sought political asylum, Paris 61; joined Le Grand Ballet du Marquis de Cuevas; appeared in Australia 64; frequent guest star at Royal Opera House, Covent Garden; appears frequently with Dame Margot Fonteyn; Choreographer and Dir. *Raymonda* 65, *Tancredi* 66, *Don Quixote* (Vienna) 66; appeared in *Jazz Calendar* 68, *Pelléas et Mélisande* 69, produced *The Nutcracker* 68, *Sleeping Beauty* 75; films include *Swan Lake* 66, *Romeo and Juliet*, *I Am a Dancer* 72, *Don Quixote* 73; Gold Star, Paris 63.
Publ. *Nureyev* 62.
Villa La Turbie, Monte Carlo, Monaco; c/o Royal Opera House, Covent Garden, London, W.C.2., England.

Nuriev, Ziya Nurievich; Soviet politician; b. 1915; ed. C.P.S.U. High School.
In education system 33-38, 40-42; Soviet Army 38-40; Party work 42-52; Second Sec. 53-57; First Sec. Bashkir Regional Party Cttee. 57-69; Deputy; mem. Presidium of U.S.S.R. Supreme Soviet 54-69; mem. U.S.S.R. Council of Collective Farms; Minister of Agricultural Procurements of U.S.S.R. 69-73; Deputy Chair. Council of Ministers 73-; mem. Central Cttee. of C.P.S.U. 61-.
U.S.S.R. Council of Ministers, The Kremlin, Moscow, U.S.S.R.

Nurjadin, Air Chief Marshal Roesmin; Indonesian diplomatist; b. 31 May 1930, Malang; *m.* Surjati Subali 1962; ed. primary and high schools, and Gajah Mada Univ.
Squadron Commdr. 53-60; Commdr.-in-Chief, Operational Command 62-64; Air Attaché, Bangkok and Moscow 64-66; Minister, Commdr.-in-Chief, Chief of Staff, Air Force 66-70; Amb. to U.K. 70-74, to U.S.A. 74-; various mil. and foreign decorations.
Leisure interests: golf, sport, reading.
Indonesian Embassy, 2020 Massachusetts Avenue, N.W., Washington, D.C. 20036, U.S.A.

Nuseibeh, Anwar Zaki, M.A.; Jordanian diplomatist; b. 20 Jan. 1913; ed. Govt. Arab Coll., Jerusalem, and Queens' Coll., Cambridge.
Land Officer, Palestine 36, Magistrate 37-42; Lecturer in Constitutional Law, Jerusalem Law Classes 36-48; fmr. mem. Jordan Parl. and Senator; Chief Arab Del., Jordan and Israel Mixed Armistice Comm. 51; Minister of Defence 53, of Educ. 54-55, of Reconstruction and Devt. 54-55; Gov. of Jerusalem, Jordan 61-62; Ambassador to U.K. 65-66; private business in Jordan 66-; Order of El Kawkab (1st Class); Assoc. Knight Order of St. John of Jerusalem; Knight of Order of Holy Sepulchre.
c/o Ministry of Foreign Affairs, Amman, Jordan.

Nuseibeh, Dr. Hazem; Jordanian politician.
Deputy Chair. of Devt. Board 58-60; Under-Sec. Ministry of Nat. Economy 59-60; Sec.-Gen. of Devt. Board 61-62; Minister of Foreign Affairs 62-63, 65-66; Minister of Reconstruction and Devt. 67-68; Amb. to Egypt 69-71, to Turkey 71-73, to Italy 73-.
Embassy of Jordan, Via Po 24, Rome, Italy.

Nyagah, Jeremiah Joseph Mwaniki; Kenyan politician; b. 24 Nov. 1920, Kigare, Embu; *s.* of Joseph Nthiga Mwonge and Mary Mbiro; *m.* Eunice Wambere 1947; five *s.* two *d.;* ed. Alliance High School, Makerere Coll. and Oxford Univ.
Teacher, Intermediate Schools and Teacher Training Coll.; secondary schools and Teacher Training Coll. teacher 54-56; Asst. Education Officer; mem., Legislative Council 58-60, 61-; Dep. Speaker 60; mem., House of Representatives 63-; Junior Minister, Ministry of Works, Communications and Power 63-64; Junior Minister, Ministry of Home Affairs 64-66; Vice-Pres. for Kenyan African Nat. Union (K.A.N.U.) E. Region March 66-; Minister of Education May 66-Jan. 68; Chair. Nat. Library Service Board April 66-; Minister of Natural Resources Jan. 68-Dec. 69; Minister of Information Dec. 69-Oct. 70; Minister of Agriculture and Animal Husbandry Oct. 70-; mem. Boards of Govs. of many schools, Univ. Coll. Council, Nairobi, E. African Univ. Council, Boy Scouts' Training Team.
Leisure interests: sports, athletics.
Ministry of Agriculture, P.O. Box 30028, Nairobi; P.O. Box 37, Embu, Kenya.

Nyamoya, Albin; Burundian politician; b. 1924, Ngozi Province; ed. Ecole Supérieure, Astrida (now Butare, Rwanda).
Qualified as veterinary surgeon; held various posts at the Ministry of Agriculture and Stockbreeding, Ruanda-Urundi 45-61, Minister of Agriculture and Stockbreeding 61-62; Minister of Interior and Information, Burundi 62-63; Prime Minister and Minister of State 64-65; Minister of State 65-66; Deputy to Nat. Assembly 63-66; various posts in Ministry of Agriculture and Stockbreeding 66-72, Dir.-Gen. 70-71, Minister 71-72; Prime Minister and Minister of the Interior July 72-73; Nat. Exec. Sec., mem. Cen. Cttee., Political Bureau, Unity and Nat. Progress Party.
P.O. Box 1017, Bujumbura, Burundi.

Nyamweya, James, LL.B.; Kenyan politician; b. 28 Dec. 1927, Kisii; *m.* Tabitha Moige 1948; four *s.* four *d.;* ed. King's Coll., London and Lincoln's Inn, London.

Legal Assistant in Ministry of Legal Affairs, Kenya 58-59; Advocate, Private Legal Practitioner, Supreme Court of Kenya 59-63; Founder-mem. and mem. Central Exec. Cttee. Kenya African Nat. Union (KANU) 59-63, Chair. Kisii 62-64; Parl. Sec. to Ministry of Justice and Constitutional Affairs 63, and in the Office of the Prime Minister 64-65; Minister of State, Provincial Admin. Civil Service, Office of the Pres. 65-66; Leader of Govt. Business in the House of Representatives May-Dec. 66; Minister of State, Foreign Affairs, Office of the Pres. and Leader of Govt. Business in Nat. Assembly Jan. 67, Minister of Power and Communications until Dec. 69, Minister of Works 69-74, of Labour Nov. 74-; Hon. LL.D. (U.S.A.).
Ministry of Labour, Nairobi, Kenya.

Nyberg, Alf Erik Gunnar, FIL.DR.; Swedish meteorologist; b. 19 June 1911, Vimmerby; *s.* of the Rev. A. E. Nyberg and Adèle Johansson; *m.* Gertrud Grenander 1938; three *d.;* ed. Universitet i Uppsala, Stockholms Universitet and Univ. of Chicago.
First State Meteorologist, Swedish Meteorological and Hydrological Inst. 45-52, Chief of Div. 52-55, Dir.-Gen. 55-; Asst. Prof. Stockholm Univ. 47; mem. Exec. Cttee. World Meteorological Org. (WMO) 55, Pres. European Regional Asscn. 56-63, Pres. WMO 63-71; UN Technical Evaporation Missions: Syria 54, E. Africa 62.
Leisure interests: gardening, fishing, sailing.
Publs. *A Synoptic-aerological Investigation* 45, *Meridional Heat Transport* 54, *An Experimental Study of the Field Variation of the Eddy Conductivity* 56, *A Study of the Evaporation and the Condensation at a Snow Surface* 65, *The Evaporation in Southern Sweden* 66, *On the Acidity of Precipitation* 70.
Rålambsvägen 19IV, S-112 59 Stockholm, Sweden.
Telephone: 08-517171.

Nyboe Andersen, Poul, DR. OECON.; Danish economist and politician; b. 23 Nov. 1913, Ladelund; *s.* of Anders Andersen and Kristine Andersen; *m.* Edith Raben 1938; three *s.* one *d.;* ed. Univ. of Aarhus.
Teacher at Krogerup Folk High School; study visit to U.S.A. 47; Asst. Prof. of Political Economy, Copenhagen Graduate School of Econs. and Business Admin. 48-50, Prof. 50-71; Chair. Board for Technical Co-operation with Developing Countries 62-68; Chair. Board of Dirs. of Danish Co-operative Wholesale Soc. 56-66; Bursar of Carlsberg Foundation and New Carlsberg Foundation 66-68; Minister for Econ. Affairs, Nordic Affairs and European Market Relations 68-71; mem. of Parliament 71-; mem. Council of Europe 71-73, Nordic Council 71-73; Minister for Econ. Affairs and Commerce 73-75; Man. Dir. Andelsbanken Danebank 76; Liberal.
Publs. *Penge og Penges Vaerd* (Money and its value) 41, *Danish Exchange Policy 1914-1939* 42, *Fra Guldfod til Clearing* (From Gold Standard to Clearing) 42, *Bilateral Exchange Clearing Policy* 46, *Laanerenten* (Loan interest) 47, *Den økonomiske Sammenhaeng* (Inter-action of Economic Forces) 47, *Kortfattet Larebog i National-økonomi* (Brief Textbook on Political Economy) 48, *Land og by* (Country and Town) 49, *Nationaløkonomi* (Political Economy) in collaboration with Bjarke Fog and Poul Winding 52, *Udenrigsøkonomi* (International Economic Relations) 55.
G1. Strandvej 19, 3050 Humlebaek, Denmark.
Telephone: 03-192703.

Nyerere, Dr. Julius Kambarage, M.A.; Tanzanian politician; b. March 1922, Butiama, Lake Victoria; *s.* of Chief Nyerere Burito; ed. Musoma Native Authority Primary School, Tabora Govt. Senior Secondary School, Makerere Coll., Uganda and Edinburgh Univ.
Teacher, St. Mary's Roman Catholic School, Tabora 46-49; student at Edinburgh Univ. 49-52; teacher, St. Francis' Roman Catholic Coll. 53-55; Founder-Pres. Tanganyika African Nat. Union (T.A.N.U.) 54-, Elected mem. Tanganyika Legislative Council 58,

leader Elected Members Org. 58-60; Chief Minister 60-61; Prime Minister May 61-Jan. 62; Pres. of Tanganyika Dec. 62-64, of Tanzania 64-; Minister of External Affairs Dec. 62-March 63, Sept. 65-72; Commdr.-in-Chief of the Armed Forces 73-; Chancellor, Univ. of East Africa 63-70, Univ. of Dar es Salaam 70-.

Publs. *Freedom and Unity—Uhuru na Umoja* 67, *Freedom and Socialism—Uhuru na Ujamaa* 68, *Ujamaa: Essays on Socialism* 69, *Freedom and Development—Uhuru na Maendelo* 73; Swahili trans. of *Julius Caesar* and *The Merchant of Venice* 69.

State House, Dar es Salaam, Tanzania.

Nyers, Rezsö; Hungarian politician; b. 1923, Budapest; m. Ilona Witz 1946; one s.

Printer until 45; now economist; mem. Parl. 47-53, 58-; Vice-Pres. Nat. Asscn. of Co-operatives 54-56; Minister of Food Industry 56-57; Pres. Nat. Asscn. of Co-operatives 57-60; Minister of Finance 60-62; Sec. Cen. Cttee. Hungarian Socialist Workers' Party 62-74; Chair. Econ. Comm. Cen. Cttee. of Hungarian Socialist Workers' Party 62-64; mem. Political Cttee. Hungarian Socialist Workers' Party 66-75; Dir. Inst. for Political Econ., Hungarian Acad. of Sciences 74-.

Publs. *The Co-operative Movement in Hungary* 63, *Gazdaságpolitikánk és a gazdasági mechanizmus reformja* (Economic Policy and Reform of Economic Management) 68, *A magyar népgazdaság a szocializmus épitésének utján* (Hungary's national economy on the road towards socialism) 73.

Leisure interests: reading, the theatre, tennis, riding, philately.

Academy of Sciences, 1387 Budapest V, Roosevelt tér 9, Hungary.

Nykopp, Johan Albert, M.A.; Finnish diplomatist and businessman; b. 27 May 1906, Le Vésinet, France; s. of Olaf Nykopp and Anna-Lisa Tilgmann; m. Marianne Achilles 1930; two s. one d.; ed. Univ. of Helsinki.

Entered Foreign Service 30; Attaché, Moscow 31-35; Vice-Consul, Leningrad 35-37; Sec. Foreign Ministry 37-39, Head of Section 39-40; Sec. and later Counsellor, Moscow 40-41; Deputy Dir. Commercial Div., Foreign Ministry 45-47, Dir. 47-51; Minister to U.S.A. 51-55, Ambassador 55-58, Minister to Mexico and Cuba 51-58, to Colombia and Venezuela 54-58; Pres. Export and Import Licence Board of Finland 49-51; Gov. for Finland, Int. Bank for Reconstruction and Development

50-51; Man. Dir. of Finnish Employers' Confederation 58-61; Pres. Tampella Ltd., Tampere 62-72; Commdr. Order of the Lion; Knight, Order of White Rose (Finland); Commdr. Order of St. Olav (Norway); Commdr. Polonia Restituta (Poland); Commdr. de la Légion d'Honneur (France); Grand Officer Order of Orange Nassau (Neths.).

Leisure interest: tennis.

2C Vatakuja, 00200 Helsinki 20, Finland.

Telephone: 931-32400 and 931-20770.

Nyman, Olle; Swedish painter; b. 24 Dec. 1909; ed. Decorative School Philip Månsson and Royal Acad. Art School, Stockholm.

Professor Royal Acad. of Arts 53-63; mem. Arts Council of Govt. 56-58; mem. Swedish Royal Acad. 53; first one-man exhbn. Stockholm 50; represented in Museum of Modern Art, Stockholm and Museum of Art, Malmö; mem. Art Cttee. School of Stockholm 58-62, and Cttee. Thiel Gallery Stockholm.

Major works include: monumental wall decorations in Stockholm at City Hospital of Medicine 51, High School of Medicine 55, roof painting for Olaus Petri Church 58, tapestry for Handelsbanken 59, Skandinaviska banken 64, Uppsala Univ. Library 67, Parliament House 71.

Strandpromenaden 61, Saltsjö-Dnäs, Stockholm, Sweden.

Nyun, U; Burmese civil servant; b. 1911; ed. Rangoon Univ., London School of Economics, London Univ. School of Oriental Studies.

Joined Indian Civil Service 31; after Burmese independence Under-Sec. and later Sec., Ministry of Commerce and Industry 48-50; Chief, Industry and Trade Div., UN Eccn. Comm. for Asia and the Far East (ECAFE) 51-57, Deputy Exec. Sec. ECAFE 57-59, Exec. Sec. 59-73.

c/o Ministry of Foreign Affairs, Rangoon, Burma.

Nzondomiyo, A'Dokpe Lingo; Zairian politician; b. 1931, Libenge-Kete; ed. Catholic seminaries.

Former schoolmaster; progressed through regional admin. to become Deputy Sec.-Gen. Mouvement populaire de la révolution (MPR); mem. Political Bureau 69-; State Commr. for Justice Oct. 72-74.

Political Bureau of the Mouvement populaire de la révolution, Kinshasa, Zaire.

O

Oakes, John Bertram, A.M., LL.D.; American journalist; b. 23 April 1913, Elkins Park, Pa.; s. of George W. Ochs-Oakes and Bertie Gans Ochs; m. Margery C. Hartman 1945; one s. three d.; ed. Princeton Univ., and The Queen's Coll., Oxford.
Reporter *Trenton Times* 36-37; Political Reporter *Washington Post* 37-41; served U.S. Army 41-46; Editor, Review of the Week, Sunday *New York Times* 46-49, mem. Editorial Board 49-61, Editorial Page Editor 61-; Carnegie Foundation Travel Award, Europe and Africa 59; Columbia-Catherwood Award (for int. journalism) 61, George Polk Memorial Award 66 (as editor), Jefferson Award of Unitarians 68 (service in cause of religious liberty); Dept. of Interior of U.S. Conservation Award 62; Silurian Soc. Award 69; Garden Club of America Award 69; Woodrow Wilson Prize (Princeton Univ.) 70; Bronze Star (U.S.); M.B.E. (U.K.); Croix de Guerre (France).
Leisure interests: sailing, walking, nature study, reading.
Publ. *The Edge of Freedom* 61.
New York Times, 229 West 43rd Street, New York N.Y.; 10036, and 1120 Fifth Avenue, New York City, N.Y., U.S.A.
Telephone: 212-556-1766 (Office); TE1-4583 (Home).

Oakeshott, Michael Joseph, M.A.; British political scientist; b. 11 Dec. 1901; ed. Caius Coll., Cambridge.
Fellow of Caius Coll. 25-; Univ. Lecturer in History, Cambridge 29-49; Fellow of Nuffield Coll., Oxford 49-50; Prof. of Political Science, Univ. of London (London School of Economics) 50-69; Muirhead Lecturer, Birmingham Univ. 53; Ludwig Mond Lecturer, Univ. of Manchester 59.
Publs. *Experience and its Modes* 33, 66, *A Guide to the Classics* 36, *Social and Political Doctrines of Contemporary Europe* 37, *Hobbes's Leviathan* (editor) 46, *The Voice of Poetry in the Conversation of Mankind* 59, *Rationalism and Politics* 62, *Of Human Conduct* 75, *Hobbes on Civil Association* 75.
16 New Row, London, W.C.2, England.

Oakeshott, Walter Fraser, M.A.; British university official; b. 10 Nov. 1903, Lydenburg, Transvaal, S. Africa; s. of Dr. Walter and Mrs. Kathleen Oakeshott (née Fraser); m. Noël Rose Moon 1928; two s. two d.; ed. Balliol Coll., Oxford.
Schoolmaster, Bec School 26-27, Merchant Taylors School 27-30, Winchester Coll. 30-38; High Master, St. Paul's School, London 38-46; Headmaster, Winchester Coll. 46-54; Rector of Lincoln Coll., Oxford 54-72; Vice-Chancellor, Oxford Univ. 62-64; Rhind Lecturer, Edinburgh Univ. 56; Master, Skinners Co. 60-61; Trustee Pilgrim Trust and Vice-Pres. Bibliographical Soc., London, Pres. 66-68.
Leisure interests: medieval books and libraries.
Publs. *Men Without Work* (co-author) 38, *Artists of the Winchester Bible* 45, *Sequence of Medieval Art* 50, *Classical Tradition in Medieval Art* 59, *The Queen and the Poet* 60, *The Mosaics of Rome from the Third to the Fourteenth Centuries* 68, *Paintings at Sigena in Spain and the Winchester Bible Artists* 72.
The Old School House, Eynsham, Oxford, England.
Telephone: Oxford 880280.

Oates, James Franklin, Jr., B.A., J.D.; American lawyer and insurance executive (retd.); b. 11 Nov. 1899, Evanston, Ill.; s. of the late James Franklin and Henrietta Jennings Oates; m. Rosalind Wright 1925; one s. one d.; ed. Phillips Exeter Acad., and Princeton and Northwestern Univs.
Member law firm of Cutting Moore & Sidley (Chicago)

and its successor Sidley, Austin, Burgess & Harper 24-48; Chief Purchase Policy, Office of the Chief of Ordnance, Washington 42-44; Chair. and Chief Exec. Officer People's Gas, Light and Coke Co., Chicago 48-57; Pres., Chair. and Chief Exec. Officer Equitable Life Assurance Soc. of the U.S. 57-70; Nat. Chair. Jobs for Veterans; mem. N.Y. State Comm. on Elementary and Secondary Educ.; Counsel, Sidley and Austin 70-74, retd.; Dir. Equitable Life and Burlington Northern Inc., Brooklyn Union Gas Co., Colgate-Palmolive Co.; Trustee Emer., Princeton Univ.; Life Trustee, Northwestern Univ., Hon. Trustee George Williams Coll.
Room 725, 401 North Michigan Avenue, Chicago, Illinois 60611, U.S.A.

Oatley, Sir Charles (William), Kt., O.B.E., M.A., F.I.E.E., F.I.E.E.E., F.R.S.; British emer. professor of electrical engineering; b. 14 Feb. 1904, Frome, Somerset; s. of William and Ada M. (née Dorrington) Oatley; m. Dorothy E. West 1930; two s.; ed. Bedford Modern School and St. John's Coll., Cambridge.
Lecturer, Univ. of London 35-39; Radar Research and Devt. Establishment 39-45, Acting Superintendent in charge of scientific work 44-45; Fellow, Trinity Coll., Cambridge 45-; Lecturer, later Reader, Dept. of Engineering, Cambridge Univ. 45-60, Prof. of Electrical Engineering 60-71, Emer. Prof. 71-; Dir. English Electric Valve Co. Ltd. 66-; mem. Council of Royal Soc. 70-72; Hon. Fellow Royal Microscopical Soc. 70; Achievement Award, Worshipful Co. of Scientific Instrument Makers 66; Royal Medal, Royal Soc. 69; Duddell Medal Inst. of Physics and Physical Soc. 69; Faraday Medal, Inst. of Electrical Engineers 70; Mullard Award, Royal Soc. 73; Hon. D.Sc. (Heriot-Watt Univ.) 74.
Leisure interest: gardening.
Publs. *The Scanning Electron Microscope* Vol. I 72; miscellaneous papers in scientific and technical journals.
16 Porson Road, Cambridge, England.
Telephone: Cambridge 56194.

Obame, Alexis André Paul; Gabonese diplomatist; b. 27 Dec. 1927, Lambaréné; ed. Inst. des Hautes Etudes d'Outre-Mer, Paris.
Former Dir. for Public Health and Population; entered diplomatic service 67; Dir. for Int. Orgs. 67-68, for Political and African Affairs 68-72; Sec.-Gen. Gabonese Council of Ministers 72-73; Perm. Rep. to UN March 73-75; rep. to UN Gen. Assembly 68-71, to several OCAM and OAU meetings.
c/o Ministry of Foreign Affairs, Libreville, Gabon.

Obasanjo, Lt.-Gen. Olusegun; Nigerian army officer and politician; b. 1937; m.; ed. Royal Mil. Coll. of Science and Engineering, Shrivenham.
Fought in Nigerian Civil War, accepted the surrender of Biafran forces Jan. 70; Fed. Commr. for Works and Housing Jan-July 75; Chief of Staff, Supreme HQ July 75-Feb. 76; mem. Supreme Mil. Council July 75-; promoted from Brig. to Lt.-Gen. Jan. 76; Head of Fed. Mil. Govt. and C.-in-C. of Armed Forces Feb. 76-.
Office of the Head of State, Lagos, Nigeria.

Obbink, Hendrik Willem, D.D.; Netherlands university professor; b. 20 March 1898, Smilde, Drente; s. of Prof. Dr. H. Th. Obbink and J. G. ten Kate; m. J. M. E. Baljon 1923; one s. one d.; ed. Univs. of Utrecht and Groningen.
Minister of Dutch Reformed Church 23-39, serving at Ootmarsum, Geldermalsen, Middelburg and Utrecht; Hon. Lecturer Hebrew and Aramaic Univ. of Utrecht 32-39, Prof. of History of Religions and Egyptian

Language 39-68; fmr. Pres. Theological Section, Academic Council of the Netherlands; Knight Order of the Netherlands Lion.

Leisure interests: little jobs, modern literature.

Publs. *The Magic Significance of the Name, Especially in Egypt* 25, *The Book of Daniel* 32, *History of the Ancient Near East* 39 and 51, *Theological Considerations on the Old Testament* 38, *Cybele, Isis, Mithras, Oriental Religions in the Roman Empire* 65.

Weteringpark 7, Flat 72, Zwolle, Netherlands.

Telephone: 05200-32767.

Oberhammer, Vinzenz; Austrian museum director; b. 23 Nov. 1901, Innsbruck; s. of Josef and Carolina Oberhammer; m. Helene Wasitzky 1934; one d.; ed. Innsbruck Univ.

Asst. Tyrolean Folk Art Inst., Innsbruck 28; Asst. Innsbruck Inst. of Art History 29, Lecturer 36, Prof. 49, Vienna 63; Curator Ferdinandeum Museum, Innsbruck 38; First Dir. and Dir. of Pictures Gallery, Kunsthistorisches Museum, Vienna 55-66, Exhbns. at Innsbruck 50, 54, Vienna 62 etc.

Publs. *Die Bronzestandbilder des Maximilian Grabmales in der Hofkirche zu Innsbruck* 35, *Der Altar von Schloss Tirol* 48, *The Vienna Gallery* 64, *Das Goldene Dachl zu Innsbruck* 70.

A-1030 Vienna, Arsenal Obj. 3/16, Austria.

Telephone: 6580615.

Oberlin, David W.; American administrator; b. 6 Jan. 1920, Atchison, Kan.; s. of William C. and Dorothy A. Wright Oberlin; m. Alida Elinor Houston 1944; two s. two d.; ed. Navy schools and Univ. of Mich. and Kansas.

Assistant Sec. and Fiscal Officer, Toledo-Lucas County Port Authority 56-67; Port Dir., Seaway Port Authority of Duluth 67-69; Admin., St. Lawrence Seaway Devt. Corpn. June 69-; fmr. Dir. American Asscn. of Port Authorities and Int. Asscn. of Port Authorities; mem. Defence Exec. Reserve, Upper Midwest Regional Export Expansion Council, Water Transportation Sub-Cttee. for Upper Great Lakes Regional Comm.; Dept. of Transportation Commr. Great Lakes Basin Comm.; U.S. Commr. Perm. Int. Asscn. of Navigation Congresses (American Section); Silver Star Medal; Dept. of Transportation's Outstanding Achievement Award with Gold Medal.

Leisure interests: golf, boating.

Office: 800 Independence Avenue, S.W., Room 814, Washington, D.C. 20591; Home: 6401 Cavalier Corridor, Falls Church, Va. 22044, U.S.A.

Telephone: 202-426-3574 (Office).

Obermayer, Adolf Max Reinout, DR.RER.POL.; German diplomatist; b. 13 July 1911, Munich; s. of Prof. Max O. Painter and Cateau Kalff; m. Gerd Sigrid Malm 1947; one s. one d.; ed. Technische Hochschule and Univ. of Munich.

Entered diplomatic service 51; Amb. of Fed. Repub. of Germany to Sweden 68-72, to the Netherlands 72-.

Embassy of Federal Republic of Germany, Groot Hertoginnelaan 18-20, The Hague, Netherlands.

Telephone: 46-92-06.

Oberth, Hermann Julius; German physicist and rocket pioneer; b. 25 June 1894, Hermannstadt, Transylvania; s. of Dr. Julius and Valerie Oberth (née Krasser); m. Mathilde Hummel 1918; two s. (one deceased), two d. (one deceased); ed. Munich, Göttingen, Heidelberg and Klausenberg Univs.

Prof. S.L. Roth College, Mediasch 25-38; experiments with gasoline and liquid air rockets; further research on rockets for army and air force Vienna Technical Univ. 38-40, Dresden 40-41; Advisory Engineer Peenemünde rocket base 41-43, Westfälisch-Anhaltische Sprengstoff A.G. 43-45; further experiments on the Brienzersee (Switzerland) 49, for Italian Navy, La Spezia 50-53, for U.S. Army Redstone Arsenal (Hunts-

ville, Ala.) 55-58; R.E.P.-Hirsch Prize (French Astronautical Soc.) 29, Medal of German Soc. for Space Research 50, Diesel Medal (Asscn. of German Inventors) 54, American Astronautical Soc. Award 55, Edward Pendray Award 56, Bundesverdienstkreuz (I Klasse) of the German Federal Republic 61, IAA Medal 69, and other decorations.

Leisure interest: horticulture.

Publs. *Die Rakete zu den Planetenräumen* 23, *Wege zur Raumschiffahrt* 29, *Forschung und Jenseits* 32, *Menschen im Weltraum* 55, *Das Mondauto* 58, *Stoff und Leben* 59, *Katechismus der Uraniden* 66.

8501 Feucht bei Nürnberg, Untere Kellerstrasse 13, Federal Republic of Germany.

Telephone: 09128-2574.

Obligado Nazar, Alberto; Argentine international official; b. 30 Sept. 1919, Buenos Aires; s. of Carlos Obligado (former Rector of Univ. of Buenos Aires); m. Susana O. de Obligado 1942; one s. nine d.; ed. Faculty of Law and Social Sciences, Univ. of Buenos Aires.

Sec. Univ. of Buenos Aires 44; Dir., Dept. of Western Culture, Inst. of Higher Culture, Buenos Aires 48-70; Prof. of History of Culture, Argentine Inst. of Hispanic Culture, Buenos Aires 65-70; Sec. of Culture and Social Action, Buenos Aires Town Hall 68-70; Chair. Int. Congress on Scientific, Cultural and Economic Ibero-American Development 68-70; Dir. Development of Latin America 68-76; Asst. Dir.-Gen. for Communication, UNESCO 70-75; Gran Cruz Alfonso El Sabio (Spain).

Publs. include *Historia de la Cultura* (3 vols.), *Cuatro Romances, La Antropología de Teilhard de Chardin, Dante e Nietzsche, El limbo en la Divina Comedia, La Ciudad y su Cultura.*

B.P. 298, Cèdex 75766, 75016 Paris, France; Córdoba 1367, Buenos Aires, Argentina.

Telephone: 42-77-75, 44-66-74.

Obote, Dr. (Apollo) Milton; Ugandan politician; b. 1924.

Labourer, clerk, salesman, Kenya 50-55; founder-mem. Kenya African Union; mem. Uganda Nat. Congress 52-60; mem. Uganda Legislative Council 57-71; formed and mem. of Uganda People's Congress 60-71; Leader of the Opposition 61-62; Prime Minister 62-66; Minister of Defence and Foreign Affairs 63-65; assumed full powers of Govt. Feb. 66; Pres. of Uganda April 66-Jan. 71; now in exile in Tanzania.

O'Boyle, H.E. Cardinal Patrick A.; American ecclesiastic; b. 1896, Scranton, Pa.; s. of Michael O'Boyle and Mary Muldoon.

Ordained Priest 21; Archbishop of Washington 48-73; created Cardinal by Pope Paul VI 67; retd. 73.

4110 Warren Street, N.W., Washington, D.C. 20016, U.S.A.

Obraztsov, Sergei Vladimirovich; Soviet puppet theatre artist; b. 5 July 1901, Moscow; trained as an artist.

Acted in Music Studies Co., Moscow Arts Theatre 22-30; started puppet variety theatre 23, Head, Central Puppet Theatre 31-; numerous tours abroad; Vice-Pres. Union Int. des Marionnettistes (U.N.I.M.A.) 57-, Pres. Soviet Section 58-; People's Artist of U.S.S.R.; State Prize 46; Orders of Red Banner of Labour 46, 61; Hero of Socialist Labour 71; Order of Lenin; "Hammer and Sickle" Gold Medal.

Principal works include: *Kashtanka* (Chekhov) 35, *By a Wave of the Hand* (Tarakhovokaya) 36, *Aladdin's Magic Lamp* 40, *Night Before Christmas* (Gogol) 41, *King Deer* (Gozz) 43, *Merry Bear-Cubs* (Polivanova) 45, *Mowgli* (Kipling) 45, *Unusual Concert* 46, *Devil's Mill* (Drda) 53, *Divine Comeay* (Shtock) 61, *I-go-go* (Speransky) 64. Publ. *My Profession.*

Central Puppet Theatre, 32A Ulitsa Gorkogo, Moscow, U.S.S.R.

Obregón, Alejandro; Colombian painter; b. 4 June 1920; ed. Stonyhurst Coll., England, Middlesex School, Concord, and Museum School of Fine Arts, Boston. Director, School of Fine Arts, Bogotá 49-51; one-man exhbns. Bogotá, Barranquilla, Cali, Paris, Milan, Washington, New York, Lima, Madrid, Barcelona, Munich, São Paulo and Rio de Janeiro; numerous prizes include 1st Nat. Prize, Guggenheim International 59; Prize at São Paulo Biennial 67; represented in numerous galleries including: Museum of Modern Art, New York, Phillips Gallery, Washington, Museo Nacional, Bogotá, Instituto de Arte Contemporáneo, Lima, Museo de Arte Moderno, Bogotá, Museo Nacional, La Paz, Galerie Creuze, Paris, Galerie Buchholz, Munich, Galeria Profili, Milan and Instituto Cultura Hispánica, Madrid.
Apartado Aéreo 37, Barranquilla, Colombia.

Obreimov, Ivan Vasilevich; Soviet physicist; b. 8 March 1894, Annecy, France; ed. Petrograd Univ.
State Optical Inst. 19-24; Leningrad Physicotechnical Inst. 24-29; Ukrainian Physicotechnical Inst. 24-29, Dir. Ukrainian Physicotechnical Inst. 29-37; Corresp. mem. U.S.S.R. Acad. of Sciences 33-58, mem 58-; in Inst. of Elementary Organic Compounds, U.S.S.R. Acad. of Sciences 44-65; at Inst. of Gen. and Inorganic Chemistry 65-; State Prize 46, Vavilov Gold Prize, U.S.S.R. Acad. of Sciences 59.
Publs. *Application of Fresnel Diffraction in Physical and Technical Measurements* 45, *Identification of Hydro-Carbons by Dispersion Curves* 55, *Double Refraction in Organic Crystals* 57, *Formation of Ultramicroscopic Heterogeneity during Plastic Deformation of Rock Salt* 56, *On Digital Coding of Scientific Concepts* 61.
Institute of General and Inorganic Chemistry, Academy of Sciences, 31, Leninsky Prospekt, Moscow, U.S.S.R.

O'Brien, Albert James, B.A., M.A., LL.B.; American business executive; b. 30 Oct. 1914, St. Louis, Mo.; s. of James Daniel O'Brien and Lydia Helena Dreher; m. Ruth Virginia Foster 1938; three s.; ed. Washington Univ. and Missouri Inst. of Accountancy and Law.
Econ. Research and Investment Analysis, First Nat. Bank of St. Louis 35-42; Special Asst. to Gen. Man. Atlas Powder Co., Weldon Springs, Mo. 42-44; Personnel Man. Production and Production Staff Man., Production Ralston Purina Co. 44-57, Sec. 57-59, Vice-Pres., Sec. and Chief Finance Officer 59-61, Exec. Vice-Pres. (Chow Marketing & Finance) 61-64, Exec. Vice-Pres. (Admin.) 64-68, Pres. 68-69, Vice-Chair. 70-, Dir. 61-72; Dir. American Investment Co., St. Louis 64-; Chair. Exec. Cttee. R. Rowland & Co.; Silver Beaver Award, Boy Scouts of America 67.
Leisure interests: tennis, golf, bicycling, stereo music.
Office: R. Rowland & Co., 720 Olive Street, St. Louis, Mo. 63101; Home: 30 Rolling Rock Court, St. Louis, Mo. 63124, U.S.A.
Telephone: 314-421-5700 (Office); 314-WY4-9126 (Home).

O'Brien, Brian, PH.B., PH.D.; American physicist; b. 2 Jan. 1898, Denver, Colo.; s. of Michael Philip O'Brien and Lina Prime O'Brien; m. 1st. Ethel Dickerman 1922 (deceased), 2nd. Mary Nelson Firth 1956; one s.; ed. Yale Univ., Mass. Inst. of Tech. and Harvard Univ.
Prof. of Physiological Optics, Univ. of Rochester, N.Y. 30-46, Research Prof. of Physics and Optics 46-54, Dir. Inst. of Optics 38-54; Vice-Pres. and Dir. of Research, American Optical Co., Mass. 53-58; Consulting Physicist and Engineer 58-; Pres. Optical Soc. of America 51-53; Chair. Div. of Physical Sciences, Nat. Research Council 53-61; mem. U.S. Air Force Scientific Advisory Board 59-; Chair. Nat. Acad. of Sciences advisory Cttee. to Air Force Systems Command 62-; Chair. Space Program Advisory Council, NASA 70-; mem. Nat. Acad. of Sciences, American Philos. Soc., American Acad. of

Arts and Sciences; U.S.A. Presidential Medal for Merit 48; Frederick Ives Medal, Optical Soc. of America 51; Sec. of Air Force Exceptional Civilian Service Medal 69, 73.
Leisure interests: fly fishing, deep sea fishing.
Publs. Approx. 60 scientific papers in physics of upper atmosphere, physical optics of metals, solar spectrum, silver halide emulsion reactions, photographic recipro-city, photographic photometry, reactions of the retina, resolution of the retina, binocular flicker phenomena, iris pulsations, etc., etc.
Box 52, North Woodstock, Conn. 06257, U.S.A.
Telephone: 203-928-7295.

O'Brien, Conor Cruise, B.A., PH.D.; Irish writer and diplomatist; b. 3 Nov. 1917, Dublin; s. of Francis Cruise O'Brien and Katherine Sheeky; m. 1st Cristine Foster 1939 (dissolved 1962), one s. two d.; m. 2nd Máire MacEntee 1962, one s. one d. (both adopted); ed. Trinity Coll., Dublin.
Entered Dept. of External Affairs of Ireland 44, Counsellor, Paris 55-56, Head UN Section and mem. Irish Del. to UN 56-60, Asst. Sec.-Gen., Dept. of External Affairs of Ireland 60; Rep. of Sec.-Gen. of UN in Katanga, May-Dec. 61; Vice-Chancellor, Univ. of Ghana 62-65; Regent's Prof. and Holder of Albert Schweitzer Chair in Humanities, New York Univ. 65-69; mem. Dáil Éireann, Dublin (Labour) 69-; Minister for Posts and Telegraphs 73-; Pro-Chancellor Univ. of Dublin 73-; Hon. D.Litt. (Bradford) 71, (Ghana) 74.
Publs. *Maria Cross* (under pseud. Donat O'Donnell) 52, *Parnell and his Party* 57, *The Shaping of Modern Ireland* (ed.) 59, *To Katanga and Back* 62, *Conflicting Concepts of the United Nations* 64, *Writers and Politics* 65, *The United Nations: Sacred Drama* 67, *Murderous Angels* (play) 68, Editor *Power and Consciousness* 69, *Conor Cruise O'Brien Introduces Ireland* 69, Editor *Edmund Burke, Reflections on the Revolution in France* 69, *Camus* 69, *A Concise History of Ireland* 72, *The Suspecting Glance* 72, *States of Ireland* 72.
Leisure interest: travelling.
Whitewater, The Summit, Howth, Dublin, Ireland.
Telephone: Dublin 322474.

O'Brien, Edna; Irish author; b. 15 Dec. 1936, Co. Clare; d. of Michael O'Brien and Lena Cleary; m. 1954 (divorced 1964); two s.; ed. convents, Pharmaceutical Coll. of Ireland.
Engaged in writing from an early age; *Yorkshire Post* Novel Award 71, Kingsley Amis Award.
Leisure interest: dancing.
Publs. *The Country Girls* 60, *The Lonely Girl* 62, *Girls in Their Married Bliss* 63, *August is a Wicked Month* 64, *Casualties of Peace* 66, *The Love Object* 68, *A Pagan Place* 70 (play 71), *Night* 72, *A Scandalous Woman* (short stories) 74.
10 Carlyle Square, London, S.W.3, England.

O'Brien, Lawrence Francis, LL.B.; American government official; b. 7 July 1917, Springfield, Mass.; s. of Lawrence O'Brien, Snr. and Myra Sweeny; m. Elva Lena Brassard 1944; one s.; ed. Cathedral Grade and High Schools, Springfield, Mass., Northeastern Univ.
United States Army 43-45; O'Brien Realty Co. (family business), Springfield, Mass. 42-52; Board Pres. and Business Man. Western Mass. Hotel and Restaurant Health Fund 52-58; State Dir. of Org. for campaigns of John F. Kennedy for Senate of U.S., Mass. 52, 58; Public Relations work, Springfield 58-60; Nat. Dir. of Org. for Democratic Nat. Cttee. and for Kennedy-Johnson campaign 60; Special Asst. to Pres. of U.S. for Congressional Relations 61-65; Postmaster-Gen. 65-68; Democratic Party Campaign Man. for Presidential Election 68; resigned as Chair. Democratic Nat. Cttee. Jan. 69, reappointed March 70-72; Chair. McGovern Presidential Campaign 72; Pres. McDonnell & Co.

(N.Y. investment banking firm) 69-; several honorary degrees.
Publ. *The O'Brien Campaign Manual.*
870 United Nations Plaza, New York, N.Y. 10017, U.S.A.

O'Brien, (Michael) Vincent; Irish racehorse trainer; b. 9 April 1917, Cork; *s.* of Daniel P. O'Brien and Kathleen (née Toomey); *m.* Jacqueline Wittenoom 1951; two *s.* three *d.*; ed. Mungret Coll., Limerick.
Started training in Co. Cork 44, moved to Co. Tipperary 51; won all principal English and Irish steeplechases, including 3 consecutive Grand Nationals, Gold Cups and Champion Hurdles; has concentrated on flat racing 59-; trained winners of 12 English classics, including 4 Derbys; trained Nijinsky, first Triple Crown winner since 1935, also winner of 2 Irish Derbys, Prix de l'Arc de Triomphe and Washington Int.
Leisure interests: golf, shooting, fishing.
Ballydoyle House, Cashel, Co. Tipperary, Ireland.
Telephone: Cashel 203.

O'Brien, Terence John, C.M.G., M.C., M.A.; British diplomatist; b. 13 Oct. 1921, Ranchi, India; *s.* of Joseph O'Brien; ed. Gresham's School, Holt, Merton Coll., Oxford.
Ayrshire Yeomanry, later Air Liaison Office with 83 Group R.A.F. 42-45; Dominions Office 47, Commonwealth Relations Office (CRO) 47-49, 52-54; Second Sec., British High Comm., Ceylon (now Sri Lanka) 49-52; Principal, Treasury 54-56; First Sec. (Financial), High Comm., Canberra 56-58; Planning Officer, CRO 58-60; First Sec. Kuala Lumpur 60-62; Sec. to Inter-Governmental Cttee., Jesselton, North Borneo (now Kota Kinabalu, Sabah, Malaysia) 62-63; Head of Chancery, New Delhi 63-66; Imp. Defence Coll. 67; Counsellor, Foreign Office, FCO 68-70; Amb. to Nepal 70-74, to Burma May 74-.
British Embassy, 80 Strand Road, Rangoon, Burma; Home: Beaufort House, Woodcutts, Salisbury, Wiltshire, England.

O'Brien of Lothbury, Baron (Life Peer) cr. 73; **Leslie Kenneth O'Brien,** G.B.E., P.C.; British banker; b. 8 Feb. 1908, London; *s.* of Charles John Grimes O'Brien and Carrie Abbot; *m.* Isabelle Gertrude Pickett 1932; one *s.*
Entered Bank of England 27, apptd. Deputy Chief Cashier 51, Chief Cashier 55-62, Dir. 62-64, Deputy Gov. 64-66, Gov. 66-73; Pres. British Bankers' Asscn. 73-; Dir. Prudential Assurance Co. Ltd. 73-, Rank Org. 74-; Consultant to J. P. Morgan and Co. 73-; Chair. Int. Advisory Council, Morgan Guaranty Trust Co. 74-, Advisory Board Unilever 73-, Advisory Council, Morgan Grenfell Co. Ltd. 74-; Dir. Bank for Int. Settlements 74-, Saudi Int. Bank; Hon. Fellow and Vice-Pres. Inst. of Bankers; Hon. D.S.; Hon. LL.D. (Univ. of Wales).
33 Lombard Street, London, EC3P 3BH, England.
Telephone: 01-283-8888.

Obukhov, Alexandr Mikhailovich, D.SC.; Soviet physicist; b. 1918; ed. Moscow State Univ.
Research Assoc., Geophysical Inst., U.S.S.R. Acad. of Sciences 40-56; Dir. Inst. of Atmospheric Physics 56-; Lecturer, Moscow State Univ. 46-49, Prof. 49-; corresp. mem. U.S.S.R. Acad. of Sciences 53-70, Academician 70-.
Institute of Atmospheric Physics, 3 Pyzhevsky pereulok, Moscow, U.S.S.R.

O'Byrne, Justin; Australian politician; b. 1 June 1912, Launceston, Tasmania; *s.* of Patrick A. O'Byrne and Mary Elizabeth Madden; *m.* Gisele Anne Crossle 1961; one *s.* two *d.*; ed. St. Patricks Coll., Launceston.
Engaged in pastoral industry, S.W. Queensland 30-39; Royal Australian Air Force Empire Training Scheme 40; Pilot Officer with R.A.A.F. Squadron in England 41-46, prisoner of war 41-44; mem. Senate 46-, Pres. 74-75; Opposition Whip 72-74; mem.

Treas. Fed. Exec. Australian Labor Party; Del. to UN Gen. Assembly 71.
Leisure interests: reading, gardening, horse riding.
The Senate, Canberra, A.C.T.; Home: 11 Ramsay Street, Launceston, Tasmania, Australia.
Telephone: 31-5506 (Home).

Obzina, Jaromír, PH.D., C.SC.; Czechoslovak politician; b. 28 May 1929, Brodek; ed. Přerov Secondary School, Cen. Political School of C.P. of Czechoslovakia.
Secretary Chrudim District Cttee., C.P. of Czechoslovakia, First Sec. Polička and Pardubice District Cttee., Instructor Pardubice Regional Cttee.; held positions on Political Board of Czechoslovak People's Army 51-53, Head of Political Dept., Deputy Commdr. for Political Affairs, Antonín Zápotocký Mil. Technical Acad. 56-64; Deputy Commdr. Klement Gottwald Mil. Political Acad. 66; mem. Cen. Cttee. C.P. of Czechoslovakia 65-, Head of Dept. for Science and Univs. 65-68; Deputy Head of Inst. for Scientific Affairs, Czechoslovak People's Army 68-69; Head of Dept. of Educ. and Science, Cen. Cttee., C.P. of Czechoslovakia 69-73; Minister of the Interior 73; Deputy House of the People, Fed. Assembly 73; several decorations incl. Medal for Distinction in Construction, Medal for Outstanding Work.
Ministry of Interior, Prague, Czechoslovakia.

O'Callaghan, (Donal N.) Mike; American state governor; b. 10 Sept. 1929, La Crosse, Wis.; *s.* of Neil T. and Olive Berry O'Callaghan; *m.* Carolyn Randall; three *s.* two *d.*; ed. Cotter High School, Winona, Minn., Univs. of Idaho and Nevada, Colorado State and Georgetown Univs. and Claremont Graduate School.
High School teacher 56-61; Chief Probation Officer and Dir. of Court Services, Clark County, Nev. 61-63; State Dir. of Health and Welfare 63-64; Project Management Dir., Job Corps Conservation Centres, Washington, D.C. 64-66; Regional Dir. Office of Emergency Planning (OEP), San Francisco 67-69; Gov. of Nevada Jan. 71-; Democrat.
Leisure interests: falconry, hiking, camping.
Office of the Governor, State Capitol, Carson City, Nevada, U.S.A.

Ocampo, Victoria, C.B.E.; Argentine writer and publisher; ed. privately.
Founder Editor *Sur* (literary magazine) 31-; Head of Management, Teatro Colón, Buenos Aires 33; Founder, Argentine Women's Union 36, Pres. 36 and 38; Vice-Pres. PEN Int.; Pres. Comm. of Letters of Nat. Foundation for the Arts in Argentina; Palmes Académiques, Officier Légion d'Honneur, Commdr. des Arts et Lettres.
Publs. *De Francesca a Beatrice* 24, *La Laguna de los nenúfares* 26, *Testimonios* (series I-VI) 35-47, *Domingos en Hyde Park* 36, *San Isidro* 41, *338.171 TE* 42, *Soledad sonora* 50, *El viajero y una de sus sombras* 51, *Lawrence Se Arabia y otros ensayos* 51, *Virginia Woolf en su diario d4, Habla el algarrobo* 59, *Tagore en las barrancas de San Isidro* 61, *Antología de Jawaharlal Nehru: Selección y Prólogo* 66, *Diálogos Con Borges* 69, *Diálogos Con Mallea* 69; trans. Camus, Colette, William Faulkner, Graham Greene, T. E. Lawrence, Dylan Thomas, John Osborne, Lanza del Vasto.
Elortondo 1811, San Isidro, Buenos Aires, Argentina.

Occhialini, Giuseppe Paolo Stanislao; Italian physicist; b. 5 Dec. 1907, Fossombrone, Urbino; *s.* of Augusto Occhialini and Etra (née Grossi); *m.* Constance Dilworth 1950; one *d.*; ed. Univ. of Florence.
Assistant in Physics, Univ. of Florence 32-37; research in Cavendish Laboratory, Cambridge Univ. 31-34, São Paulo Univ. 37-44, Wills Laboratory, Bristol Univ. 45-47; Assoc. Prof. Univ. of Brussels 48; Prof. Univ. of Genoa 50-52, Univ. of Milan 52-; Visiting Prof. M.I.T. 60; mem. Nat. Acad. Lincei, Heidelberg Acad., American Philosophical Soc., Brazilian Acad.; Foreign Fellow,

Royal Soc.; Dr. h.c. (Brussels and Bristol Univs.); Vallauri Prize, Einaudi Prize 49, Feltrinelli Int. Prize 55.
Publs. on cosmic rays, high energy physics and space research.
Viale Argonne 42, 20133 Milan, Italy.

Ochab, Edward; Polish politician; b. 16 Aug. 1906, Cracow; ed. Cracow School of Commerce and Jagiellonian Univ.
Joined Polish Communist Party 29; frequently imprisoned; co-organizer of Union of Polish Patriots and Polish Army in the Soviet Union 42-45; Minister of Public Admin. 44-45; Deputy to Seym 47-69; Chair. Cen. Council of Trade Unions 48-49; Vice-Minister of Nat. Defence 49-50; Sec. Cen. Cttee. Polish United Workers' Party 50-56, 59-64, mem. Politburo 54-68, First Sec. Cen. Cttee. 56; Minister of Agriculture 57-59; Vice-Pres. Council of State 61-64, Pres. Aug. 64-April 68; Chair. All-Polish Cttee. of Nat. Unity Front 65-68; retd.; numerous decorations.

Ochiai, Eiichi, B.SC.; Japanese trade unionist; b. 15 Feb. 1916, Kuzumaki-Machi; s. of the late Eisaburo Ochiai and Mitori Ochiai; m. Eiko Ochiai 1945; one s. one d.; ed. Yokohama Nat. Univ.
Mitsui Metal Mine Co. Ltd. 36-41, Toshiba Electric Co. 43-46; Adviser, Japan Asscn. of Science and Technology 44-47; Pres. All-Japan Electric Industry Workers Unions 46-48; mem. Exec. Board Congress of Industrial Labour Union 46-49; mem. Exec. Board Japan Socialist Party 48-49; Gen. Sec. Nat. Fed. of Industrial Orgs. 49-64; mem. Labour Problems Cttee. 61-64, Small and Medium Enterprise Retirement Counter-measure Cttee. 60-64; Dir. Tokyo Office, Int. Confederation of Free Trade Unions (ICFTU) and Special Rep. in Japan 64-; Trustee, Japan ILO Asscn. 62-.
Leisure interests: horse riding, rugby.
Publs. *Import of Foreign Capital and Production Struggle* 49, *Directory of Trade Union Administration* 49, *Earth of North America and Blood of Great Britain* 59.
Keyakidai 38-302, Nishimachi-4, Kokubumji-shi, Tokyo 185, Japan.
Telephone: 0425-36-8306.

Ochoa, Severo, M.D.; Spanish-born American biochemist; b. 24 Sept. 1905, Luarca, Spain; ed. Madrid, Glasgow, Berlin, Heidelberg and London Univs.
Lecturer Univs. of Madrid, Heidelberg, Plymouth and Oxford 31-41; Instructor and Research Assoc. Washington Univ. St. Louis 41-42; Research Assoc. New York Univ. 42, Chair. Dept. of Biochemistry 54-; U.S. citizen 56-; Visiting Prof. Univ. of Calif. 49, Univ. of Brazil 56; Foreign mem. Royal Soc. (U.K.) 65; Nobel Prize in Medicine (with Kornberg) 59; Pres. Int. Union of Biochemistry 61-67; mem. U.S. Nat. Acad. of Sciences, Acad. of Arts and Sciences, American Philosophical Soc., U.S.S.R. Acad. of Sciences, Polish Acad. of Sciences, Brazilian Acad. of Sciences, Pontifical Acad. of Sciences 74, and many other academies; numerous hon. degrees and decorations.
New York University School of Medicine, 550 First Avenue, New York, N.Y. 10016, U.S.A.

Ochsner, Alton, M.D.; American surgeon; b. 4 May 1896, Kimball, S. Dak.; m. 1st Isabel Lockwood 1923 (died 1968), three s. one d.; m. 2nd Jane Kellogg Sturdy 1970; ed. Univ. of S. Dakota and Washington Univ., St. Louis, Missouri.
Surgical practice, Chicago, Ill. 25-26; Asst. Prof. of Surgery, Univ. of Wis. Medical School and State Gen. Hosp., Madison, Wis. 26-27; Prof. Tulane Univ. School of Medicine, New Orleans, La. 27-61, Chair. Dept. of Surgery 27-56; Chief of Tulane Surgical Service to Charity Hosp., New Orleans 27-56, Senior Visiting Surgeon 27-61, now Consulting Surgeon; Dir. of Surgery, Ochsner Clinic and Ochsner Foundation

Hosp., New Orleans 42-66, now Senior Consultant; Pres. Alton Ochsner Medical Foundation, New Orleans 44-70, now Emer. Pres.; Pres. American Cancer Soc. 49-50, American Coll. of Surgeons 51-52, Int. Soc. of Surgery 62-63 (Chair. U.S. Nat. Cttee. 51-67); several consultative posts; mem. and Hon. Fellow, many medical socs. and colls.; mem. several boards of dirs.; Co-Ed. *Int. Surgical Digest* and other editorial positions; Dr. h.c., six American and three foreign univs.
Publs. *Varicose Veins* 38, *Smoking and Cancer: a Doctor's Report* 54, *Smoking and Health* 59, *Smoking and Your Life* 64, *Smoking: Your Choice between Life and Death* 70; co-author *Christopher's Minor Surgery* 55, 59; 24 sections in medical books; over 500 articles in journals.
Ochsner Clinic, 1514 Jefferson Highway, New Orleans, La. 70121, U.S.A.
Telephone: (504) 834-7070.

Ockermüller, Franz, LL.D.; Austrian banker; b. 1915; ed. Univ. of Vienna.
Chairman and Gen. Man. Österreichische Länderbank A.G.; Chair. Waagner-Biro A.G., Perlmooser Zementwerke A.G., J. M. Voith A.G., Chemiefaser Lenzing A.G., Österreichische Kontrollbank A.G.; Vice-Chair. Österreichische Kommunalkredit A.G., Vorarlberger Zementwerke Lorüns A.G., Pölser Zellulose und Papierfabrik A.G., Pöls; Dir. Esso Austria A.G., IBM Österreich Int. Büromaschinen G.m.b.H., Kabel und Drahtwerke A.G., Österreichische Brown Boveri-Werke A.G., Österreichisches Credit-Institut A.G., Österreichische Investitionskredit A.G., Steiermärkisch Elektrizitäts A.G.; Vice-Pres. Asscn. of Austrian Banks and Bankers 75; Pres. Vienna Stock Exchange Cttee.
Leisure interests: mountaineering, hiking.
2 Am Hof, Vienna; Home: 4 Schottengasse, Vienna 1, Austria.
Telephone: 631631 (Office); 638405 (Home).

O'Connor, Mgr. Martin John, A.B., S.T.D., J.C.D.; American ecclesiastic; b. 18 May 1900, Scranton, Pa.; s. of the late Martin John O'Connor and Belinda Caffrey; ed. St. Thomas Coll., Scranton, Pa., American Coll., and Urban Coll. of Propaganda, Rome.
Served in U.S. Army 18; ordained priest 24; Asst. Pastor Scranton Cathedral 25-27, Sec. to Bishop and Chancellor of the Diocese 29-35, Diocesan Consultor 32-46, Pastor 34-43, Officialis 37-46, Vicar-Gen. 38-46; Titular Bishop of Thespiae and Auxiliary Bishop of Scranton 43; Pastor, St. Mary's Church, Wilkes Barre, Pa. 43; Rector, North American Coll., Rome 46-65; Pres. Pontifical Comm. for Motion Pictures 54, Cttee. for Press Relations for Vatican Council 63-, Pontifical Comm. for Communications Media 64-71; Pres. emer., Pontifical Comm. for Social Communications 71; mem. Int. Holy Year Cttee. 50, Central Marian Year Cttee. 56, Int. Marian Acad. 58; Asst. Pontifical Throne 53-; Titular Archbishop of Laodicea in Syria 59-; Consultor, Sacred Congregation for Seminaries and Universities 54-67, Consultor, Sacred Propaganda Fide 60-; Apostolic Nuncio to Malta 65-69; Vice-Pres. Post Conciliar Comm. for Apostolate of the Laity 66-69; Consultor, Pontifical Comm. for Latin America 70; Chaplain *in gremio religionis* of the Sovereign Order of Malta 47, Kt. Commdr. with Star, Knights of the Holy Sepulchre 51, Grand Officer, Italian Order of Merit 57.
Palazzo San Carlo, Vatican City and Via di Porta Angelica 63, Rome 00193, Italy.

Oda, Shigeru, LL.D.; Japanese lawyer; b. 22 Oct. 1924; ed. Univ. of Tokyo, Yale Univ.
Research Fellow, Univ. of Tokyo 47-49; Lecturer, Univ. of Tôhoku 50-53, Asst. Prof. 53-59, Prof. 59-76; Tech. Adviser, Atomic Energy Comm. 61-64; Special Asst. to Minister of Foreign Affairs 73-76; mem. Science Council of Ministry of Educ. 69-76, of Council for Ocean Devt. in Prime Minister's Office 71-76,

Advisory Cttee. for Co-operation with UN Univ. 71-76; Judge, Int. Court of Justice Feb. 76-; del. to UN Confs. on Law of the Sea 58, 60, 73-75; Rep. at 6th Gen. Conf. of Inter-Governmental Oceanographic Comm. 69; consultative positions with bodies concerned with marine questions; Counsel for Fed. Repub. of Germany before Int. Court of Justice 68; Ed.-in-Chief, *Japanese Annual of International Law* 73-.
Publs. in Japanese: *International Law of the Sea* 56-69, *International Law and Maritime Resources* 71-75; in English: *International Control of Sea Resources* 62, *The International Law of Ocean Development* 72-74; various articles.
International Court of Justice, Peace Palace, The Hague 2102, The Netherlands.

Oda, Takio; Japanese diplomatist; b. 16 March 1907; ed. Tokyo Univ.
Secretary, Japanese Embassy, Washington; Chief Econs. Dept., Cen. Post-War Liaison Office 46; Dir. Gen. Affairs, Commercial and Research Depts.; Dir. Int. Trade and Industry Bureau 50-52; Dir. Econs. Bureau of Foreign Ministry 52-54; Minister Plenipotentiary in Britain 54-57, Minister to Denmark 57-58, Amb. to Indonesia 58-62; Vice Foreign Minister 63-64; Chair. Board Int. Public Relations Co. 66-; Pres. Japan-Denmark Soc. 66.
Central Co-operative House, Apt. 410, 15 Ageba-cho, Shinjuku-ku, Tokyo, Japan.
Telephone: 260-5041 (Home); 501-7571 (Office).

Ó Dálaigh, Cearbhall, B.A., B.L.; Irish judge and head of state; b. 12 Feb. 1911; m. Máirín Nic Dhiarmada 1934; ed. Christian Brothers' School, Dublin, Univ. Coll., Dublin.
Irish Editor, *Irish Press* 31-40; called to the Bar 34; admitted to Inner Bar 45; Attorney-Gen. 46-48, 51-53; Judge of Supreme Court 53, Chief Justice and Pres. 61-73; Judge Court of Justice of European Communities 73, Pres. First Chamber 74; Pres. of Ireland Dec. 74-; fmr. Chair. Comm. on Industrial Taxation, Comm. on Income Tax, Comm. on Accommodation Needs of the Constituent Colls. of Nat. Univ., Comm. on Higher Educ., Cultural Relations Cttee. of Dept. of Foreign Affairs, Irish Nat. Council on Alcoholism, Council for Overseas Students; Joint Pres. Alliance Française de Dublin; Pres. Irish UN Asscn., Ireland-Israel Soc.; mem. Royal Irish Acad.; Hon. F.R.C.S.; Hon. Fellow Inst. of Engineers of Ireland; Hon. LL.D., Dublin Univ., Hon. D.Litt.Celt., Nat. Univ. of Ireland; Commdr. Order of Merit (Italy), Medaglia Culturale d'Argento.
Leisure interests: Irish literature, French and Italian language, art, theatre, education, public int. law and refugee problems.
Áras an Uachtaráin, Phoenix Park, Dublin 8, Ireland.

Oddi H.E. Cardinal Silvio; Vatican diplomatist; b. 14 Nov. 1910, Morfasso.
Ordained 33; Titular Archbishop of Mesembria 53; Apostolic Delegate in Palestine, Jerusalem and Cyprus 53-56; Apostolic Internuncio in Egypt and U.A.R. 56-62; Apostolic Nuncio in Belgium and Luxembourg 62-69; cr. Cardinal March 69; Pres. of the Pontifical Comm. for the Sanctuaries of Loreto and Pompei; Pontifical Delegate for the Basilica of Assisi.
21 Via Pompeo Magno, 00192 Rome, Italy.
Telephone: 3568957.

Odegaard, Charles (Edwin), PH.D.; American university professor; b. 10 Jan. 1911; ed. Dartmouth Coll., and Harvard Univ.
Travelling Fellowship for study in France 34-35; Asst. in History, Radcliffe Coll. 35-37; Instructor to Prof. in History, Univ. of Illinois 37-48, Asst. for Humanities to Dean of Graduate Coll. 48; Exec. Dir. American Council of Learned Socs. 48-52; Prof. of History, Dean of Coll. of Literature, Science and Arts, Univ. of Michigan 52-58; Pres. Univ. of Washington, Seattle 58-74; mem. U.S. Nat. Comm. UNESCO 49-55; Pres. Int. Council of Philosophy and Humanistic Studies 59-65; U.S. Naval Reserve 42-46; mem. American Council on Educ. (fmr. Chair.), American Historical Asscn.
Publ. *Fideles and Vassi in the Carolingian Empire* 45.
University of Washington, Seattle, Wash. 98105, U.S.A.

Odelola, Amos Oyetunji, B.SC., M.A.; Nigerian economist; b. 4 March 1927, Modakeke, Ife; s. of the late Mr. and Mrs. J. Odelola; m. Bola Odeloye 1953; one s. three d.; ed. Oduduwa Coll., Ife, Univ. of Hull, England, and Yale Univ., U.S.A.
Agricultural Asst., Dept. of Agriculture, Nigeria, then Statistical Asst., Dept. of Statistics; then Admin. Officer, W. Nigerian Govt.; Special Asst. to Sec.-Gen., Comm. for Technical Co-operation in Africa (CCTA) 63-64, Acting Sec.-Gen. 64-65; Exec. Sec. Scientific, Technical and Research Comm. of Org. for African Unity (OAU) (successor to CCTA) 65-.
Leisure interests: lawn tennis, table tennis, numismatology.
Scientific, Technical and Research Commission of Organization for African Unity, Nigerian Ports Authority Building, P.M.B. 2359, Marina, Lagos, Nigeria.
Telephone: 20152, 24014.

Odero-Jowi, Joseph; Kenyan diplomatist; b. 15 Aug. 1929, S. Nyanza, Kenya; m.; ed. Delhi School of Econs., Univ. of Delhi.
Worked in Secrs. of UN Econ. Comm. for Africa, Addis Ababa and Econ. and Social Council, N.Y. 60; Lecturer, African Labour Coll., Kampala, Uganda; mem. Kenya House of Reps. 63; Asst. Minister of Labour 63, of Finance 66; Minister for East African Community in charge of Admin. and Finance; Exec. Dir. EMCO Steel Works, Kenya Ltd. and other Madhvani Groups in Kenya; Perm. Rep. to UN Oct. 70-74.
c/o Ministry of Foreign Affairs, Nairobi, Kenya.

Odinga, A. Oginga; Kenyan politician; b. 1911; ed. Alliance High School, Kikuyu, and Makerere Coll.
Former teacher; mem. Central Nyanza African District Council, Sakwa Location Advisory Council 47-49; mem. Legislative Council 57-; Vice-Pres. Kenya African Nat. Union (KANU) 60-66, founded Kenya People's Union 66 (party banned Oct. 69); Minister for Home Affairs 63-64; Vice-Pres. of Kenya Dec. 64-April 66; arrested Oct. 69, released March 71; rejoined KANU Sept. 71.
Publ. *Not Yet Uhuru* 67.
c/o KANU, P.O. Box 12394, Nairobi, Kenya.

Odlum, Floyd B., A.B., LL.B., M.B.A.; American foundation trustee; b. 30 March 1892; ed. Univ. of Colorado.
Chairman Atlas Corpn. 29-60; Chair. of Board R.K.O. Radio Pictures 37-48, Consolidated Vultee Aircraft Corpn. 47-53; Chair. Board of Trustees Lovelace Foundation for Medical Educ. and Research; Trustee Air Force Aid Soc.; Pres. Certificate of Merit, French Legion of Honour; retd.
Cochran-Odlum Ranch, Indio, California, U.S.A.

O'Donoghue, Philip; Irish lawyer; b. 15 Oct. 1896, Macroom, Co. Cork; s. of Patrick O'Donoghue and Julia MacCarthy; m. Una Ryan 1922; two s. two d.; ed. Castlenock Coll. and Nat. Univ. of Ireland.
Called to the Bar 19; Senior Counsel 39; Justice, District Court 22-29; Legal Asst. to Attorney Gen. 29-59; mem. European Comm. of Human Rights 65-71; mem. Irish Comm. on Status of Women 70-; Judge, European Court of Human Rights 71-; Commr. of Charitable Donations and Bequests for Ireland.
49 Farmhill Drive, Goatstown, Dublin 14, Ireland.
Telephone: Dublin 983584.

O'Driscoll, Timothy Joseph, B.A.; Irish tourist official; b. 6 July 1908, Cork; s. of Michael O'Driscoll and Mary Hélena Walshe; m. Elizabeth McKay 1941; three d.; ed. Presentation Coll., Cork, and Trinity Coll., Dublin.
Irish Civil Service 28-56; Irish Rep. to Int. Civil Aviation Org. 46-48, Org. for European Econ. Co-operation (OEEC) 48-50; Chair. Irish Export Board 51-55; Amb. to Netherlands 55-56; Dir.-Gen. Irish Tourist Board 56-71; mem. Board Irish Airlines; Pres. Int. Union of Official Tourist Orgs. 61-63; Executive Dir. European Travel Comm. 71-; Consultant on Tourism to UN 67-68; Chair. OECD Tourism Cttee. 64-66; Algemene Bank Nederland (Ireland) Ltd.; mem. Exec. Advisory Board Gulf Oil (Ireland); mem. Council of Design; Consultant to Indian Inst. of Public Administration 69; Pres. An Taisce Irish Nat. Trust 69-; Adviser on Tourism under UNDP to India 70, to Iran 71-; Pres. Marketing Inst. of Ireland 73-; Vice-Chair. Dublin Theatre Festival; First American Soc. of Travel Agents Hall of Fame 73; Commdr. Order of George I (Greece), Order of Prince Henry the Navigator (Portugal); Royal Danish Tourist Medal; Hon. LL.D. (Dublin Univ.).
Leisure interests: gardening, reading, photography.
P.O. Box 536, Dublin 8, Ireland.
Telephone: Dublin 01-765954 (Office); Dublin 90 6265 (Home).

Oduber Quirós, Daniel; Costa Rican politician and diplomatist; b. 25 Aug. 1921, San José; s. of Porfirio Oduber and Ana María Quirós; m. Marjorie Elliott Sypher 1950; one s.; ed. Univ. of Costa Rica, McGill Univ., Canada, and Univ. of Paris.
Ambassador to UN 49; Head of Public Relations, Partido Liberación Nacional (PLN) 51-53, Sec.-Gen. 56-58, Pres. 70-; Minister of Foreign Affairs 62-64; Head various dels. to UN Gen. Assembly; co-ordinator at the meeting of Presidents of Cen. America, United States and Panama 63; PLN Presidential Candidate 65; Pres. of Congress 70-74; Pres. of Costa Rica 74-; Grand Cross Order of Malta, Grand Cross Order of Isabel la Católica (Spain), and numerous other foreign decorations.
Leisure interests: sports, reading, travel.
Casa Presidencial, San José, Costa Rica.

Oĕ, Kenzaburo; Japanese author; b. 1935; m.; two c.
First stories published 57; Akutagawa prize for novella The Catch 58; first full-length novel Pluck The Flowers, Gun The Kids 58; represented young Japanese writers at Peking 60; travelled to Russia and Western Europe writing a series of essays on Youth in the West 61; Shinchosha Literary Prize 64; Tanizaki Prize 67.
Publs. The Catch 58, Pluck The Flowers, Gun The Kids 58, Our Age 59, Screams 62, The Perverts 63, Hiroshima Notes 63, Adventures in Daily Life 64, A Personal Matter 64 (English 69), Football in The First Year of Mannen 67.
585 Seijo-machi, Setagaya-Ku, Tokyo, Japan.
Telephone: 482-7192.

Oeftering, Heinz Maria, DR. JUR.; German railways executive; b. 31 Aug. 1903, Munich; s. of Prof. Michael and Ida (née Rattenhuber) Oeftering; m. Irmengard Hugel 1930; no c.; ed. Volksschule and Gymnasium in Munich, and Univs. of Munich, Heidelberg and Paris.
With Reichsfinanzhof, Munich 32-34; Reichsfinanzministerium, Berlin 35-45; Pres. Rechnungshof Rheinland-Pfalz, Speyer 45-50; Dir. Bundesfinanzministerium, Bonn 50-57; Chair. of Board and Pres. Deutsche Bundesbahn until 72; Pres. Admin. Council Deutsche Bundesbahn 72-; mem. various advisory boards; Hon. Prof. Univ. of Mainz; Dr. Ing. e.h.; Grosses Bundesverdienstkreuz mit Stern und Schulterband and numerous foreign orders.
Leisure interest: music.
Publs. commentaries on income tax and corporation tax, Transport Problems.

Friedrich-Ebert-Anlage 43-45, 6 Frankfurt/M, Federal Republic of Germany.
Telephone: 2651.

Oehlert, Benjamin Hilborn, B.S., LL.B.; American diplomatist; b. 13 Sept. 1909, Philadelphia, Pa.; s. of Benjamin H. Oehlert and Sarah Landis; m. Alice Naomi Greene 1937; one s. one d.; ed. Univ. of Pennsylvania.
Attorney, Mexican Claims Div., Dept. of State 35-38; Asst. Counsel, Coca Cola Co. 38-42, Asst. to Pres., Vice-Pres. 42-48, 53-65, Senior Vice-Pres. 65-67; Pres. Minute Maid Co. 61-65; Vice-Pres. W. R. Grace & Co. 48-53; Amb. to Pakistan 67-69; Nat. Dir. United Cerebral Palsy Research and Education Foundation.
Publs. The Restatement in the Courts, Eminent Domain in Pennsylvania.
The Everglades Club, 356 Worth Avenue, Palm Beach, Florida 33480, U.S.A.

Oellers, Fritz, DR. JUR.; German lawyer and diplomatist; b. 25 July 1903, Düsseldorf; s. of Dr. Alfons Oellers and Emma (née Kampmann); m. Sigrid Rabe 1932; one s. two d.; ed. Univs. of Halle and Marburg.
Practised law and served as Dir. on several industrial enterprises 30-51; mem. Economic Council, Frankfurt 48; mem. Bundestag 49-51; Ambassador to Brazil 51-56; Amb. to Turkey 56-59; co-founder Freie Demokratische Partei; prominent officer in the F.D.P., World Liberal Union and Friedrich Naumann Foundation.
Leisure interests: political literature, collecting modern art.
Frundsbergstrasse 36, 8021 Strasslach (OBB), Federal Republic of Germany.
Telephone: 08170-505.

Oelman, Robert Schantz, A.B.; American business executive; b. 9 June 1909, Dayton, Ohio; s. of William Walter and Edith (Schantz) Oelman; m. Mary Coolidge 1936; two s. two d.; ed. Dartmouth Coll., and Univ. of Vienna.
With Nat. Cash Register Co., Dayton, Ohio 33-, Asst. to Pres. 42-45, Asst. Vice-Pres. 45-46, Vice-Pres. 46-50, Exec. Vice-Pres. 50-57, Pres. 57, Chair. and Pres. 62, Chair. 64-74, Chair. Exec. Cttee. 74-, Dir. 48-; Dir. Koppers Co. Inc., Ohio Bell Telephone Co., Procter & Gamble Co., Winters Nat. Bank & Trust Co., First Nat. City Bank, New York, Ford Motor Co. etc.; fmr. Pres. and Dir. Nat. Asscn. of Manufacturers; fmr. Pres. and Dir. Business Equipment Manufacturers Asscn.; Chair. Board of Trustees Wright State Univ., Dayton; Trustee Dartmouth Coll., Nat. Safety Council, N.Y.; Hon. H.H.D. Univ. of Dayton; Hon. LL.D. Miami Univ., Hon. M.A. Dartmouth Coll., Hon. L.H.D. Wilmington Coll.
Leisure interests: reading, music, golf.
2846 Upper Bellbrook Road, Bellbrook, Ohio 45305, U.S.A.

Oetker, Rudolph-August; German industrialist and shipowner; b. 20 Sept. 1916; ed. Univs. of Hamburg and Vienna.
Owner August Oetker Nährmittelfabrik, Bielefeld, Brenner's Parkhotel, Baden-Baden, Reese-Gesellschaft, Hameln, Hamburg-Südamerikanische Dampfschiffahrts-Gesellschaft Eggert & Amsinck, Hamburg, Rudolf A. Oetker, Hamburg, Max Jordan Bauunternehmung, Ettlingen; holder of controlling interest of Bankhaus Hermann Lampe KG., Dibona Markenvertrieb KG., Ettlingen, Söhnlein Rheingold KG, Wiesbaden-Schierstein, Chemische Fabrik Budenheim, Rudolf A. Oetker, Budenheim, Noris Weinbrennereien KG, Nürnberg; numerous other business interests.
Lutterstrasse 14, 48 Bielefeld, Federal Republic of Germany.
Telephone: 1551.

O'Faoláin, Seán, M.A., A.M., D.LITT.; Irish writer; b. 1900; s. of Denis Whelan; m. Eileen Gould 1928; one s. one d.; ed. Nat. Univ. of Ireland and Harvard Univ. Commonwealth Fellow 26-28; John Harvard Fellow 28-29; Lecturer in English Boston Coll. 29, St. Mary's Coll. Strawberry Hill 29-33; Dir. Arts Council of Ireland 57-59.
Leisure interests: travel, gardening.
Publs. *Lyrics and Satires from Tom Moore* 29, *Midsummer Night Madness* 32, *Life Story of De Valera* 33, *A Nest of Simple Folk* 33, *Constance Markievicz: a Biography* 34, *There's a Birdie in the Cage* 35, *A Born Genius* 36, *Bird Alone* 36, *The Autobiography of Wolfe Tone* 37, *A Purse of Coppers* 37, *The Silver Branch* (translations) 37, *King of the Beggars* (biography) 38, *She Had to Do Something* (play) 38, *An Irish Journey* 39, *Come Back to Erin* 40, *The Great O'Neill* (biography) 42, *Story of Ireland* 43, *Teresa* 47, *The Irish* 48, *The Short Story* 48, *Summer in Italy* 49, *Newman's Way* (biography) 52, *South to Sicily* 53, *The Vanishing Hero* 56, *The Stories of Seán O'Faoláin* 58, *I Remember, I Remember* 62, *Vive Moi* 65, *The Heat of the Sun* (short stories) 66, *The Talking Trees* 70, *Foreign Affairs* (short stories) 75.
17 Rosmeen Park, Dun Laoghaire, Dublin, Ireland.

Ofer, Avraham; Israeli politician; b. 1922.
With Israeli Navy, Lt.-Col. 48; founder and Dir.-Gen. Moetzet Halul 60; Asst. Dir. Ministry of Agriculture 60, mem. Del. for negotiations towards joining European Common Market; Gen. Man. Ashdod Corpn. Ltd., Shikun Ovdim Ltd. 67-74; mem. Knesset (Parl.) 69-; Minister of Housing June 74-; Labour Party.
Ministry of Housing, Jerusalem, Israel.

Offelen, Jacques Van, D.ECON.; Belgian politician; b. 18 Oct. 1916, Isleworth, U.K.; s. of late Georges Van Offelen; m. Odette Cohen-Deswarte 1947; one s. one d. Professor at Inst. Supérieur de Commerce, Antwerp; mem. Chamber of Representatives 58-; Minister for External Trade 58-61; Minister for Econ. Affairs 66-68; Mayor of Uccle 64-; mem. European Parl. 65-; Parti pour la Liberté et le Progrès.
Publs. *La Lutte d'Anvers pour la Liberté du Commerce des Céréales* 45, *Chronique du Plan Marshall* 49, *Survivre* 55, *Deux Ans de Politique Economique* 56, *Pouvoir et Liberté* 62, *Chemins de la Politique* 71.
Rue Robert H. Jones 64, 1180 Brussels, Belgium.
Telephone: 3740599.

Offroy, Raymond, LL.D.; French diplomatist; b. 3 May 1909; m. Countess de Scaffa 1965; five c.
Attaché Bucharest 37, Sec. 38; Sec. Athens 40, Acting Consul-Gen. Salonika 41; Head of Admin. Services Free French Foreign Office, French Nat. Cttee.'s rep. to Inter-Allied War Crimes Comm. 41 and to Netherlands Govt. 42; Acting Counsellor of Embassy 42; Diplomatic Asst. to Gen. Catroux mission to Gen. Giraud, Algiers 43; Deputy Sec. to French Provisional Govt., Gen. Sec. to Economic Cttee. 44; Head of Information and Press Section, Ministry of Foreign Affairs 45-49; Consul-Gen. Milan 49-52; Diplomatic Adviser to High Commr. in Indo-China 51, Deputy Commr.-Gen. 53; Asst. Del. to Geneva Conf. 54; Ambassador to Thailand 54-57; French Rep. to S.E.A.T.O. 55-57; Dir. of Central Information Office, Paris 57-59; Head, Franco-African Community Dept., Ministry of Foreign Affairs, Chair. Franco-African Community, Cttee. of Foreign Affairs 59-60; Ambassador to Nigeria 60-61, to Mexico 61-65; Député de la Seine Maritime 67-68, 68-; Rep. for France to European Parl. 69-73; Pres. French Parl. Fed. of Friendship Groups with Arab Countries 73, European Parl. Asscn. for Euro-Arab Co-operation 74, French Asscn. How to know the Arab World 75; Officier Légion d'Honneur.
18 avenue Friedland, Paris 8e, France.
Telephone: Wagram 18-11.

O'Flaherty, Liam; Irish novelist; b. 1896, Aran Islands; ed. Rockwell Coll., Blackrock Coll., and Nat. Univ.
Publs. *Thy Neighbour's Wife, The Black Soul, The Informer, The Tent and other stories* 26, *Mr. Gilhooley* 26, *The Life of Tim Healy* 27, *The Assassin* 28, *The Mountain Tavern and other stories* 29, *A Tourist's Guide to Ireland* 29, *The House of Gold* 29, *Two Years* 30, *I Went to Russia* 31, *The Puritan* 32, *Skerrett* 32, *Shame the Devil* 34, *Hollywood Cemetery* 35, *Famine* 37, *Short Stories of Liam O'Flaherty* 37, *Land* 46, *Two Lovely Beasts* (short stories) 48, *Insurrection* 50, *The Short Stories of Liam O'Flaherty* 56.
c/o A. D. Peters, 10 Buckingham Street, London, W.C.2, England.

Ogawa, Heishiro, B.A.; Japanese diplomatist; b. 17 March 1916; ed. Tokyo Univ. Laws Dept.
Joined Ministry of Foreign Affairs 38; Consul, Hong Kong 52; Head China Div., Ministry of Foreign Affairs 54-57; Counsellor, Japanese Embassy, Washington, D.C. 57-60; Consul-Gen., Hong Kong 60-66; Dir.-Gen. Asian Affairs Bureau 66-68; Amb. to Denmark 68-72; Pres. Foreign Service Inst. 72-73; Amb. to People's Repub. of China Feb. 73-.
Embassy of Japan, Peking, People's Republic of China.

Ogawa, Masaru, B.A., M.A.; Japanese journalist; b. 1915, Los Angeles, U.S.A.; s. of Kenji Ogawa and Mine Fuijioka; m. Ayame Fukuhara 1942; one s. two d.; ed. Univ. of California at Los Angeles, Tokyo Imperial, Columbia Univs.
Domei News Agency 41-46; Kyodo News Service 46-48; *The Japan Times* 48-, Chief, political section 49, Asst. Managing Editor 50, Chief Editor 52, Managing Editor 58-64, Dir. 59-, Exec. Editor 64-68, Senior Editor 68-71, Chief Editorial Writer 69-71, Editor 71-; Lecturer, Tokyo Univ. 54-58; mem. Yoshida Int. Education Foundation 68-, Exec. Dir. 72-; mem. Japan Broadcasting Corpn. Overseas Program Consultative Council 74-, Japan Editors and Publishers Asscn., Int. Press Inst., Editorial Board *Media* Magazine, Hongkong 74; Dir. Int. Motion Picture Co. 70; Pres. Pacific News Agency 73-; life mem. Foreign Corresp. Club of Japan 73-.
Leisure interests: reading, sport.
2, 14-banchi, 5-chome, Mejiro, Toshima-ku, Tokyo, Japan.

Ogbu, Edwin Ogebe; Nigerian diplomatist; b. 28 Dec. 1926, Utonkon; s. of Chief Ogbu Iyana and Eje Alua; m. 1st Victoria Eve Ogaga 1948, 2nd Mildred Louis Johnson 1951; two s. nine d.; ed. Bethune-Cockman Coll., Florida, and Stanford Univ., California, U.S.A.
Assistant Sec. Ministry of Finance, Kaduna 57; Sec. Students Affairs, Nigerian High Comm., London 60; Sec. Fed. Public Service Comm. 60-62; Perm. Sec. Fed. Ministry of Works 62-63, Fed. Ministry of Finance 63-66, Fed. Ministry of External Affairs 66-68; Perm. Rep. to UN 68-75; High Commr. to Barbados, Jamaica, Trinidad and Tobago, Guyana 70-75.
c/o Permanent Mission of Nigeria to the United Nations, 757 Third Avenue, New York, N.Y. 10017, U.S.A.

Ogdon, John (Andrew Howard); British concert pianist; b. 27 Jan. 1937; ed. Manchester Grammar School and Royal Manchester Coll. of Music.
Concert appearances in London, Spoleto, Edinburgh, Moscow, Milan, Antwerp; Michaelangeli Festival, Brescia 66; Liszt Prize, London 61, Tchaikovsky Award, Moscow 62; Joint Dir. Cardiff Festival of Twentieth Century Music; Harriet Cohen Int. Award.
13 Chester Terrace, Regent's Park, London, N.W.1, England.

Ogg, Sir William Gammie, M.A., B.SC., B.SC. (Agric.), LL.D., PH.D., F.R.S.E.; British chemist; b. 2 Nov. 1891 Aberdeenshire, Scotland; s. of the late James Ogg; m.

Helen Hilbert 1922; one s. one d.; ed. Aberdeen Univ., and Christ's Coll., Cambridge.

Research Officer, Aberdeen Univ. Agricultural Dept. 14; Chemist, H.M. Explosives Factory Oldbury 14-16; Chief Chemist and Works Man. Explosives Factory Greetland 16-18; Research Fellow, Board of Agriculture for Scotland 19-20, working in U.S. and Canada; Research worker Christ's Coll., Cambridge 20-24; Advisory Officer in Soils, Edinburgh and East of Scotland Coll. of Agriculture 24-30; First Dir. Macaulay Inst. for Soil Research and Research Lecturer in Soil Science, Aberdeen Univ. 30-45; Dir. Rothamsted Experimental Station and Consultant Dir. Commonwealth Bureau of Soil Science 43-58; Foreign corresp. French Acad. of Agriculture, foreign mem. Royal Acad. of Agriculture of Sweden; Foreign mem. All-Union Acad. of Agricultural Sciences of the U.S.S.R.; Hon. Fellow Royal Agricultural Soc. of England.
Arnhall by Edzell, Angus, Scotland.
Telephone: Edzell 400.

Ogilvie, Richard Buell, B.A., JU.D.; American lawyer and politician; b. 22 Feb. 1923, Kansas City, Missouri; s. of Kenneth S. Ogilvie and Edna Mae Buell Ogilvie; m. Dorothy Shriver 1950; one d.; ed. Yale Univ. and Kent Coll. of Law, Chicago.
With law firm Lord, Bissell & Brook 49-54, 55-58, Partner 58; Asst. U.S. Attorney, Justice Dept. 54-55; Special Asst. to U.S. Attorney Gen. 58-61; Partner, Stevenson, Conaghan, Hackbert, Rooks & Pitts 61-62; Sheriff, Cook County 62-66; Pres. Cook County Board of Commrs. 66-69; Governor of Illinois 69-73; Partner, Isham, Lincoln & Beale 73-; Republican; Purple Heart.
Leisure interests: hunting, golf, reading.
1 First National Plaza, Chicago, Ill. 60670; Home: 1500 North Lake Short Drive, Chicago, Ill. 60610, U.S.A.

Ogilvy, David Mackenzie, C.B.E.; British advertising executive; b. 23 June 1911; ed. Fettes Coll., Edinburgh, and Oxford Univ.
Associate Director Audience Research Inst., Princeton 39; Second Sec. British Embassy, Washington 42; founder 48, since Pres., Ogilvy, Benson and Mather, New York; Chair. Ogilvy & Mather, London, March 65-; Dir. New York Philharmonic Symphony Society.
Publ. Confessions of an Advertising Man 64.
Château de Touffou, 86 Bonnes, France.

Ogmore, 1st Baron, CR. 50, of Bridgend; **Lieut.-Col. David Rees-Williams,** P.C., T.D.; British lawyer and politician; b. 22 Nov. 1903, Glamorgan, Wales; s. of William Rees Williams, F.R.C.V.S., and Jennet David; m. Alice Alexandra Constance Wills 1930; two s. one d.; ed. Mill Hill School, Univ. of Wales.
Qualified as solicitor with honours 29; fmrly. practised in Straits Settlements as mem. Bar; Lieut.-Colonel R.A. Staff Officer 1st Grade; M.P. for South Croydon 45-50; mem. Govt. Mission to Sarawak 46 on cession of Sarawak to H.M. the King; Chair. Burma Frontier Areas Cttee. of Enquiry 47; Parl. Under-Sec. of State, Colonial Office 47-50; Parl. Under-Sec. of State for Commonwealth Relations 50-51; mem. U.K. Del. to UN Assembly 50; Privy Counsellor 51; Minister of Civil Aviation 51; Chair. African Defence Facilities Conf., Nairobi 51; Pres. Liberal Party 63-64; Dir. Leo Laboratories Ltd. and other companies; Pres. Kidney Research Unit for Wales Foundation; Chair. Property Owners Building Soc.; Pres. Elizabeth House Asscn.; mem. Privy Councillor's Cttee. on Official Histories, Departmental Cttee. on Sect. 2 of Official Secrets Act 71-72, Investiture Cttee. for Investiture of H.R.H. The Prince of Wales 69; Order of Agga Maha Thray Sithu (Burma) 56, Panglima Mangku Negara (Malaya) 59.
48 Cheyne Court, Royal Hospital Road, Chelsea, London, S.W.3, England.
Telephone: 01-352-6131.

O'Gorman, Juan; Mexican architect and artist; b. 6 July 1905, Coyoacán, D.F.; s. of Cecil Crawford and Encarnación O'Gorman; m. Helen Fowler 1940; one d.; ed. National Univ. of Mexico.
With C. Obregón Santacilia and J. Villagran, Architects 26-29; private architectural practice 29-32; Prof. Polytechnic Inst., Mexico City 32-46; Head, Dept. of Architecture, Secr. of Public Educ. 32-35; Visiting critic School of Architecture, Yale Univ. 66; Works include: murals for Mexico City Airport, Patzcuaro (Mich.) Library; mosaics for Library of Univ. of City of Mexico, Secr. of Public Works and Communications buildings; stone mosaics, mural of Cuauhtemoc in the Hotel Posada de la Misión, in Taxco Guerrero, façade of Convention Centre Building, San Antonio, Texas; and murals in Castle of Chapultepec, Mexico City, Mexican Inst. of Social Security, Mexico City and Banco Internacional, Mexico City; paintings in Museum of Modern Art, New York City, Palace of Fine Arts and Museum of Modern Art, Mexico City; Elias Sourasky Nat. Art Award 67, Nat. Prize in Art 72.
Leisure interest: painting.
Calle Jardín 88, San Angel Inn, Mexico 20, D.F., Mexico.
Telephone: 48-39-19.

O'Green, Frederick W. M. S., M.S.; American industrialist; b. 25 March 1921; m. Mildred Ludlow; two s. two d.; ed. Iowa State Univ. and Univ. of Maryland.
Engineer, Naval Ordnance Laboratory 43-55; Dir. Lockheed's Agena-D project 55-62; Vice-Pres. Litton Industries 62-66, Senior Vice-Pres. 66-71, Exec. Vice-Pres. 71-72, Pres. 72-; mem. American Inst. of Aeronautics and Astronautics; mem. Board of Govs., Nat. Maritime Council; Outstanding Achievement Award, Air Force Systems Command 64, Distinguished Achievement Citation, Iowa State Univ. 73.
Litton Industries Inc., 9370 Santa Monica Boulevard, Beverly Hills, California 90210, U.S.A.

Ogston, Alexander George, M.A., D.PHIL., F.A.A., F.R.S.; British professor of biochemistry; b. 30 Jan. 1911, Bombay, India; s. of Walter H. Ogston and Josephine E. Carter; m. Elizabeth Wicksteed 1934; one s. three d.; ed. Eton Coll. and Balliol Coll., Oxford.
Demonstrator in Chemistry, Balliol Coll., Oxford 33-35; Research Fellow, London Hospital 35-37; Fellow and Tutor, Balliol Coll. 37-60; Reader in Biochemistry, Univ. of Oxford 57; Prof. of Physical Biochemistry, Australian National University 60-70; Pres. Trinity Coll., Oxford 70-; Fellow, Australian Acad. of Science 62, Hon. Fellow, Balliol Coll., Oxford 69.
Publs. scientific papers.
The President's Lodging, Trinity College, Oxford, OX1 3BH, England.

Ogura, Takakazu; Japanese agriculturist; b. 2 Oct. 1910, Fukui Prefecture; s. of Reizô and Hisako Ogura; m. Chieko Ogura 1937; three s. one d.; ed. Tokyo Imperial Univ.
Posts with Ministry of Agriculture and Forestry 34-56; Lecturer, Faculty of Agriculture, Univ. of Tokyo 47-61; Dir.-Gen. Food Agency 56-58; Sec.-Gen. Research Council on Agriculture, Forestry and Fisheries 58-60; Vice-Minister of Agriculture and Forestry 60-61; Chair. Research Council on Agriculture, Forestry and Fisheries 63-; Dir. Research Inst. on Mechanization of Agric. 65-; Pres. Inst. of Developing Economies 67-72, Chair. 72-.
Leisure interests: none in particular.
Publs. Agricultural Policy of Japan 65 (in Japanese), Agricultural Development in Modern Japan 66, Agrarian Problems and Agricultural Policy in Japan 67 (in English); articles in English and Japanese.
Institute of Developing Economies, 42 Ichigaya-Hommura-cho, Shinjuko-ku, Tokyo 162; Home: 29 Tokiwadai 1-chome, Itabashi-ku, Tokyo 174, Japan.
Telephone: Tokyo 960-1764 (Home).

Ohara, Eiichi; Japanese business executive; b. 2 Dec. 1912, Hiroshima; ed. Tokyo Univ.
With the Industrial Bank of Japan 36-63; Exec. Vice-Pres. Fuji Heavy Industries Ltd. 63-70, Pres. 70-; Chair. Fuji Robin Industries Ltd.; Pres. Transport Machine Industries Ltd.; mem. Japan Fed. of Econ. Orgs., Aircraft Industry Council; Dir. Japan Automobile Mfrs. Asscn.; Trustee, Japan Cttee. for Econ. Devt.
Leisure interests: Go, golf.
Fuji Heavy Industries Ltd., Subaru Buildings, 7, 1-chome, Nishishinjuku, Shinjuku-ku, Tokyo, Japan.

Ohin, Alexandre John, M.D., F.A.C.S., F.I.C.S.; Togolese surgeon and diplomatist; b. 20 March 1920, Anécho, Togo; s. of late John C. Ohin and late Mary Anyoko Ohin; m. Patience Ayivor 1962; two s. three d.; ed. Univ. of Dakar School of Medicine, Univ. of Calif., Washington Univ. School of Medicine (Homer G. Phillips Hospital) and New York Acad. of Medicine.
Intern, Resident and Chief Resident Surgeon, Homer G. Phillips Hospital, Washington Univ. School of Medicine 54-60; Research Fellow in Surgical Metabolism, Wash. Univ. School of Medicine 56-57; Staff mem., Research Fellow in Surgical Metabolism, Albert Einstein Coll. of Medicine, New York City 60-61; Surgeon, Chief Surgeon, Nat. Hospital Center of Togo 61-67; mem. Expert Advisory Board on Cancer for WHO 67-; Asst. Sec. Asscn. of Surgeons of West Africa 65-; Minister of Health and Justice, Togo 67; Vice-Pres. 23rd Gen. Assembly of UN; Amb. to U.S.A. and Canada, and Perm. Rep. to UN 67-71; regular guest at Nat. Cancer Inst., Bethesda, U.S.A.; Officier de l'Ordre National du Mono (Togo).
Leisure interests: international affairs, short-wave radio, classical music.
Publs. Several articles in American medical journals.
c/o Ministry of Foreign Affairs, Lomé, Togo.

Ohira, Masayoshi; Japanese politician; b. 12 March 1910; ed. Tokyo Commercial Coll.
Ministry of Finance 36, Supt. Yokohama Revenue Office 37-38, Private Sec. to Minister of Finance 49; mem. House of Reps. 52-; Chief Cabinet Sec. 60-62; Minister for Foreign Affairs 62-64; Chair. Policy Board, Liberal Democratic Party Nov. 67-68; Minister of Int. Trade and Industry 68-70, of Foreign Affairs 72-74, of Finance July 74-.
Publs. Essays: *Sugao no Daigishi* (A Parliamentarian As He Is) 54, *Random Thoughts on Public Finance* 56.
Ministry of Finance, 1-1, Kasumigaseki 3-chome, Chiyoda-ku, Tokyo 100; and 105 Komagome Hayashi-cho, Bunkyo-ku, Tokyo, Japan.

Ohno, Isamu; Japanese business executive; b. 17 March 1899, Tokyo; s. of Thoru and Mura Yokoi; m. Take Onoda 1930; three s. one d.; ed. Keio Univ.
Chairman Morinaga Milk Industry Co. Ltd.
Leisure interest: archaeology.
Morinaga Milk Industry Co. Ltd., 33-1, 5-chome, Shiba, Minato-ku, Tokyo 108, Japan.
Telephone: Tokyo (03) 456-0111.

Ohtaka, Masato, B.ARCH.; Japanese architect; b. 8 Sept. 1923; ed. Tokyo Univ.
At Maekawa-Kunio Architecture Design Office 49-61; established Ohtaka Architecture Design Office 62; also Lecturer Tokyo and Waseda Univs.
Works include Plan for new town at Tama, Tokyo, Chiba Public Hall and Agricultural Co-operative Asscns., and Tochici Govt. Building; Art Award, Ministry of Education 70.
4-13-5 Zenpuku-ji, Suginami-ku, Tokyo, Japan.

Ohtani, Ichiji; Japanese textile executive; b. 31 Aug. 1912, Kobe; s. of Kyosuke and Tama Ohtani; m. Junko Suzuki 1943; two s. one d.; ed. Kobe Univ.
Director Toyobo Co. Ltd. 64-68, Man. Dir. 68-72,

Senior Man. Dir. 72-74, Deputy Pres. 74, Pres. 74-; Dir. Toyoba Petcord Co. Ltd. 69-; Vice-Pres. Industries Unidas, S.A. 73-.
Leisure interests: sports, especially rugby and golf.
Toyobo Co. Ltd., 8 Dojima Hamadori 2-chome, Kita-ku, Osaka 530; Home: 69 Yamate-cho, Ashiya-shi 659, Japan.
Telephone: (06) 344-1331 (Office); (0797) 22-2057 (Home).

Ohya, Kazuo, LL.B.; Japanese business executive; b. 8 Sept. 1902, Higashi-Tonami-gun; m. Kaoru Ohya 1927 (deceased); three s. one d.; ed. Kyoto Univ.
Sumitomo Ltd. Partnership Co. 28; Man. Dir. Nissin Chemical Co. Ltd. (later Sumitomo Chemical Co. Ltd.) 47-56, Senior Man. Dir. Sumitomo Chemical Co. 56-63, Pres. 63-65, Counsellor 65-; Dir. Japan Exlan Co. Ltd. 63-, Chair. of Board 65-; Pres. Osaka Labour Standard Asscn. 63-; Perm. Dir. Japan Fed. of Employers' Asscn. 63-; Blue Ribbon Medal; 2nd Order of Merit with Order of the Sacred Treasure.
Leisure interests: Kendo (Japanese fencing), Go.
Office: Japan Exlan Co. Ltd., 25-1 Dojima Hamadori 1-chome Kita-ku, Osaka; Home: 2-27-6, Fujishirodai, Suita, Japan.
Telephone: Osaka (06)-344-1451 (Office); Senri (068) 32-7013 (Home).

Ohya, Shinzo; Japanese business executive; b. 5 July 1894, Gunma Prefecture; s. of Naka Ohya and Tsune Ohya (Hayakawa); m. Masako Morita 1950; two d.; ed. Tokyo Coll. of Commerce.
Entered Suzuki Shoten Co. Ltd. 18; joined Teijin Ltd. (fmrly. Teikoku Rayon Co. Ltd.) 25, Pres. 45-48, Chair. Board of Dirs. 51, Pres. 56-; mem House of Councillors 47-56; Minister of Commerce and Industry 48-49, of Finance 48-49, of Transportation 49-50; Pres. Teikin Petrochemical Industries Ltd., Teijin Chemicals Ltd., Teijin Hercules Chemical Co. Ltd., Teijin Agrochemicals Ltd., KK. Paris Nippon Kan, Iranian Petroleum Corpn. 71-; Dir. Teijin Shoju Kaisha Ltd., Teijin Seiki Co. Ltd., Sogo Stores Ltd., Nihon Soda Co. Ltd., Osaka Broadcasting Corpn., Osaka Petroleum Industries Ltd., Overseas Petroleum Corpn., Toyo Oil Devt. Corpn., Japan Synthetic Textiles Export Corpn., Private Investment Co. for Asia (PICA) S.A.; Auditor Nihon Lactam Co. Ltd., Yomiuri Telecasting Corpn.; Adviser Kobe Steels Ltd., Nissho-Iwai Co. Ltd., Nigeria Oil Co. Ltd., The Sanwa Bank Ltd.; Pres. Osaka German-Japan Soc. 67-; Japan-Belgium Soc. 69-, Japan-Madagascar Asscn. 70-, Japan-Turkey Soc. 71-, Japan-Hungary Econ. Club 71-, Japan-Thailand Trade Asscn. 72-, Tokyo Philharmonic Orchestra 72-, Kansai Kiin (Inst. of "Go") 75-; Vice-Pres. France-Japan Soc. 64-, Japan-Thailand Cultural Soc. 69-, Councillor Japan-Finland Soc. 60-; Counsellor Italy-Japan Soc. 63-, Japan-Singapore Asscn. 71-; mem. Japan-America Soc. 51-, Atlantic Inst. 69-, Japan-British Soc. 71-; several decorations.
Leisure interests: reading, golf, Go.
14-5, Kitabatake 3-chome, Abeno-ku, Osaka; 16-22, Todoroki 1-chome, Setagaya-ku, Tokyo, Japan.
Telephone: 701-4384.

Oistrakh, Igor Davidovich; Soviet violinist; b. 27 April 1931, Odessa; s. of late David Oistrakh; ed. Music School and State Conservatoire, Moscow.
Student State Conservatoire 49-55; many foreign tours, several concerts with father David Oistrakh; 1st prize, Violin competition, Budapest 52, Wieniawski competition, Poznań; Honoured Artist of R.S.F.S.R.
State Conservatoire, 13 Ulitsa Herzen, Moscow, U.S.S.R.

Oittinen, Reino Henrik, M.A.; Finnish politician and civil servant; b. 26 July 1912.
Principal of Workers' Acad. 45-50; Minister of Educ. 48-50, 51-53, 57-58, 63-64, 66-68; Dir.-Gen. Nat. Board of Schools 50-; Deputy Prime Minister 57-58, 64,

66-68; Chair. Finnish Nat. Comm. for UNESCO 57-65, mem. 66-68; prominent in workers' educational activities; mem. of numerous state and municipal cttees.; mem. Social Democratic Party; Hon. Dr. Pedagogics.
Kouluhallitus, Etelä Esplanadik. 16, Helsinki 13, Finland.

Oizerman, Teodor Ilyich; Soviet philosopher; b. 14 May 1914, Petroverovka; s. of Ilya Davidovich Oizerman and Elizabetha Abramovna Nemirovskaya; m. Genrietta Kasavina 1919; two s. one d.; ed. Moscow Inst. of History, Philosophy and Literature.
Industrial worker 30-33; Postgraduate 38-41; Army service 41-46; Asst. Prof., Moscow Inst. of Econs. 46-47; Asst. Prof., Prof. Moscow Univ. 52-, Head of Chair 54-68; corresp. mem. U.S.S.R. Acad. of Sciences 66-, Head Dept. of History of Philosophy, Inst. of Philosophy of Acad. of Sciences 71-.
Leisure interest: walking.
Publs. *Razvitije Marxistskoi teorii na opite revolutzii 1848 goda* 55, *Philosophie Hegels* 59, *Formirovanie filosofii Marxisma* 62, 74 (German edition 65), *Zur Geschichte der vormarxischen Philosophie* 61, *Die Entfremdung als historische Kategorie* 65, *Problemi istoriko-filosofskoi nauki* 69 (German edition 71, French edition 73, English edition 74), *Glavnie filosofskie napravlenija* 71, *Krisis sovremennogo idealisma* 73, *Filosofiya I. Kanta* 74.
Institute of Philosophy, U.S.S.R. Academy of Sciences, 14 Volchonka, Moscow, U.S.S.R.

Ojeda Paullada, Pedro; Mexican lawyer; b. 19 Jan. 1934, Mexico City; s. of Manuel Ojeda Lacroix and Adela Paullada de Ojeda; m. Olga Cárdenas de Ojeda 1959; two s. three d.; ed. Universidad Nacional Autónoma de Mexico
Head of Personnel and lawyer, Técnica y Fundación, S.A. de C.V. 55, Sub-Man. 55-57; Gen. Man. Industria Química de Plásticos S.A. 57-58; Dep. Dir.-Gen. Juntas Federales de Mejoras Materiales 59-65; Dir.-Gen. of Legal Affairs, SCT 66-70; Dir. Presidential Secr. 70-71; Attorney-Gen. Aug. 71-; Order of Merit (Italy).
Leisure interests: riding, swimming, shooting.
Montaña 600, Villa Alvaro Obregón, Mexico 20, D.F., Mexico.
Telephone: 521-37-14.

Ojukwu, General Chukwuemeka Odumegwu, M.A.; Nigerian army officer and politician; b. 4 Nov. 1933; ed. C.M.S. Grammar School and King's Coll., Lagos, Epsom Coll., U.K., Lincoln Coll., Oxford, Eaton Hall Officer Cadet School, U.K. and Joint Services Staff Coll., U.K.
Administrative Officer, Nigerian Public Service 56-57; joined Nigerian Army 57; at Nigerian Army Depot, Zaria 57; army training in U.K. 57-58; joined 5th Battalion Nigerian Army 58; Instructor, Royal West African Frontier Force Training School, Teshie 58-61; returned to 5th Battalion Nigerian Army 61; Maj. Army H.Q. 61; Deputy Asst. Adjutant and Quartermaster-Gen. Kaduna Brigade H.Q. 61; Congo Emergency Force 62; Lieut.-Col. and Quartermaster-Gen. 63-64; Commdr. 5th Battalion, Kano 64-66; Mil. Gov. of E. Nigeria 66-67; proclaimed Head of State of Republic of Biafra (E. Region of Nigeria) May 67-Jan. 70; sought political asylum in Ivory Coast Jan. 70; living in Ivory Coast.

Okada, Kenzo; Japanese artist; b. 28 Sept. 1902; ed. Tokyo Fine Arts Univ.
Works in Guggenheim Museum, Museum of Modern Art (both in New York City); in Dunn Int. Exhibition, Tate Gallery, London 63; Campana Memorial Prize, Art Inst. of Chicago 54, Logan Prize 55.
51 West 11th Street, New York City, N.Y. 10011, U.S.A.

Okai, Maj.-Gen. Lawrence Aboagye; Ghanaian army officer; b. Asafo-Akim, 1934; ed. Achimota Coll., Coll. of Technology and Royal Military Acad., Sandhurst.
Joined army as pioneer 53; Second Lieut. in Royal West African Frontier Force 55; Defence Attaché, Washington 68; Dir. of Mil. Intelligence 72-73; Commr. for Nat. Redemption Council Affairs 73-75; Chief of Defence Staff 75-; mem. Supreme Mil. Council Oct. 75-.
Ministry of Defence, Accra, Ghana.

Okasha, Sarwat, D. ÈS L.; Egyptian diplomatist, politician and banker; b. 1921, Cairo; m. Islah Abdel Fattah Lotfi 1943; one s. one d.; ed. Military Coll. and Cairo Univ.
Cavalry Officer 39; took part in Palestine war 48-49; Mil. Attaché, Berne 53-54, Paris 54-56; Counsellor in Presidency of Repub. 56-57; Egyptian Ambassador to Italy 57-58; U.A.R. Minister of Culture and Nat. Guidance 58-62; Chair. and Man. Dir. Nat. Bank 62-66; Deputy Prime Minister and Minister of Culture 66-67; Minister of Culture 67-71; Asst. to the Pres. 71-June 72; Pres. of Supreme Council for Literature, Art and Social Sciences; Pres. Egypt-France Asscn. 65-; numerous awards and foreign decorations.
Leisure interests: horse-riding, golf, music.
Publs. Nineteen works (including translations) 42-62, *L'Oeil écoute et l'Oreille voit* (in Arabic), studies of the works of Wagner and Gibran, *The Development of European Music* (in Arabic).
Villa 34, Rue 14, Méadi, Egypt.

Okauchi, Hideo; Japanese business executive; b. 19 Nov. 1908, Ayauta-gun, Kagawa-ken; s. of Nakataro and Ei Okauchi; m. Sumako Maeda 1937; two s. two d.; ed. Takamatsu Commercial High School (now Kagawa Univ.).
Joined Shiseido Co., Ltd. 29, Dir. 47, Man. Dir. 60, Senior Man. Dir. 66, Pres. 67-75, Chair. 75-; Exec. Counsellor, Tokyo Chamber of Commerce and Industry 67-; Rep. Dir. Tokyo Cosmetic Industry Asscn. 72-, Cosmetic Fair Trade Council 72-; Dir. Japan Cosmetic Industry Asscn. 72-, Japan Cosmetic Asscn. 71-, Japan Management Asscn. 67-.
Leisure interests: golf, Japanese calligraphy.
Shiseido Company Ltd., 5-5 Ginza 7-chome, Chuo-ku, Tokyo; Home: 5-16-7 Nishikoiwa, Edogawa-ku, Tokyo, Japan.
Telephone: 572-5111 (Office); 657-0958 (Home).

Okazaki, Chu; Japanese banker; b. 1 Oct. 1904, Tokyo; s. of Reijiro Kawashima; m. Kimi Okazaki 1931; one s. two d.; ed. Tokyo Univ.
Joined The Bank of Kobe Ltd. (now the Taiyo Kobe Bank Ltd.) 33, Man. Dir. 45-47, Pres. 47-67, Chair. 67-73, Dir. and Counsellor 73-; Blue Ribbon Medal 69; Order of the Rising Sun, Second Class 75.
Leisure interests: painting, fishing, golf.
1-3, Nishi-suma, Suma-ku, Kobe City, Japan.
Telephone: 078-731-1004.

Okero, Isaac Edwin Omolo; Kenyan politician; b. 1931, Ulumbi, Nyanza Province; s. of Ibrahim and Flora Arnolo Okero; m. Jane M. A. Okero 1964; four s. two d.; ed. Makerere Univ. Coll., Uganda, Univs. of Bombay and Leiden and Middle Temple, London.
State Counsel, Kenya 62-63, Deputy Public Prosecutor 63-65; Commr. Gen. of Customs and Excise, East African Community 65-69; mem. Parl. 69-; Minister of Health 69-73, of Power and Communications 73-; Vice-Chair. Customs Co-operatives Council; mem. Communications Council.
Leisure interests: flying, music.
P.O. Box 30582, Electricity House, Harambee Avenue, Nairobi, Kenya.

Okezie, Dr. Josiah Onyebuchi Johnson, L.S.M., F.M.C.G.P.; Nigerian physician and politician; b. 26 Nov. 1924, Umuahia-Ibeku; s. of Chief Johnson Okezie and

Esther Okezie; *m.* Rose Chioma Onwucheka 1966; four *s.* one *d.*; ed. Higher Coll., Yaba, Achimota Coll., Ghana, Yaba Coll. of Medicine, Univ. Coll., Ibadan and Royal Coll. of Surgeons (U.K.).

Assistant Medical Officer, Nigerian Civil Service 50-54; Founder and Medical Supt. Ibeku Central Hosp., Umuahia-Ibeku 58-69; Sr. Medical Officer in charge of Queen Elizabeth Hosp., Umuahia-Ibeku 70; Assoc. Editor, *The Nigerian Scientist* 61-62; Sec. E. Nigerian Science Asscn. 61-63; mem. Nigerian Medical Council 65-66; mem. E. Nigeria House of Assembly 61-66; Leader, Republican Party 64-66; Rep. of E. Central State, Fed. Exec. Council 70; Fed. Commr. for Health 70-71, for Agriculture and Natural Resources 71-75; Life mem. Nigerian Bible Soc. 72.

Leisure interests: English literature, reading poetry, gardening.

Publs. *The Evolution of Science* 59, *Atomic Radiation* 61. Federal Ministry of Agriculture and Natural Resources, 34/36 Ikoyi Road, Lagos, Nigeria.

Telephone: 22722.

Okita, Saburo; Japanese economist; b. 3 Nov. 1914, Dairen, Manchuria; *s.* of Shuji and Hana Okita; *m.* Hisako Kajii 1942; three *s.* one *d.*; ed. Tokyo Univ.

Joined Government service as engineer in Ministry of Posts 37; Econ. Stabilization Board, Chief Research Section 47; UN Econ. Comm. for Asia and the Far East 52; Chief, Econ. Co-op. Unit, Econ. Planning Agency 53, Dir.-Gen. Planning Bureau 57-, Dir.-Gen. Devt. Bureau 62-63; Pres. Japan Econ. Research Centre 64-73, Chair. 73-; mem. Pearson Comm. on Int. Devt. 69-70, OECD High-Level Experience Group on Science Policy in 1970s 70-71, the Group of Experts on the Structure of the UN 75, UN Cttee. on Devt. Planning 65-; Special Adviser Int. Devt. Centre of Japan 73-; Pres. Overseas Econ. Co-operation Fund 73-; Ramon Magsaysay Award for Int. Understanding 71; Dr. Econ. (Nagoya).

Leisure interest: golf.

Publs. *The Future of Japan's Economy* 60, *Japan's Post-War Economic Policy* 61, *Economic Planning* 62, *Conditions for a Developed Nation* 65, *Japanese Economy in the Asian Setting* 66, *Future Vision for Japanese Economy* 68, *Essays in Japan and World Economy* 71, *New Image of Japanese Economy* 71, *Role of the Economist* 73, *Resource-poor Japan and the World Economy* 75, *Japan and the World Economy* (English) 75, and numerous articles.

5-13-12 Koishikawa, Bunkyo-ku, Tokyo 112, Japan.

Telephone: 03-811-0742 and 03-814-3030.

Okogie, Mgr. Anthony Olubunmi, B.D., S.T.L., D.D.; Nigerian catholic clergyman; b. 16 June 1936, Lagos; ed. St. Gregory's Coll., Lagos, St. Peter and St. Paul's Seminary, Ibadan, Urban Univ., Rome.

Ordained priest 66; Act. Parish Priest, St. Patrick's Church, Idumagbo, Lagos; Asst. Priest, Holy Cross Cathedral, Lagos; Religious Instructor, King's Coll., Lagos; Dir. of Vocations, Archdiocese of Lagos; Man. Holy Cross Group of Schools, Lagos; Master of Ceremonies, Holy Cross Cathedral; Broadcaster of religious programmes, NBC/TV; Auxiliary Bishop of Oyo Diocese 71-72; Auxiliary Bishop to the Apostolic Admin., Archdiocese of Lagos 72-73; Archbishop of Lagos May 73-.

Holy Cross Cathedral, P.O. Box 8, Lagos, Nigeria.

Okudaira, Sen-ichi; Japanese banker; b. 20 Dec. 1910, Oita Pref.; ed. Kyoto Univ.

Director of Sumitomo Trust & Banking Co. Ltd. 57, Man. Dir. 60, Senior Man. Dir. 65, Deputy Pres. 69, Pres. 72-; Chair. Trust Co. Asscn. of Japan; Blue Ribbon Medal.

Sumitomo Trust & Banking Co. Ltd., 15, Kitahama 5-chome, Higashi-ku, Osaka; Home: 5-16, Chigusa 1-chome, Takarazuka City, Hyogo Pref., Japan.

Okun, Arthur M., A.B., PH.D.; American economist; b. 28 Nov. 1928, Jersey City, N.J.; *s.* of Louis and Rose Okun (née Cantor); *m.* Suzanne Grossman 1951; three *s.*; ed. Public Schools, Passaic, N.J., and Columbia Univ.

Instructor, Yale Univ. 52-56, Asst. Prof. 56-60, Assoc. Prof. 60-62, Prof. and Dir. of Graduate Studies in Econs., Yale Univ. 63-64; Editor *Yale Economic Essays* 63-64; Staff mem. Cowles Foundation for Research in Econs., Yale Univ. 56-64; Staff Economist, Council of Econ. Advisers 61-62, mem. Council of Econ. Advisers 64-68, Chair. 68-69; Consultant Donaldson, Lufkin and Jenrette, N.Y. 69-, Amer. Security and Trust Co., Wash. 70-; Fellow American Acad. of Arts and Sciences, Econometric Soc., American Statistical Asscn.; Senior Fellow Brookings Inst. 69-; Vice-Pres. American Econ. Asscn. 72; mem. Board of Trustees, Joint Cttee. on Econ. Educ. 71- and several other councils and committees.

Publs. Editor *The Battle Against Unemployment, An Introduction to a Current Issue of Public Policy; The Political Economy of Prosperity* 70; Co-editor *Brookings Papers on Economic Activity* 70; Co-author *Inflation: The Problems It Creates and the Policies It Requires* 70; Author: *Equality and Efficiency: The Big Tradeoff* 75; articles on economic forecasting, inflation, monetary and fiscal policy, potential GNP.

Brookings Institution, 1775 Massachusetts Avenue North-West, Washington, D.C. 20036; Home: 2809 Ellicott Street North-West, Washington, D.C. 20008, U.S.A.

Telephone: 202-797-6295 (Office); 202-363-7845 (Home).

Okuniewski, Józef, D.ECON.; Polish politician; b. 5 May 1920, Lubotyń, Poznań Voivodship; *s.* of Józef and Małgorzata Okuniewski; *m.* Krystyna Okuniewski 1942; one *s.*; ed. Łódź Univ.

Agricultural instructor, Wieluń district; worked in timber firm, Warsaw during Occupation; later became headmaster of agricultural school at Tymianka and subsequently lecturer, Agricultural Teachers' Inst., Pszczelin; mem. Polish United Workers' Party 50-, Deputy mem. Cen. Cttee. 71-; Dir. of Univ. Studies, Ministry of Higher Learning 53-54; subsequently Deputy Prof. Warsaw Univ., then Asst. Prof. and Chair. Faculty of Political Econs. 61; Under-Sec. of State Ministry of Agriculture 59-70; Minister of Agriculture 70-74; Amb. to Netherlands 74-; Order of Banner of Labour First Class 69.

Leisure interests: photography, tennis.

Embassy of Poland, Alexanderstraat 25, The Hague, Netherlands.

Okunnu, Lateef Olufemi, LL.B.; Nigerian barrister and politician; b. 19 Feb. 1933, Lagos; *s.* of M. A. and Abebi Okunnu; *m.* Lateefat Okunnu; one *d.*; ed. King's Coll., Lagos and Univ. Coll., London.

Civil Servant 53; Technical Asst. and teacher, King's Coll., Lagos 53-56; Publicity Sec., Cttee. of African Orgs., London 58-60; Editor, *Nigerian Bar Journal* 64-68; mem. Exec. Cttee. Nigerian Bar Asscn. 64-68; Fed. Commr. for Works and Housing 67-75; Commdr. Nat. Orders of Dahomey and Niger.

Leisure interests: reading, squash.

Publs. articles in *Nigerian Bar Journal*.

97 Wakeman Street, Yaba, Nigeria.

Telephone: 46280.

Okuno, Seisuke; Japanese politician; b. 12 July 1913; ed. First High School, Univ. of Tokyo.

Chief, Gen. Affairs Section, Yamanashi Pref. Govt. and Kagoshima Pref. Govt. 38; Officer Dept. of Local Govt., Ministry of Home Affairs 43; Head of Police Dept., Kochi Pref. Govt. 47; Head, Finance and Research Divs., Local Autonomy Agency 49; Dir. Bureau of Taxation, Ministry of Autonomy 53, Bureau

of Finance 58; Perm. Vice-Minister, Ministry of Autonomy 63; mem. House of Reps. 63-; Minister of Educ. 72-Dec. 74; Liberal Democratic Party.
Publs. Several articles on aspects of local government. 5-7-10 Jingumae, Shibuya-ku, Tokyo, Japan.

Ólafsson, Ragnar; Icelandic judge and accountant; b. 2 May 1906, Holtum; s. of Ólafur Ólafsson and Margrét Thordardóttir; m. Kristín Sigrídur Hinriksdóttir 1940; two s. two d.; ed. Univ. of Iceland.
Member legal staff Fed. Iceland Co-operative Socs. 31-42, mem. Board of Dirs. 73-; Advocate District and Supreme Courts, Iceland 44-; Chair. Board of Dirs. Central Bank of Iceland 73-; Govt.-apptd. mem. Power Intensive Industry Iceland 73-; Judge Labour Court 73-.
28 Hörgshlíd, Reykjavík, Iceland.
Telephone: 15715-22293 (Office).

Olang', Most Rev. Festo Habakkuk; Kenyan ecclesiastic; b. 14 Nov. 1914, Maseno; m. Eseri Olang' 1937; four s. eight d.; ed. Alliance High School, St. Pauls Theological Coll., Wycliffe Hall, Oxford.
Teacher Maseno Secondary School 36-39; on staff Butere Girls' School 40-45; ordained Deacon 45; consecrated Bishop 55; Bishop of Maseno 61-70; Archbishop of Kenya (Anglican Church) 70-.
Imani House, St. John's Gate, P.O. Box 40502, Nairobi; Home: 26 State House Avenue, P.O. Box 40502, Nairobi, Kenya.
Telephone: Nairobi 28146 (Office); Nairobi 20207 (Home).

Olav V; King of Norway; b. 2 July 1903; ed. secondary school, Oslo, Norwegian Military Acad., and Balliol Coll., Oxford.
Studied political history and political science; married Princess Märtha of Sweden 1929 (died 54); Commdr.-in-Chief, Norwegian Forces, Second World War; succeeded his father, King Haakon VII, Sept. 21, 1957.
Royal Palace, Oslo, Norway.
Telephone: 44-19-20.

Olavarria de Tezanes-Pinto, Jorge; Venezuelan diplomatist; b. 12 Dec. 1933, Caracas; s. of Jorge Olavarria y Braun and Leonor Tezanes-Pinto de Olavarria (deceased); m. Dr. Mercedes Enriqueta López-Núñez de Olavarria; one s. five d.; ed. Univ. of Madrid, Bruges and Luxembourg.
General Commdr. of Venezuela (ranking as Amb.) Brussels Universal Int. Exhbn. 58; Deputy for Caracas, Nat. Congress 63-69; Amb. to U.K. 69-70; Federal Sec. Liberal Party of Venezuela; Amb. Special Envoy to Bolivia; re-elected Deputy for Caracas 69-; Orden Francisco de Miranda, Primera Clase.
Leisure interests: riding, shooting, golf, polo.
Publs. Siete Cuentos 64, El Caso Sidor 68, Voces de Angustia sobre Nuestro Petróleo 69.
Ministerio de Asuntos Exteriores, Caracas; and La Guayabita del Peru, Calle Laom Larga, Los Guayabitos, Caracas, Venezuela.

Olcay, Osman; Turkish diplomatist; b. 17 Jan. 1924, Istanbul; s. of Seyfi Olcay; m. Necla Baran 1946; ed. St. Joseph French Coll., Istanbul, and Faculty of Political Science, Univ. of Ankara.
Joined Ministry of Foreign Affairs, Turkey 45; Lieut., Turkish Army 46; Foreign Ministry 47; Vice-Consul, London 48-50, Second Sec., London 50-52; Chief of Section, Dept. of Econ. Affairs, Ministry of Foreign Affairs 52-54; First Sec. NATO, Paris 54, Counsellor and Deputy Perm. Rep. 58-59; Asst. Dir.-Gen. NATO Dept., Minister of Foreign Affairs, Ankara 59-60, Dir.-Gen. 60-63, Deputy Sec.-Gen. 63-64; Amb. to Finland 64-66, to India and Ceylon 66-68; Deputy Sec.-Gen. of NATO, Brussels 69-71; Minister of Foreign Affairs March-Dec. 71; Perm. Rep. to UN 72-75.
c/o Ministry of Foreign Affairs, Ankara, Turkey.

Oldenbourg, Zoé; French (born Russian) writer; b. 31 March 1916; ed. Lycée Molière and Sorbonne, Paris. In France 25-; studied theology, Great Britain 38; mem. Jury of Prix Fémina 61-; Prix Fémina for La Pierre Angulaire (The Cornerstone) 53.
Publs. Argile et Cendres 46, La Pierre angulaire 53, Bûcher de Montségur 59, Les Brûlées 61, Les Cités charnelles 61, Essai historique sur les Croisades 63, Catherine de Russie 65, Saint Bernard 69, La Joie des Pauvres 70.
35 rue Poussin, Paris 16e, France.

Oldenburg, Claes; American (naturalized) pop artist; b. 28 Jan. 1929, Stockholm, Sweden; s. of Gösta Oldenburg and Sigrid E. Lindfors; m. Pat Muschinski 1960; ed. Yale Coll. and Art Inst. of Chicago.
Apprentice reporter, City News Bureau, Chicago 50-52; various odd jobs 52-53; first group exhbn., Club St. Elmo, Chicago 53; participated in other local shows, Chicago and Evanston 53-56; moved to New York 56; part-time job at Cooper Union Museum Library 56-61; exhibited in group show, Red Grooms's City Gallery 58-59; first public one-man show, Judson Gallery, N.Y. 59; two-man show with Jim Dine (q.v.), Judson Gallery Nov.-Dec. 59; has since participated in numerous exhbns. of contemporary art throughout U.S.A. and Europe; several one-man shows at Sidney Janis Gallery, N.Y.; works included in XXXII Biennale, Venice 64, IX Bienal do Museu de Arte Moderno, São Paulo 67; installed Giant Soft Fan in Buckminster Fuller's (q.v.) dome for U.S. Pavilion, Expo 67, Montreal 67; travelling one-man exhbn. sponsored by Museum of Modern Art, N.Y. shown at Tate Gallery, London and other European galleries 70.
Publs. Claes Oldenburg, Proposals for Monuments and Buildings 1965-69 69, Claes Oldenburg, Drawings and Prints 69, Notes in Hand 71.
c/o Sidney Janis Gallery, 15 East 57th Street, New York, N.Y. 10022; and 404 East 14th Street, New York, N.Y. 10009, U.S.A.

Oldenburg, Richard Erik, A.B.; American museum director; b. 21 Sept. 1933, Stockholm, Sweden; s. of Gösta Oldenburg and Sigrid E. Lindfors; brother of Claes Oldenburg q.v.; m. Harriet L. Turnure 1960; no c.; ed. Harvard Coll.
Managing Editor, The Macmillan Co. 64-69; Dir. of Publications, Museum of Modern Art, New York 69-71; Acting Dir. Museum of Modern Art Jan.-June 72, Dir. June 72-.
Leisure interest: reading.
The Museum of Modern Art, 11 West 23rd Street, New York, N.Y. 10019; Home: 447 East 57 Street, New York, N.Y. 10022, U.S.A.
Telephone: 212-956-7502 (Office).

O'Leary, Michael; Irish politician; b. 8 May 1938, Cork; s. of John O'Leary and Margaret McCarthy; ed. Univ. Coll., Cork.
Deputy Pres. Nat. Students' Union 60-61; Education Officer, Irish TUC 62-65; M.P. for Dublin North Central 65-; spokesman on Industry and Commerce, Labour, Foreign Affairs and Education 65-73; Minister for Labour 73-; Pres. 2nd European Regional Conf., ILO 74, EEC Council of Ministers for Social Affairs Jan.-June 75.
Department of Labour, 50-60 Mespil Road, Dublin 4, Ireland.
Telephone: 65861 ext. 161.

Olechowski, Tadeusz, M.A.; Polish diplomatist and politician; b. 10 Jan. 1926, Vilnius; ed. Faculty of Law, Jagiellonian Univ., Cracow and Acad. of Trade, Cracow.
Chief of Polish Trade Mission, Rangoon 55; Commercial attaché, Polish Embassy, Burma 56; Deputy Dir. Metalexport; with Ministry of Foreign Trade 58; Commercial Attaché, Rome 61-64; Vice-Minister of Foreign Trade 65-69; Amb. to France 69-72; Minister

of Foreign Trade 72-74; Amb. to Egypt Sept. 74-; mem. PZPR (Polish United Workers' Party).
Embassy of Poland, Cairo, Egypt.

Olesen, Kjeld; Danish politician; b. 8 July 1932; *m.*; two *s.*
Employed by J. Lauritzen Shipping Line 50-55; Chair. Cen. Section, Social Democratic Youth 54-56; Sec. Union of Urban Co-operative Socs. 57-58; Sec. to Social Democratic Party in Greater Copenhagen 58-62; Organizational Sec. to Social Democratic Party 62; mem. Secr. Danish Social Democratic Youth 62-67; mem. Exec. Cttee. Workers Educ. Asscn. 62-67, Social Democratic Party in Greater Copenhagen and Social Democratic Party 62-66; mem. Danish Railways Board 63-66; mem. Folketing 66-; Minister of Defence 71-73; Deputy Chair. Social Democratic Party 73-.
Socialdemokratiet, Nyropsgade 26, 1602 Copenhagen VV; and Vamdrupvej 74, 2610 Rødovre, Denmark.
Telephone: 70-94-64.

Olewinski, Marian, M.S. (ENG.); Polish engineer and politician; b. 15 Sept. 1912, Warsaw; ed. Warsaw Technical Univ.
Building trade until 39; posts in Polish Workers' Party and Polish United Workers' Party 45-51; Ministry of Transport 51-56; Vice-Minister of Transport 57-60, 71-; Minister of Building and Building Materials Industry 60-69; Vice-Pres. Council of Ministers 69-June 70; Dep.-mem. Central Cttee. 61-Dec. 71; Order of the Banner of Labour (1st Class) 64.
Publs. numerous articles in technical papers.

Ølgaard, Anders, DR.POLIT.; Danish professor of economics; b. 5 Sept. 1926, Aabenraa; *m.* Alice Christiansen 1951; three *c.*; ed. Univ. of Copenhagen.
Civil servant, Econ. Secr. 53-60; Prof. of Econs., Univ. of Copenhagen 66-; Adviser in Malaysia, Harvard Univ. Devt. Advisory Service 68-69; mem., Econ. Council 66-68, Chair. 70-.
Publ. *Growth, Productivity and Relative Prices* 66.
Institute of Economics, University of Copenhagen, 6 Studiestraede, 1455 Copenhagen; Home: 12 Lerbaekvei, 2830 Virum, Denmark.
Telephone: 02-152166 (Office); 02-851239 (Home).

Olin, John Merrill, B.S.; American businessman; b. 10 Nov. 1892; ed. Cornell Univ.
Chemical engineer, Equitable Powder Manufacturing Co. 13; chemical engineer, Western Cartridge Co. 13, Asst. to Pres. 14-18, First Vice-Pres. and Dir. 18-44, and Pres. and Dir. Olin Industries Inc. (consolidation of Western Cartridge Co., Winchester Repeating Arms Co., Olin Corpn.. etc.) 44-54; Chair. of Board, Olin Mathieson Chemical Corpn. (merger of Olin Industries Inc. and Mathieson Chemical Corpn.) 54-57, Chair. Financial and Operating Policy and Exec. Cttees. 57-62; Chair. Exec. Cttee. and Dir. Olin Mathieson Chemical Corpn. 62-63; Hon. Chair. and Dir. Olin Mathieson Chemical Corpn. 63-69; Hon. Chair. of the Board and Dir. Olin Corpn. 69-; Pres. and Dir. Illinois State Bank, East Alton; Dir. St. Louis Union Trust Co., First Nat. Bank and Trust Co., Alton; Trustee Wash. Univ. Corpn., St. Louis, Cornell Univ., American Museum of Natural History, Johns Hopkins Univ., Midwest Research Inst.; Dir. World Wildlife Fund.
Olin Corporation, 7701 Forsyth Boulevard, St. Louis, Mo. 63105; Home: Box B, Alton, Ill. 62002, U.S.A.

Oliphant, Sir Mark Laurence Elwin, K.B.E., F.R.S., F.A.A., B.SC., M.A., PH.D.; British physicist and administrator; b. 8 Oct. 1901,; Australia s. of Harold George Oliphant and Beatrice Fanny Tucker; *m.* Rosa Louise Wildbraham 1924; one *d.*; ed. Adelaide Univ., and Trinity Coll., Cambridge.
Messel Research Fellow, Royal Society 31; Lecturer and Fellow, St. John's Coll. 34; Asst. Dir. Research, Cavendish Lab., Cambridge 35; Prof. and Dir. of Dept. of Physics Birmingham Univ. 37-50, Vice-Principal Sept. 48-49; Dir. of post-graduate Research School of Physical Sciences, Australian Nat. Univ. 50-63; Prof. of Particle Physics 50-64; Pres. Australian Acad. of Sciences 54-57; Gov. of S. Australia 71-; Hon. Fellow, St. John's Coll., Cambridge 52, Australian Nat. Univ. 68-71; several honorary degrees.
Leisure interests: music, gardening, carpentry.
Government House, Adelaide, South Australia 5000, Australia.
Telephone: Adelaide 223-6166.

Olitski, Jules, M.A.; American (b. Russian) painter and sculptor; b. 27 March 1922, Snovsk, Russia; *s.* of late Jevel Demikovsky and of Anna Zarnitsky; *m.* 1st Gladys Katz 1944 (divorced 1951), one *d.*; *m.* 2nd Andrea Hill Pearce 1956 (divorced 1974), one *d.*; ed. Beaux Arts Inst., N.Y., New York Univ.
Associate Prof. of Art, State Univ. Coll., New Paltz 54-55; Curator New York Univ. Art Educ. Gallery 55-56; Art Instructor, Co-ordinator Fine Arts Dept., C. W. Post Coll., Long Island Univ. 56-63; Art Teacher, Bennington Coll., Vt. 63-67; one-man exhbns. of paintings, drawings and sculpture in U.S.A. at Corcoran Gallery, Wash., D.C. 67, 74, Metropolitan Museum of Art, N.Y. 69, retrospective exhbn. at Museum of Fine Arts, Boston 73; exhbns. at Galerie Huit, Paris 50, Kasmin Gallery, London 64-74, David Mirvish Gallery, Toronto 64-74, André Emmerich Gallery, N.Y. 66-67, Zurich 73-74; numerous group exhbns. in U.S.A., Canada, France, Fed. Repub. of Germany; chosen for Carnegie Int. 61, 67, for Venice Biennale 66; Second Prize Carnegie Int. 61, First Prize Corcoran Biennal 67.
827 Broadway, New York, N.Y. 10003, U.S.A.
Telephone: (212) 254-3699.

Olivecrona, Herbert, M.D.; Swedish surgeon; b. 11 July 1891; ed. Uppsala and Stockholm Univs.
Asst., Surgical Clinics of Leipzig, Baltimore and Stockholm 18-25; Asst. Surgeon-in-Chief, Serafimerlasarettet, Stockholm 25-35, Dir. 35-60; Associate Prof. of Surgery 24-35; Prof. of Neurological Surgery, Royal Caroline Inst. 35-60; set up clinic in Egypt at request of U.A.R. Govt. 61; Hon. M.D. (Athens and Cologne), D.S. (Gustavus Adolphus Coll., St. Peter, Minn.).
Publs. *Die chirurgische Behandlung der Gehirntumoren* 27, *On changes of the optic canals in cases of intracranial tumours* 32, *On suprasellar cholesteatomas* 32, *Die parasagittalen Meningeome* 34, *Gefässgeschwülste und Gefässmissbildungen des Gehirns* 36, *Chirurgie der Hirntumoren* 40, *Tractotomy* 42, *Parasagittal meningiomas* 47, *Surgical treatment of angina pectoris* 47, *Arteriovenous aneurysm of the brain* 48, *Hypophysectomy in cancer of the breast* 53, *Surgical treatment of intracranial tumours*, Vol. 4, *Handbuch der Neurochirurgie*.
Karolinska Sjukhuset, Stockholm 60; and Strandvägen 49, Stockholm Ö, Sweden.
Telephone: 340500/2049 (Office); 671545 (Home).

Oliveira, Gen. Araken de; Brazilian army officer; ed. Mil. School, Realengo, Command and Gen. Staff School and Catholic Univ.
Instructor, Mil. School Realengo and Command and Gen. Staff School; Gunnery Officer, then Operations Officer, First Howitzer Battalion, Brazilian Expeditionary Force; with Command and Gen. Staff, Officer in War Minister's Office; promoted to rank of Gen.; Chief, President's Office, Nat. Oil Council, later Pres.; Pres. Petrobrás Oct. 74-; Commdr. Order of Merit and several other mil. honours.
Petrobrás, Avenida Chile, Rio de Janeiro, Brazil.

Oliveira, Capt. Euclides Quandt de; Brazilian naval officer; b. 1919, Rio de Janeiro.
Joined Navy 41; naval assignments related to electronics and telecommunications; Chair. Nat. Telecom-

munications Council 65; Dir. Siemens do Brasil S.A.; Head TELEBRAS 72; Minister of Communications March 74-.
Ministério da Comunicação, Brasília, Brazil.

Oliver, Covey T., M.A., LL.M., JURIS SCI.DR.; American lawyer, diplomatist and international bank official; b. 21 April 1913, Laredo, Texas; s. of Pheneas Roan Oliver and Jane Covey Thomas; m. Barbara Frances Hauer 1946; two s. three d.; ed. Univ. of Texas and Columbia Univ.
Professor of Law, Univs. of Texas, Calif. (Berkeley) and Pennsylvania 36-41, 49-64, 66-67, 69-; U.S. Govt. official (mainly in Dept. of State) 42-49; Amb. to Colombia 64-66; Asst. Sec. of State for Inter-American Affairs and U.S. Coordinator of Alliance for Progress 67-69; U.S. Exec. Dir., Int. Bank for Reconstruction and Devt. 69; Carnegie Endowment Lecturer, Hague Acad. of Int. Law; Hubbell Prof. of Law, Univ. of Pa.; mem. Board of Editors *American Journal of Int. Law.*
Leisure interests: boating, observance of nature, psycho-diplomacy, cultural anthropology.
Publs. *The Restatement of the Foreign Relations Law of the United States* (co-author), *The Inter-American Security System and the Cuban Crisis, Law and Politics in the World Community* (co-author), *Cases and Materials on the International Legal System* (co-author); and monographs and articles in legal and foreign affairs periodicals.
The Law School, University of Pennsylvania, Philadelphia, Pennsylvania 19104; 4210 Spruce Street, Philadelphia, Pennsylvania 19104, U.S.A.
Telephone: 215-243-7925 (Office); 215-386-9116 (Home).

Oliver, Roland, M.A., PH.D.; British Africanist; b. 30 March 1923; ed. Cambridge Univ.
Lecturer, School of Oriental and African Studies, Univ. of London 48-49, 50-57, Reader 58-63, Prof. of African History 63-; organized first confs. on history and archaeology of Africa, London Univ. 53, 57, 61; founded and edited *Journal of African History* 60-73.
Publs. *The Missionary Factor in East Africa* 52, *Sir Harry Johnston and the Scramble for East Africa* 57, *The Dawn of African History* 61, *Short History of Africa* (with J. D. Fage) 62, *History of East Africa* (with G. Mathew) 63, *Africa since 1800* (with A. Atmore) 67, *Africa in the Iron Age* (with B. M. Fagan) 75, general editor *Cambridge History of Africa* 8 vols.-.
c/o School of Oriental and African Studies, University of London, London, W.C.1; Frilsham Woodhouse, Hermitage, Berkshire, England.
Telephone: Yattendon 407.

Olivetti, Arrigo, D.IUR.; Italian business executive; b. 1889, Biella; m. Elena Olivetti 1923; one s. one d.; ed. Univ. of Turin.
Former Sales Manager, Sec.-Gen., Vice-Chair. and Managing Dir. Ing. C. Olivetti & Co., S.p.A., Hon. Chair. 63-; Dir. Fergat S.p.A. (Mechanical), Soc. Autostrada Torino Ivrea Valle d'Aosta (A.T.I.V.A.), Inst. of European Studies, Turin; Pres. Piero Martinetti Foundation for Studies in Philosophy, Religion and History; mem. Central Cttee. Centre Int. Formation Européenne (CIFE), Paris; War Cross, Cavaliere del Lavoro, Gold Medal of Merit, School of Art and Culture.
Leisure interests: history and arts in general.
Via Montenavale 24, 10015 Ivrea, Italy.
Telephone: Ivrea 22-20 and 24-80.

Olivi, Beniamino, D.IUR.; Italian civil servant; b. 19 April 1925, Treviso; ed. Univ. of Padua, Univ. Inst. of Ca Foscari, Venice.
Legal Asst. to Confindustria 48-50; Judge of First Instance, Milan Tribunal 50-58; Officer, Directorate-General of Competition, Comm. of EEC 58-60; Chef de Cabinet to Vice-Pres. Comm. of EEC 60-61; Spokesman

Comm. of EEC 61-67, Comm. of European Communities 68-; Adriano Olivetti Prize 64.
Spokesman's Group, Commission of the European Communities, 200 rue de la Loi, 1040 Brussels, Belgium. Telephone: 35-00-40/35-80-40.

Olivier, Baron (Life Peer), cr. 70, of Brighton; **Laurence Kerr Olivier,** Kt.; British actor manager; b. 22 May 1907; s. of the late Rev. G. K. Olivier and Agnes Louise Crookenden; m. 1st Jill Esmond 1930 (divorced 1940), one s.; m. 2nd Vivien Leigh 1940 (divorced 1961); m. 3rd Joan Plowright (q.v.) 1961, one s. two d.; ed. St. Edward's School, Oxford.
First appearance, Shakespearian play, Stratford 22; Birmingham Repertory Company 25-28; subsequent appearances in London, New York, Paris and Denmark; Old Vic Theatre Company 44-45, 49, toured Australia and New Zealand 48; Actor-Manager, St. James's Theatre, London 50-51; Shakespeare Memorial Theatre, Stratford-on-Avon 55; Dir. Chichester Festival Theatre 62-65, The National Theatre 62-73; Hon. D.Litt. (Oxon.), Hon. LL.D. (Edin.), Hon. M.A. (Tuft's); Chevalier, Légion d'Honneur; Commdr. Order of Dannebrog (Denmark) and Grand Officer, Ordine al Merito della Repubblica (Italy); Acad. Award 48; Sonning Prize (Denmark) 66; Gold Medallion, Swedish Acad. of Literature 68; Order of Yugoslav Flag with Gold Wreath 71.
Stage appearances include many Shakespearian and classical plays, *The Entertainer*, *Rhinoceros*, *Becket*, etc.; produced and appeared in *Venus Observed*, *Caesar and Cleopatra*, *The Broken Heart*, *Uncle Vanya*, etc.; National Theatre appearances include *Uncle Vanya*, *Othello*, *Master Builder*, *Love for Love*, *The Dance of Death*, *A Flea in Her Ear*, *The Merchant of Venice*, *Long Day's Journey into Night*, *Saturday Sunday Monday*, *The Party*; Dir. *Eden's End* 74.
Films include *Wuthering Heights*, *Rebecca*, *Pride and Prejudice*, *49th Parallel*, *Carrie*, *Beggar's Opera*, *The Devil's Disciple*, *Spartacus*, *The Entertainer*, *Term of Trial*, *Khartoum*, *Othello*, *The Shoes of the Fisherman*, *The Dance of Death* 68, *Battle of Britain*, *Oh What a Lovely War*, *Three Sisters* 69, *David Copperfield*, *Nicholas and Alexandra*, *Lady Caroline Lamb*, *Sleuth;* produced, directed and played in *Henry V*, *Hamlet*, *Richard III* and *The Prince and the Showgirl*.
Television appearances include *John Gabriel Borkman*, *The Moon and Sixpence*, *The Power and The Glory*, *Long Day's Journey into Night*, *The Merchant of Venice*, *World at War* (narrator) 73, *Love among the Ruins* 74.
c/o L.O.P. Ltd., 33/34 Chancery Lane, London, WC2A 1EN, England.
Telephone: 01-836-7932.

Olivier, Louis, DR. EN DROIT; Belgian politician; b. 19 July 1923, Bastogne.
Local Councillor 58-; Mayor of Bastone 65-; Provincial Councillor 54-; Vice-Pres. Provincial Council of Luxembourg 56; Vice-Pres. Soc. de Développement Economique du Luxembourg, Conseil Economique du Luxembourg, Asscn. Intercommunale du Luxembourg pour la Valorisation de L'Eau; mem. House of Reps. for Arlon-Marche-Bastogne 65-, Intercommunale de Developpement Economique du Luxembourg; Sec. of State for Inst. Reforms and Admin. (Wallonia) Jan. 73-April 74; Minister of the Middle Classes Oct. 73-; Sec. of State for Forestry, Hunting and Fishing (Wallonia) 74-.
Ministère des Classes Moyennes, Brussels, Belgium.

Olivier-Lecamp, Max Jules Alexis Marcel; French journalist; b. 2 March 1914, Le Havre; s. of Maurice Olivier and Germaine Bredaz; m. 1st Anne Vergara 1939 (dissolved), 2nd Pyongyoo Hyun 1954; five d.; ed. Ecole Alsacienne, Paris, Univ. of Paris and Ecole Libre des Sciences Politiques, Paris.

Reporter with Havas agency 37-44; Editor, Agence France Presse (AFP) 44-45; Dir. AFP India and Afghanistan 45-50; war correspondent in Korea and Indochina 50-54; journalist with *Le Figaro* 54-; Chevalier Légion d'Honneur; Croix de Guerre, Military Cross; Prix Pierre Mille 56; Prix Albert-Londres 58; Prix Renaudot for *Les Feux de la Colère* (novel) 69.
Leisure interests: palaeography, philology.
Le Figaro, 14 Rond Point des Champs-Elysées, Paris 8e; Home: 54 Route des Gardes, 92 Bellevue-Meudon, France.
Telephone: ALMA 8000 (Office); OBS 5235 (Home).

Ollenu, Nii Amaa, G.M.; Ghanaian judge; b. 21 May 1906, Labadi, Accra; *s.* of Wilfried Kuma and Salome Anekai (née Abbey) Ollenu; *m.* Alberta Akoley Addo 1968; ed. Accra High School and Middle Temple, London.
Teacher, Accra High School 30-37; called to the Bar 40; private practice, Ghana 40-56; Judge, High Court of Ghana 56-62; Part-time Lecturer, Faculty of Law, Univ. of Ghana 62-69, Hon. Prof. of Law 62-67, 67-72; Speaker, Nat. Assembly 67-72; Chief Justice Oct. 70-72; Pres. Council, Ghana Acad. of Arts and Sciences 68-72; Coronation Medal.
Leisure interest: gardening.
Publs. *The Law of Succession in Ghana* 60, *Principles of Customary Land Law in Ghana* 62, *The Law of Testate and Intestate Succession in Ghana* 66.
Parliament House, Accra; Labadi, Accra; Home: No. 3, 5th Circular Road, Cantonments, Accra, Ghana.
Telephone: 64181 Ext. 19; 65559; 77288 (Home).

Olloqui, José Juan de; Mexican diplomatist; b. 5 Nov. 1931, Mexico City; *s.* of Fernando de Olloqui and Margarita Labastida de Olloqui; *m.* Guillermina G. de Olloqui 1962; three *s.* one *d.*
Former Prof. of Econs. at various Mexican Univs.; served in Banco de México; former Head, Dept. of Banks, Currency and Investment, Secr. of Finance and Public Credit; fmr. Dir.-Gen. of Credit; fmr. mem. Board of Dirs. of several Mexican credit insts. and technical orgs.; Exec. Dir. for Mexico, Barbados, Dominican Repub., Jamaica and Panama, Inter-American Devt. Bank 66-71; Dir. Nat. Stock Comm. 71; Amb. to U.S.A. 71-, and to Barbados 73-.
Leisure interests: hunting, weight-lifting.
Mexican Embassy, 2829 16th Street, N.W., Washington, D.C. 20009, U.S.A.
Telephone: 234-6000.

Oloitipitip, Stanley Shapashina Ole; Kenyan politician; b. 1927, Loitokitok, Kajiado District; ed. Loitokitok and Narok Govt. Schools.
Staff Sergeant, E. African Medical Corps. 42-46; Moran Leader, Masailand 47-51; Chair. Kajiado Branch, Kenya African Democratic Union (KADU) 55-60, Nat. Org. Sec. KADU 61-63; mem. Parl. for Kajiado 63-69, Kajiado South 70-; Asst. Minister for Commerce and Industry 64-69, of Health 70-74; Minister of Natural Resources Nov. 74-; Chair. Kenya African Nat. Union 65-; Elder of the Burning Spear Mil. Medal.
Ministry of Natural Resources, P.O. Box 30126, Nairobi; Home: Olgulului, P.O. Namanga, Kenya.

Olpin, A. Ray, A.B., PH.D.; American physicist; b. 1 June 1898, Pleasant Grove, Utah; *s.* of Albert Henry Olpin and Alvira Smith; *m.* Elva Chipman 1922; one *s.* three *d.*; ed. Brigham Young Univ., Provo, Utah, and Columbia Univ.
Instructor, Mathematics and Physics, Brigham Young Univ. 22-24; Asst. in Physics Columbia Univ. 24-25; mem. Technical Staff, Bell Telephone Laboratories N.Y. City 25-33; Lecturer Brooklyn Polytechnic Inst. 31-33; Dir. of Research, Kendall Mills, Charlotte, N.C.

33-39; Prof. and Dir. of Industrial Research, Field Dir. Engineering Experiment Station, and Exec. Dir. Research Foundation, Ohio State Univ. 39-46; Consultant Anthony Wayne Research Foundation 44-45; Pres. Univ. of Utah 46-64, and of Carbon Coll., Price, Utah 59-64; Pres. Emer. Univ. of Utah 64; Consultant on Devt. Planning, Seoul Nat. Univ., Korea 65-66; Assoc. Editor *Journal of Applied Physics* 37-38; Man. Editor *Science and Appliance* 39-45; Hon. D.Iur. Univ. of Utah.
102 Business Office Building, University of Utah, Salt Lake City, Utah 84112; 2431 Beacon Drive, Salt Lake City, Utah 84108, U.S.A.
Telephone: 581-7740 (Office); 582-9441 (Home).

Olsen, Poul Rovsing; Danish composer; b. 4 Nov. 1922, Copenhagen; *s.* of Alfred Rovsing and Helga Petersen; *m.* Solange Petit-Dutallis 1950; one *s.* two *d.*; ed. Aarhus and Copenhagen Univs.
Music critic on *Morgenbladet* 45-46, *Information* 49-52, *Berlingske Tidende* 53-; in Ministry of Educ. 49-60; Ethnomusicologist Dansk Folkemindesamling 60-; Lecturer Univ. of Lund 67-69, Univ. of Copenhagen 69-; leader of numerous ethnomusicological expeditions; mem. Int. Soc. for Contemporary Music, League of Danish Composers (Pres. 62-67); Carl Nielsen Prize 65, Cavaliere dell'Ordine Al Merito della Republica Italiana 69.
Works include: ballets: *Ragnarok* 48, *La Création* 52, *The Marriage* 66, *The Stranger* 70; opera: *Belisa* 64; and music for instrumental groups.
6 Birketinget, Copenhagen (Office); 179 Abrinken 2830, Virum, Denmark (Home).

Olsen, Trygve; Norwegian politician; b. 11 Nov. 1921, Havøysund, Finnmark.
Held various posts in fishermen's unions and econ. orgs.; mem. Board of Management, Fat Herring Fishermen's Sales Org.; Minister of Fisheries 72-73; mem. Labour Party until 72, now Centre Party.
c/o Senterpartiet, Arbeidergt. 4, Oslo, Norway.

Olshansky, Mikhail Alexandrovich; Soviet agronomist politician; b. 1908; ed. Maslovsky Inst. of Selection and Seed Production.
Scientist at All-Union Plant Selection and Genetic Research Inst., Odessa 28-41, Asst. Dir. 45-51; Rector Kuibyshev Agricultural Inst. 42-45; Academician, All-Union Acad. of Agricultural Sciences 48-, Vice-Pres. 51-61, Pres. 62-64; Minister of Agriculture, U.S.S.R. 60-61; Cand. mem. Central Cttee. C.P.S.U. 61-66; Order of Lenin, Order of Red Banner of Labour, State Prize laureate.
All-Union Academy of Agricultural Sciences, 7 Bolshoi Kharitonyevsky pereulok, Moscow, U.S.S.R.

Olson, H. Everett; American business executive; b. 1 Nov. 1906, Chicago, Ill.; *s.* of Harry M. Olson and Dagmar J. Nelson; ed. Northwestern Univ.
Assistant Controller, Carnation Co. 31, Treasurer 48, Dir. 50, Vice-Pres. 54, Asst. to Pres. 61, Pres. 63-73, Chair. and Chief Exec. 73-; Dir. Carnation Foods Co. Ltd., United California Bank, Suburban Gas, Containers Inc.
Carnation Company, 5045 Wilshire Boulevard, Los Angeles, Calif. 90036, U.S.A.

Olson, Harry F., B.S., M.S., E.E., PH.D., D.SC.; American physicist; b. 28 Dec. 1902, Mount Pleasant, Iowa; *s.* of Frans O. Olson and Nelly Benson Olson; *m.* Lorene E. Johnson 1935; ed. High School, Univ. and Graduate Univ.
Member Technical Staff, RCA Labs. 28-40, Dir. Acoustical Lab., RCA Labs. 40-66; Staff Vice-Pres. Acoustical and Electromechanical Research, RCA Labs. 66-; mem. Nat. Acad. of Sciences; Modern Pioneer

Award, Nat. Asscn. of Manufacturers 40; John H. Potts Medal of Audioengineering Soc. 52; Achievement Award, Inst. of Radioengineers 54; Samuel L. Warner Award, Soc. of Motion Pictures and Television Engineers 55; John Scott Medal, City of Philadelphia 56; John Ericsson Medal, American Soc. of Swedish Engineers 63; Emile Berhner Award 65; Silver Medal, Acoustical Soc. of America 74; several awards from Inst. of Electrical and Electronics Engineers.

Publs. *Acoustical Engineering, Musical Engineering, Dynamical Analogies and Music, Physics and Engineering, Modern Sound Reproduction*; over 120 articles in technical journals; holds over 100 U.S. patents.

Office: RCA Laboratories, Princeton, N.J. 08540; Home: 71 Palmer Square West, Princeton, N.J. 08540, U.S.A.

Telephone: 609-452-2700 (Office); 609-924-0790 (Home).

Olson, Horace Andrew; Canadian farmer, merchant and politician; b. 6 Oct. 1925, Iddesleigh, Alberta; s. of Carl M. Olson and Alta M. (née Perry); m. Marion Lucille McLachlan; one s. three d.; ed. Iddesleigh and Medicine Hat, Alberta.

Member for Medicine Hat, Canadian House of Commons 57-58, 72; Minister of Agriculture 68-72; Citation for Distinguished Citizenship, Medicine Hat College 68; Liberal.

Sir John Carling Building, Ottawa, Canada.

Telephone: 613-994-9691.

Olszak, Wacław, D.SC.(TECH.), D.ENG.; Polish university professor; b. 24 Oct. 1902, Karvina; s. of Dr. Wacław and Maria Olszak; m. Stefania Olszak 1952; one d.; ed. Warsaw, Vienna and Paris Univs.

Dozent Mining Coll., Cracow 37; Prof. Applied Mechanics, Cracow 46, at Warsaw Tech. Univ. 52; Head of Dept. of Mechanics of Continuous Media, Polish Acad. of Sciences 52; mem. Polish Acad. of Sciences 54, mem. Presidium 60; Dir. Inst. of Fundamental Engineering Research 63; Rector Int. Centre for Mechanical Sciences (CISM) Udine, Italy 69-; Vice-Pres. Int. Asscn. for Shell Structures (I.A.S.S.) 57; Pres. Int. Union of Testing and Research Laboratories (R.I.L.E.M.) 62; prizes for bridge and engineering structures 35, 37, 48, 53, Polish Nat. Prize 50, 55, 66; Dr. h.c. Univs. of Toulouse, Liège, Glasgow and New Brunswick, and Technical Univs. of Vienna, Cracow, Dresden and Warsaw; Foreign mem. Acad. of Sciences, Belgrade, Toulouse, Budapest, Halle, Turin, Paris, Sofia, Vienna, Bologna, Royal Swedish Acad. of Technical Sciences and Finnish Acad. of Technical Sciences.

Leisure interests: music, driving.

Publs. Research in Applied Mechanics, especially theory of plasticity and theory of structures; *Plane Elastic Problems* 34, *Prestressed Structures* 55, *Non-Homogeneity in Elasticity and Plasticity* (Editor) 59, *Recent Trends in the Development of the Theory of Plasticity* (with others) 62, *Theory of Prestressed Structures* (with others) 62; *Non-Classical Shell Problems* (Editor, with A. Sawczuk) 64, *Theory of Plasticity* (with others) 65; *Inelastic Behaviour in Shells* (with A. Sawczuk) 67.

International Centre for Mechanical Sciences (CISM), Palazzo del Torso, Piazza Garibaldi 18, 33100 Udine, Italy.

Telephone: 0432-64989 (Office).

Olszewski, Jerzy, D.ENG.; Polish politician; b. 24 March 1921, Czestochowa; ed. Silesian Technical Univ., Gliwice.

In chemical industry 49-; Dir. Chemical Factory, Bydgoszcz, subsequently Dir. Factory of Dyeing Industry "Boruta" and Chemical Factory, Oświecim; Dir. Gen., Nitric Industry Asscn., Cracow 65-71; Vice-Chair. Planning Comm. attached to Council of Ministers Feb.-Oct. 71; Minister of Chemical Industry 71-74, of Foreign Trade and Maritime Econ. Nov. 74-; Scientific worker Dept. of Organisation and Production Econ-

omics, Silesian Tech. Univ., Gliwice; mem. Polish United Workers' Party (PZPR) 48-; Deputy to Seym 57-72; Gold and Silver Crosses of Merit 51, 52, Knight's Cross of Order Polonia Restituta 58, Order of Banner of Labour 1st and 2nd Class 69, 59, Order of Builders of People's Poland 74.

Ministerstwo Handlu Zagranicznego i Gospodarki Morskiej, ul. Wiejska 10, 00-489 Warsaw, Poland.

Telephone: 21-03.

Olszewski, Kazimierz; Polish politician; b. 9 Aug. 1917, Treśniowo, Lvov, U.S.S.R.; ed. Lvov Polytechnical Univ.

Worked at State Artificial Fibres Factory, Jelenia Góra 47, later at Design Office of Artificial Fibre Industry Łódź; Dir. of Dept., Ministry of Chemical Industry 52-55, Vice-Minister of Chemical Industry 55-59; del. to COMECON, Moscow 59-62; First Vice-Chair. Cttee. on Econ. Co-operation with Foreign Countries, Council of Ministers 62-70; Asst. Rep. of Polish Govt. at COMECON 70-71; Minister of Foreign Trade 71-72; Vice-Pres., Council of Ministers March 72-; Minister of Shipping 73-74, of Foreign Trade and Maritime Econ. April-Nov. 74; mem. Cen. Cttee., Polish United Workers' Party 71-; Order of Banner of Labour, 1st Class, Polonia Restituta, Cross of Valour, etc.

Rada Ministrów PRL, Al Ujazdowskie 1/3, 00-583 Warsaw, Poland.

Olszowski, Stefan, M.A.; Polish politician; b. 28 Aug. 1931, Toruń; ed. Łódź Univ.

Former activist of Union of Polish Youth; Sec. Polish United Workers' Party (PZPR) Voivodship Cttee., Poznań 60-63; Chief PZPR Cen. Cttee. Press Bureau 63-68; Sec. Cen. Cttee. PZPR 68-Dec. 71; Deputy to Seym 69-; mem. Politburo Dec. 70-; Minister of Foreign Affairs Dec. 71-; Officer's Cross of Polonia Restituta, Order of Banner of Labour (1st and 2nd Class) and others.

Ministry of Foreign Affairs, 23 al. 1 Armii Wojska Polskiego, 00-580 Warsaw, Poland.

Omamo, Hon. William Odongo, M.SC.; Kenyan politician; b. 27 March 1929; ed. Maseno High School, Punjab Agricultural Coll., India, Punjab Univ. and Oregon State Univ.

Former officer of the Ministry of Agriculture; Deputy Principal, Egerton Coll. 65-66, Principal 66-69; mem. House of Reps. 69-74; Minister for Natural Resources 70-74.

c/o Ministry of Natural Resources, Nairobi, Kenya.

Öman, Ivar, PH.D.; Swedish politician; b. 18 April 1900, Djursholm; s. of Emil and Ebba Öman; m. Anna-Lisa Lindberg 1946; two d.; ed. Uppsala Univ.

Political Editor *Nya Dagligt Allehanda* 25-40; Conservative mem. Stockholm Town Council 31-47; M.P. 38-40; Civic Counsellor Stockholm 40-46; Pres. Stockholm Building Comm. 47; Dir. Statistical Office City of Stockholm 47-65; Gov. Rotary Int. District 134 59-60; Grand Master Swedish Order Par Bricole 70-75; Hon. Ph.D. 74.

Leisure interests: travel, card playing.

Publs. *Men of the Great War* 20, *The Ministry of Karl Staaff* 23, *English Newspaper Trusts* 30, *Statistical Office, City of Stockholm 1905-55* 55, *Great Cities and their Surroundings* 57.

Björnbo 12, 18146 Lidingö, Sweden.

Telephone: 08-7654765.

Oman, Julia Trevelyan; British theatrical designer; b. 11 July 1930, London; d. of Charles Chichele Oman and Joan Trevelyan; m. Dr. Roy Strong (q.v.) 1971; ed. Royal Coll. of Art.

Designer, BBC Television 55-67 (including TV film *Alice in Wonderland* 66); designer for theatre: *Brief Lives* (London and N.Y.) 67, 74, *Country Dance* 67, *Forty Years on* 68, *The Merchant of Venice* 70, *Othello*

71, *Getting On* 71, *A Month in the Country* 76; ballet: *Enigma Variations* (Royal Ballet, London) 68; opera: *Eugene Onegin* (Covent Garden) 71, *Un Ballo in Maschera* (Hamburg) 73, *La Bohème* (Covent Garden) 74; films: *The Charge of the Light Brigade* (art dir.) 67, *Laughter in the Dark* (art dir.) 68, *Julius Caesar* (production designer) 69, *Straw Dogs* (design consultant) 71; Dir. Oman Productions Ltd.; Silver Medal, Royal Coll. of Art; Royal Scholar, Royal Coll. of Art; Designer of the Year Award 67.

Publs. *Street Children* (with B. S. Johnson) 64, *Elizabeth R* (with Roy Strong) 71, *Mary Queen of Scots* (with Roy Strong) 72.

c/o London Management, 235/241 Regent Street, London, W1A 2JT, England; c/o Robert Lantz, The Lantz Office, 114 East 55th Street, New York, N.Y. 10022, U.S.A.

Telephone: 01-734 4192 (London); (212) 751-2107 (New York).

Omar Ali Saifuddin Sa'adul Khairi Waddin, H.H. Sultan, D.K., P.S.P.N.B., P.S.N.B., S.P.M.B., D.M.N., D.K. (Kel), D.K. (J), D.K. (Sel.), K.C.M.G.; former ruler of Brunei; b. 1916; ed. Malay Coll., Kuala Kangsar, Perak, Malaya.

Served as a Govt. official in various depts. in Brunei; First Minister or Grand Vizier and mem. of State Council 47-50; Sultan of Brunei 50-67 (abdicated in favour of his son, H.H. Sultan Hassanal Bolkiah, *q.v.*); visited U.K. and Europe 52, 53, 57, 59, 63, U.K. and America 65; on homage to Mecca 53 and 62, trip round the world 65.

Istana Darul Hana, Brunei.

Omari, Dunstan Alfred, M.B.E., B.A., DIP. ED.; Kenyan (naturalized 1972) business executive and former civil servant; b. 1922, Newala, Tanzania; s. of Rev. Alphege and Josephine Omari; m. Fidelia Shangali 1962; two s. one d.; ed. St. Joseph's Secondary School, Chidya, St. Andrew's Secondary School, Minaki, Makerere Univ. Coll. and Univ. of Wales (Aberystwyth). Education Officer (Broadcasting Duties) 53-54; District Officer 55-58, District Commr. 58-61; Tanganyika High Commr. in the U.K. 61-62; Perm. Sec., Prime Minister's Office, and Sec. to the Cabinet, Tanganyika 62; Perm. Sec., President's Office, and Sec. to the Cabinet, Tanganyika 62-63; Sec.-Gen. East African Common Services Org. 64-67, 67-68 (now called East African Community); Chair. East African Currency Board 64-72; mem. Presidential Comm. of Inquiry into the Structure and Remuneration of Public Service in Kenya 70-71; Chair. East African Railways Salaries Review Comm. 71-72; Chair. Kenya Board of Standard Bank Ltd. 74-.

Publ. *Talks on Citizenship* 54.

P.O. Box 25015, Nairobi, Kenya.

Telephone: Nairobi 48120.

Ó Moráin, Dónail; Irish public official; b. 6 Sept. 1923; m. Maire Beaumont 1949; three s. two d.; ed. Coláiste Muire, Dublin, Univ. Coll., Dublin, and King's Inns, Dublin.

Called to the Bar 46; Managing Editor of Retail Food Trade Journal 46-50; Gen. Manager, printing and publishing firm 51-63; Founder, Gael-Linn (voluntary nat. cultural and social asscn.) 53, Chair. 53-63, Dir.-Gen. 63-; Chair. Convocation of Nat. Univ. of Ireland 55-; Chair. Inisfree Handknits Group 65-; mem. Radio Telefis Éireann Authority 65-70, Chair. 70-72, 73-; mem. Consultative Council, Dept. of Finance 65-75; Dir. Glens of Antrim Tweed Co. Ltd. 67-; mem. Irish Comm. for UNESCO 66-, Irish Film Industry Comm. 67-69; Chair. Consultative Council to Radio na Gaeltachta (first local Radio service in Ireland) 71-.

32 Sydney Avenue, Blackrock, Dublin, Ireland.

Telephone: Dublin 880541.

Omwony, Maurice Peter, M.A.(ECON.); Kenyan international finance official; b. 31 Dec. 1933; m. Celestine Mary Apiyo 1958; one s. three d.; ed. Aligarh and Delhi Univs., India.

Personnel Man., Marketing Man., British American Tobacco 61-67; Personnel Man. E. African Posts and Telecommunications Corpn. 68; Alt. Exec. Dir. IMF 68-70, Exec. Dir. 70-72.

Leisure interests: golf, classical and popular music, dancing.

IBM World Trade, Nairobi; Home: P.O. Box 43950, Nairobi, Kenya.

Onana-Awana, Charles; Cameroonian politician; b. c. 1923; ed. Ecole Supérieure, Yaoundé and Ecole nationale de la France d'Outre-Mer, Paris.

With the Ministry of Finance 43-57; Head, Office of Deputy Prime Minister for the Interior 57-58; Asst.-Dir. Office of Prime Minister Feb.-Oct. 58; Perm. Sec. French Cameroons, Paris 58-59; Minister of Finance 60-61; Del. to the Presidency in charge of Finance, the Plan and Territorial Admin. 61-65; Sec.-Gen. Union Douanière et Economique de l'Afrique Centrale 65-70; Minister of Planning and Territorial Improvement 70-72, of Finance 72-75, Minister Del. to the State Inspectorate and Administrative Reform 75-; fmr. Dir. Banque Centrale de l'Afrique Equatoriale et du Cameroun; fmr. Gov. Int. Monetary Fund; Officier Ordre de la Valeur, Cameroon, Commdr. Légion d'Honneur, Ordre de la Rédemption Africaine, Ordre Tchadien.

State Inspectorate, Yaoundé, United Republic of Cameroon.

Onassis, Jacqueline Lee Bouvier; b. 28 July 1929; m. 1st John F. Kennedy 1953 (assassinated 1963), one s. one d. (and one s. deceased); m. 2nd Aristotle Onassis 1968 (died 1975); ed. Vassar Coll., George Washington Univ., and the Univ. of Paris.

Photographer *Washington Times-Herald* 52; initiated and supervised historical reconstruction of décor of the White House 61-63; Rep. of the late Pres. Kennedy on tour of India 62.

1040 Fifth Avenue, at 85th Street, New York City, N.Y. 10028, U.S.A.

O'Neal, Edward A.; American business executive; b. 9 Sept. 1905, Florence, Ala.; s. of late Edward A. O'Neal and Julia Camper; m. Mildred Pruet 1928; one s. three d.; ed. Davidson College.

Joined Swann Corpn., Anniston, Alabama 26 (acquired by Monsanto Co.) 35; Plant Man., Anniston 39-41, Plant Man. Monsanto Phosphate Div., Trenton, Mich. 41-44, Production Man. Phosphate Div. 44-46; Man. Dir. Monsanto Chemicals Ltd., London 47-52, Chair. 49-55, Dir. 64-70; Gen. Man. Monsanto Overseas Div. 53-56, Vice-Pres. 54-56, Dir. Monsanto 55-56, 61-, Vice-Pres. 62-65, mem. Exec. Cttee. 64-70, mem. Finance Cttee. 65-68, Chair. Board of Dirs. 65-68, mem. Exec. Compensation Cttee. 71-; Pres. Chemstrand Corpn. (now Monsanto Textiles Ltd.) 56-64, Chair. 64-68, Dir. 68-70; Dir. St. Louis Union Trust Co.; mem. Board of Trustees Washington Univ., Dir. Foreign Policy Asscn.

Leisure interests: hunting, golf.

Suite 2-B, 665 South Skinker Boulevard, St. Louis, Missouri 63105; (Home) 665 South Skinker Boulevard, Apt. 12F, St. Louis, Missouri 63105, U.S.A.

Telephone: 725-6626 (Office); 726-0030 (Home).

O'Neil, Michael Gerald, A.B.; American rubber executive; b. 29 Jan. 1922; ed. Coll. of Holy Cross, and Harvard Univ.

Director, The General Tire and Rubber Co. 50-, Asst. to Pres. 51-57, Vice-Pres. and Exec. Asst. to Pres. 57-60, Pres. 60-; served Second World War; official of numerous business and philanthropic orgs.

The General Tire and Rubber Co., 1 General Street, Akron, Ohio 44329, U.S.A.

O'Neill, C. William, B.A., LL.B.; American politician and lawyer; b. 14 Feb. 1916, Marietta, Ohio; m. Betty Hewson 1945; one s. one d.; ed. Marietta Coll., and Ohio State Univ. Law School.

Member, Ohio Legislature 39-50; served with U.S. Army 43-46; Speaker of Ohio House of Reps. 47-48 and Minority Leader 49-50; Attorney-Gen. of Ohio 51-56; Gov. of Ohio 57-58; private law practice 59-60; Judge, Supreme Court of Ohio 60-70; Chief Justice of the Supreme Court of Ohio 70-; Prof. of Law, Capital Univ. School of Law 71-; LL.D. h.c. from ten univs.
1560 London Drive, Columbus, Ohio 43221, U.S.A.
Telephone: 451-8828.

O'Neill, The Hon. Sir Con Douglas Walter, G.C.M.G., M.A.; British diplomatist; b. 3 June 1912, London; s. of Lord Rathcavan; ed. Eton Coll., and Balliol Coll., Oxford.

Fellow, All Souls Coll., Oxford 35-45; called to the Bar 36; entered Diplomatic Service 36; served Berlin 38; resigned from Service 38; served army 40-43; with Foreign Office 43-46; on staff of *The Times* 46-47; re-joined Foreign Office 47; served Frankfurt and Bonn 48-52; Imperial Defence Coll. 53; Head News Dept., Foreign Office 54-55; Chargé d'Affaires, Peking 55-57; Asst. Under-Sec. Foreign Office 57-60; Ambassador to Finland 61-63, to European Econ. Community 63-65; Deputy Under-Sec. in charge of Econ. Affairs, Foreign Office 65-68; Dir. Hill Samuel June 68-69; Deputy Under-Sec., Foreign Office 69-72; Leader British Del. to negotiate entry to EEC 70-72; Chair. Intervention Board for Agricultural Produce 72-74; Dir. Unigate Ltd. 74-; Dir. Britain in Europe Campaign 75.
Publ. *Our European Future* 72.
37 Flood Street, London, S.W.3, England.
Telephone: 01-352-2147.

O'Neill of the Maine, Baron (Life Peer), cr. 70, of Ahoghill in the County of Antrim; **Terence Marne O'Neill,** P.C.; British (N. Ireland) politician; b. 10 Sept. 1914; ed. Eton Coll.

Irish Guards 39-45; M.P. (N. Ireland) 46-70, Parl. Sec. Ministry of Health 48-53; Deputy Speaker and Chair. Ways and Means Cttee. 53-55; Joint Parl. Sec. Home Affairs and Health 55; Minister of Home Affairs, April-Oct. 56, of Finance Sept. 56-63; Prime Minister (N. Ireland) 63-69; mem. Comm. on Electoral Reform 75-; Dir. S. G. Warburg and Co., Int. Holdings Ltd., Phoenix Assurance; Unionist Party.
Publs. *Ulster at the Crossroads* (speeches and writings) 69, *The Autobiography of Terence O'Neill* 72.
House of Lords, London, S.W.1, England; Glebe House, Ahoghill, County Antrim, Northern Ireland.
Telephone: Ahoghill 246.

Onetti, Juan Carlos; Uruguayan writer; b. 1 July 1909; ed. High School.
Editor *Marcha* (weekly newspaper), Montevideo 39-42; Editor Reuter Agency, Montevideo 42-43, Buenos Aires 43-46; Editor *Vea y Lea* (magazine), Buenos Aires 46-55; Man. of advertising firm in Montevideo 55-57; Dir. of Municipal Libraries, Montevideo 57; Nat. Literature Prize of Uruguay 63.
Publs. novels: *El pozo* 39, *Tierra de nadie* 41, *Para esta noche* 43, *La vida breve* 50, *Un sueño realizado y otros cuentos* (stories) 51, *Una tumba sin nombre* 59, *Los adioses* 54, *La cara de la desgracia* 60, *Jacob y el otro* (story) 61, *El Astillero* 61, *El infierno tan temido* 62, *Tan triste como ella* 63, *Juntacadáveres* 65.
Gonzalo Ramírez 1497, Montevideo, Uruguay.

Ong, Tan Sri Haji Omar Yoke-Lin; Malaysian politician and diplomatist; b. 1917.
Member Kuala Lumpur Municipal Council 52-; co-founder Alliance Party; mem. Fed. Legislative Council 54-; Malayan Minister of Posts and Telecommunications 55-56, of Transport 56-57, of Labour and Social Welfare 57-59, of Health and Social Welfare 59-72; M.P. 59-72; Vice-Pres. Commonwealth Parl. Asscn. 61; Ambassador to U.S.A. and UN 62-64, to U.S.A. 64-72, also accred. to Brazil 66-72; Minister without Portfolio 64-73; Pres. of the Senate 73-; Chair. Asian Int. Merchant Bankers Bhd., Maju Jaya Industries Sdn Bhd., Kemuncak Enterprises, Syarikat Ong Yoke Lin Sdn Bhd.
Parliament House (Dewan Ra'ayat), Kuala Lumpur, Malaysia.

Onganía, Lt.-Gen. Juan Carlos; Argentine army officer and politician; b. 17 March 1914; ed. School of War.
Army career in cavalry and armoured corps; C.-in-C. of Army 63-Nov. 65; Pres. of Argentina June 66-June 70.
Buenos Aires, Argentina.

Onsager, Lars, CH.E., PH.D., SC.D., DR. TECH.; American chemist; b. 27 Nov. 1903, Oslo, Norway; s. of Erling Onsager and Ingrid (née Kirkeby); m. Margarethe Arledter 1933; three s. one d.; ed. Norges Tekniske högskole, Trondheim, and Yale Univ.
Associate in Chemistry, Johns Hopkins Univ. 28; Instructor of Chemistry, Brown Univ. (Providence, R.I.) 28-33; Sterling Fellow, Yale Univ. 33-34, Asst. Prof. 34-40, Assoc. Prof. 40-45, J. Willard Gibbs Prof. of Theoretical Chemistry, 45-72, Emeritus Prof. 72; Distinguished Univ. Prof. Miami Univ. 72-; Fulbright Scholar, Mond Laboratory, Cambridge 51-52; Visiting Prof. Univs. of California, San Diego 61, Rockefeller Univ. 67; Gauss Prof. Göttingen Univ. 68; Lorentz Prof. Leiden Univ. 70; mem. Nat. Acad. of Sciences and other Acads. in U.S.A., Norway and Sweden; Foreign mem. Royal Soc., London 75; mem. Neuro-science Associates 62-; Rumford Medal (American Acad.) 53, Lorenz Medal 58, G. N. Lewis Medal, J. G. Kirkwood Medal, Willard Gibbs Medal 62, T. W. Richards Medal 64, Debye Award 65, Belfer Award 66, National Science Medal 68, Nobel Prize for Chemistry 68; Hon. D.Sc. Harvard 54, Cambridge 70, Oxford 71, and several other univs.
Publs. articles on theory of electrolytes, reciprocal relations in irreversible processes, dipole moments in liquids, crystal statistics, interpretation of the de Haas-van Alphen effect, and electrical properties of ice.
Centre for Theoretical Studies, University of Miami, Coral Gables, Florida 33124, U.S.A.
Telephone: (305) 284-4455 (Office).

Onyeama, Charles Dadi, LL.B.; Nigerian judge; b. 5 Aug. 1917, Eke, Enugu; s. of Chief Onyeama; m. 1st Susannah Ogwudu 1950, 2nd Florence Wilcox 1966; five s. two d.; ed. King's Coll., Lagos, Achimota Coll., Gold Coast, Univ. Coll., London and Brasenose Coll., Oxford.
Cadet Admin. Officer, Nigeria 44; mem. Legislative Council of Nigeria and Eastern House of Assembly 46-51; mem. Nigerianization Comm. and mem. Gen. Conf. and Constitutional Drafting Cttee. 48-50; Chief Magistrate, Nigeria 52-56; Acting High Court Judge, W. Nigeria 56-57; High Court Judge, Lagos 57-64; Acting Chief Justice, Lagos High Court 61 and 63; Justice of Supreme Court of Nigeria 64-66; Judge Int. Court of Justice, The Hague 67-76.
Leisure interest: reading.
c/o International Court of Justice, Peace Palace, The Hague, Netherlands.

Onyonka, Zachary; Kenyan politician; b. 1938. Former Prof. of Econs., Univ. Coll., Nairobi; Minister of Econ. Planning and Devt. Dec. 69-Oct. 70, of Information 70-73, of Health 73-74, of Educ. Nov. 74-; mem. Kenya African Nat. Union (KANU).
Ministry of Education, Nairobi, Kenya.

Ooka, Shohei; Japanese writer; b. 6 March 1909, Tokyo; s. of Teisaburo and Tsuru Ooka; m. Harue Kamimura 1939; one s. one d.; ed. Univ. of Kyoto.

Translator of French literature, especially Stendhal; soldier and prisoner of war in the Philippines 44-45; novelist and critic 48-; Teacher at Meiji Univ. 52-55; visited U.S.A., England and France as Creative Fellow, Rockefeller Foundation 53-54; Yokomitsu Prize 40, Yomiuri Prize 52, Mainichi and Shincho Prize 61, Mainichi-Geijitsu Prize 72, Noma Prize 74, Asahi Prize 76.
Leisure interests: golf, Go.
Publs. Translated Alain's *Stendhal* 40, Stendhal's *Chartreuse de Parme* 49, etc.; novels: *Furyoki* (Memories of a Prisoner of War) 49, *Musashino Fujin* (A Woman of Musashino Plain) 50, *Nobi* (Fires of the Plain) 51, *Sanso* (Oxygen) 53, *Hamlet Nikki* (Diary of Hamlet) 55, *Reite Senki* (Battle of Leyte) 71, *Nakahara Chuya* (Biography) 74, etc.
7-15-12 Seijo, Setagaya-ku, Tokyo, Japan.

Oord, Willem Johan van der, C.E.; Netherlands civil engineer and United Nations official; b. 27 Sept. 1919, Haarlemmermeer; s. of Cornelis Jacob van der Oord and Marie Zanstra; m. Charee Leimsombat 1969; one s. two d.; ed. Delft Univ.
Engineer, Rijkswaterstaat, Netherlands 41-46; Water Conservancy Expert, UNRRA/FAO 46-48; Engineer-in-Charge, Rhine and Yssel Bureau, Rijkswaterstaat, Netherlands 49-50; Chief, Inland Waterway Section, ECAFE, Thailand 50-63; Chief of Public Works, ONUC, Congo 60-61; Deputy Resident Rep., UNTAB, Pakistan 63-64; Resident Rep., UNTAB, Egypt 64-65; Deputy Dir. Bureau of Operations and Programming, UNDP, New York 65-69; Exec. Agent of Cttee. for Co-ordination of Investigations of the Lower Mekong Basin (Mekong River Devt. Project) 69-; corresp. mem. Royal Netherlands Acad. of Sciences 69-.
Leisure interests: languages, electronics, sailing, swimming.
Publs. *Economic justification for expressway between the Hague and Amsterdam* 41, *Canal Plan Rhine* 43, *Experiences in river conservancy in China* 48, and co-author of several other works.
c/o Economic and Social Commission for Asia and the Pacific, Sala Santitham, Bangkok, Thailand.
Telephone: 811890.

Oorschot, Wilhelmus Petrus Hubertus van, LL.D.; Netherlands official; b. 30 April 1910, Bandoeng; m. Rita Geraldine Flemer 1944; two d.; ed. Univ. of Utrecht.
Director-Gen. Foreign Econ. Relations to the Ministry of Econ. Affairs, The Hague 57-; Chair. of GATT 61, 63; Kt. Order Netherlands Lion; Commdr. Order of Orange Nassau; Commdr. Order of the Oak Crown of Luxemburg; Grand Officer of the Order of Léopold II of Belgium; Grand Officer of the Order of the Crown of Belgium; Grand Officer of the Order of Merit of Italy; Commdr. of the Legion of Honour, France; Grand Officer of the Order of the Southern Cross of Brazil; Grand Officer Order of the Crown of Luxembourg; Grand Officer Order of Merit of Germany; Order of the Yugoslav Flag (Second Class); Grand Officer Order of Tudor Vladimirescu; Grand Officer of the Order of Dannebrog, Denmark; Grand Officer of the Order of Leopold of Belgium; Norwegian, Spanish, Tunisian, Austrian, Indonesian and Honduran awards.
Leisure interests: farming, gardening.
De Soetendaal, Bennekom, Netherlands.
Telephone: 08380-4328.

Oort, Jan Hendrik; Netherlands astronomer; b. 28 April 1900, Franeker; s. of Abraham Hermanus and Ruth Hannah Faber; m. Johanna Maria Graadt van Roggen 1927; two s. one d.; ed. Univ. of Groningen.
Assistant, Astronomical Laboratory, Groningen 21; Research Asst. Yale Univ. Observatory, U.S.A. 22-24; Astronomer Leiden Observatory 24; Prof. of Astronomy and Dir. of Observatory, Univ. of Leiden 45-70;

Gen. Sec. Int. Astronomical Union 35-48, Pres. 59-61; Foreign mem. of various Academies of Arts and Sciences; Vetlesen Prize, Columbia Univ. 66; Hon. Dr. Univs. of Copenhagen, Glasgow, Oxford, Louvain, Harvard, Brussels, Cambridge, Bordeaux, Canberra, Toruń.
Leisure interests: reading, hiking, skating.
Publs. Numerous contributions to learned journals.
President Kennedylaan 169, Oegstgeest, Netherlands.
Telephone: 071-154158.

Oparin, Alexander Ivanovich; Soviet biochemist; b. 2 March 1894, Uglich; m. Nina Oparina; ed. Moscow Univ.
Lecturer, later Prof., Univ. of Moscow 20-; founder with A. N. Bach of Biochemical Inst. U.S.S.R. Acad. of Sciences 35, Dir. of the Inst. 46-; corr. mem. U.S.S.R. Acad. of Sciences 39-46, mem. 46-; mem. U.S.S.R. Peace Cttee., Cttee. on Space Research (COSPAR) 64; Vice-Pres. World Fed. of Scientific Workers 52; Pres. Int. Soc. for the study of The Origin of Life (ISSOL) 70; mem. Bulgarian Acad. of Sciences 52; Leopoldina Acad. of Scientific Research 56; Gen. Assembly Int. Union of Biochemistry 53, Vice-Pres. 61; hon. mem. Japanese Biochemical Soc. 55; corresp. mem. Suomalaisten Kemistien Seura (Finnish Chemical Soc.) 59; Hon. Dr. Nat. Sc. Friedrich Schiller Univ. Jena 58, Hon. Dr. Univ. of Poitiers 63, Hon. Dr. Univ. of Warsaw; Hon. mem. German Acad. of Science (Berlin); Hon. mem. Acad. of Science of Cuba; Orders of Lenin (five) and of the Red Banner of Labour, Hero of Socialist Labour 69, Lenin Prize 74.
Publs. include *Proizkhoshdenie zhizni* (Origin of Life) 24, *Vozniknovenie zhizni na Zemle* (Origin of Life on Earth) 36, 57, *Zhin ee pzizoda proizkhoshednie i razvitie* (Life: Its Nature, Origin and Development) 60, *The Chemical Origin of Life* 65.
Bach Institute of Biochemistry, U.S.S.R. Academy of Sciences, 33 Leninsky Prospekt Moscow, U.S.S.R.

Opel, John Roberts, B.A., M.B.A.; American data processing company executive; b. 5 Jan. 1925, Kansas City, Mo.; s. of Norman J. Opel and Esther (Roberts) Opel; m. Julia Carole Stout 1953; two s. three d.; ed. Westminster Coll., Foulton, Mo. and Univ. of Chicago.
Joined Int. Business Machines Corpn. (IBM) 49, Sales Rep. 49, Vice-Pres. 66, Senior Vice-Pres. 69, Dir. 72-, Pres. 74-; Dir. Bank of New York, Pfizer Inc.; Trustee, Westminster Coll., Northern Westchester Hosp.
International Business Machines Corporation, Old Orchard Road, Armonk, N.Y. 10504, U.S.A.
Telephone: (914) 765-1900.

Ople, Blas F.; Philippine politician; b. 3 Feb. 1927, Hagonoy, Bulacan; s. of Felix Ople and Segundina Fajardo; m. Susana Vasquez 1949; five s. two d.; ed. Philippine public and private schools, Far Eastern Univ. and Manuel L. Quezon Univ., Manila.
Copy editor and columnist *The Daily Mirror*, Manila 50-53; Asst. to Pres. Ramon Magsaysay on labour and agrarian affairs 54-57; writer and labour leader 58-64; Head, Propaganda Div., Ferdinand E. Marcos' presidential campaign 65; Special Asst. to Pres. Marcos and Commr. Social Security System 66; Sec. of Labour 67-, concurrently Chair. Nat. Manpower and Youth Council 67-71; mem. Board of Trustees, Land Bank 68-; Chair. Govt. Group, Int. Labor Conf. 69-; Pres. Int. Labour Conference June 75-; Chair. Asian Labour Ministers' Conf. 67; various govt. and civic awards.
c/o International Labour Organization, 1211 Geneva 22, Switzerland; 61 Visayas Avenue, Project 6, Quezon City, Philippines.
Telephone: 99-67-56; 98-20-56 (Quezon City).

Oppenheim, Tan Sri Sir Alexander, S.M.N., Kt., O.B.E., M.A., PH.D., D.SC.; British mathematician; b. 4 Feb. 1903, Salford; s. of Harris Jacob Oppenheim and Fanny Ginsberg; m. Beatrice Templer Nesbitt 1930; one d.;

ed. Manchester Grammar School, and Balliol Coll., Oxford.

Commonwealth Fund Fellow Chicago 27-30; Lecturer Edinburgh Univ. 30-31; Prof. of Mathematics Raffles Coll. Singapore 31-42, 45-49, Deputy Principal 47 and 49; Prof. of Mathematics Univ. of Malaya 49-57, Dean Faculty of Arts 49, 51 and 53, Acting Vice-Chancellor 55, Vice-Chancellor 57-65; Visiting Prof. of Mathematics, Reading Univ. 65-68, Univ. of Ghana 68-73, Univ. of Benin, Nigeria 73; prisoner of war in Singapore and Thailand 42-45; Dean, Prisoner of War Univ. 42; Pres. Malayan Mathematical Soc. 51-55, 57, Singapore Chess Club 56, American Univ. Club 56, Oxford and Cambridge Soc. 52, 57; mem. Asscn. of Southeast Asian Insts. of Higher Learning 59-61, Academic Advisory Cttee., Univ. of Cape Coast 72; Pres. Mathematical Asscn. of Ghana 69-70; Fellow, Royal Soc. of Edinburgh, World Acad. of Art and Science.

Leisure interests: chess, bridge, walking, swimming.

c/o 664 Finchley Road, London, N.W.11, England.

Oppenheim, Sir Duncan Morris, Kt.; British tobacco manufacturer and solicitor; b. 6 Aug. 1904; s. of Watkins and Helen Oppenheim (née McKechnie); m. 1st Joyce Mitcheson 1932 (deceased), 2nd Susan Macnaughten 1936 (deceased); one s. one d.; ed. Repton School.

Assistant Solicitor Messrs. Linklaters & Paines, London 29; Solicitor to and Dir. of China Assoc. Co. of British-American Tobacco Co. Ltd. 34; Asst. Solicitor, British-American Tobacco Co. London 35, Solicitor 36-49, Dir. 43-, Deputy Chair. 47-49, Vice-Chair. 49-53, Chair. 53-66, Pres. 66-72; Chair. Royal College of Art Council 56-75, Pro-Provost 67-72; Chair. Council of Industrial Design 60-72; Dir. Lloyds Bank Ltd. 56-75; Chair British Nat. Cttee. of Int. Chamber of Commerce 63-74, Court of Govs., Admin. Staff Coll., Henley 63-71; Chair. Royal Inst. of Int. Affairs 66-71; mem. Advisory Cttee. Victoria and Albert Museum, London; Hon. Dr. and Senior Fellow Royal Coll. of Art; Hon. Fellow Soc. of Industrial Artists; Bicentenary Medal, Royal Soc. of Arts 69.

Leisure interests: painting, sailing.

43 Edwardes Square, London, W.8, England.

Oppenheimer, Harry Frederick, M.A.; South African industrialist; b. 28 Oct. 1908, Kimberley; s. of late Sir Ernest Oppenheimer; m. Bridget Denison 1943; one s. one d.; ed. Charterhouse and Christ Church, Oxford.

Chairman, Anglo-American Corpn. of South Africa Ltd., De Beers Consolidated Mines Ltd.; Chair. or Dir. of 68 or more subsidiary and other companies; M.P. 47-58; Chancellor, Cape Town Univ. 67-; mem. United Party until 59; Hon. D.Econ. (Natal); Hon. LL.D. (Leeds, Witwatersrand and Rhodes).

Leisure interests: golf, riding, horse racing.

Brenthurst, Federation Road, Parktown, Johannesburg, South Africa.

Orazmukhamedov, Oraz Nazarovich; Soviet politician; b. 1928; ed. Tashkent Railway Engineering Inst.

Member, C.P.S.U. 48-, cand. mem. Cen. Cttee. 71-; railway engineer 45-59; party and state work 59-61; Dep. Chair. Council of Ministers, Turkmen S.S.R. 61-66; Sec. Cen. Cttee. C.P. of Turkmen S.S.R. 66-69; Chair. Council of Ministers and Minister of Foreign Affairs, Turkmen S.S.R. 69-75; Deputy U.S.S.R. Supreme Soviet 70-; mem. Bureau of Cen. Cttee. Turkmenistan C.P.; alt. mem. C.P.S.U. Cen. Cttee. 71-.

c/o Council of Ministers of the Turkmen S.S.R., Ashkhabad, U.S.S.R.

Orbán, László; Hungarian politician; b. 1912, Nógrádveröce; ed. Law Acad. of Miskolc and Szeged Univ. Joined Communist Party 38; mem. Nat. Youth Cttee., organized independence movt., World War II; mem. Parl. 45-53, 58-; held various posts in C.P. Cen. Office

after 45, Leader Agitprop. Dept. until 50; Head of Dept., Ministry of Educ., later Deputy Minister 50-55; mem. Hungarian Socialist Workers' Party Cen. Cttee. 57-, Head of Science and Culture Dept., later of Agitprop. Dept. 56-67; First Deputy Minister of Educ. 67-74; Sec. of State; Minister of Culture 74-; mem. Agitation and Propaganda Board attached to HSWP Cen. Cttee. 75-; Red Banner of Order of Labour 62, Labour Order of Merit, Golden Degree 65, 68 Jubilee Commemorative Medal of Liberation 70.

Ministry of Culture, Szalay-utca 10/14, 1884 Budapest V, Hungary.

Telephone: 118-600.

O'Regan, (Andrew) Brendan; Irish business executive; b. 15 May 1917, Co. Clare; s. of James and Norah O'Regan; m.; two s. three d.; ed. Blackrock Coll., Dublin.

Comptroller, Sales and Catering, Shannon Airport 43-73; Chair. Bord Failte Eireann 57-73, Shannon Free Airport Devt. Co. 59-, State Agencies Devt. Co-operation Org. (DEVCO) 74-.

Leisure interests: sailing, riding.

Shannon International Free Airport, Co. Clare; Home: Fort Henry, Killaloe, Co. Clare, Ireland.

Orekhovich, Vasily Nikolayevich; Soviet biologist; b. 11 Jan. 1905, Alyeshino; ed. North Caucasus Univ.

School teacher 27-30; Postgraduate (Moscow) 30-32; Asst. Lecturer, Moscow Communist Univ. 31-35; Senior Research Worker, Moscow Inst. of Morphogenesis 33-36; mem. C.P.S.U. 39-; Head of Lab. and Deputy Dir. Moscow Inst. of Biological and Medical Chemistry, 41-48; Dir. Inst. of Medical and Biological Chemistry, U.S.S.R. Acad. of Medical Sciences 50-53; mem. U.S.S.R. Acad. of Medical Sciences, mem. Presidium 53-57; Academician-Sec. Dept. of Medico-Biological Sciences, Vice-Pres. U.S.S.R. Acad. of Medical Sciences 60-63; Head of Lab. Inst. of Natural Products Chemistry, U.S.S.R. Acad. of Sciences 59-; Vice-Pres. All-Union Biochemical Soc. and Int. Biochemistry Cttee.; mem. Presidium Moscow Biochemical Soc.; mem. Exec. Cttee. Int. Fed. for Clinical Chemistry, mem. Scientific Cttee. Perm. Int. Symposium on Proteins; Order of Red Banner of Labour 52, 61, Badge of Honour 45, 51, and other Soviet decorations; Pasteur Medal 57; French Biochemical Soc. Medal 58, Second Int. Biochemistry Congress Medal 52.

Over 160 publs. on chemistry, biochemistry, etc.

Institute of Medical and Biological Chemistry, Pogodinskaya 10, Moscow, U.S.S.R.

Orel, Admiral Alexander Yevstafievich; Soviet naval officer; b. 25 Aug. 1908, Leningrad; ed. General Staff Acad.

Merchant marine sailor, secondary technical school student, captain's mate 24-29; Naval Service 29-; Commdr. of ships and formations 41-59; Commdr. Baltic Fleet 59-67; Chief of Naval Academy 67-; mem. C.P.S.U. 37-; Deputy to U.S.S.R. Supreme Soviet until 70.

Ministry of Defence, Naberezhnaya M. Thorez 34, Moscow, U.S.S.R.

Orem, Charles Reace, B.A., LL.B.; American business executive; b. 23 Aug. 1916, Nashville, Tenn.; m. Martha Haley; one d.; ed. Columbia Univ. School of Business Administration, Fordham Univ. School of Law, Univ. of Kentucky, New York Univ. Graduate School of Business and Harvard Univ. Graduate School of Business.

With Shell Oil Co. 39-52; Man. Peat, Marwick, Mitchell & Co. 52-54; Asst. Treas. Sylvania Electric Products, Inc. 54-60; with Pickands, Mather & Co. Cleveland 60-64, during which time he was Vice-Pres. Finance and Dir.; Vice-Pres. and Controller, Armour and Co. (now subsidiary of Greyhound Corpn.) Oct. 64-65, Financial Vice-Pres. Dec. 65-67, Senior Admin. and

Financial Vice-Pres. June 67, Dir. and mem. Exec. Cttee. of the Board Feb. 68-, Pres. 68-71; now Pres. Investors Diversified Services Inc.; Dir. Greater Minneapolis Chamber of Commerce, Investors Diversified Services Inc.; U.S. Army service (attaining rank of Major) 42-46; mem. New York Bar Asscn.
Investors Diversified Services Inc., IDS Tower, Minneapolis, Minn. 55402, U.S.A.

Orescanin, Gen. Bogdan, LL.M.; Yugoslav diplomatist; b. 27 Oct. 1916, Perna; s. of Sima and Marija Orescanin; m. Sonja Dapcevic 1947; ed. Grammar School, Zagreb, Univ. of Zagreb and Belgrade Higher Mil. Acad.
Corps Commdr. and Gen., Nat. Liberation Struggle 41; Asst. and Deputy Chief of Gen. Staff and Asst. Defence Sec. 45; Mil. Attaché to U.K. 52-54; mem. Parl., Fed. Council, Chair. Cttee. for Nat. Defence, Foreign Affairs Cttee., Exec. Board of Yugoslav Group of Interparl. Union; Amb. to People's Republic of China, Democratic People's Republic of Korea, Democratic Repub. of Viet-Nam 70-73, to U.K. Sept. 73-; Order of the Nat. Hero and many other decorations.
Leisure interest: literature.
Publs. *Military Aspects of the Struggle for World Peace, National Independence and Socialism,* several studies and articles on political and military subjects.
Embassy of the Socialist Federal Republic of Yugoslavia, 5 Lexham Gardens, London W8 5JJ, England.
Telephone: 01-370 6105.

Orff, Carl; German composer; b. 10 July 1895, Munich; s. of Heinrich and Paula Orff (née Koestler); one d.; ed. Akademie der Tonkunst, Munich.
Professor and Head of Master Class of Musical Composition, Hochschule für Musik, Munich, until 60; Head of Orff Inst. at Mozarteum Acad., Salzburg 61-; mem. Bavarian Acad. of Fine Arts; mem. Swedish Acad., Acad. di Santa Cecilia, Rome, etc.; Dr. h.c.; Orden pour le Mérite (Fed. Repub. of Germany); Prize of the Goethe-Stiftung, Basle 69.
Compositions: *Carmina Burana, Catulli Carmina, Trionfo di Afrodite, Die Kluge, Der Mond, Antigone, Die Bernauerin, Ödipus der Tyrann, Astutuli, Comoedia de Christi Resurrectione, Ludus de nato Infante mirificus, Prometheus, Schulwerk, De temporum fine comoedia* 73.
St. Georgen, 8918 Diessen Ammersee, Federal Republic of Germany.

Orfila, Alejandro; Argentine diplomatist; b. 9 March 1925, Mendoza; ed. Buenos Aires, Stanford and Tulane (New Orleans) Univs.
Secretary, Ministry of Foreign Affairs 46, Moscow 46; Consul, Warsaw 47-48, San Francisco 48-49; Consul-Gen. New Orleans 49-50; Sec. Washington D.C. 51-52; Man. José Orfila, Ltda., Mendoza 52, Dir. of Information, Org. of American States (OAS) 53-58; Minister Plenipotentiary, Washington D.C. 58-60; Amb. to Japan 60-62; private consultant in int. financial and econ. affairs 62-73; Amb. to U.S.A. 73-75; Sec.-Gen. Org. of American States 75-.
Organization of American States, Washington, D.C. 20006, U.S.A.

Orgad, Ben Zion; Israeli composer; b. 1926, Germany; ed. Acad. of Music in Jerusalem and Brandeis Univ., U.S.A.
Studied violin with Kinory and Bergman and composition with Paul Ben-Haim and Josef Tal; studied in U.S.A. under Aaron Copland (q.v.) and Irving Fine; now Supervisor of Musical Education, Israel Ministry of Educ. and Culture; recipient of several awards for compositions.
Compositions include: cantatas: *The Story of the Spies* (UNESCO Koussevitsky Prize 52), *Isaiah's Vision;* works for orchestra, *Building a King's Stage, Choreographic Sketches, Movements on 'A', Kaleidoscope, Music for Horn and Orchestra; Hatsvi Israel* (Symphony for

baritone and orch.); *Out of the Dust* (for solo and instruments); *Ballada* (for violin), *Taksim* (for harp), *Monologue* (for viola); works for soloists and orchestra, songs, piano pieces, etc.
Ministry of Education and Culture, Hadar-Daphna Building, Tel-Aviv; Home: 14 Bloch Street, Tel-Aviv, Israel.
Telephone: 254122 (Office).

Organov, Nikolai Nikolayevich; Soviet party official and diplomatist; b. 1901; ed. Higher Party School, Moscow.
Full-time Party duties 23-43; Third Sec., later First Sec., Primorsk Territorial Cttee. of C.P.S.U. 47-52; Deputy to U.S.S.R. Supreme Soviet 50-; First Sec. Krasnoyarsk Territorial Cttee. of C.P.S.U. 52-58; Deputy Chair. Council of Ministers Russian Fed. Republic 58-59; Chair. Presidium Supreme Soviet Russian Fed. Republic and Deputy Chair. U.S.S.R. Supreme Soviet Presidium 59-62; mem. Central Cttee. of C.P.S.U. 52-; Amb. to Bulgaria 62-67; Head of Dept., Cen. Cttee. of C.P.S.U. 67-; mem. Foreign Affairs Comm. Soviet of Nationalities; Order of Lenin (twice).
C.P.S.U. Central Committee, 4 Staraya ploshchad, Moscow, U.S.S.R.

Örkény, István; Hungarian writer; b. 5 April 1912, Budapest; s. of Hugo Örkény and Margit Pető; m. Zsuzsa Radnóti 1964; one s. one d.; ed. Technical Univ. of Budapest.
Military service, World War II; has written short stories, novels and plays; József Attila Prize 55, 67, Kossuth Prize 73.
Leisure interests: sailing, swimming.
Publs. short stories: *Tengertánc* 41, *Lágerek népe* (The Lager People) 47, *Budai böjt* (Fasting in Buda) 48, *Idegen föld* (Alien Earth) 49, *Ezüstpisztráng* (Silver Trout) 56, *Jeruzsálem hercegnője* (Princess of Jerusalem) 67, *Nászutasok a légypapiron* (Honeymoon on the Fly-Paper) 67, *Egyperces novellák* (One Minute Stories 68, in French, Minimythes 71, in German, Der letzte Zug) 68, *Időrendben* (In Order of Time) 71; novel: *Házastársak* (Consorts) 51; plays: *Voronyezs* (Voronezh) 48, *Tóték* (The Tot Family) 67, *Macskajáték* (Cat's Play) 70, *Sötét galamb* (Dark Pigeon) 70, *Rekviem egy hadseregért* (Requiem for an Army) 73, *Vérrokonok* (Kinsfolk) 74, *Pisti a verzivatarban* (Pisti in the Holocaust) 75, *Kulcskeresok* (Searching the Key) 76.
II. Pasaréti ut 39, H-1026 Budapest, Hungary.
Telephone: 254-725.

Orlandini, Sergio; Netherlands airline executive; b. 5 May 1921; ed. Univ. of Rotterdam.
Joined KLM Royal Dutch Airlines 51, head, Long-range Planning Bureau 62-70, Man. Dir. 70-73, Pres. 73-.
Koninklijke Luchtvaart Maatschappij N.V., P.O.B. 7700, Schiphol Airport, Amsterdam, Netherlands.
Telephone: 499123.

Orlov, Georgi Mikhailovich; Soviet architect; b. 8 April 1901, Kursk; m. Irina Teodorovna Orlova; one s. one d.; ed. Moscow Higher Technical Schools.
Director of architectural group of Dnieper Hydro-Electric Power Station 27-32; Asst. Chief Architect, Central Volga Building Org. 32-35; Chief Architect, Chirchik Hydro Electric Power Station (Uzbekistan) 33-36; Chief Architect, No. 1 Architecture Studio 38-42; Chief Architect, restoration work at Dnieper Hydro-Electric Power Station 44-51; design of Kakhovskaya hydro-electric power station 51-55, Great October hydro-electric power station, Bratskaya 60-68; teacher, Moscow Architectural School 33-38, 66-, Prof. 69-; Chief Architect *Gidroenergoproject* (Hydro-power designing) Research and Designing Inst. 51-61; Exec. mem. Moscow Branch, Soviet Architects' Union 51-55, mem. Presidium Soviet Architect's Union 55-63; Vice-

Pres. U.S.S.R. Acad. of Construction and Architecture 61-63; First Sec. of Board, U.S.S.R. Union of Architects 63-; Vice-Pres. Int. Union of Architects 67-72, Pres. 72-75; State Prize, U.S.S.R. 51, R.S.F.S.R. 69; Order of Lenin, Order of October Revolution, Order of the Red Banner of Labour, Order of the Badge of Honour, and various medals; People's Architect of U.S.S.R. 70-. Leisure interests: social activities, reading, drawing, music.

Union of Architects of the U.S.S.R., 3 ulitsa Shchuseva, Moscow K-1, U.S.S.R.
Telephone: 290-16-64, 290-28-64.

Orlov, Georgi Mikhailovich; Soviet politician; b. 1903; ed. Leningrad Timber Acad.
Former engineer, cellulose and paper industry; mem. C.P.S.U. 40-; Minister of Timber Industry of U.S.S.R. 44-57, of R.S.F.S.R. 57-58; Dep. Chair. *Gosplan*, R.S.F.S.R. 58-60, First Dep. Chair. 60-62; Chair. State Cttee. for Gosplan for Timber, Pulp and Paper Industries, U.S.S.R. 62-65; Deputy Chair. U.S.S.R. Council of Ministers State Cttee. for Material and Equipment Supply 65-; Candidate mem. Central Cttee. of C.P.S.U. 52-66; Order of Lenin, Order of Red Banner of Labour.
State Committee for Material and Equipment Supply of U.S.S.R. Council of Ministers, Moscow, U.S.S.R.

Orlova, Galina Sergeyevna; Soviet farmer and politician; b. 1917; ed. special secondary school.
Member, C.P.S.U. 41-; agronomist 36-59; Chair. Exec. Cttee., village Soviet 59-61; Deputy Chair., Exec. Cttee., District Soviet 61-62; Chair. "Road to Communism" Collective Farm 62-; Deputy to U.S.S.R. Supreme Soviet 70-, and mem. Presidium 70.
"Put k Kommunizmu" Collective Farm, Taishef District, Irkutsk Region, U.S.S.R.

Ormandy, Eugene, B.A., MUS.D.; American musician; b. Hungary 18 Nov. 1899; ed. Royal State Acad. of Music, Gymnasium and Univ., Budapest.
Student of the Royal State Acad. at the age of 5; toured Hungary and later Central Europe, as child prodigy; Head of Master Classes, State Conservatorium of Music, Budapest 19; went to U.S.A. 21, naturalized 27; substituted for Toscanini as Conductor of the Philadelphia Orchestra; Conductor, Minneapolis Symphony Orchestra 31-36; Music Dir. and Conductor, Philadelphia Orchestra 36-; Commdr. de la Légion d'Honneur (France); Knight, Order of Dannebrog (Denmark); Knight of the Order White Rose (Finland); Order of Merit, Juan Pablo Duarte (Dominican Republic); Commdr., Order of Dannebrog, Commdr., Order of the Lion of Finland; Commdr. of Merit (Italy); Hon. Cross for Arts and Sciences (Austria); Sibelius Medal, Presidential Medal of Freedom (U.S. Govt.) and many hon. doctorates and awards from various acads. and univs. in the U.S.A.
c/o Philadelphia Orchestra, 230 South 15th Street, Philadelphia, Pa. 19102, U.S.A.
Telephone: 215-KI5-3830.

Ormesson, Comte Jean d'; French author, journalist and international official; b. June 1925; s. of Marquis d'Ormesson; nephew of late Comte Wladimir d'Ormesson; m. Françoise Béghin 1962; one d.; ed. Ecole Normale Supérieure.
Deputy Sec. Gen. Int. Council for Philosophy and Humanistic studies (UNESCO) 50-71, Sec.-Gen. 71-; mem. French del. to various int. confs. 45-48; mem. staff of various govt. ministers 58-66; Deputy Editor *Diogenes* (int. journal) 52-, mem. Managing Cttee. 72-; mem. Council ORTF 60-62, Programme Cttee. 73; mem. Control Comm. of Cinema 62-69; mem. Editorial Cttee. Editions Gallimard 72-74; Editor in Chief *Le Figaro* 74-; mem. Acad. Française 73; Grand Prix du Roman (Acad. Française) for novel *La Gloire de l'Empire* 71.

Publs. *L'Amour est un plaisir* 56, *Du côté de chez Jean* 59, *Un amour pour rien* 60, *Au revoir et merci* 66, *Les Illusions de la mer* 68, *La Gloire de l'Empire* 71, *Au plaisir de Dieu* 74; numerous articles in *Le Figaro*, *Le Monde*, *France-Soir*, *Paris Match*, etc.
UNESCO, 1 rue Miollis, 75732 Paris Cedex 15; *Le Figaro*, 14 Rond-Point des Champs-Elysées, 75380 Paris Cedex 08; Home: 10 avenue du Parc-Saint-James, 92200 Neuilly-sur-Seine, France.
Telephone: 577-16-10; 256-80-00.

Ornano, Comte Michel d'; French politician and administrator; b. 12 July 1924; m. Anne de Contades 1960; one s. one d.; ed. Lycée Carnot, Univ. of Paris.
Mayor of Deauville 62-74; mem. Council on Foreign Trade 56-, mem. Directing Council 63-; mem. of Parl. 67-74; Sec. Comm. of Foreign Affairs to Nat. Assembly; Sec.-Gen. Independent Republicans 74; Minister of Industry and Research May 74-.
Ministère de l'Industrie et de la Recherche, 101 rue de Grenelle, Paris 7e, France.

O'Rourke, Dennis; American lawyer and business executive; b. 31 Oct. 1914, White Clay, Neb.; s. of Frank L. and Jerene Rebbeck O'Rourke; m. Ruth Rouss 1940; two s. four d.; ed. Nebraska State Teachers Coll. and George Washington Univ. Law School, Washington, D.C.
Attorney, Office of Gen. Counsel, U.S. Dept. of Agriculture, Washington 39, rising to Chief, Basic Commodity Div.; Gen. Counsel, Holly Sugar Corpn. 45-53, Vice-Pres. 53-63, Pres. and Chief Exec. Officer 63-67, Chair. and Chief Exec. Officer 67-69, Dir. 56-69; Trustee U.S. Beet Sugar Asscn. and Dir. The Sugar Asscn. 63-69; Adviser to U.S. dels. to Int. Sugar Confs. Mexico 59, Geneva 65; Dir. Nat. Chamber of Commerce 68-70; mem. Business and Industry Advisory Cttee. OECD 69-71; U.S. Counsel, Nat. Asscn. of Sugar Producers of Mexico 70-; Partner, Rouss and O'Rourke, Attorneys, Colo. Springs and Wash. 72-; Pres. ManExec Inc. (management consultancy org.) 72-; Pres. Colo. Springs Fine Arts Center 60-62, 69-71, 73, now Trustee. mem. of Exec. Cttee.; Dir. First Nat. Bank of Colo. Springs 63-; Vice-Chair., Dir. and mem. Exec. Cttee. Colo. Public Expenditure Council 73-.
Leisure interests: fly-fishing, performing and plastic arts.
Lawyers Building, P.O. Box 572, Colorado Springs, Colo. 80901; and 1629 K Street, N.W., Washington, D.C. 20006; Home: 8 Heather Drive, Colorado Springs, Colo. 80906, U.S.A.
Telephone: 303-473-7758 (Office); 303-634-0873 (Home).

Orowan, Egon, M.A., DR.ING.; American professor emeritus of mechanical engineering; b. 2 Aug. 1902, Budapest, Hungary; s. of Berthold Orowan and Josephine Ságvári; m. Jolan Schonfeld 1941; one d.; ed. Univ. of Vienna and Technical Univ. of Berlin.
Assistant Prof. Technical Univ. of Berlin 28-33; Research Assoc. Univ. of Birmingham, England 37-39; Research Assoc. Univ. of Cambridge (Cavendish Lab.) 39-45, Nuffield Research Fellow 45-47, Reader in Physics of Metals 47-50; Prof. of Mechanical Engineering, Mass. Inst. of Technology, U.S. 50-68, Prof. of Mechanical Engineering Emer. 68-; Fellow, Royal Soc. of London; mem. Nat. Acad. of Sciences, American Acad. of Arts and Sciences; Corresp. mem. Göttingen Acad. Sciences; Dr.Ing. h.c. (Tech. Univ. Berlin); Thomas Hawksley Gold Medal of Inst. of Mechanical Engineers, London 44, Eugene C. Bingham Medal of American Soc. of Rheology 59, Carl Friedrich Gauss Medal Braunschweiger Wissenschaftliche Gesellschaft 68, Vincent Bendix Gold Medal 71, Paul Bergsøe Medal, Danish Metal Soc. 73.
Leisure interest: getting acquainted with next field of professional interest.

Publs. Papers in scientific journals and chapters in books.
44 Payson Terrace, Belmont, Mass. 02178, U.S.A.
Telephone: 617-484-8334.

Orr, David Alexander, M.C., LL.B.; British business
executive; b. 10 May 1922, Dublin; s. of Canon A. W. F.
Orr and Grace Robinson; m. Phoebe R. Davis; three d.;
ed. High School and Trinity Coll., Dublin.
With Unilever 48-; Marketing Dir., Hindustan Lever,
Bombay 55; mem. Overseas Cttee., Unilever 60; Vice-
Pres. Lever Brothers Co., New York 63, Pres. 65; Dir.
Unilever Ltd. 67-, Vice-Chair. 70-74, Chair. 74-; Vice-
Chair. of Unilever NV 74; Co-Chair. Netherlands-
British Chamber of Commerce; Vice-Pres. Liverpool
School of Tropical Medicine; Trustee Leverhulme Trust;
Fellow of Royal Soc. for the Encouragement of Arts,
Manufactures and Commerce 74.
Leisure interests: books, travel and sport.
Oakhill, Enton Green, Godalming, Surrey, England.
Telephone: Godalming 7032 (Home).

Orrick, William Horsley, Jr.; American government
official; b. 10 Oct. 1915; ed. Hotchkiss School, Yale and
Univ. of California (Berkeley).
Admitted to Calif. Bar 41; Partner, Orrick, Herrington,
Rowley and Sutcliffe, San Francisco 41-61, 65-74; Asst.
Attorney Gen. Dept. of Justice 61-62; Dep. Under Sec.
for Admin., Dept. of State 62-63; Asst. Attorney Gen.
Dept. of Justice 63-65; Chair. U.S. Del. to OECD Cttee.
on Restrictive Business Practices 63; U.S. District
Judge, North District of Calif. Aug. 74-.
450 Golden Gate Avenue, San Francisco, Calif. 94102,
U.S.A.

Országh, László, PH.D., B.A.; Hungarian philologist;
b. 25 Oct. 1907, Szombathely; ed. Budapest and
Rollins Coll., Florida.
Lecturer in English, Budapest Univ. 42-47; Prof. of
English, Debrecen Univ. 47-50, 57-69; Visiting Prof. in
American Literature, Univ. of Budapest 69-72; Head
Lexicographical Dept., Linguistic Inst. of Hungarian
Acad. of Sciences, and Ed. of the Dictionary of the
Hungarian Language 50-62; Ed. Hungarian Studies in
English 63-73; Labour Order of Merit; Diamond Jubilee
Medal of London Inst. of Linguists.
Publs. *History of American Literary History Writing,
The Rise of the English Novel, Shakespeare, English-
Hungarian/Hungarian-English Dictionary, History of
American Literature, Introduction to American Studies,
American Essays—An Anthology.*
Pálffy György u. 12, 1055 Budapest V, Hungary.
Telephone: Budapest 324-257.

Ortiz de Rozas, Carlos; Argentine diplomatist; b. 26
April 1926, Buenos Aires; s. of Alfredo Ortiz de Rozas
and Susana del Valle; m. Carmen Sarobe 1952; ed. Nat.
Univ., Buenos Aires.
Entered foreign service 48; Chargé d'Affaires, Bulgaria
52-54; Sec. Greece 54-56; mem. Cabinet, Argentine
Ministry of Foreign Affairs 58-59; Counsellor, Argentine
Mission at UN 59-61; subsequently Dir.-Gen. Policy
Dept., Ministry of Foreign Affairs and later Minister
at embassies in U.A.R. and U.K.; Chief Rep. to Conf.
of Cttee. on Disarmament, Geneva 69-74; Perm. Rep.
to UN Oct. 70-; Pres. UN Security Council 71, 72;
Rep. Ad-Hoc Cttee. on World Disarmament Conf. 74;
Chair. Del. of Conf. on Law of the Sea 73, First (Political
and Security) Cttee. of the 29th General Assembly 74;
has held several teaching posts including Prof. of Public
Law and Int. Relations, Univ. del Salvador, Buenos
Aires (now mem. Board of Dirs.); decorations from Italy,
Chile, Brazil, Greece, Japan, Peru, Thailand, Egypt,
Austria, Nicaragua and the Republic of Korea.
Permanent Mission of Argentina to United Nations,
300 East 42nd Street, 18th Floor, New York, N.Y.
10017; Home: 1 Sutton Place South, New York,
N.Y. 10022, U.S.A.
Telephone: 212-832-2884.

Ortiz Mena, Antonio, LL.L.; Mexican lawyer, politician and banker; b. 1908, Parral, Chihuahua; ed.
Escuela Nacional de Jurisprudencia.
Leading legal positions, Dept. of Fed. District and
office of Attorney-Gen.; Dir.-Gen. of Professions at the
Secr. of Public Educ.; during Second World War, mem.
of Cttee. for Political Defence of the American Con-
tinent and Adviser to Mexican Del. at the Chapultepec
Conf.; on Editorial Comms. for the Fed. Law of Civil
Procedure, to reform certain Articles of the Constitu-
tion; Deputy Dir. Banco Hipotecario Urbano y de
Obras Públicas, S.A. 48-52; Dir.-Gen. Inst. of Social
Insurance 52-58; Vice-Pres. Admin. Council, Int. Asscn.
of Social Insurance 55-59; Alt. Del. to Conf. of Ministers
of Finance and Economy, Rio de Janeiro 54, Inter-
American Conf. of Insurance, Caracas 55; Pres. Inter-
American Perm. Cttee. of Social Insurance 55; Sec. for
the Treasury and Public Credit 58-70; Pres. Inter-
American Devt. Bank 71-; numerous honours from
Belgium, France, Germany, Yugoslavia, Brazil, Nether-
lands, Chile, Italy and U.A.R.
Inter-American Development Bank, 808 17th Street,
N.W., Washington, D.C. 20577, U.S.A.

Ortoli, François-Xavier; French economist; b. 16 Feb.
1925; ed. Hanoi Faculty of Law, and Ecole Nationale
d'Administration, Paris.
Inspector of Finances 48-51; Technical Adviser to the
Office of the Minister of Economic Affairs and Informa-
tion 51-53; Technical Adviser, Office of the Minister of
Finances 54; Asst. Dir. to the Sec. of State for Economic
Affairs and Sec.-Gen. Franco-Italian Cttee. of EEC
55; Head, Commercial Politics Service of Sec. of State
for Economic Affairs 57; Dir.-Gen. of the Internal
Market Div. of EEC 58; Sec.-Gen. Inter-Ministerial
Cttee. for Questions of European Econ. Co-operation,
Paris 61; Dir. of Cabinet to Prime Minister 62-66;
Commr.-Gen. of the Plan 66-67; Minister of Works 67-
68, of Educ. 68, of Finance 68-69, of Industrial and
Scientific Devt. 69-72; Pres. Comm. of European
Communities Jan. 72-; Légion d'Honneur, Médaille
Militaire, Croix de Guerre 45; Médaille de la Résistance,
etc.
Commission of the European Communities, 200 rue de
la Loi, 1040 Brussels, Belgium; and 18 rue de Bour-
gogne, 75007 Paris, France.

Ortona, Egidio; Italian diplomatist; b. 16 Sept. 1910;
ed. Univs. of Turin and Poitiers, London School of
Economics.
Entered diplomatic service 32; mem. Italian Del. to
World Economic Conf., London 33; Consul, Cairo and
Johannesburg; Sec. of Embassy, London, Chief of
Office of Minister of Foreign Affairs 43; mem. Economic
Mission to U.S.A. 44; Counsellor, later Minister, Italian
Embassy, Washington 45-58; Permanent Rep. of Italy
to UN with Ambassador's rank 58-61; Pres. UN Security
Council 59-60; Dir.-Gen. of Econ. Affairs, Italian
Ministry of Foreign Affairs 61-66; Sec.-Gen. Ministry
of Foreign Affairs 66-67; Amb. to U.S.A. 67-75; Pres.
XIV Assembly of ICAO 62, European Conf. on Satellite
Communication 63-64.
c/o Ministry of Foreign Affairs, Piazzale della Farnesina,
00194 Rome, Italy.

Ortutay, Gyula, PH.D.; Hungarian politician and
ethnographer; b. 24 March 1910, Szabadka (now
Subotica), Yugoslavia; s. of István Ortutay and Ilona
M. Borsodi; m. Zsuzsanna Kemény 1938; one s. two d.;
ed. Szeged Univ.
On staff of Hungarian Nat. Museum and Hungarian
Radio 35-; mem. of resistance movement and Hun-
garian Nat. Independence Front; after Liberation be-
came Pres. of Hungarian Radio and mem. of Parl.;
Prof. of Folklore, Budapest Univ. 46-; Minister of
Education 47-50; Rector of the Eötvös Loránd Univ.
57-63; Gen. Sec. People's Patriotic Front 57-64, Vice-

Pres. 64-; mem. Pres. Council Hungarian People's Republic; mem. Hungarian Acad.; Dir. Hungarian Acad. of Sciences Research Group for Ethnography 75; Hon. mem. Finnish Ugrian Soc.; Editor *Magyarság-tudomány, Ethnographia, Acta Ethnographica*; on Editorial Board of *Fabula*; Dr. h.c. (Helsinki); Foreign mem. Finnish Acad. of Sciences 69; Hon. mem. Acad. of Palermo 74; Pitré Prize, Palermo 61; Banner Order of the Republic (1st Class) 70; Baumgarten Prize; Herder Prize, Vienna 72; State Prize 75.

Leisure interests: book collecting, wild game shooting.

Publs. *Székely-népballadák, Nyiri és réthözi paraszt-mesék, Magyar népismeret, Parasztságunk élete, Fedics Mihály mesél. Kis magyar néprajz, Magyar népmüvészet, Ungarische Volksmärchen, Népköltészet ès társadalom, Hungarian Folklorer.*

Pasaréti ut. 83, H-1026 Budapest II, Hungary.

Telephone: 365-359.

Osborne, John James; British playwright, actor and producer; b. 12 Dec. 1929, London; m. 1st Pamela Lane 1951 (divorced 1957), 2nd Mary Ure 1957 (divorced 1963), 3rd Penelope Gilliatt (q.v.) 1963 (divorced 1968), 4th Jill Bennett 1968; one *d.*; ed. state schools and privately.

Journalist 47-48; tour *No Room at the Inn* 48-49; actor-manager, Ilfracombe 51; repertory Leicester, Camberwell, Kidderminster, Derby, Bridgewater, etc.; also appeared London.

Leisure interests: music hall, opera, riding.

Plays: *Look Back in Anger* 56, *The Entertainer* 57, *Epitaph for George Dillon* (with Anthony Creighton) 58, *The World of Paul Slickey* 59, *A Subject of Scandal and Concern* 60, *Luther* 61, *Plays for England* 62, *Inadmissible Evidence* 64 (film 69), *A Patriot for Me* 64, *A Bond Honoured* (trans. of Lope de Vega's *La Fianza Satisfecha*) 66, *The Hotel in Amsterdam* 68, *Time Present* 68, *The Right Prospectus* 70, *Very Like a Whale* 70, *West of Suez* 71, *A Sense of Detachment* 72, *Hedda Gabler* (adaptation) 72, *The Gift of Friendship* 72, *A Place Calling Itself Rome* 73, *The Picture of Dorian Gray* (dramatization of Oscar Wilde story) 73, *The End of Me Old Cigar* 75, *Watch It Come Down* 75; screenplay for *Tom Jones* 63; *Ms or Jill and Jack* (TV play) 74.

11 Hanover Street, London, W.1, England.

Osborne, Stanley de Jongh; American businessman; b. 27 March 1905, San José, Costa Rica; s. of Edmund and Lilly de Jongh; m. Elizabeth Ide 1929; one s. two *d.*; ed. Phillips Acad., Andover, and Harvard Univ.

Dir. Publicity Harvard Athletic Asscn. 27-28; with Old Colony Trust Co., Boston 29-30; Asst. to Pres. Atlantic Coast Fisheries Co. 29-30, Treas. 30-36, 39-43, Sec. 32-42, Vice-Pres. 36-43; Vice-Pres. Eastern Airlines Inc. 44-50; Financial Vice-Pres. Mathieson Chem. Corpn., Baltimore 50-54; Exec. Vice-Pres. Olin Mathieson Chemical Corpn. 54-57, Dir. 57-64, Pres. 57-63, Chair. of Board 63-64; Partner Lazard Frères & Co. 64-69, Limited Partner 70-; Gov. and Pres. The Soc. of N.Y. Hospital; Special Adviser to the Pres. of the U.S. 63-64; mem. President's Advisory Cttee. (Supersonic Aircraft) 64-69; Special Consultant to NASA; Dir. of several companies.

1 Rockefeller Plaza, New York, N.Y. 10020; Home: 1 East End Avenue, New York, N.Y. 10021, U.S.A.

Telephone: 212-489-6600.

Osborne, W. Irving, Jr., PH.B.; American business executive; b. 19 Nov. 1904; ed. Evanston High School, and Yale Coll.

D. H. Burnham & Co., Architects, Chicago 26-29; Cornell Wood Products Co. (later Cornell Paperboard Products Co.) 29-61, Pres. Cornell Paperboard Products Co. 33-57, Chair. of Board 57-59, Chair. Cornell Paperboard Products Co. Div. of St. Regis Paper Co. 59-61; Pres. Pullman Inc. 61-72, Chair. 66-70, Chair. 70-.

Pullman Inc., 200 S. Michigan Avenue, Chicago, Ill. 60604, U.S.A.

Oscarsson, Per Oscar Heinrich; Swedish actor; b. 28 Jan. 1927, Stockholm; s. of Ing. Einar Oscarsson and Theresia Küppers; m. Bärbel Krämer 1960; one s. two *d.*; ed. Royal Dramatic School.

Royal Dramatic Theatre 47-52, Gothenburg Town Theatre 53-59, TV-Theatre 66-67; now works mainly as free-lance film-actor; Best Actor Award, Cannes 66; New York Critics Award for Best Actor 68; Silver Hugo Best Actor Award, Chicago Int. Film Festival 69; appeared on stage in *Hamlet* 53, *Candida* 61, *Waiting for Godot* 63; films: *The Doll* 62, *My Sister My Love* 65, *Hunger* 65, *Ole Dole Doff* 67, *It's Up to You* 68, *Close to the Wind* 70, *A Last Valley, Salem Comes to Supper* 71.

Leisure interests: reading and riding.

Breviksvägen 194, 135 Ol Tyresö, Sweden.

Telephone: 770-71-32.

Oshima, Nagisa; Japanese film director; b. 1932, Kyoto; ed. Kyoto Univ.

With Shochiku Co. 54-59; formed own film company 59; has also directed television films.

Films: *Ai To Kibo No Machi* (A Town of Love and Hope) 59, *Seishun Zankoku Monogatari* (Cruel Story of Youth) 60, *Taiyo No Hakaba* (The Sun's Burial) 60, *Nihon No Yoru To Kiri* (Night and Fog in Japan) 60, *Shiiku* (The Catch) 61, *Amakusa Shiro Tokisada* (The Rebel) 62, *Etsuraku* (The Pleasures of the Flesh) 65, *Yunbogi No Nikki* (Yunbogi's Diary) 65, *Hakuchu No Torima* (Violence at Noon) 66, *Ninja Bugeicho* (Band of Ninja) 67, *Nihon Shunka-ko* (A Treatise on Japanese Bawdy Song) 67, *Muri Shinju Nihon No Natsu* (Japanese Summer: Double Suicide) 67, *Koshikei* (Death By Hanging) 68, *Kaettekita Yopparai* (Three Resurrected Drunkards) 68, *Shinjuku Dorobo Nikki* (Diary of a Shinjuku Thief) 68, *Shonen* (Boy) 69, *Tokyo Senso Sengo Hiwa* (He Died After the War, or The Man Who Left His Will on Film) 70, *Gishiki* (The Ceremony) 71, *Natsu No Imooto* (Dear Summer Sister) 72.

Shibata Organization Inc., 3-4-25 Roppongi, Minatoku, Tokyo; Home: 4-11-5 Matsugaoka, Kugenuma, Fujisawa-shi, Kanagawaken, Japan.

Telephone: (03) 586-6401.

Osman, Sir (Abdool) Raman (Mahomed), G.C.M.G., C.B.E.; Mauritian judge; b. 29 Aug. 1902; s. of the late Mahomed Osman.

Called to the Bar Middle Temple 25; Senior Puisne Judge, Supreme Court Mauritius 50-61; Acting Gov.-Gen. Mauritius Aug.-Oct. 70, Dec. 71-Feb. 72, Gov.-Gen. Dec. 72-; Hon. D.C.L. (Univ. of Mauritius) 75.

Leisure interest: horticulture.

Government House, Le Reduit; Le Goulet Terrace, Tombeau Bay, Mauritius.

Osman, Ahmed, LL.B., LL.M.; Moroccan politician; b. 3 Jan. 1930, Oujda; m. H.R.H. Princess Lalla Nezha (sister of King Hassan II, q.v.) 1965; one s.; ed. Coll. and postgraduate studies, France.

Head of the Legal Section, Royal Cabinet 56; Sec.-Gen.; Defence Ministry 59; Amb. to the Fed. Republic of Germany 61; Sec. of State for Industry and Mines 62, Amb. to the U.S.A. 67-70; Minister of Civil Service 70-71; Dir., Royal Cabinet 71-72; Prime Minister Nov. 72-.

Leisure interests: bridge, sports, reading.

Prime Minister's Office, Rabat, Morocco.

Telephone: 245 54- 338 04.

Osman, Osman Ahmed, B.SC.; Egyptian civil engineer; b. 1917, Ismailia; s. of Ahmed Mohamed Osman; m. Samia Ismail Wahbi 1947; four s. one *d.*; ed. Cairo Univ.

Chairman The Arab Contractors (Osman Ahmed Osman & Co) 52-, and of its assoc. companies, Saudi Enterprises, Kuwaiti Engineering Co., The Arab Contractors (Libya), The Libyan Co. for Contracting and Devt., The Osman Ahmed Osman & Co. (Abu Dhabi, Arabian Gulf); Minister of Reconstruction 73-, and of Housing

April 75-; Republic Medal (First Class), Russian Hero of Labour Medal.

Chief works undertaken include: (in Egypt) Aswan High Dam, Suez Canal deepening and widening, Port Said Shipyard, Cairo Int. Airport, Salhia reclamation project, High Dam Electric Power Transmission Lines, Giza Bridge and Ramsis Bridge over the Nile; (in Saudi Arabia) Dhahran Airport, Riyadh Mil. Coll., Dammam Mil. Barracks; (in Kuwait) Municipality Centre, Kuwait sewer system, secondary schools, Sabahia roads and drainage system; (in Libya) Benghazi drainage system, Stadium, and Highway; (in Iraq) Kirkuk Feeder Canal No. 2 and 3; (in Jordan) Khaled Ibn El-Walid Dam and Tunnels; (in Abu Dhabi) Zayed City, Ruler's Place; Kharj Mil. Base and City, Taif Mil. Base, numerous airports, hospitals and land reclamation.

Leisure interests: fishing, football.
Publ. *The High Dam* (lecture) 66.
Ministry of Reconstruction and Housing, Ismailia, Egypt.
Telephone: 49988.

Osmańczyk, Edmund Jan; Polish journalist and author; b. 10 Aug. 1913, Jagielno; *s.* of Ryszard Osmańczyk and Feliksa Szulc; *m.* Jolanta Klimowicz 1961; one *d.*; ed. in Warsaw, Berlin and France.

Editor of Press Centre, Union of Poles in Germany 32-39; War corresp. Radio Warsaw 39; Warsaw underground 39-44; War corresp. 45; Corresp. Potsdam Conf., Nuremberg Trials; Permanent Corresp., *Czytelnik* in Berlin 46-50; Corresp. Polish Radio Moscow 56, 59-60, Diplomatic Corresp. P.A.P. and Polish Radio Washington 57-58; Dep. to Seym 52-56, 57-61, 69-72, 72-; Diplomatic Correspondent for Latin America, Polish Press Agency and Polish Radio and T.V. 61-68; mem. Polish PEN Club and Polish Writers' Union; Chair. Polish Cttee. for Solidarity with Chilean People 73-; Prize of Minister of Culture and Art 45, State Prize 55, Prize of Minister of Nat. Defence 1st Class 72; Officer's Cross of Polonia Restituta; Order of Builders of People's Poland 72; Hon. Dr. rer. pol. (Univ. of Silesia).

Publs. *Walka jest zwycięska* (The Struggle is Victorious) (verse) 45, *Sprawy Polaków* (Polish Affairs) 46, *Dokumenty pruskie* (Prussian Documents) 47, *Niemcy 1945-1950* (Germany 1945-1950) 51, *Współczesna Ameryka* (The Contemporary America) 60, *Ciekawa Historia ONZ 1945-1965* (The Interesting History of UN 1945-1965) 65, *Był rok 1945 . . .* (It was a year 1945 . . .) 70, *Nasza Europa* (Our Europe) 71, *Polacy spod znaku Rodła* (Poles of the Rodło Sign) (with Helena Lehr) 72, *Encyklopedia spraw miedzynarodowych i ONZ* (Encyclopaedia of International Affairs and the UN) 74.
Plac Zamkowy 8/5, 00-277 Warsaw, Poland.
Telephone: 31-57-97.

Osogo, James Charles Nakhwanga, M.P.; Kenyan teacher and politician; b. 10 Nov. 1932, Bukani; ed. Port Victoria Primary School, St. Mary's High School, Yala, Railway Training School, Nairobi and Kagumo Teachers' Training Coll.

Teacher, Sigalame School 55, Withur School 56, Boarding School 57, Ndenga School 58, Port Victoria School 59; Headmaster Kibasanga School 60, Nangina School 61-62; Vice-Chair. Kenya Nat. Union of Teachers, Central Nyanza 58-62; mem. Kenya House of Representatives 63-; Asst. Minister, Ministry of Agriculture 63-66; Minister for Information and Broadcasting 66-69; Minister of Commerce and Industry 69-73, also acting Minister of Agriculture May 70; Minister for Local Govt. 73-74, of Health Nov. 74-; Chair. Kenya Youth Hostels Asscn. 64-70, Patron 70-; Elder, Order of the Golden Heart (Kenya), Order of the Star of Africa (Liberia), Grand Cordon of the Star of Ethiopia, Grand Cross of the Yugoslav Flag.
Ministry of Health, Nairobi; and P.O. Port Victoria, via Kisumu, Kenya.

Ossola, Rinaldo; Italian central banker; b. 8 Nov. 1913, Lecco; ed. Bocconi Univ., Milan, and London School of Econs.

Foreign Rep. Offices of Banca d'Italia in London, Lisbon, Paris; Head of Research Dept., Int. Econ., Banca d'Italia, later Econ. Adviser 67-69, Deputy Man. Dir. 69-75, Man. Dir. 75-; Chair. Group of Ten Deputies 75; Alt. mem. Interim Cttee. of IMF 74, Alt. Gov. for Italy 75-; Alt. mem. Board of Dirs., BIS 75-; Deputy mem. Cttee. of Cen. Bank Govs. of EEC 75-; Vice-Pres. Istituto Mobiliare Italiano 75-; Grand Officier, Légion d'Honneur (France).

Publs. *La Liberazione del movimento dei capitali nell' ambito del Marcato Comune* 59, *Export credits to underdeveloped countries on a multilateral basis* 59, *Il problema della liquidità internazionale, oggi* 64, *Nouvelles reserves monétaires internationales* 69, *The European Community at the Crossroads* 70, *Towards New Monetary Relationships* 71, *The Future of Sterling: a logical approach* 71, *Convertibility, Multilateralism and Freedom* 72, *Reflections on New Currency Solutions* 72, *Il ruolo delle banche centrali nel funzionamento e nella regolazione del mercato delle eurovalute* 72, *Emphasis on World Growth in Liquidity Overlooks Many Nations Reserve Problems* 75, *The Collective Management of Floating Rates* 75.
Banca d'Italia, Via Nazionale 91, 00184 Rome, Italy.

Osswald, Albert; German politician; b. 16 May 1919, Wieseck, nr. Giessen; *m.*

Town Councillor 49; Mayor of Giessen 54; Minister of Econs. and Transport, State Govt. of Hesse 63, subsequently Minister of Finance; Minister-President of Hesse 69-; mem. Social Democratic Party, mem. Exec. Cttee. 68-; Chair. Admin. Board, Hessische Landesbank-Girozentrale until 74.
Leisure interests: hiking, fishing, swimming, and games.
62 Wiesbaden, Abeggstrasse 39, Federal Republic of Germany.

Osterbrock, Donald E., PH.D.; American astronomer; b. 13 July 1924, Cincinnati, Ohio; *s.* of William C. Osterbrock and Elsie W. Osterbrock; *m.* Irene Hansen 1952; one *s.* two *d.*; ed. Univ. of Chicago.

Instructor Princeton Univ. 52-53; Instructor, then Asst. Prof. Calif. Inst. of Technology 53-58; Asst. Prof., then Assoc. Prof., Univ. of Wis. 58-61, Prof. of Astronomy 61-73, Chair. Dept. of Astronomy 67-68, 69-72; Letters Editor Astrophysical Journal 71-73; Prof. Univ. of Calif., Santa Cruz, and Dir. Lick Observatory 72-; Guggenheim Fellow 60-61, Nat. Science Senior Foundation Fellow 68-69; mem. Nat. Acad. of Sciences, American Acad. of Arts and Sciences, Wisconsin Acad. of Arts, Science and Letters.
Leisure interests: drama, hiking, conservation.
Publs. *Astrophysics of Gaseous Nebulae* 74, numerous scientific papers in *Astrophysical Journal* and *Publications of the Astronomical Society of the Pacific*, etc.
Lick Observatory, University of California, Santa Cruz, Calif. 95064, U.S.A.
Telephone: 408-429-2991.

Österling, Anders Johan, PH.D.; Swedish author and critic; b. 13 April 1884, Hälsingborg; *s.* of Hans and Ingrid Österling (née Eneberg); *m.* Greta Sjöberg 1916; three *d.*; ed. Lund Univ.

Librarian Lund Univ. 09-19; Literary Critic *Svenska Dagbladet* 19-35, and of *Stockholms-Tidningen* 36-66; mem. Swedish Acad. 19-; Pres. Swedish PEN Club 23-36; Perm. Sec. Swedish Acad. 41-64; Chair. Nobel Literature Prize Cttee. 21.
Publs. *Preludier* 04, *Arets visor* 07, *Bäckahästen* 09, *Facklor i stormen* 13, *Idyllernas bok* 17, *De sju strängarna* 22, *Jordens heder* 27, *Tonen från havet* 33, *Skånska utflykter* 34, *Dagens gärning I-III* 21-20-31, *Minnetsvägar* 67, etc.
Blockhusringen 39, 15125 Stockholm, Sweden.
Telephone: 08-616125.

Osterrieth, Frederick; Belgian merchant and company director; b. 1903.
Honorary Pres. of Antwerp Chamber of Commerce; Pres. Anglo-Belgian Ferry Boats; Vice-Pres. Belgian Railways; Dir. Banque de Bruxelles and Banque Belge d'Afrique; Pres. Office de Récupération Economique (O.R.E.); Del. to Int. Chamber of Commerce; fmr. Vice-Pres. Office Belge du Commerce Extérieur.
Markgravestraat 12, Antwerp, Belgium.

Osterwind, Heinz; German banker; b. 28 May 1905.
Deputy Chair. Supervisory Board Deutsche Bank AG; Chair. Supervisory Board Bergmann Kabelwerke AG, Didier-Werke AG, Süddeutsche Bremsen AG; Deputy Chair. Supervisory Board Otavi Minen- und Eisenbahn-Gesellschaft; mem. Supervisory Board Banco Comercial Transatlántico, Barcelona, Deutsche Telephonwerke und Kabelindustrie AG, Horten AG, Deutsche Bank AG, 5-17 Junghofstrasse, Frankfurt-am-Main; and Buchenrodestrasse 20, 6 Frankfurt (Main)-Niederrad, Federal Republic of Germany.

Osthoff, Hans-Werner, PROF.DR.JUR.; German business executive; b. 11 Feb. 1911, Berlin; s. of Leopold Osthoff and Elisabeth Benteler; m. Inge Schmidt 1940; one s. one d.; ed. bank apprenticeship in Berlin, Univ. of Berlin.
Member of Exec. Board Wirtschaftsvereinigung Eisen und Stahlindustrie Düsseldorf 58; mem. Scientific Council of the Fed. Gov. 70; Pres. Saarländische Wirtschaftsvereinigung Eisen und Stahl 71; Pres. Verband der Eisen und Metallindustrie des Saarlandes 72; Chair. Exec. Cttee. Stahlwerke Röchling-Burbach GmbH 72-74; Hon. Prof. Faculty of Law and Econs. Univ. of the Saar; Grand Cross of the Fed. Republic of Germany.
662 Völklingen, Am Kirschenwälchen 38, Federal Republic of Germany.
Telephone: 06898/102180.

Ostrower, Fayga; Brazilian (b. Polish) painter and engraver; b. 14 Sept. 1920, Łódź, Poland; m. Heinz Ostrower 1941; one s. one d.; ed. Fundação Getúlio Vargas, Rio de Janeiro.
Lecturer in Theory of Composition and Analysis, Museum of Modern Art, Rio de Janeiro 54-70, Fed. Univ. of Minas Gerais 66-70; John Hay Whitney Lecturer, Spelman Coll., Atlanta 64; mem. Jury for Bienal of São Paulo and Nat. Show of Fine Arts, Rio de Janeiro; Vice-Pres. Brazilian Cttee., Int. Asscn. of Plastic Arts; numerous one-man exhbns. and works in collections in the Americas and Europe; Hon. mem. Accademia delle Arti del Disegno, Florence; numerous prizes including awards at São Paulo Bienal in 55, 57, 61, 63, Venice Biennale 58, 62, Venezuela Biennale 67, Rio de Janeiro City Award 69, II Biennale Internazionale della Grafica, Florence 70; Grand Int. Prize Venice; Chevalier Order of Rio Branco 72.
Leisure interest: art.
Rua do Russell 426, Apto. 302, Rio de Janeiro, Brazil.
Telephone: 225-1709.

Ostrowski, Dr. Włodzimierz; Polish biochemist; b. 21 Oct. 1925, Sosnowiec; ed. Faculty of Medicine, Jagiellonian Univ. and Medical Acad., Cracow.
Doctor 59-61, Docent 61-69, Assoc. Prof. 69-; Corresp. mem. Polish Acad. of Scs (PAN) 73-; Dean, Faculty of Medicine, Medical Acad., Cracow 69-72, Head, Dept. of Physiological Chem. 63-72, Dir. Inst. of Medical Biochemistry 72-; mem. Editorial Staff *Folia Biologica* and *Przegląd Lekarski* (Medical Review); mem. Polish Biochemical Soc., Polish Laboratory Diagnostics Soc., A.A.A.S.; State Prize, 3rd Class 57, 2nd Class 58, Gold Cross of Merit 69 and others.
Publs. numerous articles in Polish and foreign languages.
Ul. Jaracza 12 m. 6, 31-143 Cracow, Poland.

Ota, Masami; Japanese diplomatist; b. 28 Nov. 1920, Taipei; s. of Hideho Ota and Toyo Uchida; m. Kayoko Yamashita 1950; two s.; ed. Hitotsubashi Univ.
Entered Japanese Foreign Service 42, Second, afterwards First Sec. Embassy, U.S.A. 54; First Sec. Embassy, India 56; Chief, Int. Affairs Div. of Science and Technology Agency, Tokyo 58; Chief, Social Affairs Div. Ministry of Foreign Affairs 60; Japanese Permanent Del. to UNESCO, Paris 63; Counsellor, Embassy, Iran 66; Consul-Gen. Hamburg Consulate, Fed. Repub. of Germany; Councillor for Environmental Affairs with rank of Amb., Ministry of Foreign Affairs 71-; Vice-Chair. Environmental Cttee., OECD 71, Chair. 73; Del. to UN Conf. on Human Environment, Stockholm 72.
Leisure interests: collecting books, classical music.
4-1-14-405, Minami-Azabu, Minato-ku, Tokyo, Japan.
Telephone: (03)-580-3311 (Office); (03)-442-6982 (Home).

Otaiba, Mana Saeed al-, M.SC.; Abu Dhabi economist; b. 15 May 1946; m. five c.; ed. Univ. of Baghdad.
Chairman of Board, Abu Dhabi Nat. Oil Co.; mem. Abu Dhabi Planning Board; Pres. Abu Dhabi Dept. of Petroleum; Chair. of Board, Abu Dhabi Gas Liquefaction Co.; Minister of Petroleum and Mineral Resources; mem. Board six oil cos. in Abu Dhabi; has travelled on State visits, etc. throughout Arab countries, Western Europe, U.S.A., Canada.
Leisure interests: poetry, hunting, fishing.
Publs. *The Abu Dhabi Planning Board, The Economy of Abu Dhabi, Organization of the Petroleum Exporting Countries, OPEC and the Petroleum Industry.*
Ministry of Petroleum and Mineral Resources, P.O. Box 59, Abu Dhabi, United Arab Emirates.
Telephone: 62810, 61051.

Otani, Sachio, B.ARCH.; Japanese architect; b. 20 Feb. 1924, Tokyo; s. of Morisuke and Yuko Otani; m. Yoshiko Otani; one c.; ed. Univ. of Tokyo.
Architectural designer under Dr. Kenzo Tange 46-60; Lecturer in Architecture, Univ. of Tokyo 55-64; Assoc. Prof. of Urban Engineering, Univ. of Tokyo 64-; works include Kojimachi area (of Tokyo) redevelopment plan 60-64, Tokyo children's cultural centre 61-63 and Kyoto Int. Conf. Hall 63-66.
Department of Urban Engineering, Faculty of Engineering, University of Tokyo, 1-3-7 Hongo, Bunkyo-ku, Tokyo; Home: 15-22-3 Shoan, Suginami-ku, Tokyo, Japan.
Telephone: 333-6708.

Otero, Alejandro; Venezuelan artist; b. 7 March 1921; ed. School of Fine Arts, Caracas.
Early portraits in expressionist impasto, then landscapes in yellow, ochre and blue until shared a studio with Pascual Navarro in Paris 45-48; transition from figurative to abstract art through still lifes 45-48; participated in exhbn. *Les Mains Eblouies*, Galerie Maeght 47; returned to Venezuela and presented one-man exhbns. at Museum of Fine Arts, Caracas 49; Editor *Los Disidentes* after return to Paris 50; turned to optical art and collages 51; executed monumental comms. for Univ. City of Caracas 52-55; series of abstract paintings *Colour-Rhythms* 55-60; returned to Paris 60-64; Vice-Pres. Inst. of Culture and Fine Arts, Caracas 64-; collages from newspaper cuttings, in gay colours 64-; Retrospective Exhbn. *Signals*, London 66; other one-man exhbns. in Washington, D.C., Caracas, Venezuela, and Klagenfurt, Austria; numerous awards and honours.
Institute of Culture and Fine Arts, Caracas, Venezuela.

Otero de Navascués, Marqués de Hermosilla, **José María;** Spanish scientist; b. 16 March 1907, Madrid; s. of Santiago and María Otero de Navascués; m. María

Teresa Domínguez 1939; seven s. six d.; ed. San Fernando Navy Ordnance School, Madrid Univ., Eidgenössische Technische Hochschule, Zürich, Technische Hochschule, Berlin.
Head, Navy Optical Laboratory 34-36, Optics Div., Nat. Physical Laboratory 40-46; Assoc. Dir., Naval Research Laboratory 42-47, Dir. 45-55; Prof. Navy Ordnance Graduate School 47-55; Pres. Real Sociedad Española Física y Química 54-58; Vice-Pres. Spanish UNESCO Cttee. 53-57, Int. Comm. of Optics 53-59; Vice-Pres. Nuclear Energy Bd. 51-58; Pres. and Chair., Spanish Nuclear Energy Comm. 58-; Dir. Inst. of Optics "Daza de Valdés" 46-67, Chair. Tech. Admin. Board 67-; Perm. Sec. Real Academia de Ciencias 68-; mem. Board of Govs. Int. Atomic Energy Agency 69, Chair. 15th Gen. Conference 71; mem. Exec. Cttee. Spanish Nat. Council for Scientific Research 47-; Chair. Spanish Nat. Council of Physics 50; Pres. European Nuclear Energy Agency (OECD) 61; Exec. Vice-Pres. European Atomic Energy Soc. 60-62, Pres. 62-64; Vice-Pres. Bureau Int. des Poids et Mesures 64-68, Pres. 68; Fellow, Spanish Royal Acad. of Sciences 45-; mem. of Board Centre Européen de Recherches Nucléaires; many Spanish and foreign awards.
Leisure interests: history, golf.
Publs. Research papers on Physics (optics) and Nuclear Energy.
Alfonso XII 32, Madrid, Spain.
Telephone: 239-04-70.

Othman as-Said, Mohamed Ben; Libyan politician; b. Oct. 1922; ed. Libyan religious and Arabic schools.
Teacher 42-43; in Liberation Movement; Head of Fezzan Del. in Legislative Assembly 50-51; Rep. for Fezzan, U.N. Council for Libya 51; Minister of Health, Fed. Govt. 51-58, of Econ. Affairs Feb.-Oct. 60; Prime Minister Oct. 60-63; Deputy 64; private business 64-; Order of Independence (First Class).
Geraba Street 6, Tripoli, Libya.

Othman bin Wok, Enche; Singapore politician; b. 8 Oct. 1924. Singapore; m. Che Dah Mohd Noor 1949; one s. three d.; ed. Telok Saga Malay School, Raffles Inst. and London School of Journalism.
Worked on Utusan Melayu as reporter and Deputy Editor 46-63; mem. People's Action Party 54-; mem. Parl. for Pasir Panjang Constituency 63-; Minister for Social Affairs 63-65; Minister for Culture and Social Affairs 65-68; Minister for Social Affairs 68-; Capt. People's Defence Force.
Ministry for Social Affairs, Singapore.

Othmer, Donald Frederick, B.SC., M.S., PH.D.; American chemical engineer and educator; b. 11 May 1904, Omaha, Neb.; s. of Frederick George and Fredericka Darling (Snyder) Othmer; m. Mildred Jane Topp 1950; ed. Armour Inst., Chicago, and Univs. of Nebraska and Michigan.
Development Engineer Eastman Kodak Co. and Tennessee Eastman Corpn. 27-32; Prof. Polytechnic Inst. of Brooklyn 32, Head Dept. of Chemical Engineering 37-61, Sec. Graduate Faculty 48-58, Distinguished Prof. 61; consulting chemical engineer to numerous companies and govt. depts. in U.S. and abroad incl. U.S. Army, Chemical and Ordnance Corps, and Scientific Advisory Board, U.S. Navy, Special Devices Div., Depts. of State and Interior, Office of Saline Water, UN, World Health Org., U.S. Dept. of Health, Educ. and Welfare, Nat. Materials Advisory Board, National Research Council, Delaware River Basin Comm., leading financial institutions, etc.; Fellow, American Asscn. for Advancement of Science, New York Acad. of Sciences, Chair. Engineering Section 72-73, American Soc. Mechanical Eng., American Inst. of Chemists, American Inst. of Chemical Engineers (Dir. 56-59); mem. American Chemical Soc., Japan Soc. of Chemical Engineers, Nat. Panel of Arbitrators, Ameri-

can Arbitration Asscn., Soc. de Chimie Industrielle (Pres. American Section 73-74), Soc. Chemical Industry, American Soc. of Eng. Educ., Newcomen Soc., etc.; Dir. Engineers Joint Council 56-59, Chemurgic Council; inventor and licensor (over 110 U.S. and many foreign patents) of methods, processes and equipment in manufacture of chemicals, solvents, synthetic fibres, acetylene, wall-board, petroleum refining, fermentation, desalination of seawater, pollution, pipeline heating, solvents, plastics, refrigeration, wood utilization, acetic acid, evaporation, heat transfer, petrochemicals, pigments, engineering equipment, salt, pharmaceuticals, distillation, sugar refining, synthetic rubber, pulping liquor recovery, extractive metallurgy of aluminium, titanium, zinc, etc.; regent and trustee of various hospitals and univs.; Lecturer in Argentina 69, Canada 50, 71, Czechoslovakia 62, 69, France 68, Germany, Hon. Del. Achema, Frankfurt 58, 61, 64, 67, 70, 73, Greece 62, India 52, 71, Japan 55, Romania 70, Kuwait 71, Poland 64, 67, 69, 73, Puerto Rico 65, Switzerland 48, Turkey 69, Yugoslavia 63, 70, U.S. Army War Coll. 64, ASTM 66, TAPPI 66, N.Y. Acad. Sciences 71; Hon. Prof. Concepción Univ. 51; Hon. Dr. Eng. Univ. of Nebraska 62; Hon. mem. Deutsche Gesellschaft für Chemisches Apparatewesen, Barber-Coleman Award 58, Tyler Award 58, Honour Scroll AIC 70; Hon. life mem. N.Y. Acad. of Sciences 74; 1st Consultants Award, Asscn. of Chemists and Chemical Engineers 75.
Leisure interests: forestry, collecting old maps and books.
Publs. Over 320 articles in technical press; Editor Fluidization, co-Editor Kirk-Othmer Encyclopaedia of Chemical Technology (17 vols. 47-60; Vols. 1-24, 2nd edn. 63-70), Co-author Fluidization and Fluid Particle Systems 60, Adviser, Perry's Chemical Engineer's Handbook 3rd edn., Technical Editor UN Report, Technology of Water Desalination 64, Editorial Board Desalination.
333 Jay Street, Brooklyn, New York 11201; 140 Columbia Heights, Brooklyn, N.Y. 11201, U.S.A.
Telephone: MA5-1845 and 643-5120.

O'Toole, Peter Seamus; Irish actor; b. 2 Aug. 1932, Connemara, Co. Galway; m. Siân Phillips; two d.; ed. Royal Acad. Dramatic Art.
Office boy, later reporter for Yorkshire Evening News; Nat. Service as signalman, Royal Navy; studied at Royal Acad. of Dramatic Art; joined Bristol Old Vic Theatre Co., playing 73 parts 55-58; West End debut in musical play Oh, my Papa 57; toured England in play The Holiday; appeared in The Long, the Short and the Tall 59; Stratford season 60 playing Shylock, Petruchio, and Thersites; filmed Lawrence of Arabia 60; stage appearances in Pictures in the Hallway 62, Baal 63, Ride a Cock Horse, Waiting for Godot 71; Bristol Old Vic Theatre Season 73; inaugurated Britain's Nat. Theatre Co.
Films include: Kidnapped 59, The Day they Robbed the Bank of England 59, Lawrence of Arabia 60, Becket 63, Lord Jim 64, The Bible 66, What's New Pussycat? 65, How to Steal a Million 66, Night of the Generals 67, Great Catherine 67, The Lion in Winter 68, Goodbye Mr. Chips 69, Brotherly Love 70, Country Dance 70, Murphy's War 71, Under Milk Wood 72, The Ruling Class 72, Man of La Mancha 72, Rosebud 74, Man Friday 75.
c/o Keep Films, 5 Eaton Place, London, S.W.1, England.

Ottaviani, H.E. Cardinal Alfredo, D.IUR.UTR., TH.D., PH.D.; Vatican ecclesiastic; b. 29 Oct. 1890; ed. Pontifical Roman Seminary and Pontifical Inst. of Canon and Civil Law, Rome.
Ordained priest 16; created Cardinal by Pope Pius XII 53; Pro-Sec. Sacred Congregation of the Holy Office 53-59, Sec. 59-68, Bishop 62; mem. Sacred Congregation de Propaganda Fide, of the Consistory and of Extraordinary Ecclesiastical Affairs; mem. Supreme Tribunal

of the Apostolic Segnatura, Pontifical Comm. for the Authentic interpretation of the Code of Canon Law; Pres. Pontifical Comm. "de Doctrina fidei et morum" 62.
Publs. *Compendium Iuris Publici Ecclesiastici* (4th edn.) 56, *Institutiones Iuris Publici Ecclesiastici* (6th edn.) 58, *Il Baluardo*.
Piazza del Santo Uffizio 11, 00193 Rome, Italy.
Telephone: 6982.

Ottina, John R., M.A., PH.D.; American education executive; b. 5 Nov. 1931, Los Angeles; s. of Louis and Mary Maga Ottina; three s.; ed. Univ. of California, Univ. of Southern California.
Teacher, Secondary School, Los Angeles 54-56; Teacher, Adult Evening Programme, Los Angeles 56-58; mathematical analysis, Lockheed Aircraft, Los Angeles 56-58; Vice-Pres. System Devt. Corpn., Santa Monica 58-69; Exec. Vice-Pres., Computer Systems Div., King Resources Co., Chair. and Pres. Worldwide Information Systems (subsidiary co.), Los Angeles 69-70; Deputy Commr. for Devt. U.S. Office of Educ. 70-71, Deputy Commr. for Planning Evaluation and Management 71-72; Acting U.S. Commr. of Educ. 72-73; U.S. Commr. of Educ. 73-74; Asst. Sec. for Admin. and Management, Dept. of Health, Educ. and Welfare 74-.
Publs. numerous papers on planning and development and on computer management.
Department of Health, Education and Welfare, 330 Independence Avenue, S.W., Washington, D.C. 20201, U.S.A.

Otto, Frei P(aul), DR.ING.; German architect; b. 31 May 1925, Siegmar; s. of Paul and Eleonore Otto; m. 1952; one s. four d.; ed. Technische Universität, Berlin.
Director, Institut für Leichte Flächentragwerke, Univ. of Stuttgart 64-; Visiting Prof. Washington Univ., St. Louis, Yale Univ., Univ. of Calif. (Berkeley), M.I.T., and Harvard Univ. 58-62; mem. Akad. der Künste, Berlin; Hon. Fellow American Inst. of Architects; Hon. Dr. Arts and Arch. Washington Univ. of St. Louis; Berlin Art Prize 67, Prix Perret (Union Int. des Architectes) 67, Bonatzpreis, Stuttgart 71, Kölner Kunstpreis 71, Thomas Jefferson Medal and Prize, Univ. of Va. 74.
Major works: German Pavilion Expo, Montreal 67, Conference Centre, Mecca, Saudi Arabia 67, roof structure of Olympic Sports Stadium, Munich 72, Multihalle Herzogenried, Mannheim 75.
Leisure interest: gardening.
Publs. *Das hängende Dach* 54, *Zugbeanspruchte Konstruktionen*, Vol. 1 62, Vol. 2 65, Editor of series *IL1-15* on lightweight structures.
725 Leonberg 7 Warmbronn, Berghalde 19, Federal Republic of Germany.
Telephone: 0711-7843599 (Univ. of Stuttgart); 07152-41084 (Home).

Ottone, Piero; Italian journalist; b. 3 Aug. 1924, Genoa; s. of Giovanni Battista and Vittoria Ottone; m. Hanne Ottone 1958; one s. one d.; ed. Univ. of Turin.
Reporter, *Corriere Ligure* May-July 45; Reporter, *Gazzetta del Popolo* 45-48, London correspondent 48-50, Bonn correspondent 50-53; London and Moscow correspondent, *Corriere della Sera* 53-61, Special Correspondent in Italy 62, Editor-in-Chief March 72-; Editor *Secolo XIX* Dec. 68-; Palazzi Prize for Journalism 73.
Publs. *Gli industriali si confessano* 65, *Fanfani* 66, *La nuova Russia* 67, *De Gasperi* 68, *Potere economico* 68.
c/o Corriere della Sera, Via Solferino 28, Milan 20121, Italy.

Ötüken, Adnan; Turkish librarian; b. 1911, Mamastin; m. Sabiha Ötüken 1935; ed. Lycée and Univ. of Istanbul, and Staatsbibliothek, Berlin.
Asst. Turkish Language and Literature Dept., Univ. of

Istanbul 40; Dir. of Publications, Acting Asst. Dir.-Gen. of Higher Education, and Asst. Dir.-Gen. of Fine Arts, Ministry of Education 52-54; Lecturer in Library Science, Univ. of Ankara; mem. Executive Cttee. Turkish Nat. Comm. of UNESCO, and Executive Board Turkish Librarians Asscn.; Dir. Turkish Nat. Library 60-65; Under-Sec. for Cultural Affairs, Ministry of Educ. 65-67; Lecturer of Turkish Language and Lit., Lycée Teachers' Training Coll., Ankara, 67-; Gen. Sec. Turkish-Iraqi Standing Cttee. of Cultural Agreement; fmr. Turkish Cultural Attaché in Germany.
Publs. *Bibliyotek bilgisi ve bibliyografi* (Library Science and Bibliography) 40, *Istanbul Üniversitesi Yayimlari Bibliyografyasi* (Bibliography of the Publications of the University of Istanbul) 41, *Seçme eserler bibliyografyasi*. 1. cilt (Selected Bibliography, Vol. 1) 46, *Milli Kütüphane kurulurken* (Establishing the National Library) 46, *Istanbul Üniversitesi Yayimlari Bibliyografyasi, 1933-45* (Bibliography of the Publications of the University of Istanbul, 1933-45, with Acaroğlu) 47, *Dünya edebiyatından tercümeler. Klâsikler Bibliyografyasi. 1940-48* (Bibliography of classical and modern works translated and published by Turkish Ministry of Education, 1940-48) 47, 2nd edn. *1940-50* 52, *Milli Kütüphane Nasil Kuruldu* (How the Turkish National Library was founded) 55, *Türk Dilimim Başına Gelenler* 68, *Trt Igin Türkge Dersleri* 68, *Iki Yılda 600 den Fazla Yazı* 68, *Yeniden 645 Yazı* 69.
Lycée Teachers' Training College, Ankara; (Home) Memeviş sok 80/A, Kavaklıdere, Ankara, Turkey.
Telephone: 126234.

Otunga, H.E. Cardinal Maurice; Kenyan ecclesiastic; b. Jan. 1923, Chebukwa.
Ordained priest 50; consecrated titular Bishop of Tacape 57; Bishop of Kissii 60; titular Archbishop of Bomarzo 69; Archbishop of Nairobi 71-; created Cardinal by Pope Paul VI 73; Dir. Castrense for Kenya.
Archbishop's House, P.O. Box 14231, Nairobi, Kenya.

Ouazzani, Thami; Moroccan diplomatist; b. 27 Dec. 1927, Fez; s. of Driss Ouazzani and Amina Guessous; m. Zahra Ouazzani 1955; two s. two d.; ed. College Moulay Idriss, Fez, Faculté de Droit, Paris and the Sorbonne.
Called to the Bar, Casablanca 51; Minister of Industry and Mines 55-56; mem. Conseil de l'Ordre des Avocats de Casablanca 59; Amb. to Yugoslavia and Greece 61; Sec. Gen. Charte de Casablanca 62; Minister of Labour and Social Affairs 63-64, of Public Works and Admin. Reform 65; Amb. to Algeria 65-67; Minister of Tourism 68; Minister in Royal Cabinet 68-69; Amb. to Tunisia 69-71, to U.K. 71-73; Grand Cordon Alaouite and decorations from Yugoslavia and Tunisia.
Leisure interests: skiing, swimming, basketball.
c/o Ministry of Foreign Affairs, Rabat, Morocco.

Ouedraogo, Gerard Kango; Upper Voltan politician; b. 19 Sept. 1925, Ouahigouya.
Representative to French West African Fed. 52; Deputy to French Nat. Assembly 56-59; co-founder Mouvement Démocratique Voltaïque; mem. Parl. 57-65; Amb. to U.K. 61-66; Adviser, Ministry of Foreign Affairs; Pres. Union Démocratique Voltaïque 70; Prime Minister 71-74.
c/o Office of the Prime Minister, Ouagadougou, Upper Volta.

Ouellet, Hon. André, P.C., B.A., LL.L.; Canadian lawyer and politician; b. 6 April 1939, St. Pascal, Quebec; s. of Dr. Albert Ouellet and Rita Turgeon; m. Edith Pagé 1965; one s. two d.; ed. Pensionnat St. Louis de Gonzague, Quebec Seminary, Ottawa and Sherbrooke Univs.
Member of Parl. for Papineau 67-; Parl. Sec. to Minister of Nat. Health and Welfare; Postmaster Gen. 72-74;

Minister of Consumer and Corporate Affairs Aug. 74-; Liberal.
2285 Virginia Drive, Ottawa, Ont., Canada.

Ouimet, J. Alphonse, c.c., b.a., b.eng.; Canadian communications executive and engineer; b. 12 June 1908, Montreal; s. of J. Alphonse Ouimet and Marie Blanche Geoffrion; m. Jeanne Prévost 1935; one d.; ed. St. Mary's Coll., Montreal and McGill Univ.
Research Engineer Canadian Television Ltd. 32-33; Research Engineer and Dir. Canadian Electronics Co. 33-34; Research Engineer Canadian Broadcasting Corpn. (C.B.C.), Ottawa 35-36, Operations Engineer, Montreal 37-39, Gen. Supervisor of Engineering 39-40, Asst. and later Chief Engineer 41-51, Asst. Gen. Man. 51-52, Gen. Man. 53-58, Pres. 58-68; Chair. Telesat Canada 69-; Fellow Inst. of Radio Engineers; mem. Engineering Inst. of Canada, Int. Television Cttee.; Companion of the Order of Canada 69, and several other awards; Hon. Degrees from Univs. of Montreal, Acadia, Saskatchewan, McGill, Ottawa and Sherbrooke, Royal Mil. Coll. of Canada.
227 Lakeview Avenue, Pointe Claire 720, P.Q., Canada.
Telephone: 697-1922.

Ouko, Robert John; Kenyan administrator; b. 31 March 1932, Kisumu; s. of Erasto and Susanah Seda; m. Christabel Akumu Odolla 1965; one s. four d.; ed. Ogada School, Kisumu, Nyangori School, Kakamega, Siriba Coll., Haile Sellassie I and Makerere Univs.
Teacher 52-55; worked in Kisii District, Ministry of African Affairs 55-58; Asst. Sec. Foreign Affairs Dept., Office of the Prime Minister 62-63, Senior Asst. Sec. 63; Perm. Sec., Ministry of Foreign Affairs 63-64, Ministry of Works 65-69; East African Minister for Finance and Admin. 69-70, for Common Market and Econ. Affairs Nov. 70-; Pres. African Asscn. for Public Admin. and Management 71-74; mem. East African Legislative Assembly; Fellow, Kenya Inst. of Management; Hon. LL.D. (Pacific Lutheran Univ.) 71.
Leisure interests: reading, music, hunting.
Publs. essays on administration in professional journals; co-author of university textbook on management.
P.O. Box 48935, Nairobi, Kenya.
Telephone: Nairobi 27411.

Ourisson, Guy, dr.sc., ph.d.; French chemist; b. 26 March 1926, Boulogne-sur-Seine; s. of Jacques Ourisson and Colette (née de Bosredon); m. 1st Paula Baylis 1950 (deceased 1958), 2nd Nicole Heiligenstein 1959; one s. two d.; ed. Ecole Normale Supérieure, Paris, Harvard Univ.
Maître de Conférences, Univ. Louis Pasteur, Strasbourg 55-58, Prof. of Chem. 58-, Pres. of Univ. Louis Pasteur 71-75; Pres. of many scientific cttees. in France; Chair. Publications Cttee., IUPAC 73-, Sec.-Gen. 75-; Regional Editor Tetrahedron, Tetrahedron Letters 65-; Scientific Editor Bulletin de la Soc. Chimique de France 75-; Chevalier, Légion d'Honneur; Officier, Ordre Nat. du Mérite; Officier des Palmes Académiques; mem. Acad. Leopoldina (Halle), Danish Acad. of Sciences; awards from Chemical Socs. of France, Fed. Repub. of Germany, Belgium, U.K., U.S.A.; Hon. mem. Chemical Socs. of Belgium, U.K.
Leisure interests: nature, manual work, bonsai, reading, people.
Publs. about 250 publications on chemistry and on ethics of science; several books on chemistry of natural products.
Institut de Chimie, 1 rue Blaise Pascal, F67008 Strasbourg; Home: 2 rue Calmette, Mundolsheim, F 67450, France.
Telephone: (88) 61-48-02 (Work); (88) 20-01-26 (Home).

Ousmane, Sembene; Senegalese writer and film-maker; b. 1 Jan. 1923, Ziguinchor.
Plumber, bricklayer, apprentice mechanic; served in

Europe in Second World War; docker in Marseille; studied film production in U.S.S.R.; Founder Ed. first Wolof language monthly, Kaddu; first prize for novelists at World Festival of Negro Arts, Dakar 66; numerous int. awards.
Films: Borom Sarret 63, Niaye 64, La Noire de . . . 66, Mandabi 68, Taaw 71, Emitai 71, Xala 74, Ceddo 76.
Publs. novels: Le Docker Noir 56, O Pays mon Beau Peuple 57, Les Bouts de Bois de Dieu 60, Voltaïque 62, L'Harmattan 64, Vehi-Ciosane suivi du Mandat 66, Xala 74, Fot Ndioy Diop 76.
P.O. Box 8087 YOFF, Dakar, Senegal.

Outze, Børge; Danish editor; b. 18 March 1912, Odense; s. of late Oluf Outze and Cecilie Larsen; m. Ruth Lillevang 1935; two d.
Journalist in Odense 28-36, for Nationaltidende, Copenhagen 36-43; chief of Danish underground movement News Service; Editor Information (daily newspaper) 45-; awarded Croix de Guerre with Silver Star, for services in underground movement; mem. Danish PEN Club.
Publs. Denmark during the German Occupation 45, Danmarks Frihedskamp (with Ebbe Munck) 46, Spidser (with Erik Seidenfaden) 48, Danmark under den anden Verdenskrig I-IV 62-67, Sådan begyndte det 70, and translations.
Store Kongensgade 40, Copenhagen K; and Amager Strandvej 164, 2300 Copenhagen, Denmark.
Telephone: 14-14-26 (Office).

Ovando Candía, Gen. Alfredo; Bolivian army officer and politician; b. 6 April 1918, Cobija; s. of Máximo Ovando and Mercedes Candía; m. Elsa Omiste; ed. Colegio Militar del Ejército and Escuela Superior de Guerra.
Commissioned 36, Brigade Gen. 59-62, Div. Gen. 62-64, Army General 64-; fmr. Battalion Commdr. Escuela Superior de Guerra; Chief of Studies, Escuela de Estado Mayor; Military Attaché, Uruguay and Paraguay; Dir.-Gen. Studies and Planning of the Army; Dir. of Planning, Ministry of Defence; Co-Pres. of Bolivia 65-66; Chief of Staff, Commdr. of the Army, C.-in-C. of Armed Forces and Pres. of Bolivia Sept. 69-Oct. 70; Amb. to Spain 70-71; Leader of Bolivian Revolution Front.
Ministerio de Asuntos Exteriores, La Paz, Bolivia.

Óvári, Miklós; Hungarian politician; b. 24 Aug. 1925, Budapest; ed. Budapest Univ. of Liberal Arts.
Teacher, Party School 48-49, Party Acad. 49-58; in charge of Agitation and Propaganda Dept., Hungarian Socialist Workers' Party Cen. Cttee. 58-61; successive Appointments as Head of Section of Depts. of Science, Culture and Public Educ. 61-66; Head of Depts. of Science, Culture and Public Educ. 66-70; mem. Cen. Cttee., Hungarian Socialist Workers' Party 63-, Sec. Cen. Cttee. 70-, mem. Politburo 75-, Head Agitation and Propaganda Board attached to HSWP Cen. Cttee. 75-.
Leisure interest: reading.
Hungarian Socialist Workers' Party, 1387 Budapest V, Széchenyi rakpart 19, Hungary.
Telephone: 111-400.

Ovchinnikov, Yurii Anatolievich, d.sc.; Soviet biochemist; b. 2 Aug. 1934, Moscow; s. of Anatolii and Elena Ovchinnikov; m. Tatyana Kirensky 1956; two s. one d.; ed. Moscow State Univ.
Research Worker, Shemyakin Inst. of Bio-organic Chemistry, U.S.S.R. Acad. of Sciences 60, Dir. 70; Corresp. mem. U.S.S.R. Acad. of Sciences 68, mem. 70, Vice-Pres. 74, Chair. of Chem., Technological and Biological Sciences Div. 74; mem. of Acad. Leopoldina, Hon. mem. CIBA Foundation.
Publs. Membrano-aktivnye kompleksony (monograph) 74, scientific papers on synthetic and theoretical

organic chem., physical-organic chem., chem. and biochem. of peptides and proteins, membrane biology. U.S.S.R. Academy of Sciences, Leninsky prospekt 14, Moscow, U.S.S.R.

Overbeck, Egon, DR. RER. POL.; German business executive; b. 11 Jan. 1918; ed. Reform-Realgymnasium Rendsburg/Holstein, and Johann Wolfgang Goethe Universität, Frankfurt am Main.
Army service, Lt. 38, Major on Gen. Staff 44; university studies after Second World War; Deputy Dir. Metall-gesellschaft A.G., Frankfurt/Main 54; mem. Exec. Board Vereinigte Deutsche Metallgesellschaft A.G., Frankfurt/Main 56; Chair. of Management Board, Mannesmann A.G., Düsseldorf 62-; Dir. Allianz A.G., Munich, Siemens A.G., Munich, and numerous steel industry and other firms; Chair. Advisory Board DEMAG A.G., Duisburg, Advisory Council Deutsche Bank A.G.; several war decorations.
Publ. *Possibilities of Maintaining and Increasing West German Lead-Zinc Production* 51.
Mannesmann A.G., Mannesmann- Ufer 2, 4, Düsseldorf, Federal Republic of Germany.
Telephone: 8201.

Overby, Andrew Norris, M.S.; American banker; b. 27 March 1909, Cheyenne Agency, S.D.; s. of Samuel O. Overby and Anna Marie Amundson; m. Annette Picus 1928; ed. Univ. of Minnesota and Columbia Univ.
With Irving Trust Co. New York 30-41; Asst. to Vice-Pres. 36-41; Special Asst. to Vice-Pres. Fed. Reserve Bank of N.Y. 42; U.S. Army 42-46; Chief, Int. Div., Reciprocal Aid Branch 42-45; Exec. Officer to Dir. of Material, H.Q. Army Service Forces 45-46; Asst. Vice-Pres. Fed. Reserve Bank of N.Y. 46; Special Asst. to Sec. of the Treasury 46-47; U.S. Exec.-Dir. Int. Monetary Fund, and Special Asst. to the Sec., U.S. Treasury Dept. 47-49; Deputy Man. Dir. Int. Monetary Fund 49-52; Asst. Sec. Treasury Dept. 52-57; U.S. Exec.-Dir. Int. Bank for Reconstruction and Development 52-57; mem. Nat. Security Council Planning Board 52-57; Dir. The First Boston Corpn., New York City 57-; Vice-Pres. 57-64, Chair. Man. Cttee. 71-72, Vice-Chair. of Board 64-74, Consultant April-Dec. 74; Dir. Japan Soc. Inc. 70-, mem. Exec. Cttee. 71-, Chair. Exec. Cttee. 73-; Dir. Liberian Iron Ore Ltd. 65-, Int. Exec. Service Corps 65-; Trustee, Citizens' Budget Comm. Inc., N.Y. 73-; Legion of Merit, Alexander Hamilton Award (Treasury Dept.), Army Commendation Ribbon, Order of the Rising Sun (Japan) 73, etc.
Leisure interests: the theatre, music, reading, swimming.
Home: Manhattan House, 200 East 66th Street, New York 21, N.Y.; Office: 20 Exchange Place, New York 5, N.Y., U.S.A.

Overton, William Ward; American banker; b. 30 April 1897, Kansas City, Kansas; s. of William Ward and Ella May (Barnes) Overton; m. Evelyn Lucas 10 June 1924; one s. one d.; ed. private schools, Kansas City Univ. and Texas Univ.
President W. W. Overton & Co. 13-61, Chair. of Board 61-; Chair. of Board Texas Bank and Trust Co. of Dallas 47-, Pres. 61-65, Dir. 36-; Dir. and fmr. Dir. of numerous firms and business orgs. in Texas; official of numerous social, civic, educational and philanthropic orgs., particularly in Dallas.
Office: Texas Bank and Trust Co., 1 Main Place, Dallas, Texas 75226; Home: 4830 Cedar Springs, Dallas, Texas, U.S.A.
Telephone: LA1-5877.

Owe, Aage Willand; Norwegian chemical engineer; b. 9 Oct. 1894, Horten; s. of Christofer and Inga Franziska Owe; m. Marie Mathiesen 1922; one s. two d.; ed. Univ. of Oslo and Technical Univ., Trondheim.
Assistant Prof. Technical Univ. Trondheim 20-23; re-

search chemist, O. Mustad & Son, Oslo 23-27, Chief Chemist 27-35; Technical Dir. A/S Margarincentralen 35-47; Dir. of Industrial Supply, Ministry of Supply 45; Chair. A/S Nordisk Lettmetall 45-47; Chair. Govt. Fuel Comm. 40-42 and 45-50; Chair. Norsk Brenselimport A/S Oslo 40-59; Man. Dir. and Vice-Chair. A/S Ardal og Sunndal Verk, Oslo 47-64; mem. of Board O. Mustad and Son, Oslo 57-59; mem. Norwegian Energy Commission 58-69; Chair. Cttee. of Industrial-Educational Relations of the Technical Univ., Trondheim 59-67; Pres. Asscn. of Norwegian Engineers 37-46, Hon. mem.; Pres. Norwegian Chemical Soc. 50-54, Hon. mem.; Chair. Royal Norwegian Council for Scientific and Industrial Research 64-67; Chair. Norwegian Devt. Foundation 65-67, Norway-Netherlands Asscn. 66-72; mem. Royal Norwegian Soc. of Science (Trondheim), Norwegian Acad. of Science and Letters (Oslo), Norwegian Acad. of Technical Science; Orders of the North Star (Sweden), White Rose (Finland) and St. Olav (Norway) (Commander); H.M.'s Gold Medal for scientific work; The Norsk Hydro Prize of the Asscn. of Norwegian Engineers.
Leisure interests: oil painting, photography.
Øvre Ullern Terrasse 25, Øvre Ullern, Oslo 3, Norway.
Telephone: 245760.

Owen, Ray David, PH.D., SC.D.; American biologist; b. 30 Oct. 1915, Genesee, Wis.; s. of Dave Owen and Ida Hoeft Owen; m. June Johanna Weissenberg 1939; one s.; ed. Carroll Coll., Wis., Univ. of Wisconsin.
Research Fellow, Wisconsin 41-43, Asst. Prof. of Genetics and Zoology 43-47; Gosney Fellow, Calif. Inst. of Tech. 46-47, Assoc. Prof. 47-53, Prof. 53-, Chair. Div. of Biology 61-68, Vice-Pres. for Student Affairs and Dean of Students 75-; Research Participant, Oak Ridge Nat. Lab. 57-58; mem. Genetics Soc. of America (Treasurer 57-60, Vice-Pres. 61, Pres. 62), Nat. Acad. of Sciences, American Acad. of Arts and Sciences, American Acad. of Political and Social Sciences, Soc. for the Study of Evolution, American Asscn. of Immunologists; served on numerous scientific cttees.
Publs. *General Genetics* (with Srb and Edgar) 52, 65; numerous research papers.
Division of Biology, 156-29, California Institute of Technology, Pasadena, Calif. 91125, U.S.A.
Telephone: 213-795-6841.

Owings, Nathaniel Alexander, B.S.; American architect; b. 5 Feb. 1903; s. of Nathaniel Fleming and Cora Alexander; m. 2nd Margaret Wentworth 1954; ed. Univ. of Illinois, Cornell Coll. of Architecture.
Research in Egypt, India and the Far East 35-36; in partnership with Skidmore and Merrill 36, creating the firm of Skidmore, Owings and Merrill, with whom he designed numerous Govt. projects and private buildings including Oak Ridge, Tennessee, U.S. Base at Okinawa, Lever House, New York, Terrace Plaza Hotel, Cincinnati, Air Force Acad., Colorado, Chase Manhatten Bank, N.Y.C., John Hancock Western Home Office, San Francisco, Crown Zellerbach Building, San Francisco, John Hancock Tower, Chicago, Sears Tower, Chicago, etc.; Fellow, American Inst. of Architects; Trustee, American Acad. in Rome, Cttee. for Econ. Development (CED); Dir. Standard Insurance Co., Portland, Ore.; Assoc. Nat. Acad. of Design; Hon. D.D.L. (Ball State Univ.), Dr. of Humane Letters (Indiana).
Publs. *The American Aesthetic* 69, *The Spaces In Between —an Architectural Journey* 73.
1 Maritime Plaza, San Francisco, California 94111, U.S.A.

Owono, Joseph N.; Cameroon diplomatist; b. 17 Dec. 1921, Mengueme; s. of Nkudu Bene and Josepha Seng; m. Martha E. Owono 1945; three s. four d.; ed. Agricultural Coll. of Cameroon.

Agricultural Officer 43-57; Chef de Cabinet, Ministry of Finance 58-59; Chief of Div. of American Affairs in Foreign Ministry 60; Chargé d'Affaires, Washington 60; Amb. to Liberia 61-62, to U.A.R. 62-65, to U.S.A. and Canada 65-69; Perm. Rep. to UN 66-68; Amb. to U.S.S.R. 70-73; Sec.-Gen. of Ministry of Foreign Affairs 73-.
Leisure interest: film shooting.
Ministry of Foreign Affairs, P.O. Box 1732, Yaoundé, Cameroon.
Telephone: 22-01-33 (Office); 22-33-78 (Home).

Owren, Paul A., M.D., F.A.C.P., F.A.C.C.P.; Norwegian professor of medicine; b. 27 Aug. 1905, Faaberg; s. of Peder A. Owren and Anna Nermo; m. 1st Marit V. E. Roedland 1935 (deceased 1964), 2nd Kathleen M. Thrane 1968; one d.; ed. Univ. of Oslo.
Resident, Oslo City Hosps. and Rikshospitalet 40-44; Senior Resident Aker Hosp. 45-47; Research Assoc. Lister Inst. of Preventive Medicine, London 46; Senior Resident Rikshospitalet 48, Head of Medical Dept. 49-70, Head Inst. for Thrombosis Research 55-63, Researcher 71-; Prof. of Medicine Univ. of Oslo 49-70; mem. advisory panel for cardiovascular diseases, WHO 62-; Chair. Norwegian Research Council for Science and Humanities 58-61; mem. Acad. of Science and Letters (Oslo), Royal Norwegian Soc. of Science, Royal Soc. of Science (Sweden), Acad. Royale de Médecine (Belgium), Int. Soc. on Thrombosis and Haemostasis (Pres. 70), Int. Cttee. on Haemostasis and Thrombosis (Chair. 67-68), Int. Soc. of Haematology (Vice-Pres. 50-54), Int. Coll. of Angiology (Vice-Pres. 65-73), American Coll. of Chest Physicians (Gov. 68-74, Hon. Fellow), other medical and haemotogical Socs.; Commdr. Order of St. Olav 54, with Star 70; Officer, Carlos J. Finlay Nat. Order of Merit (Cuba) 54; Int. Award for Heart and Vascular Research, James M. Mitchell Foundation 69; Medical Prize, Anders Jahre Foundation 69.
Publs. *The Coagulation of Blood: Investigations on a new Clotting Factor* 47; about 200 publs. in the field.
Institute for Thrombosis Research, Rikshospitalet, Oslo; Home: Bjerkaasen 44, 1310 Blommenholm, Norway.
Telephone: 02-201050 (Office); 02-548633 (Home).

Owusu, Victor; Ghanaian politician; b. 26 Dec. 1923, Agona-Ashanti; ed. Univs. of Nottingham and London. Called to the Bar, Lincoln's Inn 52; practising barrister 52-67; M.P. for Agona-Kwabre 56-61; Attorney-Gen. 66-April 69; concurrently Minister of Justice July 67-April 69; Minister of External Affairs April 69, Sept. 69-Jan. 71; Attorney Gen. and Minister of Justice Jan. 71-Jan. 72; has served on several govt. comms. and corpns.; fmr. mem. Council of Univ. of Ghana, Legon, Council of Univ. of Science and Technology, Kumasi and Central Legal Council of Ghana; Progress Party.
Accra, Ghana.

Ozawa, Seiji; Japanese conductor; b. 1 Sept. 1935, Hoten; ed. Toho School of Music, Tokyo (under Prof. Hideo Saito), Tanglewood, U.S.A. and in Berlin under Herbert von Karajan.
Early engagements with Radio Orchestra (N.H.K.) and Japan Philharmonic; Asst. Conductor (under Leonard Bernstein), New York Philharmonic 61-62 (including tour of Japan 61); guest conductor, San Francisco Symphony, Detroit Symphony, Montreal, Minneapolis, Toronto and London Symphony Orchestras 61-65; Music Dir. Ravinia Festival, Chicago 64; Music Dir. Toronto Symphony Orchestra 65-70; toured Europe conducting many of the major orchestras 66-67; Salzburg Festival 69; Music Dir. San Francisco Symphony Orchestra 70-; Music Dir. Boston Symphony 73-; now makes frequent guest appearances with most of the leading orchestras of America, Europe and Japan; First Prize, Int. Competition of Orchestra

Conductors, France 59, Koussevitsky Memorial Scholarship 60; recordings for RCA, CBS, Polydor and EMI. Leisure interests: golf, tennis, discothèques.
c/o Ronald A. Wilford (Columbia Artists Management Inc., Conductors Division), 165 West 57th Street, New York, N.Y., U.S.A.; also c/o Harold Holt Ltd., 122 Wigmore Street, London, W.1, England.

Ozawa, Tatsuo; Japanese politician; ed. Tokyo Univ. Official, Ministry of Home Affairs; Head of Health Insurance Section, Ministry of Health and Welfare; mem. House of Reps.; fmr. Minister of Construction; Dir., Gen. Affairs Bureau and Treasury Bureau, Liberal Democratic Party; Minister of State and Dir.-Gen. Environment Agency Dec. 74-.
Government Environment Agency, Tokyo, Japan.

Özbek, Dr. Sabahattin; Turkish agronomist and politician; b. 1915, Erzincan; ed. Secondary School, Istanbul, Faculty of Agriculture, Univ. of Ankara.
Lecturer, Faculty of Agriculture, Univ. of Ankara 38, Asst. Prof. 41, Prof. 53, Dean 55-57, 65-68; Visiting Prof. Univs. of Michigan and Calif. 50-51, 57-58; Minister of Nat. Educ. 72-73, of Communications April 73-Jan. 74, Nov. 74-March 75; founded Atatürk Univ., Erzurum, later Co-Founder Faculty of Agriculture, Adana; Chair. Agricultural Cttee. for the preparation of First Five-Year Devt. Plan; mem. Turkish Atomic Energy Comm.; Prize of Professional Honour, Union of Agricultural Engineers.
Publs. 35 books in Turkish and foreign languages.
c/o Ministry of Communications, Ankara, Turkey.

Özdaş, Mehmet Nimet, DR.ING.; Turkish professor of mechanical engineering; b. 26 March 1921, Istanbul; s. of Izzet and Refia Özdaş; m. Suna Taki 1956; two s.; ed. Technical Univ. of Istanbul, Imperial Coll., London and London Univ.
Dozent, Technical Univ. of Istanbul 52, Prof. 61-73, Dir. Computation Centre 62-64; Visiting Prof. Case Inst. of Technology 58-59; Sec.-Gen. Scientific and Technical Research Council 64-67, mem. Science Board 68-71; Rep. to CENTO Science Council 65, to NATO Science Cttee. 66-73; Dir. Marmara Scientific and Industrial Research Inst. 69-73; Asst. Sec.-Gen. for Scientific and Environmental Affairs, NATO Sept. 73-.
Leisure interest: sport.
Publs. about 20 articles in English in scientific periodicals, many articles in Turkish and five books.
Scientific Affairs Division, North Atlantic Treaty Organization, 1110 Brussels; Home: 4 Clos des Oyats, 1150 Brussels, Belgium.
Telephone: 216-69-38 (Office).

Ozga-Michalski, Jozef; Polish politician and writer; b. 8 March 1919, Bieliny, Voiv. Kieleckie; s. of Władysław and Józefa Ozga-Michalski; m. Stanisława Ozga-Michalski; one s. two d.
During occupation, mem. of the leadership of the Peasant Battalions and editor of underground peasant periodicals 40-44; Organizer of Peasant Party (S.L.) and co-organizer of the Voivodship People's Council (V.P.C.), Kielce 44; after the liberation, first Chair. of V.P.C. Kielce 45-47; Chair. Central Board of Peasant Self-Aid Union 49-53; Chair. Central Union of Agricultural Circles 59-62; Vice-Chair. Polish Cttee. of Peace Defenders 50-; mem. World Peace Council 52-; Chair. Central Board of the Lay Schools Soc. 59-62, Polish-Italian Group of the Interparliamentary Union 61-; mem. Polish-Brazilian Friendship Soc. 62-74, Chair. May 74-; mem. S.L. 44-49, United Peasant Party (Z.S.L.) 49-, Sec. of S.L. Central Cttee. 49- and Z.S.L. Central Cttee. 49-55, Vice-Chair. Z.S.L. Central Cttee. 55-; mem. Home Nat. Council (K.R.N.) and Seym 47-; Vice-Marshal of Seym 52-56; mem. Council of State 57-, Vice-Chair. 72-; mem. Polish Writers' Union 45-; Vice-Chair. Presidium of All Poland Cttee.

of Nat. Unity Front 71-; Vice-Chair. Chief Council of Union of Fighters for Freedom and Democracy 72-; Vice-Chair. Cen. Board of Polish-Soviet Friendship Soc. 74-; Commdr's. Cross with the Star of the Polonia Restituta Order 64; Georgi Dymitrov Medal 72; Order of Banner of Labour, 1st Class; Grunwald Cross, 3rd Class; Partisan Cross, etc.

Leisure interest: writing.

Publs. poetry including *Poemat nowosielecki, Ludowy potok, Lutnia wiejska, Pełnia, Druga strona księżyca, Światowid, Polska, Czernek i Anna, Ta—będz, Ściernisko, Walc karnawałowy;* novels: *Młodzik, Sklepienie niebieskie, Sowizdrzał świętokrzyski;* stories: *Krajobraz rodzinny,*

Smutne i wesołe; has translated *Kalevali* into Polish. Aleja 1 Armii Wojska Polskiego 16, 00-582 Warsaw, Poland.

Telephone: 28-18-60.

Öztekin, Mukadder; Turkish politician; b. 1919, Niğde Prov.; ed. Galatasaray Lycée, Istanbul, Ankara Univ. Joined Ministry of Interior 44; Country Chief Officer in various districts, Inspector; Gov. of Adana 60; Senator for Adana 66; Minister of Public Works 71-73, of the Interior April 73-Jan. 74, Nov. 74-March 75; Officier Légion d'Honneur; Independent.

c/o Ministry of the Interior, Ankara, Turkey.

P

Paar, Jack; American television performer; b. 1 May 1918.
Radio announcer, Indianapolis, Youngstown, Pittsburgh, Cleveland, Buffalo; appeared in films: *Walk Softly Stranger* 50, *Love Nest* 51, *Down Among the Sheltering Palms* 53; TV programmes *Up to Paar* 52, TV *Morning Show* 55, *Tonight Show* 57-58, *Jack Paar Show* 58-62, *The Jack Paar Program* 62-65, *Jack Paar Tonite* 73-.
c/o ABC-TV, 1330 Avenue of the Americas, New York, N.Y. 10019, U.S.A.

Paasio, Kustaa Rafael; Finnish politician; b. 6 June 1903.
Early career as typographer, later as journalist; Editor-in-Chief *Turun Päivälehti* 42-66; mem. municipal council Turku 45-; mem. Parl. 48-, Speaker 66, 69-72; Pres. Comm. for Foreign Affairs 49-66; Candidate for Presidency 62; Pres. Social Democratic Party 63-75; Prime Minister 66-68, Feb.-Sept. 72.
Home: Virmuntie 26, Turku 53, Finland.

Pace, Frank, Jr., M.A., LL.D.; American business executive; b. 5 July 1912; ed. Princeton and Harvard Univs.
Asst. District Attorney in Arkansas 36-38; Gen. Attorney for the Revenue Dept., State of Arkansas 38-41; mem. of firm Pace, Davis & Pace 41-42; served U.S. Army Air Forces 42-46; now Lieut.-Col., Air Force Reserve; Special Asst. to Attorney-Gen. of the U.S. 46; Exec. Asst. to the Postmaster-Gen. 46-48; Vice-Pres. Universal Postal Union 47, Rep. at UN 47-48; Chief U.S. Del. to the 12th Universal Postal Congress, Paris 47; Asst. Dir. Bureau of the Budget 48-49, Dir. 49-50; mem. Cttee. on Contributions, UN 49-50, President's Advisory Cttees. on Management Improvement and on Int. Economic Growth; Defence Adviser; Chair. NATO Defence Ministers' Confs., Brussels 50, Del. Canada and Italy 51; U.S. Sec. of the Army 50-53; Exec. Vice-Pres. Gen. Dynamics Corpn., N.Y. 53-57, Dir. 53-, Pres. 57-59, Chair. and Chief Exec. Officer 59-62; Chair. Canadair Ltd. 57-62, Corpn. for Public Broadcasting 68-72; Pres. Int. Exec. Service Corps 64-; Dir. numerous other companies; Pres. Nat. Inst. of Social Sciences 56-; Hon. M.A. (Princeton), Hon. LL.D. (Louisville, Syracuse, Arkansas, Temple Univs., Dartmouth, Northland, Adelphi Colls.), Hon. Sc.D. (Lafayette, Clarkson Colls.), Hon. L.H.D. (Washington Coll.).
International Executive Service Corps, 622 Third Avenue, New York, N.Y. 10017; and Hillside Road, Greenwich, Conn., U.S.A.

Pachachi, Adnan Musahim al-, PH.D.; Iraqi diplomatist; b. 14 May 1923; ed. American Univ. of Beirut.
Joined Foreign Service 44, served Washington, Alexandria; Dir.-Gen. Ministry of Foreign Affairs 58-59; Perm. Rep. to UN 59-65, 67-69; Minister of Foreign Affairs 65-67; Minister of State, Abu Dhabi, United Arab Emirates 71-74; mem. Abu Dhabi Exec. Council 74-; Personal Rep. of Head of State of U.A.E. 74-.
c/o Manhal Palace, Abu Dhabi, United Arab Emirates.

Pachecho, Rondon; Brazilian politician; b. 31 July 1919; *m.* Maria de Freitas Pachecho 1943; one *s.* (deceased) two *d.*; ed. Univ. of Minas Gerais.
State deputy and in Secretariat of Legislative Assembly of Minas Gerais 46; sec. to Min. of Interior; Deputy Leader of União Democrática Nacional in Chamber of Deputies; mem. Constitutional and Judicial Cttee., Chamber of Deputies; Deputy Leader of Castelo Branco Govt. and of the Majority in Chamber of Deputies; Gen. Sec., Aliança Renovadora Nacional; Minister in charge of Cabinet Affairs, Costa e Silva Govt.;

Brazilian del. UN 20th Gen. Ass. 65; Pres. of Nat. Directorate, Aliança Renovadora Nacional for 1970 elections; Governor of State, Minas Gerais 71-74; Grand Cross of the Order of Merit, Brazil 67, Officer 1st Class Imperial Order of the Sacred Treasure of Japan 67, numerous other decorations.
c/o Palácio do Govêrno, Estado de Minas Gerais, Brazil.

Pacheco Areco, Jorge; Uruguayan newspaper editor and politician; b. 9 April 1920, Montevideo; *s.* of Manuel Pacheco and Lilina Areco; ed. Facultad de Derechos y Ciencias Sociales.
Assistant Editor *El Día* (Montevideo daily) until 61, Editor 61-65; Vice-Pres. of Uruguay 67; Pres. of Uruguay 67-72; Amb. to Spain 72-.
Embassy of Uruguay, Paseo del Pintor Rosales 32, Madrid, Spain.

Packard, David; American business executive and government official; b. 7 Sept. 1912, Pueblo, Colo.; *m.* Lucile Salter 1938; one *s.* three *d.*; ed. Centennial High School, Pueblo, and Stanford Univ., Calif.
Formed Hewlett-Packard Co. (to design and manufacture electronic measurement instrumentation) with William R. Hewlett 39, Pres. 47-64, Chair. of Board, Chief Exec. Officer 64-69, 72-; U.S. Deputy Sec. of Defense 69-71; fmr. mem. and Vice-Chair. Business Council; fmr. mem. Chase Manhattan Bank Int. Advisory Cttee.; fmr. Co-Chair. Stanford Mid-Peninsula Urban Coalition; Pres. Board of Trustees, Stanford Univ. 58-60; fmr. Dir. Crocker Citizens Nat. Bank, Gen. Dynamics Corpn., Stanford Research Inst., U.S. Steel Corpn., Calif. State Chamber of Commerce, Cttee. for Econ. Devt., Nat. Merit Scholarship Corpn., Univs. Research Asscn., San Francisco Bay Area Council; fmr. mem. Advisory Board Hoover Inst., Stanford Univ.; fmr. mem. Cttee. for Support of American Univs.; Dir. Standard Oil Co. 72-, Caterpillar Tractor Co. 72-, TWA 72-, Atlantic Inst. 72-; numerous awards; Hon. D.Sc. (Colorado Coll.) 64, Hon. LL.D. (Univ. of Calif.) 66.
1501 Page Mill Road, Palo Alto, Calif. 94304; and 26580 Taaffe Avenue, Los Altos Hills, Calif. 94022, U.S.A.

Packard, Vance, A.B., M.S.; American author and teacher; b. 22 May 1914, Granville Summit, Pa.; *s.* of Philip and Mabel Packard; *m.* Virginia Mathews 1938; two *s.* one *d.*; ed. Pennsylvania State Univ. and Columbia Univ.
Reporter for Boston *Record* 37; worked for four years in New York for Associated Press; editorial staff of *American Magazine* 42-56, *Collier's* Magazine 56.
Publs. *The Hidden Persuaders* 57, *The Status Seekers* 59, *The Waste Makers* 60, *The Pyramid Climbers* 62, *The Naked Society* 64, *The Sexual Wilderness* 68, *A Nation of Strangers* 72.
87 Mill Road, New Canaan, Conn. 06840, U.S.A.

Packwood, Bob; American lawyer and politician; b. 11 Sept. 1932, Portland, Ore.; *m.* Georgie Oberteuffer 1964; one *s.* one *d.*; ed. Willamette Univ., N.Y. Univ.
Practised law in Portland 58-68; mem. Oregon House of Reps. 62-68; U.S. Senator from Oregon 68-; Hon. LL.D. Willamette Univ. 69; several awards.
U.S. Senate, Washington, D.C. 20510, U.S.A.

Paço d'Arcos, Joaquim; Portuguese writer; b. 1908, Lisbon; *s.* of Henrique Corrêa da Silva (Conde de Paço d'Arcos) and Maria do Carmo Corrêa da Silva; *m.* 1st Maria Candida Magalhães Corrêa 1932 (died 1945), 2nd Maria da Graça Moura Braz 1949; three *s.*
Man. Dir. Trans-Zambesia Railway Co. Ltd.; novelist,

playwright, essayist, poet; awarded many literary prizes; work translated into various languages; Chair. Portuguese Soc. of Writers 60-62, 65-.

Publs. *The Last Hero, Ana Paula, Diary of an Emigrant, Anxiety, Loves and Voyages of Pedro Manuel, Snow over the Sea, The Accomplice, The Absent, Pathology of Dignity, United States 1942, The Novel and the Novelist, The Road to Sin, Triple Mirror, Imperfect Poems, Churchill–The Statesman and the Writer, The Forest of Concrete–Lights and Shadows of the United States, The Captive Doe, Carnival and Other Tales, Memoirs of a Banknote, Cela 27, The Long Arm of Justice, Not Too Exemplary Tales*, etc.

Avenida A.A. Aguiar 38, Lisbon; and Avenida de Pádua 218, Estoril, Portugal.
Telephone: Lisbon 43325; Estoril 261625.

Padilla Segura, Ing. José-Antonio; Mexican electrical engineer and politician; b. 12 March 1922, San Luis Potosí; *m.* María Elena Longoria de Padilla Segura 1948; eleven *c.*; ed. Escuela Superior de Ingeniería Mecánica y Eléctrica del Instituto Politécnico Nacional. Former Dir.-Gen. Instituto Politécnico Nacional, fmr. Vice-Pres. of Centre for Research and Advanced Studies, Factory Inspectorate, and Nat. Centre for Technical and Industrial Educ.; mem. Natural Sciences Cttee. (Mexico), UNESCO; mem. Managing Cttee. Nat. Technical Council for Educ.; mem. U.S.A.-Mexico Comm. for Space Research; Sec. for Communications 64-70; now Dir. Gen. Altos Hornos de México S.A., Estudios y Planeación (ESPLA), La Perla, Minas de Fierro, S.A., Cía. Carbonera La Sauceda, S.A.; Vice-Pres. Nat. Asscn. of Univs. and Insts. of Higher Educ.; mem. Mexican Asscn. of Mechanical and Electrical Engineers, Mexican Coll. of Mechanical and Electrical Engineers, Mexican Physical Soc., Franco-Mexican Asscn. of Engineers; Ordre des Palmes Académiques; Hon. D.Sc. (Univs. of Yucatán and Sinaloa).

Leisure interests: science, history, culture, art.
Plaza de la República 43-2° Piso, Mexico 1, D.F., Mexico.
Telephone: 535-33-80.

Padley, Walter Ernest, M.P.; British trade unionist and politician; b. 24 July 1916, Chipping Norton, Oxon.; *s.* of late Ernest and of Mildred Padley; *m.* Sylvia Wilson 1942; one *s.* one *d.*; ed. Chipping Norton Grammar School and Ruskin Coll., Oxford.
President, Union of Shop, Distributive and Allied Workers 48-64; M.P. 50-; mem. Nat. Exec. Cttee. of Labour Party 56-, Chair. Int. Cttee. 63-71, Chair. Labour Party 65-66; Rep. of Labour Party at Socialist Int. 63-73; Minister of State for Foreign Affairs Oct. 64-67; mem. Action Cttee. for the United States of Europe 68-70.
Publs. *The Economic Problem of the Peace* 44, *Am I My Brother's Keeper?* 45, *Britain: Pawn or Power?* 47, *Soviet Russia: Empire or Free Union?* 47.
73 Priory Gardens, Highgate, London, N.6, England.
Telephone: 01-340-2969.

Pafford, John Henry Pyle, M.A., D.LIT., F.S.A., F.L.A.; British librarian; b. 6 March 1900, Bradford-on-Avon, Wilts.; *s.* of John and Bessie Pafford (née Pyle); *m.* Elizabeth R. Ford 1941; one *d.*; ed. Trowbridge High School and Univ. Coll., London.
Library Asst., Univ. Coll., London 23-25; Librarian and Tutor, Selly Oak Colleges, Birmingham 25-31; Sub-librarian, Nat. Central Library, London 31-45; Lecturer, Univ. of London School of Librarianship 37-61; War Office, Books and Libraries for Army Education 44-45; Goldsmiths' Librarian, Univ. of London 45-67; Library Adviser, Inter-Univ. Council for Higher Educ. Overseas 60-68; Fellow, Univ. Coll. London.
Leisure interests: home, walking, book-hunting.
Publs. Bale's *King Johan* 31, *Library Co-operation in Europe* 35, *The Sodder'd Citizen* (Malone Soc.) 36,

Books and Army Education 46, *American and Canadian Libraries* 49, *W. P. Ker: A Bibliography* 50, *The Winter's Tale* (Arden Shakespeare) 63, *Isaac Watts: Divine Songs for Children* 71, *L. Bryskett: Works* 72, *Employer and Employed* (with E. R. Pafford) 74.
Hillside, Allington Park, Bridport, Dorset DT6 5DD, England.
Telephone: 0308-22829.

Pagano, Gino; Italian industrialist; b. 2 Sept. 1921, Naples; ed. Naples Univ.
Joined ANIC (Associazione Nazionale dell'Industria Chimica) 51; Vice Dir. Gen. of production, ANIC and associated factories 61-68; manager, ANIC Gela and Vice Dir. Gen. for co-ordination of ANIC S.p.A. 63-67; Gen. Man. ANIC 67, Pres. 72-, Chief Exec. 75-; co-ordinator, chemical and nuclear sector, ENI.
ANIC, San Donato Milanese, Milan, Italy.
Telephone: 02-53531.

Page, Alexander Warren, M.B.E., M.A., M.I.MECH.E.; British business executive; b. 1 July 1914, Surbiton, Surrey; *s.* of Sydney and Phyllis (née Spencer) Page; *m.* Anne Lewis Hickman 1940 (dissolved); two *s.* one *d.*; ed. Tonbridge School and Clare Coll., Cambridge.
Joined Metal Box Ltd. 36; served in army 40-45; Sales Dir. Metal Box Ltd. 57, Man. Dir. 66, Deputy Chair. 69, Chair. and Man. Dir. Feb. 70-, Chief Exec. 75-.
Leisure interests: golf, tennis, squash.
2 Montagu Square, London, W1H 1RA; Merton Place, Dunsfold, Nr. Godalming, Surrey, England.
Telephone: 01-935-9894 (London); 0486-49-211 (Country).

Page, Sir Denys Lionel, Kt., LITT.D.; British classical scholar; b. 1908, Reading, Berks.; *s.* of H. F. D. Page; *m.* Katharine Elizabeth Dohan 1938; four *d.*; ed. Christ Church, Oxford, and Vienna Univ.
Lecturer, Christ Church, Oxford 31-32, Student and Tutor 32-50; Regius Prof. of Greek, Cambridge Univ. 50-73; Master of Jesus Coll. Cambridge 59-73; attached to Foreign Office 39-45, H.Q. Supreme Allied Command, South East Asia 45-46; lecture tours in U.S.A. 57-58.
Publs. *Actors' Interpolations in Greek Tragedy* 34, *Euripides' Medea* 38, *Greek Literary Papyri* 41, *Alcman* 51, *Corinna* 53, *Sappho and Alcaeus* 55, *The Homeric Odyssey* 55, *Aeschylus' Agamemnon* (co-ed.) 57, *History and the Homeric Iliad* 59, *Poetae Melici Graeci* 62, *The Oxyrhynchus Papyri* Vol. XXIX 64, *The Greek Anthology: Hellenistic Epigrams* (co-editor) 65, *The Garland of Philip* 68, *Melica Graeca Selecta* 68, *The Santorini Volcano and the Destruction of Minoan Crete* 70, *Aeschylus* 72, *Folk Tales in the Odyssey* 73, *Supplementum Lyricis Graecis* (ed.) 75.
Thorneyburn Lodge, Tarset, Northumberland, England.

Page, Geneviève; French actress; b. 13 Dec. 1931, Paris; *m.*; two *c.*
Principal actress in the French National Theatre and the Jean-Louis Barrault company; has appeared in many famous classical and tragic stage roles; numerous film appearances include: *Ce siècle a cinquante ans, Pas de pitié pour les femmes, Fanfan la tulipe, Lettre ouverte, Plaisirs de Paris, Nuits andalouses, L'étrange désir de M. Bard, Cherchez la femme, L'homme sans passé, Foreign Intrigue, The Silken Affair, Michael Strogoff, Un amour de poche, Song Without End, Le Bal des Adieux, El Cid, Les égarements, Le jour et l'heure, L'honorable correspondence, Youngblood Hawke, Le majordome, Les corsaires, L'or et le plomb, Trois chambres à Manhattan, Grand Prix, Belle de jour, Mayerling, A Talent for Loving, The Private Life of Sherlock Holmes.*
52 rue de Vaugirard, 75006 Paris, France.

Page, John Brangwyn; British banking official; b. 23 Aug. 1923, London; *s.* of Sidney J. and Doris M. Page; *m.* Gloria Vail 1948; one *s.* one *d.*; ed. Highgate School and King's Coll., Cambridge.

Served in R.A.F. 42-46; with Bank of England 48-, Deputy Chief Cashier 68-70, Chief Cashier March 70-. Leisure interests: music, travel.
Bank of England, Threadneedle Street, London, E.C.2; Home: 74 Moor Lane, Rickmansworth, Herts., England. Telephone: 74531 (Home).

Page, Rt. Hon. (Rodney) Graham, P.C., LL.B., M.B.E., M.P.; British politician; b. 1911, Hertford; s. of late Lieut.-Col. Frank Page, D.S.O.; m. Hilda Dixon 1934; two c.; ed. Magdalen Coll. School, Oxford, London Univ. Practising solicitor 34-70, 74-; Privy Council Appeal Agent; served in Civil Air Guard and R.A.F. during Second World War; mem. Parl. for Crosby 53-; Opposition Front Bench Spokesman on Housing and Land 65-70; Minister of Local Govt. and Devt. 70-74; Chair. Commons Select Cttee. on Statutory Instruments 74-; Conservative.
Publs. Two legal textbooks and articles on law.
House of Commons, London, S.W.1; 92 Highgate Hill, London, N6 5HE, England.
Telephone: 01-340-3579.

Page, Walter Hines, A.B.; American banker; b. 7 July 1915, Huntington, N.Y.; s. of Arthur W. and Mollie (Hall) Page; m. Jane N. Nichols 1942; two s. one d.; ed. Milton Acad. and Harvard Univ.
Joined J. P. Morgan and Co. Inc. (merged with Guaranty Trust Co. of New York 59) 37; Vice-Pres. Morgan Guaranty Trust Co. 59-64, Senior Vice-Pres. 64-65, Exec. Vice-Pres. 65-68, Vice-Chair. 68-71, Dir., Pres. Morgan Guaranty Trust Co. and J. P. Morgan and Co. Inc. 71-.
Leisure interest: sailing.
Morgan Guaranty Trust Co., 23 Wall Street, New York, N.Y. 10015; Home: Cold Spring Harbor, N.Y. 11724, U.S.A.
Telephone: (212) 483-2323 (Office).

Pagliazzi, Paolo; Italian banker; b. 20 Dec. 1908, Reggello, Florence; s. of late Enrico Pagliazzi and Maria Biagi; m. Beatrice Ricci 1935; one s. one d.; ed. studies in econ. and commerce.
Deputy Gen. Man. Banca Nazionale del Lavoro 60-67; Gen. Man. Monte dei Paschi di Siena 68-75; Man. Dir. Banca Toscana 65-; Chair. Banco di Napoli 75-; has taught as Prof. of Banking at Univs. of Rome, Florence, Pisa; Dir. of ten financial institutions; Deputy Chair. Italian Int. Bank Ltd., London; Cavaliere di Gran Croce.
Publs. *Le Disposizioni sulla difesa del risparmio e sull'esercizio del credito (precedenti ed aspetti tecnici fondamentali)* 40, *Note sulla liquidità* 50, *Il Credito e la Banca* 53, *La Liquidità bancaria sotto l'aspetto aziendale* 54, *Il Credito all'Agricoltura* 58, *Problemi creditizi, monetari e di mercato* 60, *Il processo di liberalizzazione dei movimenti di capitale dalla costituzione della Comunità ad oggi* 61, *I crediti speciali* 62, *Codice della Banca Borse e Valute* 63, *Economia e Tecnica Bancaria* 67, *Risparmio, investimenti e credito nella realizzazione del programma economico* 69, *Le garanzie—aspetti economici* 74, *Il credito a lungo termine* 75.
Via Romeo Romei 35, Rome, Italy.
Telephone: 385331.

Pahang, H.H. Sultan of, Sultan Haji Ahmad Shah ibni Almarhum Sultan Sir Abu Bakar Riayatuddin Almuadzam Shah, D.K., S.P.C.M., S.P.M.J.; Malaysian Ruler; b. 24 Oct. 1930, Istana Mangga Tunggal, Pekan; m. Tengku Hajjaj Afzan binti Tengku Muhammad 1954; ed. Malay Coll. Kuala Kangsar, Worcester Coll., Oxford, Univ. Coll., Exeter.
Tengku Mahkota (Crown Prince) 44; Capt. 4th Battalion, Royal Malay Regt. 54; Commdr. of 12th Infantry Battalion of Territorial Army 63-65, Lieut.-Col.; mem. State Council 55; Regent 56, 59, 65; succeeded as Sultan; Timbalan Yang di Pertuan Agung (Deputy Supreme Head of State of Malaysia) 75-.
Pekan Lama, Kuantan, Pahang, Malaysia.

Pahlavi, Farah; Her Imperial Majesty Queen Farah Shahbanou, Empress of Iran; b. 1938; ed. Jeanne d'Arc School and Razi School, Teheran, and Ecole Spéciale d'Architecture, Paris.
Married H.I.M. the Shah 21 Dec. 59; son Reza b. 31 Dec. 60, daughter Farahnaz b. 12 March 63, son Ali Reza b. 28 April 66, daughter Leila b. 27 March 70; Foreign Assoc. mem. Fine Arts Acad., France 74; Patron Farah Pahlavi Asscn. (administration of orphanages in Iran), Iran Cultural Foundation, and 24 other educational, health and cultural orgs.
The Imperial Palace, Teheran, Iran.

Pahlavi, Mohammad-Reza; His Imperial Majesty the Shahanshah Aryamehr, Emperor of Iran; b. 26 Oct. 1919; m. 1st Princess Fawzia, sister of King Farouk of Egypt 1939 (divorced 1948), one d., Princess Shahnaz Pahlavi; 2nd Soraya Esfandiari, 1951 (divorced March 58); 3rd Farah Diba, 1959, two s., Reza Pahlavi and Ali Reza Pahlavi, and two d., Farahnaz and Leila. Succeeded to throne on the abdication of his father, Reza Shah the Great, 16 Sept. 1941; personally led the Imperial Iranian Army in liberation of province of Azerbaizhan 46; Dr. h.c. (Michigan, Columbia, Pennsylvania, California (Los Angeles), Chicago, Harvard, New York and Washington Univs., U.S.A. and Univs. of Aligarh, Bangkok, Malaya, Madras, Punjab, Agra, Beirut, Rio de Janeiro, Bucharest, Sofia, Peshawar, Istanbul and Teheran); 31 foreign decorations incl. Order of Merit (Germany), Order of Merit (Italy), Order of Isabella the Catholic (Spain), Royal Victorian Order (U.K.), Order of Al Hussein Ben Ali (Jordan), Order of Pakistan (Pakistan), Order of Independence (Tunisia), Order of Omayyad Syria (Syria), Order of Poland Restored (Poland), Order of Saint Olav (Norway), Order of the Netherlands Lion (Netherlands), Order of the Great Star of Yugoslavia (Yugoslavia), Order of the White Rose (Finland), Order of the Nile (Egypt).
Publs. *Mission for My Country* 61, *The White Revolution* 67.
The Imperial Palace, Teheran, Iran.

Pahlbod, Mehrdad, B.SC.; Iranian politician; b. Teheran; ed. Univ. of Teheran and in France.
Official, Ministry of Educ.; Supervisor, Org. of Fine Arts; Deputy Prime Minister; now Minister of Culture and Art.
Ministry of Culture and Art, Teheran, Iran.

Pai, Ei Whan, B.S., M.B.A.; Korean diplomatist and economist; b. 1907, Kimhae, Kyungsang Namdo; m. Inez Kong 1944; three s. one d.; ed. in Korea and Business Admin. Colleges in U.S.A.
With Straw Brokerage Co., U.S.A. 38-42; Dept. of Justice, U.S.A. 42; Office of Censorship, Washington, D.C. 43; Foreign Econ. Admin., Washington, D.C.; Adviser to Civil Affairs Staging Area, Monterey, Calif.; Adviser to Mil. Govt. Coll., Virginia 44-45; Asst. Dir. Dept. of Finance, Mil. Govt., Korea, Pres. of Fed. of Financial Asscns., Korea, Financial Adviser to Nat. Econ. Board, Mil. Govt. Korea 46-49; Pres. of Korean Chamber of Commerce, Hawaii, and Pres. of Far Eastern Trading Co., Hawaii 50; Gov. of Bank of Korea 60; Amb. to Japan 61, to Argentina, Chile, Paraguay and Bolivia 65, to U.K. 67-71; Amb.-at-Large 71-; Pres. Overseas Econ. Research Inst. 73-.
Leisure interests: golf, tennis, soccer.
C.P.O. Box 5795, Seoul; Overseas Economic Research Institute, C.P.O. Box 5864, Seoul, Republic of Korea.

Pai Hsiang Kuo; Chinese politician; b. Kwangtun g. People's Liberation Army Canton Units 69-70; mem. Kwangtung Provincial Revolutionary Cttee. 60-70, Vice-Chair. 70; Minister of Foreign Trade 70-73; numerous official journeys abroad, to U.S.A., France, Egypt, Pakistan, Peru, Chile, Canada and England. People's Republic of China.

Pai Ju-ping; Chinese party official; b. 1906, Shensi. Director Gen. Admin. of Handicraft Industry, State Council 54-58; Sec. CCP Shantung 58-67; Vice-Gov. of Shantung 58-63, Gov. 63-67; criticized and removed from office during Cultural Revolution 67; Vice-Chair. Shantung Revolutionary Cttee. 71; Deputy Sec. CCP Shantung 71, Second Sec. 74, First Sec. 74; mem. 10th Cen. Cttee. of CCP 73; First Political Commissar Tsinan Mil. Region, People's Liberation Army 74-. People's Republic of China.

Pai, Tonse Ananth, B.COM.; Indian politician; b. 17 Jan. 1922; ed. Sydenham Coll., Bombay, Int. Summer School of Banking, Germany.
General Man. Syndicate Bank 43-61, Man. Dir. 62-64, 66, Chair. 67-70; Chair. Food Corpn. of India 65-66, Life Insurance Corpn. of India 70-72; Minister of Railways 72-73, of Heavy Industry Feb. 73-, concurrently of Steel and Mines 73-74, of Civil Supplies 74-; mem. Madras and Mysore Legislative Assemblies, served on numerous cttees.; Chair. Board of Govs., Indian Inst. of Management, Bangalore; mem. Nat. Comm. on Agriculture; Padma Bhushan 72; Hon. LL.D. (Karnataka Univ. of Dharwar) 72; Hon. D.Litt. (Andhra Univ.).
Leisure interests: travel, reading, music.
176, Udyog Bhavan, New Delhi; Home: 2 Hastings Road, New Delhi 11, India.
Telephone: 376577 (Office); 372555 (Home).

Paige, Hilliard Wegner, B.S.; American business executive; b. 2 Oct. 1919, Hartford, Conn.; s. of Commdr. Joseph W. Paige and Ruth Hill Paige; m. Dorothea Magner 1945; one s. two d.; ed. Worcester Polytechnic Inst.
Joined General Electric Co. 41, Gen. Man. Missile and Space Div. 64, Vice-Pres. 64, Aerospace Group Exec. 67-69, Computer Group Exec. 69-70, Senior Vice-Pres. 70-71; Pres. General Dynamics Corpn. 71-73; Chair., Chief Exec., CML Satellite Corpn. 73-; Trustee Worcester Polytechnic Inst.; mem. Defense Science Board, Nat. Acad. of Eng.; Fellow American Inst. of Aeronautics and Astronautics; NASA Public Service Award, Order of Merit (Italy).
Leisure interests: tennis, skiing, scuba diving.
Publs. articles in professional journals etc.
CML Satellite Corporation, 1750 K Street, N.W., Washington, D.C. 20006; Home: 5163 Tilden Street, N.W., Washington, D.C., U.S.A.
Telephone: 202-466-2660 (Office); 202-966-6051 (Home).

Paik, General Sun Yup; Korean army officer and diplomatist; b. 1920, Seoul; s. of Yun Sang Paik and Hyo Yul Paik (Pang); m. In Suk Paik (Ro) 1944; two s. two d.; ed. Pyongyang Normal School and Mukden Mil. Acad., Manchuria.
Korean Constabulary 46-48; Repub. of Korea Army 48-60, Chief of Staff 52-54, 57-59, Gen. 53, Chair. Joint Chiefs of Staff 59-60; Amb. to Repub. of China 60-61, to France 61-65, to Canada 65-69; Minister of Transport, Repub. of Korea 69-70; Pres. Korea Gen. Chem. Industry Corpn. 71-; decorations from Korea, France, U.S.A., Belgium, Ethiopia, Thailand, Taiwan, Philippines, Upper Volta, Netherlands.
Leisure interests: golf, fishing.
68 Kyunchi-dong, Chongro-ku, Seoul; Home: 339 Huam-Dong, Yong San-Ku, Seoul, Republic of Korea.

Paine, Thomas Otten, A.B., M.S., PH.D.; American scientist-executive; b. 9 Nov. 1921, Berkeley, Calif.; s. of Commodore George Thomas Paine and Ada Louise Otten Paine; m. Barbara Helen Taunton Pearse 1946; two s. two d.; ed. Brown Univ., Providence, R.I., and Stanford Univ., Calif.
Submarine Officer, U.S. Navy 42-46; Man. Gen. Electric Meter and Instrument Laboratory 51-58; Man. Eng. Applications, Gen. Electric Research and Devt. Center 58-63; Man. Gen. Electric Center for Advanced Studies 63-68; Deputy Admin. Nat. Aeronautics and Space Admin. March-Oct. 68, Act. Admin. 68-70; Vice-Pres. Gen. Electric Co. 70-73, Senior Vice-Pres. Tech., Planning and Devt. 73-.
Leisure interests: sailing, beachcombing, skin diving, photography, book collecting and oil painting.
Publs. Numerous scientific papers.
General Electric Co., 570 Lexington Avenue, New York, N.Y. 10022, U.S.A.

Pais, Abraham, B.SC., M.SC., PH.D.; American physicist; b. 19 May 1918, Amsterdam, Netherlands; s. of Isayah Pais and Kaatje van Kleef; m. Lila Atwill 1956 (divorced); one s.; ed. Univs. of Amsterdam and Utrecht.
Oersted Fellow, Inst. of Theoretical Physics, Copenhagen 46; Fellow, Inst. of Advanced Study, Princeton 46-50, Prof. 50-63; Prof. Rockefeller Univ. 63-; Visiting Prof. Columbia Univ., New York 55; Staff mem. Lawrence Radiation Laboratory, Berkeley, Calif. 58-; Consultant Brookhaven Nat. Laboratory, Upton, N.Y.; Guggenheim Fellow 60; Fellow American Physical Soc.; mem. Nat. Acad. of Sciences, American Acad. Arts and Sciences; Corresp. mem. Royal Acad. of Sciences, Netherlands.
Leisure interests include: squash, swimming, mountaineering, theatre.
Publs. Contributions to *Physical Review, Physical Review Letters, Physics Letters, Annals of Physics* and other physics journals.
Rockefeller University, New York, N.Y. 10021; Home: 450 East 63rd Street, New York, N.Y. 10021, U.S.A.
Telephone: 212-360-1930 (Office); 212-PL3-3083 (Home).

Paish, Frank Walter, M.C., M.A.; British university professor (retd.); b. 15 Jan. 1898, Croydon, Surrey; s. of late Sir George Paish; m. Beatrice Marie Eckhard 1927; two s. one d.; ed. Winchester Coll., and Trinity Coll., Cambridge.
Served in First World War 16-19; employed in Standard Bank of S. Africa, Ltd., in London and S. Africa 21-32; Lecturer in Commerce, London School of Economics 32-38, Reader 38-49, Prof. 49-65, Prof. Emer. of London Univ. 65-; Deputy Dir. of Programmes, Ministry of Aircraft Production 41-45; Prof. of Econs. (with special reference to Business Finance) in the Univ. of London 49-65; Consultant on Econ. Affairs, Lloyds Bank Ltd. 65-70.
Leisure interests: walking, golf, gardening.
Publs. *Insurance Funds and their Investment* (with G. L. Schwartz) 34, *The Post-war Financial Problem and Other Essays* 50, *Business Finance* 53, *Studies in an Inflationary Economy* 62, *Long-term and Short-term Interest Rates* 66, Editor *Benham's Economics,* 7th 64, 8th 67, 9th edn. (with A. J. Culyer) 73, *How the Economy Works and Other Essays* 70.
The Old Rectory, Kentchurch, Herefordshire, England.

Paisley, Rev. Ian Richard Kyle, D.D., M.P.; British minister of religion; b. 6 April 1926; s. of Rev. J. Kyle Paisley and Isabella Paisley; m. Eileen E. Cassells 1956; two s. (twins) three d.; ed. Ballymena Modern School, Ballymena Technical High School and S. Wales Bible Coll. and Reformed Presbyterian Theological Coll., Belfast.
Ordained 46; Minister, Martyrs Memorial Free Presbyterian Church 46-; Moderator, Free Presbyterian Church of Ulster 51-; commenced publishing *The Protestant Telegraph* 66; mem. Parl. for N. Antrim 70-; M.P. for Bannside, Co. Antrim, Parl. of N. Ireland (Stormont) 70-72; mem. N. Ireland Assembly 73-74; mem. Constitutional Convention 75-76.
Publs. *History of the 1859 Revival* 59, *Ravenhill Pulpit* Vol. 1 66, Vol. II 67, *Exposition of the Epistle to the Romans* 68, *Billy Graham and the Church of Rome* 70.
17 Cyprus Avenue, Belfast BT5 5NT, N. Ireland.

Pajestka, Józef, M.L., DR. ECON. SC.; Polish economist and politician; b. 9 March 1924, Milówka, Żywiec district; ed. Warsaw Univ.

Worked at Cen. Planning Office, subsequently at State Comm. of Econ. Planning and Comm. of Planning attached to Council of Ministers 48-56; Dir. Inst. for Econ. Research 56-65; Dir. Inst. of Planning 65-68; Prof. Univ. of Warsaw 68-; Vice-Chair. Planning Comm., Council of Ministers 68-; Pres. Cen. Board of Polish Econ. Soc. 66-; Corresp. mem. Polish Acad. of Sciences 74-; mem. UN Planning Cttee.; mem. Cen. Cttee. Polish United Workers' Party; Gold Cross of Merit 56, Chevalier's Cross of Order Polonia Restituta 64, Commdr. Cross 69, Prize of UNO 72 and others.

Publs. *The State and Approach to Future Studies in Socialist Countries* 69, *Social Dimensions of Development* 70, *Problems, Prospects and Challenge. The Three Socio-Economic Systems towards the End of XXth Century* 72, *Examinations of Policy Measures that Contribute to Equity and Social Justice Without Substantial Sacrifice of Economic Growth* 73, *Need for Greater World-Wide Rationality* 73.

Komisja Planowania przy Radzie Ministrów, Plac Trzech Krzyży 3/5, Warsaw; Home: ul. Sulkiewicza 7, m. 20, 00-758 Warsaw, Poland.

Pak Chung Hi, Gen. (*see* Park Chung Hee).

Pal, Benjamin Peary, M.SC., PH.D., F.R.S.; Indian agricultural scientist; b. 26 May 1906, Mukandpur, Punjab; s. of Dr. R. R. and Mrs. I. D. Pal; ed. Rangoon and Cambridge Univs.

Second Econ. Botanist, Imperial Agricultural Research Inst., 33-37, Imperial Econ. Botanist 37-50; Designated as Head, Div. of Botany, Indian Agricultural Research Inst. then Dir. 50-65; fmr. Dir.-Gen. Indian Council of Agricultural Research 65-71; fmr. Chair. Special Advisory Cttee. on Food and Agriculture, Dept. of Atomic Energy; fmr. Pres. Botany and Agriculture Sections, Indian Science Congress and of many botanical and agricultural socs.; Pres. Indian Science Congress 70-71; has served on Govt. Educ. Comm., heading its Task Force on Agricultural Educ.; fmr. Chair. All India Fine Arts and Crafts Soc.; helped to establish Postgraduate School at Indian Agricultural Research Inst.; research in wheat breeding and genetics; revision work on Int. Code of Nomenclature of Agricultural and Horticultural Plants; mem. Royal Nat. Rose Soc., All Union Lenin Acad. of Agricultural Sciences 67, Linnean Soc. of London, Indian Botanical Soc., Royal Horticultural Soc. of London; Fellow Indian Nat. Science Acad., Pres. 75-; Fellow Royal Soc., London; Awards include Padma Shri 58, Rafi Ahmed Kidwai Memorial Prize of the Indian Council of Agricultural Research 60, Srinivisa Ramanujan Medal, Nat. Inst. of Sciences of India 64, Padma Bhushan 68, Birbal Sahni Medal of Indian Botanical Soc. 62; Hon. D.Sc.

Leisure interests: rose breeding, painting.

Publs. *Beautiful Climbers of India, Charophyta, The Rose in India, Wheat, Flowering Shrubs* 68, *Bougainvilleas* 74; and over 160 scientific papers.

P-11 Hauz Khas Enclave, New Delhi 16, India. Telephone: 626145.

Pál, Lénárd; Hungarian physicist; b. 7 Nov. 1925, Gyoma; s. of Imre Pál and Erzsébet Varga; m. Angela Danóczi 1963; one d.; ed. Budapest and Moscow Univs.

Department Head, Central Research Inst. for Physics, Budapest 54-56, Deputy Dir. 56-69, Dir. 70-; Prof. of Nuclear Physics, Eötvös Lorand Univ. Budapest 61-; mem. Science Council, Joint Inst. for Nuclear Research, Dubna 66-; mem. Int. Union for Pure and Applied Physics 66-; mem. European Physics Soc.—Condensed Matter Division 71-; Vice-Pres. Fed. of Technical and Scientific Socs. 72-; mem. Hungarian Pugwash Cttee. and Nat. Peace Council; Corresp. mem. Hungarian Acad. of Sciences 61-73, mem. 73-; Kossuth Prize 62; Gold Medal of the Hungarian Acad. of Sciences.

Leisure interests: music, reading, hunting.

Publs. Approximately 225 articles in Hungarian and foreign scientific journals.

H-1525 Budapest, P.O. Box 49, Hungary. Telephone: 366-394.

Palade, George Emil; American (Romanian-born) scientist; b. 19 Nov. 1912, Jassy, Romania; s. of Emil Palade and Constanta Cantemir; m. 1st Irina Malaxa 1940 (deceased); m. 2nd Marilyn Farquhar 1970; one s. one d.; ed. Hasdeu Lyceum, Buzau, Univ. of Bucharest.

Went to U.S.A. 46; naturalized U.S. citizen 52; Instructor, Asst. Prof. of Anatomy, School of Medicine, Univ. of Bucharest 35-45; Visiting Investigator, Asst. Assoc., Prof. of Cell Biology, Rockefeller Univ.; Prof. of Cell Biology, Yale Univ. 73-; Fellow American Acad. of Arts and Sciences; mem. Nat. Acad. of Sciences; Albert Lasker Basic Research Award 66, Hurwitz Prize 70, Nobel Prize for Medicine 74.

Leisure interest: history.

Section of Cell Biology, Yale University School of Medicine, 333 Cedar Street, New Haven, Conn. 06510, U.S.A.

Telephone: (203) 436-2376.

Palamarchuk, Luka Fomich; Soviet journalist and diplomatist; b. 6 Sept. 1906, Troshcha, Ukraine; ed. Kiev Univ.

Member C.P.S.U. 28-; Dir. of a School 28-29; Head of Dept., Editorial Offices *Chervony Krai* (newspaper), Vinnitsa 29-30; Deputy Editor and Editor, regional newspapers 30-37; Deputy Editor *Perets* (Kiev satirical journal) 37-41; Chair. Radio Cttee., Ukrainian Council of People's Commissars 41-42; Editor *Radyanska Ukraina* (newspaper) 42-48, 49-52; Diplomatic Service 52-; Deputy Foreign Minister of Ukrainian S.S.R. 52-54; Minister of Foreign Affairs of Ukrainian S.S.R. 54-65; Amb. to Morocco 65-72; Red Banner of Labour, Patriotic War and other awards.

Ministry of Foreign Affairs, 32-34 Smolenskaya-Sennaya ploshchad, Moscow, U.S.S.R.

Palamenghi-Crispi, Francesco; Italian finance official; b. 28 Dec. 1917, Rome; m.; four c.; ed. Univ. of Rome.

With Bank of Italy 46-49, Dir. 63; Sec., Somali Currency Board 50-59, first Gen. Dir. 59-60; Prof. of Politics and Financial Econ. Univ. of Mogadishu, Somalia 59-66; first Man. Dir. and Deputy Pres. Somali Nat. Bank 60-66; Alt. Gov. for Somalia for Int. Bank for Reconstruction and Devt. (IBRD)—World Bank 61-66; mem. Gen. Banking Panel of Experts in Trinidad and Tobago, Int. Monetary Fund (IMF) 66-67; Temp. Alt. Gov. IMF 69, 70, 72, IBRD 69; Exec. Dir. IMF for Italy (also Malta, Portugal and Spain) Dec. 67-; mem. Italian Econ. Del. to Peace Conf., Paris 46; Lecturer Univ. of Rome 46-56.

International Monetary Fund, 19th and H Streets, N.W., Washington, D.C. 20431, U.S.A.

Telephone: 202-477-3301.

Palasi, José Luis Villar; Spanish university professor and politician; b. 1923; ed. Faculty of Philosophy and Literature, Univ. of Valencia.

Professor of Admin. Law, Madrid Univ. 65-; fmr. Under-Sec. of Information and Tourism, later Under-Sec. for Commerce; Minister of Educ. 68-73.

Madrid University, Madrid, Spain.

Palazzini, H.E. Cardinal Pietro, S.T.D., J.U.D.; Vatican ecclesiastic; b. 19 May 1912, Piobbico, Pesaro; ed. Lateran Univ.

Ordained 6 Dec. 34; advocate of the Sacred Roman Rota; fmr. Asst. Dir. Pontificio Seminario Maggiore at Lateran Univ. 45-56; Under-Sec. Sacred Congregation for the Religious 56-58; Sec. Sacred Congregation for the Clergy 62; created Cardinal by Pope Paul VI 73.

Publs. *Il Monoteismo dei Padri Apostolici* 46, *Indissolubilità del Matrimonio* 52, *Il Diritto Strumento di Riforma in S. Pier Damiani* 56, *Theologia Moralis* (with A. Lanza) 4 vols. 53-63, *Principii di Teologia Morale* (Principles of Moral Theology) 3 vols. 54-62, *Morale Cattolica e Morale Protestante* 61, *La Coscienza* 63, *Morale del'Attualità* 63, *S. Pier Damiani il Superfluo* 72, *Vita Sacramentale I.P.*—*I Sacramenti dell'iniziazione cristiana* 74, *Dizionario dei concili* 6 vols. 63-67, *Dictionarium morale et canonicum* 4 vols. 62-68 (Dir.); *Vita e virtu cristiane* 75.
Via Proba Petronia 83, Rome, Italy.

Paleckis, Iustas Igno; Soviet politician; b. **22** Jan. 1899, Telshag, Lithuania; ed. Kaunas Univ.
Worker in printing works 15-22; teacher 22-26; Dir. of Lithuanian News Agency *Elta* 26-27; Corresp. of Riga papers and journals 27-39; sent to a concentration camp for opposing the Smetona dictatorship 39; Pres. of the Presidium of the Supreme Soviet of Lithuania and Vice-Pres. of the Supreme Soviet of the U.S.S.R. 40-67; Chair. of Soviet of Nationalities of the Supreme Soviet of the U.S.S.R. 67-70; Alt. mem. Central Cttee. of the C.P.S.U. 52-; awarded Order of Lenin (four times) Order of the Patriotic War, 1st Class; Hero of Socialist Labour.
Central Committee of the Communist Party of the Soviet Union, 4 Staraya Ploshchad, Moscow, U.S.S.R.

Palencia, Benjamin; Spanish painter; b. 1903; ed. primary schools at Barrax (La Mancha), private schools in Madrid.
Taught himself to paint; first One-Man Show Madrid Museum of Modern Art 23; yearly exhibitions since that year in Madrid, other Spanish cities and in America; rep. at Biennales of Venice and São Paulo; Exhbns. Paris (Galerie Pierre) 33, New York (Harriman Gallery) 34, Munich (Kunstverein), Düsseldorf (Malcasten) 58, Paris 59; Primera Medalla de Bellas Artes, Gran Premio 1st Hispano-American Art Biennale.
Publs. *Niños, Niños de mi molino, Italia con B. Palencia, Giotto, raiz viva de la Pintura (Cruz y Raya), Pintores Modernos: Pinturas de B. Palencia.*
Sagasta 19, Madrid, Spain.

Palewski, Gaston; French politician and diplomatist; b. 20 March 1901, Paris; m. Violette de Talleyrand-Périgord, Duchesse de Sagan et Dino 1969; ed. Univs. of Paris and Oxford.
On staff of Resident Gen. in Morocco 24-25; successively Chef du Cabinet of Ministry for Colonies and Justice; Dir. du Cabinet Min. of Finance 29-39; Dir. Political Affairs, Free France 40; Commdt. Free French Forces in Ethiopia and E. Africa 41-42; Dir. du Cabinet to Gen. de Gaulle 42-46; Foreign Affairs specialist, Exec. Cttee. Rassemblement du Peuple Français 47; Deputy (Seine) 51-56; Vice-Pres. R.P.F. Parl. group; formerly 1st Deputy Pres. Nat. Assembly; Minister, Deputy to the Prime Minister 55-56; Ambassador to Italy 57-62; Minister of State for Science, Atomic Questions and Space 62-65; Pres. and mem. Constitutional Council 65-74; mem. Inst. Acad. des Beaux-Arts 68-; Hon. Pres. *Revue des Deux Mondes*; Hon. Fellow, Worcester Coll., Oxford 74; Grand Croix Légion d'Honneur, Croix de Guerre Compagnon de la Libération.
1 rue Bonaparte, Paris 6e; Château de Marais, 91530 Saint-Chéron, France,
Telephone: DAN-91-35 (Paris); 491-91-26 (Saint-Chéron).

Palewski, Jean-Paul; French lawyer and politician; b. 19 July 1898; m. Anne-Marie Fouchet; three s. four d.; ed. Univ. of Paris and St. Cyr Military Acad.
Lawyer, Paris Law Courts; Deputy to Nat. Assembly 46-55, 58-, mem. Cttee. on Justice 51-55, Vice-Pres. Finance Cttee. 51-55, Pres. Nat. Assembly Cttee. on Finance, General Economy and Planning 62; Pres. High Council for Industrial Property 58, Comm. Nat. des

Secteurs Sauvegardés 65; mem. Council of Libraries of France 64-, Admin. Council Conservatoire Nat. des Arts et Métiers 64; Pres. Conseil Général de Yvelines 66-; French Rep. to UN; Commdr. Légion d'Honneur, Croix de Guerre, Médaille de la Résistance.
Publs. *Le Rôle de chef d'entreprise dans la grande industrie, L'Organisation scientifique du travail, Vies polonaises, Pensées d'un otage, L'Ame polonaise, Stanislas Auguste Poniatowski, Louveciennes, Histoire des Chefs d'Entreprise,* etc.
National Assembly, Paris 7e, France; and 27 route de Versailles, 78240 Louveciennes, France.
Telephone: 969-05-98.

Paley, William S., B.S.; American corporation executive; b. 28 Sept. 1901; ed. Univ. of Chicago, Univ. of Pennsylvania.
Chairman, CBS Inc.; Trustee Emer. Columbia Univ.; Chair. and Trustee Museum of Modern Art; Pres. and Dir. William S. Paley Foundation Inc.; Co-Chair. and Trustee Emer., N. Shore Univ. Hospital; Hon. Dir. Resources for the Future Inc.
51 W. 52nd Street, New York City, N.Y. 10019, U.S.A.

Palfrey, John Gorham; American university professor; b. 12 March 1919; ed. Milton Acad. and Harvard Univ.
Admitted to D.C. Bar 48; Office of Gen. Counsel, Atomic Energy Commission 47-50; mem. Inst. Advanced Study, Princeton 50-52; Lecturer, Columbia School of Law 52-54, Assoc. Prof. 54-56, Prof. 56-62, Dean Columbia Coll. 58-62; mem. U.S. Atomic Energy Comm. 62-66; Fellow, Inst. of Politics, Harvard Univ. 66-67; Prof. of Law and History, Columbia Univ. 67-.
15 Claremont Avenue, New York, N.Y. 10027, U.S.A.

Palgen, Rudolf, PH.D.; Luxembourg university professor; b. 23 April 1895, Echternach; s. of Nicholas Palgen and Helene von Keyserlingk; m. Hilde Maria Britz 1940; ed. Echternach (Gymnasium), Univs. of Munich, Heidelberg, Marburg-Lahn, Montpellier, and Paris.
Lecturer in French Univ. of Breslau 19-40; Prof. of Romance Philology Tübingen Univ. 40-41; Prof. at Graz, Austria 41-, also Head of Dept. of Romance Philology and of Dept. of Italian Language and Literature; hon. mem. Inst. Grand-Ducal Luxembourg; Officier Couronne de Chêne; Commdr. Ordre du Mérite, Luxembourg, Ufficiale al Merito, Repubblica Italiana.
Publs. include *Der Stein der Weisen* 22, *Villiers de l'Isle Adam* 25, *Die Weltanschauung H. Bergsons* 29, *Das mittelalterliche Gesicht der Goettlichen Komoedie* 35, *Dantes Sternglaube* 40, *Italienische Literaturgeschichte* 49, *Ursprung und Aufbau der Komödie Dantes* 54, *Werden und Wesen der Komödie Dantes* 55, *L'Origine del Purgatorio* 67, *Dantes Luzifer* 69, *Mittelalterliche Eschatologie in Dantes Komödie* 75.
Koerblergasse 83, A-8010 Graz, Austria.
Telephone: 32350.

Palkhivala, Nani Ardeshir; Indian lawyer and businessman; b. 16 Jan. 1920, Bombay; s. of Ardeshir Nanabhoy and Sheherbanoo A. Palkhivala; m. Nargesh H. Matbar 1945; ed. St. Xavier's Coll. and Govt. Law Coll., Bombay.
Senior advocate, Supreme Court of India; Chair. Assoc. Cement Cos. Ltd.; Vice-Chair. Tata Iron and Steel Co. Ltd., Tata Engineering and Locomotive Co., Assoc. Bearing Co., The Statesman Ltd.; dir. numerous other cos.; Pres. Forum of Free Enterprise; Chair. Income-tax Appellate Tribunal Bar Asscn.
Leisure interests: motoring, history, literature.
Commonwealth, 181 Backbay Reclamation, Bombay 400 020, India.
Telephone: 25-9131 (Office); 29-5963 (Home).

Pallin, Franz; Austrian judge; b. 4 April 1909, Graz; s. of Friedrich and Olga Pallin; m. Herta Pallin 1954; one s. one d.; ed. Univ. of Graz.

Judge 36-; Public Prosecutor 45; Generalanwalt 51; Generalprokurator 66-71; Vice-Pres. Supreme Court 71, Pres. 72-.
Justizpalast, Museumstrasse 12, Vienna 1; Home: Vienna 8, Breitenfeldergasse 14, Austria.
Telephone: 934511 (Supreme Court).

Palliser, Sir (Arthur) Michael, K.C.M.G., M.A.; British diplomatist; b. 9 April 1922, Reigate; s. of late Admiral Sir Arthur Palliser, K.C.B., D.S.C. and of Lady Palliser (née Margaret E. King-Salter); m. Marie M. Spaak (d. of late Paul-Henri Spaak); three s.; ed. Wellington Coll. and Merton Coll., Oxford.
Entered diplomatic service 47; Foreign Office 47-49, 51-56; posted to Athens 49-51, Paris 56-60; Head of Chancery, Dakar 60-62; Counsellor and seconded to Imperial Defence Coll. 63; Head of Planning Staff, Foreign Office 64; a Private Sec. to Prime Minister 66-69; Minister, Paris 69-71; Amb. and Head, U.K. Del. to EEC 71-72; Ambassador and U.K. Perm. Rep. to European Communities 73-75; Perm. Under-Sec., Head of Diplomatic Service Oct. 75-; Chevalier, Order of Orange-Nassau, Légion d'Honneur.
Foreign and Commonwealth Office, King Charles St., London, S.W.1, England.

Pallottino, Massimo, D.LITT.; Italian university professor; b. 9 Nov. 1909, Rome; s. of Carlo Pallottino and Margherita Perotti; m. Maria Sechi 1936; one s. two d.; ed. Univ. of Rome.
Inspector, Dept. of Antiquities of Rome 33; Dir. Museo Nazionale di Villa Giulia, Rome and excavations of Cerveteri 37; Lecturer and later Acting Prof. Univ. of Rome 38; Prof. of Classical Archaeology Univ. of Cagliari 40; Prof. of Etruscology and Italic Antiquities, Univ. of Rome 45; Pres. Inst. of Etruscan Studies, Vice-Pres. Italian Inst. of Prehistory; mem. Directorate Int. Assen. for Classical Archaeology, Academia Nazionale dei Lincei, Pontificia Accademia di Archeologia, Académie Inscriptions et Belles Lettres (Institut de France), Deutsches Archäologisches Institut, Soc. Antiquaries of London, Prehistoric Soc., London; Dir. *Studi Etruschi, Archeologia Classica.*
Publs. *Elementi di Lingua Etrusca* 36, *Tarquinia* 37, *Etruscologia* 42, 47, 55, 68, *L'Arco degli Argentari* 46, *L'Origine degli Etruschi* 47, *La Civilisation Etrusque* 50, *La Sardegna Nuragica* 50, *Etruscan Painting* 52, *Testimonia Linguae Etruscae* 54, 68, *The Etruscans* 56, *Che cos' è l'Archeologia* 63, 68, *Civiltà Artistica Etrusco-Italica* 71.
9 Via dei Redentoristi, 00186 Rome, Italy.
Telephone: 6569364.

Palme, (Sven) Olof Joachim, B.A., L.L.B.; Swedish politician; b. 30 Jan. 1927, Stockholm; m. Lisbeth Beck Friis 1956; three s.; ed. Kenyon Coll., Ohio, and Univ. of Stockholm.
Special Counsel to Swedish Prime Minister 53-63; mem. of Parl. 58-; mem. Exec. Swedish Social Democratic Youth and Workers Educational Assen. 55-61; Minister without Portfolio 63-65; Minister of Communications 65-67, of Educ. and Culture 67-69; Prime Minister 69-; mem. Exec. Swedish Social Democratic Party 64-, Chair. 69-; mem. Swedish Del. to UN 61; Chair. Comms. on Student Welfare 60-63; Hon. PH.D. Kenyon Coll. 70.
Lövångersgatan 31, Vàllingby, Sweden.

Palmén, Erik Herbert, M.SC., D.PHIL.; Finnish meteorologist and oceanographer; b. 31 Aug. 1898, Vasa; s. of Eskil Heribert and Sally Palmén; m. Synnöve Maria von Hellens 1923; one s. one d.; ed. Univ. of Helsinki.
Assistant, Finnish Inst. of Marine Research 22, Dir. 39; Prof. of Meteorology, Univ. of Helsinki 47; Prof. and mem. Acad. of Finland 48-; Visiting Prof. Univ. of Chicago 46-48, 49-50, 52 and 56, Univ. of Calif. 54; main fields of research include tropical and extra-tropical

cyclones, jet stream, structure of atmospheric fronts, general atmospheric circulation, interaction between atmosphere and oceans, and ocean currents; Pres. Finnish Scientific Society 58; Symons Memorial Gold Medal, Royal Meteorological Society 57, Carl-Gustaf Rossby Award, American Meteorological Soc. 60, Buys-Ballot Gold Medal, Royal Netherlands Academy of Sciences and Letters 64; Rossby Prize, Swedish Geophysical Soc. 66; IMO Prize, World Meteorological Org. 69.
Institute of Meteorology, University of Helsinki, Helsinki, Finland.

Palmer, Arnold Daniel; American professional golfer and business executive; b. 10 Sept. 1929, Latrobe, Pa.; s. of Milfred J. and Doris Palmer; m. Winifred Walzer 1954; two d.; ed. Wake Forest Univ., N.C.
United States Coast Guard 50-52; U.S. Amateur Golf Champion 54; professional golfer 54-; winner of 79 professional titles, incl. British Open 61, 62, U.S. Open 60, U.S. Masters 58, 60, 62, 64, and more than $3 million in prize money; mem. U.S. Ryder Cup team 61, 63, 65, 67, 71, 73, Captain 63, 75; Pres. Arnold Palmer Enterprises (div. of Nat. Broadcasting Co.), Arnold Palmer Cadillac auto agency, Latrobe Country Club and Bay Hill Club, Fla.; mem. board of dirs. Progroup Inc., Tenn., Westmoreland County (Pa.) Airport Authority, Latrobe Area Hospital, Hon. Nat. Chair. Nat. Foundation March of Dimes 71-76; Hon. LL.D.; Athlete of Decade, Associated Press 70; Sportsman of Year, Sports Illustrated 60; Hickok Belt, Athlete of Year 60.
Leisure interests: bridge, occasional hunting.
Publs. *My Game and Yours* 65, *Situation Golf* 70, *Go for Broke* 73.
One Erieview Plaza, Suite 1300, Cleveland, Ohio 44114; Home and Personal Office: P.O. Box 52, Youngstown, Pa. 15696, U.S.A.
Telephone: (216) 522-1200 (Business); (412) 537-7751 (Home).

Palmer, H(arold) Bruce; American public official; b. 16 Nov. 1908, Imlay City, Mich.; s. of Harry E. and Louise (Braman) Palmer; m. 1st Dorothy Beck 1931 (died 1967), 2nd Jean Reynolds Tuerk 1968; two d.; ed. Culver Mil. Acad. and Univ. of Michigan.
Mutual Benefit Life Insurance Co. 31-62, Vice-Pres. (Agencies) 47-48, Admin. Vice-Pres. 49-50, Exec. Vice-Pres. 51-53, Pres. 53-62; Pres. The Conference Board 63-70, Council of Better Business Bureaus 71-73; mem. Board Int. Exec. Services Corps 64-, Univ. of Mich. Devt. Council 69-; Trustee Inst. for the Future, Population Crisis Comm.; Chair. Pacific Tropical Botanical Garden 75-, Advisory Council of Los Angeles Orthopedic Hospital 75-; Assoc. Huntington Library, San Marino; Dir. First Boston Corpn., CPC Int. 71-, Emeritus, Junior Achievement; Hon. Chair. Board for Fundamental Educ.; several awards and hon. degrees.
1235 Hillside Road, Pasedana, Calif. 91105, U.S.A.

Palmer, James Lindley, A.M., C.P.A.; American retailer and museum executive; b. 12 March 1899; ed. Brown Univ., Univ. of Chicago.
Spent two years in small manufacturing business 19-21; mem. of Faculty, Univ. of Chicago School of Business 22-36; Business Consultant with various Corpns. 22-36; with Marshall Field & Co. in various exec. capacities 36-, Pres. 49-64; Pres. Chicago Natural History Museum 64-69; varied experience with several welfare organizations, incl. Community Fund of Chicago Inc., Pres. 46-49; various cttee. and advisory assignments with Federal, State and City Govts. 40-; Dir. Marshall Field, Harris Trust and Savings Bank, Int. Harvester Co., Chicago Lighthouse for the Blind, Community Fund of Chicago Inc., Gen. Candy Corpn.; Fellow Brown Univ.
921 North Hawthorne Place, Lake Forest, Illinois, U.S.A.

Palmer, Leonard Robert, M.A., D.PHIL., PH.D.; British philologist; b. 5 June 1906, Bristol; s. of William Henry Palmer and Florence Palmer (née Roberts); m. Elisabeth Weil 1930; one d.; ed. Canton High School and Univ. Coll., Cardiff, Trinity Coll., Cambridge and Vienna Univ. Assistant Lecturer in Classics, Manchester Univ. 31-35, Lecturer 35-41; attached to Foreign Office 41-45; Prof. of Greek, Head, Department of Classics, King's Coll., London Univ. 45-52; Fellow of Worcester Coll. and Prof. of Comparative Philology, Oxford Univ. 52-72, Emeritus Fellow and Prof. Emeritus 72-; Hon. Sec. Philological Soc. 47-51, Pres. 57-60; Corresp. mem. Deutsches Archäologisches Inst.
Publs. Translation of E. Zeller's *Outlines of the History of Greek Philosophy* 31; *Introduction to Modern Linguistics* 36, *A Grammar of the Post-Ptolemaic Papyri*, Vol. I (Publications of the Philological Soc.) 45, *The Latin Language* 54, *Mycenaeans and Minoans* 61, 65, *The Interpretation of Mycenaean Texts* 63, *Homer: Language and Dialect* (in *A Homeric Companion*) 62, *The Find Places of the Knossos Tablets* 63, *A New Guide to the Palace of Knossos* 69, *The Penultimate Palace of Knossos* 69, *Descriptive and Comparative Linguistics: a Critical Introduction* 72; numerous articles in British and foreign learned periodicals.
Leisure interests: gardening, mountain sports, archaeology, music.
A-60-73 Sistrans 139, Tirol, Austria.
Telephone: Innsbruck 70702.

Palmer, Philip Johnathan Gbagu; Sierra Leonean teacher and diplomatist; b. 29 June 1940, Lunsar; m.; four c.; ed. Methodist Boys High School, Fourah Bay Coll.
Teacher Methodist Boys High School, Freetown 66-69, Senior Asst. Master; Inspector of Examinations, W. African Examinations Council; Amb. to Ethiopia 70, to Israel 71, to U.S.A. 72, concurrently High Commr. to Jamaica, Trinidad and Tobago 73; Perm. Rep. to UN 74-75.
c/o Ministry of Foreign Affairs, Freetown, Sierra Leone.

Palthey, Georges Louis Claude, D.IUR.; French United Nations official (retd.); b. 26 Aug. 1910, Chalon-sur-Saône; m. 1st Marie Louise Bourdin 1938 (died 1964), 2nd Jacqueline de Roll de Hemmenholz; one s.; ed. Univs. of Lyon and Paris.
Finance Officer, Control of Expenditure Commitments, French Ministry of Finance 34-42; Chief Secretariat, Gen. Dept. of Economic Control 42-45; Deputy Financial Comptroller, French Missions in Great Britain 45-47; Deputy Dir., Personnel UN 47, Dir. 48-54; Deputy Dir., European Office of UN, Geneva 54-65; Deputy Dir.-Gen. UN Office, Geneva 65-73; Croix de Guerre.
Publ. *Le Contrôle préalable des Finances publiques.*
2 rue des Granges, Geneva, Switzerland.
Telephone: 21-32-76.

Pamplin, Robert Boisseau; American business executive; b. 25 Nov. 1911, Sutherland, Va.; s. of John R. Pamplin and Pauline Beville; m. Mary K. Reese 1940; one s.; ed. Virginia Polytechnic Inst. and Northwestern Univ.
Georgia-Pacific Corpn. (forest products) 34-, Sec. and Treas. 36-48, Financial Vice-Pres. 48-52, Admin. Vice-Pres. 52-56, Exec. Vice-Pres. 56-59, Chair., Pres. and Chief Exec. Officer 68-; Trustee Lewis and Clark Coll., Portland 56-, Chair. Board of Trustees 63-68; mem. Board of Trustees Virginia Polytechnic Institute 71-.
Leisure interests: hunting, fishing, bridge.
900 S.W. Fifth Avenue, Portland, Oregon 97204; Home: 404 S.W. Edgecliff Road, Portland, Ore. 97219, U.S.A.
Telephone: 503-222-5561 (Office).

Pan Yen; Chinese naval officer.
Chief of Staff of Navy, People's Liberation Army.
People's Republic of China.

Panǎ, Gheorghe; Romanian politician; b. 9 April 1927, Gherghiţa, Prahova County; m. Antoneta Pana; one d.; ed. Acad. of Economic Studies, Bucharest.
Joined Communist Youth Union 44, Communist Party 47; Sec. Bucharest Party Cttee. 59-64; First Sec. Braşov Regional Cttee. 66-68, Brasov County Cttee. of Romanian C.P. 68-69; mem. Exec. Cttee. of the Cen. Cttee. of R.C.P. 69-, Perm. Presidium of Cen. Cttee. 69-74; Sec. Central Cttee. of R.C.P. 69-75; Deputy to Grand Nat. Assembly 69-; mem. Nat. Council of Socialist Unity Front 68-, State Council 69-75; Chair. Gen. Trade Union Confed. 75-; Order of Labour, Star of the R.S.R. Order of 23 August, Hero of Socialist Labour 71.
General Trade Union Confederation, 14 Aleea Stefan Gheorghiu, Bucharest, Romania.

Panard, Pierre Marie Maurice; French public servant; b. 1 Nov. 1916, Dun le Palestel; m. Monique de Rigaud de Vaudreuil; ed. Univ. de Paris Faculté de Droit and Ecole Libre des Sciences Politiques.
Clerk, Ministry of Finance 41-46, Civil Admin. 46-47; transferred to Finance Comm. of Nat. Assembly 47-49, Chief, Technical Services 61-62; Chief, Office Sec. of State for Marine 49-50; Financial Comptroller 56-61; Dir. Office Minister of Public Works and Transport 62-64; Chief, Central Bureau of Finance 64; Dir.-Gen. Compagnie Générale Transatlantique 64-74; Pres. Dir.-Gen. Compagnie Générale Entretien et de Réparations; Officier Légion d'Honneur, Commdr. Ordre National du Mérite, Croix de Guerre.
Leisure interest: horse breeding.
1 ter rue Mornay, 75004 Paris, France.
Telephone: 272-13-31.

Panas, Eustace G., PH.D.; Greek professor of economics; b. Nov. 1924, Athens; s. of George and Helen Panas; m. Athena Kossifakis 1958; one d.; ed. Nat. Univ. of Athens and Harvard Univ.
Joined Ministry of Co-ordination 50, Nat. Accounts Div. 51-61, Dir. Fiscal and Monetary Matters Div. 61-69; Sec., Ministerial Economic Cttee. 62-63; Sec., Nat. Council of Economic Policy 67-69; Statistician, UN Statistical Office, Nat. Accounts Branch 56, 57, 58-59; mem. Greek Nat. Tobacco Board, Prices and Incomes Comm., Central Planning Cttee.; Assoc. Prof. Economics, Graduate School of Industrial Studies 68-72; Chair. Capital Market Cttee. 67-; Alternative Gov., IMF 69-; Chair. Export Credit Guaranty Council 69-; Deputy Gov. Bank of Greece 69-74; Prof. of Economics, Graduate School of Econ. and Business Science 72; mem. dels. to OECD, NATO, IMF; mem. American Economic Asscn., American Statistical Asscn., Royal Economic Soc., Greek Economic Soc., Int. Asscn. for Research in Income and Wealth.
Publs. articles and papers in Greek and English on economic topics.
6 Naiadon Street, Athens 516, Greece.
Telephone: 717-177 (Home).

Panayotacos, Constantine P., LL.D.; Greek diplomatist; b. 1918, Zurich, Switzerland; s. of late Panayotis Panayotacos; m. Irene Arvanitis 1957; one s.; ed. Univ. of Athens.
Professor of Int. Law, Univ. of Athens 48; joined Diplomatic Service, held several diplomatic posts 50-67, including Sec., Greek Embassy, Washington, D.C. 59-61, Counsellor, Perm. Mission to UN 65, Counsellor, Washington, D.C. 65; Amb. to India, concurrently accred. to Nepal, Ceylon, Thailand, Burma, Singapore, Malaysia, Indonesia, Repub. of Viet-Nam 68; Perm. Rep. to Council of Europe 69-70; Amb. to Cyprus 71; Under-Sec. of State for Foreign Affairs 72; Perm. Rep. to UN 73-74; Grand Officer Order of George I, Order of the Phoenix; Officer Order of the Crown (Belgium),

Order of the Oak (Luxembourg); Grand Cross Order of Holy Sepulchre and several others.

Leisure interests: reading, fishing, music.

c/o Ministry of Foreign Affairs, Athens, Greece.

Panayotakis, Konstantinos A.; Greek planning consultant; b. 1922, Athens.

Runs own planning office working on major projects (regional and town planning, buildings, utility services, archaeological restorations, landscaping) in Greece, Iraq, Saudi Arabia, Lebanon, Iran, Libya, Jordan etc.; mem. Technical Chamber of Greece, American Soc. of Civil Engineers, Associated Consulting Engineers, Union of Iraqi Architects and Engineers, Nat. Theatre Org. of Greece; Minister of Culture and Sciences Aug. 72-73.

c/o Ministry of Culture and Sciences, Athens, Greece.

Panchen Lama (Panchen Erdeni); Tibetan religious and political leader; b. 1938 in Chinghai, China.

Installed as Panchen Lama at Tashilumpo Monastery 44, not accepted in Tibet, installed as Panchen Lama in new ceremony at Kumbun Monastery, Chinghai 49; first visited Tibet 52, in charge of Shigatse sub-region; mem. N.P.C. 54-64, mem. Standing Cttee. 61-64; Vice-Chair. C.P.P.C.C. 54-64; mem. Sino-Soviet Friendship Asscn. 54-; Vice-Chair. Preparatory Cttee. for Tibetan Autonomous Region 56-59; Hon. Chair. Chinese Buddhist Asscn. 53-; Chair. Tashilumpo Monastery Democratic Admin. Cttee. 61; denounced as reactionary by Chou En-lai 64; Provisional Chair. Preparatory Cttee. for Tibetan Autonomous Region, after flight of Dalai Lama to India, March 59-65.

Shigatse, Autonomous Region of Tibet, China.

Pandit, Vijaya Lakshmi; Indian politician and diplomatist; b. 18 Aug. 1900; d. of Motilal and Sarup Rani Nehru; m. Ranjit S. Pandit 1921; three d.; ed. privately.

Joined Non-Co-operation Movement, imprisoned for one year 31; mem. Allahabad Municipal Board 36, Chair. Education Cttee. Municipal Board; Minister of Local Self-Govt. and Public Health, Uttar Pradesh Govt. 37-39, 46-47 (1st woman minister); mem. Congress Party; sentenced to three terms of imprisonment 32, 41 and 42; detained under Defence Regulations Aug. 42-June 43; sister of late Pandit Nehru; Leader of Indian Del. to UN 46-51, 63; Ambassador to U.S.S.R. 47-49, to U.S.A. 49-51; mem. Indian Parl. 52-54; Pres. UN Assembly 53-54; High Commr. for India in United Kingdom and Ambassador to Ireland 55-Aug. 61, concurrently Ambassador to Spain 58-Aug. 61; Gov. of Maharashtra 62-64; mem. Lok Sabha Nov. 64-July 68; Hon. D.C.L. (Oxford).

181B Rajpur Road, Dehra Dun, Uttar Pradesh, India.

Panichas, George Andrew, F.R.S.A., M.A., PH.D.; American university professor and writer; b. 21 May 1930, Springfield, Mass.; s. of Andrew and Fannie Dracouli Panichas; unmarried; ed. Springfield Classical High School, American Int. Coll., Trinity Coll. and Nottingham Univ., England.

Instructor in English, Univ. of Maryland 62, Asst. Prof. 63, Assoc. Prof. 66, Prof. 68-; lectures on the modern novel, the British novel between the two world wars and writes in the area of comparative literature and on interdisciplinary subjects (politics, history, philosophy and religion).

Leisure interests: hiking, keeping physically fit, listening to music.

Publs. *Adventure in Consciousness: The Meaning of D. H. Lawrence's Religious Quest* 64, *Epicurus* 67, *Mansions of the Spirit: Essays in Literature and Religion* (Editor) 67, *Promise of Greatness, The War of 1914-1918* (Editor) 68, *The Politics of Twentieth-Century Novelists* (Editor) 71, *The Reverent Discipline: Essays in Literary Criticism and Culture* 74; also numerous articles, translations, and reviews for books and journals published in U.S. and Europe; Editorial Adviser, *Modern Age: A Quarterly Review.*

Department of English, University of Maryland, College Park, Maryland 20742; Home: 4313 Knox Road, Apartment 604, College Park, Maryland 20740, U.S.A.

Telephone: 301-454-4150 (Office); 301-779-6894 (Home).

Panofsky, Wolfgang Kurt Hermann, A.B., PH.D.; American scientist; b. 24 April 1919, Berlin, Germany; s. of Erwin Panofsky and Dorothea Mosse Panofsky; m. Adele Dumond 1942; three s. two d.; ed. Princeton Univ. and California Inst. of Technology.

In U.S.A. 34-; mem. of staff Radiation Laboratory, Calif. Univ. 45-51; Asst. Prof. 47-48, Assoc. Prof. 48-51; Prof. Stanford Univ. 51-63, Dir. High Energy Physics Laboratory 53-61, Dir. Linear Accelerator Center 62-; mem. President's Science Advisory Cttee. 60-64; mem. Steering Cttee. JASON Div., Inst. for Defense Analyses 65, Atomic Energy Comm. 67-; Hon. D.Sc. (Case Inst. of Technology and Univ. of Saskatchewan); Lawrence Prize, U.S. Atomic Energy Comm. 61; Calif. Scientist of Year Award 67; Nat. Medal of Science 69, Franklin Medal 70.

Leisure interest: music.

Stanford Linear Accelerator Center, Stanford University, P.O. Box 4349, Stanford, Calif. 94305; Home: 25671 Chapin Avenue, Los Altos Hills, Calif., U.S.A.

Telephone: 854-3300.

Pansa Cedronio, Paolo, LL.D., LIC.POL.SC.; Italian diplomatist; b. 15 Nov. 1915, Naples; s. of Ciro Pansa Cedronio and Elina Stammelluti; unmarried; ed. Univs. of Naples and Florence.

Entered Italian diplomatic service 40; Sec., Italian Embassy, Washington 45-49; mem. Del. to NATO, London and Paris 51-55; Head of Service, Ministry of Foreign Affairs, Rome 55-61; Minister, Italian Embassy, London 61-66; Amb. to Chile 66-70, to Canada 70-71; Deputy Sec.-Gen. NATO Aug. 71-; Croce di Guerra, Grand' Ufficiale Ordine al Merito della Repubblica Italiana, Gran-Cruz Orden al Mérito de Chile, Officier de la Légion d'Honneur, etc.

OTAN/NATO, 1110 Brussels, Belgium.

Telephone: 241-00-40.

Pant, Apasaheb Balasaheb; Indian politician and diplomatist; b. 11 Sept. 1912, Aundh, Satara District, Maharashtra; s. of Bhawanrao and Ramabai Pant Pratinidhi; m. Nalini Natesh Dravi 1942; one s. two d.; ed. Univs. of Bombay and Oxford, and Lincoln's Inn, London.

Former Minister of Educ., Aundh State, Prime Minister 38-44, Minister 44-48; mem. All-India Congress Cttee. 48; Commr. for Govt. of India, British East Africa 48-54, concurrently Consul-Gen. in Belgian Congo and Ruanda Urundi 48-54, concurrently Commr. in Central Africa and Nyasaland 50-54; Officer on Special Duty, Ministry of External Affairs, New Delhi 54-55; Political Officer, Sikkim and Bhutan, with control over Indian missions in Tibet 55-61; Amb. to Indonesia 61-64, to Norway 64-66, to U.A.R. 66-69; High Commr. in U.K. 69-72; Amb. to Italy and High Commr. to Malta Nov. 72-; Del. to UN Gen. Assembly 51, 52, 65; Padma Shri 54.

Leisure interests: photography, yoga, tennis, skiing, riding, archaeology, music.

Publs. *Tensions and Tolerance* 65, *Aggression and Violence: Ghandian Experiments to Fight Them* 68, *Yoga* 68, *Surya Namaskar* 69, *A Moment in Time.*

Embassy of India, Lungotevere Mellini 17, Rome; Home: Via Cassia 1951, Rome, Italy.

Telephone: 878385 (Office); 6998053 (Home).

Pant, Krishna Chandra, M.SC.; Indian politician; b. 10 Aug. 1931, Bhowali, Nainital Dist.; s. of late Pandit Govind Ballabh Pant; m. Ila Pant 1957; two s.; ed. St. Joseph's Coll., Nainital, Univ. of Lucknow.

Member Parl. for Nainital 62-; Minister of Finance 67,

of Steel and Heavy Engineering 69, of Home Affairs and Head, Depts. of Electronics, Atomic Energy, Science and Technology 70; Minister of Irrigation and Power 73; First Vice-Pres. Human Rights Comm. 66; Leader del. to Int. Conf. on Human Rights, Teheran 68; del. to various other int. confs.; Hon. D.Sc. (Udaipur Univ.). Leisure interests: welfare work, reading, travelling, sports.
1 Teen Murti Marg, New Delhi, India.
Telephone: 374911, 372507.

Pant, Sumitranandan; Indian poet; b. 1900, Kausani; s. of G. Pant; Fellow of Sahitya Acad.
Jnan Pith Award 69.
Publs. *Vina Granthi* 19, *Jyotsna* (drama) 22, *Pallav* 26, *Gunjan* 31, *Uygvani-Gramya* 38, *Swarana Kiran* 46, *Uttara* 48, *Atima* 55, *Vani* 57, *Kala Aur Boodhachand* (Academy Award Winner) 59, *Lokayatan* (Epic, Soviet Nehru Award Winner) etc.
18/B.7, K. G. Marg, Allahabad, India.
Telephone: Allahabad 3540.

Panton, Verner; Danish architect and designer; b. 1926, Gamtofte; s. of Henry and Ellen Panton; m. Marianne Pherson 1964; one d.; ed. Odense Technical School, Copenhagen Royal Acad. of Fine Arts.
Study in various European countries 53-55; independent designer and architect 55-; has designed furniture, lamps, carpets, curtains, upholstery fabrics, wall decorations etc.; buildings include cardboard house 57, inn at Fyn (Denmark) 58, spherical house 60, plastic house 60; exhbns. include Dansk Köbestaevne Exhbn. 58, Bayer exposition ships *Visiona I & II*, Cologne 68, 70, Musée des Arts Décoratifs, Louvre 69; interiors include hotel at Trondheim (Norway) 60, Spiegel Publ. House, Hamburg 69, Varna Restaurant, Aarhus 71, Junior Casino, Goslar, Germany 73, Gruner and Jahr Publ. House, Hamburg 74; mem. Medlem Akademisk Arkitektverband (Denmark), Danske Arkitekters Landsforbund, Industrial Designers (Denmark), Schweizerischer Werkbund; Fellow, Royal Soc. of Arts, London; awards include PH Prize, Copenhagen 67; Rosenthal Studio Prize, Germany 67; Int. Design Award, U.S.A. 63, 68; Eurodomus 2, Italy 68, Medal of Österreichisches Bauzentrum 68, Ehrenpreis, Fourth Vienna Int. Furnishing Salon 69, 3 Bundespreise "Gute Form", Fed. Germany 72, Knight of Mark Twain, U.S.A. 73.
Rebgasse 108, 4102 Binningen, Switzerland.
Telephone: 061-39-70-66.

Panufnik, Andrzej; British composer and conductor; b. 24 Sept. 1914, Warsaw, Poland; s. of Tomasz Panufnik and Matylda Thonnes Panufnik; m. Camilla Jessel 1963; one s. one d.; ed. Warsaw State Conservatoire and the State Acad. of Music (with Felix Weingartner), Vienna.
Conductor Cracow Philharmonic Orchestra 45-46; Dir. Warsaw Philharmonic Orchestra 46-47; Vice-Pres. Polish Composers' Union 48-54; Vice-Chair. Int. Music Council of UNESCO 50-53; settled in England 54; Musical Dir. City of Birmingham Symphony Orchestra 57-59; visiting conductor leading European and South American orchestras 47-; mainly composer since 59; First Prize Chopin Competition 49; Banner of Labour 1st Class 49; State Prizewinner 51 and 52; Pre-Olympic Competition First Prize 52; First Prize for Musical Composition, Prince Rainier III of Monaco 63, Sibelius Centenary Medal 65; Knight of Mark Twain (U.S.A.) 66.
Leisure interests: travel, all arts.
Compositions: *Piano Trio* 34, *Five Polish Peasant Songs* 40, *Tragic Overture* 42, *Nocturne* 47, *Lullaby* 47, *Twelve Miniature Studies* 47, *Sinfonia Rustica* 48, *Hommage à Chopin* 49, *Old Polish Suite* 50, *Concerto in Modo Antico* 51, *Heroic Overture* 52, *Rhapsody* 56, *Sinfonia Elegiaca* 57, *Polonia—Suite* 59, *Concerto for Piano and Orchestra* 62, *Landscape* 62, *Sinfonia Sacra* 63, *Two Lyric Pieces*

63, *Song to the Virgin Mary* 64, *Autumn Music* 65, *Katyń Epitaph* 66, *Jagiellonian Triptych* 66, *Reflections for Piano* 68, *The Universal Prayer* 68-69, *Thames Pageant* 69, *Concerto for Violin and Strings* 71, *Triangles* 72, *Winter Solstice* 72, *Sinfonia Concertante* 73, *Sinfonia di Sfere* 74-75; Ballet Music: *Elegy* (N.Y. 67), *Cain and Abel* (Berlin 68), *Miss Julie* (Stuttgart 70).
Riverside House, Twickenham Middlesex TW1 3DJ, England.
Telephone: 01-892 1470.

Panyarachun, Anand; Thai diplomatist; b. 9 Aug. 1932; s. of Phya and Khunying Prichanusat; m. M. R. Sodsee Panyarachun (née Chakrabandh) 1956; two d.; ed. Bangkok Christian Coll., Dulwich Coll., London and Univ. of Cambridge.
Joined Ministry of Foreign Affairs 55; Sec. to Foreign Minister 58; First Sec. Perm. Mission to UN 64, Counsellor 66, Acting Perm. Rep. 67-72, concurrently Amb. to Canada; Amb. to U.S.A., concurrently Perm. Rep. to UN 72-75; Perm. Under-Sec. of State for Foreign Affairs Sept. 75-; del. to several sessions of UN Gen. Assembly and SEATO Council; Chair. Group of 77 on Law of Sea 73; Rep. to UN Econ. and Social Council 74-75; Chair. Thai Del. to 7th Special Session of UN Gen. Assembly; Vice-Chair. Ad Hoc Cttee. 7th Special Session.
Leisure interests: tennis, squash, reading.
Ministry of Foreign Affairs, Saranrom Palace, Bangkok, Thailand.

Pao, Yue-Kong, J.P.; Chinese shipowner; b. 1918, Chekiang, China; s. of Pao Sui-Loong and late Pao Chung Sau-Gin; m. Huang Sue-Ing; four d.; ed. Shanghai.
Banking 39-49; Chair. World-Wide (Shipping) Ltd., Head of World-Wide Shipping Group; Chair. World Finance Int. Ltd., IBJ Finance (H.K.) Ltd.; Dir. Hongkong and Shanghai Banking Corpn. 71-, Mass Transit Railway Corpn., Hong Kong; founder World-Wide Sea Training School; life mem. Court, Univ. of Hong Kong; Hon. Vice-Pres. Maritime Trust of U.K.; mem. Gen. Cttee. Lloyd's Register of Shipping, Board of Managers of American Bureau of Shipping, American Chamber of Commerce, Int. Advisory Cttee., Chase Manhattan Bank; Hon. LL.D. Hong Kong Univ. 75.
Leisure interests: swimming, golf.
World-Wide (Shipping) Ltd., Prince's Building, 21st Floor, Hong Kong; Home: 77 Deep Water Bay Road, Hong Kong.
Telephone: H-242111 (Office); H-92940 (Home).

Paolozzi, Eduardo, R.A.; British sculptor; b. 1924, Leith, Edinburgh; ed. Edinburgh Coll. of Art and Slade School of Fine Art, Oxford and London.
First exhibitions, Mayor Gallery, London 47, 48, 49; teacher of textile design, Cen. School of Art and Design 49-55; Lecturer in sculpture, St. Martin's School of Art 55-58; Visiting Prof. Hochschule für Bildende Künste, Hamburg 60-62; Visiting Lecturer, Univ. of Calif., Berkeley 68; Lecturer in ceramics, Royal Coll. of Art 68-; one-man exhbns. have included Hanover Gallery, London 58, 67, Betty Parsons Gallery, N.Y. 60, 62, Robert Fraser Gallery, London 64, 66, Museum of Modern Art, N.Y. 64, Pace Gallery, N.Y. 66, 67, Stedelijk Museum, Amsterdam 68, Tate Gallery, London 71, and other galleries in U.K., U.S.A., Canada, Netherlands, Germany; has participated in numerous group exhbns. including Venice Biennale 52, 60, São Paulo Biennale 57, 63, *New Images of Man*, Museum of Modern Art, N.Y. 59, 2nd, 3rd and 4th Int. Biennial Exhbns. of Prints, Museum of Modern Art, Tokyo 60, 62, 64, *British Art Today* (travelling exhbn., tour of U.S.A.) 62, 7th Int. Art Exhbn., Tokyo 63, Neue Realisten und Pop Art, Akademie der Künste, Berlin 64, Premier Bienniale Exhbn., Cracow 66,

Sculpture from Twenty Nations, Guggenheim Museum, N.Y. 67, *Pop Art Redefined*, Hayward Gallery, London 69, *Expo 70*, Osaka 70; British Critics' Prize 53, Copley Foundation Award 56, Bright Foundation Award 60, Blair Prize, 64th Annual American Exhbn., Chicago 61, 1st Prize for Sculpture, Carnegie Int. Exhbn., Pittsburgh 67.

107 Dovehouse Street, London, S.W.3; Gull Cottages, Landermere, Thorpe-le-Soken, Essex, England.

Pap, János; Hungarian politician; b. 23 Dec. 1925, Kaposvár; s. of János Pap and Éva Horváth; m. Mária Moravetz 1949; two d.; ed. chemical industry secondary school, Szeged, Communist Party Univ.

Chemical technician, Ajka Power Station 46-49; Head, Industrial and Transport Dept., Veszprém County Party Cttee. 49-56; First Sec. Veszprém County Party Cttee. 56-; Del. to the Nat. Ass. 58-; Minister of the Interior 61-63; Deputy Chair. Council of Ministers 63-65; mem. Central Cttee. Hungarian Socialist Workers' Party. Leisure interests: wild game shooting, mountaineering, reading.

Veszprém County Party Committee, Veszprém, Hungary.

Telephone: 123-66.

Papaconstantinou, Theophylactos; Greek author and journalist; b. 1905, Monastir, Serbia; s. of Prof. Philotheos Papaconstantinou and Paraskevi Kyriakou; m. Irene Oeconomopoulou 1932; one d.; ed. Univ. of Athens.

Editor and Contributor *Great Hellenic Encyclopaedia* 28-34; Editor and Leader-writer *Mahomeni Hellas* (Underground) 42-43; Contributor to newspapers, *Anexartitos* 33-36, *Proïa* 36-43, *Eleftheria* 45-63, *Makedonia* 58-59, *Messimvrini* 63-67; Press Dir. Hellenic Information Service, Cairo 43-44; Radio Commentator N.B.I. Athens, 50-53, 59-64; Under-Sec. to Prime Minister's Office 67; Minister of Educ. 67-69; mem. Union of Athens Daily Newspaper Journalists, Fed. Int. Journalists, Hellenic Soc. for Humanistic Studies; Athens Acad. Prize for *Anatomy of the Revolution*; Commdr. Royal Order of Phoenix, Knight Commdr. of Royal Order of George I, Gold Medal of City of Athens.

Leisure interests: gardening, swimming.

Publs. *Castoria* 30, *Falsifications of Marxism in Greece* 31, *Introduction to Dialectics* 33, *The Prussians of the Balkans* 44, *Against the Current* 49, *Anatomy of the Revolution* 52, *Manual of the Free Citizen* 55, *The New Line of Communism* 56, *Ion Dragoumis and the Political Prose* 57, *Anatomy of Fellow-travel* 60, *Problems of Our Era* 60, *Greek Philosophy* 64, *The Battle of Greece* 66, 71, *Political Education* 70; and Greek trans. of Karl Marx, Sigmund Freud, Charles Gide and Sidney Hook.

Agias Philotheis 23, Philothei, Athens, Greece.
Telephone: 6818788.

Papadimitriou, Konstantinos; Greek engineer and politician; b. 1916, Athens; m.; one d.; ed. Nat. Polytechnic "Metsovian".

Engineer, Cartridge and Power Co. 39-40; Chief, Technical Bureau of Constructions, Ministry of Social Welfare 41-55; Asst., Nat. Polytechnic "Metsovian" 47-57; Doctor at Highest School of Civil Engineers of Nat. Polytechnic "Metsovian"; Prof. of Mechanics, Aviation School 56; Prof. of Construction Polytechnic School, Univ. of Thessaloniki 59-61, mem. of Faculty 63-64; Minister of Public Works 68-73; Medal for Outstanding Acts, Knight of Royal Order of Phoenix, Commdr. Royal Order of George I.

Publs. *Study for the Calculation of Frames according to Hardy Cross, Sound Insulation, Proceedings for Experimental Laying of Influence Lines in Superstatic Structures, Statical models on Perspex, Technology of Building Materials, Building Constructions.*

c/o Ministry of Public Works, Athens, Greece.

Papadongonas, Alexandros; Greek naval officer and politician; b. 1931, Tripolis; ed. Naval Cadet School, U.S. Naval Schools, NATO Defence Coll.

Has served on Greek fleet vessels and submarines of all classes and has held staff positions in Greece and abroad; organized with others movt. of Navy against the dictatorship 68; arrested 73; mem. Parl. 74-; Minister of Merchant Shipping Nov. 74-; Medal of Mil. Valour, Commdr. Order of the Phoenix, Officer Order of George I; New Democracy Party.

Ministry of Merchant Shipping, Athens, Greece.

Papadopoulos, Georgios; Greek army officer (retd.) and politician; b. 5 May 1919, Eleochorion, Achaia; m. Nekee Vassiliadis 1941; two c.; ed. War Acad., Artillery School, and Officers' Training School in Middle East.

Second Lieut. 40, Lieut. 43, Capt. 46, Major 49, Lieut.-Col. 56, Col. 60, Brig. and retd. Dec. 67; served on Albanian front in Greek-Italian war 40; joined nat. resistance units during German occupation; Staff Officer 44-45, Intelligence Officer 45-46; Commdr. Artillery Battery 46; Training Officer, Artillery School 46-48; Commdr. 131st Mountain Artillery Unit 48, 144th Mountain Artillery Unit 48-49; then Artillery Instructor and Unit Commdr. 49-54; Intelligence Bureau, Army Gen. Staff 54; Chief of Staff, Artillery Div. 55-57; Central Intelligence Service 59-64; Commdr. 117th Field Artillery Unit 64-65, First Army Force 65-66; at Third Staff Bureau, Army Gen. Staff 66-April 67; Minister to Prime Minister's Office April-Dec. 67; Prime Minister, Minister of Defence and Minister to Prime Minister's Office 67-73, also Minister of Education 69-70, Minister of Foreign Affairs 70-73, Regent 72-73; Pres. of Repub. of Greece June-Nov. 73; arrested Oct. 74, sentenced to death for high treason and insurrection Aug. 75 (sentence commuted to life imprisonment); Commdr. Royal Order of Phoenix; Medal of Mil. Merit, and numerous other medals.

Leisure interests: ancient Greek authors, book collecting, hunting, the countryside.

Publ. *To Pistevo Mas (Credo)* 68.

Papadopoulos, Konstantinos; Greek army officer and politician; b. 1921, Achaïa; ed. Army Cadet School and Higher School of Welfare.

Commissioned 43, Col. 68; Sec.-Gen. Office of Prime Minister 68; Under-Sec. of State and Regional Gov. of Attica and the Islands 71; Minister at Prime Minister's Office responsible for Planning 72-73; arrested Feb. 75, sentenced to life imprisonment for high treason and 10 years' imprisonment for insurrection Aug. 75; Medal for Exceptional Bravery and many Greek and foreign decorations.

Papaligouras, Panayotis; Greek politician; b. 1917, Kerkyra; ed. Univs. of Athens and Geneva.

Assistant Prof. Univ. of Geneva 41; Reserve Officer, Greek Forces, World War II; Sec.-Gen., Ministry of Supply 45; Under-Sec. for Supply 45; Unity Party mem. Parl. 46, Greek Rally mem. Parl. 51, 52, Nat. Radical Union mem. Parl. 56, Populist Party mem. Parl. 58, Nat. Radical Union mem. Parl. 61, 63, 64; Under-Sec. of Commerce 52-53; Minister of Commerce 53-54, of Co-ordination 54-55, of Commerce and Industry 56-58, of Co-ordination 61-63; Gov. Bank of Greece 74; Minister of Co-ordination and Planning Nov. 74-; Knight Commdr. Order of the Phoenix, Gold Cross Order of King George I, Grand Crosses of Fed. Repub. of Germany, Ethiopia, Yugoslavia, Italy, Knight Commdr. Legion of Honour (France).

Publ. *Théorie de la Société Internationale* 41.

Ministry of Co-ordination and Planning, Athens, Greece.

Papandreou, Andreas George, PH.D.; Greek educationist and politician; b. 5 Feb. 1919, Chios; s. of the late George Papandreou (fmr. Prime Minister of Greece) and Sophia (née Mineiko); m. 2nd Margaret Chant 1951;

three *s.* one *d.*; ed. Athens Univ. Law School and Harvard Univ., U.S.A.
Associate Prof., Univ. of Minnesota 47-50, Northwestern Univ. 50-51; Prof. Univ. of Minnesota 51-55; Prof., Chair. Economics Dept., Univ. of Calif. 55-63; Dir. Centre of Economic Research, Athens, Greece 61-64; Economic Adviser, Bank of Greece 61-62; Minister to Prime Minister, Greece Feb.-Nov. 64; Minister of Econ. Co-ordination 65; Deputy from Ahaia 65-67; in prison April-Dec. 67; Founder and Chair. Pan-Hellenic Liberation Movement 68-74; Prof. Univ. of Stockholm 68-69; Prof. of Economics York Univ., Canada 69-74; returned to Greece Aug. 74; Founder and Leader of Panhellenic Socialist Movt. 74-.
Publs. *Economics as a Science* 58, *A Strategy for Greek Economic Development* 62, *Fundamentals of Model Construction in Macroeconomics* 62, *The Greek Front* 70, *Man's Freedom* 70, *Democracy at Gunpoint* 71.
Panhellenic Socialist Movement, Athens, Greece.

Papanin, Ivan Dmitrievich; Soviet polar explorer; b. 26 Nov. 1894.
Head of Polar stations at Tixi Bay on Franz Josef Land 32-33, on Cape Chelyuskin 34-35; in charge of the first Soviet drifting station in the Central Arctic 37-38; Head of the Central Northern Sea Route Admin. 38-46; Rear-Admiral; mem. Board of the U.S.S.R. I.G.Y. Cttee.; Head of Dept. of Marine Explorations and Dir. Research Inst. of Biology of Inland Waters (U.S.S.R. Acad. of Sciences); Chair. Moscow Branch of U.S.S.R. Geographical Soc.; Hero of the Soviet Union 37, 40; awarded Order of Lenin (seven times), Order of the Red Banner (twice), Order of the Red Star, Order of Nakhimov, Order of the Red Banner of Labour.
Department of Marine Explorations of U.S.S.R. Acad. of Sciences, 14 Leninsky Prospekt, Moscow, U.S.S.R.

Papaspyrou, Dimitrios; Greek lawyer and politician; b. 2 Nov. 1902; ed. Univ. of Athens.
Lawyer; Deputy for EPEK-Liberal Party 50-61, Centre Union Deputy 61-65; Minister of Justice 51-52, 63-64, 65; Minister of Agriculture 51-52; Minister of Prime Minister's Office 64; mem. of F.D.K. (Liberal Democratic Centre) 65-67; Speaker of Chamber of Deputies Nov. 65-67; under house arrest until Sept. 68; Minister of Agriculture July-Oct. 74.
79 Léoforos Vassilissis Sophias, Athens, Greece.

Papathanassiou, Aspassia; Greek actress; b. Amphissa; *m.* Costas Mavromatis 1944; ed. Dramatic Art School of National Theatre of Greece.
Played a variety of leading roles with various Greek theatrical groups; founder-mem. Piraikon Theatre; has toured extensively in Europe and N. and S. America; appeared at Int. Festivals in Berlin, Paris, Florence and Vienna; has given over 450 performances of ancient tragedy; appeared on T.V. in England, U.S.S.R., U.S.A. and several other countries; Paris Théâtre des Nations 1st Prize; Gold Medal of City of Athens 62, Silver Palladium Medal for best European actress 63.
105 Peter's Court, Porchester Road, London, W.2, England.
Telephone: 01-229-8328.

Papayannis, Costas; Greek banker; b. 16 Oct. 1901, Athens; *m.*; one *s.* two *d.*; ed. Univ. of Neuchâtel, Switzerland.
Chairman, Athens Chamber of Commerce and Industry, 39-51; Cen. Relief Comm. 40-42; Adviser Greek Relief Dept., Int. Red Cross 42-45; mem. Parl. for Athens, Populist Party 46, Greek Rally Party 52; Minister of Finance 52-54; Head of Del. GATT Confs., Geneva 53-54, NATO Conf. 53; mem. Board and Management Council, Nat. Bank of Greece 68-73; Gov. Hellenic Industrial Bank 73-74; Gov. Bank of Greece 73-74; mem. Historical and Ethnological Soc., Parnassus Literary

Soc.; Bundesverdienstkreuz (Fed. Germany), Grand Cross of Ethiopia, Grand Officier, Légion d'Honneur.
19 Dimokriton Street, Athens 136, Greece.
Telephone: 611-013.

Papi, Giuseppe Ugo; Italian economist; b. 19 Feb. 1893, Capua; *m.* Beatrice Bruni.
Professor of Economics, Messina Univ. 27, Pavia Univ. 31, Naples Univ. 35, Rome Univ. 38, Rector 53-66; Gen. Sec. Int. Inst. of Agriculture 39-48; Vice-Pres. and Pres. Food and Agriculture Cttee., OEEC; Pres. Int. Econ. Asscn. 62; Hon. LL.D. (Grenoble 55, Salonika 57, Bordeaux 58, Frankfurt 58, Paris 58, Aix-Marseille 60, Glasgow 61, Lille 65); Légion d'Honneur; Grosses Verdienstkreuz, Cavaliere di Gran Croce al Merito della Repubblica.
Leisure interests: literature, theatre.
Publs. *Cost Variations and Business Cycles* 29, *The Colonial Problem; an Economic Analysis* 38, *Elements and Directive Principles of Economic Planning* 42, *Uniformities in a Consumer's Plan* 42, *Theory of the Economic Behaviour of the Government* 56, *Principles of Economics* (3 vols.) 53-61, *International Economics* 60, 70, *Some Problems of Italian Economy* 63, *Dictionary of Economics* 67, *International Economics* 69, *The Choice of an International Monetary Measure* 70, *Agricultural Adjustment* 72, *Inflation* 74.
7 Plinio Street, Rome, Italy.
Telephone: 351-080.

Papon, Maurice Arthur Jean, L.EN D.; French politician; b. 3 Sept. 1910; ed. Lycée Louis-le-Grand and Facultés de Droit et de Lettres, Paris.
Editor, Ministry of Interior 35-36; Attaché, Cabinet of the Under-Sec. of State 36, Foreign Affairs 37-39; Sec.-Gen. Gironde 42-44; Prefect of Lands 44-45; Deputy Dir. for Algeria at Ministry of Interior 46-47; Prefect of Corsica 47-49, Constantine, Algeria 49-51; Sec.-Gen., Prefecture of Police 51-54, Protectorate of Morocco 54-55; Technical Adviser, Cabinet of Sec. of State for Interior 56; Insp.-Gen. for Admin., East Algeria 56-58; Prefect of Police, Paris 58-67; Pres., Dir.-Gen. Sud-Aviation Jan. 67-July 68; Pres. Finance Comm. of Nat. Assembly 72-, Finance Comm., Recorder 73-; Deputy for Cher; Commdr. Légion d'Honneur, Commdr. de l'Ordre du Mérite Civil and mil. awards.
Publs. *L'Ere des responsables* 54, *Vers un nouveau discours de la méthode* 65.
Office: Assemblée Nationale, Palais Bourbon, Paris 16e; Home: "La Noualla", Gretz-Armainvilliers (Seine-et-Marne), France.

Pappalardo, H.E. Cardinal Salvatore, D.S.T.; Italian ecclesiastic; b. 23 Sept. 1918, Villafranca; *s.* of the late Alfio Pappalardo and Gaetana Coco; ed. Pontifical Univ. Lateranensis.
Counsellor, Vatican Secr. of State 47-65; Apostolic Pronuncio, Indonesia 65-69; Pres. Pontifical Ecclesiastical Acad., Rome 69-70; Archbishop of Palermo 70-; created Cardinal by Pope Paul VI 73.
Via Matteo Bonello 2, Palermo, Italy.
Telephone: 21-34-42.

Pappenheimer, John Richard, PH.D.; American professor of physiology; b. 25 Oct. 1915, New York, N.Y.; *s.* of Alwin M. and Beatrice L. Pappenheimer; *m.* Helena F. Palmer 1949; three *s.* one *d.*; ed. Harvard Coll. and Cambridge Univ., England.
Demonstrator in Pharmacology, University Coll., London 39-42; Instructor in Physiology, Coll. of Physicians and Surgeons, New York 40-42; Fellow in Biophysics, Johnson Foundation, Univ. of Pennsylvania 42-45; Asst. Prof. Harvard Univ. Medical School 46-53, George Higginson Prof. of Physiology 69-; Career Investigator, American Heart Asscn. 53-; Editor *Physiological Reviews* and other scientific journals; Pres. American Physiological Soc. 64-65; mem. American Acad. of Arts

and Sciences Nat. Acad. of Sciences; Overseas Fellow (Churchill Coll.) Cantab. 71-72.
Leisure interest: violoncello.
Publs. Technical articles and reviews in physiological journals.
Department of Physiology, Harvard Medical School, 25 Shattuck Street, Boston, Mass. 02115, U.S.A.

Paradjanov, Sergei Iosifovich; Soviet film director; b. 18 March 1924, Tbilisi; ed. U.S.S.R. State Inst. of Cinematography.
Director at Kiev Dovzhenko Studios 52-; Mar del Plata Film Festival Award, Argentina, for *Shades of Forgotten Ancestors* 65.
Films include *First Lad* 56, *Ukrainian Rhapsody* 58, *Flower on the Stone* 59, *Shades of Forgotten Ancestors* 64.
Kiev A. Dovzhenko Film Studios, 110 Brest Litovskoye Shosse, Kiev, U.S.S.R.

Paraense, Wladimir Lobato, M.D., Brazilian scientist; b. 16 Nov. 1914, State of Pará; *s.* of Raymundo Horminho Paraense and Maria da Costa Paraense; *m.* Lygia dos Reis Corrêa 1972; one *d.*; ed. Colégio Estadual Pais de Carvalho, Pará, and Univ. do Recife.
Scientific Investigator, Ministry of Health, Brazil 40-; Prof. of Protozoology, Instituto Oswaldo Cruz 51, Instituto Nacional de Endemias Rurais 60; Research Assoc., Serviço Especial de Saúde Pública 54-56; mem. Pan American Health Org./WHO Working Group for Devt. of Guidance for Identification of American Planorbidae 61-; Dir. Inst. Nacional de Endemias Rurais 61-63; Active mem. Inst. of Malacology, Mich., U.S.A. 63-; mem. WHO Board of Experts in Parasitic Diseases 64-; Chief, Schistosomiasis Snail Identification Center for the Americas, Pan American Health Org. and Ministry of Health of Brazil 64-; Councillor, Nat. Research Council 68-; Dir. Inst. of Biology, Univ. of Brasília 68-72; mem. Sociedade de Biologia do Rio de Janeiro, Soc. Brasileira para o Progresso da Ciência (Councillor 59-), American Asscn. for Advancement of Science, Royal Soc. of Tropical Medicine and Hygiene (U.K.), Academia Brasileira de Ciências and other Brazilian socs., Soc. of Protozoologists, U.S.A., Int. Acad. of Zoology, India, Conchological Soc. of G.B. and Ireland, New York Acad. of Sciences, American Microscopical Soc., several medals.
Leisure interests: music, literature, history.
Publs. over 100 papers on zoological, parasitological and pathological aspects of tropical medicine, chiefly malaria, piroplamosis, leishmaniasis and bilharziasis (especially molluscan intermediate hosts).
Instituto de Ciências Biologicas, Universidade de Brasília, 70000 Brasília, Brazil.
Telephone: (0612) 72-0000 Ramal 2182 (Office); (0612) 72-1355 (Home).

Parandowski, Jan; Polish writer; b. 11 May 1895, Lwów, U.S.S.R.; *m.* Irena Parandowski 1925; two *s.* one *d.*; ed. Lwów Univ.
Civil prisoner of war in Russia 15-19; Literary Chair. Altenberg's Publishing House, Lwów 22-24; Pres. Polish P.E.N. Club 33-; Editor Literary Section Polish Radio, Warsaw 35-39; involved in underground activity during German occupation 39-45; Prof. of Comparative Literature Univ. of Lublin 45-53; Bronze Olympic Medal for novel *Dysk olimpijski* 36; State Prize 1st class 64, Great Cross of Order Polonia 65, Commdr. Ordre des Arts et des Lettres (France) 72, Medal of 30th Anniversary of People's Poland 74.
Publs. *Aspasie* 25, *Deux Printemps* 27, *Le roi de la vie* (*Oscar Wilde*) 29, *Le Disque Olympique* 32, *Visites et Rencontres* 34, *Ciel en flammes* 36, *Trois signes du Zodiaque* 38, *L'heure méditerranéenne* 49, *Voyages littéraires* 49, *Alchimie des Mots* 50, *Cadran solaire* 52, *Essais* 53, *Pétrarque, Odyssée* (translation) 59, *Souvenirs et Silhouettes* 60, *Medea* (play) 61, *Retour à la Vie*

61, *Nuit de Septembre* 62, *Quand j'étais critique théâtral* 63, *Feuillets épars* 65, *Acacia* 67, *Esquisses* 68, *My Rome* 70.
Ul. Zimorowicza 4, 02-062 Warsaw, Poland.
Telephone: 253333.

Paraskevopoulos, Ioannis; Greek economist and banker; b. 1900; ed. in Greece and at Albert-Ludwigs-Universität, Freiburg, Ludwig-Maximilians-Univ., Munich, and Univ. Leipzig.
Started with Deutsche Bank, Germany, then joined Midland Bank, England; with Nat. Bank of Greece 30-, helped organize its Industrial Credit Dept., Man., then Econ. Adviser, later Deputy Gov. 54-66, Gov. July 66-67; Prof. at Panteios School of Political and Econ. Science; fmr. Prime Minister, Minister of Supply, Nat. Economy, Commerce, Industry, Labour, Interior, Foreign Affairs, Co-ordination; Acting Prime Minister Dec. 66-March 67.
c/o National Bank of Greece, 86 Eolou Street, Athens 121, Greece.

Parbo, Arvi Hillar, B.ENG.; British mining engineer; b. 10 Feb. 1926, Tallinn, Estonia; *s.* of Aado Parbo and Hilda Rass; *m.* Saima Soots 1953; two *s.* one *d.*; ed. Estonia, Germany and Univ. of Adelaide.
Joined Western Mining Corpn. Ltd. 56, Mining Eng. 56, Underground Man. Nevoria Mine 58, Technical Asst. to Man. Dir. Western Mining Corpn. 60, Deputy Gen. Supt. W. Australia 64, Gen. Man. Western Mining Corpn. Ltd. 68, Deputy Man. Dir. 70, Man. Dir. 71-, Vice-Chair. 73, Chair. 74-.
Leisure interests: reading, carpentry.
Western Mining Corporation Ltd., 459 Collins Street, P.O. Box 860K, Melbourne, Vic. 3001; Home: Longwood, Highbury Road, Vermont South, Vic. 3133, Australia.
Telephone: 67-7556 (Office); 232-8264 (Home).

Pardee, Arthur Beck, PH.D.; American biochemist; b. 13 July 1921, Chicago, Ill.; *s.* of Charles A. and Elizabeth Beck; *m.* Ruth Sager; three *s.* one *d.*; ed. Univ. of California (Berkeley) and California Inst. of Technology.
Postdoctoral Fellow, Univ. of Wisconsin 47-49; Instructor, Asst. and Assoc. Prof. Univ. of Calif. (Berkeley) 49-61; Senior Postdoctoral Fellow, Pasteur Inst. 57-58; Prof. and Chair. Biochemical Sciences, Princeton Univ. 61-67, Prof. of Biology 67-; mem. Editorial Board *Biochimica Biophysica Acta* 62-69, *Proceedings of the Nat. Acad. of Sciences* 71-74; mem. Advisory Council, American Cancer Soc., Cttee. on Science and Public Policy Nat. Acad. Sciences; Trustee Cold Spring Harbour Lab. 63-69; mem. Nat. Acad. of Sciences 68-, American Acad. of Arts and Sciences 63-; Paul Lewis Award, American Chemical Soc. 60, Krebs Medal, European Biochemical Soc. 73, Rosensteil Award, Brandeis Univ. 75.
Leisure interests: music, sport, travel, art.
Publs. Articles on a binding site for sulphate and its relation to sulphate transport into salmonella typhimurium, enzyme synthesis in synchronous cultures of bacteria, cell division and a hypothesis of cancer; *Experiments in Biochemical Research Techniques* 57.
Sidney Farber Cancer Center, 35 Binney Street, Boston, Mass. 02115; Home: 30 Codman Road, Brookline, Mass. 02144, U.S.A.
Telephone: (617) 734-6000 (Office).

Párdi, Imre; Hungarian politician; b. 16 April 1922, Tatabánya; *s.* of Mátyás Párdi and Mária Miatton; *m.* Maria Kisfaludi 1945; one *s.* two *d.*
Former machine fitter; worked as Party official 45-, fmr. Sec. Tatabánva Town, Komárom County and Veszprém County Cttees., Hungarian Socialist Workers' Party; mem. Central Cttee. Hungarian Socialist Workers' Party 62-; Chair. Nat. Planning Office 67-73; Head Econ. Policy Dept., Cen. Cttee. of Hungarian

Socialist Workers' Party 73-75, mem. 75-; Labour Order of Merit, Golden Degree 70.
Leisure interests: reading, music.
Hungarian Socialist Workers' Party, H-1387 Budapest, Széchenyi rakpart 19, Hungary.

Pardo, Arvid; Maltese diplomatist; b. 1914; ed. Università degli Studi, Rome, and Université de Tours.
Officer-in-Charge, United Nations Archives 45-46; Dept. of Trusteeship and Information for Non-Self-Governing Territories, United Nations 46-60; Secr., Technical Assistance Board, UN, later Deputy Resident Rep. in Nigeria and Ecuador 60-64; Perm. Rep. of Malta to the United Nations 65-June 71, concurrently Amb. to U.S.A.; Co-ordinator Marine Programme, Woodrow Wilson Int. Centre for Scholars, concurrently Maltese Rep. to U.S.A. for Ocean Affairs, Prof. of Political Science and Senior Fellow Inst. Coastal Marine Studies, Univ. of S. Calif. 75-.
Publ. *The Common Heritage* 75.
University of Southern California, VKC 327, University Park, Los Angeles, Calif., U.S.A.

Pardo, Luis Mariá de Pablo; Argentine lawyer and politician; b. 15 Aug. 1912; ed. Univ. of Buenos Aires Law Faculty, postgraduate Univ. of Georgetown (Washington D.C.).
Prof. of International Law, Buenos Aires; imprisoned 51, 52, and 53 for anti-Peronist activities, exiled to Brazil until 55; Minister of the Interior designate 55, subsequently Minister for Home Affairs, Political and legal adviser to Treasury, Ambassador to Chile and adviser in the territorial settlements between Argentina and Chile; Minister of Foreign Affairs 70-72.
Publs. works on legal matters.
c/o Ministerio de Relaciones Exteriores, Buenos Aires, Argentina.

Parecattil, H.E. Cardinal Joseph; Indian ecclesiastic; b. 1 April 1912, Kidangoor; s. of Ittyrah and Eliswa Parecattil; ed. Papal Seminary, Candy, Sri Lanka.
Ordained priest 39; Editor *Sathyadeepam*; titular bishop Arathusa, installed archbishop 57; mem. Pontifical Comm.; Vice-Pres. Catholic Bishops' Conf. of India 66, Pres. 72, 74; mem. Sacred Congregation for the Oriental Churches; Cardinal 69; mem. Secr., Christian Unity, Rome 70, Secr. for Non-Christians 74-; Pres. Pontifical Comm. for revision of Oriental Canon Law 72; Pres. Syro-Malabar Bishops' Conf., Kerala Catholic Bishops' Conf.; Chancellor, Pontifical Inst. of Philosophy and Theology, Alwaye.
Archbishop's House, Post Bag 1209, Cochin 682011, Kerala, India.
Telephone: Cochin 32629.

Parekh, Hasmukh, B.A., B.SC.; Indian investment broker; b. 10 March 1911, Surat; ed. Bombay Univ., London School of Economics.
Worked as stockbroker with leading Bombay firm 36-56; Deputy Gen. Man. Industrial Credit and Investment Corpn. of India 58-68, Deputy Chair., Man. Dir. 68-71, Chair., Man. Dir. 72-73, Exec. Chair. 73-.
Leisure interests: reading, light music.
Publs. *The Bombay Money Market* 53, *The Future of Joint Stock Enterprise in India* 58, *India and Regional Development* 69, *Management of Industry in India*.
Industrial Credit and Investment Corporation of India Ltd., 163 Backbay Reclamation, Bombay 400 020; Home: Kastur Nivas No. 1, French Road, Chowpatty, Bombay 400 007, India.
Telephone: 257351 (Office); 357949 (Home).

Parente, H.E. Cardinal Pietro; Italian ecclesiastic; b. 16 Feb. 1891, Casalnuovo Monterotaro.
Ordained Priest 16; Archbishop of Perugia 55-59; Titular Archbishop of Ptolemais in Thebaide 59-;

Assessor, Sacred Congregations for Doctrine and Faith; created Cardinal by Pope Paul VI 67.
Piazza S. Calisto 16, 00153 Rome, Italy.

Park, Merle Florence, C.B.E.; British ballerina; b. 8 Oct. 1937, Salisbury, Rhodesia; m. 1st James Monahan, C.B.E. 1965, one s., 2nd Sidney Bloch 1971; ed. Elmhurst Ballet School and Royal Ballet School.
Joined Royal Ballet 54; first solo role 55; repertoire includes *Façade, Coppelia, Sleeping Beauty, La Fille Mal Gardée, Giselle, Les Sylphides, The Dream, Romeo and Juliet, Triad, The Nutcracker, La Bayadère, Cinderella, Shadow Play, Anastasia, Pineapple Poll, Swan Lake, The Firebird, Walk to the Paradise Garden, Dances at a Gathering, Shadow, Don Quixote, Deux Pigeons, Serenade, Scène de Ballet, Wedding Bouquet, Les Rendezvous, Mirror Walkers, Symphonic Variations, Daphnis and Chloë, Serenade, In the Night, Laurentia, Mamzelle Angot, Manon, Apollo, Flower Festival, Le Corsaire, The Moor's Pavane, Auriole, Elite Syncopations,* etc.; Adelaine Genée Medal and many other certificates and medals.
Leisure interests: travel, lying in the sun, listening to music.
c/o The Royal Ballet, Covent Garden, London, W.C.2, England.
Telephone: 01-240-1200.

Park Chung Hee, General; Korean army officer and politician; b. 30 Sept. 1971, Sonsan-gun, North Kyong-sang Province; s. of late Park Sung Bin and Paik Nam Ee; m. Yook Young Soo 1950 (died 1974); one s. two d.; ed. Taegu Normal School, Japanese Mil. Acad., Artillery School (U.S.A.) and Mil. Command and Gen. Staff Coll., Korea.
Teacher 37-40; Japanese Army 40-45; Korean Army 45-63; Deputy Chair. Supreme Council for Nat. Reconstruction May-July 61, Chair. July 61-Nov. 63; Acting Pres. of Repub. of Korea March 61-Nov. 63, Pres. Dec. 63- (re-elected 67, 71, 72).
Publs. *Leadership: In the Midst of the Revolutionary Process* 61, *People's Path to the Fulfilment of Revolutionary Tasks: Direction for National Movement* 61, *Our Nation's Path* 62, *The State, the Revolution and I* 63, *To Build a Nation* 71.
Ch'ong Wa Dae (Presidential Mansion), Seoul, Republic of Korea.

Park Kyung Won, M.A.; Korean civil servant; b. 3 Jan. 1923, Julanam-Do; m. Ko Kum Ok 1946; two s.; ed. U.S. Army Artillery School, Republic of Korea Command and Gen. Staff Coll., Nat. Defence Coll. and Dankuk Univ.
Minister of Home Affairs 62-63, 68-71, 74-; Dir. of Joint Staff, Rep. of Korea 63-65, Commdg. Gen. 2nd Army 65-66; Minister of Communication 66-67; Minister of Transport 67-68; Sec.-Gen. People's Council for Nat. Unification 72-74; various military and civil awards.
Leisure interests: reading, wireless operation.
102 Gea-Dong, Jongro-Gu, Seoul, Republic of Korea.
Telephone: 73-0010, 72-2400.

Parker, Eugene N., PH.D.; American physicist; b. 10 June 1927, Houghton, Mich.; s. of Glenn H. Parker and Helen M. Parker; m. Niesje Meuter 1954; one s. one d.; ed. Mich. State Univ. and Calif. Inst. of Technology.
Instructor, Dept. of Mathematics and Astronomy, Univ. of Utah 51-53, Asst. Prof., Dept. of Physics 53-55; at Univ. of Chicago 55-, Prof. Dept. of Physics 62-, Prof. Dept. of Astronomy 67-; mem. Nat. Acad. of Sciences 67-; Space Science Award, American Inst. of Aeronautics and Astronautics 64, John Adam Fleming Award, American Geophysical Union 68, Henryk Arctowski Medal, Nat. Acad. of Sciences 69, Henry Norris Russell Lecture, American Astronomical Soc. 69.

Leisure interests: hiking, history, wood-carving.
Publ. *Interplanetary Dynamical Processes* 63.
Laboratory for Astrophysics and Space Research, University of Chicago, 933 East 56th Street, Chicago, Ill. 60637; Home: 1323 Evergreen Road, Homewood, Ill. 60430, U.S.A.
Telephone: 312-753-8571 (Office); 312-798-3497 (Home).

Parker, Jack Steele; American business executive; b. 6 July 1918, Palo Alto, Calif.; *m.* Elaine Simons; one *d.*; ed. Stanford Univ.
Formerly associated with Western Pipe and Steel Co. of Calif. and Todd Shipyards; Asst. Chief Engineer American Potash and Chemical Co. 46-50; joined Gen. Electric Co. 50; Gen. Man. Aircraft Gas Turbine Div. 55; Vice-Pres. 56, in charge of Relations Services 57; Vice-Pres. and Group Exec., Aerospace and Defense Group 61; Exec. Vice-Pres. and mem. President's Office Jan. 68; Dir., Vice-Chair. of Board and Exec. Officer, Gen. Electric Co. Dec. 68-; Assoc. Fellow, Royal Aeronautical Soc.; Senior mem. American Inst. of Aeronautics and Astronautics; mem. American Soc. of Mechanical Engineers; mem. Board of Govs. and Exec. Cttee., Aerospace Industries Asscn.; Life Trustee, Rensselaer Polytechnic Inst.; mem. Advisory Council, Stanford Univ. Grad. School of Business; mem. Citizens Cttee. for Govt. Reorganization; mem. Board of Directors, Council for Financial Aid to Education; Fellow, Institute of Judicial Administration.
General Electric Co., 570 Lexington Avenue, New York, N.Y. 10022, U.S.A.

Parker, Sir Karl Theodore, Kt., C.B.E., M.A., PH.D., F.B.A.; British art historian; studied Continental art centres and British Museum.
Editor *Old Master Drawings* since inception 26; fmr. Asst. Keeper Dept. of Prints and Drawings, British Museum; Keeper Dept. of Fine Art, Ashmolean Museum, Oxford 34-35; Keeper of the Ashmolean Museum 45-62; Trustee, Nat. Gallery 62-69.
Publs. *North Italian Drawings of the Quattrocento, Drawings of the Early German Schools, Alsatian Drawings of the XV and XVI Centuries, Drawings of Antoine Watteau, Catalogue of Drawings in the Ashmolean Museums* (Vol. I, 38), *Holbein's Drawings at Windsor Castle* 45, *The Drawings of Antonio Canaletto in Windsor Castle* 48, *Antoine Watteau: Catalogue Complet de son Oeuvre dessiné* Vol. I (with J. Mathey) 57, Vol. II 58.
4 Saffrons Court, Compton Place Road, Eastbourne, Sussex, England.

Parker, Peter, M.V.O., M.A.; British company director; b. 30 Aug. 1924, Malo-les-Bains, France; *s.* of Tom and Dorothy Parker (née Mackinlay); *m.* Gillian Rowe-Dutton 1951; three *s.* one *d.*; ed. in France and China, Bedford School, London Univ. School of Oriental and African Studies, Lincoln Coll., Oxford, Cornell and Harvard Univs.
Worked for Philips Electrical 51-53; Head, Overseas Dept., Industrial Soc. 53-54; Sec., Duke of Edinburgh Study Conf. 54-56; Chair. Eng. Group, Booker McConnell 57-70; mem. Org. Cttee., later of Main Board, British Steel Corpn. 66-67; mem. Mech. Eng. EDC 66-70; Chair. British Pump Manufacturers Asscn. 66-69; mem., later Deputy Chair. Court of London Univ. 64-; Chair. Dillons Univ. Bookshop 67-75, London Univ. Computing Services 69-; mem. British Tourist Authority 69-; Vice-Chair. Rockware Group Ltd. Oct. 70-March 71, Chair. March 71-; Chair. Westfield Coll., London Univ. 70-, Econ. Devt. Cttee. for the Clothing Industry 71-, Landel Insurance Holdings Ltd. 71-75, Victoria Deepwater Terminal Ltd. 71-, H. Clarkson (Holdings) Ltd., mem. Board British Airways 71-; Dir. Int. Research and Devt. Co. Ltd. 70-75, Renold Ltd. 71-, Shipping Industrial Holdings Ltd. 71-, Fullemploy Ltd. 73; Deputy Chair. Dawnay Day Group Ltd. 71-74, Chair. Nov. 74-; Chair. Shipping

Industrial Holdings 72, Political and Econ. Planning Treas. 73; mem. British Railways Board April 76- (Chair. designate Sept. 76-); Pres. British Asscn. of Industrial Editors 71-74, British Mechanical Eng. Confed. 72-74, British Graduates Asscn. Advisory Council 72; Gov. Bedford Coll. London 70-, Inst. for Social Work Training 70-; mem. York and Humberside Devt. Asscn. Ltd., Foundation for Management Educ.; Fellow and mem. Council British Inst. of Management; mem. Eng. Industries Council 75-.
Leisure interests: browsing, swimming.
35 Brunswick Gardens, London W.8, England.
Telephone: 01-229-7547.

Parkes, Sir Alan Stirling, Kt., C.B.E., M.A., SC.D., F.R.S.; British biologist; b. 10 Sept. 1900, Rochdale, Lancs.; *s.* of E. T. Parkes; *m.* Ruth Deanesly 1933; one *s.* two *d.*; ed. Willaston School and Christ's Coll., Cambridge.
Member of scientific staff of Medical Research Council 32-61; Mary Marshall Prof. of the Physiology of Reproduction, Univ. of Cambridge 61-67; Chair. The Galton Foundation 68-; Exec. Editor *Journal of Biosocial Science* 68-.
Publs. *Marshall's Physiology of Reproduction* (Editor), 4 vols. 52-66, *Sex, Science and Society* 66; numerous papers and reviews in scientific journals.
The Galton Foundation, 7 Downing Place, Cambridge CB2 3EL, England.
Telephone: Cambridge 59729.

Parkes, Ed.; American business executive; b. 22 Nov. 1904, Bessemer, Ala.; *s.* of William Jay and Myra (Huey) Parkes; *m.* Julia Alice Washburn 1930; two *d.*; ed. Univ. of Arkansas.
Design Engineer Ark. Power & Light Co. 26-28; Engineer United Gas Pipe Line Co. 28-29, Dist. Supt. 29-30, Asst. Gen. Supt. 30-37, Gen. Supt. Field Lines 37-47, Vice-Pres. 47-56, Dir. 46-67, Pres. 56-67; Exec. Vice-Pres. United Gas Corpn. 55-58, Dir. 55-68, Pres. 58-67, Chair. of Exec. Cttee. 67-68; Dir. American Gas Asscn. 55-65, mem. Exec. Cttee. 59-65, Pres. 64; Chair. Natural Gas Reserves Cttee. 57-69; Dir. American Petroleum Inst. 56-68, mem. Exec. Cttee. 63-68, Hon. Life mem. of Board; Dir. Pennzoil United Inc. 68-, Chair. Exec. Cttee. 68-; Chair. Exec. Cttee. Pennzoil Co. 68-72, Dir. 72-; Trustee Southwest Research Inst. 61-70; Duval Corpn. 57-; United Fund Medallion 66.
Leisure interest: lapidary.
Home: 5815 Creswell Road, Shreveport, La. 71106; Office: 1525 Fairfield Avenue, Shreveport, La., U.S.A.
Telephone: 318-868-1370.

Parkinson, Charles Jay; American lawyer and business executive; b. 30 April 1909; ed. Utah and Oxford Univs.
Partner in law firms, Salt Lake City, Utah; Counsel, Basic Magnesium Inc., Henderson, Nevada 41-45; Counsel, The Anaconda Co. and affiliated companies, and Int. Smelting and Refining Co., Salt Lake City, Utah 45-55; Vice-Pres. Anaconda Aluminium Co., New York 55-57; Gen. Counsel, The Anaconda Co., New York 57-60, Exec. Vice-Pres. 60-64, Pres. 64-68, Chair. and Chief Exec. Officer 69-71; Dir. The Anaconda Co., Fansteel Metallurgical Corpn., Chase Manhattan Bank.
Creek House, West Island, Glen Cove, N.Y. 11542, U.S.A.

Parkinson, Cyril Northcote, M.A., PH.D.; British historian and author; b. 30 July 1909, Barnard Castle, Co. Durham; *s.* of William Edward Parkinson, A.R.C.A., and Rose Mary Emily (Curnow) Parkinson; *m.* 1st Ethelwyn Edith Graves 1943 (marriage dissolved 1949), one *s.* one *d.*; *m.* 2nd Elizabeth Ann Fry 1952, two *s.* one *d.*; ed. St. Peter's School, York, Emmanuel Coll., Cambridge, and King's Coll., London.
Following a period of research in London, was elected Fellow of Emmanuel Coll., Cambridge; Senior History Master, Blundell's School, Tiverton, Devon 37-39;

Master, Royal Naval Coll., Dartmouth 39-40; commissioned in Queen's Royal Regt. 40 and served as O.C.T.U. instructor, instructor and staff officer attached to R.A.F. and on Gen. Staff; Lecturer, Liverpool Univ. 46; Raffles Prof. of History, Univ. of Malaya 50-58; Visiting Prof., Illinois Univ. 59, Visiting Prof. Univ. of Calif. 60, Emer. Prof. Troy State Univ. of Ala. 70-, Fellow of the Royal Historical Soc.; Julian Corbett Prize, London Univ.
Leisure interests: painting, architecture, travel.
Publs. *Edward Pellew, Viscount Exmouth* 34, *Trade in the Eastern Seas 1793-1813* 37, *Always a Fusilier* 49, *War in the Eastern Seas 1793-1815* 54, *Parkinson's Law: The Pursuit of Progress* 57, *The Evolution of Political Thought* 58, *The Law and the Profits* 60, *British Intervention in Malaya 1867-77* 60, *In-laws and Outlaws* 62, *East and West* 64, *Ponies Plot* 65, *A Law unto Themselves* 66, *Left Luggage* 67, *Mrs. Parkinson's Law* 68, *The Law of Delay* 70, *The Life and Times of Horatio Hornblower* 70, *Devil to Pay* 73, *Big Business* 74, *The Fireship* 75.
Les Câches Hall, St. Martins, Guernsey, Channel Islands.
Telephone: Guernsey 37449.

Parks, Robert Joseph; American electrical engineer; b. 1 April 1922, Los Angeles, Calif.; s. of Joseph B. and Ruth F. Parks; m. Hanne Richter 1947; three s.; ed. California Inst. of Technology.
U.S. Army 45, later Hughes Aircraft, Culver City, later Calif. Inst. of Technology; Surveyor Project Man. 65-66; Asst. Laboratory Dir. for Flight Projects, Jet Propulsion Laboratory, Calif. Inst. of Technology (responsible for Ranger, Surveyor and Mariner Projects 60-); mem. Nat. Acad. of Engineering 73-.
Leisure interests: skiing, water skiing, tennis, flying, soaring, home workshop.
Jet Propulsion Laboratory, California Institute of Technology, 4800 Oak Grove Drive, Pasadena, California 91103, U.S.A.
Telephone: 213-354-3442.

Parlin, Charles C(oolidge), B.S., LL.B.; American lawyer; b. 22 July 1898; ed. Univ. of Pennsylvania and Harvard Univ.
Admitted to New York Bar 23; Senior Partner, Shearman and Sterling, New York City 45-; Dir. numerous companies; fmr. Lay Rep. Nat. Council of Churches, Pres. World Council of Churches 61-68; Pres. World Methodist Council 70-; Chair. Celanese Corpn. 69-71.
123 Hillside Avenue, Englewood, N.J. 07631, U.S.A.

Parmar, Y. S., B.A., M.A., LL.B., PH.D.; Indian lawyer, agriculturist and politician; b. 4 Aug. 1906; ed. Shamsher High School, Nahan, Forman Christian Coll. (Punjab Univ.), Lahore, Canning Coll. (Lucknow Univ.), Lucknow.
Sub-judge and Magistrate, Sirmur State 30-37; District and Sessions Judge, Sirmur State 37-41; Pres. Himalayan Hill States Regional Council 47; mem. Chief Commr.'s (Himachal Pradesh) Advisory Council 48-50; mem. Constituent Assembly of India 49, Provisional Parl. 50-51; Pres. Himachal Pradesh Congress Cttee. 48-50, 60-64; Standing Council for Himachal Pradesh in Supreme Court of India 60-63; mem. Himachal Pradesh Legislative Assembly and Himachal Pradesh Chief Minister 52-56, 63-67, 67-.
Publs. *Social and Economic Background of Himalayan Polyandry, Himachal Pradesh—Its Proper Shape and Status, Himachal Pradesh—Case for Statehood and Strategy for Development of Hill Areas.*
Village Bharyog, P.O. Bagthan, District Sirmur, Himachal Pradesh, India.

Parnas, Joseph, DR. MED. VET.; Danish microbiologist; b. 14 June 1909, Przemysl, Poland; s. of Leon and Etylda Parnas; m. Sophie Parnas 1937; two s.; ed. Lvov Univ.
Former Asst. Prof. of Scientific Inst., Pulawy; served Second World War; fmr. Prof. Acad. of Medicine, Lublin; Chief, Dept. of Microbiology; Founder, Chodźko Inst. of Rural Medicine; fmr. Rector, Marie Curie Univ., Lublin; Hon. Pres. Int. Asscn. of Rural Medicine, France, Polish Soc. for Microbiology, Lublin; Fellow of Royal Soc. of Medicine, Royal Soc. of Tropical Medicine and Hygiene, London; mem. American Soc. for Microbiology, Soc. of Tropical Medicine in Antwerp, Danish Soc. for Pathology, Purkyně Medical Soc., Prague, Argentine Medical Soc.; adviser to the WHO; Dr.med.h.c. Purkyně Univ.; Dr. med. vet. h.c. Brno, Czechoslovakia; Visiting Prof. Copenhagen Univ.; Prof. in State Veterinary Serum Inst. Copenhagen; Charles Darwin Medical, U.S.S.R. Acad. of Sciences; mem. Brucellosis Cttee., Int. Asscn. of Microbiological Socs.
Leisure interests: music, sport.
Publs. 3 books, 5 monographs and over 300 other items, including *Anthropozoonoses, Brucellosis, Rural Medicine and Hygiene, Leptospirosis, Tularemia,* Contrib. to *Theory of Anthropozoonoses, Colibacillopis of Newborns.*
27 Bülowsvej, DK-1870 Copenhagen, Denmark.
Telephone: AS-36-32.

Parnicki, Teodor; Polish writer; b. 5 March 1908, Berlin, Germany; ed. Lvov Univ.
Work first published 28; worked with *Kurier Lwowski* 32-34; mem. Polish Writers' Asscn.; lived in Mexico during the post-war period; Officer's Cross Order of Polonia Restituta 68, State Prize, 1st Class 72.
Publs. novels: *Trzy minuty po trzeciej* 29, *Rozkaz Nr. 94* 30, *Aecjusz, ostatni Rzymianin* 37, *Srebrne orły* 43, *Koniec Zgody Narodów* 55, *Słowo i ciało* 59, *Twarz księżyca* 61-67, *Nowa baśń* 62, *Tylko Beatrycze* 62, *I u możnych dziwny* 65, *Koła na piasku* 66, *Zabij Kleopatrę* 68, *Inne życie Kleopatry* 69, *Tożsamość* 70, *Muza dalekich podróży* 70, *Przeobrażenie* 73, *Staliśmy jak dwa sny* 73; *Opowiadania* (short stories) 58.
Ul. Zimorowicza 2 m. 10, 01-062 Warsaw, Poland.
Telephone: 25-48-35.

Parodi, Alexandre; French politician; b. 1 June 1901, Paris; s. of Dominique Parodi and Hélène Vavin; m. Anne Marie Vautier 1931; two s.
Member Council of State 26; Deputy Sec.-Gen. Nat. Economic Council 29-38; Technical Counsellor Ministry of Labour 38; Dir.-Gen. of Labour, Ministry of Labour 39-40; relieved of post by Vichy; Del.-Gen. of Provisional Govt. of Republic for Occupied France 44; Minister of Labour 44-45; Amb. of Provisional Govt. to Rome; Permanent Rep. of France, Security Council, UN 46-49; Sec.-Gen. Ministry of Foreign Affairs 49-55; Amb. and Permanent Rep. to NATO 55-57; Amb. to Morocco 57-60; Vice-Pres. Council of State 60-71; Rep. of France at Admin. Council of ILO; mem. Inst. de France 70-; retd.
102 rue de Grenelle, Paris 7e, France.
Telephone: 458-85-35.

Parodi, Anton Gaetano; Italian journalist and playwright; b. 19 May 1923, Castanzaro Lido (Calabria); s. of Luigi Parodi and Grazia Scicchitano; m. Piera Somino 1952; two c.; ed. Università degli Studi, Turin and Genoa.
Journalist 45-; professional journalist 47-; Corresp. of *Unità,* Budapest 64-; Premio nazionale di teatro Riccione 59, 65, Premio nazionale di teatro dei giovani 47 and numerous other prizes.
Plays include: *Il gatto, Il nostro scandalo quotidiano, L'ex-maggiore Hermann Grotz, Adolfo o della nagia, Filippo l'Impostore, Una corda per il figlio di Abele, Quel pomeriggio di domenica, Dialoghi intorno ad un'uovo, Una storia della notte, Pioggia d'estate, Cielo di pietra, I giorni dell'Arca, Quello che dicono.*
Via Benvenuto Cellini 34/7, Genoa, Italy.

Parr, Albert Eide, D.SC.; American (b. Norwegian) oceanographer and environmentalist; b. 15 Aug. 1900, Bergen, Norway; s. of Dr. Thomas Parr and Helga Eide; m. Ella Hage Hanssen 1925; two s. two d.; ed. Royal Univ. Oslo and Bergen.
Asst. in Zoology, Bergen Museum 18-19; Asst. Norwegian Bureau of Fisheries 24-26; Asst. N.Y. Aquarium 26; Curator Bingham Oceanographic Collection, Yale Univ. 27-42, Asst. Prof. of Zoology 31-37, Assoc. Prof. 37-38, Prof. of Oceanography 38-42; Dir. Marine Research 37-42, Dir. Peabody Museum 38-42; Dir. American Museum of Natural Hist. 42-59, Senior Scientist 59-68, Dir. Emer. 68-; Trustee Woods Hole Oceanographic Inst. 38-; Hon. Curator Peabody Museum 75-.
Leisure interest: the study of cities.
Publs. *Mostly About Museums* 59, 189 articles on oceanography, biology, museums, urban environment.
The American Museum of Natural History, Central Park West, New York 10024, N.Y., U.S.A.; 1075 Whitney Avenue, Hamden, Conn. 06517, U.S.A.
Telephone: (203)-288-5457 (Connecticut).

Parra, Nicanor; Chilean poet; b. 5 Sept. 1914, San Fabian; s. of Nicanor P. Parra and Clara S. Navarrete; m. 1st Ana Troncoso 1948, 2nd Inga Palmen; seven c.; ed. Universidad de Chile, Brown Univ., U.S.A., and Oxford.
Prof. of Theoretical Mechanics, Univ. of Chile 64-; has given poetry readings in Los Angeles, Moscow, Leningrad, Havana, Lima, Ayacucho, Cuzco; Premio Municipal de Poesía, Santiago 37, 54; Premio Nacional de Literatura 69.
Publs. Poetry: *Cancionero sin nombre* 37, *Poemas y antipoemas* 54, *La cueca larga* 58, *Antipoems* 58, *Versos de salon* 62, *Discursos* (with Pablo Neruda) 62, *Deux Poèmes* (bi-lingual) 64, *Antología* (also in Russian) 65, *Antología de la Poesía Soviética Rusa* (bi-lingual) 65, *Canciones Rusas* 67, *Defensa de Violeta Parra* 67; Scientific Works: *La Evolución del Concepto de Masa* 58, *Fundamentos de la Física* (trans. of Foundation of Physics by Profs. Lindsay and Margenau) 67, *Poems and Antipoems* 67, *Obra Gruesa* 69.
Instituto Pedagógico, Avenida Macul 774, Santiago; and Julia Bernstein, Parcela 272, Lareina, Santiago, Chile.

Parrot, André; French archaeologist; b. 15 Feb. 1901, Desandans; m. 1st Henriette Cazelles 1929, died 1955, 2nd Marie-Louise Girod 1960; two s. three d.; ed. Univ. de Paris à la Sorbonne, Ecole du Louvre and Ecole Archéologique Française de Jerusalem.
Professor, Faculty of Protestant Theology, Univ. of Paris 37-55, Ecole du Louvre 37-; Dir. Louvre Museum 68-72; Head Keeper of Nat. Museums 46-65, Insp.-Gen. 65-; Dir. of French archaeological expeditions to Mari (Syrian Repub.) and Larsa (Iraq); mem. Institut de France (Académie des Inscriptions et Belles-Lettres); Corresp. Fellow of the British Acad.; Assoc. mem. Belgian Acad.; mem. Institutum Archaeologicum Germanicum; Grand-Officier Ordre du Mérite, Commdr. Légion d'Honneur, des Arts et des Lettres; Croix de Guerre 39-45.
Publs. *Mari, une ville perdue* 36, *Archéologie mésopotamienne* 46-53, *Tello—vingt campagnes de fouilles* 48, *Ziggurats et Tour de Babel* 48, *Découverte des Mondes ensevelis* 52, *Mari—le temple d'Ishtar* 56, *Mari—le Palais* (3 vols.) 58-59, *Sumer* 60, *Assur* 61, *Abraham et son temps* 62, *Terre du Christ* 65, *Les Temples d'Ishtarat et de Ninnizaza* 67, *Le trésor d'Ur* 68, *Sumerian Art* 69, *Mari, capitale fabuleuse* 74.
11 rue du Val Grâce, Paris 5e, France.
Telephone: ODEon 75-83.

Parrott, Sir Cecil Cuthbert, K.C.M.G., O.B.E., M.A.; British diplomatist and university professor; b. 29 Jan. 1909, Plymouth, Devon; s. of Capt. J. W. A. Parrott,

R.N. and Grace Edith West; m. Ellen Matzow 1935; three s.; ed. Berkhamsted and Peterhouse, Cambridge.
Head, UN Dept., Foreign Office 50-52; Principal Political Adviser to U.K. Del. to UN 52; Counsellor, Brussels 52-54; Minister, Moscow 54-57; Librarian, Dir. of Research and Keeper of the Papers at the Foreign Office 57-60; Ambassador to Czechoslovakia 60-66; Prof. of Russian and Soviet Studies 66-71, Prof. of Central and South-Eastern European Studies 71-, Dir. Comenius Centre, Lancaster Univ. 68-; Hon. Fellow and Vice-Pres. Inst. of Linguists, Vice Chair. D'Oyly Carte Opera Trust.
Leisure interests: music, theatre, nature study.
Publs. First complete translation into English of *The Good Soldier Svejk* 73, *The Tightrope*; various articles in academic and literary journals and BBC broadcasts on cultural subjects.
Lonsdale College, University of Lancaster, Bailrigg, Lancaster, England.
Telephone: Lancaster 65201.

Parry, John Horace, C.M.G., M.B.E.; British historian; b. 26 April 1914, Handsworth, Staffs.; s. of Walter A. and Ethel (née Piddock) Parry; m. Joyce Carter 1939; one s. three d.; ed. King Edward's School, Birmingham, and Clare Coll., Cambridge.
Royal Navy 40-45; Tutor, Clare Coll., Cambridge and Univ. Lecturer in History 45-49; Prof. of Modern History, Univ. Coll. of W. Indies 49-56; Principal of Univ. of Ibadan, Nigeria 56-60, Univ. Coll. of Swansea 60-65; Vice-Chancellor, Univ. of Wales 63-65; Gardiner Prof. of Oceanic History and Affairs, Harvard Univ. Oct. 65-.
Leisure interests: fishing, sailing, ornithology, mountain walking.
Publs. *The Spanish Theory of Empire* 40, *The Audiencia of New Galicia* 48, *Europe and a Wider World* 49, *The Sale of Public Office in the Spanish Indies* 53, *A Short History of the West Indies* 56, *The Age of Reconnaissance* 63, *The Spanish Seaborne Empire* 66, *The European Reconnaissance* (ed.) 68, *Trade and Dominion* 71, *The Discovery of the Sea* 74.
Widener 45, Harvard University, Cambridge, Mass. 02138, U.S.A.

Parry, Thomas, D.LITT., F.B.A.; British university principal; b. 14 Aug. 1904, Carmel, Wales; s. of Richard and Jane Parry; m. Enid Picton Davies 1936; ed. Univ. Coll. of North Wales, Bangor.
Asst. Lecturer in Welsh and Latin, Univ. Coll., Cardiff 26-29; Lecturer in Welsh Univ. Coll., Bangor 29-47; Prof. of Welsh 47-53; Librarian of the Nat. Library of Wales, Aberystwyth 53-58; Principal Univ. Coll. of Wales, Aberystwyth 58-69; Vice-Chancellor Univ. of Wales 61-63, 67-69; Pres. Nat. Library of Wales 69-; Hon. D.Litt. Celt (N.U.I.), Hon. LL.D. (Wales).
Publs. *Hanes Llenyddiaeth Gymraeg* (History of Welsh Literature) 45, *Lladd wrth yr Allor* (Eliot's *Murder in the Cathedral*), *Gwaith Dafydd ap Gwilym* 52, *Llywelyn Fawr* (a play) 54, *Oxford Book of Welsh Verse* (Editor) 62.
2 Victoria Avenue, Bangor, North Wales.
Telephone: 0248-4460.

Parsloe, Guy; British author and administrator; b. 5 Nov. 1900, Stroud Green, Middx.; s. of Henry Edward Parsloe and Emma Jane Gamlen; m. Mary Zirphie Munro Faiers 1929; two s. one d.; ed. London Univ.
Sec. and Librarian Inst. of Historical Research 27-43; Sec. Inst. of Welding 43-67; First Sec.-Gen. Int. Inst. of Welding 48-66, Vice-Pres. 66-69; Sec. O.E.E.C. Welding Techniques Mission to U.S.A. 53; Editor-in-Chief *British Welding Journal* 54-67; Sec. British Commonwealth Welding Confs. 57, 65; Pres. Junior Inst. of Engineers 66-67; Bibliographical Consultant 68-72.
Leisure interests: gardening, historical research.
Publs. *The English Country Town, ca.* 400 bibliographies

in *Cambridge Bibliography of English Literature*; Editor *Guide to the Historical Publications of the Societies of England and Wales* 29-43, *Minute Book of the Corporation of Bedford 1647-1664*, *Wimbledon Village Club and Lecture Hall: 1858-1958—A Centenary Record*, *Wardens' Accounts of the Worshipful Company of Founders of the City of London 1497-1681.*
1 Leopold Avenue, London, SW19 7ET, England.
Telephone: 01-946-0764.

Parsons, Sir Anthony Derrick, K.C.M.G., M.V.O., M.C., M.A. (OXON); British diplomatist; b. 9 Sept. 1922, London; s. of late Col. H. A. J. Parsons; m. Sheila Emily Baird 1948; two s. two d.; ed. King's School Canterbury, Balliol Coll., Oxford.
Army service 40-54; Asst. Mil. Attaché, Baghdad 52-54; Foreign Office 54-55; at British Embassy, Ankara 55-59, Amman 59-60, Cairo 60-61; Foreign Office 61-64; British Embassy, Khartoum 64-65; British Political Agent, Bahrain 65-69; with U.K. Mission to UN 69-71; Foreign and Commonwealth Office 71-74; Amb. to Iran 74-.
British Embassy, Teheran, Iran.

Parsons, Sir Maurice Henry, K.C.M.G.; British banker; b. 19 May 1910, Ealing, London; s. of G. H. C. and Maud Parsons (née Rose); m. D. I. Warner 1937; one s. one d.; ed. Univ. Coll. School, London.
Entered Bank of England 28, Private Sec. to Gov. (Lord Norman) 38-43; Alt. Exec. Dir. for U.K. on Int. Monetary Fund 46-47, Int. Bank for Reconstruction and Devt. 47, Dir. of Operations, Int. Monetary Fund 47-50; Deputy Chief Cashier, Bank of England 50-55, Asst. to Govs. 55-57, Exec. Dir. 57-66, Deputy Gov. July 66-Feb. 70; Chair. Bank of London and South America Ltd. 70, mem. of Board 71; Alt. Gov. for U.K. on IMF 57-66; Dir. John Brown and Co. Ltd. 70-72, Globtik Tankers Ltd. 71-, Martin Cadbury Printing Group Ltd. 71-; Chair. Billing and Sons Ltd. 71-.
Leisure interests: golf, tennis, gardening.
Clifford House, Shalford, Nr. Guildford, Surrey, England.
Telephone: 0483 61523.

Parsons, Talcott, DR.PHIL., L.H.D.; American university teacher; b. 13 Dec. 1902, Colorado Springs, Colo.; s. of Edward S. Parsons and Mary Augusta (Ingersoll) Parsons; m. Helen B. Walker 1927; one s. two d. (one deceased); ed. Amherst Coll., London School of Econs., Univ. of Heidelberg.
Instructor in Econs. Amherst Coll. 26-27, Harvard Univ. 27-31, Instructor in Sociology, Harvard 31-36, Asst. Prof. 36-39, Assoc. Prof. 39-44, Prof. 44-73, Prof. Emer. 73-; Visiting Prof. Columbia Univ. 33, 35, Chicago Univ. 37, Cambridge Univ. 53-54, Chicago Univ. 70-71, 71-72, Pa. Univ. 73-74, 74-75; Chair. Comm. on Concentration in the Area of Social Science 40-46, Dept. of Sociology 44-46, Dept. of Social Relations 46-56; mem. of staff Harvard School for Overseas Admin. 43-46; mem. American Phil. Soc., American Sociological Asscn. (Pres. 49), Eastern Sociological Soc. (Pres. 41-42); Fellow Ford Center for Advanced Study in the Behavioural Sciences 57-58, American Acad. of Arts and Sciences; Hon. Dr. rer. pol. (Cologne) 63, Hon. LL.D. (Chicago) 67, Hon. Dr. Soc. Science (Boston Coll.) 69; Hon. Ph.D. (Hebrew Univ., Jerusalem) 73; Hon. LL.D. (Univ. of Pa.) 74; Hon. Dr. of Arts (Stonehill Coll.) 74.
Publs. Editor *The American Sociologist* 65-68; Author *Protestant Ethic and Spirit of Capitalism* (trans. of Max Weber) 30, *Structure of Social Action* 37, *Toward a General Theory of Action* 51, *The Social System* 51, *Essays in Sociological Theory* (revision) 54, *Structure and Process in Modern Society* 60, *Societies: Evolutionary and Comparative Perspectives* 66, *Sociological Theory and Modern Society* 67, *Politics and Social Structure* 69, *The System of Modern Societies* 71; Co-author *Working Papers in the Theory of Action* 53, *Family, Socialization and Interaction Process* 55, *Economy and Society* 56, *Theories of Society* 61, *Social Structure and Personality* 64, *Readings on Premodern Societies* 72, *The American University* 73; contributor to numerous sociological and scientific reviews.
558 William James Hall, Harvard Univ., Cambridge, Mass. 02138; Home: 62 Fairmont Street, Belmont, Mass. 02178, U.S.A.
Telephone: 495-3817 (Office); 484-5610 (Home).

Part, Sir Antony Alexander, G.C.B., M.B.E., B.A.; British civil servant; b. 28 June 1916, London; s. of late Alexander Francis Part and late Una Margaret Reynolds (née Snowdon); m. Isabella Bennett 1940; ed. Harrow School and Trinity Coll., Cambridge.
Assistant Principal, Board of Educ. 37-39; Asst. Private Sec. to successive Ministers of Supply 39-40; Army 40-44; Private Sec. to successive Ministers of Educ. 45-46; Head of Bldg. Branch, Ministry of Educ. 46-52; Commonwealth Fund Fellowship, U.S.A. 50-51, Under-Sec., Ministry of Educ. 54-60, Head of Further Educ. Branch 56-60, Deputy Sec. 60-63; Deputy Sec., Ministry of Public Bldg. and Works 63-65; Perm. Sec. 65-68; Perm. Sec. Board of Trade 68-70, Dept. of Trade and Industry 70-74, Dept. of Industry 74-; Hon. D.Tech. (Brunel) 66, Hon. D.Sc. (Aston) 74.
Leisure interest: travel.
Department of Trade and Industry, 1 Victoria Street, London, S.W.1; and Flat 5, 71 Elm Park Gardens, London, S.W.10, England.
Telephone: 01-215-5424 (Office); 01-352-2950 (Home).

Parthasarathi, Gopalaswami, B.A., M.A.; Indian diplomatist; b. 7 July 1912, Madras; s. of late Sir N. Gopalaswami Ayyengar and Komalammal Parthasarathi; m. Subur Mugaseth 1939; one s.; ed. Univ. of Madras and Oxford Univ.
Assistant Editor *The Hindu* 36-49; Chief Rep. Press Trust of India, London 49-52, Chief Ed. Press Trust of India 51-53; Chair. Int. Comm. for Cambodia 54-55; Int. Supervisory Comm. for Viet-Nam 55-56; Amb. to Indonesia 57-58, to People's Republic of China 58-61; Chair. Int. Comm. for Supervision and Control, Viet-Nam 61-62; High Commr. in Pakistan 62-65; Perm. Rep. of India to UN Aug. 65-69; Rep. to Security Council 67, 68, Pres. Security Council 67, Chair. Security Council Sanctions Cttee. on Rhodesia 68; Vice-Chancellor of Jawaharlal Nehru Univ. 69; Chair. Policy Planning Cttee., Ministry of Foreign Affairs 75-; mem. Board of Trustees UN Inst. for Training and Research 70-72.
Leisure interests: cricket, tennis, hockey, reading.
31 Aurangzeb Road, New Delhi 11, India.
Telephone: 372989.

Partos, Oedoen; Israeli composer; b. 1907, Budapest; ed. in Budapest under Hubay (violin) and Kodaly (composition).
Founding mem. Int. Soc. for Contemporary Music; Leader of viola section, Israel Philharmonic Orchestra 38-56; Dir. Israel Acad. of Music, Tel-Aviv 51-; Prof. Tel-Aviv Univ. 61-; now devotes time to musical education, composition and solo appearances.
Compositions include *Concerto* (for violin and orchestra), *Sinfonia Concertante* (for viola and orchestra), *Yiskor* (for strings), *Visions* (for flute, piano and strings), *Makamat* (for flute and string quartet), *Ein Gev* (symphonic fantasy, UNESCO Prize 52, Israel State Prize 54), *Images* (for orchestra), *Symphonic Movements*, *Five Israeli Songs*, *Tehilim* (for string quartet), *Agada* (for viola, piano and percussion), *Nebulae* (for woodwind quintet), *Iltur* (for 12 harps); piano pieces, etc.
The Israel Academy of Music, Tel-Aviv; 25, Tsimchei Hayehudim Street, Ramat Aviv, Tel-Aviv, Israel.
Telephone: 416111 (Office); 418638 (Home).

Partou, Manouchehr, LL.B.; Iranian lawyer and politician; b. July 1921, Teheran; m. Mrs. Bibi 1962; ed. Univ. of Teheran.
Former Public Prosecutor of Teheran; Public Prosecutor of the Civil Service Tribunal; Counsel to the Supreme Court; Gen. Dir. Judiciary; Parliamentary Under-Sec. Ministry of Justice; Minister of Justice 69-71; Senator 73-.
7 Partow Street, Davoudieh, Teheran, Iran.
Telephone: 771244.

Partridge, Eric Honeywood, M.A., B.LITT.; British lexicographer and writer; b. 6 Feb. 1894, New Zealand; ed. Queensland and Oxford Univs.
Served with Australian Forces 15-18; Lecturer in English Literature Manchester and London Univs. 25-27; founder and Man. Dir. Scholartis Press 27-31; served Army 40-42, R.A.F. 42-45; now engaged in revision of various works and preparation of A Dictionary of Catch Phrases; Hon. D.Litt., Queensland. Leisure interests: reading, conversing, writing reviews. Publs. Eighteenth Century English Romantic Poetry 24, Three Personal Records of the War (with R. H. Mottram and John Easton) 29, Songs and Slang of the British Soldier (with John Brophy) 30, Slang To-day and Yesterday: A History and a Study 33, Name this Child (a dictionary of Christian names) 36, 59, A Dictionary of Slang and Unconventional English 37, 7th and enlarged edn. 70, The World of Words: A General Introduction to Language 38, A Dictionary of Clichés 39, A Dictionary of Abbreviations 43, Journey to the Edge of Morning 46, Usage and Abusage: A Guide to Good English 47, Words at War: Words at Peace 48, Forces' Slang: 1939-1945 (with Wilfred Granville and Frank Roberts) 48, English: A Course for Human Beings 49, Name into Word 49, A Dictionary of the Underworld 50, Here, There and Everywhere (Essays upon Language) 50, A History of English since 1900 (with John W. Clark) 51, From Sanskrit to Brazil (Essays upon Language) 52, The "Shaggy Dog" Story 53, You Have a Point There 54, The Concise Usage and Abusage 55, What's the Meaning? 56, English Gone Wrong 57, Origins: An Etymological Dictionary 58, A Charm of Words (essays on language) 60, Adventuring Among Words 61, The Gentle Art of Lexicography 63, The Long Trail (with John Brophy) 65.
34 Orpington Road, Winchmore Hill, London, N.21, England.

Partridge, Sir (Ernest) John, K.B.E.; British business executive; b. 18 July 1908, Bristol; s. of William Henry and Alice Mary Partridge; m. 1st Madeline Fabian 1934, (died 1944), 2nd Joan Johnson 1949; two s. two d.; ed. Queen Elizabeth's Hospital, Bristol.
Assistant Sec. Imperial Group Ltd. 44-46, Sec. 46-57, Dir. 49-, mem. Exec. Cttee. 57-60, Deputy Chair. 60-64, Chair. 64-75; Dir. British-American Tobacco Co. Ltd. 63-75, Nat. Westminster Bank 68-, Tobacco Securities Trust 64-75, Gen. Accident Fire and Life Assurance Corpn. Ltd. 73-, Dunlop Holdings Ltd. 73-, Delta Metal Co. Ltd. 73-, Finance for Industry 75-; Chair. Council of Industry for Management Educ. 67-71; Pres. Confed. of British Industry 70-72, Vice-Pres. 72-; Vice-Pres. Industrial Participation Asscn. 66-; mem. Nat. Econ. Devt. Council 67-75, Council of Industrial Soc. 68-75, Int. Advisory Board of Chemical Bank, U.S.A. 72-; Pres. Foundation for Management Educ. 72-, Nat. Council of Social Service 73-; Fellow, British Inst. of Management 63-; Gov. London Graduate School of Business Studies 67-75, Nat. Inst. of Econ. and Social Research 71-; Hon. LL.D. Bristol Univ. 72, Hon. D.Sc. Cranfield Inst. of Technology 74. Leisure interests: gardening, listening to music, walking.
Imperial House, 1 Grosvenor Place, London S.W.1;

Home: Wildwood, Haslemere, Surrey GU27 1DR, England.
Telephone: 01-235 7010 (Office).

Partridge, John Walters, B.S.; American utility executive; b. 24 July 1910, Helena, Mont.; s. of Joseph W. Partridge and Maude Walters; m. Virginia Akers 1940; one s. one d.; ed. Lafayette Coll.
Engineer, Columbia Gas System 31; Pres. Charleston Group Companies 51-61; Pres. and Dir. Columbia Gas System Inc. 61-70, Vice-Chair. of Board and Chief Admin. Officer 70-71, Chair. and Chief Exec. Officer 71-. Leisure interests: golf, sport.
20 Montchanin Road, Wilmington, Del. 19807; Home: 904 Du Pont Road, Wilmington, Del. 19807, U.S.A.
Telephone: 302-429-5205 (Office); 302-654-4243 (Home).

Partridge, Mark Henry Heathcote; Rhodesian chartered accountant and politician; b. 23 Nov. 1922, East Rand, Transvaal; ed. St. George's Coll., Salisbury.
Served in King's Royal Rifle Corps, Middle East, Italy, Greece 40-45; worked in own accountants firm, Rocke, Partridge & Adair, Salisbury; mem. Parl. for Greendale 62-; Minister of Local Govt. and Housing 66-73, of Lands and Natural Resources and of Water Devt. June 73-; Independence Commemorative Decoration.
Private Bag 7726, Causeway, Salisbury, Rhodesia.

Pashkov, Mikhail Vasilyevich; Soviet trade union official; b. 22 Nov. 1917, Zhernovets, Kursk region; ed. Ukrainian Polygraphic Inst. and Higher Party School.
Komsomol official, Volchansk, Kharkovsky Region 30-34; Student, Ukrainian Polygraphic Inst.; Engineer, Printing works, Kharkov 39-40; C.P. official, Moscow 40-52; Deputy Chief of Gen. Man. Dept. of Printing and Publishing Industries, Council of Ministers of U.S.S.R. 52-53; Deputy Minister of Culture of R.S.F.S.R. 53-61; Rector, Moscow Polygraphic Inst., Chair. Scientific Technical Soc. of Printing and Publishing Industry of U.S.S.R., mem. Central Cttee. of Cultural Workers' Union 61-66, Chair. 66-; mem. All-Union Council of Trade Unions 68-.
Central Committee of Cultural Workers' Union, 42 Leninsky Prospekt, Moscow, U.S.S.R.

Pasmore, (Edwin John) Victor, C.B.E., M.A.; British artist; b. 3 Dec. 1908; ed. Harrow School and L.C.C. Central School of Arts and Crafts (evening classes).
Local Govt. service, L.C.C. County Hall 27-37; associated with "Euston Road" school of painting 37-39; Visiting Teacher Camberwell School of Art 45-49, Cen. School of Arts and Crafts 49-53; Master of Painting, Durham Univ. 54-61; Consultant Architectural Designer Peterlee New Town 55; retrospective exhibitions Venice Biennale 60, Musée des Arts Décoratifs, Paris 61, Stedelijk Museum, Amsterdam 61, Palais des Beaux Arts, Brussels 61, Louisiana Museum, Copenhagen 62, Kestner Gesellschaft, Hanover 62, Kunsthalle, Berne 63, Tate Gallery, London 65, São Paulo Biennale 65, Marlborough Gallery, London 66, 69, 72, etc.; Carnegie Prize for Painting 64.
Principal works include The Gardens of Hammersmith (Nat. Gallery of Canada), The Thames at Chiswick (Melbourne Nat. Gallery), The Snow Storm (Arts Council of Great Britain), The Inland Sea, Abstract Relief (Tate Gallery), Abstract Mural Painting (Barnsbury School, London).
12 St. German's Place, Blackheath, London, S.E.3, England.
Telephone: 01-858-0369.

Passarinho, Jarbas Gonçalves; Brazilian politician; b. 11 Jan. 1920, Xapuri, Acre; s. of Ignácio Loyola Passarinho and Júlia Gonçalves Passarinho; m. Ruth de Castro Passarinho 1945; two s. three d.; ed. Escola Militar do Realengo, Escola de Comando and Estado-Major de Exército.
Governor, State of Pará 64-66; Pres. ARENA, Pará;

Senator, State of Pará 66-67; Minister of Labour and Social Welfare 67-69; Minister of Education and Culture 69-74; Pres. Brazilian Del. to Int. Conf. UNESCO 70-71; Chief of Brazilian Del., Inter-American Council for Education, Science and Culture, Perm. Exec. Cttee. 72; Senator, Pará State 75-; numerous awards.
Leisure interest: sports.
Publs. *Terra Encharcada* (Samuel MacDowell Prize), *Roteiro 64, Amazonia—The Challenge of the Tropics* 71.
Federal Senate, Brasília, Brazil.

Passuth, László, LL.D.; Hungarian writer; b. 15 July 1900, Budapest; s. of late Francis Passuth and Emanuela Eber; m. Lola de Békésy 1936; one d.; ed. Kolozsvár, Cluj and Szeged Univ.
First novel 36; mem. Cttee. for Foreign Affairs, Asscn. of Hungarian Writers, European Community of Writers; Vice-Pres. Hungarian PEN Club; novels translated into 11 languages.
Leisure interests: archaeology, travels.
Publs. include: *The Rain-God Mourns for Mexico* 39, *Joanna of Naples* 40, *A Castle in Lombardy* 41, *Born in Purple* 43, *In Black Velvet* 47, *The Musician of the Duke of Mantua* 57, *Lagunes* 58, *The Gods Shiver in Golden Mist* 64, *The Third Majordomo, Velasquez* 65, *Exploring the Past* (autobiog.) 66, *Madrigal* 68, *Copper Age* (autobiog.) 69, *Eternal Spain* 69, *Hétszer Vágott Mezö* (Andrew II—historical novel) 71, *Encounter with The Rain God—voyage in Mexico* 72, *Gyilokjáró* (Around the Bastions—autobiog.) 73, *Speculum regis* (King-Emperor Sigismund) 74, *Emlék és folytatás* (Reminiscence and Continuation) 75.
H-1024 Budapest II, Rózsahegy u.1, Hungary.
Telephone: 355-825.

Pastore, John O., LL.B.; American lawyer and politician; b. 17 March 1907, Providence, R.I., of Italian parents; m. Elena E. Caito 1941; one s. two d.; ed. Providence Classical High School and Northeastern Univ.
Admitted to Rhode Island Bar 32; mem. House of Reps., Rhode Island Gen. Assembly 34-38; Asst. Attorney Gen., Rhode Island 37-38, 40-41; Lieut. Gov. Rhode Island 44-45, Gov. 45-50; U.S. Senator from Rhode Island 50-; mem. Joint Cttee. on Atomic Energy, Commerce and Appropriations Senate Committees; mem. U.S. Delegation to UN 55, Congressional Adviser with reference to Int. Atomic Energy Agency (I.A.E.A.); Senator-Designee, first Conf. on Peaceful Uses of Atomic Energy, Geneva 55, initiation of I.A.E.A., Vienna 57; Hon. LL.D. Providence Coll., Rhode Island Univ., Brown Univ., Northeastern Univ., Salve Regina Coll., New Bedford Inst. of Technology, Phil. Coll. of Textiles and Science, Suffolk Univ.; Villanova Univ.; Hon. Ed.D. Rhode Island Coll. of Education; Hon. Sc.D. Rhode Island Coll. of Pharmacy, Bryant Coll.; Democrat.
Leisure interests: duties as U.S. Senator.
3215 New Senate Office Building, Washington, D.C. 20510; 301 P.O. Annex, Providence, Rhode Island, U.S.A.
Telephone: 224-2921.

Pastorino Viscardi, Enrique Juan; Uruguayan trade union official; b. 6 March 1918, Montevideo; s. of Antonio and Catalina Pastorino Viscardi; m. Alba Chasate; two s. one d.; ed. primary schools.
Secretary Union of Workers of the Leather Industry 40; Sec. Gen. Union of Workers of Uruguay 50; Sec. Central Council of Workers of Uruguay 60; Sec. Nat. Convention of Workers of Uruguay 66-; Pres. World Fed. of Trade Unions (WFTU) Oct. 69-; Lenin Peace Prize 73.
Leisure interest: being with the family.
World Federation of Trade Unions, Nám. Curieovych 1, Prague, Czechoslovakia; Home: Calle Ganaderos, 4306, Montevideo, Uruguay.
Telephone: 95870 (Montevideo).

Pastrana Borrero, Misael, LL.D.; Colombian politician and diplomatist; b. 14 Nov. 1923, Neiva; s. of Misael Pastrana Pastrana and Elisa Borrero de Pastrana; m. Cristina Arango Vega; three s. one d.; ed. Pontificia Universidad Javeriana, Bogotá.
Founder and editor *El Porvenir* and Civil Law Circuit Judge 45; Sec. Colombian Embassy, The Vatican 47-49; Private Sec. to Pres. Ospina Pérez 49-50; Counsellor, Colombian Embassy, Washington, D.C. 50-52; Sec. Ministry of Foreign Affairs 53; alt. rep. at UN 54-56; Founder and Vice-Pres. Corporación Financiera Colombiana 57; Minister of Devt. 60; Minister of Public Works and Finance 61; in private business 61-65; Minister of the Interior 66-68; Amb. to U.S.A. 68-69; Pres. of Colombia 70-74; Conservative (Nat. Front Coalition).
c/o Partido Conservador, Bogotá, Colombia.

Pastyřík, Miroslav; Czechoslovak trade unionist and politician; b. 16 Aug. 1912, Břeclav.
Chairman Břeclav District Cttee. of Communist Youth 30-38; mem. C.P. of Czechoslovakia 33-; Chief Sec. Hodonín District Cttee., C.P. of Czechoslovakia 45-46; Deputy and Sec. of Communist Deputies Club in Provincial Nat. Cttee. 46-49; Sec. Gottwaldov Regional Cttee. of C.P. of Czechoslovakia 46-48, Chief Sec. 48-50; mem. Central Cttee. of C.P. of Czechoslovakia 49-71, Head of Dept. 50-63; mem. Economic Comm. of Central Cttee. C.P. of Czechoslovakia 63-66; alt. mem. Presidium and mem. Secr., Central Cttee. C.P. of Czechoslovakia 66-68; mem. and Vice-Pres. Central Council of Trade Unions 63-65, Pres. 65-68; Deputy to Nat. Assembly 64-69; Deputy to House of the People, Fed. Assembly 69-71; mem. Gen. Council, and Vice-Pres. World Fed. of Trade Unions (WFTU) 65-68; Man. Orbis Publishing House 70-; Order of 25 February, 1st Class 48; Order of the Repub. 62.
Orbis Publishing House, Prague, Czechoslovakia.

Paswan, Bhola; Indian politician; b. 1914, Bairgachhi, Bihar; s. of Dhusar Paswan; m. Devki Devi.
Member Purnea District Board 39; mem. Bihar Legis. Assembly 46; Parl. Sec. to Minister for Local Self-Govt., Bihar 46-52; Minister, Govt. of Bihar 52-63; Chief Minister 68, 69, 71-72; mem. Rajya Sabha 72; Minister of Works and Housing, Govt. of India Feb. 73-74.
Leisure interests: music, drama.
2 Western Court, New Delhi, India.
Telephone: 310481, 311973.

Pătan, Ion; Romanian economist and politician; b. 1 Dec. 1926, Daia Village, Alba County; ed. Economic Studies Acad. Bucharest.
Several posts in the Ministry of Light Industry 52-56; Dir. Ministry of Light Industry 56-62, Gen. Sec. 62-64; Deputy Minister of Light Industry 64-65; mem. Central Cttee. of R.C.P. 69-; Candidate mem. Exec. Cttee. 72; mem. Exec. Political Cttee., mem. Standing Bureau 74; Minister of Home Trade 68-69; Vice-Chair. Council of Ministers 69-; Minister of Foreign Trade 72-.
Council of Ministers, Bucharest, Romania.

Patassé, Ange; Central African Republic politician; b. 25 Jan. 1937; ed. French Equatorial Coll.
Agricultural inspector 59-65; Dir. of Agriculture 65; Minister of Devt. 65; Minister of State for Transport and Power March 69-Feb. 70, concurrently Minister of State for Devt. and Tourism Sept. 69-Feb. 70; Minister of State for Agriculture, Stock-breeding, Waters and Forests, Hunting, Tourism, Transport and Power Feb.-June 70; Minister of State for Devt. June-Aug. 70; Minister of State for Transport and Commerce 70-72, for Rural Devt. May 72-73, of Health and Social Affairs 73-74; Minister of State for Tourism, Waters, Fishing and

Hunting June 74-; Pres. Soc. Franco-Centrafricaine des Tabacs, Union Cotonnière Centrafricaine 70.
Ministère de Tourisme, Bangui, Central African Republic.

Patcèvitch, Iva; American publisher; b. 19 Nov. 1900; ed. Russian Imperial Naval Acad.
Came to U.S. 23; associated with Hemphill Noyes & Co. Jan. 24-Dec. 28; personal asst. to Pres. and Budget Dir. Condé Nast Publs. Inc. 28-32; Man. Dir. Les Editions Condé Nast Paris 32-36; Exec. Asst. to Pres. Condé Nast Publs. Inc. 36-42, Dir. 35-71, mem. Exec. Cttee. 36-71, Pres. and Chair. Board of Dirs. 42-; Liaison Officer between Russian and British troops in Persia, Turkestan and Caucasus June 18-Nov. 19; Légion d'Honneur 50.
Coopers Neck Lane, Southampton, N.Y. 11968, U.S.A.

Patel, Baburao; Indian writer, editor and film producer; b. 4 April 1904, Maswan District, Thana, Maharashtra; *s.* of Pandurang V. Patel and Jamna P. Patel; *m.* 1st 1922; 2nd 1945; five *s.* two *d.*
Began freelance journalism 22; wrote, directed and produced motion pictures, founder and Editor *Filmindia* 35-; lectured in U.S. and Europe on India's ancient culture and civilization; set up a production code and fought for revision of film censorship; Ed. *Mother India*; Man. Dir. Sumati Publications Pvt. Ltd. 58; mem. Parl. for Shajapur 67-.
Leisure interests: astrology, classical music, healing by homoeopathy.
Publs. *Grey Dust, Burning Words, The Sermon of the Lord, Prayer Book, Rosary and the Lamp, Homœopathic Lifesavers for Home and Community*; Films: (wrote and produced) *Kismet, Mahananda, Bala Joban, My Darling, Maharanee, Draupadi, Gvalan.*
Girnar, Pali Hill, Bombay 50, India.
Telephone: 261752 (Office); 533414 (Home).

Patel, Hirubhai, C.I.E., B.A., B.COM.; Indian politician; b. 26 Aug. 1904, Bombay; *s.* of Muljibhai and Hiraben Patel; *m.* Savitaben Patel 1928; ed. Oxford and London Univs.
Separation Officer, Sing 35; Finance Dept., Bombay 36; Sec. to Stock Exchange Cttee. 36-37; Trade Commr., for N. Europe, Hamburg 37-39; Deputy Trade Commr., London 39-40; Deputy Sec. Eastern Group Supply Council 41-42; Deputy Dir. Gen., Supply Dept. 42-43; Joint Sec. and Sec., Industries and Civil Supplies Dept. 43-46, Cabinet Secr. 46-47; Defence and Partition Sec. 47-53; Sec. Food and Agriculture 53-54, Dept. of Econ. Affairs, Ministry of Finance 57; Principal Finance Sec. 57-59; Chair. Life Insurance Corpn. of India 56-57; Chair. Gujarat Electricity Board 60-66; mem. Gujarat Legislative Assembly 67-71; Chair. Charutar Vidyamandal, Vallal Vidyanagar 59-; Pres. Gujarat Swatantra Party 67-72, All India Swatantra Party 71-72; mem. Lok Sabha March 71-; Hon. LL.D. (Sardar Patel Univ.).
Charutar Vidyamandal, Vallabh Vidyanagar, W. Railway, India.
Telephone: 175.

Patel, Indraprasad Gordhanbhai, B.A., PH.D.; Indian economist; b. 1924, Baroda; *s.* of Gordhanbhai Patel and Kashiben Patel; *m.* Alaknanda Dasgupta 1958; one *d.*; ed. Baroda Coll., Bombay Univ., King's Coll., Cambridge and Harvard Univ.
Professor of Econs., Maharaja Sayajirao Univ., Baroda 49-50; Economist and Asst. Chief, Financial Problems add Policies Div., Int. Monetary Fund 50-54; Dep. Econ. Adviser, Indian Ministry of Finance 54-58; Alt. Exec. Dir. for India, Int. Monetary Fund 58-61; Chief Econ. Adviser, Ministry of Finance, India 61-63, 65-67, Econ. Adviser Planning Comm. 61-63; Special Sec. Ministry of Finance 68-69, Sec. 70-; Visiting Prof., Delhi School of Economics, Delhi Univ. 64.
Leisure interest: reading.

Ministry of Finance, Department of Economic Affairs, North Block, New Delhi 1; 11 Tin Murti Lane, New Delhi 11, India.
Telephone: 372611 (Office); 611931 (Home).

Patel, Jeram; Indian painter and graphic designer; b. 20 June 1930; ed. Sir J. J. School of Art, Bombay, Central School of Arts and Crafts, London.
Reader in Applied Arts, M.S. Univ., Baroda 60-61; Reader in Visual Design, School of Architecture, Ahmedabad 61-62; Deputy Dir. All India Handloom Board 63-66; Reader in Applied Arts, M.S. Univ. Baroda 66-; mem. *Group 1890* (avant-garde group of Indian artists), Lalit Kala Akademi; one man exhbns. in London 59, New Delhi 60, 62-65, in Calcutta 66; in Tokyo Biennale 57-63, São Paulo Biennale 63; represented in Nat. Gallery of Modern Art, New Delhi, Art Soc. of India, Bombay, Sir J. J. Inst. of Applied Art, Bombay, and in private collections in U.S.A., London, Paris and Tokyo; Lalit Kala Akademi Nat. Awards 57, 64; Bombay State Award 57; Silver Medal, Bombay Art Soc. 61, Gold Medal Rajkot Exhbn.
Faculty of Fine Arts, M.S. University, Baroda 2, India.

Pathak, Gopal Swarup; Indian lawyer and politician; b. 26 Feb. 1896.
Member Lok Sabha for Uttar Pradesh; fmr. Judge Allahabad High Court; Pres. Indian Soc. of Int. Law, mem. Indian Comm. of Jurists; Minister of Law 66-67; Gov. of Mysore 67-69; Vice-Pres. of India 69-74, also Chair. Rajya Sabha 69-74.
c/o Office of the Vice-President, New Delhi, India.

Patil, Sadashiv Kanoji; Indian politician; b. 14 Aug. 1900; ed. St. Xavier's Coll., Bombay, London School of Economics and University Coll., London Univ.
Joined the Indian Nat. Congress 20 and was imprisoned for a total period of ten years for participating in freedom movt.; Gen.-Sec. Bombay Provincial Congress Cttee. 29-45 and Pres. 46-57; mem. A.I.C.C. 33-, mem. Working Cttee. 45-51, 56-57, 60-, Treas. 60-64, 68-71; mem. Congress Parl. Board 63-; mem. Bombay Legislative Assembly 37-46; mem. of the Bombay Municipal Corpn. 35-52; Mayor of Bombay three terms 49-52; mem. Constituent Assembly 47-50; mem. Provisional Parl. 50-52; mem. of Lok Sabha 52-67, 69-70; Minister for Irrigation and Power 57-58; Minister for Transport and Communications 58-59, for Food and Agriculture 59-63; Minister of Railways 64-67.
Publ. *Indian National Congress: A Case for Reorganization.*
Home: Shanti Kuteer, Marine Drive, Bombay 20, India.
Telephone: 297722 and 298877.

Patil, Veerendra, LL.B.; Indian politician and lawyer; b. 28 Feb. 1924, Chincholi, Gulbarga District; ed. Osmania Univ., Hyderabad.
Practised law 47, 50-55; mem. Hyderabad State Assembly 52, 57, 62-; Deputy Minister for Home and Industries, Mysore till 58; Minister for Excise and Rural Industries 61-62, for Public Works 62-; Chief Minister of Mysore 68-72; mem. Rajya Sabha 72-; Pres. Pradesh Congress; mem. Working Cttee.; Chair. State Advisory Board on ports; mem. Nat. Harbour Board; mem. del. to U.S.S.R. 65, Japan and S.E. Asia 70, Australia 72, U.K. and Europe 73.
23 Lower Palace Orchards, Bangalore 3, India.

Patiño, Antenor; Bolivian diplomatist and businessman; b. 12 Oct. 1898, Oruro; ed. Paris Univ. Law Faculty.
Formerly Sec. Bolivian Legation, Paris, Chargé d'Affaires, Madrid and mem. Bolivian del. to LN; Minister to U.K. 41-44; Chair. Patiño N.V.-Cie. Française d'entreprises Minières Métallurgiques et d'Investissements (COFREMMI); Pres. Consolidated Tin Smelters Ltd., Patiño Mines (Quebec) Ltd., Cía. Estanífera do Brasil (CESBRA), Cia. Espírito Santo

de Mineração (CESMI); Grand Officer Condor of the Andes, Chevalier Légion d'Honneur.

45 avenue Foch, 75116 Paris; Home: 9 avenue Maréchal Maunoury, 75016 Paris, France.

Telephone: 727-44-64 (Office); 504-52-51 (Home).

Patolichev, Nikolai Semyonovich; Soviet politician; b. 23 Sept. 1908; ed. Military Acad.

Member C.P.S.U. 28-; held exec. posts for Young Communist League in Gorky and Chelyabinsk regions 28-31; at Head Office of Central Cttee. of C.P.S.U. 37-39; First Sec. of the Yaroslavl Regional Cttee. of the Party 39-41, of the Chelyabinsk Regional Cttee. 41-46; mem. Organizational Bureau and Sec. of the Central Cttee. of the Party 46-47; Vice-Chair. of the Council for Collective Farms of the Soviet Govt. 46; Sec. Ukrainian Communist Party Central Cttee. 47; First Sec. Rostov Regional Cttee. of C.P. 47-50; First Sec. Central Cttee. of Byelorussian C.P. 50-56; mem. Central Cttee. of C.P.S.U. 41-; First Deputy Minister of Foreign Affairs of U.S.S.R. 56-58; Minister of Foreign Trade 58-; Deputy to U.S.S.R. Supreme Soviet 38-; Order of Lenin (eight times), Order of the Red Banner of Labour.

Ministry of Foreign Trade, 32-34 Smolenskaya-Sennaya ploshchad, Moscow, U.S.S.R.

Paton, Alan Stewart, B.ED., B.SC.; South African writer and politician; b. 11 Jan. 1903, Pietermaritzburg, Natal; m. 1st Dorrie Francis, two s.; 2nd Anne Hopkins 1969; ed. Pietermaritzburg Coll. and Natal Univ.

Teacher 24-36; Principal Diepkloof Reformatory for African Juvenile Delinquents, Johannesburg 36-48; Pres. Liberal Party of South Africa till 68; started a new magazine *Reality* 69; Hon. L.H.D. (Yale Univ.); Hon. D.Litt. (Kenyon Coll., Rhodes Univ., and Univ. of Natal, Harvard, Trent and Willamette Univs.; Hon. D.D. (Edinburgh Univ.); Hon. LL.D. (Witwatersrand); Freedom Award 60; Award, Free Acad. of Art, Hamburg 61.

Leisure interests: birdwatching, gardening, croquet.

Publs. *Cry, The Beloved Country* 48, *Too Late the Phalarope* 53, *The Land and People of South Africa* 55, *South Africa in Transition* 56, *Hope for South Africa* 58, *Debbie Go Home* (short stories) 61, *Hofmeyr* 65, *Instrument of Thy Peace* 68, *The Long View* 68, *Kontakion for You Departed* 69. musical *Mkhumbane* (Village in the Gulley), *Apartheid and the Archbishop* 73, *Knocking on the Door* 75.

P.O.B. 278, Hillcrest, Natal, Republic of South Africa. Telephone: Durban (Natal) 788920.

Paton, Boris Yevgeniyevich; Soviet metallurgist; b. 27 Nov. 1918, Kiev; ed. Kiev Polytechnic Inst.

Institute of Electro Welding, Ukrainian S.S.R. Acad. of Sciences, Dir. 53-; mem. C.P.S.U. 52-; Corresp. mem. Ukrainian S.S.R. Acad. of Sciences 51-58, mem. 58-, Pres. 62-; mem. U.S.S.R. Acad. of Sciences 62-, mem. Presidium 62-; Cand. mem. C.P.S.U. Central Cttee. 61-66, mem. 66-; Deputy to U.S.S.R. Supreme Soviet 62-; Vice-Chair. Union Soviet U.S.S.R. Supreme Soviet 66-; State Prize 50, Lenin Prize 57, Hero of Socialist Labour, "Hammer and Sickle" Gold Medal, Order of Lenin, Red Banner of Labour and other decorations.

E. O. Paton Institute of Electro Welding, 69 Ulitsa Gorkogo, Kiev, U.S.S.R.

Paton, Sir George Whitecross, Kt., LL.D., M.A., D.C.L.; British educationist; b. 16 Aug. 1902, Geelong, Australia; s. of Rev. Frank and Mrs. Paton; m. Alice Watson 1931; one s. three d.; ed. Univ. of Melbourne and Magdalen Coll., Oxford.

Asst. Lecturer London School of Economics 30-31; Prof. Jurisprudence Univ. of Melbourne 31-51, Vice-Chancellor 51-68; Chair. Royal Comm. on Television (Aust.) 53; Chair. Australian Vice-Chancellor's Cttee. 57-60.

Publs. *A Text Book of Jurisprudence, Bailment in the Common Law* 52.

7 Dunraven Avenue, Toorak, Victoria, Australia. Telephone: 24-1034.

Paton, Sir (Thomas) Angus (Lyall), Kt., C.M.G., F.R.S.; British civil engineer; b. 10 May 1905, Jersey, C.I.; s. of Thomas Lyall Paton and Janet Gibb; m. Eleanor Joan Delmé-Murray (died 1964); two s. two d.; ed. Cheltenham Coll. and Univ. Coll., London.

Joined Sir Alexander Gibb and Partners 25, Partner 38; work in U.K., Canada, Burma and Turkey on harbour works, hydro-electric schemes and industrial projects; responsible for design and supervision of many projects, including Owen Falls and Kariba hydro-electric schemes and Indus Basin project, W. Pakistan; Senior Partner Sir Alexander Gibb and Partners 55-; Pres. Inst. of Civil Engineers 70-71; Chair. Council of Engineering Insts. 73.

Leisure interests: walking, do-it-yourself.

Publs. numerous technical papers and articles on civil engineering; *Power from Water* 60.

Standard House, London Street, Reading, Berks.; Home: 45 Richmond Hill Court, Richmond, Surrey, England.

Telephone: Reading 586171 (Office); 01-940-1270 (Home).

Paton, William Drummond Macdonald, C.B.E., F.R.S., M.A., D.M., F.R.C.P.; British pharmacologist; b. 5 May 1917, Hendon, London; s. of Rev. William Paton and Grace Mackenzie Macdonald; m. Phoebe Margaret Rooke 1942; ed. Winchester House School, Repton School, Oxford Univ. and University Coll. Hospital Medical School.

House physician, Univ. Coll. Hospital (U.C.H.) 42; Pathologist, Midhurst Sanatorium 43; mem. staff Nat. Inst. for Med. Research 44-52; Reader, Applied Pharmacology, U.C.H. 52-54; Prof. of Pharmacology, Royal Coll. of Surgeons, London 54-59; Prof. of Pharmacology, Oxford Univ., and Fellow Balliol Coll. 59-; Sec. Physiological Soc. 51-57; Medical Research Council 63-67; Council of Royal Soc. 67-69; Joint Ed. Notes and Records of the Royal Society 71; Chair. Research Defence Soc. 72; Hon. F.F.A.R.C.S. 75; Cameron Prize (with E. J. Zaimis) 56; Gairdner Award (with E. J. Zaimis) 59; Clover Lecturer 58; Bertram Louis Abrahams Lecturer (R.C.P.) 62.

Leisure interests: music and old books.

Publs. *Pharmacological Principles and Practice* (with J. P. Payne) 68, and papers in scientific journals on diving and high-pressure biology, histamine, synaptic transmission, drug action and drug addiction.

Home: 13 Staverton Road, Oxford; University Department of Pharmacology, South Parks Road, Oxford, England.

Telephone: 58355 (Home); 57062 (Office).

Patricio, Antonio A. de Medeiros; Portuguese diplomatist; b. 30 Oct. 1930, Lisbon; s. of Emílio Patricio and Maria Augusta Goulart de Medeiros Patricio; m. Maria L. de Sousa de Camara Moraes Sarmento; three s. one d.; ed. Faculty of Law, Univ. of Lisbon.

Joined Portuguese Foreign Office 52; served with Portuguese mission in Fed. Germany, as Consul at Toronto, Canada and as First Sec. and Deputy Perm. Rep. to UN; Chargé d'Affaires, Mission of Portugal at UN 64-74.

c/o Ministry of Foreign Affairs, Lisbon, Portugal.

Patricio, Rui Manuel de Medeiros d'Espiney, LL.D.; Portuguese lawyer and politician; b. 17 Aug. 1932, Lisbon; s. of Emílio Patricio and Maria Augusta Medeiros d'Espiney; m. Maria Ignês Morais Sarmento; two s. two d.; ed. Faculty of Law, Univ. of Lisbon.

Assistant, Faculty of Law, Univ. of Lisbon 58-64; fmr.

Prof. Instituto de Estudos Sociais; Del. to Congress of Int. Chamber of Commerce 61, World Oil Congress 63; Under-Sec. of State for Overseas Devt. 65-69; Under-Sec. of State for Foreign Affairs 69-70; Minister of Foreign Affairs 70-74; Grand Cross of the Order of the Crown of Oak of Luxembourg; Grand Officer of the Legion of Honour of France; Grand Officer of Order of Merit of Fed. Germany and numerous other awards.
Avenida Infante Santo 61-6, Lisbon 3, Portugal.

Patrick, John; American dramatist; b. 17 May 1905; ed. Holy Cross Coll.
Radio writer, San Francisco 32-35, film writer, Hollywood 36-37, free-lance dramatist, London and New York 40-; served American Field Service 42-44; Pulitzer Prize 54, Drama Critics Circle Award, Tony Award and Donelson Award 54, Screen Writers Guild Award 57, Foreign Correspondent Award 57, Hon. degree Doctor of Fine Arts (Baldwin-Wallace Coll.) 72. Publs. Plays: *The Willow and I* 42, *The Hasty Heart* 45, *The Story of Mary Surratt* 47, *The Curious Savage* 50, *Lo and Behold* 51, *The Teahouse of the August Moon* 53, *Good as Gold* 57, *Everybody Loves Opal* 62, *It's Been Wonderful* 65, *Everybody's Girl* 66, *Scandal Point* 67, *Love is a Time of Day* 69, *A Barrel Full of Pennies* 70, *Opal is a Diamond* 71, *Macbeth Did It* 71, *The Dancing Mice* 71, *Lovely Ladies, Kind Gentlemen* (Musical) 71, *The Small Miracle* (TV) 72, *Hallmark Hall of Fame* (TV Script) 72, *Anybody Out There?* 72, *The Savage Dilemma* 72; films: *Enchantment* 48, *The President's Lady* 52, *Three Coins in the Fountain* 54, *Mister Roberts* 54, *A Many Splendoured Thing* 55, *High Society* 56, *Les Girls* 57, *Some Came Running* 58, *The World of Suzie Wong* 60, *Gigot* 61, *Main Attraction* 63, *Shoes of the Fisherman* 68.
c/o The Dramatist' Guild, 234 West 44th Street, New York, N.Y. 10036, U.S.A.

Patrick, Ruth, PH.D.; American limnologist; b. 26 Nov. 1907, Topeka, Kan.; d. of Frank and Myrtle (née Jetmore) Patrick; m. Charles Hodge IV 1931; one s.; ed. Coker Coll. and Univ. of Virginia.
Curator, Leidy Microscopical Soc. 37-47; Asst. Curator, Microscopy Dept., Acad. of Nat. Sciences of Philadelphia 39-47; Curator Dept. of Limnology, Acad. of Nat. Sciences of Philadelphia 47-, Chair. 47-73, Francis Boyer Chair. 73-; Chair. Board of Trustees, Acad. of Natural Sciences of Philadelphia 73-; Lecturer in Botany, Univ. of Pa. 50-70, Prof. of Biology 70-; Lecturer in Algae Course, Marine Biological Lab., Woods Hole, Mass. 51-55; mem. limnological expedition to Mexico (sponsored by American Philosophical Soc.) 47; leader of expedition to Peru and Brazil (sponsored by Catherwood Foundation) 55; Chair. panel of Cttee. on Pollution, Nat. Acad. of Sciences 66; mem. many other cttees. concerned with water pollution, environmental resources and control; mem. Nat. Acad. of Sciences, American Asscn. for the Advancement of Science, Ecological Soc. of America, American Soc. of Naturalists (Pres. 75), Int. Asscn. of Limnology etc.; Richard Hopper Day Memorial Medal, Acad. of Nat. Sciences 69, YWCA Gold Medal 70, Lewis L. Dollinger Pure Environment Award, Franklin Inst. 70, 1970 Pennsylvania Award for Excellence in Science and Tech.; Botanical Soc. of America Merit Award 71; Eminent Ecologist Award, Ecological Soc. of America 72; Philadelphia Award 73; Second Annual Tyler Int. Ecology Award 75; Hon. D.Sc. (Beaver Coll., Cedar Crest Coll., Wilkes Coll., Philadelphia Coll. of Pharmacy and Science and P.M.C. Colls.), Hon. LL.D. (Coker Coll.), L.H.D. (Chesnut Hill Coll.).
Publs. numerous articles in professional journals.
Department of Limnology, Academy of Natural Sciences of Philadelphia, 19th and The Parkway, Philadelphia, Pa. 19103, U.S.A.
Telephone: 215-567-3700.

Patsalides, Andreas, B.SC.ECONS.; Cypriot politician; b. 1922, Tseri, Nicosia; m.; two c.; ed. Greek Gymnasium, Limassol, School of Econs. and Political Science, London, and Harvard Univ., Mass.
Various posts in public service; Gen. Dir. Planning Bureau 62-68; Minister of Finance 68-.
c/o Ministry of Finance, Nicosia, Cyprus.
Telephone: Nicosia 70-213F.

Pattakos, Stylianos; Greek politician; b. 8 Nov. 1912, Crete; s. of George and Maria Pattakos; m. Dimitra Nickolaidou 1940; two d.; ed. high school, cadet school, War Coll. and Nat. Defence Acad.
Commissioned 37, promoted Maj.-Gen. Dec. 67, retd.; Minister of the Interior 67-73, Deputy Premier Dec. 67; First Deputy Premier 71-73; arrested Oct. 74, sentenced to death for high treason and insurrection Aug. 75 (sentence commuted to life imprisonment).

Patterson, Bryan; American palaeontologist; b. 10 Feb. 1909, London, England; s. of Lieut.-Col. John Henry Patterson, D.S.O., and Frances Helena Gray; m. Bernice Maurine Caine 1934; one s.; ed. Malvern Coll., England, Harvard Univ. and Univ. of Chicago.
Assistant in Palaeontology to Curator of Fossil Mammals, Chicago Natural History Museum 26-55; Alexander Agassiz Prof. of Vertebrate Palaeontology and Curator in Vertebrate Palaeontology, Harvard Univ. 55-; mem. advisory panel earth sciences Nat. Science Foundation 56-59; Guggenheim Foundation Fellow 51-53, 54-55; mem. Nat. Acad. of Sciences.
Publs. Technical articles in scientific journals.
234 Brattle Street, Cambridge, Mass. 02138, U.S.A.
Telephone: 864-3463.

Patterson, Right Rev. Cecil John, C.M.G., C.B.E., D.D., M.A.; British ecclesiastic; b. 9 Jan. 1908, London; s. of James Bruce and Alice Maud Patterson; ed. St. Paul's School and St. Catharine's Coll., Cambridge.
Deacon 31, Priest 32; London curacy 31-34; Missionary, Nigeria 34-69; Asst. Bishop 42-45, Bishop in the Niger 45-69, Archbishop of West Africa 61-69; Rep. for Archbishops of Canterbury and York for Community Relations 70-72; Hon. Asst. Bishop of London 70-.
6 High Park Road, Kew, Richmond, Surrey TW9 4BH, England.
Telephone: 01-876-4354.

Patterson, Ellmore Clark, B.S.; American banker; b. 29 Nov. 1913, Western Springs, Ill.; s. of Ellmore Clark Patterson and Harriet Emma (Wales) Patterson; m. Anne Hyde Choate 1940; five s.; ed. Lyons Township High School, Lake Forest Acad. and Univ. of Chicago.
With J. P. Morgan & Co. 35-39, 39-41, 46-59 (Vice-Pres. 51-59); following merger of J. P. Morgan & Co. and Guaranty Trust Co., became Exec. Vice-Pres. Morgan Guaranty Trust Co. of New York 59-65, Dir. and Vice-Chair. of Board 65-67, Chair. Exec. Cttee. 67-68, Pres. 69-71, Chair. 71-.
Hook Road, Bedford Village, New York 10506; 23 Wall Street, New York, N.Y. 10015, U.S.A.
Telephone: 914-BE4-7818.

Patterson, Gardner, M.A., PH.D.; American economist; b. 13 May 1916, Burt, Ia.; s. of Charles W. and Trella Gardner Patterson; m. Evelyn R. Patterson 1942; one d.; ed. Univ. of Michigan and Harvard Univ.
U.S. Treasury Rep. Africa and Middle East 41-44; U.S. Navy 44-46; U.S. mem. Greek Currency Cttee., Athens 46-48; Asst. Prof. of Econs. Univ. of Michigan 48-49; Prof. of Econs. and Dir. of Int. Finance Section, Princeton Univ. 49-57; Prof. of Econs. and Dir. of Woodrow Wilson School of Public and Int. Affairs, Princeton Univ. 57-64, Prof. of Econs. and Acting Chair. Dept. of Econs. 65-66; Asst. Dir.-Gen., General Agreement of Tariffs and Trade (GATT) 66-67, 69-73, Deputy Dir. Gen. 73-; Prof. of Econs. 68-71; Econ. Adviser, U.S. Embassy, Israel 53-54, U.S. Embassy, Ankara

55-56; Head, U.S. Econ. Survey Mission to Tunisia 61; Ford Foundation Research Fellow, Geneva 63-64; Dir. Foreign Bondholders Protective Council (U.S.A.) 63-64, 68-69.
Publ. *Survey of United States International Finance 1949-54* 50-55, *Discrimination in International Trade, The Policy Issues* 66.
General Agreement on Tariffs and Trade, CH-1211, Geneva 10, Switzerland.

Patterson, George Vaughan, B.E.E.; American engineering executive; b. 30 July 1911, Cherry Valley, Ohio; s. of William Clinton and Anna Black Patterson; m. Margaret Helen Jones 1938; two d.; ed. Ohio State Univ., Harvard Univ. Advanced Management School.
Assistant Gen. Man. Ohio Power Co. 54-60; Vice-Pres. American Electric Power Service Corpn. 61, Exec. Vice-Pres. 67, Pres., Chief Operating Officer 72-; Dir. American Electric Power Co. Inc. 66-, Pres. 72-.
Leisure interests: golf, sailing, gardening.
American Electric Power Service Corporation, Two Broadway, New York, N.Y. 10004; Home: 22 Hillside Terrace, Summit, N.J. 07901, U.S.A.
Telephone: (212) 422-4800 (Office); (201) 464-5388 (Home).

Patterson, Herbert Parsons, B.S.; American business executive; b. 3 Sept. 1925, New York; ed. Groton School and Yale Univ.
U.S. Navy 44-46; joined Chase Nat. Bank (now Chase Manhattan Bank, N.A.) 49, Asst. Man. 53 (title changed to Asst. Treas. 55), Second Vice-Pres. 56, Vice-Pres. 59, Senior Vice-Pres. 62, Exec. Vice-Pres. 65, Pres. and Chief. Admin. Officer 69-72; Consultant Marshalsed Assocs. Inc. 73-; mem. Board of Dirs. and Exec. Cttee. American Machine and Foundry Co.; Trustee Brookings Institution, Community Service Soc., mem. Board of Dirs. Standard Oil Co. (Indiana), Nat. Industrial Conf. Board; mem. Council on Foreign Relations, Trustees Cttee. New York Community Trust, New York Chamber of Commerce.
555 Madison Avenue, New York, N.Y. 10022; and 550 Park Avenue, New York, N.Y. 10021, U.S.A.

Patterson, Rex Alan, B.COMM., M.SC., PH.D.; Australian politician; b. 8 Jan. 1927, Bundaberg, Queensland; ed. Univ. of Queensland, Australian Nat. Univ., Univs. of Illinois and Chicago, U.S.A.
With Royal Australian Air Force Feb.-Sept. 45; mem. Research Staff, Bureau of Agricultural Econs. 49, Deputy Dir. 60-64; Dir. Northern Devt. Div., Dept. of Nat. Devt. until 66; mem. Parl. for Dawson 66-75; Minister for Northern Devt. 72-75, for the Northern Territory 73-75, for N. Australia 75; Labor Party.
c/o Parliament House, Canberra, A.C.T., Australia.

Pattinson, John Mellor, C.B.E.; British oil executive; b. 21 April 1899, Knutsford, Cheshire; s. of James Pearson Pattinson; m. Wilhelmina Newth 1927; two s.; ed. Rugby School, Cambridge Univ. and Royal Mil. Acad., Woolwich.
Royal Field Artillery 18-19; Anglo-Iranian Oil Co., S. Iran 22-45, Gen. Man. 37-45; Man. Dir. British Petroleum Co. Ltd. 52-65, Deputy Chair. 60-65; Dir. other oil and chemical companies; Dir. Chartered Bank; mem. Supervisory Board Erdölchemie G.m.b.H., Cologne.
Leisure interests: travel, gardening.
Oakhurst, Oakcroft Road, West Byfleet, Surrey, England.
Telephone: Byfleet 42813.

Patton, James George, LL.D.; American agriculturist; b. 8 Nov. 1902; ed. Western State Coll. of Colo.
Athletic Dir., Instructor in Physical Education, Colo. 27-29; Gen. Agent Life Insurance Co. 31; Organiser Co-operative Insurance, Colo. Farmers' Union 32-34; Sec. Colo. Farmers' Union 34-37, Pres. 38-41; Dir. Nat. Farmers' Union 37-40, Pres. 40-66; Pres. James G.

Patton & Assocs., Tucson 66-69; Pres. United World Federalists 67-69; Pres. Nat. Farmers' Union Life Insurance Co., Nat. Farmers' Union Service Corpn., Nat. Farmers' Union Auto Property and Casualty Co.; mem. Economic Stabilisation Board 42-43; mem. Nat. Labour Management Policy Comm.; fmr. mem. Advisory Board War Mobilisation and Reconversion Admin.; mem. Nat. Advisory Board Agricultural Marketing 46-53; U.S. Consultant, UN Conf., San Francisco 45, U.S. Adviser, F.A.O. Confs., Quebec 45, Copenhagen 46, Geneva 47, Washington 48; Del. Int. Fed. Agricultural Producers 46- (Vice-Pres. 55-58, Pres. 58-61).
1012 14th Street, N.W., Washington, D.C. 20005; 907 6th Street, S.W., Washington, D.C. 20024, U.S.A.

Patton, Thomas F., J.D.; American executive; b. 6 Dec. 1903, Cleveland, Ohio; s. of John T. and Anna (Navin) Patton; m. Arline Everitt 1928; two d.; ed. Ohio State Univ.
Admitted to Ohio bar 26; mem. law firm Andrews & Belden 26-32, partner in succeeding firm Belden, Young & Veach 32-36; Gen. Counsel, Republic Steel Corpn. 36-44, Vice-Pres. and Gen. Counsel 44-53, Dir. 43-, Asst. Pres., 1st Vice-Pres. 53-56, Pres. 56-68, Chief Exec. Officer 60-71, Chair. 63-71, Hon. Chair. of Board 71-; Trustee in Reorganization, Erie Lackawanna Railway Co. 72-; Chair. of Board, Chief Exec. Officer, American Iron and Steel Inst. 62-65, Dir. 61-71; Dir. Int. Iron and Steel Inst. 67-71, American Telephone and Telegraph Co., Cleveland-Cliffs Iron Co.; mem. Business Council, Exec. Cttee. Int. Iron and Steel Inst. 69-71; trustee numerous charitable, civic and business asscns.
Leisure interests: golf, hunting, spectator sports.
912 Midland Building, 101 Prospect Avenue, N.W., Cleveland, Ohio 44115; Home: 2711 Landon Road, Shaker Heights, Cleveland, Ohio 44122, U.S.A.
Telephone: 216-574-7196 (Office).

Pátzay, Pál; Hungarian sculptor; b. 17 Sept. 1896, Kapuvár; s. of József Pátzay and Ilona Szvetelsky; m. Herta Fuchs 1945; one s.; ed. Budapest and Collegium Hungaricum, Rome.
Professor Budapest Coll. of Fine Arts; early work tends towards Expressionism, becoming more classical in later periods; Franz Joseph Award of Distinction, Budapest, Kossuth Prize 50, 65; Eminent Artist of Hungarian People's Repub., Banner Order, 2nd degree, of the Hungarian People's Repub. 70.
Leisure interests: reading, conversation.
Works include: *Boy Carrying Fruit* 15, *Veiled Female Head* 16, *Grief, Wind on the Danube, Female Combing Hair,* Hussar Monument at Székesfehérvár and equestrian statue of Hunyadi at Pécs.
H-1026 Budapest II, Gábor Áron-u. 16, Hungary.
Telephone: 364-820.

Pauk, György; British violinist; b. 26 Oct. 1936, Budapest, Hungary; m. Susan Mautner 1959; one s. one d.; ed. Franz Liszt Acad. of Music, Budapest under Zathureczky, Leo Weiner and Zoltan Kodàly.
Concerts all over East Europe 52-58, and over the rest of the world; settled in Western Europe 58, Holland 58-61, England 61-; has recorded numerous concertos and the complete violin/piano music of Mozart and Schubert; Paganini Prize 56, Sonata Competition Prize, Munich 57, Jacques Thibaud Prize 59.
Leisure interests: football, tennis, theatre, reading, swimming, my family.
27 Armitage Road, London, N.W.11, England.
Telephone: 01-455-5042.

Paul VI, His Holiness Pope (Giovanni Battista Montini); b. 26 Sept. 1897, Concesio, Brescia; ed. Collegio Cesare Arici, Brescia, Liceo Arnaldo da Brescia, Seminary at Brescia, Pontifical Lombard Seminary, Pontifical Gregorian Univ., Apollinaire Juridical

Faculty, Università degli Studi and Pontifical Ecclesiastical Acad., Rome.

Ordained, Brescia 20; attaché Apostolic Nunciature, Warsaw 23-24; Sec. of State, Vatican 24-37; Chaplain to students Rome Univ.; Nat. Spiritual Dir. Italian Fed. of Catholic Univ. Students (FUCI); lecturer on the diplomatic history of the Holy See at the Ecclesiastical Acad. 31-36; Substitute Sec. of State to Cardinal Pacelli (later Pius XII) 37-39, to Pius XII 39-52, Pro.-Sec. of State 52-54; Archbishop of Milan 54-63; created Cardinal by Pope John XXIII 58; elected Pope June 63. Apostolic Palace, Vatican City.
Telephone: 6982.

Paul, Sir John Warburton, G.C.M.G., O.B.E., M.C., M.A., K.ST.J.; British overseas administrator; b. 29 March 1916, Weymouth; s. of W. G. Paul and Elizabeth née Bull; m. Kathleen Audrey Weeden 1946; three d.; ed. Weymouth Coll., and Selwyn Coll., Cambridge.
Royal Tank Regiment 37-45; Colonial Service, Sierra Leone 45-62, called to the Bar (Inner Temple) 47; Dist. Commr. 52-56; Perm. Sec. 56-59; Provincial Commr. 59-60; Sec. to the Cabinet 60-62; Gov. of the Gambia 62-65, Gov.-Gen. 65-66; Gov. of British Honduras 66-72; Gov. of the Bahamas 72-73, Gov.-Gen. July-Oct. 73; Lieut.-Gov. Isle of Man Dec. 73-.
Leisure interests: painting, fishing, shooting, sailing, cricket.
Sherrens Mead, Sherfield-on-Loddon, Hants., England.

Paula Couto, Carlos de; Brazilian geologist; b. 30 Aug. 1910, Pôrto Alegre; s. of Tito Paula Couto and Julieta Silva Couto; m. Zilah de Paula Couto 1938; two s.; ed. Colégio Militar de Pôrto Alegre.
In Brazilian Treasury Dept. 36-44; Researcher in Geology and Paleontology, Museu Nacional, Rio de Janeiro 44-60, geologist 60-, Dir. Dept. of Geology 60-66; Chief Researcher, Nat. Research Council, Brazil; Prof. Univ. Fed. do Rio de Janeiro; mem. Acad. Brasileira de Ciências, Soc. Brasileira de Geologia, Soc. Brasileira de Paleontologia, Soc. Paleontológica Argentina; Corresp. mem. Acad. Colombiana de Ciencias Exactas, Físicas y Naturales, Soc. of Vertebrate Paleontology (U.S.A.); mem. Editorial Board *Evolution* 53-55; Fellow, John Simon Guggenheim Memorial Foundation, New York 50-52, 68; Lecturer in numerous Univs. and colls.; Prize and José Bonifácio de Andrada e Silva Gold Medal, Soc. de Brasileira de Geologia 64.
Leisure interests: music, silent films, history.
Publs. *Paleontologia Brasileira (Mamiferos)* 53, and over 170 papers on vertebrate paleontology and geology.
Museu Nacional, Quinta de Bôa Vista, Rio de Janeiro, Rio de Janeiro e Guanabara, ZC-08, Brazil.
Telephone: 2-287010.

Pauley, Edwin W., M.S.; American industrialist; b. 7 Jan. 1903; ed. Georgia Mil. Acad. and Univ. of Calif.
Pres. Independent Petroleum Association 34-38; Special Rep. of California Govt. on Natural Resources Comm. 39 and Interstate Oil and Compact Comm. 40; Organiser of State of Calif. Defence Council 41; Treasurer Democratic Nat. Cttee. Sec. 41-43; Petroleum Co-ordinator for European War on Petroleum Lend-Lease Supplies for Russia and the U.K. 41; U.S. Industrial and Commercial Adviser Potsdam Conference; U.S. Rep. on Allied Comm. on Reparations (with Rank of Ambassador) 45-46; Special Adviser on Reparations to Sec. of State 47-48; Special Asst. Sec. of Army 47; Regent, Univ. of California since 39, Founder, Petrol Corpn., Los Angeles; Int. Independent Oil Producer (U.S.A., Mexico); Chair. of Board Pauley Petroleum Inc.
Home: 9521 Sunset Boulevard, Beverly Hills, Calif.; Office: 10,000 Santa Monica Boulevard, Los Angeles 67, Calif., U.S.A.

Paulinelli, Allysson; Brazilian agronomist; b. 1936, Minas Gerais.
Lecturer, later Dir. Agricultural High Inst., Minas

Gerais; Sec. of Agriculture, Minas Gerais 71; Minister of Agriculture March 74-.
Ministério da Agricultura, Esplanada dos Ministérios, Bloco 8, Brasília, DF, Brazil.

Pauling, Linus Carl, PH.D., SC.D., L.H.D., U.J.D., D.H.C.; American university professor; b. 28 Feb. 1901; ed. Oregon State Coll., Calif. Inst. of Technology and Univs. of Munich, Copenhagen and Zürich.
Full-time Asst. in Quantitative Analysis, Oregon State Coll. 19-20; part-time Asst. Chemistry, Mechanics and Materials, Oregon State Coll. 20-22; Graduate Asst., Calif. Inst. of Technology 22-23, Teaching Fellow 23-25, Research Assoc. 25-26, Nat. Research Fellow, Chemistry 25-26; Fellow John Simon Guggenheim Memorial Foundation 26-27; Asst. Prof. of Chemistry, Calif. Inst. of Technology 27-29, Assoc. Prof. 29-31, Prof. 31-64; Prof. of Chemistry, Univ. of California, at San Diego 67, Stanford Univ. 69-; Dir. Inst. of Orthomolecular Medicine 73-; Chair. Div. of Chemistry and Chemical Engineering, Calif. Inst. of Technology, Dir. of the Gates and Crellin Laboratories 36-58; George Fisher Baker Lecturer in Chemistry, Cornell Univ. 37-38; Eastman Prof. Oxford Univ. 48; Research Prof. Center for Study of Democratic Insts. 63-77; mem. Nat. Acad. of Sciences, American Acad. of Arts and Sciences, Deutsche Akad. der Naturforscher Leopoldina; hon. mem. or Fellow Chemical Soc. of London, Acad. of Sciences of Liège, Royal Inst., Swiss Chemical Soc.; Chemical Soc. of Japan, Nat. Inst. Sciences India, Royal Norwegian Scientific Society, Trondheim; foreign mem. Royal Society, Norwegian Acad. Science and Letters; Acad. of Sciences U.S.S.R.; corresp. foreign mem. Accad. delle Scienze, Lisbon Acad. Science; Foreign Assoc. Acad. des Sciences (France); Hon. Fellow, Indian Acad. Sciences, Austrian Acad. of Science, European Soc. of Haematology, etc.; hon. degrees from numerous univs., awards include: Langmuir Prize 31, William H. Nichols Medal 41, Willard Gibbs Medal 46, Theodore William Richards Medal 47, Davy Medal 47, Medal for Merit 48, Gilbert Newton Lewis Medal 51, Nobel Prize for Chemistry 54, for Peace 62, Thomas Addis Medal 55, John Phillips Memorial Award, Avogadro Medal 56, Pierre Fermat Medal, Paul Sabatier Medal 57 Lenin Prize 70, Martin Luther King, Jr. Medical Award 72, U.S. Nat. Medal of Science 74.
Publs. *The Structure of Line Spectra* (with S. Goudsmit) 30, *Introduction to Quantum Mechanics, with Applications to Chemistry* (with E. Bright Wilson, Jr.) 35, *The Nature of the Chemical Bond* 39 (2nd edn. 40, 3rd edn. 60), *General Chemistry* 47 (2nd edn. 53), *College Chemistry* 50 (3rd edn. 64), *No More War!* 58, 62, *The Architecture of Molecules* (with R. Hayward) 65, *The Chemical Bond* 67, *Vitamin C and the Common Cold* 71.
Linus Pauling Institute of Science and Medicine, 2700 Sand Hill Road, Menlo Park, Calif. 94025; and Salmon Creek, Big Sur, Calif. 93920, U.S.A.

Pauls, Dr. Rolf Friedemann; German diplomatist; b. 26 Aug. 1915, Eckartsberga; s. of Bodo Pauls and Alma Pauls (née Wilkens); m. Lilo Serlo 1951; three s.; ed. Naumburg Domgymnasium and Universität Hamburg.
Major in German Army 36-45; Sec. to Parl. Council, Bonn 48-49; Foreign Service 50-; Personal Asst. to Sec. of State for Foreign Affairs (Prof. Hallstein) 52-55; Counsellor for Political Affairs, Washington 56-60; Counsellor and Deputy Ambassador, Athens 60-63; Deputy Dir.-Gen. of Dept. for Econ. Affairs, Foreign Office, Bonn 63-65; Amb. to Israel 65-68, to U.S.A. 69-73, to People's Repub. of China 73-.
Leisure interests: reading, riding.
Embassy of Federal Republic of Germany, Peking, People's Republic of China.

Paulssen, Hans Constantin, DR. IUR.; German business executive; b. 1892, Weimar; s. of Dr. Arnold Paulssen;

m. Hertha Binswanger 1914 (died 1966); one *s.* (deceased) two *d.*; ed. Univs. of Freiburg, Munich and Jena. Chairman of Board Martinswerk G.m.b.H., Bergheim, Aluminium-Hütte Rheinfelden G.m.b.H., Aluminium-Walzwerke Singen G.m.b.H., Singen, Aluminium-Giesserei Villingen G.m.b.H., Villingen, Gothaer Feuerversicherung A.G., Cologne, Gothaer Transport-u. Rückversicherungs A.G., Cologne, Gothaer Lebensversicherung A.G., Göttingen; Hon. Senator, Univ. of Freiburg; Hon Pres. Fed. of German Employers Asscns., Cologne; Pres. Chamber of Industry and Commerce, Constance, Rheinschiffahrtsverband Konstanz e.V., Constance, Board of Trustees Ifo-Institut für Wirtschaftsforschung, Munich; mem. many other Boards, Councils, etc.; Order of Merit of German Fed. Repub. with Star and Sash.
D 7750 Constance, Hebelstrasse 4, Federal Republic of Germany.
Telephone: Constance 65075.

Paulucci di Calboli, Rinieri; Italian diplomatist and international official; b. 27 Feb. 1925, Rome; *m.* Manuela Sapuppo 1953; ed. Madrid and Rome Univs. Entered diplomatic service 51; Vice-Consul, Chicago 54-56; with Italian Embassy, Paris 56-59; First Sec., Madrid 59-62; Dir.-Gen., Economic Affairs, Ministry of Foreign Affairs 62-64; Chef de Cabinet, EEC, Brussels 64-68; Minister Counsellor, Italian Embassy, Vienna 68-70; Asst. Sec.-Gen., OECD 70-75.
c/o Ministry of Foreign Affairs, Rome, Italy.

Pauly, Jan; Czechoslovak politician; b. 22 Aug. 1910, Prague; *s.* of Josef Pauly and Marie Paulyová Krechtová; *m.* Dagmar Paulyová Jansová 1949; one *s.*; ed. Czechoslovak Commercial Acad., School of Political and Social Sciences and Coll. of Marxism-Leninism.
Provincial Bank, Prague 34-42, 45-49; Concentration Camp 42-45; Man. Spa and Recreational Services of Prague 49-55; mem. Central Nat. Cttee. of Prague 45-49; mem. Central Cttee. and Secr. of Central Cttee. of Czechoslovak People's Party 55-70, Sec.-Gen. 68-70; mem. Presidium of Union of Anti-facist Fighters 64-69; Deputy to Czech Nat. Council 68-70; Chair. Comm. for Social Questions, Central Cttee. Nat. Front of CSSR 69-70; Deputy to House of Nations, Fed. Assembly 69-71; Minister without Portfolio, Fed. Govt. 69-71; mem. Fed. Cttee. Union of Anti-fascist Fighters of CSSR 69-73; Memorial Medal of Second Nat. Resistance Movement 52, for Outstanding Work 64; Memorial Medal 20th Anniversary of the Liberation of Czechoslovakia 65; Memorial Plaque of Central Cttee., Nat. Front of CSSR 68; Hon. Medal Anti-facist Fighters of Merit 74; Memorial Medal 30th Anniversary of Liberation of Czechoslovakia.
Prague 7-Bubeneč, Nad Královskou oborou 53, Czechoslovakia.
Telephone: 376109.

Paupini, H.E. Cardinal Giuseppe; Italian ecclesiastic; b. 25 Feb. 1907, Mondavio, Fano.
Ordained 30; Titular Archbishop of Sebastopolis in Abasgia 56-; Apostolic Nuncio in Colombia 59; cr. Cardinal 69.
Palazzo Altemps, Via di S. Apollinare 8, 00186 Rome, Italy.
Telephone: 56-25-05.

Pavate, Dadasaheb Chintamani; Indian mathematician and government official; b. 2 Aug. 1899, Mandapur; *m.* Giryaderi Pavate 1918; two *s.* one *d.*; ed. Karnatak Coll., Dharwar, and Sidney Sussex Coll., Cambridge.
Professor of Mathematics, Banaras Hindu Univ. 28-30; entered Bombay Educ. Service 30; Dir. of Public Instruction, Bombay State 47-54; Vice-Chancellor Karnatak Univ. 54-67; Gov. of Punjab 67-73; mem. Official Language Comm. 55-56; Leader Indian Del. to 19th Int. Educ. Conf., Geneva 56; Padma Bhushan 67.

Publs. include *Modern College Calculus, Modern College Algebra, Memoirs of an Educational Administrator.*
c/o Office of the Governor of Punjab, Raj Bhavan, Chandigarh, India.

Pavitt, Edward, M.C., B.SC.(ENG.); South African mining engineer and executive; b. 14 July 1918, Vryburg, N. Cape; *s.* of Edward P. R. and Gertrude Pavitt (née Hornby); *m.* Elizabeth (née) Saunders 1942; three *d.*; ed. Kingswood Coll., Grahamstown and Witwatersrand Univ., Johannesburg.
Active mil. service 39-45, Maj. 11th Field Cos., S.A. Engineering Corps 44-45; Mining Eng., Union Corpn. Ltd. 46-62, Gen. Man. Leslie Gold Mines Ltd. 62-64, Consulting Eng. 64-67, Chief Consulting Eng. 67-69, Dir. Union Corpn. Ltd. 69-71, Asst. Man. Dir. 71-72, Man. Dir. 72-, Chair. 74-; Chair. St. Helena Gold Mines Ltd., Unisel Gold Mines Ltd., UC Investments Ltd. 73; Commr. Electricity Supply Comm.; Dir. Palabora Mining Co. Ltd. and numerous other companies.
Union Corporation Limited, Union Corporation Building, 74/78 Marshall Street, Johannesburg 2001; Home: 31 Fricker Road, Illovo, Johannesburg 2196, South Africa.
Telephone: 838-8281 (Office); 42-7636 (Home).

Pavlov, Aleksandr Sergeyevich; Soviet radiologist and oncologist; b. 23 June 1920, Moscow; *m.*; one *d.*; ed. Moscow Univ. and Central Inst. for Postgraduate Training.
Successively Asst. Prof., Assoc. Prof., Prof. and Chief, Dept. of Clinical Radiology, Central Inst. of Postgraduate Training, Moscow; now Dir. Herzen Cancer Research Inst. Moscow; Asst. Dir.-Gen. WHO July 71-; consultant to IAEA, Vienna; fmr. Pres. All Russian Scientific Soc. of Oncology, Moscow Soc. of Oncology; mem. U.S.S.R. Acad. of Medical Sciences.
Publs. more than 100 scientific papers and textbooks in the field of oncology and radiotherapy.
World Health Organisation, avenue Appia, 1211 Geneva, Switzerland.
Telephone: 34-60-61.

Pavlov, Georgi Sergeyevich; Soviet politician; b. 1910; ed. Dnieprodzerzhinsk Metallurgical Inst.
Second, later First Sec. Dnieprodzerzhinsk City Cttee. of C.P.S.U. 43-47; mem. staff, Central Cttee. of C.P.S.U. 47-49, 57; First Sec. Magnitogorsk City Cttee. of C.P.S.U. 49-50, of Chelyabinsk Regional Cttee. 50-51; Deputy Chair. Exec. Cttee. Kostroma Regional Soviet of Workers' Deputies 51-54; Sec., First Sec., later Second Sec. Kostroma Regional Cttee. of C.P.S.U. 54-57; First Sec. Mari Regional Cttee. of C.P.S.U. 57-63; Exec. Party and State Control Cttee. of Central Cttee. of C.P.S.U. and U.S.S.R. Council of Ministers 63-65; Head of Dept. C.P.S.U. Central Cttee. 65-; Alt. mem. C.P.S.U. Central Cttee. 61-71, mem. 71-; Deputy to U.S.S.R. Supreme Soviet 58-; several decorations.
C.P.S.U. Central Committee, 4 Staraya ploshchad, Moscow, U.S.S.R.

Pavlov, Sergey Pavlovich; Soviet politician; b. 19 Jan. 1929; ed. Technical Inst., and Moscow Inst. of Physical Culture.
Komsomol work 52-56; mem. C.P.S.U. 54-; Sec., Second Sec., First Sec., Moscow City Cttee., Komsomol 56-58; Sec. Central Cttee. Komsomol 58-59, First Sec. 59-68; Chair. Central Council of Sports Socs. June 68, U.S.S.R. Cttee. for Sports and Physical Culture 68-; mem. Central Cttee. C.P.S.U. 61-71; mem. C.P.S.U. Cen. Auditing Comm. 71-; Deputy to U.S.S.R. Supreme Soviet 62-70.
U.S.S.R. Committee for Sports and Physical Culture, 4 Skatertny pereulok, Moscow, U.S.S.R.

Pavlov, Todor Dimitrov; Bulgarian scientist; b. 14 Feb. 1890, Sofia; *s.* of Dimitar and Ekaterina Pavlov; *m.* Gana Pavlov 1910 (died 1965); one *s.* one *d.*; ed. Sofia Univ.

Teacher 10-21; Publicist 22-32; Prof. Dialectical Materialism, Moscow 32-36; mem. Regents' Council, Bulgaria 44-46; Prof. Philosophy, Sofia State Univ. 45-47; Pres. Bulgarian Acad. of Sciences 47-62, Hon. Pres. 62-; Head Inst. of Philosophy 45-; Editor-in-Chief of journal *Philosophical Thought* 45-; mem. Presidium of Nat. Assembly 62; Dep. Grand Nat. Assembly and First and Second Nat. Assemblies 46-63; mem. Politbureau of the Central Cttee. of the Bulgarian C.P. 66-, Serbian Acad. of Sciences, Belgrade, Polish Acad. of Sciences, Czechoslovak Acad. of Sciences; Hon. or foreign mem. several Acads.; mem. European Community of Writers 62, European Soc. of Culture in Venice; hon. doctor Sofia, Moscow, Prague, Berlin; Hero of Socialist Labour (twice) and many other honours.
Leisure interests: chess and backgammon.
Publs. *Theory of Reflection* 36, *General Theory of Art* 38, *Fundamental Problems of Aesthetics* 49, *Literary Science and Criticism* 54-55, *The Philosophy of Dialectical Materialism and the particular Sciences* 56, *Selected Works* 57-60, *Zur Geschichte der Ästhetik, Grundgesetze der Kunst, Informatzia, otrajenie, tvortchestvo*.
2 Dobrudja Street, Sofia, Bulgaria.

Pavlov, Vladimir Yakovlevich; Soviet politician and diplomatist; b. 1923; ed. Moscow Railway Engineering Inst.
Member, C.P.S.U. 48-, mem. Cen. Cttee. 66-; railway engineer 41-49; party and Komsomol work 49-56; First Sec., Moscow District Cttee., C.P.S.U. 56-62; Sec. Moscow City, C.P.S.U. 62-65, Second Sec. 65-71; Amb. to Hungary 71-; Dep. to U.S.S.R. Supreme Soviet 66-; Vice-Chair. Comm. for Transport and Communications Soviet of Union.
Soviet Embassy, Budapest, Hungary.

Pavlovsky, Gen. Ivan Grigorievich; Soviet army officer; b. 1909, Ternovka village, Kamenets-Podolsk Region; ed. Agricultural Technical School and Military Acad. of General Staff.
Agronomist 29-31; in Soviet Army 31-; Commdr. of Platoon, Co., Battn., Regt. 32-42; fought in Southern, Transcaucasian and Byelorussian Fronts in Second World War; Commdr. of Rifles Brigade and Div. 43-52; Corps Commdr. 52-55; Army Commdr. and First Deputy C.-in-C. Area Military Commdr. 61-67; Deputy of U.S.S.R. Minister of Defence, C.-in-C. of Land Forces and Army General 67-; mem. C.P.S.U. 39-, Central Auditing Comm. of C.P.S.U. 66-71, mem. C.P.S.U. Cen. Cttee. 71-; Deputy to U.S.S.R. Supreme Soviet 62-; mem. Foreign Affairs Comm. Soviet of Nationalities; Hero of Soviet Union, Gold Star, Red Star, Orders of Lenin (twice), of Red Banner (five times), of Suvorov, 2nd Class and other Soviet and foreign awards.
Ministry of Defence, Naberezhnaya M. Thoreza 34, Moscow, U.S.S.R.

Pawełkiewicz, Jerzy, D.SC.; Polish biochemist; b. 16 Oct. 1922, Częstochowa; ed. Poznań Univ.
Doctor 51-54, Docent 54-60, Assoc. Prof. 60-67, Prof. 67-; Corresp. mem. Polish Acad. of Sciences 67-, mem. Biochemical and Biophysical Cttee. 69-, now also mem. Scientific Councils of Inst. of Biochemistry and Biophysics and of Dept. of Dendrology, Chair. Scientific Council of Plant Genetics Dept.; Head of Biochemistry Dept., Poznań Acad. of Agriculture; mem. Polish Biochemical Soc.; worked on Vitamin B12 and biosynthesis of albumin; State Prize, 1st Class 74, Gold Cross of Merit 59, Medal of 10th Anniversary of People's Poland 55.
Publs. *Fizyko-chemiczne metody w analizie żywnościowej* (Physico-Chemical Methods in Food Analysis) 54, coauthor *Chromatografia* 57; numerous articles in Polish and other languages.
Ul. Kniewskiego 1 m. 7, 60-743 Poznań, Poland.

Payne, Rev. Ernest Alexander, C.H., D.D., LL.D.; British minister of religion; b. 19 Feb. 1902, London; s. of Alexander William Payne, F.C.A.; m. Winifred Mary Davies 1930; one d.; ed. King's Coll., London, Regent's Park Coll., London, Mansfield Coll., Oxford, and Marburg Univ., Germany.
Pastor Bugbrooke Baptist Church, Northampton 28-32; Baptist Missionary Soc. 32-40; Senior Tutor, Regent's Park Coll., Oxford 40-51, Lecturer in Comparative Religion and History of Modern Missions, Oxford Univ. 46-51; Gen. Sec. Baptist Union of Great Britain and Ireland 51-67; Vice-Chair. Cen. Cttee. World Council of Churches 54-68, Pres. World Council of Churches 68-75; mem. Free Church Fed. Council, Moderator 58-59; Vice-Pres. British Council of Churches 60-62, Chair. Exec. Cttee. 62-71; Vice-Pres. Baptist World Alliance.
Leisure interests: reading, travel.
Publs. *The Saktas* 33, *The Free Church Tradition in the Life of England* 44, *H. Wheeler Robinson: A Memoir* 46, *The Baptists of Berkshire* 51, *The Fellowship of Believers* 44, 52, *James Henry Rushbrooke—A Baptist Greatheart* 54, *The Growth of the World Church* 55, *The Baptist Union—A Short History* 59, *Free Churchmen—Unrepentant and Repentant* 65, *Out of Great Tribulation—Baptists in the U.S.S.R.* 74.
Elm Cottage, 21 Manor Road, Pitsford, Northants., England.
Telephone: 0604-880-519.

Payne, John Anson, O.B.E., M.A., F.B.I.M.; British business executive; b. 19 May 1917, London; s. of late Maj. R. L. Payne and L. M. Duncan; m. Deirdre Kelly 1949; one s. one d.; ed. St. Lawrence Coll., Ramsgate, Trinity Hall, Cambridge.
Entered Civil Service 39; served R.A.F., rank of Wing Commdr. 40-45; with Ministry of Agriculture 45; Private Sec. to Minister 47-51, Asst. Sec. 51, Under-Sec. 60-68; joined FMC Ltd. 68, Chair. 74-75.
Home: 47 Bramber Road, London, N12 9ND, England.
Telephone: 01-445-2527 (Home).

Payne, Sir Robert Frederick, Kt.; British solicitor; b. 22 Jan. 1908, Hull; s. of Frederick C. and Edith C. (née Carlton) Payne; m. Maureen R. Walsh 1951; two s. one d.; ed. Hymers Coll., Hull.
Served, Royal Air Force 40-44; Founder mem. British Acad. of Forensic Sciences 59; Pres. The Law Society of England and Wales 69-70; Chair. Mental Hospital Cttee. of Inquiry 71-72; mem. Erroll Cttee. on Liquor Licensing 71-72.
Leisure interests: music and golf.
High Woodgates, N. Ferriby, Humberside, England.
Telephone: 0482-631533.

Paynter, William; British trade unionist; b. 6 Dec. 1903; ed. Elementary Schools.
Executive, South Wales Miners' Fed. 36, South Wales Agent 39, South Wales Pres. 51; Nat. Sec., Nat. Union of Mineworkers 59-68; mem. Gen. Council T.U.C. 60-61; Communist 29-68; Comm. on Industrial Relations 69; mem. T.U.C./C.B.I. Conciliation and Arbitration Service 72-73; mem. Advisory Arbitration and Conciliation Service (when required).
Publs. *British Trade Unions and Problems of Change, My Generation* (autobiographical).
32 Glengall Road, Edgware, Middlesex, England.

Paz, Octavio; Mexican writer and diplomatist; b. 31 March 1914; ed. Univ. of Mexico.
Founder, dir. or editor several Mexican literary reviews, including *Barandal* 31, *Taller* 39, *El Hijo Pródigo* 43; Guggenheim Fellowship (U.S.A.) 44; fmr. Sec. Mexican Embassy, Paris; Chargé d'Affaires a.i., to Japan 51; posted to Secr. for External Affairs; Ambassador to India 62-68; Simón Bolívar Prof. of Latin-American Studies and Fellow. Churchill Coll., Cambridge 70-71; Charles Eliot Norton Prof. of Poetry,

Harvard Univ. 71-72; Hon. mem. American Acad. of Arts and Letters 72; Int. Poetry Grand Prix 63.
Publs. Poetry: *Luna Silvestre* 33, *Raíz del Hombre* 37, *Entre la Piedra y la Flor* 40, *A la Orilla del Mundo* 42, *Libertad bajo Palabra* 49, *Piedra de Sol* 57, *La Estación Violenta* 58, *Ladera este* 70; prose: *El Laberinto de la Soledad* 50 (*Labyrinth of Solitude* 61), *Aguila o Solé* 51, *El Arco y la Lira* 56, *Las Peras del Olmo* 57, *Conjunciones y disyunciones* (essays) 70, *Postdata* 71, *Claude Lévi-Strauss: An Introduction* 72, *Alternating Current* (essays) 73, etc.
Harvard University, Cambridge, Mass., U.S.A.

Paz Estenssoro, Victor; Bolivian politician; b. 2 Oct. 1907; s. of Domingo Paz Rojas and Carlos Estenssoro de Paz; m. 1st Carmela Cerruto Calderón 1936; one s.; one d.; m. 2nd Teresa Cortéz Velasco; three d.; ed. Univ. Mayor de "San Andrés".
Finance official 32-33; Deputy Tarija 38-39 and 40-41; Pres. Banco Minero 39; Prof. Economic History, Univ. of La Paz 39-41; Minister of Finance 41-44; Leader of Nat. Revolutionary Movement; Pres. of Republic 52-56; Amb. to the U.K. 56-59; Pres. of Republic 60-64; Prof. Economic Development Theory, Planning Inst. Nat. Engineering Univ. Lima 66-.
Leisure interest: photography.
Publs. *Esquema de la Organización Política y Administrativa de Bolivia, Aspecto de la Economía Boliviana, Revolución y Contrarrevolución, Proceso y Sentencia de la Oligarquía Boliviana, La Revolución Boliviana, Discursos Parlamentarios, Discursos y Mensajes, Contra la Restauración por la Revolución Nacional, La Obra, Maestra de los Restauradores, El Imperativo Nacional, Presencia de la Revolución Nacional.*
Universidad Nacional de Ingeniería, Casilla 1301, Lima, Peru.

Pazhwak, Abdurrahman; Afghan civil servant; b. 7 March 1919, Ghazni.
Has been successively mem. Historical Section of Afghan Acad.; Dir. Foreign Publications Section of Afghan Press Dept.; Editor daily *Islah* and acting Dir.-Gen. of Bakhtar News Agency; Pres. Pashto-Tolana (Afghan Acad. of Lit.); Dir.-Gen. Publs. Section, Afghan Press Dept.; Sec. and Press and Cultural Attaché, Afghan Embassy, London; mem. of Section of Information Dept. of ILO; Press and Cultural Attaché, Afghan Embassy, Washington; Dir. Section for East Asia and Dir. a.i., Section for UN and Int. Confs., Afghan Ministry for Foreign Affairs; Dir.-Gen. Political Affairs in Ministry of Foreign Affairs 56; Perm. Rep. to UN 58-73; Amb. to Fed. Repub. of Germany 73, to India 73-; Pres. UN Human Rights Comm. 63, 21st Session of UN Gen. Assembly 66; Special Envoy of Afghanistan to the Fourth Summit of Non-Aligned Countries, Algiers 73; Special Envoy to the Summit Conf. of Islamic Countries, Lahore 74; Special Envoy to the Pres. of Bangladesh.
Publs. *Aryana or Ancient Afghanistan, Pakhtunistan* (both in English), *Tales of the People* 58 (in Persian), and many other works.
Embassy of the Republic of Afghanistan, A-9 Ring Road, Lajrat Nagar 3, New Delhi, India.
Telephone: 24-622161.

Pazhwak, Niamatullah, PH.D.; Afghan educationist; b. 17 Aug. 1928; d. of Mr. Hafizullah and Aesha Hafizullah; m. Afifa Pazhwak 1957; two s. three d.; ed. Habibia High School, Kabul, Kabul Univ., Columbia Univ., U.S.A.
Director Teacher's Training School, Kabul 56, Habibia High School 58; Pres. Secondary Schools in Afghanistan 65; Cultural Counsellor, Royal Afghan Embassy to U.S.S.R. 68; Pres. of Compilation and Translation, Ministry of Educ. 70; Gov. Bamiyan Prov. March-

Sept. 71, Kabul Prov. 71-72; Minister of the Interior 72-73, of Educ. 73-74.
Leisure interests: sport and trips.
Publs. several articles on education in professional journals.
Ministry of Education, Kabul, Republic of Afghanistan. Telephone: 42402 (Home).

Peacock, Alan Turner, D.S.C., M.A.; British economist; b. 26 June 1922, Ryton-on-Tyne; s. of Alexander D. and Clara M. Peacock; m. Margaret Martha Astell-Burt 1944; two s. one d.; ed. Dundee High School, Univ. of St. Andrews.
Lecturer in Econs., Univ. of St. Andrews 47-48; Lecturer in Econs., London School of Econs. 48-51; Reader in Public Finance 51-56; Prof. of Econ. Science, Univ. of Edinburgh 56-62; Prof. of Econs., Univ. of York 62-; Chief Econ. Adviser, Dept. of Trade and Industry 73-; Pres. Int. Inst. of Public Finance 66-69, Hon. Pres. 75-; mem. Royal Comm. on Constitution 70-73, Social Science Research Council 71-72; mem. Council, Royal Econ. Soc., Council, London Philharmonic Orchestra; Chair. Arts Council Enquiry into Orchestral Resources 69-70; mem. Board of Dirs. English Music Theatre Ltd. 75-; Dr. h.c. (Univ. of Stirling) 74.
Leisure interest: music.
Publs. *Economics of National Insurance* 52, *Growth of Public Expenditure in United Kingdom* (with J. Wiseman) 61, *Economic Theory of Fiscal Policy* (with G. K. Shaw) 71, *The Composer in the Market Place* (with R. Weir) 75, *Welfare Economics: A Liberal Reinterpretation* (with Charles Rowley), and numerous articles in professional journals on economics, public finance, social policy.
Department of Industry, 1 Victoria Street, London, S.W.1; Home: 5 Rawcliffe Grove, York, YO3 6NR, England.
Telephone: (01) 215-4258 (Office); York 55927 (Home).

Peacock, Hon. Andrew Sharp, LL.B., M.P.; Australian politician; b. 13 Feb. 1939, Melbourne; s. of the late A. S. Peacock and of Iris Peacock; m. Susan Rossiter 1963; three d.; ed. Scotch Coll., Univ. of Melbourne.
President, Victorian Liberal Party 65-66; mem. House of Reps. for Kooyong, Vic. 66-; fmr. partner Rigby and Fielding, solicitors; fmr. Chair. Peacock & Smith Pty. Ltd., engineers; Minister for the Army and Minister Assisting the Prime Minister 69-71, Assisting the Treasurer 71-72; Minister for External Territories Feb.-Dec. 72; mem. Opposition Exec. Jan. 73, then Opposition Spokesman on Foreign Affairs and External Territories; Minister for Foreign Affairs Nov. 75-, for the Environment Nov.-Dec. 75.
Leisure interests: horse racing, Australian Rules Football, surfing, reading.
Ministry of Foreign Affairs, Canberra (Office); 30 Monomeath Avenue, Canterbury, Vic. 3126, Australia.

Peacock, Ronald, M.A., D.PHIL., LITT.D.; British university professor; b. 22 Nov. 1907, Leeds, Yorks.; s. of Arthur L. Peacock and Elizabeth Peacock (née Agar); m. Ilse G. E. Freiwald 1933; ed. Leeds Modern School, Univs. of Leeds, Berlin, Innsbruck and Marburg.
Assistant Lecturer in German, Univ. of Leeds 31-38, Lecturer 38-39, Prof. 39-45; Prof. of German Language and Literature Univ. of Manchester 45-62, Pro-Vice-Chancellor 58-62; Visiting Prof. of German Literature, Cornell Univ. 49; Visiting Prof. Univ. of Heidelberg 60-61; Prof. German, Bedford Coll., Univ. of London 62-75; Prof. Univ. of Freiburg 65, 67-68.
Leisure interests: music, travel.
Publs. *The Great War in German Lyrical Poetry* 34, *Das Leitmotiv bei Thomas Mann* 34, *Hölderlin* 38, *The Poet in the Theatre* 46, *The Art of Drama* 57, *Goethe's*

Major Plays 59, *Criticism and Personal Taste* 72, many contributions to periodicals.
Greenshade, Woodhill Avenue, Gerrard's Cross, Bucks., England.
Telephone: Gerrard's Cross 84886.

Peake, Sir Harald, Kt., M.A.; British banker; b. 28 Oct. 1899; ed. Eton and Trinity Coll., Cambridge.
Served in Coldstream Guards in First World War, subsequently Yorkshire Dragoons Yeomanry; raised and commanded No. 609 (W. Riding) Squadron, R. Aux. A.F. 36; Dir. Aux. A.F., Air Ministry 38; Dir. of Public Relations, Air Ministry 40-42, Dir. of Air Force Welfare 42-43, Special Duty List Air Ministry 43-45, retd. with rank of Air Commodore; pupil in coal mining industry 23; Rolls Royce Ltd. 37-; Dir. Lloyds Bank Ltd. 43-, Vice-Chair. 47-62, Chair. 62-69; fmr. Chair London Bd., Nat. Bank of Australasia; fmr. Dir. Bank of London and South America Ltd., fmr. Dir. Nat. Commercial Bank of Scotland; Sub-Gov. of London Assurance Co. 54, Gov. 59-64; Chair. Steel Co. of Wales Ltd. 55-62, Dir. 62-67; Dir. Lloyds and Scottish Ltd. 63-, Lloyds Bank, Europe, Ltd. 63-, Lloyds Bank Unit Trust Managers Ltd., Nat. Bank of New Zealand Ltd.; Dir. Intercontinental Banking Services Ltd. 67-; Chair. Systems Int. (U.K.) 71-.
2 Shepherds Close, Lees Place, Upper Brook Street, London, W.1, England.
Telephone: 01-629-1264.

Peal, Samuel Edward; Liberian diplomatist; b. 3 Feb. 1923; ed. Central Nat. School, White Plains, and Liberia Coll.
Former Town Clerk, Millsburg; Foreign Service, Paris, London, Hamburg; fmr. Ambassador to Netherlands, to Guinea; Amb. to U.S.A. 61-; numerous decorations.
Embassy of the Republic of Liberia, 5201 16th Street, N.W., Washington, D.C. 20011, U.S.A.

Pearce, Baron (Life Peer), cr. 62, of Sweethaws; **Edward Holroyd Pearce,** P.C., Kt., M.A., R.B.A.; British judge; b. 9 Feb. 1901, Sidcup, Kent; s. of John W. E. Pearce, F.S.A. and Irene Pearce; m. Erica Priestman 1927; two s.; ed. Merton Court School, Charterhouse and Corpus Christi Coll., Oxford.
Called to the bar 25; Q.C. 45; Judge of Probate, Divorce and Admiralty Court 48; Judge of Queen's Bench Division 54; Lord Justice of Appeal 57; Lord of Appeal in Ordinary 62-69; Treasurer of Lincoln's Inn 66; Chair. of Press Council 69-74; Chair. Appeals Cttee. Takeover Panel; Hon. Fellow, Corpus Christi Coll., Oxford 50-; Chair. British Comm. on Rhodesian Opinion 72.
Leisure interest: painting.
Sweethaws, Crowborough, Sussex, England.
Telephone: Crowborough 61520.

Pearce, Austin William, C.B.E., B.SC., PH.D.; British business executive; b. 1 Sept. 1921, Plymouth; s. of late William T. Pearce and of Florence Pearce; m. Maglona Winifred Twinn 1947 (died 1975); three d.; ed. Devonport High School for Boys, Birmingham Univ. and Harvard Business School.
Joined Esso Petroleum Co. 45, Dir. 63-68, Man. Dir. 68-71, Chair. Jan. 72-, Dir. Esso Europe Inc. 72-, Esso Africa Inc. 72-, Esso Supply Co. Inc. 72-; Chair. Irish Refining Co., Ltd. 65-71; Pres. Inst. of Petroleum 68-70, Pipeline Industries Guild 73-75; Pres. Oil Industries Club 75-; mem. Board Nat. Research Devt. Corpn., Advisory Council on Energy Conservation 74-; Dir. Williams and Glyn's Bank Ltd. 74-; mem. of Board, English Speaking Union 74-.
Leisure interests: golf, general handicrafts.
Esso House, Victoria Street, London, SW1E 5JW, England.
Telephone: 01-834-6677.

Pears, Peter, C.B.E.; British tenor; b. 22 June 1910; ed. Lancing Coll. and Univ. of Oxford.
With BBC Singers 34-37, New English Singers 36-38;

tours abroad with Benjamin Britten since 39; Sadler's Wells Opera 43-46; first performance of many new works by Benjamin Britten, Tippett and Berkeley; soloist at Lucerne Festival, Edinburgh Festivals, Holland Festival, and all Aldeburgh Festivals 47-; co-founder Aldeburgh Festival.
Important roles include Peter Grimes (*Peter Grimes*) 45, 53, Male Chorus (*The Rape of Lucretia*) 46, 51, The Evangelist (*St. Matthew Passion*) annually 47-, The Captain (*Billy Budd*) 51, Tamino (*Magic Flute*), Essex (*Gloriana*) 53, Vashek (*The Bartered Bride*) 55, Pandarus (*Troilus and Cressida*) 56, David (*Die Meistersinger*) 57, Flute (*Midsummer Night's Dream*) 60, The Mad Woman (*Curlew River*) 64, 65, Nebuchadnezzar (*Burning Fiery Furnace*) 66, The Tempter (*Prodigal Son*) 68, 69, Gustav Aschenbach (*Death in Venice*) 73.
Publ. (with Benjamin Britten) *Purcell Edition* 48-.
c/o Mrs. Susan Phipps, 8 Halliford Street, London, N.1, England.

Pearse, Henry Jesse, A.A.S.A. (Snr.), F.A.I.M.; Australian company director; b. 19 March 1915, Waratah, N.S.W.; s. of T. R. Pearce; m. Elva R. Spencer 1940; two s. one d.; ed. Newcastle, N.S.W.
Secretary John Lysaght (Aust.) Ltd. 59, Admin. Dir. 64-65, Joint Man. Dir. 65-67, Man. Dir. 67-.
42 Llandilo Avenue, Strathfield, N.S.W. 2135, Australia.

Pearson, Baron (Life Peer), cr. 65, of Minnedosa, Canada, and of the Royal Borough of Kensington; **Colin Hargreaves Pearson,** P.C., C.B.E.; British judge; b. 28 July 1899, Minnedosa, Manitoba; s. of Ernest W. and Jessie B. Pearson; m. Sophie G. H. Thomas 1931; one s. one d.; ed. St. Paul's School, London, and Balliol Coll., Oxford.
Called to the Bar 24; K.C. 49; Judge, Queen's Bench Div. 51-61; Judge, Restrictive Practices Court 57-61 (Pres. 60-61); Lord Justice of Appeal 61-65; Lord of Appeal in Ordinary 65-74; Chair. Cttee. on Funds in Court 58, Law Reform Cttee. 63-; Chair. Courts of inquiry on disputes in the Electricity Supply Industry 64, Shipping Industry 66-67, Civil Air Transport Industry 67-68, Steel Industry 68, Docks Industry 70; Chair. Royal Comm. on Civil Liability and Compensation for Personal Injury 73-.
2 Crown Office Row, Temple, London, E.C.4; House of Lords, Westminster, London, S.W.1, England.
Telephone: 01-353-5391.

Pearson, Andrall E.; American business executive; b. 3 June 1925; s. of Andrall E. Pearson and Dorothy MacDonald; m. Joanne Pope 1951; one d.; ed. Univ. of Southern Calif. and Harvard Business School.
Former Dir. McKinsey & Co. (international management consultants); Exec. Vice-Pres. PepsiCo Inc. 69-71, Pres. 71-.
Publs. *A Blueprint for Long Range Planning, An Approach to Successful Marketing Planning.*
PepsiCo Inc., Purchase, N.Y. 10577, U.S.A.
Telephone: (914) 253-3031.

Pearson, Egon Sharpe, C.B.E., M.A., D.SC., F.R.S.; British statistician; b. 11 Aug. 1895, London; s. of Karl Pearson and Maria Sharpe; m. 1st Dorothy Eileen Jolly 1934 (died 1949), 2nd Margaret Theodosia Turner 1967 (died 1975); two d.; ed. Winchester and Trinity Coll., Cambridge.
Lecturer Univ. Coll. 21; Prof. of Statistics London Univ. and Head of Statistics Dept. at Univ. Coll. 33-60, Prof. Emeritus 60-; Man. Editor *Biometrika* 36-66, Tables Editor 66-75; Assoc. mem. Emeritus Ordnance Board, Ministry of Defence 43-; Pres. Royal Statistical Soc. 55-57, Soc. Gold Medal 55; Hon. mem. Inst. of Actuaries 56.
University College, Gower Street, London, W.C.1; Home: Pendean Home, West Lavington, Midhurst, Sussex, England.
Telephone: 01-387-9244 (Office); Midhurst 4304 (Home).

Pearson, James B.; American lawyer and politician; b. 7 May 1920; m. Martha Mitchell; three s. one d. Local Government posts, Kansas City suburbs; fmr. State Senator, Kansas; fmr. State Chair. Republican Party; U.S. Senator from Kansas 62-.
5313 New Senate Office Building, Washington, D.C. 20510, U.S.A.
Telephone: 202-225-4774.

Pearson, Sir (James) Denning, Kt., J.P., B.SC.(ENG.), WH.SC., C.ENG., F.B.I.M.; British engineer and business executive; b. 8 Aug. 1908, Bootle, Lancs.; s. of James and Elizabeth (née Henderson) Pearson; m. Eluned Henry 1932; two d.; ed. Canton Secondary School and Cardiff Technical Coll.
Various appointments with Rolls-Royce since 32; Chief Exec. and Deputy Chair. Rolls-Royce Ltd., 57-68, Chief Exec. and Chair. 69-70; Pres. SBAC 63-64; mem. Nat. Econ. Devt. Council 64-66; Chair. of Govs. Derby Coll. of Technology 67-; Gov. London Graduate School of Business Studies 67-70; mem. Council, Manchester Business School, Governing Body, Admin. Staff Coll., Henley 67-73, Council, Voluntary Service Overseas; Hon. Fellow Royal Aeronautical Soc.; Dr. Ing. (Brunswick Univ.) and several honorary degrees and fellowships; Benjamin Franklin Medal 70.
Green Acres, Holbrook, Derbyshire, England.
Telephone: Derby 881137.

Peart, Rt. Hon. (Thomas) Frederick, P.C., M.P.; British politician; b. 30 April 1914; m. Sarah Elizabeth Lewis 1945; one s.; ed. Wolsingham Grammar School, Henry Smith Secondary School, Hartlepool, Bede Coll., Durham Univ. and Inner Temple.
Councillor, Easington Rural District Council 37-40; Army Service 39-45; M.P. 45-, Parliamentary Private Sec., to Minister of Agriculture and Fisheries 45-51; British Del. and Rep. Agriculture Cttee., Vice-Pres., Cttee. for Culture and Science, Council of Europe; Chair. Council of Europe's Special Cttee. dealing with Agricultural Refugees 54; Minister of Agriculture, Fisheries and Food 64-68; Lord Privy Seal and Leader of House of Commons April-Oct. 68; Lord Pres. of the Council and Leader of the House of Commons 68-70; Opposition spokesman for Agriculture, Fisheries and Food 70-72, for Defence 72-74; Leader of Labour Del. to the Council of Europe and Western European Assembly 73-74; Vice-Pres. Council of Europe 73-74; Minister of Agriculture, Fisheries and Food 74-; Labour.
Ministry of Agriculture, Fisheries and Food, Whitehall Place, London, SW1A 2HH; and House of Commons, London, S.W.1, England.

Peart, William Stanley, M.B., B.S., M.D., F.R.C.P., F.R.S.; British professor of medicine; b. 31 March 1922, South Shields; s. of J. G. and M. Peart; m. Peggy Parkes 1947; one s. one d.; ed. King's Coll. School, Wimbledon, and St. Mary's Hospital Medical School, London.
Lecturer in Medicine, St. Mary's Hospital, London 50-56, Prof. of Medicine 56-; Chair. Medical Research Soc. 68; mem. Medical Research Council 69; mem. Advisory Board for the Research Councils 73; Trustee, Wellcome Trust 75; Stouffer Prize 68.
Leisure interests: reading and tennis.
Publs. Articles in *The Biochemical Journal, Journal of Physiology, The Lancet*; chapters in textbooks on renal disease and high blood pressure.
Medical Unit, St. Mary's Hospital, London, W.2; Home: 5 Fordington Road, London, N.6, England.
Telephone: 01-262-1280 (Hospital); 01-883-9346 (Home).

Pease, Rendel Sebastian, M.A., SC.D.; British physicist; b. 2 Nov. 1922, Cambridge; s. of Michael Stewart Pease and Helen Bowen (née Wedgwood), m. Susan Spickernell 1952; two s. three d.; ed. Bedales School and Trinity Coll., Cambridge.

Scientific Officer, Ministry of Aircraft Production at Operational Research Soc. Unit. HQ, R.A.F. Bomber Command 42-46; Research at A.E.R.E., Harwell 47-61; Div. Head, Culham Lab. for Plasma Physics and Nuclear Fusion, U.K. Atomic Energy Authority (U.K.A.E.A.) 61-67, Dir. of Culham Lab. 68-; Visiting Scientist, Princeton Univ. 64-65; Asst. Dir. U.K.A.E.A. Research Group 67; Hon. D.Univ. (Surrey) 73.
Leisure interest: music.
Publs. articles in physics journals.
The Poplars, West Ilsley, Newbury, Berks., England.

Peccei, Aurelio, M.A., D.ECON.; Italian business executive; b. 4 July 1908; ed. Higher Commercial School "Quintino Sella", Turin, and Univ. of Turin.
Fiat Co., Turin 30-, Divisional Manager 46-, mem. Steering Cttee.; Founder Fiat industries in Argentina 53, Chair. of Board Fiat Concord, Buenos Aires 53-; Man. Dir. Italconsult, Rome 57-, Chair. of Board 71-; Man. Dir. Ing. C. Olivetti & Co. S.p.A., Ivrea 64-67, Vice-Chair. 67-; Chair. Cttee. for Atlantic Econ. Co-operation, Paris; Pres. Club of Rome.
Publ. *The Chasm Ahead* 69.
Ing. C. Olivetti & Co. S.p.A., Via Jervis, Ivrea, Italy.
Telephone: 525.

Peck, Sir Edward Heywood, G.C.M.G.; British diplomatist (retd.); b. 5 Oct. 1915, Hove, Sussex; s. of Lt.-Col. E. S. Peck and Doris Heywood; m. Alison Mary MacInnes 1948; one s. two d.; ed. Clifton Coll. and Queen's Coll., Oxford.
Probationer Vice-Consul, Barcelona 38-39; Foreign Office 39-40; Consulate, Sofia 40, Ankara 40-44; Consul, Adana 44, Iskenderun 44-45; Consulate-Gen., Salonica 46; with U.K. Del. to UN Special Comm. on the Balkans 47; transferred to Foreign Office 47; seconded to C.R.O. for service at New Delhi 50-52; Counsellor, Foreign Office 52-54, Berlin 55-58, Singapore 59-60; Asst. Under Sec. of State for Far Eastern and S.E. Asian Affairs, Foreign Office 61-66; High Commr. of U.K. in Kenya 66-68; Deputy Under-Sec. of State Foreign Office 68-70; Perm. Rep. of U.K. to North Atlantic Council 70-75.
Leisure interests: skiing, mountaineering, reading history.
19 The Rise, Sevenoaks, Kent, England.

Peck, Gregory, B.A.; American actor; b. 5 April 1916, La Jolla, Calif.; m.; five c.; ed. California Univ.
Member Nat. Council on Arts 65-67, reappointed 68; Pres. Acad. of Motion Picture Arts and Sciences 67-70; Medal of Freedom Award 69; Acad. Award (Oscar) best actor 62; Screen Actors' Guild Annual Award for Outstanding Achievement 70; Acad. of Motion Picture Arts and Sciences Jean Hersholt Humanitarian Award 68.
Appeared in plays including *The Doctor's Dilemma, The Male Animal, Once in a Lifetime, The Play's the Thing, You Can't Take it With You, The Morning Star, The Willow and I, Sons and Soldiers.*
Films include: *Days of Glory* 43, *Keys of the Kingdom* 44, *Spellbound* 45, *The Valley of Decision* 45, *Duel in the Sun* 46, *The Macomber Affair* 47, *Gentleman's Agreement* 47, *The Paradine Case* 48, *Yellow Sky* 49, *Twelve O'Clock High* 49, *The Great Sinner* 49, *Captain Horatio Hornblower* 51, *David and Bathsheba* 51, *The Snows of Kilimanjaro* 52, *Roman Holiday* 53, *The Purple Plain* 54, *The Man in the Grey Flannel Suit* 56, *Moby Dick* 56, *Designing Woman* 57, *The Big Country, The Bravados* 58, *Pork Chop Hill* 59, *On the Beach* 59, *Beloved Infidel* 59, *Guns of Navarone* 61, *Cape Fear* 62, *How the West Was Won* 63, *To Kill a Mocking Bird* 62, *Captain Newman, M.D.* 63, *Behold a Pale Horse* 64, *Mirage* 64, *Arabesque* 65, *The Stalking Moon* 68, *Mackenna's Gold* 69, *The Chairman* 69, *Marooned* 69, *I Walk the Line* 70, *Shoot Out* 71, *Billy Two-Hats* 72, producer *The Dove* 74.
1041 N. Formosa Avenue, Los Angeles, Calif. 90046, U.S.A.

Peck, Sir John Howard, K.C.M.G.; British retired diplomatist; b. 16 Feb. 1913; ed. Wellington Coll. and Christ Church, Oxford.
Assistant Private Sec. to First Lord of Admiralty 37-39, to Minister for Co-ordination of Defence 39-40, to Prime Minister 40-46; transferred to Foreign Service 46, served UN Dept. 46-47, The Hague 47-50; Counsellor and Head of Information Research Dept. 51-54; Counsellor (Defence Liaison) and Head of Political Div., British Middle East Office 54-56; Dir.-Gen. British Information Services, New York 56-59; U.K. Perm. Rep. to Council of Europe, and Consul-General, Strasbourg 59-62; Amb. to Senegal 62-66, and Mauritania 62-65; Asst. Under-Sec. of State, Foreign Office, later Foreign and Commonwealth Office 66-70; Amb. to Ireland 70-73.
4 Eglinton Park, Dun Laoghaire, Co. Dublin, Ireland.

Pecker, Jean-Claude; French astronomer; b. 10 May 1923, Reims; s. of Victor-Noel Pecker and Nelly Catherine Herrmann; m. 2nd Annie A. Vormser 1974; one s. two d. (by previous marriage); ed. Lycée de Bordeaux, Univ. of Grenoble and Paris (Sorbonne) and Ecole Normale Supérieure.
Research Asst. Centre National de la Recherche Scientifique (C.N.R.S.) 46-52; Asst. Prof. Univ. of Clermont-Ferrand 52-55; Asst. Astronomer Paris Observatory 55-62, Astronomer 62-65; Dir. Nice Observatory 62-69; Prof. Collège de France 63-; Asst. Gen. Sec. Int. Astronomical Union 61-63, Gen. Sec. 64-67; Pres. Comité Nat. Français d'Astronomie 70-73; Dir. Inst. Astrophysique, Paris; Pres. Soc. Astronomique de France 73-76; Commdr. Palmes Académiques; Chevalier Légion d'Honneur; Prix Forthuny, Inst. de France; Prix Stroobant Acad. des Sciences de Belgique 65; Prix Manley-Bendall de l'Acad. de Bordeaux 66; Prix des Trois Physiciens 69; Assoc. Royal Soc. of Science, Liège 67; Corresp. Bureau des Longitudes 68; Assoc. Royal Astronomical Soc. 68; Janssen Medal Astronomical Soc., France 67, Prix Jean Perrin, Soc. Française de Physique 73; Corresp. mem. Académie des Sciences, France 69; Medal Univ. de Nice 72.
Leisure interest: painting.
Publs. include *L'Astronomie au jour le jour* (with P. Couderc and E. Schatzman) 54, *Astrophysique générale* (with E. Schatzman) 59, *Le Ciel* 59, *L'Astronomie Expérimentale* 69, *Les Laboratoires Spatiaux* 69, *Papa, dis-moi: L'Astronomie, qu'est-ce que c'est?* 71, Editor *L'Astronomie nouvelle* 71.
177 rue Saint-Jacques, 75005 Paris; and Pusat Tasek, Les Corbeaux, 85350, Ile d'Yeu, France.
Telephone: 033-25-40.

Peckinpah, (David) Sam(uel), M.A.; American film director, writer and producer; b. 21 Feb. 1925, Fresno, Calif.; s. of Judge David E. Peckinpah and Fern Church; m. three times; one s. three d.; ed. Fresno State Coll. and Univ. of Southern Calif.
Films directed: *Deadly Companions* 58, *Ride High the Country* (Best Foreign Picture, Mexico and Best Picture Award, Brussels Film Festival) 60, *Major Dundee* 65, *The Wild Bunch* 68, *The Ballad of Cable Hogue* (Best Foreign Picture, Spain) 69, *The Straw Dogs* 70, *Junior Bonner* 71, *The Getaway* 72, *Pat Garrett and Billy the Kid* 73, *Bring Me the Head of Alfredo Garcia* 74, *The Killer Elite* 75; has also directed several television series.
Leisure interests: skin-diving, surfing.
Chasin Park Citron Agency, 10889 Wilshire Boulevard, Los Angeles, Calif. 90024, U.S.A.

Pedersen, Arne Fog, B.D.; Danish ecclesiastic and politician; b. 25 Aug. 1911, Hinnerup; s. of A. J. Pedersen and E. Fog; m. Mette Høyer 1939; one s. two d. Teacher, Rødding Folk High School 39-50, Principal 53-68, 71; Head of Denmark Radio's Lectures Dept. 50-53; Minister of Ecclesiastical Affairs 68-71; Chair. Liberal

Educ. Assen. 54; mem., Nat. Comm. for UNESCO 55-, Gen. Council of Norden Asscn. 56-, Govt. Cttee. to promote Danish Language and Culture Abroad 57-; Del. to UN 72; Chair. Grouseforeningen 72, Filadelfia 74; Liberal.
Publs. *Danmarks første Højskole* (Denmark's First Folk High School) 44, Editor of *Fyraften* (Knocking-Off Time) 53, Contrib. to *Højskolens ungdomstid i breve* (Early Years of the Folk High School Movement as Reflected in Contemporary Letters) Vol. 1; articles, mostly on history, North Slesvig and foreign policy.
Rødding Højskole, 6630 Rødding, Denmark.
Telephone: (04) 841568.

Pedersen, Helga, CAND.JUR.; Danish judge; b. 24 June 1911, Taarnborg; d. of J. P. Pedersen and Vilhelmine Pedersen (née Kolding); ed. Copenhagen Univ. and Columbia Univ., New York.
Danish Dept. of Justice 36-46; Judge, District Court of Copenhagen 48-50, 53-56; Minister of Justice 50-53; Judge, Court of Appeal, Copenhagen 56-64; Justice of Supreme Court, Copenhagen 64-; mem. Danish Parl. (Liberal Party) 53-64; Del. to UN and UNESCO conferences on several occasions -74; Judge, European Court of Human Rights 71-; Chair. Nat. Comm. of UNESCO -74; mem. Danish Council for Planning of Higher Educ. 68-73; Danish Council on Copyright 62-73, Special Parole Board of Danish Prison Admin. 68-73; Head Board of Danish Red Cross; Chair. Representatives of Danish State Art Foundation 65-73; Vice-Pres. Danish Welfare Asscn. 67-73; Chair. Danish Press Board 71, and Controlling Board of Danish Press Financing Inst. 73; Pres. of the Trustees, Foundation for Trees and Environment; Commdr. Order of Dannebrog (Denmark); Grand Cross Order of Orange-Nassau (Netherlands).
Leisure interests: farming, travelling, art.
Publs. *Céline and Denmark* 75, and articles on legal and political subjects.
Statholdervej 19, Copenhagen N.V. 2400, Denmark.
Telephone: Ægir 3220.

Pedersen, Johannes, PH.D., D.D.; Danish orientalist; b. 7 Nov. 1883, Lindelse, Langeland; s. of late Sören Pedersen and late Ida Pedersen (née Noiesen); m. Thora Caroline Gertz 1921 (died 1946); ed. Univ. of Copenhagen.
Studied theology and semitic languages, Copenhagen 02-08; worked on translation of Bible into Danish 08-09; continued studies in Leipzig, Leiden and Budapest 09-12; Collaborator, Arabic Dictionary, Leipzig 13-19, studied in Egypt, Palestine, Syria 20-21; Prof. of Semitic Philology, Copenhagen 22-50; mem. Royal Danish Acad. 24-, Chair. History and Philosophy Section 42-63, Pres. of the Acad. 63-69; Dir. Carlsberg Foundation 26-55, Chair. 33-55; mem. Rask-Örsted mem. numerous Danish academic orgs.; Grand Cross of Dannebrog 55.
Publs. *Der Eid bei den Semiten* 14, *Israel* Vols. I, II, (Danish 20, 34, 58, English 26, 46, 54, 59) Vols. III, IV (Danish 34, 60, English 40, 47, 53, 59); Danish *al-Azhar* 22, *Muhammedansk Mystik* 23, 52, *Hebrew Grammar* 26, 33, 50, 68, *Islams Kultur* 28, *Den Arabiske Bog* 46, *Sulami: Tabaqat Al-Sufiyya* 60 (Arabic edn. with French introduction), contributions to *Encyclopaedia of Islam*, etc.
Soendre Fasanvej 90, 2500 Copenhagen/Valby, Denmark.

Pedersen, Richard Foote, PH.D.; American diplomatist; b. 21 Feb. 1925, Miami, Ariz.; m. Nelda Newell Napier; one s. two d.; ed. Univ. of the Pacific, Stanford and Harvard Univs.
Foreign Affairs Officer, UN Econ. and Social Affairs, Dept. of State 50-53; Econ. and Social Affairs Adviser, Perm Mission to UN 53, held successive posts of Adviser on Political and Security Affairs, Senior

Adviser and Chief of Political Section, Counsellor, Senior Advisor to Perm. Rep. to UN, with rank of Amb.; Deputy U.S. Rep. in Security Council 67; Counsellor, Dept. of State 69-73; Amb. to Hungary 73-75; Hon. LL.D. (George Williams Coll.) 64, (Univ. of the Pacific) 65.
Department of State, Washington, D.C. 20520, U.S.A.

Peech, Alan James, B.A., LL.D.; British business executive; b. 24 Aug. 1905; ed. Wellington Coll. and Magdalen Coll., Oxford.
Former Dir. and Chair. United Steel Cos. Ltd.; fmr. Deputy Chair. (Operations) British Steel Corpn. and fmr. Gen. Man. Dir. Midland Group, British Steel Corpn.; Dir. and Deputy Chair. Steetley Co. Ltd.; Dir. Tinsley Wire Industries Ltd.; Independent Chair. Cement Makers' Federation 70-; Gov. Wellington Coll.; Hon. LL.D. (Sheffield Univ.).
Home: High House, Blyth, Nr. Worksop, Notts., England.

Peeters, Baron Flor; Belgian composer, organist and teacher; b. 4 July 1903, Tielen; s. of Louis Peeters and Elisabeth Deckers; m. Marieke van Gorp 1928; one s. two d.; ed. Lemmens Inst., Mechelen.
Organist, Metropolitan Cathedral of Belgium, Mechelen 23-; Prof. of Organ, Lemmens Inst., Mechelen 23-52; Royal Conservatory of Ghent 31-48; Prof. of Organ and Composition, Conservatory of Tilburg (Netherlands) 35-48; Prof. of Organ and Composition, Royal Flemish Conservatory, Antwerp 48-68; Dir. of Royal Flemish Conservatory 52-68; world-wide recitals; Editor and Publisher of *De Praestant* 51-72; mem. Royal Flemish Acad. for Fine Arts; Hon. mem. Royal Acad. of Music, London; Hon. D.Mus. (Catholic Univ. of America, Catholic Univ. of Louvain); Prix Lemmens-Tinel; Commdr. Order of Gregory the Great; Grand Officier de l'Ordre de Léopold.
Compositions: (organ) Sinfonia, Lied-Symphony, Passacaglia and Fugue, 3 preludes and fugues, 300 chorale preludes, concerto for piano and organ, concerto for organ and orchestra, concerto for piano and orchestra, concertino for positiv organ and harpsichord, chamber music, piano music and lieder; numerous gramophone recordings.
Publs. *Ars Organi* (3 vols.), *Old Netherlands Masters for the Organ* (3 vols.), *Anthologia pro organo* (4 vols.), *The Organ and its Music in the Netherlands* (with M. A. Vente) 71, *Practical Method for Plain Chant Accompaniment.*
Villa Adagio, Stuivenbergbaan 123, Mechelen, Belgium.

Pegov, Nikolai Mikhailovich; Soviet politician and diplomatist; b. 16 April 1905; ed. Industrial Acad., Moscow.
Sec. Far Eastern Territory Cttee. of the Party 38; First Sec. Maritime Territory Cttee.; held exec. post in the Central Cttee. of the C.P.S.U. 47; Sec. Central Cttee. of the C.P.S.U. 52; Sec. Presidium of the Supreme Soviet of the U.S.S.R. 53-56; Soviet Ambassador to Iran 56-63, to Algeria 63-67, to India 67-73; Vice-Minister for Foreign Affairs 73-; mem. C.P.S.U. Cen. Cttee. 39-; awarded Order of Lenin (twice), Order of the Red Banner of Labour, Order of the Patriotic War, 1st Class and other decorations.
Ministry of Foreign Affairs, Moscow, U.S.S.R.

Pei Ieoh Ming, M.ARCH., F.A.I.A.; American architect; b. 26 April 1917, Canton, China; s. of Tsu Yee Pei and Lien Kwun Chwong; m. Eileen Loo 1942; three s. one d.; ed. Shanghai, Massachusetts Inst. of Technology and Harvard Univ.
In U.S.A. 35-; naturalised citizen 54-; architectural practice 39-, Webb and Knapp Inc. 48-55, I. M. Pei & Partners 55-; Asst. Prof. Harvard Graduate School of Design 45-48; Wheelwright Fellow, Harvard Univ. 51; M.I.T. Traveling Fellowship 40; Fellow A.I.A.; mem.

Nat. Council on the Humanities 66-70, American Acad. of Arts and Sciences, Nat. Acad. of Design, Nat. Inst. of Arts and Letters, American Acad. of Arts and Letters. Urban Design Council (N.Y. City), Corpn. of the Mass. Inst. of Technology; Hon. D.F.A. (Univ. of Pennsylvania) 70, Hon. LL.D. (Chinese Univ. of Hong Kong) 70; Brunner Award, Nat. Inst. of Arts and Letters 61; Medal of Honor N.Y. Chapter A.I.A. 63.
Projects include Mile High Center (Denver), M.I.T. Earth Science Building (Cambridge, Mass.), U.S. Embassy Building (Montevideo); East-West Center, Univ. of Hawaii; redevelopment projects in New York. Philadelphia, Washington, Chicago, Pittsburgh and Singapore; Nat. Center for Atmospheric Research (Boulder, Colorado); Grave of Robert F. Kennedy; Nat. Airlines Terminal (Kennedy Int. Airport), Washington Sq. East (Philadelphia), Everson Museum of Art (Syracuse, N.Y.), Nat. Gallery of Art East Building (Washington, D.C.), Wilmington Tower (Wilmington, Del.), John Fitzgerald Kennedy Library Complex (Cambridge, Mass.), Canadian Imperial Board of Commerce Complex (Toronto, Canada), Des Moines Art Center Addition (Des Moines, Iowa), Cleo Rogers Memorial County Library (Columbus, Ind.), planning projects in Boston, Oklahoma City and N.Y. City; Master Plan Columbia Univ. (N.Y.) 70; Dallas Municipal Bldg. (Dallas); Raffles Int. Center complex (Singapore); Overseas-Chinese Banking Corpn. Tower (Singapore); Herbert F. Johnson Museum of Art (Ithaca, N.Y.).
Office: 600 Madison Avenue, New York, N.Y. 10022
Home: 11 Sutton Place, New York, N.Y. 10022, U.S.A.
Telephone: 751-3122 (Office).

Peierls, Sir Rudolf Ernst, Kt., C.B.E., PH.D., M.A., D.SC., F.R.S.; British scientist; b. 5 June 1907, Berlin, Germany; s. of Heinrich Peierls and Elisabeth (née Weigert); m. Eugenia Kannegiser 1931; one s. three d.; ed. Berlin, Munich and Leipzig Univs. and Fed. Inst. of Technology, Zürich.
Asst. Federal Technical High School, Zürich 29; Rockefeller Fellow 32; Hon. Research Fellow Manchester Univ. 33-35; Research Asst. Royal Society Mond Laboratory Cambridge Univ. 35-37; Prof. of Applied Mathematics Birmingham Univ. 37-46; work on atomic energy, Birmingham, New York, Los Alamos 40-45; Prof. of Mathematical Physics, Birmingham Univ. 46-63; Wykeham Prof. Univ. of Oxford 63-74; Foreign Hon. mem. American Acad. of Arts and Sciences 62; Foreign Assoc. U.S. Nat. Acad. of Sciences 70; Fellow, New Coll., Oxford 63-74; Hon. Fellow, Inst. of Physics 74; Lorentz Medal Royal Netherlands Acad. of Sciences 62; Council of Royal Soc., London 58; Royal Medal of Royal Soc. 59, Max Planck Medal, Asscn. of German Physical Socs. 63; Guthrie Medal, Inst. of Physics and Physical Soc. 68.
Leisure interests: travelling, photography.
Publs. *Quantum Theory of Solids, The Laws of Nature* 55.
Farleigh, Orchard Lane, Old Boar's Hill, Oxford OX1 5JH, England.

Peirano Facio, Jorge; Uruguayan politician; b. 8 Sept. 1920; m. Alba Basso; seven c.; ed. Faculty of Law and Social Sciences, Montevideo.
Assistant Prof. of Civil Law, Faculty of Law, Montevideo 47, Prof. 52; Faculty of Law and Social Sciences, Montevideo 54-59; Dir. *Revista de Derecho Jurisprudencia y Administración* 56-; Sec. Coll. of Advocates, Uruguay 49-52; Under-Sec. Ministry of Interior 50; mem. Uruguayan Del. to OAS Conf. Buenos Aires 57; Pres. Nat. Chamber of Commerce; other business and banking appointments; later became Minister of Industry and Commerce; Minister of Foreign Affairs 70-72.
Publs. include: *De los empréstitos de las Sociedades Anónimas por Emisión de obligaciones negociables* 43,

Delitos de la Muchedumbre 44, *El derecho de resistencia,*
La cláusula penal 47, *Nuestra Legislación de Desalojos*
51, *Responsabilidad Extracontractual* 54, *El Proyecto de*
G. Civil de Eduardo Acevedo 65.
c/o Ministerio de Relaciones Exteriores, Montevideo,
Uruguay.

Peive, Alexandr Woldemarovich; Soviet geologist;
b. 9 Feb. 1909, Sementsovo village, Kalinin Region;
ed. Moscow Inst. of Geology and Prospecting.
Scientific Assoc., Research Inst. of Fertilizers 29-35;
Senior Scientific Assoc., Head of Dept., Inst. of Geology,
U.S.S.R. Acad. of Sciences 35-; Corresp. mem. U.S.S.R.
Acad. of Sciences 58-64, Academician 64-; State Prize
46, 69.
Publs. numerous works on problems of regional and
theoretical tectonics.
U.S.S.R. Academy of Sciences, 14 Leninsky Prospekt,
Moscow, U.S.S.R.

Peive, Ian Woldemarovich; Soviet scientist; b. 3 Aug.
1906, Sementsevo, Toropets district, Kalinin region; s.
of Woldemar and Emma Peive; m. Ksenia Peive 1930;
two d.; ed. Moscow Timiryazev Acad. of Agriculture.
Expert on agro-chemistry and plant breeding; at the
U.S.S.R. Flax Research Inst. 30-44; Rector of the
Latvian Acad. of Agriculture 44-50; Pres. of the Acad.
of Sciences of Latvia 51-59; Chair. of the Soviet of
Nationalities of the Supreme Soviet of the U.S.S.R.
58-66; Chief Sec. U.S.S.R. Acad. of Sciences 66-;
Chair. Council of Ministers of Latvia 59-62; mem.
U.S.S.R. and Latvian S.S.R. Acads. of Sciences;
Lenin Prize, Hero of Socialist Labour, Order of Lenin
and other awards.
Leisure interest: horticulture.
Principal publs. (in Latvian): *Linkoptba* 48, *Augsnes*
pētisanas agrokimiskās metōdes 49, *Mikroelementu mēs-*
lojums lauksaimniecibā 49; (in Russian) *The Use of*
Trace Elements in Agriculture of the Non-chernosem
Zone of the U.S.S.R. 54, *Trace Elements in Plant Breed-*
ing 58, *Content of forms of Trace Elements that are*
available to Plants in the Soils of the U.S.S.R. 59, *Trace*
Elements and Enzymes 60, *Biochemistry of Soils* 61.
U.S.S.R. Academy of Sciences, Leninsky Prospekt 14,
Moscow, U.S.S.R.
Telephone: 232-50-07.

Pekeris, Chaim L., D.SC.; American applied mathe-
matician, geophysicist and educator; b. 15 June 1908,
Alytus, Lithuania; s. of Samuel Pekeris and Chaya Rivel;
m. Leah Kaplan 1933 (died 1973); ed. Mass. Inst. of
Technology.
Rockefeller Fellow 34-35; Research at Cambridge Univ.,
England 35-36; Lectured in Geophysics at Mass. Inst. of
Technology 36-40; mem. War Research Dept., Columbia
Univ. 40-45, Dir. Mathematical Physics Group 45-47;
mem. Inst. for Advanced Study, Princeton 47-48; Prof.
and Head, Dept. of Applied Mathematics, Weizmann
Inst. of Science, Rehovoth, Israel 48-73, Distinguished
Inst. Prof. 73-; mem. Israel Acad. of Sciences and
Humanities; Foreign mem. Accademia Nazionale dei
Lincei; mem. Nat. Acad. of Sciences, U.S., Israel;
Foreign Assoc. Royal Astronomical Soc., England;
Rothschild Prize in Mathematics 66.
Publs. Papers in applied mathematics and geophysics.
Weizmann Institute of Science, Rehovoth, Israel.
Telephone: 951-721.

Peled, Natan; Israeli politician; b. 3 June 1913,
Odessa; s. of Yosef and Lea Peled; m. Mania Peled 1936;
two d.; ed. secondary education.
Immigrated to Palestine 32; agricultural labourer in
Kibbutz; Sec. Gen. of Kibbutz Fed. 'Hashomer
Hatzair' 50-55; Political Sec., Mapam Party 56-58;
Minister of Israel to Bulgaria 58-60; Amb. to Austria
60-63; mem. Knesset 65-69; Minister of Immigrant

Absorption 70-74; Sec.-Gen. of Kibbutz Fed. Hashomer
Hatzair 75-.
Kibbutz Sarid, Israel.
Telephone: 065-40184.

Pelikán, Jiří; Czechoslovak fmr. television official and
diplomatist; b. 7 Feb. 1923, Olomouc; ed. Charles
Univ., Prague.
In illegal movement, Second World War, imprisoned
40; worked at Prague Regional Cttee., C.P. of Czecho-
slovakia 47-49, 52-53, at Central Cttee., C.P. of Czecho-
slovakia 49-52; Central Cttee. of Czechoslovak Youth
Union 54-63; Deputy to Nat. Assembly 48-53, 64-69;
Chair. Int. Union of Students 53-63; Gen. Dir. Czecho-
slovak Television 63-68; Counsellor, Czechoslovak
Embassy, Rome 68-69; mem. Ideological Comm. of
Central Cttee. of C.P. of Czechoslovakia 63-69; Chair.
Foreign Affairs Cttee. of Nat. Assembly 68; Deputy
House of People, Federal Assembly 69; in exile abroad
Sept. 69-; deprived of Czech citizenship 70; now living
in U.K.

Pelissier, Jacques Daniel Paul: French civil servant
and railway administrator; b. 4 Feb. 1917, Versailles;
s. of Jean Pelissier and Camille Bertrand; m. Jeanine
Picard 1946; one s.; ed. Lycée Pasteur, Lycée Hoche,
Lycée Chaptal, Inst. Nat. Agronomique.
Engineer, external service of Ministry of Agriculture
38-44; Sec.-Gen. Landes 44, Ardennes 45; Sous-préfet
hors cadre, Chef du Cabinet to Minister of Agriculture
46; Asst. Chef du Cabinet, Minister of Industry and
Commerce 48; Sec.-Gen. Indre-et-Loire 50; Sous-
préfet, Saumur 54; Dir. for Gen. Govt. of Algeria, in
Ministry for Algeria and in Gen. Del. of Govt. in Algeria
56-60; Préfet hors cadre 57; Préfet, Aude 60, Hérault
and Region of Languedoc-Roussillon 64, Ille-et-Vilaine
and Region of Brittany 67, Rhône and Region of
Rhône-Alpes 72; Préfet hors cadre, Dir.-Gen. of Admin.,
Ministry of the Interior April 74; Dir. du Cabinet for
Prime Minister May 74; Chair. Board of Dirs. Soc. Nat.
des Chemins de Fer Français Sept. 75-; Commdr.
Légion d'Honneur, Commdr. Ordre Nat. du Mérite,
Mil. Cross (39-45), Medal of the Resistance.
Société Nationale des Chemins de Fer Français, 88 rue
St. Lazare, 75436 Paris Cedex 09, France.

Peliza, Major Robert John; Gibraltar politician; b. 16
Nov. 1920, Gibraltar; s. of Robert Peliza and Emily
Victory; m. Irma Risso 1950; three s. four d.; ed.
Christian Brothers' Coll., Gibraltar.
Served in Gibraltar Regiment 39-61; company director
62; Leader, Integration with Britain Party 67; Chief
Minister of Gibraltar Aug. 69-June 72; fmr. Leader of
the Opposition 72.
Leisure interests: painting, writing, swimming, walking
and sports in general.
Buena Vista Cottage, Buena Vista Road, Gibraltar.
Telephone: 6110.

Pell, Claiborne de Borda, A.M.; American politician;
b. 22 Nov. 1918; ed. Princeton and Columbia Univs.
Limited Partner, Auchinloss, Parker and Redpath;
U.S. Coastguard 41-45; now, Capt. U.S.C.G.R.; United
States Foreign Service Officer; Instructor and Lecturer,
Naval and Mil. Govt. Schools 44-45; served State Dept.,
Czechoslovakia, Italy, Wash. 45-52; company dir. and
trustee 52-60; Consultant, Dem. Nat. Cttee. 53-60; U.S.
Del. to Inter-Govtl. Maritime Consultative Org. (IMCO)
London 59; Senator from Rhode Island 61-; Legion of
Honour (France), Crown of Italy, etc.; Democrat.
Publs. *Rochambeau and Rhode Island* 54, *Megalopolis*
Unbound 66, *Challenge of the Seven Seas* (with Harold L.
Goodwin) 66, *Power and Policy* 72.
Senate Office Building, Washington, D.C. 20510, U.S.A.

Pella, Giuseppe; Italian economist and politician;
b. 18 April 1902; ed. Univs. of Rome and Turin.
Founder and 1st Pres. of Catholic Organisation for

Secondary School Students 19; active in commercial finance until 39; participated in Int. Wool Conf. 32-39; Christian Democrat Deputy 46-; Under-Sec. of Finance 46-47, Minister 47-48; Minister of Treasury and *ad interim* Minister of Budget 48-51, of Budget 51-52, of Budget and Treasury 52-54; Prime Minister, Minister for Foreign Affairs and Budget 53-54; Deputy Prime Minister, Minister of Foreign Affairs 57-58; a Governor of Int. Monetary Fund and Rep. on O.E.E.C.; Pres. Common Assembly, European Coal and Steel Community 54-56; Minister of Foreign Affairs Feb. 59-Feb. 60; Minister of Budget July 60-62; Pres. Int. Centre of Studies and Documentation, European Communities, Nat. Inst. of Accounting; Dir. of newspaper *Stato Sociale*.
Camera dei Deputati, Palazzo Montecitorio, Rome; Via Ludovisi 35, Rome, Italy.

Pellegrino, H.E. Cardinal Michele; Italian ecclesiastic; b. 25 April 1903.
Ordained Priest 25; Archbishop of Turin 65-; created Cardinal by Pope Paul VI 67.
Via Arcivescovado 12, Turin, Italy.

Pelletier, Hon. Gérard, P.C., B.A.; Canadian journalist and politician; b. 21 June 1919, Victoriaville, P.Q.; s. of Achille Pelletier and Léda Dufresne; *m.* Alexandrine Leduc 1943; one *s.* three *d.*; ed. Nicolet and Mont-Laurier Colls., Univ. of Montreal.
Secretary-General Jeunesse étudiante catholique 39-43; Field Sec. World Student Relief, Geneva 45-47; Reporter, *Le Devoir* 47-50; Dir. of *Le Travail*, official paper of Confed. of Nat. Trade Unions 50-61; Editor of *La Presse* 61-65; Special Columnist for *Le Devoir* and group of English language dailies 65; mem. Parl. for Hochelaga 65; Parl. Sec. to Sec. of State for External Affairs 67-68; Minister without Portfolio April-June 68; Sec. of State June 68-Nov. 72; Minister of Communications 72-75; Amb. to France 75-; Liberal.
Leisure interests: boating and swimming.
Canadian Embassy, avenue Montaigne 35, Paris, France.

Pelletier, Raymond; French business executive; b. 12 Oct. 1910; ed. Ecole Polytechnique, Paris.
Joined Cie. Générale d'Electricité 32, Vice-Chair. and Man. Dir. 70; Hon. Chair. SAFT; Chair. Board Les Câbles de Lyon 72, Cie. Européenne d'Accumulateurs 73; Dir. many other companies; Officier, Légion d'Honneur; Croix de Guerre.
Cie. Générale d'Electricité, 54 rue de la Boétie, Paris 75008; Home: 36 Rue du Ranelagh, 75016 Paris, France. Telephone: 266-54-50 (Office); 647-88-61 (Home).

Pelnář, Jan; Czechoslovak politician; b. 24 April 1911, Mrákov.
Bricklayer 26-46; Sec. District Trade Union Council, Klatovy 46-47; Chair. District Nat. Cttee., Domažlice 47-49; Head of Food Supplies Dept., Regional Nat. Cttee., Pilsen 49-54; Chair. W. Bohemian Regional Nat. Cttee., Pilsen 54-68; Minister of Interior 68, Minister of Interior, Fed. Govt. 69-70; mem. Presidium Central Cttee., Nat. Front 70-71, Exec. Vice-Chair. Cen. Cttee. 70-71; mem. State Comm. for Technology 65-68, Deputy to Czech Nat. Council 68-71; mem. Presidium 68; Deputy to House of Nations Fed. Assembly 69-71; mem. Cen. Cttee. C.P. of Czechoslovakia 54-71; numerous decorations include: Medal for Distinction in Construction 55; Order of Labour 61.
Federal Assembly, Prague 7, Czechoslovakia.

Pelser, Petrus Cornelius, B.A., LL.B.; South African politician; b. 28 Feb. 1907, Reddersburg, O.F.S.; s. of late J. A. Pelser and late J. J. M. Pelser (née Olivier); *m.* Magrieta Isabella Blignaut 1934; four *s.* one *d.*; ed. Paarl Gimnasium, Univ. of South Africa (private study) and Univ. of the Witwatersrand.
Joined Public Service 25; Dept. of Mines 25-37, Dept.

of Commerce and Industry 37-43; Attorney, Klerksdorp 43; mem. Provincial Council, Klerksdorp 50; mem. Parl. 53-, Deputy Chair. of Cttees., House of Assembly 62-66, Deputy Speaker and Chair. of Cttees. 66; Minister of Justice and Prisons 66-74, retd.; Nat. Party.
Leisure interest: bowls.
Parliament Building, Pretoria, South Africa.

Pelshe, Arvid Yanovich; Soviet politician; b. 1899; ed. Institute of Red Professors.
Elected to Petrograd Soviet 17; Party duties Archangel 17-19; served in Red Army and Navy 19-29; Party duties Kazakhstan 33; Teacher at Higher Educational Insts. Moscow 37-40; mem. Central Cttee. Latvian Communist Party 40-41, Sec. 41-59, First Sec. 59-66; mem. Political Bureau of Central Cttee. of C.P.S.U. April 66-; Chair. Party Control Cttee. of C.P.S.U. Central Cttee. 66-; Deputy to U.S.S.R. Supreme Soviet 46-; Hero of Socialist Labour, Orders of Lenin, "Hammer and Sickle" Gold Medal and other awards.
Central Committee of C.P.S.U., 4 Staraya ploshchad, Moscow, U.S.S.R.

Pelt, Adrian; Netherlands international official; b. 8 May 1892, Koogaan de Zaan; s. of M. A. Pelt and D. J. Endt; *m.* Andrée Bernard 1919; three *d.*; ed. Ecole des Sciences politiques, Paris.
London corresp. 15-16, and Paris corresp. 16-19, mem. editorial staff of various Dutch newspapers; entered Information Section of League of Nations 20, becoming Dir. of this Section 34; during Second World War, organized and directed Netherlands Govt. Information Bureau, London; mem. Netherlands del. to San Francisco Conf. 45, UN Preparatory Comm., and First Session of Gen. Assembly; appointed Asst. Sec.-Gen. in charge of Dept. of Conference and Gen. Services 46; UN Commr. for Libya 49-52; Dir. UN European Office, Geneva, Sept. 52-57; Sec.-Gen. World Fed. of UN Asscns. 58-63, Pres. 63-66, Hon. Pres. 66; Rep. of Netherlands Heart Foundation with WHO; Wateler Peace Prize; Dr. h.c. Univ. of Amsterdam; Knight Order of the Lion (Netherlands); Grand Cordon of the Order of the Senussi (Libya); Hon. Citizen of N.Y.
Leisure interests: reading, walking, fishing, hunting.
Publ. *Libyan Independence and the United Nations* 70.
Le Mestral, 1248 Hermance, Geneva, Switzerland.

Pemán, José María; Spanish author; b. 1897, Cádiz; s. of Juan Pemán and María Pemartín; *m.* María del Carmen Domecq 1922; two *s.* seven *d.*; ed. Coll. San Felipe Neri and Univs. of Seville and Madrid.
Dir. of Real Academia Española 39-42 and 47-50; mem. Acad. Argentina de Letras, Lisbon Acad. of Sciences; Hispanic Soc. of America, Acad. de Cuba, Acad. de Puerto Rico; Dr. h.c. (Univ. of Santo Domingo); Juan March Prize 57; Gran Cruz Orden Alfonso X, Gran Cruz de Carlos III, Gran Cruz Orden del Mérito (Ecuador), Gran Cruz Orden del Sol (Peru), Gran Cruz de Mérito (Peru).
Leisure interests: travel, reading, music, theatre.
Publs. include essays, poems, novels and plays, in particular: *Elegía de la Tradición de España* 31, *El Divino Impaciente* (Real Academia Española Award, 1933) and his essay *Nieve en Cádiz* (Mariano de Cávia Award, 1935), *Edipo, Antigona, Hombre Nuevo.*
Felipe IV, No. 9-3°, Madrid (14); and Plaza de San Antonio, Cádiz, Spain.
Telephone: 222-14-12 (Madrid).

Peñalosa, Enrique; Colombian economist; b. 31 Aug. 1930, Soacha; s. of Vicente Peñalosa and Abby Camargo; *m.* Cecilia Londoño; four *s.* one *d.*
Economic Ed. *Semana* weekly review 52; Asst. in Nat. Planning Office 52-53; IBRD Training Course 54, missions in Colombia 55; private econ. consultant 56-61; mem. Comisión Paritaria Económica 57, City Council,

Bogotá 58-60, Nat. Council for Petroleum Affairs 58, Advisory Cttee. of Colombian Liberal Party 59; First Exec. Dir. Corporación Autónoma Regional de la Sabana de Bogotá 61; First Gen. Man. Colombia Agrarian Reform Inst. 61-68; Minister of Agriculture 68-69; Alt. Exec. Dir. Inter-American Devt. Bank 70-71, Admin. Man. 71-74; Sec.-Gen. UN Conf. on Human Settlements (Habitat) 75-; Fellow, Adlai Stevenson Inst. of Int. Affairs 72-74; Order of Orange (Netherlands); Legion of Agricultural Merit (Peru).
United Nations, New York, N.Y. 10017; 500 East 85th Street, New York, N.Y. 10028, Int. 4, Apt. 604, Bogotá, Colombia. Telephone: (212) 754-1234 (United Nations); 544611 (Bogotá).

Penderecki, Krzysztof; Polish composer and conductor; b. 23 Nov. 1933; ed. Uniwersytet Jagiellonski, Cracow and State Higher Music School, Cracow.
Studied composition first with Skolyszewski, later with Malawski and Wiechowicz, Cracow; graduated from State Higher Music School, Cracow 58; Prof. of Composition, State Higher Music School, Cracow 58-66; Prof. of Composition, Folkwang Hochschule für Musik, Essen 66-72; Musical Adviser Vienna Radio 70-71; Rector, State Higher Music School, Cracow 72-; Prof. of Composition, Univ. of Yale, U.S.A. 73-; Hon. mem. Royal Acad. of Music, London 75, Arts Acad. of German Dem. Repub. 75, Arts Acad. of W. Berlin 75, Royal Acad. of Music, Stockholm 75; Fitelberg Prize for *Threnody for the Victims of Hiroshima* 60, also UNESCO award 61, Polish Ministry of Culture Award 61; Cracow Composition Prize for *Canon* 62; North Rhine-Westphalia Grand Prize for *St. Luke Passion* 66, also Pax Prize (Poland) 66; Jurzykowski Prize, Polish Inst. of Arts and Sciences 66; Gustav Charpentier Prize 71; Dr. h.c. (Univ. of Rochester, U.S.A.) 72.
Works include: *Psalms of David* (for choir and percussion) 58, *Emanations* (for 2 String Orchestras) 58, *Strophes* (for soprano, speaker and ten instruments) 59, *Anaklasis* (for strings and percussion) 60, *Dimensions of time and silence* (for 40-part mixed choir and chamber ensemble) 60, *String Quarter* 60, *Threnody for the Victims of Hiroshima* (for 52 strings) 60, *Polymorphia* (for 48 strings) 61, *Psalms 1961 for Japes* 61, *Fluorescences* (for large orchestra) 62, *Sonata for 'cello and orchestra* 64, *Passio et mors domini nostri Jesu Christi secundum Lucam* (for soprano, baritone, bass, speaker, boys' choir, mixed chorus and large orchestra) 63-65, *Capriccio per oboe e ii archi* 65, *De natura sonoris* (for large orchestra) 66, *Dies irae* (for soprano, tenor, bass, chorus and large orchestra) 67, *Quartetto per archi II* 68, *Die Teufel von Loudon* (opera) 68, *Cosmogony* 70, *Russian Mass Utrenja* 71, *De Natura Sonoris II* (for wind instruments, percussion and strings) 71, *Partita* (for harpsichord, guitars, harp, double bass and chamber orchestra) 72, *First Symphony* 73, *Canticum Canticorum* (S'alomonis for 16 voices and chamber orchestra) 73, *Magnificat* (for bass solo, vocal ensemble, double choir, boys' voices and orchestra) 74, *When Jacob Awoke* (for orchestra) 74.
Państwowa Wyższa Szkota Muzyczna, ul. Bohaterow Stalingradu 3, 31-038 Cracow, Poland.
Telephone: 550-17.

Pendergrass, Eugene Percival, M.D., R.C.A.; American doctor; b. 6 Oct. 1895, Florence, S.C.; s. of Edward J. and Eula Ethel Smith Pendergrass; m. Rebecca Barker 1922; one s. two d.; ed. Wofford Coll., Univs. of N. Carolina and Pennsylvania.
Director Dept. of Radiology, Univ. of Pa. Hospital 39-61; Dir. Dept. of Radiology Jeanes Hosp., Philadelphia 48-61; Pres. Medical Staff, Univ. of Pa. Hospital 49-53; Prof. of Radiology, School of Medicine and Graduate School of Medicine Univ. of Pa. 36-61, Emeritus Prof. of Radiology 61-; Dir. Bicentennial Observance School

of Medicine 62-65, Wilson Prof. of Research Radiology 64-66; mem. Nat. Research Council (Cttee. on Radiology), Amer. Coll. of Radiology and Pres. 48-49; mem., Sec. 32-37, Amer. Roentgen Ray Soc., Radiological Soc. of N. America; Chair. of Board of Dirs. 52 and Pres. 54; Sec.-Gen. Fifth Inter-American Congress on Radiology 55; mem. Operation Crossroads (Bikini) 46; Consultant to Atomic Bomb Casualty Comm. 48-49, 68-; Chair. Cttee. on Cancer Control, Nat. Cancer Inst. 60; mem. Board Scientific Counsellors, Nat. Cancer Inst. 57-59, Pneumoconiosis Comm. 59-; mem. Pneumoconiosis Panel U.S. Public Health Service, Council on Health Manpower A.M.A., Govs. Conf. on Pneumoconiosis—State of Pa., Secretary's Coal Mine Health Research Advisory Council, U.S. Public Health Service 70-; del. Section in Radiology A.M.A. 57-65, Diagnostic Research Panel N.C.I. 61-62; mem. Special Medical Advisory Group, Veterans' Admin. 57-62; Pres. American Cancer Soc. 58-59, mem. of Board 60-65; Pres. Eastern Radiological Soc. 73-74; Pres. Board of Trustees Picker Foundation; Trustee Presbyterian Hospital, American Oncologic Hospital, Philadelphia; Hon. Life mem. Radiological Soc. of S. Africa 75; Gold Medal American Medical Assen. 29, award American Roentgen Ray Soc. 44, Radiological Soc. of N. America 46, 57, and of American Coll. of Radiology 56, Univ. of North Carolina Distinguished Service Award 58, Strittmatter Award, Philadelphia County Medical Soc. 65; American Cancer Soc. Annual Nat. Award 66, Pennsylvania Medical Soc. Distinguished Service Award 70; Golden Plate Award, American Acad. of Achievement 71; Hon. Dr. Sc. (Woffard Coll.) 59; Hon. D.Sc. (Hahnemann Medical Coll.) 64; Hon. LL.D. (Geneva Coll., Pa.) 70.
Leisure interests: golf, bridge, fishing.
Publs. *The Head and Neck in Roentgen Diagnosis* (with Schaeffer and Hodes) 40, *The Pneumoconiosis Problem* 58, and many medical publications.
Hospital of the University of Pennsylvania, Department of Radiology, 3400 Spruce Street, Philadelphia, Pa. 19104; and 428 Owen Road, Wynnewood, Pa. 19096, U.S.A.
Telephone: (215) 642-2760 (Home); (215) 662-3035 (Office).

Penfield, Wilder Graves, C.C., O.M., C.M.G., M.D., B.LITT., M.A., D.SC., F.R.S. (LOND.), F.R.S. (CAN.), F.R.C.S., F.R.C.P., F.R.S.M., F.R.C.S.C.; Canadian (naturalized 1934) neurosurgeon and writer; b. 26 Jan. 1891, Spokane, Wash., U.S.A.; s. of Dr. Charles Samuel Penfield and Jean Jefferson; m. Helen Katherine Kermott 1917; two s. two d.; ed. Princeton, Johns Hopkins and Oxford Univs.
Dresser, Red Cross Hospital, Paris 17; Assoc. Prof. of Surgery, Columbia Univ., New York 21-28; Asst. Surgeon, Presbyterian Hospital and New York Neurological Inst. 21-28; founded laboratory of Neuro-Cytology 24; Neuro-Surgeon, Royal Victoria and Montreal Gen. Hospitals 28-60; fmr. Chair. Neurology and Neuro-Surgery Dept., McGill Univ.; Dir. Montreal Neurological Inst. 34-60, Hon. Consultant 60-; Pres. American Neurological Assen. 51; mem. American Philosophical Soc., Polish Acad. of Sciences and Letters, Acad. Nat. de Médecine, France, Deutsche Gesellschaft für Neurologie, Nat. Acad. of Sciences, U.S.A., Acad. of Sciences, U.S.S.R., Polish Acad. of Sciences, Chinese Medical Assen., American Acad. Arts and Sciences, etc.; U.S. Medal of Freedom; Chevalier Légion d'Honneur; many hon. degrees; Médaille Lannelongue 58; Lister Medal 61; The Royal Bank Centennial Award 67; Gold Medal of Royal Soc. of Medicine 68.
Leisure interests: gardening, sailing, skiing.
Publs. *Cytology and Cellular Pathology of the Nervous System* (Editor) 32, *Epilepsy and Cerebral Localization* 41, *Manual of Military Neurosurgery* 41, *Epilepsy and*

the Cerebral Cortex of Man 50, *Epileptic Seizure Patterns* 52, *Epilepsy and the Functional Anatomy of the Human Brain* 54, *No Other Gods* 54, *The Excitable Cortex in Conscious Man* 58, *Speech and Brain Mechanisms* 59, *The Torch* 60, *Second Career* 63, *The Difficult Art of Giving, The Epic of Alan Gregg* 67, *Man and his Family* 67, *Second Thoughts* 70.
Montreal Neurological Institute, 3801 University Street, Montreal H3A 2B4; and Gleneagles Apt. C-33, 3940 Cote des Neiges, Montreal H3H 1W2, Canada.
[*Died 5 April* 1976.]

P'eng Ch'ung; Chinese party official; b. Fukien.
Mayor, Nanking 55-59; Deputy Sec. CCP Kiangsu 60-65, Sec. 65-68; Vice-Chair. Kiangsu Provincial Revolutionary Cttee. 68; Alt. mem. 9th Cen. Cttee. of CCP 69; Deputy Sec. CCP Kiangsu 71; Alt. mem. 10th Cen. Cttee. of CCP 73; First Sec. CCP Kiangsu 74.
People's Republic of China.

Peng Shao-hui; Chinese army officer; b. 1910, Hunan.
Company Commdr. Red Army 28, Div. Commdr. 33, Brigade Commdr. 38; Chief of Staff 1st Field Army 52; Deputy Commdr. N.W. Mil. Region, People's Liberation Army 54; Deputy Chief of Staff PLA 55-; Gen. 55; Deputy Dir., Gen. Training Dept., PLA 56; mem. 9th Cen. Cttee. of CCP 69, 10th Cen. Cttee 73.
People's Republic of China.

Penjor, Sangye; Bhutan diplomatist; b. 13 Feb. 1928, Bamthang; *m.*; two *s.* two *d.*; ed. local school.
Entered govt. service 45; Officer-in-charge of Royal Household of Tashichholing; Chief District Officer, Bamthang District, Deputy Chief Sec. 60; Minister for Communications 70-, also Perm. Rep. to UN 71-75.
Ministry of Communications, Thimphu, Bhutan.

Penn, Arthur; American theatre and film director; b. 27 Sept. 1922, Philadelphia.
Joined Army theatre company during World War II; worked in television 51-53; produced plays for Broadway theatre including *The Miracle Worker, All the Way Home, Toys in the Attic, Two for the Seesaw, In the Counting House, Wait Until Dark*; has since concentrated on film direction.
Films: *The Left-Handed Gun* 57, *The Miracle Worker* 62, *Mickey One* 64, *The Chase* 65, *Bonnie and Clyde* 67, *Alice's Restaurant* 69, *Little Big Man* 71, *Night Moves* 75; Co-Dir. *Visions of Eight* 73.
1860 Broadway, New York, N.Y. 10023, U.S.A.

Penn-Nouth, Samdech; Cambodian politician; b. 1906; ed. Cambodian School of Administration.
Ministry of Colonies, Paris 38; Assistant to Minister of Palace 40; Acting Minister of Finance 45; Gov. of Pnom-Penh 46-48; Minister of State 46; Minister of State without Portfolio 47; Prime Minister Sept. 48-Jan. 49, 52-55, 58; Amb. to France 58-60; Prime Minister, Minister of the Interior and Minister of Religious Affairs Jan.-Nov. 61; Prime Minister and Minister of Religious Affairs 61-62; Adviser to the Govt. 67; Prime Minister 68-69; Prime Minister of Royal Govt. of Nat. Union of Cambodia (GRUNC) 70-76 (in Phnom-Penh 75-76); numerous decorations.
c/o Office of the Prime Minister, Phnom-Penh, Cambodia.

Pennell, M. M. (Monty), C.B.E.; British oil executive; b. 1916, Devon; *m.*; one *s.* two *d.*; ed. King George V School, Southport and Liverpool Univ.
Joined British Petroleum Co., Ltd. 46 and held posts in Iran, Sicily, E. Africa, North America and Libya; Gen. Man. Exploration Dept., BP, London 66-67; Man. Dir. BP Exploration Co. 67-71; Chair. and Dir. (Technical) Exec. Cttee., BP Trading Ltd. 71; Man. Dir. British Petroleum Co. Ltd. 72-, Deputy Chair. Nov. 75-.
British Petroleum Co. Ltd., Britannic House, Moor Lane, London, EC2Y 9BU, England.

Penney, Baron (Life Peer), cr. 67, of East Hendred; **William George Penney,** O.M., K.B.E., M.A., PH.D., D.SC., F.R.S.; British scientist; b. 24 June 1909, Gibraltar; *s.* of W. A. Penney; *m.* 1st Adele Minnie Elms (deceased), 2nd Eleanor Joan Quenell; two *s.*; ed. Sheerness Technical School and Royal Coll. of Science, London Univ.
Commonwealth Fund Fellow, Univ. of Wis., U.S.A.; Senior Student of 1851 Exhibition, Trinity Coll., Cambridge 33-36; Asst. Prof. Mathematics, Imperial Coll., London Univ. 36-45; Principal Scientific Officer, Dept. Scientific and Industrial Research 44-45; Chief Supt. Armaments Research, Ministry of Supply 46-52; Dir. Atomic Weapons Research Establishment, Aldermaston 53-58; mem. for Weapons Research and Devt., U.K. Atomic Energy Authority 54-59, for Research 59-61, Dep. Chair. 61-64, Chair. 64-67; Rector Imperial Coll. of Science and Technology 67-72; Dir. Tube Investments 68-; mem. Nuclear Power Advisory Board 73-; Treas. Royal Soc. 56-60; Rumford Medal, Royal Soc. 66; Glazebrook Medal and Prize 69; Kelvin Gold Medal 71; Foreign Assoc. Nat. Acad. of Sciences U.S.A. 62; Hon. D.Sc. (Univs. of Oxford and Durham and Bath Univ. of Technology); Hon. LL.D. (Univ. of Melbourne).
Orchard House, East Hendred, Wantage, Oxon., OX12 8JT, England.

Pennigerová, Soňa, M.D.; Czechoslovak politician; b. 26 Oct. 1928, Prague; ed. Faculty of Medicine, Charles Univ, Prague.
Pediatrician, Faculty of Medicine, Charles Univ. 53-; mem. Central Cttee., C.P. of Czechoslovakia 69-, Presidium Prague City Cttee. 69-; Deputy to Nat. Assembly 64-69; Deputy to House of the People 69-; First Deputy Chair. Fed. Assembly and Chair. House of People 69-72; mem. Presidium of Fed. Assembly 69-; mem. Presidium Czechoslovak Group of Inter-Parliamentary Union 69-; Head of 3rd Children's Faculty Hosp. of Charles Univ. 72-; Award for Merit in Construction 71.
Federal Assembly, Prague, Czechoslovakia.

Pennock, Raymond William, M.A. (OXON.); British business executive; b. 16 June 1920, Redcar, Yorks.; *s.* of Frederick Henry and Harriet Anne Pennock (née Mathieson); *m.* Lorna Pearse 1944; one *s.* two *d.*; ed. Coatham School, Redcar, Yorks., and Merton Coll., Oxford.
Captain, Royal Artillery 41-46; with Imperial Chemical Industries Ltd. 47-; Dir. ICI Ltd. 72, Imperial Metal Industries Ltd. 72-75, ICI Australia Ltd. 72-, Imperial Chemicals Insurance Ltd. 73-; Deputy Chair. ICI Ltd. Feb. 75-.
Leisure interests: opera, ballet, music, tennis.
Imperial Chemical Industries Ltd., Imperial Chemical House, Millbank, London, SW1P 3JF, England.
Telephone: 01-834-4444.

Penrose, Sir Roland Algernon, C.B.E.; British artist and art critic; b. 14 Oct. 1900, London; *s.* of James Doyle Penrose and the Hon. Elizabeth Josephine Peckover; *m.* 1st Valentine Andrée Boué 1925; 2nd Lee Miller 1947; one *s.*; ed. Leighton Park School, Reading and Queens' Coll., Cambridge.
Studied and painted in France 22-34; with Surrealist Group 35-39; army 40-45; Founder, Inst. of Contemporary Arts (I.C.A.), Chair. 47-, Pres. 69-; Fine Arts Officer, British Council, Paris 56-59, mem. Fine Arts Panel 55-; mem. Arts Council 57-67; Trustee, Tate Gallery 59-66.
Leisure interest: gardening.
Publs. *The Road is Wider than Long* 39, *In the Service of the People* 45, *Picasso, His Life and Work* 58 (revised 71), *Portrait of Picasso* 58 (revised 71), *Miró, Creation in Space* 66, *The Sculpture of Picasso* 67, *The Eye of Picasso* 67, *Miró, His Life and Work* 70, *Man Ray* 75.
Farley Farm, Chiddingly, nr. Lewes, Sussex, England.
Telephone: Chiddingly 308.

Peoples, David Stuart, C.P.A.; American business executive; b. 6 June 1916, Morristown, Tenn.; s. of late J. Hansel and Mary L. (Stuart) Peoples; m. T. Kathleen Cook 1945; one s. one d.; ed. Tennessee High School, Bristol, and King Coll., Bristol.
With Ernst and Ernst 38-47; served U.S. Army 41-45; Accountant, R. J. Reynolds Tobacco Co. 47, Asst. Comptroller 53-59, Comptroller 59-66, Dir. 59-, Vice-Pres. 64-66, Exec. Vice-Pres. 66-70; Pres., Chief Admin. Officer, R. J. Reynolds Industries, Inc. 70-72, Dir. 70, Vice-Chair. 72-, Chair. of Exec. Cttee. 73-.
R. J. Reynolds Industries, Inc., Corner Fourth and Main Streets, Winston-Salem, N.C. 27102; Home: 2700 Bartram Road, Winston-Salem, N.C. 27106, U.S.A.
Telephone: 919-748-2526 (Office); 919-725-0838 (Home).

Pépin, Eugène, L. ès L., D. EN D.; French professor of law; b. 27 June 1887, Chinon; s. of Edmond Pépin and Eugénie Merlet; m. Germaine Megemont 1937; two s.; ed. Collège, Chinon, Ecole des Hautes Etudes Commerciales, Ecole des Chartes, Faculté de Droit, Paris and Faculté des Lettres, Sorbonne.
Legal Adviser, French Foreign Ministry 18-35, Int. Comm. of Air Navigation 21-44; Dir. Legal Dept. Int. Civil Aviation Org., Montreal 44-53; Dir. Inst. of Air and Space Law, McGill Univ., Montreal 54-59; Prof. of Air and Space Law, Inst. of Contemporary Int. Relations 59-; Pres. Int. Inst. of Space Law 64-; Pres. Société Archéologique Touraine; Légion d'Honneur, Croix de Guerre 1914-18; various foreign orders.
Leisure interests: skiing, music and gardening.
Publs. *Histoire de la Touraine* 37, *Droit aérien* 47, *Géographie de la Circulation Aérienne* 56, *Droit spatial* 61, *Télécommunications* 66, *La Loire au fil de ses Châteaux* 70.
51, rue Lévis, Paris 17e, France.
Telephone: WAG 06-56.

Pepin, Hon. Jean-Luc, P.C., B.A., L.PH., LL.L.; Canadian politician; b. 1 Nov. 1924; ed. Univ. of Ottawa and Institut d'Etudes politiques, Paris.
Professor, Univ. of Ottawa 51-56, 58-63; Rep., Nat Film Board, London (U.K.) 56-58; mem. Parl. 63-72; Parl. Sec. to Minister of Trade and Commerce 63; Minister without Portfolio 65; Minister of Mines and Technical Surveys (later Minister of Energy, Mines and Resources) 65-68, of Industry, Trade and Commerce 68-72; Pres. Interimco Ltd.
Interimco Ltd., 100 Bronson Avenue, Ottawa; Home: 16 Rothwell Drive, Ottawa, Ontario, Canada.
Telephone: (613) 238-1561 (Office); (613) 746-0845 (Home).

Pepler, Louis Andreas; South African administrator; b. 16 Aug. 1908, Bloemfontein; s. of H. L. Pepler and M. E. Fourie; m. M. van der Walt; one s. one d.
Civil Service 31-; Dept. of Native Affairs 49-; Dir., Bantu Agriculture 56; Dir. Bantu Devt. 61-66, Bantu and Physical Devt. of Bantu Homelands 66-71; Sr. Deputy Sec. Planning of Bantu Homelands 71-73.
Leisure interests: carpentry and bowls.
William Street 466, Brooklyn, Pretoria, South Africa.
Telephone: 785100 (Home).

Pepper, Claude Denson; American politician; b. 8 Sept. 1900, Dudleyville, Ala.; s. of J. W. and Lena Pepper; m. Mildred Webster 1936; ed. Univ. of Alabama and Harvard Univ. Law School.
Instructor in Law, Univ. of Ark. 24-25; private legal practice 25-36; mem. U.S. Senate 36-51, House of Reps. 62, 64, 66, 68, 70, 72, 74; Chair. Florida Del., Dem. Nat. Convention 40-44, alt. del. 48, 52, 56, 60, 64, del. 68; Dir. Wash. Fed. Savings & Loan Asscn., Miami; U.S. del. to various int. confs.; mem. House Rules Cttee., House Internal Security Cttee.

Leisure interests: golf, boating.
U.S. House of Representatives, Washington D.C.; 2121 North Bayshore Drive, Miami, Fla., U.S.A.

Pepping, Ernst; German composer; b. 12 Sept. 1901, Duisburg; s. of Ernst Pepping and Emma Flübers; m. Marianne Scheinpflüg 1937; ed. Hochschule für Musik, Berlin.
Teacher at Berlin Kirchenmusikschule 34; Prof. Berlin Musikhochschule 53-67; mem. Akad. der Künste, Berlin and Munich; numerous prizes include Mendelssohn Prize 26, Düsseldorf Robert Schumann Prize 55, Bremen Philharmonische Gesellschaft 62; hon. Dr. Phil. Berlin Free Univ.; hon. Dr. Theol. Berlin Kirchliche Hochschule.
Compositions include three symphonies, piano concerto, *Te Deum*, string quartet, four piano sonatas, organ concertos and partitas, *Passionsbericht des Matthäus, Deutsche Messe, Missa Dona nobis pacem* and other church music.
Publ. *Der Polyphone Satz.*
Johannesstift, Berlin-Spandau, Germany.
Telephone: 335-1274.

Peralta Azurdia, Col. Enrique; Guatemalan army officer and politician; b. 11 June 1908; ed. Polytechnic School, Guatemala City.
Guatemalan army 26, rose from Lieut. to Col.; fmr. Dir. Polytechnic School; Mil. Attaché, Mexico, Chile, Costa Rica, El Salvador and U.S.A., fmr. Ambassador to Cuba, El Salvador and Costa Rica; Dir.-Gen. Agrarian Affairs 58-59, Minister of Agriculture 59-60, of Defence 61-63, Chief of State and Minister of Defence 63-July 66.
Guatemala City, Guatemala.

Percy, Charles Harting; American business executive and politician; b. 27 Sept. 1919; ed. Univ. of Chicago.
Sales trainee, apprentice, Bell & Howell 38, Man., War Co-ordinating Dept. 41-43, Asst. Sec. 43-46, Corpn. Sec. 48-49, Pres. 49-61, Chief Exec. Officer 61-63, Chair. Board 61-66; Senator from Illinois 67-; U.S. Naval Officer 43-45; Republican.
Senate Office Building, Washington, D.C. 20510, U.S.A.

Perdigão, José de Azeredo, LL.D.; Portuguese lawyer and foundation official; b. 19 Sept. 1896, Viseu; s. of José Perdigão and Rachel Azeredo Perdigão; m. Dr. Maria Madalena Biscaia de Azeredo Perdigão 1960; two s. one d.; ed. Lisbon and Coimbra Univ.
Lawyer, Lisbon 19-26; Keeper of Registered Buildings Dept., Lisbon 26-58; Chair. Bd. of Administrators Calouste Gulbenkian Foundation 56-; fmr. Pres. Conf. of Inst. of Portuguese Lawyers; fmr. Dir. Nat. Overseas Bank; six hon. doctorates in Law, Science, Arts and Letters and other decorations; Hon. mem. Brazilian Acad. Fine Arts; corresp. mem. Acad. des Beaux Arts, Inst. de France 69 and other decorations.
Leisure interests: cultural and artistic.
Rua Marques de Fronteira, 8, 2°Dto., Lisbon, Portugal

Pereira, Aristides Maria; Cape Verde politician; b. 17 Nov. 1924, Boa Vista; one s. two d.; ed. Lycée du Cap-Vert.
Began career as radio-telegraphist; Head, Telecommunications Services, Bissau, Portuguese Guinea (now Guinea-Bissau); founded Partido Africano da Independência da Guiné e Cabo Verde (PAIGC) with the late Amílcar Cabral 56; mem. Political Bureau, Cen. Cttee., PAIGC 56-70; fled to Repub. of Guinea 60; Asst. Sec.-Gen. PAIGC 64-73, Sec.-Gen. July 73-; mem. PAIGC Council of War 65-, Perm. Comm. of Exec. Cttee. for Struggle in charge of Security, Control and Foreign Affairs 70-; Pres. Repub. of Cape Verde July 75-.
Presidência da República, Cidade de Praia, São Tiago, Cape Verde.
Telephone: 260.

Pereira, Helio Gelli, F.R.S., M.D.; British scientist; b. 23 Sept. 1918, Petropolis, Rio de Janeiro, Brazil; *s.* of R. and M. G. Pereira; *m.* Margurette Scott 1946; one *s.* two *d.*; ed. British American School, Rio de Janeiro and Faculdade Fluminense de Medicina, Niteroi and Instituto Oswaldo Cruz, Rio de Janeiro.
Assistant lecturer in microbiology Faculdade Fluminense de Medicina 42-45; British Council Scholarship, Univ. of Manchester and Nat. Inst. for Medical Research, London, 45-47; worked on rickettsial diseases and on quantitative aspects of serological reactions, Instituto Oswaldo Cruz 47-52; with Medical Research Council Common Cold Unit, Salisbury (U.K.) 52-57; with Nat. Inst. for Medical Research 57-73, Dir. World Influenza Centre 61-69, Head, Div. of Virology 64-73; Head, Div. Epidemiology, Animal Virus Research Inst. 73-.
Leisure interest: music.
Publ. *Viruses of Vertebrates* (3rd edn.) 72.
Office: Department of Epidemiology, Animal Virus Research Institute, Pirbright, Surrey; Home: 96 Millway, Mill Hill, London, N.W.7, England.
Telephone: 048-631-2441 (Office); 01-959-4112 (Home).

Pereira, Herbert Charles, PH.D., D.SC., F.R.S.; British agricultural physicist; b. 12 May 1913, London; *s.* of Mr. and Mrs. H. J. Pereira; *m.* Irene Beatrice Sloan 1941; three *s.* one *d.*; ed. Prince Albert Coll., Saskatchewan, Canada, St. Alban's School, Herts., England, London Univ. and Rothamsted Experimental Station, Herts.
War service with Royal Engineers in Western Desert, Italy and Germany; Soil Scientist Coffee Research Team Kenya 46-52; Head of Physics Div., East African Agricultural and Forestry Research Org. 52-55, Deputy Dir. 55-61; Dir. Agricultural Research Council of Cen. Africa 61-67; Consultant in Land Use Hydrology (I.H.D. Programme) Food and Agricultural Org. 68-69; Dir. East Malling Research Station, Kent, England July 69-72; Chief Scientist, Ministry of Agric., Fisheries and Food 72-; Haile Sellassie Prize for Research in Africa 66.
Publs. *Land Use and Water Resources* 73, 40 scientific papers on tillage and weed competition, soil fertility and water relations catchment area research, tropical soil structure, etc.
Great East, East Malling Research Station, Maidstone, Kent, England.
Telephone: West Malling 840195.

Pereira, Vasco Futscher; Portuguese diplomatist; b. 3 Feb. 1922, Lisbon; *s.* of Rudolf and Maria Rosa Futscher Pereira; *m.* Margarida Belmarço de Carvalho 1946; one *s.* two *d.*
Attaché, Ministry of Foreign Affairs 48; held successive diplomatic posts in Rabat, Leopoldville (now Kinshasa); Consul-Gen., San Francisco 56; Counsellor, Karachi 62; Minister, Madrid 67; Amb. to Malawi 69, to Fed. Repub. of Germany 73-75.
Leisure interests: bridge, golf.
c/o Ministry of Foreign Affairs, Lisbon, Portugal.

Pereira, William Leonard; American architect and planner; b. 25 April 1909; ed. Univ. of Illinois School of Architecture.
Associate Holabird & Root, architects, Chicago 30-32; private architectural practice, Chicago 32-38, Los Angeles 38-50; partnership, Pereira & Luckman, architects and engineers 50-58; Principal, William L. Pereira and Assocs. 58-; mem. Nat. Council on the Arts; Fellow American Inst. of Architects; numerous awards.
Principal works: design of Los Angeles County Museum of Art, Occidental Center, CBS Television City, Marineland of Pacific, Los Angeles Int. Airport (in association), research and development centres for Lockheed, Hoffman, Gen. Telephone, Astropower; campus buildings for Univ. of Calif., Los Angeles, Brigham Young Univ. and Univ. of Southern Calif.; master plans for

93,000 acre Irvine Ranch, Santa Catalina Island, 10,700 acre Mountain Park, Univ. of Calif., Irvine, Univ. of S. Calif., Occidental Coll., Hawaii Loa Coll. and Central Univ. Library, Univ. of Calif. (San Diego); new town Ivory Coast, Africa; urban centre Taipei, Taiwan; 33 block Houston Centre; new town Dearborn, Michigan; Comprehensive Development Planning Study Burlington Northern Territories; developed National Aviation Concept Plan for Fed. Aviation Admin.; campus master plan for Univ. of Missouri; Pepperdine campus Malibu; designed Mutual Benefit Life Plaza, Great Western Financial H.Q.; Transamerica World H.Q.
William L. Pereira and Associates, 5657 Wilshire Boulevard, Los Angeles, Calif. 90036, U.S.A.

Pereira dos Santos, Gen. Adalberto; Brazilian army officer; b. 11 April 1905, Taquara, Rio Grande do Sul; *s.* of Urbano Alves dos Santos and Otília Pereira dos Santos; *m.* Julieta Campos Pereira dos Santos (deceased); ed. Colégio Militar de Pôrto Alegre, Escola Militar do Realengo.
Rank of Brig.-Gen. 58, Div. Gen. 63, Gen. 65; Adjutant, Mil. Gov. of São Paulo; Officer 1st Armoured Div., U.S. Army during Italian campaign 45; Chief of Staff, Armoured Div.; Commdr. School of War Equipment; 2nd Army Sub-Chief of Staff; Army Chief of Staff; Amb., Special Mission to Chile 64; Amb., Head of Special Mission to Paraguay 68; Pres. Eighth Conf. of American Armies 68; Minister of High Mil. Tribunal, then Pres.; Vice-Pres. of Brazil 74-; numerous decorations.
Leisure interests: fencing, horse-riding.
Office of the Vice-President of Brazil, Brasília, D.F., Brazil.

Pereira Lira, Paulo H.; Brazilian economist; b. 30 Jan. 1930 Rio de Janeiro; *s.* of José Pereira Lira and Beatriz de Almeida Pereira Lira; *m.* Laís Myriam Pereira Lira 1953; one *s.* one *d.*; ed. Univ. of Brazil, Rio de Janeiro, Harvard Univ.
Professor of Micro-economics, Nat. Faculty of Econs., Univ. of Brazil 55-64; Prof. of Monetary Theory, Nat. Council of Econs. 58-61; Prof. of Advanced Courses, Getúlio Vargas Foundation 61; Pres. of Cen. Bank of Brazil March 74-; mem. Monetary Council; mem. Technical Council of Inst. of Econ. and Applied Social Research; mem. Nat. Foreign Trade Council; Alt. Gov. Int. Monetary Fund, African Devt. Fund; Commdr. Order of Rio Branco; Order of Merit Tamandaré; Order of Merit Mauá.
Leisure interest: golf.
Edifício Sede do Banco do Brasil, 6°, 70.000 Brasília, D.F., Brazil.
Telephone: (0612) 24-1503, 24-7753.

Perek, Luboš, DR.RER.NAT.; Czechoslovak astronomer; b. 26 July 1919, Prague; *m.* Vlasta Straková 1945; ed. Masaryk Univ., Brno, and Charles Univ., Prague.
Assistant, Astronomical Inst., Masaryk Univ., Brno 46, Head 53; Head, Stellar Dept., Astronomical Inst. of Czechoslovak Acad. of Sciences, Prague 56, Dir. Astronomical Inst. 68-; Vice-Pres. Comm. of the Galactic Structure and Dynamics, Int. Astronomical Union 61-64, Asst. Gen. Sec., Int. Astronomical Union 64-67, Gen. Sec. 67-70; Visiting Prof., Dearborn Observatory, Evanston, Ill. 64; Corresp. mem. Czechoslovak Acad. of Sciences 65-; mem. Czechoslovak Astronomical Soc., Astronomische Gesellschaft, Astronomical Soc. of the Pacific, Exec. Cttee. Int. Council of Scientific Unions 67-70, Vice-Pres. 68-70; silver plaque for services to Science 69.
Publs. include *Catalogue of Galactic Planetary Nebulae* (with L. Kohoutek) 67.
Astronomical Institute of Czechoslovak Academy of Sciences, Budečská 6, Prague 2, Czechoslovakia.
Telephone: 258757.

Perelman, Sidney Joseph; American writer; b. 1 Feb 1904; ed. Brown Univ.

Film script writer; articles for *New Yorker* 31-; collaborated with Marx Brothers on film scripts of *Monkey Business* 31, *Horsefeathers* 32; Best Screen Writer Award 56; mem. Screen Writers' Guild, Dramatists' Guild.
Publs. *Dawn Ginsbergh's Revenge* 29, *Parlor, Bedlam and Bath* 30, *Strictly from Hunger* 37, *Look Who's Talking* 40, *The Dream Department* 43, *Crazy Like a Fox* 44, *Keep it Crisp* 46, *Westward Ha!* 48, *Chicken Inspector No. 23* 67, *Baby, It's Cold Inside* 70; Plays: *All Good Americans* 34, *The Night Before Christmas* 41 (both with Laura Perelman), *One Touch of Venus* 43 (with Ogden Nash), *The Beauty Part* 63.
Erwinna, Bucks County, Pa., U.S.A.

Perera, Liyanagé Henry Horace, B.A.; Ceylonese international official; b. 9 May 1915, Yatiyantota, Ceylon; *s.* of L. H. Perera and Maud Mildred Sirimane; *m.* Sita Trixie Senarat 1942; one *s.* three *d.*; ed. St. Benedict's Coll., Colombo, Univ. Coll. London, Univ. of Ceylon.
Senior Master in Govt. and History, Ceylon 36-59; Asst. Registrar, Aquinas Univ. Coll., Colombo 60-61; Educ. Dir. World Fed. of UN Asscns. 61-63, Deputy Sec.-Gen. and Educ. Dir. 63-66, Sec.-Gen. 66-68, 68-73, 73-76; mem. Int. Cttee. Adult Educ. (UNESCO) 63; Pres. non-Governmental organizations in Consultative status with UN Econ. and Social Council 69-72; William Russel Award 74, Int. Asscn. of Educators for World Peace Award.
Leisure interests: swimming, tennis, photography, stamp collecting and reading.
Publs. *Ceylon and Indian History, Groundwork of Ceylon and World History, Ceylon Under Western Rule.*
World Federation of United Nations Associations, 3 rue de Varembé, P.O. Box 54, 1211-Geneva 20; Home: 22 avenue Luserna, 1203 Geneva, Switzerland.
Telephone: 34-49-60 (Office); 34-07-37 (Home).

Perera, Nanayakkarapathirage Martin, PH.D.; Ceylonese politician; b. 6 June 1905; ed. Ceylon Univ. Coll., and London School of Economics.
Lecturer, Ceylon Univ. 35-36, 45-46; Founder-mem. Lanka Sama Samaj Party 35, now Pres.; mem. Ceylon State Council 36; imprisoned 40-42, 43-45; mem. Ceylon House of Representatives 47-, Leader of the Opposition 47-52, 56-60; Minister of Finance 64-65, 70-75; Mayor of Colombo 55; Pres. Ceylon Fed. of Labour; Hon. D.Sc. (Ceylon).
Leisure interests: economics, foreign affairs, cricket.
106 Cotta Road, Colombo 8, Sri Lanka.

Peres, Shimon; Israeli politician; b. 1923, Poland; *m.* Sonia Gelman; three *c.*; ed. New York Univ., Harvard Univ.
Immigrated to Palestine 34; fmr. Sec. Hano'ar Ha'oved Movt.; mem. Haganah Movt. 47; Head of Israel Naval Service, Ministry of Defence 48; Head of Defence Mission in U.S.A.; Deputy Dir.-Gen. of Ministry of Defence 52-53, Dir.-Gen. 53-59, Deputy Minister of Defence 59-65; mem. Knesset 59-; mem. Mapai Party 59-65, founder mem. and Sec.-Gen. Rafi Party 65; mem. Labour Party after merger 68; Minister for Econ. Devt. in the Administered Areas and for Immigrant Absorption 69-70, of Transport and Communications 70-74, of Information March-June 74, of Defence June 74-.
Publs. *The Next Step* 65, *David's Sling* 70, and numerous political articles in Israeli and foreign publications.
Ministry of Defence, Tel-Aviv; 186 Arlosoroff Street, Tel-Aviv, Israel.

Peressutti, Enrico, DR.ARCH.PROF.; Italian architect; b. 28 Aug. 1908; ed. School of Architecture, Milan.
Architect 32; Visiting Prof. Architectural Association School, London 50-51, M.I.T. Cambridge, Mass. 52, Princeton, N.J. 53, 54-56, 57-59, Yale 57, 62; private

practice with Belgiojoso and Rogers in town planning, architecture, interior decoration and industrial design; works incl. Italian Merchant Navy Pavilion at Int. Exhibition, Paris 37; houses, factories, pavilions, health resort for children, Legnano 39; Post Office, Rome 39; monument in Milan cemetery 46; U.S. Pavilion at Triennale 51; Olivetti showroom, N.Y. 54; Labyrinth for Young People at Triennale 54; restoration and arrangement Castello Sforzesco Museums, Milan 56; Torre Velasca (Milan) 58; Canadian Pavilion (Venice Biennale); Italian Pavilion (Brussels World Exhibition) (in collaboration) 58, Hispano Olivetti Building, Barcelona.
Publs. *Stile* (in collab.) 36, *Piano Regolatore della Val d'Aosta* (in collab.) 43, *Piano A.R.* 45.
Studio Architetti B.B.P.R., Via dei Chiostri 2, Milan, Italy.

Peretti, Achille Antoine, L. en D.; French politician; b. 13 June 1911, Ajaccio, Corsica; *s.* of Pierre Toussaint Peretti and Madeleine Venturini; *m.* Julie Papa 1935; two *d.*; ed. Coll. Fesch d'Ajaccio and Univ. of Montpellier.
Lawyer attached to public prosecutor, Ajaccio 35-38; Commr. of Police, Sûreté Nationale 38-42; Deputy Dir., Sûreté Nationale (Algerian government) 44; Deputy Dir.-Gen. Sûreté Nationale 44; fmr. Prefect; Conseiller Gen. for Corsica 45-51, First Vice-Pres. Conseil Gen. of Corsica 45; Mayor of Neuilly-sur-Seine 47-; Conseiller de l'Union Française 52-58; Deputy for the Seine, Neuilly-Puteaux 58-67; Deputy for Hauts de Seine, Neuilly-Puteaux 67-68; mem. Accounts and Budgets Cttee.; Vice-Pres. of Nat. Assembly 64-69, Pres. 69-73, Deputy 73-; many honours and awards.
Assemblée Nationale, Palais Bourbon, Paris 7e; Home: 96 avenue du Roule, 92 Neuilly-sur-Seine, France.
Telephone: MAI.-92-11 (Home).

Pérez de Cuellar, Javier; Peruvian diplomatist; b. 19 Jan. 1920; *m.*; two *c.*; ed. Catholic Univ., Lima.
Joined Foreign Ministry 40, diplomatic service 44; served as Sec. in embassies in France, U.K., Bolivia, Brazil (later Counsellor); Dir. Legal and Personnel Dept., Ministry of Foreign Affairs 61; Amb. and Dir. of Admin., Protocol and Political Affairs 62; Amb. to Switzerland 64-66; Perm. Under Sec. and Sec.-Gen. Foreign Office 66-69; Amb. to U.S.S.R. (concurrently to Poland) 69-71; Perm. Rep. to UN 71-75; Special Rep. of UN Sec.-Gen. in Cyprus 75-; fmr. Prof. of Diplomatic Law, Academia Diplomatica del Peru and Prof. of Int. Relations, Academia de Guerra Aérea del Peru; del. to UN Gen. Assembly 46-47 and other int. confs.
Publ. *Manuale de Dercho Diplomatico* 64.
Office of the Special Representative, UN Peace-Keeping Force in Cyprus, Nicosia, Cyprus.

Pérez de la Cova, Carlos; Venezuelan diplomatist; b. 27 April 1904, Caracas; *m.* Rosa Ramírez; one *s.* one *d.*; ed. Universidad Central de Venezuela and Univ. of Tulsa, Okla., U.S.A.
Technical petroleum inspector in oil fields in Maracaibo area 30-37; Dir. of Hydrocarbons, Ministry of Devt. 37-39; special mission to U.S.A. to study technical and econ. problems related to the oil industry 39-42; Dir. of Hydrocarbons 42-43; Head, Technical Dept. of Leases and Cartography, Ministry of Devt. and mem. Presidential Comm. to revise Petroleum Law of Venezuela 43-45; Head, Lease and Lands Dept. and mem. Operating Cttee. Phillips Petroleum Co. of Venezuela 45-50; Minister-Counsellor, U.K. 50-52; Minister-Counsellor for Petroleum Affairs, U.S.A. 52-58; Minister of Mines 58; Minister for Econ. Affairs at Venezuelan Embassy, Washington, D.C. 61-70, also Deputy Chief of Mission; alt. Dir. Inter-American Devt. Bank; Amb. to U.K. Dec. 70-; del. to numerous int. confs.

Leisure interests: swimming, reading, music, theatre.
Embassy of Venezuela, Flat 6, 3 Hans Crescent, London,
S.W.1; Residence: Flat 7, 48 Grosvenor Square, London,
W.1, England.
Telephone: 01-584-4206 (Embassy); 01-499-5655 (Home).

Pérez Godoy, Gen. Ricardo Pío; Peruvian army
officer and politician; b. 9 June 1905; ed. Colegio Santo
Tomás de Aquino and Escuela de Oficiales del Ejército.
Director-Gen. of Training, Peruvian Army 56-57;
Controller-Gen. of Army 58-59; Chief of Staff of Joint
Command of Armed Forces 60-62; Prefect of Dept. of
Arequipa 52-53, 55-56; Pres. of Mil. Junta of Govt. of
Peru 62-63; mem. Centro de Altos Estudios Históricos
del Perú; now Gen. of a Division; numerous decorations.
Publs. include *Teoría de la Guerra y Doctrina de Guerra,
La Maniobra y la Batalla.*
Blasco Nuñez de Balboa 225, Miraflores, Lima, Peru.

Pérez-Guerrero, Manuel, LL.D.; Venezuelan politician;
b. 18 Sept. 1911; ed. Univ. of Paris and Ecole des
Sciences Politiques, Paris.
Member, Economics Dept., League of Nations 37-40,
Sec. Import Control Comm., Ministry of Finance,
Venezuela 40-42; mem. Economics and Statistics Sec-
tion, Int. Labor Org. 42-43; Ministry of Foreign
Relations, Venezuela 43-44; Dir. Div. of Coordination
and Liaison, UN 46-47; Minister of Finance, Venezuela
47-48; Exec. Sec. Technical Assistance Board, UN 49-53,
Resident Rep., Technical Assistance Board, Egypt 53-
57, Special Rep., Tunisia and Morocco 57-58; Dir. Non
Self-Governing Territories, UN 58-59; Chief, Office of
Co-ordination and Planning, Venezuela 59-62; mem.
Board of Dirs. Central Bank 59-63; Resident Rep.,
Technical Assistance Board, UN, Algeria 63; Minister
of Mines and Hydrocarbons Dec. 63-67; Perm. Rep. of
Venezuela to UN 67-69; Pres. of UN Econ. and Social
Council 68-69; mem. Board of Trustees of UNITAR 65-;
Sec.-Gen. UN Conf. on Trade and Devt. (UNCTAD)
69-74; Minister of State for Int. Econ. Affairs 74-;
Leader of UN Mission to Aden 67; Co-Pres. Conf. on
Int. Econ. Co-operation, Paris 75-76.
Oficina del Ministro de Estado para Asuntos Econ-
ómicos Internacionales, Palacio de Miraflores, Caracas;
and Edificio Isla Verde, Apto. c-6, Calle Valle Alto,
Colinas de Santa Fé, Venezuela.

Pérez de Bricio Olariaga, Carlos; Spanish industrial
executive and politician; b. 1927, Madrid; ed. Escuela
Técnica de Aduanas.
Several posts in the admin.; Spanish rep. at negotiations
for Brussels Tariff Nomenclature and for accession to
GATT; Asst. Dir.-Gen. Customs; Exec. Pres. Unión de
Empresas y Entidades Siderúrgicas; Vice-Pres. Iron
and Steel Heavy Industries Comm. 68-69; Pres. Iron
and Steel Sub-Cttee., OECD 69; fmr. Dir.-Gen. of
Siderometallurgical and Naval Industries; Minister of
Industry Dec. 75-.
Ministerio de Industria, Madrid, Spain.

Pérez Jiménez, Col. Marcos; Venezuelan officer and
politician; b. 1914; ed. Caracas Mil. School and Lima
War Coll.
Army Chief of Staff in Acción Democrática Govt.; mem.
of subsequent three-man Junta and Minister of Defence;
Pres. of Venezuela Dec. 52-58; extradited from U.S.A.
to Venezuela Aug. 63; imprisoned in Venezuela 63-68;
went to Madrid.

Pérez Rodríguez, Carlos Andrés; Venezuelan politi-
cian; b. 27 Oct. 1922, Rubio; m. Blanca Rodríguez de
Pérez; one s. five d.; ed. Univ. Central de Venezuela.
Private Sec. to Pres. Rómulo Betancourt 45; mem.
Chamber of Deputies 47-48, 58-74; in exile 49-58;
Chief Editor *La República*, San José 53-58; Minister of
the Interior 63-64; Sec.-Gen. Acción Democrática 68;
Pres. of Venezuela March 74-.
Oficina del Presidente, Palacio de Miraflores, Caracas,
Venezuela.

Pérez-Segnini, Ildegar; Venezuelan bank official; b.
17 March 1925, Pampán; s. of Pedro Pablo Perez and
Elena Segnini de Perez; m. Yolanda Rodriguez 1952;
five s.; ed. Escuela de Agricultura, Maracay, and
Inst. Interamericano de Ciencias Agrícolas, Costa Rica.
Joined Venezuelan civil service in Ministry of Agricul-
ture 43; Exec. Dir. Technical Inst. of Immigration and
Colonialisation 48; Senator for Cojedes 58, and Vice-
Pres. Senate Comm. on Agriculture; Pres. Inst. of
Agrarian Reform 59, Senate Comm. of Defense 62; Gov.
State of Aragua 64-68; Exec. Dir. for Chile, Colombia,
Trinidad and Tobago, and Venezuela, of Inter-American
Devt. Bank 69-75; Exec. Dir. for Barbados, Trinidad,
Tobago, and Venezuela 72.
c/o Ministry of Foreign Affairs, Caracas, Venezuela.

Perham, Dame Margery, D.C.M.G., C.B.E., D.LITT.,
F.B.A.; British scholar of colonial affairs; b. 6 Sept.
1895, Bury, Lancs.; d. of Frederick Perham and Marion
Needell; ed. St. Hugh's Coll., Oxford.
Asst. Lecturer in History Sheffield Univ.; in Somaliland
22-23; Fellow and Tutor, St. Hugh's Coll., Oxford 24-29;
Rhodes Travelling Fellowship in N. America, Polynesia,
Australia and Africa 29-31, and in West Africa 31-32;
Research Fellow, St. Hugh's Coll. 31-39; Reader in
Colonial Admin. Oxford Univ. 39-48; Dir. Oxford Univ.
Inst. of Colonial Studies 45-48; Official Fellow Nuffield
Coll., Oxford 39-; Rockefeller Travelling Fellowship of
Int. Inst. of African Languages and Culture in E. Africa
and Sudan 32; Research Lecturer in Colonial Admin.,
Oxford 35-39; mem. Advisory Cttee. on Education in
the Colonies 39-45, of Higher Education Comm. and
West Indies Higher Education Cttee. 44, of Inter-Univ.
Council on Higher Education Overseas 46-67; Reith
Lecturer 61; Pres. Univs. Mission to Central Africa
63-64; Pres. The African Studies Asscn. of Britain 63-64;
Editor *Colonial and Comparative Series* (formerly
Colonial Research Publs.) 41-; Hon. LL.D. (St. Andrews),
Hon. D.Litt. (Southampton, London, Birmingham and
Cambridge); Fellow British Acad. 61; Hon. Fellow,
Nuffield and St. Hugh's Colls., Oxford, and School of
Oriental and African Studies, London; Fellow American
Acad. of Arts and Sciences 69.
Leisure interests: gardening, animal welfare.
Publs. *Major Dane's Garden* 24, 70, *Josie Vine* 26, *The
Protectorates of South Africa* (with Lionel Curtis) 35,
Ten Africans (Ed.) 36, *Native Administration in Nigeria*
37, *Africans and British Rule* 41, *African Discovery*
(with J. Simmons) 43, *Race and Politics in Kenya* (with
E. Huxley) 44, *Studies in Colonial Legislatures* (Ed.)
46-, *The Economics of a Tropical Dependency* (Ed.) 46-
48, *The Government of Ethiopia* 48, 69, *Lugard, The Years
of Adventure* 56, ed. with Mary Bull *The Diaries of Lord
Lugard 1889-1892* 59, *1894-5, 1898* 63, *Lugard, The
Years of Authority* 60, *The Colonial Reckoning* 62,
African Outline 66, *The Colonial Sequence 1930-1949* 67,
Vol. II 70, *African Apprenticeship* 74, *Travels in East
Africa 1930* 75.

Pericot García, Luis, DR.HIST.; Spanish university
professor; b. 5 Sept. 1899; ed. Univs. of Barcelona and
Madrid.
Assistant Faculty of Philosophy and Letters, Univ. of
Barcelona 20, Asst. Prof. 23; Prof. Univ. of Santiago de
Compostela 25, Univ. of Valencia 27; Prof. of Ancient
Spanish History, Univ. of Barcelona 34-55, of Prehistory
55-, Sec. Faculty of Philosophy and Letters 34,
Vice-Dean 51-54; mem. Higher Council of Scientific
Research Regional del. Archaeological Excavations,
Barcelona; Hon. Dir. Prehistoric Research Service,
Province of Valencia; Hon. Fellow Royal Anthropo-
logical Inst. of Great Britain; Corresp. Fellow British
Acad.; Pres. 4th Int. Congress of Prehistoric and Proto-
historic Sciences; Martorell, Duque de Loubat and
Dusseigneur Prizes; Gran Cruz Alfonso X El Sabio;
Stella della Solidarietà Italiana; Chevalier Légion
d'Honneur.

Publs. *La Civilización Megalítica Catalana y la Cultura Pirenaica* 25, *España Primitiva y Romana* 34, 58, *La América Indígena I* 36, 62, *La Cueva del Parpalló* 42, *Arte Rupestre* 50, *La España Primitiva* 50, *Las Raíces de España* 52, *Prehistoria de Marruecos* 53.
Rambla de Cataluña 89-3°-2ª, Barcelona, Spain.
Telephone: 215-1760.

Périer, François (*pseudonym* of François Pillu); French actor; b. 10 Nov. 1919, Paris; *m.* Colette Boutouland 1961; one *s.* one *d.*; ed. Conservatoire Nat. d'Art Dramatique, Paris.
Co-Dir. Théâtre de la Michodière, Paris 51-65; has appeared in numerous plays including *Les Jours Heureux, Les J 3, Les Mains Sales, Bobosse, Le Ciel de Lit, Gog et Magog, La Preuve par Quatre, Le Diable et le Bon Dieu, Ne reveillez pas Madame, Le Tube*; films include: *Premier Bal* 41, *Lettres d'Amour* 42, *Un Revenant, Le Silence est d'Or* 46, *Orphée* 49, *Les Evadés* 54, *Gervaise* 55, *Le Notti di Cabiria* 56, *Bobosse* 58, *Le Testament d'Orphée* 60, *L'Amant de Cinq Jours* 61, *La Vista* 63, *Z* 68, *Le Cercle Rouge* 70, *Max et les Ferrailleurs* 71, *Juste avant la Nuit* 71, *l'Attentat* 72, *Antoine et Sébastien* 73, *Stavisky* 74; British Film Acad. Award 56, Victoire du Cinéma Français 57; Officier, Ordre des Arts et Lettres.
c/o Artmedia, 37 rue Marbeuf, Paris 8e, France.

Perin, François; Belgian politician and professor of law; b. 31 Jan. 1921, Liège; ed. Univ. of Liège.
Member of Socialist Party 43-64; Asst. Chef de Cabinet to Minister of Interior 54-57; Asst. to Prof. of Public Law 54-58; Dir. of Studies, Faculty of Law, Univ. of Liège 58, Prof. of Constitutional Law 67; Deputy to Nat. Assembly 65-; Pres. Rassemblement Wallon 68-74; Minister of Institutional Reforms June 74-.
Publs. *La Démocratie Enrayée—Essai sur le Régime Parlementaire Belge de 1918 à 1958* 60, *La Belgique au Défi: Flamands Wallons à la Recherche d'un Etat* 62, *La Décision Politique en Belgique* (co-author) 65, *Le Régionalisme dans l'Intégration Européenne* 69.
Ministère de la Réforme des Institutions, Brussels, Belgium.

Perinat, Luis Guillermo, Marqués de; Spanish diplomatist; b. 27 Oct. 1923, Madrid; *s.* of Luis Perinat and Ana Maria, Marquesa de Campo Real; *m.* Blanca Escriva de Romani, Marquesa de Alginet; two *s.* one *d.*; ed. Univs. of Salamanca and Valladolid.
Secretary, Embassy in Cairo 49-51; Deputy Consul-Gen., New York 54-56; Counsellor, Paris 62-65; Perm. Sec. Spanish-American Joint Defence Cttee. 65-70; Dir.-Gen. of North American and Far Eastern Affairs in Ministry of Foreign Affairs 73-76; Amb. to U.K. March 76-; Grand Cross, Order of Civil Merit, Knight Commdr., Order of Isabel La Católica, Knight Commdr., Order of Merito Aeronáutico, Commdr. of Order of George I (Greece), Officer, Order of Leopold (Belgium), Knight, Order of the Nile (Egypt).
Spanish Embassy, 24 Belgrave Square, London, SW1X 8QA, England; Home: Calle del Prado 26, Madrid, Spain.
Telephone: 01-235-8363 (Embassy).

Perišin, Ivo, D.ECON.; Yugoslav economist and banker; b. 4 July 1925, Split; *s.* of Dujo and Filomena Tadin Perišin; *m.* Magda Martinič 1949; two *c.*; ed. Zagreb Univ.
Professor of Economics, Zagreb Univ.; Under-Sec., Fed. Secr. for Finance; Gov. Nat. Bank of Yugoslavia (Narodna Banka Jugoslavije) 69-72; Pres. Exec. Council, Socialist Republic of Croatia 72-73, Pres. Parliament 73-; Partisan Memorial Award, Order of People's Merit, Order of the Republic, Medal for Valour.
Publs. *Money and Credit Policy* 64, 68, 72, 75, *Money and Economic Development* 61, *Economics of Yugoslavia, Inflation* 65, *Financial Dictionary* 67, *Money, Credit and Banking* 75, *Transformation of Monetary System* 75.
131 Moše Pijade, Zagreb, Yugoslavia.
Telephone: 443812.

Perkins, James Alfred, A.B., M.A., PH.D.; American educationist; b. 11 Oct. 1911, Philadelphia, Pa.; *s.* of late H. Norman Perkins and Emily (née Taylor); *m.* 1st Jean E. Bredin 1938; two *s.* three *d.*; *m.* 2nd Ruth B. Aall; ed. Swarthmore Coll. and Princeton Univ.
Instructor in political science, Princeton Univ. 37-39, Asst. Dir. School of Public and Int. Affairs 39-41; Dir. Pulp and Paper Div., O.P.A. 41-43; Asst. to Administrator, Foreign Econ. Admin. 43-45; Vice-Pres. Swarthmore Coll. 45-50; Exec. Assoc., Carnegie Corpn. 50-51, Vice-Pres. 51-63; Sec. Carnegie Foundation for Advancement of Teaching 54-55. Vice-Pres. 55-63; Pres. Cornell Univ. 63-69; Deputy Chair. Research and Development Board, Dept. of Defense 51-52; consultant Rand Corpn. 58-62, Trustee 61-; Chair. Board of Trustees United Negro Coll. Fund 65-68; Chair. Pres. Johnson's Gen. Advice Comm. on Foreign Assistance Programme 65-69; mem. various Govt. cttees. including Carnegie Comm.; mem. Board of Dirs. Overseas Devt. Council 69-; founder Centre for Educational Enquiry 69; Chair. Board and Chief Exec. Officer Int. Council for Educ. Devt. 70-; Dir. Centre for Inter-American Relations; Dir. Chase Manhattan Bank, Council on Foreign Relations, Overseas Devt. Council, Acad. for Educational Devt.; Trustee Carnegie Foundation for the Advancement of Teaching etc.; numerous hon. degrees; Gold Medal of Nat. Inst. of Social Sciences 65.
Leisure interests: golf, photography.
Publ. *The University in Transition* 66.
Office: International Council for Educational Development, 680 Fifth Avenue, New York, N.Y. 10019; Home: The North Road, Princeton, N.J. 08540, U.S.A.
Telephone: 212-JU2-3970 (Office).

Perkins, John H.; American banker; b. 28 Aug. 1921, Chicago; *s.* of Harold and Roschen Perkins; *m.* Len Welborn 1944; three *s.*; ed. Northwestern Univ., Graduate School of Banking, Univ. of Wisconsin.
Joined Continental Illinois Nat. Bank 46, Asst. Cashier, Metropolitan Div. 49, Second Vice-Pres. Bond Dept. 52, Vice-Pres. 56, Senior Vice-Pres. 65, Exec. Vice-Pres. and Dir. 68, Vice-Chair. 71, Pres. Continental Illinois Corpn. and Continental Bank March 73-.
Leisure interests: golf, tennis, curling.
Continental Illinois National Bank, 231 South LaSalle Street, Chicago, Ill. 60693; Home: 150 Birch Street, Winnetka, Ill. 66093, U.S.A.
Telephone: (312) 828-7701 (Office).

Perkins, Richard Sturgis; American banker; b. 27 June 1910, Boston, Mass.; *s.* of James H. Perkins and Katrine P. Coolidge; *m.* Adeline Havemeyer 1935; two *s.* two *d.*; ed. Hamilton Tutoring and Berkshire Preparatory Schools.
Thompson Fenn & Co. 29-32; Wood, Struthers & Co. 32-36; Harris, Upham & Co. 36-51; First Nat. City Bank (now First Nat. City Corpn.) 51-, Chair. Exec. Cttee. 59-71; Dir. of various other companies.
Office: Suite 3600, 399 Park Avenue, New York N.Y., 10022, U.S.A.
Telephone: 212-559-8833.

Perkinson, Jesse Dean, B.S., M.S., PH.D.; American science administrator and biochemist; b. 24 Oct. 1914, Etowah, Tenn.; *s.* of Jesse Dean Perkinson Sr. and Clara Bedell Perkinson; *m.* Dorothy Brumby 1943; three *d.*; ed. Univ. of Tennessee and Univ. of Rochester.
Fellow Univ. of Rochester 39-43; U.S. Navy Reserve 44-46; Research Associate, Univ. of Georgia 46-49; Senior Scientist, Oak Ridge Inst. of Nuclear Studies 49-52; Assoc. Prof. of Biochemistry, Univ. of Tenn. 52-57; Chief of Training and Educ. U.S. Atomic Energy Comm. 57-58; Exec. Sec. Inter-American Nuclear

Energy Comm. (IANEC) 58-; Dir. Dept. of Scientific Affairs, Org. of American States 58-73, Special Adviser to Sec.-Gen. 73-; mem. U.S. Dept. of Commerce, Panel on Transfer of Technology; mem. Advisory Board Pan American Devt. Foundation 69-, Population Crisis Comm. 67-; Fellow American Asscn. for the Advancement of Science; mem. American Chemical Soc., Radiation Research Soc.; Fellow Inst. of Chemists; Fellow Royal Soc. of Arts.
Special Adviser to the Secretary-General, Organization of American States, Washington, D.C. 20006; 4622 Morgan Drive, Chevy Chase, Maryland 20015, U.S.A.
Telephone: 381-8885 (Office).

Perlis, H.R.H. The Raja of; Tuanku Syed Putra ibni al-Marhum Syed Hassan Jamalullail, D.K., S.P.M.P., D.K.(M.)., D.M.N., S.M.N., D.K.(SEL), S.P.D.K., K.C.M.G.; Malaysian ruler; b. 16 Oct. 1920, Arau, Perlis; *s.* of Syed Hassan Bin Syed Mahmud Jamalullail and Cik Wan Teh Binti Edut; *m.* H.R.H. Tengku Budriah Binti al-Marhum Tengku Ismail, D.K.,D. M.N., S.M.N. 1940; eight *s.* six *d.*
Appointed Bakal Raja (Heir-Presumptive) of Perlis April 38; attached to Courts in Kangar 40; worked for a year in the Land Office, Kuala Lumpur, and for a year in the Magistrates' Court, Kuala Lumpur; in private business during Japanese occupation; Timbalan Yang di-Pertuan Agung (Deputy Paramount Ruler) of Malaya April-Sept 60, Yang di-Pertuan Agung (H.M. the Paramount Ruler) Sept. 60-Sept. 63, of Malaysia Sept. 63-65.
Leisure interests: golf, tennis, fishing and shooting.
Istana Arau, Perlis; and Istana Kenangan Indah, Perlis, Malaysia.
Telephone: 755221; 751142.

Perlman, Alfred Edward; American railway executive; b. 22 Nov. 1902; ed. Mass. Inst. Technology.
With Northern Pacific Railway, Forsyth, Mont. 23-34; Railway Div., Reconstruction Finance Corpn. 34-35; with Chicago, Burlington and Quincy Railroad 35-36; Engineer (Maintenance of Way) Denver and Rio Grande Western Railroad Co. 36-41, Chief Engineer 41-47, Gen. Man. 47-52, Exec. Vice-Pres. 52-54; Pres. Dir. New York Central System 54-68; Pres. and Chief Admin. Officer Pennsylvania New York Central Transportation Co. 68-69, Vice-Chair. 69-70; Pres. Western Pacific Railroad Co. 70-72, Chair., Chief Exec. Officer 73-74, Chair. of Board 75-.
526 Mission Street, San Francisco, Calif. 94105, U.S.A.

Perlman, Isadore, PH.D.; American professor of chemistry; b. 12 April 1915, Milwaukee, Wisconsin; *s.* of Harry Perlman and Bella Karpman; *m.* Lee Grimblat 1937; three *d.*; ed. Univ. of Calif. (Berkeley). Research Associate, Manhattan project 42-45; Assoc. Prof. Univ. of Calif. 45-49; Prof. of Chemistry, Univ. of Calif. 49-; Assoc. Dir. Lawrence Radiation Lab. 58-; Head, Nuclear Chemistry Division, Lawrence Radiation Lab. 58-; mem. American Chemical Asscn., American Physical Soc.; Calif. Section Award, American Chemical Soc. 52; Guggenheim Fellow, Copenhagen, Denmark 55, 63; E. O. Lawrence Award, Atomic Energy Comm. 60. Publs. numerous research papers and articles in scientific journals, especially *Physical Review, Journal of Biological Chemistry, Journal of the American Chemical Soc.*
University of California, Lawrence Radiation Laboratory, Berkeley, Calif. 94720; 1299 Glen Avenue, Berkeley, Calif. 94708, U.S.A.

Perlman, Itzhak; Israeli violinist; b. 31 Aug. 1945, Tel-Aviv; ed. Tel-Aviv Acad. of Music, Juilliard School, U.S.A.
Gave recitals on radio at the age of ten; went to U.S.A. 58; studied with Ivan Galamian and Dorothy De Lay; first recital at Carnegie Hall 63; has played with major American orchestras 64-; has toured Europe regularly

and played with major European orchestras 66-; debut in U.K. with London Symphony Orchestra 68; appearances at Israel Festival, South Bank Summer Concerts, London 68, 69.
c/o Harold Holt Ltd., 122 Wigmore Street, London, W1H oDJ, England.
Telephone: 01-935-2331.

Perloff, Harvey (Stephen), PH.D.; American economist and planner; b. 8 June 1915; ed. Univ. of Pennsylvania, London School of Econs. and Harvard Univ.
Economist Fed. Reserve Board 41-43; Consultant, Govt. of Puerto Rico 46-47, 50-51; Prof. of Social Science, Univ. of Chicago 47-55, Head Planning School 51-55; Consultant Presidents' Water Resources Policy Comm. 50, Tenn. Valley Authority 53-54; UN Missions to Turkey and Israel 54; Dir. Program of Regional Studies, Resources for the Future 55-61, 64-68; Consultant, State Dept. 63-65; mem. Cttee. of Nine, Alliance for Progress 61-64; Dean School of Architecture and Urban Planning U.C.L.A. 68-; mem. Comm. on the Year 2000, American Acad. of Arts and Science 65-; mem. several planning cttees. and organizations; Chair. Advisory Cttee. on Urban Planning and Development, Organization of American States; Consultant, Dept. of Housing and Urban Devt., Dept. of Health, Educ. and Welfare.
Publs. *State and Local Finance in the National Economy 44, Puerto Rico's Economic Future 50, Education for Planning—City, State and Regional 57, Regions, Resources and Economic Growth 60, Planning and the Urban Community 61, How a Region Grows 63, Regional Economic Integration in the Development of Latin America 63, Design for a Worldwide Study of Regional Development 66, Issues in Urban Economics* (ed. with L. Wingo) *68, Alliance for Progress: A Social Invention in the Making 69, Quality of the Urban Environment 69, The Future of the U.S. Government 71.*
School of Architecture and Urban Planning, University of California, Los Angeles; 930 Manning Avenue, Los Angeles, Calif. 90024, U.S.A.
Telephone: 213-474-0359 and 213-825-4091.

Perol, Gilbert; French diplomatist; b. 31 May 1926, Tunis, Tunisia; *s.* of René Perol and Jeanne Garcin; *m.* Huguette Cuchet-Cheruzel 1949; three *s.*; ed. Univ. of Paris, Ecole Nat. d'Admin.
With Ministry of Foreign Affairs, diplomatic posts in Paris, Morocco, Ethiopia, Algeria 53-62; with Office of Pres. de Gaulle 63-67; Sec.-Gen. Air France 67-74, Dir.-Gen. 74-; Chevalier Légion d'Honneur, Chevalier Ordre du Mérite.
Leisure interest: chess.
Air France, 1 square Max Hymans, Paris 15e; Home: 54 rue de Rome, Paris 8e, France.

Perón, María Estela (Isabelita) Martínez de; Argentine dancer and politician; b. 6 Feb. 1931, La Rioja Province; *m.* Gen. Juan Domingo Perón (Pres. of Argentina 1946-55, 1973-74) 1961 (died 1974).
Joined troupe of travelling folk dancers; danced in cabaret in several S. American countries; lived in Spain 60-73; returned to Argentina with Juan Perón, became Vice-Pres. of Argentina 73-74, Pres. 74-76 (deposed by mil. coup).

Perot, (Henry) Ross; American industrialist and philanthropist; b. 27 June 1930, Texarkana, Tex.; *s.* of Mr. and Mrs. Gabriel Ross Perot; *m.* Margot Birmingham 1956; one *s.* four *d.*; ed. U.S. Naval Acad.
U.S. Navy 53-57; with IBM Corpn. 57-62; formed Electronic Data Systems Corpn. 62, now Chair. of Board and Chief Exec. Officer; Chair. Board of Visitors U.S. Naval Acad. 70-; numerous awards and citations.
Leisure interest: horses.
Electronic Data Systems Corpn., 1300 EDS Center, Exchange Park, Dallas, Tex. 75235, U.S.A.
Telephone: 214-358-3171.

Perowne, Stewart Henry, O.B.E., K.ST.J., M.A., F.S.A.; British historian and orientalist; b. 17 June 1901, Worcs.; s. of Arthur William Thomson Perowne and Helena Frances Oldnall-Russell; ed. Haileybury Coll., Corpus Christi Coll., Cambridge, Harvard Univ.
English Lecturer, Govt. Arab Coll., Jerusalem 27-30; Asst. Sec. Palestine Govt. 30-32, Asst. District Commr. 32-34; Asst. Sec., Malta 34-37; Political Officer, Aden 37; Arabic Programme Organizer, B.B.C. 38; Information Officer, Aden 39-41; Public Relations Attaché, British Embassy, Baghdad 41-44; Oriental Counsellor 44-47; Colonial Sec. Barbados 47-49; Acting Gov. Mar.-Oct. 49; Adviser, Ministry of Interior, Cyrenaica 50-51; Adviser on Arab Affairs, U.K. Del. U.N. Gen. Assembly; discovered ancient Aziris 51; Hon. Asst. Jerusalem Diocesan Refugee Organisation 52; designed and supervised building of seven Arab refugee villages 52-56; mem. Church of England Council on Foreign Relations 65.
Leisure interests: archaeology and the arts.
Publs. *The One Remains* 54, *Herod the Great* 56, *The Later Herods* 58, *Hadrian* 60, *Caesars and Saints* 62, *The Pilgrim's Companion in Jerusalem and Bethlehem* 64, *The Pilgrim's Companion in Roman Rome* 64, *The Pilgrim's Companion in Athens* 64, *Jerusalem* (Famous Cities Series) 65, *The End of the Roman World* 66, *Roman Mythology* 68, *Death of the Roman Republic* 68, *The Siege Within the Walls—Malta 1940-43* 69, *Rome* 71, *The Journeys of Saint Paul* 73, *The Caesars' Wives, Above Suspicion?* 74, *The Archaeology of Greece and The Aegean* 74, *Holy Places of Christendom* 75.
44 Arminger Road, London, W12 7BB, England.
Telephone: 01-743-8363.

Perrault, Hon. Raymond Joseph; Canadian politician; b. 6 Feb. 1926, Vancouver, B.C.; s. of late Ernest Alphonse Perrault and of Florence Riebel; ed. Univ. of British Columbia.
Leader of Liberal Party, B.C. 59-68; mem. B.C. Legis. Assembly 60; mem. House of Commons 68-73; del. to UN Session 69; Parl. Sec. to Minister of Labour 70; Parl. Sec. to Minister of Manpower and Immigration 71; Asst. to Minister of Industry, Trade and Commerce in trade negotiations, Peking 71; rep. to ILO Convention, Geneva 72; mem. Senate 73-; Govt. Leader in Senate Aug. 74-.
The Senate, Parliament Buildings, Ottawa, Ont., Canada.

Perrin, Francis Henri Jean Siegfried, D. ÈS SC.; French scientist; b. 17 Aug. 1901, Paris; s. of Jean Perrin (Nobel prize winner for Physics 1926); m. Colette Auger 1926; two s. one d.; ed. Lycée Henri IV, Paris, Ecole Normale Supérieure, Univ. of Paris.
Assistant Univ. of Paris 23, Lecturer 33, Prof. 35-; Visiting Prof. Columbia Univ., New York 41-44; Rep. to Consultative Assembly Algiers, later Paris 44-45; Titular Prof. of Atomic Physics, Coll. de France 46-72; High Commr. for Atomic Energy 51-70; mem. Institut de France (Acad. des Sciences) 53-, Acad. d'Agriculture; Grand Croix Légion d'Honneur, Grand Croix Mérite National, Commandeur Palmes Académiques, Economie Nationale.
Leisure interests: sailing, skiing.
4 rue Froidevaux, 75014 Paris, France.
Telephone: 326-8558.

Perrin, René Jean Louis; French marine engineer and business executive; b. 22 Aug. 1897; ed. Ecole Polytechnique.
Former Marine Engineer and Chief Marine Engineer; Prés. d'Honneur, Compagnie Française de Raffinage; Commandeur, Légion d'Honneur.
86 avenue Raymond-Poincaré, Paris 75116, France.

Perrone, João Consani, B.SC., M.A., D.CHEM.; Brazilian protein chemist; b. 22 Jan. 1922, Passa Quatro, Estado de Minas Gerais; s. of Raphael Perrone and Adelaide Consani Perrone; m. Moema Cruz Perrone 1952; three d.; ed. Universidade do Brasil, Rio de Janeiro, and Univ. of Calif. (Berkeley).
Head of Research, Nat. Council of Research 52-60; Assoc. Prof. of Organic and Biological Chemistry, Univ. of Brazil 51-; Head, Laboratory of Protein Chemistry, Instituto Nacional de Tecnologia 52-; Prof. of Protein Chemistry and Gen. Enzymology, Instituto de Química 62-, Chair. Dept. of Biochemistry 68-72; Pres. Soc. Brasileira de Bioquímica 72-74; mem. Brazilian Acad. of Sciences.
Leisure interests: hunting, fishing.
Rua Senador Vergueiro, 99 Cobertura, Flamengo, Rio de Janeiro, RJ, Brazil.
Telephone: 225-1617.

Perroux, Prof. François, L. ès L., AGRÉGÉ DES SC. ECONS.; French professor; b. 19 Dec. 1903; ed. Coll. des Maristes, Lyons, Univ. de Lyon and Univ. de Paris à la Sorbonne.
Rockefeller Fellow 34; Prof. Collège de France 55-; Dir. of Studies, Ecole Pratique des Hautes Etudes 55-; Founder-Dir. Inst. of Applied Econ. Science 44-; Dir. Inst. of Study of Econ. and Social Devt.; mem. Exec. Cttee. for Nat. Revenue, Exec. Council for Accountancy, Statistical Soc. of Paris, Econ. and Social Council, Nat. Cttee. of Scientific Research, etc.; mem. Acad. des Sciences d'Outre-Mer, Paris, Accad. Pugliese delle Scienze, Bari, Accad. Nazionale dei Lincei, Rome, Società nazionale di lettere e belle arti, Naples, British Acad.; Foreign mem. Accad. delle scienze, Turin; Hon. mem. American Econ. Asscn.; Officier Légion d'Honneur, Commdr. Ordre des Palmes Académiques, Grand Officier Ordre Nat. du Mérite, Officier Ordre de la Couronne (Belgium), Grand Officier Ordre Nat. du Sénégal, Commendatore Ordine al Merito (Italy); Dr. h.c. São Paulo, Coimbra, Liège, Frankfurt-am-Main, Lisbon, Córdoba, Georgetown (Washington), Montevideo.
Publs. include: *Les Mythes hitlériens* 36, *Capitalisme et Communauté du Travail* 38, *Des Mythes hitlériens à l'Europe allemande* 40, *Communauté* 40, *La Valeur* 43, *Le Revenu National, son calcul et sa signification* 47, *Les Comptes de la Nation* 49, *L'Europe sans rivages* 54, *La Capitalisme* 48, 6th edn. 65, *La Coexistence pacifique* 58, *Economie et Société* 61, *Le IVe Plan français* 62, *L'Economie des jeunes nations* 62, *Industrie et Création Collective* 64, *Les Techniques Quantitatives de la Planification* 65, *l'Entreprise et l'Economie du XXe Siècle* (3 vols.) 66-67, *l'Intégration du plan scientifique et du plan de développement économique et social* 67, *le Progrès économique* 68, *le Pain et la Parole, Indépendance de la Nation, François Perroux interroge Herbert Marcuse* 69. *Masse et Classe* 72, *Pouvoir et Economie* 73, *Indépendance de l'economie nationale et Indépendance des Nations* 74.
Institut de Sciences Mathématiques et Economiques Appliquées, 11 boulevard Sébastapol, Paris 1er; Home: 9 *ter* rue Paul-Féval, Paris 18e, France.
Telephone: Louvre 91-87/91-99/93-70 (Office).

Persianinov, Leonid Semenovich; Soviet obstetrician and gynaecologist; b. 18 Aug. 1908, Staroe Village, Smolensk Region; s. of Semyon and Evdokia Persianinov; m. Vera Chernova 1931; one s.; ed. Second Leningrad Medical Inst.
Physician, Kostroma Region; Postgraduate, Research Assoc., Asst. Prof. Inst. of Postgraduate Medical Training, Kazan; Army Surgeon 41-45; Head of Chair Minsk Medical Inst. 51-58; Head of Chair Second Moscow Medical Inst. 58-67; Chief Obstetrician-Gynaecologist U.S.S.R. Ministry of Health 59-62; Dir. All-Union Inst. of Obstetrics and Gynaecology 67-; Head of Chair First Moscow Medical Inst. 67; Chair. Board U.S.S.R. Soc. of Obstetricians and Gynaecologists; WHO expert on obstetrics and gynaecology; Corresp. mem. U.S.S.R. Acad. Medical Sciences 60-65; Academician, U.S.S.R.

Acad. of Medical Sciences 65-; mem. Editorial Board *Obstetrics and Gynaecology*; mem. Int. Fed. Obstetricians and Gynaecologists; Hon. mem. Purkinye Soc., Czechoslovakia, Union of Obstetricians-Gynaecologists, Yugoclavia, Nat. Asscns. of Obstetricians and Gynaecologists in Bulgaria, German Democratic Repub., Poland, Fed. of Medical Socs., Hungary; State Prize 68; Order of Lenin, Order of Red Star, Order of October Revolution, etc.; Merited Scientist Byelorussian S.S.R., Snegirev Prize.
Leisure interests: photography, filming.
Publs. *Uterine Ruptures* 52, Editor *Manual in Obstetrics and Gynaecology* (6 vols.) 61-64, *Seminar in Obstetrics* (2 vols.) 57-60, 73, *Operative Gynaecology* 71, *Asphyxia of the Foetus and the Neonate* 61, 67, 70, *Principles of Clinical Foetal Cardiology* 67, 68, and over 350 articles on related subjects.
All-Union Research Institute of Obstetrics and Gynaecology, 2 Elansky Street, Moscow 119435, U.S.S.R.
Telephone: 246-98-41.

Pertini, Alessandro; Italian politician; b. 1896, Stella. Trained as journalist; served as lieut. during First World War; joined Socialist Party 18; arrested for anti-Fascist publication 25; imprisoned 26: emigrated to France; arrested for political disturbances and anti-Fascist activities; returned to Italy 27; imprisoned 28-35; detained in political detention camp 35-43; mem. Exec. Council, Italian Socialist Party Aug. 43; fought against German troops at Porta San Paolo, Rome, arrested but escaped Jan. 44; Sec. Socialist Party in Italy; organized insurrections, N. Italy April 45; mem. Socialist Party admin. until Jan. 48; elected to Constituent Assembly for Genoa-Florence-Naples 46; life senator 48; Chair. Socialist Parl. Group; elected to Chamber of Deputies 53, 58, 63, for Genoa constituency; Gen. Man. *Il lavoro nuovo* 45-46 and 50-June 53; Deputy Speaker, Chamber of Deputies 63-68; elected to Chamber of Deputies May 68, for Genoa constituency, Pres. 68-.
Camera dei Deputati, Rome, Italy.

Perutz, Max Ferdinand, C.H., PH.D., F.R.S.; British biochemist and crystallographer; b. 19 May 1914, Vienna, Austria; s. of Hugo and Adele Perutz; m. Gisela Peiser 1942; one s. one d.; ed. Theresianum, Vienna, and Univs. of Vienna and Cambridge.
Director Medical Research Council Unit for Molecular Biology, Cavendish Laboratory, Univ. of Cambridge 47-62; Chair. Medical Research Council Laboratory of Molecular Biology, Univ. Postgraduate Medical School, Cambridge 62-; Reader Davy Faraday Research Laboratory, Royal Inst. 54-68; Chair. European Molecular Biology Org. 63-69; Fullerian Prof. Physiology at Royal Inst. 74-(77); Hon. Dr. Phil. (Vienna and Edinburgh); Nobel Prize for Chemistry 62; Foreign Assoc. U.S. Nat. Acad. of Sciences 70-; Royal Medal, Royal Soc. 71.
Leisure interests: skiing, mountaineering.
Publs. *Proteins and Nucleic Acids: Structure and Function* 62, various papers on the structure of proteins.
MRC Laboratory of Molecular Biology, Hills Road, Cambridge; and 42 Sedley Taylor Road, Cambridge, England.
Telephone: Cambridge 48011 (Office).

Pescatore, Gabriele; Italian university professor and civil servant; b. 21 Oct. 1916; ed. Univ. of Naples.
Appointed Counsellor of State 50; Prof. of Admiralty Law, Univ. of Rome; Pres. of the Cassa del Mezzogiorno (Southern Italy Development Fund) 54-; Pres. of Section, Council of State; Vice-Pres. Int. Council of Regional Economies, Mediterranean Council of Regional Economies; Knight-Commdr. of the Pius Order; Grand Cross, Knight of the Republic's Order of Merit; Gold Medal Award for Sciences and Art.
Cassa del Mezzogiorno, Piazzale Kennedy 20, Eur, Rome; Via A. Stoppani 34, Rome, Italy.

Pescatore, Pierre, D.IUR.; Luxembourg diplomatist and professor of law; b. 20 Nov. 1919, Luxembourg; s. of Ferdinand Pescatore and Cunégonde Heuertz; m. Rosalie Margue 1948; three s. one d.
Ministry of Foreign Affairs 46-67, Sec., later mem., Del. to UN Gen. Ass. 46-52; Legal Adviser, Min. of Foreign Affairs 50-58; Dir. for Political Affairs, Min. of Foreign Affairs 58-64; Minister Plenipotentiary 59; Sec.-Gen. Ministry of Foreign Affairs 64-67; Judge, Court of Justice of the European Communities 67-; Prof. Law Faculty and Inst. for European Legal Studies, Univ. of Liège; Lectured Hague Acad. of Int. Law 61; mem. Inst. de Droit International 65-; Dr. h.c. (Nancy and Geneva Univs.).
Publs. *Essai sur la notion de la loi* 57, co-author *Aspects juridiques du Marché commun* 58, *Introduction à la Science du droit* 60, *Relations extérieures des Communautés européennes* 62, *Conclusion et effet des traités internationaux selon le droit constitutionnel du G.-D. de Luxembourg* 64, *La Fusion des Communautés européennes* 65, *L'Union économique belgo-luxembourgeoise* 65, *La Fusion des Communautés européennes au lendemain des Accords de Luxembourg* 67, *Distribución de competencias y de poderes entre los Estados miembros y las Communidas Europeas* 68, *Les droits de l'homme et l'intégration Européenne* 68, *Personnalité internationale et politique commerciale des communautés européennes* 69; co-author *Les Relations Extérieures de la Communauté européenne unifiée* 69, *Cours d'institutions internationales* 70, *L'Ordre juridique des Communautés Européennes* 73, *The Law of Integration* 74.
16 rue de la Fontaine, Luxembourg.
Telephone: Luxembourg 4762-241 (Office); 240-44 (Home).

Pesenti, Antonio; Italian economist and politician; b. 15 Oct. 1910, Verona; s. of Romeo Pesenti and Amalia Bisoffi; m. Ghiadistri Adriana 1947; ed. Univs. of Pavia, Vienna, Berne, Paris, London School of Econs.
Lecturer Sassari Univ. 35; active in underground anti-Fascist movement 30-35; took part in Italian anti-Fascist Congress in Brussels 35; arrested and sentenced to 24 years' imprisonment by special tribunal; released Sept. 43; Under-Sec., later Minister of Finance April 44-June 45; Lecturer on Finance, Univ. of Rome 45; Prof. Univ. of Parma 48, of Pisa 60-71, of Rome 71-; Ed. *Critica Economica*; mem. Italian Constituent Assembly; Pres. Economic Centre for Reconstruction; mem. Parl. 48, of Senate 53-; Communist.
Leisure interests: chess, mountaineering, rowing.
Publs. *Politica finanziaria e monetaria dell' Inghilterra* 34, *La politica monetaria delle Devisenverordnungen* 33, *I soggetti passivi dell'obbligazione doganale* 34, *Ricostruire dalle rovine* 45, *Scienza delle Finanze e diritto finanziario* 61, *Manuale d'Economia Politica*, 2 vols. 70.
Via Nomentana 372, Rome; and 41 Via Nomentana, Istituto di Economia, Rome, Italy.
Telephone: Rome 897530.

Pesenti, Carlo; Italian business executive; b. 15 June 1907, Alzano Sopra, Bergamo; ed. Politecnico di Milano.
Joined Italcementi S.p.A. 33, Man. Dir. and Dir. Gen. 42-, now also Pres.; mem. Board, Confederazione Generale dell' Industria Italiana; del. to OECD; Dir. Lancia, Instituto Bancario Italiano etc.; Cavaliere del Lavoro 62; Grande Ufficiale al merito della Repubblica italiana.
Office: Via G. Camozzi 124, Bergamo; Home: Via Porta Dipinta 15, Bergamo, Italy.

Pesmazoglu, John Stevens, PH.D.; Greek economist, banker and politician; b. 1 March 1918, Chios; s. of Stephanos G. Pesmazoglu and Angela Lorenzou; m. Miranda Economou 1945; two s.; ed. Varvakion High School, Athens, Univ. of Athens, and St. John's Coll., Cambridge.

Served in Greek Albanian campaign 40-41 and in liberation of Greece 44-45; research student, Cambridge 45-49; Lecturer in Political Economy, Univ. of Athens 50-67, Prof. 67-70; Dir. Gen. Greek Ministry of Co-ordination in charge of econ. devt. and external financial relations 51-55; Econ. Adviser Bank of Greece 55-60; Alt. Gov. for Greece, Int. Monetary Fund (IMF) 55-67; Deputy Gov. Bank of Greece 60-67; Leader of Greek mission to negotiations for European Free Trade Area and asscn. of Greece with Common Market 57-61; Chair. Interdepartmental Cttee. for European Co-operation 62-65; Trustee Royal Hellenic Research Foundation 59-68; Pres. Soc. for the Study of Greek Problems 71-72; exiled by mil. govt. May-Dec. 72; in prison April-Aug. 73; Minister of Finance July-Oct. 74; mem. Parl. Nov. 74-; Grand Commdr. Royal Order of George I; Commdr. Légion d'Honneur, Grand Commdr. of the Yugoslav Standard with Gold Crown; Grand Commdr. German Order of Merit.

Leisure interest: painting.

Publs. Studies and articles on the int. trade cycle, economic devt. and monetary policies and on European integration with special reference to Greece's asscn. with The Common Market.

6 Neophytou Vamva Street, Athens (138), Greece. Telephone: 712-458.

Petäjäniemi, (Armas) Eero (Emil); Finnish newspaper editor; b. 2 May 1907; ed. Univ. of Helsinki. London corresp. *Helsingin Sanomat* 36-39, 46-49, Berlin corresp. (also for *Berlingske Tidende* and *Dagens Nyheter*) 39-44; Editor *Valitut Palat* (Readers Digest) 45; Helsinki corresp. *New York Times* 49-57; Editor-in-Chief *Iltasonomat* 49-56, *Uusi Soumi* 56-68; Chief of Press and Information, Olympic Games, Helsinki 51-52; Chair. Helsinki Press Asscn. and Board mem. Finnish Press Asscn. 50-57; Pres. Foreign Press Asscn., Berlin 44-45; mem. State Film Board 54-, Finnish News Bureau 56-; Perm. mem. Int. Press Inst. 53-; Pres. Int. Press Inst. Finnish Cttee. 63; retired 67; White Rose (Knight), Olympic Cross of Merit I, Officer, French Black Star, Commdr. Icelandic Falcon, Medal of Merit, Finnish Press Asscn., etc.

c/o Finska Notisbyván Ab Huftvudstadsblade House, Mannerheimintie 13, 00100 Helsinki 10, Finland.

Peter, Friedrich; Austrian politician; b. 13 July 1921, Attnang/Puchheim; s. of Friedrich Aloisia; m. Anna Liselotte 1943; two d.

Former school teacher; founding mem. Freiheitliche Partei Österreichs (FPÖ); elected to Upper Austrian Diet 55; Chair. Upper Austrian branch of FPÖ 56-; Chair. Nat. Exec. of FPÖ 58-; mem. Nationalrat 66-; Leader FPÖ Parliamentary Group 70-; Grosses Goldenes Ehrenzeichen, Grosses Verdienstkreuz mit Stern (Fed. Repub. of Germany).

Leisure interest: historical-political studies.

A-1010 Vienna, Kärntnerstrasse 28, Austria. Telephone: 02-22/52-35-35.

Péter, János; Hungarian ecclesiastic and politician; b. 1910; ed. Budapest, Protestant Theological Faculty, Paris and Trinity Coll., Glasgow.

Bishop Transtibiscan Synod of the Reformed Church 49-56; Pres. Inst. of Cultural Relations 57-58; mem. of Nat. Assembly 53-, Deputy Speaker Dec. 73-; First Deputy Minister for Foreign Affairs 58-61, Minister 61-73; mem. Cen. Cttee. Hungarian Socialist Workers' Party 66-; Banner Order 1st degree of the Hungarian People's Repub. 70.

Országgyűlés, H-1357 Budapest, Kossuth Lajos tér, Hungary.

Péterfi, Ştefan, DR. RER. NAT.; Romanian biologist and politician; b. 8 March 1906, Deva; s. of Martin and Iolanda; m. Leontina Péterfi 1935; two s. one d.; ed. Cluj Univ.

Reader Cluj Univ. 29, Asst. Prof. 38, Prof. 45, Dean Faculty of Sciences 45-48, Vice-Chancellor 57-; Deputy Grand Nat. Assembly 64-; Vice-Pres. Council of State 67-; Pres. Council of Workers of Hungarian Nationality in Socialist Republic of Romania 68; mem. Romanian Acad. 63-, Int. Physiological Asscn. (U.S.A.); Hero of Socialist Labour 71; Emil Racoviţă Prize Romanian Acad. 57.

Leisure interests: gardening and pigeon-breeding.

Publs. *Creşterea şi dezvoltarea plantelor* 54, *Nutriţia plantelor* 56, *Manual de fiziologia plantelor* (co-author) Vol. I 60 and Vol. II 64, *Creşterea porumbeilor* 63, *Botanica agricolă* (co-author) 65, *Dictionar etnobotanic* 68.

Universitatea Babeş Bolyai, Str. M. Kogălniceanu, Cluj, Romania.

Peters, Sir Rudolph (Albert), Kt., M.C. (with Bar), M.D., F.R.S., F.R.C.P.; British university professor; b. 13 April 1889; ed. Wellington Coll., Berks., King's Coll. London, and Caius Coll., Cambridge, and St. Bartholomew's Hospital, London.

Benn W. Levy Student of Biochemistry, Cambridge 12-13; served R.A.M.C. in First World War; fmr. Dunn Lecturer and Senior Demonstrator in Biochemistry, Cambridge; Whitley Prof., Oxford 23-54, Emeritus 54-; mem. Scientific Staff, Agricultural Research Council 54-59; Hon. Fellow of Trinity Coll. Oxford; Hon. Fellow Gonville and Caius Coll. Cambridge; Pres. Int. Council of Scientific Unions 58-61; Pres. Cambridge Philosophical Soc. 65-67; Assoc. Sciences Naturelles, Acad. Royale Belgique 48; hon. mem. Biochemical Soc., Royal Soc. Medicine, Nutrition Soc.; Foreign mem. Royal Neths. Acad. 50; Foreign hon. mem. American Acad. of Arts and Sciences 50, Soc. of Biochemistry, Biophysics and Microbiology, Helsinki; Foreign mem. Accad. Lincei, Rome; Hon. Fellow, Royal Soc. of Medicine 59; Royal Medal of Royal Soc. 49; Cameron Prize, Edinburgh 49; Hopkins Medal 59; Hon. Fellow, Royal Soc. of Edinburgh; U.S. Medal of Freedom (with Silver Palm) 47; Hon. M.D. (Liège) 50; F.R.S.E. (Hon.); Doctor h.c. (Paris); Hon. D.Sc. (Cincinnati, London, Leeds); Hon. D.M. (Amsterdam); Hon. D.Sc. (Aust. Nat. Univ.) 61; Hon. LL.D. (Glasgow Univ.) 63, Hon. mem. Physiological Soc. 65, American Inst. of Nutrition 67; Hon. Fellow Coll. of Pathology 67; Hon. mem. group of European nutritionists, Nutrition Prize, British Nutrition Foundation 72, fmr. mem. Belgian Royal Acad. of Medicine.

Publs. *Biochemical Lesions and Lethal Synthesis* 63, contribs. to scientific journals.

3 Newnham Walk, Cambridge; Department of Biochemistry, Tennis Court Road, Cambridge, England. Telephone: 50819 (Home).

Petersen, Harald; Danish editor and politician; b. 27 Oct. 1893; ed. Magleby Realskole and Gjedved Seminarium.

Studied languages and economics until 16; journalist with the *Ringsted Folketidende* 16; Parl. reporter for *Venstres Generalkorrespondance* 18-19; with Venstre Party Press Agency 19-; Head of Venstre Parl. Secretariat 20; Sec. of Venstre Parl. Group 25; Sec. of Venstre nat. org. 29-45; mem. of Lower House 43-50; Vice-Pres. of Venstre Parl. Group 45-; Minister of Defence 45-47; Man. Dir. Mortgage Bank of Kingdom of Denmark 48-50 and 53-64; Minister of Defence 50-53; mem. Venstre (Danish Liberal Party).

Strandvej 223, Charlottenlund, Denmark.

Petersen, Howard C., B.A., J.D., LL.D.; American lawyer and banker; b. 7 May 1910, East Chicago, Ind.; s. of Hans C. and Silvia Charles Petersen; m. Elizabeth Anna Watts 1936; one s. (deceased) one d.; ed. De Pauw Univ., Univ. of Michigan Law School.

Admitted to N.Y. Bar 35; Assoc. of Cravath, de Gersdorff, Swaine & Wood (Law firm) 33-41; mem. of Nat.

Emergency Cttee. of Mil. Training Camps Asscn. **40**; one of principal drafters of Burke-Wadsworth Bill; Counsel Cttee. for drafting regulations under Selective Service Act 40; Asst. to Under-Sec. of War 41, Exec. Asst. to Under-Sec. of War, Special Asst. to Sec. of War 45, Asst. Sec. of War 46-47; Exec. Vice-Pres. and Dir. Fidelity-Philadelphia Trust Co. Pa. (now The Fidelity Bank) 47-50, Pres. 50-66, Chair. 66-; Nat. Finance Chair. Citizens Cttee. for Eisenhower 52; Chair. Board of Managers Univ. of Pa. Museum, Advisory Cttee. of Export-Import Bank; Trustee, Cttee. for Econ. Devt., Int. Legal Center; Carnegie Endowment for Int. Peace; mem. President's Cttee. on Educ. Beyond the High School 57; Special Asst. to Pres. for Trade Policy 61-62; Formulation and promotion of Trade Expansion Act 62; Negotiated conclusion of GATT tariff negotiations with EEC 60-62; Rep. on Fed. Advisory Council 60-63; Pres. Pa. Bankers' Asscn. 63-64; mem. American Philosophical Soc., Council on Foreign Relations; Dir. and Vice-Chair. Adela Investment Co. S.A.; Dir. American Acad. Political and Social Science, Insurance Co. of N. America, Greater Philadelphia Movement, Rohm & Haas Co., American Int. Bank, Banque Européenne de Financement, Paris; Medal for Merit 45, Exceptional Civilian Service Award 45, Selective Service Medal 46; Hon. LL.D. St. Joseph's Coll. 62; D.Sc. Drexel Inst. 62.
Leisure interests: bridge, reading.
Radnor, Pennsylvania 19087; The Fidelity Bank, Broad and Walnut Sts., Philadelphia Pa. 19109, U.S.A.

Petersen, Jens, DR. JUR.; German diplomatist; b. 10 Oct. 1923, Hamburg; ed. Kiel Univ.
Foreign Office, Bonn 55; Vice-Consul, Montreal 57; Amb. to Trinidad and Tobago 63, to Cyprus 66; now Perm. Del. to UNESCO.
13-15 Avenue Franklin D. Roosevelt, Paris 8e, France.

Petersen, Kristen Helveg; Danish politician; b. 29 Nov. 1909, S. Longelse, Langeland; s. of Peter L.Chr. Petersen and Sofie Augusta Petersen; m. Lilly Edith Lolk 1936; one s. two d.; ed. Skaarup Teachers Training Coll.
Principal, Youth School Odense 40-46; Inspector of Schools 53-57; State Adviser, Ministry of Educ. 57-61, Minister 61-64, Dir. of Educ. 64-65; Chair. Co-ordinating Cttee. for Educ. 64; Chair. Planning Cttee. for Higher Educ. 64; Amb. in disarmament question 66; mem. of Folketing 64-; Vice-Chair. Educ. Cttee. of Danish Comm. for UNESCO 58, Chair. 60-61; mem. numerous professional bodies; Minister for Cultural Affairs, for Technical Co-operation with Developing Countries, for Disarmament Questions 68-71; Govt. Adviser in int. educational problems 71; mem. European Parl. 73-.
Publs. text-books and articles on education.
Skindergade 28 III, 1159 Copenhagen K, Denmark.

Petersen, William E., A.B., B.S.; American banker; b. 20 Sept. 1906; ed. Columbia Coll. and Columbia School of Business.
Joined Irving Trust Co., N.Y.C. 28, Vice-Pres. 47-57, Senior Vice-Pres. 57-60, Dir. 59-, Pres. 60-70, Vice-Chair. 70-; Pres. and Dir. Irving Interamerican Bank, Irving Int. Finance Corpn., One Wall Street Corpn.; Dir. Charter New York Corpn.; Chair. Board of Trustees, Columbia Univ.; Trustee Clarkson Coll. of Technology, U.S. Council, Int. Chamber of Commerce; Dir. Westvaco Corpn.; mem. Asscn. of Reserve City Bankers, Cttee. for Corporate Support of American Univs.; Hon. D.H.L. (Clarkson Coll. of Technology, N.Y.).
Irving Trust Company, One Wall Street, New York, N.Y. 10015; Home: 18 Dellwood Circle, Bronxville, New York, N.Y. 10708, U.S.A.
Telephone: 212-487-6275 (Office).

Peterson, Martha, M.A., PH.D.; American college president; b. 22 June 1916, Jamestown, Kan.; d. of

Anton R. and Gail (French) Peterson; ed. Univ. of Kansas, Northwestern and Columbia Univs.
Instructor in Mathematics, Univ. of Kansas 42-46, Asst. Dean of Women 46-52, Dean of Women 52-56; Special Asst. to Pres., Univ. of Wisconsin 56-63, Univ. Dean for Student Affairs 63-67; Pres. Barnard Coll. 67-; mem. Exec. Board Nat. Asscn. of Women Deans and Counsellors 59-61, Pres. 65-67; Trustee, Chatham Coll. 65-; fmr. Chair., now mem. Exec. Cttee. American Council on Educ. 71-; mem. American Asscn. of Univ. Administrators; mem. many other educational cttees. etc.; holds various educational and commercial directorships; several honorary degrees.
Barnard College, 606 West 120th Street, New York, N.Y. 10027, U.S.A.
Telephone: 212-280-2021.

Peterson, Peter G., M.B.A.; American government official; b. 5 June 1926, Kearney, Neb.; s. of George and Venet Petersen; m. Sally Hornboger 1953; five c.; ed. Nebraska State Teachers Coll., Mass. Inst. of Technology, Northwestern Univ. and Univ. of Chicago.
With Market Facts 48-53, Exec. Vice-Pres. 52-53; Dir. of Marketing Services, McCann-Erickson (advertising firm) 53, later Vice-Pres. and Gen. Man. Chicago Office, Dir. 57; Exec. Vice-Pres. and Dir. Bell & Howell 58, Pres. 61, Chief Exec. Officer 63-71, Chair. of Board 68-71; Asst. to Pres. of U.S.A. for Int. Econ. Affairs 71-72; Sec. of Commerce Jan. 72-Jan. 73; Amb. and Personal Rep. of the Pres. June 73; Vice-Chair. Lehman Bros., Chair. 73-; fmr. Dir. First Nat. Bank of Chicago, American Express Co., Illinois Bell Telephone Co.; Dir. Minnesota Mining and Mfg. Co., Federated Dept. Stores, Gen. Foods Corpn., Lehman Corpn., Council on Foreign Relations, Atlantic Council, Trustee of Univ. of Chicago and Museum of Modern Art, New York.
1 William Street, New York, N.Y. 10004; and 10 Gracie Square, New York, N.Y., U.S.A.

Peterson, Roger Tory; American ornithologist; b. 28 Aug. 1908, Jamestown, N.Y.; s. of Charles Gustav Peterson and Henrietta Bader; m. 1st Mildred Washington 1936; 2nd Barbara Coulter 1943; two s.; ed. Nat. Acad. of Design.
Decorative artist 26; Science and Art Instructor, Brookline, Mass. 31-34; engaged in bird painting and illustration of bird books 34-; on admin. staff of Nat. Audubon Soc., Sec. 60-; U.S. Army 43-45; Ed. Houghton Mifflin Co. Field Guide Series 46-, Naturalist Series 65-; Art Dir. Nat. Wildlife Fed.; Hon. D.Sc. (Franklin and Marshall Coll., Ohio State Univ., Fairfield Univ., Allegheny Coll., Wesleyan Univ. 70, Colby Coll. 74); numerous medals and awards.
Leisure interests: photography (still and motion pictures), travel.
Publs. *Field Guide to the Birds* 34, *Junior Book of Birds* 39, *A Field Guide to Western Birds* 41, *Birds over America* 48, *How to Know the Birds* 49, *Wildlife in Color* 51, *A Field Guide to the Birds of Britain and Europe* (with Guy Mountfort and P. A. D. Hollom) 54, *Wild America* (with James Fisher) 55, *The Bird Watcher's Anthology* 57, *Field Guide to Birds of Texas* 60, *The Wonderful World of Birds* (with James Fisher) 64, *The Birds* 63, *Field Guide to Wildflowers* 68; co-author: *The Audubon Guide to Attracting Birds*, *Field Guide to Birds of Mexico* 73; Illustrator: *Birds of South Carolina*, *Birds of Newfoundland*, *Arizona and its Birdlife*, *Birds of Nova Scotia*, *Birds of Colorado*, *Birds of New York State* 73.
Neck Road, Old Lyme, Connecticut, U.S.A.
Telephone: 434-7800.

Peterson, Rudolph A.; American (b. Sweden) banker; b. 6 Dec. 1904; s. of Aaron and Anna (Johannsson) Peterson; m. 1st Patricia Price 1927 (deceased), 2nd Barbara Welser Lindsay 1962; one s. one d. four step c.; ed. Univ. of Calif. Coll. of Commerce.

Field Rep., successively Vice-Pres. and Gen. Man. Mexico City, Div. Operations Man., Chicago, Commercial Credit Co. 25-36; Dist. Man. Fresno, later Vice-Pres. San Francisco, Bank of America Nat. Trust and Savings Asscn. 36-46; Pres. Allied Building Credits 46-52; Vice-Pres. Transamerica Corpn. 52-55; Pres. Man. Exec. Officer, Bank of Hawaii, Honolulu 56-61; Vice-Chair. of Board of Dirs. Bank of America Nat. Trust and Savings Asscn. 61-63, Pres. 63-69; Chair. Exec. Cttee. 70-; Pres. Bank of America Corpn. 68-69, now Dir.; Dir. Alza Corpn., Communications Satellite Corpn., Bank of America Int., Standard Oil of Calif., Time Inc., etc.; Administrator UN Devt. Program (UNDP) 72-75; Commdr. Royal Order of Vasa (Sweden) 64; Grand Cross of Civil Merit 65; Order of Merit of Italian Repub. 67; Hon. D. Hum. Litt. (Univ. of Redlands), Hon. LL.D. (Univ. of Calif.).
Leisure interests: gardening, fly fishing, historical reading.
United Nations Development Program, 1 United Nations Plaza, New York, N.Y. 10017; Home: 86 Sea View, Piedmont, Calif. 94611, U.S.A.
Telephone: (212)-754-4791 (Office); (415)-547-5461 (Home).

Peterson, Russell Wilbur, PH.D.; American politician and chemist; b. 3 Oct. 1916, Portage, Wis.; s. of John Anton Peterson and Emma Marie Anthony; m. Eva Lillian Turner 1937; two s. two d.; ed. Portage High School and Univ. of Wisconsin.
With Du Pont Textile Fibers Dept. 53-68 as Asst. Plant Man. 53-54; Res. Dir. 54, Merchandising Man. 54-55, Res. Dir. 55-59, Tech. Dir. New Prod. 59-62, Dir. Res. & Devt. Div. of Devt. Dept. 63-68; Gov. of Del. 69-73; Chair. Council on Environmental Quality 73-; Chair. Comm. on Law Enforcement, Justice and Public Safety, Nat. Gov. Conf. 71, Mid-Atlantic Gov. Conf. 71; Vice-Chair. Council of State Govts. 71; Chair. President's Nat. Advisory Comm. on Criminal Justice Standards and Goals 71-72; Chair. of Board, Textile Inst.; Chair. Exec. Cttee., Comm. on Critical Choices for Americans 73; Hon. D.Sc. (Willans Coll.) 75; Vrooman Award 64, Nat. Conf. of Christians and Jews 1966 Citizenship and Brotherhood Award, Josiah Marvel Cup for Humanitarian and Civic Work; Commercial Devt. Assen. Honor Award 71; Gold Medal Award World Wildlife Fund 71, Golden Plate Award American Acad. of Achievement 71, Conservationist of the Year, Nat. Wildlife Fed. 71, Parsons Award, American Chemical Soc. 74; Republican.
Leisure interest: nature study.
Publs. various articles on autoxidation, new product developments, crime reduction, environmental quality, conservation and population.
722 Jackson Place, Washington, D.C. 20006; Home: 616 South Royal Street, Alexandria, Va. 22314, U.S.A.

Peterson, Val; American diplomatist; b. 18 July 1903, Oakland, Neb.; s. of Henry C. and Hermanda Swanberg Peterson; m. Elizabeth Howells Pleak 1929; ed. Wayne State Coll. and Univ. of Nebraska.
School teacher, Neb. 25-30; Lecturer Univ. of Neb. 30-33; Supt. of Schools, Elgin, Neb. 33-39; Publisher of *Elgin Review* 36-46; Sec. to Gov. Dwight Griswold 41-42; war service 42-46; Gov. of Nebraska 46-53; Pres. Council of State Govts. 52; Chair. Missouri River States Cttee. 48-52; Admin. Asst. to Pres. Eisenhower 53; Federal Civil Defense Administrator; Amb. to Denmark 57-61; various exec. posts McDonald Co. 61-65; Amb. to Finland 69-73; Dist. Prof. of Political Science and Political Affairs, Wayne State, Neb. 73-; Trustee, Exec. Cttee., People to People Inc.; Grand Cross of Dannebrog; many hon. degrees.
Leisure interest: flying single-engine aircraft and helicopters.
710E 7th Street, Wayne, Neb. 68787, U.S.A.

Peterson, Walter; American politician and real estate executive; b. 19 Sept. 1922, Nashua, New Hampshire; s. of Walter and Helen Reed Peterson; m. Dorothy Donovan 1949; one s. one d.; ed. New Hampton School, Coll. of William and Mary, Univ. of New Hampshire, Dartmouth.
Formed real estate firm 'The Petersons' with father and brother 48, now Realtor and Treasurer; elected to New Hampshire House of Reps. 61, Majority Leader 63, Speaker of the House 65-68; Gov. of New Hampshire Jan. 69-73; Partner Petersons Inc. 73-; Republican.
Petersons Inc., 42 Grove Street, Peterborough, N.H. 03458; and East Mountain Road, Peterborough, N.H. 03458, U.S.A.
Telephone: 603-924-3259.

Petin, Jean; French manufacturer; b. 4 Feb. 1903.
Chair. Ets. J. J. Carnaud & Forges de Basse-Indre 45-; Pres. Soc. Marocaine des Ets. J. J. Carnaud and Forges de B.I.; fmr. Pres. Soc. Europemballage; Dir. Cie. Havraise et Nantaise Péninsulaire, Int. Machinery Corpn. Belgium, Superbox, Italy, Carnaud-Galicia, Spain; fmr. Dir. Thomassen & Drijver-Verblifa, Holland, Metal Box Co. Overseas Ltd., G.B.
56 rue de Varenne, Paris 7e, France.

Petit, Daniel; French financial official; b. 4 March 1918; ed. Lycée de Rheims and Faculty of Law, Univ. of Paris.
Auditor, Court of Accounts 45; Chef de Cabinet of Min. of Armed Forces 48, Vice-Pres. of Council 48; Referendary Councillor 50; Technical Councillor to Cabinet 53-54, to Min. of Finance 54-55; Gen. Sec. La Bourse de Paris (Stock Exchange) 62-.
4 place de la Bourse, Paris 2e; and 11 rue Marbeau, Paris 16e, France.

Petit, Eugène Pierre (see Claudius-Petit, Eugène Pierre).

Petit, Pierre; French composer; b. 21 April 1922; ed. Lycée Louis-le-Grand, Université de Paris à la Sorbonne and Conservatoire de Paris.
Head of Course, Conservatoire de Paris 50; Dir. of Light Music, Office de Radiodiffusion et Télévision Française (ORTF) 60-64, Dir. of Musical Productions, ORTF 64-70, Chamber Music 70; Dir.-Gen. Ecole Normale de Musique de Paris 63; Music Critic of *Parisien-Liberé*; mem. Gov. Council Conservatoire de Paris; Officier des Arts et Lettres; Officier de l'Ordre du Cèdre du Liban; Premier Grand Prix de Rome 46.
Compositions include: Suite for four 'cellos 45, *Zadig* (ballet) 48, *Ciné-Bijou* (ballet) 52, *Feu Rouge, Feu Vert* 54, Concerto for piano and orchestra 56, Concerto for organ and orchestra 60, *Furia Italiana* 60, Concerto for two guitars and orchestra 65.
Publs. *Verdi* 57, *Ravel* 70.
2 rue de l'Amiral-Cloué, Paris 16e, France.

Petit, Roland; French dancer and choreographer; b. 13 Jan. 1924; m. Zizi Jeanmaire (q.v.) 1954; ed. Paris Opera Ballet School.
Premier Danseur Paris Opera 40-44; founded Les Vendredis de la Danse 44, Les Ballets de Champs-Elysées 45, Les Ballets de Paris 48; Dir. Paris Opera Ballet 70; founded Les Ballets de Marseilles; Chevalier des Arts et des Lettres.
Works include *Le Rossignol et la Rose, Le Jeune Homme et la Mort, Les Demoiselles de la Nuit, Deuil en Vingt-quatre Heures, Le Loup, Cyrano de Bergerac, Carmen, Les Forains, La Belle au Bois Dormant, Hans Christian Andersen, Folies Bergères, L'Eloge de la Folie, Paradise Lost, Pelléas et Mélisande, Les Intermittences du Coeur 74, La Symphonie Fantastique 75.*
69 rue de Lille, 75007 Paris, France.

Petit de Murat-Regúnaga, Ulyses Raúl; Argentine writer; b. 28 Jan. 1907, Buenos Aires; s. of Ulises Petit de Murat and Fedra Regúnaga; m. Martha King

Forelius 1932; one s. one d.; ed. Colegio Nacional de San Isidro.
Former journalist; Nat. Prize for Literature 42, 43, 44; Nat. Prize for Cinematography 43, 44; Pres. Argentine Soc. of Writers; Pres. Consejo Cine de la Sociedad General de Autores de la Argentina, Great Prize Nat. Inst. of Arts 70.
Works: Poetry: *Las Islas* (Civic Prize of Buenos Aires) 35, *Conmemoraciones* 29, *Rostros* 31, *Marea de Lágrimas* 37, *Aprendizaje de la Soledad* 42, *Las Manos Separadas* 51, *Ultimo Lugar* 65; Plays: *La Novia de Arena* 45, *Un Espejo para la Santa*, *Un Patricio del 80X*, *Ultimo Lugar* 64, *Estampas de la Tierra Purpúrea* 66, *Yrigoyen* 74; Films: *Prisioneros de la Tierra* 40, *La Guerra Gaucha* 42, *Todo un Hombre* 43, *Donde Mueren las Palabras* 46, *Su Mejor Alumno* (First Prize, Argentine Acad. of Cinematography) 44, *Tierra del Fuego* (First Prize, Argentine Acad. of Cinematography) 49, *Suburbio* 50, *La Orquidea* 51, *Reto a la Vida* 53, *Mulata* 53, *La Entrega* 54, *La Duda* 54, *En Cuerpo y Alma* 54, *Juventud Desenfrenada* 56, *Esposas Infieles* 57, *Magia Negra*, *Manicomio*, *La Rebelión de los Adolescentes* 58, *El Dinero de Dios* 59, *El Romance de un Gaucho* (Prize, Best Script, Instituto Nacional de Cine) 62, *El Perseguidor* 65, *Al Diablo con este Cura* 67, *Martin Fierro* 69, *El Santo de la Espada* 70, *Güemes* 71, *Mi hijo Ceferino Namuncurá* 72, *Andrea* 73, *Las Procesadas*, *Los Años Infames* 74; Novels: *El Balcón Hacia La Muerte*, *La Vida Fanática*, *El Miserable Amor*, *La Noche de Buenos Aires* 63; Essays: *Genio y Figura de Benito Lynch*, *Carta a Los Jovenes del año 2000* 68.
Avda. Federico Lacroze 2764, Buenos Aires, Argentina. Telephone: 771-0468.

Petitpierre, Max, Docteur en droit; Swiss barrister and notary; b. 26 Feb. 1899, Neuchâtel; s. of Edouard Ferdinand Petitpierre and Mathilde Vuithier; m. Antoinette de Rougemont 1928; three s. one d.; ed. Univ. of Neuchâtel, Zürich and Munich.
Barrister 22; Doctor of Law 24; Notary 25; Prof. of Private Int. Law and of Comparative Civil Law in Law Faculty of Univ. of Neuchâtel 26-31 and 38-44; Pres. of the Swiss Chamber of Watchmakers 43-44; Deputy to the Council of States 42-44; mem. of Federal Council 45-61; fmr. Chief of Fed. Political Dept.; Pres. Swiss Confederation 50, 55 and 60; mem. Cttee. Int. Red Cross 61-; Radical.
Leisure interests: reading, walking.
Publs. *Les Conventions conclues par la Suisse avec l'Allemagne, l'Autriche et la Tchécoslovaquie concernant la reconnaissance et l'exécution des jugements civils* 33, *Le droit applicable à la succession des étrangers domiciliés en Suisse* 29, *La reconnaissance et l'exécution des jugements civils étrangers en Suisse* 25, *Droit international privé de la Suisse*.
Port-Roulant 3a, CH-2000 Neuchâtel, Switzerland. Telephone: 038-25-14-34.

Petrassi, Goffredo; Italian composer; b. 16 July 1904, Zagarolo; s. of Eliseo Petrassi and Erminia Calzoletti, m. Rosetta Acerbi 1962; one d.; ed. Conservatorio S. Cecilia, Rome.
Superintendent Teatro Fenice, Venice 37-40; Pres. Int. Society for Contemporary Music 54-56; now Prof. of Composition, Accad. S. Cecilia.
Works include: orchestral: *Partita* 32, *First Concerto* 33, *Second Concerto* 51, *Récréation Concertante* (Third Concerto) 53, *Fourth Concerto* 54, *Fifth Concerto* 55, *Invenzione Concertata* 57, *Quartet* 57; operas and ballets: *Follia di Orlando* 43, *Ritratto di don Chisciotte* 45, *Il Cordovano* 48, *Morte dell'Aria* 50; choral works: *Salmo IX* 36, *Magnificat* 40, *Coro di Morti* 41, *Noche Oscura* 51, *Mottetti* 65; voice and orchestra *Quattro Inni Sacre* 42; chamber music: *Serenata* 58, *Trio* 59, *Suoni Notturni* 59, *Propos d'Alain* 60, *Concerto Flauto* 60, *Seconda Serenata-Trio* 62, *Settimo Concerto* 64, *Estri*

66-67, *Beatitudines* 68, *Ottetto di Ottori* 68, *Souffle* 69, *Ottavo Concerto* 70-72, *Elogio* 71, *Nunc* 71, *Ala* 72.
Via Ferdinando di Savoia 3, 00196 Rome, Italy.
Telephone: 3588264.

Petrén, Bror Arvid Sture; Swedish lawyer; b. 3 Oct. 1908, Stockholm; s. of Bror A. Petrén and Signe Anderberg; m. Gertrud Serner 1942; one s. two d.; ed. Univ. of Lund, Uppsala and Freiburg im Breisgau.
Judge Svea Court of Appeal 43; Head Legal Dept. Ministry of Foreign Affairs 49-63; Legal Adviser, Swedish Del. to UN 48-60; Deputy Vice-Pres. Labour Court of Sweden 51-63; Pres. Svea Court of Appeal 63-67; mem. European Comm. of Human Rights 54-67, Pres. 62-67; Pres. French-Spanish Arbitration Tribunal in the Lake Lanoux case 57; Judge, Int. Court of Justice 67-; mem. Perm. Court of Arbitration 55-; mem. Argentine-Chilean Court of Arbitration in the Beagle Channel Case 73; Judge, European Court of Human Rights; Assoc. Inst. of Int. Law; mem. Swedish Acad., Royal Acad. of History, Literature and Monuments of Antiquity, Acad. d'Alsace; Knight Commdr. Order of the Seraphin and other decorations.
Leisure interest: horseriding.
Publs. *La confiscation des biens étrangères et les réclamations internationales auxquelles elle peut donner lieu* 63, *History of the Svea Court of Appeal 1614-1654* 64, *Nordic and International Lawmaking* 68.
Banérgatan 3, 114 56 Stockholm, Sweden.
Telephone: 602209.

Petrén, (Bror Erik) Gustaf, D.IUR.; Swedish judge; b. 5 Dec. 1917, Lund; s. of Prof. G. Petrén and Torborg Sylwan; m. Mary Anne Jakobsson 1944; one s. four d.; ed. Lund Cathedral School and Univ. of Lund.
Assistant Judge, Town Court of Stockholm 45-51, Asst. Judge, Court of Appeal (Stockholm) 52-60, Ordinary Judge 61-71; Deputy Ombudsman 68-71, Ombudsman 71; Judge Supreme Administrative Court 72-; Asst. Prof. Stockholm Univ. 49-; mem. Int. Comm. of Jurists 69-, Chair. Swedish Section 59-74; Sec.-Gen. Nordic Council (Swedish Section) 52-71; Chair. Rättsfonden 72-, Swedish Civil Rights Movement 74-; Knight Commdr. 1st Class Order of Polar Star and Icelandic Falcon.
Leisure interests: riding, philately.
Publs. *Compulsion in Public Law* 49, Ed. *Press Legislation* 70, *Basic Laws of Sweden* 71.
Styrmansgatan 5, Stockholm, Sweden.
Telephone: 08-673301.

Petric, Jakša; Yugoslav diplomatist; b. 11 June 1922, Postire; m.; two c.
Joined Ministry of Foreign Affairs 48; Deputy Perm Rep. to UN 49; Dir. Anglo-American Dept., Ministry of Foreign Affairs 51; Minister, London 52-56; Dir. for Asia and for Information, Ministry of Foreign Affairs 56-58; Amb. to Czechoslovakia 58-61; Dir. Dept. for N. and S. America and U.K. 61-63; Sec. Comm. for Int. Co-operation and Relations of Socialist Alliance of Working People of Yugoslavia 63-65; Amb. to Romania 65-69; Asst. Fed. Sec. for Foreign Affairs 69-72, Deputy Fed. Sec. 72-74; Perm. Rep. to UN June 74-.
Permanent Mission of Yugoslavia to the United Nations, 854 Fifth Avenue, New York, N.Y. 10021, U.S.A.

Petridis, Petro; Greek composer; b. 23 July 1892, Nigde, Turkey; ed. American Robert Coll.
Corresp. *The Musical Times*, London 15, *The Christian Science Monitor* 26-28, *Vimo*, *Proia*, *Kathimerini*, Athens; Ed. *Combat* 25-28; mem. Acad. of Athens, Corresp. mem. French Acad. Fine Arts.
Compositions include: *Le Clavier Modal*, Greek and Ionic Suites, piano suites, three piano concertos, *Digenis Akritas* 37-39, five symphonies, violin and cello. concertos, oratorio *St. Paul*, *Byzantine Requiem*, opera *Zefyra*, ballet *The Pedlar*, symphonic music for *Sound*

and Light on the Acropolis, Concerts for Two Pianos, etc. 90 Queen Sophia Avenue, Athens, Greece; 84 Boulevard Pasteur, Paris 15e, France.

Telephone: 7770069 (Athens); 306-74-86 (Paris).

Petrie, Sir Charles, Bt., C.B.E., M.A., F.R.HIST.S.; British writer; b. 28 Sept. 1895, Liverpool; *s.* of Sir Charles Petrie and Lady Hannah Lindsay (née Hamilton); *m.* 1st U. Dowdall 1920, deceased; 2nd Jessie Cecilia Mason 1926; two *s.*; ed. privately and Corpus Christi Coll., Oxford.

Royal Artillery 14-19; attached Secretariat War Cabinet 18-19; mem. staff *Outlook* 25-28; Foreign Editor *English Review* 31-37; corresp. mem. Royal Spanish Acad. of History, Inst. Fernando El Católico, Saragossa; Hispanic Soc. of America; Pres. Military History Soc. of Ireland; Assoc. Editor *Empire Review* 40-41, Editor 41-43; Man. Editor *New English Review* 45-50; Editor *Household Brigade Magazine* 44-; on staff of *Illustrated London News* 58-; Hon. D.Phil. (Valladolid), Hon. Litt.D. (Nat. Univ. of Ireland).

Leisure interest: club life.

Publs. *History of Government* 29, *George Canning* 30, revised 46, *Mussolini* 31, *The Jacobite Movement* 32, 59, *Monarchy* 33, *History of Spain* (with Louis Bertrand) 34, *Spain* 34, *Letters of King Charles I* 35, *William Pitt* 35, *The Four Georges* 35, *Walter Long and His Times* 36, *Bolingbroke* 37, *Lords of the Inland Sea* 37, *The Chamberlain Tradition* 38, *Louis XIV* 38, *The Life and Letters of Austen Chamberlain* 39, 40, *Twenty Years' Armistice—and After* 40, *When Britain Saved Europe* 41, *Diplomatic History 1713-1933* 46, *Earlier Diplomatic History 1492-1713* 49, *Chapters of Life* 50, *The Marshal Duke of Berwick* 53, *Lord Liverpool and His Times* 55, *Wellington: A Reassessment* 56, *The Spanish Royal House* 58, *The Victorians* 60, *The Modern British Monarchy* 61, *Philip II of Spain* 63, *King Alfonso XIII and His Age* 63, *Scenes of Edwardian Life* 65, *Don John of Austria* 67, *The Drift to World War 1900-1914* 68, *King Charles III of Spain* 71, *A Historian Looks at His World* 72, *The Great Tyrconnel* 73, *King Charles, Prince Rupert and the Civil War* 74, *Scenes of Edwardian Life* 75.

190 Coleherne Court, London, S.W.5, England.

Telephone: 01-373 9701.

Petrilli, Giuseppe; Italian administrator; b. 24 March 1913, Naples; *m.* Angela Roberti 1939; one *s.* two *d.*; ed. Univ. of Rome.

President, Inst. Nat. d'Assurances contre les maladies 50-58; mem. Council of Economy and Work; mem. E.E.C. Commission, Pres. Social Affairs Section 58-60; Pres. Inst. for Industrial Reconstruction (IRI) 60-; Pres. Italian Council of European Movement 64-; Cavaliere del Lavoro 65.

Istituto per la Ricostruzione Industriale, Via Vittorio Veneto 89, Rome, Italy.

Petrosian, Suren Martirosovich; Soviet worker and politician; b. 1925; ed. secondary school.

Worker at S. M. Kirov plant, Erevan 40-43, foreman 48-; Soviet Army service 43-48; mem. C.P.S.U. 51-; mem. Central Cttee. of Armenian C.P.; Deputy to U.S.S.R. Supreme Soviet (Soviet of Nationalities) 62-70; Vice-Chair. of Soviet of Nationalities 66-70; Hero of Socialist Labour; Order of Lenin; Hammer and Sickle Gold Medal etc.

S. M. Kirov Plant, Erevan, Armenian S.S.R., U.S.S.R.

Petrosian, Tigran Vartanovich, M.SC. (PHIL.); Soviet chess-player; b. 1929; ed. Teachers' Coll., Erevan.

Chess Champion of Tiflis 47, later Champion of Georgia and Armenia; Moscow City Champion 51; Grand Master 52, Post-graduate Student in Philosophy, Teachers' Coll. Erevan 62-68; Int. Grand Master; World Chess Champion 63-69.

U.S.S.R. Committee for Physical Culture and Sports, 4 Skaterny pereulok, Moscow, U.S.S.R.

Petrov, Boris Nikolayevich; Soviet power engineer; b. 11 March 1913, Smolensk; ed. Moscow Power Engineering Inst.

Associate, Inst. of Automation and Telemechanics, U.S.S.R. Acad. of Sciences 39-; Instructor Moscow Aviation Inst. 44-, Prof. 48-; corresp. mem. U.S.S.R. Acad. of Sciences 53-60, mem. 60-; Dept. Head Inst. of Automation and Telemechanics, U.S.S.R. Acad. of Sciences 60-; Chief Editor *Technical Cybernetics Series*, U.S.S.R. Acad. of Sciences Bulletin; Hero of Socialist Labour; Order of Lenin, and other awards.

Publs. *The Construction and Conversion of Structural Systems* 45, *The Principle of Invariance and Conditions for its Application in Calculating Linear and Non-Linear Systems* 60, *On Evaluation of Oscillation Processes in Complex Non-Linear Systems with Different Original Deviations* 64.

Institute of Automation and Telemechanics, U.S.S.R. Academy of Sciences, 15a Kalancherskaya, Moscow, U.S.S.R.

Petrov, Georgy Ivanovich; Soviet hydro-aeromechanic; b. 31 May 1912, Pinega, Archangelsk region; ed. Moscow Univ.

Research Insts. 35-; Prof. Moscow Univ. 53-; corresp. mem. U.S.S.R. Acad. of Sciences 53-58, mem. 58-; Bureau mem. Dept. of Technical Science, U.S.S.R. Acad. of Sciences 60-; Editor-in-Chief *Izvestiya Akademii Nauk S.S.S.R., Seriya Mekhanika* (Bulletin of the U.S.S.R. Acad. of Sciences, Mechanics Series); State Prize 49.

Publs. *The Propagation of Oscillations in a Viscous Liquid, and the Inception of Turbulence* 38, *The Application of Galerkin's Method to the Problem of Flow Stability in a Viscous Liquid* 40, *Estimation of Accuracy of Approximate Calculation of Proper Value by Galerkin's Method* 57.

U.S.S.R. Academy of Sciences, 14 Leninsky Prospekt, Moscow, U.S.S.R.

Petrov, Vladimir Mikhailovich; Soviet trade corporation official; b. 20 July 1922; ed. Industrial Inst. of the Urals and Acad. of Foreign Trade.

Soviet Baltic Fleet 39-42; foundry worker 40-42; Asst. Dir., later Dir., Electrical Engineering Office, *Mashinoimport* (mining, electrical, railway goods, etc.) 49-51; other posts, *Mashinoimport*, then *Mashinoexport* 51-55; Asst. Soviet Trade Rep. in Yugoslavia 56-59; Soviet Trade Rep. in Iraq 59-61; Chair. *Autoexport* (automobiles) 61-; mem. C.P.S.U.; several decorations.

V/O Autoexport, Ministry of Foreign Trade, 32-34 Smolenskaya-Sennaya ploshchad, Moscow, U.S.S.R.

Petrovsky, Boris Vasiliyevich; Soviet surgeon; b. 27 June 1908, Essentuki; ed. First Moscow Univ.

Physician at various hospitals 30-50; mem. C.P.S.U. 42-; Head of Chair of Surgery, Second Moscow Inst. of Medicine 51-56; Head of Chair of Hospital Surgery, First Moscow Medical Inst., and Dir. Inst. of Clinical and Experimental Surgery 56-; Minister of Health of U.S.S.R. 65-; Deputy to U.S.S.R. Supreme Soviet 62-; mem. U.S.S.R. Acad. of Medical Sciences 57-; mem. U.S.S.R. Acad. of Sciences 66-; Honoured Scientific Worker of R.S.F.S.R., Lenin Prizewinner, Hero of Socialist Labour, Orders of Lenin, "Hammer and Sickle" Gold Medal and other awards.

Main works: has studied problems of blood transfusion, oncology, surgery of vessels and organs of thoracic cavity, surgical treatment of congenital and acquired heart diseases, kidney transplant.

Publs. *Drip Transfusion of Blood and Blood-Substitute Compounds* 48, *Surgical Treatment of Vascular Wounds* 49, *Surgical Treatment of Carcinoma of the Oesophagus and Cardia* 50, *Blood Transfusion in Surgery* 54, *Surgery of Mediastinum* 60, *Surgery of patent arterial duct* 63, *Cardiac aneurysms* 65, *Resection & plastic repair of bronchi* 66, *Prosthetic replacement of heart valves* 66,

Surgery of diaphragm 66, *Oesophageal diverticuli* 68, *Surgery for renovascular hypertension* 68, *Selected lectures in clinical surgery* 68, *Kidney transplantation* 69, *Surgery of aortic arch branches* 70, *Surgery of peripheral vessels* 70, *Atlas of thoracic surgery* 73-74, *Surgical hepatology* 72.
U.S.S.R. Ministry of Health, Rakhmanovsky pereulok 3, Moscow, U.S.S.R.

Petry, Heinz, DIPL.-ING.; German industrial executive; b. 12 Jan. 1919, Rheinhausen; s. of Heinrich Petry and Elise Petry (née Maas); m. Liselotte Petry (née Gebauer) 1945; two s. one d.; ed. Berlin Technical Coll., Stuttgart Univ.
Construction engineer in dredger mfg., Krupp Industrie-und Stahlbau, Rheinhausen 46, Deputy Head of Dept. 50, given proxy of firm 61, Head of Dept. 62, Deputy mem. of Man. Board 65, mem. 66, Spokesman 73; mem. Man. Board, Friedrich Krupp GmbH, Essen 74-, Deputy Chair. 75-76; Chair. 76-.
Leisure interests: hunting, golf, films.
Altendorfer Strasse 103, 4300 Essen 1, Federal Republic of Germany.
Telephone: (0201) 188-2100.

Petryanov-Sokolov, Igor Vasiliyevich; Soviet physical chemist; b. 18 June 1907, Bolshaya Yakshen, Gorky region; ed. Moscow Univ.
Professor Moscow Chemical Technological Inst. 47-; Assoc. Karpov Physico-chemical Inst., U.S.S.R. Acad. of Sciences 30-; Corresp. mem. U.S.S.R. Acad. of Sciences 53-66, mem. 66-; Chief Editor *Khimiya i zhizn* 64-; Order of Lenin; State Prize 41.
U.S.S.R. Academy of Sciences, 14 Leninsky Prospekt, Moscow, U.S.S.R.

Pettijohn, Francis J., A.B., A.M., PH.D.; American geologist; b. 20 June 1904, Waterford, Wis.; s. of John J. Pettijohn and Elizabeth Shenkenberg; m. Dorothy M. Bracken 1930; one s. two d.; ed. Univ. of Minn.
Instructor (Part-time), Macalester Coll., St. Paul, Minn. 24-25; Instructor, Oberlin Coll. 25-29 (on leave 27-29), Univ. of Minn. 28-29; Instructor, Univ. of Chicago 29-31, Asst. Prof. 31-39, Assoc. Prof. 39-46, Prof. 46-52; Prof. Johns Hopkins Univ. 52-73, Emer. Prof. 73-, Chair. Dept. of Geology 63-68; Geologist, U.S. Geological Survey 43-53; Editor *Journal of Geology* 47-52; Consultant Shell Devt. Co. 53-63; Fellow, American Acad. of Arts and Sciences; mem. Nat. Acad. of Sciences; Hon. mem. Soc. of Econ. Paleontologists and Mineralogists (Pres. 55-56); Twenhofel Medal 74; Corresp. mem. Geological Soc., Finland; Wollaston Medal Geol. Soc., London; Penrose Medal, Geological Soc. of America 75.
Leisure interests: gardening, camping.
Publs. *Manual of Sedimentary Petrography* (with W. C. Krumbein) 38, *Sedimentary Rocks* 2nd edn. 57, 3rd edn. 75, *Paleocurrents and Basin Analysis* (with P. E. Potter) 63, *Atlas and Glossary of Primary Sedimentary Structures* (with P. E. Potter) 64, *Sand and Sandstone* (with P. E. Potter and Raymond Siever) 73.
Department of Earth and Planetary Sciences, The Johns Hopkins University, Baltimore, Md. 21218, Home: 512 Woodbine Avenue, Towson, Md. 21204, U.S.A.
Telephone: 301-366-3300 (Office).

Petukhov, Valentin Afanasevich; Soviet nuclear physicist; b. 1907; ed. Leningrad Polytechnic Inst.
Teacher of Physics Kharkov Physical Inst. 34-54; Dep. Dir. High Energy Lab. Joint Inst. Nuclear Research Dubna 54-; work in cosmology and on accelerators; Lenin Prize for his part in creating 10,000 million electron volt syncrophasotron.
Joint Institute of Nuclear Research, Dubna, Moscow Region, U.S.S.R.

Peugeot, Rodolphe; French businessman; b. 2 April 1902.
Former Pres. and Man. Dir., now Dir. Société Peugeot et Cie., Société Comtoise de Participation; Dir. Soc. des Automobiles Peugeot, Ets. Peugeot Frères and of a number of other concerns; Officier Légion d'Honneur, Croix de Guerre, Médaille de la Résistance.
5 rue de Beaulieu, 25700 Valentigney, France.

Peugeot, Roland; French motor-car executive; b. 20 March 1926; ed. Lycées Janson-de-Sailly and Saint-Louis, Paris, and Harvard Business School, Mass., U.S.A.
President Etablissements Peugeot Frères; Pres. du Conseil de Surveillance de Peugeot S.A. 64-72; Vice-Pres. du Conseil de Surveillance d'Automobiles Peugeot 65-73; Dir. of subsidiaries and other companies.
170 avenue Victor-Hugo, Paris 16e, France.

Pevler, Herman H., B.S., C.E.; American transportation executive; b. 20 April 1903; s. of Chris Pevler and Bertha (Hoover) Pevler; m. Roma Mae Haines 1931; ed. Purdue Univ.
Engineer, Supervisor of Tracks, Pennsylvania Railroad Co. 27-35, Div. Engineer, Supt. 35-42, Gen. Supt. E.-Pennsylvania Div. 42-46, Gen. Man. W. Region 46, Central Region 46-48, Vice-Pres. New York Zone 48-51, Vice-Pres. W. Region 51-55, Vice-Pres. and Regional Man. N.W. Region 55-59; Pres. Wabash Railroad System 59-63; Pres. and Dir. Norfolk and Western Railway Co. and wholly-owned subsidiaries 63-70, Chair. of Board and Dir. 70-73; official of business, civic and educational orgs.; Hon. LL.D. Univ. of Akron 67; Thomas Jefferson Award for Public Service, Old Dominion Chapter, Public Relations Soc. of America.
Office: Suite 126-127, Hotel Roanoke, Roanoke, Va. 24011; Home: 15 Cardinal Road, S.W., Roanoke, Va. 24014, U.S.A.
Telephone: 345-8839 (Office); 342-7407 (Home).

Pevsner, Sir Nikolaus, Kt., C.B.E., M.A., PH.D., F.S.A., F.R.I.B.A., F.B.A.; British university teacher and art historian; b. 30 Jan. 1902, Leipzig, Germany; s. of Hugo and Annie Pevsner; m. Karola Kurlbaum 1924 (died 1963); two s. one d.; ed. St. Thomas's School, Leipzig and Univs. of Leipzig, Berlin, Munich and Frankfurt.
Assistant Keeper, Dresden Art Gallery 24-28; Lecturer, Göttingen Univ. 28-33; Prof. of Art History, Birkbeck Coll. Univ. of London 44-69, Emer. Prof. 69-; Slade Prof. of Fine Art, Univ. of Cambridge 49-55; Hon. Fellow of St. John's Coll. 67; Henry Elias Howland Memorial Prize, Yale Univ. 63; Royal Gold Medal for Architecture 67; Thomas Jefferson Medal, Univ. of Virginia 74; Albert Medal, Royal Soc. of Arts 75; 10 hon. degrees.
Publs. *The Baroque Architecture of Leipzig* (in German) 28, *Italian Painting from the End of the Renaissance to the End of the Rococo* (in German) 27-30, *Pioneers of Modern Design* 36 (revised and enlarged 60), *An Enquiry into Industrial Art in England* 37, *Academies of Art, Past and Present* 40, *German Baroque Sculpture* (with S. Sitwell and A. Ayscough) 38, *An Outline of European Architecture* 43, 63, *The Buildings of England* 51-74 (46 vols.), *The Englishness of English Art* 56, *The Planning of the Elizabethan Country House* 61, *Studies in Art, Architecture and Design* (2 vols.) 68, *Some Architectural Writers of the Nineteenth Century* 72, etc.
2 Wildwood Terrace, North End, London, N.W.3, England.
Telephone: 01-455-9369.

Peyrefitte, Alain; French diplomatist, politician and writer; b. 26 Aug. 1925, Najac Aveyron; m. Monique Luton 1948; five c.; ed. Lycée de Montpellier, Univs. de Montpellier et de Paris à la Sorbonne, Ecole Normale Supérieure, Ecole Nationale d'Administration.
Secretary, Bonn 49-52; Deputy Dir. of European Orgs.

56-58; Counsellor of Foreign Affairs 58; Deputy 58-; Mayor of Provins 65-; Rep. Assembly European Parliament and UN Gen. Assembly 59-62; Sec. of State to Prime Minister (Information) April 62, Minister for Repatriates Sept. 62; Minister for Information Dec. 62-Jan. 66; Minister for Scientific Research and Atomic Questions 66-67; Minister of Educ. April 67-May 68; Chair. Comm. of Cultural Education and Social Affairs 68-72; Rep. at UN Gen. Assembly 69-; Sec.-Gen. U.D.R. (Gaullist Party) 72-73; Minister of Admin. Reform 73-74, of Culture and the Environment March-May 74.
Leisure interests: skiing, water skiing, riding.
Publs. *Rue d'Ulm, le Sentiment de Confiance, les Roseaux froissés, le Mythe de Pénélope, Faut-il partager l'Algérie?, Le mal français, Réflexions sur la voie chinoise, Quand la Chine s'éveillera* 73.
Assemblée Nationale, Paris; Mairie de Provins, S.-et-M., France.

Peyrefitte, (Pierre) Roger, B.A.; French author; b. 17 Aug. 1907, Castres (Tarn); s. of Jean Peyrefitte and Eugénie Jamme; ed. Coll. d'Ardouane (Hérault), du Caousou (Toulouse), Lycée (Foix), Toulouse Univ., Ecole des Sciences Politiques, Paris.
Joined Diplomatic Service 31; Attaché, Ministry of Foreign Affairs 31-33, 38-40; Sec. Athens 33-38; resigned 40; re-instated 43, mem. del. of French Govt. in occupied France 43-44; dismissed 45; re-instated by judgement of Council of State 62.
Leisure interests: walking, collection of antiques.
Publs. *Les Amitiés Particulières* (Prix Théophraste Renaudot) 44-45, *Mademoiselle de Murville* 46, *Le Prince des Neiges* 47, *L'Oracle* 48, *Les Amours singulières* 49, *La Mort d'une Mère* 50, *Les Ambassades* 51, *Du Vésuve à l'Etna* 52, *La Fin des Ambassades* 53, *Les Clés de St. Pierre* 55, *Jeunes Proies* 56, *Chevaliers de Malte* 57, *L'Exilé de Capri* 59, *Le Spectateur Nocturne* 60, *Les Fils de la Lumière* 61, *La Nature du Prince* 63, *Les Juifs* 65, *Notre Amour* 67, *Les Américains* 68, *Des Français* 70, *La Coloquinte* 71, *Manouche* 72, *La Muse garçonnière* 73, *Tableaux de Chasse ou la Vie Extraordinaire de Fernand Legros* 76.
9 avenue du Maréchal Maunoury, Paris 16e, France.

Peyton, Rt. Hon. John Wynne William, P.C., M.P.; British politician; b. 13 Feb. 1919, London; m. Mary Constance Wyndham 1966; one s. one d.; ed. Eton Coll. and Trinity Coll. Oxford.
Called to the Bar 45; Conservative M.P. for Yeovil 51-; Parl. Sec., Ministry of Power 62-64; Minister for Transport Industries 70-74; Chair. Texas Instruments 74-.
Homes: 32 Chester Terrace, London N.W.1; Lytes Cary Manor, Somerton, Somerset, England.

Pfaffmann, Carl, B.A., PH.B., M.SC., PH.D., D.SC.; American physiological psychologist; b. 27 May 1913, New York City; s. of Charles Pfaffmann and Anna Haaker Pfaffmann; m. Louise Brooks Pfaffmann; two s. one d.; ed. Brown, Oxford and Cambridge Univs.
Research Assoc., Johnson Foundation, Univ. of Pennsylvania 39-40; Lieut. to Commdr., Aviation Psychologist, U.S. Naval Reserve 42-45; Asst. Prof. to Prof., Brown Univ., Providence, R.I. 45-65; Vice-Pres. and Prof. Rockefeller Univ. 65-; Visiting Prof., Psychology, Yale Univ., Visiting Prof., Harvard Univ. 62-63; Fellow American Psychological Assscn.; mem. American Physiological Soc., Soc. of Experimental Psychology, National Acad. of Sciences, American Philosophical Soc., etc.; mem. Board of Fellows, Brown Univ. Corpn.; Howard Crosby Warren Medal of Soc. of Experimental Psychologists 60, Distinguished Scientific Contribution Award of American Psychological Asscn. 63, Kenneth Craik Research Award of St. John's Coll., Cambridge.
Leisure interests: skiing, sailing.

Publs. *Gustatory afferent impulses* 41, *Taste and Smell, Handbook of Experimental Psychology* 51, *The Afferent code for Sensory Quality* (in *American Psychologist*) 59, *The Sense of Taste* (in *Handbook of Physiology* Vol. 1) 59, *The Pleasures of Sensation* (in *Psychological Review*) 60, *De Gustibus* (in *American Psychologist*) 65, *Behavioral Sciences in Basic Research and National Goals* (A Report to the Cttee. on Science Astronautics, U.S. House of Representatives) 65, *Olfaction and Taste* 3rd Int. Symposium 69.
The Rockefeller University, New York, N.Y. 10021; Home: 1 Gracie Terrace, Apt. 6-B, New York, N.Y. 10028; and Pond Meadow Road, Box 175, Killingworth, Conn., U.S.A.
Telephone: 212-360-1594 (Office); 212-744-8270 (N.Y.); 203-669-8248 (Conn.).

Pfleiderer, Otto, DR.SC.POL.; German banker; b. 17 Jan. 1904; s. of Dr. Alfred Pfleiderer and Angelika Henning; m. Dr. Hildegard Hoffmann 1937; ed. Univs. of Tübingen, Hamburg and Kiel.
Ministry of Finance, Württemberg-Baden, Stuttgart 45-48, Pres. Landeszentralbank von Württemberg-Baden 48-52, von Baden-Württemberg 53-57, in Baden-Württemberg, Stuttgart 57-72; mem. Board of Dirs. Bank deutscher Länder 48-57, Deutsche Bundesbank 57-72; Hon. Prof., Univ. of Heidelberg 47-; Alt. mem. Man. Board European Payments Union, Paris 50-51; mem. Scientific Advisory Board, Fed. Ministry of Econs., Bonn 65-; Exec. Dir. Int. Monetary Fund, Washington 52-53.
Publs. *Die Staatswirtschaft und das Sozialprodukt* 30, *Pfund, Yen und Dollar in der Weltwirtschaftskrise* 37, *Währungsordnung und europäische Integration* 64.
Rosengartenstrasse 88, D-7 Stuttgart 1, Federal Republic of Germany.
Telephone: (0711) 33-18-33.

Pflimlin, Pierre, DR. EN D.; French politician; b. 5 Feb. 1907; ed. Lycée de Mulhouse, Institut Catholique, Paris, and Strasbourg Univ.
Member of Bar, Strasbourg 33-64; served French Army 39-40; Deputy for Bas-Rhin 46-67; Under-Sec. for Nat. Economy 46; Minister of Agriculture 47-49 and 50-51; Minister for Foreign Economic Relations 51-52; Minister for Overseas Territories 52-53, of Finance 55-56 and 57-58; Prime Minister May 58; Minister of State, de Gaulle Cabinet, June 58-Jan. 59; Pres. Mouvement Républicain Populaire 56-59; Co-Pres. "Centre Démocratique" Group, Nat. Ass. 62-63; Mayor of Strasbourg 59-; Minister of Co-operation, April-May 62; Pres. of Assembly of Council of Europe 63-66; Pres. Consortium of Rhine Navigation 71-.
Publs. *Perspectives sur notre Economie, L'Industrie de Mulhouse, La Structure économique du IIIe Reich, L'Alsace—Destin et volonté* (with René Uhrich), *L'Europe communautaire* (with Raymond Legrand-Lane).
24 avenue de la Paix, 67 Strasbourg, France.

Pham Hung; Vietnamese politician; b. 1912, Vinh Long Province.
Joined Revolutionary Youth League under Ho Chi Minh in 20s; founding mem. Indochinese Communist Party 30, mem. Lao Dong (Viet-Nam Workers') Party 51-; imprisoned for 15 years by French and sentenced to death, later reprieved; mem. Cen. Cttee. Lao Dong Party with special responsibilities for activities in the South 51-; Sec. People's Revolutionary Party 62-; Commdr. and Chief Pol. Officer, Liberation Army; Chair. Cen. Office of South Viet-Nam (COSVN).
Central Office of South Viet-Nam, Saigon, South Viet-Nam.

Pham Van Dong; Vietnamese politician; b. 1 March 1906, Quang Nam Province (S. Viet-Nam).
Close collaborator of Ho Chi Minh; underground communist worker since 25; imprisoned by French autho-

rities for seven years; upon release in 36, resumed revolutionary activities; a founder of the Revolutionary League for the Independence of Viet-Nam (the *Viet-Minh*) 41; mem. *Lao Dong* (Viet-Nam Worker's) Party 51-; Minister for Foreign Affairs, Dem. Repub. of Viet-Nam 54-61, Prime Minister Sept. 55-.

Office of the Prime Minister, Hanoi, Democratic Republic of Viet-Nam.

Pham Van Ky; Vietnamese writer; b. 1916; ed. Secondary School, Hanoi, and Univ. of Paris.

Went to France 39; prepared thesis on religion for the Institut des Hautes Etudes Chinoises; Grand Prix du Roman, Académie Française 61.

Publs. *Fleurs de jade* (poems), *L'homme de nulle part* (short stories) 46, *Frères de sang* (novel) 47, *Celui qui régnera* (novel) 54, *Les yeux courroucés* (novel) 58, *Les contemporains* (novel) 59, *Perdre la demeure* (novel) 61, *Poème sur Soie* (poems) 61, *Des Femmes Assises Çà et Là* (novel) 64, *Mémoires d'un Eunuque* (novel) 66, *Le Rideau de Pluie* (play) 74.

62/2 avenue du Général de Gaulle, Maisons-Alfort 94700, France.
Telephone: 368-22-94.

Phan Huy Quat; Vietnamese physician and politician; b. 1 July 1909, Ha Tinh, Central Viet-Nam; s. of Dr. Phan Huy Tung and Tran Thi My Xuan; m. Dang Thi Ly 1931; three s. three d.; ed. Hanoi Medical School, and Univ. de Paris.

Associate Prof. of Biology Hanoi Medical School 38-43; founder mem. and 1st Pres. Hanoi Univ. Student Asscn. 34; Cabinet Dir. Prime Minister's Office 45, Minister of Educ. 49, Minister of Nat. Defense 50, 53-54; Sec.-Gen. Nat. Popular Front 52; Acting Premier 54; imprisoned 60-63; Minister of Foreign Affairs, Repub. of Viet-Nam Feb.-Oct. 64; Prime Minister Feb.-June 65; mem. Vietnam Anti-Tuberculosis Asscn. 56, Chair. 69; Vice-Chair. Viet-Nam Medical Asscn. 60-63; mem. Advisory Cttee. Int. League for Rights of Man 65.
Leisure interest: gardening (orchids).
179 Hien Vaong Street, Saigon, South Viet-Nam.
Telephone: 25674.

Phanos, Titos; Cypriot politician; b. 23 Jan. 1929, Nicosia, Cyprus; s. of Phanos Ioannides and Maria Georgallidou; m. Maro Phierou 1958; one s. two d.; ed. Pancyprian Gymnasium, Nicosia, Middle Temple, London.

Called to Bar 51; practised law 52-66; mem. EOKA fighters union during Cyprus independence campaign; mem. of Cttee. of Human Rights of the Nicosia Bar Asscn.; arrested by British administration and served 16 months as political detainee 56-58; mem. Consultative Body to Archbishop Makarios 59-60; mem. House of Reps. for Nicosia 60-66; Parl. Spokesman (Floor Leader) of pro-govt. Patriotic Front 63-66; mem. Consultative Assembly of Council of Europe 63-65; Minister of Communications and Works 66-70; Amb. to Belgium, Head of Cypriot Mission to European Communities 71-, concurrently to Luxembourg and Netherlands 73-.
Leisure interests: music, chess, sports.
Embassy of Cyprus, 83-85 rue de la Loi, Brussels, Belgium.

Philip, Kjeld, DR.ECON.; Danish economist and politician; b. 3 April 1912, Copenhagen; s. of Louis and Carli Sörine Philip; m. Inger Margrethe Nygaard, M.P., 1938; two d.; ed. Copenhagen Univ.

Instructor Aarhus Univ. 37-43 and Prof. of Social Politics and Public Finance 43-49, Prof. of Econs. and Social Politics, Stockholm Univ. 49-51; Prof. of Economics, Univ. of Copenhagen 51-57, 64, 66-69; Minister of Commerce 57-60; Minister of Finance 60-61; Minister of Econ. Affairs 61-64; Chair. Co-ordination Cttee. 55; Dir. Inst. of History and Econs. 56-60; UN Senior Econ. Adviser to Prime Minister of Somalia 65; Chair. Comm.

on East African Co-operation 65-67, Danish Board for Co-operation with developing countries 68-73, mem. 75-; Industrialization Fund for Developing Countries 68-; mem. Board of Dirs. Den danske Landmandsbank 75-; Adviser to ILO 69-71, UNECA 72.

Publs. *En fremstilling og analyse af Den danske Kriselovgivning* 31-38, 39, *Bidrag til Laeren om Forbindelsen mellem det offentliges Finanspolitik og den økonomiske Aktivitet* 42, *Staten og Fattigdommen* 47, *La Política Financiera y la Actividad Económica, Madrid* 49, *Intergovernmental Fiscal Relations* 53, *Skattepolitik* 55, second edn. 65.

Rungstedvej 91, DK-2960 Rungsted Kyst, Denmark.
Telephone: (02)-863848.

Philippe, André, DR. EN.D.; Luxembourg diplomatist; b. 28 June 1926, Luxembourg.

Barrister, Luxembourg 51-52; joined Diplomatic Service 52; Deputy Dir. of Political Affairs, Ministry of Foreign Affairs 52-54; Deputy Perm. Rep. of Luxembourg to NATO 54-61, to OECD 59-61; Dir. of Protocol and Legal Adviser, Ministry of Foreign Affairs 61-68; Amb. and Perm. Rep. to UN and Consul-Gen., New York 68-72; Amb. to U.K. and Perm. Rep. to Council of Western European Union (concurrently Amb. to Ireland and Iceland) 72-; Commdr. Order of Adolphe Nassau (Luxembourg); also holds numerous foreign decorations including Hon. G.C.V.O. 72.

Embassy of Luxembourg, 27 Wilton Crescent, London, SW1X 8SD, England.
Telephone: 01-235-6961.

Philippe, H.E. Cardinal Pierre Paul, TH.D.; French ecclesiastic; b. 16 April 1905, Paris; s. of Louis and Suzanne Adam; ed. Lycée Hoche, Versailles and Faculty of Theology Le Saulchoir.

Professor Univ. of St. Thomas, Rome 35-54; Commissary-Gen. Holy Office 55-59; Sec. Sacred Congregation of Religious 59-67; Sec. Sacred Congregation for the Doctrine of the Faith 67-73; Cardinal and Prefect of the Sacred Congregation for the Eastern Churches 73-; Chevalier, Légion d'Honneur; Grand Cross Order of Malta; Grand Cross, Order of the Holy Sepulchre.

Publs. *Le rôle de l'amitié dans la vie chrétienne selon Saint Thomas* 38, *La Très Sainte Vierge et le Sacerdoce* 46, *Les fins de la vie religieuse* 61, *Le renouveau de la vie religieuse* 64.

Via della Conciliazione 34, Rome, Italy.
Telephone: 698 4662.

Philips, Sir Cyril Henry, Kt., M.A., PH.D., D.LITT., LL.D.; British professor of oriental history; b. 27 Dec. 1912, Worcester; s. of William H. and Mary E. Philips; m. 1st Dorcas Rose 1939 (deceased); one s. (deceased) one d.; m. 2nd Joan Rosemary Marshall 1975; ed. Rock Ferry High School and Univs. of Liverpool and London. Assistant Lecturer in Indian History, School of Oriental and African Studies 36, Lecturer 39, Senior Lecturer 45; war service 40-46; Prof. of Oriental History and Head Dept. of History, School of Oriental and African Studies 46; Dir. School of Oriental and African Studies 57-; Vice-Chancellor, Univ. of London 72-; mem. Council, Chinese Univ. of Hong Kong 65-, Inter-University Council for Higher Educ. Overseas 67-; Bishop Chavasse Prize, Gladstone Memorial Fellow, Frewen Lord Prize (Royal Empire Soc.), Alexander Prize (Royal Historical Soc), Sir Percy Sykes Memorial Medal.

Publs. *The East India Company* 40, 61, *Handbook of Oriental History* 51, 60, *Correspondence of David Scott* 51, *Historians of India, Pakistan and Ceylon* 61, *The Evolution of India and Pakistan* 62, *Politics and Society in India* 63, *Fort William India House Correspondence* 64, *History of the School of Oriental and African Studies 1917-1967* 67, *The Partition of India* 70.

School of Oriental and African Studies, Malet Street, London, WC1E 7HP, England.

Philips, Frederik Jacques; Netherlands engineer, businessman and welfare worker; 16 April 1905, Eindhoven; *s.* of Dr. A. F. Philips and A. H. E. M. Philips-de Jongh; *m.* Sylvia van Lennep 1929; three *s.* four *d.*; ed. Technical Univ. of Delft.
Joined N. V. Philips' Gloeilampenfabrieken as Works Engineer 30; Man. 31, in control of mechanical workshops; Dep. Dir. 36 and Dir. 39, Vice Pres. of the Board of Management 46-61, Pres. 61-71, Chair. Supervisory Board 71-; Chair. Board of Dirs. NKF Groep BV; Companion of the Order of the Dutch Lion; Commdr. of the Order of Saint Gregory the Great, Cedar of Lebanon; Officer Cross of the French Légion d'Honneur; Commdr. of the Dannebrog Order; Grand Officer, Order of Merit (Argentine) and other honours from numerous countries.
N. V. Philips Gloeilampenfabrieken, Philips' Industries, Eindhoven, Netherlands; and De Wielewaal, Eindhoven, Netherlands.
Telephone: 040-66101 (Office); 512780 (Home).

Phillips, David Chilton, B.SC., PH.D., F.R.S.; British university professor; b. 7 March 1924, Ellesmere, Shropshire; only *s.* of late Charles Harry Phillips and Edith Harriet Phillips; *m.* Diana Kathleen Hutchinson 1960; one *d.*; ed. Ellesmere primary schools, Oswestry High School for Boys, and Univ. Coll. Cardiff (Univ. of Wales).
Sub-Lieutenant, R.N.V.R. 44-47; Post-Doctoral Fellow, Nat. Research Laboratories, Ottawa, Canada 51-53, Research Officer 53-55; Research Worker, Davy Faraday Research Laboratory, Royal Institution, London 56-66; Prof. of Molecular Biophysics, Univ. of Oxford 66-; Fellow of Corpus Christi Coll. Oxford 66-; Vice-Pres. Royal Soc. 72-73; mem. Council European Molecular Biology Org. 72-, Medical Research Council 74-; Foreign Hon. mem. American Acad. of Arts and Sciences 68; Hon. D.Sc. Leicester 74, Wales 75; Feldberg Prize 68; CIBA Medal 71; Royal Medal (Royal Soc.) 75.
Leisure interests: reading history and talking to children.
Publs. scientific papers and review articles in various journals: *Probability Distribution of X-Ray Intensities* 50, *Crystal Structures of Ephedrine and Acridine* 50, *Estimation of X-Ray Intensities* 54, *Myoglobin Structure* 58, 61, *Effects of X-Irradiation* 62, *Structure of Lysozyme* 65, *Activity of Lysozyme* 66, *Protein Crystal Chemistry* 68, *Crystalline Proteins* 69, *Vertebrate Lysozymes* 72, *Structure of Triose Phosphate Isomerase* 75.
Laboratory of Molecular Biophysics, Department of Zoology, Oxford; Home: 3 Fairlawn End, Upper Wolvercote, Oxford OX2 8AR, England.
Telephone: 56789 (Laboratory); 55828 (Home).

Phillips, Harry, A.B., LL.B.; American judge; b. 28 July, 1909, Watertown, Tenn.; *s.* of Norman C. and Bernice N. Phillips; *m.* Virginia Major 1936; four *d.*; ed. Cumberland Univ.
Admitted, Tennessee State Bar 33; practised law, Watertown, Tenn. 33-37; mem. House of Reps., Tenn. Legislature 35-57; Asst. Attorney-Gen. of Tenn. 37-43, 46-50; Naval Officer 43-46; partner, Phillips, Gullett & Steele, Nashville, Tenn. 50-63; Exec. Sec. Tenn. Code Comm. 53-63; Judge U.S. Court of Appeals 63-, Chief Judge (6th Circuit) 69-; Award of Merit, Bar Assocn. of Tenn. 60; Hon. LL.D. (Cumberland Univ.) 51.
Leisure interests: gardening, forestry.
U.S. Courthouse, Nashville, Tenn. 37203; U.S. Post Office and Courthouse, Cincinnati, Ohio; Home: 2809 Wimbledon Road, Nashville, Tenn. 37215, U.S.A.

Phillips, Sir Horace, K.C.M.G.; British diplomatist; b. 31 May 1917, Glasgow, Scotland; *s.* of Samuel and Polly Phillips; *m.* Idina Morgan 1944; one *s.* one *d.*; ed. Hillhead High School, Glasgow.
Inland Revenue Dept., London 35-39; Indian Army 40-47; Consul, Persia and Afghanistan 47-50; Foreign Office 51-53; Chargé d'Affaires, Saudi Arabia 53-56; Aden Protectorate Sec. 56-60; Counsellor. Teheran 60-64; Deputy Political Resident, Persian Gulf 64-66; Amb. to Indonesia 66-68; British High Commr. in Tanzania 68-72; Ambassador to Turkey 73-.
Leisure interests: Greece, languages, swimming, long-distance driving (especially in the Near and Middle East).
British Embassy, Ankara, Turkey; c/o Foreign and Commonwealth Office, London, S.W.1, England.

Phillips, Rev. Canon John Bertram, M.A.; British writer and broadcaster; b. 16 Sept. 1906, Barnes, London; *s.* of late Philip William Phillips, O.B.E., and late Emily Maud (Powell); *m.* Vera May Jones 1939; one *d.*; ed. Emanuel School, London, and Emmanuel Coll. and Ridley Hall, Cambridge.
Assistant Master, Sherborne Prep. School for Boys 27-28; Curate St. John's, Penge, London 30-33; Freelance journalist and Editor Sec. Pathfinder Press 34-36; Curate St. Margaret's, Lee, London 36-40, Vicar of Good Shepherd, Lee 40-44; Vicar of St. John's, Redhill 45-55; trans., writer, lecturer, broadcaster and preacher 55-; Wiccamical Prebendary of Exceit, Chichester Cathedral 57-60; Canon of Salisbury Cathedral 64-; D.D. (Lambeth) 60; Hon. D.Litt. (Exeter) 70.
Leisure interests: painting, reading, listening to music, tape-recording.
Publs. *Letters to Young Churches* 47, *Your God is too Small* 52, *The Gospels in Modern English* 52, *Making Men Whole* 52, *Plain Christianity* 54, *When God Was Man* 54, *Appointment with God* 54, *The Young Church in Action* 55, *New Testament Christianity* 56, *The Church under the Cross* 56, *St. Luke's Life of Christ* 56, *The Book of Revelation* 57, *Is God at Home?* 57, *The New Testament in Modern English* 58, *A Man Called Jesus* 59, *God our Contemporary* 60, *Good News* 63, *Four Prophets* 63, *Ring of Truth* 67, *Through the Year with J. B. Phillips* 74.
Golden Cap, 17 Gannetts Park, Swanage, Dorset, England.

Phillips, John Fleetwood Stewart, C.M.G., M.A.; British diplomatist; b. 16 Dec. 1917; ed. Worcester Coll., Oxford.
H.M. Forces 39-45; Sudan political service 45-54; First Sec., Foreign Office 55-56; Oriental Sec., Libya 57-60; H.M. Consul-Gen., Muscat 60-63; Counsellor, Amman 63-66; Imperial Defence Coll. 67; Deputy High Commr., Cyprus 68; Amb. to People's Democratic Repub. of Yemen Feb. 69-70, to Jordan 70-72, to Sudan 73-; Fellow, Royal Commonwealth Soc.; British Museum rep. on Board of Trustees, Palestine Archaeological Museum, Jerusalem 66.
British Embassy, P.O. Box 801, Khartoum, Sudan; and Records Section, Foreign and Commonwealth Office, London, S.W.1, England.

Phillips, John Frederick Vicars, D.SC., F.R.S.E., F.R.S.S.AFR.; South African ecologist, conservationist and agriculturist; b. 15 March 1899, Grahamstown, S. Africa; *s.* of the late John Roberts Phillips; *m.* Jeanie Daleigh Turnbull 1923; two *s.* three *d.*; ed. Dale Coll., King William's Town, South Africa, and Univ. of Edinburgh.
Initiated research into indigenous forests, Knysna, S. Africa 22-27; ecologist and later Dep. Dir. Tsetse Research, Tanganyika Territory; Prof. of Botany, Univ. of Witwatersrand, Johannesburg 31; Gen. Man., later Joint Gen. Man. and Chief Agricultural Adviser to Overseas Food Corpn. (East African Groundnuts Scheme) 48; Consultant in Agriculture to FAO and Int. Bank of Reconstruction and Development; British Gov. Econ. Survey Mission of High Comm. Territories, Southern Africa 59; Chair. Cttee. of Enquiry into African Educ., Nyasaland 61; Prof. of Agriculture,

Univ. Coll., Ghana and Adviser in Agricultural Educ. to Ghana Ministry of Education 52-60; Chair. Cttee. reporting on development of economic resources in Southern Rhodesia 60-62; co-ordinating agro-economic aspects of the Tugela Basin 63-; Visiting Prof. Univ. of Pa. 66; Leader of UN Survey Team, Socio-economy of Hill Tribes, Thailand 67; Pres. South African Asscn. of Advanced Science 69; Consultant in applied ecology, Loxton, Hunting and Assocs. 69-; Hon. Senior Research Fellow in applied ecology, Univ. of Natal 70-; Corresp. mem. Sociedade de Estudos Moçambique; Hon. D.Sc. Rhodes Univ.

Leisure interests: wild life studies, African history.
Publs. *The Forests of George, Knysna and the Zitzikama: A Brief History of their Management, 1778-1939, Agriculture and Ecology in Africa* 59, *Kwame Nkrumah and the Future of Africa* 60, *Development of Agriculture and Forestry in the Tropics: Patterns, Problems and Promise* 61 (2nd edn. 66).
c/o University of Natal, P.O. Box 375, Pietermaritzburg, Natal; Home: "Green Shadows", P.O. Sweetwaters, Natal, South Africa.
Telephone: (University) 21043; (Home) 25063.

Phillips, Sir John Grant, K.B.E., B.ECON.; Australian banker (retd.); b. 13 March 1911, Sydney; s. of O. Phillips; m. Mary Willmott Debenham 1935; two s. two d.; ed. Univ. of Sydney.
Research Officer, N.S.W. Retail Traders' Asscn. 32-35; Econ. Asst., Royal Comm. on Monetary and Banking System 36-37; Econ. Dept., Commonwealth Bank of Australia 37-51; Leader, Australian Del. to 6th Conf. GATT, Geneva 51; Investment Adviser, Commonwealth Bank of Australia 54-60; Deputy Gov. and Deputy Chair. of Board, Reserve Bank of Australia 60-68, Gov. and Chair. 68-75; mem. Council, Macquarie Univ. 67-; mem. Board, Howard Florey Inst. of Experimental Physiology and Medicine 71-; mem. Advisory Cttee., Australian Birthright Movement, Sydney Branch 71-; mem. Board, Medical Foundation Univ. of New South Wales 74-.
3 Cyprian Street, Mosman, N.S.W. 2008, Australia.

Phillips, O. Alfredo; Mexican international finance official; b. 2 Sept. 1935, Mexico; s. of Howard S. Phillips and Dolores Olmedo; m. Maureen Greene 1960; two s. one d.; ed. Univs. of Mexico and London and American Univ.
Deputy Chief of Dept. of Banks and Chief, Dept. of Economic and Fiscal Planning, Ministry of Finance and Public Credit, Mexico 60-65; Senior Loan Officer, Inter-American Devt. Bank, 65-66; Alternate Exec. Dir., Int. Monetary Fund (IMF) 66-68; Professor of Trade Cycles, School of Business Admin., Iberoamerican Univ., Mexico 61-63; Exec. Dir. IMF 68-70; Sec., Group of Latin American Govs. to the IMF and IBRD 68-70; Man. Bank of México 71-, Deputy Dir. 75-.
Leisure interests: golf, swimming.
Banco de México, S.A., Avenida 5 de Mayo 2, Apdo. 98 bis, México 1, D.F., Mexico.

Phillips, Lieut.-Gen. Samuel Cochran, M.S.; American air force officer; b. 19 Feb. 1921, Springville, Ariz.; s. of Clarence A. Phillips and Mabel Cochran; m. Betty Ann Brown 1942; three d.; ed. Cheyenne High School, Wyoming, Univs. of Wyoming and Michigan and Air Command and Staff School.
Commissioned 2nd Lieut. in U.S. Infantry 42; with 364th Fighter Group, Eighth Air Force, England 44-45; European Theatre H.Q., Frankfurt, Germany 45-47; Dir. of Operations, 1st AACS Wing, Langley Barracks Va. July 47-48; Dir. of Operations, Armament Laboratory, then B-52 Project Officer, then Chief of Air Defense Missiles Div. of Engineering Div., Air Materiel Command, Wright Patterson Air Force Barracks, Ohio 50-56; Chief of Logistics and Dir. of Materiel for Strategic Air Command's 7th Air Div., England 56-59: Dir.

Minuteman Systems Progrm, H.Q., Ballistic Systems Div., Air Systems Command, Los Angeles, Calif. 63-64; Deputy Program Dir. for Apollo, Nat. Aeronautics and Space Admin. (NASA), Washington, D.C. Jan. 64-Oct. 64, Apollo Program Dir., NASA Oct. 64-69; Commdr. Space and Missile Systems Org., U.S.A.F.S. Commd. 69-72; Dir. Nat. Security Agency 72-; Fellow, A.I.A.A., American Astronautical Soc., Nat. Acad. of Engineering; Board of Govs. Nat. Space Club; Senior mem. I.E.E.E.; Hon. LL.D. (Univ. of Wyoming); numerous awards include D.F.C., Croix de Guerre and Air Force Longevity Service Award with Five Oak Leaf Clusters, Langley Medal of the Smithsonian Inst., Thomas D. White U.S.A.F. Space Trophy, NASA Distinguished Service Medal.
Leisure interest: amateur radio.
HQ NSA, Fort George G. Meade, Md. 20755, U.S.A.

Phillips, Thomas L.; American business executive; b. 1924; ed. Boston Public Latin School and Virginia Polytechnic Inst.
Joined Raytheon Co. 48, Vice-Pres. and Gen. Man. Missile and Space Div. 60, Exec. Vice-Pres. 61-64, Pres. and Chief Exec. Officer, 64-75, Chair. and Chief Exec. Officer 75-; Dir. Nat. Shawmut Bank, John Hancock Mutual Life Insurance Co., State Street Investment Corpn.; mem. Nat. Acad. of Engineering; Trustee Cttee. for Econ. Devt.; Vice-Pres. and mem. of the corpn. of Joslin Diabetes Foundation Inc.; Trustee of Gordon Coll. and Northeastern Univ.; mem. Corpn. of The Museum of Science; hon. degrees from Northeastern Univ., Boston, Stonehill and Gordon Colls., and Lowell Technological Inst.
Raytheon Company, 141 Spring Street, Lexington, Mass. 02173, U.S.A.

Phillips, Warren Henry, A.B.; American newspaper executive; b. 28 June 1926, New York City; s. of Abraham and Juliette Phillips; m. Barbara Anne Thomas 1951; three d.; ed. Queens Coll.
Copyreader, *Wall Street Journal* 47-48, Foreign Corresp., Germany 49-50, Chief, London Bureau 50-51, Foreign Editor 52-53, News Editor 53-54, Man. Editor, Midwest Edition 54-57, Man. Editor, *Wall Street Journal* 57-65; Exec. Editor, Dow Jones Publications also mem. man. cttee. Dow Jones & Co.; Vice-Pres. and Gen. Man. Dow Jones and Co. Inc. 70-71, Editorial Dir. 71-, Exec. Vice-Pres. 72, Pres. 72; Dir. American Soc. of Newspaper Editors 70-; Pres. American Council on Educ. for Journalism 71-73.
Publ. *China: Behind the Mask* 73.
22 Cortlandt Street, New York, N.Y. 10004, U.S.A.

Phiri, Amock Israel, M.A.; Zambian diplomatist; b. 25 Oct. 1932, Israel village; m. 1967; one s. four d.
Lecturer in Sociology, Univ. of Zambia 67-69; mem. Parl. and Chair. Public Accounts Cttee. Nov. 68-March 69; Minister of State, Ministry of National Guidance March-Dec. 69; Minister of State for Information, Broadcasting and Tourism Jan.-Dec. 70; High Commr. to U.K. and Amb. to the Holy See 70-73; Minister of N. Western Prov. 73-75; Knight Grand Cross, Order of Pius IX 73.
Leisure interests: swimming, walks, reading, table tennis.
c/o Ministry for North-Western Province, Lusaka, Zambia.

Phomvihan, Kaysone; Laotian politician; b. 1920, Savannakhet Province; ed. Univ. of Hanoi.
Helped anti-French forces in Viet-Nam after 45; joined Free Lao Front (*Neo Lao Issara*) nationalist movement in exile in Bankok 45; attended first resistance congress; Minister of Defence in Free Lao Front resistance Govt. 50; C.-in-C. of *Pathet Lao* forces 54-57; mem. People's Party of Laos 55; mem. Lao Patriotic Front (*Neo Lao Hak Sat*) 56, Vice-Chair. 59, Vice-Chair. of Central Cttee. 64; Prime Minister of Laos

Dec. 75-; Gen. Sec. Central Cttee. Lao People's Revolutionary Party.
Office of the Prime Minister, Vientiane, Laos.

Phoumsavan, Nouhak; Laotian politician; ed. primary school.
Owner of bus and truck business; visited Peking in a *Viet-Minh* del. for Conf. of Asian and Pacific Region 52; rep. of *Pathet Lao* at Geneva Conf. on Indochina with *Viet-Minh* del. 54; became Minister of Foreign Affairs in Free Lao Front (*Neo Lao Issara*) resistance Govt.; Deputy for Sam Neua to Nat. Assembly 57; arrested 59, escaped 60; led Lao Patriotic Front (*Neo Lao Hak Sat*) del. to Ban Namone peace talks 61; mem. People's Party of Laos 55; mem. Lao Patriotic Front, mem. Standing Cttee. 64, of Central Cttee.; Deputy Prime Minister and Minister of Finance Dec. 75-.
Ministry of Finance, Vientiane, Laos.

Phongsavan, Phéng; Laotian administrator and politician; b. 19 July 1910, Ban Pakham Luang-Prabang; s. of Sisouphan and Kham Pan; m. Nang Boun Nao Phongsavan 1945; four s. five d.; ed. Pavie Coll. Vientiane.
Joined admin. service 29; Dir. Govt. Printing Office, Vientiane 43-44; Chaomuong (District Officer) of Tourakhom, Ban Keun 44-46; Rep. for Luang-Prabang, Nat. Assembly 47-51, re-elected 51, 55, 65; Vice-Minister of Interior and Sports and Youth 52-54; Minister of Nat. Econ. and Public Works 54-56; Pres. Nat. Assembly 56-58; Minister of Interior and Social Welfare 62-75; Vice-Pres. Neutralist Party; numerous nat. and foreign decorations, including Grand Cross Royal Order of Thailand 56, Civil Merit Order 69, Public Instruction Medal 72.
Leisure interest: tennis.
Ministry of the Interior, Vientiane, Laos.

Phung Van Cung; Vietnamese physician and politician; b. 1908, Vinh Long Province; ed. Faculty of Medicine, Hanoi Univ.
Director of public health service in Rach Gia Province, later in Chau Doc Province; physician, Fukien Hosp., Cholon; joined army and rose to rank of Col. under Pres. Diem; joined resistance 60; Vice-Pres. Cen. Cttee. Nat. Liberation Front (NLF); Pres. South Vietnamese Peace Cttee., NLF Red Cross Soc.; Vice-Pres. Provisional Revolutionary Govt. of South Viet-Nam, Minister of the Interior 69- (in Saigon 75-).
Ministry of the Interior, Saigon, South Viet-Nam.

Phurissara, Prince Norodom; Cambodian lawyer and politician; b. 1919.
Government Service 44-; Deputy Provincial Gov., later in Ministry of Foreign Affairs and Ministry of Planning; Deputy State Sec. of Interior 61, State Sec. 62-64; Dir. of Admin. of Council of Ministers 64-66; Dean of Faculty of Law, Royal Univ., Phnom Penh 64-66; Minister of Foreign Affairs Nov. 66-70; joined Nat. United Front of Cambodia (FUNC) 72; Minister of Justice and Judicial Reforms Royal Govt. of Nat. Union of Cambodia (GRUNC) 73-76 (in Phnom-Penh 75-76).
c/o Ministry of Justice and Judicial Reforms, Phnom-Penh, Cambodia.

P'i Ting-chun; Chinese army officer; b. 1914, Anhwei.
Lieutenant-General, People's Liberation Army 61; Deputy Commdr. Foochow Mil. Region, PLA 61; Vice-Chair. Fukien Revolutionary Cttee. 68; mem. 9th Cen. Cttee. of CCP 69; Commdr. Lanchow Mil. Region, PLA 70-73; Vice-Chair. Kansu Revolutionary Cttee. 70; Sec. CCP Kansu 71; mem. 10th Cen. Cttee. of CCP 73; Commdr. Foochow Mil. Region, PLA 74-.
People's Republic of China.

Piaget, Jean, D. ès sc.; Swiss psychologist; b. 9 Aug 1896; ed. Neuchâtel, Zürich and Paris Univs.
Private Docent 21; Prof. of Philosophy, Neuchâtel Univ.

26; Prof. of Child Psychology and History of Scientific Thought, Geneva Univ. 29-; Prof. of Gen. Psychology, Lausanne Univ. 37-54; Dir. Int. Bureau of Educ. 29-67; co-Dir. Inst. des Sciences de l'Educ. 33-71; Dir. Int. Centre of Genetic Epistemology, Geneva 55-; Foreign Assoc. U.S. Nat. Acad. of Sciences; Erasmus Prize 72. First Kittay Int. Award for Psychiatry 73, Prize of Inst. de la Vie 73; hon. degrees.
Publs. include *Le langage et la pensée chez l'Enfant, Le Jugement et le Raisonnement chez l'Enfant, La Représentation du Monde chez l'Enfant, La Causalité physique chez l'Enfant, Le Jugement moral chez l'Enfant, La Construction du Réel chez l'Enfant, La Naissance de l'Intelligence chez l'Enfant, Le Développement des Quantités chez l'Enfant, Les Mécanismes Perceptifs, Biologie et Connaissance, Logique et Connaissance Scientifique, Le Structuralisme, Mémoire et Intelligence, Psychologie et Pédagogie, L'Epistémologie génétique, L'Equilibration des structures cognitives, L'Epistémologie des Sciences de l'Homme.*
Ecole de Psychologie et des Sciences de l'Éducation, Palais Wilson, Geneva, Switzerland.

Piasecki, Boleslaw; Polish politician; b. 18 Feb. 1915, Łódź; s. of Ludomir Piasecki and Pelagia Kotnowska; m. Barbara Kolendo 1948; three s. three d.; ed. Faculty of Law, Warsaw Univ.
Active mem. of Polish resistance movt.; established weekly *Dziś i Jutro* 45; Chair. PAX Asscn. (social movt. of progressive Catholics) 52-; Deputy to Seym 65-; mem. Council of State June 71-; Order of Banner of Labour, 1st Class, Commdr. Cross with Star of Polonia Restituta, Virtuti Militari, and other decorations.
Leisure interest: collecting bears.
Krasicki Str. 7, Warsaw, Poland.
Telephone: 281985.

Piatier, André (Sylvain); French economist; b. 25 June 1914, Orne; s. of Maurice Piatier and Juliette Grenier; m. Caroline Werling 1940; one d.; ed. Univ. of Paris, London School of Econs., Inst. für Konjunkturforschung, Berlin, Hague Acad., etc.
Rockefeller Fellow and Asst., Faculté de Droit, Paris, and Sec. Inst. Int. de Finances Publiques 36-39; war and resistance, lecturer Univ. of Strasbourg, Centre d'Etudes Economiques de la Marine 39-45; Dir. Economic Studies and Research, Inst. Nat. de la Statistique, Paris 46-56; Prof. of Economic Sciences, Cairo 55-56, Teheran 65-67; Pres. of Experts, Int. Travel Inst. 48-57, Prof. Ecole Pratique des Hautes Etudes (Sorbonne), Inst. d'Etudes Politiques, Ecole Nat. d'Admin., Ecole d'Application de la Statistique, Inst. d'Etudes de Développement Economique et Social, Paris, etc.; Pres. Cttee. for Econ. Science and Devt. 60-66, Délégation gén. à la Recherche Scientifique; Officier Légion d'Honneur, Médaille de la Résistance; Dir. Centre d'Etude des Techniques Economiques Modernes (CETEM); past mem. of various int. consultative boards.
Leisure interests: painting, music.
Publ. Several works in field of economics, statistics and business studies; Dir. of collections *Observation Economique, Développement Economique, Techniques Economiques Modernes, Rythmes Economiques* etc.
11 bis, rue Vauquelin, Paris 5e, France.
Telephone: POR 2704.

Picard, Laurent A., D.B.A.; Canadian broadcasting executive; b. 27 Oct. 1927, Quebec City; s. of late Edouard Picard and Alice Gingras; m. Marie Thérèse Germain 1954; five s.; ed. Laval and Harvard Univs.
Professor, Faculty of Commerce, Laval Univ. 55-59; Research Assoc. and Asst., Harvard Business School 60-62; Prof. and Assoc. Dir. and Consultant, Ecoles des Hautes Etudes Commerciales, Montreal 62-68; Exec. Vice-Pres. Canadian Broadcasting Corpn. 68-72, Pres. and Chair. of Board 72-; mem. Board of Dirs. Nat. Theatre School of Canada, Telesat Canada, Univ.

of Montreal, Nat. Film Board; mem. Board of Trustees, Nat. Art Centre.
Publs. numerous articles.
Canadian Broadcasting Corporation, 1500 Bronson Avenue, Ottawa, Ont. K1G 3J5; Home: 591 St. Catherine Road, Outremont, Quebec, Canada.
Telephone: 731-3111 (Office).

Picart le Doux, Jean; French painter, tapestry designer and book illustrator; b. 31 Jan. 1902, Paris; s. of Charles Picart le Doux and Marguerite Bonneau; m. Annie Bellier 1930; ed. Lycée Condorcet and private Acads. of Art.
Career devoted to graphic art and since 43 to tapestry designing; Prof. École nationale supérieure des arts décoratifs, Paris; Co-founder Asscn. des Peintres-Cartonniers de tapisserie 45; one-man exhibitions since 50 in Paris, Lucerne, Geneva, Berlin, London, Zürich, Copenhagen, The Hague, Cologne, Dakar, Abidjan, etc.; has participated in over 800 group exhibitions in France and abroad including Bienal of São Paulo 58, Decorative Art Exhibition, Tokyo 60, Int. Biennale of Tapestry, Lausanne; represented in Musées Nat. d'Art Moderne, Paris and Warsaw, Univ. of Kansas, Kultusministerium Stuttgart, etc.
Major Works: over 400 patterns for tapestries; Murals: painting Polytechnic Toulouse, mosaic *Groupe Scolaire* Choisy-le-Roi, ceramic Hotel le Concorde (Toulouse), Centre Cultural Longlaville, etc.; Book Illustrations: *Paris ma rose* (Nazim Hikmet), *Le Bestiaire* (Apollinaire), *Tetrabilos* (Ptolemée).
Leisure interests: travelling, reading.
Studio: 163 avenue Victor Hugo, 75 Paris 16e; Home: 91 rue Boileau, Paris 16e, France.
Telephone: 727-93-71.

Piccard, Jacques Ernest Jean; Swiss scientist; b. 28 July 1922, Brussels, Belgium; s. of Auguste Piccard and Marianne (Denis) Piccard; m. Marie-Claude Maillard 1953; two s. one d.; ed. Univ. of Geneva and Inst. Universitaire de Hautes Etudes Internationales, Geneva.
Assistant Prof. of Econs., Geneva 46-48; consultant scientist to several American orgs. for deep sea research; collaborated with father, Prof. Auguste Piccard, in construction of bathyscaph *Trieste*; built first tourist submarine *Auguste Piccard*; has made more than 100 dives in Mediterranean and Pacific, one to 35,800 feet (deepest ever dive) in Jan. 1960; Chief Scientist, research submarine *Ben Franklin* for the Grumman-Piccard Gulf Stream Drift Mission, Summer 69; Visiting Prof. of Oceanic Engineering at Stevens Inst. of Technology, Hoboken, New Jersey; Croix de Guerre (France), U.S. Distinguished Public Service award 60, Officier Ordre de Léopold (Belgium), Hon. D.Sc. (American Int. Coll. and Hofstra Univ.).
Leisure interests: reading, walking, swimming, diving.
19 avenue de l'Avenir, 1012 Lausanne, Switzerland.
Telephone: 021-28-80-83; 021-99-25-65 (Office).

Picchia, Menotti Del, D.LITT., LL.D.; Brazilian journalist, author and civil servant; b. 1892; ed. Pôrto Alegre and São Paulo.
Former Dir. journals *Mandú, Cidade de Itapira, Tribuna de Santos, A Gazeta, O Correio Paulistano, O Anhanguera,* reviews *Nossa Revista, S. Paulo* and *A. Cigarra,* and Union of Brazilian Journalists; fmr. Dir. State of S. Paulo Credit Bank; Dir. Dept. of Propaganda and Publicity of S. Paulo State; a leader, with Graça Aranha and Ronald de Carvalho, of the "Semana de Arte Moderna" with Cassiano Ricardo and Plinio Salgado of nationalist literary movement "Verdeamarelo".
Publs. of which some are translated into other languages: *Poemas do Vicio e da Virtude, Juca Mulato, Mascaras, Angustia de D. João, Chuva de Pedra, República dos Estados Unidos do Brasil, Poemas de Amor;* ballads: *Lais, Tragedia de Zilda, A Tormenta,*

O Homem e a Morte, O Misterio do Sertão, Cummunká, Salomé; novels and stories: *A Mulher que Pecou, O Crime daquela Noite, Toda Núa, O Despertar de S. Paulo,* essays and monographs: *A Crise da Democracia, Pelo Divorcio, O Momento Literario Brasileiro;* plays: *Jesus, Suprema Conquista, Mascaras;* historical works: *Pão de Moloch, Nariz de Cleopatra;* children's books.

Piccinato, Luigi, DR. ARCHIT.; Italian architect and town planner; b. 30 Oct. 1899, Legnago, Verona; m. Ines Wild 1929; two d.; ed. High School, Padua, and Univ. of Rome.
Assistant Prof. of Town Planning, Rome 23-30; Lecturer Town Planning, Naples Univ. 27-50, Tucumán and Buenos Aires Univs. 49-50; Prof. of Town Planning Univ. of Venice 50-64, Univ. of Rome 64-; mem. Consiglio Superiore, Ministry of Works 64, Consiglio Superiore Antichità e Belle Arti, Ministry of Education 70, and numerous architectural socs.; mem. Istituto Nazionale di Urbanistica; Hon. Vice-Pres. F.I.H.U.A.T.; Olivetti First Prize for Town Planning, Golden Medal of Merit, Italian Repub.
Leisure interests: music, photography, history
Major works: town plans at Sabaudia, Padua, Matera, Pescara, Siena, L'Aquila, Catania, Bolzano, Naples, Rome 61, Venice 61, Orvieto, Macerata, Carrara and other Italian towns; Istanbul, Atakoy, Bursa (Turkey), Ezeiza (Buenos Aires), Regional Plans of Venice, Bolzano, Campania, Lazio, houses in Rome; Ivrea and Venice; Eliseo Theatre, Rome; Mediterraneo Theatre, Naples; Stadium, Pescara, C.B.D., Taranto.
Piazza Stefano Jacini 23, 00191 Rome, Italy.
Telephone: 32-03-74.

Piccoli, Flaminio; Italian politician; b. 28 Dec. 1915. Member of Chamber of Deputies 58-; Pres. of Christian Democratic Deputies 72-; Sec.-Gen. Christian Democrat Party Jan.-Nov. 69; Minister for State Participation in Industry March 70-May 72.
45 Massimi, Rome, Italy.

Pickard, Sir Cyril Stanley, K.C.M.G.; British diplomatist (retd.); b. 18 Sept. 1917, London; s. of late G. W. Pickard and Edith Pickard; m. Helen Elizabeth Strawson 1941; three s. one d.; ed. Alleyn's School, Dulwich and New Coll., Oxford.
Ministry of Home Security 39; Royal Artillery 40-41; Office of Minister of State, Cairo 41-45; UNRRA Balkan Mission 44, later with UNRRA in Germany; Home Office 45-48; Commonwealth Relations Office (C.R.O.) 48-; Office of U.K. High Commr. in India 50-52; Official Sec. to Office of U.K. High Commr. in Australia 52-55; Head, S. Asia and Middle East Dept., C.R.O. 55-58; Deputy High Commr. in New Zealand 58-61; Asst. Under Sec. of State, C.R.O. 62-66; Acting High Commr., Cyprus 64; High Commr. in Pakistan 66-71, in Nigeria 71-74.
Leisure interests: swimming, golf.
Sommer House, Oak Lane, Sevenoaks, Kent, England.

Pickavance, Thomas Gerald, C.B.E., PH.D.; British physicist; b. 19 Oct. 1915, St. Helens, Lancs.; s. of late William Pickavance and Ethel Pickavance; m. Alice Isobel Boulton 1943; two s. one d.; ed. Univ. of Liverpool.
Research on Atomic Bomb Project, Directorate of Tube Alloys, Liverpool 40-46; Lecturer in Physics, Liverpool Univ. 42-46; Head of Cyclotron Group A.E.R.E., Harwell 46; Principal Scientific Officer 47 and Senior Principal Scientific Officer 50; Deputy Head of Gen. Physics Division A.E.R.E. 55; Dir. Rutherford High Energy Laboratory, Nat. Inst. for Research in Nuclear Science 57-65, Science Research Council 65-69, Nuclear Physics Science Research Council 69-71; Fellow St. Cross Coll., Oxford 68-; Hon. D.Sc. City Univ. London 69.
Leisure interests: motoring, travel, photography.
3 Kingston Close, Abingdon, Berkshire, England.
Telephone: Abingdon 23934.

Pickering, Edward Davies; British journalist; b. 4 May 1912; ed. Middlesbrough High School.
Chief Sub-Editor *Daily Mail* 39; Royal Artillery 40-44; Staff of Supreme Headquarters Allied Expeditionary Force 44-45; Managing Editor *Daily Mail* 47-49, *Daily Express* 51-57, Editor *Daily Express* 57-62; Managing Dir. Beaverbrook Publications 62-63; Dir. Beaverbrook Newspapers 56-63; Editorial Dir. and Dir. The Daily Mirror Newspapers Ltd. 64-68; Editorial Dir. Int. Publishing Corpn. Chair. I.P.C. Newpaper Div. and Chair. Daily Mirror Newspapers Ltd. 68-70; Chair. I.P.C. Magazines Ltd. 70-74; Chair. Mirror Group Newspapers Ltd. 75-; mem. Press Council 64-69, 70-; Dir. Int. Publishing Corpn. 66; Treas. Int. Fed. of the Periodical Press 71-75; Vice-Pres. Periodical Publrs. Asscn. 71-.
Mirror Group Newspapers Ltd., Holborn Circus, London, EC1P 1DQ; Chase Warren, Tennysons Lane, Haslemere, Surrey, England.
Telephone: 01-822-3626 (Office); 0428-2541 (Home).

Pickering, Sir George White, Kt., M.D., SC.D., F.R.C.P., F.R.S.; British physician and educationalist; b. 26 June 1904, Whalton, Northumbria; s. of George and Ann Pickering; m. Mary Carola Seward 1930; one s. three d.; ed. Dulwich Coll., Pembroke Coll., Cambridge, and St. Thomas's Hospital, London.
Professor of Medicine, Univ. of London, and Dir. of Medical Clinic at St. Mary's Hospital, London 39-56; Regius Prof. of Medicine, Univ. of Oxford 56-68, Pro-Chancellor 67-69, Master of Pembroke Coll. 68-74; Foreign Assoc. U.S. Nat. Acad. of Sciences 70; Hon. Fellow, Pembroke Coll., Cambridge; Hon. mem. numerous British, Foreign and Commonwealth Medical Scientific Socs.; ten Dr. h.c. four British and foreign Univs.
Leisure interest: gardening.
Publs. *High Blood Pressure*, 1st edn. 55, 2nd edn. 68, *The Nature of Essential Hypertension* 61, *The Challenge to Education* 67, *Creative Malady* 74; and papers relating to vascular disease, high blood pressure, peptic ulcer, headache and educ.
5 Horwood Close, Headington, Oxford, OX3 7RF, England.
Telephone: Oxford 64260.

Pickering, Herbert Lorraine; New Zealand farmer and politician; b. 29 March 1919, Havelock; s. of Charles A. Pickering and Ida L. McNamara; m. Margaret P. McKenzie 1941; two s. one d.
Served in army and R.N.Z.A.F. 40-46; farmer 47-60; mem. Parl. 60-72; Minister without Portfolio and Assoc. Minister of Finance 69-72; Minister of Educ. 72.
Leisure interests: yachting, tennis, writing.
Karu, Motunau Beach, Scargill, New Zealand.
Telephone: 838 (Home).

Pickering, Thomas Reeve, M.A.; American diplomatist; b. 5 Nov. 1931, Orange, N.J.; ed. Bowdoin Coll., Brunswick, Me., Fletcher School of Law and Diplomacy, Medford, Mass., Univ. of Melbourne, Australia.
Lieutenant U.S. Navy 56-59; joined Dept. of State 59-, Intelligence Research Specialist 60, Foreign Affairs Officer 61, Arms Control and Disarmament Agency 61-62; mem. U.S. Del. to Disarmament Conf., Geneva 62-64; Principal Officer, Zanzibar 65-67; Deputy Chief of Mission, Dar es Salaam 67-69; Deputy Dir. Bureau of Politico-Mil. Affairs 69-73; Exec. Sec. Dept. of State, Special Asst. to Sec. of State 73-74; Amb. to Jordan Feb. 74-.
Department of State, Washington, D.C. 20520, U.S.A.

Pickering, William Hayward, M.S., PH.D.; American scientist; b. 24 Dec. 1910, Wellington, N.Z.; s. of Albert William and Elizabeth Hayward Pickering; m. Muriel Bowler 1932; one s. one d.; ed. Calif. Inst. of Tech.
California Inst. of Technology 36-, Prof. of Electrical

Eng. 46-, Dir. Jet Propulsion Laboratory 54-; mem. Scientific Advisory Board U.S.A.F. 45-48; Chair. Panel on Test Range Instrumentation Research and Development Board 48-49; Directed devt. of Army Corporal and Sergeant missiles 50-55, and many spacecraft, including Explorer 1; Ranger, the first U.S. spacecraft to photograph the moon; Mariner II, first spacecraft to return scientific data from the vicinity of a planet (Venus); Mariner IV, first spacecraft to photograph Mars; Surveyor, first U.S spacecraft to soft-land on the moon and return scientific data; mem. Academic Advisory Council, Univ. of Conn. Space Technology Inst., Advisory Cttee. Dept. of Aeronautics and Astronautics, Univ. of Wash., Advisory Council of Inst. of Geophysics and Planetary Physics, Univ. of Calif., U.S. Technical Panel on Earth Satellite Programs IGY 56-58, Army Scientific Advisory Panel 63-65; Pres. A.I.A.A. 63; Fellow I.E.E.E.; Hon. Fellow A.I.A.A.; mem. Nat. Acad. of Sciences, American Asscn. Univ. Profs., American Geophysical Union, Nat. Acad. of Engineering, American Asscn. for Advancement of Science, Royal Soc. of New Zealand, Int. Acad. of Astronautics; mem. Int. Astronautics Fed., Pres. 65-66; hon. mem. New Zealand Inst. of Eng., and Aerospace Medical Asscn.; Fellow American Acad. of Arts and Sciences; Hon. D.Sc. (Occidental Coll., Clark Univ.); Meritorious Civilian Service Award U.S. Army 45, Distinguished Civilian Service Award U.S. Army 59, Columbus Gold Medal 64, Prix Galabert Award 65, Robert H. Goddard Memorial Trophy 65, Crozier Gold Medal 65. Spirit of Saint Louis Medal 65, Distinguished Service Medal NASA 65, Italian Order of Merit 66, Louis W. Hill Award 68, Edison Medal (Inst. of Electrical and Electronics Engineers) 72, etc.
Leisure interests: swimming, fishing, hiking, gardening.
Jet Propulsion Laboratory, California Institute of Technology, 4800 Oak Grove Drive, Pasadena, Calif. 91103; Home: 292 St. Katherine Drive, Pasadena, Calif. 91103, U.S.A.
Telephone: 213-354-3405 (Office).

Pickersgill, John Whitney, P.C., C.C., B.LITT.; Canadian politician; b. 23 June 1905, Wyecombe, Ont.; s. of Mr. and Mrs. Frank Allan Pickersgill; m. 1st Beatrice L. Young 1936 (died 1937), 2nd M. Margaret Beattie 1939; two s. two d.; ed. Univ. of Manitoba and Oxford Univ.
Lecturer in History, Wesley Coll., Univ. of Manitoba 29-37; Third Sec. Dept. of External Affairs 37; various capacities Prime Minister's Office 37-52; Clerk of Privy Council and Sec. to Cabinet 52-53; M.P. for Bonavista-Twillingate 53-67; Fed. Sec. of State 53-54; Minister of Citizenship and Immigration 54-57; mem. Official Opposition 57-63; Sec. of State 63-64; Minister of Transport 64-67; Pres. Canadian Transport Comm. 67-72; retired.
Leisure interests: writing and travel.
Publs. *The Mackenzie King Record* (4 vols.), *The Liberal Party* 62, *Le Parti Libéral* 63, *My Years with Louis St. Laurent* 75.
550 Maple Lane East, Rockcliffe Park, Ottawa, Ontario, Canada.
Telephone: 7496101.

Pickford, Mary; American actress; b. (as Gladys Smith) 8 April 1893, Canada.
Stage debut at age of 5; fmr. organizer Pickford-Lasky Productions Inc.; Head of Mary Pickford Co., Hollywood; one of original founders of United Artists; mem. Nat. Advisory Cttee., White House Conf. on Ageing 59; Dir. American Soc. for the Aged, Inc.
Silent films include *Hearts Adrift*, *Tess of the Storm Country*, *Stella Maris*, *Daddy Long Legs*, *Pollyanna*, *Rebecca of Sunny Brook Farm*, *Poor Little Rich Girl*, *Little Lord Fauntleroy*; talking films include *Coquette*, *The Taming of the Shrew*, *Kiki*.

Publs. *Why not try God?* 34, *The Demi-Widow* 35, *My Rendezvous with Life* 35, *Sunshine and Shadow* 55.
Pickfair, Beverly Hills, Calif., U.S.A.

Pien Chiang; Chinese government official.
Vice-Minister, Sixth Ministry of Machines Building 63, Minister 75.
People's Republic of China.

Pienaar, Louis Alexander, B.A., LL.B.; South African lawyer and diplomatist; b. 23 June 1926, Stellenbosch; *s.* of Jacobus Alexander Pienaar and Eleanore Angelique Pienaar (née Stiglingh); *m.* Isabel Maud van Niekerk 1954; two *s.* one *d.*; ed. Univ. of Stellenbosch and Univ. of South Africa.
Joined legal practice in Bellville 53; mem. Provincial Council for Bellville Constituency 66-70, mem. Parl. for Belville Constituency 70-75; Amb. to France Oct. 75-.
Leisure interests: squash, youth movements.
Embassy of South Africa, 59 quai d'Orsay, 75007 Paris; Home: 5 rue Cimarosa, 75116 Paris, France.
Telephone: 555-92-37 (Office); 727-46-54 (Home).

Pieniążek, Szczepan, D.SC.; Polish pomologist; b. 27 Dec. 1913, Słup, near Garwolin; ed. Warsaw Univ.
Doctor 42-45, Docent 45-46, Assoc. Prof. 46-54, Prof. 54-; Corresp. mem. Polish Acad. of Sciences 52-64, mem. 64-, mem. Presidium 60-65, 72-, Vice-Pres. 75-; Dir. Inst. of Fruit Growing, Skierniewice 51-; mem. Polish Botanical Soc., American Soc. for Horticultural Science 38-, American Pomological Soc. 38-, American Soc. of Fruit-Growing Sciences 74, Board of Dirs. of N. Copernicus Polish Soc. of Natural Historians 69-; mem. Int. Asscn. for Horticultural Sciences 58-62, Vice-Pres. 66-70, Pres. 70-, Chair. Fruit-Growing Section 62-66; Editor *Postępy Nauk Rolniczych* and *Prace Instytutu Sadownictwa w Skierniewicach*; Foreign mem. Bulgarian Acad. of Agricultural Sciences, German Democratic Repub. Acad. of Agricultural Sciences, V. I. Lenin All-Union Acad. of Agricultural Sciences; Dr. h.c. Cracow Agricultural Acad. 73; Officer's Cross, Order of Polonia Restituta 54, Commdr's Cross 73, Medal of 10th Anniversary of People's Poland 55, Order of Banner of Labour, 2nd Class 59, State Prize, 2nd Class 50.
Publ. *Dookoła sadowniczego świata* (Round the Fruit-Growing World) 65.
Ul. Niemcewicza 24 m. 38, 02-306 Warsaw, Poland.

Pieraccini, Giovanni; Italian journalist and politician; b. 25 Nov. 1918, Viareggio; *m.* Vera Verdiani; ed. Univ. of Pisa.
Organizer, Young Socialist Federation; mem. Editorial Staff *La Nazione del Popolo* 44-46, Jt. Editor *Nuovo Corriere* 46-48; Editor *Avanti* 59-63; M.P. 48-68; fmr. mem. Finance and Treasury Comms. and Foreign Affairs Cttee.; Minister of Public Works 63-64, of Budget 64-68; Senator 68-; Minister of the Merchant Navy 73-74, of Pres. Comm. Industry, Commerce and Tourism; Minister for Scientific and Technological Affairs March-Oct. 74; Pres. of Socialist Group in Senate; Socialist Party.
The Senate, Rome; Home: 21 Via Maso di Banco, Florence, Italy.

Pierce, John Robinson, B.S., M.S., PH.D.; American electrical engineer; b. 27 March 1910, Des Moines, Ia.; *s.* of the late John S. and Harriett A. Robinson Pierce; *m.* 1st Martha Peacock 1938 (divorced 1964); 2nd Ellen Richter 1964; one *s.* one *d.*; ed. Calif. Inst. of Technology.
Bell Telephone Laboratories 36-71, Dir. of Electronics Research 52-55, Dir. of Research, Electrical Communications 55-58, Communications Principles 58-61; Exec. Dir. Research-Communications Principles and Systems Div. 61-65, Research-Communications Sciences Div. 65-71; California Inst. of Technology, Prof. of Eng. 71-; mem. Nat. Acad. of Sciences, Nat. Acad. of Engineering, American Philosophical Soc., Royal Acad. of

Sciences (Sweden); Fellow, Acoustical Soc. of America, American Physical Soc., Inst. of Electrical and Electronics Engineers, American Acad. of Arts and Sciences; Valdemar Poulsen Medal 63, President's Nat. Medal of Science 63, and many other medals and trophies.
Leisure interests: writing, science fiction, music.
Publs. *Theory and Design of Electron Beams* 54, *Traveling Wave Tubes* 50, *Electrons, Waves and Messages* 56, *Man's World of Sound* 58, *Symbols, Signals and Noise* 61, *The Research State: A History of Science in New Jersey* 64, *Electrons and Waves* 64, *Quantum Electronics* 66, *Waves and Messages* 67, *Science, Art and Communication* 68, *Almost All About Waves* 73.
California Institute of Technology, Department of Electrical Engineering, 1201 E California Boulevard, Pasadena, Calif. 91125; 931 Canon Drive, Pasadena, Calif. 91106, U.S.A.

Pierre, Abbé (*see* Groués, Henri).

Pierrot, George Francis, A.B.; American writer; b. 11 Jan. 1898, Chicago, Ill.; *s.* of Dr. George F. and Aloyse Martin Pierrot; *m.* 1st Kathryn Barnhisel 1924 (divorced 1930); one *s.* (deceased); 2nd Helen Hay Reck 1935; two *s.* two *d.*; ed. Univ. of Washington.
Reporter 19; editor *University of Washington Daily*, *Canning Age* 20; reporter *Seattle Times* 20-21; Lecturer in Journalism Univ. of Washington 21; Publicity Sec. Seattle Chamber of Commerce; Associate Editor *Business Magazine* Detroit 22; Asst. Managing Editor *American Boy Magazine* 22-24; Editor *American Boy-Youth's Companion* 24-36, staff writer 31, travelled round world; Pres. and Dir. World Adventure Series Lectures 33-; Dir. World Adventure Series, Junior Adventurers, Round-the-World; corresp. World Letters Inc. 38-39; Press Dir. Ford Motor Co., New York World's Fair 39-40; Pres. Sprague Publications Inc. 40-41; Managing Dir. Metropolitan Detroit U.S.O. 42-43; co-leader Mexican expedition 44; Exec. Sec. Medical Science Centre of Wayne Univ. 43-47; Pres. George F. Pierrot Productions 59-; Pres. G.F.P. Inc. T.V. Syndicated Shows 66-; television producer: *World Adventure* series 48-, *George Pierrot Show* 53-; *George Pierrot Presents* (daily) 58-; Pres. Sigma Delta Chi 24-25, Circumnavigators Club 62-63, Professional Travel Film Managers' Asscn. 70-; Distinguished Service Award, Wayne State Univ. 61; Stenius Award 62; Gov. of Michigan Citation 67; Michigan World Trader of the Year 68; Austrian Plaque of Merit 71, German Award of Merit 72.
Leisure interests: travel and travel writing, conversation, fishing, gardening.
Publs. *Yea, Sheriton* 25, *The Vagabond Trail* 35.
Office: Detroit Institute of Arts, Detroit, Mich. 48202; Home: 2224 Burns Avenue, Detroit, Mich. 48214, U.S.A.

Pierson, Warren Lee, A.B., LL.B.; American banker and lawyer; b. 29 Aug. 1896, Princeton, Minn.; *s.* of Lewis W. Pierson and Hilda Pearson; *m.* Eleanor Shelton Mehnert 1927; ed. Univ. of Calif. and Harvard Univ.
Served in French Army First World War; Pres. All-America Cables and Radio Inc., and The Commercial Cable Co. 45-47; Chair. Board of Dirs. Trans World Airlines Inc. 47-61; Chair. Board of Dirs. Great Western Financial Corpn. 55-67; Dir. Int. Telephone and Telegraph Corpn., Commercial Cable Co., Vertientes-Camagüey Sugar Co. of Cuba, U.S. Industries Inc. ITT World Communications Inc.; Pres. IATA 50-51; mem. Exec. Council U.S. Int. Chamber of Commerce; Dir. Molybdenum Corpn. of America 60-; Pres. Int. Chamber of Commerce 55-57; Commdr. Légion d'Honneur (France), Order of the White Rose (Finland); Commdr. Order of Southern Cross (Brazil), Order Aztec Eagle (Mexico), Order of the Star of Italian Solidarity (Italy), Commdr. Order of Christ (Portugal), Grand

Officer Order of Merit (Italy), Commdr. Order of Merit Fed. Repub. of Germany.
Office: 320 Park Avenue, New York, N.Y. 10022; Home: Further Lane, East Hampton, N.Y. 11937, U.S.A.

Pieske, Eckard, M.A., DR.RER.POL.; German economist; b. 31 May 1928, Brieg, near Breslau; s. of Dr. Erich Pieske and Beda-Johanna Pieske; m. Doris Ritter 1957; one s.; ed. Univ. of Tübingen and Western Reserve Univ., Cleveland, U.S.A.
Economist, Bank Deutscher Länder, Frankfurt 53; Investment Analyst, Allianz-Lebensversicherung-AG, Stuttgart 56; official of Fed. Ministries of Econ. Affairs and Finance 58; Ministerial Counsellor, Fed. Ministry of Finance; Exec. Dir. Int. Monetary Fund 75-.
Leisure interests: gardening, hiking.
Publ. Gold, Devisen, Sonderziehungsrechte (3rd edn.) 72.
International Monetary Fund, 19th and H Streets, Washington, D.C. 20431; Home: 6309 Long Meadow Road, McLean, Va. 22101, U.S.A.
Telephone: (202) 477-3255 (Office); 790-0055 (Home).

Pietilä, Reima Frans Ilmari; Finnish architect; b. 25 Aug. 1923, Turku; s. of Frans Viktor Pietilä and Ida Maria Lehtinen; m. Raili Inkeri Marjatta Paatelainen 1961; one c.; ed. Inst. of Technology.
Vice Chairman Asscn. of Finnish Architects 59-60, mem. Gov. Body 69-70; Foreign mem. Royal Acad. for Liberal Arts, Sweden 69-; State Prof. of Arts 71-74; Prof. of Architecture Univ. of Oulu 73-; Partner, Reima Pietilä & Raili Paatelainen, Architects; Chevalier Ordre de la Couronne (Belgium) 58; Knight Order of the Finnish Lion 67.
Major works: Finnish Pavilion at Brussels World Fair 58, Kaleva Church, Tampere 66, Students' Activity Centre, Dipoli, Congress Centre, Otaniemi 66.
Leisure interest: theoretical problems in architectural aesthetics.
Laivurinrinne 1A, 17 Helsinki 12, Finland.
Telephone: 626852.

Pieyre de Mandiargues, André; French writer; b. 14 March 1909, Paris; m. Bona Tibertelli 1950; one d.
Prix des Critiques for Soleil des loups 51; Prix Goncourt for La Marge 67.
Publs. Dans les années sordides (poems and prose) 43, Hedera ou la persistance de l'amour pendant une rêverie (poem) 45, L'Etudiante 46, Le Musée noir 46, Les Incongruités monumentales 48, Les Sept Périls spectraux 50, Les Masques de Léonor Fini 51, Soleil des loups 51, Marbre 53, Astyanax 56, Les Monstres de Bomarzo (essays) 57, Le Belvédère (essays) 58, Feu de braise 59, La Marée 59, Cartolines et dédicaces 60, Sugai 60, L'Age de craie 61, Deuxième belvédère 62, La Motocyclette (novel) 63, Saint-John Perse, A l'honneur de la chair 63, Sabine 64, Le Point où j'en suis 64, Beylamour 65, Les Corps illuminés 65, Larmes de généraux 65, Porte dévergondée 65, La Marge (novel) 67, Ruisseau des Solitudes 68, Le Marronnier 68, Troisième Belvédère 71, Mascarets 71, Bona l'amour et la peinture 71, Le Cadran lunaire 72, Isabella Morra 74, Chagall 75, Le désordre de la mémoire 75.
36 rue de Sévigné, Paris 3e, France.

Pifer, Alan (Jay Parrish); American foundation executive; b. 4 May 1921, Boston; s. of Claude Albert and Elizabeth (Parrish) Pifer; m. Erica Pringle 1953; three s.; ed. Groton School, Harvard Univ., Emmanuel Coll., Cambridge.
Executive Sec. U.S. Educ. Comm. in U.K. 48-53; Exec. Asst. Carnegie Corpn. 53-57, Exec. Assoc. 57-63, Vice-Pres. Carnegie Corpn., Carnegie Foundation for the Advancement of Teaching 63-65, Acting Pres. 65-67, Pres. 67-; mem. Man. Cttee. U.S.-S. Africa Leader Exchange Program 57-; Dir. N.Y. Urban Coalition 67-71, Nat. Assembly for Social Policy and Devt. 67-71, Council for Social Work Educ. 68-71, Fed.

Reserve Bank 71-, Council on Foreign Relations, Comm. on Private Philanthropy and Public Needs 73-, Senior Execs. Council, Conf. Board 73-74; Trustee, African-American Inst. 57-72, Vice-Chair. 64-69; Trustee, Foundation Library Center 67-70, Chair. 68-70; Trustee, Board of Overseers, Harvard Univ. 69-, Univ. of Bridgeport 73, American Ditchley Foundation 73; Fellow, African Studies Asscn., U.S. Acad. of Arts and Sciences; Hon. LL.D. (Mich. State Univ.) 71, (Hofstra Univ.) 74, Hon. Dr. Univ. (Open Univ.) 74.
437 Madison Avenue, New York, N.Y. 10022; Home: 311 Greens Farms Road, Greens Farms, Conn. 06436, U.S.A.

Pigford, Robert Lamar, PH.D., M.S.; American chemical engineer; b. 16 April 1917, Meridan, Miss.; s. of Lamar and Zula Harrington Pigford; m. Marian Pinkston; one s. one d.; ed. Mississippi State Univ. and Univ. of Illinois.
Research chemical Engineer, E.I. du Pont de Nemours & Co., Wilmington, Del. 41-47; Prof. and Chair. Dept. of Chemical Engineering, Univ. of Delaware 47-66; Prof. of Chemical Engineering, Univ. of Calif. (Berkeley) 66-75; Prof. Univ. of Delaware Sept. 75-; mem. Nat. Acad. of Sciences, Nat. Acad. of Eng.; Walker and Lewis Awards, Founders' Award, American Inst. of Chemical Engineers; Editor Fundamentals Quarterly, American Chem. Soc.
Leisure interests: music (plays the clarinet), ham radio, woodwork.
Publs. 56 articles in professional journals.
University of Delaware, Newark, Del. 19711, U.S.A.

Piggott, Stuart, D.LITT., F.B.A., F.S.A.; British university professor; b. 28 May 1910, Petersfield, Hants.; s. of G. H. O. Piggott and G. A. Phillips; ed. Churchers' Coll., Petersfield, and St. John's Coll., Oxford.
Investigator, Royal Comm. on Ancient Monuments (Wales) 28-33; Asst. Dir. Avebury Excavations (Wilts.) 34-38; war service, Lieut.-Col., Intelligence Corps 39-45; Abercromby Prof. of Prehistoric Archaeology, Univ. of Edinburgh 46-; Commr. Royal Comm. on Ancient Monuments Scotland 46; Trustee, British Museum 69-74; mem. German Archaeological Inst. 53; foreign hon. mem. American Acad. of Arts and Sciences 60; Hon. D.Litt. Hum. (Columbia Univ.).
Publs. Fire among the Ruins (poems) 48, British prehistory 49, Prehistoric India 50, William Stukeley 50, Neolithic Cultures of the British Isles 54, Scotland Before History 58, Approach to Archæology 59, Ancient Europe 65, Prehistoric Societies (with J. G. D. Clark) 65, The Druids 68, Introduction to Camden's Britannia of 1695 71; Editor The Dawn of Civilization 61.
Leisure interests: reading, eating and drinking, talking.
46 Great King Street, Edinburgh 3, Scotland.
Telephone: 556-2960.

Pignedoli, H.E. Cardinal Sergio; Italian ecclesiastic; b. 4 July, 1910, Felina di Regio Emilia.
Ordained 33; consecrated titular Archbishop of Iconio 51; Sec. of the Sacred Congregation for the Evangelization of the Peoples; created Cardinal by Pope Paul VI 73.
Segretario, S. Congregazione per l'Evangelizzazione dei Popoli, Casa 'De Propaganda Fide', Rome, Italy.

Pignon, Edouard; French painter; b. 12 Feb. 1905, Bully-Grenay (Pas de Calais); m. Hélène Parmelin; two s. one d.
Came to Paris from Marles les Mines (Pas de Calais) 27; pupil of the painter Auclair 28, of the sculptors Wlerick and Arnold 30-34; devoted himself exclusively to painting 36-; Salon des Indépendants 32-38, des Surindépendants 38, des Tuileries and d'Automne 43, de Mai (founding mem.) 44-; rep. at Paris Exhbns. 41, 42, 43, 54, 55, 56, 57; One-Man Shows Paris 46, 49, 52-56, 58,

59; Retrospective Exhbn., Musée d'Art Moderne, Paris 66; many foreign exhibitions; costumes and décor for *Scheherazade* 48, *Mère Courage* (Théâtre Nat. Populaire) 52, *Mandragore* 53, *Ce Fou de Platonov*, *Le Malade Imaginaire* 56, *On ne badine pas avec l'amour* (Théâtre Nat. Populaire) 59; retrospective exhbns. Bucarest, Budapest, Warsaw, Bologne, Luxembourg 73-75; exhbn. of 50 nudes Musée d'Art Moderne, Paris 76; works in museums at Paris (Art Moderne), Amsterdam, Brussels, Liège, London (Tate Gallery), New York (Modern Art), São Paulo, Stockholm, Gothenburg; principal series: *Les Maternités* 42-43, *Les Poissons*, *Femmes Assises* 44, *Les Catalanes* 45-46, *Le Port d'Ostende* 47, *Les Mineurs* 49, *Les Oliviers* 50, *Les Vendanges*, *Cueillettes de Jasmins* 53, *Les Electriciens* 55, *Les Paysages de Bandol* 58, *Les Combats de Coqs* 59-60, *Pousseurs de Blé* 61-62, *Batailles* 63-64, *Plongeurs* 64-67, *Têtes de Guerriers* 68, *Céramique-sculpture*, Maison de la Culture, Argenteuil 70.
Publs. Illustrations for *Les Biasons* (poem by Maurice Scève), *Arbres et Voiles* (Verdet), *Dialogue de l'Arbre* (Valéry) 57, *Jacques Le Fataliste* (Diderot).
26 rue des Plantes, Paris 14e, France.
Telephone: 540-77-21.

Pignon, Léon, L. en D.; French government official; b. 19 April 1908; ed. Ecole Coloniale.
Pupil-Administrator Tonkin 32; Ministry for the Colonies, Paris; served French Army 39-40; prisoner of war; released 42; attached to Bureau for the Colonies Algiers; attached to State Secretariat for the Colonies after creation of French Nat. Liberation Cttee.; Ministry of French Overseas Territories, Paris; political counsellor to Commr. in Indo-China with rank of Administrator First Class; Federal Commr. for Foreign Affairs 46-47; Commr. of the Republic in Cambodia 47-48; High Commr. in Indo-China 48-50; del. U.N. Trusteeship Council 50-54; Dir. Political Affairs, Ministry of French Overseas Territories 54-59; Judge French Community Court of Arbitration 59-60; Counsellor of State Jan. 62-; Pres. Central Cttee. of Overseas Territories for 5th Plan 64; Commdr. de la Légion d'Honneur; Commdr. of the Order of Léopold.
[*Died 4 April* 1976.]

Pike, Sir Philip, Kt., Q.C.; British judge; b. 6 March 1914, Jamaica; s. of Ernest B. and Dora C. (née Lillie) Pike; m. 1st Phyllis Kelvin Calder 1943, one s. one d.; m. 2nd Millicent Locke Staples 1959; ed. De Carteret School and Munro Coll., Jamaica, and Middle Temple, London.
Crown Counsel, Jamaica 47-49; Legal Draftsman, Kenya 49-52; Solicitor-Gen. Uganda 52-58; Attorney-Gen., Sarawak 58-65; Chief Justice, High Court, Borneo 65-68; Judge and Acting Chief Justice, Malawi 69-70; Chief Justice, Swaziland 70-72; Coronation Medal; decorations from Malaysia and Sarawak.
Leisure interests: golf, photography.
c/o Barclays National Bank Ltd., Adderley Street, Cape Town, S. Africa.

Pike, Marshal of the Royal Air Force Sir Thomas Geoffrey, G.C.B., C.B.E., D.F.C.; British air force officer; b. 29 June 1906; ed. Bedford School and R.A.F. Coll., Cranwell.
Joined R.A.F. 23, Squadron-Leader 37, Group Captain 41, Air Commodore 44, Air Vice-Marshal 50; Marshal of the Royal Air Force 62-; served Second World War 39-45; A.O.C. No. 11 Group, Fighter Command 50-51; D.C.S. H.Q. Air Forces, Central Europe 51-53; Dep. Chief of Air Staff 53-56; Air Officer C.-in-C. Fighter Command 56-59; Chief of Air Staff 60-63; Deputy Supreme Commdr., Allied Forces, Europe 64-67; Legion of Merit, U.S.A.
Little Wynters, Hastingwood, Harlow, Essex, England.

Pilcher, Sir John (Arthur), G.C.M.G.; former British diplomatist; b. 16 May 1912; s. of Col. A. J. Pilcher and

Edith Blair; m. Delia Margaret Taylor 1942; one d.; ed. Shrewsbury and Clare Coll., Cambridge.
Served Japan 36-39, China 39-41; Ministry of Information and Foreign Office 41-48; Press Attaché, Rome 48-51; Foreign Office 51-54; Counsellor, Madrid 54-59; Ambassador to Philippines 59-63; Asst. Under-Sec. of State, Foreign Office 63-65; Amb. to Austria 65-67, to Japan 67-72.
Leisure interests: music, literature, the arts, history.
33 The Terrace, London, S.W.13, England.
Telephone: 01-876 9710.

Pile, John Devereux, M.A., F.B.I.M.; British business executive; b. 5 June 1918, Seaford, Sussex; s. of Gen. Sir Frederick Pile, Bt. and Lady Ferguson; m. Katharine M. Shafe; two s. two d.; ed. Weymouth Coll., Dorset and Trinity Coll., Cambridge.
Joined Imperial Tobacco Group 46, Man. W. D. & H. O. Wills and Wm. Clarke & Son, Dublin 56-59, Chair. Robert Sinclair Ltd. 60-64, Churchmans 64-67, W. D. & H. O. Wills 67-71; Deputy Chair. Imperial Tobacco Group Ltd. 71-75, Chief Exec. Imperial Group Ltd. 73-, Chair. 75-.
Imperial House, Grosvenor Place, London, S.W.1; Home: Munstead, Godalming, Surrey, England.

Pilkington, Baron (Life Peer), cr. 68, of St. Helens in the County Palatine of Lancashire; **Harry Pilkington;** D.L.; British businessman; b. 19 April 1905, St. Helens, Lancs.; s. of late Richard Austin Pilkington and late Hope Cozens-Hardy; m. Mavis Joy Doreen Wilding (née Caffrey); one s. one d. one step-s. one step-d.; ed. Rugby and Magdalene Coll., Cambridge.
Director Pilkington Brothers Ltd. 34-, Chair. 49-73, Hon. Life Pres. 73-; Dir. Bank of England 55-72; Pres. Fed. of British Industries 53-55; Pres. Council of European Industrial Feds. 54-57; Chair. Nat. Advisory Council for Education for Industry and Commerce 56-67; Chair. Royal Comm. on Doctors, and Dentists' Pay 57-60, Cttee. of Inquiry into the Future of Sound and Television Broadcasting 60-62, Econ. Devt. Cttee. for Chemical Industry 68-72; Chancellor, Loughborough Univ. of Technology 66-; Dir. Business Int. Ltd. 68-; Vice-Lord Lieut. for Merseyside 74-; Fellow British Inst. of Management; Pres. British Shippers' Council 71-74, British Plastics Fed. 72-74; Businessman of the Year 73; Hon. D.S.C., LL.D., D.C.L.
Leisure interests: theatre, tennis, rose-growing.
Windle Hall, St. Helens, Merseyside, England.
Telephone: 23423.

Pilkington, Sir Lionel Alexander Bethune (known as Sir Alastair), Kt., M.A., F.R.S., F.B.I.M.; British glass-maker; b. 7 Jan. 1920, Calcutta, India; s. of late Col. G. R. Pilkington and of Mrs Pilkington; m. Patricia N. Elliot 1945; one s. one d.; ed. Sherborne School and Trinity Coll., Cambridge.
Joined Pilkington Brothers Ltd. 47, Dir. 55, Dep. Chair. 71-73, Chair. 73-; inventor of the float glass process; Dir. Bank of England 74-; mem. Court of Govs., Admin. Staff Coll. Henley 73-, Council, Liverpool Univ., Man. Cttee., Royal Liverpool Philharmonic Soc.; Fellow, Imperial Coll. of Science and Tech., London 74; Hon. Fellow UMIST 69; Hon. D.Tech. (Loughborough) 68; Hon. D.Eng. (Liverpool) 71; Toledo Glass and Ceramic Award 64, Mullard Award (Royal Soc.) 68, John Scott Award (City Trust, Philadelphia) 69, Wilhelm Exner Medal (Austrian Trade Assen.); part-time mem. British Railways Board.
Leisure interests: music, walking, carpentry, gardening and skiing.
Pilkington Brothers Ltd., St. Helens, Merseyside; Home: The Crossways, View Road, Rainhill, Prescot, Merseyside, England.
Telephone: St. Helens 28882 (Office): 051-426-4228 (Home).

Pillai, Narayana Raghavan, K.C.I.E., C.B.E., M.A., LL.B.; Indian civil servant; b. 24 July 1898, Trivandrum; s. of M. C. Narayan Pillai; m. Edith Minnie Arthurs 1928; two s.; ed. Christian Coll., Madras, and Trinity Hall, Cambridge.
Secretary, Dept. of Commerce 42; Commr.-Gen. for Economic and Commercial Affairs in Europe, Paris 48; Sec. to Cabinet 50; Sec.-Gen., Ministry of External Affairs 52-60; Hon. Fellow Trinity Hall, Cambridge; Hon. D.Litt. (Travancore).
Leisure interest: walking.
1022 St. James's Court, London, S.W.1, England.
Telephone: 01-834-0523.

Piller, Jan; Czechoslovak politician; b. 4 July 1922, Pilsen; ed. Central Political School.
Turner, Škoda Works, Pilsen 40-48; Chief Sec. District Cttee., C.P. of Czechoslovakia, Škoda Pilsen 48-50; Head of Eng., Metallurgy and Chem. Dept., Central Cttee., C.P. of Czechoslovakia, Prague 52-62; Deputy Premier 62-65; Deputy Minister of Heavy Industry 66-68; Chief Sec. Central Bohemian Regional Cttee., C.P. of Czechoslovakia 68; Alt. mem. Central Cttee. of C.P. of Czechoslovakia 58-61, mem. 62-, mem. Presidium 68-71; Deputy to Nat. Assembly 64-69; mem. Central Cttee. Bureau for directing Party Work in Czech lands 68-70; Sec. Central Cttee. Bureau 69-70; Deputy to House of People, Fed. Assembly 69-71; mem. Secr., mem. Presidium of Cen. Council of Czechoslovak Revolutionary Trade Union Movt. 70-71, Chair. Cen. Council 70-71; Awards for Merit in Construction 58.
Office: Central Council of Czechoslovak Revolutionary Trade Union Movement, Prague, Czechoslovakia.

Pilliod, Charles J., Jr.; American business executive; b. 20 Oct. 1918, Cuyahoga Falls, Ohio; m. Marie Elizabeth Pilliod; three s. two d.; ed. Kent State Univ., Ohio.
Production Trainee, Goodyear 41; Pilot U.S. Air Force, World War II; Man. Dir. Goodyear-Panama 47, Sales Man. Goodyear-Colombia 54, Man. Dir. Goodyear, Brazil 59, Man. Dir. Goodyear, U.K. 64, Dir. of Operations, Goodyear Int. 66, Vice-Pres. 67, Pres. 71; Vice-Pres. Goodyear Tire & Rubber Co. 71, Exec. Vice-Pres., Dir. 71, Pres. 72-74, Chair., Chief Exec. Officer 74-; Dir. CPC Int., Rubber Mfrs. Asscn.; Trustee Cttee. for Econ. Devt.; mem. Industry Policy Advisory Cttee. for Trade Negotiations, Washington, D.C., Business Roundtable Policy Cttee., The Conf. Board, The Business Council, Council on Foreign Relations; Hon. C.B.E. 72.
Goodyear Tire & Rubber Co., 1144 East Market Street, Akron, Ohio 44316, U.S.A.

Pillsbury, Philip Winston; American executive; b. 16 April 1903; ed. Blake School, Hotchkiss and Yale Univ. Joined The Pillsbury Co. 24, Dir. 28-, Treas. 40, Pres. and Dir. 40-52, Chair. 52-65, Chair. Finance Cttee., Exec. Cttee. 65-70; official of other companies; Hon. French Consul, Minnesota; Dir. Nat. Audubon Soc.; LL.D. (Grinnell).
300 West Ferndale Road, Wayzata, Minn., U.S.A.
Telephone: 612-473-8682.

Pilyugin, Nikolai Alekseyevich; Soviet scientist in automation and telemechanics; b. 18 May 1908, Krasnoe Selo, Leningrad region; ed. Bauman Higher Technical School, Moscow.
Worker 26-35; engineer, Dir. several research Insts. 35-; Corresp. mem. U.S.S.R. Acad. of Sciences 58-66; mem. 66-; mem. C.P.S.U. 40-; Deputy to U.S.S.R. Supreme Soviet 66-; Hero of Socialist Labour twice); Lenin Prize Winner.
Publs. Works on problems of automatic control.
U.S.S.R. Academy of Sciences, 14 Leninsky Prospekt, Moscow, U.S.S.R.

Pimen, Patriarch **(Sergei Mikhailovich Izvekov);** Soviet ecclesiastic; b. July 1910, Bogorodsk, Moscow Region.
Became monk 27; ordained priest 32; Bishop of Odessa 57, Archbishop 60; Metropolitan of Leningrad 60-63; Metropolitan of Krutitsky and Kolomna 63-71; Patriarch of Moscow and All Russia 71-; Grand Cordon, Order of the Cedar of Lebanon 72.
5 Chisty pereulok, Moscow G-34, U.S.S.R.

Pimenov, Mikhail Alexandrovich; Soviet politician; b. 1914; ed. Higher Party School.
Wood-cutter 29-30; Exec. in timber industry 30-37; in coal mining 37-39; Party work 39-52; mem. C.P.S.U. 40-; Perm. Staff, Central Cttee. C.P.S.U. 52-60; Second Sec. Central Cttee. C.P. Turkmenistan 60-63; State Cttee. for Food Industry, U.S.S.R. Gosplan 63-65; Chief Inspector, Cttee. for Party-State Control, Central Cttee. of C.P.S.U. and U.S.S.R. Council of Ministers (later U.S.S.R. People's Control Cttee.) 65-; Cand. mem. Central Cttee. C.P.S.U. 61-66.
U.S.S.R. People's Control Committee, Ulitsa Kuibysheva 21, Moscow, U.S.S.R.

Pimenov, Pyotr Timofeyevich; Soviet trade union official; b. 1915; ed. Volgograd Mechanical Inst.
Turner at a Volgograd mechanical plant 29-35; student, Volgograd Mechanical Inst. 35-40; engineer, Volgograd Mechanical Plant 40-42; scientific activity 42-44; trade union activity 44-; Sec., later Chair. Central Cttee. of Trade Union of Workers of Higher Schools and Scientific Institutions 49-51; Head of Econ., later Int. Depts., All-Union Central Council of Trade Unions 51-61; Sec. World Fed. of Trade Unions, Prague 61-63; Sec. All-Union Central Council of Trade Unions 63-; Deputy to U.S.S.R. Supreme Soviet, mem. Comm. for Foreign Affairs, Soviet of Nationalities 66-; Alt. mem. Central Cttee. of C.P.S.U. 66-.
All-Union Central Council of Trade Unions, 42 Leninsky Prospekt, Moscow, U.S.S.R.

Pimentel, George Claude, A.B., PH.D.; American professor of chemistry; b. 2 May 1922, Fresno, Calif.; s. of Emile Pimentel and Lorraine Laval; m. Betty Anne Jeffrey 1942; three d.; ed. Univ. of Calif. at Berkeley.
Instructor in Chem., Univ. of Calif. at Berkeley 49-51, Asst. Prof. 51-55, Assoc. Prof. 55-59, Prof. of Chem. 59-; Fellow American Acad. of Arts and Sciences; mem. Nat. Acad. of Science 66, American Chemical Soc.; A.C.S. Petroleum Chem. Award 59; Manufacturing Chemists College Teaching Award 71; Joseph Priestley Award 72; Pittsburgh Spectroscopy Award 74.
Leisure interests: squash, photography.
Publs. *Selected Values of Physical and Thermodynamic Properties of Hydrocarbons and Related Compounds* (with Rossini and others) 53, *Introductory Quantitative Chemistry* (with Olson and Koch) 56, *The Hydrogen Bond* (with McClellan) 60, *Radical Formation and Trapping in the Solid Phase* (in *Formation and Trapping of Free Radicals*, Edited by A. M. Bass and H. P. Broida) 60, *Chemistry: An Experimental Science* 63; *Understanding Chemical Thermodynamics* (with R. D. Spratley); *Chemical Bonding Clarified through Quantum Mechanics* (with R. D. Spratley), *Understanding Chemistry* (with R. D. Spratley); over 150 articles on molecular spectroscopy, chemical bonding, free radicals via matrix isolation, infra-red study of Mars, chemical lasers.
Department of Chemistry, University of California, Berkeley, Calif. 94720, U.S.A.
Telephone: 415-642-6330.

Pinard, Roch, B.L.; Canadian lawyer and politician b. 1910; ed. Univ. of Montreal.
Admitted to Bar 32; joined legal firm Mercier, Blain, Bissonnette and Fauteux; founded legal firm Bissonnette, Pinard and Perreault 35, changed to Bertrand, Pinard, Pigeon, Paré and Ozère and finally to Pinard,

Pigeon, Paré and D'Amour 49-; M.P. for Chambly-Rouville 45-57; mem. External Affairs Cttee. 45-57; mem. Canadian Del. to UN 53; Parliamentary Asst. to Sec. of State for External Affairs 53-54, Sec. of State 54-57; Vice-Pres. Canadian Del. to UN 55.
Messrs. Pinard, Pigeon, Paré et D'Amour, Montreal, Quebec, Canada.

Pinay, Antoine; French industrialist and politician; b. 30 Dec. 1891.
Served First World War 14-18; engaged in leather industry; Deputy from Saint Etienne (Saint Chamond) 36; Senator from Loire 38; elected to Constituent Assembly 45, to Nat. Assembly 46-58; Sec. of State for Economic Affairs, first Queuille Cabinet 48-49; Minister of Public Works and Transport in first Pleven Cabinet and subsequent cabinets 50-52; Prime Minister March-Dec. 52; Minister of Foreign Affairs Feb. 55-56; Minister of Finance and Economic Affairs, de Gaulle Cabinet, June 58-Jan. 59, Debré Cabinet Jan. 59-Jan. 60; Pres. Cie. française pour la diffusion des techniques 60-; Adviser Soc. pour l'expansion industrielle française à l'étranger 62-; Mayor of Saint Chamond; Pres. of Regional Econ. Devt. for Rhône-Alpes 64-73; Dir. Caisse d'aide à l'équipement des collectivités locales 66-; first Ombudsman of France 73-74.
87 boulevard Suchet, Paris 16e; and Route du Coin, Saint-Julien-en-Jarez, 42-Saint-Chamond, France.

Pindborg, Jens Jørgen, D.D.S.; Danish oral pathologist; b. 17 Aug. 1921, Copenhagen; m. Eva Hartz 1951; ed. Royal Dental Coll., Copenhagen, and Univ. of Illinois.
Instructor, Research Assoc. and Assoc. Prof., Royal Dental Coll., Copenhagen 43-59; Prof. and Chair. Dept. of Oral Pathology 59-; Head, Dental Dept., Univ. Hospital, Copenhagen 53-; Consultant, Danish Nat. Health Service 58-66; Chief, Dental Corps, Royal Danish Navy 46-59; Perm. Guest Lecturer, Royal Dental Coll., Malmö, Sweden; Visiting Prof. Univ. of Illinois 58, 61, Hebrew Univ. Jerusalem 69, WHO Visiting Prof. in India 63-64; Dir. Indo-Danish Oral Cancer Control Project Trivandrum 69-; Head, Collaborating Center under WHO Int. Reference Center for Oropharyngeal tumours, Agra, India 64-; Head Collaborating Center under WHO Int. Reference Center for Salivary Gland Tumours London 65-; Visiting Prof. Tata Inst. of Fundamental Research Bombay 66-; Consultant for Ministry of Health Uganda 66; Research expert for WHO to New Guinea and Fiji 66; Dir. WHO Int. Reference Centre on Odontogenic Tumours 66-; Consultant, WHO in Brazil and Colombia 67; Dir. WHO Int. Reference Centre on Oral Precancerous Conditions 67-; Consultant for WHO in Afghanistan 68; Editor-in-Chief, Danish Dental Journal 62-, Scandinavian Journal of Dental Research 70, Int. Journal of Oral Surgery 72-75; Pres. Asscn. of Hospital Dentists 54-66, Danish-Israeli Asscn. 64-69; Consultant to WHO on classification of oral diseases; mem. Danish Medical Research Council 72, Vice-Chair. 74-; Editor-in-Chief Community Dentistry & Oral Epidemiology 73; Dr. h.c. (Karolinska Inst., Stockholm) 73, (Univ. of Lund) 74; Founding mem. Int. Acad. of Oral Pathology; Fellow, American Asscn. for Advancement of Science, Royal Coll. of Surgeons; Hon. Fellow, Dental Surgery, Royal Coll. of Pathology, American Acad. of Oral Pathology 75; Hon. mem. Burmese Medical Asscn. 76; Commemoration Lecture Odontological Section, Royal Soc. of Medicine 72; K. H. Box Lecture, Toronto 64; E. J. Goddard Oration, Brisbane 70; Cordwainer's Lecturer, Univ. London 74; Isaac Schour Memorial Award 70; Elmer Best Award 72; Robertson lecture Univ. of Sheffield 75.
Leisure interest: art, archaeology.
Publs. The Dentist in Art 60, Syndromes of Head and Neck (with R. J. Gorlin) 64, Atlas of Diseases of the Oral Mucosa 68, Pathology of the Dental Hard Tissues 70, Histological Typing of Odontogenic Tumours, Cysts and Allied Lesions (with I. R. H. Kramer and H. Torloni) 72, Histology of the Human Tooth 73, Atlas of Diseases of the Jaws (with E. Hjörting-Hansen) 74, and six books in Danish and 230 papers on oral pathology, oral medicine and cancer research.
4 Universitetsparken, 2100 Copenhagen Ø, Denmark.
Telephone: 371700.

Pindling, Rt. Hon. Lynden Oscar, P.C.; Bahamian politician; b. 22 March 1930; ed. Govt. High School, Bahamas, and London Univ.
Lawyer 52-67; Leader of Progressive Liberal Party; Premier of Bahamas Jan. 67- (Prime Minister July 73-), also Minister of Internal Security and fmr. Minister of Econ. Affairs.
Office of the Prime Minister, Rawson Square, Nassau, Bahamas.

Pineau, Christian; French politician; b. 14 Oct. 1904, Chaumont; m. Blanche Bloys 1963; seven c.
Assistant Sec.-Gen. Conf. Gen. du Travail; editorial staff Le Peuple; founder clandestine "Libération Nord"; escaped to London, returned to France, arrested, again escaped to London, returned a second time, arrested and sent to Buchenwald; released 45; Deputy to Constituent Assemblies 45-46, Nat. Assembly 46-58; Minister of Food 45, of Public Works 45 and 49, of Finance 48, of Foreign Affairs 56-58; Dir.-Gen. and Pres. France-Villages, France-Môtels 63-67; Officier, Légion d'Honneur, Compagnon de la Libération, C.B.E., G.C.M.G.
Publs. Books for Children include: Contes de je ne sais quand, Plume et le Saumon, L'Ourse aux pattens verts, Comerouse le Mystérieux, Histoires de la Forêt de Bercé; Books for adults: La simple Vérité (history of the French Resistance), Mon Cher Député, L'Escalier des Ombres.
55 rue Vaneau, Paris 7e, France.
Telephone: BAB 58-20.

Pingel, Klaus G., DR.IUR.; German lawyer and civil servant; b. Grenzberg, Germany; m.; two c.; ed. Univs. of Berlin, Geneva and Kiel.
Barrister-at-law; Supervisory Officer German/Danish Border, German Customs Admin. 53; with Fed. Ministry of Finance; joined Comm. of European Communities 59, Counsellor to Customs Directorate, Head of Negotiation Team of Community in GATT; Head Customs Valuation Div. 63; Dir. Admin. of the Customs Union (fmrly. Customs Directorate) 68-.
Administration of the Customs Union, Commission of the European Communities, 200 rue de la Loi, 1049 Brussels, Belgium.

Pinget, Robert; French writer; b. 19 July 1919; ed. legal studies at univ.
Former barrister, later painter; taught French in England; literary career 51-; Prix des Critiques 63, Prix Femina 65.
Publs. Fantoine et Agapa 51, Mahu ou le Matériau 52, Le Renard et la Boussole 55, Graal Flibuste 57, Baga 58, Le Fiston 59, Lettre morte 59, La Manivelle (play) 60, Clope au dossier 61, Architruc (play) 61, L'Hypothèse (play) 61, L'Inquisitoire 62, Quelqu'un 65, Autour de Mortin (dialogue) 65, Le Libera 68, La Passacaille 69, Fable 71, Identité, Abel et Bela (play) 71.
4 rue de l'Université, Paris 7e, France.

Pinheiro de Azevedo, Vice-Admiral José Baptista; Portuguese naval officer and politician; b. 1917, Angola.
Naval Attaché, London 68-71; Commdr. Marine Corps -74; mobilized Navy support for overthrow of Caetano Govt. April 74; Chief of Navy Staff 74-75; mem. Junta of Nat. Salvation April 74-March 75, Council of State May 74-March 75; Supreme Revolutionary Council March 75-; Prime Minister Sept. 75-.
Office of the Prime Minister, Lisbon, Portugal.

Piniés, Jaime de; Spanish diplomatist; b. 18 Nov. 1917, Madrid; *m.* Luz Bianchi 1954; two *s.*; ed. Univ. of Madrid.

Law Div., Bank of Spain 41-45; joined Spanish Foreign Service 45; Sec., Cuba 45-47, U.K. 47-48, U.S.A. 48-54, Philippines 55; mem. Staff of Spanish Perm. Mission to UN 56; Dir. N. American Div., Ministry of Foreign Affairs 57-60; Deputy Perm. Rep. to UN 60-68, Perm. Rep. 68-72, 73-; Amb. to U.K. 72-73.

Permanent Mission of Spain to United Nations, 809 United Nations Plaza, 6th Floor, New York, N.Y. 10017, U.S.A.

Pinilla Fábrega, Colonel José Manuel; Panamanian army officer and politician; b. 28 March 1919, Panama; *s.* of José M. Pinilla F. and Lucila Fábrega Vda. de Pinilla; *m.* Dora Paniza de Pinilla; ed. primary school, Panama, and "Colón Eloy Alfaro" Mil. Acad., Ecuador. Second Lieut., Infantry, Nat. Guard 41, Capt. 44, Major 51, Lieut.-Col. 60, Col. 66, Second-in-Command of Nat. Guard; has been Mil. Rep. for Panama in Ecuador, Colombia, Peru, Nicaragua, Panama Canal Zone, Guatemala; Pres. of Provisional Govt. Council of Panama 68-69; numerous decorations.

Panama City, Panama.

Pińkowski, Józef; Polish politician; b. 17 April 1929, Siedlce; ed. Higher School of Econs., Poznań.

Officer Polish Army 52-56; Dir. of Dept. Ministry of Purchase, then Ministry of Agricultural Products, later Chief Insp. of Corn, Ministry of Food Industry and Purchase 56-58; Sec. Scientific Econ. Council, Voivodship Nat. Council 58-60, Vice-Chair. of Presidium 60-65, Chair. 65-71; First Vice-Chair. Planning Comm. attached to Council of Ministers 71-74; mem. Exec. Warsaw Voivodship Cttee., Polish United Workers' Party 65-71, mem. Cen. Cttee. 71-, Sec. Cen. Cttee. 74-; Deputy to Seym (Parl.) 69-; Order of Banner of Labour, 2nd Class, Knight Cross of Order of Polonia Restituta.

Komitet Centralny Polskiej Zjednoczonej Partii Robotniczej, Ul. Nowy Świat 6, 00-497 Warsaw, Poland.

Pinochet Ugarte, Gen. Augusto; Chilean army officer; b. 25 Nov. 1915; *m.* María Lucía Hiriat Rodríguez; two *s.* three *d.*; ed. Mil. Acad., School of Infantry, Acad. of War, Acad. of Nat. Defence.

Army career 33-, Col. 66, Brig.-Gen. 69, Div. Gen. 70, Gen. 73; Instructor Acad. of War 54, Deputy Dir. 64; Asst. to Under-Sec. of War 54; mem. Chilean mil. mission to U.S.A. 56; Instructor Acad. of War, Ecuador 56-59; C.-in-C. VI Army Div., Chief of Army Staff 69; C.-in-C. of Army 73-; led coup to depose President Salvador Allende Sept. 73; Pres. Gov. Council of Chile 73-74; Pres. of Chile 74-; Mil. Star, Grand Mil. Merit Cross, High Command Hon. Officer (Ecuador), Abdón Calderón Parra Medal (Ecuador), Order of Mil. Merit (Colombia), Grand Cross of Military Merit (Spain).

Publs. *Geopolitica—Diferentes Etapes para el Estudio Geopolítico de los Estados* 68, *Geografía de Chile* 68, *Geografía de Argentina, Perú y Bolivia* 72, *Guerra del Pacífico 1879—Primeras Operaciones Terrestres* 72.

Oficina del Presidente, Santiago, Chile.

Pinter, Harold, C.B.E.; British playwright; b. 10 Oct. 1930, London; *m.* Vivien Merchant 1956; one *s.*; ed. Hackney Downs Grammar School, London.

Actor, mainly in English and Irish provincial repertory 49-58; playwright 57-; Assoc. Dir. Nat. Theatre; Austrian Prize for European Literature 73.

Leisure interests: cricket, drinking.

Plays: *The Room* 57, *The Dumb Waiter* 57, *The Birthday Party* 57, *A Slight Ache* 58, *The Caretaker* 59, *A Night Out* 59, *Night School* 60, *The Dwarfs* 61, *The Collection* 62, *The Lover* 62, *Tea Party* (TV play) 64, *The Homecoming* 65, *The Basement* (TV play) 67, *Landscape* 69, *Silence* 69, *Night* (one act play) 69, *Old Times* 70, *Monologue* (one act play) 72, *No Man's Land* 75;

screen-play for *The Servant* 63, *The Pumpkin Eater* 64, *The Quiller Memorandum* 66, *Accident* 67, *The Go-Between* 69, *Langrishe Go Down* 70, *A la Recherche du Temps Perdu* 72; Dir. *The Man in the Glass Booth* London 67, N.Y. 68, *Exiles* 70, 71, *Butley* 71, (film) 73, *Next of Kin* 74, *Otherwise Engaged* 75.

7 Hanover Terrace, Regent's Park, London, N.W.1, England.

Pinto Barbosa, António Manuel; Portuguese economist and diplomatist; b. 31 July 1917; ed. Universidade Técnica de Lisboa.

Teacher 41-50; Prof., Inst. of Higher Econ. and Financial Sciences 51-; Pres. Comm. for Reorganization of Industrial Resources 51-54; Under-Sec. of State at Treasury 51-54; Minister of Finance and Gov. of Int. Bank for Reconstruction and Devt. 55-65; Gov. Bank of Portugal (Banco de Portugal) and Gov. Int. Monetary Fund 66-74; Grand Cross, Order of Christ, Order of Prince Henry and of Isabella the Catholic.

Publs. *L'Industrie des Conserves au Portugal* 41, *L'Economie, aspects positifs et aspects théologiques* 43, *L'Economie du Café* 45, *La crise des exportations métropolitaines pour l'étranger* 50, *La tâche du Ministre des Finances* 55, *Banco de Fomento Nacional* 59, *L'Activité du Ministre des Finances* 60, *La Défense de la Stabilité Financière* 62, *Communication du Ministre des Finances sur le crédit extérieur* 62, *La phase actuelle des finances portugaises* 64, *La Dévaluation de 1949 et le Commerce Extérieur Portugais* 66.

Rua Almirante António Saldanha 3, Barrio do Restelo, Lisbon, Portugal.

Pinto-Coelho, Luis da Camara; Portuguese lawyer and diplomatist; b. 12; ed. Liceu Pedro Nuñes, Univ. of Lisbon and Univ. of Rome.

Civil Governor, District of Castelo Branco 34-36; Gen. Sec. Portuguese Youth Org. 36-37; lawyer 39-61; Prof. Univ. of Lisbon 40-; Legal Adviser, Ministry of Economy 42-60; Deputy at Nat. Assembly 45-49; Nat. Commissary, Portuguese Youth Org. 46-52; Ambassador to Spain 61-68; Prof. at Univ. and Lawyer, São Paulo 69-; cultural mission for Portuguese Government in Brazil 70; several Portuguese and Spanish decorations.

Publ. *The Co-Proprietor and the Portuguese Law* 39, 42.

Avenida da Liberdade 91, 14°, São Paulo, SP, Brazil.

Telephone: 34-70-34.

Piontek, Heinz; German writer; b. 15 Nov. 1925, Kreuzburg, Silesia; *m.* Giselle Dallmann 1951; ed. Theologisch-Philosophische Hochschule, Dillingen.

Berlin Prize for Literature 57, East German Writers' Prize, Esslingen 57; mem. Bavarian Acad. of Fine Arts 60-; Rom-Preis, *Villa Massimo* 60, Münchner Literatur Preis 67, Eichendorff-Preis 71, Tukan-Preis 71, Literatur Preis des Kulturkreises im BDI 74.

Publs. *Die Furt* (poems) 52, *Die Rauchfahne* (poems) 53, *Vor Augen* (stories) 55, *Wassermarken* (poems) 57, *Buchstab-Zauberstab* (essays) 59, *Aus meines Herzens Grunde* ((anthology) 59, *John Keats: Poems* 60, *Weisser Panther* (radio play) 62, *Mit einer Kranichfeder* (poetry) 62, *Kastanien aus dem Ferer* (stories) 63, *Windrichtungen* (journey reports) 63, *Neue deutsche Erzählgedichte* (anthology) 64, *Klartext* (poetry) 66, *Die mittleren Jahre* (novel) 67, *Liebeserklärungen* (essays) 69, *Männer die Gedichte machen* 70, *Die Erzählungen* 71, *Tot oder lebendig* 71, *Deutschegedichte seit 1960* 72, *Helle Tage anderswo* 73, *Gesammelte Gedichte* 74.

Dülferstrasse 97, 8000 Munich 50, Federal Republic of Germany.

Piore, Emanuel Ruben, B.A., PH.D.; American physicist; b. 19 July 1908, Wilno, Poland; *s.* of Ruben and Olga Piore; *m.* Nora Kahn 1931; one *s.* two *d.*; ed. Univ. of Wisconsin.

Chief Scientist, U.S. Navy Office of Naval Research 51-55; Vice-Pres. for Research, Avco Corpn. 55-56; Dir. of Research, Int. Business Machines Corpn., York 56-60,

Vice-Pres. for Research and Engineering 60-63, Vice-Pres. and Group Exec. 63-65, Vice-Pres. and Chief Scientist 65-, mem. Board of Dirs.; mem. Nat. Science Board 61-; Adjunct Prof., Rockefeller Univ.; Fellow, American Physical Soc., Inst. of Electrical and Electronics Engineers, American Acad. of Arts and Sciences, American Assen. for Advancement of Science, Royal Soc. of Arts (U.K.); mem. Nat. Acad. of Sciences, Nat. Sciences Board, Nat. Acad. of Eng.; consultant to President's Science Advisory Cttee.; mem. Board American Inst. of Physics, Stark Draper Lab., Nat. Information Bureau, SIAM, N.Y. State Foundation for Science; mem. American Philosophical Soc.; visiting cttees.; Joint M.I.T.-Harvard Medical Cttee.; mem. Board Science Research Assocs., Health Advancement Inc., Paul Revere Investors, Guardian Mutual Fund; Industrial Research Inst Medal. 67, Kaplun Int. Prize; Hon. D.Sc. (Union Univ. and Univ. of Wisconsin).
International Business Machines Corporation, Armonk, N.Y. 10504, U.S.A.
Telephone: 212-ENdicott 2-1772.

Piotrovsky, Boris Borisovich; Soviet historian; b. 1908; ed. Leningrad State Univ.
Scientific worker, Head of Section, State Acad. of Material Culture (now Inst. of Archaeology), U.S.S.R. Acad. of Sciences 29-53; Dir., Leningrad Branch, Inst. of Archaeology, U.S.S.R. Acad. of Sciences 53-54; Scientific Collaborator, Scientific Dir. of Eastern Dept., and Deputy Dir. for Scientific Matters, State Hermitage Museum, Leningrad 31-61, Dir. 61-; Prof. 68-; mem. C.P.S.U. 45-; Corresp. mem. Armenian Acad. of Sciences; Honoured Art Worker of Armenia 61; Academician, U.S.S.R. Acad. of Sciences 70-; Hon. mem. Prehistory and Protohistory Soc. of Florence; Corresp. mem. British Acad. 67; State Prize, Red Banner of Labour (three times), Dr. h.c. (Univ. of Delhi).
Main works: history and archaeology of Ancient East and Caucasus; in charge of excavations at Urart Fortress, Erevan (Armenia) 39-; directed U.S.S.R. Acad. of Sciences archaeological expedition in Nubia (Egypt) 60-62; over 120 scientific works, incl. *History and Culture of Uraratu* (State Prize) 46.
State Hermitage, 34 Dvortsovaya naberezhnaya, Leningrad, U.S.S.R.

Piper, Bright Harold (Peter); British banker; b. 22 Sept. 1918, Guildford, Surrey; s. of Robert Harold Piper and Daisy Homewood; m. Marjorie Joyce Arthur 1945; one s. one d.; ed. Maidstone Grammar School.
Joined Lloyds Bank Ltd. 35, Asst. Gen. Man. 63-65, Jt. Gen. Man. 65-68, Asst. Chief Gen. Man. 68-70, Deputy Chief Gen. Man. 70-73, Group Gen. Man. 73, Group Chief Exec. Lloyds Bank Group 73-.
Leisure interest: sailing.
Blagdon House, Lower Teddington Road, Kingston upon Thames, Surrey, England.

Piper, David Towry, C.B.E., M.A., F.S.A.; British museum director and writer; b. 21 July 1918, London; s. of late Prof. S. H. Piper and Mary Piper; m. Anne Richmond 1945; one s. three d.; ed. Clifton Coll. and St. Catharine's Coll., Cambridge.
Served in Indian Army 40-45, Japanese Prisoner-of-War 42-45; Asst. Keeper Nat. Portrait Gallery, London 46-64, Dir. 64-67; Slade Prof. of Fine Art, Oxford Univ. 66-67; Dir. Fitzwilliam Museum, Cambridge 67-73, Ashmolean Museum, Oxford 73-; Fellow Worcester Coll. Oxford 73-.
Publs. *It's Warm Inside* 53, *The English Face* 57, *Trial by Battle* 59, *Catalogue of 17th Century Portraits in the National Portrait Gallery* 63, *Companion Guide to London* 64; Editor: *Enjoying Paintings* 64, *Painting in England, 1500-1880* 65, *Shades* 70, *London* (World Cultural Guides series) 71.
Ashmolean Museum, Beaumont Street, Oxford, England.

Piper, John, C.H.; British painter and author; b. 13 Dec. 1903; ed. Epsom Coll. and Royal Coll. of Art.
Exhibited London 25-; paintings bought by Tate Gallery, Victoria and Albert Museum, Contemporary Art Society, etc.; war artist, commissioned to paint ruins of House of Commons 41, and two series of water-colours for H.M. The Queen 42-43; Trustee of Tate Gallery 46-53, 54-61, 68-; mem. Royal Fine Art Comm. 59-; Trustee, Nat Gallery 67-74; designer of opera and ballet (London, Milan and Venice), of stained glass (Oundle Coll. Chapel, Coventry Cathedral, St. Andrew's, Plymouth, Eton Coll. Chapel, etc.); Retrospective Exhbn., Cologne 65; Hon. D.Litt. (Oxford and Leicester Univs.); Hon. A.R.C.A.; Hon. A.R.I.B.A.; Hon. F.R.I.B.A.
Publs. *Shell Guide to Oxfordshire* 38, *Brighton Aquatints* 39, *British Romantic Painters* 42, *Buildings and Prospects*; *Romney Marsh* (King Penguin series, with own water-colours); and with John Betjeman: *Architectural Guide to Buckinghamshire, Architectural Guide to Berkshire*; (illustrated) *The Castles on the Ground* by J. M. Richards 73.
Fawley Bottom Farmhouse, nr. Henley-on-Thames, Oxon., England.

Piper, Klaus; German publisher; b. 27 March 1911; ed. Maximilians-Gymnasium, Munich.
With R. Piper & Co., Munich (book publishers) 32-, Partner 41-53, sole Managing Dir. 53-; mem. Finance Cttee. of German Booksellers Assen., Central PEN of Fed. Repub. of Germany, Rotary Club, Assen. of Literary Publishers; Golden Cultural Medal, Italian Ministry of Foreign Affairs 63, Distinguished Service Cross, First Class, Fed. Repub. of Germany.
Publs. *Offener Horizont* 53, *Nach 50. Jahren* 54, *Stationen—Piper-Almanach 1904-1964* 64; Editor: Reinhard Piper *Mein Leben als Verleger* 64, *Erinnerungen an Karl Jaspers* (co-editor).
R. Piper & Co. Verlag, Georgenstrasse 4, 8 Munich 40, Federal Republic of Germany.

Pippard, Sir Alfred Brian, Kt., M.A., PH.D., SC.D., F.R.S.; British prof. of physics; b. 7 Sept. 1920, London; s. of Prof. A. J. S. Pippard, F.R.S. and Mrs. F. L. O. (Tucker) Pippard; m. Charlotte Frances Dyer 1955; three d.; ed. Clifton Coll., and Clare Coll., Cambridge.
Scientific Officer, Radar Research and Devt. Establishment 41-45; Demonstrator in Physics, Cambridge Univ. 46, Lecturer 50, Reader 59-60, J. H. Plummer Prof. of Physics 60-; Cavendish Prof. of Physics 71-; Pres. of Clare Hall, Cambridge 66-73; Pres. Inst. of Physics 74-76; Hughes Medal (Royal Soc.) 59, Holweck Medal 61, Dannie-Heineman Prize (Göttingen) 69, Guthrie Medal (Inst. of Physics) 70.
Leisure interest: music.
Publs. *Elements of Classical Thermodynamics* 57, *Dynamics of Conduction Electrons* 62, *Forces and Particles* 72; many papers in *Proceedings of the Royal Society*, etc.
30 Porson Road, Cambridge, England.
Telephone: Cambridge 58713.

Pipping, Hugo Edvard, DR. PHIL.; Finnish economist; b. 12 June 1895, Helsinki; s. of Prof. Knut Hugo Pipping and Anna Constance Westermarck; m. Ella Tammelander 1922; one s. one d.; ed. Univ. of Helsinki.
Assistant Librarian, Univ. Library, Helsinki 19-28; Prof. of Econ. and Statistics, Swedish Commercial Univ., Helsinki 28-41; Prof. of Econ., Univ. of Helsinki 41-58; Dean Faculty of Political and Social Science 45-50, Vice-Rector 50-58; Chancellor Åbo Acad. 58-67; Sec. Economic Soc. Finland 24-41, mem. of Board 41-68; Editor of Society's journal *Ekonomiska Samfundets Tidskrift* 48-67; mem. of Scientific Soc. Finland, Finnish Historical Soc., Royal Soc. of Arts and Sciences, Gothenburg and Scientific Soc. of Lund, Sweden; Sec.-Gen. Finnish Production Cttee. 40-42; Vice-Chair. Swedish Literary Soc. of Finland 47-66; visited U.S.A. on Rockefeller Grant 48; Grand Cross of Finnish Lion;

Commdr. of White Rose 51, of Swedish Order of North Star 48; Hon. Dr. rer. pol. (Helsinki), Ph.D. (Uppsala).
Leisure interest: music.
Publs. *Myntreformen år 1865* 28, *Jean Cronstedt* 32, *Behov och levnadsstandard* 35, *Finlands näringsliv* 36, *Landsbygdens sociala problem i Finland* 40, *Ekonomiska Samfundet i Finland 1894-1944* 44, *Standard of Living* 53, *Från pappersrubel till guldmark. Finlands Bank 1811-1877* 61, *Bankliv genom hundra år* 62, *I guldmynfotens hägn Finlands Bank 1874-1914* 69.
Kyosti Kalliovagen 8, 00570 Helsinki 57, Finland.
Telephone: 689239.

Pirbhai, Count Sir Eboo, Kt., O.B.E.; Company director; b. 25 July 1905, Bombay; s. of Pirbhai, by his wife Kuvarbai; m. Kulsumbai, d. of Karmali Nathoo 1925; three s. (one deceased) three d.; ed. Duke of Gloucester School, Nairobi.
Representative of Aga Khan in Africa; mem. Nairobi City Council 38-43; mem. Legislative Council, Kenya 52-60; Pres. Muslim Asscn.; Pres. Aga Khan Supreme Council, Africa, Europe, Canada and the U.S.A.; granted title Count by Aga Khan 54; mem. other official bodies; Brilliant Star of Zanzibar 56, Order of the Crescent Cross of the Comores 66.
P.O. Box 40898, Nairobi; and 12 Naivasha Avenue, Muthaiga, Nairobi, Kenya.

Pirelli, Leopoldo; Italian businessman; b. 27 Aug. 1925.
Chairman Pirelli S.p.A., Milano, Industrie Pirelli S.p.A.; Man. Dir. Pirelli and Co., Milan; Dir. Soc. Int. Pirelli, Basle, Dunlop Holdings Ltd., London, Dunlop Ltd., London, Mediobanca, Milan, Generale Industrie Metallurgiche, Florence, Riunione Adriatica di Sicurtà S.p.A., Milan, Ital-consult, Rome, I.S.P.I., Milan; Vice-Pres. Museo dell'Automobile, Turin.
"Centro Pirelli", Piazza Duca d'Aosta 3, Milan, Italy.

Pirenne, Comte Jacques, LL.D., PH.D.; Belgian historian; b. 1891; ed. Ghent Univ.
Tutor to Prince Leopold (now ex-King Leopold III) 20-24; Chargé de Cours Univ. of Brussels 21, Prof. 24-54; Sec. Oriental Inst. 30-; scientific mem. Oriental Inst. of Prague 33; Michonis Prof. Coll. de France 35; awarded Quinquennial Prize for Historical Sciences for work 30-35; Lecturer Univ. of Cairo 39; Prof. Univ. of Grenoble 40, Univ. of Geneva 41-44; Head, King Leopold's Secretariat with title "Secretary to the King" Aug. 45; Editor *Archives d'Histoire du Droit Oriental* 35-; mem. Académie Royal de Belgique 45-; Acad. Septentrionale (Paris) 60; Grand Croix Ordre de la Couronne, Grand Officier Ordre de Léopold, Officier Légion d'Honneur, etc.
Publs. *Histoire des Institutions et du Droit Privé de l'Ancienne Egypte* (3 vols.) 32-35, *La civilisation sumérienne* 44, *La civilisation babylonienne* 45, *Les Grands Courants de l'Histoire Universelle* (7 vols., many trans.) 44-56, *La Belgique devant le nouvel équilibre du monde* 45, *Civilisations Antiques* 50, *Histoire de l'Europe de 1500 à 1955* (3 vols.) 60-62, *Histoire de la civilisation de l'ancienne Egypte* (3 vols.) 60-63, *La Religion et la Morale de l'Egypte antique* 64, *La Société hébraïque, d'après le Bible* 64, *Les Hommes Célèbres de l'Antiquité*, 69, *Le Dossier du roi Léopold III* 69.
49 rue des Echerins, Brussels, Belgium; Château de Hierges, Ardennes, France.
Telephone: 47-54-15 (Belgium).

Pirlot de Corbion, Edmond; French engineer; b. 1 June 1916, Bournemouth, England; s. of André and Louisa (née Meeus) Pirlot de Corbion; m. Irène Voruz de Vaux 1940; three c.; ed. Ecole Saint-Louis-de-Gonzague, Lycée Janson-de-Sailly and Ecole Nat. Supérieure des Mines de Paris.
Worked for Cie. de Saint-Gobain 43; Engineer, Chantereine Glassworks 43-47, Franière Glassworks,

Belgium 47-50, Stolberg Glassworks, Germany 50-53; Principal Engineer, Chantereine Glassworks 53-56, Head Office, Cie. de Saint-Gobain 56-59; Dir.-Gen. Saint-Gobain (America) 60-64, Saint-Roch Glassworks, Belgium 65-67; Admin. Cie. de Saint-Gobain 67, Vice-Pres./Dir.-Gen. 69, Cie. de Saint-Gobain-Pont-à-Mousson 70; Pres. Saint-Gobain Industries 70; Dir. Cellulose du Pin 69-, Saint-Roch Glassworks, SAPE, Cristaleria Española S.A., Pont-à-Mousson S.A., Davum.
Leisure interests: tennis, walking, hunting.
62 boulevard Victor-Hugo, 92 Neuilly-sur-Seine; 54 avenue Hoche, 75 Paris 8e; Home: 104 boulevard de Courcelles, 75 Paris 17e, France.

Pirzada, Abdul Hafiz; Pakistani lawyer and politician; b. 24 Feb. 1935, Sukkur; ed. D. J. Sindh Govt. Science Coll. and in U.K.
Called to the Bar, Lincoln's Inn, London 57; commenced legal practice in High Court of W. Pakistan, Karachi 57 and joined Chambers of Zulfikar Ali Bhutto 57-58; Advocate, W. Pakistan High Court and Supreme Court of Pakistan; mem. Cen. Cttee. Pakistan People's Party; mem. Nat. Assembly 70-; Minister of Law and Parl. Affairs, Educ. and Provincial Co-ordination 71-74, of Educ., Science, Technology and Provincial Co-ordination Oct. 74-.
Leisure interest: sport.
Ministry of Education and Science, Rawalpindi, Pakistan.

Pirzada, Sharifuddin, LL.B., S.PK.; Pakistani lawyer and politician; b. 12 June 1923; ed. Univ. of Bombay.
Secretary Muslim Students' Fed. 43-45; Sec. Provincial Muslim League 46; Man. Editor *Morning Herald* 46; Prof., Sind Muslim Law Coll., Karachi 47-55; Adviser to Constitution Comm. of Pakistan 60; Chair. Pakistan Company Law Comm. and mem. Int. Rivers Cttee. 60; Pres. Pakistan Branch Int. Law Asscn. and Pres. Legal Aid Soc.; Pres. Karachi Bar Asscn.; Senior Advocate, Supreme Court of Pakistan; Attorney-Gen. of Pakistan 64-66, 68-71; Minister of Foreign Affairs 66-68.
Publs. include: *Evolution of Pakistan, Fundamenta, Rights and Constitutional Remedies in Pakistan, Foundations of Pakistan* Vol. I 69, Vol. II 70.
C-37, K.D.A. Scheme No. 1, Habib Ibrahim Rahimtoola Road, Karachi, Pakistan.

Pisani, Edgard; French politician; b. 9 Oct. 1918, Tunis, Tunisia; m. Isola Chazereau; three s. one d.; ed. in Tunis and Paris.
Resistance during Second World War; Prefect-Dir. de Cabinet of Chief Commr. of Police 44-45; Dir. de Cabinet of Minister of the Interior 46; Prefect, Upper Loire 46-47, Upper Marne 47-54; Senator, Upper Marne 54-61; Minister of Agriculture 61-66; Minister of Equipment 66-67; County councillor and Mayor of Montreuil-Bellay 63-75; Senator, Upper Marne 74-; mem. Comm. for Foreign Affairs and Defence; mem. Socialist Group.
Publs. *La Région: pour quoi faire?*, *Le Général Indivis.* Valpuiseaux, 91720 Maisse, France.
Telephone: 495-87-54.

Piston, Walter, A.B., MUS.D.; American composer; b. 20 Jan. 1894; ed. Harvard Univ. and in Paris.
Member Harvard Music Faculty 26-60; Walter W. Naumburg Prof. of Music 48-60, Emer. 60; Mus.D. h.c. from four univs.; mem. American Acad. of Arts and Letters; mem. American Acad. of Arts and Sciences; New York Critics' Circle Award 43; Pulitzer Prize in Music 48, 61.
Works: Eight symphonies, concertos for violin, and many other compositions.
Publs. *Harmonic Analysis* 33, *Harmony* 41, *Counterpoint* 47, *Orchestration* 55.
127 Somerset Street, Belmont, Mass. 02178, U.S.A.

Pita de Veiga y Sanz, Adm. Gabriel; Spanish naval officer; b. 31 Jan. 1909, Ferrol del Caudillo; m. Amalia Jaudenes García 1936; nine s.; ed. Naval Mil. School. Lieutenant, Spanish Navy 37, Lieut.-Commdr. 44, Commdr. 51, Capt. 62; Vice-Pres. Study and Planning Comm. of the Fleet; Rear-Adm. 67; Deputy Chief of Staff of the Navy 69; Vice-Adm. 70; Commdr.-Gen. of the Fleet 71; Adm., Chief of Staff of the Navy 72; Minister for the Navy 73-; mem. Parl. 73-; Grand Cross of Naval Merit, Order of San Hermenegildo, Order of Civil Merit (Peru), Order of Merit (Italy), and many others.
Ministerio de Marina, Paseo del Prado 1, Madrid, Spain. Telephone: 2-34-32-33.

Pitblado, Sir David B., K.C.B., C.V.O.; British government official; b. 18 Aug. 1912, London; s. of Robert P. Pitblado and Mary (née Sear); m. Edith Mary Evans 1941; one s. one d.; ed. Strand School, London, Emmanuel Coll., Cambridge and Middle Temple.
Dominions Office 35-39, Asst. Private Sec. to Sec. of State for Dominions Affairs 37; N. American Secr. War Cabinet Office 42; Treasury 42-, U.K. del. San Francisco Conf. 45, and UN meetings 46; Under-Sec. Econ. Planning Staff, Treasury 49-51; Principal Private Sec. to Prime Minister (Lord Attlee, Sir Winston Churchill, Lord Avon) 51-56; Financial Attaché, British Embassy, Wash.; Alt. Exec. Dir. Int. Bank 56-58; Vice-Chair. Management Board of European Payments Union and Monetary Agreement 58-60; Third Sec. Treasury 60; Exec. Dir. for U.K. of Int. Bank and Affiliates, and of Int. Monetary Fund; Head of U.K. Treasury and Supply Del., and Econ. Minister, British Embassy, Washington 61-63; Deputy-Sec., Ministry of Power 65-66; Perm. Sec. Ministry of Power 66-69; Perm. Sec. (Industry) Ministry of Technology 69-70; Second Perm. Sec. Civil Service Dept. June 70-71, Comptroller and Auditor-Gen. 71-(76); Hon. Fellow, Emmanuel Coll., Cambridge. 23 Cadogan Street, London, S.W.3, England.
Telephone: 01-589-6765.

Pitman, Sir (Isaac) James, K.B.E., M.A.; fmr. British publisher and politician, b. 14 Aug. 1901, London; s. of Ernest Pitman and Frances Isabel (Butler); m. Margaret Beaufort Lawson Johnson; three s. one d.; ed. Eton and Christ Church, Oxford.
Joined Sir Isaac Pitman and Sons Ltd. 23, Chair. and Man. Dir. 34-66; served R.A.F. 40-43, admin. duties, Air Ministry; Dir. Bank of England 41-45; Dir. of Organization, Treasury 43-45; Conservative M.P. for Bath 45-64; Pro-Chancellor of Bath Univ. 66-; Dir. Boots Pure Drug Co. Ltd. 51-72, Bovril Ltd. 49-71; invented and introduced the Initial Teaching Alphabet; Chair. Initial Teaching Alphabet Foundation; Hon. D.Litt. Hofstra Univ. (U.S.A.), Strathclyde Univ., Bath Univ.
Holme Wood, Chisbridge Cross, nr. Marlow, Bucks.; and 58 Chelsea Park Gardens, London, S.W.3, England.
Telephone: (Marlow) 0494-881260; (Chelsea) 01-352-7004.

Pitt, Harry Raymond, PH.D., F.R.S.; British mathematician and university administrator; b. 3 June 1914; s. of H. Pitt; m. Clemency C. Jacoby 1940; four s.; ed. King Edward's School, Stourbridge and Peterhouse, Cambridge.
Bye-Fellow, Peterhouse, Cambridge 36-39; Choate Memorial Fellow, Harvard Univ. 37-38; Univ. of Aberdeen 39-42; Air Ministry and Ministry of Aircraft Production 42-45; Prof. of Mathematics, Queen's Univ., Belfast 45-50; Dep. Vice-Chancellor, Univ. of Nottingham 50-64; Visiting Prof., Yale Univ. 62-63; Vice-Chancellor, Univ. of Reading 64-; Chair. Univs'. Central Comm. on Admissions Oct. 75-; Hon. LL.D. (Nottingham, Aberdeen).
Publs. *Tauberian Theorems* 57, *Measure, Integration*

and Probability 63; mathematical papers in scientific journals.
The University, Reading, Berks., England.
Telephone: Reading 85123.

Pittaluga, Luigi; Italian iron and steel executive; b. 1919, Genoa.
Joined Esso Standard Italiana 49; Dir. in charge of financial, administrative, fiscal and legal fields and of economic research office for business planning of the Esso Group, Italy 65-; Chair. and Man. Dir. La Columbia shipping Co.; mem. of board Raffineria Siciliana Olii Minerali; Man. Dir. SVIT (Soc. Isola del Tronchetto a Venezia); mem. of board of free shipowners' asscn.; Man. Dir. Italsider 72-; Pres. SIDERMAR S.p.a.; Grand Officer al Merito della Repubblica.
Italsider, via Corsica 4, 16128 Genoa, Italy.

Pittendrigh, Colin Stephenson, PH.D.; American professor of biology; b. 13 Oct. 1918, Whitlev Bay, Northumberland, England; s. of Alexander Pittendrigh and Florence Hemy Stephenson; m. Margaret Eitelbach 1943; one s. one d.; ed. Univ. of Durham, England.
At International Health Div. of Rockefeller Foundation 42-45; at Princeton Univ. (posts included Prof. of Zoology and Dean of Graduate School) 47-69; Prof. of Biology Stanford Univ. 69-, Prof. of Human Biology 70-; mem. Nat. Acad. of Sciences.
Leisure interest: dry-fly fishing.
Publs. include: *Life* (with George Gaylord Simpson and Lewis Tiffany) 57; and journal papers.
Department of Biological Sciences, Stanford University, Stanford, Calif. 94305; Home: 1835 Cowper Street, Palo Alto, Calif. 94301, U.S.A.
Telephone: 415-497-3511, Ext. 3511 (Office); 415-327-1293 (Home).

Pitter, Ruth; British poet; b. 7 Nov. 1897, Ilford, Essex; d. of George Pitter and Louisa R. Murrell; ed. Coborn School, London.
Junior clerk, War Office 17-18; painter of furniture, etc. Suffolk and London 18-30; own business in partnership with Kathleen O'Hara 30-43; war-work at The Morgan Crucible Co., Battersea, London 43-45; worked at home 45-; Hawthornden Prize for *A Trophy of Arms* 37; Heinemann Award 54; Queen's Medal for Poetry 55; C. Lit. 74.
Leisure interests: gardening, cosmic curiosity, cooking.
Publs. *First Poems* 20, *First and Second Poems* 27, *Persephone in Hades* (privately printed) 31, *A Mad Lady's Garland* 34, *A Trophy of Arms* 35, *The Rude Potato* 41, *The Bridge* 45, *Pitter on Cats* 46, *Urania* 51, *The Ermine* 53, *Still by Choice* 66, *Poems 1926-1946* 68, *End of Drought* 75.
Home: The Hawthorns, 71 Chilton Road, Long Crendon, Aylesbury, Bucks., England.
Telephone: Long Crendon 208373.

Pittermann, Bruno, PH.D., LL.D.; Austrian politician; b. 3 Sept. 1905; ed. Vienna Univ.
Sec. of Chamber of Labour, Klagenfurt, Carinthia 29-34, when dismissed for political reasons; Sec. Dept. of Social Welfare and Admin., later Head of Dept.; Sec.-Gen. Vienna Chamber of Labour 45; parl. dept. Nat. Assembly 45-; Parl. Deputy; Vice-Chancellor (Deputy Prime Minister) 57-66; Chair. Socialist Party until 67; mem. Consultative Vice-Pres. Assembly, Council of Europe; Pres. Socialist Int.
Parliament, Vienna 1017, Austria.

Pitts, Robert F(ranklin), PH.D., M.D.; American professor of physiology; b. 24 Oct. 1908, Indianapolis, Ind.; s. of John Franklin Pitts and Estella Coffin Pitts; m. Anna Wallace Pitts 1936; one s. one d.; ed. Butler Coll., Indianapolis, Johns Hopkins Univ., New York Univ. Medical Coll., Neurological Inst. of Northwestern Univ.

Coll. of Medicine, Johnson Foundation Univ. of Pennsylvania and Oxford Univ.
Instructor in Physiology, New York Univ. Coll. of Medicine 32-38, Asst. Prof. of Physiology 40-42; Asst. Prof. of Physiology, Cornell Univ. Medical Coll. 42-44, Assoc. Prof. 44-46, Prof. and Chair. Dept. of Physiology 50-74; Emer. Prof. 74-; Prof. and Chair. Dept. of Physiology, Syracuse Univ. Medical Coll. 46-50; Visiting Fellow, St. Catherine's Coll., Oxford 67-68; Research Prof. of Renal Medicine and Physiology, Univ. of Florida; Pres. American Physiological Soc. 59-60, Harvey Soc. of New York 60-61; Fellow, American Acad. of Arts and Sciences, American Coll. of Physicians; mem. Nat. Acad. of Sciences; Borden Prize, Asscn. of American Medical Colls. 62, New York Univ. Medical Alumni Award, Homer W. Smith Award, New York Heart Asscn. 63, American Coll. of Physicians Award 70.
Leisure interests: woodwork, amateur radio.
Publs. Over 150 scientific publications 31-; *Physiological Basis of Diuretic Therapy* 59, *Physiology of the Kidney and Body Fluids* 63, 2nd edn. 68.
Department of Renal Medicine and Physiology, University of Florida, Gainesville, Florida 32608; Home: 2000 S.W. 16th Street, Apt. 105, Gainesville, Florida 32608, U.S.A.
Telephone: (904) 392-4008 (Office); (904) 373-2658 (Home).

Pitzer, Kenneth Sanborn, PH.D.; American university professor; b. 6 Jan. 1914, Pomona, Calif.; s. of Russell and Flora S. Pitzer; m. Jean E. Mosher 1935; two s. one d.; ed. Calif. Inst. of Technology, Univ. of Calif.
At Univ. of Calif. was instructor, later Prof. of Chemistry 37-61; Technical Dir. Maryland Research Lab., Wash. 43-44; Asst. Dean, Coll. of Letters and Science 47-48; Dir. of Research, Atomic Energy Comm., Wash. 49-51; Dean, Coll. of Chemistry 51-60; Pres. and Prof. of Chemistry, Rice Univ., Houston 61-68; Pres. and Prof. of Chemistry, Stanford Univ., Calif. Dec. 68-70; Prof. of Chem., Univ. of Calif., Berkeley 71-; mem. Gen. Advisory Cttee. Atomic Energy Comm. 58-65, Chair. 60-62; Dir. Federal Reserve Bank of Dallas 65-68; Trustee RAND Corpn. 62-72, Pitzer Coll. 66-, Carnegie Fund for Advancement of Teaching 66-; mem. Board of Dirs. Owens-Illinois 67-, American Council on Educ. 67-70; Nat. Acad. of Sciences, mem. Council 64-68, 73-76; Comm. on Nat. Resources 73-74; Hon. LL.D. (Univ. of Calif. and Mills Coll.); Hon. D.Sc. (Wesleyan Univ.); Priestley Medal, American Chem. Soc. 69, Nat. Medal of Science (U.S.A.) 75.
Leisure interest: sailing.
Publs. *Selected Values of Physical and Thermodynamic Properties of Hydrocarbons and Related Compounds* 47, *Quantum Chemistry* 53, *Thermodynamics* (with L. Brewer) 61.
12 Eagle Hill, Berkeley, Calif., U.S.A.

Place, John B. M.; American business executive; b. 21 Nov. 1925; s. of Hermann G. and Angela Toland Place (née Moore); m. Katharine Smart; one s. two d.; ed. St. Paul's School, Concord, N.H., The Citadel and New York Univ.
With Chase Manhattan Bank 46-71, Asst. Treas. 50, Second Vice-Pres. 53, Vice-Pres. 56, Senior Vice-Pres. 59, with Int. Dept. 63, with Metropolitan Dept. 65, Exec. Vice-Pres. 65, Head U.S. Dept. 67, Vice-Chair., mem. Exec. Office, Head of Domestic and Int. Banking 69-71; with Anaconda Co. 71-, Pres., Chief Exec. Officer June 71-, Chair. Oct. 71-; Dir. Anaconda Co., Chemical New York Corpn., Chemical Bank, Lever Bros. Co., Metropolitan Life Insurance Co., Union Pacific Corpn., and others; Vice-Pres. Int. Copper Research Asscn. Inc.; Dir. American Mining Congress, Copper Devt. Asscn.; mem. Council on Foreign Relations, New York Chamber of Commerce; Hon. D. Eng.

(Colorado School of Mines) 73; Grand Cross Order of Civil Merit (Spain) 72.
The Anaconda Co., 25 Broadway, New York, N.Y. 10004; Home: 215 East 68th Street, New York, N.Y. 10021, U.S.A.

Plaja, Eugenio, J.D.; Italian diplomatist; b. 26 April 1914, Rome; m.; three s.
Vice-Consul, Chambéry and Cannes 38-43; diplomatic posts in Buenos Aires 46; First Sec., Santiago 50; Head EEC and NATO Affairs, Dept. of Int. Co-operation, Ministry of Foreign Affairs 52; Counsellor, later Minister Counsellor and Deputy Perm. Rep., Perm. Mission to UN 55-61; Deputy Dir.-Gen. for Political Affairs, Ministry of Foreign Affairs 62-63, Dir.-Gen. for Emigration 63-67, Dir.-Gen. of Personnel and Admin. 67-69; Amb. to Egypt 69-73; Perm. Rep. to UN Sept. 73-75, to European Communities April 76-.
Permanent Mission of Italy to European Communities, 74 rue de la Loi, Brussels, Belgium.

Plana, Efren I.; Philippine government official; b. 28 June 1928, San Juan, Rizal; s. of Gregorio Plana and Simeona Ira; m. Modesta Reyes 1954; one s. one d.
Chief Legal Counsel and Dir., Project Assistance and Supervision Dept., Board of Investments 68-70; Under-Sec. of Nat. Defence 70-72; Sec., Nat. Security Council 70-72; Acting Chair. Anti-Dummy Board 72-73; Chair. Deportation Board 72-73; Under-Sec. of Justice 72-73; Vice-Chair. Fair Trade Board 72-73; mem. Dangerous Drugs Board 72-73; mem. Petroleum Board 72-73; Dir. Nat. Computer Centre 72-73; Assoc. Justice, Court of Appeals 73-.
24 Esteban Street, Mandaluyong, Rizal, Philippines.

Planchon, Roger; French theatrical director and playwright; b. 12 Sept. 1931, Ardèche.
Founder Théâtre de la Comédie, Lyons; Dir. Théâtre de la Cité, Villeurbanne 57-; currently Dir. Théâtre Nat. Populaire; aims to popularize the theatre by extending its units and recreating the classics within a modern social context; Croix de Guerre.
Publs. Plays: *La Remise* 61, *Pattes blanches* 64, *Bleus, Blancs, Rouges ou les Libertins* 67, *Dans le Vent* 68, *L'Infâme* 70, *Le Conchon Noir* 73.
Théâtre de la Cité, 8 place de la Libération, Villeurbanne (Rhône), France.

Plant, Sir Arnold, Kt., B.COM., B.SC. (ECON.); British university professor; b. 29 April 1898; ed. London School of Econs. Univ. of London.
Professor and Dean of the Faculty of Commerce, Univ. of Capetown, S. Africa 24-30; Prof. in the Univ. of London 30-65, Prof. Emer. 65-; Temporary British Civil Servant 40-46; mem. Govt. Cttees. of Enquiry and formerly of the Monopolies and Restrictive Practices Comm.; Chair. Industrial Injuries Advisory Council; Chair. Advertising Standards Authority 62-65; Hon. Fellow, London School of Econs.; Vice-Pres. Royal Econ. Soc.; Hon. LL.D. (Cape Town).
Publ. *Selected Economic Essays and Addresses* 74.
19 Wildwood Road, London, N.W.11, England.

Planta, Louis von, DR. JUR.; Swiss pharmaceuticals executive; b. 15 March 1917, Basle; ed. Univ. of Basle.
Partner in Basle firm of lawyers 46-; mem. Board J. R. Geigy S.A. 65, Vice-Chair. 67, Chair. 68-70; Vice-Chair. of Board, Chief Man. Dir. and Chair. Exec. Cttee. CIBA-GEIGY Ltd. 70-72, Chair. of Board May 72-; Pres. Burlington AG; mem. Admin. Board, Brown, Boveri and Co., Swiss Bank Corpn.; Chair. Basle Chamber of Commerce; Pres. Swiss Soc. of Chemical Industry; mem. Bank Council, Swiss Nat. Bank; mem. Vorort, Swiss Commercial and Industrial Asscn., Swiss Chamber of Commerce.
CIBA-GEIGY Ltd., CH-4002 Basle, Switzerland.

Plantefol, Lucien, D. ès SC., LIC.PHIL.; French emeritus professor of botany; b. 24 Apr. 1891, Falaise, Calvados; ed. Ecole Normale Supérieure (Lettres et Sciences).

Second Lieut. then Lieut., of Infantry 14-18; Agrégé-préparateur, Ecole Normale Supérieure 20-23; Asst., then Asst. Dir., Coll. de France 23-37; Lecturer in Plant Biology, Sorbonne 37-42, Prof. of Botany 42-61, Prof. Emer. 61-; mem. Acad. des Sciences, Acad. royale, Belgium, Officier Légion d'Honneur, Croix de Guerre.
Leisure interest: history of science.
Publs. *La Théorie des hélices foliaires multiples* 48, *L'Ontogénie de la fleur* 49, *L'Académie des Sciences durant les trois premiers siècles de son existence, ses visages successifs, ses publications* in *Troisième Centenaire* 67.
Laboratoire de Botanique, Sorbonne, 24 rue Lhomond, Paris 5e, France.
Telephone: 329-12-25.

Plantey, Alain Gilles; French government official; b. 19 July 1924, Mulhouse; m. Christiane Wioland 1955; four d.; ed. Univs. de Bordeaux and Paris à la Sorbonne.
Staff of Council of State 49; French del. to UN 51-52; Master of Requests Council of State 56-; Legal Adviser Org. for European Econ. Co-operation (OEEC) 56-57; Prof. Ecole Royale d'Administration Cambodia 57; Gen. Sec. *Agence France-Presse* 58; Asst. Sec.-Gen. for the Community and African and Malagasy Affairs at the Presidency 61-66; Amb. in Madagascar 66-72; Asst. Sec.-Gen. WEU 72-; Conseiller d'Etat 74-; Council mem. Museum National d'Histoire naturelle; Vice-Chair. Int. Inst. of Law; numerous decorations.
Publs. *La Réforme de la Justice marocaine* 49, *La Justice Répressive et le Droit Pénal Chérifien* 50, *Au Coeur du Problème Berbère* 52, *Traité Pratique de la Fonction Publique* 56, 63 and 71, *La Formation et le Perfectionnement des Fonctionnaires* 57, *La Communauté* 62, *Indépendance et Coopération* 64-65, *Prospective de l'Etat* 75.
6 Avenue Sully-Prudhomme, Paris 7e, France.
Telephone: 555-2649.

Plaskett, Harry, F.R.S., M.A.; British astronomer; b. 5 July 1893, Toronto, Canada; s. of Dr. John Stanley Plaskett and Rebecca Hope Hemley; m. Edith Alice Smith 1921; one s. one d.; ed. Toronto Univ.
Astronomer Victoria Astrophysical Observatory 19-27; Lecturer, Associate Prof. and Prof. of Astrophysics Harvard Univ. 28-32; Savilian Prof. of Astronomy Oxford Univ. and Fellow New Coll 32-60, Emer. Prof. 60-; Pres. Royal Astronomical Soc. 45-47, Gold Medal 63.
48 Blenheim Drive, Oxford, England.
Telephone: Oxford 58109.

Plastow, David Arnold Stuart, F.B.I.M.; British business executive; b. 9 May 1932, Grimsby, Lincs.; s. of James Stuart Plastow and Marie Plastow; m. Barbara Ann May 1954; one s. one d.; ed. Culford School, Bury St. Edmunds.
Apprenticed Vauxhall Motors Ltd. 50; joined Rolls-Royce Ltd., Motor Car Div. Crewe 58, Marketing Dir. Motor Car Div. 67-71, Man. Dir. 71-72; Man. Dir. Rolls-Royce Motors Ltd. 72-74, Group Man. Dir. 74-; Vice-Pres. Soc. of Motor Mfrs. and Traders Ltd.; Regional Dir., Lloyds Bank Ltd. (N.W.); Dir. Vickers Ltd.; Vice-Pres. Inst. of Motor Industry; Patron, Coll. of Aeronautical and Automobile Eng.; Gov., Culford School, Bury St. Edmunds.
Leisure interest: golf.
Rolls-Royce Motors Limited, Pym's Lane, Crewe, Cheshire, CW1 3PL, England.
Telephone: Crewe 55155.

Platen, Baron Carl Henrik G:son von, B.A., M.POL.SC.; Swedish diplomatist; b. 14 Dec. 1913, Malmö; s. of Baron Gösta von Platen and Elsa Stina Hjorth; m.

Mildred Ax:son Johnson 1950; two s. one d.; ed. Lunds Universitet, London School of Econs. and Université de Paris à la Sorbonne.
Entered Foreign Service 39, served Moscow, Rome, Ankara, Washington, Geneva, Paris; Envoy and Perm. Rep. to UN and other int. orgs., Geneva 59, Ambassador 60-63; Ambassador at Large and Negotiator, UN Disarmament Conf. 63; Swedish Rep. to OECD, Paris 64-72, to UNESCO 65-72; Chair. OECD Industry Cttee.; Chair. Nya Asfalt AB, A. Johnson and Cie. (Paris); Chair. of Board, Binab GmbH, Hamburg.
Publ. *Diplomati och Politik* 66.
Ets. A. Johnson and Cie. (Paris), 48/50 rue Albert, 75013 Paris, and 124 boulevard Maurice Barrès, 92-Neuilly, France; Nynäs Gods Nynäshamn, Sweden.
Telephone: 583-46-21 (Office); 747-71-83 (Home); 0752/12008 (Sweden).

Plath, Werner, DR.JURIS. UTR.; German insurance executive; b. 10 Dec. 1902; ed. Univs. of Tübingen and Kiel.
General Man. National Allgemeine Versicherungs-AG, National Lebensversicherungs-AG, Stettiner Rückversicherungs-A.G. 47-69; Vice-Chair. Board of Dirs. Concordia Lebensvers.-A.G., Kölnische Rückvers.-G; Board of Dirs. Colonia National Vers.-A.G., Dresdner Bank, L. Possehl & Co. m.b.H., Nordstern Rückversicherungs A.G., Roland Rechtsschutz-Versicherungs A.G.; Grosses Verdienstkreuz.
Elsässer Strasse 36-38, 24 Lübeck, Federal Republic of Germany.
Telephone: 3101201.

Platon, Dr. Nicolas; Greek archaeologist; b. Jan. 1909, Cephallonia; m. Anastassia Logiadou 1953; one s. two d.; ed. Univ. of Athens and Ecole des Hautes Etudes pratiques supérieures, Paris.
Assistant at Heraklion Museum, Crete 30-35; Ephor of Antiquities in Beotia, etc. 35-38; Ephor of Antiquities in Crete and Dir. Heraklion Museum 38-62; Ephor of Antiquities and Dir. of Acropolis in Athens 61-65; Gen. Ephor of Antiquities 65; Prof. at Univ. of Salonika 66-74; Knight Order of Phoenix, Greece; Commendatore al Merito della Repubblica Italiana; Major works include: excavations in Crete, Beotia, Euboea, Skopelos and the great excavation of the Minoan Palace, Zakros, East Crete; Reorganization of Heraclion Museum; Hon. mem. German and Austrian Inst., of Soc. for Promotion of Hellenic Studies; mem. Greek Archaeological Soc., Soc. of Cretan Historical Studies.
Leisure interest: music.
Publs. *Crete in Archaeologia Mundi*, Geneva; *Corpus Minoischer Siegel II* 70, *Zakros, Discovery of a Lost Palace on Ancient Crete* 71, and many scientific monographs.
Léof. Alexandras 126, Athens, Greece.
Telephone: 6469092 (Athens).

Platt, Baron (Life Peer), cr. 67, of Grindleford; **Robert Platt,** Bt., M.D., F.R.C.P.; b. 16 April 1900, London; s. of William Platt and Susan Jane Willis; m. 1st Margaret Cannon, M.B., 1922 (dissolved 1974), one s. two d.; m. 2nd Sylvia Haggard 1974; ed. Univ. of Sheffield.
Physician, Royal Infirmary, Sheffield 31-45; Lieut.-Col., later Brig., Royal Army Medical Corps 41-45; Prof. of Medicine, Manchester Univ. 46-65, Emer. 65-; Physician, Manchester Royal Infirmary 46-65; mem. Medical Research Council 53-57; Pres. Royal Coll. of Physicians, London 57-62; Chair. Clinical Research Board, Medical Research Council 64-67; Chair. Manchester Chamber Concerts Soc. 52-65; Pres. Eugenics Soc. 66-68; Chair. Advisory Cttee. on Distinction Awards, Ministry of Health 67-71; mem. Assen. of American Physicians; Hon. LL.D. (Sheffield, Belfast and Manchester); Hon.

M.D. (Bristol); Hon. F.R.A.C.P., Hon. F.A.C.P., Hon. F.C.G.P.
Leisure interest: string quartet playing (cello).
Publs. *Private and Controversial* 72, and numerous medical articles.
53 Heathside, Hinchley Wood, Esher, Surrey, England.

Platt, Sir Harry, Bt., M.D., M.S., F.R.C.S., K.ST.J.; British surgeon; b. 7 Oct. 1886, Thornham; s. of Ernest and Jessie C. (Lindsay) Platt; m. Gertrude Sarah Turney 1916; one s. four d.; ed. Manchester Univ. and U.S.A.
Capt. Royal Army Medical Corps (T.F.) 15-19; Emeritus Prof. of Orthopaedic Surgery, Univ. of Manchester; Consultant Adviser in Orthopaedics, Ministry of Health 40-63; Pres. Royal Coll. of Surgeons of England 54-57; Pres. Société Int. de Chirurgie Orthopédique et de Traumatologie; Hon. Pres. Int. Fed. of Surgical Colls.; mem. American, French, Scandinavian, Italian, Neths., Australian, Argentine and Belgian Orthopaedic Societies; Hon. Fellow, Royal Coll. of Surgeons and American, Royal Edinburgh, Royal Canadian, Royal Australasian and South African Colls. of Surgeons; Hon. LL.D. (Manchester, Liverpool and Belfast Univs.); Hon. M.D. (Berne), Docteur Honoris Causa (Univ. Paris) 66.
Leisure interests: music and travel.
Publs. on orthopaedic surgery and medical education.
11 Lorne Street, Manchester 13, Lancs., England.
Telephone: 061-273-3433.

Platteel, Pieter Johannes, PH.D.; Netherlands administrator; b. 14 Aug. 1911, Utrecht; m. Margaretha Antje Laseur 1939; two s.; ed. Utrecht Univ.
Entered Netherlands Indies Civil Service 37; war service as reserve officer 40-45; Commr., Netherlands Indies Civil Service 48; Dir. Social Welfare Department, The Hague 54; Gov. Netherlands New Guinea 58-62; Burgomaster of Ede 62-68; Burgomaster of Hilversum 68-; Knight, Order of Orange-Nassau; Knight, Order of Netherlands Lion; Anti-Revolutionary Party.
Leisure interest: horse riding.
Publs. *Grondslagen der Constitutie van Nederlandsch-Indië* 36; numerous articles on political and social science in periodicals.
Town Hall, Hilversum; and s'Gravelandseweg 85c, Hilversum, Netherlands.
Telephone: 02150-45475.

Platten, Donald C.; American banker; ed. Princeton Univ.
Joined Chemical Bank 40, Asst. Sec. 50, Asst. Vice-Pres. 53, Vice-Pres. 57, Senior Vice-Pres. 64 Exec. Vice-Pres. in charge of Int. Division 67; Pres. Chemical New York Corpn. and Chemical Bank 72-73; Chair. Chemical Bank Feb. 73-; Dir. American Chain and Cable Co. Inc., Knott Hotels Corpn., Manhattan Life Insurance Co., Thompson Newspapers Inc., Otis Elevator Co.
Chemical Bank, 20 Pine Street, New York, N.Y. 10015, U.S.A.

Plattner, Karl; Italian painter; b. 13 Feb. 1919; ed. Acad. of Florence, Brera Acad. Milan and Art Acad. Paris.
One-man exhibitions at Merano, Bolzano, Verona, Innsbruck, Stuttgart, Munich, São Paulo, Rio de Janeiro, Chicago, Paris, Rome, Milan and Vienna 51-66 and other European cities; Group shows in Germany, Italy, Brazil, France, Uruguay and Sicily, including Biennali at Venice and São Paulo; numerous prizes.
Major Works: Fresco for War Memorial, Naturno, Italy 51; Fresco for Provincial Council Building, Bolzano 54-55; Panel for *Folhas* Newspaper building São Paulo and for Air France São Paulo 55-56; Panel for new Festival Hall Salzburg 60-61; Fresco for Europa Chapel, near Innsbruck 63-64; Panel for Austria A.G. Building, Vienna 65.
Piazza Borromeo 8, Milan, Italy.
Telephone: 875927.

Platts, John H.; American businessman; b. 19 Nov. 1917, Detroit, Michigan; s. of Ralph E. and Mary E. Platts; m. Dorothea M. Sleeper 1940; three d.; ed. Univ. of Toledo.
Joined Whirlpool Corpn., St. Joseph Div. as assemblyman 41, later tool engineer, buyer, Man. refrigeration plant, Dir. of purchases and Works Man.; Man. laundry sales to Sears Co.; Gen. Man. Evansville Div. 57-59; Vice-Pres., Evansville Div. July 59-July 60; Vice-Pres. Refrigeration Product Group July 60-Dec. 62; Pres. Whirlpool Corpn. Dec. 62-, also Chair. of Board and Chief Exec. Officer 71-; Dir. Whirpool Corpn. Dec. 62-; mem. American Soc. of Heating and Refrigeration Engineers; mem. of Board, Nat. Industrial Conf. 67-68; Dir. Sears Bank and Trust Co., Marathon Oil Co. 73; Trustee, Univ. of Evansville.
Whirlpool Corporation, Administrative Center, Benton Harbor, Michigan 49022; 2305 Niles Avenue, St. Joseph, Michigan 49085, U.S.A.
Telephone: 616-925-0651 (Office); 616-983-5472 (Home).

Platzer, Wilfried, G.C.V.O.; Austrian diplomatist; b. 5 April 1909, Hafslund, Norway; m. Edith von Donat 1939; one s. one d.; ed. Foreign Service School Vienna and Univ. of Vienna.
Diplomatic Service 33, Austrian Legation, Berlin 34, Foreign Office, Vienna 35-38, Counsellor Econ. Section 46-49, Political Section 49; Counsellor, Austrian Embassy, Wash. 50-54, Minister, Chief Econ. Section 54-58, Ambassador to United States 58-65; Under-Sec. for Econ. Affairs (with rank of Amb.), Ministry of Foreign Affairs 66; Sec.-Gen. for Foreign Affairs 67-70; Amb. to U.K. 70-74, retd.
Formanekgasse 40, 1190 Vienna, Austria.

Plávka, Andrej; Czechoslovak (Slovak) writer; b. 18 Nov. 1907, Liptovský Mikuláš; ed. Faculty of Law, Charles Univ. Prague.
Secretary Y.M.C.A. in Lučenec, Hradec Králové, Bratislava and Banská Bystrica 31-45; Deputy Commr., Office for Information, Bratislava 45-46, mem. Presidium of Board of Commrs. and Counsellor of Dept. 46-49; Dir. Tatran Publishing House 49-68; Sec. of Nat. Front 46-47; mem. Cen. Cttee. C.P. of Slovakia 58-66; Vice-Chair. Union of Slovak Writers 69, Chair. 69-, mem. Presidium 69-; mem. Nat. Editorial Council of Slovak Socialist Repub. 70-; Vice-Chair. Union of Czechoslovak Writers 73-; Order of Slovak Nat. Rising, Honoured Artist, Klement Gottwald State Prize 52, 72, Order of Labour 67, Vít Nejedlý Prize 69, Honoured Artist 71, Order of St. Cyril and Methodis (Bulgaria) 75.
Publs. sixteen vols. of poetry, including *Three Rods from Liptov* 40, *Bonfires on the Mountains* 47, *Green Shoot* 50, *Three Waters* 54, *Liptov Fife* 57, *Farewell My Loves* 67, *Comeback* 75; 5 prose works including *St. Paul's Conversion* 41.
Bratislava, Tvarožkova 9, Czechoslovakia.

Player, Gary (-Jim); South African professional golfer; b. 1 Oct. 1936, Johannesburg; s. of Francis Harry Audley Player and Muriel Marie Ferguson; m. Vivienne Verwey 1957; two s. four d.
First overseas player for 45 years to win U.S. Open Championship 65; Winner, British Open Championship 59, 68, 74; Piccadilly World Match Play Champion 65, 66, 68, 71, 73; U.S. Open Champion 65; U.S. Masters Champion 61, 74; U.S. Professional Golf Ascn. Champion 62, 72; third player ever to win all four major World professional titles; holds world record for lowest 18-hole score in any Open Championship (59 in the Brazilian Open 74).
Mark McCormack Agency, 82 Park Street, London, W.1, England.
Telephone: 01-493-0816.

Playfair, Sir Edward Wilder, K.C.B.; British company director and former government official; b. 17 May 1909, London; s. of Dr. E. Playfair; m. Dr. M. L. Rae

1941; three d.; ed. Eton and King's Coll., Cambridge. Inland Revenue 31-34; Treasury 34-46, 47-56 (Control Office for Germany and Austria 46-47); Perm. Under-Sec. of State for War 56-59; Perm. Sec. Ministry of Defence 60-61; Chair. Int. Computers and Tabulators Ltd. 61-65; Dir. National Westminster Bank, Equity and Law Life Assurance Soc., Glaxo Holdings, Tunnel Holdings; Trustee, Nat. Gallery 67-74 (Chair. Board of Trustees 72-74).
12 The Vale, London, SW3 6AH, England.
Telephone: 01-352-4671.

Playford, Sir Thomas, G.C.M.G.; Australian politician; b. 5 July 1896; ed. Norton Summit Public School.
Served Australian Imperial Forces First World War; M.P. for Murray District 33, for Gumeracha District 38-66; Commr. for Crown Lands and Minister of Irrigation and Repatriation, S. Australian Govt. April-Nov. 38, Premier, Treas. and Minister of Immigration, S. Australian Govt. Nov. 38-March 65; Leader of Opposition 65-66; Leader Liberal Country League.
Norton Summit, South Australia 5136, Australia.

Plaza (Lasso), Galo; Ecuadorean politician; b. 17 Feb. 1906, New York City; s. of Leonidas and Avelina (Lasso) Plaza Gutierrez; m. Rosario Pallares Zaldumbide 1933; one s. five d.; ed. Colegio Nacional Mejia, Univs. of Calif. and Maryland and Georgetown Univ. Foreign Service School.
Attaché Washington 30; mem. Municipal Council Quito 37-38, Mayor 38; Minister of Nat. Defence 39-40; Amb. to U.S.A. 44-45; Senator 47; Pres. of Republic of Ecuador 48-52; Chair. UN Observer Group in Lebanon 58, UN "BASIC" Cttee. in the Congo 60, E.C.L.A. Latin American Common Market Cttee. 58-59; UN Sec.-Gen. Rep. in Cyprus 64; UN Mediator in Cyprus 64-65; Sec.-Gen. of Org. of American States 68-75; hon. degrees, Univ. of Maryland and New School for Social Research, New York, Columbia Univ., New York, Washington Univ., Williams Coll., New Mexico and Harvard Univs., Hamilton College; decorations from U.S.A., Mexico, Venezuela, Guatemala, Colombia, Chile, Costa Rica, Cuba, Bolivia, China, Peru, Paraguay; awards include Foundation of Americas Award 55, Key Man of Americas Award 69.
Publs. *The Problems of Democracy in Latin America* 55, *The United Fruit Company in Latin America* (co-author) 58, *Latin America Today and Tomorrow* 71.
Avenida 6 de Diciembre 1300, Quito, Ecuador.

Pleasence, Donald; British actor and producer; b. 5 Oct. 1919, Worksop; s. of Thomas Stanley Pleasence; m. 1st Miriam Raymond 1941, 2nd Josephine Crombie 1956, 3rd Meira Shore 1970; five d.; ed. Ecclesfield Grammar School, Yorkshire, England.
Made first stage appearance 39; first London appearance in *Twelfth Night* at Arts Theatre 42; R.A.F. 42-46 (prisoner-of-war 44-46); returned to stage in *The Brothers Karamazov* 46, *Peter Pan* 47; Perth Repertory Theatre 47; Birmingham Repertory Theatre 48-50; Bristol Old Vic Co. 50-51; *Right Side Up* and *Saints' Day* London 51; appeared in New York with Laurence Olivier's Co. 51-52; *Hobson's Choice* Arts Theatre 52; played in own play *Ebb Tide* at Edinburgh Festival and Royal Court Theatre, London 52; Stratford-on-Avon season 53; *Antony and Cleopatra* London 53; *The Rule of the Game* 55, *The Lark* 55, *Misalliance* 56, *Restless Heart* 57, *The Caretaker* (London and New York) 60, *Poor Bitos* (co-producer), *The Man in the Glass Booth* (co-producer) 67, *Tea Party, The Basement* 70, *Wise Child* (New York) 72; numerous film appearances include *The Beachcomber, Manuela, Heart of a Child, The Caretaker, The Greatest Story Ever Told, Fantastic Voyage, The Hallelujah Trail, The Great Escape, Doctor Crippen, Cul-de-Sac, Will Penny, The Mad Woman of Chaillot, Arthur! Arthur?, Soldier Blue, Jerusalem File,*

Pied Piper, Outback, The Black Windmill, Wedding in White, The Rainbow Boys, Mutations, Henry VIII, Malachi's Cove, Escape to Witch Mountain, Journey into Fear, The Count of Monte Cristo, Doctor Jekyll and Mr. Hyde, Hearts of the West, I Don't Want to be Born, Trial by Combat, The Devil's People; numerous television appearances in Britain and America including *Armchair Theatre, Call Me Daddy, Columbo, The Captain of Köpenick;* Television Actor of the Year Award 58; London Critics Best Stage Performance Award 60; Variety Club Award; Stage Actor of 1967.
7 West Eaton Place Mews, London, S.W.1, England.

Plenderleith, Harold James, C.B.E., M.C., B.S.C., PH.D., F.R.S.E., F.S.A., F.B.A., F.M.S.; British chemist; b. 19 Sept. 1898; ed. St. Andrews Univ.
Keeper, Research Laboratory, British Museum 24-59; Prof. of Chemistry, Royal Acad. 36-58; Chair. Hon. Scientific Advisory Cttee. Nat. Gallery 44-58; Hon. Treas. Int. Inst. for the Conservation of Museum Objects 50-58, Vice-Pres. 59-65, Pres. 65-68, Hon. Fellow 71; Dir. Int. Centre for Study of Preservation and Restoration of Cultural Property, Rome 59-71, Dir. Emer. 71-; Hon. LL.D. (St. Andrews); Gold Medal Soc. Antiquaries of London 64.
Publs. *The Preservation of Antiquities, The Conservation of Prints, Drawings and Manuscripts, The Preservation of Leather Bookbinding, The Conservation of Antiquities and Works of Art.*
17 Rockfield Crescent, Dundee DD 21 JF, Scotland.
Telephone: Dundee 641552.

Plescoff, Georges; French financial adviser and international bank official; see *The International Who's Who 1975-76.*

Pleskot, Václav; Czechoslovak diplomatist; b. 1 Jan. 1921, Milostín; ed. Lycée and Univ. of Prague and Advanced School of Econs., Prague.
Director of Nat. Bank of Czechoslovakia, regional branch at Ústí 48-52; Vice-Pres. of State Cttee. for Physical Culture and Sport 52-55, Pres. 55-57; Dir. at Ministry of Finance 58; Dir. of Dept. for Western Europe, Ministry of Foreign Affairs 59-60; Amb. to France 60-66; Vice-Minister and Sec.-Gen. Ministry of Foreign Affairs 66-68; mem. Cen. Control and Auditing Comm., C.P. of Czechoslovakia 66-71; State Sec. Ministry of Foreign Affairs, Fed. Govt. of the Č.S.S.R. 69; Amb. to Algeria 70-, to Mauritanian Islamic Repub. 70-; Order of Labour 55.
Embassy of Czechoslovakia, Villa Malika, Chemin du Parc Gatliff, B.P. 999, Algiers, Algeria.

Plettner, Bernhard; German business executive; b. 2 Dec. 1914, Oberlahnstein; s. of Bernhard Christoph Plettner and Anna Maria Derstroff; m. Ursula Ganswindt 1955; ed. Humanistisches Gymnasium Oberlahnstein and Bad Kreuznach, Technische Hochschule Darmstadt.
Design engineer Industrial Div. Siemens Schuckertwerke A.G. 40-45, Head of design group 45-49, Deputy Man. Export Section 49-55, Man. Design Div. for Raw Materials Industry 55-60, Dir. 60-, Deputy Chair. Board of Dirs. 61, Chair. 62-66, Pres. and Chief Exec. Officer, Siemens AG, Berlin-Munich Oct. 71-; mem. Supervisory Board, Hamburgische Elektrizitätswerke AG, Stahl und Rohrenwerk Reishoiz GmbH, Düsseldorf-Reisholz; Deputy Chair. of Supervisory Board, Osram GmbH, München-Berlin, Bergmann Elekrizitätswerke AG, Berlin, Bosch-Siemens Hausgeräte GmbH; Chair. Board of Dirs. Siemens Overseas Inv. Ltd., Winnipeg; Vice-Pres. Board Siemens Beteiligungen AG, Zurich; mem. Presidential Cttee. of Fed. of German Industries, Cologne; mem. Board Senator, Max Planck Soc.; mem. Board Soc. of Friends of Munich Technical Univ.; mem. Soc. of Friends Darmstadt Tech. Coll., Soc. for

Freedom of Science, Univ. Erlangen Assoc.; Dr.Ing. e.h. Siemens A.G., 8000 Munich 2, Wittelsbacherplatz 2, Federal Republic of Germany.
Telephone: 2342450.

Pleven, René, D. en D.; French politician; b. 15 April 1901; m. Anne Bompard 1924 (died 1966); two d.; ed. Ecole des Sciences Politiques, Paris.
Assistant Head French Air Mission in U.S.A. 39; mem. Franco-British Co-ordination Cttee. 40; Sec.-Gen. Govt. of French Equatorial Africa 40; negotiated agreement for dispatch of war material to Free French, Washington 41; Nat. Commr. for Economy, Finance and Colonies 41-42, for Foreign Affairs and Colonies 42-43, for Colonies 43; Commr. for Colonies French Cttee. for Nat. Liberation 43-44; Minister for Colonies, French Provisional Govt. Sept.-Nov. 44; Minister of Finance 44-46; Minister of Nat. Defence Bidault Cabinet 49-50, Queuille Cabinet July 50; Prime Minister July 50-March 51; Vice-Premier Mar.-Aug. 51; Prime Minister Aug. 51-Jan. 52; Minister of Nat. Defence, Pinay Cabinet Mar.-Dec. 52, Mayer Cabinet Jan.-May 53, and Laniel Cabinet 54; Min. of Foreign Affairs 58, of Justice 69-73; Deputy (Côtes-du-Nord) 45-73; Pres. Conseil Régional de Bretagne, Conseil Général des Côtes du Nord.
Leisure interest: fishing.
Publ. *Avenir de la Bretagne*.
12 rue Châteaubriand, Dinan (Côtes du Nord), France.

Plimpton, Francis T. P., A.B., J.D.; American lawyer and diplomatist; b. 7 Dec. 1900, New York City; s. of George Arthur Plimpton and Frances Taylor Pearsons; m. Pauline Ames 1926; three s. one d.; ed. Amherst Coll. and Harvard Univ.
Admitted to Bar 26; law practice 26-31, 33-61, 65-; Gen. Solicitor, Reconstruction Finance Corpn. 32-33; Partner, Debevoise, Plimpton, Lyons and Gates (and predecessor firms) 33-61, 65-; Deputy Rep. of U.S.A. to UN with rank of Amb. 61-65, Acting Rep. July 65; Del. 15-19th UN Gen. Assemblies; Pres. Asscn. of Bar of City of N.Y. 68-70; Chair. N.Y.C. Board of Ethics 73-; Dir. of numerous financial, educational, legal and cultural orgs.; Fellow, American Acad. of Arts and Sciences; Hon. LL.D., L.H.D.
Leisure interests: tennis, travel.
299 Park Avenue, New York, N.Y. 10017; Home: 131 East 66th Street, New York, N.Y. 10021; also 168 Chichester Road, West Hills, Huntington, L.I., N.Y. 11743, U.S.A.
Telephone: PL2-6400.

Plimsoll, Sir James, C.B.E.; Australian diplomatist; b. 25 April 1917, Sydney; s. of late James Ernest and Jessie Plimsoll; ed. Sydney High School and Univ. of Sydney.
With Economic Department, Bank of New South Wales, Sydney 38-42; served in Australian Army 42-47; mem. Australian Del., Far Eastern Comm. 45-48; Rep. UN Comm. for Unification and Rehabilitation of Korea 50-52; Asst. Sec., Department of External Affairs 53-59; Perm. Rep. to UN 59-63; High Commr. in India and Ambassador to Nepal 63-65; Sec. Dept. of External Affairs 65-70; Amb. to U.S.A. 70-74, to U.S.S.R. and Mongolia 74-.
Australian Embassy, 13 Kropotkinsky Pereulok, Moscow, U.S.S.R.
Telephone: 241.20.35.

Plisetskaya, Maiya Mikhailovna; Soviet ballerina; b. 20 Nov. 1925; ed. Moscow Bolshoi Theatre Ballet School.
Soloist, Bolshoi Ballet 43, now a Principal Dancer; First Prize, Budapest Int. Competition 49; People's Artist of the R.S.F.S.R. 51; People's Artist of the U.S.S.R. 56, Lenin Prize 64.
Main ballet roles: Odette-Odile (*Swan Lake*, Tchai-

kovsky), Raimonda (*Raimonda*, Glazunov), Zaryema (*The Fountain of Bahkchisarai*, Asafiev), Kitri (*Don Quixote*, Minkus), Juliet (*Romeo and Juliet*, Prokofiev), Girl-Bird, Syunmbike (*Shuralye*, Yarullin), Laurencia (*Laurencia*, Krein), Yegina (*Spartak*, Khachaturian), Karmen (Karmen Suite Schedrin).
State Academic Bolshoi Theatre, 1 Ploshchad Sverdlova, Moscow, U.S.S.R.

Plojhar, Josef; Czechoslovak politician; b. 2 March 1902, České Budějovice; ed. theological studies.
Arrested by the Gestapo and imprisoned in Buchenwald concentration camp 39 and later in Dachau; Chair. of the organization of the Czechoslovak People's Party in České Budějovice district 45; Deputy to Nat. Assembly 45-69; Hon. Chair. 68-; Chair. Nat. Peace Cttee. Catholic Clergy 51-68; Minister of Health 48-68; Chair. of the Czechoslovak People's Party 51-68; mem. Presidium Czechoslovak People's Party 69-; mem. Presidium of Central Cttee. of Nat. Front 55-68; Deputy to House of People, Fed. Assembly 69-; Deputy Chair. Central Cttee. Czechoslovak Group of Interparliamentary Union 70-; Czechoslovak Peace Prize 66, and other decorations; Dr. Theol. h.c.
Federal Assembly, Prague, Czechoslovakia.

Plowden, Baron, (Life Peer) cr. 59; **Edwin Noel Plowden,** K.C.B., K.B.E.; British administrator; b. 6 Jan. 1907, Stachur, Argyll, Scotland; m. Bridget Horatia Richmond, J.P. (Lady Plowden, q.v.), 1933; two s. two d.; ed. Switzerland and Pembroke Coll., Cambridge.
Temporary Civil Servant Ministry of Economic Warfare 39-40; Ministry of Aircraft Production 40-46; mem. Aircraft Supply Council, Chief Exec. 45-46; Chief Planning Officer and Chair. Econ. Planning Bd. 47-53, mem. 53-59; Vice-Chair. Temporary Council Cttee. of NATO 51-52; Chair. Designate U.K. Atomic Energy Authority 53-54, Chair. 54-59; Chair. Cttee. of Enquiry into Treasury Control of Public Expenditure 59-61; Chair. Cttee. of Enquiry into Org. of Representational Service Overseas 62-63; Chair. Cttee. of Enquiry into Aircraft Industry 62-63; Chair. Standing Advisory Cttee. on Pay of Higher Civil Service 68-70; Chair. Tube Investments Ltd. 63-76, Pres. 76-; Dir. Nat. Westminster Bank Ltd., and Commercial Union Assurance Co. Ltd., Chair. Gov. Body and Council London Graduate School of Business Studies; Chair. Cttee. of Enquiry into Structure of Electricity Supply Industry 74-75; mem. Eng. Industries Council; Visiting Fellow, Nuffield Coll., Oxford 56-64; Hon. Fellow, Pembroke Coll., Cambridge 58; Hon. D.Sc. (Pennsylvania State Univ.) 58; Hon. D.Sc. (Univ. of Aston) 72.
Martels Manor, Dunmow, Essex; and 7 Cottesmore Gardens, London W.8, England.

Plowden, Lady (Bridget Horatia), D.B.E.; British administrator; d. of late Admiral Sir H. W. Richmond and Lady Richmond; m. Edwin Noel Plowden (Lord Plowden, q.v.) 1933; two s. two d.; ed. Downe House.
Director Trust House Forte Ltd. 61-72; Chair. Cen. Advisory Council for Educ. (England) 63-66, Working Ladies Guild, Professional Classes Aid Council, Advisory Cttee. for Educ. of Romany and Other Travellers, Metropolitan Architectural Consortium for Educ., Board of Govs. Philippa Fawcett Coll. of Educ. 67-, Robert Montefiore Comprehensive School 68-; co-opted mem. Educ. Cttee. Inner London Educ. Authority 67-70, Vice-Chair. ILEA School Sub-Cttee. 67-70; Vice-Chair. Gov. BBC 70-75; Chair. Independent Broadcasting Authority April 75-; Pres. Pre-Schools Playgroups Asscn. 72-; Hon. LL.D. (Leicester Univ.) 68, (Reading Univ.) 70, (Open Univ.) 75; Hon. Fellow, Coll. of Preceptors 73.
7 Cottesmore Gardens, London, W.8; and Martels Manor, Dunmow, Essex, England.
Telephone: 01-937-4238; Great Dunmow 2141.

Plowright, Joan Anne, C.B.E.; British actress; b. 28 Oct. 1929; *m.* Laurence Olivier (Lord Olivier), *q.v.*, 1961; ed. Scunthorpe Grammar School and Old Vic Theatre School.

Member Old Vic Company, toured South Africa 52-53; first leading rôle in *The Country Wife*, London 56; mem. English Stage Company 56; Best Actress (Tony) Award for *A Taste of Honey*, N.Y. 60; Best Actress (Evening Standard) Award for *St. Joan* 64.

Plays acted in include: *The Chairs* 57, *The Entertainer* 58, *Major Barbara* and *Roots* 59, *A Taste of Honey* 60, *Uncle Vanya* 62, 63, 64, *St. Joan* 63, *Hobson's Choice* 64, *The Master Builder* 65, *Much Ado About Nothing* 67, *Tartuffe* 67, *Three Sisters* 67, 69 (film 69), *The Advertisement* 68, 69, *Love's Labour's Lost* 68, 69, *The Merchant of Venice* 70, 71-72, *Rules of the Game*, *Woman Killed with Kindness* 71-72, *Taming of the Shrew*, *Doctor's Dilemma* 72, *Merchant of Venice* (TV film) 73, *Rosmersholm* 73, *Saturday Sunday Monday* 73, *Eden's End* 74, *The Sea Gull* 75, *The Bed Before Yesterday* 75.
c/o LOP Ltd., 33-34 Chancery Lane, London, WC2A 1EN, England.
Telephone: 01-836-7932.

Plumb, John Harold, PH.D., LITT.D., F.B.A.; British historian; b. 20 Aug. 1911; ed. Univ. Coll., Leicester, Christ's Coll., Cambridge.

Ehrman Research Fellow, King's Coll., Cambridge 39-46; Foreign Office 40-45; Fellow, Christ's Coll. 46-, Steward 48-50, Tutor 50-59, Vice-Master 64-68; Lecturer in History, Univ. of Cambridge 46-62, Reader in Modern English History 62-65, Prof. of Modern English History 66-73; Trustee, Nat. Portrait Gallery 61-; Visiting Prof. Columbia Univ. 60, Distinguished Visiting Prof. New York City Univ. 71-72; Editor *History of Human Society* 59-; European Advisory Editor to *Horizon* 59-; Hon. foreign mem. American Acad. of Arts and Sciences 70; Hon. D.Litt. (Leicester) 68, (East Anglia) 73, (Bowdoin Coll., U.S.A.) 74.

Publs. *England in the Eighteenth Century* 50, *West African Explorers* (with C. Howard) 51, *Chatham* 53, *Sir Robert Walpole* Vol. I 56, Vol. II 60, *The First Four Georges* 56, *The Renaissance* 61, *Men and Places* 63, *Crisis in the Humanities* 64, *The Growth of Political Stability in England 1675-1725* 67, *The Death of the Past* 69, *In the Light of History* 72, *The Commercialisation of Leisure* 74.
The Old Rectory, Westhorpe, Stowmarket, Suffolk, England.

Plummer, (Arthur) Christopher (Orme), C.C.; Canadian actor; b. 13 Dec. 1929, Toronto; *m.* 1st Tammy Lee Grimes 1956, 2nd Patricia Audrey Lewis 1962, 3rd Elaine Regina Taylor 1970; one *d.*; ed. public and private schools in Montreal, P.Q.

Professional debut as Faulkland in *The Rivals*, Ottawa Repertory Theatre; Broadway debut in *Starcross Story* 51-52; numerous appearances in theatres in U.S.A. have included: Mark Antony in *Julius Caesar*, Ferdinand in *The Tempest*, Earl of Warwick in Anouilh's *The Lark*, The Narrator in Stravinsky's *L'Histoire du Soldat*, The Devil in *J.B.*, 51-61, and *The Resistible Rise of Arturo Ui* and *The Royal Hunt of the Sun* 65-66, *The Good Doctor* 73; played many leading Shakespearian roles in productions by the Stratford Canadian Festival Co.; British debut in title role of *Richard III*, Stratford on Avon 61 and then in London as Henry II in Anouilh's *Becket;* a leading actor in The National Theatre Co. of Great Britain 71-72; has appeared in Nat. Theatre productions of *Amphytrion 38*, *Danton's Death* 71; many TV roles including Hamlet in BBC/Danish TV production, *Hamlet in Elsinore*.
Films include: *The Fall of the Roman Empire*, *The Sound of Music*, *Inside Daisy Clover*, *Triple Cross*, *Oedipus the King*, *Nobody Runs Forever*, *Lock Up Your Daughters*, *The Royal Hunt of the Sun*, *Battle of Britain*, *Waterloo*, *The Pyx*, *The Spiral Staircase*, *Conduct Unbecoming*, *The Return of the Pink Panther*, *The Man Who Would Be King*.
Leisure interests: piano, skiing, tennis, old cars.
c/o Stanley, Gorrie, Whitson & Co., 9 Cavendish Square, London, W.1, England.
Telephone: 01-580-6363.

Plumptre, Arthur Fitzwalter Wynne, C.B.E., M.A.; Canadian educationist, economist and international banking official; b. 5 June 1907; *s.* of Henry Pemberton Plumptre and Adelaide Mary Wynne Willson; *m.* Beryl Alyce Rouch 1938; one *s.* one *d.*; ed. Appleby School, Oakville, Ontario, Upper Canada Coll., Univ. of Toronto and Cambridge Univ.

Assistant Prof. of Political Economy, Univ. of Toronto 30-41; Financial Attaché, Canadian Legation, Washington, and Washington Rep., Wartime Prices and Trade Board 42-45; Sec., Wartime Prices and Trade Board, Ottawa 45-47; Assoc. Editor *Saturday Night*, Toronto 47-49; Head of Economic Div., Dept. of External Affairs, Ottawa 49-52; Minister and Dep. Head Canadian Del. to NATO Council and OEEC, Paris 52-54; Dir. Int. Economic Relations Div., Dept. of Finance, Ottawa 54; Asst. Dep. Minister, Dept. of Finance, Ottawa 55-65; Exec. Dir. for Canada, Ireland and Jamaica Int. Bank for Reconstruction and Devt. (World Bank) and Int. Monetary Fund (IMF) 62-65; Principal, Scarborough Coll., Univ. of Toronto 65-72.
Publs. *Central Banking in the British Dominions* 40, *Mobilizing Canada's Resources for War* 41.
130 Old Kingston Road, West Hill, Ontario, Canada.

Pniewski, Jerzy, D.SC.; Polish physicist; b. 1 June 1913, Płock; ed. Warsaw Univ.

Doctor 51-54, Assoc. Prof. 54-63, Prof. 63-; Prof. Inst. of Nuclear Research, Warsaw; Dir. Inst. of Experimental Physics, Warsaw Univ., specialist in high energy physics and a founder of hyper-nucleus physics; Corresp. mem. Polish Acad. of Sciences (PAN) 64-71, mem. 71-; mem. Presidium of State and PAN Cttee. for Nuclear Physics, Cen. Board of Polish Physical Soc.; mem. IUPAP, Societá Italiana di Fisica, European Physical Soc.; Corresp. mem. Heidelberg Acad. of Sciences 71-; Dr. h.c. (Lyons Univ.) 75; Gold Cross of Merit 52, Knight's Cross, Order of Polonia Restituta 54, Medal of 10th Anniversary of People's Poland, Order of Banner of Labour, 1st Class 64, State Prize, 1st and 2nd Class.
Ul. Koszykowa 75 m. 33 ,00-662 Warsaw, Poland.

Pocock, Carmichael Charles Peter, C.B.E.; British business executive; b. 25 March 1920, London; *s.* of late Joseph Albert Pocock; *m.* Nina A. H. Hearn 1943; one *s.* two *d.*; ed. Rossall, and Keble Coll., Oxford.

Joined Shell Group of Companies 46; Pres. of Compañía Shell de Venezuela 64-67; Regional co-ordinator, East and Australasia 68-69; Man. Dir. Royal Dutch/Shell Group of Companies 70-.
Leisure interests: sailing, water skiing, mountain walking.
Shell Centre, London, S.E.1, England.
Telephone: 01-934-5866.

Podgayev, Grigory Yefimovich; Soviet politician; b. 1920; ed. Tomsk Industrial Inst. and Higher Party School.

Member C.P.S.U. 40-; Engineer 40-42; with Soviet Army 42-45; Instructor, Territorial Cttee. of C.P. then First Sec. Vyazma District Cttee. of C.P. 45-58; Chief of Section Khabarovsk Territorial Cttee. of C.P., then First Sec. Khabarovsk City Cttee. of C.P. 58-61; Chair. Exec. Cttee. Regional Soviet of Jewish Autonomous Region 61-62; First Sec. Regional Cttee. of C.P. of Jewish Autonomous Region 62-70; Chair. Exec. Cttee. Khabarovsk Territorial Soviet of Deputies Working

People; Deputy to Supreme Soviet of U.S.S.R. 66-; mem. Comm. for Industry, Soviet of Nationalities 74-; mem. Legislative Proposals Cttee. 74-.
Executive Committee, Territorial Soviet of Deputies of Working People, Khabarovsk, U.S.S.R.

Podgorny, Nikolai Viktorovich; Soviet politician; b. 18 Feb. 1903, Karlovka, Poltava region, Ukraine; ed. Mikoyan Technological Inst. of Food Industry, Kiev.
Member Communist Party 30-; Engineer, later Chief Engineer of sugar factories and sugar trusts 31-39; Deputy People's Commissar of Ukrainian Food Industry 39-40, 44-46; Deputy People's Commissar of U.S.S.R. Food Industry 40-42; Dir. Moscow Technological Inst. of Food Industry 42-44; Perm. Rep. of Ukrainian S.S.R. Council of Ministers to U.S.S.R. Council of Ministers 46-50; First Sec. Kharkov District 50-53; Second Sec. Ukraine C.P. 53-57; full mem. Presidium of Central Cttee. of Communist Party of Ukrainian S.S.R. 57-63; C.P.S.U. Sec. 63-; Alt. mem. Presidium of C.P.S.U. Cen. Cttee. 58-60, mem. 60-66, mem. Political Bureau 66-; mem. Central Auditing Comm. C.P.S.U. 52-56; Deputy to U.S.S.R. (54-) and Ukrainian S.S.R. Supreme Soviets; Chair. Presidium U.S.S.R. Supreme Soviet 65-; Hero of Socialist Labour, Order of Lenin 73, Hammer and Sickle Gold Medal.
The Kremlin, Moscow, U.S.S.R.

Podzerko, Viktor Andreyevich; Soviet trade union official; b. 14 Oct. 1912, Shpikov, Vinnitsa region; Ukraine; ed. Dneprodzerzhinsk Metallurgical Inst.
Steel Plant 30-52; Sec. Cen. Cttee. of Trade Union of Workers of Metallurgical Industry 52-55, Chair. 55-64; Chair. Central Cttee. of Trade Union of Workers of Metallurgical Industry 55-64; Vice-Chair. Int. Amalgamation of Workers of Metallurgical and Machine-Building Industries 55-65; mem. All-Union Central Council of Trade Unions; Sec. World Fed. of Trade Unions 64-70; At Staff of All-Union Central Council of Trade Unions 70-; Candidate mem. Central Cttee. C.P.S.U.; two Orders of Red Banner of Labour; Badge of Honour, etc.
All-Union Central Council of Trade Unions, Leninsky Prospekt 42, Moscow, U.S.S.R.

Poehl, Karl Otto; German economist; b. 1 Dec. 1929, Hanover; m. Ulrike Pesch; one s. one d.
Head of Dept. IFO Research Inst., Munich 55-60; journalist 61-67; Sec. Fed. of German Banks 68-69; Head of Dept., Fed. Ministry of Econ. Affairs 70; Head of Econs. Dept., Fed. Chancellor's Office 71; State Sec. Fed. Ministry of Finance 72-; Pres. EEC Monetary Cttee.; Chair. Supervisory Board VIAG; Vice-Chair. of Supervisory Board, Volkswagenwerk; mem. Supervisory Board, Bayernwerke.
Publ. *Economic and Social Aspects of the Technical Progress in the United States* (in German) 67.
Ippendorfer Allee 8A, 53 Bonn, Federal Republic of Germany.
Telephone: 79-42-93 (Office); 63-67-10 (Home).

Poher, Alain Emile Louis Marie; French politician; b. 17 April 1909, Ablon-sur-Seine (S.-et-O.); s. of Ernest Poher and Louise (née Souriau); m. Henriette Tugler 1938; one d.; ed. Lycée Louis-le-Grand, Paris, Lycée Saint-Louis, Paris, and Faculty of Law, Univ. of Paris.
Ministry of Finance 35-46; Chef de Cabinet to Minister of Finance (R. Schuman) June-Nov. 46; Senator for Seine-et-Oise 46-48, 52-68, for Val-de-Marne 68-; Finance Comm. Conseil de la République 46-48; Sec. of State for Finance 48, for Budget 48; Commr.-Gen. for German and Austrian Affairs 48-50; French Del. to Int. Ruhr Authority 50-52; Pres. Higher Trade Council 53; Pres. Senate Group of Mouvement Républicain Populaire (M.R.P.) 54-57, 59-60; Pres. Transport Comm. of Coal and Steel Assembly 54-55; Pres. of Common Market Comm. 55-57; Pres. Franco-

German Governmental Comm. for Canalisation of the Moselle 55-56; Mayor of Ablon-sur-Seine 45-; Asst. Sec.-Gen. Asscn. of Mayors of France 45-60; Sec. of State Armed Forces (Naval) 57-58; Del. to European Parl. 58, Pres. Christian Democrat Group 58-66, Pres. of European Parl. 66-69; Pres. Euro-African Parl. Assembly 67-68; Pres. of Senate 68-; Acting Pres. of France April-June 69, April-May 74; Presidential Candidate June 69; Pres. World Cttee. for the Salvation of the Jews of the Middle East; Chevalier Légion d'Honneur, Croix de Guerre (39-45), Médaille de la Résistance.
9 rue du Maréchal-Foch, 94 Abion-sur-Seine, France.

Pohl, Otakar, IUR.D.; Czechoslovak banker (retd.); b. 11 Oct. 1914, Olomouc; s. of Karel Pohl and Adéla Procházková; m. Ida Červinková 1941; one s. one d.; ed. Charles Univ. and Free School of Political Sciences, Prague.
Former Deputy Man., firm of Chartered Accountants; imprisoned for anti-Nazi activity 43-45; various political and econ. posts 45-48; Deputy Chief of Econ. Section, Pres. of Republic's Office 48-50; Gen. Man., Czechoslovak State Bank 50-53, 57-69; Deputy Gen. Man. 56-57; mem. Econ. Comm. of Central Cttee. of C.P. of Czechoslovakia 63-69; mem. State Planning Comm. 64-68; mem. State Comm. for Finance, Prices and Wages 65-68; mem. Economic Council of Govt. 68-69; mem. Economic Council 69-70; Econ. Counsellor, Czechoslovak Embassy, Bulgarian People's Republic 70-71.
Leisure interest: tourism.
Milevská 837, Pankrác 1, 14700, Prague 4, Czechoslovakia.

Poignant, Raymond; French United Nations official; b. 26 Dec. 1917, Morainvilliers (S.-et-O.); s. of Jules Poignant and Marie Beaufourd; m. Suzanne Anxionnaz 1939; one s.; ed. Ecole normale d'instituteurs de Versailles, Faculté des lettres de Paris and Ecole nat. d'admin. de Paris.
Auditeur, Council of State 49; Technical adviser in Cabinet of André Marie (Minister of Educ.) 51-54, in Cabinet of René Billières (Sec. d'Etat chargé de la Fonction publique in Pierre Mendès-France govt. Nov. 54-Feb. 55 and Minister of Educ. in govts. of Guy Mollet Feb. 56-June 57, M. Bourgès-Manoury June 57-Nov. 57, and F. Gaillard Nov. 57-Apr. 58); Maître de requêtes 56; Rapporteur gén., School and Univ. Cttee. of Commissariat du Plan 56-64; Sec.-Gen. of Interministerial Cttee. for Study of Medical Training Problems, Hospital Structure and Health and Social Activities Sept. 58-; Senior Staff mem., Int. Inst. for Educ. Planning, UNESCO 63, Dir. 69-74; Conseiller d'Etat 74-; Officier de la Légion d'Honneur, Officier de l'Ordre du Mérite, Commdr. des Palmes Académiques, Officier des Arts et Lettres, Chevalier de la Santé Publique.
Leisure interests: football, tennis, gardening.
Publs. Reports on the Third French Plan 58-62, Reports on the Fourth French Plan 62-65, *Education and Development in Western Europe, the United States and the U.S.S.R., a Comparative Study*, French edn. 65, *Educational Planning in the U.S.S.R.* (co-author) 67, *The Relation of Educational Plans to Economic and Social Planning* 69, *Education in Industrialized Countries* 73.
Conseil d'Etat, Place du Palais Royal, Paris, 1er; Home: 2 avenue du Vert-Bois, Ville-d'Avray, Hauts-de-Seine, Paris, France.
Telephone: 945-59-33.

Poitier, Sidney; American actor; b. 20 Feb. 1924; ed. Western Senior High School, Nassau, Governors High School, Nassau.
Army Service 41-45; acted with American Negro Theatre 46; appeared in *Anna Lucasta* 48, *A Raisin in*

the Sun 59; Silver Bear Award, Berlin Film Festival 58; New York Film Critics Award 58; Academy Award (Oscar) Best Actor of 63; has appeared in the following films: *Cry the Beloved Country* 52, *Red Ball Express* 52, *Go, Man, Go* 54, *Blackboard Jungle* 55, *Goodbye My Lady* 56, *Edge of the City* 57, *Something of Value* 57, *The Mark of the Hawk* 58, *The Defiant Ones* 58, *Porgy and Bess* 59, *A Raisin in the Sun* 60, *Paris Blues* 60, *Lilies, of the Field* 63, *The Long Ships* 64, *The Bedford Incident* 65, *The Slender Thread* 66, *A Patch of Blue* 66, *Duel at Diablo* 66, *To Sir with Love* 67, *In the Heat of the Night* 67, *Guess Who's Coming to Dinner* 68, *For Love of Ivy* 68, *The Lost Man* 70, *They Call Me Mister Tibbs* 70, *The Organization* 71, *The Wilby Conspiracy* 75; has appeared in and directed *Warm December* 73, *Uptown Saturday Night* 74, *Let's Do It Again* 75.

c/o General Artists Corporation, 640 5th Avenue, New York City 19, N.Y., U.S.A.

Pokrovsky, Boris Alexandrovich; Soviet opera producer; b. 23 Jan. 1912, Moscow; *s.* of Alexandr Pokrovsky and Elisabet Stulova; *m.* Irina Maslennikova 1961; one *s.* one *d.*; ed. Lunachursky Inst. of Theatrical Arts. Producer of opera and ballet, Gorki Theatre 37-43; Producer Bolshoi Theatre 43-52, Chief Producer 52-63, 67-; Organized the Moscow Chamber Theatre 72; Prof. Lunacharsky Inst. 54-; People's Artist of the U.S.S.R.; State Prize 47, 48, 49, 50; Order of Lenin; Order of Kirill and Mifodiy (Bulgaria).

Productions include: *Carmen* (Bizet), *Judith* (Serov), *Eugene Onegin* (Tchaikovsky), *The Snow Maiden, Sadko* (Rimsky-Korsakov), *The Bartered Bride* (Smetana), *War and Peace* (Prokofiev), *Khovanschchina*, (Mussorgsky), *Midsummer Night's Dream* (Britten), *The Nose* (Shostakovich), *The Player* (Prokofiev).

State Academic Bolshoi Theatre, 1 Ploshchad Sverdlova; and Flat 34, Gorki Street 15, Moscow, U.S.S.R.

Pokryshkin, Marshal Alexandr Ivanovich; Soviet army officer; b. 1913; ed. Frunze Mil. Acad. and Gen. Staff Acad.

Joined Soviet Army 32; Deputy C.-in-C., U.S.S.R. Anti-Aircraft Defence 68-71; Chair. Cen. Cttee., U.S.S.R. Asscn. for Promotion of Army, Aviation, and Navy 72-; mem. Cen. Cttee. Ukraine C.P.; Deputy to U.S.S.R. Supreme Soviet 46-; mem. Foreign Affairs Comm. Soviet of Union; mem. Youth Affairs Cttee. 74-; Marshal of Aviation; Hero of Soviet Union, Orders of Lenin, Gold Star Medals (3) and other decorations.

Central Committee of U.S.S.R. Association for Promotion of Army, Aviation and Navy, 88 Volokolamskoe chaussée, Moscow, U.S.S.R.

Poláček, Karel; Czechoslovak politician; b. 7 July 1913, St. Plzenec.

Held a number of official positions and mem. of the Nat. Assembly; Minister of Heavy Eng. 53; Eng. 53-55; Deputy Prime Minister 55-58; Minister of Gen. Eng. 58-65; Minister 65-67; Chair. Perm. Eng. Comm., Council of Mutual Econ. Assistance 56-66; mem. Central Cttee. C.P. of Czechoslovakia 52-66, 68-70; Chair. Metal Workers' Trade Union 66-68; Deputy Chair. Central Council of Trade Unions 67-68, Chair. 68-69, mem. Presidium 67-69; Alt. mem. Presidium Central Cttee. C.P. of Czechoslovakia 68-69; mem. 69-70; Chair. Cen. Council Czechoslovak Revolutionary Trade Union Movement, mem. Presidium 69-70; Deputy to Czech Nat. Council 68-71; mem. Presidium of Fed. Assembly 69-; Deputy House of the People, Fed. Assembly of the C.S.S.R. 69-71; mem. Exec. Bureau WFTU; Order of Labour 71.

Federal Assembly, Prague, Czechoslovakia.

Polak, Carel Hendrik Frederik; Netherlands law professor and politician; b. 2 Sept. 1909, Rotterdam; *s.* of Maurits Polak and Bertha Oppenheim; *m.* Anneke Werker 1950; one *s.* one *d.*; ed. Rijksuniversteit, Leiden. Civil servant 34; Prof. of Agricultural Law, Agricultural

Coll., Wageningen 46; Prof. of Admin. Law, Univ. of Leiden 51; Chair. State Comm. for Water Control Legislation; Deputy Mem. Social and Econ. Council; mem. of Board of Netherlands Inst. of Administrative Sciences; Minister of Justice 67-71; mem. of the Senate; mem. European Comm. of Human Rights 73-.

Leisure interests: walking, reading.

Publs. Several legal works and articles.

Prins Hendriklaan 22, Oegstgeest, Netherlands.

Telephone: 071-153334.

Polak, Jacques Jacobus, PH.D.; Netherlands economist and international official; b. 25 April 1914, Rotterdam; *s.* of James and Elisabeth F. Polak; *m.* Josephine Weening 1937; two *s.*; ed. Gymnasium Erasmianum, Rotterdam, and Univ. of Amsterdam.

Economist, League of Nations, Geneva, and Princeton, N.J. 37-43; Economist, Netherlands Embassy, Washington, D.C. 43-44; Asst. Financial Adviser, Econ. Advisor, UN Relief and Rehabilitation Admin., Washington, D.C. 44-46; Int. Monetary Fund, Washington, D.C. 47-, Chief, Statistics Div. 47-48, Asst. Dir. Research Dept. 48-52, Deputy Dir. Research Dept. 52-58, Dir. 58-; Econ. Counsellor 66-; Professorial Lecturer, Johns Hopkins Univ. 49-50, George Washington Univ. 50-55; Fellow, Econometric Soc.

Publs. include: *The Dynamics of Business Cycles* (with Jan Tinbergen) 50, *An International Economic System* 52.

c/o International Monetary Fund, 19th and H Streets, N.W., Washington, D.C. 20431, U.S.A.

Telephone: 477-2981.

Polanski, Roman; Polish film director; b. 18 Aug. 1933; ed. Polish Film School, Łódź.

Has directed, *Two Men and a Wardrobe* 58, *When Angels Fall, Le Gros et Le Maigre, Knife in the Water* (prize at Venice Film Festival 62), *The Mammals* (prize at Tours Film Festival 63), *Repulsion* (prize at Berlin Film Festival 65), *Cul de Sac* (prize at Berlin Film Festival 66), *The Vampire Killers* 67, *Rosemary's Baby* 68, *Macbeth* 71, *What?* 72, *Lulu* (opera), Spoleto Festival 74, *Chinatown* (Best Dir. Award, Soc. of Film and TV Arts 74) 74, *The Tenant* 76.

Has acted in, *A Generation, The End of the Night, See You Tomorrow, The Innocent Sorcerers, Two Men and a Wardrobe, The Vampire Killers, What?, Chinatown, The Tenant.*

c/o Caliban Films Ltd., 140 Park Lane, London, W.1. England.

Telephone: 01-491-7211.

Poletti, H.E. Cardinal Ugo; Italian ecclesiastic; b. 19 April 1914, Omegna, Novara.

Ordained 38; consecrated titular Bishop of Medeli 58; promoted to Spoleto 67; consecrated Archbishop of Cittanova 69; Vicar General of Rome; created Cardinal by Pope Paul VI 73.

Vicariato di Roma, Piazza S. Giovanni in Laterano 6, 00184 Rome, Italy.

Polevoi, Boris Nikolayevich; Soviet writer and journalist; b. 17 March 1908, Moscow; *s.* of Nikolay Petrovich Kampov and Lidiya Vasilyevna Kampova; *m.* Yuliya Osipovna 1939; two *s.* one *d.*; ed. Kalinin industrial coll.

Technologist in Proletarska Factory, Kalinin 28; became professional journalist 28; war correspondent for *Pravda*, Finnish War 39-40, and World War 41-45; mem. C.P.S.U. 40-; Col. in Soviet Army; Deputy to Supreme Soviet R.S.F.S.R. 51-66; mem. Board U.S.S.R. Union of Writers 48-; mem. Board Union of Soviet Journalists 59-; mem. Presidium of U.S.S.R. Cttee. of War veterans 48-; Editor *Yunost* (Youth) magazine; awarded State prizes, Hero of Socialist Labour, orders of Lenin (three), Red Banner (twice), Red Star, Patriotic War 1st Class (twice), Red Banner of Labour,

Gold Medal of World Peace Council, V. Vorovsky Prize of U.S.S.R. Union of Journalists.
Leisure interest: bee-keeping.
Publs. *Goryachii tsekh* (The Hot Shop) 39, *Okrovavlennye kamni* (Blood-stained Stone) 42, *Do poslednego dykhaniya* (Till their Last Breath) 43, *Ot Belgoroda do Karpat* (From Belgorod to the Carpathians) 44, *Povest o Nastoyashchem cheloveke* (Story of a Real Man) 46, *Mysovetskie lyudi* (We Are Soviet People) 48, *Vernulsya* (He Came Back) 49, *Zoloto* (Gold) 50, *Sovremenniki* (Contemporaries) 52, *Amerikanskiye Dnevniki* (American Diaries) 56, *Za tridevyat zemel* (In the Far-away Lands) 56, *30 tyssyach li po novomu Kitayu* (Three hundred thousand li across the New China) 57, *Glubokyi Till* (Far Behind the Lines) 58, *Chelovek Cheloveku Brat* (All Men are Brothers) 60, *Blizko y Daleko* (From Near and Far) 60, *Vstrechi na perekrjesikah* (Meetings on the Cross-Roads) 61, *Nash Lenin* (Our Lenin) 62, *Na dikom brege* (On the Wild Shore) 63, *Doctor Vera* 66, *V bolshom nastuplenii* (In Great Offensive) 66, *Nuremberg Diaries* 69, *Eti chetire goda* (These Four Years) 74, *Silueti* (Profiles) 74.
13 Begovaya Street, Apt. 113, Moscow, U.S.S.R.
Telephone: 255-89-22.

Polinszky, Dr. Károly; Hungarian engineer and politician; b. 19 March 1922, Budapest; s. of Gyula Polinszky and Róza Morbitzer; m. Mária Magdolna Rézeky 1946; three s.; ed. Technical Univ., Budapest.
Assistant Lecturer Technical Univ. 44; Corresp. mem. Hungarian Acad. of Sciences 64-; Dean, later Rector Veszprém Univ. of Chemical Industry, Dir. Research Inst. for Heavy Chemistry; Deputy Minister of Educ. 63-74, Minister 74-; Vice-Pres. Awarding Cttee. for State Prize and Kossuth Prize 74-; Dr. h.c. Lensoviet Technical Univ. of Leningrad 68; Kossuth Prize 61.
Leisure interests: literature, music.
Ministry of Education, Szalay-utca 10/14, Budapest 1055, Hungary.
Telephone: 118-600.

Pollini, Maurizio; Italian pianist; b. 1942, Milan.
Has played with Berlin and Vienna Philharmonic Orchestras, Bayerischer Rundfunk Orchestra, London Symphony Orchestra, Boston, New York, Philadelphia, Los Angeles and San Francisco Orchestras; has played at Salzburg, Vienna, Berlin, Prague Festivals; recordings for Polydor Int.; First Prize Int. Chopin Competition, Warsaw 60.
c/o Harrison/Parrott Ltd., 22 Hillgate Street, London, W8 7SR, England.

Pollock, Admiral of the Fleet Sir Michael (Patrick),
G.C.B., M.V.O., D.S.C.; British naval officer; b. 19 Oct. 1916; ed. Royal Naval Coll., Dartmouth.
Entered Navy 30, specialized in gunnery 41; served in *Warspite, Vanessa, Arethusa* and *Norfolk,* Second World War; Captain, Plans Div. of Admiralty and Dir. of Surface Weapons; commanded H.M.S. *Vigo* and Portsmouth Squadron 58-59, H.M.S. *Ark Royal* 63-64; Asst. Chief of Naval Staff 64-66; Flag Officer, Second-in-Command, Home Fleet 66-67; Flag Officer, Submarines, and NATO Commdr., Submarines, E. Atlantic 67-69; Controller of the Navy 70-71; Chief of Naval Staff and First Sea Lord 71-74; First and Principal Naval Aide-de-Camp to the Queen 72-74.
The Ivy House, Churchstoke, Montgomery, Powys, SY15 6DU, Wales.

Polunin, Nicholas, M.S., M.A., D.PHIL., D.SC., F.L.S., F.R.G.S., F.R.H.S.; British biologist and author; b. 26 June 1909, Checkendon, Oxon.; s. of late Vladimir Polunin and Elizabeth Violet (née Hart); m. Helen Eugenie Campbell 1948; two s. one d.; ed. Christ Church, Oxford, and Yale and Harvard Univs.
Botanical, etc., exploring expdns. Spitsbergen, Lapland, Greenland, Iceland, Labrador, Hudson Bay and Strait, Baffin, Southampton, Devon and Ellesmere Islands 30-

38 (collections mainly in Nat. Museum of Canada, Gray Herbarium Harvard Univ., British Museum, Fielding Herbarium Oxford); explorations in Canadian North-west Territories, Alaska, Ungava-Labrador, and Arctic Archipelago (where discovered last major islands to be added to world map) 46-49; visited vicinity of magnetic North Pole 47 and flew over geographical North Pole summer 48 (demonstrating persistence of microbial life there) and winter 49; field work in Middle East 56-59, and in West Africa 62-65; U.S. Order of Polaris, Canadian Marie—Victorin Medal; Botanical Tutor various Oxford Colls. 32-47; Henry Fellow, Yale Univ. 33-34; Dept. of Scientific and Industrial Research, Senior Research Award 35-38; Research Assoc. Harvard Univ. 36-37; Foreign Research Assoc. 38-50, Research Fellow 50-53; Fielding Curator and Keeper, Univ. Herbaria, Oxford, Univ. Demonstrator and Lecturer in Botany 39-47, Univ. Moderator 41-45; Lecturer (and latterly Senior Research Fellow) New Coll., Oxford 42-47; Haley Lecturer, Acadia Univ. 50; Macdonald Prof. of Botany, McGill Univ., Montreal 47-52; Guggenheim Memorial Fellow 50-52; Lecturer in Plant Geography, Yale Univ. 53-55 while Project Dir. U.S. Air Force; Prof. of Plant Ecology and Taxonomy and Head Dept. of Botany, Dir. Univ. Herbarium, Faculty of Sciences, Baghdad 55-59; Guest Prof. Univ. of Geneva 59-61, 75-; Prof. of Botany and Head of Dept. Faculty of Science (which he established as first Dean) Univ. of Ife, Ibadan 62-66; Founder and Sec.-Gen. Int. Conf. on Environmental Future 71-; Pres. Foundation for Environmental Conservation 74-; Fellow, American Assoc. for Advancement of Science, Arctic Inst. of North America, and mem. of other learned socs.; Founding Editor *International Industry* 43-46, *World Crops Books* 54-74 and *Plant Science Monographs* 54-, *Biological Conservation* 67-74, *Environmental Conservation* 74.
Leisure interests: biological and environmental conservation, developing new ideas into plans (e.g. for world environmental council, special conferences, series of books, new journals, etc.), travel, international stock markets.
Publs. *Russian Waters* 31, *The Isle of Auks* 32, *Botany of the Canadian Eastern Arctic* (3 vols.) 40-48, *Arctic Unfolding* 49, *Circumpolar Arctic Flora* 59, *Introduction to Plant Geography and some related sciences* 60, *Eléments de Géographie botanique* 67, *The Environmental Future* (editor) 72, *Conservation of the Plant World* (2 vols. in preparation).
c/o New College, Oxford, England; 15 Chemin F. Lehmann, 1218 Grand-Saconnex, Geneva, Switzerland.
Telephone: 98 23 83/84.

Polwarth, 10th Baron, **Henry Alexander Hepburne Scott,** M.A., LL.D., F.R.S.E., F.R.S.A.; British (Scottish) chartered accountant; b. 17 Nov. 1916, Edinburgh; s. of Hon. Walter Thomas Hepburne Scott and Elspeth Glencairn Campbell; m. 1st Caroline Margaret Hay 1943 (divorced 1969), one s. three d.; m. 2nd Jean Jauncey (née Cunninghame-Graham); ed. Eton Coll. and King's Coll., Cambridge.
Deputy-Gov., Bank of Scotland 60-66, Gov. 66-72, Dir. 74-; mem. Western Hemisphere Exports Council 58-64; Partner Chiene and Tait, Edinburgh 50-68; Chair. Gen. Accident, Fire and Life Assurance Co. 68-72; Minister of State, Scottish Office 72-74; given special responsibility for oil devt. in Scotland 73-74; Chair. Oil Devt. Council for Scotland 73-74; Chair. Total Oil (G.B.) Ltd., Total Oil Marine Ltd. 75-; Dir. ICI 69-72, 74-, Halliburton Co. 74-, The Weir Group 74-, Canadian Pacific Ltd. 75-, Sun Life Assurance Co. of Canada 75-; mem. Historic Bldgs, Council for Scotland 53-66; Chancellor Univ. of Aberdeen 66-; Chair. Scottish Nat. Orchestra 75-; Hon. LL.D. (St. Andrews Univ., of Aberdeen), Hon. D.Litt. (Heriot Watt Univ.), Hon. Dr. (Univ. of Stirling).

Leisure interests: managing my family estate, country pursuits.
Harden, Hawick, Roxburghshire, Scotland.
Telephone: Hawick 2069 (Home).

Polyakov, Vasily Ivanovich; Soviet agricultural journalist and politician; b. 10 Dec. 1913, Novoivanovka village, Kursk region; ed. Agricultural Technical School, Voronezh, and Inst. of Journalism, Leningrad.
Agronomist 33-38; mem. C.P.S.U. 39-; Head of Dept. and Exec. Sec. Editorial Board *Sotsialisticheskoe Zemldelie* 38-41; Red Army, Second World War; *Pravda* 46-60; later Editor Agricultural Dept. and mem. Editorial Board; Editor *Rural Life* 60-62; Head Agriculture Dept., Central Cttee. of C.P.S.U. March-Nov. 62, Chair. U.S.S.R. Bureau of Agriculture (C.P.S.U.) 62-64; Sec. Central Cttee. of C.P.S.U. 62-64; Deputy Chief Editor *Ekonomicheskaya Gazeta* 64-; Deputy to U.S.S.R. Supreme Soviet until 70; awarded Orders of Lenin, Red Banner of Labour, Patriotic War 1st and 2nd classes, Red Star.
Ekonomicheskaya Gazeta, ulitsa Pravdy 24, Moscow, U.S.S.R.

Polyakov, Vladimir Porfirievich, PH.D.; Soviet diplomatist; b. March 1931, Smolensk; s. of Porfiry and Evdokia Polyakov; m. Nelly Polyakov 1953; one s.; ed. Inst. of Oriental Studies, Moscow.
Diplomatic Service 56-; Counsellor, Syria 61-65; various posts in Ministry of Foreign Affairs 65-67; Counsellor-Minister, Egypt 67-71; Amb. to People's Democratic Repub. of Yemen 72-74; to Egypt March 74-.
Leisure interest: politics.
Embassy of the U.S.S.R., 95 Sh. El Giza (Giza), Cairo, Egypt.

Polyansky, Dmitri Stepanovich; Soviet politician; b. 7 Nov. 1917, Slavyanoserbskoe, Ukraine; ed. Kharkov Inst. of Agriculture and Higher Party School of Central Cttee. of C.P.S.U.
Exec. work in Young Communist League, service in Soviet army and study at Higher Party School 39-42; Party work in Siberia 42-45; exec. in Central Cttee. of Party 45-49; Second Sec. Crimea regional Cttee. of Party, and Chair. Exec. Cttee. Crimea regional Soviet of Working People's Deputies 49-52; First Sec. Crimea regional Cttee. of Party 54-55; First Sec. of Chkalovsk (now Orenburg) regional Cttee. then First Sec. of Krasnodar territorial Party Cttee. 55-58; Chair. Council of Ministers of R.S.F.S.R. 58-62; Dep. Premier U.S.S.R. 62-65, First Deputy Premier 65-74; Deputy Supreme Soviet of the U.S.S.R. 64-; mem. C.P.S.U. Cen. Cttee. 56-; alt. mem. Presidium of Central Cttee. of C.P.S.U. 58-60, mem. 60-66; mem. Political Bureau 66-; Minister of Agriculture 73-76; Amb. to Japan 76-.
Publs. *Pearl of Russia* 58, *Great Plans for the Economic and Cultural Progress of the Russian Federation* 59.
Embassy of the U.S.S.R., 2-1-1 Azabudai, Minato-ku, Tokyo, Japan.

Poma, H.E. Cardinal Antonio; Italian ecclesiastic; b. 12 June 1910, Villanterio.
Ordained 33; Titular Bishop of Tagaste 51-54; Bishop of Mantua 54-68; Archbishop of Bologna 68-; cr. Cardinal 69; Pres. Italian Episcopal Conf.
Arcivescovado, Via del Monte 3, 40126 Bologna, Italy.

Pomfret, John Edwin, A.M., PH.D.; American educator; b. 21 Sept. 1898, Philadelphia; m. Sara Wise 1926; one s.; ed. Univ. of Pennsylvania.
Associate Prof. of History, Univ. of South Carolina 24-25; Instr., Asst. Prof., and Assoc. Prof. of History Princeton Univ. 25-37, also Asst. Dean 34-36; Dean of Senior Coll. and Graduate School, Vanderbilt Univ. 37-42; Pres. of the Coll. of William and Mary 42-51; Dir. H. E. Huntington Library and Art Gallery 51-66; Hon. LL.D. Univ. of Pa., Univ. of Chattanooga, Mills Coll.,

Hon. D.Litt., Univ. of Southern Calif., Claremont Graduate School, Claremont Colls.
Leisure interest: historical writings.
Publs. *The Struggle for Land in Ireland* 30, *The Geographic Pattern of Mankind* 35, *California Gold Rush* 54, *Twelve Americans Speak* 54, *Province of West New Jersey* 56, *Province of East Jersey* 62, *New Jersey Proprietors and Their Lands* 65, *History of Huntington Library and Art Gallery* 69, *Founding the American Colonies* 70, *A History of Colonial New Jersey* 73.
2436 Bayview Ave., Carmel, Calif., U.S.A.
Telephone: 408-624-6666.

Pompei, Gian Franco, DR.JUR.; Italian diplomatist; b. 31 Jan. 1915, Sète, France; s. of Raffaele Pompei (diplomat) and Countess Isabella Moroni Candelori; m. Ilde Scarpa 1939; one s. two d.; ed. Univ. of Turin.
In Diplomatic Service 39-, at Rome 39-42; Vice-Consul Neuchâtel, Switzerland 42-45; Sec., Berne 45-47; Foreign Office, Rome 47-50; Sec. then Counsellor, Paris Embassy 50-63; Perm. Del. UNESCO 53-63, elected mem. of Exec. Board 62, 66, Chair. of Exec. Board 68-70; Diplomatic Adviser to Prime Minister Rome 63-68; Head of Cabinet, Ministry of Foreign Affairs 68; Amb. to the Holy See 69-.
Leisure interests: mountaineering, skiing, chess.
166 Via Flamina, Rome; and 1e Via Bertoloni, Rome, Italy.
Telephone: 3600741 (Via Flamina); 805300 (Via Bertoloni).

Ponce Enrile, Juan, LL.M.; Philippine lawyer and public official; b. 14 Feb. 1924, Gonzaga, Cagayan; s. of Alfonso Ponce Enrile and Petra Furugganan; m. Cristina Castañer 1957; one s. one d.; ed. Ateneo de Manila, Univ. of the Philippines and Harvard Law School.
Practising corpn. lawyer and Prof. of Taxation 55-66; Under-secretary of Finance Dec. 66-Dec. 68; Acting Sec. of Finance; Acting Insurance Commr.; Acting Commr. of Customs; Sec. of Justice Dec. 68-Feb. 70; Chair., Boards of Dirs. Philippine Nat. Bank, Nat. Investment and Devt. Co., Philippine Exchange, Central Azucarera de Danao; Chair., Board of Pardons and Parole, Peace and Order Council; Vice-Chair., Peace and Order Co-ordinating Council; Acting Chair., Monetary Board, Central Bank of the Philippines; mem., Special Cttee. on Govt. Investments, Surigao Mineral Board; Acting mem., Board of Industries; Dir., Philippine Communication Satellite Corp; Trustee and Sec., Board of Trustees, Cultural Centre of the Philippines; Sec. of Nat. Defence Feb. 70-71 (resigned), 72-; Chair. Exec. Cttee., Nat. Security Council, Board of Dirs., Philippine Veterans Bank, Philippine Coconut Authority; mem. and Dir., Philippine Tax Inst.; mem. Board, Nat. Econ. and Devt. Authority; mem. numerous law and commercial asscns.
Leisure interests: reading, golf, tennis, swimming, water-skiing, fishing.
Publs. *A Proposal on Capital Gains Tax* 60, *Income Tax Treatment of Corporate Merger and Consolidation Revisited* 62, *Tax Treatment of Real Estate Transactions* 64; also various articles on law, the military and government.
Office of the Secretary of National Defence, Camp Gen. Emilio Aguinaldo, Quezon City; and Dasmariñas Village, Makati, Rizal, Philippines.
Telephone: 99-78-06 and 79-03-90.

Ponce Enriquez, Camilo; Ecuadorean politician and university professor; b. 1912; ed. Univs. of Quito and Chile.
Vice-Pres. Quito Municipal Council 43; mem. Junta Govt. 44; as Minister of Foreign Relations led Ecuadorean Dels. to San Francisco and Chapultepec Confs. 45; Vice-Pres. Nat. Assembly 46; Prof. of Constitutional Law, Catholic Univ. of Ecuador 50-; Del. to UNESCO

52; Senator 52; Minister of Government and Justice 53-56; Pres. of Ecuador 56-60; founder and leader Christian Social Movement.

Publs. *Ideas Constitucionales de Bolívar* 35, *Génesis y Ocaso de un Régimen* 42, *Parliamentary Speeches* 53-54.

Bolívar 343, Apdo. 2184, Quito, Ecuador.

Poncelet, Christian; French politician; b. 24 March 1928, Blaise; *m.* Yvette Miclot 1949; two *d.*; ed. Coll. Saint-Sulpice, Paris and Ecole Professionelle des Postes, Télégraphes et Télécommunications.

Deputy to Nat. Assembly (U.N.R.-U.D.T.) 62-; Deputy Sec.-Gen. U.D.R., responsible for social affairs; Sec. of State, Ministry of Social Affairs 72-74; Sec. of State attached to Prime Minister with responsibilities for the Civil Service Feb.-June 74; Sec. of State, Ministry of Economic Affairs and Finance June 74-.

Ministère de l'Economie et des Finances, 93 rue de Rivoli, Paris 1er, France.

Telephone: 260-33-00.

Ponge, Francis; French writer; b. 27 March 1899, Montpellier; *s.* of Armand Ponge and Juliette Saurel; *m.* Odette Chabanel 1931; one *d.*; ed. Lycée Frédéric-Mistral, Avignon, Lycée Malherbe, Caen, Lycée Louis-le-Grand, Paris, Faculty of Literature and Philosophy, Sorbonne, and Faculty of Law, Paris.

Secretary Editions Gallimard, Paris 23; with Hachette, Paris 31-37; Head of Centre "Progrès de Lyon", Bourg-en-Bresse 42; Political Traveller for Nat. Cttee. of Journalists 42-44; Literary and Artistic Dir. *Action* 44-46; Prof. at Alliance Française, Paris 52-64; Virginia C. Gildersleeve Visiting Prof., Barnard Coll. and Columbia Univ. (French Dept.), N.Y. City 66-67; mem. Bayerische Akademie der Schönen Künste; Officier Légion d'Honneur Int. Poetry Prize, Capri 59, Int. Ingram Merrill Foundation Award 72; Int. Books Abroad Literature Prize 74.

Leisure interests: listening to and reading about the universal lot.

Publs. *Douze petits écrits* 26, *Le Parti pris des choses* 42, *Proèmes* 49, *Le Peintre à l'étude* 48, *La Seine* 50, *La Rage de l'Expression* 52, *Le Grand Recueil (I Lyres, II Méthodes, III Pièces)* 61, *Pour un Malherbe* 65, *Tome Premier* 65, *Le Savon* 67, *Nouveau Recueil* 67, *Entretiens de Francis Ponge avec Philippe Sollers* 70, *La Fabrique du Pré, Introduction au Braque de Draeger* 71, *Introduction au Picasso de Draeger* 74.

34 rue Lhomond, 75 Paris 5e; Mas des Vergers, 06 Le Bar-sur-Loup, France.

Telephone: 707-03-09 (Paris); (93) 67-90-45 (Le Bar-sur-Loup).

Poniatowski, Prince Michel Casimir; French civil servant and politician; b. 16 May 1922, Paris; *s.* of Prince Charles-Casimir Poniatowski and the Princess (née Anne de Caraman-Chimay); *m.* Gilberte de Chavagnac 1946; three *s.* one *d.*; ed. Ecole des Roches, Verneuil-sur-Avre, and Univ. de Paris.

With Ministry of Finance 48-56; Financial Attaché in Washington 56-57; Asst. Dir. du cabinet to Minister of Finance 57-58; Econ. and Financial Counsellor in Morocco 58; Asst. Dir. du cabinet to Prés. du Conseil 58; Dir. du cabinet to Sec. of State for Finance, later to Minister of Finance 59-62; Dir. du Cabinet, Ministry of Finance 62; Del. for Foreign Investment, Overseas Finance Admin. 62; Head of Mission Ministry of Finance 62-65, Dir. of Insurance 63-67; Ind. Republican Deputy 67-; Sec.-Gen. Féd. des Républicains indépendants 67-70, Pres. 75-; Mayor of Isle-Adam 71-; Minister of Health and Social Security 73-74; Minister of State and of the Interior 74-; Co-founder Soc. Infipress; Chevalier de la Légion d'Honneur; Médaille militaire; Chevalier de l'ordre nat. du Mérite; Croix de Guerre 39-45; Commdr. Isabela la Católica; Officier du Ouissam alaouite.

Publs. *L'Avenir des pays sous-développés* 54, *Histoire de la Russie d'Amérique et de l'Alaska* 59, *Talleyrand aux Etats-Unis* 67, *Les Choix de l'espoir* 70, *Cartes sur table* 72, *Les Jagellons* 73, *Conduire le Changement* 75.

Ministère de l'Intérieur, Paris, France.

Telephone: LAB-90-90.

Ponnamperuma, Lakshman George, PH.D., D.I.C., F.R.I.C., M.I.CHEM.E., C.ENG.; Ceylonese chemical engineer and administrator; b. 10 Oct. 1916; *s.* of Andreas Ponnamperuma and Grace Siriwardena; *m.* Mary Frances Marcelline 1950; two *s.* one *d.*; ed. Ceylon Univ. Coll. and Imperial Coll. of Science & Technology, London Univ.

Research Officer, Dept. of Industries 41-54; Man. Ceylon Govt. Cement Works 54-58; Gen. Man. Ceylon Cement Corpn. 58-65; Chair. Petro Chemicals Planning Cttee. 60; Pres. Chemical Soc. of Ceylon 64; Chair. & Man. Dir. Ceylon Cement Corpn. 65-67; Dir. and Vice-Chair. Ceylon Inst. of Scientific & Industrial Research 67; Consultant to UNESCO on Conf. on the Application of Science & Technology to the Devt. of Asia (CASTASIA) 67; mem. Industrial Cttee. of Nat. Planning 59, ECAFE Advisory Council on Industrial Research 66; Dir. Devt. Finance Corpn. of Ceylon 65, of State Fertilizer Mfg. Corpn. 66; mem. Board of Regents, Univ. of Ceylon 66; Vice-Chair. Nat. Science Council of Ceylon 68; Special Asst. to Asst. Dir.-Gen. for Science UNESCO 70; Dir. ECAFE/UNESCO 70; Dir. ECAFE/UNESCO Science and Technology Unit 71; mem. Advisory Cttee. Tropical Products Inst. (London) 71.

Leisure interests: music, art, golf, photography, philately.

Publs. works on technical and managerial subjects.

c/o UNESCO Regional Office for Asia, P.O. Box 1425, Bangkok, Thailand.

Ponomaryov, Boris Nikolayevich; Soviet historian and politician; b. 17 Jan. 1905, Zaraisk, Ryazan region; ed. Moscow State Univ. and Red Professors' Inst.

Red Army 19, Mil. Revolutionary Cttee. Zaraisk 19-20; Young Communist League, Moscow Region 20-22; Sec. *Krasny Vostok* Factory Party Org., Moscow Region 22-23; mem. Propagandist Group, Cen. Cttee. of C.P.S.U. 26-28; Asst. Dir. Red Professors' Inst. 33-36; Exec. Cttee. Communist Int. 36-39; Asst. Dir. Marx-Engels-Lenin Inst. 43-45; Cen. Cttee. C.P.S.U. 44-46; First Dep. Chief Soviet Information Bureau, U.S.S.R. Council of Ministers 46-49; Head of Dept., Central Cttee. C.P.S.U. 49-61, mem. of Central Cttee. 56-, Sec. 61-, alt. mem. Political Bureau 72-; Deputy to U.S.S.R. Supreme Soviet 58-; Chair. Foreign Affairs Comm., Soviet of Nationalities; corresp. mem. Acad. of Sciences of U.S.S.R. 58, mem. 62-; Order of Lenin (twice); Order of Red Banner of Labour (twice), etc.

Publs. Works on history of C.P.S.U. and int. workers' movements.

Central Committee of Communist Party of Soviet Union, 4 Staraya Ploshchad, Moscow, U.S.S.R.

Pons, Bernard; French doctor and politician; b. 18 July 1926, Béziers; *s.* of Claude Pons and Véronique Vogel; *m.* Josette Cros 1952; five *d.*; ed. Faculté de Médecine, Montpellier.

General Practitioner, Cahors 52-67; Deputy to Nat. Assembly 67-; Sec. of State, Ministry of Agriculture 69-; mem. Cen. Cttee. U.N.R. 60-; Municipal Councillor, Souillac 71-.

Leisure interests: fishing, hunting, reading.

Ministère de l'Agriculture, 78 rue de Varenne, Paris 7e, France.

Telephone: 555-92-50.

Ponte, Maurice Jules Henry; French scientist and business executive; b. 5 April 1902, Voiron, Isère; *m.* Nelly Andrews 1925; three *c.*; ed. Prytanée militaire, La Flèche and Ecole normale supérieure.

Research with Henri Abraham, Sir William Bragg and

Prince Louis de Broglie 24-29; with Compagnie Générale de T.S.F. (Radio); Pres. and Dir.-Gen. 29-68, Hon. Chair. Thomson-CSF; Dir. Anvar (Agence Nationale de Valorisation de la Recherche) 68-71; Pres. of French Soc. of Electricians 48, of Radioelectricians 49, Vice-Pres. Inst. of Radio-Engineers 54; mem. Scientific Council of High Comm. for Atomic Energy; fmr. Pres. of Consultative Cttee. on Scientific Research of Asscn. for Advancement of Science 59-63; mem. Académie des Sciences, Institut de France 63-; Commandeur Légion d'Honneur, Grand Croix Ordre Nat. du Mérite, Commandeur de l'Education nationale.
Leisure interests: painting, tapestry, archaeology.
Publs. Papers on X-rays, Electronics and Radio-Electricity.
5 square Mozart, Paris 16e, France.
Telephone: 525-5783.

Pentecorvo, Bruno Maksimovich (brother of Guido Pontecorvo, q.v., and Gillo Pontecorvo); Soviet (b. Italian) physicist; b. 2 Aug. 1913, Pisa, Italy; s. of Massimo Pontecorvo and Maria (née Maroni); ed. Pisa and Rome Univs.
Instructor, Rome Univ. 33-36; at scientific institutions in France 36-40; in U.S.A. 40-43; research at Chalk River, Canada, under E. Fermi, leading to devt. of neutron physics 43-48; Assoc. Harwell Laboratory, U.K. 48-50; went to U.S.S.R. 50; mem. C.P.S.U. 55-; Corresp. mem. U.S.S.R. Acad. of Sciences 58-64, mem. 64-; in charge of team at Joint Nuclear Research Inst., Dubna; Order of Lenin 63; Lenin Prize 63.
Joint Nuclear Research Institute, Dubna, nr. Moscow, U.S.S.R.

Pontecorvo, Guido, DR.AGR., PH.D., F.R.S. (brother of Bruno Pontecorvo, q.v., and Gillo Pontecorvo); British (b. Italian) scientist and university professor; b. 29 Nov. 1907, Pisa; s. of Massimo Pontecorvo and Maria (née Maroni); m. Leonore Freyenmuth 1939; one d.; ed. Università degli Studi, Pisa, and Univ. of Edinburgh.
Assistant and later Regent of Section, Ispettorato Compartimentale Agrario, Florence 30-38; Research Student, Inst. of Animal Genetics, Edinburgh 38-40, Dept. of Zoology, Univ. of Glasgow 41-43; Lecturer, Inst. of Animal Genetics, Univ. of Edinburgh 43-45; Lecturer, Senior Lecturer, Reader, Dept. of Genetics, Univ. of Glasgow, Prof. 45-68; Hon. Dir. Medical Research Council Unit for Cell Genetics 64-68; mem. staff, Imperial Cancer Research Fund 68-75, Hon. Consultant Geneticist 75-; Jesup Lecturer, Columbia Univ. 56, Messager Lecturer, Cornell Univ. 57, Leeuwenhoek Lecturer, Royal Soc. 62; Visiting Prof. Albert Einstein Coll. of Medicine, New York 64, 65, Washington State Univ. 67; Royal Soc. Leverhulme Visiting Prof. Univ. Coll., London 68-75; Visiting Prof. King's Dept. of Biology, Pahlavi Univ., Iran 74; Visiting Prof. Univ. Coll., London 68-75; Visiting Prof. King's Coll. London 69-70; Visiting Prof. Middlebury Coll., Vermont 71; Visiting Prof. Univ. of Teheran 75; Sec. Genetical Soc. 46-52, mem. of Council 53-54, Vice-Pres. 54-57, Pres. 64-65; Vice-Pres. Inst. of Biology 69-71; mem. Council, Soc. for Gen. Microbiology 56-60; Fellow Royal Soc. of Edinburgh (mem. Council 58-61), of London (mem. Council 58-59); Fellow Linnean Soc. London 71; Foreign mem. Danish Royal Soc.; Hon. Foreign mem. American Acad. of Arts and Sciences; Hon. mem. Peruvian Soc. Medical Genetics 69; Hansen Prize 61; Hon. D.Sc. Univs. of Leicester 68, East Anglia 74, Camerino 74.
Leisure interests: alpine plant photography, mountaineering.
Publ. *Trends in Genetic Analysis.*
Imperial Cancer Research Fund, Lincoln's Inn Fields, London, W.C.2; Home: Flat 25, Cranfield House, 97 Southampton Row, London, W.C.1, England.
Telephone: 636-9441.

Ponti, Carlo, LL.D.; French (b. Italian) film producer; b. 11 Dec. 1913, Magenta, Milan; s. of the late Leone Ponti and Maria (née Zardone); m. 2nd Sophia Loren (q.v.) 1966; two s. (also one s. one d. by previous marriage); ed. Università degli Studi, Milan.
Legal practice in office of Milan barrister 35-38; film producer 38-.
Major films produced: *Roma Città Aperta* 45 (New York Critics Prize 47), *To Live in Peace* 45, *Attila* 53, *Ulysses* 53, *La Strada* 54 (Oscar), *War and Peace* 55, *Two Women* (Oscar Award for best foreign actress) 60, *Boccaccio '70* 61, *Yesterday, Today, Tomorrow* 63 (Oscar), *Marriage, Italian Style* 64, *Casanova '70* 64, *Lady L* 65, *Dr. Zhivago* 65 (six Oscars), *The 25th Hour* 66, *Blow Up* 66 (Cannes Film Festival Award), *The Girl and the General* 66, *More than a Miracle* 66, *Ghosts, Italian Style* 67, *Smashing Time* 67, *Diamonds for Breakfast* 67, *Best House in London* 68, *A Place for Lovers* 68, *Zabriskie Point* 69, *Sunflower* 69, *Priest's Wife* 70, *Love Stress* 71, *Mortadella* 71, *Red, White and . . .* 72, *Massacre in Rome* 73, *Run Run Joe* 73, *Verdict* 74, *The Passenger* 74, *Blood Money* 75.
Bürgenstock, Nidwalden, Switzerland; 32 Avenue George V, Paris 8e, France; 1 Piazza d'Ara Coeli 1, Rome, Italy.

Ponti, Gio(vanni); Italian architect and designer; b. 18 Nov. 1891, Milan; s. of Enrique Ponti and Giovanna Rigone; m. Giulia Vimercati 1921; one s. three d.; ed. Milan Polytechnic.
Designed and planned buildings in Milan, Padua, São Paulo, Buenos Aires, Baghdad, Stockholm, Caracas, Teheran, New York, Islamabad, Rome, Taranto, Beirut; with others designed Pirelli skyscraper, Milan; Consultant Architect in Paris, Lourdes, Rhodesia, Canada and Spain; worked on interior design of Italian liners (inc. *Andrea Doria*); designed costumes and settings for the La Scala Theatre, Milan, murals for Padua Univ.; contributed to the Triennale; organized Exhibitions overseas; designed furniture; Prof. of Architecture, Milan School of Architecture; mem. Nat. Acad. of St. Luke; founded and edits *Domus* (architectural magazine); Dr. h.c. (Royal Coll. of Art, U.K.).
Leisure interests: painting, travelling.
Via Dezza 49, Milan, Italy.

Pontryagin, Lev Semyonovich; Soviet mathematician; b. 3 Sept. 1908, Moscow; ed. Moscow Univ.
Has been blind 22-; Prof. of Mathematics at Moscow Univ. 35-; discovered the general law of duality 32, constructed the general theory of topological commutative groups; Corresp. mem. Acad. of Sciences of the U.S.S.R. 39, mem. 58; State prizewinner for his monograph *Continuous Groups* 38; shared Lenin Prize for monograph *Theory of Optimum Processes* 62; Hero of Socialist Labour; Order of Lenin (twice).
Publs. *The General Topological Theorem of Duality for Closed Sets* 34, *Fundamentals of Combinational Topology* 47, *Characteristic Cycles of Differential Manifolds* 47, *Vector Fields in Manifolds* 49, *Continuous Groups* 54, *Smooth Manifolds and their Application in Homotopy* 55, *Mathematical Theory of Optimum Processes* (with others) 61, *Ordinary Differential Equations* (textbook) 61, *One Probability Problem of Optimal Control* 62, *On Some Differential Games* 64.
V.I. Steklov Mathematical Institute of the Academy of Sciences of the U.S.S.R., 28 Ulitsa Vavilova, Moscow, U.S.S.R.

Poole, 1st Baron, cr. 58, of Aldgate; **Oliver Brian Sanderson Poole,** P.C., C.B.E.; British politician; b. 11 Aug. 1911; ed. Eton Coll. and Christ Church, Oxford.
Served 39-45 war; M.P. for Oswestry Division of Salop 45-50; mem. Lloyds; Joint Treasurer Conservative Party Organization 52-55, Chair. 55-57, Deputy Chair. 57-59, Jt. Chair. April-Oct. 63, Vice-Chair. Oct. 63- Oct. 64; Chair. Thomas Stephens, Poole (Holdings); Chair.

Whitehall Securities Corpn. Ltd.; Exec. Deputy Chair. Lazard Brothers Jan.-Oct. 65, Chair. Oct. 65-73; Chief Exec. S. Pearson 73-75; Dir. Reserve Bank of Rhodesia 65-; Trustee, Nat. Gallery 73-.

12 Egerton Terrace, London, S.W.3, England.

Poonacha, Cheppudira Muthana; Indian politician; b. 1910, Attur, Coorg, Karnataka State; s. of Shri Cheppudira T. Muthana and Kongetira Kaveramma; m. Gangamma Poonacha 1941; two s. two d.; ed. St. Aloysius Coll., Bangalore.

Joined Satyagraha Movement 30, imprisoned for Satyagraha activities; Sec. District Congress Cttee., Coorg 33; mem. Exec. Cttees., Karnatak and All India Congress Cttees. and Coorg District Board 38, Pres., Coorg District Board 41; mem. Exec. Cttee. Coorg Legislative Council and Leader, Congress Legislative Party in the Council 45-46; mem. Constitutent Assembly and Provisional Parl. 47-51; Chief Minister of Coorg 52-56; Minister for Industries and Commerce 57, and later for Home and Industries at Mysore; Chair. State Trading Corpn. of India 59-63; Leader of Trade Dels. to various countries 61, 63; mem. Rajya Sabha 64; Minister for Revenue and Expenditure Jan. 66; Minister of State in Ministry of Transport and Aviation 66-67; Minister of Railways 67-69, of Steel and Heavy Eng. Feb.-Dec. 69; Chair. Malabar Chemicals and Fertilizers Ltd. 70-71.

Leisure interest: agriculture.

Home Estate, Athur Post via Pollibetta, Coorg, Karnataka State, India.

Telephone: Gonicopal 85.

Popa, Dumitru; Romanian politician; b. 27 Feb. 1925, Bucharest; m. Emilia Popa; two s.; ed. Acad. of Economic Studies, Bucharest.

Joined Communist Youth 44, Communist Party 45; First Sec. Hunedoara Region Cttee. of Romanian C.P. 63-65; First Sec. Bucharest Party Cttee. and General Mayor of Bucharest 66-72; mem. Central Cttee. of R.C.P. 65; Alt. mem. Exec. Cttee. of R.C.P. 66, mem. 69-72; Deputy to Grand Nat. Assembly 61-; Sec. Grand Nat. Assembly 61-65; mem. Nat. Council of the Socialist Unity Front 68-72, Ambassador to Democratic People's Republic of Korea 72-.

Romanian Embassy, Pyongang, Democratic People's Republic of Korea.

Popa, Pretor; Romanian economist and diplomatist; b. 2 April 1922; m. Ileana Popa 1947; one d.; ed. Acad. for Economic Studies, Bucharest.

Director at Ministry for Oil Extraction and Processing 50-66; Gen. Dir. Ministry for Foreign Trade 66-70; Deputy Minister at Ministry for Foreign Trade and Vice-Pres. Chamber of Commerce and Industry, Bucharest 70-72; Amb. to U.K. 73-.

Embassy of Romania, 4 Palace Green, London, W8 4QD; and 1 Belgrave Square, London, S.W.1, England.

Popal, Ali Ahmad, PH.D.; Afghan educationist and diplomatist; b. 22 Feb. 1916, Kabul; s. of Mohammad Mukkaram Popal; m. Rabia Popal 1947; two s. three d.; ed. Nedjat Secondary School, Kabul, and Univ. of Jena. Teacher and Dir., Nedjat School, Kabul 42-46; Dir. of Teachers Training Coll. 46-47; Head of Primary Educ. Dept., Ministry of Educ. 47-49, also Teacher and Dean in Faculty of Women, Kabul Univ. 47-49; Head of Gen. Educ. Dept., Ministry of Educ. 49-51, Deputy Minister of Educ. 52-56, Minister of Educ. 56-64, Second Vice-Premier 62-64; Amb. to Fed. Repub. of Germany, also accred. to Sweden, Switzerland and Denmark 64-66; Amb. to Turkey 66-67; First Deputy Prime Minister and Minister of Educ. 67-68; Amb. to Pakistan, also accredited to Sri Lanka and Thailand 69-; Order of Maaref, 3rd Class 46, 1st Class 64; Order of Sardarie-Ahlie 58, and orders from U.A.R., Yugoslavia and German Fed. Repub.

Leisure interests: swimming, tennis.

Embassy of Afghanistan, 176 Shalimar-7-3, Islamabad, Pakistan.

Telephone: 22566.

Pope-Hennessy, Sir John Wyndham, Kt., C.B.E., F.B.A., F.S.A., F.R.S.L.; British museum director and art historian; b. 13 Dec. 1913, London; s. of late Major-Gen. L. H. R. Pope-Hennessy and late Dame Una Pope-Hennessy; ed. Balliol Coll., Oxford.

Joined staff Victoria and Albert Museum 38, Keeper Dept. of Architecture and Sculpture 54-66; Slade Prof. of Fine Art, Oxford Univ. 56-57; Robert Sterling Clark Prof. of Art, Williams Coll., Williamstown, U.S.A. 61-62; Slade Prof. of Fine Art, Cambridge Univ. 64-65; Dir. Victoria and Albert Museum 67-73, British Museum 74-76.

Leisure interest: music.

Publs. *Giovanni di Paolo* 37, *Sassetta* 39, *Sienese Quattrocento Painting* 47, *A Sienese Codex of the Divine Comedy* 47, *The Drawings of Domenichino at Windsor Castle* 48, *A Lecture on Nicholas Hilliard* 49, *Paolo Uccello* 50, *Fra Angelico* 52, *Italian Gothic Sculpture* 55, *Italian Renaissance Sculpture* 58, *Italian High Renaissance and Baroque Sculpture* 63, *Catalogue of Italian Sculpture in the Victoria and Albert Museum* 64, *Italian Bronzes in the Kress Collection* 65, *The Portrait in the Renaissance* 67, *Essays on Italian Sculpture* 68, *The Frick Collection Catalogue* Vols. III and IV, *Sculpture* 70, *Raphael* (The Wrightsman Lectures) 70.

41 Bedford Gardens, London, W.8, England.

Popescu, Dumitru; Romanian politician and writer; b. 18 April 1928, Turnu Măgurele; m. Maria Popescu; one s. two d.; ed. Acad. of Economic Studies, Bucharest. Member of the Romanian Communist Party 53-; Journalist on *Contemporanul* 50-56; Editor-in-Chief *Scinteia Tineretului* 56-60; Dir. *Agerpres* (Romanian News Agency) 60-62; Vice-Chair. State Cttee. for Culture and Art 62-65; Editor-in-Chief of *Scinteia* 65-68; Pres. of the Council of Socialist Culture and Education 71; mem. of the Cen. Cttee. of R.C.P. 65-, Alt. mem. Exec. Cttee. 68-69, mem. Political Exec. Cttee. 69-; Sec. Cen. Cttee. of R.C.P. 68-; Deputy to Grand Nat. Assembly 65-; mem. Acad. of Social and Political Sciences 70-.

Publs. *Impresii de Călător* (*Egypt, Iraq, Cuba*) 62, *Drumuri europene* 65, *Biletul la control* (essays) 68, *Pentru cel ales* (poems) 68, *Un om in Agora* (poems) 72, *Iesirea din labirint* (essays) 73, *Gustul Sîmburelui* (poems) 74.

Central Committee of the Romanian Communist Party, Council of Socialist Culture and Education, Bucharest, Romania.

Popják, George Joseph, M.D., D.SC., F.R.I.C., F.R.S.; British biochemist; b. 5 May 1914, Kiskundorozsma, Hungary; s. of late George Popják and late Maria Mayer; m. Hasel Marjory Hammond 1941; ed. Royal Hungarian Francis Joseph Univ., Szeged, Hungary, and Postgraduate Medical School, Univ. of London.

British Council Scholar 39-41; Demonstrator, Dept. of Pathology, St. Thomas's Hospital, London 41-47; Beit Memorial Fellow for Medical Research 43-47; mem. Scientific Staff, Nat. Inst. for Medical Research, London 47-53; Dir. Medical Research Council Experimental Radio-pathology Research Unit, Hammersmith Hospital, London 53-62; Visiting Scientist, Nat. Heart Inst., Nat. Insts. of Health, Bethesda, Md., U.S.A. 60-61; Joint Dir., Chemical Enzymology Laboratory, Shell Research Ltd. 62-68; Assoc. Prof. in Molecular Sciences, Warwick Univ. 65-68; Prof. of Biochemistry, Univ. of Calif. at Los Angeles Oct. 68-; Foreign mem. Royal Flemish Acad. of Sciences and Fine Arts, Belgium; mem. American Acad. of Arts and Sciences 71; Ciba Medal, Biochem. Soc. 65; Stouffer Prize 67; Davy Medal, The Royal Soc. 68.

Leisure interests: music, sculpture and gardening.

Publs. Numerous articles in scientific journals, mainly on problems of lipid metabolism; monograph *Chemistry, Biochemistry and Isotopic Trace Technique* 55.
Departments of Biological Chemistry and Psychiatry, University of California, Los Angeles, Calif. 90024; and 511 Cashmere Terrace, Los Angeles, Calif. 90049, U.S.A.
Telephone: 213-476-4536.

Popkov, Valery Ivanovich; Soviet electrical engineer; b. 3 Feb. 1908, Moscow; *s.* of Ivan Vasilievitch and Prascovija Petrovna Popkov; *m.* Anna Vasilievna 1930; one *s.* one *d.*; ed. Moscow Power Engineering Inst.
At All-Union Electrotechnical Inst. 32-36, Head of Laboratory 36-73; Assoc., Power Eng. Inst., U.S.S.R. Acad. of Sciences 43-; mem. C.P.S.U. 51-; Corresp. mem. U.S.S.R. Acad. of Sciences 53-66, mem. 66-, Vice Acad. Sec. of Dept. of Physical and Technical Problems in Engineering; Pres. Int. Electrotechnical Comm. 74; Order of Red Banner of Labour, Order of the October Revolution, Order of Lenin.
Leisure interest: rose gardening.
Publs. Works on gas discharges, high-voltage techniques and long-distance transmission.
U.S.S.R. Academy of Sciences, 14 Leninsky Prospekt, Moscow 117901, U.S.S.R.

Pople, John Anthony, M.A., PH.D., F.R.S.; British professor of theoretical chemistry; b. 31 Oct. 1925, Burnham, Somerset; *s.* of Keith Pople and Mary Jones; *m.* Joy Cynthia Bowers 1952; three *s.* one *d.*; ed. Univ. of Cambridge.
Research Fellow, Trinity Coll., Cambridge 51-54, Lecturer in Mathematics 54-58; Research Assoc., Nat. Research Council, Ottawa during summer 56, 57; Supt. Basic Physics Div., Nat. Physical Laboratory, Teddington (U.K.) 58-64; Ford Visiting Prof. of Chem., Carnegie Inst. of Tech., Pittsburgh, Pa. 61-62; Carnegie Prof. of Chemical Physics, Carnegie-Mellon Univ., Pittsburgh 64-74, Acting Head, Dept. of Chem. 67, John Christian Warner Univ. Prof. of Natural Sciences 74-; mem. American Chemical Soc. 65-, Int. Acad. of Quantum Molecular Science 67-; Fellow, American Physical Soc. 70-, American Acad. of Arts and Sciences 71-; Smith's Prizeman (Cambridge) 50, Marlow Medal of Faraday Soc. 58, American Chemical Soc., Awards: Irving Langmuir 70, Harrison Howe 71, Gilbert Newton Lewis 73, Pittsburgh 75.
Leisure interest: music.
Publs. co-author: *High Resolution Magnetic Resonance* 59, *Approximate Molecular Orbital Theory* 70; also over 200 publs. in scientific journals.
Department of Chemistry, Carnegie-Mellon University, 4400 5th Avenue, Pittsburgh, Pa. 15213; Home: 59 Holland Road, Pittsburgh, Pa. 15235, U.S.A.
Telephone: (412) 621-1100 (Office); (412) 371-9250 (Home).

Popov, Dimiter; Bulgarian politician; b. 29 March 1912, Ihtiman; *s.* of Peter Popov and Jiordana Popova; *m.* Eugenie 1938; two *d.*; ed. Sofia Univ.
Active in communist movement until arrest in 41, imprisoned 41-44; Deputy Mayor of Sofia 49, Mayor 53-61; first Vice-Pres. Planning Cttee. 62; Minister of Finance 62-; several national and foreign decorations.
Leisure interest: history.
Publs. several publications concerning the state budget.
Boulevard Klement Gottwald 58, Sofia, Bulgaria.
Telephone: 44-62-94.

Popov, Georgi Ivanovich; Soviet engineer and politician; b. 1912; ed. Leningrad Inst. of Railway Transport Engineers.
Worker in Red Triangle Factory, Leningrad 36-41, 45-52; Soviet Army 41-45; mem. C.P.S.U. 42-; political and party work, Leningrad 52-56; First Sec. Viborg Town Cttee., C.P.S.U. 56-57; Second Sec. Leningrad District City Cttee., C.P.S.U. 57-60; First Sec. Leningrad City Cttee. C.P.S.U. 60-; mem. Central Cttee. of C.P.S.U. 64-71; Deputy to U.S.S.R. Supreme Soviet 62-; mem. Cttee. U.S.S.R. Parliamentary Group; mem. Foreign Affairs Comm. Soviet of Union.
Leningrad City Committee of Communist Party of Soviet Union, Leningrad, U.S.S.R.

Popov, Olyeg Konstantinovich; Soviet actor; b. 3 Aug. 1930, Moscow; ed. Moscow State Circus School.
Clown on slack wire at Tbilisi Circus 50; clown at Saratov Circus 51; appeared in France, Britain, Poland, etc.; clown at Moscow Circus 55-; People's Artist of R.S.F.S.R. and the U.S.S.R.; Winner of Warsaw Int. Festival of Circus Art 56, Oscar Prize, Brussels 58.
All Union Organization of State Circuses, 15 Neglinnaya ulitsa, Moscow, U.S.S.R.

Popova, Nina Vasiliyevna; Soviet politician; b. 1908; ed. Chernyskevsky Inst. of History, Philosophy and Literature.
Member C.P.S.U. 32-; party work 38-45; Sec. Cen. Council of Trade Unions 45-57; Chair. Cttee. of Soviet Women, Vice-Pres. Int. Dem. Fed. of Women 57-68; Chair. All-Union Soc. for Foreign Cultural Relations, then Chair. Presidium of Union of Soviet Socs. of Friendship and Cultural Relations with Foreign Countries 57-; Cand. mem. Central Cttee. C.P.S.U. 56-61, mem. 61-; Deputy to U.S.S.R. Supreme Soviet, mem. Cttee. for Foreign Affairs, Soviet of Nationalities; Int. Lenin Prize 63.
Union of Soviet Societies for Friendship and Cultural Relations with Foreign Countries, Prospekt Kalinina 14, Moscow, U.S.S.R.

Popović, Koča; Yugoslav soldier and politician; b. 14 March 1908; ed. Univ. of Belgrade and in Switzerland and France.
Former student of literature and mem. group of progressive Yugoslav writers; volunteer in Spanish Republican Army 36; early organizer Yugoslav Liberation Army during 41-45 war; later Divisional, Corps and Army Commdr.; Chief of the Gen. Staff 46-53; Sec. of State for Foreign Affairs 53-65; Head, Comm. for Int. Econ. and Political Relations, Yugoslav C.P. 65-66; Vice-Pres. of Yugoslavia 66-69; mem. Fed. Council 69-71; mem. of Presidency of Yugoslavia 71; decorations include Order of Freedom, Spomenica 1941, etc.
Bulevar Lenjina 2, Belgrade, Yugoslavia.

Popovich, Col. Pavel Romanovich; Soviet cosmonaut; b. 5 Oct. 1930; ed. Industrial Technical School, Magnitogorsk and Zhukovsky Air Force Engineering Acad.
Joined Army 51; transferred to Air Force; Fighter Pilot; first to join cosmonaut training unit; launched into orbit around earth Aug. 12th 62, returned Aug. 15th after completing 48 orbits in space ship *Vostok 4*; piloted *Soyuz 14* mission 74; mem. Communist Party; Deputy Supreme Soviet Ukrainian S.S.R.; Eng. Pilot Cosmonaut of the U.S.S.R., Hero of Soviet Union, Order of Lenin, Gold Star Medal and other awards.
Zvezdny Gorodok, Moscow, U.S.S.R.

Popper, Sir Karl (Raimund), Kt., M.A., PH.D., D.LIT., F.B.A.; British philosopher; b. 28 July 1902, Vienna, Austria; *s.* of Dr. Simon Siegmund Carl Popper and Jenny (née Schiff); *m.* Josephine Anna Henninger 1930; ed. Vienna Univ.
Senior Lecturer in Philosophy, Canterbury Univ. Coll., Christchurch, New Zealand 37-45; Reader in Logic, London Univ. 45-48, Prof. of Logic and Scientific Method 49-69, Emeritus 69; Head, Dept. Philosophy, Logic and Scientific Method, London School of Econs. 45-66; William James Lecturer, Harvard Univ. 50; Fellow, Stanford Center for Advanced Study in the Behavioral Sciences 56-57; Annual Philosophical Lecturer, British Acad. 60; Shearman Lecturer, Univ. Coll. London 61; Herbert Spencer Lecturer, Oxford Univ. 61, 73; Visiting Prof. Calif. and Minn. Univs. 62,

Indiana 63, Univ. of Denver 66; Farnum Lecturer, Princeton Univ. 63, Inst. of Advanced Studies, Canberra 63, Inst. of Advanced Study, Vienna 64, Arthur Holly Compton Memorial Lecturer, Washington Univ. 65; Henry D. Broadhead Memorial Lecturer, Univ. of Canterbury, Christchurch, N.Z. 73; Visiting Fellow, Salk Inst. for Biological Studies 66-67; Kenan Univ. Prof., Emory Univ. 69; Ziskind Prof., Brandeis Univ. 69; James Scott Lecturer, R.S.E. 71; Romanes Lecturer, Oxford 72; William Evans Prof., Univ. of Otago 73; Visiting Erskine Fellow, Univ. of Canterbury 73; Herbert Spencer Lecturer, Oxford 73; mem. Council Asscn. for Symbolic Logic 51-55, Int. Acad. for Philosophy of Science 48-; Fellow, British Acad. 58-; Foreign Hon. mem. American Acad. Arts and Sciences 66-; Hon. mem. Harvard Chapter of Phi Beta Kappa 64-; Hon. mem. RSNZ 65; Pres. Aristotelian Soc. 58-59, British Soc. for the Philosophy of Science 59-61; Hon. LL.D. (Chicago, Denver); Hon. D.Lit. (Warwick); Hon. Litt.D. (Canterbury, N.Z.); Hon. Fellow, London School of Econs.; Corresp. mem. Institut de France; Prize, City of Vienna 65; Sonning Prize 73 (Copenhagen).
Leisure interests: music, Jane Austen, Trollope.
Publs. *Logik der Forschung, The Open Society and Its Enemies, The Poverty of Historicism, The Logic of Scientific Discovery, Conjectures and Refutations: The Growth of Scientific Knowledge, Objective Knowledge: An Evolutionary Approach, Intellectual Autobiography, Reply to my Critics, Unended Quest: An Intellectual Autobiography:* over 100 papers for periodicals and journals of learned societies.
Fallowfield, Manor Road, Penn, Bucks., England.

Porché, Wladimir; French radio and television official; b. 9 June 1910.
Joined state broadcasting service 35; organized early television programmes 35-36; television research during the occupation; Dir.-Gen. Radiodiffusion-Télévision Française 46-57, Hon. Dir.-Gen. 57-; Conseiller d'Etat 56-; Légion d'Honneur.
Publs. *Amours en Valespir, Le Chevalier Francoys.*
23 rue des Longs-Prés, 92-Boulogne-sur-Seine, France.

Porritt, Baron (Life Peer), cr. 73, of Wanganui in New Zealand and of Hampstead in Greater London; **Arthur Porritt,** Bt., G.C.M.G., G.C.V.O., C.B.E.; British surgeon and administrator; b. 10 Aug. 1900, Wanganui, New Zealand; s. of Ernest Edward and Ivy Elizabeth (McKenzie); m. 1st Molly Bond 1926, 2nd Kathleen Mary Peck; two s. one d.; ed. Wanganui Collegiate School and Otago Univ., New Zealand, Oxford Univ. and St. Mary's Medical School, London.
St. Mary's Hospital Surgical Staff 36-65; War Service with R.A.M.C. Second World War; mem. Royal Medical Household 36-67; Surgeon to Duke of York 36, to Household 37-46, to King George VI 46-52, Sergeant-Surgeon to Queen Elizabeth 53-67; Consulting Surgeon to the Army; Pres. Royal Coll. of Surgeons of England 60-63; Pres. B.M.A. 60-61; Pres. Royal Soc. of Medicine 66-67; mem. Int. Olympic Cttee. 34-67; Chair. British Commonwealth Games 48-67, now Vice-Pres.; Gov.-Gen. of New Zealand 67-72; Chair. Arthritis and Rheumatism Council 74-; African Med. Research Foundation; Pres. Medical Council on Alcoholism; Chair. Royal Masonic Hospital, African Medical and Research Foundation; Vice-Pres. Royal Commonwealth Soc.; Hon. Fellow, Royal Coll. of Surgeons of Edinburgh, Glasgow, Ireland, Australasia and Canada, and American and South African Coll. of Surgeons; Gold Medal B.M.A.; Bronze Medal 100 metres, Olympic Games 24; Hon. LL.D. (St. Andrews, Birmingham, Otago and New Zealand), Hon. D.Sc. (Oxford), Hon. M.D. (Bristol); Hon. Fellow, Royal Coll. of Physicians of U.K. and Australasia; Hon. Fellow, Royal Coll. of Obstetricians and Gynaecologists.

Publs. *Athletics* (with D. G. A. Lowe) 29, *Essentials of Modern Surgery* (with R. M. Handfield-Jones) 39.
57 Hamilton Terrace, London N.W.8, England.
Telephone: 01-286-9212.

Porsild, (Alf) Erling, M.B.E., PH.D., F.R.S.C.; Canadian (b. Danish) botanist; b. 17 Jan. 1901, Copenhagen; s. of Dr. Morten P. Porsild and Kirstine Porsild; m. Margrit Stoeffel; one d.; ed. Sorø Acad. and Copenhagen Univ.
Botanical Asst. Danish Arctic Research Station, Disko, Greenland 22-25; botanist in charge of grazing studies and introduction of domesticated reindeer from Alaska to Canada 26-35; Curator and Head of Div. of Botany, Nat. Museum of Canada, Ottawa 36-45, Chief Curator 45-67, hon. curator emeritus 68-; Canadian Consul to Greenland 41-44; has done extensive field work or led botanical expeditions to Alaska, Yukon, Arctic and Subarctic Canada, Rocky Mountains and Arctic and Alpine parts of Europe; Foreign Hon. mem. American Acad. of Arts and Sciences, and Botanical Socs. in Norway, Sweden and Finland; Massey Medal 66, George Lawson Medal, Canadian Botanical Asscn. 71.
Publs. *Botany of Southeastern Yukon* 51, *Vascular Plants of the Western Canadian Arctic Archipelago* 55, *Illustrated Flora of the Canadian Archipelago* 57, 63, *Rocky Mountains Wildflowers in Colour* 71; and over 200 scientific and popular papers and articles, mainly on the taxonomy and distribution of plants.
45 Leonard Avenue, Ottawa 1, Ontario, Canada.

Port, Arthur Tyler, LL.B.; American lawyer and administrator; b. 4 Oct. 1916, Chicago, Ill.; s. of Arthur C. Port and Helen E. Brown; m. Aline H. Gooding 1950; one s. one d.; ed. Davidson Coll. and Yale Law School.
Admitted to law practice 40; military service 42-46; attorney, Judge Advocate Div. H.Q. European Command, Frankfurt 46-48; Legal Asst. to Special Adviser to C.-in-C. and U.S. Mil. Gov. for Germany, Berlin 49; Consultant to Sec. of Army 49-50; Special Assistant to Sec. of Army 51-55; Exec. Asst. to the Asst. Sec. of Defense 55-57; Dir. Office of Security Policy, Office of Sec. of Defense 57-61; Deputy Asst. Sec. of Army for Installations and Logistics 61-67; U.S. Foreign Service Reserve Officer, Dept. of State 67-; Asst. Sec.-Gen. for Defence Support NATO 67-73; Special Asst. for Energy, Dept. of Army 73-; Chair. NATO Conf. of Nat. Armament Dirs. 68, 69-; U.S. Dept. of Defense Distinguished Civilian Service Medal; U.S. Dept. of Army Decoration for Exceptional Civilian Service; Hon. LL.D.
Leisure interests: book collecting, gardening, motor racing.
Department of the Army, Washington, D.C. 20034; Home: 6515 Hillmead Road, Bethesda, Md. 20034, U.S.A.

Porter, Arthur T., M.A., PH.D.; Sierra Leonean professor and administrator; b. 26 Jan. 1924, Freetown; s. of Guy H. and Adina A. Porter; m. Rigmor Søndergaard Rasmussen 1953; one s. one d.; ed. Fourah Bay Coll., Sierra Leone, Cambridge Univ., Inst. of Educ., London and Boston Univ., U.S.A.
Assistant, Dept. of Social Anthropology, Edinburgh Univ. 51-52; Lecturer in History, Fourah Bay Coll. 52-56; research in African Studies, Boston Univ. 56-58; Prof. of Modern History, Fourah Bay Coll., later Vice-Principal 60-64; Principal, Univ. Coll., Nairobi 64-70; UNESCO Adviser on Ministry of Educ., Educ. Planning to Kenya Govt. 70-74; Vice-Chancellor Univ. of Sierra Leone 74-; Sierra Leone Independence Medal 61; Yugoslav Flag with Gold Star.
Leisure interest: photography.
Publ. *Creoledom.*
University of Sierra Leone, Private Mail Bag, Freetown, Sierra Leone.
Telephone: Freetown 6859.

Porter, Eric Richard; British actor; b. 8 April 1928, London; s. of Richard John Porter and Phoebe Elizabeth Porter (née Spall); ed. L.C.C. and Wimbledon Tech. Coll.

First professional appearance in Shakespeare, Arts Theatre, Cambridge 45; first appearance, London stage in *Saint Joan* 46; Bristol Old Vic. Co. 54, 55-56; with Old Vic. Co. 54-55; British tour with Lynne Fontanne and Alfred Lunt 57, New York 58; joined Royal Shakespeare Co. (R.S.C.) 60: roles include Barabbas (*The Jew of Malta*), Shylock (*The Merchant of Venice*) 65; Chorus (*Henry V*) 65, Ossip (*The Government Inspector*) 66; title roles, *King Lear, Dr. Faustus* Stratford 68; toured *Dr. Faustus* with R.S.C. 69; actor and Dir. *My Little Boy—My Big Girl* 69, *The Protagonist* 71, Capt. Hook, Mr. Darling in *Peter Pan* 71; films include: *The Fall of the Roman Empire* 64, *The Pumpkin Eater* 64, *The Heroes of Telemark* 65, *Kaleidoscope* 66, *The Lost Continent* 68, *Hands of the Ripper* 71, *Nicholas and Alexandra* 71, *Anthony and Cleopatra* 72, *The Last Ten Days of Hitler, The Day of the Jackal, The Belstone Fox* 73, *Callan* 74, *Hennessy* 75; many television appearances include title role, *Cyrano de Bergerac*, Jack Tanner (*Man and Superman*), Soames Forsyte (*The Forsyte Saga*); *Separate Tables, Tolstoy, Macbeth* 70; *Evening Standard* Drama Award Best Actor of 1959, Guild of Television Producers and Directors Award to Television Actor of the Year 67.

Leisure interests: walking, swimming, gardening.

c/o International Famous Agency Ltd., 11-12 Hanover Street, London, W.1, England.

Porter, Sir George, Kt., M.A., SC.D., F.R.S.; British professor of chemistry; b. 6 Dec. 1920, Stainforth; m. Stella Brooke 1949; two s.; ed. Thorne Grammar School, Leeds Univ. and Emmanuel Coll., Cambridge.

War Service in R.N.V.R.; Demonstrator Physical Chemistry, Univ. of Cambridge 49-52, Asst. Dir. of Research 52-54; Prof. of Physical Chemistry, Univ. of Sheffield 55-63, Firth Prof. and Head of Dept. of Chemistry 63-66; Prof. of Chemistry, The Royal Institution, London 63-66; Dir. and Fullerian Prof. of Chemistry, The Royal Inst. 66-; Pres. Comité Int. de Photobiologie 68-72; Pres. Chemical Soc. 70-72, Faraday Div. 73-74, Nat. Asscn. for Gifted Children 75-; mem. Aeronautical Research Council 64-66, of Council Open Univ. 69-75, Science Museum Advisory Council 70-73; Consultant, Gen. Electric Co. 68-; Trustee, British Museum 72-74; Hon. mem. New York Acad. of Sciences 68, Leopoldina Acad. 70, Pontifical Acad. of Sciences 74; Foreign Assoc. U.S. Nat. Acad. of Sciences, Washington; Corresp. mem. Gottingen Acad. of Sciences; Hon. Fellow Inst. of Patentees & Investors 70; Hon. Fellow, Emmanuel Coll., Cambridge; Hon. Prof. Univ. of Kent; Visiting Prof., Univ. Coll., London; Corday-Morgan Medal Chemical Soc. 55; Liversidge Lecturer, Chem. Soc. 70; Nobel Prize in Chem. 67; Davy Medal, Royal Soc. 71; Hon. D.Sc. (Univ. of Sheffield 68, Univ. of Utah 68, Univs. of East Anglia, Surrey, Durham 70, Univs. of Leicester, Leeds, Heriot-Watt, City Univ. 71, Univs of Manchester, St. Andrews, London 72, Kent, 73, Oxford 74).

Leisure interest: sailing.

Publs. *Chemistry for the Modern World* 62, *Progress in Reaction Kinetics* (Editor), and numerous scientific papers; B.B.C. Television series *Laws of Disorder* 65, *Time Machines* 69-70.

The Royal Institution, 21 Albemarle Street, London, W1X 4BS, England.

Telephone: 01-493-0669; 01-493-2710.

Porter, Katherine Anne; American writer; b. 15 May 1890, Indian Creek, Brown County, Texas; d. of late Harrison Boone Porter and late Mary Alice Jones; m. 1st Eugene Dove Pressly 1933 (divorced), 2nd Albert Russel Erskine Jr. 1938 (divorced); ed. private schools and convents in southern U.S.A.

Guggenheim Fellowship for work in fiction 31-32, renewed 38-39; Fellow of Library of Congress (Fellow of Regional American Literature) 44; Vice-Pres. Nat. Inst. of Arts and Letters New York 50-52; Fulbright Lecturer, Univ. of Liège 54-55; elected mem. Nat. Acad. Arts and Letters 67; awarded Gold Medal of Soc. for the Libraries of New York Univ. 40; two-year Ford Foundation Grant 60-62; Hon. D.Litt. (Univ. of N. Carolina, Women's Coll., Smith Coll., La Salle Coll., Rutgers Univ., Maryville Coll.); Hon. D.H.L. (Univs. of Michigan and Maryland), Emerson-Thoreau Medal (American Acad. of Arts and Sciences); Nat. Book Award 66; Pulitzer Prize 66; Bronze Medal for Services to Literature (Hollins Coll.) 67.

Leisure interests: growing trees, gardening, playing ancient music on the spinet, reading, seeing friends.

Publs. *Flowering Judas* (short stories) 30, *Pale Horse, Pale Rider* (3 short novels) 39, *The Leaning Tower* (short stories) 44, *The Days Before* (collected essays) 52; *K.A.P.'s French Song Book* (trans. from French) 33; *The Itching Parrot* (novel, trans. from Spanish) 42, *Ship of Fools* (novel) 62, *Collected Stories of Katherine Anne Porter* 65, *A Christmas Story* 68, *Collected Essays* 70, *Noon Wine* (short novel).

c/o Seymour Lawrence Inc., 90 Beacon Street, Boston, Mass. 02108; and Apts. 1517-1518, 5910 Westchester Park Drive, College Park, Md. 30740, U.S.A.

Telephone: 301-345-6568.

Porter, Richard William, B.S.E.E., PH.D.; American electrical and technological executive; b. 24 March 1913, Salina, Kansas; s. of Thomas F. and Dora (Schermerhorn) Porter; m. Edith Wharton Kelly 1946; one s. two d.; ed. Univ. of Kansas and Yale Univ.

General Electric Co. 37, originated first mil. and commercial applications of amplidyne generators 37-45, responsible for aircraft automatic tracking equipment for first fire control radar 40-41; Manager Guided Missiles Dept. 50-55, Consultant Engineering Services 55-63, Gen. Electric Co., Consultant Aero Space Science and Technology 63-70, Man. Scientific & Technological Affairs, Aerospace Group 70-76; Advisory Cttee. U.S. Dept. of Defense 55-56; Scientific Advisory Board U.S. Air Force 48-51, Chair. Geophysics Panel 60-; mem. Space Science Board, Nat. Acad. of Sciences 58-70; Chair. Int. Relations Cttee. 59-70; Adviser U.S. Del. to UN 62-70; Vice-Pres. Cttee. on Space Research, Int. Council of Scientific Unions 59-71; mem. Nat. Council of Scholars 68-72; AIBS Planetary Quarantine Advisory Cttee. 70-; New York City Sciences & Technology Advisory Council to the Mayor 66-73; Private Consultant Aerospace, Energy and Environmental Science and Technology 76-; Hon. D.Sc. (Yale); numerous awards.

Leisure interests: horticulture, skiing, sailing.

Publs. *Das Amerikanische Erdsatellitenprogram* 56, *Recovery of Data in Physical Form* 56, *What the Future Holds* 58, *Preview of Scientific Progress* 59, *Weather Modification and Space Exploration* 59, *Adventures in Energy Conversion* 60.

1154-56 East Putnam Avenue, Riverside, Conn. 06878; 164 Cat Rock Road, Cos Cob, Connecticut 06807, U.S.A.

Porter, Rodney Robert, F.R.S.; British biochemist; b. 8 Oct. 1917; ed. Liverpool and Cambridge Univs.

Member of scientific staff, Nat. Inst. for Medical Research, Mill Hill, London 49-60; Prof. of Immunology St. Mary's Hosp. Medical School, London Univ. 60-67; Prof. of Biochemistry, Univ. of Oxford 67-; mem. Medical Research Council; Hon. Foreign mem. American Acad. of Arts and Sciences 68; Foreign Assoc. U.S. Nat. Acad. of Sciences 72; Nobel Prize for Medicine (jointly with G. M. Edelman q.v.) 72, Royal Soc. Medal 73. Downhill Farm, Witney, Oxon., England.

Porter, William James; American diplomatist; b. 1 Sept. 1914, England; *s.* of William and Sarah (Day) Porter; *m.* Eleanore E. Henry 1944; twin *s.* and *d.*; ed. Thibodeau Business Coll., Southeastern Mass. Univ. Entered U.S. Foreign Service 36; served in Hungary, Iraq, Lebanon, Syria, Palestine, Cyprus, Morocco, Algeria and several positions in Dept. of State 36-62; Amb. to Algeria 62-65; Deputy Amb. (with rank of Amb.) to Viet-Nam 65-67; Amb. to Repub. of Korea 67-71; Chief Negotiator, U.S. Del. to Paris talks on Viet-Nam 71-73; Under-Sec. of State for Political Affairs 73-74; Amb. to Canada 74-75, to Saudi Arabia 75-; Dept. of State Distinguished Honour Award, President's Award for Distinguished Fed. Civilian Service, Viet-Nam Service Award.
American Embassy, Jeddah, Saudi Arabia; and c/o Department of State, Washington, D.C. 20520, U.S.A.

Portmann, Adolf, DR.PHIL.; Swiss professor; b. 27 May 1897, Basle; *s.* of Adolf and Elisabeth Portmann-Rohr; *m.* Genevieve Devillers 1931; ed. Univs. of Basle, Paris, Munich, Berlin and Geneva.
Privat Dozent Univ. of Basle 26-31, Prof. of Zoology and Dir. of the Zoological Laboratory 31-67, Rector of the Univ. 47; Pres. Int. Asscn. Univ. Profs. 48-51, Pres. Rectors' Conf. (Swiss Univs.) 62-69.
Publs. *Biologische Fragmente zu einer Lehre vom Menschen* 51, 3rd edn. 69, *Einführung in die vergleichende Morphologie der Wirbeltiere* 59, *Die Tiergestalt* 60, *Das Tier als soziales Wesen* 56, *Biologie und Geist* 56, *Neue Wege der Biologie* 61, *Entlässt die Natur den Menschen* 70, *Vom Lebendigen* 73, *An den Grenzen des Wissens* 73.
Zoologisches Institut, Rheinsprung 9, Basle, Switzerland.
Telephone: 25-25-35.

Posnett, Richard Neil, O.B.E., M.A.; British barrister-at-law and diplomatist; b. 19 July 1919, Kotagiri, India; *s.* of Rev. Charles Walker Posnett and Phyllis (née Barker); *m.* Shirley Margaret Hudson 1959; two *s.* one *d.* (two *s.* one *d.* by previous marrage); ed. Kingswood School, St. John's Coll., Cambridge.
Royal Air Force 40; Colonial Admin. Service, Uganda 41-60; Chair. Uganda Olympic Cttee. 56-58; Judicial Adviser 60; Perm. Sec. for Social Devt., External Affairs, Trade and Industry 61-63; H.M. Diplomatic Service 64; Foreign Office 64-66; U.K. Mission to UN 66-70; briefly H.M. Commr., Anguilla 69; Head of West Indian Dept., Foreign and Commonwealth Office 70-72; Gov. and C.-in-C., Belize 72-; mem. Royal Inst. of Int. Affairs; Fellow, Royal Commonwealth Soc.; K. St. J. 72.
Leisure interests: skiing, growing trees.
Belize House, Belmopan, Belize; Home: Timbers, Northway, Goldaming, Surrey, England.
Telephone: 2146 (Belize).

Posokhin, Mikhail Vasilyevich; Soviet architect and politician; b. 1910; ed. Moscow Architecture Inst.
Decorator of a theatre 27-28; technician, work superintendent, architect, at construction of Kuznetsk iron and steel works 28-35; Leading Architect, Moscow Design Dept. 35-, Moscow Architecture Dept. 38-60; Moscow Chief Architect 60-; Chair. State Cttee. for Civil Engng. and Architecture and Vice-Chair. U.S.S.R. State Cttee. for Construction at U.S.S.R. Council of Ministers 63-67; Head, Main Admin. of Architecture and Planning of Moscow, Chief Architect of Moscow 67-; mem. C.P.S.U. 61-; Deputy to U.S.S.R. Supreme Soviet (Soviet of Union) 62-; mem. Comm. for Construction and Building Materials Industry, Soviet of Union; mem. Cttee. U.S.S.R. Parliamentary Group; State Prize 49, Lenin Prize 62; principal designs include multi-storeyed block of flats, Vosstaniy Square, Moscow 48; Congress Palace in the Kremlin, Moscow 61; People's Architect of U.S.S.R.
Executive Committee, Moscow City Soviet of Working People's Deputies, 13 Ulitsa Gorkogo, Moscow, U.S.S.R.

Pospelov, Pyotr Nikolayevich; Soviet politician; b. 20 June 1898, Konakovo, Kalinin region; ed. Moscow Inst. of Red Professors.
Joined Communist Party 16; worked at H.Q., Central Cttee. of Party 24-26; mem. Central Control Comm. 30, and mem. Editorial Boards of *Pravda* and of the magazine *Communist*; Asst. Head, Dept. of Propaganda, Central Cttee. of Party 37; mem. Central Cttee. 39; Editor *Pravda* 40; Dir. Marxism-Leninism Inst. of Central Cttee. 49-52, 61-; mem. and Chief, Editorial Board of Soviet Encyclopaedia 49-52; mem. Central Cttee. of C.P.S.U. 52-60; Sec. Central Cttee. 53-60; Candidate mem. Presidium, Central Cttee. of C.P.S.U. 57-61; mem. U.S.S.R. Acad. of Sciences; awarded Order of Lenin (twice), Order of the Patriotic War (1st Class), State Prize, Hero of Socialist Labour, etc.
Institute of Marxism-Leninism of Central Committee of C.P.S.U., Trety Selskokhozyaistvenny proezd 4, Moscow, U.S.S.R.

Postel-Vinay, André; French civil servant; b. 4 June 1911, Paris; *s.* of Marcel Postel-Vinay and Madeleine Delombre; *m.* Anise Girard 1946; four *c.*; ed. Univ. of Paris.
Financial Inspector 38; General Man. Caisse Centrale de Coopération Economique 44-72; Pres. de la Comm. des opérations de bourse 73-74; Commdr. Légion d'Honneur, Compagnon de la Libération, Membre du Conseil de l'Ordre de la Libération, Grand Officier de l'Ordre National du Mérite.
7 place Pinel, 75013 Paris, France.

Poswick, Charles, LL.D.; Belgian lawyer and politician; b. 6 Oct. 1924, Limbourg; *s.* of Jules Poswick and Marthe Roberti.
Attaché, Cabinet of Prime Minister Eyskens (49-50), later Asst. Chef de Cabinet, Ministry of Justice 52-54; mem. of Parl. for Namur 65-; Minister of Nat. Defence 66-68; Vice-Pres. Parti de la Liberté et du Progrès (PLP) 61-66, mem. Exec. Cttee. 68-; partner Puissant Baeyens, Poswick and Co.
Puissant Baeyens, Poswick and Co., 36 rue Ravenstein, Brussels, Belgium.

Potáč, Svatopluk, ING.; Czechoslovak banker; b. 24 March 1925; ed. School of Economics, Prague.
Entered Státní Banka Československá 52, Dept. Man. 56-58, Chief Man. 59-64, Deputy Gen. Man. 64-69, Chair. of Board and Gen. Man. 69-71, Pres. 71-; mem. Central Comm. of People's Control; mem. Scientific Council, Finance Research Inst.; mem. of Board, Int. Bank for Economic Co-operation, Moscow, Int. Investment Bank.
Františka Křížka 13, Prague 7, Czechoslovakia.

Potez, Henry Charles Alexandre; French construction engineer; b. 30 Sept. 1891; ed. Ecole Nationale Supérieure Aéronautique.
Pres. Chamber of Aeronautical industries 31-35; Pres. Société de Gestion Immobilière (fmrly. Soc. des Aéroplanes Henry Potez); Vice-Pres. de la Soc. Gaumont; Dir. various cos.; Hon. Pres. Asscn. Française des Ingénieurs et Techniciens de l'Aéronautique; Pres. Amis du Musée de l'Air; Hon. Pres. fmr. Students of Ecole Nat. Supérieure de l'Aeronautique, Union Syndicale des Industries Aéronautiques et Spatiales; Grand Officier Légion d'Honneur; Grand Croix de l'Ordre National du Mérite; Commdr. d'Economie Nationale; Médaille de l'Aéronautique; several foreign orders.
46 avenue Kléber, Paris 16e; 21 avenue du Maréchal-Maunoury, Paris 16e, France.
Telephone: 507-07-43.

Poto Ndamase, Paramount Chief Victor; South African (Transkei) politician; b. 1898, Nyandeni; s. of Paramount Chief Boklemi and Chieftainess Mangangelizwe; m. Violet Nonesi 1918; one s. two d.; ed. Healdtown Inst., C.P. and Fort Hare Coll. of Agriculture.
Paramount Chief of West Pondoland 18-; fmr. mem. Pondoland Gen. Council, United Transkeian Gen. Council, Bantu Representation Council, Transkeian Territorial Authority; defeated candidate in elections for Chief Minister of Transkei 63.
The Great Place, Nyandeni, P.O. Libode, Tranksei, South Africa.

Potter, Rev. Dr. Philip Alford, M.TH.; West Indian Methodist minister and church official; b. 19 Aug. 1921, Dominica; s. of Clement Potter (deceased) and Violet Peters; m. Doreen Cousins 1956; ed. Caenwood Theological Coll., Jamaica, Richmond Coll., England and London Univ.
Missionary and Overseas Sec., Student Christian Movement of Great Britain 48-50; Minister, Methodist Church, Haiti 50-54; World Council of Churches, Sec. Youth Dept. 54-57, Exec. Sec. 57-60, Dir. Comm. on World Mission and Evangelism 67-72, Gen. Sec., Geneva 72-; Sec. for West Africa and West Indies, Methodist Missionary Soc., London 61-66; Hon. Th.D. (Univ. of Hamburg) 71; Hon. LL.D. (Univ. of West Indies) 74.
Leisure interests: hiking and geology.
Publs. *Key Words of the Gospel* 64, *Explosives Lateinamerika* (chapter in book edited by T. Tschuy); *Review of Mission, Student World,* 10 *Fragen an die Weissen* 73, *The Love of Power or The Power of Love* 74, *Living the Christian Year* 75; numerous articles in *Ecumenical Review, International Review of Mission, Student World.*
150 route de Ferney, Geneva; 6 chemin de Tavernay, Geneva, Switzerland.
Telephone: 33-34-00 (Office); 98-20-26 (Home).

Potter, Major-Gen. William Everett, B.S.; American army officer (retd.) and business executive; b. 17 July 1905, Oshkosh; s. of William B. and Arlie Belle (Coulter) Potter; m. Ruth Elizabeth Turner 1936; two d.; ed. West Point, M.I.T., Command and Gen. Staff School, and Nat. War Coll.
Joined Corps of Engineers 28; with U.S. Army in Europe in Second World War as chief of Troops section, exec. of Propaganda and Psychological Warfare Div., Chief of Planning Branch, G-4 Section, Chief of Plans and Operations Branch G-4 Section; Asst. Chief of Engineers for Civil Works, Wash. 49-51; Nat. War Coll. 51; Div. Engineer, Missouri River Div. 52-56; Gov. Canal Zone and *ex officio* Pres. Panama Canal Co. 56-60; Exec. Vice-Pres. New York World's Fair 1964-65 Corpn. 60-65; Senior Vice-Pres. Walt Disney World Co., EPCOT Planning until 73, Consultant 73-.
Leisure interest: golf.
931 Ventura Avenue, Orlando, Fla. 32804, U.S.A.

Pöttgen, Ernst Ludwig; German theatre director; b. 1925; ed. Staatliche Hochschule für Musik, Berlin-Charlottenburg and Munich, Universität München and Universität Mainz.
Naval Officer, Second World War; Asst. Dir. Landestheater, Darmstadt 48, Bayerische Staatsoper, Munich 51, Stadttheater, Frankfurt/Main 55, Hamburgische Staatsoper 56; Dir. Hamburgische Staatsoper 56; Chief Dir. and Deputy Man. Nat. Theater Mannheim 58; Chief Dir. of Opera, Württembergisches Staatstheater, Stuttgart 61-; Dir. Teatro Colón, Buenos Aires 60, Deutsche Oper am Rhein, Düsseldorf 64, Salzburg Festival 65-, Florence Maggio Musicale Festival 65-.
Burgstrasse 59b, Stuttgart-Kaltental, Federal Republic of Germany.

Pottle, Frederick Albert, M.A., PH.D.; American university professor; b. 3 Aug. 1897, Lovell, Maine; s. of Fred Leroy Pottle and Annette (Wardwell) Kemp; m. Marion Isabel Starbird 1920; two s. one d. (deceased); ed. Colby Coll. and Yale Univ.
Served in American Expeditionary Force First World War 18-19; Asst. Prof. of English, Univ. of New Hampshire 21-23; Instructor in English, Yale Univ. 25-26, Assistant Professor 26-30, Professor 30-66, Sterling Professor of English 44-66, Professor Emeritus 66-; Fellow Davenport Coll., Yale Univ., American Acad. of Arts and Sciences, American Philosophical Soc., Provinciaal Utrechtsch Genootschap van Kunsten en Wetenschappen; Editor *The Private Papers of James Boswell* 30-37; Chair. Editorial Cttee. Yale Editions of the *Private Papers of James Boswell* 49-; Trustee Colby Coll. 32-59, 66-, and Gen. Theological Seminary 47-68; Messenger Lecturer Cornell Univ. 41; Guggenheim Fellow 45-46, 52-53; Fellow Int. Inst. Arts and Letters; Chancellor, Acad. of American Poets 50-72; Hon. Litt.D. (Colby Coll.) 41, (Rutgers Univ.) 51, LL.D. (Glasgow Univ.) 36, Hon. L.H.D. (Northwestern Univ.) 67; Wilbur Lucius Cross Medal (Yale Graduate School Asscn.) 67, William Clyde Devane Medal (Yale Coll.) 69, John F. Lewis Prize, American Philosophical Soc. 75.
Leisure interest: gardening.
Publs. *The Literary Career of James Boswell* 29, *Stretchers, the Story of a Hospital on the Western Front* 29, Vols. 7-18 of *The Private Papers of James Boswell* 30-34, *Boswell's Journal of a Tour to the Hebrides* (with C. H. Bennett) 36, 62, *The Idiom of Poetry* 41, rev. and enlarged 46; *Boswell's London Journal, 1762-63* 50, *Boswell in Holland, 1763-64* 52, *Boswell on the Grand Tour: Germany and Switzerland, 1764* 53, *Boswell on the Grand Tour: Italy, Corsica and France 1765-66* (with Frank Brady) 55, *Boswell in Search of a Wife 1766-69* (with Frank Brady) 56, *Boswell for the Defence, 1769-74* (with W. K. Wimsatt) 59, *Boswell, the Ominous Years 1774-76* (with Charles Ryskamp) 63, *James Boswell, The Earlier Years, 1740-69* 66, *Boswell in Extremes 1776-78* (with C. McC. Weis) 70.
Box 1504-A Yale Station, New Haven, Conn. 06520; and 35 Edgehill Road, New Haven, Conn. 06511, U.S.A.
Telephone: (Home) 624-8567; (Office) 436-2207.

Poujade, Pierre; French politician; b. 1 Dec. 1920, St. Céré; m. 1944; three s. two d.
Served in R.A.F., Second World War; after 45 became publisher and bookseller, also active in politics; mem. St. Céré Municipal Council 51; Founder Pres. Union de Défense de Commerçants et Artisans; Founder, Union et Fraternité Française; Founder Dir. *Union et Défense* (daily), *Fraternité Française* (weekly); Pres. Confédération Nat. des Travailleurs Indépendants 70-; Pres. Caisse Nat. d'Assurance Maladie Obligatoire 71-; creator of "La Vallée Heureuse" (gastronomic and tourist centre), Villefranche de Rowergue; Founder and Pres. Centre de Formation Avicole, and Ferme Pieste, Château de Gouzou.
Leisure interest: sport, particularly football and rugby.
Château de Gouzou 12-Sainte-Croix; "Vallée Heureuse", 12-Labastide-Leveque, France.
Telephone: Sainte-Croix 3; Labastide-Leveque 5.

Poujade, Robert; French teacher and politician; b. 6 May 1928, Moulins (Allier); s. of Henri Poujade and Edmée (née Rival); m. Marie-Thérèse Monier 1953; one s.; ed. Ecole normale supérieure.
Teacher of literature, Dijon 54; Dept. Sec. of Fed. of Union of Democrats for Fifth Republic (U.N.R.) for Côte-d'Or 58-, mem. Central Cttee. and Exec. Bureau 60-, Sec.-Gen. 68-; Technical Adviser to M. Maziol (Minister of Construction) Jan.-Feb. 63; mem. Conseil Econ. et Social 64-67; mem. Comm. for Econ. Devt. of Bourgogne Region 65-; Deputy for Côte-d'Or 67-; Sec.,

Gen. UDR 68-70; Minister for Protection of the Environment 70-74; Mayor of Dijon 71-; Chevalier de l'Ordre national du Mérite; Chevalier des Palmes Académiques.

10 boulevard Spuller, Dijon 21, France.

Poukka, (Kalle) Pentti, M.A.; Finnish newspaper editor; b. 13 Sept. 1919, Tampere; s. of Prof. Kalle Aukusti Poukka and Ina Irene Vihuri; m. Ejna Margarethe Jozua 1946; three s.; ed. Univ. of Helsinki. Public Relations Officer Yhtyneet Paperitehtaat 49-52; Research Worker, Taloudellinen Tutkimuskeskus; mem. Helsinki City Council 65-, Chair. 73-; Pres. Finnish Port Asscn. 68-74; Editor-in-Chief *Talouselämä* 54-55; Leader-writer and Economic Editor *Uusi Suomi* 55-57; Editor-in-Chief *Kauppalehti* 57-63, *Uusi Suomi* 68-.

Publs. *Teollisuuden rahoitus vv 1947-1952* (Financing Industry 1947-1952), *Huomispäivän suomalainen* (The Finn of Tomorrow), *Porvarin Päiväkirja* (Diary of a Bourgeois) 69, *Kapina Katsomossa* (Revolt of the Audience) 70, *Purkkiin pantu ihminen* (Canned Human) 72, *Tuntematon Sosialismi* (Unknown Socialism) 75.

c/o *Uusi Suomi*, 00120 Helsinki 12; Home: Armas Lindgrenintie 11, 00570 Helsinki 57, Finland.

Telephone: 647711 (Office); 688949 (Home).

Poullain, Ludwig; German banker; b. 23 Dec. 1919. Chairman, Board of Man. Dirs., Westdeutsche Landesbank Girozentrale; Pres. Deutscher Sparkassen-und Giroverband e.V., Bonn -72; Pres. Supervisory Board Preussag A.G.; mem. Supervisory Board, Deutsche Fina G.m.b.H., Fried. Krupp G.m.b.H., Hannen Brauerei, G.m.b.H., Mannesmann A.G., Ruhrkohle A.G., Stahl und Röhrenwerke Reisholz G.m.b.H., Volkswagenwerk A.G., mem. Admin. Board, Cie. de Saint-Gobain-Pont-à-Mousson S.A., Kreditanstalt für Wiederaufbau, Frankfurt/M; mem. Consultative Cttee., Petrofina S.A.; Dr. rer.pol. h.c.

Westdeutsche Landesbank Girozentrale, 4000 Düsseldorf 1, Friedrichstrasse 56, Federal Republic of Germany.

Telephone: (0211) 8261.

Pound, Robert Vivian, B.A., M.A.(HON.); American physicist; b. 16 May 1919, Ridgeway, Ont., Canada; s. of V. E. Pound and Gertrude C. Prout; m. Betty Yde Andersen 1941; one s.; ed. Univ. of Buffalo and Harvard Univ.

Research Physicist, Submarine Signal Co., Boston, Mass. 41-42; Staff mem. Radiation Laboratory, Mass. Inst. of Technology 42-46; Jr. Fellow, Soc. of Fellows, Harvard Univ. 45-48, Asst. Prof. 48-50, Assoc. Prof. 50-56, Prof. 56-68, Mallinckrodt Prof. of Physics 68-, Chair. Dept. of Physics 68-72; Visiting Prof. Coll. de France 73; B. J. Thompson Memorial Award, Inst. of Radio Engineers 48, Eddington Medal, Royal Astronomical Soc. 65.

Publs. *Microwave Mixers* 48; papers on nuclear magnetism, electric quadrupole interactions, directional correlations of gamma rays, effect of gravity on gamma rays.

87 Pinehurst Road, Belmont, Mass. 02178, U.S.A.

Powell, Anthony Dymoke, C.B.E.; British writer; b. 21 Dec. 1905, London; s. of Lt.-Col. P. L. W. Powell, C.B.E., D.S.O., and Maud Mary Wells-Dymoke; m. Lady Violet Pakenham 1934; two s.; ed. Eton and Balliol Coll., Oxford.

Served Second World War in Welch Regiment and Intelligence Corps; Orders of White Lion (Czechoslovakia), Léopold II (Belgium), Oaken Crown and Croix de Guerre (Luxembourg); James Tait Black Prize (for *At Lady Molly's*); Trustee of Nat. Portrait Gallery; Hon. D.Litt. (Sussex, Leicester); Hon. Fellow, Balliol Coll., Oxford 74; W. H. Smith Award 74.

Publs. *Afternoon Men* 31 (performed as a play 63), *Venusberg* 32, *From a View to a Death* 33, *Agents and Patients* 36, *What's Become of Waring* 39, *John Aubrey and His Friends* 48, *Selections from John Aubrey* 49, the *Music of Time* series: *A Question of Upbringing* 51, *A Buyer's Market* 52, *The Acceptance World* 55, *At Lady Molly's* 57, *Casanova's Chinese Restaurant* 60, *The Kindly Ones* 62, *The Valley of Bones* 64, *The Soldier's Art* 66, *The Military Philosophers* 68, *Books Do Furnish a Room* 71, *Temporary Kings* 73, *Hearing Secret Harmonies* 75; Plays: *The Garden God, The Rest I'll Whistle* 71.

The Chantry, near Frome, Somerset, England.

Telephone: 0373-84-314.

Powell, Sir (Arnold Joseph) Philip, Kt., O.B.E., F.R.I.B.A., A.R.A., A.A.DIPL.(HONS.); British architect; b. 15 March 1921, Bedford; s. of late Canon A. C. Powell and late Mary Winnifred (née Walker); m. Philippa Eccles 1953; one s. one d.; ed. Epsom Coll. and Architectural Asscn. School of Architecture.

In private practice 46-, as Powell and Moya, Architects (with Michael Powell and Hidalgo Moya (q.v.) 46-50, with Hidalgo Moya 50-61, with Hidalgo Moya, Robert Henley and Peter Skinner 61-; won Westminster City Council's Pimlico Housing Competition (Churchill Gardens) 46, Festival of Britain Vertical Feature (Skylon) Competition 50; R.I.B.A. Bronze Medals, R.I.B.A. Awards, Housing Medals, Civic Trust Awards; mem. Royal Fine Art Comm.

Leisure interests: travel, listening to music.

Works include: Churchill Gardens Flats, Westminster 48-62; houses and flats at Gospel Oak, London 54, houses at Chichester 50, Toy's Hill 54, Oxshott 54, Leamington 56, Baughurst (Hants.) 54; "Skylon", Festival of Britain 51; Mayfield School, Putney 55; Plumstead Manor School, Woolwich 70; extensions to Brasenose Coll. Oxford 61 and Corpus Christi Coll. Oxford 69, picture gallery and undergraduates' rooms, Christ Church, Oxford 67, new buildings at St. John's Coll. Cambridge 67; Chichester Festival Theatre 62; Public Swimming Baths, Putney 67; mental hospital extensions, Fairmile 57, Borocourt 65, hospitals at Swindon, Slough, High Wycombe and Wythenshawe; British Pavilion at *Expo 70*, Osaka, Japan; London Museum 73; Dining rooms at Bath Acad. of Art 70, Eton Coll. 74; Wolfson Coll., Oxford 74; extension to Queen's Coll., Cambridge 75.

Powell and Moya, Architects, 30 Percy Street, London, W.1; Home: 16 The Little Boltons, London, S.W.10, England.

Telephone: 01-636-7292 (Office); 01-373-8620 (Home).

Powell, John, M.A., D.PHIL.; British electronic engineer and business executive; b. 4 Nov. 1923, Islip; m. Zena Powell 1949; one s. one d.; ed. Bicester County School, No. 1 School of Technical Training, R.A.F. and Queen's Coll., Oxford.

Research Fellow, Nat. Research Laboratory, Ottawa 52-54; Section Leader, Semi-Conductor Research and Devt., Marconi Research Laboratories; joined Texas Instruments (N. Europe) Ltd. 57, Gen. Man. Technical 59, Product Group Man. 60, Asst. Man. Dir. Operations 62, Man. Dir. Northern Europe 63, Asst. Vice-Pres. Texas Instruments Inc. 68; Group Technical Dir. EMI Ltd. 71, Dir. for Commercial Electronics 72, Deputy Man. Dir. 73, Man. Dir. Nov. 74-.

Leisure interests: swimming, tennis.

EMI Limited, 20 Manchester Square, London, W1A 1ES, England.

Telephone: 01-486-4488.

Powell, Rt. Hon. (John) Enoch, P.C., M.B.E., M.P.; British politician; b. 16 June 1912, Birmingham; s. of Albert Enoch and Ellen Mary (Breese) Powell; m. Margaret Pamela Wilson 1952; four d.; ed. King Edward's School, Birmingham and Trinity Coll., Cambridge.

Fellow Trinity Coll., Cambridge 34-38; Prof. of Greek, Univ. of Sydney, N.S.W. 37-39; army service rising to rank of Brig. 39-46; Conservative mem. Parl. for Wolverhampton S.W. 50-Feb. 74, United Ulster Unionist mem. Parl. for Down, South Oct. 74-; Parl. Sec. Ministry of Housing and Local Govt. 55-57; Financial Sec. to Treasury 57-58; Minister of Health 60-63; Dir. Nat. Discount Co. 64-68.
Publs. *The Rendel Harris Papyri* 36, *First Poems* 37, *A Lexicon to Herodotus* 38, *The History of Herodotus* 39, *Casting-off, and other poems* 39, *Herodotus, Book VIII* 39, *Llyfr Blegywryd* 42, *Thucydidis Historia* 42, *Herodotus* (transl.) 49, *Dancer's End and The Wedding Gift* (poems) 51, *The Social Services, Needs and Means* 52, (jointly) *One Nation* 50, *Change is our Ally* 54, *Biography of a Nation* 55, *Saving in a Free Society* 60, *Great Parliamentary Occasions* 60, *A Nation Not Afraid* 65, *A New Look at Medicine and Politics* 66, *The House of Lords in the Middle Ages* (with Keith Wallis) 68, *Freedom and Reality* 69, *Still to Decide* 72, *No Easy Answers* 73.
33 South Eaton Place, London, S.W.1, England.

Powell, Lewis Franklin, Jr., LL.M.; American judge; b. 19 Sept. 1907, Suffolk, Va.; m. Josephine Rucker; four c.; ed. Washington and Lee Univ. and Harvard Law School.
Member of law firm, Hunton, Williams, Gay, Powell and Gibson, Richmond, Va. 37-71; Pres. American Bar Asscn. 64-65, American Coll. of Trial Lawyers 69-70; Assoc. Justice of the Supreme Court of U.S.A. Dec. 71-.
Supreme Court of the United States, Washington, D.C. 20543; Home: 1238 Rothesay Road, Richmond, Va. 23221, U.S.A.

Powell, Sir Philip (*see* Powell, Sir (Arnold Joseph) Philip).

Powell, Sir Richard Royle, G.C.B., K.B.E., C.M.G., B.A.; British civil servant (retired 1968); b. 30 July 1909, Walsall; s. of late Ernest Hartley Powell and late Florence Powell; ed. Sidney Sussex Coll., Cambridge.
Served Admiralty 31-46; Under-Sec. Ministry of Defence 46-48; Deputy Sec. Admiralty 48-50; Deputy Sec. Ministry of Defence 50-56, Perm. Sec. 56-59; Perm. Sec. Board of Trade 60-68; Deputy Chair. Permanent Cttee. on Invisible Exports 68-; Chair. Alusuisse(U.K.) Ltd. 69-, Dir. Hill Samuel Group Ltd., Sandoz Group, The Gen. Electric Co. Ltd., Wilkinson Match Ltd., National Nuclear Corpn. Ltd., BPB Industries Ltd.
Leisure interests: music, opera, theatre.
56 Montagu Square, London, W.1, England.
Telephone: 01-262-0911.

Powis, Alfred, B.COM.; Canadian business executive; b. 16 Sept. 1930, Montreal, P.Q.; ed. Westmount High School and McGill Univ.
Employee, Investment Dept., Sun Life Assurance Co. 51-55; Internal Auditor, Noranda Mines Ltd. 55, Asst. Treas. 58, Asst. to Pres. 62, Exec. Asst. 63, Dir. 64, Vice-Pres. 66, Exec. Vice-Pres. 67, Pres. and Chief Exec. Officer 68-, also Pres. and Dir., Noranda Aluminium Inc.; Chair. of Board and Dir. British Columbia Forest Products Ltd., Northwood Mills Ltd., Canadian Electrolytic Zinc Ltd., Gen. Smelting Co. of Canada Ltd.; Vice-Pres. and Dir., Northwood Pulp Ltd., Brunswick Mining and Smelting Corpn. Ltd., Bay Steel Corpn., Belledune Housing and Enterprises Ltd., Brunswick Ammonia Ltd., Chaleur Developments Ltd., Macanda Copper Mines Ltd.; Dir. Canada Wire & Cable Co. Ltd., Leaworth Holdings Ltd., Wire Rope Industries Ltd., Noranda Metal Industries, Noranda Manufacturing Ltd., Canadian Copper Refiners Ltd., Noranda Sales Corpn. Ltd., Noranda Exploration Co. Ltd., Noranda Australia Ltd., St. Lawrence Fertilizers Ltd., Quebec Smelters Ltd., Waite Amulet Mines Ltd., Amulet Dufault Mines Ltd., Gaspe Copper Mines Ltd., Empresa Fluorspar Mines Ltd., Noranda Inc., Pato

Consolidated Gold Dredging Co. Ltd., Kerr Addison Mines Ltd., Canadian Imperial Bank of Commerce, Gulf Oil Canada Ltd., Simpsons Ltd., Sun Life Assurance Co.; Trustee, Toronto Gen. Hosp.; mem. Board of Govs. of York Univ.
Noranda Mines Ltd., P.O. Box 45, Commerce Court West, Toronto, Ont., M5L IB6, Canada.
Telephone: 416-867-7111.

Powles, Sir Guy Richardson, K.B.E., C.M.G., E.D., LL.D.; New Zealand public servant; b. 5 April 1905, Otaki; s. of Col. C. G. Powles, C.M.G., D.S.O.; m. Eileen Nicholls 1931; two s.; ed. Wellington Coll., Victoria Univ. Coll.
Barrister, Supreme Court of New Zealand 27-40; War Service, to rank of Col. 40-46; Counsellor, Washington; High Commr., Western Samoa 49-60; High Commr. India 60-62, Ceylon 61-62, Ambassador to Nepal 61-62; Ombudsman, New Zealand 62-75, Chief Ombudsman 75-; Race Relations Conciliator 71-73; Pres. New Zealand Inst. of Int. Affairs 65-71; Commr. Churches Comm. on Int. Affairs, Int. Comm. of Jurists, Geneva; Patron New Zealand-India Soc., Amnesty N.Z., Environmental Defence Soc.
Telephone: 738-068.
Leisure interests: reading and gardening.
Office of the Ombudsman, Wellington; Home: 34A Wesley Road, Wellington C.1, New Zealand.
Telephone: 738-068.

Pozderac, Hakija; Yugoslav politician; b. 1919; ed. secondary technical school.
Former Sec.-Gen. of Govt. of People's Repub. of Bosnia and Herzegovina, State Under-Sec. in State Secr. for Econ. Affairs, State Sec. for Gen. Admin. and Budget, Bosnia and Herzegovina; Dir.-Gen. Yugoslav Nat. Bank; Dir. of Inst. of Econ. Planning, Bosnia and Herzegovina; Under-Sec., Fed. Sec., for Gen. Econ. Affairs until 65; Minister for Industry and Commerce 65-69; fmr. mem. Yugoslav Fed. Exec. Council.
Bulevar Lenjina 2, Belgrade, Yugoslavia.

Prabhjot Kaur; Indian poet and politician; b. 6 July 1927, Langarlal; d. of Nidhan Singh; m. Brig. Narenderpal Singh 1948; two d.; ed. Khalsa Coll. for Women, Lahore and Punjab Univ.
First collected poems published 43 (aged sixteen); represented India at numerous int. literary confs. 56-; mem. Legislative Council, Punjab 66-; mem. Central Comm. of United Nations Educational, Scientific and Cultural Org. (UNESCO), Nat. Writers Cttee. of India; received honours of Sahitya Shiromani 64 and Padma Shri 67; title of Rajya Kavi (Poet Laureate) by Punjab Govt. 64, the Sahitya Akademi Award 65, Golden Laurel Leaves, United Poets Int., Philippines 67, Grand Prix de la Rose de la France 68, Most Distinguished Order of Poetry, World Poetry Soc. Intercontinental, U.S.A. 74; Woman of the Year, U.P.L.I., Philippines 75.
Leisure interests: reading, writing.
Publs. 35 books, including: Poems *Supne Sadhran* 49, *Do Rang* 51, *Pankhru* 56, *Lala* (in Persian) 58, *Bankapasi* 58, *Pabbi* 62, *Khali* 67, *Wad-darshi Sheesha* 72, *Madhiantar* 74; Short Stories: *Kinke* 52, *Aman de Na* 74.
D-203, Defence Colony, New Delhi 110024, India.
Telephone: 626045.

Prader, Georg, LL.D.; Austrian politician; b. 15 June 1917, St. Pölten; s. of Prof. Georg Prader and Josefine Prader; m. Hertha Prader (née Hollaschke) 1943; three s. one d.; ed. Seitenstetten Hochschule and Vienna Univ.
Army Service, Second World War; with Provincial Govt. of Lower Austria 46-49; with Lower Austrian Employees Section, Fed. of Austrian Workers and Employees (ÖAAB) 49, mem. Governing Body ÖAAB 53-, Chair. Lower Austrian Employees Section 56-,

Deputy Provincial Chair. Lower Austrian Section 56-; mem. Bundesrat 54-59, Nationalrat 59-; Minister of Defence 64-70; People's Party.
Lainzer Strasse 4, 1130 Vienna, Austria.
Telephone: 43-37-10.

Prado Vallejo, Julio; Ecuadorean lawyer, diplomatist and politician; b. 3 July 1924; ed. Univ. Central del Ecuador.
Chargé d'Affaires, Brazil 53-54, U.S.A. 54-57; Pres. Inter-American Comm. for Econ. Co-operation 56; Legal Adviser on Int. Agreements at Ministry of Finance 58; Prof. at Central Univ. of Ecuador 58-; Minister of Foreign Affairs 67-68; Gran Oficial Cruzeiro do Sul (Brazil) Gran Cruz Al Mérito (Ecuador).
Publs. *Réplica a la peruanidad de Túmbez, Jaen y Mainas* 45, *Demarcación de Fronteras – Ejecución del Protocolo de Río de Janeiro de Enero 29 de 1942* 50.
Calle Tamayo 1313 y Colón, Quito, Ecuador.
Telephone: 238-375.

Prager, William, ENG.D.; American professor of engineering and applied mathematics; b. 23 May 1903, Karlsruhe, Germany; s. of Wilhelm and Helen (Kimmel) Prager; m. G. Ann Heyer 1925; one s.; ed. Technische Hochschule, Darmstadt.
Acting Dir., Inst. of Applied Mechanics, Göttingen 29-33; Prof. of Technical Mechanics, Technische Hochschule, Karlsruhe 33; Prof. of Theoretical Mechanics, Univ. of Istanbul 33-41; Prof. of Applied Mechanics, Brown Univ. 41-65, Univ. of Calif. (San Diego) 65-68; Prof. of Engineering and Applied Mathematics, Brown Univ. 68-73, Emer. Prof. 73-; Technical Editor *Journal of Applied Mechanics* 69-72; Editor *Computer Methods in Applied Mechanics and Engineering* 72-; mem. Nat. Acad. of Sciences, Nat. Acad. of Engineering, Polish Acad. of Sciences; Corresp. mem. Acad. des Sciences, Paris; numerous hon. degrees; Theodore von Kármán Medal, American Soc. of Civil Engineers 60; Panetti Prize, Acad. of Sciences, Turin 64; Timoshenko Medal, American Soc. of Mechanical Engineers 66.
Publs. *The Theory of Perfectly Plastic Solids* (with P. G. Hodge, Jr.) 51, *An Introduction to Plasticity* 59, *Introduction to Mechanics of Continua* 61, *Introduction to Basic Fortran Programming and Numerical Methods* 71, *Introduction to APL* 71.
7451 Savognin, Switzerland.

Prain, Sir Ronald Lindsay, Kt., O.B.E.; British company director; b. 3 Sept. 1907, Iquiqui, Chile; s. of Arthur Lindsay Prain and Amy (née Watson) Prain; m. Esther Pansy Brownrigg 1938; two s.; ed. Cheltenham Coll.
Controller Diamond Die and Tool Control (Ministry of Supply) 40-45, Quartz Crystal Control 43-45; Chair. Roan Selection Trust group of cos. 50-72, Merchant Bank, Zambia Ltd. 66-72; Dir. Barclays Bank Int. Ltd., Minerals Separation Ltd., Pan Holding S.A., Selection Trust Ltd., and other companies; Pres. British Overseas Mining Asscn. 52, Inst. of Metals 60-61; Hon. Pres. Copper Devt. Asscn.; Chair. Agricultural Research Council of Rhodesia and Nyasaland 59-63; mem. of Council, Commonwealth Council of Mining and Metallurgical Insts. (Chair. 61-74), Overseas Devt. Inst.; Hon. Fellow Inst. of Mining and Metallurgy, Metals Soc.; Gold Medal (Inst. of Mining and Metallurgy) 68; Inst. of Metals Platinum Medal 69.
Leisure interests: cricket, real tennis, travel.
Publs. *Selected Papers* (4 vols.), *Copper: The Anatomy of an Industry* 75.
Waverley, St. George's Hill, Weybridge, Surrey; 43 Cadogan Square, London, SW1X 0HX, England.
Telephone: Weybridge 41776; 01-235-4900.

Prakasa, Sri, B.A., LL.B., BAR.-AT-LAW; Indian politician; b. 3 Aug. 1890; s. of Dr. Bhagauandas and Shrimati Chameli Devi; m. Shrimati Anasuya Devi 1908

(died 1926); two s. two d.; ed. Allahabad and Cambridge Univs.
Connected with *Leader*, Allahabad 17-18, *Independent*, Allahabad 19, *Aj*, Banaras 20-43, *National Herald*, Lucknow 38-48, *Sansar*, Banaras 43-49; mem. A.I.C.C. 18-45; founder mem. Kashi Vidyapith 21, Chancellor 69; mem. Banaras Municipal Board 21-25; Gen. Sec. United Provinces Congress Cttee. 28-34, and Indian Nat. Congress 29-31; Pres. U.P. Political Conf. 34 and Pres. United Provinces Congress Cttee. 34-35; M.L.A. Central 34 and 45; Chair. Reception Cttee. Indian Nat. Congress 36; imprisoned for Congress activities 30, 32, 41 and 42; mem. Constituent Assembly for U.P. 46; High Commr. for India in Pakistan 47-49; Gov. of Assam 49-50; Federal Minister of Commerce 50-51, for Natural Resources and Scientific Research 51-52; Gov. of Madras 52-56; Gov. of Bombay 56-60, of Maharashtra 60-62; mem. of Lok Sabha 50-52 (resgnd.); Padma Vibushan 57.
Leisure interests: reading and writing.
Publs. *Annie Besant, As Woman and as Leader, Pakistan: Birth and Early Days* (in English and Hindi), *Grihast Gita, Sphut Vichar, Hamari antarik Gatha, Nagarik Shastra* (in Hindi), *Dr. Bhagandas as Philosopher and Man* (in English and Hindi), *Education in a Democracy, State Governors in India.*

Pramoj, Mom Rachawongse Kukrit; Thai politician; b. 20 April 1911; s. of Prince Khamrob and Mom Daeng Pramoj; brother of Seni Pramoj (q.v.); ed. Suan Kularb Coll., Trent Coll., U.K., Queen's Coll., Oxford.
With Revenue Dept., Ministry of Finance; Siam Commercial Bank; Head of Gov.'s Office, Bank of Thailand, later Head of Issue Dept.; mem. Parl. 46-76; Deputy Minister of Finance 47-48; Deputy Minister of Commerce; founded *Siam Rath* newspaper 50; Leader of Social Action Party; Speaker Nat. Assembly 73-74; Prime Minister 75-76, Minister of the Interior Jan.-April 76; Dir. of Thai Studies, Thammasat Univ.; Pres. Exec. Cttee., Foundation for the Assistance of Needy Schoolchildren.
Social Action Party, Bangkok, Thailand.

Pramoj, Mom Rachawongse Seni, B.A.; Thai lawyer and politician b. 26 May 1905, Ngor Awaga; s. of Prince Khamrob; brother of Kukrit Pramoj (q.v.); m. Usna Saligupta 1931; two s. one d.
Judge, Appeal Court; Minister, Thai Embassy, Washington, D.C., Prime Minister 45-46; law practice 46-; Leader Democratic Party 68-; mem. Parl. 69-; Prime Minister Feb.-March 75, April 76-.
Leisure interests: golf, music, painting, poetry.
Publs. several law books and English translations of Thai poetry.
219 Egamai Road, Bangkok, Thailand.
Telephone: 220191.

Prasad, Baleshwar, I.A.S., M.A.; Indian civil servant; b. 1 Jan. 1914, Chapra, Bihar; s. of Maheshwar Prasad; m. Uma Prasad; ed. Patna Univ.
Journalist 42-46; Asst. Magistrate 50; IAS Officer, Bihar 50-56; Political Adviser to Indian del. to Viet-Nam Int. Supervision and Control Comm. 56-59; Dewan (Prime Minister) of Sikkim 59-63; Chief Commr., Manipur 63-69, Lt.-Gov. 69-70; Amb. to Burma 70-71; Lt.-Gov. Tripura 71-72, Delhi 72.
Raj Niwas, New Delhi 6, India.

Prasad, P. S. Narayan; Indian economist; b. 24 Sept. 1910, Yellamanchili; s. of Sri Prasad and Sundara Bai; m. 1931; ed. Andhra, Benares Univs.
Lecturer Andhra Univ. 34-36; Prof. of Economics, Wadia Coll., Poona 37-40; Head, Economics Dept., Maharajah's Coll., Jaipur 40-45; Reserve Bank of India 46-53; Exec. Dir. for India on Int. Monetary Fund 53-57, 71-75; Asst. Dir. Economic Staff, World Bank 57-60; Chair. World Bank's Mission to Libya 58-60; Economic Adviser to Nigeria 61-63; Dir. Asian Inst. for

Econ. Devt. and Planning, Bangkok 63-70; mem. Advisory Board of the Mekong Co-ordination Cttee. 63-70; Hon. D.Litt. (Andhra) 69.

42-Pitakande, Kandy, Sri Lanka.

Telephone: 4490.

Prate, Alain; French civil servant and international official; b. 5 June 1928, Lille; m. Marie-José Alexis 1956; two s. one d.; ed. Ecole Nationale d'Administration.

Assistant Insp. of Finances 53-55, Insp. 55-58; Del. to conf. on EEC 57; Sec. of Monetary Cttee., European Econ. Community (EEC) 58-61; Dir. for Econ. Structure and Devt., Directorate-Gen. for Econ. and Financial Affairs, EEC 61-65; Dir.-Gen. of Internal Market, EEC 65; Technical counsellor for economic and financial questions in the Secretariat of the Presidency of the Repub. 67-69; Head of Service, Inspectorate-General of Finance 69-71, Dir.-Gen. Customs and Duties 71-; Admin. Air France, Soc. commerciale de réassurance; Dir. Crédit National.

93 rue de Rivoli, Paris 1er; 4 Square Thiers, Paris 75116, France.

Pratolini, Vasco; Italian writer; b. 19 Oct. 1913.

Lugano prize 47; Viareggio prize 55; Feltrinelli prize 57; Marzotto prize 63.

Publs. Novels and stories: *Via de' Magazzini* 42, *Cronaca familiare* 47, *Cronache di poveri amanti* 47, *Le ragazze di San Frediano* 50, *Metello* 55, *Lo scialo* 60, *La constanza della ragione* 63, *Allegoria e Derisione* 66.

Via Tolmino 12, Rome, Italy.

Telephone: 858435.

Pratt, Edmund T., B.S., M.B.A.; American chemical industry executive; b. 22 Feb. 1927, Savannah, Ga., s. of Edmund T. Pratt, Snr. and Rose Miller; m. Jeanette Carneale Pratt; two s.; ed. Duke Univ.; Wharton School of Commerce and Finance, Univ. of Pennsylvania.

Served with U.S. Navy, World War II; intelligence officer 52-54; Controller, IBM World Trade Corpn. 58-62; Asst. Sec. U.S. Army 62-64; joined Pfizer Inc. as controller, Vice-Pres. Operations Pfizer Int. 67-69, Chair. and Pres. 69-71; Dir. and mem. exec. cttee. Pfizer Inc. 69, Exec. Vice-Pres. 70-71, Pres. 71-72, Chair. and Chief Exec. Officer Dec. 72-; Dir. Chase Manhattan Corpn., Int. Paper Company, Nat. Asscn. of Mfrs., Int. Exec. Service Corps; Trustee Cttee. for Econ. Devt., U.S. Council of the Int. Chambers of Commerce; mem. Board Econ. Devt. Council of N.Y.C., Nat. Council on Crime and Delinquency.

Pfizer Inc. 235 East 42nd Street, New York, 10017 N.Y., U.S.A.

Telephone: 212-573-2255.

Pratt, James Davidson, C.B.E., M.A., B.SC., F.R.I.C., C.ENG., F.I.CHEM.E., C.CHEM; British chemist; b. 13 Aug. 1891, Drumoak, Aberdeenshire; s. of James Davidson and Jane Pratt; m. 1st Winifred Jean Summers 1918, 2nd Sybil Margaret Jones 1940 (both marriages dissolved); two d.; ed. Gordon's Coll. and Aberdeen Univ.

Assistant to Prof. of Chemistry, Aberdeen Univ. 13-14; served in Army 14-21; Controller, Chemical Warfare Research, War Office 23-28; Gen. Man. (later Dir.) and Sec. Asscn. of British Chemical Manufacturers 28-57; Controller, Chemical Defence Research and Development, Min. of Supply 40-45; Pres. of Chemical Defence Board 40-49; lent to Ministry of Supply to assist in organisation of explosives and chemical production for rearmament and forward planning 51-53; Chair. British Road Tar Asscn. 37-40, 44-60; Past Vice-Pres. of Inst. of Chem. Engineers, Chemical Society and Society of Chemical Industry; past mem. of Road Research Board and Chair. Road Tar Research Cttee. of Dept. of Scientific and Industrial Research 46-65; awarded American Medal of Freedom with Silver Palms 45.

Leisure interests: freemasonry and hiking.

Publ. Chemical Industry series of Monographs (joint editor) 63-72.

Hammings Bank, Oldbury Lane, Ightham, Kent, England.

Pratt, Solomon Althanasius James, B.C.L., B.LIT., LL.B., M.A., M.SC., DIP.AGR.ECONS.; Sierra Leonean politician; m.; six c.; ed. Fourah Bay Coll., St. Catherine's, Oxford Univ., Univ. of London and Inner Temple.

Economist, Sierra Leone Govt. 49-52; Int. Civil Servant, Int. Labour Office, Geneva 52-58; Chair. Riot Damages Comm. 58-61; City Solicitor, Municipality of Freetown 58-64; Gen. Man. Sierra Leone Railways and Econ. Advisor to the Govt. 64-66; arrested and detained during Mil. Rule 67; Parliamentary Rep. for Mountain Rural District 68-; Min. of Econ. Development and Planning 68-69; envoy of the Prime Min. to various countries and confs. 69-71; Min. of State and Attorney-Gen. 71, Minister of External Affairs 71-73, of Devt. and Econ. Planning 73-75; Attorney-General 75-; Pres. Sierra Leone UN Asscn.

Leisure interest: church music.

Supreme Court, Freetown, Sierra Leone.

Pratte, Yves, Q.C., B.A., LL.L.; Canadian airline executive; b. 7 Mar. 1925, Quebec City, P.Q.; s. of Garon Pratte and Georgine (Rivard) Pratte; m. Paule Gauvreau 1963; two s. one d.; ed. Coll. Garnier, Que., Laval Univ. and Univ. of Toronto.

Called to the Bar of Quebec 47; mem. of Quebec law firm, St. Laurent, Taschereau, Noel & Pratte 48-53; Senior Partner of Quebec law firm, Pratte, Côté, Tremblay, Beauvais, Bouchard, Garneau & Truchon 54-68; Dean of Faculty of Law Laval Univ. 62-65; Special Legal Counsel for Prime Ministers Jean Lesage and Daniel Johnson 65-68; mem. Royal Comm. on Security 66-68; Chair. of Board and Chief Exec. Officer Air Canada 68-75.

Leisure interests: golf, skiing.

Home: 717 Upper Lansdowne Avenue, Westmouth 217, Quebec, Canada.

Prawiro, Radius, M.A.; Indonesian economist and banker; b. 29 June 1928; ed. Senior High School, Jogjakarta, Nederlandsche Economische Hoogeschool, Rotterdam, Econ. Univ. of Indonesia.

Secretary Defence Cttee., Jogjakarta during revolution 45; with Army High Command, Jogjakarta 46-47; Angauta Tentara Pelajar (Army) 48-51; Officer in Govt. Audit Office, Ministry of Finance 53-65; Vice-Minister, Deputy Supreme Auditor, mem. Supreme Audit Office 65-66; Gov. Bank Indonesia 66; Chair. Indonesian Asscn. of Accountants 65-; Gov. Int. Monetary Fund for Indonesia 67-72, Alt. Gov. Asian Devt. Bank 67-, Gov. Int. Bank for Reconstruction and Devt. (World Bank) 72-; Minister of Trade 73-; Chair. Board of Govs. IBRD, IDA, IFC 71-72; mem. Econ. Council of the Pres. 68-, Nat. Econ. Stabilization Council 68-, Gov. Board Christian Univ. of Indonesia. Supervisory Board Trisakti Univ.

Ministry of Trade, Jakarta; Home: Jalan Imam Bonjol 4, Jakarta, Indonesia.

Praz, Mario, K.B.E., DR.JURIS., D.LITT.; Italian university professor; b. 6 Sept. 1896, Rome; s. of late Luciano Praz and late Giulia Di Marsciano; m. Vivyan Eyles 1934 (marriage dissolved 1946); one d.; ed. Rome and Florence Univs.

Came to England 23; Senior Lecturer in Italian, Liverpool Univ. 24-32; Prof. of Italian Studies, Manchester Univ. 32-34; Prof. of English Language and Literature, Univ. of Rome 34-66, Prof. Emer. 66-; mem. Standing Cttee. Int. Conf. of Univ. Profs. of English; Editor *English Miscellany* (Rome); British Acad. Gold Medallist for Anglo-Italian Studies 35; mem. Accad. dei Lincei 52-, American Acad. of Arts and Sciences 69-; hon.

mem. Modern Language Assen. of America 54; Hon. D.Litt. (Cambridge, Sorbonne and Aix-Marseille).
Leisure interests: collecting furniture, paintings and objects of the Empire period, travelling.
Publs. *Secentismo e marinismo in Inghilterra* 25, *Penisola Pentagonale* 28, *La carne, la morte e il diavolo nella letteratura romantica* (*The Romantic Agony*) 30, *Studi sul concettismo* 34, *Storia della letteratura inglese* 37, *Studi e svaghi inglesi* 37, *Studies in 17th-Century Imagery* Vol. I 39, Vol. II 48, *Gusto neoclassico* 40, *Machiavelli in Inghilterra ed altri saggi* 42, *Fiori freschi* 43, *Ricerche anglo-italiane* 44, *La filosofia dell' arredamento* 45, *Motivi e figure* 45, *Cronache letterarie anglosassoni* Vols. I, II 51, Vols. III, IV 66, *La Casa della Fama* 52, *Lettrice notturna* 52, *La crisi dell'eroe nel romanzo vittoriano* 52, *Viaggi in Occidente* 55, *The Flaming Heart* 58, *La Casa della Vita* 58; *Bellezza e bizzarria* 60, *I volti del tempo* 64, *The House of Life* 64, *An Illustrated History of Interior Decoration* 64, *Panopticon Romano* 67, *On Neoclassicism* 69, *Caleidoscopio Shakespeariano* 69, *Mnemosyne, the Parallel between Literature and the Visual Arts* 79, *Scene di Conversazione* 70, *Conversation Pieces* 71, *Il patto col serpente* 72, *Il Giardino dei sensi—Studi sul manierismo e il barocco* 75; translations from Shakespeare, Jane Austen, Lamb, Pater, G. Moore, XIXth-Century Poets; Editor new Italian trans. of Shakespeare's plays, vol. of trans. from Elizabethan dramas, etc.
Via Zanardelli 1, 00186 Rome, Italy.
Telephone: 657759.

Prebisch, Raúl; Argentine economist; b. 17 April 1901; ed. Buenos Aires Univ.
Professor of Political Economy, Buenos Aires Univ. 25-48 (retd.), Hon. Prof. 55-; Deputy Dir., Argentinian Dept. of Statistics 25-27; Dir. of Economic Research, Nat. Bank of Argentina 27-30; Under-Sec. for Finance 30-32; Adviser to Ministries of Finance and Agriculture 33-35; Organizer and first Dir.-Gen., Cen. Bank of the Republic of Argentina 35-43; Exec. Sec. UN Economic Comm. for Latin America 48-62; Dir.-Gen. of Latin American Inst. for Econ. and Social Planning 62-64, 69; Sec.-Gen. UN Conf. on Trade and Development, Geneva 64-69; Adviser to Sec.-Gen. of UN on devt. problems; Under-Sec.-Gen. of UN Emergency Operation; Hon. mem. Faculty of Econs., Univ. of Chile 56; Dr. h.c. (Columbia, Chandigarh, Los Andes (Columbia), Montevideo, Uruguay Univs.).
United Nations Secretariat, New York, N.Y. 10017, U.S.A.

Prelog, Vladimir, DR. ING.; Swiss chemist; b. 23 July 1906, Sarajevo, Yugoslavia; s. of Milan and Maria (Cettolo) Prelog; m. Kamila Vitek 1933; one s.; ed. Inst. of Technology and School of Chemistry, Prague.
Chemist, G. J. Driza Laboratories, Prague 29-35; Lecturer (Dozent), Univ. of Zagreb 35-40, Assoc. Prof. 40-41; Privatdozent Eidgenössische Technische Hochschule 42, Assoc. Prof. 47-50, Prof. of Organic Chemistry 50-, Head of Laboratory of Organic Chemistry 57-66; mem. Board CIBA-GEIGY Ltd., Basle; Foreign mem. Royal Soc. (U.K.), Acad. of Sciences of U.S.S.R., Nat. Acad. of Sciences, U.S.A., American Acad. of Arts and Sciences, etc.; Werner Prize, Marcel Benoist Prize, Roger Adams Award, Stas Medal, Medal of Honour, Rice Univ., A. W. Hofmann Medal, Davy Medal Royal Soc., Nobel Prize 75, and other prizes; Dr. h.c. (Zagreb, Liverpool, Cambridge, Brussels and Paris).
Leisure interests: swimming, skiing.
Office: Universitätsstrasse 6, 8006 Zürich; Home: Bellariastrasse 41, 8038 Zürich, Switzerland.
Telephone: 457802.

Preminger, Otto Ludwig, D.IUR.; Austrian-born American film and theatre director and producer; b. 5 Dec. 1906; ed. Vienna Univ.

Actor in Max Reinhardt's company 23; f. Comedie Theatre, Vienna 26, producer at Schauspielhaus 27, producer-dir. for Reinhardt's theatre, Josefstadt 28; dir. *Libel*, N.Y. 35, successive Broadway plays produced and directed incl. *In Time to Come, Outward Bound, My Dear Children, Margin for Error, The Full Circle* 73; Assoc. Prof. Yale Univ. 39-41; producer and dir. for 20th Century Fox 41-51, films incl. *Margin for Error* and *Laura*; producer-dir. of *The Moon is Blue* 50, *Critic's Choice* 60, both on Broadway; ind. film producer-director 51-, films incl. *The Moon is Blue* 51, *Carmen Jones* 54, *The Man with the Golden Arm* 55, *St. Joan* 56, *Bonjour Tristesse* 57, *Porgy and Bess* 58, *Anatomy of a Murder* 59, *Exodus* 60, *Advise and Consent* 62, *The Cardinal* 63, *In Harm's Way* 64, *Bunny Lake is Missing* 65, *Hurry Sundown* 66, *Too Far to Walk* 68, *Tell Me that You Love Me, Junie Moon* 70, *Such Good Friends* 72, *Rosebud* 75.
711 Fifth Avenue, New York, N.Y. 10022, U.S.A.
Telephone: 838-6100.

Prentice, Rt. Hon. Reginald Ernest, M.P., J.P.; British politician; b. 16 July 1923, Thornton Heath, Surrey; s. of Ernest George Edward Prentice and Elizabeth Prentice; m. Joan Godwin 1948; one d.; ed. Whitgift School and London School of Econs.
Temporary civil servant 40-42; Royal Artillery 42-46; student at London School of Econs. 46-49; mem. staff Transport and Gen. Workers Union, Asst. to Legal Sec., in charge of Union's Advice and Service Bureau 50-57; M.P. for East Ham (North) 57-; Minister of State, Dept. of Educ. and Science Oct. 64-66; Minister of Public Building and Works 66-67, of Overseas Devt. 67-69; Sec. of State for Educ. and Science 74-75; Minister for Overseas Devt., with Cabinet rank June 75-; Labour.
Leisure interests: walking, swimming and golf.
House of Commons, London, S.W.1; and 5 Hollingsworth Road, Croydon, Surrey, England.
Telephone: 01-657-0988 (Home).

Prentzel, Felix Alexander, DR. IUR., DIPL.-ING.; German business executive; b. 19 March 1905; ed. Technische Hochschule, Berlin-Charlottenburg, and Univ. of Erlangen.
IG-Farbenindustrie A.G., Berlin 34-47; Fed. Ministry of Commerce 47-55; mem. Management Board DEGUSSA (Deutsche Gold-und Silber-Scheideanstalt, formerly Roessler) 55-59, Chair. of the Management Board 59-73; mem. Advisory Board Farbwerke Hoechst A.G., Frankfurt, Metallgesellschaft A.G., Frankfurt, Norddeutsche Affinerie, Hamburg, Frankfurter Versicherungs-A.G., Frankfurt, Didier-Werke A.G., Wiesbaden, NSU Motorenwerke A.G., Neckarsulm, Schilde A.G., Bad Hersfeld.
Bross Strasse 11-13, 6 Frankfurt/Main, Federal Republic of Germany.

Presley, Elvis Aron; American entertainer; b. 8 Jan. 1935, Tupelo, Miss.; s. of Vernon Elvis Presley and Gladys Smith; m. Priscilla Beaulieu 1967 (dissolved); one d.; ed. East Tupelo School, L.C. Humes High School, Memphis, Tenn.
Began singing career on contract to Memphis Sun Recording Studio; transferred to RCA Corpn., first RCA record *Heartbreak Hotel* 56, also first Gold Record; has won more Gold Records than any other singer; most successful record singles incl. *Blue Suede Shoes, Love Me Tender, All Shook Up, Teddy Bear, Jailhouse Rock, I Got Stung, One Night, Stuck On You, The Girl of my Best Friend, Can't Help Falling in Love, Return to Sender, Crying in the Chapel, If I Can Dream, In the Ghetto, The Wonder of You, My Boy*; has appeared in 33 films incl. *Love Me Tender* 56, *Loving You* 57, *King Creole* 58, *G.I. Blues* 60, *Flaming Star* 61, *Wild in the Country* 61, *Blue Hawaii* 61, *Girls, Girls, Girls* 63, *That's the Way it is* 71, *Change of Habit* 71; frequent cabaret

performer; on programme televised world-wide by satellite from Hawaii.
Leisure interests: horse riding, karate, cinema.
Graceland, Elvis Presley Boulevard, Highway 51 South, Memphis, Tennessee, U.S.A.

Press, Frank, American geophysicist; b. 4 Dec. 1924, Brooklyn, New York; *s.* of Solomon and Dora (Steinholz) Press; *m.* Billie Kallick 1946; two *c.*; ed. Coll. of City of New York and Columbia Univ.
Research Associate, Columbia Univ. 46-49, Instructor Geology 49-51, Asst. Prof. of Geology 51-52, Assoc. Prof. 52-55; Prof. Geophysics, Calif. Inst. of Technology 55-65, Dir. Seismological Laboratory 57-65; Chair. Dept. of Earth and Planetary Sciences, Mass. Inst. of Technology 65-; Consultant to U.S. Navy 56-57, U.S. Dept. of Defense 58-62, NASA 60-62, and 65-; mem. U.S. del. Nuclear Test Ban Conf. Geneva 59-61, Moscow 63; Pres. Science Advisory Comm. 61-64; Chair. Board of Advisors Nat. Center for Earthquake Research of the U.S.G.S. 66-; Planetology Subcomm. NASA 66-; Chair. Earthquake Prediction Panel Office of Science and Technology 65-; Fellow American Acad. of Arts and Sciences 66; Fellow Royal Astronomical Soc., mem. Nat. Acad. of Sciences; Pres. American Geophysical Union 74-; Chair. Cttee. on Scholarly Communication with People's Repub. of China 75-; mem. U.S.—U.S.S.R. Working Group in Earthquake Prediction 73, Exec. Council Nat. Acad. of Sciences 75-; Hon. LL.D. (City Univ. of N.Y.) 72, Hon. D.Sc. (Notre Dame Univ.) 73, Townsend Harris Medal Coll. of the City of New York; Royal Astronomical Soc. Gold Medal (U.K.) 71; Day Medal Geological Soc. of America, Interior 72; NASA Award 73; Killian Faculty Achievement Award, M.I.T. 75.
Leisure interests: skiing, sailing.
Publ. *Earth* (with R. Siever) 74.
Massachusetts Institute of Technology, Department of Earth and Planetary Sciences, Cambridge, Mass.; and 26 Spring Valley Road, Belmont, Mass., U.S.A.
Telephone: 617-253-3382 and 484-1243.

Preti, Luigi; Italian politician; b. 23 Oct. 1914.
Former lawyer and Prof. of Philosophy and Pedagogy; mem. Constituent Assembly 46-; Under-Sec. of State to Treasury (War Pensions Dept.) 54; Minister for Finance 58-59, 66-68, of Foreign Trade 62-63, without Portfolio Dec. 63-66, for the Budget 68-69, of Finance 70-72, of Transport and Civil Aviation 73-74; Social Democrat.
Chamber of Deputies, Rome, Italy.

Prêtre, Georges; French conductor; b. 14 Aug. 1924; ed. Lycée and Conservatoire de Douai, Conservatoire nationale supérieur de musique de Paris and Ecole des chefs d'orchestre.
Director of Music, Opera Houses of Marseille, Lille and Toulouse 46-55, Dir. of music Opéra-comique, Paris, 55-59, at l'Opéra 59-; Dir.-Gen. of Music at l'Opéra 70-71; conductor of the symphonic asscns. of Paris and of principal festivals throughout the world; also conducted at La Scala, Milan and major American orchestras; Conductor Metropolitan Opera House, New York 64-65, La Scala, Milan 65-66, Salzburg 66.
19 rue de Montbuisson, 78430 Louveciennes, France.

Prévert, Jacques: French writer; b. 4 Feb. 1900, Neuilly-sur-Seine; ed. Ecole communale, Paris.
Wrote screenplay for *L'Affaire est dans le sac, Drôle de drame, Quai des brumes, Le jour se lève, Les enfants du paradis, Lumière d'été, Les Visiteurs du soir, Les Portes de la nuit, Les Amants de Vérone, La Bergère et le Ramoneur, Notre-Dame de Paris* etc.; has written many songs mostly set to music by Joseph Kosma.
Publs. *Paroles, Histoires, Spectacle, La Pluie et le beau temps, Choses et autres, Fatras* 73.
82 boulevard de Clichy, 75018 Paris, France.

Previn, André; American composer and conductor; b. 6 April 1929, Berlin, Germany; *s.* of Jack and Charlotte (Epstein) Previn; *m.* Mia Farrow 1970; three *s.* two *d.*; ed. Berlin and Paris Conservatories and Univ. of Calif.
Music Dir. Houston Symphony, U.S. 67-69; Music Dir. and Principal Conductor, London Symphony Orchestra 68-; composed and conducted approx. 50 film scores 50-65; Guest conductor of most major world orchestras, also Royal Opera House, Covent Garden, Salzburg, Edinburgh, Osaka, Flanders Festivals; Music Dir. London South Bank Summer Music Festival 72-74, Pittsburgh Symphony Orchestra 76-; series of television specials for BBC; Television Critics Award 72; Acad. Award for Best Film Score 59, 60, 64, 65.
Leisure interests: collecting contemporary art, fencing, American folk art.
Major works: Symphony for Strings 65, *Overture to a Comedy* 66, Suite for Piano 67, Cello Concerto 68, Four Songs, Soprano and Orchestra 68, Violin Concerto 69, *Two Serenades for Violin* 69, Guitar Concerto 70, Piano Preludes 72, Woodwind Quintet 73, *Good Companions* (musical) 74.
Publ. *Music Face to Face* 71.
c/o London Symphony Orchestra, 1 Montague Street, London, W.C.1, England.

Prévot, André-Romain, DR. en MED., DR. ès SC.; French biologist; b. 22 July 1894, Douai (Nord); *s.* of Romain Prévot and Alix Mangoux; *m.* Anna Sörensen 1918; three *s.* one *d.*; ed. Lycée de Douai, Faculté des Sciences, Lille, Faculté de Médecine, Paris.
Institut Pasteur, Paris 22- (retd. 65); fmr. Pres. Soc. française d'Hématologie, Soc. française de Microbiologie; Pres. numerous Int. Congresses; mem. Section of Rural Economy, French Acad. of Sciences; mem. Section of Biol. Sciences, Acad. of Medicine; Officier de la Légion d'Honneur; Officier de l'Ordre de la Santé Publique, Grand Officier de l'Ordre National du Mérite.
Leisure interests: bibliography of biology of humification; practical applications in an experimental garden.
Publs. *Biologie des Infections Anaérobies* 54, *Manuel de Classification des Anaérobies* 57 (American edn.), *Traité de Systématique bacterienne* 61, *Les Bactéries Anaérobies* 67, *Encyclopédie Internationale des Sciences et des techniques, départment "Bactériologique"* 69, *Humus (Biogénèse, Biochimie, Biologie)* 70, *Bactéries anaérobies mises à jour* 72.
Institut Pasteur, 28 rue du Dr. Roux, 75015 Paris; Home: 6 rue Gathelot, 92140 Clamart, France.
Telephone: 642-08-06.

Prey, Hermann; German opera and concert singer; b. 11 July 1929, Berlin; *m.* Barbara Pniok; one *s.* two *d.*; ed. Humanistisches Gymnasium "Zum Grauen Kloster", Berlin, and Staatliche Musikhochschule, Berlin.
At State Opera, Wiesbaden 52, also Hamburg, Munich, Berlin, Vienna; guest appearances at La Scala, Milan, Metropolitan Opera, New York, Teatro Colón, Buenos Aires, San Francisco Opera; has sung at Festivals at Salzburg, Bayreuth, Edinburgh, Vienna, Tokyo, Aix-en-Provence, Perugia, Berlin, etc.; now with Munich State Opera; Meistersänger-Wettbewerb, Nuremberg 52.
Leisure interests: riding, films.
D-8033 Krailling vor München, Fichtenstrasse 14, Federal Republic of Germany.
Telephone: 0811-89-65-90.

Price, Byron, A.B., A.M., LL.D.; American journalist and public servant; b. 25 March 1891, Clearspring Township, La Grange County, Ind.; *s.* of John and Emeline (Barnes) Price (British); *m.* Priscilla Alden 1920; ed. Wabash Coll.
Reporter and editor United Press Asscn. Chicago and Omaha 12; with Associated Press 12-41, News Editor Washington Bureau 22-27, Chief 27-37, Exec. News

Editor 37-41; Dir. of Censorship U.S. 41-45; personal rep. Pres. Truman on special mission to Germany 45; Vice-Pres. Motion Picture Asscn. of America; Chair. Asscn. of Motion Picture Producers 46-47; awarded Pres. Medal for Merit 46; Hon. K.B.E. 48; Asst. Sec.-Gen. for Admin. and Financial Services, United Nations 47-54; Dir. Gen. Press Congress of the World 59.
Chestertown, Maryland, U.S.A.
Telephone: 778-3588.

Price, Don Krasher, A.B., B.A., B.LITT., LL.D., L.H.D.; American university professor; b. 23 Jan. 1910, Middlesboro, Ky.; s. of Don Krasher Price and Nell Rhorer Price; m. 1st Margaret (Helen) Gailbreath 1936 (died 1970), one s. one d.; m. 2nd Harriet Sloane Fels 1971; ed. Vanderbilt and Oxford Univs.
Reporter *Nashville Evening Tennessean* 30-32; mem. staff Home Owners' Loan Corpn. 35-37, Social Science Research Council 37-39, Public Admin. Clearing House 39-53, U.S. Bureau of the Budget 45-46, Hoover Comm. on Org. of Exec. Branch of Govt. 47-48; Deputy Chair. Research and Devt. Board, U.S. Dept. of Defense 52-53; Assoc. Dir. The Ford Foundation 53-54, Vice-Pres. 54-58; Dean, John Fitzgerald Kennedy School of Govt. (fmrly. Graduate School of Public Admin.), Harvard Univ. and Prof. of Govt., Harvard Univ. 58-; mem. President's Advisory Cttee. on Govt. Org. 59-61; Consultant to Exec. Office of the Pres. 61-; Trustee, Vanderbilt Univ., Twentieth Century Fund, Rhodes Scholarship Trust; mem. American Asscn. for the Advancement of Science (Pres. 67, Chair. of Board 68); Hon. A.M., LL.D., L.H.D., Litt.D.; Faculty Prize of Harvard Univ. Press for *The Scientific Estate* 65.
Leisure interests: squash, tennis, fishing.
Publs. *City Manager Government in the United States* (with Harold and Kathryn Stone) 40, *Government and Science* 54, *The Secretary of State* (Editor) 60, *The Scientific Estate* 65.
Littauer Center 121, Harvard University, Cambridge, Mass. 02138; Home: 101 Quincy House, Cambridge, Mass. 02138, U.S.A.
Telephone: 617-876-2495 (Home).

Price, George Cadle; Belizean politician; b. 15 Jan. 1919; s. of William Cadle Price and Irene Price; ed. St. John's Coll., Belize City, and St. Augustin Seminary, Mississippi.
City Councillor 47-62; founder-mem. People's United Party (P.U.P.) 50; Sec. P.U.P. 50-56; Leader P.U.P. 56-; Pres. Gen. Workers' Union 47-52; mem. Legislative Council, British Honduras (now Belize) 54-65; mem. Exec. Council 54-57, 61-65; Mayor, Belize City 56-62; mem. House of Representatives 65-, Cabinet 65-; fmr. mem. for Nat. Resources; First Minister 61-63, leader of del. to London for self-Govt. constitutional talks; Premier 64-, Minister of Finance and Development 65-; Chair. Reconstruction and Development Corpn.
Office of the Premier, Belmopan, Belize.

Price, James Robert, D.PHIL., D.SC., F.A.A.; Australian organic chemist; b. 25 March 1912, Kadina, S. Australia; s. of E. J. Price; m. Joyce E. Brooke 1940; one s. two d.; ed. St. Peter's Coll., Adelaide and Univs. of Adelaide and Oxford.
Head, Chemistry Section, John Innes Horticultural Inst., U.K. 37; Ministry of Supply (U.K.) 39; Council for Scientific and Industrial Research (C.S.I.R.) Div. of Industrial Chem., Australia 45; Officer in charge, Organic Chem. Section, Commonwealth Scientific and Industrial Research Org. (CSIRO) 60, subsequently Chief Organic Chem. Div.; mem. Exec. CSIRO 66; Chair. CSIRO May 70-; Fellow, Australian Acad. of Science, Chair. Nat. Cttee. for Chem. 66-69; Pres. Royal Australian Chem. Inst. (R.A.C.I.) 62-64; H. G. Smith Memorial Medal (R.A.C.I.) 56, Leighton Memorial Medal (R.A.C.I.) 69.

Leisure interests: squash, growing Australian native plants.
Publs. numerous scientific papers and articles.
CSIRO, Canberra, A.C.T., Australia.

Price, Leontyne; American soprano singer; b. 10 Feb. 1927; ed. Central State Coll., Wilberforce, Ohio and Juilliard School of Music.
Appeared as Bess (*Porgy and Bess*), Vienna, Berlin, Paris, London, New York 52-54; recitalist, soloist 54-; soloist Hollywood Bowl 55-59; opera singer NBC-TV 55-58, San Francisco Opera Co. 57-59, 60-61, Vienna Staatsoper 58, 59-60, 61; recording artist RCA-Victor 58-; appeared Covent Garden 58-59, Chicago 59, 60, Milan 60-61, Metropolitan Opera, New York 61-62, 66, 69, Paris Opéra as Aida 68.
1133 Broadway (Suite 603), New York, N.Y. 10010, U.S.A.

Price, Margaret Berenice; British opera singer; b. 13 April 1941, Tredegar, Wales; d. of late Thomas Glyn Price and of Lilian Myfanwy Richards; ed. Pontllanfraith Grammar School and Trinity Coll. of Music, London.
Operatic debut with Welsh Nat. Opera in *Figaro*; renowned for Mozart operatic roles; has sung in world's leading opera houses and festivals; has made many recordings of opera, oratorio, concert works and recitals, and many radio broadcasts and television appearances; Hon. Fellow, Trinity Coll. of Music; Elizabeth Schumann Prize for Lieder, Ricordi Prize for Opera, Silver Medal of the Worshipful Co. of Musicians.
Leisure interests: cookery, reading, walking, swimming.
Major roles include Countess in *Figaro*, Pamina in *The Magic Flute*, Fiordiligi in *Così fan Tutte*, Donna Anna in *Don Giovanni*, Konstanze in *Die Entführung*, Amelia in *Simone Boccanegra*, Salud in *La Vida Breve*, Agathe in *Freischütz*, Tatiana in *Eugene Onegin*.
Flat 3, 24 Marylebone High Street, London, W1M 3PE, England.

Price, Willard DeMille, B.A., M.A., LITT.D.; American explorer, naturalist and author; b. 28 July 1887, Peterborough, Canada; m. Mary Virginia Selden 1932; one s.; ed. Western Reserve and Columbia Univs.
Editor various magazines; directed N. African expdn. to make films of Arab life 19-20; toured Indian, Burmese, Egyptian, Japanese and Philippine Univs. 30; ethnographic studies Battaks (Sumatra) 30, Bagobos (Philippines) 35; expeditions for Nat. Geographic Soc. and American Museum of Natural History to Micronesia, Egypt, Japan, etc. 36-74; foreign corresp. for American and British publs., China, Manchuria, Mongolia, Japan, Latin America and Africa 33-70; travels in 130 countries.
Publs. *Ancient Peoples at New Tasks, The Negro Around the World, Study of American influence in the Orient, Pacific Adventure, Riptide in the South Seas, Japan Reaches Out, Children of the Rising Sun, Where are you going, Japan?, Barbarian, Japan Rides the Tiger, Japan's Islands of Mystery, The Son of Heaven, Key to Japan, Roving South, Rio Grande to Patagonia, Tropic Adventure, Amazon Adventure, I Cannot Rest from Travel, South Sea Adventure, The Amazing Amazon, Journey by Junk, Underwater Adventure, Adventures in Paradise, Volcano Adventure, Roaming Britain, Whale Adventure, Incredible Africa, The Amazing Mississippi, African Adventure, Elephant Adventure, Rivers I Have Known, America's Paradise Lost, Safari Adventure, Lion Adventure, Gorilla Adventure, Odd Way Round the World, Diving Adventure, The Japanese Miracle, Cannibal Adventure, The Road Ahead, The Ironbound District.*
814N Via Alhambra, Laguna Hills, Calif. 92653, U.S.A.

Prideaux, Sir Humphrey Povah Treverbian, Kt., O.B.E., M.A.; British business executive; b. 13 Dec. 1915, London; s. of Walter Treverbian Prideaux and Marion

Fenn (née Arbuthnot); *m.* Cynthia V. Birch Reynardson 1939; four *s.*; ed. St. Aubyns, Eton and Trinity Coll., Oxford.

Regular army officer 36-53; Dir. Navy, Army & Air Force Insts. 56-, Chair. 65-73; Chair. Lord Wandsworth Foundation 56, Trustee 63-; Deputy Chair. Liebig's Extract of Meat Co. Ltd. 68-69, Dir. 66-; Chair. Oxo Ltd. 68-72; Dir. W. H. Smith & Son (Holdings) Ltd. 69, Brooke Bond Oxo Ltd. 69-70; Chair. Brooke Bond Liebig 72, Dir. 68-; Pres. London Life Asscn. Ltd. 73, Dir. 64-; Chair. London Life Managed Funds Ltd. 74. Leisure interests: riding, books.

Brooke Bond Liebig Ltd., Thames House, Queen Street Place, London, EC4R 1DH; Home: Summers Farm, Long Sutton, Basingstoke, Hants.; also 124 Marsham Court, London, S.W.1, England.

Telephone: 01-248-6422 (Office); Long Sutton 295; and 01-828-5378 (London).

Prideaux, Sir John Francis, Kt., O.B.E.; British banker; b. 1911; *m.*; two *s.* one *d.*; ed. St. Aubyns, Rottingdean and Eton Coll.

Middlesex Yeomanry, Second World War; Dir. Arbuthnot Latham and Co. Ltd. 36, Chair. 64-69, Chair. Arbuthnot Latham Holdings Ltd. 69-74; Dir. Westminster Bank Ltd. 55, Deputy Chair. 62-69; Joint Deputy Chair. Nat. Westminster Bank Ltd. 69-70, Chair. Jan. 71-; Int. Westminster Bank Ltd. 69-; Chair. and Treas., Board of Govs., St. Thomas' Hospital 64-74; Chair. Special Trustees for St. Thomas' Health District 74-; Chair. Cttee. of London Clearing Bankers 74-; Pres. Inst. of Bankers 74-.

National Westminster Bank Ltd., 41 Lothbury, London E.C.2; Home: Elderslie, Ockley, Surrey, England.

Priess, Friedrich, D.IUR.; German banker; b. 19 Oct. 1903, Bremen; *m.* Maria Büttner 1931; one *s.* three *d.*; ed. Univs. of Freiburg and Marburg.

Lawyer, Bremen and legal adviser to N.V. Philips Gloeilampenfabrieken 29-30; judge, Bremen 30-37, Hamburg 37-50; Vice-Pres. Landeszentralbank, Hamburg 50-56; Partner, M. M. Warburg-Brinkmann, Wirtz & Co., Hamburg 56-; Chair. Advisory Board, Deutsches Getreide-Kontor G.m.b.H.; mem. Advisory Board, Deutsches Schiffsbeleihungsbank A.G., Nord-Deutsche und Hamburg-Bremer Versicherungs A.G.

M. M. Warburg-Brinckmann, Wirtz & Co., Ferdinandstrasse 75, 2000 Hamburg 1, Federal Republic of Germany.

Telephone: 32-82-1.

Priestley, Charles Henry Brian, M.A., SC.D., F.A.A., F.R.S.; British meteorologist; b. 8 July 1915, Highgate, London; *s.* of Thomas Gordon Priestley and Muriel Brown; *m.* Constance Tweedy 1946; one *s.* two *d.*; ed. Mill Hill School and St. John's Coll. Cambridge.

Service in Meteorological Office, Air Ministry, at Porton (England), Suffield (Canada) and Dunstable (England), finishing as Officer-in-Charge Upper Air Analysis and Forecasting Branch 39-46; Chief, Div. of Atmospheric Physics, Commonwealth Scientific and Industrial Research Org. (CSIRO) Australia 46-73, Chair. Environmental Physics Research Laboratories 71-; Fellow, Australian Acad. of Science 54-, mem. Council 58-60, Vice-Pres. 59-60; Fellow Royal Soc. 67-; Vice-Pres. Royal Meteorological Soc. 57-59; mem. Exec. Cttee. Int. Asscn. for Meteorology and Atmospheric Physics 54-60, Vice-Pres. 67-; mem. Advisory Cttee. World Meteorological Org. 64-68. Chair. 67-68; mem. numerous other int. scientific bodies; Visiting Research Scientist, Univ. of Chicago 57; David Syme Medal, Univ. of Melbourne 56; Buchan Prize. Royal Meteorological Soc. 48, Symons Gold Medal, Royal Meteorological Soc. 67, Int. Meteorological Org. Prize 73, Rossby Research Medal 74.

Leisure interests: golf, bridge.

Publs. *Turbulent Transport in the Lower Atmosphere* 59; 60 scientific papers.

CSIRO Environmental Physics Laboratories, Aspendale, Victoria 3195; Home: 11 Coonil Crescent, Malvern, Victoria 3144, Australia.

Priestley, John Boynton, M.A., LL.D., D.LITT.; British writer; b. 13 Sept. 1894; *m.* Jacquetta Hawkes (*q.v.*) 1953; ed. Bradford and Trinity Hall Cambridge.

Pres. London P.E.N. Club 36-37; Chair. 1941 Cttee. (on War Aims); contrib. to many periodicals, "Postscripts"; B.B.C.; Chair. UNESCO Int. Theatre Inst. Conf. Paris 47, and Prague 48; Chair. British Theatre Conf. 48, Pres. Int. Theatre Inst. 49; mem. Nat. Theatre Board 65-67; Hon. Freeman of City of Bradford 73.

Publs. Criticism: *English Comic Characters, The English Novel, Meredith, Peacock, The Art of the Dramatist* 57, *Literature and Western Man* 60; Novels: *Adam in Moonshine, Benighted, The Good Companions, Angel Pavement, Faraway, Wonder Hero, They Walk in the City, The Doomsday Men, Let the People Sing, Blackout in Gretley, Daylight on Saturday, Three Men in New Suits, Bright Day, Festival at Farbridge, The Magicians, Low Notes on a High Level, Saturn over the Water, The Thirty-First of June, The Shapes of Sleep, Sir Michael and Sir George* 64, *Lost Empires* 65, *Salt is Leaving* 66, *It's an Old Country* 67, *The Image Men* (Vol. I: *Out of Town*; Vol. II: *London End*) 68; Essays: *English Journey, Midnight on the Desert, Rain upon Godshill, Thoughts in the Wilderness, Delight, Charles Dickens: A Pictorial Biography, Man and Time* 64, *Essays of Five Decades* 69; Plays: *Dangerous Corner, Eden End, Cornelius, Laburnum Grove, Bees on the Boat Deck, Time and the Conways, I Have Been Here Before, Music at Night, When We are Married, Johnson Over Jordan, Goodnight Children, They Came to a City, How are They at Home?, Desert Highway, An Inspector Calls, Ever Since Paradise, The Linden Tree, Home is To-morrow, Summer Day's Dream, Dragon's Mouth and The White Countess* (both with Jacquetta Hawkes), *Mr. Kettle and Mrs. Moon, Take the Fool Away, The Glass Cage*; assisted in dramatization of Iris Murdoch's *A Severed Head* 63; *The Pavilion of Masks* (play) 63; libretto for *The Olympians* (opera); Television plays: *Now Let Him Go, The Stone Faces, Doomsday for Dyson*; Non-fiction: *Margin Released, Trumpets over the Sea* 68, *The Prince of Pleasure* 69, *The Edwardians* 70, *Victoria's Heyday* 72, *Over the Long High Wall* 72, *The English* 73, *Outcries and Asides* 74, *A Visit to New Zealand* 74; *The Carfitt Crisis* 75, *Particular Pleasures* 75.

B3 & 4 Albany, Piccadilly, London, W.1; Home: Kissing Tree House, Alveston, Stratford-on-Avon, Warwickshire, England.

Prieto, Arnaldo da Costa; Brazilian civil engineer and politician; b. 13 Feb. 1930, Rio Grande do Sul; *s.* of Vicente B. Prieto and Henriqueta Maria Prieto; *m.* Irma Emilia Daudt Prieto; five *s.*

President of Students Union of Rio Grande do Sul State; Titular Prof., Chair of Topography, School of Eng., Pontífica Universidade Católica do Rio Grande do Sul; mem. Municipal Council, São Leopoldo 60-63; Sec. of State for Labour and Housing, Rio Grande do Sul State 63-67; Fed. Deputy 67-71, 71-75; Minister of Labour 74-.

F.H.I.S.-QL 4/9, Casa 03, Brasília, D.F., Brazil.

Telephone: 48-1044.

Prieto, Justo Pastor; Paraguayan lawyer, educationist and politician; b. 1897, Pilar; *s.* of the late Juan Pío Prieto and Concepción Rojas de Prieto; *m.* Beatriz Mernes de Prieto 1928; two *s.*; ed. Asunción Univ.

Secretary and legal adviser Police Dept. 22; Pres. Municipal Council 23; Nat. Dep. and Pres. Exec. Board Liberal Party 24; Prof. of Law Military School, Superior School of War and Escuela Normal de Profesores 24; Prof. and Dean Faculty of Law and Social Sciences

Asunción 28, Rector of Univ. 29; Minister of Justice and Educ. 32; Dir. *El Liberal;* Prof. of Sociology Faculty of Econ. Science Buenos Aires; Pres. of Senate 39; Minister of Foreign Affairs 39; Pres. of Comm. on Continental Defence at Panama Conf. 39; Prof. of Industrial Sociology, Argentine Business Coll. 66-; Extra. Prof. Sociology Univ. Mayor de San Andrés, Bolivia; Dir. of the Instituto Superior Internacional de Relaciones Públicas 65-, Prof. of Sociology and Industrial Sociology; Pres. Cttee. for Self-Determination of the People; mem. Academia Ciencias Políticas, Buenos Aires, Académie Internationale des Sciences Politiques, Geneva, Institut International de Sociologie, Societé des Americanistes de Paris, del Instituto Latino Americano de Sociología, Academia Paraguaya de la Lengua Española, Soc. Argentina de Escritores; Dr. h.c. (Rio de Janeiro).
Leisure interests: journalism, sociological studies.
Publs. *Efectos jurídicos de las obligaciones naturales* 19, *La sociología: su historia y estado actual* 27, *El tratado de Rio de Janeiro* 29, *La universidad y la solución de los problemas económicos, políticos y sociales* 31, *Misión social del profesor de Enseñanza secundaria* 34, *Síntesis sociológica* 37, *18 meses de regresión política* 37, *Ideas para la concepción de la juventud universitaria como poder espiritual* 38, *Dos Vidas Ejemplares* 39, *Valor Social de la Salud* 39, *Sentido Social de la Cultura Universitaria* 42, *El Paraguay en la empresa emancipadora* 42, *Los problemas generales de la Sociología* 43, *La Vida indómita de Augusto Comte* 44, *Estudiantes hoy, dirigentes mañana* 45, *El Problema del Paraguay Mediterráneo* 46, *Eusebio Ayala, Presidente de la Victoria* 50, *Paraguay, la Provincia Gigante de las Indias* 51, *Manual del Ciudadano Liberal Paraguayo* 53, *Los Partidos políticos en la Constitución Social* 60, *Sociología Industrial* 67, *Sociólogos argentinos en la tradición continental* 67, *Elementos de Sociología General* 71, *Diccionario Comentado del Liberalismo* 73, *Profesión de fe de una generación* 73, *Enciclopedia Británica* (Paraguayan edn.) 72, *Sociólogo del Derecho y de la Política, Prólogo a las Bases de la Organización política, Elementos ideológicos de la Emancipación americana* 75; contribs. on sociology and history to *La Prensa.*
Lima 131, Buenos Aires, Argentina; Corupayty 357, Asunción, Paraguay.
Telephone: 38-1301 (Buenos Aires); 23-538 (Asunción).

Prigogine, Ilya, PH.D.; Belgian university professor; b. 25 Jan. 1917, Moscow, U.S.S.R.; s. of Roman Prigogine and Julia Wichman; m. Marina Prokopowicz 1961; two s.; ed. Univ. Libre de Bruxelles.
Professor at Univ. of Brussels 47-; Dir. Instituts Internationaux de Physique et de Chimie, Solvay 62-; Dir. Center for Statistical Mechanics and Thermodynamics, Univ. of Texas; mem. Académie Royale de Belgique 53, Pres. 69-; Foreign Hon. mem. American Acad. of Sciences and Arts 60; Fellow Acad. of Sciences of New York 62; mem. Romanian Acad. of Science 65; mem. Royal Soc. of Sciences, Uppsala, Sweden 67; Foreign Assoc. Nat. Acad. of Sciences U.S. 67; mem. corresp. de la Soc. Royale des Sciences, Liège 67; Prix Francqui 55, Prix Solvay 65; corresp. mem. Class of Physics and Mathematics, Acad. of Sciences, Göttingen 70, Österreichische Akad. der Wissenschaften, Vienna 71; mem. Deutsche Akad. der Naturforscher Leopoldina 70, Acad. Int. de Philosophie des Sciences; Hon. mem. Chemical Soc. of Poland 71; Dr. h.c. (Univs. of Newcastle upon Tyne 66, Poitiers 66, Chicago 69, Bordeaux 72); Svante Arrhenius Gold Medal, Acad. Royale des Sciences, Sweden 69; Cothenius Medal, Deutsche Akademie des Naturforsches Leopoldina (Halle) 75.
Leisure interests: music, arts.
Publs. *Traité de Thermodynamique, conformément aux méthodes de Gibbs et de De Donder* (with R. Defay) 44, 50, *Etude Thermodynamique des Phénomènes Irréver-*

sibles 47, *Introduction to Thermodynamics of Irreversible Processes* 62, *The Molecular Theory of Solutions* (with A. Bellemans and V. Mathot) 57, *Non-Equilibrium Statistical Mechanics* 62, *Non-Equilibrium Thermodynamics, Variational Techniques and Stability* (with R. J. Donnelly and R. Herman) 66, *Kinetic Theory of Vehicular Traffic* (with R. Herman) 71, *Thermodynamic Theory of Structure Stability and Fluctuations* (with P. Glansdorff) 71.
Avenue Fond'Roy 67, 1180 Brussels, Belgium.
Telephone: 374-29-52.

Primatesta, H.E. Cardinal Raúl Francisco; Argentine ecclesiastic; b. 14 April 1919, Capilla del Señor.
Ordained 42; consecrated Bishop of Tanais 57; transferred to San Rafael 61; Archbishop of Córdoba 65-; created Cardinal by Pope Paul VI 73.
Arzobispado, Avenida H. Irigoyen 98, Córdoba, Argentina.

Prince, William Henry Wood; American businessman; b. 7 Feb. 1914, St. Louis; m. Eleanor Edwards 1940; three s.; ed. Groton School for Boys and Princeton Univ.
With First Nat. Bank of Chicago 36-42, 45-47; Sec.-Treas. Sherman Hotel, College Inn Food Products Co. Chicago 39-42; with Union Stock Yard & Transit Co. 48-57, Pres. 49-57; Dir. Armour & Co. 50-69, Chair. and Chief Exec. Officer 57-69; Pres. F. H. Prince & Co. Inc. 69-; Dir. of other companies.
F. H. Prince & Co. Inc., 1 First National Plaza, Chicago, Ill. 60603, U.S.A.
Telephone: 312 726 2232.

Pringle, John Martin Douglas, M.A.; British journalist; b. 28 June 1912, Hawick, Scotland; s. of J. Douglas Pringle; m. Celia Carroll 1936; one s. two d.; ed. Shrewsbury School, and Lincoln Coll., Oxford.
Member staff of *Manchester Guardian* 34-39; served in Army 40-44; Asst. Editor *Manchester Guardian* 44-48; joined staff *The Times* 48; Editor *Sydney Morning Herald* 52-57, 65-70; Deputy Editor *The Observer* 58-63; Managing Editor *Canberra Times* 64-65.
Publs. *China Struggles for Unity* 38, *Australian Accent* 58, *Australian Painting Today* 63, *On Second Thoughts* 72, *Have Pen: Will Travel* 73.
27 Bayview Street, McMahon's Point, North Sydney, N.S.W., Australia.
Telephone: 92-7560.

Prinz, Gerhard, DR.JUR.; German business executive; b. 1929.
Member Man. Board, Volkswagenwerk AG until 73; Chair. Man. Board, AUDI-NSU 72-.
AUDI-NSU Auto Union AG, 7107 Neckarsulm, Federal Republic of Germany.

Prior, Rt. Hon. James Michael Leathes, M.P.; British politician and farmer; b. 11 Oct. 1927, Norwich; s. of C.B.L. and A.S.M. Prior; m. Jane P. Gifford 1954; three s. one d.; ed. Charterhouse and Pembroke Coll., Cambridge.
Member of Parl. for Lowestoft 59-; Parl. Private Sec. to Pres. of Board of Trade 63, to Minister of Power 63-64, to Rt. Hon. Edward Heath 65-70; Vice-Chair. Conservative Party 65, 72-74; Minister of Agriculture, Fisheries and Food 70-72, Lord Pres. of Council 72-74; Shadow Spokesman on Home Affairs March-June 74, on Employment June 74-; Dir. F. Lambert and Sons Ltd. 58-70, IDC Group 68-70, 74-, O. G. Lywood Ltd. 69-70; Chair. Aston Boats Ltd. 68-70, 74-; Dir. Norwich Union Insurance 74-, Avon Cosmetics Ltd. 74-; United Biscuits Ltd. 74-; Adviser to the Nickerson Group Ltd. 75-.
Leisure interests: cricket, tennis, golf, gardening.
36 Morpeth Mansions, London, S.W.1; Old Hall, Brampton, Suffolk, England.
Telephone: 01-834-5543; Brampton 278.

Pritchard, Baron (Life Peer), cr. 75, of West Haddon in the County of Northamptonshire; **Derek Wilbraham Pritchard;** British business executive; b. 8 June 1910, Didsbury, Lancs.; s. of Frank Wheelton Pritchard and Ethel Annie Cheetham; m. Denise Arfor Huntbach 1941; two c.; ed. Clifton Coll., Bristol.

Took over family business of E. Halliday and Son Ltd., Manchester; Army Service, Second World War 39-46; Dir. E. K. Cole Ltd. 46-49; joined Ind. Coope Ltd. as Man. Dir. Grants of St. James's Ltd. 49-, Dir. Samuel Montagu & Co. Ltd., Midland Bank Ltd., Guardian Royal Exchange Assurance and other companies; Chair. British Nat. Export Council 66-68; Deputy Chair. Allied Breweries 67-68, Chair. 68-70; Pres. Inst. of Dirs. 68-74; non-exec. Chair. of Carreras 70-72; Chair. Rothmans International Ltd. 72-75; Pres. Abbeyfield Soc. 70-.

Leisure interests: farming, fox-hunting.
Office: 27 Baker Street, London, W.1; Home: West Haddon Hall, Northampton, NN6 7AU, England.
Telephone: 01-588-6464.

Pritchard, John Michael, C.B.E.; British conductor; b. 5 Feb. 1921, London; s. of Albert Edward Pritchard and Amy Edith Pritchard; ed. Sir George Monoux School, London.

Conductor, Glyndebourne Festivals 52-74, Principal Conductor, Glyndebourne Opera 67-; Conductor and Musical Dir. Royal Liverpool Philharmonic Orchestra 57-62; Principal Conductor and Artistic Dir. London Philharmonic Orchestra 62-66; Co-Dir. Opéra de Marseille 66-68; Musical Dir. Glyndebourne Opera Festival 69-; Music Dir. Huddersfield Choral Soc. 73-; visiting conductor with principal orchestras and opera houses throughout the world; Shakespeare Prize, F.v.S. Foundation 75.

Leisure interests: good food and wine, theatre.
Carters Corner Place, nr. Hailsham, Sussex; 1 King Street, London W.C.2, England.

Pritchard, Sir Neil, K.C.M.G.; British diplomatist; b. 14 Jan. 1911, Widnes, Lancs.; s. of the late Joseph William and Lilian Pritchard; m. Mary Devereux Burroughes 1943; one s.; ed. Liverpool Coll. and Worcester Coll., Oxford.

Dominions Office 33, Private Sec. to Perm. Under-Sec. 36-38; Asst. Sec. Rhodesia and Nyasaland Royal Comm. 38; Sec. Office of U.K. High Commr., Pretoria 41-45; Principal Sec. Office of U.K. Rep., Dublin 48-49; Asst. Under-Sec. of State, Commonwealth Relations Office (C.R.O.) 51-54; Dep. U.K. High Commr., Canada 54-57; Australia 57-60; Act. Dep. Under-Sec. of State, C.R.O. 61; High Commr. of U.K. in Tanganyika 61-63; Dep. Under-Sec. of State, C.R.O. (later Commonwealth Office) 63-67; Amb. to Thailand 67-70; retd.

Leisure interest: golf.
Little Garth, Daglingworth, Cirencester, Glos., England.

Pritchett, Sir Victor Sawdon, Kt., C.B.E.; British author, critic; b. 16 Dec. 1900, Ipswich, Suffolk; s. of Sawdon Pritchett and Beatrice Martin; m. Dorothy Rudge Roberts 1936; one s. one d.; ed. Alleyn's School.

Director of *New Statesman;* has lectured in four univs. in U.S.A. including Brandeis Univ.; Resident writer, Smith Coll. 67, 70-72; Clark Lectures, Cambridge 69; Pres. PEN Int. 74-; Hon. mem. American Acad. Arts and Letters, Nat. Inst. of Arts and Letters, N.Y.; Fellow Royal Soc. of Literature; D.Lit. (Leeds) 72; PEN Biography Award for *Balzac* 74.

Publs. *Marching Spain, Clare Drummer, The Spanish Virgin, Shirley Sanz, Nothing Like Leather, Dead Man Leading, You Make Your Own Life, In My Good Books, It May Never Happen, Why Do I Write?* (with Elizabeth Bowen and Graham Greene), *The Living Novel, Mr. Beluncle, Books in General, The Spanish Temper, Collected Short Stories, When My Girl Comes Home, London*

Perceived, The Key to My Heart, Foreign Faces, New York Proclaimed, The Living Novel and Later Appreciations, Dublin, A Cab at the Door (autobiog.) 68, *Blind Love* (short stories), *George Meredith* and *English Comedy* 70, *Midnight Oil* (autobiog. Vol. II) 71, *Balzac* 73, *The Camberwell Beauty* (stories) 74.
12 Regent's Park Terrace, London, N.W.1, England.

Prochnow, Herbert Victor, B.A., M.A., PH.D.; American banker and writer; b. 19 May 1897, Wilton, Wisconsin; s. of Adolph and Alvena Prochnow; m. Laura Virginia Stinson 1928; one s.; ed. Univ. of Wisconsin and Northwestern Univ.

Principal, Kendall (Wisconsin) High School 17; Union Trust Co., Chicago 23-29; The First Nat. Bank of Chicago 29-73, rising from asst. cashier to Dir. 60-68, Pres. 62-68, Hon. Dir. 68-73; Sec. Fed. Advisory Council of Fed. Reserve System 45-; Consultant to Sec. of State 55, 57; Deputy Under-Sec. of State for Economic Affairs 55-56; Alt. Gov. for U.S. of Int. Bank and Int. Monetary Fund 55-56; Dir. Annual Summer Graduate School of Banking, Univ. of Wisconsin 45-; Chair. U.S. Del. Gen. Agreement on Tariffs and Trade, Geneva 56; fmr. Asst. Prof. Business Admin., Indiana Univ., lectures Loyola and Northwestern Univs.; financial columnist, *Chicago Tribune* 68-70; Pres. Chicago Asscn. of Commerce and Industry 64, 65; Commdr. of the Order of Vasa of Royal Govt. of Sweden 65, Commdr. Cross of the Order of Merit of Germany 68; several awards and hon. degrees.

Leisure interests: gardening and writing.
Publs. *The Public Speaker's Treasure Chest* 42, 64, *Great Stories from Great Lives* 44, *Meditations on the Ten Commandments* 46, *The Toastmaster's Handbook* 49, *Term Loans and Theories of Bank Liquidity* 49, *The Successful Speaker's Handbook* 51, *1001 Ways to Improve your Conversation and Speeches* 52, *Meditations on the Beatitudes* 52, *The Speaker's Treasury of Stories for all Occasions* 53, *Speaker's Handbook of Epigrams and Witticisms* 55, *Speaker's Treasury for Sunday School Teachers* 55, *The Toastmasters and Speaker's Handbook* 55, *A Treasury of Stories, Illustrations, Epigrams and Quotations for Ministers and Teachers* 57, *Meditations on the Lord's Prayer* 57 (as *Inspirational Thoughts on the Lord's Prayer* 70), *The New Guide for Toastmasters and Speakers* 56, *A Family Treasury of Inspiration and Faith* 58, *The New Speaker's Treasury of Wit and Wisdom* 58, *The Complete Toastmaster* 60, *Effective Public Speaking* 60, *Speaker's Book of Illustrations* 60, *A Dictionary of Wit, Wisdom and Satire* 62, *1000 Tips and Quips for Speakers and Toastmasters* 62, *Practical Bank Credit* 63, *1400 Ideas for Speakers and Toastmasters* 64, *The Successful Toastmaster* 66, *A Treasury of Humorous Quotations. Quotation Finders* 71, *A Speaker's Treasury for Educators, Convocation Speakers,* etc., *A Tree of Life, Speakers' Source Book, 1 001 Quips, Stories and Illustrations for All Occasions* 73, *The Speaker's and Toastmaster's Handbook* 73, *The Changing World of Banking* 74; co-author: *The Next Century is America's* 38; editor *American Financial Institutions* 51, *Determining the Business Outlook* 54, *The Federal Reserve System* 60, *World Economic Problems and Policies* 65, *The Five-Year Outlook for Interest Rates* 68, *The One-Bank Holding Company* 69, *The Eurodollar* 70, *The Five-Year Outlook for Interest Rates in the U.S. and Abroad* 72.
One First National Bank Plaza, Chicago, Ill. 60670; 2950 Harrison Street, Evanston, Ill. 60201, U.S.A.

Prohaska, Carl Wilhelm, D.SC.; Danish naval architect; b. 15 Feb. 1903; ed. Technical Univ. of Denmark. Naval Architect at shipyards in Denmark and Fracen 28-36; Prof. Technical Univ. of Denmark 37-73; Dir. Hydro-Aerodynamics Laboratory, Lyngby 57-73; Dir. Danish Ship Research Inst. (incorporating Danish Shipbuilders Computing Office) 61-67; consulting Naval

Architect; Chair. FAO Fishing Boat Conf. 63, and Int. Load-Line Conf. Technical Cttee. London 66; Vice-Pres. Danish Soc. of Nat. Sciences 60-72; mem. Danish Eng. Inst. and Acad. of Technical Sciences, Swedish Eng. Acad., Acad. des Sciences, Institut de France and numerous Int. Eng. Socs.; Commdr. Order of Danneborg, and Ordre Nat. du Mérite (France); William Froude Gold Medal of Royal Inst. Naval Architects.
Publs. include *Two-Nodal Ship Vibrations* 41, *Residuary Stability* 47, *Computer Calculations in Naval Architecture* 59, *Trial Trip Analysis* 62.
Juul Steens Alle 9, Hellerup, Denmark.
Telephone: HE-7325.

Prokhorov, Aleksandr Mikhailovich; Soviet physicist; b. 11 July 1916, Atherton, Australia; s. of Mikhail Ivanovitch Prokhorov and Mariya Ivanova Prokhorova; m. Galina Alexeyevna (Shelepina); one s.; ed. Leningrad State Univ.
Physicist, P. N. Lebedev Inst. of Physics, U.S.S.R. Acad. of Sciences 39-; Academician-Sec. Dept. of Physics and Astronomy 73; Vice-Dir. P. N. Lebedev Physical Inst. 72; Corresp. mem. U.S.S.R. Acad. of Sciences (Dept. of Pure and Applied Physics) 60-66, mem. 66-; mem. C.P.S.U. 50-; Lenin Prize 59; Nobel Prize for Physics for work in field of quantum electronics 64; Chair. Soviet Nat. Cttee. U.R.S.I.; Editor in Chief of Soviet Encyclopaedia 69-; Hero of Socialist Labour, Order of Lenin (twice), etc.
P.N. Lebedev Institute of Physics, U.S.S.R. Academy of Sciences, 53 Leninsky Prospekt, Moscow, U.S.S.R.

Prokhorov, Vasili Ilich; Soviet trade union official; b. 1906; ed. Moscow Higher Technical School.
Designing Engineer 30-40; Soviet Army Service 40-41; Sec. Zhdanov District Cttee. of C.P.S.U. 41-46; Deputy U.S.S.R. Supreme Soviet 66-; Sec. Comm. for Legislative Proposals Soviet Nationalities; Sec. All-Union Central Council of Trade Unions 55-; mem. C.P.S.U. Cen. Cttee. 71-; Order of the Patriotic War 1st class, Order of the Red Banner of Labour, etc.
All-Union Central Council of Trade Unions, Leninsky prospekt 42, Moscow, U.S.S.R.

Prokofiev, Mikhail Alekseyevich; Soviet chemist and government official; b. 18 Nov. 1910, Voskresenskoe, Smolensk Region; ed. Moscow State Univ.
Member C.P.S.U. 41-; Dep. Dir. Chem. Research Unit, Moscow Univ. 39-41, 46-48; Deputy and First Deputy Minister of Higher and Specialized Secondary Educ. of U.S.S.R. 51-66; Minister of Educ. of U.S.S.R. 66-; Deputy to U.S.S.R. Supreme Soviet 66-; mem. Cttee. U.S.S.R. Parliamentary Group; mem. C.P.S.U. Cen, Cttee. 71-; mem. Acad. of Pedagogical Sciences, Corresp. mem. U.S.S.R. Acad. of Sciences 66-.
Ministry of Education of U.S.S.R., Moscow, U.S.S.R.

Prokosch, Frederic, PH.D.; American writer; b. 17 May 1908, Madison, Wis.; s. of Prof. Eduard Prokosch and Matilda Dapprich; ed. Yale Univ. and King's Coll., Cambridge.
Leisure interests: lepidoptery, book binding and printing, philately, bridge (tournament play).
Publs. Novels: *The Asiatics* 35, *The Seven Who Fled* 37, *Night of the Poor* 39, *The Skies of Europe* 41, *The Conspirators* 43, *Age of Thunder* 45, *The Idols of the Cave* 46, *Storm and Echo* 48, *Nine Days to Mukalla* 53, *A Tale for Midnight* 55, *A Ballad of Love* 60, *The Seven Sisters* 63, *The Dark Dancer* 65, *The Wreck of the Cassandra* 66, *The Missolonghi Manuscript* 68, *America, My Wilderness* 72; poems: *The Assassins* 36, *The Carnival* 38, *Death at Sea* 40, *Chosen Poems* 44, *Some Poems of Hoelderlin* (Trans.) 44.
Ma Trouvaille, 06 Plan de Grasse, France.

Promyslov, Vladimir Fedorovich; Soviet construction engineer and politician; b. 15 July 1908, Kabuzhskaya, Ozersky; ed. Moscow Construction Engineering Institute.

Member C.P.S.U. 28-; fmr. Deputy Chair. Council of Ministers, R.S.F.S.R. and Minister of Construction, R.S.F.S.R. 59-63; Chair. Exec. Cttee., Moscow City Soviet of Working People's Deputies 63-; mem. Central Cttee. C.P.S.U. 61-; Deputy U.S.S.R. Supreme Soviet 62-; mem. Foreign Affairs Comm. Soviet of Union; mem. Cttee. U.S.S.R. Parliamentary Group.
Moscow City Soviet, Ulitsa Gorkogo 13, Moscow, U.S.S.R.

Pronk, Johannes Pieter, D.ECON.; Netherlands politician; b. 16 March 1940, The Hague; s. of Johannes Pronk and Elisabeth H. v. Geel; m. Catharina Zuurmond; one s. one d.; ed. Gymnasium and Erasmus Univ.
Research Fellow, Netherlands Econ. Inst., Lecturer in Devt. Econs., Erasmus Univ. 65-71; mem. Parl. 71-73; mem. European Parl. 73; Minister of Devt. Co-operation 73-; Socialist Party.
Rondo 48, Krimpen/Yssel, Netherlands.
Telephone: 01807-2259.

Prouvost, Jean; French business executive and editor; b. 24 April 1885; m. 2nd Elisabeth Danet 1974; ed. Collège de Boulogne-sur-Mer and Beaumont Coll., England.
Manager, Soc. Prouvost and Co., La Lainière de Roubaix; Founding Pres. Filatures Prouvost Masurel; Dir.-Gen. of *Paris-Midi* and *Paris-Soir* 32-39; Minister of Information 40; now Pres., Dir.-Gen., Chief Editor of *Marie-Claire, La Maison de Marie-Claire, Paris-Match*; Dir. *Télé 7 Jours, Les Parents*; Mayor of Yvoy-le-Marron.
216 rue de Rivoli, Paris; *Paris Match*, 51 rue Pierre Charron, Paris 8e; and Domaine Saint-Jean, 41 Yvoy-le-Marron, France.
Telephone: 261-51-01.

Provenchères, Monsignor Charles de, L. ès L., L. en THÉOLOGIE; French ecclesiastic; b. 3 Sept. 1904; ed. Institut du Sacré-Coeur, Moulins, and Institut Catholique, Paris.
Ordained Priest 28; Curate at Cusset 28-31; Spiritual Dir. at Institut du Sacré-Coeur Moulins 31-38; Dir. Petit Séminaire Moulins 38-45; served French Army 39-40; Archbishop of Aix, Arles and Embrun 45-; Légion d'Honneur, Croix de Guerre, Hon. Dr. (Laval).
7 cours de la Trinité, 13625 Aix-en Provence, France.
Telephone: (91)-23-32-98.

Proxmire, William, M.A.; American politician; b. 11 Nov. 1915; ed. Yale and Harvard Univs.
U.S. Army Intelligence Service 41-46; State Assemblyman (Dem.) for Wisconsin 51-52; U.S. Senator from Wisconsin 57-; Chair. Senate Banking Cttee. 75-; Pres. Artcraft Press, Waterloo, Wisconsin 54-57; Democrat.
Senate Office Building, Washington, D.C. 20510, U.S.A.

Prŭšek, Jaroslav, PH.D., DR. SC.; Czechoslovak university professor; b. 14 Sept. 1906, Prague; ed. Oriental studies at Prague, Gothenburg, Halle, Leipzig, and in China and Japan.
Studied Chinese linguistics, literature and history; Prof. of Chinese and Japanese Literature, Charles Univ., Prague 47-69; corresp. mem. Czechoslovak Acad. of Sciences 52-55, Academician 55, and Chair. of Linguistics and Literature Section 55-61; Dir. Oriental Inst. of Czechoslovak Acad. of Sciences 54-71; Laureate of the State Prize 52 and 54; Hon. Ph.D. Humboldt Univ. Berlin 60; Hon. mem. German Acad. of Sciences; Silver Plaque of Czechoslovak Acad. of Sciences; mem. Saxon Acad. of Sciences 65, Order of Labour 66; Vice-Pres. Int. Fed. of Modern Languages and Literature 69-.
Publs. *History of Chinese Literature* 55, *Studies in Modern Chinese Literature* 64, *The Origins and the Authors of hua-pen* 68, *Three Sketches of Chinese Literature* 69, *Chinese History and Literature* 70.
Gogolova 2, Prague 1; and Oriental Institute, Lázeňská 4, Prague 1, Czechoslovakia.

Pryce, Maurice Henry Lecorney, M.A., PH.D., F.R.S.; British university professor; b. 24 Jan. 1913, Croydon, Surrey; s. of William John Pryce and Hortense E. Lecorney; m. 1st Susanne M. Born 1939, 2nd Freda M. Oldham 1961; one s. three d.; ed. Royal Grammar School, Guildford, Trinity Coll., Cambridge, and Princeton Univ., U.S.A.
Fellow, Trinity Coll. and Faculty Asst. Lecturer Cambridge 37; Reader in Theoretical Physics Liverpool Univ. 39; Admiralty Signal Establishment 41; Nat. Research Council of Canada (Atomic Energy) 44; University Lecturer and Fellow of Trinity Coll. Cambridge 45; Visiting Prof. Princeton Univ. 50-51; Wykeham Prof. of Physics, Oxford 46-54; Henry Overton Wills Prof. of Physics, Bristol 54-64; Prof. Univ. of Southern California 64-68; Prof. of Physics, Univ. of British Columbia 68-.
Leisure interests: walking, music.
Physics Department, Univ. of British Columbia, Vancouver V6T IW5; 4754 W. 6th Avenue, Vancouver 8, Canada.
Telephone: 604-224-1596 (Home).

Pryce-Jones, Alan Payan, T.D.; British writer and editor; b. 18 Nov. 1908; ed. Eton Coll. and Magdalen Coll., Oxford.
Asst. Editor *The London Mercury* 28-32; Editor *The Times Literary Supplement* 48-59; served in France, Austria, Italy, Second World War 39-45, Lieut.-Col. 45; Trustee Nat. Portrait Gallery 50-61; Dir. The Old Vic Trust 50-61; mem. Council of Royal Coll. of Music 56-61; Program Assoc. (Humanities and Arts) Ford Foundation 61-63; Book Critic *New York Herald-Tribune* 63-67; Theatre Critic *Theatre Arts* 63-.
Publs. *The Spring Journey* 31, *People in the South* 32, *27 Poems* 35, *Private Opinion* 36, *Prose Literature 1945-50*; libretto for Berkeley's opera *Nelson* 54; *The American Imagination* (edited) 60, *Vanity Fair* (libretto) 62.
46 John Street, Newport, R.I. 02340, U.S.A.

Psurtsev, Nikolai Demyanovich; (retd.) Soviet politician; b. 1900; ed. Higher Communications School and Military Electro-Technical Acad.
Member C.P.S.U. 19-; served Red Army, Chief of Communications, Soviet-Finnish War 39-40; Col.-Gen. in Second World War; Minister of Communications 48; Order of Lenin; Four Orders of the Red Banner, Order of Kutuzov, Order of Suvorov; Alt. mem. C.P.S.U. Central Cttee 61; Deputy to U.S.S.R. Supreme Soviet 54.
c/o Ministry of Communications, 7 Ulitsa Gorkogo, Moscow, U.S.S.R.

Pucci, Emilio, Marchese di Barsento, M.A., DR.SOC.SC.; Italian couturier; b. 20 Nov. 1914, Naples; s. of Orazio Pucci and Augusta Pavoncelli; m. Cristina Nannini di Casabianca 1959; one s. one d.; ed. Reed Coll., Portland (Oregon) and Florence Univ.
Air Force torpedo-bomber pilot 38-52; started his own fashion house 50; Neiman Marcus Fashion Award 54, Burdine Fashion Award 55; *Sports Illustrated* "Sporting Look" Designer's Award 61; Pres. Emilio Pucci, Paris, Florence, New York, Munich Gesellschaft, Antico Setificio Fiorentino, Nat. Asscn. Shoe Stylists, Consorzio del Chianti Classico; Vice-Pres. Richard Ginori U.S.A., Mittel (Soc. Industriale Mediterranea) Milan; mem. Board of Dirs. Richard Ginori, Italy, Wells Rich Greene Inc. New York; mem. of Parliament for Florence Liberal Party 63-72; City Counsellor Florence 64-; works under name "Emilio Pucci", Paris and New York; mem. Chamber of Deputies; Liberal.
Leisure interests: skiing, swimming, tennis, fencing and flying.
Palazzo Pucci, 6 Via dei Pucci, Florence, Italy.
Telephone: 283-061-62.

Puck, Theodore Thomas, B.S., PH.D.; American professor of biophysics; b. 24 Sept. 1916, Chicago, Ill.; s. of Joseph and Bessie Puckowitz; m. Mary R. Hill 1946; three d.; ed. Univ. of Chicago.
University Fellow, Dept. of Chem., Univ. of Chicago 38-40, Research Assoc., Dept. of Medicine 41-45, Asst. Prof. Depts. of Medicine and Biochem. 45-47; mem. Comm. on Airborne Infections, Army Epidemiological Board, Office of Surgeon-Gen. 44-46; Senior Fellow, Calif. Inst. of Technology, Pasadena 47-48; Prof. and Chair. Dept. of Biophysics, Univ. of Colorado Medical Center 48-67; Research Prof. of Biophysics, Univ. of Colorado Medical Center 67-; Research Prof. of American Cancer Soc. 66-; Dir. Eleanor Roosevelt Inst. for Cancer Research, Univ. of Colorado Medical Center 62-; mem. Nat. Acad. of Sciences 60-; Fellow American Acad. of Arts and Sciences 67-; Lasker Award 58; Borden Award 59; Stearns Award, Univ. of Colorado 59; General Rose Memorial Hospital Award 60; Nat. Acad. of Science Award 60; Distinguished Service Award of Univ. of Chicago Med. Alumni Asscn. 69; Gross Horwitz Prize of Columbia Univ. in Coll. Biology and Biochemistry 73, Inst of Med. Award 74.
Leisure interests: skiing, hiking, travel, music.
Publs. Many papers (some jointly) in the field of somatic cell genetics, concerning airborne infection, virus interaction with host cells, mammalian cell biochemical genetics, human cytogenetics and mammalian radiation biology; occasional papers dealing with interaction of science and society.
Office: University of Colorado Medical Center, 4200 East Ninth Avenue, Denver, Colo. 80220; Home: 10 South Albion, Denver, Colo. 80220, U.S.A.
Telephone: 303-394-7152 (Office); 303-333-6938 (Home).

Pudney, John Sleigh; British poet, novelist and dramatist; b. 19 Jan. 1909, Langley, Bucks.; s. of Harry William Pudney and Mabel Sleigh; m. 1st Crystal Herbert 1934 (marriage dissolved), 2nd Monica Grant Forbes 1955; one s. two d.; ed. Gresham's School, Holt.
B.B.C. writer and feature programmes producer 33; columnist *News Chronicle* 30; joined R.A.F. 40; *Daily Express* book critic 47; Literary Editor *News Review* 48-50; Editor *Pick of To-day's Short Stories* (annual).
Leisure interest: bonfires.
Publs. Poetry: *Collected Poems* 57, *Sixpenny Songs, The Trampoline* 59, *Spill Out* 67, *Spandrels* 69, *Take This Orange* 71, *Selected Poems* 67-73 73; prose: *The Green Grass Grew All Round* 42, *Who Only England Know* 43, *Air Battle of Malta* 44, *Atlantic Bridge* 45, *Laboratory of the Air* 48, *King George VI* 52, *The Queen's People* 53, *The Smallest Room* 54, *Six Great Aviators* 55, *The Seven Skies* 59, *Home and Away* 60, *The Camel Fighter* 64, *Bristol Fashion* 60, *A Pride of Unicorns* 60, *The Golden Age of Steam* 67, *De Lessep's Canal* 68 *Crossing London's River* 72, *Brunel and His World* 74, *London's Docks* 75, *Lewis Carrol and his World* 76; novels: *Estuary* 48, *Shuffley Wanderers* 49, *The Accomplice* 50, *Hero of a Summer's Day* 57, *Thin Air* 61, *The Long Time Growing Up* 71; collections of short stories: *It Breathed Down My Neck* 46, *The Europeans* 48; children's books: the "Fred and I" series 50-65, *The Grandfather Clock* 57, *Crossing the Road* 58, "The Hartwarp" series 62-67, *For Johnny* (radio documentary) 65, *The Concorde* (film script) 65, *Les Festins des Morts* (English film script) 67; plays: *Ted* 69, *Hymm to Bacchus* 69, *The Little Giant* 72, *The Break Through* 75.
4 Macartney House, Chesterfield Walk, Greenwich Park, London, SE10 8HJ, England.
Telephone: 01-858-0482.

Puech, Henri-Charles, L. ÈS L., Agrégé de l'Université; French professor; b. 20 July 1902, Montpellier; s. of Paul Puech and Madeleine Le Gras; m. Renée Chigot 1929; ed. Lycée de Montpellier, Lycée Louis-le-Grand (Paris), Ecole Normale Supérieure, Université de Paris (Sorbonne), Ecole Pratique des Hautes Etudes (Paris).

Director of Studies, Ecole Pratique des Hautes Etudes, Sorbonne 29-72; Prof. of History of Religions, Collège de France 52-72, mem. Académie des Inscriptions et Belles-Lettres 62-, Pres. 68; Pres. Institut de France 68; Vice-Pres. Int. Asscn. for Study of History of Religions 50-65; Corresp. Fellow British Acad. 70; Officier Légion d'Honneur, Commdr. Ordre Nat du Mérite, Commdr. Ordre des Palmes Académiques; Dr. h.c. (Utrecht).

Publs. *Le Traité contre les Bogomiles de Cosmas le Prêtre* 45, *Le Manichéisme: Son fondateur, sa doctrine* 49, *Histoire des Religions* (editor) 70, *L'Evangile selon Thomas*, and other Coptic Gnostic Writings of the *Nag Hammadi Library*; numerous articles and memoirs in various scientific reviews.

79 rue du Cherche-Midi, 75006 Paris, France.

Puiseux, Robert; French industrialist; b. 1 March 1892; ed. Lycée Henri IV and Lycée Saint Louis, Paris.
Former President, Soc. Anonyme André Citroën, Hon. Pres. 58-; joint Man. Dir. Compagnie Générale des Establissements Michelin 38-59, mem. Supervisory Board 59-; joint Man. Dir. Manufacture Française des Pneumatiques 51-59; Officier Légion d'Honneur, Croix de Guerre (1914-18), Commdr. de l'Economie Nat.
4 cité Chabrol, 63000 Clermont-Ferrand, France.

Puja, Frigyes; Hungarian politician; b. 1921, Batton-ya, County Békés; ed. Party Acad.
Joined Communist Party 44; Sec. of Party, District Battonya 45-46; mem. Party Cttee., Deputy Head of Appointments Cttee., County Csanád 46-49; Sub-Dept. Leader Cen. Board of Hungarian Working People's Party 49-53; Amb. to Sweden 53-55, to Austria 55-59; Deputy Foreign Minister 59-63; Head Foreign Dept., Cen. Cttee. of Hungarian Socialist Workers' Party 63-68; mem. Cen. Cttee. HSWP 66-; First Deputy Foreign Minister 68-73; Sec. of State for Foreign Affairs 73; Minister of Foreign Affairs 74-; Labour Order of Merit, golden degree 70.
Publs. *The Problems of Coexistence* 67, *Unity and Debate in the International Communist Movement* 69, *Why is the Warsaw Treaty Organization Necessary?* 70, *The Road to Security* 71, *Principles and Doctrines* 72, *Socialist Foreign Policy* 73, and various articles on int. affairs.
Ministry of Foreign Affairs, II. Bem József rakpart 47, H-1394 Budapest, Hungary.
Telephone: 350-100.

Pukhova, Zoya Pavlovna; Soviet worker and politician; b. 1936; ed. special secondary school.
Weaver, Ivanovo Spinning Mill 52-73; Dir. "8th March" Textile Factory 73-; mem. C.P.S.U. 62-; Deputy U.S.S.R. Supreme Soviet 66-, mem. Presidium 70-; Hero of Socialist Labour, Order of Lenin, "Hammer and Sickle" Gold Medal and other decorations.
Ivanovo Spinning Mill, U.S.S.R.

Pulinckx, Raymond; Belgian business administrator; b. 24; ed. Inst. supérieur de Commerce de l'Etat, Anvers.
Chef de Cabinet, Ministry of Econ. Affairs 58-61; Dir.-Gen., Fed. of Belgian Industries 61-62, Dir.-Gen. and Administrator 62-70, Exec. Vice-Pres. 70, now Man. Dir.; Chevalier de l'Ordre de Léopold, Commdr. de l'Ordre de la Couronne de Chêne, Officier de l'Ordre de la Couronne.
4 rue Ravenstein, Brussels 1, Belgium.

Pulitzer, Joseph, Jr., A.B.; American newspaper editor and publisher; b. 13 May 1913; ed. Harvard Univ.
Reporter *San Francisco News* 35; mem. staff *St. Louis Post-Dispatch* 36-48, Assoc. Editor 48-55, Editor and Publr. 55-; Vice-Pres. Pulitzer Publ. Co. 40-55, Pres. 55-; served U.S. Navy 42-45.
St. Louis Post-Dispatch, Pulitzer Publishing Co., 1133 Franklin Avenue, St. Louis, Mo. 63101, U.S.A.

Pullai, Árpád; Hungarian politician; b. 1925.
Former County Sec., Hungarian Fed. of Democratic Youth; Hungarian Working People's Party 48, fmr. First Sec. Debrecen Municipal Party Cttee., fmr. Editor *Party Life*; Sec. Central Cttee. Hungarian Communist Youth Union 58-61, First Sec. 61-64; mem. Central Cttee. Hungarian Socialist Workers' Party 62-; Sec. of Central Cttee. 66-; Chief of Party and Mass Org. Dept. of Central Cttee. of Hungarian Socialist Workers' Party 64-66; mem. Parl. 71, 75.
Hungarian Socialist Workers' Party, Szécheny rakpart 19, H-1387 Budapest V, Hungary.

Pulliam, Eugene Collins; American newspaper publisher; b. 3 May 1889; ed. Graduate Prep. School, Baker Univ. Kansas, and DePauw Univ. Ind.
Began as a reporter Kansas City (Mo.) *Star* 10-12; Editor Atchison (Kan.) *Champion* 12-15, Franklin (Ind.) *Star* 15-23; Publ. Lebanon (Ind.) *Reporter* 23; Pres. Central Newspapers Inc., Indianapolis Newspapers Inc., Muncie Newspapers Inc., Phoenix Newspapers Inc., Phoenix, Ariz.; Dir. New York Central Railroad, Associated Press, American Inst. for Foreign Trade.
307 North Pennsylvania Street, Indianapolis, Indiana, U.S.A.

Pullicino, Anthony Alfred, LL.D.; Maltese diplomatist and lawyer; b. 14 March 1917, Malta, G.C.; s. of Sir Phillip and Lady (née Maud Samut) Pullicino; m. Edith Baker 1944; three s. two d.; ed. St. Aloysius Coll., Malta and Royal Univ. of Malta.
Member, Malta Legislative Assembly 50-54, Speaker 51-52; mem. Council, Commonwealth Parl. Asscn.; High Commr. to Australia 65-69, to U.K. 70-71; Amb. to U.S.S.R. 71-; mem. Public Service Comm., Malta 71.
Leisure interest: golf.
4/191 Tower Road, Sliema, Malta.

Pumphrey, Sir (John) Laurence, K.C.M.G.; British diplomatist; b. 22 July 1916; ed. Winchester and New Coll., Oxford.
Foreign Office 45-47; Asst. Private Sec. to Prime Minister 47-50; Berlin 50-53; Foreign Office 53-60, Head of Establishment and Org. Dept. 55-60; Counsellor and Head of Chancery, Singapore 60-63, Belgrade 63-65; Deputy High Commr., Kenya 65-67; High Commr. to Zambia 67-71; High Commr. to Pakistan 71-72, Amb. Jan. 72-.
British Embassy, Islamabad, Pakistan.

Pünder, Herman (Joseph), JUR.D.; German lawyer; b. 1 April 1888; m. 1920; three s. one d.; studied law in Freiburg, London, Berlin.
Gerichtsassessor in Prussian Ministry of Justice 19; Referent in Reich Ministry of Finance 19-25; Ministerial Dir. at Reich Chancellery 25-26; State Sec. and Head of Reich Chancellery 26-32; Regional Pres. in Münster 32-33; arrested by Gestapo 44; inmate of concentration camps until liberated by U.S. Army 44; Lord Mayor of Cologne Nov. 45-May 48; Chair. of Bizonal Exec. Cttee., Frankfurt 48-49; mem. of North Rhine/Westphalia Diet 46-49; mem. Cologne City Council 45-48; mem. Centre Party 22 until dissolution by Hitler; co-founder of Christian Democratic Union in Westphalia 45; Hon. mem. Management of German Municipal League, Hon. Pres. German-Belgian-Luxembourg Chamber of Commerce Cologne; mem. Bundestag 49-57; fmr. Vice-Pres. E.C.S.C. Common Assembly, mem. Consultative Assembly, Council of Europe; Grosses Bundesverdienstkreuz mit Stern und Schulterband.
Marienburger Strasse 42, 5 Köln-Marienburg, Federal Republic of Germany.
Telephone: Cologne 384350.

Pungan, Vasile, D.ECON.SC.; Romanian university professor and diplomatist; b. 2 Nov. 1926, Bălănesti, Gorj County; one d.; ed. Inst. of Economics, Bucharest.

Dean of Faculty, Agronomical Inst. "Nicolae Bălcescu", Bucharest 54; Gen. Dir., Ministry of Agriculture and Forestry 55-58; Counsellor, Romanian Embassy, Washington 59-62; Dir. and mem. Foreign Office Coll. 63-66; Amb. to U.K. 66-72; Counsellor of the Pres. of the Socialist Repub. of Romania 73; Alt. mem. Cen. Cttee. of R.C.P., mem. 72-; Romanian decorations.
Consilul de Stat al R.S.R., Bucharest, Romania.

Puntsagnorov, Tsevegzhauyn; Mongolian diplomatist; b. 11 Aug. 1924, Ulan Bator; *m.*; three *c.*; ed. Moscow Univ.
Former lecturer, Mongolian State Univ.; served on Cen. Cttee. of Mongolian People's Revolutionary Party until 62; Editor-in-Chief *Unen* (official Govt. and Party newspaper) 62; Deputy to Great People's Khural (Parliament); Deputy Chair. Council of Ministers 63-72; Minister of Culture 71-72; Perm. Rep. to UN Sept. 72-; corresp. mem. Acad. of Sciences of Mongolia. Publs. a book on Mongolian history and numerous articles.
Permanent Mission of Mongolia to United Nations, 6 East 77th Street, New York, N.Y. 10021, U.S.A.

Purcell, Edward Mills, PH.D.; American physicist; b. 30 Aug. 1912, Taylorville, Ill.; *s.* of Edward A. Purcell and Mary E. Mills Purcell; *m.* Beth Busser 1937; two *s.*; ed. Purdue Univ., Technische Hochschule, Karlsruhe, and Harvard Univ.
Instructor in Physics, Harvard 38-40; Radiation Laboratory, Mass. Inst. of Technology 40-46 (Faculty Instructor on leave of absence, Harvard 41-45); Assoc. Prof. of Physics, Harvard 45-49, Prof. of Physics 49-58, Donner Prof. of Science 58-60, Gerhard Gade Univ. Prof. 60-; Senior Fellow, Society of Fellows, Harvard Univ. 50-71; Pres. American Physical Soc. 70; mem. Nat. Acad. of Sciences of U.S.A., American Acad. of Arts and Sciences, American Philosophical Soc.; cowinner Nobel Prize in Physics 52.
Lyman Laboratory of Physics, Harvard University, Cambridge, Mass. 02138; 5 Wright Street, Cambridge, Mass. 02138, U.S.A.
Telephone: 617-495-2860.

Purdy, James; American writer; b. 1923; ed. Chicago and Spain.
Interpreter, editor and other posts in Cuba, Mexico, Washington, D.C.
Publs. novels: *Don't Call Me by My Right Name* 56, *63: Dream Palace* 56, *Color of Darkness* 57, *Malcolm* 59, *The Nephew* 60, *Cabot Wright Begins* 63, *Eustace Chisholm and the Works* 67, *Sleepers in Moon-Crowned Valleys* (Part I *Jeremy's Version* 70, Part II *The House of the Solitary Maggot* 71), *I am Elijah Thrush* 72; play: *Children is All* 62; *An Oyster is a Wealthy Beast* (story and poems) 67, *Mr. Evening* 68 (story and poems), *On the Rebound* 70 (story and poems), *The Running Sun* (poems) 71; L.P. Recordings: *63: Dream Palace* 68, *Eventide and Other Stories* 69.
c/o Jonathan Cape Ltd., 30 Bedford Square, London, W.C.1, England.

Puri, Kanwal Raj, B.A., LL.B.; Indian banker; b. 25 Feb. 1920, Lahore (now in Pakistan); *s.* of Mukand Lal and Iqbal Devi; *m.* Abnash Puri; three *s.* one *d.* Managing Dir. Sunlight of India; Div. Man. Life Insurance Corpn. of India 56-61, Zonal Man. 61-60, Exec. Dir. 70-72, Man. Dir. 72, Chair. 72-75; Gov. Reserve Bank of India Aug. 75-.
Leisure interest: golf.
Reserve Bank of India, Central Office, Bombay; Residence: Reserve Bank House, 5 Carmichael Road, Bombay 26, India.
Telephone: 268634 (Office); 361634 (Home).

Puri, Yogendra Krishan; Indian diplomatist; b. 25 July 1916, Mardan, N.W.F.P., India (now Pakistan); *s.* of late Judge Dewan Radha Krishan Puri and Rattan

Devi; *m.* Savitri Chand 1940; one *s.* two *d.*; ed. Government Coll., Lahore, and Univ. Coll., London.
Indian Civil Service, Assam 38-46; Dep. Sec., Ministry of Finance 47; Ministry without Portfolio 47; Dir.-Gen. Ministry of Rehabilitation 48; Dep. High Commr. in Pakistan 48-51; Dep. Sec. Ministry of External Affairs 51-53; Counsellor Indian Embassy, Paris 53-55; Counsellor Indian High Comm., London 55; Jt. Sec. Ministry of External Affairs 55-60; High Commr. in Malaya 60-63, in Malaysia 63-64; Amb. to Morocco and Tunisia 64-67, to Sweden 68-69; High Commr. in Ceylon 70-72; Amb. to Fed. Repub. of Germany 72-75; Pres. Council, Colombo Plan 72-73; mem. India Del. 2nd Afro-Asian Conf., Algiers 65.
Leisure interests: literature, golf, philately.
c/o Ministry of External Affairs, New Delhi 110011, India.

Pusack, George Williams, M.S.(MECH.ENG.); American oil executive; b. 26 Sept. 1920, Michigan; *s.* of George F. Pusack and Winifred Williams; *m.* Marian Preston 1942; two *s.* one *d.*; ed. Univ. of Michigan, Univ. of Pennsylvania.
Aero Engineer, U.S. Navy 42-45; Corporal, U.S.A.F. 45-46; Tech. Service and Research Man., Mobil Oil Corpn., U.S.A. 46-53, Production Eng. Man. 53-59, Int. Supply and Distribution Man. 59-69, Vice-Pres. N. American Div. 69-73, Regional Exec. Mobil Europe, London 73-76, Chair. Mobil Oil Co. Ltd., London 76-; Tech. Adviser to U.S. Dept. of Interior, Eastern Region Administrator, Emergency Petroleum and Gas Admin. 68-73.
Leisure interests: golf, travel, teacher, layreader, vestryman and warden of Episcopal Church.
5 Cornwall House, Cornwall Gardens, London, SW7 4AE, England.
Telephone: 01-937-4275.

Pusey, Nathan Marsh, A.M., PH.D.; American administrator; b. 4 April 1907, Council Bluffs, Iowa; *s.* of John Marsh and Rosa Drake Pusey; *m.* Anne Woodward 1936; two *s.* one *d.*; ed. Harvard Univ.
Asst. Harvard Univ. 33-34; Sophomore Tutor, Lawrence Coll. 35-38; Asst. Prof. History and Literature, Scripps Coll., Claremont, Calif. 38-40; Asst. Prof. Classics, Wesleyan Univ. 40-43, Assoc. Prof. 43-44; Pres. Lawrence Coll., Appleton, Wis. 44-53; Pres. Harvard Univ. 53-71; mem. American Acad. of Arts and Sciences; Trustee, Carnegie Foundation for Advancement of Teaching; Pres. Andrew W. Mellon Foundation 71-; numerous honorary degrees.
Leisure inteserts: reading, gardening, sailing.
Publ. *The Age of the Scholar* 63.
140 West 62nd Street, New York, N.Y. 10021, U.S.A.

Pushkin, Boris Konstantinovich; Soviet foreign trade official; ed. Moscow Technical Inst. of Fisheries and the Fish Industry.
Member C.P.S.U. 40-; Official, U.S.S.R. Trade Representation in Hungary 45-47; Dir. of Office, *Tekhnoexport* Trust 47-55; Vice-Chair. *Mashinoexport* Trust 55-63; Dir. of Office, *Tekhsnabexport* 63-64; U.S.S.R. Commercial Rep. in Hungary 64-69; Chair. *Zapchastexport* 69-; Order of Red Banner of Labour (twice), Order of Patriotic War, Second Degree.
Zapchastexport, Ministry of Foreign Trade, Smolenskaya-Sennaya ploschchad 32-34, Moscow, U.S.S.R.

Putrament, Jerzy; Polish writer and journalist; b. 14 Nov. 1910, Minsk, U.S.S.R.; *s.* of Władysław Putrament and Maria Rutkowska; *m.* Anastazja Putrament; one *s.* one *d.*; ed. Univ. of Wilno.
Editor, *Rzeczpospolita*, Lublin, *Dziennik Polski*, Cracow 44-45; Amb. to Switzerland 45-47, to France 48-50; Deputy to Seym 53-61; Gen. Sec. Union of Polish Writers 50-54, Vice-Chair. 59-; mem. Cen. Cttee. Polish United Workers Party 64-; Editor, *Kultura*,

Miesięcznik Literacki, Chief Editor, *Współczesność*-71, *Literatura* 72-; State Prize 53, 55, 64; Prize of Minister of Nat. Defence 62; Commdr. Cross with Star of Polonia Restituta, Order of Builders of People's Poland 74 and many other awards.
Leisure interest: fishing.
Publs. Poems: *Wojna i wiosna* (War and Spring) 44, *Wiersze wybrane* (Selected Verse) 51; Novels: *Rzeczywistość* (Reality) 48, *Wrzesień* (September) 52, *Rozstaje* (Crossroads) 54, *Pasierbowie* (Stepchildren) 65, *Odyniec* (The Boar), *Puszcza* (The Forest), *Małowierni* (Petty Believers), *Pół wieku* (Half Century of Memoirs), *Być sobą* (To Be Oneself) 68, *Bołdyn* 69, *20 Lipca* (20th July) 73, and numerous short stories.
Zarząd Główny ZLP, Krakowskie Przedmieście 87/89, 00-079 Warsaw, Poland.

Puyan, Anushiran; Iranian physician; b. 1933, Shiraz; ed. Paris Univ.
Principal Medical Coll., Nat. Univ., Teheran 66; Chancellor of Nat. Univ. 68; Minister of Health 73-; Pres. World Health Org. Assembly 74; mem. Soc. of Surgeons, Paris; Royal Merit Award.
Ministry of Health, Teheran, Iran.

Puyana, Rafael; Colombian harpsichordist; b. 4 Oct. 1931, Bogotá; unmarried.
Studied under Wanda Landowska; now lives in Paris but gives performances throughout the world; records for Philips and CBS.
Leisure interests: collecting old keyboard instruments.

c/o Basil Douglas Ltd., 8 St. George's Terrace, London NW1 8XJ, England.
Telephone: 01-722 7142.

Puzanov, Aleksandr Mikhailovich; Soviet diplomatist; b. 25 Oct. 1926, Lezhkovka, Ivanovo Region; ed. Plesski Agricultural Technicum.
State and Econ. activity 37-52; Chair. Council of Ministers of R.S.F.S.R. 52-56; Ambassador to Dem. People's Repub. of Korea 57-62, to Yugoslavia 62-67, to Bulgaria 67-72; on staff Ministry of Foreign Affairs 72-; mem. C.P.S.U. Central Cttee. 52-.
Ministry of Foreign Affairs, 32-34 Smolenskaya-Sennaya ploshchad, Moscow, U.S.S.R.

Pyka, Tadeusz, DR.ECON.SC.; Polish politician; b. 17 May 1930, Piekary Śląskie, Tarnowskie Góry District; ed. Acad. of Mining and Metallurgy, Cracow.
Head of Casting Section, M. Buczek Foundry, Sosnowiec 51-55; with Voivodship Cttee. Polish United Workers' Party, Katowice 55-, Instructor, then Deputy Head of Econ. Dept., later Head 55-64; First Sec. Town Cttee. PUWP, Bytom 64-67; Econ. Sec., then Second Sec. Voivodship Cttee. PUWP, Katowice 67-74; Deputy to Seym (Parl.) 72-; Chair. Seym Comm. for Foreign Trade 72-74; First Vice-Chair. Planning Comm. attached to Council of Ministers March 74-; mem. Polish United Workers' Party 53-, Deputy mem. Cen. Cttee. 64-71, mem. Cen. Cttee. 71-.
Komisja Planowania Przy Radzie Ministrów, Plac Trzech Krzyży 3/5, 00-535 Warsaw, Poland.

Q

Qaboos bin Said; Omani ruler; b. 18 Nov. 1940, Salalah; *s.* of Said Bin Taimur 14th descendant of the ruling dynasty of Albusaid Family; ed. privately in U.K., Royal Mil. Acad., Sandhurst.
Sultan of Oman (following deposition of his father) July 70-.
Leisure interests: reading, horse-riding, shooting.
Sultan's Palace, Muscat, Oman.

Qaddafi, Col. Mu'ammar al- (*see* Gaddafi, Col. Mu'ammar al-).

Qader, Yahia Hasan Abd al- (*see* Kader, Yehia Abdel).

Qassim, Awn al-Sharif, M.A., PH.D.; Sudanese politician; b. 15 Oct. 1933, Halfaiat al Molook; ed. Univs. of Khartoum, London and Edinburgh.
Lecturer, School of Oriental and African Studies, London Univ. 59-61; Lecturer, Dept. of Arabic, Univ. of Khartoum 61-64, Senior Lecturer 69, Dir. Translation Section 69-70; Minister of Waqfs and Religious Affairs 71-73.
c/o Ministry of Waqfs and Religious Affairs, Khartoum, Sudan.

Qatar, Emir of, (*see* Khalifa bin Hamad al-Thani, Sheikh).

Quadros, Jânio; Brazilian politician: b. 1917 ed; São. Paulo School of Law.
Part-time high school teacher; practised law; mem. São Paulo City Council 47-59; State Deputy 50; Mayor, São Paulo City 52-55; Gov. São Paulo State 55-59; Federal Deputy 59-60; Pres. of Brazil Jan.-Aug. 61 (resigned); political rights suspended for 10 years, April 64; arrested and banished to Corumba (near Bolivian border) July 68.
Gauruja, nr. São Paulo, Brazil.

Quaison-Sackey, Alexander, M.A.; Ghanaian diplomatist; b. 9 Aug. 1924; ed. Mfantsipim School, Exeter Coll. Oxford, London School of Economics and Lincoln's Inn, London.
Former teacher at Mfantsipim School and with Gold Coast Secretariat; Labour Officer Gold Coast 52-55; Attaché British Embassy, Rio de Janeiro 56; Head of Chancery and Official Sec. Ghana High Commission, London 57-59; Perm. Rep. of Ghana to UN 59-65; Minister of Foreign Affairs 65-66; mem. Convention People's Party; Vice-Pres. UN Gen. Assembly 61-62, Pres. UN Gen. Assembly 64-65; Amb. to Cuba 61, to Mexico 62; under house arrest 66, released June 66; Hon. LL.D. (Univ. of Calif.) 65.
Publ. *Africa Unbound* 63.
Alcumbia Lodge, P.O.B. 104, Winneba, Ghana.

Quandt, Herbert; German industrialist; b. 22 June 1910, Pritzwald, Mark Brandenburg.
Chairman of Board of Dirs. Bayerische Motoren Werke AG, Munich, Varta Batterie AG, Hanover, Ceag Dominit AG, Dortmund, Busch Jaeger Gesellschaft für Industrie-Beteiligungen, Frankfurt, Byk Gulden Lomberg Chemische Fabrik GmbH, Konstanz, Milupa AG, Friedrichsdorf; Deputy Chair. of Board of Dirs. Daimler-Benz AG, Stuttgart; Dir. Deutsche Bank AG, Frankfurt; Chair. of Board of Management Varta AG, Frankfurt; Hon. D.Phil.
Seedammweg 55, 638 Bad Homburg v.d.H., Federal Republic of Germany.
Telephone: 06172-404213.

Quant, Mary, O.B.E., F.S.I.A.; British (Welsh) fashion and cosmetic designer; b. 11 Feb. 1934, London; *d.* of Jack Quant and Mildred (née Jones); *m.* Alexander Plunket Greene 1957; one *s.*; ed. Goldsmiths Coll. of Art, London.
Started career in Chelsea, London 54; retrospective exhbn. of 60's fashion 74; *Sunday Times* Int. Fashion

Award; Rex Award (U.S.A.); Annual Design Medal, Soc. of Industrial Artists and Designers; Piavolo d'Oro (Italy); Royal Designer for Industry.
Publ. *Quant by Quant* 66.
Mary Quant Ltd., 3 Ives Street, London, S.W.3, England.
Telephone: 01-584-8781.

Quastel, J. Hirsch, C.C., D.SC., PH.D., A.R.C.S., F.R.I.C., F.R.S.C., F.R.S.; British biochemist; b. 2 Oct. 1899, Sheffield; *s.* of late Jonas and Flora Quastel; *m.* 1st Henrietta Jungman 1931 (deceased 1973), two *s.* one *d.*; *m.* 2nd Shulamit Ricardo 1975; ed. Sheffield Central Secondary School, Imperial Coll. of Science, London, and Trinity Coll., Cambridge.
Served First World War; Fellow Trinity Coll. 24; Dir. of Research Cardiff City Mental Hospital 29-41; Fellow Royal Soc. London 40, Royal Soc. of Canada 52; Dir. Unit of Soil Metabolism, Agricultural Research Council 41-47; Prof. of Biochemistry McGill Univ. Montreal, Canada 47-66; Dir. McGill, Montreal Gen. Hospital Research Inst. 47-65; Dir. McGill Unit of Cell Metabolism 65-66; Prof. of Neurochemistry and Hon. Prof. of Biochemistry, Univ. of British Columbia 66-; Pres. Montreal Physiological Soc. 50; Fellow New York Acad. of Sciences, North Pacific Soc. of Neuropsychology; mem. Neurochemical Comm., Int. Brain Research Org.; North American Comm. for Study of Alcohol Problems; Hon. Fellow Japanese Pharmacological Soc., Canadian Soc. of Microbiologists, Indian Brain Research Asscn., Biochemical Soc. of U.K.; Leeuwenhoek Lecturer Royal Soc. 55, Kearney Foundation Lecturer (Univ. of Calif.), B. Priestman Lecturer (Univ. of New Brunswick); Hon. Consultant Montreal Gen. Hospital, etc.; Pres. Canadian Biochemical Soc. 63; Royal Soc. Leverhulme Visiting Prof., India 66; Seventh Jubilee Lecturer of Biochemical Soc. of U.K. 74; mem. Board Govs., Hebrew Univ., Jerusalem 50-; Meldola Medal 27, Pasteur Medal 55, Canadian Microbiological Soc. Award 65, Gairdner Int. Award for Medical Research 74, Flavelle Medal of Royal Soc., Canada 74; Hon. D.Sc. (McGill) 69, Hon. Ph.D. (Jerusalem) 70.
Publs. *Neurochemistry, Metabolic Inhibitors, Chemistry of Brain Metabolism in Health and Disease, Methods in Medical Research*, Vol. 9.
Division of Neurological Science, Department of Psychiatry, University of British Columbia, Vancouver 8, B.C.; Home: 4585 Langara Avenue, Vancouver 8, B.C., Canada.
Telephone: 228-2202; Home: 224-4755.

Quayle, Anthony, C.B.E.; British theatre director, producer and actor; b. 7 Sept. 1913, Ainsdale, Lancs.; *s.* of Arthur and Esther Overton; *m.* Dorothy Hyson 1947; one *s.* two *d.*; ed. Rugby and Royal Acad. of Dramatic Art.
First stage appearance at Q Theatre 31; joined the Old Vic Company 32; first appearance in New York at Henry Miller Theatre 36; with Old Vic at Elsinore 37, and on tour of Continent and Egypt 39; served in Royal Artillery 39-45; reappeared at the Criterion Theatre in *The Rivals* 45; produced *Crime and Punishment* at the New Theatre 46; produced and acted in Shakespeare's plays at Shakespeare Memorial Theatre, Stratford-on-Avon Feb. 48-56; Dir. Shakespeare Memorial Theatre 49-56; produced *Harvey* London 48, directed 75; produced Terence Rattigan's *Who is Sylvia*, Criterion Theatre, London Oct. 50; toured Australia with Shakespeare Memorial Theatre Company 49-50 and Jan.-Oct. 53; acted name part in *Tamburlaine* New York Jan. 56; acted in *A View From The Bridge*, London 56; European tour of *Titus Andronicus* 57; dir. and acted in *The Firstborn*, New York, acted in

Long Day's Journey into Night, Edinburgh, London and Broadway 58, *Look After Lulu, Chin-Chin* 60, *The Right Honourable Gentleman* 64, *Incident at Vichy* 66, *Sleuth*, London 70, N.Y. 70-71, *Everyman* 74; Dir. *Lady Windermere's Fan*, London 66, *Galileo*, N.Y. 67, *Harvey*, London 75; Actor/Dir. Clarence Brown Co., Tenn. 75.

Films: *Woman in a Dressing Gown, The Man Who Wouldn't Talk, Ice Cold in Alex, Serious Charge, Tarzan's Greatest Adventure, The Challenge, The Guns of Navarone, H.M.S. Defiant* 61, *Lawrence of Arabia* 62, *The Fall of the Roman Empire* 64, *Operation Crossbow, A Study in Terror, Anne of the Thousand Days, Bequest to the Nation, The Tamarind Seed*; also radio and TV plays including *Q.B.7, Moses* 74, *Great Expectations* 74, *Benjamin Franklin* 74, *David and Saul* 75; directed colour production *Caesar and Cleopatra* for Nat. Broadcasting Co. Television; producer *The Idiot* (Nat. Theatre) 70.

Leisure interest: sailing.

Publs. *Eight Hours from England, On Such a Night*.

c/o I.C.M., 22 Grafton Street, London, W.1, England.

Queen, Ellery (*see* Dannay, Frederic).

Queguiner, Jean; French international maritime official; b. 2 June 1921, Paris; m. Marguerite Gaillard 1952; one s. one d.; ed. Lycée Buffon, Collège Stanislas and Faculté de Droit, Paris, and Coll. of Admin. of Maritime Affairs, St. Malo.

Head of Maritime District of Caen 53; Deputy Head of Coll. of Admin. of Maritime Affairs 55-, Head of Safety of Navigation Section 63; Vice-Chair. Maritime Safety Cttee., UN Inter-Governmental Maritime Consultative Org. (IMCO) 65-68, Deputy Sec.-Gen. of IMCO 68-; Chevalier, Légion d'Honneur.

Office: 101-104 Piccadilly, London W.1; Home: 32 Melton Court, Old Brompton Road, London, S.W.7, England.

Telephone: 01-499-9040 (Office).

Queneau, Raymond; French writer; b. 21 Feb. 1903; ed. Univ. of Paris.

Director and Editor *Encyclopédie de la Pléiade*; mem. Acad. Goncourt.

Publs. include *Le Chiendent* 33, *Odile* 37, *Un rude hiver* 40, *Pierrot, mon ami* 42, *Exercices de style* 47, *L'instant fatal* 48, *Petite Cosmogonie Portative* 50, *Le dimanche de la vie* 52, *Zazie dans le Métro* 59, *Les Fleurs bleues* 65, *Une histoire modèle* 66, *Courir les Rues* 67, *Battre la Campagne* 68, *Le Vol d'Icare* 68, *Fendre les Flots* 69, *Le Voyage en Grèce* 73, *Morale Elémentaire* 75.

c/o Gallimard, 5 rue Sebastien-Bottin, Paris, France.

Quennell, Peter, C.B.E.; British writer; b. 9 March 1905, Bickley, Kent; s. of M. and C. H. B. Quennell; ed. Berkhamsted Grammar School and Balliol Coll., Oxford.

Former Prof. of English Literature, Tokyo Bunrika Daigaku 30; Editor *Cornhill Magazine* 44-51, *History Today* 51-.

Publs. *Baudelaire and the Symbolists, A Superficial Journey, Byron: The Years of Fame, Byron in Italy* 41, *Caroline of England, Four Portraits* 45, *Ruskin: The Portrait of a Prophet* 52, *Spring in Sicily, The Singular Preference, Hogarth's Progress* 54, *The Sign of the Fish* 60, *Shakespeare: the poet and his background* 63, *Aspects of 17th Century Verse, Memoirs of the Comte de Gramont* (trans.), *Letters of Madame de Lieven*; Editor: *Memoirs of William Hickey, Byron: A Self Portrait (1798-1824),* Mayhew's *London Labour and the London Poor* (3 vols.), *Alexander Pope: the Education of Genius* 68, *Romantic England* 70, *Marcel Proust: 1871-1922* 71; *Casanova in London* (essays) 71, *Samuel Johnson, His Friends and Enemies* 72.

History Today, 388 Strand, London, WC2R 0LT, England.

Telephone: 01-836-5444.

Quentin-Baxter, R. Q., LL.B.; New Zealand lawyer; b. 17 Jan. 1922, Christchurch; ed. Univ. of New Zealand. Joined diplomatic staff, Dept. of External Affairs 49; Deputy High Commr. in Canada 57-58; Deputy Perm. Rep. New Zealand Mission to UN 59-61; Counsellor, Tokyo 61-64; Asst. Sec. for Legal, Consular and S. Pacific Affairs 64-68, concurrently senior Commr. for New Zealand, S. Pacific Comm.; Prof. of Jurisprudence and Constitutional Law, Victoria Univ. of Wellington 68-; Rep. to Comm. on Human Rights (Chair. 69); mem. Int. Law Comm. 71-; del. to various int. confs. and several sessions of UN Gen. Assembly.

Faculty of Law, Victoria University of Wellington, P.O. Box 196, Wellington, New Zealand.

Quenum, Dr. Comlan Alfred Auguste; Benin physician; b. 1926, Ouidah; m. Angèle Desirée Lalou; five s. three d.; ed. African School of Medicine and Pharmacy, Dakar, and Faculty of Medicine, Univ. of Bordeaux. Formerly at Centre d'Etudes Nucléaires, Saclay; later Dakar Faculty of Medicine; Prof. of Histology and Embryology, Dakar Faculty of Medicine 62-64; Regional Dir. for Africa, World Health Org. 65-.

World Health Organization Regional Office for Africa, P.O. Box 6, Brazzaville, Congo People's Republic.

Telephone: 30-72, 73, 74.

Querejazu Calvo, Roberto; Bolivian diplomatist and writer; b. 24 Nov. 1913, Sucre; s. of Mamerto Querejazu and Delfina Calvo de Querejazu; m. Dorothy Lewis 1943; one s. one d.; ed. Sucre.

Director of Minister's Cabinet, Legal and Political Depts., Bolivian Foreign Service 39-42; First Sec. Embassy, Brazil 43; Counsellor, London 47, Chargé d'Affaires, London 48-52; Under-Sec. of State for Foreign Affairs, Bolivia 66; Sec.-Gen. Bolivian Del. to UN 46; Bolivian Rep. to UN Conf. on Tin 51, to Interamerican Conf. for De-Nuclearization of Latin America, Mexico 64; Del. to UN Gen. Assembly 65, Second Interamerican Conf. Extraordinary, Rio de Janeiro 65; Amb. to U.K. and also accred. to Netherlands 66-70; Cross of the Chaco and Award of Mil. Merit, Bolivia and several foreign awards.

Leisure interests: tennis, swimming.

Publs. *Masamaclay—History of the Chaco War* 65 (2nd, 3rd edns. 75), *Bolivia and the English* 72, *Llallagua—History of Tin Mining in Bolivia* 76; articles in Bolivian newspapers.

98 Great Brownings, College Road, London, SE21 7HR, England.

Telephone: 01-670-5293.

Quero-Chiesa, Luis; American artist, writer and civic leader; b. 23 Jan. 1911, Ponce, Puerto Rico; s. of Pedro Quero and Manuela Chiesa; m. Filo Santiago 1933; two d.; ed. Parsons School of Design, New York. In field of graphic arts 32-; Vice-Pres. in charge of art, Roy Blumenthal Int. Associates Inc. (int. public relations firm) 48-; Pres. Puerto Rican Inst., New York 59-; mem. Board of Higher Educ. of New York City 64-, Chair. Nov. 71-; founder, Youth Group (for young Puerto Ricans) 60; Nat. Chair. Puerto-Rican Hispanic Div., Democratic Nat. Cttee.; Academician, Acad. of Arts and Sciences of Puerto Rico; mem. Inst. of Hispanic Culture, Madrid, Ateneo Puertorriqueno of San Juan; Hon. mem. Hispanic Soc. of America; represented in travelling exhbn. of American artists; research in Puerto Rican history and culture.

Leisure interests: music, art, literature.

Publs. *An Outline of Puerto Rican Culture, Spain or the United States: A Puerto Rican Cultural Dilemma, Puerto Ricans in New York: A Transplanted Community*, several vols. of short stories, numerous articles, essays and lectures.

Roy Blumenthal International Associates Inc., 1 East 57 Street, New York, N.Y. 10022; Home: 144-45 35th Avenue, Flushing, N.Y. 11367, S.A.U.

Quijano, Raúl Alberto; Argentine diplomatist; b. 13 Dec. 1923, Santa Fé; *s.* of Mateo Quijano and Sara Aldao de Quijano; *m.* Mercedes Santander 1963; one *d.*; ed. La Salle Coll., Buenos Aires and Univ. of Buenos Aires.

Attaché, Argentine Foreign Service 47, served in Perm. Mission to UN, in India and Pakistan; Third Sec., South Africa 50; Second Sec., Perm. Mission to UN 55, First Sec. 58, Counsellor 59, Minister 63; Amb. and Dir.-Gen. of Political Affairs, Ministry of Foreign Affairs 67; Amb. and Perm. Rep. to OAS 69-75; Chair. Int. Civil Service Comm. (UN) 75-76; Minister of Foreign Affairs 76; decorations from Govts. of Chile, Italy, Norway, Japan.

Ministerio de Asuntos Exteriores, Buenos Aires, Argentina.

Quine, Willard Van Orman, M.A., PH.D., LL.D., L.H.D., D.LITT.; American philosophy professor; b. 25 June 1908, Akron, Ohio; *s.* of Cloyd R. Quine and Hattie van Orman Quine; *m.* Marjorie Boynton 1948; one *s.* three *d.*; ed. Oberlin Coll. and Harvard Univ.

Sheldon Travelling Fellow (Harvard) to Vienna, Prague and Warsaw 32-33; Junior Fellow, Soc. of Fellows, Harvard 33-36, Faculty Instructor in Philosophy 36-41, Assoc. Prof. 41-48, Prof. of Philosophy 48-56, Edgar Pierce Prof. of Philosophy, Harvard Univ. 56-; U.S. Naval Reserve 42-46; Visiting Prof. Univ. of São Paulo, Brazil 42, George Eastman Visiting Prof., Oxford Univ. 53-54; Shearman Lecturer, Univ. of London 54; Pres. Asscn. for Symbolic Logic 53-55; mem. Inst. for Advanced Study, Princeton 56-57; Fellow, Center for Advanced Study in Behavioral Sciences, Stanford 58-59; Gavin David Young Lecturer, Adelaide Univ., Australia 59; Visiting Prof. Tokyo Univ. 59; Fellow, Wesleyan Univ. Center for Advanced Study 65; Fellow, American Acad. of Arts and Sciences, American Philosophical Soc.; Corresp. Fellow British Acad.; Visiting Prof. Rockefeller Univ. 68, Collège de France 69; Paul Carus Lecturer, New York 71, Saville Fellow, Oxford 73-74; Pres. American Philosophical Asscn. 58; mem. Institut Int. de Philosophie, Académie Int. de Philosophie des Sciences, Instituto Brasileiro de Filosofia; eight hon. degrees; Butler Medal, Columbia Univ.

Leisure interests: languages, geography.

Publs. *A System of Logistic* 34, *Mathematical Logic* 40, *Elementary Logic* 41, *O Sentido da Nova Lógica* 44, *Methods of Logic* 50, *From a Logical Point of View* 53, *Word and Object* 60, *Set Theory and its Logic* 63, *The Ways of Paradox* 66, *Selected Logic Papers* 66, *Ontological Relativity* 69, *Philosophy of Logic* 70, *Web of Belief* (with J. S. Ullian) 70, *The Roots of Reference* 73.

38 Chestnut Street, Boston, Mass. 02108, U.S.A.
Telephone: 742-2813.

Quinn, Anthony Rudolph Oaxaca; American actor-director of Irish and Mexican descent; b. 21 April 1916; ed. Los Angeles.

First appeared on stage 36; has appeared in the films *Viva Zapata, Lust for Life, La Strada, Man from Del Rio, The Black Orchid, Warlock, Last Train from Gun Hill, Heller in Pink Tights, Savage Innocents, Guns of Navarone, Barabbas, Lawrence of Arabia, The Visit, Zorba the Greek, The Twenty-Fifth Hour, Guns for San Sebastian, The Secret of Santa Vittoria, The Shoes of the Fisherman, The Magus, A Dream of Kings, The Last Warrior, Flap, Across 110th Street, The Don is Dead* 73, *The Marseille Contract* 74; Dir. *The Bucaneer* 58; Venice Film Festival Award for *La Strada* 54, American Motion Picture Acad. Awards for Best Supporting Actor for *Viva Zapata* 52, and *Lust for Life* 56.

Publ. *The Original Sin* (autobiog.).

333 Las Casa Avenue, Pacific Palisades, Calif. 90272, U.S.A.

Quinn, William Francis, LL.B.; American lawyer; b. 13 July 1919, Rochester, N.Y.; *s.* of Charles Alvin and Elizabeth (Dorrity) Quinn; *m.* Nancy E. Witbeck 1942; seven *c.*; ed. St. Louis Univ. and Harvard Law School.

Served in U.S. Navy 42-46; worked with Honolulu law firm of Robertson, Castle and Anthony 47-57 and partner 50-57; admitted to practice in Territorial and Fed. Courts 48; mem. Exec. Cttee. of the Bar Asscn. of Hawaii and Advisory membership Cttee. of the American Bar Asscn.; mem. Hawaii Statehood Comm. 57; Territorial Gov. of Hawaii 57-59; first Gov. of State of Hawaii July 59-62; mem. Exec. Cttee. Nat. Govs. Conf. 59-60; Pres. Pacific Area Travel Asscn. 60-61; Partner, Quinn and Moore 62-64; Exec. Vice-Pres. Dole Co., Honolulu 64-65, Pres. 65-72; Partner, Jenks, Kidwell, Goodsill & Anderson (law firm) 72-73; Partner, Goodsill, Anderson and Quinn 73-; Republican.

Office: 16th Floor, Castle & Cooke Building, Financial Plaza of the Pacific, Honolulu, Hawaii 96813; Home: 1365 Laukahi Street, Honolulu, Hawaii 96821, U.S.A. Telephone: 531-5066 (Office).

Quinn, William John, B.A., LL.B.; American lawyer and railway executive; b. 8 May 1911, St. Paul, Minn.; *m.* Floy I. Heinen 1942; four *s.* four *d.*; ed. St. Thomas Coll. St. Paul (Minn.) and Univ. of Minnesota Law School.

Law practice St. Paul (Minn.) 35-37, Asst. District Attorney 37-40; Attorney Soo Line Railroad 40-42; Special Agent Fed. Bureau of Investigation 42-45; Asst. Commercial Counsel Soo Line Railroad 45, Commerce Counsel 46-52, Asst. Gen. Counsel 52, Gen. Counsel 52-53, Vice-Pres. and Gen. Counsel 53-54; Gen. Solicitor Chicago, Milwaukee, St. Paul and Pacific Railroad 54-55, Vice-Pres. and Gen. Counsel 55-58, Pres. 58-66, Chair. 70-; Pres. Chicago Burlington & Quincy RR Co. 66-70; Vice-Chair. Burlington Northern Inc. 70; Chair., Pres., Chicago Milwaukee Corpn. 72-; Dir. Asscn. of American Railroads, Skil Corpn., Clow Corpn., Continental Illinois Nat. Bank & Trust Co. of Chicago, Universal Oil Products Co., Continental Illinois Corpn., Peavey Co., Nat. Railroad Passenger Corpn.; Hon. LL.D. St. Thomas Coll. (St. Paul, Minn.).

Leisure interests: golf, travel, viewing sports on television.

874 Union Station Building, Chicago, Illinois 60606; Home: 1201 Chatfield Road, Winnetka, Ill. 60093, U.S.A. Telephone: 312-236-7600.

Quintana, Carlos, M.SC., M.B.A.; Mexican engineer; b. 1912, Puebla; *s.* of Miguel A. Quintana and Maria-Cruz Gomez-Daza; *m.* Lulu Pali Solomon 1944; three *s.* three *d.*; ed. Instituto Politécnico Nacional, Mexico, and Columbia and Harvard Univs., U.S.A.

Former Prof. of Engineering, Nat. Polytechnic Inst., Mexico City; in Dept. of Industrial Research, Bank of Mexico 44-50; Man. Ayotla Textile S.A., Mexico 48-49; Dir. Industrial Development Division, Econ. Comm. for Latin America (ECLA) 50-60, Exec. Sec. ECLA 67-72; Manager Industrial Programming, Nacional Financiera 60-67; mem. Governing Council, Mexican Inst. for Technological Research 61-67; mem. Govt. Econ. Missions to Yugoslavia, Czechoslovakia, U.S.S.R. and Poland; mem. FAO Advisory Comm. on Pulp and Paper, Rome 60-67; Asst. Sec.-Gen. UN 67; Chair. of Board Centro Latinoamericano de Demografía; Exec. Sec. Econ. Comm. for Latin America 67-72; Man. Fondo Nacional de Fomento Industrial (Mexico) 72; Gen. Credit Man. Nacional Financiera S.A. (official devt. bank of Mexico) 74, Gen. Man. (Technical Advice) 76.

Leisure interests: music (piano), swimming.

Isabel la Católica 51, Mexico 1, D.F.; Home: Sierra Guadarrana 155, Mexico 10, D.F., Mexico. Telephone: 520-86-99 (Home).

Quintanilla, Luis, B.S., L. ès L., PH.D.; Mexican diplomatist; b. 1900, Paris, France; s. of Luis Quintanilla Fortuno and Ana María del Valle Lerdo de Tejada; m. 1st Ruth V. Stallsmith 1922, 2nd Sara Cordero 1950; three s. one d.; ed. Sorbonne and Johns Hopkins Univ.

Entered diplomatic service 21, Protocol Div. 22; 3rd Sec. Washington 23, and Sec. Guatemala 26, Washington 29; 1st Sec. Paris 30; Sec.-Gen. Del. to League of Nations 32; Minister-Res., Washington 35, Counsellor 29, Minister 38, Ambassador 42-45; adviser to Mexican Del. at UN Conf., San Francisco 45; Ambassador to Colombia 45, to Organization of American States, Washington, D.C. 45; Rep. Inter-American Peace Comm. 48-, Chair. of Council 49-50; Chair. Inter-American Peace Commission, Washington, D.C. 48; Mexican del. to Second Gen. Assembly, UN, New York 47, and 9th Int. Conf. of American States, Bogotá, Colombia 48; Dir. Inst. Nacional de la Vivienda 59-64; Prof. Political Science Nat. Univ. of Mexico; Columnist of newspaper *Novedades*.

Leisure interests: sports, chess.

Publs. *Avión* 23, *Radio* 24, *Teatro Mexicano del Murciélago* 24, *The Other Side of the Mexican Church Question* 35, *A Latin American Speaks* 43, 46, *Pan Americanism and Democracy* 52, *Democracia y Panamericanismo* 52, *Bergsonismo y Política* 53, *The Caribbean; Contemporary Trends* 53, *The Control of Foreign Relations in Modern Nations* 57, *The Greatness of Woodrow Wilson* 57, *Pintura Moderna* 68.

Reyna 87, San Angel Inn, Mexico 20, D.F., Mexico. Telephone: 48-20-06.

Quintero, H.E. Cardinal José Humberto; Venezuelan ecclesiastic; b. 22 Sept. 1902, Mucuchíes.

Ordained priest 26; Archbishop of Acrida 53-60; Archbishop of Caracas 60-; created Cardinal and titular priest of St. Andrew and St. Gregory at Monte Celio 61; mem. Sacred Congregations of Sacraments, of Rites and of Seminaries and Univs. of Study.

Arzobispado, Apartado 954, Caracas, Venezuela.

Quiroga, Elena; Spanish writer.

Awarded Nadal Prize 50.

Publs. *Viento del Norte* 51, *La Sangre* 52, *Algo Pasa en la Calle* 54, *La Enferma* 54, *La Careta* 55, *Plácida, La Joven* 56, *La Ultima Corrida* 58, *Tristura* 60 (1960 Critics' Prize), *Escribo tu Nombre* 65 (chosen to represent Spain in the Rómulo Gallegos literary competition).

Real Academia de la Historia, Léon 21, Madrid 14, Spain.

Quizpez Asin-Mas, Carlos; Peruvian painter; b. 1906; ed. National School of Fine Arts, Lima, and San Fernando School of Fine Arts, Madrid.

Federal Art Project, Calif.; Prof. School of Fine Arts, Lima 43; Prof. of Mural Painting and Principal Teacher of Drawing and Painting; many mural paintings in public buildings in Peru; Gold Medal of Municipality of Lima for murals in Chamber of Deputies 41.

854 Los Eucaliptos, Chaclacayo, Lima, Peru.

Quoniam, Pierre; French museum director; b. 1920, Bois-Colombes; ed. Ecole des Hautes Etudes, Paris.

Curator, Musée Bardo, Tunis 48-53; Asst. in ancient history, Faculté des Lettres, Paris; Research Officer, Centre Nationale de la Recherche Scientifique (CNRS); Insp. Gen. of provincial museums 62-72; Dir. Musée du Louvre 72-.

Palais du Louvre, 75001 Paris, France.

Qureshi, Anwar Iqbal, B.A., M.A., M.SC., PH.D.; Pakistani economist; b. 10 April 1910, Jullundur; s. of Sio Albaj Mufti Mohammad Yusaf Ali; m. Zubeda Khatoon 1932; one d.; ed. Foreman Christian Coll., Lahore, London School of Economics, Trinity Coll., Dublin.

Professor, Head Econs. Dept., Osmania Univ. 37-47; Econ. Adviser, Govt. of Hyderabad 44-47; Dep. Econ. Adviser Govt. of Pakistan 47-51; Adviser, Int. Monetary Fund (Latin America, Middle and Far Eastern Dept.) 51-55; Financial and Econ. Adviser, Saudi Arabia 55-59; Econ. Adviser, Govt. of Pakistan 61-70; Pres. Pakistan Econ. Asscn.; mem. Preparatory Cttee. Asian Devt. Bank; Pakistani Rep. at numerous int. econ. confs.; Satara-i-Quait Azam 65; Additional Sec. 68; retd.; Chief Economist Sabasun Technical Services, Lahore 74-; mem. Council for Econ. Advisory Affairs, Govt. of Pakistan 75-.

Leisure interests: gardening, collection of books.

Publs. *The Farmer and His Debt* 34, *Agricultural Credit* 36, *The State and Economic Life* 37, *State Banks for India* 39, *Islam and the Theory of Interest* 46, *The Future of Co-operative Movement in India* 47, *Economic Development of Hyderabad* 48, *Development in Pakistan's Economy since the Revolution* 60, *Pakistan's March on Road to Prosperity* 65, *An Economic Appraisal of the Mujib's Six Points* 70, *Economic Problems Facing Pakistan* 71.

Al-Haniyah, 295/3 Sarwar Road, Lahore Cantt, West Pakistan.

Telephone: 70431.

Qureshi, Ishtiaq Husain, M.A., PH.D.; Pakistani scholar and politician; b. 20 Nov. 1903, Patiali; s. of Qazi Sadiq Husain Qureshi and Begum Altafunnisa Qureshi; m. Nayab Begum Qureshi 1920 (died 1965); one s.; ed. St. Stephen's Coll. (Univ. of Delhi), and Sidney Sussex Coll., Cambridge.

Lecturer in History, St. Stephen's Coll. 28; Reader in History Univ. of Delhi 40, Prof. and Head of Dept. of History 44, Dean of Faculty of Arts 45; mem. for Bengal, Constituent Assembly of Pakistan 47; Prof. of History and Head of Dept. of History, Punjab Univ. 48; Deputy Minister of the Interior, Information and Broadcasting, Refugees and Rehabilitation, Govt. of Pakistan 49, Minister of State 50, Minister for Refugees and Rehabilitation, Information and Broadcasting 51-53; Minister of Education 53-55; mem. Advisory Council of Islamic Ideology 62-63; Visiting Prof. Columbia Univ., New York 55-60; Dir. Central Inst. of Islamic Research, Karachi 60-62; Vice-Chancellor Univ. of Karachi 61-71; Star of Pakistan 64.

Leisure interests: gardening, travel.

Publs. *The Administration of the Sultanate of Delhi* 41, *The Pakistani Way of Life* 56, *The Muslim Community in the Indo-Pakistan Sub-Continent* 62, *The Struggle for Pakistan* 65, *The Administration of the Moghul Empire* 67, *Ulema in Politics* 72, *Education in Pakistan* 75.

Zeba Manzar, 1 Sharafabad, Shahid-i-Millat Road, Karachi 5, Pakistan.

Telephone: 411339.

Qureshi, Moeen Ahmad, M.A., PH.D.; Pakistani economist and international official; b. 26 June 1930, Lahore; s. of Mohyeddin Ahmad Qureshi and Khursheed Jabin; m. Lilo Elizabeth Richter 1958; two s. two d.; ed. Islamia Coll. and Govt. Coll., Univ. of Punjab and Indiana Univ., U.S.A.

Social Science Consultant, Ford Foundation, Pakistan 53; Hon. Lecturer, Univ. of Karachi 53-54; Asst. Chief, Planning Comm., Govt. of Pakistan 54-56, Deputy Chief 56-58; Economist, Int. Monetary Fund 58-61, Div. Chief 61-65, Adviser Africa Dept. 65-66, Resident Rep. Ghana 66-68, Senior Adviser 68-70; Econ. Adviser Int. Finance Corpn. 70-74, Vice-Pres. Sept. 74-.

Leisure interests: tennis, collecting antiques.

Publs. various articles in economic journals.

International Finance Corporation, 1818 H Street, N.W., Washington, D.C. 20433; Home: 11108 Gilchrist Court, Potomac Falls, Potomac, Md. 20854, U.S.A. Telephone: (202) 477-4121 (Office); (301) 299-9542 (Home).

R

Rabaeus, Bengt, M.A.; Swedish diplomatist; b. 4 May 1917, Vara; *m.* Birgitta M. Svensson 1946; three *s.*; ed. Kungliga Universitet i Uppsala.
Entered Foreign Service 46, served Prague, Paris, Swedish Del. to UN (New York); Counsellor, Swedish Del. to OEEC, Paris 57-59; Head of Political Div., Foreign Office, Stockholm 59-61; First Counsellor, Paris 61-62; Amb. to Algeria 63-66; Deputy Sec.-Gen. European Free Trade Asscn. (EFTA) 66-72, Sec.-Gen. 72-76; Deputy Perm. Under-Sec. of State, Ministry of Foreign Affairs 76-.
Ministry of Foreign Affairs, Box 16121, 103 23 Stockholm 16, Sweden.
Telephone: (08) 7631000.

Rabasa, Emilio O.; Mexican lawyer and politician; b. 23 Jan. 1925; *s.* of Oscar Rabasa and Lilia M. de Rabasa; ed. Univ. Nacional Autónoma de México.
Lecturer for 15 years, Univ. Nacional Autónoma de México; lawyer to Dept. of Banks and Money, Secr. of Finance; legal consultant to Heads of Agrarian Dept., Secr. of Agriculture and Cattle, and to Secr. of Health and Nat. Assistance; Head of Legal Dept. of Banco Nacional de Credito Ejidal; Dir. Afianzadora Mexicana; Dir. Banco Cinematográfico 65, concurrently Man. Dir. Compañiá Operadora de Teatros, Estudios Crurubusco, Películas Nacionales, CIMEX and PROCINEMEX; Amb. to U.S.A. 70; Sec. of Foreign Affairs 70-75.
c/o Secretaría de Relaciones Exteriores, México, D.F., Mexico.

Rabetafika, Joseph Albert Blaise, L. ès L.; Malagasy diplomatist; b. 3 Feb. 1932, Tananarive.
Teacher in U.K., France and Madagascar 53-59; joined Ministry of Defence, France 60; mem. Madagascar del. to independence negotiations with France 60; Counsellor in charge of cultural affairs and information, Madagascar diplomatic mission, France 60-63; Perm. del. to UNESCO, Paris 61-63; Head, Del. to IBE Confs., Geneva 61-63; mem. del. to UN Gen. Assembly 62-69; Perm. Rep. to UN 69-; Vice-Pres. ECOSOC 73.
Permanent Mission of Madagascar to the United Nations, 801 Second Avenue, Suite 404, New York, N.Y. 10017, U.S.A.

Rabi, Isidor Isaac, B.CHEM., PH.D.; American professor of physics; b. 29 July 1898; ed. Cornell and Columbia Univs.
Tutor in Physics Coll. City of N.Y. 24-27; Barnard Fellow Columbia 27-28; Int. Educ. Board Fellow Munich, Copenhagen, Hamburg, Leipzig, and Zürich 28-29; Ernest Kempton Adams Fellow 35; Lecturer Physics Columbia Univ. 29-30; Asst. Prof. Colombia Univ. 30-35, Assoc. Prof. 35-37, Prof. 37-64, Univ. Prof. 64-67, Univ. Prof. Emer. 67-; Higgins Prof. of Physics 51-64; Exec. Officer Dept. of Physics 45-49; Scientific Advisory Cttee. Ballistic Research Laboratory Aberdeen 39-65; Assoc. Dir. Radiation Laboratory M.I.T. 40-45; Chair. Vacuum Tube Devt. Cttee. (NDRC) 42-45; Consultant Los Alamos 43-45, 56-; Council American Physical Soc. 45-, Pres. 50-51; Council Nat. Acad. 46-49; Consultant Joint Research and Devt. Board 46-48; Gen. Advisory Cttee. Atomic Energy Comm. 46-56, Chair. 52-56, Consultant 56-; Trustee, Associated Universities, Inc. 46-, Pres. 61-62, Chair. 62-63; Editor Board *Physical Review* 35-38; mem. American Acad. of Sciences, Nat. Acad. 40-; del. UNESCO Conf. 50; Vice-Pres. Int. Conf. on the Peaceful Uses of Atomic Energy 55-58; mem. Presidential Science Advisory Cttee., NATO Science Advisory Cttee., I.A.E.A. Scientific Advisory Cttee., Adviser to UN Science Cttee., Council on Foreign Relations, Hudson Inst., Sigma Xi; Hon. D.Sc. Princeton, Harvard, Birmingham, Clark, Technion, Brandeis and Coimbra Univs., and Adelphi and Franklin Marshall Colls., LL.D. Dropsie Coll., Sc.D. Williams Coll., L.H.D. Hebrew Union Coll. and Oklahoma City Univ., Litt.D. Jewish Theological Seminary of America, D.Sc. Hebrew Univ., Jerusalem 72; Prize, American Asscn. for Advancement of Sciences 39; Elliot Cresson Medal, Franklin Inst. 42; Nobel Prize in Physics 44; Commdr., Order of the Southern Cross, Brazil 52; Barnard Medal 60; Priestly Memorial Award, Dickenson Coll. 64; Niels Bohr Int. Gold Medal 67; Atoms for Peace Award (U.S.) 67; Visiting Prof. UN Conf. on Peaceful Uses of Atomic Energy 71.
Work in the field of nuclear physics, quantum mechanics, and molecular beams.
Publs. *My Life and Times as a Physicist* 60, *Man and Science* 68, *Science: The Centre of Culture.*
450 Riverside Drive, New York, N.Y. 10027, U.S.A.

Rabin, Maj.-Gen. Yitzhak; Israeli army officer and politician; b. 1 March 1922, Jerusalem; ed. Agricultural School, Kfar Tabor, and Staff Coll., England.
Palmach commands 43-48, including War of Independence; represented Israel Defence Forces (I.D.F.) at Rhodes armistice negotiations; fmr. Head of Training Dept. I.D.F.; C.-in-C. Northern Command 56-59; Head, Manpower Branch 59-60; Deputy Chief of Staff and Head, Gen. Staff Branch 60-64, Chief of Staff I.D.F. 64-68; Amb. to U.S.A. 67-73; mem. Knesset Jan. 74-; Minister of Labour March-April 74; Leader Labour Party May 74-; Prime Minister June 74-, also Minister of Communications 74-75; Hon. Doctorates, Jerusalem Univ. 67, Dropsie Coll. 68, Brandeis Univ. 68, Yeshiva Univ. 68, Coll. of Jewish Studies, Chicago 69, Univ. of Miami 70, Hebrew Union Coll., Boston 71.
Office of the Prime Minister, Jerusalem, Israel.

Rabinowitz, Yehoshua; Israeli politician; b. 13 Nov. 1911; ed. Poland and Tel Aviv School of Law and Econs.
Management posts in Israeli Co-operative Movement 48-56; mem. Tel Aviv Municipal Council 56-59, Deputy Mayor 59-61, Chair. Financial, Townbuilding and Planning Cttees. 61-69, Mayor of Tel Aviv 69-74; Minister of Housing March-May 74, of Finance June 74-; Labour Party.
Ministry of Finance, Jerusalem, Israel.

Raborn, Vice-Admiral William Francis, Jr.; American naval officer (retd.); b. 8 June 1905; ed. U.S. Naval Acad.
Ensign U.S. Navy 28; Dep. Dir. Guided Missile Div., Office Chief Naval Operations 52-54; Commanding Officer U.S.S. *Bennington* 54-55; Asst. Chief Staff Commdr. Atlantic Fleet 55; Dir. Special Projects, Fleet Ballistic Missile System (*Polaris*) 55-62; Dep. Chief of Naval Operations (Devt.) 62-63; Vice-Pres. Program Management Aerojet Gen. Corpn. 63-65; Vice-Pres. Gen. Rep. Aerojet Gen. Corpn. 66-70; Dir. CIA 65-66; Private Consultant 70-; Pres. W. F. Raborn Co. Inc.
1606 Crestwood Lane, McLean, Virginia 22101, U.S.A.
Telephone: 202-659-6520.

Rabot, Louis-Georges, DIP.AGR., LIC. EN DROIT; French civil servant; b. 2 July 1913; ed. Univ. of Paris.
Director of Prices, Ministry of Agriculture 45-48; Dir. of Foreign Relations 48-54; Dir. of Agriculture and Supply Org. for European Econ. Co-operation (now

OECD) 54-58; Dir.-Gen. of Agriculture, Comm. of European Communities 58-.
Directorate-General of Agriculture, Commission of the European Communities, 200 rue de la Loi, 1040 Brussels, Belgium.

Rabotnov, Yury Nikolayevich; Soviet mechanical engineer; b. 24 Feb. 1914, Gorky; ed. Moscow Univ. Instructor, Moscow Inst. of Power Eng. 35-46; Head, Strength Laboratory, Inst. of Mechanics, U.S.S.R. Acad. of Sciences 46-58; Prof. Moscow Univ. 47-; corresp. mem. U.S.S.R. Acad. of Sciences 53-58, mem. 58-; Deputy Dir. Inst. of Hydrodynamics, Siberian Dept., U.S.S.R. Acad. of Sciences 58-; Chief Editor *Journal of Applied Mechanics and Technical Physics* 58-65; at Moscow State Univ. 65-.
Publs. *The Local Stability of Shells* 46, *The Equilibrium of an Elastic Medium with After-effects* 48, *The Technical Theory of Approximation of Elasto-Plastic Shells* 51, *Some Problems of Theory of Creep* 48, *Modelling of Creep* 61, *Unclassified Problems of Theory of Shells* 64, *Symmetric Problems of Creep of Circular Cylindrical Shells* 64.
Moscow State University, Moscow, Leninskie Gory, U.S.S.R.

Rabukawaqa, Josua Rasilau, M.V.O., C.B.E.; Fijian diplomatist; b. 2 Dec. 1917, Nabouwala, Bua; s. of Dr. Aisea Rasilau and Adi Mereoni Dimaicakau; m. Mei T. Vuiwakaya 1944; three s. two d.; ed. Queen Victoria School, Fiji, Teachers' Training Coll., Auckland, N.Z.
Teacher, Fiji 38-52; Mortar Platoon Commdr. 1st Battalion Fiji Infantry Regt. Malayan Campaign 54-55; Adjutant Fiji Mil. Forces 55-56; Asst. Econ. Devt. Officer 57-60; District Officer, Commr., Fiji 61-70; High Commr. to U.K. 70-, accred. to EEC Countries 71-.
Leisure interests: rugby, cricket, music.
41 Campden Hill Court, Campden Hill Road, London, W.8, England.
Telephone: 01-937-6538.

Race, Robert Russell, C.B.E., PH.D., F.R.C.P., F.R.C.PATH., F.R.S.; British serologist; b. 28 Nov. 1907, England; s. of late J. D. and May (née Tweddle) Race; m. 1st Monica Rotton 1938 (died 1955), 2nd Ruth Sanger q.v. 1956; three d.; ed. St. Paul's School, London, St. Bartholomew's Hospital, London, and Trinity Hall, Cambridge.
Assistant Pathologist, Hospital for Consumption and Diseases 35-37; Asst. Serologist, Galton Lab., Univ. Coll., London 37-39; Asst. Dir., Dir. Galton Lab. Serum Unit, Dept. of Pathology, Cambridge 39-46; Dir. Medical Research Council Blood Group Unit 46-73; mem. Deutsche Akademie der Naturforscher Leopoldina; Kruis van Verdeinst, Royal Neths. Red Cross, Carlos J. Finlay Medal (Cuba), Oliver Memorial Award, Karl Landsteiner Memorial Award (with Ruth Sanger); Philip Levine Award (with Ruth Sanger); Oehlecker Medal (Germany); Conway Evans Prize (London), Gairdner Award (Toronto, with Ruth Sanger); M.D. h.c. (Paris, Turku).
Publs. *Blood Groups in Man* (with Ruth Sanger) 50, 6th edn. 75; many papers in medical and genetical journals.
Medical Research Council Blood Group Unit, Wolfson House, University College London, 4 Stephenson Way, London, NW1 2HE, England.
Telephone: 01-388-7752.

Racker, Efraim, M.D.; American biochemist; b. 28 June 1913, New Sandez, Poland; m. Franziska Weiss 1945; one d.; ed. Univ. of Vienna.
Research Asst. in biochemistry, Cardiff Mental Hospital, S. Wales 38-40; Research Assoc., Dept. of Physiology, Univ. of Minn. 41-42; Intern, Pneumonia Resident and Fellow, Harlem Hospital, N.Y.C. 42-44; Instructor, then Asst. Prof. of Microbiology, N.Y. Univ. School of Medicine 44-52; Assoc. Prof. of Biochemistry, Yale Univ. School of Medicine 52-54; Chief, Div. of Nutrition and Physiology, Public Health Research Inst. of N.Y.C. 54-56; Adjunct Prof. of Microbiology, N.Y. Univ. Bellevue Medical Center; Albert Einstein Prof. and Chair. Dept. of Biochemistry and Molecular Biology, Cornell Univ. 66-; Assoc. Editor *Journal of Biological Chemistry*; Hon. Ph.D. (Univ. of Chicago); mem. Nat. Acad. of Sciences.
Leisure interests: painting, squash.
Publs. *Mechanisms in Bioenergetics* 65, *Membranes of Mitochondria and Chloroplasts* 70.
Section of Biochemistry and Molecular Biology, Cornell University, Wing Hall, Ithaca, N.Y. 14850, U.S.A.
Telephone: 607-256-4334.

Radcliffe, 1st Viscount, cr. 62, of Hampton Lucy in the County of Warwick; **Cyril John Radcliffe,** F.B.A., P.C., G.B.E., Q.C.; British lawyer; b. 30 March 1899; m. Hon. Antonia Mary Roby Tennant (née Benson) 1939; ed. Haileybury and New Coll., Oxford.
Fellow of All Souls' Coll. Oxford 22-37; called to Bar Inner Temple 24; K.C. 35; Asst. Dir.-Gen. Press and Censorship Bureau 40; Controller Press and Censorship Div., Ministry of Information 41, Deputy Dir.-Gen. of Ministry 41, Dir.-Gen. 41-45; Vice-Chair. Gen. Council of the Bar 46-49; Chair. Punjab and Bengal Boundary Comm. 47; Bencher Inner Temple 43; Lord of Appeal in Ordinary 49-64; Chair. Royal Comm. on Taxation of Profits and Income 52-55; Chair. BBC Gen. Advisory Council 52-55; Constitutional Commr. for Cyprus 56; Chair. Treasury Cttee. on Monetary and Credit Policy 57-59; Chair. Inquiry into Security Services 61; Chair. Vassall Tribunal 62; Chair. School of Oriental and African Studies 59-75; Reith Lecturer, BBC 51, Montague Burton Lecturer, Glasgow Univ. 53; Lloyd Roberts Lecturer, Royal Soc. of Medicine 55; Rede Lecturer, Cambridge Univ. 61; Romanes Lecturer, Oxford Univ. 62; Oration at London School of Econs. 65; Hon. Fellow New Coll., Oxford 49; Trustee, British Museum, Chair. of Trustees 63-68; Chair. of Trustees British Commonwealth Int. News Agency 59-; Chancellor, Univ. of Warwick 65-; mem. Court of Univ. of London 58-63; Chair. D. Notice Inquiry 67; Hon. LL.D. (Univs. of Wales, Manchester and Sussex, St. Andrews Univ., Northwestern Univ., Ill.); Hon. D.C.L. (Oxford Univ.); Hon. D.Litt. (Univ. of Warwick); Hon. M.I.C.E., Hon. Fellow, Inst. of Bankers; Life Trustee Shakespeare Birthplace Trust, Sir John Soane's Museum.
Publs. *The Problem of Power, The Law and its Compass, Censors, Mountstuart Elphinstone, Not in Feather Beds* 68.
5 Campden Hill Gate, London, W.8; and Hampton Lucy House, Warwick, England.

Rademaker Grünewald, Adm. Augusto Hamann; Brazilian naval officer and politician; b. 11 May 1905, Rio de Janeiro; s. of Jorge C. Rademaker and Anna Grünewald; m. Ruth Rademaker 1940; five c.; ed. naval college.
Served in Brazilian navy 27-64, becoming Head of Central Command, Atlantic Defence Zone; mem. Revolutionary Command 64; Minister for the Navy 64-69, also for Transport and Public Works 64-67; mem. ruling triumvirate Aug.-Oct. 69; Vice-Pres. of Brazil 69-74; numerous decorations.
Rua Candido Jaffré 131, Brasília, Brazil.

Radford, Courtenay Arthur Ralegh, M.A., D.LITT., F.S.A., F.B.A., F.R.HIST.S.; British archaeologist; b. 7 Nov. 1900, Hillingdon, Middx.; s. of late Arthur and Ada M. Radford (née Bruton); unmarried; ed. St. George's School, Harpenden and Exeter Coll., Oxford.
Inspector of Ancient Monuments for Wales and Monmouthshire under Office of Works 29-34; Dir. British School of Rome 36-40; corresp. mem. German Archaeo-

logical Inst.; mem. Royal Comm. on Ancient Monuments in Wales and Monmouthshire 35-46; mem. Royal Comm. on Historical Monuments in England 54; Pres. Prehistoric Society 54-58, Royal Archaeological Inst. 60-63, Soc. for Medieval Archaeology 69-71.
Culmcott, Uffculme EX15 3AT, Devon, England.
Telephone: Craddock 251.

Radok, Alfréd; Czechoslovak theatre and film director; b. 17 Dec. 1914; ed. Faculty of Philosophy, Charles Univ., Prague.
Imprisoned during Second World War; Dir. at various theatres in Prague and of Czechoslovak Films; Dir. at Prague Nat. Theatre 54, 66-; Artistic Dir. *Laterna Magica* (programme for Brussels Exhbn.) 58; later at Prague Municipal Theatres; directed plays *Swedish Match* (Chekhov), Vienna 65, *The Last Ones* (Gorky), Munich 65, *Donna Benarda's House* (Lorca), Berlin 67, *A Play About Love and Death* (Romain Rolland) 67, *Donna Bernarda's House* (Lorca) 69, *Mr. Pimpian's Funny Adventures* (Children's musical); State Prize 59; Honoured Artist 64, National Artist 68.
Unemocenské pojišovny 4, Prague 1, Czechoslovakia.
Telephone: 65518.

Rădulescu, Gheorghe, D.SC. (ECON.); Romanian economist and politician; b. 5 Sept. 1914, Bucharest; s. of Dumitru and Ana Rădulescu; m. Dorina Rădulescu 1938; one s.; ed. Acad. of Higher Commercial and Industrial Studies, Bucharest.
General Sec. and Deputy Minister for Foreign Econ. Relations 48-52; Dir. Inst. for Econ. Research, Romanian Acad. of Sciences 56-57; Deputy Minister of Trade and Minister of Home and Foreign Trade 57-63; Deputy Chair. Council of Ministers, and Chair. Comm. for Econ. and Tech. Collaboration and Co-operation 63-; mem. Romanian C.P. 33-; mem. Central Cttee. Romanian C.P. 60-; mem. Exec. Cttee. Central Cttee. of Romanian C.P. 65-; mem. Perm. Presidium Central Cttee. Romanian C.P. 69-74; Perm. Rep. of Romania to Exec. Cttee. of Council for Mutual Econ. Assistance (COMECON) 65-; Deputy to Grand Nat. Assembly 61-; mem. Defence Council until 74; mem. Acad. of Social and Political Sciences 70-; several Romanian orders including Hero of Socialist Labour 71.
Leisure interest: music.
Publs. Numerous econ. studies, especially on home and foreign trade.
Central Committee of the Romanian Communist Party, Bucharest, Romania.

Radzinowicz, Sir Leon, K.B., M.A., LL.D., F.B.A.; Polish-born British lawyer and penologist; b. 15 Aug. 1906, Łódź; m. 1st Irene Szereszewski 1933 (divorced 1955), 2nd Mary Ann Nevins 1958; one s. one d.; ed. Cracow, Geneva, Paris, Rome and Cambridge Univs.
Lecturer, Geneva Univ. 28-31; reported on Belgian penal system 30; Lecturer, Warsaw Free Univ. 32-36, Asst. Prof. 36-39; visited England to report on English penal system for Polish Ministry of Justice 38; Asst. Dir. of Research, Cambridge Univ. 46-49, Fellow of Trinity Coll. 48-, Dir. Dept. of Criminal Science 49-59, Wolfson Prof. of Criminology 59-73, Dir. Inst. of Criminology 60-72; mem. Gov. Body, Int. Soc. for Social Defence; Vice-Pres. Assoc. Int. de Droit Pénal, Paris 47-; Head UN Social Defence Section 47-48; mem. Royal Comm. on Capital Punishment 49-53; Home Office Advisory Council on Treatment of Offenders 50-, Royal Comm. on English Penal System 64-; Hon. Foreign mem. American Acad. of Arts and Sciences, Australian Acad. of Forensic Sciences; First Pres. British Acad. of Forensic Sciences; First Chair. Scientific Council, European Problems of Crime, Council of Europe 63-69; Assoc. Fellow, Silliman Coll., Yale Univ. 66-; Adjunct Prof. of Law and Criminology, Columbia Law School 66-; Walter E. Meyer Visiting Prof., Yale Law School 62-63; Visiting Prof. Univs. of

Virginia 68-69, of Philadelphia and Camden 68-, Univ. of Pennsylvania 70-, Rutgers Univ. 70-; Dir. Securicor 74; Visitor Princeton Inst. of Advanced Studies 75; J. B. Ames Prize and Medal, Harvard Law School 50; Chevalier, Ordre de Léopold 30, Coronation Medal 53.
Leisure interests: travelling, dinner parties.
Publs. Numerous books and articles in Polish, French, Italian and English on Criminology and Penology; *History of English Criminal Law and Its Administration from 1750* Vol. I 48, Vols. II and III 56, Vol. IV 68; *In Search of Criminology* 61, *The Need for Criminology* 65, *Ideology and Crime* 66, Editor *Cambridge Studies in Criminology* (30 vols.); ed. with Marvin E. Wolfgang *Crime and Justice* (3 vols.) 71.
Trinity College, Cambridge; 21 Cranmer Road, Cambridge, England.
Telephone: 56867.

Rae, Saul F., PH.D.; Canadian diplomatist; b. 31 Dec. 1914, Hamilton, Ont.; m.; four c.; ed. Univ. of Toronto, Univ. of London, Balliol Coll., Oxford and Princeton Univ.
Joined Canadian Dept. of External Affairs 40; served London, Algiers, Paris 43-47; First Sec., London 49, Counsellor 52; Adviser to Canadian Rep. on N. Atlantic Council 49-52; Alt. del. to Vietnam Comm., Hanoi and Adviser to Canadian Commrs. of Int. Supervisory Comms., Indo-China 55-56; Minister, Washington 56-62; Amb. and Perm. Rep., Office of UN, Geneva 62-67; Amb. to Mexico and Guatemala 67-72; Perm. Rep. to UN Oct. 72-; del. to numerous UN and other int. confs.
Permanent Mission of Canada to United Nations, 866 United Nations Plaza, Suite 250, New York, N.Y. 10017, U.S.A.

Rafael, Gideon; Israeli diplomatist; b. Germany 5 March 1913; ed. Univ. of Berlin.
Immigrated 34; mem. Kibbutz 34-43; active in Haganah and war services 39-42; Jewish Agency, Political Dept. 43; in charge of preparation of Jewish case for Jewish Agency, Political Dept., Nuremberg War Crimes Trial 45-46; mem. of Jewish Agency Comm. to Anglo-American Comm. of Enquiry 46, and of Jewish Agency mission to UN Special Comm. for Palestine 47; mem. Israel Perm. Del. to UN 51-52; alt. rep. to UN 53; rep. at UN Gen. Assemblies 47-66; Counsellor in charge of Middle East and UN Affairs, Ministry for Foreign Affairs 53-57; Amb. to Belgium and Luxembourg 57-60, to the European Econ. Community 59; Deputy Dir.-Gen. Ministry of Foreign Affairs 60; Head of Israel Del. Int. Conf. Law of the Sea, Geneva 60; Deputy Dir.-Gen. Ministry for Foreign Affairs 60-65; Perm. Rep. to UN, Geneva 65-66; Special Amb. and Adviser to Foreign Minister May 66-67; Perm. Rep. of Israel to UN 67; Dir.-Gen. Ministry for Foreign Affairs 67-71; Senior Political Adviser to Minister of Foreign Affairs 72-73; Amb. to U.K. (also accred. to Ireland) 73-; Head of Del. to UNCTAD III 72.
Embassy of Israel, 2 Palace Green, London, W8 4QB, England; and Kiryath Yovel, Jerusalem, Israel.
Telephone: 01-937-8050.

Ragghianti, Carlo Ludovico, D.LITT.; Italian art historian and critic; b. 18 March 1910; ed. Univ. of Pisa.
Founder and Dir. *La Critica d'Arte* 35-; Prof. of History of Medieval and Modern Art, Univ. of Pisa 39-; Dir. Univ. Inst. of History of Art; Founder and Dir. Studio Italiano di Storia dell' Arte, Florence 45-; Under-Sec. of State for Educ. and the Fine Arts 45; Nat. Adviser 46; mem. various Int. Acads.
Publs. include *Le Vite del Vasari* 43-47, *Impressionismo* 44, *Commenti di critica d'arte* 45, *Miscellanea di critica d'arte* 46, *Ponte a Santa Trinità* 48, *Profilo della critica d'arte* 48, *Cinema arte figurativa* 51, *L'arte e la critica* 51, *La Pittura fiorentina del Dugento* 52, *Una Lotta nel suo corso* 52, *Frank Lloyd Wright* 52, *Il mito dell'impressionismo* 52, *Disegno della liberazione italiana* 54, *Il*

pungolo dell'arte 56, *Manzu* 56, *Mondrian e l'arte del XX secolo* 62, *Pittori di Pompei* 63, *Michelangelo* 65.
Università degli Studi, Lungarno Pacinotti 43, Pisa, Italy.

Raghavan, Venkatarama, M.A., PH.D.; Indian Sanskrit scholar; b. 22 Aug. 1908, Tiruvarur, Tamilnadu; *s.* of S. Venkatarama Iyer and Minakshi; *m.* Sarada Raghavan 1938; two *s.* two *d.*; ed. Tiruvarur High School and Madras Univ.
Superintendent Sarasvati Mahal Manuscript Library, Tanjore 30; successively Research Scholar, Research Asst., Lecturer, Reader, Prof. and Head of Dept., Madras Univ. Dept. of Sanskrit 31-69; has toured widely, lecturing, attending confs.; mem. Govt. of India Sanskrit Comm. and Cen. Sanskrit Board, Indian Acad. of Letters, Fellow, Acad. of Music, Dance and Drama; Hon. corresp. mem. Ecole Française d'Extrême Orient, Austrian Acad. of Sciences; Pres. All-India Oriental Conf., Int. Asscn. of Sanskrit Studies 73; Kane Gold Medal (Bombay Asiatic Soc.) 53; awarded titles of "Kavikokila" and "Sakalakala-kalapa" by Sankaracharya 53; "Padma-bhushan" by Govt. of India 63; Indian Acad. of Letters, Award for best book on Sanskrit research 66; Jawaharlal Nehru Fellowship 69-70; Gold Medal and Membership of Noble Order of St. Martin, Austria 67; Kalidas Awards by Govts. of Uttar Pradesh and Madya Pradesh for *Anarkali* 74-75.
Leisure interests: music, dance, drama, religions, pilgrimages.
Editor *Journal of Oriental Research, Madras Music Academy Journal, Samskrita-Pratibha, Samskrita Ranga Annual, Malaya-màruta.*
Publs. include: English: *Some Concepts of Alankara Sastra* 42, *New Catalogus Catalogorum, The Indian Heritage, Sanskrit and Allied Indological Studies in Europe, Yantras or Mechanical Contrivances in Ancient India* 56, *Concept of Culture* 71, *Seasons in Sanskrit Literature* 72; Tamil: *Varalakshmivratam* (short stories) 50, *Bharata Natya* 59, *Kadaikkadal* 59, *Nataka Lakshanaratnakosa* 61. *Bhoja's Sringara Prakasa* 63, Patel Lectures: *The Great Integrators-Saint-Singers of India* 66, *Nrttaratnavali* 68, *Seasons in Sanskrit Literature* 72, *The Greater Ramayana* 73, *Sanskrit and Allied Indian Studies in U.S.* 75, *Ramayana in Greater India* 75; Sanskrit: *Rasalila, Kamasuddhi, Manunitichola, Davabandi Varadaraja, Prekshanakatrayi, Vimukti, Valmiki-pratibha, Natirpuja, Vidyanathavidambana, Anarkali* 74 (poems and plays).
7 Srikrishnapuram Street, Royapettah, Madras 14, India.
Telephone: 85091.

Raghuramaiah, Kotha, M.A., LL.B., BARR.-AT-LAW; Indian lawyer and politician; b. 1912; ed. Lucknow Univ. and the Middle Temple.
Legal practice 37-41; Provincial Judicial Service 41-51; mem. Lok Sabha 52-; Deputy Minister of Defence 57-62; Minister of State in the Ministry of Defence 62-63; Minister of Defence Production 62-64, of Supply 64-65, of Technical Devt., Supply and Social Security 65-67; Minister of State for Law 67, Minister of State in Ministry of Petroleum and Chemicals and of Social Welfare Sept. 67-68; Minister of Petroleum and Chemicals Aug. 68-69; Minister of State for Parl. Affairs, Shipping and Transport 69-71, granted Cabinet status June 70-March 71; Minister of Parl. Affairs 73-, and of Works and Housing 74-; mem. Railway Corruption Enquiry Cttee. 54; Chair. Petitions Cttee., Lok Sabha 55-57; Congress Party.
14 Asoka Road, New Delhi; Lok Sabha, New Delhi, India.

Rahal, Abdel Latif; Algerian diplomatist; b. 14 April 1922, Nedroma; *m.*; two *c.*
Former teacher; entered govt. service 62; Dir. of Cabinet, Office of the Presidency 62; Amb. to France 63; Sec.-Gen. Ministry of Foreign Affairs 64-71; Perm. Rep. to UN June 71-.
Permanent Mission of Algeria at United Nations, 750 Third Avenue, 14th Floor, New York, N.Y. 10017, U.S.A.

Rahim, Jalaluddin Abdur; Pakistani diplomatist and politician; b. 27 July 1906, Calcutta; *s.* of late Sir Abdur Rahim; one *s.*; ed. Trinity Coll., Cambridge and Univ. of Munich.
Entered Indian Civil Service and served in Madras Presidency 31; transferred to Finance Dept., Govt. of India 36; Indian Trade Commr. for Egypt and other Middle Eastern Countries 45; Chargé d'Affaires, Pakistan Embassy, Cairo 47; Joint Sec., Ministry of Foreign Affairs and Commonwealth Relations 50; Amb. to Belgium 52-53; Sec. Ministry of Foreign Affairs and Commonwealth Relations 53-55; subsequently Amb. to Federal Germany, Amb. to Spain and Amb. to France; retd. from Govt. Service 67; founder mem. Pakistan People's Party, Sec.-Gen. Dec. 69; Minister for Production and Presidential Affairs and also for Commerce 72-74.
Leisure interests: fine arts, classical Greek, Latin, painting, swimming.
Publs. *Special Hajj Enquiry Report* 44, *Outline of a Federal Constitution for Pakistan* 69.
c/o Pakistan People's Party, Islamabad, Pakistan.

Rahimtoola, Sir Fazal Ibrahim, Kt., C.I.E., B.A., J.P.; Indian industrialist; b. 21 Oct. 1895, Bombay; *s.* of late Sir Ibrahim Rahimtoola, C.B.E.; *m.* Jainab Alimahomed Fazalbhoy 1920; three *s.* five *d.*; ed. St. Xavier's High School and Coll., Bombay, and Poona Law Coll.
Chairman Bharat Line Ltd.; Dir. Ahmedabad Advance Mills Ltd., Tata Power Co. Ltd., Tata Iron and Steel Co. Ltd., Swadeshi Mills Ltd., Overseas Communications Service (Government of India), New Swadeshi Sugar Mills Ltd., Sultania Cotton Mfg. Co. Ltd., Fazalbhai, Ibrahim and Co. Prvt. Ltd., etc.; mem. Central Legislative Assembly 25-30, Legislative Assembly 37, Bombay Legislative Council 48, Indian Tariff Board 30, Acting Pres. 32, Pres. 35; Sheriff of Bombay 50; Chair. Indian Fisheries Cttee. and Deep-Sea Fisheries Station, Govt. of India; Dir. Nat. War Front; mem. War Risk Insurance Claims Cttee. of Govt. of India, Central Food Council and its Standing Cttee., Post-War Reconstruction Cttee. for Agricultural Research, Govt. Price-Fixation Cttee. (Planning Dept.), All-Indian Council for Technical Educ., UNESCO Nat. Comm. for India and its Science Sub-Comm., East India Asscn., London, etc.; Del. to UNESCO Conf., Florence 50, 52; Econ. Adviser to Junagadh State (Saurashtra); Chair. Cttee. of Hosts, 38th Int. Eucharistic Congress; Fellow, Royal Soc. of Arts (London); Hon. Consul-Gen. for Thailand in Bombay; F.R.S.A.
Leisure interests: photography, music, games, sport.
Ismail Building, 381 Dr. Dadabhoy Naoroji Road, Fort, Bombay 1, B.R., India.
Telephone: 255046 (Office); 364031 (Home).

Rahimtoola, Habib Ibrahim, B.A., LL.B., F.R.P.S.; Pakistani diplomatist and politician; b. 10 March 1912; ed. St. Xavier's School and Coll., and Government Law Coll., Bombay.
Was Dir. over 15 joint stock companies in India; Pres. Fed. of Muslim Chambers of Commerce and Industry, New Delhi 47-48; Bombay Provincial Muslim Chamber of Commerce 44-47; Bombay Provincial Muslim League Parl. Bd. for Local Bodies 45-47; Del. Prime Ministers' Confs. London 48, 49, 51, Commonwealth Conf., S.E. Asia, London 50, Afro-Asian Conf. Bandung 55; Leader Pakistan Trade Del. to British East Africa 56; High Commr. for Pakistan in Great Britain 47-52; Ambassador to France 52-53; Gov. Sind 53, Punjab 54; Minister for Commerce, Central Govt. 54-55, for Com-

merce and Industries 55-56; Chair. Karachi Development Authority 58-60, Water Co-ordination Council 58-60, Pakistan Govt. Shipping Rates Advisory Bd. 59-, Pakistan Red Cross 71-, Bandenawaz Ltd., Pakistan Oxygen Ltd., United Bank Ltd., Pakistan Chemicals Ltd., Int. Industries Ltd., Pakistan Cables Ltd., Chambon (Pakistan) Ltd., Pakistan-Japan Cultural Asscn., Royal Commonwealth Soc., Pakistan; Pakistan-Ceylon Asscn., Photographic Soc. of Pakistan. "Kulib", B/59, K.D.A. No. 1, Habib I. Rahimtoola Road, Karachi-8, Pakistan.

Rahma Brahman, Muluktla, B.E.; Indian oil executive; b. 24 Aug. 1912, Paddapuram, Andhra; s. of M. P. Dikshitulu and M. Rama Lakshmi; m.; one s. one d.; ed. Madras Univ.
Superintendent Engineer and Engineer-in-Charge, Kandla Port Trust 50-59; Chief Engineer and Gen. Man., Gauhati Refinery, Assam 59-65; Man. Dir. Madras Refineries Ltd. 65-69, Chair. and Man. Dir. 69-72, Chair. 72-; Chair. Indian Oil Corpn. Ltd. 71-73; Fellow, Inst. of Engineers; Padma Bhushan 70.
Leisure interest: reading.
Publs. technical papers in engineering journals in India and abroad.
c/o Madras Refineries Ltd., Manali, Madras 600068; Home: 131 Sunder Nagar, New Delhi, India.
Telephone: 312767 (Office); 74062 (Home).

Rahman, Hamood-ur, B.A., LL.B.; Pakistani judge; b. 1 Nov. 1910, Patna, India; s. of late Dr. Daudur Rahman; m. Rabea Ashraf Ali 1941; five s. four d.; ed. St. Xavier's Coll., Calcutta, Univ. of London and Gray's Inn, London.
Called to the Bar, London 37; joined Calcutta High Court 38; Councillor of the Calcutta Corpn. 40, Deputy Mayor of Calcutta 43; Jr. Standing Counsel, Province of Bengal 43-47; appeared for Province of E. Pakistan before Arbitration Tribunal, Delhi, India 48; Legal Adviser, State Bank of Pakistan, Dacca 50-53; Advocate-Gen. of E. Pakistan 53-54; Judge, Dacca High Court 54-60; Vice-Chancellor, Dacca Univ. 58-60; mem. Int. Court of Arbitration, The Hague 59-60; Judge, Supreme Court of Pakistan 60-68, Chief Justice 68-; Chair. Comm. on Students' Problems and Welfare 64, Law Reforms Comm. 67, War Inquiry Comm. 72; UN Cttee. on Crime Prevention and Control 72, 73.
11 Aikman Road, GOR I Estate, Lahore, Pakistan.
Telephone: 67717.

Rahman, Shaikh Abdur, B.A., M.A.; Pakistani judge; b. 4 June 1903; m. M. Mumtaz Jahan Mohammad Din 1934; three s. one d.; ed. Islamia Coll. Lahore, Govt. Coll. Lahore, and Exeter Coll., Oxford.
Joined Indian Civil Service as Asst. Commr. 28, later District and Sessions Judge and Legal Remembrancer, Punjab; Acting Judge, Lahore High Court 46; mem. Bengal Boundary Comm. 47; Custodian Evacuee Property 48; Additional Judge, Lahore High Court 48, Permanent Judge 48; Vice-Chancellor Punjab Univ. 50; Acting Chief Justice, Lahore High Court 54, Chief Justice 54-55; Chief Justice, West Pakistan High Court 55-58; Judge, Supreme Court of Pakistan 58; Chief Justice, Supreme Court of Pakistan 68 (retd.); Chair. Board for the Advancement of Literature; Vice-Chair. Bazm-i-Iqbal, Lahore; Dir. Inst. of Islamic Culture, Lahore; Hon. LL.D. (Cairo and Punjab Univs.).
Leisure interests: reading, writing.
Publs. *Tarjuman-i-Asrar* (Urdu translation), *Hadis-i-Dil* (Speeches and lectures in Urdu) 63, *Safar* (Urdu poetry) 64, *Punishment of Apostasy in Islam* 72.
65 Main Gulberg, Lahore, Pakistan.
Telephone: 80109.

Rahman, Tunku Abdul (*see* Abdul Rahman, Tunku).

Rahmsdorf, Wilhelm; German banker; b. 18 Sept. 1908, Hildesheim; m. Anneliese Knoost 1938; one d. one s.; ed. Realgymnasium, Kassel.
Deutsche Reichsbank 33-; Bank deutscher Länder, Frankfurt am Main 48; Landeszentralbank in Nordrhein-Westfalen, Düsseldorf 50-56, Vice-Pres. 62-64; Deutsche Bundesbank, Frankfurt am Main 57-61; Pres. Landeszentralbank in Niedersachsen, Hanover 64-; mem. Board of Dirs., Deutsche Bundesbank, Frankfurt am Main 64-; Grosses Bundesverdienstkreuz 68, mit Stern 73.
5 Georgplatz, D 3000 Hanover, Federal Republic of Germany.
Telephone: 1933-223.

Rahn, Hermann, PH.D.; American physiologist; b. 5 July 1912, E. Lansing, Mich.; s. of Otto Rahn and Bell S. Farrand Rahn; m. Katharine Wilson 1939; one s. one d.; ed. Cornell and Rochester, N.Y. Univs.
National Research Council Fellow, Harvard Univ. 38-39; Instructor in Physiology, Univ. of Wyoming 39-41; Asst. in Physiology, Univ. of Rochester School of Medicine 41-42, Instructor 42-46, Asst. Prof. 46-50, Assoc. Prof. 50-56; Lawrence D. Bell Prof. of Physiology and Chair. Dept. of Physiology, Univ. of Buffalo (since 62 State Univ. of N.Y. at Buffalo) 56-72; Distinguished Prof. of Physiology 73-; mem. Nat. Acad. of Sciences; Fellow, American Acad. of Arts and Sciences; Pres. American Physiological Soc. 63-64; mem. Council, Int. Union of Physiological Sciences 65-74; Vice-Pres. 71-74; hon. doctorates from Univs. of Paris, Yonsei (Seoul) and Rochester.
Publs. *A graphical analysis of the respiratory gas exchange* (with W. O. Fenn) 55, and editor of other volumes.
Department of Physiology, State University of New York at Buffalo, Buffalo, N.Y. 14214, U.S.A.
Telephone: 716-831-2619.

Raikin, Arkady Isaakovich; Soviet actor-producer; b. 24 Oct. 1911; ed. Leningrad Ostrovsky Dramatic Inst.
Actor Leningrad Komsomol Theatre 35-37; Leningrad Novy Theatre 37-39; Founded Leningrad Miniature Theatre 39; People's Artist of the U.S.S.R.; Order of Patriotic War, etc.
Leningrad State Theatre of Miniatures, Leningrad, U.S.S.R.

Raine, Kathleen Jessie, M.A.; British poet; b. 1908; m. Charles Madge; one s. one d.; ed. Girton Coll., Cambridge.
Fellow, Girton Coll., Cambridge 56-; W. H. Smith Literary Award and other English and American poetry prizes and awards; Blake scholar.
Publs. *Stone and Flower* 43, *Living in Time* 46, *The Pythoness* 49, *The Year One* 52, *Collected Poems* 56, *The Hollow Hill* (poems) 65, *Blake and Tradition* (Andrew Mellon Lectures) 69, *Selected Writings of Thomas Taylor the Platonist* (with George Mills Harper) 69, *William Blake, Selected Poems* 70, *The Lost Country* (poems) 71, *On a Deserted Shore* (poems) 72, *Faces of Day and Night* 73, *Farewell Happy Fields* (autobiog.) 73, *The Land Unknown* (autobiog.) 75; criticism: *Defending Ancient Springs* 67, *Yeats, the Tarot and the Golden Dawn* 73, *Death in Life and Life in Death* 73.
47 Paultons Square, London, S.W.3, England.

Rainier III, His Serene Highness Prince, Louis Henri Maxence Bertrand; Prince of Monaco; b. 31 May 1923; m. Grace Patricia Kelly (*q.v.*, Grace, H.S.H. Princess) 1956; one s. two d.; ed. Summerfields School, Hastings (England), Montpellier Univ., and Ecole Libre des Sciences Politiques, Paris.
Hereditary Prince of Monaco 44; succeeded his grandfather Prince Louis II 49; founded Monaco Red Cross 48, American Friends of Monaco 52, Prix Rainier 55;

Grand Master Ordre de St. Charles de Monaco, Grand Cross Légion d'Honneur, Belgian, Swedish, Greek, Lebanese, Italian, Netherlands and San Marino orders; served in French army as Lieut. and Col. 44-45.
Palais de Monaco, Monte Carlo, Principality of Monaco.

Rainwater, (Leo) James, B.S., M.A., PH.D.; American professor of physics; b. 9 Dec. 1917, Council, Ida.; s. of Leo Jasper Rainwater and Edna Eliza (Teague) Rainwater; m. Emma Louise Smith 1942; three s.; ed. Calif. Inst. of Technology and Columbia Univ., New York, N.Y.
Assistant in Physics, Columbia Univ. 39-42, Instructor in Physics 46-47, Asst. Prof. 47-49, Assoc. Prof. 49-52, Prof. of Physics 52-; Scientist Office of Scientific Research and Devt. and Manhattan Project 42-46; Dir. Nevis Cyclotron Lab. 51-53, 56-61; scientific and U.S. Naval research and research contracts with Atomic Energy Comm. and Nat. Science Foundation 47-; Fellow, American Physical Soc., A.A.A.S., Inst. of Electrical Engineers, New York Acad. of Science; mem. Nat. Acad. of Sciences, Optical Soc. of America; Ernest Orlando Lawrence Physics Award of U.S. Atomic Energy Comm.; Nobel Prize for Chemistry 75.
Leisure interests: classical music, environmental and earth sciences, astronomy, air pollution problems.
Publs. Numerous articles in *Physical Review* 46-, and other professional journals.
Nevis Laboratories, Physics Department, Columbia University, New York, N.Y. 10027; Home: 342 Mt. Hope Boulevard, Hastings-on-Hudson, N.Y. 10706, U.S.A.
Telephone: 914-LY1-8100 (Office); 914-GR8-1368 (Home).

Raisani, Sardar Ghaus; Pakistani politician; b. 6 Sept. 1924, Kanak, Baluchistan; s. of late Sir Asadullah Khan Raisani; nine s. one d.; ed. Col. Brown Public School, Dehra Dun.
Commissioned, Indian Army 45, served 45-48; Chief of his tribe, Baluchistan 49-; active in politics 49-; Convenor, Baluchistan State Muslim League; mem. W. Pakistan Assembly 56-58, Baluchistan Assembly 70-; Leader of the Opposition 72-74; founder and convenor, Baluchistan United Front 69; Gov. of Baluchistan 71-72; Fed. Minister for Food and Agriculture 72-74; Senior Minister Baluchistan Prov. Cabinet 74-; Pres. Pakistan People's Party Baluchistan 74-.
Leisure interests: farming, hunting, angling, hiking.
Baluchistan Assembly, Baluchistan; 47 Lytton Road, Quetta, Pakistan.
Telephone: 73357 (Office); 70661 and 75357 (Home).

Raiser, Ludwig, D.IUR., D.THEOL.; German university professor; b. 27 Oct. 1904; ed. Eberhard-Ludwigs-Gymnasium, Stuttgart, and Univs. of Munich, Geneva and Berlin.
Member Management Board of insurance firm in Magdeburg 37-43; Mil. Service 43-45; Prof. Univ. of Göttingen 45-51, Rector, Univ. of Göttingen 48-50; Pres. German Research Asscn., Bad Godesberg 51-55; Prof. of Civil Law, Trade and Business Law, Univ. of Tübingen 55-73; mem. German Science Council 58-65, Chair. 61-65; mem. Synod Protestant Church, Chair. 70-73; Chair. Württembergische Feuerversicherung AG, Stuttgart 75-; Corresp. Fellow, Rheinisch-West-fälische Akad. der Wissenschaften, British Acad.; Hon. D.Phil.; Grosses Bundesverdienstkreuz mit Stern.
Publs. *Die Wirkungen der Wechselerklärungen im Internationalen Privatrecht* 31, *Das Recht der Allgemeinen Geschäftsbedingungen* 35, *Lehrbuch des Sachenrechts* (with M. Wolff) 10th edn. 57, *Die Universität im Staat* 58, *Dingliche Anwartschaften* 61, *Das Bildungsziel der heutigen Universität* 65, *Deutsche Hochschulprobleme im Lichte amerikanischer Erfahrungen* 66, *Grundgesetz*

und Privatrechtsordnung 67, *Die Zukunft des Privatrechts* 71.
c/o Württembergische Feuerversicherung AG, 7 Stuttgart 1, Johannesstrasse 1-7, Federal Republic of Germany.

Raisman, Sir (Abraham) Jeremy, G.C.M.G., G.C.I.E., K.C.S.I., M.A.; British civil servant and banker; b. 19 March 1892; ed. Leeds High School and Univ., and Pembroke Coll., Oxford.
Joined Indian Civil Service 16; Asst. Magistrate and Under-Sec. Bihar and Orissa 16-22; Customs Dept. Bombay and Calcutta 22-28; Commr. Income Tax, Punjab and N.W. Frontier Province 28-31; Joint Sec. Commerce Dept. Govt. of India 31-34; mem. Central Board of Revenue 34; Dir. Reserve Bank of India 38; Sec. 38-39; Finance mem. Govt. of India 39-45; Vice-Pres. Gov.-Gen.'s Exec. Council; Hon. Fellow Pembroke Coll. 45; mem. Industrial Advisory Panel 46-; Chair. Fiscal Comm. for Fed. of Rhodesia and Nyasaland 52, Nigeria Fiscal Comm. 57-58, Econ. and Fiscal Comm. for East Africa 60-61; Dir. Lloyds Bank Ltd. 46-, Vice-Chair. 48-53, Deputy Chair. 53-63; Deputy Chair. Lloyds and Scottish Finance Ltd. 58-; Dir. Lloyds Bank Europe Ltd.; Chair. Public Works Loans Board, Commonwealth Trust Ltd.; Chair. Budget Comm. of Int. Chamber of Commerce.
Fieldhead, Shamley Green, nr. Guildford, Surrey, England.

Raj, James S.; Indian international civil servant; b. 7 Nov. 1913, Saidapet; s. of Sivaraman Vedakan James and Pushpammal Daniel; m. Hilda Gnanamuthu 1942; one s. one d.; ed. Madras Christian Coll., and Univ. Coll., London.
Former Lecturer in Econs., Univ. of Rangoon; Indian civil service, Ministries of Food and Agriculture 42-53; Chief of Multiple Currency Practices Div., Int. Monetary Fund (IMF) 53-56; Alt. Exec. Dir. for India, IMF and World Bank 56; Dir. Asian Dept., IMF 56-59; Controller of Stock Exchanges, India 59-60; Deputy Gen. Man. of Industrial Credit and Investment Corpn. of India 60-64; Gen. Man. Nigerian Industrial Devt. Bank, Lagos 64-66; Deputy Exec. Vice-Pres. Int. Finance Corpn. 66-67, Vice-Pres. 67-70; Man. Dir. Industrial Investment Trust Ltd., Bombay 70-72; Chair. Unit Trust of India 72-.
Leisure interests: stamp collecting, linguistics.
Flat 32, Sagar Tarang, B. Desai Road, Bombay 400-036, India.

Rajah, Arumugam Ponnu; Singapore lawyer and diplomatist; b. 23 July 1911; ed. St. Paul's Inst., Seremban, Raffles Inst., Singapore, and Oxford Univ.
Singapore City Councillor 47-49, 51-57; mem. Singapore Legislative Assembly 59-66, Speaker 64-66; High Commr. to U.K. 66-71, to Australia 71-73; practising lawyer in Singapore 73-.
c/o Ministry of Foreign Affairs, Singapore.

Rajapakse, Sir Lalita, Kt., Q.C., B.A., LL.D.; Sri Lanka lawyer, politician and diplomatist; b. 3 May 1900; m. Chrysobel Gunasekera 1935; one s. two d.; ed. St. Joseph's Coll., Colombo and University Coll., London.
Called to English Bar 24, Ceylon Bar 25; Lecturer, Ceylon Law Coll. 26, Examiner 27; Commr. of Assize, Supreme Court, Ceylon 47; mem., then Leader, Senate 47; Minister of Justice 47-53; Amb. to France 65-67; High Commr. in U.K. 67-69; Founded Revata Coll., Balapitiya 33; mem. Council of Legal Educ., Ceylon 39, Councils, Univ. of Ceylon 46, and Vidyodaya and Vidyalankara Univs. 59; mem. Ceylon Del. to Commonwealth Conf. on Foreign Affairs 50; Chair. Gal Oya Comm. 56; Fellow Univ. Coll. London 68.
Leisure interests: reading, agriculture.
[*Died 25 May 1976.*]

Rajaratnam, Sinnathamby; Singapore politician; b. 23 Feb. 1915, Ceylon (now Sri Lanka); ed. Raffles Inst., Singapore, King's Coll., London.
Brought to Malaya at age of six months; Assoc. Editor *Singapore Standard* 50-54; Editorial Staff *Straits Times* 54-59; mem. Malayanization Cttee. 55; mem. Minimum Standards of Livelihood Cttee. 56; Convenor and Founder-mem. of People's Action Party; Assemblyman for Kampong Glam constituency 59-; Minister for Culture 59-65; Minister of Foreign Affairs 65-, of Labour 68-71.
Ministry of Foreign Affairs, 1st Floor, Government Offices, St. Andrew's Road, Singapore 6.
Telephone: 322142.

Rakhmatov, Mirzo; Soviet politician and diplomatist; b. 1914, Jafr, Tadzhik S.S.R.; ed. All-Union Party School.
Komsomol work 34-40; mem. C.P.S.U. 40-; party work 40-48; Deputy Chair. Council of Ministers, Tadzhik S.S.R. 51-56; Sec. Cen. Cttee. C.P. of Tadzhik S.S.R. 56; Chair. Presidium of Supreme Soviet of Tadzhik S.S.R. 56-63; Minister of Culture of Tadzhik S.S.R. 63-66; Amb. to Yemen Arab Republic 66-72; Deputy Chair. Presidium of Supreme Soviet of U.S.S.R. 58-64; mem. Cen. Auditing Comm. of C.P.S.U. 61-71; Deputy to Supreme Soviet of U.S.S.R. 58-70, and Tadzhik S.S.R. 51-70.
Ministry of Foreign Affairs, 32-34 Smolenskaya-Sennaya plohschad, Moscow, U.S.S.R.

Rakowski, Mieczysław Franciszek, DR.HIST.; Polish journalist and politician; b. 1 Dec. 1926, Kowalewko, Szubin district; m. Wanda Wilkomirska q.v. 1952; two s.; ed. Higher School of Social Sciences, Cracow and Inst. of Social Sciences, Warsaw.
Worked at Cen. Cttee. of Polish United Workers' Party (PUWP) 49-52, 55-57; Sub-editor, *Polityka* 57, Editor-in-Chief 58-; Chair. Gen. Board, Polish Journalists' Asscn. 58-61; Deputy mem. Cen. Cttee., Polish United Workers Party 64-; Deputy to Seym 72-; Order of Banner of Labour, Gold Cross of Merit and other decorations.
Publs. *NRF z bliska* (Federal Republic of Germany from a Short Distance) 58, *New World* 59, *Socjaldemokratyczna Partia Niemiec w okresie powojennym 1949-54* (Social-Democratic Party of Germany in Post-war Period) 60, *Świat na zakręcie* (The World in Turning) 60, *Zachód szuka ideologii* (The West Looks for Ideology) 61, *Polityka Zagraniczna PRL* (The Foreign Policy of the Polish People's Republic) 74, *Dymisja Kanclerza* (Chancellor's Dismissal); co-author: *The Polish Upswing 1971-75* 75.
Redakcja Polityka, Stanisława Dubois 9, 00-182, Warsaw, Poland.
Telephone: 38-34-91.

Rallis, George (*see* Rhallys, George).

Ralph, Henry A. J.; American diplomatist and banker; b. 1901, San Francisco, Calif.; s. of Francis J. Ralph and Geneive L. Madden; m. Phyllis A. Puckett 1928; three d.; ed. Public Schools, Alameda, California, and American Inst. of Banking.
Vice-President and New York Rep., Bank of America NT & SA 45, Vice-Pres. and Manager, Bank of America, New York 50, Exec. Officer and Dir. 58; Vice-Pres. and Dir. Bamerical Int. Financial Corporation 61; Pres., Chief Exec. Officer and Dir., World Banking Corpn. 64-67; adviser in banking to U.S. and other govts. 67-74; Exec. in Residence, Univ. of San Francisco; now Amb. at Large; Hon. Alumnus Columbia Univ. 63; numerous decorations including Sovereign Order of Malta 56.
Leisure interests: world travel, ancient civilizations and cultures.
Publs. *Consultants' Views on Bank Management* (two

vols., in Chinese and English); and several papers on banking and management.
5255 Cribari Lane, San José, Calif. 95135, U.S.A.
Telephone: 408-274-5292.

Ram, Dr. Bharat, B.A.; Indian industrialist; b. 5 Oct. 1914; m. Sheila Bharat Ram; three s.; ed. privately and at St. Stephen's Coll., Delhi.
Joined Delhi Cloth and Gen. Mills Co. 35, Joint Man. Dir. 48, Chair. Board of Dirs. 58-; also Chair. Bengal Potteries, Shriram Bearings, Coromandel Fertilisers 67-, Indian Airlines 67-69, Indian Cotton Mills Fed. 61-63; Pres. Fed. of Indian Chambers of Commerce & Industry 63-64; Pres. Int. Chamber of Commerce 69-71; mem. Board of Govs., Delhi and Pilani Insts. of Technology; Dir. New India Assurance Co., Escorts, Bajaj Electricals.
25 Sarder Patel Road, New Delhi, India.

Ram, Hon. Jagjivan, B.SC.; Indian politician; b. 5 April 1908, Arrah, Bihar; m. Indrani Devi 1935; one s. one d.; ed. Banaras Hindu Univ. and Calcutta Univ.
General Sec. All-India Depressed Classes League until 36, Pres. 36-46; M.L.C., Bihar 36, Parl. Sec. 37-39; formed Bihar Provincial Khet Mazdoor (Agricultural Labour) Sabha 37; Sec. Bihar Provincial Congress Cttee. 40-46; Vice-Pres. Bihar Branch All India Trade Union Congress 40-46; imprisoned for political activities 40, released on medical grounds 43; Head, Del., I.L.O. Conf., Geneva, Chair. 33rd Session of Conf. 50; Chair. Preparatory Asian Regional Conf., I.L.O., New Delhi 47; Minister of Labour 46-52 (in Interim Govt. and first Indian Govt.), Minister of Communications 52-Dec. 56, 62-Aug. 63; Minister for Railways and Transport Dec. 56-April 57; Minister for Railways April 57-62, Minister of Transport 63-64; Leader of Indian Del. to Asian Labour Ministers' Conf., Manila Nov. 66, Leader of Indian Del. to FAO Conf., Rome 67, 74, 75, The Hague 70; Minister of Labour and Employment 66-67, of Food and Agriculture 67-70, of Defence 70-74, of Agriculture and Irrigation Oct. 74-; Pres. Indian Congress Dec. 69-; Chair. Indian Inst. of Public Admin. 74-; mem. Working Cttee. and Cen. Parl. Board, All-India Congress Cttee. 48-; mem. gov. bodies of several educ. insts.; Hon. D.Sc. (Vikram Univ., Ujjain).
Ministry of Agriculture and Irrigation, New Delhi; Home: 6 Krishna Menon Marg, New Delhi 110011, India.
Telephone: 381129 (Office); 376555 (Home).

Rama, Carlos M.; Uruguayan writer, lawyer, professor and editor; b. 26 Oct. 1921, Montevideo; s. of Manuel Rama and Carolina Facal; m. Judith Dellepiane 1943; one s. one d.; ed. Univs. of Montevideo and Paris.
Journalist 40-48; Exec. Sec. of Uruguayan Bar Asscn. 48-49; Prof. of Universal History in secondary schools 44-48; Editor *Nuestro Tiempo* 54-56, *Gacetilla Austral* 61-; Pres. Ateneo del Uruguay, and *El Siglo Ilustrado* S.A.; Prof. of Sociology and Social Research, Prof. of Contemporary History, Prof. of Theory and Methodology of History, Univ. of Montevideo; Commdr. Order of Liberation (Spain); Officier des Palmes Académiques (France).
Leisure interest: gardening.
Publs. *La Historia y la Novela* 47, 63, 70, *Las ideas socialistas en el siglo XIX* 47, 49, 63, 67, *Ensayo de Sociología Uruguaya* 56, *Teoría de la Historia* 59, 68, *L'Amérique Latine* 59, 67, *Las clases sociales en el Uruguay* 60, *La Crisis española del siglo XX* 60, 62, *Itinerario español* 61, *Revolución social y fascismo en el siglo XX* 62, *La religión en el Uruguay* 64, *Sociología del Uruguay* 65, *Historia del movimiento obrero y social latino americano contemporáneo* 67, 69, *Los afrouraguayos* 67, 68, 69, 70, *Garibaldi y el Uruguay* 68, *Uruguay en Crisis* 69, *Sociología de América Latina* 70.
Coronel Alegre 1340, Montevideo, Uruguay.
Telephone: 780562.

Rama Rau (*see* Rau).

Ramachandran, Gopalasamudram Narayana, M.A., M.SC., D.SC., PH.D.; Indian scientist and university professor; b. 8 Oct. 1922, Ernakulam, Kerala State; s. of G. R. Narayana Iyer and Lakshmi Ammal; m. Rajalakshmi Sankaran 1945; two s. one d.; ed. Maharaja's Coll., Ernakulam (Cochin), Indian Inst. of Science, Univs. of Madras and Cambridge.

Lecturer in Physics, Indian Inst. of Science 46-47, Asst. Prof. 49-52; 1851 Exhbn. Scholar, Univ. of Cambridge 47-49; Prof. Univ. of Madras 52-70, and Head, Dept. of Physics 52-70; Dean, Faculty of Science 64-67; Prof. of Biophysics, Indian Inst. of Science 70-; part-time Prof. of Biophysics, Univ. of Chicago 67-; Editor *Current Science* 50-58, *Journal of the Indian Institute of Science* 73-; mem. Editorial Board *J. Molecular Biology* 59-66, *Biochimica et Biophysica Acta* 65-72, *Indian Journal of Pure and Applied Physics* 63-, *International Journal of Peptide and Protein Research* 69-, *Indian Journal of Biochemistry and Biophysics* 70-, *Biopolymers* 73-; Fellow, Indian Acad. of Sciences 50-, mem. Council 53-70, Sec. 56-58, Vice-Pres. 62-64; Dir. U.G.C. Centre of Advanced Study in Biophysics 62-70; mem. Physical Research Cttee. 59-; mem. Nat. Cttee. for Biophysics 61-; Fellow, Nat. Inst. of Sciences 63-; mem. Board of Scientific and Industrial Research, India 62-65, Council Int. Union of Pure and Applied Biophysics 69-72, Comm. on Macromolecular Biophysics 69; Chair. Nat. Cttee. for Crystallography 63-70; Senior Visiting Prof., Univ. of Michigan 55-66; Jawaharlal Nehru Fellow 68-70; Hon. mem. American Soc. of Biological Chem. 65-; Hon. foreign mem. American Acad. of Arts and Sciences; Fellow, Royal Soc. of Arts, London 71-; specialist in optics, crystal physics, X-ray crystallography and biophysics; Bhatnagar Memorial Prize 61, Watumull Prize 64, John Arthur Wilson Award 67, Meghnad Saha Medal 71, Ramanujan Medal 72, J. C. Bose Award (U.G.C.) 74, (Bose Inst.) 75.

Leisure interests: Indian and Western music, detective fiction.

Publs. *Crystal Optics* (in *Handbuch der Physik*, Vol 25, Berlin), *Molecular Structure of Collagen* (in *International Review of Connective Tissue Research*, Vol. I, New York), *Conformation of Polypeptides and Proteins,* (*Advances in Protein Chemistry*, Vol. 23), *Conformation of Polypeptide Chains* (*Annual reviews in Biochemistry*, Vol. 39), *Fourier Methods in Crystallography* (New York) 70, *Advanced Methods of Crystallography* (Editor), *Aspects of Protein Structure*, London (Editor), *Treatise on Collagen* (Editor, two vols.) 67, *Conformation of Biopolymers*, Vols. I and 2 (Editor) 67, *Crystallography and Crystal Perfection* (Editor).

Molecular Biophysics Unit, Indian Institute of Science, Bangalore 560012, India.

Telephone: 34411 Ext. 461.

Ramachandran, T. N., F.A.S.; Indian archaeologist; b. 16 March 1903, Mannargudi, Tanjore District, Madras; s. of T. Narayana and Yajwa Visalakshi; m. Dr. Lalita Ramachandran; five s.; ed. Presidency Coll., Madras Univ. and London Univ. Inst. of Archaeology.

Curator Archaeological Section, Madras Govt. Museum 25-35; Asst. Superintendent Archaeological Survey of India, Calcutta 35-38, Superintendent 38-52, Deputy Dir.-Gen. Delhi 52-53, Joint Dir.-Gen. 53-58; Special Officer Nagarjunakonda Excavations, Govt. of India Dept. of Archaeology 58-61; Special Officer for Archaeology, Govt. of Madras 61-65, for Publs., H.R. & C.E. Dept. 66-68; Emer. Prof., Asiatic Soc. ICOM; Fellow, Asiatic Soc.; Narasimhacharya Prizeman, Bysany Madhava Gold Medal (Madras Univ.), Lokavedasamanvaya-kalpataru 63, Padma Bhushan 64; mem. Srinamgam Temple Renovation Cttee. 66-, Cen. Film Censor Board 67-; Tagore Prof. for Humanities, Madras Univ. 69-70.

Leisure interests: music, dance and art.

Publs. include *Buddhist Sculptures from Goli* 29, *South Indian Metal Images* 32, *The Golden Age of Indo-Javanese Art* 33, *The Royal Artist Mahendra Varman I* 33, *Three Styles of Temple Architecture* 34, *Tiruparutti-kunram and its temples* 34, *Nagarjunakonda* 38, *Jaina Monuments of India* 44, *Khandagiri and Udayagiri Caves* 50, *Nagapattinam Buddhist Bronzes* 54, *Archaeological Reconnaissance in Afghanistan* 56, *New Light on Indus Culture* 58, *Historic India and her temples* 58, *Preservation of Monuments* 55, *The Great Temple of Tanjore, The Sittannavasal Cave* 62, *Is the World Morally Progressing?*, *Buddhist India and the World, Homage to Vaisali, Asvamedha Sites Near Kalsi, Kiratarjuniya in Indian Art, Temple Inscriptions and Music* 68, *Indian Wood Carving* 68, *Temples in Madras City* 68, *Temples of Orissa and Bundelkhand* 67, *Ramasatakam* 68, *Deities of Kanchi* 64, *Kusumaksharamala* 66, *Kalpakavalli-Kapalisvara-Stuti* 66, *Thiruvanaikka Temple* 70, *Hymn To Mahabalipuram* 70.

2 Third Main Road, Nehrunagar, Adayar, Madras 20, India.

Ramalingaswami, Vulimiri, M.D., D.SC. (OXON.), F.R.C.P.; Indian medical scientist; b. 8 Aug. 1921, Srikakulam, Andhra Pradesh; s. of Shri Gumpaswami and Sundaramma Ramalingaswami; m. Surya Prabha 1947; one s. one d.; ed. Univ. of Oxford, England.

Pathologist for Indian Council of Medical Research at the Nutrition Research Laboratories, Coonor, South India 47-54; Asst. Sec. and Deputy Dir. Indian Council of Medical Research 54-57; Prof. of Pathology and Head of Dept., All-India Inst. of Medical Sciences, Ansari Nagar, New Delhi 57-69, Dir. and Prof. of Pathology 69-; Padma Bhushan 71; Silver Jubilee Research Award, Medical Council of India 74; Fellow, Indian Acad. of Medical Science 61-, Indian Nat. Science Acad. 71; Hon. Fellow, American Coll. of Physicians 70-; Foreign Assoc., Nat. Acad. of Sciences, U.S.A. 73-; D.Sc. h.c. (Andhra Univ.) 67; Hon. Dr.Med. (Karolinska Inst.) 74; Pres. Indian Assen. for Advancement of Medical Educ. 74-.

Leisure interests: music, literature, sports.

Publs. author and co-author of many papers, articles, lectures, monographs and books.

Director's Bungalow, All-India Institute of Medical Sciences, 78123 Ansari Nagar, New Delhi 110016, India.

Telephone: 78361-619481/311 (Office).

Raman, Papanasam Setlur, M.A.; Singapore diplomatist; b. 5 Oct. 1920, India; s. of P. S. Ragavachary and P. S. Kamala; m. Lim Eng Neo; one s. two d.; ed. Madras Christian Coll. and Univ. of Madras.

Former teacher; Supervisor, Pan-Malayan Indian Programme 58-59; Asst. Controller of Programmes 60-63; Deputy Dir. Broadcasting 63-65, Dir. 65-68; Amb. to Indonesia 68-69, to Australia 69-71, to U.S.S.R. 71-; Meritorious Service Medal.

Leisure interests: golf, reading, and writing aphorisms.

Embassy of Singapore, Moscow, U.S.S.R.; Home: 47 Hillside Drive, Singapore.

Ramanantsoa, Maj.-Gen. Gabriel; Malagasy army officer; b. 13 April 1906, Tananarive; ed. Lycée de Tananarive, de Marseille, Ecole Spéciale Militaire, Saint-Cyr, Inst. des Hautes Etudes de Défense Nationale.

Assistant to Chief Officer Ecole Mil. Préparatoire des Enfants de Troupe 32; assigned to Colonial Infantry Regiment of Morocco, French Army 31, 35-36; rank of Capt. 40; returned to Madagascar, organized Ecole Supérieure d'Educ. Physique, Fianarantsoa 41, 43-46; Dept. of Colonial Troops, Ministry of Defence, Paris 46, 53-59; in charge of War Veterans, Mil. Office of French High Comm., Madagascar 48-53; served with French Army in Viet-Nam 53; Lt.-Col., Col. 59, Brig.-Gen. 61, Maj.-Gen. 67; participated in Franco-Malagasy negotia-

tions for independence 60; Chief of Gen. Staff of the Malagasy Armed Forces 60-72; Head of Govt., Prime Minister, Minister of Defence, Minister of Planning 72-75.
Tananarive, Madagascar.

Ramanathan, Kalpathi Ramakrishna, M.A., D.SC.; Indian scientist; b. 28 Feb. 1893, Palghat, Kerala, South India; s. of Ramakrishna Sastry Subbalakshmi; m. Parvatti Ramanathan; two s. four d.; ed. Victoria Coll., Palghat and Presidency Coll., Madras.
Demonstrator in Physics, Trivandrum Coll. 14-21; Hon. Dir. Trivandrum Observatory; Madras Univ. Research Scholar under Prof. C. V. Raman 21-22; Lecturer in Physics, Univ. Coll., Rangoon 22-25; joined Indian Meteorological Dept. 25-48: Dir. Kodaikanal and Bombay Observatories; Supt. Meteorologist, Poona 39; Dep. Dir.-Gen. of Observatories until 48; Dir. Physical Research Lab., Ahmedabad 48-66, Prof. 67-; Pres. Indian Science Congress, Mathematics and Physics Section, Lahore 39; Founder Fellow of Indian Acad. of Sciences and of Nat. Inst. of Sciences of India; Pres. Int. Asscn. of Meteorology 51-54, Union of Geodesy and Geophysics 54-57; Chair. Radio and Telecommunications Research Cttee. 66-71, Cloud and Rain Physics and Cosmic Ray Research Cttee. 56-66; Chair. Cen. Board of Geophysics 57-; Pres. Int. Ozone Comm. 59-60, Chair. 60-67, hon. mem.; Pres. Indian Nat. Cttee. for IQSY (Int. Year of the Quiet Sun); Chair. Indian Nat. Cttee. for Int. Hydrological Decade 66-74; Chair. Int. Hydrological Programme (fmr. Int. Hydrological Decade) 74-; main fields of research: problems of molecular scattering of light in fluids, anisotrophy of molecules, atmospheric and solar radiation, study of the Indian monsoon, general circulation of the atmosphere atmospheric ozone, physics of the ionosphere and aeronomy, problems of ground-water; Hon. Fellow, Royal Meteorological Soc., London 60; Award of Int. Meteorological Org. 61; Padma Bhushan 65.
Leisure interests: gardening, cross country walking.
Physical Research Laboratory, Navrangpura, Ahmedabad 9, Gujarat, India.
Telephone: 40242-46.

Ramangasoavina, Alfred, D. EN D.; Malagasy politician; b. 2 Nov. 1917, Moramanga; m.; four c.; ed. Ecole Le Myre, Vilers and School of Political Sciences, Paris, France.
Served in Madagascan admin. 39-47; lawyer, Tananarive Appeal Court, Paris Appeal Court 52-54; served at Central Treasury for Overseas France 54-56; worked in Madagascar Exchange Office; municipal councillor for Tananarive 56; Finance Minister 57-58; Minister of Equipment 58-59; Minister of Industry and Planning 59-60; Deputy for Tananarive Province (Social Democratic Party) Sept. 60-; Minister of Justice Oct. 60-Dec. 69; Minister of Information, Tourism and Traditional Arts Dec. 69-Sept. 70; Minister of State for Commerce, Supply, Industry and Mines Sept. 70-71; Vice-Pres. and in charge of Public Health and Population, Public Works and Communications, Women's Advancement, and the Protection of Children 71-72; mem. UN Int. Law Comm.; del. to ILO and other int. confs.; Commdr. Etoile Royale de la Grande Comore, Grand Officer, Nat. Order of Ivory Coast, Commdr. Ordre de la Valeur, Cameroon.
Ministry of Public Health, Tananarive, Madagascar.

Ramanujam, G.; Indian trade unionist; b. 2 Feb. 1916.
Founder-Sec. Tamilnad Indian Nat. Trade Union Congress; Pres. Indian Nat. Textile Workers Fed. 56, Indian Nat. Plantation Workers Fed. 60; Pres. Indian Nat. Trade Union Congress 58, 59, Gen. Sec. 65-75; Man. Editor *Indian Worker* 65-75.
Publs. *From the Babul Tree, Industrial Relations—A*

Point of View, The Payment of Bonus Act, The Payment of Gratuity Act.
c/o Indian National Trade Union Congress, 17 Janpath, New Delhi, India.

Ramathan, Mustapha, B.COM.; Ugandan diplomatist; b. 29 Jan. 1936, Bombo; m. K. Nasser Ally 1968; four c.; ed. in Uganda and Cairo.
Headmaster of secondary school in Bombo 60-63; Deputy Sec. Uganda Lint Marketing Board 68-; Amb. to U.S.A. 71-73.
Leisure interests: indoor games, excursions.
c/o Ministry of Foreign Affairs, Kampala, Uganda.

Rambert, Charles Jean Julien; French architect; b. 23 March 1924, Arrigny, Marne; s. of Jean Rambert; m. Françoise Coleda 1949; three s.; ed. Lycée Pierre-Corneille, Rouen, Inst. Saint-Aspais, Melun and Ecole nationale supérieure des beaux-arts.
Architect 52-, Govt. registered architect 53; Technical Counsellor, Centre d'information et de documentation du bâtiment 55-61; Sec. Conseil d'Administration 68; Editor-in-Chief *Revêtements sols et murs* 57-64; Prof. of Construction and History of Art, Ecole de secrétariat technique du bâtiment 57-; Arbitrator-expert, Tribunal de Commerce 60, and de Grande Instance, Versailles 63, Cour d'Appel de Paris 71; Sec. Soc. of Registered Architects 54-57, Sec.-Gen. 57, 1st Vice-Pres. 68; Editor-in-Chief *L'Architecture française* 64-; Counsellor, Ordre des Architectes de Paris 64, Treas. 69; Asst. Dir. of Studies, Ecole Nationale Supérieure des Beaux Arts 65, Prof. of History of Architecture 69-; mem. Union Franco-Britannique des Architectes 69; Fellow Royal Soc. of Arts 71; Officier deArts et s Lettres 67; several awards.
Leisure interests: history of art, literature and painting.
Publs. *Constructions scolaires et universitaires* 55, *L'Habitat collectif, Problème urbain* 57, *Maisons familiales de plaisance* 59, *Magasins* 61, *Histoire de l'architecture civile en France* 63, French adaptation of *World Architecture* 64, *Architecture des Origines à Nos Jours* 68, (English translation 69), *L'Architecture Française* 69, *L'Architecture Occidentale* 74 (Audiovisual series).
35 avenue de Ségur, 75007 Paris; and 48 rue Saint-Didier, 75016 Paris, France.
Telephone: 783-35-51.

Rambert, Dame Marie, D.B.E.; British founder and director of Ballet Rambert; b. 20 Feb. 1888, Warsaw, Poland; m. Ashley Dukes 1918; two d.; ed. studies with Jacques Dalcroze and Enrico Cecchetti.
Member, Diaghilev's Ballets Russes 12; founded Rambert School of Ballet, London 20; founder and dir. Ballet Rambert 26 (reformed as Modern Dance Co. 66); founded Ballet Club at Mercury Theatre, London 30; wartime tours at home and abroad with CEMA/ENSA; teacher of Frederick Ashton, Antony Tudor, Norman Morrice and other well-known choreographers; co. has appeared in Australia, New Zealand, China, Lebanon, U.S.A., Canada, Belgium, France, Italy, Spain, Germany, Denmark, Finland, Poland, Malta, Austria, Greece, Iran and Cyprus; regular tours in Britain.
London seasons at Sadler's Wells, Young Vic, Phoenix, Duchess, Lyric and King's (Hammersmith), Stoll, Duke of York's, Arts Theatre 26-73; Dir. Mercury Theatre Trust Ltd. (controlling Ballet Rambert); mem. Grand Council Imp. Soc. of Teachers; Fellow and Vice-Pres., Royal Acad. of Dancing; Fellow, Royal Soc. of Arts; Queen Elizabeth II Coronation Award (Royal Acad. of Dancing) 56; Légion d'Honneur 57; Dip. Assoc. Manchester Coll. of Art 60; Hon. D.Litt. (Univ. of Sussex) 64.
Publs. *Quicksilver* (autobiography) 72; trans. Sizova's *Ulanova—Her Childhood and Schooldays* 62; co-author (with Mary Clarke) *Dancers of Mercury—The Story of*

the Ballet Rambert 60; gramophone recording on ballet.
Mercury Theatre Trust Limited, 94 Chiswick High
Road, London, W.4, England.
Telephone: 01-995-4246.

Ramey, James Thomas, A.B., LL.B.; American government
official; b. 5 Dec. 1914; ed. Amherst Coll., and
Columbia University School of Law.
Tennessee Valley Authority 41-47; Asst. Gen. Counsel,
Atomic Energy Comm. 47-52, Asst. Manager, Chicago
Operations Office, AEC 52-56; Exec. Dir., Joint Con-
gressional Cttee. on Atomic Energy 56-62; Commr.
U.S. Atomic Energy Comm. 62-73; Consultant Joint
Cttee. on Atomic Energy 73-.
Joint Committee on Atomic Energy, U.S. Capitol,
Washington, D.C. 20515; 6817 Hillmead Road,
Bethesda, Md., U.S.A.

Ramgoolam, Rt. Hon. Sir Seewoosagur, Kt., L.R.C.P.,
M.R.C.S., M.L.A.; British (Mauritian) administrator and
physician; b. 18 Sept. 1900, Belle Rive; *m.*; two *c.*; ed.
Royal Coll., Mauritius and Univ. Coll., London.
Municipal Councillor 40-53, 56; Deputy Mayor of Port
Louis 56, Mayor 58; mem. Legislative Council 48-;
mem. Exec. Council 48-; Liaison Officer for Educ. 51-
56; Ministerial Sec. to the Treasury 58; Leader of the
House 60-; Minister of Finance 60-72; Chief Minister
61-65, Premier 65-68, Prime Minister 68-, also Minister
of Defence, Internal Security, External Affairs, Tourism
and Immigration, and Information and Broadcasting;
Chair. Board of Dirs. *Advance* (daily); Pres. Indian
Cultural Asscn.; Editor *Indian Cultural Review*; Hon.
mem. African Psychiatric Asscn. 70-; Fellow, Univ.
Coll. 71; Dr. h.c. (Univ. of New Delhi); Médaille de
l'Assemblée Nationale française 71; Grand Croix de
l'Ordre du Mérite de la République Centrafricaine 73,
Grand Croix, Ordre National de Lion de la République
du Sénégal 73, Grand Croix National de Bénin 73,
Grand Officier de la Légion d'Honneur de la République Française 73, UN Prize for Outstanding Achievements in the field of Human Rights.
85 Desforges Street, Port Louis, Mauritius.
Telephone: 2-0460.

Ramírez Vázquez, Pedro; Mexican architect; b.
16 April 1919, Mexico; *s.* of Dolores Vázquez and Max
Ramírez; *m.* Olga Campuzano; one *s.* one *d.*; ed. Univ.
Nacional Autónoma de México.
Professor of Design and City Planning, Nat. School of
Architecture, Univ. of Mexico; Past Pres. Soc. of
Mexican Architects and Nat. Coll. of Architects of
Mexico; Chair. Organizing Cttee., Games of XIX
Olympiad; Grand Prix of Twelfth Milan Triennial for
prefabricated rural school project; Gold Medal, Eighth
São Paulo Biennial for Nat. Museum of Anthropology,
Mexico City.
Leisure interest: industrial design.
Major works include: co-author of design for Nat.
School of Medicine, University City; plans for several
cities in Mexico; numerous prefabricated schools in
Mexico (also used in S. America, Europe and Asia);
buildings in Mexico City of Ministry of Labour, Nat.
Labour Conciliation Board, Nat. Inst. for Protection
of Infancy, Ministry of Foreign Affairs, and Aztec
Stadium; Mexican pavilions at Brussels, Seattle and
New York World Fairs; museums of Ciudad Juarez and
Mexico City; Nat. Gallery of History and Nat. Gallery
of Modern Art, Mexico City; Nat. Museum of Anthro-
pology, Mexico City.
c/o Escuela Nacional de Arquitectura, Universidad
Nacional Autónoma de México, Ciudad Universitaria,
Villa Obregón, México 20, D.F., Mexico.

Ramkumar, Ramkumar, M.A.; Indian artist; b. 23
Sept. 1924; ed. Delhi Univ., Académie André Lhote,
Paris, and Acad. Montmartre, Paris (with Fernand
Léger).
Worked in bank for one year; French Govt. scholarship,

Paris 50-52; returned to India 52; exhbns. in Europe
55, 58; travelled in Europe, Afghanistan, Ceylon,
Turkey and Egypt; mem. Lalit Kala Akademi, Sahitya
Akademi; Nat. Award, Nat. Art Exhbn., India 56, 58;
one-man exhbns. in Delhi, Bombay, Calcutta, Paris,
Prague, Warsaw, Colombo 50-65; Group exhbns. with
other Indian artists in London, New York, Tokyo, etc.;
exhibited at Int. exhbns., Venice, São Paulo, Tokyo.
Publs. two novels, two collections of stories, and one
travel book.
14 A/20 W.E. Area, New Delhi 5, India.

Rammler, Erich, DR.ING.; German mining engineer;
b. 9 July 1901, Tirpersdorf, Vogtland; *s.* of Max
Rammler and Emma (née Kaiser) Rammler; widower;
ed. Bergakad., Freiberg.
Assistant in Staatliche Hütten- und Blaufarbenwerke
25-28; on staff of Laboratory for Fuel Technology
28-36; Hon. Dir. of div. of Brown Coal Research Inst.
33-38; in practice as Technical Consultant 36-45; research activity 45-49; Prof. of Fuel Technology,
Thermal Econs., etc. Bergakad., Freiberg 49-66,
Emeritus 66-; mem. Deutsche Akad. der Wissenschaften
53, Sächsische Akad. der Wissenschaften 59; Hon.
mem. Gesellschaft Deutscher Berg- und Hüttenleute
65, Brennstofftechnischen Gesellschaft der D.D.R. 67;
Nat. Prize 51; Dr. Ing. h.c. (Aachen) 58.
Leisure interests: mountaineering, philosophy.
Richard-Wagner-Strasse 12, Freiberg/Sa., German
Democratic Republic.
Telephone: 3388.

Ramo, Simon, B.S., PH.D.; American engineering
executive; b. 7 May 1913, Salt Lake City, Utah; *s.* of
Benjamin and Clara (née Trestman) Ramo; *m.* Virginia
May Smith 1937; two *s.*; ed. Univ. of Utah and Calif.
Inst. of Technology.
With Gen. Electric Co., Schenectady 36-46; Lecturer,
Union Coll. 41-46; Dir. Research Electronics Dept.,
Guided Missiles Research and Devt., Vice-Pres. and
Dir. of Operations, Hughes Aircraft Co., Culver City
46-53; Exec. Vice-Pres., Dir., Ramo-Wooldridge
Corpn., L.A. 53-58; Pres. Space Technology Laboratories
Div. Ramo-Wooldridge Corpn. 57-58; Scientific Dir.
U.S.A.F. Ballistic Missiles Programme 54-58; Dir.
TRW Inc. 54-, Exec. Vice-Pres. 58-61, Vice-Chair. 61-,
Chair. Exec. Cttee. 69-; Research Assoc. Calif. Inst. of
Technology 46-; Dir. Union Bancorp Inc., Union Bank,
Times Mirror Co., U.S. Chamber of Commerce; Trustee,
Calif. Inst. of Technology, American Museum of
Electricity; Consultant, President's Science Advisory
Cttee.; mem. White House Energy Research and Devt.
Advisory Council; mem. U.S. State Dept. Cttee. on
Science and Foreign Affairs; Fellow, American Physical
Soc., Inst. of Aeronautics and Astronautics, American
Acad. of Arts and Sciences, American Asscn. for the
Advancement of Science, American Astronautical Soc.,
Inst. for the Advancement of Eng., Inst. of Electrical
and Electronic Engineers; Founder mem. Nat. Acad.
of Eng.; mem. Nat. Acad. of Sciences 73, Int. Acad. of
Astronautics, American Philosophical Soc., Snr.
Executives Advisory Council, Nat. Industrial Conf.
Board, Advisory Council on Japan/U.S. Economic
Relations, U.S. Chamber of Commerce Council on
Trends and Perspective; (Hon.) D.Sc., D.Eng., LL.D.,
and numerous other awards.
Leisure interests: tennis, the violin.
Publs. *Fields and Waves in Modern Radio* (with J. R.
Whinnery) 44, 53, *Introduction to Microwaves* 45,
Fields and Waves in Communication Electronics (with
J. R. Whinnery and Theodore Van Duzer) 65, *Cure for
Chaos* 69, *Century of Mismatch* 70, *Extraordinary Tennis
for the Ordinary Player* 70, *The Islands of E, Cono &
My* 73.
Office: One Space Park, Redondo Beach, Calif. 90278,
U.S.A.

Ramos, Celso; Brazilian industrialist and politician; ed. Colégio Catarinense.

Founded Fed. of Industries, Santa Catarina 50, Pres. 50-61; founded Dept. of Social Service in Industry, Santa Catarina 51; founded Dept. of Nat. Service and Industrial Apprenticeship, Santa Catarina 53; Gov. of the State of Santa Catarina 62-65; Pres. (founder), Faculty of Social Service 58-; mem. Nat. Council of the Nat. Confederation of Industry.

Avenida Trompowsky 19, Florianópolis, Santa Catarina, Brazil.

Ramos, João Baptista; Brazilian lawyer and politician; b. 7 May 1910; ed. Rio Branco High School and Univ. of São Paulo.

Member Chamber of Deputies 54-; Leader of fmr. Labour Party 57; Minister of Labour 60; Parl. Observer to Int. Labour Org. Conf., Geneva 64; First Vice-Pres. Chamber of Deputies 65, 66, Pres. 66-72.

Publ. *Organic Law on Social Welfare* 60.

Chamber of Deputies, Brasília, D.F., Brazil.

Rampal, Jean-Pierre Louis; French flautist; b. 7 Jan. 1922, Marseille; m. Françoise-Anne Bacqueyrisse 1947; one s. one d.; ed. Univ. de Marseille.

World-wide tours 45-; participant in major festivals in Rio de Janeiro, Aix, Menton, Salzburg, Edinburgh, Prague, Athens, Zagreb, Granada, Tokyo, etc.; Editor for Ancient and Classical Music, Int. Music Co., New York City 58-; Prof. Conservatoire Nat. de Musique de Paris; mem. French Musicological Soc.; Chevalier Légion d'Honneur; Chevalier de l'Ordre des Arts et Lettres de France; Grand Prix du Disque 54, 56, 59, 60, 61, 63, 64; Oscar du Premier Virtuose Français 56.

Leisure interests: tennis, deep-sea diving, movie-making.

15 Avenue Mozart, 75016 Paris, France.

Telephone: 288-28-96.

Ramphal, Sir Shridath Surendranath, Kt., C.M.G., Q.C., LL.M.; Guyanese barrister, politician and international official; b. 3 Oct. 1928, New Amsterdam; s. of James I. Ramphal and Grace Ramphal (née Abdool; m. Lois Winifred King 1951; two s. two d.; ed. Queen's Coll., Georgetown, King's Coll., London, Harvard Law School.

Crown Counsel, British Guiana 52-54; Asst. to Attorney-Gen. 54-56; Legal Draftsman 56-58; Solicitor-Gen. 59-61; First Legal Draftsman, West Indies 58-59; Asst. Attorney-Gen., West Indies 61-62; Attorney-Gen., Guyana 65-73; mem. Nat. Assembly 65-75; Minister of State for External Affairs 67-72, Minister of Foreign Affairs 72-75, of Justice 73-75; Commonwealth Sec.-Gen. 75-(80); Senior Counsel, Guyana 66; Hon. LL.D. (Punjab Univ.) 75; Arden and Atkin Prize, Gray's Inn 52; John Simon Guggenheim Fellowship 62; Order of the Republic (Egypt) 73; Grand Cross, Order of the Sun (Peru) 74; Grand Cross, Order of Merit (Ecuador) 74.

Leisure interests: boating, shooting, cooking.

Publs. contributions in legal and political journals, including *International and Comparative Law Quarterly, Caribbean Quarterly, Public Law, Guyana Journal, The Round Table.*

Commonwealth Secretariat, Marlborough House, Pall Mall, London, SW1Y 5HX, England.

Telephone: 01-839 3411.

Ramphul, Radha Krishna; Mauritian diplomatist; b. 4 Jan. 1926, Curepipe; s. of Pundit Sookdev Ramphul and Rhikya Ramvarain; m. Leela Devi Lallah 1950; one s. one d.; ed. London School of Econs., and Lincoln's Inn, London.

Company Sec. and Man. Sugar Estates 46-50; helped organize Field Workers Trade Union; Dir. private firm in London 55-69; Perm. Rep. to UN 69-.

Leisure interests: riding, shooting, fishing, tennis, swimming, reading, wildlife.

Permanent Mission of Mauritius to United Nations, 301 East 47th Street, Suite 3C, New York, N.Y. 10017, U.S.A.

Rampton, Calvin L., LL.B.; American lawyer and politician; b. 6 Nov. 1913, Bountiful, Utah; m. Lucybeth Cardon; two s. two d.; ed. Davis High School, Univ. of Utah, and George Washington Univ., Washington, D.C.

Administrative Asst. to Congressman J. W. Robinson 36-38; County Attorney, Davis County, Utah 39-40; Asst. Attorney-Gen. of Utah 41, 46-48; U.S. Army, Second World War; U.S. Supreme Court 46-; Gov. of Utah 65- (re-elected 72); Democrat.

Leisure interests: golf, reading, watching sports.

1270 Fairfax Road, Salt Lake City, Utah 84103, U.S.A. Telephone: 363-1270.

Ramsbotham, Hon. Sir Peter (Edward), K.C.M.G.; British diplomatist; b. 8 Oct. 1919, London; s. of 1st Viscount Soulbury; m. Frances Blomfield 1941; two s. one d.; ed. Eton Coll. and Magdalen Coll., Oxford.

Entered diplomatic service 48; served in Political Div., Allied Control Comm., Berlin 48-50; First Sec., Foreign Office 50-53; mem. U.K. del. to UN, New York 53-57; Foreign Office 57-63; Head of Chancery, British Embassy, Paris 63-67; Foreign Office 67-69; High Commr. to Cyprus 69-71; Amb. to Iran 71-74, to U.S.A. 74-; Croix de Guerre 45.

British Embassy, Washington, D.C., U.S.A.; Home: East Lane, Ovington, Alresford, Hants., England.

Telephone: Alresford 2515 (Home).

Ramsey, Norman Foster, Jr., M.A., PH.D., D.SC.; American scientist; b. 27 Aug. 1915, Washington, D.C.; s. of Brigadier-Gen. and Mrs. Norman F. Ramsey; m. Elinor Steadman Jameson 1940; four d.; ed. Columbia, Harvard and Cambridge Univs.

Assoc. Univ. of Illinois 40-42; Asst. Prof. Columbia Univ. 42-46; Research Assoc. Massachusetts Inst. of Technology Radiation Laboratory 40-43; Expert Consultant to Sec. of War 42-45; Group Leader and Asscn. Division Head, Los Alamos Laboratory of Atomic Energy Project 43-45; Chief Scientist of Atomic Energy Laboratory, Tinian 45; Assoc. Prof. Columbia Univ. 45-47; Head Physics Dept., Brookhaven Nat. Laboratory 46-47; Assoc. Prof. Harvard Univ. 47-50; Dir. Harvard Nuclear Laboratory 48-50 and 52-53; Air Force Scientific Advisory Cttee. 47-55; Dept. Defence Panel on Atomic Energy 53-58; Prof. of Physics, Harvard Univ. 50-; Higgins Prof. of Physics, Harvard Univ. 66-; Scientific Adviser NATO 58-59; Gen. Advisory Cttee., Atomic Energy Comm. 60-; Dir. Varian Associates 63-66; Pres. Univs. Research Asscn. 66-; Eastman Prof. Oxford Univ. 73-74; mem. Nat. Acad. of Sciences, American Acad. of Arts and Sciences, American Philosophical Soc.; Trustee, Carnegie Endowment for Int. Peace 62-; Hon. D.Sc. (Case Western Reserve Univ.) 68, (Middlebury Coll.) 69, (Oxford Univ.) 73; Presidential Order of Merit, Lawrence Award 60, Davisson-Germer Prize 74.

Leisure interests: skiing, walking, sailing, swimming, tennis, reading, conversation, music.

Publs. *Nuclear Moments* 53, *Nuclear Two-Body Problems* 53, *Molecular Beans* 55, *Quick Calculus* 65; and numerous articles in the *Physical Review.*

Lyman Physics Laboratory, Harvard University, Cambridge, Mass. 02178; and 55 Scott Road, Belmont, Mass. 02178, U.S.A.

Telephone: 617-495-2864.

Ramsey of Canterbury, Baron, (Life Peer), cr. 74; **Rt. Rev. and Rt. Hon. (Arthur) Michael Ramsey,** D.D.; British ecclesiastic; b. 14 Nov. 1904, Cambridge; s. of late Arthur Stanley Ramsey, Fellow and sometime Pres. of Magdalene Coll., Cambridge; m. Joan Hamilton 1942; ed. Repton School, Magdalene Coll., Cambridge, and Cuddesdon Theological Coll.

Curate, Liverpool Parish Church 28-30; sub-Warden of

Lincoln Theological Coll. 30-36; Lecturer, Boston Parish Church 36-38; Vicar, St. Benedict, Cambridge 39-40; Canon, Durham Cathedral, and Van Mildert Prof. of Divinity, Univ. of Durham 40-50; Regius Prof. of Divinity, Univ. of Cambridge 50-52; Lord Bishop of Durham 52-56; Archbishop of York 56-61, of Canterbury 61-74; Pres. World Council of Churches 62-68; Hon. Fellow Magdalene Coll., Cambridge, Merton Coll., Oxford; Hon. D.C.L. (Oxford, Nashotah House, Wis., and Kent); Hon. S.T.D. (New York and Columbia); Hon. LL.D. (Univ. of Canterbury, New Zealand); Hon. D.D. (Cambridge, Edinburgh, Durham, Leeds, Hull, Manchester, London, Huron Coll., Trinity Coll., Toronto, King's Coll., Halifax, Pacific Lutheran Univ., Episcopal Theological School, Cambridge, U.S.A., and Virginia Theological Seminary); Hon. Dr. of Laws (Los Angeles Occidental Coll.); Dr. h.c. (Inst. Catholique, Paris), D.Litt. (New Foundland, Keele), D.Hum.Litt. (Woodstock Coll., N.Y.).
Publs. *The Gospel and the Catholic Church* 36, *The Resurrection of Christ* 45, *The Glory of God and the Transfiguration of Christ* 49, *F. D. Maurice and the Conflicts of Modern Theology* 51, *Durham Essays and Addresses* 56, *From Gore to Temple* 60, *Introducing the Christian Faith* 61, *Canterbury Essays and Addresses* 64, *Sacred and Secular* 65, *God, Christ and the World* 69, *The Christian Priest Today* 72, *Canterbury Pilgrim* 74.
The Old Vicarage, Cuddesden, Oxford, England.

Rana, Damodar Shumshere Jung Bahadur, B.A.; Nepalese social worker and politician; b. July 1928, Palpa Tansen; s. of Lieut.-Gen. Madhab Shumshere J. B. Rana and Madhubi Kumari Rana; m. Bina Rana 1956; three s. one d.; ed. Missionary School, Darjeeling, Central Hindu School, Banaras and Banaras Hindu Univ.
Executive mem. social orgs. in Nepal 54-60; Chief Admin. Morang District 61; Chair. Special Comm. Kosi Zone 61, Commr. 62-64; mem. Nat. Panchayat, mem. Exec. Cttee. and Foreign Affairs Cttee.; Amb. to the U.S.S.R. 68-69, concurrently to Poland, Hungary and Czechoslovakia; Zonal Commr. Janakpur Zone 70-71; awarded Prabala Gorkha Dakchina Bahu and Subikhyat Trisakti Patt.
Phohara Durbar, Kathmandu, Nepal.
Telephone: 11274.

Ranasinha, Sir Arthur Godwin, C.M.G., C.B.E.; Sri Lanka civil servant, banker and diplomatist; b. 24 June 1898, Colombo; s. of W. P. Ranasinha; m. Annette Hilda de Alwis (died 1968); one s. (deceased) two d.; ed. St. Thomas' Coll., Colombo and Trinity Hall, Cambridge.
Magistrate, Point Pedro, Balapitiya, Jaffna 23-28; District Judge, Avissawella 28-30, Badulla 30-32; Sec. to Minister of Agriculture and Lands 33-36; Public Trustee 36-44; Custodian of Enemy Property 39-44; Superintendent of Census 44-46; Sec. to Vice-Chair. Board of Ministers on his political Mission to London 45; Land Commr. 46-47; Permanent Sec. Ministry of Agriculture and Lands 47-50; Sec. to Cabinet and Deputy Sec. to the Treasury 50; Chair. and Leader of Ceylon Del. to Commonwealth Consultative Cttee. on Colombo Plan 50-51; Permanent Sec. Ministry of Finance, Sec. to the Treasury and Sec. to the Cabinet 50-54; Gov. Central Bank 54-59; Ambassador to Italy. and concurrently Greece and Israel 59-61; Chair. People's Bank Comm., Taxation Enquiry Comm., Tea Comm. 66-68; Knight Grand Cross of Order of Merit of Italy 61.
Leisure interests: chess, racing, writing.
Publs. *General Report on the Census of Ceylon* 46, *Memories and Musings* 72.
99/1 Rosemead Place, Colombo 7, Sri Lanka.
Telephone: Colombo 92067.

Randall, Sir John Turton, Kt., D.SC., F.R.S.; British biophysicist; b. 23 March 1905, Newton-le-Willows, Lancs.; s. of late Sidney and Hannah Cawley Randall; m. Doris Duckworth 1928; one s.; ed. Univ. of Manchester.
Research Staff of G.E.C. Ltd. Wembley 26-37; Warren Research Fellow of Royal Society in Univ. of Birmingham 37-43; Temporary Lecturer Cavendish Laboratory Cambridge 43-44; Prof. of Natural Philosophy in Univ. of St. Andrews 44-46; Wheatstone Prof. of Physics in Univ. of London (King's Coll.) 46-61, Prof. of Biophysics 61-70, Emeritus Prof.; Dir. Medical Research Council, Biophysics Unit, King's Coll. 47-70, Chair. School of Biological Science 63-69; Hon. Prof. Univ. of Edinburgh 70-; several awards.
Publs. *The Diffraction of X-rays by Amorphous Solids and Liquids* 34, *The Nature and Structure of Collagen* (Editor) 53, etc.
University of Edinburgh, Department of Zoology, West Mains Road, Edinburgh EH9 3JT, Scotland.

Randall, Michael Bennett; British journalist; b. 12 Aug. 1919; ed. St. Peter's School, Seaford, and Canford School.
Assistant Editor, *Sunday Chronicle* 52-53; Editor *Sunday Graphic* 53; Asst. Editor *Daily Mirror* 53-56; Asst. Editor *News Chronicle* 56-57; Asst. Editor *Daily Mail* 57-61, Deputy Editor 61-63, Editor 63-66; Man. Editor (News) *Sunday Times* 67-72, Senior Man. Editor 72-; Hannen Swaffer Award as Journalist of 1965-66.
Keepers, Chailey, Sussex, England.

Randers, Gunnar, M.SC.; Norwegian physicist; b. 28 April 1914, Oslo; s. of Gunnar and Lubba Randers (née Brodtkorb); m. Engelke R. Koren 1939; two s. one d.; ed. Oslo Univ.
Research Fellow, Mount Wilson Observatory, California 39-40; Instructor, Univ. of Chicago 40-42; Captain, Norwegian Army and Scientific Officer, British Ministry of Supply 42-45; Dir. Astrophysics Inst., Oslo Univ. 46-47; chief scientist, Norwegian Defence Research Establishment 47-51; Dir. Dutch-Norwegian Joint Establishment for Nuclear Energy Research 51-59; exec. Vice-Pres. European Atomic Energy Society 54-56; Chair. Norwegian Atomic Energy Council 55-68; Man. Dir. Inst. for Atomenergi, Kjeller 48-71; special adviser on atomic energy matters to the Sec.-Gen. of the U.N. 54; Scientific Adviser to Dir.-Gen. Int. Atomic Energy Agency, Vienna 58, Gov. 60; Dir. American Nuclear Society 55-57; Chair. Norwegian Agency for Int. Devt. 63-68; Pres. European Atomic Energy Soc. 66-67; Asst. Sec.-Gen. NATO 68-74; Pres. Scandpower Inc., Oslo and Washington, D.C. 76-; Visiting Investigator, Woods Hole Oceanographical Inst., U.S.A.; European Consultant for Bechtel Int. Inc.; mem. Royal Astronomical Soc., Norwegian Acad. of Science; Commdr. Norwegian Order of St. Olav, and Netherlands Orders of Orange-Nassau and House of Orange, Commdr. Finland's White Rose, and Sweden's Vasa Order, Commdr. Yugoslav Flag Order, Commdr. Order of Dannebrog.
Publs. *Atom Energy* 46, *Atoms and Common Sense* 50, *Reactors and Bombs* 68, *Lightyears* 75.
Trosterudstien 4, Oslo 3, Norway.
Telephone: Oslo 147210.

Randolph, (Asa) Philip; American labour leader; b. 15 April 1889; ed. Coll. of City of New York.
Organizer, Brotherhood of Sleeping Car Porters 25, Pres. Emer. 68; Pres. Negro-American Labor Council 60-; Vice-Pres. A.F.L.-C.I.O. 57-; Organizer and Dir. March on Washington Movement 41; Organizer and Dir. Washington Freedom March Aug. 63.
260 Park Avenue, New York City, N.Y., U.S.A.

Randolph, Jennings, A.B.; American educator, executive and politician; b. 8 March 1902, Salem, W. Va.;

s. of Ernest and Idell (née Bingman) Randolph; *m.* Mary Katherine Babb 1933; two *s.*; ed. Salem Coll.
Associate Editor *West Virginia Review* 25; Dir. Dept. of Public Speaking and Journalism, Davis and Elkins Coll. 26-32; Prof. of Public Speaking, Dir. Athletics, Southeastern Univ. 36; mem. U.S. House of Reps. 33-47; Asst. to Pres. and Dir. of Public Relations, Capital Airlines; Dean Coll. of Business and Financial Admin., Southeastern Univ.; U.S. Senator from West Virginia 58- (re-elected 72); several honorary degrees; Democrat.
Senate Office Building, Washington, D.C. 20510, U.S.A.

Ranga, N. G.; Indian professor and politician; b. 7 Nov. 1900, Nidubrolu; *m.* Bharati Devi 1924; ed. Oxford Univ., England.
College Prof. of Econs., Madras Univ., India; Founder Indian Peasant Movement 30; M.P. 34-; mem. Congress Working Cttee. 47-51; Founder Bharat Krishikar Lok (Peasant Peoples) Party 51; mem. Congress 55, Gen. Sec. Congress Parl. Party 59; Leader Swatantra Group, Lok Sabha 59-71; Hon. Principal Indian Peasants' Inst., Nidubrolu, A.P.
Publs. About 43 books, including *Credo of World Peasantry* 57, *Towards World Peace* 57, *Fight for Freedom* (autobiog.) 68, *Bapu Blesses* (talks with Gandhi) 70, *Kakatiya Nayaks* (14th Century Story of South Indian Freedom Fighters) 71.
Ponnur, Andhra Pradesh, India.
Telephone: Ponnur 106.

Rank, Sir Benjamin Keith, Kt., C.M.G., M.B., M.S., L.R.C.P., F.R.C.S., F.R.A.C.S., F.A.C.S.; Australian surgeon; b. 14 Jan. 1911, Heidelberg, Victoria; *m.* Barbara Lyle Facy 1938; one *s.* three *d.*; ed. Melbourne Univ.
War service 39-46 (Lieut.-Col.); Hon. Plastic Surgeon, Royal Melbourne Hosp. 46-66, Consulting Surgeon 66-, Chair. Board of Postgraduate Educ. 68-75, Medical Adviser to Board of Man. 71-75; Consulting Plastic Surgeon to Dept. of Repatriation, also to Queen Victoria Hosp. and Royal Victorian Eye and Ear Hosp.; Chief Reparative Surgeon, Peter MacCallum Clinic 64-; Chair. Cttee. of Man., Victorian Plastic Surgery Unit, Preston and Northcote Community Hosp.; Visiting Prof. Harvard Univ. 76; Pres. British Asscn. of Plastic Surgeons 65; Pres. Royal Australasian Coll. of Surgeons 66-68, Syme Orator 76; Foundation Chair. Australian Coll. of Speech Therapy, Hon. Fellow 65; Hon. Fellow, Royal Coll. of Surgeons of Canada 69, of Edinburgh 73; Hon. F.A.C.S. 74.
Publs. *Surgery of Repair as Applied to Hand Injuries* (co-author) 63, *Jerry Moore and Some of His Contemporaries* 75; more than 40 papers in British, American and Australian journals.
29 Royal Parade, Parkville, Victoria 3052; Home: "Mill Hill", Vine Street, Heidelberg, Victoria 3084, Australia.
Telephone: 347-1107 and 347-7050.

Rank, Joseph McArthur; British business executive; b. 24 April 1918, Kingswood, Surrey; *s.* of the late Rowland Rank and Margaret (née McArthur); *m.* The Hon. Moira, *d.* 3rd Baron Southborough; one *s.* one *d.*; ed. Loretto School.
Joined Mark Mayhew Ltd., Flour Millers 36; Royal Air Force 40-46; Joint Managing Dir. Joseph Rank Ltd. 55-; Deputy Chair. Ranks Hovis McDougall Ltd. 65-69, Chair. 69-; Chair. British Nutrition Foundation Ltd. 68-69; Chair. Millers Mutual Asscn. 69-; Pres. Nat. Asscn. of British and Irish Millers 57-58; First High Sheriff of East Sussex 74-75.
Landhurst, Hartfield, Sussex, England.

Ránki, Dezső; Hungarian pianist; b. 8 Sept. 1951, Budapest; *s.* of József Ránki and Edith Jecsmen; ed. Ferenc Liszt Music Acad., Budapest (under Pál Kadosa).
Has given recitals and appeared with several leading

orchestras throughout Europe; with Zoltán Kocsis (*q.v.*) toured U.S.A. with Budapest Symphony Orchestra under György Lehel 71; Solo tour Japan, Philippines, Singapore, India 75; First Prize, Int. Schumann Competition, Zwickau, G.D.R. 69, Grand Prix Int. du Disque (Paris) 72, Liszt Prize 2nd Degree 73.
Leisure interests: gramophone records, sound tapes, Italian and Chinese food.
H-1073, Budapest VII, Kertész-utca 50; Interconcert Agency, Budapest V, Vörösmarty tér 1, Hungary.
Telephone: 421-400 (Home); 329-580 (Agency).

Ránki, György; Hungarian composer; b. 30 Oct. 1907, Budapest; *s.* of Dr. Frigyes Reisz and Szidonia Hönig; *m.* Anna Dékány 1940; one *s.* one *d.*; ed. Budapest (under Kodály, etc.) and Paris.
Erkel Prize; Kossuth Prize 54; Merited Artist of the Hungarian People's Repub.; Gold Medal of Labour 67, Pro Arte 70.
Leisure interests: gardening, swimming, yoga.
Works include *On the Outskirts of Town* (cantata) 47, *1848* (folk-song cantata) 48, *Sword Dance* 49, *Song of Freedom* 51, *King Pomade's New Clothes* (opera, 1st and 2nd Suite for Orchestra), *Two Wonder Oxen* 56, *Pentaerophonia* (quintet for woodwind) 58, *Winner Unknown* (children's opera) 60, *Three Nights* (drama with music) 61, *1514* (fantasy for piano and orchestra) 61, *Ladies at Choice* (operetta) 61, *A Streetcar Named Desire* (incidental music) 62; *Peter in Musicland* (children's opera) 62, *A Midsummer Night's Dream* (incidental music) 64, *The Circus* (ballet) 65, *1944* (oratorio) 66, *Aurora Tempestuosa* (prelude for orchestra) 67, *Panic* (musical comedy) 67, *The Tragedy of Man* (mysterio-opera) 70, *Lament* (in memoriam Zoltán Kodály) 71, *Cantus Urbis* (oratorio) 72, *Raga di Notte* (violin and orchestra), *The Magic Drink* (ballet) 74; vocal and instrumental, educational, film and stage music 30-75.
Gülbaba-utca 36, H-1023, Budapest II, Hungary.
Telephone: 359-407.

Rankin, Dame Annabelle, D.B.E.; Australian politician and diplomatist; b. 28 July 1908, Brisbane; *d.* of the late Col. C. D. W. Rankin, mem. of Queensland Legislative Assembly; ed. Childers, Howard and Glennie Memorial School, Toowoomba.
State Sec. Queensland Girl Guides Asscn.; served in Second World War in Voluntary Aid Detachment and as Y.W.C.A. Asst. Commr. for Queensland attached to the Army; Organizer Jr. Red Cross in Queensland 46; mem. Senate 46; mem. Parl. Standing Cttee. on Broadcasting 47, Parl. Public Works Cttee. 50; Opposition Chief Whip in Senate 47-49, Govt. Whip 51-66; Vice-Pres. Liberal Party Queensland 49; Minister for Housing Jan. 66-March 71; High Commr. in New Zealand 71-74; mem. Commonwealth Parl. Del. to Canada 52; Vice-Pres. Multiple Handicapped Children's Asscn.; Patron Cystic Fibrosis Asscn.; mem. Fed. Cttee. of Outward Bound Asscn., Advisory Cttee. of Australian Broadcasting, Queensland; Liberal.
c/o Ministry of Foreign Affairs, Canberra, A.C.T., Australia.

Rankin, Bruce I.; Canadian diplomatist; b. 20 March 1918, Brandon, Man.; *m.*; three *d.*; ed. Univ. of Alberta and Nat. Defence Coll., Fort Frontenac, Kingston, Ont.
Royal Canadian Navy 41-45, discharged with rank of Lieut.-Commdr.; joined Trade Commissioner Service 45, serving in Sydney, Shanghai, Canberra, Bombay, Madrid, Berne and New York; Deputy Consul Gen., New York 59-64; Amb. to Venezuela and the Dominican Repub. 64-70; Consul Gen., New York 70-76; Gen. Assembly Second Cttee. (Econ. and Financial), Rep. 67-73; Chair. 72-; Amb. to Japan Feb. 76-.
Embassy of Canada, 3-38, Akasaka 8-chome, Minato-ku, Tokyo, Japan.

Ranković, Aleksandar; Yugoslav politician; b. 28 Nov. 1909, Draževac, Belgrade; *m.*; two *s.*
Active in trade union movements and illegal Communist Party; arrested and imprisoned for political activities 29-35; after release was in military service and active in workers' movement; arrested by Gestapo 41, but released by Partisans; mem. Supreme Staff Nat. Liberation Army 41-45; Collaborator of Marshal Tito 37-66; Gen. Col. of Yugoslav Nat. Army; Minister of the Interior and Gov. Vice-Pres. 46-52; Vice-Pres. Fed. Exec. Council 53-63; Pres. Atomic Cttee. 56-63; Vice-Pres. of Yugoslavia June 63-66; Sec. C.P. Secr. until 66; Pres. Cen. Cttee. Union of Veterans of Nat. Liberation War; Nat. Hero; many foreign and nat. decorations.
Leisure interests: hunting, chess.
Andre Nikolića No. 5, Belgrade, Yugoslavia.
Telephone: 51-882.

Rao, Calyampudi Radhakrishna, M.A., SC.D., F.N.A., F.R.S.; Indian statistician; b. 10 Sept. 1920, Hadagali, Mysore State; *s.* of C. D. Naidu and A. Laxmikanthamma; *m.* Bhargavi Rao 1948; one *s.* one *d.*; ed. Andhra and Calcutta Univs.
Research at Indian Statistical Inst. 43-46, Cambridge Univ. 46-48; Prof. and Head of Div. of Theoretical Research and Training 49-64; Dir. Research and Training School, Indian Statistical Inst. 64-71, Sec. and Dir. 72-76, Jawaharlal Nehru Prof. 76-; Fellow, Inst. of Math. Statistics; Treas. 61-65, now mem. Int. Statistical Inst., Pres.-elect 75-77, Pres. 77-79; Hon. Fellow Royal Statistical Soc.; Fellow, American Statistical Asscn., Econometric Soc.; Hon. Foreign mem. American Acad. Arts and Sciences; Pres.-elect 75-76, Pres. 76-77, Inst. of Mathematical Statistics, U.S.A.; Hon. Fellow, King's Coll., Cambridge Univ.; Editor *Sankhya* (Indian Journal of Statistics); Bhatnagar Memorial Award for Scientific Research; Padma Bhushan; Guy Silver Medal Royal Statistical Soc.; Meghnad Saha Gold Medal; Hon. D.Sc. (Andhra, Delhi and Leningrad Univs.).
Leisure interest: writing humorous essays.
Publs. include: *Advanced Statistical Methods in Biometric Research, Linear Statistical Inference and its Application, Generalized Inverse of Matrices and its Applications, Characterization Problems of Mathematical Statistics;* over one hundred research papers in mathematical statistics.
Indian Statistical Institute, 7, Shaheed Jeet Singh Sansanwal Marg, New Delhi 110029, India.
Telephone: 678823 (Office); 70113 (Home).

Rao, Chandra Rajeswar; Indian politician; b. 6 June 1914; ed. Hindu High School, Masulipatam, and Banaras Hindu Univ.
At Vizagapatam Medical Coll. 36-37; joined Communist Party, Andhra 36; mem. Central Cttee. Communist Party of India 48, Gen. Sec. 50-51, 64-; Order of Lenin 74.
Communist Party of India, Ajoy Bhavan, Kotla Road, New Delhi-1, India.
Telephone: New Delhi 271002.

Rao, Chintamani Nagesa Ramachandra, M.SC., D.SC., PH.D., F.R.I.C.; Indian professor of chemistry; b. 30 June 1934, Bangalore; *s.* of H. Nagesa Rao; *m.* Indumati Rao 1960; one *s.* one *d.*; ed. Mysore, Banaras, Purdue and California Univs.
Lecturer, Indian Inst. of Science, Bangalore 59-63; Prof., later Senior Prof., Indian Inst. of Technology, Kanpur 63-, Dean of Research and Devt. 69-72; Visiting Prof. Purdue Univ., U.S.A. 67-68, Oxford Univ. 74-75; Chair. IUPAC Cttee. on Teaching of Chem.; mem. Nat. Cttee. on Science and Tech. 70-74, Editorial Boards of seven int. journals; Fellow, Indian Acad. of Sciences, Indian Nat. Science Acad., St.

Catherine's Coll., Oxford 74-75; Jawarhalal Nehru Fellow, Indian Inst. of Tech.; Marlow Medal, Faraday Soc. 67; Bhatnagar Award 68; Padma Shri 74.
Leisure interests: swimming, gourmet cooking, general reading, watching birds.
Publs. *Ultraviolet Visible Spectroscopy* 60, *Chemical Applications of Infra-red Spectroscopy* 63, *Spectroscopy in Inorganic Chemistry* 70, *Modern Aspects of Solid State Chemistry* 70, *Solid State Chemistry* 74; nearly 200 original research papers.
Indian Institute of Technology, Kanpur 208016, India.

Rao, Kanuru Lakshmana, PH.D., F.I.C.E., F.I.STRUCT.E., F.I.E.; Indian engineer and politician; b. 15 July 1902, Kankipadu, Andhra Pradesh; *s.* of the late Shri K. Mallikharjuna Rao; *m.* K. Vara Lakshmi 1924; three *s.* two *d.*; ed. Univ. of Madras and Univ. of Birmingham.
Former Chief Engineer (Floods), Indian Central Govt.; fmr. mem. (Design and Research), Central Water and Power Comm., Govt. of India, and Pres. Central Board of Irrigation and Power; mem. Parl. 62-; Minister of State for Irrigation and Power 63-73; Pres. Int. Soc. on Soil Mechanics and Foundation Engineering; Pres. Inst. of Engineers 59-61; conferred Padma Bhushan 63 by Pres. of Indian Republic.
Leisure interests: reading, writing.
Publs. *Calculations, Designs and Testing of Reinforced Concrete, India's Water Wealth.*
7 Lodi Estate, New Delhi 3, India.
Telephone: 611073.

Rao, K. N., M.B.B.S., M.D.; Indian medical official and administrator; b. 31 Jan. 1907, Gudivada, Andhra Pradesh; *s.* of K. Venkatappiah and Ratna Desiraju; *m.* Susila Radhakrishnan 1930; two *d.*; ed. Univ. of Madras.
Entered Indian Medical Service 35; Prof. of Medical Jurisprudence, Christian Medical Coll., Vellore 48-49; Tuberculosis Adviser to Govt. of Madras 51-54; Dir. of Medical Services, Andhra Pradesh 54-63; Dir.-Gen. of Health Services, Govt. of India 64-68; Chair. Exec. Board, WHO 67-68; Pan American Health Org./WHO Consultant on Medical Educ. in Latin America 68; WHO Visiting Prof. of Int. Health, School of Hygiene, Toronto Univ. 68; Exec. Dir., Indian Asscn. for Advancement of Medical Educ. 68-70; WHO Consultant, Medical Educ. in Africa 70; Sec.-Gen., Population Council of India 70-73; Pres. World Federation of Public Health Asscns. 67-68; Visiting Prof. of Medicine, Sri Venkateswara Univ. 70-71; Editor-in-Chief *Journal of Medical Education* 70-74; Hon. consultant Population Studies Centre, Sri Venkateswara Univ.; Consultant, Pan American Health Org./WHO, Washington, D.C., on Health and Population Dynamics Oct. 73-March 74; Exec. Dir. Indian Acad. of Med. Sciences 75-; Sec. Nat. Board of Examinations 75-; official on numerous Indian and int. health orgs.; Hon. LL.D. and other hon. degrees; numerous awards.
Publs. *Recent Development in the Field of Health and Medical Education* 66, *India and World Health* 68; Gen. Editor *Text Book of Tuberculosis* 72, *Philosophy of Medicine* 68.
Indian Academy of Medical Sciences, C II/16, Ansari, Nagar, New Delhi 16; Home: D-57, Naraina, New Delhi 28, India.
Telephone: 393178 (Home).

Rao, Raja; Indian writer; b. 21 July 1909; ed. Nizam Coll., Hyderabad, Univs. of Montpellier and Paris.
Professor of Philosophy, Univ. of Texas.
Publs. *Kanthapura, Cow of the Barricades, The Serpent and The Rope, The Cat and Shakespeare;* short stories in French and English.
c/o Department of Philosophy, University of Texas, Austin, Tex., U.S.A.

Rao, Vijayendra Kasturi Ranga Varadaraja, M.A., B.A., PH.D., D.LITT.; Indian economist and government official; b. 8 July 1908, Kancheepuram; s. of K. Kasturi Ranga char and Bharathi Bai; m. 1st Pramila 1931 (died 1955); 2nd Kamala 1962; one s. two d.; ed. Wilson Coll., Bombay, and Gonville and Caius Coll., Cambridge. Principal and Prof. of Econs., L.D. Arts Coll., Ahmedabad 37-42; Prof. and Head of Dept. of Econs., Delhi Univ. 42-57; Dir. of Statistics, Govt. of India 44-45; Planning Adviser, Govt. of India 45-46; Food and Econ. Adviser, Embassy of India, Washington 46-47; Founder and Dir. Delhi School of Econs., Delhi Univ. 49-57, Vice-Chancellor, Delhi Univ. 57-60; Founder and Dir. Inst. of Econ. Growth 60-63; mem. Indian Planning Comm. 63-; Chair. UN Sub-Comm. on Econ. Devt. 47-50; mem. Parl. 67-; Union Minister for Transport and Shipping 66-69; Minister of Educ. and Youth Services 69-71; Founder, Dir. Inst. for Social and Econ. Change, Bangalore 72; Hon. D.C.L. (Oxford) 69; Hon. Fellow Gonville and Caius Coll., Cambridge 71; Padma Vibhushan Award 74.
Leisure interests: nature study, music, philosophy.
Publs. *Taxation of Income in India* 31, *An Essay on India's National Income, 1925-29* 39, *The National Income of British India, 1931-32* 40, *War and Indian Economy* 43, *India and International Currency Plans* 46, *Post-war Rupee* 48, *Foreign Aid and India's Economic Development* 62, *Essays on Economic Development* 63, *Greater Delhi—A Study in Urbanisation 1947-57* 65, *Education and Human Resource Development* 66, *Values and Economic Development, The Indian Challenge* 71, *The Nehru Legacy* 71, *Inflation and India's Economic Crisis* (co-author) 73, *Growth with Justice in Asian Agriculture, Iran's Fifth Plan—An Attempted Economic Leap* 75, *The Indian Road to Democratic Socialism—An Indian View* 76; edited: *Agricultural Labour in India* 61, *Employment and Unemployment* 65, *Bangala Desh Economy—Problems and Prospects* 72, *Planning for Change—Issues in Mysore's Development* 74.
Office: c/o Office of the Director, Institute for Social and Economic Change, Post Bag No. 4003, Bangalore 560040; "Dayanidhi", No. 1170A, 26A Main Road, 4th "T" Block, Jayanagar Bangalore 560040, India.
Telephone: 66224 (Office); 41515 (Home).

Raoul, Major Alfred; Congolese army officer and politician; b. 1930; ed. Military Acad., Saint-Cyr, France.
Adjutant to C.-in-C. of Congolese Armed Forces 63-65; Dir. of Corps of Engineers 65; Sec. in charge of Defence, Directorate of Nat. Revolutionary Council Aug. 68; Prime Minister of Congo (Brazzaville) Aug. 68-Dec. 69, concurrently Minister of Defence Sept. 68-Jan. 69, concurrently Minister of State Planning and Admin. Sept.-Dec. 69; Head of State Sept. 68-Jan. 69; Vice-Chair. Council of State Dec. 69-Dec. 71; arrested Feb. 72; fmr. mem. Political Bureau of Congolese Workers' Party (P.C.T.); 2nd Sec. Cen. Cttee. of P.C.T.
Brazzaville, People's Republic of Congo.

Raoul-Duval, Gérard; French diplomatist; b. 3 March 1908, Paris; s. of Charles Raoul-Duval and Beatrice (née Tobin); m. Monique de Vanssay 1941; one d.; ed. Lycée Janson-de-Sailly, Paris.
Ministry of Foreign Affairs 34-, French Embassy, Bucharest 34, Consulate, Los Angeles 36, Hong Kong 41, Sec. of Embassy, Ottawa 44, Consul-Gen. Salonika 45, Minister-Resident, Rangoon 48, Counsellor of Embassy, Warsaw 50, Buenos Aires 52, Minister in Charge of Consulate-Gen. Hong Kong 56-59, Counsellor, Tunis 59, Amb. to Pakistan 62-64, to Chile 65-69, to Luxembourg 71-72; Commdr., Légion d'Honneur.
Leisure interests: golf, music.
"le Mas Saint-Pierre", Chemin de Bibenas, 13 Aix-en-Provence, France.
Telephone: 47-10-91.

Rapai, Gyula; Hungarian politician and diplomatist; b. 1923; ed. Soviet Communist Party High School, Moscow.
Joined Hungarian Communist Party 45; Deputy Leader, later Head, Agitprop Dept., Hungarian Socialist Workers' Party Cen. Cttee. 59-62; First Sec. Hungarian Socialist Workers' Party County Baranya Cttee. 62-70; mem. Parl. 62-66; mem. Nat. Council of Trade Unions 66-70; Amb. to U.S.S.R. 70-.
Embassy of Hungary, Mosfilmovskaya ulitsa 62, Moscow, U.S.S.R.
Telephone: 143-86-11.

Raper, Kenneth Bryan; American professor of bacteriology and botany; b. 11 July 1908, Welcome, N.C.; s. of William Franklin Raper and Julia Crouse Raper; m. Louise Montgomery Williams; one s.; ed. Univ. of N.C. and George Washington and Harvard Univs.
Junior Mycologist Bureau of Chem. and Soils, U.S. Dept. of Agriculture (U.S.D.A.) 29-36, Asst. Mycologist Bureau of Plant Industry 36-40; Microbiologist, later Principal Microbiologist N. Regional Research Laboratory, U.S.D.A., Peoria, Ill. 40-53; Prof. of Bacteriology and Botany, Univ. of Wis. 53-, mem. Cancer Research Cttee. 56-60; Visiting Prof. of Botany, Univ. of Ill. 46-53; Trustee, American Type Culture Collection, Washington, D.C. 48-52, Chair. Exec. Cttee. 52-55; mem. Merck Fellowship Board, Nat. Research Council 53-57, Exec. Cttee. Div. of Biology and Agriculture 56-61; mem. Selection Cttee. for Senior Postdoctoral Fellowships, Nat. Science Foundation 61-64, Chair. Biological Sciences 62-64; Chair. U.S. Del. to Gen. Assembly of Int. Union of Biological Sciences (IUBS), London 58, Prague 64, Chair. U.S. Nat. Cttee. IUBS 62-64; Chair. U.S. Nat. Cttee. for Int. Botanical Congress (Vice-Pres. XI Int. Bot. Congress), Seattle 69; mem. Nat. Acad. of Sciences (mem. of Council 61-64), American Acad. of Arts and Sciences, American Philosophical Soc., American Asscn. for the Advancement of Science, Mycological Soc. of America (Pres. 51), Soc. of Industrial Microbiologists (Pres. 53), Soc. of American Microbiologists (Councillor 54-58), etc.; Lasker Award (Co-Recipient) 46, Distinguished Service Award, U.S.D.A. (Co-Recipient) 47, Charles Thom Award, Soc. for Industrial Microbiology 67.
Leisure interests: photography, gardening.
Publs. *Manual of the Aspergilli* (with Charles Thom) 45, *Manual of the Penicillia* (with Charles Thom) 49, *The Genus Aspergillus* (with Dorothy I. Fennell) 65; Research papers on Saprophytic fungi, Industrial microbiology, and cellular slime molds.
Department of Bacteriology, University of Wisconsin, Madison, Wis. 53706; Home: 4110 Chippewa Drive, Madison, Wis. 53711, U.S.A.
Telephone: 608-262-3055 (Office); 608-233-7703 (Home).

Raphael, Yitzhak, M.A., PH.D.; Israeli politician; b. 5 July 1914; ed. Hebrew Univ.
Settled in Palestine 35; mem. Exec. Jewish Agency and Head, Emigration Dept. 48-54; mem. of 2nd, 3rd, 4th, 5th, 6th and 7th Knesset; Chair. Exec. Hapoel Hamizrachi (Nat. Religious Party); mem. World Exec. Nat. Religious Party Mizrachi; Chair. Legislative Cttee. Knesset; Chair. Mossad Harav Kook (Publishers); Deputy Minister of Health 62-64; Minister of Religious Affairs 74-; Chair. Yad Harav Maimon Judaic Studies Centre.
Publs. *Sefer Hachasidith, Rishonim v'achronim, Hachasidut v'Eretz Israel*; Ed. *Encyclopaedia of Religious Zionism* 59, 60.
P.O. Box 642, Jerusalem, Israel.

Rappleye, Willard Cole, A.B., M.D.; American university professor and administrator; b. 11 Feb. 1892; ed. Univ. of Ill., and Harvard Medical School.

Worked with manufacturing companies 09-11; Instructor in Comparative Anatomy, Univ. of Ill. 13-14, in Biology 13-14; Tutor in Economics 13-14; John Harvard Hon. Scholarship 15-18; with Harvard Dental School 15-17; Asst. Physician, Foxboro State Hospital, Mass. 17-18; Mass. General Hospital, Boston 18-19; Dir. Clinical Laboratories, Univ. of Calif. 19-20, Dir. of Hospitals and Prof. of Hospital Admin. 20-22; Medical Adviser, Calif. State Board of Control 20-22; Act. Supt. Pacific Colony for Feeble-minded, Calif. 20-22; Supt. New Haven Hospital 22-26; Prof. Hospital Admin., Yale Univ. 22-26; Dir. of Study, Comm. on Medical Educ. 25-32; Dean Faculty of Med. 31-58, Emer. 58-; Prof. of Medical Economics, Columbia Univ. 31-60, Vice-Pres. in charge of Medical Affairs 49-58; Dir. N.Y. Post Graduate School 33-47; Dean School of Dental and Oral Surgery 33-45; mem. Advisory Board for Medical Specialities 33-44, Pres. 37-44, Chair. Comm. on Graduate Medical Education 37-39; Pres. Advisory Council on Medical Education 39-44; Pres. Asscn. of American Medical Colls. 38-39; Chair. Exec. Council 42-44; Commr. of Hospitals, N.Y. City 40-42; Chair. Board of Dirs., Health Insurance Plan of Greater New York 44-48; Pres. Josiah Macy Jr. Foundation 41-; Chair. William J. Matheson Comm. 31-54; Pres. William J. Matheson Foundation 54-64; Fellow N.Y. Acad. of Medicine; Hon. A.M. (Yale), Hon. Sc.D. (Trinity Coll. and Rutgers Univ.), Hon. Med.ScD. (Women's Medical Coll. of Pa.); Hon. L.H.D. (N.Y. Medical Coll.).
31 East 79th Street, New York City, N.Y. 10021, N.Y., U.S.A.

Rapson, Ralph, B.ARCH.; American architect; b. 13 Sept. 1914; ed. Alma (Mich.) Coll., Univ. of Mich. Coll. of Architecture, and Cranbrook Acad. of Art.
Practising architect 41-; Head Dept. of Architecture Chicago Inst. of Design 42-46; Assoc. Prof. of Architecture M.I.T. School of Architecture 46-54 (leave of absence to execute designs in Europe for State Dept. 51-53); Prof. and Head of School of Architecture, Univ. of Minnesota 54-; mem. American Inst. of Architects, Int. Congress of Modern Architecture; Dir. Walker Art Gallery; fmr. Chair. Editorial Board *Northwest Architect*; numerous awards include Parker Medal 51, American Inst. of Architects Honor Award for U.S. Embassy, Stockholm 54, two Merit Awards 55, Honour Award 58.
Designs include projects for U.S. Government, several churches and schools, commercial, industrial and residential buildings, particularly U.S. Embassy, Stockholm, U.S. Embassy, Copenhagen, U.S. Consulate, Le Havre, St. Peter's Lutheran Church (Edina, Minn.), Fargo (N.D.) Civic Center, St. Paul (Minn.) Arts and Science Center, American Embassy, Beirut, Dr. William G. Shepherd House, St. Paul, Tyrone Guthrie Repertory Theatre, Minn. (Designs also executed for Embassies at Athens, The Hague and Oslo.)
720 Washington Avenue, S.E., Minneapolis 14, Minn., U.S.A.

Rashid, Sheikh Mohammad, B.A., LL.B.; Pakistani lawyer and politician; b. 24 May 1915, Kalawala, Sheikhupura District; s. of late Sheikh Mehrdin; m. 1934; four s.
Joined Muslim League 40; imprisoned for political activities 47; mem. Pakistan Muslim League Council 48-50; organized Azad Pakistan Party (later re-named Nat. Awami Party), Sec.-Gen. 52; launched Kisan Morcha Movt. Lahore 56; founder mem. Pakistan People's Party; Advocate, Supreme Court of Pakistan; mem. Nat. Assembly; Minister of Social Welfare, Health and Family Planning 71-74, of Food and Agriculture, Co-operatives, Works, Underdeveloped Areas and Land Reforms Oct. 74-.
Leisure interest: reading.

8 Zaldar Road, Ichhra, Lahore; 59-9F/6-3 Islamabad, Pakistan.
Telephone: 22633 (Office); 21550 (Home).

Rashidov, Sharaf Rashidovich; Soviet politician; b. 1917; ed. Dzhizak Teachers' Training Coll., Uzbek State Univ.
Teacher 36-37; Sec. and Asst. Ed. 38-41, Ed. of the newspaper *Lenin-Yuly* 41, 43; School Dir. 42; cadres Sec. of the Samarkand Regional Cttee. of the Party 44-47; Chief Ed. of the republican newspaper *Kzyl Uzbekistan*, Pres. of the Presidium of the Uzbek Union of Soviet Writers 47-50; Deputy to Supreme Soviets of Uzbek S.S.R. and U.S.S.R. 50-; Pres. of the Presidium of the Supreme Soviet of Uzbekistan, Vice-Pres. of the Presidium of the Supreme Soviet of the U.S.S.R. 50-59; mem. 70-; one of the chief organizers of the Afro-Asian Solidarity Cttee., Cairo 57; 1st Sec. Uzbek Communist Party 59-; Alt. mem. Presidium of Cen. Cttee. of C.P.S.U. 61-66, Alt. mem. Politburo 66-; awarded Order of Lenin, Order of the Red Banner of Labour, Order of the Red Star, Badge of Honour.
Central Committee of Communist Party of Uzbekistan, Tashkent, U.S.S.R.

Rasminsky, Louis, C.C., C.B.E., B.A., LL.D., D.H.L., D.C.L.; Canadian fmr. banker; b. 1 Feb. 1908, Montreal; s. of late David and Etta Rasminsky; m. Lyla Rotenberg 1930; one s. one d.; ed. Univ. of Toronto and London School of Economics.
League of Nations official 30-39; Dir. Research and Statistical Section, Foreign Exchange Control Board of Canada 40-42; Alternate Chair. and Chief Exec. Officer of Board 42-51; Exec. Asst. to Govs. of Bank of Canada 43-54; Deputy Gov. Bank of Canada 55-61, Gov. 61-73; Pres. Industrial Devt. Bank 61; Chair. Board Int. Devt. Research Centre; mem. Canadian Del. to Bretton Woods Conf. 44, and to San Francisco Conf. of UN 45; Exec. Dir. of Int. Monetary Fund 46-62, Int. Bank 50-62, Int. Finance Corpn. 56-62; Exec. Dir. Int. Devt. Asscn. 60-62; Chair. Int. Devt. Research Centre, Ottawa 73-; Fellow, Inst. of Canadian Bankers 69; Hon. Fellow of London School of Econs.; Companion Order of Canada 68; Outstanding Achievement Award of the Public Service of Canada 68; Vanier Medal of the Inst. of Public Admin. of Canada 74.
440 Roxborough Road, Rockcliffe Park, Ottawa, K1M 0L2, Canada.
Telephone: 749-7704.

Rasmussen, Steen Eiler; Danish architect and town planner; b. 9 Feb. 1898, Copenhagen; s. of Gen. Eiler Rasmussen and Dori Jung; m. Karen M. Schrøder 1934; two d.
Member Copenhagen Acad. of Fine Arts 22; Prof. of Architecture, Royal Acad. of Fine Arts, Copenhagen 38-68; Pres. Danish Town Planning Inst. 42-48; Pres. Copenhagen Regional Planning Cttee. 44-58.
Publs. *London, The Unique City* 37, *Towns and Buildings* 51, *Experiencing Architecture* 59; and books in Danish, Swedish and German on architecture, town planning, industrial art.
Dreyersvej 9, Rungsted Kyst, Denmark.
Telephone: 02863510.

Rasmussen, Viggo J.; Danish business executive; b. 20 Jan. 1915, Aalborg; s. of C. A. and Antonie Louise Rasmussen (née Andersen); m. Lydia Hansen 1939; one s. one d.; ed. Copenhagen School of Business Science.
Danish Air Lines 32-, Vice-Pres. 47, Exec. Vice-Pres. Scandinavian Airlines System 50; Pres. and Man. Dir. United Breweries (Tuborg Breweries and Carlsberg Breweries) 62-71, mem. of the Board 71-74, mem. Board of Tuborg Foundation; mem. Board of Reps. of Privatbanken, Copenhagen; mem. Acad. of Technical Sciences; Knight First Degree, Order of Dannebrog,

Knight Order of Vasa, Commdr. Order of Merit of the Italian Republic.

Leisure interests: antiques, paintings, ships.

Tuborg Breweries Ltd., Strandvejen 50, 2900 Hellerup; Home: 23 Lundegaardsvej, 2900 Hellerup, Denmark. Telephone: 29-3311.

Rasschaert, Théo; Belgian trade unionist; b. 22 Jan. 1927, Deurne; m. Maria Belloy 1951; three d.; ed. Athenée, Antwerp, and Inst. supérieur de Commerce de l'Etat, Antwerp.

Studies Dept., Féd. du Travail de Belgique 51-59; mem. Belgian Del. to negotiations for Treaty of Rome 57-58; Sec. responsible for econ. questions and problems of collective negotiation, Secrétariat Syndical Européen (European Trade Union Secr.—CISL) 59-67, Sec.-Gen. of European Trade Union Confederation 73-. Publs. Articles on labour problems and European questions.

European Trade Union Confederation, 37-41 rue Montagne aux Herbes Potagères, Brussels 1, Belgium. Telephone: 2179141.

Rasulov, Jabar; Soviet Deputy Minister of Agriculture 55; see *The International Who's Who 1975-76.*

Ratajczak, Henryk, M.SC., PH.D., D.SC.; Polish professor of chemistry; b. 30 Sept. 1932, Kadobno; m. Halina Opryszko 1972; ed. Technical Univ., Wrocław, Wrocław Univ., Univ. of Wales, Sorbonne, Paris, Centre de Mécanique Ondulatoire Appliquée, Paris.

Assistant in Physical Chem., Univ. of Wrocław 56-59, Senior Asst. 59-63, Adjunct 63-70, Docent in Chemical Physics 70-74, Prof. of Chem. 75-, Head of Dept. of Theoretical Chem. and Chemical Physics 69-, Deputy Dir. of Research, Inst. of Chem. 70-; Scientific Sec. of Spectroscopy Cttee., Polish Acad. of Sciences 69-; Editor for Eastern Europe, *Journal of Molecular Structure, Advances in Molecular Relaxation Processes.*

Leisure interests: music, literature, sport.

Publs. *Structural Studies of some hydrogen-bonded ferroelectrics* 69, *Dipole moments of hydrogen-bonded complexes and proton transfer effect* 69, *On the nature of electron donor acceptor interactions* 72, *Charge transfer properties of the hydrogen bond* 72, 73, *CNDO/2 molecular orbital calculation of the Dewar structure of benzene* 72, *of pyridine* 74, *Relation between O-H stretching frequency and hydrogen bond energy.*

Institute of Chemistry, Wrocław University, ul. Joliot-Curie 14, 50-383 Wrocław; Home: ul. Młodych Techników 4/16, Wrocław, Poland. Telephone: 22-92-81 (Work).

Ratanov, Anatoli Petrovich; Soviet diplomatist; b. 8 March 1921, Buguruslan, Orenburg Region.

Member C.P. of Soviet Union 43-; worked for Young Communist League 43-54; Editor journal, *Molodoi Kommunist* (Young Communist) 54-58; Perm. Rep. of U.S.S.R. Cttee. of Youth Orgs. to World Fed. of Democratic Youth 58-60; First Sec., Phnom-Penh, Cambodia 60-62, Counsellor 62-63; Amb. to Cambodia 65-68; on staff at Ministry of Foreign Affairs 68-70; Amb. to Guinea 70; Order of Lenin, Red Banner of Labour, Badge of Honour, etc.

c/o Ministry of Foreign Affairs, Moscow, U.S.S.R.

Ratchford, Charles Brice, M.S., PH.D.; American university president; b. 30 July 1920, Gaston County, N.C.; s. of Earl B. and Mary E. Woods Ratchford; m. Betty Brown 1942; one s. one d.; ed. North Carolina State Coll. and Duke Univ.

Assistant Farm Management Specialist, N.C. State Coll. 42; U.S. Army 42-46; Project Leader, Extension Farm Management, N.C. State Coll. 46-48, Extension Farm Management and Marketing 48-54; Asst. Dir. N.C. Agricultural Extension Service 54-59; Dir. Co-operative Extension Service, Univ. of Missouri 59-60; Dean,

Extension Div., Univ. of Mo. System 60-65; Visiting Lecturer, Univs. of Wis. and Chicago 65-70; Interim Pres., Univ. of Mo. and on leave as Vice-Pres. for Extension 70-71; Pres. Univ. of Mo. June 71-; Distinguished Service Awards, U.S. Dept. of Agriculture and Univ. of Wis. and several other awards.

Publs. over 50 articles in professional journals.

321 University Hall, Columbia, Mo. 65201; Home 1900 South Providence Road, Columbia, Mo. 65201, U.S.A. Telephone: 314-882-2011 (Office); 314-882-4680 (Home).

Ratcliffe, John Ashworth, C.B., C.B.E., F.R.S., M.A.; British radio scientist; b. 12 Dec. 1902, Bacup, Lancs.; s. of H. H. Ratcliffe; m. Nora Disley 1930; two d.; ed. Giggleswick School and Sidney Sussex Coll., Cambridge. Lecturer, Cambridge Univ. 27-60, Reader in Physics 47-60; Dir. Radio and Space Research Station, Slough 60-66 (retd.); Hon. Pres. Int. Union of Radio Science 66-; Hon. Fellow, Sidney Sussex Coll., Cambridge 62-; Pres. Physical Soc. 59-60; Vice-Pres. Inst. of Electrical Engineers (IEE) 63-66, Pres. 66; Royal Medal, Royal Soc. 66; Faraday Medal, IEE 66; Guthrie Medal, Inst. of Physics 71.

Leisure interest: walking on the hills.

Publs. papers and books on radio waves and the ionosphere.

193 Huntingdon Road, Cambridge, CB3 0DL, England. Telephone: Cambridge 76328.

Rateb, Aisha, PH.D.; Egyptian politician· b. 22 Feb. 1928; ed. Faculty of Law, Cairo Univ.

Junior Lecturer, Faculty of Law, Cairo Univ., Lecturer 57, then Prof. of Int. Law; Minister of Social Affairs 71-; Chair. Legislative Affairs Cttee. 73-.

Ministry of Social Affairs, Cairo, Egypt.

Rathbone, Perry Townsend; American museum director; b. 3 July 1911, Germantown, Pa.; s. of Howard Betts and Beatrice (Connely) Rathbone; m. Euretta de Cosson 1945; one s. two d.; ed. Harvard Univ.

Curator, Detroit Inst. of Arts 36-40; Dir. City Art Museum, St. Louis 40-55; Dir. Museum of Fine Arts, Boston 55-72, Dir. Emer. and Consultant 72-; Dir. Christie's U.S.A. 73-; mem. American Asscn. of Museums and Asscn. of Art Museum Dirs., U.S. Nat. Comm. of Int. Council of Museums, American Acad. of Arts and Sciences, Visiting Cttee. Fogg Art Museum 55-56, Rockefeller Panel on the Performing Arts 62-63, Exec. Cttee. Art in the Embassies Prog.; Pres. Asscn. of Art Museum Dirs. 59-60, 69-70; Vice-Chair. Mass. Art Comm. Board of Overseers, Fine Arts Prog. Brandeis Univ., Fine Arts Visiting Comm. Rhode Island School of Design, Forsyth Wickes Collection; Special Adviser to the Ford Program in the Arts and Humanities; Trustee, New England Conservatory of Music, Museum of Science, Boston, Inst. of Contemporary Art, Boston, American Fed. of Arts, Boston Arts Festival, Cape Cod Art Asscn., Int. Exhibitions Foundation, Washington, D.C., Rhode Island School of Design and Charles Playhouse; Chevalier Légion d'Honneur and several hon. degrees.

Publs. *Charles Wimar: Painter of the Indian Frontier* 46, *Max Beckmann* 48, *Mississippi Panorama* 49, *Westward the Way* 54, *Lee Gatch* 60, *Handbook of the Forsyth Wickes Collection* 68.

Christie's U.S.A., 867 Madison Avenue, New York, N.Y. 10021; Home: 151 Coolidge Hill, Cambridge, Mass. 02138, U.S.A.

Rathke, Heinrich Karl Martin Hans, DR.THEOL.; German ecclesiastic; b. 12 Dec. 1928, Mölln, Kreis Malchin; s. of Paul and Hedwig (née Steding) Rathke; m. Marianne Rusam 1955; six s. one d.; ed. Univs. of Kiel, Erlangen, Tübingen and Rostock.

Parish priest, Althof bei Bad Doberan 54-55, Warnkenhagen, Mecklenburg 55-62, Rostock Südstadt 62-70; Priest in charge of community service and people's

mission, Mecklenburg 70-71; Bishop of the Evangelical-Lutheran Church of Mecklenburg 71-.
Publ. *Ignatius von Antiochien und die Paulusbriefe* 67.
27 Schwerin, Münzstrasse 8, G.D.R.

Ratliff, Floyd, B.A., M.SC., PH.D.; American university professor; b. 1 May 1919, La Junta, Colo.; s. of Charles Frederick Ratliff and Alice Hubbard; m. Orma Vernon Priddy 1942; one d.; ed. Pueblo Junior Coll., Colorado Coll. and Brown Univ.
U.S. Army 41-45; Nat. Research Council Postdoctoral Fellow, Johns Hopkins Univ. 50-51; Instructor, Harvard Univ. 51-52; Asst. Prof., Harvard 52-54; Assoc., Rockefeller Inst. 54-58, Assoc. Prof., Rockefeller Univ. 58-66, Prof. 66-; mem. Nat. Acad. of Sciences, American Acad. of Arts and Sciences, American Philosophical Soc.; mem. Editorial Board *Journal of General Physiology* 69-; mem. Board of Scientific Counsellors of Nat. Eye Inst. 70-; Hon. D.Sc. (Colo. Coll.) 75; Howard Crosby Warren Medal (Soc. of Experimental Psychologists) 66.
Leisure interests: Oriental art (Chinese ceramics of the Sung dynasty).
Publs. *Mach Bands: Quantitative Studies on Neural Networks in the Retina* 65, *Studies on Excitation and Inhibition in the Retina* (editor) 74.
Rockefeller University, York Avenue and 66th Street, New York, N.Y. 10021; Home: 500 East 63rd Street, New York, N.Y. 10021, U.S.A.
Telephone: 212-360-1214 (Office); 212-838-0060 (Home).

Ratsimamanga, Albert Rakoto, D.SC., D.MED.; Malagasy diplomatist; b. 28 Dec. 1907; ed. Univ. of Paris.
Research Dir. Centre Nat. de la Recherche Scientifique; Dir. Ecole Pratique des Hautes Etudes; Amb. of Malagasy Repub. to France 60-73, to Fed. Repub. of Germany 61-68; mem. Exec. Council, UNESCO 60, Vice-Chair. 62; corresp. mem. of l'Académie des Sciences de Paris 66; Grand Officier Légion d'Honneur, etc.
Major works: Thèse sur l'Anthropologie de Madagascar, Travaux sur la Biochimie de la Surrénale, Hormones Stéroidiques et Vitamines Hydrosolubles, Etudes expérimentales sur l'Action antituberculeuse et antilépreuse des phtalydrazides, Cicatrisants Triterpenoïdes.
c/o Ministry of Foreign Affairs, Tananarive, Madagascar.

Ratsiraka, Lieut.-Cdr. Didier; Malagasy naval officer and politician; b. 4 Nov. 1936, Vatomandry; ed. Coll. Saint Michel, Tananarive, Lycée Henri IV, Paris, Ecole Navale, Lanveoc-Poulmic (France), Ecole des Officiers "Transmissions", Les Bormettes, and Ecole Supérieure de Guerre Navale, Paris.
Had several naval postings 63-70; Mil. Attaché, Paris 70-72; Minister of Foreign Affairs May 72-Feb. 75; Pres. Supreme Council of Revolution June 75-; Prime Minister and Minister of Defence June-Dec. 75; Pres. Democratic Repub. of Madagascar Jan. 76-.
Office of the President, Tananarive, Madagascar.

Rattigan, Sir Terence Mervyn, Kt., C.B.E.; British dramatist; b. 10 June 1911; ed. Harrow and Trinity Coll., Oxford.
Publs. Plays: *First Episode* 34, *French Without Tears* 36, *After the Dance* 39, *Flare Path* 42, *While the Sun Shines* 43, *Love in Idleness* 44, *O, Mistress Mine* (N.Y. 45), *The Winslow Boy* 46 (N.Y. 47), *Playbill* 48 (N.Y. 49), *Adventure Story* 49, *Who is Sylvia?* 50, *The Deep Blue Sea* 52 (N.Y. 52), *The Sleeping Prince* 53 (N.Y. 56), *Separate Tables* 54 (N.Y. 56), *Variation on a Theme* 58, *Ross* 60 (N.Y. 61), *Man and Boy* 63, *A Bequest to the Nation* 70, *In Praise of Love* 73 (N.Y. 74); films: *Quiet Wedding* 40, *French Without Tears* 39, *Journey Together* 45, *The Way to the Stars* 46, *While the Sun Shines* 47, *The Winslow Boy* 48, *The Browning Version* 51, *The*

Sound Barrier 52, *The Final Test, The Man Who Loved Redheads, The Deep Blue Sea* 55, *The Prince and the Showgirl* 57, *Separate Tables* 59, *The V.I.P.s* 63, *The Yellow Rolls-Royce* 64, *Goodbye Mr. Chips* 69, *Conduct Unbecoming* 70-71, *A Bequest to the Nation* 71-72.
c/o Dr. Jan van Loewen, 81-83 Shaftesbury Avenue, London, W.1, England.

Rattray, Alfred Adolphus, LL.B., F.C.A., A.C.I.S.; Jamaican lawyer and diplomatist; b. 19 Jan. 1925, St. Ann; s. of Septimus Augustus Rattray and Albertha (née Bailey); m. Cynthia Louise Weston 1951; two d.; ed. Excelsior High School, London Univ., Lincoln's Inn, London, London School of Econs.
Joined Civil Service 45; Accountant and Man. Govt. Food Control Distribution Dept. 47-51, rising to Asst. Under-Sec. 53-64; with law firm Myers, Fletcher and Gordon 64-, Partner 65- (on leave of absence 75-); engaged in business 65-75; Chair. Board, Jamaica Frozen Foods Ltd., Jamaica Fashion Export Guild Ltd., Guild Productions Ltd., New Kingston Hotel Ltd.; Dir. Board Sheraton Int. (Jamaica) Ltd., Island Holidays Ltd., Windsor Foods Ltd.; Deputy Chair. Jamaica Industrial Devt. Corpn. Ltd.; Chair. Jamaica Port Authority; Pres. Jamaica Public Accountancy Board; Dir. and Vice-Chair. West Indies Shipping Corpn.; Amb. to U.S.A., also to OAS 75-; part-time lecturer, Univ. of the West Indies 61-75; mem. Excelsior School Board.
Leisure interests: cricket, table tennis, fishing, bridge, reading.
Publs. co-author: *The Jamaican Companies Act* 65, *The Public Accountancy Act* 68.
Embassy of Jamaica, 1666 Connecticut Avenue, N.W., Washington, D.C. 20009, U.S.A.
Telephone: (202) 387-1010.

Rau, Chalapathi M.; Indian newspaper editor; b. Waltair, Andhra.
Assistant Editor *National Herald*, Lucknow 38-42; Asst. Editor *Hindustan Times*, New Delhi 43-45; Joint Editor *National Herald* 45-46, and Editor 46-; Alternate rep. UNESCO Gen. Conf., New Delhi 56, Paris 60; Rep. UN Gen. Assembly 58; Vice-Pres. UNESCO Conf. on Journalism Training 56; founder, Pres. Indian Fed. of Working Journalists 50-55; mem. Indian Press Comm.; Chair. Cen. Press Advisory Board; mem. Exec. Council Nehru Univ., Nehru Trust; Nehru Award for Int. Understanding; Vice-Chair. Nehru Fund; Chair. Nehru Memorial Museum and Library; Hon. D.Litt. (Agra, Andhra Univs.), Hon. LL.D. (Sri Venkateswara Univ.).
Leisure interests: reading, writing.
Publs. *Fragments of a Revolution* 65, *Gandhi and Nehru* 67, *The Press in India* 68, *All in All* 72, *Jawaharlal Nehru* 73.
National Herald, Herald House, Bahadushah, Zafar Marg, New Delhi; and 13 Shahjahan Road, New Delhi, India.
Telephone: 271547 (Office); 383855 (Home).

Rau, Lady Dhanvanthi Rama, M.A.; Indian social worker; b. 10 May 1893; m. Sir Benegal Rama Rau (deceased); ed. St. Mary's High School, Hubli, and Presidency Coll., Univ. of Madras.
Lecturer in English, Queen Mary's Coll., Univ. of Madras 17-19; Sec. All India Child Marriage Abolition League, Simla 27-28; mem. Board, Int. Alliance of Women for Suffrage and Equal Citizenship 32-38; Pres. Bombay Branch, All India Women's Conf. (A.I.W.C.) 46, Pres. A.I.W.C. 46-47; Pres. Family Planning Asscn. of India 49-63; mem. Family Planning Programmes and Research Cttee., Ministry of Health, Govt. of India 53, Chair. Social and Moral Hygiene Enquiry Cttee. 55; mem. Central Social Welfare Board 56-61; mem. Consultative Cttee. of Planning Comm. for Third Five-Year Plan (Health) 61; Pres. Int. Planned Parenthood.

Fed. 63; Kaiser-I-Hind Gold Medal (U.K.) 38; Lasker Award (U.S.A.) 55; Padma Bhusan 59.

D/10, Mafatlal Park, Bhulabai Desai Road, Bombay 26, India.

Rau, Santha Rama; Indian writer; b. 24 Jan. 1923, Madras, Tamil Nadu; d. of late Sir Benegal Rama Rau, and Lady Rama Rau, q.v.; m. 1st Faubion Bowers 1952 (divorced 1966), one s.; m. 2nd Gurdon W. Wattles; ed. St. Paul's Girls' School, London, and Wellesley Coll., U.S.A.

Numerous journeys in Europe, India, America, Southeast Asia, Japan and Russia; fmr. teacher Hani Freedom School, Tokyo; English teacher at Sarah Lawrence Coll. 71-; Hon. doctorates from Bates, Brandeis and Roosevelt Colls.

Leisure interests: gardening, opera and swimming.

Publs. *Home to India, East of Home, Remember the House, View to the South-East, My Russian Journey, The Cooking of India* 69, *The Adventuress* 71; dramatized version of E. M. Forster's *A Passage to India, Gifts of Passage* (autobiog.).

D/10 Mafatlal Park, Bhulabhai Desai Road, Bombay 26, India; and 522 East 89th Street, New York, N.Y. 10028, U.S.A.

Rau, Walter Franz, DR. RER. POL.; German international civil servant; b. 1 Sept. 1907, Halberstadt; m.; three c.; ed. Friedrich-Wilhelm Univ., Berlin, and Christian Albrecht Univ., Kiel.

Scientific Research Dept., Inst. für Weltwirtschaft und Seeverkehr, Univ. of Kiel 32-33; Financial Editor *Kreutz Zeitung* 33-36; Deputy Dir. Econ. Research Dept., Gemeinschaftsgruppe Deutscher Hypothekenbanken 36-38; Econ. Research Dept., I.G. Farben Industry A.G. 38-45; in President's Office, Govt. of Schleswig-Holstein 46-51; Econ. Adviser, Ministry of Econs., Bonn 51-64; Deputy Sec., Ministry for Econ. Co-operation 64-67; Deputy Sec.-Gen. Org. for Co-operation and Econ. Devt. (OECD) 67-71.

c/o Ministry of the Economy, 53 Bonn, Federal Republic of Germany.

Rauchfuss, Wolfgang; German politician; b. 27 Nov. 1931.

Former mechanic; Deputy Minister of Foreign and Inner German Trade 61-65; Deputy Chair., Council of Ministers Dec. 65-, Minister for Supply of Materials 74-; mem. Cen. Cttee. Sozialistische Einheitspartei Deutschlands.

Ministerrat, Berlin, German Democratic Republic.

Rauchhaupt, Friedrich Wilhelm von, LL.D., PH.D., L. en D.; German jurist; b. 13 Aug. 1881, Wersk, West Prussia; s. of Berthold von Rauchhaupt and Susanna Nitzsche; m. Ada C. Cameron 1911; one s.

Lecturer in Law, Heidelberg Univ. 22; Visiting Prof. Buenos Aires Univ. 26, 67 and Santiago de Chile 26; Extraordinary Prof. Heidelberg since 29 (retd. 46, reinstated 56); hon. mem. of Reales Academias de Jurisprudencia y Legislación and de Ciencias Morales y Políticas, of Instituto de Estudios Políticos, Madrid, of the Facultad de Leyes y Ciencias Políticas, Santiago de Chile, Int. Inst. of Space Law in the Int. Astronautical Fed., of the Scientific Soc. for Air and Space Legal Questions, Univ. of Buenos Aires 67, Hermann Oberth-Gesellschaft, Hanover; Corresp. mem. Instituto Nacional de Derecho Aeronáutico y Espacial, Buenos Aires 67, Brazilian Soc. of Aeronautical and Space Law 70; mem. Int. Comm. for the Study of Orders of Chivalry 70-.

Leisure interests: family history, 11th Century crusades.

Publs. *Eigentümergrunddienstbarkeit* 06, *Depositenrecht* 07, *Verfassungsänderungen* 08, *Cooperation The Prize Court Rules* 14, *Handbuch der deutschen Wahlgesetze und Geschäftsordnungen* 16, *Italienische Prisenordnung* 17, *Türkei-Kapitulationen* 18, *Geschichte der spanischen Gesetzesquellen* 23, *Estudio comparativo entre el desarrollo del derecho español y el alemán* 23, *Völkerrechtliche*

Eigentümlichkeiten Amerikas, insbes. Hispanoamerikas 24, *Correlaciones en el desarrollo de los derechos de Europa y de América* 28, *Rechte Europas* (2 vols.) 31-32, *Völkerrecht* 36, *Über die Christlichen Ritterorden* 53, 56, 58, 60, 70, *Zur Geschichte der Familie v. R.* 55, *Vergleich und Angleichbarkeit der Rechte Süd- und Mittel-Amerikas* 55, *Der Aufbau des englischen Rechts,* 5th edn. 65, *Über die Atomenergie und Atomenergierecht* 57, *Die Geschichte der spanischen Gesetzgebung seit 1923* 58, *Die Hauptgebote des Neuen Testamentes: Gottesliebe, Nächstenliebe, Feindesliebe im geltenden Recht* 59, 61, *Überblick der Geschichte des Völkerrechts in den spanischsprachigen Staaten von Europa und Amerika* 59, *Die Zurückkehr zur Rechten Gotteserkenntnis* 60, *Die Wiederentdeckung des Völkerrechts durch Hugo Grotius* 61, *Über Weltraumrecht* 62 (in French and Spanish 74), *El Derecho divino y el Derecho natural en el Derecho vigente* 62, 72, *In Genealogie Handbuch des Adels U. R.* 73; contributions to the First to Eighteenth Colloquium on the Law of Outer Space 58-74, *Die Weltraumflüge und die Rechtwissenschaft* 63 (also in English), *Divine Law in Space Law* 71, and journal articles; several academic awards.

Plöck 45-49, D-69 Heidelberg, German Federal Republic.

Raunio, Eino Albin; Finnish politician; b. 18 Jan. 1909, Sääksmäki; ed. elementary school and Workers' Acad.

Began as lecturer; office manager of newspaper in Forssa 36-40; mem. of Parliament 39-; Chair. Forssa City Council 64-; Chair. Finance Cttee. of Parl. 66-; mem. Defence Council, State Science Council; Minister of Finance Jan. 68-March 70.

Helsinki, Gyldenintie 5B, Finland.

Telephone: 677197.

Rauschenberg, Robert; American artist; b. 22 Oct. 1925; ed. Kansas City Art Inst., Acad. Julien, Paris, Black Mountain Coll., North Carolina and Art Students League, New York.

Travel in Italy and North Africa 52-53; Designer of Stage-Sets and Costumes for Merce Cunningham Dance Company 55-65, Lighting for Cunningham Co. 61-65; Costumes and Sets for Paul Taylor Dance Co. 57-59; Choreography in America 62-; affiliated with Leo Castelli Gallery, New York City 57-; works in Tate Gallery, London, Albright-Knox Gallery, Buffalo, Whitney Museum of American Art, New York City, Andrew Dickson White Museum, Cornell Univ., Museum of Modern Art, N.Y., Goucher Coll. Collection, Towson, Maryland, Cleveland Museum of Art, Cleveland, Ohio, Kunstsammlung, Noedheim, Westfalen, Germany, etc.; numerous one-man shows in U.S.A. and Europe; Exhbn. at Stedelijk Museum, Amsterdam 68; First Prize, Venice Biennale 64.

c/o Leo Castelli Gallery, 4 East 77th Street, New York, N.Y. 10021, U.S.A.

Rauth, J. Donald; American business executive; b. 7 Jan. 1918; Pitman, N.J., m. Catherine Burns 1943; one s. one d.; ed. Drexel Univ., Philadelphia.

Joined Martin Company (predecessor of Martin Marietta Corpn.) 40; Vice-Pres. and Gen. Man. Denver Div. 61; Pres. Martin Marietta Aerospace 67; Pres. Harvey Aluminium (now Martin Marietta Aluminium) 69; Pres. Martin Marietta Corpn. April 72-, Chief Exec. Officer Sept. 72-.

6401 Garnett, Chevy Chase, Md. 20015, U.S.A.

Răutu, Leonte; Romanian politician; b. 28 Feb. 1910, Cernăuți; s. of Nicolae and Sofia Răutu; m. Natalia Răutu 1938; two d.; ed. Cernăuți and Bucharest.

Joined Communist Youth 29, Romanian Communist Party 31; Sec. of Bucharest District Cttee. of Romanian Communist Party 32-36; imprisoned 31, 34, 35; Editor-in-Chief of "Scînteia" 37-40; mem. Central Cttee. of R.C.P. 48-; Alt. mem. of Political Bureau of the Central Cttee. 55-65; Sec. Central Cttee. of R.C.P.

65-69, mem. Exec. Cttee. 65-; Vice-Chair. Council of Ministers 69-72; Prof. Univ. of Bucharest; Pres. Man. Council and Rector "Stefan Gheorghiu" Acad. 72-; Deputy to Grand Nat. Assembly 48-; mem. Acad. of Social and Political Sciences 70-; Hero of Socialist Labour 64.
Leisure interests: reading, travelling.
Central Committee of the Romanian Communist Party, Bucharest; and Bulevardul Armata Poporului 1-3, Bucharest, Romania.
Telephone: 313331 (Home).

Ravanel, Jean, D. en D.; French civil servant; b. 2 May 1920; ed. Faculty of Law, Grenoble Univ.
Entered Civil Service 45; Technical Adviser, Ministry of Public Works and Transport 54-55; Dir. Cabinet of Minister of Agriculture 58-62, and of Minister of Public Works and Transport 62; Chair. Gen. Commissariat for Tourism 63-70; Man. Paris Airport 63-; Conseiller d'Etat 68-; Chair. Ski France; Chevalier Légion d'Honneur, Aeronautical Medal.
48 rue de la Tour, Paris 16e, France.

Ravegnani, Giuseppe; Italian critic, journalist and author; b. 13 Oct. 1895.
Successively Literary Critic *Il Resto del Carlino*, Editor *Il Corriere Italiano*, Chief Reporter *Il Regno*, Editor *La Fiera Letteraria*, Literary Critic *La Stampa*, contributor to *Corriere della Sera* and numerous other papers; Dir. *Il Corriere Padano, Il Gazzettino, La Gazzetta di Venezia*, Chief Editor and now Literary Editor *Epoca*; Dir. Biblioteca Ariostea, Ferrara; Premio Viareggio for *Uomini Visti* 55, Premio Marzotto 56.
Publs. *Antologia di Novelle Catalane* (translation), *Uomini Visti* (2 vols.); numerous critical works on Ariosto and XIX century Italian literature.
Piazza Morbegno 5, Milan, Italy.

Ravens, Karl Friedrich; German politician; b. 29 June 1927, Achim; s. of Fritz and Anna Ravens (née Kipka); m. Inge-Lore Treichel 1953; one s.; ed. apprenticeship in aircraft building.
Car mechanic 45-52, apprentice instructor 52-61; Alderman 56-, mem. Kreistag (local council) 57-, Deputy Mayor 61-72; mem. Parl. (Bundestag) 61-; mem. Nat. Exec. Social Democratic Party (SPD) 68-69; Parl. Sec. of State to Minister for Housing and Town Planning 69-72, to Fed. Chancellor Brandt 72-74; Fed. Minister for Construction, Housing and Town Planning 74-; mem. Television Council, Second German Television (ZDF) 74-; Grand Cross, Order of St. Olav (Norway), and other decorations.
Leisure interest: gliding.
Publs. various essays on housing and urban politics in specialist periodicals.
Bundesministerium für Raumordnung, Bauwesen und Städtebau, 53 Bonn-Bad Godesberg, Deichmannsaue; Home: 2807 Achim-Bierden, Anne-Frank-Strasse 7, Federal Republic of Germany.
Telephone: 02221-8321 (Office).

Ravila, Paavo Ilmari, PH.D.; Finnish professor; b. 5 July 1902; ed. Turku and Helsinki.
Prof. of Finnish Language Univ. of Turku 34-49; Prof. of Finno-Ugric Linguistics Univ. of Helsinki 49-56, Rector 53-56; Pres. Finno-Ugric Soc.; mem. Finnish Acad. of Science and Letters 44-; mem. Acad. of Finland 56-63, Pres. 61-63; Chancellor Univ. of Helsinki 63-69.
Publs. *Das Quantitätssystem des Seelappischen Dialektes von Maattivuono* 32, *Mordwinische Volksdichtung* (Vols. I-IV) 39-45.
Ritokalliont 1, Helsinki, Finland.

Ravirosa Wade, Leandro; Mexican civil engineer; b. 11 June 1920; ed. Univ. Autónoma de México.
Head of Plano Regulador del Departamento del D.F. and afterwards head of planning in this region; Dir. of

Harbour Construction in the Secretaría de Marina and Pres. of Cámara de la Construcción; formed the building consortium, Constructora Randales, S.A. for the Netzahualcóyotl dam (Malpaso Province); Sec. of Water Resources 70-.
Secretaría de Recursos Hidráulicos, Mexico, D.F., Mexico.

Rawiri, Georges; Gabonese government official and diplomatist; b. 10 March 1932, Lambarene, Gabon; m.; two c.; ed. Protestant school, Ngomo and Lycée Jean-Baptiste Dumas, Ales.
Head, Technical Centre, Garoua Radio Station 57, Libreville Radio Station 59; a founder of Radio Gabon 59; Dir. Radiodiffusion Gabonaise 60, Radio-Télévision Gabonaise 63; Counsellor for Foreign Affairs 63; Minister of Information, Tourism, Posts and Telecommunications 63-64; Minister of State and Amb. to France 64-71, also accred. to Israel, Italy, Spain, U.K., Malta 65-71, and Switzerland 67-71; Minister of State for Foreign Affairs and Co-operation 71-74, of the Govt. Office 74-75, of Transport, Civil Aviation and the Merchant Navy April 75-; Grand Officier de l'Ordre de l'Etoile Equatoriale and decorations from Mauritania, France, Malta, and the Ivory Coast; Médaille d'Or des Arts, Sciences et Lettres; Grand Officier de l'Ordre Int. du Bien Public.
Bureau du Gouvernement, B.P. 2245, Libreville, Gabon.

Rawlings, Gen. Edwin William, B.A., M.B.A.; American corporation consultant; b. 11 Sept. 1904, Milroy, Minn.; s. of Frank Henry and Ella May Rawlings (née Frazier); m. Muriel Peterson Rawlings 1930; four s.; ed. Hamline Univ., Harvard Graduate School of Business Admin.
Entered the Army 29, progressed from flying cadet to four star Gen. 54, Head, Air Material Command, Wright-Patterson A.F.B., Dayton 51-59, retd. 59; Financial Vice-Pres. Gen. Mills, Inc. 59-60, Exec. Vice-Pres. 60-61, Pres. 61-67, Chair. of Board 67-68, retd. 69; Dir. Weyerhaeuser 68-; D.F.C., D.S.M. with Oak Leaf Cluster, Air Force Asscn.'s Citation of Honour; Hon. O.B.E.; Hon. Dr. of Business Admin. (Hamline, Tufts Univs.), Hon. D.Hum. (Dayton Univ.), Hon. LL.D. (Ohio Wesleyan, Miami Univs., Hendrix Coll.).
Leisure interests: hunting, fishing.
1903 First National Bank Building, Minneapolis, Minn. 55402, U.S.A.
Telephone: 612-338-7639.

Rawlinson, Anthony Keith, C.B., M.A.; British government official; b. 5 March 1926, Oxford; s. of Bishop Alfred Edward John Rawlinson and Mildred Ansley (née Ellis); m. Mary Hill 1956; three s.; ed. Eton College (Kings Scholar) and Christ Church, Oxford (Open Scholar).
Served Grenadier Guards 44-47, apptd. Lieutenant; entered Civil Service as Asst. Principal, Ministry of Labour and Nat. Service 51; transferred to Treasury 53, Principal 55; seconded to U.K. Atomic Energy Auth. as private sec. to chair. 58; returned to Treasury 60, Asst. Sec. 63, Under Sec. 68, Deputy Sec. 72; Economic Minister, British Embassy, Washington; U.K. Exec. Dir. IMF and World Bank 72-75; Deputy Sec., Dept. of Industry 75-.
Leisure interest: mountaineering.
Department of Industry, 1 Victoria Street, London, SW1H oET; 105 Corringham Road, London, NW11 7DL.
Telephone: 01-215-5040 (Office); 01-458-3402 (Home).

Rawlinson, Rt. Hon. Sir Peter Anthony Grayson, P.C., Q.C., M.P.; British lawyer and politician; b. 26 June 1919, Birkenhead; s. of Lieut.-Col. A. R. Rawlinson and Ailse Grayson Rawlinson; m. Elaine Angela Dominguez 1954, two s. one d.; three d. by previous marriage; ed. Downside and Christ's Coll., Cambridge. Served in Irish Guards 39-46; called to the Bar, Inner

Temple 46; mem. of Parl. 55-; Recorder of Salisbury 61-62; Solicitor-Gen. 62-64; mem. Bar Council 66-68; Attorney-Gen. 70-74; Attorney-Gen., Northern Ireland 72-74; mem. Senate, Inns of Court 68; Chair. of the Bar 75-76; Chair. of Senate, Inns of Court and Bar 75-76; Receiver of Kingston upon Thames 75-. Conservative. Leisure interests: painting, gardening.
12 King's Bench Walk, London, E.C.4, England.
Telephone: 01-353-5892.

Ray, Ajit Nath, M.A.; Indian judge; b. 29 Jan. 1912, Calcutta; s. of Sati Nath Ray and Kali Kumari Debi; m. Himani Mukherjee 1944; one s.; ed. Presidency Coll., Calcutta, Oriel Coll., Oxford and Gray's Inn, London. Formerly practised as a barrister, Calcutta High Court; Judge, Calcutta High Court 57-69; Judge, Supreme Court of India 69-73, Chief Justice 73-; Hon. Fellow, Oriel Coll., Oxford; Pres. Int. Law Asscn.
15 Panditia Place, Calcutta 29; 5 Krishna Menon Marg, New Delhi 11, India.
Telephone: 47-5213 (Calcutta); 372922 and 375439 (New Delhi).

Ray, Dixy Lee, B.A., M.A., PH.D.; American marine biologist and administrator; b. 3 Sept. 1914, Tacoma, Washington; d. of Alvis Marion Ray and Frances Adams Ray; ed. Mills Coll., Oakland, Calif., Stanford Univ.
Teacher, Oakland, Calif. public schools 38-42; John Switzer Fellow, Stanford Univ. 42-43; Van Sicklen Fellow, Stanford Univ. 43-45; Assoc. Prof. of Zoology, Univ. of Washington 45-72; Exec. Cttee. Friday Harbour Laboratories 45-60; Special Consultant biological oceanography, Nat. Science Foundation 60-62; Dir. of Pacific Science Centre, Seattle 63-72; Chief Scientist and Visiting Prof., Stanford Univ. Research ship Te Vega in Int. Indian Ocean Expedition 64; Presidential Task Force on Oceanography 69; mem. Atomic Energy Comm. 72-75, Chair. 73-75; Asst. Sec. of State 75-; mem. Marshall Fellowship Cttee.; Guggenheim Fellow 52-53; Hon. degrees Mills Coll. 67, St. Martins Coll. 72, Hood Coll. 73, Seattle Univ. 73, Ripon Coll. 74, St. Mary's Coll. 74, Puget Sound Univ. 74, Michigan State Univ. 74, Union Coll. 74, Northern Mich. Univ. 74; Seattle Maritime Award 66, William Clapp Award in Marine Biology 59, Florence K. Hutchison Medal for service in conservation 73, Francis Boyer Science Award 74, YWCA 1974 Gold Medal Award, Outstanding Woman of Science Award, ARCS Foundation 74; foreign mem. Danish Royal Soc. for Natural History 63.
Leisure interests: American Indian culture, boating, gardening, hiking.
Publs. Marine Boring and Fouling Organisms 59; numerous articles on public understanding of science and scientific papers on marine biology.
Department of State, Washington, D.C. 20520, U.S.A.
Telephone: 202/632-1554.

Ray, Man; American artist; b. 1890, Philadelphia; m. 1st Adon Lacroix, 2nd Juliet Browner.
Known as a painter, sculptor, photographer, film maker, etc.; exponent of Dada and Surrealism and pioneer of abstract art in U.S.A.; first one-man exhbn. Daniel Gallery, N.Y. 15; founding mem. Soc. Anonyme, N.Y. 20; has lived in Paris 21-; numerous exhbns. of paintings, drawings, photographs and rayographs; participated in following major exhbns., Salon Dada, Paris 22, Exposition Retrospective Dada 1916-32, Paris 32, Surrealist Exhbn., N.Y. 32, Int. Surrealist Exhbn., London 36, Paris 38, Three Surrealist Painters, Brussels 37, Objects of My Affection, Los Angeles 46, N.Y. 65, Copley Galleries Exhbn. 48, Shakespearean Equations, Paris 54, Three Surrealist Painters 56, Int. Dada Exhbn., Düsseldorf 58, Inst. of Contemporary Art, London 59, Int. Surrealist Exhbn., Paris 59, Le Surréalisme, Paris 64, Exposition Dada, Musée Nat. d'Art Moderne, Paris 66, Retrospective Exhbn., Inst.

of Contemporary Arts, London 75; exhbn. of photographs Cologne 60, Paris 62; Gold Medal, Venice Photography Biennale 61.
Films include, Emak Bakia 26, L'Etoile de mer 28, Les Mystères du Chateau de dé 29.
Publs. Les Champs délicieux (collection of photographs) 22, Facile (with Paul Eluard) 35, Les Mains Libres (with Paul Eluard) 37, To Be Continued Unnoticed (papers) 48, Alphabet for Adults (drawings) 48, Self Portrait (autobiog.) 63, Portraits (collection of photographs) 63.
2 bis rue Feron, Paris, France.

Ray, Robert D., D.JUR.; American politician; b. 26 Sept. 1928, Des Moines, Iowa; s. of the late Clark A. Ray and of Mrs. Mildred H. Ray; m. Billie Lee Hornberger 1951; three d.; ed. Drake Univ.
Chairman of Midwest Republican Chairmen's Asscn. and Nat. Advisory Cttee. of Republican State Chairmen; State Chair. of March of Dimes; mem. of county, state and Nat. Bar Asscns. and Trial Lawyers' Asscns.; mem. Nat. Acad. of Practising Law Inst., Hon. mem. Board of Trustees of American Acad. of Achievement; State Chair. of Republican Party 63-67; Gov. of Iowa 68- (re-elected 72, 74).
Leisure interests: sports, amateur photography.
State Capitol, Des Moines, Iowa 50319, U.S.A.
Telephone: 515-281-5211.

Ray, Satyajit; Indian film director; b. 2 May 1921, Calcutta; s. of Sukumar Ray and Suprabha (née Das); m. Bijoya Das 1949; one s.; ed. Ballygunge Govt. School, Presidency Coll., Calcutta.
Commercial artist in Calcutta before beginning his career in films; directed Pather Panchali 54 (Cannes Int. Film Festival Award for "the most human document" 56, Golden Laurel Award, Edinburgh Film Festival 57), Aparajito 56 (sequel to Pather Panchali, Grand Prix, Venice Film Festival 57), The Philosopher's Stone, Jalsagar (The Music Room), Apur Sansar (The World of Apu), The Goddess 61, Three Daughters 61, Abhijan 62, Kanchanjangha 62, Mahanagar 64, Charulata 65, Kapurush-o-Mahapurush 65, Nayak 66, Chiriakhana 68, The Adventures of Goopy and Bagha 69, Days and Nights in the Forest 69, Seemabaddha (Company Limited) 70, Pratidwandi (The Adversary) 71, Distant Thunder 73, Golden Fortress 74, The Middleman 75; composed the music for all his films since Three Daughters; Editor Sande, children's magazine; Magsaysay Award for Journalism and Literature 67; Berlin Film Festival Prize for Distant Thunder 73; Order of Yugoslav Flag 71; Hon. D.Litt. Royal Coll. of Art, London 74.
Leisure interests: listening to classical music (Indian and Western), reading science fiction.
Flat No. 8, 1/1 Bishop Lefroy Road, Calcutta 20, India.
Telephone: 44-8747.

Ray, Siddhartha Sankar; Indian politician; b. 20 Oct. 1920, Calcutta; m. Maya Ray; ed. Presidency Coll., Calcutta.
Called to the Bar, Inner Temple, London; fmr. Minister of Law, Govt. of West Bengal; Leader of Opposition, West Bengal Govt. 67; mem. Lok Sabha 70, West Bengal Legislative Assembly 72-; Minister of Educ., Culture and Social Welfare, Govt. of India 71-72; Chief Minister of West Bengal March 72-.
Writers' Buildings, Calcutta; and 2 Beltola Road, Calcutta 700026, India.

Raymond, Sir Stanley Edward, Kt., F.B.I.M., F.C.I.T.; British government official; b. 10 Aug. 1913; s. of Frederick George and Lilian Grace Raymond; m. Enid Buley 1938; one s.; ed. Orphanage and Grammar School, Hampton, Middlesex.
Tax Officer, Civil Service 30; Asst. Sec. Soc. of Civil Servants 39-45; Royal Artillery 42-45; joined London Passenger Transport Board 46; Chief Staff and Welfare Officer, British Road Services 47-55, Chief Officer (Org.)

52-55; Asst. Manpower Adviser, British Transport Comm. 55-56, Dir. of Establishment and Staff 56-57; Chief Commercial Manager, Scottish Region, British Railways 57-59, Asst. Gen. Manager 59-61; Traffic Adviser, British Transport Comm. 61-62; Gen. Manager, Western Region of British Railways 62-63, Chair. Western Railways Board 63; mem. British Railways Board Oct. 63-64, Vice-Chair. 64-65, Chair. 65-67; Chair. Gaming Board for Great Britain 68-; Chair. Horserace Betting Levy Board 72-74; Chair. Habit Group of Companies; Gov. Thames Polytechnic.
Leisure interests: walking, writing, reading.
124 Chiltern Court, Baker Street, London, N.W.1; 26 Cavendish House, Kings Road, Brighton, Sussex, England.
Telephone: 01-935-4503; and 0273-23084.

Rayne, Sir Max, Kt.; British company director; b. 8 Feb. 1918, London; s. of Phillip and Deborah Rayne; m. 1st Margaret Marco 1941 (dissolved 1960), one s. two d.; m. 2nd Lady Jane Antonia Frances Vane-Tempest-Stewart 1965, two s. two d.; ed. Central Foundation School and Univ. Coll., London.
Royal Air Force 40-45; Chair. London Merchant Securities Ltd. 60-; Dir. Carlton Industries Ltd. 60-, and other cos.; Gov. St. Thomas's Hospital 62-74, Special Trustee 74-; Gov. Royal Ballet School 66-, Yehudi Menuhin School 66-, Malvern Coll. 66-, Centre for Environmental Studies 67-73; mem. Gen. Council King Edward VII's Hospital Fund for London 66-; mem. Council St. Thomas's Hospital Medical School 65-; Chair. London Festival Ballet Trust 67-75, Nat. Theatre Board 71-; Founder Patron Rayne Foundation 62-; Hon. Vice-Pres. Jewish Welfare Board 66-; Hon. Fellow, Univ. Coll., London 66, London School of Econs. 74, Darwin Coll., Cambridge 66; Chevalier Légion d'Honneur 73; Hon. LL.D., London.
100 George Street, London W1H 6DJ, England.
Telephone: 01-935-3555.

Raynor, Geoffrey Vincent, M.A., D.SC., F.R.S.; British metallurgist; b. 2 Oct. 1913, Nottingham; s. of Alfred Ernest Raynor and Florence Lottie Raynor; m. Emily Jean Brockless 1943; three s.; ed. Nottingham High School and Oxford Univ.
D.S.I.R. Senior Research Award 38; research work, Oxford Univ. 40-44; I.C.I. Research Fellow, Univ. of Birmingham 45-47, Reader in Theoretical Metallurgy 47-49, Prof. of Metal Physics 49-55, Feeney Prof. of Physical Metallurgy and Head of Dept. 55-69; Deputy Dean, Faculty of Science and Eng. 63-66, Dean 66-69; Visiting Prof., Univ. of Chicago 51-52; Batelle Visiting Prof., Ohio State Univ. 62; Deputy Principal and Prof. of Physical Metallurgy, Univ. of Birmingham 69-73, Prof. of Physical Metallurgy 73-; Royal Soc. Lever-hulme Visiting Prof. Witwatersrand Univ. 74; Visiting Prof. Univ. of N.S.W., Australia 75; mem. of Council Inst. of Metallurgists 74-; Sir George Beilby Memorial Award 47; Rosenhain Medal of the Inst. of Metals 51; Heyn Medal of the Deutsche Gesellschaft für Metallkunde 56; Fellow, Royal Soc. 59; Hon. Fellow, Keble Coll., Oxford 72; Pres. Birmingham Metallurgical Soc. 65-66.
Leisure interests: gardening, walking, travel.
Publs. *Introduction to the Electron Theory of Metals* 53, *The Physical Metallurgy of Magnesium and Its Alloys* 59, *The Structure of Metals and Alloys* (with W. Hume-Rothery) 62, and numerous papers on theory of alloy formation and physical metallurgy.
Department of Physical Metallurgy and Science of Materials, University of Birmingham, P.O. Box 363, Birmingham, B15 2TT; Home: 94 Gillhurst Road, Harborne, Birmingham, B17 8PA, England.
Telephone: 021-472-1301, Ext. 3230 (Office); 021-429-3176 (Home).

Raza, Nawabzada Agha Mohammad; Pakistani diplomatist; m.; one d.; ed. Bishop Cotton's School, Simla and Royal Mil. Acad., Sandhurst.
Worked in Foreign and Political Dept., Govt. of India 30-34; served in World War II; on establishment of Pakistan was appointed Adjutant Gen. responsible for reorganization of Pakistan Army; Amb. to People's Repub. of China 51-54, 62-66, to Iran 55-59, to France 60-62, to Italy 66-69; Amb. to U.S.A. (also accred. to Mexico, Venezuela and Jamaica) 71-72; Sec. Ministry of Foreign Affairs 72-; decorations from France, Iran and The Vatican.
Leisure interests: gardening, photography.
Ministry of Foreign Affairs, Islamabad, Pakistan.

Razafimbahiny, Jules Alphonse; Malagasy jurist, economist and diplomatist; b. 19 April 1922, Mananjary; s. of Alphonse and Marguerite (née Ramasinoro) Razafimbahiny; m. Ravaoarisoa Razafy 1951; one s. one d.; ed. Institut de Droit des Affaires, Faculté de Droit, Paris, and Institut des Hautes Etudes Politiques, Paris.
President of Comm. of Overseas Countries associated with Econ. and Social Council of Common Market and EURATOM, Brussels 58-60; Technical Counsellor to Minister of State for Nat. Economy, Madagascar 60-61; Minister Plenipotentiary 62-; First Sec.-Gen. OAMCE (Org. Africaine et Malgache de Co-opération Economique) now called OCAM (Org. Commune Africaine Malgache et Mauricienne) 62-64; Dir.-Gen. Foreign Affairs (Tananarive) 64-65; Amb. to U.K., Italy, Greece and Israel 65-67; Sec. of State for Foreign Affairs (Econ. and African Affairs) 67-69; Amb. to U.S.A. 70-72, to Belgium and European Communities 73-; fmr. Pres. Admin. Council, Soc. d'Energie, Madagascar, Pan-African Inst. of Devt.; mem. Editorial Board, Soc. for Int. Devt. (Washington, D.C.), Board, Coll. of Econ. and Social Studies and Institut d'Etudes de Développement Economique et Social; Commdr. Ordre Nat. (Madagascar, Mauritania, Chad, Zaire, Comoro Islands), Officier Ordre Nat. (Upper Volta, Gabon); Grand Croix de l'Ordre de Saint Sylvestre (Vatican), Grand Croix de l'Ordre Nat. de la Répub. Italienne.
Leisure interests: music, painting, tennis.
Ambassade de Madagascar, 276 avenue de Tervueren, 1150 Brussels, Belgium.
Telephone: 770-17-26.

Razafindrabe, Armand; Malagasy diplomatist; b. 17 Sept. 1931, Tananarive; s. of Arthur Razafindrabe and Elisabeth Raheliarisoa; m. Françoise Gonin 1958; two d.; ed. Paris Univ.
Assistant Chief, Dept. of Econ. Affairs 55, Chief of Dept. 58-59; Admin. Officer, EEC 59-60; Econ. and Commercial Counsellor, Embassy in Paris 60-63; Perm. Rep. to EEC and Amb. to Belgium, Netherlands, Luxembourg and Switzerland 63-73; Amb. to Japan 74; Exec. Dir. IBRD, IFC, IDA Nov. 74-; head of del. negotiating Yaoundé Conventions with EEC 63-68, to UNCTAD 64, 68, 72, to ECOSOC 68, 70, 72; Chair. or Vice-Chair. of UN African Group, Group of 77 and other bodies 64, 66, 68, 70, 71, 72; mem. Exec. Council GATT 63-; Commdr. Ordre Nat. Malgache; Grand Officier, Ordre de la Couronne de Belgique.
Leisure interests: skiing, swimming, cooking, music, theatre.
4200 Massachusetts Avenue, N.W., Washington, D.C. 20016, U.S.A.; 13 rue Gilbert, Meyrin, Geneva, Switzerland; Home: 35 rue Rabibisoa, Antsahabe, Tananarive, Madagascar.
Telephone: (202) 244-0859 (Washington, D.C.); (022) 41-65-03 (Geneva); 212-15 (Tananarive).

Rázl, Stanislav; Czechoslovak politician; b. 13 April 1920, Sopotnice; one s. one d.; ed. School of Econs., Prague.

Worker 39-44; Technician, Asscn. for Chem. and Metallurgical Production, Ústí-on-Elbe 45-48; Technician, Gen. Management of Chem. Industries, Prague 48-51; Chief of Planning Dept., Deputy Minister, Ministry of Chem. Industry, Prague 51-56; Enterprise Man., Asscn. for Chem. and Metallurgical Production, Ústí-on-Elbe 56-63; Chief Technologist and Economist, Tech. Econs. Research Inst. 63-65; Dir. of Devt. Dept., Ministry of Chem. Industry 65-68, Minister of Chem. Industry 68; Premier of Czech Socialist Repub. Jan.-Sept. 69, Deputy Premier 69-; Minister of Planning 69-71; Chair. Czech Planning Comm. 71-; Deputy to House of Nations, Fed. Assembly of C.S.S.R. 69-; Award of Merit in Construction 60, Order of Labour 75.
Government Presidium of the Czech Socialist Republic, Prague, Czechoslovakia.

Razuvayev, Grigory Alexeyevich; Soviet organic chemist; b. 23 Aug. 1895, Moscow; s. of Alexey Grigorevich Razuvaev and Ekaterina Nikolaevna Razuvaeva; m. 2nd Elena Vladimirovna 1946; two s. one d.; ed. Leningrad Univ.
Instructor, Red Army Engineering Acad. 25-27; Laboratory Head Inst. of High Pressure, U.S.S.R. Acad. of Sciences 24-34; Prof. and Head of Chair. Gorky Univ. 46-; Dir. Chemical Research Inst., Gorky Univ. 56-, Inst. of Chemistry, Acad. of Sciences, U.S.S.R. 63-; Corresp. mem. U.S.S.R. Acad. of Sciences 58-66, mem. 66-; Hon. Life mem. New York Acad. of Sciences 75; Lenin Prize 58, State Prize 71, Hero of Socialist Labour, Order of Lenin 61, 69, 75.
Leisure interest: painting.
Institute of Chemistry, Academy of Sciences, U.S.S.R., Tropinina 49, Gorky 603600, GSP-445; Prospect Gagarina 21/5, fl 7 Gorky 603022, U.S.S.R.
Telephone: 65-49-09 (Office); 34-14-49 (Home).

Rea, 2nd Baron, cr. 35 and Baronet, of Eskdale; **Philip Russell Rea,** P.C., O.B.E., M.A., D.L., J.P.; British politician; b. 7 Feb. 1900, London; s. of 1st Baron Rea of Eskdale; m. Lorna Smith 1922; one s. (deceased) one d.; ed. Westminster School, Christ Church, Oxford, and Grenoble Univ.
Underwriting mem. of Lloyds; Dir. Rea Brothers Ltd., Scottish & Mercantile Investment Co. Ltd.; served army 14-18 and 39-45 war; with Foreign Office 46-50; Vice-Chair. Liberal Party Exec. 51-54, Pres. Liberal Party 55, Vice-Pres. 70-; Liberal Leader, House of Lords 55-67; Deputy Speaker, House of Lords; Chevalier, Légion d'Honneur; Officer Belgian Order of the Crown; Croix de Guerre with Palm; Grand Commdr. Ordre de Mérite.
Leisure interests: music and travel.
5 St. John's House, 30 Smith Square, London, S.W.1, England.

Read, Air Marshal Charles Frederick, C.B., C.B.E., D.F.C., A.F.C.; retd. Australian air force officer; b. 9 Oct. 1918, Sydney; s. of Joseph F. Read and Ethel Mary Shelton; m. Betty Elsie Bradshaw 1946; three s.; ed. Sydney Grammar School and Imperial Defence Coll.
Director Operations, Royal Australian Air Force 60-64; Commandant, R.A.A.F. Acad., Point Cook, Vic. 66-68; Officer Commanding R.A.A.F. Richmond, N.S.W. 68-69; Deputy Chief of Staff R.A.A.F. 69-72, Chief of Staff 72-75; retd. 75.
Leisure interest: yachting.
2007 Pettwater Road, Bayview, N.S.W., Australia.
Telephone: 997-1686.

Read, John Emms, F.C.A., F.B.I.M.; British business executive; b. 29 March 1918, Brighton; s. of William E. and Daysie E. (née Cooper) Read; m. Dorothy M. Berry 1942; two s.; ed. Brighton, Hove and Sussex Grammar School and Admin. Staff Coll., Henley-on-Thames.
Commander, Royal Navy 39-46; Exec., Ford Motor Co. 46-64; Exec. Dir. EMI Ltd. 65, Joint Man. Dir. 66, Chief Exec. and Man. Dir. 69-73, Deputy Chair. and

Chief Exec. 73-74, Chair. 74-; Dir. Dunlop Holdings Ltd., Thames Television, Brighton Marina Co., Capitol Industries-EMI Inc. (U.S.A.), EMI Australia, Pathé Marconi EMI France, Toshiba-EMI Japan, Post Office; mem. R.N. Film Corpn.; mem. of Court of Brunel Univ.; Fellow, British Inst. of Management, Royal Soc. of Arts; Companion Inst. of Radio Engineers.
Leisure interests: music, the arts, tennis.
EMI Limited, 20 Manchester Square, London, W1A 1ES; 21 Roedean Crescent, Brighton, England.
Telephone: 01-486-4488 (Office); 0273-63280 (Home).

Reagan, Ronald; American politician and former actor; b. 6 Feb. 1911, Tampico, Ill.; m. 1st Jane Wyman 1940 (divorced 1948), one s. one d.; m. 2nd Nancy Davis 1952, one s. one d.; ed. public schools at Tampico, Monmouth, Galesburg and Dixon, Illinois, and Eureka Coll.
Former film actor and producer, radio sports announcer and editor, Central Broadcasting Co.; operated horse-breeding and cattle ranch; Player and Production Supervisor, Gen. Electric Theater TV for eight years; fmr. Pres. Screen Actors Guild, Motion Picture Industry Council; mem. Board of Dirs. Cttee. on Fundamental Educ., St. John's Hospital; U.S. Air Force 42-46; Gov. of Calif. 67-74; Chair. Republican Govs. Asscn. 69; numerous awards; Republican.
c/o State Capitol, Sacramento, Calif. 95814, U.S.A.

Reale, Miguel; Brazilian lawyer and university administrator; b. 6 Nov. 1910, São Bento do Sapucahy; s. of Dr. Bras Reale and Felicidade Chiaradia Reale; m. Filomena Pucci Reale 1935; three c.; ed. Faculty of Law, Univ. of São Paulo.
Member, Admin. Council, State of São Paulo 42-45, Sec. of Justice 47, 63-64; Rector, Univ. of São Paulo; Pres. Brazilian Inst. of Philosophy; del. of Brazilian Govt. to ILO Conf., Geneva 51; mem. Educ. Council, State of São Paulo; mem. Comm. for Constitutional Reform 67; Moinho Santista Prize for Law 64; Teixeira de Freitas Prize, Inst. of Advocates of Brazil 68; Dr. h.c. (Geneva).
Publs. several books on legal topics.
Av. 9 de Julho, 3871 São Paulo; Rua Senador Feijó, 1769, São Paulo, Brazil.
Telephone: 81-3521; 32-6996.

Reale, Oronzo; Italian lawyer and politician; b. 24 Oct. 1902; ed. Univ. degli Studi, Rome.
Secretary, Young Republican Fed. 20-24; Founder-mem. and Exec. Partito d'Azione 42; mem. Cttee. for Nat. Liberation; mem. Exec. Cttee. Italian Republican Party (P.R.I.) 48-; mem. Chamber of Deputies 58-; Political Sec. P.R.I. 49-64; Minister of Justice 64-68, 70-71, Dec. 74-; Minister of Finance 68-69; mem. Nat. Consultative Assembly 45-46.
1 Via del Pollaiolo 5, Rome, Italy.
Telephone: 879432.

Reardon, Timothy James, Jr.; American government official; b. 18 May 1915; ed. Phillips Exeter Acad., Harvard Coll.
Worked in Boston Advertising Agency 38-41; Nat. Advertising Man., Lowell Sun Newspaper 41-42; service in U.S.A.F. attaining rank of Captain 42-46; Admin. Asst. to Senator John F. Kennedy 47-60; Special Asst. to the Pres. for Cabinet Affairs 61-64; Special Asst. to Chair. Federal Deposit Insurance Corpn. 64-65, Exec. Asst. to Board of Dirs., F.D.I.C. 65-.
Federal Deposit Insurance Corporation, Washington 25, D.C.; Home: 3134 Dumbarton Avenue, N.W., Washington, D.C. 20007, U.S.A.

Rebbeck, Denis, C.B.E., M.A., M.SC., PH.D., B.LITT., D.L., J.P.; British shipbuilder; b. 22 Jan. 1914, Belfast, N. Ireland; s. of late Sir Frederick and Lady Rebbeck; m. Rosamond Annette K. Jameson 1938; four s.; ed. Campbell Coll., Belfast and Pembroke Coll., Cambridge.

Assistant Man. Harland and Wolff Ltd., Belfast 39, Dir. 46, Deputy Man. Dir. 53-62, Man. Dir. 62-70, Chair. 65-66; Dir. D. and W. Henderson Ltd. and A. and J. Inglis Ltd. 48-68, Chair. 57-68; Dir. Iron Trades Employers Insurance Asscn. Ltd. and Iron Trades Mutual Insurance Co. Ltd. 50-, Vice-Chair. 69-72, Chair. 72-; Belfast Harbour Commr. 62-; Pres. Shipbuilding Employers' Fed. 62-63; Dir. Colvilles Ltd., Glasgow 63-67; Shipbuilding Corpn. Ltd., London 63-73, Nat. Commercial Bank of Scotland Ltd. 65-69, Royal Bank of Scotland Ltd. 69-; mem. Royal Yacht Squadron; mem. Management Board, Engineering Employers Fed. 63-75, Gen. and Technical Cttees., Lloyd's Register of Shipping; Akroyd Stuart Award, Inst. of Marine Engineers 43; mem. Research Council and Chair. Design Cttee., British Ship Research Asscn. 65-73; mem. N. Ireland Econ. Council 65-70; mem. Council of Royal Inst. of Naval Architects 64-72; mem. Court of Assts., Worshipful Co. of Shipwrights; Dir. John Kelly Ltd. 68-, Deputy Chair. 68-69, Chair. 69-; Dir. Belships Co. Ltd. 70-, Chair. 72-; Special Consultant, Swan Hunter Group Ltd. 70-.
Leisure interest: sailing.
The White House, Craigavad, Co. Down, N. Ireland; Flat 71, 49 Hallam Street, London, W.1.
Telephone: Holywood 2294 (Ireland); 01-636 6320 (London).

Rebelo de Sousa, Dr. Baltasar; Portuguese politician; b. 1922; ed. Faculty of Medicine, Univ. of Lisbon.
Under-Secretary of State for Educ. 55-61; Vice-Pres. Overseas Council 63-68; Gov.-Gen. of Mozambique 68-70; Deputy to Nat. Assembly; Minister of Health and Corpns. 70-73, of Overseas Provs. 73-74; mem. Board of Dirs. Asscn. of Social Service and Portuguese League against Cancer; fmr. Prof. Inst. of Social Service; Grand Cross Ordem do Infante D. Henrique, Grand Officer Orden de Cristo etc.
Lisbon, Portugal.

Rebeyrolle, Paul; French artist; b 3 Nov. 1926; ed. Lycée Gay-Lussac, Limoges.
Exhibitions at Salon des Indépendants, Salon d'Automne, Salon de Mai, Salon de la Jeune Peinture (France); Dir. Salon de Mai; works in collections in England, Sweden, Belgium, U.S.A., Poland, Italy, Japan, etc.; rep. at Dunn Int. Exhibition, London 63; First Prize, la Jeune Peinture 50, Fénéon Prize 51, First Prize at French Section, Paris Biennale 59.
9 rue Falguière, Paris 15e, France.

Rebinder, Pyotr Aleksandrovich; Soviet physical chemist; b. 3 Oct. 1898, St. Petersburg (now Leningrad); ed. Moscow Univ.
Associate Moscow Inst. of Physics and Bio-Physics 23-34; Prof. of Physics, Moscow Pedagogic Inst. 29-; corresp. mem. U.S.S.R. Acad. of Sciences 33-46, mem. 46-; Head Dept. of Dispersed Systems, Inst. of Physical Chemistry, U.S.S.R. Acad. of Sciences 35-; Prof. Moscow Univ. 42-; Corresp. mem. U.S.S.R. Acad. of Sciences 33-, mem. 46-; State Prize, Hero of Socialist Labour 68, Order of Red Banner of Labour, Order of Lenin, etc.
Publs. Co-author *Research on the Applied Physical Chemistry of Surface Phenomena* 36, co-author *The Physical Chemistry of Flotation Processes* 33, co-author *The Physical Chemistry of Detergent Action* 35, *New Trends in the Development of Colloidal Chemistry* 59.
U.S.S.R. Academy of Sciences, 14 Leninsky Prospekt, Moscow, U.S.S.R.

Rebling, Eberhard; German pianist and musicologist; b. 4 Dec. 1911, Berlin; m. Lin Jaldati; two d.; ed. Berlin Univ.
Emigrated to Holland 36; with resistance movement in Holland 41-45; Music Critic and Pianist, Amsterdam 45-51; Chief Editor periodical *Musik und Gesellschaft*, Berlin 52-59; Rector Deutsche Hochschule für Musik

Hanns Eisler, Berlin 59-71, Prof. 59-; Nat. Prize 54, Peace Medal 64.
Publs. *Een eeuw Nederlandse Danskunst* 50, *Den Lustelijcken Mey* 50, *Johann Sebastian Bach* 51, *Ballett gestern und heute* 56, *Ballett sein Wesen und Werden* 64, *Ballet von A-Z* 66, *Ballet Heute* 70, *Der Tanz der Völker* 72, *Ballettfibel* 74, *Marius Petipa* 75.
1251 Ziegenhals, Seestrasse 18, German Democratic Republic.
Telephone: Zeuthen 836.

Rebocho Vaz, Col. Camilo Augusto de Miranda; Portuguese army officer and administrator; b. 7 Oct. 1920, Avis; s. of Aurelio Rebocho Vaz and Marcelina da Conceição Miranda Vaz; m. Clotilde Gil da Assunção 1947; three s. two d.; ed. Univ. de Coimbra, Escola do Exército, Lisbon and Inst. de Altos Estudos Militares, Lisbon.
Military service in Portugal, Azores and Angola; 2nd Commdr., Infantry Regt., Luanda, Angola 60; Commdr. of anti-terrorist activities 61; Gov. District of Uige, Angola 61-66; Gov. of Angola 66-72; numerous military and civil decorations.
Leisure interest: collecting shells and minerals.
Publs. *Quatro Anos de Governo no Distrito do Uige, Angola 1967, Angola 1969, Dois Anos de Governo, Outros Dois Anos de Governo, Acção Governativa.*
c/o Ministério dos Negócios Estrangeiros, Lisbon, Portugal.

Reckitt, Basil Norman, M.A., T.D., D.L.; British business executive (retd.); b. 12 Aug. 1905, St. Albans; s. of Norman and Beatrice Reckitt (née Hewett); m. 1st Virginia Carre-Smith 1928 (died 1961), 2nd Mary Holmes 1966; three d.; ed. Uppingham and King's Coll., Cambridge.
Joined Reckitt & Sons Ltd., Hull 27, Dir. 37-72, later Chair.; Dir. Reckitt & Colman Ltd. 53-72, Vice-Chair. 53-65, Deputy Chair. 65-66, Chair. 66-70; Royal Artillery 38-44; Mil. Govt., Germany 44-45; Sheriff, Kingston upon Hull 70-71; Chair. of Council, Hull Univ. 71; Hon. LL.D. (Hull) 67.
Publs. *History of Reckitt & Sons Limited, Charles I and Hull, The Lindley Affair.*
The Elms, Roos, nr. Hull, Yorks., England.

Redaelli Spreafico, Enrico; Italian iron and steel executive; b. 24 April 1911, Milan; ed. "Bocconi" Univ., Milan.
Joined Soc. Dalmine in IRI Group 36; joined Finsider 38, appointed Admin. Man. of Società Rejna, a firm in Finsider group 43; Admin. Head, Società Cornigliano 50, subsequently Admin. Man. and Asst. Gen. Man.; Gen. Man. Soc. Cornigliano 58; Gen. Man. Italsider 61, Man. Dir. 62, 72, Vice-Pres. 72, Pres. 73-; Dir. of Armco Finsider, C.M.F., Deriver, C.S.M. and Accionerie di Piombino; mem. Ligurian Regional Financial Council, Vice-Pres. and mem. Exec. Cttee. Intersind; Cavaliere del Lavoro; Grand Ufficiale dell 'Ordine Equestre del Santo Sepolcro di Gerusalemme.
Office: Via Corsica 4, 16128 Genoa, Italy.
Telephone: 5999.

Redcliffe-Maud, Baron (Life Peer) cr. 67, of City and County of Bristol; **John Primatt Redcliffe Maud,** G.C.B., C.B.E., M.A., A.B.; British diplomatist and college principal; b. 3 Feb. 1906, Bristol; s. of John Primatt Maud and Elizabeth Furse; m. Jean Hamilton 1932; one s. three d. (one deceased); ed. Eton, New Coll., Oxford, and Harvard Coll.
Fellow, Univ. Coll., Oxford 29-39, Dean 32-39, Univ. Lecturer in Politics, Oxford Univ. 38-39; Councillor, Oxford City 30-35; Master, Birkbeck Coll., Univ. of London 39-43; Second Sec. Ministry of Food 43-44; Second Sec. Ministry of Reconstruction 44, Sec. 45; Permanent Sec. Ministry of Education 45-52, Ministry of Fuel and Power 52-57, Ministry of Power 57-58; mem. Economic Planning Board 52-58; First Council

Meeting, UNRRA 43; Gen. Conf. UNESCO 46, 47, 48, 49, 50, 51; Exec. Board, UNESCO 46-50; Pres. Exec. Board 49-50; High Commr. in Union of South Africa and for Basutoland, Bechuanaland Protectorate and Swaziland, Jan. 59-61, for Basutoland, Bechuanaland and Swaziland 61-63; Ambassador to South Africa 61-63; Master of University Coll., Oxford 63- (76); Chair. Royal Comm. on Local Govt. in England 66-69; High Bailiff of Westminster 67-; Hon. Fellow New Coll. 64-; Chair. Appts. Comm., Press Council 73-; Hon. LL.D. (Witwatersrand Univ. 60, Natal Univ. 63, Leeds Univ. 67, Nottingham Univ. 68); Hon. D.Soc.Sc. (Birmingham Univ.) 68; Pres. Medal, Inst. of Public Relations 74.
Publs. *English Local Government* 32, *City Government: the Johannesburg Experiment* 38; contrib. to *Oxford and the Groups* 34, *Personal Ethics* 35, *Man's Dilemma and God's Answer* 44, *Education in a Changing World* 51, *The British Tradition* 51, *English Local Government Reformed* 74, etc.
The Master's Lodgings, University College, Oxford, England.

Reddaway, William Brian, C.B.E., M.A., F.B.A.; British economist; b. 8 Jan. 1913, Cambridge; s. of William Fiddian Reddaway and Kate Waterland (née Sills) Reddaway; m. Barbara A. Bennett 1938; three s. one d.; ed. Oundle School, and King's Coll., Cambridge.
Assistant, Bank of England 34-35; Research Fellow in Econs. Univ. of Melbourne 36-37; Fellow of Clare Coll., Cambridge 38-; Board of Trade 40-47; Lecturer, Cambridge Univ. 47-55, Dir. Dept. of Applied Econs. 55-70; Reader in Applied Econs. 57-65, Prof. of Political Economy 69-; Econ. Adviser, Org. for European Econ. Co-operation (OEEC) 51-52, Confederation of British Industries 72-; Research Assoc. Centre for Int. Studies, New Delhi 59-60; Visiting Lecturer, Econ. Devt. Inst., Washington 66-67; mem. Royal Comm. on the Press 61-62; mem. Nat. Board for Prices and Incomes 67-71; Editor, *London and Cambridge Economic Bulletin* 51-74, *Economic Journal* 71-76; Adam Smith Prize, Cambridge 34.
Leisure interests: tennis, walking, skating, squash.
Publs. *The Russian Financial System* 35, *The Economics of a Declining Population* 39, *The Measurement of Production Movements* 48, *The Development of the Indian Economy* 62, *The Effects of U.K. Direct Investment Overseas* (interim report 67, final report 68), *The Effects of the Selective Employment Tax* (first report) 70, (final report) 73.
4 Adams Road, Cambridge, England.
Telephone: 0223-50041.

Reddi, Bezwada Gopala; Indian politician; b. 5 Aug. 1907, Nellore A.P.; m. B. Lakshmikanthamma; three s. one d.; ed. Visva Bharathi Santiniketan.
Elected to Madras Ass. 37, mem. 37-46; Minister of Local Govt., Madras Govt. 37-39, Minister of Finance 47; Pro-Chancellor, A.P. Univ. 51-57; Head of United Congress Legislative Party, A.P. Ass. 55-; Chief Minister A.P. 55-56, Home Minister 56, Finance Minister 57; Minister of Revenue and Civil Expenditure, Govt. of India 58-61, Minister of Housing, Works and Supply 61-62, Minister of Information and Broadcasting 62-63; Gov. of Uttar Pradesh 67-72; elected to Rajya Sabha 58-60, to Lok Sabha 62; mem. Indian Congress Party, Pres. A.P. Congress Cttee. 53; Deputy Leader Congress Party 65-67; Hon. D.Litt.
c/o Governor's Camp, Raj Bhavan, Lucknow, Uttar Pradesh, India.

Reddish, Sir Halford (Walter Lupton), Kt., F.C.A.; British chartered accountant and company director; b. 15 Aug. 1898, Coventry; s. of late Henry Lupton Reddish; m. Valerie Campbell Smith 1946 (died 1971); ed. Rugby School.

Chairman and Chief Exec. The Rugby Portland Cement Co. Ltd.; Dir. Meldrum Investment Trust Ltd., Granada Group Ltd., and of other companies; mem. Board of Referees (Inland Revenue); mem. Council, Econ. League; Underwriting mem. of Lloyd's; Freeman, City of London.
Leisure interests: business, chess.
Crown House, Rugby, Warwickshire, England.
Telephone: Rugby 2244.

Reddy, Kolli Venkata Raghunatha, M.A., LL.B.; Indian lawyer and politician; b. 4 Sept. 1924; ed. V. R. Coll., Nellore, and Annamalai Univ. and Lucknow Univ.
Member, Senate Annamalai Univ. 47-59; Advocate, Madras High Court 50, Supreme Court 58, also Andhra Pradesh High Court; mem. Rajya Sabha 62-; Union Minister of State for Industrial Devt. and Company Affairs 67-70, of Company Affairs 70-72, of Labour and Rehabilitation 73-.
Publ. *Criminal Law—Procedural and Substantial.*
Ministry of Labour and Rehabilitation, New Delhi, India.

Reddy, Kysasambally Chengalaraya, B.A., B.L.; Indian politician; b. 1902; ed. Pachaiyappa's Coll. and Law Coll., Madras, Univ. of Madras.
Member Mysore Legislature 30-52; Pres. Kolar District Board 33-37; fmr. Editor *Janavani*; Pres. Mysore Peoples' Federation 35-37; effected coalition of Peoples' Fed. with Mysore Congress 37; mem. Working Cttee., Mysore Congress 37-52, Leader Parliamentary Party 37-52, Pres. 37-38 and 46-47; mem. Exec. Council, All-India States Peoples' Conf. 44-45, Rep. to U.K. and Continent 45-46; mem. Constituent Assembly of India 47-50; launched Satyagraha for the establishment of responsible govt. in Mysore State 47; Leader Mysore Legislative Ass. (three times) and Chief Minister, Mysore State 47-52; mem. Council of States 52-57; M.P. (Lok Sabha) 57, 62-65; Gov. of Madhya Pradesh 65-71; Union Minister of Production 52-57; Minister of Works, Housing and Supply 57-61, of Commerce and Industry 61-64; LL.D. (h.c.).
Bhopal, Madhya Pradesh, India.

Reddy, Marri Channa, M.B., B.S.; Indian agriculturist and politician; b. 13 Jan. 1919; ed. Chadarghat High School and Osmania Univ.
Left medical practice to devote himself to politics in Hyderabad; held organizational posts in Indian Nat. Congress Party; leader in Hyderabad Congress; mem. Rajya Sabha 50-51; Minister of Agriculture, Andhra Pradesh 52, later Minister of Planning, Rehabilitation, Panchyat Raj, Industry and Commerce, Commercial Taxes, Education and Finance, Andhra Pradesh; Union Minister of Steel, Mines and Metals 67-68; now Gov. of Uttar Pradesh.
Office of the Governor, Lucknow, Uttar Pradesh, India.

Reddy, Neelam Sanjiva; Indian politician; b. 1913; ed. Adyar Arts Coll., Anantapur.
Secretary Andhra P.C.C. 36-46; active in Satyagraha movt.; mem., Sec. Madras Legislative Assembly 46; mem. Indian Constituent Assembly 47; Minister for Prohibition, Housing and Forests, Madras Govt. 49-51; Pres. Andhra P.C.C. 51-; mem. Rajya Sabha 52-53; mem. Andhra Pradesh Legislative Assembly 53-; Deputy Chief Minister, Andhra Pradesh 53-56; Chief Minister 56-57; Leader, Andhra Congress Legislature Party 53-; Pres. All-India Congress Party 60-62; Chief Minister, Andhra Pradesh 62-64; Minister of Steel and Mines, India 64-65, of Transport, Aviation, Shipping and Tourism 65-67; Speaker of Lok Sabha 67-69; unsuccessful Presidential candidate Aug. 69.
c/o The Lok Sabha, New Delhi, India.

Reddy, Pingle Jaganmohan, B.E., M.B.B.S., F.R.C.S., B.COM., B.SC., LL.B.; Indian doctor and engineer; b. 23 Jan. 1910, Hyderabad; s. of late Sri Pingle Venkatarama Reddy and Smt. Chaudabai; m. Pramila J. Reddy 1935; three s. one d.; ed. Univs. of Leeds and Cambridge.

Legal practice 37-46; Legal dept. Govt. of Hyderabad 46-48; District and Sessions Judge, Secunderabad 48; Puisne Judge, High Court, Hyderabad 52-56; Judge, High Court, Andhra Pradesh 56, Chief Justice 66; Judge, Supreme Court of India 69-; mem. Syndicate and Dean, Faculty of Law, Osmania Univ. 52-59.

Publs. *The Hyderabad Excess Profits Tax Act, Quest of Justice.*

11 Motilal Nehru Marg, New Delhi 11; also Lumbini Gardens, Saifabad, Hyderabad 22, India.
Telephone: 619397 (New Delhi).

Redfield, Alfred C., PH.D.; American teacher and research scientist; b. 15 Nov. 1890, Philadelphia, Pa.; s. of Robert S. Redfield and Mary T. Guillou; m. 1st Elizabeth S. Pratt 1913 (died 1920), 2nd Martha Putnam 1922; one s. two d.; ed. Haverford School, Haverford Coll., Harvard Univ., Christ's Coll., Cambridge, and Univ. of Munich.

Assistant Prof. of Physiology 19-20, Asst. Prof. 21-30, Assoc. Prof. 30-31, Prof. 31-56, Emer. 56-; Dir. Biological Lab., Harvard Univ. 34; Visiting Prof., Stanford Univ. 30; Walker Ames Prof., Univ. of Washington 40; Senior Biologist, Woods Hole Oceanographic Inst. 30-53, Senior Oceanographer 54-56, Senior Oceanographer Emer. 56-; mem. Emer. Nat. Acad. of Sciences; Hon. mem. Marine Biological Asscn. of U.K. 56-; Agassiz Medal 56; Hon. Ph.D. (Oslo) 56, Hon. D.Sc. (Lehigh) 65, (Newfoundland) 67, (Alaska) 71.

Leisure interests: boating, painting, gardening.

Publs. Numerous scientific papers in physiology, biochemistry and oceanography.

P.O. Box 106, Woods Hole, Mass., U.S.A.
Telephone: 617-548-0987.

Redford, Robert; American actor; b. 18 Aug. 1937; ed. Van Nuys High School, Univ. of Colorado.

Films include *War Hunt* 61, *Situation Hopeless But Not Serious* 65, *Inside Daisy Clover* 65, *The Chase* 65, *This Property is Condemned* 66, *Barefoot in the Park* 67, *Tell Them Willie Boy is Here* 69, *Butch Cassidy and the Sundance Kid* 69, *Downhill Racer* 69, *Little Fauss and Big Halsy* 70, *Jeremiah Johnson* 72, *The Candidate* 72, *How to Steal a Diamond in Four Uneasy Lessons* 72, *The Way We Were* 73, *The Sting* 73, *The Great Gatsby* 74, *The Great Waldo Pepper* 74, *Three Days of the Condor* 75, *All the President's Men* 76.

c/o Pickwick Public Relations, 370 Lexington Avenue, New York, N.Y. 10017, U.S.A.

Redgrave, Sir Michael (Scudamore), Kt., C.B.E., M.A., D.LITT.; British actor and author; b. 20 March 1908, Bristol; m. Rachel Kempson 1935; one s. two d.; ed. Clifton Coll., Magdalene Coll., Cambridge, Germany and France.

Liverpool Repertory Theatre 34-36; Old Vic 36-37; John Gielgud's Company 37-38; Michel St. Denis's Company 38-39, Old Vic 49-50, Stratford-on-Avon Company 51, 53, 58; appeared in *Beggar's Opera* and *Thunder Rock* 40; served in Royal Navy 41-42; appeared in *A Month in the Country* 43, *Uncle Harry* 44, *Macbeth* (London and New York) 47, *Hamlet* (London, Zürich, Elsinore and Holland Festivals) 50, *Winter Journey (Country Girl)* 52, *Merchant of Venice, King Lear* (Stratford-on-Avon), *Anthony and Cleopatra* (London, Stratford-on-Avon, Belgium, Paris) 53-54, *A Touch of the Sun, Hamlet* (Stratford-on-Avon) 58, *The Aspern Papers* 59-60, *The Tiger and the Horse* 60-61; toured Russia playing *Hamlet* 58-59, *The Complaisant Lover* 61-62, *Out of Bounds* 62, *Uncle Vanya* 62, 63; National Theatre Co. *Hamlet, Hobson's Choice,*

Uncle Vanya, The Master Builder 63-64; Dir. opening season of Yvonne Arnaud Theatre, Guildford 65; Dir. *A Month in the Country* 65, *The Old Boys* 71, *Voyage Round My Father* (London and Canada 72, Australia 73), *The Hollow Crown* (U.S.A.) 73, *Pleasure and Repentance* (U.S.A.) 74, *Shakespeare's People* (South Africa) 75; films acted in include *The Lady Vanishes, The Stars Look Down, Thunder Rock, The Way to the Stars, Dead of Night, Fame is the Spur, The Browning Version, The Importance of Being Earnest, The Dam Busters, The Innocents, The Loneliness of the Long Distance Runner, The Heroes of Telemark, The Hill, Oh! what a lovely war, Battle of Britain, Goodbye Mr. Chips, Connecting Rooms, Goodbye Gemini, The Go-Between* 71; Dir. *Werther* 66, *La Bohème,* Glyndebourne 67; Commdr. Order of Dannebrog 55.

Leisure interests: reading, music.

Publs. *The Seventh Man* (play) 36, *Actor's Ways and Means* 53, *Mask or Face* 55, *The Mountebank's Tale* (novel), *The Aspern Papers* (play) 59, *Circus Boy* (play) 63.

35 Lower Belgrave Street, London, S.W.1; c/o Hutton Management Ltd., 33 Sloane Street, London, S.W.1, England.

Redgrave, Vanessa, C.B.E.; British actress; b. 30 Jan. 1937; d. of Sir Michael Redgrave (*q.v.*); ed. Queensgate School, London, and Central School of Speech and Drama.

Evening Standard Award, Best Actress 61, and Variety Club Award 61; Award for Best Actress, Cannes Film Festival 66 for *Morgan—A Suitable Case for Treatment*; Award for Leading Actress, U.S. Nat. Soc. of Film Critics and Best Actress Award, Film Critics' Guild (U.K.) for *Isadora Duncan* 69; mem. Workers' Revolutionary Party.

Leisure interest: changing the status quo.

Stage appearances in *A Midsummer Night's Dream* 59, *The Tiger and the Horse* 60, *The Taming of the Shrew* 61, *As You Like It* 61, *Cymbeline* 62, *The Seagull* 64, *The Prime of Miss Jean Brodie* 66, *Daniel Deronda* 69, *Cato Street* 71, *Threepenny Opera* 72, *Twelfth Night* 72, *Anthony and Cleopatra* 73, *Design for Living* 73, *Macbeth* 75, *Lady from the Sea* 76.

Films include: *Morgan—A Suitable Case for Treatment* 65, *Sailor from Gibraltar* 65, *Camelot* 67, *Blow Up* 67, *Charge of the Light Brigade* 68, *Isadora Duncan* 68, *The Seagull* 68, *A Quiet Place in the Country* 68, *Dropout, The Trojan Women* 70, *The Devils* 70, *The Holiday* 71, *Mary Queen of Scots* 71, *Katherine Mansfield* (BBC TV) 73, *Murder on the Orient Express* 74, *Winter Rates* 74, *7% Solution* 75.

18 St. Peter's Square, London, W.6, England.

Reece, Hon. Eric Elliott; Australian trade unionist and politician; b. 6 July 1909, Mathinna; s. of G. O. Reece; m. Alice L. Hanigan 1935; two s. (one deceased) two d.; ed. Launceston Jr. Tech. School.

Organizer, Australian Workers' Union, W. Tasmania 35-46; mem. Fed. Exec. Australian Labor Party 40, 49-59, Fed. Pres. 52-53, 54-55, Pres. Tasmanian Section 48-59; Hon. Minister in charge of Housing and Building Supplies, Tasmania 46-47; Minister for Lands and Works, Tasmania 47-48, for Mines 47-58; Premier of Tasmania 58-69, Treas. 59-60, Minister for Mines 58-69; Leader of the Opposition 69-72; Premier, Treas., Minister for Mines, Tasmania 72-75; mem. House of Assembly for Braddon, Tasmania 46-75; Companion of Australia 75.

Leisure interest: bowls.

59 Howard Road, Glenorchy, Tasmania 7010, Australia.

Reed, Sir Carol, Kt.; British film producer; b. 30 Dec. 1906; ed. King's School, Canterbury.

First appeared on stage at Empire Theatre, London 24; acted small parts 24-27; joined Edgar Wallace as actor, stage dir. 27; left theatre for film production

30; since then has directed *Midshipman Easy, Laburnum Grove, A Girl in the News, Bank Holiday, Penny Paradise, Who's Your Lady Friend, Talk of the Devil, Climbing High, A Girl Must Live, The Stars Look Down, Night Train to Munich, Kipps, The Young Mr. Pitt, The Way Ahead, A Letter from Home, The New Lot, Odd Man Out, The Fallen Idol, The Third Man, Outcast of the Islands, The Man Between, Kid for two Farthings, Trapeze, The Key, Our Man in Havana, Running Man, The Agony and the Ecstasy, Oliver!, The Indian, The Public Eye, Follow Me;* served in army in Second World War and directed war film called *The True Glory;* Golden Thistle Award 67.
[*Died 26 April* 1976.]

Reed, Philip Dunham, B.S. in E.E., LL.B.; American corporation executive; b. 16 Nov. 1899, Milwaukee, Wis.; *s.* of William Dennis Reed and Virginia (Dunham) Reed; *m.* Mabel M. Smith 1921; one *s.* one *d.;* ed. Univ. of Wisconsin and Fordham Univ.
With law firm 21-; Vice-Pres. and Patent Counsel Van Heusen Products Inc. 22-26; with Gen. Electric Co. 26-42 and 45-59, mem. Law Dept., Asst. to Pres. and Dir. 37-39, Chair. 40-42, 45-58, Chair. of Finance Cttee. 46-59, Dir. Emer. 68-; Chair. Int. Gen. Electric Co. until merger with parent co. 45-52; Chief, Bureau of Industries, War Production Board 42-; Deputy Chief U.S. Mission for Econ. Affairs, London 42-43, Chief 43-45; Consultant to U.S. Del. to San Francisco Conf. 45; Chair. U.S. Del. Anglo-American Council on Productivity 48-52; mem. Comm. on Inf. of U.S., Inf. Agency 48-61; Pres. Int. Chamber of Commerce 49-51, now Hon. Pres.; mem. The Business Council 40-, Vice-Chair. 51-52; Trustee and mem. Research and Policy Cttee. of Cttee. for Econ. Devt. 46-, Chair. 48-49; Special Amb. to Mexico 58; Dir. Fed. Reserve Bank of N.Y. 59-65, Chair. 60-65; Dir. of numerous companies; President's Certificate of Merit Award; Commdr. de la Légion d'Honneur; Hon. LL.D. (Union Coll., Brooklyn Polytechnic Inst., Univ. of Wisconsin, Swarthmore Coll.); Hon. D.Eng. (Rensselaer Polytechnic Inst.); Hon. Dr.Comm.Sc. (N.Y. Univ.); Republican.
Home: Rye, N.Y.; Office: 375 Park Avenue, New York City 22, N.Y., U.S.A.
Telephone: 212-PL2-1550.

Reed, Thomas C., M.S.; American public official; b. 1 March 1934, New York, N.Y.; *m.* Leslie Jean Papenfus; three *c.;* ed. Cornell Univ. and Univ. of S. Calif.
First Lieutenant, U.S.A.F. 56-61; Second Engineer, Avco Research Laboratory 61; Consultant, Lawrence Radiation Laboratory, Univ. of Calif. 62-67; Gen. Man. Supercon Ltd. 63-65; Appointments Sec. Office of the Gov. of California 67; Chair., Pres., Treas. Quaker Hill Devt. Corp. 65-73; Pres. Breckenridge Co. 71-73; Asst. to Sec. and Deputy Sec. of Defence 73, Dir. of Telecommunications and Command Control Systems, Dept. of Defence 74-75, Sec. of the Air Force Dec. 75-.
Department of the Air Force, The Pentagon, Washington, D.C. 20330, U.S.A.

Reedy, George Edward, Jr.; American government official and educationist; b. 5 Aug. 1917, East Chicago, Ind.; *s.* of George E. and Mary Mulvaney Reedy; *m.* Lillian Greenwald 1948; two *s.;* ed. Univ. of Chicago.
Congressional Corresp. United Press, Washington, D.C. 38-41, 46-51; U.S. Army Air Corps 42-45; Staff Dir. U.S. Senate Minority Policy Cttee. 53-54, Majority Policy Cttee. 55-60; Special Asst. to Vice-Pres. Lyndon B. Johnson 61-63, Press Sec. to the Pres. 64-65, Aide to the Pres. 65-66, Special Consultant to the Pres. 68-69; Pegram Lecturer, Brookhaven Nat. Radiation Laboratory 71; Adjunct Prof. of Political Science, State Univ. of New York 71-72; Dean, Lucius W. Nieman Prof. of Journalism, Marquette Univ. Sept. 72-; mem. and chair. numerous govt. comms. and boards of enquiry 66-68; Vice-Pres. for Planning, Struthers Wells Corpn.

66-; Fellow, Woodrow Wilson Int. Center for Scholars 70-; Duke Univ. Fellow in Communications 73-74; Poynter Fellow, Univ. of Indiana 74.
Leisure interests: sports, fishing.
Publs. *Who Will Do Our Fighting For Us?* 69, *The Twilight of the Presidency* 70, *The Presidency in Flux* 73.
Office: College of Journalism, Marquette University, Milwaukee, Wisconsin; Home: 2307 East Newberry Boulevard, Milwaukee, Wisconsin 53211, U.S.A.
Telephone: 414-224-7132 (Office).

Rees, Albert Lloyd George, D.SC., PH.D., D.I.C., F.R.A.C.I., F.A.A.; Australian scientist; b. 15 Jan. 1916, Melbourne; *s.* of George P. Rees and Edith Targett; *m.* Marion Mofflin 1942; three *d.;* ed. Univs. of Melbourne and London.
Lecturer in Chem., Univ. of W. Australia 39; Beit Scientific Research Fellow, Imperial Coll., London 39-41; Extra-Mural Research in Chem. Defence, Ministry of Supply, U.K., 39-41; Research and Devt. Philips Electrical Industries, U.K. 41-44; with Commonwealth Scientific and Industrial Research Org. (CSIRO) 44-, Chief Div. of Chemical Physics 58-; Chair. Chem. Research Labs. 61-70; mem. Bureau and Exec. Cttee., Int. Union of Pure and Applied Chem. 63-73, Vice-Pres. 67-69, Pres. 69-71; mem. Exec. Cttee. ICSU 69-72, Gen. Cttee. ICSU 72-; Pres. Royal Australian Chem. Inst. (R.A.C.I.) 67-68; mem. Council, Australian Acad. of Science 63-68, 69-73; mem. Board of Studies, Victoria Inst. of Colls. 68-; Liversidge Lecturer, Royal Soc. of N.S.W. 52; Einstein Memorial Lecturer, Australian Inst. of Physics 70; Rennie Medal 46, H. G. Smith Medal (R.A.C.I.) 51, Leighton Memorial Medal (R.A.C.I.) 70.
Leisure interests: golf, music, gardening.
Publs. *Chemistry of the Defect Solid State* 54, and many articles in learned journals.
CSIRO, Division of Chemical Physics, P.O. Box 160, Clayton, Victoria 3168; Home: 9 Ajana Street, North Balwyn, Victoria 3104, Australia.
Telephone: 544-0633 (Office); 857-9358 (Home).

Rees, Elfan, M.A., D.D.; British United Reformed Church clergyman; b. 26 Feb. 1906, Brecon, Wales; *s.* of Thomas Rees and Charlotte Elizabeth Davies; *m.* 1st Frances Boston 1929 (deceased), 2nd Barbara Henne 1964; two *s.;* ed. Jesus Coll., Oxford and Mansfield Coll., Oxford.
Pastorates 29-34; Dir. South Wales Council of Social Service 34-44; Chair. Welsh Cttee. for Care of Refugees 38; Senior Welfare Specialist, Balkan Div., UNRRA 44, later Dir. Displaced Persons Div., UNRRA Mission to Czechoslovakia; Dir. Refugee Div., World Council of Churches 47-, Rep. in Europe of Comm. of Churches on Int. Affairs, Geneva 48-72; Consultant 72-; Refugee Adviser, World Council of Churches; Chair. Int. Cttee. for World Refugee Year 60-63; Dale Lecturer Mansfield Coll., Oxford 74; Visiting Fellow, UN Inst. of Training and Research 75-76; Awarded Nansen Ring 64.
Publs. *The Problem of Leisure* 37, *The Refugee and the United Nations* 55, *The Century of the Homeless Man* 57, *We Strangers and Afraid* 60.
8 rue de l'Hotel de Ville, 1204 Geneva, Switzerland.
Telephone: Geneva 28-80-60.

Rees, Rt. Hon. Merlyn, P.C., M.SC.(ECON.); British lecturer and politician; b. 18 Dec. 1920, Cilfynydd; *s.* of late L. D. Rees and of E. M. Rees; *m.* Colleen Faith Cleveley 1949; three *s.;* ed. Harrow Weald Grammar School, Goldsmith's Coll., London and London School of Econs.
Served R.A.F. 41-46, attained rank of Squadron Leader; Teacher, Harrow Weald Grammar School 49-60; Labour Party Head Office 60-62; Lecturer Luton Coll. of Technology 62-63; mem. Parl. for Leeds South 63-; Parl. Private Sec. to Chancellor of Exchequer 64-65; Under-Sec. Ministry of Defence 65-68, Home

Office 68-70; Opposition Spokesman for N. Ireland 70-74; Sec. of State for N. Ireland March 74-.
Leisure interest: reading.
Publ. *The Public Sector in the Mixed Economy* 73.
House of Commons, London, S.W.I, England.

Rees, Mina, PH.D.; American mathematician and university administrator; b. 2 Aug. 1902, U.S.A.; d. of Moses Rees and Alice L. Stackhouse; m. Dr. Leopold Brahdy 1955; no c.; ed. Hunter Coll., Columbia Univ. and Univ. of Chicago.
Instructor, eventually Prof. of Mathematics and Dean of Faculty, Hunter Coll. 26-43, 53-61; Technical Aide and Exec. Asst. to Chief of Applied Maths. Panel, Office of Scientific Research and Devt. 43-46; Head, Mathematical Branch, subsequently Dir., Mathematical Sciences Div., Office of Naval Research 46-53; Prof. City Univ. of New York 61-72, Prof. Emer. 72-; Dean of Graduate Studies 61-68, Provost 68-69, Pres. Graduate School 69-72, Pres. Emer. 72-; mem. Nat. Science Board 64-70; Chair. Council of Graduate Schools in U.S. 70; Pres. American Asscn. for Advancement of Science 71; numerous awards including Achievement Award, American Asscn. of Univ. Women 65, President's Medal, Hunter Coll. 70, and Elizabeth Blackwell Gold Medal 71, Chicago Univ. Alumni Medal, Chancellor's Medal City Univ. of New York 72; seventeen hon. degrees.
Leisure interest: painting.
Publs. articles in journals.
Graduate School and University Center, City University of New York, 33 West 42nd Street, New York, N.Y. 10036; Home: 301 East 66th Street, New York, N.Y. 10021, U.S.A.
Telephone: 212-790-4467 (Office); 212-879-9467 (Home).

Rees-Mogg, William; British journalist; b. 14 July 1928, Bristol; s. of Edmund Fletcher Rees-Mogg and Beatrice (née Warren); m. Gillian Shakespeare Morris 1962; two s. two d.; ed. Charterhouse and Balliol Coll., Oxford.
President Oxford Union 51; *Financial Times* 52-60, Chief Leader Writer 55-60, Asst. Editor 57-60; City Editor *Sunday Times* 60-61, Political and Econ. Editor 61-63, Deputy Editor 64-67; Editor of *The Times* 67-; Dir. The Times Ltd. 68-, mem. Exec. Board Times Newspapers Ltd. 68-.
Leisure interest: book collecting.
Publ. *The Reigning Error* 74.
Office: The Times, P.O. Box 7, New Printing House Square, Gray's Inn Road, London, WCIX 8EZ; Homes: 3 Smith Square, London, S.W.I; and Ston Easton Park, nr. Bath, Somerset, England.

Reeves, Rt. Rev. (Richard) Ambrose, M.A.; British ecclesiastic; b. 6 Dec. 1899, Norwich; s. of Mr. and Mrs. Richard Reeves; m. A. Margaret van Ryssen; two s. (one deceased) two d.; ed. Sidney Sussex Coll., Cambridge, Coll. of the Resurrection, Mirfield, and General Theological Seminary, New York.
Secretary Theological Coll. Dept. of Student Christian Movement, Curate of St. Alban's, Golders Green, London 26-31; Rector, St. Margaret's Church, Leven, Fife 31-45; Sec. World's Student Christian Fed., Geneva 35-37; Vicar St. James's Church, Haydock 37-42; Rector of Liverpool 42-49; Bishop of Johannesburg 49-61; deported from South Africa Sept. 12th, 60; Sec. Student Christian Movement 62-65; Asst. Bishop of London 62-66; St. Michael's Church, Lewes 66-72, and Asst. Bishop of Chichester 66-; Prelate Order of St. John of Jerusalem 53; S.T.D. (General Theological Seminary, New York); Fellow, Ancient Monuments Soc.; Hon. Fellow, Sidney Sussex Coll., Cambridge 60.
Leisure interests: gardening, travel and family.
Publs. *Shooting at Sharpeville: the Agony of South Africa*

60, *South Africa—Yesterday and Tomorrow* 62, *Let the Facts Speak* 62, *Calvary Now* 65.
29 Church Street, Shoreham-by-Sea, Sussex, England.
Telephone: Shoreham 62555.

Refshauge, Major-Gen. Sir William Dudley, Kt., C.B.E., E.D., M.B., B.S., F.R.C.O.G., F.R.A.C.S., F.R.A.C.P., F.A.C.M.A.; Australian health official; b. 3 April 1913, Melbourne; s. of Francis C. Refshauge and Margaret I. Brown; m. Helen E. Allwright 1942; four s. one d.; ed. Hampton High School and Scotch Coll., Melbourne and Melbourne Univ.
Resident Medical Officer, Alfred Hosp., Melbourne 39, Women's Hosp. Melbourne 46; Registrar, Women's Hosp. 46-47, Medical Supt. 48-51; Deputy Dir.-Gen. Army Medical Services 51-55, Dir.-Gen. 55-60; Commonwealth of Australia Dir.-Gen. of Health 60-73; Chair. Nat. Health and Medical Research Council 60-, Commonwealth Council for Nat. Fitness 60-, Commonwealth Health Insurance Council 60-, etc.; mem. Exec. Board, WHO 67-70, Chair. 69-70; Pres. World Health Assembly 71; Sec.-Gen. World Medical Asscn. 73-; Patron Australian Sports Medicine Asscn.
Leisure interests: bowls, gardening.
Publs. various publications in *Medical Journal of Australia* and *New Zealand Medical Journal*.
World Medical Association, Ferney-Voltain 01210, France; Home: 6 Scarborough Street, Red Hill, A.C.T. 2603, Australia.
Telephone: 81-8400 (Office); 95-7575 (Home).

Regan, Donald Thomas; American investment executive; b. 21 Dec. 1918, Cambridge, Mass.; s. of William F. Regan and Kathleen (née Ahern) Regan; m. Ann Gordon Buchanan 1942; two s. two d.; ed. Harvard Coll.
Joined Merrill Lynch 46, partner 53; Vice-Pres. Merrill Lynch, Pierce, Fenner & Smith Inc. 59, Exec. Vice-Pres. 64, Chair. of Board and Chief Exec. Officer Jan. 71-; Chair. of Board and Chief Exec. Officer Merrill Lynch and Co. Inc. 73-; Dir. Securities Investor Protection Corpn. 71-73, Beekman Downtown Hospital 69-73; Trustee, Charles E. Merrill Trust and Univ. of Pennsylvania; Hon. LL.D. Hahnemann Medical Coll. and Hospital and Tri-State Coll.
One Liberty Plaza, 165 Broadway, New York, N.Y. 10006; Home: Van Beuren Road, New Vernon, N.J. 07976, U.S.A.
Telephone: 212-766-1212.

Regan, Hon. Gerald Augustine, Q.C.; Canadian politician; b. 13 Feb. 1928, Windsor, Nova Scotia; s. of Walter E. Regan and Rose M. Greene; m. A. Carole Harrison 1956; three s. two d.; ed. St. Mary's Univ. and Dalhousie Univ.
Formerly practising lawyer; mem. Parl. for Halifax 63; Leader Liberal Party of Nova Scotia 65-; mem. Nova Scotia Legislature 67-; Premier of Nova Scotia 70-.
Leisure interests: tennis, skiing.
Province House, Halifax, Nova Scotia, Canada.
Telephone: 424-4119.

Regan, Leonard, F.B.I.M.; British business executive; b. 1 June 1917, Colne, Lancs.; s. of Harry Regan and Sarah Riley; three d.; ed. Nelson Grammar School, Nelson Tech. Coll., Manchester School of Art.
Director, Samuel Holden Ltd. 58-60, Hindley Bros. (Holdings) Ltd. 60-64, Carrington & Dewhurst Group Ltd. 68-72; Dir. Carrington Viyella Ltd. 72-74, Deputy Chair. 74-75, Chair. 75-; Chair. Gelvenor Textiles 75-; Dir. Carrington Tesit (Italy) 75-.
Leisure interests: golf, skiing, fishing, painting.
1 Sandy Hall Lane, Barrowford, Nelson, Lancs.; Flat 25, 7 Prince's Gate, London, S.W.7, England.
Telephone: Nelson 65449.

Reggiani, Serge; Italian-born French actor; b. 2 May 1922; ed. Conservatoire Nat. d'Art Dramatique.
Notable theatrical roles in *Britannicus, Les Parents Terribles, Un Homme comme les Autres, Les Trois Mousquetaires, Les Séquestrés d'Altona,* etc.; films include: *Le Carrefour des Enfants Perdus, Les Portes de la Nuit, Manon, Les Amants de Vérone, La Ronde, Casque d'Or, Napoléon, Les Salauds vont en Enfer, Les Misérables, Marie Octobre, La Grande Pagaille, La Guerre Continue, Tutti a casa, Le Doulos, Le Guépard, Marie-Chantal contre le Docteur Kah, Les Aventuriers, La 25e heure, La mafia fait la loi, L'Armée des ombres, Comptes à rebours, Touche pas la femme blanche* 74.
c/o Artmedia, 37 rue Marbeuf, Paris 8e, France.

Regnier, Charles; German actor and theatrical director; b. 1915; ed. school of dramatic art.
Acted in Vienna, Zürich, Hamburg, Cologne, Munich, Düsseldorf, Bochum and Wuppertal; appeared in many films; trans. works of Giraudoux, Cocteau, Maugham, Feydeau, Labiche, Mauriac, Colette, Barillet-Gredy, Dorin; German Critics' Prize 55.
8194 Ambach/Starnbergersee, Federal Republic of Germany.
Telephone: 08177-532; and 08151-4466.

Rehberg, Poul Kristian Brandt, M.S.C., D.PHIL.; Danish zoologist; b. 29 March 1895, Middelfart; s. of Adolf Boëtius and Marie Jakobe Rehberg (née Brandt); m. Ally Margrethe Madsen 1955; one d.
Asst. University Zoophysiological Lab., Univ. of Copenhagen 21; Reader 36; Prof. of Zoophysiology, Univ. of Copenhagen 45-65; mem. Videnskabernes Selskab 44; Defence Research Cttee. 52-60; Chair. of Danish Cttee. Int. Union of Biological Sciences 47-64; mem. Danish State Research Foundation 52-61, Chair. Nat. Science section 59-61; Chief Adviser, Civil Defence Research 50-60; mem. Board and Exec. *Politiken;* Exec. mem. Danish Atomic Energy Comm. 56, Chair. 62-70; Vice-Pres. World Asscn. of World Federalists 56, Acad. of Technical Science, Copenhagen 57; mem. NATO Science Cttee. 57-60, Danish Science Advisory Council 66-69; Board of Carlsberg Foundation 60-71, Chair. 69-72; mem. Board and Vice-Chair. United Breweries Carlsberg/Tüborg 70-71; Chair. Research Fund for Congenital Diseases 64-73; Hon. M.D. (Lund) 50, Hon. M.V.D. (Copenhagen) 58.
Publs. *Studies on Kidney Function* 26; various textbooks on physiology.
Grünersvei 19B, 2840 Holte, Denmark.
Telephone: 01-42-33-19.

Rehnquist, William H., LL.B., M.A.; American judge; b. 1 Oct. 1924, Milwaukee, Wis.; m.; ed. Stanford and Harvard Univs.
Law clerk to U.S. Supreme Court Justice R. H. Jackson 52-53; private practice, Evans, Kitchel and Jenckes, Phoenix, Ariz. 53-57, Cunningham, Messenger, Carson & Elliot 57-60, Powers & Rehnquist 60-69; Asst. Attorney-Gen., Office of Legal Counsel, Dept. of Justice 69-71; Assoc. Justice, Supreme Court of U.S.A. Dec. 71-; mem. American Bar Asscn., American Judicature Soc., etc.
Supreme Court of the United States, Washington, D.C. 20543, U.S.A.

Reich, John Theodore, PH.D.; Austrian-born American theatrical director; b. 30 Sept. 1906, Vienna; s. of Leopold Reich and Martha (Baxter) Reich; m. 1st Karoline Friederike von Kürzweil 1932 (deceased), 2nd Karen Ruth Lasker 1957; ed. Realgymnasium I, and Max Reinhardt School, Vienna, Vienna and Cornell Univs.
Dramaturgist and Asst. Producer, Burgtheater, Vienna 31-32; Dramaturgist and Producer, Max Reinhardt Theatres, Vienna 32-38; Asst. Producer, later Producer, Salzburg Festivals 34-37; Asst., later Assoc. Prof. of Drama, Ithaca Coll., N.Y. 38-45; Drama Dir.

C.B.S. Television, New York 45-46; Assoc. Prof. of Theatre, Smith Coll., Barnard Coll. 47-51; Asst., later Assoc. Prof. of Theatre, Columbia Univ., Supervisor of Production Training, New York TV Workshop and also independent producer 51-57; Head, Goodman Theatre and School of Drama, Chicago Art Inst. 57-73; Dir. Ford Foundation's Theatre Communications Group 65-72; Producing Dir. Goodman Theatre Resident Co. 69-73; Principal Guest Dir. Calif. Actors' Theatre 75-; freelance Dir. Dallas Theatre Center, Miami Ring Theatre, Penn State Theatre, etc.; Ford Foundation Award 59; Chevalier, Ordre des Arts et Lettres 64; Grand Badge of Honour, Austria 71; Dr. h.c. (Lake Forest Coll., Illinois) 72.
Leisure interests: music, hiking.
Publs. *Mary Stuart* (adaptation of Schiller's play, with Jean Goldstone) 58; numerous other adaptations and articles.
724 Bohemia Parkway, Sayville, N.Y. 11782, U.S.A.
Telephone: 516-589-5997.

Reichelderfer, Donald E.; American business executive; b. 1909, Cridersville, Ohio; m. Gladys V. Kennard; one s. one d.; ed. Ohio State Univ.
Joined Armco Steel Corpn. 29, Controller 51, Vice-Pres. 57, Exec. Vice-Pres. 63, Dir. 64-, Pres. and Chief Operating Officer Dec. 71-74; Dir. Barnitz Bank of Middletown, Central Bancorporation Inc., Central Trust Co. of Cincinnati, Monarch Machine Tool Company, Philips Industries Inc., Oglebay-Norton Co.
Armco Steel Corporation, 703 Curtis Street, Middletown, Ohio 45042; Home: 3101 Flemming Road, Middletown, Ohio 45042, U.S.A.

Reichelderfer, Francis W., A.B.; American meteorologist; b. 6 Aug. 1895, Harlan, Ind.; s. of F. A. and Mae (Carrington) Reichelderfer; m. Beatrice Hoyle; one s.; ed. Northwestern Univ., Evanston, Ill., Harvard Univ., Geophysical Inst., Bergen, Norway and Graduate School, U.S. Govt. Bureau of Standards.
Appointed Naval meteorological officer 18; Dir. Naval Meteorological Organization 22-28; qualified Airplane Pilot 19 and Airship Pilot 31; Meteorologist, First Transatlantic Flight; Int. Aviation Races, and other special assignments, and organization new services; promoted Commdr. U.S.N. 38; Chief, United States Weather Bureau 38-63; Hon. D.Sc. Northwestern Univ.; mem. American Asscn. Advancement of Science, American Geophysical Union (Vice-Pres. 49-53), Nat. Advisory Cttee. for Aeronautics (Vice-Chair. 45-55), Int. Union Geodesy and Geophysics, Nat. Acad. of Sciences, American Meteorological Society (Pres. 40-41), Inst. of Aeronautical Sciences (mem. and Hon. Fellow, Robert M. Losey award 42, Pres. Washington Section 45-46); Cleveland Abbe award 63; mem. Exec. Cttee. Int. Meteorological Org. 39-51 (Vice-Pres. 46-51); Pres. World Meteorological Org. 51-55; mem. U.S. Exec. Cttee. Int. Geophysical Year 53-59, Exec. Cttee. 54-59; Consultant, World Meteorological Org. 64-67, Nat. Oceanic and Atmospheric Admin. 63-75; Awards for role in meteorological co-operation among nations, Chile 43, Cuba 45, Japan 60, WMO Prize 66, American Meteorological Soc. special award 73; Hon. Fellow, American Asscn. for Advancement of Science, American Meteorological Soc., Royal Meteorological Soc., London; Hon. mem. American Soc. of Airways Pioneers.
Leisure interests: gardening, hiking.
3031 Sedgwick Street, N.W., (E-201), Washington, D.C. 20008, U.S.A.

Reichstein, Tadeus, DR. ING. CHEM.; Swiss chemist; b. 20 July 1897, Wloclaweck, Poland; s. of Isidor Reichstein and Gustava Brockman; m. Louise Henriette Quarls v. Ufford 1927; one d.; ed. Eidgenössische Technische Hochschule, Zürich.
Assistant Eidgenössische Technische Hochschule Zürich 22-30, Prof. of Organic Chemistry 30-38; Prof. of

Pharmacy Univ. of Basle 38-46, Prof. of Organic Chemistry 46-67, Prof. Emer. 67-; awarded Nobel Prize for Medicine and Physiology 50, Copley Medal, Royal Soc. (U.K.) 68; Dr. h.c. (Sorbonne, Geneva, Zürich, Abidjan, Basle, London and Leeds).
Leisure interests: horticulture, botany.
Institut für Organische Chemie, St. Johanns-Ring 19. CH-4056, Basle; and Weissensteinstrasse 22, CH-4059. Basle, Switzerland.
Telephone: 061-449090.

Reid, Escott Meredith, c.c.; Canadian diplomatist (retd.); b. 21 Jan. 1905 Campbellford, Ontario; s. of Rev. A. J. Reid and Morna Meredith Reid; m. Ruth Herriot; two s. one d.; ed. Toronto and Oxford Univs. Rockefeller Foundation Fellow 30-32; Nat. Sec. of Canadian Inst. of Int. Affairs 32-38; Acting Prof. of Govt. and Political Science, Dalhousie Univ., Halifax 37-38; apptd. to Dept. of External Affairs 39; served Ottawa, Washington, London; Asst. Under-Sec. of State for External Affairs 47-48; Deputy Under-Sec. 48-52; Acting Under-Sec. 48-49; High Commr. in India 52-57; Ambassador to German Fed. Repub. 58-62; Dir. S. Asia and Middle East Dept. of Int. Bank for Reconstruction and Development 62-65; Principal, Glendon Coll. and Prof. of Political Science, York Univ., Toronto 65-69; Consultant, Canadian Int. Devt. Agency, Ottawa 70-72; Skelton-Clark Fellow, Queen's Univ., Kingston 72-73; Rhodes Scholar 27-30; mem. Canadian Del. Int. Civil Aviation Conf. Chicago 44, San Francisco 45; Exec. Cttee. and Prep. Comm. of UN, London 45; First, Second and Twelfth Sessions UN Gen. Assembly; Chair. Assembly Cttee. on Procedure and Organization 47.
Publs. *The Future of the World Bank* 65, *Strengthening the World Bank* 73.
R.R.2, Ste. Cécile de Masham, Quebec JOX 2WO, Canada.
Telephone: 819-456-2805.

Reid, Sir Norman Robert, Kt., D.LITT., D.A., F.M.A., F.I.I.C.; British art gallery director; b. 27 Dec. 1915, London; s. of Edward Reid and Blanche Drouet; m. Jean Lindsay Bertram 1941; one s. one d.; ed. Wilson's Grammar School, London, Edinburgh Coll. of Art, and Edinburgh Univ.
Army Service 39-46; Tate Gallery 46-, Deputy Keeper 48-54, Deputy Dir. 54-59, Keeper 59-64, Dir. 64-; Fellow, Int. Inst. for Conservation of Historic and Artistic Works, Sec.-Gen. 63-65, Vice-Chair. 66-; Chair. British Council Fine Art Cttee. 68-; Officer, Order of Aztec Eagle (Mexico); mem. many cttees.
Leisure interests: painting, gardening.
The Tate Gallery, Millbank, London, S.W.1; Home: 50 Brabourne Rise, Park Langley, Beckenham, Kent, England.
Telephone: 01-828-1212 (Office); 01-650-7088 (Home).

Reid, Ogden Rogers, A.B.; American journalist and diplomatist; b. 24 June 1925; s. of late Helen Rogers Reid; ed. Yale Univ.
Reporter *New York Herald Tribune* 50-51, various depts. 52-53; Pres. and Editor New York Herald Tribune S.A., Paris 53-59, Dir. 53-; Vice-Pres. New York Herald Tribune Inc. 54-55; Pres. and Editor New York Herald Tribune Inc. 55-58, Dir. 50; Amb. to Israel 59-61; Chair. New York State Comm. Against Discrimination 61-62; Dir. Panama Canal Co. 56-59, Mass. Mutual Life Insurance Co. 57-60; Congressman for Westchester County, N.Y. 62-74; Nacional do Cruzeiro do Sul, Brazil 56; Chevalier of the Legion of Honour 57; Hon. LL.D., Adelphi Coll. (N.Y.); Hon. Fellow, Bar-Ilan Univ., Israel 59; Republican.
Publ. *How Strong is America? The Score on National Defense* (with Robert S. Bird) 50.
Ophir Hill, Purchase, N.Y. 10577; Home: 2901

Garfield Terrace, N.W., Washington, D.C. 20008, U.S.A.
Telephone: 202-225-6506 (Office); 202-265-8257 (Home).

Reid, Patrick M., B.A.; Canadian international banking official; b. 25 June 1931, Winnipeg, Man.; m.; three c.; ed. Upper Canada Coll., Toronto, Trinity Coll.. Univ. of Toronto, St. John's Coll., Cambridge, England and in India.
In Tariff Section, Dept. of Finance, Ottawa 56-58, Int. Programmes Div. 58-65; Alt. Exec. Dir. Int. Monetary Fund (IMF), Int. Bank for Reconstruction and Devt. (IBRD)—World Bank and Affiliates July 65, Exec. Dir. for Canada, Guyana, Ireland and Jamaica, IBRD and Affiliates 68-71; Del. to Sessions of UN Gen. Assembly and UN Confs. and Cttees.
Ministry of Finance, Ottawa, Ont., Canada.

Reid Cabral, Dr. Donald J.; Dominican politician, lawyer and businessman; b. 9 June 1923, Santiago; s. of William C. Reid and Auristela Cabral de Reid; m. Clara A. Tejera 1949; two d.; ed. Universidad de Santo Domingo.
President, Reid & Pellerano C.A. 49-; Pres. Automobile Dealers' Asscn. 49-62; Vice-Pres. Council of State 62-63; Minister of Foreign Affairs Sept.-Dec. 63; Amb. to UN 63; Amb. to Israel 63; Pres. Triumvirate which ruled Dominican Repub. 63-65; Minister of Foreign Affairs 64; Minister of Armed Forces 64-65.
Leisure interests: gardening, sailing, scuba-diving.
Calle Cervantes 8, Santo Domingo, Dominican Republic.
Telephone: 565-4481/4; 5-5677/8; 689-3389.

Reilly, Sir (D'Arcy) Patrick, G.C.M.G., O.B.E., M.A.; British diplomatist; b. 17 March 1909, Ootacamund, India; s. of Sir D'Arcy Reilly and Florence (née Wilkinson); m. Rachel Mary Sykes 1938; two d.; ed. Winchester Coll., and New Coll., Oxford.
Fellow, All Souls Coll., Oxford 32-39, 69-, Hon. Fellow, New Coll., Oxford 72; entered Diplomatic Service 33; served Teheran 35-38, Foreign Office 38, Algiers 43, Paris 44, Athens 45; Counsellor, Athens 47; Imperial Defence Coll. 49; Asst. Under-Sec. of State, Foreign Office 50-53; Minister in Paris 53-56; Deputy Under-Sec., Foreign Office 56; Amb. to U.S.S.R. 57-60; Deputy Under-Sec. Foreign Office 60-64; Official Head U.K. Del. to UN Conf. on Trade and Devt.; Amb. to France 65-68; Pres. London Chamber of Commerce 72-75; Chair. Banque Nat. de Paris Ltd. 69-, United Bank for Africa 69-74, Univ. of London Management Cttee., British Inst. in Paris 70-; Council, Bedford Coll., Univ. of London 70-75.
Leisure interests: travel, architecture, gardening.
Hampden Cottage, Ramsden, Oxford; 5 Penywern Road, London, S.W.5, England.
Telephone: Ramsden 348; 01-373-8838.

Reinert, Heinrich, DR.RER.OEC.; German business executive; b. 29 May 1920, Leipzig; m. 1952; one d.
Formerly with Bayer AG and subsequently mem. Man. Board FINA Raffinerie AG and FINA Bitumenwerk; mem. Man. Board VEBA-Chemie AG 67-; mem. Man. Board VEBA AG 74-, Chair. 73; Chair. Supervisory Board Aral AG 73-.
Leisure interest: hunting.
437 Marl, Langehegge 307, Federal Republic of Germany.
Telephone: (0209) 3663902.

Reines, Frederick, M.E., M.S., PH.D.; American physicist; b. 16 March 1918, Paterson, N.J.; s. of Israel Reines and Gussie Cohen; m. Sylvia Samuels 1940; one s. one d.; ed. Stevens Inst. of Technology and New York Univ.
Staff mem. and Group Leader, Theoretical Div., Los Alamos Scientific Laboratory 44-59; Prof. and Head, Dept. of Physics, Case Int. of Technology 59-66; Dean of Physical Sciences Univ. of Calif., Irvine 66-74, Prof.

of Physics Univ. of Calif., Irvine 66-; Fellow, American Asscn. for Advancement of Science, American Physical Soc., American Acad. of Arts and Sciences; Guggenheim Fellow 58-59; Sloan Fellow 59-63; Stevens Honor Award 71; Hon. D.Sc. (Witwatersrand).

Publs. Papers on detection of free neutrino 53-57, observation of high energy neutrinos in the cosmic radiation 65, effects of nuclear explosions 50, whole body counting of natural radioactivity in humans 53, liquid scintillation counters 52-66, stability of baryons 54-74.

2655 Basswood Street, Newport Beach, Calif. 92660, U.S.A.

Reinhardt, John Edward, M.S., PH.D.; American teacher and diplomatist; b. 8 March 1920, Glade Spring, Va.; s. of Edward Vinton Reinhardt and Alice Miller; m. Carolyn L. Daves 1947; three d.; ed. Knoxville Coll., Univs. of Chicago and Wisconsin.

Instructor in English, Knoxville Coll. 40-41, Fayetteville State Coll. 41-42; U.S. Army 42-46; graduate student 46-50; Prof. of English, Virginia State Coll. 50-56; Visiting Prof. of English, Atlanta Univ. 53; Asst. Cultural Officer, American Embassy, Philippines 56-58; Dir. American Cultural Center, Kyoto, Japan 58-62; Dir. of Field Programs, American Embassy, Tokyo 62-63; Cultural Attaché, Teheran 63-66; Deputy Asst. Dir. of U.S. Information Agency for Far East 66-68, for Africa 68-70, for Far East 70-71; Amb. to Nigeria 71-75.

Leisure interests: gardening, photography.

c/o Department of State, 2201C Street, N.W., Washington.

Reinhardt, Max; British publisher; b. 30 Nov. 1915, Istanbul; s. of Ernest Reinhardt and Frieda Reinhardt (née Darr); m. Joan MacDonald 1957; two d.; ed. Ecole des Hautes Etudes Commerciales, Paris, London School of Economics.

Chairman, Max Reinhardt Ltd. and HFL (Publishers) Ltd. 48-; Man. Dir. Bodley Head Group of Publishers 57-; Joint Chair. Chatto, Bodley Head and Jonathan Cape Ltd. 73-; mem. Council, Publishers' Asscn. 63-69, Royal Acad. of Dramatic Art 65-.

Leisure interests: tennis, swimming, bridge.

16 Pelham Crescent, London, SW7 2NR, England.
Telephone: 01-589-5527.

Reis, Maurício Rangel; Brazilian agronomist and statistician; b. 1921, Rio de Janeiro.

Former Sec.-Gen. Ministry of Agriculture; Deputy Head Inst. for Applied Econ. Research, Ministry of Planning and Gen. Co-ordination; well-known for his work in developing the Amazon region; Minister of the Interior April 74-.

Ministério do Interior, Brasília, Brazil.

Reischauer, Edwin Oldfather, A.M., PH.D.; American historian and diplomatist; b. 15 Oct. 1910, Tokyo, Japan; s. of August Karl and Helen Oldfather Reischauer; m. 1st Adrienne Danton 1935 (died 1955), 2nd Haru Matsukata 1956; one s. two d.; ed. Oberlin Coll., Harvard Univ., and Univ. of Paris.

Studied in France, Japan, China 33-38; Instructor, Harvard 38-42; Military Intelligence, Second World War; Special Asst. to Dir. Office of Far Eastern Affairs, Dept. of State 45-46; Assoc. Prof. Far Eastern Languages 46-50, Prof. 50-61; Dir. Harvard-Yenching Inst. 56-61; Amb. to Japan 61-66; Prof. Harvard Univ. 66-; Chair. Board Trustees, Harvard-Yenching Inst. 69-; Japan Foundation Prize 75.

Publs. *Selected Japanese Texts for University Students* (3 vols.-compiler, with S. Elisseeff) 42-47, *Japan Past and Present* 46, 63, 64 (new edn.), *Translations from Early Japanese Literature* (with Joseph Yamagiwa) 51, *Wanted: An Asian Policy* 55, *Ennin's Diary: The Record of a Pilgrimage to China in Search of the Law* 55, *Ennin's Travels in T'ang China* 55, *The United States*

and Japan (rev. edn.) 50, 65, *East Asia: The Great Tradition* (with John K. Fairbank) 60, *East Asia: The Modern Transformation* (with Fairbank and Craig) 65, *Beyond Vietnam: The United States and Asia* 67, *Japan: The Story of a Nation* 70, (revised edn.) 74, *East Asia: Tradition and Transformation* (with Fairbank and Craig) 73, *Toward the 21st Century: Education for a Changing World* 73.

1737 Cambridge Street, Cambridge, Mass. 02138, U.S.A.
Telephone: 495-3220.

Reisz, Karel; British film director; b. 21 July 1926, Ostrava, Czechoslovakia; s. of Dr. Josef and Frederika Reisz; m. 1st Julia Coppard (dissolved), 2nd Betsy Blair 1963; three s.; ed. Leighton Park School, Reading, and Cambridge Univ.

Came to England 39; served with Czechoslovak section of R.A.F. 44-46; free-lanced as journalist, lecturer and teacher; published *The Technique of Film Editing* 53; Films Officer, Ford Motor Co.; now film director and producer.

Leisure interest: gardening.

Films: *Momma Don't Allow* (Co-director with Tony Richardson) 54, *Every Day Except Christmas* (producer) 58, *We Are the Lambeth Boys* 58 (Both for Fords), *Saturday Night and Sunday Morning* 59, *This Sporting Life* (producer) 63, *Night Must Fall* 63, *Morgan—A Suitable Case for Treatment* 65, *Isadora* 69, *The Gambler* 74.

c/o Film Contracts, 1 Soho Square, London, W.1, England.

Rekola, Esko Johannes; Finnish lawyer and civil servant; b. 10 June 1919, Tampere; s. of Prof. Aarne Rekola and Laina Kouvo; m. 1st Raili Kilpeläinen 1945 (died 1973), three s.; m. 2nd Anna Liisa Sundquist 1974; ed. Helsinki Univ.

Chief of Taxation Dept., Ministry of Finance 57-59, Chief of Budget Dept. 59-63, 64-65; Alt. Gov. Int. Bank for Reconstruction and Devt. 62-66; Minister of Finance 63-64; Chief of the Prime Minister's Office 65-66; Gen. Man. Finnish State Railways 66-73; Sec.-Gen. Ministry of Communications 73-.

H Matinlahdenkatu 3A3, SF-02230 Espoo 23, Finland.
Telephone: 882892.

Relly, Gavin Walter Hamilton, M.A.; South African business executive; b. 6 Feb. 1926, Stellenbosch; m. Jane Margaret Glenton 1951; one s. two d.; ed. Diocesan Coll., Rondebosch and Trinity Coll., Oxford.

Joined Anglo American Corpn., Johannesburg 49, Chair. Anglo American Corpn. (Cen. Africa) 65-69; mem. Board Anglo American Corpn. of S.A. Ltd. 65, Exec. Dir. 66; Chair. Anglo American Corpn. of Canada 70-73; mem. Board Hudson Bay Mining & Smelting Co. Ltd. 70, Chair. 70-73; mem. Board Rand Selection 71, Chair. 73-; Chair. Anglo American Industrial Corpn. 73; mem. Board, Exec. Cttee. Engelhard Minerals & Chemicals Corpn. 70, mem. Board Charter Consolidated Ltd. 71.

Anglo American Corpn. of South Africa Ltd., 44 Main Street, Johannesburg, South Africa.

Remez, Brig.-Gen. Aharon; Israeli air force officer and diplomatist; b. 8 May 1919, Tel-Aviv; s. of David Remez; m. Rita Levy; one s. three d.; ed. Harvard Business School, Woodrow Wilson School, Princeton.

Agricultural training in kibbutz, Givat Haim 37-39; Emissary to Zionist Youth Movement, U.S.A. 39-41; Royal Air Force 42-47; mem. kibbutz Kfar Blum 47-; Dir. of Planning and Operations, later Chief of Staff, Israel Air Force 48; Commdr.-in-Chief Israel Air Force 48-51; Head, Ministry of Defence Purchasing Mission, U.S.A. 52-53; Aviation Adviser to Minister of Defence 53-54; Man. Dir. Solel-Boneh Koor Industries and Crafts Co. Ltd. 54-59; mem. Knesset 55-57; Admin. Dir. Weizmann Inst. of Science, Rehovot 59-60; Dir. Int. Co-operation Div., Ministry for Foreign Affairs 60-64, Adviser on Int. Co-operation to Minister for

Foreign Affairs 64-65; Amb. to U.K. 65-70; Dir.-Gen. Israel Ports Authority 70-.

Publs. articles on aviation, management and political topics.

Israel Ports Authority, Maya Building, 74 Petah-Tiqva Road, Tel-Aviv; Home: 8 San Martin Street, Jerusalem, Israel.

Remick, Lee; American actress; b. 14 Dec. 1935, Boston, Mass.; d. of Frank Remick and F. W. Packard; m. 1st William Colleran 1957 (divorced 1969), one s. one d.; m. 2nd William R. Gowans 1970; ed. Hewitt School, New York.

Stage appearances in *Anyone Can Whistle* (musical), N.Y. 64, *Wait Until Dark*, N.Y. 66; has acted in films, *Face in the Crowd* 56, *The Long Hot Summer* 57, *These Thousand Hills* 58, *Anatomy of a Murder* 59, *Wild River* 59, *Sanctuary* 60, *Experiment in Terror* (*Grip of Fear*, U.K.) 60, *Days of Wine and Roses* 61, *The Running Man* 62, *The Wheeler Dealers* 63, *The Travelling Lady* 63, *The Hallelujah Trail* 64, *No Way to Treat a Lady* 67, *The Detective* 67, *Hard Contract* 68, *A Severed Head* 69, *Loot* 69, *Sometimes a Great Notion* 70, *A Delicate Balance* 72, *Hennessy* 75, television appearances in *QB-VII*, *The Blue Knight*, *Jennie* 74; Golden Globe Award for *The Blue Knight*, Best TV Actress Award for *Jennie*, Soc. of Film and TV Arts 74.

c/o International Famous Agency, 11-12 Hanover Street, London, W.1, England.

Telephone: 01-629-8080.

Remy, Pierre-Jean (*pseudonym* of Jean-Pierre Angremy); French diplomatist and author; b. 21 March 1937, Angoulême; s. of Pierre Angremy and Alice Collebrans; m. Odile Cail 1963; one s. one d.; ed. Lycée Condorcet, Inst. d'Etudes Politiques, Paris, Brandeis Univ. (U.S.A.) and Ecole Nationale d'Administration, Paris.

Served in Hong Kong 63; Second Sec., Peking 64, London 66; First Sec. London 68; Counsellor, Ministry of Foreign Affairs 71; Dir. Programme Co-Ordination, O.R.T.F. 72; Prix Renaudot for novel *Le Sac du Palais d'Eté* 71.

Leisure interests: collecting books, music (opera), cinema.

Publs. novels: *Et Gulliver mourut de sommeil* 61, *Miste ou l'attendat* 62, *Le Sac du Palais d'Eté* 71, *Urbanisme* 72, *Une Mort Sale* 73.

30 rue Pierre Nicole, Paris 5e, France.

Telephone: 033-65-41.

Renard, H.E. Cardinal Alexandre, D. ès L.; French ecclesiastic; b. 7 June 1906; ed. Coll. Jeanne d'Arc, Grand Séminaire and Univ. Catholique de Lille.

Ordained Priest 31; Prof., college at Marcq 33-36, seminary at Haubourdin 36-38, Catholic Univ. of Lille 38-43; Chaplain to Women Students, Lille diocese 38; Diocesan Dir. of Works 47; Bishop of Versailles 53-67; Archbishop of Lyons and Primate of France 67-; created Cardinal 67; Officier Légion d'Honneur.

Publs. include *Philosophie et Pédagogie de l'école nouvelle, Possibilité de la philosophie chrétienne, Exigences spirituelles du christianisme, En équipe dans le Christ, Fidélité au Christ et présence au monde, Pour une évangélisation et une catéchèse d'Eglise, Vie Spirituelle de la religieuse aujourd'hui, Situation actuelle de l'Eglise, Prêtres Diocésains aujourd'hui, Vivre la foi en l'Eglise, La Crise et l'Espérance, Seule compte la Foi, Qu' est-ce qu'un Chrétien?, La Vie et la Foi, Liberté et Espérance, Que veut l'Eglise?*

Archevêché, 1 place de Fourvière, 69321 Lyon, Rhône, France.

Telephone: 25-12-27.

Renaud, Madeleine; French actress and author; b. 21 Feb. 1903; m. Jean-Louis Barrault (*q.v.*); ed. Lycée Racine and **Paris Conservatoire.**

Pensionnaire, Comédie Française 21-47; co-Dir. Compagnie Madeleine Renaud—Jean-Louis Barrault 47-; plays in which she has played important roles include *Le Soulier de Satin, Occupe-toi d'Amélie, Les Nuits de Colère, Christophe Colomb, La Dame aux Camélias, Harold et Maude* 73, *Oh les beaux jours* 74, *Pas Moi* 75; films include *Jean de la Lune, La Maternelle, Remorques, Le Ciel est à nous, Le Plaisir, Dialogue des Carmélites, Le Jour le plus long, Le diable par la queue* 68, *L'Humeur vagabonde* 71, *La Mandarine* 72; Chevalier Légion d'Honneur, Commdr. des Arts et des Lettres.

18 avenue du Président-Wilson, Paris 16e, France.

Renault, Mary (*pseudonym* of Mary Challans); British writer; b. 4 Sept. 1905, London; d. of Frank Challans, M.D., and Mary Challans (née Baxter); unmarried; ed. Clifton High School, Bristol, St. Hugh's Coll., Oxford, and Radcliffe Infirmary, Oxford.

Nurse during Second World War; resident in South Africa 48-; Fellow of Royal Soc. of Literature 59, Nat. Pres. PEN Club of South Africa 61, Silver Pen Award 71.

Leisure interests: conversation and dogs.

Publs. *Purposes of Love* 39, *Kind are Her Answers* 40, *The Friendly Young Ladies* 44, *Return to Night* 46, *North Face* 48, *The Charioteer* 53, *The Last of the Wine* 56, *The King Must Die* 58, *The Bull from the Sea* 62, *The Lion in the Gateway* 64, *The Mask of Apollo* 66, *Fire From Heaven* 69, *The Persian Boy* 72, *The Nature of Alexander* 75.

Delos, Glen Beach, Camps Bay, Cape Town 8001, South Africa.

Renchard, William S(hryock), A.B.; American banker; b. 1 Jan. 1908, Trenton, N.J.; s. of John A. and Lillian C. (Smith) Renchard; m. Alice Marie Fleming 1935; three d.; ed. Princeton Univ.

With the Nat. Bank of Commerce, N.Y.C. 28-29, the Guaranty Trust Co., N.Y.C. 29-30; Joined the Chemical Bank 30, Pres. and Dir. 60-66, Chair. and Chief Exec. Officer, the Chemical Bank 66-; official of many business and public bodies.

Leisure interest: golf.

Chemical Bank, 20 Pine Street, New York, N.Y. 10015, U.S.A.

Rendel, Sir George William, K.C.M.G., M.A.; British diplomatist; b. 23 Feb. 1889; s. of George Wightwick Rendel; m. Geraldine FitzGerald 1914 (died 1965); two s. two d.; ed. Downside and Queen's Coll., Oxford.

Entered Diplomatic Service 13; served Berlin, Athens, Rome, Lisbon, Madrid, and in Foreign Office 20-38; Head Eastern Dept. Foreign Office 30-38; Minister to Bulgaria 38-41, to Yugoslav Govt. in London 41-42, Ambassador 42-43; Ambassador to Belgium 48-50; Foreign Office 44-47; Chief U.K. del. for negotiations of Treaty of Brussels Feb.-Mar. 48; U.K. mem. (and Chair.) of the Tripartite Comm. on German Debts 51-53; Chair. Singapore Constitutional Comm. 53-54; U.K. Rep., Saar Referendum Comm. 55; re-employed by Foreign Office on Anglo-Egyptian Financial Agreement 59-64; Vice-Pres. Catholic Union of Great Britain 51-63; Dir. and Chair. Singer & Friedlander Ltd. 53-68; Dir. Int. Aeradio Ltd. 52-60.

Leisure interests: travelling, sketching, music.

Publ. *The Sword and the Olive* 57.

5/24 Lennox Gardens, London, S.W.1, England.

Telephone: 01-584-6645.

René, France Albert; Seychelles barrister and politician; b. 16 Nov. 1935, Seychelles; s. of Price René and Louisa Morgan; m. 1st Karen Handley 1956, one d.; m. 2nd Geva Adam 1975, one s.; ed. St. Maurice, Switzerland, St. Mary's Coll., Southampton, U.K., King's Coll., London.

Called to Bar 57; founder and Leader, Seychelles People's United Party 64-; mem. Parl. 65-; Minister of

Works and Land Devt. June 75-; Prime Minister (desig.) June 76-.
Leisure interests: gardening, fishing.
L'Exil, Mahé, Seychelles.
Telephone: 2383 (Office); 2948 (Home).

Reneker, Robert William, PH.B.; American business executive; b. 4 Aug. 1912, Chicago; ed. Calumet High School, and Univ. of Chicago School of Business.
Purchasing Dept., Swift and Co. 33-34, Office of Vice-Pres. 44, later in office of Pres.; Vice-Pres. Swift and Co. 55-64, Dir. 59-, Pres. 64-73; Pres. and Chief Exec. Officer Esmark Inc. 73, Chair. of Board and Chief Exec. Officer Oct. 73-; Dir. Continental Illinois Corpn., Continental Illinois Nat. Bank and Trust Co. of Chicago, Gen. Dynamics Corpn., Trans Union Corpn., etc.; Trustee, Univ. of Chicago; official of numerous civic orgs.
Esmark Inc., 55 East Monroe Street, Chicago, Ill. 60603; Home: 1300 Lake Shore Drive, Chicago, Ill. 60610, U.S.A.

Renger, Annemarie; German politician; b. 7 Oct. 1919, Leipzig; d. of Fritz Wildung and Martha (née Scholz) Wildung; m. 1st Emil Renger 1938 (killed in 2nd World War), one s.; m. 2nd Aleksandar Loncarevic 1965 (died 1973).
Private secretary to Dr. Kurt Schumacher 45-52; managed SPD offices Berlin May-Dec. 46; mem. Bundestag 53-; SPD Parliamentary Group Man. 69-72; Pres. Bundestag Dec. 72-; mem. SPD Presidium; mem. for ten years of advisory ass. of European Council and Ass. of West European Union; Vice-Pres. Int. Council of Social Democratic Women of the Socialist International.
53 Bonn-Bad Godesberg, Dollendorferstrasse 4, Federal Republic of Germany.

Renn, Ludwig (*pseudonym* of Arnold Vieth von Golssenau); German author; b. 22 April 1889, Dresden.
Army officer until 20; converted to Communism 27; sentenced to 2½ years imprisonment after Reichstag fire 33; emigrated to Switzerland, commanded Thälmann battalion in Spain; emigrated to Mexico; returned to Germany 47; Prof. of Anthropology 47; mem. of German Acad. of Arts; Nationalpreise 55, 61, Kinderbuchpreise 54, 55, 56, 58, 61; Dr. h.c. 49.
Leisure interests: anthropology, history of art, prehistory, war history.
Publs. *Krieg* 28, *Nachkrieg* 30, *Russlandfahrten* 32, *Vor grossen Wandlungen* 36, *Kriegführung und Propaganda* 39, *Adel im Untergang* 44, *Morelia* 50, *Vom alten und neuen Rumänien* 52, *Trini* 54, *Im Spanischen Krieg* 55, *Nobi* 55, *Herniu und der blinde Asni* 56, *Meine Kindheit und Jugend* 57, *Krieg ohne Schlacht* 57, *Herniu und Armin* 58, *Auftraggeber: Arbeiterklasse* 60, *Auf den Trümmern des Kaiserreichs* 61, *Camilo, Inflation* 63, *Zu Fuss zum Orient* 66, *Ausweg* 67; translated into many languages.
Am Kornfeld 78, 1138 Berlin Kaulsdorf, German Democratic Republic.
Telephone: Berlin 5277798.

Rennell, 2nd Baron, cr. 33, of Rodd; **Francis James Rennell Rodd,** K.B.E., C.B., M.A. (Oxon.); British banker; b. 1895; s. of Lord Rennell of Rodd and Lady Georgina Rennell; m. Mary Constance Vivion Smith; four d.; ed. Eton and Balliol Coll., Oxford.
Served First World War, France 14-15, Italy 16, Middle East 17-19; entered Diplomatic Service 19; Rome and Sofia; served Foreign Office 23-24, resgnd.; mem. Stock Exchange 26-28; mem. staff Bank of England 29-32; Man. Bank for Int. Settlements 30-31; partner in Morgan, Grenfell & Co. 31; Ministry Econ. Warfare 39-40; served British Army 40-45; Major-Gen. in charge Military admin. Italian Colonies and Chief Allied Military Govt. in Italy 43; explored Southern Sahara 22, 27; awarded Royal Geographical Society's Founders'

Medal 29; Pres. Royal Geographical Soc. 45-48, Hon. Vice-Pres. and Hon. mem. 48-; Visiting Fellow Nuffield Coll. Oxford 47-59; fmr. Dir. Morgan Grenfell & Co. and other cos. (retd.); Hon. LL.D. (Manchester).
Leisure interests: farming, geography, antiquities.
Publs. *People of the Veil, General William Eaton, British Military Administration in Africa 1940-45, Valley on the March,* and many other publs.
23 Great Winchester Street, London, EC2P 2AX, England; The Rodd, near Presteigne, Radnorshire, Wales.
Telephone: 01-588-4545 (Office); 05-44-362 (Home).

Renner, William Beach; American company executive; b. 29 Sept. 1920, Middletown, Ohio; s. of L. C. Renner and Pearl Beach Renner; m. Elizabeth Anne Kemp 1944; three s.; ed. Wittenberg Univ.
Vice-President Sales, Mill Products, Aluminum Co. of America 73-75, Pres. June 75-.
Leisure interests: golf, tennis, paddle tennis, music, reading.
Aluminum Company of America, 1501 Alcoa Building, Pittsburgh, Pa. 15219; Home: 301 Wildberry Road, Pittsburgh, Pa. 15238, U.S.A.

Rennert, Günther, DR.JUR.; German opera and theatre producer; b. 1 April 1911, Essen; s. of Dr. Alfred Rennert and Adele Nettesheim; m. Elizabeth Abegg 1955; one s. three d.; ed. law, Jura, theatrical science, Munich and Berlin.
Asst. producer films, operas and plays 33-35; producer in Frankfurt 35-37, Wuppertal 37-39, Mainz and Königsberg 39-42; head producer Charlottenburg Opera House 42-45, Munich 45-46; Opera Dir. and Dir. State Opera House, Hamburg 46-56; free-lance producer of opera and plays in Hamburg, Berlin, Stuttgart, Vienna, Frankfurt, Munich and abroad, including the Edinburgh Festival 52 and 55, 56, 58, Salzburg Festival 49-, Dublin, Naples, London, Milan, Paris, Buenos Aires, Metropolitan Opera, New York, Canada, San Francisco; Dir. State Opera House, Munich 67-; Prof. Theaterwissenschaften an der Hochschule für Musik, Munich; mem. Akademie der Künste, Berlin; Art Counsellor and Head of Production, Glyndebourne Festival Opera 59-67; Johannes-Brahms-Médaille 58, Grosses Bundesverdienstkreuz, Ehrenkreuz für Wissenschaft und Kunst, 1st class (Austria) 70, Bayrischer Verdienstorden.
Publs. stage versions of Handel, Gluck, Rossini, Monteverdi and Prokofiev operas; *Opernarbeit* 74.
8033 Krailling, Schwalbenweg 11A, Federal Republic of Germany.
Telephone: 089-871539.

Rennie, Sir John Shaw, G.C.M.G., O.B.E.; British United Nations official; b. 12 Jan. 1917, Glasgow; s. of late John Shaw and S. W. Rennie; m. Mary Winifred Macalpine Robertson 1946; one s.; ed. Hillhead High School, Glasgow Univ., and Balliol Coll., Oxford.
District Officer, Tanganyika 40-51; Dep. Colonial Sec. Mauritius 51-55; British Resident Commr. New Hebrides, Western Pacific 55-62; Gov. and C.-in-C. Mauritius 62-68; Gov.-Gen. and C.-in-C. Mauritius March-Aug. 68; Deputy Commr.-Gen. UN Relief and Works Agency for Palestine Refugees 68-71, Commr.-Gen. 71-; LL.D. (Glasgow) 72.
Leisure interests: reading, music, walking.
UNRWA, Museitbeh Quarter, Beirut, Lebanon.

Renoir, Jean; French film producer and writer; b. 15 Sept. 1894, Paris; s. of the late Pierre Auguste Renoir and Aline Charigot; m. Dido Freire 1944; one s. (by previous marriage); ed. Univ. d'Aix-en-Provence.
Served French Army 14-18; professional playwright 24-; Prof. of Dramatic Art, Univ. of Calif. 60, U.C.L.A. 64; Vice-Pres. Cinémathèque Française; Louis Delluc Prize 37, Venice Biennale 37, 46, 51; Grand Prix de l'Acad. du Cinéma 56; Golden Laurel Trophy 58; Special Oscar of

Acad. of Motion Picture Arts and Sciences, for lifetime achievement 74; mem. American Acad. of Arts and Sciences 64, Akademie der Künste, Berlin; Chevalier Légion d'Honneur, Croix de Guerre, Commandeur de l'Ordre des Arts et des Lettres; Dr. h.c. (Univ. of Calif.); Hon. Dr. Royal Coll. of Art, London 71; has produced, written and directed many films, including *La Fille de l'Eau* 24, *Nana* 26, *Tire-au-Flanc* 29, *La Chienne* 31, *Boudu Sauvé des Eaux* 32, *Madame Bovary* 34, *Le Crime de Monsieur Lange* 35, *La Grande Illusion* 37, *La Bête Humaine* 38, *La Règle du Jeu* 39, *The Southerner* 44, *Diary of a Chambermaid* 45, *The River* 50, *The Golden Coach* 52, *Eléna et les Hommes* 56, *Le Déjeuner sur l'Herbe* 59, *Le Testament de Docteur Cordellier* 59, *Le Caporal Epinglé* 61, *C'est la Révolution* 67, *Le Petit Théâtre de Jean Renoir* 69; stage plays: *Orvet, Carola, Mise en Scène Théâtrale, Jules César.*
Publs. *Orvet* 53, *Renoir, my Father* 62 (Prix Charles Blanc), *The Notebooks of Captain Georges* 66, *My Life and My Films* 74.
1273 Leona Drive, Beverly Hills, Calif., U.S.A.

Reshetnikov, Fyodor Pavlovich; Soviet painter; b. 13 July 1906, Sursko-Litovskoe, Ukraine; ed. Moscow Arts Inst.
Took part in the Sibiryakov, Chelyuskin Arctic Expeditions 32-34; war artist in Sebastopol and Kerch 41-42; Vice Pres. Acad. of Sciences U.S.S.R. 74; People's Artist of the U.S.S.R.; mem. Acad. of Arts of the U.S.S.R. 53; State prizewinner 49, 51; Order of the Red Banner of Labour, Order of the Red Star, etc.
Principal works: *Germans in Kerch (Bagerovo)* 42, *Armoured Train Zheleznyak* 43, *Home for the Holidays* 48, *First Match* 52, *Another Bad Mark* 52, *For Peace*; series of caricatures 61-62.
Academy of Arts of the U.S.S.R., 21 Kropotkinskaya ulitsa, Moscow, U.S.S.R.

Resnais, Alain; French film director; b. 3 June 1922; ed. Institut des Hautes Etudes Cinématographiques, Paris.
Short films directed (48-59) include *Van Gogh* 48, *Guernica* (with Robert Hessens) 50, *Les statues meurent aussi* (with C. Marker) 52, *Nuit et brouillard* 55; Long films include: *Hiroshima mon amour* 59, *L'année dernière à Marienbad* 61, *Muriel* 63, *La Guerre est finie* 66, *Je t'aime, je t'aime* 68, *Stavisky* 74.
70 rue des Plantes, Paris 14e, France.

Resnik, Regina; American mezzo-soprano singer; b. 30 Aug. 1922; m. Arbit Blatas 1975; ed. Hunter Coll., New York.
Concert debut, Brooklyn Acad. of Music 42; appeared as Leonore (*Fidelio*), Mexico City 43; with New York City Opera 44-45; debut at Metropolitan Opera, New York as Leonore (*Il Trovatore*); in subsequent years sang at Chicago Opera Theatre, San Francisco Opera, etc.; Bayreuth debut (as Sieglinde) 53, London debut 57; has sung at Vienna, Berlin, Stuttgart, Buenos Aires; produced *Carmen*, Hamburg State Opera 71, produced and acted in *Falstaff*, Teatr Wielki, Warsaw 75, etc.
c/o Metropolitan Opera Co., New York, N.Y. 10018, U.S.A.

Restivo, Franco; Italian politician; b. 25 May 1911.
Professor, Univ. of Palermo 43-; Pres. Sicilian Regional Parliament 49-55; mem. Chamber of Deputies 58-, Vice-Pres. Chamber of Deputies 63-66; Minister of Agriculture 66-68, of Interior 68-72, of Defence Feb.-June 72; Christian Democrat.
[*Died* 17 *April* 1976.]

Reston, James; Scottish-born American journalist; b. 3 Nov. 1909, Clydebank, Scotland; m. Sarah Jane Fulton 1935; three s.; ed. Dayton, Ohio public schools and Illinois Univ.

First brought to U.S.A. 10, permanently settled 20-; began his career on *Springfield* (Ohio) *Daily News* and as sports publicity dir. for Ohio State Univ.; travelling Sec., Cincinnati Baseball Club; Sports Writer, Associated Press, New York 34-37; Assoc. Press Corresp., London 37-39; *New York Times* London Bureau 39-41, Washington Bureau 41; Dir. Office of War Intelligence Information Service, U.S. Embassy, London 42; Asst. to Publisher, *New York Times* 43, Acting Head, London Bureau 43-45, Nat. Corresp. 45, Diplomatic Corresp. 46, Head of Washington Bureau 53-64, Assoc. Editor 64-68, Exec. Editor 68-69, Vice-Pres. 69-74, Dir. 73-, Columnist 73-; Co-publisher *Vineyard Gazette* 68-; Pulitzer Awards 44 and 57, George Polk Memorial Award 54, Raymond Clapper Award 55, etc.; Chevalier, Légion d'Honneur; Lovejoy Fellow 74; Hon. D.Litt. (Colgate and Rutgers Univs.), Hon. LL.D. (New York).
Publs. *The Artillery of the Press* 67, *Sketches in the Sand* 67.
The New York Times, 1920 L Street, N.W., Washington, D.C. 20036, U.S.A.

Rétoré, Guy; French theatre director; b. 7 April 1924; ed. Univ. of Paris.
Public Relations Dept., S.N.C.F. until 55; Actor and Producer, Théâtre de Boulevard until 55; formed "La Guilde" (theatrical company), Menilmontant, East Paris 55; opened Théâtre de Menilmontant 57; Dir. Maison de la Culture, Menilmontant 62-; Dir. Théâtre de l'Est Parisien (also gives concerts, ballets, films and conferences).
Plays produced include: *La Fille du Roi* (Cosmos) 55, *Life and Death of King John* 56, *Grenadiers de la Reine* (Farquhar, adapted by Cosmos) 57, *L'Avare* (Molière), *Macbeth* (Shakespeare), *Les Caprices de Marianne* (Musset), *La fleur à la bouche* (Pirandello), *Le Médecin malgré lui* (Molière), *Le Manteau* (Gogol, adapted by Cosmos) 63, *La Locandiera* (Goldoni), *Arden of Faversham* 64, *Monsieur Alexandre* (Cosmos) 64, *Macbeth* (Shakespeare) 64, *Turcaret* (Lesage) 65, *Measure for Measure* (Shakespeare) 65, *Le Voyage de Monsieur Perrichon* (Labiche) 65, *Live Like Pigs* (Arden), *The Silver Tassie* (O'Casey) 66-67, *Les 13 Soleils de la Rue St. Blaise* (A. Gatti).
Théâtre de l'Est Parisien, 17 rue Malte Brun, Paris 20e, France.
Telephone: PYR 94-58; and MEN-79-09.

Rettel, Jean, LL.D.; Luxembourg diplomatist; b. 12 Dec. 1925, Luxembourg; ed. Univs. of Fribourg, Switzerland and Grenoble, France.
Practising lawyer, Luxembourg Bar 50-54; joined Ministry of Foreign Affairs 54; Sec. Bonn 56-59; Counsellor and Deputy Chief, Div. of External Trade 64-68; Chief Protocol and Legal Dept. 68-69; Counsellor, Paris 69-71, also Deputy Perm. Rep. to OECD; Perm. Rep. to UN Feb. 72-; del. to meetings of ECOSOC and other int. confs.
Permanent Mission of Luxembourg to United Nations, One Dag Hammarskjöld Plaza, 17th Floor, New York, N.Y. 10017, U.S.A.

Reuter, Paul; French international lawyer; b. 12 Feb. 1911, Metz; s. of Fery Reuter; m. Christine Abram 1943; two s.
Professor, law faculties of Nancy, Poitiers, Aix-en-Provence and Paris; teacher Inst. of Political Studies, Paris 53, Acad. of Int. Law 52, 61; mem. Perm. Cen Opium Board 48-68, Vice-Chair. 53-68; mem. Int. Narcotics Control Board 68-, Chair. 74-76; legal adviser, Ministry of Foreign Affairs 48; mem. Perm. Court of Arbitration 58, European Court for Nuclear Energy 60, UN Int. Law Comm. 64-; mem. Inst. of Int. Law; mem. various conciliation comms., etc.
Leisure interests: the sea, music, gardening.
Publs. include: *Droit International public, Institutions*

internationales, Organisations européennes, La Communauté européenne du Charbon et de l'acier, Organisations européennes and other numerous books and articles.

Office: International Narcotics Control Board, Palais des Nations, Geneva, Switzerland; Home: 72 rue de Cherche-Midi, 75006 Paris, France.
Telephone: 222-07-56.

Reuter, Paul; Luxembourg diplomatist; b. 1920.
Department of Foreign Affairs 48-; Perm. Del. to Council of Europe 56-59; Perm. Del. to NATO 59-67, to OEEC 59-61, to OECD 61-67; Amb. to Netherlands 67-73.
c/o Ministère des Affaires Etrangères, Luxembourg.

Reuter, Richard Ward, B.A., L.H.D.; American international relief administrator; b. 17 Jan. 1918; ed. Amherst Coll.
Administrative positions merchandising and insurance 38-41; served (civilian) with American Friends Service Cttee. 41-45; with CARE Inc. 46-49, 51-62, Exec. Dir. 55-62; Special Asst. to Pres., Dir. U.S. "Food for Peace" Programme 62-66; joined Int. Div. of Kraft Foods 67, Vice-Pres. Purchasing 69-; several orders and decorations.
International Division, Kraft Foods, 500 Peshtigo Court, Chicago, Ill. 60690, U.S.A.

Reuter, Wolfgang Christian; German business executive; b. 26 May 1924, Duisburg; s. of Dr. Hans Reuter and Helga Gran; m. Christa Féaux de Lacroix 1960; two s. one d.
Former director of various DEMAG affiliated companies until 56; Treas. and mem. Board of Dirs. DEMAG 62, Pres. and Chair. of Board 67-75, mem. Supervisory Board 75-.
Leisure interests: sailing, golf.
DEMAG Aktiengesellschaft, 41 Duisburg, Postfach 2 and 12; Home: 4 Wittlaer/Düsseldorf, Bockumerstrasse 357, Federal Republic of Germany.
Telephone: 02131-605-2321 (Office); 0211-40-16-27 (Home).

Reuther, Victor G.; American labour union executive; b. 1 Jan. 1912; ed. Univ. of W. Virginia, Wayne Univ.
Travelled abroad 35; assembly-line worker Kelsey-Hayes Wheel Co., Detroit 35; Dir. United Automobile Workers (U.A.W.), Indiana 37, Int. Rep. 37, later Asst. Dir. War Policy Div., Dir. Educ. Programme in U.S. and Canada 51, European Rep. 51; fmr. Asst. to Pres. Congress of Industrial Orgs. (C.I.O.); Admin. Asst. to Pres. U.A.W., Dir. Int. Affairs Dept.; mem. State and Nat. Cttees. War Manpower Comm. and War Productivity Board, U.S. Govt., World War II; Co-Chair. Anglo American Council on Productivity 49; lost an eye when shot in the face by gangsters 49; mem. Commerce Technical Advisory Board; Democrat.
United Automobile Workers (U.A.W.), 1126 16th Street, N.W. Washington, D.C. 20036, U.S.A.

Reutov, Oleg Alexandrovich; Soviet organic chemist; b. 5 Sept. 1920, Makeevka, Donetsk Region; ed. Moscow Univ.
Soviet Army 41-45; Instructor, Moscow Univ. 45-54, Prof. 54-; Corresp. mem. U.S.S.R. Acad. of Sciences 58-64, mem. 64-; mem. C.P.S.U. 42-.
U.S.S.R. Academy of Sciences, 14 Leninsky Prospekt, Moscow, U.S.S.R.

Reutter, Hermann; German pianist and composer; b. 17 June 1900, Stuttgart; s. of Hermann and Clara Reutter; m. Lieselotte Lauk 1940; one s. two d.; studied music at Munich.
Director Staatliche Hochschule für Musik und Darstellende Kunst, Stuttgart 56-66; Prof. Musik-Hochschule, Munich.
Leisure interests: all arts.
Published works include choral music, cantatas, song

cycles, orchestral and solo works; operas: *Odysseus, Dr. Johannes Faust, Don Juan and Faust;* five one-act pieces: *Saul, Ballade der Landstrasse, Lübecker Totentanz, Witwe von Ephesus, Brücke von San Luis Rey, Tod des Empedokles;* ballet: *Kirmes von Delft, Notturno Montmartre.*
7 Stuttgart-Möhringen, Elfenstrasse 107, Federal Republic of Germany.
Telephone: 711597.

Revel, Jean-François; French writer; b. 19 Jan. 1924; m. Claude Sarraute 1966; two s. one d.; ed. Ecole Normale Supérieure and Sorbonne, Paris.
Teacher of French Literature, Institut Français, Mexico, later Florence 52-56; Teacher of Philosophy, Lille and Paris 56-61; Literary Adviser Editions Julliard and Pauvert 61-66, Editions Laffont 66-; Columnist of *L'Express* 66-.
Publs. novel: *Histoire de Flore* 57; essays: *Pourquoi des Philosophes?* 57, *Pour l'Italie* 58, *Le Style du Général* 59, *Sur Proust* 60, *La Cabale des Dévots* 62, *En France* 65, *Contrecensures* 66, *Histoire de la Philosophie Occidentale Vol. I* 68, *Vol. II* 70, *Ni Marx ni Jésus* 70. *Les Idées de notre Temps* 72.
55 quai de Bourbon, Paris 4e, France.
Telephone: 033-65-87.

Revelle, Roger, PH.D.; American university professor; b. 7 March 1909, Seattle, Wash.; s. of William R. and Ella R. (Dougan) Revelle; m. Ellen Virginia Clark 1931; one s. three d.; ed. Pomona Coll. and Univ. of California.
Teaching Asst., Pomona Coll. 29-30, Univ. of Calif. 30-31; Research Asst., Univ. of Calif., Scripps Inst. of Oceanography 31-36, Instructor 36-41, Asst. Prof. 41-46, Assoc. Prof. 46-48, Assoc. Dir. 48-50, Acting Dir. 50-51, Dir. 51-64, Dean of Research 63-64. Dean Emer. 64-, Prof. of Oceanography 48-64; Dir. La Jolla Campus and Dean of School of Science and Engineering, Univ. of Calif. 58-61; Science Adviser to Sec. of Interior 61-63; Univ. of Calif. Dean of Research 63-64; Richard Saltonstall Prof. of Population Policy, Faculty of Public Health, Harvard Univ. 64-; Dir. Harvard Center for Population Studies 64-75; mem. American Asscn. for Advancement of Science (Pres. 74), American Geophysical Union, Int. Asscn. of Physical Oceanography (Pres. 63-67), Nat. Acad. of Sciences, American Acad. of Arts and Sciences, American Philosophical Soc.; mem. Naval Reserve Advisory Comm. 59-, U.S. Nat. Comm. for UNESCO 58-64 (Vice-Chair. 61-64); Albatross Medal, Swedish Royal Soc. of Science and Letters 52, Agassiz Medal of Nat. Acad. of Sciences 63; Order of Sitara-i-Imtiaz (Pakistan) 64; Hon. Sc.D. (Pomona and Carleton Colls.), Hon. A.M. (Harvard).
Publs. Over 100 scientific articles in professional publications.
Office: 9 Bow Street, Cambridge, Mass. 02138; Home: 1010 Memorial Drive, Cambridge, Mass. 02138, U.S.A.
Telephone: 617-495-2021 (Office); 617-547-2551 (Home).

Reverdin, Olivier, D. ès L.; Swiss professor, politician and editor; b. 15 July 1913, Geneva; m. Renée Chaponnière 1936; three c.; ed. Univs. of Geneva and Paris, and Ecole Française d'Athènes.
School teaching, Geneva and France 38-41; Attaché Swiss Legation, Rome 41-44; Lecturer and Asst. Prof. Ancient Greek Literature, Univ. of Geneva 45-58, Ordinary Prof. 58-; Parly. Ed. *Journal de Genève,* Berne 45-54, and Man. Editor 55-59, Man. 59-67; Deputy (Liberal) of Geneva at the Conseil Nat. 55-71, at Conseil des Etats 71-; Chair. Soc. Suisse des Sciences Humaines 60-68; mem. Nat. Council for Scientific Research 63-, Chair. 68-; rep. Consultative Assembly, Council of Europe 64-, Chair. of the Cultural and Scientific Cttee. 66, of the Cttee. for Science and

Technology 67-69, Pres. of the Assembly 69-72; Vice-Pres. European Science Foundation 74-.
Publs. *La Religion de la Cité platonicienne* 45, *La Guerre du Sonderbund vue par le Général Dufour* 48, *Quatorze calvinistes chez les Topinambous* 57, *La Crète, Berceau de la Civilisation Occidentale* 60, *Connaissance de la Suisse* 64, *Polybe* 74.
8 rue des Granges, 1204 Geneva, Switzerland.
Telephone: 022-215191.

Rexroth, Kenneth; American author; b. 22 Dec. 1905, South Bend, Ind.; *s.* of Charles Marion Rexroth and Delia Reed; *m.* 1st Andree Dutcher 1926 (died 1940), 2nd Marie Kass 1940, 3rd Marthe Whitcomb Larsen 1948; two *d.*; ed. High School in Chicago.
Independent lecturer, *Classics Revisited* columns for *Saturday Review*, contributor and reviewer *New York Times*, *Nation*, etc.; Lecturer, Santa Barbara, Univ. of Calif.; two Guggenheim Fellowships, two Common-wealth Club medals, Eunice Tietjens Poetry Magazine Award, Shelley Memorial Award, Longview Founda-tion Award, Nat. Acad. of Arts and Letters Grant, Rockefeller Grant, Deutscher Akademischer Austausch-dienst Grant; mem. Nat. Inst. of Arts and Letters.
Leisure interests: skiing, mountaineering, swimming, revolution.
Publs. *In What Hour* 40, *Phoenix and Tortoise* 44, *The Selected Poems of D. H. Lawrence* 47, *New British Poets* 48, *Signature of All Things* 49, *Art of Worldly Wisdom* 49, *Dragon and Unicorn* 52, *In Defense of the Earth* 56 (verse); *Beyond the Mountains* 51 (play); *14 Poems of O. V. Lubicz-Milosz* 52, *100 Poems from the Japanese* 55, *100 Poems from the Chinese* 56, *30 Spanish Poems* 57 (translations); *A Bird in the Bush* 59 (essays); *The Homestead Called Damascus* 62, *Assays* (essays) 61, *Poems from the Greek Anthology* 62, *Natural Numbers—New and Selected Poems* 63, *An Autobiographical Novel* 66, *Collected Shorter Poems* 67, *The Heart's Garden/The Garden's Heart* 67, *The Collected Long Poems of Kenneth Rexroth* 68, *The Classics Revisited*, Vol. I (essays) 68, *Selected Poems of Pierre Reverdy, Love and the Turning Year, 100 More Chinese Poems, The Alternative Society* (essays), *With Eye and Ear* (essays), *The Orchid Boat: the Women Poets of China* (with Ling Chung) 73, *The Elastic Retort* (essays) 73.
1401 E. Pepper Lane, Santa Barbara, Calif. 93108, U.S.A.
Telephone: 969-2722.

Rey, Henri François, LIC. de PHIL.; French writer; b. 31 July 1919; ed. Lycée de Perpignan, Univ. of Montpellier.
Former journalist, broadcaster and scriptwriter.
Publs. *La Fête Espagnole* 58 (Prix des Deux Magots), *La Comédie* 60, *Les Pianos Mécaniques* 62 (Prix Interallié), *Les Chevaux Masqués* 65, *Le Rachdingue* 67, *Opéra pour un tyran* 67, *Halleluya, ma vie* 70, *le Barbare* 72, *Schizophrénie ma soeur* 73, *Dali dans son labyrinthe* 74.
44 rue Boissonade, Paris 14e, France.

Rey, Jean, D. en D.; Belgian lawyer and politician; b. 15 July 1902, Liège; *s.* of Arnold Rey; ed. Athénée Royal, Liège and Univ. of Liège.
Advocate, Liège Court of Appeal 26-; Communa Councillor, Liège 35-58; Deputy for Liège 39, 46-58; Captain of Reserves 40; prisoner of war in Germany 40-45; founder mem. Entente Libérale Wallone; Vice-Pres. Conseil Supérieur de la Famille 47; Alternative Del. UN 3rd Gen. Assembly, Paris 48, Consultative Assembly, Council of Europe, 1st Session 49, 5th Session 53; Minister of Reconstruction (Eyskens Coalition Govt.) 49-50, of Econ. Affairs 54-58; mem. and Sectional Pres. for External Relations, European Econ. Com-munity Comm. 58-67; Pres. of combined Exec. of EEC, ECSC and Euratom 67-70; mem. Supervisory Board, Philips Electrical Group; Pres. Sofina Jan. 71-; Pres.

Int. European Movt. 74-; Grand Officier, Ordre de Léopold, Grand Croix Order of Orange-Nassau, Grand Cordon Order of the Lion of Finland, Commdr. Ordre de la Couronne de Chêne, Croix de Guerre.
235 rue de la Loi, Brussels, Belgium.

Reyes, Narciso G., A.B.; Philippine journalist; b. 6 Feb. 1914; ed. Univ. of Santo Tomas.
Associate Editor *Philippines Commonweal*, Manila 35-41; mem. Nat. Language Faculty, Ateneo de Manila 39-41; Assoc. Editor *Manila Post* 45-47; Assoc. News Editor *Evening News*, Manila 47-48; Man. Editor Philippine Newspaper Guild Organ 47-48; Adviser to Philippine Mission to UN and Rep. of the Philip-pines to numerous ECOSOC sessions and UN Gen. Assemblies, and many other UN activities 48-; Philip-pine Amb. to U.K. 67-70; Chair. 19th Session UN Social Devt. Comm. 68-69; Perm. Rep. to UN 70-; Pres. United Nations Devt. Programme 74.
Philippine Mission to UN, 556 Fifth Avenue, New York, N.Y. 10036, U.S.A.
Telephone: 764-1300.

Reynaud, Roger; French trade unionist and civil servant; b. 19 May 1916.
Former Inspector, Ministry of Finance, mem. Conseil Economique, mem. Finance Comm., Modernisation and Re-equipment Plan; Sec.-Gen. French Christian Trade Union Fed. 45; Vice-Pres. Gen. Fed. of Govt. Employ-ees; fmr. mem. Council, Int. Confed. of Christian Trade Unions; mem. ECSC High Authority 58-67; Pres. Maison de l'Europe 68-71; mem. Council of Admin. of Inst. for Industrial Devt. 70-; with Ministry of Labour, Employment and Population 71-72.
10 rue Alasseur, Paris 15e, France.

Reynolds, Anna, F.R.A.M.; British opera and concert singer; b. 5 June 1936, Canterbury; *d.* of Paul Grey Reynolds and Vera Cicely Turner; ed. Benenden School, Royal Acad. of Music.
Studied with Professoressa Debora Fambri, Rome; debut Glyndebourne Festival 62, has appeared at many festivals including Spoleto and Aix-en-Provence 66, Salzburg Easter Festival 68, Vienna and Bayreuth 70; has sung with leading orchestras, debuts with Phil-harmonic Orchestra, London 63, New York Phil-harmonic 71; appearances in Rossini's *Otello*, Rome 64, with Scottish Opera 66, in Strauss's *Arabella*, Covent Garden 67, with Metropolitan Opera, New York 68, with La Scala, Milan 73, with Teatro Colón, Buenos Aires 73; recordings with Philips, Deutsche Grammo-phon.
Leisure interests: reading, piano, travel, world-wide correspondence.
37 Chelwood Gardens, Richmond, Surrey, TW9 4JG, England.
Telephone: 01-876-6164.

Reynolds, David Parham; American industrial metals executive; b. 16 June 1915, Bristol, Tenn.; *s.* of late Richard Samuel Reynolds and of Julia Louise Parham; *m.* Margaret Trezevant Harrison 1944; three *d.*; ed. Princeton Univ.
Reynolds Metals Co., Louisville 37-, Salesman 37-41, Asst. Man. Aircraft Parts Div. 41-44, Asst. Vice-Pres. 44-46, Vice-Pres. 46-58, Exec. Vice-Pres. 58-, and Gen. Man. 69-, Vice-Chair. Board 75-; Dir. other cos.
Leisure interests: golf, hunting, racing horses.
Reynolds Metals Co., 6601 W. Broad Street, Richmond, Va. 23261; 8905 Tresco Road, Richmond, Va., U.S.A.
Telephone: AT2-2311 (Office); AT2-2226 (Home).

Reynolds, John Hamilton, PH.D.; American professor of physics; b. 3 April 1923, Cambridge, Mass.; *s.* of Horace Mason Reynolds and Catharine Whitford Coffeen; *m.* Ann Burchard Arnold 1975; two *s.* three *d.* (by previous marriage); ed. Harvard Coll. and Univ. of Chicago.

Associate Physicist, Argonne Nat. Laboratory 50; Asst. Prof. to Prof. of Physics, Univ. of Calif. at Berkeley 50-61, Prof. 61-; Research Prof. Miller Inst. for Basic Research in Science 59-61, 67-68; Guggenheim Fellow, Univ. of Bristol, England 56-57, Nat. Science Foundation Senior Postdoctoral Fellow and Visiting Prof. Univ. of São Paulo, Brazil 63-64; Fulbright-Hays Research Award (Portugal) 71-72; mem. Nat. Acad. of Sciences; John Price Wetherill Medal of Franklin Inst., J. Lawrence Smith Medal of Nat. Acad. of Sciences, Leonard Medal, Meteoritical Soc., NASA Exceptional Scientific Achievement Medal.
Leisure interests: music, hiking, sailing.
Publs. Research papers and reviews in fields of mass spectroscopy, isotope studies in meteorites, geochronology, solar system chronology, extinct radioactivity, and lunar samples.
Department of Physics, University of California, Berkeley, Calif. 94720, U.S.A.
Telephone: 415-642-4863.

Reynolds, J. Louis; American business executive; b. 3 May 1910, Winston-Salem, N.C.; s. of late Richard Samuel Reynolds and of Julia Louise Parham; m. Glenn Parkinson (deceased); one d.; ed. Louisville High School, McCallie School, Chattanooga, Univ. of Pa. and Duke Univ.
Joined Reynolds Metals Co. 31, Vice-Pres. and Gen. Sales Man. 40, Vice-Pres. in charge of operations 48; Exec. Vice-Pres. and Dir. Reynolds Int. Inc. 56, Chair. and Chief Exec. 59-; Pres. and Dir. Eskimo Pie Corpn., Canadian British Aluminium Corpn., Reynolds Jamaica Mines Ltd.; Dir. British Aluminium Ltd., American Fidelity Life Insurance Co., Robertshaw Controls Co., Metropolitan Nat. Bank; Hon. LL.D. (Univ. of Arkansas).
Reynolds International Inc., Richmond, Va.; Home: 5511 Cary Street Road, Richmond, Va., U.S.A.

Reynolds, Peter William John, C.B.E.; British business executive; b. 10 Sept. 1929, Singapore; ed. Haileybury Coll.
Formerly with Walls (div. of Unilever) latterly as Chair.; Asst. Man. Dir. Ranks Hovis McDougall 71, Man. Dir. April 72-.
Leisure interests: squash, beagling, riding (occasionally), watching rugby football, reading, gardening.
Ranks Hovis McDougall Ltd., RHM Centre, P.O. Box 551, 152 Grosvenor Road, London SW1V 3JL; Home: White House, Beamond End, Amersham, Bucks., England.

Reynolds, Quentin; American business executive; b. 1906, Calif.; ed. St. Mary's Coll. of Calif.
With Safeway Stores Inc. 23-, starting as part-time Food Clerk, then through various operating and exec. posts until Man. of San Francisco Div. 56, Vice-Pres. 60, Regional Retail Man. 62, Dir. 64, Senior Vice-Pres. in Charge of all Safeway Retail Operations in U.S., and Advertising and Market Research and Grocery Merchandising Divs. at Admin. Office 64, Pres. and Exec. Officer in Charge of Company Operations 66-, Chair. 71-; appt. by Pres. Johnson to Exec. Board of Nat. Alliance of Businessmen; Dir. Calif. State Chamber of Commerce.
Safeway Stores Inc., 201 4th Street, Oakland, Calif. 94607, U.S.A.

Reynolds, Richard Samuel, Jr.; American business executive; b. 27 May 1908, Winston-Salem, N. Carolina; s. of R. S. Reynolds and Louise Parham Reynolds; m. Virginia Sargeant; two s. (one s. died 1971); ed. Univ. of Pennsylvania.
Member New York Stock Exchange 30; formed Reynolds & Co. 30; Asst. to Pres. Reynolds Metals Co. 75, Treas. 38-44, Vice-Pres., Treas. 44-48, Pres. 48-75, Chair. 63-; Dir. British Aluminium Co. Ltd., Mfrs.

Hanover Trust Co., Maniconagan Power Co., Lawyers Title Insurance Corpn., Richmond Corpn., Richmond Cen. Nat. Bank; Trustee Emer., Univ. of Pennsylvania, Virginia Museum of Fine Arts, Nat. Safety Council, many other civic and business orgs.; Hon. D.C.S. (Univ. of Richmond); Human Relations Award (American Jewish Cttee.) 68, B'nai B'rith Humanitarian Award 74; Hon. mem. American Inst. of Architects 70.
Leisure interests: horse racing, fox hunting, shooting.
Reynolds Metals Co., Richmond, Va. 23261, U.S.A.

Reynolds, William G.; American business executive; b. 17 Feb. 1913, Bristol, Tenn.; m. 1st Mary Spottswood Nicklas 1935, 2nd Charlene Moore 1974; two s. two d.; ed. Kentucky Military Inst., Hun Preparatory School, Brown School and Columbia Univ.
Joined Reynolds Metals Co. 39, now Exec. Vice-Pres. (Research and Devt.) and mem. Exec. Cttee.; Dir. several subsidiary cos. of Reynolds Metals; Pres. Reynolds Int., Inc.; mem. American Ordnance Asscn., Asscn. of U.S. Army and American Society of Metals; Medal of American Soc. of Metals.
Leisure interests: polo.
Reynolds International Inc., Richmond, Va., U.S.A.

Reyre, Jean André Marie; French banker; b. 9 Dec. 1899, Saintines, Oise; ed. Faculté de Droit de Paris and Ecole Libre des Sciences Politiques.
Entered Banque de Paris et des Pays-Bas 24, Asst. Man. 41, Man. 45, Dir.-Gen. 48, Dir. 55, Vice-Pres. Dir.-Gen. 62-67, Pres. Dir.-Gen. 67-69; Pres. Cie. financière de Paris et des Pays-Bas 68-69, Dir. 70-; Vice-Pres. Paribas Corpn.; Pres. Compagnie Centrale de Financement; Vice-Pres. Cie. Générale de Participations et d'Entreprises, C.S.F., Soc. Belge COPEBA; Pres. Soc. de Banques pour le financement et le recouvrement 71-, Compagnie int. pour le financement de l'énergie nucléaire (Cifen) 72-; Dir. several other companies; Officier Légion d'Honneur, Croix de Guerre (First World War).
96 avenue de Suffren, Paris 15e, France.

Rhallys, George J., LL.D.; Greek lawyer; b. 26 Dec. 1918; m. Helene Voultsos 1950; two d.; ed. Athens Univ.
Served Reconnaissance Groups 40-41 and Tank Corps 45-48; elected Deputy for Athens 50-58, 61-67, 74-; mem. Greek Del. to European Council, Strasbourg 53-58; Minister to Prime Minister's Office 54-56, of Public Works and Communications 56-58, of the Interior 61-63, of Public Order April 67; under house arrest April-May 67, in prison and exile May-Sept. 68; Minister to Prime Minister's Office 67, July 74-; mem. Popular Party 50, Nat. Rally 51, Nat. Radical Union 56, New Democratic Party 74; Medal of Valour, War Cross with two bars, D.S.M., and several foreign awards.
Leisure interest: golf.
Publs. *John Rhallys* 46, *The Possibility of Increasing the Yield of Greek Agriculture* 52, *Democracy and Communism* 59, *The Truth about the Greek Politicians* (in Greek) 71, *The Technique of Violence* 72.
4 Kanari Street, Athens, Greece.
Telephone: 617340.

Rham, Georges-William de, D. ès SC. MATH.; Swiss mathematician; b. 10 Sept. 1903, Roche, Vaud; s. of Léon de Rham and Marie (née DuPasquier) de Rham; ed. Collège d'Aigle, Gymnase classique de Lausanne, and Univs. de Lausanne et Paris.
Privat-Docent, Univ. of Lausanne 32, Extraordinary Prof. 36-43, Full Prof. 43-71, Hon. Prof. 71-; Extraordinary Prof. Univ. of Geneva 36-53, Full Prof. 53-73, Hon. Prof. 73-; mem. Swiss Nat. Council for Scientific Research 56-69; Visiting Prof. Harvard Univ. 49-50; temporary mem. Inst. for Advanced Study, Princeton 50, 57-58; Pres. Int. Mathematical Union 62-66;

Corresp. mem. Math. and Physics Section Acad. of Sciences, Göttingen; Foreign mem. Accad. dei Lincei; Dr. h.c. (Univs. of Strasbourg, Grenoble, Lyon and Swiss Fed. Polytechnical Inst.).
Leisure interest: alpinism.
Publs. include: *Variétés différentiables, Formes, Courants, Formes harmoniques* 55 (3rd edn. 73).
7 avenue des Bergières, Lausanne, Switzerland.
Telephone: 021-37-19-74.

Rham, Jean de, L. en D.; Swiss diplomatist; b. 24 March 1907; ed. Lausanne and Munich Univs.
Entered Fed. Political Dept. 34; served successively in London and Hamburg (Consul-Gen.); Counsellor, Rome 49-51; Chargé d'Affaires, S. Africa 51-55, Minister 55-56; Chief Int. Orgs. Dept., Fed. Political Dept. 56-61; Amb. to Japan and Repub. of Korea 61-67, to Italy 67-73.
c/o Ministry of Foreign Affairs, Berne, Switzerland.

Rhea, Alexander Dodson, III; American motor executive; b. 10 May 1919, Whitney, Tex.; m. Suzanne Menocal 1945; one s.; ed. Texas Christian Univ. and Princeton Univ.
United States Navy 41-45, Lt.-Commdr. U.S. Naval Reserve; Vice-Pres. Govt. Employees Insurance Co., Wash. 46-48; with Gen. Motors 48-, posts in S. America 48-55, in Germany and N.Y. 55-63; Regional Group Exec. 63; Man. N.Y. Staff, Gen. Motors Overseas Operations 66; Man. Dir., Gen. Motors Holden's Pty. 68; Chair. and Man. Dir. Vauxhall Motors Ltd. 70; Chair. Gen. Motors European Advisory Council and Exec. Vice-Pres. and Dir., Gen. Motors Overseas Corpn. April 74-.
Leisure interests: reading, golf.
General Motors Overseas Corporation, 77 South Audley Street, London, W.1; Home: 72 Chester Square, London, S.W.1, England.
Telephone: 01-491-3852 (Office); 01-730-5935 (Home).

Rhijn, Arie Adriaan van, J.D., D.SC., LL.D., PH.D.; Netherlands civil servant; b. 1892, Groningen; m. Engelina Maria E. van Dijk; two s. two d.; ed. Groningen and Utrecht Univs.
Deputy Sec. Court of Arbitration for Railway Personnel 17-18; Sec. Master Printers' Union 19-27; Chief of a Dept. in the Ministry of Social Affairs 28-32; Sec.-Gen. of the Ministry of Econ. Affairs 33-39; Ministry of Agric. and Fisheries 40-41; Chair. Netherlands Financial Control Board 41-45; Sec.-Gen. of the Ministry of Social Affairs 45-50; Secretary of State for Social Affairs 50-58; mem. Council of State 60-67; Knight of the Order of the Netherlands Lion; Commdr. Order of Orange Nassau; Great Commdr. Star of Romania; Knight Commdr. Order of Crown of Belgium 49.
Leisure interests: reading theology, cycling.
Publs. *Free Competition and Collective Labour Agreement* 24, *Planning* 46, *Social Security* 46, *Worker or Co-worker? New Ideas on Participation in Management in Industry* 69.
Wassenaarscheweg 76, Flat 401, The Hague, Netherlands.
Telephone: 070-248856.

Rho, Paolo; Italian railway executive and international civil servant; b. 29 June 1916, Bussoleno; m. Nella Cellesi; ed. Università degli Studi, Florence.
Army Service 40-43; Sec.-Gen., then Dir. provincial labour office, Ministry of Labour and Nat. Service 44-47; Inspector, Turin Commercial Div., Italian State Railways 47-48; Asst. Gen. Rep., Italian State Railways, Berne, Switzerland 48-50; Head, Int. Freight Rates Dept., later Head of Secr. of Asst. Dir.-Gen., Directorate-Gen. of Italian State Railways, Rome 50-58; Head of Div., Directorate-Gen. for Transport, EEC Comm., Brussels 58-63; Hon. Dir. EEC Comm. 58-63; Special duties with Dir.-Gen., Italian State Railways

63-65; Dir.-Gen. for Transport, EEC Comm. 65-68; Dir.-Gen. for Transport, Comm. of European Communities 68; Commdr. Italian Order of Merit.
Commission of European Communities, 200 rue de la Loi, 1040 Brussels, Belgium.
Telephone: 35-00-40.

Rhoads, James Berton, PH.D.; American archivist; b. 17 Sept. 1918, Sioux City, Iowa; s. of James H. and Mary K. Rhoads; m. S. Angela (Handy) Rhoads 1947; one s. two d.; ed. Univ. of Calif. (Berkeley) and the American Univ., Washington, D.C.
Held various positions in the Nat. Archives 52-65; Asst. Archivist, Civil Archives 65-66; Deputy Archivist of U.S.A. 66-68; Archivist of U.S.A. 68-; mem. Fed. Council on Arts and Humanities, Harry S. Truman Library Inst. for Nat. and Int. Affairs, Org. of American Historians, American Historical Asscn.; mem. Board of Trustees, Woodrow Wilson Int. Centre for Scholars; Fellow and Pres. Soc. of American Archivists; Vice-Pres. Int. Council on Archives and mem. numerous other related orgs.
Leisure interests: reading, philately.
Publs. numerous articles in professional journals.
Room 111, National Archives Building, 8th and Pennsylvania Avenue, N.W., Washington, D.C. 20408, U.S.A.
Telephone: 202-963-3434.

Rhodes, James Allen; American politician; b. 13 Sept. 1909, Coalton, Jackson County, O.; m. Helen Rawlins; three d.; ed. Ohio State Univ.
Former Columbus City Auditor; Mayor of Columbus, Ohio 43-52; Auditor of State, Ohio 52-62; Gov. of Ohio 63-70, 75-; Chair. Nat. Council of Vocational Educ.; mem. U.S. Olympic Cttee.; hon. degrees from Miami, Akron, Capital, Youngstown, Wilberforce, Toledo, Cincinnati, Ohio State and Ohio Univs.; Helms Foundation Award.
Publs. *The Trial of Mary Todd Lincoln* (co-author), *Johnny Shiloh* (co-author), *The Court Martial of Commodore Perry* (co-author), *Teenage Hall of Fame, Alternative to a Decadent Society.*
State Capitol, Columbus, Ohio, U.S.A.

Rhodes, John Jacob, B.S., LL.B.; American lawyer and politician; b. 18 Sept. 1916, Council Grove, Kansas; s. of John J. and Gladys Thomas Rhodes; m. Mary Elizabeth (Betty) Harvey 1942; three s. one d.; ed. Kansas State Coll., Harvard Univ.
Served World War II, Col.; Partner, Rhodes, Killian & Legg, law firm, Mesa, Ariz. 46-52; Vice-Pres., Dir. Farm Home, Life Insurance Co. 51; Vice-Chair. Ariz. State Board of Public Welfare 51-52; mem. 83rd-94th Congresses; mem. Exec. Board, Nat. Republican Congress 53-62; Chair. Special Projects Sub-Cttee., Repub. Policy Comm. 61-65; Chair. Repub. Policy Comm. 65-72; Chair. Repub. Platform Cttee. 72; Minority Leader, House of Reps. 73-.
Leisure interest: golf.
H-230, The Capitol, Washington, D.C. 20515; Home: 1114 N. Cherry, Mesa, Ariz. 85201, U.S.A.
Telephone: (202) 225-0600 (Office); (602) 833-2267 (Home).

Riad, Mahmoud; Egyptian diplomatist; b. 8 Jan. 1917; ed. Military Acad. and General Staff Coll.
Egyptian Rep. to Mixed Armistice Comm. 49-52; Dir. Dept. of Arab Affairs, Ministry of Foreign Affairs 54-55; Ambassador to Syria 55-58; President's Counsellor on Foreign Affairs 58-62; Chair. U.A.R. Del. to UN Econ. Comm. for Africa 61, Perm. Rep. to UN 62-64; Minister of Foreign Affairs under Dep. Prime Minister for Foreign Affairs 64-71; Deputy Premier and Minister of Foreign Affairs May 71-Jan. 72; Presidential Adviser Jan.-June 72; Sec.-Gen. Arab League June 72-.
Arab League, Midan Al Tahrir, Cairo, Egypt.

Ribeiro, H. E. Cardinal António, TH.D.; Portuguese ecclesiastic; b. 21 May 1928, Celorico de Basto; s. of José Ribeiro and Ana Gonçalves; ed. Seminary of Braga and Pontifical Univ., Rome.
Ordained priest 53; Prof. Univ. of Lisbon 65-67; Auxiliary Bishop of Braga 67; Auxiliary Bishop of Lisbon 70; Patriarch of Lisbon 71; Cardinal-Patriarch 73-.
Leisure interests: sport, philately, travel.
Publs. *The Aevum According to Thomas Aquinas* 58, *The Socialization* 64.
Campo dos Mártires da Pátria 45, Lisbon 1, Portugal.
Telephone: 56-39-01.

Ribeyre, Paul; French businessman and politician; b. 11 Dec. 1906, Aubagne; *m.* Andrée Offant 1939; three s.
Director La Reine Mineral Water Co.; Deputy from Ardèche to the two Constituent Nat. Assemblies 45-46; Deputy to Nat. Assembly 46-58; Senator for Ardèche 58-; Under-Sec. of State for Public Health and Population 49, Minister of Public Health 51-52, of Commerce 53, of Justice 53-54, of Industry May 58; Pres. Conseil Gen. de l'Ardèche 67-, Asscn. Parlementaire pour la Liberté de l'Enseignement, Club Européen de la Santé 70; Mayor of Val-les-Bains 45-; Chevalier de la Légion d'Honneur; mem. Directing Cttee. of Centre Democrat Party 66-.
Leisure interests: music, painting.
31 rue La Pérouse, Paris 16e, France.
Telephone: 704-50-24.

Ribičič, Mitja; Yugoslav politician; b. 1919, Trieste; ed. Univ. of Ljubljana.
Member of Communist Party 41-; mem. Central Cttee., League of Communists of Slovenia, League of Communists of Yugoslavia (LCY); mem. Presidium of Central Cttee. of LCY; mem. Slovene Del. to Chamber of Nationalities of Fed. Assembly; has held various posts in the Slovene Govt. and the Yugoslav Fed. Govt.; Pres. Fed. Exec. Council 69-71; mem. Presidency of Fed. Repub. 71-74, Vice-Pres. 73-74.
Belgrade, Yugoslavia.

Ribicoff, Abraham A. (Abe), LL.B.; American lawyer and politician; b. 9 April 1910; ed. Univ. of Chicago.
Admitted to Connecticut Bar 33; served on Conn. Legislature 39-43; Judge Hartford Municipal Court 41-43 and 54-47; mem. House of Reps. 49-53; Gov. of the State of Conn. 55-61; Sec. of Health, Education and Welfare 61-July 62; U.S. Senator from Conn. 63-; Democrat; Order of Merit (Italy).
Old Senate Office Building, Washington, D.C. 20510; and 30 Woodland Street, Hartford, Conn., U.S.A.

Riboud, Antoine Amédée Paul; French business executive; b. 24 Dec. 1918, Lyons; s. of Camille Riboud and Hélène Frachon; brother of Jean Riboud (*q.v.*); *m.* Lucette Hugonnard-Roche 1943; three s. one d.; ed. Ecole Supérieure de Commerce, Paris.
Joined Verreries Souchon-Neuvesel 43, mem. Board of Dirs. and Sec.-Gen. 52-62, Vice-Pres. 62-65, Dir.-Gen. 62-66, Pres. 65-66; Pres. and Dir.-Gen. Soc. Boussois-Souchon-Neuvesel 66-72; Pres. Boussois-Souchon-Neuvesel-Gervais-Danone 73-; Vice-Pres. Cie. Gervais-Danone 73-; later Dir.-Gen. Verreries de Giron-court 63-68; Dir., later Pres. and Dir.-Gen. Soc. des eaux minérales d'Evian-les-Bains 66-70; Vice-Pres. Glaverbel-Mecaniver, Brussels 69-; Pres. and Dir.-Gen. Soc. européenne de brasseries 70-; Pres. Soc. moderne de boissons 72-; Dir. Cie. financière de Paris et des Pays-Bas, Pricel, Cie. française Philips, Soc. des eaux minérales d'Evian, Dahlbusch, Vereenig de Glas-fabrieken (Netherlands), Soc. pour l'exploitation et la vente des produits Fruité et Eva; Pres. Centre Nat. d'information pour la productivité des entreprises 69-70, Asscn. Progrès et Environnement 71-; mem. Loan Cttee. Crédit Nat., Cercle de l'Union.

Boussois-Souchon-Neuvesel-Gervais-Danone, 22 Boulevard des Malesherbes, 75008 Paris; 126 rue Jules-Guesde, 92302 Levallois-Peret; Home: 13 rue Laurencin, 69002 Lyons, France.

Riboud, Jean; French industrialist; b. 15 Nov. 1919, Lyons; s. of Camille Riboud and Hélène (née Frachon); brother of Antoine Riboud (*q.v.*); *m.* Krishna Roy 1949; one s.; ed. Faculté de Droit, Paris, and Ecole des Sciences Politiques.
Director of Schlumberger Ltd. (oil drillings, instruments, electronics) 56-, Pres. 65-75, Chief Exec. Officer 65-, Chair. 72-; Dir.-Gen. Soc. de Prospection Electrique Schlumberger 57-65; Dir. Cie. financière de Paris et des Pays-Bas 71-.
42 rue Saint Dominique, 75007 Paris, France.

Riccardo, John Joseph; American motor company executive; b. 2 July 1924, Little Falls, N.Y.; *m.* Thelma Riccardo; five c.; ed. Univ. of Michigan.
Formerly Man. of public accounting firm; Financial Staff Exec. on Int. Operations Staff, Chrysler Corpn. 59-60, Gen. Man. Export-Import Div. 60-61, Vice-Pres., then Exec. Pres. Chrysler Canada Ltd. 61-63, Gen. Sales Man. Dodge Car and Truck Div. Dec. 63-65, also Asst. Gen. Man. Dodge Car and Truck Div. 64-65; Asst. Gen. Man. Chrysler-Plymouth Div. Nov. 65-66, Vice-Pres. Marketing, Chrysler Corpn. Oct. 66-67, Group Vice-Pres. Domestic Automotive Jan. 67-April 67, Group Vice-Pres. U.S. and Canadian Automotive April 67-70, Pres. Chrysler Corpn. 70-75, Chair. and Chief Exec. Officer 75-; served with U.S. Army Quartermaster Corps in World War II; Vice-Pres. and mem. Exec. Cttee. United Foundation of Detroit; mem. Michigan Asscn. of Certified Public Accountants, American Inst. of Certified Public Accountants.
Chrysler Corporation, 341 Massachusetts Avenue, Detroit, Mich. 48231; Home: 2243 Tottenham, Birmingham, Mich., U.S.A.
Telephone: 313-956-2894 (Office).

Ricci, Ruggiero; American violinist; b. 24 July 1918, San Francisco; s. of Pietro Ricci and Emma Bacigalupi; *m.* 1st Ruth Rink 1942, 2nd Valma Rodriguez 1957; two s. three d.; ed. under Louis Persinger, Mischel Piastro, Paul Stassévitch and Georg Kulenkampff.
Debut with Manhattan Symphony Orchestra, New York 29; first tour of Europe 32; served U.S.A.F. 42-45; now makes annual tours of U.S.A. and Europe; has made eight tours of S. America, four tours of Australia, two tours of Japan and three tours of U.S.S.R.; played the first performances of the violin concertos of Ginastera and Von Einem; specializes in violin solo literature; teacher of violin Juillard School of Music, New York.
c/o Herbert Barrett, 1860 Broadway, New York, N.Y. 10023, U.S.A.

Ricciardi, Franc M., M.A.; American business executive; b. 21 Aug. 1923, Glen Ridge, N.J.; s. of late John Ricciardi and Rose (Codella) Ricciardi; *m.* Rosemarie Stivaly 1945; three d.; ed. Rutgers Univ.
United States Army Service 42-44; Asst. Prof. of Finance, Univ. of Vermont 47-51; Assoc. Dir. N.Y. Stock Exchange Inst. 51-53; Vice-Pres. American Management Asscn. 53-58; Vice-Pres. Monroe Int. 58-64; joined Walter Kidde & Co. Inc. 64, Pres. Oct. 66-Feb. 69, Chair. Exec. Cttee. Feb. 69-; Chair. and Pres. Richton Int. Corpn. 69-; Dir. Richton Int. Corpn.
Leisure interests: hunting, gourmet cooking.
1345 Avenue of the Americas, New York, N.Y. 10019, U.S.A.
Telephone: 212-765-6480.

Rice, Oscar Knefler, B.S., PH.D.; American physical chemist; b. 12 Feb. 1903, Chicago, Ill.; s. of Oscar Guido Rice and Thekla Knefler; *m.* Hope Ernestyne

Sherfy 1947; two *d.*; ed. San Diego Junior Coll. and Univ. of Calif. at Berkeley.

National Research Council Fellow, Calif. Inst. of Technology and Univ. of Leipzig 27-30; Instructor in Chem. Harvard Univ. 30-35; Research Assoc. Univ. of Calif. at Berkeley 35-36; Assoc. Prof. of Chem. Univ. of N. Carolina 36-43, Prof. 43-59, Kenan Prof. of Chem. 59-75, Kenan Prof. Emer. 75-; Principal Chemist, Oak Ridge Nat. Laboratory 46-47; Visiting Prof. Virginia Polytechnic Inst. 68, Seydel-Woolley Visiting Prof. of Chem. Georgia Inst. of Technology 69; O. M. Stewart Lecturer Univ. of Missouri 48, Reilly Lecturer, Univ. of Notre Dame 57, Barton Lecturer, Univ. of Oklahoma 67; Distinguished Lecturer, Howard Univ. 71; Welch Lecturer 71; mem. Réunion Int. de Chimie Physique, Paris 28, 12th Solvay Congress in Chem., Brussels 62; on Chem. Panel, Nat. Science Foundation 58-61 and Army Research Office, Durham 67-72; Fellow, American Asscn. for the Advancement of Science, American Physical Soc.; mem. American Chemical Soc. (Sec. and Chair. of Div. of Physical and Inorganic Chem. 41-44), Chem. Soc. (London), Fed. of American Scientists (and on Board of Sponsors), Nat. Acad. of Sciences, etc.; American Chemical Soc. Award in Pure Chem. 32, Southern Chemist Award 61, State of N. Carolina Award in Science 66, Florida Section Award, American Chemical Soc. 67, Peter Debye Award, American Chemical Soc. 70, Charles H. Stone Award, Carolina-Piedmont Section of American Chem. Soc. 72.

Publs. *Electronic Structure and Chemical Binding* 40, *Statistical Mechanics, Thermodynamics and Kinetics* 67; articles in scientific journals.

Department of Chemistry, University of North Carolina, Chapel Hill, N.C. 27514; Home: 311 Clayton Road, Chapel Hill, N.C. 27514, U.S.A.

Telephone: 919-933-1218 (Office); 919-942-1627 (Home).

Rice, Stuart Alan, B.S., A.M., PH.D.; American professor of chemistry; b. 6 Jan. 1932, New York City; *s.* of Laurence Harlan Rice and Helen Rayfield; *m.* Marian Coopersmith 1952; two *d.*; ed. Brooklyn Coll. and Harvard Univ.

Assistant Prof. Dept. of Chem. and Inst. for the Study of Metals, Univ. of Chicago 57-59, Assoc. Prof. Inst. for the Study of Metals (later James Franck Inst.) 59-60, Prof. 60-, Dir. James Franck Inst. 62-68, Prof. Dept. of Chem. and Prof. Cttee. of Mathematical Biology 68-, Chair. Dept. of Chem. 71-; Bourke Lecturer, Faraday Soc. 64; Lecturer, numerous univs. in U.S. and abroad; Alfred P. Sloan Fellow 58-62, Guggenheim Fellow 60-61, Nat. Science Foundation Senior Postdoctoral Fellow and Visiting Prof. Univ. Libre de Bruxelles 65-66; Louis Block Prof. of Chem., Univ. of Chicago 69; Nat. Insts. of Health Special Research Fellow and Visiting Prof. H. C. Orsted Inst., Univ. of Copenhagen 70-71; Fellow, American Acad. of Arts and Sciences; mem. Nat. Acad. of Sciences; A. Cressy Morrison Prize in Natural Sciences, New York Acad. of Sciences 55, American Chemical Soc. Award in Pure Chem. 62, Marlow Medal, Faraday Soc. 63, Llewllyn John and Harriet Manchester Quantrell Award 70, Leo Hendrik Baekeland Award 71, etc.

Leisure interests: reading, carpentry.

Publs. *Polyelectrolyte Solutions* (with Mitsuru Nagasawa) 61, *Statistical Mechanics of Simple Liquids* (with Peter Gray) 65; and 285 papers on chemical physics in scientific journals.

The James Franck Institute, The University of Chicago, 5640 Ellis Avenue, Chicago, Ill. 60637; Home: 5421 Greenwood Avenue, Chicago, Ill. 60615, U.S.A.

Telephone: 753-8214 (Office); 667-2679 (Home).

Rice, Walter Lyman, A.B., LL.B.; American diplomatist; b. 29 July 1903, Peever, S. Dakota; *m.* Inger Vestergaard; one *d.*; ed. Univ. of Minnesota and Harvard Univ.

Law Practice, New York City 28-30; Special Asst. to Attorney-Gen. of U.S. 30-41; Vice-Pres. and Dir., Reynolds Metals Co. 41-68; also served as Gen. Counsel. Reynolds Metals Co. and Pres. and Dir. Reynolds Mining Corpn.; Amb. to Australia 69-73; Consultant Reynolds Int. 73-.

Lock Island, 1000 Lock Island, Richmond, Va. 23229, U.S.A.

Rich, Alexander, M.D.; American molecular biologist; b. 15 Nov. 1924, Hartford, Conn.; *s.* of Max Rich and Bella Shub; *m.* Jane Erving King 1952; two *s.* two *d.*; ed. Harvard Coll. and Medical School.

Served U.S. Navy 43-46; Research Fellow, Gates and Crellin Laboratories, California Inst. of Tech. 49-54; Chief of Section on Physical Chem., Nat. Inst. of Mental Health 54-58; Visiting Scientist, Cavendish Laboratory, Cambridge, U.K. 55-56; Assoc. Prof. of Biophysics, M.I.T. 58-61, Prof. 61-, William Thompson Sedgwick Prof. of Biophysics 74-; mem. Editorial Board *Science* 63-69, *Proceedings of the National Academy of Sciences* 73- and other journals; mem. Council of American Acad. of Arts and Sciences 67-, Chair. Nominating Cttee. 74-; mem. Biology Team of Viking Mars Mission, NASA 69-, Advisory Board of Acad. Forum, Nat. Acad. of Sciences (NAS) 75-, Scientific Advisory Board of Stanford Synchrotron Radiation Project 76-, and other cttees.; mem. American Chemical Soc. and other socs., NAS 70-; Fellow, Nat. Research Council 49-51, American Acad. of Arts and Sciences 59, Guggenheim Foundation 63, A.A.A.S. 65; Skylab Achievement Award, NASA 74.

Leisure interests: ocean sailing in small boats, growing tomato plants, collecting fossils.

Publs. *Structural Chemistry and Molecular Biology* 68; over 200 publs. in the field of molecular structure of nucleic acid components, nucleic acids and polynucleotides, physical chem. of nucleotides and polynucleotides, molecular structure of proteins, mechanism of protein synthesis, molecular biology of the nucleic acids, X-ray crystallography, origin of life.

Department of Biology, Massachusetts Institute of Technology, Cambridge, Mass. 02139; Home: 2 Walnut Avenue, Cambridge, Mass. 02140, U.S.A.

Telephone: (617) 253-4715 (Office); (617) 547-1637 (Home).

Richard, Cliff; British singer and actor; b. (as Harry Roger Webb) 14 Oct. 1940, India; *s.* of Roger and Dorothy Webb; ed. Riversmead School, Cheshunt.

First successful record *Move It* 58; plays guitar; own television series on BBC and ITV; various repertory and variety seasons; Top Box Office Star of Great Britain 62-63, 63-64; awarded Gold Discs (for sales over a million each) for *Living Doll, The Young Ones, Bachelor Boy, Lucky Lips, Congratulations, Power to All Our Friends*; also 24 Silver Discs (for sales over 250,000); films: *Serious Charge* 59, *Expresso Bongo* 60, *The Young Ones* 61, *Summer Holiday* 62, *Wonderful Life* 64, *Finders Keepers* 66, *Two A Penny* 68, *His Land, Take Me High* 73.

Leisure interests: swimming, badminton.

c/o Peter Gormley, 16 Harley House, Marylebone Road, London, NW1 4PZ, England.

Richard, Ivor Seward, M.A., Q.C.; British politician and diplomatist; b. 30 May 1932, Cardiff; *s.* of Seward Thomas and Isabella Irene Richard; *m.* Alison Mary Imrie 1962; two *s.* one *d.*; ed. Cheltenham Coll., Pembroke Coll., Oxford.

Called to the Bar 55; mem. Parl. for Barons Court 64-74; Parl. Private Sec. to Sec. of State for Defence 66-69; Under-Sec. of State for Defence for Army 69-70; Queen's Counsel 71; Perm. Rep. to UN 74-; Labour.

Leisure interests: playing piano, watching football, talking.

Publs. *Europe or the Open Sea* 71, and articles in various political journals.

Permanent Mission of United Kingdom to United Nations, 845 Third Avenue, 10th Floor, New York, N.Y. 10022, U.S.A.; Home: 47 Burntwood Grange Road, London, S.W.18, England.

Telephone: 01-870-1473 (Home).

Richard, Paul Alfred Louis; French business executive; b. 4 March 1909, Bourboule.

President Société Hotchkiss-Brandt, Société des Coffres-forts Bauche; Joint Man. Hotchkiss-Brandt-Manhurin; Admin. J. E. Johnson et Cie., SOFINEX (Société Financière pour l'expansion des entreprises), Société Brinks, France.

173 boulevard Haussmann, 75008 Paris; Home: 40 avenue Foch, 75116 Paris, France.

Richards, Arthur L.; American diplomatist (retd.); b. 21 June 1907, Emmett, Idaho; s. of Arthur A. and Sedenia (Dunford) Richards; m. Ida Elizabeth Parker; two s. one d.; ed. Pasadena Jr. Coll., George Washington Univ. and Nat. War Coll.

Joined Foreign Service 30, Mexico, Washington, Teheran, Jerusalem, Cairo, Cape Town, Pretoria, Washington, Teheran 30-52; Dir. Office of Greek, Turkish and Iranian Affairs, Dept. of State 52-54; Consul-Gen. Istanbul 54-56; Operations Co-ordinator, Dept. of State 56-58; Special Asst. to Under-Sec. of State for Law of Sea 58-60; Amb. to Ethiopia 60-62; Deputy Rep. of U.S. to 18-Nation Disarmament Cttee., Geneva 63-65; Dir. Washington Int. Centre 68-73; retd. 73.

4902 Rockmere Court, Washington, D.C. 20016, U.S.A.

Richards, Audrey Isabel, C.B.E., M.A., PH.D., F.B.A.; British anthropologist; b. 8 July 1899; d. of H. Erle Richards, Kt., and Isabel Butler; ed. Cambridge and London Univs.

Field research Bemba tribe, N.E. Rhodesia 30-34; Lecturer in Social Anthropology, London School of Economics 35-38, Senior Lecturer, Univ. of the Witwatersrand, Johannesburg 37-40; Principal, Colonial Office 41-45; Reader in Social Anthropology, London Univ. 46-50; Dir. East African Inst. of Social Research, Makerere Coll., Uganda 50-56; Smuts Reader in Anthropology, Univ. of Cambridge 61-66; Pres. Royal Anthropological Inst. 59-61; Dir. Anglia Television Co. 59-63; Pres. African Studies Asscn. 63-66; Fellow Newnham Coll. 56, now Hon. Fellow; Rivers Memorial Medal, Wellcome Medal.

Publs. *Hunger and Work in a Savage Tribe* 33, *Land, Labour and Diet in N. Rhodesia* 39, *Chisungu, a study of girls' initiation ceremonies in N. Rhodesia* 56, *The Changing Structure of a Ganda Village* 66, *The Multicultural States of East Africa* 69, *Subsistence to Commercial Farming in Buganda* 73, *Some Elmdon Families* (with Jean Robin) 75; Editor: *Economic Development and Tribal Change* 54, *East African Chiefs* 60.

Crawley House, Elmdon, Saffron Walden, Essex, England.

Telephone: Chrishall 362.

Richards, Sir Edward Trenton, Kt., C.B.E., J.P., M.P.; Bermudan politician; b. 4 Oct. 1908, Berbice, British Guiana; s. of George A. Richards and Millicent (née Williams); m. Madree E. Williams; one s. two d.; ed. Collegiate School and Queen's Coll., British Guiana.

Former teacher at Berkeley Inst., Bermuda; called to the Bar, Middle Temple, London 46; mem. Bermudan House of Assembly 48-; fmr. Chair. Public Transportation Board, Transport Control Board, Joint Parl. Cttee. investigating Racial Discrimination in Hotels and Restaurants, Berkeley Educ. Soc. 56-72; mem. Board of Health, Board of Social Welfare and numerous other

boards and cttees.; Minister for Immigration and Labour and Deputy Govt. Leader 68-71, Premier 71-75; Bermudan rep. at Commonwealth Parl. Asscn. Conf., Lagos 62, Kuala Lumpur 71; Head dels. to ILO confs., Geneva 69, 70, 71; Hon. LL.D. (Wilberforce Univ., U.S.A.) 60.

Leisure interests: sport, reading, music.

"Wilton", Keith Hall Road, Warwick East, Bermuda.

Telephone: 2-3645.

Richards, Frederic Middlebrook, PH.D.; American biochemist; b. 19 Aug. 1925, New York; s. of George and Marianna Richards; m. Sarah Wheatland 1959; one s. two d.; ed. Mass. Inst. of Technology and Harvard Univ.

Research Fellow, Physical Chem., Harvard Univ. 52-53; Nat. Research Council Fellow, Carlsberg Lab., Denmark 54; Nat. Science Foundation Fellow, Cambridge Univ., U.K. 55; Asst. Prof. of Biochemistry, Yale Univ. 55-59, Assoc. Prof. 59-62, Prof. 63, Chair. Dept. of Molecular Biology and Biophysics 63-67, Dept. of Molecular Biophysics and Biochemistry 69-73; mem. Nat. Acad. of Sciences, American Acad. of Arts and Sciences, American Chair. Soc., American Soc. of Biological Chemistry, Biophysical Soc. (Pres. 72-73), American Crystallographic Asscn.; Guggenheim Fellow 67-68; Pfizer-Paul Lewis Award 65.

Leisure interests: sailing, skiing.

Publs. various articles in scientific journals in the general field of protein and enzyme chemistry.

Department of Molecular Biophysics and Biochemistry, Yale University, P.O. Box 1937 Yale Station, New Haven, Conn. 06520; Home: 69 Andrews Road, Guildford, Conn. 06437, U.S.A.

Telephone: 203-436-2032 (Office); 203-453-3361 (Home).

Richards, Ivor Armstrong, C.H., M.A., LITT.D., F.B.A.; British literary critic; b. 26 Feb. 1893; m. Dorothy Pilley 1926; ed. Clifton and Magdalene Coll., Cambridge. Lecturer in English and Moral Sciences 22, Fellow, Magdalene Coll. 26; Visiting Prof., Tsing Hua Univ., Peking 29-30, Harvard 31; mem. Cttee., King's Medal for Poetry 33; Dir. Orthological Inst. (Basic English), China 36-38; Univ. Lecturer, Harvard 39-44, Prof. 44-63, Emer. 63; Loines Award for Poetry 62; Emerson-Thoreau Medal 70; Hon. Litt.D. (Harvard); Hon. Fellow, Magdalene Coll, Cambridge 64.

Publs. *Foundations of Aesthetics* (with C. K. Ogden and James Wood) 21, *The Meaning of Meaning* (with C. K. Ogden) 23, *Principles of Literary Criticism* 24, *Science and Poetry* 25, *Practical Criticism* 29, *Mencius on the Mind* 31, *Basic Rules of Reason* 33, *Coleridge on Imagination* 34, *Interpretation in Teaching* 38, *How to Read a Page* 42, *Basic English and its Uses* 43, *Nations and Peace* 47, *The Portable Coleridge* 50, *The Wrath of Achilles* 50, *Speculative Instruments* 55, *Goodbye Earth and other Poems* 58, *The Screens and other Poems* 60, *Tomorrow Morning, Faustus!* 62, *Why so, Socrates?* 63, abridged version *Plato's Republic* 65, *So Much Nearer* (essays) 68; *Design for Escape, World Education thru' Modern Media* 68, *Poetries and Sciences* 70, *Internal Colloquies: Collected Poems to 1970* 72, *Beyond* 73, *Poetries: Their Media and Ends* 74.

Leisure interest: Alpine Club.

Magdalene College, Cambridge; Wentworth House, 2 Chesterton Road, Cambridge, England.

Telephone: 57445 (Home).

Richardson, Burton Taylor, M.A.; Canadian journalist; b. 29 Jan. 1906, Selkirk, Manitoba; s. of Rev. Frank Richardson; m. Wanda Davidson 1931; ed. Manitoba, Syracuse (U.S.A.), and London School of Economics. Staff writer of *Winnipeg Free Press*; correspondent in Ottawa 40-44, in Washington, D.C. 45, in London, England 46; Editor of Saskatoon *Star-Phoenix* 46-48, *Winnipeg Citizen* 48; Assoc. Editor *Ottawa Citizen* 49-51; Sec. to Royal Comm. on S. Saskatchewan River 51-53;

Editor *The Telegram* (Toronto) 53-62, Special Corresp. in Washington D.C. 62-63; Special Asst. to Prime Minister Diefenbaker (later Leader of Opposition) 63-65; Consultant, Ontario Econ. Council 66-; Consulting Assoc. P. S. Ross and Partners 67-75; Hon. mem. Canadian Inst. of Int. Affairs; Fellow, Royal Canadian Geographical Soc.; Chair. Stephen Leacock Centennial Cttee. 69; Nat. Cttee. for Homage to A. Y. Jackson 72.
Leisure interests: painting, golf, travel.
Publ. *Canada and Mr. Diefenbaker* 62.
Apt. 705, 581 Avenue Road, Toronto, Canada.
Telephone: 416-481-8959.

Richardson, Sir Egerton Rudolf, Kt., C.M.G.; Jamaican government official and diplomatist; b. 15 Aug. 1912, St. Catherine; s. of James Neil and Doris Richardson (née Burton); m. 1947 (wife deceased 1966); one s. one d.; ed. Calabar High School, Kingston, Balliol Coll., Oxford.
Jamaican civil service 33-, Asst. Treas. 44, Asst. Colonial Sec. 47, Perm. Sec. Ministry of Agriculture 52-53, Under-Sec. Ministry of Finance 53-56, Financial Sec. of Jamaica 56-62; Perm. Rep. of Jamaica to the UN 62-67; Amb. to U.S.A. 67-72, and Mexico 67-72; Amb. to OAS 69-72; Perm. Sec. Ministry of Public Works 73-75; Govt. Adviser on Int. Affairs 75-.
Leisure interest: astronomy.
P.O. Box 244, Kingston 6, Jamaica.
Telephone: 92-42877

Richardson, Elliot Lee, A.B., LL.B.; American lawyer and government official; b. 20 July 1920, Boston, Mass.; s. of Dr. Edward P. Richardson and Clara Shattuck Richardson; m. Anne Francis Hazard 1952; two s. one d.; ed. Harvard Coll. and Harvard Law School.
Law Clerk, Supreme Court Justice Felix Frankfurter 48-49; Asst. Sec. (Legislation), U.S. Dept. of Health, Educ. and Welfare 57-59, Acting Sec. April-July 58; U.S. Attorney for Mass. 59-61; Special Asst. to U.S. Attorney-Gen. 61; Lieut.-Gov. of Mass. 65-67; Attorney-Gen. of Mass. 67-69; U.S. Under-Sec. of State 69-70; Sec. of Health, Educ. and Welfare 70-72, of Defense 72-73; Attorney-Gen. of U.S.A. May-Oct. 73; Dir. Study of Operations of State and Local Govt., Woodrow Wilson Int. Center 74; Amb. to U.K. 75-76; Sec. of Commerce 76-; mem. Board of Overseers Harvard Coll. 66-68; hon. degrees from Springfield Coll., Mass. Coll. of Optometry, Emerson Coll. and Univ. of New Hampshire; Hon. Bencher, Middle Temple 75.
Department of Commerce, 14th Street between Constitution and East Street, Washington, D.C. 20230, U.S.A.

Richardson, George Taylor, B.COMM., LL.D.; Canadian business executive; b. 22 Sept. 1924, Winnipeg, Manitoba; s. of late James A. and late Muriel (née Sprague) Richardson; m. Tannis Maree Thorlakson 1948; two s. two d.; ed. Grosvenor and Ravenscourt Schools, Winnipeg, and Univ. of Manitoba.
Joined family firm of James Richardson and Sons, Ltd., Winnipeg 46, Vice-Pres. 54, Pres. 66-; Senior Partner, Richardson Securities of Canada 47-; Chair. Pioneer Grain Co. Ltd., and other subsidiaries of James Richardson and Sons, Ltd.; Gov. Hudson's Bay Company 70-; Vice-Pres. and mem. Exec. Cttee., Canadian Imperial Bank of Commerce; Dir. The International Nickel Co. of Canada Ltd., Hudson's Bay Oil & Gas Co. Ltd.; mem. Toronto Stock Exchange, Midwest Stock Exchange, Winnipeg Commodity Exchange, Chicago Board of Trade and other major N. American commodity exchanges; Hon. LL.D. (Manitoba).
Leisure interests: hunting and helicopter flying.
James Richardson and Sons, Ltd., Richardson Building, 1 Lombard Place, Winnipeg, Manitoba, R3B 0Y1; Home: Briarmeade, Lot 197, St. Mary's Road, St. Germain, Manitoba, R0G 2A0, Canada.
Telephone: 988-5811 (Office); 253-4221 (Home).

Richardson, Gordon Dalyell, O.B.E., M.A., F.L.A.A.; Australian librarian (retd.); b. 23 Nov. 1917, Raymond Terrace, N.S.W.; s. of L. E. D. and Wilga (née Dale) Richardson; m. 1st Yvonne L. Spence 1940 (died 1965), 2nd Ruth Robertson 1966; one s. two d.; ed. Sydney Univ.
Assistant, Public Library, New South Wales 34-40; Infantry Officer, Australian Imperial Force 40-45; Deputy Principal Librarian, N.S.W. 54-56; Acting Principal Librarian 56-57; Mitchell Librarian 58-73; Principal Librarian and Sec. Library of N.S.W. 59-73; Exec. mem. Library Board of N.S.W. 59-73; Principal Archivist, N.S.W. 61-73; Vice-Pres. Library Assscn. of Australia 64-66, Pres. 67-68; Chair. Standing Cttee. Australian Advisory Council on Bibliographical Services 70-72.
Leisure interests: gardening, motoring.
Woondooma, Moorilda via Newbridge, N.S.W. 2741, Australia.
Telephone: Newbridge 19U.

Richardson, Rt. Hon. Gordon William Humphreys, P.C., M.B.E., B.A., LL.B.; British banker; b. 25 Nov. 1915, London; s. of John Robert and Nellie Richardson (née Humphreys); m. Margaret Alison Sheppard 1941; one s. one d.; ed. Nottingham High School, and Gonville and Caius Coll., Cambridge.
South Notts. Hussars Yeomanry 39, Staff Coll., Camberley 41; Called to the Bar, Gray's Inn 47; mem. Bar Council 51-55; Industrial and Commercial Finance Corpn. Ltd. 49-57; Dir. J. Henry Schroder and Co. 57-62; Chair. J. Henry Schroder Wagg and Co. Ltd. 62-72; Chair. Schroders Ltd. 65-73, J. Henry Schroder Banking Corpn. (U.S.A.) 67-69, Schroders AG (Switzerland) 67, Schroders Inc. (U.S.A.) 69-73; Dir. Bank of England 67-73, Gov. July 73-; Dir. Rolls-Royce (1971) Ltd. 71-73, ICI 72-73; Vice-Chair. Legal and Gen. Assurance Soc. Ltd. 59-70, Lloyds Bank Ltd. 62-66; mem. Company Law Amendment Cttee. 59-62; Chair. Cttee. on Turnover Taxation 63-64; mem. Court, London Univ. 62-65; mem. Nat. Econ. Devt. Council 71-73; Chair. Industrial Devt. Advisory Board 72-73; Hon. Master of Bench of Gray's Inn 73-; H.M. Lieut. for City of London 74-; Hon. D.Sc. (The City Univ.) 75.
Leisure interests: reading, walking.
Bank of England, London, EC2R 8AH, England.
Telephone: 01-601-4444 (Office).

Richardson, Hon. James Armstrong, P.C., M.P.; Canadian politician; b. 28 March 1922, Winnipeg; s. of James A. Richardson and Muriel Sprague; m. Shirley A. Rooper 1949; two s. three d.; ed. Queen's Univ., Kingston, Ont.
Joined James Richardson and Sons, Ltd., Winnipeg 45, Chair. and Chief Exec. until 68; mem. Parl. 68-; Minister without Portfolio July 68-May 69; Minister of Supply and Services May 69-Nov. 72; Minister of Nat. Defence Nov. 72-.
House of Commons, Ottawa, Ont.; Inn of the Provinces, Ottawa, Ont.; 5209 Roblin Boulevard, Winnipeg, Manitoba, Canada.
Telephone: 832-5433 (Winnipeg).

Richardson, Sir John Samuel, Bt., M.V.O., M.D., F.R.C.P., F.R.C.P.(EDIN.); British consultant physician; b. 16 June 1910, Sheffield; s. of Major John Watson Richardson and Elizabeth Blakeney; m. Sybil Trist 1933; two d.; ed. Charterhouse, Trinity Coll., Cambridge and St. Thomas's Hospital Medical School.
Various appointments at St. Thomas's Hospital and Royal Postgraduate Medical School; with Royal Army Medical Corps (R.A.M.C.) during Second World War; Deputy Dir. to Medical Unit, St. Thomas's Hospital; Clinical Asst. Brompton Hospital, and Endocrine Dept. of Guy's Hospital, London; Physician, Wembley and Yateley Hospitals; now Physician at St. Thomas's Hospital, Watford Gen. Hospital; Consultant Physician

to Metropolitan Police 57-, London Transport Board 64-; Chair. Gen. Medical Council 73-; Chair. Council for Postgraduate Medical Educ. in England and Wales 72-; mem. Council Royal Coll. of Physicians; fmr. Pres. Royal Soc. of Medicine, Int. Soc. for Internal Medicine, British Medical Asscn.; Past Master, Worshipful Soc. of Apothecaries of London; Hadden Prize and Bristowe Medal St., Thomas's Hospital 36, Perkins Fellowship 39-40; Hon. Bencher, Gray's Inn 74.
Leisure interest: gardening.
Publs. *The Practice of Medicine* (2nd edn.) 60, *Connective Tissue Disorders* 63, *Anticoagulant Prophylaxis and Treatment* (jointly) 65.
Alvechurch, I Hillcrest Road, London, W.5; Windcutter, Lee, North Devon, England.
Telephone: 01-997-6988 (London).

Richardson, Sir Ralph David, Kt., D.LITT. (OXON.); British actor; b. 19 Dec. 1902, Cheltenham; s. of Arthur Richardson and Lydia Russell; *m.* 1st Muriel Hewitt 1924 (died 1942), 2nd Meriel Forbes-Robertson 1944; one s.; ed. Xavierian Coll., Brighton.
First appeared on stage Brighton 21; acted in *Eden End* and *Cornelius* London 35; *Romeo and Juliet* U.S.A. 35-36; *Promise, Bees on the Boat Deck* and *The Amazing Dr. Clitterhouse* London 36-37; *Johnson over Jordan* London 38; *A Midsummer Night's Dream* and *Othello* Old Vic 38; served in Fleet Air Arm 39-44; acted at Old Vic Seasons 44-45, 45-46, 46-47 (also producing *Richard II*); toured France, Belgium and Germany with Old Vic 45, and appeared with the Company in N.Y. 46; acted and produced *Royal Circle* Wyndham's Theatre, London 48; acted in *The Heiress* Haymarket Theatre 49, *Home at Seven* Wyndham's Theatre 50, *The Three Sisters* Aldwych Theatre 51; Stratford Memorial Theatre season 52; *The White Carnation* Globe Theatre 53, *A Day by The Sea* 54; tour of Australia and New Zealand 56; *Timon of Athens* Old Vic, *Waltz of the Toreadors* New York 57; *Flowering Cherry* Haymarket Theatre 58; *The Complaisant Lover* Globe Theatre 59; *The Last Joke* 60; *School for Scandal* Haymarket Theatre 62, Broadway 63; *Six Characters in Search of an Author* Mayfair Theatre, London 63; South American tour 64; *Carving a Statue* 64, *You Never Can Tell* 66, *The Rivals* Haymarket Theatre 67, *The Merchant of Venice* Haymarket Theatre 67, *What the Butler Saw* 69, *Home* (London) 70, *Home* (New York) 70, *West of Suez* (London) 71, *Lloyd George Knew My Father* 72, *John Gabriel Borkman* 75, *No Man's Land* 75; first appeared in films in *The Ghoul* 33; since then films include: *Things to Come, The Man Who Could Work Miracles, Bulldog Drummond, South Riding, Divorce of Lady X, The Citadel, Four Feathers, Q Planes, Night of the Fire, The Silver Fleet* 42, *The Volunteer* 43, *School for Secrets* 47, *Anna Karenina* 47, *The Fallen Idol* 48, *The Heiress* (Hollywood) 48, *Outcast of the Islands* and *Home at Seven* 51, *The Sound Barrier* 52, *The Holly and the Ivy* 52, *Richard III* 55, *Smiley* 56, *The Passionate Stranger* 57, *Our Man in Havana* 59, *Exodus* 60, *Lion of Sparta* 60, *Long Day's Journey into Night* 62, *Woman of Straw* 63, *Dr. Zhivago* 65, *Khartoum* 66, *The Wrong Box* 66, *Battle of Britain* 68, *Oh! What a Lovely War* 68, *Bed Sitting Room* 68, *Midas Run* 68, *Looking Glass War* 68, *David Copperfield* 69, *Eagle in a Cage* 70, *Gingerbread House* 71, *Tales from the Crypt* 71, *Lady Caroline Lamb* 72, *A Doll's House* 73, *O Lucky Man* 73, *Whoever Slew Auntie Roo* 74, *Rollerball* 75.
Leisure interests: drawing, squash rackets, tennis.
I Chester Terrace, Regent's Park, London, N.W.1, England.

Richardson, Tony; British stage and film producer; b. 5 June 1928, Shipley, Yorks.; *m.* Vanessa Redgrave (divorced 1967); two d.; ed. Wadham Coll., Oxford.
Artistic Dir. Royal Court Theatre 56-; Dir. Woodfall Film Productions Ltd. 58-.

Plays produced or directed include: *Look Back In Anger, The Chairs, Pericles* and *Othello* (Stratford), *The Entertainer, Luther, The Seagull, St. Joan of the Stockyards, Hamlet, Threepenny Opera, I Claudius.*
Films (produced or directed): *Look Back In Anger* 58, *The Entertainer* 59, *Saturday Night and Sunday Morning* 60, *A Taste of Honey* 61, *The Loneliness of the Long Distance Runner* 62, *Tom Jones* 63, *The Loved One* 64, *Mademoiselle* 65, *The Sailor from Gibraltar* 65, *Red and Blue* 66, *The Charge of the Light Brigade* 67, *Laughter in the Dark* 68, *Hamlet* 69, *Ned Kelly* 69, *A Delicate Balance* 73, *Dead Cert* 73.
1478 North Kings Road, Los Angeles, Calif. 90069, U.S.A.

Richebächer, Kurt Alfred, DR.RER.POL.; German banker; b. 23 Sept. 1918, Karlsruhe; *m.* Anna-Maria Bienen 1949; two s. one d.; ed. High School and Univ. Correspondent *The Economist*, weekly 46-59; Dir. of Research, Berliner Bank 59-61; Dir. German Private Banking Asscn. 61-64; Exec. Man. Dresdner Bank AG 64-.
Leisure interests: literature, history.
Publ. *Börse und Kapitalmarkt.*
Dresdner Bank AG, 6 Frankfurt am Main, Gallusanlage 7-8; Home: 624 Königstein/Ts., Ölmühlweg 5d, Federal Republic of Germany.
Telephone: 263-332 (Office); 06174-4508 (Home).

Riches, Edward John, M.A.; New Zealand international civil servant (retd.); b. 30 July 1905, Timaru; s. of Edward and Sarah Riches (née Campbell); *m.* Phillis Barr Montgomery 1930; two d.; ed. Univ. of New Zealand and Univ. of Michigan.
Joined Research Div. of Int. Labour Office, Geneva 27, Asst. Econ. Adviser 41, Acting Chief, Econ. and Statistical Section 41-46, Econ. Adviser 46-60, Treas. and Financial Comptroller (Asst. Dir.-Gen.) 61-70, Special Adviser in charge of planning and construction of new headquarters 71-75.
22 avenue Krieg, 1208 Geneva, Switzerland.
Telephone: 47-86-69 (Home).

Riches, Sir Eric William, Kt., M.C., M.S., F.R.C.S.; British consulting surgeon and urologist; b. 29 July 1897, Alford, Lincs.; s. of William Riches; *m.* 1st Anne Brand 1927 (died 1952), two d.; *m.* 2nd Susan Elizabeth Ann Kitton 1954, one d.; ed. Christ's Hosp. and Middlesex Hosp. (Univ. of London).
Served World War I, Capt. and Adjutant; Emer. Surgeon and Urologist, Middlesex Hosp.; fmr. Vice-Pres. Royal Coll. of Surgeons, mem. Court of Examiners 40-46; fmr. Pres. Medical Soc. of London; fmr. Treas. *British Journal of Surgery* and Chair. Editorial Cttee. *British Journal of Urology*; Treas. Christ's Hosp., Chair. Council of Almoners 70-; Hon. Fellow, Royal Soc. of Medicine 66; mem. Int. Soc. of Surgery, Int. Soc. of Urology (Pres. 64), British Asscn: of Urological Surgeons (fmr. Pres.), Asscn. Française d'Urologie, Biological and Medical Cttee. of Royal Comm. on Population; Hon. mem. Urological Socs. of Australasia, Canada, Sweden, U.S.A., American Asscn. of Genito-Urinary Surgeons; Hon. Assoc. mem. French Acad. of Surgery 61; Hon. Librarian, Royal Soc. of Medicine.
Leisure interests: golf, music, photography.
Publs. *Modern Trends in Urology*, Series 1 53, Series 2 60, Series 3 70, *Tumours of the Kidney and Ureter* 64; contributions in *Textbook of Urology, British Surgical Practice*; articles in journals.
22 Weymouth Street, London, W1N 3FA, England.
Telephone: 01-580-4800.

Richler, Mordecai; Canadian writer; b. 1931, Montreal; s. of Moses Isaac Richler and Lily Rosenberg; *m.* Florence Wood 1960; three s. two d.; ed. Montreal Hebrew Acad., Baron Byng High School and Sir George Williams Univ.

Canada Council Junior Arts Fellowship 59, 60; Fellowship in Creative Writing, Guggenheim Foundation, New York 61, Canada Council, Senior Arts Fellowship 67, Paris Review Humour Prize 68, Writer-in-residence, Sir George Williams Univ. 68-69; Visiting Prof. Carleton Univ., Ottawa 72-74; Canadian Gov.-Gen.'s Award for Fiction 69, 72, Golden Bear, Berlin Film Festival 74.
Leisure interest: poker.
Publs. (novels) *The Acrobats* 54, *Son of a Smaller Hero* 55, *A Choice of Enemies* 57, *The Apprenticeship of Duddy Kravitz* 59, *The Incomparable Atuk* 63, *Cocksure* 68, *St. Urbain's Horseman* 71; (stories) *The Street* 72; (film scripts) *No Love for Johnnie*, *Life at the Top*, *The Apprenticeship of Duddy Kravitz*, etc.; (TV plays) *The Trouble with Benny*, etc.; (essays) *Hunting Tigers under Glass* 69, *Shovelling Trouble* 73; *Canadian Writing Today* (editor) 70; (for children) *Jacob Two-Two Meets the Hooded Fang* 75.
218 Edgehill Road, Westmount, Quebec, Canada.
Telephone: 514-488-4774.

Richmond, Sir John Christopher Blake, K.C.M.G.; British diplomatist; b. 7 Sept. 1909, Hitcham; *s.* of Ernest Tatham and Margaret Muriel Richmond (née Lubbock); *m.* Diana Margaret Lyle Galbraith 1939; two *s.* three *d.*; ed. Lancing Coll., Hertford Coll., Oxford, and Univ. Coll., London.
On archaeological expeditions, Beisan, Jericho, Tel El Duweir, Ithaca 31-36; H.M. Office of Works 37-39; served in Middle East in Second World War 39-46; Dept. of Antiquities, Palestine Govt. 46-47; British Foreign Service, Oriental Sec., Baghdad 47-51; Foreign Office 51-53; Counsellor, Amman 53-55; Consul-Gen. Houston, Texas 55-58; British Property Comm., Cairo 59; Political Agent, Kuwait Oct. 59-61; Amb. to Kuwait 61-63; Supernumerary Fellow, St. Antony's Coll., Oxford 63-64; Amb. to Sudan 65-66; Lecturer in Modern Near East History, Durham Univ. 66-74, retd.
Leisure interest: carpentry and joinery.
20 The Avenue, Durham, England.

Richter, Curt Paul, B.S., PH.D.; American psychologist; b. 20 Feb. 1894, Denver, Colo.; *s.* of Paul Ernst Richter and Martha Dressler; *m.* Leslie Prince Bidwell 1936; two *s.* three *d.*; ed. Denver, Dresden, Harvard and Johns Hopkins Univs.
Director, Psychobiology Laboratory, Phipps Psychiatric Clinic, Johns Hopkins Univ. 23-; Prof. Emer., Psychobiology, Johns Hopkins Medical School 57-; Harvey Lecturer 42-43; mem. Nat. Acad. of Sciences, American Philosophical Soc., American Acad. of Arts and Sciences, Halsted Soc., Century Asscn.; Hon. mem. American Neurological Asscn.; Hon. D.Sc. (Univ. of Chicago) 68; Hon. LL.D. (Johns Hopkins Univ.) 70; Distinguished Citizen of Denver; Warren Soc. Medal; American Psychopathological Soc. Medal.
Leisure interests: tennis, squash, skiing, archaeology.
Publs. *Animal Behavior and Internal Drives* 27, *Harvey Lecture* 42-43, *Rats, Man, and the Welfare State* 59, *Biological Clocks in Medicine and Psychiatry* 65.
Johns Hopkins Hospital, 601 North Broadway, Baltimore, Md. 21205; Home: 14 Meadow Road, Baltimore, Md. 21212, U.S.A.
Telephone: 955-3128 (Office); Dr. 7-9894 (Home).

Richter, Hans Werner; German writer; b. 12 Nov. 1908.
Prisoner-of-war in U.S.A., Second World War; freelance writer 46-; Founder, founder mem. Group 47.
Publs. *Die Geschlagenen* 49, *Sie fielen aus Gottes Hand* 51, *Spuren im Sand* 53, *Du sollst nicht töten* 55, *Linus oder Der Verlust der Würde* 58, *Almanach der Gruppe 47 1947-1962* 62, *Bestandsaufnahme—Eine deutsche Bilanz* 62, *Walther Rathenau—Reden und Schriften* 64, *Plaedoyer für eine neue Regierung oder Keine Alternative* 65, *Menschen in freundlicher Umgebung* 65, *Doda* 66, *Blinder Alarm* 70, *Rose weiss, Rose rot* 71.

München-Pasing, 7 Rembrandtstrasse, Federal Republic of Germany.
Telephone: Munich 880486.

Richter, Hermann, DR. RER. POL.; German business executive; b. 29 Jan. 1903; ed. Freiburg, Bonn and Cologne Univs.
Chairman, Dresdner Bank A.G. 72-, Gold-u. Silberscheideanstalt (Degussa), Frankfurt/M., Brown Boveri & Cie. AG, Mannheim, Metallgesellschaft AG, Frankfurt/M., Kempinski Hotelbetrieb AG, Berlin, Kienzle apparate Bag GmbH, Villingen; Vice-Chair. Farbwerke Hoechst AG, Frankfurt/M., Audi-NSU Auto-union AG, Neckarsulm; mem. Advisory Board Volkswagenwerk AG, Wolfsburg, Hapag-Lloyd AG, Hamburg-Bremen, Henkel and Cie. GmbH; Pres. Aktionsgemeinschaft, apparate Bag G.m.b.H., Villingen; Vice-Chair. Farbwerke Hoechst AG, Frankfurt/M., Audi-NSU Auto-union AG, Neckarsulm; mem. Advisory Board Volkswagenwerk AG, Wolfsburg, Hapag-Lloyd AG, Hamburg-Bremen; Pres. Aktionsgemeinschaft, Deutsches Steinkohlenrevier G.m.b.H., Düsseldorf.
Fahneburgstrasse 21, Düsseldorf, Federal Republic of Germany.
Telephone: 62-63-37.

Richter, Karl; German conductor, organist and harpsichordist; b. 1926, Plauen, Saxony; ed. Kreuz-Gymnasium, Dresden and Leipzig Conservatory (under Karl Straube and Günther Ramin).
Organist, Thomaskirche, Leipzig 49-51; joined faculty of the Musikhochschule, Munich 51; organist, Markuskirche, Munich and Dir. *Munich Bach Choir* 53; founded *Munich Bach Orchestra* 53; now frequently tours Europe, North and South America with the choir and orchestra; has recorded many of Bach's works including *St. Matthew* and *St. John Passions*, *Mass in B Minor*, *Magnificat* and numerous cantatas and orchestral works.
c/o Rudolf Vedder Konzertdirektion, Mauerkirchenstrasse 8, 8 Munich 80, Federal Republic of Germany.

Richter, Svyatoslav Theofilovich; Soviet pianist; b. 20 March 1915, Zhitomir, Ukraine; ed. Moscow State Conservatoire.
Won First Prize at the Third U.S.S.R. Competition of Executant Musicians 45; extensive tours all over the world; State and Lenin prizewinner; People's Artist of the U.S.S.R.; Order of Lenin, Hero of Socialist Labour 75, etc.
Repertoire includes works by Bach (cycle of 48 Preludes and Fugues), Beethoven, Schubert, Rachmaninov, Scriabin, Prokofiev, Ravel, Debussy, Mozart, Schumann, Rubinstein, Myaskovsky, Shostakovich, etc.
c/o Victor Hochhauser Ltd., 4 Holland Park Avenue, London, W.11, England; Moscow State Philharmonic Society, 31 Ulitsa Gorkogo, Moscow, U.S.S.R.

Rick, Charles Madeira, Jr., PH.D.; American professor and geneticist; b. 30 April 1915, Reading, Pa.; *s.* of Charles M. Rick and Miriam C. (Yeager) Rick; *m.* Martha Elizabeth Overholts 1938; one *s.* one *d.*; ed. Pennsylvania State and Harvard Univs.
Assistant Plant Breeder, W. Atlee Burpee Co., Lompoc, Calif. 37-40; Instructor and Asst. Geneticist, Univ. of Calif. at Davis 40, other Academic ranks, then Prof. and Geneticist 55-; mem. Genetics Study Section of Nat. Insts. of Health 58-62; Co-ordinator Tomato Genetics Co-operative 50-; Visiting Lecturer, N. Carolina State Univ. 56, Univ. de São Paulo, Brazil 65, Faculty Research Lecturer, Univ. of Calif. 61, Carnegie Visiting Prof., Univ. of Hawaii 63; Visiting Scientist, Univ. of Puerto Rico 68; Guggenheim Fellow 48, 50; mem. Panel in Genetic Biology, Nat. Science Foundation 71-72; Centennial Lecturer Ontario Agricultural Coll., Univ. of Guelph 74; mem. Nat. Acad. of Sciences; Vaughan Research Award of American Soc. for Horticultural Science 46, Campbell Award of A.A.A.S.

59, M. A. Blake Award, American Soc. Horticultural Science 74.
Leisure interests: gardening, photography.
Publs. 96 papers in research journals; and 106 research notes in *Reports* of Tomato Genetics Co-operative.
Department of Vegetable Crops, University of California, Davis, Calif. 95616; 8 Parkside Drive, Davis, Calif. 95616, U.S.A.
Telephone: 916-752-1737 (Office); 916-756-1387 (Home).

Rickett, Sir Denis Hubert Fletcher, K.C.M.G., C.B.; former British civil servant and banker; b. 27 July 1907, Sutton, Surrey; *s.* of Hubert Cecil Rickett and Mabel Fletcher; *m.* Ruth Pauline Armstrong 1946; two *s.* one *d.*; ed. Rugby and Balliol Coll., Oxford.
Joined staff of Economic Advisory Council 31; Offices of the War Cabinet 39; Private Sec. to Minister of Production 43-45; Asst. (for work on atomic energy) to Chancellor of the Exchequer 45-47; transferred to Treasury 47; Principal Private Sec. to the Prime Minister 50-51; Minister (economic) to U.S.A. and Head of U.K. Treasury and Supply Del. 51-54; Third Sec., Treasury 54-60, Second Sec. 60-68; Vice-Pres. World Bank 68-74; Dir. Schroder Int. 74-, De La Rue Co. 74-; Adviser J. Henry Schroder Wagg & Co. 74-; Fellow of All Souls Coll., Oxford 29-49.
Leisure interest: music.
The Maltings, Ugley, nr. Bishop's Stortford, Herts., England.

Rickover, Admiral Hyman George; American naval officer; b. 1900; *m.* Eleonore A. Bednowicz 1974; ed. U.S. Naval Acad.
Commissioned 22; in charge of atomic submarine project, Atomic Energy Comm. 46-47, Navy Dept. 47-; currently Dir. AEC Div. of Naval Reactors; Deputy Commdr. Naval Ships System Command for Nuclear Propulsion; responsible for the programme for designing and building the world's first atomic ship U.S.S. *Nautilus*; Adm. 73; Special Gold Congressional Medal 59; Enrico Fermi Award 64.
Publs. *Education and Freedom* 58, *Swiss Schools and Ours* 61, *American Education, A National Failure* 63.
c/o Bureau of Ships, Department of the Navy, Washington, D.C., U.S.A.

Riddick, Gerard Galloway; British Chief Executive of The De La Rue Co. Ltd.; see *The International Who's Who 1975-76*.

Ride, Sir Lindsay Tasman, Kt., C.B.E., E.D., M.A., D.M., B.CH. (OXON), M.R.C.S., L.R.C.P.; British educationist; b. 10 Oct. 1898, Newstead, Victoria, Australia; *s.* of Rev. W. Ride and Eliza Mary Best; *m.* 1st M. M. L. Fennety 1925, 2nd V. M. Witchell 1954; two *s.* two *d.*; ed. Scotch Coll., Melbourne, Melbourne Univ., New Coll., Oxford, and Guy's Hospital Medical School, London.
Former Demonstrator in Physiology and Pharmacology, Guy's Hospital, London; Prof. of Physiology, Univ. of Hong Kong 28-52, Dean of Medical Faculty and Vice-Chancellor 49-64, Dir. of Inst. of Modern Asian Studies 60-64, Prof. Emer. 65-; Chair. Asscn. of Univs. of British Commonwealth 60-61; Vice-Pres. Asscn. of S.E. Asian Institutions of Higher Learning 63-64; Research Assoc., Inst. of Social Studies, Chinese Univ. of Hong Kong 65-68; Hon. LL.D. (Toronto, Melbourne, London and Hong Kong); Hon. R.A.M.
Leisure interests: music, sport, bird watching, S.E. Asian history.
Publs. *Genetics and the Clinician* 40, *Morrison, The Scholar and the Man* 58, *Biographical Note on James Legge* 61, *The Old Protestant Cemetery, Macao* 63, and various papers on human genetics.
Villa Monte Rosa, E2/11, 41A Stubbs Road, Hong Kong.

Ridge, Anthony Hubert, B.A. (CANTAB.); British international civil servant; b. 5 Oct. 1913, London; *s.* of Timothy L. and Magdalen Ridge (née Hernig); *m.* Marjory J. Sage 1938; three *s.* one *d.*; ed. Christ's Hospital, Jesus Coll., Cambridge.
Held posts in Gen. Post Office Personnel 37-44; Principal Private Sec. Postmaster-Gen. 47; Deputy Regional Dir. London Postal Region 50; Asst. Sec. Overseas Postal Services 51; Dir. Clerical Mechanization and Bldg., GPO 60; Deputy Dir.-Gen. Int. Bureau, Universal Postal Union 64-73, Dir.-Gen. 73-74.
Leisure interests: music, gardening, walking, "popular" science, transport systems.
Staple, Postling, Hythe, Kent, England.
Telephone: (0)303-862315.

Ridgway, General Matthew B., D.S.C. (with O.L.C.), D.S.M. (with 3rd O.L.C.); American army officer; b. 3 March 1895, Fort Monroe, Va.; *s.* of Thomas Ridgway and Ruth Starbuck Bunker; *m.* Mary Princess Anthony 1947; one *s.* (deceased); ed. U.S. Military Acad.
Commissioned Lieut. U.S. Army 17 and advanced through grades to Lieut.-Gen. 45, Gen. 51; technical adviser to Gov.-Gen. of Philippines 32-33; Asst. Chief of Staff 6th Corps Area 35-36, Deputy Chief of Staff Second Army 36; Asst. Chief of Staff Fourth Army 37-39; accompanied Gen. Marshall to Brazil 39; War Plans Div., War Dept. Gen. Staff 39-42; Asst. Div. Commdr. 82nd Infantry Div. 42, Div. Commdr. 42; Commdg. Gen. 82nd Airborne Div., Sicily, Italy, Normandy 42-44; Commdr. 18th Airborne Corps, Belgium, France, Germany 44-45; Commdr. Luzon Area 45; Commdr. Mediterranean Theatre of Operations and Deputy Supreme Allied Commdr. Mediterranean Sept. 45-Jan. 46; senior U.S. Army mem. Mil. Staff Cttee., U.N. 46-48; Chair. Inter-American Defence Board 46-48; C.-in-C. Caribbean Commd. 48-49; Deputy Army Chief of Staff for Admin. 49-50; Commdr. Eighth Army in Korea 50-51; Commdr. U.N. Command in Far East, C.-in-C. Far East and Supreme Commdr. Allied Powers in Japan 51-52; Supreme Allied Commdr., Europe 52-53; Chief of Staff U.S. Army 53-55; Chair. Board of Trustees, Mellon Inst. of Industrial Research 55-60.
Leisure interests: hunting, fishing, gardening, travel.
Publs. *Soldier* 56, *The Korean War* 67.
Home: 918 West Waldheim Road, Fox Chapel, Pittsburgh, Pa. 15215, U.S.A.
Telephone: 412-781-4833.

Riding, Laura (Jackson); American writer; b. 16 Jan. 1901, New York City; *d.* of Nathaniel S. and Sarah Reichenthal; legally adopted surname Riding 1926; *m.* Schuyler B. Jackson 1941 (died 1968); ed. Cornell Univ.
Member Fugitives (Southern U.S. poets) in early career; writing activities long centred in poetry; expanded linguistic norm of poems, affecting style of many other poets; lived abroad 26-39, seeking in varied writing and work with others, including printing, publishing (partner in Seizin Press), to outline ground of moral unity for modern sensibility; renounced poetry and literary affiliations on return to U.S.A., seeing language itself as essential moral meeting-ground; long work with husband of language-study issued in book part finished when he died, completed alone under a Guggenheim fellowship.
Publs. include, *The Close Chaplet* (first of 9 vols. of poems) 26, *Contemporaries and Snobs* 27, *Survey of Modernist Poetry* (with Robert Graves) 27, *Anarchism is Not Enough* 28, *Experts are Puzzled* 30, *Progress of Stories* 35, *Essays and Critical Notes, Epilogue* 35-37, *A Trojan Ending* 37, *Collected Poems* 38, *Lives of Wives* 39; edited *Epilogue* 35-37, *The World and Ourselves* 38; later publs., contrib. to *Chelsea* 62, 64, 66, 67, 72, 74, *Civiltà delle Macchine* 63, *Art and Literature* 65, *The Private Library* 72, 73, *Denver Quarterly* 74, 75, 76, *Antaeus* 74, 75, 76; *Selected Poems: In Five Sets* U.K.

70, U.S.A. 73; *The Telling* (expanded book form) U.K. 72, U.S.A. 73; contribs. in anthology *Revolution of the Word* 75; *Rational Meaning: a New Foundation for the Definition of Words* (publ. pending); *It Has Taken Long*, Selected Writings (volume-length, *Chelsea*) 76.
Box 35, Wabasso, Fla. 32970, U.S.A.

Riegner, Gerhart M.; Swiss administrator; b. 12 Sept. 1911, Berlin; ed. Univs. of Berlin, Freiburg, Heidelberg, Paris, Graduate Inst. of Int. Studies, Geneva, and Acad. for Int. Law, The Hague.
Legal Sec. World Jewish Congress 36-39, Dir. Geneva Office 39-48, mem. World Exec. 48-60, Dir. of Coordination 60-65, Sec.-Gen. 65-; Int. Chair. World Univ. Service 49-55; Pres. Conf. of non-Govt. Orgs. at UN 53-55, Conf. of non-Govt. Orgs. in Consultative Status with UNESCO 56-58.
Publs. articles on legal matters, Jewish affairs and Christian-Jewish relations.
World Jewish Congress, 1 rue Varembé, Geneva; Home: 25 Avenue Wendt, Geneva, Switzerland.

Riemsdijk, H. A. C. van; Netherlands business executive; b. 1911, Aerdenhout; brother-in-law of Frits Philips *q.v.*
Joined Philips 34; Deputy Man. Philips Nederland N.V. 46, Man. 49, Gen. Man. 56; mem. Man. Board, N.V. Philips Gloeilampenfabrieken 63-, Vice-Pres. 68-71, Pres. 71-.
N.V. Philips Gloeilampenfabrieken, Eindhoven, Netherlands.

Rienäcker, Günther, DR.PHIL.; German chemist; b. 13 May 1904, Bremen; *s.* of Franz and Frieda (née Kröger) Rienäcker; *m.* Lotte Christiansen 1931; two *s.* one *d.*; ed. Univ. of Munich.
Professor Univ. of Göttingen 37; Prof. and Dir. Inst. of Inorganic Chem., Univ. of Rostock 42; Prof. of Inorganic Chem., Univ. of Berlin 5-, Dir. 1st Chemical Inst. 54-62; mem. Deutsche Akad. der Wissenschaften, Dir. of its Inst. for Research into Catalysts 51-69, Gen. Sec. 57-68; mem. Exec. Council, Kulturbund der D.D.R., Deutsche Akad. der Naturforscher Leopoldina; Hon. mem. Hungarian Acad. of Sciences; Foreign mem. Acad. of Sciences, U.S.S.R.; mem. Inst. d'Egypte, Cairo; Nat. Prize 55, many other prizes and awards; Dr. Rer. Nat. h.c. (Rostock) 69, (Leuna-Merseburg) 74; Editor *Zeitschrift anorganische allgemeine Chemie*.
Leisure interests: chemistry, music.
DDR-111 Berlin-Niederschönhausen, Tschaikowskistrasse 40-42, German Democratic Republic.
Telephone: 4829741.

Riese, Otto, LL.D.; German judge; b. 27 Oct. 1894, Frankfurt-am-Main; ed. Lausanne, Leipzig and Frankfurt Univs.
Attached to Frankfurt-am-Main Court 23, Ministry of Justice 25; Prof. of Law, Lausanne Univ. 35, Dean, Faculty of Law 50; Senatspräsident, High Court of Justice, Karlsruhe 51; Judge, E.C.S.C. Court 52-58, Vice-Pres. 53 and 56; Judge, Court of the European Communities 58-63; Vice-Pres. 58, 62-63; Dir. Inst. of Comparative Law, Lausanne Univ. (retd. Oct. 66).
Leisure interest: collecting Japanese prints.
Publs. *Das internationale Recht der Zivilen Luftfahrt unter besonderer Berücksichtigung des Schweizerischen Rechts* 49, *Der Entwurf zur internationalen Vereinheitlichung des Kaufrechts* 56, *Une juridiction supranationale pour l'interprétation du droit unifié?* 61.
61 bis ave. des Cerisiers, 1009 Pully (Vd), Lausanne, Switzerland.
Telephone: (021) 28-11-32.

Riesman, David, A.B., LL.B., LL.D., D.LIT., ED.D.; American social scientist; b. 1909, Philadelphia, Pa.; *s.* of Dr. David and Eleanor F. Riesman; *m.* Evelyn Hastings Thompson 1936; two *s.* two *d.*; ed. Harvard Univ. and Harvard Law School.

Law clerk to Mr. Justice Brandeis, Supreme Court 35-36; Practised law 36-37; Prof. of Law, Buffalo Univ. 37-41; Deputy Asst. Dist. Attorney, New York County 42-43; Asst. Treasurer, Sperry Gyroscope Co. 43-46; Prof. Social Sciences, Chicago Univ. 46-58; Prof. Social Sciences, Harvard 58-; mem. Carnegie Comm. on Future of Higher Educ. 67-; Fellow, Center for Advanced Study in the Behavioral Sciences, Stanford 68-69; mem. Inst. for Advanced Study, Princeton 71-72; on board of editors, *Sociology of Education, Technology and Culture, Universities Quarterly*; Nat. Sponsor, Cttee. for a Sane Nuclear Policy; Dir. Nat. Movement for Student Vote.
Publs. *The Lonely Crowd* 50, *Faces in the Crowd* 52, *Thorstein Veblen: A Critical Interpretation* 53, *Individualism Reconsidered* 54, *Constraint and Variety in American Education* 56, *Abundance for what?* 64, *The Academic Revolution* (with Christopher Jencks) 68, *Academic Values and Mass Education* (with Joseph Gusfield and Zelda Gamson) 70.
Department of Social Relations, William James Hall 280, Harvard University, Cambridge, Mass. 02138, U.S.A.
Telephone: 617-495-3822.

Rietz, Hans; German politician; b. 1914; ed. secondary school, Bitterfeld.
Former locksmith; I. G. Farben 32-39; Mil. Service, Second World War; mem. Dem. Peasants' Party (D.B.D.) 49-; mem. Volkskammer 54-; now Vice-Chair. Council of State.
Volkskammer, Berlin, German Democratic Republic.

Rifaat, Kameleddin; Egyptian politician.
Minister of Labour, United Arab Repub. 61-62; mem. Presidency Council 62-64; Dep. Prime Minister for Scientific Affairs 64-65; mem. Supreme Exec. Arab Socialist Union 65-; Minister of Labour June 67-71; Amb. to U.K. 71-74.
c/o Ministry of Foreign Affairs, Cairo, Egypt.

Rifa'i, Abdul Monem; Jordanian diplomatist; b. 1917, Tyre, Lebanon; *m.*; ed. American Univ. of Beirut.
In Service of King Abdullah 38; Chief Sec. of Govt. and Chief Censor 40; Asst. Chief of Royal Court 41-42; Consul-Gen. in Cairo, Lebanon and Syria 43-44; Del. to Treaty Conf. with Great Britain 46; Counsellor in Washington, and Del. to U.N. 49; Minister to Iran and Pakistan 49; Ambassador to United States 53-57, to Lebanon 57-58, to Great Britain 58; Dir. of Radio, Press and Tourism 58-59; Rep. to UN 59-65; Ambassador to United Arab Republic 66-67 (withdrawn Feb. 67); Minister of Foreign Affairs 67-69; Prime Minister March-Aug. 69, June-Sept. 70; Deputy Prime Minister and Minister of Foreign Affairs 69-70; Personal Rep. to H.M. King Hussein 72-73; Perm. Rep. to Arab League 73; Amb. to Egypt 73-74.
c/o Ministry of Foreign Affairs, Amman, Jordan.

Rifai, Rashid M. S. al-, M.S.ENG., PH.D., M.I.E.E.; Iraqi electrical engineer; b. 1 May 1929; ed. American Univ. of Beirut, Lebanon, Univ. of Bristol, England, Purdue and Rice Univs., U.S.A.
Engineer, Directorate Gen. of Posts, Telephones and Telegraph 54-62; Chief Engineer, Gen. Co. for Electrical Industries 68; Minister for Presidential Affairs July 68, of Oil and Minerals 68-69; Minister of State 69-71; Minister of Planning 71-72, of Communications 72-74, of Work and Housing Nov. 74-.
Ministry of Works and Housing, Baghdad, Iraq.

Rifa'i, Zaid al-, M.A.; Jordanian diplomatist: b. 27 Nov. 1936, Amman; *s.* of Samir Pasha al-Rifa'i and Alia Shukry; *m.* Muna Talhouni 1965; one *s.* one *d.*; ed. Victoria Coll., Cairo, and Harvard and Columbia Univs.
Joined diplomatic service 57; served at embassies in Cairo, Beirut and London and at the Permanent

Mission of Jordan at UN; Chief of Royal Protocol 65; Sec.-Gen. of Royal Court and Private Sec. to H.M. King Hussein 67; Chief of Royal Court 69; Amb. to U.K. 70-72; Political Adviser to King Hussain March 72; Prime Minister and Minister for Foreign Affairs and Defence May 73-.

Leisure interests: music, reading, bridge, water-skiing, sailing, tennis.

Prime Minister's Office, Amman, Jordan.

Rifbjerg, Klaus; Danish author; b. 15 Dec. 1931, Copenhagen; *s.* of Thorvald Rifbjerg and Lilly Nielsen; *m.* Inge Merete Gerner 1955; one *s.* two *d.*; ed. Princeton Univ., U.S.A., and Univ. of Copenhagen.

Literary critic, *Information* 55-57, *Politiken* 59- (Copenhagen daily newspapers); Aarestrup Medal 64, Danish Critics' Award 65, Grant of Honour from the Danish Dramatists 66, Danish Acad. Award 66, Golden Laurels 67, Soren Gyldendal Award 69, Nordic Council Award 70, Grant of Honour from the Danish Writers' Guild 73. Publs. novels: *Den Kroniske Uskyld* 58, *Operaelsken* 66, *Arkivet* 67, *Lonni Og Karl* 68, *Anna (Jeg) Anna* 70, *Marts 1970* 70, *Leif den Lykkelige JR.* 71, *Til Spanien* 71, *Lena Jorgensen, Klintevej 4, 2650 Hvidovre* 71, *Brevet til Gerda* 72, *R.R.* 72, *Spinatfuglene* 73, *Dilettanterne* 73, *Du skal ikke vaere ked af det Amalia* 74, *En hugorm i solen* 74, *Vejen ad hvilken* 75, *Tak for turen* 75, *Kiks* 76; short stories: *Og Andre Historier* 64, *Rejsende* 69, *Den Syende Jomfru* 72, *Sommer* 74; non-fiction: *I Medgang Og Modgang* 70; plays: *Gris Pa Gaflen* 62, *Hva' Skal Vi Lave* 63, *Udviklinger* 65, *Hvad en Mand Har Brug For* 66, *Voks* 68, *Ar* 70, *Narrene* 71, *Svaret Blaeser i Vinden* 71; several vols. of poetry; twenty radio plays.

c/o Gyldendal Publishers, 3 Klareboderne, 1001 Copenhagen; Home: Tesseboelle, 4681 Herfoelge, Denmark.

Rigby, Sir Ivo Charles Clayton, Kt.; British judge; b. 2 June 1911; *s.* of the late James and Elisabeth Rigby; *m.* 1st Agnes Bothway 1937, 2nd Kathleen Turquand Young (née Jones) 1954; no *c.*; ed. Magdalen Coll., Oxford and Inner Temple.

Called to the Bar 32; Magistrate, Gambia 35-38; Chief Magistrate, Crown Counsel and Pres. of District Court, Palestine 38-48; Asst. Judge, Nyasaland 48-54; Pres. of Sessions Court, Malaya 54-55; Puisne Judge, Malaya 52-61; Senior Puisne Judge, Hong Kong 61-70, Chief Justice of Hong Kong and Brunei 70-73, now Chief Justice, Court of Appeal, Brunei; Recorder of the Crown Court 75-.

Leisure interests: squash, cricket, bridge.

Publs. *The Law Reports of Nyasaland* 34-52.

8 More's Garden, Cheyne Walk, London, SW3 5BB, England.

Telephone: 01-352-0120.

Riggs, Lorrin Andrews, A.B., M.A., PH.D.; American psychologist; b. 11 June 1912, Harput, Turkey; *s.* of Ernest Wilson and Alice (Shepard) Riggs; *m.* Doris Robinson 1937; two *s.*; ed. Dartmouth Coll. and Clark Univ.

N.R.C. Fellow, Biological Sciences, Univ. of Pennsylvania 36-37; Instructor Univ. of Vermont 37-38, 39-41; with Brown Univ. 38-39, 41-, Research Assoc., Research Psychologist Nat. Defence Research Cttee., Asst. Prof., Assoc. Prof. 38-51, Prof. of Psychology 51-; L. Herbert Ballou Foundation Prof. of Psychology 60-68, Edgar J. Marston Univ. Prof. of Psychology 68-; Guggenheim Fellow, Univ. of Cambridge 71-72; Assoc. Editor, *Journal* of Optical Soc. of America, *Experimental Psychology*; mem. American Eastern Psychological Asscn. (Div. Pres. 62-63, Pres. 75-76), American Assen. for the Advancement of Science (Chair. and Vice-Pres. Section 1 64), Optical Soc. of America, Nat. Acad. of Sciences, American Physiological Soc., Int. Brain Research Org., Soc. for Neuroscience, Int. Soc. of Clinical Electroretinography, Soc. of Experi-

mental Psychologists, American Acad. of Arts and Sciences, Asscn. for Research in Vision and Ophthalmology (Trustee 71-); Howard Crosby Warren Medal, Soc. of Experimental Psychologists 57, Jonas S. Friedenwald Award, Asscn. for Research in Opthalmology 66, Edgar D. Tillyer Award, Optical Soc. of America 69, Charles F. Prentice Award, American Acad. of Optometry 73, Distinguished Scientific Contribution Award, American Psychological Asscn. 74.

Publs. Numerous scientific articles on vision and physiological psychology.

Hunter Laboratory of Psychology, Brown University, Providence, R.I. 02912, U.S.A.

Telephone: 401-863-2512.

Riker, Albert Joyce, PH.D.; American plant pathologist; b. 1894, Wheeling, W. Va.; ed. Oberlin Coll., Univ. of Wisconsin and in Paris and London.

Taught Botany, Univ. of Cincinnati; Bacteriologist, Cincinnati Base Hospital during First World War; joined Staff of Univ. of Wisconsin 42, retd. as Prof. 64; Fellow, A.A.A.S., American Acad. of Microbiology; mem. numerous learned socs. including Nat. Acad. of Sciences (Chair. Botany Section 59-62), American Asscn. for Cancer Research, American Phytopathological Soc., Botanical Soc. of America, Indian Phytopathological Soc.; awarded American Men of Science Star 44 and Eighth Int. Botanical Congress Medal, Paris 54.

Publs. *Introduction to Methods of Doing Research in Plant Pathology*; and more than 300 technical papers (in co-operation with students and colleagues).

2760 East Eighth Street, Tucson, Ariz. 85716, U.S.A.

Telephone: 325-6235.

Rikhye, Maj.-Gen. Indar Jit; Indian businessman, educator and former army officer; b. 30 July 1920, Lahore; *s.* of the late Raisahib Dr. Madan Lal Rikhye and of Raj Rani (née Sudan) Rikhye; *m.* 1st Usha Erry 1946 (divorced 1974), 2nd Cynthia de Haan 1974; two *s.*; ed. Govt. Coll., Lahore and Indian Military Acad.

Served 6 DCO Lancers, Iraq, Iran, Syria, Lebanon, Palestine, Italy 39-45, North-West Frontier (India) 45-47; fmr. Commdr. Royal Deccan Horse, Jammu and Kashmir; Commdr. Indian Contingent, UN Force, Gaza 57-58, Chief of Staff UN Emergency Force 58-60; Commdr. Infantry Brigade, Indian Army 60; Mil. Adviser to Sec.-Gen. of UN 60-68; with UN Force in Congo, West Irian, Yemen and Cyprus, established a UN Military Training Team in Ruanda-Urundi 60-61; UN Supervisor in Netherlands New Guinea 62, Adviser to Sec.-Gen. of UN on Cuba 62, Palestine 65, and Dominican Repub. 65-66; Commdr. UNEF Gaza Feb. 66-Dec. 67; Mil. Adviser to Sec.-Gen. of UN 68; Pres. Int. Peace Acad.

Leisure interests: golf, tennis, swimming, writing.

445 East 86th Street, New York, N.Y. 10028, U.S.A.

Telephone: 212-427-2704.

Riklis, Meshulam; American (b. Turkish) business executive; b. 1923; ed. High School, Israel, Univ. of Mexico and Ohio State Univ.

Co-Director Youth Activities and Military Training, Hertzlia High School, Tel-Aviv 42; went to U.S. 47, naturalized 55; Teacher of Hebrew, Talmud Torah School, Minneapolis 51; Research Dept., Piper, Jaffray and Hopwood 51-53, Sales Rep. 53-56; Chair., Chief Exec. Officer Rapid Electrotype Co., American Colortype Co. 56-57; Pres. Rapid-American Corpn. 57-58, Chair. 58-; Chair. McCrory Corpn., Glen Alden Corpn. 65-.

Rapid American Corporation, 711 Fifth Avenue, New York, N.Y. 10022; 7 Shelter Bay Drive, Kings Point, Long Island, N.Y., U.S.A.

Riley, Bridget, C.B.E., A.R.C.A.; British artist; b. 24 April 1931, London; *d.* of John Fisher Riley and Bessie Louise (née Gladstone); ed. Cheltenham Ladies'

Coll., Goldsmiths Coll. of Art and Royal Coll. of Art, London.

First one-man exhibition in London at Gallery One 62, followed by others in England and America; has exhibited in group shows in Australia, Italy, France, Holland, Germany, Israel, America, Japan and Argentina; represented Great Britain at Biennale des Jeunes, Paris 65, at Venice Biennale 68; retrospective exhbn. Europe and U.K. 70-72; paintings, drawings, and prints in public collections in England, Ireland, America and Australia; AICA Critics Prize 63; Prize in Open Section, John Moores Liverpool Exhbn. 63; Peter Stuyvesant Foundation Travel Bursary to U.S.A. 64; Major Painting Prize, Venice Biennale 68; founder mem. and Dir. S.P.A.C.E. Ltd.; mem. Royal Soc. London, England.

Riley, Richard A.; American business executive; b. **27** March 1916, Fall River, Mass.; *m.* Helen Fox 1941; one *s.* one *d.*; ed. Providence Coll., R.I.

Joined Firestone Tire and Rubber Co. 39; Pres. Firestone Rubber and Latex Products Co. 60-65, Synthetic Rubber and Latex Co. 65-68; Pres. Firestone Steel Products Co. 68; Vice-Pres. Firestone Tire and Rubber Co. 68, Dir. 70-, Exec. Vice-Pres. 71, Pres. 72-, Chief Exec. Officer 73-; mem. Board of Dirs. Rubber Mfrs. Asscn.; Hon. D.Sc. (Bradford Durfee Coll. of Technology) 61; Hon. D.B.A. (Providence Coll.) 69.

Firestone Tire and Rubber Co., 1200 Firestone Parkway, Akron, Ohio 44317, U.S.A.

Rimalt, Elimelech, PH.D.; Israeli politician; b. 1 Nov. 1907, Bochnia, Poland; *s.* of Samuel and Cilli Rimalt; *m.* Wilmer Gelmann 1933; two *s.*; ed. Hebrew High School, Cracow, Poland, Univ. of Vienna and Rabbinical Seminary, Vienna, Austria.

Emigrated to Palestine from Austria 39, and served as Head of Schools in Ramat Gan, Israel and Dir. of Educ. Dept. of Ramat Gan Municipality; Deputy Mayor of Ramat Gan 55-59; Minister of Posts, Israel Govt. 69-Aug. 71; Founder Union of Gen. Zionist (now Liberal) Workers; mem. Knesset; Chair. Liberal Party in fifth Knesset; Co-Chair. Herut-Liberal bloc (Gahal), Knesset 65-68; Past Chair. or mem. of numerous Parl. Cttees.; Chair. Liberal Party, Co-Chair. Likud block.

Leisure interests: history, philosophy, research on Aramaic Dialects.

Publs. Scientific works in the field of Semitic languages.
Ramat-Gan 19, Haam Hatsarfatt Boulevard, Tel Aviv, Israel.

Telephone: 03-790507.

Rimington, Claude, M.A., PH.D., D.SC., F.R.S.; British university professor; b. 17 Nov. 1902, London; *s.* of George Garthwaite Rimington and Hilda Klyne; *m.* Soffi Andersen 1929; one *d.*; ed. Cambridge and London Univs.

Biochemist, Woollen Industries' Research Asscn., Leeds 28-31; Empire Marketing Board Research Fellow at Onderstepoort Veterinary Research Laboratory, Pretoria, South Africa 31-36; Scientific Research Officer, Div. of Veterinary Services, Govt. of Union of S. Africa 36-37; Biochemist on staff of Nat. Inst. for Medical Research of Medical Research Council of Great Britain 37-45; Prof. of Chemical Pathology, Univ. of London, and Head of Dept. of Chemical Pathology, Univ. Coll. Hospital Medical School 45-67, Emer. Prof. Univ. of London; Hon. F.R.C.P.(E).

Leisure interests: literature, languages.
c/o Department of Chemical Pathology, University College Hospital Medical School, London, W.C.1, England.

Rinchin, Lodongiyn; Mongolian agronomist and politician; b. 25 July 1929, Gobi Altai; ed. Agricultural Inst., U.S.S.R.

Agronomist, Chief of Dept., Chief Agronomist. Ministry of Livestock Husbandry 55-60; Deputy Minister, First Deputy Minister, Ministry of Agriculture 60-67; Chair. Supreme Council, Agricultural Co-operative Board 67-70; Minister of Foreign Affairs 70-; mem. Cen. Cttee. Mongolian People's Revolutionary Party 61-; Deputy to the Great People's Hural; various state orders and medals.

Ministry of Foreign Affairs, Ulan Bator, Mongolia.

Ring, Sir Lindsay Roberts, G.B.E., J.P., D.SC.; British executive; b. 1 May 1914, London; *s.* of George Arthur Ring and Helen Rhoda Mason Ring (née Stedman); *m.* Hazel Doris Nichols 1940; two *s.* one *d.*; ed. Dulwich Coll. and Mecklenburg, Germany.

Served Europe and Middle East, Maj., Royal Army Service Corps 39-45; Underwriting mem. Lloyd's 64; Chair. Ring and Brymer (Birchs) Ltd.; Chair. Hotel and Catering Trades Benevolent Asscn. 62-71; mem. Board of Verge of Royal Palaces; Gov. Farrington's School; Hon. Treas. Church Army Housing; mem. Court of Assts., Armourers' and Braziers' Co., Master 72; Common Councilman for Ward of Bishopsgate, City of London 64-68, Alderman for Ward of Vintry 68; Sheriff, City of London 67-68; Lord Mayor of London 75-76; Freeman, City of London 35; Fellow, Hotel and Catering Inst.; K.St.J.

Leisure interest: gardening.
Chalvedune, Wilderness Road, Chislehurst, Kent, BR7 5EY, England.

Telephone: 01-467-3199.

Ringadoo, Sir Veerasamy, Kt., BAR.-AT-LAW; Mauritius politician; b. 1920, Port Louis; *m.* Lydie Vadamootoo 1954; one *s.* one *d.*; ed. Port Louis Grammar School and London School of Economics, England.

Called to the Bar 49; elected Municipal Councillor 56; elected mem. Legis. Council for Moka-Flacq 51-67; Minister for Labour and Social Security 59-64, for Educ. 64-67, of Agriculture and Natural Resources 67-68, of Finance June 68-; attended London Constitutional Conf. 65; First mem., Legislative Assembly (M.L.A.) for Quartier Militaire and Moka 67- (Lab.); Officer, Ordre National Malgache.

Ministry of Finance, Port Louis; Home: corner of Farquhar and Sir Celicourt Antelme Streets, Quatre-Bornes, Mauritius.

Rinkel, Andreas; Netherlands ecclesiastic; b. 10 Jan 1889; ed. Old Catholic Seminary, Amersfoort.

Ordained Priest 14; Vicar, Enkhuizen 14-20, Amersfoort 20-37; Prof. of Theology, Ethics and Liturgy 20-48; Canon of the Metropolitan Chapter of Utrecht 26-70, Hon. Canon 70-; Archbishop of Utrecht 37-70; Editor of *Geloof en Leven* 15-20, of *De Oud-Katholiek* 20-36, of *Internationale Kirchliche Zeitschrift* 20-37; Hon. D.Th. (twice).

Publs. *Handboek voor geloofs—en Zedeleer* 30, *Die Heilige Eucharistie*; Sermons: *Van heerlijkheid tot heerlijkheid* 23, *Uit den rijkdom zijner genade* (3 vols.) 25, *De moeilijke weg* 30, *De gave Gods* 30; Essays: *Psalter* (2 vols.) 37, *Dogmatic Lectures* 56; composer of liturgical church music, masses and hymns.

Emmalaan 8, Utrecht, Netherlands.
Telephone: 030-516989.

Rinnooy Kan, Alfred, LL.D.; Netherlands international finance official; b. 16 June 1913, Amsterdam; *m.*; three *c.*; ed. Gymnasium Haganum, The Hague and Municipal Univ., Amsterdam.

Assistant to Treas.-Gen. Ministry of Finance 35-40, Dept. of Monetary Affairs 40-45, Legal and Custodians Dept. 45-59; Deputy Treas.-Gen. Ministry of Finance 59-71; Exec. Dir. IBRD, IFC and IDA 71-75; mem. Council for Pure Scientific Research; mem. Board of Dirs. Royal Netherlands Iron and Steel Works, Foundation for Devt. of Mechanized Agriculture in

Surinam, Netherlands Credit Insurance Co., Nat. Investment Bank, Netherlands Finance Co. for Developing Countries; Knight, Order of Netherlands Lion, Commdr. Order of the Oak Crown (Luxembourg), Officier, Légion d'Honneur (France).
c/o International Bank for Reconstruction and Development, 1818 H Street, N.W., Washington, D.C. 20433, U.S.A.

Rinser, Luise; German author; b. 30 April 1911, Pitzling/Oberbayern; d. of Joseph and Luise Rinser; m. 1st Horst-Guenther Schnell 1939 (deceased), 2nd Carl Orff (q.v.); two s.
School teacher 35-39; imprisoned during 3rd Reich; after Second World War became literary critic of *Neue Zeitung*, Munich; now free-lance writer; mem. Akad. der Künste, Berlin, PEN, etc.
Leisure interests: politics, theology.
Publs. novels: *Die gläsernen Ringe* 40, *Mitte des Lebens* 50, *Daniela* 53, *Abenteuer der Tugend* 57, *Tobias* 68; *Der schwarze Esel* 74; short stories: *Ein Bündel weisser Narzissen* 56; essays: *Schwerpunkt, Über die Hoffnung, Vom Sinn der Traurigkeit, Unterentwickeltes Land Frau, Wie, wenn wir ärmer würden* 74, *Dem Tode geweiht* 74; letters: *Hochzeit der Widersprüche* 73; diaries: *Baustelle* 70, *Grenz-Übergänge* 72; play: *Philemon*; travel: *Süd Korea* 76; children's: *Bruder Feuer* 75.
Rocca di Papa, Rome, Italy.
Telephone: 94-90-87.

Riopelle, Jean-Paul; Canadian painter; b. 1923, Canada.
Settled in Paris 47; participated in *L'Imaginaire* exhbn., Gallerie du Luxembourg 47, Surrealist exhbn., Galerie Maeght 47; one-man shows, Paris 49, New York 54, London 56; chosen by J. J. Sweeney for Younger European Painters Exhbn., Guggenheim Museum, N.Y. 53-54; works in the Tate Gallery and Nat. Gallery of Canada and in private collections; Canada Council Medal 66.
c/o Galerie Maeght, rue du Teheran, Paris 8e, France; c/o Arthur Tooth & Sons Ltd., 31 Bruton Street, London, W.1, England.

Rios, Juan; Peruvian poet, dramatist and dramatic critic; b. 28 Sept. 1914, Barranco, Lima; s. of Rogelio Ríos and Victoria Rey (de Ríos); m. Rosa Saco 1946; one d.
National Prize for Playwriting 46, 50, 52, 54, 60; Nat. Poetry Prize 48, 53; Writers' Fellowship, UNESCO, Europe and Egypt 60-61; writer for *Oiga*; mem. Academia Peruana de la Lengua Correspondiente a la Española.
Publs. *Canción de Siempre* 41, *Malstrom* 41, *La Pintura Contemporánea en el Perú* 46, *Teatro* (I) 61, *Ayar Manko* 63.
Dos de Mayo 657, Miraflores, Lima 18, Peru.
Telephone: 255218 (Lima).

Ripamonti, Camillo; Italian politician; b. 25 May 1919, Gorgonzola; ed. Milan Polytechnic.
Member, district cttee. of Christian Democrat Party, Milan 45; Deputy to Chamber of Deputies 58-68; Pres. Nat. Inst. of Urban Planning 60; Senator 68-; Minister of Public Health Dec. 68-69, of Science 70-72, of Foreign Trade 72-73, without Portfolio, in charge of Cultural Heritage 73-74, of Tourism March-Oct. 74.
c/o Ministry of Tourism, Rome; and Via S. Sofia, 18-Milan, Italy.
Telephone: 860228.

Ripley, S. Dillon, B.A., PH.D.; American museum director and zoologist; b. 20 Sept. 1913, New York City; s. of Louis Arthur Ripley and Constance Ballie (Rose); m. Mary Moncrieffe Livingston 1949; three d.; ed. St. Paul's School, Concord, N.H., and Yale and Harvard Univs.

Zoological Collector, Acad. of Natural Science, Phila. 36-39; Voluntary Asst. American Museum of Natural History, N.Y. 39-40; Asst. Harvard Univ. 41-42; Asst. Curator Birds, Smithsonian Inst. 42, Sec. 64-; Lecturer Yale Univ. 46-52, Asst. Prof. 49-55, Assoc. Prof. Zoology 55-61, Prof. of Biology 61-64; Fellow or mem. of numerous scientific socs. in U.S. and abroad, including Nat. Acad. of Sciences and British Ornithologists' Union; Hon. M.A. (Yale Univ.), Hon. D.H.L. (Marlboro Coll., Williams Coll.), Hon. D.Sc. (George Washington Univ., Catholic Univ., Maryland Univ., Cambridge Univ. and Brown Univ.), Hon. LL.D. (Dickinson Coll., Hofstra Univ., Yale Univ.); New York Zoological Soc. Medal 66, Royal Zoological Soc. of Antwerp Medal 70, Order of White Elephant and Freedom Medal, Thailand, Officier, Ordre Français des Arts et Lettres, France.
Leisure interests: travel, observing and collecting waterfowl, especially watching ducks.
Publs. *The Trail of the Money Bird* 42, *Search for the Spiny Babbler* 52, *A Paddling of Ducks* 57, *A Synopsis of the Birds of India and Pakistan* 61, *Ornithological Books in the Yale Library* (Co-Author) 61, *Land and Wildlife, Tropical Asia* 64, *Handbook of the Birds of India and Pakistan* (Co-Author), Vol. I 68, Vols. II and III 69, Vol. IV 70, Vol. V 72, Vol. VI 71, Vol. VII 72, Vol. VIII, Vol. IX 73, Vol. X 74, *The Sacred Grove/ Essays on Museums* 69, *The Paradox of the Human Condition* 75; contributions to numerous journals.
Smithsonian Institution, Washington, D.C. 20560; Home: 2324 Massachusetts Avenue, N.W., Washington, D.C. 20008; Summer: Paddling Ponds, Litchfield, Conn. 06759, U.S.A.
Telephone: 202-381-5005 (Office); 202-232-3131 (Home); 203-JO7-8208 (Summer).

Rippon, Rt. Hon. Geoffrey, P.C., Q.C., M.A., M.P.; British barrister and politician; b. 28 May 1924; ed. King's Coll., Taunton, and Brasenose Coll., Oxford.
Called to Bar, Middle Temple 48; mem. Surbiton Borough Council 45-54, Mayor 51-52; mem. London County Council 52-61; Mem. of Parl. for Norwich 55-64, for Hexham 66-; Parl. Sec. Ministry of Aviation 59-61; Joint Parl. Sec. Ministry of Housing and Local Govt. 61-62; Minister of Public Building and Works 62-64; Dir. Fairey Co. Ltd.; Dir. Bristol Aeroplane Co.; Dir. and Chair. Holland and Hannen & Cubitts 64-70; Pres. British section, Council of European Municipalities 56-; Pres. British section, European League for Econ. Co-operation 69-; Deputy Chair. Drake & Scull Ltd. 64-70; mem. Court, Univ. of London 58-; Minister of Technology June-July 70; Chancellor of Duchy of Lancaster in charge of negotiations for British entry to Common Market 70-72; Sec. of State for the Environment 72-74; Conservative.
Publs. *Forward from Victory* (co-author) 43, *The Rent Act* 57.
House of Commons, London, S.W.1, England.

Rishtya, Kassim; Afghan civil servant and diplomatist; b. 1913; ed. Istiqlal High School, Kabul.
Clerk in Press Section, Ministry of Foreign Affairs 32; Chief Clerk Foreign Relations Section, Ministry of Communications 32; trans. at Afghan Acad. of Literature 33, mem. 34, Dir. Publs. Div. 36, Vice-Pres. 38; Dir.-Gen. of Publs., Press Dept. 40-44, Pres. 48; Pres. Govt. Econ. Planning Board 49, Govt. Co-operative Org. 52, Bakhtar News Agency 54; Minister of Information 56-60; Afghan Del. to UN 10th Gen. Ass.; headed Press Del. to U.S.S.R. 56; Amb. to Czechoslovakia, Poland and Hungary 60-62, to United Arab Repub. 62-67, to Japan 70-73; (retd.); Editor *Kabul Almanach* and *Kabul Magazine* 36-38.
Publs. *Afghanistan in the 19th Century, Jawani Afghan*, and several novels.
c/o Ministry of Foreign Affairs, Kabul, Afghanistan.

Riško, Ján; Czechoslovak journalist and politician; b. 6 Feb. 1930, Lúky; *s.* of Anton and Júlia Riškovi; *m.* Katarína Rišková; ed. Commercial Coll. and Faculty of Social Sciences, Coll. of Political and Econ. Sciences, Prague.

Member editorial staff of youth daily *Mladá fronta*, Prague 53-56; Head of news dept. Slovak youth daily *Smena*, Bratislava, 56-59; Head of news dept. *Pravda* (C.P. daily), Bratislava 60-67; Correspondent, Czechoslovak News Agency, Moscow 67-Jan. 70; official, Secr. Central Cttee. C.P. of Czechoslovakia 70; Gen. Dir. Czechoslovak Radio Sept. 70-; Deputy, House of the People, Czechoslovak Fed. Assembly 71; Order of Merit in Construction 70.

Czechoslovak Radio, Vinohradská 12, 12099 Prague 2, Czechoslovakia.
Telephone: 225835.

Risterucci, Jean, L. en D.; French civil servant and diplomatist; b. 11 April 1911, Bustanico, Corsica; *s.* of Paul M. Risterucci and Marie D. Renucci; *m.* Micheline Gérard 1944; five *c.*; ed. Ecole Nat. de la France d'Outre-Mer.

Official in Indochina Civil Service 35-52; Political Adviser to High Commr. 50-52; High Commr. in Cambodia 52-54; Dir. du Cabinet to Sec. of State for Armed Forces (Air); Inspector-Gen. (Admin. Affairs), French West Africa; High Commr. in Gabon 59-60, High Rep. 60-62; Dir. of Overseas Territories 63; High Commr. in Pacific and New Hebrides and Gov. of New Caledonia 65-69; retd. 73; Pres. and Dir.-Gen. Soc. de la mise en valeur agricole de la Corse 74-; Commdr. Légion d'Honneur, Croix de Guerre, Médaille de l'Aéronautique; Commdr. or Grand Officier in Cambodian, Vietnamese and Laotian orders; Grand Officier of the Equatorial Star (Gabon).

78 rue Charles Laffitte, 92200 Neuilly-sur-Seine, France.
Telephone: 722-70-90.

Ritblat, John Henry, F.S.V.A., British business executive; b. 1935; *m.* Isabel Ritblat 1960; two *s.* one *d.*; ed. Dulwich Coll., Coll. of Estate Management.

Chairman British Land Co. Ltd., W. Crowther & Sons Ltd., C. E. Coates & Co. Ltd., Bankers; Senior Partner, Conrad Ritblat & Co., Consultant Surveyors and Valuers.

Leisure interests: golf, skiing, squash, books, architecture.
14 Manchester Square, London, W.1, England.
Telephone: 01-935-4499.

Ritchie, Albert Edgar, B.A.; Canadian diplomatist; b. 20 Dec. 1916, Andover, N.B.; *s.* of Stanley W. and Beatrice (Walker) Ritchie; *m.* Gwendolin Perdue 1941; two *s.* two *d.*; ed. Mount Allison and Oxford Univs.

Deputy Under-Sec. of State for External Affairs 64-66; Amb. to U.S.A. 66-70; Under-Sec. of State for External Affairs, Ottawa 70-74; Special Adviser to Privy Council 74; Hon. LL.D. (Mount Allison Univ.) 66, (St. Thomas Univ.) 68.

Leisure interests: skating, walking, fishing.
16 Carlyle Avenue, Ottawa, K1S 4Y3, Ont., Canada.

Ritchie, Charles Stewart Almon; Canadian diplomatist; b. 23 Sept. 1906; ed. Halifax, Oxford, Harvard and Paris Univs.

Third Sec., Dept. of External Affairs 34-36, Washington 36-39; Second Sec., London 39-43; First Sec., London 43-45, Ottawa 45-47; Counsellor, Paris 47-50; Asst. Under-Sec., Ottawa 50-52; Deputy Under-Sec. 52-54; Amb. to German Fed. Repub. and Head of Mil. Mission, Berlin 54-58; Perm. Rep. to UN 58-62; Amb. to U.S.A. 62-66; Perm. Rep. to NATO 66-67; Canadian High Commr. in U.K. 67-71; Special Adviser to Privy Council, Canada 71-73.

Publ. *The Siren Years: Undiplomatic Diaries 1937-45* 75.

Apt. 10, 216 Metcalfe Street, Ottawa, Ont., Canada.

Ritchie, James Martin; Scottish business executive; b. 29 May 1917, Glasgow; *s.* of Sir James and Lady Ritchie; *m.* Noreen M. L. Johnston 1939; three *s.*; ed. Strathallan School.

Joined Andrew Ritchie & Son Ltd., Glasgow (family business) 34, Dir. 38; war service 39-45; rejoined Andrew Ritchie & Son Ltd. 45, Man. Dir. 50; Gen. Man. Bowater-Eburite Ltd. (after merger) 56; Dir. Bowater Paper Corpn. Ltd. 59, Man. Dir. 64, Deputy Chair. 67, Chair. 69-72; Vice-Chair. British Enkalon Ltd. 74-75, Chair. 75-; Dir. Vickers Ltd., British Enkalon Ltd., Haymills Holdings Ltd., Sun Alliance and London Insurance Group.

Leisure interest: golf.
The Court House, Fulmer, Bucks., England.
Telephone: Fulmer 2585.

Ritchie, Kenneth Gordon, C.M.G.; British diplomatist; b. 19 Aug. 1921; ed. Arbroath High School and St. Andrew's Univ.

Served British Embassy, Ankara 44-47; Foreign Office 47-49; Khorramshahr, Iran 49-50; Second Sec. Information, Teheran 50-52; Second Sec. Commercial Dept., Djakarta 52-55; Foreign Office 55-57; First Sec. Commercial Dept., Peking 57-62; First Sec. and Head of Chancery, Santiago 62-64; Consul, Elisabethville, Congo 65-66; Deputy High Commr., Lusaka 66; High Commr. to Guyana 67-70; Head of Perm. Under-Sec.'s Dept., Foreign and Commonwealth Office 70-73; High Commr. to Malawi 73-.

British High Commission, P.O. Box 30042, Lilongwe, Malawi.

Ritchie, Robert James, C.B.E.; Australian airline executive; b. 5 Nov. 1915, Hurlstone Park, N.S.W.; *s.* of R. L. H. Ritchie; *m.* Gwendoline Rose Lester 1937; four *s.* one *d.*; ed. Cleveland Street High School, Sydney.

Joined Amalgamated Wireless (Australasia) Ltd. 29, later flew with Kingsford Smith Aerial Services Ltd., Sydney, and Mandated Airlines Ltd., New Guinea; Pilot, W. R. Carpenter & Co. 38; First Officer, Qantas Airways Ltd. 43, Capt. 44, Flight Capt. 46; Flight Capt. (Constellations) 47-48; Flight Supt., Kangaroo Service 47-48; Asst. Operations Man., Qantas 49-55, Technical Man. 55-59, Dir. of Technical Services 59-61, Deputy Chief Exec. and Deputy Gen. Man. 61-67, Gen. Man. 67-, Dir. 70-.

Leisure interests: golf, swimming.
Office: Qantas House, 70 Hunter Street, Sydney, New South Wales; Home: 12 Graham Avenue, Pymble, N.S.W., Australia.

Ritchie-Calder, Baron (Life Peer), cr. 66, of Balmashannar; **Peter Ritchie Ritchie-Calder,** C.B.E., M.A.; British writer and university professor; b. (Peter) Ritchie Calder, 1 July 1906, Forfar; *s.* of David Lindsay Calder and Georgina Ritchie; *m.* Mabel Jane Forbes McKail 1927; three *s.* two *d.*; ed. Forfar Acad., Scotland.

Police Court Reporter, *Dundee Courier* 22, *Daily News* (London) 26-30, *Daily Chronicle* 30, *Daily Herald* 30-41; Dir. of Plans of Political Warfare, Foreign Office 41-45; Special Adviser, Supreme H.Q. 45; Science Editor *News Chronicle* 45-57; Editorial Staff, *New Statesman* 45-57; mem. Council, British Asscn. 45-60, U.K. Del. UNESCO 46, 47, 66, 68; Special Adviser, FAO Famine Conf. 46, UN and Specialized Agencies Missions for Deserts 49-50, S.E. Asia 51, 62, Arctic 55, Congo 60; UN Sec. Atoms for Peace Conf. 55, 58; Prof. of Int. Relations, Edinburgh Univ. 61-67; Visiting Prof. Heriot Watt Univ. 73-; Chair. Edinburgh Univ. Settlement; Fellow World Acad. of Arts and Science; U.K. Metrication Board 69-72; Founder mem. and fmr. Chair. Asscn. British Science Writers; mem. Gen. Council, Open Univ. 69-; Senior Fellow, Center for Study of Democratic Insts., Santa Barbara, Calif. 72-; UNESCO Kalinga Prize 60, Victor Gollancz Award 69; D.Univ. (Open Univ.) 75.

Publs. *The Birth of the Future* 34, *Conquest of Suffering*

35, *Roving Commission* 35, *The Lesson of London* 41, *Carry on London* 41, *Start Planning Britain Now* 41, *Profile of Science* 51, *Men Against the Desert* 51, *The Lamp is Lit* 51, *Men Against Ignorance* 53, *Men Against the Jungle* 54, *Science Makes Sense* 55, *Medicine and Man* 57, *Men Against the Frozen North* 58, *Ten Steps Forward* 58, *The Hand of Life* 59, *From Magic to Medicine* 59, *The Inheritors* 61, *Agony of the Congo* 61, *Living With the Atom* 62, *The Life Savers* 62, *Commonsense about a Starving World* 62, *Two-Way Passage* 64, *Man and the Cosmos* 68, *Evolution of the Machine* 68, *Leonardo and the Age of the Eye* 71, *How Long Have We Got?* 72, *Pollution of the Mediterranean* 72.

1 Randolph Place, Edinburgh 3, Scotland; 10 Denny Crescent, London, S.E.11, England.

Telephone: 031-225-5565; 01-735-8969.

Rithaudeen al-Haj bin Tengku Ismail, Y.M. Tengku Ahmad; Malaysian lawyer and politician; b. 1933; mem. of Royal family of Kelantan; ed. Nottingham Univ.
Member of Kelantan State Parl. for Kota Bharu; fmr. legal adviser to Kelantan State Govt., resigned to enter private practice; Minister with Special Functions Assisting Prime Minister on Foreign Affairs 73-75; mem. Supreme Council, United Malays' Nat. Org. June 75-; Minister for Foreign Affairs Aug. 75-; Chair. Farmers' Org. Authority.
Ministry of Foreign Affairs, Kuala Lumpur, Malaysia.

Ritschard, Willi; Swiss politician; b. 28 Sept. 1918, Deitingen/So.; s. of Ernest F. Ritschard and Frieda Ryf; m. Greti Hostettler 1941; one s. one d.; ed. Schweizerische Arbeiterschule.
Member of the Municipal 43; Mayor 47-59; mem. City Council, Solothurn Canton 45-63; Nat. Councillor 55-63; mem. Council of States for Solothurn Canton 64-73; mem. Fed. Council 73-; Head Dept. of Transport, Communications and Power 73-; Social Democrat.
Leisure interests: gardening, mountain walking.
Département des transports et communications et de l'énergie, 3003 Berne, Bundeshaus–Nord, Amthausgasse 15, Switzerland.

Ritt, Martin; American film director; b. 2 March 1920, New York; s. of Morris and Rose Ritt; ed. Elon Coll.
Numerous Broadway acting appearances 37-55; appeared in *Winged Victory* (film) 44; directed numerous productions on Broadway incl. *Mr. Peebles and Mr. Hooker* 46, *Yellow Jack* 47, *The Big People* 47, *Set My People Free* 48, *The Man* 50, *Cry of the Peacock* 50, *Golden Boy* 54, *Boy Meets Girl* 54, *The Front Page* 54, *A View from the Bridge* 55, *A Memory of Two Mondays* 55; films directed: *A Man is Ten Feet Tall* 56, *Edge of the City* 56, *The Down Payment* 57, *The Long Hot Summer* 57, *The Sound and the Fury* 58, *The Black Orchid* 59, *Five Branded Women* 60, *Paris Blues* 61, *Adventures of a Young Man* 62, *Hud* 63, *The Outrage* 64, *The Spy Who Came in from the Cold* 65, *Hombre* 67, *The Brotherhood* 68, *The Molly Maguires* 69, *The Great White Hope* 70, *Sounder* 72, *Pete'n'Tillie* 72, *Conrack* 74; mem. Screen Dirs. Guild, American Fed. of TV and Radio Artists, Screen Actors Guild; Peabody Award.
c/o Paramount Pictures, 1501 Broadway, New York, N.Y. 10036, U.S.A.

Ritter, Kurt, DR.AGR.; German university professor; b. 13 April 1894, Berlin; m. Irmgard Benda 1921; one s.
Prof. of Constitutional Law, Univ. of Berlin 28-34; independent activities 35-45, administrative activities 45-51; Prof. and Dir. of Inst. for Agricultural Policy and Agricultural History, Humboldt Univ. Berlin 51-57; Dir. of Inst. for Agricultural History of Deutsche Akad. der Landwirtschaftswissenschaften, Berlin 57-61; mem. Deutsche Akad. der Landwirtschaftswissenschaften, Berlin; Nat. Prize 56, Vaterländischer Verdienstorden in Gold 70.
Leisure interest: writing novels under pseudonym.
Publs. *Die Einwirkung des weltwirtschaftlichen Verkehrs*

auf die Entwicklung und den Betrieb der Landwirtschaft, insbesondere in Deutschland 21, *Deutschlands Wirtschaftslage und die Produktionssteigerung der Landwirtschaft* 22, *Agrarzölle* 24, *Weltproduktion und Welthandel der Molkereierzeugnisse* 30, *Svetová Krise Zemedelská* 30, *Die Krise der deutschen Agrarpolitik* 31, *Die Schweinehaltung der Welt und der Handel mit ihren Erzeugnissen* 31, *Die Produktion und Aussenhandel der Vereinigten Staaten von Amerika an Gartenbauerzeugnissen* 31, *Die Standardisierung landwirtschaftlicher und gartenbaulicher Erzeugnisse in den Vereinigten Staaten von Amerika* 31, *Weltproduktion und Welthandel an frischen Südfrüchten* 33, *Agrarpolitische Aufsätze und Vorträge* (18 vols.) 24-33, *Muss ein grosser Teil der Menschheit weiter hungern?* 56, *Agrarwirtschaft und Agrarpolitik im Kapitalismus* Vol. I (2nd edn.) 56, Vol. II 59, *Zu einigen aktuellen Tendenzen und Widersprüchen in der kapitalistischen Landwirtschaft* 59.
Dorfstrasse 29, Altenhof via Eberswalde, German Democratic Republic.

Ritter-Aislán, Eduardo, PH.D.; Panamanian diplomatist and educator; b. 11 Sept. 1916, Panama; s. of Federico Ritter and Juana Aislán de Ritter; m. 1st Elida Domingo 1939 (died 1956), 2nd Katherine Mason 1958; three s. three d.; ed. Univ. of Panama and Pontificial Catholic Javeriana Univ. of Bogotá, Colombia.
Private Sec. to Pres. of Repub. of Panama 51; Prof. of Languages, Washington and Jefferson Coll., Wash., Pa. 46-47; Prof. of Romance Languages, Howard Univ., Wash., D.C. 47-49; Prof. of Philosophy, Univ. of Panama 49-53, 55-57, 63-65; Amb. to Colombia 57-58, 60-61; Alt. Amb. to UN 58-60; Amb. to Org. of American States 65-71, Chair. Council of Org. of American States (OAS) 66-67; decorations from Govts. of Panama, Colombia, Peru, Nicaragua, Vatican, and from Orgs. in U.S.A., Greece, Denmark, France and Italy.
Leisure interests: chess, weight-lifting, painting.
Publs. *Umbral* 40, *Crisalida* 41, *Nenúfares: Poemas Orientales* 41, *Mastil* 47, *Poemas* 50, *Espigas al Viento* 51, *Rosicler* (First Prize in Nat. Contest "Ricardo Miró") 55, *Silva de Amor y otros poemas* 57, *Tornasol* 67, *Así hablaba Bem Asser* 68.
Betania 783, Panama City, Panama.

Ritz, Charles C.; Swiss hotel executive; b. 1891; ed. Univ. of Commerce, Geneva.
Chairman, Ritz Hotel, Paris; Dir. Ritz Hotel, London, Ritz Hotel, Lisbon, Ritz Carlton, Boston; manufacturer of fishing tackle.
Publs. *A Fly Fisher's Life, Pris sur le vif, Erlebetes Fliegenfischer, A la mouche*.
Hotel Ritz, 15 place Vendôme, 75001 Paris, France.
Telephone: OPEra 28-30.

Ritzel, Gerhard Albert Johannes, DR. RER. POL.; German diplomatist; b. 12 April 1923, Michelstadt; s. of Heinrich G. and Elisabeth (née Lack) Ritzel; m. Ursula Fastenrodt 1966; two d.; ed. Univs. of Basle, Geneva, Zürich and Heidelberg.
Deputy Chief of Research, Jelmoli S.A., Zürich; entered foreign service 51, posted to Bombay, Colombo, New York and Los Angeles; Foreign Office, Bonn 60, Chef de Cabinet 67; Chancellor's Office 69; Amb. to Norway 70-74, to Czechoslovakia 74-.
Leisure interests: music, horseback riding.
c/o Ministerium des Ausseren, Bonn, Federal Republic of Germany.

Rivero, Admiral Horacio, Jr.; American diplomatist and fmr. naval officer; b. 16 May 1910, Ponce, Puerto Rico; s. of Horacio Rivero and Margarita DeLucca; m. Hazel Hooper 1941; one d.; ed. Univ. Naval Acad., and Mass. Inst of Technology.
Commissioned ensign, U.S. Navy 31, served in *U.S.S. San Juan* 42-44, in *U.S.S. Pittsburgh* 44-45; with Staff Office, Atomic Defence, Navy Dept. 45-48; Commdg.

Officer *U.S.S. W.C. Law* 48; with Weapons Systems Evaluation Group 49-51; Commdg. Officer *U.S.S. Noble* 51-52; Nat. War Coll. 53; Staff C.-in-C. Pacific Fleet 53-55; Deputy Chief Armed Forces Special Weapons Project 55-57; Commdr. Destroyer *Flotilla* 57-58; Dir. Long Range Objectives, Navy Dept. 58-60; Deputy Chief Staff C.-in-C. Atlantic Command and Fleet 60-62, Commdr. Amphibious Force 62-65; Vice-Chief Naval Operations 65-68; C.-in-C. Allied Forces, S. Europe 68-72; Amb. to Spain 72-74; D.S.M., Legion of Merit and decorations from Ecuador, Brazil, Spain, Greece, Italy and Turkey.
1424 Tenth Street, Coronado, Calif., U.S.A.

Rivett, Rohan Deakin, B.A.; Australian journalist; b. 1917, Melbourne; s. of Sir David and Lady Rivett (née Deakin); m. Nancy Ethel Summers 1947; two s. one d.; ed. Wesley Coll., Melbourne, Queen's Coll., Melbourne Univ. and Balliol Coll., Oxford.
Reporter, *Melbourne Argus* 39-40; War Corresp. Radio Singapore 41-42; Prisoner of War 42-45; Reporter, *Melbourne Herald* 46-48, Melbourne Herald Cable Service, China, Britain and Europe 48-51; Editor *Adelaide News* 51-60; Dir. News Ltd. of Australia 52-60; Foreign Affairs Commentator ABC 48-; Columnist *Canberra Times* 64-, *Nation Review* 70-; Chair. Australian Cttee. Int. Press Inst. (IPI) 54-62; Dir. IPI Zurich 62-64; Commentator on int. affairs (TV and radio) 64-; mem. Council of Authors 65-; Pres. Melbourne Press Club 74-76; Coronation Medal, Commonwealth Literary Award 67; Fellow Queen's Coll. Univ. of Melbourne 66-; Fellow Royal Soc. of Arts, London 72.
Leisure interest: watching test cricket.
Publs. *Behind Bamboo* 46, *The Migrant and the Community* 58, *Australia 1970 and Beyond* (Co-Author) 58, *Australia Looks Ahead* (Co-Author) 61, *Australian Citizen: Herbert Brookes 1867-1963* 65, *Australia* (OUP Modern World Series) 68, *Writing about Australia* 69, *David Rivett: Fighter for Australian Science* 72.
147 Wattle Valley Road, Camberwell, Victoria, 3124 Australia.
Telephone: Melbourne 29-39-13.

Rivette, Jacques; French film director; b. 1 March 1928; ed. Lycée Corneille, Rouen.
Journalist and Critic on *Cahiers du Cinéma* 53-; Asst. to Jacques Becker and Jean Renoir 54; Dir. of Films 56-. Films: *Le coup du berger* (director) 56, *Paris nous appartient* (author and director) 58-60, *La Religieuse* (director) 66, *L'Amour fou* 68, *Out One: Spectre* 73, *Céline et Julie vont en bateau* 74, *Le Vengeur*.
20 boulevard de la Bastille, 75012 Paris, France.

Rivière, Georges Henri; French ethnographer and museologist; b. 1897, Paris.
Honorary Chief Keeper of Musée national des arts et traditions populaires; Perm. Adviser of Int. Council of Museums; Officer, Legion of Honour.
ICOM, Maison de l'Unesco, 1 rue Miollis, 75015 Paris; 7 rue Pierre Louÿs, 75016 Paris, France.
Telephone: 527-79-62 (Home).

Rivlin, Moshe; Israeli executive; b. 16 Jan. 1925, Jerusalem; s. of Yitzhak and Esther Rivlin; m. Ruth Moav (Horbaty) 1960; two d.; ed. Teachers' Seminary, Graduate Aluma Inst. for Jewish Studies and School for Political Science, Jerusalem.
Director, Information Dept., The Jewish Agency 58-60, Sec.-Gen. 60-66, Dir.-Gen. and Head of Admin. and Public Relations Dept. 66-71; elected Dir.-Gen. of reconstituted Jewish Agency 71; Assoc. mem. Exec., World Zionist Org. 71; Nat. Chair. Haganah Veterans Asscn. in Israel; mem. Board of Governors Ben-Gurion Univ., Coll. for Public Admin., Jewish Telegraphic Agency; mem. Exec. Cttee. Yad Ben-Zvi, mem. Council Yad Ben-Gurion; mem. Board of Dirs. *Jerusalem Post*.

The Jewish Agency, P.O. Box 92, Jerusalem; 34 Hapalmach Street, Jerusalem, Israel.
Telephone: 223706 (Office).

Roa Bastos, Augusto; Paraguayan writer and journalist; b. 1917; ed. Asunción.
Awarded John Simon Guggenheim Memorial Foundation 71.
Publs. Poetry: *El Ruiseñor y la Aurora* 36, *El Naranjal Ardiente* 47-49; Novels: *El Trueno entre las Hojas* 53, *Hijo de hombre* 60, *El Baldío* 66, *Los Pies sobre el Agua* 67, *Madera Quemada* 67, *Moriencia* 69, *Cuerpo Presente y otros cuentos* 71, *Yo el Supremo* 74, *Los Congresos* 74; Screen plays: *El Trueno entre las Hojas* 55, *Hijo de Hombre* 60, *Shunko* 60, *Alias Gardelito* 63, *Castigo al Traidor* 66, *El Señor Presidente* 66, *Don Segundo Sombra* 68.
Berutti 2828, Martínez, Buenos Aires, Argentina.

Roa García, Dr. Raúl; Cuban author, professor and politician.
Lecturer in Law and Social Sciences, then Prof. Univ. of Havana; Dean of Social Sciences 48-59; Cuban Rep., Org. of American States 56-58; Minister of Foreign Affairs 59-; Guggenheim Fellow 45-46; Nat. journalism award Justo de Lara 54.
Publs. *Historia de las Doctrinas Sociales* 48, *Quince Años Después* 50, *Viento Sur* 53, *Retorno a la Alborada* 64.
Ministerio de Asuntos Exteriores, Havana, Cuba.

Robarts, David John; British banker; b. 1906; ed. Eton and Magdalen Coll., Oxford.
Chairman Nat. Provincial Bank Ltd. 54-68; Dir. Nat. Westminster Bank Ltd. (Chair. 69-71), Robert Fleming and Co. Ltd., Union Discount Co. of London Ltd. and other companies; Chair. Cttee. of London Clearing Bankers until 70.
Lillingstone House, Buckingham, England.

Robarts, Eric Kirkby; British dairy executive; b. 1908, Northwood, Middx.; s. of Charles Martin Robarts and Flora Kirkby; m. Lucy Iris Swan 1930; five d.; ed. Bishops Stortford College and Hertfordshire Inst. of Agriculture, St. Albans.
Producer-retailer with C. M. Robarts & Son., which was acquired by Express Dairy 42; Dir. Express Dairy 47, Man. Dir. 60, Deputy Chair. 66-67, Chair. 67-73; fmr. Chair. Middlesex Agricultural Exec. Cttee.; Deputy Chair. Herts. Agricultural Exec. Cttee., Nat. Milk Publicity Council; Dir. Grand Metropolitan Hotels Ltd. 69-73.
Leisure interests: hunting, shooting, tennis.
Frithcote, Watford Road, Northwood, Middx., England.

Robarts, John Parmenter, Q.C., P.C.; Canadian politician; b. 1917; ed. Univ. of Western Ontario and Osgoode Hall Law School.
Naval service 40-45; Called to the Bar of Ontario 47, Q.C. 54; mem. London Ontario City Council 50; mem. Ontario Legislature 51, 55, 59; Minister of Educ. 59-62; Prime Minister of Ontario 61-71; Dir. Reed Shaw Osler Ltd. (insurance brokers) 71-, Canadian Imperial Bank of Commerce 71-; partner Robarts, Betts, McLennan and Flinn; Hon. LL.D. (Univ. of Toronto, Univ. of Ottawa).
366 Richmond Street, London, Ont.; and Suite 5220, Commerce Court West, P.O. Box 85, Toronto, Ont.; Home: 1084 The Parkway, London, Ont., Canada.

Robbe-Grillet, Alain; French writer and agronomist; b. 18 Aug. 1922, Brest; s. of Gaston Robbe-Grillet and Yvonne Canu; m. Catherine Rstakian 1957; ed. Lycée Buffon, Lycée St. Louis and Inst. Nat. Agronomique, Paris.
Chargé de Mission, Inst. Nat. de la Statistique 45-48; Engineer Inst. des Fruits Tropicaux (Guinea, Morocco, Martinique and Guadeloupe) 49-51; Literary Adviser Editions de Minuit.

Publs. Novels: *Les Gommes* 53, *Le Voyeur* 55, *La Jalousie* 57, *Dans le Labyrinthe* 59, *La Maison de Rendez-vous* 65, *Projet pour une Révolution à New York* 70, *Topologie d'une Cité Fantôme* 76; essay: *Pour un Nouveau Roman* 64; films: *L'Année Dernière à Marienbad* 61, *L'Immortelle* 63, *Trans-Europe Express* 66, *L'Homme qui Ment* 68, *L'Eden et Après* 70, *Glissements Progressifs du Plaisir* 73, *Le Jeu avec le Feu* 75; short stories: *Instantanés* 62.
18 boulevard Maillot, 92 Neuilly-sur-Seine, France.
Telephone: 722.31-22.

Robbins, Baron (Life Peer), cr. 59, of Clare Market; **Lionel Charles Robbins,** C.B., C.H., B.SC.(ECON.), M.A., F.B.A.; British economist; b. 22 Nov. 1898; s. of late Rowland Richard Robbins, C.B.E.; m. Iris Elizabeth Gardiner 1924; one s. one d.; ed. Univ. Coll., London, and London School of Economics.
Served First World War 16-19; Lecturer, New Coll., Oxford 24, London School of Economics 25-27; Fellow and Lecturer, New Coll., Oxford 27-29; Prof. of Economics in Univ. of London 29-61; Hon. Fellow Univ. Coll., London, London School of Econs., London Graduate School of Business Studies, Manchester Coll. of Science and Technology; Dir. Econ. Section Offices of the War Cabinet 41-45; mem. Council Royal Econ. Soc., Board of Trustees, Nat. Gallery 52-59, 60-74, Tate Gallery 53-59, 62-67; Dir. Royal Opera House, Covent Garden 56-; Chair. *Financial Times* 61-Jan. 71; Pres. British Acad. 62-67; Chair. Prime Minister's Cttee. on Higher Educ. 61-63; Chancellor, Univ. of Stirling 68-; Chair. Court of Govs., London School of Economics 68-74, mem. 74-; mem. Accad. dei Lincei, American Philosophical Soc., American Acad. of Arts and Sciences; Hon. L.H.D. (Columbia); Hon. D.Litt. (Durham, Exeter, Strathclyde, Sheffield, Heriot Watt); Hon. LL.D. (Strasbourg, Exeter, Leicester and Cambridge Univs. and Univ. of Calif.); Doutor en Ciências Económicas e Financeiras (Tech. Univ., Lisbon); Hon. D.Sc.(Econ.) (London), and numerous other hon. degrees.
Leisure interest: the arts.
Publs. *An Essay on the Nature and Significance of Economic Science, The Great Depression, Economic Planning and International Order, The Economic Basis of Class Conflict and Other Essays in Political Economy, The Economic Causes of War, The Economic Problem in Peace and War, The Theory of Economic Policy in English Classical Political Economy, The Economist in the Twentieth Century, Robert Torrens and the Evolution of Classical Economics, Politics and Economics, The University in the Modern World, The Theory of Economic Development in the History of Economic Thought, The Evolution of Modern Economic Theory, Autobiography of an Economist, Money, Trade and International Relations, Political Economy Past and Present.*
10 Meadway Close, London, N.W. 11, England.

Robbins, Frederick Chapman, A.B. B.S., M.D.; American scientist and university professor; b. 25 Aug. 1916, Auburn, Ala.; m. Alice Havemeyer Northrop 1948; two d.; ed. Univ. of Missouri and Harvard Medical School.
Served U.S. Army 42-46; Senior Fellow, Nat. Research Council 48-50; Research Fellow, Harvard Medical School 48-50; Instructor, Harvard Medical School 50-51, Assoc. (Pediatrics) 51-52; Assoc., Research Div. of Infectious Disease, Children's Medical Center, Boston 50-52; Assoc. Physician and Assoc. Dir. of Isolation Services, Children's Hospital, Boston 50-52; Research Fellow, Boston Lying-in Hospital 50-52; Asst. Children's Medical Service, Mass. Gen. Hospital, Boston 50-52;. Dir. Dept. of Pediatrics and Contagious Diseases, Cleveland Metropolitan Gen. Hospital 52-66; Prof. of Pediatrics, Case Western Reserve Univ. School of Medicine, Cleveland 52-, Dean 66-; Assoc. Pediatrician Univ. Hospitals, Cleveland 52-; mem. Nat. Acad. of Sciences 72, American Philosophical Soc. 72; Bronze Star 45; First Mead Johnson Award (jointly) 53; Nobel Prize (jointly) 54; Medical Mutual Honor Award for 1969; Hon. D.Sc. (John Carrol and Mo. Univs.); Hon. LL.D. (Univ. of New Mexico) 68.
Publs. various scientific papers related to virus and rickettsial diseases, especially "Q" fever in the Mediterranean area and cultivation of poliomyelitis viruses in tissue culture.
Case Western Reserve University, 2119 Abington Road, Cleveland, Ohio 44106; and 2467 Guilford Road, Cleveland Heights, Ohio 44118, U.S.A.
Telephone: 216-368-2820.

Robbins, Harold (*pseudonym* of Francis Kane); American author; b. 21 May 1916, New York; m. 1st Lillian Machnivitz (dissolved); m. later Grace Palermo; two d.; ed. George Washington High School, New York.
Food and commodity dealer, New York until 40; Shipping Clerk, later Dir. of Budget and Planning, Universal Pictures, New York 40-46.
Publs. *Never Love a Stranger* 48, *The Dream Merchants* 49, *A Stone for Danny Fisher* 52, *Never Leave Me* 53, *79 Park Avenue* 55, *Stiletto* 60, *The Carpetbaggers* 61, *Where Love Has Gone* 62, *The Adventurers* 66, *The Inheritors* 69, *The Betsy* 71, *The Pirate* 74.
c/o Paul Griffin, 7 West 51st Street, New York, N.Y. 10019, U.S.A.

Robbins, Jerome; American choreographer and director; b. 1918; ed. New York Univ.
Dancer in Broadway choruses 38-40; American Ballet Theatre soloist 41-46; Assoc. Artistic Dir., New York City Ballet 49-; formed Ballets: U.S.A.; touring U.S. and Europe 58-; Antoinette Perry (Tony) Award for *Fiddler on the Roof* 65.
Choreographed: Ballets: *Fancy Free* 44, *Interplay* 45, *Facsimile* 47, *Pas de Trois* 47, *The Cage* 51, *Fanfare* 53, *Afternoon of a Faun* 53, *The Concert* 56, *N.Y. Export op. Jazz* 58, *Moves* 61, *Events* 61, *Les Noces* 65, *Dances at a Gathering* 70, *Requiem Cantides* 72, *In the Night, The Dybbuk Variations* 74, *Mother Goose* 75, and many others; Musicals include: *On the Town* 45, *High Button Shoes* 47, *Call Me Madam* 50, *The King and I* 51 (film 56), *The Pajama Game* (co-dir.) 54, *Bells are Ringing* (dir.) 56, *West Side Story* (dir. and choreographer) 57, (film 60), *Gypsy* (dir. and choreographer) 59, *Oh Dad, Poor Dad* (dir.) 62, *Fiddler on the Roof* (dir. and choreographer) 64; Opera: *The Tender Land* 54.
c/o New York City Ballet, Center of Music and Drama, 131 West 55th Street, New York, N.Y. 10019, U.S.A.

Robbins, John Dennis, O.B.E., T.D., F.C.A.; British accountant, company executive and merchant; b. 28 July 1915, London; s. of Duncan Ross Robbins and Harriette Winifred Robbins (née Goodyear); m. Joan Mary Mason 1942; one s. two d.; ed. Aldenham School.
Commissioned Middlesex Regt. 39; Served Middle East and twice mentioned in dispatches; retd. as Lieut.-Col. 46; Partner, Kay Keeping & Co. (chartered accountants) 46-49; Dir. The British Metal Corpn. Ltd. 50, Man. Dir. 63; Dir. Amalgamated Metal Corpn. Ltd. 65, Chair. 75-; Dir. Aluminium Bahrain 67, Chair. 69; Dir. Smith & Nephew Associated Cos., Norddeutsche Affinerie, Hamburg, London Board of Advice, Nat. Bank of Australasia Ltd.
Leisure interests: gardening, shooting, fly-fishing.
Inworth Hall, Kelvedon, near Colchester, Essex, England.
Telephone: Kelvedon (0376) 70318.

Robbins, John Everett, M.A., PH.D.; Canadian diplomatist (retd.); b. 9 Oct. 1903, Hampton, Ont.; s. of John and Gertrude (Brown) Robbins; m. Catherine Saint-Denis 1934; two s.; ed. schools in Ontario and Manitoba and Univs. of Manitoba and Ottawa.

Director of Educ. and Information Divs., Dominion Bureau of Statistics 30-51; Dir. of Educ. for Palestine Refugees (UNESCO) in Middle East 51-52; Editor-in-Chief *Encyclopedia Canadiana* 53-58; Sec.-Treas. Humanities Research Council of Canada and Social Science Research Council of Canada 58-60; Pres. Brandon Coll. 60-67, Brandon Univ. 67-69; First Amb. of Canada to the Vatican 70-73; Chair. of Exec. Amnesty Int. Canada 73-74, Treas. 74-75; Dir. Canadian Writers' Foundation, Pres. 76-.
Leisure interests: United Nations Asscn., Canadian Asscn. for Adult Educ., Canadian Citizenship Council, Humanities Research Council of Canada and Social Science Research Council, Amnesty International, Canada.
Publs. Numerous reports, monographs and articles.
336 Island Park Drive, Ottawa K1Y OA7, Ontario, Canada.
Telephone: 728-3061.

Robbins, William Jacob, A.B. (Lehigh), HON. SC.D., PH.D. (Cornell), SC.D. (Fordham); American botanist; b. 22 Feb. 1890, North Platte, Nebraska; s. of Frederick Woods Robbins and Clara J. Federhoof; m. Christine Chapman 1915; three s.; ed. Lehigh and Cornell Univs. Instructor in Biology, Lehigh Univ. 10-11; Summers Asst., Marine Biology Laboratory, Woods Hole 12-14; Instructor Plant Physiology Cornell Univ. 12-16; Prof. Botany Alabama Polytechnic Inst. and Plant Physiologist Agricultural Experiment Station 16-17; Soil Biochemist, Bureau Plant Industry, U.S. Dept. of Agriculture 19; Prof. Botany Missouri Univ. 19-37, Dean Graduate Faculty 30-37; Prof. Botany, Columbia 37-58; Dir. N.Y. Botanical Garden 37-58, Prof. and Dir. Emeritus 58-; mem. Nat. Acad. of Sciences and Nat. Research Council 48-, Treas. 48-60; mem. American Philosophical Soc. of Philadelphia 41; Trustee Rockefeller Univ. 56-70; Pres. American Philosophical Soc. 56-59, Exec. Officer 59; Assoc. Dir. Nat. Science Foundation 62-63; Pres. Fairchild Tropical Garden 62-69.
Leisure interests: fishing, reading.
Publ. *General Botany.*
Rockefeller University, 66th Street and York Avenue, New York, N.Y. 10021; Home: 301 East 66th Street, New York, N.Y. 10021, U.S.A.
Telephone: 212-360-1563 (Office).

Robens of Woldingham, Baron, cr. 61 (Life Peer), of Woldingham in the County of Surrey; **Alfred Robens,** P.C., D.C.L., LL.D.; British politician; b. 18 Dec. 1910, Manchester; s. of George and Edith Robens; m. Eva Powell 1937; ed. Council School.
Official of Union of Distributive and Allied Workers 35-; Manchester City Councillor 42-45; Labour M.P. for Wansbeck Div. of Northumberland 45-50, Blyth 50-60; Parl. Private Sec. to Minister of Transport 45-47; Parl. Sec. Minister of Fuel and Power 47-51; Minister of Labour April-Oct. 51; Labour Relations Consultant, Atomic Power Construction Ltd. 60; Dep. Chair. Nat. Coal Board 60-61, Chair. 61-71; Chair. Johnson Matthey and Co. Ltd. 71-, Vickers Ltd. 71-; mem. Nat. Econ. Devt. Council (N.E.D.C.) 62-71; Pres. Advertising Asscn. 63-67; Chair. Foundation on Automation and Employment 70; Chair. Council of the Manchester Business School 70-; mem. Royal Comm. on Trade Unions and Employers' Asscns. 65-68; Chair. Govt. Enquiry into Safety and Health of People at Work; Chair. Engineering Industries Council 75-; Gov. Queen Elizabeth's Training Coll. for the Disabled 51-; Chair. of Govs. Guy's Hosp. June 65; Dir. J. H. Sankey and Son Ltd., Bank of England 66-, St. Regis Paper Co. (U.K.) 71-, Trust-Houses-Forte Ltd., Times Newspapers; Chancellor, Univ. of Surrey 66-; Hon. D. Civil Law (Newcastle Univ.), Hon. LL.D. (Leicester and Man-

chester Univs.); Dir. Times Newspapers Ltd.; Chair. Joint Econ. Mission to Malta 67.
Leisure interest: gardening.
Publs. *Human Engineering* 70, *Ten Year Stint* 71.
Walton Manor, Walton-on-the-Hill, Surrey, England.

Robert, Louis; French archaeologist; b. 15 Feb. 1904, Laurière, Haute-Vienne; s. of Léon and Valentine Robert; m. Jeanne Vanseveren 1938; ed. Paris Univ., Ecole Normale Supérieure.
Member French School, Athens 27-32; Dir. of Studies, Ecole des Hautes Etudes 32-74; Prof. of Greek Epigraphy and Antiquities, Coll. de France 39-74; dir. excavations at Amyzon 49 and Claros (Temple of Apollo) 50-61; mem. Acad. des Inscriptions et Belles Lettres (Pres. 55 and 66) and of numerous foreign acads.; Officier Légion d'Honneur.
Publs. *Villes d'Asie Mineure, Etudes Anatoliennes, Les Gladiateurs dans l'Orient Grec, Etudes de Numismatique Grecque, Hellenica* (13 vols.), *Noms Indigènes dans l'Asie Mineure, La Carie* (with his wife, Jeanne Robert), *Monnaies antiques en Troade, Monnaies grecques, Opera Minora Selecta* (4 vols.), etc.
31 avenue René Coty, 75014 Paris, France.

Roberthall, Baron (Life Peer), cr. 69, of Silverspur, Queensland, and Trenance, Cornwall; **Robert Lowe Hall,** K.C.M.G., C.B., M.A., B.ENG.; British economist; b. 6 March 1901, Tenterfield, N.S.W., Australia; s. of Edgar and Rose Hall; m. 1st Laura Margaret Linfoot 1932 (dissolved 1968), two d.; m. 2nd Perilla Thyme Nowell-Smith 1968; ed. Univ. of Queensland and Magdalen Coll., Oxford.
Lecturer in Econs., Trinity Coll., Oxford 26-27; Fellow of Trinity Coll., Oxford 27-49; temporary civil servant 39-45; Dir. Econ. Section, Cabinet Office 47-53; Econ. Adviser to Her Majesty's Govt. 53-61; mem. of Econ. Planning Board 47-61; Vice-Pres. Royal Econ. Soc. (Pres. 58-60); Advisory Dir. Unilever Ltd. 61-May 71; Adviser, Tube Investments Ltd. 61-; Principal, Hertford Coll., Oxford 64-67; Pres. Soc. of Business Economists 68-73.
Leisure interest: gardening.
Publs. *Earning and Spending* 34, *The Economic System in a Socialist State* 36, *The Place of the Economist in Government* (Sidney Ball Lecture, Oxford) 56, *Planning* (Rede Lecture, Cambridge) 63.
7A Carey Mansions, Rutherford Street, London, S.W.1; and Trenance, Newquay, Cornwall, England.
Telephone: St. Mawgan 242.

Roberti, H.E. Cardinal Francesco; Vatican ecclesiastic; b. 1889.
Ordained priest 13; created Cardinal by Pope John XXIII 58; mem. Sacred Congregations of Sacraments, of the Council, De Propaganda Fide; Prefect Emeritus Supreme Tribunal of the Apostolic Signature 59-; mem. Comm. for the Interpretation of Canon Law; Pres. Court of Cassation.
Piazza San Callisto 16, 00153 Rome, Italy.

Roberto, Holden (*see* Holden, Roberto).

Roberts, Chalmers McGeagh, A.B.; American journalist; b. 18 Nov. 1910; m. Lois Hall 1941; two s. one d.; ed. Amherst Coll.
Reporter *Washington Post*, D.C. 33-34, Associated Press, Pittsburgh Bureau 34-35, *Toledo News-Bee* 36-38, *Japan Times*, Tokyo 38-39; Asst. Man. Editor *Washington Daily News* 39-41; Sunday Editor *Washington Times-Herald* 41; Office of War Information, London and Washington 41-43; U.S. Army Air Force 43-46; *Life* magazine 46-47; *Washington Star* 47-49; *Washington Post* 49-, Chief Diplomatic corresp. 54-71, Columnist 71-; Hon. Dr. of Humane Letters 63.
Publs. *Washington Past and Present* 50, *Can We Meet the Russians Half Way?* 58, *The Nuclear Years: the*

Arms Race and Arms Control, 1945-70 70, *First Rough Draft: a Journalist's Journal of Our Times* 73.
Washington Post, 1150 15th Street, N.W., Washington, D.C. 20005; Home: 6699 MacArthur Boulevard, Washington, D.C. 20016, U.S.A.

Roberts, Sir Denys Tudor Emil, K.B.E., Q.C., M.A., B.C.L.; British barrister and administrator; b. 19 Jan. 1923, London; ed. Aldenham School, Wadham Coll., Oxford and Lincoln's Inn.
Captain, Royal Artillery 43-46; English Bar 50-53; Crown Counsel, Nyasaland (now Malawi) 53-59; Attorney-Gen., Gibraltar 60-62; Solicitor-Gen., Hong Kong 62-66, Attorney-Gen. 66-73; Colonial Sec., Hong Kong 73-.
Publs. five novels 55-65.
Colonial Secretariat, Hong Kong; Home: Victoria House, 15 Barker Road, Hong Kong.

Roberts, Sir Frank Kenyon, G.C.M.G., G.C.V.O., M.A.; British diplomatist (retd.); b. 27 Oct. 1907, Buenos Aires, Argentina; s. of Henry George Roberts and Gertrude Kenyon; m. Celeste Leila B. Shoucair 1937; ed. Bedales and Rugby Schools and Trinity Coll., Cambridge.
Third Sec. Foreign Office 30-32, British Embassy, Paris 32-35; Second Sec. Cairo 35-37, Foreign Office 37-45 (First Sec. 41, Head of Central Dept. 41-45, Acting Counsellor 43); Chargé d'Affaires to Czechoslovak Govt. in London 43; Minister to U.S.S.R. 45-47; Private Sec. to Foreign Sec. 47-49; mission to Moscow 48; Deputy High Commr. in India 49-51; Deputy Under-Sec. of State, Foreign Office 51-54; Amb. to Yugoslavia 54-57; U.K. Perm. Rep. on N. Atlantic Council Feb. 57-60; Amb. to U.S.S.R. 60-62, to Fed. Repub. of Germany 63-68; Advisory Dir. Unilever Ltd., Dir. Dunlop Ltd., Adviser on Int. Affairs to Lloyds; Pres. British Atlantic Cttee., Vice-Pres. Atlantic Treaty Asscn. 73-; Chair. European-Atlantic Group 70-73, Pres. 73-; mem. Review Cttee. on Overseas Representation; mem. Council of the Royal Inst. for Int. Affairs; Pres. German Chamber of Industry and Commerce 71-74; Grand Cross of German Order of Merit.
Leisure interests: golf, reading, travelling, international relations.
25 Kensington Court Gardens, London, W8 5QF, England.
Telephone: 01-937-1140.

Roberts, George A., D.SC.; American business executive; b. 18 Feb. 1919, Uniontown, Pa.; s. of Jacob Earle Roberts and Mary Mildred Bower; m. Jeanne Polk Roberts 1971; two s. one d.; ed. Carnegie Inst. of Technology.
President and Chair. of the Board, Vasco Metals Corp. until 66; Pres. and mem. of the Board of Dirs., Teledyne Inc. 66-; formerly Int. Pres. American Soc. for Metals, Pres. American Soc. for Metals Foundation for Education and Research, Trustee Council for Profit Sharing Industries, Trustee Trade Relations Council and Chair. of the Board Metallurgy-Ceramics Foundation Inc.; mem. Board of Trustees, Carnegie-Mellon Univ.; Fellow of the Metallurgical Soc. of the American Inst. of Mining, Metallurgical and Petroleum Engineers and the American Soc. for Metals.
Publs. *Tool Steels*; many technical papers.
Teledyne Inc., 1901 Avenue of the Stars, Los Angeles, Calif. 90067, U.S.A.

Roberts, Henry Reginald, B.A.; American (b. Canadian) life assurance executive; b. 2 June 1916, Toronto, Ont.; s. of Alfred Reginald and Mary Margaret (Creighton) Roberts; m. Margaret Elizabeth Fisher 1940; two s. two d.; ed. Univ. of Toronto.
With Mfrs. Life Insurance Co., Toronto 37-42; went to U.S. 45, naturalized 54; joined Connecticut Gen. Life Insurance Co., Hartford 45, Second Vice-Pres. 58-60,

Exec. Vice-Pres. and Dir. 60-61, Pres. and Chief Exec. Officer 61-; Chair. of Board Aetna Insurance Co. (affiliate) 66, Chair. Investment Cttees. both cos. 66; Pres. and Dir. Conn. Gen. Insurance Corpn. (parent co.) 67; Dir., Gen. Foods Corpn., S. New England Telephone Co., Greater Hartford Corpn.; mem. Advisory Cttee. on Business Programs, Brookings Inst.; Dir. Int. Exec. Service Corps; Trustee, Rensselear Polytechnic Inst. of Conn., Conn. Public Expenditure Council, Kingswood-Oxford School; mem. advisory board, Council for Financial Aid to Educ.; fmr. Dir. Health Insurance Inst., Inst. of Life Insurance; Chair. Insurance Asscn. of Conn.; mem. Special Cttee. on Capital Funding of Atomic Energy Devt. of American Life Insurance Asscn.; Fellow, Soc. of Actuaries; Hon. L.H.D. (Clarkson Coll. of Technology), Hon. LL.D. (Trinity Coll., Univ. of Hartford).
Connecticut General Life Insurance Company, Hartford, Conn. 06152; 171 Bloomfield Avenue, Hartford, Conn., U.S.A.
Telephone: 203-243-8811.

Roberts, John Alexander Fraser, C.B.E., M.A., M.D., D.SC., F.R.C.P., F.R.S.; British geneticist; b. 8 Sept. 1899, Denbigh.; s. of Robert H. and Elizabeth M. Roberts; m. 1st Doris Breamer Hare 1941, 2nd Margaret Dorothy Ralph 1975; two d.; ed. Univs. of Cambridge, Edinburgh, Bristol and Univ. Coll. of N. Wales, Bangor.
Research Asst. Animal Breeding Research Dept., Univ. of Edinburgh 22-28; Biologist, Wool Industries Research Asscn. 28-31; Macaulay Research Fellow, Univ. of Edinburgh 31-33; Dir. of Research, Burden Mental Research Dept., Bristol 33-57; Surgeon-Commdr. R.N.V.R. and Consultant, Medical Statistics, Royal Navy 42-46; Dir. Clinical Genetics Research Unit, Medical Research Council 57-64; Consultant in medical genetics, Great Ormond Street Children's Hospital, London; Geneticist, Paediatric Research Unit, Guy's Hospital, London 64-; Hon. Consultant in Medical Genetics 64-.
Leisure interest: mountain walks.
Publs. *An Introduction to Medical Genetics* (6th edn.) 80; papers in medical and genetical journals.
Paediatric Research Unit, Guy's Hospital Medical School, London, S.E.1; 10 Aspley Road, Wandsworth, London, S.W.18, England.
Telephone: 01-407-7000, Ext. 477; Home: 01-874-4826.

Roberts, John D., PH.D.; American chemist and educator; b. 8 June 1918, Los Angeles, Calif.; s. of Allen Andrew Roberts and Flora Dombrowski; m. Edith M. Johnson 1942; three s. one d.; ed. Univ. of Calif. at Los Angeles.
Instructor Univ. of Calif. at Los Angeles; Nat. Research Fellow in Chem., Harvard Univ. 45-46, Instructor 46; Instructor Mass. Inst. of Technology 46-47, Asst. Prof. 47-50; Assoc. Prof. 50-53; Guggenheim Fellow, Calif. Inst. of Technology 52-53, Prof. of Organic Chem. 53-72, Inst. Prof. of Chem. 72-, Chair. Div. of Chem. and Chemical Engineering 63-68, Acting Chair. 72-73; Visiting Prof. Ohio State Univ. 52, Harvard Univ. 59-60, Univ. of Munich 62; Distinguished Visiting Prof. Univ. of Iowa 67; Visiting Prof. Stanford Univ. 73; mem. Nat. Acad. of Sciences, Chair. Section of Chem. 68-71; mem. American Philosophical Soc. 74; Dr. h.c. (Univ. of Munich and Temple Univ.); American Chemical Soc. Award in Pure Chem. 54, Harrison Howe Award 57, Roger Adams Award 67, Univ. of Calif. at Los Angeles Alumni Achievement Award 67, Nichols Medal 72, Richard C. Tolman Medal 75.
Leisure interests: tennis, skiing, sailing, classical music, colour-photography.
Publs. *Nuclear Magnetic Resonance* 58, *Spin-Spin Splitting in High-Resolution Nuclear Magnetic Resonance Spectra* 61, *Molecular Orbital Calculations* 61, *Basic Principles of Organic Chemistry* 65, *Modern*

Organic Chemistry 67, *Organic Chemistry, Methane to Macromolecules* 71; and numerous articles 40-.
Gates and Crellin Laboratories, California Institute of Technology, Pasadena, Calif. 91125, U.S.A.
Telephone: 213-795-6841.

Roberts, Walter Orr, PH.D.; American solar astronomer; b. 20 Aug. 1915, West Bridgewater, Mass.; s. of Ernest Marion and Alice Elliot Orr Roberts; *m.* Janet Naomi Smock 1940; three s. one d.; ed. public schools, Brockton, Mass., Amherst Coll. and Harvard Univ.
Established and directed solar coronagraph station of Harvard Coll. Observatory, Climax, Colorado 40-46; Dir. High Altitude Observatory, Boulder, Colorado 46-60; Dir. Nat. Center for Atmospheric Research, Boulder 60-68; Pres. Univ. Corpn. for Atmospheric Research, Boulder 67-73, Past Pres. and Trustee 73-; Pres. American Asscn. for Advancement of Science 68; Trustee The MITRE Corpn., Amherst Coll. 64-70, Kettering Foundation 64-70, Max C. Fleischmann Foundation, Aspen Inst. for Humanistic Studies 70-, Int. Fed. of Insts. for Advanced Study 72-; Dir. Program on Science, Technology and Humanism, Aspen Inst. for Humanistic Studies 74-; Head Subcttee. of U.S.-U.S.S.R. Co-operative Programme on Man's Impact on the Environment 73-; mem. Editorial Board *Journal of Planetary and Space Science*, U.S.-Japan Cttee. on Scientific Co-operation 68-, Environmental Group, UN Asscn. of U.S.A. 70-; fmr. mem. Advisory Cttee. World Meteorological Org., Geophysics Board of Nat. Acad. of Sciences; Gen. mem. Board of Dirs., Int. Inst. for Environmental Affairs 71-; mem. Cttee. on Int. Environmental Programs of the Nat. Acad. of Sciences 71-, Defense Science Board, Dept. of Defense 72-; Trustee, Upper Atmosphere Research Corpn. 71-; Hon. D.Sc. (Ripon Coll., Amherst Coll., The Colorado Coll., C. W. Post Coll. of L.I. Univ., Carleton Coll., Southwestern at Memphis, Univ. of Colorado, Univ. of Denver); Hodgkins Medal, Smithsonian Inst. 73.
Leisure interests: music, gardening, flying.
National Center for Atmospheric Research, Boulder, Colorado 80303, U.S.A.
Telephone: 303-494-5151.

Robertson, Harold Rocke, C.C., B.SC., M.D., C.M., F.R.C.S., F.A.C.S., F.R.S.C., D.C.L., LL.D., D.SC.; Canadian surgeon; b. 4 Aug. 1912, Victoria, B.C.; s. of Harold Bruce Robertson and Helen McGregor Rogers; *m.* Beatrice Roslyn Arnold 1937; three s. one d.; ed. St. Michael's School, Victoria, B.C., Ecole Nouvelle, Coppet, Switzerland, Brentwood Coll., Victoria, B.C., and McGill Univ.
Chief of Surgery, Shaughnessy Hospital, D.V.A., Vancouver 45-59; Chief of Surgery, Vancouver Gen. Hospital 50-59; Prof. of Surgery Univ. of British Columbia 50-59; Surgeon-in-Chief Montreal Gen. Hospital 59-62; Prof. of Surgery, Chair. of Dept., McGill Univ. 59-62; Principal and Vice-Chancellor McGill Univ. 62-70; Pres. Conf. of Rectors and Principals of Quebec Univs. 68-.
Leisure interests: tennis, fishing, gardening, golf.
Publs. Numerous articles in medical journals and medical textbooks.
301 Buena Vista Road, Ontario K1M 0W1, Canada.
Telephone: (613) 746-5409.

Robertson, James Louis; American government official; b. 31 Oct. 1907, Broken Bow, Neb.; *m.* Julia Jensen 1928; three s.; ed. Grinnell Coll., Iowa, George Washington Univ., and Harvard Law School.
U.S. Senate Post Office 27; later Special Agent, Fed. Bureau of Investigation; admitted to Court of Appeals Bar, D.C. 31, to Supreme Court of United States 35; Office of Comptroller of Currency 33-43; U.S. Naval Reserve 43-44; Dep. Comptroller of Currency 44-52;

mem. Board of Govs. Fed. Reserve System 52-, Vice-Chair. 66-73.
Leisure interests: reading, tennis, squash.
Office: Federal Reserve Board, Washington, D.C. 20551; 5114 Brookview Drive, Westhaven, Md., U.S.A.
Telephone: RE 7-1100, Ext. 217 (Office).

Robertson, Sir James Wilson, K.T., G.C.M.G., G.C.V.O., K.B.E., M.A.; British overseas administrator; b. 27 Oct. 1899, Broughty Ferry, Angus; s. of James Robertson and Margaret Eva Wilson; *m.* Nancy Walker 1926; one s. one d.; ed. Merchiston Castle School, Edinburgh and Balliol Coll., Oxford.
Asst. District Commr. Sudan Political Service 22; District Commr. 33; Compensation Commr. Jebel Aulia Dam 36; Sub. Gov. White Nile Province 37; Deputy Gov. Gezira Province 39, Acting Gov. 40-41; Asst. Civil Sec. 41-42; Deputy Civil Sec. 42-45, Civil Sec. 45-53 (periodically Acting Gov.-Gen. of the Sudan); Chair. British Guiana Constitutional Comm. 54; Dir. Uganda Co. Ltd. 54-55, 61-69; Hon. Fellow, Balliol Coll. 53-; Gov.-Gen. and C.-in-C. Nigeria 55-Nov. 60; Chair. Commonwealth Inst. 61-68; Dir. Barclays Bank D.C.O. 61-71; Commr. Kenya Coastal Strip Inquiry 61, Chair. Royal Overseas League 62-68; Deputy Chair. Nat. Cttee. for Commonwealth Immigrants 65-68; Gov. Queen Mary Coll., Univ. of London 61-72; mem. Exec. Council, Royal Commonwealth Soc. for the Blind 61-; Hon. LL.D. (Leeds).
Leisure interests: walking, gardening.
Publ. *Transition in Africa from Direct Rule to Independence.*
The Old Bakehouse, Cholsey, Oxfordshire, England; Douglas Cottage, Killichonan, Rannoch Station, Perthshire, Scotland.
Telephone: Cholsey 651234; Bridge of Gaur 242.

Robertson, John Monteath, C.B.E., M.A., PH.D., D.SC., LL.D., F.R.I.C., F.INST.P., F.R.S., F.R.S.E.; British university professor; b. 24 July 1900, Perthshire, Scotland, s. of William Robertson and Jane Monteath; *m.* Stella Kennard Nairn 1930; two s. one d.; ed. Perth Acad., and Glasgow Univ.
Commonwealth Fellow, U.S.A. 28-30; mem. of staff, Davy Faraday Research Laboratory, The Royal Institution, London 30-39; Senior Lecturer in Physical Chemistry, Univ. of Sheffield 39-41; Scientific Adviser (Chemical) H.Q. Bomber Command, R.A.F. 41-42; Gardiner Prof. of Chemistry and Dir. of the Chemical Laboratories, Univ. of Glasgow 42-70, Emeritus Prof. 70; mem. Univ. Grants Cttee. 60-64; mem. Turin Acad. of Sciences; Davy Medal, Royal Soc. 60, Longstaff Medal, Chemical Soc. 66, Paracelsus Medal, Swiss Chemical Soc. 71; Pres. Chemical Soc. 62-64; Hon. LL.D. (Aberdeen), Hon. D.Sc. (Strathclyde).
Leisure interest: travel.
Publs. *Organic Crystals and Molecules* 53, *Organic Structure Reports* (Editor) 40-53, 57, 60, 61, *Computing Methods and the Phase Problem* (Editor) 61, *International Review of Science, Physical Chemistry* Vol. II (Editor) 72, 75; about 300 research papers in *Journal of the Chemistry Society* and *Proceedings of the Royal Society*, etc.
42 Bailie Drive, Bearsden, Glasgow; and The University, Glasgow, W.2., Scotland.
Telephone: 041-942-2640 (Home).

Robertson, Sir Rutherford Ness, Kt., C.M.G., D.SC., PH.D., F.R.S.; Australian botanist; b. 29 Sept. 1913, Melbourne; s. of Rev. J. Robertson; *m.* Mary Rogerson 1937; one s.; ed. St. Andrew's Coll., Christchurch, New Zealand, Sydney Univ., and St. John's Coll., Cambridge.
Assistant Lecturer, later Lecturer in Botany, Sydney Univ. 39-46; Senior Research Officer, later Chief

Research Officer, Commonwealth Scientific and Industrial Research Org. (C.S.I.R.O.), Div. of Food Preservation 46-59, mem. Exec. of C.S.I.R.O. 59-62; Visiting Prof. Univ. of California 58-59; Prof. of Botany, Univ. of Adelaide 62-69; Chair. Australian Research Grants Cttee. 65-69; Master, Univ. House, Australian Nat. Univ., Canberra 69-72; Dir. Research School of Biological Sciences 72-; Fellow, Australian Acad. of Science 54, Pres. 70-74; Foreign Assoc. U.S. Acad. of Sciences 62; Pres. Australian and New Zealand Asscn. for the Advancement of Science 65; Foreign mem. American Philosophical Soc. 71, Hon. mem. Royal Soc. of New Zealand 71, Hon. Foreign mem. A.A.A.S. 73, Hon. Fellow St. John's Coll. Cambridge 73; Clarke Memorial Medal, Royal Soc. of New South Wales 54; Farrer Memorial Medal 63; A.N.Z.A.A.S. Medal 68; Mueller Medal 70; Burnet Medal 75.
Leisure interests: riding, watercolours.
Publ. *Electrolytes in Plant Cells* (co-author) 61, *Protons, Electrons Phosphorylation and Active Transport* 68.
Research School of Biological Sciences, Australian National University, Canberra, A.C.T. 2600, Australia.
Telephone: 49-2469.

Robichaud, Hédard J., M.P.; Canadian politician; b. 1911; ed. Académie Sainte-Famille, Tracadie, Sacred Heart Coll. and Saint Joseph Univ.
Inspector of Fisheries, Dominion Govt. 39-46; Dir. of Fisheries, New Brunswick 46-52; M.P. 53-68, Minister of Fisheries 63-68; Senator 68-; Lieut.-Gov. New Brunswick 72-; Liberal.
Government House, Fredericton, New Brunswick, Canada.

Robichaud, Hon. Louis Joseph, Q.C.; Canadian politician; b. 21 Oct. 1925, St. Anthony, Kent County, N.B.; s. of Amedee and Annie (née Richard) Robichaud; ed. Sacred Heart and Laval Univs.
Private law practice 51-60; mem. New Brunswick Legislature 52-, Leader of Opposition 58-60; Premier of New Brunswick 60-70, Minister of Youth 68; Hon. Dr. of Commerce (Univ. of Moncton); Liberal.
2365 Georgina Drive, Ottawa, Ont., Canada.

Robinson, Sir Albert Edward Phineas, Kt., M.A.; British (Rhodesian) business executive; b. 1915; ed. Durban High School and Stellenbosch, London, Cambridge and Leiden Univs.
Barrister-at-Law, Lincoln's Inn; Imperial Light Horse, N. Africa 40-43; mem. Johannesburg City Council and Leader United Party in Council 45-48; United Party M.P., South African Parl. 47-53; perm. resident in S. Rhodesia 53-; Dir. banks, building socs., several financial and industrial cos. 53-61; Chair. Cen. African Airways Corpn. 57-61; mem. Monckton Comm. 60; High Commr., Fed. of Rhodesia and Nyasaland in the U.K. 61-63; Chair. Johannesburg Consolidated Investment Co. Ltd., Rustenburg Platinum Mines Ltd.; Exec. Dir. Anglo-American Corpn. of South Africa Ltd.; Dir. Anglo-American Corpn. Rhodesia Ltd., and other companies in Rhodesia and South Africa.
P.O. Box 2341, Salisbury, Rhodesia; P.O. Box 590, Johannesburg, South Africa.

Robinson, (Arthur Napoleon) Raymond, M.A., LL.B., M.P.; Trinidadian politician; b. 11 Dec. 1926, Calder Hall; s. of James Andrew Robinson and Emily Isabella Robinson; m. Patricia Jean Rawlins 1961; one s. one d.; ed. Bishop's High School, Tobago, St. John's Coll., Oxford and, Inner Temple, London.
M.P. West Indies 58-61; Rep. of Trinidad and Tobago Council of Univ. of West Indies 59-61; Minister of Finance and Governor for Trinidad Board of Govs. of Int. Monetary Fund and Int. Bank for Reconstruction and Development 61-67; Deputy Leader, People's National Movement 67-70; Minister of External Affairs 67-68; Consultant to the Foundation for the Establishment of an Int. Criminal Court 71; Chair.

Democratic Action Congress 71-; Studentship Prize, Inner Temple.
Leisure interests: walking, swimming, travel.
Publs. *The New Frontier and the New Africa* 61, *Fiscal Reform in Trinidad and Tobago* 66, *The Path of Progress* 67, *The Teacher and Nationalism* 67, *The Mechanics of Independence* 71.
21 Ellerslie Park, Maraval, Trinidad, Trinidad and Tobago.
Telephone: 62-25544.

Robinson, Sir (Edward) Austin (Gossage), Kt., C.M.G., O.B.E., F.B.A., M.A., British economist; b. 20 Nov. 1897, Farnham; s. of Rev. A. G. Robinson (Canon of Winchester Cathedral) and Edith (née Sidebotham) Robinson; m. Joan Maurice (q.v. Joan Robinson) 1926; two d.; ed. Marlborough Coll. and Christ's Coll., Cambridge.
Fellow of Corpus Christi Coll. Cambridge 23-26; Tutor to H.H. the Maharajah of Gwalior 26-28; Univ. Lecturer Cambridge 29; Fellow of Sidney Sussex Coll. Cambridge 31-; mem. Econ. Section War Cabt. 39-42; Chief Econ. Adviser and Head of Programmes Div., Ministry of Production 42-45; mem. Reparations Mission, Moscow and Berlin 45; Econ. Adviser, Board of Trade 45-46; Cen. Econ. Planing Staff 47-48; mem. U.K. Del. to OEEC 48; Reader in Econs. Univ. of Cambridge 49, Prof. of Econs. 50-65, now Emer.; Sec. Royal Econ. Soc. 46-72; Treas. Int. Econ. Asscn. 50-59, Pres. 59-62; mem. Exec. Council Dept. Scientific and Industrial Research 54-59; OEEC Adviser on Italian Development 54-58; Chair. OEEC Energy Advisory Comm. 57-60; Dir. of Econs., Ministry of Power 67-68; Joint Editor *The Economic Journal* 44-72; Fellow, British Acad.
Leisure interest: visiting developing countries.
Publs. *The Structure of Competitive Industry* 32, *Monopoly* 40; Editor or Joint Editor: *Economic Consequences of the size of Nations* 60, *Economic Development of Africa South of the Sahara* 63, *Problems in Economic Development* 65, *The Economics of Education* (with J. E. Vaizey) 66, *Backward Areas in Advanced Countries* 69, *Economic Development in South Asia* 70, *Economic Prospects of Bangladesh* 73.
Sidney Sussex College, Cambridge, England.
Telephone: Cambridge 57815.

Robinson, Forbes; British opera singer; b. 21 May 1926, Macclesfield, Cheshire; s. of Wilfred and Gertrude Robinson; m. Marion Stubbs 1952; two d.; ed. Kings School, Macclesfield, St. Pauls Coll., Cheltenham, and Loughborough Coll.
Trained in Leicester, Manchester and at La Scala, Milan 52-53; Debut, Covent Garden 54, and Promenade Concerts 57; Principal Bass, Royal Opera House, Covent Garden 54-; has sung in opera and concerts in Europe, Argentina and the U.S.A. and many festivals in Europe, also in four television operas and own radio series; created title role *King Priam* (Tippett) and was the first to play the speaking role of Moses in *Moses and Aaron* (Schönberg) in English; first British singer to sing *Don Giovanni* at Covent Garden for over 100 years 70; guest artist with Handel Opera, Sadler's Wells Opera, Scottish Opera and Welsh Nat. Opera; won Great Caruso Voice Contest 52, Opera Medal 63.
Leisure interests: swimming, walking.
225 Princes Gardens, London, W.3, England.
Telephone: 01-992-5498.

Robinson, Prof. Joan Violet; British economist; b. 31 Oct. 1903; m. Edward A. G. Robinson (q.v.) 1926; two d.; ed. St. Paul's Girls' School, London and Girton Coll., Cambridge.
Assistant Lecturer in Econs., Cambridge Univ. 31, Lecturer 37-49, Reader 49-Oct. 65, Prof. 65-71; retd. 73; Special Prof. Stanford Univ., Spring 69.
Publs. *Economics of Imperfect Competition* 33, *Essays in*

the *Theory of Employment* 37, *Introduction to the Theory of Employment* 37, *Essay on Marxian Economics* 42, *Collected Economic Papers* Vols. I to IV 51-73, *The Rate of Interest and Other Essays* 52, *The Accumulation of Capital* 56, *Essays in the Theory of Economic Growth* 62, *Economic Philosophy* 63, *Economics: An Awkward Corner* 66, *The Cultural Revolution in China* 69, *Freedom and Necessity* 70, *Economic Heresies* 71, *Introduction to Modern Economics* (with John Eatwell) 73.
62 Grange Road, Cambridge, England.

Robinson, Rt. Rev. John Arthur Thomas, M.A., PH.D., B.D., D.D.; British ecclesiastic and writer; b. 15 June 1919, Canterbury; s. of Rev. Canon A. W. and Mrs. Beatrice Robinson; m. Ruth Grace 1947; one s. three d.; ed. Marlborough Coll., Jesus and Trinity Colls., Cambridge, and Westcott House, Cambridge.
Curate, St. Matthew, Moorfields, Bristol 45-48; Chaplain, Wells Theological Coll. 48-51; Fellow and Dean, Clare Coll., Cambridge 51-59; Lecturer in Divinity, Cambridge Univ. 53-59; Examining Chaplain to Archbishop of Canterbury 53-59; Six Preacher, Canterbury Cathedral 58-68; Bishop Suffragan of Woolwich 59-69; Asst. Bishop of Southwark 69-; Proctor in Convocation, Diocese of Southwark 60-70; Fellow and Dean of Chapel, Trinity Coll., Cambridge 69-; Hulsean Lecturer, Cambridge Univ. 70.
Publs. *In the End, God . . .* 50 (revised edn. 68), *The Body* 52, *Jesus and His Coming* 57, *On Being the Church in the World* 60, *Christ Comes In* 60, *Liturgy Coming to Life* 60, *Twelve New Testament Studies* 62, *Honest to God* 63, *The Honest to God Debate* 63, *Christian Morals Today* 64, *The New Reformation?* 65, *But that I can't Believe!* 67, *Exploration into God* 67, *Christian Freedom in a Permissive Society* 70, *The Difference in Being a Christian Today* 72, *The Human Face of God* 73, *Redating the New Testament* 76.
Trinity College, Cambridge, England.
Telephone: Cambridge 58201.

Robinson, John Foster, C.B.E., D.L., T.D.; British business executive; b. 2 Feb. 1909, Bristol; s. of late Sir Foster Gotch Robinson and late Marguerite Victoria M. Clarke; m. Margaret Paterson 1935; two s. two d.; ed. Harrow and Christ Church, Oxford.
Director E. S. and A. Robinson Ltd. 43-48, Man. Dir. 48-58, Deputy Chair. 58-61, Chair. E. S. and A. Robinson (Holdings) Ltd. 61-; Deputy Chair. Dickinson Robinson Group Ltd. 66-68, Chair. 68-74, Hon. Vice-Pres. 74-; Chair. John Dickinson and Co. Ltd. 68-74; Dir. Eagle Star Insurance Co. Ltd. 68-; Chair. South-West Regional Board Nat. Westminster Bank Ltd. 69-; Dir. Bristol and West Building Soc.
Leisure interests: shooting, fishing, cricket, golf.
St. George's Hill, Easton-in-Gordano, near Bristol, England.

Robinson, Rt. Hon. Kenneth, P.C.; British politician; b. 19 March 1911, Warrington; s. of late Clarence Robinson and of Marion Robinson (née Linnell); m. Helen Elizabeth Edwards 1941; one d.; ed. Oundle School.
Insurance Broker, Lloyds' 27-40; Naval service 41-46; Company Sec. 46-49; M.P. 49-70; Asst. Whip 50-51, Opposition Whip 51-54; Minister of Health 64-68; Minister for Planning and Land, Ministry of Housing and Local Govt. Nov. 68-Oct. 69; Vice-Pres. Asscn. for Mental Health 58-; mem. Exec. Cttee. The Nat. Trust 51-64, 71-, Council 70-; Chair., Sadler's Wells Opera 71-; Man. Dir. Personnel, British Steel Corpn. 71-74; Chair. London Transport Exec. 75-; Labour.
Publs. *Wilkie Collins, a Biography* 51, *Policy for Mental Health* 58, *Patterns of Care* 61, *Look at Parliament* 62.
12 Grove Terrace, London, N.W.5, England.

Robinson, Kenneth Ernest, C.B.E., M.A., D.LITT., LL.D., F.R.HIST.S.; British historian and university administrator; b. 9 March 1914, London; s. of late Ernest and

Isabel Robinson; m. Stephanie Christine S. Wilson 1938; one s. one d.; ed. Monoux Grammar School, Walthamstow, Hertford Coll., Oxford, and London School of Economics.
Entered Colonial Office 36; Asst. Sec. 46-48, resgnd.; Fellow of Nuffield Coll. 48-57, Librarian 51-57; Reader in Commonwealth Govt., Oxford 48-57; Leverhulme Research Fellow 52-53; Visiting Lecturer, School of Advanced Int. Studies, Johns Hopkins Univ. 54, Duke Univ. 63, Acadia Univ. 63; part-time mem., Directing Staff, Civil Service Selection Board 51-56, Chairman Panel 72-; Prof. of Commonwealth Affairs and Dir. of Inst. of Commonwealth Studies, Univ. of London 57-65; mem. Colonial Econ. Research Cttee. 49-62, Colonial Social Science Research Council 58-62, Council of Overseas Devt. Inst. 60-65, Royal Inst. of Int. Affairs 62-65, Int. African Inst. 60-65, African Studies Asscn. of U.K. 63-65, Asscn. of Commonwealth Univs. 67-69, Royal Asiatic Soc. Hong Kong Branch 65-69, Hong Kong Management Asscn. 66-72, Council, Univ. of Cape Coast 72-, Inter-Univ. Council for Higher Educ. Overseas 73-; Gov. London School of Econs. 59-65; Vice-Chancellor, Univ. of Hong Kong 65-72; Halls-worth Res. Fellow, Manchester Univ. 72-74; Dir. Survey of Resources for Commonwealth Studies, Univ. of London 74-75; J.P. Hong Kong 67-72; corresp. mem. Acad. des Sciences d'Outre-Mer, Paris; Hon. LL.D. (Chinese Univ. of Hong Kong) 69; Editor *Journal of Commonwealth Political Studies* 61-65; Special Commonwealth Award, Ministry of Overseas Devt. 65.
Publs. *Africa Today* (co-author) 55, *Africa in the Modern World* (co-author) 55, *Five Elections in Africa* (with W. J. M. Mackenzie) 60, *Essays in Imperial Government* (with A. F. Madden) 63, *The Dilemmas of Trusteeship* 65, *A Decade of the Commonwealth* (with W. B. Hamilton and C. Goodwin) 66, *University Co-operation and Asian Development* (co-author) 67, *L'Europe au XIXe et XXe siècles*, Vol. VII (co-author) 67.
The Old Rectory, Church Westcote, Oxford, OX7 6SF; 10c St. Augustine's Road, London, NW1 9RN, England.
Telephone: Shipton under Wychwood 830586; 01-485-1198.

Robles, Marco Aurelio; Panamanian politician; b. 8 Nov. 1905.
Former government official; Minister of Govt. and Justice 60-64; Pres. of Panama 64-68; Partido Liberal.
Partido Liberal, Panama City, Panama.

Robson, Dame Flora McKenzie, D.B.E.; British actress; b. 28 March 1902, South Shields, Durham; d. of D. M. Robson and Eliza McKenzie; ed. Palmers Green High School, London.
D.Litt. h.c. (Durham, London, Oxford Univs. and Univ. of Wales); Hon. Fellow, St. Anne's Coll., Oxford 75, Sunderland Tech. Coll. 75; Orders of White Lion and White Rose, Finland.
Leisure interests: gros-point needlework, reading.
Appearances include *Will Shakespeare* 21, *Desire Under the Elms* 31, *Dangerous Corner* 32, *For Services Rendered* 32, *All God's Chillun* 32, Shakespeare productions at the Old Vic 32-33; plays: *Ladies in Retirement*, *Black Chiffon* and *Macbeth* in New York; *The House by the Lake* 56-58, Ibsen's *Ghosts* 58-59, *The Aspern Papers* 59-60, *Time and Yellow Roses* 61, *The Corn is Green* 61, *Close Quarters* 63, *John Gabriel Borkman* 63, *Importance of Being Earnest* 68, 75, *The Old Ladies* 69 in London; *Brother and Sister* 67 on tour; *Ring Round the Moon* 68 in London; also films in London and Hollywood, film *Alice in Wonderland*.
Marine House, 14 Marine Gardens, Brighton 7, Sussex, England.

Robson, Sir Hugh Norwood, Kt., M.B., CH.B., F.R.C.P. (LONDON), F.R.C.P.(EDINBURGH), F.R.A.C.P.; British physician and university administrator; b. 18 Oct.

1917, Langholm, Scotland; *s.* of Hugh Robson and Elizabeth Warnock; *m.* Alice Eleanor Livingstone 1942; one *s.* two *d.*; ed. Langholm and Dumfries Academies, Edinburgh Univ.

Surgeon-Lieut., R.N.V.R. 42-46; Lecturer in Medicine, Univ. of Edinburgh 47-50; Senior Lecturer and Asst. Physician, Univ. of Aberdeen 50-52; Prof. of Medicine and Physician, Univ. of Adelaide 53-65; Vice-Chancellor Univ. of Sheffield 66-74; Principal and Vice-Chancellor, Univ. of Edinburgh 74-; Honeyman Gillespie Lecturer 49, 59, Listerian Lecturer 54, Bancroft Lecturer 65, Keith Inglis Memorial Lecturer 68; Fellow, Royal Soc. of Edinburgh; Hon. D.Sc. (Pennsylvania) 75; Hon. LL.D. (Sheffield) 75.

Leisure interests: golf, reading, carpentry.

Publs. *Idiopathic Thrombocytopenic Purpura* 49, *Observations on Kuru* 58, *Human Chromosomal Aberration* 63, *International Medical Care* 72.

Principal's Office, Old College, South Bridge, Edinburgh, EH8 9YL; Home: 14 Heriot Row, Edinburgh, EH3 6HP, Scotland.

Telephone: 031-667-1011 (Office); 031-556-6959 (Home).

Robson, William Alexander, PH.D., LL.M., B.SC. (ECON.); British jurist and political scientist; b. 14 July 1895, London; *s.* of late Jack Robson; *m.* Juliette Alvin 1929; two *s.* one *d.*; ed. London School of Economics and Political Science.

Barrister; Founder and Joint Editor *The Political Quarterly* 30-75; Prof. of Public Admin. London School of Econs. 47-62; Principal, Mines Dept. 40-42, Ministry of Fuel and Power 42-43; Asst. Sec. Air Ministry 43, Civil Aviation 45; mem. Council Town and Country Planning Asscn., Vice-Pres. Inst. of Public Admin., Dept. Cttee. Greater London Planning Admin., Cttee. on training in Public Admin. for Overseas Countries; Pres. Int. Political Science Asscn. 52-55; Vice-Pres. Political Studies Asscn.; Chair. Greater London Group; Hon. Fellow, London School of Econs.; Dr. h.c. (Paris, Lille, Grenoble, Algiers); Hon. D.Litt. (Durham and Manchester Univs.); Hon. D.Soc.Sc. (Birmingham Univ.); Consultant to Govts. of Lebanon, Nigeria, Turkey, Japan, Isle of Man, UNICEF and State Charter Revision Comm. for N.Y.C.

Leisure interests: walking, swimming, tennis, theatre, cinema, reading.

Publs. *The Town Councillor* (with Rt. Hon. C. R. Attlee), *Justice and Administrative Law, The Development of Local Government, The Relation of Wealth to Welfare, The Law of Local Government Audit, A Century of Municipal Progress, Civilization and the Growth of Law, The British Civil Servant, Public Enterprise, The Government and Misgovernment of London, Social Security, The British System of Government, Planning and Performance, The War and the Planning Outlook, Population and the People, British Government since 1918, Problems of Nationalised Industry, The University Teaching of Political Science, Great Cities of the World, The Civil Service in Britain and France, Nationalised Industry and Public Ownership, The Governors and the Governed, Local Government in Crisis, Politics and Government at Home and Abroad, Man and the Social Sciences, Welfare State and Welfare Society.*

48 Lanchester Road, London, N.6, England.

Telephone: 01-883-1331.

Roca, Edwardo Alejandro; Argentine lawyer and diplomatist; b. 15 Dec. 1921, Buenos Aires; *s.* of Marcos Roca and María Teresa Hunter; *m.* Magdalena Figueroa 1947; three *s.* three *d.*; ed. State Univ. of Buenos Aires School of Law.

Has specialized in commercial law, insurance and financial matters, and taught modern languages; mem. drafting cttee. of Arbitration Tribunal of Commodity Exchange; Legal Advisor to Ministry of Interior; Chief Secr. of Minister of Justice and Inspector of Corpns.;

Under-Sec. of Justice; presided over comm. that proposed reforms to Argentina's commercial laws; mem. Exec. Cttee. of Argentine Inst. of Commercial Law; Rep. of Argentina on Council of OAS 66-68; Amb. to U.S. Sept. 68-Oct. 69.

Sarmiento 643, Buenos Aires (Office); Cerrito 1154, Buenos Aires, Argentina (Home).

Roca Calderío, Blas; Cuban politician; b. 1908, Manzanillo-Oriente; ed. Grammar School.

Former cobbler; official Cuban Shoe Workers' Union 29-30; Sec.-Gen. Communist Party of Cuba (IC Section) 34-39; Del. Constituent Assembly 39-40; M.P. 40-52; Sec.-Gen. Popular Socialist Party 42-60; mem. Central Cttee., Political Bureau and Secr. Communist Party; Dir. *Hoy* 62-65.

Publs. *Los Fundamentos del Socialismo en Cuba, Aclaraciones* (3 vols.), *Martí Revolucionario Radical* (pamphlet 48), *Veneno en "La Quincena"* 61.

Prado y Teniente Rey, Havana, Cuba.

Rocaut-Quillet, Jean; French publisher; b. 6 May 1898.

Sec.-Gen. Publishing Co., Aristide Quillet 31-50, Deputy Dir. 50, Pres., Dir.-Gen. 55-; Pres., Dir.-Gen. *Les Dernières Nouvelles de Strasbourg* 61-; Vice-Pres. Syndicat des Quotidiens Régionaux; Commdr. Légion d'Honneur, Croix de Guerre.

Home: 4 rue André-Colledeboeuf, Paris 16e; Office: 278 Boulevard St. Germain, Paris. 7e, France.

Rocha, Antonio; Mexican politician; b. 1912; ed. Univ. Autónoma de San Luis Potosí.

Lawyer 35-; Justice Attorney for State of San Luis Potosí; Sec.-Gen. Govt. of State of Tamaulipas; Deputy to Union Congress; Senator; Pres. of Senate and Senate Comms. on Legislative and Constitutional Matters; Prof. of Penal Law and Procedure; fmr. Attorney-Gen. of Mexico; Rep. of Mexican Govt. at various int. confs. in Latin America; mem. Mexican Acad. of Penal Sciences, Int. Asscn. of Penal Law and Mexican Soc. of Geography and Statistics.

The Senate, Mexico City, Mexico.

Rocha-e-Silva, Mauricio, DR.MED.; Brazilian pharmacologist and biochemist; b. 1910, Rio de Janeiro; *s.* of João Olavo da Rocha e Silva and Alzira Couto Rocha e Silva; one *s.* two *d.*; ed. Univ. of Rio de Janeiro.

Research Asst., Faculty of Sciences of São Paulo Univ. 35-37; Asst. Instituto Biológico, São Paulo 37-42, Head of Dept. of Biochemistry and Pharmacodynamics 42-; Lecturer, Univs. of Brazil and São Paulo 52; Prof. Pharmacology, Univ. of São Paulo 57-; Co-founder and Pres. Brazilian Asscn. for Advancement of Science; Fellow of Guggenheim Foundation, N.Y. for research work in U.S.A. 40-42; Fellow of British Council for research work in London 46-47; Fogarty Scholar, Nat. Inst. of Health, Bethesda, Md. 73-74; full mem. Brazilian Acad. of Sciences; Hon. mem. American Acad. of Allergy.

Leisure interests: photography, painting, travel.

Publs. *Histamine and Anaphylaxis* 46, *Bradykinin* 49, *Histamine, its Role in Anaphylaxis and Allergy* 55, *Histamine and Antihistaminics* (section of book) 66, *Foundations of Pharmacology* 61, 68, 69, 73, *Kinin Hormones* 70, *Chemical Mediators of Acute Inflammatory Reaction* 72, *Fondamenti di Farmacologia* (Italian edn.) 74, *A Bradykinin Anthology* 75, *Histamine and Antihistaminics* (part II).

Department of Pharmacology, University of São Paulo, Ribeirão Preto, São Paulo, Brazil.

Rocha Lagoa, Francisco de Paulo da; Brazilian politician and physician; b. 24 Oct. 1919, Rio de Janeiro; *s.* of João Pereira da Rocha Lagoa and Marie Amália Abreu Rocha Lagoa; *m.* Beatriz Toja da Rocha Lagoa 1949; one *s.* one *d.*; ed. Colégio Bicalho, Juiz da Fora, Universidade Federal do Rio de Janeiro, Instituto Osvaldo Cruz, and Instituto Superior de Guerra.

Secretary, Instituto Osvaldo Cruz 43-48; Dir. Instituto Ezquiel Dias, Belo Horizonte 53-56; Prof. of Virology, Escola Média de São Paulo and Universidade Católica de Rio de Janeiro 59; mem. Int. Cttee. on Bacteriological Nomenclature 50-58, Soc. American Bacteriologists, Soc. Belge de Médicine Tropicale; Minister of Health 69-72; Nat. Order of Merit (Paraguay), Knight, Order of Holy Sepulchre (Jerusalem), Knight of the Sovereign Mil., Order of Malta and many Brazilian decorations.

Leisure interests: reading, sports.
Publs. 58 articles, mainly on bacteriology and virology.
186 Epitácio Pessoa Avenue, Ipanema, Rio de Janeiro, Brazil.
Telephone: 2520169; 2525807.

Rochdale, Viscount, cr. 60, 2nd Baron, cr. 13; **John Durival Kemp,** O.B.E., T.D., D.L., B.A.; British industrialist; b. 5 June 1906, Rochdale, Lancs.; m. Elinor Dorothea Pease 1931; one s.; ed. Eton Coll., and Trinity Coll., Cambridge.
Manager and later Dir., Kelsall & Kemp Ltd., Rochdale 28-39; served with British Expeditionary Force in France 39-40; attached to U.S. Forces in Pacific with rank of Colonel 44; later with Combined Operations Command, India; Brigadier 45; mem. Cen. Transport Consultative Cttee. 52-57; Pres. Nat. Union of Manufacturers 53-56; Vice-Pres. British Productivity Council 55-56; Gov. B.B.C. 54-59; Dir. Consett Iron Co. 56-67; Chair. The Cotton Board 57-62; Chair. Kelsall & Kemp Ltd., Rochdale 50-71, Harland and Wolff Ltd., Belfast 71-75 (resgnd.); Dir. Nat. and Commercial Banking Group Ltd. 71-; Chair. Cttee. of Enquiry into the Major Docks of Great Britain 61-62; Deputy Chair. William & Glyn's Bank Ltd. 73-; Pres. British Legion (North Western Area) 54-61, Econ. League 63-69; Pres. Lancashire and Merseyside League 63-69; Vice-Pres. Lancashire and Merseyside Industrial Devt. Asscn.; mem. Western Hemisphere Exports Council 53-64; mem. Past Upper Bailiff, Worshipful Co. of Weavers; Chair. Nat. Ports Council 63-67, Cttee. of Inquiry into Shipping Industry 67-70.
Leisure interests: forestry, gardening.
Lingholm, Keswick, Cumberland, England.
Telephone: Keswick 72003.

Roche, (Eamonn) Kevin; American architect; b. 14 June 1922, Dublin, Ireland; s. of Eamon and Alice (Harding) Roche; m. Jane Tuohy 1963; two s. three d.; ed. Nat. Univ. of Ireland and Illinois Inst. of Technology.
With Eero Saarinen & Associates 50-66, Chief Designer 54-66; Partner, Kevin Roche, John Dinkeloo and Associates 66-; mem. Nat. Inst. of Arts and Letters, American Acad. in Rome 68-71; mem. Fine Arts Comm., Washington, D.C.; Academician Nat. Acad. of Design; mem. Board of Trustees, Woodrow Wilson Int. Center for Scholars, Smithsonian Inst.; Brunner Award, Nat. Acad. of Arts and Letters 65, Brandeis Univ. Creative Arts Award 67, and other awards.
Major works include: IBM World Fair Pavilion, N.Y.; Oakland Museum; Rochester Inst. of Technology; Ford Foundation Headquarters, N.Y.; Fine Arts Center, Univ. of Mass.; Power Center for the Performing Arts, Univ. of Mich.; Creative Arts Center, Wesleyan Univ., Middletown, Conn.; Nat. Fisheries Center and Aquarium, Washington, D.C. (with Charles Eames, q.v.); Coll. Life Insurance Co. of America Headquarters, Indianapolis; Fed. Reserve Bank of New York, N.Y.; Major Expansion Program, Master Plan, Metropolitan Museum of Art, New York; Fiat H.Q., Turin, Italy; Office Complex, UN Devt. Corpn., New York, N.Y.; Denver Center for the Performing Arts, Denver, Colo.
Kevin Roche, John Dinkeloo & Associates, 20 Davis Street, Hamden, Conn. 06517, U.S.A.
Telephone: 203-777-7251.

Roche, Emile; French international civil servant; b. 24 Sept. 1893.
Journalist, Editor of Cri des Flandres 27, Dir. of La République, 29-39 La Semaine Economique et Financière 48-50; Pres. Radical-Socialist Fed. of the North 32-56; mem. of Econ. Council 51-, Pres. 54-59; mem. French Econ. and Social Council 59, Pres. 59-; Pres. Econ. and Social Cttee. of European Econ. Community (EEC) and of Euratom 62-64; Grand Officier Légion d'Honneur.
Publs. Caillaux que j'ai connu, L'or n'est plus roi, On a voté . . . . et maintenant, Perspectives franco-marocaines, L'Ere des métamorphoses.
92 avenue Henri-Martin, 75116 Paris, France.

Roche, James M.; American motor executive; b. 16 Dec. 1906, Elgin, Ill.; s. of Thomas E. and Gertrude (Bull) Roche; m. Louise McMillan 1929; two s. one d.; ed. La Salle Univ., Chicago.
General Motors 27-; Statistician, Cadillac Sales and Service Branch, Chicago 27; Head of Business Management Dept., Cadillac Motor Car Div., Detroit 35; Gen. Sales Manager, Cadillac Motor Car Div. 50-57, Gen. Manager 57-60; Vice-Pres. Gen. Motors 57-60, Vice-Pres. (Gen. Motors Marketing Staff) 60-62, Exec. Vice-Pres. and Dir. 62-65; Pres., Chief Operating Officer, Chair. Exec. Cttee., Dir. and mem. Finance Cttee. Gen. Motors June 65-Oct. 67, Chair. Oct. 67-72, now Dir.; Dir. Pepsico Inc., Chicago Board of Trade, New York Stock Exchange.
Leisure interests: reading, music, fishing.
425 Dunston Road, Bloomfield Hills, Mich. 48013, U.S.A.

Roche, Jean Casimir Henri Hilaire, D. EN MED., D. ÈS S.; French university professor; b. 14 Jan. 1901, Sorgues; s. of Gaston Roche and Marie Lointier; m. Elsa Barman 1937; three s. (one deceased) two d. (one deceased).
Assistant in Physiology, Montpellier Univ. 20-23; Lecturer in Biochemistry, Univ. of Strasbourg 25-30; Prof. of Biochemistry, Univ. of Lyon 30-31; Marseilles Univ. 31-47; Hon. Prof. 48; Dir. of Laboratory Comparative Biochemistry, Ecole des Hautes Etudes, Paris 41-; Prof. of Biochemistry, Collège de France, Paris 47-72; Rector, Univ. of Paris 61-69; Dir. of Laboratoire Maritime du Collège de France, Concarneau, Brittany and Pres. Int. des Hautes Etudes, Tunis (Univ. of Paris); Rector, Gen. Del. of Minister of Educ. to Univ. Int. Affairs; Vice-Pres. Int. Asscn. of Univs.; mem. Acad. des Sciences, Acad. de Médecine; Hon. mem. Accademia dei Lincei (Rome), Royal Acad. of Sciences, Sweden, Denmark, Nat. Acad. of Sciences (Argentina), Belgian Acad. of Sciences, Bulgarian Acad., Hungarian Acad., Romanian Acad.; Hon. D.C.L. (Oxford), Hon. D.SC. (London, Frankfurt, New York, Bucharest, Montreal, Southampton, Pamplona, Bradford), D.Med. (Naples, Liège, Buenos Aires, São Paulo-Campinos), D. Phil. (Tel Aviv).
Leisure interest: archaeology.
Publs. Essai sur la Biochimie générale et comparée des pigments respiratoires 36, Précis de Chimie 34.
6 boulevard Jourdan, Paris 14e, France.
Telephone: 589-92-60.

Roche, John P., A.B., A.M., PH.D., LITT.D.; American professor of politics and history; b. 7 May 1923, Brooklyn, N.Y.; s. of Walter John and Ruth Pearson Roche; m. Constance Ludwig 1947; one d.; ed. Hofstra Coll. and Cornell Univ.
Instructor, then Assoc. Prof. of Political Science, Haverford Coll. 49-56; Prof. of Politics and History, Brandeis Univ. 56-73, Chair. Dept. of Politics 56-59, 61-65, Dean, Faculty of Arts and Sciences 58-60, Henry R. Luce Prof. of Civilization and Foreign Affairs, Fletcher School of Law and Diplomacy 73-; Visiting appts.: Swarthmore Coll., Cornell and Columbia Univs. and Mass. Inst. of Technology and Lecturer,

Univ. of Aix-en-Provence; Fellow, Fund for the Advancement of Educ. 54-55, Rockefeller Foundation 61-62, 65-66; Nat. Chair. Americans for Democratic Action 62-65; Consultant, Vice-Pres. Hubert H. Humphrey and U.S. Dept. of State 64-66; Special Consultant to the Pres. of the U.S. 66-68; mem. Presidential Comm. on Int. Radio Broadcasting 72-73; Trustee, Woodrow Wilson Center for Scholars, Smithsonian Inst., Dubinsky Foundation; mem. U.S. Board for Int. Broadcasting 74-; mem. Council of Foreign Relations.
Publs. *The Dynamics of Democratic Government* (with Murray S. Stedman, Jr.) 54, *Aspects of Liberty* 58, *Courts and Rights* 61, revised edn. 66, *The American Image: the Political Process* (with Leonard W. Levy) 63, *The Quest for the Dream: The Development of Civil Liberties and Human Relations in Modern America* 63, *Shadow and Substance: Essays on the Theory and Structure of Politics* 64, *The Crossroad Papers* 65, *The Dynamics of Modern Government* (with Meehan and Stedman) 66, *John Marshall. Major Opinions and Other Writings* (Editor) 67, *Sentenced to Life: Reflections on Politics, Education and Law* 74, *The American Revolution—A Heritage of Change* (co/author) 75; numerous articles on law and politics.
Fletcher School of Law and Diplomacy, Medford, Mass. 02155; Home: 15 Bay State Road, Weston, Mass. 02193, U.S.A.
Telephone: 617-628-5000 (Office), 617-899-5085 (Home).

Roche, Josephine, A.M.; American industrialist; b. 2 Dec. 1886; ed. Vassar Coll., and Columbia Univ.
Exec. Sec. Colorado Progressive Service 13-15; Special Agent England and U.S., Comm. for Relief in Belgium 15; Dir. Girls' Dept. Juvenile Court, Denver 15-18, Referee 25-27; Investigator Nat. Consumers' League 18, Pres. 39-; Dir. Foreign Language Information Service 18-23, New York and Washington; Dir. Editorial Div. U.S. Children's Bureau 23-25; with Rocky Mountain Fuel Co. 27-50, Vice-Pres. 28-29, Pres. 29-34, Pres. and Gen. Man. 37-50; mem. Nat. Board Dirs. Federal Reemployment Service 33; Asst. Sec. U.S. Treas. 34-37, Rep. Pres. Cabinet Cttee. on Economic Security; Chair. Interdeptl. Cttee. to Co-ordinate Health and Welfare Activities, Fed. Govt. 34-40; Chair. Nat. Health Conf. 38; Dir. United Mine Workers of America Welfare and Retirement Fund 48-71, Trustee 50-71; Hon. D.Litt., etc.
1711 Massachusetts Avenue, N.W., Washington, D.C. 20036, U.S.A.

Roche, Marcel, M.D., M.A., B.S.; Venezuelan parasitologist; b. 15 Aug. 1920, Caracas; s. of Luis and Beatrice Roche; m. 1st María Teresa Rolands 1948 (deceased), one s. three d.; m. 2nd Flor Blanco-Fombona 1972; ed. Coll. Sainte Croix de Neuilly, St. Joseph's Coll., Philadelphia, Johns Hopkins Univ., Baltimore, and Harvard School of Medicine, Boston.
Intern, Johns Hopkins Hospital, Baltimore 46-47; Asst. Resident, Peter Bent Brigham Hospital, Boston 47-48; Research Fellow, Harvard School of Medicine, Boston 48-50; Research work, New York Public Health Research Inst. 50-51; Dir. Luis Roche Inst. for Medical Research 52-58; Dir. Venezuelan Inst. for Scientific Research 58-69, Chief of Dept. of Physiopathology 58-; Pres. Consejo Nacional de Investigaciones Científicas y Tecnológicas 69-72; Simón Bolívar Prof. of Latin American Studies, Univ. of Cambridge 70-71; D.Sc. (h.c.).
Leisure interest: playing the cello.
Avenida Luis Roche 41, Altamira, Caracas, Venezuela.
Telephone: 322366.

Rochester, George Dixon, M.SC., PH.D., F.R.S., F.INST.P.; British professor of physics (emer.); b. 4 Feb. 1908, Wallsend; s. of Thomas and Ellen Rochester; m. Idaline Bayliffe 1938; one s. one d.; ed. Wallsend

Grammar School, Univs. of Durham, Stockholm and California.
Earl Grey Scholar, Durham Univ. 26-29; Earl Grey Fellow, Stockholm Univ. 34-35; Commonwealth Fund Fellow, Univ. of Calif. 35-37; Asst. Lecturer, Manchester Univ 37-46, Lecturer 46-49, Senior Lecturer 49-53, Reader 53-55, Prof. of Physics 55-73, Emer. 73-; Scientific Adviser in Civil Defence, N.W. Region 52-55; mem. Council for Nat. Academic Awards (CNAA) 64-74; Second Pro-Vice-Chancellor, Durham Univ. 67-69, Pro-Vice-Chancellor 69-70; Hon. D.Sc. (Newcastle) 73, (CNAA) 75; C. V. Boys Prizeman 56; Symons Memorial Lecturer, Meteorological Soc. 62.
Leisure interests: gardening, travel.
Publs. (with J. G. Wilson) *Cloud Chamber Photographs of the Cosmic Radiation* 52; also scientific papers on elementary particles, cosmic rays and spectroscopy.
18 Dryburn Road, Durham, DH1 5AJ, England.
Telephone: Durham 64796.

Rochet, Waldeck; French agriculturist and politician; b. 5 April 1905, Sainte-Choix.
Market gardener; Deputy to Nat. Ass. 36-40, 54-72; Del. to Provisional Consultative Ass. 44; Pres. Agricultural Cttee., Nat. Ass. 46-47; Dir. of *La Terre*; Pres. Communist Party in Nat. Ass. 58-59, 62-64; Deputy Sec.-Gen. of Communist Party until 64, Sec.-Gen. 64-72, Hon. Pres. 72-.
14 rue Jules-Gauthier, 92000 Nanterre, France.

Rock, John; American physician; b. 24 March 1890, Marlborough, Mass.; s. of Frank S. Rock and Ann Jane Murphy; m. Anna Thorndike 1925; one s. four d.; ed. Harvard Coll., and Harvard Medical School.
Practised obstetrics at Boston and Brookline, Mass. 21-44, gynaecology 21-; Surgeon, Free Hospital for Women, Brookline 24-56, Consulting Gynaecologist 56-; Dir. Fertility and Endocrine Clinic 26-56; Clinical Prof. of Gynaecology, Harvard Medical School, Boston 47-56, Emeritus Prof. 56-; mem. Board of Consultation, Massachusetts Gen. Hospital, Boston 45-60, Hon. Surgeon 60-; Dir. Rock Reproductive Clinic, Inc. (fmrly. Rock Reproductive Study Center) 56-69; Lasker Award of Planned Parenthood Fed. of America, Ortho Award of American Soc. for the Study of Sterility; Oliver Bird Medal 63, Modern Medicine Award 66; Hon. Sc.D. Amherst Coll.; Dr. h.c. Univ. of San Marcos, Lima; Hon. LL.D. Harvard Univ.
Leisure interests: reading, writing, clinical research in human reproduction.
Publs. *The Time Has Come, A Catholic Doctor's Proposals to End the Battle Over Birth Control* 63; Co-author *Voluntary Parenthood* 49, and numerous articles.
Temple, New Hampshire 03084, U.S.A.
Telephone: 603-878-1722.

Rockefeller, David, B.S., PH.D.; American banker; b. 12 June 1915, New York; s. of John Davison Jr. and Abby Greene (née Aldrich) Rockefeller; m. Margaret McGrath 1940; two s. four d.; ed. Harvard Univ. and Univ. of Chicago.
Secretary to Mayor Fiorello H. La Guardia, N.Y. 40-41; Asst. Regional Dir. U.S. Office of Defence 41-42; Officer of Defence, Health and Welfare, U.S. Army 42-45; Foreign Dept. Chase Nat. Bank 46-48, 2nd Vice-Pres. 48-49. Vice-Pres. 49-51, Snr. Vice-Pres. 51-55; Exec. Vice-Pres. Chase Manhattan Bank 55-57, Dir. 57-, Vice-Chair. Board of Dirs. 57-61, Pres. and Chair. Exec. Cttee. 61-69, Chair. and Chief Exec. Officer 69-; Chair. Rockefeller Univ., Council on Foreign Relations and other chairmanships; Vice-Chair. Museum of Modern Art; Trustee Rockefeller Brothers Fund, Vice-Chair. 69-, Rockefeller Family Fund, John F. Kennedy Library, Chicago Univ., Life Trustee 66-; Dir. Rockefeller Center Inc., N.Y. Clearing House, Int. Exec. Service Corps, Chair. 64-68,

Council of the Americas, Chair. 65-70, Center for Inter-American Relations, Chair. 66-70; Hon. LL.D. from eight univs.; numerous American and foreign awards.
Publs. *Unused Resources and Economic Waste* 40, *Creative Management in Banking* 64.
1 Chase Manhattan Plaza, New York, N.Y. 10015, U.S.A.

Rockefeller, James S.; American businessman; b. 8 June 1902, New York; *s.* of William G. and Elsie (Stillman) Rockefeller; *m.* Nancy Carnegie 1925; two *s.* two *d.*; ed. Yale Univ.
Worked with Brown Brothers & Co. 24-30; joined Nat. City Bank of New York (now First Nat. City Bank) 30, Asst. Cashier 31, Asst. Vice-Pres. 33, Vice-Pres. 40, Senior Vice-Pres. 48, Exec. Vice-Pres. 52, Pres. and Dir. 52-59, Chair. and Dir. 59-67; served with U.S. Army 42-46; Dir. First Nat. City Trust Co. (Bahamas) Ltd., Kimberly-Clark Corpn., Pan American World Airways, Cranston Print Works Co.; Vice-Pres. and Dir. Indian Spring Land Co.; mem. Board of Managers of the Memorial Hosp. for Cancer and Allied Diseases, New York; Trustee of Estate of William Rockefeller, American Museum of Natural History.
Leisure interests: farming, shooting, fishing.
c/o First National City Bank, Room 2900, 399 Park Avenue, New York, N.Y. 10022, U.S.A.
Telephone: 212-559-4444.

Rockefeller, John Davison, III, B.S.; American executive and philanthropist; b. 21 March 1906, New York; *s.* of John Davison Jr. and Abby Greene (née Aldrich) Rockefeller; *m.* Blanchette Ferry Hooker 1932; one *s.* three *d.*; ed. Princeton Univ.
Served in U.S.N.R. 42-45; Consultant to Dulles Mission to Japan 51; Adviser U.S. Del. to Japanese Peace Conf. San Francisco 51; Established Rockefeller Public Service awards 51; Dir. Rockefeller Inst. (now Univ.) 32-49, Rockefeller Center Inc. 32-63, N.Y. Life Insurance Co. 49-59, Phelps Memorial Hosp. Asscn. 53-68, Foreign Policy Asscn. 54-61; Chair. Colonial Williamsburg 39-53, Gen. Educ. Board 52-64, Nat. Council United Negro Coll. Fund 58-65, Hon. Chair. 65-69, Rockefeller Foundation, Comm. on Population Growth and the American Future, Population Council (founder), Japan Soc., Asia Soc.; Chair. Agricultural Devt. Council 67-73, Trustee of same; Pres. JDR 3rd Fund (founder); Dir. Lincoln Center for the Performing Arts, Chair. 61-70; Trustee Rockefeller Family Fund, Rockefeller Brothers Fund, Pres. 40-56, Educ. Broadcasting Corpn., Princeton Univ. 37-67; numerous American and foreign awards.
Home: 1 Beekman Place, New York, N.Y. 10022; Office: 30 Rockefeller Plaza, New York, N.Y. 10020, U.S.A.

Rockefeller, Laurance Spelman, O.B.E., A.B.; American conservationist and business executive; b. 26 May 1910, New York; *s.* of John Davison Jr. and Abby Greene (née Aldrich) Rockefeller; *m.* Mary French 1934; one *s.* three *d.*; ed. Princeton Univ.
Served in U.S.N.R. 42-45; Dir. Eastern Airlines 38-61; Chair. Rockefeller Center 53-56, 58-66, Hudson River Valley Comm. 65-66, N.Z. Zool. Soc., Rockefeller Brothers Fund, Citizens' Advisory Cttee. on Environmental Quality 69-73; Pres. American Conservation Asscn.; Jackson Hole Preserve Inc., Palisades Interstate Park Comm.; Trustee, Princeton Univ., Alfred P. Sloan Foundation, Nat. Geog. Soc., N.Y. State Historic Trust, Nat. Park Foundation; mem. Nat. Cancer Advisory Board, State Council of Parks and Outdoor Recreation; Commdr. Ordre Royal du Lion (Belgium) 50 and several American awards.
Home: 834 Fifth Avenue, New York, N.Y. 10021; Office: 30 Rockefeller Plaza, New York, N.Y. 10020, U.S.A.

Rockefeller, Nelson Aldrich, A.B.; American public servant and politician; b. 8 July 1908, Bar Harbor, Me.; *s.* of John Davison Jr. and Abby Greene (née Aldrich) Rockefeller; *m.* 1st Mary Todhunter Clark 1930 (divorced 1962), three *s.* (one deceased) two *d.*; *m.* 2nd Margaretta Fitler Murphy 1963, two *s.*; ed. Lincoln School, New York and Dartmouth Coll.
Co-ordinator Inter-American Affairs and mem. Nat. Foreign Intelligence Advisory Board 40-44, 69-74; Asst. Sec. of State for American Repub. Affairs 44-45; Pres. Int. Basic Econ. Corpn. 47-53, 56-58, Chair. 58 (founder); Chair. Int. Devt. Advisory Board 50-51; Under-Sec. of Health, Educ. and Welfare 53-54; Special Asst. to Pres. 54-55; Gov. of New York 59-73; Vice-Pres. of U.S.A. Dec. 74-; Dir. Rockefeller Center Inc. 31-58, Chair. 45-53, 56-58, Pres. 38-45, 48-51; Chair. Museum of Modern Art 57-58, Pres. 39-41, 46-53; Chair. President's Advisory Cttee. on Govt. Org. 53-58; Pres. Museum of Primitive Art (founder); Trustee, Rockefeller Brothers Fund, Pres. 56-58; Dir. American Inst. Asscn. for Econ. and Social Devt.; Chair. Comm. on Critical Choices for Americans, Nat. Comm. on Water Quality 73-; Order of Merit, Chile 45; Nat. Order of Southern Cross, Brazil 46; Order of Aztec Eagle, Mexico 49; Ramon Magsaysay Award, Philippines 59 and several American awards.
Publs. *The Future of Federalism* 62, *Unity, Freedom and Peace* 68, *Our Environment Can Be Saved* 70.
Pocantico Hills, North Tarrytown, New York, U.S.A.

Rockwell, Stuart Wesson; American diplomatist; b. 15 Jan. 1917, New York; *s.* of Charles Kellogg and Vera Wesson Rockwell; *m.* Rosalind H. Morgan 1956; two *s.* one *d.*; ed. Harvard Univ.
Third Sec., Panama 41-44; military service 44-46; Second Sec., Ankara 46-48; Officer-in-charge, Palestine-Israel-Jordan Affairs, Dept. of State 48-52; First Sec., Madrid 52-55; Dir. Office of Near Eastern Affairs, Dept. of State 56-60; Minister, Teheran 60-65; Deputy Asst. Sec. of State 65-70; Amb. to Morocco 70-73; Deputy Chief of Protocol of the U.S.A. 74-.
Leisure interests: fishing, shooting, skiing, gardening.
Department of State, 2201 C Street, Washington, D.C., U.S.A.

Rockwell, Willard Frederick, Jr., B.S.; American industrialist; b. 3 March 1914, Boston; *s.* of Willard F. and Clara Thayer Rockwell; *m.* Constance Templeton 1942; four *s.* one *d.*; ed. Pennsylvania State Univ.
Cost Accountant, Pittsburgh Equitable Meter Co. 35-36, Accountant 37-39, Vice-Pres., Controller 39-43, Vice-Pres., Gen. Man. 45-47; Asst. to Controller, Timken-Detroit Axle Co. 33-37; Pres., Rockwell-Standard Corpn. 63-67; Chair. of Board North American Rockwell (now Rockwell Int. Corpn.) 67-, Chief Exec. Officer 70-74; Rockwell Mfg. Co. 47-64, Vice-Chair. 64-71, Chair. 71-73; Dir., Allegheny Ludlum Industries Inc., Mellon Bank N.A., Realty Growth Co., El Paso Natural Gas Co., Kearney and Trecker Corpn.; Advisory Dir. El Paso Products Co., Odessa, Texas; mem. Citizens' Advisory Cttee. on Environmental Quality; Vice-Chair. Nat. Industrial Pollution Control Council, Chair. 73; Dir. and mem. of Exec. Cttee. of Pennsylvania Chamber of Commerce; U.S. Dir., U.S.-U.S.S.R. Trade and Econ. Council, New York; mem. Nat. Council Foreign Policy Asscn.; mem. American Inst. of Industrial Engineers, American Petroleum Inst., etc.; mem. Board of Trustees, Univ. of S. Calif. 73; Trustee Midwest Research Inst., Kansas City, Southwest Research Inst., San Antonio; Hon. LL.D. (Grove City Coll.), Hon. D.Eng. (Tufts Univ., Washington and Jefferson Coll.).
Rockwell International Corpn., 600 Grant Street, Pittsburgh, Pa. 15219, U.S.A.

Roddis, Louis, Jr.; American business executive; b. 9 Sept. 1918, Charleston, S.C.; ed. U.S. Naval Acad. and Mass. Inst. of Technology.
Former U.S. Naval Officer; helped to develop a prototype ship propulsion reactor and participated in design of U.S.S. *Nautilus* and other early naval nuclear projects; with Div. of Reactor Devt., U.S. Atomic Energy Comm. 55-58; Pres. Pennsylvania Electric Co. (subsidiary of Gen. Public Utilities Corpn.) 58-67, Chair. of Board 67-69; Dir. Nuclear Activities of Gen. Public Utilities Corpn. 67; Pres. and mem. Board of Trustees, Consolidated Edison Co. of New York Inc. 69-73, Vice-Chair. 73-74, mem. Board of Trustees 73-; active in a wide variety of public services, charitable, industrial and trade orgs.; consultant to several govt. agencies; Dir. and Past Pres. Atomic Industrial Forum, American Nuclear Soc.; mem. Nat. Acad. of Engineering and other professional socs.; Outstanding Service Award, U.S. Atomic Energy Comm. 57.
Consolidated Edison Co. of New York Inc., 4 Irving Place, New York, N.Y. 10003, U.S.A.

Rode, Ebbe; Danish actor; b. 10 May 1910.
Member staff Dagmarteatret 31, Royal Theatre, Copenhagen 32-57, 65-; guest actor at theatres in Aarhus, Aalborg, Odense, Oslo and Copenhagen; Knight of the Order of Dannebrog.
Leading roles in plays including: *Etienne, Topaze, Winterset, Ah! Wilderness, Waterloo-Bridge, Caesar and Cleopatra, Dolls House, Pygmalion, Otto Frank, The School for Scandal, The Price, The Father*; has acted in numerous films and on television and radio.
Publs. *My Meeting with Albert Schweitzer in His Hospital*, numerous speeches, poems, memoirs, articles and books about actors and acting.
Solbakken 28, 2830 Virum; The Royal Theatre, Copenhagen, Denmark.

Rodenbourg, Eugène; Luxembourg lawyer; b. 18 Sept. 1895, Luxembourg.
Advocate 20; Justice of Peace, Rédange 27; Judge, District Court, Kiekirck 27, Luxembourg (City) 29; Advocate-Gen. 37; Public Prosecutor 45; Pres. District Court of Luxembourg 46; Vice-Pres. High Court of Justice 59-60, Hon. Vice-Pres. 60-; Councillor of State 47-, Vice-Pres. Council of State 69-; Judge, European Court of Human Rights 58-.
20 rue des Roses, Luxembourg.

Rodenstock, Rudolf (Rolf), DR.RER.POL.; German manufacturer; b. 1 July 1917; ed. Technical Univ., Munich.
Prof. with special duties, Univ. of Munich 56; proprietor of Optische Werke G. Rodenstock, Munich; Pres. Landesverband der Bayerischen Industrie, Munich; mem. Presidency, Bundesvereinigung der Deutschen Arbeitgeberverbände, Cologne; Vice-Pres. Bundesverband der Deutschen Industrie, Cologne; mem. Board Deutsche Allgemeine Spiegelglas A.G., Münchener Rückversicherungs-Ges., Bayernwerk A.G., Messe- u. Austellungs A.G., Industriekreditbank A.G., Gesellschaft der Freunde der Bayerischen Akad. der Wissenschaften, Munich, Deutsches Industrieinstitut, Cologne.
Romanstrasse 32, Munich 19; and c/o Optische Werke G. Rodenstock, Isartalstrasse 39-43, Munich 5, Federal Republic of Germany.

Röder, Franz-Josef, DR.PHIL.; German politician; b. 22 July 1909, Merzig, Saar; s. of Franz Josef and Emilie (Gräber) Röder; m. Magdalene Spiess 1937; one s. four d.; ed. Univs. of Freiburg i. Breisgau, Innsbruck and Münster.
Schoolteacher abroad 37-45; Chief Interpreter German Fed. Railways 46-48, later Dir. Dillingen Gymnasium; mem. Saar Landtag (Land Parliament) 55-; Minister of Education, Culture, Saar Land Govt. 57-65, Minister Pres. 59-; mem. Bundestag Jan.-Sept. 57; Pres.

Bundesrat 59-60, 69-70; Chair. Saar Christian Democratic Union 59-.
Am Ludwigsplatz 14, 66 Saarbrücken, Federal Republic of Germany.
Telephone: 5947.

Rodgers, John, M.S., PH.D.; American professor of geology; b. 11 July 1914, Albany, N.Y.; s. of Henry D. and Louise W. (Allen) Rodgers; unmarried; ed. Albany Acad., Cornell and Yale Univs.
Assistant, Dept. of Geology, Cornell Univ. 35-36, Instructor 36-37; Field Geologist, U.S. Geological Survey 38-, in full time employment 40-46; Scientific Consultant, U.S. Army Corps. of Engineers 44-46; Instructor, Yale Univ. 46-47, Asst. Prof. 47-52, Assoc. Prof. 52-59, Prof. 59-, Silliman Prof. of Geol. 62-; Gen. Sec. Int. Comm. on Stratigraphy 52-60; Senior Fellow, Nat. Science Foundation 59-60; Commr. Connecticut Geol. and Nat. History Survey 60-71; Visiting Lecturer, Coll. de France 60; Exchange scholar Soviet Union 67; Asst. Editor, *American Journal of Science* 48-54, Editor 54-; mem. Nat. Acad. of Sciences; Hon. mem. Geol. Soc. of London; Pres. Conn. Acad. of Arts and Sciences 69, Geol. Soc. of America 70; Hon. mem. Soc. Géologique de France 73; John Simon Guggenheim Fellow (Australia) 73-74; Medal of Freedom, U.S. Army.
Leisure interests: music (piano), travel, reading (history, philosophy).
Publs. *Principles of Stratigraphy* (with C. Dunbar) 57, *The Tectonics of the Appalachians* 70; many articles on geology.
Department of Geology, Yale University, New Haven, Conn. 06520, U.S.A.

Rodgers, Sir John (Charles), Bart., M.A., F.S.S., F.B.I.M., F.R.S.A., F.I.S., D.L., M.P.; British administrator and politician; b. 5 Oct. 1906, York; m. Betsy Aikin-Sneath, J.P. 1931; two s.; ed. St. Peter's, York, Ecole des Roches, France, and Keble Coll., Oxford.
Sub-Warden, Mary Ward Supplement, London 29; Lecturer and Admin. Asst. Hull Univ. 30; Foreign Office 39, 44 and 45; Special Mission to Portugal Dec. 45; Ministry of Information 39-41; Dept. of Overseas Trade 41-42; with Ministry of Production 42-43; Gov. Admin. Staff Coll. 48-; BBC Gen. Advisory Council 46-52; M.P. 50-; Parl. Private Sec. to Sir David (now Viscount) Eccles at Ministries of Works, Educ., and Board of Trade 51-57; Parl. Sec. to Board of Trade and Minister for Regional Devt. and Employment 58-60; Select Cttee. on Public Accounts 70-, on Expenditure 74-; mem. Exec. Cttee. British Council 57-58, Tucker Cttee. on Evidence before Examining Justices 57; mem. of Council and leader Parl. Panel Inst. of Dirs. 55-58; Dir. British Film Inst. 58-59; Int. Pres. Centre Européen de Documentation et Information 66-69; Vice-Pres. INFRA (Int. Freedom Acad.) 66-68; Council Exec. Foundation for Management Educ. 60-, Council British Inst. of Management 65-69; Vice-Chair. Exec. Cttee. PEP (Political and Econ. Planning) 62-69; U.K. Del. and leader of Conservative group, Gen. Assembly Council of Europe, Western European Union 69-; Chair. Anglo-Finnish, Anglo-Taiwan, Anglo-Mexican and Anglo-Spanish All-Party Parl. groups; Chair., Caribbean Sub-Cttee. Conservative Foreign and Commonwealth Cttee.; Vice-Pres. British Section, European League for Econ. Co-operation 72-; Deputy Lieut. County of Kent 73; fmrly. Deputy Chair. J. Walter Thompson Co. Ltd.; Dir. Cocoa Merchants Ltd., History Today Ltd., etc.; Grand Cross of Liechtenstein, Commdr., Order of Dom Infante Henrique (Portugal), Knight Grand Cross of Civil Merit, Spain; Conservative.
Leisure interests: travel and theatre.
Publs. *Mary Ward Settlement: a History* 30, *Marketing Survey of the United Kingdom* (joint) 36-38, *The*

Old Public Schools of England 38, *The English Woodland* 42, *Industry Looks at the New Order* (joint) 42, *English Rivers* 45, *Tobias and Raphael* 48, *York* 51, *One Nation* (joint) 51; Editor: *Poems of Thomas Gray* 53, *Change is our Ally* 55, *Automation and the Consumer* (joint) 57, *Monopolies and the Consumer's Interests* (joint) 63, etc.

72 Berkeley House, Hay Hill, London, W.1; and The Dower House, Groombridge, Kent, England.
Telephone: 01-629-5220; Groombridge 213.

Rodgers, Richard; American composer; b. 28 June 1902, New York; *s.* of Dr. and Mrs. William Rodgers; *m.* Dorothy Feiner 1930; two *d.*; ed. Columbia Univ. and Inst. of Musical Art, New York.
Produced various shows; Pres. Dramatists' Guild 43-47; mem. Authors League of America; Pres. and Producing Dir., Lincoln Center for the Performing Arts Music Theatre; mem. Nat. Inst. of Arts and Letters; Award, Entertainment Hall of Fame 75.
First score *Lido Lady* 26; later shows include *Pal Joey* 40, *Oklahoma* (Pulitzer Award) 43, *Carousel* 45, *Allegro* 47, *South Pacific* (Pulitzer Prize) 49, *The King and I* 51, *Me and Juliet* 53, *Pipe Dream* 55, *Cinderella* (TV) 57, *Flower Drum Song* 58, *The Sound of Music* 59, *No Strings* 63, *Do I Hear a Waltz?* 65, *Androcles and the Lion* (TV) 67, *Two by Two* 70; scores for films *Love Me Tonight*, *State Fair* and others; scores for TV series *Churchill*, *Victory at Sea*, *The Valiant Years*.
c/o Rodgers and Hammerstein, 598 Madison Avenue, New York, N.Y. 10022, U.S.A.

Rodino, Peter Wallace, Jr.; American congressman; b. 7 June 1909, Newark, N.J.; *m.* Marianna Stango 1941; one *s.* one *d.*; ed. New Jersey Law School.
Admitted to New Jersey Bar 38; mem. House of Reps. for New Jersey 48-; Chair. House Judiciary Cttee. 73-; Del. North Atlantic Asscn.; Knight Order of the Crown (Italy), Grand Knight Order of Merit (Italy), and others.
House of Representatives, Washington, D.C. 20515, U.S.A.

Rodinò di Miglione, Marcello; Italian broadcasting official; b. 17 April 1906; ed. Univ. of Naples.
Former Dir.-Gen. Southern Italy Power Co. (S.M.E.); fmr. Treas. Nat. Asscn. of Electrical Companies; fmr. Del. Manager Radiotelevisione Italiana (R.A.I.); fmr. Del. Man. S.I.P.R.A. (advertising agency)), M.C.M. (Southern Cotton Mfg.); Pres. Telespazio; fmr. Pres. European Broadcasting Union; Pres. Associazone Società Italiane per Azione (ASSONIME); Cavaliere del Lavoro and other decorations.
Telespazio, Corso d'Italia 42, 00198 Rome; Assonime, Piazza Venezia 11, 00187 Rome, Italy.

Rodionov, Aleksey Alekseyevich; Soviet diplomatist; b. 27 March 1922, Pesochnoe, Gorky Region; ed. U.S.S.R. Finance and Economics (Correspondence) Inst.
Young Communist League and C.P. work 40-64; First Sec. Omsk City Cttee., C.P.S.U. 53-60; Sec. Omsk Regional Cttee., C.P.S.U. 60-62; Diplomatic Service 64-; Counsellor-Minister, New Delhi 64-66; Amb. to Burma 66-68; Minister of Foreign Affairs of R.S.F.S.R. 68-; Orders of Red Banner (thrice).
Ministry of Foreign Affairs of R.S.F.S.R., Prospekt Mira 79, Moscow, U.S.S.R.

Rodionov, Nikolay Nikolayevich; Soviet politician; b. 1915; ed. Moscow Steel Inst.
Engineer, Magnitogorsk and Leningrad 41-48; mem. C.P.S.U. 44-; party work, Leningrad 48-54; Second Sec. Leningrad City Cttee. C.P.S.U. 54-56, First Sec. 56-60; Second Sec. Central Cttee. C.P. Kazakhstan 60-62; Dep. Chair. Council of National Economy, Leningrad Econ. Region 62-65; First Sec. Chelyabinsk Regional Cttee. of the C.P.S.U. 65-70; Deputy Minister of U.S.S.R. for Foreign Affairs 70-; Alt. mem. Cen. Cttee.

C.P.S.U. 61-66, mem. 66-; Deputy to U.S.S.R. Supreme Soviet 58-70.
U.S.S.R. Ministry of Foreign Affairs, 32-34 Smolenskaya-Sennaya ploshchad, Moscow, U.S.S.R.

Rödönyi, Károly; Hungarian engineer and politician; b. 1911, Budapest; *s.* of Károly Rödönyi and Mária Vida; *m.* 1948; two *c.*; ed. Technical Univ. of Budapest.
Joined Communist Party 46; with Weiss Manfred Iron and Metal Works, Csepel 36; Railway Engineer 38, Official at local railway management sections of Budapest, Debrecen and Szeged; with Hungarian State Railways 51, Deputy Gen. Dir. 57-63, Gen. Dir. 63-74; Deputy Minister, Ministry of Posts and Communications 63-70, First Deputy Minister and State Sec. 71, Minister 74-; mem. Hungarian Acad. of Sciences Railway Cttee.; Pres. Fed. for Communication Science 63-; Chair. Int. Railway Asscn. 71-72; awards from railway authorities of U.S.S.R., Czechoslovakia, German Democratic Repub. and Poland; Medal of Merit for Socialist Labour 55, 56, Labour Order of Merit 63.
Ministry of Posts and Communications, Dob-utca 75/81, 1400 Budapest, Hungary.
Telephone: 220-220.

Rodríguez, Carlos Rafael; Cuban journalist, writer and politician.
Member Communist Party 32-, Exec. Cttee. 40-; Dir. Havana Univ. Econ. School 60-62; Editor *Hoy* 59-62; Pres. Nat. Land Reform Inst. 62-65; mem. Central Cttee. and Nat. Secr. Cuban C.P. 66; Minister, Pres. Comm. for Econ. and Technical Collaboration 66-; Vice-Pres. Council of Ministers 71-; mem. Exec. Cttee. for Foreign Affairs 72-; Perm. Rep. of Cuba to COMECON 72-.
Central Committee of the Communist Party, Plaza de la Revolución, Havana, Cuba.

Rodríguez de Miguel, Luis; Spanish lawyer and politician; b. 1914; ed. Univs. of Barcelona and Madrid.
Civil Gov. Baleares 41, Guipúzcoa 42; Dir.-Gen. of Posts and Telecommunications 44-56; Pres. Int. Telecommunications Union 55; Under-Sec. Ministry of the Interior 56-69, June-Dec. 73; Minister of Housing Dec. 73-75; Grand Cross Order of Isabel la Católica, Medal of the Old Guard.
c/o Ministerio de la Vivienda, Madrid, Spain.

Rodríguez de Valcarcel y Nebreda, Alejandro; Spanish lawyer and politician; b. 27 April 1917, Burgos; *s.* of Alejandro and Irene (née Nebreda) de Valcarcel; *m.* María Victoria Gavilán Alonso 1945; no *c.*; ed. schools in Burgos and Salamanca Univ.
President, Santander Congress; Civil Gov. and Provincial Head of the Falange in provinces of Burgos and Baleares; Sec.-Gen. Nat. Finance Inst.; Vice-Pres. Nat. Supplies Inst.; Dir. of Social Welfare, Nat. Industrial Inst.; Head, State Lawyers' Office, Delegación de Hacienda, Madrid; mem. Cortes; Gen. Vice-Sec. of Falange; Spokesman for State Council; Nat. Councillor; Pres. Cortes Nov. 69-; Gran Cruz del Mérito Civil, several mil. medals and other awards.
Publs. Several speeches and political works.
Avenida de Alberto Alcocer 13, 1° piso izq., Madrid, Spain.
Telephone: 2-50-31-09.

Rodríguez Lara, Maj.-Gen. Guillermo; Ecuadorean army officer; b. 4 Nov. 1923; ed. Quito Mil. Acad. and studies abroad.
Commander-in-Chief of Army 71; President of Ecuador (following *coup d'état*) Feb. 72-Jan. 76.

Rodríguez Monegal, Emir; Uruguayan writer; b. 28 July 1921; ed. Lycée Français, Montevideo, and Univ. of Montevideo.
Teacher of general literature, secondary schools,

Montevideo 45-52; Prof. of English Literature, Instituto de Profesores, Montevideo 52-62; Visiting Prof. of Latin American Literature, El Colegio de México, Mexico 64; Visiting Prof. Harvard Univ. 65; Editor *Mundo Nuevo* (literary magazine), Paris 65-.
Publs. *El juicio de los parricidas* 56, *Obras completas de José Enrique Rodó* (Editor) 57, *Las raíces de Horacio Quiroga* 60, *Literatura uruguaya del medio siglo* 66, *El viajero inmóvil: Introducción a Pablo Neruda* 66, *Vínculo de Sangre* 69.
Mundo Nuevo, 97 rue Saint Lazare, Paris 9e, France.

Rodríguez Ramos, Manuel, A.B., LL.B., M.C.L.; American writer, lawyer and law professor; b. 1908, San Juan, Puerto Rico; ed. Univ. of Puerto Rico and Tulane Univ. of Louisiana.
Private law practice 32-36; Under-Sec. of Justice of Puerto Rico 36-44; law lecturer (*ad honorem*) Coll. of Law, Univ. of Puerto Rico; Visiting Prof. Coll. of Law, Tulane Univ. 46-47; Visiting Prof. Luxembourg Univ.; Dean, Faculty of Law, Univ. of Puerto Rico 44-60, Dean Emer. 61-; Dir. Legal Aid Soc. of Puerto Rico; fmr. Gov. Puerto Rico Rotary Int.; Chief Editor *Revista Jurídica de la Universidad de Puerto Rico* 32, and Faculty Adviser 44-; Adviser to *Revista de Legislación y Jurisprudencia de Puerto Rico*; Order of the Coif; Hon. LL.D.
Publs. books and articles on comparative and administrative law.
P.O. Box 1175, Hato Rey, Puerto Rico 00919, U.S.A.

Rodríguez y Rodríguez, Jesús; Mexican financial official; b. 2 March 1920, Mexico City; ed. Universidad Nacional Autónoma de México.
Joined Secretariat of Finance and Public Credit 42, Under-Sec. for Finance and Credit 59-70; Exec. Dir. for Mexico, Panama and Dominican Repub., IDB Feb. 71-; Prof. of Admin. Law, Univ. Nacional Autónoma de México; First Vice-Pres. Inter-American Econ. and Social Council; Acting Chair. Inter-American Cttee. on Alliance for Progress; del. to numerous int. confs.
Inter-American Development Bank, 808 17th Street, N.W., Washington, D.C. 20577, U.S.A.

Roeder, Kenneth David, M.A.; American professor of physiology; b. 9 March 1908, England; s. of Carl David Roeder and Grace (Phillips) Roeder; m. Sonja von Cancrin 1931; one s. one d.; ed. Bembridge School, Isle of Wight, England and Cambridge and Toronto Univs. Member of Biology Dept., Tufts Univ., Mass. 31-, Prof. of Physiology 48-, Chair. of Biology Dept. 59-64; Fellow, American Acad. of Arts and Sciences; mem. Nat. Acad. of Sciences; Hon. Fellow, Royal Entomological Soc. (London); Hon. D.Sc. (Tufts Univ.).
Leisure interests: research, photography.
Publs. *Insect Physiology* 53, *Nerve Cells and Insect Behavior* (2nd edn.) 67; and about 70 papers on insect neurophysiology and behaviour.
Department of Biology, Tufts University, Medford, Mass. 02155; Home: 454 Monument Street, Concord, Mass. 01742, U.S.A.
Telephone: 617-628-5000, Ext. 332 (Office); 617-369-9451 (Home).

Roem, Mohammad; Indonesian politician; b. 1908; ed. Law School, Jakarta.
Solicitor in private practice, Jakarta 39-45; fmr. leader of Islamic Youth Movement; Indonesian Minister of the Interior 46-48; Del. to Round Table Conf. with Netherlands Govt. 49; first High Commr. of Indonesia to the Netherlands 50; Minister of Foreign Affairs 50-51, of Home Affairs 52-53; First Vice-Premier 56-57; mem. Exec. Cttee. Masjumi Party 57-59, 3rd Deputy Chair. 59; Pres. Islamic Univ., Medan; detained Jan. 62; founder-mem. Partai Muslimin Indonesia 67, Chair. 68. c/o Jalan Tjhik Ditiro 58, Jakarta, Indonesia.

Roemer, Karl Josef; German lawyer; b. 30 Jan. 1899, Völklingen, Saar; m. Brita Weyer 1948; one s.; ed. Cologne, Munich, Freiburg i. Br. and Bonn Univs.
Worked for a private bank 21-24, later Assessor and Judge, Cologne; official banking inst. in Berlin 32-48, Chief of External Relations Dept., Advocate 36-46; Advocate, Courts of First Instance and Appeal, Saarbrücken 47-53; attached to Bonn Govt. Services for study of problems of economic re-organization; mem. Sonderstelle Geld und Kredit (monetary reform); Counsellor to Govt. on int. law and foreign jurisdiction 47-53, on judicial missions abroad for Fed. Govt. 48-52; Advocate Gen. E.C.S.C. Court 52-58, Court of Justice to European Communities 58-72; German Red Cross, Golden Grand Cross, Grosses Verdienstkreuz mit Stern und Schulterband of Fed. Repub. of Germany; Ordre de Mérite du Grand Duchy of Luxembourg (1st Class), Grande Ufficiale dell'Ordine al Merito della Repubblica Italiana; Légion d'Honneur; Dr. jur. h.c., Univ. of Munich.
26 rue Frantz-Clément, Luxembourg.
Telephone: 26 793 (Home).

Roemers, D., D.ECON.; Netherlands politician; b. 1915; ed. Amsterdam Univ.
Formerly in Price-Control Dept. of State Textile Office; Economic Adviser Industrial Tobacco Group 45-47; Dir. Scientific Research Bureau, Netherlands Fed. of Trade Unions (N.V.V.) 47-52, Sec. 52-56, Vice-Pres. 56-59, Pres. 59-65; mem. Netherlands Social Econ. Council 50-59, Vice-Pres. 59-65; M.P. 52-67; Burgomaster of Vlissingen (Flushing) 67-; Labour.
Mozartlaan 12, Vlissingen, Netherlands.

Rogers, Benjamin, B.A., M.SC.(ECON.); Canadian diplomatist; b. 3 Aug. 1911, Vernon, B.C.; s. of Reginald Heber and Anna (Fraser) Rogers; m. Frances Morrison 1939; one s.; ed. Dalhousie Univ., and Univ. of London.
With Royal Inst. of Int. Affairs, London 35-36; Acting Nat. Sec. Canadian Inst. of Int. Affairs 37-38; entered Dept. of External Affairs 38; served Australia 39-43, U.S.A. 43-44, Brazil 44-48, Dept. of External Affairs 48-50; Chargé d'Affaires, Prague 50-52; Dept. of External Affairs 52-55; Amb. to Peru 55-58, Amb. to Turkey 58-60; Deputy High Commr. to U.K. 60-64; Amb. to Spain and Morocco 64-69; Amb. to Italy and High Commr. to Malta 70-72; Chief of Protocol, Dept. of External Affairs 72-75; retd.
Leisure interests: painting, skiing, writing.
Publ. *Canada Looks Abroad* (with R. A. MacKay) 38.
450 Piccadilly Avenue, Ottawa K1Y OH6, Canada.
Telephone: 728-0914.

Rogers, (N.) Ernesto, DR. ARCH.; Italian architect; b. 16 March 1909; ed. School of Architecture, Milan.
Prof. of Theory of Architecture at Milan Polytechnic; Private practice with others in Town Planning, Architecture, Interior Decoration and Industrial Design, Milan; works include houses, factories, pavilions, health resort for children at Legnano 39; Post Office, Rome 39; monument to the dead in German concentration camps at Milan Cemetery 46; Olivetti Showroom, Fifth Ave., N.Y.; Italian Merchant Navy Pavilion at Int. Exhibition, Paris 37, U.S. Pavilion at Triennale 51; restoration of Sforza Castle Museums 56; Torre Velasca, Milan; Canadian Pavilion, Venice Biennale; Italian Pavilion (in collaboration), Brussels Int. Exhibition 58; town planning studies (in collaboration): Pavia 33, Milan 45, regional plan for Valle d'Aosta 36-37, Elba Island 40; Consultant for Town Planning, Buenos Aires 48; Adviser for Town Planning, Lima 48; Visiting Prof. Lausanne Univ. 44-45, Geneva Univ. 45, Tucuman Univ. 48, Architectural Asscn. School, London 49; Prof. Italian Culture Univ. of Calif. 59; lecturer other univs. and cultural centres, Europe, America and Asia; mem. Council CIAM (Congrès Int. d'Architecture Moderne); mem. Cttee. of Five Architects, UNESCO;

Accademia di S. Luca, Rome, World Acad. of Art and
Science; Editor *Domus* magazine 46-47, *Casabella-Continuita* magazine 54-64.
Publs. *Stile* (with Banfi, Belgiojoso, Peressutti) 36; in
collaboration: *Piano regionale della Valle d'Aosta* 43,
Piano A.R. 45, *The Heart of the City* 52, *Auguste Perret
Esperienza dell'Architettura* 58, *Utopia della Realtà* 65
(with others).
**Studio Architetti B.D.P.R., Via dei Chiostri 2, Milan,
Italy.**

Rogers, Ginger (Virginia McMath); American actress;
b. 16 July 1911, Independence, Mo.; *m.* G. William
Marshall (divorced).
Commenced dancing career as performer in stage shows
on cinema circuit, later graduating to musical shows on
Broadway, and films; Acad. Award Best Actress for
Kitty Foyle 40.
Stage appearances include *Top Speed, Girl Crazy,
Hello Dolly, Mame* (London) 69.
Films include: *Young Man of Manhattan, Flying Down
to Rio*, the first of eleven musicals co-starring Fred
Astaire (q.v.), *Golddiggers of 1933, Forty-Second Street,
Gay Divorce, Roberta, Top Hat, Follow the Fleet, Swing
Time, Stage Door, The Life of Vernon and Irene
Castle, Kitty Foyle, Lady in the Dark, It had to be You,
Barkleys of Broadway, Storm Warning, Dream Boat,
Monkey Business, Forever Female, Twist of Fate, Black
Widow, Teenage Rebel, Tight Spot, Oh Men, Oh Women.*
Leisure interests: oil painting, tennis, golf.
**Rogers Rogue River Ranch, Route 1, Box 472, Eagle
Point, Ore. 97524, U.S.A.**

Rogers, Paul; British actor; b. 22 March 1917; ed.
Newton Abbot Grammar School, Devon and Michael
Chekhov Theatre Studio.
First stage appearance at Scala Theatre 38; Stratford on
Avon Shakespeare Memorial Theatre 39; Royal Navy
40-46; with Bristol Old Vic Co. 47-49, London Old Vic
49-53, 55-56; shows include *The Merchant of Venice* 52,
The Confidential Clerk 53, *Macbeth* 54, *The Taming of
the Shrew*; toured Australia as Hamlet 57; *The Elder
Statesman* 58, *King Lear* 58, *Mr. Fox of Venice* 59, *The
Merry Wives of Windsor* 59, *A Winter's Tale* 59, *One
More River* 59, *JB* 61, *Photo Finish* 62, *The Seagull* 64,
Season of Goodwill 64, *The Homecoming* 65, N.Y. 67,
Timon of Athens (Stratford) 65, *The Government
Inspector* 66, *Henry IV* (Stratford) 66, *Plaza Suite* 69,
The Happy Apple 70, *Sleuth* (London 70, New York 71),
Othello (Old Vic) 74, *Heartbreak House* (Nat. Theatre)
75; Films: *A Midsummer Night's Dream , The Looking-
Glass War.*
9 Hillside Gardens, Highgate, London, N.6, England.

Rogers, William P., LL.B.; American lawyer and
government official; b. 23 June 1913, Norfolk, N.Y.;
m. 1936; three *s.* one *d.*; ed. Canton High School, New
York, Colgate Univ. and Cornell Univ. Law School.
Joined law firm of Cadwalader, Wickersham and Taft,
New York 37; Asst. District Attorney, New York
County 38-42, 46-47; officer in U.S. Navy 42-46; Chief
Counsel, Senate War Investigating Cttee. 47-48,
Senate Permanent Investigating Cttee. 48-50; mem.
law firm of Dwight, Royall, Harris, Koegel and Caskey
50-53; Deputy Attorney Gen. of the U.S. 53-57,
Attorney Gen. 57-61; U.S. Rep., Gen. Assembly UN
65; U.S. Rep., UN Ad Hoc Cttee. on S.W. Africa 67;
mem. Pres. Comm. on Law Enforcement and Admin.
of Justice 65-67; with Royall, Koegel, Rogers and Wells
61-69; U.S. Sec. of State 69-73; with law firm of Rogers
and Wells 73-.
200 Park Avenue, New York, N.Y. 10017, U.S.A.

Rohal-Ilkiv, Ivan, LL.D.; Czechoslovak diplomatist;
b. 16 Feb. 1917, Lukov; *s.* of Juraj Rohal-Ilkiv and
Julia Džmurová; *m.* Olga Vološinovičová 1942; three *s.*
one *d.*; ed. Law School of Comenius Univ., Bratislava.
Deputy, Czechoslovak Provisional Nat. Assembly
45-46; Deputy, Czechoslovak Nat. Assembly 48-49;
Vice-Pres. Slovak Nat. Council 48-54; Prof. of Political
Science, Coll. of Technology, Bratislava 52-56; joined
diplomatic service 56; Czechoslovak Amb. to Romania
56-60; mem. del. to XVth Session, UN Gen. Assembly
60; Head, African Dept., Ministry of Foreign Affairs
61-62; Amb. to India, also accred. to Ceylon and Nepal
62-65; Head of Asian Dept., Ministry of Foreign
Affairs 65-68; Amb. to Canada 68-69, to U.S.A. 69-71;
Deputy Minister of Foreign Affairs 71-75; Amb. to
Italy and Malta 75-; Order of Slovak Nat. Uprising;
Medal of Slovak Nat. Uprising; Order of Merit (Czechoslovakia).
Leisure interests: tourism, skiing, fishing, hunting.
Publs. Articles on political science in Czechoslovak
journals.
**Embassy of Czechoslovakia, Rome, Italy; Ulrychova
ulice 1, Prague 6, Czechoslovakia.**

Rohde, Helmut; German journalist and politician;
b. 9 Nov. 1925, Hanover; *m.* Hanna Müller 1950; one
s.; ed. Acad. for Labour, Political Studies and Econs.
Journalist, German Press Agency; Press Officer,
Ministry for Social Affairs, Lower Saxony; mem. Parl.
(Bundestag) 57-; mem. European Parl.; Parl. State
Sec., Fed. Ministry of Labour and Social Affairs 69;
Chair. Social Democratic Party Working Group for
Issues Concerning Employees 73-; Fed. Minister for
Educ. and Science May 74-; Paul Klinger Prize 74,
Gold Medal, Asscn. of War-Blinded.
Leisure interests: modern art, music, modern jazz.
Publs. *Sozialplanung—Theorie und Praxis der deutschen
Sozialdemokratie, Gesellschaftspolitische Planung und
Praxis, Für eine soziale Zukunft*, and numerous articles
on social and education policy.
**53 Bonn-Bad Godesberg, Stresemannstrasse 2, Federal
Republic of Germany.**
Telephone: 57/2000.

Rohlíček, Rudolf, D.SC.; Czechoslovak politician; b.
14 July 1929, Malacky; ed. School of Economics,
Bratislava.
Head of Dept., Investment Bank, Bratislava 48-58;
Chief Sec. District Cttee., C.P. of Slovakia 58-60; post-
graduate studies 60-63; official, Central Cttee., C.P. of
Czechoslovakia 63-64; various offices, Central Cttee.,
C.P. of Slovakia 64-67; Head of Dept., Central Cttee.,
C.P. of Czechoslovakia 67-69; Minister of Finance, Fed.
Govt. 69-73, Deputy Prime Minister 73-; Head of
Czechoslovak del. to CMEA Perm. Comm. for Financial
Questions 70-73, Perm. Rep. to CMEA 73-; Deputy,
House of People, Fed. Ass. Č.S.S.R. 71-; Chair. Č.S.S.R.
Govt. Comm. for Questions of Rationalization of State
Admin. 70; Chair. Council for Int. Econ. and Scientific
Tech. Co-operation 74-; mem. Central Cttee. of C.P. of
Czechoslovakia 71-; Order of Labour 73.
Publ. *Finance and Technical Progress* 66, *Finance and
Efficiency* 74.
**Government Presidium of Czechoslovakia, nábř. kpt.
Jaroše 4, Prague, Czechoslovakia.**

Rohmer, Eric (*pseudonym* of Jean-Marie Maurice
Scherer); French film director; b. 1 Dec. 1920, Nancy;
s. of Lucien Scherer and Mathilde Bucher; ed. in Paris.
School teacher until 42, then journalist until 51; film
critic of *Revue du cinéma, Arts, Temps modernes, La
Parisienne*; founded (with others) and former co-
editor of *La Gazette du cinéma* (review); contributed to
and former co-editor of *Cahiers du cinéma*; co-dir. Soc.
des Films du Losange; directed *Journal d'un scélérat* 50,
Nadja à Paris 64; made educational films for French
TV 64-66; wrote script for *Une Etudiante d'aujourd'hui*
66; wrote and directed *Présentation ou Charlotte et son
steak* 51, *Les Petites Filles modèles* 52, *Bérénice* 54,
La Sonate à Kreutzer 56, *Véronique et son cancre* 58, *Le
Signe du Lion* (first feature) 59, *La Boulangère de
Monceau* 62, *La Carrière de Suzanne* 63, *La Place de*

l'Etoile 65, *La Collectionneuse* 66, *Fermière à Montfaucon* 68, *Ma Nuit chez Maud* 69, *Le Genou de Claire* 70, *L'Amour l'après-midi* 72; Prix Max-Ophuls 70 (for *Ma Nuit chez Maud*); Prix Louis-Delluc 71, Prix du Meilleur Film du Festival de Saint-Sébastien 71, Prix Méliès 71 (all for *Le Genou de Claire*).
Publs. *Alfred Hitchcock, Charlie Chaplin* 73, *Six contes moraux* 74.
30 rue de Bourgogne, Paris 7e, France.

Rohrer, Herbert, DR.RER.POL.; German businessman; b. 3 June 1901; ed. Univs. of Munich and Erlangen. Member of Board of Execs. Schering A.G., Berlin 34-39; Pres. Osram G.m.b.H. 39-45; Pres. Feldmühle A.G. 57-63, mem. of the Board 64-, Vice-Chair. 65, Chair. 68; Chair. Troisdorf/Köln 68, Krauss-Maffe A.G., Munich 67-; mem. Board Rothesay Paper Corpn., St. John, Intercontinental Pulp Co. Ltd., Vancouver.
81 Garmisch-Partenkirchen, Gsteig 46, Federal Republic of Germany.
Telephone: 08821-3417.

Röhrs, Karl, DR.RER.POL.; German business executive; b. 14 Dec. 1910, Freilingen, Niedersachsen; s. of August and Emma (née Sasse) Röhrs; m. Marga Dücker 1936; ed. Univs. of Berlin and Hamburg.
Joined Vereinigte Aluminium-Werke A.G. (VAW) 37; Deputy mem. Man. Board 46, mem. 51, Chair. Man. Board 62-68, Chair. Advisory Board 69-; mem. Man. Board, Vereinigte Industrie-Unternehmungen A.G. 51-.
Gerichtsweg 48, 53 Bonn, Federal Republic of Germany.

Roiseland, Bent; Norwegian farmer and politician; b. 11 Oct. 1902, Mandal; s. of Bent and Otilde Roiseland; m. Bertha Langeland 1929; five s. one d.
Member of the Storting (Parl.) 45-73; Pres. of the Lagting (Upper House) 54-58, 61-62, 65-69; Chair. of Norges Venstrelag (Liberal Party) 52-64; Chair. of the Liberal group in the Storting 54-70; mem. Board of Auditors for State Accounts 54-74.
Mandal, Norway.

Rojas de Moreno Díaz, María Eugenia; Colombian politician; b. 1934; d. of the late Gen. Gustavo Rojas Pinilla (Pres. of Colombia 1953-57); m. Samuel Moreno Díaz; two s.
Member of the Senate; Majority Leader, Bogotá City Council; Leader, Alianza Nacional Popular (ANAPO).
The Senate, Bogotá, Colombia.

Roll, Sir Eric, K.C.M.G., C.B., PH.D., B.COM.; British banker and former civil servant; b. 1 Dec. 1907, Austria; s. of Mathias and Fany (Frendel) Roll; m. Winifred Taylor 1934; two d.; ed. Univ. of Birmingham.
Assistant Lecturer, Univ. Coll., Hull 30, Prof. of Econs. and Commerce 35-39; Special Fellow, Rockefeller Foundation 39-41; Dep. mem., Combined Food Bd. 41-46; Asst. Sec. Ministry of Food 46-47, The Treasury 47, Under-Sec. 48-53; Chair. Econ. Cttee., OEEC 48-53. Minister, U.K. Del. to NATO 52-53; Under-Sec. Ministry of Agriculture, Fisheries and Food 53-57; Exec; Dir. Int. Sugar Council 57-59; Dep. Sec. Ministry of Agriculture, Fisheries and Food 60-61; Dep. Leader, U.K. Del. to EEC Brussels Conf. 61-63; Econ. Minister and Head of U.K. Treasury Del., Washington 63-65; Exec. Dir. for U.K., Int. Monetary Fund (I.M.F.). Perm. Under-Sec. of State, Dept. of Econ. Affairs 64-66; Chair. S. G. Warburg & Co. Ltd. 74-; Chair. Mercury Securities 74-; Dir. Chrysler (U.K.) Ltd., Times Newspapers Ltd., Bunzl Pulp & Paper Ltd., Bank of England; Hon. Chair. Book Devt. Council; Chancellor, Southampton Univ. 74-; Hon. D.Sc. (Hull, Birmingham), Hon. LL.D. (Southampton).
Leisure interests: reading, music.
Publs. *An Early Experiment in Industrial Organization* 30, *Spotlight on Germany* 33, *About Money* 34, *Elements of Economic Theory* 35, *Organized Labour* (co-author)

38, *The British Commonwealth at War* (co-author) 43, *The Combined Food Board* 57, *The World after Keynes* 68, *A History of Economic Thought* 73.
c/o S. G. Warburg and Co., Ltd., 30 Gresham Street, London, EC2B 2EP, England.

Roll, Lyle Charles; American business executive; b. 13 Sept. 1907, Easton, Ill.; ed. Illinois Wesleyan Univ. Kellogg Co. 27-, Sales Manager, Kellogg Co. of Canada 47-49, Asst. to Pres. Kellogg Co. 49-52, Vice-Pres. 52, Exec. Vice-Pres. 53-57, Pres. Gen. Man. 57-68, Chair. 63-; Dir. Consumers Power Co., Grocery Mfrs. of America, Smucker Co.; Trustee, W. K. Kellogg Foundation; Dir. *The Banker's Life*, Des Moines, Iowa.
Kellogg Company, Battle Creek, Mich. 49016, U.S.A.

Rollefson, Ragnar, M.A., PH.D.; American physicist; b. 23 Aug. 1906, Chicago, Ill.; s. of Carl J. and Marie (Krohn) Rollefson; m. Erna Brambora 1936; two s. two d.; ed. Univ. of Wisconsin.
Instructor in Physics, Univ. of Wisconsin 30-36, Asst. Prof. 36-42, Assoc. Prof. 42-46, Prof. 46-, Chair. Physics Dept. 47-51, 52-56, 57-61; with Radar Laboratory, Mass. Inst. of Technology (M.I.T.) 42-45; Chief Scientist, Naval Research Laboratory Field Station 46, Chief Scientist, U.S. Army 56-57; Act. Dir. Univ. Research Asscn. Devt. Laboratory 57-60; Dir. Int. Scientific Affairs, State Dept. 62-64.
Leisure interests: sports, travel.
Department of Physics, University of Wisconsin, Madison, Wis.; Home: 4206 Wanetah Trail, Madison, Wis., U.S.A.
Telephone: 274-0635.

Rollier, François; French motor executive; b. 2 Feb. 1915, Paris; m.; five c.; ed. Faculté de Droit, Paris.
Admitted to Annecy Bar; joined Soc. Michelin 56; Man. Cie. Générale des Etablissements Michelin, Manufacture Française des Pneumatiques Michelin; Deputy Chair. Citroën S.A. June-Dec. 70, Chair. Jan. 71-.
Citroën S.A., 133 quai Citroën, 75 Paris 15e, France.

Rollins, Reed Clark, B.S., M.A., PH.D.; American botanist; b. 7 Dec. 1911, Lyman, Wyoming; s. of William Clarence Rollins and Clara Rachel Slade Rollins; m. Alberta Fitz-Gerald 1939; one s. one d.; ed. A.B. Univ. of Wyoming, S.M. State Coll., Washington, Harvard Univ. Teaching Fellow, State Coll., Washington 34-36; teaching asst., summer school Univ. of Wyoming 35, biology, Harvard 36-37; instructor biology, asst. curator, Dudley Herbarium, Stanford 40-41; asst. Prof., curator 41-47,-assoc. Prof., curator 47-48; assoc. geneticist, Guayule Res. Proj., Dept. of Agriculture 43-45; principal geneticist, Stanford Research Inst. 46-47; geneticist div. rubber plant investigations, Dept. Agriculture 47-48; Assoc. Prof., botany and Dir., Gray Herbarium, Harvard Univ. 48-54; Asa Gray Prof. of Systematic Botany, Dir., Gray Herbarium, Supervisor, Bussey Inst., Harvard Univ. 54-; Fellow, Soc. of Fellows, Harvard Univ.; mem. N.A.S., American Soc. of Naturalists (Vice-Pres. 60, Pres. 66), A.A.A.S. American Inst. of Biological Sciences, Genetics Soc. of America; Centenary Medal, French Botanical Soc., Certificate of Merit, Botanical Soc. of America, Congress Medals XI and XII Int. Botanical Congress.
Leisure interests: golf, gardening, outdoor activities.
Publs. Revised edition of Fernald and Kinsey's *Edible Wild Plants of Eastern North America*, *The Genus Lesquerella (Cruciferae) in North America* (with E. Shaw), articles and technical papers in professional journals.
Gray Herbarium, 22 Divinity Avenue, Cambridge, Mass. 02138; Home: 19 Chauncy Street, Cambridge, Mass. 02138, U.S.A.
Telephone: 617-495-2364 (Office); 617-876-5442 (Home).

Rolshoven, Hubertus, DR. ING.; German mining executive; b. 15 Feb. 1913, Schellerten; s. of Franz and Therese (Meulenbergh) Rolshoven; m. Sofie Dorothea von Wunsch; four *s.*; ed. Univs. of Tübingen and Bonn, Technische Hochschulen Aachen and Berlin.

Engineer, Bochum 45-47; Works Man. Consolidation Colliery, Gelsenkirchen 47-53; Man. Mining Works, Essen 53-56; Man. Dir. Management Board, Hansa Bergbau A.G., Dortmund 56-57; Chair. of Management Board Saarbergwerke A.G., Saarbrücken 57-69; Prof. Saarland Univ.; Dir. European Acad. Otzenhausen; Pres. Inst. für regional-politische Zusammenarbeit in innergemeinschaftlichen Grenzräumen.

Leisure interests: hunting, riding.

Publs. *Beobachtungen über die Geologie des Kunnitales und des oberen Ramistales im Cercergebirge* 39, *Der Steinkohlenbergbau an der Saar* 60, *Wirtschaftsgrundlagen im Montandrück Saar-Lothringen-Luxemburg* 65, *Das Industriedreieck Saar-Lothringen-Luxemburg, Rohstoffwirtschaft und Rohstoffpolitik* 68, *Rohstoffe für die Welt von morgen, Mineralrohstoffe Grundlage der Industriewirtschaft* 72.

Saargemünder Strasse 226A, Haus Blauberg, 66 Saarbrücken, Federal Republic of Germany.
Telephone: 405-3203.

Roman, Herschel Lewis, PH.D.; American professor of genetics; b. 29 Sept. 1914, Szumsk, Poland; *s.* of Isadore Roman and Anna Bluwstejn; *m.* Caryl Kahn Roman 1938; two *d.*; ed. Univ. of Missouri.

Instructor to Prof. of Botany, Univ. of Washington, Seattle, Wash. 42-52; Prof. of Botany, Univ. of Washington 52-59, Prof. and Chair. Dept. of Genetics 59-; mem. Nat. Acad. of Sciences, American Acad. of Arts and Sciences; Pres. Genetics Soc. of America 68; Guggenheim Fellow, Univ. of Paris 52-53, Fulbright Scholar 56-57; Visiting Prof. Australian Nat. Univ., Canberra 66.

Leisure interests: gardening, tourism.

Publs. papers on cytogenetic studies in maize 47-51, on the genetics of yeast 51-.

Department of Genetics, University of Washington, Seattle, Wash. 98105; 5619 77th N.E., Seattle, Wash. 98115, U.S.A.
Telephone: 206-543-1657 (Office); 206-LA5-8224 (Home).

Romanov, Aleksandr Iosifovich; Soviet diplomatist; b. 18 Oct. 1912, Shchepino, Vladimir Region; *m.*; two *d.*; ed. Higher Engineering and education in the Humanities.

Former Engineer; Foreign Service 46-, Ministry of Foreign Affairs, and Minister-Counsellor, London 60-64; Amb. to Nigeria 64-70; Ministry of Foreign Affairs 70-73; Amb. to Netherlands 73-.

Andries Bickerweg 2, The Hague, The Netherlands.
Telephone: 333875.

Romanov, Aleksey Vladimirovich; Soviet journalist and politician; b. 16 Feb. 1908, Byelev, Tula Region; ed. Higher Literary Courses and Higher Party School.

Member C.P.S.U. 39-; successively journalist, Sec. *Pravda,* Editor *Gorkovskaya Kommuna,* and *Sovyetskaya Byelorussia* 29-49; Deputy Chief Editor *For A Lasting Peace, For a People's Democracy* 49-55; on staff of Cen. Cttee. C.P.S.U. 55-65; mem. Bureau Cen. Cttee. of R.S.F.S.R. 61-72; Chair. State Cttee. on Cinematography 62-72; Editor-in-Chief *Sovyetskaya Kultura* 72-; Cand. mem. Cen. Cttee. C.P.S.U. 61-; Deputy to U.S.S.R. Supreme Soviet 62-74.

Sovyetskaya Kultura, 73 Novoslobodskaya ulitsa, Moscow, U.S.S.R.

Romanov, Pavel Konstantinovich; Soviet publishing official; b. 1913; ed. Leningrad Inst. of Transport Engineering, and Higher Party School, Moscow.

With Soviet Army 41-45; Staff of C.P.S.U. Central Cttee. 45-57; fmr. Head of *Glavlit* (censorship org.) until 63; Chair. State Cttee. on the Press and Publishing Aug. 63-65, First Deputy Chair. 65-.

State Committee on the Press and Publishing, 26 Petrovka, Moscow, U.S.S.R.

Romanovsky, Sergei Kalistratovich; Soviet politician; b. 21 Oct. 1923, Novoseltsy, Rudnya District, Smolensk Region; ed. Moscow Inst. of Int. Relations.

Deputy Chair. U.S.S.R. Cttee. for Youth Orgs. 48-57; Secretary of *Komsomol* (Young Communist League) 57-59; Dep. Minister of Culture, U.S.S.R. 59-60; Dep. Chair. Cttee. for Cultural Relations with Foreign Countries 60-62, Chair. 62-Dec. 67; Chair. U.S.S.R. Comm. for UNESCO 62-68; Amb. to Norway 68-; Deputy to U.S.S.R. Supreme Soviet until 70.

U.S.S.R. Embassy, Oslo, Norway.

Romány, Pál, D.SC.; Hungarian agronomist and politician; *s.* of Pál Romány and Jolán Tasi; *m.* Erzsébet Markó, 1957; one *d.*; ed. Gödöllő Univ. of Agronomy.

Joined Hungarian Communist Party 49; various posts in Ministry of Agric. and in State Farm Admin., Pest-Nógrád County 52-58, later Chair. Board for State Farms, Borsod-Heves County; Deputy Leader, Dept. of Political Econ., Hungarian Socialist Workers' Party, Sec. Cen. Cttee. Board on Co-operative Policy 67-70, Pres. 74-75; First Sec. Bács-Kiskun County Cttee. 70, mem. Cen. Cttee. 70-, Head of Cen. Cttee. Dept. for Regional Econ. Devt. 73-75; Minister of Agric. and Food 75-; Chair. Comm. for Agric. History, Hungarian Acad. of Sciences 71-; Gold Award, Labour Order of Merit 67, 75; Tessedik Sámuel Memorial Medal 73.

Leisure interest: swimming.

Ministry of Agriculture and Food, 1055 Budapest, Kossuth L. tér 11, Hungary.
Telephone: 113-000.

Romero, José E., A.B., LL.B.; Philippine diplomatist and attorney-at-law; b. 1897, Bais, Negros Oriental; *s.* of Francisco Romero and Josefa Muñoz; *m.* 1st Pilar G. Sinco (died 1923), one *s.*; *m.* 2nd Elisa Villanueva 1930, four *s.* three *d.*; ed. Univ. of the Philippines.

Elected mem. of Provincial Board of Oriental Negros 25-31; House of Reps. and Nat. Assembly 31-46; Chair. of Cttee. on Public Instruction, House of Reps., and *ex-officio* mem. Board of Regents, Univ. of the Philippines 34-36; elected to Constitutional Convention and Chair. of Cttee. on Rules and Floor Leader 34-35; Floor Leader of Nat. Assembly 36-38; mem. Joint Philippine-American Cttee. on Philippine Affairs 37-38; Chair. Cttee. on Economic Readjustment 38-41; Chair. Cttee. on Foreign Relations and of Joint Congressional Cttee. on Rehabilitation and Reconstruction 45-46; elected to Philippine Senate 46; Minister to Great Britain and concurrently to Norway, Sweden and Denmark 49-54; Rep. Philippines Sugar Asscn., Washington, D.C. 54-57; Sec.-Treas. Philippine Sugar Asscn. 57-59; Sec. of Educ. 59-61; Sec.-Treas. Philippine Sugar Asscn. 61-74, Senior Consultant 75-; Vice-Pres. Philippine Asscn.; Pres. Asscn. of Surviving Delegates to the First Constitutional Convention 60-; Pres. Philippine Constitution Asscn. 63-64; mem. Board of Regents. Univ. of the Philippines 59-69; mem. Bar of U.S. Supreme Court; mem. American Soc. of Int. Law; Patron Int. Bar Asscn.; Pres. Philippine Ambs. Asscn. 75.

Leisure interests: hiking, swimming.

Philippine Sugar Association, R-809 Sikatuna Bldg., Ayala Avenue, Makati, Rizal; 15 Galaxy Street, Bel-Air III, Makati, Rizal, Philippines.
Telephone: 88-60-82 (Office); 87-72-96 (Home).

Romero, José Luis; Argentine historian; b. 24 March 1909, Buenos Aires; *s.* of Francisco Romero and Aurora Delgado de Romero; *m.* Teresa Basso de Romero 1933; one *s.* two *d.*; ed. Univ. de la Plata, Argentina.

Former Prof. of History, Univs. of La Plata, Buenos Aires and Montevideo; Founder-Dir. of review *Imago Mundi*; Founder and Dir. Centre for Study of Social History, Univ. of Buenos Aires until 65; Hon. Prof. Univs. of Buenos Aires and Montevideo 65-, Rector of

Univ. of Buenos Aires 55-56, Dean of Faculty of Philosophy and Letters 62-65; Visiting Lecturer, Univs. of Chile, San Marcos de Lima, Toulouse, Caen, Poitiers, Ecole des Hautes Etudes (Paris), and Columbia Univ., New York; mem. Board UN Univ. 74; fmr. Pres. Argentine Soc. of Writers; fmr. mem. Exec. Cttee. Socialist Party; Dr. h.c. Univ. of Montevideo; Officier des Palmes Académiques (France).

Publs. *La Cultura occidental*, *La historia y la vida*, *Sobre la biografía y la historia*, *La Edad Media*, *Ensayos sobre la burguesía*, *Maquiavelo historiador*, *Las ideas políticas en Argentina*, *Argentina imágenes y perspectivas*, *El desarrollo de las ideas en la sociedad argentina del siglo XX*, *La revolución burguesa en el mundo feudal*, *El Pensamiento Político de la Derecha Latino Americana*, *Latinoamérica: Las ciudades y las ideas*. 75.

Cerreti 928, Adrogué (B.A.), Argentina.

Telephone: 294-1256.

Romita, Pier Luigi, DR.ENG.; Italian politician; b. 27 July 1924, Turin; s. of Giuseppe Romita and Maria Stella; m. Antonia Magri 1961; one d.; ed. University of Rome.

Member of Italian Parl. 58-; Prof., Milan Univ. 63-; Under-Sec. for Public Works 63, for Public Educ. 66, for Internal Affairs 68, for Public Educ. 70; Minister of Scientific and Technological Research 72-73.

c/o Camera dei Deputati, Rome, Italy.

Telephone: 482889; 487278; 4754980.

Romney, George Wilcken; American businessman and politician; b. 8 July 1907, Chihuahua, Mexico; s. of Gaskell and Anna (Pratt) Romney; m. Leonore La Fount 1931; two s. two d.; ed. Latter-Day Saints Univ. and Univ. of Utah.

Mormon missionary in U.K. 27-28; Tariff Specialist to U.S. Senator David I. Walsh 29; joined Aluminium Co. of America 29, later its Rep. and also of Aluminium Wares Asscn., Washington, D.C.; Detroit Man. Automobile Manufacturers' Asscn. 39, Gen. Man. 42-48; Man. Dir. Automotive Council for War Production 41, also connected with Automotive Council for Air Defense; U.S. Employer Del. to ILO Metal Trades Industries Confs. Toledo (Ohio), Stockholm and Geneva 46-49; Asst. to Pres. Nash-Kelvinator Corpn. 48-50, Vice-Pres. 50-54, Exec. Vice-Pres. and Dir. 54; Pres. and Chair. American Motors Corpn. (successor co. to Nash-Kelvinator Corpn.) 54-62; Gov. of Michigan 63-68; U.S. Sec. of Housing 69-72; Chair., Nat. Cen. for Voluntary Action 73-; fmr. Chair., Redisco Inc.; Dir., Redisco of Canada Ltd., Kelvinator Ltd. (Great Britain), Kelvinator of Canada Ltd., American Motors of Canada Ltd., Douglas Aircraft Corpn.; numerous awards include Vermilye Medal (Franklin Inst. of Philadelphia) 59; Pres., Detroit Stake, Church of Jesus Christ of Latter Day Saints (Mormon); Hon. LL.D. (Wayne State Univ. and Brigham Young Univ.); Industry's "Man of the Year", Associated Press 58, 59, 60; Republican.

National Center for Voluntary Action, 1735 I Street, N.W., Washington, D.C. 20006; Home: East Valley Road, Bloomfield Hills, Mich. 48013, U.S.A.

Rompe, Robert, DR.PHIL.; German physicist; b. 10 Sept. 1905; ed. Technical Univ., Berlin-Charlottenburg. On staff of Inst. Buch 45; Prof. of Physics and Dir. II Physical Inst. of Humboldt Univ., Berlin 46-; mem. Deutsche Akad. der Wissenschaften and Dir. of its Inst. für Strahlungsquellen 49-; mem. Exec. Cttee. Forschungsgemeinschaft der naturwissenschaftlichen, technischen und medizinischen Institut der Deutsche Akad. der Wissenschaften; mem. Research Council of DDR; Deputy Pres. Council for Peaceful Use of Atomic Energy; Foreign mem. Czechoslovak Acad. of Sciences; Nat. Prize 51; Vaterländischer Verdienstorden (silver); Euler Medal of U.S.S.R. Acad. of Sciences 57.

Ekhoffstrasse 27, Berlin-Köpenick, Germany.

Romualdez, Eduardo Z.; Philippine politician; b. 22 Nov. 1909, Tolosa, Leyte; m. Concepción A. Veloso; ed. Univs. of the Philippines and Santo Tomás, and Georgetown Univ., Washington, D.C.

President, Bankers Asscn. of the Philippines 50-53; Dir. Chamber of Commerce of the Philippines 50-52; Vice-Pres. American Bankers' Asscn. 51-56; Chair. Board of Dirs., Philippine Air Lines (PAL) 54-62, Pres. 61-62; Alt. Gov. IMF 56-61, IBRD 56-61, IFC 57-61; Pres. Philippine Trust Co. 47-54, 62-, Fidelity and Surety Co. of the Philippines Inc. 47-54, 62-; Sec. of Finance, Repub. of the Philippines 65-70; Chair. Asian Devt. Bank 67-68; Amb. to U.S.A. 71-; mem. numerous cttees., etc., and del. to many int. confs.

Embassy of the Philippines, 1617 Massachusetts Avenue, N.W., Washington, D.C. 20036, U.S.A.

Romulo, Brig.-Gen. Carlos Peña; Philippine writer, educator and diplomatist; b. 14 Jan. 1899; ed. Univ. of the Philippines and Columbia Univ.

Associate Prof. of English, Univ. of the Philippines 26-30, mem. Board of Regents 31-41; Editor-in-Chief TVT Publications 31, Publisher DMHM Newspapers 37-41; Staff of Gen. MacArthur and Sec. of Information and Public Relations, Philippine War Cabinet in U.S.A. 43-44, Brigadier Gen. 44; Acting-Sec. of Public Instruction 44-45, Chief Del. to UN 45-55, Pres. 49-50, Security Council 57; Sec. of Foreign Affairs 50-52; Ambassador to the U.S.A. 52-53, 55-62, Special Envoy 54-55, concurrently Minister to Cuba 59; Pres. Univ. of the Philippines 62-68, Philippine Acad. of Sciences and Humanities; Presidential Adviser on Foreign Affairs; Sec. Dept. of Educ. 66-68; Sec. of Foreign Affairs 68-; numerous decorations, honours, hon. degrees and awards.

Publs. *I saw the Fall of the Philippines* 42, *Mother America* 43, *My Brother Americans* 45, *Crusade in Asia* 55, *The Meaning of Bandung* 56, *The Magsaysay Story* 56, *Friend to Friend* 58, *I Walked with Heroes (An Autobiography)* 61, *Contemporary Nationalism and World Order* 64, *Mission to Asia* 64, *Identity and Change* 65, *Evasions and Response* 66, *The University and External Aid* 67, *Clarifying the Asian Mystique* 69.

Department of Foreign Affairs, Padre Faura, Manila; and 74 McKinley Road, Forbes Park, Makati, Rizal, Philippines.

Ronan, Sean G., M.A., LL.B.; Irish civil servant; b. 11 Jan. 1924, Cork; s. of John Ronan and Mary Hogan; m. Brigid Teresa McGuinness 1949; two s. two d.; ed. Nat. Univ. of Ireland, Univ. Coll., Dublin.

Executive Officer Revenue Commrs. 42-46; Admin. Officer Ministry of Finance 46-49; Third Sec. Ministry of Foreign Affairs 49-51, First Sec. 51-55; Consul-Gen., Chicago 55-60; Counsellor Ministry of Foreign Affairs 60-64; Asst. Sec.-Gen. for Political, UN and Cultural Affairs and Information, Ministry of Foreign Affairs 64-72; Amb. to Fed. Repub. of Germany 72-73; Dir.-Gen. for Information, Comm. of European Communities 73-; Great Order of Merit with Star of Fed. Rep. of Germany 73.

Leisure interests: literary and cultural.

Directorate-General for Information, Commission of the European Communities, 200 rue de la Loi, 1049 Brussels, Belgium.

Telephone: 735-00-40/735-80-40.

Ronchi, Vasco; Italian professor of physics; b. 19 Dec. 1897, Florence; s. of Giorgio Ronchi and Maria Bartoli; m. Edda Suckert 1926; two d.; ed. Univs. of Pisa and Florence and Scuola Normale Superiore, Pisa.

Army service 15-19; Reader, Inst. of Physics, Florence Univ. 20-27; Founder-Dir. Istituto Nazionale di Ottica di Firenze-Arcetri 27-; Pres. of Council, Int. Union of History and Philosophy of Science of ICSU 57-69; Pres. Italian Optical Asscn. 39-, Asscn. of Astronautical Sciences 56-, Italian Group of Scientific

History 57-, Giorgio Ronchi Foundation 45-, Industrial School Benvenuto Cellini 43-, Ignazio Porro Foundation 67; mem. of numerous cttees. of Consiglio Nazionale delle Ricerche and int. comms.; mem. numerous Nat. and Int. Acads.; Fellow Optical Soc. of America; Chevalier, Légion d'Honneur, France; Cavaliere di Gran Croce del Ordine al Merito, Italy; numerous medals.

Major work: Inventor of Ronchi test for interferential testing of optical instruments.

Publs. *Lezioni di Ottica Ondulatoria, Storia della luce, Optics, the Science of Vision, Critica dei fondamenti dell'acustica e dell' ottica, Sul modo di sperimentare, Galileo e il suo cannocchiale, The Nature of Light, New Optics, Two Thousand Years of Conflict between Reason and Sense, Perspective based on New Optics*, etc.
1 Largo E. Fermi, 50125 Florence, Italy.
Telephone: 22-11-63.

Rood, Henry Fairbank, A.B., A.M.; American insurance executive; b. 14 Sept. 1906, Port Chester, N.Y.; s. of Henry Martin Rood and Grace S. F. (Mellen) Rood; m. Ruth N. Winchester 1929; three s.; ed. Oberlin Coll. and Univ. of Michigan.
With Lincoln Nat. Life Insurance Co., Fort Wayne, Ind. 31-71, Actuary 49-58, Second Vice-Pres. 48-52, Vice-Pres. 54-58, Senior Vice-Pres. 58-64, Pres. 64-68, Chair. and Chief Exec. Officer 68-71, Dir. 54-; Chair. and Chief Exec. Officer Lincoln Nat. Corpn. 68-71, Hon. Chair. 72-; Hon. Chair., Lincoln Nat. Life Insurance Co. of New York 72-; Chair. American States Insurance Co., American Economy Insurance Co., American States Life Insurance Co., American Union Insurance Co. of New York, American States Insurance Co. of Texas 68-71; Dir. N. Atlantic Reassurance Co., Paris 63-71, Dominion-Lincoln Assurance Co., London 65-71, Lincoln Nat. Bank & Trust Co., Fort Wayne 65-; Chicago Title and Trust Co. 70-71; LNC Devt. Corpn. and LNC Land Sales Inc.; Fellow, Soc. of Actuaries 37-, Past Pres. 66-67; official of numerous other insurance orgs.; U.S. Naval Reserve 43-46; Distinguished Hoosier Award 71.
Leisure interests: reading, bridge, golf.
Office: 1505 Lincoln Bank Tower, Fort Wayne, Ind. 46802; Home: 5505 Old Mill Road, Fort Wayne, Ind. 46807, U.S.A.
Telephone: 219-422-1766 (Office); 219-744-5363 (Home).

Rood, Johannes (Jon) Joseph Van, PH.D., M.D.; Netherlands immunologist; b. 7 April 1926, The Hague; s. of Albert van Rood and Rientje Röell; m. Sacha Bsse van Tuyll van Serooskerken 1957; one s. two d.; ed. Univ. of Leiden.
Worked in bloodbanking 52-; in charge of Bloodbank and foundation of Dept. of Immunohaematology, Univ. Hospital, Leiden 57; work in tissue typing 58-; worked on antibody synthesis in Public Health Research Inst., New York 62; Lecturer in Immunohaematology, Univ. of Leiden 65-, Prof. in Internal Medicine 69-; Founder Eurotransplant 67.
Leisure interests: sailing, swimming, skiing, photography.
Publs. *Leukocyte Antibodies in Sera of Pregnant Women 58, Platelet Survival 59, Erythrocyte Survival with DFP 32 61, Leukocyte Grouping, a Method and its Application 62, Leukocyte Groups, the Normal Lymphocyte Transfer Test and Homograft Sensitivity 65, Platelet Transfusion 65, The Relevance of Leukocyte Antigens 67, A Proposal for International Co-operation: EUROTRANSPLANT 67, Transplantation of bone-marrow cells and fetal thymus in an infant with lymphonenic immunological deficiency 69, The 4a and 4b Antigens: Do They or Don't They? 70, Anti HL-A 2 inhibitor in normal human serum 70, HL-A identical phenotypes and genotypes in unrelated individuals 70, HL-A and the Group Five System in Hodgkin's Disease 71, The (Relative) Importance of HL-A Matching in Kidney Transplantation 71.*
Department of Immunohaematology, University Hospital, Leiden, Netherlands.
Telephone: 01710-47222-2091.

Rooke, Denis Eric, C.B.E., B.SC.(ENG.); British engineer and executive; b. 2 April 1924, London; s. of F. G. Rooke; m. Elizabeth Brenda Evans 1949; one d.; ed. Westminster City School, Addey and Stanhope School, Univ. Coll., London.
Served with Royal Electrical and Mechanical Engineers in U.K. and India 44-49; joined S.E. Gas Board 49, Asst. Mechanical Engineer 49, Deputy Man. of Works 54, Devt. Engineer 59; seconded to N. Thames Gas Board 57; mem. technical team aboard *Methane Pioneer* 59; Devt. Engineer, Gas Council 60 (name changed to British Gas Corpn. 73), mem. for Production and Supply 66-71, Deputy Chair. 72-76, Chair. (designate) June 76-; mem. Advisory Council on Research and Devt. for Fuel and Power 72-, Advisory Council for Energy Conservation 74-, Offshore Energy Tech. Board 75-; Fellow, Univ. Coll., London 72, Inst. of Chemical Engineers, Inst. of Gas Engineers (Pres. 75-76), Inst. of Mechanical Engineers.
Leisure interests: photography, listening to music.
Publs. numerous papers to learned socs. and professional asscns.
British Gas Corporation, 59 Bryanston Street, London, W1A 2AZ; Home: 23 Hardy Road, Blackheath, London, SE3 7NS, England.
Telephone: 01-723-7030 (Office).

Roolvink, Bauke; Netherlands politician and former trade union official; b. 31 Jan. 1912, Wijtgaard, Friesland; m. G. S. Schouten; three s. three d.; ed. Trade Unions Training Coll. of the Protestant National Federation of Trade Unions.
Bench fitter; Second Chair. Protestant Trade Union for the Metal Industry 46-52; Sec. Protestant Nat. Fed. of Trade Unions 52-59; State Sec. for Social Affairs and Public Health 59-63; mem. Second Chamber of the States-Gen. July 63-67; Minister of Social Affairs and Public Health 67-71; Knight, Order of Netherlands Lion, Grand Cross, Order of Léopold II of Belgium, Grand Cross, Order of the Crown of Belgium, Grand Cross, Order of the Yugoslav Flag, Special Social Welfare Distinction 1st Class of Belgium.
26 Uytenbosch, Baarn, Netherlands.

Room, Thomas Gerald, SC.D., F.R.S., F.A.A.; British mathematician; b. 10 Nov. 1902, London; s. of Ernest W. Room and E. Elisabeth Henry; m. Jessie Bannerman 1937; one s. two d.; ed. Alleyn's School, London, St. John's Coll., Cambridge.
Lecturer in Mathematics, Liverpool Univ. 25-27; Fellow, St. John's Coll., Cambridge 26-29; Lecturer in Mathematics, Cambridge Univ. 27-35; Prof. of Mathematics, Sydney Univ. 35-68, Dean Faculty of Science 52-56, 60-65; Visiting Prof. of Mathematics, Univ. of Washington 48, Univ. of Tennessee 49, Univ. of Sussex 66, Univ. of London 69-70; mem. Princeton Inst. of Advanced Study 48 and 57; Visiting Senior Fellow, Westfield Coll., Univ. of London 69-70; Staff Tutor, Open Univ. 71, Visiting Prof. 72-74.
Publs. *Geometry of Determinantal Loci 39, The Sorting Process 66, A Background to Geometry 67, Miniquaternion Geometry 71.*
High Walden, St. Ives, N.S.W., Australia.
Telephone: (Sydney) 449-5743.

Roos, Joseph Marie-Philippe; French public servant; b. 13 March 1906, Paris; s. of Joseph Roos and Aimée Bègue; m. Suzanne Pellet 1932; two d.; ed. Ecole Polytechnique, and Ecole Supérieure Aéronautique.
Dir. of Air Transport, Min. of Public Works 46-47; Gen. Man. Société des Usines Chausson 47-55, Chair. 55-61;

Pres. Air France 61-67; Pres. Inst. of Air Transport 60-72; Commdr. Légion d'Honneur, Croix de Guerre.
37 rue Chardon-Lagache, 75016 Paris, France.

Roosa, Robert V., A.B., M.A., PH.D.; American banker and fmr. government official; b. 21 June 1918, Marquette, Mich.; s. of Harvey Mapes Rosa and Ruth Lagerquist; m. Ruth Grace Amende 1946; two d.; ed. Univ. of Michigan.
Teacher of Economics, Michigan, Harvard, Mass. Inst of Tech. 39-43; Fed. Reserve Bank of New York 46-60, Vice-Pres. Research Dept. 56-60; Under-Sec. for Monetary Affairs, U.S. Treasury 61-64; Partner Brown Bros. Harriman and Co. 65-; Dir. American Express Co. 66. Anaconda Co. 67, Texaco Inc. 69, Owens-Corning Fiberglas Corpn. 69, Brown Harriman and Int. Banks Ltd. (London) 69; Trustee, The Rockefeller Foundation 67; mem. American Acad. of Arts and Sciences, American Philosophical Soc.; Independent Democrat.
Leisure interests: music, opera, reading (especially history, politics, diplomacy).
Publs. *Money, Trade and Economic Growth* (Editor) 51. *Federal Reserve Operations in the Money and Government Securities Markets* 56, *Monetary Reform for the World Economy* 65, *The Dollar and World Liquidity* 67, *The Balance of Payments: Free Versus Fixed Exchange Rates* (with Milton Friedman) 67.
30 Woodlands Road, Harrison, N.Y 10528; and 59 Wall Street, New York City 10005, N.Y., U.S.A.
Telephone: 914-967-7646 (Home); 212-483-1818 (Office).

Roosa, Col. Stuart A.; American astronaut; b. 16 Aug. 1933, Durango, Colo.; m. Joan C. Barrett; three s. one d.; ed. Univ. of Colorado.
Entered U.S Air Force 53; commissioned after graduation from Aviation Cadet Program, Williams Air Force Base, Arizona; flew F-84F and F-100 aircraft, Langley Air Force Base, Va.; then attended Univ. of Colorado; later Chief of Service Engineering, Tachikawa Air Base, Japan; maintenance test pilot, Olmsted Air Force Base, Pa. 62-64; graduated from Air Force Aerospace Research Pilot School 65; experimental test pilot; Edwards Air Force Base, Calif. 65-66; selected by NASA as astronaut April 66; flew in *Apollo XIV* Jan.-Feb. 71, served as backup pilot for *Apollo XVI* and *XVII* 72; on course Harvard Business School 73; now assigned to Space Shuttle Program.
NASA Johnson Space Center, Houston, Tex. 77058, U.S.A.

Roosevelt, Franklin Delano, Jr.; American lawyer and politician; b. 17 Aug. 1914; s. of the late Franklin Delano Roosevelt (31st President of the U.S.) and Eleanor Roosevelt; ed. Harvard, and Univ. of Virginia.
United States Naval service 41-45; mem. U.S. House of Reps. 49-53; Pres., Roosevelt Automobile Co. 58-63; Under-Sec. of Commerce 63-65; Chair. Equal Employment Opportunity Comm. 65-66; Cand. for Gov. of New York 66; Democrat.
45 E. 66th Street, New York, N.Y., U.S.A.

Rootes, 2nd Baron (cr. 59) of Ramsbury; William Geoffrey Rootes, F.B.I.M., F.R.S.A.; British company director; b. 14 June 1917; s. of 1st Baron Rootes, G.B.E.; m. Marian Slater (née Hayter) 1946; one s. one d.; ed. Harrow and Christ Church, Oxford.
War Service 39-45, R.A.S.C.; rejoined Rootes Motors 46, Man. Dir. 62-67, Deputy Chair. 65-67, Chair. 67-70; Chair. Chrysler United Kingdom (now Rootes Motors Ltd.) 67-73; Dir. First Nat. City Trust Co. (Bahamas) Ltd.; Pres. Motor and Cycle Trades Benevolent Fund 68-70, Motor Industry Research Asscn. 70-71, Inst. of Motor Industry 73-; mem. Nat. Advisory Council, Motor Mfg. Industry 64-71, Nat. Econ. Devt. Cttee., Motor Mfg. Industry 68-73, British Nat. Export Council (Chair. American Cttee. 69-71), Council Confed. of British Industry 67-74, Europe Cttee., CBI 72-, Council Inst. of Dirs., Council Warwick Univ. 56-74, Council Soc. of Motor Mfrs. (Pres. 60-61, Chair. Exec. Cttee. 72-73), Council of the Cranfield Inst. of Technology; Dir. Joseph Lucas (Industries) Ltd. 73-, Ranks Hovis McDougall Ltd. 73-; Chair. Game Conservancy May 75-.
Leisure interests: shooting, tennis, skiing, fishing.
Halkin House, 5-6 Halkin Street, London, S.W.1; North Standen House, Hungerford, Berks., England; Glenalmond House, Glenalmond, Perthshire, Scotland.
Telephone: 01-235-8845.

Rootes, Sir Reginald Claud, Kt.; British engineer and business executive; b. 20 Oct. 1896; ed. Cranbrook School, Kent.
President Soc. of Motor Manufacturers and Traders 45-46, Deputy Pres. 46-50; Pres. Motor Industry Research Asscn. 52-53; Chair. Rootes Motors Ltd. 65-67; retd.
Polla House, Hothfield, Ashford, Kent, England.

Roquemaurel, Marquis Ithier de; French business executive; b. 15 Sept. 1914, Villetoureix, Dordogne; s. of late Marquis de Roquemaurel and Madeleine Meunier du Houssoy; m. Claude du Pouget de Nadaillac; two s. one d.; ed. Collège Stanislas, Paris and Ecole Centrale des Arts et Manufactures, Paris.
President/Dir.-Gen. Brodard and Taupin (printers) 50-; Dir. Ancienne Société Anonyme de Rotogravure d'Art, Brussels 54-, Librairie Hachette 55-, Agence and Messageries de Presse, Belgium (also Pres.) 59-, Société d'Etudes and de Publications Economiques 62-, Réalités in America (also Pres./Dir.-Gen.) 62-, Office d'Editions Générales-Presse 63-; Man. F.E.P. (France Editions & Publications) 64-; Deputy Dir.-Gen. Librairie Hachette 64-67, Pres./Dir.-Gen. 67-76; Man. Société de Gérance des Messageries 67-, Télé-7 Jours 68-; Dir. Crédit Foncier Franco-Canadien 68-, Cie. Française d'Exploitations Commerciales 68-, Femmes d'Aujourd'hui, Belgium 68-, Sociedad General Española de Librería, Spain 68-; Officier, Légion d'Honneur, Ordre du Cèdre, Chevalier, Ordre de Léopold, Croix de Guerre and many other decorations.
Leisure interests: yachting, equitation, golf.
Libraire Hachette, 24 boulevard St. Michel, Paris 6e; Home: 82 rue de l'Université, Paris 7e, France.

Rosales, H.E. Cardinal Julio R.; Philippine ecclesiastic; b. 18 Sept. 1906, Calbayog City, Samar.
Ordained 29; First Bishop of Tagbiliran 46-49; Archbishop of Cebú 61-65, 74-76; Pres. Bishops' Conf. of Philippines 61-65, 74-76; cr. Cardinal 69; mem. Sacred Congregation of the Clergy and Sacred Congregation of Catholic Educ., Rome; Grand Cross of Isabel la Católica (Spain), Grand Cross, Order of St. Raymundo de Pennafort, Knight Order of Corpus Christi in Toledo; LL.D. (Univ. of San Carlos), D.H. (De La Salle Coll.).
Archbishop's Residence, P.O. Box 52, Cebú City, Philippines.

Rosania, Luca, D.ECON.; Italian financial executive; b. 19 March 1908, Barranquilla; m. Lea Ballini; ed. Univ. of Florence.
Assistant Prof. of Financial Science and Econs., University of Florence; Research Dept. Banca d'Italia 37, Head of Dept. 60, with Operational Dept. (dealing with securities) 64, Gen. Man. Milan Branch 68; mem. Cttee. for Reform of the Stock Exchange, Ministry of Finance; Chair. of Cttee., Milan Stock Exchange 68; Expert, Cttee. for the Right of Establishment of Banks in the EEC; Vice-Chair. European Investment Bank 70-.
European Investment Bank, 2 place de Metz, Luxembourg; and 10 avenue Guillaume, Luxembourg; Home: 131 via Friggeri, Rome, Italy.
Telephone: 43-50-11 (Office); 47-18-53; 34-72-92 (Home).

Rosanov, Anatoly Anatolievich; Soviet diplomatist; b. 25 April 1921, Ryazan; ed. Moscow Machine Tool and Instrument Building Inst. and High Diplomatic School, Ministry of Foreign Affairs.
Official, Soviet Section, Allied Council on Japan 47-51; Ranking Official, Central Staff, Ministry of Foreign Affairs, U.S.S.R. 51-57; First Sec. Tokyo Embassy 57-61, Counsellor 63-68; at Ministry of Foreign Affairs 61-63, 68-70; Amb. to Thailand 70-73.
c/o Ministry of Foreign Affairs, Moscow, U.S.S.R.

Rösch, Jean; French astronomer; b. 5 Jan. 1915-s. of Dr. Gabriel Rösch and Lucile Forgues; m. Ray; monde Postel 1937; ed. Lycée in Algiers and Ecole Normale Supérieure, Paris.
Astronomical Asst. Observatory of Bordeaux 40-43, Asst. Astronomer 43-47, Dir. Pic du Midi Observatory (now Observatoires du Pic du Midi et de Toulouse) 47-; Lecturer, Univ. of Bordeaux 43-63; Prof. of Astronomy, Univ. de Paris à la Sorbonne (now Univ. de Pierre et Marie Curie) 64-; research on astronomical subjects including binocular vision, the solar system and telescopic images, and choice of sites for observatories; Pres. and mem. numerous astronomical comms.; Pres. Soc. Astronomique de France 66-69; Corresp. Bureau des Longitudes 68-; Chevalier Légion d'Honneur; Prix Benjamin Valz 42, Médaille Janssen 44; Prix Ancel, Acad. des Sciences 71, Prix des Trois Physiciens 74.
Leisure interest: mountaineering.
Publs. Numerous works on astronomy.
Observatoires du Pic du Midi et de Toulouse, 65200 Bagnères-de-Bigorre; and Institut d'Astrophysique, 98 bis boulevard Arago, 75014 Paris, France.
Telephone: 62-95-00-69.

Rösch, Otto; Austrian politician; b. 24 March 1917, Vienna; s. of Otto and Maria (née Gusenbauer) Rösch; m. Elfriede Rösch 1938 (dissolved); one s. three d.; ed. Volksschule, Vienna, Bundeserziehungsanstalt Traiskirchen, and Univs. of Vienna and Graz.
Military service 40-45; Sec. (for region of Styria) to Asscn. of Socialist Municipal Reps. 49; mem. Bundesrat 51; mem. Styrian Ass. 53; mem. Lower Austrian Assembly and Sec. of State, Fed. Ministry of Defence 59-66; mem. Lower Austrian Provincial Govt. 66; Fed. Minister of Interior April 70-; Grosses Silbernes Ehrenzeichen, Silbernes Komturkreuz; Socialist Party.
Leisure interests: films, skiing.
Publs. articles in the press and political documents.
Liechtensteinstrasse 91/7a, 1090 Vienna, Austria.
Telephone: 345252.

Rose, Bram, M.D., PH.D., F.R.S.(C.); Canadian physician; b. 21 April 1907; m. Rosa Mary Johnson 1940; two s. one d.; ed. Westmount High School and McGill Univ.
Research Asst. McGill Univ. Clinic 36-39, Research Assoc. 39-40; R.C.A.F. 40-46; Asst. Physician, Royal Victoria Hospital, Montreal 42; Asst. Prof. of Medicine, McGill Univ. Clinic 50; Assoc. Physician Royal Victoria Hospital 51; Assoc. Prof. of Medicine, McGill Univ. Clinic 55; Physician, Royal Victoria Hospital 61; Prof. of Experimental Medicine, McGill Univ. Clinic 63-; Consultant in Allergy and Dir. of Allergy Laboratory, Queen Mary Veterans Hospital 49-; Hon. Consultant in Medicine, Jewish Gen. Hospital, Montreal 57-; Regional Cons., Jewish Nat. Home for Asthmatic Children, Denver 59-; Dir. Div. of Immunochemistry and Allergy, Univ. Clinic, Royal Victoria Hospital 55-; Pres. Canadian Soc. of Immunology; Past Pres. of Canadian and American Acads. of Allergy, Int. Asscn. of Allergology; mem. Training Grant Cttee., Nat. Inst. of Allergy and Immunology, Nat. Inst. of Health, Bethesda, Maryland; Centennial Medal 67.
Leisure interests: music, skiing, electronics.
Publs. Over 150 works, on histamine, cardiac catheterization, metabolism, shock, (blackout) acceleration in aircraft, ACTH, cortisone, immunoglobulins, and immune mechanisms in disease; Section Editor of *Immunological Diseases* 66, 71.
Division of Immunochemistry and Allergy, 11th Floor Medical Wing, Royal Victoria Hospital, Montreal 2, Quebec; Home: 687 Pine Avenue West, Montreal 112, Quebec, Canada.
Telephone: 842-1251.

Rose, Eliot Joseph Benn; British publisher; b. 7 June 1909, London; s. of Col. E. A. and Mrs. Julia E. Rose; m. Susan P. Gibson 1946; one s. one d.; ed. Rugby, and New Coll., Oxford.
Served R.A.F. 39-45; Literary Editor *The Observer* 48-51; Dir. Int. Press Inst., Zürich 52-62; Dir. Survey of Race Relations in Britain 63-69; Editorial Dir., Westminster Press 70-74, Chair., Penguin Books Ltd., Viking Penguin Inc.
Leisure interest: music.
Publ. *Colour and Citizenship* 69.
37 Pembroke Square, London, W.8, England.
Telephone: 01-937-3772.

Rose, Leonard; American cellist; b. 27 July 1918, Washington, D.C.; s. of Harry Rose and Jennie Frankel Rose; m. Xenia Petschek Rose 1965; one s. one d.; ed. Miami, Florida, Curtis Inst. of Music.
Assistant Solo Cellist, NBC Symphony Orchestra 38; Solo Cellist, Cleveland Orchestra 39-43, New York Philharmonic Orchestra 43-51; Cello Teacher, Juilliard School 43-, Curtis Inst. 51-62; Cello Soloist in recitals and with most major orchestras in N. and S. America, Europe, Middle East, Far East; recorded with CBS Records; performing trio with Isaac Stern and Eugene Istomin; Ford Foundation Grant 63; Hon. D.Mus. (Hartford Univ.) 65.
Leisure interests: cooking, golf, painting, antiques, reading.
Publs. Edited major portion of cello literature for Int. Music Co. of New York.
19 Overlook Road, Hastings-on-Hudson, N.Y. 10706, U.S.A.

Rose, William Cumming, B.S., PH.D.; American professor of biochemistry; b. 4 April 1887, Greenville, S.C.; s. of Rev. John M. Rose and Mary Santos; m. Zula F. Hedrick 1913; ed. Davidson Coll., Yale Univ. and Univ. of Freiburg.
Instructor in Physiological Chem., Univ. of Pa. 11-13; Assoc. Prof. of Biochem., Coll. of Medicine of Univ. of Texas 13-14, Prof. of Biochem. and Head of Dept. 14-22; Prof. of Biochem. at Univ. of Ill. 22-53, Research Prof. 53-55, Research Prof. Emer. 55-; mem. of Editorial Board *Journal of Nutrition* 35-39, *Journal of Biological Chemistry* 36-49; Pres. American Soc. of Biological Chemists 37-39, American Inst. of Nutrition 45-46; mem. of numerous scientific advisory bodies 36-57, including Scientific Advisory Cttee. of Nutrition Foundation Inc. 43-57; discovered, isolated, identified and established the spatial configuration of the dietary essential amino acid, Threonine; Fellow American Asscn. for the Advancement of Science; mem. Nat. Acad. of Sciences, American Chemical Soc.; Hon. mem. Harvey Soc. of New York; Hon. Sc.D. (Davidson Coll., Yale Univ. and Univs. of Chicago and Ill.); Osborn Mendel Award of American Inst. of Nutrition 49, American Chemical Society's Willard Gibbs Medal 52 and Charles F. Spencer Award 57, Twentieth Anniversary Award of Nutrition Foundation 61, Nat. Medal of Science awarded by the Pres. of U.S.A. 66.
Leisure interests: photography, amateur ornithology.
Publs. Numerous scientific articles on the metabolism of creatinine, creatinine purines, and amino acids.
Apartment 204, The Oaks, 405 West University Avenue, Champaign, Ill. 61820, U.S.A.
Telephone: 217-352-7709.

Roseman, Alvin, A.B., M.A., J.D.; American university professor; b. 31 March 1910, Cleveland, Ohio; s. of Benjamin D. and Ruth (Stern) Roseman; m. Edith Freund 1935; one s. one d.; ed. Western Reserve Univ., and Univ. of Chicago.

Staff Consultant, Public Welfare Asscn. 33-35; Exec Officer, Social Security Board 35-39; Asst. to Fed Security Administrator 39-41; Asst. Dir., U.S. War Manpower Comm. 41-43; Dep. Chief of Mission to Middle East (UNRRA) and Balkans 43-45; Chief, International Activities, U.S. Bureau of the Budget 45-49; U.S. Rep. to U.N. agencies at Geneva 49-51; Dep. Chief, U.S. Econ. Mission to Greece 51-53; Dir., Public Services, International Co-operation Admin. 53-57; Dir., U.S. Econ. Mission to Cambodia 57-59; Regional Dir. for the Far East, International Co-operation Admin. 59-60; Asst. Dir.-Gen., UNESCO 60-63; Assoc. Dean and Prof. of Int. Affairs, Univ. of Pittsburgh Graduate School of Public and International Affairs 63-; Asst. Dir. for Population Affairs, U.S. Aid Mission to India 70-72; Outstanding Public Service Citation 57; Distinguished Career Award 59.

Leisure interests: tennis, small boat sailing.

Publs. *Shelter Care and the Homeless Local Man* 35, *International Professional Education for Business and Public Administration* (co-author) 67, *American Universities and Development Assistance* (co-author) 67, and numerous articles in professional journals.

University of Pittsburgh, Pittsburgh, Pa.; Home: 148 Maple Heights Drive, Pittsburgh 32, Pa., U.S.A. Telephone: 683-5743 (Home).

Roseman, Saul, M.S., PH.D.; American biochemist; b. 9 March 1921, Brooklyn, N.Y.; s. of Emil and Rose (née Markowitz) Roseman; m. Martha Ozrowitz 1941; one s. two d.; ed. City Coll. of N.Y. and Univ. of Wisconsin.

Instructor to Asst. Prof., Univ. of Chicago 48-53; Asst. Prof. to Prof. of Biological Chemistry, Univ. of Mich. 53-65; Prof. of Biology, Johns Hopkins Univ. 65-, Chair., Dept. of Biology 69-73, Dir., McCollum-Pratt Inst. 69-73; Ralph S. O'Connor Prof. of Biology; Consultant, Nat. Cystic Fibrosis Research Foundation, American Cancer Soc., Hosp. for Sick Children, Toronto; mem. American Soc. of Biological Chemists, American Acad. of Arts and Sciences, American Chem. Soc., Nat. Acad. of Sciences, A.A.A.S., Biophysical Soc., American Asscn. of Univ. Profs.; Scientific Counsellor to Nat. Cancer Inst.; Counsellor to American Soc. of Biological Chemists; awarded Sesquicentennial Award (Univ. of Michigan) 67, 15th Annual T. Duckett Jones Memorial Award, Helen Hay Whitney Foundation 73, Rosensteihl Award (Brandeis Univ.) 74.

Leisure interests: sailing, music, reading, athletics.

Publs. over 100 original articles in scientific journals.

Department of Biology and McCollum-Pratt Institute, The Johns Hopkins University, Md. 21218; Home: 8206 Cranwood Court, Baltimore, Md. 21208, U.S.A. Telephone: 366-3300 (Office); 486-7439 (Home).

Rosen, Charles, PH.D.; American pianist; b. 5 May 1927, New York City; s. of Irwin Rosen and Anita Gerber; ed. Juilliard School of Music, Princeton Univ.

Studied piano with Moriz Rosenthal and Hedwig Kanner-Rosenthal 38-45; recital debut, N.Y. 51; first complete recording of Debussy Etudes 51; première of Double Concerto by Elliott Carter, N.Y. 61; has played recitals and as soloist with orchestras throughout America and Europe; has made over 25 recordings including Stravinsky: *Movements* with composer conducting 62, Schumann: *Davidsbündlertänze* 63, Bach: *Art of Fugue, Two Ricercars, Goldberg Variations* 71, Beethoven: *Last Six Sonatas* 72, Boulez: *Piano Music, Vol. I*; Prof. of Music, State Univ. of N.Y. 72-; Nat. Book Award 72; Phi Beta Kappa Visiting Scholar

73-74; Guggenheim Fellowship 74; Messenger Lectures, Cornell Univ. 75.

Publs. *The Classical Style: Haydn, Mozart, Beethoven* 71, *Schoenberg* 75, and several articles on music.

101 West 78th Street, New York, N.Y. 10024, U.S.A.; and 3 place Boulnois, Paris 17e, France.

Rosen, Martin M., M.A.; American executive and economist; b. 7 Aug. 1919, Cincinnati, Ohio; s. of Samuel Rosen and Sarah Fradkin; m. Judith Jacobs 1949; two s. four d.; ed. Univs. of Cincinnati and Minnesota.

Economist, U.S. Treasury Dept. 41-42; served with U.S. Army 42-46; Deputy Chief, Finance Division U.S. Element, Allied Comm. for Austria 45-46; mem. of Economic Staff, Int. Bank 46; on leave to be Consultant to W. A. Harriman, U.S. Special Rep. in Europe 48-; Acting Chief Economist 48, Chief Economist 50, Asst. to Dir. Economic Staff 51, Asst. Dir. Dept. of Operations, Europe, Africa and Australasia 52, Asst. Dir. Dept. of Technical Operations 55, Dir. Dept. of Operations, Far East, Int. Bank for Reconstruction and Development 57-61; Dir. Dept. of Operations, Far East, Int. Development Asscn. (IDA) 60-61; Exec. Vice-Pres. Int. Finance Corpn. 61-69; Chair. and Dir. First Washington Securities Corpn. 69-; Pres. Model, Roland and Co. Inc. 72-73, Co-Chair. 73-74; Vice-Chair. Shields Model Roland Inc. 74-; decorated by Govts. of Columbia, Japan, Mauritania and Senegal.

First Washington Securities Corpn., 1211 Connecticut Avenue, N.W., Washington, D.C. 20036; Home: 2115 Paul Spring Road, Alexandria, Va. 22307, U.S.A. Telephone: 296-2394 (Office); 768-7751 (Home).

Rosen, Milton William, B.S.; American engineer and physicist; b. 25 July 1915, Philadelphia, Pa.; s. of Abraham and Regina (Weiss) Rosen; m. Josephine Haar 1948; three d.; ed. Univ. of Pennsylvania, Univ. of Pittsburgh, and California Inst. of Technology.

Engineer Westinghouse Electric and Mfg. Co. 37-38; Engineer-physicist Naval Research Laboratory, Wash. 40-58, Scientific Officer Viking Rocket 47-55, Head Rocket Development Branch 53-55, Technical Dir. Project Vanguard (earth satellite) 55-58; Engineer Nat. Aeronautics and Space Admin. (NASA) 58-; Chief Rocket Vehicle Development Programs 58-59, Dep. Dir. Launch Vehicle Programs 60-61, Dir. Launch Vehicles and Propulsion 61-63; Senior Scientist, Office of DOD and Interagency Affairs, Nat. Aeronautics and Space Admin. 63-72; Deputy Assoc. Admin. for Space Science (Eng.) 72-; Chair. Greater Washington Asscn. of Unitarian Churches 66-68.

Leisure interests: music, tennis.

Publ. *The Viking Rocket Story* 55.

Office: NASA Headquarters, Washington, D.C. 20546; Home: 5610 Alta Vista Road, Bethesda, Maryland 20034, U.S.A. Telephone: 202-755-3944 (Office); 301-530-1497 (Home).

Rosen, Shlomo; Israeli politician; b. 21 June 1905.

Active in Histadrut, missions abroad; mem. Exec. Cttee., Jewish Agency; mem. Exec. Comm., Mapam (United Workers' Party); mem. Knesset (Parl.), Deputy Speaker 65-; Sec. Kibbutz Movement; Minister for Immigration and Absorption March 74-.

Ministry of Immigration and Absorption, Jerusalem, Israel.

Rosenberg, Ludwig; German trade union official; b. 29 June 1903, Berlin; m. Margot (née Mützelburg) 1933; ed. State Coll. of Economics and Admin., Düsseldorf.

Secretary, Clerical Workers' Union 28-33; political refugee in Great Britain 33-46; Trades Union Liaison Office, Bielefeld 46-47; Trades Union Council, Frankfurt/Main 48-50; Exec. Cttee. DGB (German Fed. of Trade Unions), Chief, Foreign Relations Dept. 50-53,

Vice-Pres. Exec. Cttee. 59-62, Pres. 62-69, retd.; Pres. Econ. and Social Cttee., EEC and Euratom 60-62, Vice-Pres. 58-60, 62-63; mem. of Monnet Cttee., United States of Europe; mem. various nat. and int. insts.; German and Italian decorations; Social Democratic Party.

Publs. *Decisions for Tomorrow* 69, *Trade Union Policy for Today* 69, *Aphorismen* 72, *Purpose and Aim of Trade Unions, Tradition and Future* 73.

Fernholz 2, 403 Ratingen-Hösel, Federal Republic of Germany.

Rosenblith, Walter Alter; American scientist and university professor; b. 21 Sept. 1913, Vienna, Austria; *s.* of David A. and Gabriele (Roth) Rosenblith; *m.* Judy O. Francis 1941; one *s.* one *d.*; ed. Berlin, Lausanne, Paris, Bordeaux Univs.

Research, Paris 38-39, N.Y. Univ. 39-40, Univ. Calif. (Los Angeles) Grad. Scholar and Asst. in Physics 40-43; Asst. Prof., Assoc. Prof., Acting Head, Dept. of Physics, South Dakota School of Mines and Technology 43-47; Research Fellow, Harvard Univ., Psycho-Acoustic Laboratory 47-51; Assoc. Prof., Communications Biophysics, Massachusetts Inst. of Technology (M.I.T.) 51-57, Prof. 57-; Research Assoc. in Otology, Harvard Medical School and Massachusetts Eye and Ear Infirmary 57-; Chair. M.I.T. Faculty 67-69; Assoc. Provost M.I.T. 69-71, Provost 71-; Fellow, American Acad. of Arts and Sciences, Acoustical Soc. of America, World Acad. of Art and Science, New York Acad. of Sciences, Inst. of Electrical and Electronic Engineers; mem. Nat. Acad. of Eng., Nat. Acad. of Sciences Inst. of Medicine (also Council mem.), Council Int. Union for Pure and Applied Biophysics, Cen. Council, Exec. Cttee. and Hon. Treas. Inst. Brain Research Org. (UNESCO); Inaugural Lecturer, Tata Inst. for Fundamental Research 62; Weizmann Memorial Lectures 62; Consultant, WHO 64-65; President's Cttee. on Urban Housing 67-68; Dir. Kaiser Industries 68-.

Publs. *Noise and Man* (with K. N. Stevens) 53, *Processing Neuroelectric Data* (Editor) 59, *Sensory Communication* (Editor) 61.

Massachusetts Institute of Technology, Room 3-240, Cambridge, Mass. 02139; 164 Mason Terrace, Brookline, Mass. 02146, U.S.A.

Telephone: 617-734-1110 (Home).

Rosenne, Shabtai, LL.B., PH.D.; Israeli lawyer and diplomatist; b. 24 Nov. 1917; ed. London Univ. and Hebrew Univ. of Jerusalem.

Advocate (Israel), Political Dept., Jewish Agency for Palestine 46-48; Legal Adviser, Ministry of Foreign Affairs 48-66; Deputy Perm. Rep. to UN 67-71; Perm. Rep. to UN, Geneva 71-74; Ministry of Foreign Affairs 74-; mem. Israeli Del. to UN Gen. Assemblies 48-74, Vice-Chair. Legal Cttee. Gen. Assembly 60; mem. Israeli Del. to Armistice Negotiations with Egypt, Jordan, Lebanon and Syria 49; mem. Israel Del. to UN Conf. on Law of the Sea 58, 60, 73-75; Chair. Israel Del. to UN Conf. on Law of Treaties 68, 69, mem. other UN confs.; Govt. Rep. before Int. Court of Justice in several cases; mem. Int. Law Comm. 62-71, UN Comm. on Human Rights 68-70; Assoc. Inst. of Int. Law 63-; Rapporteur, Termination and Modification of Treaties 65; Israel Prize 60, Certificate of Merit, American Soc. of Int. Law 68.

Publs. *International Court of Justice* 57, *The Time Factor in Jurisdiction of the International Court of Justice* 60, *The Law and Practice of the International Court* (2 vols.) 65, *The Law of Treaties: Guide to the Vienna Convention* 70; *The World Court: What it is and how it works* 73; and numerous articles, mainly on law.

Ministry of Foreign Affairs, Jerusalem, Israel.

Rosenstein-Rodan, Paul N., DR.RER.POL., B.COMM.; British economist and university professor; b. 19 April 1902; ed. Vienna Univ.

Assistant Vienna Univ. 26-29; Editor *Zeitschrift f. Natoek.*, Vienna 28-32; Library of Economics, Allen and Unwin, London 36-56; Lecturer, Reader, Head of Dept. of Political Economy Univ. Coll., Univ. of London 31-47; Asst. Dir. Economics Dept. and Head Economics Advisory Staff, Int. Bank for Reconstruction and Development, Washington, D.C. 47-53; Prof. of Economics, Mass. Inst. of Technology and Center for Int. Studies, Cambridge (Mass.) 53-70; Prof. Univ. of Texas at Austin 70-; Consultant, UN Comms. for Latin America, Asia and the Far East and for FAO; mem. Panel of Experts, Alliance for Progress; Fellow, American Acad. of Arts and Sciences; Italian Order of Merit.

Publs. *Marginal Utility* 26, *The Role of Time in Economic Theory* 34, *Complementarietà . . .* 34, *Problems of Industrialization of Eastern and Southeastern Europe* 43, *Notes on the Theory of the Big Push* 55, *International Aid for Underdeveloped Countries* 61.

University of Texas, Austin, Texas 78701, U.S.A.

Rosenthal, Abraham Michael; American newspaperman; b. 2 May 1922, Sault St. Marie, Ont., Canada; *m.* Ann Marie Burke 1949; three *s.*

New York Times 44-, UN Bureau 46-54, New Delhi 54-58, Warsaw 58-59, Geneva 59-61, Tokyo 61-63, Metropolitan Editor 63-66, Asst. Man. Editor 66-68, Assoc. Man. Editor 68-69, Man. Editor 69-; Pulitzer Prize 60.

Publs. *38 Witnesses, One More Victim* (co-author).

New York Times, 229 West 43rd Street, New York City 36, N.Y., U.S.A.

Telephone: 556-1234.

Rosenthal, Philip, M.A.; German ceramics and glass executive and politician; b. 23 Oct. 1916, Berlin; *s.* of Dr. Philipp Rosenthal and Maria (née Frank); *m.* Lavinia McLeod Day; two *s.* three *d.*; ed. Wittelsbacher Gymnasium, Munich, St. Laurence Coll., Ramsgate, and Exeter Coll., Oxford.

Chairman, Management Board Rosenthal A.G., Selb 58-70; Chair. Advisory Board Rosenthal Isolatoren G.m.b.H., Selb until 70; SPD mem. of Parliament 69-; Parl. Sec. of State at Ministry of Econs. and Finance Sept. 70-Oct. 71; mem. Advisory Board, Messe und Ausstellungs G.m.b.H., Hanover; fmr. Chair. Asscn. of Ceramics Industry; Deputy Chair. Design Council of Fed. of German Industries; fmr. Chair. of Presidium of Labour Council of Ceramics Industry; fmr. Pres. Féd. Européenne des Industries de Porcelaine et la Faïence de Table et d'Ornamentation, Brussels.

Leisure interests: mountaineering, walking.

8672 Erkersreuth, Schloss Erkersreuth, Federal Republic of Germany.

Telephone: Selb 721.

Roshchin, Aleksey Aleksandrovich; Soviet diplomatist; b. 2 Jan. 1905, Moscow; ed. Leningrad Inst. of National Economy.

Member C.P.S.U. 28-; Diplomatic Service 36-; Asst. Head, later Head, Third Western Dept., U.S.S.R. Foreign Ministry 38-39; Counsellor to Chief Soviet Rep. on European Consultative Comm., London 44-46; Deputy Head, later Head, U.S.S.R. Foreign Ministry UN Dept. 46-52; Senior Counsellor Soviet Mission to UN 52-53; Deputy Head U.S.S.R. Foreign Ministry UN Dept. 53-54, Deputy Head, Int. Orgs. Dept. 54-56; Counsellor-Minister, London 56-59; Counsellor, Office of U.S.S.R. Foreign Minister 59-64; Head of Second European Dept., U.S.S.R. Foreign Ministry 64-66; Soviet Rep. on Eighteen-Nations Disarmament Cttee., Geneva 66-; Orders and medals of U.S.S.R.

Eighteen-Nations Disarmament Committee, Geneva, Switzerland.

Rosholt, Aanon Michael; South African chartered accountant and business executive; b. 1920, Johannesburg; *m.* Beatrice Ash 1948; three *s.*

Commissioned as Lieut., Natal Field Artillery, World War II, prisoner-of-war 42-45; joined firm of C.A.'s Goldby, Panchaud and Webber, and later became Senior Partner; non-exec. mem. of the Board, Thos. Barlow and Sons Ltd. 61-63, Dir. 63, Joint Deputy Chair. 63-68, Man. Dir. 68-72; Vice-Chair. and Chief Exec., Barlow Rand Ltd. Nov. 72-; Dir. of various cos. in the Barlow Rand Group; Dir. The Standard Bank of S.A., S.A. Breweries Ltd. and several other cos.; Chair. Babcok and Wilcox Africa and Ash Brothers; Gov. Michaelhouse School; Chair. Finance Cttee., African Children's Feeding Scheme.
Leisure interests: squash, golf, deep-sea fishing, photography.
Barlow Rand Ltd., P.O. Box 4862, Johannesburg, South Africa.

Rosický, Bohumir, DR.RER.NAT., D.SC.; Czechoslovak professor of parasitology; b. 18 April 1922, Brno; ed. Charles Univ., Prague.
Member of staff, *Rovnost* (Brno daily paper) 45-46; Chemical Research Worker, Lab. Head in chemical industry 47-50; specialist, Cen. Biological Inst., Prague 50-53; Head, Dept. of Parasitology, Biological Inst., Czechoslovak Acad. of Sciences, Prague 54-61; Dir. Inst. of Parasitology, Prague 62-; Prof. Natural Sciences, Comenius Univ., Bratislava 65-; corresp. mem. Czechoslovak Acad. of Sciences 60-70, Academician 70-, Vice-Pres. 70-; Deputy to Czech Nat. Council 69-, mem. Presidium 69-; WHO Consultant, India 64-65; mem. Joint WHO/FAO UN Panel of Zoonoses; Corresp. mem. Bulgarian Acad. of Sciences 74; State Prize 54; Klement Gottwald State Prize (with team) 56, 72, G. Mendel Gold Medal 70, Silver Plaque of Czechoslovak Acad. of Sciences 72, Order of Cyril and Method (Bulgaria) 72, Krzyz Oficerski (Poland) 73.
Publs. *Modern Insecticides* (co-author) 51, *Czechoslovak Fauna-Aphaniptera* 57, *Parasitologische Arbeitsmethoden* (co-author) 65; 130 papers on ecology, taxonomy, entomology, medical zoology and parasitology.
Institute of Parasitology of Czechoslovak Academy of Sciences, Flemingovo nám. 2, 166 32 Prague 6, Czechoslovakia.

Rosini, Giuseppe; Italian shipping executive; b. 1901. Engineer, later Deputy Manager Soc. Grandi Fucine Italiane Gio'Fossati & Co. 27; later Manager Stabilimento Fossati, and Fonderie Ghisa e Metalli , of Ansaldo Co.; Consultant Cantieri Riuniti dell' Adriatico, Cantieri del Quarnaro, Motomeccanica, Stabilimento di S. Eustacchio 45-46; Gen. Man. Soc. Industriale S. Giorgio-Genoa 48; Man. Dir. and Gen. Man. Ansaldo Co. 49-59; Pres. FINMARE 59-; numerous decorations.
c/o FINMARE, Via Barberini n. 22, Rome, Italy.

Ross, Alan Strode Campbell, M.A.; British philologist; b. 1 Feb. 1907, Brecon; s. of Archibald Campbell Carne Ross and Millicent Strode Cobham; m. Elizabeth Stefanyja Olszewska 1932 (deceased 1973); one s.; ed. Malvern Coll., and Balliol Coll., Oxford.
Won Henry Skynner Scholarship in Astronomy to Balliol Coll. Oxford 24; Asst. Lecturer in English Language Leeds Univ. 29-36, Lecturer 36-39; seconded to Foreign Office 40-45; Lecturer in English Language Birmingham Univ. 46, Reader 47, Prof. 48-51, Prof. of Linguistics 51-74; Corresp. mem. Société Finnoougrienne.
Leisure interests: land rovering, croquet.
Publs. *The Dream of the Rood* (with B. Dickins) **34,** *Studies in the Accidence of the Lindisfarne Gospels* **37,** *The 'Numeral-signs' of the Mohenjo-daro Script* **38,** *The 'Terfinnas' and the 'Beormas' of Ohthere* **40,** *Essentials of Anglo-Saxon Grammar* **48,** *Tables for Old English Sound-changes* **51,** *Ginger* **52,** *Noblesse Oblige* (with Nancy Mitford and others) **56,** *Lindisfarne Gospels,* Urs Graf Edition (with several others) **57, 61,** *Etymology* **58,** *Essentials of German Grammar* **63,**

Essentials of English **64,** *The Pitcairnese Language* (with A. W. Moverley) **64,** I. I. Revzin's *Models of Language* (trans. with N. F. C. Owen) **66,** *Arts v. Science* (Editor) **67,** *What are U?* (with several others) **69,** *Durham Ritual* (with others) **70,** *How to Pronounce it* **70,** *Don't Say It* **73.**
37 Phoenix Way, Southwick, Sussex, BN4 4HP, England.
Telephone: Brighton 595027.

Ross, Sir Archibald David Manisty, K.C.M.G., M.A.; British businessman and fmr. diplomatist; b. 12 Oct. 1911, Budleigh Salterton, Devon; s. of John Archibald Ross, I.C.S., and Dorothea Manisty; m. Mary Melville Macfadyen 1939; one s. one d.; ed. Winchester, and New Coll., Oxford.
Diplomatic Service 36-71; Minister, Rome 53-56; Asst. Under-Sec. of State 56-60; Ambassador to Portugal 61-66, to Sweden 66-71; Chair., Alfa-Laval Co. Ltd., Saab-Scania (U.K.), Datasaab.
Leisure interests: tennis, music.
17 Ennismore Gardens, London, S.W.7, England.
Telephone: 01-584-2524.

Ross, Colonel The Hon. Frank Mackenzie, C.M.G., M.C., K.ST.J., LL.D.; Canadian businessman; b. 14 April 1891, Glasgow, Scotland; s. of David and Grace (Archibald) Ross; m. Phyllis Gregory Turner; ed. Royal Acad., Tain, Scotland.
Served with Canadian Army First World War; Chair. Int. Paints (Canada) Ltd., Grosvenor-Laing (B.C.) Ltd., Lafarge Cement of N. America Ltd., Deeks McBride Ltd., Canadian Allied Property Investments Ltd., McCord Street Sites Ltd., Guildford Devt. Corpn. Ltd., Mayfair Shopping Centre Ltd., Third Properties Ltd.; Pres. T. C. Gorman Construction Co. Ltd., Vancouver Iron & Engineering Works Ltd., West Coast Shipbuilders Ltd.; Dir. Inter City Papers Ltd.; Vice-Pres. and Dir. Canadian Imperial Bank of Commerce, Toronto; Dir. R.C.A. Victor Co. Ltd. (Montreal), Canada Trust Co. Ltd., and many other companies; Lieut.-Gov. of British Columbia 55-60; Hon. degrees: Univs. of New Brunswick, British Columbia, Aberdeen and St. Francis Xavier Univ. (Nova Scotia).
Home: 2002 Robson Street, Vancouver 5, B.C.; Office: 1101 West 6th Avenue, Vancouver 9, B.C., Canada.
Telephone: 224-1212 (Home); 731-1112 (Office).

Ross, Rt. Hon. William, P.C., M.B.E., M.P.; British politician; b. 7 April 1911; ed. Ayr Acad., and Glasgow Univ.
Former schoolmaster; Army service, Second World War; M.P. for Kilmarnock 46-; Sec. of State for Scotland 64-70, 74-76; Labour.
House of Commons, Westminster, London, S.W.1, England; and 10 Chapelpark Road, Ayr, Scotland.

Ross Williamson, Hugh, F.R.S.L.; British writer; b. 2 Jan. 1901, Romsey, Hants.; s. of Hugh and Grace (Walker) Williamson; m. Margaret Cox 1941; one s. one d.
Member editorial staff *Yorkshire Post* 25-30; Editor *Bookman* 30-34; Acting Editor *Strand Magazine* 34.
Leisure interest: listening to music.
Publs. *The Poetry of T. S. Eliot* 32, *John Hampden* 33, *King James I, Gods and Mortals in Love* 36, *George Villiers, Duke of Buckingham* 37, *Who Is For Liberty?* 38, *A.D. 33* 41, *Captain Thomas Schofield* 42, *Charles and Cromwell* 46, *The Arrow and the Sword* 47, *Were You There . . ?* 47, *The Silver Bowl* 48, *Four Stuart Portraits* 49, *The Seven Christian Virtues* 49, *The Gunpowder Plot* 51, *Sir Walter Raleigh* 51, *Jeremy Taylor* 52, *The Walled Garden* (autobiography) 53, *The Ancient Capital* 53, *Canterbury Cathedral* 53, *The Children's Book of (British, French, Italian, Spanish) Saints* 53, 54, 56, *The Great Prayer* 55, *Historical Whodunits* 55, *James by the Grace of God* 55, *Enigmas of History* 57, *The Day They Killed*

the King 57, *The Beginnings of the English Reformation* 57, *The Sisters* 58, *A Wicked Pack of Cards* 61, *The Day Shakespeare Died* 62, *The Flowering Hawthorn* 63, *Guy Fawkes* 64, *The Butt of Malmsey* 67, *The Marriage Made in Blood* 68, *A Matter of Martyrdom* 69, *The Cardinal in Exile* 69, *The Cardinal in England* 70, *The Florentine Woman* 70, *The Last of the Valois, Paris is Worth a Mass, The Modern Mass, The Great Betrayal* 71, *Kind Kit* 72, *Catherine de Medici* 73, *Lorenzo the Magnificent* 73, *Letter to Julia* 75, *The Princess a Nun!* 76; plays: *In a Glass Darkly* 31, *After the Event* 33, *Rose and Gloves* 34, *The Seven Deadly Virtues, Monsieur Moi* 35, *Various Heavens, Cinderella's Grandchild* 36, *Mr. Gladstone* 37, *Stories from History* 38, *The Death of Don Juan* 43, *Paul, a Bondslave* 45, *Queen Elizabeth* 46, *The Story Without an End* 47, *Odds Beyond Arithmetic* 47, *The Pilgrim's Progress* (dramatic version) 48, *The Cardinal's Learning* 50, *Gunpowder, Treason and Plot* 51, *Conversation with a Ghost* 52, *Diamond Cut Diamond* 52, *His Eminence of England* 53, *The Elder Brother* 53, *Wild Grows the Heather* (musical version of J. M. Barrie's *Little Minister*) 56, *King Claudius* 57, *Test of Truth* 58, *The Mime of Bernadette* 58, *Heart of Bruce* 59, *Teresa of Avila* 61, *Quartet for Lovers* (with Ian Burford) 62, *Pavane for a Dead Infanta* 68.
c/o Savage Club, 86 St. James's Street, London, S.W.1; and 11a St. Barnabas Road, Cambridge, England. Telephone: 01-262-7138.

Rössel, Mrs. Agda; Swedish diplomatist; b. 4 Nov. 1910; ed. Swedish Inst. Social Politics.
Secretary, Union of Women Employees, Nat. Telephone Co. 39-41; various advisory posts 41-50; mem. Int. Fed. of Business and Professional Women 47-, Vice-Pres. 50-52; mem. Swedish del. to U.N. 52-58, Perm. Rep. 58-64; Amb. to Yugoslavia 64-69, to Czechoslovakia 69; Chair. Swedish Del. Human Rights Conf., Teheran 68.
c/o Ministry of Foreign Affairs, Stockholm, Sweden.

Rossel, Marie-Thérèse; Belgian newspaper director; b. 1910.
Director, *Le Soir*, Rosselet et Cie. S.A., Imprimerie M.Th. Rossel; Officier de l'Ordre de Léopold, Officier de l'Ordre de la Couronne, Chevalier de la Légion d'Honneur, Officier de l'Ordre au Merite d'Italie.
112 rue Royale, Brussels; and 28 avenue des Phalènes, Brussels, Belgium.

Rosseland, Svein; Norwegian astronomer; b. 31 March 1894, Kvam, Hardanger; s. of Isak and Ragna Rosseland; m. Ragna Michelsen 1924; one s.; ed. Oslo Univ.
Prof. of Astronomy, Oslo Univ. 28-64, Dir. and Founder, Univ. Inst. of Theoretical Astrophysics 34; Visiting Prof. Harvard Univ. 29-30; Prof. of Astronomy Princeton Univ. 41-46; Exec. Cttee. mem. Royal Norwegian Council of Scientific and Industrial Research 46-53, Vice-Pres. 47-51; Chair. Research Cttee., Central Inst. of Industrial Research 50-56, Vice-Chair. of Board 56-; mem. Norwegian Acad. of Sciences and Letters, Pres. 48-60, and Vice-Pres. 49-59, Dean Faculty of Science 51-53; founded Oslo Solar Observatory 54; founded *Astrophysica Norvegica* 34; Dir. and Founder Oslo Space Track Facility 60; contrib. to *Handbuch der Astrophysik*; mem. NATO Science Cttee. 58-65; mem. scientific socs. in Norway, Sweden, Denmark, Belgium, England, U.S.A. and India; Commdr. with Star Royal Order of St. Olaf; Hon. D.Sc. (Copenhagen and Stockholm).
Leisure interest: photography.
Publs. *Astrophysik auf atomtheoretischer Grundlage* 31, *Theoretical Astrophysics* 36, *The Pulsation Theory of Variable Stars* 49.
Institute of Theoretical Astrophysics, Box 1029, Blindern, Oslo 3; Home: Ovenbakken 18c, 1345 Österås, Norway.
Telephone: Oslo 244760 (Home).

Rossellini, Renzo; Italian composer and musical critic; b. 2 Feb. 1908; ed. Conservatorio di Musica di S. Cecilia, Rome.
Director, Musical Inst. G. B. Pergolesi, Varese 33-40; then Vice-Dir. and Prof. of Composition Conservatorio G. Rossini, Pesaro; Music Critic *Il Messaggero*, Rome; mem. Nat. Council of UNESCO 58-; mem. Management Cttee., Nat. Orchestra of Monte Carlo 65-, Italian Authors and Writers Soc. 66-; mem. Accad. Nazionale di S. Cecilia, Accad. Cherubini, Florence, Accad. Filarmonica, Bologna.
Compositions: Lyric operas: *La Guerra* 56, *Il Vortice* 58, *La Campane* 59, *Uno Sguardo dal Ponte* 61, *Il Linguaggio dei Fiori* 63, *La Leggenda del Ritorno* 66, *L'Avventuriero* 67.
Publs. *Polemica Musicale* 62, *Pagine di un Musicista* 64.
Palais Héraclès, Monte Carlo, Monaco; and 12 Via Lisbona, Rome, Italy.

Rossellini, Roberto; Italian film and operatic director, b. 8 May 1906.
Sound effects technician for films 34-; Operatic productions include *Jeanne d'Arc au Bûcher* (Honegger) 53, *La Figlia di Jorio* (Pizzetti) 54; films directed include *Prélude à l'Après-midi d'un Faune* 38, *Il Tacchino Prepotente, La Vispa Teresa* 39, *La Nave Bianca* 41, *L'Uomo della Croce* 42, *Desiderio* 43, *Roma Città Aperta* 45, *Paisà* 46, *Germania Anno Zero* 48, *Stromboli* 50, *Dov'è la Libertà?* 52, *Viaggio in Italia* 54, *Giovanna d'Arco al rogo* 55, *Il Generale della Rovere* 59, *Vanina Vanini* 61, *Anima Nera* 62, *La Prise de Pouvoir par Louis XIV* 66, *Socrate* 70, *Year One, La Messie* 75.
Viale B. Buozzi 49, Rome, Italy.

Rossi, H.E. Cardinal Agnelo; Brazilian ecclesiastic; b. 4 May 1913.
Ordained priest 37; Bishop of Barra do Pirai 56; Archbishop of São Paulo 64; created Cardinal 65; now Prefect, Sacred Congregation for the Evangelization of the People.
Collegio Urbano di Propaganda Fide, Via Urbano VIII, 16 Rome, Italy.
Telephone: 560331.

Rossi, Bruno B.; American professor; b. 13 April 1905, Venice, Italy; s. of Rino Rossi and Lina Minerbi Rossi; m. Nora Lombroso 1938; one s. two d.; ed. Univs. of Padua and Bologna.
Assistant Univ. of Florence 28-32; Prof. Univ. of Padua 32-38; Assoc. Prof. Cornell Univ., Ithaca, N.Y. 40-43; Staff mem. Los Alamos Laboratory, Los Alamos, N.M. 43-46; Prof. of Physics Mass. Inst. of Technology 46-66, Inst. Prof. 66, Inst. Prof. Emer. 70-; Hon. Prof. Univ. Mayor de San Andres, La Paz, Bolivia; Hon. Fellow Tata Inst. Fundamental Research, Bombay 71; Dr. h.c. Univ. of Palermo, Univ. of Durham 74; Research Corpn. Scientific Award; Order of Merit of the Repub. of Italy; Italian Physical Soc. Gold Medal 70; Int. Feltrinelli Award, Accademia dei Lincei, Cresson Medal, Franklin Inst., Philadelphia 74.
Publs. *Ionization Chambers and Counters* (Co-Author) 49, *High Energy Particles* 52, *Optics* 57, *Cosmic Rays* 64, *Introduction to the Physics of Space* (Co-Author) 70; about 150 papers.
Massachusetts Institute of Technology, 77 Massachusetts Avenue, Cambridge, Mass., U.S.A.
Telephone: 253-4283.

Rossides, Zenon George; Cypriot diplomatist; b. 8 Feb. 1895; ed. Limassol Coll. and Middle Temple, London.
Called to bar 23; law practice in Cyprus and England 25-54; mem. Nat. Del. of Cyprus to London 29; rep. Nat. Council of Cyprus in London 30-31; arrested by Colonial Admin. during nat. uprising 31, confined to Kythrea village 31-33; mem. Ethnarchy Council of Cyprus 46-48, 50-59; mem. Nat. Del. to London 46;

observer for Cyprus to UN Gen. Ass. 51-52, 54-58; attended Afro-Asian Conf., Bandung 55; Chief Rep. of Greek Cypriots at London Conf. for Establishment of Repub. of Cyprus 59-60; Amb., Perm. Rep. of Cyprus to UN, Chair. of Del. to Gen. Ass. 60-; Amb. to U.S.A. 60-73; attended Founding Conf. of Non-Aligned Countries, Belgrade 61, Second Conf., Cairo 64; Vice-Pres. UN Gen. Ass. 61, 63, 66, 71; Chair. UN Special Cttee. on Territories under Portuguese Admin. 62, Legal Cttee. of Gen. Ass. 71, UN Cttee. on Relations with the Host Country 71-, UN Special Cttee. on Definition of Agression 72; mem. UN Admin. Tribunal 66-, UN Cttee. on Elimination of Racial Discrimination 69-71, Int. Law Comm. 71-, Preparatory Cttee. on Conf. on Human Environment.

Publs. *Self-determination and other aspects of the Question of Cyprus* 30, *The Island of Cyprus and Union with Greece* 51, *The Problem of Cyprus, its Political and Legal Aspects* 58; various articles on political and legal subjects, and poetry.

Permanent Mission of Cyprus to the United Nations, 820 Second Avenue, 12th Floor, New York, N.Y. 10017, U.S.A.

Rossini, Frederick Dominic, M.S., PH.D., D.SC., D.ENG.SC., LITT.D.; American chemist; b. 18 July 1899, Monongahela, Pa.; m. Anne K. Landgraff 1932; one s.; ed. Carnegie Inst. of Technology, and Univ. of Calif. Asst. in Physics, Carnegie Inst. of Technology 23-24, Asst. in Mathematics 24-26; Teaching Fellow in Chemistry, Univ. of Calif. 26-28; Physical Chemist, Nat. Bureau of Standards 28-50, Chief of Section on Thermochemistry and Hydrocarbons 36-50; Silliman Prof., Head Dept. of Chemistry, Dir. Chemical and Petroleum Research Lab., Carnegie Inst. of Technology 50-60; Dir. American Petroleum Inst. Research Projects 35-60; Lecturer in Chemical Thermodynamics, Graduate School Nat. Bureau of Standards 34-50; Dean, Coll. of Science and Assoc. Dean Graduate School, Univ. of Notre Dame 60-67, Vice-Pres. for Research 67-71; Prof. of Chemistry, Rice Univ. 71-; Board of Editors *Journal of American Chemical Society* 46-56; Comm. on Thermochemistry, International Union of Pure and Applied Chemistry 34-61; Pres. Comm. on Chemical Thermodynamics 52-61; Consultant Nat. Science Foundation 52-62; Chair. Div. of Petroleum Chemistry, American Chemical Soc. 54; Marburg Lecturer, American Soc. for Testing Materials 53; Chair. Div. Chemistry and Chemical Tech., Nat. Research Council 55-58; Pres. Albertus Magnus Guild 61-65, Soc. Sigma Xi 63-64, Asscn. Midwest Univ. 67-68, Cttee. on Data for Science and Technology of the Int. Council of Scientific Unions 66-70, World Petroleum Congresses 67-75; Vice-Pres. Argonne Univ. Asscn. 68-70; mem. Nat. Acad. of Science; Dr. h.c. Univ. of Lund, Sweden 74; received Hillebrand Award of Chemical Soc. of Wash. 34 and U.S. Dept. of Commerce Gold Medal for Exceptional Service 50; Pittsburgh Award, American Chemical Soc. 59; Laetare Medal (Univ. of Notre Dame) 65, John Price Wetherill Medal (Franklin Inst.) 65, William H. Nichols Medal (American Chemical Soc.) 66, Priestley Medal (American Chem. Soc.) 71, Redwood Medal (Inst. of Petroleum) 72, and other awards. Publs. 11 books and 238 papers.

Department of Chemistry, Rice University, Houston, Tex. 77001; Home: 3614 Montrose Boulevard, Houston, Tex. 77006, U.S.A.

Rossiter, Roger James, B.SC., B.A., D.PHIL., B.M.B.CH., M.A., D.M., F.R.I.C., F.C.I.C., F.R.S.C.; British biochemist; b. 1913, Glenelg, South Australia; s. of James Leonard and Margaret (née Sparkman) Rossiter; m. Helen Margaret Randell 1940; three s. one d.; ed. Univs. of Western Australia and Oxford.

Demonstrator in Biochemistry and Tutor in Physiology, Oxford Univ. 38-46; Carnegie Research Scholar 41;

served in R.A.M.C. 43-46; now Prof. of Biochemistry, Vice-Pres. Health Sciences Univ. of Western Ontario, and Consultant in Biochemistry, Westminster Victoria and St. Joseph's Hospitals, London, Ont.; mem. Biochemical Soc., American Soc. of Biochemical Chemists, Canadian Physiological Soc., Soc. for Experimental Biology and Medicine, Canadian Biochemical Soc., Canadian Soc. for Clinical Chemistry; Fellow Royal Soc. of Medicine, Royal Soc. of Canada and Chemical Inst. of Canada; Hon. LL.D. (York Univ., Toronto).

Vice-President Health Sciences, University of Western Ontario, London, Ont. N6A 5C1, Canada.

Telephone: 519-679-2664.

Rosta, Endre, D.IUR.; Hungarian jurist; b. 18 July 1909, Berettyószéplak; m. Simone Pasche 1946; three d.; ed. Budapest and Graz.

Official, Central Cttee. Hungarian C.P. 45-48, later Hungarian Working People's Party; Head of Press Dept. of Prime Minister's Office; Judge, later Vice-Pres. High Court for Econ. Affairs; Exec. Chair. Inst. for Cultural Relations 61-69, Chair. 70-; Labour Order of Merit golden degree.

Leisure interests: logic, mathematics.

Office: Kulturális Kapcsolatok Intézete (Institute for Cultural Relations), H-1051 Budapest V, Dorottya-utca 8, Hungary.

Telephone: 183-890.

Rostand, Jean; French writer and biologist; b. 30 Oct. 1894.

Member Acad. Française 59-; Kalinga Prize (UNESCO) 59.

Author of *La loi des riches, Les Familiotes, Deux Angoisses, Le Mariage, Valère ou l'Exaspéré, Julien ou une Conscience, De la Vanité, Hommes de vérité, Journal d'un caractère, Ignace ou l'Écrivain, Les Chromosomes, L'Aventure humaine, La Vie des Crapauds, La Vie des Libellules, La Vie des Vers à soie, La Vie et ses problèmes, La Parthénogenèse des Vertébrés, La Nouvelle Biologie, L'Homme, Pensées d'un biologiste, Les Idées nouvelles de la génétique, La Formation de l'être, L'Evolution des espèces, La genèse de la Vie, L'Avenir de la Biologie, Science et Génération, Esquisse d'une histoire de la biologie, Ce que je crois,* etc.

29 rue Pradier, 92 Ville d'Avray (Seine-et-Oise), France. Telephone: 926-4331.

Rostoft, Sverre Walter; Norwegian business executive and politician; b. 12 Dec. 1912, Glemmen; ed. Univ. of Oslo.

Managing Dir. Kristiansands Mekaniske Verksted (shipyard), Kristiansand 45-65; mem. Oddernes Municipal Council 52-55; mem. Storting 54-57, 65-; fmr. Dir. several industrial concerns in Norway and Sweden; Minister of Industries 65-71; Past Pres. Norwegian Asscn. of Industries; mem. Nat. Asscn. of Shipbuilders, Nat. Asscn. of Mechanical Engineering Firms; Conservative.

Storting, Oslo, Norway.

Rostow, Eugene Victor, LL.D. (brother of Walt Whitman Rostow, *q.v.*); American lawyer, economist and government official; b. 25 Aug. 1913, Brooklyn, N.Y.; s. of Victor A. and Lillian Rostow; m. Edna B. Greenberg 1933; two s. one d.; ed. Yale Coll., King's Coll., Cambridge, and Yale Law School.

Admitted to N.Y. Bar 38, practised in New York City 37-38; mem. Faculty, Law School, Yale 38-, Prof. of Law 44-, Sterling Prof. of law and public relations 64-, Dean 55-65 (on leave 66-69); Visiting Prof., Univ. of Chicago 41; Pitt Prof. of American History and Insts., Professorial Fellow, King's Coll., Cambridge 59-60; Guggenheim Fellow 59-60; Adviser to Dept. of State 42-44. 61-66; Asst. Exec. Sec. Econ. Comm. for Europe, UN 49-50; Under-Sec. of State for Political

Affairs, Dept. of State 66-69; Eastman Visiting Prof. and Fellow of Balliol Coll., Oxford 70-71; Pres. Atlantic Treaty Asscn. 73-; Fellow, American Acad. of Arts and Sciences; Hon. LL.D. (Cambridge); Kt. Commdr. Order of the Crown, Belgium.
Publs. *Planning for Freedom* 59, *The Sovereign Prerogative* 62, *Law, Power and the Pursuit of Peace* 68, *Peace in the Balance* 72, Editor *Is Law Dead?* 71.
208 St. Ronan Street, New Haven, Conn. 06511; and (summer) Peru, Vermont 05152, U.S.A.

Rostow, Walt Whitman, PH.D.; American economist; b. 7 Oct. 1916, New York, N.Y.; *s.* of Victor A and Lillian H. Rostow; brother of Eugene Rostow (*q.v.*); *m.* Elspeth Vaughan Davies 1947; one *s.* one *d.*; ed. Yale and Oxford Univs.
Instructor in Economics Columbia Univ. 40-41; served as Major, 42-45; Asst. Chief German-Austrian Econ. Div. State Dept. 45-46; Harmsworth Prof. of American History, Oxford Univ. 46-47; Asst. to Exec. Sec. UN Econ. Comm. for Europe 47-49; Pitt Prof. of American History Cambridge Univ. 49-50; Prof. of Econ. History M.I.T. and Staff mem. M.I.T. Center for Int. Studies 51-60; Dep. Special Asst. to the President for Nat. Security Affairs Jan.-Nov. 61; Counsellor and Chair. Policy Planning Council, Dept. of State Dec. 61-66; Special Asst., The White House 66-69; currently Prof. of Econs. and History, Univ. of Texas; Legion of Merit, Hon. O.B.E. (U.K.), Presidential Medal of Freedom (with distinction) 69.
Publs. *The American Diplomatic Revolution* 47, *Essays on the British Economy of the XIX Century* 48, *The Process of Economic Growth* 52, *The Growth and Fluctuation of the British Economy 1790-1850* (with A. D. Gayer and A. J. Schwartz) 53, *The Dynamics of Soviet Society* (with A. Levin and others) 53, *The Prospects for Communist China* (with others) 54, *An American Policy in Asia* (with R. W. Hatch) 55, *A Proposal: Key to an Effective Foreign Policy* (with Max F. Millikan) 57, *The United States in the World Arena* 60, *The Stages of Economic Growth* 60 (2nd edn.) 71; *View from the Seventh Floor* 64, *A Design for Asian Development* 65, *East-West Relations: Is Detente Possible?* (with William E. Griffith) 69, *Politics and the Stages of Growth* 71, *The Diffusion of Power* 72, *How It All Began* 75.
1 Wildwind Point, Austin, Tex., U.S.A.

Rostropovich, Mstislav Leopoldovich; Soviet 'cellist; b. 27 March 1927, Baku, Azerbaizhan S.S.R.; *m.* Galina Vishnevskaya; ed. Moscow Conservatoire.
First Concert 42; First Prize, All-Union Concourse of Musicians 45; First Prize, International Cellists Competition, Prague; numerous concert tours in U.S.S.R. and abroad, particularly as 'cellist in trio with Emil Gilels and Leonid Kogan; Prof. Moscow and Leningrad Conservatoires 60-; debut in U.S.A. 75; State Prize 51; People's Artist of R.S.F.S.R. 64; People's Artist of the U.S.S.R.; Lenin Prize 64; Gold Medal, Royal Philharmonic Soc. 70; Hon. D.Mus., (Cambridge) 75.
c/o Victor Hochhauser, 4 Holland Park Avenue, London, W.11, England.

Rota, Francesco; Italian business executive; b. 28 May 1909, Turin; ed. Istituto Tecnico, Turin and Univ. of Turin.
Joined Istituto Bancario S. Paolo di Torino 28, Sec.-Gen. 45, Dir.-Gen. 57-68, Hon. Dir.-Gen. 68-; Deputy Dir.-Gen. Fiat S.p.A. 68-69, Co-Dir.-Gen. 69-; Dir. Mediocredito Centrale; mem. Board, Banque Française et Italienne pour l'Amérique du Sud, IFI, Locat FISPAO, and Italo-Soviet Chamber of Commerce; Dir. Citroën S.A. 71-; Cavaliere del Lavoro.
Fiat S.p.A., Corso Marconi 10, Turin; Home: Corso Rosselli 9, Turin, Italy.

Rota, Giorgio, B.POL.SC.; Italian civil servant and international banking official; b. 29 Nov. 1913, Gorizia;

s. of Oscar and Irma Collioud; *m.* Elena Cambi 1947; two *s.*; ed. Ca' Foscari, Venice Univ.
Civil Servant 40; Welfare Officer, then Dir. Refugee Camps in Southern Italy, UN Relief and Rehabilitation Admin. (UNRRA) 45-46; in charge of Import-Export Problems, Ministry of Foreign Trade 47-50; Gen. Treasury Admin., Overseas Dept. of Ministry of the Treasury 50-68, Alt. to Minister of the Treasury in the Group of Ten 63-68; Exec. Dir. for Italy, Portugal and Spain of Int. Bank for Reconstruction and Devt. (IBRD)—World Bank, Int. Finance Corpn. (IFC) and Int. Devt. Asscn. (IDA) Nov. 68-; Italian Rep. at confs. of Int. Monetary Fund (IMF), IBRD, IFC, etc. since 50.
Leisure interest: photography.
International Bank for Reconstruction and Development, 1818 H Street, N.W., Washington, D.C. 20433, U.S.A.
Telephone: 477-2391.

Rotberg, Eugene Harvey, LL.B.; American World Bank official; b. 19 Jan. 1930, Philadelphia, Pa.; *s.* of Irving Bernard Rotberg and Blanche Grace Rotberg; *m.* Dr. Iris Sybil Comens 1954; two *d.*; ed. Temple Univ. and Univ. of Pennsylvania.
Member Pennsylvania and D.C. Bar; with U.S. Securities and Exchange Comm. 57-68, Chief Counsel, Office of Policy Research, Sec. 63-66; Assoc. Dir. Markets and Regulation, Sec. 66-68; Treas. IBRD and affiliates (Int. Devt. Asscn. and Int. Finance Corpn.) Jan. 69-; professorial Lecturer in Law, George Washington Univ. Law School 65-; Distinguished Service Award, U.S. Govt. (Securities and Exchange Comm.) 68; Alumni Award, Temple Univ. 69; Distinguished Scholar Award, Hofstra Univ.
Leisure interests: theatre, travel.
International Bank for Reconstruction and Development, 1818 H Street, N.W., Washington, D.C. 20433; Home: 10822 Childs Court, Silver Spring, Md. 20901, U.S.A.
Telephone: 477-2213 (Office); 593-4134 (Home).

Rotblat, Joseph, C.B.E., M.A., D.SC., PH.D.; British (b. Polish) physicist; b. 4 Nov. 1908, Warsaw; ed. Univ. of Warsaw.
Research Fellow, Radiological Laboratory of Scientific Soc. of Warsaw 33-39; Asst. Dir. of Atomic Physics, Inst. of Free Univ. of Poland 37-39; Oliver Lodge Fellow, Univ. of Liverpool 39-40; Lecturer, later Senior Lecturer, Dept. of Physics, Univ. of Liverpool 40-49; Dir. of Research in Nuclear Physics, Univ. of Liverpool 45-49; Prof. of Physics in Univ. of London, at St. Bartholomew's Hospital Medical Coll. 50-; mem. Polish Acad. of Sciences, American Acad. of Arts and Sciences; Sec.-Gen. the Pugwash Confs.; Editor *Physics in Medicine and Biology*; Pres. Hosp. Physicists' Asscn. British Inst. of Radiology; Pres. Int. Youth Science Fortnight.
Leisure interests: travel, music.
Publs. *Atomic Energy, a Survey* 54, *Atoms and the Universe* 56, 73, *Science and World Affairs* 62, *Aspects of Medical Physics* 66, *Pugwash* 67, *Scientists in the Quest for Peace* 72.
8 Asmara Road, London, N.W.2, England.
Telephone: 01-435-1471.

Roth, Klaus Friedrich, B.A., M.SC., PH.D., F.R.S.; British mathematician; b. 29 Oct. 1925, Breslau, Germany; *s.* of Dr. Franz Roth and Mathilde Roth (née Liebrecht); *m.* Dr. Melek Khairy 1955; ed. St. Paul's School, London, Peterhouse, Cambridge, and Univ. Coll., London.
Assistant Master Gordonstoun School 45-46; Postgraduate student Univ. Coll., London 46-48; mem. Mathematics Dept. Univ. Coll., London 48-66 (title of Prof. in Univ. of London conferred 61); Prof. of Pure Mathematics (Theory of Numbers), Imperial Coll., London 66-; Visiting Lecturer Mass. Inst. of Technology 56-57, Visiting Prof. 65-66; Fellow of Royal Soc. 60-;

Foreign Hon. mem. American Acad. of Arts and Sciences 66-; Fields Medal Int. Congress of Mathematicians 58.
Leisure interests: chess, cinema.
Publs. Papers in journals of learned societies.
Department of Mathematics, Imperial College of Science and Technology, Exhibition Road, London, S.W.7; Home: 24 Burnsall Street, London, S.W.3, England.
Telephone: 01-589-5111 (Dept. of Mathematics); 01-352-1363 (Home).

Roth, Sir Martin, Kt., M.D., F.R.C.P., F.R.C. PSYCH.; British professor of psychiatry; b. 6 Nov. 1917, Budapest, Hungary; s. of Samuel Simon Roth and late Regina Roth; m. Constance Heller 1945; three d.; ed. St. Mary's Hospital Medical School, London and McGill Univs.
Director of Clinical Research, Graylingwell Hosp. 50-55; Visiting Asst. Prof. McGill Univ. 54; Prof. of Psychological Medicine, Univ. of Newcastle-upon-Tyne (fmrly. Durham Univ.) 56-; Hon. Physician Royal Victoria Infirmary, Newcastle-upon-Tyne 56-; mem. Medical Research Council 64-68; mem. Clinical Research Board 64-70, Chair. Cttee. 68-70; Co-Editor *British Journal of Psychiatry* 68-; mem. Cen. Health Services Council, Standing Medical Advisory Cttee., Dept. of Health and Social Security 68-75; Visiting Prof. Swedish univs. 67; Mayne Guest Prof. Univ. of Queensland 68; Pres. Section of Psychiatry, Royal Soc. of Medicine 68-69; First Pres. Royal Coll. of Psychiatrists 71-75; Hon. mem. Soc. Royale de Médicine Mentale de Belgique 70, Canadian Psychiatric Asscn. 72; Corresp. mem. Deutsche Gesellschaft für Psychiatrie und Nervenheilkunde 70; Adolf Meyer Lecturer, American Psychiatric Asscn. 71; Distinguished Fellow American Psychiatric Asscn. 72; Hon. Fellow Australian and New Zealand Coll. of Psychiatrists 74, Royal Coll. of Psychiatrists 75.
Leisure interests: English, French and Russian literature of the 19th and 20th Centuries, contemporary and classical music, visual arts, travel, swimming.
Publ. *Clinical Psychiatry* (with W. Mayer-Gross and Eliot Slater) 54, 3rd edn. 69, Italian, Spanish, Portuguese and Chinese transls.
Elmfield Lodge, 35 Elmfield Road, Gosforth, Newcastle-upon-Tyne, NE3 4BA, England.
Telephone: (0632) 854019.

Roth, Philip, M.A.; American writer; b. 19 March 1933, Newark, N.J.; s. of Bess Finkel Roth and Herman Roth; ed. Bucknell Univ. and Univ. of Chicago.
In U.S. Army 55-56; Lecturer in English, Univ. of Chicago 56-58; Visiting Lecturer, Univ. of Iowa Writers' Workshop 60-62; Writer-in-Residence, Princeton Univ. 62-64, Univ. of Pennsylvania 65, 66, 70, 71-; Visiting Lecturer, State Univ. of N.Y., Stony Brook 67, 68; Houghton Mifflin Literary Fellow 59; Guggenheim Fellowship Grant in Rome 59-60, Rockefeller Grant 65, Ford Foundation Grant 66; mem. Nat. Inst. of Arts and Letters 70-; Daroff Award of Jewish Book Council of America 59, Award of Nat. Inst. of Arts and Letters 59, Nat. Book Award for Fiction 60.
Publs. *Goodbye Columbus* (novella and stories) 59; novels: *Letting Go* 62, *When She Was Good* 67, *Portnoy's Complaint* 69, *Our Gang* 71, *The Breast* 72, *The Great American Novel* 73, *My Life as a Man* 74, *Reading Myself and Others* (essays) 75.
c/o Farrar, Straus and Giroux, 19 Union Square, New York, N.Y., U.S.A.

Roth, William V., Jr.: American politician; b. 22 July 1921; ed. Univ. of Oregon and Harvard Univ.
Admitted to Del. Bar and U.S. Supreme Court; fmr.

Congressman from Delaware; mem. Republican Nat. Cttee. 61-64; Senator from Delaware 71-.
New Senate Office Building, Washington, D.C. 20525, U.S.A.

Rotha, Paul; British film producer, writer and journalist; b. 3 June 1907, London; ed. Highgate School and Slade School of Art, London.
Painter and designer; art critic, *The Connoisseur* 27-28; produced documentary films for Empire Marketing Board, *The Times*, Shell-Mex, etc.; formed own cos. 41 and 44; awarded gold medals Venice Film Festival 34; Brussels Film Festival 35; British Film Acad. award 48, UN award 53, Top Award, Leipzig 63; mem. Council British Film Acad. 47-51, Fellow 51, Chair. of Council 51; Head of Television Documentary BBC 53-55; Simon Senior Research Fellow, Univ. of Manchester 67-68; Fellow Royal Soc. of Arts; Hon. mem. Critics' Circle, London 69.
Leisure interests: walking, gardening.
Productions include: *The World is Rich, World of Plenty, Land of Promise, Total War in Britain, A City Speaks, Contact, To-day We Live, Cover to Cover, The Future's in the Air, The Face of Britain, New Worlds for Old, The Fourth Estate, World Without End* (with Basil Wright); *No Resting Place* 50, *Cat and Mouse* (features) 57, *Cradle of Genius* 59, *The Life of Adolf Hitler* 60, 61, *De Overval* (*Silent Raid*) (Dutch Feature) 62.
Publs. *The Film Till Now* 30, 49, 60, 63, 64, 67, *Celluloid: The Film Today* 31, *Documentary Film* 35, 39, 52, 64, *Movie Parade* 36, 50, *Portrait of a Flying Yorkshireman* 52, *Television in the Making* 56, *Rotha on the Film* 58, *The Innocent Eye*, biography of Robert J. Flaherty (with Basil Wright and A. Calder-Marshall) 63, *Documentary Diary, A History of the British Documentary Film* 73.
c/o John Farquarson Ltd., 13 Red Lion Square, London, W.C.1, England.

Rothé, Jean-Pierre-Edmond, D. ES SC.; French university professor; b. 16 Nov. 1906, Nancy; s. of Edmond Rothé; m. Marguerite Méjan 1942; two s. two d.
Assistant, Faculty of Sciences, Strasbourg Univ. 28; Asst. Prof. 37, Prof. 45-; Dir. Inst. de Physique du Globe de Strasbourg 46-; Hon. Sec.-Gen. Int. Asscn. of Seismology of Int. Union of Geodesy and Geophysics; Dir. Int. Bureau of Seismology; Chevalier, Légion d'Honneur.
Leisure interests: tennis, skiing.
Publs. *Contribution à l'étude des anomalies de champ magnétique terrestre* 37, *Séismes et Volcans* 46, 58, 62, 68, 72, *Prospection géophysique*, Vol. I 49, Vol. II 51, *La radioactivité des Vosges hercyniennes* 57, *The Seismicity of the Earth (1953-1965)* 69, *Earthquakes and reservoir loadings* 69, *Séismes artificiels* 70, *Séismicité de la France* 72.
77 rue du Général Conrad, 67000 Strasbourg, France.
Telephone: 616296.

Rothenberger, Anneliese; German opera singer (soprano); b. 19 June 1926; ed. Real and Musikhochschule, Mannheim.
Debut, Coblenz Theatre 47; Hamburg Opera House 48; Vienna State Opera 57-; has sung at La Scala, Milan, Metropolitan Opera, New York, Salzburg Festival, etc. Films *Die Fledermaus* 55, *Der Rosenkavalier*.
Vienna State Opera, Vienna, Austria.

Rothenstein, Sir John Knewstub Maurice, Kt., C.B.E., M.A., PH.D., LL.D., F.M.A.; British writer and art director; b. 11 July 1901, London; s. of Sir William Rothenstein and Alice M. Knewstub; m. Elizabeth Kennard Smith 1929; one d.; ed. Bedales School, Worcester Coll., Oxford, and Univ. Coll., London.
Assistant Prof. of Art History Univ. of Kentucky 27-28, Univ. of Pittsburgh 28-29; Dir. of City Art Galleries Leeds 32-34, Sheffield 33-38; Dir. and Keeper Tate

Gallery 38-64; mem. British Council 38-64; mem. Exec. Cttee. Contemporary Art Soc. 38-64; mem. Art Panel, Arts Council Great Britain 42-52, 54-56; mem. Advisory Cttee. on decoration of Westminster Cathedral 53-; mem. Council Friends of the Tate Gallery 58-; Hon. Fellow, Worcester Coll., Oxford 63-; Rector Univ. of St. Andrews 64-67; Pres. Friends of Bradford Art Galleries and Museums 72-; Editor *The Masters* 65-67; **Visiting Prof. of Art History, Fordham Univ., N.Y.** 67-68, Agnes Scott Coll., Georgia 69-70; Distinguished Prof., Brooklyn Coll. of the City Univ., New York 71 and 72; Regents' Lecturer, Univ. of Calif. at Irvine 73; Kt. Commdr., Order of Aztec Eagle (Mexico) 53.

Publs. *The Portrait Drawings of William Rothenstein, 1889-1925* 26, *Eric Gill* 27, *The Artists of the 1890's* 28, *Morning Sorrow* (novel) 30, *Sixteen Letters from Oscar Wilde* (editor) 30, *British Artists and the War* 31, *Nineteenth Century Painting* 32, *An Introduction to English Painting* 33, *The Life and Death of Conder* 38, *Augustus John* 44, *Edward Burra* 45, *Manet* 45, *Foreign Pictures in the Tate Gallery* 49, *Turner* 49, 60, *London's River, an Anthology* (with Father Vincent Turner, S.J.) 51, *Modern English Painters*, Vol. I, *Sickert to Smith* 52, Vol. II, *Lewis to Moore* 56, Vol. III, *Wood to Hockney* 74, *The Moderns and their World* (introduction) 57, *The Tate Gallery* 58, 62, *British Art since 1900: an Anthology* 62, *Matthew Smith* 62, *Paul Nash* 62, *Augustus John* 63, *Sickert* 63, *Turner* (with Martin Butlin) 64, *Francis Bacon* (with Ronald Alley) 64, *Summer's Lease* (autobiography I) 65, *Brave Day, Hideous Night* (II) 66, *BBC TV: Collection and Recollection* 68, *Churchill the Painter* (COI) 68, *Time's Thievish Progress* (III) 70, *Walter Greaves* 76.

Beauforest House, Newington, Dorchester-on-Thames, Oxfordshire, OX9 8AG; and 8 Tryon Street, London, SW3 3LH, England.

Rothermere, 2nd Viscount, cr. 19, of Hemsted; **Esmond Cecil Harmsworth;** British newspaper proprietor; b. 29 May 1898; ed. Eton.

Conservative M.P. for the Isle of Thanet 19-29; Chair. Associated Newspapers Ltd. 32-71, Pres. and Dir. of Group Finance 71-; Chair. Daily Mail General Trust Ltd.; Chair. Newspaper Proprietors Asscn. Ltd. 34-61; for a short time Dir. of Press Relations, Ministry of Information 39, resigned; mem. Ministry Advisory Council; succeeded to title 40; Dir. Reuters 45-; Chancellor Newfoundland Memorial Univ. 52-61.

Warwick House, St. James's, London, S.W.1, England.

Rothfels, Hans, PH.D.; German historian; b. 12 April 1891, Kassel; *m.* 1st Hildegard Consbruch 1918 (died 1961); 2nd Ada Freiin v.d. Bussche 1963; two *s.* one *d.*; ed. Freiburg, Munich, Berlin and Heidelberg Univs.

Lecturer Berlin Univ. 24-26; Prof. of Modern History Koenigsberg Univ. 26-34; Research Fellow St. John's Coll., Oxford 39-40; Visiting Prof. Brown Univ., Providence (U.S.A.) 40-46; **Prof. of Modern** European History, Univ. of Chicago 46-56, of Modern History, Tübingen Univ. 51-59, Prof. Emer. 59-; Chair. German Historical Asscn. 58-62; Editor *Vierteljahrshefte für Zeitgeschichte* 53-, *Akten zur deutschen Aussenpolitik* 61-; mem. Heidelberg Akad., Corresp. mem. Göttingen Akad.; Dr. Iur. h.c.; Grosses Bundesverdienstkreuz (with Star); mem. Order "Pour le Mérite" in Sciences and Arts.

Leisure interests: general reading, gardening.

Publs. *C. von Clausewitz: Politik und Krieg* 20, *Bismarcks englische Bündnispolitik* 24, *Bismarck und der Staat* 25, *Th. Lohmann und die Kampfjahre der staatlichen Sozialpolitik* 26, *Prinzipienfragen der Bismarckschen Sozialpolitik* 29, *Ideengeschichte und Parteigeschichte* 30, *Bismarck und der Osten* 34, *Th. von Schön, Friedrich Wilhelm IV und die Revolution von 1848* 36, *The German Opposition to Hitler* 48, (German edn. 49, new edn. 58, 69, new English edn. 62, 70), *Gesellschaftsform u.*

Ausw. Politik 53, *Bismarck-Briefe* 55, *Zeitgeschichtliche Betrachtungen* 59, *Bismarck, der Osten und das Reich* 60, *Krieg und Menschlichkeit* 60, *Bismarck, Vorträge und Abhändlungen* 70, *Tagebuch der Reise d. preussischen Kronprinzen nach d. Morgenland 1869* (ed.) 71, *1848— Betrachtungen im Abstand von 100 Jahren* 72.

18 Waldhäuserstr., 74 Tübingen, Germany. Telephone: 07122 and 63016.

Rothschild, 3rd Baron, cr. 85; **Nathaniel Mayer Victor Rothschild,** G.B.E., G.M., F.R.S., PH.D., SC.D.; British; b. 31 Oct. 1910, London; *s.* of Nathaniel C. Rothschild and Rozsika v. Wertheimstein; *m.* 1st Barbara J. Hutchinson 1933, 2nd Teresa G. Mayor 1946; two *s.* four *d.*; ed. Harrow and Trinity Coll., Cambridge.

Fellow of Trinity Coll., Cambridge 35-39; Mil. Intelligence 39-45; Dir. B.O.A.C. 46-48; Chair. Agric. Research Council 48-58; mem. B.B.C. Gen. Advisory Council 52-56; Asst. Dir. of Research, Dept. of Zoology, Cambridge Univ. 50-70; Research Co-ordinator of Royal Dutch Shell Group of Companies 65-70; Vice-Chair. Shell Research Ltd. 61-63, Chair. 63-70; mem. Council for Scientific Policy 65-67, Central Advisory Council for Science and Technology; Dir.-Gen. Central Policy Review Staff, Cabinet Office 71-74; mem. Board, Chair. N. M. Rothschild & Sons 75-; Hon. Fellow, Trinity Coll., Cambridge, Weizmann Inst. of Science, Israel, Bellairs Research Inst. of McGill Univ., Barbados, Univ. Coll., Cambridge, Inst. of Biology, Imperial Coll. of Science and Tech.; Hon. D.Sc. (Newcastle, Manchester, Technion, Haifa, City Univ., London), Hon. Ph.D. (Tel-Aviv Univ., Hebrew Univ.); American Legion of Merit, American Bronze Star.

Leisure interests: golf, jazz.

Publs. *A Classification of Living Animals, Fertilization,* and a number of scientific papers.

11 Herschel Road, Cambridge, England. Telephone: 50488.

Rothschild, Baron Alain James Gustave Jules de; French banker; b. 7 Jan. 1910; ed. Univ. de Paris.

Partner in Banque de Rothschild Frères 46-67; Vice-Pres. Banque Rothschild 68-; Pres. Soc. d'investissement du Nord 63-67, Cie. du Nord 68-, Consistoire Central Israélite de France 67; fmr. Mayor of Chamant; Officier, Légion d'Honneur, Croix de Guerre.

21 rue Laffitte, Paris 9e, France.

Rothschild, Edmund Leopold de; British merchant banker; b. 2 Jan. 1916, London; *s.* of Lionel N. de Rothschild and Marie Louise Beer; *m.* Elizabeth E. Lentner 1948; two *s.* two *d.*; ed. Harrow and Trinity Coll., Cambridge.

Royal Artillery 39-46; Chair. N. M. Rothschild & Sons Ltd., Pres. 75-; Chair. Tokyo Pacific Holdings (Seaboard) N.V., Tokyo Pacific Holdings N.V., Straflo Ltd.; Dir. Alliance Assurance Co. Ltd., Sun Alliance and London Insurance Ltd., Sun Insurance Office Ltd., Brinco Ltd., Carreras Rothmans Ltd., Rothmans Int. Ltd., Alfred Dunhill Ltd., Five Arrows Securities Co. Ltd., Sun Alliance and London Assurance Co. Ltd., Exbury Gardens Ltd.; Pres. Asscn. of Jewish Ex-Servicemen and Women; Vice-Chair. Cen. British Fund for Jewish Relief and Rehabilitation; mem. Council Royal Nat. Pension Fund for Nurses; Trustee, Queen's Nursing Inst., British Freedom from Hunger Campaign; Joint Hon. Treas. Council of Christians and Jews, Friends of Hebrew Univ.

Leisure interests: gardening, shooting, fishing, photography.

Publ. *Window on the World.*

N. M. Rothschild & Sons Ltd., New Court, St. Swithins Lane, London, EC4P 4DU, England.

Rothschild, Baron Elie Robert de; French banker; b. 29 May 1917, Paris; *s.* of Baron Robert de Rothschild and Nelly Beer; *m.* Liliane Fould-Springer 1942; one *s.*

two d.; ed. Lycée Louis le Grand, Faculty of Law, Univ. de Paris.

President and Dir.-Gen. de P.L.M., La Fédération Continentale; Vice-Pres., Dir.-Gen. Banque Rothschild; Dir. New Court Securities Corpn., Five Arrows Security Co. Ltd., Canada, Assicurazioni Generali Trieste, Cie. du Nord; Vice-Pres. Cie. d'assurances "La Concorde"; Pres. Rothschild Bank, Zürich; Dir. Tokyo Capital Holdings; Officier Légion d'Honneur, Croix de Guerre, Ufficiale Ordine Al Merito della Repubblica Italiana.

Leisure interests: shooting, yachting.

21 rue Laffitte, Paris 9e; Home: 11 rue Masseran, Paris 7e, France.

Telephone: 523-47-47 (Office); FON 90-90 (Home).

Rothschild, Baron Guy Edouard Alphonse Paul de; French banker; b. 21 May 1909, Paris; m. 1st Alix Schey de Koromla, 2nd Baronne Marie-Hélène van Zuylen van Nyevelt; two s.; ed. Lycées Condorcet and Louis le Grand, Univ. de Paris.

Chairman Banque Rothschild, Société Minière et Métallurgique de Peñarroya, Second Continuation Ltd.; Dir. and Chair. Exec. Cttee. Compagnie du Nord; Dir. Sté. Le Nickel, The Rio-Tinto-Zinc Co. Ltd. (London), S.A. de Gérance et d'Armement (Saga), Cie. franco-africaine de recherches pétrolières (Francarep), S.A. Femmes d'Aujourd'hui (Brussels), Rothschild Intercontinental Bank Ltd., New Court Securities Corpn., European Property Co. Ltd. (London), Franco-Britannique de Participations; Chair. Board Five Arrows Security Co. Ltd., Canada; Non-Exec. Dir. N. M. Rothschild & Sons Ltd.; Officier Légion d'Honneur, Croix de Guerre.

Leisure interests: breeding and racing horses.

10 rue de Courcelles, Paris 8e, France.

Rothschild, Robert, DR.RER.POL.; Belgian diplomatist; b. 1911, Brussels; s. of Bernard Rothschild and Marianne von Rynveld; one d.; ed. Univ. of Brussels and Acad. of Int. Law, The Hague.

Entered Foreign Office 37; served Lisbon 41, Chungking 44, Shanghai 46, Washington, D.C. 50; Deputy Permanent Rep. to NATO 52; Chef de Cabinet, Foreign Office 54-58; Amb. to Yugoslavia 58-60; Deputy Chief of Diplomatic Mission to the Republic of Congo 60; Chef de Cabinet, Foreign Office 61-64; Ambassador to Switzerland 64-66, to France 66-73, to U.K. and Perm. Rep. to W.E.U. Council 73-; awards include Commdr. Order of Leopold (Belgium), Commdr. Légion d'Honneur (France), Hon. K.C.M.G. (U.K.).

Belgian Embassy, 103 Eaton Square, London, SW1W 9AB; Residence: 36 Belgrave Square, London, SW1X 8QB, England; 51 Avenue Général de Gaulle, Brussels, Belgium.

Telephone: 01-235-5422 (Office); 01-235-1752 (Residence).

Rotov, Boris Georgievich (Most Rev. Nikodim); Soviet ecclesiastic; b. 16 Oct. 1929, Frolovo, Korablinsk District, Ryazan Region; ed. Ryazan Pedagogic Inst., Leningrad Theological Seminary and Theological Acad.

Ordained monk and deacon 47, hierodeacon 47; worked in Yaroslavl and Uglich 49-52; priest, Yaroslavl Cathedral and Sec. to Archbishop 52-54, Dean 54-56; Russian Orthodox Mission in Jerusalem 56-59; Chief, Moscow Patriarchate Chancellery, Deputy Chair. Dept. for Foreign Ecclesiastical Relations 59-60, Chair. 60-; Bishop of Podolsk, Vicar of Moscow Eparchy 60-, Archbishop 61-; mem. Comm. for Inter-Christian Relations 60-; Head Moscow Patriarchate Publishing House 60-; perm. mem. Holy Synod 61-; Metropolitan of Minsk and Byelorussia 63-, of Leningrad and Ladoga 63-; mem. Central Cttee. and Exec. Cttee. of World Council of Churches; Vice-Pres. Christian Peace Conf.; Orders of Eastern Patriarchs.

Publs. *History of the Russian Orthodox Mission in Jerusalem, Christian Liturgy and Churches at the time of St. John Chrysostom.*

Moscow Patriarchate, 18 Ryleev Street, Moscow, U.S.S.R.

Rottier, Antoine Cyrille Julien; Netherlands business executive; b. 13 March 1910, St. Janssteen; s. of Honoré J. Rottier and Emilia S. Vael; m. Else H. Retera 1940; five s. two d.; ed. Univ. of Economic Science, Tilburg.

With Ministry of Econ. Affairs; DSM (Staatsmijnen) Limburg 36-, Man. Dir. 49-62, Chair. 62-73; Knight, Order of Netherlands Lion; Hon. Dr. (Univ. of Tilburg).

Leisure interests: fishing, walking, music.

Publ. *De beambte in onderneming en maatschappij.*

31 Valkenburgerweg, Heerlen, Netherlands.

Rötzsch, Helmut, PH.D.; German librarian; b. 1923; ed. Buchhändler-Lehranstalt, Leipzig, and Karl-Marx Univ., Leipzig.

Director of Acquisition Dept., Deutsche Bücherei 55-58, Dep. Director, Deutsche Bücherei 59-61, Dir.-Gen. 61-; Town Councillor, Leipzig 61-; Pres. Bibliotheksverband der D.D.R. 68-74, mem. of presidency 74-; Distinguished Service Medal of German Democratic Republic 59, Nat. Order for Distinguished Services 64; Titular Prof. Librarianship and Information Science 70; Wilhelm Bracke Gold Medal 73.

Publs. *Der Börsenverein der deutschen Buchhändler zu Leipzig und die Deutsche Bücherei 62, Die Deutsche Bücherei—die Deutsche Nationalbibliothek 62, Anton Graff und seine Buchhändlerporträts 65*; Editor: *Deutsche Bücherei 12-62, Jahrbuch der Deutschen Bücherei 65-, Beiträge zur Geschichte des Buchwesens 65-.*

Karl-Rothe-Strasse 15, 7022 Leipzig, German Democratic Republic.

Telephone: 52206.

Rouamba, Tensoré Paul; Upper Voltan diplomatist; b. 28 March 1933, Ouagadougou; m. Jeanne Zongo; two s. two d.; ed. Univs. of Bordeaux, Grenoble and Paris.

Former mem. Constitutional Chamber of Supreme Court of Upper Volta; fmr. Asst. Prof., Centre of Tropical Geography, Univ. of Abidjan; Prof. at Normal School, Ouagadougou 63-65; Perm. Rep. of Upper Volta to UN 66-72; Amb. to U.S.A. and Canada 66-72, to Nigeria 72, to Ghana 72-.

Leisure interests: basketball, bridge, horse-riding.

Embassy of Upper Volta, House No. 772/3, Asylum Down, Off Farrar Avenue, P.O. Box 651, Accra, Ghana.

Roubault, Marcel Edouard, D. ès sc.; French geologist; b. 11 May 1905, Angoulême (Charente); s. of Henri Roubault and Anne Marie (née Dupuy); m. Henriette Lacostère 1929; two s.; ed. Ecole Normale Supérieure and Faculté des Sciences, Paris.

Geology Dept., Ecole Normale Supérieure 30-35; Faculty of Sciences, Paris 35-38; Titular Prof. of Geology Univ. of Nancy 38-, Dean of Faculty of Sciences 61-64, Hon. Dean 64-; Hon. Pres. de l'Institut Nat. Polytechnique de Nancy 71; Hon. Dir. Ecole Nat. Supérieure de Géologie Appliquée et de Prospection Minière, Nancy 38-71; Hon. Dir. Centre de Recherches Pétrographiques et Géochimiques de Centre Nat. de la Recherche Scientifique 52-73; Hon. Dir. Centre de Recherches Radiogéologiques, Univ. of Nancy 56-73; Dir. of Research and Mineral Exploitation, Atomic Energy Comm. 48-52, Pres. Cttee. of Mines 52-71, Hon. Adviser to High Commr. on geological and mineralogical questions 52-; Principal Consultant on Geol. Map of France Service; mem. Acad. des Sciences 67-; Pres. Soc. Géologique de France 66; Vice-Pres. Soc. française de Minéralogie 43; numerous other scientific appointments; Officer Légion d'Honneur, Assoc. mem. Royal Acad. Belgium 70, and other awards.

Leisure interest: horticulture.

Publs. *La Kabylie de Collo: Etude Géologique, L'emploi du Microscope Polarisant* (with L. Bertrand), *Le Granite et les Réactions à l'état solide* (with R. Perrin), *La genèse des Montagnes, Géologie de l'uranium, Détermination des Minéraux des roches au microscope polarisant, Peut-on prévoir les catastrophes naturelles?, La dérive des continents.*

c/o Académie des Sciences, 23 Quai de Conti, Paris 6e, France.

Rougemont, Denis de, L. ÈS L.; Swiss author; b. 8 Sept. 1906, Neuchâtel; *s.* of Georges de Rougemont and Alice-Sophie Bovet; *m.* Anahite Repond 1952; one *s.* one *d.*

Lecturer, Univ. of Frankfurt-on-Main 35-36; Prof. Ecole Libre des Hautes Etudes, New York 41; one of the founders of the Personalist Movement in Paris 33; contrib. to leading periodicals in Europe, North and South America; Dir. Centre Européen de la Culture; Chair. Exec. Cttee. Congress for Cultural Freedom 51-66; Chair. Round Table Council of Europe 53, 55; Chair. European Asscn. of Music Festivals, Prof. Inst. Univ. d'Etudes Européennes, Geneva; Corresp. mem. Acad. des Sciences morales et politiques, Paris.

Leisure interest: dry-stone walling.

Publs. *Politique de la Personne, Penser avec les Mains, Journal d'un Intellectuel en Chômage, Journal d'Allemagne, L'Amour et l'Occident* (new version 56), *Nicolas de Flue, Mission ou Démission de la Suisse, The Heart of Europe, La Part du Diable, Les Personnes du Drame, Lettres sur la Bombe Atomique, Vivre en Amérique, Journal des Deux-Mondes, L'Europe en Jeu, Doctrine fabuleuse, Suite Neuchâteloise, Lettres aux Députés Européens, La Confédération Helvétique, L'Aventure Occidentale de l'homme, Comme toi-même, Vingt-huit siècles d'Europe, Les Chances de l'Europe, The Christian Opportunity, La Suisse ou l'histoire d'un peuple heureux, Journal d'une époque (1926-1946), Lettre ouverte aux Européens, Le cheminement des Esprits (1946-1970), L'Un et le Divers, L'Amour et l'Occident, Les Méfaits de l'Instruction Publique.*

01.630 St. Genis-Pouilly, France.

Telephone: (50) 41.13.85.

Rouhani, Fuad, LL.M.; Iranian lawyer and executive; b. 23 Oct. 1907, Teheran; *s.* of Ali Akbar Rouhani; *m.* Rohan Fath-Aazam 1927; two *d.*; ed. Teheran, London Univ.

Anglo-Iranian Oil Co., Legal and Admin. Branches 26-51; Chief Legal Adviser, Nat. Iranian Oil Co. 51-54, Dir. 54-, Man. Dir., Dep. Chair. 56-; Sec.-Gen. and Chair. Board of Govs., Org. of Petroleum Exporting Countries (OPEC) 61-64; Prof. of Iranian Studies at Columbia Univ. 64-65; Sec.-Gen., Org. of Regional Co-operation for Devt. between Iran, Pakistan and Turkey 65-68; Amb. 65; Adviser to Prime Minister of Iran; now in private practice as expert on Iranian and int. law; part-time Legal Adviser to Cen. Bank of Iran 72; D. en D. (Paris) 68.

Leisure interests: music, philosophy, religions, languages.

16 Kh. Rasht (Behjatabad), Teheran, Iran.

Telephone: 43807.

Rouhani, Mansour, M.SC.; Iranian politician; b. 1921, Teheran; ed. Univs. of Teheran and London.

Chairman and Gen. Dir. Technical Dept., Teheran Water Supply Org.; fmr. Minister of Water and Power; Minister of Agric. 71-, and Natural Resources 74-.

Ministry of Agriculture, Teheran, Iran.

Rouleau, Joseph-Alfred; Canadian bass singer; b. 26 Feb. 1929, Matane, Quebec; *s.* of Joseph-Alfred Rouleau and Florence Bouchard; *m.* Renée Moreau 1952; one *s.*

two *d.*; ed. Coll. Jean De Brebeuf, Montreal, Univ. of Montreal, Conservatoire of Music, Province of Quebec.

Three years in Milan for singing studies; debut in Montreal 55, at Royal Opera House, Covent Garden 57-, has sung over 30 roles at Covent Garden; guest artist at principal Opera Houses all over the world; tours of Canada 60, Australia (with Joan Sutherland) 65, Russia 66, 69, Romania, S. Africa 74, 75, 76; Paris Opera 75; recordings for E.M.I. include: Scenes from *Anna Bolena, Ruddigore, Romeo et Juliette* (Gounod); for L'oiseau lyre: *l'Enfance du Christ* (Berlioz); for Decca: *Semiramide, Boris Godunov, Renard* (Stravinsky), and recording of French operatic arias with Royal Opera House Orchestra; several awards including Prix Calixa-Lavallée 67 (La Société St. Jean Baptiste, Montreal).

Major roles include: Boris Godunov (*Boris Godunov*), Philip II (*Don Carlo*), Basilio (*Barber of Seville*), Mephisto (*Faust*), Dosifei (*Khovanschina*), Don Quixote (*Don Quixote*).

Royal Opera House, London, W.C.2; Home: 2 Laverock, Manor Park, Chislehurst, Kent, England.

Telephone: 01-467-5315.

Roumajon, Yves Pierre Jean; French psychiatrist; b. 13 Dec. 1914, Aix-en-Provence; *s.* of late Joseph Roumajon and Camille Guilbaud; *m.* 1954; one *s.*; ed. Lycée Champollion, Grenoble, Collège Municipal de Chalons-sur-Marne, Lycée Faidherbe, Lille, and Lycée Louis-le-Grand, Paris.

Former Intern, Hôpitaux Psychiatriques de la Seine; Medical Head of Psychiatric Service, Choquan Hospital, S. Viet-Nam 50-52; Head of Clinic, Faculty of Medicine 53; Doctor, Seine Centre for Educational Guidance for Children and Adolescents 53-60; Psychiatrist, Educ. Service for Young Prisoners, Fresnes Prison 58-70; medical Dir. C.M.P. Vauhallan 70; Expert at Paris Court of Appeal 58-, and Court of Cassation 63-; mem. Board of Dirs. Int. Soc. of Criminology 63, Treas. 72; Pres. Assen. française de Criminologie 69; Officier Légion d'Honneur, Croix de Guerre 39-45, etc.

5 rue Cambon, Paris 1er, France.

Telephone: 260-81-10.

Rountree, William Manning, LL.B.; American diplomatist; b. 28 March 1917, Swainsboro, Georgia; *s.* of William M. and Clyde B. Rountree; *m.* Suzanne McDowell 1946; one *d.*; ed. Atlanta Technological High School, and Columbus Univ., Washington, D.C.

Accountant and Auditor U.S. Treasury Dept. 35-41; Budget Officer and Dep. to Asst. Admin. Lend Lease Admin. 41-42; Gen. Asst. to Dir. U.S. Economic Operations in Middle East 42-45; Special Asst. and Economic Adviser to Head of Near Eastern, South Asian and African Div., State Dept. 46-48; Special Asst. U.S. Ambassador to Greece 48-49; Dep., later Dir. Office of Greek, Turkish and Iranian Affairs 49-52; Counsellor of Embassy, Ankara 52-53; Minister Counsellor Teheran 53-55; Dep. Asst. Sec. of State for Near Eastern, South Asian and African Affairs 55-56, Asst. Sec. 56-59; Ambassador to Pakistan 59-62, to the Sudan 62-65, to the Republic of South Africa 65-70, to Brazil 70-73.

6307 S.W. 35th Way, Gainsville, Fla., U.S.A.

Rous, Sir Stanley Ford, Kt., C.B.E., J.P.; British sports administrator; b. 25 April 1895, Mutford, Suffolk; *s.* of George S. and Alice Rous; *m.* Adrienne Gacon 1924; ed. St. Luke's Coll., Exeter.

Served European War 14-18; Asst. Master Watford Grammar School 21-34; Sec. of the Football Assen. 34-61; Vice-Pres. European Football Fed. 60; Chair. The Central Council of Physical Recreation 46-73, Hon. Vice-Pres. 73-; mem. Int. Fed. of Assen. Football, Pres. 61-74, Hon. Life Pres. 74-; Vice-Pres. Arts Educational Schools; Chevalier, Couronne de Chêne, Luxembourg; Chevalier de la Légion d'Honneur

France; Commendatore dell'Ordine al merito della Repubblica Italiana; Commdr. de l'Ordre du Ouissam Alaouite (Morocco) 68; Commdr. Ordre Nat. du Lion (Senegal) 75; Grand Cross of Merit, Order of Merit, Fed. Repub. of Germany 74.
115 Ladbroke Road, London, W.11, England.
Telephone: 01-727-4113.

Rouse, Irving, B.S., PH.D.; American professor of anthropology; b. 29 Aug. 1913, Rochester, N.Y.; s. of B. Irving Rouse and Louise Bohachek; m. Mary Mikami 1939; two s.
Assistant, then Assoc. Curator, Peabody Museum of Natural History, Yale Univ. 38-62, Instructor to Assoc. Prof. 39-54, Prof. of Anthropology 54-; fmr. Chair. Dept. of Anthropology; Pres. Soc. for American Archaeology 52-53, American Anthropological Asscn. 67-68; Charles J. MacCurdy Prof. of Anthropology (Yale Univ.) 69-; mem. American Acad. of Arts and Sciences, Nat. Acad. of Sciences, New York Acad. of Sciences, Royal Anthropological Inst.; A. Cressy Morrison Prize in Natural Sciences, Viking Fund Medal in Anthropology.
Leisure interests: singing, swimming.
Publs. *Prehistory in Haiti* 39, *Culture of the Ft. Liberté Region, Haiti* 41, *Archeology of the Maniabón Hills, Cuba* 42, *A Survey of Indian River Archeology, Florida* 51, *Porto Rican Prehistory* 52, *An Archeological Chronology of Venezuela* (with J. M. Cruxent) 58, *Venezuelan Archeology* (with J. M. Cruxent) 63, *Introduction to Prehistory* 72.
Department of Anthropology, Yale University, New Haven, Conn. 06520; Home: 12 Ridgewood Terrace, North Haven, Conn. 06473, U.S.A.
Telephone: 203-436-8421.

Rousseau, Jacques, D.SC., F.R.S.C.; Canadian botanist and ethnographer; b. 5 Oct. 1905; ed. Univ. of Montreal, and Cornell Univ.
Lecturer, Institut Botanique, Montreal Univ. 28-35; Prof. 35-44; Asst. Dir., Montreal Botanical Garden 38-44, Dir. 44-57; Dir. Canadian Museum of Human History 57-59; Assoc. Prof., Sorbonne 59-62; Research Prof. Centre d'Etudes Nordiques and Prof. Univ. Laval, Quebec 62-.
Publs. Books, pamphlets and articles on geography, flora and ethnology of Quebec-Labrador Peninsula, etc.
5208 Côte St. Antoine, Montreal 260, Canada.
Telephone: 482-4230.

Roussel, Claude; French journalist; b. 7 Feb. 1919, Paris; s. of Pierre Roussel; m. Aasa Billquist 1955; one s. one d.; ed. Lycée Louis-le-Grand, Ecole Normale Supérieure.
French Resistance 41-44; co-founder Agence Information et Documentation and of Agence France-Presse 44; Asst. Sec.-Gen., later Sec.-Gen. Agence France-Presse 44-51, Dir. in Scandinavia 51-54, Sec.-Gen. 54-75, Chair. and Man. Dir. June 75-; Pres. Union Européenne des Agences Photographiques 60-65.
Leisure interests: tennis, swimming, skiing.
Agence France-Presse, 11 Place de la Bourse, 75002 Paris, France.

Rousselet, Marcel, D. EN D., D. ès L.; French lawyer; b. 6 Dec. 1893; ed. Nancy and Paris Univs.
Entered Magistracy 20; Deputy at Tribunal de la Seine 32; Pres. Tribunal de la Seine 44-50; Pres. Paris Court of Appeal 50-62, First Hon. Pres. Sept. 62-; mem. l'Institut de France, Acad. des Sciences Morales et Politiques 59-; Commdr. de la Légion d'Honneur.
Publs. *Les Livres fonciers en Alsace Lorraine* 20, *La Magistrature sous la Monarchie de Juillet* 37, *L'Affaire du Duc de Praslin et la Magistrature* 37, *Histoire de la Justice* 43, *Les Souverains devant la Justice* 46, *Histoire de la Magistrature Française des Origines à nos Jours* 57,

Berryer devant la Cour d'Assises 65, *Les cas de Conscience du Magistrat* 67.
52 rue des Ecoles, Paris 5e, France.

Roussin, André Jean Paul, B. ès L.; French playwright; b. 22 Jan. 1911; ed. Inst. Mélizan, Marseilles.
Left journalism to found *"Le Rideau Gris"* with Louis Ducreux; mem. Académie Française 73-; Officier de Mérite Nat.; Commdr. des Arts et Lettres; Chevalier de la Légion d'Honneur.
Plays include: *Am-Stram-Gram, Une grande fille toute simple, Jean-Baptiste le Mal-Aimé, Le Tombeau d'Achille, La Sainte Famille, La Petite Hutte, Les Oeufs d'Autriche, Nina, Bobosse, Lorsque l'enfant paraît, La Main de César, Le Mari, la Femme et la Mort, L'Amour Fou, La Mamma, Une femme qui dit la vérité, Les Glorieuses, L'Ecole des Autres, Un amour qui ne finit pas, La Voyante, La Locomotive, On ne sait jamais, Le Claque;* (essays) *Patience et Impatiences, Un contentement raisonnable.*
12 Place des Victoires, Paris 2e, France.

Roux, Abraham Johannes Andries, DR. ENG., D.SC., B.SC.; South African nuclear scientist; b. 18 Oct. 1914, Bethlehem, Orange Free State; s. of Abraham J. A. Roux and Anna S. Naude; m. Ulrica Prinsloo 1939; one s. one d.; ed. Univ. of the Witwatersrand.
Lecturer, Dept. of Mechanical Engineering, Witwatersrand Univ. 39-44; Senior Lecturer, Stellenbosch Univ. 44-46; Principal Research Officer, Nat. Building Research Inst., Council for Scientific and Industrial Research (C.S.I.R.) 46-52, Officer in Charge C.S.I.R. Mech. Engineering Research Unit 52; Dir. Nat. Physical Research Lab. 52-55, Nat. Mech. Engineering Research Inst., C.S.I.R. 55-57, Vice-Pres. C.S.I.R. 57-60; Part-time Dir. Atomic Energy Research Programme 56-59, Dir. of Research, Atomic Energy Board 59-60, Dir. Atomic Energy Board 60-64, Dir.-Gen. 64-67, Chair. 67-70, Pres. 70-; Chair. Nat. Inst. for Metallurgy 67-, UCOR 70-; mem. Board of Dirs. Nuclear Fuels Corpn.; mem. Prime Minister's Scientific Advisory Council 62-75, Univs. Advisory Cttee. 66-74, C.S.I.R. 66-, S.A. Council of Professional Engs. 68, Prime Minister's Planning Advisory Cttee. 68, Cttee. on Energy Policy, Dept. of Planning and the Environment 74-; D.Sc. h.c.; Hendrik Verwoerd Award.
Leisure interest: golf.
Publs. *Mechanical Engineering Research in South Africa* 52, *Mechanical Engineering in Relation to Industry* 55-57, *Developments in the Field of Nuclear Power and their Impact on South Africa* 58, *The Atomic Energy Research and Development Programme of South Africa* 59, *Science, Industry and the Professional Society* 60, *The First Reactor Installation of the Republic of South Africa* 62, *South Africa's Programme of Nuclear Research* 62, *The Scope of Research and Development in the Field of Radioisotopes and Nuclear Radiation in South Africa* 64, *Nuclear Engineering in South Africa* 64, *Power Generation in South Africa with Special Reference to the Introduction of Nuclear Power* (Co-author) 66, *Nuclear Energy in South Africa* 67, *Energy for the Coming Century—Nuclear Energy* 69, *Policy Aspects of the Introduction of Nuclear Power in South Africa* (Co-author) 69, *South Africa's Position in the World Energy Picture* 73.
Atomic Energy Board, Private Bag X256, Pretoria 0001, South Africa.
Telephone: 79-4441, Ext. 200.

Roux, Ambroise Marie Casimir; French business executive; b. 26 June 1921, Piscop, Val d'Oise; s. of André Roux and Cécile Marcilhacy; m. Françoise Marion 1946; one s. one d.; ed. Collège Stanislas, Paris, Ecole Polytechnique, Ecole des Ponts et Chaussées, Ecole Supérieure de l'Electricité.
Engineer, Civil Eng. Dept. 44-51; Exec. Dir. Office of

Sec. of State for Industry and Commerce, Industry Dept. 52-55; Senior Vice-Pres. Compagnie Générale d'Electricité, Paris 55-63, Pres. 63-, Dir. 66-, Chair. of Board 70-; Vice-Chair. Crédit Commercial de France 74-; Dir. and Hon. Chair. Pétrofigaz; Chair. of Board, Cie. Industrielle des Télécommunications CITAL-CATEL 66-, Cie. Electro Financière 69-, AFNOR 72-; Dir. Alsthom, Crédit National, Société La Radiotechnique, Péchiney Ugine Kuhlmann, Cie. Financière de Paris et des Pays-Bas, Soc. Nat. d'Investissement; Dir. Cinémathèque; Vice-Chair. Fed. French Industries 66-74, 1st Vice-Chair. 75-; Commdr. Légion d'Honneur; Commdr. Mérite Commercial; Officier de l'Instruction Publique.

54 rue La Boétie, 75382 Paris Cedex 08; Home: 17 place des Etats-Unis, 75116 Paris, France.
Telephone: 266-54-60.

Roux, Jacques; French diplomatist; b. 1 March 1907, Avignon; s. of Pierre Roux and Jeanne Sivan; m. Consuelo Eyre 1964; ed. Collège Saint-Joseph, Avignon, Facultés de droit d'Aix en Provence et de Paris, Ecole libre de sciences politiques.
Diplomatic Service, London 34-37; Ministry of Foreign Affairs 37; Sec. Chungking 45, Counsellor Nanking 46; Dir. of Asian Dept., Ministry of Foreign Affairs 52-56, Asst. Dir.-Gen. of Political Affairs 56, 57-63, Asst. Dir. Office of Minister 56-57; Amb. to United Arab Republic 63-68, to Switzerland 69-72; Minister of Monaco 74; Commdr. Légion d'Honneur.
25 rue de Constantine, Paris 7e, France.

Rowicki, Witold; Polish conductor and composer; b. 26 Feb. 1914, Taganrog, U.S.S.R.; s. of Jan and Nadieżda Rowicki; m. Joanna Nowak 1939; one s. one d.; ed. Cracow Conservatoire.
Debut as conductor 32; appearances as soloist and in chamber ensembles 32-45; Founder, Musical Dir. and Chief Conductor Radio Symphony Orchestra, Katowice 45-50; Prof. Superior School of Music, Warsaw 52-54; organizer, Musical Dir. and Chief Conductor Warsaw Philharmonic Orchestra, now Nat. Philharmonic Orchestra 50-55, 58-; Dir. Teatr Wielki Opera Centre 65-70; conducted in many European, African, Asian, North and South American countries and Australia; Grand Prix du Disque, Acad. Charles Cros, Paris 59, Ministry of Culture and Art Prize 63, Grand Prix Belge 65, Edison Prize, Amsterdam 65, Grand Prix Nat. du Disque, Paris 66, State Prize 66, Award of Union of Composers 62, Officers Cross of Polonia Restituta, Order of the Banner of Labour, etc.
Ul. Chocimska 35, m. 12, 00-791 Warsaw, Poland.
Telephone: 49-80-64.

Rowland, Air Marshal James Anthony, D.F.C., A.F.C., B.E., C.ENG., F.R.AE.S.; Australian air force officer; b. 1 Nov. 1922, Armidale, N.S.W.; s. of Commdr. Louis Claude Rowland and Elsie Jean Wright; m. Faye Alison Doughton 1955; one d.; ed. Univ. of Sydney.
Master Bomber, Pathfinder Force, Bomber Command R.A.F. 44; with R.A.A.F.: Chief Test Pilot, Aircraft Research and Devt. Unit 51-54, C.O. 58-60; Officer Commanding Research and Devt. 58-60; Chief Tech. Officer, No. 82 Wing 57, Mirage Mission, Paris 61-64; Commanding No. 3 Aircraft Depot, Amberley 67-68; Senior Tech. Staff Officer, HQ Operational Command 69-70; with Dept. of Air: Dir.-Gen. of Aircraft Eng. 72, Air Mem. for Tech. Services 73-74; Chief of Air Staff, R.A.A.F. 75-; Councillor, Royal Aeronautical Soc., Australian Branch 73-75.
Leisure interests: carpentry, history, skiing, surfing.
Publs. official reports, contributions to journals.
Department of Defence, Russell Offices, Canberra, A.C.T.; Home: 4 Galway Place, Deakin, A.C.T. 2600, Australia.
Telephone: 65-5474 (Office); 813483 (Home).

Rowland, John Russell; Australian diplomatist; b. 10 Feb. 1925, Armidale, N.S.W.; s. of L. C. and E. J. Rowland; m. Moira Enid Armstrong 1956; one s. two d.; ed. Cranbrook School, Sydney, and Univ. of Sydney.
Department of External Affairs 44-, served Moscow 46-48, Saigon 52, 54-55, Washington 55-56, London 57-59; Asst. Sec., Dept. of External Affairs 61-65; Amb. to U.S.S.R. 65-68, First Asst. Sec. Dept. of External Affairs 69; High Commr. to Malaysia 69-72, Amb. to Austria, Czechoslovakia, Hungary and Switzerland 73-74; Deputy Sec., Dept. of Foreign Affairs 75-.
Publs. *The Feast of Ancestors* 65, *Snow* 71 (poetry).
Department of Foreign Affairs, Administrative Building, Canberra, A.C.T. 2600, Australia.

Rowland, Raymond Edgar, B.S. (Agriculture); American businessman; b. 8 Dec. 1902, Kansas, Ill.; s. of William E. Rowland and Lula P. Estes; m. Connie L. Melton 1928; one s. two d.; ed. Univs. of Illinois and Wisconsin.
Joined Ralston Purina Co. as Junior Salesman 26, later various sales and production positions, Asst. Vice-Pres. 40-43, Vice-Pres. 43-56, Dir. 51-, Pres. 56-64, Chair. of Board 64-68; Dir. Mercantile Trust Co. (St. Louis); mem. Univ. of Wis. Foundation; Trustee, Cen. Presbyterian Church, Wisconsin Alumni Research Foundation; David Ranken Jr. School of Mechanical Trades; Chair. Board of Dirs., Barnes Hosp.
Leisure interest: breeding pedigree polled Hereford cattle.
The Whitehall, Apartment 21A, 710 South Hanley Road, Clayton, Miss. 63105, U.S.A.
Telephone: 314-863-1010.

Rowling, Wallace Edward, M.A.; New Zealand politician; b. 15 Nov. 1927, Motheha, South Island; m. Glen Elna Reeves 1951; two s. two d.; ed. Nelson Coll. and Canterbury Univ.
Former Educ. Officer, New Zealand Army; mem. Parl. for Buller 62-72, Tasman 72-; Pres. Labour Party 70-73; Minister of Finance 72-74; Prime Minister 74-75, also Minister of Foreign Affairs, of Legislative Dept., in charge of N.Z. Security Intelligence Dept., the Audit Dept.
Leisure interests: golf, badminton.
Parliament Buildings, Wellington, New Zealand.

Rowse, Alfred Leslie, D.LITT., F.R.S.L.; British historian and writer; b. 4 Dec. 1903, St. Austell, Cornwall; ed. in Cornwall, and Christ Church, Oxford.
Fellow British Acad., All Souls Coll., Oxford 25-74.
Leisure interests: seeing historic places, music, gardening.
Publs. *Sir Richard Grenville of the Revenge* 37, *Tudor Cornwall* 41 (revised edn. 69), *Poems of a Decade 31-41, A Cornish Childhood* 42, *The Spirit of English History* 43, *Poems Chiefly Cornish* 44, *The English Spirit* 44, *West Country Stories* 45, *The Use of History* 46, *Poems of Deliverance* 46, *The End of an Epoch* 47, *The England of Elizabeth* 50, *The English Past* 51 (revised edn. entitled *Times, Persons, Places* 65), Lucien Romier's *History of France* trans. and completed 53, *The Expansion of Elizabethan England* 55, *The Early Churchills* 56, *The Later Churchills* 58, *Poems Partly American* 59, *The Elizabethans and America* 59, *St. Austell: Church, Town, Parish* 60, *Appeasement: A Study in Political Decline* 61, *Ralegh and the Throckmortons* 62, *William Shakespeare: A Biography* 63, *Shakespeare's Sonnets* 64 (rev. edn.) 73, *Christopher Marlowe: A Biography* 64, *A Cornishman at Oxford* 65, *Shakespeare's Southampton* 65, *Bosworth Field and the Wars of the Roses* 66, *Poems of Cornwall and America* 67, *Cornish Stories* 67, *A Cornish Anthology* 68, *The Cornish in America* 69, *The Elizabethan Renaissance: Vol. I The Life of the Society* 71, *Vol. II The Cultural Achievement* 72, *The Tower of London in the History of*

the Nation 72, *Shakespeare the Man* 73, *Simon Forman: Sex and Society in Shakespeare's Age* 74, *Windsor Castle in the History of the Nation* 74, *Peter, The White Cat of Trenarren* 74, *Victorian and Edwardian Cornwall* (with Sir John Betjeman) 74, *Oxford in the History of the Nation* 75, *Discoveries and Reviews from Renaissance to Restoration* 75, *Jonathan Swift—Major Prophet* 75, *A Cornishman Abroad* 76, *Brown Buck: A Californian Fantasy* 76, *Matthew Arnold: Poet and Prophet* 76, *Shakespeare the Elizabethan* 76.
Trenarren, St. Austell, Cornwall, England.

Roy, Sir Asoka Kumar, Kt., M.A., B.L.; Indian lawyer; b. 9 Sept. 1886, Calcutta; *s.* of Akshoy Roy Chaudhury and Soroshi Roy Chaudhurani; *m.* Charu Hasini 1908 (died 1963); one *s.* one *d.*; ed. Doveton, Presidency and Ripon Colls., Calcutta.
Called to Bar, Middle Temple 12; Standing Counsel, Bengal 29, fmr. Act. Judge High Court, Calcutta 32 and 33-34; Kt. 37; Advocate-Gen. Bengal 34-43; Law mem. Viceroy's Exec. Council 43-46; Dir. Jardine Henderson Ltd. 50-70, Bengal Coal Co. Ltd. 50-70, Braithwaite & Co. (India) Ltd. 50-70, Anglo India Jute Mills Co. Ltd. 50-70 and 10 other companies 50-70.
Leisure interests: gardening, walking.
3 Upper Wood Street, Calcutta 17, India.
Telephone: 44-5440.

Roy, Bhabesh Chandra, D.I.C., M.SC., DR.ING.; Indian geologist; b. 1 Aug. 1907; ed. Imperial Coll., London, Univ. of Nancy, and Univ. of Freiberg, Germany.
Joined Geological Survey of India 37, Dir. 58-61, Dir.-Gen. 61-65; UN Fellow in U.S.A. and Canada 57; mem. Oil and Natural Gas Comm. 64-65; Del. to ECAFE Mineral Confs. in Tokyo 55, Kuala Lumpur 58, U.S.S.R., U.K., France and Germany 55, Rome and Bandung 63, Vienna 64, Antwerp 66, Mexico City 67, New Zealand 70; Leader Del. Int. Geological Congress, Copenhagen 60; and numerous other int. geological meetings; Pres. Geological, Mining and Metallurgical Inst. of India 58-59, Indian Asscn. Geohydrologists 70-71; Co-ordinator Geological Map for Asia and Far East 58-68; Vice-Pres. Int. Union of Geological Sciences 61-68; Sec.-Gen. Int. Geol. Congress, New Delhi 64; Chair. Dept. of Geology, Univ. of Nigeria 66-67, U.G.C. Prof., Presidency Coll., Calcutta 68-; Editor *Journal of Mines, Metals and Fuels* 68-; Vice-Pres. I.G.C. Comm., History of Geol. Sciences 68-; Fellow, Nat. Inst. of Sciences of India; Medallist Czechoslovak Acad. Sciences 69.
Leisure interests: music, photography.
Publs. include: *Mineral Resources of Bombay* 51, *Economic Geology and Mineral Resources of Saurashtra* 53, *The Nellore Mica Belt* 56, *The Economic Geology and Mineral Resources of Rajasthan and Ajmer* 57; numerous articles on Geology and Mineral Resources.
37/3, Southend Park, Calcutta 29, India.
Telephone: 46-3189.

Roy, Claude; French writer; b. 28 Aug. 1915; ed. Univ. of Paris.
War service 39-40; imprisoned and escaped 40; in the Free Zone of France 40-43; contributed to the review *Poésie* 40, 41, etc., and to the review *Fontaine;* mem. Resistance in Southern Zone, Les Etoiles movement; contributed to the clandestine Press *Les Lettres Françaises;* War Corresp. after the Liberation; Croix de Guerre; Prix Fémina-Vacaresco 70.
Publs. *L'Enfance de l'Art* 41, *Clefs pour l'Amérique, Clefs pour la Chine, Descriptions Critiques, La Nuit est le manteau des pauvres, Le Soleil sur la Terre, Le Malheur d'Aimer, Le journal des Voyages, L'Homme en Question, Gérard Philipe* (with Anne Philipe), *Léone et les Siens, L'Amour du théâtre, La Dérobée, Jean Vilar, Défense de la littérature* 68, *Le Verbe Aimer* 69, *Moi je* (memoirs) 69, *Nous* (memoirs 1944-56) 72, *Le Soleil des Roman-tiques* 74, *Enfantasques* 74, *Somme Toute* 75 (memoirs 1955-75).
Editions Gallimard, 5 rue Sébastien-Bottin, Paris 7e, France.

Roy, H.E. Cardinal Maurice, D.D., D.PH.; French Canadian ecclesiastic; b. 25 Jan. 1905, Quebec; *s.* of the Hon. Justice Ferdinand Roy and Mariette Legendre; ed. Laval Univ., Quebec, Inst. Angelicum, Rome, and Inst. Catholique and Sorbonne, Paris.
Ordained Priest 27; Prof. of Theology, Laval Univ. 30-46; Army Chaplain (Canadian Army Overseas) 39, 45; Rector of Grand Seminary (School of Theology), Laval Univ. 46; Bishop of Trois Rivières, Quebec 46-47; Archbishop (R.C.) of Quebec 47-; Bishop Ordinary to Canadian Armed Forces; Primate of Canada 56-; cr. Cardinal by Pope Paul VI 65; Chair. Council of Laity and Pontifical Comm. for Justice and Peace 67-.
Leisure interests: painting, canoeing.
Archevêché, C.P. 459, Quebec 4, Quebec, Canada.

Roy, Maurice; French engineer; b. 7 Nov. 1899; ed. Ecole Polytechnique, and Ecole Nat. Supérieure des Mines.
Engineer Corps des Mines 22; Prof. Ecole Nat. des Ponts et Chaussées 26-50, concurrently Prof. Ecole Nat. Supérieure de l'Aéronautique; Dir. *La Science Aérienne* 30-35; Prof. Ecole Polytechnique 47-69; Dir. Office Nat. d'Etudes et de Recherches Aéronautiques 49-62; Hon. Chair. Int. Council of Aeronautical Sciences; fmr. Pres. Int. Union of Theoretical and Applied Mechanics, now Vice-Pres.; Pres. Cttee. on Space Research; fmr. Pres. French Mathematical Soc.; mem. Acad. des Sciences; Grand Officier Légion d'Honneur; F.I.Ae.S. (U.S.), F.R.Ae.S. (U.K.).
Publs. include papers on jet propulsion and theory of flight.
86 avenue Niel, Paris 17e, France.
Telephone: 924-01-02.

Roy, Raja Tridiv; Pakistani politician; b. 14 May 1933, Rajbari, Rangamati; *s.* of late Raja Nalinaksha Roy and Rajmata Benita Roy; *m.* Rani Arati Roy 1953; three *s.* two *d.*
Called to the Bar, Lincoln's Inn, London 51; Chief Chakma Community 53; mem. E. Pakistan Provincial Assembly 62-70; mem. Nat. Assembly 70-; Minister of Minority Affairs and of Tourism 71-74; Rep. of Pakistan to 6th World Buddhist Council, Rangoon and 2500th Buddha Jayanti celebrations, New Delhi 56, 10th Conf. of World Fellowship of Buddhists, Colombo 72; Del. to World Food Congress 63, UN Gen. Assembly 64, 72, Colombo Plan Consultative Cttee., Wellington 73; Special Envoy to S. Asian countries 71, to Latin America, U.S.A. and Caribbean 74-75; Adviser to Prime Minister on Tourism 75-.
Leisure interests: writing, photography.
National Assembly, Rawalpindi; Home: 248-B, F. 6/2, Margalla Road, Islamabad, Pakistan.
Telephone: 24597 (Office); 22526 (Home).

Roy Chowdhury, Devi Prasad, M.B.E.; Indian sculptor and painter; b. 15 June 1899, Rangpur (now Bangladesh); *s.* of Uma Prasad and Himangni Devi Roy Chowdhury; *m.* Charulata Banerji 1929; one *s.*
Principal Govt. Coll. of Arts and Crafts, Madras 29-57; fmr. Chair. Lalita Kala Akad., New Delhi; Dir. and Pres. Art Seminar of UNESCO, Tokyo 55; many prizes in Nat. Modern Sculpture exhbns., Govt. of India; Hon. Dr. of Lit. (Rabindra Bharati Univ., Calcutta) 68; Padma Bhusan 58.
Sculptures include: *Martyrs' Memorial* in Bronze at Bihar, *Triumph of Labour* at Madras and New Delhi, *Mahatma Gandhi* at Madras and Calcutta, *Rhythm,* Nat. Museum, New Delhi, *Motilal Nehru* at Parl. House, Delhi, currently executing *Martyrs' Memorial* consisting

of eleven double life size figures in bronze, New Delhi, numerous awards for sculpture.

Leisure interest: big game hunting.

Publs. Eleven books of short stories and novels, and novels and articles on art.

63 Shambhu Nath Pandit Street, Calcutta 25, India. Telephone: 47-2921.

Royer, Jean; French politician; b. 31 Oct. 1920, Nevers; *s.* of Léon-Antoine Royer and Odette Bourgoin; *m.* Lucienne Leux 1944; two *s.* two *d.*; ed. Ecole primaire supérieure Paul-Louis-Courier, Tours and Univ. de Poitiers.

Teacher at Langeais 45-48, at Sainte-Maure 50-54, at Tours 54-58; del. of R.P.F. (Rassemblement du Peuple Français) 47-51; Ind. Deputy 58-; Mayor of Tours 59-; Gen. Counsellor for Tours-ouest district 61-; Minister of Commerce, Trades and Crafts 73-74, of Posts and Telecommunications March-May 74.

37 Saint-Avertin, France.

Royle, Sir Lancelot Carrington, K.B.E.; British company director; b. 31 May 1898, Elstree, Herts.; *s.* of Rev. Vernon Royle; *m.* Barbara R. Haldin 1922; two *s.* one *d.*; ed. Harrow School and Royal Military Acad., Woolwich.

Served in France First World War 18; resgnd. commission 21; took up appt. with Van den Berghs Ltd., subsequently by amalgamation Lever & Unilever Ltd., recalled to Army Second World War 39-45; appt. mem. of Macharg/Royle Cttee. by Treasury 40; Chair. Navy, Army and Air Force Insts. 41-53; Chair. and Managing Dir. Home and Colonial Stores Ltd. 47-58; Chair. Lipton Ltd. 52-58, Liptons Overseas Ltd. 59-63; Dir. Liptons Ltd. 52-63, Allied Suppliers Ltd. 59-62, Clowes Walker Ltd. 59-65, U.P.M. Ltd. 59-65, Malgavita Ltd. 65-68, British Match Corpn. 60-68, Oxo Ltd. 60-68, Bryant and May Ltd. 60-70, Liebigs Extract of Meat Co. Ltd. 60-68; Pres. Multiple Shops Fed. 60-63; Gov. of Harrow School 47-62.

Leisure interests: athletics (silver medallist, 1924 Olympics), cricket, association and rugby football, gardening.

31 Elsworthy Road, London, N.W.3, England. Telephone: 01-722-5445.

Royster, Vermont Connecticut, A.B., LL.D.; American journalist; b. 30 April 1914, Raleigh, N.C.; *s.* of Wilbur H. and Olivette B. Royster; *m.* Frances Claypole 1937; two *d.*; ed. Univ. of North Carolina.

Reporter New York City News Bureau 36, *Wall Street Journal* 36; Washington corresp. *Wall Street Journal* 36-41, 45-46, Chief Washington corresp. 46-48; Editorial Writer and Columnist 46-48, Assoc. Editor 48-51, Senior Assoc. Editor 51-58, Editor 58-71, Contrib. Editor and Columnist 71-; Vice-Pres. Dow Jones & Co. Inc. 65-, Senior Vice-Pres. and Dir. 70; Pres. American Soc. of Newspaper Editors 65-66; Kenan Prof. Journalism and Public Affairs, Univ. of N. Carolina 71-; served U.S. Navy 41-45; mem. Pulitzer Board for Prizes in Journalism and Letters; Hon. Litt.D. (Temple Univ., Phila.), Hon. L.H.D. (Elon Coll., N.C.); Pulitzer Prize for editorial writing 53.

Leisure interest: boating.

Publs. *Journey through the Soviet Union* 64, *A Pride of Prejudices* 67.

Dow Jones & Co. Inc., 22 Cortlandt Street, New York, N.Y. 10007, U.S.A. Telephone: 212-285-5000.

Rozenko, Pyotr Akimovich; Soviet politician; b. 1907; ed. Donetsk Mining Inst.

Mining Engineer 31-54; mem. C.P.S.U. 43-; Dep. Minister of Coal Industry, Ukraine 54; Dep. Chair. Council of Ministers Ukraine 54-57, 59-; First Dep. Chair. State Planning Comm. of Ukraine 57-59, Chair. 59-63, 67-; First Deputy Chair. Ukrainian S.S.R.

Council of Ministers 63-; mem. Cen. Cttee. of C.P.S.U. 61-66, alt. mem. 66-; Deputy to U.S.S.R. Supreme Soviet 58-, Chair. Planning and Budgetary Comm.

Council of Ministers of the Ukrainian S.S.R., Kiev, U.S.S.R.

Różewicz, Tadeusz; Polish poet and playwright; b. 9 Oct. 1921, Radomsko; ed. Univ. of Cracow.

Former factory worker and teacher; State Prize for Poetry 55, 56; Literary Prize, City of Cracow 59; Prize of Minister of Culture and Art 62, State Prize 1st Class 66, Commdr. Cross of Order Polonia Restituta 70, Medal of 30th Anniversary of People's Poland 74.

Publs. 15 vols. of poetry including *Niepokój* (*Faces of Anxiety*), *Czerwona rękawiczka* (*The Red Glove*), *Czas który idzie* (*The Time Which Goes On*), *Równina* (*The Plain*), *Srebrny kłos* (*The Silver Ear*), *Rozmowa z księciem* (*Conversation with the Prince*), *Zielona róża* (*The Green Rose*), *Nic w płaszczu Prospera* (*Nothing in Prosper's Overcoat*), *Twarz* (*The Face*); Plays include *Kartoteka* (*The Card Index*), *Grupa Laokoona* (*Laocoon's Group*), *Świadkowie albo nasza mała stabilizacja* (*The Witnesses*), *Akt przerywany* (*The Interrupted Act*), *Śmieszny staruszek* (*The Funny Man*), *Wyszedł z domu* (*Gone Out*), *Spaghetti i miecz* (*Spaghetti and the Sword*), *Stara kobieta wysiaduje* (*The Old Woman Broods*); some prose collections.

Ul. Januszewicka 13 m. 14, 53-136, Wrocław, Poland. Telephone: 643-38.

Rozhdestvensky, Gennadi Nikolayevich; Soviet conductor; b. 1931, Moscow; ed. Moscow State Conservatoire.

Assistant Conductor, Bolshoi Theatre 51, Conductor 56-60; Chief Conductor of U.S.S.R. Radio and TV Symphony Orchestra 61-; Principal Conductor Bolshoi Theatre 64-70; has been guest conductor for numerous orchestras throughout Europe, America and Asia; Merited and People's Artist of the R.S.F.S.R., Lenin Prizewinner 70.

U.S.S.R. Radio and T.V. Symphony Orchestra, Moscow, U.S.S.R.

Ruark, Arthur Edward, M.A., PH.D.; American physicist; b. 9 Nov. 1899, Washington, D.C.; *s.* of Oliver M. and Margaret G. Ruark; *m.* Sarah G. Hazen 1927 (died 1967); four *d.*; ed. Johns Hopkins Univ.

Worked at Bureau of Standards 21-26; Asst. Prof. Yale Univ. 26-27; Mellon Inst. of Industrial Research 27-29; Head of Physics Division, Gulf Research Laboratory 29; Prof. of Physics, Univ. of Pittsburgh 30-34; Head of Physics Dept. and Kenan Research Prof. Univ. of North Carolina 34-44; Consultant, Naval Research Laboratory 44-46; Head Research Division, Applied Physics Laboratory of Johns Hopkins Univ. 46-47; Asst. Dir. Inst. for Co-operative Research, Johns Hopkins Univ. 48-49; Head Navy Research Project, Johns Hopkins Univ. 49-52; Temerson Prof. of Physics, Univ. of Alabama 52-56; Chief, Controlled Thermonuclear Branch, U.S. Atomic Energy Comm. 57-60; Asst. Dir. of Research, U.S. Atomic Energy Comm. 61-65, Senior Assoc. Dir. of Research 66-69.

Publs. *Atoms, Molecules and Quanta* (with Harold C. Urey), *Atomic Physics* (with mems. of the Pittsburgh Physics Staff) and articles on Atomic Physics.

7952 Orchid Street, N.W., Washington, D.C. 20012, U.S.A.

Rubayyi, Salem Ali; Southern Yemeni politician; b. 1934, Southern Arabia; ed. in Aden.

Formerly school-teacher and in private law practice; participated in activities of Nat. Front for the Liberation of Occupied Southern Yemen (FLOSY) 63-67; mem. Gen. Command of Nat. Front Nov. 67; in exile 68-69; Chair. Presidential Council June 69-, also Supreme Commdr. of the Armed Forces.

Presidential Council, Aden, People's Democratic Republic of Yemen.

Rubbra, Edmund, C.B.E., M.A., D.MUS., LL.D.; British composer; b. 23 May 1901, Northampton; s. of Edmund J. Rubbra and Mary J. Bailey; m. 2nd Colette Yardley 1975; two s.; ed. Reading Univ., Royal Coll. of Music. Lecturer in Music, Oxford Univ. 47-68; Senior Research Fellow, Worcester Coll., Oxford 68-71, Hon. Fellow 71-; Hon. Fellow of Guildhall School of Music and Drama, London; Hon. mem. Royal Acad. of Music, London; Hon. Fellow, Int. Poetry Soc. 73; Orchestral works include: ten Symphonies, two Overtures and *Farnaby Improvisations*; Concertos for piano, violin and viola; vocal works include: sets of songs for tenor and baritone (with strings) and Ode for Contralto and Orchestra; motets, madrigals and masses for unaccompanied voices; seven works for chorus and orchestra; chamber music includes: sonatas for violin, 'cello and oboe with piano, three string quartets, piano quintet, two piano trios, and works with recorder; songs with string quartet, harp or piano; preludes for piano, works for solo harp.
Leisure interests: reading, gardening.
Publs. *Counterpoint* 60, *Collected Essays on Gustav Holst* 74.
Lindens, Bull Lane, Gerrard's Cross, Bucks., England. Telephone: Gerrards Cross 84650.

Rubel, John H.; American business executive; b. 27 April 1920, Chicago, Ill.; s. of Harry W. Rubel and Hermine Baum; m. Dorothy J. Rosenkranz 1942; two s. one d.; ed. California Inst. of Technology.
Research Laboratory, Gen. Electric Co. 42-45, Lockheed Aircraft Corpn. 45-46, Hughes Aircraft Co. (and Dir. Airborne Systems Laboratories) 46-59; Dept. of Defense 59-63, Asst. Dir. Defense Research and Engineering for Strategic Weapons 59-63, Asst. Dir. of Defence, Research and Engineering and Act. Dir. 60-63, Asst. Sec. Defence, Research and Engineering 61-63; Vice-Pres. and Dir. Technical Planning, Litton Industries Inc. 63-65, Vice-Pres. and Dir. Fast Deployment Logistic Ship Project 66-, Vice-Pres. and Dir. Advanced Marine Technology Div. 67-68, Senior Vice-Pres. 68-.
Leisure interests: swimming, gardening, painting.
Litton Industries Inc., 360 Crescent Drive, Beverly Hills, Calif.; Home: 416 South Bristol Avenue, Los Angeles, Calif. 90049, U.S.A.

Ruben, Vitali Petrovich; Soviet politician; b. 26 Feb. 1914, Moscow; ed. Yaroslav Agricultural Coll., Higher Party School.
Worked as agronomist and teacher until 41; party work 41-44; worked with Central Cttee. Latvian C.P. 44-47; Second Sec. Daugavpils Regional Cttee. Latvian C.P. 47-48; attended C.P.S.U. School 48-51; Central Cttee. Latvian C.P., Councils of Agric. and Gosplan of Latvia 51-61; Dep. Chair. Council of Ministers, Latvian S.S.R. 61-62, Chair. 62-70; Chair. Presidium of Supreme Soviet of Latvian S.S.R. 70-; Vice-Chair. Presidium of U.S.S.R. Supreme Soviet 70-; Alt. mem. Cen. Cttee. C.P.S.U. 66-; Deputy to U.S.S.R. Supreme Soviet 62-; Chair. Soviet of Nationalities, U.S.S.R. Supreme Soviet 74-.
Presidium of Supreme Soviet of Latvian S.S.R., Riga, U.S.S.R.

Ruben, Yury Yanovich; Soviet politician; b. 1925; ed. Latvian State Univ. and Higher Party School of C.P.S.U. Cen. Cttee.
Member C.P.S.U. 53-; engaged in party work 52-60; First Sec. Liepaia City Cttee., Latvian C.P. 60-63, First Sec. Riga City Cttee. 63-66; Sec. Cen. Cttee., Latvian C.P. 66-70; Chair. Council of Ministers of Latvian S.S.R. 70-; Deputy to U.S.S.R. Supreme Soviet 70-; Alt. mem. Cen. Cttee. C.P.S.U. 71-.
Council of Ministers of Latvian S.S.R., Riga, U.S.S.R.

Rubey, William Walden, D.SC., LL.D.; American geologist; b. 19 Dec. 1908, Moberly, Mo.; s. of Ambrose Burnside and Alva Beatrice Walden Rubey; m. Susan

Elsie Manovill 1919; three d. (one deceased); ed. Missouri, Johns Hopkins and Yale Univs.
Geological Aide to Asst. Geologist, U.S. Geological Survey 20-22; Instructor in Geology, Yale Univ. 22-24; Assoc. Geologist to Research Geologist, U.S. Geological Survey 24-60; Emer. Prof. of Geology and Geophysics, Dept. of Geology and Inst. of Geophysics and Planetary Physics, Univ. of Calif. (Los Angeles) 60-; Dir. Lunar Science Inst. 68-71; Chair. Nat. Research Council 51-54 (Chair. Div. of Geology and Geography 43-46); Visiting Prof., UCLA 54, Calif. Inst. of Technology 55, Johns Hopkins Univ. 56; mem. Nat. Science Board 60-66; Trustee, Science Service 56-64, Carnegie Inst., Washington 62-, Woods Hole Oceanographic Inst. 66-; mem. Nat. Acad. of Sciences, American Philosophical Soc., Geological Soc. of America (Pres. 50); Award of Excellence 43 and Distinguished Service Award 58, U.S. Dept. of Interior; Penrose Medal, Geological Soc. of America 63; Nat. Medal of Science 65.
Leisure interests: bird-watching, camping, horseback-riding, history of American northwest.
Publs. Numerous articles in *U.S. Geological Survey Bulletin, Geological Society of America Bulletin.*
Department of Geology, University of California, Los Angeles, Calif. 90024, U.S.A.
Telephone: 213-825-4384.

Rubinstein, Artur; Polish pianist virtuoso; b. 28 Jan. 1887, Łódź; s. of Ignace and Félice (Heyman) Rubinstein; m. Aniela Mlynarska 1932; two s. two d.; ed. Warsaw and Berlin Acad. Music.
First concert in Berlin 01; with Philadelphia Philharmonic Orchestra 06; tours in Europe, South America, Australia, China, Japan; recitals throughout the world; Hon. mem. Accademia de Santa Cecilia, Rome and Brazil, Acad. of Stockholm, etc.; Assoc. mem. Acad. des Beaux Arts (France) 71-; Hon. Citizen of Philadelphia, Chicago, Columbia; Grand Croix de la Légion d'Honneur; Commdr. des Arts et Lettres Order of Leopold, Chilean Merit, Officer of Santiago (Portugal), Polonia Restituta, Leopold 1st of Belgium, Order of Grand Cross of Alfonso el Sabio (Spain), etc.; Hon. Dr. Mus. (Northwestern, Yale, Brown, Rutgers, Columbia Univs., Hebrew Univ. (Jerusalem), etc.).
Publ. *My Young Years* (autobiog.) 73.
c/o Wilfrid Van Wyck, Troon, Old Mill Lane, Bray, SL6 2BG, Berks., England; and 22 square de l'avenue Foch, Paris 16e, France.

Rubottom, Roy Richard, Jr.; American diplomatist; b. 13 Feb. 1912, Brownwood, Tex.; s. of Roy Richard Rubottom and Jennie Eleanor Watkins; m. Billy Ruth Young 1938; two s. one d.; ed. Southern Methodist and Texas Univs.
In commerce 35-37; Asst. Dean, Student Life Texas Univ. 37-41; served in U.S. Navy (Commander) 41-46; Naval liaison officer, Mexico 43-45; Naval Attaché, Paraguay 45-46; Appointed Foreign Service Officer 47; Embassy Sec. and Consul Bogotá 47-49; in charge Mexican Affairs, State Dept. 50-52; Dir. Mid-American Affairs 52-53; 1st Sec., Madrid Embassy 53-54; Dir. Operations Mission, Madrid 54-56; Dep. Asst. Sec. and Acting Asst. Sec., of State for Inter-American Affairs 56; Asst. Sec. 57-60; Ambassador to Argentina 60-61; faculty adviser for State Dept., Naval War Coll. 61-64; Vice-Pres. Southern Methodist Univ., Texas 64-71; Pres. Univ. of the Americas 71-; Hon. LL.D. (Southwestern Coll., Winfield, Kansas) 68.
Leisure interests: swimming, travel, reading.
University of the Americas, Apartado 507, Puebla, Mexico.
Telephone: Puebla 3-16-50.

Rucinski, Joseph; American (b. Polish) economist; b. 13 Aug. 1907, Kiev, Ukraine; s. of Roman and Maria Rucinski: m. Wanda Zofia Princess Lubomirska 1965;

ed. Inst. Supérieur de Commerce, Antwerp, and Univ. of Geneva.

Member of the Money and Credit Dept. of the Polish Ministry of Finance 32-39; Financial Counsellor of the Polish Embassy, London 39-42; Economic Adviser to the Polish Foreign Office in London 42; went to the U.S. 45; joined staff of the Int. Bank 46; Asst. Dir. of the Dept. of Operations for Asia and the Middle East 52 and Dir. 55; Dir. of the Dept. of Operations for South Asia and the Middle East 57-61; Vice-Pres. Kaiser Industries Dec. 61-67; Vice-Pres. Allied Chemical Corpn. 67-70, Consultant 71-.

Leisure interests: music, photography, deep-sea fishing.
Allied Chemical Corporation, 61 Broadway, New York, N.Y. 10006; Hawthorne Towers, 36 Hawthorne Place, Montclair, N.J. 07042, U.S.A.
Telephone: 422-7300, Ext. 2273 (Office); 201-746-2764 (Home).

Ruckelshaus, William Doyle; American government official; b. 24 July 1934, Indianapolis, Ind.; s. of John K. and Marion (Doyle) Ruckelshaus; m. Jill E. Strickland 1962; one s. four d.; ed. Portsmouth Priory School, R.I. and Princeton and Harvard Univs.

Served with U.S. Army 53-55; Admitted to Indiana Bar 60; joined family firm Ruckelshaus, Bobbit & O'Connor 60-69; Partner Ruckelshaus, Beveridge, Fairbanks & Diamond (fmrly. Ruckelshaus, Beveridge & Fairbanks); Deputy Attorney-Gen., Ind. 60-62; Minority Attorney, Ind. State Senate 65-67; mem. Indiana House of Reps. 67-69; Asst. Attorney-Gen., U.S. Civil Div. 69-70; Dir. Environmental Protection Agency 70-73; Acting Dir. Fed. Bureau of Investigation 73; Deputy Attorney-Gen. 73; mem. Board of Dirs. Cummins Engine Co., Inc., Peabody-Galion Corpn., Church and Dwight Co. Inc.; mem. several U.S. bar asscns.

Publ. *Reapportionment—A Continuing Problem* 63.
(Office) 1 Farragut Square South, Washington, D.C. 20006; (Home) 11124 Luxmanor Road, Rockville, Md. 20852, U.S.A.

Ruda, José Maria, LL.D.; Argentine lawyer and diplomatist; b. 9 Aug. 1924, Buenos Aires; s. of José María Ruda and Margarita Comas de Ruda; m. María Haydée Arnold 1949; five c.; ed. Univ. de Buenos Aires and New York Univ.

Office of Legal Affairs, UN Secr. 51-55; Sec. of State, Salta Province, Argentina 56-57; Counsellor, La Paz 57-60; mem. Argentine Del. to UN 59-, Chair. Argentine Del. 65, Perm. Rep. to UN 66-70; Assoc. Prof. of Int. Law, Univ. of Buenos Aires 59-71, Prof. of Int. Law 71-; Under-Sec. of State for Foreign Affairs and Worship 70-; Visiting Prof. Colegio de Mexico 63; mem. Int. Law Comm. of UN 64-; Judge, Int. Court of Justice 73-; Del. to numerous int. confs.

Publs. include *The Powers of the General Assembly of the UN in Political and Security Matters* 56, *Jurisdiction of the International Court* 59, *Relations Between the United Nations and the Organization of American States in Connexion with International Peace and Security* 59, *A Study in Politics and Law: The United Nations* 62, *The Evolution of International Law.*
International Court of Justice, Peace Palace, The Hague, Netherlands; Callao 1707, Buenos Aires, Argentina.

Rudberg, Erik Gustav, D.SC.; Swedish physicist; b. 17 Nov. 1902, Stockholm; s. of Dr. Albert Rudberg and Emma Teresia Frederika (née Munck); m. Birgit Holmgren 1930; ed. Stockholm Univ., Göttingen Univ., King's Coll., London Univ.

Assistant, Stockholm Univ. 22-24, Lecturer 29; Asst. Nobel Inst. 24-30; Instructor in physics, M.I.T. 31-32, Asst. Prof. 32-36; Dir. of Applied Physics Research Laboratory, Allmänna Svenska Elektriska Aktiebolaget

36-39; Prof. and Head of Physics Dept., Chalmers Univ. of Tech., Gothenburg 39-45; Dir. Swedish Inst. of Metal Research 45-59; Perm. Sec. Royal Swedish Acad. of Sciences 59-72, Prof. Emer. 73-; Pres. European Physical Soc. 70-71; mem. Swedish Eng. Acad., Royal Acad. of Sciences; Hon. mem. Swedish Soc. of Metallurgy, Swedish Soc. of Mountaineers, Soc. française de Métallurgie; Foreign mem. Romanian Acad. of Sciences, Indian Acad. of Sciences; Liljevalch Fellow, Göttingen 24; Ramsay Fellow, London 25-27; Rockefeller Fellow, Franklin Inst., Philadelphia 30-31; Fellow, American Physical Soc.

Leisure interests: sailing, skiing, mountaineering, wildlife studies, carpentry.
Publs. scientific papers on electroemission, electron theory of metals, electron collisions, vapour pressure of metals, metallography, chemical reaction velocities, solid state physics.
Sjoevretsvaegen 48, S-15024 Roenninge, Sweden.

Rudenko, Roman Andreyevich; Soviet lawyer; b. 30 July 1907, Ukraine; ed. Moscow Legal Academy.

At the Procurator's Office 29-; Chief Soviet Prosecutor at the Nuremburg Trials 45-46; Procurator of the Ukraine 44-53; State Judiciary Counsellor, Procurator-Gen. of the U.S.S.R. 53-; Alt. mem. C.P.S.U. Cen. Cttee. 56-61, mem. 61-; Deputy to U.S.S.R. Supreme Soviet 50-; has attended Confs. of the Int. Asscn. of Democratic Lawyers; LL.D. (h.c.) Charles Univ. Prague and Humboldt Univ. Berlin; awarded Order of Lenin (five times), Order of the Red Banner of Labour, etc.

Office of the Procurator-General of the U.S.S.R., 15a Pushkinskaya Street, Moscow, U.S.S.R.

Rudenko, Marshal Sergei Ignatievich; Soviet air force officer; b. 20 Oct. 1904, Korob, Chernigov Region, Ukraine; ed. Zhukovsky Air Force Acad.

Commander of an air army, taking part in the fighting at Stalingrad, Kursk, Berlin, in Byelorussia 41-49; Chief of Staff of Air Force 49-58, First Deputy C.-in-C. Soviet Air Force 56-58; Chief of Gagarin Air Force Acad. 68-; Marshal of Aviation 55-; Hero of the Soviet Union; awarded Order of Lenin (four times), Gold Star Medal, Suvorov (three times), Red Banner (four times), Kutuzov, also Polish honours.

Ministry of Defence, 34 Maurice Thorez Embankment, Moscow, U.S.S.R.

Rudhart, Hans Wilhelm, DR. RER. POL.; German business executive; b. 30 Sept. 1902.

Vice-Pres. Gutehoffnungshütte Aktienverein and Gutehoffnungshütte Sterkrade AG; Pres. Employers' Feds.; mem. of management of German Industry Inst., Fed. Asscn. of German Industry, Trade Asscn. of Iron and Steel Industry, etc.; mem. or Pres. of Board of Dirs. Schwäbische Hüttenwerke G.m.b.H., Zahnräderfabrik Augsburg Renk AG, Eisenwerk Nürnberg AG, Vereinigte Aluminiumwerke AG, Bonn Gutehoffnungshütte Schwerte G.m.b.H., UTMAL, India, The Libyan Drilling and Servicing Co. Ltd., Associated Tunnelling Co. Ltd., London.

Publ. *Die preussische Staatsbank mit besonderer Berücksichtigung der letzten zwei Jahrzehnte.*
43 Essen-Bredeney, Am Tann 7, Federal Republic of Germany.

Rudnev, Konstantin Nikolayevich; Soviet politician; b. 1911; ed. Tula Engineering Inst.

Electrical fitter 29-30; Chief Eng. 35-48; Sr. Exec. Ministry of Defence Equipment 48-58; Chair. State Cttee. of Defence Equipment 58-61; Chair. State Cttee. for Co-ordination of Scientific Research Work 61-65; Deputy Chair. U.S.S.R. Council of Ministers 61-65; Minister of Instrument Making, Automation and Control Devices Industry 65-; mem. C.P.S.U. Central Cttee. 61-; Deputy, U.S.S.R. Supreme Soviet 62-; Hero of

Socialist Labour, Orders of Lenin, "Hammer and Sickle" Gold Medal, etc.
Ministry of Instrument Making, Automation and Control Devices Industry, Moscow, U.S.S.R.

Rudnicki, Adolf; Polish writer; b. 19 Feb. 1912, Warsaw; ed. Commercial School, Warsaw.
Soldier, Polish campaign 39; mem. resistance 42-44, Warsaw insurrection 44; Co-editor *Kuźnica* 45-49; State Prize 55, 66, Officer's Cross Order of Polonia Restituta 56.
Publs. *Szczury* (Rats), *żołnierze* (Soldiers), *Niekochana* (The Unloved One), *Lato* (Summer), *Ucieczka z Jasnej Polany* (Flight from Yasna Polyana), *żywe i martwe morze* (Living and Dead Seas), *Pałeczka czyli każdemu to na crym mu mniej zależy* (The Baton, or To Each What He Least Cares For), *Niebieskie kartki* (Blue Pages, 8 vols. of short stories and essays), *Krowa* (The Cow), *Złote okna* (Golden Windows), *Młode cierpienia* (The Young Sufferings), *Manfred* (drama), *50 opowiadań* (50 stories).
Ul. Kanonia 16/18m. 4, 00-278 Warsaw, Poland.
Telephone: 31-3609.

Rudolf, Tadeusz, M.ECON.; Polish politician; b. 22 Jan. 1926, Bochnia; ed. High School of Social Sciences, Party School, Polish United Workers' Party, and Univ. of Warsaw.
Worked in Cable Factory, Cracow 44; active mem. Fighting Youth Union and Polish Youth Union; First Sec. PUWP Town Cttee., Zakopane 48-50; Chair. Comm. for Youth Questions, PUWP Town Cttee., Warsaw 57; Sec. Cen. Cttee., Socialist Youth Union; Deputy Chief Organizational Dept., Cen. Cttee. of PUWP; 1st Sec. Voivodship Cttee., Kielce 68-72; Deputy to Seym 69-; Deputy mem. Cen. Cttee., PUWP 68-71, mem. 71-; Vice-Chair. Cen. Council of Trade Unions 72-74; Chair. Seym Comm. of Econ. Plan, Budget and Finance 73-74; Minister of Labour, Pay and Social Services Nov. 74-; Order of Banner of Labour 1st Class and others.
Ministerstwo Pracy, Płac i Spraw Socjalnych, ul. Nowogrodzka 1/3, 00-513 Warsaw, Poland.
Telephone: 28-77-34 (Office).

Rudolph, Paul Marvin, M.ARCH.; American architect; b. 23 Oct. 1918; ed. Alabama Polytechnic Inst., and Harvard Univ.
Fellow in Architecture, Harvard Univ. 41-42; Officer in Charge, Ship Construction, U.S. Naval Reserve, Brooklyn Navy Yard 43-46; partner, architectural firm of Twitchell & Rudolph, Sarasota (Florida) 47-51; architectural practice Sarasota, Cambridge, Newhaven 52-65; Boston, N.Y. 65-; Chair. Dept. of Architecture, Yale Univ. 58-65; numerous honours and awards including Best House of the Year Award, America Inst. of Architects 49, Outstanding Young Architects Award, São Paulo Int. Competition 54, House chosen by *Architectural Record* as one of fifty most significant buildings completed since 1900 56, Arnold Brunner Prize in Architecture, American Acad. of Arts and Letters 58, Boston Arts Festival Award for Commercial Building; Award of Merit A.I.A. Honors Award 62, 64, First Honor Award A.I.A. Honors Award 64, *Architectural Record* Award of Excellence for House Design 63.
Important projects include Good Design Exhibition (Chicago Merchandise Mart and New York Museum of Modern Art) 51, U.S. Embassy, Amman, Jordan 54, Art, Music and Drama Building, Wellesly Coll., Mass., Junior-Senior High School, Sarasota, Blue Cross-Blue Shield Inc. Headquarters Building, Boston, Greeley Memorial Laboratory, Yale Forestry School 57, Arts and Architecture Building, Yale Univ., Church Street Redevelopment Project, New Haven, Conn., Tuskegee Inst., Montgomery, Ala. 58, work at Yale 60, Auburn 61, and Endo Laboratories, Garden City, N.Y., Parking Garage, New Haven, Conn., I.B.M. Components Div.

Facilities, East Fishkill, N.Y., Elderly Housing, New Haven, Creative Arts Center for Colgate Univ., N.Y., New Town of Stafford Harbor, Virginia 67, Orange County Govt. Center, Goshen, N.Y. 67, New Haven Govt. Center 68.
26 West 57th Street, New York, N.Y., U.S.A.

Rudowski, Witold Janusz; Polish professor of surgery; b. 17 July 1918, Piotrków Trybunalski; s. of Maksymilian Rudowski, judge of Supreme Court of Poland and Stefania Rudowska; m. Irena Rutkowska 1940; two s. one d.; ed. Clandestine Univ., Warsaw.
Associate Prof. of Surgery, Warsaw Univ. 54-61, Prof. 61-; Consultant Surgeon and Senior Research Worker, Madame M. Curie Cancer Insts. in Warsaw 48-64; Dir. and Head, Dept. of Surgery, Inst. of Hematology and Blood Transfusion, Warsaw 64-; Chair. Scientific Council to Minister of Health and Social Welfare 70-; Expert WHO 75-; Vice-Pres. Int. Fed. of Surgical Colls., Pres. 75-; Corresp. mem. Polish Acad. of Sciences 73-, N. Pacific Surgeons' Soc. 74, Italian Soc. of Surgical Investigations 75; Hon. mem. W. African Coll. of Surgeons 75; Dr. h.c. Poznań Medical Acad. 75; Hon. Fellow, American Coll. of Surgeons 71, Royal Coll. of Surgeons of Edinburgh 72, Royal Coll. of Surgeons of England 73, Royal Coll. of Physicians and Surgeons of Canada 74; Gold Cross of Merit 56, Knight's Cross Order of Polonia Restituta 67, Partisans' Cross 70, Medal for Warsaw 70.
Leisure interests: literature, music.
Publs. 250 papers in Polish and other languages on cancer, clinical pathophysiology, burns and blood transfusion.
Aleja Armii Ludowej 17-1, 07632 Warsaw, Poland.
Telephone: 25-44-39 (Home); 49-85-06 (Office).

Rudziński, Witold; Polish musicologist and composer; b. 14 March 1913, Siebież; s. of Henryk and Maria Rudziński; m. Nina Rudzińska 1958; one s. two d.; ed. Wilno and Paris.
Professor, Wilno Conservatoire 39-42, Łódź Conservatoire 45-47; Dir. Dept. of Music, Ministry of Culture 47-48; Editor *Muzyka* 50-56; Prof. State Superior School of Music, Warsaw 57-; Officer and Commdr. Cross of Polonia Restituta, etc.
Works include Piano Concerto, two Symphonies, Symphonic Suite, two String Quartets, two Sonatas for piano and violin, cantata, flute quartet, song cycle, chamber works for piano, flute, 'cello, woodwind and percussion instruments; Operas: *Janko Muzykant*, *Komendant Paryża* (Commander of Paris), *Odprawa posłów greckich* (Dismissal of the Greek Envoys), *Sulamita* (Sulamith), *Chłopi* (The Peasants); Music poem *Dach świata* (Roof of the World) for recitative and orchestra; *Gaude Mater Polonia* for solo voice, choir, recitative and orchestra.
Leisure interests: history, linguistics.
Publs. Musical encyclopaedia, monographs on Moniuszko and Bartok.
Państwowa Wyższa Szkoła Muzyczna, ul. Okólnik 2, Warsaw; ul. Narbutta 50 m.6, 02541 Warsaw, Poland.
Telephone: 45 34 77.

Rueff, Jacques Léon; French economist; b. 23 Aug. 1896; ed. Ecole Polytechnique, Paris.
Inspector of Finance 23; mem. of Economic and Financial Section, L.N. Secretariat 27; Financial attaché to French Embassy, London 30; Prof. of Economics, Ecole libre des Sciences politiques, Paris 31; Asst. Dir. Mouvement Général des Fonds 34, Dir. 36; Vice-Gov. Bank of France 39-40; Pres. of Economic and Financial Del. to Mil. Mission for German and Austrian Affairs Dec. 44; economic adviser to C.-in-C., Germany 45; French Del. to Reparations Comm., Moscow July 45; Pres. of Paris Conf. on Reparations Dec. 45; Pres. of Inter-allied Reparations Agency in Brussels Jan. 46; Del. to Peace Conf. in Paris and to second Assembly of

U.N.; mem. of U.N. Economic and Employment Comm.; Judge Court of Justice of European Steel and Coal Community 52-58; Judge, Court of European Communities 58-62; Pres. Cttee. for Reform of French Financial Situation 58, Cttee. for Suppression of Obstacles to Econ. Expansion 59; mem. Econ. and Social Council 62; Hon. Pres. Société d'Economie Politique de Paris; Prof. of Econs., Institut des Sciences politiques, Paris; Hon. Vice-Gov. Bank of France; mem. Académie Française, Acad. des Sciences morales et politiques, Chancelier de l'Institut de France; Grand Croix Légion d'Honneur; Croix de Guerre (3 citations).
Publs. include: *Des Sciences physiques aux Sciences morales* 22 (translated into English), *Théorie des Phénomènes monétaires* 27, *L'Assurance-chômage* 31, *L'Ordre social* 45, *Epître aux dirigistes* 49, *Une cause du désordre mondial: l'état actuel du système des paiements internationaux*, *La régulation monétaire et le problème institutionnel de la monnaie* 53, *Discours sur le Crédit*, *L'Age de l'inflation* 63 (trans. into English), *Le lancinant problème de la balance des paiements* 65 (trans. into English), *Discours de reception à l'Académie française*, *Les fondements philosophiques des systèmes économiques* 67, *Les Dieux et les Rois* 67 (trans. into English), *Des Sciences physiques aux Sciences morales: un essai de 1922 reconsideré en 1969*, *Le péché monétaire de l'Occident* 71 (trans. into English), *Combat pour l'ordre financier* 72, *La Réforme du système monétaire international* 73, *La Création du Monde, Comédie-ballet en cinq journées*.
51 rue de Varenne, Paris 7e, France.

Ruehmann, Heinz; German actor and stage director; b. 7 March 1902, Essen; *m.* Hertha Feiler 1939; one *s.*; ed. Secondary Modern School.
Stage actor, Breslau, Hanover, Berlin and Munich 22-60; with Theatre of Vienna 60-; acted in films: *Der Mann der nicht nein sagen konnte, Der eiserne Gustav, Die Pauker, Menschen im Hotel, Ein Mann geht durch die Wand, Der Jugendrichter, Mein Schulfreund, Der brave Soldat Schwejk, Das schwarze Schaf, Der Lügner, Max der Taschendieb: Lauter Lügen, Lauter Liebe, Sophienlund, Der Engel mit dem Saitenspiel, Die kupferne Hochzeit, Hauptmann von Köpenick*; Hon. mem. Inst. Artists' Lodge; Grosses Verdienstkreuz; Kunstpreis of Berlin 57, Ernst-Lubitsch Prize of Screenwriters Club 59, German Film Critics' Prize for *Der brave Soldat Schwejk* 61, Filmband in Gold Prize of the Film Fed. for *Das Schwarze Schaf*.
8022 Geiselgasteig/Obb., Robert Kochstr. 20, Federal Republic of Germany.

Ruete, Hans-Helmuth, DR.JUR.; German diplomatist; b. 21 Dec. 1914, Petersburg; *s.* of Dr. med. Alfred E. and Margarita (née Bohnstedt) Ruete; *m.* Ruth Arfsten 1948; one *s.* two *d.*; ed. Univs. of Marburg, Kiel, Lausanne and Tokyo.
Assistant, Univ. of Marburg 46-49; Judge 49; Ministry of Justice 50; joined diplomatic service 52; Second Sec., Tokyo 52-56; Foreign Office, Bonn 56-60; Prof. Univ. of Marburg 56-60; Harvard Univ. Center for Int. Affairs 60-61; Consul-Gen., Calcutta 61-64; Deputy Head of Political Dept., Ministry of Foreign Affairs 64, Head of Political Dept. II 66-70; Amb. to France June 70-72, to Poland 72-.
Leisure interests: literature, music (plays piano and 'cello), theatre.
Publ. *Der Einfluss des abendländischen Rechts auf die Rechtsgestaltung in China und Japan* 40.
Embassy of the Federal Republic of Germany, Dąbrowiecka 30, Warsaw, Poland.
Telephone: 17-30-12.

Ruf, Sep; German architect; b. 9 March 1908; ed. Technische Hochschule, Munich.
Freelance architect 31-; Prof., Acad. of Fine Arts,

Nuremberg 47, Acad. of Fine Arts, Munich 53-; Cultural Prize of City of Nuremberg
Major works include: branches of Bayerische Staatsbank, Nuremberg and Erlangen; new buildings for Acad. of Fine Arts, Nuremberg; Maxburg Admin. Buildings (with Prof. Theo Pabst), Munich; German Pavilion, Brussels World Fair (with Prof. Egon Eiermann); new building for Church of St. John of Capistran, Munich; Max-Planck-Institut für Physik und Astrophysik (Heisenberg Inst.), Munich; renovation and extensions of the Germanische Nationalmuseum, Nuremberg; admin. bldgs. of the Deutsche Forschungsgemeinschaft, Bad Godesberg and Berliner Handelsgesellschaft, Frankfurt/Main; reception rooms for residence of Federal Chancellor, Bonn; extensions to the Bayerische Staatsbibliothek, Munich; Seminarkapelle, Fulda; München Hilton Hotel, Esso Motor-Hotel München, IBM Rechenzentrale u. Verwaltungsgebäude München, Technisches Zentrum und Verwaltungsgebäude Bayerische Vereinsbank München.
8022 Grünwald/Obb., Hubertusstrasse 66, Federal Republic of Germany.
Telephone: 6-49-21-66.

Rugambwa, H.E. Cardinal Laurian; Tanzanian ecclesiastic; b. 12 July 1912; *s.* of D. Rushubirwa and A. Mukaboshezi; ed. Katigondo Seminary, De Propaganda Fide Univ., Rome.
Ordained priest 43; missionary work in East Africa; studied canon law in Rome; Bishop of Rutabo 52; created Cardinal by Pope John XXIII 60; transferred to Bukoba Diocese 60, to Dar es Salaam Archdiocese 69; Hon. LL.D. Univ. of Notre Dame, St. Joseph's Coll., Philadelphia, Rosary Hill Coll., Hon. H.L.D. Coll. of New Rochelle. Hon. Dr. Catholic Univ. of America, Georgetown Univ., Washington; mem. Comm. for Revision of Canon Law; mem. Knights of Columbus, Sacred Congregation for the causes of saints.
St. Joseph, P.O. Box 167, Dar es Salaam, Tanzania, East Africa.
Telephone: Dar es Salaam 22031.

Ruggiero, Renato; Italian diplomatist; b. 9 April 1930, Naples; ed. Univ. of Naples.
Entered Diplomatic Service 55; First Vice-Consul, São Paulo 56; Second Sec., Italian Embassy, Moscow 59, First Sec., Washington, D.C. 62; with Ministry of Foreign Affairs 64-65; Counsellor, Italian Embassy, Belgrade 66; Chef de Cabinet, Ministry of Foreign Affairs 68; First Counsellor for Social Affairs, Perm. Mission to European Communities 69; Chef de Cabinet, then Principal Counsellor to Pres. Comm. of European Communities 70-73; Dir.-Gen. of Regional Policy 73-; Knight, Order of Merit.
Directorate-General of Regional Policy, Commission of the European Communities, 200 rue de la Loi, 1049 Brussels, Belgium.

Ruiz Jarabo, Francisco; Spanish judge and politician; b. 1902; *m.*; seven *c.*; ed. Cardinal Cisneros Inst., Madrid, Univ. Central de Madrid.
Judicial career 25-; Labour Magistrate 39-42, Dir.-Gen. of Labour 42-44; Judge Fourth Tribunal, Supreme Court 44-51; Under-Sec. Ministry of Labour 51-54; Pres. Sixth Tribunal, Supreme Court 54-67; Pres. Supreme Court 68-73; Minister of Justice 73-75; mem. Royal Acad. of Jurisprudence and Legislation 61-; Prof. of Procedural Labour Law, Escuela Social de Madrid; Grand Cross, Order of Isabel la Católica, Order of San Raimundo de Penafort, of Civil Merit, Order of Cisneros.
c/o Ministerio de Justicia, Madrid, Spain.

Rujirawongse, Gen. Prasert; Thai army officer and politician; b. 4 Dec. 1911, Chadaburi; *s.* of Nim and Jongjin Rujirawongse; *m.* Khunying Noi Rujirawongse; four *s.* five *d.*; ed. Royal Mil. Cadet Acad., Artillery School for Officers and Nat. Defence Coll.

Commissioned 32; Deputy Dir.-Gen. of Police 57, Dir.-Gen. 63, also Deputy Minister of Interior 63; Minister of Public Health 69, 72-73; Dir. of Civil Admin. Nov. 70; Dir. of Public Health and Educ. of Nat. Exec. Council 71-72; Chair. Bank of Ayudhya; Knight Grand Cordon, Order of Crown of Thailand, Order of White Elephant; Victory Medal, Chakra Mala Medal and other decorations.
Leisure interests: fund raising for hospitals, health clinics, schools and temples and for aiding poor students.
Bank of Ayudhya Ltd., P.O. Box 491, Bangkok, Thailand.
Telephone: 49254 (Home).

Rukmini, Devi; Indian dancer and arts patron; b. 1904, Madurai; d. of Nilakanta and Seshammal Sastri; m. Dr. G. S. Arundale 1920 (deceased).
Started dancing under Anna Pavlova; extensive tours throughout India and Europe with dance recitals and lectures; lecture visits to U.S.A.; also lectures and writes on Theosophy, Religion, Art, Culture, Educ., etc.; Dir. Arundale Training Centre for Teachers, Int. Soc. for the Prevention of Cruelty to Animals, London for India, Dr. V. Swaminatha Iyer Tamil Library; Head Int. Theosophical Centre, Huizen, Holland; Pres. The Bharata Samaj, Indian Vegetarian Congress, Kalakshetra (Int. Art Centre), Besant Centenary Trust, Young Men's Indian Asscn.; Chair. Animal Welfare Board and mem. of various int. animal welfare orgs.; fmr. mem. of Rajya Sabha (Parl.); decorations: Padma Bhushan 56, Sangit Natak Akademi Award 57, Queen Victoria Silver Medal of R.S.P.C.A. 58, Prani Mitra (Animal Welfare Board) 68; D.H. (Wayne Univ.) 60; hon. doctorate (Rabindra Bharathi Univ.) 71; Desikothama (Viswabharati Univ.) 72; Fellowship, Sangit Natak Akademi 68.
Productions: *The Light of Asia, Incidents from the Life of Bishma, Karaikal Ammayar* (Tamil), *Kutrala Kuravanji* (temple drama), *Kumara Sambhavm, Sita Swayamvaram, Sri Rama Vanagamanam Paduka Pattabhishekham, Sabari Moksham, Choodamani Pradhanam, Maha Pattabhishekham, Gita Govindam, Usha Parinayam, Andal Charitram, Kannapar Kuravanji, Rukmini Kalajanam, Shyama, Krishnamari Kuravanii, Dhruva Charithram.*
Publs. *Yoga: Art or Science, Message of Beauty to Civilisation, Women as Artists, Dance and Music, The Creative Spirit, Art and Education.*
Animal Welfare Board of India, Gandhinagar, Madras-20; Kalakshetra, Madras-41, India.
Telephone: 74307 (Office); 74836 (Home).

Rumbold, Sir (Horace) Algernon (Fraser), K.C.M.G., C.I.E.; British government official (retd.); b. 1906, North Berwick, Scotland; s. of Col. William Edwin Rumbold, C.M.G.; m. Margaret Adél Hughes 1946; two d.; ed. Wellington Coll., and Christ Church, Oxford.
Assistant Principal, India Office 29, Private Sec. to Parl. Under-Sec. of State for India 30-33, to Perm. Under-Sec. of State 33-34, Principal 34, Asst. Sec. 43; Commonwealth Relations Office 47; Deputy High Commr. in South Africa 49-53; Asst. Under-Sec. of State, Commonwealth Relations Office 54-58, Deputy Under-Sec. of State 58-66; Chair. Cttee. on Inter-Territorial Questions, Central Africa 63; Deputy Chair. Air Transport Licensing Board 71-72.
Shortwoods, West Clandon, Surrey, England.
Telephone: Clandon 757.

Rumiantsev, Aleksey Matveyevich; Soviet journalist and politician; b. 16 Nov. 1905, Mintsovo, Galich District, Kostroma Region; ed. Kharkov Economics Inst.
Commissariat of Agriculture, later Justice, Ukraine 26-30; Dir. Inst. of Econs., U.S.S.R. Acad. of Sciences, Head Social Science Dept., Ukrainian Acad. of Sciences 30-43; mem. C.P.S.U. 40-; party work, Kharkov Regional Cttee., Communist Party of Ukraine 43-52;

on staff of Central Cttee. of C.P.S.U. 52-56; Editor-in-Chief *Kommunist* 55-58, *Problemy Mira i Sotsialisma* (Problems of Peace and Socialism) 58-64, *Pravda* Nov. 64-65; Sec. Econ. Branch of the U.S.S.R. Acad. of Sciences 65-67; Vice-Pres. U.S.S.R. Acad. of Sciences 67-71; Dir. Inst. of Concrete Investigations, Acad. of Sciences 68-71; mem. Presidium U.S.S.R. Acad. of Sciences 71-; mem. Cen. Cttee. of C.P.S.U. 52-; corresp. mem. U.S.S.R. Acad. of Sciences 60-66, mem. 66-, Vice-Pres. 66.
U.S.S.R. Academy of Sciences, 14 Leninsky Prospekt, Moscow, U.S.S.R.

Rumor, Mariano; Italian politician; b. 16 June 1915, Vicenza (Venezia).
Member of Parl. 48-; Deputy Sec. Christian Democrat Party 54-64, Sec.-Gen. 64-65, now Political Sec.; fmr. Under-Sec. for Agriculture, fmr. Under-Sec. to the Presidency; Minister of Agriculture 59-63, of Interior 63; Pres. European Union of Christian Democrats 65-; Prime Minister of Italy 68-69, 69-70, March-July 70, 73-74; Minister of Interior 72-73, of Foreign Affairs Nov. 74-.
Ministry of Foreign Affairs, Piazzale della Farnesina, Rome, Italy.

Rumsfeld, Donald H.; American government official; b. 9 July 1932, Chicago; s. of George and Jeannette Rumsfeld; m. Joyce Pierson 1954; one s. two d.; ed. Princeton Univ.
Administrative Asst. to Congressman Dennison 58; mem. 88th-91st Congresses; Republican; Dir. Office of Econ. Opportunity 69-70; Dir. Cost of Living Council, Counsellor to Pres. 71-73; Amb. to NATO 73-74; Asst. to Pres. Ford 74-75; Sec. of Defense Nov. 75-; mem. Cabinet 69-72, 74-.
Leisure interests: sports, history and reading.
Department of Defense, The Pentagon, Washington, D.C. 20301, U.S.A.

Runciman, The Hon. Sir Steven (James Cochran Stevenson), Kt., M.A., F.B.A.; British historian; b. 7 July 1903, Northumberland; s. of 1st Viscount Runciman and Hilda Stevenson; ed. Eton Coll., and Trinity Coll., Cambridge.
Fellow Trinity Coll., Cambridge 27-38; Lecturer Cambridge Univ. 31-38; Press Attaché, British Legation, Sofia 40-41; Prof. of Byzantine Studies, Istanbul Univ. 42-45; Rep. of British Council, Greece 45-47; Chair. Anglo-Hellenic League 51-67; Trustee, British Museum 60-67; Pres. British Inst. of Archaeology at Ankara 60-75; Fellow British Acad. 57; Hon. Fellow Trinity Coll., Cambridge; Foreign mem. American Philosophical Soc. 65; Kt. Commdr. Order of the Phoenix (Greece); Hon. Litt.D. (Cambridge, Chicago, Durham, London, Oxford, St. Andrews and Birmingham); Hon. LL.D. (Glasgow); Hon. D.Phil. (Salonika); Hon. D.D. (Wabash, U.S.A.); Silver PEN award 69; Apptd. by Oecumenical Patriarch, Grand Orator of the Great Church 70.
Publs. *The Emperor Romanus Lecapenus* 29, *The First Bulgarian Empire* 30, *Byzantine Civilisation* 33, *The Medieval Manichee* 47, *History of the Crusades* (3 vols.) 51-54, *The Eastern Schism* 55, *The Sicilian Vespers* 58, *The White Rajahs* 60, *The Fall of Constantinople 1453* 65, *The Great Church in Captivity* 68, *The Last Byzantine Renaissance* 70, *The Orthodox Churches and the Secular State* 72, *Byzantine Style and Civilization* 75.
Elshieshields, Lockerbie, Dumfriesshire, Scotland.
Telephone: Lochmaben 280.

Runciman of Doxford, 2nd Viscount, cr. 37; **Walter Leslie Runciman,** Bt., A.F.C., O.B.E., M.A.; British shipowner and industrialist; b. 26 Aug. 1900, Newcastle upon Tyne; s. of 1st Viscount Runciman of Doxford, P.C.; m. Katherine Schuyler Garrison 1932; one s.; ed. Eton and Trinity Coll., Cambridge.
Chairman, Walter Runciman & Co. Ltd., Anchor Line Ltd.; Pres. Royal Inst. of Naval Architects 51-61;

Chair. North of England Shipowners' Asscn. 31-32; Chair. Council, Armstrong Coll., Durham Univ. 35-37; Dir.-Gen. British Overseas Airways Corpn. 40-43; Air Attaché, Teheran 43-46; Pres. Chamber of Shipping of the U.K. 52, Chair. Gen. Council of British Shipping 52; Chair. Trustees Nat. Maritime Museum 63-73; Hon. D.C.L. (Durham).
Leisure interests: sailing, shooting.
46 Abbey Lodge, Park Road, London, N.W.8, England.

Runcorn, Stanley Keith, M.A., SC.D., PH.D., F.R.S.; British physicist; b. 19 Nov. 1922, Southport, Lancs.; s. of W. H. Runcorn and Lily Idena Roberts; unmarried; ed. George V Grammar School, Southport and Gonville and Caius Coll., Cambridge.
Experimental Officer, Radar Research and Devt. Establishment, Malvern 43-46; Asst. Lecturer, Univ. of Manchester 46-48, Lecturer 48-49; Asst. Dir. of Research in Geophysics, Cambridge Univ. 50-55; Fellow, Gonville and Caius Coll., Cambridge; Prof. of Physics and Head of School of Physics, Univ. of Newcastle upon Tyne; recipient lunar samples from *Apollo* missions; Rutherford Memorial Lecturer, Kenya, Tanzania and Uganda 70; Hon. D.Sc. Utrecht 69 and Ghent Univs. 71; Vetlesen prize, Columbia Univ. 71; Napier Shaw Prize, Royal Meteorological Soc. 59, Charles Chree Medal and Prize, Inst. of Physics 69.
Publs. Editor of *Continental Drift* 62, *Methods & Techniques in Geophysics* (2 vols.) 66, *Mantles of the Earth and Terrestrial Planets* 68, *The Application of Modern Physics to the Earth & Planetary Interiors* 69, *Palaeogeophysics* 70; Co-Editor of *Physics and Chemistry of the Earth* (Vols. 1-7) 56-66, *Methods in Palaeomagnetism* 67, *Magnetism and the Cosmos* 67, *Palaeogeophysics* 70, *The Moon* 71; author of approximately 80 scientific papers.
School of Physics, University of Newcastle upon Tyne, Newcastle upon Tyne, NE1 7RU; Home: 16 Moorside Court, Fenham, Newcastle upon Tyne, England.
Telephone: Newcastle 28511 (Office).

Rupert, Anthony Edward, M.SC.; South African business executive; b. 4 Oct. 1916, Graaff Reinet; s. of John P. Rupert and Hester A. van Eeden; m. H. Goote 1941; two s. one d.; ed. Volks High School, Graaff Reinet, and Univs. of Pretoria and South Africa.
Lecturer in Chemistry, Pretoria Univ. 39-41; Founder, Chair. and Managing Dir. Rembrandt Group of Companies (tobacco) 48-; Chair. Technical and Industrial Investments Ltd. 50-; Pres. S.A. Nature Foundation, Nat. Devt. and Management Foundation; Chair. Historical Homes of South Africa Ltd.; Fellow, Int. Acad. of Management; Dir. South African Reserve Bank; Hon. Fellow, Coll. of Medicine of South Africa; mem. South African Chemical Inst., Exec. Council World Wildlife Fund, South African Inst. of Management, South African Acad. for Arts and Science; Hon. Industrial Adviser to the Govt. of Lesotho; Hon. Prof. Univ. of Pretoria 64-; Hon. D.Sc. (Pretoria), Hon. D.Comm. (Stellenbosch).
Leisure interests: research, art.
Publs. *Progress through Partnership, Leaders on Leadership, Inflation—How to Curb Public Enemy Number One*.
Office: Alexander Street, Stellenbosch; Home: 13 Thibault Street, Mostertsdrift, Stellenbosch, South Africa.
Telephone: Stellenbosch 2331 (Office).

Ruppel, Aloys (**Leonhard**), DR.PHIL.; German professor; b. 21 June 1882, Neuhof, near Fulda; s. of Kilian and Luzia Ruppel; m. Thea Baumeister 1919; two s. two d.; ed. Univs. of Würzburg, Marburg, Berlin, Münster and Strasbourg.
Scholarship, Prussian Historical Inst., Rome 09-10; Asst. and Dir. State Archives for Lorraine, Metz 11-19; Dir. Country Library Fulda 19-20; Dir. City Library and Archives, Mainz 20-34 and 44-50; Dir. Gutenberg

Museum 20-62; Prof. Emer. Univ. of Mainz 47-; Great Gold Medal, Ibero-American Exhbn., Seville 30; Grand Prix Int. Exhbn. Paris 37; Gutenberg Medal City of Mainz 47; O.M. German Fed. Repub. 52; mem. Acad. at Erfurt; Hon. Fellow, Pierpont Morgan Library, N.Y.; Hon. Citizen of Mainz, Oberrodenbach and Neuhof; Goldener Ehrenring, Int. Gutenberg-Gesellschaft; Bundesverdienstorden, Grosses Bundesverdienstkreuz; Chevalier, Légion d'Honneur, Officier de l'Ordre de la Couronne de Belgique; Chevalier Ordre Nat. de la République du Sénégal; Commdr., Order du Cèdre du Liban; Dr. Litt. h.c., Dr. Litt. et jur. h.c.
Publs. include: *Johannes Gutenberg, sein Leben und sein Werk* 47, *Grosse Drucker* 53, *Haben die Chinesen und Koreaner die Buchdruckerkunst erfunden?* 55, *Druckte Gutenberg vor seiner Bibel ein grösseres Werk?* 55, *The Wandering Legend of the Theft of the Art of Printing, Rettet das Grab Gutenbergs* 56, *Gutenberg—Kleine Biographie* 57, *Die Technik Gutenbergs und ihre Vorstufen* 62, *Gutenberg und Columbus, die Väter der Neuzeit* 64, *Die Stadt Mainz und ihr grosser John Gutenberg* 64, *Wer war der wirkliche Erfinder der Druckkunst* 64, *40. Jahre Gutenberg—Jahrbuch* 69, *Vollständige Bibliographie von Widman* 70; Editor *Int. Gutenberg Jahrbuch* 26-.
Fischtorplatz 15, 65 Mainz, Federal Republic of Germany.
Telephone: 26278 (Home).

Rush, Kenneth, A.B., J.D.; American lawyer, diplomatist and businessman; b. 17 Jan. 1910, Walla Walla, Wash.; s. of David C. and Emma K. Kidwell Rush; m. Jane Gilbert Smith 1937; three s. one d.; ed. Univ. of Tennessee, and Yale Univ. Law School.
Associate Chadbourne, Stanchfield & Levy (now Chadbourne, Parke, Whiteside & Wolff) 32-36; joined Union Carbide Corpn. April-Sept. 36 and Aug. 37-July 69, Vice-Pres. 49-61, Exec. Vice-Pres. 61-66, Pres. 66-69, mem. Exec. Cttee. 66-69; Dir. Union Carbide Corpn. 58-69; Asst. Prof. of Law, Duke Univ. Law School 36-37; Dir. U.S. Council Int. Chamber of Commerce 55-59, American Sugar Co. (now Amstar Corpn.) 62-69, Foreign Policy Asscn. 64-69; Dir. and mem. Exec. Cttee., Manufacturing Chemists Asscn. 65-67, Chair. 66-67; Dir. Bankers Trust Co. 66-69, Bankers Trust New York Corpn. 66-69; Trustee Inst. of Int. Educ. 68-69; Gov. The Pinnacle Club 66-69; Sec.-Treas. and Trustee Grand Central Art Galleries Inc. 51-69; mem. American Bar Asscn., Devt. Council, Univ. of Tennessee, Council on Foreign Relations, Industries Advisory Cttee. of the Advertising Council Inc. 66-69, Public Advisory Cttee. on U.S. Trade Policy of L. B. Johnson 68-69, U.S. Dept. of Commerce Advisory Cttee. on Foreign Direct Investment Program 69, Pilgrims of the United States; Amb. to Fed. Germany 69-72; Deputy Sec. of Defense 72-73; Deputy Sec. of State 73-74; Acting Sec. State Sept. 73; Counsellor to the Pres. for Economic Policy 74; mem. Nat. Security Council; Chair. Council on Int. Econ. Policy, the President's Cttee. on East-West Trade Policy, President's Food Cttee., Council for Wage and Price Stability 74; Chair. Joint Presidential-Congressional Steering Cttee. for Conference on Inflation Sept. 74; Amb. to France 74-; Gov. American Red Cross 72-74; Chair. Board of Foreign Service 73-74; Grand Cross, Order of Merit, Germany 72; Dept. of Defense Medal for Distinguished Public Service 73.
Leisure interest: golf.
American Embassy, 2 avenue Gabriel, 75008 Paris, France.
Telephone: 265-7400.

Rushton, William Albert Hugh, F.R.S., M.R.C.S. (LOND.), SC.D., PH.D.; British physiologist; b. 8 Dec. 1901, London; s. of William Rushton and Alice née Amsler; m. Marjorie Glasson Kendrick 1930; two s. two d.; ed. Gresham's School, Holt, Emmanuel Coll., Cambridge, and Univ. Coll. Hospital, London.

Stokes Student, Pembroke Coll., Cambridge 27-29; Johnson Foundation Fellow, Univ. of Pennsylvania 29-31; Research Fellow, Emmanuel Coll., Cambridge 30-32, 35-37, Lecturer in Physiology, Univ. of Cambridge 35-53, Dir. of Medical Studies, Trinity Coll., Cambridge 36-66, Fellow of Trinity 38-; Reader in Physiology, Univ. of Cambridge 53-56, Prof. of Visual Physiology 66-68; Distinguished Research Prof. Florida State Univ. 68-75; Visiting Resident Prof. Univ. of Sydney and Australian Nat. Univ. Canberra 73-74; Pres. Soc. Psychical Research 69-71; Fellow of the Royal Soc. 48; Foreign Hon. mem. American Acad. of Arts and Sciences 63, Swedish Royal Soc. 69; awarded Prentice Medal of American Acad. of Optometry 63, Newton Medal of the Colour Group 65, Feldberg Prize 67, Royal Medal of Royal Soc. for Biological Sciences 70, Acad. Medal for Journalism 70, Proctor Medal of American Asscn. for Research in Opthalmology 71, Silliman Lecturer, Yale Univ. 66, Waynflete Lecturer, Oxford 68; Fogarty Scholar (American Nat. Inst. of Health) 72-73; Hon. D.Sc. (Case Western Reserve Univ.) 69.
Leisure interest: music (viola and bassoon).
Publs. include 35 papers in *Journal of Physiology* on nerve excitation and conduction 27-51, 140 on visual pigments and mechanism of vision 51-.
Trinity College, Cambridge, England.
Telephone: Cambridge 58201.

Rusinek, Michał; Polish writer; b. 29 Sept. 1904, Cracow; s. of Piotr and Maria Rusinek; m. Josephine Rusinek 1932; two d.; ed. Cracow Univ.
Director Acad. of Letters, Warsaw 34-39; prisoner at Mauthausen concentration camp during the war; Head of Dept. Ministry of Culture and Art 46-48; Sec.-Gen. of Polish PEN Club 46-; Vice-Pres. Polish Writers Union, Warsaw 56-; Vice-Pres. Union of Polish Authors and Composers; Hon. Chair. Int. Writers' Fund, London PEN Club; Vice-Pres. Centre Société Européenne de Culture (SEC); Man. Dir. Authors Agency; Editor-in-Chief *Polish Literature—Littérature Polonaise*; Literary Prize of Cracow 34; Gold Cross of Merit 47; Chevalier's Cross of Polonia Restituta 56, Commdr.'s Cross 59; Order of Banner of Labour, 2nd Class 67, etc.
Leisure interests: chess, gardening (roses).
Publs. novels: *Burza nad brukiem, Człowiek z bramy, Ziemia miodem płynąca, Pluton z Dzikiej Łąki, Z barykady w doline głodu, Wiosna admirała, Muszkieter z Itamariki, Królestwo pychy, Niebieskie ptaki, Zielone złoto, Kolorowe podróże, Prawo jesieni, Igraszki Nieba, Malowane życie, Opowieści niezmyślone, Ziemia Kopernika, Dzika Plaża;* plays: *Kobieta we mgle, Pawilon pod sosnami, Jedna ojczyzna, Dwie Ewy;* screenplay for *Pierwszy start.*
Ul. Odolańska 44, 02-562 Warsaw, Poland.
Telephone: 45-03-21.

Rusk, Dean, M.A.; American former Secretary of State; b. 9 Feb. 1909; ed. Davidson Coll., N.C., St. John's Coll., Oxford, and Univ. of Calif. Law School.
Associate Prof. of Govt., Mills Coll. Calif. 34-38, Dean of Faculty 38-40, mil. service 40-46; Asst. Chief Div. of Int. Security Affairs, U.S. Dept. of State 46; Special Asst. to Sec. of War 46-47; Dir. of Office of UN Affairs 47-49, Asst. Sec. of State 49, Deputy Under-Sec. of State 49-50, Asst. Sec. of State for Far Eastern Affairs 50-52; Pres. The Rockefeller Foundation 52-61; Sec. of State 61-69; Prof. of Int. Law, Univ. of Georgia 69-; Pres. Gen. Educ. Board 52-61; mem. Asscn. of American Rhodes Scholars, American Soc. of Int. Law, Council on Foreign Relations; awards include Legion of Merit with Oak Leaf Cluster and Cecil Peace Prize 33; Hon. LL.D. (18 univs. and colls.); Hon. L.H.D. (3 univs. and colls.); Hon. D.C.L. Oxon. 62, Hon. Fellow (St. John's Coll., Oxford); Democrat.
University of Georgia, Athens, Georgia, U.S.A.

Russell, Sir Archibald Edward, Kt., C.B.E., D.SC., F.R.AE.S., F.A.I.A.A., F.R.S.; British aircraft engineer and executive; b. 30 May 1904, Wotton-under-Edge, Glos.; ed. Bristol Univ.
Joined The Bristol Aeroplane Co. Ltd. 26, Chief Engineer of Aircraft Div. 43, elected to the Board 51, assumed title of Chief Engineer (Aircraft) 55, Dir. and Chief Engineer of Bristol Aircraft Ltd. 56, Technical Dir. Filton Div. of British Aircraft Corpn. 60-69, Man. Dir. Filton Div. 66-69, then Chair. 67-69; fmr. Dir. of British Aircraft Corpn. Ltd. and British Chair. of Anglo-French Concorde Cttee. of Dirs. (Aircraft).
Glendower House, Clifton Park, Bristol 8, England.

Russell, Donald Joseph; American businessman; b. 3 Jan. 1900, Denver, Colo.; s. of Donald M. Russell and Josephine Nunan; m. Mary L. Herring 1921; two d.; ed. Stanford Univ.
With Southern Pacific Co. 20-72, Asst. to Pres. 41, Vice-Pres. 41-51, Exec. Vice-Pres. 51, Pres. 52-64, Chair. 64-72, Hon. Dir. 72-; Hon. Dir. Emer. Tenneco Inc.; Founding Dir. Stanford Research Inst.; mem. Tulane Univ. Board of Visitors; Hon. mem. The Business Council.
Home: 2298 Pacific Avenue, San Francisco, Calif. 94115; Office: One Market Street, San Francisco, Calif. 94105, U.S.A.

Russell, Donald Stuart; American lawyer and politician; b. 22 Feb. 1906; ed. Univ. of Michigan.
Admitted to S. Carolina Bar 28; legal practice 30-42; mem. Price Adjustment Board, War Dept., Wash. 42; Asst. to Dir. Econ. Stabilisation 42, Asst. to Dir. War Mobilisation 43; U.S. Army 44; Deputy Dir. Office of War Mobilisation Reconversion 45; Asst. Sec. of State 45-47; Pres. Univ. of S. Carolina 52-57; legal practice 57-62; Gov. of S. Carolina 62-65; Senator from S. Carolina 65-66; Fed. Judge (Fourth Circuit) 66-; Democrat.
716 Otis Boulevard, Spartanburg, South Carolina 29302, U.S.A.

Russell, Francis Henry, A.B., LL.B., LL.D.; American lawyer and diplomatist; b. 1 Oct. 1904, Cambridge, Mass.; s. of James P. Russell and Edith B. Pratt; m. Ruth A. Libbey 1932; one s. one d.; ed. Tufts Coll., and Harvard Law School.
Private Law practice 29-41; Chief Div. of World Trade Intelligence Dept. of State 41-45; Dir. Office of Public Affairs 45-52, and Chair. Nat. Conf. on American Foreign Policy Dept. of State 49-50-51; Counsellor, Embassy, Tel-Aviv 52-53, Chargé d'Affaires 53-54; Special Asst. to the Sec. of State 55-56; Amb. to New Zealand 57-61, to Ghana 61-62, to Tunisia 62-69; U.S. del. Colombo Plan Ministerial Conf. 59; Amb. in Residence, Fletcher School of Law and Diplomacy, Tufts Univ. 70-.
Leisure interests: archaeology, farming.
55 Hill Road, Belmont, Mass., U.S.A.
Telephone: 617-484-1971.

Russell, George, B.S.; American automobile executive; b. 15 March 1905, Glasgow, Scotland; s. of James C. Russell and Elizabeth S. Chapman; m. Mary Love Rose 1936; one s. one d.; ed. Univ. of Minnesota.
Treasurer, Gen. Motors Corpn. 51-56, Vice-Pres. (Finance) and Dir. 56, Exec. Vice-Pres. and Dir. 58, Vice-Chair. of Board and Chair. Finance Cttee. 67-70, Dir. mem. Finance Cttee. and Public Policy Cttee. 70-74; Dir. Kennecott Copper Corpn., S.S. Kresge Co., Nat. Bank of Detroit; Trustee, Kresge Foundation; Hon. LL.D. (Univ. of Strathclyde).
Leisure interests: golf, travel.
283 Lone Pine Road, Bloomfield Hills, Mich. 48013, U.S.A.
Telephone: 313-644-8154.

Russell, Admiral James Sargent; American naval officer; b. 22 March 1903, Tacoma, Wash.; s. of Ambrose J. Russell and Loella J. Sargent; m. 1st Dorothy Johnson 1929 (deceased 1965), 2nd Geraldine Haus Rahn 1966; two s.; ed. Naval Acad., Annapolis and Calif. Inst. of Technology.
Merchant Marine 18-22; U.S. Navy 26-65, Naval Aviator 29-65, Admiral 58-65; Aircraft Carrier Desk, Bureau of Aeronautics 39-41, Dir. of Military Requirements 43-44; Commdg. Officer, Aircraft Squadron 42; Chief of Staff to Commdr. Carrier Div. 2, Pacific Campaigns 44-45; Commdg. Officer U.S.S. Bairoko 46-47, U.S.S. Coral Sea 51-52; Dep. Dir., Military Application, Atomic Energy Comm. 47-51; Office of Chief of Naval Operations 52-54; Commdr. Carrier Div. 17 and 5, Pacific Fleet 54-55; Chief, Bureau of Aeronautics 55-57; Dep. Commdr. Atlantic Fleet 57-58; Vice-Chief of Naval Operations 58-61; C.-in-C. NATO Forces in Southern Europe 62-65; recalled to active duty to direct review of safety in aircraft-carrier operations 67, and to Chair an evaluation group in Viet-Nam 68; Consultant to Boeing Co. 65-; Dir. Alaska Airlines 65-70, Airtronics Inc. 65-72; Collier Trophy 56; D.F.C., D.S.M., etc.
Leisure interests: aviation, swimming, sailing, gardening.
7734 Walnut Avenue, S.W., Tacoma, Washington 98498, U.S.A.
Telephone: 206-588-9356.

Russell, Sir John Wriothesley, G.C.V.O., C.M.G.; retd. British diplomatist; b. 23 Aug. 1914, Wollaton, Notts.; s. of Sir Thomas Russell Pasha; m. Aliki Diplarakos 1945; one s. one d.; ed. Eton Coll., and Trinity Coll., Cambridge.
Foreign Service 37-74, served Vienna, Foreign Office, Moscow, Washington, Warsaw, Brussels, Rome, New York 36-53; First Dir.-Gen. Brussels Treaty Perm. Org., London 48; Counsellor 53, Dir.-Gen. British Information Services, New York 53-56; Counsellor, Teheran 56-59; Foreign Office Spokesman (Head of News Dept., Foreign Office) 59-62; Amb. to Ethiopia 62-66, to Brazil 66-69, to Spain 69-74.
80 Chester Square, London, S.W.1, England.

Russell, Ken; British film director; b. 1927, Southampton; m. Shirley Russell; five c.; ed. Nautical Coll., Pangbourne.
Former actor and free-lance magazine photographer; has directed many television documentaries for BBC which have been widely shown all over the world; has directed the following films: Elgar, Bartok, Debussy, Henri Rousseau, Isadora Duncan, Delius, Richard Strauss, French Dressing, Billion Dollar Brain, Women in Love, The Music Lovers, The Devils, The Boyfriend, Savage Messiah 72, Mahler 73, Tommy 74, Lisztomania 75.
c/o Warner Bros., 135/141 Wardour Street, London, W.1, England.

Russell, Sir (Sydney) Gordon, C.B.E., M.C., R.D.I., F.S.I.A.; British industrial designer; b. 20 May 1892, London; s. of S. B. and Elizabeth Russell; m. Constance Denning 1921; three s. one d.; ed. Campden Grammar School.
Served with Worcestershire Regt. 14-19; partner Russell & Sons 19; Chair. Gordon Russell Ltd.; Chair. The Lygon Arms Ltd.; mem. Art Workers' Guild 26-; Master 62; elected Royal Designer for Industry 40, Master of Faculty 47-49; mem. Utility Furniture Cttee. and Furniture Production Cttee., Board of Trade 43-47; original mem. Council of Industrial Design (now Design Council) 44, Dir. of Council of Industrial Design 47-59, mem. 60-; mem. Design Panel, British Railways Board 56-66; Pres. Design and Industries Assen. 59-62; mem. Bank Note Design Cttee. of Bank of England 60-70, Arts Advisory Cttee. of UNESCO Nat. Comm., U.K. 60-66, Nat. Council for Diplomas in Arts

and Design 61-68, Crafts Advisory Cttee. 71-; Albert Medal of Royal Soc. of Arts 62; Hon. F.R.I.B.A., Senior Fellow, R.C.A.; Hon. A.I.L.A.; Hon. LL.D. (Birmingham Univ.) 60; Hon. Dr. (York Univ.) 69; Officer Order of Vasa (Sweden); Commdr. Order of St. Olav (Norway).
Leisure interests: gardening and handwork of many kinds.
Publs. The Story of Furniture 47, The things we see: Furniture 48, Looking at Furniture 64, Designer's trade (autobiography) 68.
Kingcombe, Chipping Campden, Gloucestershire, England.
Telephone: Evesham 840253.

Russell of Liverpool, 2nd Baron, cr. 1919; **Edward Frederick Langley Russell,** C.B.E., M.C.; British author; b. 10 April 1895, Liverpool; m. 1st Alix de Bréviare d'Alaincourt 1946 (died 1971); m. 2nd Selma Brayley 1972; ed. Liverpool Coll., and St. John's Coll., Oxford.
Served in British Army in France 14-18, later with Indian Cavalry; served in office of Judge Advocate-Gen. 34-54; during Second World War Dep. Judge Advocate-Gen. to B.E.F., First Army, Allied Force H.Q. and British Army of the Rhine; responsible for all War Crimes trials in British Zone of Germany 46-51; awarded Mil. Cross (2 bars).
Publs. The Scourge of the Swastika 54, Though the Heavens Fall 56, The Knights of Bushido 58, That Reminds Me 59, If I Forget Thee 60, The Royal Conscience 61, The Trial of Adolf Eichmann 62, Knight of the Sword 64, Deadman's Hill: Was Hanratty Guilty? 65, Caroline the Unhappy Queen 67, Return of the Swastika 68, Henry of Navarre 69, The French Corsairs 70.
House of Lords, London, S.W.1, England; 1 avenue George V, Dinard, France.
Telephone: 46-1871.

Russo, Carlo; Italian politician; b. 19 March 1920. Former mem. Nat. Cttee. of Liberation, Savona; mem. Chamber of Deputies 48-; Under-Sec. to Presidency of Council of Ministers 54, 55-57, 59-60; Under-Sec. for Defence 58-59; Under-Sec. for Foreign Affairs 60-62; Minister of Posts and Telecommunications 62-65, of Foreign Trade June-Dec. 68; Minister without Portfolio for Parl. Relations Dec. 68-69, for Implementation of Regions Feb. 71-72, for Parl. Relations and Pres. of Italian Del. to UN 72; Christian Democrat.
Camera dei Deputati, Rome, Italy.

Rust, Josef, DR.JUR.; German business executive; b. 12 Nov. 1907, Bremen-Blumenthal; ed. Univs. of Göttingen, Munich and Berlin.
Assessor, Oldenburg Bar; with State Ministry of the Economy 34; again at Oldenburg Bar 45-48; Finance Ministry of Lower Saxony 48; Dir. Dept. of Econ. and Finance, Fed. Chancellory 49-52; Dir. Dept. of Raw Materials Industry, Fed. Ministry of the Economy 52-55; Sec. of State, Fed. Ministry of Defence 55; Chair. Man. Board, Wintershall A.G. 59, now Chair. Supervisory Board; mem. Supervisory Board, Volkswagenwerk A.G., Chair. 66-74; mem. supervisory boards of various other German industrial companies.
35 Kassel-Wilhelmshöhe, Steinhoferstrasse 4, Federal Republic of Germany.

Rustomji, Nari Kaikhosru, M.A.; Indian civil servant; b. 16 May 1919, Lahore; s. of K. J. Rustomji and Homai Cooper; m. 1st Hilla Master 1951 (died 1953), 2nd Avi Dalal 1963; three d.; ed. Bedford School and Christ's Coll., Cambridge, England.
Joined Indian Civil Service 41; Under-Sec. Assam Home and Political Dept. 44; Adviser to Gov. of Assam 48; Dewan (Prime Minister) of Sikkim, Speaker, Sikkim Council, Pres. Sikkim Exec. Council 54-59; Adviser to Governor of Assam for North East Frontier Agency

and Nagaland 59; Adviser to Govt. of Bhutan 63-66; Chief Sec. to Gov. of Assam 66, to Govt. of Meghalaya 71; Ford Foundation Fellowship 64.
Leisure interests: music, writing.
Publ. *Enchanted Frontiers: Sikkim, Bhutan and India's North-eastern Borderlands.*
"Lumpyngad", Bivar Road, Shillong, India.
Telephone: Shillong 3083.

Rutstein, David Davis, M.D.; American physician and professor; b. 5 Feb. 1909, Wilkes-Barre, Pa.; s. of Harry and Nellie (née Davis) Rutstein; m. 1st Mazie E. Weissman 1935, one d. one s.; 2nd Ruth E. Rickel 1951; ed. Harvard Univ.
Assistant and Research Fellow, Harvard Medical School 36-47, Prof. of Preventive Medicine and Head of Dept. 47-69, Ridley Watts Prof. 66-; Visiting Inst. Lecturer, M.I.T. 70-71; Asst. Prof. Albany Medical Coll. 40-43, Asst. Attending Physician, Albany Hosp. 39-42; various assoc. and consulting posts; mem. and chair. comms. of WHO 56, 58, 66, and other int. confs. and programmes; Foreign Corresp. mem. Acad. Nat. de Médecine (France); mem. Royal Soc. of Medicine (U.K.), various American asscns.; Vice-Pres. American Heart Asscn. (Gold Heart Award 59); Chevalier, Légion d'Honneur (France); Benjamin Franklin Magazine Award 57; Jubilee Medal, Swedish Medical Soc. 66.
Publs. *Lifetime and Health Record* 58, *The Coming Revolution in Medicine* 67, *Engineering and Living Systems* 70, *Blueprint for Medical Care* 74; also scientific papers.
25 Shattuck Street, Boston, Mass. 02115; Home: 98 Winthrop Street, Cambridge, Mass. 02138, U.S.A.

Rutten, Franciscus Josephus Theodorus, DR. PSYCH., DR. LIT.; Netherlands psychologist; b. 15 Sept. 1899, Schinnen; m. Hilda Elisabeth Cornelia Leën 1927; one s. four d.; ed. Univs. of Utrecht and Louvain, Sorbonne, Leipzig and Vienna Univs.
Teacher, St. Ignatius Coll., Amsterdam; Asst. Psychological Laboratory, Univ. of Nijmegen; Extra. Prof. Univ. of Nijmegen 30, Ord. Prof. 33, Rector Magnificus 40, Dir. of Psychological Laboratory; arrested by Germans 44; Minister of Education, Arts and Sciences 48-52; Catholic Party; mem. New York Acad. of Sciences; Commdr. Order of Orange Nassau; Grand Cross Order of the Crown (Belgium); Grand Cross Order of Phoenix (Greece); Oak Crown (Luxembourg); Dr. h.c. Univ. of Athens.
Leisure interests: belles lettres, taking a walk.
Publs. *Felix Timmermans* 28, *Psychologie der waarneming* (Psychology of Perception) 30, *Symposion over het probleem der psychologie* (Symposium of Psychological Problems) 39, *Training en opleiding tot vakman* (Training and Instruction for Craftsmen) 47, *De overgang van het agrarische volkstype in het industriele type* (The transition of an agricultural worker into an industrial worker) 47, *Persoonlijkheid in de spiegel der samenleving* (Personality reflected in the Community) 47, *Menselijke Verhoudingen* (Human Relations) 55, *Analyse gebarentaal doofstommen* 57, *De geschiedkundige ontwikkeling der Sociale psychologie in Nederland* 58, *Inter-human relations: How do they stand today?* 60, *De methode van Nijmegen* (The Method of Nijmegen), *De ontwikkeling in het onderwijs van doven* (The development of education of deaf men), *Qu'en est-il des relations interhumaines?* (What about inter-human relations?), *Une étude de cas concernant le peuple Néerlandais* (A case study about Dutch people), *Zelfstandigheid en afhankelijkheid van bejaarden* (Independency and dependency of aged people), *Psychologie van het toerisme* (Psychology of tourism), *Mensbeelden in de theoretische psychologie* (Conception of men in psychological theories).
Pater Brugmanstraat 1, Nijmegen, Netherlands.

Růžek, Miloslav, PH.DR.; Czechoslovak diplomatist; b. 25 Jan. 1923, Kamenná Lhota; m. Věra Černohlávková 1949; two s. two d.; ed. Charles Univ., Prague.
Local Govt. 45-49, Ministry of Education and Culture 49-50, Foreign Trade 50-54, of Foreign Affairs 54-; Counsellor, London 54-57; Section Head, Ministry of Foreign Affairs 57-59, 63-66; Amb. to U.S.A. 59-63, to U.K. 66-71; Deputy Minister of Foreign Affairs 71-.
c/o Ministry of Foreign Affairs, Prague, Czechoslovakia.

Ruzicka, Leopold; Croatian-born Swiss chemist; b. 1887; ed. Inst. of Technology, Karlsruhe.
Former Professor of Organic Chemistry Zürich Fed. Inst. of Technology; awarded Nobel Chemistry Prize (with Adolph Butenandt) 39, for works on polymethylenes and the higher terpene compounds; Foreign mem. Royal Soc., London 42; Foreign Assoc. U.S. Nat. Acad. of Sciences 44.
Freudenbergstrasse 101, Zürich 8044, Switzerland.

Ryabinkina, Yelena Lvovna; Soviet ballet dancer; b. 1941, Moscow; ed. Bolshoi Theatre Ballet School.
Joined Bolshoi Theatre Ballet Company 59; Hon. Actress of R.S.F.S.R.
Principal roles: Odette-Odille (*Swan Lake*), Raimonde (*Raimonde*), Mirta (*Giselle*), Kitri (*Don Quixote*), Vanina Vanini (*Vanina Vanini*), Persian Dance (*Khovanshchina*), Zarema (*Fountain of Bakhchisarai*), etc.
State Academic Bolshoi Theatre of the U.S.S.R., Ploshchad Sverdlova, Moscow, U.S.S.R.

Ryan, Most Rev. Dermot, D.D., B.D., S.T.L., L.S.S., M.A.; Irish ecclesiastic; b. 27 June 1924, Dublin; s. of Dr. Andrew and Theresa (née McKenna) Ryan; ed. Belvedere Coll., Dublin, Holy Cross Coll., Clonliffe, Univ. Coll. Dublin, St. Patrick's Coll., Maynooth, St. John Lateran Univ., Rome, Gregorian Univ., Rome, and Pontifical Biblical Inst., Rome.
Professor of Fundamental Dogmatic Theology, Holy Cross Coll., Clonliffe 55-57; part-time Prof. of Eastern Languages, Univ. Coll., Dublin 57; Visiting Prof. (Old Testament Studies), Clonliffe Coll. 67; appointed to Chair. of Semitic Languages, Univ. Coll., Dublin 69; Archbishop of Dublin and Primate of Ireland Feb. 72-.
Leisure interests: golf, squash.
Publs. *Group Study of Bible in Europe* 57, *Sacraments Foreshadowed* 64, *The Mass in Christian Life* 65, *Teaching Scripture* 66, *Commentaries on the Old Testament books of Hosea, Amos, Micah and Zachariah* 69.
Archbishop's House, Dublin 9, Ireland.
Telephone: 373732.

Ryan, Gen. John Dale; American air force officer; b. 10 Dec. 1915, Cherokee, Iowa; s. of Edward T. Ryan and Mabel C. Dubel; m. Jo Guidera 1939; two s. one d.; ed. U.S. Military Acad., West Point.
Served Second World War; Dir. of Training, Advanced Bombardment School, Midland Field, Tex. 42-Aug. 43; Operations Officer H.Q. Second Air Force, Colorado Springs Aug. 43-Jan. 44; Commdr. Second Bombardment Group and Operations Officer, 5th Bombardment Wing, 15th Air Force in Italy Jan. 44-Feb. 45; Air Training Command at Carswell, Tex. and participation in Bikini Atoll nuclear weapons tests April 45-Sept. 46; Eighth Air Force Dir. of Operations and commdr. at various U.S. bases Sept. 46-June 56; with Strategic Air Command June 56-57; U.S.A.F. Insp.-Gen. Aug. 63-Aug. 64; Vice-C.-in-C. Aug. 64-Nov. 64, C.-in-C. Dec. 64-67; C.-in-C. Pacific Air Force 67-68; Vice-Chief of Staff U.S.A.F. 68-69, Chief of Staff U.S.A.F. 69-73; numerous decorations, including D.S.M., Legion of Merit and Croix de Guerre avec palme, Gallantry Cross (Viet-Nam); Hon. LL.D. (Creighton Univ., Omaha) 66, (Akron Univ., Ohio) 67.
H.Q. U.S.A.F. (A.F.C.C.S.), Room 4E929, The Pentagon, Washington, D.C. 20330; Home: Quarters 5, Fort Myer, Va. 22211, U.S.A.

Ryan, Peter Allen, B.A., M.M.; Australian publisher; b. 4 Sept. 1923, Melbourne; s. of Emmett F. and Alice D. Ryan; m. Gladys A. Davidson 1947; one s. one d.; ed. Malvern Grammar School, Melbourne and Univ. of Melbourne.
Military Service 42-45; Dir. United Service Publicity Pty. Ltd. 53-57; Public Relations Manager, Imperial Chemical Industries of Australia and New Zealand Ltd. 57-61; Asst. to Vice-Chancellor, Univ. of Melbourne 62; Dir. Melbourne Univ. Press 62-.
Leisure interests: reading, writing, riding.
Publs. *Fear Drive My Feet* 59, *The Preparation of Manuscripts* 66, *Encylopaedia of Papua and New Guinea* (Gen. Editor) 72, *Redmond Barry* 73.
932 Swanston Street, Carlton, Victoria 3053, Australia. Telephone: 347-3455.

Ryan, Richie, T.D., B.A.; Irish politician and solicitor; b. 1929, Dublin; s. of James R. Ryan and Irene Boyle; m. Mairéad King 1956; three s. two d.; ed. Synge St. Christian Brothers' School, Dublin, Univ. College, Dublin, Inc. Law Soc. of Ireland Law School.
Auditor of Literary and Historical Soc., Univ. Coll., Dublin 50-51; Personal Asst. to Minister for Justice 54-57; Chair. Dublin Health Authority 57-58; mem. Dublin City Council 60-73; Comm. of Irish Lights 60; Del. to Consultative Assembly of Council of Europe 67-73; mem. of European Parl. 73; Trustee of Fine Gael Party 73; Minister for Finance, Minister for the Public Service 73-; mem. Inc. Law Soc. of Ireland, Dublin Grand Opera Soc., Royal Dublin Soc., An Taisce, Royal Zoological Soc. of Ireland, Amnesty Int. (Irish Section); Inc. Law Soc. of Ireland Gold Medallist.
Leisure interests: reading, theatre, music.
Government Buildings, Merrion Street, Dublin 2; Home: St. Mary's, 127 Templeogue Road, Terenure, Dublin 6, Ireland.
Telephone: 767571 (Office).

Ryan, Robert Joseph; American diplomatist; b. 1914; Hatfield, Mass.; s. of Thomas W. and Hannah W. Ryan; m. Mary O'Leary 1938; two s.; ed. Massachusetts State Coll. and Columbus Univ.
Member D.C. Bar; Deputy of State 37-; Exec. Dir. Bureau of Near Eastern, South Asian and African Affairs 55-58; Nat. War Coll. 58; Admin. Counsellor, Paris 59-64; Amb. to Niger 64-68; Deputy Asst. Sec. for Org. and Management 68-69, Dir. Admin. Man. Services, UN 69-72; Asst. Sec.-Gen. for Gen. Services, UN April 72-.
United Nations Secretariat, New York, N.Y. 10017, U.S.A.

Rybakov, Boris Aleksandrovich; Soviet historian and archaeologist; b. 1908; ed. Moscow Univ.
Director archaeological expeditions at Vyshgorod, Moscow, Zvenigorod, Chernigov, etc. 32-; Assoc. Inst. of History of Material Culture, U.S.S.R. Acad. of Sciences 36-39; Lecturer, Moscow Univ. 38-43, Prof. 43-; Dir. Inst. of History of Material Culture, now Inst. of Archaeology, U.S.S.R. Acad. of Sciences 43-; corresp. mem. U.S.S.R. Acad. of Sciences 53-58, mem. 58-; Bureau mem. Dept. of Historical Science, U.S.S.R. Acad. of Sciences 57-; Bureau mem. Nat. Cttee. of Soviet Historians 57-; Foreign mem. Czechoslovak Acad. of Sciences; State Prize 49, 52.
Publs. include *The Radimichians* 32, *Chernigov Antiquities* 49, *Russian Systems of Linear Measurements from 11th–15th Century* 49, *Handicraft of Ancient Rus* 48.
Institute of Archaeology, U.S.S.R. Academy of Sciences, 19 D. Ulyanov, Moscow, U.S.S.R.

Rybicki, Marian; Polish lawyer and politician; b. 11 Feb. 1915, Warsaw; m. 1943; one s. one d.; ed. Univ. of Warsaw.
Head Legal Bureau of The Seym 47-48; Dir. Educational Section, Cen. Exec. Cttee., Polish Socialist

Party and Sec. Cen. Exec. Cttee. 48; mem. Cen. Cttee. Polish United Workers Party 48-68; First Sec. Voivodship Cttee., Cracow 49-50; Head of Chancellery of State Council 50-52, Sec. to State Council 52-56; Deputy to Seym 52-65; Procurator-Gen. 56-57; Minister of Justice 57-65; Prof. of Law, Inst. of Legal Sciences, Polish Acad. of Sciences 65-; Sec. All-Polish Cttee. of the Nat. Unity Front 67-; Order of Banner of Labour 1st Class.
Publs. in Polish, *Lay Judges in the Courts of Poland* 68, *Principles of the Administration of Justice in European Socialist Constitutions* 69, *The Federal Constitution of Switzerland* 70, *Social Courts in European Socialist States* 74, *Front of National Unity* 75.
Instytut Nauk Prawnych P.A.N., Warsaw, Ul. Nowy Świat 72, Pałac Staszica; Home: Aleja I Armii Wojska Polskiego 16 m. 33, Warsaw, Poland.
Telephone: 26-78-53 (Office); 21-48-10 (Home).

Rybicki, Zygmunt, M.A., LL.D.; Polish university rector; b. 15 May 1925, Panki; s. of Stanisław and Maria Górska; m. Maria Warowna 1952; two d.; ed. Univ. of Warsaw.
In Polish Partisan Army 42-45; Civil Office of Pres. of Poland 47; Scientific worker Acad. of Political Sciences 48-50, Faculty of Law, Warsaw Univ. 50; Prof. of Admin. Law, Univ. of Warsaw 59; Dept. Dir. Ministry of Higher Educ. 63-65; Deputy Rector Warsaw Univ. 63-69, Rector 69-; Pres. Popular Knowledge Soc. 69-; Deputy mem. Cen. Cttee., Polish United Workers' Party 71-; Pres. Cttee. of Legal Science, Polish Acad. of Sciences 72-; mem. Int. Political Sciences Asscn., American Asscn. for Public Admin. Sciences, Asscn. du Droit Comparé; Knight and Officer Order of Polonia Restituta, Cross for Valour, Partisan Cross, Golden Cross of Merit, S. Vavilov Medal (U.S.S.R.) 73, Commdr. Nat. Order of Merit (France) 75.
Leisure interest: touring.
Publs. *Council of Workers' Delegates in Poland 1918-19* 62, *The Structure and Functioning of People's Councils in the Polish People's Republic* 65, *Administrative Law: Aspects of Planned Economy* 68, *System of Local Government in Poland* 71, *Economic Administration in COMECON Countries (Council of Mutual Economic Assistance)* 74, *Economic Administration in Poland* 75.
Uniwersytet Warszawski, Krakowskie Przedmieście 26/28, 00-325 Warsaw; Home: Grażyny 22, Flat 7, 02 548 Warsaw, Poland.
Telephone: 26-18-47 (Office); 45-30-17 (Home).

Rydbeck, Olof, B.A., B.L.; Swedish diplomatist and radio administrator; b. 15 April 1913, Djursholm; s. of Oscar Rydbeck and Signe Olson; m. Monica Schell 1940; one s. one d.; ed. Djursholm Secondary School, Uppsala Univ.
Attaché Ministry for Foreign Affairs 39, Berlin 40, Ankara 41; Second Sec. Ministry for Foreign Affairs 43-45, Washington 45-46; First Sec. Washington 46-50, Bonn 50-53; Head of Press Section Ministry for Foreign Affairs 53-55; Dir.-Gen. Swedish Broadcasting Corpn. 55-70; mem. Board for Psychological Defence Preparedness 54-70, Board of Dirs. Stockholm Concert Soc. 55-62, Cen. Cttee. Swedish Red Cross 55-70, Council Swedish Inst. 56-, Royal Acad. of Music 62-; Board of Dirs. T.T. (Swedish Central News Agency) 67-70, Inst. of Int. Affairs 67-; Chair. Int. Broadcasting Inst. 67-70, mem. 70-, UNESCO Advisory Cttee. on Outer Space Communications 67-70; Pres. European Broadcasting Union 61-64, Hon. Chair. 64-; Perm. Rep. to UN 70-.
Leisure interests: music, literature.
Permanent Mission of Sweden to the UN, 825 Third Avenue, 38th Floor, New York, N.Y. 10022, U.S.A.
Telephone: PL1-5900.

Ryder of Eaton Hastings, Baron (Life Peer), cr. 75; **Sydney Thomas (Don) Ryder,** Kt.; British business executive; b. 16 Sept. 1916, Ealing, London; s. of John Ryder; m. Eileen Winifred Dodds 1950; one s. one d.

Editor *Stock Exchange Gazette* 50-60; Joint Man. Dir. Kelly Iliffe Holdings and Assoc. Iliffe Press 60-61, Sole Man. Dir. 61-63; Dir. Int. Publishing Corpn. 63-70; Man. Dir. Reed Paper Group 63-68, Chair., Chief Exec. Reed Int. 68-74, Nat. Enterprise Board 75-; Industrial Adviser, Cabinet Office Dec. 74-; Dir. Metropolitan Estate Property Corpn. Ltd. 72-75; part-time mem. British Gas Corpn. 73-; mem. of Council, British Inst. of Management 70-, Cranfield Inst. of Technology 70-, Industrial Soc. 71-, Nat. Econ. Devt. Council 75-; Pres. Nat. Materials Handling Centre 70-; Vice-Pres. Royal Soc. for Prevention of Accidents 73-.
Leisure interests: sailing, squash, chess.
National Enterprise Board, 12/18 Grosvenor Gardens, London, SW1W 0DW; Home: 121 Century Court, Grove End Road, St. John's Wood, London, NW8 9LD; Eaton Hastings House, Eaton Hastings, nr. Faringdon, Berks., England.
Telephone: 01-730 9600 (Office); 0367-20646 (Berks.).

Rydin, Bo, B.SC.; Swedish business executive; b. 5 July 1932.
With Stockholms Enskilda Bank 56-57; Marma-Långrör AB 57-60; A.B. Gullhögens Bruk 60, Pres. and Chief Exec. Officer 65-71; Pres. and Chief Exec. Officer Svenska Cellulosa Aktiebolaget 72-; mem. Board Borås Invest AB, Svenska Handelsbanken, AB Industrivärden, Mölnlycke AB, Papierwerke Waldhof-Aschaffenburg AG, Papeteries Léon Clergeau SA, Papelera Navarra SA; Chair. Sundsvall Chamber of Commerce.
Svenska Cellulosa Aktiebolaget, 851 88 Sundsvall, Sweden.

Ryelandt, Baron Daniel-Benoit, D. EN D.; Belgian barrister; b. 1903; ed. Univ. of Louvain.
Barrister, Brussels Court of Appeal 27; Sec. to Prime Minister 32; Head of Secretariat of Ministries of Interior and Agriculture 34-38; Gen. Manager of Agence-Télégraphique Belge de Presse (Belga) 38-, now Chair.; mem. of Cttee. of *Revue Générale Belge* (monthly).
Agence Belga, 1 blvd. Charlemagne, 1040 Brussels; 6 rue de la Science, Brussels, Belgium.

Ryerson, Knowles Augustus, M.S., LL.D.; American horticulturalist and educationist; b. 17 Oct. 1892, Seattle, Wash.; s. of Will A. Ryerson and Jessie Knowles; m. 1st Emma Mary Freeman (deceased), 2nd Edith Palmer Popenoe 1969; one s. (deceased); ed. Univ. of Calif.
Agricultural damage investigator, American Peace Comm. 19; mem. staff Univ. of California Agricultural Extension Service 19-25; Horticulturalist Haiti Agricultural Experimental Station 25-27; Horticultural Survey of Palestine 27; Dir. Div. of Foreign Plant Introduction U.S. Dept. of Agriculture 28-34; Chief Bureau of Plant Industry 34; fmrly in charge Tropical and Sub-Tropical Fruit Investigations U.S. Dept. of Agriculture 35-37; Dir. and Prof. of Horticulture Coll. of Agriculture Univ. of California, Davis Campus 37-52; Dean Coll. of Agriculture, Berkeley Campus 52-60; on leave, serving as Special Rep. Pacific Ocean Area, Board of Economic Warfare, Foreign Economic Admin. 42-44; Chair. Pacific Science Board, Nat. Research Council (U.S.) 46-53; mem. Hopkins Comm. Civil Govt., Guam and Samoa 47; mem. Research Council, South Pacific Comm. 48-53 63-, Commr. 53-56, Senior Commr. 56-63; Admin. Board Inter-American Inst. of Agricultural Sciences, Costa Rica 45-54, Chair. 50-54; Sr. Agricultural Officer ECA, Bangkok, Thailand 50-51; U.S. Rep. Pacific Science Council 50-63; U.S. Rep. UN/South Pacific Comm. Jt. Project Rhinoceros Beetle Control Operations Board 63-; Special Asst. to Chancellor, Santa Cruz Campus (South Pacific Studies) and to Chancellor, Davis Campus (Arboretum), Univ. of Calif.; Fellow, American Asscn. for the Advancement of

Science, Washington Acad. of Science; Berkeley Fellow; President's Citation 46; Chevalier de Mérite Agricole (France), Ouissam Alouite (Morocco), Bronze Medal Soc. d'Acclimatation (France), Frank L. Meyer Medal for Plant Exploration, Centennial Award Distinguished Service (Santa Cruz Campus and Berkeley Campus, Univ. of Calif.).
Leisure interests: gardening, amateur astronomy.
106 Giannini Hall, University of California, Berkeley, Calif. 94720, U.S.A.
Telephone: 415-526-0230.

Rykalin, Nikolai Nikolaievich, D.TECH.SC.; Soviet physicist and chemist; b. 29 Sept. 1903, Odessa; ed. Far Eastern Univ.
Welder, Technician, Chief Engineer, Ussuryskaya Railway 23-33; Chief of Faculty, Far East Polytechnic Inst. 33-37; Research Worker 37-53; Prof. 46-; Head of Lab. A. A. Baikov Inst. of Metallurgy, U.S.S.R. Acad. of Sciences 53-; Academician, U.S.S.R. Acad. of Sciences 68-; Vice-Chair. Council on New Methods of Producing and Processing Metals; Chair. Nat. Welding Cttee.
Publs. Research works in the field of metal processing and joining.
The Baikov Institute of Metallurgy, Moscow, U.S.S.R.

Ryland, Sir (Albert) William (Cecil), Kt., C.B., C.I.E.E.; British posts and telecommunications executive; b. 10 Nov. 1913, Tunbridge Wells; m. Sybil Wookey 1946; one s. one d.; ed. Gosforth County Grammar School.
Assistant Traffic Supt. 34, Asst. Surveyor 38; war service 39-45; Principal 49, Principal Private Sec. to Postmaster-Gen. 54; Asst. Sec. 55, Dir. of Establishments and Org. 58; Dir. of Inland Telecommunications 61-65; Dep. Dir.-Gen. 65-67; Man. Dir. Telecommunications 67-69; Deputy Chair. and Chief Exec. The Post Office 69-71, Chair. and Chief Exec. 71-; Hon. C.G.I.A.
23 Howland Street, London, W1P 6HQ; Home: 13 Mill View Gardens, Croydon, CR0 5HW, England.
Telephone: 01-631-2345 (Office); 01-656-4224 (Home).

Ryle, Gilbert, M.A.; British philosopher; b. 19 Aug. 1900; ed. Brighton Coll., and Queen's Coll., Oxford.
Philosophy Tutor, Christ Church, Oxford 24; officer in Welsh Guards during Second World War; Waynflete Prof. of Metaphysical Philosophy and Fellow of Magdalen Coll., Oxford 45-68, now Hon. Fellow; Editor *Mind* 47-71; Foreign Hon. mem. American Acad. of Arts and Sciences 68.
Publs. *The Concept of Mind* 49, *Dilemmas* 54, *Plato's Progress* 66, *Collected Papers* 71.
Magdalen College, Oxford; and The Orchard, North Street, Islip, Oxon., England.
Telephone: Kidlington 3277.

Ryle, Sir Martin, Kt., M.A., F.R.S.; British physicist and astronomer; b. 27 Sept. 1918; ed. Bradfield Coll., and Christ Church, Oxford.
Worked at Telecommunications Research Estab. 39-45; ICI Fellowship, Cambridge 45; Univ. Lecturer 48; Fellow of Trinity Coll., Cambridge 49-; Reader in Physics, Cambridge Univ. 57-59, Prof. Radio Astronomy 59-; Dir. Mullard Radio Astronomy Observatory 58-; mem. Soviet Acad. of Sciences 71-; Henry Draper Medal, U.S. Nat. Acad. of Sciences 65; Astronomer Royal 72-; Royal Soc. Medal 73, Nobel Prize for Physics (with Antony Hewish, *q.v.*) 74.
5A Herschel Road, Cambridge, England.

Ryrie, William Sinclair, M.A.; British civil servant and international official; b. 10 Nov. 1928, Calcutta, India; s. of Rev. Dr. Frank and Mabel M. Ryrie; m. 1st Dorrit Klein 1953 (dissolved 1969), two s. one d.; m. 2nd Christine G. Thomson 1969, one s.; ed. Heriots School, Edinburgh, Edinburgh Univ.
Army service, Lieut. Intelligence Corps in Malaya 51-53 (dispatches 53); joined Colonial Office as Asst.

Principal 53; seconded to Govt. of Uganda 56-58; Principal, UN Affairs, Colonial Office 59-63; Principal, Balance of Payments Div. of H.M. Treasury 63-66, Asst. Sec. for Int. Monetary Affairs 66-69; Principal Private Sec. to Chancellor of the Exchequer 69-71; Under-Sec., Public Sector Group in Treasury 71-75; Econ. Minister, Embassy in U.S.A. and Exec. Dir. of IMF, IBRD, IDA, IFC Oct. 75-.
Leisure interests: music, hill walking.
76 Kalorama Circle, N.W., Washington, D.C. 20008, U.S.A.
Telephone: (202) 477-3186 (Office); (202) 462-6212 (Home).

Rysanek, Leonie; Austrian soprano; b. 14 Nov. 1928, Vienna; *d.* of Peter and Josefine (née Hoeberth) Rysanek; *m.* Ernst Ludwig Gausman 1968; ed. Vienna Conservatory.
Roles include Sieglinde (*Die Walküre*) Bayreuth 51, Senta (*Der fliegende Holländer*) San Francisco 56, Lady Macbeth Metropolitan Opera 59, Chrysothemis (*Elektra*) Paris 73, Medea, Athens 73, Gioconda, Berlin 74, die Kaiserin (*Die Frau ohne Schatten*) Salzburg Festival 74, Orange (*Salome* 74, *Die Walküre* 75); also frequent appearances in New York, Munich, Milan, London, Edinburgh, Aix en Provence, Hamburg, Budapest, Vienna, Paris, Moscow, San Francisco, Bayreuth; Kammersängerin of Austria and Bavaria; Chappel Gold Medal of Singing (London), Silver Rose (Vienna Philharmonic), Austrian Gold Cross (1st Class) for Arts and Science; hon. mem. Vienna Staatsoper.
8201 Altenbeuern über Rosenheim, Federal Republic of Germany.

Ryssdal, Rolv Einar Rasmussen, CAND.JUR.; Norwegian judge; b. 27 Oct. 1914, Bergen; *s.* of Anders Rasmussen Ryssdal and Martha Seim; *m.* Signe Marie Stray 1954; two *s.* one *d.*; ed. Oslo Univ.
Deputy Crown Prosecutor, Attorney-Gen.'s Office 45; called to the Bar of the Supreme Court 48; Under-Sec. of Justice 56; Justice, Supreme Court 64, Chief Justice 69-; fmr. Judge European Court of Human Rights; Commdr. with Star, Order of St. Olav (Norway); Commdr. 1st Class, Order of Dannebrog (Denmark); Commdr. Order of Nordstjerne (Sweden).
Supreme Court, Grubbegt. 1, Oslo 1; Home: Øvre Ullern terrasse 34, Oslo 3, Norway.

Rytkheu, Yuri Sergeevich; Soviet writer; b. 8 March 1930, Uellen, Chukotka N.O., Magadan Region; ed. Leningrad Univ.
Foremost Chukchi writer; works have been translated into Russian; started writing for the newspaper *Soviet Chukotka* 47; Badge of Honour.
Publs. Short stories: *Friends and Comrades, People of our Coast* 53, *When the Snow Melts* (novel) 60, *The Sorceress of Konerga* 60, *The Saga of Chukotka* 60, *Farewell to the Gods* (short stories) 61, *Nunivak* (tales) 63, *The Magic Gauntlet* (novel) 63, *In the Vale of the Little Sunbeams* (novel) 63, *The Walrus of Dissent* (stories) 64, *Blue Peppers* (stories) 64, *Wings Are Becoming Stronger in Flight* (novel) 64, *Bear Stew* (verses) 65.
Union of Writers of the U.S.S.R., Ul. Vorovskogo 52, Moscow, U.S.S.R.

Ryzhov, Nikita Semyonovich; Soviet diplomatist; b. 8 June 1907, Baryatino, Smolensk Region; ed. Moscow Industrial Acad.
Former U.S.S.R. Minister of Textile Light Industry; Diplomatic Service 57-; Amb. to Turkey 57-66, to Italy 66-; mem. Central Auditing Comm. of C.P.S.U. 66-.
U.S.S.R. Embassy, Via Gaeta 5, Rome, Italy.

S

Sá Carneiro, Dr. Francisco; Portuguese lawyer and politician; b. 19 July 1934, Oporto; s. of José Gualberto and Maria Francisca Sá Carneiro; m. Isabel Nunes Matos Sá Carneiro 1956; three s. two d.; ed. Law Faculty, Lisbon Univ.
Co-founder, *Confronto* co-operative; Pres. *Revista dos Tribunais*; Independent mem. Nat. Assembly, author of eight major legislative proposals 69-73, resigned 73; worked with *Expresso* and other newspapers; Founder and Sec.-Gen. Popular Democratic Party (PPD) May 74-; Minister without Portfolio May-July 74.
Leisure interests: swimming, tennis, reading.
Publs. *Uma Tentativa de Participação Política* 71, *Revisão da Constituição Política* 71, *As Revisões da Constituição Política* 73, *Ser ou Não Ser Deputado?* 73, *Por uma Social-Democracia* 75, *Poder Civil, Autoridade Democrática e Social-Democracia* 75.
Rua Marechal Saldanha No. 337—2° E, Porto, Portugal.
Telephone: 557102.

Saad, Dr. Ahmed Bey Saad; Egyptian lawyer and politician; b. 21 Feb. 1900, Belbeis; s. of Joseph Saad and Farida Ibrahim; m. Hoda Ruffet 1940; ed. Univ. de Paris à la Sorbonne.
Assistant Attorney-Gen. of Egypt 22-29; Consul, Genoa 29-31; Consul-Gen. Hamburg 31-33, Liverpool 33-37, Dublin 33-37; Chargé d'Affaires, Baghdad 37-38; 1st Sec. Egyptian Embassy, London 38; Dir. Dept. for Alien Affairs, Cairo 39-44; Postmaster-Gen. 44; Under-Sec. of State, Ministry of Finance 45-51; Gov. Nat. Bank of Egypt 51-52, 55-57; Gov. for Egypt of IBRD 46-52, 55, Chair. Board of Govs. 55, 62; Exec. Dir. IMF 46-70, Gov. 46-52, 58, Principal Rep. 64; Special counsellor to King of Saudi Arabia 57; LL.B. Univ. of Cairo 22; J. D. Univ. of Paris 28.
c/o Ministry of Finance, Cairo, Egypt.

Sa'ad, Farid, B.SC.; Jordanian business executive and politician; b. 1908, Umm el Fahm, Palestine; s. of Ali Sa'ad and Almaza Ownallah; m. Khadijeh Yousef Khalidi 1943; one s. three d.; ed. American Univ. of Beirut.
Teacher 28-35; District Gov., Palestine Govt. 35-43; Dir. Arab Bank in Haifa 43-48; mem. Board of Dirs. Jordan Tobacco Co. 49-55, Pres. 55; Minister of Finance 72-73; mem. Board of Trustees, American Univ. of Beirut, Univ. of Jordan.
Leisure interests: sports, mainly walking.
Jordan Tobacco and Cigarette Co. Ltd., P.O. Box 59, Amman, Jordan.
Telephone: 36345.

Saam, Mohammad, M.A., PH.D.; Iranian educationist and politician; b. 1924, Kerman, Iran; ed. Univs. of Teheran, Nebraska and S. Calif., U.S.A.
Former teacher; Dir. Dept. of Educ.; Del. of Dept. of Educ. to Near East Inst.; Admin. Consultant to Cen. Bank of Iran; mem. Parl.; Gov. Gen. of Gilan and Isfahan; fmr. Minister of Information; Minister of Interior 72-74.
c/o Ministry of Interior, Teheran, Iran.

Saarinen, Aarne; Finnish politician; b. 5 Dec. 1913, Degerby; s. of Armas R. Saarinen and Maria Tomminen; m. Helmi Aho 1933; three c.
Former mason; fmr. mem. Social-Democratic Party; Joined Finland-U.S.S.R. Soc. 40; mem. Finnish Communist Party 44, mem. Central Cttee. 57-, mem. Political Bureau 64-, Chair. Finnish Communist Party 66-; Officer Building Workers' Union 45, Sec. for Educ. 47-50, Pres. 54-66; mem. Gen. Council of World Fed. of Trade Unions 61-; mem. Diet 62-; mem. Gen. Council of World Fed. of Trade Unions 61-69; Vice-Pres. Finnish Peace Supporters' Org.
Suomen Kommunistiner Puolue, Sturenkatu 4, Helsinki, Finland.
Telephone: 483022.

Saba, Elias, B.LITT.; Lebanese economist and politician; b. 1932, Lebanon; s. of Shukri Saba and Guilnar Abou Haidar; m. Hind Sabri Shurbagi 1960; five d.; ed. American Univ. of Beirut and Univ. of Oxford.
Economic Adviser to Ministry of Finance and Petroleum, Kuwait and Kuwait Fund for Arab Econ. Devt. 61-62; Chair. Dept. of Econs., American Univ. of Beirut 63-67; Assoc. Prof. of Econs., American Univ. of Beirut 67-69; Deputy Prime Minister of the Lebanon, Minister of Finance and of Defence 70-72; Econ. and Financial Adviser to the Pres. 72-73; Chair., Gen. Man. St. Charles City Centre S.A.L. 74-; Chief Exec. Arab Int. Finance Co. (ARINFI) S.A., Switzerland 74-.
Publ. *Postwar Developments in the Foreign Exchange Systems of Lebanon and Syria* 62.
P.O. Box 9500, Beirut, Lebanon.
Telephone: 302885, 363271, 350350/1.

Saba, Hanna, D. EN D.; Egyptian jurist and diplomatist; b. 23 July 1909, Damietta; s. of S. Saba Bey and Catherine Facks; m. Carmen Sednaoui 1937; one s. two d.; ed. Coll. of Jesuit Fathers, Cairo, Faculté de Droit, Paris, and Ecole libre des Sciences politiques, Paris.
Ministry of Foreign Affairs, Cairo 42, Counsellor 46, Minister 52; Dir. of Treaties Div., UN Secr. 46-50; Juridical Adviser, UNESCO 50-67; Asst. Dir.-Gen. of UNESCO 67-71, Alt. Chair. Appeals Board 73; Grand Officer of Merit (Egypt); Officer of the Nile.
Leisure interest: golf.
Publs. *L'Islam et la nationalité* 32, *L'évolution dans la technique des traités, Les droits économiques et sociaux dans le projet de pacte des droits de l'homme, Les ententes et accords régionaux dans la Charte des Nations Unies* (Course at Acad. of Int. Law, The Hague 52), *L'Activité quasi-législative des Institutions spécialisées des Nations Unies* (Course at Acad. of Int. Law, The Hague 64).
3 boulevard de la Saussaye, Neuilly (Hauts de Seine), France.

Sabah, His Highness Sheikh Jaber al-Ahmad al-Jaber al-; the Crown Prince and Prime Minister of the State of Kuwait; b. 1928, Kuwait; ed. Almubarakiyyah School, Kuwait and private tutors.
Governor of Ahmadi and Oil areas 49-59; Pres. Dept. of Finance and Economy 59; Minister of Finance, Industry and Commerce 63; Minister of Finance and Oil; Prime Minister 65-; appointed Crown Prince 66.
Office of the Prime Minister, Council of Ministers, Kuwait; Dasman Palace, Kuwait City, Kuwait.
Telephone: 422205 (Office); 432001. (Residence)

Sabah, Sheikh Sabah al-Ahmad al-Jaber al; Kuwaiti, politician; b. 1929; ed. Mubarakiyyah National School, Kuwait and privately.
Member Supreme Cttee. 55-62; Minister of Public Information and Guidance and of Social Affairs 62-63; Minister of Foreign Affairs 63-, acting Minister of Finance and Oil 65.
Ministry of Foreign Affairs, Kuwait.

Sabah, Sheikh Sabah al-Salim al-; Amir of Kuwait, 12th ruler of the Sabah Dynasty; b. 1913, Kuwait; ed. under private tutors.

Head of the Police Dept. 38-59; mem. Supreme Council of the Principality 55-61; Minister of Foreign Affairs and Deputy Prime Minister 61-63; Heir Apparent and Prime Minister 63-65; succeeded his brother Sheikh Abdulla al-Salem al-Sabah as Head of the State of Kuwait Nov. 65.
Leisure interests: literature, poetry.
Sief Palace, Amiry Diwan, Kuwait (official residence).

Sabah, Sheikh Salim al Sabah al-; Kuwait diplomatist; b. 18 June 1937; s. of Sheikh Sabah al-Salim al-Sabah, Amir of Kuwait (q.v.); ed. Secondary School, Kuwait, Gray's Inn, London, and Christ Church, Oxford.
Joined Foreign Service 63; fmr. Head Political Dept. Ministry of Foreign Affairs; Ambassador to the U.K. 65-70; also to Norway, Denmark and Sweden 68-70; Amb. to U.S.A. 70-75, also accred. to Canada; rep. of Kuwait to confs. in Middle East and Africa, including Arab Summit Conf., Casablanca Oct. 65.
Embassy of Kuwait, 2940 Tilden Street, N.W., Washington, D.C., U.S.A.

Sabatier, Robert; French writer; b. 17 Aug. 1928.
Former manual worker and factory executive; produced journal *la Cassette*; lauréat de la Soc. des gens de lettres 61; Grand Prix de Poésie de l'Académie française 69 for *Chateaux de millions d'années*; Antonin-Artaud Prize and Prix Appollinaire for poems *les fêtes solaires*; mem. l'Académie Goncourt.
Publs. *Alain et le nègre* 53, *le Marchand de sable* 54, *Le Goût de la cenón* 55, *Les Fêtes solaires* 55, *Boulevard* 56, *Canard au sang* 58, *Saint Vincent de Paul, Dédicace d'un navire* 59, *la Sainte-Farce* 60, *la Mort d'un figuier* 62, *Dessin sur un trottoir* 64, *les Poisons délectables* (poems) 65, *Le Chinois d'Afrique* 66, *Dictionnaire de la mort* 67, *Les Châteaux de millions d'années* (poems) 69, *les Allumettes Suédoises* 69, *Trois sucettes à la menthe* 72, *Noisettes sauvages* 74, *Histoire de la poésie Française des origines à nos jours* (2 vols.) 75.
23 rue Fantin Latour, Paris 16e, France.

Sábato, Ernesto; Argentine writer; b. 24 June 1911, Rojas; m. Matilde Kusminsky-Richter; two s.; ed. Universidad Nacional de la Plata.
Former Dir. of Cultural Relations, Argentina; has lectured in following Univs.: Paris, Columbia, Berkeley, Madrid, Warsaw, Bucharest, Bonn, Milan, Pavia, Florence, etc.; mem. the Club of Rome, Ribbon of Honour, Argentine Soc. of Letters; Chevalier, Ordre des Arts et des Lettres de la République Française, Prize of the Inst. of Foreign Relations (Stuttgart) 73, Grand Prize of Argentine Writer's Soc. 74.
Publs. *Uno y el Universo* 45, *Hombres y Engranajes* 51, *Heterdoxia* 53, *El escritor y sus fantasmas* 63, *Tres Aproximaciones a la Literatura de Nuestro Tuempo* 69 (essays); *El Túnel* 47, *Sobre Héroes y Tumbas* 61 *Abaddon el Exterminador* (novels).
Severino Langeri 3135, Santos Lugares, Argentina.
Telephone: 757-1373.

Sabin, Albert B(ruce), B.S., M.D.; American virologist; b. 26 Aug. 1906, Bialystok, Russia; s. of Jacob and Tilly Krugman Sabin; m. 1st Sylvia Tregillus (deceased) 1935, 2nd Jane Blach Warner (divorced) 1967, 3rd Heloisa Dunshee de Abranches 1972; two d.; ed. New York Univ.
Research Assoc. in bacteriology, New York Univ. Coll. of Medicine 26-31; House Physician, Bellevue Hospital, New York City 32-33; Fellow in Medicine, Nat. Research Council, Lister Inst. (England) 34; Asst., Rockefeller Inst., N.Y.C. 35-37; Assoc. 37-39; Assoc. Prof. of Research Pediatrics, Univ. of Cincinnati Coll. of Medicine 39-46, Prof. 46-60, Distinguished Service Prof. 60-70; Pres. Weizmann Inst. of Science 70-72; Fogarty Scholar, Nat. Insts. of Health, U.S.A. 73-; Expert Consultant Nat. Cancer Inst. 73-74; Distinguished Research

Prof. of Biomedicine, Medical Univ. South Carolina 74-; Consultant, Surgeon Gen., U.S. Army 74-, Consultant to Asst. Sec. for Health, Dept. of Health, Educ. and Welfare (U.S.A.) 75-, WHO Advisory Panel 75-; developer of oral polio vaccine; Medical Corps U.S. Army, Second World War; mem. U.S. Army Medical Research and Devt. Advisory Panel 74-, Advisory Panel on Medical Research, Pan American Health Org. (Washington D.C.) 75-; mem. Nat. Acad. of Sciences (U.S.A.), American Acad. of Arts and Sciences (Fellow), A.A.A.S.; hon. mem. numerous acads. and socs.; numerous hon. degrees; Hon. Fellow, Royal Soc. of Health, London; Int. Antonio Feltrinelli Prize 64, Lasker Award 65, Royal Soc. of Health Gold Medal 69, Nat. Medal of Science (U.S.A.) 71, Distinguished Civilian Service Medal, U.S. Army 73, Statesman in Medicine Award 73, and numerous awards and honours for work in medical research.
Leisure interests: foreign affairs, music, art, philosophy.
Medical University of South Carolina, Charleston, South Carolina 29401, U.S.A.
Telephone: (803) 792-2165.

Sabo, Boukary; Niger politician; b. 1924, Dan-Amario, Maradi; m.; ed. Frédéric Assomption Teachers' Training Coll., Katibougou, Mali.
Teacher, Frédéric Assomption Secondary School, Katibougou, Mali 50-59; M.P. for Tessoua in Nat. Assembly 59-65; Minister of Information, Youth and Sports 65-70, of Civil Service and Labour 70-72, of Foreign Affairs 72-74; Commdr. Nat. Order of Niger; Parti Progressiste Nigérien.
Leisure interests: sports, modern literature.
c/o Ministère des Affaires Etrangères, Niamey, Niger.

Sabri, Wing-Cmmdr, Ali; Egyptian air force officer and politician; b. 30 Aug. 1920.
Fought in Palestine War 48; Minister for Presidential Affairs, Egypt 57-58, U.A.R. 58-62; Pres. Exec. Council 62-64, Prime Minister 64-65; Vice-Pres. of Republic Oct. 65-67; Sec.-Gen. Arab Socialist Union Oct. 65-67, 68-70; Deputy Prime Minister and Minister of Local Govt. June-Oct. 67; Resident Minister for Suez Canal Zone Oct. 67-68; Vice-Pres. of Egypt 70-71; charged with treason and sentenced to death Dec. 71; sentence later commuted to life imprisonment.

Sacher, Paul; Swiss musician; b. 28 April 1906, Basle; m. Maja Stehlin 1934; ed. Univ. and Conservatoire of Basle.
Founder of Basle Chamber Orchestra 26, with Chamber Choir 28; founder of Schola Cantorum Basiliensis 33; conductor of Collegium Musicum Zürich 41-; Dir. Basle Acad. of Music 54-69; has conducted in almost all European countries; Hon. Pres. Asscn. of Swiss Musicians; Hon. mem. I.S.C.M.; Dr. Phil. h.c. of Basle Univ.; Schönberg Medal 53; Mozart Medal 56, *Litteris et artibus* Medal 1st Class (Vienna) 72.
Leisure interests: trees, gardening, books.
Publs. Articles in reports of Basle Chamber Orchestra, and book on *Adolf Hamm* (organist).
Schönenberg, 4133 Prattelen BL, Basle, Switzerland.
Telephone: 061-815100.

Sachs, Robert Green, PH.D.; American professor of physics; b. 4 May 1916, Hagerstown, Md.; s. of Henry M. and Anna (Green) Sachs; m. 1st Selma Solomon 1941, 2nd Jean K. Woolf, 3rd Carolyn L. Wolf 1968; two s. three d., one step s. two step d.; ed. Baltimore City Coll., and Johns Hopkins Univ.
Research Fellow, George Washington Univ. 39-41; Instructor, Purdue Univ. 41-43; Section Chief, Ballistic Research Lab. Aberdeen (Md.) Proving Ground 43-45; Dir. Theoretical Physics Div., Argonne National Lab. 45-47; Assoc. Prof. of Physics, Univ. of Wisconsin 47-48, Prof. 48-64; Assoc. Dir. Argonne Nat. Lab. 64-68; Prof. of Physics, Univ. of Chicago 64-, Dir. Enrico Fermi

Inst. 68-73; Vice-Pres. Chair. A.A.A.S., Physics Section 70-71; Dir. Argonne Nat. Laboratory 73-; Visiting Prof., Princeton Univ. 55-56, Univ. of Paris 59-60; mem. Nat. Acad. of Sciences; Fellow, American Acad. of Arts and Sciences; Guggenheim Fellowship 59-60; Hon. D.Sc. (Purdue Univ.) 67.
Leisure interest: sailing.
Publ. *Nuclear Theory* 53; numerous articles in scientific journals.
Argonne National Laboratory, 9700 South Cass Avenue, Argonne, Ill. 60439; Home: 5490 South Shore Drive, Chicago, Ill. 60615, U.S.A.
Telephone: 312-739-7711, ext. 4567 (Office); 312-752-2077 (Home).

Sadaqiani, Reza; Iranian politician; b. 1917, Sabzevar; ed. Karaj Agricultural Coll., Syracuse Univ., N.Y.
With Ministry of Agriculture 39, Procurement Officer, Section Head; with Crown Lands and Rural Estates 40; Asst. Dir. Forestry Agency; Head of Karkheh Devt. Authority; Head of Agriculture Div., Plan Org.; Under-Sec., Ministry of Agriculture; Head of Agricultural Bank of Iran; Gov.-Gen. Khuzistan 73; Minister of Co-operatives and Rural Affairs 73-; Founder-mem. Iran Novin Party.
Ministry of Co-operatives and Rural Affairs, Teheran, Iran.

Sadat, Col. Mohamed Anwar El-; Egyptian army officer and politician; b. 25 Dec. 1918, Tala Dist., Menufia Governorate; *s.* of Mohamed El-Sadat; *m.* Jihan Sadat; one *s.* six *d.*; ed. Military Coll.
Commissioned 38; fmr. Gen. Sec. Islamic Congress; fmr. Editor *Al Jumhuriya* and *Al Tahrir* 55-56; Minister of State 55-56; Vice-Chair. Nat. Assembly 57-60, Chair. 60-68; Gen. Sec. Egyptian Nat. Union 57-61; Chair. Afro-Asian Solidarity Council 61; mem. Presidential Council 62-64; Vice-Pres. of Egypt 64-66, 69-70; interim Pres. of Egypt, Sept.-Oct. 70, Pres. Oct. 70-, Prime Minister 73-74; proclaimed Military Gov.-Gen. March 73; Pres. Council Fed. of Arab Repubs. 71-; Chair. Arab Socialist Union 70-; Sinai Medal 74.
The Presidency, Cairo, Egypt.

Sadawi, A. M. Suhail Al; Libyan oil executive; b. 1928, Beirut; ed. American Univ. of Beirut.
With Gulf Oil Corpn., Libya 58-61; Int. Labour Office, Geneva 62-63; Head, Gen. Econ. Section, Org. of Petroleum Exporting Countries (OPEC) 63; participated in negotiations for amendment of Libyan Petroleum Law 65; mem. Pricing Comm., Libya 67, Chair. 68; Asst. Under Sec., Libyan Ministry of Petroleum 68; Deputy Dir. Gen. Libyan Nat. Petroleum Corpn. 68; Sec.-Gen. Org. of Arab Petroleum Exporting Countries 70-73.
Arab Economists Petroleum Affairs (Consultants), P.O. Box 8840, Beirut, Lebanon.
Telephone: 352319.

Sadek, Gen. Mohammed Ahmed; Egyptian army officer; ed. Frunze Military Academy, U.S.S.R.
Served in Egyptian army, World War II, Palestine War 48, Suez Campaign 56; Mil. Attaché, Egyptian Embassy to Fed. Repub. of Germany 64; Dir. of Studies, Mil. Acad., Cairo 65-67; Dir. of Information, Army Intelligence Dept. 67; Chief of Staff of the Army Sept. 69; Minister of War and Mil. Production May 71-72; Deputy Premier for Nat. Defence Jan.-Oct. 72; mem. Supreme Council of the Armed Forces.
Ministry of War, Cairo, Egypt.

Sadiq, Issa, PH.D.; Iranian educationist; b. 1894, Teheran; *m.* Badry Heravi 1925; two *s.* two *d.*; ed. Univs. of Paris, Cambridge (England), and Columbia (New York).

Directed various depts. Ministry of Educ. 19-30; mem. Nat. Constituent Assembly 25, 49, 67; Pres. and Prof. Nat. Teachers' Coll.; Dean of Faculties of Arts and Science, Teheran Univ. 32-41, Prof. 32-72, Prof. Emer. 72-; Chancellor of Univ. 41; Minister of Educ. 41, 43-45, 47, 60-61; Vice-Pres. Persian Acad. 37-70; mem. Board of Governors, Nat. Bank of Persia 37-52; Senator for Teheran 49-52, 54-60, 63-67, 67-71, 75-; Pres. Persia-America Relations Soc. 49-53; founding mem. Nat. Soc. for Physical Educ. 33-54, Soc. for Preservation of Nat. Heritage 44-, Nat. Soc. for Protection of Children 53-; mem. High Educ. Council 34-41, 51-58, 72-, Royal Cultural Council 62-, Higher Council Nat. Org. for the Protection of Historical Monuments 65-, mem. Acad. of Iran language 70-, mem. Higher Council of Culture and Art 72-.
Leisure interests: walking in the country, reading.
Publs. *Principles of Education, New Methods in Education, History of Education, Modern Persia and her Educational System* (in English), *A Year in America, The March of Education in Persia and the West, A Brief Course in the History of Education in Iran, A History of Education in Europe, History of Education in Persia from the Earliest Time till Today, Forty Lectures, Memoirs* (autobiography, 3 vols.), eleven essays, etc.
316 Avenue Hedayat, Valiabad, Teheran; and The Senate, Teheran, Iran.
Telephone: 318266.

Sadler, Donald Harry, O.B.E., M.A.; British astronomer; b. 22 Aug. 1908, Dewsbury, Yorkshire; *s.* of James W, Sadler and Gertrude Needham; *m.* Flora Munro McBain 1954; ed. Trinity Coll., Cambridge.
Entered H.M. Nautical Almanac Office 30, Deputy Superintendent 33, Superintendent 36-71; Sec. Royal Astronomical Society 39-47; Pres. Inst. of Navigation 53-55; Gen. Sec. Int. Astronomical Union 58-64; Vice-Pres. Council of Fed. of Astronomical and Geophysical Services 66-68, Pres. 68-70; Pres. Royal Astronomical Soc. 67-69; retd. 72.
Leisure interests: bridge, chess.
8 Collington Rise, Bexhill-on-Sea, Sussex, England.
Telephone: Cooden 3572.

Sadli, Mohammad, M.SC., PH.D.; Indonesian politician; b. 10 June 1922; ed. Univs. of Gadjah Mada and Indonesia, Massachusetts Inst. of Technology, Univ. of California (Berkeley) and Harvard Univ.
Lecturer, later Prof. of Econs., Univ. of Indonesia 57-, Army Staff Coll. 58-65, Navy Staff Coll. 58-65; Dir. Inst. of Econ. and Social Research, Faculty of Econs., Univ. of Indonesia 57-63; Asst. to Pres., Univ. of Indonesia 63-64; mem. Gov. Council, UN Asian Inst. of Devt. and Planning 63-64; Chair. Indonesian Economists Asscn. 66-72; Chair. Tech. Cttee. for Foreign Investment 67-73; Minister of Manpower 71-73, of Mines 73-; mem. U.N. Group on Multinational Cos. 73-74.
Ministry of Mines, Merdeka Selatan 18, Jakarta; Home: Brawijaya IV, 24 Kebayoran Baru, Jakarta-Selatan, Indonesia.
Telephone: 50232 (Office); 72599 (Home).

Sadove, A. Robert, PH.D.; American international finance official; b. 8 Sept. 1921, Lake Placid, N.Y.; *m.*; one *s.* three *d.*; ed. Harvard Univ.
Staff economist, Gass, Bell and Associates (Consulting Economists) 50-56; Adviser, German-Israel Reparations Mission, Cologne 52-53; Industrial Devt. Adviser, Govt. of Israel 53-54; Asst. Prof. of Economics, George Washington Univ. 54-56; Economist, Transportation Div., Public Utilities Div. and Economics Dept. IBRD 56-62, Economic Adviser Projects Dept. 62-68, Dir. Transportation Projects Dept. and Acting Dir. Tourism Projects Dept. 68-69; Dir. Special Projects Dept. IBRD

69-72, Urban Projects Dept. 72-74, Special Studies, East Asia and Pacific 74-.
International Bank for Reconstruction and Development, 1818 H Street, N.W. Washington, D.C. 20433, U.S.A.

Sadovsky, Mikhail Alexandrovich; Soviet physicist; b. 6 Nov. 1904, Leningrad; ed. Leningrad Polytechnical Inst.
Scientific Worker, U.S.S.R. Acad. of Sciences Seismological Inst. 30-41; mem. staff Presidium U.S.S.R. Acad. of Sciences 41-46; Deputy Dir. U.S.S.R. Acad. of Sciences Inst. of Chemical Physics 46-60; Dir. U.S.S.R. Acad. of Sciences Schmidt Inst. of Earth Physics 60-; Corresp. mem. U.S.S.R. Acad. of Sciences 58-66, mem. 66-; mem. C.P.S.U. 41-; Hero of Socialist Labour; State Prize (4 times); Academician-Sec. U.S.S.R. Acad. of Sciences Section of Earth-Science 66.
O. Y. Schmidt Institute of Earth Physics, B. Gruzinskaya ulitsa 10, Moscow, U.S.S.R.

Sádovský, Štefan; Czechoslovak politician; b. 13 Oct. 1928, Vlkas; ed. Coll. of Economy, Bratislava.
Secretary West Slovak Regional Cttee., C.P. of Slovakia 62-66; Chair. West Slovak Regional Nat. Cttee. 66-67; Deputy, Slovak Nat. Council 66-; mem. Central Cttee. C.P. of Slovakia 70; mem. Central Cttee. C.P. of Czechoslovakia 66-; Candidate mem. Presidium Central Cttee. of C.P. of Czechoslovakia 66-68; Sec. Central Cttee. C.P. of Czechoslovakia 67-68; Chair. Agricultural Comm., Central Cttee. C.P. of Czechoslovakia 67-69; Sec. Central Cttee. C.P. of Slovakia, mem. Secretariat of Central Cttee. C.P. of Slovakia 68-69; mem. Central Cttee. Presidium 68-70, First Sec. May 69-Jan. 70; mem. Secr. Cen. Cttee. C.P. of Czechoslovakia April-Aug. 68, Oct. 69-Jan. 70, and mem. Exec. Cttee. of Presidium 68-69; Premier of Slovak Socialist Republic Jan.-May 69, Deputy Premier Feb. 70-Dec. 70; Deputy to House of Nations, Fed. Assembly 68-; Chair. Legislative Council, Govt. of S.S.R. 70; mem. Legislative Council, Govt. of C.S.S.R. 70; Chair. Slovak Govt. Council for Nat. Cttees. 70-.
Government Presidium of Slovak Socialist Republic, Bratislava, Czechoslovakia.

Sadovsky, Vissarion Dmitryevich; Soviet metallurgist; b. 6 Aug. 1908, Omsk; ed. Kazan State Univ.
Head of Laboratory, Zlatoust Instrumental Plant 30-35; Research Worker, Head of Lab., Inst. of Metal Physics, U.S.S.R. Acad. of Sciences 35-, Prof. 46; mem. U.S.S.R. Acad. of Sciences 70-.
Publs. scientific works in the field of physical metallurgical science and the heat treatment of steel.
Institute of Metal Physics, Sverdlovsk, U.S.S.R.

Sadron, Charles Louis; French research scientist; b. 12 May 1902, Cluis, Indre; m. 1st Marie-Louise Eck 1931 (died), 2nd Geneviève Aubel; one d.; ed. Lycée de Chateauroux and Univs. of Poitiers and Strasbourg.
Professor at Lycées of Troyes 27-28 and Strasbourg 28-31; engaged on aeronautical research 31-33; Rockefeller Scholar (Inst. of Technology Pasadena) 33-34; research sponsored by Nat. Research Fund 34-37; Prof. Univ. of Strasbourg, 37-62, Muséum Nat. d'Histoire Naturelle, Paris 62-75; Scientific Adviser to UNESCO 46-47; Dir. Centre de Recherches sul res Macromolécules, Strasbourg 47-67; Sec. Int. Comm. on Macromolecular Chemistry 52-57; mem. Consultative Cttee. of Scientific and Technical Research 58-60; Hon. Dir. Centre de Biophysique Moléculaire, Orléans; mem. Acad. Royale Scientifique, Liège; Lauréat de l'Institut; Fellow, New York Acad. of Science; Dr. h.c. Univs. of Montreal, Uppsala; Officier de la Légion d'Honneur, Croix de Guerre, Commdr. des Palmes Académiques.
Leisure interests: music, hunting, fishing.
Publs. About 170 publications on magnetism, mechanics

of fluids, physical chemistry of macromolecules, particularly biological macromolecules, biophysics.
Centre de Biophysique Moléculaire, avenue de la Recherche Scientifique, 45045 Orléans 02, France.
Telephone: (38) 63 10 14.

Sadykov, Abid Sadykovich; Soviet chemist; b. 15 Nov. 1913, Tashkent, Uzbekistan; ed. Central Asia State Univ.
Teacher, Uzbek State Univ. 39-41, Central Asia State Univ. 41-46; Dir. Inst. of Chemistry, Uzbek Acad. of Sciences 46-50; Rector, Tashkent State Univ. 58-66; Prof. mem. Uzbek Acad. of Sciences 47-, Pres. 66-; Corresp. mem. U.S.S.R. Acad. of Sciences 66-73, mem. 73-; mem. C.P.S.U. 46-; mem. Cen. Cttee. C.P. of Uzbekistan; Orders and medals of U.S.S.R.
Publs. *The Chemistry of Alkaloids, Cotton Leaves as Valuable Chemical Raw Material.*
Uzbek S.S.R. Academy of Sciences, Ul. Kuibysheva 15, Tashkent, U.S.S.R.

Saeland, Einar; Norwegian scientist; b. 3 April 1915, Trondheim; s. of the late Prof. Sem Saeland and Gudrun Schöning, M.D.; m. Elsebe Stoltenberg 1951; one s. one d.; ed. Oslo Univ. and Coll. de France.
Research Chemist, Norsk Hydro 39-42; Research Scientist, Norwegian Defence Research Establishment 47-50; Research Scientist and Head of Isotope Dept., Netherlands-Norwegian Joint Establishment for Nuclear Energy Research 51-57; Dep. Dir OECD Nuclear Energy Agency (NEA) 58-62, Deputy Dir.-Gen. 62-64, Dir.-Gen. 64-.
Publs. Scientific works on nuclear chemistry, radiation chemistry and application of radioactive isotopes.
Nuclear Energy Agency, 38 boulevard Suchet, 75016 Paris, France.
Telephone: 524-96-50.

Safdie, Moshe, B.ARCH.; Canadian (b. Israeli) architect; b. 14 July 1938, Haifa, Palestine; s. of Leon Safdie and Rachael Esses; m. Nina Nusynowicz 1959; one s. one d.; ed. McGill Univ. Montreal, Canada.
With Van Ginkle & Assocs., Montreal 61-62; Louis I. Kahn, Philadelphia 62-63; architect, planner Canadian Corpn. for 1967 World Exhbn. 63; Moshe Safdie & Assocs., Montreal 64-, commissioned to execute Habitat '67 64; Visiting Prof. McGill Univ. 70-71; Davenport Prof. of Architecture, Yale Univ. 71-72; Lieut.-Gov. Gold Medal (Canada) 61, Massey Medal for Architecture (Canada) 69, A.R.I.A. Sinergy Award (U.S.A.) 70.
Publs. *Beyond Habitat* 70, *The Japan Architect* 70, *The Coldspring Presentation* 72, *Horizon* 73, *For Everyone a Garden* 74.
1315 de Maisonneuve Boulevard W., Montreal, H3G 1M4, Quebec; Home: 1011 Habitat '67, Cité du Havre, Montreal 103, Quebec, Canada.
Telephone: 514-849-2381 (Office); 514-871-9549 (Home).

Saffar, Salman Mohamed Al, PH.D.; Bahrain diplomatist; b. 1931, Bahrain; m. ed. Baghdad Univ., Iraq and Sorbonne, Paris.
Permanent Rep. to UN Sept. 71-.
Permanent Mission of Bahrain at United Nations, 747 Third Avenue, New York, N.Y. 10017, U.S.A.

Safronchuk, Vasily Stepanovich; Soviet diplomatist; b. 16 Feb. 1925, Lozovatka, Dnepropetrovsk region, Ukraine; ed. Moscow Inst. of International Relations.
Lecturer, researcher at Moscow Inst. of Int. Relations 55-59; First Sec. Counsellor at Soviet Embassy in U.K.; Deputy Chief Second European Dept. Foreign Ministry; Amb. to Ghana 67-71; Deputy Perm. Rep. of U.S.S.R. to UN 71-.
U.S.S.R. Permanent Mission of the UN, 136 East 67th Street, New York, N.Y. 10021, U.S.A.

Sagan, Carl, PH.D., SC.D.; American scientist and author; b. 19 Nov. 1934, New York; s. of Samuel and Rachel Sagan; m. Linda Salzman 1968; three s.; ed. Univ. of Chicago.

Assistant Prof. of Genetics, Stanford Univ. Medical School 62-63; Asst. Prof. of Astronomy, Harvard Univ., and Astrophysicist, Smithsonian Astrophysical Observatory 63-68; Dir., Laboratory for Planetary Studies, Cornell Univ. 68-, Prof. of Astronomy and Space Sciences 70, Assoc. Dir. of Center for Radiophysics and Space Research 75-; Visiting Assoc., California Inst. of Tech. 71-72, 76-77; Chair. Div. for Planetary Sciences, American Astronomical Soc. 75-76, Astronomy Section of A.A.A.S. 75-76; Editor-in-Chief *ICARUS: International Journal of Solar System Studies* 68-; Vice-Chair. Working Group on Moon and Planets of Cttee. on Space Research (COSPAR) of ICSU 68-75; mem. various advisory boards, NASA 59-, Investigator of interplanetary missions 62, 71-72, 76; mem. or Fellow Int. Astronomical Union, American Astronomical Union, American Geophysical Union, American Physical Soc., Int. Acad. of Astronautics, Int. Soc. for Study of Origins of Life, NASA Medal 72, Prix Galabert 73, Campbell Award 74, K. Roberts Prize 74, Joseph Priestley Award 75.

Publs. *Intelligent Life in the Universe* 66, *Planets* 66, *Planetary Exploration* 70, *The Air War in Indochina* 71, *UFOs: A Scientific Debate* 72, *The Cosmic Connection* 73, *Communication with Extraterrestrial Intelligence* 73, *Mars and the Mind of Man* 73, *Other Worlds* 75; 350 scientific papers and articles.

Laboratory for Planetary Studies, Center for Radiophysics and Space Research, Cornell University, Ithaca, N.Y. 14853, U.S.A.

Telephone: (607) 256-4971, 4972.

Sagan, Françoise (*pseudonym* of Françoise Quoirez); French writer; b. 21 June 1935; ed. Couvent des Oiseaux and Couvent du Sacré Coeur, Paris.

Prix des Critiques for *Bonjour Tristesse* 54.

Publs. *Bonjour Tristesse* 54, *Un certain sourire* 56, *Dans un mois, dans un an* 57, *Aimez-vous Brahms . . .* 59, *la Chamade* 65, *le Garde du coeur* 68, *Un peu de soleil dans l'eau froide* 69, *Des bleus à l'âme* 72, *Il est des parfums* (with Guillaume Hanoteau) 73, *les Merveilleux Nuages* 73, *Un profil perdu* 74, *Réponses* 75; scenario for the ballet *Le Rendez-vous Manqué* (with Michel Magne); own film adaption of *Dans un Mois, dans un An*; Plays: *Château en Suède* 59, *les Violons parfois . . .* 61, *la Robe mauve de Valentine* 63, *Bonheur, impair et passe* 64, *le Cheval évanoui* 66, *l'Echarde* 66, *Un piano dans l'herbe* 70, *Zaphorie* 73.

Editions Flammarion, 26 rue Racine, 75006 Paris, France.

Sagdeyev, Roald Zinnurovich, D.SC.; Soviet physicist; b. 26 Dec. 1932; ed. Moscow State Univ.

Research Worker, Inst. of Atomic Energy, U.S.S.R. Acad. of Sciences 56-61; Head of Laboratory, Inst. of Nuclear Physics, Siberian Dept., Acad. of Sciences 61-; Prof. Novosibirsk State Univ. 64-; Academician, U.S.S.R. Acad. of Sciences 68-.

U.S.S.R. Academy of Sciences, 14 Lenin Prospect, Moscow, U.S.S.R.

Saget, Louis Joseph Edouard; French government official; b. 27 April 1915, Paris; m. Anne Vincens 1940; five c.; ed. Univ. de Paris.

Mayor of Tananarive 54-56; First Counsellor, French Embassy, Madagascar 59-60; High Commr. in Comoro Islands 60-62; Commissaire aux Comptes, European Launcher Devt. Org. 63-66; Gov. of French Somaliland 66-67; High Commr. in Djibouti 67-69; Conseiller maître à la Cour des Comptes 70-; Pres. Agence nationale pour l'amélioration de l'habitat 71-, Comm. de terminologie du ministère de la Défense 73-; Investigator, Comité central d'enquête sur le coût et le rendement des services publics 74-; Officier Légion d'Honneur, Croix de Guerre, Commdr. de l'Etoile Noire, Commdr. de l'Ordre Nat. Malgache, Grand Commdr. of the Order of the Star of Ethiopia, Commdr. de l'Etoile Equatoriale de Gabon, Nat. Order of Upper Volta, Order of the Leopard of Zaire.

Leisure interest: nature.

Office: 13 rue Cambon, 75001 Paris; Home: 1 rue de Laborde, 91660 Méréville, France.

Sagør, Odd; Norwegian politician; b. 2 July 1918, Meldal.

With Norwegian Fire Insurance Fund 36-70, Regional Dir. for Møre and Trøndelag 69; mem. Trondheim City Council 46-70, Mayor 63-70; mem. several civic orgs.; Exec. Dir. of Finance, Trondheim 70; mem. Exec. Cttee., Working Cttee., Cen. League of Norwegian Municipalities 72-; Minister for Consumer Affairs and Govt. Admin. 73-; Labour.

Ministry of Consumer Affairs, Oslo Dep., Norway.

Sahay, Bhagwan, B.SC.; Indian civil servant and diplomatist; b. 15 Feb. 1905; ed. Univ. of Allahabad and School of Oriental Studies, London.

Joined Indian Civil Service 29; District Magistrate 35-37; Deputy Sec. Industries Dept., United Provinces 37-39, Commr. Census Operations 39-41; Sec. Indian Council of Agricultural Research, New Delhi 41-43; Joint Sec. Dept. of Agriculture, Govt. of India 44-45; Commr. of Food and Civil Supplies 46-49; Chief Sec., United Provinces 49-51; Chief Commr. of Himachal Pradesh 51-52, of Bhopal State 52-54; Ambassador to Nepel 54-59; Chief Commr. of Delhi 59-63; Lieut.-Gov. of Himachal Pradesh 63, then Kerala; Gov. of Padma Bhushan 61, Jammu and Kashmir 67-73.

c/o Office of the Governor, Srinagar, Jammu and Kashmir, India.

Saheki, Isamu, LL.B.; Japanese transport executive; b. 25 March 1903, Ehime Prefecture; m. Chiyoko Saheki; one s. two d.; ed. Tokyo Imperial Univ.

Executive, Kinki Nippon Railway Co. 25-, Vice-Pres. 47-51, Pres. 51-73, Chair. 73-; Chair. Kintetsu Business Group-Kintetsu Miyako hotels, Kinki Nippon Tourist Co., Kintetsu Motors Co., Kintetsu Dept. Stores; Pres. Osaka Chamber of Commerce and Industry; Vice-Pres. Fed. of Econ. Orgs.; Adviser Japan Airlines; founder of Yamato Bunka-Kan Museum; Blue Ribbon Medal.

Leisure interests: Kiyomoto (Japanese music), golf.

6-1-1 Uehommachi, Tennoji-ku, Osaka; Home: 2-1-4 Tomigaoka, Nara City, Japan.

Telephone: 06(771)3331, 0742(45)4550 (Home).

Sahgal, Mrs. Nayantara; Indian writer; b. 10 May 1927, Allahabad; d. of Ranjit Sitaram and Vijaya Lakshmi Pandit; m. Gautam Sahgal 1949 (divorced 1967); one s. two d.; ed. Wellesley Coll., U.S.A.

Scholar-in-Residence, holding creative writing seminar, Southern Methodist Univ., Dallas, Texas 73; Adviser English Language Board, Sahitya Akademi (Nat. Acad. of Letters), New Delhi.

Leisure interests: reading (novels, politics, philosophy), music (Indian, Western, Classical), walking

Publs. *Prison and Chocolate Cake* 54, *A Time to be Happy* 58, *From Fear Set Free* 62, *This Time of Morning* 65, *Storm in Chandigarh* 69, *History of the Freedom Movement* 70, *The Day in Shadow* 72.

10 Massey Hall Jai Singh Road, New Delhi 110001, India.

Sahm, Heinz-Ulrich, DR.JUR.; German diplomatist; b. 13 Oct. 1917, Bochum; s. of Heinrich and Dora (née Rolffs) Sahm; m. Insea Hohlt 1949; four s. two d.; ed. Städtisches Gymnasium, Danzig, Kaiserin-Augusta-Gymnasium, Berlin, Klosterschule Roszleben and Univs. of Munich, Kiel and Freiburg.

Joined diplomatic service 51; Amb. to U.S.S.R. 72-.

Embassy of the Federal Republic of Germany, Moscow, ul. Bol. Grusinskaja 17, U.S.S.R.

Said, El-Said Mostafa El-, LL.B., LL.D.; Egyptian lawyer and professor; b. 7 Oct. 1908; ed. Mansourah Secondary School and Cairo Univ.
Public Prosecutor 29-38; Lecturer and Asst. Prof. of Criminal Law, Cairo Univ. 32-42; Prof. of Criminal Law, Alexandria Univ. 42; Dean of Faculty of Law, Alexandria Univ. 46; Attorney-Gen., Alexandria Court of Appeal 49; Prof. of Criminal Law, Cairo Univ. 50, Dean of Faculty of Law, Cairo Univ. 52; Rector of Alexandria Univ. 54-58; Rector of Cairo Univ. 58-61; Amb. to Portugal 62-64, to Somalia 64-68, to German Democratic Repub. 72-; Chair. of Supreme Council of the Univs.
Publs. *On the Scope and Exercise of Marital Rights* 36, *The Egyptian Penal Code Annotated*, 3rd edition 37, *Crimes of Forgery Under the Egyptian Law*, 4th edition 53, *Principles of Criminal Law*, 4th edition 62, *The Expansion of Higher Education in the United Arab Republic* 60, *International Study of University Admissions, the United Arab Republic* 62.
Egyptian Embassy, Warmbader Strasse 50-52, Berlin-Karlshorst, German Democratic Republic.

Said, Faisal al-; Omani diplomatist; b. 1927, Muscat. Attached to Ministry of Foreign Affairs, Muscat 53-57; lived abroad 57-70; Perm. Under-Sec. Ministry of Educ. 70-72; Minister of Econ. Affairs 72; Perm. Rep. to UN, Amb. to U.S.A. 72-73; Minister of Educ. 73-.
Ministry of Education, Muscat, Oman.

Said, Hakim Mohammed; Pakistani physician; b. 9 Jan. 1920; s. of late Hakim Adul Majeed; ed. Ayurvedic and Unani Tibbia (Medical) Coll., Delhi.
Founder, Sec.-Gen. Soc. for Promotion of Eastern Medicine 56; Founder, Pres. Coll. of Eastern Medicine, Karachi 58; Pres. Inst. of Health and Medical Research; Pres. Hamdard Nat. Foundation; Pres. Soc. for the Promotion and Improvement of Libraries; mem. Cen. Advisory Cttee. Pakistan Broadcasting Corpn.; organized Health of the Nation Conf., Karachi 71, formed Nat. Health Cttee.; Consultant mem. Technical Devt. Board, Union Int. d'Education pour la Santé, Paris until 76; participant, organizer many int. confs. and congresses; Sitara-i-Imtiaz (Award for Social and Educ. Service, Govt. of Pakistan) 66.
Publs. *Medicine of China, Europe Nama, Germany Nama, Wonders of the Human Body, Health of the Nation, The Employer and Employee, Tazkara-i-Muhammad, Pharmacopoeia of Eastern Medicine, Main Currents of Contemporary Thought in Pakistan* (2 vols.).
Hamdard National Foundation, Hamdard Centre, Nazimabad, Karachi 18; Home: Hamdard Manzil, 58/1 Shikarpur Colony, New Town, Karachi 5, Pakistan.

Saif al-Islam Mohamed al-Badr, H.R.H.; fmr. Imam of the Yemen; b. 1927; ed. Coll. for Higher Education, Sana'a (Yemen).
Minister for Foreign Affairs 55-61, and Minister of Defence and C.-in-C. 55-62; succeeded to Imamate on the death of his father, Imam Ahmed Sept. 62; in hills, Yemen, leading Royalist Forces in civil war 62-68; replaced by Imamate Council May 68; in exile in Saudi Arabia 68-.
Jeddah, Saudi Arabia.

Saifudin; Chinese (Uighur) politician; b. 1916, Artush, Sinkiang; ed. Cen. Asia Univ., Moscow.
Leader of Uighur Uprisings 33, 44; Minister of Educ., E. Turkistan Repub. 45; Deputy Chair. Sinkiang People's Govt. 49-54, Chair. 55-68; Deputy Commdr. Sinkiang Mil. Region, People's Liberation Army 49; Second Sec. CCP Sinkiang 56-68; Alt. mem. 8th Cen. Cttee. of CCP 56; Pres. Sinkiang Univ. 64; Vice-Chair. Sinkiang Revolutionary Cttee. 68, Chair. 72; mem. 9th Cen. Cttee. of CCP 69; Second Sec. CCP Sinkiang 71, First Sec. 73; Alt. mem. Politburo, 10th Cen. Cttee. of CCP 73; Political Commissar Sinkiang Mil. Region, PLA 74-.
People's Republic of China.

Saigol, Mohammed Rafique; Pakistani business executive; b. 1933, Calcutta; m.; one d. three s.; ed. Aitchison Coll., Lahore and Clemson Coll., S.C., U.S.A. Formerly Man. Dir. Kohinoor Textile Mills, Lyallpur and Chair. Cen. Board of Management of the Saigol Group; mem. Nat. Assembly; Parl. Sec. to Govt. 65-69; Chair. All-Pakistan Textile Mills Asscn. 67-69; Pres. Lahore Chamber of Commerce and Industry 68-69; Pres. Lahore Stock Exchange 71; Man. Dir. Pakistan Int. Airlines 72-73; mem. Exec. Cttee. Int. Air Transport Asscn.; Chair. Saigol Bros. Ltd., Nat. Construction Co. (Pakistan) Ltd.; Dir. State Bank of Pakistan; mem. Advisory Council on Econ. Affairs, Govt. of Pakistan; Man. Trustee Saigol Foundation Trust; has served on numerous advisory bodies to Govt. of Pakistan.
6 Egerton Road, Lahore; Home: 91-E-1, Gulberg 3, Lahore, Pakistan.

Sainsbury, Baron (Life Peer), cr. 62, of Drury Lane; **Alan John Sainsbury;** British retail executive; b. 13 Aug. 1902; s. of John Benjamin and Mabel Miriam Sainsbury; m. 1st Doreen Davan Adams (dissolved) 1925; three s.; 2nd Anne Elizabeth Lewy 1944; one d.; ed. Haileybury School.
J. Sainsbury Ltd. (grocery and provision firm) 21-, Joint Pres. 67-; mem. Williams' Cttee. on Milk Distribution 47-48; mem. Food Research Advisory Cttee. 60-70, Chair. 65-70; mem. Econ. Devt. Cttee. for the Distributive Trades (N.E.D.C.) 64-68; Vice-Pres. Royal Soc. for Encouragement of Arts, Manufactures and Commerce 62-66, The Asscn. of Agriculture 65-; Pres. Grocer's Inst. 63-66, Dir. 66-; Pres. Pestalozzi Children's Village Trust 63-, Multiple Shops Fed. 63-65, Royal Inst. Public Health and Hygiene 65-70; Chair. Cttee. of Inquiry into relationship of pharmaceutical industry with Nat. Health Service 65-67; mem. Labour Party 45-; mem. Court of Univ. of Essex 66-; Gov. City Literary Inst. 67-69; Pres. Distributive Trades Educ. and Training Council 75-; Chair. of Trustees, Overseas Students Advisory Bureau; mem. Exec. Cttee. of PEP 70-; mem. Council English Stage Co. 75-, Writers and Scholars Educational Trust 75-; Hon. Fellow Inst. of Food Science and Technology.
Stamford House, Blackfriars, London, S.E.1, England.
Telephone: 01-928-3355.

St. John-Stevas, Norman Antony Francis, M.P.; British politician, barrister, author and journalist; b. 18 May 1929; ed. Ratcliffe, Cambridge, Christ Church, Oxford and Yale.
Barrister, Middle Temple 52; Lecturer, King's Coll., London 53-56; Tutor in Jurisprudence, Christ Church, Oxford 53-55, Merton Coll., Oxford 55-57; Founder mem. Inst. of Higher European Studies, Bolzano 55; Legal Adviser to Sir Alan Herbert's Cttee. on Book Censorship 54-59; Legal and Political Corresp., *The Economist* 59-64; Conservative M.P. 64-; Sec. Conservative Party Home Affairs Cttee. 69-72; mem. Fulbright Comm. 61; Parl. Select Cttee. Race Relations and Immigration 70-72; Parl. Under-Sec. for Educ. and Science 72-73; Minister of State for the Arts 73-74; Civil List 71-; mem. Shadow Cabinet 74-, Opposition Spokesman on Educ., Science and the Arts; Vice-Chair. Cons. Parl. N. Ireland Cttee. 72-; Vice-Chair. Cons. Group for Europe 72-; founder mem. Christian-Social Inst. of Culture, Rome 69; Hon. Sec. Fed. of Conservative Students 71-73; Editor *The Dublin (Wiseman Review)* 61; Kt. St. Lazarus of Jerusalem 63; Cavaliere Ordine al Merito della Repubblica (Italy) 65; F.R.S.L. 66.
Leisure interests: reading, talking, listening to music, travelling, walking, appearing on television.

Publs. *Obscenity and the Law* 56, *Walter Bagehot* 59, *Life, Death and the Law* 61, *The Right to Life* 63, *Law and Morals* 64, *The Literary Essays of Walter Bagehot* 65, *The Historical Essays of Walter Bagehot* 68, *The Agonising Choice* 71, *The Political Essays of Walter Bagehot* 74.
1 Hampstead Square, London, N.W.3, England.
Telephone: 01-435-7080.

Saint Laurent, Yves (Henri Donat Mathieu); French couturier; b. 1 Aug. 1936, Oran, Algeria; s. of Charles Mathieu Saint Laurent and Lucienne Andrée Wilbaux; ed. Lycée d'Oran.
Career dedicated to haute couture; designer; partner and successor of Christian Dior 54; shareholder Yves Saint Laurent S.A. 62-; works include: costume sketches for Roland Petit's ballets *Chants de Maldoror* 62, *Adagio and Variations, Notre Dame de Paris* 65; sketches for costumes for *le Mariage de Figaro* (Compagnie Madeleine Renaud—Jean Louis Barrault) 64, scenery and costumes for Zizi Jeanmaire's shows at the Alhambra 62 and Théâtre National de Paris 63, costumes for Edward Albee's *A Delicate Balance* (Théâtre de France) 67; films: costumes for Luis Buñuel's *Belle de Jour* 67, *La Chamade* (from the novel of Françoise Sagan) 68, Alain Resnais' *Stavisky*; Oscars from Neiman-Marcus (Dallas) 58 and Harper's Bazaar 66.
Publ. illustrated book *La Vilaine Lulu* 67.
5 avenue Marceau, 75016 Paris; and 55 rue de Babylone, 75007 Paris, France.

Sainteny, Jean; French banker and politician; b. 29 May 1907.
Banking career in Indochina 29-31, and Paris 32-39; Resistance Movement 39-45; French Commr. to China 45, to Tonkin and Annam 45-47; Gov. of the Colonies 46; Del.-Gen. to N. Viet-Nam 54-58; Commr.Gen. for Tourism 59-62; Minister for Ex-Service Men 62-66; Dir. 68-; Dir. Int. Inst. of Public Admin. 67-; mem. Constitutional Council 68-.
Publs. *Histoire d'une Paix Manquée: Indochine 1945-47* 53, *Face à Ho-Chi-Minh* 70.
204 rue de Rivoli, 75001 Paris, France.

Saito, Eiichi; Japanese newspaper executive; b. 3 Dec. 1910, Osaka; m. Aiko Saito; two d.; ed. Osaka Higher Commercial School.
Reporter, *Mainichi Shimbun*, Osaka 31; Overseas correspondent, London 41; Asst. City News Editor, Osaka 42; Chief, Kyoto Branch Office 45; City News Editor, Osaka 47; Editorial Writer 50; overseas correspondent, U.S.A. 51; Asst. Man. Editor 54; Chief, London Office 56, Gen. Man. European Office 57; Man. Editor, Osaka 61, Tokyo 63; mem. Board of Dirs. 64; Man. Dir. and Exec. Editor 68-.
Leisure interest: golf.
Mainichi Shimbun, 1-1-1, Hitotsubashi, Chiyoda-ku, Tokyo; New Akasaka Corporas, 12-4, Akasaka 8-chome, Minato-ku, Tokyo, Japan.

Saito, Kiyoshi; Japanese wood print artist; b. 1907, Fukushima Pref.; m. Fumiko Kamiya 1932; one d.
First specialized in oil painting and held many exhbns. in Japan; later turned to wood printing, often using Haniwa (Ancient Clay Image) as material; one-man exhbn. Corcoran Gallery of Art, Washington, D.C. 57; numerous exhbns. throughout U.S.A. 57-59; took part in Asia and Africa Art exhbn. sponsored by Egyptian Govt. and won prize 57; one-man exhbns. at Nordness Gallery, New York 62, Sydney and Melbourne 65, Fine Arts Gallery of San Diego 69; two-man exhbn. Hawaii Museum 64; awarded the Int. Biennial Exhbn. of Prints in Yugoslavia; awarded Prize for Japanese Artist at Int. Arts Exhbn., Brazil.
1-23-14, Nishimikado, Kamakura City, Kanagawa Pref., Japan.
Telephone: 0467-22-2170.

Saito, Kunikichi; Japanese politician; b. 1909.
Specialized in welfare and medical affairs, Labour Ministry; mem. for Fukushima Prefecture, House of Representatives; Deputy Sec.-Gen. Liberal Democratic Party (LDP), Chair. House of Representatives Finance Cttee., Deputy Chief Cabinet Sec., Parl. Vice-Minister of Finance, Minister of Health and Welfare 72-Dec. 74.
House of Representatives, Tokyo, Japan.

Saito, Nobufusa, D.SC.; Japanese atomic scientist; b. 28 Sept. 1916, Tokyo; m. Haruko Umeda 1944; one s. two d.; ed. Tokyo Imperial Univ.
Former Asst. Prof., Kyushu and Seoul Univs., Prof. of Inorganic Chem., Tokyo Univ. 56-; Chief Researcher, Inst. of Physical and Chemical Research 59-; fmr. Consultant to Int. Atomic Energy Agency (I.A.E.A.), Dir. of Isotopes Div. 63-65; Prof. Inorganic and Nuclear Chem., Tokyo Univ. 65-, Dir. Radioisotope Centre 70-; Dir. Japan Radioisotopes Asscn. 67-; Technical Adviser, Japan Atomic Energy Research Inst. 66-; mem. Chemical Soc. of Japan, American Chemical Soc., Atomic Energy Soc. of Japan, Japan Soc. for Analytical Chem.; Co-Editor *Int. Journal of Applied Radiation & Isotopes*; Chem. Soc. of Japan Award 74.
Leisure interests: music, travel.
5-12-9, Koshigoe, Kamakura, Japan.
Telephone: 0467-31-3178.

Saito, Noburo; Japanese politician; b. 1903, Mie Prefecture; ed. Tokyo Imperial Univ.
Former Gov. of Yamanashi Prefecture; fmr. Vice-Minister for Home Affairs; fmr. Chief of Metropolitan Police; fmr. Dir.-Gen., Police Headquarters; fmr. Minister of Transport; Minister of Health and Welfare Nov. 68-Jan. 70, 71-72; mem. House of Councillors; Liberal Democrat.
Koseisho, 2-1 Kasumigaseki, Chiyoda-ku, Tokyo, Japan.

Saito, Ryoei; Japanese business executive; b. 17 April 1916; ed. Nihon Univ.
President, Daishowa Paper Manufacturing Co., Ltd.
Daishowa Paper Manufacturing Co., Ltd. 133 Imai, Fuji City, Shizuoka Prefecture, Japan.

Saito, Shizuo; Japanese diplomatist; b. 1914, Tokyo; s. of Kichinosuke and Sanko Saito; m. Akiko Saito née Araki 1950; two s.; ed. Tokyo Imperial Univ.
Counsellor, London 59-62; Minister in Bangkok 62-63; Dir. UN Bureau 63-64; Amb. to Indonesia 64-66, to Australia 70-74, concurrently to Fiji 72-74 and to Nauru 72-74; Perm. Rep. to UN 74-.
Leisure interests: painting, golf.
Permanent Mission of Japan to the United Nations, 866 United Nations Plaza, 2nd Floor, New York, N.Y. 10017, U.S.A.

Saito, Shoichi; Japanese automobile executive; b. 1 June 1908, Chikusa, Aichi-gun; s. of Yoshihiro and Taka Saito; m. Mitsu Kawamoto 1938; three s.; ed. Tohoku Univ.
Executive; Vice-Pres. Toyota Motor Co. Ltd. 67-73, Chair. 73-; Dir. Toyota Motor Sales U.S.A. Inc. 67-; Dir. Toyota Central Research and Devt. Laboratories Inc. 68-; Pres. Soc. of Automotive Engineers of Japan 68-72; Auditor Toyota Automatic Loom Works Ltd., Aisin Seiki Co. Ltd., Towa Real Estate Co. Ltd. 73-; Hon. Blue Ribbon Medal 70.
Leisure interests: skating, tennis, golf, music.
Toyota Motor Co. Ltd., 1 Toyota-cho, Toyota-shi, Aichi-ken; Home: 26 Takamine-cho, Showa-ku, Nagoyashi, Aichi-ken, Japan 471.
Telephone: 0565-28-2121 (Office).

Saiyidain, Khwaja Ghulam, B.A., M.ED.; Indian educationist; b. 14 Feb. 1904, Panipat; s. of Khwaja Ghulam Saqlain; m. Aziz Jahan Begum 1930; four d.; ed. Univs. of Aligarh and Leeds.
Prof. of Education Aligarh Muslim Univ. 26-39; Dir. of

Education Jammu and Kashmir State 39-46; Educational Adviser to Rampur Government 46-47; Educational Adviser to Bombay Government 47-50; joint Educational Adviser to Government of India 51-54; Additional Sec. Min. of Education 54-55; Sec. and Education Adviser to the Government of India, Ministry of Education 56-60, on special duty 60-61; Visiting Prof. Columbia, Wisconsin and Stanford Univs.; Educational Adviser to Jammu and Kashmir Govt. 62; Senior Scholar, East West Center, Hawaii 63-64; mem. Educ. Comm. 64-66; Dir. Asian Inst. of Educational Planning and Admin. 64-68; Acad. of Letters Award 64; Padma Bhushan 66; D.Litt. h.c.
Leisure interests: reading, writing, music.
Publs. *The School of the Future, Principles of Education, Iqbal's Educational Philosophy, Problems of Educational Reconstruction, Andhi Men Charagh* (award winning book), *Universities and the life of the mind, Humanistic Tradition in Indian Educational thought, Lamps in the storm, Principles of Education, Faith of an educationist.*
P.O. Jamianagar, New Delhi 25, India.
Telephone: 63202.

Sakamoto, Isamu; Japanese business executive; b. 23 Oct. 1911; s. of Tanekichi and Fusa Sakamoto; m. Chizuko Takeuchi 1937; four c.; ed. Kyoto Univ.
Director and Man. Engineering Div. and Research and Devt. Labs., Sumitomo Electric Industries, Ltd. (SEI) 58; Man. Dir. SEI 61, Exec. Vice-Pres. May 69, Pres. 69-73, Chair. of Board Nov. 73-; Chair. Nuclear Fuel Industries Ltd.; Dir. Meidensha Ltd., Sumitomo-3M Co. Ltd.; Vice-Chair. Japan-U.S. Soc. of Osaka; Chair. Int. Wrought Copper Council.
5-3, 2-chome, Fujishirodai, Suita City, Osaka Pref., Japan.
Telephone: 06-872-2837.

Sakata, Michita; Japanese politician; b. 1916, Kyu-Shu; s. of Michio and Yo Sakata; m. Michiyo Sakata 1948; two s. two d.; ed. Tokyo Imperial Univ.
Former Private Sec. to Minister of Commerce and Industry; fmr. Parl. Vice-Minister for Transport; fmr. Minister of Health and Welfare; fmr. Minister of Education; mem. House of Reps.; Dir. Defence Agency Dec. 74-; Liberal Democrat.
Leisure interests: music, painting.
Dai-ichi Gi-in-kaikan, 2-2-1, Nagato-cho, Chiyoda-ku, Tokyo, Japan.
Telephone: Tokyo 581-4877.

Sakharov, Andrei Dimitrievich; Soviet nuclear physicist; b. 21 May 1921, Moscow; m. 2nd Elena Bonner 1971; one s. one d.; ed. Moscow State Univ.
Physicist, P.N. Lebedev Physics Inst., Acad. of Sciences 45-; mem. Acad. of Sciences of U.S.S.R. (Dept. of Nuclear Physics) 53-; mem. American Acad. of Arts and Sciences 69-, Nat. Acad. of Sciences 72-; with Igor Tamm achieved important breakthrough in field of controlled nuclear fusion leading to devt. of Soviet hydrogen bomb; formed Human Rights Cttee. 70; Eleanor Roosevelt Peace Award 73, Cino del Duca Prize 74, Reinhold Niebohr Prize, Univ. of Chicago 74, Nobel Peace Prize 75.
Publs. include *Progress, Peaceful Co-existence and Intellectual Freedom* 68, *Sakharov Speaks* 74, *My Country and the World* 75, and basic works on problems of theoretical physics.
U.S.S.R. Acad. of Sciences, Leninsky prospekt 14, Moscow, U.S.S.R.

Sakombi, Inongo; Zairian politician; b. 1940, Akula; ed. Université Libre de Bruxelles.
Secretary for Mobilization, European Section, Mouvement populaire de la révolution (MPR) 67-69; Dir. Cabinet of the Minister of Information 69-70; State

Commr. for Information 70-75; mem. Political Bureau of MPR.
Political Bureau of the Mouvement populaire de la révolution, Kinshasa, Zaire.

Sakurada Takeshi; Japanese textile executive; b. 17 March 1904, Hiroshima; s. of Sai and Naka Sakurada; m. Fumi Yokoyama 1932; two s. one d.; ed. Tokyo Univ.
Nisshin Spinning Co. Ltd. 43-; Man. Dir. 44-45, Pres. 45-64, Chair. of Board 64-70, Adviser 70-; Dir. The Industry Club of Japan 49-; Adviser Japan Broadcasting Co. Ltd. 54-; Auditor Fuji Television Broadcasting Co. Ltd. 67-; Dir. New Japan Radio Co. Ltd. 59-, Toho Rayon Co. Ltd. 66-; Promotor and Auditor Arabian Oil Co. Ltd. 58-; mem. Public Security Comm. 64-; Deputy Chair. Fiscal System Council 65-. Chair. Toho Rayon Co. Ltd. 69-; fmr. Pres. Japan Fed. of Employers' Asscns.
Leisure interests: oil painting, golf.
8, 22-Kamiyamacho, Shibuya-ku, Tokyo, Japan.

Sakurai, Toshiki, B.ENG.; Japanese business executive; b. 1 April 1893, Tokyo; m. 1922; four s. one d.; ed. Tokyo Imperial Univ.
With Mitsubishi Shipbuilding & Engineering Co. Ltd. 19-43; Gen. Man. Nagoya Engine Works, Mitsubishi Heavy Industries Ltd. 43-45, Gen. Man. Fourth Engineering Works 45, Gen. Man. Kyoto Engineering Works 45-46, Dir. and Gen. Man. Kyoto 46-49, Man. Dir. and Gen. Man. 49; Man. Dir. Mitsubishi Heavy Industries 49-50; Exec. Vice-Pres. Mitsubishi Nippon Heavy Industries Ltd. 50-52, Pres. 52-61, Chair. Board of Dirs. 61-64; Counsellor, Mitsubishi Heavy Industries Ltd. 64-; Adviser, The Shipbuilders' Asscn. of Japan; Blue Ribbon Medal; Second Order of Merit.
5-1, Marunouchi 2-chome, Chiyoda-Ku, Tokyo, Japan.

Sakurauchi, Yoshio; Japanese politician; b. 1912; ed. Keio Univ.
Member of House of Reps. Liberal Democratic Party (LDP); Minister of Int. Trade and Industry July 64-65; Minister of Agriculture and Forestry 72-73; fmr. Chair. LDP Policy Affairs Council; Chair. House of Reps. Foreign Affairs Cttee. 71.
Agriculture and Forestry Ministry, House of Representatives, Tokyo, Japan.

Salacrou, Armand Camille; French playwright; b. 9 Aug. 1899; ed. Faculty of Medicine, Faculty of Letters, Faculty of Law, Paris.
Thirty plays produced in Paris, first performance in Théâtre de l'Oeuvre 25, first included in repertoire of Comédie-Française 44; fmr. Pres. Société des Auteurs et Compositeurs Dramatiques; fmr. Pres. of Int. Theatre Inst. (UNESCO); mem. Acad. Goncourt; Commandeur de la Légion d'Honneur.
Plays. *Le Pont de l'Europe* 27, *Atlas-Hotel* 31, *Une femme libre* 34, *L'Inconnue d'Arras* 35, *La Terre est ronde* 38, *Histoire de rire* 39, *Les Fiancés du Havre* 44, *Les Nuits de la colère* 46, *L'Archipel Lenoir* 47, *Les Invités du Bon Dieu, Sens Interdit* 53, *Le Miroir, Une Femme trop honnête* 56, *Boulevard Durand* 60, *Comme les Chardons* 64; etc.
Villa Maritime, 8 rue Guy de Maupassant, 76600 Le Havre, France.

Salah, Abdullah A.; Jordanian diplomatist; b. 31 Dec. 1922; ed. Bishop Gobat's School, Jerusalem, and American Univ. of Beirut.
Field Educ. Officer, UN Relief and Works Agency (UNRWA), Jordan 52-62; Amb. to Kuwait 62-63, to India 63-64, to France 64-Dec. 66, 67-70; Minister of Foreign Affairs Dec. 66-67, 70-72; Amb. to U.S.A. (also accred. to Canada) 73-; several decorations.
Embassy of Jordan, 2319 Wyoming Avenue, N.W., Washington, D.C., U.S.A.

Salam, Abdus, M.A., PH.D., D.SC., F.R.S.; Pakistani university professor; b. 29 Jan. 1926, Jhang; ed. St. John's Coll., Cambridge and Govt. Coll., Lahore.
Professor of Mathematics, Govt. Coll., Lahore 51-54; Head, Mathematics Dept., Panjab Univ., Lahore 52-54; Lecturer, Univ. of Cambridge 54-56; Prof. of Theoretical Physics, Imperial Coll. of Science and Technology, Univ. of London 57-; mem. Pakistan Atomic Energy Comm. 59-74, Pakistan Science Council 62-, Chief Scientific Adviser to Pres. 61-74; Gov., Int. Atomic Energy Agency 62-63; Dir. Int. Centre for Theoretical Physics, Trieste 64-; mem. UN Advisory Cttee. on Science and Technology 64, Chair. 71; Vice-Pres. IUPAP 73; mem. Scientific Council Stockholm Int. Peace Research Inst. (SIPRI) 70-; mem. London and American Physical Socs.; Fellow, Royal Swedish Acad. of Sciences 70; Foreign mem. U.S.S.R. Acad. of Sciences, American Academy of Arts and Sciences; many awards including Atoms for Peace Award 68.
Publs. about 150 articles.
Department of Physics, Imperial College of Science and Technology, London, S.W.7, England and International Centre for Theoretical Physics, P.O. Box 586, 34100, Trieste, Italy.
Telephone: 01-589-5111, ext. 2513; and Trieste 224281.

Salam, Saeb; Lebanese politician; b. 1905, Beirut; s. of Selim and Koulthoum Salam; m. Tamima Mardam Bey 1945; three s. two d.; ed. American Univ. of Beirut, London School of Economics.
Elected Provisional Head, Lebanese Govt. 43; Deputy 43-47, 51, 60-; Minister of Interior 46, 60-61, 70-73, of Foreign Affairs 46; Prime Minister 52, 53, 60-61, 70-73, concurrently Minister of Defence 61; pioneer Lebanese civil aviation 45; Pres. Middle East Airlines Co., Beirut 45-56; Pres. Nat. Fats and Oil Co. Ltd., Beirut.
Leisure interests: hunting, swimming, reading, riding.
Abu Bakr Al Saddik Street, P.O. Box 3147, Mousaitbeh, Beirut, Lebanon.
Telephone: 231716; 293975.

Salan, Raoul Albin Louis; French army officer; b. 1899; ed. Coll. de St. Cyr.
2nd Lieut. 19, Lieut. 21, Capt. 30, Commandant 38, Lieut. Col. 41; Head, Deuxième Bureau, French West Africa 41-43; Col. 43; Gén. de Brigade, commanding 9th Division of Colonial Infantry, later 14th Div. of Infantry 44; Commdr. French troops in China and at Tongkin 45-46; Gén. de Division, commanding Tongkin troops 47; Commandant Supérieur, French troops in Far East 48; Gén. de Corps d'Armée, C.-in-C. Indochina 52-53; Inspector Gen., Land Defence 53; mem. Conseil Supérieur de la Guerre et des Forces Armées 55; Commdr. 10th Army District, Supreme Commdr., Algeria 56-May 58; Del. Gen. of French Govt., C.-in C., Algeria May-Dec. 58; Military Gov. of Paris 59-60; in exile 60-61; implicated in Algiers revolt April 61, sentenced to death in absentia July 61, captured in Algiers April 62; sentenced to life imprisonment and stripped of military honours May 62; granted pardon June 68; Médaille Militaire, Grand Croix de la Légion d'Honneur, Croix de Guerre (14-18 and 39-45), Croix de Guerre T.O.E., C.B.E., D.S.C. (U.S.A.).
Publs. Etude sur les langues "Lu" du Haut-Laos, memoirs Fin d'un Empire (4 vols., 5th in preparation), O.A.S. mon dernier combat, Indochine Rouge, le message d'Hô Chi Minh.
41 boulevard Raspail, Paris 7e, France.

Salas, Rafael M., M.P.A., LL.B.; Philippine international administrator; b. 7 Aug. 1928, Bago, Negros Occidental; s. of Ernesto S. Salas and Isabel Montinola; m. Carmelita J. Rodriguez 1967; one s.; ed. Univ. of the Philippines, Harvard Univ.
Chair. Presidential Consultative Council of Students 54; Univ. of the Philippines, Lecturer in Political

Science and Econs. 55-59, in Law 63-66, Asst. Vice-Pres. 62-63, mem. Board of Regents 66-69; Lecturer in Econ., Graduate School, Far Eastern Univ. 60-61; Asst. to Exec. Sec., Office of Pres. 54-55; Tech. Adviser to Pres. 56-57; Supervising Economist, Nat. Econ. Council 57-60, Exec. Dir. (cabinet rank) 60-61, Acting Chair. 66, 68; Special Asst. to Pres., Local Govts. and to Sec. of Agric. and Natural Resources 61; Gen. Man. The Manila Chronicle 63-65; Board Chair., Govt. Service Insurance System 66; Action Officer Nat. Rice and Corn Sufficiency Prog. 66-69; Nat. Projects Overall Co-ordinator and Action Officer 66-69; Chair. Govt. Reorganization Comm. 68-69; Exec. Sec. of the Philippines 66-69; Under Sec.-Gen., Exec. Dir. UNFPA (UN Fund for Population Activities) 69-, Dir. 69-71, Asst. Sec.-Gen. 71-72; UN Official in charge of World Population Year 74; Exec. Sec. UNESCO Nat. Comm. of the Philippines 57; Asst. Sec.-Gen. 2nd Asia Productivity Conf., Manila 60; Adviser, Philippine Del., 17th, 18th, 19th Gen. Sessions of ECAFE (New Delhi 61, Tokyo 62, Manila 63); Amb. to Indonesia, Merdeka Day 67; Vice-Pres. UN Int. Conf. on Human Rights, Teheran 68; mem. Philippine Del., 23rd Session UN Gen. Assembly 68; Hon. Ph.D., D.H.L.; many foreign orders; numerous awards incl. Management Man of the Year Award, Management Asscn. of the Philippines 66.
Leisure interest: reading.
Publs. numerous articles on govt. management and population issues.
UNFPA, United Nations Plaza, New York, N.Y. 10017, U.S.A.

Salas, Xavier de, DR. EN FIL. Y LETRAS, LIC. EN DER.; Spanish art historian; b. 4 June 1907, Barcelona; s. of Francisco Javier de Salas y de Milans and of Maria Teresa Bosch Tintorer; m. Maria del Carmen de Ortueta 1940; three s. one d.; ed. Univs. of Madrid, Barcelona, Vienna and Berlin.
Assistant Prof., Faculty of Philosophy and Letters, Barcelona 31-40, Temp. Asst. Prof. of History of Art 40-43, Prof. 43-45; Prof. of History of Art, Univs. of Barcelona 45-, and Madrid 63-; Dir. Museo de Cataluña, Barcelona 40-47; Deputy Dir. Cttee. of Museums of Barcelona 40-47; Dir. Spanish Inst., London and Cultural Attaché, Spanish Embassy, London 47-63, Hon. Attaché 63-; Deputy Dir. Museo del Prado 61-70, Dir. 70-; mem. Real Academia de Buenas Letras de Barcelona 43-56, Corresp. mem. 56-; mem. Real Academia Artes de San Fernando 67; corresp. mem. Hispanic Soc., New York and several Spanish acads.; hon. Academician, Royal Acad., London; Assoc. mem. Royal Flemish Acad. of Language and Literature; Pres. Spanish Cttee. of Int. Council of Museums (ICOM); Pres. Consultative Cttee. of ICOM 71-74; Pres. Int. Cttee. of Art History 73.
Leisure interests: driving and walking.
Publ. Miguel Angel y El Greco 67 and over 100 articles on painting and sculpture in learned journals.
Pedro de Valdivia No. 4, Madrid 6, Spain; also Upper 5A Albany, Piccadilly, London, W.1, England.

Salazar López, H.E. Cardinal José; Mexican ecclesiastic; b. 12 June 1910, Ameca, Guadalajara.
Ordained 34; consecrated titular Bishop of Prusiade 61; transferred to Zamora 67; Archbishop of Guadalajara 70-; created Cardinal by Pope Paul VI 73.
Palacio Arzobispal, Apartado Postal I-331, Guadalajara, Mexico.

Salazar Navarrete, Fernando; Costa Rican diplomatist; b. 22 April 1930, San José; ed. Univ. of Costa Rica.
Official Mayor, Univ. of Costa Rica 58; Sec.-Gen. Youth of the Nat. Liberation Party 58-64; Deputy to Legislative Assembly 62-66; Vice-Pres. Comm. of Int. Affairs, Nat. Liberation Party 67-68; Amb. to Colombia

70-72; Vice Minister of Foreign Affairs 72-73; Perm. Rep. to UN Nov. 73-.
Permanent Mission of Costa Rica to the United Nations, 211 East 43rd Street, Room 1002A, New York, N.Y. 10017, U.S.A.

Salcedo-Bastardo, José Luis; Venezuelan writer and diplomatist; b. 1926, Carúpano; m. María Avila 1968; four s.; ed. Universidad Central de Venezuela, Univ. of Paris and London School of Economics.
Teacher of Social Sciences 45; Chief Ed. *Revista Nacional de Cultura* 48-50; Asst. Lecturer, Universidad Central de Venezuela 49; Founder Rector, Univ. of Santa Maria, Caracas 53; Senator for Estado Sucre, mem. Senate Foreign Relations Cttee. 58; Ambassador to Ecuador 59-61, to Brazil 61-63; Prof. of Sociology, Univ. Central de Venezuela 64; Pres. Nat. Inst. of Culture and Fine Arts 65-67; Vice-Pres., Supreme Electoral Council 70-74; Sec.-Gen. to Presidency 76-.
Leisure interest: travelling abroad.
Publs. *Por el Mundo Sociológico de Cecilio Acosta* 45, *En Fuga hacia la Gloria* 47, *Visión y Revisión de Bolívar* 57, *Biografía de Don Egidio Montesinos* 57, *Tesis para la Unión* 63, *Bases de una Acción Cultural* 65, *Historia Fundamental de Venezuela* 70, *La Concienciadel Presente* 71, *Carabobo: Nacionalidad e Historia* 72, *Bolívar: Un Continente y un Destino* 72.
Apartado Postal 2777, Caracas, Venezuela.

Saleh, Jehanshah, M.D., F.I.C.S., F.R.C.O.G.; Iranian surgeon, gynaecologist and politician; b. 20 April 1905, Kashan; s. of Hassan and Khorshid Saleh; m. Mae 1933; four s.; ed. Syracuse Univ., N.Y.
Intern, St. Joseph's Hospital, Syracuse, N.Y. 33, Orange Memorial Hospital, N.J. 34, Resident Surgeon 35; Prof. of Anatomy, Teheran Univ. Faculty of Medicine 36-41, Prof. of Gynaecology 40-47, Dean 47-54; Dir. and Chief of Gynaecological and Obstetrical Service, Vaziri Hospital, Teheran 36-37; Dir. and Chief Surgeon, Women's Hospital, Teheran 37; Minister of Public Health 50, 53, 54, 55, 56 and 60-61; Minister of Education March-May 61; Chancellor Teheran Univ. 62, Senator 69; mem. Board of Dirs. and Chief of Public Health Section, Red Lion and Sun (analogous to the Red Cross) 38-; Fellow, Int. Coll. of Surgeons, Hon. F.R.C.O.G.; Pres. Iranian Asscn. of Obstetricians and Gynaecologists, and of Iran-America Medical Soc.; mem. American Medical Asscn., Iranian Central Council of Sanitation, Central Council for Education and Teheran Univ. Council; WHO expert adviser in medical education and auxiliary branches 52-; Hon. LL.D. (Syracuse Univ.) 63, Dr. h.c. (Bordeaux Univ.), Hon. M.D. (Univ. of Vienna) 72; Palmes Académiques, France; Grand Officier Ordre de Mérite, France, Ordre du Mérite Social, Belgium 72.
Leisure interests: horseback riding, gardening.
Publs. *The Relation of Diet to the Preservation of Teeth* 31, *Morphine Addiction and its Treatment* 32, *Diseases of Women* 41, *Normal and Abnormal Obstetrics* 42, *Recent Advances in Gynaecology* 60, *Text Book of Gynaecology* 64, 70, and numerous papers and articles.
West Takhte Jamshid Avenue No. 10, Teheran, Iran.
Telephone: 42211; 880133.

Salem, Gen. Mamdouh Muhammad; Egyptian police officer, administrator and politician; b. 1918, Alexandria; ed. Police Acad.
Police Commdr., Alexandria 46-68; Gov. of Assiyut 68-70, of Alexandria 70; Deputy Prime Minister, Minister of the Interior 71-75; Prime Minister April 75-.
Office of the Prime Minister, Cairo, Egypt.

Salibayev, Khatam Khakimovich; Soviet politician; b. 21 April 1910, Leninabad; ed. Central Asian Cotton Irrigation Polytechnic Inst. and Higher Party School.
Director of Leninabad Agricultural Technical Coll.

31-35; Dir. Teachers' Training Coll. 35-37; Vice-Chair. Leninabad Regional Soviet of Working People's Deputies 39-40; Chair. State Planning Comm. Tadjik S.S.R. Council of People's Commissars 40-42, People's Commissar for Educ. 42-43; Vice-Chair. Tadjik Council of People's Commissars 43-45; Chair. Kurgan-Tyube City Soviet of Working People's Deputies 47-51; Minister of Municipal Economy of Tadjik S.S.R. 51-53; Chair. Dushanbe City Soviet of Working People's Deputies 56-57; Rector Dushanbe Shevchenko State Inst. of Pedagogical Sciences 57-61; Perm. Rep. of Tadjik S.S.R. Council of Ministers to U.S.S.R. Council of Ministers 61-; mem. Central Cttee. Tadjik C.P. 61-; Deputy to Tadjik Supreme Soviet; Order of Lenin, Red Banner of Labour (twice), Badge of Honour (twice), etc.
Permanent Representation of Tadjik S.S.R. Council of Ministers to U.S.S.R. Council of Ministers, Skatertny pereulok 19, Moscow, U.S.S.R.

Salifou, Illa; Niger diplomatist; b. 17 Feb. 1932, Madaoua; m.; seven c.; ed. Univ. Inst. for Higher Int. Studies.
Director Admin. and Legislative Div., Ministry of Justice 60-61; First Sec., later Counsellor, Washington, D.C. until 66; Dir. de Cabinet, Ministry of Foreign Affairs 68-70, Technical Counsellor, Dir. Consular and Admin. Affairs 70-71; Perm. Rep. to UN Aug. 74-.
Permanent Mission of Niger to the United Nations, 866 United Nations Plaza, Suite 570, New York, N.Y. 10017, U.S.A.

Salim, Khalil; Jordanian politician and banker; b. 1921, El-Husn; s. of Dalleh Salim; m. Mary Salfity; two s. four d.; ed. American Univ. of Beirut, Univs. of London and Columbia Univ.
Teacher in Secondary Schools 41-49; Lecturer Teachers' Coll. 50; Dir. Cultural Affairs 52; Sec. Jordan Nat. Comm. for UNESCO 50-58; Asst. Under-Sec. of Educ. 55-62; Minister of Social Affairs 62; Minister of State, Prime Minister's Office 62-63; Chair. Authority for Tourism and Antiquities 62-63, Minister of Nat. Economy 62-63; Gov. Cen. Bank of Jordan 63; Chair. Board of Jordan Co-operation Union 65-68; Amb. to France (also accred. to Belgium) 74-; mem. Jordan Devt. Board and mem. Board of Trustees Univ. of Jordan; Deputy Chair. ALIA; Chair. Gen. Insurance Corpn.; Sec.-Gen. Royal Scientific Soc.; Chair. Inst. of Banking Studies; Deputy Chair. Council of Scientific Research; mem. Higher Exec. Cttee. Jordanian Nat. Union.
Leisure interests: reading-writing, bridge.
Publs. *Re-organization of Educational Administration in Jordan* 60, 15 textbooks on mathematics and numerous articles on mathematics, popular science, education, economics and banking.
Jordanian Embassy, 80 boulevard Maurice Barrès, 92200 Neuilly, France.

Salim, Salim Ahmed; Tanzanian diplomatist; b. 1942, Zanzibar; ed. Lumumba Coll., Zanzibar and Univ. of Delhi.
Publicity Sec. of UMMA Party and Chief Editor of its official organ *Sauti ya UMMA* 63; Exec. Sec. United Front of Opposition Parties and Chief Editor of its newspaper; Sec. Gen. All-Zanzibar Journalists Union 63; Amb. to United Arab Republic 64-65; High Commr. to India 65-68; Dir. African and Middle East Affairs Div., Ministry of Foreign Affairs 68-69; Amb. to People's Republic of China and Democratic People's Republic of Korea June-Dec. 69; Perm. Rep. to UN Feb. 70-, also High Commr. to Jamaica, accred. to Guyana, Trinidad and Tobago, and Amb. to Cuba April 71-; fmr. del. of Tanzania at UN Gen. Assembly and other int. confs.
Permanent Mission of Tanzania to the United Nations, 201 East 42nd Street, 8th Floor, New York, N.Y. 10017, U.S.A.

Salinger, J(erome) D(avid); American author; b. 1919; ed. Manhattan public schools and a military coll. Travelled in Europe 37-38; army service with 4th Infantry Division (Staff Sergeant) 42-46.
Publs. *The Catcher in the Rye, Franny and Zooey, Raise High the Roof Beam, Carpenters* 63 (novels), *For Esmé with Love and Squalor* (stories); numerous stories, mostly in the *New Yorker* 48-.
c/o Harold Ober Associates Inc., 40 E 49th Street, New York, N.Y. 10017, U.S.A.

Salinger, Pierre Emil George, B.S.; American journalist and politician; b. 14 June 1925, San Francisco; s. of the late Herbert Edgar Salinger and of Jehanne Bietry Carlson; m. Nicole Helene Gillmann 1965; three s. one d.; ed. Univ. of San Francisco.
San Francisco Chronicle 42-55; U.S. Navy Second World War; Press Officer, Calif., Stevenson for Pres. Campaign 52, Richard Graves for Gov. (Calif.) 54; West Coast Ed., Contributing Ed. *Collier's Magazine* 55-56; Investigator, Senate Labor Rackets Cttee. 57-59; Press Sec. to Senator John F. Kennedy Sept. 59-Jan. 61, to Pres. John F. Kennedy Jan. 61-Nov. 63, to Pres. Lyndon Johnson Nov. 63-March 64; U.S. Senator from Calif. 4 Aug. 64-Jan. 65; Dir. Nat. Gen. Productions 65-; Vice-Pres. Nat. Gen. Corpn. 65-, Continental Airlines 65-68; Chair. Great America Management and Research Co. Int. (GRAMCO) 68-, Deputy Chair. GRAMCO (U.K.) Ltd. 70-71; Senior Vice-Pres. AMPROP Inc. 69; Roving Editor *L'Express*, Paris 73-; lecturer at over 60 U.S. univs. and colls. 65-69; Trustee of Robert F. Kennedy Memorial Foundation; Democrat. Publs. *With Kennedy* 66, Ed. *A Tribute to John F. Kennedy* 64, *A Tribute to Robert F. Kennedy* 68, *On Instructions of my Government* 71, *For the Eyes of the President Only* (novel) 71, *Je suis un Américain* 75.
9101 Hazen Drive, Beverly Hills, Calif. 90211, U.S.A.; Home: 248 rue de Rivoli, 75001 Paris, France.

Salis, Jean Rodolphe de, D. ès L.; Swiss professor; b. 12 Dec. 1901, Berne; m. Elsie Huber 1940; one s.; ed. Gymnase de Berne and Univs. of Montpellier, Berne, Berlin and Paris.
Corresp. of *Der Bund* in Paris 30-35; syndic of the foreign press in Paris 31-35; Prof. of History, Swiss Inst. of Technology, Zürich 35-68; commentator of Radio Beromuenster ("Weltchronik") 40-47; observer at First Gen. Assembly of UNESCO 46; Prof. Univ. of Vienna, Summer 47; mem. of University Comm. (Germany, British Zone) 48; Del. to UNESCO Gen. Conf. 54, 60; Pres. Pro Helvetia Foundation 52-64; Officier Légion d'Honneur; Grosses Silbernes Ehrenzeichen Oesterreich; Dr. h.c. Univ. Geneva 59.
Leisure interests: music, theatre, hunting.
Publs. *Sismondi, La vie et l'oeuvre d'un Cosmopolite philosophe* (2 vols.) 32, *Rainer Maria Rilkes Schweizer Jahre* 36, *Giuseppe Motta, Dreissig Jahre Eidgenössische Politik* 41, *Fritz Wotruba* 47, *Weltgeschichte der Neuesten Zeit*, Vol. I 51, Vol. II 55, Vol. III 60, *Im Lauf der Jahre* 62, *Weltchronik* 39-45, *Schwierige Schweiz* 68.
Schloss Brunegg, Aargau, Switzerland.
Telephone: 56-11-44.

Salisbury, Sir Edward James, Kt., C.B.E., D.SC., LL.D., F.R.S., F.L.S., V.M.H., V.P.R.H.S.; British botanist; b. 16 April 1886, Harpenden, Herts.; s. of James W. Salisbury; m. Mabel Elwin-Coles 1918 (died 1956); ed. Univ. Coll. School and Univ. Coll. London.
Senior Lecturer East London Coll. 14-18; Lecturer Univ. Coll. 18, Fellow 20, Reader in Plant Ecology 24, Quain Prof. of Botany 28 Hon. Fellow Botanical Soc. of Edinburgh 38; Fellow Queen Mary's Coll. 38; Fellow Wye Coll.; fmrly. Gov Royal Holloway Coll., Queen Mary Coll., East Malling Research Station; Trustee Rothamsted Experimental Station; Vice-Pres. Royal Society 42-55; Dir. Royal Botanic Gardens, Kew 43-56; mem. Senate Univ. of London 34-44; Sec.

Royal Soc. 45-55; Chair. Joint Comm. of Agricultural Research Council and Agricultural Improvement Council 45-56; Percy Sladen Trustee; Chair. Commonwealth Bursaries Comm. 53-65; Fullerton Prof. of Physiology, Royal Inst. 47-52; Hon. LL.D. (Edinburgh and Glasgow); Hon. Fellow Inst. of Biology; Royal Medal 45.
Leisure interest: gardening.
Publs. *An introduction to the Study of Plants* 14-38, *Botany for Medical Students* 21, *The East Anglian Flora* 33, *The Living Garden* 35, *Plant Form and Function* 38, *The Reproductive Capacity of Plants* 42, *Downs and Dunes* 52, *Weeds and Aliens* 60, *The Biology of Garden Weeds* 62, etc.
Croindene, 8 Strandway, Felpham, Sussex, England.

Salisbury, Harrison Evans, B.A.; American journalist; b. 14 Nov. 1908; s. of Percy P. and Georgiana E. Salisbury; m. 1st Mary Hollis 1933 (divorced), 2nd Charlotte Rand 1964; two s.; ed. Univ. of Minnesota.
United Press Int. 30-48; Moscow Corresp., *New York Times* 49-54, Nat. Affairs Editor 61-63, Asst. Man. Editor 64-72, Assoc. Editor 72-; mem. American Acad. of Arts and Sciences 69-, Nat. Inst. of Arts and Letters 72- (Pres. 75); Pulitzer Prize for Int. Correspondence 55; George Polk Memorial Journalism Award 58, 67.
Publs. *Russia on the Way* 46, *American in Russia* 55, *The Shook-Up Generation* 59, *To Moscow—and Beyond* 60, *Moscow Journal* 61, *A New Russia?* 62, *The Northern Palmyra Affair* 62, *Orbit of China* 67, *Behind the Lines—Hanoi* 67, *The Soviet Union: The 50 Years* 67, *The 900 Days, The Siege of Leningrad* 69, *The Coming War Between Russia and China* 70, *The Many Americas Shall be One* 71, *The Eloquence of Protest* 72, *To Peking—and Beyond* 73.
The New York Times, 229 West 43rd Street, New York, N.Y. 10036; Home: 349 East 84th Street, New York N.Y. 10028, U.S.A.

Salk, Jonas Edward, B.SC., M.D.; American scientist; b. 28 Oct. 1914; s. of Daniel Salk and Dora Press; m. 1st Donna Lindsay 1939 (dissolved 1968), 2nd Françoise Gilot 1970; three s.; ed. New York Univ. Coll. of Medicine and Coll. of New York City.
Fellow in Chemistry, N.Y. Univ. Coll. of Medicine 35-36, Christian A. Herter Fellow 37-38, Fellow in Bacteriology 39-40; at Mt. Sinai Hospital, New York 40-42; Nat. Research Council Fellow, School of Public Health, Univ. of Michigan 42-43, Research Fellow in Epidemiology 43-44, Research Assoc. in Epidemiology 44-46, Asst. Prof. 46-47; Assoc. Prof. of Bacteriology and Dir. of Virus Research, School of Medicine, Univ. of Pittsburgh 47-49, Research Prof. 49-55; Prof. Preventive Medicine 55-56; Commonwealth Prof. Preventive Medicine 56-57; Commonwealth Prof. Experimental Medicine 57-63; Dir. and Fellow, Salk Inst. for Biological Studies 62-; Consultant to Sec. of Army in Epidemic Diseases 47-52; on Consulting Staff, Municipal Hosp. for Contagious Diseases 48-56; Adjunct Prof. of Health Sciences, Dept. of Psychiatry, Community Medicine and Medicine, Univ. of California 70; specialist polio research; mem. American Epidemiological Society, Society of American Bacteriologists, American Asscn. of Immunologists, American Society for Clinical Investigation, Society for Experimental Biology and Medicine; Fellow of American Public Health Asscn., American Asscn. for the Advancement of Science, Asscn. American Physicians.
The Salk Institute for Biological Studies, P.O. Box 1809, San Diego, Calif. 92112, U.S.A.
Telephone: 714-453-4100.

Sallal, Marshal Abdullah as-; Yemeni army officer and politician; b. 1917; ed. in Iraq.
Returned to Yemen from Iraq 39; imprisoned 39; Army Service 40-48, 55-67; imprisoned 48-55; Gov. of Hodeida 59-62; Chief of Staff to Imam Mohammed 62; Pres. of the Revolutionary Council, Commdr.-in-Chief of the

Republican forces, Yemeni Civil War Sept. 62-Nov. 67, concurrently Prime Minister Sept. 66-Nov. 67; now living in Egypt.

Sallé, Jean-Paul; French international civil servant; b. 16 March 1910, Raincy; s. of Gen. Gaston Sallé and Yvonne de La Marnierre; m. Françoise Cheysson 1934; one s. one d.; ed. Ecole Sainte-Geneviève, Versailles and Ecole Nationale Supérieure des Mines, Paris.
Engineer, Ets. Skoda, Prague 35; Dir. Franco-Yugoslav Bureau for Econ. Research 39; Division Chief in mil. govt. in Austria 45; Adviser, IMF, Washington, D.C. 46; Dir. IMF European Office 63-; Croix de Guerre.
Office: 12 place du Panthéon, 75005, Paris; Home: 231 rue Saint-Honoré, 75001 Paris, France.

Sallinger, Rudolf; Austrian building contractor; b. 3 Sept. 1916; ed. Technische Hochschule, Vienna.
Proprietor of stonemason's firm, Vienna 43-; Head of Guild of Stone-Masons, Vienna 50, later Deputy Head of Fed. of Guilds; Chair. Trade Section, Chamber of Commerce, Vienna; Pres. Chamber of Commerce, Vienna 60-64; Pres. Fed. of Chambers of Commerce 64-; Pres. Austrian Nat. Cttee. for Int. Trade; mem. Nationalrat 66-; Pres. Fed. Econ. Chamber 66-; numerous decorations.
1050 Vienna, Nikolsdorfergasse 37, Austria.

Salmon, Baron (Life Peer), cr. 72, of Sandwich, Kent; **Cyril Barnet Salmon,** P.C.; British judge; b. 28 Dec. 1903, London; s. of Montagu Salmon and Marian Trevor; m. 1st Rencie Anderfelt 1929 (died 1942), 2nd Jean, Lady Morris 1946; one s. one d.; ed. Mill Hill and Pembroke Coll., Cambridge.
Called to the Bar, Middle Temple 25, Master, Treasurer 72, Hon. Fellow; Q.C. 45; Judge, High Court of Justice, Queen's Bench Div. 57-64; Lord Justice of Appeal 64-72; Lord of Appeal in Ordinary 72-.
Leisure interests: fishing, golf.
Manwood Place, Sandwich, Kent, England.

Salmon, Brian Lawson, C.B.E.; British business executive; b. 30 June 1917, London; s. of Julius Salmon and Emma Constance Gluckstein; m. Annette Wilson Mackay 1946; two s. one d.; ed. Malvern Coll.
Joined J. Lyons & Co. 35, Dir. 61-, Joint Man. Dir. 67-69, Deputy Chair. 69-72, Chair. 72-; Vice-Chair., Board of Govs., Westminster Hospital Group 63-74; a Vice-Chair. Royal Coll. of Nursing 72; Chair. Cttee. on Sr. Nursing Staff Structure 63-66, Camden and Islington Area Health Authority (Teaching) 74.
Leisure interests: theatre, ballet.
J. Lyons & Co. Ltd., Cadby Hall, London, W14 OPA, England.
Telephone: 01-603 2040.

Salmon, Geoffrey Isidore Hamilton, C.B.E.; British businessman; b. 14 Jan. 1908, London; s. of Harry and Lena (née Gluckstein) Salmon; m. Peggy Rica (née Jacobs) 1936; two s. one d.; ed. Malvern Coll. and Jesus Coll., Cambridge.
Hon. Catering Adviser to the Army 59; Chair. J. Lyons & Co. Ltd. 68-71, Pres. 72-.
10 Stavordale Lodge, 12 Melbury Road, London, W14 8LW, England.

Salmon, Robert; French journalist; b. 6 April 1918; ed. Lycée Louis le Grand, Ecole Normale Supérieure and at the Sorbonne.
Member Provisional Consultative Assembly 44, First Constituent Assembly 45; Founder Pres. and Dir. Gen. *France-Soir* 44-; Pres. Soc. France-Editions (*Elle, Le Journal de Dimanche, Paris-Presse,* etc.); Pres. Soc. de Publications Economiques (*Réalités, Connaissance des Arts, Entreprise,* etc.); Sec.-Gen. Féd. Nat. de la Presse; Hon. Pres. French Cttee. Int. Press Inst.; mem. Fondation Nationale des Sciences Politiques; Prof. Inst. d'Etudes Politiques, Univ. de Paris, etc.
Publs. *Le sentiment de l'existence chez Maine de Biran*

43, *Notions élémentaires de psychologie* 47, *L'organisation actuelle de la presse française* 55, *Information et Publicité* 56, *L'Information économique, clé de la prosperité* 63.
100 rue Réaumur, 75002 Paris, France.

Salmon, Sir Samuel Isidore, Kt., M.A.; British company executive; b. 18 Oct. 1900, London; s. of Sir Isidore and Lady Salmon; m. Lallah W. Benjamin; one s. one d.; ed. Bedales School and Jesus Coll., Cambridge.
J. Lyons & Co. Ltd. (catering and food manufacturing business) 22-, Dir. 33-, Man. Dir. 49-65, Chair. 65-68, Pres. 68-72; mem. London County Council 49-65, Greater London Council 65-67; Mayor of Hammersmith 68; Vice-Chair. Metropolitan Water Board 69, Chair. 70-.
Leisure interests: reading, bridge.
14 Carlos Place, London W.1, England.
Telephone: 01-629-6217.

Salmon, Thomas P., LL.B., LL.M.; American lawyer and politician; b. 19 Aug. 1932, Cleveland Ohio; s. of Thomas A. and Luch Conlon Salmon; m. 1958; one s. three d.; ed. Boston College, Boston College Law School, New York Univ. Law School.
Judge of Municipal Court, Bellows Falls, Vermont 63-65; mem. Vt. House of Representatives 65-70; Minority leader, mem. House Rules Cttee., Chair., House Judiciary Cttee. 69-70; Gov. of State of Vt. 72-; Chair. New England Govs.' Conf. 74; State. Co.-Chair. New England Regional Comm. Jan. 75; mem. Exec. Council Nat. Govs.' Conf. June 74; mem. of American County and Local Bar Asscn.; American Trial Lawyers Asscn.; Democrat.
Leisure interests: sports, music, hiking, cross-country skiing, golf.
State House, Montpelier, Vermont 05602; Home: 39 Square, Bellows Falls, Vermont 05101, U.S.A.
Telephone: 802-828-2222; 802-463-4234.

Salonen, Olavi Oskar, M.A.; Finnish business executive; b. 28 Aug. 1914, Helsinki; s. of Oskar and Hilma (née Pakkala) Salonen; m. Paula Oterma 1939; two s. one d.
Entered Keskusuuslike OTK service 34, Head of Dept. 47-57, Asst. Man. 57-58, Man. Food Dept. 59, Board of Dirs. and Admin. Vice-Chair. 68; Chair. Board of Dirs. Oil Refinery Ltd. 58, Renlund Ltd. 59, NAF 72; mem. Parl. Cttee., Bank of Finland 66-; Deputy Gen. Man. Foodstuffs Industry 68-; Minister of Trade and Industry 66-71; Alt. mem. Board of Admin. Int. Bank for Reconstruction and Devt. 66-68; Minister of Co-operation for Nordic Countries 66-68; mem. State Council for Science 66-68; mem. Defence Council 66-68; Chair. Econ. Council 68; Chair. GATT 67-68; Chair. UNCTAD II, New Delhi 68; Vice-Chair. Outokumpu Ltd. 66 ; Chair. Board of Commrs. State Inst. for Technical Research; Chair. Finnish-Hungarian Trade Asscn. 68-.
Solnantie 21, Helsinki 33, Finland.
Telephone: 487277.

Salpeter, Edwin E., M.SC., PH.D.; American physicist and professor; b. 3 Dec. 1924, Vienna, Austria; s. of Jakob L. and Friedericke Salpeter; m. Miriam M. Mark 1950; two d.; ed. Sydney Boys' High School, Australia and Univ. of Birmingham, England.
Department of Scientific and Industrial Research Fellow, Univ. of Birmingham, England 48-49; Research Assoc., then Assoc. Prof., Cornell Univ., U.S. 49-56, Prof. of Physics and Astrophysics 56-; Visiting Prof. Australian Nat. Univ. 54, Sydney Univ. 60, Cambridge Univ. 68; mem. Nat. Acad. of Sciences, American Acad. of Arts and Sciences; Hon. D.Sc. (Chicago and Case Western Reserve Univs.).
Leisure interests: tennis, skiing, photography.
Publs. One book and over 100 scientific papers on

quantum mechanics, plasma physics and theoretical astrophysics.

Office: Laboratory of Nuclear Studies, Cornell Univ., Ithaca, New York 14850; Home: 116 Westbourne Lane, Ithaca, N.Y. 14850, U.S.A.

Telephone: 607-273-9179.

Salt, George, S.D., PH.D., SC.D., F.R.S.; British zoologist; b. 12 Dec. 1903, Loughborough; s. of Walter Salt and Mary Cecilia Hulme; m. Joyce Laing 1939; two s.; ed. Univs. of Alberta, Harvard and Cambridge.

Entomologist with United Fruit Co., Repub. of Colombia 26-27, with Imperial Inst. of Entomology 28-31; Royal Soc. Moseley Research Student 32-33; Fellow, King's Coll., Cambridge 33-; Lecturer in Zoology, Cambridge Univ. 37-65; Dean, King's Coll. 39-45, Tutor for Advanced Students 45-51; Reader in Animal Ecology, Univ. of Cambridge 65-71; Visiting Prof. Univ. of Calif. 66; Murchison Grant, Royal Geographical Soc. 51; Fellow of Royal Sec. 56; Pres. Cambridge Philosophical Soc. 70-72.

Leisure interests: mountaineering, gardening, calligraphy and illumination.

Publs. *Experimental Studies in Insect Parasitism 1-16 34-72, Ecology of Upper Kilimanjaro 54, Defence Reactions of Insects to Metazoan Parasites 63, Resistance of Insect Parasitoids to the Defence Reactions of their Hosts 68, The Cellular Defence Reactions of Insects 70,* and numerous scientific papers.

King's College, Cambridge; Home: 21 Barton Road, Cambridge, England.

Telephone: 50411 (King's Coll.).

Saltzman, Charles Eskridge, B.S., B.A., M.A.; American investment banker; b. 19 Sept. 1903, Zamboanga, Philippines; s. of Major Gen. Charles McKinley Saltzman and Mary Eskridge Saltzman; m. 1st Gertrude Lamont 1931 (divorced), 2nd Cynthia Southall Myrick 1947 (divorced); one s. two d.; ed. Cornell Univ., U.S. Military Acad., and Oxford Univ.

With N.Y. Telephone Co., successively Commercial Engineer, Commercial Asst. Man., Commercial Man., Directory Production Man. 30-35; with N.Y. Stock Exchange 35-49, beginning as Asst. to Exec. Vice-Pres., later Sec. and Vice-Pres.; on mil. leave of absence 40-46; served as 2nd Lieut. Corps of Engineers, U.S. Army 25-30; Commissioned 1st Lieut. N.Y. Nat. Guard 30, advanced to Lieut.-Col. 40, on active duty in U.S. Army 40-46; serving overseas 42-46, Brig.-Gen. 45; Major-Gen., retd.; on leave of absence from New York Stock Exchange for government service 47-49; Special Asst. to Sec. of State 47; Asst. Sec. of State in charge of occupied areas 47-49; Gen. Partner, Henry Sears & Co. June 49-56 (on leave of absence for govt. service June 54-Jan. 55); Under-Sec. of State for Admin. June 54-Jan. 55; partner Goldman Sachs & Co. 56-; Dir. A. H. Robins Co., Inc., Nat. Pres. English-Speaking Union of United States 61-66; awarded D.S.M. (U.S.), L.M. (U.S.), O.B.E. (U.K.), Croix de Guerre (France), Bronze Medal (Italy), Ouissam Alouitte (Morocco), Cross of Merit (Poland), The War Medal (Brazil); Grand Officer, Order of the Crown of Italy.

Leisure interests: travel, tennis.

55 Broad Street, New York, N.Y. 10004; Home: 101 East 69th Street, New York 10021, U.S.A.

Telephone: (Office) (212) 676-8360; (Home) (212) RE4-5400.

Salvador y Diaz-Benjumea, Lt.-Gen. Julio; Spanish air force officer and politician; b. 22 May 1910, Cadiz; s. of Luis and María Teresa; m. María Teresa Martínez Bidón 1939; four s. three d.; ed. Toledo Infantry Acad. Commissioned 28, Lieut.-Col. 45, Col. 52, Brig.-Gen. 63, Gen. of Div. 66; fmr. Dir. Fighter Pilots' School; Military attaché (air), Washington; Dir. Military Air Acad.; Second-in-Command, Alto Estade Mayor;

Minister of Aviation 69-73; numerous military awards and medals.

c/o Ministry of Aviation, Madrid, Spain.

Telephone: 243-24-20.

Salvat, Augustin, LIC. EN DERECHO; Mexican lawyer and government official; b. 23 Oct. 1908; ed. Escuela Benito Juárez, Salina Cruz, Oaxaca and Univ. Nacional Autónoma de México.

With Compañía Mexicana de Luz y Fuerza Motriz 24-39; Sec. Mexican Electrical Workers' Union 35; lecturer in world history 42-43; qualified in law 44; directed youth org. in Manuel Avila Camacho's Campaign; later held various admin. posts in Govt. of Fed. District; Treas., later Sec. of Finance for twelve years, Partido Revolucionario Institucional (PRI); Head of Mexican Govt. Tourism Dept. 64-73; Pres. Int. Union of Official Travel Orgs. 67-69.

Publs. include *Industria Eléctrica, Desarrollo Industrial y el Ahorro Popular, Justicia Social y Revolución Mexicana, Israel, Breve relato de un Gran Pueblo.*

Cerro Dos Conejo 10, Frac. Romero de Terreros, Coyoacán, Mexico 18, D.F., Mexico.

Salvetti, Carlo; Italian physicist; b. 30 Dec. 1918, Milan; m. Piera Pinto 1951; two d.; ed. Univ. of Milan.

Former Prof. of Theoretical Physics, Univ. of Bari; Dir.-Gen. Nuclear Study Centre, Ispra 57-59; Dir. Int. Atomic Energy Agency (IAEA) Research Div. 59-62; Gov. for Italy to IAEA 62-64, 68-70, Chair. Board of Govs. IAEA 63-64; Chair. European Atomic Energy Soc. 67-68, mem. EAES Council 63-72; Chair. Euratom Scientific and Technical Cttee. 69-70, mem. 67-73; Chair. ENEA-OECD Steering Cttee. 69-73, ANS, Italian Section; Prof. of Gen. Physics, Univ. of Milan; Vice-Chair. and mem. Board of Dirs., Italian Nat. Cttee. for Nuclear Energy (C.N.E.N.) 64-; Vice-Chair. Italian Forum for Nuclear Energy (FIEN) 65-; Chair. Italian Nuclear Soc. (SNI) 75-; mem. Board European Nuclear Soc. (ENS) 75-; Fellow, American Nuclear Soc. 70-.

Viale Regina Margherita 125, CNEN, 00198 Rome, Italy.

Telephone: 8528 ext. 200.

Salzman, Pnina; Israeli pianist; b. Tel-Aviv; m. Igal Weissmann 1947; one d.; ed. Ecole normale de musique and Conservatoire national de musique, Paris.

Gave first concert in Paris at age of twelve; since then has given concerts in Israel, Japan, U.S.S.R., S. Africa, Australia, New Zealand, France, Britain, Belgium, Denmark, Sweden, Norway, Finland, U.S.A., etc., under baton of Sir Malcolm Sargent, Charles Munch, Koussevitsky, etc.; over 300 concerts with Israeli orchestras and regular performances with orchestras all over the world; Prof. of Piano, Tel-Aviv Univ.

Leisure interests: gardening, painting, graphology.

A20 Dubnov Street, Tel-Aviv, Israel.

Telephone: 261993.

Samarakis, Antonis; Greek author; b. 16 Aug. 1919, Athens; s. of Evripidis Samarakis and Adriani Pantelopoulos; m. Eleni Kourebanas 1963; ed. Univ. of Athens.

Chief of Emigration, Refugees and Technical Assistance Depts., Ministry of Labour 35-40, 44-63; active in resistance movt. during second World War; has served on many humanitarian missions in many parts of the world for ILO, UNHCR, ICEM and Council of Europe; Expert on social and labour problems (many African countries, chiefly Guinea) ILO 68-69; denied a passport Oct. 70; mem. PEN, Nat. Soc. of Authors; Officier, Ordre de Léopold II (Belgium); hon. citizen of San Francisco and New Orleans; Greek Nat. Book Award 62, Greek Prize of the Twelve 66, Grand Prix de la Littérature Policière (France) 70.

Leisure interest: travel.

Publs. short stories: *Wanted: Hope* 54, *I Refuse* 61, *The Jungle* 66, *The Passport* (in *Nea Kimina* 2) 71; novels: *Danger Signal* 59, *The Flaw* 65; contributor to *The Child's Song* (anthology of poems for children); works have been translated into 16 languages and frequently adapted for cinema and television.
53 Taygetou and Ippolytu Streets, Athens 806, Greece.
Telephone: 202-9044 (Home).

Samaran, Charles, LITT.D.; French historian and paleographer; b. 28 Oct. 1879, Cravencères, Gers; *s.* of Victor Bertrand Samaran and Prospérie Baurens; *m.* Marie C. Taffanel 1912; three *d.*; ed. Ecole des Chartes and Ecole des Hautes Etudes.
Former mem. French School in Rome; mem. Société Nationale des Antiquaires since 30; mem. Cttee. of Historical Works 28-; Prof. of Latin and French Paleography, Ecole des Hautes Etudes 27-; Prof. of Bibliography and Archive Administration, Ecole des Chartes 33-52; Dir. Archives de France 41-48, Hon. Dir. 48-; Pres. Int. Council of Archives 48; mem. Acad. des Inscriptions et Belles-Lettres 41; Pres. Int. Coll. of Paleography 52; Pres. Comm. Supérieure des Archives 58, History and Philology Sec., Comité des Travaux historiques et scientifiques 59, Conseil de perfectionnement de l'Ecole des Chartes 61; Editor *Histoire Littéraire de la France* 61, *Du Journal des Savants* 65; Grand Prix Littéraire de la Ville de Paris 70, Prix Osiris, Inst. de France 74.
Leisure interest: history.
Publs. *La Fiscalité pontificale en France au XIVe siècle* (Bordin Prize 05), *La Maison d'Armagnac au XVe siècle* (Gobert Prize 07), *Les Diplômes originaux des Mérovingiens* 08, *D'Artagnan, capitaine des mousquetaires du roi* 12 (Montyon Prize of Acad. Française), *Jacques Casanova, Vénitien* 14, *Jean de Bilhères-Lagraulas, cardinal de Saint-Denis* 21, *Chronique latine inédite de Jean Chartier* 28, *Thomas Basin, Histoire de Charles VII et de Louis XI* (5 vols.) 33, 44, 63, 66, 72, *Auctarium Chartularii Universitatis Parisiensis* (Estrade-Delcros Prize) (4 vols.) 35, 37, 38, 42, *Etudes Sandionysiennes* 44, *Aspects de l'Université de Paris* 48, *Balzac Livre du Centenaire* 52, *Alexandre Dumas, Trois Mousquetaires* 56, *Les Institutions féodales en Gascogne au moyen âge* 57, *Manuscrits latins datés* (10 vols.) 59, 62, 65, 68, 74, *L'Histoire et ses méthodes* (with others) 61, *Pierre Bersuire* 62, *Vocation Universitaire de Paris* 62, *Alexandre Dumas: Vingt Ans Après* 62, *De Rousseau à Nerval* 64, *Chartes de Gascogne* 66, *Actes de l'Abbaye de Bonnefont* 70, *La Commanderie de l'Hôpital-Sainte-Christie* 73, *Thomas Basin, Apologie* 74.
8 avenue Gourgaud, Paris 75017, France.
Telephone: 754-90-23.

Samayoa Chinchilla, Carlos; Guatemalan writer; b. 10 Dec. 1898, Guatemala City; *s.* of Ing. Luis C. Samayoa and Josefina de Samayoa; *m.* Amelia Evangelina Paz 1947; one *d.*; ed. Instituto Nacional de Varones and Escuela Politecnica.
Editor *Diario de Centro América* 22-28; Secr. of Presidency 32; Under-Sec. of the Presidency 44; Minister of Guatemala to Colombia 44-46; Dir. Nat. Library 47-48; Ambassador to Venezuela 48; Dir. *Diario del Pueblo* 50, voluntary exile in El Salvador 50-54, Co-founder Gen. Directorate of Fine Arts of El Salvador; Dir. Guatemala Inst. of Anthropology and History 54-; Founder "Santiago" Museum, "Libro Antiguo" Museum, and Museum of Arts and Crafts; numerous medals.
Publs. *Madre Milpa* 34, *Cuatro Suertes* 36, *La Casa de la Muerta* 41, *El Dictador y Yo* 50, *Estampas de la Costa Grande* 54, *El Quetzal no es Rojo* 56, *Chapines de Ayer* 57, *The Art of the Ancient Maya* 59, *Aproximación al Arte Maya* 64.
Instituto de Antropología e Historia, Edificio No. 5 La Aurora, Zona 13, Guatemala City; Home: 4a Calle 14-22, Zona 13, Guatemala City, Guatemala.

Sambasivan, Dr. G.; Indian malariologist.
Malariologist, Travancore 35; World Health Organization 49-, Senior Malaria Adviser, South East Asia Regional Office of WHO, New Delhi 61-64; Dir. WHO Malaria Eradication Activities 64-.
World Health Organization, Palais des Nations, Geneva, Switzerland.

Samii, Abdol Hossein, M.A., PH.D.; Iranian professor of medicine; b. 20 June 1930; *s.* of Mehdi and Zahra Samii; *m.* Shahla Kosrowshahi 1967; one *s.* one *d.*; ed. Univ. of Calif., Los Angeles, Cornell Univ.
Intern, Resident in Medicine, N.Y. Hosp., Peter Bent Brigham Hosp., Mass. Gen. Hosp.; Fellow, Rockefeller and Helen Hay Whitney Foundations; Prof. of Medicine, Nat. Univ. of Iran 63; Deputy Minister of Health 64; Chair. Dept. of Medicine, Medical Dir., Firouzgar Medical Centre 64; mem. Exec. Board, Social Insurance Org. 67; Dir. Pars Hosp. 70; Assoc. Prof. of Medicine, Univ. of Rochester 72; Adjunct Prof. of Medicine, Cornell Univ. 74; Minister of Science and Higher Educ. 74-; Chancellor of Reza Shah Kabir Univ.
Leisure interests: music, writing, tennis, collecting antiques, archaeology.
Publs. 16 papers in *American Journal of Physiology*, *Annual, N.Y. Acad. of Sciences, etc.*
Ministry of Science and Higher Education, Villa Avenue, Teheran, Iran
Telephone: 827234.

Samkalden, Ivo; Netherlands civil servant and university professor; b. 10 Aug. 1912; ed. Univ. of Leiden.
Sec. Comm.-Gen. for Neths. E. Indies 46; Asst. Prof. of Public Law, Leiden Univ. 47-48; Head of Legislative and Juridical Dept., Ministry of Agriculture, Fisheries and Food 48-52; Prof. of Law and Political Science, Agricultural Univ., Wageningen 52-56; Minister of Justice of the Netherlands 56-58, 65-66; Prof. Int. Law, Leiden Univ. 58-65, 67; Mayor of Amsterdam Aug. 67-; mem. Partij van de Arbeid (Labour Party).
Herengracht 502, Amsterdam C, Netherlands.
Telephone: 220200.

Sammet, Rolf, DR.RER.NAT.; German chemicals executive; b. 21 Feb. 1920, Stuttgart; *s.* of Dr. Paul and Else (née Hillman) Sammet; *m.* Hilde Beckerwerth; one *s.* two *d.*; ed. Gymnasium and Technische Hochschule, Stuttgart and Technische Hochschule, Munich.
Assistant, Inst. for Organic Chemistry 45-47, joined Hoechst AG 49; Divisional Adviser, Dept. of Technical Management 52-54, Man. 57, Departmental Dir. 60; Deputy mem. of Board, Hoechst AG 62, Chief Exec. Officer 66-, Chair. of Board 69-.
Hoechst AG, 623 Frankfurt/Main—80, Federal Republic of Germany.
Telephone: Frankfurt 305-7892.

Samoré, H.E. Cardinal Antonio; Vatican ecclesiastic: b. 4 Dec. 1905, Bardi (Parma); *s.* of Gino Samoré and Giuseppina Basini.
Ordained 28; Archbishop 50-; Cardinal 67; Prefect Sacred Congregation for the Discipline of the Sacraments; librarian and archivist to the Holy Roman Church (Santa Romana Chiesa).
The Vatican, Rome, Italy.
Telephone: Vatican 698, Ext. 3301, 4938 (Office), Ext. 3164 (Home).

Sampedro, José Luis; Spanish economist and novelist; b. 1 Feb. 1917, Barcelona; *s.* of Luis and Matilde Sampedro; *m.* Isabel Pellicer Iturrioz 1944; one *d.*; ed. Madrid Univ.
Civil Service, Ministry of Finance 35-50, 57-62; Asst. Prof. of Econ. Structure, Madrid Univ. 47-55, Prof. 55-69; Economist, Ministry of Commerce 51-57; Adviser to Spanish Del. to UN 56-58; Special Prof. of Econ. Sociology, Madrid Univ. 62-65; Asst. Gen. Dir. Banco

Exterior de España 62-69; Visiting Prof. Univ. of Salford 69-70, Univ. of Liverpool 70-71; Econ. Adviser Customs Bureau, Ministry of Finance 71-; Spanish Nat. Award for new playwrights 50.
Leisure interest: human communication.
Publs. Economics: *Principles of Industrial Location 54, Effects of European Economic Integration 57, Economic Reality and Structural Analysis 58, The European Future of Spain 60, Regional Profiles of Spain 64, Decisive Forces in World Economics 67, Economic Structure 69, Conscience of Underdevelopment 73*; Fiction: *Congreso en Estocolmo* (Congress in Stockholm) 52, *El Río que nos lleva* (The River which Carries Us) 62, *El Caballo Desnudo* (The Naked Horse) 70; plays: *La Paloma de Cartón* (The Paper Dove) 50, *Un sitio para vivir* (A Place to Live in) 56.
Marqués de Urquijo 11, Madrid 8, Spain.
Telephone: 2472416.

Samper, Armando; Colombian agricultural economist; b. 9 April 1920, Bogotá; s. of late Daniel Samper Ortega and of Mayita Gnecco de Samper; m. Jean K. de Samper 1945; two s. two d.; ed. Cornell Univ.
Research and teaching posts in agricultural econs., Colombia 43-49; Inter-American Inst. of Agricultural Sciences of Org. of American States (O.A.S.), Turrialba, Costa Rica 49-69, Head of Scientific Communications Service 49-54, Dir. of Regional Services 55-60, Dir. of Inst. 60-69; Visiting Prof. Univ. of Chicago 54-55; Minister of Agriculture of Colombia 66-67, 69-70; Agricultural Adviser, Bank of Repub., Bogotá 70-72; Chancellor Univ. of Bogotá 71; FAO Asst. Dir.-Gen. for Latin American Affairs, Santiago, Chile 72-74; Pres. Nat. Corpn. for Forestry Research and Devt. (CONIF), Bogotá 75-; mem. Latin American Plant Science Asscn., Colombian Asscn. of Professional Agriculturists, Soc. for Int. Devt., Int. Asscn. of Agricultural Econs., Econ. Soc. of Friends of the Country, Int. Inst. of Tropical Agriculture, Amazonia 2,000 Foundation.
Publs. *Importancia del Café en el Comercio Exterior de Colombia 48, A Case Study of Cooperation in Secondary Education in Chile 57, Política de Transformación Rural 67, Memoria del Ministro de Agricultura al Congreso Nacional 66-67, Desarrollo Institucional y Dessarrollo Agrícola* (III vols.) *69, El Cuartrenio de la Transformación Rural 66-70.*
Corporación Nacional de Investigación y Fomento Forestal (CONIF), Calle 84 Número 20-05, Apartado Aéreo 091676, Bogotá; Calle 122 Número 20-60, Bogotá, Colombia.
Telephone: 36-15-73 (Office); 54-44-84 (Home).

Sampson, Anthony (Terrell Seward) M.A.; British writer and journalist; b. 3 Aug. 1926, Billingham, Durham; s. of Michael Sampson and Phyllis (née Seward); m. Sally Bentlif 1965; one s. one d.; ed. Westminster School and Christ Church, Oxford.
Served with Royal Navy 44-47; Sub Lieut. R.N.V.R. 46; Editor *Drum* magazine, Johannesburg 51-55; Editorial Staff, *The Observer* 55-66, Chief American Corresp. 73-74, Editor *The Observer Colour Magazine* 65-66; Assoc. Prof. Univ. of Vincennes, Paris 68-70.
Leisure interest: gardening.
Publs. *Drum, a Venture into the New Africa 56, The Treason Cage 58, Commonsense about Africa 60,* (with S. Pienaar), *Anatomy of Britain 62, Anatomy of Britain Today 65, South Africa: Two Views of Separate Development 66, Macmillan: a Study in Ambiguity 68, The New Anatomy of Britain 71, The Sovereign State: the Secret History of ITT 73, The Seven Sisters 75.*
27 Ladbroke Grove, London W.11; 2 Valley Farm, Walberswick, Suffolk, England.
Telephone: 01-727 4188 (London); Southwold 2080 (Suffolk).

Samuel, 2nd Viscount, cr. 37, of Mount Carmel and of Toxteth, Liverpool; **Edwin Herbert Samuel,** C.M.G.;

British lecturer and author; b. 1898, London; s. of Herbert Louis, 1st Viscount Samuel; m. Hadassah Goor 1920; two s.; ed. Westminster School, Balliol Coll., Oxford Univ., and Columbia Univ., New York.
Second Lieut. Royal Field Artillery 17; Palestine Civil Service 20-48; Visiting Prof., Dropsie Coll., Philadelphia 48-49, State Univ., New York 63; Principal, Israel Inst. of Public Admin. 49-; Senior Lecturer on British Institutions, Hebrew Univ. of Jerusalem 52-69; Lecturer Witwatersrand Univ. 55; Visiting Prof. Pittsburgh 70, Miami 71; European Dir., "Conquest of the Desert" Exhibition, Jerusalem 51-53; Dir., *Jewish Chronicle* (London) 51-70, Vallentine Mitchell (publishers), London 65-; Adviser, Magen David Adom (Israeli Red Cross) 57-; Dir. Ellern Investment Corpn., Tel Aviv 64-, Moller Textile Corpn., Nahariya 65-.
Leisure interest: short-story writing.
Publs. *A Primer of Palestine 32, Handbook of the Jewish Communal Villages in Palestine 38, 45, The Theory of Administration 47, Problems of Government in the State of Israel 56, British Traditions in the State of Israel 60, The Structure of Society in Israel 69, Anglo-Israel Relations 1948-1968: A Catalogue 69, A Lifetime in Jerusalem: Memoirs 69, See How They Run: The Administration of Venerable Institutions 75*; short stories: *A Cottage in Galilee 57, A Coat of Many Colours 60, My Friend Musa 63, The Cucumber King 65, His Celestial Highness 68, The Man Who Liked Cats 74*; for children: *Capt. Noah and His Ark.*
House of Lords, London, S.W.1, England; 15 Rashba Road, Jerusalem, Israel.
Telephone: 33871 (Israel).

Samuels, Nathaniel; American government and international official; b. 20 Oct. 1908, Chicago, Ill.; s. of Maurice and Sarah Altman Samuels; m. Mary Elizabeth Hyman 1952; two s.; ed. Harvard Univ.
Admitted Ill. bar 35, practised law 35-42; war service 42-46; assigned to Mission for Economic Affairs, London 45-46; various exec. posts, SOFINA engineering and investment firm, Brussels 46-55; Special Adviser, later Dir. of Div. of Industrial Resources, Mutual Security Agency, Paris 52-53; various posts Kuhn, Loeb & Co. 55-69, 72-; Deputy Under-Sec. of State for Economic Affairs 69-72; Dir. Int. Basic Economy Corpn. 63-69, Chair. 72-; fmrly. mem. Cttee. on Int. Monetary Relations and Cttee. on Foreign Investment and Economic Devt.; mem. Council on Foreign Relations of New York.
Publs. articles in *Foreign Affairs* and *Columbia Journal of World Business.*
40 Wall Street, New York, N.Y. 10005; Home: 775 Park Avenue, New York, N.Y. 10021, U.S.A.

Samuelson, Paul Anthony, PH.D., LL.D., D.LITT., D.SC.; American economist; b. 15 May 1915, Gary, Ind.; s. of Frank Samuelson and Ella Lipton; m. Marion E. Crawford 1938; four s. (including triplets) two d.; ed. Hyde Park High School Chicago, Univ. of Chicago and Harvard Univ.
Professor of Econs. at Massachusetts Inst. of Technology 40-, Inst. Prof. 66-, mem. Radiation Laboratory Staff 44-45; Consultant to Nat. Resources Planning Board 41-43, to War Production Board 45, to U.S. Treasury 45-52, 61-, to Rand Corpn. 49-, to Council of Economic Advisers 60-68, to Federal Reserve Board 65-, to Loomis, Sayles & Co. Boston and to Burden Investors Services Inc.; Research Advisory Board Cttee. for Economic Devt. 60; Advisory Board to Pres. Eisenhower's Comm. on Nat. Goals 60; Nat. Task Force on Economic Educ. 60-61; Special Comm. on Social Sciences of Nat. Science Foundation 68-; Comm. on Money and Credit; Economic Adviser to Pres. Kennedy during election campaign; author of report to Pres. Kennedy on State of American Economy 61; on Editorial Board of *Econometrica*; Guggenheim Fellow

48-49; numerous honorary degrees; mem. American Acad. of Arts and Sciences, American Economic Asscn. (Pres. 61), Int. Economic Asscn. (Pres. 65-68, lifetime hon. Pres.); Fellow American Philosophical Soc., Econometric Soc. (Council mem., Vice-Pres. 50, Pres. 51); Corresp. Fellow British Acad; several awards including Nobel Prize for Economic Science 70, Albert Einstein Commemorative Award 71.
Leisure interest: tennis.
Publs. *Foundations of Economic Analysis* 47 (2nd edn. 61), *Economics* 48, 52, 55, 58, 61, 64, 67, 70, 73, 76 (21 translations), *Readings in Economics* (with R. L. Bishop and J. R. Coleman) 52, 55, 58, 67, 73, *Linear Programming and Economic Analysis* 58, *Collected Scientific Papers*, I and II 66, III 72, *Collected Scientific Papers of Paul A. Samuelson* (vols. I-III) 65, 72; author and joint author of numerous articles on economics.
Massachusetts Institute of Technology, Cambridge, Mass. 02139; Home: 75 Clairemont Road, Belmont, Mass. 02178, U.S.A.
Telephone: 617-253-3368 (M.I.T.).

San Sebastian, Rubens Guillermo; Argentine lawyer; b. 2 Feb. 1927, Buenos Aires; s. of Guillermo San Sebastian and Angela Sara Reggio de San Sebastian; m. Marta Isolda Lleonart 1951; two s.; ed. Univ. of Buenos Aires.
Director-General of Labour Relations, Ministry of Labour 60-66; Sec. of State for Labour 66-70, March-May 71; Minister of Labour 71-73; decorations from Spain and Chile.
Leisure interests: sport, music, theatre, cinema; reading.
Office: Corrientes 456, Piso 5°, Buenos Aires; Home: Echeverría 2096, Piso 15°, Buenos Aires, Argentina.
Telephone: 40-6992/46-7317/46-9216/46-8967 (Office).

San Yu, Brig.-Gen.; Burmese army officer and politician; b. 1919, Prome; ed. Univ. of Rangoon and an American mil. coll.
Commissioned 42, served in Second World War; Mil. Sec. to Chief of Gen. Staff 56-59; Officer commanding the North and Northwest mil. areas; mem. Revolutionary Council, Deputy Chief of Gen. Staff, Commdr. of Land Forces and Minister of Finance and Revenue 63; Gen. Sec. Cen. Organizing Cttee., Burmese Socialist Programme Party 65-; Minister of Nat. Planning, Finance and Revenue 69-72; Deputy Prime Minister 71-74; Minister of Defence 72-74; Chief of Gen. Staff 72-74; Sec. Council of State 74-.
Council of State, Rangoon, Burma.

Sananikone, Phoui; Laotian politician; b. 1903.
Head of Province 41-46; Pres. Chamber of Deputies 48-50, 60-74; Prime Minister and Pres. of the Council of Ministers Feb. 50-Nov. 51, 58-Dec. 59; Minister of Foreign Affairs 53-54, 54-56, 57-58, 59; Vice-Pres. Council of Ministers 53-56; numerous other cabinet posts; Pres. Nationalist group, Rassemblement du Peuple Lao 62-74; sentenced to death *in absentia* Sept. 75; Grand Croix Ordre Royal du Million d'Eléphants et du Parasol Blanc; Commdr. Légion d'Honneur; Croix de Guerre avec palme.

Sanbar, Moshe, M.A.(ECON.); Israeli banker and economist; b. 29 March 1926, Kecskemét, Hungary; s. of Shlomo and Miriam (Klansner) Sandberg; m. Bracha Rabinovich 1951; two d.; ed. Univ. of Budapest and Hebrew Univ., Jerusalem.
Immigrated to Israel 58; Project Dir., Israel Inst. of Applied Social Research and later Deputy Dir. 51-58; Lecturer in Statistics, Hebrew Univ., Jerusalem 57-61; Deputy Dir. Internal State Revenue Div., Ministry of Finance 58-63; Econ. Adviser to Ministry of Finance 63-68; Dir. of the Budgets, Ministry of Finance 64-68; Deputy Chair. and later Chair., Industrial Devt. Bank

of Israel 68-71; Chief Econ. Adviser to Minister of Finance 69-71; Acting Deputy Minister of Commerce 70-71; Gov. Bank of Israel Nov. 71-.
Publs. *My Longest Year* (Yad Vashem Prize) 66; numerous articles in professional journals.
Bank of Israel, Mizpa Building, 29 Jaffa Road, Jerusalem; Home: 44 Pincas Street, Tel-Aviv, Israel.
Telephone: 22 7026 (Office); 441992 (Home).

Sançar, Ilhami, B.A.; Turkish lawyer; b. 1909, Göredes; m.; ed. secondary school, Izmir, Univ. of Ankara.
Appointed bailiff 34; Attorney-Gen. for Menemen 36, for Urgüp 39; worked as lawyer in local govt. 39; practised as barrister 40; mem. National Assembly 61; Deputy for Istanbul 61, 65-; Minister of National Defence 61-65, 73-74, 74.
Tunali Hilmi Caddesi No. 90/7 Kavaklidere, Ankara, Turkey.

Sancar, Gen. Semih; Turkish army officer; b. 1911, Erzurum; m.; two c.; ed. Artillery School, War Acad.
Served in Turkish Army as Commdr. of Artillery Battery and Battalion, Asst. Commdr. Army Corps Artillery, Dept. Chief, Branch Section Dir. in Land Forces and Gen. Staff H.Q.; then Instructor War Acad.; Dir. of Personnel, Dir. of Operations Turkish Gen. Staff; promoted to rank of Gen. 69; Commdr. of Gendarmerie 69; Commdr. 2nd. Army; Commdr. Turkish Land Forces 72-73; Chief of Gen. Staff 73-.
General Staff Headquarters, Ankara, Turkey.

Sánchez, Luis Alberto, PH.D., LIT.D., HIST.D.; Peruvian university professor and politician; b. 1900; ed. Sacré Coeur, Universidad Mayor de San Marcos.
Assistant Director, Nat. Library of Peru 28-30; Dean, Faculty of Philosophy, History and Literature, Univ. Mayor de San Marcos, Lima 46, 61, Rector 46-48, 61-64; mem. of the Chamber of Deps. 31-36, 45-48, Pres. 45; Special Ambassador to Colombia 46, Mexico 60-61; Dir. Editorial Ercilla, Santiago, Chile 35-45; mem. Exec. Nat. Cttee. of the Partido Aprista Peruano (APRA Party) 31-34, 45-49, 56-; mem. Board of Trustees, American Inst. for Free Labor Development, Washington 62-; exiled 32-33, 34-45, 48-56; Nat. Culture Prize 59, 60; Peruvian and foreign honours.
Publs. *La Literatura Peruana* (6 vols.) 51, *Historia General de América* (2 vols.) 42, 6th edn. 58, *Proceso y Contenido de la Novela Hispano-Americana* 53, *Historia de la Literatura Americana* 51, *Escritores Representativos de América* (2 vols.) 57, *Examen Espectral de América Latina* 62.
P.O. Box 673, Lima, Peru.

Sánchez-Bella, Alfredo, D.HIST.SC.; Spanish diplomatist and politician; b. Tordesilos, Guadalajara 1916; s. of Hipólito Sánchez Sánchez and Filomena Bella; m. Isabel Carswell 1950; two s.; ed. Univ. of Valencia.
Chair. of Youth Div. of Catholic Action and a mem. of its Nat. Council; also held posts of Deputy Sec. of Fed. of Catholic Studies and Sec.-Gen. of Pax Romana; also Prof. of Faculty of Philosophy and Letters, Valencia Univ. and of Faculties of Philosophy and Letters and Economic Science of Madrid Univ.; fmr. Editor of Valencian newspaper *Avance* (now *Levante*), and Founder-Editor of magazines *Mundo Hispánico* and *Cuadernos Hispanoamericanos*; Dir. Radio Valencia and Radio Mediterráneo 39-40; Deputy Sec.-Gen. Higher Council for Scientific Research 40-41; Deputy Dir. Giménez de Cisneros Coll., Madrid Univ. 41-45; Sec.-Gen., Deputy Dir., then Dir., Inst. of Hispanic Culture 46-56; Amb. to Dominican Republic 56-58, to Colombia 58-62, to Italy 62-69, concurrently to Malta 68-69; Minister of Information and Tourism 69-73; Pres. Banco Hipotecario de España; fmr. Del. at UN Assemblies, and to UNESCO and other int. orgs.; Grand

Cross of Isabella the Catholic, Grand Cross of Civil Merit and numerous South American decorations.
Paseo de la Castellana 72, Madrid 1, Spain.
Telephone: 2614342.

Sánchez-Gavito, Vicente, A.B., LL.B.; Mexican diplomatist; b. 25 May 1910, Mexico City; s. of Vicente Sánchez-Gavito and María Pina y Aguayo; m. María Murguia 1936; six d.; ed. Univ. Nacional Autónoma de México and Escuela Libre de Derecho.
Entered Diplomatic Service of Mexico 35-; Counsellor, Embassy in Washington 43-47; Dir.-Gen. Diplomatic Service, Foreign Office 47-51; Minister, Washington 56-58, Amb. 59; Amb. to Brazil 65-70, to U.K. 70-73, to Fed. Repub. of Germany 75-; mem. UN Tribunals in Libya and Eritrea 51-55; Mexican Rep., Council of Org. of American States (OAS) 59-65, Chair. of Council 60, Chair. Interamerican Peace Cttee. 61, Honduras-Nicaragua Mixed Comm. 61; mem. Mexican Dels. to numerous Foreign Ministers' Meetings and Extraordinary Interamerican Confs. of OAS (Pres. of Mexican Dels. to 9th Foreign Ministers' Meeting and to 1st Extraordinary Interamerican Conf.); Orders of the Southern Cross (Brazil), Liberator (Venezuela), Ethiopian Star, Cedar of Lebanon, Orange-Nassau (Netherlands).
Leisure interest: chess.
Mexican Embassy, Eugen-Langenstrasse 10, 5 Cologne S1, Federal Republic of Germany.

Sánchez Hernández, Col. Fidel; Salvadorian army officer and politician; b. 7 July 1917.
Military Attaché, Washington 60-62; Minister of Interior 62-66; Pres. of El Salvador 67-72; Leader of Partido de Conciliación Nacional (P.C.N.).
San Salvador, El Salvador.

Sánchez Méndez, Jorge; Costa Rican economist and politician; ed. School of Econ. and Social Services, Costa Rica.
Representative on Exec. Council of Gen. Treaty of Cen. American Econ. Integration 65; Prof. Cen. American Econ. Univ.; head of dels. to ECLA, LAFTA 67; Deputy Minister of Econs., Industry and Commerce 70-72, Minister 72-73, 74-.
Ministerio de Economía, Industria y Comercio, San José, Costa Rica.

Sánchez Quell, H., LL.D.; Paraguayan politician and diplomatist; b. 1907; ed. Univ. of Asunción.
Member Colorado Party 30; fmr. Editor *Patria, La Unión, Rumbos, La Prensa, Jornada*; fmr. posts incl. Prof. Univ. of Asunción, Dir.-Gen. of Nat. Archives, Vice-Pres. Chamber of Reps., Ambassador to Mexico; Paraguayan Rep. to UN until 54; Minister of Foreign Affairs 54-57; Ambassador to Brazil 57-59, to France 59-62; mem. Permanent Arbitration Court of The Hague, Pan American Inst. of Geography and History, Paraguayan Inst. of Historical Research, Argentine Inst. of Law, Argentine Acad. of Sociology, Historical and Geographical Inst. of Uruguay, Mexican Athenaeum of Sciences and Arts.
c/o Ministry of Foreign Affairs, Asunción, Paraguay.

Sánchez-Vilella, Roberto; Puerto Rican politician; b. 19 Feb. 1913, Mayaguez; s. of Luis Sánchez-Frasqueri and Angela Vilella-Vélez; m. Jeanette Ramos-Buonomo 1967; one s. two d.; ed. Ohio State Univ.
Sub-Commissioner of the Interior 41-42; Dir. Transportation Authority of Puerto Rico 42-45; Special Asst. to Pres. of Senate 46-47; Resident Engineer Caribe Hilton Hotel 47-48; Exec. Sec. to Govt. 49-51; Sec. of State 52-64; Gov. Puerto Rico 65-69; Pres. People's Party; mem. Puerto Rico Coll. of Engineers, American Soc. of Public Administrators; Hon. LL.D. (Ohio State Univ.) 66.
Leisure interests: reading, dominoes.

156 F. D. Roosevelt Avenue, Hato Rey, Puerto Rico 00918.
Telephone: 765-06240.

Sandage, Allan Rex, PH.D., D.SC.; American astronomer; b. 18 June 1926, Iowa City; s. of Charles H. Sandage and Dorothy M. Briggs; m. Mary L. Connelly 1959; two s.; ed. Univ. of Illinois and California Inst. of Technology.
Staff mem. Mount Wilson and Palomar Observatories 52-; Asst. Astronomer Hale Observatories, Calif. 52-56, Astronomer 56-; Visiting Lecturer, Harvard Univ. 57; Consultant, Nat. Science Foundation 61-63; mem. Cttee. on Science and Public Policy 65; mem. Nat. Acad. of Sciences; Philips Lecturer, Haverford Coll. 68; Research Assoc. Australian Nat. Univ. 68-69; Helen Warner Prize of American Astronomical Soc. 60; Eddington Medal, Royal Astronomical Soc. (U.K.) 63; Pope Pius XI Gold Medal, Pontifical Acad. of Sciences 66; Gold Medal, Royal Astronomical Soc. (U.K.) 67, Rittenhouse Medal 68, Nat. Medal of Scientific Merit 71.
Leisure interest: gardening.
Publs. Numerous scientific papers and *Hubble Atlas of Galaxies*.
8319 Josard Road, San Gabriel, Calif. 91775, U.S.A.
Telephone: 213-285-5086.

Sandberg, Willem; Netherlands museum director; b. 24 Oct. 1897, Amersfoort; m. Alida Swaneveld 1926; one s. two d.; ed. Acad. of Fine Arts, Amsterdam, Univs. of Vienna and Utrecht.
Designer in Amsterdam 28-38; Asst. Dir. Municipal Museums, Amsterdam 38-45, Dir. 45-62; Head, Int. Section "Art since 1950" U.S. World's Fair, Seattle, Wash. 62; Chair. Exec. Cttee. Israel Museum, Jerusalem 64-68, 71-72; Erasmus Lecturer, Harvard Univ., U.S.A. 69; Co-founder Fed. of Professional Artists in the Netherlands 45, Pres. 47-51; Vice-Pres. Netherlands Arts Council 48-60; Pres. Acad. Council, Jerusalem 73-; Hon. degree Univ. of Buffalo, N.Y. 62; Gold Medallist American Inst. of Graphic Arts, City of Amsterdam, Dutch State Prize for Graphic Design 68; Erasmus Prize 75; many foreign decorations.
Leisure interest: designing.
Publs. many articles on art and museum building; Co-editor *Pioneers of Modern Art*.
Dirk Schaeferstraat 37, Amsterdam, Netherlands.
Telephone: 725385.

Sandblom, (John) Philip, M.D., M.S., F.A.C.S., F.R.C.S.; Swedish professor of surgery and university administrator; b. 29 Oct. 1903, Chicago, Ill.; s. of Dr. John N. Sandblom and Ellen Chinlund; m. Grace Schaefer 1932; three s. two d.; ed. Northwestern Univ. and Karolinska Institutet, Stockholm.
Associate Prof. of Surgery, Karolinska Institutet, Stockholm 44; Surgeon-in-Chief, Crown Princess Louise's Children's Hospital 45-50; Prof. of Surgery and Head of Dept. of Surgery, Lund Univ. 50-70, Vice-Chancellor of Lund Univ. 57-68; Visiting Prof. Univ. of Calif., San Diego 72-73, Univ. of Lausanne 73-; mem. of Board Soc. for Modern Art 36-46, Gen. Art Soc. 43-70; Treas. Swedish Surgical Soc. 46-52, Pres. 57-58, 70; mem. Insurance Advisory Board 47-50; Assoc. mem. Asscn. Française de Chirurgie, corresp. mem. Deutsche Gesellschaft für Chirurgie, and Norwegian Surgical Soc.; Pres. Soc. Int. de Chirurgie 67; Hon. Fellow, American Coll. of Surgeons, Royal Coll. of Surgeons in Edinburgh and Ireland; Hon. mem. American Surgical Asscn., Southern Surgical Asscn., Soc. Int. de Chirurgie, Swedish, Danish, Italian, Northern and Finnish Surgical Socs.; many hon. degrees.
Leisure interests: collecting works of modern art, sailing, skiing.
Publs. *Function of the Human Gall Bladder, Function of*

the Sphincter Oddi., Tensile Strength of Healing Wounds, Hemobilia, The Responsibility of Society to Surgery, The Role of the University in the World of Violence, The Difference in Men, Portal Hypertension, and various papers.
2 Chemin des Bluets, 1012 Lausanne, Switzerland.
Telephone: 021-296877.

Sander, Bruno Hermann Max; Austrian geologist; b. 23 Feb. 1884, Innsbruck; *s.* of Max Sander and Marie Rizzoli; *m.* Elisabeth Holzknecht 1920; one *d.*; ed. Gymnasium Innsbruck and Leopold-Franzens Universität, Innsbruck.
Assistant, Technische Hochschule of Vienna 09-; Lecturer in Geology, Univ. of Innsbruck 12-14, Univ. of Vienna 14-22; Geologist, Geological Inst., Vienna 13-22; Prof. of Mineralogy and Petrography, Univ. of Innsbruck 22-55, Emeritus 55-; mem. Acads. of Vienna, Bologna, Modena, Uppsala, Berlin, Halle, Nat. Acad. of Sciences, Washington; Corresp. mem. Geol. Soc. of America, Geol. Soc. of Finland, Geological Soc. of London; Int. Prize of Accad. dei Lincei, Rome; numerous medals; Dr. h.c. Göttingen 37, Vienna 65.
Leisure interests: sociology, religions.
Publs. *Gefügekünde der Gesteine* 30, *Einführung in die Gefügekünde der Geologischen Körper* (2 vols.) 48-50; geological maps and treatises on geology and petrography; other books and treatises under pseudonym *Santer*.
Kaiserjosefstr. 13, 6020 Innsbruck, Austria.
Telephone: 25476.

Sanders, Donald Neil, B.ECON.; Australian central banker; b. 21 June 1927, Sydney; *s.* of L. G. Sanders; *m.* Betty Elaine Constance 1952; four *s.* one *d.*; ed. Univ. of Sydney.
Commonwealth Bank of Australia 43-60; Australian Treasury 56; Bank of England 60; with Reserve Bank of Australia 60-, Supt., Credit Policy Div. of Banking Dept. 64-66, Deputy Man. of Banking Dept. 66-67, of Research Dept. 67-70, Chief Man. of Securities Markets Dept. 70-72, of Banking and Finance Dept. 72-74, Adviser and Chief Man. of Banking and Finance Dept. 74-75, Deputy Gov. and Deputy Chair. of Board 75-.
Reserve Bank of Australia, 65 Martin Place, Sydney, N.S.W. 2000; Home: 27 Marjorie Street, Roseville, N.S.W. 2000, Australia.

Sanders, William; American lawyer and diplomatist; b. 14 April 1903; ed. Stanford, George Washington, Columbus and Oxford Univs.
International Telephone and Telegraph Corpn., New York 29-32; admitted to D.C. Bar 35, legal practice 35-36; Chief, Juridical Div., Pan-American Union 36-41; Principal Attorney, Co-ordinator of Inter-American Affairs 42; Alt. mem. Emergency Advisory Cttee. for Political Defense, Montevideo 42-43, mem. 44-45; Assoc. Chief, Div. of Int. Org. Affairs, Office of Special Political Affairs, Dept. of State 45-48; Special Asst. Bureau of UN Affairs, Dept. of State 48-52, Acting Deputy Asst. Sec. of State 50-52; U.S. del. conferences Inter-American system, NATO and UN 45-58; U.S. rep. I.A. Council of Jurists 48-58; Counsellor and Deputy Chief Mission, Chile 53-56; Asst. Sec.-Gen. Org. of American States 58-68; fmr. Pres. Pan American Devt. Foundation.
Publs. *Improvement and Co-ordination of Inter-American Peace Instruments* 40, *Sovereignty and Interdependence in the New World* 48.
c/o Pan American Union, 19th Street and Constitution Avenue, Washington, D.C. 20006, U.S.A.
Telephone: DU 1-8205.

Sandilands, Sir Francis Edwin Prescott, Kt., C.B.E., M.A.; British insurance executive; b. 11 Dec. 1913, Chatham; *s.* of Lt.-Col. Prescott Sandilands and Gladys Baird Murton; *m.* Susan Gillian Jackson 1939; two *s.*; ed. Eton and Corpus Christi Coll., Cambridge.

Joined Commercial Union Group of insurance cos. 35, Chief Exec. 58-72, Vice-Chair. 68-72, Chair. 72-; Chair. Royal Trust Co. of Canada (U.K.) 74-, British Insurance Asscn. 65-67, Cttee. on Inflation Accounting (Sandilands Cttee.) 74-75; Dir. Finance for Industry Ltd., Imperial Chemicals Industries Ltd., Kleinwort, Benson Lonsdale Ltd., Plessey Co. Ltd., Trafalgar House Investments Ltd., Royal Opera House 75-; Pres. Royal Insurance Inst. of London 69-70; Treas. Univ. Coll., London 73-; Gov. Admin. Staff Coll., Henley 73-; Hon. Fellow, Corpus Christi Coll., Cambridge 75; Commdr. Order of Crown of Belgium.
Leisure interests: music, medieval history, gardening.
Commercial Union Insurance Company Ltd., St. Helen's, 1 Undershaft, London E.C.3; Home: 53 Cadogan Square, London, S.W.1, England.
Telephone: 01-283 7500 (Office); 01-235 6384 (Home).

Sandoungout, Marcel; Gabonese trade unionist and diplomatist; b. 25 Oct. 1927.
Former trade unionist, Gabon; fmr. Chef de Cabinet to Minister of Planning for Agriculture; Chief, Div. for Int. Orgs., Ministry of Foreign Affairs 60; mem. Nat. Assembly 61, Chair. Cttee. for Foreign Affairs and Defence, 61, 62; Del. to Defence Council of African and Malagasy Union 61, 62; Minister of Health and Social Affairs May-Dec. 62, for Public Works, Tourism and Posts and Telecommunications 63-64; Amb. to German Fed. Repub., Belgium, Netherlands, Norway, Denmark, Sweden and Luxembourg 64-66; Perm. Rep. to GATT and EEC 64-66; Perm. Rep. to UN 67-68; Amb. to Dahomey and Senegal 69-71, to Ivory Coast 71-72, to France (also accred. to Switzerland) 72-.
Embassy of Gabon, 26 bis avenue Raphael 75016 Paris, France.

Sanford, Terry, A.B., J.D., LL.D., LITT.D.; American university president, lawyer and politician; b. 20 Aug. 1917, Laurinberg, N.C.; *s.* of late Cecil L. Sanford and of Elizabeth Martin; *m.* Margaret Rose Knight 1942; one *s.* one *d.*; ed. Presbyterian Junior Coll., Univ. of North Carolina and Univ. of N.C. School of Law.
Attorney at Law and partner in private law firm N.C. 48-60; mem. N.C. State Ports Authority 50-53; N.C. State Senator 53-55; Gov. N.C. 61-65; mem. Board of Trustees Berea Coll., Methodist Coll. Fayetteville 58- (Chair. 58-68), Shaw Univ., Univ. of N.C. 61- (Chair. 61-65); Pres. Duke Univ. 69-; Trustee Howard Univ. 71-74; Trustee and mem. numerous orgs. mainly concerned with educ., children's welfare, govt., regional and urban problems; mem. Advisory Board Nat. Asscn. for Retarded Children 65-; mem. Board of Dirs. Arts Council of America 65-70; Trustee Nat. Council on Crime and Delinquency 69-; mem. Advisory Cttee. for Institutional Rels. of Nat. Science Foundation 71-; mem. American Bar Asscn. Special Cttee. on Co-ordination of Judicial Improvements 71-72; Chair. Board of Dirs. Nat. Council of Independent Colls. and Univs. 71-; mem. American and N.C. Bar Asscns., American Judicature Soc., American Acad. of Political Science; several honorary degrees.
Publs. *But What About People* 66, *Storm Over the States* 67.
Office of the President, Duke University, Durham, N.C. 27706, U.S.A.

Sanger, Elrich, DR. IUR.; Indonesian lawyer and international official; b. 14 Jan. 1927, Gorontalo; *s.* of J. B. Sanger and N. Karaseran; *m.* Maria Louise Sara Sanger 1959; two *s.*; ed. Dutch schools in Indonesia, Bonn Univ. and Inst. for Int. Law and Politics, Bonn.
Joined Ministry of Industry, Indonesia 59, Head of Legal Dept., Bureau of Oil Affairs; mem. Board for Distribution of Oil Products 60; Sec.-Gen. of Co-ordinating Comm. for Indonesian Nat. Oil Companies 61; Sec. Indonesian Oil Negotiating Cttee. until 63; Chief of Staff of Nat. Oil Co., Permina 64; Under-Sec.,

Oil Ministry 64-67; Dir. in charge of Legal Affairs, Foreign Relations and Int. Marketing 66-68; Sec.-Gen. Org. of the Petroleum Exporting Countries (OPEC) 69-70.
Leisure interests: reading, gardening.
Publ. *Indonesian Nationality*.
c/o Pertamina Perwira 2, Jakarta, Indonesia.

Sanger, Frederick, C.B.E., B.A., PH.D., F.R.S.; British research biochemist; b. 13 Aug. 1918, Rendcomb, Glos.; s. of Frederick Sanger and Cicely Crewdson; m. Joan Howe 1940; two s. one d.; ed. Bryanston School and St. John's Coll., Cambridge.
Biochemical research at Cambridge 40-; Beit Memorial Fellowship 44-51; mem. Scientific Staff, Medical Research Council 51-; Fellow, King's Coll., Cambridge 54-; Hon. Foreign mem. American Acad. of Arts and Sciences 58-; hon. mem. American Soc. of Biological Chemists, Japanese Biochemical Soc.; corresp. mem. Association Quimica de Argentina; mem. Acad. of Science of Argentina and Brazil, World Acad. of Arts and Science; foreign assoc. Nat. Acad. of Sciences (U.S.A.); Corday-Morgan Medal and Prize, Chemical Soc. 51, Nobel Prize for Chemistry 58, Alfred Benzon Prize 66; Royal Medal (Royal Soc.) 69; Hopkins Memorial Medal 71; Gairdner Foundation Annual Award 71; Hon. D.Sc. (Leicester, Oxford, Strasbourg).
Leisure interests: boating, skiing, gardening.
Publs. Various papers on protein and nucleic acid structure and metabolism in scientific journals.
Medical Research Council Laboratory of Molecular Biology, Hills Road, Cambridge, England.
Telephone: Cambridge 48011.

Sänger, Fritz Paul; German journalist; b. 24 Dec. 1901, Stettin; s. of Paul Sänger and Ida Kempe; m. Susanne Kühne 1936; one s. two d.; ed. Univ. of Berlin.
Sub-editor *General Anzeiger* (Stettin) 21; with Pressestelle Deutscher Beamtenbund 23-27; editor *Preussische Lehrerzeitung* 27-33, dismissed by Hitler; with the *Frankfurter Zeitung* 35-43 and *Neues Wiener Tagblatt* 43-44; Editor *Braunschweiger Neue Presse/Braunschweiger Zeitung* 45-46; Editor and founder *Sozialdemokratischer Pressedienst* 46-47; Editor-in-Chief Deutscher Presse-Dienst (D.P.D.), later merged in the Deutsche Presse-Agentur (D.P.A.) 47-59; mem. Board of Dirs. Deutschlandfunk; mem. Deutscher Presserat, mem. Sozialdemokratische Partei Deutschands (S.P.D.) since 20; mem. Bundestag 61-69.
Leisure interests: history (particularly modern history), international contacts.
Publs. *Handbuch des Deutschen Bundestages* 49, 52, 54 and 58, *Soziale Demokratie, Bemerkungen zum Grundsatzprogramm der SPD* 60, 62, 64, *Erich Ollenhauer, Reden und Aufsätze* 64, *Politik der Täuschungen, Missbrauch der Presse im Dritten Reich, Weisungen, Informationen, Notizen 1933-39* 75.
Erlenweg 28, 2000 Wedel, Federal Republic of Germany.
Telephone: 04103-3716.

Sanger, Ruth Ann, PH.D., F.R.S.; British medical research scientist; b. 6 June 1918, Southport, Queensland; d. of Hubert Sanger and Katharine M. Ross (Cameron); m. Robert Russell Race, C.B.E., F.R.C.P., F.R.S. (q.v.) 1956; no c.; ed. Abbotsleigh, Sydney and Sydney and London Univs.
Member of scientific staff, Red Cross Blood Transfusion Service, Syndey 41-46, Medical Research Council Blood Group Unit, Lister Inst., London 46-, Dir. 73-; Karl Landsteiner Award, American Asscn. of Blood Banks (with Dr. R. R. Race) 57, Philip Levine Award, American Soc. of Clinical Pathologists (with Dr. R. R. Race) 70, Gairdner Award, Toronto 72, Oliver Memorial Award 73.
Leisure interests: boating, gardening.
Publs. *Blood Groups in Man* (with Dr. R. R. Race) 50,

6th edition 75; many papers on blood groups in medical and scientific journals.
Medical Research Council Blood Group Unit., Wolfson House, University College London, 4 Stephenson Way, London NW1 2HE; Home: 22 Vicarage Road, East Sheen, London, SW14 8RU, England.
Telephone: 01-388-7752 (Office); 01-876-1508 (Home).

Sangster, John Young; British industrialist; b. 29 May 1896, Birmingham; s. of Charles Sangster; ed. Hurstpierpoint Coll.
Practical experience in German and French cycle and motor car factories 13-14; war service 14-18; produced prototype 8 h.p. air-cooled car which, sold to the Rover Co., became the famous Rover-8 19; Asst. to Works Man., Rover Co. 20-21; joined Ariel Works 23, Joint Man. Dir. 26; acquired Ariel Motor Cycle Co. and set up Ariel Motors Ltd. 32; acquired Triumph Motor Cycle Co. and set up Triumph Engineering Co. Ltd. 36; Triumph factory, Coventry, completely destroyed in air raids 40, rebuilt at Allesley, near Coventry; sold Ariel Motors Ltd. to Birmingham Small Arms Co. Ltd. 45, Triumph Engineering Co. Ltd. 51; Dir. Birmingham Small Arms Co. Ltd. 51-70; Chair. Birmingham Small Arms Co. Ltd. 56-61; Pres. British Cycle and Motor Cycle Industries Asscn. 53-54.
Leisure interests: yachting, skiing, cycling, motor cycling.
34 Ennismore Gardens, London, SW7 1AE, England.
Telephone: 01-589-2561.

Sanguineti, Edoardo; Italian writer; b. 9 Dec. 1930, Genoa; s. of Giovanni Sanguineti and Giuseppina Cocchi; m. Luciana Garabello 1954; three s. one d.; ed. Univ. degli Studi, Turin.
Former Prof. of Italian Literature, Univ. of Genoa.
Publs. *Laborintus* 56, *Opus metricum* 60, *Interpretazione di Malebolge* 61, *Tre studi danteschi* 61, *Tra liberty e crepuscolarismo* 61 and 65, *Alberto Moravia* 62, *K. e altre cose* 62, *Passaggio* 63, *Capriccio italiano* 63, *Triperuno* 64, *Ideologia e linguaggio* 65, *Il realismo di Dante* 66, *Guido Gozzano* 66, *Il Giuoco dell' Oca* 67, *Le Baccanti di Euripide* (trans.) 68, *Fedra di Seneca* (trans.) 69, *T.A.T.* 69, *Teatro* 69, *Poesia Italiana del Novecento* 69, *Il Giuoco del Satyricon* 70, *Orlando Furioso* (with L. Ronconi) 70, *Renga* (with O. Paz, J. Roubaud, C. Tomlinson) 71, *Storie Naturali* 71, *Wirrwarr* 72, *Catamerone* 74, *Le Troiane di Euripide* (trans.) 74.
Via Cabella 11, 16122 Genoa, Italy.
Telephone: 010-813263.

Sanguinetti, Alexandre; French politician; b. 27 March 1913; ed. Coll. Stanislas, Paris and Ecole de Droit, Cairo.
War service, Second World War; Head of Office, Ministry of Information 59-61, Ministry of the Interior 61-62; mem. Chamber of Deputies 62-; Minister for Veterans 66-67; Vice-Pres. Comm. for Nat. Defence 62-66, Pres. 68-; Pres. regional council of Midi-Pyrénées (U.D.R.) 70-; Sec.-Gen. Union des Démocrates pour la République 73-74; Chevalier Légion d'Honneur, Médaille Militaire, Croix de Guerre.
Publ. *La France et l'Arme atomique*.
c/o Union des Démocrates pour la Republique, 123 rue de Lille, Paris 7e, France.

Sanminiatelli, Bino; Italian artist and writer; b. 7 May 1896, Florence; s. of Count Senator Donato Sanminiatelli and Countess Marta Camerini; m. Contessa Elena dei Principi di Castelbarco Albani 1921; one s. two d.; ed. Univs. of Padua, Rome and Siena.
Member Futurist and Dada movements, Dir. with painter Prampolini of avant-garde magazine *Noi*; represented with etchings in important int. and nat. exhbns. in Venice and Rome; works hung in Galleria Nazionale d'Arte Moderna Rome, Florence and Turin; etchings published by Ceschina and De Luca; Vice-Pres. Dante Alighieri Soc.; Pres. Cento Amici del Libro;

Viareggio Prize 33, Encomio della Reale Accad. d'Italia 35, Rustichello Prize 61, Marzotto Prize 63. Leisure interests: literature, art, wine-making. Publs. *Fiamme a Monteluce* 38, *L'Omnibus del Corso* 40, *Cervo in Maremma* 42, *Gente in Famiglia* 51, *Le Proibizioni* 54, *Il Viaggiatore sedentario* 53, *Mi dico addio* 59, *La Mora* 61, *Il Permesso di Vivere* 63, *Vita di Michelangelo* 64, *Quasi un uomo* 68.
Vignamaggio, 50022 Greve in Chianti, Florence, Italy.
Telephone: 055-85007.

Sansbury, Rt. Rev. Cyril Kenneth, D.D.; British ecclesiastic; b. 21 Jan. 1905; ed. St. Paul's School, London, Peterhouse, Cambridge, and Westcott House, Cambridge.
Ordained Deacon 28, Priest 29; Curate, Diocese of Southwark 28-32; Missionary in Japan 32-41; Prof. Central Theological Coll., Tokyo, and Chaplain, St. Andrew's Church, Tokyo 34-41; Chaplain, Royal Canadian Air Force 41-45; Warden, Lincoln Theological Coll. 45-52; Canon and Prebendary, Lincoln Cathedral 48-53; Warden, St. Augustine's Coll., Canterbury 52-61; Hon. Canon of Canterbury 53-61; Bishop of Singapore and Malaya 61-66; Gen. Sec. British Council of Churches 66-73; Asst. Bishop, Diocese of London 66-73; Priest-in-charge St. Mary in the Marsh and Hon. Minor Canon, Norwich Cathedral.
Publ. *Truth, Unity and Concord, Anglican Faith in an Ecumenical Setting* 67, *Combating Racism, The British Churches and the World Council of Churches Programme to Combat Racism* 75.
53 The Close, Norwich, NR1 4EG, England.
Telephone: 0603-618808.

Santa Cruz, Hernán, LIC. EN DER.; Chilean diplomatist; b. 8 Feb. 1906, Santiago; s. of Joaquín Santa-Cruz and Josefina Barcelo; m. Adriana Garcia de la Huerta 1929; three s. two d.; ed. Univ. of Chile and Catholic Univ. of Chile.
Permanent Rep. of Chile at UN 47-52, Pres. ECOSOC 50-51; Pres. and Rapporteur, UN Comm. on Racial Situation in S. Africa 53-55; Consultant to Sec.-Gen. of UN and Dir.-Gen. of FAO 55-56; Asst. Dir.-Gen. FAO and Dir. Regional Office in Latin America 59-67; Amb. and Perm. Rep. of Chile to int. orgs. in Geneva 67-; del. to FAO Council 67-72; Chair. FAO Conf. 69; Pres. Gov. Council UNDP 71; del. to UN Gen. Assembly and other int. confs.; Dag Hammarskjöld Prize for Int. Co-operation 69; Commdr. Légion d'Honneur (France) and decorations from Ethiopia, Panama, Brazil, Argentina, Ecuador.
Publs. *FAO Role in Rural Welfare* 58, *Discrimination on Political Rights* 63.
Office: 56 rue Moillebeau, Geneva; Home: 139 rue de Lausanne, Geneva, Switzerland.
Telephone: 345130 (Office); 315528 (Home).

Santa Maria, Luigi; Italian business executive; b. 20 Nov. 1912, Naples; s. of Alberto and Elena Monarine; m. Cesarina Pica; two s. one d.; graduated in law.
Pres. Lombard Union of Mfrs. of Artificial Textile Fibres; mem. Exec. Council Gen. Confederation of Industry 70-73; Chair. Snia Viscosa S.p.A.
Via Serbelloni 14, 20121 Milan, Italy.
Telephone: 709795.

Santaella, Dr. Héctor; Venezuelan economist, banker and diplomatist; b. 18 May 1920, Rio Caribe; s. of Juan Santalla and Carmen Guerra; m. Margarita Telleria 1943; one s. three d.; ed. Colegio La Salle, Caracas, Liceo Andrés Bello, Caracas, and Universidad Central de Venezuela, Caracas.
General Counsellor and Founder of Metalanca (Nat. Steel Rolling Mills); Chief of Econ. Section, Directorate of Econ. Policy, Venezuelan Foreign Service 43; later Head of Dept. of Econ. Information, Ministry of Foreign Affairs; fmr. Venezuelan Gov. Int. Bank for Reconstruc-

tion and Devt.; fmr. Alt. Dir. Int. Monetary Fund; Amb. to U.S.A. 58; Sec. of Govt. Junta, Republic of Venezuela 58-59; mem. Nat. Congress 64-; Pres. Chamber of Deputies 64-65; Amb. to U.K. 65-66; Minister of Communications 66-67; Pres. Melalanca (Nat. Steel Rolling Mills) 71-; fmr. Chair. Inveco, Bank of Repub., Bank of S. America; fmr. Sec. Nat. Banking Council; Dir. Venezuelan Fed. of Chambers and Asscns. of Commerce and Production; fmr. Pres. Asscn. of Venezuelan Exporters; fmr. Prof. of Econ. Theory, Venezuelan Central Univ.; numerous decorations.
Home: Transversal 5, No. 10-Sebucán, Caracas; Office: Apartado 1846, Caracas, Venezuela.
Telephone: (Home) 343648; (Office) 55888.

Santas Elordy, Andrés Adolfo; Argentine professor of surgery; b. 9 Aug. 1913, Buenos Aires; s. of Manuel Santos and Catalina Elordy; m. Margarita M. Nicholson 1939; one s.; ed. Faculty of Medicine, Univ. of Buenos Aires.
Head Surgeon of Policlínico del Hospital Hacienda; Deputy Dir. of Surgical Inst. of Hospital de Clinicas; Asst. Professor of Surgery 55; Dean of Faculty of Medicine, Univ. of Buenos Aires 66-69; Rector of Univ. of Buenos Aires 69-71; Pres. Third Pan-American Conf. on Medical Education; Gold Medallist of Univ.
Publ. *Revista Argentina de Cirugía* (Founder and Director).
Avda. Quintana 116, 1° Piso, Buenos Aires, Argentina.
Telephone: 41-8026.

Santorini, Paul E.; Greek scientist and engineer, emeritus professor of physics; b. 8 June 1893, Odessa; m. 1st Gertrude Bonn, 1922; one s.; 2nd Anastasie Pierrakou, 1967; ed. Eidgenössische Technische Hochschule, Zürich (engineering) and Univ. of Zürich (physics).
Engineer, Löntschwerk Hydro-electric plant, Glarus, Switzerland 18-19; Engineer, Ministry of Communications, Athens 19-22; Dir. Athens Construction Co. 22-30; Dir. Dept. of Hydrometry, Ministry of Agriculture 30-46; Extraordinary Prof. of Applied Physics, Athens Univ. 35; invented High-frequency Absorbomicrometer 29, Absorbomicrometric Balance 34; discovered "Elastic Inertia Effect" in concrete mass under deformation 30; Electronic Weapons Research, Greek Army Gen. Staff, Athens 36-40; built Greece's Radar, the first centimetric wavelength radar 36-39 and the first Proximity Fuse 36; discovered natural and obtained artificial propagation of centimetric electromagnetic waves beyond optical line of sight, by Dispersion Effect on top of natural obstacles (S.-Effect) 37; holds the two basic patents for the "Electronic Brain H" for automatic guiding of missiles type Nike 42; established lowest duration limit of observable physical phenomena in nature 58; proposed new hypothetical Universe Continuum, Nice (France) 69, proposed new theory of emergence of Universe ("*Small*" Bang of infinitesimal original Continuum Particle, as opposed to Lemaître's "*Big*" Bang), Nice (France) 70; Ordinary Prof. of Experimental Physics and Dir. of Experimental Physics Laboratory, The Nat. Technical Univ. of Athens 46-64, Prof. Emer. 64-; Chief Greek Govt. Del. to numerous Int. Scientific Congresses 31-; Hon. Pres. 7th Int. Congress Philosophy, Nice 69; Pres. Hellenic Soc. for Research and Invention 69-71; Fellow, New York Acad. of Sciences 65; Fellow of Royal Soc. of Arts (London); mem. or corresp. mem. many Acads. of Sciences, Insts. and Learned Socs. 60-; recipient of numerous hon. degrees and awards; medals include Gold Medal, Royal Inst. Agricultural Sciences 60; Fermat Medal, Acad. of Sciences of Toulouse 61; Vermeil Medal, French Soc. for Research and Invention (Paris) 68; Hon. Vermeil Medal, French Soc. for Encouragement au Progrès (Paris) 69; Grand Gold Medal "Archimedes" for Research and Invention 70; Commdr.

Royal Order of George I and Commdr. Royal Order of Phoenix (Greece) and many foreign decorations.
Leisure interest: classical music.
Publs. about 300, the most recent being: *Evolution de la Pensée vers une nouvelle conception panthéistique de l'Univers* 68, *Considérations philosophiques sur un Nouveau Continuum Hypothétique Espace-Temps-Matière-Esprit et sur le sens physique du "Rien" absolu* 69, *Considérations sur la Naissance de l'Univers, conduisant à une Théorie de sa Croissance Progressive à partir d'une hypothétique Particule Primitive de Continuum Espace-Temps-Matière-Esprit* 70, *Essai d'un traitement philosophique de la Création de l'Univers comme système physiquement non-clos* 71, *Les Points Noirs de Schwarzschild et les Points Blancs de Hjellming considérés comme deux étapes successives d'un seul phénomène dans un Univers en croissance progressive* 71, *L'Intelligence Humaine—une modeste étape à l'échelon terrestre dans l'évolution de l'Esprit Absolu Universel* 71, *Philosophical considerations in connection with the Emergence of the Universe* 73, *New Theory* 73.
P.O. Box 49, Athens, Greece.
Telephone: 546-902.

Santos, João Oliveira, LL.D.; Brazilian international trade and banking expert; b. 26 Oct. 1914, Rio de Janeiro; *s.* of João Barbosa dos Santos and Albertina de Oliveira Santos; *m.* Margarita Beatriz Williams 1959; two *s.* one *d.*; ed. Universidade do Brazil and American Univ., Washington, D.C.
At Ministry of Labour, Industry and Commerce, Brazil 35, 42, 50-54; on active service in Brazilian Air Force 43-45; Lecturer American Univ., Washington 45-46; Deputy Dir. and Acting Dir. Dept. of Econ. and Social Affairs, Gen. Secr. of Org. of American States (OAS), Washington, D.C. 55-58; Sec.-Gen. Latin American Coffee Agreement 58-59, Coffee Study Group, Wash. 58-, Int. Coffee Agreement 59-63; Exec. Dir. Int. Coffee Org., London 63-68; Operations Man. and Vice-Pres. in charge of the fund for Special Operations, Inter-American Devt. Bank, Washington, D.C. 68-; Consultant on Commodities for UN 62; Order of the Sun of Peru, Order of Honour, Merit of Haiti and Order of Ruben Dario of Nicaragua, Order of San Carlos (Colombia), Order of Merit (Ecuador), Order of José Matías Delgado (El Salvador), Order of Duarte Sánchez y Mella (Dominican Republic), and others.
Publs. numerous articles on trade and economics.
7214 Park Terrace Drive, Alexandra, Virginia 22307, U.S.A.; Office: 808 17th Street, N.W. Washington, D.C. 20577, U.S.A.
Telephone: (Home) 765-3092; (Office) 382-8708.

Santos Blanco, Alfredo; Spanish economist and politician; b. 1914; *m.*; four *s.*; ed. Univ. of Madrid.
Assistant Lecturer, Faculty of Econ. Science and Escuela Social, Madrid; mem. Inst. of Political Studies; Gen. Sec. (technical) Ministry of Labour; Deputy Dir.-Gen. Compañía Telefónica Nacional de España; Pres. Empresa Nacional de Artesanía; Minister of Industry 73-March 75; Grand Cross of Civil Merit.
Publs. Co-author *Sindicatos y Solidaridad Nacional, Los Capitales Exteriores en el Desarrollo Económico de España.*
Ministerio de Industria, Madrid, Spain.

Santos e Castro, Fernando A.; Portuguese administrator and agricultural engineer; b. 1912, Funchal, Madeira; ed. Luanda, Angola.
Worked in Ministry of Agriculture; Chair. Lisbon Municipal Council; Gov.-Gen. of Angola 72-74.
c/o Ministério dos Negócios Estrangeiros, Lisbon, Portugal.

Santry, Arthur J., Jr.; American business executive; ed. Williams Coll. and Harvard Law School.
Former Partner, Putnam, Bell, Santry and Ray (law firm), Boston, Mass.; joined Combustion Engineering

Inc. 56, Dir. 57, Pres. and Chief Exec. Officer 63-; Dir. American Arbitration Asscn., Bristol-Myers Co., Emhart Corpn., Jenney Oil Co., Inc., North American Reassurance Co., Putnam Trust Co., N. American Reinsurance Corpn., Arkwright-Boston Mfrs., Mutual Insurance Co.
Combustion Engineering Inc., 900 Long Ridge Road, Stamford, Conn. 06902, U.S.A.

Sanz de Santamaría, Carlos; Colombian civil engineer and economist.
Former Minister of Economy, Minister of Finance, Minister of Foreign Affairs; Colombian Ambassador to Brazil and twice Colombian Ambassador to the U.S.; Chair. Inter-American Cttee. on the Alliance for Progress (CIAP) 64.
Inter-American Committee on the Alliance for Progress, 1725 Eye Street, N.W., Washington, D.C. 20006, U.S.A.

Saouma, Edouard; Lebanese agricultural engineer and international official; b. 6 Nov. 1926, Beirut; *m.* Inès Ferero; one *s.* two *d.*; ed. St. Joseph's Univ. School of Eng., Beirut, Ecole Nat. Supérieure d'Agronomie, Montpellier, France.
Director, Tel Amara Agricultural School 52-53, Nat. Centre for Farm Mechanization 54-55; Sec.-Gen. Nat. Fed. of Lebanese Agronomists 55; Dir.-Gen. Nat. Inst. for Agricultural Research 55-62; mem. Governing Board, Nat. Grains Office 60-62; Deputy Regional Rep. for Asia and Far East, FAO 62-65, Dir. Land and Water Devt. Div. 65-75, Dir.-Gen. of FAO 76-; Minister of Agric., Fisheries and Forestry Oct.-Nov. 70; Order of the Cedar (Lebanon), Said Akl Prize (Lebanon); Chevalier du Mérite Agricole (France).
Publs. technical publs. in agriculture.
Food and Agriculture Organization of the United Nations, Via delle Terme di Caracalla, 00100 Rome, Italy.
Telephone: 5797.

Sapeika, Norman, M.D., PH.D., F.R.S.S.AF.; South African professor of pharmacology; b. 17 Jan. 1909, Oudtshoorn; *s.* of Raphael and Leah Sapeika; *m.* Simone Gusta Silverberg 1942; two *s.* one *d.*; ed. Boys High School, Kimberley and Univ. of Cape Town.
Wernher Beit Asst. in Pharmacology, Univ. of Cape Town 33-47, Senior Lecturer 44-55, Assoc. Prof. 56-65; Prof. of Pharmacology 65-74; Pres. Royal Soc. of S. Africa 72-74; Pres. Athenaeum Trust 70-; Medical Dir., R & C Pharmaceuticals (Pty.) Ltd.; mem. Drugs Control Council 66-71.
Publs. *Actions and Uses of Drugs* 43, 9th edn. 72, *Food Pharmacology* 69, and chapters in books.
R. & C. Pharmaceuticals (Pty.) Ltd., Old Mill Road, Pinelands, Cape, South Africa.

Sapena Pastor, Raúl, B.SC., B.LITT., LL.D.; Paraguayan university professor and politician; b. 9 Oct. 1908; ed. Univ. of Paraguay.
Former mem. Supreme Court of Justice of Paraguay, Pres. Civil and Commercial Court of Appeals, Attorney-Gen., Judge Civil and Criminal Courts; Minister to Bolivia 41, to Uruguay 42-44; Ambassador to Argentina 48-49; Del. to numerous Inter-American and Int. Confs.; fmr. Prof. of Public Int. Law and Prof. of Political Economy, School of Law and Social Sciences and Dean of the School, Prof. of Private Int. Law at School of Econ. Sciences, Univ. of Paraguay; Rector Nat. Univ. of Paraguay 54-55; Counsellor of State 47-48, 56-; fmr. Pres. Bank of Paraguay, Dir. Bank of Republic of Paraguay, Sec. to Ministry of Economy, Legal Adviser to Foreign Ministry; Minister of Foreign Affairs 56-76; mem. Perm. Court of Arbitration, The Hague 45-; Paraguayan Rep. Inter-American Council of Jurisprudence since its inception; Vice Pres. Gen. Assembly of UN 57; Pres. Paraguayan Del. to Gen. Assembly of UN 58-; Pres. Nat. Comm. for Codification of Int. Law, Nat. Council Foreign Trade; Prof. Private Int. Law,

School of Law and Social Sciences; Vice-Pres. Paraguayan Acad. Law and Social Sciences; mem. American Soc. Int. Law; hon. mem. Inst. Spanish Culture, Madrid; numerous foreign decorations.

Publs. include *Derecho Internacional Privado*, Vol. I 44.

Ministerio de Relaciones Exteriores, Venezuela 157, Asunción, Paraguay.

Telephone: 60-488.

Saporta, Marc, B.A., PH.M., LL.D.; French writer; b. 20 March 1923; ed. Univs. of Paris and Madrid.

Worked in the Dept. of Cultural Activities UNESCO 48-53, Asst. Editor *Informations et Documents* 54-71, Editor 71-; Literary Critic *L'Express* 54-71, *La Quinzaine Littéraire* 66-71.

Publs. *Les Lois de l'Air* 53, *La convention universelle du droit d'auteur de l'UNESCO* 52, *Le Grand Défi: U.S.A.-U.S.S.R.*, I 67, II 68 (Editor and Co-Author), *Histoire du Roman Américain* 70, *La Vie Quotidienne Contemporaine aux U.S.A.* 72; Novels: *Le Furet* 59, *La Distribution* 61, *La Quête* 61, *Composition Numéro Un* 62, *Les Invités* 64.

9 rue Saint-Didier, Paris 16e, France.

Saraceno, Pasquale, PH.D.; Italian economist; b. 14 June 1903; ed. Milan Univ.

Joined Istituto per la Ricostruzione Industriale (I.R.I.) 33, now General Economic Adviser; Prof. of Industrial Econs., Univ. Inst. of Venice 59-; Pres. SVIMEZ (Southern Italy Industrial Development Asscn.); Pres. ITALSIEL (Electronic Information Systems); mem. of Board, Cassa per il Mezzogiorno; Gold Medal Benemeriti Scuola, Cultura ed Arte, Gran Croce al merito della Repubblica Italiana.

Publs. *Elementi per un piano economico 1949-52* 48, *Lo sviluppo economico dei paesi sovrapopolati* 52, *L'IRI-Origini, ordinamente e attività* 56, *Iniziativa privata e azione pubblica nei piani di sviluppo economico* 59, *Lo Stato e l'Economia* 63, *La produzione industriale* 67, *Ricostruzione e Pianificazione 1943-1948* 69, *L'economia dei Paesi industrializzati* 70, *La programmazione negli anni 70* 69, *La produzione industriale* 73, *Il governo delle aziende* 73.

Via Fratelli Ruspoli 8, Rome, Italy.

Telephone: 4677 (Office).

Saragat, Giuseppe; Italian politician; b. 19 Sept. 1898; ed. Università degli Studi, Turin.

Bank Clerk 19-26; joined Socialist Party 22; Sec. Turin Branch 22, associated with party magazine *Rivoluzione Liberale*; lived in exile first in Vienna 26-35, then Paris 35-43; associated with Italian Socialist weeklies *Rinascità* and *Libertà*; returned to Italy 43, mem. executive of Socialist Party; Minister without Portfolio 44; Pres. Constituent Assembly 46; Ambassador to France 45-47; Sec. Italian Socialist Labour Party 47-64; Deputy Prime Minister 47-49, 54-57; Minister of Merchant Marine 47-49; Minister of Foreign Affairs 63-64; fmr. mem. of the Senate; Pres. of Italian Repub. 64-71; Pres. Social Democratic Party 75-76, Dec. 76-; Life Senator.

Publs. *L'humanisme marxiste, Socialismo e libertà* 44, *Quaranta anni di lotta per la democrazia, scritti e discorsi 1925–1965* 66.

c/o Partito Socialista Democratico, Via Santa Maria in Via 12, 00187 Rome, Italy.

Sarasin, Pote; Thai lawyer, politician and international administrator; b. 25 March 1907, Bangkok; m.; five s. one d.; ed. Wilbraham Acad., Mass., and Middle Temple, London.

Practised law in Thailand 33-45; mem. Senate 48-50; Deputy Minister of Foreign Affairs 48, Minister of Foreign Affairs 48-50; represented Thailand on UN Korea Commission 50; Ambassador to U.S.A. 52-57; Del. to UN 52-55; Prime Minister Sept. 57-Jan. 58; Sec.-Gen. SEATO 57-63; Minister of Econ. Affairs and Nat. Devt., Thailand 63-68; Minister of Econ.

Affairs Feb. 68-69; Vice-Chair. United Thai People's Party 68; Deputy Prime Minister and Minister of Nat. Devt. 69-71; mem. Nat. Exec. Council and Dir. Econ., Finance and Industry Affairs 71-72; mem. Thai Bar Asscn.

Saha-Pracha-Thai, 1/226, Sri Ayudhya, Dusit, Bangkok, Thailand.

Sarc, Omer Celâl, DR.RER.POL.; Turkish professor and administrator; b. 1901, Istanbul; s. of Celâl Bey (former Cabinet Minister); m. Cenan Paker 1937; one s.; ed. Robert Coll., Istanbul, Handelshochschule, Berlin, and Univ. of Berlin.

Assistant Prof. of Econs., Univ. of Istanbul 26, Assoc. Prof. of Applied Econs. and Statistics 33, Prof. of Applied Econs. and Statistics 38-55; 57-, Dean of Faculty of Economics 36-48, Rector of the Univ. 49-51, 63-65 Pro-Rector 51-53, 63-, Visiting Prof., Columbia Univ., School of Int. Affairs 54-55, 67-68; Chief, Middle East Unit, Dept. of Econ. Affairs, United Nations, New York 55-56; Dir. Econ. and Social Affairs, Council of Europe 59-61; Officer French Legion of Honour, German Great Cross of Merit; Hon. Dr. Jur. (Fouad I Univ., Cairo).

Publs. *Agricultural and Industrial Policy* 34, *Theory of Statistics* 35, *The Foundations of Turkish Economy* 50.

University of Istanbul, Istanbul; Home: Kalipci Sok 156-I, Divan AP, Tesvikiye, Istanbul, Turkey.

Telephone: 477867.

Sardanis, Andreas Sotiris; Zambian company director; b. 13 March 1931, Cyprus; m. Danae Gavas 1962; two s.; ed. in Cyprus.

Emigrated to Zambia 50; managerial posts in trading and transport undertakings 50-62; Chair. and Man. Dir. Industrial Devt. Corpn. June 65-April 70; Perm. Sec. Ministry of Commerce, Industry and Foreign Trade 68; later Perm. Ministry of Trade, Industry and Mines, and Perm. Sec. Ministry of Devt. and Finance; Man. Dir. Zambia Industrial and Mining Corpn. Ltd. (ZIMCO) and Chair. of its subsidiaries, Indeco Ltd. and Mindeco Ltd. April 70-71; Perm. Sec., Ministry of State Participation April 70-Dec. 70; Joint Man. Dir. of new co. to streamline Lonrho's interests W. of the Zambesi, Jan.-May 71; Man. Dir. Sardanis Assocs. 71-.

P.O. Box 2943 Lusaka, Zambia; and Excel House, 42 Upper Berkeley Street, London W1H 7PL, England.

Telephone: 73027 (Lusaka).

Sarell, Sir Roderick Francis Gisbert, K.C.M.G., K.C.V.O.; British diplomatist; b. 23 Jan. 1913, Dunkirk, France; s. of Philip Charles Sarell; m. Pamela Muriel Crowther-Smith 1946; three s.; ed. Radley and Magdalen Coll., Oxford.

Consular Service 36-46, Vice-Consul, Persia 37, Italian E. Africa 39, Iraq 40-42, Second Sec. Addis Ababa 42-46; Foreign Service 46-73, Rome, Bucharest, Foreign Office, Rangoon 46-56; Consul-Gen., Algiers 56-59; Counsellor, Foreign Office 59-63; Ambassador to Libya 64-69, to Turkey 69-73.

Leisure interests: walking, swimming, music.

The Litten, Hampstead Norreys, Newbury, Berks., England.

Telephone: Hermitage 274.

Sargant, William Walters, M.A., M.B., F.R.C.P., D.P.M. British psychiatrist and author; b. 1907, Highgate; s. of Norman Sargant and Alice Walters; m. Margaret Gien 1940; ed. Leys School, St. John's Coll., Cambridge and Geraldine Harmsworth School, St. Mary's Hospital, Paddington.

Assistant to Medical Professorial Unit, St. Mary's Hospital 32-34; Medical Officer and Physician Maudsley Hospital, London 35-49; Asst. Clinical Dir. Sutton Emergency Hospital 39-47; Physician in Charge of Dept. of Psychological Medicine, St. Thomas's Hospital, London 48-72; Rockefeller Travelling Fellow and Research Fellow, Harvard Medical School, U.S. 38-39;

Visiting Prof. of Neuropsychiatry, Duke Univ. Medical School, U.S. 47-48; Registrar Royal Medico-Psychological Asscn.; Pres. Section of Psychiatry, Royal Soc. of Medicine 56-57; Examiner in Psychological Medicine, Conjoint Board of England 60-63; Assoc. Sec. World Psychiatric Asscn. 61-66; Lecturer American Soc. of Biological Psychiatry and New York Coll. of Medicine 64; Starkey Medal, Royal Soc. of Health 73, Mark Twain Award 75.
Publs. Psychiatric papers in medical journals; *Physical Methods of Treatment in Psychiatry* 44, 4th edn. 63, *Battle for the Mind* 57, *The Unquiet Mind* 67, *The Mind Possessed* 73.
23 Harley Street, London, W.1, England.
Telephone: 01-636-5161.

Sargent, Francis Williams; American fmr. state governor; b. 29 July 1915, Hamilton, Mass.; s. of Francis W. and Margery (Lee) Sargent; m. Jessie Fay 1938; one s. two d.; ed. Noble and Greenough School, and Mass. Inst. of Technology.
Architect, Coolidge, Shepley, Bullfinch and Abbot 39-41, Sargent & Sweeney 41-42; served, U.S. Army 42-45; founder-owner Goose Hummock Shop Inc., Orleans 46; Dir. Mass. Div. of Marine Fisheries 47-56; U.S. Commr., Int. Comm. for the Northwest Atlantic Fisheries 51-62; Chair., Atlantic States Marine Fisheries Comm. 56-59; Mass. Water Resources Comm. 56-59; Commr. Mass. Dept. of Natural Resources 56-59; Exec. Dir. U.S. Outdoor Recreation Resources Review Comm. 59-62; Chair. Merrimac Valley Flood Control Comm. 56-59; Dir. Mass. Div. of Fisheries and Game 63; Adviser, Calif. Park and Recreation 64-68; Assoc. Commr. Mass. Dept. of Public Works 63-65, Commr. 65-66; Lieut. Gov. of Mass. 66-69; Gov. of Mass. 69-74; Sr. Lecturer Harvard Graduate School of Design, M.I.T. School of Architecture and Planning, M.I.T.-Harvard Joint Center for Urban Studies 75-76; Fellow, Inst. of Politics, John F. Kennedy School of Govt., Harvard 75; Republican mem. or trustee of various educ. and other public orgs.; numerous hon. degrees.
Leisure interests: skiing, boating, fishing, golf.
16 Arlington Street, Boston, Mass. 02116, U.S.A.
Telephone: 617-247-0006.

Sargent, John Turner; American publisher; b. 26 June 1924.
Doubleday and Co. Inc., Editor 49-50, Advertising and Publicity, Trade Sales Manager 50-60, Vice-Pres. and Dir. 60-61, Pres. 61-; Trustee East River Savings Bank. New York Public Library, New York Zoological Soc.
Doubleday and Co. Inc., 227 Park Avenue, New York City, N.Y. 10017; Home: 5 Beekman Place, New York City, N.Y. 10022, U.S.A.
Telephone: 212-826-2000 (Office).

Sarin Chhak, Dr.; Cambodian diplomat and politician. Former Amb. to Egypt; Minister of Foreign Affairs, Royal Govt. of Nat. Union 70-76 (in Phnom-Penh 75-76).
c/o Ministry of Foreign Affairs, Phnom-Penh, Cambodia.

Sarkar, Amal Kumar; Indian judge; b. 29 June 1901, Dacca; s. of Kali Kumar Sarkar and Basenta Kumari Sarkar; ed. Univ. of Calcutta and Lincoln's Inn, London.
Practised as Advocate of the High Court, Calcutta 30-48; Judge of the High Court, Calcutta 49-57; Judge of the Supreme Court of India 57-66, Chief Justice 66.
55 Baghbazar Street, Calcutta 3, India.
Telephone: 55-2477.

Sarkis, Elias, L. EN D.; Lebanese banker and politician.
Former Magistrate, Cour des Comptes; Pres. Management Cttee. of Intra Bank 67-; fmr. Dir.-Gen. Cabinet of Presidency; Gov. Bank of Lebanon June 68-76; Pres. Elect of Lebanon May 76-; Pres. Comm. Supérieure des Banques; Medal of Independence 1st Class, Jordan.

Office of the President, Beirut, Lebanon; Home: rue Notre-Dame de Lourdes, Beirut, Lebanon.
Telephone: 280-561 (Home).

Sarlós, István; Hungarian politician; b. 30 Oct. 1921, Budapest; s. of István Sarlós and Erzsébet Till; m. Róza Benk 1946; one d.; ed. Budapest Univ.
Joined Working-Class Movement and the Social Democrat Party 39; held various mass organizational and Party positions 45-59; First Sec. of 6th District Cttee. Hungarian Socialist Workers' Party 59-63, mem. Central Cttee. 66-; Chair. Budapest Metropolitan Council Exec. Cttee. 63-70; head of editorial board daily *Népszabadság* 70-74; Gen. Sec. Patriotic People's Front 74-; mem. Politburo, HSWP Central Cttee. March 75-; Labour Order of Merit, golden degree 70.
Leisure interest: reading.
National Council of the Patriotic People's Front, Belgrád rakpart 24, 1360 Budapest V, Hungary.
Telephone: 182-850.

Sarmento Rodrigues, Rear-Admiral Manoel Maria, K.C.V.O., O.B.E.; Portuguese naval officer and overseas administrator; b. 20 June 1899, F.E. Cinta; s. of A. M. Rodrigues and Isabel Morais Sarmento; m. Margarida Guerra Jungueiro 1935; one s. two d.; ed. Univ. of Coimbra and Naval School, Lisbon.
Lieutenant 22; Commdg. Officer torpedo boat *Lis* 24; A.D.C. to Gov.-Gen. of Portuguese India 25; Commdg. Officer gunboat *Faro* 29; Port Capt., Chinde, Portuguese E. Africa 31; Commdg. Officer river gunboat *Tete* 32; Port Capt. Quelimane, Portuguese E. Africa 35; Naval Staff 38; Chief of Staff, Light Flotilla 39, Home Fleet 40; Commdg. Officer destroyer *Lima* 41; Gov. of Portuguese Guinea 45; Prof. Colonial School, Lisbon 49-; Deputy for Mozambique, Nat. Assembly 49-57; Portuguese Del. Comm. of Technical Co-operation in Africa South of the Sahara 49, 50; Commdg. Officer Fleet Air Arm 50; Minister for Overseas Provinces 50-55; Pres. I.N.C.I.D.I. 55-57; Commdg. Officer Portuguese Naval Squadron 55-; Commdr. Portuguese Naval Group, Supt. Naval Acad. 57-61; Pres. African Advisory Cttee. ILO 59; Advisory Cttee. Bilderberg Meetings 59; Gov.-Gen. and C.-in-C. Armed Forces, Mozambique 61-64; Pres. Center of Maritime Studies, Lisbon; Grand Cross Portuguese Orders of Christ, Empire, Avis and Prince Henry; Commdr. Légion d'Honneur; U.S. Legion of Merit; Grand Cross Lion Belgique, Gregorius Magnus Vatican; Crown of Thailand, Cedar of Lebanon, Naval Merit of Spain, D. S. y Mella Dominican Repub.; mem. Acad. des Sciences d'Outre Mer, Paris, Acad. Marine, Paris and Acad. of Sciences, Lisbon.
Leisure interests: sailing, big game hunting in Africa, whaling in Azores.
Publs. *The Heroic Life of Nelson* 41, *The Battle of the Atlantic* 42, *Anchorages of the Azores Islands* 43, *The Government of Guinea* 49, *Unity of the Portuguese Nation* 56, *The Presence of Mozambique in the Life of the Nation* 65, and several other books and articles.
R. Jorge Alvares, 3-5° Lisbon 3, Portugal.
Telephone: 612381.

Sarnoff, Robert W.; American electronics and communications executive; b. 2 July 1918, New York; s. of late Gen. David Sarnoff and Lizette Hermant; m. Anna Moffo (q.v.) 1974; three d. (by two previous marriages); ed. Harvard Univ. and Columbia Univ. Law School.
With Radio Div., New York World's Fair 39; Office of the Co-ordinator of Information 41; served in U.S. Navy, including duty in South Pacific 42-45; exec. in Cowles publishing and broadcasting enterprises in Des Moines and New York 45-48; with Nat. Broadcasting Co. 48-66, Vice-Pres. 51-, mem. Board of Dirs. 53-, Exec. Vice-Pres. 55-58, Chair. and Chief Exec. Officer 58-66; Dir. RCA Corpn. 57, Pres. 66-71, Chief Exec. Officer 68-75, Chair. of Board 70-75; Dir. RCA Global Communications, Inc., Hertz Corpn., Banquet Foods

Corpn., Coronet Industries, Mfrs. Hanover Trust Co., N.Y. Stock Exchange, American Home Products Inc.; Trustee, John Fitzgerald Kennedy Library Corpn.; Chair. Board of Business Cttee. for the Arts; mem. U.S. Foundation for Int. Scouting; mem. Econ. Club of N.Y.; Fellow, Imperial Coll. of Science and Technology 73-; Hon. Fellow, Royal Television Soc. 73-; Officer of French Order of Arts and Letters 66; Commdr. Italian Order of Merit 68; Belgian Order of Crown 71; Commdr. Cross, First Class, Austria; other int. awards; hon. doctorates from 16 American colls. and univs.
30 Rockefeller Plaza, New York, N.Y., U.S.A.
Telephone: 212-CO-5-5900.

Sareyan, William; American writer; b. 31 Aug. 1908. Publs. short stories: *The Daring Young Man on the Flying Trapeze* 34, *Inhale and Exhale, Three Times Three, The Gay and Melancholy Flux* 36, *Little Children* 37, *Love, Here is My Hat, The Trouble with Tigers* 38, *Peace, It's Wonderful* 39, *Saroyan's Fables, My Name is Aram* 40, *Dear Baby* 44, *The Assyrian* 50, *The Whole Voyald* 57; plays: *My Heart's in the Highlands, The Time of Your Life* (Pulitzer Prize) 39 (film 47), *Love's Old Sweet Song* 40, *The Beautiful People* 41, *Sweeney in the Trees, Across the Board on Tomorrow Morning* 41, *Razzle Dazzle* (16 plays) 42, *Get Away, Old Man* 46, *Jim Dandy, Fat Man in a Famine* 47, *The Slaughter of the Innocents* 52, *The Cave Dwellers* 56, *Sam, The Highest Jumper of Them All* (or *The London Comedy*) 60, *Here Comes There Goes You Know Who* (autobiography) 62; novels: *The Human Comedy* 43 (film 44), *The Adventures of Wesley Jackson* 46, *Rock Wagram* 51, *Tracy's Tiger* 52, *The Laughing Matter* 55, *Papa, You're Crazy* 57, *Boys and Girls Together* 63, *One Day in the Afternoon of the World* 64, *Not Dying* 66, *Look at Us* (with A. Rothstein) 67, *I Used to Believe I Had Forever, Now I'm Not So Sure* (short stories) 68, *Letters from 74 Rue Taitbout, or Don't Go, But If You Must, Say Hello to Everybody* 69, *Days of Life and Death and Escape to the Moon* 71, *Places Where I've Done Time* (autobiography) 73.
2729 W. Griffith Way, Fresno, Calif. 93705, U.S.A.

Sarpaneva, Timo Tapani; Finnish designer; b. 31 Oct. 1926; ed. Industrial Art Inst., Helsinki.
Designer for A. Ahlström Oy, Iittala Glassworks 50-; Teacher in Textile Printing and Design, Industrial Art Inst., Helsinki 53-57; Design Consultant Porin Puuvilla Cotton Mill 55-66; Design Consultant, AB Kinnasand Textile Mill, Sweden 64-; invited by Brazilian Govt. to Lecture on and exhibit Finnish art glass 58; Exhbn. architect for Finnish industrial art exhbns. in most European countries, Japan and U.S.A.; architect for Finnish Section, Expo 67, Montreal; private exhbns. in Helsinki, Stockholm, Copenhagen, London, Paris, New York, Amsterdam, Reykjavík; numerous awards, including three Grand Prix at Milan Triennali; Hon. Dr. of Design, Royal Coll. of Art, London 67.
Sarpaneva Studio, Laivastokatu 8-10 p 657113, Helsinki, Finland.

Sarraute, Nathalie, L. ÈS L., L. EN D.; French writer; b. 18 July 1902, Ivanovo, Russia; d. of Ilya Tcherniak and Pauline Chatounovski; m. Raymond Sarraute 1925; three d.; ed. Univs. of Paris and Oxford.
Prix International 64.
Publs. *Tropismes* 39, *Portrait d'un Inconnu* 48, *Martereau* 53, *L'Ere du Soupçon* 56, *Le Planétarium* 59, *Les Fruits d'Or* 63, *Le Silence et le Mensonge* 67, *Entre la vie et la mort* 68, *Isma* 70, *Vous les Entendez?* 71, *C'est beau* 73.
12 avenue Pierre I de Serbie, Paris 16e, France.

Sarre, Claude-Alain; French industrialist; b. 10 April 1928, Douai; s. of Henri Sarre and Claudine Vau; m. Simone Allien 1952; two s. one d.; ed. Inst. d'Etudes Politiques, Paris.

With Cie. Air France; joined Soc. André Citroën 55, Commercial Dir. Jan. 68, Chair., Man. Dir. Soc. Automobiles Citroën and Soc. Commerciale Citroën Aug. 68; joined Lainière de Roubaix-Prouvost Masurel S.A. 70, Chair., Man. Dir. Dec. 71-; Chair., Man. Board, Comptoir de l'Industrie Textile de France (Boussac Group) 75.
25 Avenue Gustave Delory, Roubaix, France.
Telephone: 70-05-08.

Sarrüf, Füad, B.A., LL.D.; Lebanese author and university official; b. 20 Dec. 1900; s. of Hanna Sarrüf and Helen Juraidini; m. Lily Majdalany 1928; one d.; ed. Shwaifat Nat. Coll., and American Univ. of Beirut.
Teacher and Headmaster, Lebanon 19-22; Asst. Editor *Al-Muqtaf* (monthly), Cairo 22-27, Editor 27-44; Editor *Al-Mukhtar* (Arabic edition of *Reader's Digest*), Cairo 43-47; Columnist, *Al-Ahram* (daily), Cairo 48-51; Vice-Pres. in charge of Univ. Relations, American Univ. Beirut 52-68; Editor *Al-Abhath* (Univ. Quarterly), Beirut 59-65; started Dept. of Journalism, American Univ., Cairo 35-43; Vice-Pres. Lebanese Nat. Comm. for UNESCO; mem. Exec. Board of UNESCO 66-, Chair. 72-74; fmr. mem., later Sec., Vice-Pres. Egyptian Asscn. for the Advancement of Science 30-52; mem. Lebanese Nat. Research Council, Baalbek Int. Festival Cttee.; Hon. LL.D. (Univ. of The Pacific, Calif.) 58; several decorations.
Leisure interests: reading science, bridge.
Publs. *Conquests of Modern Science, Pillars of Modern Science* 35, *Horizons of Modern Science* 39, *The Conquest Goes On* 44, *Horizons Without End* 58, *Man and the Universe* 61, *Modern Science in Modern Society* 66, *The Eternal Fire,* numerous other books.
UNESCO, Place de Fontenoy, Paris 7e, France; Home: 55 rue du Caire, Hamra, Beirut, Lebanon.
Telephone: 566-57-57 (Office); 343-919 (Home).

Sartre, Jean-Paul; French writer; b. 21 June 1905; ed. Lycée Henri IV and Ecole Normale Supérieure, Paris. Taught at Lycée du Havre, and later travelled in Egypt, Greece and Italy 29-34; at Inst. Français, Berlin 34; taught philosophy at Lycée Pasteur de Neuilly-sur-Seine 35-39 and Lycée Condorcet; army 39-41 (prisoner of war 40-41); active in resistance movement 41-44; resgnd. from teaching 44; Founder Dir. *Les Temps Modernes*; was offered, but declined, Nobel Prize for Literature 64; Dir. *Ce Que Nous Voulons: Tout.*
Publs. Philosophy: *L'Imagination* 36, *Esquisse d'une théorie des émotions* 39, *L'Imaginaire, psychologie phénoménologique de l'imagination* 40, *L'Etre et le Néant* 43, *Critique de la raison dialectique* 60, *La Transcendence de l'Ego* 65; Novels: *La Nausée* 38, *Le Mur* 39, *Les Chemins de la Liberté* 45; Plays: *Les Mouches* 43, *Huis-clos* 44, *Morts sans sépulture* 46, *La Putain Respectueuse* 46, *Les Mains sales* 48, *Le Diable et le Bon Dieu* 51, *Nekrassov* 55, *Les Séquestrés d'Altona* 60; Essays: *L'existentialisme est un humanisme* 46, *Situations* 47-72, *Qu'est-ce que la littérature?* 47, *Baudelaire* 47, *Saint Genet, comédien et martyr* 52, *Merleau-Ponty vivant* 61, *Le Peintre sans privilège* 62, *Marxisme et existentialisme* (with Roger Garaudy) 63, *Les Communistes et la Paix* 69, *Le Spectre de Staline* 69, *L'Idiot de la Famille* (vol. III of biography of Flaubert) 72; Screenplays: *Les Jeux sont faits* 47, *L'Engrenage* 49; *Les Mots* (memoirs) 64.
42 rue Bonaparte, Paris 6e, France.

Sasaki, Kunihiko; Japanese banker; b. 20 Dec. 1908, Formosa; s. of late Mikisaburo and Matsuko Sasaki; m. Shizue Shigemura 1937; two s. one d.; ed. Tokyo Imperial Univ.
Joined the Yasuda Bank Ltd. 32, Man. Customer Relations Dept. 47; name of bank changed to The Fuji Bank Ltd. 48; Chief Man. Int. Div. 51; Dir. and Chief Man. Business Devt. Div. 54, Chief Man. Head Office Business Div. 56; Man. Dir. 57, Deputy Pres. 63, Chair.

of Board and Pres. The Fuji Bank Ltd. 71-75, Hon. Chair. 75-.
Leisure interest: reading.
The Fuji Bank Ltd., 5-5, 1-chome Otemachi,Chiyodaku, Tokyo; Home: 18-10, 6-chome Matsubara, Setagaya-ku, Tokyo, Japan.
Telephone: 328-1258.

Sasaki, Tadashi; Japanese banker; b. 19 May 1907, Sendai City; s. of Totaro and Tane Sasaki; m. Kusuko Tsukasaki (deceased); one s. one d.; ed. Dept. of Econs., Tokyo Imperial Univ. (now Tokyo Univ.).
Joined the Bank of Japan 30, Chief Personnel, Dept. 46-47, Chief, Co-ordination Dept. 47-51, Chief, Business Dept. 51-54, Exec. Dir. 54-62, Vice-Gov. 62-69; Gov. The Bank of Japan Dec. 69-74; Chair. Keizai Doyukai (Japan Cttee. for Econ. Devt.) 75-.
Leisure interests: reading, golf.
4-6 Marunouchi 1-chome, Chiyoda-ku, Tokyo; Home: 5-34-10 Yoyogi, Shibuya-ku, Tokyo 151, Japan.

Sasaki, Yoshitake; Japanese politician.
Director, Atomic Energy Comm. 56; mem. Liberal Democratic Party, fmr. Head of LDP Cttee. on Science and Technology; mem. House of Reps. (five times); Dir. Science and Technology Agency Dec. 74-.
House of Representatives, Tokyo, Japan.

Sassen, Emmanuel Marie Joseph Antony, DR. JUR.; Netherlands politician and international administrator; b. 8 Sept. 1911, 's-Hertogenbosch; m. Sophie Marie Louise Romme 1939; one s. two d.; ed. Roman Catholic Univ., Nijmegen.
Lawyer at 's-Hertogenbosch; mem. of Provincial Govt. of Noord-Brabant; mem. of Second Chamber; Vice-Pres. of Roman Catholic Democratic Party 46-48; Minister for Overseas Territories 48-49; Senator 52-58; rep. Joint Assembly of European Coal and Steel Community 52-58; mem. Euratom Comm. 58-67; mem. Combined Exec. of EEC, ECSC and Euratom 67-70; Perm. Rep. of Netherlands to European Communities 71-.
Leisure interests: music, swimming, and painting.
62 rue Belliard, 1040 Brussels, Belgium.
Telephone: 13-65-70.

Sathe, Ramchandra, M.D., F.R.C.P., M.R.C.P.; Indian physician; b. 28 Nov. 1905, Ahmedabad; s. of Vishwanath Mahadeo and Laxmibai Vishwanath Sathe; m. Dr. Kashibai R. Sathe 1935; one s. one d.; ed. Elphinstone High School, Elphinstone Coll., Grant Medical Coll., Bombay, and St. Bartholomew's Hospital, London.
Emeritus Prof. of Medicine, Grant Medical Coll., Bombay; Hon. Dir. of Postgraduate Studies in Medicine, Grant Medical Coll., Bombay; Pres. Asscn. of Physicians of India 60, Indian Medical Asscn. 62, World Medical Asscn. 62-63; Vice-Chancellor Bombay Univ. 63-66; Deputy Pres. Elect, World Conf. on Medical Educ. 66; Pres. Diabetic Asscn. of India; mem. Health Survey and Planning Cttee., Drugs and Equipment Standards Cttee., Indian Pharmacopoeia Cttee., Nat. Formulary Cttee., Govt. of India; J. J. Gold Medal for Clinical Medicine; Hewlett Prize for Hygiene.
Publs. include articles on nutritional oedema, cirrhosis of liver, treatment of hypertension, diabetes, jaundice, etc.
Nagindas Mansion, Girgaum Road, near Opera House, Bombay 400 004, India.
Telephone: 356465.

Sato, Mitsugi, B.SC., M.SC.; Japanese dairy executive; b. 14 Feb. 1898, Sapporo, Hokkaido; s. of Zenshichi and Fuji Sato; m. Chiyo Tsujimura 1925; one s. four d.; ed. Colls. of Agriculture, Hokkaido Imperial Univ. and Ohio State Univ.
Managed dairy plant, Dept. of Dairying, Ohio State Univ. 22; Plant Man. and Technical Chief, Fed. of

Hokkaido Co-op Creamery Asscns. 25-37, Senior Exec. Dir. Hokkaido Kono-Kosha 41-45; Staff mem. and Adviser Econ. Stabilization Board 47-50; Area Dir. Dairy Soc. Int. 49-57, Vice-Pres. 58-; Pres. Hokkaido Co-op Dairy Co. 49; Pres. Snow Brand Milk Products Co. 50-63, Chair. 63-71, Adviser 71-; Dir. Hokkaido Broadcasting Co. 51-, Sapporo Co-op Bank 51-, Chair. 57-58; mem. Exec. Cttee. Fed. of Japan Employers' Asscn. and Sapporo Chamber of Commerce 61-; Pres. Hokkaido Employer's Asscn. 62-; Pres. Rakuno Gakuen Coll. of Dairying 66-69; Chair. Board of Trustees of Coll. of Dairying 66-; past official various Hokkaido asscns.; Del. int. dairy asscns.; awards include Ranju Decoration 60 and Dairy Soc. Int. Certificate of Honour as "Herald" 1965, Kun 3-to Zui-Ho-Sho (3rd Class Decoration of Sacred Treasure) 68, Alumni Award, Dept. of Dairy Technology, Coll. of Agriculture, The Ohio State Univ. 60, Commdr. Royal Order of Saint Olav (Norway) 69, Ohio State Univ. Centennial Achievement Award 70.
Leisure interests: golf, Go (Japanese chess).
Publs. *What We Should Eat* 29, *Dairy Industry in New Zealand and Australia* 42, *Zenshichi Sato and Self-help* 68, *Food Problem and Promotion of Dairying* 70.
580 Nishi 8, Minami 16, Sapporo, Chuoku 064, Japan.
Telephone: (011) 511-4772.

Satpathy, Nandini; Indian politician, social worker and short-story writer; b. 9 June 1931, Cuttack; d. of Padma Bhushan and Kalindi Charan Panigrahi; m. Shri Debendra Satpathy; two s.; ed. Ravenshaw Coll., Cuttack.
Leader of the students' movements in Orissa and Sec. Girls Students' Asscn. 48-49; took part in many welfare activities, organized and became Sec. of the Orissa Women's Relief Cttee.; organized Orissa branch, Asscn. of Social and Moral Hygiene in India 58; associated with numerous nat. welfare, literary and other orgs.; mem. Rajya Sabha (Upper House) 62-72; Deputy Minister for Information and Broadcasting (Orissa) 66-69; Deputy Minister attached to Prime Minister 69-70, Minister of State for Information and Broadcasting 71-72; Leader Indian film del. to Moscow 66, 68 and Taskent 72; del. Gen. Conf. UNESCO, Paris 72; mem. Indian del. to Commemorative Session UN, N.Y.C. 70; Chief Minister of Orissa 72-73, 74-; mem. Working Cttee. of the All India Congress Cttee. and Advisory Council Youth Congress; Chair. Orissa Flood and Cyclone Relief Cttee.; Chair. Children's Film Soc., Bombay; mem. Board of Dirs. Int. Centre of Films for Children and Young People, Paris 68-; Editor *Dharitri* (Mother Earth) and *Kalana* (Assessment), monthly magazines; received many literary prizes.
Leisure interests: reading and story writing.
Publs. *Ketoti Katha*, collection of short stories.
Office of the Chief Minister, Bhubaneswar, Orissa, India.
Telephone: 51100 (Office); 50200 (Home).

Satre, Pierre Henri; French fmr. aeronautical engineer; b. 4 May 1909, Grenoble; s. of Alfred Satre and Maria (Fauché) Satre; m. Marie-Jeanne Servant 1941; two s. three d.; ed. Lycée Thiers, Marseille.
Engineer, Centre d'essais du matériel aérien, Villacoublay 34-36, service technique aéronautique 36-41; Chief Engineer Toulouse engineering office of Soc. Sud Aviation 41-59, Technical Dir. Sud Aviation 59-69, Aircraft Technical Dir. 70-73, Deputy to Aircraft Div. Dir. 74; research on the following aeroplanes Armagnac 49, Grognard 50, Caravelle 55, Durandal 56, Concorde 69; retd. 74; Laureate Acad. des Sciences; Commdr. Légion d'Honneur, Médaille de l'Aéronautique, Commdr. Ordre Nat. du Mérite.
2 Allée du Lac Supérieur, 78110 Le Vesinet, France.
Telephone: 224-84-00 (Paris); 976-11-86.

Sattar, Abdul; Maldivian diplomatist; b. 18 June
1936; ed. St. Peter's Coll., Colombo, Ceylon (now Sri
Lanka).
Under-Secretary, Dept. of External Affairs, Maldive
Islands 58-59; Deputy to Minister of External Affairs
and Minister of Educ. 59-60; Maldive Islands Rep. in
Ceylon 60-66, Amb. to Ceylon 66-67; Perm. Rep. to UN
and Amb. to U.S.A. 67-70.
c/o Ministry of External Affairs, Malé, Maldive Islands.

Satterthwaite, Joseph Charles, A.M.; American diplomatist; b. 4 March 1900, Tecumseh, Michigan; s. of
J. Newton Satterthwaite and Eva Perry Satterthwaite;
m. Leyla Ilbars 1945; one d.; ed. Univ. of Michigan.
Entered U.S. Foreign Service 24, first post at Stuttgart;
Dept. of State, Washington 26-27; Guadalajara, Mexico
27-29; Mexico City 29-34; Buenos Aires 34-37; Baghdad
37-40; Ankara 40-44; Chargé d'Affaires, Damascus
44-45; Office of Near Eastern and African Affairs,
Dept. of State 45; Sec. U.S. Dels., North and Central
American Regional Radio Conf., Mexico City 33, and
Inter-American Conf. for the Maintenance of Peace,
Buenos Aires 36; Sec.-Gen., U.S. Del., Int. Tele-
communications Conf., Cairo 38; Minister and Chief of
U.S. Special Diplomatic Mission to the Kingdom of
Nepal 47; Dir. Office of Near Eastern and African
Affairs 48-49; Amb. to Ceylon 49-53; Diplomatic Agent
at Tangier, Morocco (with Rank of Minister) 53-55;
Amb. to Burma 55-57; Dir.-Gen. of Foreign Service
57-58; Asst. Sec. of State for African Affairs 58-61;
Amb. to South Africa 61-65; private consultant 66-;
Pres., Diplomatic and Consular Officers, Retired
(DACOR, Inc.); mem. Board of Dirs. Int. Student
House; mem. Washington Inst. of Foreign Affairs;
Hon. LL.D. (Univ. of Michigan) 58.
Leisure interests: travel, music.
Home: 5120 Upton Street, N.W., Washington, D.C.
20016, U.S.A.
Telephone: 362-7260 (Home).

Satyukov, Pavel Alekseyevich; Soviet journalist; b. 23
July 1911, Gorky; ed. Gorky Teacher Training Inst.,
and C.P.S.U. Higher Party School.
Began career on Gorky youth newspaper 30-; later con-
tributor to *Komsomolskaya Pravda*; served in Air Force
during Second World War and edited an Air Force
paper; worked in Press Dept. of Central Cttee. C.P.S.U.,
Asst. Editor and later Editor *Kultura i Zhizn* (Culture
and Life) 46-49; Chief Sec. *Pravda* 49-55, Asst. Editor
55, Editor-in-Chief 56-64; mem. Editorial Board *Party
Life* (organ of C.P.S.U.) 64-; mem. C.P.S.U. 39-, mem.
Central Cttee. 61-66; Order of Lenin, Order of Red
Banner of Labour; Lenin Prize.
Partiinaya Zhizn (Party Life), 5 ulitsa Marxa-Engelsa,
Moscow, U.S.S.R.

Saul, Ralph Southey, B.A., LL.B.; American lawyer and
stock exchange official; b. 21 May 1922, Brooklyn, N.Y.;
s. of Walter Emerson and Helen Douglas; m. Bette Jane
Bertschinger 1956; one s. one d.; ed. Univ. of Chicago
and Yale Law School.
War Service, U.S. Naval Reserve 43-46; Attached to
American Embassy, Prague 47-48; Admitted to District
of Columbia Bar 51, to New York Bar 52; Assoc. firm
of Lyeth and Voorhees, New York City 51-52; Asst.
Counsel to Gov. of New York State 52-54; Staff
Attorney, Radio Corpn. of America 54-58; with
Securities and Exchange Comm. 58-65, Dir. Div. of
Trading and Markets 63-65; Vice-Pres. for Corporate
Devt., Investors Diversified Services, Inc. 65-66; Pres.
American Stock Exchange 66-71; Vice-Chair. First
Boston Corpn. 71-.
275 Manor Road, Ridgewood, New Jersey, U.S.A.

Saunders, Sir John Anthony Holt, Kt., C.B.E., D.S.O.,
M.C.; British banker; b. 1917, London; s. of E. B.
Saunders; m. Enid M. D. Cassidy 1942; two d.; ed.
Bromsgrove School.

British Army 40-45; rejoined Hongkong and Shanghai
Banking Corpn. 45, Chair. 64-72, Chair. London
Advisory Cttee. 72-; mem. Exec. Council Hong Kong
Govt. 66-72; Chair. of Stewards, Royal Hong Kong
Jockey Club 67-72; Chair. Int. Commercial Bank Ltd.
72-; Dir. The British Bank of the Middle East, P & O
SN Co., Highlands & Lowlands Para Rubber Co. Ltd.,
Rediffusion Ltd., World Shipping and Investment Co.,
Hong Kong, World Maritime Ltd., Bermuda, World
Finance Int. Ltd., Bermuda; Hon. D.Sc. (Hong Kong)
69; Commdr. Order of Prince Henry the Navigator
(Portugal) 66.
Leisure interest: travel.
17 Hyde Park Gate, London, S.W.7; Home: The
Dairy House, Maresfield Park, Uckfield, Sussex, Eng-
land.

Saunders, Stuart Thomas, A.B., LL.B.; American
lawyer and transport executive; b. 16 July 1909; ed.
Roanoke Coll. and Harvard Univ. Law School.
Law practice, Washington, D.C. 34-39; mem. firm
Douglas, Obear and Campbell 36-39; Asst. Gen.
Solicitor Norfolk & Western Railway Co. 39-54, Gen.
Counsel 54-56, Exec. Vice-Pres. 56-58, Pres. 58-63;
Chair. Board and Chief Exec. Officer Pa. Railroad Co.
63-70, Consultant 71-; Dir. Chase Manhattan Bank,
U.S. Steel Corpn., Equitable Life Assurance Soc.,
Georgia-Pacific Corpn., First Pa. Banking and Trust
Co., Bell Telephone Co. of Pa., First Nat. Exchange
Bank of Va., Philadelphia Saving Fund Soc., Virginia
Hot Springs Inc., Philadelphia Orchestra Assn.; Trus-
tee several educational orgs.; mem. President's Ad-
visory Cttee. on Labour-Management Policy.
801 East Main Street, Richmond, Va. 23219; Home:
202 Nottingham Road, Richmond, Va. 23221, U.S.A.

Sauvagnargues, Jean Victor; French diplomatist; b. 2
April 1915, Paris; m. Lise Marie L'Evesque 1948; two s.
two d.; ed. Ecole Normale Supérieure.
Ministry of Foreign Affairs 41-, attached to French
Embassy, Bucharest, later on staff of Gen. de Gaulle
45-46; Head of Political Service for German Affairs
46-49, Deputy Dir. for Central Europe 49-54; in office of
Antoine Pinay, Minister of Foreign Affairs 55-56; Dir.
Gen. for Moroccan and Tunisian Affairs Jan.-March 56;
Ambassador to Ethiopia 56-60; Dir. for Middle Eastern
Affairs and African Affairs; Amb. to Tunisia 62-70; Amb.
to Fed. Germany 70-74; Minister of Foreign Affairs
May 74-; Officier, Légion d'Honneur.
Ministère des Affaires Etrangères, Quai d'Orsay, Paris;
and 8 rue Lalo, Paris 16e, France.

Sauvé, Jeanne (Benoit); Canadian journalist and
politician; b. 26 April 1922, Prud'Homme, Sask.; d. of
Charles Albert Benoit and Anna Vaillant; m. Maurice
Sauvé 1948; one s.; ed. Univs. of Ottawa and Paris.
National Pres., Jeunesse Etudiante Catholique,
Montreal 42-47; Founder and Del. to int. confs.,
Fédération des Mouvements de Jeunesse du Québec 47;
Student, London and French Teacher, London Co.
Council 48-50; Asst. to Dir., Youth Section, UNESCO,
Paris 51; Journalist and Broadcaster, CBC, Contrib.
to CTV, NBC and CBS 52-72; Union des Artistes,
Montreal, mem. of the Board 61-, Vice-Pres. 68-70;
Canadian Inst. on Public Affairs, Vice-Pres. 62-64,
Pres. 64; mem. Canadian Centennial Comm. 66; Gen.
Sec., Fédération des Auteurs et des Artistes du Canada
66-72; mem. of the Board, Montreal YMCA 68; Dir.,
Bushnell Communications Ltd., Ottawa 69-72; Dir.,
CKAC Radio Station, Montreal 69-72; Free-lance
editorial contribs. to *Montreal Star* and *Toronto Star*
70-72; M.P. for Montreal-Ahuntsic 72-; Minister of
State in charge of Science and Technology 72-74, for
Environment 74-75, of Communications 75; lecture
tours in Canada and U.S.A.; named one of seven
founding mems. of the Inst. of Political Research by

the Rt. Hon. Pierre Trudeau 72; D.Sc.h.c. (New Brunswick Univ.) 74.
281 Avenue McDougall, Montreal H2V 3P3, Quebec, Canada.

Sauvy, Alfred; French economist, sociologist and demographer; b. 31 Oct. 1898, Villeneuve de la Raho; *s.* of Louis Sauvy and Jeanne Tisseyre; *m.* Marthe Lamberet 1932; one *d.*; ed. Ecole Polytechnique.
Director Institut de Conjoncture 37-45; Sec.-Gen. for Family and Population 45; Dir. Institut National d'Etudes Démographiques 45-62; mem. UN Statistical Comm. 46-47; Pres. UN Population Comm. 50-53; Pres. Société de Statistique de Paris 47; Prof. of Econs. and Opinion, Inst. of Political Studies 42-58; mem. Int. Statistical Inst.; Pres. Int. Population Union 61-63; Dr. h.c. Geneva, Brussels, Liège, Utrecht and Montreal Univs.; Prof. Social Demography (Life of Populations), Collège de France 59-69; fmr. Dir. Institut de Démographie de l'Université de Paris 57-69; Prof. of Economy and Population, Univ. Paris 62-, Univ. of Louvain 74-; Commandeur de la Légion d'Honneur.
Leisure interests: theatre, humour, skiing, ancient books on economy and population and village life.
Publs. Principal works: *Essai sur la conjoncture et la prévision économique* 38, *Richesse et population* 44, *Le pouvoir et l'opinion* 49, *Théorie Générale de la Population* 52-66, *L'Opinion Publique* 56, *La Bureaucratie* 56, *La Nature Sociale* 57, *La Montée des Jeunes* 59, *Le plan Sauvy* 60, *Les Limites de la Vie Humaine* 61, *Fertility and Survival* 61, *Malthus et les deux Marx* 63, 66, *Mythologie de notre temps* 65, 71, *Histoire économique de la France entre les deux guerres* Vol. I (*1918-1931*) 65, Vol. II *De Pierre Laval à Paul Reynaud* 67, Vol. III 71, Vol. IV 75, *Les quatres roues de la fortune* 68, *Socialisme en Liberté* 70, *General Theory of Population* 70, *La Révolte des Jeunes* 70, *De Paul Reynaud à Charles de Gaulle* 72, *Croissance Zéro?* 73, 2nd edn. 75, *Vers l'Enseignement pour tous* 74, *La Fin des Riches* 75, *L'économie du diable* 76.
76 rue Lepic, 75018 Paris, France.

Savalas, Telly (Aristotle), B.A.; American actor; b. 21 Jan. 1923, Long Island, N.Y.; *s.* of the late Nicholas Constantine and of Christina (née Kapsallis) Savalas; *m.* 2nd Marilynn Gardner 1955 (divorced 1974), three *d.*; *m.* 3rd Sarah Adams 1974, one *s.*; ed. Columbia Univ.
Worked with *Voice of America* radio broadcasts; joined U.S. State Dept., became Exec. Dir. of Information Services; worked on television network documentaries; began film acting career 60; appeared in television series *Kojak* in U.S.A. 73-, in U.K. Aug. 74-; films include: *Birdman of Alcatraz* 62, *Genghis Khan* 65, *The Battle of the Bulge* 65, *The Greatest Story Ever Told* 65, *Beau Geste* 66, *The Dirty Dozen* 67, *The Scalphunters* 68, *Buona Sera Mrs. Campbell* 68, *The Assassination Bureau* 68, *On Her Majesty's Secret Service* 69, *Crooks and Coronets* 69, *Mackenna's Gold* 69, *Kelly's Heroes* 70, *A Town Called Bastard* 70, *Pancho Villa* 71, *Horror Express* 72, *Inside Out* 75, *Diamond Mercenaries* 75.
c/o International Creative Managements, 22 Grafton Street, London W.1, England; and Alexander Tucker, 9200 Sunset Boulevard, Los Angeles, Calif. 90069, U.S.A.
Telephone: 01-629 8080 (London Agent).

Savang Vatthana, H.M. Boroma-setha Khatya Sourya Vongsa Phra Maha Sri, L. EN D.; fmr. King of Laos; b. 13 Nov. 1907; ed. Paris Univ.
Took active part in politics during the lifetime of his father; Chief Del. Arbitration Comm. Washington 47, Japanese Peace Treaty Conf. San Francisco 51; appointed Regent Aug. 59; succeeded his father King Sisavang Vong Oct. 59, abdicated when monarchy was abolished Dec. 75; Supreme Adviser to Pres. of Laos Dec. 75-.
c/o Office of the President, Vientiane, Laos.

Savić, Pavle; Yugoslav physical chemist; b. 10 Jan. 1909, Salonika, Greece; ed. Univ. Belgrade.
Assistant Prof., Univ. of Belgrade 32-34; worked with Mme. Joliot-Curie at Inst. for Radium, Paris, 34-39; discovered together fission of uranium nucleus and thence basis for practical use of nuclear energy; lecturer, Univ. of Belgrade 40-41; active in People's Liberation War 41-45; Prof. of Chemistry, Univ. of Belgrade 45-66; Inst. for Physical Problems, Acad. of Sciences of U.S.S.R. 45-46; Head, Physical Chem. Inst., Univ. of Belgrade, 47-66; founder of Boris Kidrič Inst. for Nuclear Sciences, Vinča, Pres. the Scientific Council 48-58; Vice-Pres. Fed. Comm. for Nuclear Energy 55-60; Pres. Serbian Acad. of Sciences and Arts 71-; mem. Yugoslav Acad. of Sciences, U.S. Nat. Acad. of Sciences; foreign mem. Acad. of Sciences of U.S.S.R.; hon. mem. Hungarian Acad. of Sciences; corresp. mem. Slovenian Acad. of Sciences and Arts; mem. Acad. of Sciences and Arts of Bosnia and Herzegovina, N.Y., Athens Acads. of Sciences; numerous Yugoslav and foreign awards and decorations, including Order of Labour, First Class 54 and Officier de la Légion d'Honneur 65.
Publs. *The Behaviour of Materials under High Pressures,* Vols. I-IV (with R. Kašanin) 62-64, *Od atoma do nebeskih tela* 70; also many papers on nuclear physics.
Bulevar Revolucije 257/III, Entrance 5, Flat 32, Belgrade, Yugoslavia.

Savimbi, Dr. Jonas; Angolan nationalist leader; ed. Univ. of Lausanne.
Former Sec.-Gen. União das Populações de Angola (U.P.A.); Foreign Minister of Governo Revolucionário de Angola no Exílio (G.R.A.E.) 62-July 64; resigned from G.R.A.E. at OAU meeting, Cairo July 64; studied at Univ. of Lausanne 64-65; moved to Lusaka; founded União Nacional para a Independência Total de Angola (U.N.I.T.A.) near Luso, March 66; Pres. U.N.I.T.A. March 66-; Leader U.N.I.T.A. forces in guerrilla war against the Portuguese and in Angolan civil war against M.P.L.A. forces after Portuguese withdrawal in Nov. 75; proclaimed Pres. of People's Dem. Repub. of Angola Nov. 75 (not recognized internationally).

Savkar, Dattatraya Sitaram, B.A., M.COM.; Indian economist and international civil servant; b. 17 Jan. 1909, Belgaum; *s.* of S. K. Savkar and Janaki S. Savkar; *m.* Nalini Savkar 1935; three *s.*; ed. Bombay Univ.
Professor, H.L. Coll. of Commerce, Ahmedabad 36-45; Reserve Bank of India 45-67; Deputy Dir. of Research 45-51, Dir. of Research 51-59, Econ. Adviser 59-67; Alt. Exec. Dir. for India, Int. Monetary Fund 48-51, Dir. Asian Dept., Int. Monetary Fund 59-72; mem. Economist Panel, Planning Comm., Govt. of India 54-59.
Leisure interest: reading.
Publs. *Joint Stock Banking in India* 38, *Modern Economic Development of Great Powers* 43.
4437 45th Street N.W., Washington, D.C. 20016, U.S.A.

Saw, U Ba; Burmese politician; b. 17 Nov. 1914, Ramree; *s.* of U Lu Pyu and Daw Nwe Ma Pyu; *m.* Daw Pyu Pyu 1935; two *s.* two *d.*; ed. Govt. High School, Kyaukpyu, and Ananda Coll., Colombo, Ceylon.
Joint Editor Burma Propaganda Office, British Ministry of Information (Far-Eastern Bureau), New Delhi 43; guerrilla warfare training in India and Ceylon 44; parachuted to Kyaukpyu District as leader of Resistance campaign in Southern Arakan 44; formed Kyaukpyu District Anti-Fascist People's Freedom League and People's Volunteer Org. (Pres. and mem. Exec. both orgs.); mem. Constituent Assembly for Kyaukpyu North 48-50; Special District Commr. Kyaukpyu District 50-51; elected to Union Parl. for Kyaukpyu (South) 51-62; Minister for Minorities and

Refugee Welfare 52-53, for Relief Resettlement and Social Welfare 53-56, for Religious Affairs and Social Welfare 56-58, for Social Welfare and Religious Affairs, Union Culture, Health, Immigration and Nat. Registration 60-62; Amb. to Thailand and the Philippines 62-64, to U.S.S.R., Romania, Poland, Czechoslovakia and Hungary 64-68, to United Kingdom, Sweden, Norway and Denmark 68-71, to Fed. Repub. of Germany 71, concurrently accred. to Finland 72, and to EEC 73.
Leisure interests: gardening, painting, reading.
Burmese Embassy, Am Hofgarten 1-2, Bonn, Federal Republic of Germany.
Telephone: 6/35-135.

Sawada, Setsuzo, LL.B.; Japanese diplomatist and administrator; b. 1884, Tottori-Ken; s. of Nobugo Sawada; m. Miyo Ohyama 1911; four s.; ed. Tokyo Imperial Univ.
Foreign Service 09-; Sec. Japanese Embassy, London 12-18; Counsellor, Washington 25-29; Consul Gen. N.Y. 29-31; Minister to League of Nations 31-33; Amb. to Brazil 34-38; Pres. Nippon-Brazilian Central Asscn. 45-75; Chair. and Adviser, Asscn. of Foreign Service Men of Japan 41-; Adviser, Japan Red Cross Soc. 64-; Diplomatic Adviser to Prime Minister Suzuki 45; Pres. Tokyo Univ. for Foreign Studies 49-56; Vice-Pres. Nat. Comm. for UNESCO 52-59; Pres. Govt. Council for Overseas Emigration 59-62, Inst. of World Economy 39-; Grand Cordon of Cruzeiro do Sul, Brazil 38, First Class of Sacred Treasure, Japan 37, Grand Cordon, First Class of Rising Sun, Japan 40.
Leisure interests: daily walking, reading and writing.
Inamuragasaki, 3-chome 10-25, Kamakura, Japan.
Telephone: 0467 (22) 2355.

Sawallisch, Wolfgang; German conductor; b. 26 Aug. 1923, Munich; ed. Wittelsbacher Gymnasium, Munich. Studied under Profs. Ruoff, Haas and Sachsse; mil. service 42-46, prisoner of war in Italy; conductor Augsburg 47-53; Musical Dir. Aachen 53-58, Wiesbaden 58-60, Cologne Opera 60-63; Conductor Hamburg Philharmonic Orchestra 60-73; Principal Conductor Vienna Symphony Orchestra 60-70; Prof. Staatliche Hochschule für Musik, Cologne 60-63; Musical Dir. Bayerische Staatsoper Munich 71-; Perm. conductor Teatro alla Scala Milan; Conducted at many Festivals; Recordings in U.S.A. and Britain; Hon. Conductor NHK Symphony Orchestra, Tokyo; Artistic Dir. Suisse Romande Orchestra, Geneva 73; Accademico Onorario Santa Cecilia; Österreichisches Ehrenkreuz für Kunst und Wissenschaft.
8211 Grassau, Federal Republic of Germany.
Telephone: 08641-2315 (Home).

Sawamura, Kaichi; Japanese business executive; b. 1 Jan. 1916; ed. Chiba Univ.
Joined Toppan Printing Co., Ltd. 36, Dir. 59, Man. Dir. 60, Exec. Man. Dir. 65, Pres. 67-; Chair. Toppan Printing Co. (Hong Kong) Ltd.; Pres. Toppan Printing Co. (Singapore) Pte., Ltd., Toppan Printing Co. (America) Inc.; Chair. Kwangmyong-Toppan Printing Co. Ltd.; Auditor, Nippon Cultural Broadcasting Inc.; standing mem. Tokyo Chamber of Commerce; Asst. Chair. Cttee. of Industry, Chamber of Commerce; Chair. Japan Printers' Asscn., Chair. Printing Dept.
Toppan Printing Co. Ltd., 1-5-1 Taito, Taitoku, Tokyo, Japan.

Sawamura, Takayoshi, B.COM.SC.; Japanese business executive; b. 6 Feb. 1913; ed. Kobe Univ.
Joined Nippon Express Co. Ltd., Dir. 64, Man. Dir. 66, Senior Man. Dir. 66, Pres. 68-; Ministry of Transport Award 72.
3-12-9, Soto-Kanda, Chiyoda-ku; Home: 5-15-5, Shimoigusa, Suginami-ku, Tokyo, Japan.

Sawaya, Paulo; Brazilian scientist; b. 1903; ed. Faculty of Medicine, Univ. of São Paulo.
Assistant Prof. of Zoology, Univ. of São Paulo 37, Assoc.

Prof. 38, Prof. of Gen. and Animal Physiology 39-, Head of Dept., Dean Faculty Science, Philosophy and Letters 39-70; Dean, Institute of Bio-sciences 71-; Consultant, Nat. Research Council Rio de Janeiro 56 and Brasília Univ.; Pres. Technical Council of Education, São Paulo; Dir. Marine Biological Inst., Univ. of São Paulo; main fields of research: colour changes in animal neurosecretion, muscular physiology of invertebrates.
Universidade de São Paulo, Cidade Universitária "Armando de Salles Oliveira", Caixa Postal 11230, São Paulo 9, Brazil.

Sawyer, Ralph Alansen, A.B., PH.D.; American professor of physics; b. 5 Jan. 1895, Atkinson, N.H.; s. of George Alanson and Lillie Elvira (Noyes) Sawyer; m. 1st Martha Green 1919 (died 1957), 2nd Frances Tracy Hay 1964; one s. one d.; ed. Dartmouth Coll. and Univ. of Chicago.
Fellow and Asst. in Physics, Univ. of Chicago 17-18; Served Signal Corps 18; Ensign U.S.N.R.F., engaged in design of optical instruments for the Bureau of Ordnance 18-19; Instr. in Physics, Univ. of Michigan 19, Asst. Prof. of Physics 22-27, Assoc. Prof. 27-30, Prof. 30-64; on leave from Univ. of Mich. to serve in the U.S.N.R. as Lieut.-Commdr. in Charge of the Armour and Projectile Laboratory at the Naval Proving Ground, Dahlgren, Va. 41-45; Commdr. U.S.N.R. and Experimental Laboratories Officer 43-45; Technical Dir. of Joint Task Force One, engaged in carrying out the "Crossroads" Atomic Bomb Test at Bikini Atoll 46; Dean, Horace H. Rackham School of Graduate Studies, Univ. of Mich. 46-64; mem. Nat. Research Council 49-52, 59-71; Capt. U.S.N.R. 50; Dir. Michigan Memorial-Phoenix Project 51-59; Dir. Optical Society of America 41-45, Vice-Pres. 53-55, Pres. 55-57; Pres. Asscn. of Graduate Schools in the Asscn. of American Universities 57; mem. of Gov. Board of American Inst. of Physics 54-59, Chair. 59-71, Acting Dir. 64-65, 66; Vice-Pres. for Research Univ. of Michigan 59-64; Consultant Goddard Space Flight Center, Nat. Aeronautics and Space Admin. 64-65; Executive Secretary National Academy of Sciences Advisory Panels to Nat. Bureau of Standards 66-69; Chair. U.S. Del. to Brazil, U.S. Comm. on Brazilian Industrial Standards and Specifications 67-69; mem. American Asscn. for the Advancement of Science; Navy Commendation Ribbon; Frederic Ives Medal, Optical Soc. of America; Hon. Sc.D. (Dartmouth Coll. and Michigan Coll. of Mining and Technology), Hon. LL.D. (Wayne Univ.); Spectroscopy Soc. of Pittsburgh Award 61, Medal Soc. of Applied Spectroscopy, New York Section 66; Karl Taylor Compton Medal of American Inst. of Physics 71.
Leisure interest: golf.
Publ. *Experimental Spectroscopy* 44, 3rd. edn. 63.
Home: 1208 Wells Street, Ann Arbor, Mich., 48104; Office: University of Michigan, Ann Arbor, Mich., U.S.A.
Telephone: 313-662-1248.

Saxbe, William B., LL.B.; American politician; b. 25 June 1916, Mechanicsburg, Ohio; m. Ardath (Dolly) Kleinhans 1940; two s. one d.; ed. Mechanicsburg High Schools and Ohio State Univ.
Member Ohio House of Reps. 47-54 (Majority Leader 51-52, Speaker of the House 53-54); Chair. Ohio Program Comm. 53; Ohio Attorney-Gen. 57-58, 63-68; Chair. Ohio Crime Comm. 69-70; Senator 69-73; Attorney-Gen. 73-74; Amb. to India 75-; mem. Cttee. on Armed Services, Govt. Operations, Post Office, Civil Service and Special Cttee. on Ageing; Republican.
American Embassy, Shantipath, Chanakyapuri, New Delhi, India.

Saxena, Surrendra Kumar, M.A., M.SOC.SC., PH.D.; Indian international Co-operative official; b. 3 April 1926; m. Ingalill Gunnel Amanda Friberg; one s. two d.; ed. Univ. of Agra, Inst. of Social Studies, The Hague, Municipal Univ., Amsterdam.

Assistant Prof., Dept. of Econs., Birla Coll. 49-52; Research Fellow, Inst. of Social Studies, The Hague 55-56; with ICA Regional Office and Educ. Centre for S.E. Asia 59-61, Regional Officer 61-68; Dir. Int. Co-operative Alliance (ICA) 68-; Dr. h.c. Univ. of Sherbrooke, Canada.
Leisure interests: golf, Indian music.
Publs. *Nationalisation and Industrial Conflict: Example of British Coal Mining* 55, *Agricultural Co-operation in S.E. Asia* 61, *Role of Foreign Aid in Development of Co-operative Processing* 65, *Activities and Role of the International Co-operative Alliance in S.E. Asia* 66, *The International Co-operative Alliance and Co-operative Trade* 67.
International Co-operative Alliance, 11 Upper Grosvenor Street, London, W1X 9PA; Home: 6 Hoe Meadow, Seelys Estate, Beaconsfield, Bucks., England.
Telephone: 01-499-5991. (Office)

Saxild, Jorgen, M.SC.; Danish civil engineer; b. 6 June 1891, Copenhagen; s. of late J. F. Saxild and late Ingeborg Lassen; m. 1st Gudrun Hassel 1918 (died 1953), 2nd Birte Hansen 1958; one s. two d.
Employed by various English and French engineering firms 14-17; Man. Dir. Kampmann, Kierulff & Saxild A/S (Kampsax), civil engineers and contractors, Copenhagen 17-; Man. Dir. Saxild & Partners, London 23-26; Dir. Peter Lind Holding Co. Ltd. London 35-55; Man. Dir. Danish-Swedish Consortium for construction of railways in Turkey and Iran 27-39; Dir. Kampsax-Invest A/S, Copenhagen 41; Dir. East Asiatic Co. Ltd., Copenhagen, and other companies 48-; Chair. Danish Govt. Cttee. for Technical Assistance (UN) 51-62; Managing Dir. Kampsax Holding A/S 57-; Pres. Danish Soc. for Civil Engineers 48-52; mem. Acad. for Technical Sciences 41, Council mem. 58-61; mem. Danish Council for Technical Co-operation with Developing Countries 62-66; Grand Cross of the Order of Dannebrog, and holder of several other Scandinavian and foreign decorations.
Granhøjen 1, 2900 Hellerup, Denmark.
Telephone: Gentofte 5101.

Say, Rt. Rev. Richard David, D.D.; British ecclesiastic; b. 4 Oct. 1914, London; s. of Commdr. Richard Say, O.B.E., R.N.V.R., and Kathleen Mary Wildy; m. Irene Frances Rayner, J.P., 1943; two s. (one deceased) two d.; ed. Univ. Coll. School, Christ's Coll., Cambridge and Ridley Hall, Cambridge.
Curate of St. Martin-in-the-Fields 43-50, Gen. Sec., Church of England Youth Council 44-47; Gen. Sec., British Council of Churches 47-55; Rector of Hatfield and Domestic Chaplain to Marquess of Salisbury, K.G. 55-61; Hon. Canon of St. Albans 57-61; Bishop of Rochester 61-; Church of England del. to World Council of Churches 48, 54, and 61; Sub-Prelate of the Order of St. John of Jerusalem; Chaplain to the Pilgrims of Great Britain 68-; mem. House of Lords 69-; High Almoner to H.M. the Queen 70-.
Leisure interests: sailing and travel.
Bishopscourt, Rochester, Kent, ME1 1TS, England.
Telephone: Medway 42721.

Sayem, Abusadat Mohammad, B.A., B.L.; Bangladesh judge; b. 1 March 1916; ed. Rangpur Zilla School, Presidency Coll., Calcutta, Carmichael Coll., Rangpur, Univ. Law Coll., Calcutta.
Advocate, Calcutta High Court 44; joined Dacca High Court Bar 47; Examiner in Law, Dacca Univ.; mem. Local Board, State Bank of Pakistan until 56; Sponsor, Gen. Sec. and Vice-Pres. East Pakistan Lawyers Asscn.; fmr. Sec. and Vice-Pres. High Court Bar Asscn.; Advocate, Fed. Court of Pakistan 51-59; Senior Advocate, Supreme Court of Pakistan 59-62; mem. Bar Council until 62; Judge High Court, Dacca 62; mem. of various legal comms. of enquiry; mem. East Pakistan Election Comm. for Nat. and Pro-

vincial Assemblies 70-71; Chief Justice, High Court of Bangladesh Jan.-Dec. 72, Supreme Court Dec. 72-75; President of Bangladesh, Chief Marshal Law Admin., Minister of Defence, of Law, of Parliamentary Affairs and Justice of Foreign Affairs, of Agric. Nov. 75-.
Office of the President, Dacca, Bangladesh.

Sayer, Guy Mowbray, J.P.; British banker; b. 18 June 1924; ed. Hong Kong, Shrewsbury School, England.
With The Hongkong and Shanghai Banking Corpn. 61-, Accountant, Rangoon Branch 61, Man. 63, Man. Osaka Branch 64, Monkok Branch 65, Staff Controller, Head Office 68, Gen. Man. 69, Dir. 70, Deputy Chair. 71, Chair. April 72-; Chair. Mercantile Bank Ltd., Hong Kong, The Hong Kong Bank of Calif., San Francisco, Hongkong Finance Ltd., Sydney; Unofficial mem. Exec. Council ,Hong Kong Govt.; Treas., Univ. of Hong Kong; mem. Exchange Fund Advisory Cttee., Hong Kong; Fellow, Inst. of Bankers, London; Liveryman, Worshipful Company of Innholders, Freeman of the City of London.
The Hongkong and Shanghai Banking Corpn., 1 Queen's Road Central, Hong Kong; Home: Skyhigh, 10 Pollocks Path, Hong Kong.

Sayushev, Vadim Arkadievich; Soviet politician; b. 16 Jan. 1930, Novosibirsk; ed. Leningrad Mining Inst.
Member C.P.S.U. 52-; Sec., Sverdlovsk Dist. (Leningrad) Cttee. Komsomol 54-58, Leningrad Regional Cttee. 55-58; Second Sec., then First Sec., Leningrad Regional Cttee., Komsomol 58-61; Sec., Cen. Cttee. Komsomol 61-64; Vice-Chair. U.S.S.R. Council of Ministers State Cttee. for Vocational Training 64-67, First Vice-Chair. 67-; Deputy U.S.S.R. Supreme Soviet 62-66; Cand. mem. Cen. Cttee. C.P.S.U. 61-66; awarded Orders of Red Banner of Labour, Badge of Honour and other decorations.
U.S.S.R. Council of Ministers State Cttee. for Vocational Training, Sadovosukharevskaya ulitsa, 16, Moscow, U.S.S.R.

Scaglia, Giovanni Battista; Italian journalist and politician; b. 20 Sept. 1910; ed. Collegio Ghislieri and Università di Pavia.
President of Catholic Action 45-49; Editor *Studium* (magazine) 49-; mem. Chamber of Deputies 48-; Under-Sec. of Educ. 54-59; Deputy Sec. of Christian Democrat Party 59-64; Minister without Portfolio for Parl. Liaison 64-68, of Educ. 68-69, Tourism and Entertainment Feb.-June 72.
3 Via Antonio Rosmini, Bergamo, Italy.

Scalfaro, Oscar Luigi; Italian lawyer and politician; b. 9 Sept. 1918; ed. Università Cattolica del Sacro Cuore, Milan.
Christian Democrat mem. Chamber of Deputies 48-; Under-Sec., Ministry of Works and Social Security 54, at the Presidency of the Council of Ministers 55, Ministry of Justice 55-58, Minister of the Interior 59-62; fmr. Sec. then Vice-Pres. of Christian Democrats in Chamber of Deputies, Vice Political Sec. 65-66; Minister of Transport and Civil Aviation 66-69, Feb.-June 72, of Educ. 72-73.
Camera dei Deputati, Rome, Italy.

Scali, John Alfred, B.S.; American diplomatist; b. 27 April 1918, Canton, O.; s. of Paul M. and Lucy (Leone) Scali; m. 1st Helen Lauinger Glock 1945, 2nd Denise Scali 1973; three d.; ed. Boston Univ.
Reporter Boston Herald 42 and Boston Bureau, United Press (UP) 42-43; Associated Press, War Corresp. European Theatre of Operations 44 and later Diplomatic Corresp., Wash. Bureau 45-61; Diplomatic Corresp. ABC Television and Radio, Wash. 61-71; Special Consultant for Foreign Affairs to the Pres. 71-73; Amb., Perm. Rep. to UN 73-75; mem. A.F.T.R.A.; Journalism Award, Univ. of S. Calif. 64; special award, Wash. Chapter Nat. Acad. of Arts and Sciences 64;

John Scali award created by Wash. Chapter of A.F.T.R.A. 64; Man of the Year award in Journalism, Boston Univ. 65; special award Overseas Press Clubs 65; Rizzuto Gold Medal Award 74; Hon. degrees (Malone and York Colls.) 74.
c/o Department of State, Washington, D.C. 20520, U.S.A.

Scammon, Richard M.; American psephologist; b. 17 July 1915, Minneapolis, Minn.; s. of Dr. Richard E. and Mrs. Julia (Simms) Scammon; m. Mary Stark Allen 1952; one d.; ed. Univ. of Minnesota, London School of Economics, Univ. of London and Univ. of Michigan.
Research Sec., Radio Office, Univ. of Chicago 39-41; Army Service 41-46; Chief, Political Activities Branch, Civil Admin. Div., Office of Military Govt. United States (Germany) 46-48; Chief, Div. of Research for Western Europe, Dept. of State 48-55; Dir. Elections Research Center, Governmental Affairs Inst., Washington 55-61, 65-; Dir. of the Census 61-65; Chair. U.S. Del. to Observe Elections in U.S.S.R. 58, Chair. President's Comm. on Registration and Voting Participation 63, OAS Electoral Mission to the Dominican Repub. 66; Pres. Nat. Council on Public Polls 69-70; Chair. Select Comm. on Western Hemisphere Immigration 66-68; mem. U.S. Del. to UN Gen. Assembly 73.
Publs. Editor, *America Votes* Vol. 1 56, Vol. 2 58, Vol. 3 60, Vol. 4 62, Vol. 5 64, Vol. 6 66, Vol. 7 68, Vol. 8 70, Vol. 9 72, Vol. 10 73, Vol. 11 75, Editor *America at the Polls* 65, Co-Author *This U.S.A.* 65, *The Real Majority* 70.
5508 Greystone Street, Chevy Chase, Maryland 20015, U.S.A.
Telephone: 202-387-6066.

Scamp, Sir (Athelstan) Jack, Kt., D.L., J.P., F.I.P.M., F.B.I.M., C.I.E.E.; British company director; b. 22 May 1913, Birmingham; s. of Edward H. and Jane Scamp; m. Jane Kendall 1939; one s. one d.; ed. Birmingham. Chief Personnel Officer, Plessey Co., Ltd. 53-58; Personnel Dir. Massey-Ferguson (U.K.) Ltd. 58-62; Dir. The General Electric Co. Ltd. 62-; mem. Industrial Court (later Industrial Arbitration Board) 64-; Chair. Motor Industry Joint Labour Council 65-68; Industrial Adviser, Dept. of Econ. Affairs 65-66; Dir. A.E.I. Ltd. 67-72; Dir. Fairfields (Glasgow) Ltd., 67-68; Gov. William Temple Coll. 67-73; Dir. Urwick, Orr & Partners Ltd. 69-; Chair. Urwick, Orr and Partners Ltd. 73-; mem. Lord Devlin Cttee. of Inquiry on the Docks 64; Chair. Courts of Inquiry, Footplate Staff, British Railways 65; Transporter Drivers, Longbridge Group of Delivery Agents 66, Motor Vehicle Collections Ltd. 66; Maintenance Workers, Birmingham Aluminium Castings Ltd. 67; British Airline Pilots' Asscn. 67; Coal Trimmers, N.E. Ports 67; Liverpool Docks Dispute 67; Time Workers, Pressed Steel Fisher Ltd. 68; Hill Precision Castings 68; Sewing Machinists, Ford Motor Co. 68; Vickers Ltd., Barrow in Furness 69; Coal Trimmers, Immingham 70; Local Authorities Dispute 70; Chair. Coventry City Football Club; Dir. Coventry Broadcasting Ltd. 73-, Nat. Nuclear Corpn. Ltd. 73-, GEC Schreiber Ltd. 74-.
Leisure interests: association football, cricket, tennis.
Flax Hill, Ufton, Leamington Spa, Warwicks., England.
Telephone: Harburg 612-799.

Scanlon, Hugh Parr; British trade unionist; b. 26 Oct. 1913, Australia; m. Nora Markey 1943; two d.; ed. Stretford Elementary School, Nat. Council of Labour Colls.
Apprentice; Instrument Maker; Shop Steward, Convener Associated Electrical Industries, Trafford Park; Div. Organizer Amalgamated Engineering Union, Manchester 47-63, mem. Exec. Council AEU, London 63-67; Pres. Amalgamated Union of Engineering Workers (AUEW) 67-; mem. Trades Union Congress

Gen. Council, TUC Econ. Cttee.; Vice-Pres., mem. Exec. Cttee. IMF; mem. Nat. Econ. Devt. Council (NEDC) 71-; mem. Metrication Board 73-; Pres. European Metalworkers' Fed. 74-; Chair. Eng. Industry Training Board 75.
Leisure interests: golf, swimming, gardening.
30 Crown Woods Way, Eltham, London, S.E.9, England.

Scarascia-Mugnozza, Carlo, DR.JUR.; Italian lawyer; b. 19 Jan. 1920, Rome.
Member Chamber of Deputies 53; Vice-Pres. Christian Democrat Parliamentary Group 58-62; Leader, Italian del. to UNESCO 62; Sec. of State for Educ. 62-63, for Justice June-Dec. 63; mem. European Parl. 61, Chair. Political Cttee. 71-72; Vice-Pres. of Comm. of the European Communities, Commr. for Agriculture 72-73; Commr. for Press and Information, Transport Policy, Environment and Consumer Protection, Relations with the European Parl. 73-.
Commission of the European Communities, 200 rue de la Loi, 1049 Brussels, Belgium.

Scarfe, Gerald A.; British cartoonist; b. 1 June 1936, London.
Has contributed cartoons to *Punch* 60-, *Private Eye* 61-, *Daily Mail* 66-, *The Sunday Times* 67-, *Time* 67-; exhibited at Grosvenor Gallery (group exhbns.) 69, 70, Pavilion d'Humour, Montreal 69, *Expo 70*, Osaka 70; one-man exhbns. Waddell Gallery, New York 68, 70, Vincent Price Gallery, Chicago 69, Grosvenor Gallery 69, Nat. Portrait Gallery 71; animation and film directing BBC 69-; Zagreb Prize for BBC film *Long Drawn Out Trip* 73.
Leisure interests: drawing, painting, sculpting.
Publs. *Gerald Scarfe's People* 66, *Indecent Exposure* 73, *Expletive Deleted: The Life and Times of Richard Nixon* 74.
10 Cheyne Walk, London, S.W.3, England.

Scelba, Mario, D.JUR.; Italian politician; b. 5 Sept. 1901, Caltagirone; m. Nerina Palestini 1929; one d.; ed. Rome Univ.
Founder mem. Italian People's Party 19; practised as lawyer after suppression of People's Party 26-; re-entered politics 41 and became one of founders of Christian Democrat Party and newspaper *Il Popolo*; Minister for Posts and Telecommunications 45-47; Minister of the Interior 47-53, 60-62; Prime Minister and Minister of the Interior 54-55; mem. Chamber of Deputies; Deputy to the European Parliamentary Assembly 58-, Pres. 69-71; Pres. Nat. Council of the Christian Democrat Party 66; mem. Senate; Pres. Senate's Comm. on Foreign Affairs; hon. degrees Univ. of Ottawa, Columbia Univ. (Washington), Fordham Univ. and St. John's Univ. (New York).
European Parliament, Centre Européen, Kirchberg, Luxembourg; and Via Barberini 47, Rome, Italy.
Telephone: 48-54-56 (Rome).

Scerri, Arthur J.; Maltese politician and diplomat; b. 31 Jan. 1921, Senglea; m. Ruby (née Howell); one d.; ed. St. Mary's Coll., Cospicua and technical studies.
Draughtsman, G.E.C. Elliot Co. Ltd. 50-71; draughtsman Procon (London) Ltd. Jan.-July 71; High Commr. for Malta (also accred. to U.S.S.R.) in London July 71-; Amb. to U.S.S.R. 72; Amb. to Iran 72; High Commr. to Cyprus 72; Rep. Malta Labour Party in U.K. 54-71; London corresp. Voice of Malta 54-71; fmr. Sec. and Chair. Labour Party (Hampstead); Sec. Mediterranean and Middle East Cttee. of the Movement for Colonial Freedom; fmr. Chair. Maltese Labour Movement in England, assisted in organizing Malta Freedom Fund.
Leisure interests: politics, reading, philately (Maltese).
Malta High Commission, Malta House, 24 Haymarket, London, SW1Y 4DJ, England.
Telephone: 01-930-9851.

Schaaf, C(arl) Hart, A.B., PH.D.; American United Nations official; b. 14 Jan. 1912, Ft. Wayne, Ind.; s. of Albert H. and Bertha May Hart Schaaf; m. Barbara J. Crook 1945; two s.; ed. Univ. of Michigan, Montpelier, Stockholm.
Associate Professor of Administration, Coll. of William and Mary (Richmond Div.) 40-42; State Rationing Admin., Virginia 42-43; Asst. Deputy Dir.-Gen. and Chief, Supply for Europe, UN Relief and Rehabilitation Admin. 44-47; Assoc. Prof. of Admin., School of Business and Public Admin., Cornell Univ. 47-49; Exec. Dir., United World Federalists 49; Deputy Exec. Sec. UN/ECAFE 49-54; Resident Rep. in Israel for UN/TAB 54-57, in the Philippines 57-59; Exec. Agent Cttee. for Co-ordination of Investigations of the Lower Mekong Basin 59-70; Dir. Career Secr. of UN; Resident Rep. in Sri Lanka and the Maldives 69-.
Leisure interests: golf, piano.
Publs. *Fiscal Planning at the State Level* 41, *Economic Co-operation in Asia* 50, *The United Nations Economic Commission for Asia and the Far East* 53, *The Lower Mekong* (with Russell Fifield) 63, *Burke's Idea or Partition* (play) 48.
United Nations, P.O. Box 1505, Colombo, Sri Lanka.

Schachman, Howard Kapnek, B.S., PH.D.; American educator and biochemist; b. 5 Dec. 1918, Philadelphia, Pa.; s. of Morris H. Schachman and Rose Kapnek Schachman; m. Ethel H. Lazarus 1945; two s.; ed. Mass. Inst. of Technology and Princeton Univ.
Fellow, Nat. Insts. of Health 46-48; Instructor (Biochem.), Univ. of Calif., Berkeley 48-50, Asst. Prof. 50-54, Assoc. Prof. 55-59, Prof. of Biochem. and Molecular Biology 59-, Research Biochemist to Virus Lab. 59-; Chair. Dept. of Molecular Biology and Dir. Virus Lab. 69-; mem. Nat. Acad. of Sciences; Calif. Section Award, American Chemical Soc. 58; E. H. Sargent & Co. Award for Chemical Instrumentation, American Chemical Soc. 62; John Scott Award, City of Philadelphia 64; Warren Triennial Prize, Mass. Gen. Hosp. 65; Hon. D.Sc. (Northwestern Univ.) 74.
Leisure interest: sports.
Publs. *Ultracentrifugation in Biochemistry* 59; articles.
Molecular Biology and Virus Laboratory, University of California, Berkeley, Calif. 94720, U.S.A.
Telephone: 642-7046.

Schacht Aristeguieta, Efraín; Venezuelan lawyer and politician; b. Caracas; ed. Cen. Univ. of Venezuela.
Lecturer, School of Int. Studies, Cen. Univ.; Lecturer Free School of Journalism; Lecturer in Int. Public Law, Cen. Univ. Law School; Co-founder, Pres. Colegio de Internacionalistas de Venezuela; Minister of Foreign Affairs 74-75; Sec.-Gen. of the Presidency Jan. 75-.
Publs. *Elements of International Law, The International Concept of Liberty, International Juridical Questions.*
Office of the President, Caracas, Venezuela.

Schadewaldt, Wolfgang Otto Bernhard, DR. PHIL.; German classicist; b. 15 March 1900, Berlin; s. of Otto Schadewaldt and Agnes Trensky; m. Maria Mayer 1928; one s. four d.; ed. Universität zu Berlin.
Private Lecturer, Berlin 27; Prof. of Classics, Königsberg 28, Freiburg i. Br. 29, Leipzig 34, Berlin 41; Prof. of Classics, Eberhard-Karls-Universität, Tübingen 50-; Visiting Prof., Univ. of Mich., U.S.A. 68; mem. PEN Club, Acad. for German Language and Poetry, Darmstadt, Acads. of Leipzig, Berlin, Heidelberg, Königsberg, Erfurt and Vienna; hon. mem. Greek Humanistic Soc.; mem. Cen. Directorate German Archaeological Inst.; Knight Order Pour le Mérite for Sciences and Arts 62, Reuchlin Prize of Pforzheim 63, Grand Cross of Merit with Star (Fed. Repub. of Germany) 64, Translator Prize, Acad. for German Language and Poetry, Darmstadt 65.
Leisure interests: music, photography.
Publs. *Ilias-Studien* 38, *Von Homers Welt und Werk* (4th edition) 65, *Sappho* 50, *Griechische Sternsagen* 57, *Homer, Odyssee* (trans. into German prose) 58, *Hellas und Hesperien* 60 (2nd ed. 70), *Goethe-Studien, Natur und Altertum* 63, *Griechisches Theater* (trans. of Aeschylus, Sophocles, Aristophanes, Menander) 64, Editor *Goethe-Wörterbuch* Parts 1-7, 66-72.
65 Stauffenbergstrasse, 74 Tübingen, Federal Republic of Germany.
Telephone: 07122-22500.

Schaeberle, Robert M.; American business executive; b. 1923, N.J.; m.; three c.; ed. Dartmouth Coll.
Served U.S. Navy, World War II (rank of Lieut.-Commdr.); joined Nabisco Inc. 46, Controller 60, Vice-Pres. and Asst. to Pres. 62, Vice-Pres. for Finance 64, Exec. Vice-Pres. 64-66, Pres. 66-73, Chief Operating Officer 72-73, Chair. of Board and Chief Exec. Officer June 73-, Dir. and mem. Exec. Cttee.; Dir. Libbey-Owens-Ford Co.; mem. Advisory Board, Chemical Bank New York Trust Co., Emergency Cttee. for American Trade; Dir. of several cos.
Nabisco Inc., East Hanover, New Jersey 07936, U.S.A.

Schaefer, Alfred, LL.D.; Swiss banker; b. 30 Jan. 1905, Aarau; s. of Adolf Schaefer (architect) and Martha Brugger; m. Dorrit E. Hunziker 1932; one s. one d.; ed. Univs. of Geneva, Zurich and Rome.
With Union Bank of Switzerland 31-, Deputy Man. 34-37, Man. Jan. 37-41, Gen. Man. Mar. 41-53, Chief Gen. Man. 53, Chair. Board of Dirs. 64-; Chair. and mem. of many other companies.
Leisure interests: riding, history.
Publs. numerous publs. on banking problems.
Union Bank of Switzerland, 45 Bahnhofstrasse, 8021 Zurich, Home: Seestrasse 14, 8702 Zollikon, Switzerland.
Telephone: 051-29-44-11 (Office).

Schaefer, Walter Erich, DR.PHIL.; German theatre director and playwright; b. 16 March 1901, Hemmingen/Württemberg; s. of Friedrich Schaefer and Hildegard née Speidel; m. Irmgard Sigel 1926; two s. two d.; ed. Karls-gymnasium, Stuttgart, and Eberhard-Karls-Universität, Tübingen.
Writer, Lecturer at Stuttgarter Musikhochschule; Dramatic Producer, Stuttgart 29-33, Mannheim 34-38; Dir. and Chief Dramatic Producer, Kassel 39-47, Augsburg 48-49; Supt. then Gen. Supt. Württembergische Staatstheater, Stuttgart 49-72; Dir. Wiener Staatsoper 62-63; Grosses Verdienstkreuz 59, with Star 71; Officier de l'Ordre des Arts et des Lettres 65.
Publs. novels: *Die 12 Stunden Gottes* 26, *Die letzte Wandlung* 28; theatre: *Günther Rennert—Regisseur in dieser Zeit* 62, *Martha Moedl* 67, *Wieland Wagner* 70; *Die Stuttgarter Staatsoper* 72, *Gespräche mit Cranko* 74; plays: *Richter Feuerbach* 30, *Der 18 Oktober* 32, *Schwarzmann und die Magd* 33, *Die Reise nach Paris* 36, *Theres und die Hoheit* 40, *Das Feuer* 41, *Die Verschwörung* 49, *Aus Abend und Morgen* (Hora Mortis) 52, radio: plays *Malmgren* 29, *Die fünf Sekunden des Mahatma Gandhi* 49, *Der Staatssekretär* 49, *Spiel der Gedanken* 50, *Konferenz in Cristobal* 52, *Die Himmelfahrt des Physikers M.N.* 58, *Die Nacht im alten Hotel* 69.
7000 Stuttgart-Sonnenberg, Feuerreiterweg 32, Federal Republic of Germany.
Telephone: 763673.

Schaefers, Wolfgang Friedrich Wilhelm, DR.ING.; German engineer and executive; b. 11 Dec. 1930, Oberhausen; s. of Friedrich Schaefers and Adele (née Verhufen); m. Christel Weingarten 1954; two s.; ed. Rheinisch-Westfälische Technische Hochschule, Aachen.
Works Man. with Mannesmann AG 61-62; mem. Man. Board Verein Deutscher Eisenhüttenleute 62-64 (also currently); Technical Works Man. Rheinstahl Hüttenwerke AG 64-69; mem. Man. Board Rheinstahl AG 69-75, Spokesman 75-76, Chair. Jan. 76-; Chair.

Supervisory Board Rheinstahl Nordseewerke GmbH, Rheinstahl Schalker Verein GmbH, Rheinstahl Giesserei AG; Chair. Advisory Board Rheinstahl AG Transporttechnik; mem. one Advisory Board, four Supervisory Boards in steel industry; Cttee. or Board positions with nine firms and asscns. in steel and other sectors.
Leisure interests: sailing, hunting.
Publs. numerous publs. on technical subjects, including steel production.
Rheinstahl AG, Am Rheinstahlhaus 1, D 4300 Essen; Home: Pöppinghausstrasse 8, D 4660 Gelsenkirchen-Buer, Federal Republic of Germany.
Telephone: 0201 1063000 (Office); 0209 396581 (Office).

Schaeffer, Claude Frédéric Armand (*see* Schaeffer-Forrer, Claude).

Schaeffer, Pierre; French engineer, writer and composer; b. 14 Aug. 1910; *m.* Jacqueline de Lilsle 1963: one *d.*; ed. Ecole Polytechnique.
Director of Research, Office de Radiodiffusion-Télévision Française 59-; a leader of movement for development of musique concrète (works include *Symphonie pour un Homme Seul* and music for films); mem. Centre Nat. de la Recherche Scientifique; Assoc. Prof., Conservatoire nat. de Musique; Chevalier Légion d'Honneur, Chevalier des Palmes Académiques.
Leisure interest: philosophy.
Publs. *Amérique, nous t'ignorons* (essay) 46, *Les Enfants de coeur* (novel) 49, *A la Recherche d'une Musique concrète* 52, *Traité des Objets musicaux* 66, *La Musique concrète* 67, *Solfège de l'objet sonore* 67, *Le Gardien de Volcan* 69, *L'Avenir à reculons* 70, *Machines à communiquer* vol. I 70, vol. II 72.
13 rue des Petits-Champs, 75001 Paris, France.

Schaeffer-Forrer, Claude F. A., M.A.; French archaeologist; b. 6 March 1898, Strasbourg (Alsace), Bas Rhin; *s.* of Heinrich Schaeffer and Irma Wiernsberger; *m.* Odile Forrer 1923; one *s.* two *d.*; ed. Strasbourg and Paris Univs.
Curator Prehistoric, Roman and Early Medieval Museum, Palais Rohan, Strasbourg 21-32; Curator Coins and Medals Dept. Strasbourg Univ. 26-32; Curator French Nat. Museums 33-46; Dir. of Research at Nat. Centre of Scientific Research, Paris 46-54; Prof. Collège de France 54-69; Vice-Pres. Comm. des Fouilles, Direction des Relations Culturelles, Ministry of Foreign Affairs; Dir. expedition Ras Shamra, Syria 29-70 (discovered Canaanite alphabetic cuneiform records); Cyprus 32, 34, 35, 46, 47, 49-70, Malatya, Turkey 46, 47, 48, 50; mem. Archaeological Cttee. Min. of Educ.; Hon. Fellow St. John's Coll., Oxford; mem. Académie des Inscriptions, Inst. de France; Hon. mem. Nat. Society of Antiquaries France, Royal Acad. Denmark; corresp. mem. Belgian Royal Acad.; corresp. Fellow of British Acad.; Hon. Fellow Royal Anthropological Inst. of Great Britain and Ireland, Royal Asian Soc., etc.; Hon. mem. Deutsche Morgenländische Gesellschaft; served as Capt. Corvette with Free French Naval Forces 40-45; D.Litt. h.c. (Oxon.), D.C.L. h.c. (Glasgow); Hon. F.S.A.; Gold Medal, Soc. of Antiquaries 58, Scientific and Philological Soc., Famagusta, Cyprus 65; Hon. Citizen of Lattaquie (Syria) and Famagusta (Cyprus).
Leisure interests: travel, mountains, research in forestry.
Publs. *Haches néolitiques* 24, *Tertres funéraires préhistoriques dans la forêt de Haguenau* (2 vols.) 26, 30, *Missions en Chypre* 36, *Ugaritica I* 39, *Cuneiform Texts of Ras Shamra-Ugarit* 39, *Stratigraphie comparée et Chronologie de l'Asie occidentale* 48, *Ugaritica II* 49, *Enkomi-Alasia* 52, *Ugaritica III* 56, *IV* 61, *V* 68, *VI* 69, *VII* 76, *Alasia I* 71.

Le Castel Blanc, 16 rue Turgot, 78100 St. Germain-en-Laye; La Chaumière, 67 Fréland, Alsace; L'Escale, P.O. Box 16, 83 La Croix-Valmer, France.
Telephone: 963-4225, 97-62-14(94).

Schaetzel, John Robert; American writer and business consultant; b. 28 Jan. 1917, Holtville, Calif.; ed. Pomona Coll., California, Univ. of Mexico and Harvard Univ.
Administrative Asst., Bureau of the Budget 42; Special Asst. to Dir. of Office of Int. Trade Policy, Dept. of State 45-50; Special Asst. to Asst. Sec. of State for Econ. Affairs 50-54; Nat. War Coll. 54-55; Officer in charge of peaceful uses of atomic energy, Office of Special Asst. to Sec. for Disarmament and Atomic Energy 55-59; mem. Presidential Task Force 60-61; Special Asst. to Under-Sec. of State for Econ. Affairs 61, to Under-Sec. of State 61-62; Deputy Asst. Sec. of State for Atlantic Affairs 62-66; Amb. to European Communities 66-72, resigned; Chair. Task Force on Consultation for Trilateral Comm.; Vice-Pres. Atlantic Visitors, Johns Hopkins Bologna Center; mem. Council on Foreign Relations, N.Y.; mem. Board and Consultant Honeywell Inc.; Sr. Fellow, Woodrow Wilson on Foreign Relations; N.Y.; mem. Board and Consultant Honeywell Inc.; St. Fellow, Woodrow Wilson Fellowship Foundation; Rockefeller Public Service Award 59
Publs. *The Unhinged Alliance—America and the European Community* 75; numerous articles for many journals.
2 Bay Tree Lane, Washington, D.C. 20016, U.S.A.
Telephone: (301) 229-5316.

Schaff, Adam, PH.D.; Polish sociologist and philosopher; b. 1913, Lwów; *s.* of Maks Schaff and Ernestina Schaff de domo Felix; *m.* Anna Schaff 1935; one *d.*; ed. Lwów Univ. and Ecole des Sciences Politiques et Economiques, Paris.
Scientific work in U.S.S.R. 40-45; Prof. Łódź Univ. 45-48; Prof. of Philosophy, Warsaw Univ. 48-70; Dir. Polish United Workers' Party Inst. of Social Sciences 50-57; mem. Polish Acad. of Sciences (Chair. Philosophy Cttee. 51-68, Dir. Inst. of Philosophy and Sociology 57-68); Visiting Prof., Univ. of Vienna 69-72, Hon. Prof. of Philosophy 72-; mem. Bulgarian Acad. of Sciences; mem. Cen. Cttee. Polish United Workers' Party 59-68; mem. Exec. Cttee. Int. Fed. of Philosophical Asscns.; mem. of Int. Inst. of Philosophy, Paris; Pres. Board of Dirs. of the European Centre for Social Sciences in Vienna; Dr. h.c. Michigan Univ., Ann Arbor 67; Editor *Myśl Współczesna* (Contemporary Thought) 46-51, *Myśl Filozoficzna* (Philosophical Thought) 51-56; Dr. h.c. Sorbonne 75.
Leisure interest: tennis.
Publs. *Pojęcie i słowo* (Concept and Word) 46, *Wstęp do teorii marksizmu* (Introduction to the Theory of Marxism) 47, *Narodziny i rozwój filozofii marksistowskiej* (Birth and Development of Marxist Philosophy) 49, *Z zagadnień marksistowskiej teorii prawdy* (Some Problems of the Marxist Theory of Truth) 51, *Obiektywny Charakter Praw Historii* (The Objective Character of Historical Laws) 55, *Wstęp do Semantyki* (Introduction to Semantics) 60, *Filozofia Człowieka* (A Philosophy of Man) 62, *Język i poznanie* (Language and Cognition) 63, *Marksizm a jednostka ludzkz* (Marxism and the Human Individual) 65, *Szkice a filozofii języka* (Essays in the Philosophy of Language) 67, *Historia i Prawda* (History and Truth) 70, *Gramatyka generatywna a koncepcja wrodzonych idei* (Generative Grammar and Conception of Innate Ideas) 72, *Strukturalizm i Marksizm* (Structuralism and Marxism) 75.
Aleja I Armii W.P. 2/4, Warsaw, Poland.
Telephone: 28-18-32.

Schäffer, Bogusław; Polish composer; b. 6 June 1929, Lvov, U.S.S.R.; ed. State Higher School of Music, Jagiellonian Univ., Cracow.

Wrote first dodecaphonic music for orchestra, *Music for Strings: Nocturne* 53; Prof. State Higher School of Music, Cracow 63-; Chief Editor *Forum Musicum* 67-; G. Fitelberg Prize 59, 60, 64; A Malawski Prize 62; Minister of Culture and Arts Prize 71.

Publs. *Nowa Muzyka. Problemy współczesnej techniki kompozytorskiej* (New music. Problems of contemporary technique in composing) 58, *Klasycy dodekafonii* (Classics of dodecaphonic music) 64, *Leksykon kompozytorów XX wieku* (Lexicon of 20th century composers) 65, *W kręgu nowej muzyki* (In the sphere of new music) 67.

Ul. Kolorowe 4, 31-938 Cracow, Poland.
Telephone: 419-60.

Schaffner, Hans; Swiss lawyer and politician; b. 16 Dec. 1908; ed. Universität Bern.

Advocate 34; Sec. High Court of Berne 38-41; Lawyer to Directorate of Fed. Industry, Trade and Labour Office 38-41; Head of Cen. Office for War Econ. 41-45; Del. of Fed. Council for Trade Agreements 45-61; Dir. Div. of Commerce, Fed. Dept. of Public Economy 54-61; mem. Steering Board for Trade of OEEC 53-61; mem. Fed. Council, Head of Fed. Dept. of Public Economy 61-69; Vice-Pres. Fed. Council Jan.-Dec. 65, Pres. Jan.-Dec. 66; Vice-Chair. Sandoz Basle; Pres. Ministerial Council of Org. for Economic Co-operation and Devt. (OECD) 65; mem. UN Group on Multinationals 73; Dr. h.c. (Berne) 59.

Junkerngasse 59, Berne, Switzerland.

Schairer, George Swift, M.S.; American aircraft and missile design engineer; b. 19 May 1913, Wilkinsburg, Pa.; s. of Otto Sorg Schairer and Elizabeth Blanch Swift Schairer; m. Mary Pauline Tarbox 1935; two s. two d.; ed. Oakmont Public School, Oakmont, Pa., Summit New Jersey High School, Swarthmore Coll., Mass. Inst. of Technology, and Advanced Management Program, Hawaii Univ.

Automotive Engineer, Bendix Aviation Corpn., South Bend, Ind. 35-37; Engineer, Consolidated Vultee Aircraft Corpn., San Diego 37-39; Chief Aerodynamist, Boeing Co. 39-46, Staff Engineer (Aerodynamics and Power Plant) 46-51, Chief of Technical Staff 51-56, Asst. Chief Engineer 56-57, Dir. of Research 57-59, Vice-Pres. (Research and Devt.) 59-71, Vice-Pres. Research 71-; mem. Nat. Acad. of Sciences 68-; Hon. Fellow, American Inst. of Aeronautics and Astronautics; mem. Nat. Acad. of Engineering; mem. Int. Acad. of Astronautics; official of numerous other orgs.; Sylvanus Albert Reed Award, Inst. of Aeronautical Sciences 49; Daniel Guggenheim Medal 67; Hon. D.Eng. (Swarthmore Coll.) 58.

Leisure interests: sailing, model airplane building, photography, fine arts.

Publs. Numerous papers on aeronautics and related subjects.

Office: The Boeing Company, P.O. Box 3707, Seattle, Wash. 98124; Home: 4242 Hunts Point Road, Bellevue, Wash., U.S.A.

Schaper, Lieut.-Gen. Heye; Netherlands air force officer; b. 8 Sept. 1906, Joure; s. of Johan Schaper and Wietske van der Zee; m. T. Feenstra 1942; three s.

Sub-Lieut. Netherlands Naval Reserve 30; served with submarine and later naval aviation Holland and Dutch East Indies 38; Flying Instructor and Test Pilot, Holland 40; evacuated to England and served as pilot in R.A.F. 40-42; prisoner of war 42-45; Commanding Officer, Netherlands Naval Air Service, Dutch East Indies 45-46; Head of naval aviation, Ministry of Navy, Holland 46-49; Rear-Adm. and Flag Officer Air, Royal Netherlands Navy 49; transferred to Royal Netherlands Air Force as Deputy Chief of Staff, in rank of Major-Gen. 54; Chief of Staff, Royal Netherlands Air Force Lieut.-Gen. 56-61; Chair. Joint Chiefs of Staff 57-59; Chief of the Mil. House of H.M. Queen Juliana 62; Sec. of State for Air 66-67; Chief of the Mil. House of H.M. Queen Juliana 67-; Willemsorde and D.F.C.; Chancellor, Netherlands Orders of Knighthood 59-.

Leisure interests: sailing, game-shooting.

Noordeinde 68, The Hague, Netherlands.
Telephone: 070-630206.

Scharf, Kurt Franz Wilhelm, TH.D., D.D.; German ecclesiastic; b. 21 Oct. 1902, Landsberg/Warthe; s. of Johannes Scharf and Margarethe Rüdel; m. 1st Ingeborg Sommerwerck 1928 (died 1929), 2nd Renate Scharf 1933; one s. four d.; ed. Tübingen, Jena and Halle/Saale Univs.

Pastor Friesack 28, Sachsenhausen 33; Präses Brotherhood of Brandenburg Confessional Churches 35; Chair. Conf. of Brotherhoods of Confessional Churches in Germany 37; several times arrested and forbidden to preach and publish by Nazi regime; Präses Brandenburg Confessional Synod 35; Provost Berlin-Brandenburg Province 45; Chair. Utd. Evangelical Church 55, Dep. Chair. 61-; Chair. Evangelical Church in Germany 61-67; Bishop of Berlin-Brandenburg (Evangelical Church) 66-; Vice-Pres. United World Bible Soc. 66-69; mem. Cen. Cttee. World Council of Churches 68-; Publisher *Rundbriefe der Bekennenden Kirche* 33-45 (illegal 35-45); Hon. Th.D. Humboldt Univ. Berlin; Hon. D.D. Eden Seminary Webster Groves (Mass.); Buber-Rosenzweig Medal, Jüdisch-Christlicher Koordinierungsrat.

Leisure interest: chess.

Bachstrasse 1-2, Berlin 21, Federal Republic of Germany.

Telephone: 3991-1.

Scharrer, Berta Vogel, PH.D.; American professor of anatomy; b. 1 Dec. 1906, Munich, Germany; d. of Karl Vogel and Johanna Greis; m. Dr. Ernst Albert Scharrer 1934 (deceased); ed. Univ. of Munich.

Research Assoc., Univ. of Frankfurt Neurological Inst. 34-37, Univ. of Chicago, U.S. 37-38, Rockefeller Inst. 38-40, Western Reserve Univ., Cleveland, Ohio 40-46; Asst. Prof. (Research) and John Simon Guggenheim Fellow, Univ. of Colorado 46-54; Prof. Albert Einstein Coll. of Medicine, N.Y. 55-; mem. Nat. Acad. of Sciences, American Acad. of Arts and Sciences, Deutsche Akad. der Naturforscher Leopoldina, Royal Netherlands Acad. of Arts and Sciences.

Leisure interests: music, reading.

Publs. *Neuroendocrinology* (with E. Scharrer) 63; and other publications in the fields of comparative neuroendocrinology and neurosecretion.

Department of Anatomy, Albert Einstein College of Medicine, 1300 Morris Park Avenue, Bronx, N.Y. 10461, U.S.A.

Telephone: 212-430-2835.

Schaum, Gustav, DR. PHIL.; German chemist; b. 6 Jan. 1908, Marburg/Lahn; s. of Dr. Karl Schaum and Eleonore Schaum (née Winter); m. Erna Traumüller 1934; one s. one d.; ed. Gymnasium, Giessen, and Univs. of Marburg, Vienna, Munich and Giessen.

Entered AGFA-Photofabrik 33; Chair. Management Board AGFA A.G. 60-, Pres. Supervisory Board of AGFA-Gevaert A.G. Vice-Pres. Supervisory Board AGFA-Gevaert N.V., Chair. Management Board of AGFA-Gevaert A.G. 64; Hon. Prof., Univ. of Bonn; Hon. Fellow, Univ. of Bonn; Hon. mem. numerous Socs.; Gold Medal of Vienna Photographic Soc.

AGFA-Gevaert A.G., 5090 Leverkusen-Bayerwerk, 62 Wiesbaden, Gluckstrasse 10, Federal Republic of Germany.

Telephone: 02172-30-5676 (Office); 06121-525544 (Home).

Schaus, Eugène, DR.JUR.; Luxembourg lawyer and politician; b. 11 May 1901; ed. Univs. of Brussels, Berlin, and Paris.

Lawyer 25-; Pres. Corpn. of Barristers; Minister of the Interior, of Justice and of Physical Education 45-51, Deputy Prime Minister and Minister of Foreign Affairs and Defence 59-66; Deputy Prime Minister, Minister of Justice, of Interior, of Armed Forces 69-74; mem. Council of Europe 51-; mem. Assembly Coal and Steel Community 51-58, of European Parl. 58-.

Grande rue 56, Luxembourg.

Schaus, Lambert, D. EN D.; Luxembourg lawyer and politician; b. 1908.

Legal practice in Luxembourg 32-52; mem. Luxembourg City Council 36-40; deported by occupying power to Germany 40-45; mem. Constituent Assembly, Chief Alderman, City of Luxembourg 46; Sec. Christian Social Party 46; Minister of Supply and Economic Affairs 46-48, of Armed Forces 47-48; mem. Council of State 48-53; Minister to Belgium 52-55, Amb. 55-58; mem. European Economic Community Comm. 58-67; Perm. Rep. to NATO Council 67-73, also Amb. to Belgium.

8 rue des Girondins, Luxembourg.

Schawlow, Arthur Leonard, M.A., PH.D., LL.D., D.SC.; American professor of physics; b. 5 May 1921, Mount Vernon, N.Y.; s. of Arthur and Helen (Mason) Schawlow; m. Aurelia Keith Townes 1951; one s. two d.; ed. Univ. of Toronto.

Postdoctoral Fellow and Research Assoc., Columbia Univ. 49-51; Research Physicist, Bell Telephone Laboratories 51-61; Visiting Assoc. Prof., Columbia Univ. 60; Prof. of Physics, Stanford Univ. 61-, Chair. Dept. of Physics 66-70; Dir. Optical Soc. of America 66-69, Pres. 75; mem. Council, American Physical Soc. 66-70, Chair. Div. of Electron and Atomic Physics 74-; mem. Nat. Acad. of Sciences; Fellow, American Acad. of Arts and Sciences; Thomas Young Medal and Prize (Inst. of Physics and Physical Soc. U.K.), Ballantine Medal (Franklin Inst.), Liebmann Prize (Inst. of Electrical and Electronic Engineers), Calif. Scientist of the Year 73, Geffrey Frew Fellowship (Australian Acad. of Sciences) 73; hon. doctorates from Univs. of Ghent, Toronto, Bradford.

Leisure interest: jazz music.

Publs. *Microwave Spectroscopy* (with C. H. Townes) 55, and over 100 scientific papers.

Department of Physics, Stanford University, Stanford, Calif. 94305; Home: 849 Esplanada Way, Stanford, Calif. 94305, U.S.A.

Scheel, Walter; German politician; b. 8 July 1919, Solingen; m. Dr. Mildred Scheel 1969; two s. two d.; ed. Reform-Gymnasium, Solingen.

Served German Air Force, World War II; fmr. head of market research org.; fmr. mem. Landtag North Rhine-Westphalia; mem. Bundestag 53-74, Vice-Pres. 67-69; Fed. Minister for Econ. Co-operation 61-66; Chair. of Free Democrats 68-74; Vice-Chancellor, Minister of Foreign Affairs 69-74; Pres. Fed. Repub. of Germany July 74-.

Leisure interest: modern art.

Publs. *Konturen einer neuen Welt* 65, *Formeln deutscher Politik* 68, *Warum Mitbestimmung und wie* 70, *Die Freiburger Thesen der Liberalen* (with K.-H. Flach and W. Maihofer) 72, *Bundestagreden* 72, *Reden und Interviews* 72.

Villa Hammerschmidt, Bonn, Federal Republic of Germany.

Scheele, Leonard Andrew, A.B., M.D.; American physician; b. 25 July 1907, Fort Wayne, Ind.; s. of Martin F. Scheele and Minnie C. Vogely; m. Frances K. McCormick 1929; one s. two d.; ed. Michigan and Wayne Univs.

Various appointments in United States Public Health Service, Surgeon-General 48-56; Pres. Warner Chilcott Laboratories 56-60; Senior Vice-Pres. Warner-Lambert Co. 60-72, Dir. 57-62, 63-68; Pres. Warner-Lambert Research Inst. 65-68; served in Second World War, holding assignments in military govt. and civil affairs in Africa, Italy, and later in N.W. Europe 43-45.

Leisure interests: photography, gardening, travel.

700 New Hampshire Avenue, N.W., Washington, D.C. 20037, U.S.A.

Telephone: 202-338-2273.

Schell, Maximilian; Swiss actor; b. 8 Dec. 1930, Vienna; s. of Hermann Ferdinand Schell and Margarete Noe von Nordberg; ed. Humanistiches Gymnasium, Basle, Freies Gymnasium, Zürich, and Univs. of Zürich, Basle and Munich.

Corporal, Swiss Army 48-49; various appearances on stage in Switzerland and Germany 52-55; German debut in *Children, Mothers and the General* 55; American film debut in *Young Lions* 57, on Broadway stage in *Interlock* 58; Critics Award (Broadway) 58; New York Critics Award 61; Golden Globe Award 61; Acad. Award 61, 70; Silver Award San Sebastian 70; Bundesfilmpreis 70; Film Critics' Award, Chicago 73; Golden Globe 74; Goldene Schale 74, Silver Shell San Sebastian 75.

Principal films acted in: *Judgment at Nuremberg* 61, *Five Finger Exercise* 61, *Reluctant Saint* 62, *Condemned of Altona* 62, *Topkapi* 64, *Return from the Ashes* 65, *Beyond the Mountains* 66, *The Deadly Affair* 66, *Counterpoint* 66, *Krakatoa, East of Java* 67, *The Castle* 68, *First Love* 69, *Pope Joan* 71, *Paulina 1880* 71, *The Pedestrian* 73, *The Odessa File* 74, *The Man in a Glass Booth, Assassination* 75; Producer, Dir. *First Love* 69, Dir. *End of the Game* 75.

Principal plays acted in: *Hamlet, Prince of Homburg, Mannerhouse, Don Carlos, Sappho* (Durrell), *A Patriot for Me, The Twins of Venice, Old Times*; Dir. *All for the Best, A Patriot for Me, Hamlet, Pygmalion, La Traviata* 75.

Office: c/o William Morris Agency, New York City, U.S.A.; Home: Keplerstrasse 2, 8 Munich 80, Federal Republic of Germany.

Telephone: 089-478577 (Home).

Schelle, Carel Jan van, LL.D.; Netherlands diplomatist; b. 26 Aug. 1913, Wassenaar; m. Elsie R. Headde; ed. Leyden Univ.

Joined Ministry of Foreign Affairs 40; dismissed by occupation authorities 41; served with the Ministry of Foreign Affairs 45-46; attached to Netherlands Embassy, Paris 46-50; mem. Netherlands delegation to Indonesian-Dutch negotiations 48-50; Head Political Section, Netherlands High Commissioner's Office, Jakarta 50-54; NATO Defence Coll., Paris 54-55; Counsellor, Netherlands Embassy, Ottawa 55-58; Minister Plenipotentiary and Head Financial and Econ. Section, Netherlands Del. to NATO, Paris 58-61; Head European Div., Ministry of Foreign Affairs 61-63, Head of Personnel 63-69; Private Sec. to T.R.H. Princess Beatrix and Prince Claus of the Netherlands 65-66 and temporarily attached to H.R.H. Princess Beatrix during two world tours; Amb. to Belgium 69-; Commdr. Order of the House of Orange; Knight Order of the Netherlands Lion; Officer Order of Orange Nassau; Grand Officer Order of Merit, Luxembourg; Grand Cross of Merit Order of Merit of the Fed. Repub. of Germany; Officer Légion d'Honneur.

Royal Netherlands Embassy, 35 rue de la Science, 1040 Brussels, Belgium.

Telephone: 5113960.

Schelling, Friedrich Wilhelm Eugen Eberhard von; German banker; b. 3 May 1906, Berlin; s. of Ulrich and Lina (von Jagemann) von Schelling, great-grandson of F. W. J. von Schelling, philosopher (1775-1854); m. Hildegard Oelkers 1932; one s. one d.; ed. Kaiserin

Augusta Gymnasium, Berlin and Univs. of Heidelberg and Berlin.
Judge, Berlin 31-32; Reichsbank, Berlin 32-45; Reichsbankdirektor, Hamburg 46-48; Bank deutscher Länder, Frankfurt (Main) 48-57; Pres. of Landeszentralbank of Free and Hanseatic City of Hamburg 57-74.
Kaspar-Ohm-Weg 16, 2 Hamburg-Wellingsbüttel, Federal Republic of Germany.
Telephone: 5-36-11-90 (Home).

Schelsky, Helmut, DR. PHIL.; German sociologist; b. 14 Oct. 1912; ed. Univs. of Königsberg and Leipzig. Privatdozent of Philosophy and Sociology, Univ. of Königsberg; Assoc. Prof., Univ. of Strasbourg 43-44; German Red Cross and journalism 44-48; Prof. of Sociology, Akademie für Gemeinwirtschaft, Hamburg 48-53; Prof. of Sociology, Univ. of Münster and Dir. Sozialforschungstelle, Dortmund.
Publs. *Arbeitslosigheit und Berufsnot der Jugend* (2 vols.) 53, *Wandlungen der deutschen Familie in der Gegenwart, Aufgaben und Grenzen der Betriebssoziologie* 54, *Arbeiterjugend gestern und heute* 55, *Soziologie der Sexualität* 55, *Die sozialen Folgen der Automatisierung* 57, *Schule und Erziehung in der industriellen Gesellschaft* 57, *Die skeptische Generation* 57, *Ortsbestimmung der deutschen Soziologie* 59, *Die soziale Idee der deutschen Universität* 60, *Anpassung oder Widerstand?* 61, *Der Mensch in der wissenschaftlichen Zivilisation* 61, *Einsamkeit und Freiheit, Idee und Gestalt der deutschen Universität und ihrer Reformen* 63, *Auf der Suche nach Wirklichkeit* 65, *Grundzüge einer neuen Universität* 66, *Abschied von der Hochschulpolitik* 69, *Zur Theorie der Institution* 70, *Friede auf Zeit, die Zukunft der Olympischen Spiele* 73, *Systemüberwindung, Demokratisierung und Gewaltenteilung*, 3rd edn. 73, *Die Arbeit tun die Anderen, Klassenkampf über Priesterherrschaft der Intellektuellen* 75.
Pleistermühlenweg 101, Münster/Westf. 44, Federal Republic of Germany.

Schenck, Michael U. R. von, DR. IUR.; Swiss diplomatist; b. 21 April 1931, Basle; s. of Dr. Ernst von Schenck and Selma Oettinger; m. Annagret Nussbaumer 1967; ed. Humanistisches Gymnasium and Univ., Basle, and in Lausanne.
Swiss Trade Fair 50-55; *Die Woche* 50-55; Swiss Foreign Ministry 57-67, Del. to OECD 58, Del. to UN 59-61, UN Narcotics Conf. 61, Swiss Technical Assistance Authority 61-67; Founder and Dir. Swiss Volunteers for Devt. 62-67; Sec.-Gen. Int. Secr. for Volunteer Service (ISVS) 67-71; Harvard Univ. 72-73; Rep. to IAEA and UNIDO, Swiss Embassy, Vienna, 73-.
Leisure interests: skiing, hiking.
Publs. *Der Statutenwechsel im internationalen Obligationenrecht* 55, *Volunteer Manpower for Development* 67, *Conferencia Regional sobre Servicio Voluntario* 68, *An International Peace Corps* 68, *Youth Today* 68, *Youth's Role in Development* 68, *International Volunteer Service* 69.
Embassy of Switzerland, Prinz Eugen Strasse, Vienna, Austria.

Schendel, Arthur F. E. Van, PH.D.; Netherlands museum director; b. 18 May 1910, Ede; s. of Arthur van Schendel (author); m. J. E. Reesink 1941; two s. two d.; ed. High School, Florence, Italy, and Univ. of Paris.
Assistant, Dept. of Paintings, Rijksmuseum, Amsterdam 35, later Curator and Dir. of Dept., Gen. Dir., Rijksmuseum 59-; Pres. Int. Inst. for the Conservation of Historic and Artistic Works 61-64; Pres. Int. Council of Museums 65-72; has published articles on Rembrandt in *Oud-Holland*, etc.
Publs. *Le Dessin en Lombardie jusqu'au 15ème siècle* 38, *G. H. Breitner* 39, *The Rijksmuseum* 66.
Rijksmuseum, Stadhouderskade 42, Amsterdam; Home: Vossiusstraat 44, Amsterdam, Netherlands.
Telephone: 79-22-21 (Home).

Scheraga, Harold A., PH.D.; American professor of chemistry; b. 18 Oct. 1921, Brooklyn, N.Y.; s. of Samuel and Etta Scheraga; m. Miriam Kurnow 1943; one s. two d.; ed. City Coll. of New York and Duke Univ.
American Chemical Soc. Postdoctoral Fellow, Harvard Medical School 46-47; Instructor of Chem., Cornell Univ. 47-50, Asst. Prof. 50-53, Assoc. Prof. 53-58, Prof. 58-, Todd Prof. 65-, Chair. Chem. Dept. 60-67; Guggenheim Fellow and Fulbright Research Scholar, Carlsberg Lab., Copenhagen 56-57, Weizmann Inst., Rehovoth, Israel 63; Nat. Inst. of Health Special Fellow, Weizman Inst., Rehovoth, Israel 70; Visiting Lecturer, Wool Research Labs., C.S.I.R.O., Australia Dec. 59; mem. Nat. Acad. of Sciences, American Acad. of Arts and Sciences; Vice-Chair. Cornell Section, American Chemical Soc. 54-55, Chair. 55-56, Councillor 59-62; mem. Advisory Panel in Molecular Biology, Nat. Science Foundation 60-62; mem. Editorial Board numerous scientific journals; mem. Biochem. Training Cttee., Nat. Insts. of Health 63-65; mem. Comm. on Molecular Biophysics, Int. Union for Pure and Applied Biophysics 67-69; mem. Comm. on Macromolecular Biophysics, Int. Union for Pure and Applied Biophysics 69-75, Pres. 72-75; mem. Comm. on Subcellular and Macromolecular Biophysics, Int. Union for Pure and Applied Biophysics 75- (78); mem. Exec. Comm., Div. of Biological Chem., American Chemical Soc. 66-69; Vice-Chair. Div. of Biological Chem., American Chemical Soc. 70, Chair. 71; mem. Council Biophysical Soc. 67-70; mem. Research Career Award Cttee. Nat. Inst. of Health 67-71; mem. Board of Governors, Weizmann Inst., Rehovoth, Israel 70-; Eli Lilly Award in Biochem. 57; Welch Foundation Lecturer 62; Harvey Lecturer 68; Gallagher Lecturer 68-69; Hon. Sc.D. (Duke Univ.) 61; Townsend Harris Award C.C.N.Y. 70; Nichols Medal, N.Y. Section, American Chem. Soc. 74.
Leisure interests: golf, skiing.
Publs. *Protein Structure* 61, *Theory of Helix-Coil Transitions in Biopolymers* 70; 400 articles; research on physical chem. of proteins and other macromolecules; structure of water; chemistry of blood clotting.
Department of Chemistry, Cornell University, Ithaca, N.Y. 14853; Home: 212 Homestead Terrace, Ithaca, N.Y. 14850, U.S.A.
Telephone: 607-256-4034 (Office); 607-272-5155 (Home).

Scherer, H.E. Cardinal Vicente; Brazilian ecclesiastic; b. 5 Feb. 1903, Bom Princípio, Rio Grande do Sul; s. of Pedro Scherer and Ana Oppermann Scherer; ed. primary school, Seminário Central de São Leopoldo and Pontifical Gregorian Univ., Rome.
Ordained priest in Rome 26; Private Sec. to Archbishop of Pôrto Alegre 27-33; organizer of Parishes of Tapes and Barra do Ribeiro 33-35; Paris Priest, São Geraldo, Pôrto Alegre 35-46; Auxiliary Bishop of Pôrto Alegre 46; Archbishop of Pôrto Alegre 46-; cr. Cardinal 69.
Residência Arquiepiscopal, Rua Espírito Santo 95, Pôrto Alegre, Rio Grande do Sul, Brazil.

Scherger, Air Chief Marshal Sir Frederick Rudolph Williams, K.B.E., C.B., D.S.O., A.F.C.; Australian air force officer; b. 18 May 1904, Ararat, Victoria; s. of Frederick Hermann Scherger and Sarah Jane Chamberlain; m. Thelma L. Harricks 1929 (deceased); one d.; ed. Royal Mil. Coll., Duntroon.
Transferred to R.A.A.F. 24; Flying Instructor 25-34 and Chief Flying Instructor 34-39, Point Cook; R.A.A.F. Chief Test Pilot 39; Dir. of Training 38-40; A.O.C. New Guinea 43-44; Task Force Commdr. Allied Air Forces in attacks and landings at Aitape and Noemfoor; A.O.C. First Tactical Air Force, New Guinea 45; attended Imperial Defence Coll. 46; Deputy Chief of Air Staff 47-51; Head, Australian Joint Services Staff, Washington 51-52; loaned to R.A.F. as A.O.C. Malaya 52-54; Air mem. for Personnel 54-57; Chief of Air Staff,

R.A.A.F. 57-60; Chair. Chiefs of Staff Cttee. 60-66; Chair. Australian Nat. Airlines Comm. 66-75, Constructors John Brown (Aust.), Mono Pumps (Aust.); Dir. ICL (Aust.), Plessey Pacific, Mutual Acceptance, Assoc. Broadcasting Services.
Leisure interests: golf, shooting.
45 Stephens Street, North Balwyn, 3104 Vic., Australia.

Schermerhorn, W.; Netherlands politician; b. 17 Dec. 1894, Schermeer; s. of Teun Schermerhorn and Tryntje Honig; m. Barbara Rook 1909; three s. one d.; ed. Delft Technical Univ.
Assistant Prof. Heuvelink until 26; Prof. in Surveying, Levelling and Geodesy at Delft Univ. 26; instituted the "Geodetisch Bureau" (Inst. of Geodesy) 23; surveying-Adviser to Public Works and management of "Meetkundige Dienst" (Surveying Service) 31; consultant to K.L.M. (Royal Dutch Airlines); introduced aerial photogrammetry into Holland; Sec. of State Committee of Geodesy; Chair. Int. Society for Photogrammetry 38-48; Chair. anti-Fascist Organization E.D.D. (Eenheid door Democratie) until May 10th 40; during German occupation spent considerable time in hostage camp; played important part in Netherlands Resistance Movement; Chair. "Nederlandsche Volksbeweging"; Prime Minister and Minister for the Co-ordination of the War Effort June 45-46; Chair. Gen. Comm. for the Netherlands Indies Sept. 46-Nov. 47; mem. of Parliament 48-51; mem. of the Senate 51-63; Dean, Int. Training Centre for Aerial Survey, Delft 51-65; Dr. h.c. (Ghent) 46, (Zürich) 63, (Milan) 64, (Glasgow) 65, (Hanover) 67.
Leisure interests: political and religious literature, sailing, farming.
Zandvoorter Allee 304, Haarlem, Netherlands.
Telephone: 023-287259.

Scherrer-Bylund, Paul, PH.D.; Swiss librarian; b. 18 Aug. 1900, St. Gallen; s. of Gustav Hermann Scherrer and Sophie Gehrig; m. 1st Tamara Wintsch 1929, 2nd Barbro Bylund 1963; two s. one d.; ed. Univs. of Munich, Berlin and Glasgow.
Asst. Librarian, Univ. Library of Basle 28-31, Librarian 31-47; Chief Librarian, Library of Swiss Fed. Inst. of Technology, Zürich 47-52, Dir. 53-62; Dir. Central Library, Zürich Univ. 63-71; fmr. Vice-Pres. Swiss Asscn. of Librarians and fmr. Pres. Swiss Soc. of Bibliophiles; fmr. Pres. Gottfried-Keller-Gesellschaft; Hon. mem. Int. Asscn. Bibliophily, Swiss Soc. of Bibliophiles, Naturforschende Gesellschaft, Zürich; Award of Kulturförderungskommission, Zurich 73.
Leisure interest: book-collecting.
Publs. include *Thomas Murners Verhältnis zum Humanismus, untersucht auf Grund seiner "Reformatio poetarum"* 29, *Zwei neue Schriften Thomas Murners* 29, *Zum Kampfmotiv bei Thomas Murner* 35, *Erasmus im Spiegel von Thomas Murners Reformationspublizistik* 36, *Die Toten in der deutschen Lyrik zweier Weltkriege* 44, *Sub aeternitatis specie* 53, *Vom Werden und von den Aufgaben der Bibliotheken technischer Hochschulen* 55, *Die Gründung des Eidg. Polytechnicums und das schweizerische Nationalbewusstsein* 55, *Bibliotheken und Bibliothekare als Träger kultureller Aufgaben* 56, *Epigonen-Angst* 57, *Vornehmheit, Illusion und Wirklichkeit als Grundmotive des "Felix Krull"* 58, *Bruchstücke der Buddenbrooks-Urhandschrift* 58, *Die Bibliothek des deutschen Patentamtes und die kulturellen Aufgaben technischer Bibliotheken* 59, *Aus Thomas Manns Vorarbeiten zu den Buddenbrooks* 59, *Thomas Manns Mutter liefert Rezepte für die Buddenbrooks* 59, *Thomas Mann und die Wirklichkeit* 60, *Ueber den Sinn des Thomas Mann Archivs* 61, *Von der Macht und der Sendung des Buchdrucks* 61, *Die Zeit im bibliothekarischen Beruf* 65, *Die Stellung des Bibliothekars in der modernen Gesellschaft* 67, *Schweizerische Gesichtspunkte zum Problem der Universal-*

bibliothek 67, *Tradition und Technik in den Bibliotheken* 68, *Gottfried Keller und die Buchillustration* 72.
Home: Beckhammer 32, Zürich 8057, Switzerland.
Telephone: 01-28-27-10.

Scheyven, Baron Louis Maurice Emile Marie; Belgian diplomatist; b. 13 Dec. 1904; ed. Louvain Univ.
Held diplomatic posts in Cairo 31-34, Berlin 35, Peking 37, Cairo 42-44, Counsellor in Paris 44; Belgian rep. on Allied High Comm., Bonn; Head of Belgian Mil. Mission, Berlin 49-51; Head Political Dept. Ministry Foreign Affairs 51-53, Sec.-Gen. with rank of Ambassador 53-59; Ambassador to U.S.A. 59-70; Grand Officier Ordre de Léopold II, Ordre de la Couronne, Grand Officer, Order of the Nile, of the Légion d'Honneur, of the Couronne de Chêne (Luxembourg), and of the Order of Orange-Nassau; Grand Commdr., Order of the Aztec Eagle (2nd Class) (Mexico); Grand Cross, 2nd Class, Order of Merit of the German Federal Republic, Grand Cross Nat. Order of Southern Cross (Brazil), etc.
Ministry of Foreign Affairs, Brussels, Belgium.

Scheyven, Raymond, D. en D.; Belgian politician; b. 1911, Brussels; ed. Univ. Catholique de Louvain.
Former lawyer and company exec.; Social-Christian Deputy 46-; Minister of Econ. Affairs 58; Minister without Portfolio in charge of Econ. and Financial Affairs of Belgian Congo and Rwanda-Urundi 59-60; Minister of Co-operation for Devt. 68-71; Chair. UN Econ. and Social Council 69-70.
Chambre des Deputés, Brussels, Belgium.

Schieder, Theodor, DR. PHIL.; German historian; b. 11 April 1908, Oettingen, Bavaria; s. of Heinrich Schieder and Marga (née Autenrieth); m. Eva Rogalsky 1934; three s. one d.; ed. Gymnasium bei St. Anna, Augsburg, and Univs. of Munich and Berlin.
Dozent in History, Univ. of Königsberg 40-42, Prof. of History 42-45; Guest Prof., Univ. of Cologne 47-48, Prof. of Medieval and Modern History, Univ. of Cologne 48-; mem. Acad. of Sciences and Literature, Mainz, Bavarian Acad. of Sciences, Munich, Rhine-Westphalia Acad. of Sciences, Düsseldorf; Kongel Danske Videnskabernes Selskab Copenhagen; Pres. of Historical Comm. of Bavarian Acad. of Sciences, Munich; Grosses Verdienstkreuz der Bundesrepublik Deutschland mit Stern; Orden pour le Mérite für Wissenschaften und Künste.
Publs. *Staat und Gesellschaft im Wandel unserer Zeit* 58, 70, *Das Deutsche Kaiserreich von 1871 als Nationalstaat* 61, *Begegnungen mit der Geschichte* 62, *Nietzsche und Bismarch* 63, *Der Nationalstaat in Europa als historisches Phänomen* 64, *Geschichte als Wissenschaft* 65, 68, *Handbuch der Europäischen Geschichte* (Ed.), Vol. VI 68, Vol. IV 68, Vol. III 71, *Zum Problem des Staatenpluralismus in der modernen Welt* 69, *Reichsgründung 1870-71* 70, *Hermann Rauschnings "Gespräche mit Hitler" als Geschichtsquelle* 72, Editor *Historische Zeitschrift*.
5000 Köln 41 (Lindenthal), Gyrhofstrasse 21, Federal Republic of Germany.
Telephone: 415820.

Schiff, Dorothy; American newspaper publisher; b. 11 March 1903; ed. Bryn Mawr Coll.
Editor-in-Chief and publisher *New York Post*, owner 39-; French Legion of Honour 47.
New York Post, 75 West Street, New York 6, N.Y., U.S.A.

Schiff, Emile Louis Constant; Netherlands diplomatist; b. 2 March 1918; ed. Rijksuniversiteit, Leiden.
Second Sec., Washington 45-49; Second, later First Sec., Madrid 49-52; Private Sec. to Ministers of Foreign Affairs, The Hague 52-54; Counsellor, Perm. Mission to UN 55-59; Minister, Washington 59-64; Ambassador to Indonesia 65-68; Sec.-Gen. Ministry of Foreign

Affairs 68-; Knight, Order of Netherlands Lion and many foreign awards.
Leisure interest: golf.
Ministry of Foreign Affairs, The Hague, Netherlands.
Telephone: 614941.

Schiffer, Menahem Max, PH.D.; American professor of mathematics; b. 24 Sept. 1911, Berlin, Germany; s. of Chaim Schiffer and Miriam née Alpern; m. Fanya Rabinovics 1937; one d.; ed. Oberrealschule, Berlin, Berlin Univ. and Hebrew Univ., Jerusalem.
Junior Asst., Hebrew Univ., Jerusalem 34-38, Senior Asst. 38-43, Lecturer 43-46; Visiting Lecturer, Harvard Univ. 46-49, Princeton Univ. 49-50; Prof., Hebrew Univ., Jerusalem 50-51; Prof. of Mathematics, Stanford Univ. 51-; mem. Nat. Acad. of Sciences, American Acad. of Arts and Sciences; Foreign mem. Finnish Acad. of Sciences 75; Hon. D.Sc. (Israel Inst. of Technology) 73.
Leisure interests: history, philosophy, rare books, walking, travel.
Publs. Co-author: *Kernel Functions in Mathematical Physics* 53, *Functionals of Finite Riemann Surfaces* 54, *Introduction to General Relativity* 65; numerous articles in mathematical journals.
3748 Laguna Avenue, Palo Alto, Calif. 94306, U.S.A.
Telephone: 415-493-9154.

Schiller, Karl, DR. RER. POL.; German economist and politician; b. 24 April 1911, Breslau; ed. Univs. of Kiel, Frankfurt/M., Berlin and Heidelberg.
University Asst., Heidelberg 34-35; Head of Research Group, Inst. for World Econs., Kiel 35-41; Army Service 41-45; Visiting Prof. Univ. of Kiel 45-46; Prof. of Econs., Dir. of Social Econ. Seminars and Inst. for Foreign Trade and Overseas Commerce, Univ. of Hamburg 47-, Rector, Univ. of Hamburg 56-58; mem. Council of Scientific Advisers, Fed. Ministry of Econs. 47-; mem. Council of Scientific Advisers, Fed. Ministry of Econ. Co-operation 63-66; Senator for Econs., Hamburg 48-53, Berlin 61-65; mem. Bundesrat 49-53; Deputy Chair. Econ. Cttee., Exec. Cttee. of Social Democrat Party (S.P.D.) 62-64, Chair. 64-72, mem. Exec. Cttee. S.P.D. 64-72, mem. Presidium 66-72, mem. Bundestag, Deputy Chair. and Econ. Spokesman of S.P.D. Parl. Group 65-; Fed. Minister of Econs. 66-71, of Econs. and Finance 71-72; Pres. Econ. Devt. of Equatorial and Southern Africa (EDESA) 73-.
Publs. *Aufgaben und Versuche: Zur neuen Ordnung von Wirtschaft und Gesellschaft* 53, *Der Ökonom und die Gesellschaft: Das freiheitliche und soziale Element in der Wirtschaftspolitik* 64, *Berliner Wirtschaft und deutsche Politik, Reden und Aufsätze 1961-1964* 64, *Reden zur Wirtschafts- und Finanzpolitik* 66, *Aufgeklärte Marktwirtschaft-Kollektive Vernunft in Politik und Wirtschaft* 69; numerous economic and political articles.
Am Klostergarten 1, 53 Bonn-Endenich, Federal Republic of Germany.

Schilpp, Paul Arthur, M.A., B.D., PH.D.; American (German-born) university professor, philosopher and writer; b. 1897, Dillenburg, Hessen; s. of the Rev. Hermann and Emilie (Dittmar) Schilpp; m. E. Madelon Golden 1950; one s. one d.; ed. Bayreuth Gymnasium, Baldwin-Wallace Coll. (Ohio), Northwestern Univ., Garrett Theol. Seminary, Evanston, and Stanford Univ.
Professor of Psychology and Religious Education, Coll. of Puget Sound 22-23, Prof. of Philosophy, Coll. of the Pacific 23-34; Lecturer, Associate Prof. and (since 50) Prof. of Philosophy, Northwestern Univ. 36-65, Emeritus 65-; Distinguished Visiting Prof. of Philosophy, Southern Ill. Univ., Carbondale 65-; Visiting Professor, Ohio State Univ. 31, Univ. of Munich 48, Pacific Philosophy Inst. 54; Founder, Pres. and Editor Library of Living Philosophers; Watumull Foundation

Research Fellowship for India 50-51; Pres. American Philosophical Asscn. (Western Div.) 58-59; Distinguished Service Medal of Chicago Area Phi Beta Kappa chapters 74; Hon. Litt.D. (Baldwin-Wallace Coll.); Hon. L.H.D. (Springfield Coll., Kent State Univ., Ohio) 75.
Leisure interests: travel, music.
Publs. *Do We Need a New Religion?* 29, *Kant's Pre-Critical Ethics* 38, *The Quest for Religious Realism* 38, *Lamentations on Christmas* 45, *Human Nature and Progress* 54, *The Crisis in Science and Education* 63; Editor and Contributor *Higher Education Faces the Future* 30, *Theology and Modern Life* 40, *Library of Living Philosophers* (14 vols. so far published), *The Student Seeks an Answer* 60, *New Frontiers of Christianity* 62, *In Albert Schweitzer's Realms* 62, *Religion Ponders Science* 64, *The World of Philosophy* (Pakistan) 66, *The Critique of War* 69, *Value and Valuation* 72.
9 Hillcrest Drive, Carbondale, Ill.; and Department of Philosophy, Southern Illinois University, Carbondale, Ill. 62901, U.S.A.
Telephone: 618-536-6641 (Office); 618-549-6335 (Home).

Schiöttz-Christensen, Alf Krabbe, B.A., B.LITT.; Danish journalist; b. 12 Feb. 1909, Nörresundby; s. of Lauritz Alexander Schiöttz-Christensen and Thora Anna Krabbe; m. 1st Ebba Jorgensen 1944 (died 1964), 2nd Inger Larsen 1967; ed. Univ. of Copenhagen and Columbia Univ.
On staff of *Seattle Times* 31; Corresp. to Danish newspapers, League of Nations 32-33; Editorial Staff, *Aalborg Stiftstidende* newspaper 33, Dir., Chief Editor 40-, Publr. 50-; Dir. Aalborg Stiftsbogtrykkeri (printing works) 40-; Pres. Nordjyske Distriktsaviser 75; Vice-Pres. Danish Newspaper Publishers Asscn.; mem. Exec. Cttee. Fed. Int. des Editeurs de Journaux (FIEJ) 61, Vice-Pres. 74-; mem. Exec. Cttee. Int. Newspaper and Colour Asscn.—FIEJ Inst. 69, Treas. 75; several foreign decorations.
Leisure interest: aviation.
Aalborg Stiftstidende, 7 Nytorv, 9100, Aalborg, Denmark.
Telephone: 08-12-58-00 (Office); 08-12-57-92 (Home).

Schiotz, Fredrik Axel, TH.M., TH.D., D.D., LL.D., LITT.D., L.H.D., J.C.D.; American ecclesiastic; b. 15 June 1901, Chicago; s. of Jacob Schiotz and Stina Akerholt; m. Dagny Aasen 1928; three s. one d.; ed. St. Olaf Coll., Northfield, Minnesota, and Luther Theological Seminary, St. Paul, Minnesota.
Pastor Lutheran congregations 30-38, 45-48; Exec. Sec. Student Service Comm. of American Lutheran Conf. 38-45; Exec. Sec. Comm. on Younger Churches and Orphaned Missions of Nat. Lutheran Council 48-54; Pres. Evangelical Lutheran Church 54-60; Chair. Comm. on World Mission of Lutheran World Fed. 49-57, Vice-Chair. 57-63; Chair. Board for Lutheran World Fed. Broadcasting Service 60-64; Pres. American Lutheran Church 61-70, Pres. Emer. 71-; Pres. Lutheran World Fed. 63-70; mem. Nat. Lutheran Council Exec. Cttee. 55-70; mem. Lutheran Council, U.S.A., Exec. Cttee. 67-71; mem. World Council of Churches Cen. Cttee. 61-71; Commdr. with star, Order of St. Olav.
Leisure interests: reading, walking, sports, fishing.
Publ. *Release* 35.
Home: 5567 Waldeck Crossing, Minneapolis, Minn. 55432; Office: The American Lutheran Church, 422 South Fifth Street, Minneapolis, Minnesota 55415, U.S.A.
Telephone: 338-3821 (Office); 574-1212 (Home).

Schippers, Thomas; American conductor; b. 9 March 1930, Portage, Michigan; m. Elaine Phipps 1965; ed. Curtis Inst. Philadelphia, Juilliard School of Music and Yale Univ.
Has conducted orchestras in many American cities and Europe; resident conductor New York City Opera

Company 51-54, Metropolitan Opera 55-; guest conductor principal orchestras and opera houses Europe, U.S., Asia; Dir. Spoleto Int. Festival, Italy 58-; debut at Rome opera 69; Musical Dir. Cincinatti Orchestra 70. Leisure interest: sailing.

c/o Director of Public Relations, Capital Records Inc., 1750 North Vine Street, Hollywood, Calif. 90028, U.S.A.

Schirmer, Hans Heinrich Theodor, DR.PHIL.; German diplomatist; b. 9 Jan. 1911, Berlin; s. of Lt.-Gen. Hermann Schirmer and Henrietta née Hansen; m. Gabrielle Achard 1951; one s. one d.; ed. Univ. of Heidelberg.

Foreign Service, Berlin 39-43; mil. service and prisoner-of-war 43-46; Head, Foreign Affairs Div., Press and Information Office of German Fed. Govt. 50-55; Counsellor, Cairo 55-60; Consul-Gen. Hong Kong 61-62; Asst. Sec. Press and Information Office 66-68; Amb. to Australia 68-70, to Austria 70-74; Rep. of Fed. Republic of Germany in European-Arab Dialogue. Leisure interests: history, ornithology, sport (swimming).

Auswärtiges Amt, Bonn, Federal Republic of Germany. Telephone: (02221) 171.

Schirra, Capt. Walter Marty, Jr.; American former astronaut; b. 12 March 1923, Hackensack, N.J.; s. of late Walter Schirra, Sr. and of Mrs. Schirra; m. Josephine Fraser; one s. one d.; ed. Newark Coll. of Engineering and Naval Acad., Annapolis.

Military Flight Training 45; fighter-pilot, Korea; Project Mercury, National Aeronautics and Space Admin. 59-, made six orbital flights of the earth in spaceship *Sigma VII* 3 Oct. 62; in charge of Operations and Training Astronaut Office 63-; backup command pilot for *Gemini III* mission; command pilot *Gemini VI* flight, successfully achieved rendezvous with *Gemini VII*, 15-16 Dec. 65; Commdr. *Apollo VII* flight, first televised transmission of onboard crew activities, 11-22 Oct. 68; retd. from N.A.S.A. and US Navy 69; Chair. of Board and Chief Exec. Officer ECCO 70-; Chair. SERNCO, Inc. 73-74; Exec. Johns-Manville Corpn.; Fellow, Soc. of Exp. Test Pilots, Fellow, American Astronautical Soc.; mem. American Inst. Aeronautics and Astronautics; Distinguished Service Medal 68; numerous decorations and awards. Leisure interests: skiing, hunting, sailing, sports cars.

Johns-Manville Corpn., Greenwood Plaza, Denver, Colo. 80217, U.S.A.

Schjelderup, Kristian Vilhelm Koren, B.D., D.D.; Norwegian ecclesiastic; b. 18 Jan. 1894; ed. Univs. of Oslo, Marburg, Berlin and Strasbourg.

Assoc. Prof. of Theology, Univ. of Oslo 21-27; mem. The Christian Michelsen Inst. for Science and Spiritual Freedom, Bergen 30-35; Founder and first Pres. the Norwegian Academy of Humanism (Nansen-skolen) 38-45; ordained Minister of Norwegian Church 45; Bishop of Hamar 47-64; mem. Int. Psychoanalytical Asscn. 28-; Pres. Norwegian Polio Asscn.; Commdr. Order of St. Olav.

Publs. *Religionens sandhet i lys av den relativitetsteoretiske virkelighetsopfatning* 21, *Der mennesker blir guder* 23, *Hvem Jesus var og hvad kirken har gjort ham til* 24, *Religion og religioner* 26, *Die Askese* 28, *Über drei Haupttypen der religiösen Erlebnisformen* 32, *Toleransens og fordragelighetens problem* 34, *På vei mot hedenskapet* 35, *Guds hus i fangeleiren* 45, *Oppgjor med nazismens ideologi* 45, *Tiden kaller på kirken* 48, *Den grunn hvor på jeg bygger* 57, *Ved Dören* 60, *Veien jeg måtte gå* 62, *Lys i mörket* 65.

Peder Claussönsgt. 19, Kristiansand 5, Norway. Telephone: 26336.

Schlauch, Margaret, A.B., M.A., PH.D.; Polish (b. American) philologist; b. 25 Sept. 1898, Philadelphia; d. of William Storb Schlauch and Margaret Brosnahan

Schlauch; ed. Barnard Coll. and Columbia Univ., New York.

Assistant Prof., New York Univ. 27-31, Assoc. Prof. 31-40, Full Prof. 40-51; Prof. of English Philology, Warsaw Univ., Poland 51-68, Chair. of Dept. 53-68, Prof. Emeritus 68-; Visiting Prof., Univ. of Connecticut 66-70; Pres. Soc. for Polish-Icelandic Friendship; Corresp. mem. Polish Acad. of Sciences; Officer's Cross of Order of Polonia Restituta, Knight, Order of the Falcon, Iceland.

Publs. *Chaucer's Constance* 27, *Medieval Narrative* 28, *The Saga of the Volsungs* 30, *The Gift of Tongues* 42, *English Medieval Literature and its Social Foundations* 56, *Modern English and American Poetry* 56, *Zarys wersyfikacji angielskiej* (Outline of English Versification) 58, *The English Language in Modern Times* 59, *Antecedents of the English Novel* 63, *Language and the Study of Languages Today* 67, Polish trans. 67.

Ul. Brzozowa 10 m. 12, Warsaw, Poland. Telephone: 31-78-12.

Schlenker, Rudolf; German tobacco executive; b. 18 June 1915, Dortmund; m. Liselotte Riesenberg 1944; two s. one d.; ed. business management studies, Cologne.

Adviser, Provincial Economy Office, Württemberg/Baden, and in Provincial Parl. after Second World War, later in Econ. Admin. Office, Frankfurt; in Fed. Ministry of Economy, Bonn 49-51, in Washington, D.C. 51-53; mem. Management Board H. F. and Ph. F. Reemtsma 53-, Spokesman of Management Board 58, Chair. of Management Board 62-75; Chair. Cigarette Industry Asscn.; Vice-Pres. Hamburg Chamber of Commerce; Pres. CORESTA Centre de Coopération pour les recherches scientifiques relatives au tabac, Paris: mem. Advisory Board Deutsche Bank A.G., Badische Anilin & Sodafabrik A.G., Hapag-Lloyd A.G., Nord-Deutsche und Hamburg-Bremer Versicherungs-Aktien-gesellschaft; mem. Advisory Council Aachener und Münchener Feuer-Versicherung A.G., Gerling-Konzern, Henkel G.m.b.H., Hermes Kreditversicherungs A.G.

H. F. and Ph. F. Reemtsma, Hamburg-Gr. Flottbek, Parkstrasse 51 (Office); (Home) Frenssenstr. 54, 2000 Hamburg 55 (Blankenese), Federal Republic of Germany. Telephone: (Home) 0411-86-29-76.

Schlesinger, Arthur, Jr. A.B.; American writer and educator; b. 15 Oct. 1917, Columbus, Ohio; s. of Arthur Meier and Elizabeth Bancroft Schlesinger; m. 1st Marian Cannon 1940, two s. two d.; 2nd Alexandra Emmet 1971, one s.; ed. Phillips Exeter Acad., Harvard Univ. and Peterhouse, Cambridge, England.

Society of Fellows, Harvard 39-42; with Office of War Information 42-43; Office of Strategic Services 43-45; U.S. Army 45; Assoc. Prof. of History, Harvard Univ. 46-54, Prof. 54-61; Special Asst. to Pres. of U.S.A. 61-64; Schweitzer Prof. of the Humanities, City Univ. of N.Y. 66-; Consultant, Econ. Co-operation Admin. 48, Mutual Security Admin. 51-52; mem. Adlai Stevenson campaign staff 52 and 56; mem. American Historical Asscn., Nat. Inst. of Arts and Letters, Board of Trustees John F. Kennedy Center for the Performing Arts, Board of Dirs. John F. Kennedy Library, Harry S. Truman Library Inst., American Civil Liberties Union etc.; Pulitzer Prize for History 46, for Biography 66, Bancroft and Parkman Prizes 58; Nat. Book Award 66; Gold Medal, Nat. Inst. of Arts and Letters 67; Hon. Litt.D. (Muhlenberg) 50, Hon. LL.D. (Bethany) 56, (New School for Social Research) 66; Hon. D.C.L. (New Brunswick) 60; Hon. L.H.D. (Tusculum Coll.) 66, Hon. L.H.D. (Rhode Island Coll.) 69, Hon. Litt.D. (Aquinas Coll.) 71, Hon. LL.D. (Western New England Coll.) 74.

Leisure interests: tennis, films.

Publs. *Orestes A. Brownson: A Pilgrim's Progress* 39, *The Age of Jackson* 45, *The Vital Center* (English title *The Politics of Freedom*) 49, *The General and the*

President (with R. H. Rovere) 51, *The Age of Roosevelt:*
Vol. I *The Crisis of the Old Order* 57, Vol. II *The Coming
of the New Deal* 58, Vol. III *The Politics of Upheaval* 60,
Kennedy or Nixon 60, *The Politics of Hope* 63, *Paths of
American Thought* (ed. with Morton White) 63, *A
Thousand Days: John F. Kennedy in the White House*
65, *The Bitter Heritage: Vietnam and American Democracy 1941-1966* 67, *The Crisis of Confidence* 69, *History
of American Presidential Elections* (ed. with F. L. Israel)
71, *The Imperial Presidency* 73.
Office: City University of New York, 33 West 42nd
Street, New York, N.Y. 10036, U.S.A.
Telephone: 790-4261.

Schlesinger, James Rodney, M.A., PH.D.; American
economist; b. 15 Feb. 1929, New York City; s. of Julius
and Rhea (Rogen) Schlesinger; m. Rachel Mellinger
1954; four s. four d.; ed. Harvard Univ.
Asst. Prof. and Assoc. Prof., Univ. of Virginia 55-63;
Senior Staff mem. RAND Corpn. 63-67, Dir. Strategic
Studies 67-69; Asst. Dir., Office of Management and
Budget 69-71; Chair. U.S. Atomic Energy Comm. 71-73;
Dir. Cen. Intelligence Agency Feb.-May 73; Sec. of
Defence 73-75; Distinguished Service Medal from U.S.
Intelligence Community 76.
c/o Department of Defence, The Pentagon, Washington,
D.C. 20301, U.S.A.

Schlesinger, John Richard, C.B.E.; British film and
theatre director; b. 16 Feb. 1926, London; s. of Dr.
Bernard Schlesinger and Winifred Henrietta Regensburg; ed. Uppingham School and Balliol Coll. Oxford.
Early career as actor on television and in films *Singlehanded, Battle of the River Plate, Brothers in Law* and
numerous others; directed shorts for *Tonight* and
Monitor; made films for BBC Television including
part of *The Valiant Years*; joined Sapphire Films for
Four Just Men; Assoc. Dir. Nat. Theatre 73-.
Major films: *Terminus* (Venice Golden Lion 62) 61,
A Kind of Loving (Berlin Golden Bear) 62, *Billy Liar*
63, *Darling* (New York Film Critics' Award) 65, *Far
From the Madding Crowd* 67, *Midnight Cowboy* (Dirs.
Guild of America Award, Acad. Award for best Dir.
and British Film Acad. Award) 69, *Sunday Bloody
Sunday* 70 (David Donatello Award), *Marathon-
Olympics* 72, *Visions of Eight* 73, *The Day of the Locust*
74; plays: *No Why* (John Whiting), Aldwych Theatre
64, *Timon of Athens*, Royal Shakespeare Theatre,
Stratford 65, *Days in the Trees* (London) 66, *I and
Albert*, Piccadilly Theatre 72-73, *Heartbreak House*,
Nat. Theatre 75.
10 Victoria Road, London, W8 5RD, England.
Telephone: 01-937-3983.

Schlesinger, John Samuel; South African business
executive; b. 1923; ed. Michaelhouse and Harvard
Univ.
United States Army Air Corps, Second World War;
Dir. Schlesinger group of insurance, banking and
property cos. in U.K. including Schlesinger European
Investments Ltd., Throgmorton Securities Ltd.,
Trident Insurance Co. Ltd., London Consolidated
Properties Ltd., Dorrington Investment Ltd.
Schlesinger Organization, P.O. Box 1182, Johannesburg,
South Africa.

Schlesinger, Theodore; American retail executive;
b. 27 Oct. 1908; ed. City Coll. of New York and
Fordham Univ.
Allied Stores Corpn. 29-, Asst. to Pres. 39-45, Vice-Pres.
45-59, Pres. and Chief Exec. Officer 59-, Dir. 55-.
Allied Stores Corporation, 401 Fifth Avenue, New York
City, N.Y., U.S.A.

Schlieder, Willy, LL.D.; German lawyer; b. 21 Nov.
1926, Farnstädt; ed. Univs. of Halle and Marburg.
Lawyer and Legal Counsellor, Confed. of German Trade
Unions 54-58; Principal Admin., Directorate-Gen. of

Competition, Comm. of the EEC 58-60, Head of Dept.
62-67; Chef de Cabinet of Pres. of the Econ. and Social
Cttee., EEC 60-62; Chef de Cabinet of Wilhelm Haferkamp, Vice-Pres. of the Comm. of EEC 67-70; Dir.-
Gen. of Competition, Comm. of the European Communities 70-.
Directorate-General of Competition, Commission of the
European Communities, 200 rue de la Loi, 1040
Brussels, Belgium.

Schlieker, Willy Hermann: German industrialist;
b. 1914; ed. Elementary and High School in Hamburg.
Sales Rep. German export firm in Haiti 36-38; Export
Man. Ruhr steel construction firm 39; with raw material
dept. Vereinigte Stahlwerke, Düsseldorf 40-42; Steel
Controller, Ministry of War Production 43-45; industrial adviser 46-47; since 48 built up the Schlieker
Group, comprising Schlieker Yard (shipbuilding),
Schlieker Kessel-u. Maschinenbau (engines and boilers),
Reederei Willy H. Schlieker & Co. (shipping) (all Hamburg), Walzwerk Neviges (electrical sheet-mill), Metall-
und Kaltwalzwerk Langenberg (strip mill), Schlieker
Eisenhandel GmbH (steel), Schrottverwertung Niederrhein GmbH (scrap), Schlieker Anlagen-Export GmbH,
Düsseldorf.
Fischers Allee 97, Hamburg-Altona, Federal Republic
of Germany.

Schlier, Heinrich; German university professor; b.
1900, Neuburg; s. of H. Schlier and Paula Puls; m.
Erna Haas 1927; two s. two d.; ed. Univs. of Leipzig
and Marburg.
Pastor 27; Reader, Jena 28; Marburg Univ. 30; Lecturer,
Theological School, Elberfeld 35; Pastor, Lutheran
Church, Elberfeld 37; Prof. of the New Testament and
Church History Bonn Univ. 45, Hon. Prof. 52; Dr. h.c.
Leisure interest: world literature.
Publs. *Religionsgeschichtliche Untersuchungen zu den
Ignatiusbriefen* 29, *Christus und die Kirche im Epheser-
brief* 30, *Der Brief an die Galater* 51, 62, 65, *Der Brief
an die Epheser* 57, 59, 61, 63, 65, 68, *Die Zeit der Kirche*
63, 65, 72, *Besinnung auf das NT* 64, 68, *Über die
Auferstehung Jesu Christi* 68, 69, *Das Ende der Zeit* 71.
Wegelerstrasse 2, Bonn, Federal Republic of Germany.
Telephone: 02221/653416.

Schlosser, Hermann; German business executive; b.
8 Oct. 1889; ed. Landgraf-Ludwigs-Gymnasium,
Giessen.
Commercial studies, Hamburg 08-10; commercial posts,
Calcutta and New Delhi 10-14; joined Deutsche Gold-
und Silber-Scheidenanstalt (Degussa) 15; Military
Service 15-18; Degussa 18-, mem. Board of Dirs. 26-39,
Chair. Board of Dirs. 39, Chair. Supervisory Board 59,
Hon. Chair. 65-; Hon. mem. Asscn. of the Chemical
Industry.
Degussa, 6 Frankfurt am Main, Weissfrauenstrasse 9,
Postfach 2644, Federal Republic of Germany.
Telephone: 218-2300.

Schmaus, Michael, DR. THEOL.; German theologian
and university professor; b. 17 July 1897; ed. Gymnasium Rosenheim and Univ. Munich.
Ordained 22; Lecturer Philosophische-theologische
Hochschule und Seminar, Freising 24-29; Lecturer
Munich Univ. 27-29; Prof. of Dogmatic Theology,
German Univ. in Prague 29-33; Prof. Univ. Münster
33-46, Munich 46-65, Emer. 65-; Rector Munich Univ.
51-52; Peritus of Second Vatican Council 60-65; mem.
Bavarian Acad. of Sciences; Commdr. of Greek Order
of Phoenix; Commdr. Spanish Order of Civil Merit;
Bayerischer Verdienstorden; Grosses Bundesver-
dienstkreuz.
Publs. *Die psychologische Trinitätslehre des Heiligen
Augustinus* 27, *Der Liber propugnatorius des Thomas
Anglicus* 30, *Katholische Dogmatik*, 8 Vols. 38-64,
Handbuch der Katholischen Dogmatik 69-70, *Die*

Denkform Augustins in seinem Werk "De Trinitate" 62, *Wahrheit als Heilsbegegnung* 64, articles, translations and several series.
8035 Gauting bei München, Junkerstrasse 5, Federal Republic of Germany.
Telephone: Munich 850 2800.

Schmeisser, Kurt; German foreign trade official; b. 21 May 1909.
Head of China and Glass, and Machine Export Trade Corpns. 50-58; Foreign Trade Rep. of German Democratic Republic (D.D.R.) in Iraq and Sweden 58-62; Gen. Dir. of Int. Leipzig Trade Fair 62-71.
Leipziger Messeamt, Markt 11/15, 701 Leipzig, German Democratic Republic.
Telephone: 2030.

Schmelzer, W. K. Norbert; Netherlands politician; b. 22 March 1921; *m.*; three *c.*; ed. Catholic Univ., Tilburg.
With Unilever N.V., Rotterdam 47-50; Ministry of Econ. Affairs 50-56; State Sec. for Home Affairs 58-59, for Gen. Affairs 59-63; mem. Second Chamber of Parl.; Minister of Foreign Affairs 71-73; Industrial Adviser 73-; Grand Officer, Order of Orange-Nassau; Commdr. Order of Netherlands Lion; Catholic People's Party.
Ministry of Foreign Affairs, The Hague, Netherlands.

Schmid, Erich, DR. PHIL.; Austrian scientist; b. 4 May 1896, Bruck a. d. Mur; *s.* of Dr. med. K. Schmid and A. Monschein; *m.* Margarete Ludwig 1922; one *s.* three *d.*; ed. Univ. Wien.
Member staff Kaiser Wilhelm-Inst. für Faserstoffchemie 22-24; metallurgist, Metallgesellschaft A.G., Frankfurt 24-28; Head of Physics Dept., Kaiser Wilhelm-Inst. für Metallforschung, Berlin-Dahlem 28-32; Teacher at Technische Hochschule, Berlin 32; Prof. and Head of Physics Inst., Univ. of Fribourg (Switzerland) 32-36; Head of Metal Laboratories, Metallgesellschaft A.G., Frankfurt 36-45; Head of Laboratories of Vacuumschmelze A.G., Hanau am Main 46-51; Prof. of Physics and Head of Second Physics Inst., Univ. of Vienna 51-67, Emer. 67-; Pres. Austrian Acad. of Sciences 63-73, Vice-Pres. 66-67, 73-; mem. Deutsche Akad. der Naturforscher Leopoldina, Akad. der Wissenschaften der D.D.R., Sächsische Akad. der Wissenschaften zu Leipzig, New York Acad. of Sciences; Hon. mem. Österreichische Physikalische Ges., Japanese Soc. of Metallurgy; Foreign mem. Max-Planck Inst. für Metallforschung, Stuttgart; Dr. Mont. h.c., Dr. Rer. Nat. h.c.; numerous medals and decorations.
Leisure interests: music, mountains.
Publs. *Kristallplastizität* (with W. Boas) 35, *Gleitlager* (with R. Weber) 53, *Texturen in Metallen und Legierungen* (6th edition) 57, *Bedeutung von Korpuskularbestrahlung für die Eigenschaften von Festkörpern* (with K. Lintner) 55, *Werkstoffe des Reaktorbaues* (with K. Lintner) 62, *Radiation Damage* 70, *Behaviour of Insonated Metals* (with K. Lintner) 70.
A 1090 Vienna, Universitätsstrasse 10, Austria.
Telephone: 42-40-062.

Schmid, Karl (Carlo), DR. JUR.; German lawyer, writer and politician; b. 3 Dec. 1896, Perpignan, France; *s.* of Josef Schmid and Anna (Erra) Schmid; *m.* Lydia (Hermes) Schmid 1921; three *s.* (one deceased) one *d.*; ed. Univ. of Tübingen and Kaiser Wilhelm Inst. of Foreign Public and Int. Law.
Lawyer 24, Judge 25; Dozent Univ. of Tübingen 29; Prof. of Public Law 45-50; Pres. of Social Democratic Party in Württemberg 46-; mem. Central Cttee. of SPD 47-; Minister of State in Württemberg 45-52; mem. of Diet 46-; mem. of Parl. Council in Bonn 48-49; mem. and Vice-Pres. Fed. Parl. 49-73; Prof. of Political Science Univ. of Frankfurt 53, now Emer.; Minister for Bundesrat and the Länder 66-69; mem. Council of Europe; mem. PEN; Presidential candidate 59; Pres.

Parl. Assembly of the Western European Union; Goethepreis der Stadt Frankfurt/Main 67; Hanseatischer Goethepreis 75; Dr. h.c. (Sorbonne, Paris) 73.
Publs. *Machiavelli* 56, *Politik und Geist* 62; trans. of Baudelaire and Calderón, trans. of Malraux's *Anti-mémoires* 68; *Gesammelte Werke* 73.
5340 Bad Honnef 6, Paul-Keller-Strasse 34, Federal Republic of Germany.
Telephone: 02224-80088.

Schmidheiny, Max, DIPL.ENG.; Swiss engineer and industrialist; b. 3 April 1908; *m.* 1942; four *c.*; ed. Gymnasium Trogen and Eidgenössische Technische Hochschule, Zürich.
President and Dir. of many companies in Switzerland and abroad; fmrly Nat. Councillor and mem. Swiss Chamber of Commerce; fmr. Chair. Brown, Boveri; Chair. Holder Bank Financière Glarus Ltd. 74-; Hon. Freeman of Pagig/Gr.; Dr. h.c. (Univ. of Basle, High Commercial School, St. Gall).
Leisure interest: flying.
Holder Bank Financière Glarus Ltd., Glarus, Switzerland.

Schmidt, Adolph William; American diplomatist; b. 1904; *m.* Helen Sedgeley Mellon 1936; one *s.* one *d.*; ed. Univs. of Princeton, Harvard, Dijon, Berlin and Paris.
With Mellon Nat. Bank & Trust Co. 29-38; with A. W. Mellon, Pittsburgh 38-42; war service 42-46; Gov. T. Mellon & Sons 46-69; Chair. Pa. State Planning Board 55-67, etc.; U.S. Del., Conf. on North Atlantic Community 57 and Atlantic Congress 59; mem. U.S. Citizens Comm. on NATO 61-62; U.S. Del. Atlantic Convention of NATO nations 62; Dir. Atlantic Council of U.S. 62-69; Adviser U.S. Del., Economic Comm. for Europe 67; mem. Board of Governors, Atlantic Inst., Paris 60-69; Amb. to Canada 69-74; Hon. LL.D. (Univs. of Pittsburgh and New Brunswick), Hon. L.H.D. (Chatham Coll.).
R. D4, Ligonier, Pa. 15658, U.S.A.

Schmidt, Aleksander; Polish politician; b. 6 May 1919, Wiszkup, near Ostróda; ed. grammar school at Nakło.
Participated in September Campaign and in the defence of Warsaw; mem. United Peasants' Party (ZSL) 45-, mem. Presidium of Bydgoszcz Voivodship Cttee. 50-58, mem. Chief Cttee. 59-, Presidium of Chief Cttee. 73-; Vice-Chair. Presidium of Bydgoszcz Voivodship Nat. Council 50-58, Chair. 58-71; Chair. Bydgoszcz Voivodship Cttee., Nat. Unity Front 56-71, mem. All-Poland Cttee. 59-73; Deputy to Seym 61-; Pres. Cen. Union of Agricultural Co-operatives 71-; mem. Council of State 72-; Medal of 10th Anniversary of People's Poland, Order of Banner of Labour, 1st and 2nd Class, Knight's Cross, Order of Polonia Restituta.
Kancelaria Rady Państwa, ul. Wiejska 4/6/8, 00-489 Warsaw, Poland.

Schmidt, Arno Otto; German novelist; b. 18 Jan. 1914, Hamburg; *s.* of Otto Schmidt and Klara Ehrentraut; *m.* Alice Murawski 1937; ed. Univ. of Breslau.
Employed 34-39; Soldier and Prisoner of War 39-45; Writer 46-; Grand Prize for Literature, Akademie für Wissenschaft und Literatur, Mainz 50; Fontanepreis 64, Grand Award for Literature, Fed. German Industries 65, Goethe Prize 73.
Publs. *Leviathan* 49, *Brands' Haide* 51, *Aus dem Leben eines Fauns* 53, *Das steinerne Herz* 56, *Die Gelehrtenrepublik* 57, *Dya na sore* 58, *Rosen und Porree* 59, *Kaff* 60, *Belphegor* 61, *Kühe in Halbtrauer* 64, *Die Ritter vom Geist* 65, *Trommler beim Zaren* 66, *Der Triton mit dem Sonnenschirm* 69, *Zettels Traum* 70, *Die Schule der Atheisten* 72, *Abend mit Goldrand* 75; Biography: *Fouqué und einige seiner Zeitgenossen* 58, *Sitara und der Weg dorthin* (Karl May) 63; translations from English

(Hunter, Ellin, Faulkner, Poe, Cooper, Collins, Joyce, E. Bulwer-Lytton, etc.).
3101 Bargfeld Krs. Celle Nr. 37, Federal Republic of Germany.
Telephone: Steinhorst 500.

Schmidt, Carl Frederic, A.B., M.D.; American physician, pharmacologist, physiologist; b. 29 July 1893, Lebanon, Pa.; s. of Jacob Charles Schmidt and Mary Ellen (Greth) Schmidt; m. Elizabeth Viola Gruber 1920; one s. one d.; ed. Lebanon Valley Coll. and Univ. of Pennsylvania.
Instructor, Dept. of Pharmacology, Univ. of Pa. 19; Assoc. in Pharmacology, Peking (China) Union Medical Coll. 22-24; Asst. Prof., Dept. of Pharmacology, Univ. of Pa. 24-29, Assoc. Prof. 29-31, Prof. 31-39, Head of Dept. of Pharmacology 39-59, Emer. 59-; Man. Editor *Circulation Research* 57-62; Research Dir. Aerospace Medical Research Dept., U.S. Naval Air. Devt. Center 62-69; Clinical Prof. of Pharmacology, Univ. of S. Florida 70-; Pres. American Soc. of Pharmacology and Exp. Therapeutics 48-50; Sec. Int. Council of Pharmacologists 53-59; Vice-Pres. Int. Union of Physiological Sciences, Pres. Section on Pharmacology 59-65; Chair. Panel on Physiology, U.S. Research and Devt. Board 48-50, Pharmacology Study Section, U.S. Nat. Insts. of Health 47-51, Advisory Cttee. Life Insurance Medical Research Fund 54-55, Cttee. on Continuing Medical Educ. of Drug Research Board of U.S. Nat. Acad. of Sciences 64-69; Hon. Pres. Int. Union of Pharmacology 66-; Hon. Sc.D. (Lebanon Valley Coll.) 55, (Univ. of Pa.) 65; Hon. Med.Sc.D. (Charles Univ., Prague) 63; Hachmeister Award, Georgetown Univ. 51; Schmiedeberg Plakette, German Pharmacological Soc. 63.
Leisure interests: fishing, gardening, photography, hiking, motoring.
Major works: *Ephedrine and other Chinese drugs* 23-26; Physiology and pharmacology of: respiration 26-68, of aerospace medicine 42-66, of cerebral circulation 28-66; section on respiration in Bard-Macleod's *Textbook of Physiology* 46-56; reviews or monographs on cerebral circulation 50-60, respiratory control 40, 41, 45, 51, aerospace pharmacology 61, 65, continuing medical education 69, education on drug abuse 70.
2361 East Vina del Mar Boulevard, St. Petersburg Beach, Florida 33706, U.S.A.
Telephone: 813-360-0935.

Schmidt, Chauncey Everett, B.S., M.B.A.; American banker; b. 7 June 1931, Oxford, Ia.; s. of Walter F. Schmidt and Vilda Saxton; m. Anne Garrett McWilliams 1954; one s. two d.; ed. U.S. Naval Acad., Harvard Graduate School of Business Admin.
With First Nat. Bank of Chicago 59-, Vice-Pres. 65, Gen. Man., London 66, Gen. Man. for Europe, Middle East and Africa 68, Senior Vice-Pres. 69, Exec. Vice-Pres. 72, Vice-Chair. 73, Pres. 74-; Trustee Art Inst. of Chicago, Chicago Symphony Orch., Hadley School for the Blind; mem. Asscn. of Reserve City Bankers.
Leisure interests: tennis, swimming.
The First National Bank of Chicago, One First National Plaza, Chicago, Ill. 60670; Home: 2122 Middlefork Road, Northfield, Ill. 60093, U.S.A.
Telephone: 212-732-8026 (Office); 212-446-0325 (Home).

Schmidt, Helmut Heinrich Waldemar; German economist and politician; b. 23 Dec. 1918, Hamburg; s. of Gustav and Ludovica Schmidt; m. Hannelore Glaser 1942; one d.; ed. Univ. Hamburg.
Manager of Transport Admin. of State of Hamburg 49-53; mem. Social Democrat Party 46-; mem. Bundestag 53-62, 65-; Chair. Social Democrat (S.P.D.) Parl. Party in Bundestag 67-69; Vice-Chair. Social Democratic Party (S.P.D.) 68-; Senator (Minister) for Domestic Affairs in Hamburg 61-65; Minister of Defence 69-72, for Econ. and Finance July-Dec. 72, of Finance 72-74; Fed. Chancellor May 74-.

Publs. *Defence or Retaliation* 62, *Beiträge* 67, *Strategie des Gleichgewichts* 69 (English edition "*Balance of Power*" 70).
Bundeskanzleramt, Adenauerallee 139-141, Bonn 1, Federal Republic of Germany.

Schmidt, Maarten, PH.D., SC.D.; Netherlands astronomer; b. 28 Dec. 1929, Groningen; s. of W. Schmidt and A. W. Haringhuizen; m. Cornelia J. Tom 1955; three d.; ed. Univs. of Groningen and Leiden.
Scientific Officer, Univ. of Leiden Observatory 49-59; Carnegie Fellow Mt. Wilson Observatory, Pasadena 56-58; Assoc. Prof. Calif. Inst. of Technology 59-64; Prof. of Astronomy 64-; discovered large red shifts in spectra of quasi-stellar radio sources (quasars); Rumford Award, American Acad. of Arts and Sciences 68.
Leisure interest: classical music.
California Inst. of Technology, Pasadena, Calif. 91109, U.S.A.
Telephone: 213-795-6841.

Schmidt, Werner P., DR.RER.POL.; German business executive; b. 5 July 1932, Borken, Westphalia; m. Annely Bresser 1957; one s. one d.; ed. Univ. of Münster, Kalamazoo Coll., Michigan, Univ. of Cologne.
Sales Planning Man., Marketing Man., Domestic Sales Man., Ford Werke AG 56-67; Export Man., Volkswagen Werk AG 67-71; Pres. Volkswagen do Brasil 71-73; Chair. Management Board, Audi NSU Auto Union AG 73-75, mem. Management Board, Volkswagen AG 75-.
Volkswagen AG, 3180 Wolfsburg, Federal Republic of Germany.

Schmidt-Clausen, Kurt Hermann, DR. THEOL.; German international church official; b. 1 Oct. 1920, Hanover; m. Erika Rokahr 1943; one s. one d.; ed. Hanover Gymnasium, Univs. of Vienna and Göttingen, Christ Church Coll., Oxford, and Loccum Preachers' Seminary.
Pastor, City Parish, Hanover 51-52; mem. Admin. Staff Evangelical Lutheran Church of Hanover 52-55; Pastor, Wunstorf Suburban Parish (near Hanover) 55-60; Asst. Exec. Sec., later Acting Exec. Sec., Lutheran World Fed. 60-61, Exec. Sec. 61-64, Gen. Sec. 64-65; Chair. Ecumenical Comm., Evangelical Lutheran Church of Hanover; Chair. Ecumenical Comm., United Evangelical Lutheran Church of Germany; Editor *Lutherische Monatshefte* (monthly); Landessuperintendent of Osnabrück Diocese.
Leisure interest: Roman archaeology.
Publs. *Vorweggenommene Einheit* 64, *Reformation als Oekumenisches Ereignis* 70.
4500 Osnabrück, Bismarckstrasse 8, Federal Republic of Germany.

Schmidt-Nielsen, Knut, DR. PHIL.; American professor of physiology; b. 24 Sept. 1915, Norway; s. of Sigval and Signe Torborg (Sturzen-Becker) Schmidt-Nielsen; ed. Oslo and Copenhagen Univs.
Research Fellow, Carlsberg Labs., Copenhagen 41-44; Research Fellow, Univ. of Copenhagen 44-46; Research Assoc., Swarthmore Coll., Dept. of Zoology 46-48; Research Assoc., Stanford Univ., Dept. of Physiology 48-49; Docent, Univ. of Oslo 47-49; Asst. Prof., Univ. of Cincinnati Coll. of Medicine 49-52; Prof. of Physiology, Dept. of Zoology Duke Univ. 52-, James B. Duke Prof. of Physiology 63-; mem. Nat. Acad. of Sciences, Royal Norwegian Soc. of Arts and Science 73, Royal Danish Acad. 75; Fellow, American Acad. of Arts and Sciences, N.Y. Acad. of Science, American Asscn. for Advancement of Science; Guggenheim Fellow, Algeria 53-54; Brody Memorial Lecturer, Univ. of Mo. 62; Harvey Soc. Lecturer 62 (Hon. mem. 62); Regents' Lecturer, Univ. of Calif. (Davis) 63; Hans Gadow Lecturer, Cambridge Univ. 71; Visiting Agassiz Prof., Harvard Univ. 72; mem. numerous scientific Cttees, including Advisory Board to the Physiological Research Laboratory, Scripps Inst. of Oceanography 63-69, Chair.

68-69; U.S. Nat. Cttee. for Int. Union of Physiological Sciences 66-, Vice-Chair. 69-; Biomedical Engineering Advisory Cttee., Duke Univ. 68-; Animal Resources Advisory Cttee., Nat. Institute of Health 68; mem. Organizing Cttee., First Int. Conf. Comparative Physiology 72, Pres. 72-; mem. Advisory Board, Bio-Medical Sciences, Inc. 73-74; mem. Editorial Board several scientific journals.

Publs. *Animal Physiology* (1st edn.) 60, (2nd edn.) 64 (Japanese, French, Swedish, Polish, German, Spanish, Norwegian, Indian, Hebrew, Hindi translations) (3rd edn.) 70, *Desert Animals, Physiological Problems of Heat and Water* 64, *How Animals Work* 72, *Animal Physiology, Adaptation and Environment* 75; numerous articles.

Department of Zoology, Duke University, Durham, N.C. 27706, U.S.A.
Telephone: 919-684-2687.

Schmit, André, L. EN DR.; French civil servant; b. 12 Feb. 1915, Geneva; *m.* Nicole Delmas 1942; two *s.* one *d.*; ed. Ecole des Sciences Politiques, Ecole Nat. de la France d'Outre-Mer (Indo-China) and Cambridge Univ.

Colonial Administration (Indo-China) 41-45; Asst. Dir. Press Relations, Ministry of Information 36, Inspector Gen. 46; Dir. Press Council 47; Dir. Nouvelles Messageries de la Presse Parisienne 49-; Chef de Cabinet, Ministry of Public Works and Reconstruction 54-55; Chef de Cabinet, Ministry of State 56-57, Ministry of Defence 57; Chef de Cabinet of Pres. of Nat. Assembly 58-; Directeur du Cabinet of Pres. of Nat. Assembly June 69-; Officier, Légion d'Honneur, Lt.-Col. de Réserve, diplômé d'Etat-Major.

48 avenue de New York, Paris 16e, France.

Schmitt, Francis Otto, PH.D.; American neurobiologist; b. 23 Nov. 1903, St. Louis, Mo.; *s.* of Otto Franz and Clara Elizabeth (Senniger) Schmitt; *m.* Barbara Hecker 1927; two *s.* (one deceased) one *d.*; ed. Univ. Coll., London, Kaiser Wilhelm Inst., Berlin-Dahlem, Washington Univ., Univ. of Calif., Berkeley, St. Louis Univ.

Assistant Prof. of Zoology, Washington Univ. 29-34, Assoc. Prof. 34-38, Prof. 38-40, Head of Dept. 40; Prof. of Biology, Mass. Inst. of Technology 41, Head of Dept. 42-55, Inst. Prof. 55-69, Inst. Prof. Emer. 69-, Chair. Neurosciences Research Program 62-; mem. Nat. Acad. Sciences, Nat. Research Council's Cttee. on Neurobiology 45, Cttee. on Growth 46-50, Cttee. on Radiation Cataracts 49-53, Cttee. on Atherosclerosis 53-54, Biology Council 54-56, Nat. Advisory Health Council U.S.P.H.S. 59-63, Nat. Advisory Gen. Medical Sciences Council 69-71; mem. Board of Science Consultants of Sloan-Kettering Inst. of Cancer Research 63-71, Cttee. for Fellowships for Basic Neuroscience Research, Sloan Foundation 71-, Nat. Advisory Council Marine Biomedical Inst., Univ. of Texas 73; Trustee and exec. mem. of several insts.; Fellow, American Acad. of Arts and Sciences (Council mem. 50-52, 64-65), A.A.A.S., New York Acad. of Sciences; mem. numerous scientific socs. including Soc. of Gen. Physiologists, American Philosophical Soc. (Council mem. 64-66, Vice-Pres. 73-), Soc. for Growth and Devt. (Treas. 45-46, Pres. 47), Biophysical Soc. (Council mem.), Electron Microscope Soc. of America (Dir. 44-47, Pres. 49), Nat. Acad. of Sciences, Swedish Royal Acad. of Sciences, Soc. Philomathique de Paris; Hon. D.Sc. (six univs.), Hon. M.D. (Univ. of Gothenburg, Sweden), Hon. LL.D. (Wittenburg Univ. and Juniata Coll.); Alsop Award of American Leather Chemical Asscn. 47, Lasker Award of American Public Health Asscn. 56, T. Duckett Jones Memorial Award of Helen Hay Whitney Foundation 63.
Leisure interest: music.
Publs. *Fundamental Transfer Processes in Aqueous*

Biomolecular System 60, *Macromolecular Specificity and Biological Memory* 62, *Neurosciences—A Study Program* 67, *Neurosciences—Second Study Program* 70, *Neurosciences—Third Study Program* 73, *Neurosciences Research Symposium* Vols. I-VII 66-74, *Functional Linkage in Biomolecular Systems* 74.
Massachusetts Institute of Technology, Neurosciences Research Program, 165 Allandale Street, Jamaica Plain, Mass. 02130; Home: 72 Byron Road, Weston, Mass. 02193, U.S.A.
Telephone: 617-522-6700 (Office); 617-235-6976 (Home).

Schmitt, Harrison H.; American astronaut; b. 3 July 1935, Santa Rita, N.M.; ed. Calif. Inst. of Technology, Univ. of Oslo, Norway, and Harvard Univ.

Fulbright Fellowship 57-58, Kennecott Fellowship in Geology 58-59, Harvard Fellowship 59-60, Harvard Travelling Fellowship 60, Parker Travelling Fellowship 61-62, Nat. Science Foundation Postdoctoral Fellowship, Dept. of Geological Sciences, Harvard 63-64; has done geological work for Norwegian Geological Survey, Oslo, and for U.S. Geological Survey, N.M. and Montana; with U.S. Geological Survey Astrogeology Dept. until 65; project chief on photo and telescopic mapping of moon and planets; selected as scientist-astronaut by NASA June 65; completed flight training 66; Lunar Module pilot *Apollo XVII* Dec. 72; Chief, Astronaut Office, Science and Applications, Johnson Space Center 74; Asst. Admin., Energy Programs, NASA, Washington, D.C. 74-.
National Aeronautics and Space Administration, Washington, D.C. 20546, U.S.A.

Schmitt-Vockenhausen, Hermann, DR.JUR.; German politician and publisher; b. 31 Jan. 1923, Vockenhausen; *s.* of Valentin and Katharina (née Wolf) Schmitt; *m.* Ruth Schulz 1951; one *d.*; ed. Goethe-Gymnasium, Frankfurt-am-Main and Univ. of Frankfurt.

Adviser, Hessisches Innenministerium 45-48; joined Max Gehlen Verlag 50; head of own publishing houses; mem. Bundestag (SPD) 53-, Chair. Inner Council 61-69, Vice-Pres. 69-; Pres. Deutscher Städte -und Gemeindebund 73-; Pres. Deutsch-Ibero-Amerikanische Gesellschaft; mem. Zentral Komitee der Deutschen Katholiken.
Leisure interests: football, stamps.
Publ. *Die Wahlprüfung in Bund und Ländern unter Einbeziehung Österreichs und der Schweiz.*
6232 Bad Soden (Taunus), Oranienstrasse 20, Federal Republic of Germany.
Telephone: 06196/23129.

Schmitz, Wolfgang, LL.D.; Austrian economist and banker; b. 28 May 1923, Vienna; *s.* of Dr. Hans Schmitz and Maria Habel; *m.* Dr. Elisabeth Mayr-Harting 1951; one *s.* four *d.*; ed. Univs. of Vienna and Fribourg (Switzerland), Catholic Univ., Washington, D.C.

Legal practice 49-50; Austrian Fed. Econ. Chamber 50-64, Sec. Econ. Policy Dept. and Sec. Austrian Nat. Cttee. of Int. Chamber of Commerce 50-64; Chair. Beirat für Wirtschafts-und Sozialfragen 63-64; Head of Econ. Policy Dept. Jan.-April 64; Fed. Minister of Finance 64-68; Pres. Austrian Nat. Bank 68-73, Inst. for Advanced Studies 68-; Gov. of World Bank for Austria 64-68, of IMF 68-73; Dir. Austrian Inst. for Econ. Research 68-73; Hon. Pres. Austro-American Soc., Austro-Japanese Soc., Inst. für Bildungs und Beratungsforschung; Lecturer, Univ. Vienna; Chair. of Ed. Cttee. Europäische Rundschau, Vienna; Hon. LL.D. (St. John's Univ., New York).

Publs. *Der Ausgleich der Familienlasten–Allgemeine Theorie und praktische Verwirklichung in Österreich* 55, *Die Österreichische Wirtschaftspolitik im Zeichen der Europäischen Integration* 60, *Die Österreichische Wirtschafts- und Sozialpolitik, Würdigung, Kritik, Ansatzpunkte* 61, *Geldwertstabilität und Wirtschaftswachstum— Währungspolitik im Spannungsfeld des Konjunktur-*

veraufs (editor) 70, *Convertibility, Multilateralism and Freedom—World Economic Policy in the Seventies* (editor) 72, *International Investment—Growth and Crisis* 75, *Die antizyklische Konjunktur-politik—eine Illusion* 76, and numerous articles on economic, financial and social policy matters.

c/o Austrian Federal Economic Chamber, 10 Biber-strasse, 1010 Vienna; Home: Gustav Tschermak Gasse 3/2, A-1180 Vienna, Austria.

Telephone: 522216 (Office); 343333 (Home).

Schmücker, Kurt; German politician; b. 10 Nov. 1919, Löningen; s. of Friedrich and Gertrud Schmücker; m. Ilse Varelmann 1944; two s. four d.; ed. Secondary School and Trade School.

Apprentice to printing and journalism; military service 39-46; printing works, Oldenburg 46-, owner 54-; mem. Bundestag 49-72, Chair. Econ. Policy Cttee; Minister of Economics 63-66, for Fed. Property 66-69; Christian Democrat.

Leisure interest: classical music.

4573 Löningen/Oldberg, Allee, Federal Republic of Germany.

Schmücker, Toni; German business executive; b. 23 April 1921, Frechen; m. Edith Schmücker; two s.

Member of Board, Ford-Werke AG 61-68, Rheinstahl AG March-July 68; Chair. of Board, Rheinstahl AG 68-74; Chair. of Management Board, Volkswagenwerk AG 75-; mem. Management Board Audi NSU Auto Union 75.

Leisure interests: tennis, climbing.

Volkswagenwerk AG, 318 Wolfsburg; Home: 4300 Essen-Stadtwald, Vittinghoffstrasse 51, Federal Republic of Germany.

Telephone: 05361/221 (Office).

Schneider, Alan Leo (Abram Leopoldovitch); American (b. Russian) theatre director and lecturer; b. 12 Dec. 1917, Kharkov, Russia; s. of Leo V. and Rebecka (Malkin); m. Eugenie Muckle 1953; one s. one d.; ed. Forest Park High School, Baltimore, Maryland, Maryland Inst. of Art, Baltimore, Johns Hopkins Univ., Univs. of Maryland and Wisconsin and Cornell Univ.

Office of War Information 43-44; Instructor, Speech and Drama Dept., The Catholic Univ. of America 41-47, Asst. Prof. 49-52; Artistic Dir. Arena Stage, Washington, D.C. 52-53, Assoc. Dir. 61-63, 72-; Drama Critic *The New Leader* 62-63; Assoc. Dir. Tyrone Guthrie Theatre 64; Artistic Dir. Ithaca Festival Theater 63-, Actors Studio Theatre 62-; mem. Board of Dirs. Theatre Communications Group 63-; Prof. of Theatre Arts, Boston Univ. 72-; mem. Advisory Board New Dramatists Cttee. 55-, *Tulane Drama Review* 62-, N.Y. State Council on the Arts 65-, Nat. Theatre Conf. 65, Exec. Board Soc. of Stage Dirs. and Choreographers 72-; mem. Advisory Board Nat. Endowment for the Arts 74-; Assoc. Dir. Drama Div., Juilliard School of Music 75-76; Lecturer at major univs. in U.S. 45-; recent awards include Antoinette Perry Award for *Virginia Woolf* 63, "Obie" Award for Pinter plays 63, Prix Filmcritica, Venice 65, Prix Special du Jury, Tours 66, Preis der Kurzfilmtage, Oberhausen 66; Hon. L.H.D. (Hofstra Univ.) 74.

Leisure interests: swimming, walking, reading, being home.

Plays directed include: (U.S.A.) *Happy Days* 61, *The Caucasian Chalk Circle* 61, *The Dumbwaiter* and *The Collection* 62, *Who's Afraid of Virginia Woolf?* 62, *The Ballad of the Sad Café* 63, *Tiny Alice* 64, *Herakles* 65, *Slapstick Tragedy* 66, *A Delicate Balance* 66, *You Know I Can't Hear You When the Water's Running* 67, *I Never Sang for My Father* 67, *Box-Mao-Box* 68, *Not I* 72, *Madness of God* 76, *The Texas Trilogy* 76; (Israel) *The Cherry Orchard* 66; (England) *The Trip to Bountiful* 56, *Who's Afraid of Virginia*

Woolf? 64; (France) *The Skin of Our Teeth* 55, *Waiting for Godot* 56, 71, *Endgame* 58, *The Birthday Party* 67, *Inquest* 70, *Saved* 70, *Moonchildren* 71, *Uptight* 72, *The Foursome* 72, *Enemies* 73; (U.S.S.R.) *Our Town* 73, *The Madness of God* 74, *The Last Meeting of the Knights of the White Magnolia* 75.

Films and TV: *Oedipus the King* 56, *The Life of Samuel Johnson* 57, *The Years Between* 58, *The Secret of Freedom* 59, *Waiting for Godot* 60, *Film* 64, *Act Without Words, II* 65, *Eh, Joe?* 66, *Krapp's Last Tape* 71, *The Madness of God* 75.

30 Scenic Drive, Hastings-on-Hudson, N.Y. 10706, U.S.A.

Schneider, Liliane Louise Hélène; French company executive; b. 26 Sept. 1902.

Cinematographer 31; Dir. of Schneider and Co. 60; Dir. of Usines Schneider 60-70; Dir. and Hon. Pres. Schneider S.A. 66-; Chevalier Légion d'Honneur.

42 rue d'Anjou, 75008 Paris, France.

Schneider, William George, B.SC., M.SC., PH.D., F.R.C.S., F.R.S.; Canadian physical chemist; b. 1 June 1915, Wolseley, Saskatchewan; s. of Michael Schneider and Phillipina Kraushaar; m. Jean Purves 1940; two d.; ed. Saskatchewan, McGill and Harvard Univs.

Research Physicist, Oceanographic Inst., Woods Hole, Mass., U.S. 43-46; Research Chemist, Div. of Pure Chem., Nat. Research Council of Canada, Ottawa 46, Dir. Div. of Pure Chem. 63-66, Vice-Pres. (Scientific) 65-67, Pres. 67-; Hon. LL.D. (Alberta, Laurentian); Hon. D.Sc. (Memorial, Saskatchewan, Moncton, McMaster, Laval, York, New Brunswick, Montreal, McGill); Henry Marshall Tory Medal of the Royal Soc. of Canada; Chemical Inst. of Canada Medal, Montreal Medal 73.

Leisure interests: skiing, tennis.

Publs. *High Resolution Nuclear Magnetic Resonance* (with J. A. Pople and H. J. Bernstein) 59; 125 scientific papers.

National Research Council of Canada, Ottawa, Ont. K1A 0R6, Canada.

Telephone: 613-993-2024.

Schneiderhan, Wolfgang; Austrian violinist; b. 28 May 1915; m. Irmgard Seefried (q.v.); two d.; studied under Prof. Julius Winkler and Prof. Ottokar Sevcik.

Professor at Mozarteum, Salzburg 36-56, at Musik-hochschule, Vienna 39-50, at Conservatoire, Lucerne 49-; leader of master classes; Beethoven Plakat 60.

Reckenbühlstrasse 20, Lucerne, Switzerland.

Schnitzer, Moshe, M.A.; Israeli diamond exporter; b. 21 Jan. 1921; ed. Balfour High School, Tel-Aviv, Hebrew Univ. of Jerusalem.

Chairman, Asscn. of Diamond Instructors 43-46; Vice-Pres. Israel Diamond Exchange 51-66, Pres. 66-; Pres. Israel Exporters' Asscn. of Diamonds 62-; World Pres. Int. Fed. of Diamond Exchanges 68-72; partner, Diamond Export Enterprise 53-; mem. Consulting Cttee. to Minister of Commerce and Industry 68-; Editor *The Diamond*; Most Distinguished Exporter of Israel 64.

Publ. *Diamond Book* (in Hebrew) 46.

Israel Diamond Exchange, 3 Jabotinsky Road, **Ramat** Gan; and 78 Sharet Street, Tel-Aviv, Israel.

Schnurre, Wolfdietrich; German writer; b. 22 Aug. 1920, Frankfurt am Main; s. of Dr. Otto Schnurre; m. Marina Schnurre 1966; one s.; ed. Humanistisches Gymnasium.

Army Service 39-45; Freelance writer 45-; Founder-mem. "Group 47" 47; mem. Akademie für Sprache und Dichtung 59, West German PEN 58-61; Young Generation Prize, City of Berlin 58, Immermann Prize, Düsseldorf 59, George Mackensen Literature Prize 62.

Leisure interest: drawing.

Publs. *Aufzeichnungen des Pudels Ali* (satire) 51, 62, *Kassiber* (poems) 56, 64, *Abendländler* (satirical poems) 57, *Protest im Parterre* (fables) 57, *Eine Rechnung, die Nicht Aufgeht* (short stories) 58, *Als Vaters Bart noch Rot War* (novel) 58, *Das Los Unserer Stadt* (novel) 59, *Man Sollte Dagegen Sein* (short stories) 60, *Die Mauer des 13 August* (documentary) 61, *Berlin—eine Stadt Wird Geteilt* (documentary) 62, *Funke im Reisig* (short stories) 63, *Schreibtisch unter freiem Himmel* (essays) 64, *Ohne Einsatz kein Spiel* (short stories) 64, *Die Erzählungen* (stories) 66, *Spreezimmer möbliert* (radio plays) 67, *Die Zwengel* (for children) 67, *Was ich für mein Leben gern tue* (collection of prose pieces) 68, *Ein Schneemann für den grossen Bruder* (for children) 69, *Gocko* (for children) 70, *Die Sache mit den Meerschweinchen* (for children) 70, *Schnurre heiter* (short stories) 70, *Die Wandlung des Hippipotamos* (satire) 70, *Immer mehr Meerschweinchen* (for children) 71, *Der Spatz in der Hand* (tales and verse) 71, *Wie der Koalabär wieder lachen lernte* (for children) 71, *Der Meerschweinchendieb* (for children) 72, *Auf Tauchstation* (prose pieces) 73, *Ich frag ja bloss* (dialogue) 73, *Der wahre Noah* (satire) 74, *Schnurren und Murren* (for children) 74.
Goethestrasse 29, 1 Berlin 37, Germany.
Telephone: 802-80-63.

Schnyder, Felix; Swiss diplomatist; b. 5 March 1910, Burgdorf; *m.* Sigrid Bucher 1941; one *d.*; ed. Berne Univ.
Served in Swiss Foreign Service, Berne, Moscow, Berlin, Washington 40-57; Swiss Minister to Israel 57-58; Perm. Swiss observer at UN 58-60; Chair., Exec. Cttee. UNICEF 60; UN High Commr. for Refugees 61-65; Amb. to U.S.A. 66-75.
Leisure interests: chess, gardening, mountaineering.
c/o Department for Foreign Affairs, Berne, Switzerland.

Schocken, Gershom Gustav; Israeli editor and publisher; b. Sept. 1912; ed. Univ. of Heidelberg and London School of Economics.
Joined staff of *Haaretz* (daily newspaper) 37; publisher and editor 39-; Dir. Schocken Publishing House Ltd.; mem. Knesset (Parliament) 55-59.
Haaretz Building, 21 Salman Schocken Street, P.O. Box 233, Tel-Aviv, Israel.
Telephone: Tel-Aviv 623311.

Schoeman, Barend Jacobus, M.INST.T.; South African politician; b. 19 Jan. 1905, Johannesburg; *m.* H. B. van Rooyen; two *s.*; ed. Forest Secondary School, Johannesburg.
Leader Witwatersrand National Party 40-66; fmr. Minister of Labour, Minister of Public Works, Minister of Forestry; Nat. M.P., Maraisburg 48-74; Minister of Labour and Public Works 50; Minister of Transport 54-74; retd.; Leader, Nat. Party in Transvaal until Sept. 72.
Leisure interest: big-game hunting.
c/o House of Assembly, Cape Town, South Africa.

Schoeman, Hendrik; South African politician; b. 11 June 1927, Delmas, Transvaal; *m.* Christelle Loedolff; two *s.* one *d.*; ed. Afrikaans Boys' High School, Pretoria.
Member for Standerton, Nat. Party, 66-; Deputy Minister of Agriculture Aug. 68-July 72, Minister July 72-; fmr. Chair. of Board, Langeberg Co-operative; Chair. of Delmas Agricultural Corpn., Delmas Consumer Corpn.; mem. of Co-operative Council and Maize Cttee., Transvaal Agricultural Union; widespread farming interests.
Ministry of Agriculture, Pretoria, Republic of South Africa.

Schoenhofen, Leo H., Jr.; American business executive; b. 8 Aug. 1915; ed. Univ. of Wisconsin and Northwestern Univ.
Oklahoma Gas and Electric Co., Oklahoma City 36-38;

Container Corpn. of America, Chicago 40-, Vice-Pres. 52-54, Senior Vice-Pres. 56-61, Pres. and mem. Exec. Cttee. 61-64, Pres. and Chief Exec. Officer 64-68, Chair. and Chief Exec. Officer 68-; U.S. Naval Reserve 43-46.
Container Corporation of America, 1 First National Plaza, Chicago, Ill. 60670, U.S.A.

Scholander, Per Fredrik, M.D., PH.D.; American scientist; b. 29 Nov. 1905, Orebro; *s.* of Torkel F. and Agnethe Faye-Hansen Scholander; *m.* Susan Irving Scholander 1951; ed. Univ. of Oslo.
Botanical explorations in Greenland and Spitsbergen 30-32; Research Fellow in Physiology, Univ. of Oslo 32-39; Rockefeller Fellow 39-41; Research Assoc. Dept. of Zoology, Swarthmore Coll. 39-43; U.S. Air Force 43-46; Research Biologist 46-49; Research Fellow, Harvard Medical School 49-51; Physiologist, Woods Hole Oceanographic Inst. 52-55; Prof. of Physiology and Dir. Inst. of Zoophysiology, Univ. of Oslo 55-58; Prof. of Physiology, Scripps Inst. of Oceanography, Univ. of Calif. 58-; Dir. Physiological Research Lab., Univ. of Calif. at San Diego 63-70; mem. Royal Swedish Acad. of Sciences 74; Guggenheim Fellowship 69; mem. Nat. Acad. of Sciences, American Philosophical Soc. etc.; Hon. D.Sc. (Univ. of Alaska) 73.
Publ. *Tensile Water in Osmotic Processes* (co-author) 76.
Physiological Research Laboratory, Scripps Institution of Oceanography, University of California, San Diego, La Jolla, Calif. 92037, U.S.A.
Telephone: 714-452-2933.

Scholem, Gershom, PH.D.; Israeli professor; b. 5 Dec. 1897, Berlin, Germany; *s.* of Arthur Scholem and Betty née Hirsch; *m.* Fania Freud; ed. Berlin, Jena, Berne and Munich Univs.
Lecturer, Hebrew Univ., Jerusalem 25, Prof. of Jewish Mysticism 33-65; Dean, Hebrew Univ. 41-43, now Prof. Emer. Inst. of Jewish Studies; Visiting Prof., Jewish Inst. of Religion, New York 38, 49, Brown Univ., Providence, R.I. 56-57, Hebrew Union Coll., Cincinnati 66; Pres. Israel Acad. of Sciences and Humanities 68-74; mem. Dutch Acad. of Sciences, American Acad. of Arts and Sciences (Boston), American Acad. for Jewish Research, Westfälische Akad. der Wissenschaften; Israel State Prize 58, Rothschild Prize 62, Reuchlin Prize 69, Harvey Prize 74, Literature Prize, Bavarian Acad. of Arts 74.
Publs. several books on Judaism and Jewish Mysticism (in Hebrew, German and English).
The Israel Academy of Sciences and Humanities, P.O. Box 4040, Jerusalem; Home: 28 Abarbanel Street, Jerusalem, Israel.
Telephone: 36211 (Office); 32693 (Home).

Scholey, Robert; British engineer; b. 8 Oct. 1921, Sheffield; *s.* of Harold and Eveline Scholey; *m.* Joan Methley 1946; two *d.*; ed. King Edward VII School, Sheffield Univ.
Joined Steel, Peech & Tozer 47, held various engineering posts until 58, Works Man. Railway Materials 58, Works Man. Re-rolling Mills 59, Works Man. Steelmaking and Primary Mills 66, Dir., Gen. Works Man. 68; Works Man. Heavy Depts., Samuel Fox & Co. Ltd. 65-66; with British Steel Corpn. 68-, Dir. Rotheram Div., Midland Group 68, Dir. Special Steels Div., Steelworks Group 70, Man. Dir. Operations 72, Man. Dir. Strip Mills Div. 72-73, Chief Exec., mem. of Board Nov. 73-.
Leisure interests: history of the arts, reading, photography, camping, gardening.
British Steel Corporation, 33 Grosvenor Place, London, SW1X 7JG; Home: The Coach House, Much Hadham, Herts., England.
Telephone: 01-235-1212 (Office); Much Hadham 2908 (Home).

Scholl, Günther; German diplomatist; b. 11 Jan. 1909, Stettin; s. of Hermann Scholl and Hertha née Krause; m. 1st Brunhild Meister (died 1969), two d.; m. 2nd Dr. Anna Elisabeth Wolff 1971; two d.; qualified in law.
Scientific Asst., Foreign Office 39-45; at Diergardt-Mevissen III coal mine 45-50; Ministry of Interior 50-52; rose through German Diplomatic Service, Belgrade 54-56, Foreign Office 56-60, Moscow 60-63; Amb. to Pakistan 63-70, to Denmark 70-73; Commdr., Order of Phoenix, Grosses Bundesverdienstkreuz mit Stern, Hilal-i-Quaid-i-Azam (Pakistan), Grand Cross of Dannebrog (Denmark).
Leisure interests: art, history, music, sport.
Munich 8000, Beckmesserstrasse 4, Federal Republic of Germany.
Telephone: 916166.

Schon, Baron (Life Peer), cr. 76, of Whitehaven in the County of Cumbria; **Frank Schon,** Kt.; British industrialist; b. 18 May 1912, Vienna, Austria; s. of Dr. Frederick Schon and Henriette (née Nettel); m. Gertrude Secher 1936; two d.; ed. Rainer Gymnasium, Univ. of Prague, Univ. of Vienna.
Co-founder Marchon Products Ltd. 39, Solway Chemicals Ltd. 43, Chair. and Man. Dir. of both until 67; mem. Nat. Research Devt. Corpn. 67-, Chair. 69-; Chair. Cumberland Devt. Council 64-68; Dir. Albright & Wilson Ltd. 56-67, Associated Portland Cement Mfrs. Ltd. 67-; mem. Council, King's Coll., Newcastle, in Durham Univ. 59-63; mem. Council, Univ. of Newcastle upon Tyne 63-66; mem. Univ. Court 63-; mem. Northern Econ. Planning Council 65-68, Industrial Reorganization Corpn. 66-71, Advisory Council of Tech. 68-70; Part-time mem. Northern Gas Board 63-66; Hon. D.C.L. (Durham Univ.) 61; Freeman of Whitehaven 61.
Leisure interests: golf, reading.
Spaniards Field, Wildwood Rise, London, NW11 6SY, England.
Telephone: 01-455 3729.

Schonberg, Harold C.; American music critic; b. 29 Nov. 1915; ed. Brooklyn Coll. and New York Univ.
Associate Editor *American Music Lover* 46-48; Music critic *New York Sun* 46-50; Contributing Editor and Record Columnist *Musical Courier* 48-52; Music and Record Critic *New York Times* 50-60, Senior Music Critic 60-; columnist for *The Gramophone* (London) 48-60; U.S. Army service 42-46; Pulitzer Prize for Criticism 71.
Publs. *The Guide to Long-Playing Records: Chamber and Solo Instrument Music* 55, *The Collector's Chopin and Schumann* 59, *The Great Pianists* 63, *The Great Conductors* 67, *Lives of the Great Composers* 70, *Grandmasters of Chess* 73, contributing Editor *International Cyclopedia of Music and Musicians*.
New York Times, Times Square, New York, N.Y. 10036, U.S.A.

Schönberg, Mario; Brazilian university professor; b. 2 July 1916; ed. Univ. de São Paulo and Escola Politecnica of Univ. de São Paulo.
Instructor in Physics, Polytechnic, São Paulo 36; Asst. Prof. Theoretical Physics, Univ. of São Paulo 37; worked in Rome, Zürich, Coll. de France, Paris, Washington, D.C., Princeton Univ., and Yerkes Observatory 38-42; returned to Brazil 42-48, 53-; Prof. of Pure, Celestial and Higher Mechanics, Univ. of São Paulo 44-, Prof. of Quantum Mechanics 44-62, Dir. Dept. of Physics 53-61; with Free Univ. of Brussels 48-53; mem. Brazilian Acad. of Sciences 42.
Publs. 80 papers on theoretical, mathematical and experimental physics and astrophysics, and pure mathematics; articles on art criticism.
Universidade de São Paulo, Caixa Postal 9105, São Paulo; Home: Rua São Vicente de Paulo 501, Apto. 105, São Paulo, Brazil.

Schöner, Josef Andreas Carl, LL.D., DR. RER. POL.; Austrian diplomatist; b. 18 Feb. 1904, Vienna; s. of Andreas Carl Schöner and Lina Eder; m. Henrietta Welz 1965; ed. Vienna Univ.
Service in Austrian law courts; Foreign Service 33-70; Attaché, Washington 34; Ministry of Foreign Affairs 34-38; dismissed 38; worked for private firms 38-41; war service 41-45; returned to Foreign Service 45; Counsellor, London 47-48, Washington 48-50; Chief, Austrian Liaison Offices, Bonn 50-52; Minister, Bonn 52-53; Dir., **Political Affairs Dept., Foreign Office 53-55; Sec.-Gen.** Foreign Affairs 55-58; Ambassador to Fed. Repub. of Germany 58-66; Amb. to U.K. and Malta 66-70; retd.; Grosses Silbernes Ehrenzeichen mit Stern; Grand Officer Legion of Honour; Grand Crosses, Germany; Hon. G.C.V.O. 66; Order Knights of Malta, etc.; mem. Union Yacht Club.
Leisure interests: sailing, photography, painting.
13 Seilerstaette, 1010 Vienna, Austria.

Schorer, Mark, PH.D., LL.D.; American writer and teacher; b. 17 May 1908, Sauk City, Wis.; s. of William Carl and Anna Walser Schorer; m. Ruth Tozier Page 1936; one s. one d.; ed. Univ. of Wisconsin and Harvard Univ.
Briggs-Copeland Faculty Instructor, Harvard Univ. 40-45; Assoc. Prof. of English Univ. of Calif., Berkeley 45-46, Prof. of English 46-73, Emer. Prof. 73-, Chair. Dept. of English 60-65; Fulbright Lecturer, Univ. of Pisa 52-53, Univ. of Rome 64.
Leisure interest: music.
Publs. *A House Too Old* 35, *The Hermit Place* 41, *William Blake: The Politics of Vision* 46, *The State of Mind: Thirty-Two Stories* 47, *The Wars of Love* (novel) 54, *Sinclair Lewis: An American Life* 61, *The World We Imagine: Selected Essays* 68, *D. H. Lawrence* 69, *The Literature of America: Twentieth Century* 70.
68 Tamalpais Road, Berkeley, Calif. 94708, U.S.A.
Telephone: 415-848-8789.

Schotman, Johan Wilhelm, M.D.; Netherlands psychiatrist, philosopher, poet and writer; b. 10 March 1892, Hoogeveen; s. of M. Schotman and J. W. Veltman; m. 1st Constance Kokke 1917 (deceased), 2nd Maria Yanchevskaya 1923 (divorced), 3rd Hendrika van den Wyngaard 1935; two s. three d.; ed. Leyden Univ.
Practised as Physician 19-21; Hydrographic Expedition to Lunghai Railroad, China 21-27; Asst. Psychiatrist, Santpoort Mental Hospital 27-28; Psychiatrist, Maasoord Mental Hospital, Poortugaal near Rotterdam 28-37; Practice as Consultant Psychiatrist Gouda 37-39; Bussum 39-48; retd.; Pres. Nederlandsche Vertalingen Society 31-41; Dir. Zwolle Historical Museum 54-62; mem. Netherlands Soc. of Literature, PEN Club; Pres. Zwolle Branch Dickens Fellowship; Dir. Art School "Gerard Terboch".
Leisure interests: gardening, carpentry.
Publs. Poetry: *Der Geesten Gemoeting* 27, *Cloisonné* 36, *Hellevaart* 47; Philosophy and Psychology: *De schone gave* 27, *Naar open water* 36, *Jodulphus en de Kater* 39, *De macht tot Vrijheid* 46, *China Ongereed* 41; Prose: *Het Vermolmde Boeddhabeeld* I 27, II 28, III 29, *Wind in Bamboestengels* 46, *Arcadië en Asfalt*; Essays: *Analysen en Retouches* 53; and several other works; translations of about 45 works from English, French, German, Latin and in 69 the *Sji Sjing* in verse from Chinese.
Willemskade 11, Zwolle, Netherlands.
Telephone: 05200 141941.

Schöttle, Erwin; German politician; b. 18 Oct. 1899.
Former employee in printing trade; later became a journalist; emigrated to Switzerland 33, later to U.K.; in German Service of B.B.C. 41-46; later became a leading mem. of Social Democratic Party (S.P.D.), Württemberg; mem. Bundestag 49-72, Vice-Pres. 61-69; Deputy Chair. of S.P.D. in Bundestag 69-72.
Wannenstrasse 52, 7 Stuttgart, Federal Republic of Germany.

Schou, August, M.A.; Norwegian historian; b. 19 Nov. 1903, Oslo; *s.* of Aage Schou and Hallfrid Hall; *m.* Harriet Haaland 1937; two *d.*; ed. Univ. of Oslo. Secretary of review *Samtiden* 30-47; Teacher, Mercantile Gymnasium of Oslo 34-44; Dir. Norwegian Nobel Inst. 46-74; mem. Alliance Française; Knight, Legion of Honour.

Leisure interests: literature, art.

Publs. *Histoire de l'Internationalisme*, Vol. II 54, Vol. III 63, *Economics—a History* 44, *History of the Norwegian Posts* 47, *History of the Nobel Peace Prize* 50, *Aschehougf's History of the World*, Vol. IV 55.

c/o Norwegian Nobel Institute, 19 Drammensveien, Oslo, Norway.

Schouwenaar-Franssen, Johanna Frederika; Netherlands teacher and politician; b. 3 May 1909, Rotterdam; *m.* A. J. Schouwenaar 1945 (died 1962); two *s.* one *d.*; ed. Univ. of Leyden.

Teacher of classics; mem. Rotterdam Town Council, Benelux Parl. Conf., European Parl.; mem. Parl. (First Chamber); Minister of Social Welfare 63-65; Netherlands del. to the 24th and 25th Assemblies of the UN; Liberal; Knight Order of Netherlands Lion; Grand Officer in The Order of Merit of the Italian Repub.; Grand Officer in The Order of Merit of the Kingdom of the Hellenes.

24 Beethovenlaan, Bilthoven, Netherlands.

Telephone: 030-783623.

Schram-Nielsen, Erik, PH.D.; Danish diplomatist; b. 6 June 1911, Copenhagen; *s.* of Ejnar Schram-Nielsen; *m.* Grethe Volkert 1939; two *d.*; ed. Metropolitan School, Copenhagen and Univ. of Copenhagen.

Entered Foreign Service 36; studied in the Middle East 37-38; Deputy Under-Sec. of State, Ministry of Foreign Affairs 59-61; Perm. Rep. to NATO 61-66; Ambassador to France 66-71, to Sweden 71-.

Leisure interests: riding, shooting.

Publ. *System of Damages in Islamic Law* 45.

Royal Danish Embassy, 14 Gustaf Adolfstorg, Stockholm, Sweden.

Schramm, Wilbur, A.M., PH.D., LITT.D.; American educationist; b. 5 Aug. 1907, Marietta, Ohio; *s.* of A. A. and Louise Schramm; *m.* Elizabeth Donaldson 1934; one *s.* one *d.*; ed. Marietta Coll., and Harvard and Iowa Univs.

Newspaper reporter and desk editor, corresp. of Associated Press 24-30; Asst. Prof., Assoc. Prof. and later Prof. of English, Univ. of Iowa 35-41; Editor, Harcourt, Brace & Co. (publishers) 41; Dir. of educational services, U.S. Office of War Information 42-43; Educational Consultant to Navy Dept. 43; Educational Adviser to War Department 43-46; Dir. School of Journalism, Univ. of Iowa 43-47; Asst. to the Pres., Dir. Inst. of Communications Research, Dir. Univ. Press, and Prof. Univ. of Ill. 47-55, Dean, Div. of Communications 50-55; Prof. Communications Stanford Univ. 55-73, Dir. Inst. for Communication Research 58-73; Janet M. Peck Prof. of Int. Communications 62, Prof. of Educ. 67-73; Dir. East-West Communication Inst., 73-76; Distinguished Center Researcher 76-; Chair. U.S. Nat. Council on Research in Journalism; Fellow, Center for Advanced Study in the Behavioral Sciences 59-60; mem. Nat. Acad. of Educ., Editorial Board *Public Opinion Quarterly*, *Journalism Quarterly* and *Communications Review*.

Publs. *Approaches to a Science of English Verse* 35, *American Medley* (stories) 37, *Francis Parkman* 38, *Literary Scholarship* 41, *Windwagon Smith and Other Yarns* 47, *The Lost Train* 48, *The Reds Take a City* 51; Editor: *The Story Workshop* 39, *Two Creative Traditions* 40, *American Literature* 46, *Iowa Studies in Newspaper Reading* 46-47, *Communications in Modern Society* 48, *Process and Effects of Mass Communication* 54, 71, *Four Theories of The Press* 56, *Responsibility in Mass Communications* 57, *One day in the World's Press* 59, *The Impact of Educational Television* 60, *Television in the Lives of our Children* 61, *The Science of Human Communication* 63, *The People Look at Educational Television* 63, *Mass Media and National Development* 64, *Communication and Change in the Developing Countries* 66, *The New Media: Memo to Educational Planners* 67, *Communications in Family Planning* 71, *Quality in Instructional Television* 73, *Men, Messages, Media: A Look at Human Communication* 73, *Handbook of Communication* (with Pool) 73, *Communication and Change—the Last Ten Years* 76, *Big Media, Little Media* 76.

Apartment 3009, Yacht Harbor Towers, 1650 Ala Moana Boulevard, Honolulu, Hawaii 96815; East-West Communication Institute, East-West Center, Honolulu, Hawaii 96822, U.S.A.

Telephone: 808-947-4157 (Home); 808-948-8624 (Office).

Schreiber, Marc, LL.D., LIC. POL. SC.; Belgian United Nations official; b. 5 Sept. 1915; *m.* Myriam E. Nassaux 1940; one *s.* one *d.*; ed. Brussels Univ.

Scientific Assoc., Inst. of Sociology Solvay, Univ. of Brussels 38; mem. Brussels Bar 39; Asst. Belgian Programme Organizer B.B.C., London 40-41; Exec. Asst. to Belgian Minister of Foreign Affairs and Information 41-43; Asst. Legal Adviser, Belgian Ministry for Foreign Affairs and Chargé de Mission 43-45; Assoc. Chief, Legal Section and Chief, Drafting and Co-ordination Section, UN Preparatory Comm. 45; Legal Adviser, UN Secr. 46-48, Senior Legal Adviser 53; Deputy Dir.-Gen. Legal Div. 53-66; Dir. UN Information Centre, Paris 60-61; Scientific Assoc. Columbia Univ. N.Y. 65-; Dir. Div. of Human Rights UN 66-; has acted as legal adviser or as Sec. or Rep. of the Sec.-Gen. at many UN meetings, confs. and field missions, Exec. Sec. International Conf. on Human Rights, Teheran 68.

Leisure interests: music, reading, walking.

Publs. *Belgium* 45, and contributions to various publs.

12 Avenue de Budé, Geneva, Switzerland.

Telephone: 33-96-62.

Schreyer, Edward Richard, B.A., B.PED., B.ED., M.A.; Canadian politician; b. 21 Dec. 1935, Beausejour, Manitoba; *s.* of John J. Schreyer and Elizabeth Gottfried; *m.* Lilly Schulz 1960; one *s.* two *d.*; ed. Cromwell Public School, Beausejour Collegiate, United Coll., St. John's Coll. and Univ. of Manitoba.

Teacher of Political Science and Int. Relations, Univ. of Manitoba; mem. for Brokenhead, Manitoba Legislature 58, re-elected 59, 62; mem. Parl. for Springfield Constituency 65-68, for Selkirk 68; Leader, Manitoba New Democratic Party June 69-; Premier of Manitoba, Pres. of the Council and Minister of Dominion-Provincial Relations July 69-, Minister of Industry and Commerce July-Dec. 69, of Finance 75-; mem. Canadian Asscn. of Univ. Teachers, Commonwealth Parliamentary Asscn., Inter-Parliamentary Union.

Leisure interests: reading, baseball, squash, hockey.

Office of the Premier, Winnipeg, Manitoba; 3069 Henderson Highway, East St. Paul, Winipeg, Manitoba, Canada.

Telephone: 204-338-4214.

Schrieffer, John Robert, M.S., PH.D.; American professor of physics; b. 31 May 1931, Oak Park, Ill.; *m.* Anne Grete Thomson 1960; one *s.* two *d.*; ed. Mass. Inst. of Technology and Univ. of Illinois.

National Science Foundation Fellow, Univ. of Birmingham, U.K., and Univ. Inst. for Theoretical Physics, Copenhagen 57-58; Asst. Prof., Univ. of Chicago 57-60, Univ. of Illinois 59-60; Assoc. Prof., Univ. of Ill. 60-62; Univ. of Pennsylvania 62-, Mary Amanda Wood Prof. of Physics 64-; Andrew D. White Prof. Cornell Univ. 70; mem. Nat. Acad. of Sciences, American Acad. Arts and Sciences; Buckley Prize 68; Comstock Prize (Nat. Acad. of Sciences) 68; hon. doctorates, Univ. of Geneva,

Technische Hochschule, Munich, Univs. of Pa. and Ill.; Nobel Prize in Physics (with J. Bardeen (*q.v.*) and L. N. Cooper) 72; Guggenheim Fellow 67-68.
Department of Physics, University of Pennsylvania, Philadelphia, Pa. 19104; Home: 1303 Club House Road, Gladwyne, Pa. 19035, U.S.A.
Telephone: 215-594-7003 (Office); 215-LA5-8993 (Home).

Schröder, Dr. Gerhard; German lawyer and politician; b. 11 Sept. 1910; ed. Kaiser-Wilhelm-Gymnasium in Trier and Univs. of Königsberg, Edinburgh, Berlin and Bonn.
Assistant Law Faculty Bonn Univ. and Kaiser-Wilhelm Inst. for Int. Private Law, Berlin 33-36; practice in Berlin 36-39; served 39-45 war; served *Land* Govt. Nordrhein-Westfalen 45-47; mem. post-war Comm. on Electoral Law; practice in Düsseldorf since 47; concerned with reorganization of mining and iron and steel industries 47-53; mem. (Christian Democratic Union) Federal Parl. 49-; mem. Central Exec. Cttee. CDU; Chair. Protestant Working Group CDU/CSU; Minister of the Interior 53-61, of Foreign Affairs 61-66, of Defence 66-69; Chair. Foreign Affairs Cttee. of Parl. Nov. 69-. Publ. *Decision for Europe* 64.
Pappelweg 25a, 53 Bonn-Bad Godesberg, Federal Republic of Germany.
Telephone: 161.

Schroder, Gerhard; German public servant; b. 3 March 1921; ed. Marburg Univ.
Officer, Radio, Film and Press Affairs, Ministry of Education, Lower Saxony 52-59; Head of Arts Dept., Ministry of Education, Lower Saxony 60-61; mem. Admin. Council, North German Radio 55-61; Dir.-Gen. Norddeutscher Rundfunk (North German Radio and TV) 61-74; Chair. of ARD (Assen. of German Broadcasting Orgs.) 70-71; Chair. Radio Bremen 74-.
Radio Bremen, Heinrich-Hertz-Strasse 13, 28 Bremen 33, Postfach, Federal Republic of Germany.

Schröder, Kurt, DR. PHIL.; German mathematician; b. 31 July 1909, Berlin; *s.* of Otto Schröder and Anna Paul; *m.* Ruth Hase 1937; one *s.* one *d.*; ed. Friedrich-Wilhelms Universität, Berlin.
Lecturer, Berlin 40; Prof. of Applied Mathematics and Dir. Mathematical Inst., Humboldt Universität zu Berlin 46-72, Pro-Rector for Research 51, Rector of Univ. 59-65; mem. E. Berlin Acad. of Sciences 52-; mem. Research Council of Council of Ministers of D.D.R. 57-; Dir. Inst. Advanced Mathematics, Inst. of Engineering, Machinery and Mechanics of the Deutsche Akademie der Wissenschaften zu Berlin; Pres. Mathematical Soc. of D.D.R. 63-72; Vaterländischer Verdienstorden in Gold; Nationalpreis.
Leisure interest: art.
1187 Berlin-Karrlinenhof, Rehfeldstrasse 6, Berlin, German Democratic Republic.

Schroeder, Hermann; German composer; b. 26 March 1904, Bernkastel/Mosel; *m.* Gisela Fassbinder 1940; ed. Universität Innsbruck and Musikhochschule Köln.
Teacher, Rheinische Musikschule, Cologne 30-38; Organist, Trier Cathedral 38, Head of City Music Acad., Trier 40-46; Teacher, Musikhochschule, Cologne 46-48, Prof. 48-; Lecturer, Univ. of Bonn 46-, Univ. of Cologne 56-61; Acting Dir. of Musikhochschule, Cologne 58-61; Leader, Cologne Bach Soc. 47-61; Robert Schumann Prize (City of Düsseldorf) 52; Arts Prize (Rheinland-Pfalz Province) 56; Order of Gregory the Great; Dr. h.c. (Univ. Bonn) 74.
Compositions include: organ music, operatic and orchestral music.
5 Köln-Bayenthal, Bernhardstrasse 145, Federal Republic of Germany.
Telephone: 0221-386338.

Schulberg, Budd; American novelist and scriptwriter; b. 27 March 1914, N.Y.C.; *s.* of Benjamin P. and Adeline (Jaffe) Schulberg; *m.* 1st Virginia Ray 1936 (divorced 1942), one *d.*; *m.* 2nd Victoria Anderson 1943 (divorced 1964), two *s.*; *m.* 3rd Geraldine Brooks 1964; ed. Deerfield Acad. and Dartmouth Coll.
Short-story writer and novelist 36-; Screenwriter for Samuel Goldwyn, David O. Selznick and Walter Wanger, Hollywood, Calif. 36-40; Lieut. U.S. Navy 43-46, assigned to Office of Strategic Service; taught writing courses and conducted workshops at various institutes in the U.S.; mem. Authors Guild, Dramatists Guild, American Civil Liberties Union, American Soc. Composers Authors and Publishers, Sphinx, Nat. Board Nat. Book Cttee.; Founder Watts Writers Workshop; Pres. Douglass House Foundation 65-; numerous awards for writings.
Publs. (novels) *What Makes Sammy Run?* 41, *The Harder They Fall* 47, *The Disenchanted* 50, *Waterfront* 55, *Sanctuary V* 69; *Some Faces in the Crowd* (short stories) 53, *From the Ashes: Voices of Watts* (Editor and author of introduction) 67, *Loser and Still Champion: Muhammad Ali* 72, *The Four Seasons of Success* 72; (plays) *Winter Carnival* (with F. Scott Fitzgerald) 39, *The Pharmacist's Mate* 51, *On the Waterfront* 54, *A Face in the Crowd* 57, *Wind Across the Everglades* 58, *The Disenchanted* 58, *What Makes Sammy Run?* (television play 59, stage 64); stories and articles in numerous anthologies; contrib. to *Newsday Syndicate, Esquire, Saturday Review, Life, Harper's, Playboy, Intellectual Digest, The New Republic*.
300 E. 57th Street, New York, N.Y. 10022; Home: Versailles 21, México 6, D.F., Mexico.

Schuller, Gunther; American composer and conductor; b. 22 Nov. 1925, New York; *s.* of Arthur E. and Elsie (Bernatz) Schuller; *m.* Marjorie Black; two *s.*; ed. St. Thomas Choir School, N.Y.C. and Manhattan School of Music.
Soloist, French horn, Metropolitan Opera Orchestra 45-59; Teacher, Manhattan School of Music 50; Music Dir. First Int. Jazz Festival, Washington 62; Pres. New England Conservatory of Music 67-; Artistic Dir. Summer Activities, Boston Symphony Orchestra, Tanglewood 69-; mem. Nat. Inst. of Arts and Letters, Nat. Endowment for the Arts, Mass. Council on the Arts and Humanities; Creative Arts Award, Brandeis Univ. 60; Nat. Inst. Arts and Letters Award 60; Guggenheim Grant 62-63; ASCAP Deems Taylor Award 70; Rogers and Hammerstein Award 71; Hon. D.Mus. (Northeastern Univ. 67, Colby Coll. 69).
Compositions include: *Concerto for Horn and Orchestra* 44, *Symphony for Brass and Percussion* 50, *Fantasy for Unaccompanied Cello* 51, *Recitative and Rondo for Violin and Piano* 53, *Dramatic Overture* 51, *Music for Violin, Piano and Percussion* 57, *Woodwind Quintet* 58, *Concertino for Jazz Quartet and Orchestra* 59, *Seven Studies on Themes of Paul Klee* 59, *Spectra* 58, *Conversations* 60, *Variants* (ballet with choreography by Balanchine) 61, *Music for Brass Quintet* 61, *String Quartet* 65, *Sacred Cantata* 66, *Gala Music* (Concerto for Orchestra) 66, *The Visitation* (opera commissioned by Hamburg State Opera) 66, *Movements for Flute and Strings, Six Renaissance Lyrics, Triplum* 67, *Shapes and Designs* 68, *Fisherman and his Wife* 70, *Capriccio Stravagante* 72.
Publs. *Horn Technique* 62, *Early Jazz, its Roots and Musical Development*, Vol. I 68.
c/o New England Conservatory of Music, 290 Huntington Avenue, Boston, Mass. 02115, U.S.A.
Telephone: 617-262-1120.

Schultheisz, Emil, M.D.; Hungarian physician and politician; b. 1923, Budapest; ed. Univ. of Liberal Arts, Kolozsvár (now Cluj, Romania), and Medical Univs. of Debrecen and Budapest.
Practised in Budapest Hospitals 50-54; qualified as

specialist for internal diseases 54; Chief of Internal Dept., Cen. State Hospital 60, Vice-Dir., later Dir. 70-72; Deputy Minister of Health, later First Deputy Minister and Sec. of State for Health 72; Minister of Health 74-; Chief Dir. Semmelweis Museum of Medical History until 73; mem. numerous medical socs. in Hungary and abroad.

Publs. one book and more than 100 medical articles.

Ministry of Health, V. Akadémia-utca 10, 1361 Budapest, Hungary.

Telephone: 114-600.

Schulthess, Felix W.; Swiss banker; b. 1909, Zürich; ed. in Switzerland, New York and Buenos Aires.

Joined Swiss Nat. Bank after Second World War; Gen. Man. Swiss Credit Bank 51, Chair. Man. Board 63-; mem. advisory boards of dirs. of many major Swiss and other concerns.

Swiss Credit Bank, Paradeplatz, Zürich, Switzerland.

Schultze, Charles Louis, PH.D.; American economist and government official; b. 12 Dec. 1924; ed. Georgetown Univ. and Univ. of Maryland.

U.S. Army 43-46; Admin. Asst. Democratic Nat. Cttee. 48; Research Specialist, Army Security Agency 48-49; Instructor, Coll. of St. Thomas (St. Paul, Minn.) 49-51; Economist, Office of Price Stabilization 51-52, Council of Econ. Advisers 52-53, 55-59, Machine and Allied Products Inst. 53-54; Assoc. Prof. of Econs., Indiana Univ. 59-61; Prof. of Econs., Univ. of Maryland 61-62, 68-; Asst. Dir., Bureau of the Budget 62-65, Dir. 65-Jan. 68; Senior Fellow, Brookings Inst.

Publs. *Recent Inflation in the United States* 59, *Prices, Costs and Output for the Postwar Decade* 59, *National Income Analysis* 64.

Home: 5826 Nevada Avenue, N.W., Washington, D.C. 20015, U.S.A.

Schulz, Peter; German lawyer; b. 25 April 1930, Rostock; s. of Albert Schulz and Emmi Munck; m. Dr. Sonja Planeth 1955; one s. one d.; ed. Univ. of Hamburg.

Member of Hamburg City Council 61-, Senator for Justice 66-71; fmr. Deputy Regional Chair. Social Democratic Party, Hamburg-North; Second Burgomaster of Hamburg and Deputy Pres. of the Senate and Dept. of Educ. 70-71; Chief Burgomaster of Hamburg and Pres. of Senate 71-74.

Senat der Freien und Hansestadt Hamburg, Senatskanzlei, 2 Hamburg 1, Rathaus, Federal Republic of Germany.

Schulze, Rudolph; German pharmacist and politician; b. 1918.

Member of Presidium, Christlich-Demokratische Union (CDU); Deputy Chair. Council of Ministers and Minister of Posts and Telecommunications.

Ministerrat, Berlin, German Democratic Republic.

Schuman, Frederick Lewis, PH.D.; American political scientist; b. 22 Feb. 1904, Chicago, Ill.; s. of August and Ella Schulze Schuman; m. Lily Caroline Abell 1930; two s.; ed. Chicago Univ.

Instructor in Political Science, Chicago Univ. 27-32; Fellow, Acad. Political and Social Science, Berlin 33; Woodrow Wilson Prof. of Govt., Williams Coll. 36-68, Prof. Emer. 68-; Prof. of Political Science, Portland State Univ. 68-69; Fellow, Social Science Research Council 29-30, American Acad. Political and Social Science 33; mem. American Political Science Asscn., American Society Int. Law; Principal Political Analyst, Foreign Broadcast Intelligence Service, Fed. Communications Comm. 42-43; Visiting Lecturer in Int. Relations, Harvard 38, California 39 and 55, Cornell 44, Columbia 46, Chicago 56, Central Washington Coll. 59, Portland State Coll. 61, Stanford 63, Hawaii 63.

Leisure interests: travel, photography, swimming.

Publs. *American Policy toward Russia since 1917* 28, *War and Diplomacy in the French Republic* 31, *International Politics* 33, *Conduct of German Foreign Affairs* 34, *Rotary?* 34, *Hitler and the Nazi Dictatorship* 35, *Germany since 1918* 37, *Europe on the Eve* 39, *Night Over Europe* 41, *Design for Power* 42, *Soviet Politics* 46, *The Commonwealth of Man* 52, *Russia since 1917* 57, *International Politics* 58, *Government in the Soviet Union* 61, *The Cold War: Retrospect and Prospect* 62, *International Politics* (7th edition) 69.

Williams College, Williamstown, Mass.; Home: 1205 S.W. Cardinell Drive, Portland, Ore. 97201, U.S.A.

Telephone: 227-4863.

Schuman, William Howard, B.S., M.A.; American musician; b. 4 Aug. 1910; ed. Columbia Univ. and privately.

Lecturer and Dir. of Chorus, Sarah Lawrence Coll., Bronxville 35-45; Dir. of Publications, G. Schirmer Inc. 45-51; Pres. Juilliard School of Music 45-62, Pres. Emer. 62-; Pres. Lincoln Center for the Performing Arts 62-69, Pres. Emer. 69-; Chair. of Board Videorecord Corpn. 70-; Honorary doctorates from Chicago Musical Coll., Univ. of Wisconsin, Philadelphia Conservatory of Music, Cincinnati Coll. of Music, Columbia Univ., Hartt Coll. of Music, Colgate Univ., Allegheny Coll., New York Univ., Brandeis Univ., Oberlin Coll., Adelphi Coll., Northwestern Univ., Bates Coll. and others; Hon. mem. Royal Acad. of Music; Pulitzer Prize for Music, Guggenheim Fellowships, Award of Nat. Inst. of Arts and Letters, League of Composers Award, New York Critics Circle Award and Award of Merit of Nat. Asscn. of American Composers and Conductors.

Compositions include: nine symphonies, four string quartets, *"Amaryllis" Variation for String Trio, American Festival Overture, Credendum, New England Triptych, Circus Overture, Concerto for Piano and Orchestra, Concerto for Violin and Orchestra, A Song of Orpheus* fantasy for 'cello and orchestra, *The Witch of Endor, In Praise of Shahn,* secular cantatas and music for ballets, band works and piano music.

Videorecord Corporation of America, 180 East State Street, Westport, Conn. 06880, U.S.A.

Schumann, Horst; German politician; b. 6 Feb. 1924; ed. elementary school.

Former piano-maker, fmr. mem. Kommunistische Partei Deutschlands; mem. Sozialistische Einheitspartei Deutschlands (S.E.D.) 45-; District Sec. Freie Deutsche Jugend (F.D.J.), Leipzig 47-48; Sec. for Pioneer Questions in Saxon F.D.J. 49-50; First Sec. Saxon F.D.J. 50-52; First Sec. F.D.J. District Headquarters 52-55; mem. Bureau of Cen. Cttee. of F.D.J. 55-, Cen. Cttee. S.E.D. 59-; First Sec. Cen. Cttee. F.D.J. 59-; mem. State Council 60-, Volkskammer 63-; Freie Deutsche Jugend, Unter den Linden 36-38, Berlin W.8, Germany.

Schumann, Maurice; French writer and politician; b. 10 April 1911; m. Lucie Daniel 1944; three d.

With Havas News Agency 32-40; Chief Official Broadcaster, B.B.C. French Service 40-44; Liaison Officer with Allied Expeditionary Forces from D-Day until liberation of Paris; mem. of French Provisional Consultative Assembly Nov. 44-July 45; mem. of both Constituent Assemblies Oct. 45-May 46 and June-Nov. 46; Chair. of Popular Republican Movement (M.R.P.) 45-49; Deputy for Nord 45-73; Sec. of State for Foreign Affairs 51-54; Pres. Foreign Affairs Comm. of Nat. Assembly 59; Minister of State attached to the Prime Minister's Office (Territorial Planning) April-May 62; Minister of State for Scientific Research 67-68; Minister of Social Affairs 68-69, of Foreign Affairs 69-73; Senator, Département du Nord 74-; chief contrib. to *L'Aube;* mem. Acad. Française 74; Compagnon de la Libération; Chevalier Légion d'Honneur, Order of Léopold; Croix de Guerre; Hon. LL.D. (Cantab.) 72.

Publs. *Le germanisme en marche* 38, *Mussolini* 39, *Les problèmes ukrainiens et la paix européenne* 39,

Honneur et Patrie 46, *Le vrai malaise des intellectuels de gauche* 57, *Le Rendezvous avec quelqu'un* (novel) 61, *La voix du couvre-feu* (novel) 64, *Les Flots roulant au loin* (novel) 73, *La Communication* (novel) 74, *La mort née de leur propre vie: essai sur Péguy, Simone Weil et Gandhi* 74.
53 avenue Maréchal-Lyautey, 75016 Paris, France.

Schürer, Gerhard; German politician; b. 1921.
Former machine fitter; mem. Sozialistische Einheitspartei Deutschlands (S.E.D.) 48-; Dept. Head for Planning, Dept. of Planning and Finance, Central Cttee. of S.E.D. 55-61, Head of Dept. of Planning and Finance 61-62; Deputy Chair. State Planning Comm. 62-63, First Deputy Chair. 63-65, Chair. 65-; mem. Council of Ministers 63, now Deputy Chair.; mem. Cen. Cttee. of S.E.D. 63 .
State Planning Commission, Berlin, German Democratic Republic.

Schürmann, Leo, D.IUR.; Swiss jurist and central banker; b. 1917, Olten; m. Cécile Baur 1943; one s. one d.; ed. Univ. of Basle.
Advocate and Notary, Clerk of Court and Legal Sec., Canton of Soleure 40; engaged in banking 47; own law office 49; Chief Justice, Canton of Soleure 53-74; Habilitation at Fribourg Univ. 56, Extraordinary Prof. 64-; Chair. Swiss Cartel Comm., also of various Fed. and Cantonal Cttees. of Experts 64-74; Cantonal Councillor 57-69; Nat. Councillor 59-74; mem. Board of Gen. Mans. Swiss Nat. Bank July 74-.
Publs. *Textbook on the Economic Articles of the Federal Constitution.* Author of bills, inter alia on the laws on town and country planning and on housing devt., of the Fed. Decree on measures against abuses in the rental system, of an executive order related to the environmental protection article, of a new press article in the Fed. Constitution and a press-promoting law, of the Fed. law on investment assistance to mountain areas, of the law enacted by the canton of Soleure on admin. judicature, of the law on disaster provisions and of communal decrees 64-74.
Banque Nationale Suisse, Börsenstrasse 15, 8022 Zurich, Switzerland.
Telephone: 01/23 47 40.

Schuschnigg, Kurt von; Austrian politician and professor; b. 14 Dec. 1897; s. of Arthur von Schuschnigg and Anna (née Wopfrier); m. 1st Hermione Masere 1924 (died 1935), 2nd Vera Countess Czernin 1938; one s. one d.; ed. Fribourg and Innsbruck.
Attorney at Law; Deputy 27; Founder and Chief of *Ostmärkische Sturmscharen*, patriotic organization for defence of Austrian independence; Min. of Justice in Buresch Cabinet Jan.-May 32 and in Dollfuss Cabinet May 32-July 34, also of Education Sept. 33-July 34; Federal Chancellor after assassination of Dollfuss July 34; Chancellor, Min. of Defence and Foreign Affairs 36-38; Min. for Public Security 37; fmr. mem. Christian Social Party; Leader of Patriotic Front May 36-38; arrested after Nazi Putsch Mar. 38; imprisoned; liberated by Allied Advance May 45; Prof. Political Science, St. Louis Univ., Mo. 48-68.
Leisure interests: travelling, reading.
Publs. *Farewell Austria* 38, *Austrian Requiem* 47, *The Law of Peace* 59, *The Brutal Takeover* 69.
6162 Mutters, Austria.

Schuster, Günter, D.SC.; German scientist; b. 17 Dec. 1918, Bonn; ed. Univs. of Göttingen and Bonn.
Assistant, Bonn Univ. 48-50, Scientific Asst. Inst. of Applied Physics 50-55, Head of Physical Studies 56-65; Adviser, Ministry of Scientific Research 65-67; Dir. Nuclear Research and Technique Div., Ministry of Education and Science 68-71; Deputy Dir.-Gen. of Industrial, Technological and Scientific Affairs Comm. of the European Communities 71-73, Dir.-Gen. of Research, Science and Educ. 73-.

Directorate-General of Research, Science and Education, Commission of the European Communities, 200 rue de la Loi, 1040 Brussels, Belgium.
Telephone: 735-00-40.

Schut, Willem Fredrik; Netherlands civil engineer and politician; b. 21 Aug. 1920, Amsterdam; m. G. E. Boot 1945; two s. six d.; ed. Secondary School, Amsterdam and Technological Inst., Delft.
Planner, Inst. of Town and Country Planning, South Holland 43, Deputy Dir. 45-46, Dir. Jan. 46-67; Private Planning Consultant, Middleburg 56-67; Minister of Housing and Physical Planning 67-71; Dir. Town and Country Planning; mem. Scientific Council for Govt. Policy; Bronze Cross 46; Grand Cross in Order of Merit of Luxembourg 67; Grand Cross Order of the Crown of Belgium 69, Knight, Order of Lion of the Netherlands 71.
Town and Country, Delftsestraat 15B, Rotterdam; Home: Mr. P. D. Kleylaan I, Nieuwerkerk aan den Ijssel, Netherlands.
Telephone: 146922 (Office); 01803-4734 (Home).

Schüttenhelm, Emile A.; Netherlands broadcasting executive; b. 23 Nov. 1909, The Hague; s. of Abraham Schüttenhelm and Helena van Went; two s. one d.; ed. Delft Technical Coll. and Utrecht Univ.
Lieutenant, Military Police 37-40; Asst. Inspector for Social Welfare 40-45; Dir. Roman Catholic Youth Movement 45-48; Deputy Dir. for Youth and Adult Educ., Ministry for Educ. and Sciences 48-55, Dir. Dept. for Youth and Adult Educ. and Social Pedagogic Training 55-59; Pres., Netherlands Television Foundation (N.T.S.) 59-69, Netherlands Broadcasting Foundation (N.O.S.) 69-75; Adviser for Int. Affairs and New Bldgs., Netherlands Broadcasting Foundation 75-; Chair. Interdept. Comm. for Open-Air Recreation and Tourism, Liturgical Ecumenical Centre, Soc. for the Queen Wilhelmina Cancer Research Fund, Dutch Camping Council, Foundation of the Green Heart of Amsterdam, Nat., Dutch Carillon Museum, Royal Dutch Land Devt. Soc., Amsterdam; Vice-Pres. Foundation for Civic Educ.; mem. Belgium-Netherlands Technical Comm. Cultural Agreement; Knight, Order of the Lion of the Netherlands, Officer Order of Orange-Nassau, Knight Order of St. Gregory the Great, Commdr. de la Couronne (Belgium).
Leisure interests: sailing, golf, camping.
Koningslaan 12, Bussum, Netherlands.
Telephone: 02159-45310.

Schütz, Klaus; German politician; b. 17 Sept. 1926; m. Heide Schütz; ed. Paulsen-Real-Gymnasium, Humboldt Univ. zu Berlin and Harvard Univ., U.S.A.
War service, seriously wounded 44-45; Asst., Inst. für Politische Wissenschaften, Freie Univ., Berlin 51; mem. City Assembly 54-57; mem. Bundestag 57-61; Liaison Senator between Berlin Senate and Bonn Govt. 61-66; mem. Bundesrat 61-, Pres. 67-68; Under-Sec. Ministry of Foreign Affairs 66-67; Governing Mayor of West Berlin 67-; Chair. Berlin Social Democratic Party 68-.
Berlin 31, Johannisberger Strasse 34, Germany.
Telephone: 7801-3300.

Schütz, Paul, DR. RER. POL.; German banker; b. 27 June 1910, Tholey, Saar; s. of Nikolaus Schütz and Barbara Schütz (née Simon); m. Christiane Waelder 1947; ed. Univs. of Würzburg, Berlin and Freiburg im Breisgau.
Industrial posts 36-46; Chair. of Management Board of a credit house 47-61; Pres. of Saarland Asscn. of Savings and Deposit Banks 55-61; Pres. of Landeszentralbank im Saarland 61-; mem. of Board of Deutsche Bundesbank, Frankfurt.
Willi-Graf-Strasse 30, 66 Saarbrücken 3, Federal Republic of Germany.
Telephone: 5-30-14.

Schuurmans, Constant, LL.D., PH.D.; Belgian diplomatist; b. 8 Dec. 1914, Achel, s. of Antoine and Clemence Meyers.
Foreign Service 46-; Second Sec., later First Sec., Paris 48-52; Sec. to Sec.-Gen. of Ministry of Foreign Affairs 52-58; Chef de Cabinet, Ministry of Foreign Affairs 58-61; Ambassador to Greece 62-65; Perm. Rep. to UN 65-70; Amb. to Fed. Repub. of Germany 70-76; Amb. and Perm. Rep. to NATO Council March 76-.
Home: "Commende", 53 Bonn-Bad Godesberg, Federal Republic of Germany.
Telephone: 33-18-51 (Home).

Schuyler, Gen. Cortlandt Van Rennsselaer; American army officer; b. 22 Dec. 1900; ed. U.S. Mil. Acad. and Command and Gen. Staff School.
Served Coast Artillery 22-27; Instructor in Maths. U.S. Mil. Acad. 27; retd. Coast Artillery 31; Prov. Marshal Chesapeake Bay 34; Grad. Coast Artillery School 36, Command and Staff School 37; office of Chief Coast Artillery 39; Exec. Officer, later Asst. Chief of Staff, H.Q. Anti-Aircraft Comm. 42; Chief of Staff 43; C.O. Anti-Aircraft Artillery Training Centre 43; Chief U.S. Mil. Rep. Control Comm. for Romania 44; U.S. Gen. Staff Appts. 47-51; assigned to SHAPE 51; C.G. 28th Infantry Div. 53; Chief of Staff SHAPE 53-59 (retd.); Exec. Asst. to Gov. of N.Y. State 59-63; Commr. of Gen. Services 60-71; retd. 71; Distinguished Service Medal, Legion of Merit, Commdr. Légion d'Honneur, Grand Officier Légion d'Honneur (France), Distinguished Service Cross with Cluster (Germany), Grand Officer Order of Merit (Italy), Grand Officer Order of Orange Nassau (Netherlands), Grand Officer Order of Léopold (Belgium), Grand Officer Order of Crown of Oak (Luxembourg).
14 Chestnut Hill North, Loudonville, N.Y. 12211, U.S.A.

Schwabe, Kurt, DR. ING. HABIL.; German engineer; b. 29 May 1905, Reichenbach, Saxony.
Teacher, Technische Hochschule Dresden 33, Prof. of Physical and Electrical Chemistry 49-70, Rector (now Technische Universität Dresden) 61-65; mem. Acad. of Sciences of German Dem. Repub., E. Berlin, Saxon Acad. of Sciences, Leipzig (now Pres.); Nat. Prize (First Class), Order of Banner of Labour, Hero of Labour; Dr. rer. nat. h.c. (Karl-Marx-Stadt, Merseburg and Dresden).
Sächsische Akademie der Wissenschaften zu Leipzig, 701 Leipzig, Goethestrasse 3-5; Meinsberg 70, Post DDR-7305 Waldheim, German Democratic Republic.
Telephone: Waldheim 667.

Schwalb López Aldaña, Fernando; Peruvian politician; b. 26 Aug. 1916, Lima; m. three c.; ed. Catholic Univ. of Peru.
Entered Ministry of Foreign Affairs 33; entered diplomatic service 39; Second Sec., Washington, D.C. 44-45, First Sec. 45-48, Minister Counsellor 48; private law practice 49-50, 50-53, 68-69; alt. Exec. Dir. IBRD 50; Senator from Lima 62 (prevented from taking office by coup d'état); Minister of Foreign Affairs 63-65; Chair. Council of Ministers 63-65; Chair. Peruvian Del. to Gen. Ass. of UN 63; Pres. Central Reserve Bank of Peru 66-68; Rep. of Pres. to Bogotá Meeting of Presidents 66; Banco de la República, Bogotá 69; Consultant, Cen. Banking Service, IMF 69-; mem. Partido Acción Popular.
Jirón Carabaya 940- Of. 201, Lima, Peru.
Telephone: 281020.

Schwartz, Stanislav Semenovich; Soviet zoologist; b. 1 April 1919, Dnepropetrovsk, Ukraine; s. of Semion Jakovlewitch Schwartz and Evgenia Stanislavovna Schwartz; m. Faina Michailovna Schwartz 1945; one d.; ed. Leningrad Univ.
Research Assoc., Head of Laboratory, Dir. Inst. of Biology, Urals Branch, U.S.S.R. Acad. of Sciences 46-, Prof. 57; Dir. Inst. of Plant and Animal Ecology 66-; Editor-in-Chief Ecologia journal 72-; mem. C.P.S.U. 66-; corresp. mem. U.S.S.R. Acad. of Sciences 66-70, mem. 70-; Fellow of Zoological Acad. of Agra (India); Severtzov Prize 72.
Leisure interest: collecting articles of folk-art of northern peoples.
Publs. Evolutionary Ecology 69, Principles and Methods of Modern Ecology 60, Ways of Adaptation of Mammals in the Subarctic 63, Intraspecies Variability of Vertebrates and Micro-evolution (Ed.) 66, Experimental Investigations of the Species Problems (Ed.) 73.
Institute of Plant and Animal Ecology, Ul. Pervomaiskaya 91, Sverdlovsk-Oblastnoi, U.S.S.R.
Telephone: 223409.

Schwarz, Rudolf, C.B.E.; British conductor; b. 29 April 1905, Vienna, Austria; s. of Josef Schwarz and Bertha Roth; m. Greta Ohlson 1950; two s. one d.; ed. in Vienna.
Conductor, Opera House, Düsseldorf 23-27, Opera House, Karlsruhe 27-33; worked for Jewish Cultural Organisation in Berlin 36-41; Conductor, Bournemouth Municipal Orchestra 47-51, City of Birmingham Symphony Orchestra 51-57; Conductor-in-Chief B.B.C. Symphony Orchestra 57-62; Conductor Northern Sinfonia Orchestra, Newcastle upon Tyne 64-73; Principal Guest Conductor Bournemouth Symphony Orchestra and Northern Sinfonia Orchestra; Hon. D.Mus. (Univ. Newcastle upon Tyne).
24 Wildcroft Manor, London, S.W.15, England.

Schwarz, Štefan, DR. RER. NAT., D.SC.; Czechoslovak mathematician; b. 18 May 1914, Nové Město nad Váhom; ed. Universita Karlova, Prague.
Assistant, Charles Univ., Prague 37; Docent, Univ. of Bratislava 45; Professor, Technical Univ., Bratislava 47-; mem. Czechoslovak Acad. of Sciences 60-, Vice-Pres. 65-70; mem. Slovak Acad. of Sciences 53-, Vice-Pres. 58-65, Pres. 65-70, mem. Presidium 72-; Dir. Mathematical Inst. 63-; mem. Cen. Cttee. of C.P. of Czechoslovakia 66-71 and of Slovakia 66-68; State Prize 55; Order of Labour 64; Hon. Gold Plaque of Czechoslovak Acad. of Sciences for Services to Science and Mankind 69; Gold Medal, Slovak Acad. of Sciences 74.
Publs. Three books and about 75 papers, mostly on algebra and number theory, in particular on theory of semi-groups.
Porubského 10, Bratislava, Czechoslovakia.

Schwarzkopf, Elisabeth; German singer; b. 9 Dec. 1915, Janotchin; d. of Friedrich and Elisabeth (née Fröhlich) Schwarzkopf; m. Walter Legge; ed. Berlin Conservatoire and in England.
Debut in Parsifal 38; Zerbinetta in Ariadne auf Naxos 41; sang at inauguration of post-war Bayreuth Festival; since 47 principal soprano at Vienna State Opera, La Scala Milan, Covent Garden, San Francisco; Metropolitan Opera, N.Y. 64-66; guest singer, Salzburg Festival 47-64; created Anne Trulove in Stravinsky's Rake's Progress; principal roles include Contessa, Le nozze di Figaro, Marschallin, Rosenkavalier, Fiordiligi, Così fan Tutte, Eva, Meistersinger, Donna Elvira, Don Giovanni, Gräfin, Capriccio, etc.; in recent years has concentrated on recitals of German songs; Hon. D.Mus. (Cambridge) 75.
Leisure interests: tennis, mountain walking.
c/o Musical Adviser Establishment, Vaduz, Liechtenstein.

Schwarzschild, Martin, PH.D.; American professor of astronomy; b. 31 May 1912, Potsdam, Germany; s. of Karl Schwarzschild and Else (Rosenbach) Schwarzschild; m. Barbara Cherry 1945; ed. Gymnasium and Univ. of Göttingen.
Research Fellow, Univ. of Oslo, Norway 36-37, Harvard Univ. 37-40; Lecturer, Asst. Prof., Columbia Univ.

40-47; Prof., Princeton Univ. 47-; Vice-Pres. Int. Astronomical Union 64-70, American Astronomical Soc. 67-69, Pres. 70-72; Fellow, American Acad. of Arts and Sciences; mem. Akad. der Naturforscher Leopoldina, Nat. Acad. of Sciences, Norwegian Acad. of Science and Letters; Life mem. Astronomical Soc. of the Pacific, Royal Astronomical Soc. of Canada; Foreign mem. Royal Netherlands Acad. of Sciences and Letters, Royal Danish Acad. of Sciences and Letters; Corresp. mem. Soc. Royale des Sciences de Liège; Assoc. Royal Astronomical Soc.; Hon. D.Sc. (Swarthmore Coll.); Draper Medal, Nat. Acad. of Sciences, Eddington Medal and Gold Medal, Royal Astronomical Soc., Bruce Medal, Astronomical Soc. of the Pacific, Albert A. Michelson Award, Case Western Reserve Univ., Dannie Heinemann Prize, Akad. der Wissenschaften zu Göttingen.
Leisure interests: collecting minerals and fossils, bird-photography.
Publs. *Structure and Evolution of the Stars*; numerous articles on research on internal constitution and evolution of stars, and on astronomical observations with telescopes carried by balloons into stratosphere.
Princeton University Observatory, Peyton Hall, Princeton, N.J. 08540; Home: 12 Ober Road, Princeton, N.J. 08540, U.S.A.
Telephone: 609-452-3802 (Office); 609-924-4369 (Home).

Schwedhelm, Karl; German writer and broadcasting official; b. 14 Aug. 1915, Berlin; s. of Adolf and Charlotte Schwedhelm; m. Hildegard Bühler, 1941; one s. one d.; ed. Universität Berlin.
Former librarian; with Süddeutscher Rundfunk 47-, now Dir. of Dept. of Literature; mem. PEN, Acad. of Sciences and Literature, Mainz.
Leisure interests: archaeology, speleology.
Publs. *Dichtungen der Marceline Desbordes-Valmore* 47, *Fährte der Fische* 55, *E. Glissant: Carthago* 59, *Nelly Sachs* 68, *Propheten des Nationalismus* 69, *Hagia Sophia* (Coll." Lynkeus")73.
7057 Winnenden, Bachstrasse 10, Federal Republic of Germany.
Telephone: 07195-3115.

Schweickart, Russell L.; American astronaut; b. 25 Oct. 1935, Neptune, N.J.; m. Clare G. Whitfield; five c.; ed. Mass. Inst. of Technology.
Pilot, U.S. Air Force 56-60, 61; Research Scientist, Experimental Astronomy Lab., Mass. Inst. of Technology 61-63; selected by NASA as astronaut Oct. 63; pilot of Lunar Module on *Apollo IX* Flight March 69; now Dir. of User Affairs.
Office of Applications, NASA H.Q., Washington, D.C.

Schweiker, Richard Schultz; American politician; b. 1 June 1926, Norristown, Pa.; s. of Malcolm A. Schweiker and Blanche Schultz; m. Claire Joan Coleman 1955; two s. three d.; ed. Pennsylvania State Univ.
Business exec. 50-60; mem. U.S. House of Reps. 60-68; U.S. Senator from Pennsylvania 69-; Republican.
U.S. Senate, Washington, D.C. 20510, U.S.A.
Telephone: 202-225-4254.

Schweikher, Paul, B.F.A., M.A.; American architect; b. 28 July 1903, Denver, Colo.; s. of Frederick Schweikher and Elizabeth Ann Williams; m. Dorothy Mueller 1923; one s.; ed. Colorado and Yale Univs.
Private architectural practice 33-; co-founder, Chicago Workshops 33-35; Lieut. Commdr. in U.S. Naval Reserve 41-45; Partner, Schweikher and Elting 45-53; Visiting Critic in Architecture, Yale Univ. 47-51, Prof. of Architecture, Chair. Dept. of Architecture 53-56; Prof. Head, Dept. of Architecture, Carnegie Mellon Univ. 56-69, Prof. Emer. 69-; lecturer, panellist and juror at many educ. and professional insts. 46-; mem. Fulbright Fellowships in Architecture selection cttee. 53-55, interviewing cttee. for American Acad. in

Rome fellowships 55; Adviser, Memphis (Tenn.) **Arts Center Competition** 56; **Consultant on master** planning, Yale Univ. 53-56, Maryville Coll., Tenn. 54-58; Buffalo Univ. 55-57; mem. Arts Club of Chicago (Board of Dirs. 39-56), Pittsburgh Planning Comm. 61-63; mem. Advisory Council, Princeton Univ. School of Architecture 60-70; Adviser, Allegheny Square Competition, Pittsburgh 64; Visiting Prof. Princeton 60-61; Ford Foundation research grant for theatre design 60-61; life mem. Chicago Art Inst. 46-; Fellow, Silliman Coll., Yale 54-55; architectural work at exhbns. New York Museum of Modern Art and several other museums and insts. 33-; Distinguished Citizen Award, Denver 58, Architect of the Year, Pittsburgh 66, Artist of the Year, Pittsburgh 68, and other awards.
Leisure interests: painting, sculpture, travel.
P.O. Box 1408, Sedona, Arizona 86336, U.S.A.
Telephone: 602-282-3722.

Schweitzer, Pierre-Paul; French banker; b. 29 May 1912, Strasbourg; s. of Paul and Emma (Munch) Schweitzer; m. Catherine Hatt 1941; one s. one d.; ed. Univs. of Strasbourg and Paris.
Official, French Treasury 36-47; alt. Exec. Dir. for France, IMF 47-48; Sec.-Gen. Interministerial Comm. European Econ. Co-operation 48-49; Financial Attaché, French Embassy, Washington, D.C. 49-53; Dir. of Treasury, Ministry of Finance 53-60; Deputy Gov. Bank of France 60-63; Man. Dir., Chair. Exec. Board IMF 63-73; Inspecteur général honoraire des finances; Chair. Bank of America Int., Luxembourg 74-, Banque Petrofigaz, Paris, Cie de Participations et d'Investissements Holding, Luxembourg Advisory Dir. Bank of America, New York and Unilever N.V., Rotterdam 74; Dir. Robeco Group Rotterdam 74; Hon. LL.D. (Yale) 66, (Harvard) 66, (Leeds) 68, (New York) 68, (George Washington Univ.) 72, (Univ. of Wales) 72, (Williams Univ.) 73; Grand Officier Légion d'Honneur, Croix de Guerre, Médaille de la Resistance.
Bank of America International, 31 rue Danielle Casanova, Paris 1e; Home: 19 rue de Valois, Paris 1e, France.
Telephone: 261-21-65 (Office); 261-48-85 (Home).

Schwinger, Julian Seymour, PH.D.; American physicist; b. 12 Feb. 1918; ed. Columbia Univ.
National Research Council Fellow 39-40; Research Assoc. Univ. of Calif. (Berkeley) 40-41; Instructor, later Asst. Prof. Purdue Univ. 41-43; staff mem. Radiation Lab., Mass. Inst. of Technology 43-46; mem. staff Metallurgy Lab., Univ. of Chicago 43; Assoc. Prof. Harvard Univ. 45-47, Prof. 47-72, Higgins Prof. 66-72; Prof. of Physics, Univ. of Calif. 72-; mem. Nat. Acad. of Sciences, American Acad. of Arts and Sciences, American Physical Soc., Civil Liberties Union; Editor *Quantum Electrodynamics* 58; Nobel Prize for Physics (with R. Feynman and S. Tomonaga) 65, and other awards.
Department of Physics, University of California at Los Angeles, Calif. 90024, U.S.A.

Schwyzer, Robert, DR. PHIL.; Swiss molecular biologist; b. 8 Dec. 1920, Zürich; s. of Robert Schwyzer and Rose Schätzle; m. Rose Nägeli 1948; two s. one d.; ed. primary school, Nathan Hale, Minneapolis, U.S.A., Canton High School (A), Zürich, and Dept. of Chemistry, Univ. of Zürich.
Privatdozent, Univ. of Zürich 51-59, Asst. Prof. 60-63; initiation of Polypeptide Research, Head of Polypeptide Research Group, Ciba Ltd., Basle 52-63, Asst. Man. 60-63; Prof. and Head of (new) Dept. of Molecular Biology, Swiss Fed. Inst. of Technology, Zürich 63-; Werner Award, Swiss Chemical Soc. 57; Ruzicka Prize, Swiss Fed. Inst. of Technology 59; Otto Nägeli Award, Switzerland 64; Vernon Stouffer Award, American Heart Asscn., Cleveland 68.
Leisure interests: mountain climbing, skiing, literature.

Publs. Scientific papers on syntheses of biologically active polypeptides; structure activity relationships in this field; structure-conformation-activity relationships; structure-receptor relationships.

Laboratorium für Molekularbiologie, Eidgenössische Technische Hochschule, 8006 Zürich; Home: 8180 Bülach, Switzerland.
Telephone: 01-575770 (Lab.); 01-807111 (Home).

Sciascia, Leonardo; Italian writer; b. 8 Jan. 1921; ed. Istituto Magistrale Caltanissetta.
Has won many prizes including Premio Crotone, Premio Libera Stampa Lugano, and Premio Prato.
Publs. *Le parrocchie di Regalpetra* 56, *Gli zii di Sicilia* 58, *Il giorno della civetta* 61 (Mafia Vendetta 63), *Pirandello e la Sicilia* 61, *Il consiglio d'Egitto* 63, *A ciascuno il suo* 63, *Morte dell'inquisitore* 64, *Feste religiose in Sicilia* 65, *Recitazione della controversia liparitana* 69, *Il contesto* 71, *Il mare colore del vino* 73.
Via Redentore 131, Caltanissetta, Italy.

Scofield, Paul, C.B.E.; British actor; b. 21 Jan. 1922; m. Joy Parker; one *s*. one *d*.; trained London Mask Theatre Drama School.
Birmingham Repertory Theatre 41 and 43-46; Stratford-on-Avon Shakespeare Memorial Theatre 46-48; Arts Theatre 46; Phoenix Theatre 47; with H. M. Tennent 49-56; Assoc. Dir. Nat. Theatre 70-71; Hon. LL.D. (Glasgow Univ.), Hon. D.Lit. (Kent Univ.) 73.
Has appeared in Chekhov's *Seagull*, Anouilh's *Ring Round the Moon*, Charles Morgan's *The River Line*; *Richard II, Time Remembered, A Question of Fact, Hamlet* (also in Moscow), *Power and the Glory, Family Reunion, A Dead Secret, Expresso Bongo, The Complaisant Lover, A Man for all Seasons*, Stratford Festival, Ont., Canada 61, *Coriolanus, Don Armado* New York 61-62, *A Man for All Seasons* London 62-63, *King Lear* 63 (E. Europe, Helsinki, Moscow, New York 64), *Timon of Athens* 65, *The Government Inspector* London 66, *Staircase* 67, *Macbeth* 68, *The Hotel in Amsterdam* 68, *Uncle Vanya* 70, *The Captain of Köpenik* 71, *Rules of the Game* 71, *Savages* 73, *The Tempest* 74, 75.
Films: *The Train* 63, *A Man for All Seasons* 67 (Oscar and New York Film Critics Award, Moscow Film Festival and British Film Acad. Awards), *King Lear* 70, *Scorpio* 72, *A Delicate Balance* 72.
The Gables, Balcombe, Sussex, England.

Scott, Sir (Arleigh) Winston, G.C.M.G., G.C.V.O., B.SC., M.D., L.R.C.P., L.R.C.S. (EDIN.), L.R.F.P.S. (GLAS.), K.ST.J.; Barbadian administrator; b. 27 March 1900, Barbados; *s*. of late Walter Scott and Edith Hall; *m*. Rosita May Hynam 1936; three *d*.; ed. Harrison Coll., Barbados, Howard Univ., U.S.A.
Physician, Surgeon Woodside Nursing Home 34-67; mem. Senate 64-66; appointed to Privy Council of Barbados 66; Gov.-Gen. of Barbados 67-; Hon. LL.D. (Howard Univ.) 72.
Leisure interest: reading.
Government House, Barbados.

Scott, Bernard Francis William, C.B.E., T.D., F.I.MECH.E., F.B.I.M., F.R.S.A.; British business executive; b. 19 Nov. 1914, Kings Norton; *s*. of Francis William Robert Scott and Agnes Edith Kett; *m*. Charlotte Kathleen Laidlow 1942; one *s*. two *d*.; ed. Bishop Vesey's Grammar School, Epsom Coll.
Joined Joseph Lucas Ltd. 31; Personal Asst. to Oliver Lucas 36; army service in World War II, mentioned in despatches 44; Sales Dir. Joseph Lucas (Electrical) Ltd. 47; Vice-Chair., Gen. Man. CAV Ltd. 59; Dir. Joseph Lucas (Industries) Ltd. 68, Chair. Lucas Industries Ltd. 74-; Chair. European Components Service, British Nat. Export Council 66-71; Exec. Cttee., Council, Soc. of Motor Mfrs. & Traders 71-, British Overseas Trade Board 73-; mem. Council Confed. of British Industry 74; Dir. Lloyds Bank 75-.

Leisure interests: sailing, gardening.
Lucas Industries Ltd., Lucas House, 46 Park Street, London, W1Y 4DJ; and Burchetts Green House, Burchetts Green, Berks., England.

Scott, Sir David Aubrey, K.C.M.G.; British diplomatist; b. 3 Aug. 1919, London; *s*. of the late H. S. and of Barbara E. Scott, J.P.; *m*. Vera Kathleen Ibbitson 1941; two *s*. one *d*.; ed. Charterhouse and Birmingham Univ.
Royal Artillery 39-47; Chief Radar Adviser, British Mil. Mission to Egyptian Army 45-47; Commonwealth Relations Office 48-50, South Africa 51-53; Cabinet Office 54-56; Singapore 56-58; British Deputy High Commr. in Fed. of Rhodesia and Nyasaland 61-63; Imperial Defence Coll. 64; Deputy High Commr. in India 65-67; High Commr. in Uganda 67-70; Amb. to Rwanda (non-resident) 67-70; Asst. Under-Sec. of State, Foreign and Commonwealth Office 70-72; High Commr. New Zealand and Gov. of Pitcairn Island 73-75; Amb. to S. Africa 76-.
Leisure interests: bird-watching, music, theatre.
23 Petersham Mews, London, S.W.7, England; British Embassy, 91 Parliament Street, Cape Town; and Hill Street, Pretoria, South Africa.
Telephone: 01-589-0424 (London).

Scott, David R.; American astronaut; b. 6 June 1932, San Antonio, Tex.; *s*. of Brig.-Gen. Tom W. Scott; *m*. Ann Lurton Ott; one *s*. one *d*.; ed. U.S. Military Acad. and Mass. Inst. of Technology.
Received flight training and attended Air Force Experimental Test Pilot School and Air Force Aerospace Research Pilot School; selected by NASA as astronaut Oct. 63; pilot of *Gemini VIII* flight 66; pilot of Command Module *Apollo IX* flight March 69; Commdr. *Apollo XV* mission July-Aug. 71; NASA Exceptional Service Medal; American Inst. of Aeronautics and Astronautics Award 66.
NASA Johnson Space Center, Houston, Tex. 77058, U.S.A.

Scott, George Campbell; American actor, producer and director; b. 18 Oct. 1927, Wise, Va.; *s*. of George C. Scott and late Helena Scott; ed. Redford High School and Univ. of Missouri.
Appeared in *Richard III*, New York Shakespeare Festival 56; subsequent theatrical appearances included *As You Like It, Children of Darkness* and *Comes A Day* (Broadway); formed Theater of Michigan Company 62; produced, directed and appeared in *General Seeger* and produced *Great Day in the Morning*; Dir. *Death of a Salesman*, N.Y. 75, *All God's Chillun Got Wings* 75.
Films include: *The Hanging Tree, Anatomy of a Murder, The Andersonville Trial, The Wall, The Hustler, Dr. Strangelove, The List of Adrian Messenger, The Yellow Rolls-Royce, The Flim-Flam Man, Petulia, Patton, They Might be Giants, The Hospital, Precinct 45, Oklahoma Crude, Rage* (also directed), *Day of the Dolphin, Bank Shot* (also dir.), *The Savage is Loose* (also dir.), *Hindenberg;* refused Acad. Award (Oscar) for *Patton*.
c/o Warner Bros.-Seven Arts, 200 Park Avenue, New York, N.Y. 10017, U.S.A.

Scott, Rev. G(uthrie) Michael; British ecclesiastic; b. 30 July 1907, Lowfield Heath, Sussex; *s*. of Rev. Perceval Caleb Scott and Ethel Maud Burn; ed. King's Coll., Taunton, St. Paul's Coll., Grahamstown, South Africa, and Chichester Theological Coll.
Curate of Slaugham 30-32, St. Stephen's, Kensington 32-34; Domestic Chaplain to Bishop of Bombay 35-37; Chaplain to St. Paul's Cathedral, Calcutta 37-38, Kasauli 38-39; Curate to St. Alban's Coloured Mission, Johannesburg 43-46; Rep. of Herero, Berg, Damara and Nama Tribes of South-West Africa at UN 48; prohibited from South Africa 50; Hon. Dir. Africa Bureau, London 52-68; mem. Nagaland Peace Mission 64-66, expelled by

India 66; special licence to officiate in the Diocese of Chichester 49-; Hon. Doctor Sacred Theology, Gen. Theological Seminary, U.S.A. 72; Hon. Canon, St. George's Cathedral, Windhoek, Namibia 75-.
Leisure interests: walking, reading, listening, swimming.
Publs. *Shadow over Africa* 50, *Attitude to Africa* 51, *The Orphans' Heritage* 58, *A Time to Speak* 58, *The Nagas: India's Problem or the World's.*
c/o Lloyd's Bank, 6 Pall Mall, London, S.W.1, England.
Telephone: 01-722-5787.

Scott, Hugh, A.B., LL.B.; American lawyer and politician; b. 11 Nov. 1900; *m.* Marian Huntington Chase; one *d.*; ed. Pennsylvania Univ., Randolph-Macon Coll. and Virginia Univ.
Asst. District Attorney, Philadelphia 26-41; mem. U.S. House of Reps. (6th Pa. District) 40-42, 44-58; served in U.S. Merchant Marine and Navy (Commdr.) in Second World War and in Navy in Korean War; fmr. Gen. Counsel, Republican Nat. Cttee.; Nat. Chair., Republican Nat. Cttee. 48-49; Chair. of Regional Organization, Eisenhower campaign and on personal staff, Chair. Eisenhower Headquarters Cttee. 52; U.S. Senator from Pennsylvania 58-; mem. Judiciary, Foreign Relations and Rules Cttees.; Republican Minority Leader in Senate 69-(77); del. by Presidential designated at numerous int. confs.; Vice-Chair. U.S. Del. to Interparl. Union; Counsel to firm of Obermayer, Rebmann, Maxwell and Hippel, Philadelphia; mem. Philadelphia and American Bar Asscns., Pennsylvania Bar Asscn. (fmr. Chair. Criminal Law Cttee.), American Soc. of Int. Law, Comm. on Critical Choices for America, Phila. Museum of Art Oriental Art Cttee.; 29 hon. degrees from American univs. and colls.; Commdr. Royal Order of Phoenix; Grand Cross, Order of El Quetzal, Order of Service Merit; Gold Medal, Pa. Soc. 73; Republican.
Leisure interest: collecting Chinese art.
Publs. *Scott on Bailments* 31, *How to Go into Politics* 49, *Politics, U.S.A.* (co-author) 60, *The Golden Age of Chinese Art* 67, *Come to the Party* 68, *How to Run for Public Office and Win* 68.
Senate Office Building, Washington, D.C. 20510, U.S.A.
Telephone: 225-6324.

Scott, Sir Ian Dixon, K.C.M.G., K.C.V.O., C.I.E.; fmr. British diplomatist; b. 6 March 1909, Inverness; *s.* of Thomas Henderson Scott, M.I.C.E., O.B.E., and Mary Agnes (née Dixon); *m.* Hon. Anna Drusilla Lindsay 1937; one *s.* four *d.*; ed. Queen's Royal Coll., Trinidad, Balliol Coll., Oxford, London School of Econ.
Entered Indian Civil Service 32; joined Indian Political Service 35; Asst. Dir. of Intelligence, Peshawar 41; Principal Islamia Coll., Peshawar 42-45; Deputy Private Sec. to the Viceroy 45-47; with John Lewis Partnership 48-50; Foreign Service, London 50, First Sec. Foreign Office 50-51; British Legation, Helsinki 52; First Sec. and Head of Chancery, Lebanon 54, Counsellor 56, Chargé d'Affaires 56-58; Imperial Defence Coll. 59; Amb. to Congo 60-61, to Sudan 61-65, to Norway 65-68; Dir. Clarksons Holiday Holdings Ltd. 69, Chair. 72-73; Chair. Davell and Rufford (Holdings) Ltd. 70-72; Chair. Dr. Barnardo's 72-, Board of Govs., Felixstowe Coll. 72-, Suffolk Area Health Authority 73-.
Leisure interest: sailing.
Publ. *Tumbled House* 69.
Ash House, Alde Lane, Aldeburgh, Suffolk, England.

Scott, J. L.; American business executive; b. 2 Feb. 1930; *m.*; two *c.*; ed. Coll. of Idaho, Harvard Univ.
With Western Enterprises Inc. 52-53; Gen. Supervisor Albertson's Inc. 53-61, Exec. Vice-Pres. 61-66, Pres., Dir. 66-72, Vice-Chair., Chief Exec. Officer 72-74; Vice-Chair., Dir. Great Atlantic & Pacific Tea Co. Inc. Jan. 75, Chair., Chief Exec. Officer Feb. 75-; Dir. Morrison-

Knudsen Co., Idaho Power Co., Idaho First Nat. Bank, Home Fed. Savings and Loan Asscn. (Boise).
The Great Atlantic & Pacific Tea Co. Inc., Two Paragon Drive, Montvale, N.J. 07645, U.S.A.

Scott, John Vivian, LL.B.; New Zealand diplomatist; b. 19 Nov. 1920; *m.*; three *d.*; ed. Victoria Univ., Wellington.
Joined New Zealand Dept. of External Affairs 47; has served in Canberra, New York and London; mem. New Zealand Perm. Mission at UN 51-55; Amb. to Japan 65-69; Perm. Rep. to UN 69-73; Deputy Sec. of Foreign Affairs 73-.
c/o Ministry of Foreign Affairs, Wellington, New Zealand.

Scott, Michael, F.R.I.A.I., H.F.R.S.U.A., H.F.I.A.A., H.DIP.ARCH., D.LITT., D.R.C.A.; Irish architect; b. 24 June 1905, Drogheda, Co. Louth; *s.* of William Scott and Hilda Daly; *m.* Patricia Nixon 1932; four *s.* one *d.*; ed. Belvedere Coll., Dublin.
Architectural pupil with Messrs. Jones & Kelly, Dublin; Partner, Scott, Tallon, Walker Architects (fmrly. Michael Scott & Partners) 29-; Chair. Irish Directions, Cttee., Bldg. Centre of Ireland, Dublin Theatre Festival, ROSC 67, 71; mem. Stamp Design Advisory Comm., Council of Bolton Street Coll. of Technology, Council of Royal Coll. of Art, London, Arts Advisory Cttee. of Dublin Corpn., An Taisce Council; Past Pres. Architectural Asscn., Belvedere Coll. Union; Fellow, Royal Inst. of Architects of Ireland 46, Hon. Fellow, Royal Soc. of Ulster Architects 67, Hon. Fellow, American Inst. of Architects 72; Dr. h.c. Royal Coll. of Art 69, Hon. D.Litt. Trinity Coll., Dublin 70; RIAI Triennial Gold Medal for Bus Terminus and offices of CIE, Dublin 53-55; Royal Inst. of British Architects Gold Medal 75; Knight's Cross, Order of Icelandic Falcon 74.
Leisure interests: drawing, theatre, music, sunbathing, swimming.
19 Merrion Square, Dublin 2; Home: Geragh, Sandycove Point, Sandycove, Co. Dublin, Ireland.
Telephone: 760621 (Office); 803515 (Home).

Scott, Sir Peter (Markham), C.B.E., D.S.C., M.A.; British artist and ornithologist; b. 14 Sept. 1909, London; *s.* of late Capt. Robert Falcon Scott and Kathleen Bruce; *m.* 1st Elizabeth J. Howard 1942 (divorced 1951); one *d.*; *m.* 2nd Philippa Talbot-Ponsonby 1951; one *d.*; ed. Oundle School, Trinity Coll., Cambridge, Munich State Acad., and Royal Acad., London.
Founded, now Hon. Dir., The Wildfowl Trust 46; rep. Great Britain in Olympic Games, in single handed sailing (bronze medal) 36; served in Navy during 39-45 War; Pres. Int. Yacht Racing Union 55-69; Chair. Olympic Int. Yacht Racing Jury, Melbourne 56, Naples 60, Tokyo 64; 1st Vice-Pres. and Chair. World Wildlife Fund; Vice-Pres. Inland Waterways Asscn.; mem. Council of Winston Churchill Memorial Trust; Pres. Wildlife Youth Service; Chair. Survival Service Comm. of Int. Union for the Conservation of Nature and Natural Resources; Chancellor Birmingham Univ. 74-; Hon. LL.D. (Aberdeen and Exeter); Cherry Kearton Medal R.G.S. 67; Albert Medal, R.S.A. 70; Bernard Tucker Medal B.O.U. 70; Arthur Allan Medal Cornell Univ. 71; Gold Medal, N.Y. Zoological Soc. 74; Icelandic Order of Falcon 69.
Leisure interests: exploring, bird-watching.
Publs. *Morning Flight* 35, *Wild Chorus* 38, *The Battle of the Narrow Seas* 45, *Portrait Drawings* 49, *Key to the Wild Fowl of the World* 49, *Wild Geese and Eskimos* 51, *A Thousand Geese* (with James Fisher) 53, *The Eye of the Wind* 61; illustrated many books incl. *Bird in the Bush* (Lord Kennet), *Grey Goose*, and *Through the Air* (Michael Bratby), *The Snow Goose* (Paul Gallico), *The*

Swans (with the Wildfowl Trust) etc.; Joint Editor and Illustrator of Wildfowl Trust Annual Reports 48-.
The Wildfowl Trust, Slimbridge, Glos., GL2 7BT, England.
Telephone: Cambridge (Glos.) 333.

Scott, Robert Walter; fmr. American state governor; b. 13 June 1929, Alamance Co., N.C.; s. of W. Kerr Scott (fmr. Gov. of N.C. and U.S. Senator) and Mary Elizabeth (White) Scott; m. Jessie Rae Osborne 1951; one s. four d.; ed. Duke and North Carolina State Univs.
Served in Counter Intelligence Corps U.S. Army 53-55; fmr. Lieut.-Gov. of North Carolina; Gov. of North Carolina Jan. 69-73; Past Chair. or mem. of numerous state cttees.; Exec. Vice-Pres. North Carolina Agribusiness Council 72-75; Pres. Scott Enterprises, Govt. Relations and Acceptance Group, Inc. 75-.
1 Haw River, N.C. 27258, U.S.A.

Scott, Stuart Nash, A.B., LL.B.; American lawyer; b. 6 Dec. 1906, Madison, Wis.; s. of William Amasa and Nellie Irene Nash Scott; m. Katherine Leavelle Miller 1928; one d.; ed. Phillips Acad., Andover, Mass., Yale and Harvard Univs.
Assistant Prof. of Law, Harvard Law School 30-31; admitted to Bar, New York 32; practised in law firm, Dewey, Ballantine, Bushby, Palmer & Wood 31-73; Counsel, French Purchasing Comm. 39-40; Navy Dept. 41-44, Gen. Counsel Surplus War Property Admin., Office of War Mobilization 44; Nat. Chair. Harvard Law School Fund 59-61; Chair. Temporary State Comm. to Study Govt. Operation of N.Y.C. 71-73; Amb. to Portugal Jan.-Nov. 74; mem. American Bar Asscn.; Distinguished Civilian Service Award 44.
c/o Department of State, Washington, D.C. 20520, U.S.A.

Scott, William George, C.B.E.; British artist; b. 15 Feb. 1913, Scotland; m. Hilda Mary Lucas 1936; two s.; ed. Enniskillen, Belfast School of Art and Royal Acad. Schools, London.
Exhibitions at Leger Gallery 42, 44, 46, Leicester Gallery 48, 51, Hanover Gallery 53, 56, 61, 65, 67, 69, Tate Gallery 63 (all in London); Martha Jackson Gallery, New York 54, 58, 73, 75; Venice Biennale 58; São Paulo, Brazil 53, 61; Retrospective exhbn. Tate Gallery 72; exhbn. Gimpel Fils, London 74; Hon. Dr. R.C.A.
Leisure interest: farming.
13 Edith Terrace, Chelsea, London, S.W.10, England.
Telephone: 01-352-8044.

Scott, William L.; American lawyer and politician; b. 1 July 1915, Williamsburg, Va.; s. of William David Scott and Nora Bell Ingram; m. Ruth Inez Huffman 1940; two s. one d.; ed. Nat. Univ.
Admitted to Va. bar; Trial Attorney, Dept. of Justice 42-60; Special Asst. to solicitor, Dept. of Interior 60-61; private law practice, Fairfax, Va. 61-66; Republican Senator from Va. Nov. 66-.
Longworth House Office Building, Washington, D.C. 20515; Home: 3930 West Ox Road, Fairfax County, Virginia 22030, U.S.A.

Scott, Wilton E., B.S.; American business executive; b. 3 Jan. 1913, Elgin, Tex.; s. of Samuel S. Scott and Clara Schuerman; m. Loradean Allen 1942; one s. two d.; ed. Univ. of Texas.
Surface Geologist, Standard Oil of New Jersey in Venezuela 36-38; Geologist Cities Service, New Mexico 38-40, District Geologist 40-44; Chief Geologist Buffalo Oil Co., Dallas, Tex. 44-54, Vice-Pres. for Oil and Gas Exploration in Midland, Tex. 54-55; Oil and Gas Exploration Man. Tenneco Inc. 55, Vice-Pres. 56-60, Senior Vice-Pres. Tenneco Oil Co., subsidiary 60-61, Pres. Tenneco Oil Co. 61-70, Senior Vice-Pres. Tenneco

Inc. 66, Dir. 66, Exec. Vice-Pres. 70-73, Vice-Chair. Jan.-April 74, Pres., Chief Exec. Officer 74-75, Chair. Pres. and Chief Exec. Officer 75-.
Leisure interests: fishing, hunting, golf.
Tenneco Inc., P.O. Box 2511, Houston, Tex. 77001; and 5602 Sugar Hill, Houston, Tex. 77027, U.S.A.
Telephone: (713) 229-4251 (Office); (713) 622-5852 (Home).

Scotto, Renata; Italian soprano; b. 1934; ed. under Ghirardini at Milan.
Joined La Scala Opera Company after debut in *La Traviata* at Teatro Nuovo, Milan 53; then studied under Merlino and Mercedes Llopart; known for roles in *La Sonnambula, I Puritani, L'Elisir d'amore, Lucia di Lammermoor, Falstaff, La Bohème, Turandot, I Capuleti,* etc.
c/o presso Il Teatro alla Scala, via Filodrammatici 2, Milan, Italy.

Scowcroft, Lieut.-Gen. Brent, B.S., M.A., PH.D.; American air force officer and government official; b. 19 March 1925, Odgen, Utah; m. Marian Horner 1951; one d.; ed. U.S. Mil. Acad., West Point, and Columbia Univ.
Operational and Admin. positions in U.S. Air Force 48-53; taught Russian history as Asst. Prof., Dept. of Social Sciences, U.S. Mil. Acad., West Point 53-57; Asst. Air Attaché, U.S. Embassy, Belgrade 59-61; Assoc. Prof., Political Science Dept., U.S. Air Force Acad., Colorado 62-63, Prof., Head of Dept. 63-64; Plans and Operations Section, Air Force HQ, Washington 64-66; various Nat. Security posts with Dept. of Defense 68-72; Mil. Asst. to Pres., The White House 72, Deputy Asst. to Pres. for Nat. Security Affairs 73-75, Asst. to Pres. for Nat. Security Affairs Nov. 75-; D.S.M., Legion of Merit.
The White House, Washington, D.C. 20500, U.S.A.
Telephone: (202) 456-1414.

Scranton, William W., A.B., LL.B.; American lawyer and politician; b. 19 July 1917, Madison; s. of Worthington and Marion Margery Warren Scranton; m. Mary Lowe Chamberlin 1942; three s. one d.; ed. Hotchkiss School, Yale Univ. and Yale Univ. Law School.
U.S. Army Air Force 41-45; Pennsylvania bar 46; Assoc. O'Malley, Harris, Harris and Warren 46-47; Vice-Pres. Int. Textbook Co., Scranton, Pa. 47-52, later Dir. and mem. Exec. Cttee.; Pres. Scranton-Lackawanna Trust Co. 54-56; Chair. Board and Dir. Northeastern Pennsylvania Broadcasting Co. 57-61; Special Asst. to U.S. Sec. of State 59-60; mem. U.S. House of Reps. 60-62; Gov. of Pennsylvania 63-67; Special Envoy to Middle East on behalf of Pres.-elect Nixon Dec. 68; Chair. President's Commission on Campus Unrest 70; Special Consultant to the Pres. 74; Perm. Rep. to UN Feb. 76-; mem. U.S. Railway Assen. Board 74; Chair. of Board Northeastern Bank of Pa.; Dir. Scott Paper Co., IBM, Sun Oil, Mutual of N.Y.; numerous hon. degrees; Republican.
Box 116, Dalton, Pennsylvania; Office: 799 United Nations Plaza, New York, N.Y. 10017, U.S.A.

Scribner, Charles, Jr., A.B.; American publisher; b. 13 July 1921, Quogue, N.Y.; s. of Charles Scribner and Vera (Bloodgood) Scribner; m. Joan Sunderland 1949; three s.; ed. St. Paul's School and Princeton Univ.
In U.S. Navy 43-46, 50-52; Advertising Man., Charles Scribner's Sons 46-48, Production Man. 48-50, Pres. 52-; Pres. Princeton Univ. Press 57-68, American Book Publisher's Council 66-68; Trustee, Princeton Univ. 69-.
Charles Scribner's Sons, 597 Fifth Avenue, New York, N.Y. 10017; Home: 791 Park Avenue, New York, N.Y. 10021, U.S.A.

Scrimshaw, Nevin Stewart, M.D., PH.D.; American professor of nutrition; b. 20 Jan. 1918, Milwaukee, Wis.; s. of Stewart and Harriet F. S. Scrimshaw; m. Mary

Ware Goodrich 1941; four *s.* one *d.*; ed. Ohio Wesleyan Univ., Harvard Univ. and Univ. of Rochester.

Consultant in Nutrition, Pan American Sanitary Bureau, Regional Office of the Americas, WHO 48-49, Regional Adviser in Nutrition 49-53; Dir. Inst. of Nutrition of Cen. America and Panama (INCAP), Guatemala 49-61, Consulting Dir. 61-65, Consultant 65-; Adjunct Prof., Public Health Nutrition, Columbia Univ. 59-61, Visiting Lecturer 61-65; Visiting Lecturer on Tropical Public Health, Harvard Univ. 68-; Prof. of Human Nutrition and Head, Dept. of Nutrition and Food Science, Mass. Inst. of Technology 61-, Dir. Clinical Research Center 62-66, Principal Investigator 62-; Fellow, American Asscn. for Advancement of Science; mem. Nat. Acad. of Sciences and numerous other nat. and foreign scientific socs. and asscns.; mem. numerous cttees. and advisory panels to UN agencies and other orgs.; Int. Award, Inst. of Food Technologists 69, Goldberger Award in Clinical Nutrition, American Medical Asscn. 69, First James R. Killian Jr. Faculty Achievement Award, M.I.T., 72 etc.

Publs. over 300 scientific articles on various aspects of human and animal nutrition, nutrition and infection, agricultural and food chemistry, and public health.

Department of Nutrition and Food Science, Massachusetts Institute of Technology, Cambridge, Mass. 02139, U.S.A.

Telephone: 617-253-5101.

Scripps, Charles Edward; American newspaper publisher; b. 27 Jan. 1920; ed. William and Mary Coll. and Pomona Coll.

Reporter, Cleveland Press, Ohio 41; Successor-Trustee, **Edward W. Scripps Trust 45,** Chair., Board of Trustees **48-,** Vice-Pres., Dir., E. W. Scripps Co. 46-, Chair. of Board 53-; Chair. Scripps-Howard Newspaper Group.

Scripps-Howard Newspaper Group, Zoo Park Avenue, New York, N.Y. 10071; Union Central Building, Cincinnati 2, Ohio, U.S.A.

Scrivener, Ronald Stratford, C.M.G.; British diplomatist; b. 29 Dec. 1919, London; *s.* of late Sir Patrick Scrivener, K.C.M.G. and Margaret M. Scrivener (née Dorling); *m.* 1st Elizabeth Drake-Brockman 1947 (dissolved 1952), 2nd Mary O. A. S. J. Hohler (née Lane); two step *s.* two step *d.*; ed. Westminster School, St. Catharine's Coll., Cambridge and privately in France and Austria.

Entered diplomatic service Dec. 45; has served in Berlin, Buenos Aires, Vienna, Caracas, Berne, Bangkok; Amb. to Panama 69-70, to Czechoslovakia 71-74; Asst. Under-Sec. of State, Foreign and Commonwealth Office 74-.

Leisure interests: travel, fishing.

72 Bedford Gardens, London, W.8, England.

Scully, Vincent William Thomas, C.M.G., F.C.A.; Canadian company executive (retd.); b. 9 Jan. 1900, Ballymahon, Ireland; *s.* of James and Katherine (Monaghan) Scully; *m.* Sylvia Grier 1930; one *s.*; ed. Christian Brothers School, New Ross (Ireland), and Trinity Coll., Dublin.

Practised as chartered accountant with Clarkson, Gordon, Dilworth and Nash, Toronto 25-32; chartered accountant Ontario 29; Dir. and Sec.-Treas. J. D. Woods & Co. Ltd. 32-45; Comptroller and Sec.-Treas., York Knitting Mills Ltd. 32-45; Sec.-Treas. Plateau Co. Ltd. (Crown Co.) 40-41; Treas. and subsequently Pres., War Supplies Ltd. (Crown Co.) 41-44; Pres. Victory Aircraft Ltd. (Crown Co.) 44-45; Deputy Minister of Reconstruction and Supply and Vice-Pres. Nat. Research Council 45-47; Deputy Minister of Nat. Revenue for Taxation, Canada 48-51; Comptroller The Steel Co., Canada Ltd. 51, Pres. 57-66, Chair. of Board 66-71, Chair. Exec. Cttee. of Board 71-74; Dir. Sun Life Assurance Co. of Canada, Royal Canadian Geographical

Soc.; Dir. Moore Corpn. Ltd.; awarded United States Medal of Freedom (Bronze Palm).

Leisure interests: reading, golf, photography.

117 Rochester Avenue, Toronto, Ontario, M4N 1N9, Canada.

Sculthorpe, Peter Joshua, M.B.E.; Australian composer; b. 29 April 1929, Launceston, Tasmania; *s.* of Joshua Sculthorpe and Edna Moorhouse; ed. Launceston Grammar School, Univ. of Melbourne and Wadham Coll., Oxford.

Senior Lecturer in Music, Univ. of Sydney 63-; Visiting Fellow, Yale Univ. 65-67; Reader in Music, Univ. of Sydney 68; Visiting Prof. of Music, Univ. of Sussex 71-72; comms. from bodies including Australian Broadcasting Comm., Birmingham Chamber Music Soc., Australian Elizabethan Theatre Trust and Australian Ballet.

Compositions published include: *The Loneliness of Bunjil* 54, *Sonatina* 54, *Violin Sonata* 55, *Irkanda* I 55, II 59, III 60, IV 61, *Ulterior Motifs,* a musical farce and music for various revues 57-59, *Sonata for Viola and Percussion* 60, *Orchestral Suite* (from film *They Found a Cave*) 62, *Sonata for Piano* 63, *The Fifth Continent* 63, *String Quartet No. 6* 65, *South by Five* 65, *Sun Music* I 65, *Sun Music for Voices* 66, *Sun Music* III 67, IV 67, *Morning Song for the Christ Child* 66, *Red Landscape* 66, *Tabuh Tabuhan* 68, *Autumn Song* 68, *Sea Chant* 68, *Sun Music* II 69, *Orchestral Suite* from film *The Age of Consent* 68, *Sun Music Ballet* 68, *Ketjak* for orchestra 69, *String Quartet Music* 69, *Love 200* for pop group and orchestra 70, *The Stars Turn* 70, *Music for Japan* 70, *Rain* 70, *Dream* 70, *Rain* 65-70, *Snow, Moon & Flowers* 71, *Landscape* 71, *Stars* 71, *How The Stars Were Made* 71, *Ketjak* 72, *Koto Music* 72, *Rites of Passage* 73, *Music of Early Morning* 74; various works for radio, television, theatre and film.

147B Queen Street, Woollahra, Sydney, New South Wales 2025, Australia.

Telephone: 324701.

Seaborg, Glenn T(heodore), B.A., PH.D.; American chemist; b. 19 April 1912, Ishpeming, Mich.; *s.* of H. Theodore and Selma (Erickson) Seaborg; *m.* Helen L. Griggs 1942; four *s.* two *d.*; ed. Univ. of California.

Research Assoc., Univ. of Calif. 37-39, Instructor 39-41, Asst. Prof. 41-45, Prof. of Chemistry 45-71, Dir. Nuclear Chemical Research, **Lawrence Radiation Laboratory** 46-58, 72-75, Assoc. Dir. Lawrence Radiation Laboratory 54-61, Chancellor, Univ. of Calif., Berkeley 58-61; on leave of absence to head plutonium work of Manhattan Project at Univ. of Chicago Metallurgical Laboratory 42-46; on leave of absence to serve as Chair. U.S. Atomic Energy Comm. 61-71; Univ. Prof. 71-; Assoc. Dir. Lawrence Berkeley Laboratory 72-; Chair. Steering Cttee., Chemical Educ. Material Study (CHEM Study), Nat. Science Foundation 59-; Pres. Board of Trustees, Science Service 66-; mem. Board of Trustees, Educational Broadcasting Corpn. 70-73; mem. Nat. Programming Council for Public Television 70-72; Pres. American Asscn. for the Advancement of Science 72, Chair. of the Board 73; Pres.-elect American Chem. Soc. 75, Pres. 76; co-discoverer of elements 94 (plutonium), 95 (americium), 96 (curium) 97 (berkelium), 98 (californium), 99 (einsteinium), 100 (fermium), 101 (mendelevium), 102 (nobelium) and 106; author of actinide concept of heavy element electronic structure; Nobel Prize in Chem. 51; Enrico Fermi Award 59; Franklin Medal 63; Arches of Science Award 68; fmr. mem. ten nat. acads. of science, including U.S.S.R.; Officier Légion d'Honneur 73; other awards include more than 40 hon. degrees.

Leisure interests: golf, hiking.

Publs. *The Transuranium Elements: Research Papers* (ed. with J. J. Katz and W. M. Manning) 49, *Production and Seperation of* U^{233} (ed. with L. I. Katzin) 51,

The Actinide Elements (ed. with J. J. Katz) 54; *Comprehensive Inorganic Chemistry* Vol. I (with others) 53, *The Chemistry of the Actinide Elements* (with J. J. Katz) 57, *The Transuranium Elements* 58, *Elements of the Universe* (with E. G. Valens) 58, *Man-made Transuranium Elements* 63; *Education and the Atom* (with D. M. Wilkes) 64, *The Nuclear Properties of the Heavy Elements*, Vol. I: *Systematics of Nuclear Structure and Radioactivity*, and Vol. II: *Detailed Radioactivity Properties* (with E. K. Hyde and I. Perlman) 64, *Man and Atom* (with W. R. Corliss) 71, *Nuclear Milestones* 72; more than 200 papers on nuclear chemistry and physics, etc.
Lawrence Berkeley Laboratory, University of California, Berkeley, Calif. 94720, U.S.A.
Telephone: 415-843-2740.

Seamans, Robert Channing, Jr.; American scientist and government official; b. 30 Oct. 1918; s. of Robert Channing and Pauline (Bosson) Seamans; m. Eugenia Merrill 1942; three s. two d.; ed. Harvard and Mass. Inst. of Technology.
Massachusetts Inst. of Technology 41-55, teaching and project management positions, successively Assoc. Prof. Dept. of Aeronautical Engineering, Chief Engineer Project Meteor, Dir. Flight Control Laboratory; Radio Corpn. of America 45-60, successively Man. Airborne Systems Lab., Chief Systems Engineer Airborne Systems Dept., Chief Engineer Missile Electronics and Control Div.; Assoc. Administrator and later Deputy Administrator Nat. Aeronautics and Space Admin. (NASA) 60-68; Consultant to Admin. (NASA) 68-69; Sec. of Air Force 69-73; Visiting Prof. of Aeronautics and Astronautics and of Management, Mass. Inst. of Technology 68-; mem. Nat. Acad. of Eng. 68-, Pres. 73-74; Admin., Energy Research and Devt. Admin. 74-75; mem. Scientific Advisory Board, U.S. Air Force 57-62, Assoc. Adviser 63-67; Nat. del. to AGARD; mem. Int. Acad. of Astronomy, American Acad. of Arts and Sciences, Nat. Space Club, Council on Foreign Relations, Board of Trustees Nat. Geographic Soc., Nat. Acad. of Eng., American Asscn. for Advancement of Science; Fellow, American Astronomical and Astronautical Socs., Inst. of Aeronautics and Astronautics, Inst. of Electrical and Electronic Engs.; Board of Overseers, Harvard Coll.
Leisure interests: tennis, sailing, skiing.
National Academy of Engineering, 2101 Constitution Avenue, N.W., Washington, D.C. 20418, U.S.A.

Searle, Humphrey, M.A., C.B.E., F.R.C.M.; British composer; b. 26 Aug. 1915, Oxford; s. of Humphrey Frederic Searle, I.C.S., and Charlotte Mathilde Mary Schlich; m. 1st Margaret Gillen Gray 1949 (died 1957), 2nd Fiona Elizabeth Anne Nicholson 1960; ed. Winchester Coll., New Coll., Oxford, and Royal Coll. of Music.
Studied privately with Anton Webern; mem. BBC Music Dept. 38-40; army service 40-46; Producer BBC Music Dept. 46-48; Gen. Sec. Int. Soc. for Contemporary Music 47-49; mem. Sadler's Wells Ballet Advisory Panel 51-57; Hon. Sec. Liszt Soc. 50-62; Resident Composer, Stanford Univ., Calif., U.S.A. 64-65; Prof. of Composition, Royal Coll. of Music, London 65-; Guest Composer Aspen Music Festival, Colorado, U.S.A. 67; Guest Prof. Staatliche Hochschule für Musik, Karlsruhe 58-72.
Compositions include First Piano Concerto 44, *Trilogy* on Texts of Edith Sitwell and James Joyce 49-52, *Poem* for 22 Strings 50, Piano Sonata 51, First Symphony 53, Second Piano Concerto 55, *Noctambules* (ballet) 56, *The Great Peacock* (ballet) 58, *The Diary of a Madman* (opera) 58, Second Symphony 58, Third Symphony 60, Fourth Symphony 62, *Dualities* (ballet) 63, *The Photo of the Colonel* (opera) 64, Fifth Symphony 64, *Scherzi* for Orchestra 64, *The Canticle of the Rose* 65, *Oxus* scena

67, *Hamlet* (opera) 68, *Sinfonietta for nine instruments* 69, *Jerusalem* (Blake) 70, *Hamlet Suite* 70, *Zodiac Variations* 70, *Labyrinth* 71, *Cello Fantasia* 72, *Les Fleurs du Mal* 72, *Fantasy-Toccata* for organ 73, *Kubla Khan* 74, *Five for Guitar* 74, *Skimbleshanks* (T. S. Eliot) 75, *Contemplations* 75; music for stage, radio, TV and films.
Leisure interest: travel.
Publs. *The Music of Liszt* 66, *Twentieth Century Counterpoint* 54, *Ballet Music: An Introduction* 73, *20th Century Composers* 3 72.
44 Ordnance Hill, London, N.W.8, England.
Telephone: 01-722-5182.

Searle, Ronald, A.G.I., F.S.I.A.; British artist; b. 3 March 1920, Cambridge; s. of William James and Nellie (Hunt) Searle; m. 1st Kaye Webb (dissolved 1967); one s. one d.; 2nd Monica Koenig 1967; ed. Central School, Cambridge and Cambridge School of Art.
First drawings published 35-39; served with Royal Engineers 39-46; prisoner-of-war in Japanese camps 42-45; contributor to nat. publs. 46-; mem. *Punch* 'Table' 56-; special features artist *Life* magazine 55-, *Holiday* 57, *The New Yorker* 66-; One-Man Exhbns. Leicester Galleries (London) 50, 54, 57, Kraushaar Gallery (New York) 59, Bianchaar Gallery (New York) 63, Kunsthalle (Bremen) 65, in Paris 66, 67, 68, 69, 70, 71, Bibliothèque Nationale 73, in Munich 67, 68, 69, 70, 71, 73, in London 68, etc.; work rep., in Victoria and Albert Museum and British Museum (London), Bibliothèque Nationale, Paris and in several German and American museums; designer of several films including *John Gilpin*, *On the Twelfth Day*, *Energetically Yours* (awards at Venice, Edinburgh, San Francisco and other film festivals), *Germany 1960*, *Toulouse-Lautrec*, *Dick Deadeye, or Duty Done* 75; designed animation sequences for films *Those Magnificent Men in their Flying Machines* 65, *Monte-Carlo or Bust!* 69, *Scrooge* 70; Los Angeles Art Dirs. Club Medal 59, Philadelphia Art Dirs. Club Medal 59, Nat. Cartoonists' Soc. Award 59, 60, Gold Medal, III Biennale, Tolentino, Italy 65, Prix de la Critique Belge 68, Grand Prix de l'Humour noir (France) 71, Prix d'Humour Festival d'Avignon 71, Medal of French Circus 71, Prix Internationale "Charles Huard" 72, La Monnaie de Paris Medal 74.
Publs. *Forty Drawings* 46, *John Gilpin* 52, *Souls in Torment* 53, *Rake's Progress* 55, *Merry England* 56, *Paris Sketchbook* 57, *The St. Trinian's Story* (with Kaye Webb) 59, *U.S.A. For Beginners* 59, *Russia for Beginners* 60, *The Big City* 58 (all with Alex Atkinson) *Refugees 1960* 60, *Which Way did he Go?* 61, *Escape from the Amazon* 63, *From Frozen North to Filthy Lucre* 64, *Those Magnificent Men in their Flying Machines* 65, *Haven't We Met Before Somewhere?* (with Heinz Huber) 66, *Searle's Cats* 67, *The Square Egg* 68, *Hello—Where did all the People Go?* 69, *Secret Sketchbook* 70, *The Second Coming of Toulouse-Lautrec* 70, *The Addict* 71, *More Cats* 75, *Designs for Gilbert and Sullivan* 75, etc.
c/o Hope Leresche and Steele, 11 Jubilee Place, London, SW3 3TE, England; John Locke Studio, 15 East 76th Street, New York, N.Y. 10021, U.S.A.
Telephone: 01-352-4311 (London); BU-8-8010 (N.Y.).

Sears, Ernest Robert, B.S., M.A., PH.D.; American geneticist; b. 15 Oct. 1910, Oregon; s. of Jacob P. Sears and A. Estella McKee; m. 1st Caroline F. Eichorn 1936, 2nd Lotti M. Steinitz 1950; two s. two d.; ed. Oregon State Coll. and Harvard Univ.
Geneticist, U.S. Dept. of Agriculture 36-; mem. Nat. Acad. of Sciences; Agronomy Soc. Award 51, Hoblitzelle Award 58, Gamma Sigma Delta Award 58, U.S. Dept. of Agriculture Superior Service Award 58, Mo. Sigma Xi Research Award 70, Ore. State Univ. Distinguished Service Award 73; Hon. D.Sc. (Göttingen).

Publs. 63 papers and articles on wheat cytogenetics. Curtis Hall, University of Missouri, Columbia, Mo. 65201, U.S.A.
Telephone: 314-882-7225.

Sears, Paul Bigelow, B.SC., B.A., M.A., PH.D.; American ecologist; b. 17 Dec. 1891, Bucyrus, Ohio; s. of Rufus Victor and Sallie Harris Sears; m. W. Marjorie Lea McCutcheon 1917; one s. two d.; ed. Ohio Wesleyan Univ., Univ. of Nebraska, and Univ. of Chicago.
Instructor in Botany, Ohio State Univ. 15-19; Asst. Prof. Univ. of Nebraska 19-25, Assoc. Prof. 25-27; Prof. and Head of Dept. of Botany, Univ. of Oklahoma 27-38, Oberlin Coll. 38-50; Dir. of Conservation, Yale Univ. 50-60; Chair. Botany Dept., Yale 53-55; Pres. American Asscn. for the Advancement of Science 56, Chair. of Board of Dirs. 57; mem. Nat. Science Board 58-64; Hon. Pres. Nat. Audubon Soc.; Trustee, Pacific Tropical Botanical Garden 63-71; Hon. D.Sc. (Ohio Wesleyan); Hon. Litt.D. (Marietta Coll.); Hon. LL.D. (Arkansas, Nebraska and Wayne State Univs.); Hon. D.Sc. (Oberlin Coll. and Bowling Green State Univ.), citations and medals for ecology and conservation.
Leisure interests: farming, sketching, writing and lecturing on ecology.
Publs. *Deserts on the March* 35, *This is Our World* 37, *Life and Environment* 39, *Charles Darwin* 50, *Where There is Life* 62, *The Living Landscape* 66, *Lands Beyond the Forest* 68, *Wild Wealth* (co-author) 71; numerous technical and general articles on ecology.
17 Las Milpas, Taos, N. Mex. 87571, U.S.A.
Telephone: 1-505-758-4637.

Seawell, William Thomas, B.S., J.D.; American airline executive; b. 27 Jan. 1918, Pine Bluff, Ark.; s. of George M. Seawell and Hattie A. Aldridge; m. Judith T. Alexander 1941; one s. one d.; ed. U.S. Military Acad. and Harvard Law School.
Served U.S.A.F. 42-63, retd. Brig. Gen.; Vice-Pres. (Operations) Air Transport Asscn. 63-65, Senior Vice-Pres. (Operations) American Airlines Inc. 65-68; Pres. Rolls-Royce Aero Engines Inc. 68-71; Pres. and Chief Operating Officer, Pan American World Airways Inc. Dec. 71-March 72, Chair. and Chief Exec. Officer March 72-; Silver Star, Distinguished Flying Cross, Air Medal, Croix de Guerre.
Pan American World Airways Inc., Pan Am Building, New York, N.Y. 10017; Home: 151 East 79th Street, New York, N.Y. 10021, U.S.A.
Telephone: 212-973-6207 (Office); 212-879-1934 (Home).

Sebai, Youssef Mohamed; Egyptian writer; b. 1917; ed. Military Acad. and Cairo Univ.
Began writing while at school; teacher of military history 43-52, Dir. Military Museum 52-53; Editor-in-Chief *Arissala al Gadida* 53-56; Sec.-Gen. High Council of Arts, Letters and Social Sciences 56, Afro-Asian People's Solidarity Org. 57-73; Minister of Culture 73-75, of Culture and Information 75-; Italian and Egyptian decorations; Ministry of Culture Prize for best film story (for *Rodda Qalbi* and *Gamila*) (*Rodda Qalbi* also won a prize for the best dialogue).
Publs. novels: *Na'eb Azra'il*, *Ard el Nifaq* (Land of Hypocrisy), *Inny Rahila* (I am Going Away), *Bein el Atlal* (Among the Ruins), *El Sakka Mat* (Death of a Water Carrier), *Rodda Qalbi, Tarik el Awda* (The Return), *Nadia*; short stories: *Ya Ommatun Dahikat* (A Nation that Laughed), *A Night of Wine, Sheikh Zo'orob*; plays: *Om Ratiba, Behind the Curtain, Stronger than Time.*
Ministry of Culture and Information, Cairo; Home: Villa Sebai, Mokatam City, Cairo, Egypt.

Sébilleau, Pierre; French diplomatist; b. 16 Sept. 1912; ed. Lycée de Nantes, Univ. de Paris à la Sorbonne and Ecole Libre des Sciences Politiques.
Embassy, Warsaw 38; Counsellor, Rome 45-55;

Minister Plenipotentiary, Head of Service of Bilateral Agreements, Econ. Dept., Ministry of Foreign Affairs 55, later Dir. of East Africa Dept.; Ambassador to Libya 60-62, Syria 62-64, Brazil 64-65, Denmark 66-70, to Yugoslavia 70-; Officier Légion d'Honneur.
French Embassy, Pariska II, Belgrade, Yugoslavia.

Seck, Assane; Senegalese politician; b. 1 Feb. 1919, Inor, Sedhiou; ed. Univ. of Paris.
Lecturer, Faculty of Literature, Univ. of Dakar and Prof. Lycée Maurice-Delafosse 56; Deputy, Assemblée constituante 57-; Asst. Sec.-Gen., Parti du regroupement africain Sénégal 57-58; Minister of Cultural Affairs 66-68; Minister of Nat. Educ. 68-73; Minister of Foreign Affairs April 73-.
Ministry of Foreign Affairs, Dakar, Senegal.

Secomski, Kazimierz, DR.ECON.SC.; Polish economist and politician; b. 26 Nov. 1910, Kamieńsk, Piotrków Trybunalski District; ed. economic studies.
Professor, Univ. of Łódź 47, Main School of Planning and Statistics, Warsaw 48-; mem. Polish Acad. of Sciences 61-, Head Cttee. of Econ. Sciences, mem. Presidium 72-; Vice-Chair. State Comm. of Econ. Planning 55-56; Vice-Chair. Econ. Council, Council of Ministers 57-62; Vice-Chair. Planning Comm., Council of Ministers 57-Dec. 68, First Vice-Chair. Feb. 71-; Chair. Chief Council of Polish Economic Soc.; State Prize; Order of Builders of People's Poland 74; Dr. h.c. (Warsaw Univ.) 75.
Publs. *Planowanie inwestycji* 54-55, *Wstęp do teorii rozmieszczenia sił wytwórczych* 56, *Studia z zakresu efektywności inwestycji* 57, *Podstawy planowania perspektywicznego* 66, *Elementy polityki ekonomicznej* 70, *Prognostyka* 71.
Komisja Planowania przy Radzie Ministrów, Plac Trzech Krzyży 3/5, Warsaw, Poland.

Seddon, Sir Herbert (John), Kt., C.M.G., D.M., F.R.C.S., F.A.C.S.; British orthopaedic surgeon; b. 13 July 1903, Derby; s. of the late John and Ellen Seddon; m. Mary Lorene Lytle 1931; one s. one d.; ed. William Hulme's Grammar School, Manchester, St. Bartholomew's Hosp. Medical Coll., London.
Junior appointments, St. Bartholomew's Hosp., London 25-29; Instructor in Surgery, Univ. Hosp., Ann Arbor, Mich., U.S.A. 30; Resident Surgeon, Country Branch, Royal Nat. Orthopaedic Hosp. 31-39; Prof. of Orthopaedic Surgery and Fellow of Worcester Coll., Oxford 40-48; Surgeon and Dir. of Studies, Royal Nat. Orthopaedic Hosp., later Prof. of Orthopaedic Surgery, Univ. of London 48-64; now Hon. Consulting Surgeon, Royal Nat. Orthopaedic Hosp.; Univ. Gold Medal, London; Robert James Medal, British Orthopaedic Asscn.; Lebanese Order of Merit, First Class.
Leisure interests: painting, gardening.
Publs. *Peripheral Nerve Injuries* (Medical Research Council Report, Editor) 54, *Surgical Disorder of the Peripheral Nerves* 72; many papers in medical journals.
Lakes House, 24 Gordon Avenue, Stanmore, Middlesex, HA7 3QD, England.
Telephone: 01-954 0827.

Sedney, Jules; Surinam politician; b. 28 Sept. 1922, Paramaribo; ed. Graaf van Zinzendorfschool, Mulo and Univ. of Amsterdam.
Former teacher; held senior post with Cen. Bank of Surinam 56-58; Minister of Finance 58-63; Dir. Industrial Devt. Comm. of Surinam and Nat. Devt. Bank 63; left Nationale Partij Suriname (NPS) and joined Progressieve Nationale Partij (PNP) 67; Prime Minister and Minister of Gen. Affairs 70-73.
Progressieve Nationale Partij, Keizerstraat 195, Paramaribo, Surinam.

Sedov, Leonid Ivanovich; Soviet foreign trade corporation official; b. 7 Jan. 1917; ed. Moscow Mining Inst.

Mineworker, Khabarovsk Territory 40-41; Red Army 41-44; *Soyuzpromexport* 44-46; Soviet Trade Mission in Britain 46-51; U.S.S.R. Ministry to Foreign Trade 51-55; Trade Counsellor, Soviet Embassy, Indonesia 55-56, Trade Rep. in Indonesia 56-60; Chair. *Soyuzpromexport* (coal and mineral) 60-64; Head of Dept. U.S.S.R. Ministry of Foreign Trade 64-; mem. C.P.S.U.; Badge of Honour, etc.
U.S.S.R. Ministry of Foreign Trade, 32/34 Smolenskaya-Sennaya ploshschad, Moscow, U.S.S.R.

Sedov, Leonid Ivanovich; Soviet scientist; b. 14 Nov. 1907, Rostov-on-Don; *s.* of Ivan and Raisa Sedov; *m.* Galia Tolstova 1931; one *s.* one *d.*; ed. Moscow Univ.
At the Aero-hydro-dynamics Inst. 31-; Prof. at Moscow Univ. 37-; at the Central Aircraft Engine Designing Inst. 47-; mem. U.S.S.R. Acad. of Sciences 53-; Chief Editor *Cosmic Research;* Pres. Int. Astronautic Fed. 59-61, Vice-Pres. 61-; awarded five Orders of Lenin, two Orders of Red Banner, Chaplygin Prize 46, State Prize 52, Lomonosov Prize 54, Hero of Socialist Labour 67; Belsch Prize 68, Légion d'Honneur 70; Liapounov Medal 74; hon. mem. of a number of foreign acads. and univs.
Publs. *Extension of Powerful Blasts, Some Unsteady Movements in Compressible Liquid* 45, *Two Dimensional Problems in Hydro-dynamics and Aerodynamics, Similarity and Dimensional Methods in Mechanics* 51, *Nonlinear Mechanics of Continuous Media* 62, *Introduction to Continuous Mechanics* 62, *Mechanics of Continuous Media,* Vols. I and II 73.
Moscow B-234, Leninski Gory MGU, Zona II, kv. 84, U.S.S.R.

Sedwitz, Walter J., M.A., PH.D.; American economist; b. 14 April 1925, Austria; *s.* of Emil H. Sedtwitz and Anna de Pitt; *m.* Jacqueline Maltaire 1951; two *s.*; ed. Univ. de Paris à la Sorbonne and Columbia Univ.
Former Dir. of Latin American Studies, Council on Foreign Relations; Economist, UN 49, U.S. Dept. of Commerce 51-53; Research Fellow, Council on Foreign Relations 53-54; Dir. of Research Dept., Fed. Reserve Bank of New York 53-59; Adviser to several Latin American countries in econ. and financial sphere 53-59; Prof. of Econs. and Senior Research Fellow, Boston Univ., Dir. Dept. of Econs., Pan American Union, Org. of American States (OAS) Washington 61-63; Asst. Sec. for Econ. and Social Affairs, OAS 63-; Exec. Sec. Inter-American Econ. and Social Council, OAS 63-; Exec. Sec. Inter-American Cttee. on Alliance for Progress; Trustee, Panamerican Devt. Foundation; mem. Council on Foreign Relations, Center for Interamerican Relations, American Econ. Asscn.
Leisure interests: piano, winter sports.
Publs. *Inflexible Interest Rates and Monetary Policy, Monetary Controls in Underdeveloped Countries, The Mexican Devaluation of 1954, Toward a Latin-American Common Market, The Alliance for Progress and Multilateral Economic Cooperation.*
Inter-American Economic and Social Council, General Secretariat, Washington, D.C. 20006; Home: 6704 Tulip Hill Terrace, Bethesda, Maryland, U.S.A.
Telephone: 652-1848.

Seebohm, Baron (Life Peer), cr. 72, of Hertford; **Frederic Seebohm,** Kt.; British banker; b. 18 Jan. 1909, Hitchin, Herts.; *s.* of Hugh Exton Seebohm and Leslie Gribble; *m.* Evangeline Hurst 1932; one *s.* two *d.*; ed. Leighton Park School, Reading, and Trinity Coll., Cambridge.
Barclays Bank Ltd. 29-, Sheffield, York and Birmingham, Dir. 47-, Deputy Chair. 68-74; Dir. Barclays Bank D.C.O., now Barclays Bank Int., 51-55, Vice-Chair. 55-59, Deputy Chair. 59-65, Chair. 65-72, Chair. London Cttee. 65-72; Chair. Finance for Industry Ltd., Industrial and Commercial Finance Corpn. Ltd., Finance Corpn. for Industry Ltd., ICFC Trustee Co. Ltd., Tech.

Devt. Capital Ltd., Gardens Pensions Trustees Ltd., Ship Mortgage Finance Co. Ltd., Finance for Shipping Ltd; holds numerous directorships; Pres. Inst. of Bankers 66-68; Chair. Export Guarantees Advisory Council 67-72; High Sheriff of Hertfordshire 70-71; Gov. London School of Econs. and Political Science; official of commercial, social and educational orgs.
Leisure interest: painting.
Finance for Industry Ltd., 91 Waterloo Road, London, SE1 8XP; Home: Brook House, Dedham, Nr. Colchester, Essex, England.
Telephone: 01-928-7822 (Office); Dedham 3372 (Home).

Seefehlner, Egon Hugo, DR.IUR.; Austrian opera director; b. 3 June 1912, Vienna; *s.* of Dr. Egon Ewald Seefehlner and Charlotte de Kerpely-Krassó; ed. Theresianum, Univ. of Vienna, Konsularakademie.
Co-founder and Gen. Sec. Austrian Cultural Asscn. 45; Chief Editor *Der Turm* (cultural) magazine 45; also in Ministry of Educ.; organized art exhbns., especially modern painting and sculpture; Gen. Sec. Wiener Konzertgesellschaft 46-61; Founded and organized Vienna Int. Festivals; Deputy Dir. Vienna State Opera 54-61, Gen. Man. (desig.) Sept. 76-; Deputy Gen. Man. and Gen. Sec. Deutsche Oper, Berlin 61-72, Gen. Man. 72-76; Commdr.'s Cross, Papal Order of Silvester; Officier Ordre des Arts et des Lettres; Goldenes Ehrenzeichen für Verdienste um das Land Wien; Österreichisches Ehrenkreuz für Wissenschaft und Kunst, 1st Class.
Staatsoper, Vienna, Austria; Olympische Strasse 10, 1 Berlin 19, Federal Republic of Germany.

Seefelder, Matthias, DR.RER.NAT.; German industrial executive; b. 1920, Boos, Kreis Memmingen, Bavaria; ed. Humanistisches Gymnasium, Univ. of Munich.
Joined BASF AG 67, Deputy mem. Man. Board 71, mem. Man. Board 73, Chair. Man. Board 74-; mem. Eastern Cttee. of Deutsche Wirtschaft/Arbeitskreis UdSSR, Board of Dirs. of Hack-Stiftung; Hon. Prof., Faculty of Chemistry, Univ. of Heidelberg 74.
BASF Aktiengesellschaft, Ludwigshafen am Rhein, Federal Republic of Germany.

Seefried, Irmgard; Austrian singer; *m.* Wolfgang Schneiderhan (*q.v.*); two *d.*; ed. Augsburg Conservatoire.
Aachen 40-43; Vienna State Opera 43-; numerous concert tours, incl. Scala Milan, Covent Garden London, Metropolitan New York, Salzburg, Lucerne and Edinburgh Festivals; numerous recordings; Mozart Ring 48, Mozart Medal, Lehmann Medal, Österreichisches Ehrenkreuz für Wissenschaft und Kunst, Officer's Cross of Royal Danish Dannebrog Order.
State Opera House, Vienna, Austria.

Seeiso, Constantine Bereng (see H.M. King Moshoeshoe II).

Seelye, Talcott Williams; American diplomatist; b. 6 March 1922, Beirut; *s.* of Laurens and Kate C. Seelye; *m.* Joan Hazeltine 1950; one *s.* three *d.*; ed. Deerfield Acad., Amherst Coll. and George Washington Univ.
Army service 43-46; teacher, Deerfield Acad., Deerfield, Mass. 47-48; speech writer, Washington 48-49; joined State Dept. 49; served in Germany, Jordan and Lebanon; Consul, Kuwait 56-60; Chargé d'Affaires, Saudi Arabia 65-66, Deputy Chief of Mission 66-68; Amb. to Tunisia 72-; White House Commendation; Hon. LL.D. (Amherst Coll.) 74.
Leisure interests: sport, music, archaeology.
Publs. articles in various journals.
American Embassy, Tunis, Tunisia.
Telephone: 282-566.

Sefrin, Max; German politician; b. 21 Nov. 1913; ed. Oberrealschule.
Served as pilot, Second World War; prisoner of war in U.S.S.R.; on return worked as man. of private firm;

Hon. Councillor for Trade and Supply, City Council of Jueterborg 46-; mem. Volkskammer 52-; mem. Christian Dem. Union (CDU), Deputy Gen. Sec. and Pres. of its Parl. group in Volkskammer; Deputy Chair. Council of Ministers and Minister of Health 58-71; Chair. CDU Viet-Nam Cttee.; Vaterländischer Verdienstorden (bronze).
Christian Democratic Union, Otto-Nuschke-Strasse 59-60, Berlin, W.8, German Democratic Republic.

Segal, Ronald Michael, B.A.; South African author; b. 14 July 1932, Cape Town; s. of Leon and Mary Segal; m. Susan Wolff 1962; one s. two d.; ed. Univ. of Cape Town and Trinity Coll., Cambridge.
Dir. Faculty and Cultural Studies Nat. Union of South African Students 51-52; Pres. Univ. of Cape Town Council of Univ. Socs. 51; won Philip Francis du Pont Fellowship to Univ. of Virginia (U.S.A.) 55 but returned to South Africa to found *Africa South* quarterly), 56; helped launch economic boycott April 59; banned by South African Govt. from all meetings July 59; in England with *Africa South in Exile*, April 60-61; Gen. Ed. Penguin African Library 61-; Hon. Sec. South African Freedom Asscn. 60-61; Convenor, Int. Conf. on Econ. Sanctions against South Africa 64, Int. Conf. on S.W. Africa 66.
Leisure interest: day-dreaming.
Publs. *The Tokolosh* (a fantasy) 60, *Political Africa: A Who's Who of Personalities and Parties* 61, *African Profiles* 62, *Into Exile* 63, *Sanctions Against South Africa* (Editor) 64, *The Crisis of India* 65, *The Race War* 66, *South West Africa: Travesty of Trust* (Editor) 67, *America's Receding Future* 68, *The Struggle against History* 71, *Whose Jerusalem? The Conflicts of Israel* 73, *The Decline and Fall of the American Dollar* 74.
The Old Manor House, Manor Road, Walton-on-Thames, Surrey, England.
Telephone: Walton-on-Thames 27766.

Ségalat, André; French executive; b. 10 Aug. 1910; ed. Ecole des Sciences Politiques.
Conseiller d'Etat; Sec.-Gen. of the Govt. 46-58; Chair. Board of Dirs. of the Société Nat. des Chemins de Fer Français 58-75; Grand Officier Légion d'Honneur.
88 rue Saint Lazare, 75436 Paris Cedex 09, France.

Ségard, Norbert, D.SC.; French scientist and politician; b. 3 Oct. 1922, Aniche (Nord); m.; three c.
Founder Dir. Inst. Supérieur d'Electronique du Nord, Dir. des Hautes Etudes Industrielles; Pres. Féd. des Ecoles Supérieures d'Ingénieurs et de Cadres; mem. Council, Scientific Soc. of Brussels, Pres. 70-71; Dir. Eng. Section, Inst. Européen pour la formation Professionnelle, Paris 61, Milan 63, Munich 65, Paris 67; Dir. Fondation pour l'Innovation; mem. many French and foreign professional socs.; mem. High Council of Nat. Educ., Nat. Council of Higher Educ. and Research; mem. Nord Regional Council; Deputy for Lille 73; Sec. of State for Foreign Trade 74-75, Minister Feb. 75-Jan. 76; Sec. of State for Posts and Telecommunications 76-; several decorations.
Ministère des Postes et Télécommunications, Paris, France.

Segawa, Minoru; Japanese investment executive b. 31 March 1906; ed. Osaka Commercial Univ.
Nomura Securities Ltd. 29-, Dir. 46-, Man. Dir. 48-52, Exec. Vice-Pres. 52-59, Pres. 59-68, Chair. 68-; Dir. Tokyo Securities Dealers Asscn. 62-, Tokyo Stock Exchange 62- (now Chair.), Mainichi Broadcasting Co. Ltd. 53-, Nippon Koka Railway Co. Ltd. 61-; Auditor, Toho Distiller Co. Ltd. 53-, Tokyo Koku Precision Instrument Co. 57-.
Nomura Securities Co. Ltd., 1 Nihonbashi 1-chome, Chuo-ku, Tokyo 103; and 15-14, Minami-Aoyama 1-chome, Minato-ku, Tokyo, Japan.

Segers, Paul Willem; Belgian politician; b. 21 Dec. 1900, Antwerp; ed. Catholic Univ. of Louvain.
Secretary, Gen. Fed. of Christian Workers 27-47, Pres. 47; mem. City Council of Antwerp 32-; Alderman of City of Antwerp 39-49; Senator 49-; Minister of Communications 49-54, 58-61; Minister of Nat. Defence 61-65, Vice-Pres. of Council and Minister in charge of Co-ordination of Social Policies 65-66; Minister of State 67, of Nat. Defence 68-71; Christian Socialist Party; seven Belgian and foreign awards.
Avenue Rubens 1, Antwerp, Belgium.

Segerstedt, Torgny, D.PHIL.; Swedish university administrator; b. 11 Aug. 1908, Mellerud; s. of Prof. Torgny and Augusta Segerstedt; m. Marie Louise Karling 1934; one s. two d.; ed. Lund Univ.
Asst. Prof. in Moral Philosophy, Lund Univ. 34-38; Prof. of Moral Philosophy, Uppsala Univ. 38, of Sociology 47, Dean of Faculty of Philosophy 47-54, and Rector 55-; Chair. Social Science Research Council; Chair. Univ. Comm. 57-63; Chair. Bank of Sweden Research Council 65-; G.C. Order of Northern Star; Commdr. of the Order of Finnish White Rose; Officer French Legion of Honour; Dr. h.c. (Univ. of Helsinki, Univ. of Uppsala Coll., U.S.A.).
Publs. *Value and Reality in Bradley's Philosophy* 34, *The Problem of Knowledge in Scottish Philosophy* 35, *Common-Sense-Skolan* 37, *Värde och Verklighet* (*Value and Reality*) 38, *Demokratins Problem* 39, *Ordens Makt* 44, *Människan i industrisamhället* 52, 55, *The Nature of Social Reality* 66, *Gesellschaftliche Herrschaft als Soziologisches Konzept* 68.
Uppsala Universitet, P.O. Box 256, 75105 Uppsala, Sweden.
Telephone: 018/137009.

Seghers, Anna; German author; b. 19 Nov. 1900.
Mem. Deutsche Akad. der Künste; Pres. German Writers' Asscn.; Kleist Prize 28; Nat. Prize 51, 59; mem. Lenin Peace Prize Cttee.; Lenin Peace Prize.
Publs. *Der Aufstand der Fischer von Sankt Barbara* 28, *Die Gefährten* 32, *Das siebte Kreuz* 42, *Transit* 48, *Die Toten bleiben jung* 49, *Der Mann und sein Name* 52, *Der Bienenstock* 53, *Brot und Salz* 58, *Die Entscheidung* (novel) 59, *Das Licht auf dem Galgen* (story) 61, *Karibische Geschichten* (stories) 62, *Über Tolstoi—Über Dostojewski* (essays) 63, *Die Kraft der Schwachen* (novel) 65, *Das wirkliche Blau* (stories) 67, *Das Vertraune* (novel) 68, *Sonderbare Begegnungen* (stories), etc.
Aufbau Verlag, Französischestrasse 32, Berlin, W.8, German Democratic Republic.

Seghers Pierre, D. ÈS L.; French writer, poet and literary editor; b. 5 Jan. 1906, Paris; s. of Charles and Marthe (Lebbe) Seghers; m. Colette Peugniez 1968; one d.; also one s. one d. (by previous marriage); ed. Coll. de Carpentras (Vaucluse) and Univ. of Paris.
While serving with the army (39) founded magazine *Poètes Casqués* published yearly as *Poésie* 40, 41, etc. until 48; active in production and distribution of clandestine publications 40-44, founder mem. Comité National des Ecrivains; early collaborator on *Parisien Libéré*; f. *Autour du Monde* (anthology of foreign poets) 52; two films with Felix Labisse (q.v.), television and radio productions; Prix Apollinaire 58; Chevalier de la Légion d'Honneur; Officier des Arts et des Lettres.
Publs. *Bonne Espérance* 39, *L'Homme du Commun, ou Jean Dubuffet* 44, *Le Domaine Public* 45, *Le Futur Antérieur* 47, *Jeune Fille* 49, *Six Poèmes pour Véronique* 50, *Poèmes Choisis* 52, *Le Coeur-Volant* 54, *Racines* 57, *Les Pierres* 58, *Chansons et Complaintes* (4 vols.) 59-70, *Piranèse* 60, *Le Livre d'or de la Poésie Française* 62, *Dialogues* 67, *Les Mots Couverts* 70, *Clavé* 72, *Les Poètes maudits* 72, *Dis-moi, ma vie* 73, *La Résistance et ses Poètes* 74.
228 boulevard Raspail, 75014 Paris, France.
Telephone: 325-28-88.

Segovia, Andrés; Spanish guitarist; b. 18 Feb. 1894; *m.* Emilia Segovia; two *s.*
Concerts throughout the world 14-; has taught at Santiago de Compostela and Acad. Chigi, Siena; has adapted works of Bach, Haydn, Mozart and other composers for the guitar; Gold Medal for Meritorious Work (Spain); Hon. D.Mus. (Oxon.) 72.
c/o Ibbs and Tillett Ltd., 124 Wigmore Street, London, W.1, England.

Segre, Beniamino, DR.MATH.; Italian university professor; b. 16 Feb. 1903, Turin; *s.* of Samuele and Leonilda Segre; *m.* Fernanda Coen 1932; three *c.*; ed. Coll. Colonna and Finzi, Technical Inst. C. Someiller and Univ. of Turin.
Assistant, Univ. of Turin 23-26; Fellow (Libero Docente), Univ. of Rome 27; Asst., Univ. of Rome 27-31; Prof. of Geometry, Univ. of Bologna 31-50, Univ. of Rome 50-; Pres. Accademia Nazionale dei Lincei 67-73, Vice-Pres. 73-; Pres. Accademia Nazionale dei XL 74-; mem. several Italian and foreign academies, including Acad. des Sciences de l'Institut de France and Pontificia Acad. Scientiarum; Dr. h.c. (Univs. of Bologna and Bratislava); several medals and prizes; Grand Cross of the Order of Merit of the Italian Republic; Commdr. Légion d'Honneur.
Leisure interests: mountaineering, gardening, chess.
Publs. *The non-singular cubic surfaces* 42, *Arithmetical questions on algebraic varieties* 51, *Forme differenziali e loro integrali I, II,* 51, 56, *Some properties of differentiable varieties* 57, 71, *Lectures on modern geometry* 61, *Prodromi di Geometria algebrica* 72; also more than 300 scientific papers.
Via di Salé 3, 00044 Frascati (Rome), Italy.
Telephone: (06) 942-7219.

Segrè, Emilio, PH.D.; American physicist; b. 1 Feb. 1905, Tivoli, Rome, Italy; *s.* of Giuseppe and Amelia (Treves) Segrè; *m.* 1st Elfriede Spiro 1936 (deceased), one *s.* two *d.*; *m.* 2nd Rosa Mines 1972; ed. Univ. of Rome.
Assistant Prof. Univ. of Rome 28-35; Prof. of Physics and Dir. Physics Laboratory Palermo Univ. 36-38; Research Asst. and Lecturer Univ. of Calif., Berkeley 38-42; Group Leader Los Alamos Scientific Laboratory 42-46; naturalized U.S. citizen 44; Prof. of Physics Univ. of Calif., Berkeley 46-, Emeritus 72; Prof. of Physics, Univ. of Rome 74-75; mem. Nat. Acad. of Sciences, American Philosophical Soc., Accad. dei Lincei, Heidelberg Acad. of Sciences, American Acad. of Arts and Sciences, Indian Acad. of Sciences, etc.; Hoffman Medal (German Chemical Soc.), Cannizzaro Medal (Accad. dei Lincei), Nobel Prize in Physics (with Owen Chamberlain) 59; Hon. D.Sc. Palermo Univ., Gustavus Adolphus Coll., S. Marcos Univ., Lima, Tel Aviv Univ. etc.; Grand Ufficiale al Merito della Repubblica (Italy); co-discoverer of the elements Technetium, Astatine and Plutonium, of the slow neutrons and the anti-proton.
Leisure interests: hiking, fishing.
Publs. Numerous papers on atomic and nuclear physics in *Physical Review, Proceedings of the Royal Society* (London), *Nature, Nuovo Cimento*; books: *Nuclei and Particles, Enrico Fermi physicist,* etc.
Department of Physics, University of California, Berkeley, Calif. 94720; Home: 36 Crest Road, Lafayette, Calif. 94549, U.S.A.

Seguy, Georges; French trade unionist; b. 16 March 1927.
Apprentice typographer 42; mem. French C.P. 42-; arrested by Gestapo and deported to Mauthausen Concentration Camp 44; electrician, S.N.C.F. (French Railways) 45; Sec. of Fédération C.G.T. des Cheminots 49-65, Sec. of C.G.T. 65-67; Sec.-Gen. of Confédération Générale du Travail (C.G.T.) 67-.

Confédération Générale du Travail, 213 rue Lafayette, Paris 10e, France.
Telephone: BOT 86-50 (Office).

Sehgal, Amar Nath, B.SC., M.A.; Indian sculptor; b. 5 Feb. 1922, Campbellpur, West Pakistan; *s.* of Ram Asra Mal and Parmeshwari Devi; *m.* Shukla Dhawan 1954; two *s.*; ed. Punjab Univ., Govt. Coll., Lahore, and New York Univ.
One-man exhbns. New York 50-51, Paris 52, East Africa and India; Hon. Art Consultant to Ministry of Community Devt., Govt. of India 55-66; organized sculpture exhbns. in Belgrade 64, Musée d'Art Moderne, Paris 65, Paulskirche Frankfurt 65, Haus am Lutzoplatz, West Berlin 66, Musées Royaux D'Art et Histoire, Brussels 66, Musée Etat Luxembourg 66, Wiener Secession, Vienna 66, Flemish Acad. Arts 67, Tokyo Int. Fair 73, etc.; retrospective exhbn. Nat. Gallery of Modern Art, New Delhi 72, City Hall Ottawa 73, Aerogolf, Luxembourg 75; participated in Sculpture Biennale, Musée Rodin, Paris 66 and UNESCO Conf. on role of art in contemporary society 74; Sculpture Award, Lalit Kala Academy 57; President's Award, Lalit Kala Academy 58 (donated to Prime Minister Nehru during Chinese invasion).
Major works: *Voice of Africa* (Ghana) 59, *A Cricketer* 61, *Mahatma Gandhi,* Amritsar, *To Space Unknown* (bronze, Moscow) 63; commissioned to decorate Vigyan Bhawan (India's Int. Conferences Building) with bronze sculptural mural depicting rural life of India; Bronze work *Conquest of the Moon* in White House Collection 69; *Anguished Cries* (bronze) monument, W. Berlin 71; Gandhi monument, Luxembourg 71; Monument to Aviation, New Delhi Airport, 72; works in Jerusalem, Vienna, Paris, West Berlin, Antwerp, New Delhi.
Leisure interests: writing poetry, photography.
Publs. *Arts and Aesthetics, Organising Exhibitions in Rural Areas, Der Innere Rhythmus* (poems) 75.
J-23 Jangpura Extension, New Delhi 14, India.
Telephone: 79206.

Seibert, Donald Vincent; American retail executive; b. 17 Aug. 1923, Hamilton, Ohio; *s.* of Carl F. Seibert and Minnie L. Wells; *m.* Verna S. Stone 1944; one *s.* two *d.*; ed. Univ. of Cincinnati.
Joined J. C. Penney Co. Inc. as shoe salesman 47, Store Man. 57, District Man. 59, Dir. of Planning and Research 63, of Catalogue Operations 64, of Int. Operations 72, of Corporate Planning and Devt. 73, Chair. and Chief Exec. Officer 74-; Dir. Continental Can Co. Inc. 75-; Chair. Board of Trustees, Nyack Coll. 72; William Howard Taft Award, Univ. of Cincinnati 75; Hon. LL.D., Hon. D.C.S.
Leisure interests: music, art, reading, tennis.
J. C. Penney Co., Inc., 1301 Avenue of the Americas, New York, N.Y. 10019; Home: Murray Hill, N.J., U.S.A.
Telephone: (212) 957-5753 (Office).

Seidenfaden, Erik; Danish writer and college warden; b. 24 April 1910, Hasle; *s.* of Aage Seidenfaden and Annalise Teilmann Harck; *m.* 1st Jytte Kaastrup Olsen 1935 (dissolved), 2nd Lone Knutson 1953; one *s.* two *d.*; university education.
With *Nationaltidende,* Copenhagen 31-34; London corresp. of *Berlingske Tidende* 35-37; city editor of *Politiken* 37, Rome corresp. 40; during German occupation of Denmark was head of Free Danish information services in Stockholm; Editor-in-Chief of independent daily *Information* and monthly review of foreign affairs *Fremtiden* 46-66; Warden Danish Students' Coll., La Cité Int. de l'Université, Paris 66-; contributor on foreign affairs to Scandinavian, English and American newspapers and periodicals; Diplomatic Columnist *Berlingske Tidende* 67-; Copenhagen Corresp. *The*

Times, London; mem. Council of the Inst. for Strategic Studies, London; Pres. Students Asscn., Copenhagen Univ. 64-65; mem. Conseil d'Administration and Asst. Del.-Gen. de la Cité Int. de la Université de Paris 70; Hon. M.B.E. (U.K.); Knight of Dannebrog (Denmark). Leisure interest: gardening.

Publs. *Borgerkrig i Spanien* (Civil War in Spain) 36, *Hitler beskyddar Danmark* (Hitler Protects Denmark) 43 (published in Stockholm), *Spidser* 48, *Den hellige krig om det hellige land* 56, *Nuclear Arms and Foreign Policy* 60, *Disengagement* 61, *Disarmament* 62, *Nato and Denmark* 68, *The Roads Towards Europe* 70.

La Fondation Danoise, 9 boulevard Jourdan, Paris 14e, France.

Telephone: 589-2947.

Seidenfaden, Gunnar, D.PH. & SC.; Danish scientist and diplomatist; b. 24 Feb. 1908, Varde; s. of Aage Seiden- faden and Annalise Teilmann Harck; m. Alix Arnstedt 1939; one s. four d.; ed. Copenhagen Univ.

Expeditions to Greenland 28-34, Thailand 34-35, Spitzbergen 38; U.S.A., Canada, Alaska 47-49, South America 50, Far East 55-57, China and Japan 58, Thailand 64-73; Danish Foreign Service 40-73, Washing- ton 45-50, Ministry of Foreign Affairs, Copenhagen 50-55, Amb. S.E. Asia 55-59, to U.S.S.R. 59-61; Deputy Under-Sec. of State 61-67; Chair. Nat. Security Cttee. 68-70; Amb. for Environment Problems 70-73; mem. Royal Danish Acad. of Sciences and Letters; Danish and foreign awards.

Leisure interests: East-Asiatic orchids.

Publs. *Modern Arctic Exploration* 38, *The Orchids of Thailand* (with Tem Smitinand) 59-65.

Borsholmgård pr. 3100 Hornbak, Denmark.

Telephone: 03240106.

Seidler, Harry, O.B.E., M.ARCH.; Australian architect; b. 25 June 1923, Vienna, Austria; s. of Max and Rose Seidler; m. Penelope Evatt 1958; one s. one d.; ed. Wasagymnasium, Vienna, Austria, Cambridge Tech- nical School, U.K., Univ. of Manitoba, Canada, Harvard Univ. and Black Mountain Coll., U.S.A.

Post graduate work under Walter Gropius, Harvard Univ. 46; study with painter Josef Albers, Black Moun- tain Coll. 46; Chief Asst. with Marcel Breuer, New York 46-48; Principal Architect, Harry Seidler and Assocs., Sydney, Australia 48-; Sir John Sulman Medal 51; Architecture and Arts Building of the Year Award 60. Major Works: flats and housing units in Australia, urban redevelopment projects for McMahons Point 57, city centre redevelopment "Australia Square", Sydney 62-66; Commonwealth Trade Office Complex, Canberra 70-72; High Rise Apartments, Acapulco 70; M.L.C. Center, Martin Place, Sydney 72-75; Conzinc Rio Tinto H.Q. Melbourne 72-75; Australian Embassy, Paris 73-; Hon. Fellow, American Inst. of Architects 66; Hon. Fellow, Royal Australian Inst. of Architects; Wilkinson Award 65, 66, 67; Sir John Sulman Medal 67, Civic Design Award 67, Pan Pacific Citation of the American Inst. of Architects 68.

Publs. *Houses, Interiors and Projects 1949-1954, Harry Seidler 1955-63, Architecture in the New World, The Work of Harry Seidler by Peter Blake* 73.

Office: 2 Glen Street, Milsons Point, New South Wales 2061; Home: 13 Kalang Avenue, Killara, N.S.W. 2071, Australia.

Telephone: 9221388 (Office); 4985986 (Home).

Seifert, Jaroslav; Czechoslovak poet; b. 23 Sept. 1901, Prague; m. Marie Ulrichová 1928; one s. one d.; ed. secondary school, Prague.

Writer and journalist for various Prague dailies and periodicals; Co-founder *Devětsil* Art Asscn. 20; Editor *Rovnost*, Brno 22, *Sršatec* (periodical) 22-25; Editor in Chief *Nová scéna* (theatre monthly) 30; Editor *Pestré Květy* (weekly) 31-33, *Ranní noviny* (daily) 33-39, *Národní práce* 39-45, *Práce* (daily) 45-49; State Prizes

36, 55, 68; Acting Chair. Union of Czechoslovak Writers 68-69, Chair. 69-70; Nat. Artist 66.

Leisure interest: botany.

Publs. include: *Ruce Venušiny* (Venus' Hands—State Prize) 36, *Maminka* (Mother—State Prize) 54, *Koncert na ostrové* (Concert at the Island—State Prize) 68, *Odlévání zvonů, Halleyova kometa, Morový sloup* (un- published), *Světlem oděná*, etc.

Břevnov U Ladronky 23/1338, Prague 6, Czechoslovakia.

Telephone: 35-78-71.

Seifert, Robin (Richard), J.P., F.R.I.B.A., DIP.ARCH.; British architect; b. 25 Nov. 1910, Switzerland; s. of William Seifert; m. Josephine Jeannette Harding 1939; two s. one d.; ed. Central Foundation School, London and Univ. Coll., London.

Commenced architectural practice 34; Corps of Royal Engineers 40-44; Indian Army 44-46; Hon. Lt.-Col. 46; private practice 48-; Principal of R. Seifert and Partners, formed April 58; Liveryman, City of London; mem. British Waterways Board 71-74, Home Office Cttee. of Management for Homeless Discharged Prisoners, Council R.I.B.A.

Principal works include: Centre Point, St. Giles Circus; Drapers Gardens; Nat. Provincial Bank H.Q.; Royal Garden Hotel, Kensington; Tolworth Towers, Surbiton; Woolworth House, Marylebone Rd.; I.C.T. H.Q., Putney; Kellogg House, Baker Street (all in London area).

Leisure interests: chess, violin.

Office: R. Seifert and Partners, 34 Red Lion Square, London, W.C.1; Home: Eleventrees, Milespit Hill, Mill Hill, London, N.W.7, England.

Telephone: 01-242-1644 (Office); 01-959-3397 (Home).

Seigner, Louis; French actor; b. 23 June 1903; ed. Lycée de Lyon and Conservatoires d'Art dramatique de Lyon et de Paris.

Actor, Théâtre des Celestins, Lyon 19-23, Théâtre de l'Odéon, Paris 23-39; Pensionnaire, Comédie Française 39-43, Sociétaire 43, Doyen 60, Hon. Sociétaire 71; Prof. Conservatoire National d'Art Dramatique 62-; Officier Légion d'Honneur, Commdr. des Arts et des Lettres.

Plays acted in include: *Le Roi soleil, Madame Sans- Gêne, Cyrano de Bergerac, Pelléas et Mélisande, Le Chevalier Canepin, Le Dindon.*

Films acted in include: *La Symphonie fantastique, Nous sommes tous des assassins, La Belle Otéro, Marguerite de la nuit, Le Bourgeois gentilhomme, La Verité, L'Eclipse, Les Amitiés particulières, Le Soleil Noir, Prêtres inter- dits, la Race des Seigneurs.*

12 rue Pierre-Curie, Paris 5e, France.

Seignoret, Eustace Edward, B.SC.; Trinidadian diplomatist; b. 16 Feb. 1925, Curepe, Trinidad; m.; two s. one d.; ed. Howard Univ., Washington, D.C. and Univ. of Wales, Bangor.

Agricultural Officer, Dept. of Agriculture, Trinidad & Tobago 53-58; Admin. Asst., West Indies Fed. Public Service 58-60, Asst. Sec. 60, Deputy Sec. 60-62; Asst. Sec. Trinidad & Tobago Public Service 62; First Sec., Perm. Mission of Trinidad & Tobago to UN 62, Coun- sellor 65-68; Deputy High Commr. to U.K. 69-71; Perm. Rep. to UN 71-75.

c/o Ministry of Foreign Affairs, Port of Spain, Trinidad, Trinidad and Tobago.

Seip, Helge Lunde; Norwegian journalist and politi- cian; b. 5 March 1919, Surnadal; s. of Torkel Arup S. Seip and Helga Lunde; m. Therese Holth 1943; three d.; ed. Oslo, Harvard (U.S.A.) and Cambridge (England) Univs.

Assistant Oslo Univ. 39; Statistical Sec. Norwegian Leather Board 41; Consultant Rieber A/S 42, Ministry of Finance 45; Div. Head Ministry of Commerce 48, Central Bureau of Statistics 52; Chief Political Editor *Dagbladet* (Oslo daily) 54, Editor-in-Chief 54-65; mem.

Norwegian Parliament 53-61 and 65-73; mem. Nordic Cultural Comm. 55-61, Nordic Council 58-62, 71-73; Minister of Labour and Local Affairs 65-71; Chair. Liberal Party 71-73; Sec.-Gen. Nordic Council 71-.
Leisure interests: fishing, travelling, stamp collecting.
Publ. *Kommunenes Ökonomi 49.*
Secretariat of the Nordic Council, Nordisk Rad, Fack, 103 10 Stockholm, Sweden; and Gl. Drammensveg 146, Blommenholm, Norway.

Seitz, Frederick, A.B., PH.D.; American physicist; b. 4 July 1911, San Francisco; s. of Frederick and Emily Seitz; m. Elizabeth K. Marshall 1935; ed. Stanford and Princeton Univs.
Instructor of Physics, Univ. of Rochester 35-36, Asst. Prof. 36-37; on staff of Research Laboratory of Gen. Electric Co. 37-39; Asst. Prof., Univ. of Pa. 39-41; Assoc. Prof. 41-42, Prof. and Head of Dept. of Physics, Carnegie Inst. of Technology 42-49; Prof. Physics Univ. of Ill. 49-57, Head of Dept. 57-64, Dean Graduate Coll. and Vice-Pres. of Research 64-65; NATO Science Adviser 59-60; mem. American Philosophical Soc., Full-time Pres. Nat. Acad. of Sciences 62-69, American Physics Soc. 61; Pres. Rockefeller Univ. 68-; mem. American Acad. of Arts and Sciences, President's Science Advisory Cttee., Naval Research Advisory Cttee., and numerous other advisory cttees.; mem. Board of Trustees, Rockefeller, Univ., etc.; Nat. Medal of Science 73-; several hon. degrees.
Publs. *The Modern Theory of Solids* 40, *The Physics of Metals* 43, *Solid State Physics* 55.
Rockefeller University, 66th Street and York Avenue, New York, N.Y. 10021, U.S.A.
Telephone: (212) 360-1234.

Sekyi, Henry Van Hien; Ghanaian diplomatist; b. 15 Jan. 1928; m. Maria Joyce Tachie-Menson 1958; one s. one d.; ed. Univ. Coll. of the Gold Coast (now Univ. of Ghana), King's Coll. Canbridge Univ. and London School of Econs.
Entered Foreign Service 57; successively Third Sec., Second Sec. and First Sec., Ghana Embassy, Wash. 58-61; First Sec. and later Counsellor, Ghana Embassy, Rome 62; Ministry of Foreign Affairs, Dir. divs. of Eastern Europe and China, Middle East and Asia, UN Affairs, Personnel and Admin. 62-65; Acting Principal Sec. 65; Ghana High Commr. to Australia 66-70; Amb. to Italy 70-72; High Commr. to U.K. 72-75.
Leisure interests: classics, music, Africana, gymnastics.
c/o Ministry of Foreign Affairs, Accra, Ghana.

Sela, Michael (Salomonowicz), M.SC., PH.D.; Israeli chemist and immunologist; b. 6 March 1924, Tomaszow, Poland; s. of Jakob and Roza Salomonowicz; m. Margalit Liebman 1948 (died 1975); two d.; ed. Hebrew Univ., Jerusalem and Geneva Univ.
Head Dept. of Chemical Immunology, Weizmann Inst. of Science 62-75, Vice-Pres. 70-71, Dean Faculty of Biology 70-73, mem. Board of Govs. 70-, Pres. 75; W. W. Garfield Weston Prof. of Immunology; mem. Israel Acad. of Sciences and Humanities 71, Pontifical Acad. of Science 75, N.Y. Acad. of Sciences; mem. Council Int. Union of Immunological Socs., Vice-Pres. 74-; mem. Advisory Board, Dept. of Basic and Clinical Immunology, Medical Univ. of S.C., Scientific Advisory Cttee., European Molecular Biology Lab., Heidelberg; mem. Int. Union Pure and Applied Biophysics, Int. Cell Research Org.; Foreign mem. Max-Planck-Inst. für Immunbiologie; mem. Board of Trustees, Inst. de Biologie Physico-Chimique, Paris; Chair. Council European Molecular Biology Org. 75; serves on many editorial boards, including *European Journal of Immunology, European Journal of Biochemistry, and Immunogenetics*; Hon. mem. American Soc. Biological Chemists, American Asscn. of Immunologists, Scandinavian Soc. for Immunology, Harvey Soc.; Foreign Hon. mem. American Acad. Arts and Sciences; Fogarty Scholar-

in-Residence, Nat. Insts. of Health, Bethesda, Md. 73-74; Israel Prize Natural Science 59, Rothschild Prize for Chemistry 68, Otto Warburg Medal 68, Emil von Behring Prize 73.
Publs. over 400 in immunology, biochemistry and molecular biology; Ed. *The Antigens* (three vols. published).
Weizmann Institute of Science, Rehovot, Israel.
Telephone: 951132.

Selecman, Charles E.; American business executive; b. 17 Sept. 1928, Dallas, Tex.; m.; three d.; ed. Southern Methodist Univ.
Formerly employed by Gen. Motors Corpn. and Chance Vought Aircraft; Divisional Personnel Man., Axelson Div., U.S. Industries Inc. 56, Exec. Vice-Pres., Axelson Div. 66; Vice-Pres. U.S. Industries Inc. 67, Exec. Vice-Pres. and Dir. 68, Pres. 70-73, Vice-Chair. and Chief Exec. 73-.
U.S. Industries Inc., 250 Park Avenue, New York, N.Y. 10017, U.S.A.

Selem, Kam; Nigerian police officer; b. 1924, Dikwa, North-Eastern State; s. of Mallam Bashir; m. Amne Shettima 1953; three s. three d.; ed. Dikwa Elementary School and Bornu Secondary School.
Enlisted in Nigeria Police Force April 42; trained at Police Coll., Kaduna; Detective, Kano until 50; Sub-Insp. of Police 50-53; Asst. Supt. 53-55; Deputy Supt. 55-59; attended Officers' Course, Ryton-on-Dunsmore, U.K. 56; Supt. of Police 59-60; Chief Supt. 60-61; Asst. Commr. of Police 61-62; Deputy Commr. March-Sept. 62; Commr. of Police in command of Northern Region 62-65; Deputy Insp.-Gen. 65-66; Insp.-Gen. 66-75; mem. Supreme Mil. Council and Fed. Exec. Council 66-75; Fed. Commr., Internal Affairs 67-75; Pres. Nigeria Branch of Int. Police Asscn.; mem. Int. Asscn. of Chiefs of Police; Defence Medal; Colonial Police Meritorious Service Medal; Queen's Police Medal for distinguished service; Nigerian Independence Medal; Nigeria Police Medal for Long Service; Commdr. Order of St. John.
Leisure interests: lawn tennis, hunting, swimming, farming, golf.
Force Headquarters, The Nigeria Police, Moloney Street, Lagos, Nigeria.

Seligman, Henry, O.B.E., PH.D.; British scientist; b. 25 Feb. 1909, Frankfurt-am-Main, Germany; s. of Milton Chase Seligman and Marie Gans; m. Lesley Bradley 1941; two s.; ed. Liebigschule, Frankfurt-am-Main, Univs. of Lausanne, Paris and Zürich.
Joined Atomic Energy Team, Cavendish Laboratory, Cambridge 41; worked on atomic research with N.R.C., Canada 43-46; founded Isotope Div., Harwell 47, Deputy Dir.-Gen. of Research and Isotopes at the Int. Atomic Energy Agency, Vienna 58-69, Scientific Adviser 69-; Pres. Joint Cttee. on Applied Radioactivity, Int. Council of Scientific Unions (ICSU) 57-69; Pres. and Dir. Exec. AG, Basle 74-; Cultural Medal of Monaco.
Leisure interests: skiing, music, modern art.
Scherpegasse 8/VI/4, 1190 Vienna, Austria.
Telephone: 32 47 764.

Selkirk, 10th Earl of; George Nigel Douglas-Hamilton, P.C., G.C.M.G., G.B.E., A.F.C., Q.C.; Scottish advocate and politician; b. 4 Jan. 1906, Dorset; m. Darell Sale Barker 1949; ed. Eton, Balliol Coll., Oxford, and Univs. of Edinburgh, Bonn, Vienna and Paris.
Admitted to Faculty of Advocates 34; commanded 603 Squadron A.A.F. 34-38; mem. Edinburgh Town Council 35-40; Commr. for Gen. Board of Control (Scotland) 36-39 and for Special Areas (Scotland) 37-39; served R.A.F. 39-45; elected Scots Rep. Peer 45-63; served successively in Churchill, Eden and Macmillan govts. 51-60; Paymaster Gen. 53-55; Chancellor of the Duchy of Lancaster 55-57; First Lord of the Admiralty

57-59; U.K. Commr. for Singapore and Commr.-Gen. for S.E. Asia, Singapore 59-63; U.K. Council Rep. to South-East Asia Treaty Org. 60-63; Chair. Conservative Commonwealth Council 65-72, Victoria League 71-76; Pres. Building Socs. Asscn., Nat. Ski Fed. of Great Britain 64-68, Royal Soc. for Asian Affairs 65-76; Freeman of Hamilton 37.

60 Eaton Place, London, S.W.1, England.

Telephone: 01-235 6926.

Sellers, Peter Richard Henry, C.B.E.; British actor; b. 8 Sept. 1925; ed. St. Aloysius Coll., Highgate.

Debut at Windmill Theatre 48; toured 49-54; radio shows include *Ray's a Laugh, The Goon Show;* television shows *Idiots Weekly, A Show Called Fred, Son of Fred;* films *The Ladykillers, The Smallest Show on Earth, The Naked Truth, Tom Thumb, Carleton Browne of the F.O., The Mouse that Roared, I'm Alright Jack, Up the Creek, Two Way Stretch, Battle of the Sexes, Never Let Go, The Millionairess, Mr. Topaze, The Running, Jumping and Standing Still Film, Only Two Can Play, The Waltz of the Toreadors, Lolita, The Wrong Arm of the Law, Heavens Above!, Dr. Strangelove, The Pink Panther, The World of Henry Orient, What's New, Pussycat?, A Shot in the Dark, After the Fox, Casino Royale, The Bobo, The Party, I Love You Alice B. Toklas, The Magic Christian, A Day at the Beach, Hoffman, There's A Girl in My Soup, Where Does it Hurt?, Alice's Adventures in Wonderland, The Blockhouse, The Optimists of Nine Elms, Soft Beds and Hard Battles, The Great McGonagall, Ghost in the Noonday Sun, The Return of the Pink Panther, Murder by Death, The Pink Panther Strikes Again;* British Film Acad. Award 59, Golden Gate Trophy 59, San Sebastian 62, Award for Best Actor, Iran Film Festival 73.

c/o Theo Cowan Ltd., 45 Clarges Street, London, W.1, England.

Sellers, Robert Vernon; American business executive; b. 26 March 1927, Bartlesville, Okla.; s. of C. Vernon and Helen (Weeks) Sellers; m. Anna Marie Hughes 1950; two s. two d.; ed. Univ. of Kansas.

Joined Cities Service Oil Co. 51; Man. Planning and Devt. Dept., Cities Service Co. 63-66, Staff Vice-Pres. (Corporate Planning Dept.) 66-68, Asst. Treas. 68, Treas. 68-69, Vice-Pres. 69-71, Dir. and mem. Exec. Cttee. 69-, Vice-Chair. 71-72, Chair. of Board, Chief Exec. Officer and Chair. Exec. Cttee. 72-, Chair. Finance Cttee. 73-; Dir. John Hancock Mutual Life Insurance Co., First Nat. Bank and Trust Co. of Tulsa.

Cities Service Company, Box 300, Tulsa, Okla. 74102; Home: 2131 East 29th Street, Tulsa, Okla. 74114, U.S.A.

Sellick, Phyllis, O.B.E., F.R.A.M.; British concert pianist; b. 16 June 1911, Newbury Park, Essex; m. Cyril Smith 1937 (died 1974); one s. one d.; ed. Glenarm Coll., Ilford, Royal Acad. of Music and in Paris.

Professor, Royal Coll. of Music, London; Hon. F.R.C.M.

Leisure interests: gardening, cooking, yoga.

33 Fife Road, London, SW14 7EJ, England.

Sellin, (Johan) Thorsten, A.M., PH.D., LL.D.; American sociologist; b. 26 Oct. 1896, Örnsköldsvik, Sweden; s. of Jonas and Martha Westman; m. Amy J. Anderson 1920; three s.; ed. primary and secondary schools in Sweden, Augustana Coll., Rock Island, Illinois and Univs. of Pennsylvania, Minnesota and Paris.

Assistant Prof., Univ. of Pa. 22-30, Prof. of Sociology 30-67, Emeritus Prof. 67-; Lecturer, Columbia Univ. 35-46; Visiting Prof. Univs. of Uppsala, Stockholm and Lund 46-47, Princeton Univ. 49, Univ. of Calif 58; Queen's Coll., New York 68-69; Fulbright Lecturer, Cambridge Univ. 59-60; Sec.-Gen. Int. Penal and Penitentiary Comm. 50-51, 12th Int. Penal and Penitentiary Congress 50; Consultant, Swedish Penal Code Comm. 46-47, American Law Inst. Youth Correc-

tion and Model Penal Code projects; Official, UN Comms. of Experts on Prevention of Crime and Treatment of Offenders 49-56; Pres. Int. Soc. of Criminology 56-66, Int. Penal and Penitentiary Foundation 65-71; Pres. Fourth Int. Congress of Criminology 60 (Hon. Pres. Fifth Congress 65); Gen. Rapporteur First UN World Congress on Prevention of Crime and Treatment of Offenders; Editor *Annals* of the American Acad. of Political and Social Science 29-68; mem. American Philosophical Soc., Social Science Research Council, Royal Soc. of Humanistic Knowledge (Lund), History of Law Soc. (Paris), Mexican Acad. of Penal Sciences; Grand Officer Order of North Star (Sweden); Penitentiary Medal (France); Gold Medal German Criminological Soc.; Hon. Dr. (Augustana Coll. and Univs. of Uppsala, Pennsylvania, Copenhagen and Leiden).

Publs. *Crime in the Depression* 37, *Culture Conflict and Crime* 38, *The Criminality of Youth* 40, *Pioneering in Penology* 44, *The Death Penalty* 59, *The Measurement of Delinquency* (co-author) 64, *Delinquency in a Birth Cohort* (co-author) 72, *Slavery and the Penal System* 76; Editor: *Capital Punishment* 67.

Gilmanton, N.H. 03237, U.S.A.

Telephone: 1-603-267-6309.

Sellner, Gustav Rudolf; German theatre director; b. 25 May 1905, Traunstein, Upper Bavaria; s. of Gustav and Frieda (Elliesen) Sellner; m. Ilse Pässler 1951; one s. one d.; ed. Gymnasium, Univ. of Munich, and drama training at Kammerspiele, Munich.

Actor, Producer, Stage Dir. and Dir., Oldenburg, Göttingen, Hanover 24-38; Producer at Kiel, Essen and Hamburg 45-51; Dir. Hessisches Landestheater, Darmstadt 51-, Deutsche Oper, Berlin 61-72; numerous awards and prizes.

First performances include: *Alkmene* (Giselher Klebe) Berlin 61, *Dir Orestie* (Darius Milhaud) Berlin 63, *Montezuma* (Roger Sessions) Berlin 64, *Der Junge Lord* (Hans Werner Henze) Berlin 65, *Die Bassariden* (Henze) Salzburg 66, *Zwischenfälle bei einer Notlandung* (Boris Blacher) Hamburg 66, *Prometheus* (Carl Orff) Stuttgart 68, *Odysseys* (Luigi Dallapiccola) Berlin 68, *200,000 Taler* (Boris Blacher) Berlin 69, *Melusine* (Aribert Reimann) Berlin/Schwetzingen 71; leading part in film *The Pedestrian* 73.

Leisure interests: modern arts, architecture.

Publs. include *Theatralische Landschaft* (with Werner Wien) 62.

7741 Koenigsfeld-Burgberg, Prof. Domagkweg 106, Federal Republic of Germany.

Telephone: 07725/7674.

Selmer, Ragnhild Elisabeth Schweigaard; Norwegian judge and politician; b. 18 Oct. 1923, Oslo; d. of Niels Schweigaard and Betty Reimers; m. Prof. Knut S. Selmer; one s. one d.; ed. Univ. of Oslo.

Assistant Judge, Municipal Court of Asker and Baerum 50-55; mem. Oslo City Council 51-55; Law Section, Ministry of Justice 55-65; Judge, Court of Probate, Oslo 65; Minister of Justice 65-70; Supreme Court Judge 71-; Conservative.

Leisure interests: reading, family life.

Supreme Court of Norway, Oslo, Norway.

Selormey, Col. Anthony Hugh; Ghanaian army officer and politician; b. 2 March 1937, Volta Region; m.; four c.; ed. Catholic Mission School, Bishop Herman Secondary School.

Joined Army 1961; Officer Cadet, Ghana Mil. Acad.; Commissioned 1962, Reece Regiment, Ghana Army; courses at Royal Armoured Corps Centre, Bovington Camp, England, Joint Services Staff Coll., Latimer, England, U.S. Adjutant-Gen.'s Dept., U.S. Intelligence School, U.S. Armour School 67; Ghana Army: Support Troop Leader, Sabre Troop Leader, Intelligence

Officer, Commdg. Officer of 2nd Reece Squadron, Staff Capt. to Mil. Sec., Instructor at Ghana Mil. Acad., Officer commdg. Reece Regiment, Accra; Commr. for Transport and Communications 72-73, for Health 74-75; mem. Nat. Redemption Council 72-75.
Leisure interests: hunting, gardening, music.
c/o Ministry of Health, Accra, Ghana.

Selwyn-Lloyd, Baron (Life Peer), cr. 76, of Wirral in the County of Merseyside; (**John**) **Selwyn Brooke Lloyd**, PC., C.H., C.B.E., T.D., Q.C., D.L.; British politician; b. 28 July 1904; ed. Fettes and Magdalene Coll., Cambridge. Barrister 30-, Master of the Bench, Gray's Inn 51; served army 39-45; elected as Conservative M.P. for Wirral Div. of Cheshire 45, re-elected 50, 51, 55, 59, 64, 66, 70, 74; Recorder of Wigan 48-51; Minister of State Foreign Office 51-54; Minister of Supply 54-55, of Defence April-Dec. 55; Sec. of State for Foreign Affairs 55-60; Chancellor of the Exchequer 60-62; Chair. Nat. Econ. Devt. Council 62; Lord Privy Seal and Leader of the House of Commons Oct. 63-Oct. 64; Speaker of the House of Commons 71-76; Dir. Alliance Assurance, Sun Alliance Insurance 62-63, 65-70, Rank Org. 63, 65-70, English and Caledonian Investment Co. Ltd. 65-70; Legion of Merit; Hon. D.C.L. (Oxford).
Hilbre House, Macdona Drive, West Kirby, Wirral, Cheshire, England.

Selye, Hans, PH.D., D.SC., M.D., F.R.S.C.; Canadian university professor; b. 26 Jan. 1907, Vienna, Austria; s. of Dr. Hugo Selye and Maria Felicitas Langbank; m. Gabrielle Grant; three s. one d.; ed. Prague, Paris, Rome and McGill Univs.
Asst. in Experimental Pathology at Univ. of Prague 29-31; Rockefeller Research Fellow in Biochemical Hygiene, Johns Hopkins Univ. 31; Rockefeller Research Fellow in Biochemistry, McGill Univ. 32-33, Lecturer 33-34, Asst. Prof. 34-37; Asst. Prof. of Histology, McGill Univ. 37-41, Assoc. Prof. 41-45; Prof. and Dir. of Institute of Experimental Medicine and Surgery, Univ. of Montreal 45-; Guest Lecturer U.S.A. and Canada 50-; consultant to Surgeon-Gen., U.S. Army 47-57; Hon. Prof. Guatemala, Univ. of San Carlos; Fellow, N.Y. Acad. of Sciences and American Asscn. for the Advancement of Science, American Geriatrics Soc., Int. Coll. of Surgeons (Hon.), and numerous other North and South American and European Acads. and Socs.; numerous honorary degrees; awards include: Casgrain and Charbonneau prize; Gordon Wilson medal; Heberden Research Medal; Medal of Accad. Medico Fisica of Florence; Semmelweiss Medal (New York), Henderson Gold Medal, American Coll. of Angiology Award 59, Western Soc. of Periodontology Award 60, Samuel Charles Miller Memorial Award 60, B'nai B'rith Humanitarian Award 61; Hon. Citizen of Verona 55.
Publs. *The Steroids* 43, *Ovarian Tumors* 46, *Textbook of Endocrinology* 49, *Stress* 50, *On the Experimental Morphology of the Adrenal Cortex* 50, *First Annual Report on Stress* 51, *Second Annual Report on Stress* 52, *The Story of the Adaptation Syndrome* 52, *Third Annual Report on Stress* 53, *Fourth Annual Report on Stress* 54, *Fifth Annual Report on Stress* 55, *The Stress of Life* 56 (2nd edn. 76), *The Chemical Prevention of Cardiac Necroses* 58, *The Pluricausal Cardoipathies* 61, *Calciphylaxis* 62, *From Dream to Discovery* 64, *The Mast Cells* 65, *Thrombohemorrhagic Phenomena* 66, *In Vivo* 67, *Anaphylactoid Edema* 68, *Experimental Cardiovascular Diseases* 70, *Hormones and Resistance* 71, *Stress without Distress* 74, *Stress in Health and Disease* 76, *The Stress of My Life* 76 and many other scientific papers.
Institut de Médecine et de Chirurgie Expérimentales, Université de Montreal, P.O. Box 6128, Montreal; and 659 Milton Street, Montreal, Quebec, Canada.
Telephone: 343-6378/9.

Sema, Hokishe, B.A.; Indian politician; b. March 1921, Apitomi; s. of late Sukiye Sema and of Hevili Sema; m. Shitoli Sema 1951; five s. one d.; ed. Mokokchung High School, Serampur Coll., W. Bengal, and St. Anthony's Coll., Shillong.
Founder-Leader of Youth orgs. for unity and understanding among the various Naga tribes 42-48; opponent of secessionist policy and movement 48-52; Educ. Service 52-55; Admin. Service 56-58; mem. Sema Public Orgs. and mem. Naga People's Convention 58-60; mem. Select and Drafting Cttees. of Naga People's Convention 60-61; Exec. Councillor, Finance (Nagaland) 61-63; elected to Nagaland Legislative Assembly, Minister of Finance and Health 64-68; re-elected for Legislative Assembly as Leader of Nagaland Nationalist Org. 69; Chief Minister of Nagaland 69-74.
Leisure interests: reading, gardening, hunting, singing.
c/o Office of Chief Minister of Nagaland, P.O. Kohima, India.
Telephone: KMA: 239, 357, 254.

Semega-Janneh, Bocar Ousman, M.B.E.; Gambian diplomatist; b. 21 July 1910; s. of late Ousman Semega-Janneh and Koumba Tunkara; m. 1936; several c.; ed. Mohammedan Primary School and Methodist Boy's High School.
Joined Gambia Surveys Dept. 31, Senior Surveyor 48, Dir. 53-66; mem. Bathurst City Council 51-67, Mayor 65-67; High Commr. to Senegal 67-71, also accred. as Amb. to Mali, Mauritania, Guinea and Liberia and High Commr. to Sierra Leone 69-71; High Commr. to U.K. 71-, also accred. as Amb. to Fed. Germany, France, Austria, Sweden, Switzerland; del. to UN Gen. Assembly and to OAU 68-; Grand Officer, Order of Merit (Senegal, Mauritania).
Leisure interests: football, cricket, lawn tennis, golf.
The Gambia High Commission, 60 Ennismore Gardens, London, S.W.7, England.

Semichastny, Vladimir Yefimovich; Soviet politician; b. 1924; ed. Kemerovo Chemical Technological Inst.
Former First Sec., Communist League of Youth; fmr. senior official, Soviet Communist Party, Moscow; fmr. Sec., Communist Party of Azerbaijan; Chair. State Security Cttee. of Council of Ministers of U.S.S.R. 61-67; First Vice-Chair. Ukrainian Council of Ministers June 67-; Alt. mem. Central Cttee. C.P.S.U. 56-64, mem. 64-71.
Council of Ministers of Ukrainian S.S.R., Kiev, U.S.S.R.

Semkow, Jerzy (Georg), M.A.(MUS.); Polish conductor; b. 12 Oct. 1928, Radomsko; s. of Alexander and Valerie Sienczak Semkow; ed. Jagiellonian Univ. of Cracow, High School of Music, Cracow and Leningrad Music Conservatoire.
Assistant Conductor, Leningrad Philharmonic Orch. 54-56; Conductor, Bolshoi Opera and Ballet Theatre, Moscow 56-58; Artistic Dir. and Principal Conductor, Warsaw Nat. Opera 59-61; Perm. Conductor, Danish Royal Opera, Copenhagen 66-71; Musical Dir. and Principal Conductor St. Louis Symphony Orchestra 75-; guest conductor of London Philharmonic, New York Philharmonic, Chicago Symphony, Boston Symphony and many other leading European and American orchestras; engagements at Covent Garden, La Scala, Berlin, Vienna, Madrid, Paris, Rome, etc.; Commdr. Cross of Polonia Restituta.
Leisure interests: reading, yachting.
"Propaganda Musicale", Via Sicilia 154, Rome, Italy; c/o W. Hansen Koncertdirektion, Gothersgade 9-11, Copenhagen, Denmark; Ul. Dynasy 6/1, 00-354 Warsaw, Poland.
Telephone: 11-7888 (Copenhagen); 26-37-82 (Warsaw).

Semyonov, Nikolay Nikolayevich, D.SC.; Soviet scientist; b. 15 April 1896, Saratov; ed. Leningrad State Univ.

Assistant Dir. and Laboratory Man. Physico-Technical Inst., Leningrad 20-30; Asst. Prof. Leningrad Polytechnic Inst. 28; Dir. Inst. of Chemical Physics, Leningrad 31-; Prof. Moscow State Univ. 44-; Deputy to U.S.S.R. Supreme Soviet; mem. CPSU 47-; mem. U.S.S.R. Acad. of Sciences 32-, Vice-Pres. 63, mem. Presidium, Academician, Sec. Dept. of Chemical Sciences 57-; Cand. mem. Cen. Cttee. CPSU 61-66; mem. Chemical Soc. of England 43-; foreign mem. Royal Soc. of England 58; hon. mem. Indian Acad. of Sciences 59; mem. German Acad. of Naturalists (Leopoldina) 59; hon. mem. Hungarian Acad. of Sciences 61; hon. life mem. New York Acad. of Sciences 62; Foreign associate, Nat. Acad. of Sciences, U.S.A. 63; hon. mem. Czech. and Romanian Acads. of Sciences 65; Corresp. mem. German Acad. of Sciences Berlin; hon. Fellow Royal Soc. of Edinburgh 66; Dr. h.c. Oxford 60, Brussels 62, Milan 64, Budapest, Prague, London 65; Orders of Lenin (five); Order of Red Banner of Labour; Nobel Prize 56; State Prize 41; Lomonosov Gold Medal (U.S.S.R. Acad. of Sciences) 69; Hero of Socialist Labour 66.

Publs. *Chain Reactions* 34, *Some Problems of Chemical Kinetics and Reactivity* 54 (2nd edn. revised and translated into English 58), and over 200 articles in the field of chemical physics.

U.S.S.R. Academy of Sciences, 14 Leninsky Prospekt, Moscow, U.S.S.R.

Semyonov, Vladimir Semyonovich; Soviet diplomatist and politician; b. 16 Feb. 1911, Krasnoslobodskoe, Tambov Region; ed. Moscow Inst. of Philosophy, History and Literature.

Counsellor in Kaunas 39-40, Berlin 40-41, Stockholm 42-45; Political Adviser Berlin 45-53; rank of Minister 45, of Amb. 49; High Commr. in Germany 53-54; Deputy Foreign Minister 55-; mem. Central Auditing Comm. C.P.S.U. 61-66; Alt. mem. C.P.S.U. Central Cttee. 66-; Head U.S.S.R. Del. to Strategic Arms Limitations Talks (SALT) 69-.

Ministry of Foreign Affairs, 32-34 Smolenskaya-Sennaya ploshchad, Moscow, U.S.S.R.

Sen, Amartya Kumar, M.A., PH.D.; Indian economist; b. 3 Nov. 1933, Santiniketan, Bengal; *s.* of Ashutosh and Amita Sen; ed. Presidency Coll., Calcutta and Trinity Coll., Cambridge.

Professor of Econs., Jadavpur Univ., Calcutta 56-58; Fellow, Trinity Coll., Cambridge 57-63; Prof. of Econs., Univ. of Delhi 63-71, Chair. Dept. of Econs. 66-68; Hon. Dir. Agricultural Econs. Research Centre, Delhi 66-68, 69-71; Prof. of Econs. London School of Econs. 71-; Visiting Prof., Univ. of Calif., Berkeley 64-65; Harvard Univ. 68-69; Fellow, Econometric Soc.

Publs. *Choice of Techniques: An Aspect of Planned Economic Development* 60, *Growth Economics* 70, *Collective Choice and Social Welfare* 70, *On Economic Inequality* 73, *Employment, Technology and Development* 75; articles in various journals in econs., philosophy and political science.

London School of Economics and Political Science, Houghton Street, Aldwych, London, W.C.2, England. Telephone: 01-405 7686.

Sen, Dr. Binay Ranjan; Indian diplomatist and international administrator; b. 1 Jan. 1898, Dibrugarh, Assam; *s.* of the late Dr. K. M. Sen and Mrs. Saudamini Sen; *m.* Chiroprava Chatterjee 1931; four *d.*; ed. Calcutta and Oxford Univs.

District Magistrate, Midnapore 37-40; Revenue Sec., Govt. of Bengal 40-43, Dir. of Civil Evacuation 42-43; Relief Commr. 42-43; Dir.-Gen. of Food, Govt. of India 43-46, Sec., Dept. of Food 46-47; Minister in Washington 47-48; Sec. Ministry of Agriculture 48; Chargé d'Affaires and Minister in Washington 48-50; Indian Ambassador to Italy and Yugoslavia 50-51 and 52-55, to U.S.A. 51-52; Ambassador to Japan 55-56; Dir.-Gen.

Food and Agriculture Org. of UN (FAO) 56-67; several hon. doctorates; Hon. Fellow, St. Catherine's Coll., Oxford; Knight Commdr. of the Ordine Piano; Knight Grand Cross of the Order of Pope S. Silvestri; Padma Vibhusan; decorations from govts. of Morocco, South Korea, Ivory Coast, Chad, Gabon and Lebanon.

Leisure interests: western music and reading.

14/2 Palm Avenue, Calcutta 19, India. Telephone: 44-0757.

Sen, Samarendranath, B.A., B.SC.; Indian diplomatist; b. 10 Aug. 1914; *m.*; two *s.* two *d.*; ed. Univs. of Calcutta and London.

Joined Indian Civil Service 38; held several posts in Bengal 39-46; Under-Sec., Dept. of External Affairs; Liaison Officer to UN 46-48; Deputy Sec., Ministry of External Affairs and Commonwealth Relations; Head of Chancery, High Comm., London 49; Deputy Sec. in charge of External Publicity, Ministry of External Affairs 51-53; Consul-Gen., Geneva 53-55; Chair. Int. Supervision and Control Comm., Laos 55-57; Joint Sec. Ministry of External Affairs 57-59; High Commr. in Australia and New Zealand 59-62; Amb. to Algeria 62-64, to Lebanon, Jordan and Kuwait and High Commr. to Cyprus 64-66; High Commr. to Pakistan 66-69; Perm. Rep. to UN 69-74; High Commr. to Bangladesh 74-; Kaiser-i-Hind 43, Padma Shri 57.

Indian High Commission, Road 2, Dhanmondi, Dacca, Bangladesh.

Sen, S. R., PH.D.; Indian international bank official; b. 2 July 1916, Noakhali; *s.* of late Satya R. Sen and of Ashalata Sen; *m.* Anita Sen 1948; two *s.*; ed. Calcutta Univ., Univ. of Dacca and London School of Econs.

Taught economics, Univ. of Dacca 40-48; Deputy Econ. Adviser, Govt. of India 48-51; Econ. and Statistical Adviser, Ministry of Food and Agric., Govt. of India 51-58; Joint Sec. (Plan Co-ordination and Admin.), Planning Comm. 59-63; Adviser (Programme Admin.) and Additional Sec., Govt. of India 63-69; Vice-Chair. Irrigation Comm., Govt. of India 69-70; Amb. and Exec. Dir. IBRD, IFC and IDA 70-; has taken part in and led numerous Indian and int. agric. and devt. comms., and delegations; Pres. Int. Asscn. of Agric. Economists 70.

Leisure interest: photography.

Publs. *Strategy for Agricultural Development, Economics of Sir James Steuart, Population and Food Supply, Planning Machinery in India, Growth and Instability in Indian Agriculture, Politics of Indian Economy.*

International Bank for Reconstruction and Development, 1818 H Street, N.W., Washington, D.C. 20433, U.S.A.

Telephone: 477-2223 (Office); 229-9200 (Home).

Sen, Satyendra Nath, M.A., PH.D.; Indian university administrator; b. April 1907; ed. London Univ.

Former Dean of Faculties of Arts and Commerce, Univ. of Calcutta, Prof. of Econs. 58-, Vice-Chancellor 68-; Visiting Prof. Princeton and Stanford Univs. 62-63; mem. Gov. Body, Research and Training School, Indian Statistical Inst., Calcutta; mem. Board of Trustees, Indian Museum, Victoria Memorial, Mahajati Sadan (all in Calcutta); Chair. Cttee. for the Review of Univ. and Coll. Teachers' Salaries; mem. various govt. advisory bodies, etc.

Publs. *Central Banking in Underdeveloped Money Markets* 52, *The City of Calcutta: A Socio-economic survey 1954-55 to 1957-58* 60, *The Co-operative Movement in West Bengal* 66, *Industrial Relations in the Jute Industry in West Bengal* (with T. Piplai) 68.

Office of the Vice-Chancellor, University of Calcutta, Calcutta, India.

Sen, Sukumar, M.A., PH.D., J.P.; Indian philologist; b. 30 Jan. 1900, Calcutta; *s.* of Harendranath and Navanalini Sen; *m.* Sunila Ghosh 1928; one *s.* one *d.*; ed. Raj Coll., Burdwan, Sanskrit Coll. and Univ. of Calcutta.

Research Student Univ. of Calcutta 24-26, Khaira Research Scholar 27-29, Lecturer 30-54, Khaira Prof. of Indian Linguistics and Phonetics and Head of Dept. of Comparative Philology 54-64; Pres. Linguistic Soc. of India 54; Fellow Asiatic Soc.; Chair. Paribhaska Samsad, Govt. of W. Bengal.
Leisure interest: reading detective fiction.
Publs. English: *History of Brajabuli Literature* 35, *Old Persian Inscriptions of the Akhaemenian Emperors* 41, *History and Prehistory of Sanskrit* 57, *History of Bengali Literature* 59, etc.; Bengali: *History of Bengali Literature*, 4 vols. 41-58, *History of Indian Literature*.
403 Grand Trunk Road, Burdwan; 10 Raja Rajkissen Street, Calcutta 6, India.
Telephone: (Bur) 144; (Calcutta) 557783.

Senanayake, Maithripala; Ceylonese politician; b. 1916; ed. St. Joseph's Coll., Anuradhapura, St. John's Coll., Jaffna, and Nalanda Vidyalaya, Colombo.
Joined Govt. Service 40, Cultivation Officer 40-47; mem. Parl. 47-; Minister of Transport and Works 56-Dec. 59; Minister of Industries, Home Affairs and Cultural Affairs July 60-July 63; Minister of Commerce and Industries July 63-June 64, of Rural and Industrial Devt. 64-65, of Irrigation, Power and Highways 70-; Leader of the House; Sri Lanka Freedom Party.
121 MacCarthy Road, Colombo 7, Sri Lanka.

Senard, Jacques, L. EN D.; French diplomat; b. 21 Nov. 1919, Corgoloin, Côte d'Or; s. of Daniel Senard and Magdeleine Mistral Bernard; m. Mireille de la Croix de Chevrières de Sayve; two s. one d.; ed. Ecole Nationale d'Administration.
Press Service, Ministry of Foreign Affairs 47-49; attached to Ministry of Foreign Affairs 50; attached to Cen. Admin. 51; attached to Ministry of Foreign Affairs 51-56; attached to Cen. Admin. for Europe 56-61; attached to NATO 61-64; attached to Cen. Admin. 64-65; First Councillor, Cairo 65-67; attached to Gen. Secr., Ministry of Foreign Affairs 67-69; Head of Protocol 69-72; Amb. to Netherlands 72-.
Smidsplein 1, The Hague, Netherlands; 2 rue d'Andigné, Paris 16e, France.
Telephone: 469453 (Office); 469257 (Home, The Hague).

Sender, Ramón José, LIC. EN FIL. Y LET.; Spanish-born American author and educator; b. 3 Feb. 1901; ed. Colegio de la Sagrada Familia, Reus (Catalonia), Inst. de Zaragoza, Inst. de Teruel and Madrid Univ.
Infantry Officer, Morocco 23-24; Editor *El Sol*, Madrid 24-31; free-lance writer 31-36; Major on Gen. Staff, Spanish Republican Army 36-39; Prof. of Spanish Literature, Amherst Coll., Mass. 43-44, Denver Univ. 44; Prof. of Spanish Literature, New Mexico Univ. 47-63, Prof. Emer. 63; Visiting Prof. Ohio State Univ. 51, Univ. of Calif. 62; Medal of Morocco, Spanish Mil. Cross of Merit; Planeta Prize 69.
Publs. *Pro Patria* 34, *Seven Red Sundays* 35, *Mr. Witt among the Rebels* 36, *Counter-attack in Spain* 38, *A Man's Place* 40, *Dark Wedding* 43, *Chronicle of Dawn* 44, *The King and the Queen* 48, *The Sphere* 49, *The Affable Hangman* 54, *Before Noon* 57, *Requiem for a Spanish Peasant* 60, *Exemplary Novels of Cíbola* 63, *Tres Ejemplos de Amor y Una Teoria* 69, *Aventura equinoccial de Lope de Aguirre* 70, *Nocturno de los 14*, 70, *Tanit* 70, *El Angel Anfibio* 71, *Las criaturas saturnianas* 71, *La Luna de los perros* 72, *La antesala* 73, *El fugitivo* 73.
American Literary Agency, 11 Riverside Drive, New York, N.Y. 10023, U.S.A.

Sendler, Hans-Jörg; German steel executive; b. 16 Sept. 1910, Malmédy (now in Belgium); s. of Dr. Carl and Olga (née Kalthoff) Sendler.
Joined Otto Wolff-Konzern 31; mem. Man. Board, Düsseldorfer Eisenhüttengesellschaft AG, Ratingen

(subsidiary of Otto Wolff-Konzern) 35; mem. Man. Board, Eisen- und Hüttenwerk Thale AG, Cologne (Otto Wolff-Konzern) 40, Chair. Man. Board 46; mem. Man. Board, Stahlwerke Bochum AG 47, Chair. 55; mem. Man. Board Klöckner-Werke AG, Duisburg 56, Chair. 70-74, mem. Supervisory Board 74-; mem. numerous supervisory boards.
Freytagstrasse 6, 4 Düsseldorf, Federal Republic of Germany.

Senghor, Blaise; Senegalese diplomatist; b. 30 May 1932, Joal; s. of René Philippe Senghor and Marie-Hélène Konté; m. 1961; one s. one d.; ed. Univ. of Dakar, Lycée Louis-le-Grand, Paris, Univ. of Paris and Institut des Hautes Etudes Cinématographiques.
Producer of publicity films, Films Pierre Remont, Paris, later Asst. Producer, Drama programmes, Office de Radiodiffusion et Télévision Française 60-61; Founder Société de Production de Films, Union Cinématographique africaine 61, now Admin.; Technical Adviser to the Minister for Information, Senegal 62-65; Adviser, Senegalese Embassy, Paris 65-68; Perm. Del. of Senegal to UNESCO 68-69, Minister Plenipotentiary 69-72, Amb. 72-; mem. Exec. Board, UNESCO 70-72, Vice-Chair. Nov. 72-; Sec.-Gen. Comm. inter-africaine du Cinéma 63-66; Pres. Soc. Sénégalaise d'importation, de distribution et d'exploitation cinématographiques (SIDEC) 73-; represented Senegal at numerous int. confs. on cinema and television; mem. of the jury at African and int. film festivals; Officier Ordre Nationale du Mérite Français; Silver Bear for short film, Festival of Berlin 61; Silver Medal of the City of Paris for co-production of film *Liberté I* 62.
Leisure interests: tennis, photography.
52 rue Madame, 75006 Paris, France.
Telephone: 544-0745.

Senghor, Léopold Sédar; Senegalese writer and politician; b. 9 Oct. 1906; m. Colette Hubert 1957; ed. Lycée de Dakar, Lycée Louis le Grand, Paris and Paris Univ.
Classics Teacher, Lycée Descartes, Tours 35-44, Lycée Marcelin Berthelot, Paris 44-48; mem. Constituent Assemblies 45-46; Deputy from Senegal to Nat. Assembly 46-58; Prof., Ecole Nat. de la France d'Outre-Mer 48-58; Sec. of State, Présidence du Conseil 55-56; mem. Consultative Assembly, Council of Europe; Pres. Fed. Assembly, Mali Fed. of Senegal and Sudan 59-60, Pres. Senegal Repub. 60-, also Minister of Defence 68-69; Sec.-Gen. Union Progressiste Sénégalaise, nat. party of Parti Fédéraliste Africain (P.F.A.); mem. Inst. Français, Acad. des Sciences morales et politiques 69; Dag Hammarskjöld Prize 65; Peace Prize of German Book Trade, Frankfurt; Haile Sellassie African Research Prize 73; Apollinaire Prize for Poetry 74.
Publs. *Chants d'ombres* (poems) 45, *Hosties noires* (poems) 48, *Chants pour Naëtt* (poems) 49, *Ethiopiques* (poems) 56, *Nocturnes* (poems) 61, *Langage et poésie négro-africaine* 54, *L'Apport de la poésie nègre* 53, *Esthéthique négro-africain* 56.
Office of the President, Dakar, Senegal, West Africa.

Sengoku, Jo, LL.B.; Japanese business executive; b. 26 Jan. 1904, Osaka; m. Tetsuko Sasaki 1935; no c.; ed. Tokyo Univ.
Director, Kuraray Co. Ltd. 42, Man. Dir. 45, Senior Man. Dir. 48, Vice-Pres. 61, Pres. 68-75; Pres. Kyowa Gas Chemical Industry Co. 61-; Dir. Keihanshin Real Estate Co. 52-, Sanyo Broadcasting Co. 69-, Hotel Plaza 69-; Man. Dir. Kuraishiki Cen. Hosp. 73-; Standing Dir. Fed. of Econ. Orgs. 68-; Kansai Fed. of Employers' Asscns. 68-; Blue Ribbon Medal 67; Second Order of Merit with the Order of the Sacred Treasure 74.
Leisure interests: golf, race-horse owner, music.
1-37, Kumoicho, Nishinomiya, Hyogo Prefecture, Japan.

Senoussi, Badreddine, M.A., LL.M.; Moroccan diplomatist; b. 30 March 1933, Fez; s. of Ahmed and Zineb Senoussi; m. Touria Kerdoudi 1958; three s.; ed. Lycée Rabat, and Univs. of Rabat and Paris.
Counsellor, High Tribunal of Rabat 56; with Ministry of State in charge of admin. 57; Gen. Sec. Nat. Tobacco Office 58; Chief of Royal Cabinet 63; Under-Sec. of State for Commerce, Industry, Mines and Merchant Marine 64, for Admin. Affairs 65; Minister of Post Offices and Telecommunications 66; Minister of Youth, Sport and Social Affairs 70; Deputy to House of Reps. 70; Amb. to U.S.A. 71-74; numerous foreign awards and decorations.
Leisure interests: tennis, water skiing, hunting.
c/o Ministry of Foreign Affairs, Rabat, Morocco.

Šeper, H.E. Cardinal Franjo, PH.D., TH.D.; Yugoslav ecclesiastic; b. 2 Oct. 1905, Osijek; s. of Alois Šeper and Maria Kelemen; ed. Gregorian Univ., Rome.
Secretary to Archbishop of Zagreb 34-41; Rector Zagreb Major Seminary 41-51, Church of Christ the King, Zagreb 51-54; Archbishop Coadjutor to Cardinal Stepinac 54-60; Archbishop of Zagreb 60-69, cr. Cardinal 65; Prefect of the Sacred Congregation for the Doctrine of the Faith, Rome 68-; Hon. LL.D.
Piazza della Città Leonina 1, 00193, Rome, Italy.
Telephone: 654-27-95.

Sépinski, Augustin Joseph Antoine, B.C.L., D.TH.; French ecclesiastic; b. 26 July 1900, St. Julien-les-Metz; ed. Franciscan Studium (Metz) and Strasbourg Univ.
Entered Order of Friars Minor (Franciscans) 19, ordained priest 24; Dir. Coll. St. Antoine, Metz 29-33, Phalsbourg 33-38; Minister Provincial, Metz 38-45; Del. Gen. for Southern France 43-45; Definitor Gen., Rome 45-51; Minister Gen. of the Order 51- (re-elected 57); Titular Archbishop of Assura 65; Apostolic Del. of Jerusalem, Palestine, Cyprus 65; Apostolic Nuncio to Uruguay 69-75; retd.; Chevalier Légion d'Honneur; Dr. h.c. Univs. of St. Bonaventure (New York) and Dublin and Quincy Coll. (Ill.).
Publ. La Psychologie du Christ chez Saint Bonaventure 48; trans. Cristo Interiore secondo San Bonaventura 64.
Convento S. Maria Immacolata "La Palma", Salita Mauro 14, 80136 Naples, Italy.

Seppala, Richard Rafael, Barrister-at-Law; Finnish diplomatist; b. 15 Jan. 1905; ed. Turku Lyceum, Hamina Reserve Officers' School, Helsinki Univ.
Entered Foreign Service 30; served in Riga, Rio de Janeiro and London; Chief of Bureau, Ministry of Foreign Affairs 42-43, Asst. Dir. and Dir. Political Dept. 43-48; Consul Gen. and Permanent Observer, UN 48-53; Sec.-Gen. Ministry of Foreign Affairs 53, Sec. of State 54-56; Amb. to France 56-58, 65-72, to U.S.A. 58-65; Perm. Rep. to UNESCO 67-72, OECD 68-69; Grand Commdr. White Rose of Finland, Crown of Belgium, French Legion of Honour, Icelandic, Netherlands, Polish, Brazilian, Mexican and British decorations.
Jt, Puistotie 11 B18, Helsinki, Finland.

Seraphim, His Beatitude Archbishop; Greek ecclesiastic; b. 1913, Artesianon, Karditsa, Thessaly; ed. Theological School, Univ. of Athens.
Ordained 38; participated in Nat. Resistance against Nazi occupation; Clerk, later Sec. of Holy Synod; Metropolitan of Arta 49, of Ioannina 58; Archbishop of Athens and All Greece 74-; participated in First Pan-Orthodox Conf. of Rhodes.
c/o Holy Synod of the Church of Greece, Athens, Greece.

Serber, Robert, PH.D.; American physicist; b. 14 Mar. 1909, Philadelphia, Pa.; ed. Lehigh Univ. and Univ. of Wis.
National Research Fellow, Univ. of Calif. 34-36, Re-search Assoc. 36-38, Prof. 46-51; Asst. Prof. Univ. of Illinois 38-40, Assoc. Prof. 40-45, Prof. 45; Prof. Columbia Univ. 51-; Consultant, Metallurgical Laboratory, Chicago 42-43, Brookhaven Nat. Lab. 51-; Senior Scientist Los Alamos Lab. 43-45; Dir. Physics Measurements, Atomic Bomb Mission to Japan 45; mem. Atomic Bomb Group, Marianas 45, Solvay Conf., Brussels 48; Vice-Pres. American Physical Soc. 69; Guggenheim Fellow; mem. of Advisory Cttee. to Nat. Accelerator Lab. 67, and of numerous other scientific cttees.; mem. Nat. Acad. of Sciences.
Department of Physics, Columbia University, New York, N.Y. 10027, U.S.A.

Sereni, Emilio; Italian agronomist and politician; b. 13 Aug. 1907, Rome; m. 1st Xenia Silberberg 1928, 2nd Silvana Pecori 1953; five d.; ed. Rome and Univ. of Naples.
Graduated in agricultural science at Portici Univ. 27; Dir. of the Observatory for Rural Economics, Portici 28; joined Communist Party 28; sentenced to 15 years' imprisonment by Fascist Special Court 30, released 36; Editor of Italian daily paper La Voce degli Italiani, Paris 37-43; re-arrested 43-44; mem. Nat. Liberation Cttee. for Northern Italy 44-45; Commr. for Home Ministry in Northern Italy 45; mem. of Constituent Assembly 46; Ministry of Post-War Assistance 46-47; Minister for Public Works 47; Senator 48; Gen. Sec. Italian Movement of Partisans of Peace 50; mem. Bureau, World Peace Council 51; mem. Central Cttee. and of Directorate of Italian Communist Party; Senator 53-63; Pres. Nat. Peasant Alliance 55; Prof. of History of Agriculture, Rome Univ. 60; mem. Chamber of Deputies 63-68; Editor Critica marxista 66.
Leisure interest: music.
Publs. I Comitati di Liberazione Nazionale nella cospirazione, nell'insurrezione, nella ricostruzione 45, La questione agraria nella rinascita nazionale italiana 46, Il capitalismo nelle campagne 47, Il Mezzogiorno all'opposizione 48, Scienza marxismo cultura 49, Comunità rurali nell'Italia antica 56, Vecchio e nuovo nelle campagne italiane 57, Storia del paesaggio agrario italiano 61, Due linee di politica agraria 62, Per la storia delle più antiche tecniche e della nomenclatura della vite e del vino 65, Capitalismo e mercato nazionale in Italia 66.
Camera dei Deputati, Rome, Italy.
Telephone: 536979.

Sereni, Vittorio, LAUR. IN LETT.; Italian writer and publisher; b. 27 July 1913, Luino (Varese); s. of Enrico Sereni and Maria Colombi; m. Maria Luisa Bonfanti 1940; three d.; ed. Univ. of Milan.
Literary Dir. Arnoldo Mondadori Editore 58-; Premio Libera Stampa 56, Premio Montefeltro 65, Premio Antonio Feltrinelli 72 per la poesia (Accademia Nazionale dei Lincei).
Leisure interest: football.
Publs. Frontiera 41, 66, Poesie 42, Diario d'Algeria 47, 65, Gli Immediati Dintorni 62, L'opzione 64, Gli Strumenti Umani 65, 75, Ventisei 70, Sei Poesie e Sei Disegni 72, Poesie scelte 73, Un posto di Vacanza 73, Letture Preliminari 73.
via Paravia 37, 20148 Milan, Italy.
Telephone: 40-33-701.

Sergent, René Edmond; French civil servant; b. 16 Jan. 1904, Paris; m. Monique Schweisguth 1931; three s. three d.; ed. Ecole Polytechnique.
With Ministry of Finance 29-37; Financial Dir. Nat. Societies for Aeronautical Construction 37-40; mem. and later Dir. Foreign Trade Dept., Ministry of Finance 40-44; Chair. French Economic and Financial Dept., Berlin Control Comm. 45-47; Financial Attaché, French Embassy, London 47; Asst. Sec.-Gen. (Economics and Finance), N.A.T.O. 52-55; Sec.-Gen. Organisation for European Economic Co-operation 55-60; Vice-Pres. Syndicat Gén. de la Construction Electrique 60-69,

Pres. Groupement des Industries de la Construction Electrique 69-75, Soc. Bancaire de Paris 70-72; Officier Légion d'Honneur.

1 boulevard de Beauséjour, 75016 Paris, France.
Telephone: 288-30-31.

Serisawa, Kojiro; Japanese author; b. 5 May 1897; s. of Tsumehal and Haru Serisawa; m. Kanae Serisawa 1927; three d.; ed. Tokyo and Paris Univs.
Administrative Official Ministry of Agriculture 22-25; Prof. at Chuo Univ. 30-32; Pres. Japanese PEN Club 48-; mem. of Japanese Acad.; awarded Prix des Amitiés Françaises 59, Prix of Japanese Gov. 70, of Japanese Acad. 72.
Publs. *Death in Paris* 40, *One World* 54, *Mrs. Aida* 57, *Under the Shadow of Love and Death* 53, *House on the Hill* 59, *Parting* 61, *Love, Intelligence and Sadness* 62, *Fate of Man* (14 vols.) 62-71.
5-8-3 Higashinakano, Nagano-ku, Tokyo, Japan.
Telephone: 03-361-2913.

Serkin, Rudolf; American pianist; b. 28 March 1903, Eger, Bohemia; m. Irene Busch 1935; two s. four d.
Debut with the Vienna Symphony Orchestra 15; with Adolf Busch in a series of sonatas for violin and piano; American debut 33; appeared with Toscanini 34, 36, with Nat. Orchestral 37; Asscn. annual tours of the U.S.A. 34-; Head Piano Dept., later Dir., Curtis Inst. of Music; Artistic Dir. and Pres. Marlboro School of Music; mem. American Acad. of Arts and Sciences, Nat. Council on the Arts, Carnegie Comm. Report; Presidential Medal of Freedom 63; Hon. mem. Philharmonic Soc. of New York 71, Neue Bachgesellschaft, Bonn, Acad. of St. Cecilia, Rome, Verein Beethoven Haus, Bonn, Rieminschneider-Bach Inst.; Fifth annual Pa. award for Excellence in the Field of Performing Arts 71; Dr. h.c. Curtis Inst., Temple Univ., Univ. of Vermont, Williams Coll., Oberlin Coll., Univ. of Rochester, Harvard Univ.
R.F.D.3, Brattleboro, Vermont, U.S.A.

Serlachius, Ralph Erik; Finnish industrialist; b. 24 Jan. 1901, Mänttä; s. of Gösta and Sigrid (Serlachius) Serlachius; m. Brita Idman 1931; one s. two d.; ed. Dresden Technical Univ. and Ecole des Hautes Etudes Commerciales, Paris.
Chairman G. A. Serlachius Ltd. 42-, Man. Dir. 42-68; Chair. The Art Foundation of Gösta Serlachius; Chair., Deputy Chair. or Dir. many other companies and asscns.; Counsellor of Mines 48; Minister of Communications and Public Works 53-54; Dr. Tech. h.c. (Åbo Acad.); Cross of Liberty, 3rd and 4th class; Commdr. with Grand Cross and Chancellor, Orders of the White Rose of Finland and of the Lion of Finland; Commdr. Légion d'Honneur, and other foreign decorations.
Leisure interests: fishing, shooting.
Honkahovi, Mänttä, Finland.
Telephone: Mänttä 47131.

Serocki, Kazimierz; Polish composer; b. 3 March 1922, Torun; ed. Warsaw, Łódź and Paris.
State Artistic Prize 52; Prize of Minister of Culture and Art 1st Class 63, State Prize 1st Class 72; Award of Tribune Internationale des Compositeurs UNESCO 65; G. Fitelberg Prize 56, 58, 60; Prize of the Union of Polish Composers 65 and many other int. and nat. prizes; numerous decorations including Commdr. Cross Order of Polonia Restituta.
Compositions include two symphonies 52, 53 (one choral), Sinfonietta for two string orchestras 56, *Heart of the Night* 56, *Eyes Of Air* (song cycles) 57, Musica concertante for chamber orchestra 58, Episodes for strings and three groups of percussion 59, Segments for seven instrumental groups 61, Symphonic frescoes 64, *Niobe* for two voices, choir and orchestra, Continuum for percussion 66, *Forte e Piano* (for 2 pianos and Orchestra) 67, *Dramatic Story* (for orchestra) 68-71,

Poesies (for soprano and chamber orchestra) 69, *Swinging Music* (for clarinet, trombone, bass and piano) 70, *Fantasmagoria* (for piano and percussion) 70-71, *Fantasia Elegiaca* (for organ and orchestra) 71-72, *Impromptu Fantasque* (for recorders, mandolins, guitars, percussion and piano) 73, *Concerto alla Cadenza* (for recorder and orchestra), *Arrangements* (for 1-4 recorders); chamber and piano music.
Post Box 63, 00-770 Warsaw, Poland.
Telephone: 410796.

Serpan, Iaroslav, D. ès sc.; French artist and biologist; b. 4 June 1922, Prague, Czechoslovakia; m. Lucienne Baudry 1947; one d.; ed. Lycée de Versailles, and Univ. of Paris.
Studied biology and mathematics at Paris Univ.; research in biology; began painting 40; active mem. of Paris surrealist group 46-48; since leaving this group in 48, one of representatives of earlier "informal cut"; now one of leaders of avant-garde trends in modern European painting; paintings in main European and American collections; group exhibitions in Europe, South America, Japan and the U.S.A.; one-man exhibitions in Paris, Brussels, Milan, Venice, Rome, New York, Tokyo, Copenhagen and in Germany 51-; Mural decoration for Besançon Univ. (enamelled lava); Marzotto Prize 63; began investigations in sculpture (painted wood, metal, plastics) 67.
Leisure interests: mountaineering, modern music.
Publ. *Contre-Espace* (poems) 51.
45 avenue d'Aligre, F-78230 Le Pecq, France.
Telephone: 976-63-37.

Serrano-Camargo, Gabriel; Colombian architect; b. 24 March 1909; s. of Angel M. Serrano and Paulina Camargo; m. Stella Navia 1946; three s. two d.; ed. Univ. Nacional de Colombia.
Founder and for 33 years collaborator and Dir. of Dept. of Architecture Cuellar Serrano Gómez Arq.; Pres. Colombian Del. to congresses in Mexico, Moscow, London and Washington, D.C.; Counsellor and Prof. Nat. Univ. of Colombia; mem. Comm. for Regulatory Plan of Bogotá; Pres. Board of Dirs. Museum of Modern Art, Bogotá; Pres. Soc. of Architects; Pres. Pan-American Fed. of Architectural Socs.; Hon. Pres. Colombian Soc. of Architects; mem. American Inst. of Architects, Colls. of Architects of Brazil, Chile, Venezuela, Puerto Rico, Uruguay, Paraguay; Cruz de Boyaca; Nat. Engineering Prize 48, Nat. Architects Prize 62.
Edif. Seguros Bolívar, Carrera 10A 16-39, piso 15, Bogotá, Colombia.
Telephone: 410-612.

Sert, José Luis, M.ARCH.; American architect; b. 1 July 1902, Barcelona, Spain; s. of Francisco and Genara (López) Sert; m. Ramona Longas 1938; one d.; ed. Barcelona Escuela Superior de Arquitectura.
Worked with Le Corbusier, Paris 29-30; private practice in Barcelona 29-38; settled in U.S. 39; co-Founder and Partner Town Planning Associates, New York 41-56; naturalized U.S. citizen 51; Co-Founder and Partner, Sert, Jackson and Associates (fmrly. Sert, Jackson and Gourley) 57-; Dean and Prof. Harvard Univ. Graduate School of Design 53-69; mem. Int. Congress of Modern Architecture (Pres. 47-56); Fellow American Inst. of Architects; mem. American Inst. of Planners, American Acad. Arts and Sciences, Nat. Inst. Arts and Letters; Hon. mem. R.I.B.A., Peruvian Inst. of Urbanism, Soc. Colombiana de Arquitectos; Hon. M.A., Hon. Art.D. (Harvard Univ.); Hon. Litt.D. (Boston Coll.).
Projects include: U.S. Embassy, Baghdad, Harvard Univ. Holyoke Center, Married Students Dormitories, Undergraduate Science Center, Center for Study of World Religions; Boston Univ. Student Union, Mugar Library, Law and Educ. Bldgs.; Archdiocese of Boston,

St. Botolph's Chapel; Cambridge, Mass., Martin Luther King Jr. Elementary School, Negea Service Corpn.; Mass. Bay Transportation Authority, Bowdoin Square Station, North Quincy Rapid Transit Station; Worcester, Mass., Urban renewal plan for cen. business district; Besançon, France, School of Fine and Applied Arts; Chalon-sur-Saône, France, Carmelite Convent; Maeght, France, Musée Foundation; Design Consultant Univ. of Guelph Admin. and Liberal Arts Bldgs., Library, Univ. Center; Master Plans for Havana, Bogotá, etc. Publs. *Can Our Cities Survive?* 47, *The Heart of the City* (with Rogers and Tyrwhitt) 52, *Antoni Gaudi* (with Sweeney) 60.
Home: 64 Francis Avenue, Cambridge, Mass. 02115; Office: 26 Church Street, Cambridge, Mass. 02138, U.S.A. Telephone: 617-876-4015.

Sertoli, Giandomenico, IUR.D.; Italian international civil servant and banker; b. 26 Sept. 1922, Vicenza; s. of Giovanni F. and Angela Maddalena Sertoli; m. Marianne Roblin 1946; two s.; ed. Univ. of Padua and Institut des Hautes Etudes Internationales, Geneva.
Assistant to the Pres. and Sec. Board of Dirs., ARAR, Rome 46-54; mem. Finance Dept., European Coal and Steel Community, Luxembourg 54-58; Deputy Man. Finance and Treasury Dept., European Investment Bank 58-60, Man. 60-68; Financial Adviser to Banca Commerciale Italiana 68-, Deputy Gen. Man. 69.
Leisure interests: tennis, skiing, bridge.
Banca Commerciale Italiana, 20121 Milan, Piazza della Scala 6; Piazza E. Duse, 2, 20122 Milan, Italy.
Telephone: 8850; 707169.

Servais, Léon; Belgian trade unionist and politician; b. 7 Nov. 1907.
Member Confédération des Syndicats Chrétiens 28-; Pres. Mouvement Ouvrier Chrétien 47-50; mem. Senate 50-74; Minister for Social Security 58-61, of Labour and Employment 61-68; Pres. Walloon Wing of Christian Socialist Party 68-72; Minister for Public Health 72-Jan. 73, Minister of State 74-.
51 quai de Rome, Liège, Belgium.

Servan-Schreiber, Jean-Claude, L. EN DR.; French newspaperman; b. 11 April 1918; ed. Oxford and Sorbonne Univs.
Served World War II in Flanders 40, in Resistance 41-42, in North Africa 43, France 44, Germany 45; with *Les Echos* 46-, Gen. Man. 57, Dir. 63-65; Deputy for Paris 65-67; Asst. Sec.-Gen. U.N.R.-U.D.T.; mem. Board Jacques de Saint Phalle et Cie. (advertising agency), Paris; Pres. Rassemblement français pour Israël May 67; Dir.-Gen. Régie française de publicité; mem. Bureau du Comité pour un nouveau contrat social et Pres. Comm. de contrôle et des statuts du mouvement pour le socialisme par la participation 71-; Officier de la Légion d'Honneur, Mil. Medal, Croix de Guerre, Croix du Combattant Volontaire de la Résistance, Legion of Merit (U.S.A.).
10 rue du Haut-Bourgeois, 54000 Nancy, France.

Servan-Schreiber, Jean-Jacques; French journalist and writer; b. 13 Feb. 1924; ed. Ecole Polytechnique, Paris.
Joined as a volunteer the Free French Army of General de Gaulle as fighter pilot 43 (U.S. Air Force); diplomatic editor of *Le Monde* 48-51; founder and Dir. of *L'Express* 53-; Sec.-Gen. Social Radical Party 69-71, Pres. Radical Party 71-75; Deputy for Nancy 70-; founder Mouvement Réformateur (with Jean Lecanuet, q.v.) 72; Minister of Reforms May-June 74; Pres. Council of Lorraine 76-; Croix de la Valeur Militaire.
Publs. *Lieutenant en Algérie* 57, *Le Défi Américain* 67, *Le Réveil de la France* 69, *Ciel et Terre* 70, *Forcer le destin* 70, *Le Pouvoir régional* 71, *Appel à la réforme* 72, *Le Project Réformateur* 73.
Assemblée Nationale, Paris 7e; Home: 8 place de la Carrière, 54-Nancy, France.

Servolini, Luigi, D.LIT., D.F.A.; Italian xylographer, writer and art critic; b. 1 March 1906, Leghorn (Livorno), Tuscany; s. of Carlo Servolini; m. Odetta Andreoni 1930; one s. one d.; ed. Pisa Univ., Acad. of Fine Arts, Carrara.
Professor of Xylography and Lithography, R. Istituto del Libro di Urbino, and Dir. of Library, Urbino Univ. 30-39; Dir. artistic and cultural insts. at Forli 39-53; Dir. Istituto Poligrafico Rizzoli, Milan 53-56; Prof. History of Art; Headmaster; Prof. Special School for Art Historians, Istituto Storia d'Arte, Univ. of Pisa 69-72; Gen. Sec. "Incisori d'Italia" Asscn.; also painter and lithographer and has since 26 taken part in many important exhbns.; works represented in 80 European and American Public Galleries; has won several prizes; Hon. mem. Accademico Disegno, Florence; Editor "Comanducci" Dictionary; mem. Ordine dei Giornalisti (Rome) 35; Editor *La Voce degli IDIT* (fortnightly); Grand Officer Italian Repub.
Leisure interests: ancient and modern prints, ex libris, hypnotism.
Publs. *Ugo da Carpi* 29, *La Xilografia a chiaroscuro italiana nei secoli XVI, XVII e XVIII* 30, *Tecnica della Xilografia* 35, *A. Bosse* 37, *Problemi e aspetti dell'Incisione* 39, *J. de'Barbari* 43, *Pittura gotica romagnola* 44, *Xilografia giapponese* 49, *La Xilografia* 50, *Incisione italiana di cinque secoli* 51, *Incidere* 52, 61, *Dizionario Incisori ital. moderni e contemporanei* 55, *Mosaico di Romagna* 57, *Autobiografia di Bodoni* 58, *I procedimenti artistici e industriali della Grafica* 59-63, *Gli Incisori d'Italia* 60, *Il Comanducci: Dizionario dei Pittori* (5 vols.) 4th edn. 71-73, *Acqueforti di Giovanni Fattori* 66, *Athena: Storia dell' Arte classica e italiana* (3 vols.) 66-68, *Dalla pietra litografica alla stampa offset* 68, *L'Arte di Incidere* 3rd edn. 70, *La Serigrafia Originale* 73, *Gli Incisori d'Italia*, Vol. II, 74, *Tecnica della Xilografia giapponese* 75.
Piazza della Liberta 33, Cecina, Livorno 57023, Italy.
Telephone: Cecina (Li) 0586/642632.

Seshadri, Tiruvenkata Rajendra, M.A., PH.D., F.R.S.; Indian chemist; b. 3 Feb. 1900, Kulittalai, Madras State; s. of R. T. and Namagiri Iyengar; m. Kamala Seshadri 1924; three d.; ed. Univs. of Madras, Manchester, London, Edinburgh, Graz.
Professor Univ. of Andhra 33-49, Univ. of Delhi 49-; has acted as adviser to Ministries of Educ., Agriculture, Industry and Defence, to Council of Scientific and Industrial Research, Indian Council of Agricultural Research, Indian Council of Medical Research, Univ. Grants Comm., Dept of Defence Research and Dept. of Atomic Energy; Past Pres. Indian Nat. Science Acad., Indian Science Congress, Indian Pharmaceutical Asscn., Indian Pharmaceutical Congress, Indian Chem. Soc.; Past Chair. North India Section, Royal Inst. of Chem.; Pres. Oil Technologists Asscn. of India; Vice-Pres. Indian Acad. of Sciences; awarded title of Padma-Bhushan, Govt. of India; mem. Deutsche Akademie der Naturforscher, Leopoldina; Bhatnagar and Saha Medals, Indian Nat. Science Acad.; Acharya Ray Medal, Indian Chem. Soc.; Hon. D.Sc. (Univs. Andhra, Banaras, Delhi, Osmania, Venkateswara).
Publs. approximately 1,100 articles on chemistry, utilization of Indian natural resources, agricultural commodities and forest products, in Indian and foreign scientific journals.
Department of Chemistry, University of Delhi, Delhi 7; Home: No. 4a Model Town, Delhi-9, India.
Telephone: 228348 (Home).

Sessions, Roger Huntington, A.B., B.M.; American composer and teacher; b. 28 Dec. 1896; ed. Harvard Coll., Yale Univ. School of Music and private studies with Ernest Bloch.
Assistant, later Instructor, Smith Coll. 17-21, Teacher and Asst. to Dir., Cleveland Inst. of Music 21-25;

Guggenheim Fellowship, Florence 26-28, Walter Damrosch Fellowship, American Acad. in Rome 28-31, Carnegie Foundation Fellowship, Berlin 31-33; Lecturer, New School for Social Research, N.Y., and Teacher, Malkin Conservatory, Boston 33-34; Lecturer, Boston Univ. Coll. of Music, and Teacher, Dalcroze School of Music, N.Y. 34-35; private teaching, musical composition, N.Y. 35-45; Instructor, Asst. Prof. and Assoc. Prof., Princeton Univ. 35-45; Prof. of Music, Univ. of Calif., Berkeley 45 (sabbatical leave, Fulbright Award, Florence 51-52); William Shubael Conant Prof. Music Princeton Univ. 53-65; mem. faculty Juilliard School of Music 65-; mem. Int. Soc. for Contemporary Music, Pres. U.S. Section 34-42, Nat. Inst. of Arts and Letters 38-, American Acad. of Arts and Letters 53-, Akad. der Künste, Berlin 60-, American Acad. of Arts and Sciences 61-; Hon. D. Mus. (Wesleyan, Rutgers, Harvard Univs.); Pulitzer Special Citation for Music 74. Compositions include *Concerto for Violin and Orchestra* 37, *String Quartet No. 1 in E Minor* 38, *Duo for Violin and Piano* 48, *String Quartet No. 2, Sonata No. 2 for Pianoforte* 48, *Symphony No. 2* 49, *Symphony No. 3* 57, *No. 4* 58, *String Quintet* 58, *Divertimento for Orchestra* 60, *Montezuma* (opera) 63, *Symphony No. 5* 64, *No. 6* 66, *Six Pieces for Violin Solo* 66, *Symphony No. 7* 67, *Symphony No. 8* 68, *Rhapsody for Orchestra* 70, *Concertino for Chamber Orchestra* 72.
Publs. *The Intent of the Artist* 41, *The Musical Experience of Composer, Performer, and Listener* 50, *Harmonic Practice* 51, *Questions About Music* 70.
63 Stanworth Lane, Princeton, N.J. 08540, U.S.A.

Setalvad, Motilal Chimanlal, B.A., LL.B.; Indian lawyer; b. 12 Nov. 1884, Ahmedabad, State of Gujarat; s. of Chimanlal and Krishnagavri Setalvad; m. June 1907; one s. one d.; ed. Elphinstone Coll., and Government Law Coll.
Advocate Bombay High Court 11; Advocate-Gen., Bombay 37; resigned 42; mem. Indian del. to the Gen. Assembly of the UN 47, 48, 49 (Leader); Principal Rep. of India for the Kashmir question at the Security Council Session 52; Attorney-Gen. of India 50-62; Chair. Law Comm. 55; mem. All-India Bar Cttee.; Vice-Pres. Indian Branch Int. Law Asscn.; India Comm. of Jurists; Leader Indian Del. Asian-African Legal Consultative Cttee. 57, 58, 60, 61, 62; Presented Indian case (v. Portugal) Int. Court of Justice 58-60; mem. Rajya Sabha 66-72; Hon. LL.D. (Banaras Hindu Univ.) 67; Padma Vibhushan.
Leisure interests: general reading, literature, history, economics.
Publs. *Civil Liberties, Common Law in India* (Hamlyn Lectures 60), *Law and Culture* 63, *Role of English Law in India* 66, *Secularism* 66, *The Indian Constitution 1950-65* 67, *United Nations and World Peace* 67, *Bhulabhai Desai* 69, *My Life, Law and Other Things* 70, *Tagore Law Lectures* 73.
Nirant, Juhu, Bombay 54, India.
Telephone: 532119.

Seter, Mordecai; Israeli composer; b. 1916, Russia; s. of Itzhac and Beraha Seter; m. Dina Pevsner 1939; two c.
Studied Paris with Paul Dukas and Nadia Boulanger 32-37; Assoc. Prof. Israel Acad. of Music, Tel Aviv; Tel-Aviv Municipality Prize 45, 54; Prix Soc. d'Auteurs et de Compositeurs 56; Prix Italia 62; Israel State Prize 65.
Works include: *Sabbath Cantata* 40, *Three Motets* 51, *Midnight Vigil* 62, *Dithyramb* 65 (choral music); *Ricercar* 56, *Variations* 59-67, *Jephthah's Daughter* 65, etc. (symphonic music); *The Legend of Judith* 62 (ballet); *Partita* for violin and piano 51; *Jerusalem* 66, *Fantasia* (chamber music) 64, *Yemenite Suite* (chamber music) 67, *Rounds* (chamber music) 68, *Chamber Music* 70 (six works for different instrumental combinations) 70;

Soliloquio, Cappricci, Intervals, Senza Nomine, Janus (for piano) 72-73; *Concertante* (for violin, oboe, horn and piano) 73; *Trio* (for violin, 'cello and piano) 73; *Wood-Wind Trio* 74; *Quintet* (for violin, 'cello, flute, horn and piano) 75; *Ensemble* (for six instruments) 75; violin sonatas, educ. music, etc.
The Israel Academy of Music, Tel Aviv; Home: 1 Karny Street, Ramat Aviv, Tel Aviv, Israel.
Telephone: 416111 (Office); 417766 (Home).

Sethi, Shri Prakash Chandra, B.A., LL.B.; Indian politician; b. 19 Oct. 1920, Jhalrapatan, Rajasthan; s. of Shri Bhanwarlal Sethi; m. 1939; five d.; ed. Madhav Coll., Ujjain and Holkar Coll., Indore.
President Madhav Nagar Ward Congress 47, Ujjain District Congress 51, 54, 57, Textile Clerks Asscn. 48-49; Madhya Bharat Employees Asscn. Vice-Pres. 42, 49, 52; Treas. Madhya Bharat Congress 54-55; mem. Ujjain District and Madhya Bharat Congress Cttee. Exec. 53-57; Dir. Ujjain District Co-operative Bank 57-59; A.I.C.C. Zonal Rep. for Karnatak, Maharashtra, Bombay and Gujarat 55-56; observer for Bihar Dec. 66; elected to Rajya Sabha Feb. 61, April 64, to Lok Sabha Feb. 67; Deputy Minister for Steel, Heavy Industries and Mines, Cen. Govt. 62-67, Minister of State 67-69; Minister for Revenue and Expenditure 69-70; Minister of Defence Production 70-71; Minister of Petroleum and Chemicals 71-72; Chief Minister Madhya Pradesh 72-75; Minister of Fertilizers and Chemicals Dec. 75-; Rep. Govt. of India at Commonwealth Finance Ministers' Conference, Barbados 69; leader of del. to Colombo Plan Conf., Victoria 69; Gov. for India, Asian Devt. Bank, Manila, and Int. Bank for Reconstruction and Devt. 69.
Leisure interests: tennis, travel, music, and reading.
Ministry of Fertilizers and Chemicals, New Delhi, India.

Sethna, Homi Nusserwanji, B.SC., M.S.E., D.SC.; Indian engineer; b. 24 Aug. 1923; ed. St. Xavier's School and Coll., Bombay, Univ. of Bombay, and Michigan Univ.
Works Man. Indian Rare Earths Ltd. (Govt. Co.) 49-50; joined Atomic Energy Establishment, Trombay (now Bhabha Atomic Research Centre) 59, Dir. 66; constructed Monazite Plant, Alwaye, Kerala, Thorium and Uranium Metal Plants and Plutonium Plant, Trombay, Bombay, and Uranium Mill, Jadugoda, Bihar; Deputy Sec.-Gen. of UN Conf. on Peaceful Uses of Atomic Energy, Geneva 58; Chair. Fertilizer Corpn. of India Ltd. until 73, Madras and Rajasthan Atomic Power Project Boards; mem. Scientific Advisory Cttee. to Cabinet 61; mem. Int. Atomic Energy Agency (IAEA) 66, UN Cttee. of Specialists on Nuclear Technology and the developing countries; mem. for Research and Devt., Atomic Energy Comm. 66-, Dir. 66; Sec. to Govt. of India, Dept. Atomic Energy; Chair. Atomic Energy Comm. 72; mem. Cttee. on Scientific Research, Planning Comm.; mem. Board of Govs. Indian Inst. of Tech. 71-74, Tata Memorial Centre, Indian Rare Earths Ltd., Electronics Corpn. of India Ltd.; mem. Gov. Council Tata Inst. of Fundamental Research; mem. Scientific study team, Govt. of India; mem. UN Scientific Advisory Cttee., Scientific Advisory Cttee., IAEE; mem. Indian Inst. of Chemical Engineers, Inst. of Engineers; Life mem. Indian Acad. of Science; Fellow, Indian Nat. Science Acad.; Dr. h.c. (Marathwada Univ.) 73; Hon. LL.D. (Bombay) 74; Hon. Dr. Tech. (Jawaharlal Nehru Tech. Univ.) 74; Hon. D.Sc. (Roorkee Univ.) 75; Padma Shri Award 59, Shanti Swarup Bhatnagar Memorial Award 60, Padma Bhushan 66, Sesquicentennial Award, Univ. of Michigan 67, Sir Walter Puckey Award 71, Sir William Jones Memorial Medal 74, Padma Vibhushan 75.
Old Yacht Club, Chhatrapati Shivaji Maharaj Marg, Bombay 400 039; Home: 12th Floor, Dept. of Atomic Energy Officers' Apartments, Little Gibbs Road No. 2, Malabar Hill, Bombay 400 006, India.

Sethness, Charles O., A.B., M.B.A.; American investment banker and international official; b. 24 Feb. 1941, Evanston, Ill.; s. of C. Olin Sethness and Alison Louise Burge; m. Ann Worcester 1964; one s.; ed. Princeton Univ. and Harvard Business School.
Senior Credit Analyst, American Nat. Bank and Trust Co. of Chicago 63-64; Research Asst. Harvard Business School 66-67; with Morgan Stanley and Co. 67-73, Vice-Pres. 72-73; Head of Corporate Finance Dept., Morgan & Cie. Int. S.A., Paris 71-73; Exec. Dir. IBRD, IFC, IDA 73-75; Special Asst. to Sec. of Treasury July 73-.
c/o International Bank for Reconstruction and Development, 1818 H Street, N.W., Washington, D.C. 20433; Home: 4437 Cathedral Avenue, N.W., Washington, D.C., U.S.A.

Setoh, Shoji; Japanese electrical engineer; b. 18 March 1891, Wakayama Prefecture; s. of Sadanosuke Setoh; m. 1st Masumi Iwasaki 1917; m. 2nd Sadako Tachikawa 1952; two s. two d.; ed. Imperial Univ., Tokyo.
Assistant Prof., Tokyo Imperial Univ. 18-23; sent abroad by Japanese Govt. to study electrical engineering in Germany, Switzerland, U.K., and U.S.A. 23-25; Prof. Tokyo Imperial Univ. 25-51, Prof. Emeritus 51-, Dean of Engineering 42-45, 48-51; with Inst. of Physical and Chemical Research Tokyo 25-47; Pres. Inst. of Electrical Engineers of Japan 41-42; Vice-Pres. Nat. Research Council of Japan 47-49; Pres. Japanese Electrotechnical Cttee. 47-51; Dir. Electric Power Engineering Research Inst., Japan Electric Power Generation and Transmission Co. 47-49; Pres. Japan Society of Electronmicroscopy 48-54; Man. Dir. Tokyo Shibaura Electric Co. 51-62; Counsellor, Atomic Energy Comm. of Japan 56-67; Vice-Pres. Japan Radio-Isotope Asscn. 55-; Pres. Nippon Atomic Industry Group Co. Ltd. 58-67, Adviser 68-; Chair. Tokyo Electrical Engineering Coll. 59-; Man. Dir. Japan Atomic Industrial Forum 62-; Pres. Atomic Energy Soc. of Japan 63-65; Order of Cultural Merit 73.
Kitasawa 1-24-15, Setagaya-ku, Tokyo, Japan.
Telephone: 03-468-0539.

Setshogo, Boithoko Moonwa, B.A.; Botswana civil servant and diplomatist; b. 16 June 1941, Serowe; m. Jennifer Tlalane 1971; two d.; ed. Moeng Coll. and Univ. of Botswana, Lesotho and Swaziland.
District Officer, Kanye 69-70; First Sec., High Comm. in London 70-72; Clerk to the Cabinet 72-73; Under-Sec., Ministry of Commerce and Industry 73-75; High Commr. to U.K. Sept. 75-.
Leisure interests: music, sport, reading, theatre, films, opera.
Botswana High Commission, 162 Buckingham Palace Road, London, S.W.1; Residence: 95 Platts Lane, London, N.W.3, England.
Telephone: 01-930 5216/7/8/9 (High Commission); 01-437 6807 (Residence).

Sette Camara, José; Brazilian diplomatist; b. 4 April 1920, Alfenas, Minas Gerais; ed. Univ. of Minas Gerais and McGill Univ., Canada.
Brazilian Diplomatic Service 45-; Third Sec. Washington 47; Vice-Consul, Montreal 47-50; Third Sec. UN, New York 50-52; Sec. to Civil Household of Pres. of Brazil 52-55, Deputy Head of Civil Household 56-59, Head 59-60; Consul, Florence 55-56; Provisional Gov., State of Guanabara 60; Head Perm. Del. of Brazil to UN, Geneva 60-61; Ambassador to Canada 61-62; Mayor of Brasília 62-63; Ambassador to Switzerland 63-64; Perm. Rep. to UN 64-68; Publr. *Jornal do Brasil* 69-; mem. UN Int. Law Comm. 70-.
Jornal do Brasil, Avda. Brasil 500, Rio de Janeiro, RJ, Brazil.

Sevareid, Eric; American news correspondent; b. 26 Nov. 1912, Velva, N.D.; ed. Univ. of Minesota.
Reporter, *Minneapolis Journal* 36; joined Columbia Broadcasting System (CBS) 39; war correspondent, France and London 39-40; CBS Wash. Bureau 40-43; war corresp. China 43; subsequently covered final stages of war in Europe; returned to U.S.A. to cover founding of UN, San Francisco Conf. 45; attached to CBS Wash. Bureau 46-59; roving European corresp., London 59-61; returned to New York and served as moderator for various broadcasts 61-64; Nat. Corresp., CBS News, Wash., D.C. 64-; War Corresp. Vietnam 66; George Foster Peabody Award 50, 64, 67; Order of the Crown (Belgium); Freedom Medal (Norway); Alfred I. DuPont Award; George Polk Award and numerous other awards and decorations; several hon. degrees.
Publs. Several books, essays and articles.
CBS News, 2020 M Street, Washington, D.C. 20036, U.S.A.

Sevastianov, Vitaly Ivanovich, CAND. ENG.; Soviet cosmonaut; b. 8 July 1935, Krasnouralsk, Sverdlovsk Region; ed. Moscow Aviation Inst.
Engineer in a designing office, postgraduate student, Moscow Aviation Inst. 59-64; mem. C.P.S.U. 63-; at cosmonaut training detachment 64; engineer of spaceship *Soyuz* 9 in long orbital flight 1-19 July 70; participated in long orbital flight July 75; twice Hero of Soviet Union, Gold Star Medal, Order of Lenin, K. E. Tsiolkovsky Gold Medal of U.S.S.R. Acad. of Sciences; Pilot-Cosmonaut of U.S.S.R.
Zvezdny Gorodok, Moscow, U.S.S.R.

Severny, Andrei Borisovich, D.SC.; Soviet astrophysicist; b. 11 May 1913, Tula; one s. one d.; ed. Moscow State Univ.
Director Crimean Astrophysical Observatory, U.S.S.R. Acad. of Sciences; Vice-Pres. Int. Astronomical Union 64-70; designed optical scheme of large tower Sun telescope; expert on solar physics and stellar magnetism; mem. Royal Astronomical Soc.; corresp. mem. Heidelberg Acad. (Fed. Repub. of Germany); mem. Göttingen Acad. of Sciences, Int. Astronautical Acad.; Academician, U.S.S.R. Acad. of Sciences 68-; State Prize; Hero of Socialist Labour; Dr. h.c. (Univ. Newcastle, Wrocław Univ., Poland.)
Poselok Nauchny, Crimean Region 334413, U.S.S.R.
Telephone: 166; 107 (Observatory).

Sevilla Sacasa, Guillermo; Nicaraguan diplomatist, jurist and congressman; b. 1908, León, Nicaragua; ed. Inst. Nacional de Occidente, Univ. Centenaria de León; m. Doña Lillian Somoza de Sevilla Sacasa; nine c.
Began diplomatic career 34; Amb. to U.S.A. 43-; Perm. Rep. to UN; Del. to San Francisco Conf. 45; signed UN Charter; Pres. Council of OAS 46; Amb. to Canada; Dean, Diplomatic Corps accredited to the White House 58-; fmr. Amb. to Dominican Republic and Cuba; Perm. Rep. to OAS; Amb. of Nicaragua to numerous governments, including Japan, China, Korea; rep. Nicaragua in more than 125 Int. Confs.; Head of Delegation to special meetings commemorating 10th, 20th and 25th anniversaries of the UN Charter; attended all General Assemblies of UN; Vice-Pres. of General Assembly 68; Pres. of Security Council July 70-Oct. 71; Pres. Special Mission, Security Council, to Senegal 71; Pres. of various Inter-American Confs.; Gov. for Nicaragua at World Bank and IMF; fmr. Prof. Int. and Civil Law and Judge; fmr. Pres. Nat. Congress of Nicaragua; awarded more than 45 foreign decorations; mem. many Insts.; Hon. Pres. Pan-American Society, U.S.A.
Publ. *Expropriación.*
Nicaraguan Embassy, 1627 New Hampshire Avenue, N.W., Washington, D.C. 20009; Home: 3200 Ellicot Street, N.W., Washington, D.C. 20008, U.S.A.

Seydewitz, Max; German politician; b. 19 Dec. 1892. In youth apprenticed to printing trade; Ed. of Social Democratic newspaper in Halle 18; Chief Ed. *Sächsisches Volksblatt*, Zwickau 20; elected to Reichstag 24; co-publisher and Ed. *Der Klassenkampf* (fortnightly) 27; left Social Democratic Party (SPD) and helped to found Socialist Workers' Party (SAP) 31; emigrated to Czechoslovakia 33, Norway 38, Sweden 40; returned to Germany 45; Editor of periodical *Einheit*; Dir. Berlin Radio 46; Prime Minister of Saxony 47; mem. Volkskammer 49, Pres. of Economic and Financial Cttee.; Dir.-Gen. State Art Collection 55-; Hon. Pres. Museum Council, Ministry of Culture; mem. Socialist Unity Party (SED).
Publs. *Todesstrahlen und andere Kriegswaffen* 34, *Stalin oder Trotzki?* 36, *Hakenkreuz über Europa* 38, *Den tyska hemmafronten* 43, *Civil Life in Wartime Germany* 44, *Es geht um Deutschland* 49, *Jde o Nemecko* 50, *Wo blieben unsere Männer?* 54, *Dresden mahnt Europa* 55, *Niemiecka Republika Demokratyczna* 55, *Die Unbesiegbare Stadt* 55, *Der Antisemitismus in Westdeutschland* (with Ruth Seydewitz) 56, *Mezi Odrou a Rynem* 57, *Das DresdenerGaleriebuch* and *Die Dresdener Kunstschätze* (with Ruth Seydewitz) 57, *Deutschland-Zwischen Oder und Rhein* 58, *Die grosse Kraft* 61, *Goethe und der General Winter* 62, *Germania meschdu Odrom i Rejnom, Moskau* 60, *Die Dame mit dem Hermelin* (with Ruth Seydewitz, trans. into 5 languages) 63, *Die Dresdener Gemäldegalerie Alte und Neue Meister, Der verschenkte Herkules* (with Ruth Seydewitz), *Dresden—Musen und Menschen* 71.
8051 Dresden-Heideflügel 18, German Democratic Republic.

Seydoux Fornier de Clausonne, François, L. ès L., L. en D.; French diplomatist; b. 15 Feb. 1905, Berlin; s. of Jacques Seydoux; brother of Roger Seydoux Fornier de Clausonne (*q.v.*); m. Beatrice Thurneyssen 1930; one s. four d.; ed. Ecole Libre des Sciences Politiques, Paris Univ. Law Faculty.
Secretary, Berlin 33, Counsellor 38; mem. Bureau d'Etudes Clandestin, Ministry of Foreign Affairs 43; First Counsellor, Brussels 45; Sec.-Gen. French del. to UN Gen. Assembly, Paris 46; Dir. European Affairs, Ministry of Foreign Affairs 49-55; Amb. to Austria 55-58, to Fed. Repub. of Germany 58-62, to NATO 62-64, to Fed. Repub. of Germany 65-70; Amb. de France 65; Admin., State rep. of Havas agency 69; State Councillor 70-; Prés. de la Maison de l'Europe 71-; Pres. Conseil supérieur de l'Agence France-Presse 71-; mem. Council of Admin. ORTF 71-72; Grand Officier Légion d'Honneur; Prix Charlemagne 70.
Leisure interests: reading, walking.
Conseil d'Etat, place du Palais-Royal, Paris 1er; Home: 21 boulevard Jules-Sandeau, Paris 16e, France.

Seydoux Fornier de Clausonne, Roger, L. EN D.; French diplomatist; b. 28 March 1908; s. of Jacques Seydoux; brother of Francois Seydoux Fornier de Clausonne (*q.v.*).
Asst. to Financial Attaché, French Embassy, London 31-32; Asst., Office of French Resident-Gen., Morocco 33; Sec.-Gen. Ecole des Sciences Politiques, Paris 34-45, Dir. 42; Dir. Inst. d'Etudes Politiques de l'Université de Paris 47; Head of Cultural Relations, French Foreign Office 47-50; Vice-Pres. UNESCO 48; Consul-Gen. New York 50-52; Minister in Washington 52-54; Minister in Tunisia 54-56; High Commr. in Tunisia 55-56, Amb. 56-57; Dir.-Gen. of Culture and Technical Affairs, Ministry of Foreign Affairs 56; Amb. to Morocco 60-62; Amb. and Perm. Rep. to UN 62-67; Perm. Rep. to NATO 67-68; Amb. to U.S.S.R. 68-72; Amb. de France 70; Admin., Fondation Nationale des Sciences Politiques; Pres. Banque de Madagascar et des Comores 73-; Grand Officier Légion d'Honneur; Croix de Guerre.
18 rue de Bourgogne, Paris 7e, France.

Seynes, Philippe de; French United Nations official; b. 4 Jan. 1910; ed. Ecole Libre des Sciences Politiques. Ministry of Finance 35-45; mem. French Mission in Germany, later Dep. Sec.-Gen. Allied Reparations Agency Brussels 45-49; Financial Adviser to French Del. to U.N. 49-54, on staff of Minister of Foreign Affairs 54 (Adviser to M. Mendès-France); Under-Sec. for Econ. and Social Affairs, United Nations 55-68, Under-Sec.-Gen. 68-74; Dir. Programme for the Future 75-; Chevalier, Légion d'Honneur, Croix de Guerre.
United Nations Secretariat, New York, N.Y. 10017, U.S.A.

Sforza, Galeazzo-Sforza; Italian international official; b. 6 Sept. 1916, Corfu; s. of Count Carlo Sforza and Valentine de Dudzeele; m. Anne Spehner 1969; ed. Massimo Coll., Rome, Inst. St.-Boniface and Coll. St.-Louis, Brussels, and Louvain, Aix-en-Provence and Columbia Univs.
Editor of European political affairs with NBC, New York 41-42; returned to Italy after 15 years exile 43; Foreign Press Attaché, Prime Minister's Office 45-46; sculptor in Paris and contributor to Italian weeklies 46-49; mem. Secretariat, Council of Europe 49, Head Private Office of Sec. Gen. 53, Head Dept. of External Rels. 56-, Deputy Clerk of Consultative Assembly 63-; Deputy Sec.-Gen. Council of Europe 68-.
Leisure interest: sculpture.
Publs. contribs. to newspapers, radio and magazines.
Council of Europe, Place Lenôtre, Strasbourg; 4 rue de la Carpe Haute, La Robertsau 67, Strasbourg; 13 rue Grégoire de Tours, Paris 6e, France; and La Dogana Estense, 1 via Lucca Ronchi (Massa e Carrara), Italy. Telephone: 31-08-57 (Strasbourg); DAN. 25-49 (Paris); 290-33 (Massa).

Sha Feng; Chinese government official. Minister of Agriculture and Forestry 69-. People's Republic of China.

Shaabi, Qahtan Muhammed al-; Southern Yemen politician; b. 1920; ed. school in Aden, and studied agricultural engineering, Khartoum Univ.
Director of Agriculture, Lahej State 55-58; joined South Arabian League 58, Public Relations Officer 59-60; Adviser to Ministry of South Yemen Affairs, Govt. of Yemen People's Repub. 63; founder-mem. Nat. Liberation Front (N.L.F.) 63, later Sec.-Gen.; mem. N.L.F. Del. to Geneva talks on independence of S. Arabia Nov. 67; Pres. of People's Repub. of Southern Yemen, also Prime Minister and Supreme Commdr. of Armed Forces Nov. 67-June 69.
Aden, People's Democratic Republic of Yemen.

Shackleton, Baron (Life Peer), cr. 58; **Edward Arthur Alexander Shackleton,** K.G., P.C., O.B.E., M.A.; British politician; b. 15 July 1911; s. of the late Sir Ernest Shackleton, Antarctic explorer; ed. Radley Coll. and Magdalen Coll., Oxford.
Surveyor, Oxford Univ. Expedition to Sarawak 32; Organizer and Surveyor, Oxford Univ. Expedition to Ellesmereland 34-35; Royal Air Force 40-45; M.P. 46-55; Parl. Private Sec. to Minister of Supply 45-50, to Lord Pres. of Council 50-51, to Foreign Sec. 51; Minister of Defence for the Royal Air Force 64-67, Minister without Portfolio and Deputy Leader House of Lords 67-68; mem. Cabinet 68-70; Leader, House of Lords 68-70; Lord Privy Seal Jan.-April 68, 68-70; Paymaster-Gen. April-Nov. 68; Leader of Opposition, House of Lords 70-74; Chair. RTZ Development Enterprises etc.; Exec. Dir. Rio Tinto-Zinc Corpn. Ltd., Dep. Chair. 75-; fmr. Pres. Asscn. of Special Libraries and Information Bureaux; Pres. Royal Geographical Soc. 71-74; Pres. Arctic Club 60; Vice-Pres. Parl. and Scientific Cttee.; mem. British Overseas Trade Board; Cuthbert Peek Award, Royal Geographical Soc. 33, Ludwig Medallist, Munich Geog. Soc. 38; Labour.

Publs. *Arctic Journeys, Nansen the Explorer, Borneo Jungle* (part author).
Long Coppice, Canford Magna, Wimborne, Dorset, England.
Telephone: Broadstone 3635.

Shafei, Col. Hussein Mahmoud El-; Egyptian army officer and politician; b. 8 Feb. 1918, Tanta; *s.* of Mahmoud El-Shafei; *m.* Magda Gubr 1948; two *s.* one *d.*; ed. Mil. Coll., Cairo.
Commissioned as 2nd Lieut. 38; took part in Palestine hostilities 48; graduated from Staff Officers' Coll. 53 and apptd. Officer-in-Charge Cavalry Corps; Minister of War and Marine 54, of Social Affairs (Egypt) 54-58; Minister of Labour and Social Affairs, U.A.R. 58-61; Vice-Pres. of U.A.R. and Minister of Social Affairs and Waqfs 61-62; mem. Presidency Council 62-64; Vice-Pres. of U.A.R. (Egypt) 64-67, 70-75; Deputy Prime Minister and Minister of Religious Institutions (Waqfs) 67-70; Pres. Egyptian del. to OAU Summit Conf. 73-74; participated in preparing constitution of federation between Egypt, Syria and Libya.
Leisure interests: riding, tennis, swimming, drawing.
6 Sharai Wizaret, El Ziraä Dokki, Giza, Egypt.
Telephone: 811244.

Shaffer, George Wilson, A.B., PH.D.; American psychologist; b. 23 Nov. 1901, Baltimore, Md.; *s.* of George E. Shaffer and Alice M. Wilson; *m.* Margaret Cowles 1931; ed. Johns Hopkins Univ.
Director Physical Educ., Playground Athletic League, Baltimore, Md. 17-28; Prof. of Psychology, Univ. of Baltimore 28-34; Lecturer Psychology and Dir. of Health of Physical Educ., Johns Hopkins Univ. 34-; Dean, Coll. of Arts and Sciences 42-; Prof. of Psychology 41-, Dean of Univ. 47; Chief Psychologist Sheppard Pratt Mental Hospital 28-; Visiting Prof. of Psychology, William and Mary Coll. (Summers) 33 and 34, Goucher Coll. 44, Univ. of Calif. 54; Board of Examiners Nat. Comm. of Clinical and Experimental Hypnosis; Editor *International Journal of Clinical and Experimental Hypnosis*; Adviser to House and Senate on mental health problems; Fellow, American Psychological Asscn., American Psychopathological Asscn., etc.; Diploma Abnormal and Clinical Psychology; Distinguished Psychology Award 69; Eisenhower Medal 71.
Leisure interests: sports, bridge.
Publs. *Textbook of Abnormal Psychology* 34, *Case Histories in Clinical and Abnormal Psychology* 47, *Fundamental Concepts in Clinical Psychology* 52, etc.
Home: De Sota Apartments, 3409 Greenway, Baltimore, Md. 21212; Office: Johns Hopkins University, Baltimore, Md., U.S.A.
Telephone: Bel 59205 (Home).

Shaffer, John Hixon, M.SC.; American transportation executive; b. 25 Feb. 1919, Everett, Pa.; *m.* Joan Van Vleck 1943; one *s.* two *d.*; ed. Franklin and Marshall Acad., Lancaster, Pa., U.S. Military Acad., West Point, U.S. Air Force Engineering School, Dayton, Ohio and Columbia Univ.
Production Project Officer, Air Force B-50 Program 46-48, Weapons System Program Man. of B-47 Program Sept. 48-54; resigned Air Force comm. as Lieut.-Col. 54; Gen. Production Man. and Asst. Plant Man. of Mercury Assembly Plant, Ford Motor Co., Metuchen, N.J. Jan. 54, Asst. to Group Vice-Pres., Automotive, T.R.W. Jan. 57-58, Vice-Pres. Marketing and Sales of Equipment Group (Defense) Jan. 58-62, Corporate Vice-Pres. (Customer Requirements) 62-69; Administrator, Fed. Aviation Admin., Washington, D.C. 69-73; Pres. Pioneer Van Lines Inc.; Dir. Beech Aircraft Corpn., TRE Inc.; Wright Brothers Memorial Trophy 72; Distinguished Service Medal 72; Sec. of Transportation Outstanding Performance Medal 73.

Leisure interests: golf, hunting, fishing, reading.
4608 Ingraham Street, Hyattsville, Md. 20781, U.S.A.
Telephone: (301) 277-1344.

Shaffer, Peter Levin; British playwright; b. 15 May 1926; ed. St. Paul's School, London, and Trinity Coll., Cambridge.
Evening Standard Drama Award 58; New York Drama Critics Circle Award 59-60; Antoinette Perry Award for Best Play (*Equus*) 75.
Plays: *Five Finger Exercise* 58, *The Private Ear* and *The Public Eye* 62, *The Royal Hunt of the Sun* 64, *Black Comedy* 65, *White Liars* 67, *The Battle of Shrivings* 70, *Equus* 73; also television plays.
18 Earls Terrace, Kensington High Street, London, W.8, England.
Telephone: 01-937-7972.

Shaffer, Raymond F.; American business executive; b. 6 April 1912, Harding, Kan.; ed. Kansas Univ.
Joined Greyhound Corpn. 46, Corporate Exec. Vice-Pres. 64, Dir. 66-, Pres. Greyhound Lines Inc. 67, mem. Exec. Cttee. 69, Pres. May 70-.
The Greyhound Corporation, Greyhound Tower, Phoenix, Ariz. 85077, U.S.A.

Shafiq, Mohammad Musa, M.A.; Afghan politician; b. 1924, Kabul; ed. Ghazi High School, Al Azhar Univ., Cairo and Columbia Univ., U.S.A.
Joined Ministry of Justice 57, later became Dir. Legislative Dept.; also taught at Faculty of Law and Political Science, Kabul Univ.; Partner, private law firm, Kabul 61; Deputy Minister of Justice 63-66; Adviser, Ministry of Foreign Affairs 66-68; Amb. to Egypt, also accred. to Lebanon, Sudan and Ghana 68-71; Minister of Foreign Affairs 71-72; Prime Minister 72-73.
c/o Office of the Prime Minister, Kabul, Afghanistan.

Shagari, Shehu Usman Aliu; Nigerian educationist and politician; b. 1925, Shagari; ed. Middle School, Sokoto, Barena Coll., Kaduna, Teacher Training Coll., Zarta.
Science Teacher, Sokoto Middle School 45-50; Headmaster, Argungu Senior Primary School 51-52; Senior Visiting Teacher, Sokoto Prov. 53-58; mem. Fed. Parl. 54-58; Parl. Sec. to the Prime Minister 58-59; Fed. Minister of Econ. Devt. 59-60, of Est. 60-62, of Internal Affairs 62-65, of Works 65-66; Sec. Sokoto Prov. Educ. Devt. 66-68; State Commr. for Educ., Sokoto Prov. 68-70; Fed. Commr. for Econ. Devt. and Reconstruction 70-71, for Finance 71-75.
Publ. *Wakar Nijeriya* (poetry) 48.
6a Okoli'e Eboh Street, Ikoyi, Lagos, Nigeria.

Shah, Shri Kodardas Kalidas, B.A., LL.B.; Indian lawyer and politician; b. 27 Oct. 1908, Goregaon, Kolaba; *s.* of Shri Kalidas Bechardas Shah; *m.* Madhuben K. Shah 1944; two *s.* three *d.*; ed. Gujarat Coll. and New Poona Coll.
Joined Nat. Movement 30, in custody 32, detained for participation in "Quit India" Campaign 42; Fellow S.P. Coll., Poona; Teacher, Poddar High School, Santa Cruz, Bombay; started legal practice, Bombay 34; Legal Adviser to Maharajah of Baroda 48; mem. Bombay Legislative Assembly 52, Rajya Sabha (Upper House of Parl.) 60-; Gen. Sec. Bombay Pradesh Cttee., Vice-Pres. 55-57, Pres. 57-60; Gen. Sec. All-India Congress Cttee. 62-63; Union Minister of Information and Broadcasting 67-69; Union Minister of Health, Family Planning, Works, Housing and Urban Devt. 69-71; Union Minister of Health and Family Planning March 71-72; Gov. of Tamil Nadu May 71-; Sec. Bombay Famine Relief Cttee.; Leader Indian Del. to Apartheid Conf., London 64; Count Bernadotte Medal, Red Cross 70.

Leisure interests: cricket, tennis, swimming, riding, cards.

Raj Bhavan, Madras-22, Ootacamnnd Camp; Home: 8 Dr. Rajendra Prasad Road, New Delhi, 1 India.

Shah, Manubhai, B.SC.(CHEM.), B.SC.(TECH.); Indian politician; b. 1 Nov. 1915, Surendranagar; s. of Mansukhlal Maneklal Shah; m. Vidyaben Shah 1945; three s. one d.; ed. Baroda Coll. and Univ. of Bombay.

Senior Technical and Admin. Posts, Delhi Cloth and Gen. Mills 37-48; mem. Saurashtra Legislative Assembly 48-56, Minister of Finance, Industries and Planning, Govt. of Saurashtra 48-56; Union Minister of Industry 56-62; Minister of Int. Trade 62-64, Minister of Commerce 64-67; Chair. Cen. Board of Rehabilitation, Gujarat Industrial Devt. Corpn., Gujarat Industrial Investment Corpn. 67-70; mem. of Parl. 56-67, 70-.

Leisure interests: public work, writing, politics, development of science and technology.

10 Haily Road, New Delhi-1; Home: 8 Teen Murti Lane, New Delhi 11, India.

Telephone: 386369 (Office); 372551 (Home).

Shah, Rishikesh; Nepalese politician and diplomatist; b. 1925, Tansen, Palpain Province; s. of Raja Tarak Bahadur Shaha and Madan Dibeshwari; m. Siddhanta Rajyalakshmi 1946; one s.; ed. Patna Univ. and Allahabad Univ., India.

Lecturer in English and Nepalese Literature, Tri-Chandra Coll. 45-48; Opposition Leader, First Advisory Assembly 52; Gen. Sec., Nepalese Congress 53-55; Perm. Rep. (with rank of Amb.) to UN 56-61; Amb. to U.S.A. 58-61; Chair. UN Int. Comm. investigating death of Dag Hammarskjöld 61; Minister of Finance, Planning and Economic Affairs 61-62, of Foreign Affairs July-Sept. 62; Amb.-at-large 62-63; Chair. Standing Cttee., Council of State 63-64; Visiting Prof. East-West Center Univ. of Hawaii 65-66; mem. Parl. 67-.

Leisure interests: reading, writing, big game hunting.

Shri Nivas, Kamal Pokhari, Kathmandu, Nepal.

Telephone: 11766.

Shahi, Agha, M.A., LL.B.; Pakistani diplomatist; b. 25 Aug. 1920, Bangalore; s. of Agha Abdullah; ed. Madras Univ. and Allahabad Univ.

Indian Civil Service 43; Pakistan Foreign Service 51-; Deputy Sec., Ministry of Foreign Affairs, in charge of UN and Int. Confs. Branch 51-55; First Counsellor and Minister, Wash. 55-58; Deputy Perm. Rep. to UN 58-61; Dir.-Gen. in charge Divs. of UN and Int. Conf. Affairs, Soviet, Chinese and Arab Affairs, Ministry of Foreign Affairs 61-64; Additional Foreign Sec. 64-67; Perm. Rep. to UN 67-72; Chair. Pakistan Del. UN Gen. Assembly; Pakistan Rep. to Security Council 68-69; Pres. UN Security Council Jan. 68; Pres. Governing Council for UN Devt. Programme 69; Pakistan Rep. to Conf. of the Cttee. on Disarmament 69; Foreign Sec. 72-.

Leisure interests: riding, reading.

Ministry of Foreign Affairs, Islamabad, Pakistan.

Shakespeare, Frank J., Jr.; American communications executive and government official; b. 9 April 1925, New York City; s. of Frank J. Shakespeare Sr. and Frances Hughes Shakespeare; m. Deborah Ann Spaeth Shakespeare 1954; one s. two d.; ed. Holy Cross Coll., Worcester, Mass.

Liberty Mutual Insurance Co., Washington, D.C. 47-49; Procter and Gamble Co. 49-50; Radio Station WOR, New York 50, Columbia Broadcasting System 50; Gen. Man. WXIX-TV, Milwaukee, Wis. 57-59; Vice-Pres. and Gen. Man. WCBS-TV, New York 59-63; Vice-Pres. and Asst. to Pres. CBS-TV Network 63-65; Exec. Vice-Pres. CBS-TV Stations 65-67; Pres. CBS Television Service Div. 67-69; Dir. U.S. Information Agency 69-73; Exec. Vice-Pres. Westinghouse Electric Co. 73-75; Pres. RKO Gen. 75-; Young Man of Year, New York City 60.

RKO General, 1440 Broadway, New York, N.Y., U.S.A.

Shakirov, Midkhat Zakirovich; Soviet engineer and politician; b. 1916; ed. Bezhitsa Machine-Building Inst.

Fitter at a factory 34-41, Engineer, Chief Engineer and Deputy Dir. 41-47; mem. C.P.S.U. 44-; Sec. C.P.S.U. District Cttee. and Chief Engineer, Bashkirian A.S.S.R. Ministry of Local Industry 47-52; Chief Engineer, Head, Oil Main Pipeline Construction Org. 52-63; First Sec., Ufa City Cttee., C.P.S.U. 63-69; First Sec., Bashkir Regional Cttee., C.P.S.U. 69-; Deputy to U.S.S.R. Supreme Soviet 66-; mem. Presidium 70-; mem. Cen. Cttee., C.P.S.U. 71-.

Bashkir Regional Cttee. of C.P.S.U., Ufa, U.S.S.R.

Shako, Juxon Levi Madoka; Kenyan politician; b. 1918, Taita district; s. of Mwakio Kiwinda and Mrs. Constance M. Kidelo; m. 1937; four s. six d.; ed. Alliance High School.

Teacher, Teachers' Training Centre, Machakos, teacher and headmaster at various schools 37-52; joined provincial admin. 52; Asst. District Officer 53-55; District Asst., Kisii District 55-Jan. 60; District Officer Jan. 60-62; District Commr. for Kitui 62-Jan. 63; Senior District Commr. Jan. 63-Jan. 64; Amb. to Fed. Repub. of Germany and to France Jan. 64; Perm. Sec. Ministry of Defence 67; Chair. East African Harbour Corpn. 68-69; Minister of Tourism and Wildlife 69-74.

Leisure interests: gardening and music.

Ministry of Tourism and Wildlife, Nairobi, Kenya.

Shamoya, Leonard Hantebele, B.A., M.TECH.; Zambian diplomatist; b. 20 Dec. 1936, Mazabuka; s. of Chiyupa Shamoya and Kavumbu Shamoya; m. 1964; two s. three d.; ed. Univ. of London and Brunel Univ.

Secretarial Asst., Roan Consolidated Mines Ltd., Ndola 63-69, Chief Personnel Officer 70-75; mem. Ndola City Council 66-75, Mayor 66-68, 70-75; Dir. Bank of Zambia 66-75, Zambia Nat. Building Soc. 72-75, Shell and BP Ltd. 74-75; Deputy Chair. Local Govt. Asscn. 67-75; Constituency Sec., Ndola North, United Nat. Independence Party (UNIP) 70-75; Deputy Chair. Zambia Inst. of Personnel Management 64-75; High Commr. in U.K., non-residential Amb. to Netherlands 75-.

Leisure interests: football, rowing.

Zambian High Commission, 7-11 Cavendish Place, London, W1N 0HB, England.

Telephone: 01-580 0691.

Shane, Charles Donald, A.B., PH.D.; American astronomer; b. 6 Sept. 1895, Auburn, Calif.; s. of Charles Nelson Shane and Annette Futhey; m. 1st Ethel Haskett 1917 (died 1919), one s.; 2nd Mary Lea Heger 1920, one s.; ed. Univ. of California.

Instructor, Univ. of Calif. 20-24, Asst. Prof. 24-29, Assoc. Prof. 29-35, Prof. 35-45; Astronomer, Lick Observatory, Univ. of Calif. 45-63, Dir. 45-58; Asst. Dir. Radiation Laboratory, Univ. of Calif. 42-44; Dir. of Personnel Los Alamos 44-45; Pres. Asscn. of Univs. for Research in Astronomy Inc. 57-62; Hon. LL.D.

Leisure interests: gardening, travel, serious literature especially historical.

P.O. Box 582, Santa Cruz, Calif., U.S.A.

Telephone: 408-438-1142.

Shankar (Shankar Pillai, K.); Indian newspaper cartoonist; b. 31 July 1902.

Former cartoonist for *Hindustan Times*, New Delhi; founded *Indian News Chronicle*, Delhi 47; Founder and Editor *Shankar's Weekly* 48-; initiated Shankar's Int. Children's Art Competition 49; founded Children's Book Trust 57 of which he is now Exec. Trustee; founder and Ed. Children's World Magazine 68; Dir. Int. Dolls Museum; founder and Dir. Children's Library and Reading Room.

9 Purana Kila Road, New Delhi 1, India.

Shankar, Ravi; Indian sitar player and composer; b. 7 April 1920; ed. under Ustad Allauddin, Khan of Maihar.

Trained in the *Guru-Shishya* tradition; pupil of Ustad Allauddin Khan 38; solo sitar player; fmr. Dir. of Music All-India Radio and founder of the Nat. Orchestra; Founder-Dir. Kinnara School of Music, Bombay 62-; Founder, Int. Dolls Museum and Children's Library and Reading Room; many recordings of traditional and experimental variety in India, U.K. and the U.S.A.; Concert tours in Europe, U.S.A. and the East; Visiting Lecturer Univ. of Calif. 65; appeared in film, *Raga* 74; Silver Bear of Berlin; Award of Indian Nat. Acad. for Music, Dance and Drama 62; award of Padma Bhushan 67.

Film Scores: *Pather Panchali, The Flute and the Arrow, Nava Rasa Ranga, Charly,* etc. and many musical compositions.

Publ. *My Music, My Life* 69.

c/o K. C. Vajifdar, 17 Warden Court, Second Floor, Gowalia Tank Road, Bombay-36, India.

Telephone: 350586.

Shankar, Uday, A.R.C.A.; Indian dancer and artist. Joined Anna Pavlova's Company, London 22, touring America, Canada, British Columbia and Mexico; formed own troupe, numerous tours all over the world; founded Uday Shankar India Culture Centre for dance, drama and music, Almora, closed during Second World War, reopened Calcutta 65; composed ballets; produced and directed film *Kalpana* (Imagination); created innumerable dance dramas and two shadow plays, *Ramleela* and *Lord Buddha*; Fellow, Sangeet Natak Akad.; Nat. Award as Creative Artist; Hon. D.Lit., Rabindra Bharati Univ.; Padma Vibhushan 71.

82/9 Ballygunge Place, Flat 20, Floor 10, Calcutta 19, India.

Shanks, Carrol Meteer, LL.B., B.A.; American lawyer and insurance executive; b. 14 Oct. 1898, Fairmont, Minn.; s. of Edgar Beeson Shanks and Lilly Meteer; m. Martha S. Taylor 1921; one s. two d.; ed. Univ. of Washington and Columbia Univ. School of Law.

Lecturer Columbia Univ. School of Law 25-27; with law firm of Root, Clark, Buckner and Ballantine (New York) 25-29, 31-32; Assoc. Prof. of Law Yale Univ. 29-30; Asst. Solicitor Prudential Insurance Co. of America 32, Gen. Solicitor 38, Vice-Pres. and Gen. Solicitor 39, Exec. Vice-Pres. 44, Pres. 46-60; Pres. Universal Controls, Inc. 62-67; Partner Shanks, Davis and Remer.

Leisure interests: music, North American big game hunting.

Publs. *Cases on Corporate Reorganization* 31, *Cases and Materials on Business Units,* 3 vols. 31-32 (both with William O. Douglas).

575 Park Avenue, New York, N.Y. 10021, U.S.A.

Shanks, Michael; British economist; b. 1927, London; m.; ed. Balliol Coll., Oxford.

Lecturer in Econs., William Coll., Mass. 50-51; Leader, Feature Writer, then Labour Corresp., Industrial Editor *Financial Times* 53-64; Econ. Corresp. *Sunday Times* 64-65; Industrial Policy Co-ordinator Dept. of Econ. Affairs 65-67; Econ. Adviser Leyland Motors Ltd. 67-68; Dir. Marketing Services and Econ. Planning, British Leyland Motor Corpn. 68-71; Chief Exec. Finance and Planning, British Oxygen 71-72, Dir. Group Strategy 73-75; Dir.-Gen. for Social Affairs, Comm. of European Communities 73-; Visiting Prof. Brunel Univ. 73-; Fellow British Inst. of Management; mem. Acad. Council of Wilton Park, mem. Council, Foundation of Management Educ.; Visiting Fellow Univ. of Lancaster.

Publs. *The Stagnant Society* 60 (2nd edn. 71), *Britain and the New Europe* (with John Lambert) 62, *The Innovators* 67, *The Lessons of Public Enterprise, The Quest for Growth* 73.

Directorate-General for Social Affairs, Commission of the European Communities, 200 rue de la Loi, 1040 Brussels, Belgium.

Shann, Keith Charles Owen, C.B.E., B.A.; Australian diplomatist; b. 22 Nov. 1917, Kew, Victoria; s. of Frank Shann and Eileen Caplen Hall; m. Betty Evans 1944; two s. one d.; ed. Trinity Grammar School, Kew, and Trinity Coll., Melbourne Univ., Australia.

Treasury 39, Dept. of Labour and Nat. Service 40-46; United Nations Div., Dept. of External Affairs 46-49; Australian Mission to UN, New York 49-52; Head, UN Branch, Dept. of External Affairs 52-55; Australian Minister to the Philippines 55-56, Ambassador 56-59; Rapporteur UN Comm. on Hungary 57; Australian External Affairs Officer, London 59-62; Amb. to Indonesia 62-66; First Asst. Sec. Dept. of External Affairs 66-70; Deputy Sec., Dept. of Foreign Affairs 70-74; Amb. to Japan 74-.

Leisure interests: gardening, golf, music.

11 Grey Street, Deakin, Canberra, 2600, Australia.

Telephone: 73-1042.

Shannon, Claude Elwood, PH.D.; American applied mathematician; b. 30 April 1916; ed. Univ. of Michigan and Massachusetts Inst. of Technology.

Research mathematician Bell Telephone Laboratories 41-56, Consultant 57-; Visiting Prof. of Communication Sciences Massachusetts Inst. of Technology 56, Prof. of Communication Sciences and Mathematics 57-58, Donner Prof. of Science 58-; Fellow Center for Advanced Study in the Behavioral Sciences, Stanford, Calif. 57-58, Inst. of Radio Engineers; mem. Nat. Acad. of Sciences, American Acad. of Arts and Sciences, I.R.E., American Mathematical Soc.; Alfred Noble Prize A.I.E.E., Morris Liebman Award I.R.E., Stuart Ballantine Medal, Franklin Soc., Research Corpn. Award, Harvey Prize, Technion, Haifa, Israel.

Publs. *Mathematical Theory of Communication* 49; numerous technical papers; Editor (with J. McCarthy) *Automata Studies* 56.

Research Laboratory of Electronics, Massachusetts Institute of Technology, Cambridge, Mass. 02139, U.S.A.

Shannon, James Augustine, A.B., M.D., PH.D.; American medical research administrator; b. 9 Aug. 1904, Hollis, N.Y.; s. of James A. Shannon and Anna Maraison Shannon; m. Dr. Alice Waterhouse 1933; one s. one d.; ed. Coll. of Holy Cross, Worcester, Mass. and New York Univ. Coll. of Medicine and Graduate School.

Assistant Prof. of Physiology, New York Univ. 35-41, Asst. Prof. of Medicine 41-42, Assoc. Prof. of Medicine 42-46; Consulting Physician N.Y. hospitals 38-44; Dir. Squibb Inst. for Medical Research, New Brunswick, New Jersey 46-49; Chair. Malaria Study Section, Nat. Insts. of Health, Bethesda, Maryland 46-47, Assoc. Dir. Nat. Heart Inst. 49-52, Assoc. Dir. Nat. Inst. of Health 52-55, Dir. 55-68; Special Consultant to Surgeon-Gen., U.S. Public Health Service 46-49; mem. WHO Advisory Comm. on Medical Research 59-63; Consultant, President's Science Advisory Comm. 59-65, Advisory Comm. on Research to AID 63-, PAHO Advisory Comm. on Medical Research 62-; mem. U.S. Nat. Acad. of Sciences 65-, Philosophical Soc. 65-; mem. American Acad. of Arts and Sciences 65-; special adviser to Pres. Nat. Acad. Sciences 68-; Presidential Medal for Merit 48, Nat. Acad. of Science Public Welfare Medal 62; Rockefeller Public Service Award 64, Presidential Distinguished Fed. Civilian Service Award 66; several hon. degrees; chair. and mem. of numerous cttees. of Nat. Research Council.

Rockefeller University, New York, N.Y. 10021, U.S.A.

Shanqiti, Sheikh Mohammed Amin; Jordanian politician and diplomatist.

Former Minister of Education; Amb. to Saudi Arabia and the Sudan July 63-70, to Saudi Arabia 71-; mem. Joint Comm. for Border Disputes 66-.

Embassy of the Hashemite Kingdom of Jordan, Jeddah, Saudi Arabia.

Shantaram, V(ankudre); Indian film director, producer and actor; b. 18 Nov. 1901; ed. Kolhapur High School.
Worked in film industry 20-; Founder mem. Prabhat Film Co., Poona; fmr. Chief Producer Govt. of India Films Div., mem. Censor Board, Film Advisory Board, Film Enquiry Cttee.; has directed and produced over 60 films 26-, including *King of Ayodhya, Chandrasena, Duniya-na-mane, Shakuntala* (first Indian film released in U.S.A.), *Ramjoshi, Amar Bhoopali, Jhanak Jhanak Payal Baaje* and *Do Ankhen Barah Haath* (11 awards incl. Berlin Gold Bear, Int. Catholic Award and Hollywood Foreign Press Award).
Rajkamal Kalamandir Private Ltd., Parel, Bombay 12, India.

Shapiro, Ascher H(erman), S.B., SC.D.; American mechanical engineering educator and consultant; b. 20 May 1916, New York City; s. of Bernard Shapiro and Jennie (Kaplan) Shapiro; m. 1st Sylvia Helen Charm 1939, 2nd Regina Julia Lee 1961; one s. three d.; ed. Mass. Inst. of Technology.
Member of Teaching Faculty, Mass. Inst. of Technology 38-, Ford Prof. of Engineering 62-75, Chair. of Faculty 64-65, Head of Dept. of Mechanical Engineering 65-74, Inst. Prof. 75-; Visiting Prof., Cambridge Univ. 55-56; Founder and First Chair. Nat. Cttee. for Fluid Mechanics Films 62-69; mem. U.S. Air Force Scientific Advisory Board 64-66; Councillor, American Acad. of Arts and Sciences 66-69; Consultant to Govt. and Industry in propulsion, compressors and turbines, fluid dynamics; mem. Board of Govs., Israel Inst. of Tech.; Fellow, American Acad. of Arts and Sciences, A.S.M.E., A.I.A.A.; mem. Nat. Acad. of Sciences, Nat. Acad. of Engineering; Naval Ordnance Devt. Award 45, Joint Certificate for Outstanding Contribution, War and Navy Depts. 47, Richards Memorial Award of A.S.M.E. 60, Worcester Reed Warner Medal of A.S.M.E. 65.
Leisure interests: gardening, sailing, photography.
Publs. *The Dynamics and Thermodynamics of Compressible Fluid Flow* Vol. I 53, Vol. II 54, *Physical Measurements in Gas Dynamics and Combustion* (Contrib. to) 54, *Shape and Flow: The Fluid Dynamics of Drag* 61, *Handbook of Fluid Dynamics* (Contrib. to) 61; and numerous technical articles in fields of thermodynamics, propulsion, gas dynamics, fluid mechanics, educational films, biomedical engineering.
Headquarters, Mechanical Engineering Department, Massachusetts Institute of Technology, 77 Massachusetts Avenue, Cambridge, Mass. 02139; Home: 111 Perkins Street, Jamaica Plain, Mass. 02174, U.S.A.
Telephone: 617-253-2201 (Office); 617-522-4418 (Home).

Shapiro, Eli, PH.D.; American economist and business executive; b. 13 June 1916, New York; s. of Samuel Shapiro and Pauline Kushel Shapiro; m. Beatrice Ferbend 1946; one s. one d.; ed. Brooklyn Coll., Columbia Univ.
Professor of Finance, Univ. of Chicago 46-51; Prof. of Finance and Assoc. Dean, M.I.T. 52-61; Sylvan C. Coleman Prof. of Financial Management, Harvard Univ. 62-70 (leave of absence 70-72); Chair. Finance Cttee., The Travelers Corpn. 71-.
Publs. *Personal Finance Industry and its Credit Standards* (with others) 39, *Money and Banking* (with Steiner) 41, *Development of Wisconsin Credit Union Movement* 47, *Money and Banking* (with Steiner and Solomon) 58, *Corporate Sources and Uses of Funds* (with Meiselman) 63, *Money and Banking* (with Solomon and White) 68, *The Role of Private Placements in Corporate Finance* (with Wolf) 72.
The Travelers Corporation, One Tower Square, Hartford, Conn. 06115; Home: 59 Ledyard Road, West Hartford, Conn. 06117, U.S.A.

Shapiro, Harry L(ionel), A.B., A.M., PH.D.; American anthropologist; b. 19 March 1902, Boston, Mass.; s. of Jacob Shapiro and Rose Clemens Shapiro; m. Janice Sandler Shapiro 1938 (deceased 1962); two s. one d.; ed. Harvard Univ.
Tutor, Harvard Univ. 25-26; Asst. Curator, American Museum of Natural History 26-31, Assoc. Curator 31-42, Chair. of Dept. of Anthropology and Curator 42-70, Curator Emer. 70; Research Prof., Hawaii 30-35; Prof., Columbia Univ., New York City 38-73; Assoc., Bishop Museum, Honolulu; mem. Board of Dirs. Louise Wise Services 58-; Sec. American Soc. of Physical Anthropology 35-39, Vice-Pres. 41-42; Pres. American Anthropological Asscn. 48, American Ethnological Soc. 42-43, American Eugenics Soc. 56-63; Fellow, Nat. Acad. of Sciences, American Acad. of Sciences; mem. Social Science Research Council, American Eugenics Soc.; Hon. mem. Die Anthropologische Gesellschaft, Vienna; mem. Board of Field Foundation; Professor Univ. of Pittsburgh 70; Theodore Roosevelt Distinguished Service Medal 64.
Leisure interests: music, literature, gardening.
Publs. *Heritage of the Bounty* 36, *Migration and Environment* 39, *Aspects of Culture* 56, *Man, Culture and Society* (Editor) 56, *The Jewish People* 60, *Peking Man* 75.
American Museum of Natural History, New York, N.Y. 10024; Home: 26 East 91st Street, New York, N.Y., U.S.A.

Shapiro, Irving S., LL.B.; American business executive; b. 15 July 1916, Minneapolis, Minn.; s. of Samuel and Frieda Shapiro; m. Charlotte Farsht 1942; one s. one d.; ed. Univ. of Minnesota.
With U.S. Office of Price Admin. 42-43; U.S. Justice Dept. 43-51; E. I. du Pont de Nemours & Co. 51-; Legal Dept. 51-65, Asst. Gen. Counsel 65, Vice-Pres., Dir., mem. Exec. Cttee. 70, Senior Vice-Pres. 72, Vice-Chair. Board of Dirs. 73-74, Chair., Chief Exec. Officer 74-.
E. I. du Pont de Nemours & Co., 9000 du Pont Building, Wilmington, Delaware 19898, U.S.A.

Shapiro, Jacob Shimshon, LL.B.; Israeli lawyer and politician; b. 1902, Russia; ed. Kharkov Univ. and Law School, Jerusalem.
Went to Palestine 24; Co-founder Kibbutz Givat Hashlosha; First Attorney-Gen., Govt. of Israel 48-49; Minister of Justice 66-72, 72-73; Israeli Labour Party.
10 K.K.L. Boulevard, Tel-Aviv, Israel.

Shapiro, Karl Jay; American poet; b. 10 Nov. 1913; s. of Joseph and Sara Shapiro; m. 1st 1945, 2nd 1967; one s. two d.; ed. Johns Hopkins Univ.
Served with U.S. Army 41-45; Consultant in poetry, Library of Congress 46-47; Assoc. Prof. of Writing, Johns Hopkins Univ. 47-50; Ed. *Poetry* 50-55; Prof. of Writing, Univ. of Nebraska 56-66; Prof. of English, Univ. of Illinois at Chicago Circle 66-68; Prof. of English Univ. of Calif. at Davis 55-56, 68-; Editor *Prairie Schooner* 56-63; Jeanette S. Davis Prize 42; Levinson Prize 43; Contemporary Poetry Prize 43; American Acad. of Arts and Letters Grant 44; Pulitzer Prize (Poetry) 45; Shelley Memorial Prize 45; Guggenheim Fellowship 45-46, 53-54; Fellow in American Letters, Library of Congress; mem. Nat. Inst. of Arts and Letters, American Acad. of Arts and Sciences; Hon. D.H.L. Wayne State Univ. 60; Hon. D.Litt. Bucknell Univ. 72; Bollingen Prize for Poetry.
Leisure interest: painting.
Publs. *Poems* 35, *Person, Place and Thing* 42, *The Place of Love* 42, *V-Letter and Other Poems* 44, *Essay on Rime* 45, *Trial of a Poet* 47, *Bibliography of Modern Prosody* 48, *Poems 42-53* 53, *Beyond Criticism* 53, *Poems of a Jew* 58; Ed. *Newberry Library Bulletin* 53-, *In Defence of Ignorance* 60, *American Poetry Anthology* 60, *The Bourgeois Poet* 64, *A Prosody Handbook* (with Robert Beum) 65, *To Abolish Children* 68, *White-haired Lover* 68,

Selected Poems 68, *Edsel* (novel) 71, *The Poetry Wreck* (selected essays) 75, *Adult Bookstore* (poems) 76.
313 Sproul Hall, University of California at Davis, Davis, Calif. 95616; Home: 1119 Bucknell Drive, Davis, Calif. 95616, U.S.A.
Telephone: 756-2378 (Home).

Shapleigh, Warren McKinney; American business executive; b. 27 Oct. 1920, St. Louis, Mo.; *m.* Jane Smith 1945; two *d.*; ed. St. Louis Country Day School, Yale Univ.
United States Navy 42-46; Vice-Pres. Buying & Merchandising, Shapleigh Hardware Co. 46-56; Pres. Warhington Land & Mining Co. 56-63; Pres. Hipolite Co. 56-59; Vice-Pres. Sterling Aluminium Products 59-61; Man. Diversification Planning, Ralston Purina Co. 61-63, Vice-Pres. Consumer Products Div. 63-70, Dir. 66-, Exec. Vice-Pres. 68-72, Pres. Consumer Products Group 70-72, Pres. 72-; Dir. Brown Group Inc., St. Louis 69-, St. Louis Union Trust Co. 72-, First Nat. Bank, St. Louis 72-, J. P. Morgan & Co. 74-, Morgan Guaranty Trust 74-, and other cos.; mem. Grocery Mfrs. of America 61-, Exec. Cttee. Cereal Inst. 62-72, Board of Dirs., Pet Food Inst. 62-72; mem. Board of Trustees, Washington Univ. 66-, Yale Univ. Devt. Board 71-, Govt. Research Inst., St. Louis 72-, The Brookings Inst., Washington, D.C. 72-, and many other civic orgs.
Leisure interests: skiing, tennis, sailing, gardening.
Ralston Purina Co., Checkerboard Square, St. Louis, Mo. 63188; Home: 1310 Mason Road, St. Louis, Mo. 63131, U.S.A.

Shapp, Milton Jerold; American state governor; b. 25 June 1912, Cleveland, Ohio; *s.* of Aaron and Eva Smelsey Shapiro; *m.* Muriel Matzkin Shapp 1947; one *s.* two *d.*; ed. Case Inst. of Technology, Cleveland, Ohio.
Founded the Jerrold Corpn. (pioneer company in the community antenna television business) 46, resigned to stand as governor 66; Gov. of Pennsylvania Jan. 71-; numerous awards and citations; Democrat.
Leisure interests: music, art.
Publs. various reports.
626 S. Bowman Avenue, Merion, Pa. 19066; Executive Mansion, 2035 North Front Street, Harrisburg, Pa., U.S.A.
Telephone: 603-924-6928.

Sharaf, Abdul Hamid; Jordanian diplomatist.
Former Head, Arab and Palestine Affairs, Ministry of Foreign Affairs; Dir. Broadcasting Service 63-64; Dir., Political Dept., Ministry of Foreign Affairs; Asst. Chief of Royal Cabinet 64-65; Minister of Information 65-67; Amb. to U.S.A. 67-72, to Canada 69-72; Perm. Rep. to UN 72-.
Permanent Mission of Jordan to the United Nations, Room 550-552, 866 United Nations Plaza, New York, N.Y. 10017, U.S.A.

Sharbaugh, H. Robert, M.S.; American business executive; b. 22 Oct. 1928, Pittsburgh, Pa.; *s.* of Olliver M. and Sadie M. (Wingenroth) Sharbaugh; *m.* Ivy Gallagher 1951; two *s.* one *d.*; ed. Carnegie Inst. of Technology and Mass. Inst. of Technology.
Joined Sun Oil Co. as junior engineer 48, Pres., Chief Operating Officer 69-74, Pres. 74-, Chair 75-; mem. Board of Dirs. American Petroleum Inst., Sun Int., Great Canadian Oil Sands Ltd., Girard Co. and Girard Bank Subsidiary; Hon. D.Sc. (Ursinus Coll., Pa.).
Sun Oil Company, 240 Radnor-Chester Road, St. Davids, Pa. 19087, U.S.A.

Sharef, Ze'ev; Israeli politician; b. 1906, Bukovina, Romania; *m.*; three *s.* one *d.*
Went to Palestine 25, worked as labourer; joined Kibbutz Givat Brenner 29; Sec. Israel Sports Org. of Gen. Fed. of Labour in Israel (Histadrut); active in Hagana 40; Sec. of Political Dept. of Jewish Agency

43-47; worked on admin. blueprint of Jewish State 47-48; Sec. of Israel Govt. 48-57; Dir.-Gen. of Prime Minister's Office 48-49; Civil Service Commr. 51-52; Dir. of State Revenue, Ministry of Finance 54-61; Special Adviser to Prime Minister 64-65; mem. Knesset 65-; Chair. of Ports Authority 62-66; Minister of Commerce and Industry 66-69, Minister of Finance Aug. 68-Dec. 69; Minister of Housing 69-74; Mapai.
Publ. *Shlosha Yamin* (Three Days).
25 Shemariahu Levin Street, Jerusalem, Israel.

Sharif, Omar (Michael Chalhoub); Egyptian actor; b. 10 April 1932, Cairo; *s.* of Claire and Joseph Chalhoub; *m.* Faten Hamama 1967; one *s.*; ed. Victoria Coll., Cairo.
Salesman, lumber-import firm; made first film *The Blazing Sun* 53; starred in 24 Egyptian films and two French co-production films during following five years; commenced int. film career with *Lawrence of Arabia*.
Films include: *Lawrence of Arabia, The Fall of the Roman Empire, Behold a Pale Horse, Genghis Khan, The Yellow Rolls-Royce, Doctor Zhivago, Night of the Generals, Mackenna's Gold, Funny Girl, Cinderella-Italian Style, Mayerling, The Appointment, Che, The Last Valley, The Horsemen, The Burglars, The Island, The Tamarind Seed, Juggernaut, Funny Lady, Ace Up My Sleeve.*
Leisure interests: bridge and horse racing.
c/o Pfeiffer, Bury, Tromans Ltd., Flat 2, 10 Connaught Place, London, W.2, England.

Sharif-Emami, Jaffar, G.C.M.G.; Iranian engineer and politician; b. 8 Sept. 1910, Teheran; *s.* of Haji Mohamed Hossein and Kobra; *m.* Mrs. Eshrat Moazzami 1946; one *s.* two *d.*; ed. Secondary School, Teheran, German Central Railway School and Boras Technical School, Sweden.
Joined Iranian State Railways 31; Technical Deputy Gen. Dir. Iranian State Railways 42-46; Chair. and Man. Dir. Independent Irrigation Corpn. 46-50; Under-Sec. of State to Ministry of Roads and Communications, Minister of Roads and Communications 50-51; Gen. Dir. Iranian State Railways 50-51; mem. High Council, Plan Org. 51-52, Man. Dir. and Chair. High Council, Plan Org. 53-54; Senator from Teheran 55-57, 63-; Minister of Industry and Mines 57-60; Prime Minister Aug. 60-May 61; Deputy Custodian Pahlavi Foundation 62-; Chair. Industrial and Mining Devt. Bank 63-; Pres. of the Senate 63-; Pres. Iranian Asscn. of World Federalists 63-; Pres. Iranian Engineers Asscn. 66-; Deputy Chair. of Red Lion and Sun of Iran 66-; Pres. Third Constituent Assembly 67-, Pres. of 22nd Int. Conf. of the Red Cross 73; Pres. Int. Bankers Asscn. 75; mem. American Soc. of Civil Engineers 46-, Board of Dirs. Royal Org. of Social Services 62-, Red Lion and Sun 63 (Vice-Pres. 63), Board of Trustees, Pahlavi Univ. 62, Nat. Univ. Teheran 62, Aria Mehr Technical Univ., Teheran 65, Queen Pahlavi's Foundation 66; mem. of Board of Founders of Soc. for Preservation of Nat. Monuments 66; Iranian decorations incl. Order of Homayoun (3rd and 1st Class), Order of Tadj (1st Class) and many foreign decorations incl. Grosses Kreuz Verdienstorden (Germany), Grand Officer Légion d'Honneur (France), Grand Croix Ordre de la Couronne (Belgium), Order of Rising Sun, 1st Class (Japan), Order of St. Michael and St. George (U.K.).
Leisure interests: sport, swimming, riding, reading.
Darroos, Ehteshamieh 48, Teheran, Iran.
Telephone: 881994.

Sharifi, Ahmad-Hushang, PH.D.; Iranian educationist; b. 1925, Teheran; ed. France.
With Iranian Consulate, Paris; mem. Perm. Del. to UNESCO; French Language Translator, Teheran Univ. 57, Finance Teacher 58, Lecturer in Political Science 60, Prof. of Political Science 66; Financial and Admin. Adviser to Ministry of Educ. 64, Under-Sec. of Educ.

64; Principal, Teachers Training Coll. 68; Chancellor Nat. Univ., Teheran 73; Minister of Educ. 74-; mem. Iran Novin Party.
Ministry of Education, Teheran, Iran.

Sharipov, Adiy, M.SC.; Soviet politician and writer; b. 1912; ed. Kazakh Pedagogical Inst.
Teacher, secondary school, and special secondary school 31-40; Soviet Army Service 40-41; anti-Nazi guerrilla warfare, Byelorussia 41-44; mem. C.P.S.U. 45-; Deputy Minister, Minister of Educ., Kazakh S.S.R. 44-63; Vice-Chair. Council of Ministers and Minister for Foreign Affairs, Kazakh S.S.R. 63-66; First Sec. Board of Kazakh S.S.R. Union of Writers 66-; mem. Central Cttee. Kazakh C.P. 58-; Deputy to U.S.S.R. Supreme Soviet 66-70; Vice-Chair. Soviet of Union, U.S.S.R. Supreme Soviet 66-70; Merited Teacher of Kazakh S.S.R.
Publs. include: *Guerilla's Daughter* (novel) 61, *Creative Activity of Jumgali Sain* (monograph) 63.
Kazakh Union of Writers, Alma-Ata, U.S.S.R.

Sharma, Shanker Dayal, M.A., LL.M., PH.D.; Indian barrister and politician; b. 19 Aug. 1918; ed. Lucknow Univ., Cambridge Univ. and Lincoln's Inn.
Lawyer 42-; mem. All India Congress Cttee. 50-; Pres. Bhopal State Congress Cttee. 50-52; Chief Minister of Bhopal 52-56; mem. Cen. Advisory Board of Educ. 52-64; mem. Consultative Cttees. on Legislation, Bhopal and Madhya Pradesh Legislative Assemblies 52-64; Minister, Madhya Pradesh Govt. 56-67; Gen. Sec. Indian Nat. Congress 68-72; Pres. All India Congress Cttee. 72-74; mem. Lok Sabha (Parl.) 71-; Minister of Communications Oct. 74-; served as Chair. and mem. of numerous parl. cttees.; Editor-in-Chief *Light and Learning, Ilm-au-Noor*; Editor *Lucknow Law Journal*; Hon. Ph.D. (Cambridge), D.P.A. (London), LL.D. (Vikran and Bhopal Univs.).
Leisure interests: travel, reading, swimming.
Publ. *Congress Approach to International Affairs*.
Sardar Patel Bhavan, Parliament Street, New Delhi; Home: 135/1 Professor's Colony, Bhopal, India.

Sharon, Major-Gen. Ariel; Israeli army officer (retd.) and politician; b. 1928.
Active in Hagana since early youth; Instructor, Jewish Police units 47; Platoon Commdr. Alexandroni Brigade; Regimental Intelligence Officer 48; Co. Commdr. 49; Commdr. Brigade Reconnaissance Unit 49-50; Intelligence Officer, Cen. Command and Northern Command 50-52; studies at Hebrew Univ. 52-53; in charge of Unit 101, on numerous reprisal operations until 57; studies Staff Coll., Camberley, U.K. 57-58; Training Commdr., Gen. Staff 58; Commdr. Infantry School 58-69; Commdr. Armoured Brigade 62; Head of Staff, Northern Command 64; law studies, Tel-Aviv Univ. 66; Head Brigade Group during Six-Day War 67; resigned from Army July 73; recalled as Commdr. Cen. Section of Sinai Front during Yom Kippur War Oct. 73, forged bridgehead across Suez Canal; with others formed Likud Front Sept. 73; mem. Knesset (Parl.) 73-74; Adviser to Prime Minister 75-.
Prime Minister's Office, Jerusalem, Israel.

Sharp, Margery, B.A.; British writer; ed. London Univ.
Publs. *The Flowering Thorn, Four Gardens* 35, *The Nutmeg Tree* 37 (play, U.S.A. 40, England 41), *Cluny Brown* 44, *Britannia Mews* 46, *The Foolish Gentlewoman* 48 (play, England 49), *Lise Lillywhite* 51, *The Gypsy in the Parlour* 54, *The Eye of Love* 57, *The Rescuers* 59, *Something Light* 60, *Martha in Paris* 62, *Miss Bianca* (for children) 62, *The Turret* 63, *Martha, Eric and George* 64, *The Sun in Scorpio* 65, *Miss Bianca in the Salt Mines* (for children) 66, *Lost at the Fair* (for children) 67, *In Pious Memory* 68, *Rosa* 69, *Miss Bianca in the Orient* (for children) 70, *Miss Bianca in the Antarctic* (for children) 71, *The Innocents* 71, *Miss*

Bianca and the Bridesmaid (for children) 72, *The Los Chapel Picnic* 73, *The Faithful Servants* 75.
c/o William Heinemann Ltd., 15-16 Queen Street, London, W1X 8BE, England.

Sharp, Hon. (William) Mitchell, B.A., M.P.; Canadian economist and politician; b. 11 May 1911, Winnipeg, Manitoba; s. of Thomas and Elizabeth (Little) Sharp; m. Daisy Boyd 1938 (deceased); one s.
Director Econ. Policy Div. of Dept. of Finance 47; fmr. Deputy Minister of Trade and Commerce; fmr. Vice-Pres. Brazilian Traction Co.; Minister of Trade and Commerce 63-65, of Finance 65-68; Sec. of State for External Affairs 68-74; Pres. of Privy Council, Leader of House of Commons Aug. 74-; Liberal.
House of Commons, Ottawa, Canada.

Shashin, Valentin Dmitrievich; Soviet oil executive and politician; b. 1916; ed. Moscow Petroleum Inst.
Worked at oilfields in Bashkiria 31-61; mem. C.P.S.U. 45-; Head of Chief Admin. of Oil and Gas Industry of Econ. Council of R.S.F.S.R. 60-65; Minister of Oil Industry, U.S.S.R. 65-; mem. Central Auditing Cttee. C.P.S.U. 66-71, Alt. mem. C.P.S.U. Cen. Cttee. 71-; Deputy to U.S.S.R. Supreme Soviet 66-; Order of Lenin, Order of Red Banner of Labour and other decorations.
U.S.S.R. Ministry of Oil Industry, 26/1 Maurice Thorez Naberezhnaya, Moscow, U.S.S.R.

Shatalov, Col. Vladimir Alexandrovich; Soviet cosmonaut; b. 8 Dec. 1927; ed. Mjasnikov School of Military Pilots, Kacha and Military Air Force Acad.
Pilot-Instructor, School of Military Pilots, Kacha 49-53; Officer Soviet Air Force 53-63; mem. C.P.S.U. 53-; with Cosmonaut Training Unit 63-, Commdr. of space ship *Soyuz-4*, which orbited Earth, forming first manned orbital station with *Soyuz-5* Jan. 69; Commdr. of space ship *Soyuz-8*, which made a group flight with *Soyuz-6* and *Soyuz-7* Oct. 69; awards include Hero of Soviet Union (twice), Gold Star (twice), Order of Lenin, Pilot-Cosmonaut of the U.S.S.R., K. Tsiolkovsky Gold Medal of U.S.S.R. Acad. of Sciences, Y. A. Gagarin Gold Medal of F.A.I.
Zvezdny Gorodok, Moscow, U.S.S.R.

Shaub, Harold A.; American business executive; b. 28 Nov. 1915, Lancaster County, Pa.; s. of Arthur and Clara Cramer Shaub; m. Eileen Baire 1939; two s. two d.; ed. Drexel Univ.
Assistant Plant Man., Campbell Soup Co., Chicago 56-57; Vice-Pres.-Gen. Man., Campbell Soup Co., Ltd., Toronto 57-60, Pres. 60-66; Pres. Pepperidge Farm Inc., Norwalk, Conn. 66-68; Senior Vice-Pres., Campbell Soup Co., Camden, N.J. 68-70, Exec. Vice-Pres. and Dir. 70-72, Pres. and Chief Exec. Officer 72-.
Leisure interests: golf, curling, fishing, hunting.
Campbell Soup Company, Campbell Place, Camden, N.J. 08101, U.S.A.

Shaw, Irwin, B.A.; American writer; b. 27 Feb. 1913, New York City; one s.; ed. Brooklyn Coll.
Formerly worked on radio; served in U.S. Army in Europe and Africa during Second World War; contributor to *The New Yorker, Esquire*, etc.
Publs. Plays: *Bury the Dead, Siege, The Gentle People, Retreat to Pleasure, Sons and Soldiers, The Assassin, The Survivors* (with Peter Viertel), *Children from their Games*; Short Stories: *Sailor off the Bremen, Welcome to the City, Act of Faith, Mixed Company, Tip on a Dead Jockey, Whispers on Bedlam, Love on a Dark Street*; Novels: *The Young Lions, The Troubled Air, Lucy Crown, Two Weeks in Another Town, Voices of a Summer Day, Rich Man, Poor Man* 70, *Evening in Byzantium* 73, *Nightwork* 75; *In the Company of Dolphins* (travel).
P.O. Box 39, Klosters, Switzerland; c/o Weidenfeld and Nicolson, 11 St. John's Hill, London, S.W.11, England.

Shawcross, Baron (Life Peer), cr. 59, of Friston; **Hartley William Shawcross,** Kt., P.C., C.M.G., Q.C., LL.M.; British jurist, politician and businessman; b. 4

Feb. 1902, Giessen, Germany; s. of John and Hilda Shawcross; m. Joan Winifred Mather (died 1974); two s. one d.; ed. Dulwich Coll. and abroad.

Called to Bar 25; Senior Law Lecturer Liverpool Univ. 27-34; Deputy Regional Commr. S.E. Region 41; Regional Commr. N.W. Region 42-45; Recorder of Salford 41-45; Chair. Catering Wages Comm. 43-45; Asst. Chair. East Sussex Quarter Sessions 41; Labour M.P. for St. Helens 45-58; Attorney-General 45-51; Pres. Board of Trade April-Nov. 51; Judge of Int. Court of Arbitration, The Hague; Chair. Royal Comm. on the Press 61-62; Chair. British Medical Research Council 62-65; Chair. "Justice" (British branch of Int. Comm. of Jurists) 56-73; Chief Prosecutor, Nuremberg Trials 45-46; U.K. del. UN 45-49; withdrew from Labour Party 58; mem. Monckton Comm. 59-June 60 (resigned); Pres. Rainer Foundation until 72; Chair. Dominion Lincoln Assurance Co. Ltd., Thames Television Co. Ltd. 69-74, Upjohn and Co. Ltd., European Enterprises Devt. Co. SA, City of London Panel on Takeovers and Mergers 69-, Press Council 74-, London and Continental Bankers 74-; Dir. Shell Transport and Trading Co. Ltd. until 73, EMI Ltd. European, Enterprises Devt. Co. S.A. (Luxembourg), Hawker Siddeley Group Ltd., Times Newspapers Ltd. 67-74, Ranks, Hovis Macdougall Ltd., Caffyns Ltd., Morgan et Cie. S.A., Morgan et Cie. International S.A., European Enterprises Development Co. S.A.; Special Adviser to Morgan Guaranty Trust Co. of N.Y.; mem. Court of London Univ.; Sussex Univ. Exec. Council, Pro-Chancellor 62-65, Chancellor 65-; mem. Int. Cttee. of Jurists, Board of Trustees, American Univ. of Beirut, Council of Int. Chambers of Commerce; Hon. mem. New York and American Bar Asscns.; Hon. LL.D. (Columbia, Bristol, Michigan, Lehigh, Liverpool, Hull Univs.); Hon. D.C.L. (New Brunswick Univ.).
Leisure interest: yachting.
Friston Place, Sussex; 12 Grays Inn Square, London, W.C.1, England.
Telephone: East Dean 2206; and 01-242-5500.

Shawn, William; American editor; b. 31 Aug. 1907; ed. Univ. of Michigan.
Reporter, Las Vegas (N.M.) *Optic* 28; Midwest Editor *Int. Illustrated News*, Chicago 29; reporter *The New Yorker* 33-35, Assoc. Editor 35-39, Man. Editor 39-52, Editor *The New Yorker* 52-.
Home: 1150 Fifth Avenue, New York 28, N.Y.; Office: 25 West 43rd Street, New York 36, N.Y., U.S.A.

Shazly, Lt.-Gen. Saad Mohamed el-Hosseiny el-, M.POL.SC.; Egyptian army officer; b. 1 April 1922, Cairo; s. of Mohamed el-Hosseiny el-Shazly and Tafida Ibrahim el-Shazly; m. Zeinat Mohamed Metwally 1942; ed. Khedive Ismail Secondary School, Cairo, Cairo Univ., Mil. Coll., and in U.S.S.R.
Officer of the Guards 43-48; Platoon Commdr. Arab-Israeli War 48; Commdr. of Parachute School 54-56; Commdr. of Parachute Battalion 56-58; Commdr. United Arab Repub. Contingent, UN, Congo 59-60; Defence Attaché, London 61-63; Brig. Commdr. in Yemen Civil War 65-66; Commdr. Shazly Group, Egyptian-Israeli War 67; Commdr. of Special Forces 67-69; Commdr. Red Sea District 70-71; Chief of Staff of Egyptian Armed Forces 71-73; Amb. to U.K. 74-75, to Portugal Sept. 75-; holder of twenty-two decorations including Order of the Repub., 1st Class, Etoile d'Hónneur, Médaille Mil. du Courage, Médaille du Congo, Knight, Syrian Order of Honour.
Leisure interests: gliding, shooting, fencing, golf, camping, chess.
Embassy of Arab Republic of Egypt, Rua das Amoreiras, 80-4 Dto., Lisbon 1, Portugal; and 39 Gamal Eldin Eldessuky, Helipolis, Cairo, Egypt.

Shchelokov, Nikolai Anisimovich, M.SC.; Soviet politician; b. 1910; ed. Dnepropetrovsk Metallurgical Inst.

Member C.P. of Soviet Union 31-; Miner 26-32; Engineer 33-38; Local Govt. and Party work 38-41; Army service 41-46; Head of Dept., Central Cttee. of C.P. of Ukraine 47-51; First Vice-Chair., Council of Ministers of Moldavian S.S.R. 51-62; Chair. Moldavian Council of Nat. Econ. 62-65; Second Sec., Central Cttee. of Moldavian C.P. 65-66; U.S.S.R. Minister of Public Order 66-69, of Internal Affairs 69-; Alt. mem. C.P.S.U. Cen. Cttee. 66-68, mem. 68-; Deputy to U.S.S.R. Supreme Soviet 54-; numerous Soviet and foreign orders and medals.
Ministry of Internal Affairs, 5 Ulitsa Ogareva, Moscow, U.S.S.R.

Shcherbachevich, Aleksey Florianovich; Soviet diplomatist; b. 12 Oct. 1913, Leningrad; ed. Novosibirsk Inst. of Geodesy Engineers and High Diplomatic School, Ministry of Foreign Affairs.
At Ministry of Foreign Affairs, U.S.S.R. until 54; Second Sec. Soviet Embassy, Finland 54-56; ranking official, Ministry of Foreign Affairs 56-60, 64-67; First Sec., Soviet Embassy, Argentina 60-64; Counsellor Soviet Embassy, Chile 67-70; Amb. to Bolivia 70-75.
c/o Ministry of Foreign Affairs, Moscow, U.S.S.R.

Shcherbitsky, Vladimir Vasiliyevich; Soviet politician; b. 1918; ed. Dnepropetrovsk Chemical Engineering Inst.
Instructor, Young Communist League District Cttee. 34; served Soviet Army Second World War; joined Communist Party 41; Candidate mem. Ce itral Cttee., Ukraine Supreme Soviet 35; mem. Presidium Ukraine Communist Party 56, Sec. Central Cttee. 57-61; Prime Minister of Ukraine 61-63 and Oct. 65-May 72; alternate mem. of Presidium of the Central Cttee. of C.P.S.U. 61-63, Alt. mem. Political Bureau 66-71, mem. 71-; First Sec. Dnepropetrovsk Industrial Regional Cttee. of Ukraine Communist Party 63-64; First Sec. Dnepropetrovsk Regional Cttee. Ukraine C.P. 64-65; mem. Cen. Cttee. of C.P.S.U. 61-; First Sec., Cen. Cttee. of Ukraine C.P. May 72-; Deputy to U.S.S.R. Supreme Soviet 58-; mem. Presidium of U.S.S.R. Supreme Soviet 72-.
Central Committee of the Communist Party of the Ukraine, Kiev, U.S.S.R.

Shchukin, Aleksandr Nikolayevich; Soviet radio engineer; b. 22 July 1900, Leningrad; ed. Leningrad Electrotechnical Inst.
Instructor, Leningrad Electrotechnical Inst. 29-39, Prof. 33-; Leningrad Naval Acad. 33-45; Corresp. mem., U.S.S.R. Acad. of Sciences 46-53, mem. 53-; mem. Communist Party 44-; Presidium mem. Lenin Prize Cttee. for Science and Technology 60-; Order of Lenin and other decorations.
Publs. numerous works on radio engineering.
U.S.S.R. Academy of Sciences, 14 Leninsky Prospekt, Moscow, U.S.S.R.

Shea, Joseph Francis; American scientist; b. 5 Sept. 1926; ed. Univ. of Michigan.
Instructor, Eng. Mechanics, Univ. of Mich. 48-50, 53-55; Research Mathematician, Bell Telephone Laboratory 50-53, Development Engineer 55-59; Dir., Advanced System R. and D., and Man. Titan Inertial Guidance Program, A.C. Spark Plug 59-61; Space Program Dir., Space Technology Lab. 61-62; Deputy Dir., Manned Space Flight (Systems), Nat. Aeronautics and Space Admin. 62-63, Program Manager Apollo Spacecraft, Manned Spacecraft Center 63-67; Deputy Assoc. Man. for Manned Space Flight April-July 67; Vice-Pres. Polaroid Corpn. 67-68; Sen. Vice-Pres. and Gen. Man. equipment division, Raytheon Co. 68-.
Boston Post Road, Wayland, Mass. 01778, U.S.A.

Shearer, Rt. Hon. Hugh Lawson; Jamaican politician; b. 18 May 1923, Martha Brae, Trelawny; ed. St. Simon's Coll.
Journalist *Jamaica Worker* 41-47; mem. Kingston and

St. Andrew Corpn. 47-51; mem. House of Reps. 55-59; mem. Legislative Council (now Senate) 61-66; Minister without Portfolio and Leader of Govt. Business in the Senate 62-67; Deputy Leader Jamaica Labour Party 67-; Jamaican del. to UN 62-72; Prime Minister, Minister of Defence and Minister of External Affairs 67-72; Leader of the Opposition March 72-; Island Supervisor, Bustamante Industrial Trade Union 53, Vice-Pres. 60-; Hon. LL.D. Howard Univ.

Jamaica Labour Party, 7 Retirement Road, Kingston 5, Jamaica.

Sheares, Benjamin Henry, M.D., M.S., F.R.C.O.G., F.A.C.S.; Singapore Head of State; b. 12 Aug. 1907, Singapore; s. of Edwin H. Sheares and Lilian J. Gomes; m. Yeo Seh Geok; two s. one d.; ed. St. Andrew's School, Raffles Inst., and King Edward VII Coll. of Medicine, Singapore.

Assistant Medical Officer, Outram Road Gen. Hospital 29-31; Head Dept. of Obstetrics and Gynaecology, Kandang Kerbau Hosp., also Medical Supt. 42-45; Acting Prof. King Edward VII Coll. of Medicine 45; Hon. Consultant, British Military Hosp. 48; Prof. of Obstetrics & Gynaecology, Univ. of Malaya in Singapore 50-60; private practice 60-; Hon. Consultant Kandang Kerbau Hosp. 60-; Pres. of the Repub. of Singapore Jan. 71-; Hon. Fellow Royal Soc. of Medicine 75-; G.C.B.; Dato of Kedah and also of Kelantan (Malaysia); Litt. D. h.c.

Leisure interests: swimming, theatre and movies.
Publs. about 20 articles on obstetrics and gynaecology in professional journals.
The Istana, Singapore 9.
Telephone: 375522.

Sheehan, John C(lark), PH.D.; American professor of organic chemistry; b. 23 Sept. 1915, Battle Creek, Mich.; m.; three c.; ed. Univ. of Mich.

Research Assoc., Nat. Defense Research Cttee. Project Michigan 41; Research Chemist Merck and Co., N.J. 41-46; Asst. Prof. of Chemistry, Mass. Inst. of Technology 46-49, Assoc. Prof. 49-52, Prof. of Organic Chemistry 52-, Camille Dreyfus Prof. of Chemistry 69-; held editorial posts on scientific journals; fmr. Consultant to Arms Control and Disarmament Agency, U.S. State Dept.; Consultant to the President's Scientific Advisory Cttee. (Office of Science and Technology); Reilly Lecturer Univ. of Notre Dame 53, Swiss-American Foundation Lecturer 58, McGregory Lecturer 58; fmr. mem. and Chair. of numerous scientific cttees.; mem. American Chemical Soc. (Chair. Div. of Organic Chemistry 59-60, Past Chair. Grants and Fellowships Cttee., mem. Nat. Finance Cttee., Chair. Int. Activities Cttee.), Nat. Acad. of Sciences, American Acad. of Arts and Sciences, New York Acad. of Arts and Sciences, Chemical Soc., London; Hon. D.Sc. Univ. of Notre Dame; American Chemical Soc. Award in Pure Chemistry 51, American Chemical Soc. Award for Creative Work in Synthetic Chemistry 59, John Scott Award and Medal of City of Philadelphia 64, Synthetic Organic Chemical Mfrs. Asscn. Medal 69.

Leisure interests include: tennis, boating, colour photography.
Department of Chemistry, Massachusetts Institute of Technology, Cambridge, Mass. 02139; Home: 10 Moon Hill Road, Lexington, Mass. 02173, U.S.A.

Sheen, Most Rev. Fulton John, J.C.B., PH.D., S.T.D.; American Roman Catholic bishop; b. 8 May 1895, El Paso, Ill.; s. of Newton and Delia Fulton Sheen; ed. St. Viator Coll., Catholic Univ. of America, Angelicum Coll., Rome, and Louvain Univ., Belgium (Agrégé en Philosophie).

Ordained 19; Papal Chamberlain 34; Domestic Prelate 35; Nat. Dir. Society for the Propagation of the Faith 50-66; Prof. of Philosophy, Catholic Univ. of America 26-50; Auxiliary Bishop of New York 51-66; Bishop of Rochester 66-69; Titular Archbishop of Newport 69-; Titular Bishop of Caesariana 51-; radio and television series for many years; editor *World-mission* and *Mission*; Episcopal Synod 67; Hon. LL.D., Hon. Litt.D., Hon. L.H.D.; Cardinal Mazella Philosophy Medal (Georgetown Univ.).

Leisure interests: tennis, reading.
Publs. *God and Intelligence* 25, *Life of All Living* 29, *Divine Romance* 30, *Eternal Galilean* 34, *Moral Universe* 36, *Cross and Beatitudes* 37, *God and Country* 41, *Declaration of Dependence* 41, *God and War and Peace* 42, *Love One Another* 44, *Communism and the Conscience of the West* 48, *Lift Up Your Heart* 50, *Way to Happiness* 54, *God Love You* 55, *Life is Worth Living*, IV and V, 56 and 57, *Life of Christ* 58, *This is the Mass* 58, *This is Rome* 60, *Go to Heaven* 60, *This is the Holy Land* 61, *These are the Sacraments* 62, *The Priest is not his own* 63, *Missions and the World Crisis* 63, *The Power of Love* 64, *Christmas Inspirations* 66, *Lenten and Easter Inspirations, Guide to Contentment, The Quotable Bishop Sheen, Footprints in a Darkened Forest* 67, etc.
50 Chestnut Street, Rochester, N.Y. 14604, U.S.A.

Shehan, H.E. Cardinal Lawrence Joseph; American ecclesiastic; b. 18 March 1898; ed. St. Charles Coll., Catonsville, St. Mary's Seminary, Baltimore and North American Coll., Rome.

Ordained priest 22; Asst. St. Patrick's Church, Washington, D.C. 22-45, parish priest 41-45; named Titular Bishop of Lydda and Auxiliary to the Archbishop of Baltimore and Washington 45; Pastor of St. Philip and St. James Church, Baltimore 45-53; first Bishop of Bridgeport, Connecticut 53-61; Co-adjutor Archbishop of Baltimore 61, Archbishop 61-; created Cardinal 65; mem. Secretariat for Promotion of Christian Unity 64-; Consultor, Comm. for Revision of Code of Canon Law 64-; Chair. Bishops' Comm. for Ecumenical Affairs 64-; Press Dept. Nat. Catholic Welfare Conf. 64-.
408 North Charles Street, Baltimore, Md. 21201, U.S.A.

Shehu, Mehmet; Albanian politician; b. 10 Jan. 1913; ed. Tirana Technical Coll., higher studies in France.
Fought in Spanish Civil War; Chief of Staff Albanian Nat. Army 46; mem. Political Bureau Albanian Workers' Party 48-; Vice-Pres. Council of Ministers and Minister of the Interior 48-54; Chair. Council of Ministers 54-, Minister of Defence 74-.
Office of the Council of Ministers, Tirana, Albania.

Sheikhly, Abdul Kareem Abdul Sattar Al-; Iraqi politician; b. 14 June 1937, Baghdad; m. Sawsaw Al-Sheikhly 1971; one s. one d.
Political emigré in Cairo 60-63; Asst. Attaché Iraqi Embassy, Beirut 63-64; Minister of Foreign Affairs 68-71; Perm. Rep. to UN 71-.
Permanent Mission of Iraq to the United Nations, 14 East 79th Street, New York, N.Y. 10021, U.S.A.

Shelepin, Aleksandr Nikolayevich; Soviet politician and trade union official; b. 18 Aug. 1918, Moscow; ed. Moscow Inst. of History, Philosophy and Literature.
Held exec. positions in Moscow City Cttee. of Young Communist League 43-52; Sec. Cen. Cttee. of Young Communist League, and also mem. U.S.S.R. Cttee. for Physical Culture and Sports under U.S.S.R. Council of Ministers 45-53; First Sec., Cen. Cttee. of the Lenin Young Communist League 52; mem. Cen. Cttee. C.P.S.U. 52; Deputy to U.S.S.R. Supreme Soviet 54-; mem. U.S.S.R. Slav Cttee.; Chair. State Security Cttee. Dec. 58-61; mem. Secr. of the Presidium of the Cen. Cttee. of C.P.S.U. 61-64, 66-Sept. 67, of Presidium 64-66, of Political Bureau 66-75; Chair. C.P. Cttee. of Party State Control 62-65; Deputy Chair. Council of Ministers 62-65; Chair. All-Union Council of Trade Unions 67-75; awarded Order of Lenin (twice), Order of the Red Star, and other decorations.
All-Union Council of Trade Unions, 42 Leninsky Prospekt, Moscow, U.S.S.R.

Shelest, Pyotr Yefimovich; Soviet politician; b. 1908; ed. Mariupol Metallurgical Inst.

Member C.P.S.U. 28-; Engineer, Mariupol and Kharkov 32-41; party work, Chelyabinsk, Moscow, Suratov, Leningrad and Kiev 41-54; Second Sec., Kiev City Cttee., Ukraine C.P., later Second Sec. Kiev Regional Cttee. 54-57, First Sec. 57-62; mem. Presidium Cen. Cttee. of Ukraine C.P. 61, Sec. Cen. Cttee. 62-63, First Sec. 63-65, 66-72; mem. Cen. Cttee. of C.P.S.U. 61-; Candidate mem. 63-64, Presidium mem. 64-66, mem. Political Bureau 66-; mem. Presidium of Supreme Soviet of U.S.S.R. 66-72; Deputy Chair. U.S.S.R. Council of Ministers 72-73; Hero of Socialist Labour 68, Orders of Lenin, Hammer and Sickle Gold Medal, and other decorations.
Council of Ministers, The Kremlin, Moscow, U.S.S.R.

Shemin, David, B.S., A.M., PH.D.; American professor of biochemistry; b. 18 March 1911, U.S.A.; s. of Louis Shemin and Mary Bushkoff Shemin; m. 1st Mildred Sumpter (died 1962), 2nd Charlotte Norton 1963; two d.; ed. Coll. of City of New York and Columbia Univ.
Assistant Prof. of Biochem., Columbia Univ. 45-49, Assoc. Prof. 49-53, Prof. 53-68; Prof. of Biochem., Northwestern Univ. 68-, Chair. Dept. of Biochemistry; mem. Nat. Acad. of Sciences; Fellow, American Acad. of Arts and Sciences; Guggenheim Fellowship, Commonwealth Fund Fellow.
Leisure interests: reading, music, photography, gardening, tennis, swimming, snorkling and jogging.
Publs. *Biosynthesis of Porphyrins* (Harvey Lecture) 55; Editor *Biochemical Preparations* Vol. 5 57; about 100 publs. in scientific journals dealing with amino acid metabolism, porphyrin and B12 synthesis, enzymology.
Department of Biochemistry and Molecular Biology, Northwestern University, Evanston, Ill. 60201; 902 Lincoln Street, Evanston, Ill. 60201, U.S.A.
Telephone: 312-492-5060 (Office); 312-491-9898 (Home).

Shen, James, C.H., M.A.; Chinese diplomatist; b. 15 June 1909; ed. Yenching Univ., Peiping, Univ. of Missouri, Columbia, U.S.A.
Editor Cen. News Agency, Nanking 36-37; Chief Editorial Section, Int. Dept., Ministry of Information, Chungking 38-43; Dir. Pacific Coast Bureau, Ministry of Information 43-47; Dir. of Int. Dept., Govt. Information Office 47-48, Dir.-Gen. 61-66; Sec. to Pres. of Repub. of China, Taipei 56-59; Dir. of Information Dept., Ministry of Foreign Affairs, Taipei 59-61; Amb. to Australia 66-68; Vice-Minister of Foreign Affairs 68-71; Amb. to U.S.A. April 71-; Faculty-Alumni Gold Medal (Univ. of Missouri) 72.
Embassy of Taiwan, 2311 Massachusetts Avenue, N.W., Washington, D.C. 20008; Home: 3225 Woodley Road, N.W., Washington, D.C. 20008, U.S.A.

Shenouda III, Anba, B.A., B.D.; Egyptian ecclesiastic; b. 3 Aug. 1923; ed. Cairo Univ. and Coptic Orthodox Theological Coll.
Theological teacher and writer; fmr. Bishop and Prof. of theology, Orthodox Clerical Coll., Cairo; 1st Chair., Asscn. of Theological Colls. in the Near East; 117th Pope of Alexandria and Patriarch of the See of St. Mark of Egypt, the Near East and All Africa (Coptic Orthodox Church) 71-.
Coptic Orthodox Patriarchate, Anba Ruiess Building, Ramses Street, Abbasiya, Cairo, Egypt.

Shepard, Alan B., Jr.; American astronaut; b. 18 Nov. 1923, E. Derry, N.H.; m. Louise Brewer; two d.; ed. U.S. Naval Acad.
Destroyer service in Pacific, U.S. Navy, Second World War; naval flight experience 47-58; graduated from Naval War Coll., Newport, R.I. 58; Air Readiness Officer, Staff of C.-in-C. Atlantic Fleet 58-59; selected by NASA as astronaut April 59; pilot of *Mercury-Redstone III* (sub-orbital flight, and first American in space) 61; now Chief, Astronaut Office; Commdr.

Apollo XIV Jan.-Feb. 71; NASA Distinguished Service Medal 61; U.S. Nat. Space Hall of Fame Award 69, Langley Medal 69.
NASA Johnson Space Center, Houston, Tex. 77058, U.S.A.

Shepard, Horace Armor; American business executive; b. 15 Nov. 1912, Purvis, Miss.; s. of Horace and Carolyn (Hand) Shepard; m. Lucy Dunbar 1937; three d.; ed. Murphy High School and Auburn Univ.
U.S. Air Force 35-51, Brig. Gen. 47; Dir. of Procurement and Engineering U.S.A.F. Headquarters 50-51; Vice-Pres., Asst. to Gen. Manager, Thompson Ramo Wooldridge Inc. 51-57, Vice-Pres. and Gen. Manager 61-62, Pres. 62-69, Chair. of Board 69-; Legion of Merit.
TRW Inc., 23555 Euclid Avenue, Cleveland, Ohio 44117; 2731 Shelly Road, Shaker Heights, Ohio 44122, U.S.A.
Telephone (Home): 464-0253.

Shepheard, Peter Faulkner, C.B.E., B.ARCH.; British architect, town planner and landscape architect; b. 11 Nov. 1913, Birkenhead; s. of Thomas Faulkner Shepheard, F.R.I.B.A.; m. Mary Bailey 1943; one s. one d.; ed. Birkenhead School, Liverpool School of Architecture.
Assistant to Derek Bridgwater 37-40; Royal Ordinance Factories, Ministry of Supply 40-43; Technical Officer on Greater London Plan, later on Research and Master Plan, Stevenage New Town, Ministry of Town and Country Planning 43-47; Deputy Chief Architect and Planner, Stevenage Devt. Corpn. 47-48; private practice 48-; Visiting Prof. of Landscape Architecture, Univ. of Pennsylvania 59, 62-67; mem. Council Royal Inst. of British Architects 50-56, 57-62, 63-, Pres. 69-71; Pres. Architectural Asscn. 54-55, Inst. of Landscape Architects 65-66; mem. Royal Fine Art Comm. 68-71, Countryside Comm. 68-71; Dean Graduate School of Fine Arts, Univ. of Pennsylvania 71-; R.I.B.A. Distinction in Town Planning 56; Hon. Fellow, Royal Architectural Inst. of Canada 72, American Inst. of Architects 73.
Leisure interests: music, poetry, drawing, gardening, study of natural science.
Publs. *Modern Gardens* 63, *Gardens* 69, Illustrator *A Book of Ducks and Woodland Birds.*
Shepheard, Epstein and Hunter, 60 Kingly Street, London, W1R 6EY, England.
Telephone: 01-734-8577.

Shepherd, 2nd Baron, cr. 46, of Spalding; **Malcolm Newton Shepherd,** P.C.; British politician; b. 27 Sept. 1918, Blackburn; s. of George Robert and Ada Shepherd; m. 1941; two s.; ed. Friends' School, Saffron Walden.
Opposition Chief Whip, House of Lords 63-64, Govt. Chief Whip 64-67, Minister of State, Commonwealth Office 67-68, Foreign and Commonwealth Office 68-70; Deputy Leader of House of Lords 67-70, Deputy Leader of the Opposition, House of Lords 70-74; Lord Privy Seal, Leader of House of Lords 74-; Labour.
House of Lords, London, S.W.1; 29 Kennington Palace Court, London, S.E.11, England.
Telephone: 01-735-0031.

Shepilov, Dmitri Trofimovich; Soviet journalist and politician.
Dir. Propaganda and Agitation Dept., Central Cttee. of the Communist Party 49, full mem. Central Cttee. 52, and one of its Secs. 54; Chief Editor *Pravda* 52-56; mem. Supreme Soviet Council of Nationalities 54 and Chair. Foreign Affairs Comm.; mem. Soviet Del. to China 54, to Yugoslavia 55, and to Egypt 55 and 56; Minister of Foreign Affairs 56-57; Dir. Inst. of Econ. Acad. of Sciences of Kirghiz S.S.R. 57-62; engaged in scientific work 62-.
Academy of Sciences, Moscow, U.S.S.R.

Shepley, James Robinson; American publishing executive; b. 16 Aug. 1917, Harrisburg, Pa.; ed. Dickinson Coll.

Reporter *Daily Patriot*, Harrisburg, Pittsburgh *Press* and *United Press*; Washington correspondent *Time* and *Life* magazines 42-45; Capt. and Staff Officer Potsdam Conf. 45; attached U.S. Chief of Staff 45-46; with *Time* 46, Chief Washington news bureau 48-57, Chief *Time-Life* U.S. and Canadian bureaux 57-60; with Nixon Presidential campaign 60; Asst. publisher *Life* 60, publisher *Fortune* 64; Vice-Pres. Time Inc. 64; publisher *Time* 67, Pres. Aug. 69-; War Dept. Citation.
Publ. *The Hydrogen Bomb* 54 (co-author).
Time-Life Building, Rockefeller Center, New York, N.Y. 10020, U.S.A.

Sheppard, Percival Albert, C.B.E., F.R.S.; British meteorologist; b. 12 May 1907, Box, Wilts.; s. of A. E. Sheppard and Flora Archard; m. Phyllis Blanche Foster 1933; two s.; ed. City of Bath Boys School and Bristol Univ.
Demonstrator, Physics Dept. Bristol Univ. 27-29; Resident Observer, Kew Observatory, Meteorological Office 29-32; Int. Polar Year, British Party, N.W.T., Canada 32-33; Professional Asst. Meteorological Office, U.K. 33-39; Reader in Meteorology, Imperial Coll., London Univ. 39-52; seconded Meteorological Office for war duties 39-45; Prof. of Meteorology, Imperial Coll. 52-74, now Emer.; Chair. Meteorological Research Cttee., U.K. 58-68; Pres. Royal Meteorological Soc. 57-59; Chair. Space Policy and Grants Cttee., Science Research Council 65-71; Chair. Scientific and Technical Cttee., European Space Research Org. 67-70; mem. Science Research Council, U.K. 67-71; Chair. Meteorological Research Grants Cttee. 69-72; mem. Council of Royal Society 70-72; Hon. Dr. Leningrad Univ., Hon. A.R.C.S.; Symons Gold Medal, Royal Meteorological Soc.
Leisure interests: music and arts.
Publs. Papers in various journals on meteorology and atmospheric electricity.
Office: Imperial College, London, S.W.7; Weathering, Longbottom, Seer Green, nr. Beaconsfield, Bucks., England.
Telephone: 01-589-5111, Ext. 1870 (Office); 04946-71297 (Home).

Sheppard, Richard, C.B.E., R.A., F.R.I.B.A.; British architect; b. 2 July 1910, Bristol; s. of William Sheppard and Hilda (née Kirby-Evans); m. Jean Shufflebotham, A.R.I.B.A. 1938; one s. one d.; ed. Bristol Grammar School, Royal West of England Acad. School of Architecture, Bristol, Architectural Asscn. School of Architecture.
Assistant in various offices 34-37; Staff, Architectural Asscn. School of Architecture 37-41; private practice 37-, Senior Partner Richard Sheppard, Robson & Partners; numerous Royal Inst. of British Architects Awards and Civic Trust Awards (Architecture).
Buildings designed by partnership include, City Univ., London; Brunel Univ.; Science and Arts Bldgs., Univ. of Newcastle; Churchill Coll., Cambridge; Manchester Polytechnic; Worcester Technical Coll.; Campus West, Theatre and Social Amenities Centre, Welwyn Garden City; Gwent Square, Cwmbran New Town, Monmouthshire; Waltham Cross Cen. Area Redevt.; West Midlands Teachers' Training Coll., Walsall.
Leisure interest: looking at the work of others.
Publs. *Building for the People* 45, *Prefabrication and Building* 46, and many technical articles.
Richard Sheppard, Robson & Partners, 77 Parkway, London, NW1 7PU; Home: The Old Rectory, Little Berkhamsted, nr. Hertford, Herts., England.
Telephone: 01-485-4161 (Office); Cuffley 5066 (Home).

Sherer, Albert William, Jr., LL.B.; American diplomatist; b. 16 Jan. 1916, Wheaton, Ill.; s. of Albert W. Sherer and Linda van Nostrand; m. Carroll Russell Sherer 1944; three c.; ed. Yale and Harvard Univs.
Ambassador to Togo 67-70, to Guinea 70-72, to

Czechoslovakia 72-75 and concurrently Chief U.S. Del. to Conf. on Security and Co-operation in Europe, Geneva 74-75; mem. U.S. Mission to UN 75-, Dep. U.S. Rep., Security Council 75-.
Leisure interests: tennis, golf, gardening.
United States Mission to the United Nations, 799 United Nations Plaza, New York, N.Y. 10017, U.S.A.
Telephone: 826-4488.

Sherfield, 1st Baron, cr. 64; **Roger Mellor Makins,** G.C.B., G.C.M.G.; British diplomatist, public servant and business executive; b. 3 Feb. 1904; s. of Brig.-Gen. Sir Ernest Makins, K.B.E., D.S.O. and Florence Mellor; m. Alice Davis 1934; two s. four d.; ed. Winchester and Christ Church, Oxford.
Barrister 27; Foreign Service 28, Washington and Oslo; mem. Staff Resident Minister in W. Africa 42, of Resident Minister, Allied Force H.Q. Mediterranean 43-44; Minister in Washington 45-47; Asst. Under-Sec. of State for Foreign Affairs 47-48, Deputy Under-Sec. 48-52; Ambassador to U.S.A. 52-56; Joint Perm. Sec. to Treasury 56-59; Chair. U.K. Atomic Energy Authority 60-64; Chair. Industrial and Commercial Finance Corpn. 64-74, Estate Duties Investment Trust 66-73, Ship Mortgage Finance Co. 66-74, Hill Samuel Group Ltd. 66-70, Technical Devt. Capital Ltd. 66-74, A. C. Cossor Ltd. 68-, Raytheon Europe Int. Co. 70-, Wells Fargo Ltd. 72-, Finance for Industry Ltd. 73-74, Finance Corpn. for Industry Ltd. 73-74; Fellow, All Souls Coll., Oxford; Warden and Fellow, Winchester Coll.; Chair. Governing Body Imperial Coll. of Science and Technology 62-74; Chair. Marshall Aid Commemoration Comm. 66-73; Trustee, Kennedy Memorial Trust 64-74; Chancellor, Univ. of Reading 70-; Pres. Parl. and Scientific Cttee. 69-73; Pres. British Standards Inst. 70-73; Warden Winchester Coll. 74-; Hon. D.C.L. (Oxford), Hon. F.I.C.E., Hon. D.Litt. (Reading), Hon. LL.D. (London); Hon. Student, Christ Church (Oxford).
Leisure interests: shooting, gardening.
Sherfield Court, Basingstoke, Hants., England.

Sherman, Frank (Howard); Canadian iron and steel executive; b. 4 Oct. 1916, Bellevue, Pa., U.S.A.; s. of Frank A. Sherman; m. Catherine Audrey Carpenter 1941 (deceased 1972); two s.; ed. Westdale Secondary School, Hamilton, Ont. and Queen's Univ.
Metallurgical Asst., Dominion Foundries and Steel, Ltd. (Dofasco) 39-40, in Devt. and Operation of Armaments Dept. 40-44, Asst. Works Man. 45-47, Works Man. 47-49, Vice-Pres. and Works Man. 49-52, Exec. Vice-Pres. 52-57, Gen. Man. 57-59, Pres. and Gen. Man. 59-64, Pres. and Chief Exec. Officer 64-; Directorships include American Iron and Steel Inst., Bank of Nova Scotia, Crown Life Insurance Co., Dominion Foundries and Steel Ltd., and Wabush Lake Railway Co. Ltd.; mem. Board of Govs. McMaster Univ. and Art Gallery of Hamilton.
Leisure interests: golf, photography, boating, fishing, skeet shooting, hunting, wood-working, horse-racing.
P.O. Box 460, 1330 Burlington Street East, Hamilton, Ont. L8N 3J5, Canada.
Telephone: 416-544-3761.

Sherrill, Rt. Rev. Henry Knox, D.D.; American ecclesiastic; b. 6 Nov. 1890; ed. Hotchkiss School, Yale Univ. and Episcopal Theological School, Cambridge, Mass.
Deacon 14, Priest 15, Protestant Episcopal Church; Asst. Minister, Trinity Church, Boston 14-17; Red Cross and U.S. Army Chaplain in France 17-19; received Medal of Merit (U.S.); Rector Church of Our Saviour, Brookline, Mass. 19-23; Trinity Church, Boston 23-30; Bishop of Mass. 30-47; Presiding Bishop 47-58; Pres. Nat. Council of Churches of Christ in U.S.A. 50-52; Pres. World Council of Churches 54-61; mem. President's Comm. on Civil Rights 47; Fellow Corpn., Yale Univ.; Fellow American Acad. Arts and Sciences; Trustee Boston Univ.; Hon. LL.D. (Boston);

Hon. D.D. (Harvard, **Trinity Coll.,** Philadelphia Divinity School, Princeton, Columbia, Hobart Coll., Univs. of Edinburgh and Rochester, Seabury **Western** Theological Seminary); Hon. S.T.D. (Gen. Theological Seminary); Hon. D.C.L. (Union Coll.).
Publs. *William Lawrence—Later Years of a Happy Life, The Church's Ministry in Our Time* 48, *Among Friends* 62.
Boxford, Mass. 01921, U.S.A.

Sherrill, William Wayne, B.B.A., M.B.A.; American government official; b. 23 Aug. 1926, Houston, Tex.; *m.* Sue Poer; three *d.*; ed. Univ. of Houston and Harvard Graduate School of Business.
Served in Second World War with U.S. Marine Corps; with Southwestern Bell Telephone Co. until 54; Admin., City Court System of City of Houston; Exec. Asst. to the Mayor; Chief Admin. Officer and City Treas.; Investment Analyst; Pres. of Homestead Bank and Exec. Vice-Pres. of Jamaica Corpn. in Houston 63; Dir. Fed. Deposit Insurance Corpn. 66-67; mem. Board of Govs., Fed. Reserve System 67-71; Pres. Associated Corpn. of N. America 71-.
Leisure interests: tennis, boating.
1700 Mishawaka Avenue, South Bend, Ind. 46624; Home: Mishawaka, Ind. 46544, U.S.A.

Sherrod, Robert Lee, A.B.; American writer; b. 8 Feb. 1909; ed. Univ. of Georgia.
Newspaper reporter 29-35; Corresp. *Time* and *Life* 35-52; Far East Corresp. *Saturday Evening Post* 52-55, Managing Editor 55-62, Editor 62-63, Editor-at-Large 63-65; Vice-Pres. and Editorial Co-ordinator, Curtis Publishing Co. 65-66; contract writer, *Life* 67-72; Benjamin Franklin award 55.
Publs. *Tarawa, The Story of a Battle* 44, *On to Westward* 45, *'Life's' Picture History of World War II* 50, *History of Marine Corps Aviation* 52, *Kobunsha's History of the Pacific War* 50.
c/o Curtis Publishing Company, 641 Lexington Avenue, New York 22, N.Y., U.S.A.

Sherwood, Thomas Kilgore, S.M., SC.D.; American chemical engineer; b. 25 July 1903, Columbus, Ohio; *s.* of Milton W. and Sadie D. (Tackaberry) Sherwood; *m.* 1st Betty MacDonald 1927 (died 1950), 2nd Virginia Howell 1953; two *s.* one *d.*; ed. McGill Univ. and Mass. Inst. of Technology.
Assistant and Research Asst., Mass. Inst. of Technology 24-28; Asst. Prof. Worcester Polytechnic Inst. 28-30; Asst. Prof. Mass. Inst. of Technology 30-33, Assoc. Prof. 33-41, Prof. of Chem. Eng. 41-46, Dean of Eng. 46-52, Prof. of Chem. Eng. 52-66, Lammot DuPont Prof. 66-69; Visiting Prof. Univ. of Calif. (Berkeley) 58-59, 66-67; Technical Aide, Section Chief, Div. Mem. Nat. Defence Research Cttee. 40-46; Consultant, Baruch Cttee. 42, War Dept. 44; Trustee Assoc. Univs. Inc. 48-52; Priestley Lecturer Pennsylvania State Univ. 59; Fellow American Acad. of Arts and Sciences; mem. American Chemical Soc., American Inst. of Chemical Engineers (Fellow), American Soc. Mechanical Engineers, Nat. Acad. of Sciences (Chair. Sec. of Eng. 62-65), Nat. Research Council, Cttee. on Air Quality Man. (Chair. 69-71), etc.; Founder and mem. Nat. Acad. of Eng.; Hon. senior mem. Chemical Inst. of Canada; William H. Walker Award 41; W. K. Lewis Award 72, Founders' Award, American Inst. of Chemical Engineers 64; E. V. Murphree Award, American Chemical Soc. 73; U.S. Medal for Merit 48; Hon. D.Eng. (Northeastern Univ.), Hon. D.Sc. (McGill Univ.), Hon. D.Tech. (Technological Univ., Denmark) 74.
Leisure interests: travel, mountains, shopwork.
Publs. *Absorption and Extraction* 37, 2nd edn. (with R. L. Pigford) 52, *Applied Mathematics in Chemical Engineering,* 2nd edn. (with H. S. Mickley and C. E. Reed) 57, *Properties of Gases and Liquids* (with R. C. Reid) 58, 68, *The Role of Diffusion in Catalysis* (with

C. N. Satterfield) 64, *Process Design* 64, *Mass Transfer* (with R. L. Pigford and C. R. Wilke) 75.
Department of Chemical Engineering, University of California, Berkeley, Calif. 94720; Home: 17 Senior Avenue, Berkeley, Calif., U.S.A.
Telephone: 415-642-4899.

Shevchenko, Arkady Nikolayevich, D.JUR.; Soviet diplomatist; b. 11 Oct. 1930, Gorlovka, Ukraine; *m.* Leongina Shevchenko 1951; one *s.* one *d.*; ed. Moscow State Inst. of Int. Relations.
Joined Ministry of Foreign Affairs 56, held senior diplomatic posts in Dept. of Int. Orgs. 56-63; Counsellor, then Senior Counsellor, Perm. Mission to UN 63-70; Adviser to Minister of Foreign Affairs, with rank of Amb. 70-73; part-time Senior Research Fellow, Inst. of U.S. Studies, U.S.S.R. Acad. of Sciences 70-73; UN Under Sec.-Gen. for Political and Security Council Affairs April 73-; several U.S.S.R. decorations.
Leisure interests: research, journalism.
Publs. *Struggle of the Soviet Union for Disarmament* 61, *Current Problems of Disarmament* 65, and about 100 articles in various Soviet scientific magazines.
Department of Political and Security Council Affairs, United Nations Secretariat, New York, N.Y. 10017; Home: 160 East 65th Street, Apartment 26D, New York, N.Y. 10021, U.S.A.
Telephone: 734-8525 (Home).

Shibata, Yuji; Japanese inorganic chemist; b. 28 Jan. 1882, Tokyo; *s.* of Shokei and Chika Shibata; *m.* Nami Sugimura 1914; one *s.*; ed. Imperial Univ. of Tokyo, Univs. of Leipzig, Zürich and Paris.
Professor of Inorganic Chemistry, Univ. of Tokyo 13-42; Prof. Univ. of Nagoya 42-48; Rector Tokyo Metropolitan Univ. 49-57; mem. Japan. Acad. 44, Pres. 62-70; Hon. mem. Romanian Acad.; Sakurai Medal, Japan Chemical Soc. 19, Imperial Medal of Japan Acad. 27.
Major works include: study of colour change of salt solutions, study of absorption spectra of the metal complexes, works on spectrochemistry, co-ordination chemistry and geochemistry.
1-30-8 Ookayama, Megurogu, Tokyo, Japan.

Shiga, Yoshio; Japanese journalist; b. 8 Jan. 1901, Kitakyushu-City; *s.* of Fudesuke and Tama Kawamoto; *m.* Taeko Watanabe 1927; ed. Imperial Univ., Tokyo.
Joined Communist Party 23; Editor *Marxism* 26; elected mem. of Central Cttee. of Communist Party 27; imprisoned for political reasons 28-45; re-elected mem. of Central Cttee. 45; mem. of House of Representatives 46-47 and 49-50; removed from public office by Gen. MacArthur, June 50; underground activity 50-54; re-elected mem. House of Reps. 55-; mem. Presidium Central Cttee. Japanese Communist Party, expelled from Party 64; founded the Voice of Japan; Chief Editor newspaper *Nihon-no-Koe*; mem. editorial Cttee. Moscow Peace Manifesto 57.
Publs. *Eighteen Years of Imprisonment* 47, *On the State* 49, *Japanese Revolutionaries* 56, *On Japan* 60, *I Appeal Against the Atomic Bomb* 64, *Japanese Imperialism* 72, *Collective Security of Asia* 73, *Problems of Communist Movement in Japan* 74, *Kuril Problems* (2 vols.) 75.
26-15, Minamicho-3, Kichijoji, Musashino City, Tokyo, Japan.
Telephone 0422-43-8374.

Shiguer, Muhammad Hadou; Moroccan politician; b. 1932; ed. Mohammed V Univ.
Taught for 12 years; mem. Nat. Assembly; Minister of Posts and Telecommunications 64-66, of Agriculture 66-67, of the Royal Cabinet 67, of Defence 67-68, of Primary Educ. 68-72, of Nat. Educ. 72-73, of the Interior May 73-.
Ministry of the Interior, Rabat, Morocco.

Shiina, Etsusaburo, LL.D.; Japanese politician; b.1898; ed. Tokyo Univ.
Former Pres. Tohoku Wool Manufacturing Co. and Dir. Toho Bussan Trading Co.; mem. House of Reps.; Sec.-Gen. of Cabinet 59-60; Minister of Int. Trade and Industry 60-61, 67-68; Minister of Foreign Affairs 64-Dec. 66; Chair. Liberal Dem. Party Exec. Board Dec. 66-; Order of the Rising Sun, First Class, 68; Liberal Democrat.
14 Hanezawa-cho, Shibuya-ku, Tokyo, Japan.

Shilling, John Woollerton; South African mining official; b. 9 June 1913, S. Africa; s. of late Rev. and Mrs. W. W. Shilling; m. 1st Eileen P. Hargreaves 1942 (deceased), one s. two d.; m. 2nd Maureen Yardley (née Watt) 1971; ed. Kingswood Coll., Grahamstown, C.P.
Member of Side Bar 34-39; Legal Adviser, Transvaal and O.F.S. Chamber of Mines 46-53; Dir./Man. Anglo-American Corpn. of S. Africa Ltd. 53-74; Chair. of several gold mining companies in Anglo-American Group; Chair. Nuclear Fuels Corpn. of S. Africa Ltd. 69-74; Pres. S. African Chamber of Mines 71-72; retd. Sept. 74.
Leisure interests: shooting, fishing, tennis.
109 Boundary Lane, Parkmore, Johannesburg 2196, South Africa.

Shilo, Nikolai Alexeyevich; Soviet geologist; b. 7 April 1913, Pyatigorsk, Stavropolye Region; s. of Aleksey Vasilyevich and Akulina Dmitrievna Shilo; m. Valeria Arsentyevna Shilo 1954; one s. two d.; ed. Leningrad Prospecting Inst.
Geologist in gold fields in north-eastern district of U.S.S.R. 37-49; Scientific Assoc., U.S.S.R. Research Inst. of Gold and Rare Metals 49-60; Dir. North-Eastern Complex Research Inst., Siberian Dept. of U.S.S.R. Acad. of Sciences 60-; corresp. mem. U.S.S.R. Acad. of Sciences 64-70, Academician 70-; mem. C.P.S.U. 41-; U.S.S.R. Acad. of Sciences, Far Eastern Branch 70-.
Leisure interests: politics, economics.
NECRI, Portovaya Street 16, Magadan 685000; Home: Gorky Square 6, Apt. 39, Magadan 685000, U.S.S.R.
Telephone: 3-06-11 (Office); 2-37-05 (Home).

Shima, Shigenobu; Japanese former diplomatist; b. 1907, Inchon, Korea; s. of Shigeharu and Sada (Nishimura) Shima; m. Sanaye Shimasuye 1935; two d.; ed. Univ. of Tokyo.
Entered diplomatic service 30; served London 31-35; Private Sec. to Foreign Minister 36-37; Peking, Tientsin and Tsingtao 37-41; Foreign Ministry 42-47; Dir. Osaka Liaison Office 48-51; Counsellor (European Affairs), Foreign Ministry 51-53; Minister in Washington 54-57; Amb. to Sweden 57-59; Deputy Vice-Minister for Foreign Affairs 59-62, Vice-Minister 63-64; Amb. to U.K. 64-68; Grand Master of Ceremonies, Imperial Japanese Court 68-73.
Leisure interests: music, hi-fi.
Shirogane 4-10-11, Minato-ku, Tokyo 108, Japan.
Telephone: (03) 443-0677.

Shimoda, Takeso; Japanese judge; b. 1907; ed. Tokyo Imperial Univ.
Entered Japanese Diplomatic Service 31, served Nanking, Moscow, The Hague; Dir. Treaties Bureau Ministry of Foreign Affairs 52-57; Minister to U.S.A. 57-60; Adviser to Minister of Foreign Affairs 60-61; Ambassador to Belgium and Chief of Japanese Del. to European Communities 60-63; Ambassador to U.S.S.R. 63-65; Vice Minister of Foreign Affairs 65-67; Amb. to U.S.A. 67-70; Justice of the Supreme Court 70-; Judge, Perm. Court of Arbitration 72-; Dir. Japanese Asscn. of Int. Law, Japanese Asscn. of Maritime Law; Hon. mem. American Bar Asscn.; Hon. LL.D. (Univ. of Nebraska); numerous foreign decorations.
S-16-12, Yayoi-cho, Nakano-ku, Tokyo, Japan.

Shinde, Annasaheb P., B.A., LL.B.; Indian lawyer and agriculturist; b. 21 Jan. 1922, Padali, Maharashtra Province; s. of Shri Pandurang Vithoba Shinde; m. Shrimati Hirabai 1947; three s. one d.; ed. Law Colls., Poona and Ahmedabad.
Practised law before political imprisonment 44; organized landowning farmers who had leased land to private sugar factories for nominal rents and became heavily involved in educational and agricultural projects; Chair. Maharashtra State Co-operative Sugar Factories Federation, Poona; Vice-Chair. Pravara Co-operative Sugar Factory, Pravaranagar, Pravara Agricultural and Industrial Devt. Co-operative Soc. Ltd.; mem. Man. Cttees., All India Co-operative Sugar Factories Fed., New Delhi, Maharashtra State Co-operative Union; Dir. Land Mortgage Bank, Ahmednagar; mem. All India Congress Cttee. and Maharashtra Pradesh Congress Cttee.; mem. Lok Sabha 62-67; Parl. Sec. to Minister of Food and Agriculture 62-63, to Minister for Community Devt. and Co-operation 64-65; Deputy Minister for Food, Agriculture, Community Devt. and Co-operation 66-67; Minister of State for Food, Agriculture, Community Devt. and Co-operation 67-71; Minister of State for Agriculture 71-.
Leisure interests: gardening, reading.
Publs. *Problems of Indian Agriculture and Food, The Indo-Pakistan Conflict.*
1 Motilal Nehru Marg, New Delhi, India.

Shindo, Sadakazu; Japanese business executive; b. 4 March 1910; ed. Kyushu Univ.
Pres., Mitsubishi Electric Corpn.
Mitsubishi Electric Corpn., 2-2-3 Marunouchi, Chiyoda-ku, Tokyo; 1-12-8 Gotokuji, Setagayaku, Tokyo, Japan.
Telephone: 03-425-2500 (Home).

Shinichi, Ishino; Japanese banker; b. 13 March 1912, Kobe; m. Kazuko Ujiie 1936; ed. Tokyo Imperial Univ.
Deputy Vice-Minister of Finance 57; Dir.-Gen. Banking Bureau 59, Budget Bureau 61, Vice-Minister 63, retd. from Ministry of Finance 65; Pres. Bank of Kobe Ltd. 67-73, The Taiyo Kobe Bank Ltd. (following merger of Bank of Kobe Ltd. with Taiyo Bank) 73-.
Leisure interests: golf, haiku, "Go" game.
5-31 Rokuban-Cho, Kuraken, Nishinomiya City, Hyogo Pref., Japan.
Telephone: 0798-33-1020.

Shinn, Richard Randolph; American insurance executive; b. 7 Jan. 1918, Lakewood, N.J.; s. of Clayton Randolph and Carrie McGravey Shinn; m. Mary Helen Shea; one s. two d.; ed. Lakewood public schools and Rider Coll., Trenton, N.J.
Joined Metropolitan Life's Group Insurance Div. May 39; Asst. to Group Sales Man. 48-50, Asst. Man. on group staff 50-52, responsible for group sales unit 52-53; Asst. Vice-Pres. 53-57; Third Vice-Pres. 57-59, Second Vice-Pres. 59-63, Vice-Pres. 63-64, Senior Vice-Pres. 64-65, Admin. Vice-Pres. 65-66, Exec. Vice-Pres. Oct. 66-May 68, Senior Exec. Vice-Pres. May 68, with exec. responsibility for Exec. Office for Personal Insurance; Pres. and mem. Board of Dirs. 69-73, Pres. and Chief Exec. Officer 73-; mem. Board of Dirs. Chase Manhattan Bank, May Dept. Stores Co., Allied Chemicals and Board of Trustees, American Coll. of Life Underwriters.
Leisure interests: outdoor sports, including yachting and golf.
Metropolitan Life Insurance Company, 1 Madison Avenue, New York, N.Y. 10010; Home: 31 Lindsay Drive, Greenwich, Conn. 06830, U.S.A.

Shinohara, Shuichi; Japanese banker; b. 13 Oct. 1906, Nagano-shi, Nagano Pref.; s. of Shigetaro and Hana Shinohara; m. Shizu Miyajima 1932; two d.; ed. Faculty of Law, Univ. of Tokyo.
Joined The Bank of Japan 30, Chief, Statistics Dept. 46,

Man. Sendai Branch 47, Deputy Chief, Personnel Dept. 52, Chief, Business Dept. 54, Chief, Bank Relations and Supervision Dept. 57-58; Deputy Pres. The Kyowa Bank Ltd. 58-62, Pres. 62-71, Chair. 71-.
Leisure interest: golf.
The Kyowa Bank Ltd., 5-1, 1-chome, Marunouchi, Chiyoda-ku, Tokyo; 7-13, Nishiogi Kita 1-chome, Suginami-ku, Tokyo, Japan.
Telephone: 390-4080.

Shinwell, Baron (Life Peer), cr. 70, of Easington, Durham; **Emanuel Shinwell,** P.C., C.H.; British politician; b. 18 Oct. 1884, London.
Labour M.P. for Linlithgow 22-24, 28-31, Seaham 35-50, Easington 50-70; Financial Sec., War Office 29-30; Parl. Sec. to Dept. of Mines 24, 30-31; Minister of Fuel and Power 45-47; Sec. of State for War 47-50; Minister of Defence 50-51; fmr. Chair. and mem. Nat. Exec. Labour Party; Chair. Parl. Labour Party 64-67.
Publs. *The Britain I Want* 43, *When the Men Come Home* 44, *Conflict without Malice* 55, *The Labour Story* 63, *I've Lived Through It All* (autobiog.) 73.
House of Lords, London, S.W.1, England.

Shiomi, Shunji; Japanese politician; b. 1907; ed. Tokyo Univ.
Deputy Sec.-Gen. Liberal-Democratic Party; Parl. Vice-Minister of Defence; Minister of Home Affairs; mem. House of Councillors; Minister of Health and Welfare 72-74; founded Shiomi Library, Kochi City 72.
Ministry of Health and Welfare, Tokyo, Japan.

Shirer, William Lawrence, B.A., LITT.D.; American author and journalist; b. 23 Feb. 1904, Chicago, Illinois; ed. Coe Coll.
Foreign corresp. various American newspapers, Europe, Near East and India 25-45; Pres. Authors' Guild 56-57; contrib. various publs.; Légion d'Honneur.
Leisure interests: music, gardening, sailing, hiking.
Publs. *Berlin Diary* 41, *End of a Berlin Diary* 47, *The Traitor* (novel) 50, *Midcentury Journey* 52, *Stranger Come Home* (novel) 54, *The Challenge of Scandinavia* 55, *The Consul's Wife* (novel) 56, *The Rise and Fall of the Third Reich* 60, *The Rise and Fall of Adolf Hitler* 61, *The Sinking of the Bismarck* 62, *The Collapse of the Third Republic* 69.
7 West 43rd Street, New York City, N.Y., U.S.A.

Shirley, George; American tenor; b. 18 April 1934, Indianapolis, Ind.; *s.* of Irving E. and Daisy (née Bell) Shirley; *m.* Gladys Lee Ishop 1956; one *s.* one *d.*; ed. Wayne State Univ., Wilberforce Univ.
Debuts with Metropolitan Opera, N.Y.C. Opera, Festival of Two Worlds (Spoleto, Italy), Santa Fé Opera 61, Teatro Colón, Buenos Aires 65, La Scala, Milan 65, Glyndebourne Festival 66, Royal Opera, Covent Garden, Scottish Opera 67, Vienna Festival 72; Nat. Arts Club Award 60, Concorso di Musica e Danza (Italy) 60.
Leisure interests: tennis, sketching and cartoons, writing.
c/o Shaw Concerts, 233 W. 49th Street, Suite 800, New York, N.Y. 10019, U.S.A.; Artists International Management, 5 Regent's Park Road, London, NW1 7TL, England; and Ann Summers Dossena, Via Maria dei Fiori 42, 00187 Rome, Italy.
Telephone: (212) 581-4654 (U.S.A.); 01-485-1099 (England); 678-5747 (Italy).

Shirley-Quirk, John, C.B.E., B.SC.; British concert and opera singer; b. 28 Aug. 1931, Liverpool; *s.* of Joseph Stanley and Amelia Shirley-Quirk; *m.* Dr. Patricia Hastie 1952; one *s.* one *d.*; ed. Holt School, Liverpool, and Liverpool Univ.
Flying Officer, R.A.F. (Educ. Branch) 52-55; Asst. Lecturer, Acton Tech. Coll. 56-60; Vicar Choral, St.. Paul's Cathedral 60-61; professional singer 61-; Hon. R.A.M. 72; many recordings and first performances, particularly works of Benjamin Britten.

Leisure interests: clocks, canals.
White House, 82 Heath End Road, Flackwell Heath, Bucks., HP10 9ES, England.
Telephone: 06285 21325.

Shitikov, Aleksey Pavlovich; Soviet politician; b. 1912; ed. Gorki Agricultural Inst. and Higher Party School.
Member C.P.S.U. 39-; party work, Soviet army 41-45; Apparatus, Khabarovsk Territorial Cttee. C.P.S.U. 45-48, 50-52; Sec. Kamchatka Regional Cttee. C.P.S.U., the First Sec. Jewish Autonomous Region 48-55; Sec. Khabarovsk Territorial Cttee. C.P.S.U. 55-57, First Sec. 57-70; Chair. Soviet of Union, U.S.S.R. Supreme Soviet 70-, U.S.S.R. Parliamentary Group of Interparliamentary Union 70-; mem. Central Cttee. C.P.S.U. 61-; Deputy to U.S.S.R. Supreme Soviet 54-; mem. Cttee. for Foreign Affairs, Soviet of Union-70; Chair. Soviet Cttee. for European Security and Co-operation 71-.
Presidium of the U.S.S.R. Supreme Soviet, The Kremlin, Moscow.

Shklovsky, Iosif Samuilovich; Soviet astrophysicist; b. 1 July 1916, Glukhov, Ukraine; ed. Moscow Univ.
Head, Dept. of Radio Astronomy, Shternberg Astronomical Inst., Moscow 38-; Prof. Moscow Univ.; Lenin Prize 60; Corresp. mem. U.S.S.R. Acad. of Sciences 66-.
Publs. *The Solar Corona* 51, *The Nature of the Aurora Polaris' Radiance* 52, *The Origin of Cosmic Rays and Radio Astronomy* 53, *The Origin of the Crab Nebula's Radiance* 53, *Radio Astronomy* 55, *Cosmic Radio-Frequency Emission* 56, *The Nature of the Earth's Third Radiation Belt* 60, *On the Distant Planet of Venus* 61, *The Universe, Life and Reason* 62.
Moscow State University, Leninskie Gory, Moscow, U.S.S.R.

Shkuratov, Ivan Fyodorovich; Soviet trade union official; b. 9 Jan. 1912, Bolshaya Krasnastavka, Voronezh Region; ed. Moscow Zootechnical Inst.
State-Farm Zootechnician 35-40; Soviet Army 41-46; State Farm Dir. 46-49; U.S.S.R. Ministry of State Farms 49-56; Dep. Chair. Cen. Cttee. of Agricultural and Procurement Workers' Union 56-58, Sec. 58-62, Chair. 62-; Sec. All-Union Central Council of Trade Unions 64-68; mem. Presidium All-Union Central Council of Trade Unions 68-; mem. C.P.S.U.; Order of Red Star, Red Banner of Labour, Badge of Honour, etc.
Central Committee of Agricultural and Procurement Workers' Union, 42 Leninsky Prospekt, Moscow, U.S.S.R.

Shoaib, Mohamed, H.PK., M.B.E., M.A., LL.B.; Pakistani diplomatist and banker; b. 5 Sept. 1905, Jaunpur, India; *s.* of Mohammad Abdussatar and Ayesha; *m.* Hameeda Fatima Shoaib 1959; four *s.* one step-*s.* two *d.* two step-*d.*; ed. Allahabad Univ.
Appointed to Provincial Admin. Service 26, to Indian Mil. Accounts Dept. 29; Chief Controller Army Factory Accounts, Govt. of India 42; after Partition appointed Adviser on Mil. Finance; Special Del. Sterling Accounts Settlement Confs.; Exec. Dir. Int. Bank for Reconstruction and Devt. representing Pakistan, U.A.R., Ethiopia, Iran and Middle Eastern countries 52-58; Minister of Finance, Govt. of Pakistan Nov. 58-62; Minister of Econ. Co-ordination Feb.-May 62; Exec. Dir. World Bank June 62-Feb. 63, Vice-Pres. 66-75; Minister of Finance (Pakistan) Dec. 62-66; Fellow, Inst. of Cost and Management Accountants (London), Inst. of Costs and Works Accountants (India), Inst. of Industrial Accountants (Pakistan); mem. Nat. Asscn. of Accountants, New York.
Leisure interests: bridge, reading, sport.
[*Died* 13 *May* 1976.]

Shockley, William (Bradford), B.SC., PH.D.; American scientist; b. 13 Feb. 1910, London, England of American parents; *s.* of William Hillman and May (née Bradford)

Shockley; *m.* 1st Jean Alberta Bailey 1933; two *s.* one *d.*; *m.* 2nd Emmy Lanning 1955; ed. California Inst. of Technology, Massachusetts Inst. of Technology.
Member Technical Staff 36-42, Dir. Solid State Physics Research Program 45-54 and Dir. Transistor Physics Research 54-55, Bell Telephone Laboratories; Dir. of Research, anti-submarine Warfare Operations Research Group U.S. Navy 42-44; Expert Consultant, Office of the Sec. of War 44-45; Visiting Lecturer Princeton Univ. 46; Scientific Adviser, Policy Council, Joint Research and Devt. Board 47-49; Scientific Advisory Panel, U.S. Army 51-63; Visiting Prof. California Inst. of Technology 54-55; Deputy Dir. and Dir. of Research, Weapons Systems Evaluation Group, Dept. of Defence 54-55; Dir. Semi-conductor Laboratory of Beckman Instruments Inc. 55-58; Pres. Shockley Transistor Corpn. 58-60; Dir. Shockley Transistor (unit of Clevite Transistor) 60-63; Mem. of President's Science Advisory Comm. on Scientific and Technical Manpower 62; Alexander M. Poniatoff Prof. of Engineering and Applied Science, Stanford Univ. 63-75, Emer. Prof. 75-; mem. Air Force Scientific Advisory Board 58-62; Exec. Consultant to Bell Labs. 65-75; Sr. Consultant to Army Scientific Advisory Panel; holder of over 90 U.S. patents; mem. Scientific and Tech. Advisory Comm. to NASA, Nat. Acad. of Sciences, American Inst. of Physics, Inventors Hall of Fame of Nat. Council of Patent Law Asscn.; Fellow I.E.E.E.; Hon. Dr. (Univ. Pa.) 55, (Rutgers) 56, (Gustavus Adolphus Coll.) 63; numerous awards 46-69 including Medal for Merit 46, Nobel Prize for Physics 56; NASA Certificate of Appreciation 69 and NASA Public Service Group Achievement Award 69.
Leisure interests: swimming, skin diving, mountain climbing.
Publs. *Electrons and Holes in Semi-conductors* 50, *Imperfections of Nearly Perfect Crystals* 52; *Mechanics* (co-author) 66, and many articles.
Stanford Electronics Laboratories, Department of Electrical Engineering, McC 202 Stanford University, Stanford, Calif. 94305; 797 Esplanada Way, Stanford, Calif. 94305, U.S.A.
Telephone: 321-2300, Extension 4675.

Shogo, Watanabe; Japanese executive; b. 31 Aug. 1915; ed. Tokyo Univ.
With the Industrial Bank of Japan Ltd. 38-62; Man. Dir. Nikko Securities Co. 62, Senior Man. Dir. 63, Vice-Pres. 66, Pres. 70-; Pres. Nikko Research Centre Ltd. 70-.
Nikko Research Centre Ltd., 3-1, Marunouchi 3-chome, Chiyoda-ku, Tokyo; Home: 6-2, Eifuku 3-chome, Suginami-ku, Tokyo, Japan.
Telephone: (03) 328-4205 (Home).

Shokin, Alexandr Ivanovich; Soviet politician; b. 1909; ed. Bauman Higher Technical School, Moscow.
Engineer, Ministry of Shipbuilding Industry 32-38, Chief Engineer, Ministry of Shipbuilding Industries 38-43; State work 43-49; Dep. Minister, U.S.S.R. Communications Industry 49-53, First Dep. Minister 54-57; First Dep. Chair. State Cttee. of Council of Ministers for Electronics 58-61, Chair. 61-65; U.S.S.R. Minister of Electronics Industries 65-; Alt. mem. Cen. Cttee. of C.P.S.U. 61-66, mem. 66-; Deputy to U.S.S.R. Supreme Soviet 62-; State Prize 52, 53.
U.S.S.R. Ministry of Electronics Industries, Moscow, U.S.S.R.

Sholokhov, Mikhail Alexandrovich; Soviet novelist; b. 24 May 1905, Khutor Kruzhilin, Rostov Region (fmrly. Region of Don Kossak Army).
Member Acad. of Sciences of U.S.S.R. 39-; mem. C.P.S.U. 32-; awarded State Prize 41; corresp., broadcaster; Deputy to Supreme Soviet 46-; mem. Comm. for Foreign Affairs, Soviet of Nationalities; mem. Presidium Union of Soviet Writers 54-; mem. C.P.S.U.

Cen. Cttee. 61-; Nobel Prize for Literature 65; Hero of Socialist Labour 67; Lenin Prize; Order of Lenin (eight times); Hon.D.Iur. (St. Andrews 75).
Publs. *Dvukhmuznaya* (Woman with two husbands) 25, *Alyoshkino Serdtse* (The Heart of Alyoshka) 25, *Donskiye Razkazy* (Stories of the Don) 26, *Tikhy Don* (And Quiet Flows the Don) (4 vols.) 28-40, *Podnyataya Tselina* (Virgin Soil Upturned) 32-33, 2nd vol. 59, *They Fought for their Country* 66, *One Man's Destiny* 67; Short stories: *Smertelnyi Vrag* (The Mortal Enemy), *Chervotochina* (Dry Rot), *Semeynyi Chelovek* (The Family Man), *Zherebyonok* (The Colt), *Collected Works* (Vols. 1-8) 59-62.
U.S.S.R. Union of Writers, Ulitsa Vorovskogo 52, Moscow, U.S.S.R.

Shone, Sir Robert Minshull, C.B.E., M.A., M.ENG.; British economist; b. 1906, Birkenhead; ed. Sedbergh School, Liverpool Univ. and Univ. of Chicago.
Industrial work 28-32; Commonwealth Fellow (U.S.A.) 32-34; Lecturer, London School of Econs. 35-36; Gen. Dir. Ministry of Supply, Iron and Steel Control 42-45; Dir. British Iron and Steel Fed. 50-53; exec. mem. Iron and Steel Board 53-61; Dir.-Gen. Nat. Econ. Devt. Council 62-66; Dir. White Drummond Co. Ltd. 66-; Visiting Prof. of Applied Econs., City Univ. (London) 67-; Dir. Rank Org. Ltd. 68-, A.P.V. Holdings Ltd. 70-; Special Prof. Nottingham Univ. 71-73.
Leisure interest: golf.
Publs. *Problems of Investment* 71, *Price and Investment Relationships* 75, and numerous articles in journals.
7 Windmill Hill, London, N.W.3, England.
Telephone: 01-435 1930.

Shonfield, Andrew Akiba; British economist; b. 10 Aug. 1917, Tadworth, Surrey; *s.* of Dr. Avigdor Schonfeld and Rachel Lea Sternberg; *m.* Zuzanna Maria Przeworska; one *s.* one *d.*; ed. Magdalen Coll. Oxford Univ.
Army service World War II; Econ. Affairs Commentator on radio, television and in newspapers 47; Foreign Editor, Financial Times 49-57; Econ. Editor, The Observer 58-61; Dir. of Studies, Royal Inst. of Int. Affairs 61-68, Dir. 72-; Chair., Social Science Research Council 69-71; mem. Royal Comm. on Trade Unions and Employers' Asscns. 65-67; mem. Duncan Cttee. on British Overseas Representation 68-69; mem. Vedel Cttee. on EEC Insts., European Commission 71-72; Reith Lecturer 72; Hon. D.Lit. (Loughborough); Cortina-Ulysse Prize (*Europe: Journey to an Unknown Destination*) 74.
Publs. *British Economic Policy since the War* 58, *The Attack on World Poverty* 60, *A Man Beside Himself* (novel) 64, *Modern Capitalism: the Changing Balance of Public and Private Power* 65, *Europe: Journey to an Unknown Destination* 73.
Royal Institute of International Affairs, Chatham House, 10 St. James's Square, London, S.W.1, England.
Telephone: 01-930-2233.

Shonin, Col. Georgy Stepanovich; Soviet cosmonaut; b. 2 Aug. 1935, Rovenki, Ukraine; ed. School of Naval Military Pilots and Zhukovsky Air Force Engineering Acad.
Air Force Fighter Pilot in Baltic and North Fleets 57-63; mem. C.P.S.U. 57-; with Cosmonaut Training Unit 63-; Commdr. of space ship *Soyuz*-6, which made a group flight with *Soyuz*-7 and *Soyuz*-8 Oct. 69; Hero of Soviet Union, Gold Star, Order of Lenin, Pilot-Cosmonaut of the U.S.S.R., K. Tsiolkovsky Gold Medal of U.S.S.R. Acad. of Sciences.
Zvezdny Gorodok, Moscow, U.S.S.R.

Shono, Senkichi, LL.B.; Japanese banker; b. 22 Sept. 1913, Tokyo; *s.* of Danroku and Shige Shono; *m.* Yuki Minoda 1943; one *s.* two *d.*; ed. Tokyo Univ.
Joined The Mitsui Trust and Banking Co., Ltd. 37, Dir. and Man., Security Dept. 59, Dir. and Man. Nagoya

Branch 62, Man. Dir. and Man., Head Office Business Dept. 65, Senior Man. Dir. 68, Pres. 71-; Dir. Japan Fed. of Employers Asscn. 71-, Fed. of Econ. Orgs. 71-, Mitsui Devt. Co. 72-, Mitsui Kanko Devt. Co. Ltd. 73-, Mitsui Memorial Hosp. 74-.
Leisure interests: listening to music, reading, golf.
Mitsui Trust & Banking Co. Ltd., 1-1 Nihonbashi-Muromachi, 2-chome, Chuo-ku, 103 Tokyo; Home: 1605 Fueta, Kamakura-shi, Kanagawa Pref., 248 Japan.
Telephone: 03-270-9511 (Office); 0467-31-1647 (Home).

Shoppee, Charles William, M.A., D.PHIL., PH.D., D.SC., F.R.S.; British university professor; b. 24 Feb. 1904, London; elder *s.* of J. W. and Elizabeth Shoppee; *m.* Eileen Alice West 1929; one *d.*; ed. Stationers' Company School, London, and Univs. of London, Leeds and Basle.
Senior Student of Royal Comm. for Exhbn. of 185 26-28; Asst. Lecturer and Lecturer in Organic Chem., Univ. of Leeds 29-39; Rockefeller Research Fellow, Univ. of Basle 39-45; Reader in Chem., Univ. of London, at Royal Cancer Hospital 45-48; Prof. of Chem., Univ. of Wales, at Univ. Coll., Swansea 48-56; Prof. of Organic Chem., Univ. of Sydney 56-69, now Emer.; Robert A. Welch Prof. of Chem., Texas Technological Univ. 70-75; Reilly Lecturer, Univ. of Notre Dame 51; Visiting Prof. of Organic Chem., Duke Univ. 63, Univ. of Georgia 66, Univ. of Miss. 68; Fellow, Royal Soc. 56-, Fellow, Australian Acad. of Science 58-.
Leisure interests: bowls, music.
Publs. Some 200 scientific papers in *Journal of Chemical Society* (London), *Journal of American Chemical Society* and *Helvetica Chimica Acta.*
Department of Chemistry, Texas Technological Univ., Lubbock, Texas 79409, U.S.A.; Home: 41 Kenthurst Road, St. Ives, N.S.W. 2075, Australia.
Telephone: 806-743-3200 (Univ.); 449-1176 (Home).

Shore, Rt. Hon. Peter (David), P.C., M.P.; British politician; b. 20 May 1924; *m.* Elizabeth Catherine Wrong 1948; two *s.* two *d.*; ed. Quarry Bank High School, Liverpool, and King's Coll., Cambridge.
Member Labour Party 48-; Head of Research Dept., Labour Party 59-64; M.P. for Stepney 64-74, for Tower Hamlets, Stepney and Poplar 74-; Parl. Private Sec. to Prime Minister 65-66; Joint Parl. Sec. Ministry of Technology 66-67; Sec. of State for Econ. Affairs 67-69; Minister without Portfolio 69-70; Labour Party Spokesman on European Affairs 71-74; Sec. of State for Trade 74-76, for the Environment April 76-; Pres. British Overseas Trade Board 74-76.
Leisure interest: swimming.
Publ. *Entitled to Know* 66.
House of Commons, London, S.W.1, England.

Shore, Thomas Spencer, A.B., B.J., M.B.A.; American industrialist; b. 24 June 1903; ed. Univ. of Missouri and Harvard Univ.
With Goldman, Sachs & Co. N.Y. (Investment Bankers) 26-31; Vice-Pres. and Treas. The General Tire & Rubber Co., Akron, Ohio 31-43; Gen. Partner, Goldman, Sachs & Co. N.Y. 43-48; Pres. Eagle-Picher Industries Inc., Cincinnati, (fmrly Eagle-Picher Co.) 49-68, Chair. 68-; Dir. Cen. Trust Co., Cincinnati, Gas and Electric Co., Cluett, Peabody & Co., Kroger Co., Federated Dept. Stores Inc., Cincinnati Reds Inc., Armco Steel Corpn., Middletown, Ohio.
Office: American Building, Cincinnati, Ohio 45202; Home: Edwards and Walsh Roads, Cincinnati, Ohio 45208, U.S.A.

Shores, Louis, A.B., B.S. in L.S., M.S., PH.D.; American librarian, editor and writer; b. 14 Sept. 1904, Buffalo, N.Y.; *s.* of Paul and Ernestine (Lutenber) Shores; *m.* Geraldine Urist 1931; ed. Toledo, Columbia Univs., City of New York Coll., Chicago Univ. and George Peabody Coll.
Served in New York Public Library 26-28; Fisk Univ.

28-33; Dir. and Prof., Library School, George Peabody Coll. 33-46; Dean, Library School, Florida State Univ. 46-67, Dean Emer. 67-; Visiting Prof. McGill Univ. 30, Univ. of Dayton 31, Colorado State Coll. 36, Univ. of Southern Ill. 68, Univ. of Colorado 69, Dalhousie Univ. 70; Editor-in-Chief, *Colliers Encyclopedia* 60-; Legion of Merit; Fulbright Fellow, U.K. 51-52; Isadore Gilbert Mudge Award in reference librarianship 67; Beta Phi Mu Int. Library Science Honorary in Library Educ. 67; Hon. Dr. Humanistic Letters (Dallas Baptist Coll.).
Leisure interests: hiking, reading, book collecting, extrasensory perception.
Publs. *Origins of the American College Library* 34, *Bibliographies and Summaries in Education* (with another) 36, *Basic Reference Books* 37, 39, *How to Study* (with another) 48, *General Education* (with others) 49, *Highways in the Sky* 47, *Challenges to Librarianship* 53, *Basic Reference Sources* 54, *Instructional Materials* 60, *Mark Hopkins Log* 65, *The Library College* (with others) 66, *Tex-Tec* (with others) 68, *Library-College U.S.A.* 70, *Looking Forward to 1999* 72, *Library Education* 72, *Audiovisual Librarianship* 73.
Florida State University, Tallahassee, Florida; 2013 W. Randolph Circle, Tallahassee, Florida, 32303 U.S.A.
Telephone: 599-3132 (Office); 385-12708 (Home).

Short, Rt. Hon. Edward Watson, P.C., M.P.; British politician; b. 17 Dec. 1912; ed. Bede College, Durham. Served Second World War and became Capt. in Durham Light Infantry; Headmaster, Princess Louise County Secondary School, Blyth, Northumberland 47; Leader Labour Group, Newcastle City Council 50; M.P. for Newcastle upon Tyne Central 51-; Opposition Whip (N. Area) 55-62; Deputy Chief Opposition Whip 62-64; Parl. Sec. to Treasury and Govt. Chief Whip 64-66; Postmaster-Gen. 66-68; Sec. of State for Educ. and Science 68-70; Deputy Leader of Labour Party April 72-; Lord Pres. of Council, Leader of House of Commons 74-76.
House of Commons, London, S.W.1; 4 Patterdale Gardens, Newcastle upon Tyne 7, England.

Shoukry, Mohammed Anwar; Egyptian egyptologist; b. 1905; ed. Cairo Univ. Inst. of Egyptology and Univ. of Göttingen.
Assistant Prof. of Egyptology Cairo Univ. 48-52, Prof. 52-; Chief Archaeologist Cen. of Documentation of Egyptian Art and Civilisation 56-59; Dir.-Gen. Dept. of Egyptian Antiquities 59-66; Asst. Under-Sec. of State, Ministry of Culture and Nat. Guidance 61-70.
Publ. *Die Grabstatue im Alten Reich.*
c/o Ministry of Culture, Cairo, Egypt.

Showering, Keith Stanley; British business executive; b. 6 Aug. 1930, Shepton Mallet, Somerset; *s.* of late Herbert M. V. Showering and of Ada A. Showering; *m.* Marie Sadie Golden 1954; four *s.* two *d.*; ed. Wells Cathedral School.
Joined Showerings Ltd., Cidermakers and Brewers 47, Dir. 51; Founder Dir. Showerings, Vine Products & Whiteways Ltd. 61, Deputy Chair. 64-71, Chief Exec. 71; Man. Dir. Harveys of Bristol Ltd., John Harvey & Sons Ltd. 66-71; Chair. John Harvey & Sons Ltd. 71; Dir. Allied Breweries Ltd. 68, Vice-Chair. 69-75, Deputy Chair., Chair. 75; Dir. Guardian Royal Exchange 71, Vice-Chair. 74.
Leisure interests: farming, shooting.
Allied Breweries Ltd., 160 St. John Street, London, EC1P 1AR; Home: 16 Belgrave Mews West, London, S.W.1; and Sharcombe Park, Dinder, Wells, Somerset, BA5 3PG, England.

Shpedko, Ivan Fadeevich; Soviet ambassador to Pakistan 56-60, to Canada 63-68; see *The International Who's Who 1975-76.*

Shrimali, Kalu Lal, M.A., PH.D., LL.D., D.LITT.; Indian educationist and politician; b. 30 Dec. 1909, Udaipur, Rajasthan; *s.* of R. L. and K. Shrimali; *m.* Gangabai

Shrimali 1926; two s. three d.; ed. Banaras Hindu Univ., Calcutta Univ. and Columbia Univ., New York.
Life mem. Vidya Bhawan Soc. 31-; Dean, Faculty of Educ. Univ. of Rajputana 51-54; Parl. Sec. Ministry of Educ. New Delhi 53-55, Dep. Minister for Educ. 55-57, Minister of State in Ministry of Educ. and Scientific Research 57-58, Minister of Education 58-63; Vice-Chancellor Univ. of Mysore 64-69; Vice-Chancellor, Banaras Hindu Univ. 69-; Chair. Asscn. of Commonwealth Univs. 69-70; mem. Admin. Board, Int. Asscn. of Univs. 70-74; Chair. Inter-Univ. Board of India 72-73; Pres. All-India Fed. of Educ. Asscns.; Leader Indian Del. to U.S.S.R. (sponsored by Nat. Cttee., Indo-Soviet Cultural Soc.) June 73; Hon. D.Litt. (Banaras Hindu Univ. and Mysore Univ.), Hon. LL.D. (Vikram Univ.), Hon. D.Sc. (Kiev Univ.).
Leisure interest: gardening.
Publs. *Bachon Ki Kuch Samasyayen* (Hindi), *Shiksha aur Bhartiya Loktantra* (Hindi), *The Wardha Scheme*, *Adventures in Education, Problems of Education in India, Education in Changing India, The Prospects for Democracy in India, A Search for Values in Indian Education.*
Banaras Hindu University, Varanasi 5, India.
Telephone: 62339.

Shriver, (Robert) Sargent, Jr., B.S., LL.D.; American executive and public servant; b. 9 Nov. 1915, Westminster, Maryland; m. Eunice Kennedy 1953; four s. one d.; ed. Yale Univ.
Admitted to New York Bar 41; served U.S. Navy 41-45; Asst. Editor *Newsweek* 45-46; Exec. Dir. The Joseph P. Kennedy, Jr. Foundation 55-; Asst. Gen. Man. The Merchandise Mart 48-61; mem. Chicago Board of Educ. 55-60 (Pres. 56-60); Dir. The Peace Corps 61-66, Office of Econ. Opportunity 64-68; Special Asst. to the Pres. 64-68; Amb. to France 68-March 70; Democratic Vice-Presidential Candidate 72; Partner, Fried, Frank, Harris, Shriver & Jacobson; Official of numerous educational bodies; Hon. LL.D., Hon. L.H.D., Hon. D.C.L., etc. from numerous univs.; Golden Heart Presidential Award (Philippines), Médaille de Vermeil (City of Paris) and many national awards.
c/o Fried, Frank, Harris, Shriver & Jacobson. 120 Broadway, New York, N.Y. 10005; and 600 New Hampshire Avenue, N.W., Washington, D.C., U.S.A.
Telephone: 212-964-6500 (N.Y.); 202-965-9440.

Shtemenko, Gen. Sergei Matveyevich; Soviet army officer; b. 1907; ed. Artillery Coll., Military Acad. of Mechanization and Motorization and Military Acad. of General Staff.
Soviet Army Officer 29-; mem. C.P.S.U. 30-; Gen. Staff 40-; Chief of Operative Dept., Deputy Chief of Gen. Staff 43-48; Chief of Gen. Staff 48-52; Chief of Staff, Soviet Forces in Germany 53; Chief of Staff and First Deputy C.-in-C. 53-62; Chief of Main Staff of Land Forces 62-64; Deputy Chief of Gen. Staff of U.S.S.R. Mil. Forces 64-, and Chief of Joint Armed Forces of Warsaw Pact Countries 68-; awards include Orders of Lenin, of Red Banner (twice), of Suvorov 1st Class (twice) and 2nd Class, of Kutuzov 1st Class.
Publs. *General Staff in War Years* 68, and other works.
[*Died 22 April* 1976.]

Shuckburgh, Sir Evelyn, G.C.M.G., C.B.; British diplomatist; b. 26 May 1909, London; s. of Sir John Shuckburgh, K.C.M.G., C.B.; m. Hon. Nancy Brett 1937; two s. one d.; ed. Winchester Coll. and King's Coll., Cambridge.
Joined Foreign Office 33; served Cairo 37-39, Ottawa 40-42, Buenos Aires 42-45, Prague 45-47; Head of South American Dept., Foreign Office 47-48, Western Dept., Western Organisations Dept. 49-51; Private Sec. to Sec. of State for Foreign Affairs 51-54; Asst. Under-Sec. of State, Foreign Office 54-56; seconded to Imperial

Defence College as civilian instructor 56-58; Asst. Sec.-Gen. (Political Affairs) NATO 58-60; Dep. Under-Sec. Foreign Office, responsible for NATO, Western European Union, Council of Europe and West European Countries 60-62; Perm. Rep. to NATO 62-66; Amb. to Italy 66-69; Chair. Exec. Cttee., British Red Cross Soc. 70-; mem. Standing Comm. Int. Red Cross 73-.
Leisure interests: music, cabinet making.
High Wood, Watlington, Oxford, England.
Telephone: Watlington 2433.

Shuleikin, Vasily Vladimirovich; Soviet geophysicist; b. 13 Jan. 1895, Moscow; ed. St. Petersburg Polytechnic Inst.
Research devoted to problems of marine physics; founded the Black Sea Hydrophysical station in the Crimea 29, the Hydrophysical Marine Laboratory 35, the Chair of Marine Physics at Moscow Univ. 45; mem. U.S.S.R. Acad. of Sciences 46-; State prizewinner 42; awarded Order of Lenin (twice), Semyonov-Tyanshan Medal of Geographical Soc. of the U.S.S.R.
Publs. *Outline of Marine Physics* 49, *Marine Physics* 53, *Theory of Marine Waves* 56, *Short Course of Marine Physics* 59, *Physical Investigation of Oceans and Seas* 60.
Moscow State University, Leninsky Gory, Moscow, U.S.S.R.

Shull, Harrison, PH.D.; American professor of chemistry; b. 17 Aug. 1923, Princeton, N.J.; s. of Prof. George H. Shull and Mary J. Nicholl; m. 1st Jeanne L. Johnson 1948 (dissolved 1962), 2nd Wil J. Bentley 1962; five s. three d.; ed. Princeton Univ. and Univ. of Calif. (Berkeley).
National Research Council post-doctoral Fellow, Univ. of Chicago 48-49; Asst. Prof., Iowa State Univ., Ames, Iowa 49-54; Assoc. Prof., Indiana Univ. 55-58, Prof. 58-61, Research Prof. 61-; Dir. Research Computing Center 59-63, Dean Graduate School 65-72; Nat. Science Foundation Senior post-doctoral Fellow 68-69; Guggenheim Fellow 54-55; Alfred P. Sloan Research Fellow 56-58; Vice-Chancellor for Research and Development, Indiana Univ. 72-; mem. Nat. Acad. of Sciences; Fellow, Amer. Acad. of Arts and Sciences.
Publs. numerous articles in *Journal of Chemical Physics, Physical Review, Journal of Physical Chemistry* etc.
Chemistry Department, Indiana University, Bloomington, Ind. 47401; Home: RR 3, Box 25A, Bloomington, Ind. 47401, U.S.A.
Telephone: 812-337-6605 (Office); 812-336-3450 (Home).

Shultz, George Pratt, B.A., PH.D.; American economist, educator and government official; b. 13 Dec. 1920, New York; s. of Birl E. and Margaret Lennox Pratt Shultz; m. Helena M. O'Brien 1946; two s. three d.; ed. Princeton Univ. and Mass. Inst. of Technology.
Associate Prof. of Industrial Relations, Mass. Inst. of Technology 55-57; Senior Staff Economist, President's Council of Econ. Advisers 55-56; Prof. of Industrial Relations, Graduate School of Business, Univ. of Chicago 57-68; Consultant to Office of U.S. Sec. of Labor 59-60; mem. Illinois Governor's Cttee. on Unemployment 61-62; Consultant to Pres. Advisory Comm. on Labor-Management Policy 61-62; Dean, Graduate School of Business. Univ. of Chicago 62-68; Chair. U.S. Dept. of Labor Task Force on U.S. Employment Service 65-68; mem. U.S. Dept. of Labor Nat. Manpower Policy Task Force 66-68; Pres. Industrial Research Asscn. 68; U.S. Sec. of Labor 69-70; Dir. Office of Management and Budget, Exec. Office of the Pres. 70-72; U.S. Sec. of Treasury 72-74; Chair. Council on Econ. Policy 73-74; Exec. Vice-Pres. Bechtel Corpn. 74-; Prof. of Management and Public Policy, Graduate School of Business, Stanford Univ. 74-; mem. Foreign Intelligence Advisory Board 74-; mem. Treasury Advisory Cttee. on Reform of Int. Monetary System 75-; Dir. J. P. Morgan 74-, Borg-Warner Corpn., J. I. Case

Co., Stein Roe and Farnham Stock Fund and Balanced Fund, Fellow, Center for Advancement of Study in the Behavioral Sciences, Stanford, Calif.
Leisure interests: golf, tennis.
Publs. *The Dynamics of a Labor Market, Management Organization and the Computer, Strategies for the Displaced Worker, Guidelines, Informal Controls and the Market Place.*
5731 Blackstone Avenue, Chicago, Ill. 60637, U.S.A.

Shuman, Charles B.; American farmer and agricultural executive; b. 27 April 1907, Sullivan, Ill.; *s.* of Bliss and Grace Baker Shuman; *m.* 1st Ida Wilson 1933 (died 1954), 2nd Mabel Ervin 1956; four *s.* one *d.*; ed. Coll. of Agriculture, Univ. of Illinois.
Engaged in farming, Ill. 29-; mem. Board of Dirs., Ill. Agricultural Asscn. 40-45, Pres. 45-54; Pres. American Farm Bureau 54-70; mem. President's Highway Safety Comm. 53-61; Pres. American Agricultural Mutual Insurance Co. 54-70; American Agricultural Marketing Asscn. 60-70; Farm Bureau Trade Development Corpn. 60-69; mem. Nat. Livestock and Meat Board 55-69; Comm. on Money and Credit 59-61; mem. Export-Import Advisory Cttee. 70-71; mem. Board of Trustees, Millikin Univ.; Board of Regents Northern Ill. Univ., Ill. State Univ., Samgamon State Univ., Board of Dirs. Ill. Power Co., Gen. Telephone Co. of Ill., Advisory Cttee. Chicago Mercantile Exchange, Board of Dirs., U.S. Railway Asscn.
Leisure interests: fishing, gardening.
RFD No. 1, Sullivan, Ill., U.S.A.
Telephone: 217-728-7235.

Shumauskas, Moteyus Yuozo; Soviet politician; b. 15 Nov. 1905, Kaunas City, Lithuania; ed. Int. Lenin School.
Member Communist Party 24; forced labour and concentration camps 29, 31-37, 39-40; Deputy, People's Seym, Lithuania 40-; Deputy-Chair. Council of Lithuanian People's Commissariat; Chair. Lithuanian Planning Cttee. 45-50; Deputy, U.S.S.R. Supreme Soviet 46-; mem. Lithuanian S.S.R. Supreme Soviet 47-; First Sec. Sjauljay Party Cttee. 50-53; First Deputy-Chair., Lithuanian Council of Ministers 53, Chair. 56-67; Pres. of Presidium of Supreme Soviet of Lithuanian S.S.R. 67-75; Vice-Chair. Presidium of Supreme Soviet of U.S.S.R. 67-75 (retd.); Deputy to U.S.S.R. Supreme Soviet 46-, mem. Bureau Cen. Cttee. Lithuanian C.P. 49-63, 66-, mem. Presidium 63-66; Alt. mem. Cen. Cttee. C.P.S.U. 56-; Order of Lenin 43, 51, 58, 65; Order of the Red Banner of Labour; Order of the Great Patriotic War (1st Class); Order (2nd Class) of the Cross of Grunvald, Poland.
Presidium of Supreme Soviet of Lithuanian S.S.R., Vilnius, U.S.S.R.

Shumway, Forrest N.; American business executive; b. 21 March 1927; ed. Stanford Univ.
In U.S. Marine Corps; Senior Law Clerk and Deputy County Counsel, Los Angeles until 57; joined Legal Dept., Signal Oil and Gas Co. (now Signal Companies Inc.) 57, Sec. 59-60, Asst. Gen. Counsel 60-61, Vice-Pres. and Gen. Counsel 61-64, Dir. 61-, Pres. 64-; Dir. The Garrett Corpn., Mack Trucks Inc., W. R. Grace & Co., Transamerica Corpn., United Calif. Bank; official of civic orgs.
Signal Companies Inc., 9665 Wilshire Boulevard, Beverly Hills, Calif. 90212, U.S.A.

Shumway, Norman Edward, M.D., PH.D.; American surgeon; b. 1923, Kalamazoo, Mich.; *m.* Mary Lou Sturman; one *s.* three *d.*; ed. Vanderbilt Univ. and Univ. of Minnesota.
Intern, Univ. of Minnesota Hospitals 49-50, Medical Fellow in Surgery 50-51, 53, 54; Nat. Heart Inst. Research Fellow 54-56, Special Trainee 56-57; mem.

Surgical Staff, Stanford Univ. Hospitals 58-, Asst. Prof. of Surgery 59-61, Assoc. Prof. 61-, Head of Div. of Cardiovascular Surgery 64, Prof. of Surgery 65, Prof. Cardiovascular Surgery 74; Chair. Dept. of Cardiovascular Surgery, Stanford Univ. Medical Center 74-; has performed heart transplant operations.
Division of Cardiovascular Surgery, Department of Surgery, Stanford University Medical Center, Stanford, Calif. 94305, U.S.A.
Telephone: (415) 497-5771.

Shuster, George Nauman, A.B., A.M., C.D'APT., PH.D.; American educationist; b. 27 Aug. 1894; ed. Univ. of Notre Dame. Université de Poitiers, Colombia Univ.
Chairman, Dept. of English, Univ. of Notre Dame 20-24; Man. Ed. *Commonweal* 25-37; Fellow, Carl Schurz Foundation 33-34; Fellow, Social Science Research Council 37-38; Pres. Hunter Coll. of the Research Council 37-38; Pres. Hunter Coll. of the City of New York 39-60, Pres. Emeritus 60-; Asst. to the Pres. and Prof. of English, Univ. of Notre Dame 61-; mem. Gen. Advisory Cttee., Div. of Cultural Relations, U.S. Dept. of State 41-44; Land Comm. for Bavaria, Dept. of State 50-51; U.S. rep., Exec. Board UNESCO 58-64; Trustee, Carnegie Endowment for Int. Peace; mem. Board of Editors, *Encyclopaedia Britannica*; several foreign awards and hon. degrees.
Publs. *Catholic Spirit in Modern English Literature 22, Catholic Spirit in America 26, The Germans 31, Strong Rules 34, The English Ode from Milton to Keats 39, Short History of Germany* (with A. Bergstraesser) *39, Religion behind the Iron Curtain 52, In Silence I Speak 58, Education and Moral Wisdom 60, The Ground I Walked On 61, UNESCO: Assessment and Promise 63, Catholic Education in a Changing World 67.*
2819 York Road, South Bend, Ind. 46614, U.S.A.

Siassi, Ali-Akbar, PH.D.; Iranian psychologist and politician; b. 1896, Teheran; *s.* of Mohammad Hassan and Sedigheh Sadeghi; *m.* Roshan Maleh Bayat 1932; three *s.* one *d.*; ed. Persia and France.
Professor Univ. of Teheran 27-; Head Dept. of Advanced Studies of the Min. of Educ. 32; Chancellor of the Univ. of Teheran 42; Min. of Educ. 43; drafted bill and law for national compulsory free education, and took necessary measures for its enforcement 43; Min. of State without portfolio 45; Minister of Education 48-50; Minister of Foreign Affairs 50; mem. of the Supreme Council of Educ.; del. III Int. Congress of Persian Art and Archaeology 35, UN Conf. San Francisco 45; Pres. Iranian del. UNESCO Conf. Paris 49, Int. Conf. of Univs. 50, UNESCO Conf. Paris 51, Int. Conf. of Univs., Mexico City 60, Royal Soc. Tricentenary Celebrations, London 60; Perm. mem. of the Persian Acad.; Hon. Pres. Univ. of Teheran; mem. Int. Cttee. Scientific and Cultural History of Humanity; Pres. Iranian Psychological Asscn., Iranian Council of Philosophy and Human Sciences, Irane-Djavan Asscn., Board of Trustees Girls' Coll. of Iran; mem. Royal Cultural Council, Int. Council of Psychologists, Int. Asscn. of Applied Psychology and others; Commdr. Légion d'Honneur; Commdr. Palmes Académiques, Nishane-Elmy and others; Hon. degrees, Univ. Charles I, Prague, Strasbourg Univ., France, etc.
Leisure interests: reading, writing, travelling, tennis, bridge.
Publs. include: *L'Education en Perse 21, La Perse au Contact de l'Occident 31, La Méthode des Tests 31, Le Génie et l'Art iraniens aux prises avec l'Islam 35, De l'Unesco à la Sorbonne 53, L'Iran au XIXe siècle* (all in French); *Psychology 38, Educational Psychology for Teachers' Colleges 41, Introduction to Philosophy 47, Logic and Methodology 48, Mind and Body 53, The Psychology of Avicenna and its similarities with the Modern Psychology 54, Logic 56, Ethics 57, Logic and Philosophy 58, Intelligence and Reason 62, Criminal*

Psychology 64, *Psychology of Personality* 70, *Theories of Personality* 75 (all in Persian).
President Roosevelt Avenue, Namdjou Street, Teheran, Iran.
Telephone: 826776.

Sibley, Antoinette, C.B.E.; British ballerina; b. 27 Feb. 1939, Bromley, Kent; *d.* of Edward G. Sibley and Winifred Smith; *m.* 1st Michael Somes 1964 (separated 1969), 2nd Panton Corbett 1974.
Joined the Royal Ballet 56, Soloist 59, Principal Ballerina 60-; dances leading roles in: *Swan Lake, Sleeping Beauty, Coppelia, The Nutcracker, La Fille Mal Gardée, Romeo and Juliet, Jabez and the Devil* (created role of Mary), *The Dream* (created Titania), *Jazz Calendar* (created Friday's Child), *Enigma Variations* (created Dorabella), *Thais* (created Thais), *Triad* (created the Girl), *Manon*, etc.
Leisure interests: doing nothing, opera, cinema, reading.
c/o The Royal Ballet, Covent Garden, London, W.C.2, England.

Sibley, Shermer L.; American business executive; b. 24 Sept. 1913, Oakland, Calif.; *m.* Mary Horwinski 1942; two *s.* one *d.*; ed. Technical High School, Oakland and Univ. of Calif.
Joined Pacific Gas and Electric Co. 36, Vice-Pres. and Asst. Gen. Man. 55, Vice-Pres. and Gen. Man. 58, Pres. and Chief Operating Officer 65, Pres. and Chief Exec. Officer 69, Chair. of Board and Chief Exec. Officer 72-; Dir. Del Monte Corpn., Gen. Motors Corpn.; mem. Inst. of Electrical and Electronics Engineers, Edison Electric Inst.; mem. The Business Council; mem. numerous civic and educational cttees. etc.
Leisure interests: hunting, fishing, tennis.
Pacific Gas and Electric Co., 77 Beale Street, San Francisco, Calif. 94106, U.S.A.

Sicat, Gerardo P., M.A., PH.D.; Philippine professor of economics and government official; b. 7 Oct. 1935; *s.* of Eloy S. Sicat and Flora C. Pasión; *m.* Loretta S. Makasiar 1958; one *s.* three *d.*; ed. Univ. of the Philippines and Massachusetts Inst. of Technology.
Professor of Economics, Univ. of the Philippines 69-, Regent 72-; Chair. Nat. Econ. Council 70-72; Dir.-Gen. Nat. Econ. and Devt. Authority, Govt. of the Philippines 72-.
Leisure interests: tennis, swimming, running.
Publs. *Production Functions in Philippine Manufacturing* 64, *Regional Economic Development in the Philippines* 70, *Philippine Development and Economic Policy* 72 and several other works.
National Economic and Development Authority, Padre Faura Street, Ermita, Manila, Philippines.
Telephone: 59-48-75; 58-56-14; 59-70-91.

Sickinghe, Jonkheer Feyo Onno Joost, LL.D.; Netherlands business executive; b. 1 May 1926, The Hague; *s.* of Jonkheer D. W. Sickinghe and Jonkvrouwe W. J. M. E. Radermacher Schorer; *m.* M. C. van Eeghen 1952; two *s.* two *d.*; ed. Univ. of Utrecht.
Solicitor 52-55; various staff functions within VMF Stork 55-67; Man. Dir. Koninklijke Machinefabriek Stork N.V. 67; mem. Board of Management, Verenigde Machinefabrieken Stork N.V. 69, Chair. 71-; mem. Board of Dirs. De Nederlandsche Bank N.V., Hagemeijer N.V., European Community Trust N.V. 73-, Amrobank N.V. 74; Pres. Utrecht Univ. Foundation; mem. Board, Protestant Political Party (CHU), Advisory Board, R. J. Reynolds Industries Inc.; Exec. mem. Fed. of Netherlands Industry.
Leisure interests: sailing, theatre.
Oud Blaricummerweg 7, Naarden, Netherlands.
Telephone: 02159-43728.

Siclait, Raoul, LIC. EN DROIT; Haitian diplomatist; b. 3 April 1921, Petit-Goave; ed. Nat. Schools of Agriculture, Accounting and Journalism, and Univ. of Haiti.

Assistant, Dept. of Foreign Affairs 57; Dir. Int. Congresses and Confs. Dept. 58; First Sec., Santo Domingo 60, Consul-Gen., Chargé d'Affaires 61; Minister-Counsellor, Del. to OAS 62, Perm. Mission to UN 63; Deputy Perm. Rep. to UN 64-73, Perm. Rep. Feb. 73-; rep. to UN Gen. Assembly 63-; Vice-Chair. Special Cttee. on Apartheid 72-.
Permanent Mission of Haiti to United Nations, 801 Second Avenue, Room 300, New York, N.Y. 10017, U.S.A.

Sidarouss, H.E. Cardinal Stephanos I; Egyptian ecclesiastic; b. 22 Feb. 1904, Cairo; ed. Jesuits' Coll. Cairo, Univ. de Paris and Ecole libre des sciences politiques.
Barrister Egypt 26-32; Vincentian Priest 39-; Prof. Seminaries at Evreux, Dax and Beauvais (France); Rector Coptic Catholic Seminary, Tahta 46, Tanta 47-53, Maadi 53-58; Auxiliary Bishop to the Patriarch of Alexandria, 47-58, Patriarch 58-; created Cardinal 65.
34 Ibn Sandar Street, Koubbeh Bridge, Cairo, Egypt.
Telephone: 821-740; 827-816.

Siddall, Norman, C.B.E., C.ENG., F.I.MIN.E., F.B.I.M., F.R.S.A.; British mining engineer; b. 1918; ed. King Edward VII School, Sheffield, Sheffield Univ.
With B.A. Collieries Ltd. as Undermanager, then Asst. Man. of Gedling Colliery, later as Man. of Bestwood Colliery, Nottingham 36-47; Area Gen. Man. of No. 5 Area in East Midlands Div.; Area Gen. Man. of No. 1 (Bolsover) Area 57; Chief Mining Eng., H.Q. Production Dept. 66; Dir.-Gen. of Production 67; mem. Nat. Coal Board 71, Deputy Chair. 73-; mem. American Inst. of Mining Engs.
National Coal Board, Hobart House, Grosvenor Place, London, SW1X 7AE, England.
Telephone: 01-235-2020.

Siddiqi, M. Raziuddin, M.A., PH.D., D.S.; Pakistani educationist; b. 7 April 1905; ed. Osmania, Cambridge, Berlin, Göttingen, Leipzig, Paris Univs.
Professor of Mathematics, Dir. of Research and Vice-Chancellor, Osmania Univ. 31-50; Dir. of Research and Vice-Chancellor, Peshawar Univ. 50-58; Vice-Chancellor, Univ. of Sind 59-64; Pres. Pakistan Acad. of Sciences 61-73, Sec. 73-; Vice-Chancellor, Univ. of Islamabad 65-73; Joint Sec. (in charge) Scientific and Technological Research Div., President's Secretariat.
Publs. *Lectures on Quantum Mechanics* 37, *Boundary Problems in Non-linear Partial Differential Equations* 38, *Theory of Relativity* 40, *Problems of Education* 43.
University of Islamabad, 77-E, Satellite Town, Rawalpindi, Pakistan.

Siddiqui, Salimuzzaman, M.B.E., D.PHIL., F.R.S.; Pakistani scientist; b. 19 Oct. 1897, Subeha, U.P., India; *s.* of late Shaikh Mohammad Zaman and Maqbul-Un-Nisa; *m.* Shakira Khatoon 1926; three *s.*; ed. Muslim Univ., Aligarh, India, Univ. Coll. London and Univ. of Frankfurt-am-Main.
Director Research Inst., Ayurvedic and Unam Tibbi Coll., Delhi 28-40; Organic Chemist, Council of Scientific and Industrial Research (India) 40-44, Acting Dir. 44-47; Dir. Nat. Chemical Lab. (India) 47-51; Dir. Dept. Scientific and Industrial Research (Pakistan) 51-66; Dir. and Chair. Pakistan Council of Scientific and Industrial Research 51-66; Chair. Nat. Science Council 62-66; Dir. Postgraduate Inst. of Chem., Univ. of Karachi, Pakistan 66-; Pres. Pakistan Acad. of Sciences 67; mem. Vatican Acad. of Sciences and Pontifical Academician; Gold Medal, Russian Acad. of Sciences 58; President's Pride of Performance Medal (Pakistan) 66; Hon. D.Sc. (Karachi and Leeds); D.Med. h.c. (Frankfurt).
Leisure interests: painting, chess.
Publs. Over a hundred research papers and memoirs on chemical studies relating to alkaloids, also studies on natural resins, plant bitters and plant colouring

matters. Granted over 50 patents to processes concerned with utilization of natural products.

Postgraduate Institute of Chemistry, University of Karachi, Karachi; 8 A, Karachi University Campus, Country Club Road, Karachi 32, Pakistan.
Telephone: 413414 (Office); 416993 (Home).

Sidenbladh, Göran; Swedish architect and town planner; b. 19 March 1912, Stockholm; s. of Karl E. Sidenbladh and Gertrud Bernström; m. Suzanne Hedenlund 1944; two d.; ed. Royal Institute of Polytechnics, Stockholm.
Assistant Planner, Stockholm County Council; Consultant and with Göteborg City Planning Dept. 36-43; Senior Planner, Stockholm Planning Dept. 44-55, Dir. 55-73; Consultant, Prof., Nordic Institute for Planning, Stockholm 73-76; mem. Royal Swedish Acad. of Engineering Sciences 62-; corresp. mem. RIBA 63.
Leisure interests: dendrology, roses.
Publs. articles on town planning.
Mäster Mikaels G 11, 116 45 Stockholm, Sweden.
Telephone: (08) 420313.

Sidi Baba, Dey Ould; Moroccan diplomatist; b. 1921, Atar, Mauritania; m.; five c.
Counsellor, Ministry of Foreign Affairs, Morocco 58-59; Head of African Div. 59-61; mem. Moroccan Dels. to UN Gen. Assembly 59-64; Amb. to Guinea 61-62; Acting Perm. Rep. of Morocco to UN 63-65, Perm. Rep. 65-67; Vice-Pres. of Gen. Assembly of UN 66; Minister of Royal Cabinet 67-71, Dir. 72-73; Amb. to Saudi Arabia 71-72; Minister of Educ. 73-74, of Waqfs and Islamic Affairs April 74-; Commdr. du Trône alaonite 65.
Ministry of Waqfs and Islamic Affairs, Rabat, Morocco.

Sidki, Aziz, B.ENG., M.A., PH.D.; Egyptian politician; b. 1 July 1920, Cairo; ed. Cairo Univ., Univ. of Oregon and Harvard Univ.
Taught Cairo Univ.; Technical Counsellor to the President 53; Ministry for Industry 56-63, Deputy Prime Minister and Minister for Industry and Mineral Wealth 64-65; Minister for Industry, Petroleum and Mineral Wealth 68-71; Deputy Prime Minister 71-72; Prime Minister 72-73; Acting Gen. Sec. Arab Socialist Union 71-73; Personal Asst. to Pres. Sadat 73-75; has participated in various int. confs. on industrial affairs.
c/o The Presidency, Cairo, Egypt.

Sidorenko, Aleksandr Vasiliyevich; Soviet geologist and administrator; 19 Oct. 1917, Novo-Nikolaevka, Melovsk district; s. of Vasily Ivanovich Sidorenko and Pelageya Fedortovna Sidorenko; m. Kaleria Petrovna Sidorenko; one s. two d.; ed. Voronezh State Univ.
Head, Laboratory Turkmen branch Soviet Acad. of Sciences 43-50, Kola Branch 50-61, Chair. Presidium Kola Branch 50-61; Vice-Chair. R.S.F.S.R. State Cttee. for Co-ordination of Scientific Research Work 61-62; Minister of Geology and Mineral Wealth Protection 62-63; Chair. State Cttee. for Geology 63-65; Minister of Geology 65-75; Deputy to U.S.S.R. Supreme Soviet 66-; Corresp. mem. U.S.S.R. Acad. of Sciences 53-66, mem. 66-; Alt. mem. C.P.S.U. Cen. Cttee. 66-; Chief Editor *Geology of the U.S.S.R.* (40 vols.) 64.
Leisure interest: geology.
Publs. numerous articles and papers on geological subjects including *Principal Characteristics of Mineral Formation in Deserts* 56, *Preglacial Erosion Crust of Kola Peninsula* 58, *To the Problem of Litological Investigation of Metamorphic Rocks* 61, *Organic Matter in the Precambrian Sedimentary-Metamorphic Rocks* 75.
c/o Ministry of Geology, Bolshaya Gruzinskaya ul. 4/6 Moscow 123242, U.S.S.R.

Siebold, Klaus; German mining engineer and politician; b. 1930.
Former Minister of Raw Materials Industry; Minister for Coal and Power 71-.
Ministerrat, Berlin, German Democratic Republic.

Sieff, (Joseph) Edward; British business executive; b. 28 Nov. 1905; s. of Ephraim Sieff; brother of late Lord Sieff; m. 1st Maisie Marsh 1929, two d.; m. 2nd Lois Ross 1952, one s. one d.; ed. Manchester Grammar School and Manchester Univ.
Joined Marks and Spencer Ltd. 33, Dir. 39-, Asst. Man. Dir. 46-63, Joint Man. Dir. 63-72, Deputy Chair. 65-67, Chair. 67-72, Pres. 72-; Hon. Vice-Pres. Zionist Fed. of Great Britain and N. Ireland; Chair. Joint Palestine Appeal (now Joint Israel Appeal) 61-65, Pres. 65-; Pres. Zionist Fed. 74-.
Marks and Spencer Ltd., Michael House, Baker Street, London, W1A 1DN, England.

Sieff, Sir Marcus Joseph, Kt., O.B.E., B.A.; British business executive; b. 2 July 1913; s. of late Lord Sieff; nephew of J. Edward Sieff (q.v.); m. 1st Rosalie Fromson 1937 (dissolved 1947), 2nd Elsie Gosen 1951 (dissolved 1951), 3rd Brenda M. Beith 1956 (dissolved 1962), 4th Mrs. Pauline L. Moretzki (née Spatz) 1963; one s. two d.; ed. Manchester Grammar School, St. Paul's, and Corpus Christi Coll., Cambridge.
Director, Marks and Spencer Ltd. 54-, Asst. Man. Dir. 63-65, Vice-Chair. 65-67, Joint Man. Dir. 67-71, Deputy Chair. 71-72, Chair. and Joint Man. Dir. 72-; Pres. Anglo-Israel Chamber of Commerce; Vice-Pres. Joint Israel Appeal, Political and Econ. Planning; Deputy Chair. and Hon. Fellow, Weizmann Inst., Corpus Christi Coll., Cambridge Univ.
Marks and Spencer Ltd., Michael House, Baker Street, London, W1A 1DN, England.

Siegbahn, Karl Manne Georg, D.SC.; Swedish physicist; b. 3 Dec. 1886; ed. Lund Univ.
Prof. of Physics, Lund Univ. 14-23, Uppsala Univ. 24-37; Dir. Nobel Inst. for Physics, Royal Acad. of Sciences 37-75; mem. Swedish, Danish, Norwegian, Finnish Acads., Int. Cttee. Weights and Measures 37-59, Hon. mem. 59-; Nobel Prize for Physics 25, Hughes Medal 34, and Rumford Medal of Royal Society, London 40, for pioneer work in high-precision X-ray spectroscopy and its application; Duddel Medal, Physical Society of London 48; foreign mem. Acad. des Sciences, Paris; hon. mem. Royal Society, Edinburgh; foreign mem. Royal Soc. London; Dr. h.c. (Freiburg, Bucharest, Oslo, Paris Univs.).
Publs. *The Spectroscopy of X-rays* 25, *Spektroskopie der Röntgenstrahlen* 31.
Roslagsvägen 98, 10405 Stockholm, Sweden.
Telephone: 08-153011.

Siegel, Milton P.; American international official and educationist; b. 23 July, 1911, Des Moines, Ill.; s. of Barney and Silvy (Levinson) Siegel; m. Rosalie Rosenberg 1934; one s. two d.; ed. Drake Univ., Des Moines.
Director of Finance and Statistics, Iowa Emergency Relief Admin., Treasurer, Iowa Rural Rehabilitation Admin. 33-35; Regional Finance and Business Manager, Farm Security Admin., U.S. Dept. of Agriculture 35-41, Chief Fiscal Officer 42-44; Asst. Treasurer, Dir. Office for Far East, UNRRA 44-45; Asst. Dir., Fiscal Branch, Production and Marketing Admin., U.S. Dept. of Agriculture 45-47; Asst. Dir.-Gen. World Health Org. 47-71; Visiting Prof. Univ. of Michigan 67-; mem. Perm. Scale of Contributions Comm. LRCS-; Visiting Prof., Univ. of North Carolina 70-; Consultant to Carolina Population Center 70-; Prof. of Int. Health, Health Science Center, Univ. of Texas at Houston 71-75.
1 Rue Viollier, 1207 Geneva, Switzerland.
Telephone: (022) 36-36-09.

Siegfried, Charles A.; American business executive. b. 27 Aug. 1908, Orwigsburg, Pa.; m. Marjorie Young, one s. one d.; ed. Franklin and Marshall Coll.
Actuarial Clerk, Metropolitan Life Insurance Co. 30, Manager of Ordinary Policy Contract Bureau of Actuarial Div. 36, Asst. Actuary 42-51, Assoc. Actuary 51-53, Actuary May 53, Second Vice-Pres. in Group

Insurance Div. 53-60, Vice-Pres. 60-63, Sr. Vice-Pres. and Chief Actuary Feb. 63-65, Exec. Vice-Pres. 65-66, Dir. April 66, Pres. Oct. 66-69, Vice-Chair. of Board and Chair. of Exec. Cttee. May 69-; Insurance Business Rep. on Fed. Govt.'s Advisory Council on Welfare and Pension Benefit Plans 62; mem. Advisory Council on Social Security of Dept. of Health, Educ. and Welfare 69; Dir. The Anaconda Co.; mem. Board of Trustees of Franklin and Marshall Coll., Board of Govs. of Soc. of Actuaries 70; Fellow Soc. of Actuaries.
Metropolitan Life Insurance Company, 1 Madison Avenue, New York, N.Y. 10010; Home: 29 Hillcrest Road, Madison, N.J. 07940, U.S.A.

Siemens, Ernst Albrecht von; German industrialist; b. 9 April 1903; ed. Munich Univ.
Member Supervisory Board, Siemens AG, Hon. Dr. Eng. Munich Technical High School.
Wittelsbacherplatz 2, 8000 Munich 2, Federal Republic of Germany.

Siemens, Dr. Peter von; German business executive; b. 29 Jan. 1911, Berlin; s. of Werner Ferdinand and Katrin (née Heck) von Siemens; m. Julia Lienau 1935; one s. one d.; ed. Realgymnasium, Berlin-Lankwitz, and Universität Rostock.
Entered Siemens and Hakels AG 34; in Sales Dept. of Siemens-Reiniger-Werke AG, mainly in South America 36-50; transferred to Siemens-Schuckertwerke AG, Erlangen 50; Gen. Man. Siemens-Schuckertwerke AG 57, Deputy mem. of Management Board 59, elected to Supervisory Board 63; Deputy Chair. Supervisory Board of Siemens AG 67-71, Chair. 71-; mem. Supervisory Board of Allianz AG, München, Deutsche Bank AG, Frankfurt, Bayer AG, Leverkusen, Hamburg-Amerika Linie HAPAG, Hamburg, Mannesmann AG, Düsseldorf, J. M. Voith GmbH, Heidenheim; Hon. mem. Presidium Cen. Cttee. of Electrotechnical Industry; Hon. Citizen of Erlangen; Bavarian Order of Merit.
8 Munich 2, Wittelsbacherplatz 2, Federal Republic of Germany.
Telephone: 2342750.

Sievers Wicke, Hugo K.; Chilean veterinary physician and politician; b. 1903, Rengo; m. Elena Kutz Schroer 1931; ed. Colegio Alemán, Santiago and Univs. of Chile, Buenos Aires, La Plata, Rio de Janeiro, Inst. Pasteur and Inst. Curie, Paris, Inst. of Tropical Medicine, Hamburg.
Assistant at Inst. for Veterinary Research 24-27; Prof., School of Agriculture 27-28; Mil. Veterinary Physician 26-32; Dir. Inst. of Veterinary Research, Ministry of Agriculture 30-42; Dean School Veterinary Medicine, Univ. of Chile 36-61; Vice-Rector Univ. of Chile 53-61, now Prof. Emer.; Minister of Agriculture, Lands and Colonization 55; Perm. Del. Int. Congress of Veterinary Medicine 36-59; Pres. Chilean Soc. of Sciences 64-; Founder mem. Soc. of Veterinary Physicians of Chile (and past Pres.), Chilean Natural History Soc., Anatomical Soc.; mem. Chilean Acad. Natural Sciences; Hon. mem. Soc. of Veterinary Science, Peru; Hon. Prof. Central Univ. of Quito, and Univ. Nat. of San Marcos, Lima; Dr. h.c. Univ. Austral de Chile; Decoration of the Rising Sun Japan 59; Decoration Eloy Alfaro Int. Foundation, Gold Medal Camara di Commercio, Industria e Agricultura, Trento, Italy.
Publs. *La vuelta al Mundo con 10 Estudiantes, Rutas Patagónicas, Chilenos en la Amazonia, Max Westenhöfer 1871-1951* (biography), *Domingo Amunátegui Solar* (biography), *Teliatria, Nosotros y la Comunidad, Proteinas y Alimentación.*
Las Trinitarias 6881, Las Condes, Santiago 10, Chile.
Telephone: 480717.

Signoret, Simone (*pseudonym* of Simone Kaminker), German-born French actress; b. 25 March 1921; m. 1st Yves Allegret, 2nd Yves Montand (*q.v.*) 1951.

Films include *Le Couple Idéal, Dédée d'Anvers, La Ronde, Casque d'Or, Thérèse Raquin, Les Diaboliques* (The Fiends), *La Mort en ce Jardin, Les Sorcières de Salem, Room at the Top* ("Oscar" for best actress), *Adua* 61, *Term of Trial* 62, *Dragées au Poivre, Ship of Fools, The Sleeping Car Murder, Games, The Deadly Affair, The Seagull, L'Aveu* 70, *L'Armée des Ombres* 71, *Le Chat* 71, *Rude Journée pour la Reine* 73.
15 Place Dauphine, Paris 1er, France.

Sigrist, Helmut, DR. RER. POL.; German diplomatist; b. 1919, Frankfurt/Main; m.; four c.; ed. Humanistisches Gymnasium Gelsenkirchen-Schalke, Philosophisch-theologische Hochschule, Bamberg, and Univs. of Heidelberg and Denver, Colo., U.S.A.
National Labour Service 37; Mil. Service and Prisoner-of-war 37-45; univ. studies 45-50; entered Diplomatic Service 51; Second Sec., later Sec., Washington 53-55, Sec., Rome 57-62, New Delhi 62-64; Dir. of Training Centre for Senior Foreign Service Officials, Bonn 55-57; Deputy Exec. Sec. of EEC Comm. 64-67; Deputy Sec.-Gen. of Comm. of European Communities, Brussels 67; Dir.-Gen. for External Relations, Comm. of European Communities Dec. 68-72.
147 avenue des Statuaires, 1180 Bruxelles-Uccle, Belgium.

Sigurdsson, Halldór; Icelandic politician; b. 9 Sept. 1915, Snaefellssýsla; m. Margrét Gísladóttir; two s. one d.; ed. Co-operative Coll. of Iceland.
Farmer in Dalasýsla 37-55; Mayor of Borgarnes 55-68; mem. Central Cttee. Progressive Party 53-; mem. Althing 56-; Parliamentary Auditor of Nat. Revenue and Expenditure 65-; Minister of Finance and Agriculture 71-74, of Agriculture and Communications Aug. 74-.
Ministry of Agriculture, Reykjavík, Iceland.

Sigurdsson, Jon; Icelandic lawyer and civil servant; b. 29 Oct. 1934, Reykjavík; s. of Sigurdur Jonsson and Ingebjör Palsdottir; m. Bergljot Jonatansdottir 1955; one s. two d.; ed. Univ. of Iceland and Univ. of Southern California School of Public Admin.
Assistant to Sec.-Gen., Ministry of Fisheries and Agriculture 58-62, Chief of Div. 62-66; Adviser to Minister of Finance 65-66; Budget Dir., Ministry of Finance 66-67; Sec.-Gen. 67-; Exec. Dir. for Denmark, Finland, Iceland, Norway, Sweden, IBRD (on leave of absence from Icelandic Govt.) 74- (Nov. 76).
12313 Falls Road, Potomac, Md. 20854, U.S.A. (until Nov. 1976); 6 Bakkaflöt, Gardahreppur, Iceland (after Nov. 1976).

Sigurdsson, Niels P.; Icelandic diplomatist; b. 1926, Reykjavik; s. of Sigurdur B. Sigurdsson and Karitas Einarsdóttir; m. Olafia Rafnsdóttir; two s. one d.; ed. Univ. of Iceland.
Joined Diplomatic Service 52; First Sec. Paris Embassy 56-60; Deputy Perm. Rep. to NATO and OECD 57-60; Dir. Int. Policy Div. Ministry of Foreign Affairs, Reykjavik 61; Del. to the UN Gen. Assembly 65; Amb. and Perm. Rep. of Iceland to North Atlantic Council; Amb. to Belgium and the EEC 68; Amb. to UK. 71-76, to Fed. Repub. of Germany 76-.
Leisure interests: swimming, riding.
Icelandic Embassy, Kronprinzenstrasse 6, Bonn-Bad Godesberg, Federal Republic of Germany.

Sihanouk, Prince Norodom (*see* Norodom Sihanouk, Prince).

Siilasvuo, Lieut.-Gen. Ensio; Finnish army officer; b. 1 Jan. 1922, Helsinki; s. of Lieut. Gen. Hjalmar Siilasvuo and Salli Kolsi; m. Salli Paldanius 1947; three s.; ed. Lycée of Oulu, Finnish Mil. Acad., Finnish Command and Staff Coll.
Platoon Commdr., Infantry Co. Commdr. and Chief of Staff, Infantry Regiment 11 41-44; Company Commdr., Infantry Regiment 1 45-50; attended Command and

Staff Coll. 51-52; various staff appointments in mil. districts of N. Finland 53-57; Commdr. Finnish Contingent, UN Emergency Force 57; Mil. Observer, UN Observation Group in Lebanon 58; Finnish Defence Attaché in Warsaw 59-61; Staff Officer Third Div. 62-64; Commdr. Finnish Contingent, UN Force in Cyprus 64-65; Instructor, Nat. Defence Coll. 65-67; Chief, Foreign Dept. GHQ 67; Senior Staff Officer, UN Truce Supervision Org. in Palestine 67-70; Chief of Staff, UN Truce Supervision Org. in Palestine 70-73, Commdr. UN Emergency Force 73-75; Chief Co-ordinator of UN Peace-Keeping Missions in Middle East 75-; Commdr. of the Order of the Lion of Finland 1st Class; Finnish Cross of Freedom 3rd and 4th Class; Knight of the Order of the White Rose of Finland 1st Class.
Leisure interests: UN peace-keeping affairs, history of the Middle East.
UNCC, P.O. Box 490, Jerusalem, Israel.
Telephone: 36223/4/5.

Sijthoff, Hendrik Albert Henri; Netherlands publisher; b. 1915; ed. Univs. of Leipzig and Lausanne.
Pres.-Dir. of *Het Financieele Dagblad*; Pres.-Dir. of Hendrik Sijthoff's Financieele Bladen N.V.
Office: Weesperstraat 85, Amsterdam C, Netherlands; Home: 20 Mansion Place, Greenwich, Conn., U.S.A.

Sik, Endre; Hungarian diplomatist, politician and writer; b. 2 April 1891; ed. Budapest Univ.
Prisoner-of-War, First World War; teacher, Oriental Univ., Moscow 24-36; mem. staff Historical Inst., U.S.S.R. Acad. of Sciences 38-41, Ethnographic Inst. 43-45; returned to Hungary 45; First Counsellor, Hungarian Legation, later Minister, Washington 46-49; Chief of Dept., Ministry of Foreign Affairs 49-53, Deputy Minister 54-54, First Deputy Minister 55-58; Minister of Foreign Affairs 58-61; mem. Central Cttee. Hungarian Socialist Workers' Party 59-70; Pres. Hungarian Nat. Peace Council; mem. Exec. Council Soc. Européenne de Culture; State Prize 65, Lenin Peace Prize for 1967/68; Banner, Order 1st degree of Hungarian People's Repub. 70.
Publs. *History of Black Africa, Racial Problems and Marxism*, and literary works.
Pentelei Molnár u. 12, 1025 Budapest II, Hungary.
Telephone: 155-266.

Šik, Ota, DR.SC.; fmr. Czechoslovak economist (deprived of Czech citizenship 70); b. 11 Sept. 1919, Plzeň; s. of Oswald and Marie Šik; m. Lilli Grünfeld 1947; two s.
Director Econ. Inst. of Czechoslovak Acad. of Sciences 63-68; Chair. of Scientific Collegium of Econ. Czechoslovak Acad. of Sciences 63-69; Corresp. mem. Czechoslovak Acad. of Sciences 60; mem. Cen. Cttee. of Communist Party of Czechoslovakia 62-69; mem. Econ. Comm., Central Cttee. of Communist Party of Czechoslovakia 62-69; mem. State Comm. for Management and Org. 63-68; mem. State Planning Comm.; Deputy Prime Minister 68; mem. Econ. Council 68-69; Deputy to Czech Nat. Council 68-69; now lecturing at Univ. of St. Gallen; Order of 25th February 1948; Klement Gottwald State Prize 66; Dr. h.c. (Univ. of Lancaster); granted political asylum in Switzerland April 70.
Leisure interest: sport.
Publs. include: *Economics, Interests, Politics, On the Question of Socialist Commodity Relations, Plan and Market under Socialism, Facts about the Czechoslovakian Economy, Democratic and Socialist Economy, Structural Changes of the Economic Systems in East-Europe*.
Hochschule St. Gallen, Dufourstrasse 50, 9000 St. Gallen, Switzerland.

Sikivou, Semesa Koroikilai, C.B.E., M.A.; Fijian diplomatist; b. 13 Feb. 1917, Rewa, Fiji; s. of Navitalai Tubuna and Ateca Canavusa; m. 1st Seini Ratuvou 1944 (deceased), 2nd Salote Tabuanitoga 1957; five s.

one d.; ed. schools in Fiji, Auckland Training Coll. and Auckland Univ., and London Univ. Inst. of Educ.
Teacher 35-42; Mil. Service 42-46; Asst. Master, Queen Victoria School, 49, 51-59; Educ. Officer 60-62; Asst. Dir. of Educ., Fiji 63-66, Deputy Dir. 66-70; Perm. Rep. to UN Oct. 70-; High Commr. to Canada 71-; Amb. to U.S.A. 71-, Vice-Pres. of 28th Session of UN Gen. Assembly 73; mem. Fiji Broadcasting Comm. 55-62, 66-70; mem. Fiji Legislative Council 56-66; mem. Fijian Affairs Board 55-66, 69-70, Fijian Devt. Fund Board 56-66, Native Land Trust Board 65-70; mem. Advisory Council on Educ. 54-70; mem. Council of Chiefs 52-70; mem. many other govt. and civic bodies.
Leisure interests: reading and walking.
Permanent Mission of Fiji to the United Nations, 845 Third Avenue, 19th Floor, New York, N.Y. 10022; Home: 1155 Park Avenue at 92nd Street, New York, N.Y., U.S.A.
Telephone: 355-7316 (Office); 860-4400 (Home).

Sikorski, Kazimierz; Polish composer and teacher; b. 28 June 1895, Zurich, Switzerland; widower; one s. one d.; ed. Warsaw Conservatoire and Paris and Warsaw Univs.
Former Prof. of composition in Łódź, Poznań and Warsaw; Rector, State Higher School of Music, Warsaw 57-66; Pres. Union of Polish Composers 54-59; State Music Prize 37, State Prize 51, Union of Polish Composers Prize 51, Minister of Culture and Art Prize 55; City of Warsaw Prize 60; numerous decorations including Commdr. Cross Order of Polonia Restituta. Compositions include four symphonies, concertos for clarinet, flute, horn, oboe, trumpet and bassoon, three string quartets, string sextet, *Stabat Mater*, symphonic poems, works for choir, film music, etc.; Editor of *Polish music from 17th and 18th centuries*, and orchestration of Moniuszko operas, *Straszny dwór* and *Halka*.
Publs. Handbooks: *Harmony* (3 vols.), *Counterpoint* (3 vols.), *Musical Instruments*.
Ul. Kozietulskiego 6/6, 01-571, Warsaw, Poland.
Telephone: 33-5546.

Sikri, Hon. Sarv Mittra; Indian judge; b. 26 April 1908, Lahore (Pakistan); s. of late Dr. Nihal Chand; m. Leila Sikri; one s.; ed. Trinity Hall, Cambridge and Lincoln's Inn, London.
Started practice, Lahore High Court 30; Asst. Advocate Gen., Punjab 49, Advocate-Gen. 51-64; Judge, Supreme Court of India 64-71; Chief Justice of India Jan. 71-April 73; Pres. Indian Law Inst., Indian Branch, Int. Law Asscn.; Hon. Pres. Indian Soc. of Int. Law; mem. Indian Comm. of Jurists; del. to various int. confs.
Leisure interests: golf, tennis, bridge.
B-18 Maharani Bagh, New Delhi, India.

Silberman, Laurence Hirsch, LL.B.; American lawyer and diplomatist; b. 12 Oct. 1935, York, Pa.; s. of William and Anna Hirsch; m. Rosalie Gaull 1957; one s. two d.; ed. Dartmouth Coll., Harvard Law School.
With Moore, Torkildson & Rice, Quinn & Moore, law firm 61-64; Partner Moore, Silberman & Schulze 64-67; Lawyer Nat. Labor Relations Board 67-69; Solicitor, Labor Dept. 69-70, Under-Sec. for Labor Affairs 70-73; Partner Steptoe & Johnson 73-74; Deputy Attorney Gen., Dept. of Justice 74-75; Amb. to Yugoslavia 75-.
U.S. Embassy, Kneza Milosa 50, Belgrade, Yugoslavia.
Telephone: 645-555.

Siles Zuazo, Hernán, D.IUR.; Bolivian lawyer, politician and diplomatist; b. 1914; ed. San Andres Univ.
Sergeant in Chaco War 32; legal practice in La Paz 39-, M.P. for La Paz 43-46; in exile in Argentina and Chile, where he worked as translator for U.S. news agencies 46-51; Vice-Presidential candidate 51; a leader of the revolution of 52; Vice-Pres. of Bolivia 52-56, Pres. 56-60; Amb. to Uruguay 60-63, to Spain 63-64; in exile 64-.

Silex, Karl, D.PHIL.; German journalist; b. 6 July 1896; ed. Stettin Gymnasium, Kiel and Berlin Univs. Naval officer during both World Wars; London corresp. *Deutsche Allgemeine Zeitung* 25, Chief Editor 33; Naval officer 43; Publisher *Deutsche Kommentare* (weekly) 49, *Bücher-Kommentare* (literary quarterly) 52; Chief Editor *Der Tagesspiegel* (Berlin) 55-63; freelance journalist 63-.
Publs. *John Bull At Home* 29, *Patriot Macdonald* 32, *Mit Kommentar* (autobiography) 69.
1 Berlin 28, Ludolfingerweg 18, Federal Republic of Germany.
Telephone: 401 45 43.

Silkin, Rt. Hon. John Ernest, P.C., M.P., M.A., LL.B.; British politician and solicitor; b. 18 March 1923, London; s. of Lord Silkin and Rosa (née Neft) Silkin; m. Rosamund Jones 1950; one s.; ed. Dulwich Coll., Univ. of Wales, and Trinity Hall, Cambridge.
Member of Parl. for Deptford 63-74, for Lewisham, Deptford 74-; Asst. Govt. Chief Whip 64-66; Treas. of the Household April-July 66; Govt. Chief Whip 66-69; Minister of Public Building and Works 69-70; Minister for Planning and Local Govt. 74-; Dir. Pergamon Press 71-74; Labour.
Leisure interests: chess, golf, history, theatre.
7 Storey's Gate, London, S.W.1, England.
Telephone: 01-839-4222.

Silkin, Jon, B.A.; British writer and editor; b. 2 Dec. 1930, London; s. of Joseph Silkin and Dora Silkin (née Rubenstein); m. Lorna Tracy 1975; three s.; ed. Wycliffe and Dulwich Colls., Leeds Univ.
Journalist 47; nat. service as teacher in Educ. Corps 48-49; worked as manual labourer 49-55; taught English to foreign students 55-57; Gregory Fellowship in Poetry (non-academic fellowship given to a practising poet), Univ. of Leeds 58-60, graduated 62, research 62-65; Editor *Stand* magazine, Newcastle upon Tyne 65; visited U.S.A., giving poetry reading tours; Visiting Lecturer, Denison Univ., Ohio; taught at Writers' Workshop, Univ. of Ia. 68-69; Visiting Writer, Australian Arts Council and Univ. of Sydney 74; Geoffrey Faber Memorial Prize for *Nature With Man* 66.
Publs. *The Peaceable Kingdom* 54, *The Two Freedoms* 58, *The Re-ordering of the Stones* 61, *Nature With Man* 65, *Penguin Modern Poets 7* (with Richard Murphy and Nathaniel Tarn) 65, *Poems New and Selected* 66, *Killhope Wheel* 70, *Amana Grass* 71, *Out of Battle* (criticism) 72, *Poetry of the Committed Individual* (Co-editor) 73, *The Principle of Water* 74, *The Little Time-Keeper* 76.
58 Queens Road, Newcastle upon Tyne, NE2 2PR, England.
Telephone: Newcastle 812614.

Silkin, Rt. Hon. Samuel Charles, B.A., Q.C.; British barrister-at-law; b. 6 March 1918, Neath, Glam.; s. of late Lewis Silkin, C.H., P.C., 1st Baron Silkin, and Rosa Neft; brother of John Silkin (q.v.); m. Elaine Violet Stamp 1941; two s. two d.; ed. Dulwich Coll., Trinity Hall, Cambridge.
Called to the Bar, Middle Temple 41; served World War II 39-45, Lieut-Col. (mentioned in despatches); mem. Parl. for Camberwell, Dulwich 64-74, for Southwark, Dulwich 74-; Queen's Counsel 63; mem. Royal Comm. on Penal System for England and Wales 65-66; Chair. Parl. Labour Party Group on EEC and European Affairs 66-70; Recorder of Bedford 66-71; Leader del. to Assembly, Council of Europe 68-70; Opposition Spokesman on Law Officer Matters 70-74; Attorney-Gen. March 74-; mem. Soc. of Labour Lawyers 64-71, Vice-Pres. 71-; Bencher, Middle Temple 69.
House of Commons, Westminster, London, S.W.1.

Sillitoe, Alan; British author; b. 4 March 1928, Nottingham; s. of Christopher Archibald Sillitoe and Sylvina Burton; m. Ruth Esther Fainlight 1959; one s.

one d. (adopted); ed. elementary school, Radford, Nottingham.
Worked in various factories, Nottingham 42-46; served wireless operator, R.A.F., Malaya; lived several years in France and Spain; editorial adviser W. H. Allen Co. Ltd.; Hawthornden Prize 60.
Leisure interests: geography, navigation, travel.
Publs. (novels) *Saturday Night and Sunday Morning* 58, *The General* 60, *Key to the Door* 61, *The Death of William Posters* 65, *A Tree on Fire* 67, *A Start in Life* 70, *Travels in Nihilon* 71, *Raw Materials* 72, *The Flame of Life* 74; (stories) *The Loneliness of the Long Distance Runner* 59, *The Ragman's Daughter* 63, *Guzman, Go Home* 68, *Men, Women and Children* 73; (essays) *Mountains and Caverns* 75; (poems) *The Rats and Other Poems* 60, *A Falling Out of Love* 64, *Love in the Environs of Voronezh* 68, *Barbarians and Other Poems* 74, *Storm and other poems* 74; (travel) *Road to Volgograd* 64, *All Citizens are Soldiers* 69 (trans. of Lope de Vega play *Fuenteovejuna*, with Ruth Fainlight).
W. H. Allen & Co. Ltd., 44 Hill Street, London, W1X 8LB, England.

Sills, Beverly; American coloratura soprano; b. 25 May 1929, Brooklyn; m. Peter Bulkeley Greenough 1956; five c.; ed. pupil of Estelle Liebling.
Debut at San Francisco Opera as Helen of Troy in *Mefistofele* 53, at New York City Opera as Rosalinda in *Die Fledermaus* 55; with New York City Opera 55-; debut at the Vienna State Opera as Queen of the Night (*Die Zauberflöte*) 67, at La Scala, Milan in *The Siege of Corinth* 69, at Royal Opera House, Covent Garden in title role of *Lucia di Lammermoor* 70, Metropolitan Opera, New York as Pamira in *Siege of Corinth* 75; other best known roles include Cleopatra (*Julius Ceasar*), Queen Elizabeth I (*Roberto Devereux*), all three heroines in *The Tales of Hoffmann*, Manon (*Manon*), Violetta (*La Traviata*), Marie (*Daughter of the Regiment*), Rosina (*Barber of Seville*); title roles in *Anna Bolena* and *Maria Stuarda, Norma, Lucrezia Borgia;* recordings for Columbia, RCA, Angel, ABC—Audio Treasure; has appeared at most of the major opera houses of Europe and Latin America and given numerous recitals with leading orchestras throughout U.S.A.
c/o Edgar Vincent Associates, 156 East 52nd Street, New York, N.Y. 10022, U.S.A.

Silone, Ignazio; Italian writer; b. 1 May 1900; ed. private and public schools.
In Italian Socialist Youth Movement 17-21; mem. Cen. Cttee. Italian C.P. and editor various newspapers 21-29; left C.P. 30; exile Switzerland 30-44; mem. Exec. Cttee. Italian Socialist Party 41; Sec. Union Ind. Socialists 48; Sec. Unitary Socialist Party 50; Founder and Pres. Teatro del Popolo (People's Theatre) 45; Editor of *Avanti* (Socialist daily newspaper); hon. corresp. mem. American Acad. of Arts and Letters 50; mem. Exec. Cttee. Int. Congress for Cultural Freedom 50; Editor *Tempo Presente;* Marzotto Prize 65; Campiello Award 68.
Publs. *Fontamara* (novel) 30, *Fascism* (history) 34, *Mr. Aristotle* (short stories) 35, *Bread and Wine* (novel) 37, *The School for Dictators* (dialogues) 38, *Mazzini* (essay) 39, *The Seed Beneath the Snow* (novel) 41, *And He did Hide Himself* (play) 44, *The God that Failed* (symposium) 50, *A Handful of Blackberries* (novel) 52, *The Choice of Comrade* 55, *The Fox and the Camelias* (novel) 60, *Uscita di sicurezza* 65, *L'avventura d'un povero cristiano* 68.
Via di Villa Ricotti 36, Rome, Italy.

Silsoe, 1st Baron, cr. 63, of Silsoe; **(Arthur) Malcolm Trustram Eve,** Bt., G.B.E., M.C., T.D., Q.C.; Gentleman Usher of the Purple Rod in the Order of the British Empire 60-69; British lawyer and administrator; b. 8 April 1894, Bedford; s. of Sir Herbert Trustram Eve, K.B.E. and Fanny Jean Turing; m. 1st Marguerite

Nanton 1927 (died 1945), 2nd Margaret Elizabeth Robertson; twin s.; ed. Winchester and Christ Church, Oxford.
Served First World War, Gallipoli 15, Egypt and Palestine 16-19; Capt. Royal Welch Fusiliers; G.S.O. 53rd Div. 17; Brig. Maj. 159th Infantry Brigade 18-19; commanded 6th Battn. Royal Welch Fusiliers 27-31; Col. (T.A.) 31; A/Q 53 Div. 39-40; Brig. 40; called to Bar 19, K.C. 35, Bencher Inner Temple 42, Reader Inner Temple 65, Treas. Inner Temple 66; Chair. Air Transport Licensing Authority 38-39, War Damage Comm. 41-49; Building Apprenticeship and Training Council 43-47, War Works Comm. 45-49, Local Govt. Boundary Comm. 45-49, Central Land Board 47-49, Burnham Cttees. on Teachers' Salaries 50-53, Police Council on Police Salaries 51, St. George's Hospital Medical School 48-54, Lord Mayor's Nat. Flood and Tempest Distress Fund 53, Prime Minister's Cttee. on Admin. of Crown Lands 55; mem. Church Assembly 52-57; Electoral Boundaries Comm., Mauritius 57; Pres. Ski Club of Great Britain 50-54; First Church Estates Commr. 54-69 (Third Church Estates Commr. 53-54); First Crown Estate Commr. 55-62; Ind. Chair. Cement Makers' Fed. 51-70, Cembureau West European Cement Asscn. 52-70; Dir. Yorkshire Insurance Co. 49-66; Gov. Peabody Trust 57-65; Dir. St. Martin's Property Corpn. Ltd. 61-70; Pres. Kandahar Ski Club 65-69; Chair. Fiji Sugar Inquiry Comm. 61, Fiji Coconut Industry Inquiry Comm. 63; Hon. Treas. Royal Coll. of Nursing 64-70.
Leisure interests: travelling, and gardening.
Lower Ballacottier, Kirk Onchan, Isle of Man.
Telephone: 0624-5687.

Siluyanov, Vasily Grigorievich; Soviet trade union official; b. 10 April 1909, Borisoglabsk, Voronezh Region; s. of Grigori Andreyevich and Pelageya Grigorievna Siluyanova; m. Polina Antonovna Siluyanova; three d.; ed. Moscow Inst. for Mechanization and Electrification in Agriculture.
Member C.P.S.U. 32-; Railway Worker 24-30; Designer, Shop Supt., Chair. of Works Cttee. and Dir. Chelyabinsk Tractor Works 35-46; Trade Union Official 42-; Chair. Cen. Cttee. Transport Eng. Workers' Union 46-48; Man. of Section of All-Union Council of Trade Unions 48-56, mem. 47, mem. Presidium 62-72; Chair. All-Union Council of Scientific and Technical Socs. 56-68, First Vice-Chair. 68; Order of Lenin, Order of Red Banner of Labour (twice), Red Star and other Soviet decorations.
Leisure interests: sport, reading.
All-Union Council of Scientific and Technical Societies, Ul. Krzhizhanovskogo 20/30 Kor. 5, Moscow, U.S.S.R.
Telephone: 125-77-32.

Silva Henríquez, H.E. Cardinal Raúl; Chilean ecclesiastic; b. 3 July 1907; ed. Universidad Católica de Chile and Ateneo Salesiano, Turin.
Former Prof. Canon and Moral Law, Salesian Study Centre, La Cisterna and Pres. Fed. of Catholic Colls., Chile; Pres. Caritas, Chile, Caritas Internacional and organizer of other social welfare projects; Diocesan Bishop, Valparaíso 59-61; Archbishop of Santiago 61-, cr. Cardinal 62; Chancellor, Universidad Católica de Chile; Hon. LL.D. (Univ. of Notre Dame).
Publ. *La Misión Social del Cristianismo: Conflicto de Clases o Solidaridad Cristiana.*
Palacio Arzobispal, Casilla 30-D, Santiago, Chile.

Silva Muñoz, Federico, LL.D.; Spanish politician; b. 1923; ed. Universidad de Madrid.
Former Prof. of Political Economy, Central Univ. and was apptd. to Nat. Lawyers' Council and Lawyers of the Council of State; fmr. Pres. Higher Coll. of San Pablo and Rector, Centre of Univ. Studies; fmr. Dir. Sociology Studies, Univ. Menéndez Pelavo, Santander, Prof., School of Taxation Studies and Prof., Santa

María de la Rábida Univ.; mem. Perm. Comm. of Inst. of Political Studies and various comms. on Devt. Plans; also Vice-Pres. Third Section, Fiscal Policy and Credit of Official Chamber of Commerce, Madrid; Procurator, Cortes 61-; Minister of Public Works 66-April 70, 71-72; mem. various religious cttees.
Las Cortes Españolas, Madrid, Spain.

Silva V., Rodolfo, M.A.; Costa Rican diplomatist; b. 13 Sept. 1932, San José; s. of Enrique Silva and Mariana Vargas; m. Margaret Nealey 1959; one s.; ed. Univ. of Costa Rica, Univ. of North Carolina.
Urban Planner, Nat. Inst. of Housing and Urban Planning 58-62; Dir. of Co-ordination and Nat. Planning, Office of the Pres. 63-66; Exec. Vice-Pres. Cen. American Bank for Econ. Integration, Honduras 66-71; Minister of Public Works and Transportation 71-74; Amb. to U.S.A. (also accred. to Canada) and OAS 74-; Dir. Professional Coll. of Eng. 60; Dir. Interamerican Planning Soc. 73-74.
Leisure interests: tennis, chess, stamps, travel.
Publs. *Water Consumption Related to Land Use in Urban Areas* 58, *Traffic Studies in San José* 60, *National Development Plans for Costa Rica* 65, *The Central American Integration* 68, *Multinational Planning of Physical Infrastructure* 74.
2112 South Street, N.W., Washington, D.C. 20008, U.S.A.; P.O.B. 1188, San José, Costa Rica.
Telephone: 332-9325 (Office); 21-31-95.

Silver, Robert Simpson, C.B.E., M.A., B.SC., PH.D., D.SC.; British mechanical engineer; b. 13 March 1913, Montrose, Scotland; s. of Alexander Clark Silver and Isabella Simpson; m. Jean MacIntyre Bruce 1937; two s.; ed. Montrose Acad. and Glasgow Univ.
Research Physicist, I.C.I. Ltd. 36-39; Head of Research Dept., G. & J. Weir Ltd. 39-46; Asst. Dir. of Research, Gas Research Board 46-48; Dir. of Research, Federated Foundries Ltd. 48-54; Chief Designer, John Brown Land Boilers Ltd. 54-56; Technical Dir. G. & J. Weir Ltd. 56-62; Prof. of Mechanical Engineering, Heriot-Watt Univ., Edinburgh 62-66; James Watt Prof. of Mechanical Engineering, Univ. of Glasgow Jan. 67-; Inst. of Mechanical Engineers Prizes: George Stephenson Prize 45, Thomas Lowe Gray Prize 64, James Clayton Prize 65; Memorial Award, American Soc. of Mechanical Engineers 63; UNESCO Science Prize 68.
Leisure interest: fly fishing.
Publs. *An Introduction to Thermodynamics* 71; many papers on thermodynamics and mechanical engineering of power and process plant with particular reference to desalination in later work.
Department of Mechanical Engineering, University of Glasgow, Glasgow, W.2; Home: 14 Beech Avenue, Glasgow, S.1, Scotland.
Telephone: 041-339-8855, Ext. 302 (Univ.); 041-427-1322 (Home).

Silverstein, Abe; American aeronautical engineer; b. 15 Sept. 1908; ed. Rose Polytechnic Inst.
Junior Engineer, Langley Laboratory, Nat. Advisory Cttee. for Aeronautics (now Nat. Aeronautics and Space Admin., N.A.S.A.) 29-40, successively, Head Full-Scale Wind Tunnel, Chief Engine Installation Div., Chief Wind Tunnel and Flight Div., Chief of Research; Assoc. Dir., Lewis Flight Propulsion Lab. 40-58; Dir. of Space Flight Programs, N.A.S.A. 58-61; Dir. Lewis Research Center 61-Nov. 69; involved in environmental planning, Repub. Steel Corpn. 70-; mem. Int. Acad. of Astronautics, Nat. Acad. of Eng.; Fellow, American Inst. of Astronautics, American Astronautical Soc., Royal Aeronautical Soc.; numerous awards; five hon. degrees; author of some fifty scientific papers.
21160 Seabury Avenue, Fairview Park, Ohio 44126; and Republic Building, Cleveland, Ohio 44135, U.S.A.

Simão, José Veiga, PH.D.; Portuguese physicist and politician; b. 13 Feb. 1929, Guarda; ed. Universidade de Coimbra and Univ. of Cambridge, England.
With Dept. of Nuclear Physics, Cavendish Lab., Univ. of Cambridge 53-57; Prof. of Physics, Univ. de Coimbra 59-62; Rector, Univ. of Mozambique 62-70; Minister of Educ. 70-74; Perm. Rep. to UN 74-75.
c/o Ministério dos Assuntos Exteriores, Lisbon, Portugal.

Simatupang, Lieut.-Gen. Tahi Bonar; Indonesian international church official and retd. army officer; b. 28 Jan. 1920, Sidikalang; s. of late Simon Mangaraja Soaduon and of Mina Boru Sibuea; m. Sumarti Budiardjo 1949; two s. one d.; ed. Mil. Acad.
Director of Org., Gen. Staff of Indonesian Nat. Army 45-48; Deputy Chief of Staff, Armed Forces of Repub. of Indonesia 48-49, Acting Chief of Staff 49-51, Chief of Staff 51-54; Mil. Adviser to Govt. of Indonesia 54-59; retd. from mil. service 59; Pres. Council of Churches in Indonesia 71-, Christian Conf. in Asia 72-, World Council of Churches 75-; mem. Supreme Advisory Council, Republic of Indonesia 73-; D.Hum.Litt. (Tulsa Univ.) 69.
Leisure interest: reading.
Publs. *Pioneer in War, Pioneer in Peace* (Role of the Armed Forces in Indonesia) 54, *Report from Banaran—Experiences during the People's War* 59, *Christian Task in Revolution* 66.
Jalan Diponegoro 55, Jakarta, Indonesia.
Telephone: 48234.

Simba, Iddi, B.SC., C.E.R.; Tanzanian banking official; b. 8 Oct. 1935, Usumbura; m. Mrs. Khadija Simba; one s. two d.; ed. Panjab Univ., Pakistan, and Univ. of Toulouse, France.
Agricultural Field Officer, Ministry of Agriculture 61-62; Asst. Dir. of Planning, Ministry of Econ. Affairs and Planning; Alt. Exec. Dir. IBRD 66-68; Chair. and Dir.-Gen. East African Devt. Bank Feb. 68-; Fellow Int. Bankers' Asscn., and Econ. Devt. Inst. (IBRD).
Leisure interests: music, light reading.
Publs. *Planning of a typical peasant farm to meet complete dietary and cash needs of a five-member peasant family* 62, *The use of a national centre for the collection of Agricultural Statistics in the planning of peasant agriculture in Tanzania* 64.
East African Development Bank, P.O. Box 7128, Kampala, Uganda.
Telephone: Kampala 30021.

Simenon, Georges; Belgian novelist; b. 13 Feb. 1903, Liège; s. of Désiré and Henriette (née Brull) Simenon; m. Denise Ouimet 1950; three s. one d.; ed. Coll. St. Servais, Liège.
Mem. Acad. Royale de Langue et de Littérature Française, Brussels.
Publs. 212 novels including 80 in the Maigret series; books translated into 47 languages and published in 32 countries.
155 avenue de Cour, 1007 Lausanne, Switzerland.
Telephone: Lausanne 33-39-79 (Office).

Simkin, William E.; American labour arbitrator and mediator; b. 13 Jan. 1907, Merrifield, N.Y.; s. of Alfred E. Simkin and Florence Manchester; m. Ruth Commons 1929; two s.; ed. Earlham Coll. and Univ. of Pennsylvania.
Principal, Cen. High School, Sherwood 28-30; Teacher Brooklyn Friends School 30-32; Rep. in W. Virginia, American Friends Service Cttee. 32-37; Instructor Wharton School of Finance and Commerce, Pennsylvania Univ. 37-39; Labor Arbitrator 39-61 and 69-; Assoc. Impartial Chair. Philadelphia Men's Clothing Industry 40-61, Philadelphia Dress Industry 47-61; Arbitrator, American Viscose Corpn. 47-61, Sun Shipbuilding Co. 45-49, and for many other firms; Pres. Nat. Acad. of Arbitrators 50; Dir. Fed. Mediation and Conciliation Service 61-69; Chair. Basic Steel Industry Incentive Study Group 69-70; Chair. Labor Relations Panel, Fed. Reserve System 70-; Chair. Foreign Service Grievance Board 71-; Lecturer and Fellow, Harvard Univ. 69-73.
Leisure interests: woodwork, golf.
5210 N. Nina Drive, Tucson, Arizona 85704, U.S.A.
Telephone: (602) 888-4091.

Simms, Most Rev. George Otto, PH.D., D.D.; Irish ecclesiastic; b. 4 July 1910, Dublin; s. of John Francis Arthur and Ottilie Simms; m. Mercy Felicia 1941; three s. two d.; ed. Cheltenham Coll. and Trinity Coll., Dublin.
Ordained Deacon 35, Priest 36; Curate-Asst., St. Bartholomew's, Dublin 35-38; Chaplain, Lincoln Theological Coll. 38-39; Dean of Residence, Trinity Coll., Dublin 39-52; Chaplain, Church of Ireland Training Coll. 43-52; Dean of Cork 52; Bishop of Cork 52-56; Archbishop of Dublin, Bishop of Glendalough and Kildare, Primate of Ireland 56-69; Archbishop of Armagh and Primate of all Ireland 69-; Chair. Irish Council of Churches 72-74; mem. Royal Irish Acad.
Publs. Joint Editor, Facsimile Edition of the *Book of Kells* 51, Facsimile Edition of the *Book of Durrow* 60; *For Better, for Worse* 45, *The Book of Kells: a short description* 50, *The Bible in Perspective* 53, *Memoir of Michael Lloyd Ferrar* 62, *Christ within Me* 75.
The Palace, Armagh, Ireland.
Telephone: Armagh 522851.

Simon, Claude; French writer; b. 10 Oct. 1913, Tananarive (Madagascar); ed. Collège Stanislas, Paris.
Prix de l'Express for *La Route des Flandres* 60; Prix Médicis for *Histoire* 67.
Publs. *Le Tricheur* 45, *La Corde Raide* 47, *Le Vent* 57, *L'Herbe* 58, *La Route des Flandres* 60, *La Palace* 62, *Histoire* 67, *La Bataille de Pharsale* 69, *Orion Aveugle* 70, *Les Corps Conducteurs* 71, *Triptyque* 73.
Editions de Minuit, 7 rue Bernard-Palissy, 75006 Paris; 3 place Monge, 75005 Paris; place Vieille, Salses, 66600 Rivesattes, France.
Telephone: 587-10-59 (Paris).

Simon, Herbert A., PH.D.; American social scientist and professor; b. 15 June 1916, Milwaukee, Wis.; s. of Arthur Simon and Edna (Merkel) Simon; m. Dorothea Pye 1937; one s. two d.; ed. Univ. of Chicago.
Staff mem. Int. City Managers' Asscn. 37-39; mem. Research Staff, Univ. of Calif. at Berkeley 39-42, Asst. Prof., later Prof., Ill. Inst. of Technology 42-49, Chair. of Dept. 46-49; Prof. of Admin., then Chair. of Dept. and Assoc. Dean, Carnegie-Mellon Univ. 49-66, Richard King Mellon Prof. of Computer Science and Psychology 66-; Chair. Board of Dirs. Social Science Research Council 61-66, Div. of Behavioral Sciences of Nat. Research Council 68-70; Ford Lecturer, New York Univ. 60, Vanuxem Lecturer, Princeton Univ. 61, William James Lecturer, Harvard Univ. 63, Harris Lecturer, Northwestern Univ. 67, Compton Lecturer, Mass. Inst. of Technology 68; mem. President's Science Advisory Cttee. 68-72, Nat. Acad. of Sciences, American Philosophical Soc., Board of Trustees, Carnegie-Mellon Univ. 72-; Distinguished Scientific Contributions Award, American Psychological Asscn. 69; A. M. Turing Award, Asscn. for Computing Machinery 75; Hon. D.Sc. (Yale Univ., Case Inst. of Technology), Hon. LL.D. (Univ. of Chicago, McGill Univ.), Hon. Fil.D. (Lund Univ.), Hon. Dr. Econ.Sc. (Erasmus Univ.).
Leisure interests: hiking, music.
Publs. *Administrative Behavior* 47, 57, *Public Administration* 50, *Models of Man* 57, *Organizations* 58, *The Shape of Automation* 60, 65, *The Sciences of the Artificial* 69, *Human Problem-Solving* 72.
Carnegie-Mellon University, Pittsburgh, Pa. 15213, U.S.A.
Telephone: 412-621-2600.

Simon, Ing. Josef; Czechoslovak economist and politician; b. 10 March 1921, Medlešice.
Head of Dept., Regional Cttee. C.P. of Czechoslovakia 48-50; Dir. nat. enterprise Tatra, Kopřivnice 51-52; Head of Dept., Ministry of Engineering 53-57; Dir. Skoda enterprise, V.I. Lenin Works, Pilsen 58-62; Head of Dept., Ministry of Heavy Engineering 62-66; Dir. AZNP Motor Car Works, Mladá Boleslav 66-69; fmr. Minister of Industry, Czech S.R.; Deputy to Czech Nat. Council and Fed. Assembly 69-71; to House of Nations, Fed. Assembly 69-; mem. Cen. Cttee. of C.P. of Czechoslovakia 71-; Minister of Metallurgy and Eng. 71-73, of Metallurgy and Heavy Eng. 73-74; Chair. CMEA Standing Cttee. for Eng. 74-; Vice-Premier of Czechoslovakia 74-; Order of Labour, Order of Friendship between Nations (U.S.S.R.) 74, and other awards.
Federal Government, Prague, Czechoslovakia.

Simon, Neil; American playwright; b. 1927.
Wrote for various television programmes 56-60; author of plays: *Come Blow Your Horn* 61, *Little Me* (musical) 62, *Barefoot in the Park* 63, *The Odd Couple* 65, *Sweet Charity* 66 (musical), *The Star-Spangled Girl* 66, *Plaza Suite* 68, *Promises, Promises* 68, *The Last of the Red Hot Lovers* 69, *The Gingerbread Lady* 70, *Charlie Bobby, The Good Doctor* 73, *The Prisoner of Second Avenue, The Sunshine Boys* 73, *God's Favorite* 74; mem. Dramatists Guild; Emmy Award 56; Antoinette Perry (Tony) Award Best playwright 65.
225 East 57th Street, New York, N.Y. 10022, U.S.A.

Simon, Pál, D.SC.; Hungarian engineer and politician; b. 1929, Miscolc; ed. Budapest Technical Coll.
Joined Hungarian Communist Party 47; Mil. Engineer, Ministry of Defence 52-55; worked in Moscow Inst. for Light Chemistry 55-59; Deputy Dir. Hungarian Petroleum and Natural Gas Research Inst. 59-62; Dir.-Gen. Nat. Petroleum and Gas Industry Trust 73; Deputy Minister of Heavy Industry, Minister July 75-; Dir. Danube Oil Refinery; mem. CMEA Perm. Cttee. for Petroleum and Gas Industry 65-; mem. Budapest Cttee. Hungarian Socialist Workers' Party 75-; Titular Lecturer, Veszprém Univ. of Chemical Eng.; Gold Award, Labour Order of Merit.
Ministry of Heavy Industry, 1055 Budapest, Markó-utca 16, Hungary.
Telephone: 114-250.

Simon, William Edward; American financier and government official; b. 27 Nov. 1927, Patterson, N.J.; m. Carol Girard; two s. five d.; ed. Lafayette Coll., Easton, Pennsylvania.
Joined Union Securities, N.Y. 52, Asst. Vice-Pres., Man. Municipal Trading Dept. 55; Vice-Pres. Weedon & Co. 57-64; joined Salomon Bros. 64, later Partner; Deputy Sec. U.S. Treasury Dept. Jan. 73-74, Head of Federal Energy Office Dec. 73-74; Sec. of the Treasury April 74-; Chair. Econ. Policy Board Oct. 74-; Chair. Council on Wage and Price Stability 75-; mem. Board of Govs., Exec. Cttee. Investment Bankers' Asscn. of America until 72; mem. Board of Dirs., Exec. Cttee. Securities Industry Asscn. 72, Chair. Public Finance Council; Founder, Past Pres. Asscn. of Primary Dealers in U.S. Govt. Securities; Nat. Chair. Fund Raising, U.S. Olympic Cttee.; Chair. Debt Management Cttee. of N.Y.; Trustee, Lafayette Coll., Mannes Coll. of Music, Newark Acad.
U.S. Treasury Department, 15th Street and Pennsylvania Avenue, N.W., Washington, D.C. 20220, U.S.A.

Simon of Glaisdale, Baron (Life Peer), cr. 70; **Jocelyn Edward Salis Simon,** Kt., P.C.; British judge; b. 15 Jan. 1911, London; s. of Frank Cecil Simon and Claire Evelyn Simon, M.B.E.; m. Fay Elizabeth Leicester Pearson 1948; ed. Gresham's School, Holt and Trinity Hall, Cambridge.
Member of Parliament (Conservative) 51-62; Joint Parl. Under-Sec. of State, Home Office 57-58; Financial Sec. to Treasury 58-59; Solicitor-Gen. 59-62; Pres. of Probate, Divorce and Admiralty Div. of High Court 62-71; Lord of Appeal in Ordinary 71-.
Publs. Co-author of *Change is our Ally* 54, *Rule of Law* 55, *The Church and the Law of Nullity* 55.
Home: Midge Hall, Glaisdale Head, nr. Whitby, Yorkshire, England.

Simonen, Aarre Edvard, LL.B., LL.L.; Finnish politician; b. 18 Nov. 1913, Helsinki; s. of Edward Simonen and Ida Alina Hagstedt-Haapala; m. Leni Lahja Nikkinen 1945; one s. two d.; ed. Univ. of Helsinki.
Sec. of Welfare Offices in Helsinki 36, Chief of Legal Dept. 37-42; First Sec. of Asscn. of Finnish Cities 42-46, Gen. Sec. 46, Chair. 47-57; Minister of Interior 48-50; mem. of Parl. 51-62; Chair. State House Admin. 51-53; Minister of Trade and Industry 54-56, of Finance 56-57; mem. Board of Govs., Bank of Finland 57-, Dep. Gov. 72-; Deputy Prime Minister 57; Minister of Justice 66-70; Chair. Social Dem. Workers and Smallfarmers Union 64-70, Socialist Workers Party 73-; mem., Sec. and Chair. of numerous municipal and State Cttees.
Rauhankatu 13.A, Helsinki 17, Finland.

Simonet, Henri François, D. EN D., D. ÈS SC.; Belgian politician; b. 10 May 1931, Brussels; m. Marie-Louise Angenent 1960; one s. one d.; ed. Univ. Libre de Bruxelles and Columbia Univ., U.S.A.
Assistant, Univ. Libre de Bruxelles 56-58, now Prof.; Financial Adviser, Inst. National d'Etudes pour le Développement du Bas-Congo 58-59; Legal Adviser, Comm. of Brussels Stock Exchange 59-60; Deputy Dir. Office of Econ. Programming 61; Dir. of Cabinet of Ministry of Econ. Affairs and Power 61-65; Dir. of Cabinet of Deputy Prime Minister responsible for Co-ordination of Econ. Policy 65; Mayor of Anderlecht 66-; Deputy from Brussels 68-; Minister of Econ. Affairs Jan. 72-73; mem., Vice-Pres. Comm. of the European Communities 73-.
Publs. Various books and articles on economics, financial and political topics.
Commission of the European Communities, 200 rue de la Loi, 1040 Brussels, Belgium.

Simonetta; b. Duchess Colonna di Cesaro; d. of Duke Giovanni Colonna di Cesaro and Countess Barbara Antonelli; m. 1st Count Galeazzo Visconti di Modrone 1944, one d.; m. 2nd Alberto Fabiani (fashion designer) 1952, one s.; separated Feb. 1970 and has taken back her maiden name of Duchess Colonna di Cesaro.
Opened fashion Atelier, Rome 46; transferred fashion business to Paris 62; Philadelphia Fashion Group Award 53, Davison Paxon Award, Atlanta 59, Fashion Oscar from Filene's of Boston 60; after five consecutive years in list of world's best dressed women is in "Hall of Fame"; Hon. citizen of Austin, New Orleans and Las Vegas.
Publ. *A Snob in the Kitchen* 67.
Office: 40 rue François 1er, Paris 8e, France.
Telephone: 359-5671 (Office).

Simonnet, Maurice-René; French lawyer and politician; b. 4 Oct. 1919, Lyons; m. Jeanne-Marie Montagne; eight c.; ed. Ecole des Sciences Politiques, Paris, Faculty of Law, Lyons.
Deputy for Drôme 46-62; Sec. of State for the Merchant Marine 57-58; Sec.-Gen. Mouvement Républicain Populaire (M.R.P.) 55-62; Prof. of Int. Law, Univ. of Lyons; Officier Légion d'Honneur, Croix de Guerre (39-45), Croix de Combattant Volontaire de la Résistance.
65 Avenue Victor-Hugo, 26000 Valence, France.
Telephone: (75) 44-31-46.

Simonov, Konstantin Mikhailovich (real name Kirill); Soviet journalist and writer; b. 28 Nov. 1915, Tver (now Kalinin); ed. M. Gorky Literary Inst., Moscow.
War corresp. for *Red Star* and *Pravda* 38; mem. C.P.S.U.

42-; Deputy to Supreme Soviet 46-54; Editor *Literaturnaya gazeta* (Literary Gazette) 50-53; Editor *Novy Mir* (New World) 46-50, 54-58; mem. Sec. Union of Soviet Writers 46-59; six State Prizes, Order of Lenin, Red Banner of Labour, Badge of Honour and other decorations.

Publs. include poems: *Real Men* 38, *Ice Blood Battle* 38, *Pavel Cherny* 38, *A Son of an Artilleryman* 42, *Friends and Enemies* 48, *Selected Poems* 60, 64, *Three Note Books* 64; plays: *A Story of Love* 40, *Fellow from Our Town* 42, *The Russians* 42, *Under the Chestnut Trees* 45, *Russian Question* 46, *Alien Shadow* 49, *The Fourth* 62; novels: *Days and Nights* 44, *Collected Works* (3 vols.) 53, *Comrades in Arms* 53, *Those Alive and Those Dead* 59, *Over there, where were once . . .* 64, *Soldiers are not Born* 64, *From Lopatin's Notes* 65, *Collected Works* 66.
U.S.S.R. Union of Writers, Ulitsa Vorovskogo 52, Moscow, U.S.S.R.

Simonov, Yevgeny Rubenovich; Soviet theatrical producer; b. 21 June 1925; ed. Maly Theatre School.
Art Dir. worker theatre club Kauchuk 48-54; Producer, E. Vakhtangov Theatre 55-62, Chief Stage Dir. 68-; Chief Stage Dir. Maly Theatre 62-68; Teacher B. Schukin Theatre School 54-; Honoured Artist of the R.S.F.S.R.
Main productions: Maly Theatre: *Two Gentlemen of Verona* (Shakespeare) 52, *Filumena Marturano* (De Filippo) 56, *Town at Daybreak* (Arbuzov) 57, *Irkutsk Story* (Arbuzov) 59, *Little Tragedies* (Pushkin) 59; E. Vakhtangov Theatre: *Misfortune from Intellect* (Griboedov) 63, *They are Waiting for Us Somewhere* (Arbuzov) 63, *Clever Things* (Marshak) 65.
E. Vakhtangov Theatre, 26 Arbat, Moscow, U.S.S.R.

Simonov, Yuri Ivanovich; Soviet conductor; b. 4 March 1941, Saratov; ed. Leningrad Conservatoire.
Conductor, Kislovodsk Philharmonic Soc. 67-69; Conductor, State Bolshoi Opera and Ballet Theatre, Moscow 69-70, Chief Conductor 70-; in Bolshoi Theatre conducts: *The Marriage of Figaro, Aida, Boris Godunov, Prince Igor, Pskovityanka*; has toured solo and with Theatre in France, Italy and German Democratic Republic; Laureate of 2nd U.S.S.R. Competition of Conductors, Moscow 66; First Prize, 5th Int. Competition of Conductors, Santa Cecilia Acad., Rome 68.
Bolshoi State Academic Theatre, 1 ploshchad Sverdlova, Moscow, U.S.S.R.

Simonsen, Mário Henrique; Brazilian engineer and economist; b. 19 Feb. 1935, Guanabara; s. of Mario Simonsen and Carmen Roxo Simonsen; m. Iluska Pereira da Cunha Simonsen; ed. Univ. of Brazil, Univ. of Rio de Janeiro.
Lecturer Instituto de Matemática Pura e Aplicada 58, Escola Nacional de Engenharia 58-60; Dir. Crédito, Financiamento e Investimento S.A. 62-63; Dir. Econs. Dept. Confederação Nacional da Indústria 61-65; Dir. Post-Graduate School of Econs., Fundação Getúlio Vargas, 65-; mem. Board Banco Nacional de Habitação 65-; mem. Board Mercedes Benz do Brasil 68-; Vice-Pres. Banco Bozano, Simonsen de Investimentos 69-; Pres. Fundação MOBRAL—Movimento Brasileiro de Alfabetização 70-; Minister of Finance 74-.
Publs. *Ensaios sobre Economia e Política Econômica* 61, *Teoria Microeconômica* 67-69, *Brasil 2001* 69, *Brasil 2002* 72, and various essays and monographs.
Ministério das Finanças, Esplanada dos Ministérios, Brasília D.F., Brazil.

Simpson, Alan, M.A. D.PHIL.; American (b. British) educator and administrator; b. 23 July 1912, Gateshead; s. of George and Isabella Graham Simpson; m. Mary M. McEldowney 1938; one s. two d.; ed. Dame Allan's School, Newcastle-on-Tyne, Worcester Coll. and Merton Coll., Oxford, and Harvard Univ.
Senior Lecturer in Modern British History and American History, Univ. of St. Andrews, Scotland 38-46; Lecturer in Constitutional Law, Univ. Coll., Dundee, Scotland 38-46; Royal Artillery 41-45; Asst. Prof. of History, Univ. of Chicago 46-54, Assoc. Prof. 54-59, Thomas E. Donnelley Prof. of History, and Dean of Coll., Univ. of Chicago 59-64; Pres. of Vassar Coll. 64-; L.H.D. (Nat. Coll. of Educ., Evanston, Univ. of Rochester); LL.D. (Knox College).
Leisure interest: planting trees.
Publs. *The People Shall Judge: Readings in the Formation of American Policy* (2 vols.) (co-author) 49, *Puritanism in Old and New England* 55, *The Wealth of the Gentry 1540-1660: East Anglian Studies* 61, *Diary of King Philip's War (1675-76) by Colonel Benjamin Church* (with Mary Simpson) 75.
The President's House, Vassar College, Poughkeepsie, N.Y. 12601, U.S.A.

Simpson, George Gaylord, PH.D.; American biologist, geologist and palaeontologist; b. 16 June 1902, Chicago, Ill.; s. of Joseph Alexander and Helen Julia (Kinney) Simpson; m. 1st Lydia Pedroja 1923, 2nd Anne Roe 1938; four d.; ed. Colorado and Yale Univs.
Fellow Nat. Research Council 26-27; Asst. Curator American Museum of Natural History, New York 27-28, Assoc. Curator 29-42, Curator 42-59, Chair. Geology and Palaeontology Depts. 44-58; Prof. Columbia Univ. 45-59; Alexander Agassiz Prof. of Vertebrate Palaeontology, Museum of Comparative Zoology, Harvard Univ. 59-70; Geosciences Prof., Univ. of Arizona 67-; Trustee and Pres. Simroe Foundation, Tucson, Ariz. 68-; mem. Nat. Acad. of Sciences; foreign mem. Royal Soc. (London); Lewis Prize 42, Thompson Medal 43 and Elliott Medal 44, 64, Gaudry Medal 47, Penrose Medal 52, André H. Dumont Medal 53, Commemorative Medal 58, Darwin Plaquette 59, Verrill Medal (Yale Univ.) 66 Distinguished Achievement Medal (American Museum) 66, Wilbur Cross Medal 69; Hon. Sc.D. (Yale, Princeton, Oxford, Durham, Chicago, Kenyon, Cambridge, New Mexico, York (Canada), Colorado Univs.); Hon. LL.D. (Glasgow Univ.); Dr. h.c. (Univ. of Paris); Linnean Soc. Gold Medal 62, Royal Soc. Darwin Medal 62; Nat. Medal of Science 65, etc.
Publs. include *American Mesozoic Mammalia* 29, *Quantitative Zoology* (with Anne Roe) 39, *Tempo and Mode in Evolution* 44, *The Meaning of Evolution* 49, *Life of the Past* 53, *The Major Features of Evolution* 53, *Evolution and Geography* 53, *Life: An Introduction to Biology* (with Beck) 57, 65, *Behavior and Evolution* (with Anne Roe) 58, *Principles of Animal Taxonomy* 61, *This View of Life* 64, *Biology and Man* 69.
5151 E. Holmes Street, Tucson, Arizona 85711, U.S.A. Telephone: 602-326-1345.

Simpson, Norman Frederick; British playwright; b. 29 Jan. 1919, London; s. of George Frederick Simpson; m. Joyce Bartlett 1944; one d.; ed. Emanuel School, London, and Birkbeck Coll., Univ. of London.
Teacher in adult education until 63; full-time playwright 63-.
Plays: *A Resounding Tinkle* 58, *The Hole* 58, *One Way Pendulum* (also film) 59, *The Form* 61, *The Cresta Run* 65, *Some Tall Tinkles* 68; Co-Author *Diamonds for Breakfast* (film) 68, *Was He Anyone?* 73; novel: *Harry Bleachbaker* 76.
Leisure interests: reading, walking.
c/o Robin Dalton Associates, 18 Elm Tree Road, London, N.W.8, England.

Sims, Ivor D., B.SC.; American business executive; b. 1912, Coquimbo, Chile; m. Christine Buchman; one d.; ed. Lehigh Univ.
Joined Bethlehem Steel Corpn. as junior buyer 33; purchasing agent in associated Philadelphia, Bethlehem and New England Railroad Co. 36-37, buyer Bethlehem Steel Corpn. 40-44, Asst. purchasing agent 44-50, purchasing agent 50-57, Dir. and Asst. Vice-Pres. Purchasing Dept. 57, Vice-Pres. (Admin.) 63, Exec. Vice-

Pres. 66-73, retd. 73; Dir. Int. Nickel Co. of Canada Ltd. 69-73; mem. Office of Price Stabilization Ferro-Manganese Industry Advisory Cttee. 51-53, Manganese Industry Advisory Cttee. 55, Board of Trustees, Lehigh Univ. 64, American Iron and Steel Inst., Newcomen Soc.; Dir. Nat. Asscn. of Mfrs. 69-73; Hon. LL.D. (Univ. of Liberia) 67; Knight Commdr. of the Liberian Humane Order of African Redemption 65; Commdr. of Star of Equatorial Africa 69; L-in-Life Award from Lehigh Club of N.Y. 70; Hon. LL.D. Lehigh Univ. 70.
1723 Cloverleaf Street, Bethlehem, Pa. 18017, U.S.A.

Simson, Otto von, PH.D.; German scholar; b. 17 July 1912, Berlin; m. Louise von Schönburg-Hartenstein 1936; two s.; ed. Arndt Gymnasium, Berlin and Munich Univ.
Professor of the History of Art, Chicago Univ. 45-57; Perm. Del. of the Fed. Repub. of Germany to UNESCO 59-; mem. Exec. Board UNESCO 60-64; First Counsellor, Embassy of the Fed. Repub. of Germany, Paris 59-64; Prof. Inst. History of Art, Freie Univ. Berlin; Foreign hon. mem. American Acad. of Arts and Sciences; Vice-Pres. German Nat. Comm. for UNESCO; Officier Légion d'Honneur, Commdr., Ordre Nat. de Mérite.
Publs. *Zur Genealogie der weltlichen Apotheose im Barock* 36, *Sacred Fortress: Byzantine Art and State-craft in Ravenna* 48, *The Gothic Cathedral* 56, 62, *Die Kunst des Hohen Mittelalters* 72..
1 Berlin 33, Max-Eyth-Strasse 26, Germany.
Telephone: 8312082.

Sinatra, Frank; American singer, actor and composer; b. 12 Dec. 1915, Hoboken, N.J.; m. 1st Nancy Barbato 1939 (divorced), one s. two d.; m. 2nd Ava Gardner (*q.v.*) 1951 (divorced); m. 3rd Mia Farrow (*q.v.*) 1966 (divorced); ed. Drake Inst.
Sang with Harry James and Tommy Dorsey Bands; Jean Hersholt Humanitarian Award, Motion Picture Acad. 71; Hon. citizen of Chicago 75; appeared in the films *Las Vegas Nights, Ship Ahoy*; played leading roles in the films *Higher and Higher, Anchors Aweigh, It Happened in Brooklyn, From Here to Eternity, Guys and Dolls, Not as a Stranger, The Tender Trap, The Man with the Golden Arm, Johnny Concho, The Pride and the Passion, Pal Joey, Some Came Running, Kings Go Forth, A Hole in the Head, Never So Few, The Jimmy Durante Story, Can-Can, The Devil at 4 o'clock, Sergeants Three, Robin and the Seven Hoods, Von Ryan's Express, Assault on a Queen, The Naked Runner, On the Town, High Society, The Joker is Wild, Ocean's 11, Come Blow Your Horn, Suddenly, The Manchurian Candidate, Tony Rome, Dirty Dingus Magee*, etc.; American Motion Picture Acad. Award for Best Supporting Actor for *From Here to Eternity*.
4000 Warner Boulevard, Burbank, Calif. 91503, U.S.A.

Sinclair, Ernest Keith, C.M.G., O.B.E., D.F.C., F.R.G.S.; Australian journalist; b. 13 Nov. 1914, Hawthorn, Victoria; s. of J. E. and F. Sinclair; m. Jill Nelder 1949; one s.; ed. Melbourne High School.
Served R.A.F., Second World War; C.O. 97 Pathfinder Sqdn. 44-45; Foreign Corresp., Europe 38, 46; Editor *The Age* 59-66; Chair. Australian Assoc. Press 65-66; Dir.-Gen. Television Corpn. 59-66; Consultant to Dept. of Prime Minister and Cabinet 67-74; Dir. Australian Paper Manufacturers, Hecla-Rowe Ltd., Hecron Ltd.; Deputy Chair. Australian Tourist Comm. 69-75; Vice-Pres. Library Council of Australia; Assoc. Commr. Industries Assistance Comm.
Leisure interests: swimming, reading.
138 Toorak Road West, South Yarra, Victoria 3141, Australia.
Telephone: 26-4331 (Melbourne).

Sinclair, Ian David, Q.C., B.A., LL.B.; Canadian lawyer and railway executive; b. 27 Dec. 1913, Winnipeg, Manitoba; s. of John David and Lillian Sinclair; m.

Ruth Beatrice Drennan 1942; two s. two d.; ed. public schools, Winnipeg and Univ. of Manitoba.
Assistant Solicitor, Canadian Pacific Railway Co. Ltd. 42, Solicitor 46, Asst. to Gen. Counsel 51, Gen. Solicitor 53, Vice-Pres. Gen. Council 60, Vice-Pres. Law 60, Vice-Pres. and Dir., mem. Exec. Cttee. 61; Pres. Canadian Pacific Railway Co. Ltd. 66-72, Chief Exec. Officer 69-, Chair. 72-; Dir. and Officer Canadian Pacific Air Lines Ltd., Midland Simcoe Elevator Co. Ltd., Canadian Pacific Investments Ltd., Pancanadian Petroleum Ltd., Royal Bank of Canada, Canadian Pacific Securities Ltd., Cominco Ltd.; Dir. numerous other companies; mem. Int. Advisory Cttee., Chase Manhattan Corpn., Canadian Chamber of Commerce, Montreal Board of Trade, Canadian Advisory Board, Sun Alliance and London Insurance Group, Conf. Board, N.Y.; Hon. LL.D. (Univ. of Manitoba) 67.
Leisure interests: reading, motoring.
Canadian Pacific Ltd., Windsor Station, Montreal, Quebec H3C 3E4, Canada.

Sinclair, Hon. Ian McCahon, B.A., LL.B.; Australian politician; b. June 1929, Sydney; s. of George and Hazel Sinclair; m. 1st Margaret Tarrant 1956 (died 1967), 2nd Rosemary Edna Fenton 1970; two s. two d.; ed. Knox Grammar School, Wahroonga and Sydney Univ.
Barrister 52-; mem. Legislative Council in N.S.W. Parl. 61-63, House of Reps. 63-; Minister for Social Services 65-68; Minister Assisting Minister for Trade and Industry 65-71; Minister for Shipping and Transport 68-71, for Primary Industry 71-72; Deputy Leader Country Party (now Nat. Country Party) 71-, Party Spokesman on Defence, Foreign Affairs, Law and Agric. 73-, Opposition Spokesman on Agric., Leader of Opposition in House of Reps. 74-75; Minister for Agric. and Northern Australia Nov.-Dec. 75; Leader of Govt. in House of Reps. Dec. 75-; Dir. Farmers' and Graziers' Co-operative Co. Ltd. 62-65; National Country Party.
Leisure interests: squash, sailing, surfing.
Parliament House, Canberra, A.C.T.; Home: Glenclair, Bendemeer, N.S.W., Australia.

Sinclair, Sir Ronald Ormiston, K.B.E., LL.M.; British lawyer; b. 2 May 1903, Dunedin, New Zealand; s. of W. A. Sinclair; m. Ellen Isabel Entrican 1935; two s.; ed. Auckland Univ. Coll. and Balliol Coll., Oxford.
Joined Nigerian Administrative Service 31, Magistrate 36; Resident Magistrate, Northern Rhodesia 38; Puisne Judge, Tanganyika 46-53; Chief Justice, Nyasaland 53-56; Vice-Pres. East African Court of Appeal 56-57; Chief Justice of Kenya 57-62; Pres. H.M. Court of Appeal for Eastern Africa 62-64; Pres. Court of Appeal for the Bahamas Islands Feb. 65-70, Court of Appeal for Bermuda June 65-70, Court of Appeal for British Honduras May 68-70; Chair. Industrial Tribunals, England and Wales 65-69.
Leisure interest: bird watching.
158 Victoria Avenue, Remuera, Auckland, 5, New Zealand.
Telephone: 546-391.

Sinclair of Cleeve (1st Baron, cr. 57), of Cleeve in the County of Somerset; **Robert John Sinclair,** K.C.B., K.B.E., M.A.; British industrialist; b. 29 July 1893; ed. Glasgow Acad. and Oriel Coll., Oxford.
Commissioned in 5th Battalion K.O.S.B. Aug. 14; served Gallipoli (wounded, despatches); seconded to Min. of Munitions 16, Deputy Dir., Insp. of Munitions 17-19; mem. Prime Min.'s Advisory Panel of Industrialists Jan. 39; Dir.-Gen. of Army Requirements, War Office 39-42; mem. Supply Council 39-42; mem. Army Council 40-42; Deputy for Min. of Production on Combined Production and Resources Board, Washington 42-43; Chief Exec. Min. of Production 43-45; Chair. Imperial Tobacco Co. Ltd. 47-59, Pres. 59-67; Chair. Bristol Waterworks Co. 60-71; Pres. Fed. of British

Industries 49-50, 50-51; mem. Security Comm. 65-; Pro-Chancellor Bristol Univ. 46-70; U.S. Medal of Freedom with Gold Palm; Hon. LL.D. (Bristol); Hon. Fellow, Oriel Coll., Oxford 59.
Cleeve Court, Cleeve, nr. Bristol, England.
Telephone: Yatton 832124.

Sindermann, Horst; German politician; b. 5 Sept. 1915, Dresden; *m.*; two *c.*
Member Communist Union of Youth, Saxony 29; political imprisonment 34-45 (including Sachsenhausen concentration camp); later Chief Editor *Volksstimme* (Voice of the People), Chemnitz (now Karl-Marx-Stadt); later Chief Editor, Press Service of Sozialistische Einheitspartei Deutschlands (S.E.D.); Editor S.E.D. District paper *Freiheit* (Freedom), Halle/Saale; staff of Central Cttee. S.E.D. 55-63, Cand. mem. Central Cttee. S.E.D. 58-63, mem. 63-, mem. Politburo 67-; First Deputy Chair. Council of Ministers 71-73, Chair. 73-; mem. Volkskammer 63-.
Ministerrat, Berlin, German Democratic Republic.

Sindona, Michele, D.IUR.; Italian financial lawyer; b. 8 May 1920; ed. Univ. of Messina.
Legal practice, Sicily 40-46, Milan (tax, company and finance) 46-; controls Fasco A.G. (int. financial group); Pres. Banca di Messina Keyes S.p.A.; Vice-Pres. Acciaierie Crucible Vanzetti, Banca Privata Italiana (merger of Banca Unione with Banca Privata Finanziaria); Dir. Snia Viscosa, Remington Rand Italia, Chesebrough Pond's Italia, Stabilimenti Tessili Italiani (S.T.I.), Reeves S.p.A., Società Industriale Agricola per la Produzione di Cellulosa (S.I.A.C.E.) and other companies.

Singer, Isaac Bashevis, D.H.L.; American journalist and author; b. 14 July 1904, Radzymin, Poland; *s.* of Pinchos Menachem and Bathsheba née Zylberman; *m.* Alma Haimann 1940; one *s.*; ed. Rabbinical Seminary, Warsaw.
Came to U.S.A. 35; on staff of *Jewish Daily Forward* 35-; Nat. Inst. of Arts and Letters grant 59, Nat. Council on the Arts grant 66; mem. Nat. Inst. of Arts and Letters, American Acad. of Arts and Sciences; Louis Lamed Prize (twice), Creative Arts Award of Brandeis Univ. 70, Nat. Book Award 70.
Leisure interest: walking in the bad air of New York City.
Publs. *The Family Moskat* 50, *Satan in Goray* 55, *Gimpel the Fool and other Stories* 57, *The Magician of Lublin* 59, *The Spinoza of Market Street* 61, *The Slave* 62, *Short, Friday* 64, *Zlateh the Goat and Other Stories* 66, *In My Father's Court* 66, *The Manor* 67, *The Seance* 68, *The Estate* 69, *A Friend of Kafka and Other Stories* 70, *Enemies, A Love Story* 72, *Crown of Feathers* 74.
209 West 86th Street, New York, N.Y. 10024, U.S.A.
Telephone: 212-877-5968.

Singer, Isadore Manuel, PH.D.; American mathematician; b. 4 May 1924, Detroit, Mich.; *s.* of Simon Singer and Freda Rose; *m.* Sheila Ruff 1961; two *s.* one *d.*; ed. Univs. of Michigan and Chicago.
C.L.E. Moore Instructor at Mass. Inst. of Technology (M.I.T.) 50-52; Asst. Prof. Univ. of Calif. (Los Angeles) 52-54; Visiting Asst. Prof. Columbia Univ. 54-55; Visiting mem. Inst. for Advanced Study, Princeton 55-56; Asst. Prof. M.I.T. 56, Assoc. Prof. 58, Prof. of Mathematics 59-, Norbert Wiener Prof. of Mathematics 70; mem. Nat. Acad. of Sciences, American Mathematical Soc., Mathematical Asscn. of America, American Acad. of Arts and Sciences; Sloan Fellow 59-62, Guggenheim Fellow 68-69; Bôcher Memorial Prize 69, 75-76.
Leisure interests: literature, hiking, tennis.
Publs. *Lecture Notes on Elementary Topology and Geometry;* author of research articles in functional analysis, differential geometry and topology.

Department of Mathematics, Massachusetts Institute of Technology, Cambridge, Mass. 02139, U.S.A.
Telephone: 617-253-2945.

Singh, Air Chief Marshal Arjan, D.F.C.; Indian air force officer; b. 15 April 1919; ed. Government Coll., Lahore, R.A.F. Coll., Cranwell, and Imperial Defence Coll., London.
Wing Commdr. 45, Group Capt. 47, Air Commodore 50, Air Vice Marshal 59, Air Marshal 64, Air Chief Marshal 66; Chief of Air Staff 64-69; Amb. to Switzerland 71-74; High Commr. to Kenya 74-; Patron, All India Fed. of the Deaf; Padma Vibhushan.
Indian High Commission, Nairobi, Kenya; and c/o Grindlays Bank Ltd., New Delhi, India.

Singh, Dinesh, B.A.; Indian politician; b. 19 July 1925, Kalakankar, Uttar Pradesh; *s.* of Raja Avadhesh Singh and Rani Lakshami Kumari; *m.* Rani Neelima Kumari Singh 1944; six *d.*; ed. Doon School, Dehra Doon, and Colvin Coll., Lucknow Univ.
Member of Parl. 57-; fmr. Private Sec. to Prime Minister; fmr. Sec. to the High Comm. for India in London, to the Embassy in Paris; leader Indian Dels. to FAO, ECAFE, ECOSOC and UN; Deputy Minister for External Affairs 62-Jan. 66; Minister of State for External Affairs 66-67; Minister of Commerce 67-69; Pres. of UNCTAD II 68-72; Minister of External Affairs 69-70, of Industrial Devt. and Internal Trade 70-71.
Leisure interest: photography.
1 Thyagaraja Marg, New Delhi 11; and Raj Bhavan, Kalakankar, Dist. Pratapgarh (U.P.), India.
Telephone: 371766 (New Delhi); 40 (Kalakankar).

Singh, Hukam; Indian politician; b. 30 Aug. 1895; ed. Govt. High School, Montgomery, Khalsa Coll., Amritsar and Law Coll., Lahore.
Lawyer; fmr. Pres. Singh Sabha, Montgomery; Man. Khalsa High School, Montgomery 41, 43-45; Pres. Shiromani Akali Dal; imprisoned 23-25, 55; Puisne Judge, State High Court, Kapurthala 47-48; mem. Constituent Assembly 48-50, Provisional Parl. 50-52, Lok Sabha (Parl.) 52-57, 57-; Deputy Speaker, Lok Sabha 56-62, Speaker 62-67; Gov. of Rajasthan 67-72; Del. to Commonwealth Parl. Confs. 59, 61, 62; Hon. Litt.D.; Congress Party.
Publs. *Russia as I Saw It, Russia Today, Some Reflections.*
c/o Governor's Office, Jaipur, Rajasthan, India.

Singh, Dr. Jogendra; Indian politician; b. 30 Oct. 1903, Rai Bareli.
Elected Cen. Legislative Ass. 37; mem. Public Accounts and Estimate Cttees.; Opposition Chief Whip; leader Indian Del. to FAO, Rome 58; mem. Constituent Assembly Provisional Parl., Lok Sabha and Rajya Sabha 34-63; Chair. Indian Refineries 63-64; mem. for Rajya Sabha 65-71; mem. Agricultural Comm. and Chair. House Cttee. Rajya Sabha; Chair. Delhi Sikh Gurdwaras Board 71-75; Gov. of Orissa 71-72; Gov. of Rajasthan 72-.
Office of the Governor, Jaipur, Rajasthan, India.

Singh, Karan, M.A., PH.D.; Indian politician; b. 9 March 1931, Cannes, France; *s.* of Lieut.-Gen. H.H. Maharaja Sir Hari Singhji, G.C.S.I., G.C.I.E., G.C.V.O., and Maharani Tara Devi, C.I.; *m.* Princess Yasho Rajya Lakshmi of Nepal 1950; two *s.* one *d.*; ed. Doon School, Univ. of Jammu and Kashmir, and Delhi Univ.
Appointed Regent of Jammu and Kashmir 49; elected Sadar-i-Riyasat (Head of State) by Jammu and Kashmir Legislative Assembly Nov. 52; recognized by Pres. of India and assumed office 17 Nov. 1952, re-elected 57 and 62, Gov. 65-67; Union Minister for Tourism and Civil Aviation 67-73, for Health and Family Planning 73-75; Vice-Pres. World Health Assembly 75-; Sec.

Jawaharlal Nehru Memorial Fund; Chair. Indian Board for Wild Life.

3 Nyaya Marg, Chanakyapuri, New Delhi 11, India.

Telephone: 371744.

Singh, Kewal, B.A., LL.B.; Indian diplomatist; b. 1 June 1915, Lyallpur (West Pakistan); s. of late S. Mihan Singh; m. Shamie Grewal; one d.; ed. Forman Christian Coll., Lahore, Law Coll., Lahore, and Balliol Coll., Oxford.

Joined Indian Civil Service 38; Indian Civil Service appointments 40-48; First Sec. Indian Embassy, Ankara 48-49; Indian Military Mission, Berlin 49-51; Chargé d'Affaires, Lisbon 51-53; Consul-General, Pondicherry 53-54; Chief Commr., State of Pondicherry, Karaikal, Mahe and Yanam 54-57; awarded Padma Shri for distinguished services leading to merger of French Possessions with India; Amb. to Cambodia 57-58, to Sweden, Denmark and Finland 59-62; Deputy High Commr. in U.K. 62-65; High Commr. in Pakistan 65-66; Amb. to U.S.S.R. 66-68; Sec. Ministry of External Affairs 68-70; Amb. to Fed. Repub. of Germany 70-72; Foreign Sec. 72-.

Ministry of External Affairs, Government of India, South Block, New Delhi, India.

Telephone: 372318.

Singh, Khushwant, LL.B.; Indian author; b. 1915; ed. Government Coll., Lahore, King's Coll. and Inner Temple, London.

Practised, High Court, Lahore 39-47; joined Indian Ministry of External Affairs 47; Press Attaché, Canada and then Public Relations Officer, London 48-51; Ministry of Information and Broadcasting; edited *Yojana*; Dept. of Mass Communication, UNESCO 54-56; commissioned by Rockefeller Foundation and Muslim Univ., Aligarh to write a history of the Sikhs 58; Grove Press Award; Padma Bhushan 74; Editor *The Illustrated Weekly of India*.

Publs. *Mark of Vishnu* 49, *The Sikhs* 51, *Train to Pakistan* 54, *Sacred Writings of the Sikhs* 60, *I shall not hear the Nightingale* 61, *Umrao Jan Ada—Courtesan of Lucknow* (trans.) 61, *History of the Sikhs (1769-1839)* Vol. I 62, *Ranjit Singh: Maharaja of the Punjab* 62, *Fall of the Sikh Kingdom* 62, *The Skeleton* (trans.) 63, *Land of the Five Rivers* (trans.) 64, *History of the Sikhs (1839-Present Day)* Vol. II 65, *Khushwant Singh's India* 69.

The Illustrated Weekly of India, Times of India Building, Dr. Dadabhai Naoroji Road, Bombay 1, India.

Telephone: 268271.

Singh, Nagendra, M.A., LL.D., D.LITT., D.PHIL., D.SC., D.C.L.; Indian civil servant and international lawyer; b. 18 March 1914, Dungarpur, Rajasthan; ed. Agra and Cambridge Univs. and Gray's Inn, London.

Entered Indian Civil Service 38; recent posts include: Special Sec. Ministry of Information and Broadcasting 64, Ministry of Transport Aug. 64; Sec. Ministry of Transport and Dir.-Gen. of Shipping 66; Sec. to Pres. of India 66-; Constitutional Adviser to Govt. of Bhutan 70-; Chair. Govt. Shipping Corpn. 62, The Mogul Line Ltd. 60-61, 63-67, The Hindustan Shipyard Ltd. 62-67 (Dir. 56-67); mem. Indian Constituent Assembly 47-48; Justice of the Peace, Bombay 48-; Nehru Prof. of Int. Law and Co-operation, Graduate Inst. of Int. Studies, Univ. of Geneva; Prof. of Human Rights and Int. Co-operation, Univ. of Tribhuban, Nepal; Prof. of Int. Law and Maritime Law, Univ. of Madras; mem. Perm. Court of Arbitration, The Hague 67; mem. Int. Law Comm. 66-, Vice-Chair. 69; Vice-Chair. UN Comm. on Int. Trade Law 69, Chair. 71; Judge, Int. Court of Justice 73-, Vice-Pres. 76-(79); mem. Panel of Legal Experts, IAEA; founder mem. Int. Council for Environmental Law 69; Assoc. Inst. de Droit International; Vice-Pres. Indian Soc. of Int. Law, Maritime Law Asscn. of India; mem. American Soc. of Int. Law, Indian

Inst. of Public Admin., India Int. Centre, etc.; Visiting Prof. Univs. of Delhi, Udaipur, Bombay and Banaras and has lectured at Univs. of Cairo, Baghdad, Belgrade and Cambridge among others; Pres. IMCO Assembly 63-65; Chair. or mem. many other int. cttees. and leader, Indian del. to numerous confs., etc.; Padma Vibushan Award 73.

Publs. *Termination of Membership of International Organizations* 58, *Nuclear Weapons and International Law, Defence Mechanism of the Modern State* 63, *The Concept of Force and Organization of Defence in the Constitutional History of India* 69, *Achievements of UNCTAD I and II in the field of Invisibles* 69, *India and International Law* 69, *Bhutan* 71; several vols. of lectures and numerous articles on questions of int. law, etc.

International Court of Justice, Peace Palace, The Hague, Netherlands; 6 Akbar Road, New Delhi, India.

Singh, Raja Roy; Indian educationist; b. 5 April 1918, Pithoragarh; s. of Th. Durg Singh; m. Zorine Bonifacius 1943; two s. three d.; ed. Univ. of Allahabad.

Entered Indian Admin. Service 43; fmr. Dir. of Educ., Uttar Pradesh; fmr. Joint Sec., Fed. Ministry of Educ., New Delhi; fmr. Joint Dir. Indian Council of Educational Research and Training, Nat. Inst. of Educ.; at Office of Educational Planning, UNESCO Headquarters, Paris 64-65; Dir. UNESCO Regional Office for Educ. in Asia 65-.

Leisure interests: art, theatre, music.

Publ. *Education in the Soviet Union.*

UNESCO Regional Office for Education in Asia, P.O. Box 1425, Darakarn Building, 920 Sukhumvit Road, Bangkok, Thailand.

Telephone: 918474.

Singh, Ram Subhag, M.A., PH.D.; Indian politician; b. 7 July 1917, Arrah, Bihar; ed. Varanasi, Missouri Univ.

Joined Congress Party 35; mem. of Parl. 50-71; Chief Whip, Parl. Congress Party 67-69; Sec. Congress Parl. Party 55-62; Minister of State in the Ministry of Agriculture 62-64, in Ministry of Social Security and Cottage Industries 64-66; Minister of State for Railways 64-67; Minister of Parl. Affairs and Communications 67-69; Minister of Railways Feb.-Nov. 69; Leader of Opposition in Lok Sabha 69-71.

Leisure interests: riding, gardening.

Khajuria, Arrah (Bihar), India.

Singh, Sher, M.A.; Indian agriculturist and politician; b. 18 Sept. 1917, Baghpur Dist. Rohtak (Haryana); s. of Ch. Sis Ram; m. Smt. Prabhat Shobha 1942; one s. two d.; ed. Delhi Univ.

Former Lecturer, M.S.J. Coll., Bharatpur and Lecturer in Mathematics, Jat Coll., Rohtak; elected to Punjab Legislative Assembly 46, 52, 57, to Punjab Legislative Council 62; Parl. Sec. Punjab 48-51; Deputy Leader Congress Legislature Party, Punjab 56-57; Minister of Irrigation and Power, Punjab 56-57; mem. Lok Sabha 67; Minister of State, Ministry of Educ. 67-69; Minister of State, Ministry of Information and Broadcasting Communications 69-71; Minister of State for Agriculture 71-74, for Communications 74-; Chancellor of Gurukl, Jhajjar; mem. of Syndicate of Gurukl Kangri Univ.; fmr. Founder-Pres. Haryana Lok Samiti; del. to several int. confs.

New Delhi, India.

Singh, Swaran, M.SC., LL.B.; Indian politician; b. 19 Aug. 1907; ed. Govt. Coll., Lahore, and Lahore Law Coll.

Elected Punjab Legislative Assembly 46; Minister of Devt., Food, Civil Supplies 46-47; mem. Gov's. Security Council, then Partition Cttee. 47; Minister of Home, Gen. Admin., Revenue, Irrigation and Electricity in first Punjab Congress Ministry 47-49; resigned

to resume legal practice; Minister of Capital Projects and Electricity 52; Minister for Works, Housing and Supply (Cen. Govt.) 52-57; elected to Rajya Sabha; initiated Subsidized Industrial Housing Scheme; Lok Sabha (Parl.) 57-; Minister for Steel, Mines and Fuel 57-62; Minister for Railways 62-Aug. 63, of Food and Agriculture Aug. 63-June 64, of Industry, Engineering and Technical Devt. June-July 64, of External Affairs 64-66, 70-74, of Defence 66, 70, 74-75; led Indian del. to UN Gen. Assembly 64-66, 70-73, ECOSOC 54, 55; Rep. to Commonwealth Prime Ministers' Conf. 71, 73.
7 Hastings Road, New Delhi, India.

Singh, Tarlok, B.A., B.SC.; Indian economist; b. 26 Feb. 1913, Gujranwala; s. of Gurmukh Singh and Gyan Kaur; m. Kamla Verma 1939; three s.; ed. St. Vincent's School and Deccan Coll., Poona, Gujarat Coll., Ahmedabad and London School of Economics.
Indian Civil Service 37-62; Colonization Officer, Nili Bar Colony, Punjab 43; Finance Dept., Govt. of India 44-46; Private Sec. to Vice-Pres. Interim Govt. and to Prime Minister 46-47; Dir.-Gen. of Rehabilitation 47-49; mem. Planning Comm. 62-67, Additional Sec. and other positions 50-62; Fellow, Inst. for Int. Econ. Studies, Univ. of Stockholm 67 and 69-70; Visiting Research Economist, Woodrow Wilson School, Princeton Univ. 68; Deputy Exec. Dir. (Planning) UNICEF 70-74; Hon. Fellow, London School of Econs.; Padma Shri 54, Padma Bhushan 62, Swedish Royal Acad. Sciences Söderström Medal 70.
Leisure interest: rural studies.
Publs. *Poverty and Social Change* 45 (2nd edn. 69), *Resettlement Manual for Displaced Persons* 52, *Towards an Integrated Society* 69, *India's Development Experience* 74.
110 Sundar Nagar, New Delhi, India.

Singh Deo, Rajendra Narayan; Indian former Maharaja of Patna; b. 31 March 1912, Seraikella; m. the Maharani Kailash Kumari Devi 1932; two s. four d.; ed. Mayo Coll., Ajmer and St. Columba's Coll., Hazaribagh.
Ruler of Patna State 33-, later becoming the first ruler to sign the merger agreement with the Indian Union; formed political party Ganatantra Parishad 49 (merged with Swatantra Party 62); elected to Lok Sabha 52; Leader of Opposition, Orissa Legislative Assembly 57-59; Deputy Leader, Coalition Govt. and Finance Minister 59-61; re-elected to Orissa Legislative Assembly as Leader of Opposition 61-66, 72-; Chief Minister of Orissa 67-70; Deputy Chief Minister, Minister of Industries 71-72; fmr. Chair. Eastern States Board of Forestry and Agriculture, Vice-Pres. Council of Rulers of Eastern States Agency, mem. Standing Cttee. Eastern States Union; Pres. Orissa Unit of Swatantra Party and mem. of its Gen. Council, Nat. Exec. and Cen. Parl. Board.
Bhubaneshwar, Orissa, India.

Singhania, Lakshmipat (brother of Sir Padampat Singhania, q.v.); Indian businessman; b. 23 Feb. 1910.
Entered business 29; Dir.-in-charge Aluminium Corpn. of India Ltd., Straw Products Ltd.; Chair. J. K. Steels and Industries Ltd.; Dir. J. K. Cotton Spinning and Weaving Mills Co. Ltd., Nav Bharat Vanijya Ltd., Bengal and Assam Investors Ltd., J. K. Industries Private Ltd., J. K. Iron and Steel Co. Ltd.; Pres. Nat. Insurance Co. Ltd.; fmr. Pres. Merchants' Chamber of U.P., Kanpur 46 and 47, and Bharat Chamber of Commerce, Calcutta 48-49; mem. Coal Control Board, Bharat Chamber of Commerce, Indian Central Jute Cttee., Joint Consultative Board of Industry and Labour, Indian Inst. of Social Welfare and Business Management, All-India Board of Technical Studies in Commerce and Business Admin., etc.; Underwriter, Lloyd's Society of London; fmr. Pres. Fed. Indian Chamber of Commerce and Industry, Indian Nat.

Cttee. of the Int. Chamber of Commerce (58); Pres. All-India Organization of Industrial Employers.
Leisure interests: racing, rowing.
Home: J. K. House, 12 Alipore Road, Calcutta 700027; Office: 7 Council House Street, Calcutta 700001, India.

Singhania, Sir Padampat, Kt. (brother of Lakshmipat Singhania, q.v.); Indian industrialist; b. 1905; ed. privately.
President J.K. Org. (Juggilal Kamlapat Group of Mills), Kanpur; a pioneer of cotton and woollen textiles, rayon, nylon, jute, sugar, hosiery, iron and steel, aluminium, plastic, strawboard, chemical, mining and oil industries; Founder Merchants' Chamber of U.P.; fmr. Pres. Federation of Indian Chambers of Commerce and Industries; mem. 1st Indian Parl.; Chair. Indian Inst. of Technology, Kanpur; Hon. D. Lit. Kanpur Univ.
Leisure interest: philanthropy.
Kamla Tower, Kanpur, India.
Telephone: 62532.

Singhuber, Dr. Kurt; German engineer and politician; b. 1932.
Minister of Mining and Metallurgy and Potash, Govt. of G.D.R.
Ministerrat, Berlin, German Democratic Republic.

Singier, Gustav Henri; Belgian-born French artist; b. 11 Feb. 1909, Warneton, Belgium; m.; one d.
Foundation mem. of the Salon de Mai 45-; has exhibited in Paris, Stockholm, Brussels, Hanover, New York, London, Turin and Venice; has exclusive contract with Galerie de France, Paris; works in museums at Paris, New York, Vienna, Brussels, Basle, Johannesburg, Essen, Wellington, Tate Gallery, London, etc.; numerous tapestries, theatre sets and costumes; teacher of painting Acad. Ranson 51-54, and Ecole Nationale des Beaux Arts, Paris.
203 rue de Vaugirard, 75015 Paris, France.
Telephone: SEGur 64-05.

Singleton, Henry E.; American business executive; see *The International Who's Who 1975-76*.

Sinha, Satya Narain; Indian politician; b. 1900, Shambhupath, Bihar; ed. Patna Univ.
Joined Non-Violence Movement and imprisoned 20; mem. Bihar Legislature 26-30; Pres. Darbhanga District Congress Cttee. 30-47; mem. Indian Constituent Ass. 26-47, of Lok Sabha 47-; Minister of State for Parl. Affairs 49-52; Minister for Parl. Affairs 52-67, of Information and Broadcasting Sept. 63-June 64, of Civil Aviation June 64, of Communications 64-67; Minister without Portfolio 67-Nov. 67; Minister of Health, Family Planning and Urban Devt. Nov. 67-69; Minister of Information, Broadcasting and Communications 69-71; Gov. Madhya Pradesh 71-; Pres. Indian Council of Medical Research; Chief Whip Congress Party in Cen. Assembly and Constituent Assembly.
Raj Bhavan, Bhopal, India.

Sinitsin, Ivan Flegontyevich; Soviet politician; b. 1911; ed. Gorky Industrial Inst.
Gorky Motor Works 29-36; worker at other enterprises, Gorky 36-46; Dir. Volgograd Tractor Works 50-57; later Head of Econ. Councils, Volgograd Region 57-60; Minister of Tractor and Farm Machine Building 65-; Alt. mem. C.P.S.U. Cen. Cttee. 66-; Deputy to U.S.S.R. Supreme Soviet 54.
Ministry of Tractor and Farm Machine Building, Moscow, U.S.S.R.

Sinker, Sir (Algernon) Paul, K.C.M.G., C.B.; British civil servant; b. 13 April 1905, Slough, Bucks.; s. of Rev. R. Sinker; m. Ruth Longland 1929; two s. two d.; ed. Haileybury Coll. and Jesus Coll., Cambridge.
Fellow of Jesus Coll. 27-49, Tutor 29-40; civil servant Admiralty 40-45, Treasury 45-50; Adviser to Egyptian Govt. on Civil Service reform 50; First Civil Service Commr. 51-54; Dir. Gen. of the British Council 54-68;

Chair. Council for Small Industries in Rural Areas 68-; Crafts Advisory Cttee. 71-; Hon. Fellow, Jesus Coll. 55; Hon. LL.D. (Exeter) 61, (Southampton) 67.
Leisure interests: country pursuits.
39 Berwick Road, Shrewsbury, England.
Telephone: Shrewsbury 3176.

Sinsheimer, Robert Louis, S.B., S.M., PH.D.; American biologist; b. 5 Feb. 1920, Washington, D.C.; s. of Allen and Rose Davidson Sinsheimer; m. 1st Flora Joan Hirsch 1943 (divorced 1972), 2nd Kathleen Mae Reynolds 1972; one s. two d.; ed. Massachusetts Inst. of Technology.
Research Assoc., Biology, Mass. Inst. of Technology 48-49; Assoc. Prof. of Biophysics, Iowa State Coll. 49-55, Prof. 55-57; Prof. of Biophysics, Calif. Inst. of Technology 57-, Chair. Div. of Biology 68-; mem. Nat. Acad. of Sciences, U.S.A.; Calif. Scientist of the Year Award 68, Beijerinck Medal of the Royal Netherlands Acad. of Sciences 69; Pres. Biophysical Soc. 70-71; mem. Council of Nat. Acad. of Sciences, U.S.A. 70-73, Chair. Board of Editors, NAS *Proceedings* 72-.
Leisure interests: camping, hiking and photography.
Publs. More than 200 scientific papers 46-75.
Division of Biology, California Institute of Technology, Pasadena, Calif. 91125; Home: 2770 Winrock Avenue, Altadena, Calif. 91001, U.S.A.
Telephone: 213-795-6811 (Office); 213-794-1203 (Home).

Sipilä, Helvi Linnea; Finnish lawyer and United Nations official; b. 5 May 1915, Helsinki; m.; four c.; ed. Univ. of Helsinki.
Acting judge, rural district courts 41-42; Sec. Ministry of Supply 42-43; held various legal posts in Supreme Court and Supreme Admin. Court 41-51; Dir. and founder of law office 43-72; mem. various Finnish govt. cttees. on matrimonial legislation, protection of children, social benefits for children, citizenship educ. and int. devt. aid 50-; mem. World Cttee. of World Asscn. of Girl Guides and Girl Scouts 57-66; Chief Commr. of Finnish Girl Guides 52-69; Rep. of Finland, UN Comm. on Status of Women 60-68, 71-72, Vice-Chair. 63-66, Chair. 67; mem. Council, Human Rights Inst., Strasbourg 69-; Pres. Int. Fed. of Women Lawyers 54-56, ZONTA Int. 68-70; Vice-Pres. Int. Council of Women 70-; Chair. Finnish Refugee Council 65-72; mem. Finnish del. to UN Gen. Assembly 66-72, Chair. Third Cttee. 71; Asst. Sec.-Gen. (for social and humanitarian matters), UN 72-; Gen. Sec. UN Int. Women's Year 75.
United Nations, First Avenue, New York, N.Y. 10017, U.S.A.

Sippel, Heinz, DR.RER.POL.; German banker; b. 7 Nov. 1922, Leverkusen; m. Christa Dausel 1953; one d.; ed. Carl Duisberg Gymnasium, Leverkusen, Cologne Univ.
Kreditanstalt für Wiederaufbau 51-56; Man., Regional Credit Dept., Commerzbank AG, Düsseldorf 57-61; Head of Credit Dept., Bankhaus Friedrich Simon, Düsseldorf 61-62; joined Rheinische Girozentrale und Provinzialbank as Head of Essen Branch 62, Alt. mem. Man. Board 67, mem. Man. Board 68; mem. Man. Board, Westdeutsche Landesbank Girozentrale 69; Chair. Man. Board, Hessische Landesbank Girozentrale 75; Dir. Banque Worms, BCL Banque Continentale du Luxembourg S.A.; DGZ Deutsche Girozentrale Deutsche Kommunalbank, DSGV Deutscher Sparkassen- und Giroverband, IHB Investitions- und Handelsbank AG, LZB Landeszentralbank in Hessen, MHB Mitteleuropäische Handelsbank AG, Overseas Investors Inc.
Leisure interests: hiking, gardening, classical music.
6 Frankfurt (Main) 1, Wiesenau 22, Federal Republic of Germany.

Siracusa, Ernest Victor; American diplomatist; b. 30 Nov. 1918, Coalinga, Calif.; s. of Sisti and Caterina Cazzola Siracusa; m. Jacq Bachman 1951; one s. two d.; ed. Fullerton Junior Coll., Stanford Univ. and Mass. Inst. of Technology.

Joined foreign service 41; has served in Mexico, Honduras, Guatemala, Argentina, Italy and Peru; Adviser, Latin American Affairs, U.S. Perm. Mission to UN, New York 62-63; Deputy Chief of Mission, U.S. Embassy, Lima 63-69; Amb. to Bolivia 69-73, to Uruguay 73-.
Leisure interests: yachting, flying, painting in oils, horseback riding, motorcycling.
United States Embassy, Lauro Muller 1776, Montevideo, Uruguay.

Siraud, Pierre; French diplomatist; b. 11 Oct. 1907; ed. Ecole des Sciences politiques, Faculty of Law, Paris.
With Ministry of Foreign Affairs 35-40; mem. Résistance Second World War; Second Counsellor, Washington 45-51; Deputy Sec.-Gen., Rabat 51-55; Counsellor, Ankara 55-56; Deputy Dir. Personnel and Gen. Admin. Ministry of Foreign Affairs 56-59, Chief of Protocol 61-65; Head, French Embassy, Guinea 59-60; Amb. to the Netherlands 65-68, to Canada 68-72; Commdr. Légion d'Honneur, Commdr. Ordre Nat. du Mérite and foreign honours.
2 place Rodin, Paris 16e, France.

Siregar, Melanchton; Indonesian teacher and politician; b. 7 Aug. 1913, Pea-Arung Numbang, N. Tapanuli; m. 1st Bertha Ramian Siburian 1940 (died 1947), 2nd Setjawan Siburian 1948; ed. Christian Teachers' Training Coll. (H.I.K.), Solo and Coll. for Headmasters' Degree, Bandung.
Teacher and Headmaster in various schools 38-45; Dir. Higher Technical School, Pematang Siantar 45-47; Head of Gen. and Vocational Training Divs. of Service of Education, Instruction and Culture, Pematang Siantar, Sumatra 47, similar senior appts. in Education Service and Inspector of Secondary Schools in N. Sumatra 47-51; Co-ordinator of Office for Inspection of Education of N. Sumatra Region, Medan 52-56; mem. of Exec., North Sumatra Representative Council 48-50; mem. Parl. 56-71; Gen. Chair. in N. Sumatra and Co-ordinator in Sumatra, PARKINDO 50-60, Vice-Chair. Man. Board 60-64, Gen. Chair. of Exec. Board 64-67. Gen. Chair. 67-; Vice-Chair. Peoples' Congress of Republic of Indonesia (MPRS) 66-72; mem. of Indonesian Dels. to UN 57, 67.
Leisure interest: reading about politics, literature and theology.
59 H.O.S. Tjokroaminto Street, Jakarta, Indonesia.
Telephone: 45322-3.

Siren, Heikki; Finnish architect; b. 5 Oct. 1918, Helsinki; s. of Prof. J. S. and Sirkka Siren; m. Kaija Siren (q.v.) 1944; two s. two d.
Started private practice with Kaija Siren, Arkkitehtitoimisto Kaija & Heikki Siren 49-; mem. Finnish Acad. of Technical Sciences 71; Hon. Citation and Medal São Paulo Biennal 57, Medal São Paulo Biennal 61, Hon. Citation "Auguste Perret", Union Int. des Architectes 65; Prof. h.c. 70; Officier Nat. Order of Merit (France) 71, SLK (Finland) 74.
Leisure interests: sailing, theatre, art, music.
Major works include, Little Stage of Nat. Theatre, Helsinki 54, Concert House, Lahti 54, Chapel in Otaniemi 57, Church in Orivesi 60, Office Buildings, Helsinki 65, Housing Area in Boussy St. Antoine, Paris 67, "Round Bank" Kop, Helsinki, Schools, Sports Centres, Offices, Industrial Bldgs., Housing, Holiday Centres, etc. 68, Brucknerhaus Concert Hall, Linz, Austria 73, Golf complex, Karuizawa, Japan 74.
Lounaisväylä 8, Helsinki 20, Finland.
Telephone: 673032 (Office); 672445 (Home).

Siren, Katri (Kaija) Anna-Maija Helena; Finnish architect; b. 23 Oct. 1920, Kotka; d. of Gottlieb and Lydia Tuominen; m. Heikki Siren (q.v.) 1944; two s. two d.
Private practice in partnership with Heikki Siren, Arkkitehtitoimisto Kaija & Heikki Siren 49-; Hon.

Citation and Medal São Paulo Biennal 57, Medal São Paulo Biennal 61, Hon. Citation "Auguste Perret", Union Int. des Architectes 65.
Leisure interests: out-of-doors life, theatre, music.
Major works include, Little Stage of Nat. Theatre, Helsinki 54, Concert House, Lahti 54, Chapel in Otaniemi 57, Church in Orivesi 60, Office Bldgs., Helsinki 65, Housing Area in Boussy St. Antoine, Paris 67, "Round Bank" Kop, Helsinki, Schools, Sports Centres, Offices, Industrial Bldgs., Housing, Holiday Centres, etc. 68, Brucknerhaus Concert Hall, Linz, Austria 73.
Lounaisväylä 8, Helsinki 20, Finland.
Telephone: 673032 (Office); 672445 (Home).

Siri, H.E. Cardinal Giuseppe; Italian ecclesiastic; b. 20 May 1906; ed. Episcopal Seminary, Genoa and Pontifical Gregorian Univ., Rome.
Ordained priest 28; Titular Bishop of Livias 44; Archbishop of Genoa 46-; created Cardinal by Pope Pius XII 53; Pres. Episcopal Dir. Comm., Italian Catholic Action, Episcopal Conference of Italy (C.E.I.) 59-61; Chair. Italian Episcopal Conf. 55-65; mem. Sacred Congregations of Sacraments of the Council and of Seminaries and Univs. of Study.
Publs. *Corso di Teologia per Laici* 42, *La Strada passa per Cristo* 56.
Palazzo Arcivescovile, Piazza Mateotti 4, 16123 Genoa, Italy.

Sirica, John J.; American judge; b. 1904; ed. Georgetown Univ.
Former mem. Hogan & Hartson, Washington; Chief Judge U.S. District Court for District of Columbia; Adjunct Prof. of Law, Georgetown Univ. Law Center; mem. American Bar Asscn.
U.S. Court House, Washington, D.C. 20001, U.S.A.

Siriwardane, Codippilliarachchige Don Stanislaus; Ceylonese diplomatist; b. 26 March 1911; ed. Ananda Coll., Colombo and London Univ.
Advocate of Supreme Court, Ceylon; Major, The Ceylon Light Infantry; mem. Royal Comm. on Educ. 61; mem. Royal Comm. on Buddhist Affairs 57; mem. Ceylon Senate 61-67; Amb. to U.S.S.R., Czechoslovakia, Poland, Hungary, Romania and German Democratic Repub. 73-74, to Pakistan (also accred. to Iran) 74-.
Embassy of Sri Lanka, 468-F, Sector G-6/4, Islamabad, Pakistan; Home: Longdon Place, Colombo 7, Sri Lanka.

Sisco, Joseph John, PH.D.; American government official; b. 31 Oct. 1919; ed. Knox Coll. and Univ. of Chicago.
U.S. Army 41-45; Central Intelligence Agency 50-51; Dept. of State 51-; Officer-in-Charge, UN Political Affairs 51-58, Deputy Dir. Office of UN Political and Security Affairs 58-60, Dir. 60-62; Deputy Asst. Sec. 62-65; Asst. Sec. of State for Int. Org. Affairs, Dept. of State July 65-69; Asst. Sec. State, Middle East-S. Asia 69-74; Under-Sec. of State for Political Affairs 74-76; Pres. American Univ. in Washington 76-; Rockefeller Public Service Award 71.
5344 Falmouth Road, Washington, D.C. 20016, U.S.A.

Šiška, Karol, M.D., D.SC.; Czechoslovak medical scientist and surgeon; b. 19 March 1906, Selenča, Yugoslavia; s. of Samuel and Maria (Lekar) Šiška; m. 1942; four s.; ed. Charles Univ., Prague.
Head, Second Surgical Clinic, Medical Faculty, Comenius Univ. Bratislava 51, Prof. of Medical Faculty 53-; Dir., Inst. of Experimental Surgery, Slovak Acad. of Sciences 64-; Academician, Slovak Acad. of Sciences 55- (Vice-Pres. 61-65, Pres. 70-74), Czechoslovak Acad. of Sciences 62- (Vice-Pres. 71-74); mem. of Presidium, Czechoslovak Acad. of Sciences 61-65, Slovak Acad. of Sciences 65-; mem. Cen. Cttee. of C.P. of Slovakia 58-62, and of Czechoslovakia 62-74; Deputy to Slovak Nat. Council 69-; Deputy Chair. Czechoslovak Cttee.

for European Security 70-71; Chair. Cttee. for Klement Gottwald State Prize 71-74; Hon. Chair. Slovak Medical Soc. 73-; designed heart and lung machines for use during operations; Foreign mem. Acad. of Medical Sciences of the U.S.S.R. 69-, Acad of Sciences of U.S.S.R. 73, Acad. of Sciences of German Democratic Repub. 74; J. E. Purkyně Medal 56, Order of Labour 61, and many other scientific honours.
Leisure interests: medicine, swimming, tourism.
Publs. Papers on chest surgery and cardiosurgery.
Institute for Experimental Surgery, Slovak Academy of Sciences, Dárbravská ceska Patrónka 2, Bratislava; and Kuzmányho 5, Bratislava, Czechoslovakia.

Sithole, Rev. Ndabaningi; Rhodesian clergyman and politician; b. 1920; ed. Waddilove Inst., Marandellas and Newton Theological Coll., U.S.A.
Teacher 41-55; U.S.A. 55-58; Ordained at Mount Silinda Congregationalist Church 58; Principal, Chikore Cen. Primary School; Pres. African Teachers Asscn. 59-60; Treas. Nat. Dem. Party (NDP) 60; Del. to Fed. Review Conf. London Dec. 60; fmr. Chair. Zimbabwe African People's Union (ZAPU) S. Rhodesia, Pres. July-Aug. 63; Leader Zimbabwe African Nat. Union (ZANU) Rhodesia 63-, incorporated in African Nat. Council Dec. 74; sentenced to 12 months imprisonment Dec. 63, sent to Wha Wha Restriction Camp May 65; tried and sentenced to six years hard labour for incitement to murder Ian Smith Feb. 69, released Dec. 74; in exile in Zambia with Section of the African National Congress (ANC) led by Bishop Muzorewa.
Publs. *African Nationalism* 69, 67, *The Polygamist* 73.
c/o African National Council Headquarters, Lusaka, Zambia.

Sitnin, Vladimir Xenofontovich; Soviet politician; b. 1907; ed. Moscow Inst. of Nat. Economy.
Economist and consultant, U.S.S.R. State Bank 28-31; Economist, U.S.S.R. Ministry of Finance 31-41; army service 41-50; Exec. Ministry of Finance 50-60, Deputy Minister and First Deputy Minister 60-65; Chair. State Prices Cttee., U.S.S.R. Planning Comm. 65-70; Chair. State Prices Cttee., U.S.S.R. Council of Ministers 70-74; Lecturer, Moscow Inst. of Nat. Economy; mem. C.P.S.U. 45-; Deputy to U.S.S.R. Supreme Soviet 70-.
c/o State Prices Committee, U.S.S.R. Council of Ministers, Moscow, U.S.S.R.

Sitwell, Sir Sacheverell, 6th Bt., cr. 1808; British writer; b.1897; brother of the late Dame Edith Sitwell and the late Sir Osbert Sitwell; ed. Eton and Balliol Coll., Oxford.
Publs. include: *The People's Palace, Doctor Donne and Gargantua, The Hundred and One Harlequins, Four Essays on Baroque Art, Actor Rehearsing and Other Poems, The Thirteenth Caesar, Canons of Giant Art, Life of Liszt, Touching the Orient, Dance of the Quick and the Dead, Collected Poems, La Vie Parisienne, Narrative Picture, Roumanian Journey, Trio, Mauretania, Poltergeists* 40, *Of Sacred and Profane Love* 40, *Valse des Fleurs* 41, *Primitive Scenes and Festivals* 42, *Splendour and Miseries* 43, *British Architects and Craftsmen* 45, *Selected Poems* 48, *Cupid and the Jacaranda* 52, *Truffle Hunt with Sacheverell Sitwell* 53, *Portugal and Madeira* 54, *Denmark* 56, *Arabesque and Honeycomb* 57, *Austria* 59, *Journey to the Ends of Time,* Vol. I: *Lost in the Dark Wood* 59, *The Bridge of the Brocade Sash: Travels and Observations in Japan* 59, *Golden Wall and Mirador* 61, *The Red Chapels of Banteai Srei* 62, *Great Palaces* 64, *Monks, Nuns and Monasteries* 65, *Southern Baroque Revisited* 68, *Gothic Europe* 69, *For Want of the Golden City* 73.
Weston Hall, Towcester, Northants., England.

Sivadon, Paul Daniel; French psychiatrist; b. 10 Jan. 1907, Moncoutant; m. Renée Nodot 1930; three c.; ed. Lycée Blaise Pascal, Clermont Ferrand and Univ. de Paris.

Head, Clinic for Mental Illness, Faculté de Paris 35-36; Dir. Colonie Familiale, Seine 36-43; Head Dr. Psychiatric Hospital, Ville-Evrard 43-58; Prof. of Psychiatry and Medical Psychology, Univ. of Brussels 59-; Dir. Psychiatric Services for Nat. Educ. 58-72; Consultant WHO 51-65; fmr. Pres. World Fed. for Mental Health 60-61; Pres. French League for Mental Hygiene 61-; Soc. Médico Psychologique 75; Officier Légion d'Honneur, Officier de la Santé Publique, Commdr. Ordre de la Couronne, Grand Officier Ordre Léopold II.
Publs. include: *Psychoses puerpérales* 33, *Rééducation Corporelle des Fonctions Mentales* 65, *Psychopathologie du Travail* 69, *Traité de Psychologie Médicale* (three vols.) 73, and over 400 scientific articles.
8 rue de L'Alboni, Paris 16e, France.
Telephone: 870-64-87.

Sivara, Gen. Kris; Thai army officer.
Secretary-General Nat. Exec. Council until 72; Minister of Industry 72-73; C.-in-C. of the Army Sept. 73-; Dir. for Maintenance of Peace and Order Oct. 73-.
[*Died 23 April 1976.*]

Siverd, Clifford David, B.S.; American business executive; b. 25 June 1912, Cumberland, Md.; s. of Norman Elder Siverd and Eva V. Mause; m. Elizabeth Ann Klink 1939; two s. one d.; ed. Johns Hopkins Univ.
Assistant Gen. Man. Agricultural Div., American Cyanamid Co. 58-60, Gen. Man. 60-65, Vice-Pres. 65-67, Pres. and Chief Exec. Officer 67-72, Chair. and Chief Exec. Officer 72-75; fmr. Chair. Nat. Plant Food Inst., Pres. Animal Health Inst. and other orgs.; Dir. Public Service Electric and Gas Co., Continental Corpn.; Chair. Foundation of the New Jersey Inst. of Technology; mem. Nat. Industrial Pollution Control Council 70-; Trustee, Johns Hopkins Univ.
Leisure interests: golf, bridge.
American Cyanamid Company, Wayne, N.J. 07470, U.S.A.
Telephone: 201-831-1234.

Siwabessy, Gerrit Agustinus; Indonesian radiologist and politician; b. 19 Aug. 1914, Saparua, Moluccas; s. of Enos Siwabessy and Naatje Manuhutu; m. 1st Reny Poetiray 1942 (divorced); 2nd Paulina Margaretha Putuhena (died 1968); five c.; ed. Univ. of Medicine, Jakarta and Univ. of London.
Radiologist, Cen. Hosp., Surabaja 42-45, Cen. Hosp., Malang 45-47, Cen. Hosp., Jakarta 48; Chief Doctor, Cen. Hosp., Jakarta, concurrently Doctor at Mil. Hosp. 53; Head, Indonesian Inst. of Radiology 54; Dir.-Gen. Indonesian Inst. of Atomic Energy 58-73; Lecturer, Univ. of Indonesia 56; mem. Nat. Council 57; mem. Indonesian Nat. Planning Council 59; Minister of Health 66-; del. to several int. radiology and atomic energy confs.
Ministry of Health, Jakarta, Indonesia.

Six, Robert Forman; American airline executive; b. 25 June 1907, Stockton, Calif.; m. Audrey Meadows 1961; ed. public schools in Stockton.
District Circulation Man. *San Francisco Chronicle* 33-35; owner, Mouton & Six 35-37; Pres. and Dir. Continental Airlines 38-, Chair. of Board Continental Air Services 66-75, Chair. of Board and Chief Exec. Officer 75-; Hon. D.Sc (Univ. Colo.).
Leisure interest: ranching.
Continental Airlines, Los Angeles International Airport, Los Angeles, Calif. 90009, U.S.A.

Siyad Barre, Maj.-Gen. Muhammad; Somali army officer; b. 1919, Lugh District.
Chief Insp., Somali Police Force; Col., Vice-Commdt. Somali Nat. Army 60, Commdt. 65, Maj.-Gen. 66, C.-in-C. of the Armed Forces; Pres. of the Supreme Revolutionary Council since the coup of Oct. 69; Chair. OAU Assembly of Heads of State 74-75.
Supreme Revolutionary Council, Mogadishu, Somalia.

Sizov, Gennady Fedorovich; Soviet politician; b. 1903; ed. K. A. Timiryazev Agricultural Inst.
Member C.P.S.U. 26-; Dean of Faculty and Dir. Inst. of Dairy-Cattle Breeding, Moscow 33-41, 47-52; Soviet Army 41-47; staff of Kurgan District Cttee., C.P.S.U. 52-54; Chair. Exec. Cttee. Kurgan District Council of Working People's Deputies 54-55; First Sec. Kurgan District Cttee., C.P.S.U. 55-66; Alt. mem. Central Cttee. C.P.S.U. 56-64, mem. 64-66; Chair. Central Auditing Comm. of C.P.S.U. 66-; Deputy to U.S.S.R. Supreme Soviet 58-.
Central Auditing Commission of C.P.S.U., 4 Staraya ploshchad, Moscow, U.S.S.R.

Sizova, Alla Ivanovna; Soviet ballet dancer; b. 1939; ed. Leningrad School of Ballet.
Joined Leningrad Kirov Theatre of Opera and Ballet 58-; honoured artist of the R.S.F.S.R.
Major roles: Masha (*Nutcracker*), Mirta (*Giselle*), Pas de trois (*Corsair*), Katerina (*Stone Flower*), Waltz and Mazurka (*Chopiniana*), Pas de trois (*Swan Lake*), Aurora (*Sleeping Beauty*), Maria (*Fountain of Bakhchisarai*), Juliet (*Romeo and Juliet*).
State Kirov Academic Theatre of Opera and Ballet, ploshchad Iskusstv 1, Leningrad, U.S.S.R.

Sjöberg, Alf Sven Erik; HON. DR. PHIL.; Swedish theatrical and film producer; b. 21 June 1903, Stockholm; m. 1st Marta Esktrom, 2nd Elsa Ahlsell; one s. one d.; ed. Royal Theatre School.
Actor, Royal Theatre 25-29, producer 30-; studied and acted abroad; Swedish radio; produced Swedish films; Grand Prix for *Miss Julie*, Cannes 52; Litteris et Artibus; St. Erik-Medaljen.
Theatre productions include works by Shakespeare, Strindberg, Ibsen, O'Neill, Brecht, Gombrowicz.
Leisure interests: sailing, skiing.
Kungliga Dramatiska Teatern, Stockholm; Andreég 5, Stockholm, Sweden.
Telephone: 614757 (Home).

Sjoberg, Sigurd A., B.S.; American space flights director; b. 9 Sept. 1919, Minneapolis, Minn.; s. of John and Anna Charlotte Sjoberg; m. Elizabeth Jane Ludwig 1944; three s.; ed. Univ. of Minnesota.
Aeronautical engineer, Nat. Aeronautics and Space Admin. (NASA, then called Nat. Advisory Cttee. for Aeronautics) 42, joined Manned Spacecraft Center (MSC) 59, Deputy Dir. Flight Operations 63-69, Dir. 69-72, Deputy Dir. 72-; U.S. Rep. to Féd. Aéronautique Int. (FAI); mem. American Inst. of Aeronautics and Astronautics (Houston Chapter), American Astronautical Soc., Nat. Acad. of Engineering; MSC Superior Achievement Award 66; NASA Exceptional Service Medal Jan. 69, Oct. 69; NASA Certificate of Commendation 70; NASA D.S.M. 71; Hon. D.Sc. (De Pauw Univ.) 72; Outstanding Achievement Award (Univ. of Minnesota) 73.
Leisure interests: golf, reading.
Publs. *Flight Control and Monitoring and Recovery* 63, *Flying Qualities Associated with several types of Command Flight Control System* 59; and numerous NACA and NASA published reports.
NASA-Johnson Space Center, Houston, Texas 77058, U.S.A.
Telephone: 713-483-5309.

Skachkov, Semyon Andreyevich; Soviet engineer and politician; b. 1907; ed. Kharkov Engineering Inst.
Worked at Kharkov Steam Locomotive Works, rising to be Chief Metallurgist 30-41; worked in the Urals during the Second World War; later Dir. of Leningrad Diesel Engine Works, Nizhny-Tagil Works and Chelyabinsk Tractor Works; First Deputy Minister of Transport Machine Building Industry 54-57; Chair. Kharkov Economic Council 57-58; Chair. State Cttee. for External Econ. Relations 58-; Alt. mem. C.P.S.U. Cen. Cttee. 61-71, mem. 71-; Deputy to Supreme Soviet

of the U.S.S.R. 50-; Order of Lenin, four Orders of the Red Banner of Labour, Order of the Red Star, Order of the Patriotic War and other decorations.
State Committee for External Economic Relations, Ovchinnikovskaya naberezhnaya 18/1, Moscow, U.S.S.R.

Skak-Nielsen, Niels Verner, CAND. POL.; Danish international civil servant; b. 18 Feb. 1922, Århus; s. of Jens and Thora Skak-Nielsen; m. Birthe Reinwald 1947; two s. two d.; ed. Univ. of Copenhagen.
Joined Foreign Service 47; Econ. Secr. of Danish Govt. 49-51; Dep. Chief of Section, Ministry of Foreign Affairs 51-53; Sec., Del. to NATO 53-56; Chief of Section, Ministry of Foreign Affairs 56-59; Counsellor, Del. to OEEC 59-60; Minister and Perm. Rep. to EFTA and European Office of UN 60-66, Amb. 63-66; Asst. Under-Sec. of State for Econ. Affairs, Ministry of Foreign Affairs 66; Chief Statistician of Denmark 66-; mem. of Board of Chairmen of Econ. Council 67-73.
Danmarks Statistik, Sejerøgade 11, Copenhagen Ø, Denmark.
Telephone: 01-298222.

Skautrup, J. Peter A., DR. PHIL.; Danish university professor; b. 21 Jan. 1896, Grove; s. of Niels Jensen Skautrup and Anne Kirstine Pedersen; m. Ester Bengtsson 1921; one s. three d.; ed. Københavns Universitet.
Editor at Great Danish Dictionary 22-28; Tutor, Univ. of Århus 28-34, Prof. of Scandinavian Languages 34-66, Rector 32-34, 53-55; Chief Editor at Jysk Ordbog; Commdr. Order of Dannebrog, Cross of Honour; several prizes; Hon. Dr. Phil. (Stockholm).
Leisure interest: gardening.
Publs. *Et Hardsysselmål* Vol. I 27-29, Vol. II 30, *Hardiske mål* Vol. I 30, Vol. II 42, *Den jyske Lov* 41, *Det danske sprogs historie* Vols. I-IV 44-68, *Jysk Sinnelaw. Antologi.* 50, *Bondesind* 50, *Arv og gæld i ordenes samfund* 58, *Jyske Lov* 64, *Det danske sprogs historie, Registerbind* 70, *Jysk Ordbog* Vol. I 1-3 70-74, *Corpus Codicum Danicorum Medii Aevi* Vol. IX 72, X 73.
Stationsgade 23, 8240 Risskov, Denmark.
Telephone: Århus 179514.

Skeat, Theodore Cressy, B.A., F.B.A.; British papyrologist; b. 15 Feb. 1907, St. Albans, Herts.; s. of Walter William Skeat and Theodora Duckworth; m. Olive Martin 1942; one s.; ed. Whitgift School, Christ's Coll., Cambridge, and British School of Archaeology, Athens.
Assistant Keeper, Dept. of Manuscripts, British Museum 31-48, Deputy Keeper 48-61, Keeper 61-72; Cromer Greek Prize 32.
Publs. *Fragments of an Unknown Gospel* (with H. I. Bell) 35, *Scribes and Correctors of the Codex Sinaiticus* (with H. J. M. Milne) 38, *The Reigns of the Ptolemies* 54, *Papyri from Panopolis* 64, *Catalogue of Greek Papyri in the British Museum* 74.
63 Ashbourne Road, London, W5 3DH, England.
Telephone: 01-998-1246.

Skeen, Brig. Andrew, I.C.D., O.B.E.; Rhodesian soldier and politician and diplomatist; b. 3 Oct. 1906, Desolali, India; s. of Gen. Sir Andrew Skeen; m. Honor Quintin Skeen 1939; one s. one d.; ed. Wellington Coll. and Royal Mil. Coll., Sandhurst.
British Army Service 26-47 (mentioned in despatches); Pres. Manicaland Publicity Asscn.; mem. Rhodesian Forestry Comm., Rhodesian Tourist Board, Labour Conciliation Boards, Umtali Odzi Road Council, Vumba Town Planning Authority; Chair. Manicaland Div. Rhodesian Front Party; High Commr. for Rhodesia in London 65; mem. Rhodesian Parl. 66-74.
Leisure interests: swimming, trap shooting and gardening.
Publ. *Prelude to Independence.*

19 Granta Road, Vainona, P.O. Borrowdale, Salisbury, Rhodesia.
Telephone: Salisbury 882097.

Skeggs, Leonard Tucker, A.B., M.S., PH.D.; American research biochemist; b. 9 June 1918, Fremont, Ohio; s. of late Leonard T. Skeggs, Sr. and Frances E. Wolfe; m. Jean Hossel 1941; one s. two d.; ed. Youngstown State Univ. and Western Reserve Univ. (now Case Western Reserve Univ.).
Research Fellow in Clinical Biochem., Western Reserve Univ. 48-49, Instructor in Biochem. 50-51, Senior Instructor in Biochem. (Dept. of Pathology) 51-52, Asst. Prof. 52-59, Assoc. Prof. 59-69, Prof. 69-; Chief of Biochem. Section and Co-Dir. Hypertension Research Laboratory, Veterans' Admin. Hospital, Cleveland, Ohio 47-68, Dir., Principal Investigator 68-; U.S. Navy 43-46; mem. American Soc. of Biological Chemists, American Chemical Soc., Board of Editors *Clinical Chemistry* 67; Fellow, American Asscn. of Clinical Chemists, New York Acad. of Sciences, American Heart Asscn. Council on High Blood Pressure; Arthur S. Flemming Award 57, Van Slyke Medal 63, American Chemical Soc. Award for Chemical Instrumentation 66, Ames Award 66, Middleton Award 68, Career Service Award (Greater Cleveland Growth Asscn.) 68, Stouffer Award 68; mem. American Heart Asscn. Council on Basic Sciences; Bendetti-Pichler Award in microchemistry 71; John Scott Award for invention of the Auto Analyzer 73.
Leisure interests: hiking, backpacking, breeding Arabian horses.
Major fields of work include: Hypertension, automatic chemical analysis, multiple automatic analysis; over fifty-nine scientific publications.
Veterans' Administration Hospital, 10701 East Boulevard, Cleveland, Ohio 44106, U.S.A.
Telephone: 216-791-3800. Ext. 547.

Skempton, Alec Westley, D.SC., F.I.C.E., F.G.S., F.R.S.; British professor of engineering; b. 4 June 1914, Northampton; s. of A. W. Skempton and Beatrice Edridge Payne; m. Mary Wood 1940; two d.; ed. Northampton Grammar School and Univ. of London.
Building Research Station 36-46; at Imperial Coll., Univ. of London, was Univ. Reader in Soil Mechanics 46-54, Prof. of Soil Mechanics 55-57, Prof. of Civil Eng. and Head of Dept. 57-; Lecturer in Copenhagen, Paris, Harvard Univ., Univs. of Illinois, Stockholm, Madrid, Florence; Special Lecturer, Architectural Asscn. 48-57; Visiting Lecturer, Cambridge Univ. School of Architecture 62-66, Edinburgh Univ. School of Architecture 68-; Chair. Joint Cttee. on Soils, Ministry of Supply and Road Research Board 54-59; Pres. Int. Soc. Soil Mechanics and Foundation Eng. 57-61; mem. Council Inst. of Civil Eng. 49-54, Vice-Pres. Inst. of Civil Eng.; mem. Cathedrals Advisory Cttee. 64-69, Council N.E.R.C.; Consultant to Binnie & Partners, John Mowlem & Co. Ltd.; Fellow, Royal Soc. 61; Hon. D.Sc. (Durham) 68; James Alfred Ewing Medal 68, Lyell Medal 72, Dickinson Medal 74.
Leisure interests: architectural travel, music.
Publs. Over 80 papers on soil mechanics, geology and history of civil engineering.
Department of Civil Engineering, Imperial College, London, S.W.7; 16 The Boltons, London, S.W.10, England.
Telephone: 01-589-5111 (Office); 01-370-3457 (Home).

Skibine, George; Russian-born American dancer and choreographer; b. 17 Jan. 1920; m. Marjorie Tallchief (q.v.) 1947; two s.; ed. Lycée Albert de Mun.
Joined Ballet Russe de Monte Carlo 38, Ballet Theater (New York) 40; Master Sergeant, U.S. Military Intelligence during Second World War; First Dancer and Choreographer, Ballets du Marquis de Cuevas 47-57; First Dancer and Choreographer, Paris Opera Ballet

57, Ballet Master and Dir. 58-; Artistic Dir. Rebekah Harkness Foundation and Dir. Harkness Ballet Co., New York 64-; Grand Prix de la Critique 58; Bronze Star (U.S.), Nisham Iftikar (Tunisia).
Ballets: Monte Carlo: *Tragedy in Verona*; Marquis de Cuevas: *Annabel Lee, Prisoner of the Caucasus, Achille, Ange Gris, Idylle, Pastorale*; Opéra Comique: *Concerto*; Paris Opera: *Daphnis and Chloé, Atlantide, La Péri*.
Office: Harkness Foundation, 15 E. 69th Street, New York, N.Y., U.S.A.; Home: 58 rue des Fontenelles, Sèvres (Seine-et-Oise), France.

Skibniewska, Halina, D.ENG.; Polish architect and town planner; b. 10 Jan. 1921, Warsaw; d. of Wacław and Ewelina (Kuczowska) Erentz; m. Zygmunt Skibniewski 1951; ed. Warsaw Technical Univ.
Worked at Bureau for Rebuilding of the Capital, Warsaw 45-47; Asst. Warsaw Technical Univ. 45-54, Lecturer 54-62, Prof. 62-; Chief Architect, Design Office 53-; Deputy to Seym 65-, Vice-Marshal of Seym Feb. 71-; Chair. Cen. Board of Soc. for Polish-French Friendship 72-; State Prize 1st Class 72; chief works include schools, housing estates and Nat. Theatre, Warsaw; mem. Asscn. of Architects of Polish Republic 51-, Asscn. of Polish Urban Planners; Commdr. and Knight's Cross, Order of Polonia Restituta, Grand Officier de la Légion d'Honneur 72, Cross of Order of Labour (2nd Class) 74, Medal of 30th Anniversary of People's Poland 74 and other decorations.
Publs. *Dziecko w mieszkaniu i osiedln* 69, *Wyniki badań w zakresie budownictwa w Polsce dia ludzi z ciężkim uszkodzeniem narządow ruchu* 68, *Rodzina a mieszkanie* 74.
Seym PRL, Ul. Wiejska 2/6, 00-489 Warsaw; Home: Ul. Frascati 14m. 2, 00-483 Warsaw, Poland.

Skilling, Hugh Hildreth, A.B., S.M., PH.D.; American professor of electrical engineering; b. 2 Sept. 1905, San Diego, Calif.; s. of William Thompson and Bird Hildreth Skilling; m. Hazel Dillon 1932; one d.; ed. Stanford Univ. and Mass. Inst. of Technology.
Construction Dept. Southern Calif. Edison Co., Los Angeles Calif. 27-29; Instr. to Prof., Electrical Engineering Faculty, Stanford Univ. 29, 31-; Dept. Head 41-64 (act. 41-45); act. Dean of Engineering 44-46; Lecturer on electric power transmission, Mass. Inst. of Technology 34; Dir. Electrical Engineering War Research, and Electrical Engineering War Training, Stanford Univ. 41-45; Scientific Observer, atomic bomb tests, Bikini Atoll 46; Visiting Lecturer in electrical eng. Cambridge Univ. 51-52, for Consejo Superior de Investigaciones Científicas, Madrid 52, Univ. of Chile 57; Consultant Dartmouth Coll. and Univ. of Hawaii 58; mem. review team, Univ. of the Philippines 53, King's Coll., Cambridge 51-; Consultant, Univ. of Alaska 64, Univ. of Washington 66; visiting Prof. Electrical Eng., Cambridge Univ. 65; awarded Medal for Educ. Inst. of Electrical and Electronics Engineers, N.Y. 65.
Leisure interest: writing.
Publs. *Transient Electric Currents* 37, *Fundamentals of Electric Waves* 42, *Prelude to Bikini* 47, *Exploring Electricity* 48, *Electric Transmission Lines* 51, *Electrical Engineering Circuits* 57, *A First Course in Electromechanics* 60, *Electromechanics* 62, *Do you Teach?* 69, *Electric Networks* 74; several works trans. into Spanish, Russian, Polish, Vietnamese and Thai.
672 Mirada Road, Stanford, California, U.S.A.
Telephone: 323-5638.

Skinner, Burrhus Frederic, A.B., M.A., PH.D., SC.D., LITT.D., L.H.D., L.L.D.; American professor of psychology; b. 20 March 1904, Susquehanna, Pa.; s. of William and Grace (née Burrhus) Skinner; m. Yvonne Blue 1936; two d.; ed. Hamilton Coll. and Harvard Univ.
With Nat. Research Council, Harvard 31-33; Jr.

Fellow, Harvard 33-36; Instructor, Minnesota Univ. 36-37, Asst. Prof. 37-39, Assoc. Prof. 39-45 (war research 42-43); Prof. and Chair. Dept. of Psychology, Indiana Univ. 45-48; Prof., Harvard Univ. 48-57, Edgar Pierce Prof. 58-74, Edgar Pierce Prof. Emer. 74-; Fellow, American Psychological Asscn., American Philosophical Soc., Nat. Acad. of Sciences, American Acad. of Arts and Sciences, Swedish Psychological Soc., British Psychological Soc., Royal Soc. of Arts; numerous hon. degrees.
Leisure interest: music.
Publs. *Behavior of Organisms* 38, *Walden Two* 48, *Science and Human Behavior* 53, *Verbal Behavior* 57, *Schedules of Reinforcement* 57 (with C. B. Ferster), *Cumulative Record* 59, 61, *Analysis of Behavior* (with James G. Holland) 61, *The Technology of Teaching* 67, *Contingencies of Reinforcement: A Theoretical Analysis* 69, *Beyond Freedom and Dignity* 71, *About Behaviorism* 74, *Particulars of My Life* 76.
Office: Department of Psychology and Social Relations, Harvard University, William James Hall, 33 Kirkland Street, Cambridge; Home: 11 Old Dee Road, Cambridge, Mass. 02138, U.S.A.
Telephone: 864-0848 (Home).

Skinner, Cornelia Otis; American writer and actress; ed. Bryn Mawr Coll., Sorbonne, Paris.
Studied drama in Paris; played on American stage in *Candida, Lady Windermere's Fan, The Pleasure of His Company*, etc.; wrote and produced *The Wives of Henry VIII, The Empress Eugénie, The Loves of Charles II, Mansion on the Hudson*; dramatized and produced *Edna, His Wife*; Hon. degrees Temple, Clark, St. Lawrence, Rochester and New York Univs., Tufts, Mills and Hofstra Colls.
Publs. *Captain Fury* (play) 25, *Tiny Garments, Excuse It, Please!, Dithers and Jitters, Soap Behind the Ears, Our Hearts were Young and Gay* (with Emily Kimbrough) 42, *Family Circle* 48, *That's Me All Over* (omnibus) 48, *Nuts in May* 50, *Bottoms Up* 55, *The Ape in Me* 59, *Elegant Wits and Grand Horizontals* 63, *Madame Sarah* 67.
131 East 66th Street, New York, N.Y., U.S.A.

Skinner, Hon. James John, Q.C.; Irish judge; b. 24 July 1923; ed. Trinity Coll., Dublin and King's Inn, Dublin.
Called to the Irish Bar 46, joined Leinster Circuit; called to the English Bar, Gray's Inn 50, to the Northern Rhodesia Bar 51; Queen's Counsel, N. Rhodesia 64; mem. Parl. for Lusaka East 64-68; Minister of Justice, Lusaka 64-65; Attorney-Gen. 65-69; Minister of Legal Affairs 67-68; Chief Justice of Zambia March-Sept. 69; Chief Justice of Malawi 70-; Grand Commdr., Order of Menelik II, Ethiopia 65.
The High Court of Malawi, P.O. Box 30244, Chichiri, Blantyre 3, Malawi.

Skládal, Josef; Czechoslovak physician and physiologist (retd.); b. 16 March 1889, Vienna, Austria; ed. Prague and Paris Univs.
Former Assistant at the Medical Faculty, Univ. of Paris and Brno and Prague Physiological Insts.; Lecturer in Gen. and Experimental Pathology 36; Head of Chest Dept., Bulovka Hospital, Prague 37; Lectured Royal Society of Medicine and Physiological Society, London 41, Palais de la Découverte, Paris 47, Moscow 57; titular mem. Int. Union against Tuberculosis; fmr. Editor *Rozhledy v tuberkulose*; Chair. Czechoslovak Health Council in London during Second World War; Prof. of Clinical Physiology, Charles Univ. Prague 45-56, of Pathological Physiology 56-70; Dir. Research Inst. of Clinical Physiology 68; Pres. Czechoslovak Pneumological and Phthisiological Soc. 46; special mem. Czech. Soc. of Sciences 51; mem. Scientific Council, Ministry of Health 53; Order of Labour 68.
Publs. *The Pleuro-subpleural Zone* (Cambridge Univ.

Press) 42, *Syndrome cortico-pleural* (Masson et Cie, Paris), *Quelques aspects nouveaux de l'exploration physique du poumon* 47, *La cinédensigraphie du diaphragme chez l'homme* 70 (Traité de biologie appliquée); papers on postural function of the human diaphragm 69, 70, 71.
Londýnská 20, Prague 2, Czechoslovakia.
Telephone: 250638 (Home).

Skobeltsyn, Dmitry Vladimirovich; Soviet nuclear and cosmic ray physicist; b. 24 Nov. 1892, St. Petersburg (now Leningrad); ed. Petrograd Univ.
Worked at the Leningrad Polytechnic and Physico-Technical Inst., Moscow Univ. 40-60; mem. U.S.S.R. Acad. of Sciences 46-; Dir. of the Inst. of Physics of the Acad. of Sciences of the U.S.S.R. 51-73; Chair. of the Cttee. for the award of Int. Lenin Peace Prizes 50-74; mem. Comm. for Foreign Affairs of the U.S.S.R. Supreme Soviet; Deputy to U.S.S.R. Supreme Soviet 54-74; State prizewinner 51; awarded Order of Lenin (six times), Vavilov Gold Medal of the Acad. of Sciences of the U.S.S.R. 52, Hero of Socialist Labour, Order of Red Banner of Labour (twice); Mendeleyev Prize of U.S.S.R. Acad. of Sciences 36.
Publs. *Research into Recoil Effect of Scattered Gamma Rays* 25, *Cosmic Rays* 27-29, 36, *Nature of Cosmic Radiation* 50, etc.
Academy of Sciences of the U.S.S.R., 14 Leninsky prospekt, Moscow, U.S.S.R.

Sköld, Per; Swedish business executive; b. 29 Dec. 1922, Stockholm; s. of Per Edvin Sköld (*q.v.*) and Edit Sköld; m. Anna-Christina Neumuller; two s. one d.; ed. Royal Swedish Coll. of Forestry.
District Forest Officer, Swedish Forest Service 56, Chief District Forest Officer 61, Dir. in Chief 64, Dir.-Gen. 65; Vice-Pres. Statsföretag AB 70, Pres. 71-.
Statsföretag AB, Fack, Hamngatan 6, 103 80 Stockholm 40; Home: Grävlingsvägen 35, 161 37 Bromma, Sweden.
Telephone: (08) 24-29-00 (Office); (08) 25-93-60 (Home).

Sköld, Per Edvin, B.A.; Swedish politician, economist and agriculturist; b. 25 May 1891; m. Edit Sköld; ed. Lund Univ.
Deputy 18-64; Under-Sec. of State in Ministry of Agriculture 24-26; mem. editorial staffs of various labour papers; Dir. Bank of Sweden 31-32 and 36; Minister of Agriculture 32-36, of Commerce 36-38, of Defence 38-45, of Agriculture 45-48, of Economic Co-ordination 48-49, of Finance 49-55; Chair. Board of Dirs. Bank of Sweden 57-64; Social-Democrat.
Box 3335, Höör (Summer); Strandvägen 27, Stockholm O (Winter), Sweden.
Telephone: 0413-50114 (Summer); 08-618350 (Winter).

Skolimowski, Jerzy; Polish film director; b. 5 May 1938, Warsaw; m. Joanna Szczerbic; ed. Warsaw Univ. and State Superior Film School, Łódź.
Wrote scripts for Wajda's *Innocent Sorcerers* and Polanski's *Knife in the Water*; directed, designed, scripted, edited and appeared in *Rysopis* 64; scripted directed and appeared in *Walkover* 65; scripted and directed *Barrier* 66; directed *Le Départ* 67; scripted, directed and appeared in *Hands Up* 67; directed *Adventures of Gerard* 69; Grand Prix for *Barrier* Int. Film Festival, Bergamo 66.
Films: *Rysopis* (Identification Marks: None) 64, *Walkover* 65, *Bariera* (Barrier) 66, *Le Départ* 67, *Ręce do góry* (Hands Up) 67, *Dialogue 20-40-60* 68, *Adventures of Gerard* 69, *The Deep End* 71, *King, Queen, Knave* 72.
Publs. Poetry *Gdzieś blisko siebie* (Somewhere close to oneself), Play *Ktoś się utopił* (Somebody got drowned).
c/o Film Polski, ul. Mazowiecka 6/8, 00-048 Warsaw, Poland.

Skoog, Folke (Karl), PH.D.; American plant physiologist; b. 15 July 1908, Sweden; s. of Karl (G.) Skoog and Sigrid (Person) Skoog; m. Birgit Anna Lisa Bergner 1947; one d.; ed. Calif. Inst. of Technology and Univ. of Calif.
Instructor and Research Assoc., Harvard Univ. 37-41; Asst. Prof., Assoc. Prof. of Biology Johns Hopkins Univ. 41-44; Technical Rep. (Chemist), U.S. Army 44-46; Assoc. Prof. of Botany, Univ. of Wisconsin 47-49, Prof. of Botany 49-; mem., American Soc. of Plant Physiologists (Vice-Pres. 56-57, Pres. 57-58), Botanical Soc. of America (Chair. Physiology Section 54-55), Nat. Acad. of Sciences, American Acad. of Arts and Sciences, Soc. of Gen. Physiologists (Pres. 57-58), Soc. of Devt. Biology (Pres. 70-71), Royal Soc. of Sciences, Sweden, Royal Acad. of Sciences, Sweden. Akad. Leopoldina, Germany; Hon. Ph.D. (Univ. of Lund, Sweden); Stephen Hales Medal of American Soc. of Plant Physiologists 55, Certificate of Merit of Botanical Soc. of America 56, Reid Barnes Award, American Soc. of Plant Physiologists 70.
Leisure interests: farming, sports.
Publs. *Plant Growth Substances* (Editor) 51; author and co-author of many scientific articles on plant growth, auxins and cytokinins 33-76.
Institute of Plant Development, Birge Hall, University of Wisconsin, Madison, Wis. 53706; Home: 2134 Chamberlain Avenue, Madison, Wis. 53705, U.S.A.
Telephone: 608-262-2790 (Office); 608-233-1948 (Home).

Skriabin, Georgy Konstantinovich; Soviet biochemist and microbiologist; b. 17 Sept. 1917, Leningrad; s. of K. I. and E. M. Skriabin; m. I. B. Skriabin; two s.; ed. Kazan Veterinary Inst. and Moscow Veterinary Acad.
Soviet Army 43-46; Senior Research Worker, Head of Dept., Inst. of Microbiology, U.S.S.R. Acad. of Sciences 49-62, Dir. Inst. of Biochemistry and Physiology of Micro-organisms, Acad. of Sciences 62-, Dir. Scientific Centre of Biological Investigations, Acad. of Sciences 67-74; Vice-Pres. All-Union Microbiological Soc.; corresp. mem. U.S.S.R. Acad. of Sciences 68, State Prize 71.
Institute of Biochemistry and Physiology of Micro-organisms, Puschino-on-Oka, Moscow region 142292, U.S.S.R.

Skrinsky, Aleksandr Nikolayevich, D.SC.; Soviet physicist; b. 15 Jan. 1936, Orenburg; ed. Moscow State Univ.
Research Worker, Head of Laboratory, Inst. of Nuclear Physics, Siberian Dept., U.S.S.R. Acad. of Sciences 59-; Prof. Novosibirsk Univ. 67; corresp. mem. U.S.S.R. Acad. of Sciences 68-70, mem. 70-; Lenin Prize 67.
Publs. scientific works in the field of speed technology and nuclear physics.
Akademgorodok, Novosibirsk, U.S.S.R.

Skrowaczewski, Stanisław; Polish conductor and composer; b. 3 Oct. 1923, Lwów; s. of Pawel and Zofia (Karszniewicz) Skrowaczewski; m. Krystyna Jarosz 1956; two s. one d.; ed. Lwów and Cracow.
Conductor, Wrocław Philharmonic Orchestra 46-47; further composition studies with Nadia Boulanger and P. Klecki, Paris 47-49; Artistic Dir. and First Conductor, Silesian Philharmonic Orch. 49-54; First Conductor, Cracow Philharmonic Orch. 55-56; Dir. Nat. Philharmonic Orch., Warsaw 57-59; Musical Dir. Minnesota Orchestra 60-; tours in Europe, N. and S. America, Israel; State Prize, First Prize, Int. Conductor's Competition, Rome 56; D.H.L. h.c. (Hamline Univ., St. Paul, Minnesota) 63; D.Mus. h.c. (Macalester Coll., St. Paul, Minn.) 73.
Compositions include Symphony for String Orchestra, three other symphonies, *Muzyka Nocą* (Music by Night, suite of nocturnes), four string quartets, two overtures, *Cantique des Cantiques* (voice and orch.), *Prelude,*

Fugue, Post-Ludium (orch.), English Horn Concerto 69, opera, ballet, film and theatre music.
Orchestra Hall, 1111 Nicollet Mall, Minn. 55403, U.S.A.

Skwirzyński, Tadeusz; Polish politician; b. 29 Sept. 1923, Iwonicz, Krosno District; ed. Warsaw Univ.
Soldier of Peasants' Battalions, Rzeszów District, organizer of underground educ. 39-45; with CRS "Sampomec Chłopska" (Agricultural Centre of Co-operative "Peasants' Self-Help") 48-53; Head of Dept., Cen. Board of Corn Plants 53-57, Deputy Dir. of Investment Affairs 57-58; Dir. Union of Plants of Fodder Industry (Bacutil) 58-67; Under-Sec. of State for Agricultural Products, Ministry of Food Industry and Purchase 67-69; Vice-Chair. Planning Comm. attached to Council of Ministers 69-71; Chair. Presidium of Voivodship Nat. Council, Bydgoszcz 71-73; Minister of Forestry and Wood Industry 73-; mem. Chief Cttee. of United Peasants' Party; Deputy to Seym (Parl.) 72-; Knight's, Officer's Cross and Commdr. Order of Polonia Restituta, Silver Cross of Merit and other decorations.
Ministerstwo Leśnictwa i Przemysłu Drzewnego, Ul. Wawelska 52/54, 02-067 Warsaw, Poland.

Skytte, Karl; Danish politician and farmer; b. 31 March 1908; ed. agricultural schools.
Member Cen. Cttee. Nat. Union of Radical Youth 29-43, Chair. 33-37; mem. Cen. Cttee. Radical Party (Det radikale Venstre) 33-; mem. Govt. Cttee. on Land Settlement 42-57; mem. of Parliament 47-; Minister of Agriculture 57-64; Chair. of Govt. Cttee. on Land Settlement; mem. Hillerslev Parish Council, Svendborg County Council; Chair. House of Parliament (Folketing) 68-.
Bregnehøjgaard, 5750 Ringe, Denmark.

Slaoui, Driss; Moroccan politician and banker.
Minister of Commerce and Industry 59-61; Dir. of Royal Cabinet March 62; Minister of Public Works July 62-Jan. 63; Minister of Finance Jan. 63-64, of Nat. Economy and Agriculture Nov. 63-64; Gov. Banque du Maroc 64-68; Minister of Justice 68-69; Dir. of the Royal Cabinet 69-71; Perm. Rep. to UN 74-.
Permanent Mission of Morocco to UN, 757 Third Ave., 23rd Floor, New York, N.Y. 10017, U.S.A.

Slater, James Derrick, F.C.A.; British company director; b. 13 March 1929, Wirral, Cheshire; s. of Hubert and Jessie Slater; m. Helen Wyndham Goodwyn 1965; two s. two d.; ed. Preston Manor County School.
Director, A.E.C. Ltd. 59; Deputy Sales Director, Leyland Motor Corpn. 63; acquired with associates, H. Lotery and Co., Ltd., which was then renamed Slater, Walker Securities Ltd., and appointed Chair. and Man. Dir. 64-72, Chair., Chief Exec. Officer 72-75.
Leisure interests: chess, backgammon, reading, golf, tennis.
Home: High Beeches, Blackhills, Esher, Surrey, England.

Slater, John Clarke, PH.D.; American university professor; b. 22 Dec. 1900, Oak Park, Ill.; s. of John Rothwell and Katherine Chapin Slater; m. 1st Helen L. Frankenfield 1926, 2nd Rose C. L. Mooney 1954; two s. one d.; ed. Univ. of Rochester and Harvard Univ.
Instructor, Asst. Prof. and Assoc. Prof. of Physics, Harvard 24-30; Prof. of Physics and Head of Dept., Mass. Inst. of Technology 30-51, Inst. Prof. 51-66; Graduate Research Prof. Univ. of Florida 64-; mem. Technical Staff, Bell Telephone Laboratories Inc. (on leave from M.I.T.) 43-44; mem. staff Brookhaven Nat. Laboratory (on leave from M.I.T.) 51-52; Nat. Medal for Science 71.
Publs. *Introduction to Theoretical Physics* (with N. H. Frank) 33, *Introduction to Chemical Physics* 39, *Microwave Transmission* 43, *Mechanics*, and *Electromagnetism* (with N. H. Frank) 47, *Microwave Electronics* 50,

Quantum Theory of Matter 51 (2nd edn. 68), *Modern Physics* 55, *Quantum Theory of Atomic Structure* I and II 60, *Quantum Theory of Molecules and Solids* I, II, III, IV, 63, 65, 67, 74, *Solid-State and Molecular Theory: A Scientific Biography* 75.
Office: University of Florida, Gainesville, Fla.; Home 623 S.W. 27th Street, Gainesville, Fla. 32601, U.S.A.
Telephone: 376-7449 (Home).

Slater, Joseph Elliott; American administrator; b. 17 Aug. 1922, Salt Lake City, Utah; m.; two c.; ed. Univ. of California.
Naval Reserve Officer, Mil. Govt. Planning Officer, Berlin, London and Paris 43-46; U.S. Sec. of Econ. Directorate, Allied Control Comm. for Germany; Asst. U.S. Sec. of Allied Control Council Econ. and Financial Affairs 45-48; mem. UN Affairs Planning Staff, Dept. of State, Wash. 49; Sec.-Gen. Allied High Comm. for Germany, Bonn 49-52; Exec. Sec. Office of U.S. Special Rep. in Europe, U.S. Sec. to NATO and mem. U.S. Del. to OEEC 52; Chief Economist, Creole Petroleum Corpn., Caracas 54-57; Sec. to President's Comm. on Foreign Assistance 59; Assoc. Dir., Int. Affairs Program, Program Officer (Office of Int. Relations), Ford Foundation 57-67; Asst. Man. Dir. Devt. Loan Fund 60-61, and Deputy Asst. Sec. of State on Educ. and Cultural Affairs 61-62; Pres. Salk Inst. 65-72; Pres. Aspen Inst. for Humanistic Studies 69-; Pres. Anderson Foundation 69-72; Special Fellow, Salk Inst.; Consultant to Int. Affairs Program, Ford Foundation; Visiting Prof. Univ. of Colorado; mem. Council on Foreign Relations, New York, Center for Inter-American Affairs, New York Inst. for Strategic Studies, London Int. Affairs Cttee. of Nat. Planning Asscn.; UN Policy Studies Group and Environment Group; Trustee of Inst. of Religion and Mental Health, Aspen Center of Contemporary Art, Aspen Center for Physics, Int. Broadcast Inst., World Affairs Council, San Diego TIAA-CREF, Acad. for Educ. Devt., Int. Inst. for Environmental Affairs, Int. Assoc. for Cultural Freedom; Dir. Overseas Devt. Council, American Council on Germany; Hon. LL.D.
717 Fifth Avenue, New York, N.Y. 10022; Home: 870 UN Plaza, New York, N.Y. 10017, U.S.A.
Telephone: (212) 759-1053.

Slater, Layton Ernest Alfred; South African printing and publishing executive; b. 27 Jan. 1916, Johannesburg; s. of Joseph Slater and Marguerita Hildebrandt; m. Elizabeth Anne Ledger 1940; two d.; ed. St. Aidan's Coll., Grahamstown.
Military service Middle East and Italy 40-45; Chair. Nat. Industrial Council of the Printing and Newspaper Industry of South Africa 66-75; Chair. and Man. Dir. Argus Printing & Publishing Co. Ltd. 67- (proprietors of seven daily and many weekly newspapers in South Africa); Pres. Newspaper Press Union of South Africa 72-73; Trustee, Nat. Development and Management Foundation; Vice-Chair. South Africa Nature Foundation.
Leisure interests: golf, reading, fishing.
4 Melville Road, Illovo, Johannesburg, South Africa.
Telephone: 42-4033.

Slater, Richard Mercer Keene, C.M.G.; British diplomatist; b. 27 May 1915, India; s. of Samuel H. Slater, C.M.G., C.I.E.; m. Barbara J. Murdoch 1939; four s.; ed. Eton Coll., and Magdalene Coll., Cambridge.
Indian Civil Service (Punjab Comm.) 39-47; joined H.M. Diplomatic Service 47; served in Karachi (on secondment to Commonwealth Relations Office), Lima, Moscow, Rangoon and Foreign Office; Amb. to Cuba 66-70; High Commr. to Uganda 70-72, concurrently Amb. to Rwanda; retd. 73; Adviser, Commercial Union Assurance Co.
Vicary's, Odiham, Hampshire, England.
Telephone: Odiham 2648.

Slater, Robert E.; American financial executive; b. 25 Oct. 1916, New York; s. of David and Sarah Brown Slater; m. Roberta Gillies 1946; one s. three d.; ed. Harvard Business School, and Aspen Inst. for Humanistic Studies.
Research Asst. John Hancock Mutual Life Insurance Co., Boston 46, Controller 49, Vice-Pres. 53, Senior Vice-Pres. and Dir. 61, Exec. Vice-Pres. 65, Pres. and Chief Exec. Officer 66-69; Pres. and Chief Exec. Officer IOS, Ltd. 70-71; Chair. Nat. Liberty Corpn. 71-; Fellow, Soc. of Actuaries; Hon. LL.D. (Gordon Coll.); Hon. D. Comm. Sc. (Suffolk Univ.).
Leisure interests: golf, hunting.
Publs. various articles on automation for *Harvard Business Review*.
Investors' Overseas Services (IOS) Ltd., Geneva, Switzerland.

Slattery, Rear-Admiral Sir Matthew Sausse, K.B.E., C.B., F.R.AE.S.; British company director; b. 12 May 1902, Chislehurst, Kent; s. of H. F. Slattery and Agnes Cuddon; m. Mica Mary Swain 1925; two s. one d.; ed. Stonyhurst Coll., and R.N. Colls. of Osborne and Dartmouth.
Joined R.N. 16; Dir. of Air Material, Admiralty 39-41; in command H.M.S. *Cleopatra* and *Danae* 41-42; Dir.-Gen. Naval Aircraft Devt. and Production (Ministry of Aircraft Production) 41, and Chief Naval Rep. 43; Vice-Controller (Air) and Chief of Naval Air Equipment (Admiralty) and Chief Naval Rep. Supply Council (Ministry of Supply) 45-48; retd. from R.N. with war service rank of Rear Admiral 48; Man. Dir. Short Bros. & Harland Ltd. 48-52, Chair. and Man. Dir. 52-60; Chair. S.B. Realisations Ltd. 52-60, Bristol Aircraft Ltd. 57-60; Dir. Bristol Aeroplane Co. Ltd. 57-60; Special Adviser to Prime Minister on Transport of Middle East Oil 57-59; Chair. BOAC 60-63, BOAC/Cunard 62-63; Dir. (fmr. Chair.) R. & W. Hawthorn, Leslie & Co. Ltd.; Hon. D.Sc.; Legion of Merit (U.S.A.).
Leisure interests: living in the country, gardening.
Harvey's Farm, Warninglid, Sussex, England.
Telephone: Warninglid 291.

Slavsky, Efim Pavlovich; Soviet politician; b. 1898; ed. Moscow Inst. of Non-Ferrous Metals and Gold.
Engineer, Workshop Man., Chief Engineer, Dir., Electrozinc Plant, Odjonikidze 38-40; Dir. Dnieper Aluminium Plant 40, Urals Plant 41-45; Deputy People's Commissar of Non-Ferrous Metallurgy 45-46; at staff of U.S.S.R. Council of Ministers 46-53; Deputy Minister, First Deputy Minister of Medium Machine Building 53-57, Minister 57-; mem. C.P.S.U. 18-; mem. C.P.S.U. Cen. Cttee. 61-; Deputy to U.S.S.R. Supreme Soviet 58-; State Prize (twice); Hero of Socialist Labour, Order of Lenin, Hammer and Sickle Gold Medals (3).
U.S.S.R. Ministry of Medium Machine Building, Moscow, U.S.S.R.

Slayton, Donald K.; American astronaut; b. 1 March 1924, Sparta, Wis.; m. Marjorie Lunney; one s.; ed. Univ. of Minn. and Mich. Technological Univ.
Entered U.S. Air Force 42, pilot 43; flew 56 combat missions, Second World War; aeronautical engineer, Boeing Co., Seattle, Wash. 49-51; recalled to 12th Air Force H.Q. 51; attended Air Force Flight Test Pilot School, Edwards Air Force Base, Calif. 55, experimental test pilot, Edwards Air Force Base 56-59; selected by NASA as astronaut 59; named as pilot of MA-7 flight 61, but prevented from flying by heart condition; astronaut and Dir. Flight Crew Operations, NASA Johnson Space Center 63-; mem., docking module pilot Joint U.S.-U.S.S.R. Soyuz-Apollo Manned Space Flight July 75; NASA Distinguished Service Medal 65.
NASA Johnson Space Center, Houston, Tex. 77058, U.S.A.

Slessor, Marshal of the Royal Air Force Sir John Cotesworth, G.C.B., D.S.O., M.C., D.L.; British air force officer; b. 3 June 1897, Rhanikhet, India; s. of Major A. K. Slessor; m. Hermione Guinness 1923; one s. one d.; ed. Haileybury.
Served with Royal Flying Corps France, Egypt, Sudan 15-18; served India 21-22; R.A.F. Staff Coll. 24-25; Commdr. No. 4 Squadron 25-28; Air Staff, Air Ministry 28-30; Instructor Staff Coll. Camberley 31-34; served India 35-37, Commd. No. 3 Indian Wing Quetta and N.F.W.P.; served Waziristan Operations 36-37; Dir. of Plans Air Ministry 37-41; Air Officer Commanding No. 5 (Bomber) Group 41-42; Asst. Chief of Air Staff 42; Air Officer C.-in-C. Coastal Command 43; C.-in-C. R.A.F. Mediterranean and Middle East and Deputy to Allied Air C.-in-C. 44-45, Air Member for Personnel 45-47; Commandant Imperial Defence Coll. 48-49; Chief Air Staff Jan. 50-52; Vice-Pres. Inst. of Strategic Studies, British Atlantic Cttee., Anglo-German Soc.; mem. English-Speaking Union, R.A.F. Benevolent Fund; fmr. mem. Somerset County Council; High Sheriff of Somerset 65-66.
Leisure interest: leisure.
Publs. *Air Power and Armies* 36, *Strategy for the West* 54, *The Central Blue* 56, *The Great Deterrent* 57, *What Price Co-existence* 62, *These Remain* (essays) 69.
Rimpton Manor, Yeovil, Somerset, England.

Slichter, Charles Pence, B.A., M.A., PH.D.; American professor of physics; b. 21 Jan. 1924, Ithaca, N.Y.; s. of Sumner Huber Slichter and Ada Pence Slichter; m. Gertrude Thayer Almy 1952; three s. one d.; ed. Brown and Nichols School, Cambridge, Mass. and Harvard Univ.
Instructor, Univ. of Ill. 49-51, Asst. Prof. of Physics 51-54, Assoc. Prof. 54-55, Prof. 55-, mem. Center for Advanced Study, Univ. of Ill. 68-; Morris Loeb Lecturer, Harvard Univ. 61; mem. President's Science Advisory Cttee. 65-69, Cttee. on the Nat. Medal of Science 69-74; Alfred Sloan Fellow 57-63; mem. Nat. Acad. of Sciences 67, American Acad. of Arts and Sciences 69, Corpn. of Harvard Univ. 70, American Philosophical Soc. 71, Nat. Science Board 75-, Board of Dirs. Polaroid Corpn. 75-; Langmuir Prize of American Physical Soc. 69.
Publs. *Principles of Magnetic Resonance* 63; articles on solid state physics, chemical physics and magnetic resonance.
311 Physics Building, University of Illinois, Urbana, Ill. 61801; Home: 3012 Valley Brook Drive, Champaign, Ill. 61820, U.S.A.
Telephone: 217-333-3834 (Office); 217-359-7795 (Home).

Slichter, Louis Byrne, PH.D., D.SC., LL.D.; American geophysicist; b. 19 May 1896, Madison, Wis.; s. of Charles Sumner and Mary Louise (Byrne); m. Martha Merry Buell 1926; two d.; ed. Univ. of Wis. and Calif. Inst. of Technology.
Ensign, U.S. Naval Reserve 17-19; Submarine Signal Corpn. 22-24; Mason, Slichter and Gauld, geophysical exploration 24-31; Assoc. Prof. of Geophysics, Mass. Inst. of Technology 31-32, Prof. 32-45; mem. Div. 6, Office of Scientific Research and Devt. 42-45; Prof. of Geophysics, Univ. of Wis. 46-47; Dir. Inst. of Geophysics, Univ. of Calif. 47-62, Assoc. Dir. 67-, Prof. of Geophysics 47-63, Emer. 63-; mem. American Acad. of Arts and Sciences, Nat. Acad. of Sciences; Presidential Certificate of Merit 48; Distinguished Service Citation, Univ. of Wis. 57; Jackling Award, American Inst. of Mining, Metallurgy and Petroleum Engineers 60; Wm. Bowie Medal, American Geophysical Union 66; Hon. Sc.D. (Univ. of Wis.) 67, Hon. LL.D. (U.C.L.A.).
Leisure interests: sailing, swimming, camping.
Publs. *Interpretation of Seismic Travel Time Curves* 32, *Interpretation of the Resistivity Prospecting Method for Horizontal Structures* 33, *Inverse Boundary Value Problem in Electrodynamics* 33, *Cooling of the Earth* 41,

Electromagnetic Interpretation Problem for the Sphere 52, *Seismic Interpretation Theory for an Elastic Earth* 54, *Aspects of Mineral Exploration* 59, *Need of a New Philosophy of Prospecting* 60, *Observations of the Free Oscillations of the Earth* 61, *Earth-Tide Observations Made During the International Geophysical Year* 63, *Secular Effects of Tidal Friction upon the Earth's Rotation* 63, *An Experiment Concerning Gravitational Shielding* 65, *Gravity Observations and the Dynamics of the Earth* 66, *Spheroidal Oscillations of the Earth* 67, *Free Oscillations of the Earth* 67, *The Residual Daily Earth Tides at the South Pole* (with B. V. Jackson) 74. University of California at Los Angeles, Calif. 90024; Home: 1446 North Amalfi Drive, Pacific Palisades, Calif. 90272, U.S.A.
Telephone: 213-825-1384 (Office); 213-454-7450 (Home).

Slim, Taieb; Tunisian politician and diplomatist; b. 19 Jan. 1919, Tunis; s. of Abed Slim and Habiba Beyram; m. Leyla Zaouche 1959; two d.; ed. Tunis Lycée and Univ. of Paris.
Member Néo-Destour Party, detained 41-43; Arab Maghreb Bureau, Cairo 46-49; Head, Tunisian Office, Cairo 49, established Tunisian offices, New Delhi, Djakarta, Karachi; Head, Foreign Affairs, Presidency of Council of Ministers 55-56; Ambassador to U.K. 56-62; Perm. Rep. to UN 62-67; Sec. of State, Personal Rep. of Pres. 67-70; Amb. to Morocco 70-71; Minister of State 71-73; mem. Political Bureau Destour Socialist Party 70-74; Amb. and Perm. Rep. to UN, Geneva 73-74; Amb. to Canada 74-.
Leisure interest: sailing.
Embassy of Tunisia, 515 O'Connor Street, Ottawa, Ont. K1S 3P8; Home: 8 Crescent Road, Ottawa, Ont., Canada.
Telephone: 746-7603.

Slipyj-Kobernickyj-Dyčkowsky, H.E. Cardinal Joseph; Vatican ecclesiastic; b. 17 Feb. 1892, Zazdrist, District of Terebovlia, Western Ukraine; s. of Ivan Kobernyckyj Slipyj and Anastasia Dyčkowska; ed. Univ. of Innsbruck and Gregorianum, Angelicum and Oriental Inst., Rome.
Ordained 17; Prof. of dogmatic theology 22; Rector Theological Seminar, Lviv 25; Pres. Theological Scientific Soc. 23; founded and edited *Boholovia*; Rector of Theological Acad. 29; Titular Archbishop of Serre 39; Archbishop of Lviv and Metropolitan of Halyc 44; arrested and deported to Siberia 45; released to Vatican City 63; recognized as Major Archbishop of Ukrainian Rite Catholic Church 63; founded Ukrainian Catholic Univ. Research Centre of St. Clement in Rome 63; mem. Sacred Congregation for the Oriental Churches 63, Pontifical Comm. for compilation of Oriental Codex of Canon Law, Taras Shevcenko Literary Soc.; edited *Blahovistnik* and *Monumenta Ucrainae Historica* 64; cr. Cardinal 65; mem. Tiberian Acad. of Rome; Pontifical Comm. for Revision of the Code of Canon Law, built Church of St. Sophia in Rome for Ukrainians 69; established Ukrainian parish of SS. Sergius and Bacchus in Rome 71; visited Ukraine communities in Canada, U.S.A., S. America, Australia, etc. 68-69; Hon. degrees from Loyola Univ. Chicago, Catholic Univ. Washington, Innsbruck Univ., etc.
Publs. since 63, 70 vols. in fields of philosophy, history, theology, etc.
Palazzino dell' Arciprete, Vatican City, 00120 Rome, Italy.
Telephone: Vatican City 3321.

Śliwiński, Marian; Polish physician and politician; b. 2 Feb. 1932, Strzelce Wielkie; ed. Medical Acad., Łódź.
Member of PZPR (Polish United Workers Party) 48-; mem. of youth orgs.; Asst. Physiological Inst. Med. Acad., Łódź 52-55; Asst., later lecturer II Surgical Clinic, Medical Acad. Łódź; Dir. Clinical Hospital, Łódź 55-64; doctorate 63; Asst. Prof. 65; Deputy mem. Cen. Cttee. PZPR 71-; Dir. Educ. and Scientific Dept., Ministry of Health and Social Welfare 64-70, Vice-Minister 70-72, Minister 72-; scientific prize of Łódź City; mem. of nat. and int. medical socs.; several Polish decorations.
Publs. numerous papers on surgery of the thorax and cardiosurgery.
Ministerstwo Zdrowia i Opieki Społecznej, ul. Miodowa 15, 00-246 Warsaw, Poland.

Śliwiński, Zdzisław; Polish theatre and music executive; b. 20 July 1910, Dolina; s. of Jan and Maria Śliwiński; m. Alicja Woszczyńska; one s. one d.; ed. High School, Lwów, and Higher Coll. of Commerce, Warsaw.
Head of Section in Dept. of Music, Ministry of Art and Culture 45-46; Vice-Dir. Polish Music Publication, Cracow 46-47; Dir.-Gen. Poznań Philharmonic Orchestra 46-58, Nat. Philharmonic Orchestra, Warsaw 58-69; Dir.-Gen. of Grand Opera House (Teatr Wielki), Warsaw Jan. 65-Oct. 66, 70-; mem. Organizing Cttee. of Int. Chopin Competition 49-, Presidium of "Autumn in Warsaw" Int. Festivals of Contemporary Music 58-; Pres. Organizing Cttee. Int. Henryk Wieniawski Violin Competition, Poznań 52, 57; mem. Polish Authors' Agency; Gold Cross of Merit; Knight's and Officer's Cross of Polonia Restituta.
Leisure interest: cars.
Teatr Wielki, ul. Moliera 5, Warsaw, Poland.
Telephone: 26-32-89.

Sloman, Albert Edward, M.A., D.PHIL.; British university administrator; b. 14 Feb. 1921, Launceston, Cornwall; s. of Albert Sloman and L. F. Brewer; m. Marie B. Bergeron 1948; three d.; ed. Launceston Coll. and Wadham Coll., Oxford.
Lecturer, Univ. of Calif. (Berkeley) 46-47; Reader in Spanish, Univ. of Dublin 47-53; Fellow, Trinity Coll., Dublin 50-53; Prof. of Spanish, Univ. of Liverpool 53-62; Vice-Chancellor, Univ. of Essex 62-; Pres. Conf. of European Rectors and Vice-Chancellors 69-74; Vice-Pres. Int. Asscn. of Univs.; mem. Econ. and Social Cttee. EEC 73-.
Leisure interest: travel.
Publs. *The Sources of Calderón's El Príncipe Constante* 50, *The Dramatic Craftsmanship of Calderón* 58, *Calderón, La Vida Es Sueño* (Editor), 60, *Bulletin of Hispanic Studies* (Editor) 53-62, *A University in the Making* 64.
University of Essex, Wivenhoe Park, Colchester, Essex, England.
Telephone: Colchester 44144.

Słonimski, Antoni; Polish writer; b. 15 Oct. 1895, Warsaw; ed. Acad. of Fine Arts, Warsaw and Munich.
Counsellor, Head of Section of Letters, UNESCO Prep. Comm.; Dir. Polish Cultural Inst., London 49-51; returned Poland 51; Chair. Polish Writers' Union 56-59, State Prize 1st Class 55, Literary Prize of Warsaw 56; Officer's Cross Order of Polonia Restituta 52, Commdr. 54.
Publs. include poems *Harmonja, Sonety, Parada, Godzina Poezji, Okno bez krat, Alarm, Liryki, Rozmowa z gwiazdą, Popiół i wiatr;* plays: *Rodzina, Murzyn Warszawski, Wieża Babel, Lekarz Bezdomny;* vol. articles *Walki nad Bzdurą, Heretyk na ambonie, Moja Podróż do Rosji, Jawa i Mrzonka, Wiersze zebrane, Jedna strona medalu, Kroniki tygodniowe 1927-1939, Wspomnienia warszawskie, Artykuły pierwszej potrzeby, W oparach absurdu* (with Julian Tuwin), *Załatwione odmownie, Torpeda czasu* (novel), *138 wierszy* (138 verses) 73, *Alfabet wspomnień* (Alphabet of Recollections) 74.
Aleja Róż 6 m. 13, 00-556 Warsaw, Poland.
Telephone: 21-4118.

Ślopek, Stefan; Polish microbiologist; b. 1 Dec. 1914, Skawa, near Cracow; ed. Medical Faculty, Lvov Univ. Doctor 45-48, Docent 48-50, Assoc. Prof. 50-57, Prof. 57-; Dir. Inst. of Immunology and Experimental Therapy, Polish Acad. of Sciences (PAN) 56-, Corresp. mem. PAN 65-73, mem. 73-, mem. Presidium 72-, Chair. Cttee. of Immunology; now Prof. Inst. of Bio-structure, Medical Acad. in Wrocław; mem. Silesian Medical Acad. 49-56; Vice-Chair. Polish Soc. of Micro-biologists; Dr. h.c. Silesian and Poznań Medical Acads.; State Prize, 2nd Class 52, 1st Class 70, Knight's and Officer's Crosses, Order of Polonia Restituta, Order of Banner of Labour, 1st Class 69, The Armed Forces in the Service of the Fatherland Silver Medal 71.
Publs. *Immunologia* 63, *Schorzenia ropne skóry* (Sup-purant Diseases of the Skin) (co-author) 67, *Mikro-biologia lekarska. Podręcznik dla studentów Akademii Medycznych* (Medical Microbiology. Handbook for Medical Academy Students) 72; Editor *Immunologia praktyczna* (Practical Immunology) 70; numerous articles in Polish and foreign languages.
Pl. Muzealny 5 m.I, 50-035 Wrocław, Poland.

Slyussarenko, Pyotr Konstantinovich; Soviet diplo-matist; b. 5 Oct. 1912, Taganrog; ed. Moscow Inst. of Technology.
Diplomatic service 39-; fmr. First Sec. Netherlands; fmr. Counsellor, Democratic Republic of Viet-Nam; Minister Counsellor, Cairo 61-64; Amb. to Jordan 64-68; Ministry of Foreign Affairs 68-70; Amb. to Togo 70-.
Embassy of the U.S.S.R., P.O. Box 634, route d'Atak-pamé, Lomé, Togo.

Smale, John G., B.S.; American business executive; b. 1 Aug. 1927, Listowel, Ont., Canada; s. of Vera G. and Peter G. Smale; m. Phyllis Anne Weaver 1950; one s. two d.; ed. Univ. of Miami.
Worked for Vick Chemical Co., New York 49-50; with Bio-Research Inc., New York 51-52; with Procter and Gamble Co. 52-, Dir. 72-, Pres. 74-; Hon. LL.D. (Kenyon Coll.) 74.
The Procter and Gamble Company, 301 East Sixth Street, Cincinnati, Ohio 45202, U.S.A.
Telephone: (513) 562-1100.

Smale, Stephen, M.S., PH.D.; American professor of mathematics; b. 15 July 1930, Michigan; s. of Lawrence and Helen Smale; m. Clara Davis 1955; two c.; ed. Univ. of Mich.
Professor, Columbia Univ. 61-64; Prof., Univ. of Calif., Berkeley 64-; mem. Nat. Acad. of Sciences; Veblen Prize; Fields Medal, Int. Union of Mathematicians.
Leisure interests: mineral collector, skin diving.
Publs. *Differential Equations, Dynamical Systems and Linear Algebra* (with M. Hirsch) 74, various articles on topology and global analysis.
Department of Mathematics, University of California, Berkeley, Calif. 94720, U.S.A.
Telephone: 642-4367.

Small, Charles John; Canadian economist; b. 19 Dec. 1919, Chengtu, Szechuan, China; s. of Rev. and Mrs. Walter Small; m. Jean McNeel 1946; four d.; ed. Ontario Agricultural Coll. and Univ. of Toronto.
Royal Canadian Navy serving in North Atlantic, Mediterranean, Normandy and Australia; mem. Dept. of Trade and Commerce 49, serving in The Hague 50-55; Dept. of External Affairs 55-; studying Chinese Language at Univ. of Toronto 56-57, seconded to Dept. of Trade and Commerce and apptd. Canadian Govt. Trade Commr., Hong Kong 58-61, Ottawa 61-63; Counsellor, Karachi 63-65; Perm. Rep. to OECD 65-69; Amb. to Pakistan 69-73, also to Afghanistan; Amb. to People's Repub. of China 72-, concurrently to Democratic Repub. of Viet-Nam 75-; LL.D. h.c. (Univ. of Guelph) 75.
Leisure interests: tennis, golf, swimming.
c/o Department of External Affairs, Ottawa, Ont., Canada.

Smallpeice, Sir Basil, K.C.V.O., F.C.A., B.COM.; British businessman; b. 18 Sept. 1906, Rio de Janeiro, Brazil; s. of Herbert Charles Smallpeice and Georgina Ruth (née Rust); m. 1st Kathleen Ivey Singleton Brame 1931 (deceased 1973), 2nd Rita Barbara Mary Burns 1973.
With Bullimore and Co., chartered accountants 25-30; Accountant, Hoover Ltd. 30-37; Chief Accountant and Sec., Doulton & Co. 37-48; Dir. of Costs and Statistics, British Transport Comm. 48-50; Financial Comptroller, British Overseas Airways Corpn. 50, mem. of Board 53, Deputy Chief Exec. 54, Managing Dir. 56-63; Man. Dir. BOAC-Cunard Ltd. 62-63; Dir. Cunard Steamship Co. 64-71, Chair. 65-71; Chair. Assoc. Container Transportation (Australia) 69-; Admin. Adviser, Queen's Household 64-; mem. Cttee. for Ex-ports to U.S.A. 64-66; Dir. Charterhouse Group 65-69; Chair. English-Speaking Union of the Commonwealth 65-68; Chair. British Inst. Management 70-72, Vice-Pres. 72-; Dir. Barclays Bank, London Local Board (fmr. Martins Bank) 66-74; Deputy Chair. Lonrho Ltd. 72-73.
Leisure interests: golf, gardening.
ACT (Australia) Ltd., 136 Fenchurch Street, London, E.C.3; Home: Reed Thatch, 25 Clare Hill, Esher, Surrey, England.
Telephone: 01-626-3233 (Office); Esher 63020 (Home).

Smallwood, Joseph R., D.C.L., LL.D.; Canadian politician; b. 24 Dec. 1900; ed. Bishop Field Coll., St. John's.
Journalist and author; launched and led movement to make Newfoundland a province of Canada; Premier of Newfoundland 49-72, concurrently Minister of Economic Development 56-72; Liberal.
Canada House, St. John's, Newfoundland, Canada.

Smathers, George A.; American lawyer and politician; b. 4 Nov. 1913; ed. Univ. of Florida.
Practising lawyer 38-; served U.S. Marine Corps 42-45; mem. House of Reps. (Democrat Florida) 46-50; U.S. Senator from Florida 50-68; U.S. del. Int. Tariff Conf. 66; Senior Partner Smathers & Thompson, Miami 69-, Smathers & Merrigan, Washington 69-; mem. Board Junior Chambers of Commerce.
2451 Brickell Avenue, Miami, Fla., U.S.A.

Smedley, Harold, C.M.G., M.B.E.; British diplomatist; b. 19 June 1920, Hove, Sussex; s. of late Ralph Davies Smedley, M.D.; m. Beryl Harley Brown 1950; two s. two d.; ed. Aldenham School and Pembroke Coll., Cambridge.
Royal Marine Commandos, Second World War; Dominions Office 46, British High Commission in New Zealand 48-50, S. Rhodesia 51-53, India 57-60; Private Sec. to Commonwealth Sec. 54-57; later Head of News Dept., Commonwealth Relations Office; High Commr. in Ghana 64-65 and 66-67; Amb. to Laos 67-70; Asst. Under-Sec. of State, Foreign and Commonwealth Office 70-72; Sec.-Gen. Comm. on Rhodesian Opinion 71-72; British High Commr. to Sri Lanka and Amb. (non-resident) to the Repub. of Maldives 73-75, High Commissioner to New Zealand 76-, concurrently Gov. of Pitcairn Island.
Leisure interest: gardening.
British High Commission, Reserve Bank Building, 2 The Terrace, P.O. Box 1812, Wellington, New Zealand; Sherwood, Oak End Way, Woodham, Weybridge, Surrey, England.
Telephone: Byfleet 43715 (England).

Smedt, Rt. Rev. Bishop Aemilius Josephus de, D.PHIL., D.THEOL.; Belgian ecclesiastic; b. 30 Oct. 1909; ed. Univ. Gregorianum, Rome.
Auxiliary Bishop, Malines 50; Bishop of Bruges 52-; mem. Secretariat for Christian Unity, Rome; Knight, Order of Leopold.
Publs. *Le Mariage, Le grand Mystère, Le Christ dans le Quartier, Le Sacerdoce des Fidèles, L'Amour Conjugal,*

Pour un dialogue "Parents-Adolescents", Pour un Climat de Liberté.
4 H. Geeststraat, 8000 Bruges, Belgium.
Telephone: 050-359-06.

Smelyakov, Nikolai Nikolayevich; Soviet foreign trade official; b. 14 April 1911; ed. Moscow Engineering Inst.
Member C.P.S.U. 39-; engineering 34-55; Minister of Engineering 56-57; Chair. Gorki Econ. Council 57-58; First Sec. Gorki Regional Cttee. of C.P. 58-59; Pres. Amtorg Joint-Stock Soc. in U.S.A. 59; Deputy Minister of Foreign Trade 59; Order of Red Banner of Labour (six times), Order of Red Star, Honour Badge, Order of the Great Patriotic War (1st Degree).
U.S.S.R. Ministry of Foreign Trade, 32-34 Smolenskaya-Sennaya ploshchad, Moscow, U.S.S.R.

Smetáček, Václav, PH.D.; Czechoslovak conductor and professor of music; b. 30 Sept. 1906, Brno; s. of Judr Rudolf Smetáček and Eleonora Smetáčková; m. Miloslava Kočvarová 1948; two s. two d.; ed. Acad. of Music, Prague and Charles Univ., Prague.
Founder and oboist Prague Wind Quintet 28-56; Conductor Prague Hlahol Singing Choir 34-46, Prague Broadcasting Corpn. 34-43; Artistic Dir. and First Conductor Prague Symphony Orchestra 43-72; Prof. Prague Conservatoire 45-67; has conducted orchestras in all continents of the world; numerous recordings for Suprafon, Deutsche Grammophongesellschaft, Panton, Opus and Musica Sacra; Officer Order Polonia Restituta; Honoured Artist of Czechoslovakia; Prize of the City of Prague, Order of Labour 66.
Major works: *Ballet on the Eve of a Summer Day, Vivat Olympia* (Solemn March), *Wedding March* and several Wind Quintets.
Klidná 6, Prague 6, Czechoslovakia.
Telephone: 35-05-92.

Šmid, Ladislav; Czechoslovak diplomatist; b. 16 July 1925, Kladno; m.; one d.
Associate Prof. of Modern History, Social Sciences and Econs., Charles Univ., Prague until 56; entered foreign service; with Czechoslovak Embassy, New Delhi 57-59; Deputy Head of Dept. for Int. Orgs., Ministry of Foreign Affairs 60-62; Deputy Perm. Rep. to UN 62-65, Perm. Rep. Aug. 73-; Head of Div., Ministry of Foreign Affairs 66-73; mem. of del. to numerous UN bodies and specialized agencies; Vice-Chair. UNCTAD Preparatory Board 63-64; Vice-Pres. UNCTAD Trade and Devt. Board 69-70, 72-73; Vice-Pres. ECOSOC 74, 75, Chair. ECOSOC Social Cttee. 74.
Permanent Mission of Czechoslovakia to United Nations, 1109-1111 Madison Avenue, New York, N.Y. 10028, U.S.A.

Smiley, Donald B., LL.B.; American business executive; b. 6 April 1915, Albany, Illinois; s. of Ralph Smiley and Etta Sorrowfree; m. Ruth Dick Cutter 1942; one s. three d.; ed. Augustana Coll. and Northwestern Univ. Law School.
Naval service during Second World War; Asst. Gen. Attorney, R. H. Macy & Co. Inc., Gen. Attorney and Sec. 53, Dir. 56, then apptd. Vice-Pres. and Treas., latest Chair. of the Board and Treas. 68-, Chief Exec. Officer 71-; Trustee Cttee. for Econ. Devt.; Dir., Texasgulf, Inc., Ralston Purina Co., Charter New York Corpn., Foreign Policy Asscn., RCA Corpn., N.B.C., Metropolitan Life Insurance Co., Fidelity Union Bancorpn., American Arbitration Asscn., United States Steel Corpn.; mem. Bar Asscns., City and State of New York.
Leisure interests: tennis, golf, music, theatre and literature.
R. H. Macy & Co. Inc., Herald Square, New York, N.Y. 10001; Home: 1 Putnam Hill, Greenwich, Conn. 06830, U.S.A.
Telephone: 203-869-1230.

Smirnov, Andrei Andreyevich; Soviet diplomatist; b. 8 Oct. 1905, Khovostovo, Yaroslavl Region; ed. Leningrad Planning Inst.
Joined Diplomatic Service 36; served in Germany 40-41; Amb. to Iran 41-43; at U.S.S.R. Ministry of Foreign Affairs 43-46; Deputy Minister of Foreign Affairs of R.S.F.S.R. 46-49; Amb. to Austria 56-57, to German Fed. Repub. 57-66, to Turkey 66-68; Deputy Minister of Foreign Affairs 68-.
Ministry of Foreign Affairs, Smolenskaya-Sennaya ploshchad 32-34, Moscow, U.S.S.R.

Smirnov, Leonid Vasiliyevich; Soviet politician; b. 1916; ed. Novocherkassy Industrial Inst.
Engineer, Foreman, Head of Electrical Dept., Factory Dir. 39-61; Deputy Chair., later Chair. State Cttee. for Defence Equipment, U.S.S.R. Ministry of Defence Equipment 61-63; mem. Cen. Cttee. of C.P.S.U. 61-; Vice-Chair. Council of Ministers 63-; Deputy to U.S.S.R. Supreme Soviet 62-; Hero of Socialist Labour 61, Orders of Lenin, Hammer and Sickle Gold Medal, Lenin Prize 60.
Council of Ministers, The Kremlin, Moscow, U.S.S.R.

Smirnov, Nikolai Ivanovich; Soviet diplomatist; b. 21 May 1918, Moscow; ed. Moscow Inst. of Oriental Studies.
State Service until 59; First Sec., Soviet Embassy, Pakistan 59-61; Deputy Head of South Asia Dept., Ministry of Foreign Affairs 61-66; Counsellor, Soviet Embassy, India 66-69; Amb. to Burma 69-71; Deputy Minister of U.S.S.R. Foreign Affairs 71-; Chair. U.S.S.R. Cttee. for UNESCO 71-; Order of Red Banner of Labour and Medals.
Ministry of Foreign Affairs, 32-34 Smolenskaya-Sennaya ploshchad, Moscow, U.S.S.R.

Smirnov, Vladimir Ivanovich, D.SC.; Soviet geologist; b. 31 Jan. 1910, Moscow; ed. Moscow Inst. of Exploration Geology.
Post-graduate Student and Asst., Moscow Inst. of Exploration Geology 34-39, Reader and Dean of Geology Faculty 39-41; Chief Geologist, Cinnabar Mines, Cen. Asia 41-44; Reader and Dir. of Research Activities, Moscow Inst. of Exploration Geology 44-46; Vice-Minister of Geology, U.S.S.R. 46-51; Prof. and Head, Dept. of Econ. Geology, Moscow State Univ. 51-; mem. U.S.S.R. Acad. of Sciences 62-, Head Div. of Geology, Geophysics and Geochemistry, mem. Presidium U.S.S.R. Acad. of Sciences 69-; Vice-Pres. Int. Asscn. on the Genesis Ore Deposits 64, Int. Union of Geological Sciences 68-; two Orders of Lenin, the Lenin Award 72.
Publs. *Ore Deposits of Central Asia* 37, *Types of the Hydrothermal Ore Deposits Connected with the Magmatic Differentiation at Tian Shan* 44, *Geology of the Cinnabar Deposits* 47, *Estimation of Ore Reserves* 50, *Geological Basis of Prospecting and Exploration of Ore Deposits* 54, *Six Types of Primary Zoning in Hydrothermal Ore Deposits* 57, *Convergence of Pyritic Ore Deposits* 60, *Metallogenesis in Geosynclines* 62, *Outlines of Metallogenesis* 63, *Geology of Mineral Deposits* 65, 69, 75.
U.S.S.R. Academy of Sciences, 14 Leninsky Prospekt, Moscow V-71, U.S.S.R.

Smirnov, Vladimir Ivanovich; Soviet mathematician; b. 10 July 1887, Leningrad; ed. Petersburg Univ.
Research devoted to the theory of the functions of the complex variable and to mathematical physics; Prof. at Petersburg Univ. 15; at the Insts. of Seismology and Mathematics of the Acad. of Sciences of the U.S.S.R. 29-35; Dir. Inst. of Mathematics and Mechanics, Leningrad Univ. 37-; mem. Acad. of Sciences of the U.S.S.R. 43-; State prizewinner 48; awarded Order of Lenin (thrice); Hero of Socialist Labour.
Publs. *Higher Mathematics Course* (6 vols.) 24-57, *Sur les formules de Cauchy et de Green* 32, *Solving Limited*

Problems of the Theory of Elasticity in the Case of Circle and Sphere 37, *On Conjugate Functions in Manifold Euclidian Space* 57, *Constructure Theory of Functions of Complex Variable Value* 64, etc.
U.S.S.R. Academy of Sciences, 14 Leninsky Prospekt, Moscow V-71, U.S.S.R.

Smirnovsky, Mikhail Nikolayevich; Soviet engineer and diplomatist; b. 7 Aug. 1921, Kalinin; ed. secondary school, Kalinin, and Moscow Aviation Inst.
Former engineer, Moscow; Diplomatic Service 48-; joined staff of U.S.S.R. Representation in Far East Comm. 49; later Third and First Sec., Washington; Asst., later Deputy Head, U.S. Dept., Ministry of Foreign Affairs 55-58; Counsellor, later Counsellor-Minister, Washington 58-62; Head of U.S. Dept., Ministry of Foreign Affairs, and mem. Collegium of Ministry of Foreign Affairs 62-66; Amb. to U.K. 66-73 and to Malta 67-73; mem. Cen. Auditing Comm. of C.P.S.U. 66-; numerous awards.
c/o Ministry of Foreign Affairs, 32-34 Smolenskaya Sennaya ploshchad, Moscow, U.S.S.R.

Smith, Albert Charles, PH.D.; American biologist; b. 5 April 1906, Springfield, Mass.; s. of Henry J. and Jeanette R. (Machol) Smith; m. 1st Nina Grönstrand 1935, one s. one d.; 2nd Emma van Ginneken 1966; ed. Columbia Univ.
Assistant Curator, N.Y. Botanical Garden 28-31, Assoc. Curator 31-40; Curator, Herbarium Arnold Arboretum, Harvard Univ. 40-48; Curator, Div. of phanerogams, U.S. Nat. Museum, Smithsonian Inst. 48-56; Program Dir. Systematic Biology, Nat. Science Foundation 56-58; Dir. Museum of Nat. History, Smithsonian Inst. 58-62, Asst. Sec. 62-63; Prof. of Botany and Dir. of Research, Univ. of Hawaii 63-65, Wilder Prof. of Botany 65-70; Ray Ethan Torrey Prof. of Botany, Univ. of Massachusetts 70-; mem. Nat. Acad. of Sciences; Fellow, American Acad. of Arts and Sciences, A.A.A.S., etc.
Department of Botany, University of Massachusetts, Amherst, Mass. 01002, U.S.A.

Smith, Arnold Cantwell, C.H., M.A., D.C.L., LL.D.; Canadian diplomatist; b. 18 Jan. 1915, Toronto; s. of Victor Arnold Smith; m. Evelyn Hardwick Stewart 1938; two s. one d.; ed. Upper Canada Coll., Toronto, Lycée Champoléon, Grenoble, Univs. of Toronto, Oxford (Christ Church) and Gray's Inn, London.
Journalist and univ. lecturer; diplomatic service 39-, Tallinn 39-40, Cairo 40-43, Moscow 43-45, Brussels 50-53; mem. Del. to UN 47, 49, 51, 54; Alt. Rep. UN Security Council and Atomic Energy Comm. and Senior Adviser to Perm. Del. 49-50; Int. Truce Commr. Cambodia 55-56; Minister to U.K. 56-58; Amb. to U.A.R. 58-61, to U.S.S.R. 61-63; Asst. Under-Sec. of State for External Affairs 63-65; elected first Sec.-Gen. of the Commonwealth June 65, re-elected 70-75; Visiting Centenary Prof. Toronto Univ. 67; Lester B. Pearson Prof. of Int. Relations, Carleton Univ., Ottawa Jan. 76-; Hon. D.C.L. (Univ. of Michigan, Oxon.), Hon. LL.D. (Ricker Coll. of North-West, Queen's Univ., Toronto Univ., New Brunswick Univ., British Columbia Univ., Leeds Univ.).
Leisure interests: photography, farming in France, travelling.
The Norman Paterson School of International Affairs, Carleton University, Ottawa, Ont., Canada.
Telephone: (613) 231-5524.

Smith, Arthur Edward, B.S.; American aircraft executive; b. 7 July 1911, Malden, Mass.; s. of George August and Mary Wardwell Smith; m. Frances Kenworthy 1936; two s. one d.; ed. South High School, Worcester, Mass. and Worcester Polytechnic Inst.
Test Engineer, Int. Motors 33-34; sales, Manning, Maxwell & Moore 34-35; joined Pratt & Whitney

Aircraft, East Hartford 35 as Test Engineer, later Asst. Project Engineer, Project Engineer; Chief Engineer, Pratt & Whitney, Missouri 42-44; Asst. Chief Engineer, Pratt & Whitney Aircraft, East Hartford 44-49, Chief Engineer 49-52, Asst. Eng. Man. 52-56, Eng. Man. 56-57, Div. Exec. Vice-Pres. 57-67, Div. Pres. April-Dec. 67, Exec. Vice-Pres. Jan.-Sept. 68, Pres. and Chief Admin. Officer United Aircraft Corpn. Oct. 68-71, Chair. Exec. Cttee. Sept. 71-; Robert H. Goddard Award of Worcester Polytechnic Inst. 67.
United Aircraft Corporation, East Hartford, Conn. 06108; Home: 28 Raymond Road, Manchester, Conn. 06040, U.S.A.
Telephone: 203-565-7262 (Office).

Smith, Cyril Stanley, D.SC., D.LITT., SC.D.; American metallurgist and historian of technology; b. 4 Oct. 1903, Birmingham, England; s. of Joseph Seymour Smith and Frances (Norton) Smith; m. Alice Marchant Kimball 1931; one s. one d.; ed. Univ. of Birmingham and Mass. Inst. of Technology.
Research Assoc. Mass. Inst. of Technology 26-27; Research Metallurgist American Brass Co. 27-42; Research Supervisor Nat. Defense Research Cttee. 42-43; Assoc. Div. Leader (Metallurgy) Los Alamos Scientific Laboratory 43-46; Dir. Inst. for the Study of Metals, Chicago Univ. 46-57, Prof. of Metallurgy 46-61; Inst. Prof. Mass. Inst. of Technology 61-69; Prof. Emer. 69-; mem. Gen. Advisory Cttee., U.S. Atomic Energy Comm. 46-52; mem. Materials Advisory Board 54-56, President's Science Advisory Cttee. 59, Cttee. on Science and Public Policy of Nat. Acad. of Sciences 65-67, Smithsonian Inst. Council 66-; Visiting Fellow, St. Catherine's Coll. Oxford 68; Pres. Soc. for the History of Technology 63-64; mem. Akademie der Wissenschaften, Göttingen; American Philosophical Soc., Nat. Acad. of Sciences; Medal for Merit 46, Clamer Medal (Franklin Inst.) 52, American Soc. of Metals Gold Medal 62, American Inst. Mining and Metallurgical Engineers Douglas Medal 63, Leonardo da Vinci Medal 66, Inst. of Metals (London) Platinum Medal 70; naturalized U.S. citizen 40.
Leisure interest: Oriental art.
Publs. *A History of Metallography* 60, *Sources for the History of the Science of Steel* 68; translations (in collaboration) of *Pirotechnia* (Biringuccio) 42, 59, 66, *Treatise on Ores and Assaying* (Lazarus Ercker) 51, *On Divers Arts* (Theophilus) 63, *Mappae Clavicula* 74; Editor *Sorby Centennial Symposium on the History of Metallurgy* 65.
Room 14N-317, Massachusetts Institute of Technology, Cambridge, Mass. 02139; Home: 31 Madison Street, Cambridge, Mass. 02138, U.S.A.
Telephone: (617) 253-3722 (Office); (617) 491-1916 (Home).

Smith, Cyrus R.; American airline executive; b. 9 Sept. 1899; ed. Univ. of Texas.
Public Accountant, Peat, Marwick Mitchell and Co. 21-26; Asst. Treas. Texas-Louisiana Power Co., Fort Worth 26-28; Vice-Pres. Texas Air Transport Inc., Fort Worth 29-30; Vice-Pres. American Airlines Inc. 34-42; U.S. Army Air Force, rising to Maj.-Gen. 42-45; Pres. American Airlines Inc. 45-64, Chair. and Chief Exec. 64-68, 73-74; U.S. Sec. of Commerce 68-69; Gen. Partner Lazard Frères, New York 69-73; D.S.M., Legion of Merit, Hon. C.B.E. (U.K.).
510 Park Avenue, New York City, N.Y., U.S.A.

Smith, Darwin Eatna, B.S., LL.B.; American business executive; b. 16 April 1926, Garrett, Ind.; s. of Kay B. Smith and Hazel R. Sherman; m. Lois Claire Archbold 1950; twin s. and d. and one s. one d.; ed. Indiana Univ. and Harvard Law School.
Employee, Sidley & Austin (law firm), Chicago 55-58; joined Kimberley Clarke Corpn. 58, Gen. Attorney 59, Vice-Pres. 62, Vice-Pres. (Finance and Law) 67, Exec.

Vice-Pres. 69, Pres. 70, Chair. of Board and Chief Exec. Officer 71-.
Kimberley-Clark Corporation, Neenah, Wis. 54956; Home: Route 1, Box 211, Menasha, Wis. 54952, U.S.A.

Smith, Dodie (*pseudonym* C. L. Anthony); British dramatist and novelist; b. Bury, Lancs.; *d.* of late Ernest Smith and Ella Furber; *m.* Alec Macbeth Beesley 1939; ed. St. Paul's School for Girls and Royal Acad. of Dramatic Art.
Former actress; buyer at Heal and Son until 31.
Leisure interests: reading, music.
Plays: As C. L. Anthony: *Autumn Crocus* 31, *Service* 32, *Touch Wood* 34; As Dodie Smith: *Call It a Day* 35, *Bonnet Over the Windmill* 37, *Dear Octopus* 38 (revived 67), *Lovers and Friends* 43, *Letter from Paris* 52, *I Capture the Castle* 54, *These People—Those Books* 58; Novels: *I Capture the Castle* 48, *The New Moon with the Old* 63, *The Town in Bloom* 65, *It Ends with Revelations* 67, *A Tale of Two Families* 70; Children's Books: *The Hundred and One Dalmatians* 56, *The Starlight Barking* 67; Autobiography: *Look Back With Love* 74.
The Barretts, Finchingfield, Essex, England.
Telephone: 037-181-260.

Smith, Emil L., B.S., PH.D.; American biochemist and biophysicist; b. 5 July 1911, New York City; *s.* of Abraham and Esther Smith; *m.* Esther Press 1934; two *s.*; ed. Columbia, Cambridge and Yale Univs.
Instructor, Columbia Univ. 36-38; Fellow, Rockefeller Inst. 40-42; Senior Biochemist and Biophysicist, E. R. Squibb & Sons 42-46; Assoc. Prof. and Prof., Univ. of Utah 46-63; Prof. and Chair. Dept. of Biological Chem., Univ. of Calif., Los Angeles 63-; mem. Nat. Acad. of Sciences, American Acad. of Arts and Sciences, American Philosophical Soc., etc.; Guggenheim Fellow (Cambridge and Yale) 38-40.
Leisure interests: music, literature, art.
Publs. *Principles of Biochemistry* (co-author) 54 (5th edn. 73); many articles in biochemistry and biophysics.
Department of Biological Chemistry, University of California, School of Medicine, Los Angeles, Calif. 90024, U.S.A.
Telephone: 213-825-6494.

Smith, George Ivan, M.A.; Australian United Nations administrator; b. 1915; ed. Sydney Univ.
Editor of Talks, Australian Broadcasting Comm. 37-39; Dir. Australian Short-Wave Service 39-41; Dir. BBC Pacific Service 41-45; Int. Affairs Films 45-47; UN Information Services, Lake Success 47-49; UN Dir. Information Centre, London 49-58; Dir. External Relations, UN, New York; Sen. Dir. of Public Information, UN 61-62; UN Rep. Katanga 61-62; Personal Rep. of UN Sec.-Gen. in East and Central Africa; Regional Dir. UN Technical Assistance Programmes in Central Africa 62-66; Visiting Prof. Princeton Univ. and Fletcher School of Law and Diplomacy Boston (on special leave from UN) 66-68; Dir. UN Office, London 68-74; Senior Consultant, Int. Inst. for Environment and Devt. 74-.
17 Ashley Court, Morpeth Terrace, London, S.W.1, England.

Smith, Gerard Coad, LL.B.; American government official and lawyer; b. 4 May 1914, New York City; *s.* of John T. Smith and Mary A. (Smith) Smith; *m.* Bernice Latrobe Maguire 1941; three *s.* one *d.*; ed. Canterbury School, New Milford, Yale Coll. and Yale Law School.
Lawyer, N.Y.C. 39-50; U.S. Navy 41-45; Special Asst., U.S. Atomic Energy Comm. 50-54, to Sec. of State for Atomic Affairs 54-57; Deputy Chief, U.S. Del. negotiating IAEA Treaty 55-56; Chief U.S. Political Adviser to first Atoms-for-Peace Conf. and to talks with U.S.S.R. on safeguards against diversion of nuclear materials to weaponry 55; State Dept. Liaison Officer to Senate Foreign Relations Cttee. on Disarmament Affairs 57; Chief Aide to Sec. of State, London Disarmament Conf.

57; originated nuclear test restraint concept agreed upon at Bermuda Heads of Govts. meeting 57; Asst. Sec. of State and Dir. Policy Planning Staff Dept. of State 57-61; originated Washington-Moscow "Hot Line" concept 59; Consultant, State Dept. Policy Planning Council 61-68; Foreign Policy Consultant, Washington Centre Foreign Policy Research 61-69; mem. Council on Foreign Relations 61-; mem. Exec. Cttee. Yale Law School Asscn. 62-; Special Adviser to Sec. of State for Multilateral Force Negotiations 62, 64; Dir. U.S. Arms Control and Disarmament Agency 68-72; Head, U.S. Del. to Strategic Arms Limitation Talks (SALT), Helsinki 69-72; Chair. Trilateral Comm. 73-; Dir. American Security and Trust Co. 64-68, Atlantic Council 67-68; Publisher, *Interplay* magazine 67-68; Dir. School of Advanced Int. Studies, Johns Hopkins Univ. 67.
Leisure interests: tennis, golf, yachting.
2425 Tracy Place, N.W., Washington, D.C. 20008, U.S.A.

Smith, Henry Nash, M.A., PH.D.; American professor of English; b. 9 Sept. 1906, Dallas, Texas; *s.* of Loyd Bond and Elizabeth Nash Smith; *m.* Elinor Lucas 1936; one *s.* two *d.*; ed. Southern Methodist Univ. and Harvard Univ.
Instructor to Assoc. Prof. of English, Southern Methodist Univ. 27-41; Prof. of English and American History, Univ. of Texas (Austin) 41-47; Prof. of English, Univ. of Minnesota 47-53; Prof. of English, Univ. of Calif. (Berkeley) 53-, Chair. Dept. of English 57-60; Fellow American Acad. of Arts and Sciences 65-; Pres. Modern Language Asscn. of America 69; John H. Dunning Prize, American Historical Asscn. and Bancroft Prize, Columbia Univ. for *Virgin Land* 51; Award for distinguished scholarship in the humanities, American Council of Learned Socs. 60; Hon. Litt.D., Southern Methodist Univ. 66; Hon. LL.D., Colorado State Univ. 70.
Leisure interests: walking, photography.
Publs. *Virgin Land: The American West as Symbol and Myth* 50, *Mark Twain: The Development of a Writer* 62, *Mark Twain's Fable of Progress* 64; Editor: *Mark Twain of the "Enterprise"* 57, *Popular Culture and Industrialism 1865-1890* 67, *Mark Twain-Howells Letters* 60.
Dept. of English, University of California, Berkeley, Calif. 94720; Home: 1725 LeRoy Avenue, Apt. 5, Berkeley, Calif. 94709, U.S.A.
Telephone: 642-2738 (Office); 845-0895 (Home).

Smith, Sir Howard Frank Trayton, Kt., K.C.M.G.; British diplomatist; b. 15 Oct. 1919, Brighton, Sussex; *s.* of Frank Howard Smith; *m.* Mary Cropper 1943; one *d.*; ed. Polytechnic Secondary School, London, and Sidney Sussex Coll., Cambridge.
Foreign Office 39-47; Second Sec., Oslo 47-50; First Sec., Washington 50-53, Caracas 53-56; Foreign Office 56-61; Counsellor, Moscow 61-63; Head of N. Dept., Foreign Office 64-68; Amb. to Czechoslovakia 68-71; Special Rep. of British Govt. in Ulster 71-72; Deputy Sec. to Cabinet Office 72-75; Amb. to U.S.S.R. 76-.
British Embassy, Nab. Maurice Thorez 14, Moscow, U.S.S.R.

Smith, Howard Kingsbury, B.A.; American journalist; b. 12 May 1914, Ferriday, La.; *m.* Benedicte Traberg 1942; one *s.* one *d.*; ed. Tulane Univ., New Orleans, Heidelberg Summer School, and Oxford Univ.
Reported for *New Orleans Item* 36-39; in United Press, London then Berlin 39-41; Columbia Broadcasting System (Berlin, Berne, 9th U.S. Army, Germany, and finally as Chief European Corresp. in London 46-57) 41-59; C.B.S. Washington Corresp. 57-61; News Commentator, American Broadcasting Co. (A.B.C.), Wash. 62-; Hon. LL.D. (Tulane, Roosevelt, Maryland Univs. and Centenary Coll., La.); D.Litt. (St. Norbert's Coll.); Dr. of Humane Letters (Alfred Univ. and Thiel,

Pikeville, and St. Michael's Colls.); recipient of many awards for radio and television, including Overseas Press Award for best radio and TV reporting from abroad 51-54, George Polk Memorial and Emmy awards for documentary "The Population Explosion", and *Radio-TV Daily* award as Commentator of the Year 60, Overseas Press Award, best radio interpretation of foreign affairs 61, Du Pont award 55, 63.

Publs. *Last Train from Berlin* 42, *The State of Europe* 49, *Washington D.C.* 67.

Office: American Broadcasting Co., 1124 Connecticut Avenue, Washington, D.C. 20036, U.S.A.

Telephone: 202-393-7700.

Smith, Ian Douglas; Rhodesian politician; b. 8 April 1919; ed. Chaplin School, Gwelo, Rhodesia and Rhodes Univ., Grahamstown, S. Africa.

Royal Air Force 41-46; farmer; mem. S. Rhodesia Legislative Assembly 48-53, 62-, Parl. of Fed. of Rhodesia and Nyasaland 53-61; fmr. Chief Whip United Fed. Party; foundation mem. and Vice-Pres. Rhodesian Front 62, Pres. 64-; Deputy Prime Minister and Minister of Treasury S. Rhodesia Dec. 62-April 64; Minister of Defence 64-65, of External Affairs April-Aug. 64; Prime Minister of Rhodesia April 64-; proclaimed Rhodesia's independence Nov. 65; Independence Decoration 70.

8 Chancellor Avenue, Salisbury, Rhodesia; Gwenoro Farm, Selukwe, Rhodesia.

Smith, J. Stanford; American business executive; b. 4 Jan. 1915, Terre Haute, Ind.; *m.* Elaine Showalter; two *s.* two *d.*; ed. DePauw Univ.

Joined Gen. Electric Co. 36, Vice-Pres. Information Systems Group 66-69, Vice-Pres. Int. Group 69-72, Senior Vice-Pres. for Corporate Admin. 72-73; Vice-Chair. Int. Paper Co. 73, Chair., Chief Exec. Officer Jan. 74-; Vice-Chair. Board of Trustees, DePauw Univ.; Dir. Nat. Asscn. of Mfrs., Gen. Crude Oil Co., Chase Manhattan Bank; mem. Nat. Industrial Energy Conservation Council, Dept. of Commerce, U.S. Business Council; fmr. mem. many educ., community and church bodies; Hon. LL.D. (DePauw Univ.) 68; Phi Beta Kappa.

International Paper Co., 220 East 42nd Street, New York, N.Y. 10017; Home: Round Hill Road, Greenwich, Conn., U.S.A.

Smith, Maj.-Gen. James Desmond Blaise, C.B.E., D.S.O., C.D.; Canadian army officer; b. 7 Oct. 1911, Ottawa; *s.* of William George Smith and Anna O'Brien; *m.* Miriam Irene Blackburn 1937 (died 1969); two *s.*; ed. Univ. of Ottawa, Royal Military Coll., Canada, Staff Coll., Camberley, Imperial Defence Coll.

Joined Royal Canadian Dragoons 33; served Defence H.Q. Ottawa and 1st Infantry Div. 40; War Course, Staff Coll. Camberley 40; Directing Staff, first Canadian Army Staff Course 40-41; Brigade Major 41-42; C.O. Royal Canadian Dragoons 42; G.S.O. I, 5th Armoured Div. 42-43; Commanded 4th Armoured Brigade 43-44, 5th 44; Gen. Staff, 1st Canadian Corps, Italy 44; G.O.C. 1st Canadian Infantry Div. 44-45; Commdt. Royal Mil. Coll. and Canadian Army Staff Coll. 45-46; Hon. A.D.C. to the Gov.-Gen. 46; I.D.C. 46-47; Sec. Chiefs of Staff Cttee. and Mil. Sec. Cabinet Defence Cttee. 48-50; Quartermaster Gen. 50-51; Chair. Joint Staff, Canadian Mil. Rep. at SHAPE and Perm. Canadian Rep. to NATO Council 51-54; Commdt., Nat. Defence Coll., Canada 54-58; Adjutant-Gen. 58-62; Col., H.M. Regiment of Canadian Guards 61-66; Chair. and Chief Exec. Pillar Eng. Ltd.; Dir. RTZ Industries Ltd. and numerous other companies; Vice-Pres. Eng. Industries Asscn.; Légion d'Honneur, Croix de Guerre, Legion of Merit (U.S.A.), Italian, Greek and Canadian decorations.

Leisure interests: tennis, skiing.

Pillar Engineering Ltd., Cleveland House, 19 St.

James's Square, London, SW1Y 4JG; Home: 20 Eaton Place, Belgravia, London, S.W.1, England.

Telephone: 01-930-2399.

Smith, James Eric, C.B.E., M.A., SC.D., PH.D., F.R.S.; British zoologist; b. 23 Feb. 1909, Hull, Yorks.; *s.* of Walter Smith and Elsie K. Pickett; *m.* Thelma A. Cornish; one *s.* one *d.*; ed. Hull Grammar School and King's Coll., London.

Assistant Lecturer, Manchester Univ. 32-35; Lecturer, Sheffield Univ. 35-38, Cambridge Univ. 38-50; Prof. of Zoology, Queen Mary Coll., London 50-65; Dir. Plymouth Lab. and Sec., Marine Biological Asscn. of U.K. 65-74; mem. Science Research Council 63-66; Chair. Trustees of British Museum (Natural History) 69-74; Chair. Special Cttee. on Problems of the Environment, ICSU 70-73; mem. Advisory Board for Research Councils 74-; Fellow, Queen Mary Coll., London, King's Coll., London; Hon. D.Sc. (Exeter).

Leisure interests: travel, gardening.

Publs. Various papers on the ecology, nervous system and behaviour of echinoderms and other marine invertebrates.

The Laboratory, Citadel Hill, Plymouth, Devon; Home: Wellesley House, Coombe Road, Saltash, Cornwall, England.

Telephone: Plymouth 21761; Saltash 2495.

Smith, J(ames) Henry, B.A.; American insurance executive; b. 29 March 1910, Chestertown, Md.; *s.* of Rev. Tilghman Smith and Clara Murray; *m.* Roberta Foard 1931; three *s.* one *d.*; ed. Univ. of Delaware.

With Equitable Life Assurance Soc., N.Y.C. 30-35; Travelers Ins. Co. 35-42; Equitable 42-, Vice-Pres. and Assoc. Actuary 53-57, Underwriting Vice-Pres. 58-65, Vice-Pres. and Actuary 65-67, Pres. 67-73, Chair. 73-75; mem. Board of Alfred Univ., Brooklyn Methodist Hospital, N.Y. Heart Asscn.; Fellow, Soc. of Actuaries; mem. American Acad. of Actuaries, President's Comm. on Income Maintenance; Hon. LL.D. (Alfred and Delaware Univs.).

Leisure interest: golf.

c/o The Equitable Life Assurance Society, 1285 Avenue of the Americas, New York, N.Y. 10019, U.S.A.

Telephone: 212-554-3273.

Smith, Rev. Dr. John Coventry; American ecclesiastic; b. 1903, Canada.

Missionary, Japan 29-42; Assoc. Gen. Sec. for Japan, Korea, Philippines and Thailand, Comm. on Ecumenical Mission and Relations (COEMAR), United Presbyterian Church in U.S.A.; Gen. Sec. COEMAR 59-70; Moderator 180th Gen. Assembly of United Presbyterian Church 68-69; mem. Central Cttee. of World Council of Churches (WCC) 61-, Vice-Chair. Divisional Cttee. on World Mission and Evangelism; Pres. of WCC 68-.

World Council of Churches, 150 route de Ferney, 1211 Geneva 20, Switzerland.

Smith, John Lucian, B.S.C.; American business executive; b. 24 Oct. 1918, West Point, Mississippi; *m.* Claire Davis; one *s.* one *d.*; ed. Univ. of Mississippi, Oxford, Mass.

Joined The Coca-Cola Co. 40; army service in Air Corps, World War II; Sales Man. Western Coca-Cola Bottling Co. 47, Field Sales Man. Bottler Sales Dept. 58, Vice-Pres. 61, Gen. Man. Bottler Sales Devt. Dept. 62, Asst. Marketing Dir. for Carbonated Beverages 65-67, Pres. Duncan Foods Co. Div. 67, Pres. Coca-Cola U.S.A. 71, Dir. The Coca-Cola Co. 72-, Senior Vice-Pres. 74, Pres. May 74-.

The Coca-Cola Co., 515 Madison Avenue, New York, N.Y. 10022, U.S.A.

Smith, Leslie Edward, F.C.A.; British business executive; b. 15 April 1919, London; *s.* of Edward V. Smith and Doris E. Browning; *m.* 1st Lorna Pickworth 1943, 2nd Cynthia Holmes 1964; one *s.* three *d.*; ed. Christ's Hospital.

Chief Exec., Finance, The British Oxygen Co. Ltd. (now BOC Int. Ltd.) 61-65, Dir. (Commercial) 65-67, Joint Man. Dir. 67-69, Group Man. Dir. 69-72, Chair. March 72-.
Leisure interest: reading.
BOC International Ltd., Hammersmith House, London, W.6; Home: Cookley House, Cookley Green, Swyncombe, nr. Henley-on-Thames, Oxon., RG9 6EN, England.
Telephone: 01-748-2020 (Office); Nettlebed 258 (Home).

Smith, Lloyd Bruce; American business executive; b. 13 Oct. 1920, Milwaukee, Wis.; s. of Lloyd Raymond and Agnes (Gram) Smith; m. Lucy Anne Woodhull; three s. one d.; ed. Sheffield Science School, Yale.
With A. O. Smith Corpn., Milwaukee 42-, successively Asst. to Pres., then Vice-Pres., Dir., Man. Home Appliances division, Asst. Gen. Man., Pres. 51-67, Chair. and Chief Exec. Officer 67-; Dir. A. O. Smith, Inland Inc., A. O. Smith Harvestore Products Inc.; Dir. First Wisconsin Nat. Bank of Milwaukee, First Wisconsin Corpn., Goodyear Tire and Rubber Co., Medical Coll. of Wis., Deere and Co., Continental Can Co., Milwaukee Voluntary Equal Employment Council; mem. Business Council; distinguished Life Mem. American Soc. for Metals.
3533 North 27th Street, Milwaukee. Wis. 53201, U.S.A.
Telephone: 414-873-3000.

Smith, Maggie Natalie, C.B.E.; British actress; b. 28 Dec. 1934, Ilford, Essex; m. 1st Robert Stephens (q.v.) 1967 (dissolved 1975), two s.; m. 2nd Beverly Cross 1975; ed. Oxford High School for Girls.
First appeared with Oxford Univ. Dramatic Soc. (O.U.D.S.) in *Twelfth Night* 52; appeared in revue *New Faces* N.Y. 56, *Share My Lettuce* 57, *The Stepmother* 58; with Old Vic Co. 59-60 playing in *The Double Dealer, As You Like It, Richard II, The Merry Wives of Windsor, What Every Woman Knows*; other appearances include *Rhinoceros* 60, *Strip the Willow* 60, *The Rehearsal* 61, *The Private Ear and The Public Eye* 62, *Mary, Mary* 63; with Nat. Theatre played in *The Recruiting Officer* 63, *Othello* (Desdemona) 64, *The Master Builder* 64, *Hay Fever* 64, *Much Ado About Nothing* 65, *Miss Julie* 65, *A Bond Honoured* 66, *The Beaux' Stratagem* 70, *Hedda Gabler* 70, *Three Sisters, Design for Living* (Los Angeles) 71, *Private Lives* London 72, U.S.A. 74-75, *Peter Pan* 73, *Snap* 74.
Films include: *The V.I.P.s* 63, *The Pumpkin Eater* 64, *Young Cassidy* 65, *Othello* 66, *The Honey Pot* 67, *Hot Millions* 68, *The Prime of Miss Jean Brodie* 69, *Travels with My Aunt* 72, *Love and Pain and the Whole Damn Thing* 73; Awards: Evening Standard Best Actress Award 62, 70; Variety Club Actress of the Year 63; L.A. Critics Award Best Actress 70; Variety Club Award Best Stage Actress 72 (plays); Academy Award for Best Actress 69; Best Actress Award from Soc. of Film and Television Arts (U.K.) 69; Best Actress Award from Film Critics' Guild (U.S.A.) 69 (films).
c/o Fraser & Dunlop, 91 Regent Street, London, W1R 8RU, England.

Smith, Margaret Chase; American politician; b. 14 Dec. 1897; ed. Skowhegan High School.
Began career as teacher; with *Independent Reporter* 19-28, Daniel E. Cummings Co. 28-30; Treasurer, New England Process Co. 28-30; mem. House of Reps. 40-48; Senator from Maine 48-72; mem. Senate Appropriations, Armed Services, and Aeronautical and Space Sciences Cttees.; Republican.
Norridgewock Avenue, Skowhegan, Maine 04976, U.S.A.

Smith, Preston Earnest; American state governor; b. 8 March 1912, Williamson County, Tex.; s. of Charles K. and Effie Smith; m. Ima Smith 1935; one s. one d.; ed. Lamesa High School and Texas Technological Coll., Lubbock.

State Rep., Texas House of Reps. 44-50; State Senator 56-62; Lieut.-Gov. 62-68; Gov. of Texas Jan. 69-73; Democrat.
Leisure interests: fishing (particularly stream fishing), hunting, golf, bridge.
105 University Avenue, Lubbock, Texas, U.S.A.
Telephone: 806-765-9641.

Smith, Richard, C.B.E.; British artist; b. 1931, Letchworth, Herts.; ed. Luton School of Art, St. Albans School of Art and Royal Coll. of Art.
Lived in New York 59-61, 63-65; teacher St. Martin's School of Art, London 61-63; Artist-in-Residence, Univ. of Virginia 67; Grand Prix São Paulo Bienal 67; one-man exhbns. at the Kasmin Gallery 63, 67, Whitechapel Gallery 66; participated in the Pittsburgh Int. 61, New Shapes in Colour, Amsterdam, Berne and Stuttgart 66-67 and in exhbns. at Guggenheim Museum, Tate Gallery, etc.; works represented in Tate Gallery, Stuyvesant Foundation, Contemporary Art Soc., the Ulster Museum, Belfast, the Walker Art Center, etc.
c/o Kasmin Art, 8 Gloucester Gate, London, S.W.1, England.

Smith, Robert Allan, C.B.E., PH.D., F.R.S.E., F.R.S.; British physicist; b. 14 May 1909; ed. Edinburgh and Cambridge Univs.
Carnegie Research Fellow, St. Andrew's Univ. 35-38; Lecturer, Reading Univ. 38-39; worked for Royal Radar Est. 39-60, Head of Physics Dept. 47-60; Prof. of Physics, Sheffield Univ. 61-62; Prof. of Physics and Dir., Center for Materials Science, Mass. Inst. of Technology, U.S.A. 62-68; Principal and Vice-Chancellor, Heriot-Watt Univ. 68-74; Fellow, Royal Soc., American Acad. of Arts and Sciences, American Physical Soc., Royal Soc. Edinburgh.
Publs. *Radio Aids to Navigation* 47, *Aerials for Metre and Decimetre Wavelengths* 49, *The Physical Principles of Thermodynamics* 52, *Semiconductors* 59, *The Wave Mechanics of Crystalline Solids* 61, *The Detection and Measurement of Infra-red Radiation* 68, numerous articles in scientific journals.
Heriot-Watt University, Chambers Street, Edinburgh EH1 1HX, Scotland.
Telephone: 031-449-5111.

Smith, Sylvester Richard; American government official (retd.); b. 30 Aug. 1906, Dolton, S. Dakota; s. of Lydia Dirks and Frank Albert Schmidt; m. Olive Theona Nash 1930; one s. one d.; ed. State Univ. of Montana and Univ. of California.
Economic Analyst, Dept. of Agriculture 34-38; Chief Citrus Section, Fruit and Vegetable Div., Surplus Marketing Admin. 38-40; Chief Econ. Analysis Section, Fruit and Vegetable Div. 40-42, Asst. Chief Fruit and Vegetable Div. 42; Asst. Chief Fruit and Vegetable Branch, Agricultural Marketing Admin., U.S. Dept. of Agriculture 42-43; Asst. Dep. Dir. Food Distribution Admin., War Food Admin. 43, Deputy Dir. Office of Distribution 43-44; Deputy Dir. Civilian Programs, Office Marketing Services 45; Assoc. Dir. Fruit and Vegetable Branch, Production and Marketing Admin., Dept. of Agriculture 45-46, Dir. 46-53; Dir. Fruit and Vegetable Div. Agricultural Marketing Service 53-61; Admin., Agricultural Marketing Service 61-65, Consumer and Marketing Service 65-68; Distinguished Service Award, U.S. Dept. of Agriculture 56; Univ. of Montana Alumni Asscn. Distinguished Service Award 65.
Leisure interests: golf, travel, reading financial periodicals and historical fiction.
Home: 4507 31st Street South, Arlington, Va. 22206, U.S.A.
Telephone: 931-2409 (Home).

Smith, Wilfred Cantwell, M.A., PH.D., D.D.; Canadian university professor; b. 21 July 1916, Toronto; s. of Victor Arnold Smith and Sarah Cantwell; m. Dr. Muriel Struthers 1939; three s. two d.; ed. Upper Canada Coll.,

Univ. of Grenoble, Univ. of Madrid, American Univ., Cairo, Univ. of Toronto, Cambridge and Princeton Univs.

Served as rep. among Muslims of the Canadian Overseas Missions Council, chiefly in Lahore 40-49; Lecturer in Indian and Islamic History, Forman Christian Coll., Lahore 41-45; Prof. of Comparative Religion 49-63, and Dir. Inst. of Islamic Studies, McGill Univ. 51-63; Pres. American Soc. for the Study of Religion 66-69; Visiting Prof., London Univ. 60, Princeton Univ. 65, Toronto 68; Prof. of World Religions and Dir. Center for the Study of World Religions, Harvard Univ. 64-73; now McCulloch Prof. of Religion, Dalhousie Univ., Halifax, Canada and part-time Visiting Prof., Harvard Univ.; Fellow, Royal Soc. of Canada, Pres. Humanities and Social Sciences 72-73, American Acad. of Arts and Sciences; Chauveau Medal, Royal Soc. of Canada 74. Leisure interests: canoeing, hiking.

Publs. *Modern Islam in India* 43 (revised edns. 47, 65), *Islam in Modern History* 57, *Meaning and End of Religion* 63, *Faith of Other Men* 63, *Questions of Religious Truth* 67.

Dalhousie University, Halifax, Nova Scotia; Home: 6010 Inglis Street, Halifax, Nova Scotia, Canada.
Telephone: 902-424-3579 (Office).

Smith-Rose, Reginald Leslie, C.B.E., D.SC., PH.D., F.C.G.I., F.I.C., A.R.C.S., C.ENG., F.I.E.E., F.I.E.E.E.; British scientist; b. 2 April 1894, London; *m.* Elsie Masters 1919; two *d.*; ed. Imperial Coll. of Science and Technology, Univ. of London.

Assistant Engineer, Messrs. Siemens Bros. 15-19; Scientific Officer Electricity Div., Nat. Physical Lab. 19-33, Principal Scientific Officer, Radio Div. 33-39, Supt. Radio Div. 39-47; Dir. of Radio Research, Dept. of Scientific and Industrial Research, London 47-60; Chair. Eng. Advisory Cttee. BBC 70-73; Fellow of Inst. of Radio Engineers, New York, Vice-Pres. 48; Fellow of Inst. of Electrical and Electronic Engineers N.Y. 62-; Treas. U.K. and Irish Repub. branch of same 63-; Vice-Pres. Inst. of Electrical Engineers, London 61-65; Pres. Int. Scientific Radio Union 60-63, Radio Soc. of Great Britain 59; Sec.-Gen. Inter-Union Comm. on Frequency Allocations for Radio Astronomy and Space Science 60-72; awarded Coronation Medals 37, 53, U.S. Medal of Freedom with Silver Palm 47; conducted research into problems fundamental to radio applications including electrical measurements, radio direction finding, and the propagation of radio waves. Leisure interests: reading, writing, motoring, foreign travel.

Publs. *James Clerk Maxwell*; many scientific papers.
21 Tumblewood Road, Banstead, Surrey, England.
Telephone: Burgh Heath 51697.

Smithers, Sir Peter Henry Berry Otway, Kt., D.PHIL.; British politician and international civil servant; b. 9 Dec. 1913, Moor Allerton, Yorks.; *s.* of Lt.-Col. H. Otway Smithers, J.P. and Ethel M. M. Berry; *m.* Dorothy Jean Sayman 1943; two *d.*; ed. Harrow School and Magdalen Coll., Oxford.

Called to Bar, Inner Temple 36, joined Lincoln's Inn 37; Naval Service 39-45; M.P. 50-64; Parl. Private Sec. to Minister of State for Colonies 52-56, to Sec. of State for Colonies 56-59; Vice-Chair. Conservative Parl. Foreign Affairs Cttee. 58-62; Parl. Under-Sec. of State, Foreign Office 62-64; U.K. Del. to UN Gen. Assembly 60-63; Consultative Assembly, Council of Europe 52-56, 60; Vice-Pres. European Assembly of Local Autherities 59-62; Sec.-Gen. Council of Europe 64-69; Senior Fellow, UNITAR, New York 69-; Gen. Rapporteur, the European Conf. of Parliamentarians and Scientists 71-; Chevalier, Légion d'Honneur; Order Mexicana de la Aguila Azteca; Humboldt Gold Medal (for int. work on conservation of nature and natural resources) 70; Hon. Dr.jur. (Zurich) 70; Conservative.

Leisure interests: horticulture and astronomy.
Publ. *Life of Joseph Addison.*
6911 Vico Morcote, Switzerland.

Smithson, Alison Margaret, DIP.ARCH.; British architect; b. 22 June 1928, Sheffield; *d.* of Ernest Gill and Alison Jessie Malcolm; *m.* Peter Denham Smithson (*q.v.*) 1949; one *s.* two *d.*; ed. Sunderland, South Shields, George Watson's Ladies Coll., Edinburgh and Univ. of Durham.

Assistant with London County Council 49-50; in private practice as architect with Peter Smithson 50-. Principal works: Hunstanton School, Economist Bldg., London; Robin Hood Gardens, G.L.C. Housing in Tower Hamlets, Garden Bldg. St. Hilda's Coll., Oxford. Publs. *Young Girl* (novel), *Urban Structuring Studies* (with P. Smithson), *Team 10 Primer* (Editor), *Euston Arch, Ordinariness and Light, Without Rhetoric* (all with P. Smithson).

Cato Lodge, 24 Gilston Road, London, SW10 9SR, England.
Telephone: 01-373-7423 and 01-373-3838.

Smithson, Peter Denham; British architect; b. 18 Sept. 1923, Stockton-on-Tees; *s.* of William Blenkiron Smithson and Elizabeth Denham; *m.* Alison Margaret Gill (Smithson, *q.v.*) 1949; one *s.* two *d.*; ed. Stockton-on-Tees Grammar School, Univ. of Durham and Royal Acad. Schools, London.

Assistant at L.C.C. 49-50; in private practice as architect with Alison Smithson 50-.

Principal works: Hunstanton School; Economist Bldg., London; Robin Hood Gardens, G.L.C. Housing in Tower Hamlets; Garden Bldg. St. Hildas's Coll. Oxford. Publs. *Urban Structuring Studies, Euston Arch, Ordinariness and Light, Without Rhetoric* (all with A. Smithson), *Walks Within the Walls.*

Cato Lodge, 24 Gilston Road, London SW10 9SR, England.
Telephone: 01-373-7423 and 01-373-3838.

Smoktunovsky, Innokenty Mikhailovich; Soviet actor; b. 1925; ed. Pushkin Dramatic Theatre Studio, Krasnoyarsk.

Soviet Army 43-45; Leningrad Gorky Bolshoi State Drama Theatre 57-; worked in cinema 60-; Honoured Artist of R.S.F.S.R., Lenin Prize 65.

Principal stage roles: Prince Myskin in *The Idiot,* Sergei in *Irkutsk Story.*

Films include: *9 Days in One Year, Hamlet* 64, *Be Aware of a Car* 66, *Tchaikovsky* 69.
Bolshoi State Drama Theatre, Leningrad, U.S.S.R.

Smoquina, Giorgio; Italian diplomatist; b. 1915.
Chief Spokesman, European Econ. Communities (EEC) 55-61; Chief Press Officer, Ministry of Foreign Affairs, Rome 61-68; Amb. to Int. Orgs. in Geneva 68-70; mem. Combined Comm. of EEC, ECSC and Euratom July 70; Chair. of Session, GATT 71-72; Amb. to Turkey 73-. Atatürk Bulvari, 118, Ankara, Turkey.
Telephone: 18-93-66.

Smyth, Charles Phelps, A.B., A.M., PH.D.; American physical chemist; b. 10 Feb. 1895, Clinton, N.Y.; *s.* of Charles Henry Smyth, Jr., and Ruth Phelps Smyth; *m.* Emily Ellen Vezin 1955; ed. Princeton and Harvard Univs.

Assistant Chemist, U.S. Bureau of Standards 17; First Lieut. U.S. Army 18; Instructor in Chem., Princeton Univ. 20-23, Asst. Prof. 23-27, Assoc. Prof. 27-38, Prof. 38-58, David B. Jones Prof. of Chem. 58-63, Emer. 63-; Chemist on Atom Bomb Project 43-45; Expert Consultant, serving with U.S. Army, Germany 45; Lieut.-Commdr. U.S. Naval Reserve 37-41; Consulting Chemist, Office of Naval Research 63-; Visiting Prof., Japan 65; Liaison Scientist, Office of Naval Research, London 69-70; Hon. Chair. Gordon Conf. 70; Visiting Prof., Salford 74-; mem. Nat. Acad. of Sciences,

American Philosophical Soc. (Council 18-71); Fellow, American Physical Soc.; Nichols Medal (American Chemical Soc.); Medal of Freedom (U.S. Army); Hon. D.Sc. (Salford) 70; Certificate of Appreciation, War Dept., Certificate in Recognition of Public Service, U.S. Dept. of State, Cert. of Merit, O.S.R.D.
Leisure interests: fly-fishing, walking, riding, reading, music, travel.
Publs. *Dielectric Constant and Molecular Structure* 31, *Dielectric Behavior and Structure* 55; 303 scientific papers and book chapters 17-74.
Frick Chemical Laboratory, Princeton Univ., Princeton, N.J. 08540; Home: 245 Prospect Avenue, Princeton, N.J. 08540, U.S.A.
Telephone: 609-452-3902 (Frick Chemical Lab.); 609-921-6525 (Home).

Smyth, Craig Hugh, A.B., M.F.A., PH.D.; American art historian and educationist; b. 28 July 1915, New York; *s.* of George Hugh Smyth and Lucy Salome Humeston; *m.* Barbara Linforth 1941; one *s.* one *d.*; ed. Hotchkiss School, Princeton Univ.
Research Asst. Nat. Gallery of Art, Wash., D.C. 41-42; Officer-in-Charge, Dir. Cen. Art Collecting Point, Munich 45-46; Lecturer Frick Collection, New York 46-50; Asst. Prof. of Fine Arts, Inst. of Fine Arts, New York Univ. 50-53, Assoc. Prof. 53-57, Prof. 57-73, Acting Dir. 51-53, Dir. 53-73; Prof. of Fine Arts, Harvard Univ. 73-; Dir. Harvard Univ. Center for Italian Renaissance Studies, Florence 74-; Hon. Trustee, Metropolitan Museum of Art; Chevalier Légion d'Honneur.
Publs. *Mannerism and Maniera* 63, *Bronzino as Draughtsman* 71.
Harvard University Center for Italian Renaissance Studies, Villa I Tatti, Via di Vincigliata, 50135 Florence, Italy.
Telephone: 603-251, 608-909.

Sneath, William S., M.B.A.; American business executive; b. 29 March 1926, Buffalo, N.Y.; *m.* Nancy Thornton; three *s.* three *d.*; ed. Williams Coll. and Harvard Graduate School of Business Admin.
Joined Union Carbide Corpn. 50, Treas. 61, Vice-Pres., Treas. and Chief Financial Officer 65, Dir. 69, Pres. April 71-.
Leisure interests: skiing, golf, sailing.
Union Carbide Corporation, 270 Park Avenue, New York, N.Y. 10017, U.S.A.

Snedden, Rt. Hon. Billy Mackie, Q.C., M.P.; Australian lawyer and politician; b. 31 Dec. 1926, Perth; *s.* of Alan Snedden; *m.* Joy Forsyth 1950; two *s.* two *d.*
Admitted to Supreme Court 51, Victorian Bar 55; Migration Officer Italy, England 52-54; mem. House of Reps. Bruce, Victoria 55-; Commonwealth Attorney-Gen. 63-66; Leader, House of Reps. 66; appointed Q.C. 64; Chair. First Commonwealth Law Ministers Conf., Canberra 65; Minister for Immigration Dec. 66-69; Minister for Labour and Nat. Service and Leader of the House of Reps. 69-71, Treasurer 71-72; Deputy Leader Liberal Party 71-72, Leader 72-75; Leader of Opposition 72-75.
22 Pine Crescent, Ringwood, Victoria, Australia.

Sneider, Richard Lee, A.B., M.I.A.; American diplomatist; b. 29 June 1922, New York; *s.* of late Leopold T. and Frances M. Sneider; *m.* Lea Ruth Tartalsky 1944; two *s.* one *d.*; ed. Brown Univ., Columbia Univ.
Japan and Korea Research Officer, Dept. of State 48-52; Special Asst. UN Affairs, Dept. of State 52-54; First Sec., Tokyo 54-58; Officer-in-Charge, Japanese Affairs, Dept. of State 58-61; Nat. War Coll. 61-62; Political Counsellor, Karachi 62-65; Public Affairs Officer, East Asia Bureau, Dept. of State 65-66, Country Dir. for Japan 66-68; Senior Staff mem. Nat. Security Council 69; Deputy Chief of Mission, Minister for Okinawan Reversion Negotiations, Tokyo 69-72;

Deputy Asst. Sec. of State, East Asia Bureau 72-74; Amb. to Repub. of Korea 74-; Superior Honor Awards, Dept. of State 70, 72.
Leisure interests: golf, skiing, tennis.
Publ. *North Korea: Case Study of a Soviet Satellite* (co-author) 61.
American Embassy, Seoul, Republic of Korea; and 4930 30th Street, N.W., Washington, D.C., U.S.A.

Snell, Bruno, DR.PHIL.; German Hellenist; b. 18 June 1896, Hildesheim; *s.* of Otto Snell and Anna Struckmann; *m.* 1st Herta Schräder 1925; two *d.*; 2nd Liese-Lotte Cahn 1970; ed. Lüneburg Johanneum and Univs. of Edinburgh, Leiden, Berlin, Munich and Göttingen.
Lector Pisa Univ. 25; Privatdozent Hamburg Univ. 25, Prof. 31-60, now Emer.
Publs. *Die Entdeckung des Geistes* 46 (4th edn. 75), *Der Aufbau der Sprache* 52, 61, *Griechische Metrik* 55 (3rd edn. 62), *Poetry and Society* 61, *Scenes from Greek Drama* 64; Editions of Bacchylides 34 (4th edn. 61) and Pindar 53, 59, 63, 64; and *Fragmenta Tragicorum Graecorum Minorum* 71.
Heimhuderstrasse 80, 2 Hamburg 13, Federal Republic of Germany.
Telephone: 440756.

Snell, Esmond Emerson, B.A., M.A., PH.D.; American professor of biochemistry; b. 22 Sept. 1914, Salt Lake City, Utah; *s.* of Heber C. Snell and Hedwig Ludwig; *m.* Mary Caroline Terrill 1941; two *s.* one *d.*; ed. Brigham Young Univ. and Univ. of Wis.
Assistant Prof. of Chem., Univ. of Texas 41-42, Assoc. Prof. 43-45, Prof. 53-56, Assoc. Dir. Clayton Foundation, Biochemical Inst. of Univ. of Texas 54-56; Assoc. Prof. of Biochem., Univ. of Wis. 45-47, Prof. 47-53; Prof. of Biochem., Univ. of Calif. at Berkeley 56-, Chair. Dept. of Biochem. 56-62; Editor *Annual Review of Biochemistry* 62-64, 68-; Walker-Ames Visiting Prof. of Biochem., Univ of Wash., Seattle 53; Guggenheim Fellow, Univs. of Cambridge, Copenhagen and Zurich 54-55, Max-Planck Inst. für Zellchemie Munich 62-63, Hebrew Univ., Jerusalem, and Univs. of Freiburg and Würzburg 70; mem. Nat. Acad. of Sciences, American Soc. of Biological Chemists (Pres. 61-62); Eli Lilly Award in Bacteriology and Immunology 45, Meade-Johnson Vitamin B Complex Award 46, Osborn Mendel Award 51, Kenneth A. Spencer Award in Agricultural Chem. (American Chemical Soc.) 73.
Leisure interests: skiing, hiking, gardening.
Publs. Over 300 research papers in scientific journals, including *Journal of Biological Chemistry*, *Journal of Bacteriology*, *Biochemistry*, *Proceedings* of Nat. Acad. of Sciences, *Journal* of American Chemical Soc. 37-; *Biochemical Preparations*, Vol. III (Editor) 53, *Methods in Enzymology* (Contributor) 57, 67, *Comprehensive Biochemistry* (Contributor) 63, 64, 71, *International Union of Biochemistry Symposium Series*, Vol. 30 63, Vol. 35 68 (Co-Editor).
Department of Biochemistry, University of California, Berkeley, Calif. 94720, U.S.A.
Telephone: (415) 642-0594.

Snell, Foster Dee, B.S., M.A., PH.D.; American chemist and chemical engineer; b. 29 June 1898, Binghamton, N.Y.; *s.* of Dayton A. and Bertha V. (Hickling) Snell; *m.* Cornelia A. Tyler 1921; one *d.*; ed. Colgate Univ. and Columbia Univ.
Teacher of Chem. Columbia Univ. 19-20; Teacher of Chem. Coll. of City of N.Y. 20-23; in charge of Technical Chem. Pratt Inst. 23-28; Office of Production Research and Devt. 41-45; Chair. Emer. Board Foster D. Snell Inc.; Chair. of Board, 29 West 15th St. Corpn. 64-68, trustee in liquidation 68-; fmr. Vice-Pres. Soc. of Chemical Industry; Vice-Chair. American Section 40-42, Chair. 42-44; Pres. American Inst. of Chemists 46-48; Vice-Pres. American Oil Chemists' Soc. 40-43; Vice-Pres. Fat and Oil Comm. of Int. Union of Pure

and Applied Chemistry 47-51, Pres. 51-53; Pres. Asscn. Consulting Chemists and Chemical Engineers 52-54; Vice-Pres. Chemists' Club (New York) 56-57, Pres. 62-64; Trustee, Columbia Univ. 64; Nat. Council, Colgate Univ. 73-; Soc. of Chemical Industry Medal for 1949; American Inst. of Chemists Award 52, etc.; Hon. mem. American Inst. of Chemists 59; Hon. Sc.D. (Colgate Univ.) 63; Chemical Pioneer Award A.I.C. 70. Leisure interests: bridge, reading.

Publs. *Colorimetric Methods of Analysis* 23 (3rd edn. in 4 vols. 49-54, supplementary vols. 59, 61, 67, 70), *Chemicals of Commerce* 39 and 52, *Chemistry Made Easy* (4 vols.) 43, 59, 60 (all with Dr. Cornelia T. Snell), *Commercial Methods of Analysis* (with Frank M. Biffen) 2nd edn. 64; *Dictionary of Commercial Chemicals* 62; Editor-in-Chief *Encyclopedia of Industrial Chemical Analysis* (20 vols.), first 3 vols. 66, 2 vols. 68, 1 vol. 69, 3 vols. 70, 3 vols. 71, 2 vols. 72, 2 vols. 73, 2 vols. 74.

Home: 860 United Nations Plaza, New York, N.Y. 10017; Office: 245 Park Avenue, New York, N.Y. 10017, U.S.A.

Telephone: 486-1393 (Home); 697-1900 (Office).

Snell, George Davis, D.SC.; American research geneticist; b. 19 Dec. 1903, Haverhill, Mass.; s. of Cullen Bryant and Katherine Davis Snell; m. Rhoda Carson 1937; three s.; ed. Dartmouth Coll. and Harvard Univ. Instructor in Zoology, Dartmouth Coll. 29-30, Brown Univ. 30-31; Nat. Research Council Fellow, Univ. of Texas 31-33; Asst. Prof., Washington Univ., St. Louis 33-34; Research Assoc., The Jackson Laboratory 35-56; Science Admin. 49-50; Guggenheim Fellow, Univ. of Texas 53-54; Senior Staff Scientist, The Jackson Laboratory 57-69, Senior Staff Scientist Emeritus 69-; fmr. mem. Nat. Inst. of Health Allergy and Immunology Study Section 58-62; Fellow, American Asscn. for the Advancement of Science; mem. American Acad. of Arts and Sciences, Nat. Acad. of Sciences, Transplantation Soc.; Editor-in-Chief, *Immunogenetics*; Bertner Foundation Award 62; Gregor Mendel Medal, Czechoslovak Acad. of Sciences 67; Hon. M.D. (Charles Univ., Prague) 67, Hon. Sc.D. (Dartmouth Coll.) 74; Hon. mem. British Transplantation Soc. Leisure interests: gardening, forestry.

Publs. numerous papers in technical journals and books; Ed. *The Biology of the Laboratory Mouse* 41.

The Jackson Laboratory, Bar Harbor, Maine 04609; 21 Atlantic Avenue, Bar Harbor, Maine 04609, U.S.A.

Snodgrass, William DeWitt, B.A., M.A., M.F.A.; American poet, critic and teacher; b. 5 Jan. 1926; s. of Bruce DeWitt Snodgrass and Helen J. Murchie; m. Camille Rykowski 1967; one s. two d.; ed. State Univ. of Iowa. Instructor, English Dept., Cornell Univ., Ithaca 55-57, Univ. of Rochester 57-58; Prof. English Dept., Wayne State Univ. 59-68; Prof. English and Speech, Syracuse Univ. 68-; Leader, Poetry Workshop, Morehead, Kentucky 55, Yellow Springs, Ohio 58, 59; mem. Nat. Inst. of Arts and Letters 72-; mem. Acad. American Poets 73-; Guggenheim Fellow 72-73; Pulitzer Prize for Poetry 60, and other awards. Leisure interest: translating medieval music to be sung, playing the lute, woodcarving.

Publs. *Heart's Needle* 59, *After Experience* 68, *In Radical Pursuit* (critical essays) 75.

English Department, Syracuse University, Syracuse, N.Y. 13210, U.S.A.

Snow, Baron (Life Peer), cr. 64, of Leicester; **Charles Percy Snow** (husband of Pamela Hansford Johnson, *q.v.*), Kt., C.B.E., PH.D.; British writer; b. 15 Oct. 1905; one s.; ed. Univ. Coll., Leicester, and Christ's Coll., Cambridge. Fellow of Christ's Coll., Cambridge 30-50 (in residence 30-40), Hon. Fellow 66-; Technical Dir. Ministry of Labour 40-44; Civil Service Commr. 45-60; Dir. English Electric Co. Ltd. 47-64; Parl. Sec. Ministry of Technology 64-66; Hon. LL.D. (Leicester, Liverpool, St. Andrews, Brooklyn Polytechnic Inst., Bridgeport, York, Toronto), Hon. D.Litt. (Dartmouth, Bard, Temple, Syracuse, Pittsburgh, Ithaca, Westminster Colls.); Hon. D.H.L. (Kenyon Coll., Wash., Mich., Alfred and Akron Univs.); Hon. D.Sc. (Pa. Mil. Coll.); Dr. of Phil. Sc. (Rostov-on-Don); Hon. mem. American Acad. Inst.; foreign hon. mem. American Acad. of Arts and Sciences; Extraordinary Fellow, Churchill Coll., Cambridge; Fellow, Morse Coll., Yale Univ.; Diamond Jubilee Medal, Catholic Univ. of America; Centennial Eng. Medal, Pa. Mil. Coll.; Resolution of Esteem, Congressional Cttee. on Science and Astronautics; mem. Arts Council of Great Britain 71-74.

Publs. Novels: *Death Under Sail* 32, *New Lives for Old* 33, *The Search* 34, *Strangers and Brothers* 40, *The Light and the Dark* 47, *Time of Hope* 49, *The Masters* 51, *The New Men* 54, *Homecoming* 56, *The Conscience of The Rich* 58, *The Affair* 60, *Corridors of Power* 64, *The Sleep of Reason* 68, *Last Things* 70, *The Malcontents* 72, *In Their Wisdom* 74; Lectures: *The Two Cultures and the Scientific Revolution* (Rede Lecture) 59, *Science and Government* (Godkin Lectures) 61; *Variety of Men* (biographical portraits) 67, *Public Affairs* (collected essays) 71, *Anthony Trollope* 75; Plays: *View over the Park* 50, *The Affair, The New Men, The Masters* (adapted by Ronald Millar) 61, 62, 63.

c/o Macmillan & Co. Ltd., Little Essex Street, London, W.C.2; 85 Eaton Terrace, London, S.W.1, England.

Snowdon, 1st Earl of, cr. 61; **Antony Charles Robert Armstrong-Jones,** G.C.V.O.; b. 7 March 1930; s. of late Ronald Owen Lloyd Armstrong-Jones, M.B.E., Q.C., D.L., and the Countess of Rosse; m. H.R.H. The Princess Margaret (*q.v.*) 1960; one s. one d.; ed. Eton Coll. and Jesus Coll., Cambridge.

Consultant, Council of Industrial Design; Editorial Adviser, *Design* magazine; Artistic Adviser to *The Sunday Times* and Sunday Times Publications Ltd. 62-; Constable of Caernarvon Castle 63-; Fellow, Inst. of British Photographers, Soc. of Industrial Artists and Designers, Royal Photographic Soc.; Hon. mem. North Wales Soc. of Architects, South Wales Inst. of Architects; mem. Council, Nat. Fund for Research for the Crippled Child; Patron Nat. Youth Theatre, Metropolitan Union of YMCA's, British Water Ski Fed., British Theatre Museum; designed Snowdon Aviary, London Zoo 65, Chairmobile 72; television documentaries *Don't Count the Candles* (six awards) 68, *Love of a Kind* 70, *Born to be Small* 71, *Happy being Happy* 73, *Mary Kingsley* 75, *Burke and Wills* 75; exhbns. *Photocall*, London 58, *Assignments*, Cologne, London, Brussels 72, U.S.A., Canada, Japan, Australia.

Publs. *London* 58, *Malta* (in collaboration) 58, *Private View* (with John Russell and Bryan Robertson) 65, *Assignments* 72, *Venice* (with Derek Hart) 72.

Kensington Palace, London, W.8, England.

Snoy et d'Oppuers, Baron Jean-Charles; Belgian economist; b. 2 July 1907, Bois-Seigneur-Isaac, Brabant; s. of Baron Thierry Snoy et d'Oppuers and Viscountess Claire de Beughem de Houtem; m. Countess Nathalie d'Alcantara 1935; two s. five d.; ed. Univ. of Louvain and Harvard Univ.

Entered banking business in Belgium 31; became Attaché to Minister for Economic Affairs 34, Dir., Int. Treaty Section, Ministry of Economic Affairs 36, Sec.-Gen. of the Ministry 39; dismissed from post by the Germans and active in Resistance Movement during Second World War; re-assumed duties after Liberation and became Pres. Four Party Supply Cttee. of Belgium; played prominent part in creation of Benelux Economic Union and was Chair. Council for Econ. Union; also contributed to work leading to creation of O.E.E.C,

in 48; Chair. O.E.E.C. Council 48-50, Steering Board for Trade O.E.E.C. 52, 60; Chief Belgian del. 55 to Int. Cttee. set up at Messina Conf., which later became Int. Conf. for Common European Market and Euratom; Pres. Interim Cttee. for European Common Market and Euratom 57; Sec.-Gen. Ministry of Economic Affairs until 60; Perm. Rep. to European Economic Community 58-59; Man. Dir. Cie. Lambert pour l'Industrie et la Finance 60-68; Partner Banque Lambert 65-68; mem. Lower House of Parl. 68-71; Minister of Finance June 68-Jan. 72; several Belgian and foreign decorations including Grand Officer, Order of Leopold and Grand Officer Order of the Crown (Belgium); Grand Cross Order of Crown of Oak (Luxembourg), Royal Order George I (Greece), Order of Merit (Italy), Grand Cross Order of Orange-Nassau (Netherlands), Hon. K.B.E. (U.K.), Grand Cross Order of Merit (German Fed. Repub.).
Leisure interests: shooting, alpinism, tennis.
Château de Bois-Seigneur-Isaac, 1421 Ophain B.S.I., Belgium.
Telephone: 067-22-22-27.

Snyder, John Wesley; American banker; b. 21 June 1895; ed. Vanderbilt Univ.
Banker in Arkansas and Missouri 19-30; Bank Receiver and Conservator, Office of Comptroller of the Currency, St. Louis 31-37; Man. St. Louis Agency, Reconstruction Finance Corpn. 37-43; Exec. Vice-Pres. and Dir. Defense Plant Corpn., Washington 40-43; Asst. to Board of Dirs. R.F.C. 40-44; Vice-Pres. First Nat. Bank of St. Louis 43-45; Fed. Loan Administrator 45; Dir. Office of War Mobilization and Reconversion 45; Sec. of Treasury 46-53; Chair. Nat. Advisory Council on Int. Monetary and Financial Problems 46-53; U.S. Gov. of Int. Monetary Fund and Int. Bank for Reconstruction 46-53; Senior U.S. Financial Rep. in admin. of Anglo-American Financial Agreement 46, and financial, rehabilitation and aid programmes, Philippines, France, Italy, Austria, Turkey, Greece, Germany, Japan and Marshall Plan operations; mem. U.S. Nat. Security Council 51-52, NATO Council 49-53; del. to numerous int. financial confs.; Pres. Overland Corpn., Toledo 53-66, Dir. 66-; Medal for Merit 47; Hon. LL.D. (Ouachita Coll., George Washington Univ., Univ. of Arkansas, Univ. of Toledo, Georgetown Univ.); Hon. D.Sc. (Bryant Coll.).
Home: 8109 Kerry Lane, Chevy Chase, Md. 20015; Office: Overland Corporation, Investment Bankers, 500 Security Building, Toledo, Ohio, U.S.A.

Snyder, Laurence Hasbrouck, M.S., S.D., H.H.D., D.SC.; American university president; b. 23 July 1901, Kingston, N.Y.; s. of DeWitt Clinton and Gertrude Wood Snyder; m. Guldberg M. Herland 1923; two d.; ed. Rutgers Univ. and Harvard.
Instructor in Zoology, N. Carolina State Coll. of Agriculture and Eng. 24-25, Asst. Prof. 25-27, Assoc. Prof. 27-30; Assoc. Prof. of Zoology, Ohio State Univ. 30-33, Prof. 33-47; Prof. of Medical Genetics, Ohio State Univ. Coll. of Medicine 33-47, Chair., Dept. of Zoology and Entomology 42-47; Dean of Graduate Coll. Univ. of Okla. 47-58; Pres. Univ. of Hawaii 58-66, Emeritus 66-; mem. Nat. Research Council, Eugenics Research Asscn., American Soc. of Zoologists, A.A.A.S. (Pres. 57), Genetics Soc. of America (Pres. 48), American Soc. Human Genetics (Pres. 50).
Leisure interests: tropical gardening, piano playing.
Publs. include *Medical Genetics* 41, *Genetics, Medicine and Man* (with Muller and Little) 47, *Principles of Heredity*, 5th edn. 57.
2885 Oahu Avenue, Honolulu, Hawaii 96822, U.S.A.

Soames, Rt. Hon. Sir Christopher, G.C.M.G., G.C.V.O., C.B.E.; British politician and diplomatist; b. 12 Oct. 1920, Penn, Bucks.; m. Mary Spencer Churchill 1947;

three s. two d.; ed. Eton Coll. and Royal Mil. Coll., Sandhurst.
Captain Coldstream Guards, served in France, Italy and Middle East 39-45; Asst. Mil. Attaché, Paris 46-47; Conservative M.P. for Bedford 50-66; Parl. Private Sec. to the Prime Minister 52-55; Parl. Under-Sec. of State to Air Ministry 55-57, and to Admiralty 57-58; Sec. of State for War 58-60; Minister of Agriculture, Fisheries and Food 60-64; Exec. Dir. Decca 66-68; Amb. to France 68-72; mem., Vice-Pres. Comm. of European Communities 73-; Croix de Guerre, Grand Officier Légion d'Honneur, Grand Cross Order of St. Olav; Robert Schuman Prize 75.
Commission of the European Communities, 200 rue de la Loi, 1040 Brussels, Belgium.

Soares, Mário Alberto Nobre Lopes, L. ÈS L., D. EN D.; Portuguese lawyer, historian and politician; b. 7 Dec. 1924, Lisbon; s. of João Lopes Soares and Elisa Nobre Soares; m. Maria Barroso Soares 1949; one s. one d.; ed. Univ. of Lisbon and Faculty of Law, Sorbonne, Paris.
Leader MUD Juvenil (United Democratic Youth Movement), mem. MUD Cen. Cttee. 45-48; Sec. presidential candidature of Gen. Norton da Mattos 49; mem. Exec. of Social Democratic Action 52-60; mem. Campaign Cttee. for Delgado in presidential elections 58; Democratic Opposition candidate for Lisbon in legislative elections 65, 69; rep. of Portuguese socialists at various European socialist congresses and 11th Congress of Socialist International, Eastbourne 59; Portuguese rep. Int. League of Rights of Man; imprisoned 12 times on political grounds; in exile in Paris 70-74, returned to Portugal after coup April 74; Minister of Foreign Affairs 74-75; Minister without Portfolio March-July 75; corresp. *República* (Lisbon), *Ibérica* (New York).
Leisure interests: bibliophile and collector of contemporary Portuguese paintings.
Publs. *As Ideias Políticas e Sociais de Teófilo Braga* 51, *A Justificação Jurídica da Restauração e a teoriá da origem popular do poder político* 56, *Oliveira Martins e o Fontismo* 60, *Direito a Casa* 65, *Escritos Políticos* 69, *Le Portugal Baillonné* 72.
Partido Socialista, Rua Emenda 46, Lisbon, Portugal.
Telephone: 761074 (Lisbon).

Sobell, Sir Michael, Kt.; British business executive; b. 1 Nov. 1892, Borislaw, U.S.S.R.; s. of Lewis and Esther Sobell; m. Anne Rakusen 1917; two d.; ed. Cen. London Foundation School.
Director, Gen. Electric Co. 60-67; Chair. Gen. Electric (Radio & Television) Ltd. 68-; Pres. British Technion Soc. 58-66, Nat. Soc. for Cancer Relief 64-; Freeman and Liveryman, Carmen Company; Hon. Fellow, Jew's Coll., Bar Ilan Univ.
Leisure interests: racing, charitable work.
Bakeham House, Englefield Green, Surrey, TN20 9TX, England.
Telephone: Egham 4111.

Sobhi, Mohamed Ibrahim, B.SC.; Egyptian international official; b. 28 March 1925, Alexandria; s. of Gen. Ibrahim Sobhi; m. Laila Ahmed Sobhi 1950; two s. one d.; ed. Cairo Univ.
Director-General Int. Bureau of Universal Postal Union Jan. 75-; Order of Merit, 1st Class (Egypt).
Leisure interests: reading, philately, music.
Bureau International de l'Union Postale Universelle, Weltpoststrasse 4, 3000 Berne 15; Home: Jupiterstrasse 29, 3015 Berne, Switzerland.
Telephone: (031) 43-22-11 (Office).

Sobhuza II, H.R.H. King; King (Ngwenyama) and Head of State of Swaziland; b. 22 July 1899; s. of King Ngwane V; ed. Zombodze, Swaziland, Lovedale Inst. (Cape).
Installed as constitutional ruler 21; led deputation to London to petition against land lost under the Partitions

Proclamation of 1907 Dec. 22; petitioned King George VI of England 41; officially recognized by Britain as King and Head of State April 67, assumed all exec. powers in Swaziland April 73; Chancellor Univ. of Lesotho, Botswana and Swaziland.

Official Residence of the King, Lozithehlezi, Kwaluseni, Swaziland.

Telephone: Kwaluseni 50.

Sobolev, Sergei Lvovich; Soviet mathematician; b. 6 Oct. 1908, Leningrad; ed. Leningrad Univ.

Research devoted to mechanics, the dynamics of the resilient body and theoretical mathematics; mem. Acad. of Sciences of U.S.S.R. 39-; Dir. Inst. of Mathematics and Computing Centre of the Siberian Dept. of the Acad. of Sciences of the U.S.S.R. 59-; Prof. at Moscow Univ. 35; awarded Order of Lenin; Editor-in-Chief *Bulletin of Siberian Department of U.S.S.R. Academy of Sciences;* Hon. Fellow Royal Soc. of Edinburgh 63.

Publs. *Some Applications of Functional Analysis in Mathematical Physics* 50, *Equations of Mathematical Physics* 54, *Lectures on Theory of Cubic Formulae* 64. Akademgorodok, Novosibirsk, U.S.S.R.

Sobolev, Vladimir Alexeyevich; Soviet foreign trade official; b. 15 July 1912; ed. Moscow Textile Inst.

Member C.P.S.U. 46-; official, foreign trade orgs. 40-48; Dir. of Office, *Exportlyon* 48-50, 53-63; U.S.S.R. Commercial Rep. in Iran 50-51; official, Ministry of Agriculture 51-53; Deputy, later Commercial Rep. of U.S.S.R. in India 63-70; Chair. All-Union Asscn. for export and import of natural fibres 70-; Order of Red Banner of Labour.

All-Union Asscn., "Exportlyon", Ulitsa Vlasova 33, Moscow, U.S.S.R.

Sobolev, Vladimir Stepanovich; Soviet geologist; b. 30 May 1908, Voroshilovgrad, Ukraine; ed. Leningrad Inst. of Mines.

Geologist, Cen. Scientific Research Exploration, Inst. of Mines, Leningrad 29-41, Prof. of Inst. 39-45; Prof. Univ. of Lvov 45-58; Dep. Dir. Inst. of Geology and Geophysics, Novosibirsk 58-; mem. U.S.S.R. Acad. of Sciences 58-, and Ukrainian S.S.R., Mineralogical Socs. of the U.S.S.R., Hungary and Czechoslovakia, Soc. géologique de France; State Prize 50.

Publs. *Petrology of Traps of the Siberian Platform, Petrology of Korosten Pluton, Introduction into Mineralogy of Silicates, Geology of Diamond Deposits, Phedorov's Method, Petrography of Igneous rocks of the Soviet Carpathians, Physical-Chemical Principles of Petrography of Igneous Rocks, Map of Metamorphic Facies of U.S.S.R.;* Ed. *Diamond Deposits of Jakutiya.* Akademgorodok, Novosibirsk, U.S.S.R.

Sobukwe, Robert Maugatiso; South African politician; b. 1924; ed. Univ. Coll. of Fort Hare.

Former Lecturer, Witwatersrand Univ., Johannesburg; fmr. mem. African Nat. Congress; Pres. South African Pan Africanist Congress 59-; in detention March 60-63, 63-May 69, 69-May 74, banning order renewed for 5 years 74; now restricted to Kimberley; refused permission to leave S. Africa 70, 74.

Kimberley, South Africa.

Sochava, Viktor Borisovich, D.SC.; Soviet geographer; b. 20 July 1905, Leningrad; ed. Leningrad Agricultural Inst.

Lecturer, Leningrad Agricultural Inst., Gertsen Leningrad Pedagogical Inst.; Research Worker, V. L. Komarov Botanical Inst. of U.S.S.R. Acad. of Sciences, Inst. of Reindeer-Breeding, Lenin All-Union Acad. of Agricultural Sciences; Head of Dept., Inst. of the Arctic and Antarctic; Prof. Zhdanov State Univ., Leningrad; Chair. Scientific Council on Taiga Regions and Dir. Inst. of Geography of Siberia and Far East, Siberian

Dept. of U.S.S.R. Acad. of Sciences 59-; Academician, U.S.S.R. Acad. of Sciences 68-.

Institute of Geography of Siberia and Far East, Siberian Department of Academy of Sciences of U.S.S.R., Irkutsk, U.S.S.R.

Soderberg, C. Richard, D.ENG.; American mechanical engineer; b. 3 Feb. 1895, Ulvöhamn, Sweden; s. of Jonas Axel Söderberg and Johanna Kristina (Nordquist) Söderberg; m. Sigrid Kristina Lofstedt 1921; two s. one d.; ed. Chalmers Inst. of Technology, Gothenburg, Sweden, Mass. Inst. of Technology and Tufts Univ., Mass., U.S.A.

Development Engineer, Westinghouse Electric and Mfg. Co., East Pittsburgh, Pa. 22-28, Chief Turbine Engineer 31-38; in charge of turbo generators, Asea, Västerås, Sweden 28-30; Prof. of Mechanical Eng., Mass. Inst. of Technology 38-59, Head of Dept. of Mechanical Eng. 47-54, Dean of Eng. 54-59, Inst. Prof. 59-61, Inst. Prof. Emer. 61-; Fellow American-Scandinavian Foundation 19-20; Fellow, American Acad. of Arts and Sciences, American Inst. of Aeronautics and Astronautics, American Soc. of Mechanical Engineers, Nat. Acad. of Sciences, Ingeniörvetens-kapakademiens, IVA, Sweden; mem. A.A.A.S., Brit. Inst. of Mechanical Engineers, Svenska Teknologförenigen, etc.; Joseph H. Linnard Prize (co-recipient) of Soc. of Naval Architects and Marine Engineers 44, John Ericsson Gold Medal of American Soc. of Swedish Engineers 52, Medal of American Soc. of Mechanical Engineers 60, Gustaf DeLaval Medal of IVA 68, Gustaf Dalen Medal of Chalmers Inst. of Technology, Gothenburg 70.

Publs. Numerous monographs in American and European journals on dynamics, vibrations, design of turbines and generators, gas turbines, etc.

6 Joy Street, Boston, Mass. 02108, U.S.A.

Söderberg, Erik Axel Olof R:son, M.SC.; Swedish business executive; b. 17 Nov. 1926, Stockholm; s. of Ragnar O. Söderberg (*q.v.*), and Ingegerd A. Wallenberg; m. Helene M. Schultz 1948; two s. two d.; ed. Univ. of Commerce, Göteborg and Columbia Univ., New York.

Director, Söderberg & Haak AB, Stockholm 52, Vice-Pres. 54-66; Man. Dir. Förvaltnings AB Ratos, Stockholm (investment co.) 58-69; Man. Dir. AB Nordiska Kompaniet 66-; Man. Dir. AB Turitz & Co. 71, now Chair. of Board; Hon. R.V.O., Hon. C.B.E. 69.

Leisure interests: golf, skating, skiing, reading, race-horse owner.

Strandvägen 63, Stockholm, Sweden.

Telephone: 23-63-00 (Office).

Söderberg, Ragnar; Swedish businessman; b. 13 April 1900, Stockholm; s. of Consul Gen. Olof Söderberg and Otilia Herzog; m. 1st Ingegerd Wallenberg 1922, 2nd Barbro Rålamb 1941; three s. one d.; ed. Stockholm Univ. of Commerce.

Chairman AB Electrolux, Esselte AB, Förvaltnings AB Ratos, Holmens Bruk AB, Söderberg & Haak AB, Försäkringsaktiebolaget Skandia; fmr. Vice-Chair. ASEA, AB Iggesunds Bruk, Skandinaviska Enskilda Banken; Hon. D.Econ.

Djurgärdsvägen 150, 11521 Stockholm, Sweden.

Telephone: 24-20-00.

Söderström, Elisabeth Anna; Swedish soprano opera singer; b. 7 May 1927; m. Sverker Olow 1950; three s.; studied singing under Andrejewa de Skilonz and Opera School, Stockholm.

Engaged at Royal Opera, Stockholm 50-; appearances at Salzburg 55, Glyndebourne 57, 59, 61, 63, 64, Metropolitan Opera, New York 59, 60, 62, 63; frequent concert and TV appearances in Europe and U.S.A.; toured U.S.S.R. 66; mem. Royal Acad. of Music; Singer of the Court (Sweden) 59; Order of Vasa; Stelle della Solidarieta dell'Italia; Prize for Best Acting, Royal Swedish Acad. 65, "Literis et Artibus" award 69, Commdr. of the Order of Vasa 73.

Leisure interests: sailing, literature, embroidery.
Roles include: Fiordiligi (*Cosi Fan Tutte*), Countess and Susanna (*Figaro*), Countess (*Capriccio*); sang three leading roles in *Der Rosenkavalier* 59.
c/o Royal Opera House, Stockholm, Sweden.

Sofonov, Georgi Petrovich; Soviet trade union official; b. 15 Sept. 1919, Chelyabinsk; ed. Rostov Inst. of Railway Engineering.
Mechanical Engineer, Dep. Shop Superintendent, Chair. Trade Union Factory Cttee. Moscow Likhachov Motor Works 42-62; Sec.-Gen. Cttee. Engineering Workers Trade Union 62-63, Chair. Central Cttee. 63; mem. Presidium All-Union Central Cttee. of Trade Unions; mem. C.P.S.U.; Order of Red Banner of Labour.
Central Committee of Engineering Workers Trade Union, 42 Leninski Prospekt, Moscow, U.S.S.R.

Soglo, Gen. Christophe; Benin army officer and politician, b. 1909.
Joined French Army 31, 2nd Lt. Second World War; later fought in Indo-China becoming Capt. 50, Maj. 56; Col. of Armed Forces of Dahomey 61, Gen. 64; Head of Provisional Govt. Oct. 63-Jan. 64; Chief of Staff, Dahomeyan Army Jan. 64-Dec. 65; Pres. of the Repub. and Prime Minister Dec. 65-67, also Minister of Defence and for Rural Devt. Dec. 66-67.
Cotonou, Benin.

Sohl, Hans-Günther; German businessman; b. 2 May 1906, Danzig; m. Annelis Baronin von Wrede 1938; one *s.* one *d.*; ed. Technical Univ. Berlin-Charlottenburg.
President August Thyssen-Hütte AG, Chair. of Supervisory Board 73-; Pres. Duisburg-Hamborn; Vice-Chair. Wirtschaftsvereinigung Eisen und Stahlindustrie, Düsseldorf; Pres. Bundesverband der Deutschen Industrie e.V., Cologne; mem. of numerous boards in steel industry and other firms; Grosses Verdienstkreuz; Hon. Dr. Ing. (Technische Hochschule, Aachen); hon. mem. American Iron and Steel Inst., British Iron and Steel Inst.
Leisure interests: music, art.
August Thyssen-Hütte AG, 41 Duisburg-Hamborn, Kaiser-Wilhelm-Str. 100, Postfach 67, German Federal Republic.
Telephone: 5401.

Soilih, Ali; Comoros politician and agronomist; ed. Inst. of Agriculture, Madagascar, and Nat. Inst. of Tropical Agronomy, Nogent, France.
Deputy in Comoro Is. Territorial Assembly 68-70; Minister of Supplies 70-72; helped found UMMA opposition party; led coup against Pres. Abdallah Aug. 75; Minister of Defence and Justice Aug. 75-Jan. 76; Pres. Jan. 76-.
Office of the President, Moroni, Grande-Comore, Comoros.

Sokoine, Edward Moringe; Tanzanian politician; b. 1938.
Worked as Exec. Officer of Masai District Council until 65; mem. Nat. Assembly for Masai, Tanganyika African Nat. Union (TANU) 65-; Parl. Sec. to Ministry of Communications, Transport and Labour Aug. 67; Minister of State in Second Vice-Pres. Office Nov. 70; Minister of Defence and Nat. Service Feb. 72-; Chair. Masai Range Devt. Comm. 65-67, Transport Licensing Authority 67-70.
Ministry of Defence, Dar es Salaam, Tanzania.

Sokolov, Boris Sergeyevich, D.SC.; Soviet paleontologist and geologist; b. 9 April 1914; ed. Leningrad State Univ.
Laboratory State Asst., Asst. Lecturer, Leningrad State Univ. 37-41, Lecturer 45-60; Chief of Geological search party, Senior Research Worker, Head of Dept., All-Union Oil Research Geological Inst. 43-60; Head of Dept., Inst. of Geology and Geophysics, Siberian Dept. of U.S.S.R. Acad. of Sciences 60-; Academician, U.S.S.R. Acad. of Sciences 68-; Lenin Prize.
Akademgorodok, Novosibirsk, U.S.S.R.

Sokorski, Włodzimierz; Polish writer and journalist; b. 2 July 1908, Aleksandrowsk; ed. Univ. of Warsaw.
General Sec. Polish Socialist Party "Left Wing" 29-31; Col., Polish Army Second World War; Vice-Minister 48-53, Minister of Culture and Art 53-56; Pres., Cttee. for Radio and Television 56-72; Chief Editor *Literature Monthly* 65-; Vice-Pres. Polish UNESCO Cttee.; Deputy mem. Cen. Cttee. Polish United Workers' Party 48-; Deputy to Seym 47-; numerous Govt. and Army awards including Virtuti Militari, Order of Lenin (U.S.S.R.), Banner of Labour, 1st Class, Order of Polonia Restituta, 4th and 3rd Class.
Publs. *Rozdarty bruk* (The Torn Pavement—novel) 36, *Problemy polityki kulturalnej* (Problems of Cultural Policy) 47, *Sztuka w walce o socjalizm* (Arts for Socialism) 50, *Dziennik podróży* (The Journey Diary) 54, *Grubą kreską* (Drawing Thick Lines—essay) 58, *Zakręty* (Curves—essay) 59, *Okruchy* (Crumbs—short stories) 61, *Escapes* (play) 61, *Współezesność i młodzież* (The Present Day and Youth) 63, *Współezesna kultura masowa* (The Modern Mass Culture) 67, *Spotkania* (The Meeting—play), *Milczenie* (Silence—play), *Polacy pod Lenino* (Poles of Lenino—war memoirs) 71, *Notatki* (Notes—Memoirs) 75, *Nie ma powrotów tych samych* (Returning is Never the Same—play) 75, *Piotr* (Peter—novel) 76; numerous radio and television plays.
Redakcja "Miesięcznik Literacki", Plac Zwycięstwa 9, Warsaw; Home: Aleja Róż 6/5, Warsaw, Poland.
Telephone: 274182.

Solá, Alberto; Argentine economist; b. 1924; ed. Univ. of Buenos Aires and Univ. of Madrid.
Director, Ministry of Commerce 55-56; Nat. Dir. Politics and Finance 56-57; Under-Sec. of Finance 57-58; Prof. of Political Economy, Univ. of Buenos Aires 57-59; Dep. Dir. of Trade Affairs, Econ. Comm. for Latin America (ECLA) 58-62; Asst. Exec. Sec. Latin American Free Trade Assцn. (LAFTA) 62, Exec. Sec. 62-66; Sec. Industry and Commerce (Argentina) 67-69; mem. Inter-American Cttee. on the Alliance for Progress.
Julio A. Roca 651, 2° piso, Buenos Aires, Argentina.
Telephone: 34-3768.

Solages, Mgr. Bruno de, L. ÈS L., D.THEOL., DR.JUR. CANONICI; French ecclesiastic; b. 8 Aug. 1895, Mézens, Tarn; *s.* of Comte Henri de Solages and Anne-Marie du Parc; ed. Inst. Catholique de Paris, Séminaire de Saint-Sulpice and Ecole Biblique, Jerusalem.
Ordained 22; Chaplain of St. Louis des Français, Rome 22; Prof. of Rhetoric 25 and of Philosophy 28, Petit Séminaire de Saint-Sulpice; Editor-in-Chief *Revue Apologétique* 26; Rector Inst. Catholique de Toulouse 32-64 and Apostolic Protonotary 32, Hon. Rector 64-; Vice-Pres. des Semaines Sociales de France 45-56; mem. Higher Council of Nat. Education 46-54; Docteur h.c. (Univ. of Montreal).
Publs. *Camille Dupin* 20, *Le Procès de la Scolastique* 28, *Le Problème de l'Apostolat dans le monde moderne* 32, *Le Christianisme dans la Vie Publique* 37, *Pour rebâtir une chrétienté* 38, *Discours interdits* 46, *Dialogue sur l'analogie* 46, *La Théologie de la guerre juste* 47, *Essai sur l'ordre politique national et international* 47, *Billets de Christianus* 48, *L'âme, Dieu, la destinée* 55, *Synopse grecque des Evangiles* 58, *Initiation Métaphysique* 62, *Teilhard de Chardin* 67, *Critique des Evangiles et Méthode Historique* 72, *La Composition des Evangiles de Luc et de Mathieu et leurs Sources* 73, *Comments sont nés les Evangiles* 73.
31 rue Fondeville, Pouvourville, 31400 Toulouse (Haute-Garonne), France.
Telephone: 52-14-54.

Solaiman, Mohammed Sidky; Egyptian engineer and politician; b. 1919.
Studied eng. and mil. science; rose to Col. in Egyptian Army; Minister of Aswan High Dam 62-66; Prime Minister 66-June 67; Deputy Prime Minister and Minister of Industry, Electricity and the Aswan Dam June 67-70, 71; Pres. Soviet-Egyptian Friendship Soc.; Order of Lenin.
Cairo, Egypt.

Solandt, Omond McKillop, O.B.E., C.C., M.D., D.SC., LL.D., F.R.C.P., F.R.S.C., F.A.A.A.S., D.ENG.; Canadian physiologist; b. 2 Sept. 1909, Winnipeg, Man.; s. of Donald McKillop and Edith (Young) Solandt; m. 1st Elizabeth McPhedran 1941 (died 1971); one s. two d.; m. 2nd Vaire Pringle 1972; ed. Univ. of Toronto.
Lecturer in Physiology, Univ. of Cambridge 39; Dir. S.W. London Blood Supply Depot 40; Dir. Physiological Laboratory, Armoured Fighting Vehicle School 41; Dir. Tank Section, Army Operational Research Group 42; Deputy Superintendent, Army Operational Research Group 43, Superintendent 44; Chair. Defence Research Board 46-56; Asst. Vice-Pres., Research and Devt., Canadian Nat. Railways 56, Vice-Pres. 57-63; Vice-Pres. Research and Devt. and Dir. de Havilland Aircraft of Canada Ltd. 66; Vice-Chair. Board of Electric Reduction Co. of Canada Ltd. 66-70; Dir. other cos.; Chancellor Univ. of Toronto 65-71; Chair. Science Council of Canada 66-72; Dir. Expo 67; Public Gov. Toronto Stock Exchange 71; Fellow Royal Soc. of Canada, Royal Coll. of Physicians (London) 48; Companion Order of Canada 70; Dir. William F. Mitchell and Co. Ltd., and Mitchell, Plummer & Co. Ltd. 71-; hon. mem. Engineering Inst. of Canada; Hon. D.Sc. (British Columbia, Manitoba, Laval, McGill and St. Francis Xavier, Royal Mil. Coll., Univ. of Montreal), Hon. LL.D. (Toronto, Dalhousie, Sir George Williams Univ., Saskatchewan), Hon. D.Eng. (Waterloo); Medal of Freedom (with Bronze Palm).
Leisure interests: skiing and canoeing.
Suite 1107, 18 King Street East, Toronto, Ont., M5C 1C4; Home: The Wolfe Den, R.R.1, Bolton, Ont. L0P 1A0, Canada.
Telephone: 363-3074.

Solano López, Miguel; Paraguayan diplomatist; b. 16 May 1911.
Director-Gen. of Culture, Paraguay 44-45; Dir. Dept. of Organizations and Treaties, Ministry of Foreign Affairs 54; mem. Paraguayan Dels. to UN Gen. Assembly 55-; Rep. of Paraguay to UN Trusteeship Council 59-61; Alt. Rep. to UN 57-65, Perm. Rep. to UN 65-73; Amb. to U.S.A. 73-.
Embassy of Paraguay, 2400 Massachusetts Avenue, N.W., Washington, D.C. 20008, U.S.A.

Solberg, Halvor Skappel, DR. PHIL.; Norwegian meteorologist; b. 5 Feb. 1895; ed. Univ. of Oslo.
Meteorologist in Norwegian Meteorological Service 18; Lecturer in Applied Mathematics, Univ. of Oslo 22, Prof. of Theoretical Meteorology 30-64; Dean Faculty of Science 42-46; Pres. Norwegian Cttee. of Geodesy and Geophysics 46-58; Norwegian Cttee. of Mechanics 50-55, Norwegian Cttee. of Int. Geophysical Year, Norwegian Cttee. of Computing Machinery; mem. Int. Council of Scientific Unions 46-49, Vice-Pres. 49-55; mem. Norwegian Acad. of Sciences and Letters (Gen. Sec. 46-53), Royal Danish Soc. of Sciences; Hon. mem. American Meteorological Soc., Polish Meteorological and Hydrological Soc.
Publ. *Hydrodynamique physique* 33.
Jonas Reinsgate 6, Oslo 3, Norway.
[*Deceased.*]

Soldati, Mario, D.LITT.; Italian writer, film director and actor; b. 17 Nov. 1906; ed. Turin and Columbia Univs.

Former corresp. of *Il Lavoro*; essays on art, articles in various papers and magazines, column in *Il Giorno*, Milan; films include *Piccolo mondo antico, Eugenia Grandet, Malombra, La Provinciale, La Donna del Fiume, La Mano dello Straniero, Policarpo*; TV appearances.
Publs. include *America Primo Amore, Racconti, A Cena col Commendatore, Lettere da Capri, La Messa dei Villeggianti, Il Vero Silvestri, La Confessione, Storie di Spettri, La Busta Arancione, Le due Città* 64, *L'Attore* 70, *The Malacca Cane* 71.
c/o Arnoldo Mondadori Editore, Via Bianca di Savoia 20; Home: Via Cappuccio 14, 20123 Milan, Italy.

Soldatov, Aleksandr Alekseyevich; Soviet diplomatist; b. 27 Aug. 1915, Prigorody, Vologda Region; ed. Liebkneht Pedagogical Inst., Moscow.
Formerly Counsellor, Canberra, Senior Political Adviser to Soviet Del. to UN, Rep. to UN Trusteeship Council; mem. del. to UN 52-55; Dir. American Dept. Ministry of Foreign Affairs 55-60; Dep. Del. Geneva Foreign Ministers Conf. 59; Ambassador to United Kingdom 60-66; Deputy Minister of Foreign Affairs 66-68; Amb. to Cuba 68-70; mem. C.P.S.U. Central Auditing Comm. 66-71; Rector, Inst. of Int. Relations 71-.
Moscow State Institute of International Relations, 53 Metrostroevskaya ulitsa, Moscow, U.S.S.R.

Soldevila Zubiburu, Ferran; Spanish writer; b. 24 Oct. 1894, Barcelona; s. of Charles M. Soldevila and Mercè Zubiburu; m. Helène Yvonne Lepage 1924; one s.; ed. Univs. of Barcelona and Madrid.
Secretary-Editor Historical Section Institut d'Estudis Catalans 14-20; mem. Archives, Libraries and Museums 22-38, and 54-64; Lecturer in Spanish Liverpool Univ. 26-28; Prof. of Catalan History at School of Librarianship, Barcelona 29-38, at Univ. of Barcelona 31-38, and at Estudis Universitaris Catalans 43-; mem. Inst. d'Estudis Catalans; mem. Acad. de Buenas Letras, Centro Int. di Studi Sardi, etc.; Archiviste de la Corona de Aragon; Premi Patxot, Premi de l'Escola Catalana d'Art Dramatic; Dr. h.c. (Montpellier Univ.).
Publs. *Pere II el Gran: el desafiament amb Carles d'Anjou* 19, *Historia de Catalunya* (in collab. with F. Valls-Taberner) 22-23 (2nd edn. 69), *La Reina Maria, Muller del Magnanim* 28, *Historia de Catalunya* (3 vols.) 34-35 (2nd edn. 62-63), *Barcelona sense Universitat 1714-1836* 38, *Pere el Gran* (4 vols.) 49-, *Els almogàvers* 52, *L'almirall Ramon Marquet* 53, *Jaume I i Pere el Gran* 55, *Ramon Berenguer IV* 55, *Resum d'Historia de Catalunya* 56, *Historia de España* (8 vols.) 52-57 (2nd edn. 61-64), *Vida de Jaume I el Conqueridor* 58, *Un Segle de Vida Catalana 1814-1930* (2 vols.; editor and part author), *Vida de Pere el Gran i Alfons el Liberal* 63, *Què Cal Saber de Catalunya* 68; Belles-Lettres: *Poema de l'Amor Perdut, Exili, Càntics, La Ruta Invisible, Hores Angleses, Matilde d'Anglaterra, Guifré, l'Hostal de l'Amor, Albert i Francina, Don Joan, L'Aprenent de Suicida, L'Amador de la Gentilesa.*
Teodora Lamadrid 34, Barcelona, Spain.
[*Deceased.*]

Solh, Rashid; Lebanese lawyer and politician; b. 1926, Beirut; ed. Coll. des Frères des Ecoles Chrétiennes, Coll. Al Makassed, Faculty of Law, Beirut.
Successively Judge, Pres. of the Labour Arbitration Council, Examining Magistrate, Attorney-Gen. of the Charéi Tribunal; Independent mem. Parl. for Beirut 64, 72; Prime Minister Oct. 74-May 75.
Chambre des Députés, Place de l'Etoile, Beirut, Lebanon.

Solh, Takieddine; Lebanese politician and diplomatist; b. 1909; ed. American Univ. of Beirut, and Univ. Saint Joseph, Beirut.
Former Civil Servant; fmr. Counsellor, Embassy to United Arab Republic, and to the Arab League; mem.

of Parl. 57, 64-; Pres. Foreign Affairs Comm. 64-; Minister of the Interior 64-65; Prime Minister, Minister of Finance 73-74; Pres. L'Appel Nat. Party (*Al Nida'a El Quaoumi*).

rue de Damas, Beirut, Lebanon.

Solis Ruiz, José; Spanish politician and trade unionist; b. 1913.

Barrister and military lawyer; fmr. mem. Falange labour and trade union organizations, organized First Nat. Congress of Workers 46; fmr. Civil Gov., Pontevedra and Guipuzcoa; Nat. Delegate of Syndicates 51-57; Minister and Sec.-Gen. of Falange 57-69, Minister of Labour Dec. 75-.

Alcalá 44, Madrid, Spain.

Sölle, Horst; German politician; b. 3 June 1924; ed. Karl Marx Univ., Leipzig.

Official, Ministry of Transport of D.D.R.; later mem. staff Central Cttee. of Socialist Unity Party (S.E.D.); later Sec. of State, Ministry of Foreign and Inter-German Trade of D.D.R.; now Minister of Foreign Trade, D.D.R.; Medal of Merit of D.D.R.; Patriotic Order of Merit in Gold, Order Banner of Labour.

Ministerium für Aussenwirtschaft, 108 Berlin, Unter den Linden 46/60, German Democratic Republic.

Sollero, Lauro; Brazilian pharmacologist; b. 23 Jan. 1916; ed. Ginásio Raul Soares, Ubá, Minas Gerais, and Universidade do Brasil.

Professor in Dept. of Pharmacology, School of Medicine and Surgery, Rio de Janeiro 53-, Faculty of Medicine, Univ. of Brazil 63-; Fellow, Guggenheim Foundation, Rockefeller Foundation.

Publs. include: *Curarização, Orgão elétrico do Electrophorus electricus, Serotonina, Bloqueadores A-drenérgicos.*

Laboratório de Farmacologia, Faculdade Nacional de Medicina, Avda. Pasteur 458, Rio de Janeiro, Brazil.

Solodovnikov, Aleksandr Vasiliyevich; Soviet theatrical director and journalist; b. 14 Aug. 1904; ed. Moscow Inst. of Literature, Philosophy and History.

Designer in shoe factory 24-30; editor of local paper 30-34; student 34-37; on staff of *Pravda* 37-38; Deputy Chair. Art Cttee. U.S.S.R. Council of Ministers 38-45; with Tass Agency 45-48; Dir. Bolshoi Theatre Moscow 48-51; Deputy Editor *Sovietskaya Kultura* 51-54; with Ministry of Culture 54-55; Dir. Moscow Arts Theatre 55-63; Adviser to Ministry of Culture 63-67; Dir. Malyi Theatre 67-; mem. Collegium, Ministry of Culture; mem. C.P.S.U.; Order of the Red Banner of Labour; three medals.

Malyi State Academic Theatre, 1/6 Ploshchad Sverdlova, Moscow, U.S.S.R.

Solomentsev, Mikhail Sergeyevich; Soviet politician; b. 1913; ed. Leningrad Polytechnic Inst.

Member C.P.S.U. 40-; Engineer, Workshop Foreman, Chief Engineer, Factory Dir., Lipetsk and Chelyabinsk Regions 40-54; Sec., later Second Sec. Chelyabinsk Regional Cttee. of C.P.S.U. 54-57; Chair. Chelyabinsk Nat. Econ. Council 57-59; First Sec. Karaganda Regional Cttee., C.P. of Kazakhstan 59-64; First Sec. Rostov District Cttee. of C.P.S.U. 64-66; Sec. C.P.S.U. Central Cttee. 66-67; Head of Dept. of Heavy Industry, C.P.S.U. Central Cttee. 67-71; Chair. Council of Ministers of R.S.F.S.R. July 71-; mem. Central Cttee. of C.P.S.U. 61-; alt. mem. Politburo 71-; Deputy to U.S.S.R. Supreme Soviet 58-.

R.S.F.S.R. Council of Ministers, 3 Delegatskaya ulitsa, Moscow, U.S.S.R.

Solomon, Arthur Kaskel, PH.D., D.PHIL., SC.D.; American professor of biophysics; b. 26 Nov. 1912, Pittsburgh, Pa.; s. of Mark K. Solomon and Hortense Nattans; m. Mariot Fraser Mathews 1972; one s. one d. from previous m.; ed. Univs. of Princeton, Harvard and Cambridge.

Research Fellow, Cavendish Lab., Cambridge 37-39;

Research Assoc., Physics and Chem., Harvard Univ. 39-41; Research Fellow, Biological Chem., Harvard Medical School 40-42, Asst. Prof. Physiological Chem. 46-56, Assoc. Prof. Biophysics 57-68, Prof. 68-; Chair. Comm. on Higher Degrees in Biophysics, Harvard 59-; Fellow, American Acad. of Arts and Sciences; Sec.-Gen. Int. Union for Pure and Applied Biophysics 61-72; mem. Exec. Cttee., Int. Council of Scientific Unions 66-72; mem. U. S. Nat. Comm. for UNESCO 69-74, Science Policy Adviser to Thai Govt. 69-72; mem. Editorial Board *Journal of General Physiology*; Pres. Read's Inc.; Trustee, Inst. of Contemporary Art; Order Andrés Bello, Venezuela 74.

Leisure interests: art, travel.

Publs. *Why Smash Atoms* 40, and over two hundred scientific articles.

Biophysical Laboratory, Harvard Medical School, 25 Shattuck Street, Boston, Mass.; Home: 27 Craigie Street, Cambridge, Mass., U.S.A.

Telephone: 617-566-3057 (Office); 617-876-0149 (Home).

Solomon, Ezra, PH.D.; American professor of finance and government official; b. 20 March 1920, Rangoon, Burma; m. Janet Cameron 1950; three d.; ed. Univs. of Rangoon and Chicago.

Faculty Member, Univ. of Chicago 48-60; Prof. of Finance and Dir., Int. Center for Advancement of Management Educ., Stanford Univ. 61-65; Dean Witter Prof. of Finance, Stanford Univ. 65-71; mem. Council of Econ. Advisers to Pres. Nixon 71-73 (resigned).

Publs. *The Management of Corporate Capital* 60, *Metropolitan Chicago—An Economic Analysis* 60, *The Theory of Financial Management* 63, *Money and Banking* (5th edn.) 68, *Wall Street in Transition* 74, *The Anxious Economy* 75.

775 Santa Ynez, Stanford, Calif. 94305, U.S.A.

Solomon, Patrick Vincent Joseph; Trinidadian diplomat, politician and physician; b. 12 April 1910; ed. St. Mary's Coll., Trinidad, Queen's Univ., Belfast.

Practised medicine in Scotland, Ireland, Wales, Leeward Islands and Trinidad 34-43; mem. Legislative Council, Trinidad 46-50, 56-61; Deputy Pol. Leader, People's Nat. Movement 56-66; Minister of Educ. and Culture 56-60; Minister of Home Affairs 60-64; Deputy Prime Minister 62-66; Minister of Foreign Affairs 64-66; Perm. Rep. of Trinidad and Tobago to UN 66-71, Vice-Pres. Gen. Assembly 66, Chair. Fourth Cttee. of Gen. Assembly 68, Vice-Chair. Sea-Bed Cttee. 71-; High Commr. to U.K. and Amb. to Norway, Finland, Denmark, Switzerland, Fed. Repub. of Germany, France, Netherlands, Italy, Luxembourg 71-73, EEC and Belgium 71-73; Pres. of Assembly, IMCO 76-.

c/o IMCO, 101-104 Piccadilly, London, W1V 0AE, England.

Solomon, Richard L., A.B., M.SC., PH.D.; American professor of psychology; b. 2 Oct. 1918; s. of Frank Solomon and Rose Roud; divorced; two d.; ed. Brown Univ.

Instructor, Brown Univ. until 47; Prof. Harvard Univ. until 60; Prof. Psychology, Univ. of Pennsylvania 60-; American Acad. of Arts and Sciences; Nat. Acad. of Sciences.

Leisure interests: hiking, mountaineering, summer camp counselling.

3815 Walnut Street, Philadelphia, Pa. 19104, U.S.A.

Soloukhin, Vladimir Alexeyevich; Soviet writer; b. 14 June 1924, Alepino Stavrovsky; ed. Gorky Inst. of Literature.

Order of Red Banner of Labour, Badge of Honour.

Publs. (first publs. 45): verse: *Rain in the Steppes* 53, *Saxifrage, Streamlets on the Asphalt* 59, *Tale of the Steppes* 60, *How to Drink the Sun* 61, *Postcards from Viet-Nam* 62; novels: *Birth of Zernograd* 55, *The Goldmine* 56, *Beyond the Blue Seas* 57, *Country Roads of Vladimir*

(lyrical diary) 58, *The Drop of Dew* 63, *A Lyrical Story* 64, *Mother—Stepmother*; short stories: *The Loaf of Bread* 65, *White Grass* 71; poetry: *Don't seek shelter from the rain* 67.
Union of U.S.S.R. Writers, 52 Ulitsa Vorovskogo, Moscow, U.S.S.R.

Solovyov, Yury Vladimirovich; Soviet ballet dancer; b. 1940; ed. Leningrad School of Ballet.
Joined Kirov State Theatre of Opera and Ballet 58; Honoured Artist of the R.S.F.S.R.
Principal roles include: Prince Désiré (*Sleeping Beauty*), Siegfried (*Swan Lake*), Frondoso (*Laurencia*), The Poet (*Chopiniana*), Andrei (*Taras Bulba*), Danila (*Stone Flower*), Farkhad (*Legend of Love*), Prince (*Nutcracker*), Albert (*Giselle*), Prince Charming (*Cinderella*).
Kirov State Academic Theatre of Opera and Ballet, 1 Ploshchad Iskusstv, Leningrad, U.S.S.R.

Solovyov-Sedoy, Vasily Pavlovich; Soviet composer; b. 25 April 1907, Leningrad; ed. Central School of Music and Leningrad Conservatoire.
Honoured Worker of Arts of the R.S.F.S.R. 56, People's Artist of the R.S.F.S.R. 57, of the U.S.S.R. 67; Sec. R.S.F.S.R. Union of Composers.
Principal compositions: *Taras Bulba* (ballet) 40, revised 45, *True Friend* (operetta) 45, *The Russian Enters Port* (ballet) 62; and many songs, including *Moscow Nights*.
Leningrad Branch of R.S.F.S.R. Composers' Union, 45 Ulitsa Herzena, Leningrad, U.S.S.R.

Solow, Robert Merton, PH.D.; American economist; b. 23 Aug. 1924, Brooklyn, N.Y.; s. of Milton and Hannah Solow; m. Barbara Lewis 1945; two s. one d.; ed. Harvard Univ.
Assistant Prof. of Statistics, Massachusetts Inst. of Technology 49-53, Assoc. Prof. of Economics 54-57, Prof. of Economics 58-73, Inst. Prof. 73-; Senior Economist, Council of Economic Advisers 61-62; Marshall Lecturer, Cambridge Univ. 63-64; De Vries Lecturer, Rotterdam 63, Wicksell Lecturer, Stockholm 64; Eastman Visiting Prof., Oxford Univ. 68-69; mem. Nat. Comm. on Technology, Automation and Econ. Progress 64-65, Presidential Comm. on Income Maintenance 68-69; mem. Board of Dirs. Fed. Reserve Bank of Boston 75-; Fellow, Center for Advanced Study in Behavioral Sciences 57-58; Vice-Pres. American Econ. Asscn. 68, American Asscn. for Advancement of Science 70; Pres. Econometric Soc. 64; mem. American Acad. of Arts and Sciences, Nat. Acad. of Sciences; corresp. mem. British Acad.; David A. Wells Prize, Harvard Univ. 51, John Bates Clark Medal, American Econ. Asscn. 61; Hon. LL.D. (Univ. of Chicago) 67, (Brown Univ.) 72, Hon. Litt.D. (Williams Coll.) 74, Dr. h.c. (Paris) 75, Hon. D.Litt. (Univ. of Warwick) 76.
Leisure interest: dinghy sailing.
Publs. *Linear Programming and Economic Analysis* 58, *Capital Theory and the Rate of Return* 63, *Sources of Unemployment in the United States* 64, *Price Expectations and the Behavior of the Price Level* 70, *Growth Theory: An Exposition* 70.
Department of Economics, Massachusetts Institute of Technology, Cambridge, Mass.; Home: 528 Lewis Wharf, Boston, Mass., U.S.A.
Telephone: 617-253-5268; 617-227-4436.

Solti, Sir Georg, K.B.E.; British (naturalized) musician; b. 21 Oct. 1912, Budapest; s. of Mor Stern Solti and Teresa Rosenbaum; m. 1st Hedwig Oeschli 1946; m. 2nd Anne Valerie Pitts 1967; two d.; ed. High School of Music, Budapest, and studied with Zoltan Kodaly, Bela Bartok and Ernst von Dohnanyi.
General Music Dir., Munich State Opera 46-52; Gen. Music Dir., Frankfurt Opera, Permanent Conductor of Museum Concerts 52-61; Music Dir., Royal Opera House, Covent Garden 61-71, Guest Conductor 71-; Music Dir. Chicago Symphony Orchestra 68-, Orchestre

de Paris 72-75; has also appeared as Guest Conductor in Europe with Berlin and Vienna Philharmonic Orchestras, Vienna Symphony Orchestra, Orchestre Nationale and Conservatoire Orchestra, Paris, at Salzburg Festival, with London Philharmonic Orchestra, London Symphony Orchestra, at Edinburgh Festival, at Glyndebourne Festival, at Covent Garden; has appeared in U.S.A. with San Francisco Opera, Philadelphia Orchestra, New York Philharmonic Orchestra, Chicago Lyric Opera, Los Angeles Symphony Orchestra, Chicago Symphony Orchestra, and at Metropolitan Opera; First Prize as a pianist, Concours International, Geneva 42; Grand Prix du Disque 59, awarded 8 times; and numerous other record awards; Hon. C.B.E. 68, Hon. K.B.E. 71; Hon. D.Mus. (Univs. of Leeds, Oxford and Yale); Commdr. Légion d'Honneur (France) 74.
Chalet Haut Pré, Villars-sur-Ollons, Vaud, Switzerland.

Solvay, Jaques Ernest; Belgian business executive; b. 4 Dec. 1920, Ixelles; s. of Ernest-John Solvay and Marie Graux; m. Marie-Claude Boulin 1949; one s. three d.; ed. Univ. of Brussels.
Joined Solvay Cie. 50, mem. Board 55, Chair. of Board June 71-; Dir. Société Générale de Banque 65-, Allied Chemical 66-; Pres. Fédération des Industries Chimiques de Belgique; Pres. Belgo-British Union; Chevalier de l'Ordre de Léopold; Hon. C.B.E.
Leisure interest: orchid growing.
Solvay Cie. S.A., rue de Prince Albert 33, B-1050 Brussels; Home: Le Long Fonds, B-1310 La Hulpe, Belgium.

Sølvhøj, Hans, M.A.; Danish politician and radio administrator; b. 11 July 1919, Copenhagen; s. of Johannes Sølvhøj and Dagmar Elizabeth Sølvhøj; m. Ruth Finsen 1952; one s.; ed. Elsinore Public School, Univ. of Copenhagen.
Teacher at Elsinore Public School 45-47; Producer, Radio Denmark 47, Dir., Talks and Current Affairs Dept. 53-61, Dir.-Gen. 61-64; Sec. of State for Cultural Affairs 64-66, Joint Minister of State for Foreign Affairs 66-68; Dir.-Gen. Danish Radio 68-; Pres. Danish-German Soc.; Commdr., Danish Order of Dannebrog.
Leisure interests: tennis, gardening, reading.
Rødehns, Mødrup, Espergaerde, Denmark.
Telephone: 03232115.

Solzhenitsyn, Aleksandr Isayevich; Soviet writer; b. 11 Dec. 1918, Rostov-on-Don; m. 1st Natalya Reshetovskaya (separated 1970), 2nd Natalya Svetlova; three s.; ed. Rostov Univ. and Correspondence Course in Literature, Moscow Univ.
Joined Army 41, attended artillery school, commissioned 42, served at front as Commdr. of Artillery Battery, and twice decorated for bravery; sentenced to eight years in a forced labour camp 45-53; contracted, later cured of cancer; in exile in Siberia 53-57; officially rehabilitated 57; taught mathematics at secondary school, Ryazan; expelled from Writers' Union of U.S.S.R. Nov. 69; mem. American Acad. of Arts and Sciences 69-; expelled from U.S.S.R. Feb. 74; Prix du Meilleur Livre Etranger (France) for *The First Circle* and *Cancer Ward* 69; Nobel Prize for Literature 70; Hon. U.S. Citizen 74; Hon. Fellow, Hoover Inst. 75.
Publs. *One Day in the Life of Ivan Denisovich* 62 (film 71), *Matryona's Home* (short story), *For the Good of the Cause* (short story), *The First Circle* (publ. U.S.A. and U.K. 68), *Cancer Ward* (U.S.A. and U.K. 68), *The Easter Procession* (short story), *The Love Girl and the Innocent* (play, U.K.) 69, *In the Interests of the Cause* 70, *Stories and Prose Poems* 71, *August 1914* 71, *The Gulag Archipelago* Vol. I 73, Vol. II 74, Vol. III 76, *Letter to Soviet Leaders* 74, *Candle in the Wind* (play), *When the Calf Horns the Oak* revised edn. 75, *Lenin in Zürich* 75.
Stapferstrasse 45, 8033 Zürich, Switzerland.

Somare, Michael Thomas; Papua New Guinea politician; b. 9 April 1936; ed. Sogeri Secondary School, Admin. Coll.

Teacher various schools 56-62; Asst. Area Educ. Officer, Madang 62-63; Broadcasts Officer, Dept. of Information and Extension Services, Wewak 63-66, Journalist 66-68; mem. House of Assembly for East Sepik Regional 68-; Parl. Leader Pangu Party 68-; Deputy Chair. Exec. Council 72-73, Chair. 73-; Chief Minister Papua New Guinea 72-75, Prime Minister Sept. 75-; Chair. Board of Trustees, P.N.G.; mem. Second Select Cttee. on Constitutional Devt. 68-72, Australian Broadcasting Comm. Advisory Cttee.

Office of the Prime Minister, P.O. Box 2501, Konedobu; Home: Karan, Murik Lakes, East Sepik, Papua New Guinea.

Telephone: 44501 (Office).

Sommaruga, Cornelio, LL.D.; Swiss diplomatist; b. 29 Dec. 1932, Rome, Italy; s. of Carlo Sommaruga and Anna-Maria Valagussa; m. Ornella Marzorati 1957; two s. four d.; ed. Rome, Paris, Univ. of Zürich.

Bank trainee, Zürich 57-59; joined Diplomatic Service 60; Attaché, Swiss Embassy, The Hague 61; Sec. Swiss Embassy, Bonn 62-64, Rome 65-68; Deputy Head of Del. to EFTA, GATT and UNCTAD, Geneva 69-73; Asst. Sec.-Gen. EFTA July 73-75.

Publs. *La posizione costituzionale del Capo dello Stato nelle Costituzioni francese ed italiana del dopoguerra* 57, and numerous articles in journals and periodicals.

Office of the Assistant Secretary-General, European Free Trade Association, 9-11 rue de Varembé, 1211 Geneva 20; Home: 7 Chemin A. Bétems, 1218 Grand-Saconnex, Switzerland.

Telephone: 34-90-00 (Office); 34-91-42 (Home).

Sommer, Charles H., B.S.; American chemical executive; b. 24 Sept. 1910, St. Louis, Mo.; s. of Charles H. Sommer and Mary Duella Steele Sommer; m. Jane S. Scudder 1940; one s.; ed. Univs. of Mich. and Ariz.

Joined Monsanto Co. 34, Man. Plasticizer and Intermediate Sales 39-51, Gen. Man., Merrimac Div. 51-54, Gen. Man. and Vice-Pres. Organic Chemicals Div. 54-59, mem. Exec. Cttee. 59-, Dir. 59-, Exec. Vice-Pres. 59-60, Pres. 60-68, Chair. Board of Dirs. 68-; Trustee St. Louis Univ. 69-; mem. Board of Dirs. Trans World Airlines, St. Louis Union Trust Co.; mem. Business Council, American Chemical Soc., American Inst. of Chemical Engineers; Vice-Pres. and mem. Exec. Board Boy Scouts of America St. Louis Area Council; mem. emer. Civic Progress Inc.

Monsanto Company, P.O.B. 526, St. Louis, Mo. 63166, U.S.A.

Telephone: 314-694-3013.

Sommer, Theo, DR.PHIL.; German journalist; b. 10 June 1930, Constance; s. of Theo and Else Sommer; m. Elda Tsilenis 1952; four s.; ed. Schwäbisch-Gmünd, Tübingen, Chicago and Harvard Univs.

Local Editor, Schwäbisch-Gmünd 52-54; Political Editor *Die Zeit* 58, Deputy Editor-in-Chief 68, Editor-in-Chief 73-; Lecturer in Int. Relations, Univ. of Hamburg 67-70; Head of Planning Staff, Ministry of Defence 69-70; mem. Deutsche Gesellschaft für Auswärtige Politik, mem. Council Int. Inst. for Strategic Studies; Contrib. Editor *Newsweek*; Commentator German TV, Radio; Theodor-Wolf-Preis 66.

Publs. *Deutschland und Japan zwischen den Mächten 1935-40, Vom Antikominternpakt zum Dreimächtepakt* 62, *Reise in ein fernes Land* 64, Editor *Denken an Deutschland* 66, Editor *Schweden-Report* 74.

Die Zeit, Pressehaus, Speersort, Hamburg 1; Home: Zabelweg 17, Hamburg 67, Federal Republic of Germany.

Telephone: 32-80-210 (Office); 603-73-00 (Home).

Sommerfelt, Søren Christian; Norwegian diplomatist; b. 9 May 1916, Oslo; s. of Søren Christian Sommerfelt and Sigrid Nicolaysen; m. Frances Bull Ely 1947; one d.; ed. Oslo Economic High School and Oslo Univ.

Entered Norwegian Foreign Service 41; UN Secr. Div. for Refugees and Displaced Persons 46-48; First Sec., Copenhagen 48-50; Counsellor, Norwegian Perm. Del. to NATO 51-52; Deputy Head, Politico-Econ. Dept., Norwegian Ministry of Foreign Affairs 53-56, Head 56-60; Amb., Head, Norwegian Perm. Del. to EFTA, European Office of UN and other int. orgs. at Geneva 60-68, to Fed. Repub. of Germany 68-73, to U.S.A. 73-; leader numerous trade dels., leader Norwegian del. to negotiations establishing EFTA 59; Chair. EFTA Perm. Council 62, 66; Chair. GATT Perm. Council 63-64, leader Norwegian del. to GATT Tariff negotiations (Kennedy Round) 64-67; Chair. GATT Contracting Parties 68; Norwegian Rep. CERN Council 60-68; Chair. Norwegian Del. in negotiations with EEC 70-72; Order of St. Olav (Norway), Grosses Verdienstkreuz (Fed. Repub. of Germany), North Star (Sweden), Dannebrog (Denmark), Falcon (Iceland), Leopold II (Belgium), Ethiopian Star.

Leisure interests: Skiing, tennis, shooting.

Royal Norwegian Embassy, 3401 Massachusetts Avenue, N.W., Washington, D.C., U.S.A.

Somoza Debayle, General Anastasio; Nicaraguan army officer and politician; b. 5 Dec. 1925, León; s. of late Gen. Anastasio Somoza García (Pres. of Nicaragua) and Salvadora Debayle Sacasa; brother of late Col. Luis Somoza Debayle (Pres. of Nicaragua 56-63); m. Hope Portocarrero Debayle; three s. two d.; ed. Inst. Pedagógico de Managua, La Salle Military Acad., New York, and U.S. Military Acad., West Point.

Entered Guardia Nacional (Nicaraguan Army) 41, rose progressively to Gen. of Div. 41-64; Head of Nat. Guard; Special envoy of Nicaragua on several Diplomatic Missions; Chair. Board Nicaragua Merchant Marine; Pres. Board LANICA Airlines; Pres. several commercial enterprises (cotton textiles, cement, real estate, etc.); Pres. of Nicaragua 67-72; Chair. Nat. Emergency Cttee. 73-74; Pres. of Nicaragua Dec. 74-; several Nicaraguan and foreign decorations.

Leisure interests: the army, aviation, sports.

c/o Residencia de El Retiro, Managua, Nicaragua.

Son Sann; Cambodian financial administrator; b. 1911, Phnom-Penh; m. Nema Machhwa 1940; five s. two d.; ed. Ecole des Hautes Etudes Commerciales de Paris.

Deputy Gov. Provinces of Battambang and Prey-Veng 35-39; Head of Yuvan Kampuchearath (Youth Movement); Minister of Finance 46-47; Vice-Pres. Council of Ministers 49; Minister of Foreign Affairs 50; Mem. of Parl. for Phnom-Penh and Pres. Cambodian Nat. Assembly 51-52; Gov. of Nat. Bank of Cambodia 54-68; Minister of State (Finance and Nat. Economy) 61-62; Vice-Pres., in charge of Economy, Finance and Planning 65-67, Pres. Council of Ministers May-Dec. 67; First Vice-Pres. in charge of Econ. and Financial Affairs 68; Grand Croix de l'Ordre Royal du Cambodge, Séna yayasedth, Commdr. du Sowathara (Mérite économique), Grand Officier Légion d'Honneur, Commdr. du Monisaraphon, Médaille d'or du Règne, Grand Officier du Million d'Eléphants (Laos).

Leisure interest: Buddhist books.

Sondheim, Stephen Joshua; American song writer; b. 22 March 1930, New York City; s. of Janet Fox and Herbert Sondheim; ed. George School, Newtown, Pa., Williams Coll., Williamstown, Mass., private instruction.

President, Dramatists' Guild 73; Antoinette Perry Award for *Company* 71, *Follies* 72, *A Little Night Music* 73; Drama Critics Award 71, 72, 73; television: *Topper* (co-author) 53, *Evening Primrose* (music and lyrics) 67; lyrics: *West Side Story* 57, *Gypsy* 59, *Do I Hear a Waltz?* 65, *Candide* 74; music and lyrics: *A Funny Thing*

Happened on the Way to the Forum 62, *Anyone Can Whistle* 64, *Company* 70, *Follies* 71, *A Little Night Music* 73, *The Frogs* 74, *Pacific Overtures* 76; screenplay: (with Anthony Perkins) *The Last of Sheila* 73; film score: *Stavisky* 75.

c/o Flora Roberts, 65 East 55th Street, Suite 702, New York, N.Y. 10022, U.S.A.

Sondheimer, Franz, M.A., PH.D., F.R.S.; British professor of organic chemistry; b. 17 May 1926, Stuttgart, Germany; s. of Max and Ida Sondheimer; m. Betty J. Moss 1958; one step d. (deceased); ed. Highgate School, Imperial Coll. of Science, London, and Harvard Univ.
Associate Dir. of Chemical Research, Syntex S.A., Mexico City 52-56, Vice-Pres. of Research 61-63; Head of Organic Chem. Dept., Weizmann Inst. of Science 56-64, Rebecca and Israel Sieff Prof. of Organic Chem. 60-64; Royal Society Research Prof., Univ. of Cambridge and Fellow Churchill Coll. 64-67; Royal Soc. Research Prof., Univ. Coll., London 67-; Israel Prize in the Exact Sciences 60, Corday-Morgan Medal and Prize, Chem. Soc. 61, Adolf-von-Bayer Denkmünze, Gesellschaft Deutscher Chemiker 65, Synthetic Organic Chem. Award, Chem. Soc. 73, A.C.S. Award for Creative Work in Synthetic Organic Chem. 75.
Leisure interests: collecting old chemical books, music, travel.
Publs. Scientific papers in chemical journals.
Chemistry Department, University College London, Gordon Street, London, W.C.1; Home: 43 Green Street, London, W1Y 3FJ, England.
Telephone: 01-387-7050 (Office); 01-629-2816 (Home).

Song Yo Chan, Gen.; Korean army officer and politician; b. 1919.
Former Commander 1st Field Army and Army Chief of Staff; Martial Law Commdr. April 60; Minister of Defence June-July 61; Prime Minister July 61-62, Minister of Foreign Affairs Aug.-Oct. 61; Chair. of Econ. Planning Board 62; Pres. Inchon Iron and Steel Co., Ltd. 70-.
14-5 Songbuk-tong, Songbuk-ku, Seoul, Republic of Korea.

Sonne, Karl-Heinz, DR. ECON.; German business executive; b. 3 June 1915; ed. Wirtschaftshochschule Berlin.
Member of Management Board Concordia Electrizitäts A.G., Dortmund 48-56, Chair. of Management Board 56-62; Chair. of Management Bd. Bayerische Motoren Werke A.G. Munich 62-65; Chair. Management Board Klöckner-Humboldt-Deutz A.G. 65-.
4600 Dortmund-Lücklemburg, Heideblick 70, Federal Republic of Germany.

Sonneborn, Tracy M., A.B., PH.D.; American zoologist; b. 19 Oct. 1905, Baltimore, Md.; s. of Lee and Daisy (Bamberger) Sonneborn; m. Ruth Meyers 1929; two s.; ed. Johns Hopkins Univ.
Fellow of Nat. Research Council, Johns Hopkins Univ. 28-30, Research Asst. 30-31, Research Assoc. 31-33, Assoc. in Zoology 33-39; Assoc. Prof. of Zoology, Indiana Univ. 39-43; Prof. of Zoology, Indiana Univ. 43-53, Distinguished Service Prof. 53-, Chair. Div. of Biological Sciences 63-64; mem. Editorial Board *Journal of Experimental Zoology* 48-60, *Genetics* 47-62, *Journal of Morphology* 46-49, *Annual Review of Microbiology* 54-58, *Physiological Zoology* 48-60, *Cytologia, Experimental Cell Research* 53-63; Treas. American Soc. of Naturalists 45-47, Vice-Pres. 48, Pres. 49; Vice-Pres. Genetics Soc. of America 48-, Pres. 49; Pres. American Soc. of Zoologists 56; Vice-Pres. Soc. for Study of Evolution 58; Pres. American Inst. of Biological Science 61; hon. mem. Faculty of Biology and Medical Science, Univ. of Chile, Visiting Prof. 51; mem. Exec. Cttee. American Soc. of Cell Biology 63-65, Council Nat. Acad. of Sciences 63-66; Foreign mem. Royal Soc. 64; Hon. D.Sc. (Johns Hopkins Univ.) 57, (Univ. of

Geneva) 75, (Northwestern Univ.) 75; co-winner of Annual $1,000 Prize for Research, A.A.A.S. 46; co-winner of Newcomb-Cleveland Prize; Kimber Genetics Award of the Nat. Acad. of Sciences 59; Mendel Centennial Medal, Czechoslovak Acad. of Sciences 65.
Publs. Over 200 papers and abstracts, chiefly on genetics of paramecium.
Office: Department of Zoology, 220 Jordan Hall, Indiana University, Bloomington, Ind. 47401; Home: 1305 Maxwell Lane, Bloomington, Ind. 47401, U.S.A.
Telephone: 812-336-5796 (Home).

Sonnenfeldt, Helmut, M.A.; American government official; b. 13 Sept. 1926, Berlin, Germany; s. of Dr. Walther H. Sonnenfeldt and Dr. Gertrud L. Sonnenfeldt; m. Marjorie Hecht 1953; two s. one d.; ed. Univ. of Manchester, Johns Hopkins Univ.
Went to U.S.A. 44; mem. Counterintelligence Corps, U.S. Army, Pacific and European Theaters; with Dept. of State 52-69, Policy Officer, U.S. Disarmament Admin. 60-61, Director Office of Research and Analysis for the U.S.S.R. and E. Europe 66-69; Senior Staff mem. for Europe and East-West Relations, Nat. Security Council 69-74; Counsellor of Dept. of State Jan. 74-; Lecturer on Soviet Affairs, Johns Hopkins Univ. School of Advanced Int. Studies; Consultant Washington Center for Foreign Policy Research; Senior Fellow, Russian Inst., Columbia Univ.; mem. Int. Inst. of Strategic Studies, London, Council of Foreign Relations; govt. rep. to numerous confs. and meetings abroad.
Department of State, Washington, D.C. 20520; Home: 4105 Thornapple Street, Chevy Chase, Md. 20015, U.S.A.
Telephone: (202) 632-4404 (Office); (301) 656-6731 (Home).

Soper, Baron (Life Peer), cr. 65, of Kingsway; **Rev. Donald O. Soper,** M.A., PH.D.; British Methodist minister; b. 31 Jan. 1903, London; s. of Ernest Frankham Soper and Caroline Amelia Pilcher; m. Marie Gertrude Dean 1929; four d.; ed. St. Catharine's Coll., Cambridge, Wesley House, Cambridge, and London Univ.
Minister to the South London Mission 26-29, to the Central London Mission 29-36; Superintendent of the West London Mission 36-; Pres. of the Methodist Conf. 53; Alderman, L.C.C. 58-65; Chair. Shelter 74-; Hon. Fellow, St. Catharine's Coll., Cambridge 66.
Leisure interests: music, most games.
Publs. *Christ and Tower Hill, Question Time on Tower Hill, Answer Time on Tower Hill, Christianity and its Critics, Popular Fallacies about the Christian Faith, Will Christianity Work?, Practical Christianity To-Day, Questions and Answers in Ceylon, Children's Prayer Time, All His Grace, It is Hard to Work for God, The Advocacy of the Gospel, Tower Hill, 12.30.*
West London Mission, Kingsway Hall, London, W.C.2, England.
Telephone: 01-405-3246.

Sopwith, Sir Thomas Octave Murdoch, Kt., C.B.E.; British aeronautical engineer; b. 1888.
Founded Sopwith Aviation Co. 12; now Pres. Hawker Siddeley Group Ltd.; Hon. F.R.Ae.S.
Compton Manor, Kings Somborne, Hampshire, England.

Sorato, Dr. Bruno, D.ECON.; Italian business executive; b. 7 May 1922, Venice; m. Giovanna Coin 1949; one d.; ed. in Rome.
Executive SAVA, Venice 47-64; Exec. AISA São Paulo 65-66; Man. Dir. NABALCO Pty. Ltd., Sydney 67-72; mem. Exec. Cttee. Swiss Aluminium Ltd. 72-74, Exec. Vice-Pres. 75-.
Swiss Aluminium Ltd., Feldeggstrasse 4, CH-8034, Zurich, Switzerland.
Telephone: 34-90-90.

Sørensen, Holger R., Kt.; Danish editor; b. 8 Sept. 1909, Nyborg; m. Marie Kirstine Larsen 1935; no c.
Journalist since 29; with *Fyns Tidende* 32-39; Parl.

Reporter and Copenhagen Editor 36-39; mem. of staff of Editors of Danish Broadcasting News Service 39-45; act. Chief Ed. 45; Press Agent, Provincial Chamber of Commerce 42-45; Venstres Landsorganisation 45-56; Sec. Parl. Group of Liberal Party, Cttee. of Reps. and Exec. Cttee. of party organization; mem. of Exec. Cttee. of Information Organization, mem. Party Cen. Board 57-71; Chair. Propaganda Cttee. 45-56; Ed. *Venstres Maanedsblad* (monthly) and *Den Liberale Almanak* (yearly) 45-56, Chief Ed. *Ringkjöbing Amts Dagblad* 56-62; Chief Ed. *Fyns Tidende* 62-66; lecturer in Danish policy Danmarks Journalisthøjskole 66; Dir Dansk Pressemuseum og Arkiv Århus 66; mem. Danish Press Council 64-67.

Leisure interests: fishing, hunting, sailing.

Bredkaer Tvaervej 63, 8250 Egaa, Denmark.

Telephone: 06 220938.

Sørensen, Max, DR.JUR.; Danish university professor; b. 19 Feb. 1913, Copenhagen; s. of Jens Martin Sørensen and Christophine (née Poulsen); m. Ellen Jacobsen 1940; ed. Univ. of Copenhagen and Geneva Post-graduate Inst. for International Studies.

Entered Danish Foreign Office 38; Attaché, Danish Legation, Berne 43-44, Sec., London 44-45; Asst. Chief of Section, Foreign Office, Copenhagen 45-47; Prof. of Int., Constitutional and Administrative Law, Univ. of Aarhus 47-72; Rep. of Danish Govt. on Human Rights Comm. of UN 48-51, and Comm. on Int. Criminal Jurisdiction 51; Adviser to Danish Minister for Foreign Affairs at meetings of Cttee. of Ministers, Council of Europe 49-50; Lecturer, Acad. of Int. Law, The Hague 52, 60; Chair. U.N. Sub-Cttee. on Prevention of Discrimination and Protection of Minorities 54-55; mem. of European Comm. on Human Rights 55-72 (Pres. 67) and of ILO Cttee. on Application of Int. Labour Conventions 54-62, Judge *ad hoc* Int. Court of Justice 68-69 (North Sea continental shelf cases); mem. Perm. Court of Arbitration, The Hague; mem. Inst. de Droit Int.; Legal Adviser to Danish Ministry for Foreign Affairs 56-72; Judge in Court of Justice of European Communities 73-; Dr. Jur. h.c. (Univ. of Kiel) 64.

Publs. *Les sources du droit international* 46 *Elements of International Organization* (in Danish) 52, *Denmark and the United Nations* 56, *Manual of Public International Law* 68, *Constitutional Law* (in Danish) 69.

Tretommervej 21, 8240 Risskov, Denmark; 29 rue F-B Esch, Luxembourg.

Telephone: Århus 06-17-82-64; Luxembourg 47-17-73.

Sorensen, Theodore Chaikin, B.S.L., LL.B.; American lawyer and government official; b. 8 May 1928, Lincoln, Nebraska; s. of Christian A. and Annis Chaikin; m. Gillian Martin 1969; three s. one d.; ed. Univ. of Nebraska.

Attorney, Federal Security Agency 51-52; Staff Researcher, Joint Cttee. on Railroad Retirement 52-53; Asst. to Senator John F. Kennedy 53-61; Special Counsel to Presidents Kennedy and Johnson 61-64; now lawyer, Paul, Weiss, Rifkind, Wharton & Garrison, New York City; Editor-at-Large *Saturday Review* 66-69; Democrat.

Publs. *Decision-Making in The White House* 63, *Kennedy* 64, *The Kennedy Legacy* 70, *Watchmen in the Night: Presidential Accountability After Watergate* 75.

345 Park Avenue, New York, N.Y. 10022, U.S.A.

Telephone: (212) 644-8000.

Sorgenicht, Klaus, DR.RER.POL.; German politician; b. 24 Aug. 1923, Wuppertal-Elberfeld; m.; one c.; ed. Volksschule and Deutsche Akad. für Staats- und Rechtswissenschaft.

Mayor of Güstrow 46, mem. local council 46-49; Head of Dept., Mecklenburg Ministry of Interior 49-51; Head of Dept., Ministry of Interior of German Democratic Republic 51-52; Head of Dept. for Co-ordination and Control of Labour in admin. service of GDR 52-54;

Head of Dept., Cen. Cttee. of Sozialistische Einheitspartei Deutschlands (SED) 54-; mem. Volkskammer 58-; mem. Comm. on Law and Constitution 63-; mem. State Council 63-; Vaterländischer Verdienstorden, Order of Banner of Labour (2) and other decorations.

Staatsrat der Deutschen Demokratischen Republik, 102 Berlin, Marx-Engels-Platz, German Democratic Republic.

Soriano, Raphael S., B.ARCH.; American architect; b. 1 Aug. 1907; ed. Coll. St. Jean, Rhodes and Univ. of Southern California.

Went to U.S. 24; naturalized 30; engaged on City Planning Project with Neutra 33; carried out special projects for Los Angeles County Regional Planning Comm. 35; private architectural practice 36-; Prof. Washington Univ. 62-63; developed industrialized packaged structures of aluminium, steel and plastic, steel houses; works exhibited at Paris Int. Exhbn. 37, New York Museum of Modern Art 52, VII Pan-American Congress, Havana, VIII, Mexico City, São Paulo Int. Exhbn. 53, Munich Int. Exhbn. 55, Toledo (Ohio) Museum of Art 56, Moscow Int. Congress 58; Speaker World Design Conf., Tokyo 60; Honor Awards Judge for Mexican Architecture 64; Fellow American Inst. of Architects; mem. American Asscn. Univ. Profs.; hon. mem. Soc. de Arquitectos Mexicanos; VII Pan-American Congress Award 51, American Inst. of Architects Nat. Awards 51, 56, 58, 60, Progressive Architecture Award, A.I.A. Sunset Awards 57, 59, *Architectural Record* Award 56, S. Calif. A.I.A. Awards 49, 51, 57, *House and Home* Award 60, Life-A.I.A. Award 62, A.I.A. and City of Los Angeles Grand Prix Award 67.

Projects: Site planning, apartments, hospitals, harbour facilities, research laboratories, office and medical buildings, community centres, horticultural centres and shops.

P.O. Box 128, Belvedere, Tiburon, Calif. 94920, U.S.A.

Telephone: 415-435-0472.

Šorm, František, D.SC., DR. TECH. ING.; Czechoslovak scientist; b. 28 Feb. 1913, Prague; s. of František Šorm and Kamila Durdilová; m. Zora Drápalová 1940; one s. one d.

Professor of Organic Chemistry, Charles Univ., Prague; mem. Czechoslovak Acad. of Sciences 52-, Gen. Scientific Sec. 52-60, Vice-Pres. 61, Pres. of the Acad. 62-69; Deputy to Nat. Assembly 60-69; mem. Central Cttee. C.P. of Czechoslovakia 62-69; mem. Ideological Comm. of Central Cttee. 63-69; Deputy to House of the People Fed. Assembly Jan.-Dec. 69; Dir. of the Academy's Inst. of Organic Chemistry and Biochemistry 50-70, Inst. of Organic Chemistry and Biochemistry 70-; hon. mem. Romanian and Hungarian Acads. of Sciences; mem. U.S.S.R., German, Leopoldina, Bulgarian, Polish, Bavarian and Royal Danish Acads. of Sciences; hon. mem. British and Belgian Chemical Socs.; Foreign mem. U.S. Nat. Acad. of Sciences; Laureate of the State Prize 50, 52, 58; Fritzsche Medal, American Chemical Soc. 59; Stas Medal, Belgian Chemical Soc. 62, etc.; Dr. h.c. (Univ. Libre de Bruxelles, Lomonosov Univ., Moscow); Order of Labour 58, 63; Hon. Gold Plaque of Czechoslovak Acad. of Science for services to science and to mankind 68.

Institute of Organic Chemistry and Biochemistry, Flemingovo nám. 2, Prague 6; Korejská 9, 160-00 Prague 6, Czechoslovakia.

Sorokos, Lieut.-Gen. (Rtd.) Ioannis A.; Greek army officer (retired) and diplomatist; b. 1917, Amphissa; s. of A. and P. Sorokos; m. Pia Madaros 1954; one s.; ed. Military Acad. of Greece, Staff and Nat. Defence Colls., Staff Coll., U.K. and U.S. Military School.

Company Commdr., Albania 40-41, El Alamein 42-43; Army Div. Staff Officer and Battalion Commdr. during guerrilla war 47-49; Staff Officer, Army H.Q. and Armed Forces H.Q. 52-53; Staff Officer, NATO Allied Forces,

Southern Europe 57-59; Regt. Commdr. 65; Mil. Attaché, Greek Embassies, Washington and Ottawa 66-68; Div. Commdr. 68; Deputy Commdr. Greek Armed Forces 69; Amb. to U.K. 70-72, to U.S.A. 72-74; Gold Medal for Gallantry (twice), Mil. Cross (twice), Medal for Distinguished Service (thrice), Mil. Medal of Merit; Commdr., and Silver and Gold Cross, Order of George I; Commdr. Order of Phoenix; Officer, Legion of Merit (U.S.A.).
Leisure interests: horses, boating, fishing.
Mimnermou 2, Athens (138), Greece.

Soronics, Franz; Austrian politician; b. 28 July 1920, Eisenstadt; s. of Stefan and Theresia Soronics; m. Gertrud Baier 1944; one d.; ed. primary, secondary and trade schools, Eisenstadt.
Local Govt. work, Eisenstadt 50-62; mem. Bundesrat 56-66, State Sec. Ministry of Interior 63-66; State Sec. Ministry for Social Affairs 66-68; Minister of Interior 68-72; Provincial Head of Austrian League of Workers and Employees 64-; Head of Burgenland Section of Austrian People's Party 68-, Grosses Silbernes Ehrenzeichen am Bande and other decorations.
7000 Eisenstadt, Meierhofgasse 4, Austria.
Telephone: 02682/2865; 63-17-41.

Sorsa, (Taisto) Kalevi; Finnish politician; b. 21 Dec. 1930, Keuruu; s. of Kaarlo O. Sorsa and Elsa S. (née Leinonen); m. Elli Irene Lääkäri 1953; ed. School of Social Science (now Univ. of Tampere).
Chief Editor, Vihuri 54-56; Literary Editor Tammi (publishing house) 56-59; Programme Asst. Specialist UNESCO 59-65; Sec.-Gen. of Finnish UNESCO Cttee. 65-69; Sec.-Gen. Social Democratic Party 69-75, Pres. 75-; mem. Parl. 70-; Minister for Foreign Affairs Feb.-Sept. 72; Prime Minister 72-75; Deputy Prime Minister and Minister for Foreign Affairs Nov. 75-; Grand Decoration of Honour (Austria), Grand Cross, Order of the Dannebrog (Denmark), Golden Star of the Order of Star of Friendship between Peoples (German Democratic Repub.), Grand Cross of the Order of Orange-Nassau (Netherlands), Grand Cross of the Order of Merit of Polish People's Repub., Grand Cross of the Order of St. Marinus, Grand Cross of the Order of Merit of Senegal, Grand Cross of the Royal Order of the Northern Star (Sweden).
Leisure interests: the arts, social and international questions, outdoor life.
Ministry of Foreign Affairs, Helsinki, Finland.

Sorsby, Arnold, C.B.E., M.D., F.R.C.S.; British surgeon and ophthalmologist; b. 10 June 1900, Bialystock, Poland; s. of Jacob and Elka Sourasky; m. Charmaine V. Guinness 1943; ed. Leeds, London and Edinburgh Univs.
Dean Medical School Royal Eye Hospital 34-38; Ophthalmic Surgeon London Jewish Hospital 27-43; Hampstead Gen. Hospital 28-43; and West End Hospital for Nervous Diseases 33-38; Hunterian Prof. Royal Coll. of Surgeons 33 and 41; Pres. London Jewish Hospital Medical Society 37; Middlemore Prize, British Medical Asscn. 36; Montgomery Lecturer, Royal Coll. of Surgeons 33 and 41; Pres. London Hospital 31-66; Research Prof. Ophthalmology, Royal Coll. of Surgeons and Royal Eye Hospital 43-66; Vice-Pres. Int. League against Trachoma 52-60; mem. Expert Advisory Panel on Trachoma, WHO 54-69; Hon. Dir. Wernher Group for Research in Ophthalmological Genetics Research, Medical Research Council 53-66; Dir. Medical Ophthalmology Unit, Lambeth Hospital 63-66; Hon. Adviser in Ophthalmology, Royal Nat. Inst. for the Blind 63-66; Emer. Research Prof. in Ophthalmology, Royal Coll. of Surgeons 66-; Consultant Adviser, Ministry of Health 66-71; Keith Medal Royal Coll. of Surgeons 66, Grimshaw award Nat. Fed. of the Blind 67.
Publs. A Short History of Ophthalmology 33, 48, Modern

Trends in Ophthalmology Vol. I 40, Vol. II 48, Vol. III 55, Vol. IV 67, Vol. V 73, Medicine and Mankind 42, 50, Ophthalmia Neonaturum 45, The Causes of Blindness in England and Wales 50, Ophthalmic Genetics 51, 70, Systemic Ophthalmology 51, 58, Clinical Genetics 53, 73, The Causes of Blindness in England 1948-1950 53, The Causes of Blindness in England 1951-1954 56, Emmetropia and its Aberrations 57, Antibiotics and Sulphonamides in Ophthalmology 60, Refraction and its Components during the Growth of the Eye 61, Refraction and its Components in Twins 62, Modern Ophthalmology (4 vols.) 63-64, 70, The Incidence and Causes of Blindness in England and Wales 1948-1962 66. A longitudinal study on refraction and its components during growth 70, The Incidence and Causes of Blindness in England and Wales 1963-68 73, Tenements of Clay 74, Diseases of the Fundus Oculi 75.
19 Parham Court, Grand Avenue, Worthing BN11 5AH, Sussex, England.
Telephone: Worthing 40607.

Sosa de la Vega, Manuel; Mexican airline executive; b. 24 July 1916, San Luis Potosí; s. of Manuel Sosa Gómez and the late Raquel De la Vega de Sosa; m. Cristina Elízaga 1945; two s. three d.; ed. Mexico and complementary courses in U.S.A.
Joined Mexicana Airlines 39-, Pres. and Chief Exec. 67-; Pres. IATA 76-(77); Cavalliere della Repubblica Italiana.
Leisure interests: golf, swimming.
Balderas 36—Piso 12°, México 1, D.F.; Home: Avenue Glorieta Sur 29, Club de Golf México, México 22, D.F., Mexico.

Sosnowski, Leonard, D.SC.; Polish physicist; b. 19 Feb. 1911, Tver (now Kalinin), U.S.S.R.; ed. Warsaw Univ. Docent 48-50, Assoc. Prof. 50-56, Full Prof. 56-; Corresp. mem. Polish Acad. of Sciences 60-69, mem. 69-, Chair. Scientific Council of Inst. of Physics and of Inst. of Nuclear Research; Head of Dept. of Solid State Physics, Inst. of Applied Physics of Warsaw Univ. 53-; mem. Editorial Staff Acta Physica Polonica, Solid State Electronics; mem. Polish Physical Soc. 32-, IUPAP (Chair. 75-, Chair. Polish Nat. Cttee.); Knight's Cross, Order of Polonia Restituta 54, Officer's Cross 58, Commdr.'s Cross 64; Medal of 10th Anniversary of People's Poland 55; Order of Banner of Labour, 1st Class 70; State Prize, 1st Class 72; Medal of 30th Anniversary of People's Poland 74; research on propagation of charged molecules under operation of various external agents.
Ul. Puławska 1 m. 8, 02-515 Warsaw, Poland.

Sötér, István; Hungarian university professor, literary historian and novelist; b. 1913, Szeged; m. Veronika Jász 1939; ed. Budapest, Univ. de Paris à la Sorbonne and Ecole Normale Supérieure, Paris.
Director, Inst. of Literary History, Hungarian Acad. of Sciences 57-; Rector, Lóránd Eötvös Univ. Budapest 63-66; Pres. Int. Comparative Literature Asscn. ICLA 70-73; mem. Hungarian Acad. of Sciences; Kossuth Prize; Dr. h.c. (Paris) 73, Officier Ordre des Arts et Lettres (Paris) 74.
Leisure interest: gardening.
Publs. novels and short stories: Fellegjárás (Walking in the Clouds) 39, A templomrabló (The Robber of the Church) 42, A Kisértet (The Ghost) 46, Bünbeesés (The Fall) 47, Hidszakadás (The Broken Bridge) 48, Edenkert (The Eden) 61, Az elveszett bárány (The Lost Lamb) 74; critical essays and historical monographs: Jókai Mór 40, Játék és valóság (Play and Reality) 46, Eötvös József 53, Világtájak 57, Madártávlat 59, Nemzet és haladás (Nation and Progress) 63, Romantika és realizmus 65, Aspects et parallélismes de la littérature hongroise 66, Tisztuló tükrök 66, Az ember és müve 71, The Dilemma of Literary Science 73.
1118 Budapest, Ménesi ut 11-13, Hungary.
Telephone: 451-156.

Soteriades, Antis; Cypriot lawyer and diplomatist; b. 10 Sept. 1924; *m.*; one *s.* one *d.*; ed. London Univ. and Gray's Inn, London.
In legal practice, Nicosia 51-56; detained on suspicion of assisting EOKA 56; escaped and became EOKA leader for Kyrenia district; mem. Exec., Edma Party May 59; Ambassador to U.K. Oct. 60-Feb. 61, High Commr. Feb. 61-66; Amb. to Egypt 66-, concurrently accred. to Syria and Lebanon 67-; Knight of the Order of St. Gregory the Great (Vatican) 63.
16 Cleopatra Road, Heliopolis, Cairo, Egypt.

Soto, Jesús-Rafael; Venezuelan artist; b. 5 June 1923; ed. School of Fine Arts, Caracas.
Director, School of Fine Arts, Maracaibo, Venezuela 47-50; in Paris since 50; early exponent of "optical art"; various films made on works in field of kinetic art and vibrations since 58; one-man exhbns. at Caracas 49, 57, 61, Paris 56, 59, 62, 65, Brussels 57, Essen 61, Antwerp 62, Stuttgart 64, New York 65, Retrospective Exhbn., Signals, London 65; represented in perm. collections including: Tate Gallery, London, Museum of Fine Arts, Caracas, Albright-Knox Art Gallery, Buffalo, Cali Inst. of Fine Arts, Cali, Colombia, Stedelijk Museum, Amsterdam, Museum of Contemporary Arts, São Paulo, Moderna Museet, Stockholm, Kaiser Foundation, Cordoba, Argentina, Palace of Fine Arts, Brussels, Kröller-Müller Museum, Otterlo, Holland, Museum of Modern Art, Jerusalem; numerous prizes including Wolf Prize, São Paulo Bienal 63, David Bright Foundation Prize, Venice Biennale 64.
Major works include: sculpture for garden of School of Architecture, Univ. City of Caracas, two murals and sculpture for Venezuelan pavilion, Brussels Exhbn. 58.
68 rue de Turenne, Paris 3e, France.

Sotomayor, Antonio; Bolivian painter; b. 1904, Chulumani; *s.* of Carmen Celina Meza and Juan Sotomayor; *m.* Grace La Mora Andrews 1926; ed. La Paz School of Applied Arts.
Awarded first prize of Nat. Exposition of Painting 21; F.R.S.A.
Works include: *El Crucifijo, Copacabana, Lavanderas, Funeral Aimara, Alacitas, Madre, Rezando Reposo,* Historical Murals Palace Hotel and Sharon Building, San Francisco, Murals at Sonoma Mission Inn, Calif., Mural *El Tigero,* Hillsborough, Calif.; murals Peruvian Pavilion and terra cotta fountain Pacific Area, Theme Building, Golden Gate, Int. Exposition 39-40, Murals, Stage Door Canteen, S.F.; American Women's Voluntary Services Canteen; Art Faculty, Mills Coll. and California School of Fine Arts; Mural Altarpiece St. Augustine Church, Pleasanton, Calif., Glass Mosaic Facade, Hillsdale Methodist Church, Calif.; Mural, Matson Navigation Co., San Francisco, Calif.; backdrop for San Francisco Civic Auditorium Concerts.
Leisure interests: music, travel.
Publs. *Pinturas interpretativas de indígenas de Bolivia* 29, *Pinturas con motivos mejicanos* 30, *Khasa Goes to the Fiesta* 67, *Balloons* 72.
3 Le Roy Place, San Francisco, Calif. 94109, U.S.A.
Telephone: 415-673-6193.

Sotoudeh, Fathollah, M.S.; Iranian engineer and politician; b. 1924, Teheran; *s.* of Ali Akbar and Mah Talat; *m.* Azar Hamidi 1960; one *s.* one *d.*; ed. Teheran Polytechnic and New York Univ., U.S.A.
Former employee, Plan Org.; Acting Dir. Vanak Metalworks 59-64; Chair. of Board, Iranian Fisheries 64; Minister of Posts, Telegraph and Telephone 64-74; Chair. Board of Dirs. Construction Bank, Iranian Nuclear Energy Co.
Leisure interests: study in fields of engineering and management; sport, especially hunting and mountaineering.
Old Shemiran Road, Seh Rahe Zarrab-Khaneh; and Saltanat-Abad Road, Koocheh Laleh No. 12, Iran.
Telephone: 772771.

Soulages, Pierre; French painter; b. 24 Dec. 1919, Rodez; *m.* Colette Llaurens 1942; ed. Lycée de Rodez.
Exhibited abstract painting since 47 in Salon des Surindépendants, Salon de Mai et Réalités Nouvelles; one-man exhbn., Lydia Conti Gallery, Paris 49, Birch Gallery, Copenhagen 51, Stangl Gallery, Munich 52, Kootz Gallery, New York 54-65, Gimpel Gallery, London 55, Galerie de France, Paris 56, 60, 63, Knoedler Gallery 68; exhibited in int. festivals including Biennales of Venice and São Paulo, and the itinerary of the Guggenheim Collection, the Carnegie Inst., Pittsburgh, The New Decade at the Museum of Modern Art, New York, Tate Gallery, London, etc.; also décors for theatres and ballet; and lithographs and engravings.
Works in Museums of Modern Art, Paris, and N.Y., Tate Gallery, London, Guggenheim Museum, N.Y., Phillips Gallery, Washington, Museum of Modern Art, Rio de Janeiro, museums in many American cities and in Europe; retrospective exhbns. Hanover, Essen, The Hague, Zürich 60-61, Massachusetts Inst. of Technology 62, Copenhagen Glyptothek 63, Fine Arts Museum, Houston 66, Musée Nat. d'Art Moderne, Paris 67; Carnegie Inst., Pittsburgh, Albright Knox Art Gallery, Buffalo, Musée de Québec, Musée d'Art Contemporain, Montreal 68, Oslo, Aalborg, Neuchâtel, Charleroi 73, Musée Dynamique, Dakar 74, Gulbenkian Foundation, Lisbon, Museo de arte contemporaneo, Madrid, Musée Fabre, Montpellier, Museo de Arte Moderno, Mexico City 75, Museu de Arte Moderna, Rio de Janeiro, Museo de Arte Moderno, Caracas 76; retrospective exhbn. of engravings Ljubljana 61; Carnegie Prize 64; Rembrandt Prize 76.
18 rue des Trois-Portes, Paris 5e, France.

Soulioti, Stella; Cypriot lawyer and politician; b. 1920, Limassol; sister of Michael Cacoyannis (*q.v.*); *d.* of Panayiotis Cacoyannis; *m.* Demetrios Souliotis 49; one *d.*; ed. Cyprus, Egypt and Gray's Inn, London.
Joined Women's Auxiliary Air Force, Nicosia and served in Middle East 43-46; called to the Bar, London 51; law practice, Limassol 52-60; Minister of Justice 60-70, concurrently Minister of Health 64-66; Law Commr. 71; LL.D. (Honoris Causa) Nottingham Univ. 72; Pres. Cyprus Red Cross, Cyprus Scholarship Board; Vice-Pres. Cyprus Anti-Cancer Soc.; Hon. Vice-Pres. Int. Fed. of Women Lawyers.
Leisure interests: reading, music, theatre.
97 Ayii Omoloyitae Street, Nicosia, Cyprus.

Soupault, Philippe; French writer; b. 2 Aug. 1897, Chaville; *m.* Renée Niemeyer 1937; two *d.*; ed. Univ. de Paris à la Sorbonne.
Winner of Strassburger Prize 32, Prix Italia 58, 63; fmr. Prof. Swarthmore Coll., Pa., U.S.A.
Leisure interest: reading.
Publs. Poetry: *Les Champs Magnétiques* 19, *Westwego* 22, *Georgia* 26, *Poésies complètes* 37, *L'arme secrète* 47, *Message de l'île déserte* 48, *Chansons* 50, *Sans phrases* 53, *Poèmes et Poésies* 73; novels: *Le Bon apôtre* 23, *Les frères Durandeau* 25, *En joue!* 25, *Le Coeur d'or* 27, *Le Nègre* 27, *Les dernières nuits de Paris* 28, *Les Moribonds* 34, biographies of *Henri Rousseau, Charles Baudelaire* 27, *Paolo Uccello* 28, *William Blake* 29, *Lautréamont* 31, *Souvenirs de James Joyce* 43; plays: *La fille qui faisait des miracles* 51, *Comment dresser une Garce* 54, *Tous ensemble au bout du monde* 55, *Rendezvous* 57, *La nuit du temps* 62, *Alibis* 69; essays: *Profils Perdus* 63, *Eugène Labiche* 64, *Le Sixième Coup de Minuit* 72.
11 rue Chanez, 75016 Paris, France.
Telephone: MIR. 8400.

Souphanouvong, Prince; Laotian politician; b. 1902; half-brother of Prince Souvanna Phouma (*q.v.*); ed. Lycée Saint-Louis (Paris), Ecole Nationale des Ponts et Chaussées.
Studied engineering in France; returned to Laos 38 and

became active in the Nationalist Movement; joined Pathet Lao and fought against the French; formed Nationalist Party (Neo Lao Hak Sat) in Bangkok 50; Leader of the Patriotic Front; Minister of Planning, Reconstruction and Urbanism 58; arrested 59, escaped May 60, rejoined Pathet Lao Forces, became Leader; Pathet Lao del., Geneva Conf. on Laos 61-62; Vice-Premier and Minister of Econ. Planning 62, absent, returned 74; Chair. Joint Nat. Political Council 74-75; Pres. of Lao People's Democratic Repub. Dec. 75-.
Office of the President, Vientiane, Laos.

Soustelle, Jacques, D. ès L.; French scientist and politician; b. 3 Feb. 1912, Montpellier; s. of Jean Soustelle and Germaine (Blatière) Soustelle; m. Georgette Fagot 1931; ed. Ecole normale supérieure.
Various scientific missions to Mexico 32-34, 35-36, 39; Asst. Dir. Musée de l'Homme, Paris 37; joined Gen. de Gaulle in London 40; French Nat. Cttee. Del. in Central America, Mexico and West Indies 41-42; Nat. Commr. for Information 42-43; Dir.-Gen. Special Services, Algiers 43-44; Commissaire of Repub., Bordeaux 44; Minister of Information 45; Minister for the Colonies 45; mem. Constituent Assembly 45-46; Sec.-Gen. of Rassemblement du Peuple Français 47-51; mem. French Parl. for Lyon 51-59; Gov.-Gen. of Algeria 55-56; leader, Gaullist group in Nat. Assembly 56-58; returned to Algeria May 58; Minister of Information July 58-Jan. 59; Minister attached to Prime Minister as Minister for Sahara and Atomic Questions Jan. 59-Feb. 60; mem. Cen. U.N.R. 58-60; Del.-Gen. Org. commune des régions sahariennes 59-60; Pres. Information centre on Problems of Algeria and Sahara 60; Political Dir. *Voici Pourquoi* 60; warrant issued for arrest for subversion 62; in exile, mainly in Italy and Switzerland 61-68; returned to France after general amnesty Oct. 68; Dir. of Studies, Ecole Pratique des Hautes Etudes 69-; Founder-Pres. Mouvement Nat. Progrès et Liberté 70; mem. Nat. Council of Scientific Research 71-; mem. Lyons City Council 71-; mem. Parl. for Lyon 73-; joined Reformist group in Nat. Ass. 74; French rep. to Council of Europe 73-; in charge of Special Mission to Prime Minister 75; Officier Légion d'Honneur; Hon. C.B.E.
Publs. *La Vie quotidienne des Aztèques* 55, 62, *Aimée et souffrante Algérie* 56, *L'espérance Trahie* 62, *Sur une route nouvelle* 64, *La Page n'est pas tournée* 65, *L'Art du Mexique ancien* 66, *Les Quatre Soleils* 67, *Vingt-huit ans de Gaullisme* 68, *The Long March of Israel* 69, *Les Aztèques* 70.
c/o 25 rue du Président-Edouard-Herriot, Lyons 1er, (Rhône), France.
Telephone: 28-17-55.

Southam, Gordon Hamilton, B.A.; Canadian civil servant; b. 19 Dec. 1916, Ottawa; s. of Wilson Mills Southam and Henrietta Alberta (née Cargill); m. 1st Jacqueline Lambert-David 1940 (dissolved 1968), three s. one d.; 2nd Gro Mortensen 1968, one s. one d.; ed. Ashbury Coll. School, Trinity Coll., Toronto and Christ Church, Oxford.
Officer, Second World War, British and Canadian Armies; Reporter *The Times*, London 45-46; Editorial Writer *Ottawa Citizen* 46-47; joined Dept. of External Affairs 48; Second Sec., Stockholm 49-Aug. 53, Ottawa 53-59; Chargé d'Affaires, Warsaw Mar. 59-60, Amb. May 60-62; Head, Information Div., Dept. of External Affairs Aug. 62-64; Dir. Southam Press Ltd. 64-; Co-ordinator, Nat. Arts Centre 64-67, Dir. Gen. 67-.
Leisure interests: the arts, sailing, tennis, skiing.
300 Queen Elizabeth Driveway, Apartment 7c, Ottawa K1S 3M6, Canada.
Telephone: 238-6611.

Southard, Frank Allan, Jr., B.A., PH.D.; American economist; b. 17 Jan. 1907, Cleveland, Ohio; s. of

Frank A. Southard and May L. Bowsher; m. Mary I. Hay 1941; ed. Pomona Coll., and Univ. of Calif.
Instructor in Economics, Univ. of Calif. 30-31, Asst. Prof. of Economics, Cornell Univ. 31-39, Prof. 39-48, Chair. of Dept. of Economics 46-48; Researcher in Int. Finance, Carnegie Endowment 34; Senior Economic Analyst, U.S. Tariff Comm. 35; Guggenheim Fellow, Latin America 40; Asst. Dir., Div. of Monetary Research, Treasury Dept. 41-42; served U.S. Naval Reserve, principally as Financial Adviser, Allied Force H.Q. Mediterranean 42-46; Dir. Office of Int. Finance, Treasury Dept. 47-48; Assoc. Dir. of Research and Statistics, in charge of int. work, Board of Govs. Fed. Reserve System 48-49; Special Asst. to Sec. of Treasury and U.S. Exec. Dir. Int. Monetary Fund 49-62; Deputy Man. Dir. IMF 62-74; Alt. Gov. IMF and IBRD 48-62; Prof. of Econ. Florida Atlantic Univ. 73-; Senior Assoc. Kearns Int., Washington; Officer Legion of Merit, Officer Legion of Honor (France); Hon. O.B.E.
Leisure interests: snorkeling, swimming, shell collecting.
Publs. *American Industry in Europe* 31, *Canadian-American Industry* (with others) 36, *Foreign Exchange Practice and Policy* (with others) 40, *Some European Currency and Exchange Experiences 43-46* 47, *Finances of European Liberation—With Special Reference to Italy* 46; various articles and published speeches.
Office: 1701 Pennsylvania Avenue, N.W., Washington, D.C. 20015; Home: 4620 North Park Avenue, Chevy Chase, Md. 20015, U.S.A.
Telephone: (202) 387-7500 (Office); (301) 986-1263 (Home).

Southborough, 3rd Baron, cr. 17; **Francis John Hopwood,** Kt.; British company director; b. 7 March 1897, London; s. of Francis J. S. Hopwood, 1st Baron Southborough and Florence Emily Black; m. Audrey E. D. Money 1918; one s. one d.; ed. Westminster School.
Sub-Lieut., R.N.V.R. in First World War, served at Admiralty and Foreign Office, seconded to staff of Irish Convention, Dublin 17; later Sec. to War Trade Advisory Cttee.; joined Royal Dutch Shell Group 19; Pres. Asiatic Petroleum Corpn., in U.S.A. (also rep. Petroleum Board) 42-46; Man.-Dir. Shell Petroleum Co. Ltd. and N. V. de Bataafsche Petroleum Maatschappij 46-57; Chair. Shell Oil Co. 51-57; Dir. The Shell Transport and Trading Co. Ltd. 46-70, Man. Dir. 51-70; fmr. Dir. The Shell Petroleum Co. Ltd., Shell Petroleum N.V.; Commdr. of the Order of Orange Nassau.
Leisure interests: reading, gardening, architecture, furniture.
Bingham's Melcombe, Near Dorchester, Dorset, England.
Telephone: Milton Abbas 202.

Soutou, Jean Marie Léon; French diplomatist; b. 18 Sept. 1912; ed. Univ. de Paris à la Sorbonne.
Entered Ministry of Foreign Affairs 43, served Switzerland 43-44, Yugoslavia 45; Administrator to Minister of Foreign Affairs 50; Sec. of Foreign Affairs 51; Asst. Dir. Cabinet of M. Mendès-France 54-55; E. European Sub-Dir. to Minister of Foreign Affairs 55-56; Minister-Counsellor, Moscow 56-58; Consul-Gen., Milan 58-61; Dir. European Affairs, Ministry of Foreign Affairs 61-62, Dir. African Affairs 62-66; Insp.-Gen. Diplomatic and Consular Corps 66-71; Amb. to Algeria 71-75; Perm. Rep. to the European Communities 75-; Chevalier, Légion d'Honneur.
42 Boulevard du Régent, 1000 Brussels, Belgium.

Souvanlasy, Khamking, L. en D.; Laotian government official and diplomatist; b. 14 Sept. 1926, Không, Laos; s. of Thao Phay and Nang Sô Souvanlasy; m. Sivaly Abhay 1954; two s. two d.; ed. Collège Pavie, Vientiane, and Univ. of Paris.
Head of Dept., Ministry of Foreign Affairs 53-54,

Ministry of Nat. Educ. 54-55; Under-Sec. to Pres. of Council of Ministers 55-56; Counsellor, Laotian Embassy, Tokyo 56-58, Chargé d'Affaires a.i. 58-59; Sec. of State in Presidency of Council of Ministers (in charge of Foreign Affairs and Nat. Information) 59; Sec. of State for Foreign Affairs 60; Adviser, Ministry of Foreign Affairs 61-62; Amb. to People's Republic of China 63-65, to U.S.A. 66-70; Perm. Rep. of Kingdom of Laos to UN 66-70; Acting Minister of Justice 70-74, Minister 74-75; Grand Officier of Laos, National Order; Ordre du Règne; Hon. Phagna Kittikhoun Sounthone. Leisure interests: hunting, fishing.
c/o Ministry of Justice, Vientiane, Laos.

Souvanna Phouma, H.H. Prince; Laotian engineer and politician; b. 7 Oct. 1901; half-brother of Prince Souphanouvong (q.v.); ed. Coll. Paul Bert and Lycée Albert Sarraut, Hanoi, Univs. of Paris and Grenoble.
Entered Public Works Service of Indo-China 31; Engineer at Phoukhoun 40-41, at Luang Prabang 41-44; Chief Engineer, Bureau à la Circonscription Territoriale des Travaux Publics du Laos 44-45; Principal Engineer (1st Class) of the Public Works Service of Indo-China; Minister of Public Works 50-51; Prime Minister, Pres. of the Council, Minister of Public Works and of Planning 51-54; Vice-Pres. of the Council and Minister of Nat. Defence and Ex-Servicemen 54-56; Prime Minister, Pres. of the Council, Minister of Nat. Defence and Ex-Servicemen, of Foreign Affairs and of Information 56-57, Prime Minister 57-58; Amb. to France 58-59; Pres. National Assembly 60; Prime Minister, Minister of Defence and Foreign Affairs Aug.-Dec. 60; Leader of Neutralist Govt. 60-62; Prime Minister 62-75; Adviser to the Government Dec. 75-; Minister of Defence and Veterans' Affairs 62, Minister of Foreign Affairs 64, Minister of Rural Devt. 71 (all concurrently); Grand Cross Order of a Million Elephants, Commdr. Légion d'Honneur, etc.
c/o Office of the Prime Minister, Vientiane, Laos.

Souza, Francis Newton; Indian painter; b. 12 April 1924, Goa; s. of Joseph Newton Souza and Lily Mary Antunes; m. 1st Maria Figueredo 1947 (divorced 1964); one d.; 2nd Liselotte Kristian (in common law); three d.; 3rd Barbara Zinkant 1965; one s.; ed. St. Xavier's Coll. and J. J. School of Art, Bombay, Central School of Art, London, École des Beaux Arts, Paris.
One Man Exhbns. in London and major cities of England, in Paris, Stockholm, Copenhagen, Johannesburg and principal cities of Germany and U.S.A.; Retrospective Exhbns. in London 51, New Delhi 65, Leicester 67, Detroit 68; Minneapolis Int. Art Festival 72; represented in Baroda Museum, Nat. Gallery, New Delhi, Tate Gallery, London, Wakefield Gallery, Haifa Museum, Nat. Gallery, Melbourne, etc.; several awards.
Leisure interest: cogitating the *Bhagavad Gita*.
Publs. *Nirvana of a Maggot* in Encounter, *Words and Lines* (autobiography) 59.
148 West 67 Street, New York City, N.Y., U.S.A.
Telephone: 212-874-2181.

Souza Lopes, Hugo; Brazilian entomologist; b. 5 Jan. 1909, Rio de Janeiro; s. of Carlos H. de Souza Lopes and Mathilde G. de Souza Lopes; m. Jurema Carvalho Lopes 1934; two d.; ed. Escola Nacional de Veterinaria da Universidade Rural do Brasil.
Qualified Veterinary Practitioner 33; Asst. Prof. Univ. Rural do Brasil 33-38, Prof. of Parasitology 38-64, Prof. Emer. 64-; Biologist, Instituto Oswaldo Cruz 50-70, Chief of Entomology Section 61-64; mem. Brazilian Acad. of Sciences; Premio Costa Lima (Brazilian Acad. of Sciences).
Leisure interest: postal stamps.
Publs. research into insects (Diptera: Sarcophagidae, Calliphoridae, Acalypteratae and Memestrinidae) and molluscs.

Academia Brasileira de Ciencias, Caixa Postal 229-2C-00, Rio de Janeiro; Home: Rua Desembargador Isidro 6, apt. 601, Tijuca, Rio de Janeiro, Brazil.
Telephone: 2686238.

Souzay, Gérard (Gérard Marcel Tisserand); French singer; b. 8 Dec. 1920; ed. Coll. de Chinon, Lycée Hoche (Versailles), Lycée Carnot (Paris).
Debut 45; since then numerous tours and appearances in Europe, North and South America, South Africa, Australia and Japan; radio and television performances; Premier Prix d'Excellence, Paris Conservatoire.
26 rue Freycinet, Paris 16e, France.

Sowemimo, Hon. George Sodeinde, LL.B.; Nigerian judge; b. 8 Nov. 1920, Zaria, North Central State; ed. C.M.S. Grammar School, Lagos and Univ. of Bristol, England.
Magistrate 51-56; Chief Magistrate 56-59; Chief Registrar Supreme Court 60; Judge of High Court, Lagos 61-70, Justice of Supreme Court 70-.
Supreme Court of Nigeria, Lagos; Home: 26 Luggard Avenue, Ikoyi, Lagos, Nigeria.

Soyinka, Wole, B.A.; Nigerian playwright and lecturer; b. 13 July 1934, Abeokuta; s. of Ayo and Eniola Soyinka; m.; one s. three d.; ed. Univ. of Ibadan, Nigeria, and Univ. of Leeds, England.
Worked at Royal Court Theatre, London; Research Fellow in Drama, Univ. of Ibadan 60-61; Lecturer in English, Univ. of Ife 62-63; Senior Lecturer in English, Univ. of Lagos 65-67; Political Prisoner 67-69; Artistic Dir. and Head Dept. of Theatre Arts, Univ. of Ibadan 69-; Artistic Dir. Orisun Theatre, 1960 Masks; Literary Editor Orisun Acting Editions; Prisoner of Conscience Award, Amnesty International, Jock Campbell-*New Statesman* Literary Award 69.
Publs. plays: *The Lion and the Jewel* 59, *The Swamp Dwellers* 59, *A Dance of the Forests* 60, *The Trials of Brother Jero* 61, *The Strong Breed* 62, *The Road* 64, *Kongi's Harvest* 65, *Madmen and Specialists* 71, *Before the Blackout* 71, *Jero's Metamorphosis* 73, *Death and the King's Horsemen*; novels: *The Interpreters* 64, *The Forest of a Thousand Demons* (trans.), *Idanre and Other Poems* 67, *A Shuffle in the Crypt* 72; non-fiction: *The Man Died* (prison memoirs) 72.
Department of English, University of Ife, Ile-Ife, Nigeria.

Spaak, Fernand Paul Jules, D. EN D., B.A.; Belgian international civil servant; b. 8 Aug. 1923; ed. Univs. of Brussels and Cambridge.
National Bank of Belgium 50-52; Sec. Econ. Div., High Authority of European Coal and Steel Community 52-54, Exec. Asst. to Pres. of High Authority 54-58, Dir. Cartels and Concentration Div. 58-60; Gen. Dir. Supply Agency and Dir. a.i. Safeguards and Controls Euratom 66-68; Dir.-Gen. for Energy, Comm. of EEC; Head, Del. of Comm. of European Communities to U.S.A. 75-.
Commission of the European Communities, 200 rue de la Loi, 1040 Brussels, Belgium.

Spadavekkia, Antonio Emmanuilovich; Soviet composer; b. 3 June 1907, Odessa; ed. Moscow Conservatoire.
Honoured Worker of the Arts of the R.S.F.S.R. 63; Order of Badge of Honour 67.
Principal compositions: *Djangar* (symphonic suite) 40, Concerto for Piano and Orchestra 44; Operas: *The Hotel Mistress* 47, *Calvary* 53, *The Gadfly* 59, *Brave Soldier Schweik* 61; Ballet: *Coast of Happiness* 48; Incidental music for films: *Cinderella* 46, *For Those at Sea* 47, *India-rubber Boy* 50, *The Brave* 50, *Mountain Halt* 52, *The Unsubdued* 59; Music for plays: *The Minor, Katrine Lefevre, The Tamer Tamed, Fairy Kiss, The Green Trunk, The Tale of a Tale, Adventures of Chipol-*

lino, Buratino. Three Musketeers, The Great Wizard; romances, songs, instrumental music.
Moscow Branch of R.S.F.S.R. Composers' Union, 4/6 Third Miusskaya ulitsa, Moscow, U.S.S.R.

Spadolini, Giovanni, LL.D.; Italian journalist and politician; b. 21 June 1925, Florence.
Writer for *Il Messaggero*; Political Editor *Gazzetta del Popolo* 50-52, of *Corriere della Sera* 53-55; Editor *Resto del Carlino* 55-68; Editor *Corriere della Sera* and *Corriere d'Informazione* 68-72; Teacher of Contemporary History, Faculty of Political Science, Florence; Minister of the Environment Nov. 74-Jan. 76; Uff. della Legion d'Onore; Cavaliere di Gran Groce dell'Ordine al Merito della Repubblica.
Publs. *Sorel* 47, *Il 1848 realtà e leggenda di una rivoluzione* 48, *Ritratto dell'Italia moderna* 49, *Lotta sociale in Italia* 49, *Il papato socialista* 50, *L'opposizione cattolica da Porta Pia al '98* 54, *Giolitti e i cattolici* 60, *I radicali dell'Ottocento* 62, *I repubblicani dopa l'Unità* 62, *Un dissidente del Risorgimento* 62, *Firenze Capitale* 67, *Il Tevere più largo* 67, *Storia Fiorentina, Carducci nella storia d'Italia, Il Mondo di Giolitti* 69, *Il 20 Settembre nella storia d'Italia* 70, *Autunno del Risorgimento* 71.
c/o Ministry of the Environment, Rome, Italy.

Spaght, Monroe Edward, PH.D.; American oil executive; b. 9 Dec. 1909, Eureka, Calif.; s. of Frederick E. and Alpha (Light) Spaght; three c.; ed. Stanford Univ.
Research Chemist, Technologist, Shell Oil Co., **Martinez** and Wilmington, Calif. 33-40, Man. (Development and Mfg.) 40-45; Vice-Pres. Shell Development Co., **New** York City 46-49, Pres. Emeryville, Calif. 49-53; **Exec.** Vice-Pres. and Dir., Shell Oil Co. 53-60, Pres. and Dir. 60-65, Chair. 65-70, Dir. 70-; a Man. Dir. Royal Dutch Petroleum Co., Shell Petroleum N.V., Shell Petroleum Co. Ltd. 65-70, Dir. 70-; Dir. The Boston Co., American Standard Inc., Wells Fargo Ltd., European Enterprises Devt. Co. SA; mem. Int. Advisory Board of Chemical Bank; Dir. Inst. Int. Educ (Chair. 71-74); official, scientific and educational orgs.; Commdr. Order of Orange-Nassau 70, Order of Francisco de Miranda (Venezuela) 68.
c/o Shell Centre, London, S.E.1, England.

Spagnolli, Giovanni; Italian politician; b. 26 Oct. 1907; ed. Univ. Cattolica del Sacro Cuore, Milan.
Former official, Banca Commerciale Italiana; fmr. Sec. Nat. Cttee. of Liberation, Milan; Sec. Christian Democrat Party 45-48; Senator 53-; Under-Sec. for Foreign Trade 58-60; Vice-Pres. Finance and Treasury Comm. of Senate 60-63; Minister of Merchant Marine 63-66, of Posts and Telecommunications 66-68, of Merchant Marine 68; Pres. of Christian Democrat Party in Senate 69-73; Pres. of Senate 73-.
Via dei Monti Parioli 53/A, Rome, Italy.
Telephone: 874588.

Spahr, Charles Eugene, B.S.; American oil executive; b. 8 Oct. 1913; ed. Univ. of Kansas and Harvard Univ. Business School.
Joined Standard Oil Co. (Ohio) 39, Vice-Pres. (Transportation) 51, Exec. Vice-Pres. and Dir. 55, Pres. 57-69, Chair. 70-; Major in Army Corps of Engineers 42-45; Dir. Supply and Distribution Div. Petroleum Admin. for Defense 52, White Motor Corpn., Cleveland, Electric Illuminating Co., Nat. City Bank of Cleveland, American Petroleum Inst., Cleveland and Ohio Chambers of Commerce, Ohio Bell Telephone Co.; Trustee Lutheran Hospital, Cleveland Devt. Foundation; mem. Exec. Cttee. Board of Trustees Case Inst. of Technology; Chair. Board of Trustees Baldwin-Wallace Coll.; mem. Exec. Cttee. of the Greater Cleveland Growth Board; mem. Nat. Petroleum Council; Chair. Plans for Progress Advisory Council; Dir. Repub. Steel Corpn.; Hon. Dr. Ing. (Fenn Coll.), Hon. LL.D. (Baldwin-Wallace Coll.),

Citation for Distinguished Service (Univ. of Kansas).
The Standard Oil Co., 1750 Midland Bldg., Cleveland, Ohio 44115, U.S.A.
Telephone: 216-621-7400.

Spanos, Marcos; Cypriot politician; b. 6 Aug. 1932, Lefkonico; ed. Famagusta Greek Gymnasium, American Acad., Larnaca, Gray's Inn, London.
Called to the Bar 56; practised law in Nicosia 57; Dir.-Gen. Office of the Pancyprian Cttee. of Human Rights 58, resident corresp. Int. League for the Rights of Man 59; Recorder, Supreme Constitutional Court 62-64, Counsel of the Repub., Legal Dept. 64-67; seconded to Ministry of Labour to establish Arbitration Tribunal 67, Chair. Arbitration Tribunal 68; Minister of Labour and Social Insurance 72-74, Jan. 75-; founder mem. UN Asscn. of Cyprus; Chair. Consultative Cttee. to Cyprus Athletic Org. 69.
Ministry of Labour and Social Insurance, Nicosia, Cyprus.

Spark, Muriel Sarah, O.B.E.; British author; b. Edinburgh; d. of Bernard Camberg and Sarah Elizabeth Maud (Uezzell); m. S. O. Spark 1937 (dissolved); one s.; ed. James Gillespie's High School for Girls, Edinburgh.
Foreign Office 44-45; Editor *The Poetry Review* 47-49; Gen. Sec. Poetry Soc., London; *The Observer* story prize 51, Italia Prize 62, James Tait Black Memorial Prize for *The Mandelbaum Gate* 65.
Leisure interests: poetry, friends, music.
Publs. *The Fanfarlo and Other Verse* 52, *John Masefield* (a critical study) 53, *The Comforters* 57, *Robinson* 58, *The Go-Away Bird and Other Stories* 58, *Memento Mori* 59 (play 64), *The Bachelors* 60, *The Ballad of Peckham Rye* 60, *The Prime of Miss Jean Brodie* 61 (play 66, film 69), *Voices at Play* 61, *Doctors of Philosophy* (play) 63, *The Girls of Slender Means* 63, *The Mandelbaum Gate* 65, *Collected Stories* Vol. I 67, *Collected Poems* Vol. I 67, *The Public Image* 68, *The Very Fine Clock* 68, *The Driver's Seat* 70 (film 74), *Not to Disturb* 71, *The Hothouse by the East River* 73, *The Abbess of Crewe* 74, *The Takeover* 76 and several critical and biographical works.
c/o Macmillan & Co. Ltd., Little Essex Street, London, W.C.2, England.

Sparkman, John J., LL.B., A.M.; American politician; b. 20 Dec. 1899; ed. Univ. of Alabama.
Admitted to Alabama Bar 25; Y.M.C.A. Sec., Univ. of Alabama 23-25; Instructor, Huntsville Coll. 25-28; practised as attorney, Huntsville 25-36; U.S. Commr. 30-31; mem. Congress 37-47; U.S. Senator from Alabama 46-; Democratic nomination for Vice-Presidency 52; Chair. Senate Foreign Relations Cttee. 75-.
Home: Huntsville, Ala.; Office: Senate Office Building, Washington, D.C., U.S.A.

Spassky, Boris Vasiliyevich; Soviet journalist and chess-player; b. 30 Jan. 1937, Leningrad; m. Marina Stcherbatcheff 1975; ed. Faculty of Journalism, Leningrad State Univ.
In Leningrad Section of Voluntary Sport Soc., Trud 59-61; Trainer, Leningrad Section of Voluntary Sport Soc., Locomotiv 64-; played in numerous individual and command int. chess tournaments; U.S.S.R. Grand Master, Int. Grand Master and World Chess Student Champion 56, U.S.S.R. Chess Champion 62, World Chess Champion 69-72; several decorations.
State Committee for Sports and Physical Culture of U.S.S.R. Council of Ministers, Skatertny pereulok 4, Moscow, U.S.S.R.

Spater, George Alexander, J.D.; American airline executive (retd.); b. 3 May 1909, Detroit, Mich.; s. of Alexander M. and Julia (née Robinson) Spater; m. Hope W. Clark 1936; four s. one d.; ed. Univ. of Michigan.
Admitted to N.Y. Bar 35; Partner Chadbourne, Wallace, Parke and Whiteside 42-58; Exec. Vice-Pres. Gen.

Counsel, American Airlines, Inc., 59-67, Vice-Chair. of Board 67-68, Pres. and Chair. 68-73; Senior Fellow, Univ. of Sussex; Hon. LL.D. (Monmouth Univ.).
Juggs Way, Kingston, Lewes, Sussex, England.
Telephone: Lewes 6656.

Speaight, Robert William, C.B.E., M.A., F.R.S.L.; British actor, critic, theatre director and author; b. 14 Jan. 1904, St. Margaret's Bay, Kent; s. of Frederick William and Emily Isabella Speaight; m. Bridget Laura Bosworth-Smith 1951; two s.; ed. Haileybury Coll. and Lincoln Coll., Oxford.
Principal parts: Becket in T. S. Eliot's *Murder in the Cathedral*; leading Shakespearian parts for the Old Vic.; Christ in Dorothy Sayers' *Man Born to be King*, More in *A Man for All Seasons*; principal productions: *Antony and Cleopatra*, Geneva; *The Madwoman of Chaillot*, London; *Murder in the Cathedral*, Montreal; guest artist with Australian Broadcasting Comm. 53 and with Australian Elizabethan Theatre Trust 60, 62-63; Officer Legion of Honour.
Leisure interests: reading and walking.
Publs. *Mutinous Wind* 32, *The Lost Hero* 34, *The Angel in the Mist* 36, *Thomas Becket* 38, *The Unbroken Heart* 39, *Acting* 39, *Drama since 1939* 48, *George Eliot* 54, *William Poel and the Elizabethan Revival* 54, *Nature in Shakespearian Tragedy* 55, *Hilaire Belloc* 57, *Letters of Hilaire Belloc* (editor) 58, *Christian Theatre* 60, *William Rothenstein* 63, *Ronald Knox The Writer* 65, *Eric Gill* 66, *Teilhard de Chardin* 67, *The Property Basket* (autobiography) 70, *Vanier* 70, *Shakespeare on the Stage* 73, *Georges Bernanos* 73, *Companion Guide to Burgundy* 75, *François Mauriac* 76.
Campion House, Benenden, Kent, England.
Telephone: 058-082-617.

Spear, Ruskin, R.A., A.R.C.A.; British artist; b. 30 June 1911, London; s. of Augustus Spear and Jane (née Lemon); m. Hilda Mary Hill 1935; one s.; ed. Royal Coll. of Art.
Elected London Group 42, Pres. 50; Visiting Teacher of Painting, Royal Coll. of Art; paintings exhibited in many English and Australian art galleries; works purchased by The Chantrey Trustees, The British Council, The Arts Council, Stratford Memorial Theatre, St. Clement Dane's R.A.F. Memorial Church; executed murals for liner *Canberra*; numerous portraits incl. Duke of Westminster, Lord Goodman, Harold Wilson, Chief Justice Dalton-Wells of Toronto, Lord Adrian, Lord Rothermere, Archbishop of Canterbury, Dowager Duchess of Devonshire, Sir Aubrey Lewis, Sir Ian Jacob, Lord Oliver, Barbara Castle, Sir Hugh Carleton-Greene, Lord Netherthorpe, Sir Maurice Bridgeman, Lord Redcliffe-Maude; travelling exhbns. in U.S.; exhbn. in Pushkin Museum, Moscow 57.
Leisure interest: music.
20 Fielding Road, London, W.4, England.
Telephone: 01-995-9736.

Spedding, Frank Harold, B.CH.E., M.S., PH.D.; American chemist, physicist and metallurgist; b. 22 Oct. 1902, Hamilton, Ont., Canada; s. of Howard Leslie Spedding and Mary Ann Elizabeth Marshall Spedding; m. Ethel Annie MacFarlane 1931; one d.; ed Univs. of Mich. and Calif.
Teaching Asst., Univ. of Mich. (Analytical Chem.) 23-25, Fellow, Analytical Chem. 25-26; Teaching Fellow in Chem., Univ. of Calif. 26-29, Instructor in Chem. 29-30, 32-34, Nat. Research Fellow in Chem. 30-32; Guggenheim Professorship, England, Germany, Russia 34-35; George Fisher Baker Asst. Prof., Cornell Univ., Ithaca, N.Y. 35-37; Assoc. Prof. of Physical Chem., Head of Physical Chem. Section, Iowa State Univ. 37-41, Dir. Atomic Project 42-47, Dir. Inst. for Atomic Research 45-68, Dir. Ames Lab. of Atomic Energy Comm., Iowa State Univ. 47-68, Prof. of Physics, Iowa State Univ. 50-, Prof. of Metallurgy 62-,

Principal Scientist, Ames Lab. of Atomic Energy Comm. (now Energy Research and Devt. Admin.), Iowa State Univ. 68-; mem. Cttee. on Radioactive Waste Management Nat. Acad. of Science 68-; mem. Nat. Acad. of Sciences, Soc. for Applied Spectroscopy; Hon. mem. Soc. of Austrian Chemists; numerous awards including Francis J. Clamer Medal of the Franklin Inst.
Leisure interests: mountain climbing, camping, gardening, golf.
Publs. Editor *The Rare Earths* 61; over 230 articles in scientific journals.
Ames Laboratory, Energy Research and Development Administration (ERDA), Iowa State University, Ames, Iowa 50011; Home: 520 Oliver Circle, Ames, Iowa 50010, U.S.A.
Telephone: 515-294-2785 (Office); 515-292-2785 (Home).

Speer, Edgar Boyle; American business executive; b. 28 July 1916, Pittsburgh, Pa.; s. of Edgar B. Speer and Gladys (Kelly) Speer; m. Arlene R. Kline 1946; four s.; ed. Widener Coll., Univ. of Pennsylvania, Harvard Univ.
Joined U.S. Steel Corpn. 38, Gen. Supt. Fairless Works 56-58, Gen. Man. Steel Operations, Pittsburgh 58-59, Admin. Vice-Pres. Central Operations 59-64, Admin. Vice-Pres. Steel Operations 64-67, Exec. Vice-Pres. Production 67-69, Dir. 68-, Pres. 69-73, Chair. and Chief Exec. Officer 73-; Dir. American Iron and Steel Inst.
Office: U.S. Steel Corporation, 600 Grant Street, Pittsburgh, Pa. 15230; Home: Edgewood Road, Fox Chapel, Pittsburgh, Pa. 15215, U.S.A.
Telephone: 412-433-1101 (Office); 412-782-0582 (Home).

Speidel, Gen. Hans, DR.PHIL.; German army officer; b. 28 Oct. 1897, Metzingen; s. of Emil Speidel and Amalie née von Klipstein; m. Ruth Stahl 1925; one s. two d.; ed. Univs. of Tübingen and Berlin, Technische Hochschule Stuttgart, Kriegsakademie.
Regular army officer 14-45; served 14-18 war in König Karl Grenadier Regt. and 39-45 war mainly in staff appts., finally as Chief of Staff to an Army Group under Rommel; arrested by the Gestapo Sept. 44; Lecturer, Univ. of Tübingen 49-55; Head of Mil. del. to CED and NATO confs. 51-55; C.-in-C. German Armed Forces 55-57; Commdr. Allied Land Forces Central Europe 57-63; Special Counsellor to Fed. Govt. 63-64; Pres. of Foundation Sciences and Politics (Wissenschaft und Politik) 64-; Ritterkreuz Königlich-Württembergischen Militärverdienstorden (14-18), Ritterkreuz des Eisernen Kreuzes (39-45), Grosses Verdienstkreuz mit Stern und Schulterband 63, Prof. h.c. 71; Ehrenbürger der Stadt Metzingen.
Leisure interests: history, literature, music.
Publs. *Invasion 1944—Ein Beitrag zu Rommels und des Reiches Schicksal* 49, Beck's *Studien* (editor) 55, *Zeitbetrachtungen: Ausgewählte Reden* 69, *Gedanken zu antikem und modernem Feldherrntum* 70; essays on Theodor Heuss, Neidhart von Gneisenau, etc.
Am Spitzenbach 21, 534 Bad Honnef/Rhein, Federal Republic of Germany.
Telephone: Bad Honnef (02224) 3150.

Spence, Sir Basil Urwin, Kt., O.M., O.B.E., T.D., R.A., R.D.I., P.P.R.I.B.A.; British architect; b. 13 Aug. 1907, Bombay, India; s. of Urwin Spence and Daisy Crisp; m. Mary Joan Ferris 1937; one s. one d.; ed. George Watson's Coll., Edinburgh, schools of architecture in London and Edinburgh Univs.
Silver medallist R.I.B.A. 31; Arthur Cates Prizeman (Town Planning) 32; Pugin student 33; R.I.B.A. Distinction in Town Planning 61; served in army 39-45 war; built large country houses before war, since then housing estates, theatres, schools, university buildings, churches and factories; Adviser to Board of Trade for B.I.F. 47, 48 and 49; won competition for new Coventry Cathedral 51; Saltire Award for fishermen's houses, Dunbar 52; Newhaven 61; Planning Consultant

for Edinburgh Univ. 54, Southampton Univ. 55, apptd. to design new Town Halls for Slough, Basildon and Hampstead, new Univ. of Sussex, and various univ. science buildings, British Embassy, Rome, Hyde Park Cavalry Barracks, Civic Centre, Kensington, London, British Pavilion *Expo 67*, Montreal; Consultant architect for extension to Palais des Nations, Geneva, and int. airport at Baghdad; R.I.B.A. Council mem. 52-63, Vice-Pres. 54-55, Hon. Sec. 56, Pres. 58-60; mem. Fine Art Comm. 56-70; Prof. of Architecture, Royal Acad. 61-68, Treas. 62-64; Pres. Building Centre 60-67; Festival of Britain 1951 Award for Sunbury-on-Thames Housing Estate; Hon. mem. Accad. di San Luca, Rome 73; Hon. Fellow, American Inst. of Architects, Royal Architectural Inst. of Canada, Inst. of South Africa Architects, Royal Coll. of Art; Hon. D.Litt. (Leicester, Southampton); Hon. LL.D. (Manitoba).
Leisure interests: painting, sailing.
Publ. *Phoenix at Coventry* 62.
1 Canonbury Place, London, N.1, England.
Telephone: 01-226-7175.

Spencer, Donald Clayton, PH.D., SC.D.; American professor of mathematics; b. 25 April 1912, Boulder, Colo.; *s.* of Frank Robert Spencer and Edith (Clayton) Spencer; *m.* 1st Mary J. Halley 1936, 2nd Natalie Robertson Sanborn 1951; one *s.* two *d.*; ed. Univ. of Colo., Mass. Inst. of Technology and Univ. of Cambridge.
Instructor, Mass. Inst. of Technology 39-42; Assoc. Prof., Stanford Univ. 42-46, Prof. 46-50, 63-68; Assoc. Prof., Princeton Univ. 50-53, Prof. 53-63, 68-, Henry Burchard Fine Prof. 72-; mem. Applied Mathematics Group, Nat. Defense Research Cttee., New York Univ. 44-45; mem. Nat. Acad. of Sciences, American Acad. of Arts and Sciences; Bocher Prize of American Mathematical Soc. (joint recipient) 48; Sc.D. h.c. Purdue Univ. 71.
Leisure interests: conservation, hiking.
Publs. (Monographs): *Coefficient Regions for Schlickt Functions* (with A. C. Schaeffer), *American Mathematical Society Colloquium Publications* Vol. 35 50, *Functionals of Finite Riemann Surfaces* (with M. Schiffer) 54, *Advanced Calculus* (with H. K. Nickerson and N. E. Steenrod) 59, *Lie Equations Vol. I: General Theory* (with A. Kumpera) 72; articles in mathematical journals.
Fine Hall, Princeton University, Princeton, N.J. 08540; Home: RD No 4, Box 832, Lake Road, Princeton, N.J. 08540, U.S.A.
Telephone: 609-452-4188 (Office); 609-452-9220 (Home).

Spencer, Edson W.; American President and Chief Executive Officer, Honeywell Inc. 74; see *The International Who's Who 1975-76*.

Spencer, William I.; American banker; b. 24 July 1917, Mesa County, Colo.; *s.* of Eugene W. Spencer and Nellie Haviland; *m.* Kathryn M. Cope 1953; no *c.*; ed. Mesa Coll., Colorado Coll., Colorado Springs and Columbia Univ.
Vice-Pres., Special Industries Div., First National City Corpn. 54; Senior. Vice-Pres. in charge of Special Industries Group 59; Exec. Vice-Pres. in charge of Specialized Industries Div. 65, in charge of Operating Group 68; Pres. First National City Bank and CITICORP May 70-.
Leisure interests: hunting, golf, photography.
CITICORP, 399 Park Avenue, New York, N.Y. 10022; Home: 12 Beekman Place, New York, N.Y. 10022, U.S.A.
Telephone: 212-559-4941 (Office); 212-PL2-3096 (Home).

Spender, Sir Percy Claude, K.C.V.O., K.B.E., KT.ST.J., Q.C., B.A., LL.B.; Australian diplomatist, international judge, company director and writer; b. 5 Oct. 1897, Sydney; *s.* of Frank Henry Spender and Mary Spender (née Murray); *m.* Jean Maud Henderson 1925, (died 1970); two *s.*; ed. Sydney Univ.

Entered public service as Clerk, Sydney Town Hall 15; enlisted A.I.F. 18; called to N.S.W. Bar 23; K.C. 35; mem. House of Reps. for Warringah N.S.W. 37-51; mem. Fed. Exec. Council 39, Vice-Pres. Exec. Council 40; Minister without Portfolio 39; Acting Treas. 39, Treas. 40; Minister for Army 40-41; mem. Australian War Cabinet 40-41; mem. of Govt. and later Opposition mem.. Australian Advisory War Council 41-45; Lieut.-Col. Active List, Australian Mil. Forces 42-45; Minister for External Affairs 49-51; Ambassador to U.S.A. 51-58; Chair. Australian del. to British Commonwealth Foreign Ministers Conf., Colombo 50, and to UN 50; Vice-Pres. Fifth Gen. Assembly 50-51; Vice-Chair. Australian del. to Seventh, Eighth, Ninth, Tenth and Eleventh Gen. Assemblies, later Chair. 52-56; Vice-Pres. Japanese Peace Treaty Conf. San Francisco 51; Chair. Australian del. to Twelve Power Conf. to settle Draft Statute for Int. Atomic Energy Agency 56 and to several other int. confs.; Australian Gov. Int. Monetary Fund and Int. Bank 51-53 and 56, Alternate Gov. Int. Monetary Fund 54-55; Judge of the Int. Court of Justice 58-67, Pres. 64-67; Leader Australian Del. to 2nd Suez Conf. 66; mem. Gen. Council, Assicurazione Generali, Italy; Hon. LL.D., D.C.L., Litt.D.; retd.
Leisure interests: swimming, reading, gardening and travelling.
Publs. *Company Law and Practice* 39, *Foreign Policy—the Next Phase* 44, *Exercises in Diplomacy* 69, *Politics and a Man* 72.
Headingley House, 11 Wellington Street, Woollahra, Sydney, N.S.W. 2025, Australia.
Telephone: 32 32 52; 328 71 71.

Spender, Stephen, C.B.E.; British writer; b. 28 Feb. 1909; ed. Univ. Coll. School, London, and Univ. Coll., Oxford.
Poet and critic; Co-editor *Horizon* 39-41; Counsellor, Section of Letters UNESCO 47; Co-editor *Encounter* 53-66, Corresp. Editor 66-67; Consultant in Poetry in English to U.S. Library of Congress 65-; Visiting Prof. of English, Univ. of Connecticut; Prof. of English, Univ. Coll., London Oct. 70-; Hon. D.Litt. (Montpellier Univ.); Queen's Gold Medal for Poetry 71.
Publs. Poems in *New Signatures* 33, *Poems* (2 editions), *The Destructive Element* 34, *The Burning Cactus* (stories), *Forward From Liberalism* 36, *The Trial of a Judge* 37, *The Still Centre* 39, trans. Ernst Toller's *Pastor Hall* 39, *The Backward Son* 40, *Ruins and Visions* 42, *Life and the Poet* 42, *Citizens in War and After* 44, *European Witness* 46, *Poems of Dedication* 46, *The Edge of Being* 49, *World Within World* (autobiography) 51, *The Creative Element* 53, *Collected Poems* 55, *Engaged in Writing* 57; translation of Schiller's *Mary Stuart* 58; *The Struggle for the Modern* 62, *Selected Poems* 64, *The Year of the Young Rebels* 69, *The Concise Encyclopedia of English and American Poets and Poetry* (edited with Donald Hall) 70, *The Generous Days* 71, Editor *A Choice of Shelley's Verse* 71, Editor *D. H. Lawrence: Novelist, Poet, Prophet* 73, *Love-Hate Relations: A Study of Anglo-American Sensibilities* 74, *T. S. Eliot* 75, Editor *W. H. Auden: A Tribute* 75.
15 Loudoun Road, London, N.W.8, England.

Sperry, Roger Wolcott, A.B., M.A., PH.D.; American professor of psychobiology; b. 20 Aug. 1913, Hartford, Conn.; *s.* of Frances Bushnell Sperry and Florence Kramer; *m.* Norma Deupree 1949; one *s.* one *d.*; ed. Oberlin Coll., Univ. of Chicago and Harvard Univ.
Research Assoc., Yerkes Laboratories Primate Biology 42-46; Asst. Prof. of Anatomy, then Assoc. Prof. of Psychology, Univ. of Chicago 46-52; Section Chief, Developmental Neurology, Nat. Insts. of Health 52-53; Hixon Prof. of Psychobiology 54-; Fellow, American Acad. of Arts and Sciences, American Asscn. for the Advancement of Science, American Asscn. of Psychologists; mem. Nat. Acad. of Sciences; Warren Medal,

Soc. of Experimental Psychologists 69, Distinguished Scientific Contribution Award of American Psychological Asscn. 71; Calif. Scientist of the Year Award 72; Co-recipient 1st William Thompson Wakeman Research Award of Nat. Paraplegic Foundation 72; Hon. D.Sc. Univ. of Cambridge 72; Passano Award 73.
Leisure interests: sculpture, sketching, palaeontology.
Publs. Numerous scientific publications in professional journals and textbooks.
California Institute of Technology, 1201 East California Boulevard, Pasadena, Calif. 91109; Home: 1369 Boston Street, Altadena, Calif. 91001, U.S.A.
Telephone: 795-6841 (Office); 794-0784 (Home).

Sperti, George Speri, E.E., SC.D.; American scientist; b. 17 Jan. 1900, Covington, Ky.; s. of George and Caroline (Speri) Sperti; ed. Univ. of Cincinnati.
Assistant Chief Meter Laboratories U.G. & E., Cincinnati 22; Asst. Research Dir. Duncan Electrical and Manufacturing Co., Lafayette 23; Research Asst. Univ. of Cincinnati 24-25; Research Prof. and Dir. of Research (also co-founder) Basic Science Research Laboratory Univ. of Cincinnati 25-35; mem. Board of Dirs. Gen. Development Laboratories Inc., New York 30-35, Sperti Lamp Corpn. 30-40, Sperti Drug Products Inc.; Dir. Sperti Lamp Corpn. 35-; Research Prof., Dir. of Research, mem. Board of Trustees, mem. Board of Regents and Pres. St. Thomas Inst.; Principal Consultant War Production Board 42; mem. Pontifical Acad. Science, American Asscn. for Advancement of Science, American Physical Society; mem. Royal Soc. of Arts, London; Founding mem. American Soc. for the Aged and mem. of its Medical & Scientific Cttee.; Board of Dirs. American Council for Int. Promotion of Democracy under God Inc. 59; Dir. Franklin Corpn.; mem. Emeritus Hall; Hon. mem. Società Italiana de Fisica; mem. Académie Internationale de Philosophie des Sciences, Brussels; mem. Engineering Soc. of Cincinnati; mem. Academia de Doctores, Madrid; Catholic Action Medal 42, Mendel Medal 43, Christian Culture Award 47; Star of Solidarity Third Class of the Italian Repub. 56; Gold Medal Univ. Int. degli Studi Sociali "Pro Deo" 58, William Howard Taft Award 70, Cincinnati Scientist Engineer-of-the-Year Award 70; Hon. Sc.D. (Univ. of Dayton 34, Duquesne Univ. 36, Bryant Coll. 57); developed type of therapeutic lamp; other developments with selective irradiation and on fluorescent lighting; discovered biological substances Biodynes; specialist in cancer research.
Leisure interests: farming, horseback riding.
Publs. *Probiotics*; co-author *Quantum Theory in Biology* 27, and *Correlated Investigations in the Basic Sciences*; Editor *Studies Inst. Divi Thomae*.
St. Thomas Institute, 1842 Madison Road, Cincinnati, Ohio 45206, U.S.A.
Telephone: 513-861-3460.

Spicer, Sir John Armstrong, Kt., Q.C.; Australian lawyer; b. 5 March 1899, Melbourne; s. of late Henry Spicer and late Helen Jane Armstrong; m. Lavinia May Webster; one s.; ed. in Torquay (England) and Melbourne.
Admitted Barrister and Solicitor 21; K.C. 48; Senator Commonwealth Parl. 40-44, and 49-56; Attorney-Gen. 49-56; Chief Judge Australian Industrial Court (fmrly. Commonwealth Industrial Court) 56-.
Leisure interests: walking, swimming, reading.
153 Glen Iris Road, Glen Iris, Melbourne, Victoria, Australia.
Telephone: 25-2882.

Spiegel, Samuel P.; American film producer (born in Austria); b. 11 Nov. 1904; ed. Univ. of Vienna.
Went to U.S.A. 39; Pres. Horizon American Pictures Inc. 48-; two Academy Awards (*Oscars*); films produced include *Tales of Manhattan, The Stranger, African*

Queen, We Were Strangers, On the Waterfront, The Strange One, The Bridge on the River Kwai, The Chase, Suddenly Last Summer, Lawrence of Arabia, Mister Innocence, The Night of the Generals, The Swimmer.
475 Park Avenue, New York City, N.Y., U.S.A.

Spiegelman, Sol, PH.D., D.SC.; American microbiologist; b. 14 Dec. 1914, New York; s. of Max Spiegelman and Eva Kramer Spiegelman; m. Helen Wahala; two s. one d.; ed. Coll. of City of New York, Columbia Univ. and Washington Univ., St. Louis.
Lecturer in Physics at Wash. Univ. 42-44, in Applied Mathematics 43-44, Lecturer in Bacteriology School of Medicine, Wash. Univ. 45-46, Asst. Prof. 46-48; Special Fellow U.S. Public Health Service 48-49; Prof. of Microbiology, Univ. of Ill. 49-69; member Center of Advanced Study Univ. of Ill. 64-69; Dir. Inst. of Cancer Research; Prof. of Human Genetics and Development, Coll. of Physicians and Surgeons, Columbia Univ. 69-; mem. Nat. Cancer Advisory Board 72-; Fellow American Acad. of Arts and Sciences; mem. Nat. Acad. of Sciences, American Soc. for Microbiology, Soc. for Gen. Microbiology (U.K.), Genetics Soc. of America, German Acad. of Sciences etc.; foreign mem. Nat. Acad. of Medicine of Brazil; Pasteur Award, Ill. Soc. for Microbiology 63; Alumni Citation Award, Washington Univ. St. Louis 66; Bertner Foundation Award in Cancer Research 68; numerous guest lectureships; Hon. D.Sc. (Rensselaer Polytechnic Inst., Northwestern, St. Louis, Chicago and Glasgow Univs.).
Publs: author and co-author of 250 publications on cell physiology, genetics, developmental biology and molecular biology.
College of Physicians & Surgeons of Columbia Univ., Inst. of Cancer Research, Francis Delafield Hospital, 99 Fort Washington Ave., New York, N.Y. 10032, U.S.A.
Telephone: 212-795-1660; 212-579-8582.

Spierenburg, Dirk P.; Netherlands international official (retd.); b. 4 Feb. 1909, Rotterdam; m. Milja Ilitch; two s.; ed. Netherlands School of Economics, Rotterdam.
Mem. Netherlands Ministry for Economic Affairs 35-; Dir. Netherlands Bureau for Repartition of Metals and Metal Products during the war; Dir. for trade agreements with Western European countries 45-47, Head, Permanent Mission to O.E.E.C., Paris 47-48; Dir.-Gen. of Foreign Trade and Deputy Govt. Commr. for American Aid 48; Netherlands mem. of Council of Presidents of Benelux; Pres. Council of O.E.E.C. 50 and 51; Netherlands mem. 52-, and Vice-Pres. E.C.S.C. High Authority 58-63; Head, Perm. Rep. of Netherlands to European Econ. Community and EURATOM 63-70; Perm. Rep. to NATO 71-74.
c/o Ministry of Foreign Affairs, The Hague, Netherlands.

Spilhaus, Athelstan Frederick, M.S., D.SC.; American (naturalized) meteorologist and oceanographer; b. 25 Nov. 1911, Cape Town, South Africa; s. of Karl Antonio and Nellie (Muir) Spilhaus; m. Gail Griffin 1964; two s. three d.; ed. Univ. of Cape Town and Mass. Inst. of Technology.
Went to America 31, naturalized 46; research Asst. M.I.T. 33-35; Asst. Dir. of Technical Services, Union of South Africa Defence Forces 35-36, Woods Hole Oceanographic Inst. 36-37, Investigator in Physical Oceanography 38-60, Assoc. 60, now Hon. Staff mem.; Asst. Prof. New York Univ. 37-38, Assoc. Prof. 39-41; Prof. of Meteorology 42-48, started Dept. of Meteorology and Oceanography, Chair. 38-47; Capt. U.S.A.F. 43, Major 44, Lieut.-Col. 46; Dir. of Research New York Univ. 46-48; Meteorological Adviser to Govt. of Union of South Africa 47; Dean and Prof. Inst. of Technology, Univ. of Minnesota 49-66; Prof. School of Physics, Univ. of Minnesota 66; Pres. Franklin Inst. 67-69. Aqua Int. Inc. 69-70; Fellow Woodrow Wilson

Int. Center for Scholars 71-, Royal Meteorological Society, American Inst. of Aeronautics and Astronautics, A.A.A.S.; mem. American Meteorological Society, Royal Society of South Africa, American Geophysical Union, Amer. Soc. of Limnology and Oceanography, Amer. Phil. Soc.; mem. U.S. Nat. Cttee. Int. Geophysical Year; mem. Nat. Science Board, Cttee. on Science and Astronautics, House of Reps.; Trustee Woods Hole Oceanographic Inst., Int. Oceanographic Foundation, Science Service Inc., Aerospace Corpn. 63-; Dir. Donaldson Co. Inc., Amer. Dynamics Corpn.; U.S. Rep. UNESCO Exec. Board 54-58; U.S. Commr. Seattle World's Fair 61-63; inventor of bathythermograph 38; Legion of Merit 46; Exceptional Civilian Service Medal, U.S.A.F. 52; Patriotic Civilian Service Award, Dept. of the Army 59; Berzelius Medal 62; Proctor Prize, Scientific Research Soc. of America 68; ten Hon. Degrees from U.S.A. and U.K.
Publs. *Workbook in Meteorology* (textbook) 42, *Weathercraft* (for children) 51, *Meteorological Instruments* (with W. E. K. Middleton) 53, *Satellite of the Sun* 58, *Turn to the Sea* 59, *The Ocean Laboratory* 66, *Experimental Cities* 66-, *Waste Management, The Next Industrial Revolution* 66-; *Our New Age* (daily and Sunday feature); more than 200 articles in journals and magazines.
2815 28th Street, N.W., Washington, D.C. 20008, U.S.A.
Telephone: 202-232-4809.

Spinelli, Altiero; Italian EEC official; b. 31 Aug. 1907, Rome; s. of Carlo and Maria Spinelli-Ricci; m. Ursula Hirschmann 1944; three d.; ed. Univ. of Rome.
Spent ten years in prison and six years in confinement on account of political activities 27-43; f. European Federalist Movement, Milan 43; mem. political secr. N. Italian Action Party 43; organized first int. federalist confs. Geneva, July 44, Paris, Feb. 45; mem. Nat. Political Secr., Action Party 45-46; Sec.-Gen. European Federalist Movement in Italy 48-62; also mem. exec. cttee. and gen. del. of European Union of Federalists, Paris; Visiting Prof., Bologna Centre of School for Advanced Int. Studies, Johns Hopkins Univ. 62-66; Dir. Inst. of Int. Affairs, Rome 66-70; Adviser on European Affairs to Pietro Nenni, Minister of Foreign Affairs, 68-69; mem. Comm. of European Communities 70-, in charge of industrial policy and technology; Robert Schumann Prize, F.V.S. Foundation 74.
Leisure interests: reading and swimming.
Publs. *Problems of European Federation* (with E. Rossi) 44, *From Sovereign States to the United States of Europe* 50, *The European Federalist Manifesto* 57, *Germans at the Crossroads* 60, *Che fare per l'Europe* 65 (publ. in English as *The Eurocrats* 66), *Il lungo monologo* 68, *L'Avventura Europea*.
Commission of the European Communities, 200 rue de la Loi, 1949 Brussels, Belgium.
Telephone: 735-00-40.

Spínola, Gen. Antonio Sebastião Ribeiro de; Portuguese retd. army officer; b. 11 April 1910, Estremoz; ed. Mil. Schools, Lisbon, Univ. of Lisbon.
Promoted to rank of Capt. 44, Maj. 56, Lt.-Col. 61, Col. 63, Brig. 66, Gen. 69; held various posts in Portuguese Army; Deputy Commdr., later Commdr. 2nd Lancers Regt. 61; Commdr. 345th Cavalry Group, Angola 61-64; Provost Marshal 64-65; High Command Course 65-66; Cavalry Insp. 66-67; Deputy Commdr. Nat. Republican Guard 67-68; Gov., C.-in-C. of the Armed Forces of Portuguese Guinea 68-73; Deputy Chief of Staff of the Armed Forces 73-74; Head Junta Nacional de Salvação 74; Pres. of Portugal May-Sept. 74; retd. from Army Nov. 74; in exile in Brazil 75-; Dir. Sociedade Hípica Portuguesa (Equestrian Soc.) 40-44, Pres. 67; mem. Board of Dirs. Siderurgia Nacional (Nat. Steel Works Co.) 55-64; Commdr. Order

of Aviz 59, Gold Medal for Exemplary Conduct 65, of Mil. Merit with Laurels 72, Tower and Sword with Palms 73, and many other mil. decorations.
Publs. *Por Uma Guiné Melhor* (For a Better Guinea) 70, *Linha de Accão* (Line of Action) 71, *No Caminho do Futuro* (On the Path to the Future) 74.

Spinoy, André; Belgian politician; b. 1906; ed. L'Athénée de Malines.
Secretary, Fed. of Malines 30-36; Provincial Counsellor, Antwerp 36-44; fmr. Mayor of Malines; M.P. 44-; Minister of Nat. Defence 54-58, of Econ. Affairs 61-65; Deputy Prime Minister and Co-ordinator of Econ. Policy 65-66; Socialist.
100 ave. Reine Astrid, Malines, Belgium.

Spirin, Aleksandr Sergeyevich; Soviet biochemist; b. 4 Sept. 1931, Moscow Region; m. Lydia Pavlovna Gavrilova; one s.; ed. Moscow State Univ.
Member of Staff, Bakh Inst. of Biochemistry 58-62, Head of Laboratory 62-73; Prof. Moscow State Univ. 64-73, Head of Chair. of Plant Biochemistry 73-; Head of Laboratory and Dir. Inst. of Protein Research 67-; Corresp. mem. U.S.S.R. Acad. of Sciences 66-70, Academician 70-; mem. Deutsche Akad. der Naturforscher Leopoldina 74; Sir Hans Krebs Medal 69; Dr. h.c. Univ. of Granada, Spain 72.
Leisure interest: hunting.
Publs. *Macromolecular Structure of Ribonucleic Acids* 64, *The Ribosome* 69.
Biological Faculty, Moscow State University, Moscow; Institute of Protein Research, U.S.S.R. Academy of Sciences, Poustchino, Moscow Region, U.S.S.R.

Spiro, Sidney, M.C.; South African business executive; b. 1914, South Africa; s. of Marcus and Clara Spiro; m. Diana D. M. Susskind; two d.; ed. Grey Coll., Bloemfontein and Cape Town Univ.
Joined Anglo American Corpn. S.A. Ltd. 53, Exec. Dir. 61; Vice-Chair. and Man. Dir. Charter Consolidated Ltd. 69, Chair. and Man. Dir. 71-72, Chair. Oct. 72-.
Leisure interests: shooting, golf, tennis.
Charter Consolidated Ltd., 40 Holborn Viaduct, London, E.C.1, England.

Spitsyn, Viktor Ivanovich; Soviet scientist; b. 25 April 1902, Moscow; ed. Moscow State Univ.
Worked at chemical plant 18; Instructor, Inorganic Chemistry, Moscow State Univ. 23-31; Research Chemist, Moscow Electrical Plant 23-28; Senior Research Chemist, Inst. of Applied Mineralogy and Nonferrous Metallurgy 28-31; Prof. Inorganic Chemistry, Moscow State C. Liebknecht Pedagogical Inst. 32-42; Prof. Inorganic Chemistry, Moscow State Lomonossov Univ. 42-, Vice-Rector 42-48; Vice-Dir. Inst. of Physical Chemistry, Acad. of Sciences of the U.S.S.R. 49-53, Dir. 53-; mem. Acad. of Sciences of the U.S.S.R. 58-; mem. Scientific Advisory Cttee. IAEA; Hon. Fellow, Polish Chemical Soc., Indian Chemical Soc.; Hero of Socialist Labour; Order of Lenin (three times), Order of the Red Banner of Labour; Order of the October Revolution.
Publs. *The Reduction of Tungstates* 25, *The Chlorination of Oxides* 30, *The Organisation of Soviet Beryllium Production* 33, *The Methods of Use of Radioactive Tracers* 55, *The Migration of Radioelements in Soil* 58, 60, *The Action of Radioactive Radiation of Solids on their Physico-Chemical Properties* 58, *Soviet Chemistry Today* 61, *Investigations in the Chemistry of Uranium* 61, *Radioactive Catalysts* 63, *Investigation in the Chemistry of Technetium* 73.
U.S.S.R. Academy of Sciences, 14 Leninsky Prospekt, Moscow, U.S.S.R.

Spitzer, Lyman, Jr., B.A., PH.D.; American astronomer; b. 26 June 1914; s. of Lyman Spitzer and Blanche Brumback Spitzer; m. Doreen D. Canaday 1940; one s. three d.; ed. Phillips Acad., Andover, Mass., and Yale, Cambridge, Princeton and Harvard Univs.
Instructor in Physics and Astronomy Yale Univ. 39;

Scientist Special Studies Group 42, and Dir. Sonar Analysis Group 44, Columbia Univ., Division of War Research; Associate Prof. of Astrophysics Yale Univ. 46; Prof. of Astronomy, Chair. of Dept. and Dir. of Observatory, Princeton Univ. 47-, Charles A. Young Prof. of Astronomy 52-; Dir. Project Matterhorn 53-61; Chair. Exec. Cttee. Plasma Physics Laboratory 61-66; Chair. Univ. Research Board 67-72; mem. Nat. Acad. of Sciences 52-, Royal Astronomical Soc., American Astronomical Soc., Physical Soc., American Acad. of Arts and Sciences, American Philosophical Soc., American Alpine Club; Pres. American Astronomical Soc. 60-62; Assoc. Royal Astronomical Soc. 73-; NASA Medal 72, Bruce Medal 73, Henry Draper Medal, U.S. Nat. Acad. of Sciences 74, James Clerk Maxwell Prize, American Physical Soc. 75; Hon. D.Sc. (Yale Univ., Case Inst., Harvard Univ.), Hon. LL.D. (Toledo Univ.). Leisure interests: mountain climbing, skiing.
Publs. *Physics of Sound in the Sea* (Editor) 46, *Physics of Fully Ionized Gases* 56, 62, *Diffuse Matter in Space* 68, and many articles.
Princeton University, Princeton, N.J. 08540, U.S.A. Telephone: 609-452-3800.

Spivakovsky, Tossy; Russian-born American violinist; b. 4 Feb. 1907, Odessa, U.S.S.R.; s. of David and Rahel Spivakovsky; m. Erika Lipsker 1934; one d.; ed. Hochschule für Musik, Berlin.
Brought to Berlin 09; concert debut 17; recitals and solo performances in Europe 17-33; concert tour, Australia and New Zealand 33; settled in Melbourne, taught at Melbourne Univ. Conservatory Master Class; settled in U.S.A. 43-; yearly concert tours U.S.A., Canada and Europe; apart from classical and romantic repertoire, is well known for his introductory performances of concertos by Bartok, Stravinsky, Menotti, Miklos Rozsa, Leonard Bernstein, Roger Sessions, Carl Nielsen, William Schuman, Leroy Robertson, Frank Martin and others; numerous recordings.
Leisure interest: reading.
American Manager: Columbia Artists Management, 165 West 57th Street, New York 19, N.Y., U.S.A.; European Manager: Wilfred Van Wyck, Troon, Old Mill Lane, Bray, Berks., SL6 2BG, England; Home: 70 Weston Road, Westport, Conn., U.S.A.
Telephone: 203-227-9057 (Home).

Spock, Benjamin, B.A., M.D.; American pediatrician; b. May 1903, New Haven, Conn.; s. of Benjamin Ives Spock and Mildred Stoughton Spock; m. Jane Cheney 1927; two s.; ed. Yale Coll., Coll. of Physicians and Surgeons, Columbia Univ.
Pediatrical practice, Cornell Medical Coll., New York Hosp. and New York City Health Department 33-47; served in U.S. Navy 44-46; mem. staff, Rochester (Minn.) Child Health Inst., Mayo Clinic and Univ. of Minnesota; organized teaching programme in child psychiatry and development, Pittsburgh Univ. Medical School 51-55; Prof. of Child Development, Western Reserve Univ. 55-67; specializes in application of psychoanalytic principles to pediatric practice; Spokesman, Cttee. for Sane Nuclear Policy (SANE); Candidate for U.S. Presidency, People's Party, 72.
Leisure interest: sailing.
Publs. *Baby and Child Care* 46, revised edns. 57, 68, 76, *A Baby's First Year* (with John Reinhart and Wayne Miller) 55, *Feeding Your Baby and Child* (with Miriam E. Lowenberg) 55, *Dr. Spock Talks with Mothers* 61, *Problems of Parents* 62, *Caring for your Disabled Child* (in collaboration) 65, *Dr. Spock on Vietnam* (with Mitchell Zimmermann) 68, *Decent and Indecent* 70, *A Teenager's Guide to Life and Love* 70 (U.K.: *A Young Person's Guide to Life and Love* 71), *Raising Children in a Difficult Time* 74.
538 Madison Avenue, New York, N.Y. 10022, U.S.A. Telephone: 212-421-1085.

Spoehr, Alexander, PH.D.; American anthropologist; b. 23 Aug. 1913, Tucson, Ariz.; s. of Herman A. and Florence M. Spoehr; m. Anne D. Harding 1941; one s. one d.; ed. Stanford Univ. and Univ. of Chicago.
Assistant Curator, Field Museum of Natural History 40-44, Curator 45-52; Dir. Bernice P. Bishop Museum 53-61; Prof. of Anthropology, Yale Univ. 53-61; Chancellor, East-West Center, Hawaii 62-63; U.S. Commr. South Pacific Comm. 59-60; Prof. of Anthropology, Univ. of Pittsburgh 64-; mem. Nat. Acad. of Sciences; Guggenheim Fellow 52.
Leisure interests: gardening, swimming.
Publs. *Majuro* 49, *Saipan* 54, *Marianas Prehistory* 57, *Zamboanga and Sulu: An Archaeological Approach to Ethnic Diversity* 73.
Department of Anthropology, University of Pittsburgh, Pittsburgh, Pa. 15213, U.S.A.
Telephone: 621-1395.

Spohr, Arnold Theodore, O.C.; Canadian ballet director, teacher and choreographer; b. 26 Dec. 1927; ed. St. John's High School and Winnipeg Teachers Coll.
Piano Teacher 46-51; Principal Dancer Royal Winnipeg Ballet 47-54; Canadian Broadcasting Corpn. Television Choreographer and performer 55-57; Choreographer Rainbow Stage 57-60; Artistic Dir. Royal Winnipeg Ballet 58-; Dir.-Teacher Royal Winnipeg Ballet School 58-; Dir. Nelson School of Fine Arts Dance Dept. 64-67; Artistic Dir. Dance Dept. Banff School of Fine Arts 67-; mem. Board of Dirs. Canadian Theatre Centre; many awards including Molson Prize, Canada Council 70, Centennial Medal, Gov. of Canada 67; Hon. LL.D. (Univ. of Manitoba) 70.
Choreography: *Ballet Premier* 50, *Intermede* 51, *E Minor* 59, *Hansel and Gretel* 60, and 18 musicals for Rainbow State.
Leisure interests: sports, piano, travel-research for study of every type of dancing.
289 Portage Avenue, 2nd Floor, Winnipeg, Manitoba R3B 2B4, Canada.

Spong, William Belser, Jr., LL.B.; American lawyer and politician; b. 29 Sept. 1920, Portsmouth, Va.; m. Virginia Wise Galliford 1950; one s. one d.; ed. Hampden-Sydney Coll., Virginia and Univs. of Virginia and Edinburgh.
Admitted to the Bar, Va. 47; Lecturer in Law and Govt., Coll. of William and Mary, Williamsburg, Va. 48-49; mem. Va. House of Delegates 54-55, Va. State Senate 56-66; Senator from Virginia 67-73; Democrat.
316 North Street, Portsmouth, Va. 23704, U.S.A.

Sporn, Philip; American engineer and executive; b. 25 Nov. 1896, Austria; s. of Isak and Rachel (Kolker); m. Sadie Posner 1923; two s. one d.; ed. Columbia Univ. School of Engineering.
Joined American Electric Power Co. 20, Chief Electrical Engineer 27, Chief Engineer 33, Vice-Pres. (Engineering) 34, Exec. Vice-Pres. (and Exec. Vice-Pres. American Electric Power Service Corpn.) 45, Pres. American Electric Power Co. and all subsidiaries 47-61; Pres. Ohio Valley Electric Corpn., Indiana-Kentucky Electric Corpn. 52-67; Chair. E. Central Nuclear Group Research and Devt. Cttee. 58-67, U.S. Nat. Cttee. C.I.G.R.E.; Chair. Seawater Conversion Comm. Israel Govt. 59; Chair. System Devt. Cttee., Dir. and mem. Exec. Cttee. American Electric Power Co. 61-67, Dir. and Consultant 67-69, Consultant 61-71; Chair. Exec. Advisory Cttee. Fed. Power Comm. Nat. Power Survey 62-65; Chair. Nat. Acad. of Sciences Advisory Board on Hardened Power Systems 62-70; Visiting Prof. Cornell Univ. 63, 65; mem. Nat. Comm. on Technology, Automation and Econ. Progress 64-66; Lecturer, M.I.T. 67, Visiting Prof. 70; Lecturer and Visiting Prof., Manhattan Coll. 75; Gov. Weizmann Inst. of Science; Trustee and mem. Research and Policy Cttee., Cttee. for Econ. Devt.;

mem. Advisory Councils Columbia Graduate School of Business, Columbia School of Engineering and Applied Science, Cornell Coll. of Engineering; mem. Visiting Comm., Dept. of Electrical Engineering M.I.T.; Fellow and Hon. mem. American Inst. of Electrical and Electronic Engineers; Fellow and Hon. mem. American Soc. of Mechanical Engineers; Hon. Fellow, Inst. of Mechanical Engineers; Fellow, American Soc. of Civil Engineers; Fellow, American Nuclear Soc.; mem. Nat. Acad. of Sciences; mem. Nat. Acad. of Eng.; awards include Edison Medal 45, John Fritz Medal 56, Faraday Medal 69; Hon. degrees from Stevens Inst. of Technology, Ill. Inst. of Technology, Univ. of Grenoble, Ohio State Univ., Haifa Technion, Columbia Univ. 66, Rensselaer Poly. Inst. 68, and other insts.; Chevalier Légion d'Honneur.
Leisure interests: walking, swimming, reading, theatre, listening to music, writing, lecturing.
Publs. *Heat Pumps* (with Ambrose and Baumeister) 47, *The Integrated Power System* 50, *Energy—Its Production, Conversion and Use in the Service of Man* 63, *Foundations of Engineering* 64, *Fresh Water from Saline Waters* 66, *Research in Electric Power* 66, *Vistas in Electric Power* 69, *Technology Engineering and Economics* 69, *The Social Organization of Electric Power Supply in Modern Societies* 71; series of critiques on nuclear power economics in the U.S.A. for J.C.A.E. 62-70.
320 East 72nd Street, New York, N.Y. 10021, U.S.A.

Spotswood, Marshal of the Royal Air Force Sir Denis, G.C.B., C.B.E., D.S.O., D.F.C.; British air force officer; b. 26 Sept. 1916, England; s. of F. H. and M. C. Spotswood; m. Ann Child 1942; one s.
Joined Royal Air Force 36; service in Squadrons U.K. and N. Africa 37-43; Dir. of Plans, H.Q. Supreme Allied Commdr., S.E. Asia 44-46; Stations (Fighter) 48-50, 54-56; Commdt. and Air Officer Commanding (A.O.C.) R.A.F. Coll. Cranwell, 58-61; Asst. Chief of Staff (Air Defence) SHAPE 61-63; C.-in-C. R.A.F. Germany and Commd. 2nd Allied Tactical Air Force 65-68; C.-in-C. Strike Command 68-71; Chief of Air Staff 71-74; Vice-Chair. Rolls-Royce (1971) Ltd. 74-; A.D.C. to H.M. The Queen 57-61, Air A.D.C. to H.M. The Queen Aug. 70-74; U.S. Legion of Merit.
Leisure interests: shooting, bridge, rugby (spectator), golf.
c/o Williams and Glyn's Bank Ltd., Kirkland House, Whitehall, London, S.W.1, England.

Sprague, George F., PH.D., D.SC.; American research agronomist; b. 3 Sept. 1902, Crete, Neb.; s. of E. E. Sprague and Lucy K. Manville; m. 1st Mary S. Whitworth 1926, 2nd Amy M. Millang 1945; two s. two d.; ed. Univ. of Nebraska and Cornell Univ.
Junior Agronomist, U.S. Dept. of Agriculture 24-28, Asst. Agronomist 28-34, Assoc. Agronomist 34-39, Agronomist 39-42, Senior Agronomist 42-58, Principal Agronomist 58, Leader of Corn and Sorghum Investigations 58-; Fellow, A.A.A.S., American Soc. of Agronomy; mem. Nat. Acad. of Sciences, Washington Acad. of Sciences; Crop Science Award.
Publs. *Corn and Corn Improvement* 56, *Quantitative Genetics in Plant Improvement* 66; and over 100 research papers in scientific journals.
S 12 Turner Hall, Department of Agronomy, University of Illinois, Urbana, Ill. 61801; Home: 2212 S. Lynn, Urbana, Ill. 61801, U.S.A.
Telephone: 333-4254 (Office); 344-6685 (Home).

Springer, Axel; German publisher; b. 2 May 1912, Hamburg-Altona; s. of Hinrich and Ottilie Springer; divorced; two s. one d.; ed. Realgymnasium, Hamburg-Altona.
Printing and publishing apprenticeships with provincial newspapers; received journalistic training with WTB news agency and on his father's paper *Altonaer Nach-*

richten; founded own publishing company 45; now sole proprietor Axel Springer Publishing Group, consisting of Axel Springer Verlag A.G., the Ullstein and Propyläen book publishing companies and Ullstein AV (production and distribution of audio-visual publications); publs. include *Die Welt, Bild Zeitung, Hamburger Abendblatt, Berliner Morgenpost, BZ* (daily papers); *Bild am Sonntag, Welt am Sonntag* (Sunday papers); *Hör Zu, Funk Uhr* (radio and television programme magazines); Hon. Fellow, Weizmann Inst., Israel; Hon. D.Hum.Litt. (Temple Univ.); Dr.phil. h.c. (Bar-Ilan Univ., Israel); Grosses Bundesverdienstkreuz, Bayerischer Verdienstorden.
Publ. *Von Berlin aus Gesehen* 71 and numerous articles and speeches.
1 Berlin 61, Kochstrasse 50, Germany.

Springer, Sir Hugh Worrell, K.C.M.G., C.B.E., M.A., D.SC., SOC.; Barbadian barrister and educationist; b. 22 June 1913, Barbados; s. of Charles Wilkinson Springer and Florence Springer; m. Dorothy Drinan Gittens 1942; three s. one d.; ed. Harrison Coll., Barbados, Hertford Coll., Oxford and Inner Temple, London.
Practised at Bar of Barbados 39-47; mem. House of Assembly, Barbados 40-47; mem. Exec. Cttee., Barbados 44-47; mem. Educ. Board, Barbados 44-47; Gen. Sec. Barbados Labour Party 40-47; Organizer and first Gen. Sec. Barbados Workers' Union 40-47; Registrar, Univ. of West Indies 47-63; mem. Educ. Authority of Jamaica 50-56, ILO Cttee. of Experts on Social Policy in Non-Metropolitan Territories 53-58, W. Indies Trade and Tariff Comm. 57-58, Univ. Grants Cttee., Ghana 59, Jamaica Public Service Comm. 59-63, W. Indies Fed. Service Comm. 60-61; Guggenheim Fellow and Fellow Harvard Centre for Int. Affairs 61-62; Senior Visiting Fellow, All Souls Coll., Oxford 62-63; Acting Gov. of Barbados 64; Dir. Inst. of Educ. of Univ. of W. Indies 63-66; Chair. Commonwealth Caribbean Medical Research Council 65-; Sec. Commonwealth Educ. Liaison Cttee. and Dir. Commonwealth Educ. Liaison Unit 66-67; Commonwealth Asst. Sec.-Gen. (Educ.) 67-70; mem. Council of Bernard van Leer Foundation 67-; Fellow, Royal Soc. of Arts 68-; mem. of Bermuda Civil Disorders Comm. 68; Sec.-Gen. Asscn. of Commonwealth Univs. 70-; Chair. Commonwealth Human Ecology Council 72-, Commonwealth Foundation 74-; Pres. Education Section of British Asscn. 74-75; Hon. Fellow, Hertford Coll., Oxford 74; Hon. LL.D. (Victoria Univ., British Columbia, Univ. of West Indies), Hon. D.Litt. (Warwick Univ., Ulster Univ.).
Leisure interests: walking, reading and conversation.
Publs. *Reflections on the Failure of the First West Indian Federation* 62, *Problems of National Development in the West Indies* 65, *Barbados as a Sovereign State, University Government Relations in the West Indies* 67, *Relevance or Respectability in Education—The Rural Problem* 70, *Educational Aspects of Human Ecology and Development* 71, and articles in journals.
22 Kensington Court Gardens, London, W8 5QP, England.
Telephone: 01-937-4626.

Springer, Konrad Ferdinand, DR. PHIL.; German publisher; b. 25; ed. Staatliches Kaiserin Augusta-Gymnasium, Berlin, Staatliches Kant-Gymnasium, Berlin, and Univ. of Zürich.
Partner Springer Verlag, Berlin, Heidelberg and New York 63-, J. F. Bergmanns Verlagsbuchhandlung, Munich 63-, Lange and Springer Scientific Bookshop, Berlin 63-, Springer-Verlag, Minerva Wissenschaftl. Buchhandlung, Vienna 65.
Neuenheimer Landstrasse 28-30, 69 Heidelberg 1, Federal Republic of Germany.
Telephone: 487-215.

Spühler, Willy; Swiss economist and politician; b. 31 Jan. 1902; ed. Gymnasium of Zürich and Univs. of Zürich and Paris.

Statistician, Zürich 31-34; Head of Employment Bureau, Zürich 35-42; Head, Cen. Office of War Economy 39-48; mem. Zürich Town Council 42-59; mem. Nat. Council, Fed. Assembly 38-55, mem. Council of States, Fed. Assembly 55-59; mem. Fed. Council 59-70, Pres. Jan.-Dec. 63, Jan.-Dec. 68, Vice-Pres. Jan.-Dec. 67; Head of Transport, Communications and Power Dept. 59-65; Head of Fed. Political (Foreign Affairs) Dept. 66-Jan. 70; Pres. of Foundation "Pro Helvetia" 71.
Hirschengraben 20, Zürich, Switzerland.
Telephone: 01-471133.

Spuler, Bertold, DR. PHIL.; German university professor; b. 5 Dec. 1911, Karlsruhe, Baden; s. of Dr. Rudolf Spuler and Natalena (née Lindner); m. Gerda Roehrig 1937; two s. one d.; ed. Univs. of Heidelberg, Munich, Hamburg and Breslau.
Collaborator, Society for Silesian History 34-35; Asst. Dept. of East European History, Univ. of Berlin and Co-editor *Jahrbücher für Geschichte Osteuropas* 35-37; Asst. Dept. of Near Eastern Studies, Univ. of Göttingen 37-38, Dozent 38-41; Full Prof. Univ. of Munich 42, Göttingen 45, Hamburg 48-; Editor *Der Islam* 49-, *Handbuch der Orientalistik* 52-, *Studien zur Sprache, Geschichte und Kultur des Islamischen Orients* 65-; Co-editor *Das Historisch-Politische Buch* 53-; Hon. Dr. Theol. (Berne), Hon. D. ès Lettres (Bordeaux).
Leisure interests: collaboration in church work, hiking.
Publs. include *Die europäische Diplomatie in Konstantinopel bis 1739* 35, *Die Minderheitenschulen der europäischen Türkei von der Reformzeit bis zum Weltkriege* 36, *Die Mongolen in Iran: Politik, Verwaltung und Kultur der Ilchanzeit 1220-1350,* 3rd edn. 68 (Turkish edn. 56), *Die Goldene Horde, Die Mongolen in Russland, 1223-1302* 43, 2nd edn. 65, *Die Gegenwartslage der Ostkirchen in ihrer staatlichen und volklichen Umwelt* 48, 2nd edn. 69, *Geschichte der islamischen Länder im Überblick I: Chalifenzeit; II: Mongolenzeit* 52-53, *Iran in frühislamischer Zeit: Politik, Kultur, Verwaltung und öffentliches Leben 633-1055* 52 (Persian edn. 70), *Regenten und Regierungen der Welt* 53, 62-66, 71, *Wissenschaftl. Forschungsbericht: Der Vordere Orient in islamischer Zeit* 54, *The Age of the Caliphs* 60, 68, *The Age of the Mongols* 60 (twice), *Geschichte der Morgenländischen Kirchen* 61, *Innerasien seit dem Aufkommen der Türken* 66, *Les Mongols et l'Europe* 61 (Spanish edn. 66, English edn. 71), *Wüstenfeld-Mahlersche Vergleichungstabellen zur muslimischen, iranischen und orient-christlichen Zeitrechnung,* 3rd edn. 61, *Die islamische Welt* (Saeculum Weltgeschichte III-VII, 67-75), *Die Orthodoxen Kirchen No. 72* 75, *Geschichte der Mongolen nach östlichen und europäischen Zeugnissen* 68 (English edn. 70), *Die historische und geographische Literatur in Persischer Sprache* 68, *Kulturgeschichte des Islams (östlicher Teil)* 71, *Die Kunst des Islam* (with J. Sourdel-Thomine) 73.
Mittelweg 90, 2 Hamburg 13; Rothenbaumchaussee 36, 2 Hamburg 13, Federal Republic of Germany.
Telephone: 4123-3180.

Spychalski, Marian; Polish architect and politician; b. 6 Dec. 1906, Łódź; s. of Józef and Franciszka (née Leśkiewicz) Spychalski; m. Barbara Skrzypczyk 1935; two d.; ed. Warsaw Polytechnic.
Joined Polish Communist Party 31; awarded Grand Prix at Paris Int. Exhibition for his plan for development of Warsaw 37; during occupation of Poland, became leader in left-wing of resistance movement; mem. Polish Workers' Party 42-48; Mayor of Warsaw 45; mem. Exec. Cttee. P.W.P. 45-48; Deputy Minister of Nat. Defence 45-48; mem. Politburo, Polish United Workers' Party 48-49, 56-70; expelled from Party 49, rehabilitated 56; Minister of Nat. Defence 56-68;

Marshal of Poland 63-; Pres. of Council of State 68-70; Chair. of All Poland Cttee. of Nat. Unity Front 68-70; Deputy to Seym 57-72; retd.; Grunwald Cross (2nd Class) 45, Order of the Banner of Labour 59, Order of the Builders of People's Poland.
Warsaw, Poland.

Spyridakis, Constantinos, PH.D.; Cypriot politician; b. 21 May 1903, Nicosia; s. of Spyridon and Aglaia Spyridakis; m. Thalia Kissonerghis 1937; two s.; ed. Pancyprian Gymnasium, Nicosia, and Univs. of Athens and Berlin.
Teacher, Pancyprian Gymnasium, Nicosia 23-31, 34-35, Asst. Headmaster 35-36, Principal 36-60; Chair. Greek Board of Educ. 59-60; Pres. Greek Communal Chamber 60-65; Minister of Educ. 65-70; mem. and official of numerous Academic and Scientific orgs.; Greek Grand Cross of Royal Order of Phoenix, Gold Medal of Goethe Inst., Munich, Gold Medal of St. Barnabas, and other decorations; Hon. Ph.D. Univ. of Salonika.
Leisure interest: collecting antiquities.
Publs. *Evagoras the First, King of Salamis* (German 35, Greek 45), *An Outline of the History of Cyprus* 58, *The Kings of Cyprus* (Greek) 63, *A Brief History of Cyprus* (English 63, Greek 64 enlarged new edn., Greek 72, English 74), *Studies and Lectures* (Greek I 1-2) 72, etc.
St. Helen Street 8b, Nicosia, Cyprus.
Telephone: Nicosia 63834.

Spyropoulos, Jannis; Greek artist; b. 12 March 1912, Pylos, Peloponese; s. of Georges J. Spyropoulos and Phigalia G. J. Spyropoulos; m. Zoe Margaritis 1954; ed. School of Fine Arts, Athens, and Ecole des Beaux Arts, Paris.
Numerous one-man exhbns. in Europe, U.S.A. and Australia 50-; on touring exhbns. of Greek Art, Rome 53, Belgrade 54, Malmö and Gothenburg 59, Canada 59, Cyprus 60, Helsinki 61; participated in Alexandria Biennale 55, São Paulo Bienal 57, Venice Biennale 60, Carnegie Internationals 61, 64; Documenta III (Kassel) 64, etc.; represented in Guggenheim Museum, New York, Museum of Contemporary Art, Dallas, Bezallel Nat. Museum, Jerusalem, Museum of Contemporary Art, Belgrade, Museum of Fine Arts, Ostend, Toronto Art Gallery, Nat. Art Gallery of Athens, Museum of Modern Art, Paris, Israel Museum, Jerusalem, Museum of Modern Art, Brussels, in galleries Nebraska, Rochester, Vermont, New Jersey, Washington, D.C. (U.S.A.), Nuremburg, Mainz (Fed. Repub. of Germany), Sydney (Australia), Auckland (New Zealand), and at Expo 67 (Montreal) and 70 (Osaka); Commdr. Royal Order of Phoenix; UNESCO Prize 60.
Leisure interest: photography.
11 Sarantaporou Street, Athens 905, Greece.
Telephone: 281-182.

Srb, Adrian Morris, M.S., PH.D.; American professor of genetics; b. 4 March 1917, Howells, Neb.; s. of Jerome Ve. Srb and Viola Morris; m. Jozetta Marie Helfrich 1940; one s. two d.; ed. Howells High School, Univ. of Nebraska, Stanford Univ. and Calif. Inst. of Technology.
Civilian, Office of Scientific Research and Devt. 44; Asst. Prof. of Biology, Stanford Univ. and Research Fellow, Calif. Inst. of Technology 46-47; Assoc. Prof. Plant Breeding, Cornell Univ. 47-51; Research Assoc., Calif. Inst. of Technology 49; Prof. of Plant Breeding, Cornell Univ. 51-63, Prof. of Genetics 65-; Fulbright Research Scholar and Guggenheim Fellow, Univ. of Paris 53-54; Nat. Science Foundation Senior Postdoctoral Research Fellow, Centre Nat. de la Recherche Scientifique, Gif-sur-Yvette, France 60-61, Univ. of Edinburgh, Scotland 67-68; mem. Nat. Acad. of Sciences; Fellow, American Acad. of Arts and Sciences; Hon. Foreign Fellow, Edinburgh Botanical Soc.; Fellow, N.Y. Acad. of Sciences, American Asscn. for Advancement of Science; Trustee, Cornell Univ. 75-;

Distinguished Teacher Award 67; Hon. D.Sc. (Univ. of Nebraska) 69.

Leisure interests: music, collecting juvenile books, gardening.

Publs. *General Genetics* (with R. D. Owen) 52, *Pathways to the Understanding of Genetics* 53, *Adaptation* (with B. Wallace) 61, 64, *General Genetics* (with R. D. Owen and R. S. Edgar) 65, Editor *Genes, Enzymes, and Population* 73; over 100 research papers in scientific journals.

Section of Genetics, Development and Physiology, Cornell University, Ithaca, N.Y. 14850; Home: 411 Cayuga Heights Road, Ithaca, N.Y. 14850, U.S.A.

Telephone: 256-3145 (Office); 272-8492 (Home).

Srivastava, Chandrika Prasad, LL.B., M.A.; Indian international civil servant; b. 8 July 1920, Unnao; s. of B. B. Srivastava and Mataji Srivastava; m. Nirmala Salve 1947; two d.; ed. Univ. of Lucknow.

Deputy Dir.-Gen. of Shipping, Govt. of India 54-57; Joint Sec. to Prime Minister 64-66; Chair. State Shipping Corpn. of India 66-73; Pres. Indian Nat. Shipowners' Asscn. 71-73; Dir. Reserve Bank of India 73-74; Pres. UN Diplomatic Conf. of Plenipotentiaries on a Code of Conduct for Liner Confs. 73-74; Sec.-Gen. Inter-Governmental Maritime Consultative Org. (IMCO) Jan. 74-; Gold Medal for English (Univ. of Lucknow); Padma Bhushan 72.

Leisure interest: music.

Publs. contributions to maritime journals.

Inter-Governmental Maritime Consultative Organization, 101-104 Piccadilly, London, W1V 0AE; 2 Parklands, Ice House Wood, Oxted, Surrey, England.

Staats, Elmer Boyd, PH.D.; American economist and government official; b. 6 June 1914, Richfield, Kansas; s. of Wesley F. and Maude (Goodall) Staats; m. Margaret S. Rich 1940; one s. two d.; ed. McPherson Coll., and Univs. of Kansas and Minnesota.

Research Asst., Kansas Legislative Council 36; mem. Staff, Public Admin. Service, Chicago 37-38; Fellow, Brookings Inst. 38-39; Asst. to Dir., Bureau of the Budget 47, Asst. Dir. (Legis. Reference) 47-49, Exec. Asst. Dir. 49-50, Asst. Dir. 58-59, Deputy Dir. 50-53, 59-66; Research Dir., Marshall Field & Co., Chicago 53; Exec. Officer Operations Co-ordinating Board, Nat. Security Council 53-58; Comptroller Gen. of the United States 66-; mem. numerous public orgs. including Pres. American Soc. for Public Admin. 61-62; mem. Board of Dirs. of American Acad. of Political and Social Science 66, Board of Govs. Int. Org. of Supreme Audit Insts. 69-, Visiting Cttee. John F. Kennedy School of Gov., Harvard Univ. 74-; President's Comm. on Budget Concepts; Hon. mem. of Faculty, Industrial Coll. of the Armed Forces 73-; Rockefeller Public Service Award 61; Hon. LL.D. (McPherson Coll.) 66.

Publ. *Personnel Standards in the Social Security Program* 39.

5011 Overlook Road, N.W., Washington, D.C. 20016, U.S.A.

Stacey, Col. Charles Perry, O.C., O.B.E., C.D., A.M., PH.D., LL.D., D.LITT., F.R.S.C.; Canadian army officer; b. 30 July 1906, Toronto; s. of Dr. C. E. Stacey and Pearl Perry; m. Doris Newton Shiell 1939 (died 1969); ed. Univs. of Toronto, Oxford and Princeton.

On Canadian Army Reserve 29-40; mem. Princeton Univ. History Dept. 34-40; Historical Officer, Canadian Mil. Headquarters, London 40-45; Pres. Canadian Historical Asscn. 52-53; Pres. Canadian Writers' Foundation 58-59; Dir. Historical Section, Canadian Army Gen. Staff 45-59; Hon. Sec. Royal Soc. of Canada 57-59, Hon. Editor 64-68; Pres. Section II Royal Soc. of Canada 68-69; Special Lecturer in History, Univ. of Toronto 59-60, Prof. 60-, Univ. Prof. 73-; on leave while acting as Dir. of History, Canadian Forces H.Q., Ottawa 65-66.

Publs. *Canada and the British Army 1846-1871* 36 (2nd edn. 63), *The Military Problems of Canada* 40, *The Canadian Army 1939-1945: an Official Historical Summary* 48, *Introduction to the Study of Military History for Canadian Students* 55, *Six Years of War* 55, *Quebec 1759: The Siege and the Battle* 59, *Records of the Nile Voyageurs 1884-1885* 59, *The Victory Campaign* 60, *Arms, Men and Governments: The War Policies of Canada 1939-1945* 70, *The Arts of War and Peace, 1914-45* (*Historical Documents of Canada*, Vol. V) 72, *A Very Double Life: The Private World of MacKenzie King* 76.

Department of History, University of Toronto, Toronto, Ont. M5S 1A1; 89 Tranmer Avenue, Toronto, Ont. M5P 1E3, Canada.

Telephone: 928-8745 (Office); 481-4885 (Home).

Stacey, Maurice, C.B.E., PH.D., D.SC., F.R.S.; British professor of chemistry; b. 8 April 1907, U.K.; m. Constance Mary Pugh 1937; two s. two d.; ed. Adams School, Shropshire, Birmingham Univ., London Univ. and Columbia Univ., New York.

Beit Memorial Research Fellow, London Univ. 33-37; Lecturer, Birmingham Univ. 37-46, Prof. of Chem. 46-56, Mason Prof. of Chem. 56-, Head of Dept. 56-74; Meldola Medal 33; Virtanen Medal; U.S. Nat. Acad. Science Award 50; John Scott Medal and Award 69; Hon. D.Sc. (San Marcos Univ., Peru).

Leisure interests: collector of antiques, travel, horticulture.

Publs. 400 publs. on chemical and biochemical topics, two books (with S. A. Barker) on Polysaccharides.

Department of Chemistry, Birmingham University, Birmingham, England.

Telephone: 021-472-1301, Ext. 100; 021-475-2065.

Staden, Berndt Von; German diplomatist; b. 24 June 1919, Rostock; m. Wendelgard von Neurath; three c.; ed. Bonn. Univ., Hamburg Univ.

Military service 40-45; studied law, Hamburg Univ. 46-48; Junior Barrister 48-51; worked for Foreign Ministry 51; Third Sec., Embassy, Brussels 53-55; Dir. Desk of Soviet Affairs, Foreign Office, Bonn 55-58; Staff mem. EEC Comm., Brussels, Head of Office of Pres. of Comm. 58-63; Counsellor, First Class, Embassy, Washington 63-68; Deputy Asst. State Sec., Foreign Office 68-70, Asst. State Sec., Head of Political Dept. 70-73; Amb. to U.S.A. April 73-.

Leisure interests: music, horseback riding.

Embassy of the Federal Republic of Germany, 4645 Reservoir Road, N.W., Washington, D.C. 20007, U.S.A.

Stadtman, Earl R., PH.D.; American biochemist; b. 15 Nov. 1919, Carrizozo, N.M.; s. of Walter W. Stadtman and Minnie Ethyl Stadtman; m. Theresa Campbell Stadtman 1943; ed. Univ. of Calif.

Research Asst. Dept. of Food Technology, Univ. of Calif. 43-46, Research Asst., Div. of Plant Nutrition 48-49; Atomic Energy Comm. Fellow, Biochemical Research Lab., Mass. Gen. Hospital 49-50; Chemist (Biochem.) GS-15-Lab. for Cellular Physiology and Metabolism Nat. Insts. of Health (NIH) 50-58, Chief of Enzyme Section, Lab. of Cellular Physiology and Metabolism, NIH 58-62, Chief, Lab. of Biochem., Nat. Heart Inst., NIH 62-; mem. Nat. Acad. of Sciences, American Acad. of Arts and Sciences, U.S. Cttee. for Int. Union of Biochemistry, Council of American Soc. of Biological Chemists; Paul Lewis Award in Enzyme Chem. 52, Wash. Acad. of Sciences Annual Award in Biological Chem. 57; Superior Service Award of Dept. of Health, Educ. and Welfare 68, Distinguished Service Award 70; Hillebrand Award of American Chem. Soc. of Wash. 69, Award in Microbiology, Nat. Acad. of Sciences 70.

Leisure interests: gardening, bowling, badminton, travelling.

Publs. Numerous scientific articles 53-.

National Institutes of Health, Bethesda, Md. 20014; Home: 16907 Redland-Derwood Road, Derwood, Md. 20855, U.S.A.
Telephone: 301-496-4096 (Office); 301-869-1747 (Home).

Staebler, Neil; American businessman and politician; b. 11 July 1905, Ann Arbor, Mich.; s. of Edward W. and Magdalena (Dold) Staebler; m. Burnette Bradley 1935; one s. one d.; ed. Univ. of Michigan.
Treasurer, Staebler-Kempf Oil Co. 26-51; Partner, Staebler and Son 26-; Chief, Building Materials Branch, Office of Price Admin. 42-43; U.S. Navy Service 43-45; Chair. Dem. State Central Cttee. of Mich. 50-61, Dem. Nat. Ctee.-man from Mich. 61-68, 72-; Assoc. Dem. Nat. Cttee.-man from Mich. 69-72; mem. Dem. Nat. Finance Council 71-, Dem. Charter Comm. 73-74; mem. Fed. Election Comm. 75-; Visiting Prof. of Govt., Univ. of Mass. 62; mem. U.S. House of Reps. 62-64; Pres. Michigan Capital & Service Inc. 66-; Fellow, Kennedy Inst. of Politics 75-; Trustee, Citizens Research Foundation 68-; Hon. LL.D. (Univ. of Mich.).
Publ. *How to Argue with a Conservative* (co-author) 66.
408 Wolverine Building, Ann Arbor, Michigan 48104, U.S.A.
Telephone: (313) 662-4406.

Staehelin, Ernst; Swiss ecclesiastic; b. 3 Oct. 1889; s. of Pastor Ernst Staehelin and Sibylla née Merian; m. Gertrud Kutter 1921; two s. three d.; ed. Basle, Göttingen, Berlin and Marburg Univs.
Pastor of Reformed Church, Thalheim (Aargau) 20; Extra. Prof. of Church History and Dogmatics Basle Univ. 24, Prof. 27, Rector Univ. 33, 39 and 60; Pastor Olten 26; Hon. D.Theol. (Berne, Lausanne), D.Phil. (Basle).
Publs. include: *Der Jesuitenorden und die Schweiz* 23, *Das Buch der Basler Reformation* 29, *Das theologische Lebenswerk Johannes Oekolampads* 39, *Johann Caspar Lavaters ausgewählte Werke* 43, *Alexandre Vinets ausgewählte Werke* 44-45, *Johann Ludwig Frey, Johannes Grynaeus und das Frey-Grynaeische Institut in Basel* 47, *Die Stimme der schweizerischen Kirchen zum Sonderbundskrieg und zur Gründung des schweizerischen Bundesstaates* 48, *Die Verkündigung des Reiches Gottes in der Kirche Jesu Christi* (7 vols. 51, 53, 55, 57, 59, 63, 65), *Die Jesuitenfrage* 55, *Dewettiana, Forschungen und Texte zu Deswettes Leben und Werk* 56, *Die Wiederbringung aller Dinge* 60, *Overbeckiana: Übersicht über die auf der Universitätsbibliothek Basel aufbewahrte Korrespondenz Franz Overbecks* 62, *Professor Friedrich Lachenal* 65, *Die Korrespondenz des Basler Professors Jakob Christoph Beck 1711–1785* 68, *Die Christentumgesellschaft in der Zeit der Aufklärung und der beginnenden Erweckung* 70, *Die Christentumsgesellschaft in der Zeit von der Erweckung bis zur Gegenwart* 74.
Ob. Heuberg 33, Basle, Switzerland.
Telephone: 061-251345.

Staercke, André Marie de, DR.JUR.; Belgian diplomatist; b. 1913; ed. Coll. St. Barbe, Ghent, and Univs. of Namur, Louvain and Paris.
Secretary to Prime Minister and Cabinet 43, to Prince Regent 45-50; Rep. to Council of NATO 51, Perm. Rep. 52-; Head Belgian Del. to EDC Conf. Paris 51; awards include Commdr. Légion d'Honneur, Ordre du Christ, Ordre du Chêne, Medal of Freedom (U.S.A.) and Grand Cross Order of Orange-Nassau; Officer Order of Leopold.
14 rue Vaneau, Paris 7e, France.

Staerke, Roger De (*see* De Staerke).

Staffa, H.E. Cardinal Dino; b. 14 Aug. 1906, Lugo, Italy; s. of Dominic and Gualandi Emilia Staffa.
Ordained 29; Titular Archbishop of Caesarea 60-; fmr. Sec. of Sacred Congregation of Seminars and Univs.; Prefect of Supreme Tribunal of the Apostolic Signatura; Pres. Corte di Cassazione of Vatican State; mem.

Pontifical Comm. for Revision of Codex of Canon Law; cr. Cardinal by Pope Paul VI 67.
16 Piazza San Calisto, 00153, Rome, Italy.

Stafford, Godfrey Harry, M.SC., PH.D.; British physicist; b. 15 April 1920, Sheffield; s. of Henry and Sarah Stafford; m. Helen Goldthorp 1950; one s. two d.; ed. Rondebosch Boys' High School, Univ. of Cape Town, Gonville and Caius Coll., Cambridge.
South African Naval Forces 41-46; A.E.R.E., Harwell 49-51; Head of Biophysics Subdivision, Commonwealth Scientific and Industrial Research Org., Pretoria 51-54; Cyclotron Group, A.E.R.E. 54-57; Head of Proton Linear Accelerator Group, Rutherford Laboratory 57, Head of High Energy Physics Div. 63, Deputy Dir. 66, Dir. 69-; Dir. of Atlas Laboratory 75-; Visiting Fellow, St. Cross Coll., Oxford 71; Ebden Scholar, Cambridge Univ.
Publs. papers and articles in learned journals on biophysics, nuclear physics and high energy physics.
Ferry Cottage, North Hinksey Village, Oxford, OX2 0NA, England.
Telephone: Abingdon 21900 Extension 469 (Office); Oxford 47621 (Home).

Stafford, Brig. Gen. Thomas P.; American astronaut; b. 17 Sept. 1930, Weatherford, Okla.; m. Faye L. Shoemaker; two c.; ed. U.S. Naval Acad.
Commissioned U.S. Air Force, completed flight training and advanced interceptor training; served five years as fighter-interceptor pilot; graduated from Air Force Experimental Flight Test School 59; selected by NASA as astronaut Sept. 62; pilot of *Gemini VI* (rendezvous with *Gemini VII*, first rendezvous in space) Dec. 65; command pilot *Gemini IX* mission 66; commander *Apollo X* May 69 (first lunar module flight to the moon and first rendezvous around the moon, prelude mission to the lunar landing); selected Chief of Astronaut Group Aug. 69; Deputy Dir. Flight Crew Operations 71-; NASA Exceptional Service Medal (twice); NASA Distinguished Service Medal; American Astronautical Soc. Flight Achievement Award 66; Harmon Int. Aviation Trophy 66.
Publs. Co-author: *Pilot's Handbook for Performance Flight Testing, Aerodynamics Handbook for Performance Flight Testing.*
NASA Johnson Space Center, Houston, Tex. 77058, U.S.A.
Telephone: 713-483-3586.

Stafleu, Frans Antonie; Netherlands professor of systematic botany; b. 8 Sept. 1921, Velsen; s. of Frans J. Stafleu and Elisabeth S. Ladan; m. Charlotte A. M. Corporaal 1947; two s.; ed. Univ. of Utrecht.
Geneticist Java Sugar Experimental Station 48-50; Scientific Officer, Univ. of Utrecht 50-66, Prof. of Botany 66;- Sec.-Gen. Int. Asscn. for Plant Taxonomy 53-; Treas. Int. Union of Biological Sciences 64-67, Sec.-Gen. 67-70; Sec.-Gen. Int. Council of Scientific Unions 70-74; mem. and Treas.-Gen. Royal Netherlands Acad. of Sciences; Foreign mem. Linnean Soc. of London; Dr. h.c. Univ. of Bergen, Norway.
Leisure interests: walking, book collecting.
Publs. *A Monograph of the Vochysiaceae* 1-5 48-53, *Index nominum genericorum* (editor and part author) 55-, *Taxonomic Literature* 67, *Linnaeus and the Linnaeans* 71; series *Taxon and Regnum vegetabile* (editor and author).
Department of Botany, Room 1904, Tweede Transitorium, Uithof, Utrecht; Home: 33 Weg naar Rhynauwen, Utrecht, Netherlands.
Telephone: 030-513372 (Home).

Ståhle, Anders Nils Oscar Kåse, LL.B.; Swedish diplomatist and public servant; b. 12 June 1901, Helsingborg; s. of Isaac W. Ståhle and Karin Trapp; m. Birgit Olsson 1926; one s. three d.; ed. Univ. of Lund.

Entered Swedish Foreign Service 27; served home and abroad until 48; Executive Dir. Nobel Foundation 48-72; represented Sweden in post-war int. confs. on shipping and trade; Del. Maritime Transport Cttee., OEEC Paris 47-59; Chair. Int. Fed. of Insts. for Advanced Study 72-74; board mem. several banking and industrial companies; holds Swedish and foreign decorations; Dr.Iur. h.c.
Leisure interest: riding.
Nobel House, Sturegatan 14, 11436 Stockholm, Sweden. Telephone: 633787.

Stahle, Hans, M.A., M.B.A.; Swedish business executive; b. 8 Aug. 1923; ed. Uppsala Univ., Stockholm School of Economics and IMEDE Management Devt. Inst., Lausanne.
Deputy Managing Dir. Alfa-Laval AB (machinery) until 60, Managing Dir. 60-.
Hamra, Tumba, Sweden.

Stahlman, James Geddes, A.B.; American journalist; b. 28 Feb. 1893; ed. Webb School, Bell Buckle, Tenn., Vanderbilt Univ., Nashville, Tenn., and Univ. of Chicago.
President and Publisher *Nashville Banner* 30-72; Chair. of Board Newspaper Printing Corpn. 37-72; private U.S. Army, First World War; Captain, U.S.N.R., Second World War; Pres. Southern Newspaper Publishers' Asscn. 32-33, Chair. of Board 33-34; Pres. American Newspaper Publishers' Asscn. 37-39, Inter American Press Asscn. 55-56; Trustee, Vanderbilt Univ.; mem. Nat. Council Boy Scouts of America; Hon. LL.D. (Atlanta Law School).
Home: 815 Tyne Boulevard, Nashville, Tenn. 37220, U.S.A.

Stahr, Elvis J., Jr., M.A., B.C.L.; American conservationist, lawyer and university official; b. 9 March 1916, Hickman, Ky.; s. of Elvis J. and Mary A. (McDaniel) Stahr; m. Dorothy Howland Berkfield 1946; two s. one d.; ed. Univ. of Kentucky, Oxford Univ., Yale Univ.
With New York law firm; served U.S. Army, Second World War; Assoc. Prof. of Law, Univ. of Kentucky 47-48, Prof. and Dean of Law Coll. 48-54; served Dept. of Army in Korean War; Provost, Univ. of Kentucky 54-56; Exec. Dir. President's Cttee. on Educ. Beyond Secondary School Level 56-57; Vice-Chancellor, Univ. of Pittsburgh 57-59; Pres. West Virginia Univ. 59-61; Sec. of the Army 61-62; Pres. Indiana Univ. 62-68; Pres. Nat. Audubon Soc. 68-; mem. U.S. Del. to UN Conf. on Human Environment, Stockholm 72; mem. Joint U.S.-U.S.S.R. Cttee. on Co-operation for Protection of the Environment, Washington 73; fmr. Deputy Chair. of Board Fed. Reserve Bank of Chicago; mem. Presidential Aviation Advisory Comm.; Trustee, C.E.D., Transylvania Coll., American Cancer Soc.; mem. Board of Dirs. Acacia Mutual Life Insurance Co.; Hon. LL.D. (Univ. of Maryland, Univ. of Pittsburgh, Louisiana State Univ., Texas Christian Univ., Univ. of Kentucky, Univ. of Notre Dame, West Virginia Wesleyan Coll., Concord Coll., Waynesburg Coll., Rose Polytechnic Inst.), Hon. D.Mil.Sc. (Northeastern Univ.), Hon. D.Pub.Admin. (Bethany Coll.), Hon. D.H.L. (DePauw Univ.), and other hon. degrees.
Leisure interests: tennis, books, sun and surf.
National Audubon Society, 950 Third Avenue, New York, N.Y. 10022; Home: Martin Dale, Greenwich, Conn. 06830, U.S.A.
Telephone: 212-832-3200 (Office).

Staiger, Emil, D.PHIL.; Swiss university professor and writer; b. 8 Feb. 1908, Kreuzlingen; s. of Richard Staiger and Emma Seiler; m. Sibylle Zwicky 1938; one s. one d.; ed. Univs. of Geneva, Zürich and Munich.
Professor of German Literature, Zürich Univ. 43-; mem. Deutsche Akad. and Vetenskaps-Societeten, Lund,

Finnish Acad. of Sciences; hon. mem. Modern Language Asscn. of America, Order "Pour le Mérite".
Publs. *Die Zeit als Einbildungskraft des Dichters* 39, *Meisterwerke deutscher Sprache* 43, *Grundbegriffe der Poetik* 46, *Goethe* Vol. I 52, Vol. II 56, Vol. III 59, *Die Kunste der Interpretation* 55, *Stilwandel* 63, *Geist und Zeitgeist* 64, *Schiller* 67; trans. (into German) *Sophokles Tragödien* 44, *Griechische Epigramme* 46, *Euripides Ion* 47; (Greek and German with E. Howald) *Callimachi opera omnia* 56, *Aischylos Oresti* 59, *Theokrit* 70.
Universität Zürich, Rämistrasse 71, 8006 Zürich, Switzerland.

Staiger, John Gustav, B.A.; American business executive; b. 20 March 1910, Chase, Wis.; m. Jane Emily Crawford 1936; one s.; ed. Univ. of Dubuque, Iowa.
Assistant to Exec. Vice-Pres. Nash Kelvinator (now American Motors) 56; joined Massey-Ferguson, Asst. to Pres. 57, Vice-Pres., Asst. to Pres. 60, Vice-Pres., Gen. Man. N. American Operations 61, Vice-Pres. Admin., Office of Pres. 62, Group Vice-Pres. Farm Machinery 66, Senior Vice-Pres. Corporate Admin. 69, Senior Vice-Pres. 72-; Pres., Chief Exec. Officer, Dir. Massey-Ferguson Credit Corpn.; Chair., Pres., Dir. Massey-Ferguson Leasing Corpn., Distribution Holdings Inc.; fmr. Chair., Dir. Farm and Industrial Equipment Inst.; Dir. several Massey-Ferguson subsidiaries; Trustee, Iowa Methodist Hospital, Simpson Coll., Iowa, Canadian Opera Co.
Massey-Ferguson Ltd., 200 University Avenue, Toronto, Canada; and 600 Island Drive, Palm Beach, Fla. 33480, U.S.A.
Telephone: (316) 367-3766 (Canada); (305) 655-9212 (U.S.A.).

Stakman, Elvin Charles, B.A., M.A., PH.D.; American plant pathologist and agricultural botanist; b. 17 May 1885, Algoma, Wis.; s. of Frederick and Emelia Eberhardt Stakman; m. Louise Jensen 1917 (deceased); ed. Univ. of Minn.
Department of Plant Pathology and Botany, Univ. of Minn. 09-53, Chief of Dept. 40-53, Prof. Emer. 53-; Consultant, Rockefeller Foundation 53-; Agent in charge of stem rust epidemiology studies at Fed. Rust Lab., St. Paul, in co-op. with the Univ. 17-55; Guest Prof., Univ. of Halle-Wittenberg, Germany 30-31; Hitchcock Prof., Univ. of Calif. 55; Scientific Adviser, Firestone Plantations Co., Liberia 30; Leader of rubber survey to N.W. South America, U.S. Dept. of Agriculture 41; mem. Agricultural Survey Party to Mexico 41; Scientific Mission to Japan, Supreme Command for Allied Powers 48; mem. Nat. Comm. UNESCO 50-56, Nat. Science Board 51-54; mem. Advisory Cttee. on Biology and Medicine, U.S. Atomic Energy Comm. 51-54, Chair. Advisory Cttee. 53-54, Consultant 54-59; mem. Nat. Acad. of Sciences, American Acad. of Arts and Sciences, Det Norske Videnskaps-Akad., Oslo, etc.; Pres. American Phytopathological Soc. 22, American Asscn. for Advancement of Science 49; numerous awards and hon. degrees.
Leisure interests: general reading, sports.
Publs. *Principles of Plant Pathology* (with J. G. Harrar) 57, *Campaigns against Hunger* (with Bradfield and Mangelsdorf) 67; approx. 300 scientific or educ. articles in various bulletins and journals.
Institute of Agriculture, University of Minnesota, St. Paul, Minn. 55101; Home: 1411 Hythe Street, St. Paul, Minn. 55108, U.S.A.

Staley, Edward, A.B.; American businessman; b. 2 Oct. 1903; ed. Miami and Harvard Univs.
With W. T. Grant Co. 26; Regional Man. and Asst. Gen. Merchandising Man. Montgomery Ward 33; Merchandising Dir. W. T. Grant Co. 40, Vice-Pres. 43, Gen. Man. and Dir. 50, Pres. 52, Vice-Chair. 55-, Chief Exec. Officer 59-, Chair. Board 66-73, Chair. Exec.

Cttee. 73-; Pres. New York City Commerec and Industry Asscn. 56-58, Dir. 59-; Trustee, Grant Foundation 54-.
Home: 3 Chalford Lane, Scarsdale, N.Y. 10583; Office: 1515 Broadway, New York, N.Y. 10036, U.S.A.

Stambolić, Petar; Yugoslav politician; b. 12 July 1912; ed. Univ. of Belgrade.
Member Young Communist League 33, C.P. of Yugoslavia 35-; organized resistance in Serbia 41; Sec. Central Cttee. of National Liberation for Serbia 41; Commdr. H.Q. Nat. Liberation Army and partisan units for Serbia 43; Deputy and mem. Presidium, Antifascist Council of Nat. Liberation of Yugoslavia 43; mem. Central Cttee. of C.P. of Serbia 45, Sec. 48-57; First Vice-Chair. Council of Ministers, Serbia 45-47; Pres. Exec. Council, Serbia 48-53, Pres. Serbian Assembly 53-57; Minister of Agriculture and Forests, Yugoslavia 47-48; Pres. Fed. People's Assembly 57-63; Pres. Fed. Exec. Council 63-67; mem. Collective Presidency of Yugoslavia 74-, Vice-Pres. 74-75; mem. Central Cttee. of C.P. of Yugoslavia 48-, mem. Politbureau 51-68, and Exec. Cttee. 52-68, Central Cttee. League of Communists of Yugoslavia, Chair. Ideological Comm. 48-63; mem. Presidium of Central Cttee. of League of Communists of Yugoslavia 66-; mem. Council of Fed. 63-; Pres. Central Cttee. L.C. of Serbia 68-; Order of Hero of the People and other decorations.
Collective Presidency of Yugoslavia, Belgrade, Yugoslavia.

Stammati, Gaetano; Italian banker; b. 5 Oct. 1908, Naples; *s.* of Gennaro Stammati and Anna d'Auria; *m.* Maria Fiore 1937; one *s.* one *d.*; ed. Univ. of Naples.
Former Chief of Cabinet of Minister of Foreign Trade and Minister of Finance; Sec.-Gen. Econ. Council and Dir.-Gen. of Taxation, Ministry of Finance; Dir.-Gen. Ministry of State Participation; Chief of Cabinet of Minister of the Treasury and Dir.-Gen. of Treasury; Auditor-Gen. 67-72; Pres. Banca Commerciale Italiana April 72-; Minister of Finance Feb. 76-; Cavaliere di Gran Croce al Merito.
Publs. *Capitalismo e Socialismo di fronte al problema del costo, Il problema economico della ricostruzione, Calmieri, tesseramenti e controllo della produzione, Imposta generale sulla entrata, La finanza pubblica, Il sistema monetario internazionale.*
Piazza SS. Apostoli 53, Rome, Italy.
Telephone: 6780141.

Stamp, Hon. Arthur Maxwell, M.A.; British economic consultant; b. 20 Sept. 1915, Twickenham, Middx.; *s.* of 1st Baron Stamp, G.C.B., G.B.E.; *m.* Alice Mary Richards 1944; one *s.* two *d.*; ed. Leys School, Cambridge, Zürich and Lausanne, and Clare Coll., Cambridge.
Called to the Bar (Inner Temple) 39; war service as Lieut.-Col. in Intelligence Corps 40-46; Financial Adviser and Dir. John Lewis Partnership Ltd. 47-50; Acting Adviser to Bank of England 50-53; Alternate Exec. Dir. for the U.K. Int. Monetary Fund 51-53; Dir. of European Dept., Int. Monetary Fund 53-54; Adviser to Bank of England 54-57; Chair. Maxeast Ltd., Maxwell Stamp Associates Ltd.; Dir. Philip Hill, Higginson, Erlangers Ltd. 58-65, Hill, Samuel & Co. Ltd. 65-, The De La Rue Co. Ltd. 60-, Triplex Holdings Ltd. 63-75; Godfrey Bonsack Ltd.; Gov. London School of Economics; mem. Exec. Cttee. Nat. Inst. of Econ. and Social Research; mem. Civil Aviation Authority 76-; Chair. Home Office Cttee. on Taxi-cab Trade 67; Chair. The Rehearsal Orchestra.
Leisure interests: music, photography.
Ebb's House, Combs, Near Stowmarket, Suffolk; and 19 Clarence Gate Gardens, Glentworth Street, London N.W.1, England.
Telephone: 044-92-2553 (Suffolk); 01-723-9538 (London).

Stamper, Malcolm T.; American aviation executive; b. 4 April 1925, Detroit; *m.* Mari Guinan; six *c.*; ed. Univ. of Michigan, Georgia Technical Coll.
With Gen. Motors 48-62; joined Boeing Co. 62, Vice-Pres., Gen. Man. fmr. Boeing Turbine Div. 65, Man. Boeing Everett Branch (now 747 Div.) 66, in charge of 747 programme 66-69, Gen. Man. Commercial Airplane Group 69-71, Senior Vice-Pres. Operations 71-72, Pres. 72-.
The Boeing Co., P.O. Box 3707, Seattle, Washington 98124, U.S.A.

Stamprech, Franz, DR.PHIL.; Austrian journalist; b. 30 May 1906, Vienna; *m.* Helene Wanke 1934; one *d.*; ed. Vienna Univ.
Editor *Kleines Volksblatt* 29-55; Chief Editor *Wiener Zeitung* 55-72; retd.
Publs. *Tierhotel* (for children) 46, *Hans Kudlich* 47, *Frühlingsstimmen* 48, *Leopold Kunschak* (biography) 52, *Der grosse Schlosser* (publ. in newspaper), *Ignaz Franz Castelli: Untermieter im Parnass* (biography) 58, *Die älteste Tageszeitung der Welt* 74.
Rotenturmstrasse 27, 1010 Vienna, Austria.
Telephone: 6350215.

Stanbury, Hon. Robert Douglas George, P.C., Q.C., M.P.; Canadian politician, barrister and solicitor; b. 26 Oct. 1929, Exeter, Ont.; *s.* of James George Stuart Stanbury and Elizabeth Jean (Hardy); *m.* Miriam Voelker 1952; two *s.* two *d.*; ed. Exeter and St. Catharines public schools, St. Catharines Coll. Inst., Univ. of Western Ont. and Osgoode Hall Law School.
Member North York Board of Educ. 61-64, Vice-Chair. 62, Chair. 63-64; mem. Metropolitan School Board, Toronto 63-64 and Metropolitan Toronto Planning Board 63; mem. of Parl. 65-; Parl. Sec. to Sec. of State of Canada 68-69; Minister without Portfolio responsible for Citizenship 69-71, for Information Canada 70-71; Minister of Communications 71-72; Minister of Nat. Revenue 72-74; Del. to UN Gen. Assembly 74, 75; Chair. Canadian Group Inter-Parliamentary Union 74-; Liberal.
House of Commons, Ottawa, Ont.; Box 6888, Station A, Toronto, Ont., Canada.
Telephone: 992-7624; 924-1626.

Štancel', Michal; Czechoslovak politician; b. 20 Oct. 1921, Malý Čepčin; ed. Commercial Acad., Martin, and Party School, Prague.
Workers' Social Insurance Co., Bratislava 42-45; Nat. Insurance, Bratislava 45-51, Dir. 51-52; Deputy Chair. Slovak Social Security Office 53-60; Deputy Chair. State Social Security Office, Prague 60-63, Chair. 63-68; Chair. State Population Comm. 63-68; Minister of Labour and Social Affairs 68; mem. Central Cttee. C.P. of Czechoslovakia 68-; Minister of Labour and Social Affairs, Fed. Govt. of Č.S.S.R. 69-, mem. Legislative Council 69-; several decorations.
Ministry of Labour and Social Affairs, Prague 2, nábř. B. Engelse 42, Czechoslovakia.

Stanfield, Hon. Robert Lorne, B.A., LL.B., Q.C., LL.D.; Canadian politician; b. 11 April 1914; ed. Ashbury Coll., Ottawa, Dalhousie and Harvard Univs.
Governor, Dalhousie Univ. 49-56; Premier, Minister of Educ., Nova Scotia 56-67; mem. Parl. for Halifax, Nova Scotia 68-; fmr. Leader Progressive Conservatives, Nova Scotia; Leader of Opposition, Leader Nat. Progressive Conservative Party of Canada 67-76.
Stornoway, 541 Acacia Avenue, Rockcliffe Park, Ottawa, Ont., Canada.

Stankiewicz, Witold, DR.HIST.HABIL.; Polish librarian, editor, and historian; b. 30 Aug. 1919, Kargoszynek; ed. Warsaw Univ.
Official in co-operative societies; mem. Scientific Council, Co-operative Research Inst.; mem. History Inst. and Presidium of Cttee. of Historical Sciences, Polish Acad. of Sciences; Chief Dir. Nat. Library 62-; Chief Editor

The National Library Yearbook 65-; Vice-Chair. Nat. Library Council 69-; Chair. Polish Librarians Asscn. 72-.
Publs. *People's Newspaper Publications in the Polish Kingdom 1905-1914* 57, *History of the Polish People's Movement in Outline* (co-author) 63, 70, *Social Conflicts in Rural Poland 1918-1920* 63, *Source Materials to the History of the Peasant Movement* (co-author) 66, *Programmes of the People's Parties* (co-author) 69, *The Political Archives of Ignace Jan Paderewski*, Vols. 1-4 (co-editor) 73-74, and numerous articles on Polish history.
Biblioteka Narodowa, ul. Hankiewicza 1, 00-973 Warsaw, Poland.

Stanley, Henry Sydney Herbert Cloete, C.M.G.; British diplomatist; b. 5 March 1920; s. of Sir Herbert Stanley and Reniera Cloete; m. Margaret Dixon 1941; three s.; ed. Eton and Balliol Coll., Oxford.
Commonwealth Relations Office 47; served in Pakistan 50-52, Swaziland and S. Africa 54-57, U.S.A. 59-61, Tanganyika 61-63, Kenya 63-65; Inspector, H.M. Diplomatic Service 66-68, Chief Inspector 68-70; High Commr. to Ghana 70-75.
c/o Foreign and Commonwealth Office, London, S.W.1, England.

Stanovnik, Janez; Yugoslav politician and international official; b. 4 Aug. 1922, Ljubljana; s. of Ivan Stanovnik and Ana Jeglich; m. Dragica Dragovich 1953; four s.; ed. Faculty of Law, Ljubljana Univ., and Inst. for Social Sciences, Belgrade.
Took part in Nat. Liberation Struggle 41-45; fmr. Dir. of Exec. Office of Vice-Pres. and Foreign Minister 45-52; Econ. Counsellor to Yugoslav Perm. Mission in New York 52-55; Dir. of Inst. for Econs. and Policy in Belgrade 55-61; Prof. of Econs. Ljubljana Univ. 61-65; special adviser Sec.-Gen. UNCTAD 65-67; mem. of Yugoslav Fed. Parl. and Govt. mem. (in charge of foreign trade) 67-68; leader of del. to UNCTAD II (Delhi) 68; Exec. Sec. of UN Econ. Comm. for Europe 68-.
Leisure interest: mountain climbing.
Publs. dealing with problems of the world economy from point of view of developing countries.
Economic Commission for Europe, Palais des Nations, Geneva; Home: 9 avenue Krieg, 1208 Geneva, Switzerland.
Telephone: 34-60-11 (Office); 47-83-10 (Home).

Stans, Maurice Hubert, C.P.A., LL.D.; American investment banker and government official (retd.); b. 22 March 1908, Shakopee, Minn.; s. of J. Hubert Stans and Mathilda Nyssen; m. Kathleen Carmody 1933; two s. two d.; ed. Northwestern Univ., Columbia Univ.
Joined Alexander Grant and Co., Chicago 28; exec partner 40-55; Dir. ten other business corpns. 35-55; Financial Consultant to U.S. Postmaster General 53-55; Deputy Postmaster General 55-57; Dir. Bureau of the Budget, U.S. Govt. 58-61; Pres. Western Bancorporation 61-62; Vice-Chair. United California Bank 61-62; Senior partner, William R. Staats & Co. 63-65; Pres. Glore Forgan, Wm. R. Staats Inc. 65-69; Finance Chair. Nixon for President Cttee. 68-69; Chair. Republican Nat. Finance Cttee. 68-69, 72-73, Finance Cttee. to Re-elect the President 72-73; indicted by U.S. District Court May 73, found not guilty April 74; Trustee and Dir. several cos.; U.S. Sec. of Commerce 69-72; fmr. Pres. American Inst. of Certified Public Accountants 54; Outstanding Service citation, American Inst. of C.P.A.'s and American Accounting Asscn. 52; elected Accounting Hall of Fame 60-62; Republican; Tax Foundation Public Service Award 59, Great Living American Award of U.S. Chamber of Commerce 61; twelve hon. degrees.
Leisure interests: fishing, hunting.
5114 North 40th Street, Phoenix, Ariz. 85018, U.S.A.

Stanton, Frank, PH.D.; American administrator; b. 20 March 1908, Muskegon, Mich.; s. of Frank Cooper Stanton and Helen Josephine Schmidt; m. Ruth Stephenson 1931; ed. Ohio State Univ.
President (also Dir.) Columbia Broadcasting System Inc. 46-71, Vice-Chair. of Board and Dir. 71-73, Dir. 73-; Chair. American Nat. Red Cross 73-, Vice-Chair. League of Red Cross Socs., Geneva; Licensed Psychologist, N.Y.; Diplomate, American Board of Professional Psychology; Dir. New York Life Insurance Co., Atlantic Richfield Co., Pan American World Airways Inc., American Electric Power Co. Inc., New Perspective Fund, Inc.; Trustee, American Crafts Council 57-75, Inst. for Architecture and Urban Studies 70-75, New York City Rand Inst. 69-75, Rockefeller Foundation 61-73, The Rand Corpn., Carnegie Inst. of Washington; Founding Chair. and Trustee, Center for Advanced Study in the Behavioural Sciences 53-71; Chair. U.S. Advisory Comm. on Information 64-73; Co-Founder, Office of Radio Research, Princeton Univ. 37; Chair., Panel on Int. Information, Educ. and Cultural Relations, Georgetown Univ. 74-75; Dir. Lincoln Center for the Performing Arts, The Roper Public Opinion Research Center, Business Cttee. for the Arts, Municipal Art Soc. of New York; mem. The Business Council; Fellow, American Asscn. for the Advancement of Science, American Psychological Asscn., American Acad. Arts and Sciences, New York Acad. of Science; mem. Architectural League of N.Y., Council on Foreign Relations Inc., Inst. of Electrical and Electronic Engineers, Nat. Acad. of Television Arts and Sciences, Radio-Television News Dirs. Asscn., Int. Radio and Television Soc.; numerous medals and awards; many hon. degrees.
Leisure interests: photography, design, crafts.
Publs. *Students' Guide—The Study of Psychology* (co-author) 35, *Radio Research 1941*, *Radio Research 1942-43*, *Communications Research 1948-49* (co-editor); Films: *Some Physiological Reactions to Emotional Stimuli* 32, *Factors in Visual Depth Perception* 36.
Office: 10 East 56 Street, New York, N.Y. 10022; American National Red Cross, Washington, D.C., 20006, U.S.A.
Telephone: (212) 752-4445; (202) 857-3443.

Stapp, Col. John Paul, B.A., M.A., PH.D., M.D., SC.D.; American fmr. air force officer and aerospace scientist; b. 11 July 1910, Bahia, Brazil; s. of late Rev. and Mrs. Charles F. Stapp; m. Lillian Lanese 1957; ed. Baylor Univ. (Texas), Univs. of Texas and Minnesota and School of Aviation Medicine.
Joined U.S. Air Force Medical Corps 44; pioneer of research on effects of mechanical force on living tissues, especially with regard to high-speed flight and space flight; conducted rocket sled deceleration tests on himself; planned and directed high-altitude (102,000 feet) manned balloon flights 57; organized Aeromedical Facility (Edwards Air Force Base, Calif.) and Aeromedical Field Laboratory (Holloman Air Force Base, N.M.); Chief Aerospace Medical Laboratory, Wright Air Development Div. (Wright-Patterson Air Force Base, Ohio) 58-60; Special Asst. Advanced Studies, Aerospace Medical Center (Brooks Air Force Base, Tex.) 60-61, Chief Scientist 61-65; Chief of Impact Injury, Armed Forces Inst. of Pathology 65-67; retired from U.S. Air Force 70; Chief Scientist (Medicine) Nat. Highway Safety Traffic Admin. 67-; Vice-Pres. Int. Astronautical Fed. 60-; Chair. Annual Stapp Car Crash Conf. 55-; Pres. Civil Aviation Medical, Asscn. 68; Adjunct Prof. Univ. of Southern Calif. Systems Management Center; Fellow, American Inst. Aeronautics and Astronautics, British Inter-planetary Soc.; mem. Int. Acad. Astronautics, Int. Acad. Aviation and Space Medicine, American Medical Asscn., Nat. Research Council, Int. Acad. Aviation Medicine, etc.;

many awards include: John Jefferies Award 53, Cheney Award 55, Liljenkrantz Award 57, Gorgas Medal 57, Commdr. Legion of Merit 55, Distinguished Service Medal (U.S.A.F.) 71, Elliot Cresson Medal of Franklin Inst. 73, Excalibur Award, Nat. Motor Vehicle Safety Council 75.

Publs. *Human Exposure to Linear Deceleration* (Journal of Aviation Medicine) 50, *Crash Protection in Air Force Transports* (Aeronautical Engineering Review) 53, *Effects of Mechanical Force on Living Tissue* (Journal of Aviation Medicine) 55, 56 and 58, *Space Cabin Landing Impact Vector Effects on Human Physiology* 64, *Biomechanics of Injury in the Prevention of Highway Injury* 67, *Voluntary Human Tolerance Levels in Impact Injury and Crash Protection* 70, *Biodynamics of Deceleration, Impact and Blast in Aerospace Medicine* 71.
P.O. Box 553, Alamogordo, N.M. 88310, U.S.A.
Telephone: 505-437-3645.

Star Busmann, Eduard, LL.D.; Netherlands diplomatist; b. 1904, Bussum; *m.* Jonkvrouwe Ariane Röell 1929; two *d.*; ed. Utrecht Univ.
Attaché, Berlin 29; Second Sec., Paris 32; Second Sec., Berlin 35, First Sec. 36; First Sec., Copenhagen 37; First Sec., Pretoria 38, Counsellor 40; Head, Legal Dept., Neths. Foreign Office, London, also Neths. rep. with Fighting French and Judge Neths. Maritime Court 41; Head of Political Dept., Neths. Foreign Office 45; Minister at Embassy, Paris 46; Sec.-Gen. Brussels Treaty Organisation, London 48-53; Ambassador to Austria 53-58; Ambassador to U.A.R., concurrently accred. to Libya 58-63, to U.S.S.R. 63-65, to Switzerland 66-69; Del. San Francisco Conf. 45, Paris Conf. 46, Geneva Conf. on Law of the Sea 58; Officer, Order of Orange Nassau (Neths.); Grand Officier, Légion d'Honneur (France); Commdr. Order of St. Olav (Norway); Grand Officer Order of Leopold II (Belgium); Chevalier, Order of Netherlands Lion; Grand Cross, Order of Merit (Austria) and Order of the Oak Crown (Luxembourg).
1781 Cordast, Switzerland.
Telephone: (037) 341753.

Starewicz, Artur; Polish politician; b. 20 March 1917, Warsaw; *m.* Maria Rutkiewicz 1947; four *c.*; ed. Lvov Technical Univ.
Member revolutionary youth orgs., incl. Communist Union of Polish Youth (K.Z.M.P.); arrested 35 and 36; studied in France 37-38; chemical engineer in Soviet electrotechnical industry 43-44; mem. Polish Workers Party (P.P.R.) 44-48, Polish United Workers' Party (P.Z.P.R.) 48-; worked in P.P.R. Voivodship Cttee. at Rzeszow, then Cracow and Warsaw, First Sec. of P.P.R. Voivodship Cttee. in Wrocław 46-48; Head of Propaganda, P.Z.P.R. Central Cttee. 48-53; Sec. of Central Council of Trade Unions 54-56; Deputy Editor-in-Chief of daily *Trybuna Ludu* 56; Alt. mem. P.Z.P.R. Central Cttee. 54-59, mem. 59-71, Head of Press Office 57-63, Sec. 63-71; Amb. to U.K. 71-; mem. Seym 57-72; Chair. Polish Group of Interparliamentary Union -72; Order of the Banner of Labour, First Class 54, 64, and others.
Leisure interest: aquatic sport.
Polish Embassy, 47 Portland Place, London, W1N 3AG, England.
Telephone: 01-580-4324.

Staribacher, Josef, DR.RER.POL.; Austrian politician; b. 25 March 1921, Vienna; *s.* of Josef and Marianne (née Ine) Staribacher; *m.* Gertrude Mayerhofer 1943; two *s.*; ed. Univ. of Vienna.
Joined Vienna Chamber of Labour 45. Deputy Dir. 61-68, Dir. 68; Leader, Food and Refreshment Workers' Union 61; mem. Nationalrat 61-; Minister for Commerce and Industry April 70-; Socialist Party.
Leisure interests: sports (walking, cycling).
Ministry for Commerce and Industry, Vienna, Austria.

Stark, Sir Andrew Alexander Steel, K.C.M.G., C.V.O., M.A.; British diplomatist; b. 30 Dec. 1916, Fauldhouse, Scotland; *s.* of Thomas Bow Stark and Barbara Black Stark; *m.* Rosemary Helen Oxley Parker 1944; three *s.* (one deceased); ed. Bathgate Acad. and Univ. of Edinburgh.
British Army 40-46; entered Diplomatic Service 48, First Sec., British Embassy, Vienna 51-53; Asst. Private Sec. to Sec. of State 53-56; First Sec., British Embassy, Belgrade 56-58, Rome 58-60; Counsellor, Head of Establishment and Org. Dept., Foreign Office 60-63; Counsellor British Embassy, Bonn 64-68; Amb. British Mission to UN 68; UN Under-Sec.-Gen. (Admin. and Management) 68-71; Amb. to Denmark 71-76; Grosses Verdienstkreuz, Fed. Repub. of Germany 65, Grand Cross, Order of the Dannebrog 74.
Leisure interests: reading, music, skiing, tennis, golf.
c/o Foreign and Commonwealth Office, London, S.W.1; Home: 41 Eaton Place, London, S.W.1, England.
Telephone: 01-235-7624 (Home).

Stark, Dame Freya Madeline, D.B.E.; British explorer and writer; b. 31 Jan. 1893, Paris, France; *d.* of Robert Stark and Flora (née Stark); *m.* Stewart Perowne 1947 (separated); ed. School of Oriental Studies and privately.
Travelled in Middle East and Iran 27-31 and in South Arabia 34-35, 37-38; joined Min. of Information Sept. 39, sent to Aden 39, Cairo 40, Baghdad 44, U.S.A. and Canada 44; Hon. LL.D. (Glasgow Univ.) 52, Hon. D.Litt. (Durham Univ.) 70; Founder's Medal, Royal Geographical Soc., Mungo Park Medal, Royal Scottish Geographical Soc., Sir Percy Sykes Medal, Royal Central Asian Soc., Burton Medal, Royal Asiatic Soc.
Leisure interests: gardening, embroidery.
Publs. *The Valleys of the Assassins* 34, *The Southern Gates of Arabia* 36, *Baghdad Sketches* 37, *Seen in the Hadhramaut* 38, *A Winter in Arabia* 40, *Letters from Syria* 42, *East is West* 45, *Perseus in the Wind* 48, *Traveller's Prelude* 50, *Beyond Euphrates* 51, *The Coast of Incense* 53, *Ionia: A Quest* 54, *The Lycian Shore* 56, *Alexander's Path* 58, *Riding to the Tigris* 59, *Dust in the Lion's Paw* 61, *The Journey's Echo* 63, *Rome on the Euphrates* 66, *The Zodiac Arch* 68, *Space, Time and Movement in Landscape* 69, *The Minaret of Djam* 70, *Turkey: Sketch of Turkish History* 71, *Selected Letters* (2 vols.) 74, 75.
Via Canova, Asolo, Treviso, Italy; and c/o John Murray, 50 Albemarle Street, London, W.1, England.

Starke, H. F. Gerhard, DR. PHIL.; German newspaper editor; b. 16 Aug. 1916, Berbersdorf; *s.* of Richard Starke and Elsbeth née Burghaus; *m.* Ingeborg Bechmann-Baumgarten 1941; ed. Univs. of Leipzig and Geneva.
Editor *Deutsche Allgemeine Zeitung*, Berlin 39-45; Editor *Prisma* and *Thema* (cultural periodicals), Munich and Gauting 46-49; Chief Editor and Chief Political Dept., Nordwestdeutscher Rundfunk (NWDR) and Norddeutscher Rundfunk (NDR), Hamburg 49-61; Dir. Deutschlandfunk, Cologne 61-66; Chief Editor *Die Welt*, Hamburg Sept. 66-68; agent in Bonn for Axel Springer publishing group 69.
Leisure interests: philosophy and political sciences.
5300 Bonn-Bad Godesberg, Deutschherrenstrasse 7, Federal Republic of Germany.
Telephone: 33-00-31.

Starke, Dr. Heinz; German politician; b. 27 Feb. 1911, Schweidnitz; *s.* of Fritz Starke and Margarete Dorn; *m.* Madeleine Nuel 1958; ed. Univs. of Berlin, Breslau and Jena.
Worked for Econ. Admin. Body of British Zone of Occupation; fmr. Dir. Bayreuth Chamber of Commerce; mem. European Assembly 58-; mem. Bundestag 53-; Minister of Finance 61-62; mem. Free Democratic Party until 70, Christian Social Union 70-.

Leisure interest: history and history of the arts.
Europastrasse 6, 53 Bonn/Bad Godesberg, Federal
Republic of Germany.
Telephone: Bonn 375049.

Starker, Janos; American (b. Hungarian) cellist;
b. 5 July 1924; s. of Margit and Sandor Starker; m. Rae
Busch Starker 1960; two d.; ed. Franz Liszt Acad. of
Music, Budapest.
Solo cellist, Budapest Opera House and Philharmonic
Orchestra 45-46; Solo cellist Dallas Symphony Orchestra
48-49, Metropolitan Opera Orchestra 49-53, Chicago
Symphony Orchestra 53-58; Resident cellist and Prof.
of Music, Indiana Univ. 58-; Grand Prix du Disque 48;
Distinguished Prof. of Music, hon. D.Mus.; world-wide
concert tours, numerous recordings and magazine
articles.
Publs. *Method* 64, *Bach Suites* 71.
Indiana University Music Department, Bloomington,
Indiana 47401, U.S.A.

Starkie, Walter Fitzwilliam, C.M.G., C.B.E., M.A.,
LITT.D., M.R.I.A., F.R.S.A., F.R.S.L.; British literary his-
torian; b. 9 Aug. 1894, Dublin; s. of Rt. Hon. W. J. M.
Starkie and May C. Walsh; m. Augusta Porchietti 1921;
one s. one d.; ed. Shrewsbury and Trinity Coll., Dublin.
Served First World War; Lecturer in Romance Lan-
guages, Trinity Coll. 20, in Modern Spanish Drama,
King's Coll., London 23; Fellow, Trinity Coll., Dublin
24-47; Dir. Irish National (Abbey) Theatre 27-42;
Lecturer Madrid 24, 28, Florence 26, Sweden 26,
U.S.A. and Canada 29, 30, France 31, 32, Italy, Austria
48, Portugal 49, Central and S. America 50; Visiting
Prof. of Romance Languages, Univ. of Chicago 30;
Lord Northcliffe Lecturer in Literature, Univ. Coll.,
London 36; Prof. of Spanish and Lecturer in Italian
Literature, Dublin Univ. 26-47; Dir. British Inst.
Madrid 40-54; Visiting Prof. Univ. of Texas 57, 58,
New York Univ. 59, Univ. of Kansas 60, Colorado 61;
Prof. in Residence, Univ. of California (Los Angeles)
64-68; Rep. of British Council in Spain 40-54; Chevalier
Légion d'Honneur; Commdr. Order of Isabel la Católica.
Leisure interests: violin playing and wandering.
Publs. *Jacinto Benavente* 25, *Raggle-Taggle* 33, *Spanish
Raggle-Taggle* 34, *Luigi Pirandello* 37, *The Waveless
Plain* 38, *Grand Inquisitor* 40, *In Sara's Tents* 53, *The
Road to Santiago* 57, *Spain: A Musician's Journey
through Time and Space* (2 vols., with 4 L.P. records
in English, French and German) 58, *Scholars and Gyp-
sies* 63, trans. of *Don Quixote* (Cervantes) 63, *Six Exemp-
lary Novels of Cervantes* 64, *Eight Plays of the Spanish
Golden Age* 64.
Apartamentos Melia 15/12, 25 Calle de la Princesa,
Madrid 8, Spain; and The Athenaeum, London, S.W.1,
England.

Starnes, John Kennett; Canadian diplomatist (retd.);
b. 5 Feb. 1918, Montreal; s. of Henry Kennett Starnes
and Altha Ella McCrea; m. Helen Gordon Robinson
1941; two s.; ed. Trinity Coll. School, Port Hope,
Institut Sillig, Switzerland, Univ. of Munich and
Bishop's Univ.
Canadian Army 40-44; Dept. of External Affairs 44-70;
Adviser, Canadian Del. to UN 48-50; First Sec., later
Counsellor, Bonn 53-56; Deputy Exec. Sec. North
Atlantic Council, Paris 56-58; Amb. to Fed. Repub. of
Germany and Head of Canadian Mil. Mission, Berlin
62-66; Amb. to United Arab Repub. 66-67 and to
Repub. of Sudan 67; Asst. Under-Sec. of State for
External Affairs 67-70; Dir.-Gen. Security Service,
Royal Canadian Mounted Police 70-73; mem. Council,
Int. Inst. for Strategic Studies, London 75-; D.C.L. h.c.,
Bishop's Univ. 75.
Leisure interests: skiing, philately, photography.
Fleury Road, Chelsea, P.Q., Canada.
Telephone: 827-0889 (Home); 993-1049 (Office).

Starr, Isaac, B.S., M.D.; American university medical
scientist; b. 6 March 1895, Philadelphia, Pa.; s. of
Isaac and Mary Barclay Starr; m. Edith Nelson Page
1922; three s. one d.; ed. Princeton Univ. and Univ. of
Pennsylvania.
House Officer, Mass. Gen. Hospital 20-22; Instr. in
Pharmacology, Univ. of Pennsylvania 22-28, Asst.
Prof. of Clinical Pharmacology 28-33; Hartzell Re-
search Prof. of Therapeutics 33-45 and 48-61; Prof. of
Therapeutic Research, Univ. of Pennsylvania 45-48;
Dean of the School of Medicine 45-48, Emeritus Prof.
Therapeutic Research 61-; during the Second World
War served as Chair. Sub-Cttee. on Pharmacy, Sec.
Sub-Committee on Essential Drugs, Committee on
Medical Supplies, Nat. Research Council; Responsible
Investigator, O.S.R.D.; Project on Convalescence, In-
vestigator Aviation Medicine and Anti-malarials; mem.
Cttee. on Narcotics and Drug Addiction (Chair. 47-60),
Cttee. on Problems of Alcohol, National Research
Council; Chair. Council on Drugs, American Medical
Assen. 60-63; mem. Cardiovascular Study Section, Nat.
Inst. of Health 46-51; Consultant U.S. Navy A.M.A.L.
49-64, U.S. Army Chemical, Biological and Radiological
Agency 62-66; Editor Board *Circulation* 49-53, 55-59;
Selective Service Medal; Lasker Award, American
Heart Assen. 57; Kober Medal, Assen. American
Physicians 67; Burger Medal, European Ballistocardio-
graphic Soc. 75.
Leisure interests: gardening, fly fishing.
Publs. Over 100 publications on renal physiology, drug
action in man, cardiac output in man, action of derivatives of choline in man, peripheral vascular disease
and its treatment, the ballistocardiogram and its
utility, the pulse derivative and cardiac contractility;
Ballistocardiography in Cardiovascular Research (in
collaboration with A. Noordergraaf) 67.
851 Gates Memorial Pavilion, University Hospital, 36th
and Spruce Streets, Philadelphia, Pa. 19104, U.S.A.
Telephone: 662-3328.

Starr, Ringo (Richard Starkey), M.B.E.; British
entertainer; b. 7 July 1940, Dingle, Liverpool; m.
Maureen Cox 1965 (divorced 1975); two s. one d.; ed.
Dingle Vale Secondary Modern School.
Plays drums; formerly an apprentice engineer; played
with Rory Storme's *Hurricanes* 59-62; joined *The
Beatles* Aug. 62; appeared with *The Beatles* in the
following activities: performances in Hamburg 62;
toured Scotland, Sweden, U.K. 63, Paris, Denmark,
Hong Kong, Australia, New Zealand, U.S.A., Canada
64, France, Italy Spain, U.S.A. 65, Canada, Spain,
Philippines, U.S.A. 66; attended Transcendental Medi-
tation Course at Maharishi's Acad., Rishikesh, India
Feb. 68; formed Apple Corps Ltd., parent org. of The
Beatles Group of Companies 68; following break-up of
group, now records solo.
Films by *The Beatles*: *A Hard Day's Night* 64, *Help!* 65,
Yellow Submarine (animated colour cartoon film) 68,
Let it be 70; TV film *Magical Mystery Tour* 67.
Individual appearances in films: *Candy* 68, *The Magic
Christian* 69, *200 Motels* 71, *Blindman* 71, *That'll be the
Day* 73, *Born to Boogie* (also directed and produced) 74,
Son of Dracula (also produced) 75, *Lisztomania* 75.
c/o Apple Corps Ltd., 3 Savile Row, London, W.1,
England.

Starrenburg, Willem F. G. L.; Netherlands oil executive; b. 1908; ed. Technische Hogeschool Te Delft.
Joined Royal Dutch/Shell 32, early service as development engineer; Man. Western Div. Venezuela 50-56;
Head, Production Dept. The Hague 56-57, Co-ordinator
Exploration and Production 57-60; Regional Co-
ordinator (Oil), Caribbean, Central and S. America
60-61; Dir. of Co-ordination (Chemical) 61-62; Asst.
Man. Dir. Royal Dutch Petroleum Co. 62-63, Man. Dir.

63-68; Dir. Shell Petroleum N.V.; Dir. Shell Research
N.V. 64-68.
Wassenaarseslag 2, Wassenaar, Netherlands.

Starý, Oldřich, M.D., D.SC.; Czechoslovak neurologist;
b. 15 June 1914, Plzeň; ed. Charles Univ., Prague.
First Internal Clinic, Prague 39-41; Neurological Clinic,
Prague 41-52; Asst. Prof. of Neurology 55-61, Prof. 61-
71, Dean, Faculty for Gen. Medicine, Charles Univ.,
Prague 61-63, Rector, Charles Univ., Prague 66-69;
Chief Editor *Czechoslovak Neurology*; Corresp. mem.
Czechoslovak Acad. of Sciences 60-; mem. Ideological
Comm. Central Cttee. C.P. of Czechoslovakia 62-69,
mem. Central Cttee. C.P. of Czechoslovakia 66-70;
mem., Pres. State Cttee. for Univs. 66-69; Pres. mem.
Scientific Council, Ministry of Health 67-68; mem.
Neurological Cttee., J. E. Purkyně Medical Soc. 53-,
Soc. Française de Neurologie 65-, U.S.S.R. Acad. of
Medical Sciences, Advisory Cttee. for Rehabilitation of
WHO 67-.
Publs. *Some Problems of the Pathogenesis of Disorders
due to Changes in an Intervertebral Disc* 59, and 110
papers on vertebrogenous disorders, the objective sub-
strate of the regularity in the central analysis of pain,
neurological problems, especially immunological pathogenesis of multiple sclerosis and problems of allergical
and non-allergical migraines, reflex therapy of spastic
paralysis.
c/o Československá Akademie Věd, Národní Tř. 3,
Prague 1, Czechoslovakia.

Stasi, Bernard, L. EN D.; French politician; b. 4 July
1930, Reims; ed. Institut d'Etudes Politiques, Paris
and Ecole Nationale d'Administration.
Attached to the Cabinet of the Pres. of the Nat.
Assembly 55; Civil Admin., Ministry of Interior 59;
Chef de Cabinet to the Prefect of Algiers 59-60; Head
of Section, Directorate-Gen. of Political Affairs and
Territorial Admin., Ministry of Interior 60-62; Technical
Adviser, Cabinet of the Sec. of State for Youth and
Sports 63-65; Directeur de Cabinet to the Sec. of Over-
seas Depts. 66-68; Deputy from Marne, Nat. Assembly
68-73, mem. Comm. on Cultural, Social and Family
Affairs; charged with missions to Israel, Great Britain,
Cuba and Chile; Mayor of Epernay 70-; Vice-Pres.
Centre Démocratie et Progrès 69-; Minister for Over-
seas Depts. and Territories 73-74; Pres. Fédération
française de course d'orientation 70-; Founder, Groupe
d'études parlementaires pour l'aménagement rural 70;
Board of Dirs. Association des Maires de France; mem.
various municipal orgs.; fmrly. active mem. of youth
movements; Officier de Réserve, Chevalier des Palmes
Académiques, Officier du Mérite Sportif.
Leisure interests: football, tennis, skiing, sailing.
11 allée des Pyramides, 51200 Epernay; 20 rue du
Commandant-Mouchotte, 75014 Paris, France.
Telephone: 51-34-30.

Stasiak, Ludomir; Polish state official; b. 3 Oct. 1919,
Góry, Puławy; ed. Higher School of Social Services,
Warsaw.
Active in ZMW (Rural Youth Union—"Wici") 38;
during Second World War fought with Peasant Battns.,
Commdr. Peasant Battn. region and mem. Editorial
Board of illegal paper *Orle ciosy*; after War was Sec. of
Cen. Board of "Wici" and Co-organizer and Vice-Chair.
of its Nat. Cttee. for Democratic Action; Sec. Central
Board of ZMP (Polish Youth Union) 48; Sec. Central
Cttee. of ZSL (United Peasant Party) 51-54, 56-69,
mem. Praesidium ZSL Central Cttee. 69-; Deputy to
Seym 52-; Sec. Council of State 69-; mem., Pres.
All Polish Cttee. of Nat. Unity Front 56-, Sec. 58-;
decorations include Order of Banner of Labour 1st
Class, Commdr. Cross of Order of Polonia Restituta,
Grunwald Cross 3rd Class, Silver Cross of Merit.
Kancelaria Rady Państwa, ul. Wiejska 2/4/6, 00-489
Warsaw, Poland.

Stassen, Harold E., A.B., LL.B.; American lawyer and
politician; b. 13 April 1907; ed. Univ. of Minnesota.
Member law firm of Stassen & Ryan, South St. Paul,
Minn. 30-38; County Attorney, Dakota Co. 31-38; Gov.
of Minn. 38-42; Chair. Nat. Governors' Conf. 41 and 42;
Chair. Council of State Govts. 40-41; resigned as Gov.
to enter U.S. Navy as Lieut.-Commdr. 43; served on
staff of Admiral Halsey in Pacific Theatre as Halsey's
Flag Sec. and later as Asst. Chief of Staff for Admin.
of Third Fleet 43-45; mem. U.S. del. to San Francisco
Conf. 45; Pres. Univ. of Pa. 48-53; Dir. Foreign
Operations Admin. 53-55; Special Asst. to Pres. on
Disarmament Problems (with cabinet rank) 55-58;
partner Stassen, Kephart, Sarkis and Scullin 58-; Pres.
Int. Council of Religious Educ. 42-50; Vice-Pres. Nat.
Council of Churches 50-52; Pres. American Baptist
Convention 63-64; Chair. Int. Law Cttee. of Phila-
delphia Bar Asscn. 73; Hon. LL.D., Hon. L.H.D.;
Legion of Merit; Bronze Star; Republican.
Publs. *Where I Stand* 47, *Man was Meant to be Free* 51.
Office: Fidelity Bldg. Philadelphia, Pa. 19109; Home:
Penn Towers, Philadelphia, Pa. 19103, U.S.A.

Stassinopoulos, Michael; Greek politician, university
professor and judge; b. 27 July 1905, Calamata; s. of
Demetrios Stassinopoulos and Catherine Scopetou; m.
Stamatia Ritsoni 1942; one d.; ed. Athens Univ.
Lecturer in Admin. Law, Athens Univ. 37-68; Prof.
Admin. Law, High School of Political Sciences, Athens
39-68, Dean 51-58; State Council Adviser 43-58; Political
Adviser to Dodecanese Gov. 47; Chair. Cttee. for the
Civil Servants Code 48; Minister of the Press and sub-
sequently Minister of Labour 52; Chair. Hellenic Nat.
Broadcasting Inst. Admin. Board 53; Chair. Nat.
Opera Admin. Board 53-63; Minister of the Press 58;
Vice-Pres. State Council 63, Pres. 66-69; mem. Parl.
Nov.-Dec. 74; Pres. of Greece Dec. 74-June 75; mem.
Acad. of Athens 68; Chief Justice until 74; Dr. h.c.
(Univ. of Bordeaux) 57, Dr. h.c. (Univ. of Paris) 74,
Order of St. George (First Class).
Leisure interests: poetry, cinema, gardening.
Publs. *The States' Civil Responsibility* 49, *Administra-
tive Acts Law* 50, *Civil Service Laws* 51, *Administrative
Disputes Laws* 53, *Principles of Administrative Law* 54,
Principles of Public Finance 56, *Traité des actes
administratifs* (in French), *Poems* 49, *The Land of
the Blue Lakes* 50, *Harmonia* (poems) 56, *Thought and
Life* (essays) 70, *The Wolf's Law* (essays) 72.
Taygetoy Street 7, (Psichicon), Athens, Greece.

Stătescu, Constantin, LL.D.; Romanian lawyer and
politician; b. 27 Nov. 1927, Curtea de Argeş; ed. Faculty
of Law, Univ. of Bucharest.
Member of Staff, Faculty of Law, Bucharest 50-66, Prof.
67-; Justice, Supreme Court of Romanian S.R. 64-67,
Vice-Pres. Civil Section 64-67; mem. Grand Nat.
Assembly 65-; Sec. State Council 67-75; mem. Acad. of
Social and Political Sciences 70-.
Publs. Works and textbooks on Common Law, *State
Arbitration and Arbitration Practice* 62, *Civil Law* 67, 70.
Academia de Stiinte Sociale si Politico, Str. Onesti 9-11,
Bucharest, Romania.

Stavropoulos, Constantin Anghelos; Greek lawyer,
politician and fmr. United Nations official; b. 15 Aug.
1905, Athens; m. Giannina Colquhoun 1969; ed. Univ.
of Athens and London School of Economics.
Private legal practice 29-33, 36-39; Sec.-Gen. and Acting
Gov. Epirus 33-36; Legal Adviser, Royal Greek
Embassy, London 41-46, Pres. Greek Maritime Court
in U.K. 42-46; UN War Crimes Comm. 43-46, UN
Legal Dept. 46-74; Under-Sec., Legal Counsel, Office of
Legal Affairs 55-74; Acting Commr. for South West
Africa 66-69; Under-Sec.-Gen. with responsibility for
Gen. Assembly Affairs 69-71; Under-Sec.-Gen., Special
Rep. of Sec.-Gen. to UN Conf. on the Law of the Sea

73-74; mem. Parl. Nov. 74-; Commdr. Order of George I (Greece).
Leisure interests: golf, swimming.
Parliament, Athens, Greece.

Stażewski, Henryk; Polish painter and graphic artist; b. 9 Jan. 1894, Warsaw; ed. Warsaw Acad. of Fine Arts.
Member of Block Group 24-26, Praesens Group 26-30, Cercle et Carré Int. Group 29-30, "a.r." Group 32-39, Abstraction-Création Int. Group 33-39, Union of Polish Painters 35-39, European Artistic Vanguard -39; one-man exhbns.: Galleria dell'Incontro, Rome 56, Kordegarda, Warsaw 59, Musée d'Art et d'Histoire, Geneva, Grabowsy Gallery, London 63, Kazimir Gallery, Chicago 69, Nat. Gallery, Prague 70; Collections: Museum of Modern Art, New York, Tate Gallery, London, Univ. Art Museum, Berkeley, Galérie Denise René, Paris, Museum der Stadt, St. Gallen, Nat. Galleries of Warsaw, Cracow, Poznań; State Prize, 1st Class 65, Gold Cross of Merit 55, Officer's Cross of Order of Polonia Restituta 65; works include painting, relief, spacial compositions, geometrical abstraction, book typography, interior architecture, scenography.
Publs. Co-Editor: *Blok, Praesens, L'Art Contemporain, Cercle et Carré, Europa, Pion, Nike, Wiadomości Literackie, Grafika, Kuźnica.*
Ul. Świerczewskiego 64 m. 118, 00-240 Warsaw, Poland.

Stearns, Robert Lawrence, B.A., LL.B. American institution executive; b. 3 Oct. 1892, Halifax, Nova Scotia; s. of John L. Stearns and Ella Powell Stearns; m. Amy Pitkin 1920; four d.; ed. Univ. of Colorado and Columbia Univ.
Admitted to Colorado Bar 16; mem. Lewis and Grant, Denver 22-35; Asst. in History Univ. of Colorado 13-14; Instr. in History, Univ. of Denver, summer 21; mem. Faculty of Univ. of Denver Law School 20-31; Prof. of Law, Univ. of Colo. 31-39, Act. Dean of Law School 31-33, Dean 35-39, Pres. of Univ. 39-53; mem. Educ. Council U.S. Navy 42-46; Operations Analyst U.S. Air Forces 42-46; mem. Board of Visitors U.S. Air Forces Academy; Chair. American Council on Educ. 52; Pres. Boettcher Foundation 53-62; Pres. Webb-Waring Inst. for Medical Research 63-71; Hon. LL.D. (Columbia Univ. and Univs. of Denver, New Mexico, Colorado and Colorado Coll.); medals include U.S. Medal of Freedom and U.S. Air Force Exceptional Civilian Service medal.
Publ. Compiler *Colorado Law of Wills and Estates* 38.
918 Race Street, Denver, Colo., U.S.A.
Telephone: 333-4635.

Stearns, Russell Bangs; American industrialist; b. 9 Feb. 1894, Chicago, Ill.; s. of Robert Bangs and Emma (Owens) Stearns; m. 1st Edna Dilley 1918 (died 1950), 2nd Mrs. Andrée Beauchamp Ryan 1958; ed. Univ. of Mich.
With North America Co. 16-17, with Arthur Perry & Co. 20, Partner 26-30, Pres. 30-38; Dir. and Chair. Exec. Cttee. Colonial Stores Inc.; Dir. of numerous other companies; Vice-Chair. of Corpn. and Board of Dirs. and mem. of Exec. Cttee., Northeastern Univ., Civic Educ. Foundation, Tufts Univ., Boston Hospital for Women, Museum of Science, Univ. of Michigan; mem. of Presidents' Club, Boston Opera Asscn., Trustee and mem. of Exec. Cttee. Museum of Science, etc.
Office: 24 Federal Street, Boston, Mass. 02110; Home: 50 Haven Street, Dedham, Mass. 02026, U.S.A.
Telephone: 617-326-1329 (Home); 617-542-3435 (Office).

Stebbins, George Ledyard, PH.D.; American professor of genetics; b. 6 Jan. 1906, Lawrence, N.Y.; s. of George Ledyard and Edith Candler; m. 1st Margaret Chamberlaine 1931 (divorced 1958), 2nd Barbara Jean Brumley

1958; two s. (one deceased), one d.; ed. Cate School, Carpinteria, Calif., and Harvard Univ.
Instructor in Biology, Colgate Univ. 31-35; Junior Geneticist, Univ. of Calif., Berkeley 35-39, Asst. Prof. 39-40, Assoc. Prof. 40-47, Prof. of Genetics 47-, moved from Berkeley to Univ. of Calif., Davis 50; mem. Nat. Acad. of Sciences, Linnaeus Soc. London, Royal Swedish Acad. of Sciences, Deutsche Akademie Leopoldina; Jessup Lecturer, Columbia Univ. 46; Prather Lecturer, Harvard Univ. 58; Hon. D.Sc. (Paris) 52.
Leisure interests: hiking, mountain climbing, plant collecting, music as listener.
Publs. *The Human Organism and the World of Life* (with C. W. Young) 38, *Variation and Evolution in Plants* 50, *Processes of Organic Evolution* 66, *The Basis of Progressive Evolution* 69, *Chromosomal Evolution in Higher Plants* 71, *Flowering Plants: Evolution above the Species Level* 74.
Office: Department of Genetics, University of California, Davis, Calif. 95616; Home: 1009 Ovejas Avenue, Davis, Calif. 95616, U.S.A.
Telephone: 916-752-0200 (Office); 916-753-2665 (Home).

Stedtfeld, Fritz, DR.JUR.; German international finance official (retd.); b. 6 June 1908, Cappel, Westphalia; m. one s. one d.; ed. Univs. of Munich and Berlin.
Assistant in Commercial Law, Univ. of Berlin 33; with Ministry of Economics 33-70, Deputy Asst. Sec. responsible for gen. trade policies 56-70; Exec. Dir. IBRD, IFC and IDA 70-73.

Steel, David Edward Charles, D.S.O., M.C., T.D.; British company director; b. 29 Nov. 1916; m. Ann Price 1956; one s. two d.; ed. Rugby School and Univ. Coll., Oxford.
Officer, Q.R. Lancers, serving in France, the Middle East, N. Africa and Italy 40-45; admitted as Solicitor 48; worked for Linklaters and Paines 48-50; in Legal Dept., British Petroleum Co. Ltd. 50-56; Pres. British Petroleum (N. America) Ltd. 59-61, Regional Co-ordinator, Western Hemisphere, B.P. Co. Ltd. 61-62; Man. Dir. Kuwait Oil Co. Ltd. 62-65, Dir. 65-; a Man. Dir. British Petroleum Co. Ltd. 65-72, Deputy Chair. 72-75, Chair. 75-76; Chair. B.P. Oil 76-.
18 Princes Gate, London, S.W.7, England.
Telephone: 01-589-2406.

Steel, Sir (Joseph) Lincoln (Spedding), Kt., F.R.S.A., M.A., J.P.; British business executive; b. 24 March 1900, Liscard; s. of Joseph Steel and Esther Spedding; m. 1st Cynthia Smith 1928 (died 1929), one s.; m. 2nd Barbara Goldschmidt 1938, one s.; ed. Christ's Hospital and St. John's Coll., Oxford.
Joined Brunner Mond and Co. Ltd. 22; Del. Dir. I.C.I. (Alkali) Ltd. 32, Man. Dir. Alkali Div. of I.C.I. Ltd. 42, Chair. Alkali Div. of I.C.I. Ltd. 43; Dir. Imperial Chemical Industries Ltd. (I.C.I.) 45-60; Deputy Chair. Triplex Holdings Ltd. 60-61, Chair. 61-66; Chair. British Nat. Cttee., Int. Chamber of Commerce 51-63, Pres. Int. Chamber of Commerce 63-65; mem. Consultative Cttee. EFTA 60-69; Dir. Charterhouse Investment Trust Ltd. 60-74; Chair. Overseas Cttee. Fed. of British Industries 50-65; Hon. Pres. Int. Chamber of Commerce; mem. Central Council European League for Econ. Co-operation 66-69.
Leisure interests: gardening, walking, travel.
The Warren, Chesham Bois, Bucks., England.
Telephone: Amersham 6406.

Steen, Reiulf; Norwegian politician; b. 16 Aug. 1933, Saetre.
Factory worker 51; joined *Fremtiden* as journalist 55; Sec. AVF (Labour Party Junior Org.) 58, Chair. 61-64; Sec. Labour Party Parl. Group 64, Vice-Chair. Labour Party 65-75, Chair. April 75-; Deputy mem. Storting 61-65; Minister of Communications March 71-Oct. 72.
Arbeiderpartiet, Youngstorget 2, Oslo, Norway.

Steenbeck, Max, DR. PHIL.; German scientist; b. 21 March 1904, Kiel; ed. Realgymnasium, Kiel and Univ. of Kiel.
Siemens-Schuckert, Berlin 27-45, in Soviet Union 45-56; returned to Jena 56; Dir. of Inst. for Magneto-Hydrodynamics, Jena 56-59, Chief of Atomic Reactor building 57-63; Pres. of Research Council of German Democratic Republic 65-; Prof. Jena Univ.; mem. German Acad. of Sciences, Berlin, U.S.S.R. Acad. of Sciences; Hon. Dr. rer. nat.
Kernbergstrasse 3, Jena, German Democratic Republic.

Steeves, John Milton, B.A., M.A.; American diplomatist; b. 6 May 1905, Brinsmae, North Dakota; s. of Andrew Wellington Steeves and Sarah Jane Saisbury; m. Anna Jean Berstresser 1945; one c. (deceased); ed. Walla Walla Coll. and Univ. of Washington.
Educational Work, India 27-43; Dept. of State 45-, served New Delhi, Tokyo, Djakarta 48-55; Foreign Relations Consultant to High Commr. of Ryukyu Islands, Consul Gen. in Naha, Counsellor in Tokyo 55-57; Political Adviser to C.-in-C. Pacific 57-59; Consul-Gen. in Hong Kong 59; Deputy Asst. Sec. of State for Far Eastern Affairs 59-62; Amb. to Afghanistan 62-66; Dir.-Gen. Foreign Service, Dept. of State 66-69; Exec. Dir. Center for Strategic and Int. Studies, Georgetown Univ. 70-71, Chair. 71-73.
Leisure interests: writing, golf, riding, travel.
Box 153, Fairfield, Pa. 17320, U.S.A.

Stefanopoulos, Constantine; Greek lawyer; b. 1926, Patras; s. of Demetrius and Vrisiis Stefanopoulos; m. Eugenia El. Stounopoulou 1959; two s. one d.
Private law practice; mem. Parl. (Nat. Radical Union) for Achaia 64; Under-Sec. of Commerce July-Oct. 74; Minister of the Interior Nov. 74-.
Ministry of the Interior, Athens, Greece.
Telephone: 600-514.

Steffe, Horst-Otto, D.ECON.; German economist; b. 27 Aug. 1919, Berlin; m. Margareta Spangl; three c.; ed. Leipzig and Vienna Univs.
Military Service 37-45; Economist, Austrian Inst. for Econ. Research 48; Asst., then Deputy Section Head, Fed. Ministry of Econ. Affairs 52; Man. Dir. Gemeinschaft zum Schutz der deutschen Sparer 58; Dir. Nat. Econ. and Econ. Trends, EEC Comm., Brussels, Chair. EEC Cttee. for Business Cycle Analysis and of Working Parties on Econ. Budgets, Cyclical Statistics and Econ. Tendency Surveys 60; mem. Short Term Econ. Policy and Budgetary Policy Cttees.; alternative mem. Monetary Cttee.; Man. Econ. and Research Dept., European Investment Bank 67, Vice-Chair. 72-.
Publs. numerous works on economics, investment and related subjects.
European Investment Bank, 2 place de Metz, Luxembourg; Home: 4 rue Nicolas Gredt, Luxembourg-Cessange.
Telephone: 43-50-11 (Office); 49-09-02 (Home).

Steger, Otfried; German civil engineer and politician; b. 1926.
Member, Cen. Cttee. Sozialistische Einheitspartei Deutschlands (SED); Minister for Electrical Engineering and Electronics.
Ministerrat, Berlin, German Democratic Republic.

Steiger, Rod; American actor; b. 14 April 1925; m. 1st Claire Bloom q.v. (divorced), one d.; m. 2nd Sherry Nelson 1973; ed. public schools.
Berlin Film Festival Award 64; British Film Acad. Award; Acad. Award (Oscar) Best Actor 67.
Stage appearances include Night Music 51, An Enemy of the People 53, Rashomon 59; numerous film appearances include On the Waterfront 53, Big Knife 55, Oklahoma 56, Jubal 57, Across the Bridge 58, Al Capone 59, Seven Thieves 59, The Mark 60, The World in my Pocket 60, The Tiger Among Us 61, The Longest Day 61,

Convicts 4 61, The Time of Indifference 62, Hands on the City 63, The Pawnbroker 64, The Loved One 64, Doctor Zhivago 66, In the Heat of the Night 67, No Way to Treat a Lady 68, The Illustrated Man 68, The Sergeant 68, Three into Two Won't Go 69, Waterloo 70, The Lolly Madonna War, Lucky Luciano 73, The Heroes 74, Les Innocents aux Mains Sales 75, Hennessy 75.
c/o Jess S. Morgan & Co. Inc., 6399 Wilshire Boulevard, Los Angeles, Calif. 90048, U.S.A.

Stein, Herbert, PH.D.; American government official; b. 27 Aug. 1916, Detroit; ed. Williams Coll. and Univ. of Chicago.
Economist, U.S. Govt. 38-45; Economist, Cttee. for Econ. Devt. 45-48, Assoc. Dir. of Research 48-56, Dir. of Research 56-66, Vice-Pres. and Chief Economist 66-67; Senior Fellow, Brookings Inst. 67-69; mem. President's Council of Econ. Advisers 69-, Chair. 72-74; A. Willis Robertson Prof. of Econs., Univ. of Va. 71-.
Department of Economics, University of Virginia, Charlottesville, Va. 22903, U.S.A.

Stein, William H(oward), B.S., PH.D.; American biochemist; b. 25 June 1911, New York City; s. of Fred M. and Beatrice B(org) Stein; m. Phoebe Hockstader 1936; three s.; ed. Lincoln School of Teachers Coll., New York City, Phillips Exeter Acad., Exeter, N.H., Harvard Coll. and Coll. of Physicians and Surgeons, Columbia Univ.
Assistant in Biochem., Rockefeller Inst. (now Rockefeller Univ.) 39-43, Assoc. 43-49, Assoc. mem. 49-52, mem. and Prof. 52-; Visiting Prof., Univ. of Chicago 60, Harvard Univ. 64; Chair. Editorial Cttee. American Soc. of Biological Chemists 57-60, U.S. Nat. Cttee. for Int. Union of Biochemists 65-68; mem. Editorial Board Journal of Biological Chemistry 61-, Assoc. Editor 64-68, Editor 68-71; Councillor, Nat. Inst. of Neurological Diseases and Blindness, Nat. Insts. of Health 61-66; Trustee, Montefiore Hospital, N.Y.; Harvey Lecturer 57, Shaffer Lecturer 65; American-Swiss Foundation Fellow 56; mem. Nat. Acad. of Sciences, American Acad. of Arts and Sciences; American Chemical Soc. Award in Chromatography and Electrophoresis 64; Nobel Prize for Chem. with C. B. Anfinsen (q.v.) and S. Moore (q.v.) 72; Richards Medal of American Chem. Soc., Kaj Linderstrøm-Lang Award, Copenhagen (with Stanford Moore) 72; D.Sc. h.c., Columbia Univ., N.Y.C., Albert Einstein Coll. of Medicine of Yeshiva Univ., N.Y.C. 73; Award of Excellence Medal, Columbia Univ. 73.
Leisure interests: travel, music.
Publs. Numerous articles in various biochemical and chemical journals 39-.
Rockefeller University, 66th and York, New York, N.Y. 10021; Home: 530 East 72nd Street, New York, N.Y. 10021, U.S.A.

Steinberg, Saul; American (b. Romanian) artist and architect; b. 15 June 1914; ed. Milan Polytechnic School.
Cartoonist 36-39; practising architect 39-41; moved to U.S. 42; illustrator for the New Yorker 42-; represented in Museum of Modern Art N.Y.
Publs. All in Line 45, The Art of Living 49, The Passport 54, The Labyrinth 60, The Inspector 73.
3 Washington Square, Village, New York, N.Y. 10012, U.S.A.

Steinberg, William; American conductor; b. 1 Aug 1899, Cologne, Germany; s. of Julius and Bertha (Matzdorf) Steinberg; m. Lotti Stern 1934 (deceased); one s. one d.; ed. School of Higher Musical Studies, Univ. of Cologne, and privately.
Conductor Cologne Opera House 20-25; Opera Dir. German Theatre, Prague 25-29; later Gen. Musical Dir. Frankfurt Opera House and Museumsgesellschaft Frankfurt; guest conductor Berlin State Opera House and Czech Philharmonic, Prague; founder conductor

Palestine Orchestra 36-38; went to U.S.A. 38; regular conductor with N.B.C.; guest conductor Vancouver Symphony, Chicago Symphony, Minneapolis Symphony, Cleveland Symphony, L.A. Philharmonic, N.Y. Philharmonic, San Francisco Symphony, Brazilian Symphony, Havana Philharmonic orchestras; conductor with San Francisco Opera 44-52; Music Dir. Buffalo Philharmonic Orchestra 45-52; Musical Dir. Pittsburgh Symphony Orchestra 52-76, London Philharmonic Orchestra 58-59, Boston Symphony 69-72; many recordings.
11C Gateway Towers, Pittsburgh, Pa. 15222, U.S.A.

Steinberger, Jack, PH.D.; American physicist; b. 25 May 1921, Germany; s. of Ludwig Steinberger and Bertha (May) Steinberger; m. 1st Joan Beauregard 1943, 2nd Cynthia Eve Alff 1961; two s.; ed. Univ. of Chicago.
Visiting mem. Inst. of Advanced Study, Princeton 48-49; Research Asst., Univ. of Calif. (Berkeley) 49-50; Prof. Columbia Univ., New York City 50-71, Higgins Prof. 67-71; Staff mem. Centre Européen pour la Recherche Nucléaire 68-; mem. Nat. Acad. of Sciences 67-, Heidelberg Acad. of Sciences 67-, American Acad. of Arts and Sciences 69-; Hon. Prof., Heidelberg 68.
Leisure interest: mountaineering.
Publs. *Muon Decay* 49, *Pi Zero Meson* 50, *Spin of Pion* 51, *Parity of Pion* 54, 59, 2° *Hyperon* 57, *Properties of "Strange Particles"* 57-64, *CP Violating Effects in K° Decay* 66-.
CERN, Geneva 23, Switzerland; and Les Maladières, Gex, France.

Steiner, George, B. ès L., B.A., M.A., D.PHIL., F.R.S.L.; American writer and scholar; b. 23 April 1929, Paris, France; s. of Dr. and Mrs. F. G. Steiner; m. Zara Shakow 1955; one s. one d.; ed. Univs. of Paris and Chicago, Harvard Univ. and Balliol Coll., Oxford.
Editorial Staff *The Economist*, London 52-56; Fellow, Inst. for Advanced Study, Princeton 56-58; Gauss Lecturer, Princeton Univ. 59-60; Fellow and Dir. of English Studies, Churchill Coll., Cambridge 61-69, Extraordinary Fellow 69-; Albert Schweitzer Visiting Prof., New York Univ. 66-67; Visiting Prof. Yale Univ. 70-71; Prof. of English and Comparative Lit., Univ. of Geneva 75-(77); delivered Massey Lectures 74; Pres. The English Asscn. 75-76; O. Henry Award 58, *Jewish Chronicle* Book Award 68, Zabel Prize of Nat. Inst. of Arts and Letters 70, Le Prix du Souvenir 74.
Leisure interests: chess, music, mountain walking.
Publs. *Tolstoy or Dostoevsky* 59, *The Death of Tragedy* 61, *Anno Domini: Three Stories* 64, *Language and Silence* 67, *Extraterritorial* 71, *In Bluebeard's Castle* 71, *The Sporting Scene: White Knights in Reykjavik* 73, *Fields of Force* 74, *A Nostalgia for the Absolute* (Massey Lectures) 74, *After Babel* 75; Editor *Penguin Book of Modern Verse Translation* 67.
32 Barrow Road, Cambridge, England; Harvard Club, New York City, U.S.A.

Stella, Frank; American painter; b. May 1936, Malden, Mass.; ed. Phillips Acad. and Princeton Univ.
Frequent exhbns. at Leo Castelli Gallery, New York; one-man exhbns. include Galerie Lawrence, Paris 61, 64, Ferus Gallery, Los Angeles 63, 65, Kasmin Ltd., London 64, 66, 68, David Mirvish Gallery, Toronto 66, 68, Galerie Bischofberger, Zurich 67, Irving Blum Gallery 68, 69, Univ. of Puerto Rico 69; Retrospective exhbns. Museum of Modern Art, N.Y. 70, Hayward Gallery, London 70; work has also appeared in *Sixteen Americans* exhbn., Museum of Modern Art, N.Y., *Abstract Expressionist and Imagists*, Guggenheim Museum, N.Y. and in major exhbns. in Oberlin Houston, Seattle World Fair 62, Brandeis Univ. and in many other countries including Switzerland 63, The Venice Biennale 64, Argentina 65, São Paulo Biennale, Brazil 65, Holland 66, 67, Ninth Int. Exhbn.,

Tokyo, Japan 67, India 66, Germany 68, 69, Helsinki 69; First prize, Ninth Int. Exhbn., Tokyo 67.
c/o Leo Castelli Gallery, 4 East 77 Street, New York, N.Y., U.S.A.

Stella-Richter, Mario, D.IUR.; Italian judge; b. 11 Dec. 1906, Rome; s. of Vitaliano Stella-Richter and Olimpia Falasconi; m. Laura Tonni-Bazza 1934; two s.; ed. Univ. of Rome.
Judge of First Instance, Pretura-Court, Rome 29-34; Asst. Judge, Tribunal of Brescia 34-36; Sec. Civil Code Reform Comm., Ministry of Justice 36-40; Asst. Judge, Tribunal of Rome 40-49; Justice of Appeal, Acting Justice of Supreme Court of Cassation 49-54; Asst. Justice, Supreme Court of Cassation 54-63, Presiding Justice 63-72; Pres. Superior Tribunal of Public Waters 72-73; Procurator-Gen., Supreme Court of Cassation 73-74, Chief Justice 74-; Chair. Asscn. for Cultural Exchange between Italian and German Jurists 74-; Medal, Educ. Surveillé, and Medal, Admin. Pénitentiaire, French Dept. of Justice 74.
Leisure interest: history of arts.
Publs. *Rassegna di Giurisprudenza sul Codice Civile* (Editor) 69, *Rassegna di Giurisprudenza sul Codice di Procedura Civile* (Editor) 73.
Palazzo di Giustizia, Piazza Cavour, 00100 Rome, Italy.

Stelling-Michaud, Sven, DR. ÈS L.; Swiss historian; b. 15 Aug. 1905, Copenhagen; s. of Erwin Stelling and Jeanne Michaud; two s.; ed. Univs. of Zürich and Lausanne, Sorbonne and Ecole des Chartes, Paris.
Archaeological expeditions in Persia 29, Turkey 32; Int. Affairs Editor for *Journal de Genève* 42-47; Prof. of Modern History and History of Political Theories, Univ. of Geneva 43-58, Principal Interpreters' School 51-, Prof. of Modern History 58-, Prof. of Philosophy of History 62-.
Publs. include *Visage de la Perse* 30, *St. Saphorin et la politique étrangère de la Suisse pendant la guerre de succession d'Espagne* 35, *Unbekannte schweizer Landschaften aus dem 17. Jahrhundert* 37, *Etudes d'histoire diplomatique* 43, *Les Partis politiques et la guerre* 45, *L'Université de Bologne et la Suisse aux XIII° et XIV° siècles*, 2 vols. 55, 60, *Livre du Recteur de l'Académie de Genève 1559-1878* (editor) Vol. I 59, Vol. II 66, Vol. III 72, Vol. IV 75, *Journal politique du Comte Ciano 1939-1943* (editor) 2 vols. 46, Jacob Burckhardt *Considérations sur l'histoire universelle* (translation) 65, 2nd edn. 73, *Matériaux pour une histoire des sciences sociales à Genève* (with G. Busino) 65, *Autour d'Alexandre Herzen* (editor) 73.
14 ave. de Thônex, Chêne-Bourg, Geneva, Switzerland. Telephone: 022-480500.

Stelmakh, Mikhail Afanasyevich; Soviet writer; b. 24 May 1912, Dyakovtsy, Ukraine; s. of Afanasy Demyanovich and Anna Ivanovna Stelmakh; two s. one d.; ed. Vinnitsa Pedagogical Inst.
Teacher 32-39; service in Soviet Army 39-45; began literary work 36; Deputy to Supreme Soviet U.S.S.R.; mem. Comm. for Foreign Affairs, U.S.S.R. Supreme Soviet; Lenin and State Prizes 51, 61; Order of Lenin (twice), of Red Banner of Labour 62; Red Star Patriotic War 2nd class; Hero of Socialist Labour.
Leisure interests: fishing, collecting mushrooms.
Publs. (trilogy) *Bread and Salt, Blood is Thicker than Water, The Big Family, Truth and Falsehood* (novel) 61, *Goose-swans are flying* (children's story) 64, *The Evening is Generous* 67, *The Poppy is in Blossom* (Collected Poetry) 68, *Family of Burunduk* 68, *With the Thought of You* (novel) 69, *Collected Works* (6 vols.) 72-73.
Ap. 70, Lenin Street 68, Kiev 154, U.S.S.R.
Telephone: 25-30-65.

Stennis, John Cornelius, B.S., LL.B.; American politician; b. 3 Aug. 1901, Kemper Co., Miss.; s. of Hampton Howell and Cornelia Adams Stennis; m. Coy H.

Stennis 1929; one *s*. one *d*.; ed. Mississippi State Coll. and Univ. of Virginia Law School.

Member Miss. House of Reps. from Kemper County 28-32; District Prosecuting Attorney, Sixteenth Judicial District 31 and 35; apptd. Circuit Judge, Sixteenth Judicial District 37 and elected 38, 46; U.S. Senator from Mississippi 47-; Democrat.

Leisure interests: hunting, fishing, reading, sporting events.

Senate Office Building, Washington, D.C., U.S.A.

Stensiö, Erik Helge Oswald; Swedish university professor; *b*. 2 Oct. 1891; ed. Univ. of Uppsala.

Professor of Palaeozoology at the Swedish Museum of Natural History, Stockholm 23-59, Emer. 59-; Foreign mem. of Royal Soc., London; Hon. mem. Royal Soc. of Edinburgh; Hon. mem. Acad. Sciences, New York; Foreign mem. U.S.S.R. Acad. Sciences, etc.; Wollaston Medal, Gold Medal of Linnean Soc., London, Daniel Elliott Giraud Medal, Washington; Darwin-Wallace Medal, Linnean Soc., Gold Medal, Royal Acad. of Science, Stockholm, Dumont Medal, Belgian Geological Soc.; Dr. h.c. Paris, Copenhagen, Oslo and Tübingen.

Swedish Museum of Natural History, Stockholm 50, Sweden.

Telephone: 150240.

Stepakov, Vladimir Ilich, M.SC.; Soviet journalist and diplomatist; *b*. 1912; ed. Lenin Pedagogical Inst., Moscow and Acad. of Social Sciences of C.P.S.U. Central Cttee.

Former metal craftsman and wood cutter; Soviet Army 35-37; mem. C.P.S.U. 37-; staff of People's Commissariat for Means of Communication 37-40; in machine-building factory 41-45; party and political work, Moscow 44-59; Head of Dept., Central Cttee. of C.P.S.U. 59-61; Head of Ideological Dept., Communist Party of C.P.S.U. 61-64; Chief Editor *Izvestia* 64-65; Head of Propaganda and Agitation Dept. of Central Cttee. of C.P.S.U. 65-70; Amb. to Yugoslavia 71-; mem. C.P.S.U. Cen. Auditing Comm. 61-66; mem. Cen. Cttee. of C.P.S.U. 66-; Deputy to U.S.S.R. Supreme Soviet 62-70.

Embassy of U.S.S.R., Deligradska 32, Belgrade, Yugoslavia.

Stephani, Christakis, B.COMM., F.C.A.; Cypriot banker; *b*. 28 Sept. 1926, Cyprus; *m*. Vera Halliday 1951; one *s*. two *d*.; ed. London School of Econs. and Political Science.

Accountant-General of the Repub. of Cyprus 60-65; Gov. Cen. Bank of Cyprus 65-.

Central Bank of Cyprus, P.O. Box 1087, Nicosia, Cyprus.

Stephanopoulos, Stephanos; Greek lawyer and politician; *b*. 1898; ed. Univs. of Athens and Paris.

Deputy for Elis 30; Under-Sec. in Ministry of Economy and Labour in 1st Populist Govt., Minister of Nat. Econ. in 2nd; resistance in Greece during 41-44 occupation; Minister of Transport in 1st Nat. Govt. 44, of Economic Co-ordination in Populist Govt. 46; left Populist Party 50, formed independent group which joined Kanellopoulos' Unionist-Populist Party, formed and disbanded (on Papagos' election) 51; joined Greek Rally Party 51; Minister of Foreign Affairs 52-55; Second Deputy Prime Minister Dec. 63-Feb. 64; Deputy Prime Minister Feb. 64-65, also Minister of Co-ordination June 64-65; Prime Minister Sept. 65-Dec. 66; Leader Social Populist Party 59 (later mem. Central Union Party), founded Liberal Democratic Centre Party Dec. 65.

Publs. include *Social Insurance* 32, *Economic and Social Studies* 35, *Philosophy and Social Systems* 36.

Athens, Greece.

Stephens, Frederick James; British retd. oil executive; *b*. 30 July 1903, Bristol; *s*. of John Frederick Douglas Stephens and Frances Mary (née Mirrlees);

m. Sara Clark 1948 (died 1954); no *c*.; ed. Marlborough Coll., Grenoble Univ., France, and Pembroke Coll., Cambridge.

Joined Royal Dutch Shell Group of Companies 26, served Venezuela, London and U.S.A.; Dir. and Exec. Vice-Pres. Asiatic Petroleum Corpn., New York 46-68; returned to London 48; Man. Dir. Shell Petroleum Co. 51-61, Chair. 61-71; Dir. Shell Transport and Trading Co. 51-, Man. Dir. 57-71, Chair. 61-67; Man. Dir. Shell Int. Petroleum Co. Lte. 59-61; Dir. Bataafse Petroleum Maatschappij N.V.; Commdr. Order of Orange-Nassau.

Leisure interests: gardens, golf.

Noel House, Les Ruisseaux, St. Brelade, Jersey, Channel Islands.

Telephone: Central 41444.

Stephens, Olin James II; American naval architect and yacht designer; *b*. 13 April 1908, New York City; *s*. of Roderick Stephens and Marguerite Dulon; *m*. Florence Reynolds 1930; two *s*.; ed. Massachusetts Inst. of Tech.

Partner, Sparkman & Stephens 28; Chief Designer, Vice-Pres. and Dir., Sparkman & Stephens Inc. 29-64, Chief Designer, Pres. and Dir. 64-; Hon. M.S. (Stevens Inst. of Tech.) 45; Hon. M.A. (Brown Univ.) 59; some yachts designed: *Dorade* 30, *Stormy Weather* 34, (with W. Starling Burgess) *Ranger* 37, *Vim, Goose, Bolero* 38, *Finisterre* 54, *Columbia* 58, *Constellation* 64, *Intrepid* 67, *Morning Cloud* 69, 71, 73, 75, *Courageous* 74.

Sparkman and Stephens Inc., 79 Madison Avenue, New York, N.Y. 10016; Home: Underhill Road, Scarsdale, New York, N.Y. 10583, U.S.A.

Telephone: (212) 689-3880 (Office); (914) 723-4641 (Home).

Stephens, Robert; British actor; *b*. 14 July 1931; *m*. Maggie Smith (*q.v.*) 1967 (dissolved 1975); two *s*.

Member English Stage Co., Royal Court 56-62; joined Nat. Theatre Co. 63; Assoc. Dir. Nat. Theatre 69-; Stage appearances include *Hay Fever* 64, *The Royal Hunt of the Sun* 64, *Much Ado About Nothing* 65, Lindsay in *Armstrongs' Last Goodnight* 65, Tom Wrench (*Trelawney of the Well's*) 65, Leonido (*A Bond Honoured*) 66, Harold Goringe (*Black Comedy*) 66, Kurt (*The Dance of Death*) 67, Vershinin (*Three Sisters*) 67, Jacques (*As You Like It*) 67, Tartuffe (*Tartuffe*) 67, Frederick (*Home and Beauty*) 68, *Beaux Stratagem* 70, *Design for Living* 70, *Private Lives* 72, *The Seagull, Ghosts, Hamlet* 74, *Murderer, Zoo Story, Sherlock Holmes* 75, *Othello, Private Lives* 76; directed one of a triple bill *A Most Unwarrantable Intrusion* 68; appeared in and co-directed *Macrune's Guevara* 69; directed and appeared in *Apropos the Falling Sleet*; Films: *The Prime of Miss Jean Brodie* 69, *The Private Life of Sherlock Holmes* 70, *The Asphyx* 72, *Travels with my Aunt* 72, *Luther* 72; numerous T.V. appearances; Assoc. Dir. Nat. Theatre.

c/o Film Rights Ltd., 113 Wardour Street, London, W.1, England.

Telephone: 01-437-7151.

Stephens, Robert Porritt, B.A., B.A.OXON.; Swaziland politician; *b*. 20 Feb. 1905, Laingsburg, South Africa; *s*. of Dr. H. W. Stephens and Mabel Browne Stephens; *m*. Coral Maria Barnes 1932; one *s*. two *d*.; ed. Diocesan Coll., Rondebosch, Cape Town, Univ. of Cape Town and Oxford Univ.

Forester, Dept. of Forestry, S. Africa 29-46; served with S. African Engineers, Kenya and Western Desert 39-43; Man. Dir. and Chair. Peak Timbers Ltd., Swaziland 47-68; mem. European Advisory Council 58-63; mem. Legislative Council 63-67; mem. House of Assembly 67-; Minister of Finance 72-; Rhodes Scholar 23.

Leisure interests: big game fishing, shooting (Bisley .303), cattle farming.

Publs. several articles on forestry in technical journals.
P.O. Box 443, Mbabane; P.O. Box 3, Piggs Peak,
Swaziland.
Telephone: Mbabane 2141 (Office); Piggs Peak 9 (Home).

Stephenson, Gordon, C.B.E., M.C.P., B.ARCH.,
L.F.R.A.I.A., L.F.R.A.P.I., F.R.I.B.A., F.I.L.A., F.R.T.P.I.;
British architect and town planner; b. 6 June 1908,
Liverpool; s. of Francis Edwin and Eva Eliza Stephen-
son; m. Flora Bartlett Crockett 1938; three d.; ed.
Liverpool Inst., Univs. of Liverpool and Paris, Massa-
chusetts Inst. of Technology.
With Le Corbusier and Pierre Jeanneret 30-32; Lec-
turer, Univ. of Liverpool 32-36; Commonwealth Fellow,
Mass. Inst. of Technology 36-38; Master, Architectural
Asscn. School of Architecture 39-40; Div. Architect,
Royal Ordinance Factory and War Hostels 40-42;
Sr. Research Officer and Chief Planning Officer,
Ministry of Town and Country Planning 42-47; Prof.
of Civic Design and Editor *Town Planning Review,*
Univ. of Liverpool 48-53; Consultant to Govt. of W.
Australia, City of Perth and Univ. of W. Australia 54-
55; consultant to cities of Toronto, Ottawa and Kings-
ton, Ontario and Halifax, Nova Scotia 55-60; Prof. of
Town and Regional Planning, Univ. of Toronto 55-60;
Consultant Architect and Prof. of Architecture, Univ. of
W. Australia 60-72, Emer. Prof. 72-; partner in
Ferguson and Stephenson, Architects, Planners and
Landscape Architects, Perth 72-; mem. Nat. Capital
Planning Cttee., Canberra 67-73.
Publs. (with Flora C. Stephenson) *Community Centres*
40, (with J. A. Hepburn) *Plan for the Metropolitan
Region of Perth and Fremantle* 55, *A Redevelopment
Study of Halifax, Nova Scotia* 57, (with G. G. Muirhead)
A Planning Study of Kingston, Ontario 59, (with
R. J. Ferguson) *Physical Planning Report, Murdoch
University* 73, *The Design of Central Perth* 75.
78 Kingsway, Nedlands, Western Australia 6009.
Telephone: 86-5058.

Sterky, Håkan Karl August, DR. TECH.; Swedish
electrical engineer; b. 7 April 1900, Stockholm; s. of
Carl Edvard Sterky and Hilma Almén; m. Kerstin Tottie
1927; two s. one d.; ed. Royal Inst. of Technology, Stock-
holm, and Harvard Univ., Cambridge., Mass., U.S.A.
Radio engineer, ASEA 23-24; Transmission engineer,
Royal Board of Swedish Waterfalls 26-27, Svenska
Radio AB 27-31, and L. M. Ericsson Telephone Co. 31-
33; Head of Design Dept., L.M. Ericsson Telephone Co.
33-37; Asst. Prof. of Telegraphy and Telephony 34-37;
Prof. *pro tem.* 37-39, Ord. Prof. 39-42, and Vice-Principal
42, of Royal Inst. of Technology, Stockholm; Dir.-Gen.
Royal Board of Swedish Telecommunications 42-65;
Pres. Swedish Nat. Comm. Int. Scientific Radio Union
46-69, Board of Trustees, Swedish Nat. Comm. of Int.
Electro-technical Comm. 48-71; mem. Board of Atomic
Energy Co. 47-69, Pripp Breweries Co. 50-69, Scania
Vabis Co. 66-72, IBM Swedish Co. 66-71, Inter-Union
Cttee. on Frequency Allocations for Radio Astronomy
and Space Sciences (I.C.S.U.) 60-72; mem. Royal
Swedish Acad. of Engineering Sciences, Royal Swedish
Acad. of Sciences, Royal Swedish Academy of Military
Sciences, Science Soc. of Uppsala and Danish Acad. of
Technical Sciences; Polheim Gold Medal and Hon. mem.
Swedish Asscn. of Engineers and Architects; I.V.A.
Gold Medal 69.
Leisure interests: skiing, handicraft.
Publs. *The Use of Thermionic Valves for Generating
Multiple Frequencies* 30, *Methods of Computing and
Improving the Complex Effective Attenuation, Load
Impedances and Reflexion Coefficients of Electric Wave
Filters* 33, *Frequency Multiplication and Division* 37,
Puissance et affaiblissement dans les circuits électriques
40, *Fernwirkbetrieb in Stromversorgungsnetzen* 41,
*Uebertragungsverhältnisse auf bespülten und wahlrufs
betriebenen Fernsprechleitungen* 43, *Telecommunications*

in Sweden, present and future 50, *Past, Present and
Future Telecommunication Standardization* 54, *The
First Century of Swedish Telecommunications and what
we can learn from it* 56, *The Foundation of Agriculture
and Industry in Modern Sweden* 57, *Trends of Develop-
ment in the Swedish Telecommunication Services* 60,
Swedish Telecommunications 65, *A Tele-Vision: Com-
munity Planning and Telecommunications* 72.
Sibyllegatan 43-45, 11442 Stockholm, Sweden.
Telephone: 08-600606.

Stern, Curt, PH.D.; American professor of zoology and
genetics; b. 30 Aug. 1902, Hamburg, Germany; s. of
Barned Stern and Anna (Liebrecht) Stern; m. Evelyn
Sommerfield 1931; three d.; ed. Univ. of Berlin.
Investigator, Kaiser Wilhelm Inst. 23-33; Fellow, Int.
Educ. Board 24-26; Privatdozent, Univ. of Berlin 28-33;
Research Assoc. in Zoology, Univ. of Rochester, U.S.
33-35, Asst. Prof. 35-37, Assoc. Prof. 37-41, Prof. and
Chair. Dept. of Zoology and Chair. Div. of Biological
Sciences 41-47; Prof. of Zoology, Univ. of Calif. at
Berkeley 47-58, Prof. of Zoology and Genetics 58-,
Emer. Prof. 70-; Prather Lecturer, Harvard Univ. 65;
mem. Nat. Acad. of Sciences; Hon. Sc.D. (McGill Univ.)
58, Hon. Dr.Rer.Nat. (Munich Univ.) 72; Kimber
Genetics Award 63, Mendel Silver Medal of Czechoslo-
vak Acad. of Science 65, Fred Lyman Adair Award of
American Gynaecological Soc. 67.
Leisure interest: reading.
Publs. *Multiple Allelie* 30, *Faktorenkoppelung und
Faktorenaustausch* 33, *Principles of Human Genetics* 49,
60, 73, *Origin of Genetics* (Editor with E. Sherwood) 66,
Genetic Mosaics and Other Essays 68; about 200 papers
in scientific journals.
Department of Zoology, University of California,
Berkeley, Calif. 94720, U.S.A.
Telephone: 642-2919 (Office); 525-5313 (Home).

Stern, Isaac; American violinist; b. 21 July 1920,
Russia; s. of Solomon and Clara Stern; m. Vera Linden-
blit 1951; two s. one d.; studied San Francisco, notably
with Naoum Blinder.
Debut, San Francisco Symphony 35; New York debut
37; world tours every year 47-; appearances with major
orchestras; extensive recordings; frequent appearances
major festivals—Edinburgh, Casals, Berkshire, etc.;
Pres. Carnegie Hall; Chair. Board of Dirs., American
Israel Cultural Foundation; fmr. mem. Nat. Arts Council;
founded Jerusalem Music Centre 73; awarded first
Albert Schweitzer Music Award 75.
1370 Avenue of the Americas, New York, N.Y. 10022,
U.S.A.

Stern, Leo, DR. RER. POL.; German (b. Austrian) his-
torian and university professor; b. 27 March 1901,
Woloka, Austria; m. Alice Stern 1945; one s. one d.; ed.
Vienna Univ.
Emigrated from Austria to Czechoslovakia and U.S.S.R.
34; fought in Spanish Civil War; Prof. of History,
Moscow 40; Officer in Red Army 41-45; Guest Prof.,
Univ. of Vienna 45; Prof. of Modern History, Martin
Luther-Universität, Halle-Wittenberg 50, Rector 53-59;
fmr. Vice-Pres. German Acad. of Sciences, Dir. Histori-
cal Research Dept. 68-; Nat. Prize; several hon.
degrees.
Leisure interest: scientific history of the 19th and 20th
centuries.
Publs. include: *Archivalische Forschungen zur Geschichte
der deutschen Arbeiterbewegung* (24 vols.); *Philipp
Melanchthon—Humanist, Reformator, Praeceptor Germaniae; Oktoberrevolution und Wissenschaft; 450 Jahre
Reformation; Geschichte der Akademie der Wissenschaften
der DDR von 1900-1945.*
1199 Berlin-Adlershof, Rudower Chaussee 5, German
Democratic Republic.
Telephone: 67-0-28-41/2514.

Sternberger, Dolf, DR. PHIL.; German writer and professor of political science; b. 28 July 1907, Wiesbaden; s. of Georg Sternberger and Luise Schauss; m. Ilse Rothschild 1931.

Professor of Political Science, Heidelberg Univ.; Dir. Inst. für Politische Wissenschaft; fmr. Chair. German Asscn. of Political Science; Pres. German PEN Club; Vice-Pres. German Acad. of Language and Literature; mem. German UNESCO Comm.

Publs. *Der verstandene Tod, eine Untersuchung zu Martin Heideggers Existential-Ontologie* 34, *Panorama oder Ansichten vom 19. Jahrhundert* 38, 55, *13 Politische Radioreden* 47, *Figuren der Fabel* 50, *Aus dem Wörterbuch des Unmenschen* 55, 68, *Lebende Verfassung, Studien über Koalition und Opposition* 56, *Über den Jugendstil und andere Essays* 56, *Indische Miniaturen* 57, *Begriff des Politischen* 61, *Grund und Abgrund der Macht* 62, *Ekel an der Freiheit* 64, *Die Grosse Wahlreform* 64, *Kriterien Ein Lesebuch* 65, *Ich wünschte ein Bürger zu sein* 67.

6 Frankfurt/M., Grüneburgweg 153, Federal Republic of Germany.

Telephone: 72 64 40.

Sternfeld, Reuben; American financial official; b. 5 May 1924, New York; ed. Univs. of Maryland and Michigan.

Held various positions with Bureau of the Budget 49-60; Special Asst. to Under-Sec. of State and Exec. Sec. President's Task Force on Foreign Econ. Assistance 60-61; Officer, Bureau of Latin-American Affairs, Agency for Int. Devt. 61-65; Assoc. U.S. Co-ordinator, Alliance for Progress 65; Alt. Exec. Dir. IDB 66-73; Asst. Dir. Council on Econ. Policy, Office of Pres. of U.S.A. 73-74; Exec. Vice-Pres. IDB 75-.

Inter-American Development Bank, 808 17th Street, N.W., Washington, D.C. 20577, U.S.A.

Stevenius-Nielsen, Hans Henrik, M.SC.; Danish company director; b. 1902, Soroe; s. of Daniel Nielsen and Eva Petersen; m. Grete Rasmussen 1927 (deceased); no c.; ed. Univ. of Copenhagen and Royal Danish Technical Coll.

Chemical Asst. Danish Sulphuric Acid and Superphosphate Works Ltd. 25-26; Asst. Royal Veterinary and Agricultural Coll. 26-27; Chief of Research Laboratory, Danish Sulphuric Acid and Superphosphate Works Ltd. 27-33, Asst. to Technical Dir. 33-40, Technical Dir. 40-45, Man. Dir. 45-64, Dir. 64-73; mem. Board Dirs. Hellesens Ltd. 52-73, The Great Northern Telegraph Co. Ltd. 54-73 (Chair. 60-73), Kastrup Glass Works Ltd. 61-73, The Cryolite Co. Oeresund Ltd. 63-73; mem. Advisory Cttee. Royal Greenland Trade Dept. 50-65, Chair. 63-65; mem. Atomic Energy Comm. 55-71, Brewery Advisory Cttee. of the Carlsberg Foundation 53-73; Pres. Asscn. of Chemical Industries in Denmark 45-52; Pres. Fed. of Danish Industries 52-56; Pres. Int. Superphosphate Manufacturers' Asscn. 59-62; mem. Acad. of Technical Sciences 41-, Vice-Pres. 43-48; mem. Royal Physiographical Society, Sweden 45-, Royal Swedish Acad. of Engineering Sciences 53-; Hon. Foreign mem. Society of Chemical Industry (U.K.) 56-, The Fertiliser Soc. (U.K.) 58-; mem. High Court (*Rigsretten*) 54-72; Commdr. 1st Class Order of Dannebrog (Denmark), Commdr. de la Légion d'Honneur (France), Commdr. Order of Vasa (Sweden), Commdr. Order of Ouissam Alaouite (Morocco), Commdr. Order of Belgian Crown; Commdr. 1st class Norwegian Order of St. Olav. Leisure interest: chamber music (active 'cellist).

Palaegade 4, 1261 Copenhagen K, Denmark.

Telephone: (01) 032235.

Stevens, John Paul, J.D.; American judge; b. 20 April 1920, Chicago, Ill.; m. Elizabeth Jane Sheeren; four c.; ed. Univ. of Chicago, Northwestern Univ. School of Law.

Served U.S. Navy (Bronze Star Medal) 42-45; Co-Ed. of Law Review at Northwestern Univ. School of Law -47; Law Clerk to Supreme Court Justice Wiley Rutledge 47; worked with Poppenhusen, Johnston, Thompson and Raymond law practice 48-51, 52; Partner, Rothschild, Stevens, Barry and Myers 52-70; Circuit Judge, Seventh Circuit Court of Appeals 70-75; Judge, U.S. Supreme Court Dec. 75-; Assoc. Counsel, Monopoly Power Sub-Cttee. of House of Reps. Judiciary Cttee. 51; mem. Attorney Gen.'s Nat. Cttee. on Antitrust Laws 53-55; part-time teacher, North-western Univ. School of Law, later Univ. of Chicago Law School 42-56; admitted to Ill. Bar 49, to U.S. Supreme Court 54.

Publs. numerous articles on commercial monopoly affairs.

United States Supreme Court, Washington, D.C. 20543, U.S.A.

Stevens, Robert T., B.A.; American executive; b. 31 July 1899, Fanwood, N.J.; s. of John P. and Edna Ten Broeck Stevens; m. Dorothy Goodwin Whitney 1923; four s. one d. (deceased); ed. Philipps Acad., Andover, Mass. and Yale Univ.

Entered employment of J. P. Stevens & Co. Inc. 21; Admin. Rep. in industry section of Nat. Recovery Admin. 33; Head of Textile Section, Nat. Defence Advisory Comm. 40; District Co-ordinator of defence contract service, Office of Production Management N.Y. area 41; Class B. Dir. Fed. Reserve Bank of N.Y. 34-42, Class C. Dir. and Chair. 48-53; Chair. Business Advisory Council of U.S. Dept. of Commerce 51-52; Secretary of the Army Feb. 53-55; served in both World Wars, Col. 42, serving in Procurement Div., Office of Quartermaster-Gen., Washington, D.C. 42-45, temporary duty, European Theatre 45; Chair. Board J. P. Stevens & Co. Inc. 45-53, 62-64, Pres. 55-69, Chief Exec. Officer 62-69, Chair. Exec. Cttee. 69-74; Dir. Emer. Gen. Electric Co.; mem. Dir. Advisory Council, Morgan Guaranty Trust Co. of New York; Trustee, Mutual Life Insurance Co. of New York; D.S.M.; Legion of Merit; numerous hon. degrees.

Stevens Building, 1460 Broadway, New York, N.Y. 10036, U.S.A.; Home: 1 Woodland Avenue, South Plainfield, N.J. 07080, U.S.A.

Stevens, Sir Roger Bentham, G.C.M.G.; British diplomatist; b. 8 June 1906, Lewes; s. of F. Bentham Stevens and Cordelia Wheeler; m. Constance Hipwell 1931; one s.; ed. Wellington Coll. and Queen's Coll., Oxford.

Entered Consular Service 28; served Buenos Aires, New York, Antwerp; Ministry of Information 39-42; Consul in Denver, U.S.A. 42-44; Sec. British Civil Secretariat, Washington 44-46; Foreign Office 46-51; Ambassador to Sweden 51-54, to Iran 54-58; Dep. Under-Sec. Foreign Office 58-63; Vice-Chancellor, Leeds Univ. 63-70; Chair. Yorks. and Humberside Economic Planning Council 65-70; mem. Panel of Enquiry into Greater London Devt. Plan 70-72; mem. UN Admin. Tribunal 72-; Chair. Cttee. on Minerals Planning Control 72-74; Dir. British Bank of the Middle East 64-.

Publ. *The Land of the Great Sophy* 62 (revised edn. 72).

Hill Farm, Thursley, Surrey, England.

Telephone: Elstead 2115.

Stevens, Siaka Probyn; Sierra Leonean politician; b. 24 Aug. 1905, Moyamba; m. Rebecca Stevens 1940; seven s. two d.; ed. Albert Acad., Freetown, and Ruskin Coll., Oxford (47-48).

Sierra Leone Police Force, rising to rank of First Class Sergeant and Musketry Instructor 23-30; railway worker, rising to Station Master, later mine worker with Sierra Leone Devt. Co. (DELCO) 30-43; Sec. Marampa Mineworkers Union 43, later Gen. Sec. United Mineworkers Union; mem. Protectorate Assembly, Bo 45; at Ruskin Coll., Oxford 47-48; mem. Legis. Council 51-57, Minister of Lands, Mines and Labour 51; Founder

mem. Sierra Leone Org. Soc., later Sierra Leone People's Party; Deputy Leader People's Nat. Party 58-60; Leader All People's Congress 60-; political imprisonment 61; Mayor of Freetown 64-65; Prime Minister March 67; in exile 67-68; Prime Minister 68-71; President 71-; D.C.L. h.c. (Univ. of Sierra Leone) 69; Chancellor Univ. of Sierra Leone 73-; Grand Commdr. Order of the Republic 73.
Leisure interest: walking.
Office of the President, State House, Freetown, Sierra Leone.

Stevens, Ted, LL.B.; American lawyer and politician; b. 18 Nov. 1923, Indianapolis, Ind.; s. of George A. Stevens; m. Ann Cherrington 1952; three s. two d.; ed. High School, Redondo Beach, Calif., Univ. of Calif. at Los Angeles, and Harvard Law School.
United States Attorney, Fairbanks, Alaska 53-56; Legis. Counsel, Dept. of Interior, Washington, D.C. 56-58; Asst. to Sec. of Interior 58-60; Solicitor of Interior Dept. 60; private law practice, Anchorage, Alaska 61-68; Senator from Alaska 68-; U.S. Senate del. to Int. Law of the Sea Conf., to Canadian-U.S. Inter-parliamentary Conf.; Republican.
Office: 411 Russell Senate Office Building, Washington, D.C., U.S.A.
Telephone: 202-224-3004.

Stevens, Wayne Mackenzie, B.S., M.B.A., PH.D., C.P.A.; American economist, business consultant and executive; ed. Univ. of Ill., Northwestern and American Univs.
Sales Man., chain store supervisor, govt. marketing specialist; Prof. Marketing and Financial Management, La. State Univ. till 37; Dean, Coll. of Business Admin. Univ. of Md. 37-42; Partner, Mackenzie Stevens & Co., Int. Business Consultants 38-; Pres. Int. Div. Assoc. Manufacturers, Inc. 46-49; adviser and consultant to Govt. and commercial organizations in U.S. and abroad 34-; Economic Commr., Korea, and ECA Dir. Trade and Finance Div. 49-50; mem. State Dept. Far-Eastern Conf., Tokyo, and Dir. Trade Mission in fifteen countries of Asia, Australia and Far East 50; Dir. School of World Business and Consultant on Int. Devt., San Francisco State Coll. (now Univ.) 50-; Chair. World Investment and Trade Corpn. 53-65, 68-; mem. U.S. Sec. of Commerce Regional Export Expansion Council 62-65, Int. Economist and Project Evaluator, Nat. Planning Office, Govt. of Nicaragua Nat. Econ. Council 65-67; Emeritus Prof. of Business and Project Dir., Devt. of Improved Employment and Utilization of Older Persons, Calif. State Univ. at San Francisco 68-.
Publs. *Financial Organization and Administration* 34, *Practical Accounting* 35, *Effective Structural Organization for Cooperatives* 36, *Warehousing and Storage of Agricultural Products* 37, *Cooperative Sugar Association, A Basis for Democratizing Tropical Agriculture* 38, *Production and Marketing of Industrial Goods Co-operatively* 42, *Management Analysis Applied to Industrial Cooperation* 43, *Effective Utilization of Private Capital in Foreign Economic Development* 44, *Training of Chinese Technicians in American Methods* 45, *The So-Called Dollar Shortage* 47, *Trade, Not Aid* 48, *Currency Exchange and Pricing Policies* 50, *Public Finance* (co-author) 59, *How to Utilize Older Persons More Effectively* 73.
3 Skyline Drive, Daly City, Calif. 94015, U.S.A.
Telephone: 415-755-0600; and 415-755-2100.

Stevenson, Adlai E., III; American senator; b. 10 Oct. 1930, Chicago, Ill.; s. of late Adlai Stevenson II (fmr. Gov. of Illinois, presidential candidate and Amb. to UN); great-grandson of Adlai E. Stevenson (Vice-Pres. of U.S.A. 1893-97); m. Nancy Anderson 1955; two s. two d.; ed. Milton Acad., Mass., and Harvard Univ.
Law clerk to a justice of Illinois Supreme Court 57; joined Chicago law firm of Mayer, Friedlich, Spiess, Tierney, Brown and Platt 58, subsequently partner

until 70; elected to Ill. House of Reps. 64; State Treas. of Ill. 66-70; Senator from Illinois Nov. 70-; Democrat.
New Senate Office Building, Washington, D.C. 20510, U.S.A.

Stever, Horton Guyford, PH.D.; American government official; b. 24 Oct. 1916, Corning, N.Y.; s. of Ralph Raymond Stever and Alma Matt; m. Louise Risley 1946; two s. two d.; ed. Colgate Univ. and Calif. Inst. of Technology.
Member of Staff Radiation Lab. and Instructor, Officers' Radar School, Mass. Inst. of Technology (M.I.T.) 41-42; Science Liaison Officer, London Mission, Office of Scientific Research and Devt. 42-45; Asst. Prof. of Aeronautical Eng. M.I.T. 46-51, Assoc. Prof. 51-56, Prof. 56-65; Chief Scientist, U.S.A.F. 55-56; Assoc. Dean of Eng. M.I.T. 56-59, Head Depts. of Mechanical Eng. Naval Architecture and Marine Eng. 61-65; Pres. Carnegie-Mellon Univ. 65-72; Chair. U.S.A.F. Scientific Advisory Board 62-69; mem. exec. cttee. Defense Science Board, Dept. of Defense 62-69; mem. Panel on Science and Technology, U.S. House of Reps. Comm. on Science and Technology 59-72; Trustee, Colgate Univ. 62-72, Sarah Mellon Scaife Foundation 65-72, Shady Side Acad. 67-72; Dir. Fisher Scientific Co. 65-72, Koppers Co. 65-72, System Devt. Corpn. 65-70, United Aircraft Corpn. 66-72; Chair. Aeronautics and Space Eng. Board Nat. Acad. of Eng. 67-69; mem. Nat. Science Board 70-72; Dir. Nat. Science Foundation 72-; Science Adviser and Chair. Fed. Council for Science and Technology, Exec. Cttee. Nat. Science Board, Energy R & D Advisory Council; U.S. Chair. U.S.-U.S.S.R. Joint Comm. on Scientific and Technical Co-operation; mem. U.S.-Japan Cttee. on Scientific Co-operation, Fed. Council on the Arts and Humanities, Nat. Council on Educational Research, and many other Govt. bodies; President's Certificate of Merit 48, Exceptional Civilian Service Award, U.S.A.F. 56, Scott Gold Medal of American Ordnance Asscn. 60, Alumni Distinguished Service Award Calif. Inst. of Technology 66, Distinguished Public Service Medal, Dept. of Defense 69; thirteen hon. degrees.
Leisure interests: skiing, fishing, golf, hiking.
Publ. *Flight* (with J. J. Haggerty) 65.
National Science Foundation, Washington, D.C. 20550, U.S.A.
Telephone: 202-632-4001.

Stewart, Andrew, B.S.A., M.A.; Scottish-born Canadian educator and radio administrator; b. 17 Jan. 1904; ed. Daniel Stewart's Coll., East of Scotland Agricultural Coll., Edinburgh and Manitoba Univ.
Lecturer in Agricultural Economics, Manitoba Univ. 32-33; Lecturer in Political Economy, Alberta Univ. 35, Prof. of Political Economy 46, Dean of Business Affairs 49, Pres. 50-59; Chair. Board of Broadcast Govs. 58-68; Chair. Alberta Univs. Comm. 68-70; Educational Adviser, Univ. of Ibadan, Nigeria 70-72; retd. 73; mem. Royal Comm. on Natural Gas (Province of Alberta) 48, on Econ. Prospects (Canada) 55-57; Chair. Royal Comm. (Canada) on Price Spreads of Food Products 58-59; Fellow, Royal Soc. of Canada, Agricultural Inst. of Canada; Hon. LL.D. (Manitoba, New Brunswick, Melbourne and Alberta Univs.), Hon. D.Econ. (Laval Univ.).
10435 Allbay Road, Sidney, B.C., Canada.
Telephone: 656-2953.

Stewart, D. S., O.B.E.; Australian mechanical and electrical engineer; b. 18 Dec. 1919, Brisbane; ed. Queensland Univ.
Fomer Man. Britannia Production and Devt., Bristol Aircraft Co.; Dir., Gen. Man. Hestair Group; Dir. of Eng., Clyde Eng. Pty. Ltd., Chief Exec., Hadfields-Goodwin-Scotts Group; Man. Dir. Hamersley Holdings Ltd. and Hamersley Iron Pty. Ltd. March 73-; Fellow,

Inst. of Engs., Australia; Assoc. Fellow, Royal Aeronautical Soc.

Hamersley Iron Pty. Ltd., 95 Collins Street, Melbourne, 3000 Australia.

Stewart, Sir Dugald Leslie Lorn, K.C.V.O., C.M.G.; British diplomatist; b. 10 Sept. 1921, London; s. of Allan W. and Marjorie Stewart; m. Sibyl Anna Sturrock, M.B.E.; three s. one d.; ed. Eton and Magdalen Coll., Oxford.

Entered the diplomatic service 42; served in Belgrade 45-48, Berlin 48-50, Amara, Iraq 50-51, Cairo 51-53, Foreign Office 53-56, Belgrade 56-59, Foreign Office 59-62, Moscow 62-64; Imperial Defence Coll. 65; Inspector, Diplomatic Service 66-69; Counsellor, Cairo 69-71; Amb. to Yugoslavia 71-.

Leisure interests: shooting, fishing, golf.

British Embassy, Belgrade, Yugoslavia; Home: Braevallich, by Dalmally, Argyll, Scotland.

Telephone: Ford 243.

Stewart, Francis Eugene; Australian politician; b. 20 Feb. 1923; s. of late P. F. Stewart and Mrs. M. M. Stewart; m. Maureen N. Smith 1952; one s. five d.; ed. Christian Brothers' Coll., St. Mary's Cathedral, Sydney.

Clerk, Transport Dept., N.S.W. Govt. 39; Army Service 41-46; Transport Dept. 46-53; mem. House of Reps. for Lang 53-; mem. Fed. Parl. Labor Party Exec. 69-; Minister of Tourism and Recreation Dec. 72-Nov. 75, concurrently Minister Assisting the Treasurer 73-75; Vice-Pres. of Exec. Council 73-75; Labor Party.

Leisure interests: tennis, bowls.

2A Wilson Avenue, Belmore, N.S.W.; and Shop 2, The Boulevarde, Lakemba, N.S.W., Australia.

Stewart, Frederick Henry, K.B., B.SC., PH.D., D.SC., F.R.S., F.R.S.E.; British geologist; b. 16 Jan. 1916, Aberdeen; s. of Frederick R. Stewart and Hester Alexander; m. Mary Florence Elinor Rainbow 1945; ed. Fettes Coll., Edinburgh, Univ. of Aberdeen, Emmanuel Coll., Cambridge.

Mineralogist in Research Dept., ICI Ltd. 41-43; Lecturer in Geology, Durham Univ. 43-56; Regius Prof. of Geology, Edinburgh Univ. 56-; Chair. Natural Environment Research Council 71-73, Advisory Board for the Research Councils 73-; Lyell Fund Award, J. B. Tyrrell Fund, Lyell Medal, Geological Soc. of London; Mineralogical Soc. of America Award; Clough Medal, Geological Soc. of Edinburgh.

Leisure interest: fishing.

Publs. papers in *Mineralogical Magazine, Journal of Geological Society of London* and other journals dealing with igneous and metamorphic petrology and salt deposits.

Grant Institute of Geology, University of Edinburgh, West Mains Road, Edinburgh, EH9 3HJ; Home: 79 Morningside Park, Edinburgh, EH10 5EZ, Scotland.

Stewart, Sir Herbert Ray, Kt., C.I.E., M.SC., F.R.C.SC.I., D.I.C., N.D.A.; British international agricultural consultant; b.10 July 1890, Cambridge, Mass., U.S.A.; s. of Hugh Stewart and Rebecca Stewart (née Rea); m. 1st Evangeline Rea 1917 (died 1955); 2nd Elsie Pyne 1957; one d.; ed. Royal Coll. of Science for Ireland and Imperial Coll. of Science and Technology, London.

Served in France First World War 15-18; apptd. to Indian Agricultural Service 20; Prof. of Agriculture Punjab 21-27; Asst. Dir. of Agriculture Punjab 27-32, Dir. of Agriculture 32-43; Fellow Univ. of Punjab 27-43; Dean of Faculty of Agriculture 32-43; Agricultural Commr. with Govt. of India 43-46; Vice-Chair. Imperial Council of Agricultural Research India, Pres. Board of Agriculture and Animal Husbandry India; Chair. All-India Central Cttees. for Cotton, Jute, Lac, Sugar-cane, Tobacco, Coconuts and Pres. Indian Coffee Board 44-46; Agricultural Adviser British Middle East Office

Cairo 46-51; Agricultural Adviser, UN Economic Survey Mission for the Middle East 49, UN Relief and Works Agency for Palestine Refugees 50-51; Chief, Agricultural Mission of Int. Bank for Reconstruction and Development to Colombia 55-56, Agricultural Consultant Economic Missions of Int. Bank to Pakistan 56 and 58, Italy 57, Yugoslavia 60, Uganda 60-61, Kenya 61-62.

Leisure interest: gardening.

29 Alyth Road, Bournemouth, BH3 7DG, Dorset, England.

Telephone: 0202-764782.

Stewart, Sir Iain Maxwell, Kt., B.SC.; British company director; b. 16 June 1916, Glasgow; s. of W. Maxwell Stewart; m. Margaret Jean Walker 1941 (dissolved 1967); two s. two d.; ed. Loretto School and Glasgow Univ.

Director, Thermotank 41-46, Man. Dir. 46-50, Chair. 50-64; Chair. Hall-Thermotank 59-60 and 64-; Dir. BEA, Beaverbrook Newspapers, Eagle Star Insurance Co., Royal Bank of Scotland, Lyle Shipping Co., Dorchester Hotel, Dunbar & Co., Industrial Communications Ltd.; Chair. Higher Productivity (Organization and Bargaining) Ltd.; Capt. Royal and Ancient Golf Club of St. Andrew's 72-73.

Leisure interest: golf.

Lochbrae House, Bearsden, Dunbartonshire, Scotland.

Telephone: 041-445-2444.

Stewart, James, D.F.C., B.S.; American actor; b. 20 May 1908; ed. Mercersburg Acad. and Princeton Univ.

Films since 35 include *You Can't Take It With You, Made for Each Other, Mr. Smith Goes to Washington, Destry Rides Again, Philadelphia Story, Pot O' Gold, The Stratton Story, Winchester 73, Broken Arrow, Harvey, No Highway, Rear Window, The Greatest Show on Earth, Rope, Naked Spur, The Glenn Miller Story, The Man from Laramie, Strategic Air Command, Spirit of St. Louis, Anatomy of a Murder, The FBI Story, Two Rode Together, Cheyenne Autumn, Shenandoah, The Rare Breed, The Cheyenne Social Club, Fool's Parade, Dynamite Man from Glory Jail,* etc.; American Motion Picture Acad. Award for *Philadelphia Story* 40, New York Critics' Award for *Mr. Smith Goes to Washington* 39, Volpi Cup, Venice 59, for performance in *Anatomy of a Murder.*

Stage performances: *Harvey,* New York 47, London 75.

P.O. Box 550, Beverly Hills, Calif. 93301, U.S.A.

Stewart, John Young (Jackie), O.B.E.; Scottish racing driver (retd.); b. 11 June 1939, Milton, Scotland; s. of the late Robert Paul Stewart and of Jean Clark Young; m. Helen McGregor 1962; two s.; ed. Dumbarton Acad.

First raced 61; competed in 4 meetings driving for Barry Filer, Glasgow 61-62; drove for Ecurie Ecosse and Barry Filer, winning 14 out of 23 starts 63, 28 wins out of 53 starts 64; drove formula 1 for British Racing Motors (BRM) 65-67, for Ken Tyrell 68-73; has won Australian, New Zealand, Swedish, Mediterranean, Japanese and many other non-championship major int. motor races; set new world record by winning his 26th World Championship Grand Prix (Zandvoort) 73, 27th (Nürburgring) 73; Third in World Championship 65, 2nd in 68 and 72, World Champion 69, 71, 73; British Automobile Racing Club Gold Medal 71, *Daily Express* Sportsman of the Year 71, 73, BBC Sports Personality of the Year 73, Scottish Sportsman of the Year 73, U.S. Sportsman of the Year 73, Segrave Trophy 73; film: *Weekend of a Champion* 72.

Leisure interests: shooting, golf, tennis.

Publ. *Faster!* (with Peter Manse) 72.

Clayton House, 1268 Begnins, Vaud, Switzerland.

Telephone: Geneva (022) 61.01.52.

Stewart, Rt. Hon. Michael (*see* Stewart, R. M. M.).

Stewart, Sir Michael (Norman Francis), K.C.M.G., O.B.E.; British diplomatist; b. 18 Jan. 1911; s. of Sir Francis and Lady Stewart; m. Katherine Damaris Houssemayne du Boulay 1951; one s. two d.; ed. Shrewsbury and Trinity Coll., Cambridge.
Assistant Keeper, Victoria and Albert Museum 35-39; Ministry of Information 39-41; Press Attaché, British Embassy, Lisbon 41-44, Rome 44-48; Foreign Office 48-51; Counsellor, Office of Commr.-Gen. for U.K. in S.E. Asia 51-54; Counsellor, Ankara 54-59; Chargé d'Affaires, Peking 59-62; Senior Civilian Instructor, Imperial Defence Coll. 62-64; Minister, Washington 64-67; Amb. to Greece 67-71; Dir. of Ditchley Foundation 71-.
c/o Brooks's Club, St. James's Street, London, S.W.1; The Ditchley Foundation, Ditchley Park, Enstone, Oxford, England.

Stewart, Potter, B.A., LL.B.; American judge; b. 23 Jan. 1915, Jackson, Mich.; s. of James Garfield Stewart and Harriet Loomis Potter; m. Mary Ann Bertles 1943; two s. one d.; ed. Hotchkiss School, Cambridge (England) and Yale Univ.
Admitted to Ohio Bar 41, New York Bar 42; Assoc. Debevoise, Stevenson, Plimpton and Page (New York) 41-42, 45-47; Assoc., Dinsmore, Shohl, Sawyer and Dinsmore (Cincinnati) 47, Partner 51-54; service in U.S. Naval Reserve 41-45; mem. Cincinnati City Council 50-53, Vice-Mayor 52-53; Judge, U.S. Court of Appeals (Sixth Circuit) 54-58; Assoc. Justice, U.S. Supreme Court 58-; mem. Court Admin. Cttee., Judicial Conf. of the U.S. 55-58; mem. American, Ohio, Cincinnati, City of New York Bar Asscns., American Law Inst., American Judicature Soc., etc.
Supreme Court of the United States, Washington, D.C. 20543; Home: 5136 Palisade Lane, N.W., Washington, D.C. 20016, U.S.A.
Telephone: 202-393-1640.

Stewart, Rt. Hon. (Robert) Michael Maitland, P.C., C.H., M.P.; British politician and author; b. 6 Nov. 1906, Bromley, Kent; s. of Robert and Eva Stewart; m. Elizabeth Birkenshaw (Baroness Stewart of Alvechurch) 1941; ed. Brownhill Road LCC School, Christ's Hospital and St. John's Coll., Oxford.
Member of Parl. 45-, Govt. Whip 45-47, Under-Sec. of State for War 47-51, Parl. Sec. Ministry of Supply 51; Sec. of State for Education and Science 64-65, for Foreign Affairs 65-66; First Sec. of State 66-68; Sec. of State for Econ. Affairs 66-67, for Foreign and Commonwealth Affairs 68-70; Leader, British Labour Del. to European Parl. 75-; Labour.
Leisure interests: chess, painting.
Publs. *The Forty Hour Week* 36, *Bias and Education for Democracy* 37, *The British Approach to Politics* 38, *Modern Forms of Government* 59.
House of Commons, London, S.W.1, England.
Telephone: 01-219-4429.

Stewart, Stanley Toft, C.M.G.; Singapore official; b. 13 June 1910, Penang; m. Therese Zelie de Souza 1935; seven d.; ed. St. Xavier's Inst. and Raffles Coll., Singapore.
Teacher, Malay Coll., Kuala Kangsar, Perak 33-34; joined Straits Settlements Civil Service 34; Asst. District Office, Butterworth 36-39, Balik Pulau 39-41; Rural Board, Province Wellesley 47, also mem. Penang State Legis. Council; later Chair. Province Wellesley War Exec. Cttee., mem. State War Exec. Cttee.; in Singapore 52-; Deputy Chair. Rural Board, Singapore 52-54, Chair. 54-55; Deputy Sec. Ministry of Local Govt. Lands and Housing 55-57, Deputy Chief Sec. 57-59; Perm. Sec. Ministry of Home Affairs 59-63, Perm. Sec. to Prime Minister 61-66, later also Perm. Sec. to Deputy Prime Minister and Head of Civil Service; Singapore High Commr. in Australia 66-69; Perm. Sec., Ministry of Foreign Affairs, Singapore

69-72; Exec. Sec. Singapore Nat. Stadium 73, Chair., Dir. 74; Singapore State Meritorious Service Medal 62.
Leisure interests: cricket, tennis, walking.
103 Holland Road, Singapore 10.
Telephone: 623232.

Stewart, Thomas; American opera singer; b. San Saba, Tex.; m. Evelyn Lear (q.v.); ed. Baylor Univ., Juilliard School of Music.
Joined Berlin Opera 58; first performance at Bayreuth Festival 60; has performed at Metropolitan Opera, San Francisco Opera, Royal Opera House, Covent Garden; has given many recitals with Evelyn Lear.
Major roles include: Wotan in *Das Rheingold*, Ford in *Falstaff*, Escamillo in *Carmen*, Golaud in *Pelléas et Mélisande*, Amfortas in *Parsifal*, Kurvenal in *Tristan and Isolde*.
c/o Ingpen & Williams Ltd., 14 Kensington Court, London, W.8, England.

Stewart, Thomas Dale, A.B., M.D.; American physical anthropologist; b. 10 June 1901, Delta, Pa.; s. of Thomas Dale and Susan Price Stewart; m. 1st Julia Cable Wright 1932, 2nd Rita Frame Dewey 1952; one d.; ed. George Washington Univ. and Johns Hopkins Medical School.
Aid, Div. of Physical Anthropology, U.S. Nat. Museum 27-31, Asst. Curator 31-39, Assoc. Curator 39-42, Curator 42-61, Head Curator, Dept. of Anthropology 61-62; Dir. Nat. Museum of Natural History 62-65, Snr. Physical Anthropologist, Dept. of Anthropology 66-71, Anthropologist emer. 71-; Hon. D.Sc. (Univ. of Cuzco, Peru) 49; Viking Fund Medal and Award 53.
Leisure interests: gardening, portrait-painting.
Publs. over 190 scientific articles in the fields of anthropometry, paleopathology and forensic anthropology.
National Museum of Natural History, Smithsonian Institution, Washington, D.C. 20560; Home: 1191 Crest Lane, McLean, Va. 22101, U.S.A.
Telephone: 381-5456 (Office); 522-4328 (Home).

Steyn, Lucas Cornelius, B.A., LL.D.; South African judge; b. 21 Dec. 1903; ed. Kroonstad Secondary School and Stellenbosch Univ.
Attorney-General, South West Africa 31; Senior Law Adviser, Union Govt. 44; Judge of Appeal 55; Chief Justice of South Africa 59-71.
Publ. *Uitleg van Wette*.
33 Waverley Road, Bloemfontein, South Africa.

Steyn, S. J. Marais, B.A., LL.B.; South African politician; b. 25 Dec. 1914, Cape Prov.; s. of M. H. Steyn; m. Susan E. Moolman; two s. two d.; ed. Univ. of Cape Town, Univ. of Witwatersrand.
Journalist 38-40; Govt. Information Services 40-42; Political Sec. 42-48; mem. Parl. 48- (United Party to 74); defected from United Party and joined Nat. Party 74; Minister of Tourism and Indian Affairs 75-, of Community Devt. Jan. 76-.
Leisure interests: bowls, sound recordings.
Private Bag X364, Pretoria, 0001, South Africa.
Telephone: Pretoria 37171.

Sticht, J. Paul; American business executive; b. 3 Oct. 1917, Clairton, Pa.; s. of Joseph P. and Adah M. Sticht; m. A. Ferne Cozad 1940; two s.; ed. Grove City Coll. and Univ. of Pittsburgh Graduate School.
Started as shipping clerk, U.S. Steel Co., industrial engineer 41-44; Air Transport Command, TWA airlines div. 44-48; various posts Campbell Soup Co. 48-60; various posts Federated Dept. Stores 60-65, Pres. 67-72; Chair. Exec. Cttee. and Dir. R. J. Reynolds Industries Inc. 72-73, Pres., Chief Operating Officer and Dir. 73-; Dir. Celanese Corpn., S. C. Johnson & Son, Inc., Grocery Manufacturers of America Inc., Foremost-McKesson Inc., The Wachovia Corpn.; mem. The Conference Board Inc.; Founding mem. Rockefeller Univ. Council; Visitor, Bowman Gray School of

Medicine, Grad. School of Business of Univ. of Pittsburgh, Grad. School of Business Admin. of Duke Univ.; Trustee, Grove City Coll., Old Salem Inc.

Leisure interests: golf, boating, fishing.

Office: Reynolds Building, Fourth and Main Streets, Winston-Salem, N.C.; Home: 2705 Bartram Place, Winston-Salem, N.C., U.S.A.

Telephone: 919-748-7100 (Office); 919-748-1100 (Home).

Stieler von Heydekampf, Gerd, DR.ING.; German business executive; b. 5 Jan. 1905, Berlin; s. of Kurt Stieler von Heydekampf and Frieda née Gelau; m. Elizabeth Heuschen 1931; one s. two d.; ed. public schools and Technische Hochschule, Brunswick.

Research engineer in U.S.A. 30-33; joined Adam Opel AG 33, mem. of Board 36; Man. Dir. Henschel & Sohn GmbH, Kassel 42; joined NSU Motorenwerke 48, mem. of Board 50, Chair. of Board 53-69. Chair. of Board AUDI NSU 69-71; mem. Advisory Board AUDI-NSU 72-, Fried. Krupp GmbH 68-74, Frankfurter Versicherung 69-74.

Leisure interests: golf, literature, natural sciences.

Publs. scientific papers (engineering) 27-33.

7100 Heilbronn, Alexanderstrasse 24, Federal Republic of Germany.

Telephone: 73135.

Stigler, George Joseph; American professor of economics; b. 17 Jan. 1911, Renton, Wash., U.S.A.; s. of Joseph Stigler and Elizabeth Hungler; m. Margaret Mack 1936 (deceased); three s.; ed. Univs. of Washington, Chicago and Northwestern Univ.

Assistant Prof. Iowa State Univ. 36-38, Univ. of Minnesota 38-41, Associate Prof. 41-44, Prof. 44-46; Prof. Brown Univ. 46-47; Prof. Columbia Univ. 47-57, Center for Advanced Study in Behavioral Sciences 57-58, Univ. of Chicago 58-; Pres. American Economic Association 64; Vice-Chair. Securities Investor Protection Corpn.; Alumnus Summa Laude Dignatus, Univ. of Washington 69; Hon. Dr. Sc. Carnegie-Mellon Univ. 73, Rochester Univ. 74.

Leisure interests: golf, tennis, photography.

Publs. many books and papers.

University of Chicago, Chicago, Ill. 60637; Home: 2621 Brassie Avenue, Flossmoor, Ill. 60422, U.S.A.

Telephone: 312-753-3606 (Office); 312-799-5823 (Home).

Stikker, Dirk Uipko, DR.JUR.; Netherlands politician and diplomatist; b. 5 Feb. 1897; ed. Univ. of Groningen.

Former Man. Dir. of branches of Twentsche Bank at Leyden and Haarlem; Man. Dir. of Heineken Lagerbeer Brewery Co. Ltd. 35-48; Dir. of S.A. des Bières Bomonti & Pyramides, Cairo; mem. of board of Société Internationale de Brasserie, Brussels; Founder and Chair. Neths. Foundation of Labour; Founder (46) and Pres. of Party of Freedom and Democracy; mem. of Senate; Minister of Foreign Affairs 48-52; Political Conciliator, later Chair., OEEC 50-52; Amb. to Great Britain 52-58; Minister, later Amb., to Iceland 54-58; Head, combined Dutch perm. representation to North Atlantic Council and OEEC with rank of Amb. 58-61, Sec.-Gen. of NATO 61-64; Dir. Royal Dutch Shell Group 64-67; fmr. Dir. some 15 companies; fmr. Chair. Employers' Org.; retd.; Consultant to UNCTAD; Hon. LL.D. (Brown Univ.); Hon. G.C.V.O., Hon. G.B.E.

Publ. *Men of Responsibility* 66; reports and articles for UNCTAD and Asian Devt. Bank on private investment in developing countries.

Villa "Belfaggio", Menaggio-Loveno, Lago di Como, Italy.

Telephone: 32361.

Stinson, George Arthur, A.B., LL.B.; American lawyer and business executive; b. 11 Feb. 1915; ed. Northwestern Univ. and Columbia Univ.

U.S. Air Force 41-45; Special Asst. to Attorney-Gen., Washington, D.C. 47-48; Partner in law firm Cleary, Gottlieb, Friendly and Hamilton, New York, Washing-

ton, D.C., and Paris 48-61; Nat. Steel Corpn., Pittsburgh 61-, Pres. and Dir. 63-, Chief Exec. Officer 66-, Chair. of Board of Dirs. 72-; mem. of Board Hanna Mining Co., Mutual Life Insurance Co. of N.Y.; Legion of Merit.

Office: National Steel Corporation, Grant Building, Pittsburgh, Pa. 15219; Home: 420 Oliver Road, Sewickley, Pa. 15143, U.S.A.

Stirling, Alfred, C.B.E., M.A., LL.B.; Australian diplomatist; b. 8 Sept. 1902; s. of Robert Andrew and Isabel Stirling; ed. Scotch Coll., Melbourne, Univ. of Melbourne, and Univ. Coll., Oxford.

Head, Pol. Div., Australian Dept. of External Affairs 36; External Affairs Officer, London 36-45; Counsellor, Australian Legation to Netherlands 43-45; Australian High Commr. to Canada 45-47; Minister, Australian Embassy, Washington 47-48; Australian High Commr. in S. Africa 48-50; Amb. to the Netherlands 50-55, to France 55-59, to Philippines 59-62, to Italy 62-67 (also to Greece 64-65); Grand Cross of Order of St. Gregory.

Publs. *Victorian* (with John Oldham) 34, *Joseph Bosisto* 70, *The Italian Diplomat* 71, *Gang Forward, A Stirling Note-Book* 72, *On the Fringe of Diplomacy* 73, *Lord Bruce of Melbourne: The London Years* 74, *A Distant View of the Vatican* 75.

30 St. Ives, 166 Toorak Road West, South Yarra, Victoria 3141, Australia.

Telephone: 267-1140.

Stirling, Duncan Alexander; British banker; b. 6 Oct. 1899; s. of Major William Stirling, D.L., J.P. and Charlotte Eva Mackintosh; m. Lady Marjorie Murray 1926; two s.; ed. Harrow and New Coll., Oxford.

Partner with H. S. Lefevre and Co. 29-49; Dir. Westminster Bank (now Nat. Westminster Bank Ltd.) 35-74, Deputy Chair. 48-61, Chair. 62-69; Dir. of Westminster Foreign Bank 35-74, Chair. 62-69; Chair. Cttee. of London Clearing Bankers 66-68; Dir. London Life Asscn. 35-, Pres. 52-66; fmr. Pres. Inst. of Bankers; Dir. Mercantile Investment Trust 37-74, Baring Foundation.

28 St. James's Place, London, S.W.1; Hinton Ampner Place, Alresford, Hants, England.

Stirling, James, DIP.ARCH., A.R.I.B.A.; British architect and town planner; b. 1926, Glasgow; s. of Joseph Stirling and Louisa Frazer; m. Mary Shand 1966; one s. two d.; ed. Liverpool School of Art, Liverpool Univ. School of Architecture.

With Asscn. of Town Planning and Regional Research, London 50-52; Asst. Lyons Israel and Ellis 53-56; mem. Inst. of Contemporary Art Independent Group 52-56; private practice 56-, with James Gowan 56-63, with Michael Wilford 71-; exhbns. New York 69, London 74; Hon. mem. Akad. der Kunst, Berlin 69, American Inst. of Architects 75; Charles Davenport Visiting Prof., Yale Univ. 70; has lectured in Europe, U.S.A. 60-.

Major works: Flats, Ham Common 55-58, Leicester Univ. Engineering Building (U.S.A. Reynolds Award) 59-63, Cambridge Univ. History Faculty 64-67, Andrew Melville Hall, St. Andrews Univ. 64-68, Dorman Long Steel Co. Head Office 65, Runcorn New Town Housing 68-, Florey Building, Queen's Coll., Oxford 67-71, Redevt. Plan of West Mid-Town Manhatten for New York Planning Comm. 68-69, Olivetti Training School 69-72, Olivetti Head Office, U.K. 70-, Arts Centre, St. Andrew's Univ. 71-.

Publs. include *Buildings and Projects 1950-74, R.I.B.A. Drawings Catalogue.*

75 Gloucester Place, London, W1H 3PF, England.

Telephone: 01-486-4257/8.

Stirn, Olivier, L. EN D.; French civil servant; b. 24 Feb. 1936, Boulogne Billancourt; m. Marine Saunier 1961; two s.; ed. Univ. of Paris.

Deputy for Calvados 68-; Councillor General, Mayor of Vire 70-; Sec. of State for Parl. Relations 73, for Overseas Territories 74-.
7 place Furstenberg, Paris 6e, France.

Stockhausen, Karlheinz; German composer; b. 22 Aug. 1928, Moedrath bei Köln; s. of Simon Stockhausen and Gertrud Stupp; m. 1st Doris Andreae 1951, 2nd Mary Bauermeister 1967; two s. four d.; ed. Cologne State Music High School, Univs. of Cologne and Bonn.
Worked with Olivier Messiaen and with the "Musique Concrète" Group in Paris 52-53; with Westdeutscher Rundfunk Electronic Music Studio, Cologne 53-, Artistic Dir. 63-; first composition of purely electronic music (*Studie I* for sinewaves) 53; Co-editor *Die Reihe* (Universal Edn.) 55-58; Dozent for composition and analysis at the Int. Summer School for New Music, Darmstadt 57-; concert tours throughout the world since 58; Founder, composition classes in *Kölner Kurse für Neue Musik* 63-68; founder of ensemble for electronic live music 64; exclusive contract with Deutsche Grammophon for interpretation of own works 68-; Int. World Fair *Expo 70*, Osaka; Prof. for Composition Staatliche Hochschule für Musik, Cologne, 71-.
Compositions: *Frühe Noten* 50, *Kreuzspiel* 51, *Formel* (orchestra) 51, *Schlagtrio* 52, *Spiel* (orchestra) 52, *Punkte* (orchestra) 52 (new version 62), *Klavierstücke I-IV* 52-53, *Kontra-Punkte* 52-53, *Elektronische Studien* 53-54, *Klavierstücke V-X* 54-61, *Zeitmasze* 55-56, *Gruppen* (three orchestras) 55-57, *Klavierstück XI* 56, *Gesang der Jünglinge* (electronic) 55-56, *Zyklus* (percussionist) 59, *Refrain* (three players) 59, *Carré* (four orchestras and chorus) 59-60, *Kontakte* (piano, percussion and electronic sounds) 59-60, *Originale* (musical theatre) 61, *Momente* (soprano, four choral groups and 13 instrumentalists) 62-64, *Plus Minus* 63, *Mikrophonie I* (tam-tam, two microphones, two filters and regulator) 64, *Mixtur* (orchestra, four sine-generators and ring-modulators) 64, *Mikrophonie II* (choir, Hammond organ and ring-modulator) 65, *Stop* (orchestra) 65, *Telemusik* (electronic music) 66, *Solo* (melodic instrument and feed-back) 66, *Adieu* (wind quintet) 66, *Hymnen* (electronic and concrete music with soloists) 66-67, *Prozession* (tam-tam, viola, electronium, piano, two filters and regulator) 67, *Ensemble* (Prozessplanung) 67, *Kurzwellen* (six players) 68, *Stimmung* (six vocalists) 68, *Aus den sieben Tagen* 68, *Musik für ein Haus* (Prozessplannung) 68, *Spiral* (soloist) 68, *Fresco* (four orchestral groups) 69, *Dritte Region* (hymns with orchestra) 69, *Pole* (two pianists) 70, *Expo* (three pianists) 70, *Mantra* (two pianists) 70, *Sternklang*, *Trans* (orchestra) 71, *Für Kommende Zeiten* (17 texts of intuitive music) 68-70, *Alphabet* 72, "*Am Himmel wandre ich*" (12 Indian songs) 72, *Ylem* (19 or more players) 72, *Atmen gibt das Leben* 74, *Inori* (Adorations for mime and orchestra) 73-74, *Herbstmusik* 74, *Musik im Bauch* (percussion and musical boxes) 75, *Tierkreis* (12 melodies of the star-signs) 75, *Harlekin* (clarinette) 75, *Sirius* (electronic music and trumpet, bass-clarinet, soprano and bass) 75.
Publs. *Texte* (3 vols.) 63-64, 71.
Studio für Elektronische Musik, Westdeutscher Rundfunk, Wallrafplaz 5, Cologne; 5073 Kürten, Federal Republic of Germany.
Telephone: 02283-6639.

Stockwood, Rt. Rev. (Arthur) Mervyn, M.A.; British ecclesiastic; b. 27 May 1913; s. of late Arthur and Beatrice Ethel Stockwood; ed. Kelly Coll., Christ's Coll. and Westcott House, Cambridge.
Ordained 36; Curate, St. Matthew Moorfields, Bristol, and Blundell's School Missioner 36-41, Vicar 41-45; Hon. Canon, Bristol 53-55; Vicar, St. Mary the Great, Cambridge 55-59; Bishop of Southwark 59-; Church Comm. 72-; D.D. (Lambeth), D.Litt. (Sussex); Labour

mem. Bristol City Council 46-55, Cambridge City Council 56-59.
Leisure interests: fishing, walking.
Publs. *There is a Tide* 46, *Whom they Pierced* 48, *I Went to Moscow* 55, *The Faith Today* 59, *Cambridge Sermons* 59, *Bishop's Journal* 65.
Bishop's House, 38 Tooting Bec Gardens, London, S.W. 16, England.

Stoecker, Dietrich, DR.JUR.; German lawyer and diplomatist; b. 11 Nov. 1915, Cologne; s. of Otto Stoecker and Ina Rottenburg; m. Ingrid Bergemann 1942; four s.; ed. Marburg/Lahn and Lausanne Univs.
Assistant Judge Hanseatic Court of Appeals, Hamburg 46-48; Official, High Court for Combined Econ. Area, Cologne 48-49; Official, Fed. Ministry of Justice 49-52; Diplomatic Service 53-; Counsellor, German Embassy, Luxembourg 54-57; Vatican 57-61; Consul-Gen., Gothenburg 61-68; Head Admin. Dept., Foreign Office, Berlin 68-72; Amb. to Sweden 72-.
Leisure interests: numismatics, philately.
Publs. *Kommentar zum Gesetz über Ordnungswidrigkeiten* 52, *Das Deutsche Obergericht für das Vereinigte Wirtschaftsgebiet in Gedächtnisschrift für Herbert Ruscheweyh* 66.
Embassy of Federal Republic of Germany, Skarpögatan 9, 115 27 Stockholm, Sweden.
Telephone: (08) 63-13-80.

Stoessel, Walter John, Jr.; American diplomatist; b. 24 Jan. 1920, Kansas; s. of Walter John and Katherine (Haston) Stoessel; m. Mary Ann Ferrandou 1946; three d.; ed. Lausanne, Stanford Univs., Russian Inst. of Columbia Univ., Harvard Center for Int. Affairs.
Joined U.S. Foreign Service 42, served in Caracas, Moscow, Bad-Nauheim; Officer in charge of U.S.S.R. and E. European Affairs, Dept. of State 52-56; Special Asst. to Presidential Adviser on Foreign Affairs 56-61; Political Adviser, SHAPE, Paris 61-63; Minister-Counsellor, Moscow 63-65; Deputy Asst. Sec. for European Affairs, Dept. of State 65-68; Amb. to Poland 68-72; Asst. Sec. for European Affairs 72-73; Amb. to U.S.S.R. Dec. 73-.
Leisure interests: tennis, skiing, swimming, painting.
American Embassy, Ul. Chaikovskogo 19/23, Moscow, U.S.S.R.; and Moscow, Department of State, Washington, D.C. 20520, U.S.A.

Stoica, Gheorghe; Romanian politician; b. 20 July 1900, Dorohoi.
Member Central Cttee., Union of Communist Youth 22, mem. Romanian Communist Party 21-; 1st Sec. Communist Party Cttee. Dobrogea Region 46-47. Bucharest and its region 50-53; Sec.-Gen. Fed. of Labour 47-50; alt. mem. Central Cttee. of Romanian Communist Party 48, mem. 52-; Amb. to German Democratic Repub. 53-56; Dir. Office for local organization problems of state admin. 61-65; mem. State Council 65-; alt. mem. Exec. Cttee. 67, mem. 68; Deputy to Grand Nat. Assembly 48-, Sec. of Presidium 57-61; mem. Exec. Bureau of Nat. Council of Socialist Unity Front 68-; mem. Acad. of Social and Political Sciences 70; Hero of Socialist Labour.
The State Council, Bucharest, Romania.

Stokes, Baron (Life Peer), cr. 69, of Leyland in the County Palatine of Lancaster: **Donald Gresham Stokes,** Kt., T.D., D.L., C.ENG., F.I.MECH.E.; British engineer and business executive; b. 22 March 1914, London; s. of Harry Potts Stokes; m. Laura Lamb 1939; one s.; ed. Blundell's School and Harris Inst. of Technology, Preston.
Student engineer Leyland Motors 30-33; Technical Asst. 33-39; Export Man. Leyland Motors 46-50, Dir. 54; Man. Dir. Leyland Motors Corpn. 63, Chair. 67; Man. Dir. British Leyland Motor Corpn. 68-73, Chair. 68-75, Chief Exec. 73-75, Pres. British Leyland Ltd. 75-; fmr. Chair. British Leyland U.K. Ltd., NV

Leyland Industries Belgium S.A., NV British Leyland (Belgium) S.A., British Leyland Motors Inc. U.S.A.; fmr. Dir. British Leyland Motor Corpn. of Australia Ltd., Leyland Motor Corpn. of South Africa Ltd., N.Z. Motor Corpn., Ashole Leyland Ltd. India, Ennore Foundries Ltd. India, British Leyland Motors Canada Inc., Automóviles de Turismo Hispano Ingleses S.A., Metalúrgica de Santa Ana, British Leyland France S.A., Leyland Motor Corpn. (Malawi) Ltd., Nat. Westminster Bank Ltd. 69; Chair. A.E.C. Ltd. 65; Vice-Pres. Empresa Nacional de Auto-camiones S.A. (Spain) 69-73; mem. Council of Soc. of Motor Manufacturers and Traders 53, Vice-Pres. 61, Pres. 62, Deputy-Pres. 63; mem. Worshipful Company of Carmen 64, North West Econ. Planning Council 65-70, E.D.C. for the Motor Mfg. Industry 67, Nat. Advisory Council for the Motor Mfg. Industry 67, Confed. of British Industry Council; Vice-Pres. Eng. Employers Fed. 67-, Inst. of Motor Industry 67-; Vice-Pres. Univ. of Manchester Inst. of Science and Technology 68, Pres. 72; Deputy Lieut. for the Lancashire County Palatine 68-; Deputy Chair. Ind. Reorganization Corpn. 68-71; Vice-Pres. Inst. of Mechanical Engineers 71, Pres. 72; Hon. Fellow, Keble Coll., Oxford 68; Fellow, Inst. of Road Transport Engineers 68; Officer, Ordre de La Couronne (Belgium); Commdr. Ordre de Léopold II (Belgium) 72; Hon. LL.D. (Lancaster Univ.), Hon. D.Tech. (Loughborough), Hon. D.Sc. (Southampton and Salford); U.K. Marketing Award 64.
Leisure interest: yachting.
25 St. James's Place, London, S.W.1, England.

Stokes, Colin, B.S.; American industrial executive; b. 4 April 1914, Winston-Salem, N.C.; s. of Henry Straughan and Eloise Brown Stokes; m. Mary Louise Siewers 1943; two s. one d.; ed. Univ. of North Carolina. Joined R. J. Reynolds Tobacco Co. 35, Supt. of Mfg. 56-59, Dir. 57-, Exec. Vice-Pres. 61-70, Chair. of Board 70-72; Dir. R. J. Reynolds Industries Inc. 70-, Pres. 72-73, Chair. and Chief Exec. Officer 73-.
R. J. Reynolds Industries Inc., Winston-Salem, N.C. 27102; Home: 2701 Reynolds Drive, Winston-Salem, N.C. 27104, U.S.A.
Telephone: (919) 748-2366 (Office); (919) 722-4792 (Home).

Stokowski, Leopold (Boleslawowicz Stanislaw Antoni), F.R.C.M., B.MUS. (OXON.); American musician; b. 18 April 1882, London, England; s. of Boleslaw Kopernik Stokowski; ed. Royal Coll. of Music, London, and France and Germany.
Organist and Choirmaster, St. James's, London 02-05, St. Bartholomew's, New York 05-08; Conductor, Cincinnati Orchestra 09-12, Philadelphia Orchestra 12-36; Organizer and Conductor, All-American Youth Orchestra 40-41; Co-Conductor, NBC Symphony Orchestra 41-43; Founder and Conductor, New York City Symphony Orchestra 44-45; Conductor, Hollywood Bowl Symphony Orchestra 45-46, New York Philharmonic Orchestra 47-50; Music Dir., Houston Symphony Orchestra 55-60; Founder and Music Dir., American Symphony Orchestra, N.Y. 62-72; films: *A Hundred Men and a Girl* 37, *The Big Broadcast of 1937* 37, *Fantasia* 40, *Carnegie Hall* 46; many symphonic transcriptions of works of Bach; numerous recordings; Hon. Fellow, Queen's Coll., Oxford; Hon. D.Mus. (Pennsylvania Univ.), LL.D. (California Univ.).
Publ. *Music for All of Us* 43.
555 Madison Avenue, New York, N.Y. 10022, U.S.A.

Stoltenberg, Gerhard, DR.PHIL.; German scientist and politician; b. 29 Sept. 1928, Kiel; ed. Grammar School, Bad Oldesloe, and Kiel Univ.
Scientific Asst., Kiel Univ. 54-60, Lecturer 60-65; Deputy Chair. Christian Democratic Union, Schleswig-Holstein 55, Chair. 71-; Fed. Chair. "Junge Union" 55-61; mem. Schleswig-Holstein Parl. 54-57, 71-; mem. Bundestag 57-71; Fed. Vice-Chair. Christian Demo-

cratic Union 69-; Prime Minister Land Schleswig-Holstein 71-; mem. Board of Management Fried. Krupp, Essen 65; Fed. Minister for Scientific Research Oct. 65-69.
23 Kiel, Landeshaus, Federal Republic of Germany.
Telephone: 0431-5961 (2000).

Stone, Dewey D.; American businessman; b. 31 Aug. 1900; ed. Brockton Grammar School, Brockton High School and Coll. of Business Admin., Boston Univ.
Sergeant-Major, American Army, First World War; Chair. Harodite Finishing Co., N. Dighton, Mass. 52-; Chair. Board of Govs., Weizmann Inst. of Science, Rehovoth, Israel 45; Dir. Converse Rubber Co., Crosby Valve & Gage Co., Ashton Valve Co., T. Toonan Sons Co., Leumi Financial Corpn., and foreign companies; Hon. Nat. Chair. United Israel Appeal, United Jewish Appeal; official of many Israeli orgs. in America and Israel; Hon. D.Hum. (Boston Univ.), Hon. LL.D. (Stonehill Coll.); Hon. Fellow, Weizmann Inst. of Science.
53 Arlington Street, Brockton, Mass. 02109; Office: North Dighton, Mass. 02715, U.S.A.

Stone, Donald Crawford, A.B., M.S., LL.D.; American government official and educator; b. 17 June 1903, Cleveland, Ohio; s. of Alfred W. and Mary R. Stone; m. Alice Kathryn Biermann 1928; one s. three d.; ed. Colgate, Syracuse, Cincinnati and Columbia Univs.
Staff mem. Cincinnati Bureau of Governmental Research 27-28, Inst. of Public Administration N.Y. 29-30; Dir. of Research, Int. City Management Asscn., Chicago 30-33; Exec. Dir., Public Administration Service, Chicago 33-39; Asst. Dir. Bureau of the Budget, Exec. Office of the Pres., Washington 39-48; Dir. of Admin., E.C.A., Washington, D.C. 48-51, M.S.A. 51-53; Pres. Springfield Coll. 53-57; Adviser to U.S. Del., to UN Conf., San Francisco 45, to U.S. Del. to UNESCO Organizing Conf., London 45, to Gen. Assembly of UN London 46, and New York 47, to U.S. Rep. to Economic and Social Council N.Y. 46; U.S. Rep. to UNESCO Preparatory Commission, London 46; mem. UN Standing Cttee. on Administration and Budgetary Affairs 46-48; Dean, Graduate School of Public and Int. Affairs, Pittsburgh Univ. 57-69, now Prof. School of Urban and Public Affairs, Carnegie-Mellon Univ., Advisory assignments or studies in approx. 25 countries; Consultant to UN 70-74; Chair. Cttee. on Leaders and Specialists and mem. Comm. on Educ. and Int. Affairs, American Council on Educ. 55-61; Chair. Int. Asscn. of Schools and Insts. of Admin. 61-, Cttee. on Int. Admin., Nat. Acad. of Public Admin. 74-; Green Chair. Prof., Texas Christian Univ. 76.
Leisure interests: sports, music, religious activities.
Publs. numerous articles, monographs and books on government, international development and education.
School of Urban and Public Affairs, Carnegie-Mellon Univ., Pittsburgh, Pa. 15213, U.S.A.
Telephone: 412-621-2600.

Stone, Edward Durell, B.A., D.F.A.; American architect; b. 9 March 1902; ed. Harvard Univ. and M.I.T. Architecture Schools.
Architectural practice 35-; Instructor Advanced Design for New York Univ. 37-42; served in U.S. Army 42-45; Assoc. Prof. of Architecture, Yale Univ. 46-52; Visiting Critic, Yale Univ. 51-52; mem. Architectural Advisory Cttee., Fed. Public Housing Authority; Rotch Travelling Scholarship in Architecture; Architectural League Silver Medal for Domestic Architecture 50, Gold Medal for Museum of Modern Art 50, Gold Medal for Hotel El Panama 50; Honourable Mention for Univ. of Arkansas Fine Arts Center 52; Amer. Inst. of Architects Honor Award for Univ. of Arkansas Medical Center 52, New York Chapter Medal of Honor 55, First Honor Award for Stuart Company California 58, Award of Merit for U.S. Pavilion, World's Fair, Brussels 58, A.I.A.

Awards for U.S. Embassy, New Delhi 61 and Peninsula Community Hosp., Calif. 63, John F. Kennedy Award, Inst. of North American Studies, Barcelona 66; elected Nat. Inst. of Arts and Letters 58, American Acad. of Arts and Sciences 60, Royal Soc. of Arts 60-.

Principal works include: Museum of Modern Art 37 (Philip Goodwin, Associate); El Panama Hotel, Panama City 51; Univ. of Arkansas Fine Arts Center 51; Hospital for Peruvian Government Lima 57; Graf Residence, Dallas 57; U.S. pavilion, Brussels 58; U.S. Embassy, New Delhi 59; The Stuart Company, California 58; Huntington Hartford Gallery of Modern Art, New York; Stanford-Palo Alto Medical Center 60; Akron Downtown Redevelopment, Akron, Ohio; Univ. of Chicago Center for Continuing Education, Chicago 61; Nat. Cultural Center, Washington, D.C.; Pakistan Inst. of Nuclear Science and Technology, Islamabad, Pakistan 61; Nat. Geographic Soc. Office Building, Washington, D.C. 61; Int. Coll., Beirut 61; Perpetual Savings and Loan Assen. Building, Los Angeles 61; Peninsula Community Hosp., Carmel, Calif. 63; John F. Kennedy Center for the Performing Arts, Washington, D.C. 63; N.Y. State Univ. at Albany 63, N.Y. Civic Center (Eggers and Higgins Assoc.) 63; General Motors Building, N.Y.C. (Emery Roth and Sons, Assoc.) 64; NASA Electronics Research Centre, Cambridge, Mass. (Giffels, Maguire Associates) 64; Projects in U.S., Saudi Arabia, Nicaragua and Pakistan 66; Outdoor Amphitheatre for Garden State Arts Center, nr. New Brunswick, N.J.; Standard Oil Co. (Indiana), Chicago. 745 Fifth Avenue, New York, N.Y. 10021, U.S.A.

Stone, Rear-Admiral Ellery Wheeler; American communications executive and naval officer (Reserve); b. 14 Jan. 1894, Oakland, Calif.; s. of Edgar Parkman Stone and Florence Pickering Weeks; m. Heidi Margareta Bertel 1963; one s. (deceased) four d. (by previous marriages), ed. Univ. of California.

U.S. radio inspector 14-17; Lieut U.S. Naval Reserve and district Communications supt. 17-19; Pres. Fed. Telegraph Co. 24-31; operating Vice-Pres. and Dir. Mackay Radio and Telegraph Co. 31-37; Vice-Pres. All-American Cables and Radio Inc. 37-38; Pres. and Dir. Postal Telegraph Inc. and Postal Telegraph-Cable Co. 42-; Pres. and Dir Postal Telegraph Sales Corpn. 40; Commdr. U.S. Naval Reserve 39, Capt. 42, Commodore 43, Rear-Admiral 43; mem. Tech. Cttees. Defence Communications Board 40; Chief Commr. Allied Comm. for Italy 44-47; Chief of Italian Mil. Affairs Section of A.F.H.Q. 47; Vice-Pres. and Dir. Int. Telephone and Telegraph Corpn.; Chair. of Board American Cable and Radio Corpn., Commercial Cable Co., Mackay Radio & Tel. Co., All-American Cables & Radio Inc.; Pres. ITT Europe Inc., Brussels 61-65, Vice-Chair. 65-69; awarded U.S. Army and U.S. Navy D.S.M.s; K.B.E.; Grand Cross St. Maurice and St. Lazarus and Grand Officer Crown of Italy (Italy); Grand Cross of San Marino; Cross of Merit, 1st Class, with Crown, Knights of Malta; Officier, Légion d'Honneur; Commdr. Order of Leopold II; Commdr. 1st Grade Order of Isabella the Catholic (Spain); Campaign Medals World Wars I and II; Fellow, U.S. Inst. of Electric and Electronics Engineers and U.S. Naval Inst.; F.R.S.A.

Leisure interests: motor cars, hi-fi.

Publ. *Elements of Radio Communication* (3rd edn.) 26. 491 River Road, Nutley, N.J. 07110, U.S.A. Telephone: 201-667-4400.

Stone, Irving, A.B., M.A., CAND. PH.D.; American writer; b. 14 July 1903, San Francisco, Calif.; s. of Charles and Pauline (Rosenberg) Tennenbaum; m. Jean Factor 1934; one s. one d.; ed. Univ. of California, Univ. of Southern California.

Teaching Fellow, Univ. of Southern California 23-24, Univ. of California 24-26; Creative Writing, Indiana 48,

Washington 61, Univ. of Southern California 66; Lecturer California State Colleges 66; book reviews, magazine contributions; mem. numerous cultural, literary socs.; numerous awards; founder Irving and Jean Stone prizes for biog. and historical novels 68-; Hon. D.Lit. (Univ. of S. Calif., Coe Coll., Calif. State Colls.), Hon. LL.D. (Univ. of Calif. at Berkeley).

Publs. *Pageant of Youth* 33, *Lust for Life* (Vincent Van Gogh) 34, *Dear Theo* (Van Gogh's autobiography) 37, *Sailor on Horseback* (Jack London) 38, *False Witness* 40, *Clarence Darrow for the Defense* 41, *They also Ran* (Defeated Presidential Candidates) 43, *Immortal Wife* (Jessie and John Fremont) 44, *Adversary in the House* (Eugene Debs) 47, *Earl Warren* 48, *The Passionate Journey* (John Noble) 49, *We Speak for Ourselves* (A Self-Portrait of America) 50, *The President's Lady* (Rachel and Andrew Jackson) 51, *Love is Eternal* (Mary Todd Lincoln) 54, *Men to Match My Mountains* (opening of the Far West) 56, *The Biographical Novel* 57, *The Agony and the Ecstasy* (Michelangelo) 61, *Lincoln, A Contemporary Portrait* (Editor) 62, *I, Michelangelo, Sculptor* (Michelangelo's Letters) 62, *The Irving Stone Reader* 63, *Story of Michelangelo's Pietà* 64, *The Great Adventures of Michelangelo* 65, *Those Who Love* (Abigail and John Adams) 65, *There Was Light: Autobiography of a University, Berkeley, 1868-1968* 70, *The Passions of the Mind* (Sigmund Freud) 71, *Clarence Darrow—A One Man Play* 74, *Mary Todd Lincoln: A Final Judgment?* 74, *The Greek Treasure* (Henry and Sophia Schliemann) 75.

c/o Doubleday & Co. Inc., 501 Franklin Avenue, Garden City, New York, N.Y. 11530, U.S.A.

Stone, John O., B.SC., B.A.; Australian financial executive; b. 31 Jan. 1929, Perth; s. of Horace and Eva Stone (née Hunt); m. Nancy Hardwick 1954; four s. one d.; ed. Univ. of Western Australia and New Coll., Oxford.

Assistant to Australian Treasury Rep. in London 54-56, Australian Treasury Rep. in London 58-61; in Research and Information Div., Gen. Financial and Econ. Policy Branch, Dept. of Treasury, Canberra 56-57, in Home Finance Div. 61-62, Asst. Sec. Econ. and Financial Surveys Div. 62-66; Exec. Dir. for Australia, New Zealand and South Africa, Int. Monetary Fund (IMF) and Int. Bank for Reconstruction and Devt. (IBRD—World Bank) 67-70; First Asst. Sec., Revenue, Loans and Investment Div., Treasury 71; Sec. Australian Loan Council, Sec. Australian Nat. Debt Comm. 71; Deputy Sec. (Econs.) Treasury 71-; mem. Australian Dels. to GATT and IMF annual meetings, etc.

Leisure interests: reading, tennis, wine and food. The Treasury, Canberra, A.C.T. 2600, Australia. Telephone: Canberra 63 3740.

Stone, (John) Richard (Nicholas), C.B.E.; British economist; b. 30 Aug. 1913; ed. Westminster School and Gonville and Caius Coll., Cambridge.

With C. E. Heath and Co. (Lloyd's Brokers) 36-39; Ministry of Economic Warfare 39-40; offices of War Cabinet, Central Statistical Office 40-45; Dir. Dept. of Applied Economics, Cambridge 45-55; Leake Prof. of Finance and Accounting, Cambridge 55-; Fellow, King's Coll., Cambridge 45, Econometric Soc. (fmr. Pres.); mem. Int. Statistical Inst.; Fellow British Acad. 56; Foreign Hon. mem. American Acad. of Arts and Sciences 68; Sc.D. 57, Dr. h.c. (Oslo and Brussels) 65, (Geneva) 71, (Warwick) 75.

Publs. *The Role of Measurement in Economics* 51, *The Measurement of Consumers' Expenditure and Behaviour in the United Kingdom 1920-1938* Vol. I (with others) 54, Vol. II (with D. A. Rowe) 66, *Quantity and Price Indexes in National Accounts* 56, *Social Accounting and Economic Models* (with Giovanna Croft-Murray) 59, *Input-Output and National Accounts* 61, *National Income and Expenditure* (with Giovanna Stone) 61

(ninth edn.) 72, *A Programme for Growth* (with others) 62, *Mathematics in the Social Sciences and Other Essays* 66, *Mathematical Models of the Economy and Other Essays* 70, *Demographic Accounting and Model Building* 71.
13 Millington Road, Cambridge, England.

Stone, Marshall Harvey, B.A., M.A., PH.D.; American mathematician and educator; b. 8 April 1903, New York; *s.* of Harlan Fiske Stone and Agnes Harvey Stone; *m.* 1st Emmy Portman 1927, 2nd Ravijojla Kostić (née Perendija) 1962; three *d.* one step *d.*; ed. Harvard Univ.
Instructor Columbia Univ. 25-27; Instructor, Harvard Univ. 27-28, Asst. Prof. 28-31, Assoc. Prof. 33-37, Prof. 37-46; Assoc. Prof., Yale Univ. 31-33; Andrew MacLeish Distinguished Service Prof., Univ. of Chicago 46-68, Prof. Emer. 68-; George David Birkhoff Prof. of Mathematics, Univ. of Mass. 68-73, Prof. 73-; Visiting Lecturer many countries; Hon. Prof. of Mathematics, Madurai Univ., India; mem. Nat. Acad. of Sciences, American Philosophical Soc.; Hon. D.Sc. (seven times). Leisure interest: travel.
Publs. *Linear Transformations in Hilbert Space and Their Applications to Analysis* (American Mathematical Soc.) 32; numerous papers on mathematics and mathematical education.
Department of Mathematics, 202 Arnold House, University of Massachusetts, Amherst, Mass. 01002; Home: 260 Lincoln Avenue, Amherst, Mass. 01002, U.S.A. Telephone: 545-1311 (Office); 253-3016 (Home).

Stone, Richard; (*see* Stone J. R. N.).

Stonehouse, Rt. Hon. John Thomson, P.C., M.P.; British politician; b. 28 July 1925, Southampton; *s.* of late W. M. Stonehouse and Alderman Mrs. R. M. Stonehouse; *m.* Barbara J. Smith 1948; one *s.* two *d.*; ed. Springhill and Tauntons Schools, Southampton and London School of Economics.
Assistant to Senior Probation Officer, Southampton 41-44; R.A.F. pilot and education officer 44-47; Sec. and Man. to co-operative Socs., Uganda 52-54; Dir. London Co-operative Soc. 56-62, Pres. 62-64; mem. Parl. for Wednesbury 57-74, for Walsall North 74-; Parl. Sec. Ministry of Aviation 64-66; Parl. Under-Sec. of State for the Colonies 66-67; Minister of Aviation, subsequently Minister of Technology 67-68; Postmaster-Gen. 68-69; Minister of Posts and Telecommunications 69-70; Chair. Export Promotion and Consultancy Service Ltd. 70, Global Imex Ltd. 72, British Bangladesh Trust Ltd. 72; disappeared Nov. 74; reappeared in Australia Dec. 74; extradited July 75; resigned from Labour Party, joined English National Party 76.
Leisure interests: music, desmology, reading, chess.
Publs. *Prohibited Immigrant* 60, *Gangrene* (co-author) 64, *Death of an Idealist* 75.
House of Commons, London, S.W.1, England.
Telephone: 01-219-3000.

Stopford, Rt. Rev. and Rt. Hon. Robert Wright, P.C., K.C.V.O., C.B.E., D.D., D.C.L., M.A.; British ecclesiastic; b. 20 Feb. 1901, Liverpool; *s.* of John Stopford and Ethel Stopford (née Wright); *m.* 1st Winifred Morton 1935 (deceased), 2nd Kathleen Holt 1945 (deceased); two *s.* one *d.*; ed. Liverpool Coll. and Hertford Coll., Oxford.
Senior History Master and Chaplain, Oundle School 25-34; Principal, Trinity Coll., Kandy, Ceylon 35-40, Achimota Coll., Gold Coast 41-45; Rector of Barnet 46-47; Moderator, Church Training Colls. 47-55; Chaplain to H.M. Queen Elizabeth 52-55; Bishop of Fulham 55-56 (also Rep. of Archbishop of Canterbury in North and Central Europe); Sec. of Schools Council and Nat. Soc. 52-55; Chair. Schools Council 56-58; Hon. Canon of Canterbury 51-55; Bishop of Peterborough 56-61, of London 61-73; Vicar-Gen. Anglican Archbishopric of Jerusalem 74-76; Bishop of Bermuda 76-; Chair.

Church of England Board of Educ. 58-73; Chair. Joint Comm. for Anglican-Methodist Union 65; Hon. Fellow, Hertford Coll., Oxford; Fellow, King's Coll., London. Leisure interest: gardening.
Publs. include *None of us Liveth to Himself* 64.
Bishop's Lodge, P.O. Box 769, Hamilton 5, Bermuda.

Stoph, Willi; German politician; b. 9 July 1914, Berlin; *m.*; four *c.*
Worked as a mason and foreman bricklayer, later as a technical architect, following extra-mural studies; mem. Communist Party of Germany 31-; active anti-fascist resistance 33-45; mem. Central Cttee. Socialist Unity Party (SED) 50-, mem. Political Bureau of SED Central Cttee. 53-; mem. People's Chamber 50-; mem. Council of State 63-, Deputy Chair. 64-73, Chair. 73-; Minister of the Interior 52-55; Minister of Nat. Defence (rank of Gen. of Army) 56-60; Deputy Chair. Council of Ministers 54-64, Chair. Council of Ministers 64-73; Patriotic Order of Merit (Gold); Hero of Labour, Order of Banner of Labour, Order of Lenin 74, etc.
Klosterstrasse 47, 102 Berlin, German Democratic Republic.

Stoppard, Tom; British writer; b. 3 July 1937, Czechoslovakia; *m.* 1st 1965, 2nd 1972; four *s.*; ed. Pocklington Grammar School, Yorks.
Journalist, Bristol 54-60; free-lance journalist, London 60-64; John Whiting Award, Arts Council 67, New York Drama Critics Best Play Award 68, Antoinette Perry Award 68, Evening Standard Awards 67, 72, 74; Italia Prize (radio drama) 68; Hon. M.Litt. (Bristol).
Publs. plays: *Rosencrantz and Guildenstern are Dead* 67, *The Real Inspector Hound* 68, *Enter a Free Man* 68, *After Magritte* 70, *Dogg's Our Pet* 72, *Jumpers* 72, *Travesties* 75; radio plays: *The Dissolution of Dominic Boot* 64, *M is for Moon among other things* 64, *Albert's Bridge* 67, *If You're Glad I'll be Frank* 68, *Where Are They Now?* 70, *Artist Descending a Staircase* 72; short stories: *Introduction 2* 63; novel: *Lord Malquist and Mr. Moon* 66; screenplay: *The Romantic Englishwoman* (co-author) 75.
c/o Fraser & Dunlop, 91 Regent Street, London, W.1; Home: Fernleigh, Wood Lane, Iver Heath, Bucks., England.

Stopper, Edwin, DR.ECON.SC.; Swiss banker; b. 14 Aug. 1912, Winterthur; ed. Univs. of St. Gall, London, Paris and Geneva.
Formerly in export trade and banking; Asst. to Dir. Commercial Dept., Swiss Fed. Ministry for Econ. Affairs 39-45; Sec. Central Office of Swiss Asscn. for Trade and Industry, Zürich; Acting Man. and Deputy to Central Man. for Finance, Nestlé Alimentana Ltd., Vevey 52-53; Del. for Trade Agreements, Commercial Dept. of Fed. Ministry for Econ. Affairs 54-60, rank of Minister 55-60; Dir. Swiss Fed. Finance Dept. 60-61; Dir. Swiss Fed. Commercial Dept. (rank of Amb.) 61-66; Pres. Board of Gen. Management and Chief of Dept. I, Swiss Nat. Bank 66-74; mem. Board of Dirs. B.I.S. 66-; Hon. Lecturer in Econs., Basle Univ.
Winkelwiese 6, 8001 Zurich, Switzerland.

Storey, David; British author and playwright; b. 1933, Wakefield; *m.*; four *c.*; ed. Wakefield Grammar School, Wakefield Coll. of Art and Slade School of Art.
Publs. novels: *This Sporting Life* (MacMillan Award) 60, *Flight into Camden* (John Llewellyn Rhys Memorial Prize 61, Somerset Maugham Award 63) 60, *Radcliffe* 63, *Pasmore* (Faber Memorial Prize 72) 72, *A Temporary Life* 73; plays: *The Restoration of Arnold Middleton* (Evening Standard Award 67), *In Celebration* 69, *The Contractor* (New York Critics' Prize 74) 69, *Home* (Evening Standard Award, New York Critics' Prize) 70, *The Changing Room* (New York Critics' Prize) 71, *Cromwell* 73, *The Farm* 73, *Life Class* 74.
c/o Jonathan Cape Ltd., 30 Bedford Square, London, WC1B 3EL, England.

Storey, Robert Gerald, B.A.; American lawyer; b. 4 Dec. 1893, Greenville, Tex.; s. of Dr. and Mrs. F. W. Storey; m. 1st Hazel Porter 1917 (died 1962), 2nd Jewel Osborn 1965; ed. Univ. of Texas and Southern Methodist Univ.

Partner Storey, Armstrong & Steger (Dallas) 34-; Dean Southern Methodist Univ. Law School 47-59; Pres. Southwestern Legal Foundation 47-; Asst. Attorney Gen. of Texas 21-23; Regent Univ. of Texas 24-30; U.S. Exec. Trial Counsel, Nuremberg Major Axis War Crimes Trials 45-46; mem. Hoover Comm. 53-55; Adviser to Govt. of South Korea 54; Rep. of State Dept. in Far and Middle East 54-55; Chair. Board of Foreign Scholarships (Int. Education Exchange) 56-62; Vice-Chair. Civil Rights Comm. 57-63; Pres. Dallas Bar Asscn. 34, State Bar of Texas 48-49; American Bar Asscn. 52-53, Inter-American Bar Asscn. 54-56; mem. Int. Bar Asscn. 52-; Vice-Chair. and mem. U.S. Sea Level Canal Study Comm.; mem. President's Comm. on Law Enforcement and Improvement in Admin. of Justice; Chair. Lakewood State Bank; Dir. Southwestern Bell Telephone Co.; Dir. and Gen. Counsel Sabine Royalty Corpn.; 2nd Lieut. in Heavy Artillery during First World War, Col. in Air Corps during Second World War; Gold Medal American Bar Asscn. 56; decorations include Legion of Merit, Medal of Freedom, Légion d'Honneur, Bronze Star, Lawyer of the World award from World Peace through Law Center 64; Democrat.
Leisure interests: hunting, fishing and travel.
Publs. *Professional Responsibility* 58, *Our Unalienable Rights* 65, *The Final Judgment: Pearl Harbour to Nuremberg*; numerous articles and reviews.
4100 Republic Bank Tower, Dallas, Texas 75201, U.S.A. Telephone: 748-0211.

Storheill, Vice-Admiral Skule Valentin; Norwegian naval officer (retd.); b. 17 Aug. 1907, Brønnøysund; s. of Johannes Storheill and Aasta Moe; m. Cecilia Redman 1947; two s. one d.; ed. Norwegian Naval Coll. and Royal Naval Staff Coll., Greenwich.
Sub-Lieut. 28, Lieut. 31, Commdr. 41, Commodore 46, Vice-Admiral 51; served in submarines 31-36; Instructor Royal Norwegian Naval Coll. 36-40; active service during Second World War 40-45; staff appt., Norwegian Admiralty 45; Chief of Staff 46-49; C.-in-C. Norwegian Training Squadron 49-51; C.-in-C. Norwegian Navy Oct. 51-54; mem. Mil. Reps. Cttee. NATO 54-58; Commdr. Allied Task Force North Norway 58-67; Dir. Norwegian Nat. Defence Coll. 67-69; retd.; War Cross with Sword, Commdr. with Star, Royal Order of St. Olav, St. Olav Medal with Oak Leaf and Norwegian War Medal; D.S.C. with 2 bars (U.K.); Commdr. de la Légion d'Honneur, Croix de Guerre (France), Grand Cross, Orange Nassau, Hausorder (Netherlands), Officer Legion of Merit (U.S.A.), Commdr. Order of Dannebrog.
Leisure interests: sport, fishing.
1440 Droebak, Norway.
Telephone: 93-06-64.

Stork, Gilbert, PH.D.; American professor of chemistry; b. 31 Dec. 1921, Brussels, Belgium; s. of Jacques Stork and Simone Weil; m. Winifred Elizabeth Stewart 1944; one s. three d.; ed. Univ. of Wisconsin.
Instructor, Harvard Univ. 46-48, Asst. Prof. 48; Assoc. Prof., Columbia Univ. 53-55, Prof. 55-67, Eugene Higgins Prof. of Chemistry 67-; Kharasch Visiting Prof. Univ. of Chicago; Distinguished Visiting Prof. Case Inst. of Technology 66, Univ. of Iowa 68; Visiting Scholar Fisk Univ. 57; numerous Lectureships, including Coover Lecturer, Iowa State Univ. 58, Treat B. Johnson Lecturer Yale Univ. 64, Karl Pfister Lecturer Mass. Inst. of Tech. 69; Consulting Editor *Advanced Chemistry Series* McGraw-Hill 58-; mem. Editorial Board, *Accounts of Chemical Research* 68-, *Organometallics in Chemical Synthesis* 70-; mem. of Visiting Cttee. Chemistry Dept. of Tufts Univ.

and of Advisory Council of Chemistry Dept., Princeton Univ. 65-; Consultant Nat. Insts. of Health 67-; invited Plenary Lecturer Int. Union Pure Applied Chem., Kyoto 63, London 68, Boston 71; mem. Nat. Acad. of Sciences, American Acad. of Arts and Sciences; Hon. D.Sc. Lawrence Coll.; Award in Pure Chemistry of American Chemical Soc. (A.C.S.) 57, Baekeland Medal of N. Jersey Section of A.C.S. 61, Harrison Howe Award 62, Edward Curtis Franklin Memorial Award of Stanford Univ. 66, A.C.S. Award in Synthetic Organic Chemistry 67.
459 Next Day Hill Drive, Englewood, N.J.07631, U.S.A. Telephone: 201-871-4032.

Storti, Bruno; Italian trade unionist; b. 9 July 1913. Former mem. of the directing Cttee. Confederazione Generale Italiana del Lavoro; co-founder Confederazione Italiana Sindicati Lavoratori (C.I.S.L.) 50, Sec.-Gen. C.I.S.L. 59-; Pres. Int. Confed. of Free Trade Unions (ICFTU) 65-72; mem. Chamber of Deputies 58-; mem. Parl. of Europe 59.
Confederazione Italiana Sindicati Lavoratori, Via Po 21, Rome, Italy.

Storz, Gerhard, DR.PHIL.; German university professor; b. 19 Aug. 1898, Rottenacker, Württemburg; s. of Otto Storz and Hanna Storz (née Majer); m. Edith Baum 1944; one s. one d.; ed. Humanistisches Gymnasium, Esslingen, and Eberhard-Karls-Universität, Tübingen.
Actor and producer in various German theatres, particularly Nationaltheater, Mannheim 23-35; schoolteacher 35-45, Headmaster 45-58; Minister of Culture, Baden-Württemberg 58-64; Hon. Prof. Univ. of Tübingen 64-; Pres. Deutsche Akad. für Sprache und Dichtung, Darmstadt 66-; Grosses Bundesverdienstkreuz 63; Konrad Duden Prize, City of Mannheim 66; Schiller-Gedächtnis Prize of Baden Württemberg 71; Hon. D.Litt. (Middleburg Coll., U.S.A.) 65.
Leisure interest: sport (fencing and swimming).
Publs. *Umgang mit der Sprache* 37, *Das Drama Schillers* 38, *Das Wörterbuch des Unmenschen* (with Dolf Sternberger and W. E. Süskind) 45-48, *Goethe—Vigilien* 53, *Sprache und Dichtung, Versuch einer Poetik* 53, *Der Dichter Friedrich Schiller* 59, *Figuren und Prospekte* 63, *Eduard Mörike* 67, *Schwabische Romantik* 67, *Der Vers in der Deutschen Dichtung* 70, *Heinrich Heines Lyrische Dichtung* 71, *Klassik und Romantik in der deutschen Literatur* 72, *Im Lauf der Jahre* (autobiography) 73, *Sprachanalyse ohne Sprache* 75.
Eugen Hegele Weg 4, 725 Leonberg/Württ., Federal Republic of Germany.
Telephone: 43496.

Stowe, Leland, M.A.; American journalist; b. 10 Nov. 1899; ed. Wesleyan Univ.
Member staff *Worcester Telegram* 21; Foreign Editor Pathé News 24; Paris corresp. *New York Herald Tribune* 26-35; Pres. Anglo-American Press Club of Paris 35-35; awarded Pulitzer Prize for best foreign correspondence 30; reporter in North and South America for *New York Herald Tribune* 35-38; war corresp. *Chicago Daily News* Scandinavia, U.S.S.R. Balkans, Egypt and Far East 39-42, Europe 44-45. News Analyst, American Broadcasting Co. 44-45; Greek Mil. Cross 45; Lecturer-Writer N.Y. Post Syndicate; Foreign Editor *The Reporter Magazine* 48-50; Dir. News and Information Service, Radio Free Europe, Munich 52-54; Roving Editor *The Reader's Digest* 55-; Prof. of Journalism, Univ. of Michigan 57-70; Hon. D.Litt. (Wesleyan Univ., Hobart Coll.).
Publs. *Nazi Means War* 33, *No Other Road to Freedom* 41, *They Shall Not Sleep* 44, *While Time Remains* 46, *Target: You* 49, *Conquest by Terror: The Story of Satellite Europe* 52, *Crusoe of Lonesome Lake* 57.
2126 Woodside Road, Ann Arbor, Mich. 48104, U.S.A.

Støylen, Kaare, D.D.; Norwegian ecclesiastic; b. 3 Oct. 1909, V. Aker; s. of Bernt Støylen and Kamilla Heiberg; m. 1st Agnes Stray 1932 (died 1943), 2nd Honoria Faye 1945; one s. two d.; ed. Univ. of Oslo.

Pastor, Norwegian Seamen's Mission, London 32-35, Oslo 35-40; Chaplain, Cathedral Church, Bergen 40-47; Rector, St. Jacob's Church, Bergen 47; Sec.-Gen. Norwegian Seaman's Mission 53; Bishop Agder, Kristiansand 58; Bishop of Oslo 73-; Commander of North Star (Sweden), Commander with Star of St. Olav (Norway). Lesiure interest: music.

Publs. *Peder Palladius Visitasbook* 45, *Johan Nordahl Brun* 45, *Claus Frimann* 55, *Arv og Ansvar* 58.

St. Halvards pl. 3, Oslo 1, Norway.

Strachan, Douglas Alan; American international official (retd.); b. 6 Aug. 1903, London, England; s. of John Strachan and Minnie Conboy; m. Evelyn Berglund 1933; two d.; ed. Paddington Technical Inst. and Willesden Polytechnic, London.

Apprentice, British Thompson-Houston Co., London 19-26; emigrated to U.S. 26; toolmaker, automobile industry, Detroit 26-37; Sec. Michigan Labor Non-Partisan League 37-39; Field Rep., Fed. Cttee. on Apprenticeship, U.S. Dept. of Labor 39-40; Dir. United Automobile Workers Union, Willow Run Bomber Plant 42-43; Deputy Vice-Chair., Office of Labor Production, War Production Board 43-45; Dir. United Automobile Workers Union Office, Washington 45-47; Labor Adviser, American Mission for Aid to Greece (later known as Marshall Plan) 47-53; Chief, Labor Training Div., Office Labor Affairs, Agency for Int. Devt. (AID), Washington 54-59; Provincial Dir., Lahore, AID Mission, Pakistan 59-62; Deputy Dir. AID Mission, Cairo 62-64; Asst. to Dir. for Special Projects, AID, Saigon 65; Dir. Colombo Plan Bureau 66-69; Dir. Welfare and Grievance Staff AID, Washington 70-72, Special Asst. for Labour Relations 72-73. Leisure interests: tennis, music, reading.

403 N. Street, S.W., Washington, D.C. 20024, U.S.A.

Stradling, Rt. Rev. Leslie Edward, M.A., D.C.L.; British ecclesiastic; b. 11 Feb. 1908; ed. Oxford Univ., Westcott House, Cambridge.

Curate in London 33-38, Vicar 38-45; Bishop of Masasi 45-52, of S.W. Tanganyika 52-61, of Johannesburg, South Africa 61-74; retd.

Publs. *A Bishop on Safari* 60, *"The Acts" through Modern Eyes* 63, *An Open Door* 66, *A Bishop at Prarey* 71.

197 Main Road, Kalk Bay, Cape, South Africa 7975. Telephone: 8-5588.

Straight, Whitney Williard, C.B.E., M.C., D.F.C.; British company director; b. 6 Nov. 1912, U.S.A.; s. of Major W. D. Straight and Mrs. Dorothy Whitney Elmhirst; m. Lady Daphne Finch Hatton 1935; two d.; ed. Lincoln School, U.S.A., Dartington Hall, Devon, and Trinity Coll. Cambridge.

Former professional motor car driver; gave up motor racing to enter civil aviation 34; started a number of companies; served in Auxiliary Air Force Second World War 39-45; Additional Air A.D.C. to the King 44; Deputy Chair. British European Airways 46; Man. Dir. (Chief Exec.) British Overseas Airways Corpn. 47, Deputy Chair. BOAC 49-56; Dir. Midland Bank 56-; Exec. Deputy Chair. Rolls-Royce Ltd. 57-71; Chair. 71; Chair. Arran Trust Ltd.; Deputy Chair. Post Office 69-74; Dir. British Aircraft Corpn. (Holdings) 71; Vice-Pres. Royal Air Force Asscn.; mem. Insts. of Transport, Navigation and Directors; Fellow, Royal Geographical Soc.; Vice-Pres. British Light Aviation Centre; Hon. Companion Royal Aeronautical Soc.; Chair. Exec. Cttee. Alexandra Rose Day; Fellow, Royal Soc. of Arts. Leisure interests: flying, underwater exploration, skiing, music, art and industrial design.

The Aviary, Windmill Lane, Southall, Middx., England. Telephone: 01-574-2711.

Strakhov, Nikolai Mikhailovich; Soviet geologist; b. 15 April 1900, Bolkhov, Oryel Region; ed. Moscow State Univ.

Assistant, Moscow Geological Prospecting Inst. 30-31, Asst. Prof. 31-37, Prof. 44-46; Prof. Moscow State Univ. 51-53; Geological Inst. of U.S.S.R. Acad. of Sciences 34-; Corresp. mem. U.S.S.R. Acad. of Sciences 47-53, mem. 53-; Man. Lithological Dept. of Geological Inst. of U.S.S.R. Acad. of Sciences 37-58, Man. Laboratory of Geochemistry and Sedimentary Rocks, Geological Inst. 59-; Chief Editor *Lithology and Mineral Resources;* State Prize 48, Lenin Prize 61.

Publs. *Principles of Historical Geology* (2 vols.) 37, 38, 48, *Iron-ore Facies and their Analogues in the History of the Earth* 47, *Calcareous-dolomitic Facies in Modern and Ancient Basins* 54, *On the Geochemistry of Upper Paleozoic Deposits of Humidic Type* (with Glagoleva and Zalmanzon) 59, *Principles of the Theory of Lithogenesis* (Vols. 1-3) 60-62 (English edn. 67), *Lithogenetical Types and Their Evolution in the History of Earth* 63.

Geological Institute of the U.S.S.R. Academy of Sciences, Pyzhevsky per. 7, Moscow, U.S.S.R.

Strang, 1st Baron, cr. 54; **William Strang,** G.C.B., G.C.M.G., M.B.E.; British diplomatist; b. 2 Jan. 1893, Rainham, Essex; s. of James Strang; m. Elsie Jones 1920 (died 1974); one s. one d.; ed. Palmer's School, Univ. Coll., London, Sorbonne.

Served First World War; entered Foreign Office 19, 3rd Sec. Belgrade 19, 2nd Sec. 20, Foreign Office 22, 1st Sec. 25, Counsellor Moscow Embassy 30, Foreign Office 33, Asst. Under-Sec. of State Foreign Office 39-43; United Kingdom rep. with rank of Amb., European Advisory Comm. 43-45; Political Adviser to C.-in-C., British Zone, Germany 45-47; Permanent Under-Sec., Foreign Office (German Section) 47-49; Permanent Under-Sec. Foreign Office 49-53; Chair. Nat. Parks Comm. 54-66; Chair. Food Hygiene Advisory Council 55-71; Chair. Royal Inst. of Int. Affairs 58-66.

Publs. *The Foreign Office* 55, *Home and Abroad* 56, *Britain in World Affairs* 61, *The Diplomatic Career* 62.

14 Graham Park Road, Gosforth, Newcastle upon Tyne, NE3 4BH, England. Telephone: 0632-857455.

Sträng, Gunnar Georg Emmanuel: Swedish politician; b. 23 Dec. 1906; ed. Stockholm.

Labourer 21-27; rep. on Workers' Asscn. 27-32; official, T.U.C.; Chair. Agricultural Workers' Union; Minister without portfolio 45-47; Minister of Supply 47; Minister of Agriculture 48-51; Minister of Social Affairs 51-55; Minister of Finance 55-; Social Democratic Labour.

Finansdepartementet, Stockholm, Sweden.

Stranski, Iwan N., DR. PHIL.; German professor of chemistry; b. 2 Jan. 1897, Sofia, Bulgaria; s. of Nikola Stranski and Maria (née Krohn); m. Martha Pötschke 1926; ed. Gymnasium, Sofia, and Univs. of Vienna, Sofia and Berlin.

Dozent, Sofia 26; Asst. Prof., Univ. of Sofia until 37, Prof. 37-44; Scientific mem. Kaiser-Wilhelm-Inst. for Physical Chem., Berlin-Dahlem 44-, later Fritz-Haber-Inst. of Max-Planck Gesellschaft; Prof. and Dir. Max-Volmer-Inst. of Physical Chem., Tech. Univ., Berlin 45-63, Emer. 63-; Hon. Prof., Free Univ. of Berlin 49-; Deputy Dir. Fritz-Haber-Inst. of Max-Planck-Gesellschaft 53-67; Dir. of Dept. of Physical Chem. 54-67; Corresp. mem. Göttingen Acad. of Sciences; mem. Bavarian Acad. of Sciences, German Leopoldina Acad., Halle; Foreign mem. Royal Swedish Soc. of Science and Literature, Bulgarian Acad. of Sciences; Galvani Medal, Univ. of Bologna 38; Silver Hoffman Medal, German Chemical Soc. 39; Kyrillus Methodius Prize. Bulgarian Acad. of Sciences 40; Grosses Bundesverdienstkreuz and decorations from Bulgaria and Poland; several hon. degrees.

Publs. Numerous publs. on growth of crystals, problems of condensation and evaporation, formation of stalactites, etc.

1 Berlin 33-Dahlem, Faradayweg 8, Germany.

Telephone: 76-64-64.

Strasberg, Lee; American theatrical director; b. 17 Nov. 1901.

Emigrated to U.S. from Austria 09; first directed and acted N.Y. 25, becoming professional 25; Actor and Asst. Stage Man. with Theatre Guild 25; founded Group Theatre N.Y. 30 and acted in many productions including *House of Connelly, Night over Taos, Success Story, Men in White, Gold Eagle Guy, Johnny Johnson;* directed *All the Living, Clash by Night, Fifth Column, Skipper next to God, The Big Knife;* Artistic Dir. Actors Studio, N.Y. 48-, Actors Studio Theatre Inc. 63-66; film debut *The Godfather, Part II* 75; lecturer on the theatre at various univs.; Pulitzer Prize for *Men in White;* Kelcey Allen Award 61; Centennial Gold Medal Award for Excellence in Dramatic arts, Boston Coll. 63.

135 Central Park West, New York, N.Y. 10023, U.S.A.

Strassman, Fritz, DR.ING.; German chemist; b. 22 Feb. 1902, Boppard; ed. Oberrealschule an der Scharnhorststrasse, Düsseldorf, Technische Hochschule, Hanover, and Kaiser Wilhelm Institut für Chemie, Berlin-Dahlem. Assistant, Inst. for Physical Chemistry, Technische Hochschule, Hanover 29; scholar, Kaiser Wilhelm Inst. for Chemistry, Berlin-Dahlem 29; worked with Prof. O. Hahn and L. Meitner, Kaiser Wilhelm Inst. for Chemistry, Berlin; Head of Chemistry Dept., Kaiser Wilhelm Inst. for Chemistry, Tailfingen, Mainz (Max-Planck-Institut) 46-52; Dir. Inst. of Inorganic Chemistry and Nuclear Chemistry, Univ. of Mainz 46-70; Enrico Fermi Prize 66; Hon. Citizen of Mainz 72.

65 Mainz-Universität, Johann Friedrich von Pfeifferweg 6, Federal Republic of Germany.

Telephone: 31919.

Straten-Waillet, François-Xavier van der; Belgian politician and diplomatist (retd.); b. 22 Jan. 1910, Antwerp; s. of Baron A. van der Straten-Waillet and Irene Bosschaert de Bouwel; m. 1935; three s. three d.; ed. Collège de St. André and Univ. of Louvain.

Barrister 34-38; Dir. Employers Organization 39-45; mem. of Parl. 46-52; Minister of Commerce 47-48 and of Public Health 48-49; Pres. Christian Social Party 49-50; Del. to various sessions of the UN, UNESCO, etc.; Minister to Argentina 52, Amb. 53-55; Amb. to Netherlands 55-66; Dir.-Gen. Political Affairs, Foreign Office, Brussels 66-70; Amb. to Italy 70-74; retd. 75; Grand Cross, Order of Netherlands Lion, Orange-Nassau, House of Orange; Orders of Merit from Italy, Argentina and Chile; Grand Officier Order of Leopold etc.

Leisure interest: bird watching.

Duindak, Stabroek (Anvers), Belgium.

Telephone: 031-686673 (Home).

Strathalmond, 2nd Baron, cr. 55, of Pumpherston in the County of Midlothian; **William Fraser,** C.M.G., O.B.E., T.D.; British oil executive; b. 8 May 1916, Glasgow, Scotland; s. of 1st Baron Strathalmond; m. Letitia Krementz 1945; one s. two d.; ed. Loretto and Clare Coll., Cambridge.

Served in army 39-45; Barrister-at-Law, in private practice 46-50; joined The British Petroleum Co. Ltd. 50, rep. in New York 56-58; Man. Dir. Kuwait Oil Co. 59-62; Man. Dir. British Petroleum Co. Ltd. 62-72, Dir. 72-74; Chair. Govan Shipbuilders 72-74; Dir. Prudential Insurance 73-, Burmah Oil Co. 75-.

Leisure interests: horse-racing, golf.

Hillfields Farm, Lower Basildon, near Pangbourne, Berks., England.

Stratos, Christoforos; Greek politician; b. 1924, Athens; m. Sofia C. Katsambas; two s. one d.; ed. Univ. of Athens.

Vice-President of Social Security Foundation; Vice-Pres. Fed. of Greek Industries 55-57; Minister of Educ. 61, 63, of Transport 64, of Interior 66; arrested Dec. 67, May 73; Minister of Public Works July 74-; Commdr. Order of the Phoenix, Nat. Resistance Medal, Knight Commdr. Order of Orthodox Crusaders of Holy Sepulchre.

Publs. *The Greek Problem* 58, *The Free Man in the Twentieth Century* 60, *Man's Position in Contemporary Society* 61, *The Administration: Its New Duties and Sacrifices* 61, *The Economy and the State* 61, *The National Consciousness and Reassurance of the Citizens* 61, *Greece and Europe* 61, *Youth and Greek Development* 62, *National Dangers and Policy on National Foundations* 66.

Ministry of Public Works, Athens, Greece.

Stratton, Sir (Francis) John, Kt., C.B.E.; British business executive; b. 18 Jan. 1906, Gamlingay; s. of Ernest W. Stratton and Annie A. Peters; m. Christine Harrison 1936; one d.; ed. Fitzwilliam House, Cambridge.

Eastern Associated Telegraph Co. Ltd. 22-28; Lewis's Ltd. 32-39; Man. Dir. Dolcis Ltd. and associated cos. 47-57, Chair. 52-57; Dolcis (Canada) Ltd. 47-57; Chair. F.M.C. Ltd., F.M.C. (Meat) Ltd., F.M.C. (Products) Ltd., Fatstock Finance Ltd., Marsh & Baxter Ltd., C. & T. Harris (Calne) Ltd. and associated companies 58-74, Pres. 74-.

Leisure interest: farming.

F.M.C. Ltd., 19 Knightsbridge, London, S.W.1; Home: Rotherwood, Fittleworth, nr. Pulborough, Sussex, England.

Telephone: Fittleworth 396.

Stratton, Julius A., SC.D., S.M., S.B.; American physicist; b. 18 May 1901, Seattle, Wash.; s. of Julius and Laura Stratton; m. Catherine Coffman 1935; three d.; ed. Univ. of Washington, Mass. Inst. of Technology, Eidgenössische Technische Hochschule, Zürich.

With M.I.T. 24-; Asst. Prof. Dept. of Electrical Engineering 28-31, Asst. Prof. of Physics 31-35, Assoc. Prof. 35-41, Prof. 41-51, Dir. Research Laboratory of Electronics 45-49, Provost, M.I.T. 49-56, Vice-Pres. 51-56, Chancellor 56-59, Acting Pres. 57-59, Pres. 59-66, Pres. Emer. 66-; Chair. of Board, The Ford Foundation Jan. 66-71; Trustee, Boston Museum of Science; Chair. Comm. on Marine Science, Engineering and Resources 67-69; mem. Nat. Advisory Cttee. on Oceans and Atmosphere 71-73; numerous hon. degrees and awards and decorations.

Publs. *Electromagnetic Theory* 41, *Science and the Educated Man* 66, also numerous papers.

Massachusetts Institute of Technology, Cambridge, Mass. 02139; Home: 100 Memorial Drive, Cambridge, Mass. 02142, U.S.A.

Stratton, Richard James, C.M.G., M.A.; British diplomatist; b. 16 July 1924, London; ed. The King's School, Rochester, Merton Coll., Oxford.

Joined Foreign Service 47; Private Sec. to Minister without Portfolio, Foreign Office 63-64, to Minister of State for Foreign Affairs 64-66; Counsellor and Head of Chancery, British High Comm., Rawalpindi, Pakistan 66-69; Imperial Defence Coll. 70; Head UN (Political) Dept., Foreign and Commonwealth Office 71-72; Political Adviser to the Gov. of Hong Kong 72-74; Amb. to Zaire 74-, concurrently accred. to Congo and Burundi.

British Embassy, B.P. 8049, Kinshasa, Zaire; and c/o Foreign and Commonwealth Office, King Charles Street, London, S.W.1, England.

Straub, F. Bruno; Hungarian biochemist; b. 1914. University prof.; Vice-Pres. Nat. Peace Council 58-62; mem. Hungarian Acad. of Sciences, Vice-Pres. 70-72;

Dir. Biology Centre of Hungarian Acad. of Sciences; Vice-Pres. ICSU 71; Vice-Pres. Int. Union of Biochemistry (IUB); work mainly concerns studies of muscle function, cell respiration and protein synthesis; Kossuth Prize 48, 58; Labour Order of Merit, golden degree 70, Banner Order of Hungary, 2nd degree 74; Dr. h.c., Humboldt Univ., Berlin 75.
Publs. *Inorganic and Analytical Chemistry* 50, *Organic Chemistry* 52, *Biochemistry* 58.
Hungarian Academy of Sciences, Roosevelt tér 9, Budapest V; Home: Endrödi Sándor-u. 18/a, H-1026 Budapest II, Hungary.
Telephone: 668-858 (Office); 353-353 (Home).

Straub, Robert W., M.S.; American politician; b. 6 May 1920, San Francisco; ed. Dartmouth Univ.
Member Oregon State Senate 59; State Treasurer 64-72; Gov. of Oregon Jan. 75-; Democrat.
State Capitol, Salem, Oregon, U.S.A.

Straus, Jack I., B.A.; American merchant; b. 13 Jan. 1900, New York City; s. of Jesse I. and Irma (née Nathan) Straus; m. Virginia Megear 1975; one s. two d.; ed. Harvard Coll.
Entered R. H. Macy & Co. Inc., Training Squad 21, Exec. Vice-Pres. 26-33, Sec. 29-33, Vice-Pres. 35-39, Acting Pres. 39-40, Pres. 40-56, Chair. 56-68, Chair. of Exec. Cttee. 68-; mem. Board of Trustees, Greenwich Savings Bank; fmr. mem. Board of Overseers Harvard Coll.; fmr. Dir. L.I. Railroad, Mutual Broadcasting System Inc., Gen. Teleradio Inc., Safeway Stores Inc.; Hon. Dir. Greater N.Y. Fund; fmr. Dir. Fidelity Union Trust Co., Continental Can Co.; Dir. First Empire Bank New York, United Fund of Greater New York; Chair of the Board, Roosevelt Hospital 65-74, Chair. of the Advisory Board of Trustees 75-, Chair. of the Building Cttee. 74-; fmr. Public Gov., N.Y. Stock Exchange; mem. Nat. Public Advisory Cttee. on Regional Economic Devt. 70; hon. Fellowship American Coll. of Hospital Administrators 68; Officer Order of Leopold II (Belgium) 51; Chevalier de la Légion d'Honneur (France) 51; Commendatore Order of Merit of the Italian Republic 69; Star of Italian Solidarity 52; Hon. LL.D. (Adelphi Coll.) 55; Hon. Dr. Comm. Sc. (New York Univ.) 58.
Home: 19 East 72nd Street, New York, N.Y. 10021; Office: R. H. Macy & Co., Inc., 151 West 34th Street, New York, N.Y. 10001, U.S.A.

Straus, William L., Jr., PH.D.; American anatomist and physical anthropologist; b. 29 Oct. 1900, Baltimore, Md.; s. of William L. Straus and Pauline Gutman; m. 1st. Henrietta S. Hecht 1926 (died 1954), 2nd Bertha L. Nusbaum 1955; one d.; ed. Harvard and Johns Hopkins Univs.
Instructor in Anatomy, Johns Hopkins Univ. 27-30, Assoc. in Anatomy 30-43, Assoc. Prof. of Anatomy 43-52, Prof. of Physical Anthropology 52-57, of Anatomy and Physical Anthropology 57-66; Prof. Emer. 66-; mem. Nat. Acad. of Sciences; Viking Medal and Award in Physical Anthropology 52.
Leisure interests: painting, history of art, history of science.
Publs. 78 publications on anatomy, zoology, physical anthropology, palaeontology and history of science 23-.
Department of Anatomy, School of Medicine, The Johns Hopkins University, Baltimore, Md. 21205; Home: 7111 Park Heights Avenue, Baltimore, Md. 21215, U.S.A.
Telephone: 955-3240 (Office); 358-6249 (Home).

Strauss, Franz Josef; German politician; b. 6 Sept. 1915, Munich; m. Marianne Zwicknagl 1957; two s. one d.; ed. Univ. of Munich.
Served Second World War 39-45; mem. Bavarian Christian Social Union Party (C.S.U.) 45-, Deputy Chair. 52, Chair. 61-; mem. Bundestag (Fed. Parl.) 49-; Fed. Minister for Special Tasks 53-55, for Atomic

Questions 55-56, of Defence 56-62, of Finance 66-Oct. 69.
Leisure interests: reading, sports.
Publs. *The Grand Design* 65, *Herausforderung und Antwort* 68, *Finanzpolitik, Theorie und Wirklichkeit* 68, *Bundestagsreden* 68, *Die Zukunft Deutschlands* 69.
Munich 2, Lazarettstrasse 33, Federal Republic of Germany.
Telephone: 120710.

Strauss, Paul; German carpenter and politician; b. 1923.
Member Cen. Cttee. Sozialistische Einheitspartei Deutschlands; mem. Council of State.
Staatsrat, Berlin, German Democratic Republic.

Strausz-Hupe, Robert, A.M., PH.D.; American diplomatist; b. 25 March 1903, Vienna; m. Eleanor de Graff Cuyler (died 1976); ed. Univ. of Pennsylvania.
Engaged in investment banking 27-37; Assoc. Editor, *Current History* 39-41; Assoc. Prof. of Political Science, Univ. of Pennsylvania 46-52, Prof. 52-, Dir. Foreign Policy Research Inst. 55-69; Amb. to Ceylon and Repub. of Maldives 70-72, to Belgium 72-74, to Sweden 74-75; Perm. Rep. to North Atlantic Council 76-; fmr. Dir. Atlantic Council of U.S.A.; mem. Council on Foreign Relations, American Political Science Asscn.; Fellow, Royal Geographical Soc.
Publs. *The Russian-German Riddle* 40, *Axis-America* 41, *Geopolitics* 42, *The Balance of Tomorrow* 45, *International Relations* 50, *The Zone of Indifference* 52, *Power and Community* 56, *Protracted Conflict* (co-author) 59, *A Forward Strategy for America* 61 (co-author), *Building the Atlantic World* (co-author) 63, *In My Time* 67.
North Atlantic Council, NATO, 1110 Brussels, Belgium.

Streat, Sir Edward Raymond, K.B.E.; British industrialist; b. 7 Feb. 1897; ed. Manchester Grammar School.
Served First World War (Lieut., 10th Manchester Regt.); Asst. Sec. Manchester Chamber of Commerce 19; Dir and Sec. 20-40; Hon. Dir. Lancashire Industrial Development Council 31-40; Pres. Manchester Statistical Soc 36-38; Sec. Export Council, Board of Trade 40; Pres. Textile Institute 46-48; Chair. Cotton Board Manchester 40-57; mem. Advisory Council D.S.I.R. 42-47; Chair. Manchester Joint Research Council 48-51; Treasurer of Council of Manchester Univ. 50-57, Chair. 57-65; Chair. North Western Electricity Consultative Council and mem. North Western Electricity Board 60-68; Visiting Fellow Nuffield Coll., Oxford 44-59, Hon. Fellow 59.
4 Mill Street, Eynsham, Oxford, England.
Telephone: Oxford 881562.

Street, Anthony Austin; Australian politician; b. 8 Feb. 1926, Victoria; s. of Brig. the Hon. G. A. Street, M.C.; m. V. E. Rickard 1951; three s.; ed. Melbourne Grammar.
Royal Australian Navy; primary producer; mem. for Corangamite, House of Reps. 66; Sec. Govt. Mems. Defence and Wool Cttees. 67-71; mem. Joint Parl. Cttee. on Foreign Affairs 69; Chair. Fed. Rural Cttee. of Liberal Party 70-74; mem. Fed. Exec. Council 71; Asst. Minister of Labour and Nat. Service 72; mem. Liberal Party Shadow Cabinet for Social Security, Health and Welfare 73, for Primary Industry, Shipping and Transport 73, for Science and Tech. and A.C.T. 74, for Labour 75; Minister for Labour and Immigration Nov.-Dec. 75; Minister for Employment and Industrial Relations, and Minister Assisting the Prime Minister in Public Service Matters Dec. 75-.
Leisure interests: flying, cricket, golf, tennis.
Department of Employment and Industrial Relations, 239 Bourke Street, Melbourne, Victoria; and Parliament House, Canberra, A.C.T.; Home: Eildon, Lismore, Victoria, Australia.

Street, Robert, PH.D., D.SC.; Australian professor of physics; b. 16 Dec. 1920, Wakefield, England; m. Joan Marjorie Bere 1943; one s. one d.; ed. Univ. of London. Scientific Officer, Dept. of Supply, U.K. 42-45; Lecturer, later Senior Lecturer, Dept. of Physics, Univ. of Nottingham 45-54; Senior Lecturer, Dept. of Physics, Univ. of Sheffield 54-60; Foundation Prof. of Physics, Monash Univ., Melbourne, Victoria 60-74; Dir. Research School of Physical Sciences, Australian Nat. Univ. 74-; fmr. Pres. Australian Inst. of Nuclear Science and Eng.; mem. and Chair. Australian Research Grants Cttee. 70-; Chair. Nat. Standards Comm. 67-; Fellow, Australian Acad. of Science 73, Treas. 76-. Leisure interests: fly fishing, golf.
Research School of Physical Sciences, Australian National University, P.O. Box 4, Canberra, A.C.T. 2600; Home: 47 Curlewis Crescent, Garran, A.C.T. 2605, Australia.

Streich, Rita; German singer; b. 18 Dec. 1926, Barnaul, Russia; m. Dieter Berger 1949; one s.
Studied with Erna Berger and Maria Ivogün; with Berlin State Opera, first important role Olympia (*Tales of Hoffmann*) 47; with Städtische Oper, Berlin 50-53, with Vienna Staatsoper 53-; sang at Bayreuth Festival 52, 53, Salzburg 54-62 and 65-, Aix-en-Provence 55, Glyndebourne 58; guest appearances in Europe, U.S.A. and Buenos Aires; concerts in Europe and U.S.A., Japan, Australia and New Zealand; numerous recordings and broadcasts; has appeared on television in Germany, Great Britain, on the Ed Sullivan Show (New York), etc., own television show in Germany; notable roles include the Queen of the Night (*The Magic Flute*), Konstanze (*Il Seraglio*), Susanna (*The Marriage of Figaro*), Zerbinetta (*Ariadne auf Naxos*), Sophie (*Der Rosenkavalier*), Gilda (*Rigoletto*), Rosina (*The Barber of Seville*), etc.; Bundesverdienstkreuz 1st class 71.
Publ. *Österreichische Kammersängerin.*
Kärntnerstrasse 23, Vienna I, Austria; and Palazzo Olimpo, Ascona, Switzerland.

Streisand, Barbra; American actress and singer; b. 24 April 1942, Brooklyn, N.Y.; ed. Erasmus Hall High School.
Nightclub debut at *Bon Soir* 61; appeared in off-Broadway revue *Another Evening with Harry Stoones* 61; appeared at Caucus Club, Detroit and Blue Angel, N.Y. 61; played in musical comedy *I can get it for you Wholesale* 62; began recording career with Columbia records 63; appeared in musical play *Funny Girl*, N.Y. 64, London 66; television programme *My Name is Barbra* shown in England, Holland, Australia, Sweden, Bermuda and the Philippines, winning five Emmy awards; second programme *Color Me Barbra* also shown abroad; numerous concert and nightclub appearances; N.Y. Critics Best Supporting Actress Award 62; Grammy recording awards; London Critics' Musical Award 66; Academy Award (Oscar) for film *Funny Girl* 68; American Guild of Variety Artists' Entertainer of the Year Award 70.
Films: *Funny Girl* 68, *Hello Dolly* 69, *On a Clear Day you can see Forever* 69, *The Owl and the Pussycat* 71, *What's Up Doc?* 72, *Up the Sandbox* 73, *The Way We Were* 73, *For Pete's Sake* 74, *Funny Lady* 75.
c/o 20th Century Fox Studios, Beverly Hills, California, U.S.A.

Streit, Clarence K.; American journalist; b. 21 Jan. 1896, California, Mo.; s. of Louis Leland and Emma Kirshman Streit; m. Jeanne Defrance 1921; one s. two d.; ed. Montana and Oxford Univs.
Rhodes Scholar Oxford 20; Foreign Corresp. 21-; fmr. *New York Times* Corresp. for L.N.; Pres. Int. Asscn. of Journalists accredited to the League 32; Pres. Federal Union Inc. 39-; Editor *Freedom and Union* 46-;

Pres. Int. Movement for Atlantic Union 59-; Kefauver Union of the Free Award 68.
Leisure interests: hiking in the mountains, fly fishing, writing verse, reading.
Publs. *Where Iron Is, There Is the Fatherland* 20, *Hafiz: The Tongue of the Hidden* 28, *Union Now* 39, *Union Now with Britain* 41, *Union Now* (post-war edn.) 48, *The New Federalist* (in collaboration) 50, *Freedom Against Itself* 54, *Freedom's Frontier—Atlantic Union Now* 61.
Home: Ontario Apartments, 2853 Ontario Road, N.W., Washington, D.C. 20009; Office: Federal Union Inc., 1736 Columbia Road, Washington, D.C. 20009, U.S.A. Telephone: 202-AD4-2211 (Office); 202-AD4-3232 (Home).

Streit, Josef; German lawyer; b. 9 June 1911.
In Czechoslovakia until 45; mem. Czechoslovak Communist Party 38-45, Sozialistische Einheitspartei Deutschlands 45-; Area Youth Leader, Schönberg/ Mecklenburg 45; Chief Adviser, Ministry of Justice 49; Public Prosecutor, Office of Public Prosecutor-Gen. of D.D.R. 51-53; staff of Central Cttee., S.E.D. 53-62, mem. Central Cttee. S.E.D. 63-; Public Prosecutor-Gen. of D.D.R. 62-; Vaterländischer Verdienstorden in Silber.
Generalstaatsanwalt der Deutschen Demokratischen Republik, 104 Berlin, Hermann-Matern-Strasse 33-34, German Democratic Republic.

Streitwieser, Andrew, Jr., M.A., PH.D.; American professor of chemistry; b. 23 June 1927, Buffalo, N.Y.; s. of Andrew Streitwieser and Sophie Morlock; m. 1st Mary Ann Good 1950 (died 1965), 2nd Suzanne Cope 1967; one s. one d.; ed. Stuyvesant High School and Columbia Univ.
Atomic Energy Comm. Postdoctoral Fellow, Mass. Inst. of Technology 51-52; Instructor in Chem. Univ. of Calif. at Berkeley 52-54, Asst. Prof. 54-59, Assoc. Prof. 59-63, Prof. of Chem. 63-; Guggenheim Fellow 69; mem. Nat. Acad. of Sciences; American Chemical Soc. awards: Calif. Section 64, Award in Petroleum Chem. 67; Humboldt Senior Scientist Award 76.
Leisure interests: music, wine, photography.
Publs. *Molecular Orbital Theory for Organic Chemists* 61, *Solvolytic Displacement Reactions* 62, *Supplemental Tables of Molecular Orbital Calculations* (with J. I. Brauman) Vols. I and II 65, *Progress in Physical Organic Chemistry* (Co-editor) Vols. I-XI 63-74, *Dictionary of π-Electron Calculations* (with C. A. Coulson) 65, *Orbital and Electron Density Diagrams* (with P. H. Owens) 73, *Introduction to Organic Chemistry* (with C. H. Heathcock) 76.
Department of Chemistry, University of California, Berkeley, Calif. 94720, U.S.A.
Telephone: 415-642-2204.

Strengers, Jan; Netherlands diplomatist; b. 22 April 1914, Utrecht; s. of Theodoor Strengers; m. Jonkvrouw Marie A. de Beaufort 1946; ed. Utrecht State Univ.
Worked at banking inst. 40-48; Ministry of Econ. Affairs 48-52; Directorate-Gen. for Econ. Co-operation, Ministry of Foreign Affairs 52-58; Minister Plenipotentiary, Head of OECD Section of Netherlands Perm. Del. to OECD and NATO 58-67; Amb. Perm. Del. to OECD 67-69; Consul-Gen. to Istanbul 69-74; Amb. to Morocco 74-.
Embassy of Netherlands, 38 rue de Tunis, Rabat, Morocco.

Strickland, The Hon. Mabel Edeline, O.B.E., C.ST.J.; Maltese journalist and politician; b. 8 Jan. 1899, Malta; d. of Lord Strickland (1st and last Baron Strickland and 6th Count della Catena, Malta) and Lady Edeline Sackville; ed. St. Mary's Coll., Hobart, Tasmania.
With Naval Cypher Office, Malta 17-18; Asst. Sec. Constitutional Party 21-45, mem. Maltese Nat. Ass. 44, Malta Legislative Assembly 50, 51-53, 62-64; Malta Chamber of Commerce 54; Managing Dir. Allied

Malta Newspapers Ltd. 38-55, Chair. 66-; Editor *Times of Malta* 35-50, *Sunday Times of Malta* 35-56; Chair. Xara Palace Hotel 49-61, 66-; Leader Progressive Constitutional Party 53-; mem. House of Reps. 64-66.
Leisure interests: gardening, poultry, swimming.
Publs. *A Collection of Essays on Malta* 55, *Maltese Constitutional and Economic Issues 1955-59* 59.
Villa Parisio, Lija, Malta.
Telephone: 41286.

Strobel, Kate; German politician; b. 23 July 1907, Nuremberg; *m.* Hans Strobel 1928; two *d.*; ed. primary and technical schools, Nuremberg.
Member Social Democrat Party (SPD) 25-; State Chair. of SPD youth org. in Bavaria; mem. Bundestag 49-72; mem. European Parl. 58-66, Vice-Pres. 62-64, Chair. Social Democratic Group 64-66; Fed. Minister of Health 66-72, Fed. Minister of Youth, Family and Health 69-72; Grosses Bundesverdienstkreuz mit Stern und Schulterband 72.
85 Nürnberg, Julius-Lossmann-Strasse 108, Federal Republic of Germany.

Stroessner, Gen. Alfredo; Paraguayan army officer and politician; b. 1912; ed. Military Coll., Asunción.
Entered Paraguayan army; commissioned 32, served through all ranks to Gen.; C.-in-C. of Armed Forces 51; Pres. of Paraguay 54-; mem. Partido Rojo; Cruz del Chaco, Cruz del Defensor, decorations from Argentina and Brazil.
Casa Presidencial, Avenida Mariscal López, Asunción, Paraguay.

Strom, Harry Edwin; Canadian politician; b. 7 July 1914, Burdett, Alberta; *m.* Ruth Strom; six *c.*
Member Alberta Legislative Assembly 55-, Minister of Agriculture 62, Minister of Municipal Affairs 68; Premier of Alberta 68-71; Leader of the official opposition 71-; Chair. Human Resources Devt. Authority; Dir. Rural Electrification Asscn., Western Canada Reclamation Asscn.; Pres. Home and School Asscn., Agricultural Improvement Asscn.; mem. South Alberta Water Conservation Asscn.
Leisure interests: skiing and outdoor sports.
205 Legislative Building, Edmonton, Alberta, Canada.
Telephone: 2293803.

Strömgren, Bengt Georg Daniel, PH.D.; Danish astronomer; b. 21 Jan. 1908; ed. Univ. of Copenhagen.
Lecturer, Univ. of Copenhagen 33, Prof. 38-40, Dir. Observatory 40; Asst. Prof. of Astrophysics, Univ. of Chicago 36-37; Assoc. Prof. 37-38; Prof. Dir. Yerkes and MacDonald Observatory, Williams Bay, Wis. 47-57; mem. Inst. for Advanced Study, Princeton 57-67; Prof. of Astronomy, Univ. of Copenhagen 67-; Pres. Danish Acad. of Sciences and Letters; Foreign mem. Nat. Acad. of Sciences (U.S.A.) 71-; mem. American Acad. of Arts and Sciences, Soc. Royale des Sciences de Liège, Royal Swedish Acad. of Sciences, Koninklijke Nederlandse Akademie van Wetenschappen, Int. Astron. Union (Gen. Sec. 48), ICSU (mem. Exec. Cttee. 48); Assoc. Royal Astron. Soc.; Hon. mem. American Astron. Soc.; Augustinus Prize Royal Soc. Gold Medal, Ole Rømer Medal.
Department of Astronomy, Københavens Universitet, Frue Plads, 1168 Copenhagen K, Denmark.

Strong, Maurice F.; Canadian international official; b. 29 April 1929, Oak Lake, Manitoba; *s.* of Frederick Milton Strong and Mary Fyfe Strong (deceased); *m.* Pauline Olivette Williams 1950; five *c.*
Served in UN Secr. 47; Pres. or Dir. of various Canadian and int. corpns. 54-66; also involved in leadership of various private orgs. in field of devt. and int. affairs; Dir.-Gen. External Aid Office of Canadian Govt. 66; (office subsequently redesignated as Canadian Int. Devt. Agency); Chair. Canadian Int. Devt. Board;

Alt. Gov. IBRD, ADB, Caribbean Devt. Bank; UN Under-Sec. Gen. with responsibility for environmental affairs 71-73, Chief Exec. for 1972 Conf. on Human Environment, Stockholm, June 72; Exec. Dir. UN Environment Programme 73-75; Chair. Petro Canada 76-; Trustee, Rockefeller Foundation 71-; several hon. degrees.
P.O. Box 2855, Calgary, Alberta, T2 P 2 M7, Canada.

Strong, Most Rev. Philip Nigel Warrington, K.B.E., C.M.G., C.ST.J., D.D., M.A., TH.D.; British ecclesiastic; b. 11 July 1899, Etwall; *s.* of late Rev. John Warrington Strong and late Rosamond Marian (née Wingfield-Digby) Strong; ed. King's School, Worcester, Selwyn Coll., Cambridge, and Bishop's Coll., Cheshunt.
Served with Royal Engineers (Signal Service) 18-19; Deacon 22, Priest 23; Curate of St. Mary's, Tyne Dock 22-26; Vicar of Christ Church, Leeds 26-31, of St. Ignatius the Martyr, Sunderland 31-36; Proctor of Convocation of York and mem. Church Assembly for Archdeaconry of Durham 36; Bishop of New Guinea 36-63; Senior Chaplain to Australian Army 43-45; mem. Legislative Council, Territory of Papua and New Guinea 55-63; Archbishop of Brisbane and Metropolitan of Queensland, Australia 63-70; Primate of Australia 66-70; Hon. Fellow Selwyn Coll., Cambridge 66-; Sub-Prelate Order of St. John of Jerusalem 67-.
Publ. *Out of Tribulation* 47.
11 Cathedral Close, Wangaratta, Victoria 3677, Australia.
Telephone: Wangaratta 215603.

Strong, Roy Colin, PH.D.; British museum director; b. 23 Aug. 1935, London; *s.* of George Edward Clement Strong and Mabel Ada Smart; *m.* Julia Trevelyan Oman (*q.v.*) 1971; ed. Queen Mary Coll., Univ. of London and Warburg Inst.
Assistant Keeper, Nat. Portrait Gallery, London 59-67, Dir. 67-73; Dir. Victoria and Albert Museum, London 74-; Organizer of Exhibitions incl. *The Elizabethan Image* (Tate Gallery) 69, *The Destruction of the Country House* (Victoria and Albert Museum) 74.
Publs. *Portraits of Queen Elizabeth I* 63, *Holbein and Henry VIII* 67, *Tudor and Jacobean Portraits* 69, *The English Icon: Tudor and Jacobean Portraiture* 69, *Van Dyck: Charles I on Horseback* 72 (with S. Orgel), *Inigo Jones: The Theatre of the Stuart Court* 72, *Splendour at Court: Renaissance Spectacle and the Theatre of Power* 73, *Nicholas Hilliard* 75, *A Garland for Elizabeth* 76.
c/o Victoria and Albert Museum, London, S.W.7, England.
Telephone: 01-589-6371.

Stronge, Rt. Hon. Sir Charles Norman Lockhart, Bt., P.C. (Northern Ireland), M.C.; British (Northern Ireland) politician; b. 23 July 1894, Bryansford; *s.* of Sir Charles E. Stronge and Marion Iliff Bostock; *m.* Gladys Olive Hall; one *s.* two *d.*; ed. Eton.
War service 14-19; M.P. for Mid-Armagh, N. Ireland Parl. 38-69; Asst. Parl. Sec. Ministry of Finance 41-42; Parl. Sec. and Chief Whip 42-44; Speaker N. Ireland House of Commons 45-69; Dir. Commercial Insurance Co. of Ireland Ltd.; Chair. Armagh County Council 45-56; Lord Lieut. Co. Armagh 39-; Pres. Royal Overseas League (N. Ireland), British Legion N. Ireland Area 49-; Hon. Col. 5th Bn. Royal Irish Fusiliers 50-63; Commdr. Order of Leopold (Belgium) 46, Belgian Croix de Guerre 18, Knight of St. John; mem. of Unionist Party.
Tynan Abbey, Tynan, Co. Armagh, N. Ireland.

Štrougal, L'ubomir, LL.D.; Czechoslovak politician; b. 10 Oct. 1924, Veselí nad Lužnicí; ed. Charles Univ., Prague.
Member C.P. of Czechoslovakia 45-; Sec. České Budějovice Regional Cttee., C.P. of Czechoslovakia 55-57, Chief Sec. 57-59; mem. Central Cttee., C.P. of Czechoslovakia 58-, Secr. of Central Cttee. 59-61; Minister of Agriculture and Forestry 59-61, of the Interior 61-65;

Deputy, Nat. Assembly 60-69; Sec. Central Cttee., C.P. of Czechoslovakia 65-68; Deputy Prime Minister 68; mem. Comm. for Questions of Living Standards, Central Cttee. 66-69, Chair. 67-68; Chair. Econ. Council 68-69; mem. Presidium, Central Cttee. of C.P. of Czechoslovakia 68-, Sec. and mem. Secr. 68-70, mem. Exec. Cttee. 68-69; Chair. Bureau for directing Party work in the Czech lands, Central Cttee. C.P. of Czechoslovakia 68-70; Deputy to Czech Nat. Council 68-; Deputy to House of the People, Fed. Assembly 69-; Prime Minister of Czechoslovak Socialist Repub. Jan. 70-; Commdr. Czech People's Militia 69; Order of Merit for Construction 58, Dimitrov Order (Bulgaria) 70, Order Stara Planina 1st Class (Bulgaria) 72, Order Victorious 73, Order of Sukhe Bator (Mongolia) 73, Order of State Banner, 1st Class (Democratic People's Republic of Korea) 73, Order of May Revolution (Argentina) 74.
Govt. Presidium of C.S.S.R., Prague, Czechoslovakia.

Stroux, Karl-Heinz; German theatre director; b. 25 Feb. 1908, Hamborn; s. of Heinrich Stroux and Maria Guinotte; m. Eva-Maria Raffel 1942; two s.; ed. Landfermanngymnasium Duisburg, Universität Berlin, and Drama School of Volksbühne, Berlin.
Actor and Asst. Dir. Volksbühne, Berlin 27-30; freelance Dir. various Berlin theatres 30-38; at Burgtheater, Vienna 38-40, Staatstheater Berlin 40-45; founded Heidelberger Kammerspiele 45; Dramatic Dir. Landestheater Darmstadt 46; Dramatic Dir. Staatstheater Wiesbaden 47-49, also Film Producer and Dir. (Nova-Film) 47-49; Dramatic Dir. Hebbeltheater, Berlin 49-51; freelance Dir. Hamburg, Vienna and Düsseldorf, and Dramatic Dir. Schiller Theater, Berlin 52-55; Financial, Dramatic and Producing Dir. Schauspielhaus, Düsseldorf 55-72; free-lance Dir. of opera and drama 72-.
Leisure interests: history, modern art, cybernetics.
4 Düsseldorf 30, Paul von Hasestrasse 14, Federal Republic of Germany.

Strowger, Gaston Jack, C.B.E.; British business executive; b. 8 Feb. 1916, Kessingland, Suffolk; s. of A. H. Strowger and Lily Ellen Tripp; m. Katherine Ellen Gilbert; two s. one d.; ed. Lowestoft Grammar School.
Joined London Electricity Supply Co. 34; served with 24th Lancers, Eighth Army 39-43; Accountant, Thorn Electrical Industries Ltd. 43, Group Chief Accountant 52, Exec. Dir. 61, mem. Board 66, Financial Dir. 67, Man. Dir. Jan. 70-, Chair. Engineering Div. 72-.
Leisure interests: gardening, fishing.
Thorn Electrical Industries Ltd., Cambridge House, Great Cambridge Road, Enfield, Middlesex, England.
Telephone: 01-363-5353.

Struminsky, Vladimir Vasilievich, D.SC.(ENG.); Soviet 5 Oct. 1925, Moscow; ed. Bolshoi Theatre Ballet School.
Soloist, Bolshoi Theatre Ballet Group 44-; People's Artist of U.S.S.R.
Principal roles include: Cinderella (*Cinderella*, Prokofiev), Juliet (*Romeo and Juliet*, Prokofiev), Giselle (*Giselle*, Adan), Princess Aurora (*Sleeping Beauty*, Tchaikovsky), Odette-Odile (*Swan Lake*, Tchaikovsky), Kitri (*Don Quixote*), Parasha (*Copper Rider*, Glier), Tao Khoa (*Red Poppy*, Glier), Maria (*Fountain of Bakhsisarai*, Asafyev), Janne, also Diana de Mirrel (*Flames of Paris*, Asafyev), Gayane (*Gayane*, Khachaturyan), Vakchanka (*Walpurgisnacht*, Gounod), etc.
State Academic Bolshoi Theatre, 1 ploshchad Sverdlova, Moscow, U.S.S.R.

Struminsky, Vladimir Vasilievich, D.SC.(ENG.); Soviet scientist (Mechanics); b. 29 April 1914, Orenburg; ed. Moscow State Univ.
Scientific work in Central Inst. of Aerohydrodynamics 41-66; Prof. Moscow Physical-Technical Inst. 47-66; Dir. U.S.S.R. Acad. of Sciences Siberian Dept. Inst. of

theoretical and applied mechanics 66-; corresp. mem. U.S.S.R. Acad. of Sciences 58-66, mem. 66-; State Prize (twice) and Lenin Prize.
Akademgorodok, Novosibirsk, U.S.S.R.

Struycken, Antonie Arnold Marie, LL.D.; Netherlands lawyer and politician; b. 27 Dec. 1906, Breda; s. of H. J. L. Struycken and M. Bogers; m. Mathea Feldbrugge 1935; six s. two d.; ed. Catholic Univ. of Nijmegen.
Solicitor in Breda 32; Alderman of Breda and mem. Prov. States 38; Head Social Services of N.V. Hollandse Kunstzijde Unie 41-45; Deputy Burgomaster Breda 45-50; Minister of Justice 50-51, 58-59, 66-67; Gov. Netherlands Antilles 51-56; Deputy Prime Minister and Minister of the Interior 56-59; mem. Council of State; Knight Order of Netherlands Lion; Grand Cross British Empire, Grand Cordon Simon Bolívar; Grand Officer Order of Orange Nassau; Catholic People's Party.
Leisure interests: stamps, golf, sailing, history.
Jan Muschlaan 54, The Hague, Netherlands.
Telephone: 245240.

Struyev, Aleksandr Ivanovich; Soviet politician; b. 1906.
Soviet and party work 25-; mem. C.P.S.U. 27-; Chair. Exec. Cttee. Donets Regional Soviet of Workers' Deputies C.P. of Ukraine 44-47, First Sec. Donets Regional Cttee. 47-53; First Sec. Perm Regional Cttee., C.P.S.U. 54-58; Deputy Chair. Council of Ministers of R.S.F.S.R. 58-63; Chair. Council of Ministers of U.S.S.R. State Cttee. for Trade 63-65; Minister of Trade 65-; mem. Central Auditing Comm., C.P.S.U. 52-56, mem. Central Cttee. of C.P.S.U. 56-61, 66-, Alt. mem. 61-66; Deputy to U.S.S.R. Supreme Soviet 46-62, 66-; Deputy to R.S.F.S.R. Supreme Soviet 62-66.
Ministry of Trade, 14 Ulitsa Razina, Moscow, U.S.S.R.

Stuart, Jesse Hilton, B.A.; American writer; b. 8 Aug. 1907; ed. Lincoln Memorial and Vanderbilt Univs. and Peabody Coll., Nashville.
Teacher, Secondary Schools; Coll. and Univ. Lecturer; Officer U.S. Naval Reserve; fmr. Visiting Prof., American Univ., Cairo.
Publs. 25 books, 279 short stories, over 1,600 poems.
Route 1, W-Hollow, Greenup, Kentucky 41144, U.S.A.

Stubbe, Hans, DR. AGR.; German geneticist; b. 7 March 1902, Berlin; ed. Landwirtschaftliche Hochschule, Berlin, and Univ. of Göttingen.
Agricultural employment 22-25; asst. at Inst. für Vererbungsforschung, Berlin 27; asst. and departmental dir. Kaiser-Wilhelm-Inst. für Züchtungsforschung, Müncheberg 29-36; Kaiser-Wilhelm-Inst. für Biologie 36-43; Dir. Kaiser-Wilhelm-Inst. für Kulturpflanzenforschung, Vienna 43-45; Prof. of General and Special Genetics and Dir. Inst. of Genetics, Univ. of Halle; Hon. Pres. Akad. der Landwirtschaftswissenschaften der D.D.R., Berlin; mem. Akad. der Wissenschaften der D.D.R. and Emer. Dir. of its Zentral-Inst. für Genetik und Kulturpflanzenforschung, Gatersleben; mem. other acads. and research bodies; Nat. Prize 49, 60, Vaterländischer Verdienstorden (silver) 54, (gold) 61; Dr. h.c., Dr. agr. h.c., Dr. Sc. h.c.
Publs. books on genetics.
4325 Gatersleben, Krs. Aschersleben, Schmiedestr. 1, German Democratic Republic.
Telephone: Gatersleben 212.

Stubblefield, Sir (Cyril) James, Kt., F.R.S., D.SC. (LOND.), A.R.C.S.; British geologist; b. 6 Sept. 1901, Cambridge; s. of James and Jane Stubblefield; m. Emily Muriel Elizabeth Yakchee 1932; two s.; ed. Perse School (Cambridge), Chelsea Polytechnic and Royal Coll. of Science, London.
Demonstrator, Geology Dept. Imperial Coll. of Science and Technology 23-28; with Geological Survey of Great

Britain and Museum of Practical Geology 28-66, Chief Palaeontologist 47-53, Asst. Dir. 53-60, Dir. 60-66; Dir. Geological Survey of N. Ireland 60-66; Pres. 6th Int. Congress Carboniferous Stratigraphy and Geology, Sheffield 67; Pres. Geological Soc., London 58-60; Pres. Palaeontographical Soc. 66-71; Gov. Chelsea Coll. of Science and Technology 58-; Corresp. mem. Paleontological Soc., U.S.A., Geological Soc., Stockholm, Geological Soc. of France, Senckenbergischen Naturforschenden Gesellschaft; Hon. Fellow, Palaeontological Soc. of India; Fellow Imperial Coll.; Hon. D.Sc. (Southampton Univ.).
Publs. *Handbook of Geology of Great Britain* (co-editor) 29, A. M. Davies's *Introduction to Palaeontology* (revised, 3rd edn.) 61.
35 Kent Avenue, Ealing, London, W13 8BE, England. Telephone: 01-997-5051.

Stücklen, Richard; German electrical engineer and politician; b. 20 Aug. 1916; ed. primary school and engineering school.
Former Industrial Dept. Man.; Army Service 40-44; then Man. in family business; mem. Bundestag 49-; Deputy Chair. Christian Democratic Union/Christian Socialist Union (C.S.U.) Group and Parl. Leader of C.S.U. 53-57, 67-; Fed. Minister of Posts and Telegraphs 57-66; awards include Grosskreuz des Verdienstordens der Bundesrepublik Deutschland, Bayerische Verdienststorden.
Bundeshaus, 53 Bonn; Home: 8832 Weissenburg, Eichstätter Strasse 27, Federal Republic of Germany.

Stummvoll, Josef Leopold, M.SC., SC.D., PH.D.; Austrian librarian; b. 19 Aug. 1902, Baden, Vienna; s. of Josef Stummvoll and Maria Gassler; m. Luise Thorngren 1939; one s. two d.; ed. Univs. of Vienna, Kiel and Leipzig.
Research Librarian and Dir. Reading Dept., Deutsche Bücherei, Leipzig 25-33, 37-39; Dir. and organizer, Library of Coll. of Agriculture and Veterinary Medicine (Yüksek Ziraat Enstitüsü) Ankara 33-37; Research librarian, Library of the Patent Office, Berlin 39-43; non-combatant war service 43-45, P.O.W. 45; Librarian (Oberstaatsbibliothekar), Austrian Nat. Library May 46, Deputy Dir.-Gen. Sept. 46, Dir.-Gen. Oct. 49-67; on leave as UNESCO Expert for development of Iranian libraries 52-53; on leave as Dir. UN Library, New York 59-63; Chair. Fed. Board of Examination in Library Science 49-69; Chair. Council on Librarianship (Austrian Ministry of Educ.) 56-67; Past Pres. Asscn. of Austrian Librarians; Pres. Int. Inst. for Youth Literature 65-72, Hon. Pres. 72-; Pres. Österreichisches Inst. für Bibliotheksforschung 66-; merit awards from Austria, Lower Austria, Italy and Vienna; Golden M.Sc. 75; Chief Editor *Biblos (Österreichische Zeitschrift für Buch und Bibliothekswesen, Dokumentation, Bibliographie und Bibliophilie)* 52- and *Biblos-Schriften* (85 vols.), *Die Österreichische Nationalbibliothek, Festschrift J. Bick* 48, *Denkmäler des Theaters, Anton Bruckner, Collected Works* (19 vols.), *Museion* Publications of the Austrian Nat. Library (20 vols.), *Corpus Papyrorum Raineri, Mitteilungen aus der Papyrussammlung* (5 vols.), *Codices Selecti* (45 vols.), *Geschichte der Österreichischen National Bibliothek 1368-1967* (2 vols.) 68-73, etc.
Leisure interests: swimming, walking, music (piano, accordion), reading (at all times).
Publs. Books on librarianship, history of science, documentation, etc., *Festschrift J. Stummvoll zum 50. Geburtstag* 52, *Bibliothek der Zukunft* 65, *Festschrift J. Stummvoll zum 65. Geburtstag* (2 vols.) 70, *Dira Necessitas* 68, *Elektronik in Bibliotheken* 69, *Die Gutenberg-Bibel, Eine Census-Übersicht* 71, *Die Österreichische National-Bibliothek im Handbuch der Bibl. Wissenschaft* 71, *J. Stummvoll: Leben und Werk* 71, *Am Beispiel eines Bibliothekars Zum* 70, *Geburtstag* 72, *Technikgeschichte u. Schrifttum* 75.

Home: Flamminggasse 36, A 2500 Baden; Office: Josefplatz 1, A 1014 Vienna, Austria.
Telephone: 02252-36565 (Home); 0222-52-52-55 (Office).

Stuyt, L. B. J., M.D., F.R.C.P.(LOND.); Netherlands politician; b. 16 June 1914, Amsterdam; m. Jkvr. E. van Ryckevorsel van Kessel 1956; three s.; ed. medical studies in Amsterdam and Leiden.
Former consultant physician, The Hague; mem. Board Catholic Univ. Nijmegen; mem. Nat. Health Council; Pres. Netherlands Soc. of Internal Med.; Minister of Public Health and Environment 71-May 73; Pres. Netherlands Central Org. for Applied Scientific Research TNO, The Hague.
Leisure interests: music, tennis, gardening.
Van Soutelandelaan 149, The Hague, Netherlands.
Telephone: 241800.

Styrikovich, Mikhail Adolfovich, D.SC.(ENG.); Soviet specialist in heat engineering; b. 16 Nov. 1902, Leningrad; ed. Leningrad Technical Inst.
Engineer, Leningrad optical glass factory 26-28; scientific worker of Central Turbine and Boiler Inst. 28-46; U.S.S.R. Acad. of Sciences Inst. of Energetics 38-60; Head, Laboratory of Research Inst. of High Temperatures 61-; Corresp. mem. U.S.S.R. Acad. of Sciences 46-64, mem. 64-; Academician-Sec. of the U.S.S.R. Acad. of Science Dept. for Physical Engineering Problems and for Energetics.
U.S.S.R. Academy of Sciences, 14 Leninsky prospekt, Moscow, U.S.S.R.

Styron, William, A.B.; American writer; b. 11 June 1925, Newport News, Va.; s. of William Styron and Pauline Abraham; m. Rose Burgunder 1953; one s. three d.; ed. Davidson Coll., Duke Univ.
Member Nat. Inst. of Arts and Letters; mem. Editorial Board, *The American Scholar*; Fellow, Silliman Coll., Yale Univ.; Pulitzer Prize for best novel 68; Howells Medal for Fiction 70; Hon. D.Hum. (Wilberforce Univ.) 67, Hon. D.Litt. (New School for Social Research, Tufts Univ., Duke Univ., Fairfield Univ.); Fellow, American Acad. of Arts and Sciences; Hon. Consultant, Library of Congress.
Leisure interests: tennis, sailing.
Publs. *Lie Down in Darkness* 51, *The Long March* 55, *Set this House on Fire* 60, *The Confessions of Nat Turner* 67, *In the Clap Shack* (play) 73.
R.F.D., Roxbury, Conn. 06783; Summer: Vineyard Haven, Mass. 02568, U.S.A.
Telephone: 203-354-5939.

Su Chen-hua; Chinese party official; b. 1909, Hunan; ed. Red Army Acad.
Joined Red Army 29; on Long March 34-35; Political Commissar 7th Army Corps, 2nd Field Army 49; Sec. CCP Kweichow 50; Deputy Political Commissar of Navy, People's Liberation Army 53, Political Commissar 57-; Adm. 56; Alt. mem. 8th Cen. Cttee. of CCP 56; Alt. mem. Politburo, 10th Cen. Cttee. of CCP 73.
People's Republic of China.

Su Yu; Chinese politician and fmr. army officer; b. 1909, Fukien; ed. Hunan Prov. No. 2 Normal School, Changte.
Commander Training Battalion, Red Army Coll. 31; Deputy Commdr. N. Kiangsu Command, New 4th Army 39; Alt. mem. 7th Cen. Cttee. of CCP 45; Deputy Commdr. 3rd Field Army 48; Acting Mayor of Nanking 49; Chief of Staff People's Liberation Army 54-58; Gen. 55; mem. 8th Cen. Cttee. of CCP 56; Vice-Minister of Nat. Defence 59-; mem. 9th Cen. Cttee. of CCP 69, 10th Cen. Cttee. 73.
People's Republic of China.

Suárez, Adolfo; Spanish lawyer and civil servant; b. 25 Sept. 1932.
Civil Gov. of Segovia until 69, then Dir.-Gen. Radio

and TV; Pres. Empresa Nacional de Turismo; now Pres. Unión del Pueblo Español; Vice Sec.-Gen. Falange until 75, Sec.-Gen. 75-.
Falange Española Tradicionalista y de las Juntas de Ofensiva Nacional-Sindicalistas, Madrid, Spain.

Suárez, Eduardo, LL.D.; Mexican lawyer and diplomatist; b. 3 Jan. 1895; ed. Colegio Municipal de Texcoco, Colegio Inglés, Tacubaya, Escuela Nacional Preparatoria, and Escuela de Jurisprudencia de la Univ. Nac. Autónoma de México.
Superintending Under-Sec., State of Hidalgo; Pres. Central Conciliation and Arbitration Board, Mexico City; Prof. of Jurisprudence, Nat. Univ. of Mexico, various times 16-48; Counsel for Mexico in claims between Mexico and U.S.A. 26-27, in claims between Mexico and the U.K. 28; mem. Arbitration Tribunal between Mexico and France; Head of Legal Dept., Ministry of Foreign Affairs 29-31, 31-34, 35; Minister of Finance and Public Credit 35-46; Amb. to U.K. 65-Aug. 70; Chevalier Légion d'Honneur; Grand Cross Order of Merit (Chile); Dr. h.c. (Nat. Univ. of Mexico). Paseo de la Reforma 645, Lomas, México 10, D.F., Mexico.

Subandrio, Dr.; Indonesian politician, diplomatist and surgeon; b. 1914; ed. Medical Univ., Jakarta.
Active in Nat. Movement as student and gen. practitioner; worked with underground anti-Japanese Forces during Second World War; forced to leave post at Jakarta Central Hospital and then established a private practice at Semarang; following Declaration of Independence abandoned practice to become Sec.-Gen., Ministry of Information and was later sent by Indonesian Govt. as special envoy to Europe; established Information Office, London 47; Chargé d'Affaires, London 49, Ambassador to Great Britain 50-54, to U.S.S.R. 54-56; Foreign Minister 57-66; Second Deputy First Minister 60-66, concurrently Minister for Foreign Econ. Relations 62-66; sentenced to death Oct. 66; sentence commuted to life imprisonment April 70. Jakarta, Indonesia.

Subba Rao, K.; Indian judge; b. 1902, Rajahmundry; s. of Subrahmaneswara Rao; m. Parijatham 1925; one s. one d.; ed. Govt. Arts Coll., Rajahmundry and Madras Law Coll.
Practice at Madras Bar 26-48; Judge, Madras High Court 48-54; Chief Justice, Andhra High Court 54-56, Andhra Pradesh High Court 56-58; Justice, Supreme Court of India 58-67, Chief Justice of India 66-67; Chancellor, Venkateswara Univ. 54, Pro-Chancellor Delhi Univ. 66-67; Hon. LL.D. (Univs. of Osmania and Bangalore).
Publs. *Fundamental Rights, Philosophy of Indian Constitution, Some Constitutional Problems, Man and Society, The Conflicts in Indian Polity, The Centre and State Relations, The Indian Democracy.*
7 Rest House Crescent, Bangalore 1, India.
Telephone: 51774.

Subbulakshmi, Madurai Shanmugavadivu; Indian singer; b. 1916; m. T. Sadasivam; ed. privately.
Recitals with mother, Veena Shanmugavadivu, 28-32, independent concerts and recitals in India 32-, and at Edinburgh Int. Festival; in London, Frankfurt, Geneva and Cairo; concert tour U.S.A. 66; numerous recordings and film appearances; Padma Bhushan decoration (Govt. of India) 54; Pres. Award for Classical Carnatic Music 56; Ramon Magsaysay Award 74; Padma Vibhushan 75; Hon. D.Lit., Shri Venkateswara Univ. 71; Hon. D.Mus., Delhi 73.
Kalki Buildings, Chetput, Madras 600031, India.

Subono, Admiral Richardus; Indonesian diplomatist and former naval officer; b. 27 June 1927, Yogjakarta; s. of R. S. Suryosumarno and R. Sukimah; m. Veronica Umboh 1959; one s. three d.; ed. naval schools.

Various appointments in the fleet, shore establishments and Naval Headquarters 50-61; Deputy C.-in-C. Theatre Command for Liberation of West Irian 62; Dir.-Gen. of Planning, Naval HQ 63; Deputy Gov. Nat. Defence Coll. 64; Deputy Chief of Staff of Navy 66; Chief of Gen. Staff, Armed Forces HQ, Ministry of Defence and Security 69; Chief of Staff of the Navy 73; Amb. to U.K. 74-; numerous medals.
Leisure interests: reading, golf.
Indonesian Embassy, 38 Grosvenor Square, London, W.1, England.

Subramaniam, Chidambaram, B.A., B.L.; Indian politician; b. 30 Jan. 1910, Pollachi, Coimbatore District of Tamil Nadu; ed. Madras Univ.
Joined Satyagraha Movement and imprisoned 32; started legal practice Coimbatore 36; political imprisonment 41, 42; Pres. Coimbatore District Congress Cttee. and mem. Working Cttee. of All-India Congress Cttee.: mem. Constituent Assembly of India 46-51, Madras Legislative Assembly 52-62; Minister of Finance, Educ. and Law, Madras State 52-62; mem. Lok Sabha 62-67, 71-; Minister of Steel 62-63, of Steel, Mines and Heavy Eng. 63-64, of Food and Agriculture 64-66, of Food, Agriculture, Community Devt. and Co-operation 66-67, of Planning, Science and Technology 71-72, of Industrial Devt., Science and Technology 72-74, of Finance 74-; Chair. Nat. Comm. on Agriculture 70; Deputy Chair. Nat. Planning Comm. 71; mem. Governing Council of Int. Wheat and Maize Improvement Centre, Mexico; mem. Board of Govs. Int. Rice Research Inst., Manila.
Publs. Travelogues in Tamil: *Countries I Visited, Around the World, India of my Dreams.*
Ministry of Finance, New Delhi; and River View, Guindy, Madras 25, India.

Subroto, M.A., PH.D.; Indonesian politician; b. 19 Sept. 1928, Surakarta; ed. Univ. of Indonesia, McGill, Stanford and Harvard Univs.
Former Dir.-Gen. of Research and Devt., Ministry of Trade; Prof. in Int. Econs., Univ. of Indonesia; Minister of Manpower, Transmigration and Co-operatives Sept. 71-.
Publs. numerous books on econ. topics.
Ministry of Manpower, Transmigration and Co-operatives, Jakarta, Indonesia.

Sucharitkul, Sompong, M.A., D.PHIL., LL.M.; Thai diplomatist and international lawyer; b. 4 Dec. 1931, Bangkok; ed. Univs. of Oxford and Paris, Harvard Law School, Middle Temple, London and Int. Law Acad., The Hague.
Lecturer in Int. Law and Relations, Chulalongkorn Univ. 56, also lecturer in Int. Econ. Law, Thammasat Univ.; mem. Nat. Research Council 59-70; joined Ministry of Foreign Affairs 59, Sec. to Minister 64-67, Dir.-Gen. Econ. Dept. 68-70; Amb. to Netherlands (also accred. to Belgium and Luxembourg) 70-73, to Japan 74-; Rep. to Thailand, UN Comm. on Int. Trade Law (UNCITRAL) 67; mem. Civil Aviation Board of Thailand; del. to various int. confs., etc.
Publs. various books and articles on int. law and int. trade law.
Royal Thai Embassy, 14-6, Kami-Osaki, 3-chome, Shinagawa-ku, Tokyo, Japan.

Suchodolski, Bogdan, PH.D.; Polish educator and philosopher; b. 27 Dec. 1903, Sosnowiec; s. of Kazimierz and Helena (Sułowska) Suchodolski; m. Maria Bartczak 1946; one d.; ed. Univs. of Warsaw, Cracow, Berlin and Paris.
Professor of Educ., Warsaw Univ. 46-68; Dir. Inst. of Pedagogical Sciences, Warsaw Univ. 58-68; Head, Inst. of History of Science and Technology, Polish Acad. of Sciences 58-73; mem. Polish Acad. of Science,

mem. Presidium 69-74; mem. Int. Asscn. for Advancement of Educational Research, Pres. 69-73; mem. European Asscn. of Comparative Educ., Vice-Pres. 64-71; mem. Int. Acad. for History of Science, Vice-Pres. 68-71; Prof. Emer. 74-; Order of Banner of Labour 1st Class, Commdr. Cross of Order Polonia Restituta and others.

Leisure interests: motor cars, travel, dogs.

Publs. *Uspolecznienie kultury* (Dissemination of Culture) 37, 47, *Wychowanie dla przyszłości* (Educ. for the Future) 47, 59, 68 (trans. into Hungarian, Italian and Spanish), *U podstaw materialistycznej teorii wychowania* (Foundations of the materialist theory of education) 57 (trans. into German, Spanish and Italian), *La pédagogie et les grands courants philosophiques* 60 (trans. into Italian and Romanian), *Narodziny nowożytnej filozofii czołwieka* (Origins of Modern Philosophy of Man) 63, 68 (trans. into Serbian and French), *Rozwój nowożytnej filozofii człoweika* (Devt. of Modern Philosophy of Man) 67, *Podstawy wychowania socjalistycznego* (Foundations of Socialist Education) 67, (trans. into Italian and Czech), *Trzy pedagogiki* (Three Pedagogies) 70 (trans. into Serbian), *La Scuola Polacca* 71, *Labirynty współczesności* (Labyrinths of the Present Time) 72, *Nasza współczesność a wychowanie* (Our Present Time and Education) with Irena Wojnar 72, *Oświata i człowiek przyszłości* (Education and Man of the Future) 74, *Kim jest człowiek?* (Who is man?) 74, *Theorie der sozialistischen Bildung* 74; editor *Wielka Encyklopedia Powszechna* (Great Encyclopaedia, 13 vols.) 62-70, *Historia Nauki Polskiej* (History of Polish Science, 5 vols.) 70-.

Ul. Smiała 63 A, 01-526 Warsaw, Poland.
Telephone: 39-20-27.

Suchoň, Eugen; Czechoslovak composer; b. 25 Sept. 1908, Pezinok; s. of Ladislav Suchoň and Serafina Suchoňová Balga; m. Herta Schischitz 1940; two c.; ed. Acad. of Music and Drama, Bratislava and Prague Conservatoire.

Professor of Composition Acad. of Music and Drama, Bratislava 33; Prof. at the Dept. of Musicology and Music Pedagogy, Bratislava Univ. 49-60, Prof. Philosophical Faculty 60-; mem. Presidium, Union of Slovak Composers 70-, Chair. 72-; mem. Cttee. Union of Czechoslovak Composers; Deputy to Slovak Nat. Council 68; Prof. Coll. of Music and Dramatic Art, Bratislava 71-; founder of the Slovak Nat. Opera; corresp. mem., Acad. of Arts of D.D.R.; Czechoslovak State Prize (3 times), Nat. Artist 58, Order of Labour 68; Kl. Gottwald State Prize 73; Dr. h.c. Univ. of Bratislava 69.

Works include: *Sonata for Violin and Piano* 30, *String Quartet* 31, *Serenade for Wind Quintet* 31, *Serenade for String Orchestra* 32, *Nox et Solitudo* (mezzo-soprano and orchestra) 32, *Little Suite with Passacaglia* (orchestra or piano) 32, *Piano Quartet* 33, *Fantasy and Burlesque for Violin and Orchestra* 33, 48, *King Svätopluk* (overture) 34, *Ballad Suite* 36, *Sonatina for Violin and Piano* 37, *Psalm of Carpathian Country* (chorus and orchestra) 38, *Svätopluk* (opera) 37-39, *From the Hills* (four male-voice choirs a capella) 40, *Krútňava* (opera, *The Vortex*) 41-49, *Metamorphoses* (orchestra) 51-52, *Pictures of Slovakia* (six cycles for piano or various instrumental and vocal ensembles) 55-56, *Sinfonietta Rustica* (orchestra) 56, *Ad Astra* (soprano and orchestra) 61, *Five Songs of Men* (mixed chorus a capella) 62, *Six Pieces for String Orchestra* 63, *Six Pieces for String Quartet* 63, *Poème Macabre* (violin and piano) 63, *Contemplazioni* (reciter and piano) 64, *Partita Rapsodica* (piano and orchestra) 65, *Kaleidoskop* (six cycles for piano or for string orchestra, percussion and piano) 68-71, *Toccata for Piano* 73, *Symphonic Fantasy on B-A-C-H for Organ, String Orchestra and Percussion* 75, *Concertino for Clarinet and Orchestra* 75.

Union of Czechoslovak Composers, Valdštejnské nám.

4, Prague I; and Bradlanská ul. 19, Bratislava, Czechoslovakia.
Telephone: Bratislava 31340.

Sucksdorff, Arne Edvard; Swedish film producer; b. 3 Feb. 1917; ed. Stockholm.

Films include the documentaries *Shadow over the Snow*, *Cliff Face*, *The Open Road*, *Rhythm of a City*, *Summer Interlude*, *Indian Village*, and *The Divided World*; also the feature films *The Great Adventure*, *The Flute and the Arrow*, *The Boy in the Tree*.

Copacabana, Casa Cabardi, Alghero, Sardinia, Italy.

Sudreau, Pierre Robert, L. en D.; French politician; b. 13 May 1919; m. France Brun 1939; two s. one d.; ed. Ecole des Sciences Politiques, Law and Letters Faculties, Paris Univ.

Served 2nd World War, prisoner in Buchenwald; Dir. de Cabinet, Sec. d'Etat à la Présidence du Conseil 46; Joint Dir. Gen., Dir. of Admin. and Gen. Affairs, Sûreté Nationale 47; Dir. Financial Services, Ministry of the Interior 49; Prefect, Loir-et-Cher 51-55; Sec. Gen. Seine Préfecture, Commr. for Reconstruction and Town Planning, Paris Region 55-58; Minister of Housing (De Gaulle cabinet) 58-59; Minister of Construction (Debré cabinet) Jan. 59-62, of Educ. (Pompidou cabinet) 62; Deputy for Loir-et-Cher 67-; mem. Union Centriste group in Nat. Assembly; Pres. Fédération des Industries Ferroviaires; Pres. Conseil français du mouvement européen 68-72, Hon. Pres. 72-; Pres. Comité Nat. pour l'aménagement du territoire français 70-; Mayor of Blois 71-; Pres. Cttee. on Industrial Reform 74; Commdr. Légion d'Honneur, Croix de Guerre, Médaille de la Résistance.

12 rue Bixio, Paris 7e, France.

Sudyets, Marshal Vladimir Aleksandrovich; Soviet army officer; b. 23 Oct. 1904, Nizhnedneprovsk, Ukraine; ed. Soviet Armed Forces Technical School and Acad. of General Staff.

Member C.P.S.U. 24-; Soviet Army 25-, held successively command posts in Soviet Fighter and Bomber Commands; Chief of Gen. Staff and Dep. C.-in-C. Soviet Air Forces 46-49; Head, Officer Training, then Commdr. Air Army 51-55; Deputy C.-in-C. Soviet Air Force, Commdr. Long Range Bomber Force 58-62; C.-in-C. Anti-Aircraft Defences and Deputy Minister of Defence U.S.S.R. 62-66; Insp.-Gen. Ministry of Defence 66-; Candidate mem. Central Cttee. C.P.S.U. 61-66; Deputy to U.S.S.R. Supreme Soviet 61-66; Hero of the Soviet Union 45, Orders of Lenin (4), Gold Star Medal Suvorov (2), Kutuzov, Red Banner (4), Red Star; Hon. K.B.E.; Marshal of Aviation 55-.

Ministry of Defence, Naberezhnaya M. Thoreza 34, Moscow U.S.S.R.

Suenens, H.E. Cardinal Leon-Joseph, D.D., PH.D., B.C.L.; Belgian ecclesiastic; b. 16 July 1904, Ixelles; ed. Pontifical Gregorian Univ., Rome.

Ordained Priest 27; Teacher, Institut Sainte-Marie, Brussels 29; Lecturer in Philosophy, Malines Seminary 30-40; Vice-Rector, Louvain Univ. 40-45; Private Chamberlain to Pope 41; Auxiliary Bishop and Vicar-Gen. of Archdiocese of Malines 45-61; Archbishop of Malines-Brussels and Primate of Belgium 61-; Created Cardinal 62; Moderator of Vatican Council 62-65; mem. Pontifical Comm. for Revision of Canon Law 62-; Pres. Belgian Bishops' Conf. 66-; Templeton Foundation Prize 76.

Publs. *Theology of the Legion of Mary, Edel-Mary Quinn, The Right View on Moral Re-armament, The Gospel to Every Creature, Mary the Mother of God, Love and Control, The Nun in the World, Christian Life Day by Day, Co-responsibility in the Church, The Future of the Christian Church, A New Pentecost?*

Aartsbisdom, Wollemarkt 15, 2800 Mechelen, Belgium.
Telephone: 015-21-65-01.

Suess, Hans Eduard, PH.D.; American professor of geochemistry; b. 16 Dec. 1909, Vienna, Austria; s. of Franz Eduard Suess and Olga Frenzl; m. Ruth V. Teuteberg 1940; one s. one d.; ed. Univ. of Vienna.
Instructor, Univ. of Vienna 33-35; Research Asst., Fed. Technical High School, Zurich, Switzerland 35-36, Univ. of Hamburg, Germany 37-39; Asst. Prof. 40-47; Assoc. Prof. 48-50; Research Fellow, Univ. of Chicago, U.S. 50-51; Physical Chemist, U.S. Geological Survey, Washington, D.C. 51-55; Research Chemist, Scripps Inst. of Oceanography, La Jolla, Calif. 55-58; Prof. of Geochem., Univ. of Calif., San Diego 58-; Guggenheim Fellow 66; mem. American Acad. of Arts and Science, N.A.S., Austrian and Heidelberg Acads. of Sciences, Max Planck Soc.; Gold Medal of American Geochem. Soc. (Goldschmidt Medal) 74.
Publs. 130, in Geochemistry, Oceanography, Nuclear Physics and Cosmochemistry.
Department of Chemistry, University of California, San Diego, La Jolla, Calif. 92037, U.S.A.
Telephone: 714-453-0183.

Sueyoshi, Toshio, B.A.(ECON.); Japanese business executive; b. 13 Feb. 1907, Tokyo; s. of Yasuma Sueyoshi and Masu Hamada; m. Hiroko Watanabe 1936; three s. one d.; ed. Tokyo Univ. of Commerce.
Mitsui Mining Co. 30-31; Miike Nitrogen Industries Co. 31-37; Toyo Koatsu Industries Inc. 37-68, Dir. 47-55; Man. Dir. 55-57, Vice-Pres. 57-68; Vice-Pres. Mitsui Toatsu Chemicals Inc. 68-70, Pres. 70-; Pres. Japan Phosphatic and Compound Fertilizers Mfrs. Asscn. 71; Blue Ribbon Medal 68.
Leisure interests: golf, mahjong, "Go".
Mitsui Toatsu Chemicals Inc., 2-5, Kasuimgaseki 3-chome, Chiyoda-ku, Tokyo; Home: 45-7, Kitasenzoku 2-chome, Ohta-ku, Tokyo, Japan.
Telephone: 581-6111 (Office); 729-2270 (Home).

Sugaï, Kumi; Japanese painter; b. 1919; ed. Osaka School of Fine Arts.
One-man shows, Galerie Cruen, Paris, Palais des Beaux Arts, Brussels 54, St. George's Gallery, London 55, Galerie Legendre, Paris 57; rep. at Pittsburgh Carnegie Int. Exhbn. 55, and Salon des Réalités Nouvelles 56, 57, Salon de Mai 57, 58, Salon Biennale 57 (all Paris) and Dunn Int. Exhbn., London 63; Int. Painting Prize, São Paulo Bienal 65.
Publ. La Quête sans Fin.
37 rue de la Tombe Issoire, Paris 14e, France.

Sugitani, Takeo, B.L.; Japanese banker; b. 7 Aug. 1903, Miyagi Pref.; s. of Taizan and Tai Sugitani; m. Miho Tayui 1928; one d.; ed. Tokyo Imperial Univ.
Joined the Mitsui Trust Co. Ltd. 26; Dir. The Tokyo Trust & Banking Co. Ltd. 48; Man. Dir. The Mitsui Trust and Banking Co. Ltd. 53, Pres. 60-68, Chair. 68-71, Counsellor 71-; Auditor, Mitsui Petrochemical Industries Ltd. 67-; Adviser, Mitsui Real Estate Co. Ltd. 61-, Mitsui Mining Co. Ltd. 64-; Counsellor, Auditor Japan Women's Univ. 73.
Leisure interests: reading, golf.
The Mitsui Trust & Banking Co. Ltd., 1-1 Muromachi, 2-chome, Nihonbashi, Chuo-ku, Tokyo; 14-5 Meguro 3-chome, Meguro-ku, Tokyo, Japan.
Telephone: 03-712-1600.

Sugiura, Binsuke; Japanese banker; b. 13 Nov. 1911, Tokyo; m. Chizuko Hayashida 1939; three d.; ed. Tokyo Univ.
Director, Long-Term Credit Bank of Japan Ltd. 58-61, Man. Dir. 61-68, Senior Man. Dir. 68-69, Deputy Pres. 69-71, Pres. 71-.
Leisure interest: golf.
The Long Term Credit Bank of Japan Ltd., 2-4, Otemachi 1-chome, Chiyoda-ku, Tokyo 100; Home: 31-5, Kami-Meguro 3-chome, Meguro-ku, Tokyo 153, Japan.
Telephone: 211-5111 (Office); 719-5505 (Home).

Suharto, Lt.-Gen. T. N. J.; Indonesian army officer and politician; b. 8 June 1921, Kemusa, Yogjakarta; m. Siti Hartinah 1947; eight c.; ed. military schools and Indonesian Army Staff and Command Coll.
Officer in Japanese-sponsored Indonesian Army 43; Battalion, later Regimental, Commdr. Yogjakarta 45-50; Regimental Commdr., Central Java 53; Brig.-Gen. 60; Deputy Chief of Army Staff 60-65; Chief of Army Staff 65-68, Supreme Commdr. 68-73; Minister of Army 65; Deputy Prime Minister for Defence and Security 66; Chair. of Presidium of Cabinet 66-67, in charge of Defence and Security, also Minister of Army July 66; Full Gen. 66; Acting Pres. of Indonesia 67-68; Prime Minister 67-, concurrently Minister for Defence and Security 67-73; Pres. of Indonesia March 68-.
Presidium Office, 15 Jalan Merdeka Utara; Home: 8 Jalan Tjendana, Jakarta, Indonesia.

Suhrbier, Max, DR. IUR.; German lawyer and politician; b. 12 Oct. 1902, Rostock; m. Edith Wick 1929; one s. one d.; ed. Realgymnasium and Univ. Rostock.
Councillor for Finance, Govt. of Mecklenburg 45-48, Minister of Finance, Mecklenburg 48-52; Deputy Chair. Council of Schwerin District 52-59; mem. Länderkammer 49-50; mem. Volkskammer 50-58, 63-; Deputy Minister of Finance of German Dem. Repub. (D.D.R.) 59-60; Chair. Liberal-Demokratische Partei 60-67, Hon. Chair. 67-; Deputy Chair. Council of Ministers of D.D.R. 60-65; mem. Council of Nat. Front; Ehrenspange zum Vaterländischen Verdienstorden in Gold, Banner der Arbeit.
Leisure interest: literature.
Liberal-Demokratische Partei Deutschlands, Taubenstrasse 48-49, Berlin, W.8, German Democratic Republic.

Suitner, Otmar; Austrian conductor; b. 16 May 1922, Innsbruck; s. of Karl Suitner and Maria Rizzi; m. Marita Wilckens 1948; ed. Pädagogium Innsbrück, Mozarteum Salzburg.
Music Dir. in Remscheid 52-57; Gen. Dir. of Pfalzorchester in Ludwigshafen/Rh. 57-60; Gen. Dir. of State Opera Dresden 60-64; Gen. Dir. German State Opera Berlin 64-; Hon. Conductor Nippon Hoso Kyokai Orchestra, Tokyo 73; Guest Conductor San Fransisco, Tokyo, Vienna, Bayreuth Festival, etc.; many recordings; led course for conductors, Int. Summer Acad. Univ. Mozarteum, Salzburg 75, 76; Prof. 68; Commendatore, Gregorian Order 73.
Berlin-Niederschönhausen, Platanenstr. 13, German Democratic Republic; and Innsbruck, Stamserfeldstr. 1, Austria.

Suits, Chauncey Guy, B.A., D.SC.; American physicist; b. 12 March 1905; ed. Univ. of Wisconsin and Swiss Fed. Inst. of Technology.
Physics Consultant, U.S. Forest Products Laboratory, Madison, Wis. 29-30; Research Physicist, Gen. Electric Co., Research Laboratory, Schenectady, N.Y. 30-40, Asst. to Dir. 40-45; Vice-Pres. and Dir. of Research 45-66; Chief, Div. 15 of Nat. Defence Research Cttee. of Office of Scientific Research and Development, Govt., and mem. Div. 14 of N.D.R.C. of O.S.R.D. 42-46; mem. Naval Research Advisory Cttee. 56-64, Chair. 58-61; mem. N.Y. State Science and Tech. Foundation 65-, Vice-Chair. 68-; Consultant Industrial Research Management; mem. Nat. Acad. of Sciences, American Philosophical Soc., Nat. Acad. of Engineering; Silliman Lecturer, Yale Univ. 52; H.M. Medal for Service in the Cause of Freedom 48; Medal for Merit 48; Procter Prize Award—RESA 58; Hon. D.Sc. (Union and Hamilton Colls., Drexel Inst. of Technology, Marquette Univ.), Hon. D.Eng. (Rensselaer Polytechnic Inst.) 50.
Home: Crosswinds, Pilot Knob, N.Y. 12844, U.S.A.

Suk, Josef; Czechoslovak violinist; b. 1929, Prague; great-grandson of Antonin Dvořák; grandson of Josef

Suk; ed. Prague Conservatory and studied with Jaroslav Kocian.

First violinist, Prague String Quartet 50; founded Suk Trio 52; has performed as a soloist or with trio throughout the world; Grand Prix du Disque 60, 66, 68, 74, Czechoslovak State Prize 64, Edison Prize 72, Wiener Flötenuhr 74.

Karlovo Namesti 5, 12000 Prague 2, Czechoslovakia. Telephone: 299407.

Sukati, Samuel Thornton Msindazwe, M.B.E., B.A.; Swazi diplomatist; b. 11 June 1910, Manzini District; s. of Chief Lomadokola and Landvwako Sukati; m. Grissel Thokozile (née Nkumane) 1937; four s. four d.; ed. school at Zombodze and Lovedale Inst., Cape Province, South Africa.

First Swazi Revenue Clerk, Swaziland Govt. 35; Senior Liaison Officer between Swazi King and Central Govt. 44; First Establishment Officer, Swaziland Govt., and first Swazi to be in Senior and Pensionable Service 50; attended Overseas Civil Service Course, London School of Econs. 55; Chair. Council of Univ. of Botswana, Lesotho and Swaziland 66; First Speaker House of Assembly 67; Amb. of Kingdom of Swaziland to U.S.A., Amb. and Perm. Rep. to UN, and High Commr. in Canada 68-73; mem. UN Cttee. for Elimination of all forms of racial discrimination 69-73; Exec. Chair. Nat. Industrial Devt. Corpn. of Swaziland 73-; Certificate of Honour and Badge 45; Hon. LL.D. 68.

Leisure interest: reading.

National Industrial Development Corporation of Swaziland, P.O. Box 866, Mbabane, Swaziland. Telephone: Mbabane 2833.

Sukhadia, Mohan Lal, L.E.E.; Indian politician; b. 1916, Jhalawar, Rajasthan; s. of Shri Purshottamdras; m. Smt Indubala Sukhadia; two s. five d.; ed. Nathdwara (Udaipur) and Bombay Univ.

Active mem. Praja Mandal organization in former Mewar State 39-; interned during "Quit India" movement 42; fmr. Minister for Civil Supplies, Post-War Development, Relief and Rehabilitation, Mewar State 46; Minister of Development when State of Rajasthan was first formed; mem. Rajasthan Legislative Ass.; Minister for Civil Supplies, Agriculture and Irrigation 51-52, Minister for Revenue (except Forests and Co-operation) and Famine Relief 52-54; Chief Minister, Rajasthan 54-71; Gov. of Karnataka (fmrly. Mysore) 72-75; Gov. of Andhra Pradesh 75-; LL.D. h.c., Univ. of Udaipur 74; Congress Party.

Leisure interests: cricket, indoor games, social studies.

Office of the Governor, Hyderabad, Andhra Pradesh, India.

Sukselainen, Vieno Johannes; Finnish economist and politician; b. 12 Oct. 1906, Paimio; m. Elma Bonden 1938; three s. one d.

Lecturer, School of Social Sciences, Helsinki 39; Sec. to Prime Minister 41-45; teacher of political economics, Univ. of Turku 45-47; Prof. School of Social Sciences, Univ. of Tampere 47-54, Rector 53-54, Chancellor 69-; Pres. of the Agrarian Union 45-64; mem. Finnish Parl. 48-70, 72-, Speaker 56-57, 58-59, 68-70, 72-; Minister of Finance 50-51 and 54; Minister of Interior 51-53; Gen. Dir. People's Pension Inst. 54-71; Prime Minister May-Nov. 57, 59-61; mem. Nordic Council, Pres. 72.

Leisure interest: agriculture.

Tapiola, Finland.
Telephone: Helsinki 462189.

Suleiman, Ahmed; Sudanese diplomatist; b. 1924; ed. Faculty of Law, Cairo Univ.

Minister of Agriculture 64; Deputy to Constituent Assembly; fmr. Chair. Sudan Peace Cttee.; Amb. to U.S.S.R. 69-Oct. 69; Minister of Economy and Foreign Trade Oct. 69-June 70; Minister of Industry and Mining 70-71, of Justice 71-73; Amb. to U.K. 73-75; has

attended many int. confs. sponsored by World Peace Council and Afro-Asian People's Solidarity Org.

c/o Ministry of Foreign Affairs, Khartoum, The Sudan.

Sulek, Miroslav; Czechoslovak journalist; b. 15 March 1918, Tábor; ed. Charles Univ., Prague.

Imprisoned and in underground movement 40-45; worked in youth and students orgs. 45-46; posts in District Orgs. of Communist Party of Czechoslovakia, later Central Cttee. 46-62; Gen. Dir. Czechoslovak News Agency 62-68; mem. Presidium, Central Cttee. Union of Czechoslovak Journalists 63-68; Chair. of Board, Photo Int. 65-68; Amb. to Romania 70-; Order of 25th Feb. 1948, Resistance Award, Award for Merit in Construction 65, Order of Labour 68, Bulgarian Order of Labour.

Embassy of Czechoslovakia, Strada Ion Ghica 11, Sector 4, Bucharest, Romania.
Telephone: 15-91-41.

Suliotis, Elena; Greek soprano opera singer; b. 28 May 1943, Athens; d. of Constantino Souliotis and Gallia Cavalengo; m. Marcello Guerrini 1970; ed. Buenos Aires and Milan.

Grew up in Argentina; went to Milan and was introduced to Gianandrea Gavazzeni 62; studied singing with Mercedes Llopart; debut in Cavalleria Rusticana, Teatro San Carlo, Naples 64; sang Amelia in Un Ballo in Maschera, Trieste 65 and has since sung frequently throughout Italy; debut at La Scala as Abigail in Nabucco 66; U.S. debut as Helen of Troy in Mefistofele, Chicago 66; debut at Covent Garden as Lady Macbeth 69; has also appeared at Teatro Colon, Buenos Aires and in Rio de Janeiro, São Paulo, Mexico City, New York, Dallas, Philadelphia, San Antonio, Montreal, Paris, Kiel, Lübeck, Höchst, Tokyo, Lisbon, Athens and Madrid; repertoire includes Manon Lescaut, La Gioconda. Macbeth, Norma, Otello, Aida, Luisa Miller, Il Trovatore, Tosca, Loreley, la Forza del Destino, etc.; has recorded Norma, Cavalleria Rusticana, Nabucco, Anna Bolena, Macbeth and arias for Decca; recipient of several prizes.

Leisure interests: country life, looking after plants and animals.

Villa il Poderino, Via Incontri 38, Florence, Italy; Herbert H. Breslin, Inc., 119 West 57th Street, Room 1505, New York 10019, U.S.A.

Sullivan, Charles Andrew; American business executive; b. 3 Nov. 1920, Washington; s. of Michael Francis and Gertrude Lavinia (Miller) Sullivan; m. Katherine Reynolds McCarthy 1943; ed. George Washington Univ. and Cambridge, England.

Commercial specialist Treasury Dept. 40-43; served U.S. Army 43-46; economist, Reconstruction Finance Corpn., War Assets Admin. 46-48; int. economist Munitions Board 48-51; staff office Sec. of Defence for Int. Security Affairs 51-57, Chief Far East Div. 51-52, Chief Western Hemisphere Far East and South Asian Affairs 52-53, Dir. Office Int. Affairs 55-57; Asst. Dir. Office of Defence Mobilization 57-59, Deputy Special Asst. to Under-Sec. of State for Disarmament and Atomic Energy 59-60; Special Asst. to Under-Sec. of State Dept., State 60-61; Asst. to Treasury 61-66; Pres. and Chair. Board of Dirs. Hispano Corpn. of America 67-71; Pres. and Chair. Board of Dirs. Charles A. Sullivan Assoc. Inc. 70-; mem. Board of Dirs. Chemalloy Minerals Ltd., Canada, Templet Industries Inc., New York; mem. Board Int. Advisory Cttee., American Security and Trust Co., Washington, D.C.; Chair. Industrial Mobilization Cttee. NATO 50-51; Defence Adviser to del. of ANZUS, NATO and SEATO councils 52-57; mem. numerous other dels, and cttees.

Barr Building, 910 17th Street, N.W., Washington, D.C. 20006; Home: 1539 29th Street, N.W., Washington, D.C. 20007, U.S.A.

Sullivan, Eugene John, B.S., M.B.A.; American business executive; b. 28 Nov. 1919, New York; s. of Cornelius and Margaret Sullivan; m. Gloria Roesch; three s. one d.; ed. St. John's Univ. and New York Univ.
With Borden Chemical 46-, Vice-Pres. Sales 57, Exec. Vice-Pres. 58-64, Pres. 64, Vice-Pres. Borden Co. 64-67, Exec. Vice-Pres. 67-73, Dir. 67-, Pres. 73-; Adjunct Prof. St. John's Univ. Business School 74-; Trustee Emigrant Savings Bank; Dir. St. Francis Hospital, Long Island; mem. Council, St. John's Univ. Alumni Asscn.; Hon. Ph.D. (St. John's Univ.) 73. Leisure interest: carpentry.
Borden, Inc., 277 Park Avenue, New York, N.Y. 10017; Home: 465 Manhasset Woods Road, Manhasset, N.Y. 11030, U.S.A.
Telephone: (212) 573-4176 (Office).

Sullivan, Fred R., B.S., M.B.A.; American business executive; b. 22 Aug. 1914, Fort Wayne, Ind.; s. of Walter H. and Grace P. Sullivan; m. Judith O. Omanoff 1967; one s. two d.; Rutgers and New York Univs. Joined Monroe Calculating Machine Co. 34, Pres. 53; Monroe merged with and became Div. of Litton Industries Inc. 58; Senior Vice-Pres. and Dir. Litton Industries 58-64; Pres. Walter Kidde & Company Inc. 64-, Chair. of Board 66-.
Walter Kidde & Company Inc., 9 Brighton Road, Clifton, N.J. 07012, U.S.A.
Telephone: 201-777-6500.

Sullivan, John Lawrence, A.B., LL.B.; American lawyer; b. 16 June 1899, Manchester, N.H.; s. of Patrick and Ellen Sullivan; m. Priscilla Manning 1928; one s. two d.; ed. Dartmouth Coll. and Harvard Univ. Served in U.S. Navy, First World War 18; admitted to New Hampshire Bar 23; began practice in Manchester, N.H., as mem. of firm Sullivan and White 24; County Solicitor Hillsborough County 29-33; Partner, Sullivan and Sullivan 30; became sole owner 31; now senior partner Sullivan & Wynot, Manchester, N.H., and Sullivan, Shea & Kenney, Washington, D.C.; Asst. to Commr. of Internal Revenue Sept. 39; Asst. Sec. of the Treasury Jan. 40-Nov. 44; Asst. Sec. of Navy for Air July 45-June 46; Under-Sec. of the Navy June 46-47; Sec. of the Navy 47-49; Dir. Aluminium Ltd., The Martin Marietta Corpn., Brown Co., Nat. Savings and Trust Co., M.G.M., Naval Historical Foundation, Navy League of the U.S.; mem. Nat. Advisory Council, Foundation for Religious Action in Social and Civil Order; mem. Advisory Board, Inst. of Contemporary Russian Studies, Fordham Univ.; Hon. LL.D. (Duquesne, New Hampshire, Portland Univs., Dartmouth, Loyola Colls.); Democrat.
1330 Union Street, Manchester, N.H. 63104, U.S.A.
Telephone: 202-338-1000 (Washington, D.C.).

Sullivan, Walter Seager; American journalist and author; b. 12 Jan. 1918, New York City; s. of Walter S. and Jeanet E. L. Sullivan; m. Mary E. Barrett 1950; one s. two d.; ed. Groton School and Yale Univ.
Field Work, Alaska, American Museum of Natural History 35; New York Times 40-; U.S. Navy 40-46; Foreign Corresp., Far East, New York Times 48-50; UN 50-52, Germany and Berlin 52-56, U.S. Antarctic Expeditions 46-47, 54-55, 56-57, Science News Editor 60-63, Science Editor 64-; Gov. Arctic Inst. of North America 59-66; Councillor, American Geographical Soc. 59-; Fellow, American Asscn. for Advancement of Science; Hon. H.L.D. (Yale), (Newark Coll. of Eng.) 73; Hon. D.Sc. (Hofstra Univ.) 75; Westinghouse Award of American Asscn. for Advancement of Science 63, 68, 72; George Polk Memorial Award, New York 59; Int. Non-Fiction Book Prize, Frankfurt 65, Grady Award, American Chemical Soc. 69, American Inst. Physics U.S. Steel Foundation Award in Physics and Astronomy 69, Washburn Medal, Boston Museum of Science 72,

Daly Medal, American Geographical Soc. 73, Ralph Coats Roe Medal, American Soc. Mech. Eng. 75.
Leisure interest: chamber music.
Publs. Quest for a Continent 57, White Land of Adventure 57, Assault on the Unknown 61, We Are Not Alone 64, Continents in Motion 74.
Office: New York Times, Times Square, New York; Home: 66 Indian Head Road, Riverside, Conn., U.S.A.
Telephone: 203-637-3318.

Sullivan, William Healy; American diplomatist; b. 12 Oct. 1922; ed. Brown Univ. and Fletcher School of Law and Diplomacy.
U.S. Navy 43-46; Foreign Service 47-, served Bangkok 47-49, Calcutta 49-50, Tokyo 50-52, Rome 52-55, The Hague 55-58; Officer-in-Charge, Burma Affairs, Dept. of State 58-59; Foreign Affairs Officer 59; UN Adviser, Bureau of Far Eastern Affairs 60-63; Special Asst. to Under-Sec. for Political Affairs 63-64; Amb. to Laos 64-69; Deputy Asst. Sec. of State for E. Asia (with special responsibility for Viet-Nam); Amb. to the Philippines 73-.
American Embassy, Roxas Boulevard, Manila, Philippines.

Sullo, Fiorentino; Italian politician; b. 29 March 1921, Paternopoli, Avelloni; m. Elvira di Laurentiis 1961; one d.
Member of Constituent Assembly 46-48, of Chamber of Deputies 48-; fmr. Under-Sec. for Defence, Under-Sec. for Industry and Commerce, Under-Sec. for State Participation; Minister of Transport 60, of Labour and Social Insurance 60-62, of Public Works and Regions 62-63, of Educ. 68-69; Minister without portfolio for scientific and technological research 72-73, for regions 73; Editor Le Discussione 66-69; Pres. Christian Democrat group in Parl. 68; resigned from Christian Democrat Party 74; mem. Social Democrat Party 74-.
Leisure interest: tennis.
Camera dei Deputati, Montecitorio, Rome, Italy.
Telephone: (06) 345-10-31.

Sulman al-Khalifah, H. H. Shaikh Isa bin (see Isa bin Sulman al-Khalifah, H.H. Shaikh).

Sultan, Syed Abdus, B.A., LL.B.; Bangladesh politician; b. 1 Feb. 1917, Bangladesh; s. of Syed Adbur Rauf (deceased) and Lutfun Nisa (deceased); m. Begum Kulsum 1938; two s. two d.; ed. Calcutta and Dacca Univs.
Advocate of the Supreme Court of fmr. Pakistan, now Bangladesh, and mem. of the fmr. Pakistan Bar Council; elected to Nat. Assembly 62 and became Deputy Leader of the Opposition; attended and participated in the Inter-Parl. Union Conf., Belgrade 63; fmr. Senior Vice-Pres. Pakistan Postal Union, fmr. Pres. E. Pakistan Postal Union; political disciple of late Hussain Shahid Suhrawardy, worked in close asscn. with late Sheikh Mujibur Rahman; Awami League Rep. to the Nat. Assembly and mem. Awami League's Constitution Drafting Cttee. 70-71; played an important part in the training of the Mukti Bahini and for the projection of the cause of Bangladesh to various int. forums, incl. the UN Gen. Assembly and the Security Council; High Commr. for the People's Repub. of Bangladesh in the U.K. 72-75; Senior mem. Bengali Acad., Dacca, mem. Writers Guild of fmr. Pakistan.
Leisure interest: literature.
Publs. Pancha Nadir Palimati, Monirag, Juge Juge Manush (historical work), Taruner Jinnah (biography), Ibne Sina (biography), Sabuj Kahini (juvenile), Genocide in Bangladesh; translation of American short stories into Bengali.
c/o Ministry of Foreign Affairs, Dacca, Bangladesh.

Sulzberger, Arthur Ochs; American newspaper executive; b. 5 Feb. 1926, New York; s. of Arthur Hays and Iphigene Ochs Sulzberger; ed. Columbia Univ.

U.S. Marine Corps., Second World War and Korean War; The New York Times Co., New York City 51-, Asst. Treas. 58-63, Pres. and Publisher 63-; Dir., Times Printing Co., Chattanooga, Spruce Falls Power and Paper Co. Ltd., Gaspesia Pulp and Paper Co. Ltd. of Canada; Chair. Teaching Systems and Resources Corpn.; Trustee Columbia Univ., mem. Coll. Council.
229 West 43rd Street, New York City, N.Y. 10036, U.S.A.
Telephone: 556-1234.

Sulzberger, Cyrus Leo, B.S.; American journalist; b. 27 Oct. 1912; ed. Harvard Univ.
Columnist for *New York Times*.
Publs. *Sit Down with John L. Lewis* 38, *The Big Thaw* 56, *What's Wrong with U.S. Foreign Policy* 59, *My Brother Death* 61, *The Test: de Gaulle and Algeria* 62, *Unfinished Revolution* 65, *History of World War II* 66, *A Long Row of Candles, Memoirs and Diaries 1934-54* 69, *The Last of the Giants* 70, *The Tooth Merchant* 73, *Unconquered Souls—The Resistentialists* 73, *The Age of Mediocrity* 73, *The Coldest War— Russia's Game in China* 74, *Postscript with a Chinese Accent* 74.
New York Times, 3 rue Scribe, Paris 9e, France.

Sulzer, Georg; Swiss mechanical engineer and business executive; b. 29 Dec. 1909, Winterthur; m. Lilo Schwarzenbach 1943; one s. two d.; ed. Kantonsschule, Winterthur, and Eidgenössische Technische Hochschule, Zürich.
Direct descendant (fourth generation) of founders of Sulzer Brothers; joined Sulzer Brothers 34, started in Technical Draftsman's School, spent three years with Sulzer Brothers, Paris; Man. Diesel Engine Sales Dept., Sulzer Brothers 45-48, Man. Dir., Sulzer Brothers 48-75, Chair. of Board 59-; mem. Board of Swiss Nat. Bank.
Rychenbergstrasse 85, CH-8400 Winterthur, Switzerland.
Telephone: 22-14-43.

Summer, James A.; American business executive; b. 12 June 1923, Dallas, Tex.; m.; four c.; ed. Southern Methodist Univ., and U.S. Mil. Acad. and Univ. of Michigan.
Former Officer, U.S.A.F.; Export Man. Lycoming Div., Avco Corpn. 57, subsequently directed radar and satellite systems projects, Advanced Research and Devt. Div. until 60; joined Gen. Mills Inc. 60, Gen. Man. Electronics Div. 62, Corporate Controller 65; Man. Dir. Smiths Food Group Ltd., U.K. (now a subsidiary of Gen. Mills) 67-; Dir., Exec. Vice-Pres. and Chief Operating Officer, Gen. Mills 68, Pres. and Chief Operating Officer 69-, Vice-Chair. of Board, Chief Devt. and Financial Officer 73-; Dir. Northwestern Nat. Bank of Minneapolis.
General Mills Inc., P.O. Box 1113, Minneapolis, Minn. 55440, U.S.A.

Summerskill, Baroness (Life Peeress) cr. 61, of Ken-Wood in the County of London; **Edith Clara Summerskill**, P.C., C.H., LL.D.; British physician and politician; b. 1901, London; d. of William and Edith Summerskill; m. Dr. E. Jeffrey Samuel 1925; one s. one d.; ed. King's Coll., London, and Charing Cross Hospital.
Qualified Doctor 24; Vice-Pres. Socialist Medical Asscn.; Labour M.P. for West Fulham 38-55, Warrington 55-61; Chair. of Labour Party 55; mem. Middx. County Council for Green Lanes Div. of Tottenham; mem. Cttee. on Women's Services 42, Women's Consultative Cttee. to Ministry of Labour, Women-Power Cttee.; Pres. Married Women's Asscn.; Parl. Sec. Ministry of Food 45-50; Minister of Nat. Insurance 50-51.
Publs. *Women, Fall In* 41, *Babies Without Tears* 41, *The Ignoble Art* 56, *Letters to my Daughter* 58, *A Woman's World* 67.
Pond House, Millfield Lane, Highgate, London, N6 6YD, England.

Summerson, Sir John Newenham, C.B.E., F.B.A., F.S.A., A.R.I.B.A.; British architectural historian; b. 25 Nov. 1904, Darlington; s. of Samuel Summerson and Dorothea Newenham; m. Elizabeth Hepworth 1938; three s.; ed. Univ. Coll., London.
Served in architects' offices and taught Edinburgh Coll. of Art 29-30, took up architectural journalism; on staff *Architect and Building News* 34-40; Deputy Dir. Nat. Bldgs. Record 40-45; Curator Sir John Soane's Museum 45-; mem. Royal Comm. on Historical Monuments, Historic Bldgs. Council Dept. of Environment); Chair. Nat. Council for Diplomas in Art and Design 60-69; Lecturer in History of Architecture, Birkbeck Coll. 61-70; Slade Prof. of Fine Art, Oxford 58-59; Ferens Prof. of Fine Art, Hull 60-61, 70-71, Slade Prof. of Fine Art, Cambridge 66-67; Bampton Lecturer, Columbia 67-68; Hon. mem. American Acad. of Arts and Sciences; Hon. D.Litt. (Leicester, Oxford, Hull and Newcastle), Hon. D.Sc. (Edinburgh).
Publs. *John Nash* 34, *Georgian London* 45, *Heavenly Mansions* 49, *Sir John Soane* 52, *Sir Christopher Wren* 53, *Architecture in Britain 1530-1830* (Pelican History of Art) 53, *The Classical Language of Architecture* 64, *Book of John Thorpe* (Walpole Soc., Vol. XL) 66, *Inigo Jones* 66, *Victorian Architecture* 70.
1 Eton Villas, London, N.W.3, England.
Telephone: 01-722-6247.

Sun Chien; Chinese government official.
Vice-Premier, State Council 75.
People's Republic of China.

Sun Yat-sen, Madame (see Sung Ch'ing-ling).

Sunay, Gen. Cevdet; Turkish army officer and politician; b. 10 Feb. 1900; ed. Kuleli Military Lyceum, Istanbul and Military Acad.
With Turkish Army 16-66; served in Palestine 17, later under Atatürk; Capt. 30; Officer Operations Dept. Gen. Staff 33; Teacher Mil. Acad. 42-47; Commdr. Artillery Regt. 47; Chief Operations Dept. Gen. Staff; Gen. 59; Deputy Chief Gen. Staff Aug. 58-May 60; C.-in-C. Land Forces 60, Chief of Staff Aug. 60-66; Senator 66, 73-; Pres. of Turkey 66-73; Hon. K.C.B. 67.
Akbaş sok. Botanik Apt. 2/5, Çankaya-Ankara, Turkey.

Sundaravadivelu, Neyyadupakkam Duraiswamy, M.A.; Indian educational administrator; b. 15 Oct. 1912, Neyyadupakkam, Madras (now Tamil Nadu); s. of Duraiswamy Mudaliar and Saradambal; m. Kanthamma 1940; ed. Univ. of Madras.
District Educ. Office 42-51; Deputy Dir. of Public Instruction 51-54, Dir. of Public Instruction and Public Libraries 54-65; Dir. of Public Libraries and of Higher Educ., Tamil Nadu 65-66; Joint Educ. Adviser to Govt. of India, Ministry of Educ. 66-68, Chief Educ. Adviser, Dir. of Higher Educ. and of Public Libraries, Additional Sec. to Govt. 68-69; Vice-Chancellor, Univ. of Madras 69-75 (retd.); Padma Shri 61; Tamil Nadu State First Prize for Best Travelogue in Tamil 68.
Leisure interest: writing.
Publs. 13 children's books, 16 adult books; major works: *Sindanai Malargal* 68, *Ellorum Vazhvom* 70, *Valluvan Varisai* 59-62, *Ulagath Thamizh* 72, *Valluvar Voimozhi* 73, *Methai Meganathan* 73.
90-C Shenoynagar, Madras-600 030, India.
Telephone: 612516.

Sundblad, Erik; Swedish business executive; b. 26 Jan. 1929, Hudiksvall; s. of Dr. Gunnar Sundblad and Hildur Aberg; m. Brita Bergman 1954; four s.; ed. Royal Univ. of Technology.
Assistant Technical Man., Uddeholms AB 53-61; Pres. Wifstavarfs AB 61-66; Pres. Stora Kopparbergs Bergslags AB 66-.
Stora Kopparbergs Bergslags AB, Fack, S-791 01 Falun 1, Sweden.
Telephone: 023-80000.

Sundby, (Carl) Olof (Werner), B.A., D.D.; Swedish ecclesiastic; b. 16 Dec. 1917, Karskloga; s. of Josef Sundby and Gerda Gustafson; m. Birgitta Nordfors 1944; one s. three d.; ed. Univ. of Lund.
Ordained 43; Parish Curate; Mil. Chaplain; Prison Chaplain; Diocesan Youth Pastor, Karlstad 44; Senior Lecturer on Theological Ethics, Univ. of Lund 59; Rector of St. Peter, Lund 60; Bishop of Växjö 70; Archbishop of Uppsala 72-; Pres. Swedish Ecumenical Council; Chair. Swedish Section, Lutheran World Fed.; mem. Cen. Cttee., mem. Exec. Cttee., World Council of Churches; mem. Presidium Dec. 75-.
Leisure interests: tennis, skiing.
Publs. *Lutheran Conception of Marriage* 59, *Pastoral Letter to the Diocese of Växjö* 70.
P.O. Box 640, 751 27 Uppsala 1, Sweden.
Telephone: (018) 10-39-16; (018) 15-53-40 (Office).

Sunderland, Sir Sydney, Kt., C.M.G., D.SC., M.D., B.S., F.R.A.C.P., F.R.A.C.S., F.A.A.; Australian anatomist; b. 31 Dec. 1910, Brisbane; m. Nina Johnston 1939; one s.; ed. Melbourne Univ.
Senior Lecturer in Anatomy, Melbourne Univ. 36-37; Asst. Neurologist Alfred Hospital Melbourne 36-37; Demonstrator Dept. of Human Anatomy Oxford 38; Prof. of Anatomy and Histology Melbourne Univ. 39-61, of Experimental Neurology 61-75, Dean Medical Faculty 53-71, Prof. Emer. 76-; Visiting Specialist, injuries of the peripheral nervous system, Australian Gen. Mil. Hosp. 41-45; Visiting Prof. of Anatomy, Johns Hopkins Univ. 53-54; mem. Nat. Health and Medical Research Council of Australia 53-69; Foundation Fellow and Sec. for Biological Sciences, Australian Acad. of Sciences 55-58; Trustee, Nat. Museum of Victoria 54-, Van Cleef Foundation 71; mem. Zool. Board of Victoria 44-65; Deputy Chair. Advisory Cttee. of Victorian Mental Hygiene Authority 52-63; rep. Pacific Science Council 57-69; mem. Defence Research and Devt. Policy Cttee. 57-75, Medical Services Cttee. 57-, Commonwealth Dept. of Defence; Nat. Radiation Advisory Cttee. 57-64, Chair. 59-64; Chair. Safety Review Cttee. 61-74, Australian Atomic Energy Comm.; Medical Research Advisory Cttee. of Nat. Health and Medical Research Council 53-69, Chair. 64-69; Chair. Protective Chemistry Research Advisory Cttee., Dept. of Supply 64-73; mem. Scientific Advisory Cttee. Australian Atomic Energy Comm. 62-63; Australian Univs. Comm. 62-, Cttee. of Management Royal Melbourne Hosp. 63-71, Victorian Medical Advisory Cttee. 62-71, Advisory Medical Council of Australia 70-71; Fogarty Scholar-in-Residence, Nat. Insts. of Health, Bethesda, U.S.A. 72; Gov. Ian Potter Foundation 64-; mem. Board, Walter and Eliza Hall Inst. 68-75; Hon. M.D. (Tasmania) 70, (Queensland) 75; Hon. LL.D. (Melbourne) 75.
Leisure interest: tennis.
Publ. *Nerves and Nerve Injuries* 68.
Department of Experimental Neurology, University of Melbourne, Parkville 3052, Victoria, Australia.
Telephone: 3451844.

Sunderland, Thomas Elbert, A.B., LL.B., J.D.; American lawyer and business executive; b. 28 April 1907, Ann Arbor, Mich.; s. of Prof. Edson R. and Hannah Dell Read Sunderland; m. Mary Louise Allyn 1946; three d.; ed. Univs. of Michigan, California and Harvard.
Legal practice, Detroit 30-31, New York City 31-48, Chicago 48-59; U.S. Air Force 42-46; Gen. Counsel Pan American Petroleum and Transport Co., American Oil Co. 40-48; Dir., mem. Exec. Cttee. Pan American Petroleum and Transport Co. 47-54; Gen. Counsel, Dir. Standard Oil Co. (Ind.) 48-60; Vice-Pres., mem. Exec. Cttee. 54-60; Pres. and Dir. United Fruit Co. 60-65, Chair. of Board and Dir. 65-69; Dir. Nat. Cash Register Co., Johns-Manville Corpn., Liberty Mutual Insurance Co., First Nat. Bank of Boston; Univ. of Michigan

Nat. Business Leadership Award 66, Outstanding Achievement Award 70.
Office: c/o Snell and Wilmer, Attorneys, 3100 Valley Center, Phoenix, Ariz. 85073; Home (winter): 5840 East Starlight Way, Scottsdale, Ariz. 85253; (summer): 66 Fernwood Road, Chestnut Hill, Mass. 02167, U.S.A.
Telephone: 602-257-7262 (Office).

Sunesen, Frede; Danish banker; b. 11 May 1915, Tulstrup; m. Karen Hansen 1938; ed. Commercial Coll., Århus.
Bank official 31-50; Manager Veile Bank 50-57; mem. Board of Govs., Nat. Bank of Denmark 57-; mem. Boards of Mortgage Fund for Danish Agriculture 60, Danish Airlines 57 and Manufacturing and Manual Industries Finance Corpn. 58; Commander's Cross.
Øresundshøj 24, DK 2920 Charlottenlund, Denmark.
Telephone: Or. 4014.

Sung Chih-kuang; Chinese diplomatist; b. April 1916, Kwangtung Province; ed. univ.
Counsellor, Embassy in German Democratic Repub.; Deputy Dir. Dept. of W. European Affairs, Ministry of Foreign Affairs; Counsellor, Embassy to France; Amb. to German Democratic Repub. 70-72, to U.K. 72-.
Embassy of the People's Republic of China, 31 Portland Place, London, W1N 3AG, England.

Sung Ch'ing-ling; Chinese former government official; b. 1894, Shanghai; m. Sun Yat-sen 1915 (died 1925); ed. Wesleyan Coll., U.S.A.
Secretary to Sun Yat-sen 15; led Left Kuomintang after Kuomintang-CCP split 27; in Moscow 27-29; Vice-Chair. Cen. People's Govt. 49-54; Vice-Chair. People's Repub. of China 59-74; Chair. China Welfare Inst.; Stalin Peace Prize 51.
Publ. *The Struggle for New China* 52.
People's Republic of China.

Sung Pei-chang; Chinese party official.
Deputy Political Commissar, Anhwei Mil. District, People's Liberation Army 68; Vice-Chair. Anhwei Revolutionary Cttee. 68, Chair. 75-; Sec. CCP Anhwei 71, First Sec. 75-.
People's Republic of China.

Suomalainen, Heikki, D.SC.; Finnish biochemist and microbiologist; b. 26 Jan. 1917, Helsinki; s. of Vihtori Suomalainen and Aleksandra (Sanni) Lähde; m. Toini Irma Toivonen 1950; two s.; ed. Univ. of Helsinki.
Biochemist, Finnish State Alcohol Monopoly 41-43, Chief of Biochemical Dept. 43-51, Head of Research Laboratories 51-58, Man. of Rajamäki Factories 55-58, mem. Board of Dirs. and Dir. of Industrial Production and Chem. Research 58-, Deputy Gen. Man. 72-; Asst. Prof. of Microbiology, Univ. of Helsinki 49-, of Biochemistry and Food Chem., Helsinki Univ. of Tech. 58-; Pres. Finnish Yeast Producers' Corpn. 59-; mem. Board, Finnish Acad. of Tech. Sciences 73-; mem. Finnish Acad. of Sciences and Letters 74-; Prof. h.c. 69, Dr. Ing. h.c. (Free Univ. Berlin) 74.
Leisure interests: book collecting, pictorial arts.
Publs. about 270 reports on biological chemistry, particularly fermentation chemistry, in int. journals.
Alko, Box 350, SF-00101 Helsinki 10, Finland.
Telephone: 60911.

Suomela, Vilho Samuli, PH.D.; Finnish agricultural economist; b. 27 July 1918, Pertteli; s. of Theodor Suomela and Signe Lehtiö; m. Hilkka Soidinsuo 1946; two s.; ed. Helsinki Univ.
Fellow, Helsinki Univ. 46-50; Manager of Experimental Farm, Helsinki Univ. 50-52; Dir. of Research Inst. of Agric. Econs. 52-; Sec. Finnish Acad. 57-59; Minister of Agriculture 63-64; Planning Dir. Ministry of Agriculture 69-71; Dir.-Gen. Board of Agriculture 71-; Minister of Agriculture and Forestry 71-72; Chair. of the Comm. on Int. Agricultural Affairs.

Leisure interest: fly fishing.

Publs. *On the Influence of the Location of Fields on Farming* 50, *Development of Productivity in Finnish Agriculture* 58.

Palotie 14E, Helsinki 44, Finland.
Telephone: Helsinki 661771 (Office).

Suorttanen, Sulo, BARR.-AT-LAW; Finnish politician; b. 13 Feb. 1921, Valkeala; s. of Elias Suorttanen and Amånda Askola; m. Lea Annikki Laakso 1949; one s.
Assistant Police-Inspector, Kymi Admin. District 58-62; mem. of Parl. 62-70, 72-; held numerous high positions in local govt. and in co-operative orgs.; Minister of Defence 66-70.
Leisure interests: horse racing, motoring.
Parliament Building, Helsinki, Finland.

Suphamongkhon, Konthi, LL.B.; Thai lawyer and diplomatist; b. 3 Aug. 1916; ed. Univ. of Moral and Political Sciences, Bangkok and Faculté de Droit, Paris.
Chief of Section, Political Div., Ministry of Foreign Affairs 40-42; Second Sec., Tokyo 42-44; Chief of Political Div., Western Affairs Dept., Ministry of Foreign Affairs 44-48, Dir.-Gen. Western Affairs Dept. 48-50, Dir.-Gen. United Nations Dept. 50-52; Minister to Australia 52-56, Ambassador to Australia, concurrently to New Zealand 56-59; Dir.-Gen. Dept. of Int. Orgs., Ministry of Foreign Affairs 59-63; Adviser on Foreign Affairs to Prime Minister 62-64; Sec.-Gen. South East Asia Treaty Organisation (SEATO) 64-65; Amb. to German Fed. Repub. 65-70, to U.K. May 70-; numerous decorations.
Publ. *Thailand and Her Relations with France* 40.
Royal Thai Embassy, 30 Queen's Gate, London, SW7 5JB, England.
Telephone: 01-589-0173.

Šupka, Ladislav, ING.; Czechoslovak economist and politician; b. 1 Aug. 1928, Stará Turá; ed. Polytechnic Inst., Sverdlovsk, U.S.S.R.
Chief technologist, factory man., Dep. Dir., Technical Dir., Škoda nat. enterprise, V.I. Lenin Works, Pilsen 55-65; mem. Econ. Comm. Cen. Cttee. C.P. of Czechoslovakia 63-69; mem. State Comm. for Econ., Scientific and Technological Co-operation 65-67; Deputy Minister for Heavy Industry 65-69; Deputy Minister-Chair. Fed. Cttee. for Industry 69; Head, Econ. Dept. Cen. Cttee., C.P. of Czechoslovakia 69-70; Minister-Chair. Fed. Cttee. for Technological and Investment Devt. 70-71; Minister for Technological and Investment Devt. of C.S.S.R. Jan. 71-; Order for Outstanding Work 59.
Ministry for Technological and Investment Development, Slezská 9, Prague 2, Czechoslovakia.

Suppes, Patrick, B.S., PH.D.; American educationist; b. 17 March 1922, Tulsa, Okla.; m. 1st Joan Farmer 1946 (divorced 1970), 2nd Joan Elizabeth Sieber 1970; one s. two d.; ed. Univ. of Chicago and Columbia Univ.
Instructor, Stanford Univ. 50-52, Asst. Prof. Dept. of Philosophy, Stanford Univ. 52-55, Assoc. Prof. 55-59, Assoc. Dean, School of Humanities and Sciences 58-61, Dir. Honors Program in Quantitative Methods in the Behavioral Sciences 58-, Prof. Dept. of Philosophy 59-, Prof. of Philosophy and Statistics 60- also of Educ. 67-, Dir. Inst. for Mathematical Studies in the Social Sciences, Stanford 59-, Chair. Dept. of Philosophy 63-69; Fellow American Asscn. for Advancement of Science, American Psychological Asscn.; mem. Nat. Acad. of Educ. 65, American Acad. of Arts and Sciences 68; Palmer O. Johnson Memorial Award 67; Award for distinguished contributions to Educational Research, AERA 71.
Publs. *Introduction to Logic* 57, *Decision Making: An Experimental Approach* (with D. Davidson and S. Siegel) 57, *Axiomatic Set Theory* 60, *Markov Learning Models for Multiperson Interactions* (with R. C. Atkin-

son) 60, *First Course in Mathematical Logic* 64, *Experiments in Second-Language Acquisition* (with E. Crothers) 67, *Computer Assisted Instruction: Stanford's 1965-66 Arithmetic Program* (with M. Jerman and D. Brian) 68, *Studies in the Methodology and Foundations of Science* 70, *A Probabilistic Theory of Casuality* 70, *Foundations of Measurement* (with D. Krantz, R. D. Luce, A. Tversky) Vol. I 71.
Ventura Hall, Stanford University, Stanford, Calif. 94305, U.S.A.
Telephone: 415-321-2300, Ext. 3111.

Surganov, Fyodor Anisimovich; Soviet politician; b. 7 June 1911; ed. Byelorussian Agricultural Inst.
Komsomol and Partisan work 39-45; Mem. staff of Cen. Cttee. of Communist Party of Byelorussia 45-47; Second Sec., Minsk Regional Cttee., C.P. of Byelorussia 47-54, First Sec. 55-56; Chair. Exec. Cttee. of Minsk Regional Soviet of Workers' Deputies 54-55; Sec. Central Cttee. of Communist Party of Byelorussia 56-65, Second Sec. 65-71; Alt. mem. Central Cttee. of C.P.S.U. 56-61, mem. 61-; Deputy to Supreme Soviet, U.S.S.R. 54-; Chair. Presidium, Byelorussian S.S.R. Supreme Soviet 71-; Vice-Chair. Presidium Supreme Soviet 71-.
Presidium of the Byelorussian S.S.R. Supreme Soviet, Minsk, U.S.S.R.

Surkov, Aleksey Aleksandrovich; Soviet poet; b. 14 Oct. 1899, Srednevo, Yaroslavl Region; ed. Inst. of Red Professors, Moscow.
Alternative mem. Central Cttee. of the C.P.S.U. 56; first Sec. Writers' Union of the U.S.S.R. until 59, Sec. 59-; Pres. U.S.S.R.-Great Britain Soc. 58-; Deputy to U.S.S.R. Supreme Soviet; mem. Comm. for Public Educ., Science and Culture; State Prizewinner 46, 51; awarded Orders of Lenin (four times), Red Banner, Red Star (twice), Badge of Honour, Hero of Socialist Labour; Gold Medal 'Hammer and Sickle'.
Publs. *Let's Sing* 30, *Peace to the World* 50; poems: *Moscow is at our Backs, Flame Beats in the Small Stove* 42, *Victory!* 43; *Collected Works* (two vols.) 54, 59, *Songs of Mankind* 58-61, *Bullet is Frightened by Brave Man* 64, *The Voice of Time* 65, *Relay Race of Friendship* (collection of translations) 68.
Writers' Union of the U.S.S.R., Ul. Vorovskogo 52. Moscow, U.S.S.R.

Suromihardjo, Maj.-Gen. Suadi; Indonesian army officer and diplomatist; b. 1921; ed. Staff Coll., Quetta, Pakistan, Fort Bliss, U.S.A.
Department of Interior 39; 1st. Lieutenant Indonesian Army 42; C.O. (Lt.-Col.) 1st Regiment 10th Div. 45; mem. U.N. Comm. for Indonesia 47; Dep. Chief of Staff Diponegoro Div., Central Java 50; C.O. 21st Regiment, VI Div., South Kalimantan 51; C.O. 23rd Regiment VII Div. South Sulawesi 54; C.O. Indonesian Contingent U.N.E.F. Egypt 57; Commandant Indonesian Command and General Staff Coll., Bandung 59; Amb. to Australia 61-64, to Ethiopia 64-69; Gov. Indonesia Nat. Defence Council 68-.
Lembaga Pertahanan Nasional, Jalan Kebon Sirih 28, Jakarta, Indonesia.

Surrey, Stanley Sterling; American professor and lawyer; b. 3 Oct. 1910, New York, N.Y.; m. Dorothy Mooklar 1938; one s.; ed. Coll. of City of New York and Columbia Univ. Law School.
Admitted to New York Bar 33; Research Asst., Columbia Univ. Law School 32-33; Attorney, Proskauer, Rose and Paskus, New York 33; Nat. Recovery Admin. Wash. 33-35; Nat. Labor Relations Board, Wash. 35-37; U.S. Treasury Dept. 38-44, 46-47; Prof. Univ. of Calif. Law School 47-50, Harvard Law School 50-61, 69-; Asst. Sec. for Tax Policy, U.S. Treasury Dept. 61-69; mem. American Acad. of Arts and Sciences.
Leisure interests: sailing and photography.

Publs. Co-Editor *Legislation, Cases and Materials* 55, *Federal Income Taxation, Cases and Materials* Vol. I 72, Vol. II 73, *Federal Estate and Gift Taxation, Cases and Materials* 76; Author *Pathways to Tax Reform* 73.
Office: Harvard Law School, Cambridge, Mass. 02138; Home: 54 Buckingham Street, Cambridge, Mass. 02138, U.S.A.
Telephone: 617-495-4635.

Suryadhay, Phagna Prasith Inpèng; Laotian diplomatist; b. 13 Feb. 1923, Khong; s. of Thao Nouphuoc and Nang South Suryadhay; m. Nang Bounlay Kykèo 1947; one s. two d.; ed. Pavie Coll. Vientiane, Lycée Sisowath, Phnom Penh, Inst. d'Etudes Politiques, Paris.
First Sec. Embassy of Laos, Washington, D.C. 53-55; Sec.-Gen. Council of Ministers 55-58; Sec. of State for Justice 58-59, for Educ. 59-60; mem. of Parl. 60-; Minister of Finance and Nat. Econ. 60-62, of Finance 62; Editor *The Nation* daily newspaper 62-71; Vice-Pres. Nat. Assembly 62-63; Minister of Justice in charge of Planning and Devt. Co-operation 64-71; Amb. to U.K. 71-75; Order of the Reign of Sisavang Vong-Sisavang Vatthana, Officer Mérite Civique, Grand Officer Million Elephants and Order of the Great Friendship (Khmer Repub.).
Leisure interests: reading, historical and social studies.
c/o Embassy of Laos, 5 Palace Green, London W8 4QA, England.
Telephone: 01-937-9519/10.

Suslov, Mikhail Andreyevich; Soviet politician; b. 21 Nov. 1902, Shakhovskol, Ulyanovsk Region; ed. Moscow Inst. of Nat. Economy.
Joined Communist Party 21; lecturer at Moscow Univ. and at Industrial Acad. 29-31; exec. post, Central Control Comm. of C.P.S.U. and People's Commissariat for Workers' and Peasants' Inspection 31-36; Sec. Rostov Regional Cttee. of Party 37-39; First Sec. Stavropol Territorial and City Cttee. of C.P.S.U. 39-44; during war, mem. Mil. Council for North Caucasus front and Chief of Staff, Stavropol Territory partisan detachments; Chair. C.P.S.U. Central Cttee. Bureau for Lithuania 44; held executive positions in Central Cttee. of Party during 46; Sec. of Central Cttee. 47-; Ed.-in-Chief *Pravda* 49-50; mem. Presidium of U.S.S.R. Supreme Soviet 50-54; Deputy of U.S.S.R. Supreme Soviet; Chair. Foreign Comm., Soviet of Union of Supreme Soviet of U.S.S.R. 54-; mem. Presidium, Central Cttee. of C.P.S.U. 55-66, Political Bureau 66-; awarded Order of Lenin (three times), Order of the Patriotic War (1st Class), Hero of Socialist Labour; Hammer and Sickle Gold Medal (two); and other decorations.
C.P.S.U. Central Committee, 4 Staraya ploshchad, Moscow, U.S.S.R.

Sussekind, Arnaldo Lopes; Brazilian lawyer and retd. public servant; b. 9 July 1917, Rio de Janeiro; s. of Frederico and Sylvia Lopes Sussekind; m. M. Santos Sussekind 1940; one s. one d.; ed. Colégio Mallet Soares, Rio de Janeiro, and Univ. do Brasil, Rio de Janeiro.
Federal Public Service 38-, Asst., Nat. Council of Labour; Regional Attorney, São Paulo 41-44, Rio de Janeiro 44-51; mem. Comm. on Labour Laws 43-64; Dir. of Recreation and Cultural Assistance 51-53; Dir. Dept. of Nat. Security, Ministry of Labour 55-61; Pres. Perm. Comm. on Social Laws 60-61; Attorney Gen. of Labour Justice 61-62; Minister of Labour and Social Welfare 64-65; Judge Superior Labour Court 65-71; mem. of Cttee. of Experts on the Application of Conventions and Recommendations—Int. Labour Office Nov. 69-; several decorations.
Publs. numerous works on labour laws.
Rua Timoteo da Costa 135, Ap. 401, Rio de Janeiro, ZC-20, G.B., Brazil.
Telephone: 227-1364.

Süssenguth, Hans, DIPL.ING.; German aviation executive; b. 8 Sept. 1913, Neustadt/Coburg; s. of Franz H. and Rosalie Süssenguth; m. Christa Reischel 1942; one s. one d.; ed. Oberrealschule, Coburg and Technische Hochschule, Darmstadt.
Technician in Research and Devt. and Maintenance and Operations Depts. Deutsche Lufthansa A.G., Berlin 39-45; Engineer in father-in-law's business 45-50; Engineer at Gummi-Werke Fulda 50-52; rejoined Lufthansa in Engineering Div., Hamburg 52, Technical Dir. 54, Head of Traffic Division 58, Deputy mem. Exec. Board 59, mem. 63-, responsible for sales, worldwide field org., in-flight services and marketing; Chair. Lufthansa Service GmbH (LH-Catering Co.), Lufthansa Intercontinental Hotel Verwaltungs-gesellschaft mbH, Lufthansa Commercial Holding GmbH, Cologne; Deputy Chair. Delvag Luftfahrtversicherungs-AG; mem. of Board Condor Flugdienst GmbH; DSG-Deutsche Schlafwagen-und Speisewagen-GmbH Frankfurt, Frankfurt Intercontinental Hotels GmbH; mem. Exec. Board and Vice-Pres., German Tourist Board; mem. Advisory Board, Intercontinental Package Tours Inc., Airtours Int.; mem. Board of Trustees, Hessian Inst. for Aviation; mem. Chartered Inst. of Air Transport, London, Soc. for Study of Automation in Transport and Tourism (START), Frankfurt, Foundation for Aid of Sport in Germany; Hon. Consul Repub. of Togo; Hon. Prof. Technische Univ., Berlin.
Deutsche Lufthansa AG, 6 Frankfurt/Main-Flughafen, Lufthansa-Basis; Home: 6242 Kronberg/Taunus, Taunusstrasse 2, Federal Republic of Germany.
Telephone: (0611) 696-2200 (Office); (06173) 3298 (Home).

Susskind, David Howard; American television producer; b. 19 Dec. 1920; ed. Harvard Univ.
Publicity Dept., Warner Bros. also with Universal Picture Corpn. 46-48; Talent Agent, Century Artists, and Music Corpn. of America 49-52; Co-owner and Pres. Talent Assocs. Ltd., New York 52-; Chair. TV Discussion programme *Open End* 58-67; The David Susskind Show 67-, producer TV programmes incl. duPont Show of the Month, Philco Playhouse, and Kraft Theater; Hallmark Hall of Fame *The Price* 71; numerous TV awards.
Produced Broadway plays: *A Very Special Baby* 56, *Rashomon* 59, *Handful of Fire* 58, *Kelly* 65, *All in Good Time* 65.
Films: *Edge of the City* 56, *Raisin in the Sun* 60, *Requiem for a Heavyweight* 61, *All the Way Home* 63, *Lovers and Other Strangers* 70, *Pursuit of Happiness* 71, *Straw Dogs* 72; T.V. Programmes: *Festival of Performing Arts, Play of the Week, East Side, West Side.*
Talent Associates-Norton Simon Inc., 444 Madison Avenue, New York City, N.Y., U.S.A.

Susskind, (Jan) Walter; British (b. Czechoslovak) musician; b. 1 May 1913; s. of Bruno and Gertrud Seger Susskind; m. Janis Susskind 1973; one s.; ed. State Acad. of Music, Prague.
Conductor German Opera, Prague 33-38; pianist London Czech Trio 33-42; Principal Conductor, Royal Carl Rosa Opera Co., England 43-45; Principal Guest Conductor; Sadler's Wells Opera Co. and Glyndebourne Opera (at First Edinburgh Festival) 45-47; Principal Conductor, Scottish Nat. Orchestra 46-52; Principal Conductor, Victorian Symphony Orchestra, Melbourne 53-55; Music Dir. Mendelssohn Choir, Toronto 56-64; Musical Dir. and First Conductor, Toronto Symphony Orchestra, Toronto, Canada 56-65; Music Dir. Aspen, Colo., Music Festival 61-68; Dir. Nat. Youth Orchestra of Canada; Music Dir. and Conductor Mississippi River Festival 69-75; Music Dir. St. Louis Symphony Orchestra 68-75; Principal Conductor, Int. Festival of Youth Orchestras, Switzerland 70-71; also Guest Conductor of many leading orchestras in the world; over 200 record-

ings on various labels; frequent piano soloist; orchestral arrangements of piano works by Prokofiev and Debussy; known for his work with youth orchestras and youth conductors; Hon. doctorate (Humanities) Univ. of S. Ill. 69, Hon. Dr. of Fine Arts, Washington Univ. 75.

Works include various compositions for piano, violin and orchestra, also songs, instrumental music to films and plays.

c/o Ingpen and Williams, 14 Kensington Court, London, W.8, England.

Sutami, Dr.; Indonesian engineer and politician; b. 19 Oct. 1928, Surakarta, Cen. Java; ed. Inst. of Technology, Bandung.

Employee Hollandse Beton Maatschappij N.V. 56-58; Dir. Hutama Karya Co. 59; mem. Indonesian Nat. Research Inst.; Asst. Dean, Technical Faculty, Univ. of Indonesia 64; Minister of Public Works 66-, also of Energy 68-; mem. Indonesian Council of Science 68.

Ministry of Public Works, Jakarta, Indonesia.

Sutcliffe, Reginald Cockcroft, C.B., O.B.E., F.R.S., B.SC., PH.D.; British meteorologist; b. 1904, Wrexham, North Wales; s. of late O. G. Sutcliffe and late Jessie Sutcliffe (née Cockcroft); m. Evelyn Williams 1929; two d.; ed. Whitcliffe Mount Grammar School, Cleckheaton, Leeds Univ. and Univ. Coll., Bangor.

Professional Asst., Meteorological Office 27, Met. Office appts. in Malta 28-32, Felixstowe 32-35, Air Ministry 35-37, Thorney Island 37-39; Sqdn.-Ldr. R.A.F.V.R., France 39-40; Senior Met. Officer No. 3 Bomber Group, R.A.F. 41-44; Group Capt.; Chief Met. Officer Allied Expeditionary Air Force (later British Air Forces of Occupation), Germany 44-46; Research, Met. Office 46-, Dir. of Research 57-65; Prof. of Meteorology Reading Univ. 65-70, Prof. Emer. 70-; Symons Gold Medal 55, Buchan Prize 56, Charles Chree Medal of Physical Soc. 59, Int. Met. Org. Prize 63.

Leisure interests: golf, gardening.

Publs. *Meteorology for Aviators* 38, *Weather and Climate* 66, meteorological papers in journals.

Green Side, Winslow Road, Nash, Milton Keynes, Bucks., MK17 0EJ, England.

Sutermeister, Heinrich; Swiss composer; b. 12 Aug. 1910, Feuerthalen; m. Verena-Maria Renker 1948; one d.; studied philology at Paris and Munich, and music at the Acad. of Music at Munich.

Professor, Hochschule für Musik, Hanover 63-; Pres. Schweizerische Mechanlizenz; Salzburg Opera Prize 65, Asscn. of Swiss Composers' Prize 67.

Operas include: *L'araignée noire, Romeo and Juliet, The Tempest, Niobe, Raskolnikoff* (Stockholm and Scala, Milan), *Botte Rouge, Titus Feuerfuchs* (opera burlesque) (Basle and Brussels) 58, *Seraphine, The Canterville Ghost* (for television) *Madame Bovary* (Zürich) 67; other works: *Missa da Requiem* 53, three piano concertos 54, cello concerto 55, *La Croisade des Enfants* 69 (for television), *The Bottle Imp* (for television); two divertimenti, eight cantatas, two cello concerti, *Te Deum* 75.

Leisure interest: dog breeding (Belgian shepherd dogs).

Vaux-sur-Morges, Switzerland.

Telephone: 021-712833.

Sutherland, Sir Gordon Brims Black McIvor, Kt., M.A., B.SC., PH.D., SC.D., F.R.S.; British scientist; b. 8 April 1907, Watten, Scotland; s. of Peter Sutherland and Eliza Sutherland (née Morrison); m. Gunborg Wahlstrom 1936; three d.; ed. St. Andrews Univ. and Trinity and Pembroke Colls., Cambridge.

Fellow Pembroke Coll. 35-49; Leverhulme Fellow 39; Asst. to Dir. of Scientific Research in Ministry of Supply 40-41; head of group doing infra-red research for various Govt. depts. 41-45; Asst. Dir. in Colloid Science, Cambridge Univ. 44-47; mem. Council of Senate, Cambridge Univ. 46-49; Reader in Spectroscopy, Cambridge Univ.

47-49; Prof. of Physics, Univ. of Michigan 49-56; Guggenheim Fellow 56; Dir. Nat. Physical Laboratory, Teddington Sept. 56-64; Master of Emmanuel Coll., Cambridge 64-; Gov. London School of Econs. 57-65, Northampton Coll. of Advanced Technology 60-65; mem. Governing Body Coll. of Aeronautics 57-63; Pres. Triple Comm. for Spectroscopy 62-63; Vice-Pres. Int. Org. for Biophysics 61-64, Royal Soc. 61-63, Int. Union of Pure and Applied Physics 63-69; Pres. Inst. of Physics and the Physical Soc. 64-66, Glazebrook Medal 72; mem. of Council for Scientific Policy 65-68; Syndic of Cambridge Univ. Press 65-; Pres. Section X of British Asscn. 68; Trustee of Nat. Gallery 71-; Foreign Hon. mem. American Acad. of Arts and Sciences 68; Hon. Fellow, Pembroke Coll., Cambridge; Hon. LL.D. (St. Andrews), Hon. D.Sc. (Strathclyde).

Leisure interest: golf.

Publs. include *Infra-red and Raman Spectra* 35.

The Master's Lodge, Emmanuel College, Cambridge, England.

Telephone: Cambridge 65411.

Sutherland, Graham Vivian, O.M.; British artist; b. 24 Aug. 1903; ed. Epsom Coll., Goldsmiths Coll. School of Art and London Univ.

Exhibited XXI Gallery 25 and 28, First Int. Surrealist Exhibition London; Exhibition Rosenberg and Helft Gallery 38, Leicester Galleries 40, Curt Valentin, Buchholz Gallery New York 46, Musée Nat. de l'Art Moderne, Paris 52, Stedelijk Museum, Amsterdam, Kunsthaus, Zürich, Tate Gallery, London 53, Galleria d'Arte Moderna, Turin 65, Haus der Kunst, Munich 67, Cologne 67, Marlborough 68, 73, Milan 73; works in Tate Gallery, British Museum, Victoria and Albert Museum, London, Museum of Modern Art, New York, Musée de l'Art Moderne, Paris, Musée des Beaux-Arts, Brussels, Albertina, Vienna; Official War Artist during Second World War; Trustee, Tate Gallery 48-54; designed tapestry *Christ in Majesty* for Coventry Cathedral 62; Hon. mem. American Acad. of Arts and Letters 72; Commdr. Ordre des Arts et des Lettres 72; Hon. D.Litt. (Oxford) 62, (Leicester) 65; Prize, Museum of Modern Art, São Paulo.

La Villa Blanche, Route de Castellar, 06 Menton, France.

Sutherland, Joan, C.B.E.; Australian opera singer; b. 7 Nov. 1926, Sydney; d. of William McDonald Sutherland and Muriel Beatrice (née Alston); m. Richard Bonynge (q.v.) 1954; one s.; ed. St. Catherine's School, Waverley, Sydney.

Début as Dido in Purcell's *Dido and Aeneas*, Sydney 47; Royal Opera Co., Covent Garden, London 52-; has sung leading soprano roles at the Vienna State Opera, La Scala, Milan, Teatro Fenice, Venice, the Paris Opera, Glyndebourne, San Francisco and Chicago Operas, The Metropolitan, New York, etc.; Hon. life mem. Australia Opera Co. 74, Companion Order of Australia 75.

Leisure interests: reading, needlepoint.

c/o Ingpen and Williams Ltd., 14 Kensington Court, London, W.8, England

Sutherland, Dame Lucy Stuart, D.B.E., F.R.S.A., F.B.A., M.A., D.LITT.; British university professor and public servant; b. 21 June 1903, Geelong, Victoria, Australia; d. of Alexander Sutherland and Margaret Sutherland (née Goddard); ed. Univ. of Witwatersrand, South Africa, and Somerville Coll., Oxford.

Fellow and Tutor in Economic History and Politics, Somerville Coll., Oxford 27-45; Principal and then Asst. Sec. Board of Trade 41-45; Principal, Lady Margaret Hall, Oxford 45-71; Hon. Fellow 71; Pro-Vice-Chancellor, Univ. of Oxford 60-69; Chair. Lace Working Party 46; mem. Royal Comm. on Taxation, Profits and Income 51-55, mem. Univ. Grants Cttee. 63-68; Hon. Litt.D. (Cantab.) 63, (Kent) 67, Hon. LL.B. (Smith Coll., Northampton, Mass.) 64, Hon. D.Litt. (Glasgow)

66, (Keele) 69, Hon. D.Lit. (Belfast) 70, Hon. D.C.L. (Oxford) 72.
Leisure interests: travel, reading.
Publs. *A London Merchant (1695-1774)* 33, *The East India Company in Eighteenth-Century Politics* 52; edited (with M. McKisack) *Mediaeval Representation and Consent* 36, ed. *The Correspondence of Edmund Burke*, Vol. II 60, edited *Studies in History, British Academy Lectures* 66, *The University of Oxford in the Eighteenth Century* 73, etc.
59 Park Town, Oxford, England.
Telephone: Oxford 56159.

Šutka, Stefan, ING., LL.D.; Czechoslovak politician; b. 30 Oct. 1921, Velké Vozokany; ed. Faculty of Law, Slovak Univ., Bratislava, School of Economics, Bratislava, and Transport Coll., Žilina.
Deputy Minister of Transport, Posts and Telecommunications of Slovak Socialist Republic 69, Minister 69-70; Minister of Transport of Č.S.S.R. 71-; Head of del. to CMEA Perm. Comm. for Transport 71-; Award of Merit in Construction 67, Order of Labour 71.
Ministry of Transport, Na příkopě 33, Prague 1, Czechoslovakia.

Sutton, George Paul, A.A., B.S., M.S.; American engineer; b. 5 Sept. 1920, s. of Frederick and Augusta Sutton; m. Yvonne Barnes; two d.; ed. Los Angeles City Coll. and California Inst. of Technology.
Manager of Advanced Design, Rocketdyne (N. American Aviation Inc.), Canoga Park, Calif. 46-58; Hunsaker Prof. of Aeronautical Engineering, Mass. Inst. of Technology 58; Chief Scientist Advanced Research Projects Agency (Dept. of Defense) 59-60; Dir. Advanced Research Projects Div. (Inst. of Defense Analyses) 59-60; Asst. to Pres. North American Rockwell Corpn. 60-69; Vice-Pres. Envirotech Corpn. 69-; Exec. Vice-Pres. Sumitomo Jukikai Envirotech, Inc. 70-74; Vice Pres. Johnston Pump Co. 74-; Fellow American Inst. of Aeronautics and Astronautics; mem. Int. Acad. of Astronautics, several professional socs.; E. G. Pendray Award, American Rocket Soc. 51.
Leisure interests: skiing, stamp collecting.
Publs. *Rocket Propulsion Elements* 49, 54, 63, *Advanced Propulsion Systems* (co-editor) 59.
Johnston Pump Co., 1775 E. Allen Avenue, Glendora, Calif. 91770, U.S.A.

Sutton, Leslie Ernest, M.A., D.PHIL., F.R.S.; British chemist; b. 22 June 1906, London; s. of Edgar W. Sutton and Margaret L. W. (Heard) Sutton; m. 1st Catharine V. Stock 1932 (died 1962); two s. one d.; m. 2nd Rachel A. Long (née Batten) 1963; two s.; ed. Watford Grammar School, Lincoln Coll., Oxford, Leipzig Univ., and Calif. Inst. of Technology.
Fellow, Magdalen Coll., Oxford 32-36; Univ. Lecturer, Oxford 45-62; Vice-Pres. Magdalen Coll. 47-48; Fellow and Tutor Magdalen Coll., Oxford 36-73; Reader in Physical Chem. 62-73; retd. 73; Sec. Chemical Soc. 51-57, Vice-Pres. 57-60; Visiting Prof. Heidelberg Univ. 60, 64, 67; Baggesgaard Rasmussen Lecturer, Copenhagen 74; Rockefeller Fellow 33-34; Meldola Medal (Royal Inst. of Chem.) 32, Harrison Prize (Chem. Soc.) 35, Tilden Lecturer (Chem. Soc.) 40; Hon. D.Sc. (Salford Univ.) 73.
Leisure interests: music, photography.
Publs. papers in scientific and chemical journals.
62 Osler Road, Headington, Oxford, OX3 9BN, England.
Telephone: Oxford 66456.

Sutton, Sir (Oliver) Graham, C.B.E., D.SC., LL.D., F.R.S.; British mathematical physicist; b. 4 Feb. 1903, Cwmcarn; s. of Oliver and Rachael Sutton; m. Doris Morgan 1931; two s.; ed. Univ. Coll. of Wales, Aberystwyth, and Jesus Coll., Oxford.
Lecturer, Univ. Coll. of Wales, Aberystwyth 26-28;

Professional Asst., Meteorological Office 28-41; Supt. of Research, Chemical Defence Experimental Establishment, Porton 42-43; Supt. Tank Armament Research 43-45; Chief Supt. Radar Research and Development Establishment, Malvern 45-47; Chair. Atmospheric Pollution Research Cttee. 50-55; Scientific Adviser to the Army Council 51; Dean of Royal Mil. Coll. of Science, Shrivenham 52-53; Bashforth Prof. of Mathematical Physics 47-53; Pres. Royal Meteorological Soc. 53-55; mem. Exec. Cttee. World Meteorological Organisation 53-65, Chair. Nat. Cttee. Geodesy and Geophysics 60-66, Natural Environment Research Council 65-71; Dir.-Gen. of British Meteorological Office 53-65; Vice-Pres. Univ. Coll. of Wales 67-; Int. Meteorological Org. Prize 68.
Publs. *Atmospheric Turbulence* 48, *The Science of Flight* 49, *Micrometeorology* 53, *Mathematics in Action* 54, *A Compendium of Mathematics and Physics* (with D. S. Meyler) 58, *Understanding Weather* 60, *The Challenge of the Atmosphere* 61, *Mastery of the Air* 66, *The Weather* 74.
4 The Bryn, Sketty Green, Swansea, SA2 8DD, Wales.
Telephone: Swansea 21005.

Suwayyil, Ibrahim Al-; Saudi Arabian diplomatist; b. 1916; ed. Saudi Inst., Mecca, and Coll. of Sciences, Cairo.
Minister of Foreign Affairs 60-62; Adviser to King Saud and Head of Political Office in Royal Diwan Jan.-Nov. 62; Minister of Agriculture Nov. 62-Aug. 64; Amb. to United States, also accred. to Mexico 64-75.
c/o Ministry of Foreign Affairs, Jeddah, Saudi Arabia.

Suy, Erik, DR.IUR., DR.SC. POL.; Belgian international lawyer; b. 15 Aug. 1933, Ghent; m. Ute Stenzel 1962; one d.; ed. Univs. of Ghent, Geneva and Vienna.
Member of UN Conf. on Diplomatic Intercourse 61, on Law of Treaties 68-69; Adviser to Ministry for Foreign Affairs 67-73; mem. del. to UN Gen. Assembly 69-72; Chair. Sixth Cttee. Gen. Assembly 72; Under-Sec.-Gen. Legal Counsel, UN 74-; Prof. Int. Law, Univ. of Leuven; mem. Int. Law Asscn., American Soc. of Int. Law, German Soc. of Int. Law, Perm. Court of Arbitration; Chevalier Crown Order (Belgium), Officer Order of Merit (Austria).
Publs. *Les Actes Juridiques Unilatéraux en Droit International Public* 62, *The Concept of Jus Cogens in International Law* 67.
United Nations Secretariat, New York, N.Y. 10017; Home: 45 East 89th Street, Apartment 31B, New York, U.S.A.
Telephone: PL4-1234 (Office); (212) 534-3761 (Home).

Suyumbaev, Akhmatbek Suttubaevich; Soviet politician; b. 1920; ed. All-Union Extra-Mural Financial and Econ. Inst.
Accountant, Chief Accountant, Osh City Financial Dept. 38-39; Soviet Army Service 39-47; mem. C.P.S.U. 42-; Head, District and Osh Region Financial Dept. 47-55; Minister of Finance, Kirghiz S.S.R. 55-60; Chair. Exec. Cttee., Osh Region, Soviet of Working People's Deputies 60-62; First Sec. Osh Region Cttee. of C.P.S.U. 62-67; Chair. of Council of Ministers of Kirghiz S.S.R. 68-; Deputy to U.S.S.R. and Kirghiz S.S.R. Supreme Soviets 62-; mem. Cen. Cttee. of Kirghiz C.P. 62-.
Kirghiz S.S.R. Council of Ministers, Frunze, U.S.S.R.

Suzman, Helen, B.COM., M.P.; South African politician; b. Germiston, Transvaal; m. Dr. M. M. Suzman 1937; two d.; ed. Parktown Convent, Univ. of Witwatersrand.
Assistant statistician, War Supplies Board 41-44; part-time lecturer. Dept. of Econs. and Econ. Hist., Univ. of Witwatersrand 44-52; mem. Parl. Houghton 53-; United Party) 53-61, Progressive Party (now Progressive Reform Party) 61-; mem. South African Inst. of Race Relatiobs; Hon. Fellow St. Hugh's Coll., Oxford 73,

London School of Econs. 75; Hon. D.C.L. (Oxford) 73. Leisure interests: golf, bridge.
49 Melville Road, Hyde Park, Sandton, 2146 Transvaal, South Africa.

Suzman, Janet, B.A.; South African actress; b. 9 Feb. 1939, Johannesburg; d. of Saul Suzman and Betty Sonnenberg; m. Trevor Nunn 1969; ed. Kingsmead Coll., Univ. of the Witwatersrand, London Acad. of Music and Dramatic Art.
Moved to Britain 60; Best Actress, Evening Standard Drama Award 73; roles and plays for Royal Shakespeare Co. include: Lady Anne, La Pucelle, Lady Percy, Luciana, Lulu in *The Birthday Party* 63-64, Portia, Rosaline 65, Carmen in *The Balcony, She Stoops to Conquer* 66, Katharina, Celia and Berinthia in *The Relapse* 67, Beatrice, Rosalind 68-69, Cleopatra, Lavinia, Hester in *Hello and Goodbye* 72-73; films: *A Day in the Death of Joe Egg* 70, *Nicholas and Alexandra* 71; television plays since 66 include *Saint Joan* 68, *The Three Sisters* 69, *Macbeth* 70, *Hedda Gabler* 72, *Twelfth Night* 73, *Miss Nightingale, Clayhanger* (serial) 75-76, *The Family Re-Union.*
William Morris Agency (U.K.) Ltd., 147-149 Wardour Street, London, W1V 3TB, England.
Telephone: 01-734-9361.

Suzuki, Gengo; Japanese banker; b. 11 Feb. 1904, Mino-Kamo City; s. of Seijiro Suzuki and Sumi Kani; m. Hide Motoda 1929 (died 1975); two c.; ed. Taihoku Coll. of Commerce and Univ. of Wisconsin.
Instructor then Prof. Econs. Taihoku Coll. of Commerce, Taihoku, Taiwan 30-45; Prof. Econs. Taiwan Nat. Univ. 45-48; Deputy Financial Commr. Ministry of Finance 49-51, Financial Commr. 51-57; Financial Minister, Embassy of Japan, Washington, D.C. 57-60; Special Asst. to Minister of Foreign Affairs and to Minister of Finance 60-66; Exec. Dir. Int. Monetary Fund and Int. Bank for Reconstruction and Devt. 60-66; Japan's Rep. to Group of Ten Deputies and Working Party 3 of OECD 63-66; Auditor, Bank of Japan, Tokyo 66-70; mem. Advisory Board Mekong Comm. ESCAP 68-; Chief Finance Mission on Ryukyu Islands 68-69; mem. World Bank's Investment Dispute Conciliation Panel 68-74; Trustee, Int. Christian Univ., Tokyo 68-; Chair. Board Associated Japanese Bank (Int.) Ltd. London 70-; Rep. Dir. Int. Devt. Journal Ltd. 70-; Gov. and Steering Cttee. mem., Atlantic Inst. for Int. Affairs (Paris) 71-; mem. European Atlantic Group 71-; mem. Council of Int. Chamber of Commerce (Paris) 74-.
Leisure interest: golf.
Office: 29-30 Cornhill, London, E.C.3; Home: Flat 38, London House, 7-9 Avenue Road, London, N.W.8, England; and 2-5-13 Nukuikita-machi, Koganeishi, Tokyo, Japan.
Telephone: 01-623-5661 (London Office); 01-586-2721 (London Home); 0423-83-5751 (Tokyo Home).

Suzuki, Haruo, LL.B.; Japanese business executive; b. 31 March 1913, Hayama, Kanagawa Pref.; s. of Chuji and Masu Suzuki; m. Itoko Hibiya 1941; two d.; ed. Tokyo Univ.
With Nomura Securities Co. Ltd., 36-39; joined Showa-Denko K.K. 39, Exec. Vice-Pres. 59-71, Pres. 71-; Chair. AA Chemical Co., Showa Neoprene K.K., Showa Yuka K.K. 71-, Showa Unox K.K. 75-; Pres. Tokuyama Petrochem. Co. 71-; Dir. N.Z. Aluminium Smelters Ltd. 72-, Industria Venezolana de Aluminio C.A. 73-; Chair. Japan Carbon Asscn., Abrasive Industry Asscn.; Vice-Pres. Japan Light Metal Smelters' Asscn.; Dir. Int. Primary Aluminium Inst.; Chair. Industrial Policy Cttee., Keidanren (Japan Fed. of Econ. Orgs.); Vice-Chair. Japan-German Dem. Repub. Econ. Cttee., Japan-Southern U.S. Asscn.; mem. Industrial Structure Council and Electric Utility Industry Council of Minis-

try of Int. Trade and Industry, Cttee. on Financial Systems Research of Ministry of Finance.
Leisure interests: reading, art appreciation, golf.
Publ. *Chemical Industry* 68.
Showa Denko K.K., 13-9, Shiba Daimon 1-chome, Minato-ku, Tokyo; Home: Chateau Mita (Rm. 810) 7-1, Mita 2-chome, Minato-ku, Tokyo, Japan.
Telephone: 432-5111 (Office).

Suzuki, Hideo; Japanese investment banker; b. 4 June 1917, Hayama, Kanagawa Pref.; m.; two c.; ed. Univ. of Tokyo.
Entered Ministry of Finance 40; Deputy Supt. of Kobe Customs, Ministry of Finance 53-55; Head, Treasury Div., Financial Bureau, Ministry of Finance 55-57; Head Govt., Investment Div., Financial Bureau, Ministry of Finance 57-58, Co-ordinating Div., Foreign Exchange Bureau 58-59; Financial Counsellor, Japanese Embassy, Consul in New York and Rep. of Ministry of Finance in New York 59-62; Deputy Dir. Int. Finance Bureau Ministry of Finance 62-64; mem. Policy Board, Bank of Japan, concurrently Deputy Dir. Int. Finance Bureau, Ministry of Finance 64-65; Dir. Int. Finance Bureau 65-66; Special Adviser to Minister of Finance and Special Asst. to Minister of Foreign Affairs 66-74; Exec. Dir. IMF 66-72; Vice-Chair., Deputies of Cttee. of 20, IMF 72-74; Adviser, Nomura Securities Co.; Chair., Nomura Securities International Inc.; Chair. Nomura Europe, N.V. 74-.
The Nomura Securities Co., 1-9-1, Nihoubashi, Chuo-ku, Tokyo 103, Japan.

Suzuki, Hiroaki, LL.B.; Japanese business executive; b. 15 Feb. 1916, Kyoto; s. of Kijuro and Asa Suzuki; m. Emiko Kosuga 1944; two s.; ed. Kyoto Univ.
With Kobe Steel Ltd. 43, Dir. 69-70, Dir. and Exec. Officer 70-72, Dir. and Senior Exec. Officer 72-74, Dir. and Vice-Pres. 74, Dir. and Pres. 74-.
Leisure interests: golf, reading.
5-17-603, 6-chome, Okamoto, Higashinada-ku, Kobe, Japan.
Telephone: Kobe 452-1800.

Suzuki, Jitsujiro; Japanese business executive; b. 29 Nov. 1913, Fujieda, Shizuoka; m. Ai Suzuki 1940; three s. three d.; ed. Hamamatsu Technical School.
With Suzuki Motor Co. Ltd. 40-, Dir. 48-, Man. Dir. 61-67, Senior Man. Dir. 67-73, Pres. 73-; Ranjyu Hosho (Japan Nat. Prize) 74.
Leisure interest: golf.
4-27-26, Kamoe, Hamamatsu, Shizuoka, Japan.
Telephone: 0534-52-0579.

Suzuki, Kyoji, M.A.; Japanese business executive; b. 18 March 1909, Kyoto; s. of Tanaka and Hajime Suzuki; m. Sakae Suzuki; one s. three d.; ed. Tokyo Imperial Univ.
With Dai-Ichi Bank Ltd. 31-48; Dir. Ajinomoto Co. Inc. 48, Exec. Vice-Pres. 59, Exec. Dir. Ajinomoto-Insud S.p.A., Rome 63; Pres. Ajinomoto Inc. 65-73, Chair. 73-75; Auditor May 75-; Chair. Knorr Food Products (Japan) Ltd.; Blue Ribbon Medal.
Leisure interest: reading books, especially history.
Ajinomoto Co. Inc., 1-6 Kyobashi, Chuoku; Home: 3-8-2-chome Shoto, Shibuya-ku, Tokyo, Japan.
Telephone: 03-272-1111.

Suzuki, Shunzo; Japanese business executive; b. 24 May 1903; ed. Shizuoka Univ.
President, Suzuki Motor Co. Ltd. until 73, Chair. 73-.
Suzuki Motor Co. Ltd., 300 Takatsuka, Kamimura, Hamaganun, Shizuoka Prefecture, Japan.

Suzuki, Ziro; Japanese business executive; b. 8 Nov. 1912; ed. Tokyo Inst. of Tech.
Chairman of Board, Furukawa Electric Co. Ltd. Nov. 74-.
Office: Furukawa Electric Co. Ltd., 6-1, Marunouchi

2-chome, Chiyoda-ku, Tokyo 100; Home: 13-5, Nakadai, Higashi Terao, Tsurumi-ku, Yokohama 230, Japan. Telephone: 03-213-0811 (Office); 045-581-6285 (Home).

Svart, Anker; Danish diplomatist; b. 15 Sept. 1918, Taps; s. of Jakob Svart and Helene (née Olsen); m. Nina Jonsson 1949; no c.; ed. Aarhus Universitet and Univ. of Sheffield, England.

Attaché, Danish Legation, Iceland 44-45; Ministry of Foreign Affairs, Copenhagen 45-52; Sec. Danish Legation, Canada 52-55; Counsellor, Moscow 56-60, Bonn 60-62; Amb. to Repub. of China (Peking) 62-65; Head of Dept., Econ. Div., Ministry of Foreign Affairs 65-66; Amb. to U.S.S.R. (also accredited to Mongolia) 66-73; Amb. to NATO (also accredited to Belgium and Luxembourg) 73-.

Leisure interests: photography, motoring, music, skating.

Danish Delegation to NATO, Boulevard Léopold III, B-1110 Brussels, Belgium.

Sveinsson, Einar Olafur, DR. LITT. ISL.; Icelandic university professor; b. 12 Dec. 1899, Höfdabrekka; s. of Sveinn Olafsson and Vilborg Einarsdóttir; m. Kristjana Thorsteinsdóttir Manberg 1930; one s.; ed. Univs. of Copenhagen and Iceland.

Various posts at Univ. of Iceland 31-, Head of Univ. Library 40-45, Prof. of Icelandic Literature 45-70; Head of Manuscript Inst. of Iceland 62-70; mem. various Cttees.; Editor *Skirnir* 44-53; Editor-in-Chief *Islenzk Fornrit* 52-62; Co-Editor *Arv,* Uppsala 53-; Chair. Icelandic Presidium *Kulturhistorisk leksikon för nordisk Middelalder* 62-; Editor-in-Chief Publs. of Manuscript Inst. of Iceland 62-70; Chair. Icelandic Literary Soc. 63-67; mem. Societas Scientiarium Islandica 34-, Royal Swedish Gustav Adolf Acad. 34-, Medieval Acad. of America 49- (Fellow 61), Norwegian Acad. of Letters and Sciences 55, Royal Danish Acad. of Letters and Sciences 55, Acad. Septentrionale, Paris 68-, Royal Swedish Acad. of Letters 69, etc.; Hon. mem. Modern Languages Asscn. America 58; Hon. Fil. dr. (Uppsala), Hon. D.Litt. (Dublin), Dr. phil. h.c. (Oslo); Commdr. Order of Falcon (Iceland), Royal Swedish Nordstjärna Order; Chevalier Ordre des Arts et Lettres.

Leisure interest: sleep.

Publs. *Verzeichnis isländischer Märchenvarianten* 29, *Um Njálu* 33, *Sagnaritun Oddaverja* 37, *Um islenzkar thjóðsögur* 40, *Sturlungaöld* 40, *Á Njálsbúd* 43 (translated into Norwegian and English), *Landnám í Skaftafellspingi* 48, *Studies in the Manuscript Tradition of Njálssaga* 53, *The Age of the Sturlungs* 53 (translated into Chinese), *Vid uppspretturnar* 56, *Dating the Icelandic Sagas* 58, *Handritamálid* 59, *Njáls saga* 59, *Les sagas islandaises* 61, *Islenzkar bókmenntir í fornöld I* 62, *Ferd og förunautar* 63, *Ritunartimi Islendingasagna* 65, *Ljód* (poems) 68 (translated into French); also worked as editor and translator.

Oddagötu 6, Reykjavik, Iceland. Telephone: 13431.

Svenningsen, Nils Thomas; Danish diplomatist; b. 28 March 1894, Stockholm, Sweden; s. of Anders Svenningsen and Anna Bennet; m. Eva Larsen 1922 (died 1960); one d.; ed. Univ. of Copenhagen.

Ministry of Justice 18; Ministry of Foreign Affairs 20; Sec., Berlin 24-30; various depts., Ministry of Foreign Affairs 30-41; Sec.-Gen., Ministry of Foreign Affairs 41-45; Ambassador to Sweden 45-50, to France 50-51; Sec.-Gen. Ministry of Foreign Affairs 51-61; Ambassador to Great Britain 61-64; Head of Swedish-Norwegian Commission on Research of Reindeer Grazing in North Scandinavia 64-67; mem. UN Register for fact-finding experts in international disputes 68-; Grand Cross Order of Dannebrog (Denmark), Hon. G.B.E. (U.K.) and other foreign orders.

Leisure interest: riding.

Overgaden oven Vandet 50, Copenhagen K, Denmark. Telephone: Asta 15-66.

Sveshnikov, Aleksandr Vasilyevich; Soviet musician; b. 1890; ed. Moscow People's Conservatoire.

Choirmaster in schools and theatres 09-28; Organizer, Artistic Adviser, Conductor and Dir., All-Union Broadcasting Cttee. Choir 28-36; Artistic Adviser, Conductor and Dir. U.S.S.R. State Choir 36-37, Leningrad Academic Choir 37-41; Organizer, Artistic Adviser, Conductor and Dir., U.S.S.R. Academic Choir of Russian Songs 41-46; Prof., Moscow Conservatoire 46-74, Rector 48-74; mem. C.P.S.U. 50-; People's Artist of U.S.S.R. 56; U.S.S.R. State Prize 46, R.S.F.S.R. State Prize 67; Hon. mem. Royal Acad. of Music (England) 67; Hero of Socialist Labour 70, Orders of Lenin and other awards.

Principal works: numerous arrangements of Russian and other folk songs and compositions of Russian, Soviet and foreign composers.

c/o Moscow Conservatoire, 13 Ulitsa Gertsena, Moscow, U.S.S.R.

Sveshnikov, Mefodii Naumovich; Soviet economist and banker; b. 1911; ed. Financial and Econ. Inst.

State Bank of U.S.S.R. 29-, Branch Manager, Office Manager, Dir. of Dept., mem. Board of Dirs., Dep. Chair. Board of Dirs.; Chair. Board of Dirs. of Bank for Foreign Trade of U.S.S.R. 57-69; Chair. Board of U.S.S.R. State Bank 69-.

The State Bank of the U.S.S.R., 12 Neglinnaya ulitsa, Moscow, U.S.S.R.

Švestka, Bedřich, M.D., Czechoslovak scientist and politician; b. 16 Jan. 1912, Švermov; ed. Faculty of Medicine, Charles University, Prague.

Dean, Faculty of Hygiene, Charles Univ. Prague 57-59; Amb. to Yugoslavia 60-62; Amb. to Algeria 62-64; Dean, Faculty of Hygiene, Charles Univ. Prague 66-69; Rector, Charles Univ. Jan. 70-; mem. Bureau of Central Cttee. C.P. of Czechoslovakia for directing Party work in the Czech Lands 70-71; Chair. Czechoslovak Cttee. for European Security 70-; Dir. Inst. of Work Hygiene and Professional Diseases 71-; Corresp. mem. Czechoslovak Acad. of Sciences 70-, mem. Presidium 70-; Alt. mem. Cen. Cttee. of C.P. of Czechoslovakia 71-; Hon. mem. Deutsche Gesellschaft für die gesamte Hygiene (D.D.R.); Award for Merit in Construction 58; J. E. Purkyné Medal 70; J. A. Comenius Medal 72.

Publs. scientific papers on occupational medicine and work safety.

Charles University, Prague, Czechoslovakia.

Švestka, Oldřich; Czechoslovak journalist; b. 24 March 1922, Pozorka; ed. Commercial Acad.

Member of underground movement 38-45; joined *Rudé právo* 45, fmr. Deputy Editor, Editor 58-68, Chief Editor 75-; Chief Editor *Tribuna,* weekly of Cen. Cttee. C.P. of Czechoslovakia 69-71; mem. Cen. Cttee. C.P. of Czechoslovakia 62-, Sec. 70-, mem. Ideological Comm. of Cen. Cttee. 63-69, mem. Presidium of Cen. Cttee. April-Aug. 68, mem. Bureau for directing Party work in Czech Lands 69-70, Sec. 70-; Deputy to House of the People, Fed. Assembly 71-; Order of February 1948 First Class 49; Medal for Distinction in Construction 55; Order of Labour 70; Czechoslovak Journalists Prize 70; Order of the Repub. 72; Order of Victorious February 73.

Central Committee, Communist Party of Czechoslovakia, nábř. Kyjevské brigády 12, Prague 1, Czechoslovakia.

Svetlanov, Yevgeni Fyodorovich; Soviet composer and conductor; b. 6 Sept. 1928, Moscow; ed. Gnesiny Music Education Inst. and Moscow Conservatoire.

Conductor, Moscow Radio 53; Conductor, Bolshoi Theatre, Moscow 54-62, Chief Conductor 62-65; Conductor U.S.S.R. State Symphony Orchestra 65-; People's Artist of R.S.F.S.R.

Compositions include: Symphony, Tone-Poems *Festival* 50, *Daugava* 53, *Siberian Fantasy* 53, Rhapsody 54, Cantata *Home Fields* 49, Concerto 51, five Sonatas

46-52, five Sonatinas 46-51, Preludes 45-51; about 50 Romances and Songs.

Has conducted *Rusalka* (Dargomyshski), *Pskovityanka, The Czar's Bride, Sadko, Snow-Maiden* (Rimsky-Korsakov), *Prince Igor* (Borodin), *The Sorceress* (Tchaikovsky), *Not Only Love* (Shchedrin), *Boris Godunov* (Mussorgsky), *October* (Muradelya), *Storm Along the Path* (Karaev), *Paganini* (Rachmaninov), *Swan Lake* (Tchaikovsky), *Night Town* (Bartok), *Pages of Life* (Belanchivadze), *Chopiniana* (Chopin).

U.S.S.R. State Symphony Orchestra, 31 Ulitsa Gorkogo, Moscow, U.S.S.R.

Svetzov, Nikolai Pavlovich; Soviet engineer and trade union official; b. 5 Sept. 1912, Rostov-on-Don; ed. Novocherkask Industrial Inst.

Member C.P. of Soviet Union; Chair. Central Cttee. of Oil and Chemical Workers' Union 65-; mem. All-Union Council of Trade Unions; Order of Red Star.

Central Committee of Oil and Chemical Workers' Union, 42 Leninsky Prospekt, Moscow, U.S.S.R.

Sviridov, Georgy Vasilievich; Soviet composer; b. 16 Dec. 1915, Fatezh, Kursk Region; ed. Leningrad Conservatoire.

Secretary, Union of Composers of U.S.S.R. 62-; State prizewinner 46, 68; Lenin prizewinner 60, People's Artist of R.S.F.S.R. 63; Order of Lenin 65.

Works: romances set to pieces by A. Pushkin 35, M. Lermontov 38, songs to words by Shakespeare 44, a song cycle *My Homeland* 50, songs to poems by Burns 55, a symphonic poem *In Memory of Sergei Esenin* 56, *A Pathetic Oratory* (words by Mayakovsky) 60, *Kursk Songs* for chorus and symphony orchestra 63, also composed a trio for piano, violin and 'cello, and music for films and theatre.

Union of U.S.S.R. Composers, 8-10 Ulitsa Nezhdanovoi, Moscow, U.S.S.R.

Svoboda, Josef; Czechoslovak architect and stage designer; b. 10 May 1920, Čáslav; s. of Růžena and Josef Svoboda; m. Libuše Hrubešová 1948; one d.; ed. Special School for Interior Architecture, Prague and School of Fine and Applied Arts, Prague.

Stage designer, Nat. Theatre, Prague 47, Head Designer 51-; Prof. Acad. of Applied Arts 68-; mem. Union of Czech Dramatic Artists 75-; Gen. Sec. Int. Org. of Scenographers and Theatre Technicians 71-; Artistic Dir. of Laterna Magica 73; created over 320 stage sets in Czechoslovakia and for theatres in Belgium, France, Italy, Germany, U.S.S.R., U.K., U.S.A., etc.; State Prize 54, Order of Labour 63, Honoured Artist 66; Best Stage Designer Art Biennale São Paulo 61, London Theatre Critics' Award for the Best Stage Set (*The Insect Comedy*, Čapek and *Tempest*, Ostrovsky) 66, Nat. Artist 68, Nederlands Sikkenprijs 69; Hon. Degree Royal Coll. of Art 69.

Leisure interest: motoring.

National Theatre, Divadelní 6, Prague 1; Home: Na-Květnici 850/6, Prague-Nusle, Czechoslovakia.

Telephone: 27-72-69 (Office); 43-22-60 (Home).

Svoboda, Gen. Ludvík; Czechoslovak army officer and politician; b. 25 Nov. 1895, Hroznatín.

Fought in Czechoslovak Legions in First World War 15-20; in Czechoslovak Army 22-39, Company Commdr. 36, later Infantry Battalion Commdr., teacher at Mil. Acad.; fought in U.S.S.R. in Second World War; organized and commanded Czechoslovak Army Unit 39-45; Minister of Nat. Defence and organized new Czechoslovak People's Army 45-50; Deputy Premier 50-51; Chief of Mil. Acad. 54-58, retd. 59; Pres. of Republic 68-75; mem. Nat. Assembly 48-68, mem. Presidium Nat. Assembly 60-64; mem. Presidium Czechoslovak-Soviet Friendship Union 45-; mem. Presidium and Deputy Chair. Central Cttee. of Union of Anti-Fascist Fighters 48-68; mem. Central Cttee. C.P. of Czecho-

slovakia; mem. Central Cttee. Presidium; mem. Exec. Cttee. of Presidium of Central Cttee. C.P. of Czechoslovakia 68-69; C.-in-C. Czechoslovak Armed Forces 68-75; Lenin Prize 68, 69, Czechoslovak Peace Prize 68; numerous decorations including Order of Klement Gottwald 70, Order of the October Revolution (U.S.S.R.) 70, Order of the Banner, 1st Class with Diamonds (Hungary) 70, Order Stara Planina with Ribbon (Bulgaria) 72, Order of Victorious February 73, Hero of Czechoslovak Socialist Repub. 70, 75.

Publ. *From Buzuluk to Prague* 60.

c/o Communist Party of the Czechoslovak Socialist Republic, Nábř. Kyjevské brigády 12, 125 II Prague I, Czechoslovakia.

Svolinský, Karel; Czechoslovak painter and graphic artist; b. 14 Jan. 1896, Kopeček; ed. School of Fine and Applied Arts, Prague.

Professor, Coll. of Fine and Applied Arts, Prague 45-70; Grand Prix, Paris 25, 37, Milan 40, Brussels 58; Gold Medals, Paris 37 and two at Leipzig 65; State Prize 52; Honoured Artist 56; Nat. Artist 61.

Works include stained glass windows and mosaics in St. Vitus Cathedral, Prague; work for Paris Exhbn. 37, Brussels Exhbn. 58; book illustrations and layout; costumes and stage sets, Nat. and other Theatres Prague, Vienna and Moscow; at int. exhbns. in Lugano 54, Leipzig 27, 59, 65, Venice 56, São Paulo 60 Paris 63, 75, Belgrade 65, Mainz 65, etc., one-man shows Kassel 64, Vienna 65, Offenbach/M. 66, Olomouc 66, 73, Amsterdam 69, Prague 67, 71, 75.

Na Zátorce 13, Prague 6, Czechoslovakia.

Telephone: 372-676.

Swai, Asanterabi Zephaniah Nsilo, B.A.; Tanzanian politician and diplomatist; b. 20 April 1925, Kilimanjaro; s. of Zephaniah Jacob Swai and Miriam Lazaro Muro; m. Victoria Ely Joseph Mawalla 65; three d.; ed. Makerere Coll. and Univs. of Bombay and Delhi.

Assistant Warden, Makerere Coll. 52-54; Gen. Man. Meru Co-operative Union 58-60; Provincial Chair., Tanganyika African National Union (T.A.N.U.), Northern Province 58-60; Chair. T.A.N.U. Economics and Social Devt. Cttee. 60-62, Nat. Treas. 62-67; mem. Legislative Council 60-; Minister of Commerce and Industry 60; Minister of Health and Labour Jan.-Mar. 62; Minister without Portfolio and Perm. Rep. to UN 62; Minister of Development Planning, Tanganyika 62-63, Minister of State, President's Office, Directorate of Devt. and Planning 64-65; Minister of Industries, Mineral Resources and Power Sept. 65-March 67; Minister of Econ. Affairs and Devt. Planning, Chair. Nat. Devt. Corpn. March 67-June 67; Minister for E. African Affairs 67; E. African Community Minister for Communications, Research and Social Services 67-68; mem. E. African Legislative Assembly 67-68.

P.O. Box 1077, Arusha, Tanzania.

Telephone: Moshi Machame 24.

Swaminathan, Jagdish; Indian painter; b. 21 June 1928, Simla; m. Bhavani 1955; two s.; ed. Delhi Polytechnic and Acad. of Fine Arts, Warsaw.

Early career of freedom fighter, trade unionist, journalist, and writer of children's books; mem. Delhi State Cttee. of Congress Socialist Party and Editor of its weekly organ, *Mazdoor Awaz*; Senior Art Teacher, Cambridge School, New Delhi; Founder-mem. *Group 1890* (avante-garde group of Indian artists); mem., Nat. Cttee., Int. Asscn. of the Arts 67-, Exec. Cttee. Delhi Slipi Chakra 67-, also Founder-Editor monthly journal, *Contra 66* and full-time painter; one-man exhbns. in New Delhi 62, 63, 64, 65, 66, in Bombay 66; in group shows Warsaw 61, Saigon 63, Tokyo Biennale 65, *Art Now in India*, London, Newcastle and Brussels 65-66, *Seven Indian Painters*, London 67; Jawaharlal

Nehru Research Fellow; represented in various public and private collections in India and abroad.

c/o Gallery Chemould, Jahangir Art Gallery, Mahatma Ghandi Road, Bombay 1; 6/17 W.E.A., New Delhi 5, India.

Swank, Emory Coblentz, M.A.; American diplomatist; b. 29 Jan. 1922, Frederick, Md.; s. of late George P. Swank and of Ruth Coblentz McCollough; m. Margaret K. Whiting; no c.; ed. Franklin and Marshall Coll., Harvard Univ. and Nat. War Coll., Washington, D.C. Served in U.S. Army 43-46; Instructor in English, Franklin and Marshall Coll. 46; joined foreign service 46; appointments in China, Indonesia and U.S.S.R.; Deputy Chief, U.S. Embassy, Bucharest 58-60; Special Asst. to Sec. of State 60-63; Deputy Chief, U.S. Embassy, Vientiane, Laos 64-67; Minister, Moscow 67-69; Deputy Asst. Sec. for European Affairs, Dept. of State 69-70; Amb. to Khmer Repub. 70-73; Political Adviser to C.-in-C., Atlantic, and Supreme Allied Commdr., NATO Atlantic Forces 73-; Bronze Star.

Leisure interests: swimming, golf, music, literature.

POLAD—CINCLANT, Norfolk, Va. 23411, U.S.A.

Swann, Donald Ibrahim, M.A.; British composer, pianist and entertainer; b. 30 Sept. 1923, Llanelly, Wales; s. of Herbert Swann and Naguimé Piszóva; m. Janet Oxborrow 1955; two d.; ed. Westminster School and Christ Church, Oxford.

Musical contributor to London revues, including *Airs on a Shoestring* 53-54; joint leader writer, musical play *Wild Thyme* 55; with Michael Flanders in two-man revues, *At the Drop of a Hat*, and *At the Drop of Another Hat* (singer and accompanist of own songs); toured Australia, New Zealand, America and Canada; other works include *London Sketches* 58, *Festival Matins* 62, *Perelandra* (opera) 61-62, settings of John Betjeman's poems 64; since 1966 has appeared in own concert/entertainments *Set by Swann* (settings of poetry by Tolkien and others), *An Evening in Crete* (Greek songs), *Soundings by Swann* (church music), *Between the Bars* (musical autobiography) 70, *A Crack in Time* (a concert in search of peace) 73; recordings include Flanders and Swann material (Parlophone), religious music (Argo, Galliard), Tolkien Songs (Caedmon).

Leisure interest: going to the laundrette.

Publs. *Sing Round the Year* (carols for children) 65, *The Road goes ever on* (with J. R. R. Tolkien), *The Space Between the Bars* 67, *Requiem for the Living* (choral work, with C. Day Lewis) 70, *Song of Caedmon* (narration with songs) 71, *The Rope of Love* (more carols) 73, *Swann's Way Out* 75.

13 Albert Bridge, London, SW11 4PX, England.

Telephone: 01-622-4281.

Swann, Sir Michael Meredith, Kt., M.A., PH.D., F.R.S., F.R.S.E., F.R.C.S.(E.), LL.D., D.SC., D.UNIV.; British academic and administrator; b. 1 March 1920; s. of M. B. R. Swann; m. Tess Gleadowe 1942; two s. two d.; ed. Winchester and Gonville and Caius Coll., Cambridge.

Army Service 40-46; Demonstrator, Dept. of Zoology, Univ. of Cambridge 46-52; Prof. of Natural History, Univ. of Edinburgh 52-62; Dean of Faculty of Science, Univ. of Edinburgh 62-65; Principal and Vice-Chancellor, Univ. of Edinburgh 65-73; mem. Medical Research Council 62-65; mem. Cttee. on Manpower Resources 65-68; mem. Council for Scientific Policy 65-69, Science Research Council 70-73; Chair. BBC Jan 73-; Chair. Council for Science and Society 73-; Trustee Wellcome Trust 73-; Queen's Lecture, Berlin 75.

Leisure interests: gardening, sailing.

Broadcasting House, London, W.1.; and Ormsacre, 41 Barnton Avenue, Edinburgh 4, Scotland.

Swart, Charles Robberts, B.A., LL.B.; South African lawyer, journalist and politician; b. 5 Dec. 1894, Morgenzon; s. of H. B. Swart and A. C. Swart (née

Robberts); m. Nellie de Klerk 1924; one s. one d.; ed. Grey University Coll., Bloemfontein, Univ. of South Africa and Columbia Univ., New York.

Advocate Supreme Court of South Africa 19-48; fmr. Organising Sec. Nat Party of Orange Free State 19-28; Leader Nat. Party of O.F.S. 40-59; fmr. mem. Federal Nat. Party Council; fmr. Lecturer in Law and Agricultural Legislation; M.P. for Ladybrand 23-38, Winburg 41-59; Minister of Education, Arts and Science 49-50; Minister of Justice 48-59; Deputy Prime Minister and Leader, House of Ass. 54-59; Gov.-Gen. 60-61; State Pres. Republic of South Africa 61-67; Chancellor, Univ. of Orange Free State 51-; Hon. Col. Oos-Vrystaat Regt. 53-, Regt. Univ. Oranje-Vrystaat 62-; Hon. LL.D. (Univ. of Orange Free State, Rhodes Univ. and Potchefstroom Univ.); Hon. Fellow Coll. of Medicine S. Africa; Hon. mem. S. Africa Acad. of Science and Art; Hon. Fellow, S. African Inst. of Architects; Hon. Pres. Automobile Asscn. S. Africa; Hon. LL.D.; Life Patron-in-Chief Voortrekker Youth Movement; freeman of numerous S. African towns; decoration for Meritorious Service 72.

Leisure interests: farming and agriculture.

Publs. *Kinders van Suid-Afrika* 33, *Die Agterryer* 39.

P.O. Box 135, Brandfort, Orange Free State, Republic of South Africa.

Swart, Karel, B.CHEM.ENG.; Netherlands oil company executive; b. 26 May 1921, Singapore; m. Wilhelmina A. Bruinsma 1950; ed. Delft Univ.

With Royal Dutch Shell-Laboratory, Amsterdam 48; Shell Berre 53; Start-up Team, Bombay 54, Geelong 55; Central Office, The Hague 56; Adviser, Technical Service, Refinery Asst., Man. Cardón Refinery, Venezuela 58; Gen. Man. Curaçao 65; Dir. Manufacturing and Supply, Venezuela 67; Special Assignment Central Office, The Hague 68; Man. Dir. N.V. Koninklijke Nederlandsche Petroleum Maatschappij (Royal Dutch) and of Shell Petroleum Co. Ltd., and Principal Dir. Shell Petroleum N.V. 70-; Knight Order of Netherlands Lion.

Royal Dutch Petroleum Co., Carel van Bylandtlaan 30, The Hague; Home: Brouwerlaan 6, Voorschoten, The Netherlands.

Swartz, Col. Hon. Sir Reginald William Colin, K.B.E., E.D.; Australian politician; b. 14 April 1911; ed. Toowoomba and Brisbane Grammar Schools.

Parliamentary Under-Sec. Ministry of Commerce and Agriculture 52-56; Parl. Sec. Ministry of Trade 56-61; Minister for Repatriation 61-64; Minister for Health 64-66; Minister for Social Services 65-66, for Civil Aviation 66-69, for Nat. Devt. 69-72; Leader of House of Reps. 71-72; Liberal.

31 Furlong Street, Rio Vista, Surfers Paradise, Queensland 4217, Australia.

Telephone: Gold Coast 317186.

Swe, U Ba; Burmese politician; b. 19 April 1915, Tavoy; s. of U Tun Hlaing and Daw Pe Lay Swe; m. Daw Nu Nu Swe 1944; six s. four d.; ed. Rangoon Univ.

President Rangoon Univ. Students' Union 40-41; one of the founders of People's Revolutionary Party 39; Exec. mem. of Party in Mergui District during Japanese occupation; Chief of Civil Defence in the "Kebotai" 42-45; one of leaders of Anti-Japanese Resistance Movement, in charge of Rangoon, Hanthawaddy and Insein districts 44-45, arrested and detained by Japanese; Pres. Socialist Party (originally People's Revolutionary Party) 45, later Sec.-Gen.; Pres. Asia Socialist Conf. 52-56, 56-60; Sec.-Gen. Anti-Fascist People's Freedom League 47-58; Leader of "Stable" Group 58; fmr. mem. Parl. from Taikkyi; Minister of Defence 52-58, concurrently Prime Minister 56; Deputy Prime Minister 57-58; Leader of Opposition 58-; under political arrest 63-66.

Leisure interests: gardening, billiards, writing.
84 Innes Road, Rangoon, Burma.
Telephone: 31323.

Swearingen, John Eldred, M.S.; American business-man; b. 7 Sept. 1918, Columbia, S.C.; s. of John E. and Mary (née Hough) Swearingen; m. 1st Rolly A. Ost-berger 1942, 2nd Bonnie Bolding; three d.; ed. Univ. of South Carolina and Carnegie Mellon Univ.
Chemical Engineer, Standard Oil Co. (Indiana) 39-47; various positions Stanolind Oil and Gas Co. (now Amoco Production Co.) 47-51 and Dir. 51-; Gen. Man. Production, Standard Oil Co. (Indiana) 51, Dir. 52, Vice-Pres. 54, Exec. Vice-Pres. 56, Pres. 58-65, Chair. of Board 65-; Dir. Chase Manhattan Bank, Midwest Oil Corpn.; Dir. American Petroleum Inst., Northwestern Memorial Hosp., Chicago, Highway Users Fed. for Safety and Mobility, McGraw Wildlife Foundation; Trustee, Carnegie Mellon Univ., DePauw Univ.; mem. Nat. Petroleum Council, Advisory Board Hoover Inst. for War, Revolution and Peace; mem. Nat. Acad. of Engineering, American Chemical Soc., American Inst. of Mining and Metallurgical Engineers; Fellow, Ameri-can Inst. of Chemical Engineers; Hon. D.Eng. (S.D. School of Mines and Technology), Hon. LL.D. (DePauw Univ., Univ. of S. Carolina, Knox Coll., Butler Univ., Illinois Coll.), Hon. D.L.H. (Nat. Coll. of Educ.).
Leisure interests: reading, fishing, hunting, golf.
200 E. Randolph Drive, Chicago, Ill. 60601; Home: 1420 Lake Shore Drive, Chicago, Ill., U.S.A.

Sweden, King of (see Carl XVI Gustaf).

Sweeney, James Johnson, A.B.; American museum director; b. 30 May 1900, New York; s. of Patrick Sweeney and Mary Johnson; m. Laura Harden 1927; three s. two d.; ed. Georgetown Univ., Jesus Coll., Cambridge (England), Sorbonne (Paris) and Siena Univs.
Lecturer New York Univ. Inst. of Fine Arts 35-40, Salzburg Seminar in American Studies 47 and 49; Visiting Scholar Univ. of Georgia 50-51; Dir. of Painting and Sculpture New York Museum of Modern Art 45-46, Solomon R. Guggenheim Museum, New York 52-60; Gallery Consultant, Nat. Gallery, Canberra; Dir. Houston Museum of Fine Arts 61-68, Consultant Dir. 68-; Dir. Iran America Soc. 64-; Lecturer Harvard Univ. 61; Vice-Pres. Int. Art Critics Asscn. 48-57, Pres. 57-63; Vice-Pres. Edward MacDowell Asscn. 53-54, Pres. 55-62, Counsellor 62-; Trustee American Acad. in Rome 62-, Nat. Council of the Arts 65-68, The Arts Council (Dublin) 66-, Mediaeval Acad. of America, Councillor 66; Art Adviser, Israel Museum, Jerusalem 72-; mem. Phi Beta Kappa, American Acad. of Arts and Sciences; Art in America Award 63; Chevalier Légion d'Honneur, Officier Ordre des Arts et des Lettres; Hon. A.I.A. (American Inst. of Architects), Hon. D.F.A. Univ. of Mich., Hon. L.H.D. Georgetown Univ. and Univ. of Miami and numerous other hon. degrees.
Publs. *Plastic Redirections in XXth Century Painting* 34, *African Negro Art* (editor) 35, *Joan Miró* 41, *Alexander Calder* 43, 51, 66, *Stuart Davis* 45, *Marc Chagall* 45, *Henry Moore* 47, *African Folk Tales and Sculpture* (with Paul Radin) 52, 64, *Burri* 55, *The Miró Atmosphere* 59, *Antoni Gaudi* (with José Luis Sert) 60, *Irish Illuminated Manuscripts* 65, *Vision and Image* 68, *Calder* 71, *Pierre Soulages* 72, *African Sculpture* 70; *Joan Miró* 71; numerous articles in various journals.
120 East End Avenue, New York, N.Y. 10028, U.S.A.
Telephone: BU80602.

Sweeting, William Hart, C.M.G., C.B.E.; British banker; b. 18 Dec. 1909, Nassau, Bahamas; s. of Charles C. and Clara M. Sweeting; m. Isabel J. Woodall 1950; ed. Queen's Coll., Nassau and Univ. of London.
Assistant Receiver-Gen. and Treas., Bahamas 46;

Financial Sec., Dominica 50-52; Receiver-Gen. and Treas., Bahamas 55; Chair. Bahamas Currency Commrs. 55-63; Chair. Bahamas Broadcasting and Television Comm. 56-62; mem. Legislative Council, Bahamas 60-64; Chief Sec., Bahamas 64, Deputy Gov. 69; Chair. Bank of London and Montreal (BOLAM) 70-.
Leisure interests: swimming, painting, music, bird-watching.
Bank of London and Montreal Ltd., Bolam House, King & George Streets, P.O. Box 1262, Nassau; Ryswick, P.O. Box N573, Nassau, Bahamas.
Telephone: 3-1518.

Sweetman, Seamus George, B.A.; British business executive; b. 7 Nov. 1914, Dublin; s. of James M. Sweetman, K.C., and Agnes Fottrell; m. Mary Giblett 1939; one s.; ed. Beaumont Coll., St. John's Coll., Cambridge.
Joined Unilever Group 36; War Service (Lt.-Col., The Buffs) 39-45; Unilever subsidiaries, U.K. 46-55; Uni-lever appointments, Continental Europe 55-61; Dir. Unilever NV 61-; Dir. Unilever Ltd. 61-, Vice-Chair. 74-.
Leisure interests: gardening, mountain walking, reading, history.
Unilever Ltd., Unilever House, Blackfriars, London, E.C.4; Home: Greenloaning, West Common Close, Harpenden Herts., England.

Swiderski, Jan; Polish actor and theatre director; b. 14 Jan. 1916, Chmielniec; m.; ed. State Inst. of Thea-trical Arts, Warsaw.
Debut at Teatr Polski, Poznań 38-39; Teatr Miejski, Lublin 45, Teatr Wojska Polskiego, Łódź 46-49, Teatr Polski, Warsaw 49-55, Teatr Dramatyczny, Warsaw 55-67, Teatr Ateneum, Warsaw 67-; Vice-Pres. Cen. Board, Asscn. of Polish Theatre and Film Actors 70-; State Prize 1st Class 64, Order of Banner of Labour 1st Class 64, Artistic Prize of City of Warsaw 70, Ministry of Culture and Arts 1st Class 73, Commdr. Cross with Star, Order of Polonia Restituta 76; roles incl.: Arnolf in *L'Ecole des femmes* by Molière, Macbeth, Voivode in *Mazepa* by J. Słowacki, Baron in *The Lower Depths* by Gorky, Poet in *Wesele* by S. Wyspiański, Old Man in *The Chairs* by Ionesco, Romulus the Great by Dürrenmatt, Gregory Solomon in *The Price* by A. Miller, Cup-Bearer in *The Revenge* by A. Fredro, Captain Edgar in *The Dance of Death* by Strindberg, Borkman in *John Gabriel Borkman* by Ibsen.
Ul. Krzywe Koło 8/10 m. 4, 00-270 Warsaw, Poland.
Telephone: 31-37-08.

Swift, A. Dean; American business executive; ed. Univ. of Illinois.
Joined Sears, Roebuck and Co. 40, Gen. Man. India-napolis, Ind. 64-67, Detroit Area 67-69, Vice-Pres. Southern Area 69, Dir. 69-, Pres. Feb. 73-; Dir. Allstate Insurance Cos., Homart Devt. Co., Sears Roebuck Acceptance Corpn., First Chicago Corpn., Common-wealth Edison Co.; Chair. Nat. Corpns. Cttee., United Negro Coll. Fund; mem. Business Advisory Board, Chicago Metropolitan Area, Nat. Alliance of Business-men; Dir. Sears Roebuck Foundation; Trustee Museum of Science and Industry, Northwestern Univ., mem. advisory council Graduate School of Man., Northwest-ern Univ.; Dir. and Mem. Exec. Cttee., Nat. Retail Merchants Asscn.
Sears, Roebuck and Co., 925 South Homan Avenue, Chicago, Ill. 60624, U.S.A.

Swigert, John Leonard, Jr., M.SC., M.B.A.; American astronaut; b. 30 Aug. 1931, Denver, Colo.; s. of the late Dr. and of Mrs. Leonard Swigert; ed. Univ. of Colorado, Rensselaer Polytechnic Inst. and Univ. of Hartford.
United States Air Force 53-56; fighter pilot in Japan and Korea; engineering test pilot, Pratt and Whitney Aircraft 57-64; engineering test pilot, N. American

Aviation Inc. 64-66; selected by NASA as astronaut April 66; mem. crew of *Apollo XIII* April 70; Exec. Dir., Cttee. on Science and Technology, U.S. House of Reps. 73-; Co-recipient American Inst. of Aeronautics and Astronautics Octave Chanute Award for his participation in demonstrating the Rogallo Wing as a feasible land landing system for returning space vehicles and astronauts 66; Medal of Freedom 70; NASA Distinguished Service Medal; AIAA Haley Astronautics Award 71; American Astronautical Soc. Flight Achievement Award 71; Gold Medals of cities of New York, Houston, Chicago; Antonian Gold Medal 72; Hon. D.Sc. (American Int. Coll. and W. Michigan Univ.), Hon. LL.D. (Western State Univ.).
Leisure interests: sports, photography, golf.
Committee on Science and Technology, U.S. House of Representatives, Washington, D.C. 20515, U.S.A.

Swings, Pol, PH.D., D.SC.; Belgian university professor; b. 24 Sept. 1906, Ransart; *m.* Christiane Borgerhoff 1932; one *s.*; ed. Univ. of Liège.
Assistant in Astronomy, Univ. of Liège 28-32, Asst. Prof. 32-36, Prof. 36-; Visiting Prof. Univ. of Chicago 39-43, 46-52; War Research Assignment U.S.A. 43-45; mem. Royal Acad. of Belgium, American Acad. Arts and Sciences, American Philosophical Soc., Nat. Acad. of Sciences U.S.A., Bavarian Acad. of Sciences., Acad. dei Lincei, Rome; Assoc. Inst. de France; Pres. Int. Astronomical Union 64-67; Francqui Prize 48; Decennial Physics Prize 60; Hon. D.Sc. (Aix-Marseille Univ., Bordeaux Univ., Charles Univ., Prague, York Univ., Toronto); Solvay Prize 70.
Leisure interest: gardening.
Department of Astrophysics, University of Liège Ougrée; Home: 23 Avenue Léon Souguenet, 4050 Esneux, Belgium.
Telephone: 041-801135 (Home).

Swinnerton, Frank Arthur; British novelist and literary critic; b. 12 Aug. 1884, Wood Green; *s.* of Charles Swinnerton and Rose Cottam; *m.* Mary Dorothy Bennett 1924; two *d.*
President, Royal Literary Fund 62-66.
Leisure interests: reading, gardening.
Publs. include: *Nocturne* 17, *The Georgian House, The Georgian Literary Scene* 36, 70, *Swinnerton: An Autobiography* 37, *The Bookman's London* 51, *Background with Chorus* 56, *Death of a Highbrow* 61, *Figures in the Foreground* 63, *Quadrille* 65, *A Galaxy of Fathers* 66, *Sanctuary* 66, *The Bright Lights* 68, *Reflections from a Village* 69, *On the Shady Side* 70, *Nor All Thy Tears* 72, *Rosalind Passes* 73, *Some Achieve Greatness* 76.
Old Tokefield, Cranleigh, Surrey, England.
Telephone: Cranleigh 3732.

Swinnerton-Dyer, Sir Henry Peter Francis, Bt., M.A., F.R.S.; British mathematician and university professor; b. 2 Aug. 1927, Ponteland; *s.* of the late Sir Leonard Dyer; ed. Eton and Trinity Coll., Cambridge.
Research Fellow, Trinity Coll. 50-54; Commonwealth Fund Fellow, Univ. of Chicago 54-55; College Lecturer in Mathematics, Trinity 55-71, Dean 63-70; Lecturer in Mathematics, Cambridge Univ. 60-71, Prof. of Mathematics 71-, Master of St. Catharine's Coll. 73-; Visiting Prof. Harvard Univ. 70-71.
Leisure interests: tennis, squash, chess.
Publs. *Analytic Theory of Abelion Varieties* 74, and papers in learned journals.
Master's Lodge, St. Catharine's College, Cambridge, England.
Telephone: Cambridge 59445.

Sydow, Erik von, B.L.; Swedish diplomatist; b. 2 Sept. 1912, Göteborg; *s.* of Oscar von Sydow and Mary (née Wijk) von Sydow; *m.* Lia Akel 1940; one *s.* one *d.*; ed. Uppsala Univ.
Ministry of Foreign Affairs 36; early service Germany

and Baltic States; Sec. Legation to Japan 40, Chargé d'Affaires 45-46; Head of Div., Ministry of Foreign Affairs 47-49; Perm. Rep. to OEEC 49-53; Counsellor, U.S.A. 54-56; Asst. Under-Sec. Commercial and Econ. Affairs, Ministry of Foreign Affairs 59-63; Ambassador and Perm. Rep. to EFTA and other Int. Orgs. in Geneva 64-71; Amb. to the EEC, Brussels 72-; Chair. numerous bilateral and multilateral trade negotiations.
Swedish Delegation to the EEC, 6 Rond-Point Robert Schuman, B 1040 Brussels; Home: 28 avenue du Prince d'Orange, B 1180 Brussels, Belgium.
Telephone: 73690 30 (Office); 374 12 04 (Home).

Sydow, Max von; Swedish actor; b. 10 April 1929, Lund, Sweden; *s.* of Carl Sydow and Greta Rappe; *m.* Christina Olin 1951; two *s.*; ed. Royal Dramatic Theatre School, Stockholm.
Norrköping-Linköping Theatre 51-53, Hälsingborg Theatre 53-55, Malmö Theatre 55-60, Royal Dramatic Theatre, Stockholm 60-; Sorrento Prize 68.
Leisure interest: nautical history.
Plays acted in include: *Peer Gynt, Henry IV* (Pirandello), *The Tempest, Le Misanthrope, Faust, Ett Drömspel, La Valse des Toréadors, Les Sequestrés d'Altona, After the Fall, The Wild Duck.*
Films acted in include: *Bara en mor* 49, *Miss Julie* 50, *Det sjunde inseglet* (The Seventh Seal) 57, *Ansiktet* (The Face) 58, *The Virgin Spring* 60, *Såsom i en spegel* (Through a Glass Darkly) 61, *Nattvardsgästerna* (Winter Light) 63, *The Greatest Story Ever Told* 63, *4×4* 65, *Hawaii* 65, *Quiller Memorandum* 66, *The Hour of the Wolf* 66, *The Shame* 67, *A Passion* 68, *The Emigrants* 69, *The New Land* 69, *The Exorcist* 73, *Steppenwolf* 73, *Trompe l'Oeil* 75, *Heart of a Dog* 75, *Foxtrot* 75, *The Voyage of the St. Louis* 76, *The Desert of the Tartars* 76.
c/o Filmhuset, Box 27126, 102 52 Stockholm 27, Sweden.

Syed Putra bin Syed Hassan Jamalullail (*see* Perlis).

Syed Zahiruddin bin Syed Hassan, Tan Sri, P.S.M., G.C.V.O., J.M.N., S.P.M.P., P.J.K.; Malaysian government official; b. 11 Oct. 1918, Perak; *m.* Halimah Binti Haji Mohd. Noh 1944; ten *c.*; ed. Raffles Coll., Singapore.
Malay Officer 45-47; Deputy Asst. District Officer, Krian 48, Asst. District Officer 51; Asst. District Officer, Tanjong Malim 53, Ipoh 54; Second Asst. State Sec., Perak 55, Registrar of Titles and Asst. State Sec. (Lands) 56; District Officer, Batang Padang, Tapah 57; Deputy Sec. Public Services Comm. 58; Principal Asst. Sec., Fed. Establishment Officer 60; State Sec. Perak 61; Perm. Sec. Ministry of Agriculture and Co-operatives 63, Ministry of Educ. 66; Dir.-Gen. Public Services Comm. 69; retd. 72; High Commr. in U.K. 74-; Chair. Railway Services Comm. 72-, Special Cttee. on Superannuation, Board of Govs. Malay Coll., Interim Council of Nat. Inst. of Technology, Central Board.
Leisure interest: golf.
Malaysian High Commission, 45 Belgrave Square, London, SW1X 8QT; Residence: 1 Templewood Gardens, Hampstead, London, N.W.3, England.
Telephone: 01-435-7074 (Residence).

Sykes, Peter, B.SC., M.SC., PH.D., F.R.I.C.; British chemistry teacher; b. 19 Feb. 1923, Manchester; *s.* of Charles Hyde Sykes and Alice Booth; *m.* Joyce Tyler 1946; two *s.* one *d.*; ed. Rydal School, Colwyn Bay, Univ. of Manchester, Clare Coll., Cambridge.
Research Fellow, St. John's Coll., Cambridge 47-50, Univ. Demonstrator in Organic Chem. 47-55, Lecturer 55-, Official Fellow and Dir. of Studies in Chem., Christ's Coll. 56-; Visiting Research Prof., Coll. of William and Mary, Williamsburg, Va. 70-71; Visiting Prof., Univ. of Cape Town 74.
Leisure interests: chamber music, church architecture, talking, German wine.
Publs. *A Guidebook to Mechanism in Organic Chemistry*

(4th edn.) 61, *The Search for Organic Reaction Pathways* 72 (both trans. in numerous languages).

University Chemical Laboratory, Lensfield Road, Cambridge, CB2 1EW; and Christ's Coll., Cambridge, CB2 3BU, England.

Telephone: 0223 66499 (Laboratory); 0223 67641 (College).

Syme, Sir Colin York, Kt., LL.B.; Australian businessman; b. 22 April 1903, Claremont; *s.* of Francis Mark Syme; *m.* Patricia Baird 1933; three *s.* one *d.*; ed. Perth and Melbourne Univs.

Partner firm of Hedderwick, Fookes and Alston 28-66; Dir. Broken Hill Pty. Co. Ltd. 37-71, Chair. 57-71, Dir. of Admin. 66-71; Chair. Tubemakers of Australia Ltd. 66-73; Pres. Walter and Eliza Hall Inst. of Medical Research; Dir. Australian Industry Devt. Corpn.; Chair. Inquiry into Hosp. and Health Services in Victoria; Hon. D.Sc.

Leisure interest: trout fishing.

22 Stonnington Place, Toorak, Victoria 3142, Australia. Telephone: 20-5254.

Syme, Sir Ronald, Kt., O.M., F.B.A.; British university professor; b. 11 March 1903, Eltham, New Zealand; ed. New Zealand and Oriel Coll. Oxford.

Fellow and Tutor, Trinity Coll., Oxford 29-49; Press Attaché, British Legation, Belgrade 40-41, Ankara, 41-42; Prof. of Classical Philology Univ. of Istanbul 42-45; Camden Prof. of Ancient History Univ. of Oxford 49-70; Pres. Int. Fed. Classical Societies 51; Pres. Soc. for the Promotion of Roman Studies 48-52; Sec.-Gen. Int. Council for Philosophy and the Humanities 52, Pres. 71; Foreign mem. Royal Danish Acad., American Phil. Soc., American Acad. of Arts and Sciences, American Historical Soc.; mem. Lund Soc. of Letters, etc.; Hon. D.Litt. (N.Z.) 49, Durham 52, Belfast 59, Emory 62, Graz 62; Hon. D. ès. L. Paris 62, Lyon 67; Hon. Fellow Oriel Coll. 58, Trinity Coll. 71.

Publs. *The Roman Revolution* 39, *Tacitus* 58, *Colonial Elites* 58, *Sallust* 64, *Ammianus and the Historia Augusta* 68, *Ten Studies in Tacitus* 70, *Emperors and Biography* 71, *The Historia Augusta: a call for Clarity* 71, *Danubian Papers* 71.

Wolfson College, Oxford, England.

Symington, Stuart; American politician; b. 26 June 1901, Amherst, Mass., U.S.A.; *s.* of William Symington and Emily Harrison; *m.* Evelyn Wadsworth 1924 (deceased); two *s.*; ed. Yale Univ. and Int. Correspondence School.

With Symington companies, Rochester, N.Y. 23-30; Pres. Colonial Radio Co., Rochester 30-35, Rustless Iron & Steel Co., Baltimore 35-37; Pres. and Chair. Board Emerson Electric Manufacturing Co., St. Louis 38-45; Surplus Property Admin., Washington, D.C. 45-46; Asst. Sec. of War for Air 46-47; Sec. of Air Force, Nat. Defense 47-50; later Chair. Nat. Security Resources Board and Admin. Reconstruction Finance Corpn.; U.S. Senator from Missouri 53-; Democrat.

Senate Office Building, Washington, D.C. 20510. U.S.A.

Symonette, Sir Roland Theodore, Kt.; Bahamian business executive and politician; b. 16 Dec. 1898; ed. Current Eleuthera, Bahamas.

Shipyard Owner and Contractor; mem. House of Assembly 35-, Exec. Council 49-; Parl. Leader United Bahamian Party; Prime Minister of Bahamas 64-67.

601 Bay Street, Nassau, Bahamas.

Synge, Henry Millington; British stockbroker; b. 4 April 1921, Liverpool; *s.* of Richard Millington Synge and Eileen B. N. Hall; *m.* Joyce Helen Topping 1947; two *s.* one *d.*; ed. Shrewsbury School.

With Merchant Navy 39-46; Dir. Union Int. Co. Ltd. 56, Chair. 69-; Man. Liverpool Trustee Savings Bank 56-71, Chair. 68-69; Man. West Midlands Trustee Savings Bank 70-; Partner, Tilney & Co. Stockbrokers, Liverpool, London and Shrewsbury.

Leisure interests: fishing, aviation, amateur radio.

4 St. Alkmonds Place, Shrewsbury, SY1 1UJ, 385 Sefton House, Liverpool, L2 3RT and Finsbury House, 22-23 Blomfield Street, London, EC2M 7AL; Home: Wilcot House, Nesscliffe, Shrewsbury, SY4 1BJ, England.

Synge, John Lighton, M.A., SC.D., F.R.S., M.R.I.A.; Irish mathematician; b. 23 March 1897, Dublin; *s.* of Edward and Ellen Synge (née Price); *m.* Elizabeth Allen 1918; three *d.*; ed. Trinity Coll., Dublin.

Lecturer in Mathematics Trinity Coll. Dublin 20; Asst. Prof. of Mathematics. Univ. Toronto 20-25; Fellow and Univ. Prof. of Natural Philosophy. Trinity Coll. Dublin 25-30; Prof. of Applied Mathematics, Toronto Univ. 30-43; Prof. of Mathematics Ohio State Univ. 43-46; Prof. of Mathematics Carnegie Inst. of Technology 46-48; Prof. Inst. for Advanced Studies, Dublin 48-72, Emer. Prof. 72-; Visiting Lecturer Princeton 39, Visiting Prof. Brown Univ. 41, Univ. of Maryland 51; Pres. Royal Irish Acad. 61-64; Hon. Fellow, Trinity Coll., Dublin; Hon. LL.D. (St. Andrews) 66; Hon. D.Sc. (Belfast) 69; Hon. D.Sc. (Nat. Univ. of Ireland) 70.

Leisure interests: reading, motoring, walking.

Publs. *Mathematical Papers of Sir W. R. Hamilton, Vol. I* (Editor, with A. W. Conway) 31, *Geometrical Optics* 37, *Principles of Mechanics* (with B. A. Griffith) 42, *Tensor Calculus* (with A. Schild) 49, *Science: Sense and Nonsense* 51, *Geometrical Mechanics and de Broglie Waves* 54, *Relativity: the Special Theory* 56, *The Relativistic Gas, Kandelman's Krim, The Hypercircle in Mathematical Physics* 57, *Relativity: The General Theory* 60, *Talking About Relativity* 71.

Torfan, Stillorgan Park, Blackrock, Co. Dublin; Institute for Advanced Studies, 10 Burlington Road, Dublin, Ireland.

Telephone: 881251.

Synge, Richard Laurence Millington, B.A., PH.D., F.R.I.C., F.R.S.E., F.R.S.; British biochemist; b. 28 Oct. 1914, Liverpool; ed. Winchester Coll. and Trinity Coll., Cambridge.

International Wool Secretariat Student in Biochemistry, Univ. of Cambridge 38 (transferred to Wool Industries Research Asscn., Leeds 39); Biochemist, Wool Industries Research Asscn., Leeds 41-43; Staff Biochemist, Lister Inst. of Preventive Medicine, London 43-48 (studied at Inst. of Physical Chemistry, Uppsala 46-47); Head of Dept. of Protein Chemistry, Rowett Research Inst., Bucksburn, Aberdeen, Scotland 48-67; Biochemist, Food Research Inst., Norwich 67-; Hon. Prof. School of Biological Sciences, Univ. of East Anglia 68-; shared Nobel Prize for Chemistry with A. J. P. Martin 52 (for invention of partition chromatography 41); mem. Editorial Board *Biochemical Journal* 49-55; Visiting biochemist Ruakura Animal Research Station, Hamilton. N.Z. 58-59; John Price Wetherill Medal. Franklin Inst. Philadelphia, U.S.A. (with others) 59; Hon. mem. Royal Irish Acad., Royal Soc. N.Z., American Soc. of Biological Chemists.

Agricultural Research Council's Food Research Institute, Colney Lane, Norwich, NR4 7UA, England.

Telephone: 56122.

Szabelski, Bolesław; Polish composer; b. 3 Dec. 1896, Radoryż, near Łuków; ed. Warsaw Conservatoire under R. Statkowski, K. Szymanowski and M. Surzynski.

Professor of Composition and Organ Music, State Higher School of Music, Katowice 29-; Prize of City of Katowice 48, State Prizes 53, 62, 66, Prize of Polish Composers' Asscn. 60, Prize of Katowice Voivod 63.

Works include: *Symphony No. 2* (for Soprano solo, Choir and Orchestra) (folk text) 34, *Suite* (for Orchestra) 38, *Study* (for Orchestra) 39, *Sonata* (for Organ) 43, *Sinfonietta* (for String Orchestra and Percussion) 46,

Symphony No. 3 51, *Concerto grosso* 54, *String Quartet* 56, *Symphony No. 4* 56, *Sonnets* (for Orchestra) 58, *Improvisations* (for Mixed Choir and Chamber Orchestra) 59, *Verses* (for Piano and Orchestra) 61, *"9", Aphorisms* (for Chamber Ensemble) 62, *Preludes* (for Chamber Orchestra) 63, *Concerto* (for Flute and Orchestra) 64, *Symphony No. 5* (for Mixed Choir and Orchestra) 68.
Ul. Nad Jarem 9, 40-625 Katowice Ochojec, Poland.

Szabó, Magda; Hungarian authoress; b. 5 Oct. 1917, Debrecen; *d.* of Alex Szabo and Madeleine Jablonczay; *m.* Tibor Szobotka 1948.
Graduated as a teacher 40; worked in secondary schools 40-44, 50-59; started literary career as poetess and has since written novels, plays, radio dramas and film scripts; works have been translated into 22 languages including English, French, German, Italian, Russian, Polish, Swedish; Józoef Attila Prize 59 and 72.
Publs. poems: *Neszek* (Noises); autobiography: *Ókut* (Old Well); novels for children: *Szigetkék* (Island-Blue), *Tündér Lala* (Lala the Fairy), *Abigél* (Abigail); novels: *Az öz* (The Fawn), *Fresko* (Fresco), *Disznótor* (Night of Pig-Killing), *Pilatus* (Pilate), *A Danaida* (The Danaid), *Mózes* 1.22 (Genesis 1.22), *Katalin utca* (Kathleen Street), *A szemlélök* (The Onlookers).
Leisure interest: pets.
H-1026 Budapest II, Julia-utca 3, Hungary.

Szabó, Zoltán, M.D.; Hungarian physician and politician; b. 17 Feb. 1914, Patalom; *s.* of Béla Szabó and Mária Klapp; *m.* Erzsébet Nagy 1948; one *s.* one *d.*; ed. Pécs Univ.
Assistant Lecturer, Univ. Medical School, Pécs 45, Univ. Medical Clinic, Budapest 57, Asst. Prof. 63; Pres. Physicians and Health Workers Union 52, Gen. Sec. 63; First Deputy Minister of Health 63; Minister of Health 64-74; mem. Cen. Cttee. Hungarian Socialist Workers' Party 62-75; Gen. Sec. World Fed. of Hungarians 74-; Red Banner Order of Merit 74.
II. Sarolta-u. 12, H-1028 Budapest, Hungary.
Telephone: 150-627.

Szádeczky-Kardoss, Elemér; Hungarian geochemist and geologist; b. 1903; *m.* Julia Lengyel.
University Prof.; mem. Hungarian Acad. of Sciences, Pres. Dept. for Geology and Mining Science; mem. World Acad. of Arts and Sciences, Austrian Acad. of Sciences; made fundamental discoveries in fields of sediment formation, coal petrology, magmatic rock genesis and geochemistry; law of the Universal cyclicities; Kossuth Prize 49, 52, Labour Order of Merit, golden degree 53, 73.
Leisure interests: philosophy, music.
Publs. *Coal Petrology* 52, *Geochemistry* 55, *Structure and Evolution of the Earth* 68, *Mechanism of the New Global Tectonics and its Relations to the Evolution of the Earth and Life* 71, *Geonomics* 74.
Geokémiai Kutató Laboratorium, Budaörsi ut. 43-45, H-1112 Budapest XI, Hungary.
Telephone: 850-777/159, 162.

Szafrański, Henryk; Polish politician; b. 1 Nov. 1905, Warsaw; ed. Warsaw Polytechnic.
Employed at Lilpop factory, then at machine tool factory at Pruszków, then at Ursus works; participated in September Campaign 38; returned to Ursus works 45; mem. Polish Workers' Party (PPR) 42-48, Cen. Cttee. 45-48; Deputy to Nat. People's Council; Sec. Bydgoszcz Voivodship Cttee., Polish United Workers' Party (PZPR) 48, Warsaw Voivodship Cttee. 49, 56-67, First Sec. Warsaw Voivodship Cttee. 67-71; mem. Cen. Cttee., PZPR 64-; mem. Council of State 71-; Chair. Warsaw Voivodship Cttee. of Nat. Unity Front 72-; Order of Builders of People's Poland 74, Order of Banner of Labour, 1st Class, Commdr.'s Cross with Star, Order of Polonia Restituta, Grunwald Cross, 3rd Class.
Kancelaria Rady Państwa, ul. Wiejska 4/6/8, 00-489 Warsaw, Poland.

Szajna, Józef; Polish theatre director, scenographer and painter; b. 13 March 1922, Rzeszów; *s.* of Julian and Karolina Szajna; *m.* Bożena Sierosławska; one *s.*; ed. Cracow Acad. of Fine Arts.
Lecturer, Acad. of Arts, Cracow 54-68; Co-founder and scenographer Teatr Ludowy, Nowa Huta 55-63, Man. Dir. 63-66; Dir. and Scenographer, Teatr Stary, Cracow 66-70; Man. Dir. Teatr Klasyczny, now Art Gallery and experimental theatre called Teatr Studio, Warsaw 71-; Prof. Acad. of Arts, Warsaw, and Dir. School for Stage Designers 71-; Dir. *Faust* 71, *Replika* 73, *Gulgutiera* 73, *Dante* (scenario) 74; Reviewers, Award 57, ITI Distinction Award for decorations and costumes, Paris 58; Nowa Huta Artistic Award 59, First Prize for All-Polish Short-Feature Film Festival, Cracow 62, Prize of Minister of Culture and Art 63, 71, Annual Award of Arkady Gallery, Cracow 71, Gold Medal of "Quadriennale", Prague 71, First Prize and Gold Medal, IV Art Festival, Warsaw 72; numerous decorations.
Spasowskiego 14/8, 00-389 Warsaw, Poland.
Telephone: 26-4752.

Szakács, Ödön, LL.D.; Hungarian judge; b. 1912.
Graduated as Doctor of Law and Political Science 42; Judge of district court Makó 42, County Court Szeged; Pres. County Court Debrecen 51-53, Szeged 53-55; leader Criminal Dept., Ministry of Justice 55-56; Pres. Budapest Metropolitan Court 57-62; Vice-Pres. 62-68, then Pres. of Supreme Court of Justice 68-.
c/o Supreme Court of Justice of the Hungarian People's Republic, H-1251 Budapest I, Fö-utca 1, Hungary.
Telephone: 160-075.

Szalay, Sándor, B.A., M.A., PH.D., D.SC.; Hungarian physicist; b. 4 Oct. 1909, Nyiregyháza; *s.* of Sandor Szalay and Gizelle Niedermayer; *m.* Eva Csongor 1948; two *s.*; ed. Budapest and Leipzig Univs., Technical High School, Munich, and Cavendish Laboratory, Cambridge; mem. Hungarian Acad. of Sciences 65-; Titular Prof. Experimental Physics, Kossuth Univ.; Head, Inst. Nuclear esRearch of Debrecen 54-; Dr. h.c. (Marie-Curie-Skłodowska Univ., Lublin) 70; Kossuth Award 52; Gold Medal of Hungary 69.
Leisure interests: tennis, angling, photography, skiing, etc.
Institute of Nuclear Research, 18c, Bem tér, 4001 Debrecen, Hungary.
Telephone: Debrecen 133-87.

Szarka, Karoly; Hungarian diplomatist; b. 1923, Budapest; *m.*; two *c.*
Entered foreign service 48; served in Hungarian embassies in London 49-50, New Delhi 51-53, Washington, D.C. 53-56; Deputy Minister for Foreign Affairs 56-68; Amb. to Egypt 68-70; Perm. Rep. to UN 70-74; Deputy Minister of Foreign Affairs 74-; Order of Merit (Hungary), Order of Homayoun (Iran) 1st Class, and several other decorations.
c/o Ministry of Foreign Affairs, 1394 Budapest II., Bem József rakpart 47, Hungary.

Szasz, Thomas Stephen, M.D.; American psychiatrist, psychoanalyst, author and lecturer; b. 15 April 1920, Budapest, Hungary; *s.* of Julius Szasz and Lily Wellisch; *m.* (divorced); two *d.*; ed. Cincinnati Univ. and Medical Coll.
Staff mem., Chicago Inst. for Psychoanalysis 51-56; mil. service with U.S. Naval Hosp., Bethesda (attained rank of Commdr.) 54-56; Prof. of Psychiatry, State Univ. of New York, Upstate Medical Center 56-; Co-founder and Chair. Board of Dirs., American Asscn. for the Abolition of Involuntary Mental Hospitalization Inc.; mem. Board of Dirs., Nat. Council on Crime and Delinquency; Consultant, Cttee. on Mental Hygiene, New York State Bar Asscn. and other advisory positions; mem. A.A.A.S. and other asscns. Int. Editorial Board *The International Journal of the Addictions*, *Contemporary Psychoanalysis*, Editorial Board *Journal*

of Humanistic Psychology, *The Humanist*, also consulting positions with journals; Hon. Pres. Int. Comm. for Human Rights 74; D. Sc. h.c. (Allegheny Coll.) 75.
Leisure interests: swimming, hiking, literature.
Publs. *Pain and Pleasure* 57, *The Myth of Mental Illness* 61, 74, *Law, Liberty and Psychiatry* 63, *Psychiatric Justice* 65, *The Ethics of Psychoanalysis* 65, *Ideology and Insanity* 70, *The Manufacture of Madness* 70, *The Age of Madness* 73, *The Second Sin* 73, *Ceremonial Chemistry* 74, *Heresies* 76, *Schizophrenia: the Sacred Symbol of Psychiatry* 76, *Karl Kraus and the Soul-Doctors* 76.
Department of Psychiatry, State University of New York, Upstate Medical Center, 750 East Adams Street, Syracuse, N.Y. 13210; Home: 4739 Limberlost Lane, Manlius, N.Y. 13104, U.S.A.
Telephone: (315) 473-5630 (Office); (351) 673-8918 (Home).

Szczepański, Jan, PH.D.; Polish sociologist; b. 14 Sept. 1913, Ustron, Cieszyn district; s. of Paweł and Ewa Szczepański (née Cholewa); m. Eleonora Poczobut 1937; one s. one d.; ed. Univ. of Poznań.
Asst. Poznań Univ. 35-39; during Nazi occupation forced labour in Germany; Asst. Łódź Univ. 45-52, Extraordinary Prof. 52-63, Prof. 63-; Chief Sociological Dept. Inst. of Philosophy and Sociology, Polish Acad. of Sciences 57-68, Deputy Dir. 61, Dir. 68-; mem. Polish Acad. of Sciences 64-, Vice-Pres. 72-; Pres. Int. Sociological Asscn. 66-70; Vice-Chair. All-Polish Cttee. of Nat. Unity Front 71-; Deputy to Seym 57-60, 72-; Chair. Chief Council of Science, Higher Educ. and Technology, Ministry of Science, Higher Educ., and Technology 73-; Chair. Scientific Council of Intercollegiate Inst. for Research on Higher Educ. 73-; Dr. h.c. Brno Univ. 69, Łódź Univ. 73; mem. Board UNRISD, Asscn. Int. de Sociologie (AIS); foreign mem. Finnish Acad. of Science and Literature; hon. mem. American Acad. of Exact Sciences and the Humanities 72; Commdr. Cross with Star of Order Polonia Restituta 69, Order of the Builders of People's Poland 74, and others.
Leisure interest: philately.
Publs. *Structure of Intelligenzia in Poland* (in Polish) 60, *History of Sociology* (in Polish) 61, *Sociological Problems of Higher Education* (in Polish, French, Hungarian) 63, edited *Studies in Polish Class Structure* (28 vols.), *Introduction to Sociology* (in Polish, Czech, Russian, Hungarian and Finnish) 63, *Problems of Contemporary Sociology* (in Polish) 65, *Industry and Society in Poland* (in Polish) 69, *Sociology and Society* (in Bulgarian) 70, *Changes of the Present Time* (in Polish) 70, Co-editor *Social Problems of Work Production* (in Polish, Russian) 70, *Considerations on the Republic* (in Polish) 71, *Reflections on Education* (in Polish) 73, *Changes of Polish Community in the Process of Industrialization* 73.
00-543 Warsaw, Mokotowska 46a/23, Poland.
Telephone: 28-21-93.

Szekér, Gyula; Hungarian engineer and politician; b. 24 Sept. 1925, Szombathely; ed. Technical Univ. Joined Communist Party 48; mem. Central Cttee. Hungarian Socialist Workers Party; important posts in Ministry of Heavy Industry 54-75, First Deputy Minister 63, Minister 71-75; Deputy Pres. Council of Ministers 75-.
Council of Ministers, Parliament Building, Kossuth Lajos tér., Budapest, Hungary.
Telephone: 123-500.

Szénási, Géza; Hungarian jurist; b. 23 Nov. 1919, Budapest; s. of Géza Szénási and Mária Genczy; m. Marta Beregi 1945; one s.
Administrative econ. positions 45-56; mem. Hungarian Communist Party 45-; mem. Cen. Cttee. 62-; Chief Public Prosecutor 56-75; Amb. to Bulgaria 75-.

Leisure interests: wild game shooting, angling, philately.
Hungarian Embassy, ul. 6 Septemvri 47, Sofia, Bulgaria.

Szent-Györgyi, Albert, M.D., PH.D.; Hungarian-born American biochemist; b. 16 Sept. 1893, Budapest; s. of Nicholas Szent-Györgyi and Josephine Lenbossek; one d.; ed. Univ. of Budapest and Cambridge Univ.
Professor of Medical Chem., Szeged Univ. 31-45; Prof. of Biochemistry, Univ. of Budapest 45-47; Dir. of Research, Inst. of Muscle Research, Marine Biological Laboratories 47-; fmr. Pres. Acad. of Sciences, Budapest; fmr. Vice-Pres. Nat. Acad., Budapest; awarded Nobel Prize for Medicine 37.
Leisure interests: sports, music.
Publs. *Oxidation, Fermentation, Vitamins, Health and Disease* 39, *Muscular Contraction* 47, 51, 53, *The Nature of Life* 47, *Bioenergetics* 57, *Submolecular Biology* 60, *Bioelectronics* 68, *The Crazy Ape* 70, *What Next?* 71, *The Living State* 72.
Marine Biological Laboratories, P.O. Box 187, Woods Hole, Mass. 02543, U.S.A.
Telephone: 548-1879.

Szentágothai, János, M.D.; Hungarian professor of anatomy; b. 31 Oct. 1912, Budapest; s. of Gustav and Margaret (Antal) Schimert; m. Alice Biberauer 1938; three d.; ed. Univ. of Budapest.
Research Asst., Dept. of Anatomy, Univ. of Budapest 35-37, Lecturer 37-40, Reader 40-47; Prof. and Head, Dept. of Anatomy, Univ. of Pécs 47-63, Univ. of Budapest 63-; Editor, Journal *Hinforschung* 63; experimental brain research 66; mem. Hungarian Acad. of Sciences 48; Deutsche Akad. der Naturforscher Leopoldina 64, Akad. der Wissenschaften und der Literatur, Mainz 69, Acad. Royale de Médecine de Belgique 70, Nat. Acad. of Sciences, Washington 72, American Acad. of Arts and Sciences 73; Kossuth State Prize 50, Hufeland Memorial Medal 69, State Award 1st Class 70, Karl Spencer Lashley Prize 73, Gold Medal of Milan 73.
Leisure interests: water colour sketching, scientific illustration, gardening.
Publs. *Die Rolle der einzelnen Labyrinthrezeptoren bei der Orientation vom Augen und Kopf in Raume* 52, *Hypothalamic Control Anterior Pituitary* (with others) 62, *The Cerebellum as a Neuronal Machine* (with others) 67, *Functional Anatomy* 71, *Atlas of Human Anatomy* 46-75; author numerous articles.
Department of Anatomy, Semmelweis University Medical School, 58 Tüzoltó utca 1450 Budapest IX, Home: 2/3 Magyar Jakobinusok tér 1122 Budapest XII, Hungary.
Telephone: 138-806 (Office); 359-506 (Home).

Szeryng, Henryk; Mexican violinist; b. 22 Sept. 1921, Warsaw, Poland; s. of Szymon Szeryng and Aline Woźnicka; studied with Carl Flesch, Berlin, and Gabriel Bouillon, Paris Conservatoire, and with Nadia Boulanger.
Liaison officer Polish Govt. in exile, London and translator for Gen. Sikorski 39-45; played over 300 concerts for Allied Armed Forces during this period in Britain, Canada, U.S.A., Mexico, Panama, Trinidad, Brazil, Persian Gulf, N. Africa, Italy and France; apptd. Prof. Faculty of Music, Mexican Nat. Univ. Dec. 45; Mexican citizen 46-; global concerts and goodwill tours 56-; apptd. Goodwill Ambassador by Mexican Govt. 56; Special Musical Adviser to Mexican Perm. Del. to UNESCO 70; Grand Prix du Disque 55, 57, 60, 61, 67-69, Knight Polish Order Polonia Restituta 56, Romanian Cultural Merit (First Class) 64, Officier des Arts et Lettres (France). Commdr., Finnish Order of Red Lion 68, Chevalier, Légion d'Honneur (France) 71, Mozart Medal (Austria) 71, etc.
Leisure interests: reading, linguistic research; collecting rare books, violin bows.
Publs. Works for piano, violin, chamber music; several

publs. on aspects of violin technique and interpretation.
Permanent Mexican Delegation, UNESCO, 1 rue Miollis, 75 Paris 15e, France.

Szigeti, George; Hungarian physicist; b. 29 Jan. 1905, Szentes; s. of Dr. Julius Szigeti and Ilona Huth; m. Susanne Ziffer 1935; one s. one d.; ed. Tech. Univ. of Budapest.
Engineer, Tungsram (United Incandescent Lamp and Electrical Co.) 26-28, Physicist in Research Laboratory 28-48, Head of Research Laboratory 48-58; mem. Hungarian Acad. of Sciences 58, Dir. of Research Inst. for Tech. Physics 58-74, retd., now Scientific Adviser; Hon. mem. Indian Acad. of Sciences, Bangalore 61, European Physical Soc. 75 (Vice-Pres. 74-75); Pres. Hungarian Roland Eötvös Physical Soc. 68; Chair. Solid State Comm. of IUPAP 75; Fellow, Inst. of Physics, London 70; Zipernovszky Medal, Hungarian Electrotechnical Soc. 49, Medal of Hungarian People's Repub. 51, Medal of Labour 53, 56, Order of Labour 65, Kossuth Prize 59, Prize of Union of Hungarian Scientific Socs. 68, Flag Order of Hungarian People's Repub. 74; several electrotechnical patents.
Leisure interests: tourism, rowing.
Publs. author and co-author of scientific papers, editor conf. proceedings.
Research Institute for Technical Physics of the Hungarian Academy of Sciences, H-1325 Budapest, P.O. Box 76; Home: Nyár utca 94, H-1045 Budapest, Hungary.
Telephone: 880-376 and 880-130 (Office); 492-205 (Home).

Szijártó, Károly, DR.; Hungarian lawyer; b. 26 Jan. 1927, Székesfehérvár; s. of Károly Szijártó and Magdolna Langmár; m. Magdolna Gerber 1949; one s. one d.; ed. Budapest Univ. of Liberal Arts.
Joined Hungarian Communist Party 45; Pres. Budapest Mil. Court of Law 65-71; Vice-Pres. Hungarian Supreme Court 71-75; Chief Public Prosecutor 75-.
Office of the Chief Public Prosecutor, 1369 Budapest, Apáczai Csere János-utca 10, Hungary.
Telephone: 187-850.

Szilágyi, Béla; Hungarian diplomatist; b. 30 Oct. 1908, Budapest; m. Eva Szilágyi 1946; one s. one d.; ed. Gymnasium and High School for Textile Industry.
Financial Director, State Coal Mines 46; Dir. State Textile Industries 48; Commercial Counsellor in India 50; Head of inter-state Depts. (Western Countries), Ministry of Foreign Trade 52; Minister to U.K. 59-63, Deputy Minister of Foreign Affairs Dec. 63-70; Amb. to Greece 70-; Distinguished Worker of Foreign Trade 57, Order of Labour 56, 58, 61, 65, Order of Freedom 57, Order of Hungarian People's Republic 49, Order for the Socialist Fatherland 67, Order of Labour 68, 70, Grand Officer Order of White Rose of Finland.
Leisure interests: music, theatre, art, cinema.
Athens 73, Rue Marathonodromu, Psichikon, Greece.
Telephone: 6715-515.

Szlachcic, Franciszek, M.ENG.; Polish politician; b. 5 Feb. 1920, Byczyno, near Chrzanów; ed. Acad. of Mining and Metallurgy, Cracow.
Former miner; mem. People's Guard and People's Army during occupation; mem. Polish Workers' Party 43-48; mem. Polish United Workers' Party (PZPR) 48-, deputy mem. Cen. Cttee. 64-68, mem. 68-75, Sec. Cen. Cttee. 71-74, mem. Political Bureau 71-75; Deputy Minister of Home Affairs 62-71, Minister Feb.-Dec. 71; Deputy Chair. Council of Ministers 74-76; mem. Council of State 72-74; Deputy to Seym 72-; Order of Banner of Labour, 1st and 2nd Class, Grunwald Cross, Cross of the Brave, Medal of 30th Anniversary of People's Poland 74
c/o Rada Ministrów, Al. Ujazdowskie 1/3, 00-583 Warsaw, Poland.

Sznajder, Edward; Polish politician; b. 29 Oct. 1920, Cracow; ed. Jagiellonian Univ., Cracow.
During Second World War took part in Sept. Campaign 39; managerial posts in state enterprises and cen. insts. 45-52; Deputy Head, Cen. Office of Economy of Materials 52-55; Deputy Chair. State Comm. of Econ. Planning 55-58, Comm. of Planning attached to Council of Ministers 63-65; Deputy Minister of Internal Trade 58-63; Minister of Internal Trade Dec. 65-72, of Internal Trade and Services 72-75; mem. Polish United Workers' Party 48-, deputy mem. Cen. Cttee. 71-; decorations include Order of Banner of Labour 1st and 2nd Class, Officier's Cross Order of Polonia Restituta, Gold Cross of Merit.
Ministerstwo Handlu Wewnętrznego i Usług, Plac Powstanców Warszawy 1, Warsaw, Poland.

Szokolay, Sándor; Hungarian composer; b. 30 March 1931, Kunágota; s. of Balint Szokolay and Erzsébet Holecska; m. 1st Sári Szesztay 1952, 2nd Maja Weltler 1970; four s.; ed. Budapest Music Acad.
Has won prizes in Warsaw, Moscow, Vienna.
Leisure interests: car driving, mountaineering.
Works include: *Blood Wedding* (opera) 63, *Hamlet* (opera) 68, *Az iszonyat balladája* (The Ballad of Horror), *Tetemrehivás* (Ordeal of the Bier), *Samson* (opera) 73; Oratorios: *A tüz márciusa* (March Fire), *Istár pokoljárása* (Ishtar's Descent to Hell); has also written cantatas, songs, chamber music and choral works.
H-1119 Budapest, Szabados S.-ucta 90, Hungary.
Telephone: 263-109.

Szönyi, Erzsébet; Hungarian musician; b. 25 April 1924; d. of Jenő Szőnyi and Erzsebet Piszanoff; m. Dr. Lajos Gémes 1948; two s.; ed. Music Acad. Budapest and Paris Conservatoire.
Teacher of music at a Budapest grammar school 45-48, Music Acad. Budapest 48-; leading Prof. Music Acad. 60-; Vice-Pres. Int. Soc. for Music Educ. 70-74; mem. Chopin Soc. of Warsaw, Liszt Soc. of Hungary; Erkel Prize 59.
Leisure interests: gardening, cooking.
Works: *Concerto for Organ and Orchestra*; symphonic works: *Musica Festiva, Divertimento 1 and 2*; opera: *Tragedy of Firenze*; chamber music, vocal compositions, etc.
Publs. *Methods of Musical Reading and Writing, Kodály's Principles in Practice.*
Tamás-utca 3, H-1124 Budapest XII, Hungary.
Telephone: 258-576.

Szopa, Jerzy, M.SC.; Polish engineer and politician; b. 29 Jan. 1930, Piotrków Trybunalski; ed. State Nautical School and Gdańsk Technical Univ.
Stoker, then Officer, on cargo ships: Chief Mechanic, then Technical Man., Polish Ocean Lines; Under-Sec. of State, Ministry of Shipping 65-69; Minister of Shipping 69-73, retd.; mem. Polish United Workers' Party (PZPR); mem. Cen. Cttee. 71-; Order of Banner of Labour 2nd Class 69.
Warsaw, Poland.

Szurdi, István; Hungarian politician; b. 1911, Nagyszöllös; s. of Istvan Szurdi; m. Marta Kreisler 1935; two s.
Manual industrial worker, later technician until 45; mem. Hungarian Socialist Democratic Party 36-, full-time party functionary 46-; mem. Nat. Assembly 48-; Sec. Central Cttee. Hungarian Socialist Workers' Party 63-66; Minister of Internal Trade 66-; Pres. Nat. Council of Tourism.
Leisure interest: sports.
Ministry of Home Trade, V. Vigadó-utca 6, H-1368 Budapest, Hungary.
Telephone: 469-399.

Szydlak, Jan; Polish politician; b. 24 Nov. 1925, Siemianowice, Silesia; ed. Party School, Cen. Cttee., Polish United Workers' Party (PZPR), Warsaw.

Member, Katowice Voivodship Cttee., Polish Workers' Party (PPR) 47; Vice-Chair. Voivodship Board, Polish Youth Union, Kielce 48, subsequently in Szczecin; Head, Propaganda Dept., PZPR Voivodship Cttee., Katowice 51, Sec. 52-54; Sec. Cen. Board of Polish Youth Union 54-57; Sec. PZPR Voivodship Cttee., Katowice 57-60; First Sec. PZPR Voivodship Cttee., Poznań 60-68; mem. Cen. Cttee. PZPR 64-; alt. mem. Politburo 68-70, Sec. Cen. Cttee. of PZPR 68-; mem. Politburo 70-; Deputy to Seym 61-; mem. Presidium All-Polish Cttee. of Nat. Unity Front 70-; Chair. Cen. Board of Polish-Soviet Friendship Soc. 71-, Party-State Comm. on Econ. Modernization 71-; Order of Banner of Labour (1st and 2nd Class), Commdr. Cross of Polonia Restituta.

Biuro Polityczne KC, Polska Zjednoczona Partia Robotnicza, Nowy Świat 6, Warsaw, Poland.

Szymborska, Wisława; Polish poetess, translator and literary critic; b. 2 July 1923, Prowent-Bnin near Poznań; *m.*; ed. Jagiellonian Univ., Cracow.

First work published 45; mem. Polish Writers' Asscn. 52-; mem. Editorial Staff *Życie Literackie* (weekly) 53-; Gold Cross of Merit 55, Knight's Cross, Order of Polonia Restituta 74.

Publs. poetry: *Dlatego żyjemy* 52, *Wołanie do Yeti* 57, *Sól* 62, *Sto pociech* 67, *Poezje* 70, *Wszelki wypadek* 72, *Wybór wierszy* (Selected Poems) 73.

Ul. 18 Stycznia 82/89, 30-079 Cracow, Poland.

Szyr, Eugeniusz; Polish economist and politician; b. 16 April 1915, Ładygowice, Żywiec district; *m.*; one *d.*

Member Union of Polish Communist Youth 30-34, later Polish Communist Party 34-36; Spanish Civil War 36-38; prisoner in concentration camps in France and Algeria 40-43; Polish Army, U.S.S.R. 44; Under-Sec. in Ministry of Industry and Commerce 46-49; Deputy Chair. State Comm. for Econ. Planning 49-53, Chair. 54-56; Sec. of Econ. Cttee., Council of Ministers 57-59; Vice-Pres. Council of Ministers 59-72; Chair. Cttee. of Science and Technology 63-68; mem. Cen. Cttee. Polish United Workers' Party; mem. Politburo 64-68; Deputy to Seym 52-56, 61-68, 72-; Vice-Chair. Chief Council of Union of Fighters for Freedom and Democracy 48-; Chair. State Council of Economy of Materials 72-; Grunwald Cross 49, Order of Banner of Labour 50, 64, Order of Builders of People's Poland 72.

Państwowa Rada Gospodarki Materiałowej, Warsaw, Poland.

Telephone: 213-850.

Szyszło, Fernando de; Peruvian painter; b. 5 July 1925; ed. School of Fine Arts, Catholic Univ., Lima.

Professor of Art, Catholic Univ. of Lima and Coll. of Architecture, Nat. Univ. of Engineering; Visiting Critic Cornell Univ. 62-63; Visiting Lecturer Yale Univ. 66; First one-man exhbn., Lima 47, later in New York, Washington, Ithaca, Rio de Janeiro, São Paulo, Mexico, Buenos Aires, Santiago de Chile, Bogotá, Caracas, Florence and Paris; group exhbns. include Biennali at Venice and São Paulo; represented in museums and public collections in North and South America; Carnegie Prize 58, Guggenheim Int. Prize 64.

Avenida Diagonal 550, Miraflores, Lima, Peru.

T

Tabard de Grièges, (Léon Maurice) Dominique; French former Inspector of Finances; b. 16 Feb. 1911; ed. Lycée Condorcet.

With Ministry of Finance, Budget Dept. 35-46; joined Compagnie Universelle du Canal Maritime de Suez 46, then Compagnie Financière de Suez, Dir.-Gen. 57-; now Chair. and Gen. Man. Soc. Nat. d'Investissement; Chair. and Gen. Man. Suez Int.; Vice-Chair. Cie. Financière de Suez; Chair. Suez Finance Co. (London) Ltd., Suez Finance and Real Estate Co. of Canada Ltd., Soc. de Financement Int. de la Cie. de Suez (SOFIS S.A.); Dir. Banque de Suez (U.K.) Ltd., Cie. de St.-Gobain-Pont-à-Mousson, Selected Risk Investments S.A.; mem. Supervisory Board Banque de l'Indochine et de Suez; Officier Légion d'Honneur; Hon. C.B.E. (U.K.).

1 rue d'Astorg, Paris 8e, France.
Telephone: 265-15-90.

Tabatoni, Pierre, DR.ECON.; French professor; b. Feb. 1923, Cannes; s. of Joseph and Rose Tabatoni; m. Jacqueline Ferrat 1949; two c.; ed. Lycée de Cannes, Faculties of Letters and Law, Aix-en-Provence, London School of Econs., Harvard Univ.

Associate Prof. Univs. of Algiers and Aix-en-Provence 50-54; Prof. Aix-Marseilles Univ., Dir. of Inst. of Business Admin. 54-61; Prof. Univ. of Paris 61-; Counsellor for Higher Educ., Ministry of Educ. 69-73; Dir. of Cultural Affairs, French Embassy, Washington, D.C. 73-75; Dir. for Int. Univ. Relations for State Sec. for Univs. July 75-; Chevalier, Légion d'Honneur, Officier, Palmes Académiques, Dr. h.c. (Brussels Univ.).
Leisure interest: sailing.
Publs. *Economics of Financial Institutions* (co-author) 63, *Policy and Structures in Management Systems* (co-author) 75, *Problems of European Management of Enterprises* (Platt Report, OECD) 60.
173 Boulevard Saint Germain, 75006 Paris, France.
Telephone: 548-44-50.

Tabibi, Abdul Hakim, M.A., PH.D.; Afghan diplomatist; b. 7 Oct. 1924, Kabul; ed. Habibia High School, Kabul Univ., and George Washington and American Univs., U.S.A.

Entered Ministry of Foreign Affairs 54; First Sec. Perm. Mission to UN 56-58, Counsellor 59-61, Minister Counsellor 61-64; Amb. to Yugoslavia and Bulgaria 64-65; Minister of Justice and Attorney-Gen. 65-66; Amb. to Japan and the Philippines 67-70, to India, Nepal and Burma 70-; Gov. Asian Devt. Bank 67; mem. UN Int. Law Comm. 71-; del. to various UN and other int. confs.; decorations from Afghanistan, Yugoslavia and Japan.
Publs. *Law of the Sea and its relation to the countries without sea coast* 59, *Free Access to the Sea for Land-locked Countries* 58, *The Right of Transit* 70, and various articles.
Embassy of Afghanistan, 9A Ring Road, Lajpat Nagar III, New Delhi, India.

Tabor, David, B.SC., PH.D., SC.D., F.R.S.; British physicist; b. 23 Oct. 1913, London; s. of Charles Tabor and Rebecca Weinstein; m. Hannalene Stillschweig 1943; two s.; ed. Royal Coll. of Science, London, Cambridge Univ.

Tribophysics, CSIRO, Melbourne, Australia 40-46; Asst. Dir. of Research, Cambridge Univ. 46-61, Lecturer in Physics 61-64, Reader 64-73, Prof. 73-, Head of Physics and Chem. of Solids, Cavendish Lab. 69-; Int. Fellow, Stanford Research Inst. 56; UNESCO Visiting Prof., Israel 61; Russell Springer Visiting Prof. Univ. of Calif., Berkeley 70; Nat. Award, American Soc. for Lubrication Engineers 55, Wilson Award, American Soc. of Metals 69, Inaugural Gold Medal for Tribology, Inst. of Mechanical Engineers 72, Mayo D. Hersey Award, American Soc. of Mechanical Engineers 74, Guthrie Medal, Inst. of Physics 74.
Publs. *Hardness of Metals* 51, *Gases, Liquids and Solids* 69, (with F. P. Bowden) *Friction and Lubrication of Solids*, Part I 50, revised edn. 54, Part II 64, *Friction—an Introduction to Tribology* 73; contributions to learned journals on friction and adhesion.
8 Rutherford Road, Cambridge, CB2 2HH, England.
Telephone: (0223) 66477 (Work); (0220-21) 3336 (Home).

Tabor, Hans Rasmussen, DR.RER.POL.; Danish diplomatist; b. 25 April 1922, Copenhagen; s. of S. Rasmussen; m. Inger Petersen 1945; two d.; ed. Birkerød Statsskole and Univ. of Copenhagen.

Secretary, Gen. Secr. Organisation for European Economic Co-operation (OEEC), Paris 48-50; Sec. Ministry of Foreign Affairs, Copenhagen 50-52; Asst. Head Danish Del. to OEEC 52-56; Branch Head Ministry of Foreign Affairs 56, 57-59; Dep. Sec.-Gen. Suez Canal Users' Asscn., London 57; Econ. Counsellor, Asst. Head Danish Mission to the European Communities 59-61, Minister and Head 61-64, Ambassador 63-64; Perm. Rep. to the UN 64-67; Minister of Foreign Affairs 67-68; Rep. of Denmark on the UN Security Council 67-68; Amb. to Italy (also accred. to Malta) 68-74; Perm. Rep. to UN 74; Amb. to Canada Jan. 75-.
Leisure interests: tennis, swimming, reading.
Publs. *Danmark og Marshallplanen* (Denmark and the Marshall Plan) 61, *De Seks og det økonomiske samarbejde i Vesten* (The Six and Economic Co-operation in the Western World).
Danish Embassy, Suite 702, 85 Range Road, Ottawa, Ont., Canada.

Tabor, Peder; Danish editor; b. 23 Nov. 1891, Vejen; m. Johanne Rune 1928.
Journalist on staff of *Social-Demokraten* Fredericia 07-10; with *Social-Demokraten* Silkeborg 10-23; ed. of Social Dem. papers in Silkeborg, Herning and Skanderborg 23-30; editor of Sunday edition of *Social-Demokraten* 30; co-editor of *Social-Demokraten* (now *Aktuelt*) 34; Chief Editor 41-59; Pres. Jutland Soc. for Modern Art 24-30; mem. exec. cttee. of Copenhagen Editors' Soc. (Pres. 43-45), of Danish-British Society 46; mem. Joint Representative Council of Danish Daily Newspapers; mem. Broadcasting Council 42-; Pres. Danish nat. news agency Ritzaus Bureau 55-59.
Leisure interests: history, art and cricket.
Publs. *Malurt* (a vol. of aphorisms) 19, *Naerbilleder* (memoirs) 61, *Randbemaerkninger* (political aphorisms) 63, *Situationer Og Profiler* 67.
Hans Egedes Gade 23, Copenhagen N, Denmark.
Telephone: 398093.

Tack, Juan Antonio, LIC. FIL. Y LETRAS; Panamanian government official and diplomatist; b. 16 Nov. 1934; m.; two d.; ed. Univ. of Panama.
With Ministry of Foreign Affairs 60-; Dir. Diplomatic Dept. 60-64; Alt. del. to OAS 64; Alt. del. to UN, Geneva 64-66; Minister-Counsellor, Paris, Alt. del. to UNESCO 66-68; Vice-Minister of Foreign Affairs 69-70, Minister 70-76; mem. History Acad., Panama; del. to many UNESCO, ILO, ITU confs., numerous awards and decorations.
Leisure interests: reading, his home.
Publs. many articles on the history of Panama.
c/o Ministerio de Relaciones Exteriores, Panama City, Panama.

Taft, Charles Phelps, B.A., LL.B., LL.D., D.C.L.; American lawyer; b. 20 Sept. 1897, Cincinnati; *s.* of William Howard Taft (27th President of U.S.A.) and Helen Herron; ed. Taft School, Watertown, Conn., and Yale Univ.
Prosecuting Attorney, Hamilton County, Ohio 27-28; Govt. Arbitrator Toledo strikes 34; mem. Cincinnati City Council 38-42, 48-51, 55-, Mayor 55-57; Dir. Community War Services, Fed. Security Agency 41-43; Dir. War-time Economic Affairs, Dept. of State 44-45; Pres. Fed. Council of Churches 47-48; mem. Central Cttee. World Council of Churches 48-54; Medal for Merit 46; Republican.
Publs. *City Management—The Cincinnati Experiment* 33, *You and I—and Roosevelt* 36, *Why I am for the Church* 47, *Democracy in Politics and Economics* 50.
1071 Celestial Street, Cincinnati, Ohio 45202, U.S.A.
Telephone: 513-621-4227.

Taft, Robert, Jr.; American politician; b. 26 Feb. 1917; ed. Yale and Harvard Univs.
Admitted to Ohio Bar; partner, Taft, Stettinius & Hollister, Cincinnati 46-67; mem. Ohio House of Reps. 55-62; mem. 88th, 90th and 91st U.S. Congresses; Senator from Ohio 71-; Republican.
United States Senate, Washington, D.C. 20510, U.S.A.

Taguchi, H.E. Cardinal Paul Yoshigoro; Japanese ecclesiastic; b. 20 July 1902, Shittsu, Nagasaki; *s.* of Melchior and Cathrine Taguchi.
Ordained priest 28; Bishop of Osaka 41-69, Archbishop July 69-; cr. Cardinal by Pope Paul VI Feb. 73.
Archbishop's House, Koyoen Nishiyama-cho No. 1-55, Nishinomiya-shi (662), Hyogo-Ken, Japan.
Telephone: 0798-33-0921.

Taguchi, Renzo; Japanese shipbuilding executive; b. 3 Feb. 1906, Yamagata Prefecture; *s.* of Keiji and Sei Taguchi; *m.* Sadako Taguchi 1933; three *s.* three *d.*; ed. Yonezawa Coll. of Technology.
President Ishikawajima Heavy Industries Co. Ltd., now Chair.; Pres. Japan Machinery Fed., Japan Consulting Inst.; Vice-Pres. Tokyo Chamber of Commerce and Industry.
Leisure interest: painting.
Ishikawajima-Harima Heavy Industries Co. Ltd. (IHI), New Ohtemachin Building, 2-chome 2-1, Ohtemachi, Chiyoda-ku, Tokyo 100, Japan.

Taha, Mohammed Fathi; Egyptian meteorologist; b. 15 Jan. 1914, Cairo; ed. Cairo Univ. and Imperial Coll. of Science and Technology, London.
Under-Secretary of State and Chair. Board of Dir. Egyptian Meteorological Authority 53-75; Meteorological Counsellor to Ministry of Civil Aviation 76-; Vice-Pres. Int. Meteorological Org. (IMO) Cttee. for Africa 47, Int. Aeronautical Fed. (IAF) 65; mem. WMO Exec. Cttee. 55-71, Second Vice-Pres. 59-63, Pres. 71-75; Pres. Perm. Meteorological Cttee. of Arab League Org. 71-77; Chair. Nat. Cttee. on Geodesy and Geophysics 67-75; mem. Outer Space Exploration Cttee. for Peaceful Uses; mem. Nat. Cttee. Int. Council of Scientific Unions and many other nat. cttees. dealing with scientific research in Egypt.
Egyptian Meteorological Authority, Koubry El-Quobba P.O., Cairo, Egypt.

Taher, Abdulhady, PH.D.; Saudi Arabian government official; b. 1930, Medina; ed. Ain Shams Univ., Cairo, and Univ. of California.
Entered Saudi Arabian Govt. service 55; Dir.-Gen. Ministry of Petroleum and Mineral Resources 60; Gov., Gen. Petroleum and Mineral Org. (PETROMIN) 62-; Man. Dir. Saudi Arabian Fertilizers Co. (SAFCO); Dir. Arabian American Oil Co. (ARAMCO), Saudi Govt. Railways Corpn.; Trustee, Coll. of Petroleum and Minerals; mem. Industrial Research and Devt. Center

Saudi Arabia; Hon. mem. American Soc. of Petroleum Engineers.
Publs. *Income Determination in the International Petroleum Industry* 66, *Development and Petroleum Strategies in Saudi Arabia* (Arabic); lectures and papers on economic and petroleum affairs.
General Petroleum and Mineral Organization (PETROMIN), P.O. Box 757, Riyadh, Saudi Arabia.

Taimur al-Said, Tarik; Omani diplomatist; b. 2 July 1923; ed. English High School for Boys, Istanbul, Robert Coll., Istanbul, and Germany.
Commissioned in Muscat Army 41-44; Chair. Admin., Muscat Mutrah Municipality 45-57; in charge of Operational Area in Jabal War 58-59; self-exile 62-70; Prime Minister 70-71; Personal Adviser for Diplomatic Affairs to Sultan of Oman, Senior Amb. Extraordinary and Plenipotentiary 72-; Order of Oman, 1st Class.
P.O. Box 202, Muscat, Oman; and Leuchtturmweg 21, Hamburg 56, Federal Republic of Germany.

Tairova, Taira Akperovna, M.SC. (ENG.); Soviet engineer and politician; b. 7 Nov. 1913; ed. Azerbaijan Industrial Inst.
Engineer, Oil Industry, then Dir. Azerbaijan Research Inst. of Oil 40-42; Head of Dept., Deputy Sec. on Oil Azerbaijan C.P. Central Cttee., then Sec. Azerbaijan C.P. Baku Cttee. 42-49; Dozent Azerbaijan Oil and Chemical Inst. 49-53; Chair. Azerbaijan Council of Trade Unions 53-57; Sec. Azerbaijan Peace Cttee. 48-53; mem. of Presidium 48-65; Deputy Supreme Soviet of the U.S.S.R. 54-58; del. World Women's Congress, Lausanne 55; mem. Soviet Parl. Dels. to Czechoslovakia 55, Belgium 56; Chair. Azerbaijan Scientific Technical Cttee. 57-62; mem. Soviet Del. to 13th Session of UN Gen. Assembly 59; Minister of Foreign Affairs, Azerbaijan S.S.R. 59-; Deputy Chair. Azerbaijan Council of Ministers 63-68; Deputy, Supreme Soviet of Azerbaijan S.S.R. 59-; mem. Soviet Del. to India, Burma, Indonesia, Afghanistan 60, to Tunisia 62, to Tunisia and Algeria 64; mem. Soviet Del. to UN 23rd Session Gen. Assembly 68, to 30th Session 75; Order of Lenin, Order of Red Banner of Labour (six times), Badge of Honour and other awards.
Ministry of Foreign Affairs of Azerbaijan S.S.R., Baku, U.S.S.R.

Taittinger, Jean; French vintner and politician; b. 25 Jan. 1923, Paris; *s.* of Pierre Taittinger.
Deputy for Union pour la Nouvelle République (U.N.R.), later for Union Démocratique Ve République, for Union des Démocrates pour la République (U.D.R.) 58-; Mayor of Rheims 59; Nat. Sec. U.N.R.-U.D.T. (Union Démocratique du Travail) 67; mem. Exec. Office and Nat. Treas. U.D.R. Feb.-Oct. 68, Deputy Sec.-Gen. Dec. 74-; Vice-Pres. Finance Comm. of Nat. Assembly until 68, Pres. 68-71; Sec. of State, Ministry of Finance and Econ. Affairs 71-73; Minister of Justice 73-74; Minister of State for Justice March-May 74; Vice-Pres. Soc. de l'hôtel Terminus-Saint-Lazare; Admin. Soc. de l'hôtel Lutétia and Louvre dept. stores; mem. Comm. for Econ. Devt. of Champagne-Ardennes region.
c/o Union des Démocrates pour la République, 123 rue de Lille, Paris 7e, France.

Tajitsu, Wataru; Japanese banker; b. 25 March 1902, Tokyo; *s.* of Toyokichi Sakai and Teruko Tajitsu; *m.* Aiko Kusuda; one *s.* one *d.*; ed. Tokyo Univ.
Joined The Mitsubishi Bank Ltd. 26, Dir. 55-, Man. Dir. 59, Deputy Pres. 61, Pres. 64-70, Chair. 70-75; Dir. The Tokyo Marine and Fire Insurance Co. Ltd., Kirin Brewery Co. Ltd., Kikkoman Shoyu Co. Ltd.; Chair. The Mitsubishi Foundation; Exec. Dir. Japan Fed. of Employers Asscn., Fed. of Econ. Org.; Blue Ribbon Medal.
6-41, Akasaka 7-chome, Minato-ku, Tokyo, Japan.

Takeda, Chobei; Japanese business executive; b. **29** April 1905; ed. Keio Gijuku Univ.
President, Takeda Chemical Industries Ltd. until 74, Chair. 74-.
Takeda Chemical Industries, 27 Doshomachi 2-chome, Higashi-ku, Osaka, Japan.

Takeiri, Yoshikatsu; Japanese politician; b. 10 Jan. 1926, Nagano Prefecture; *m.* Kiku Takeiri 1951; one *s.* two *d.*; ed. Inst. of Politics (Seiji Daigakko).
With Japan Nat. Railways 48-59; Bunkyo Ward Assembly Tokyo 59; Tokyo Metropolitan Assembly 63-67; Vice-Sec.-Gen. Komeito (Clean Govt.) Party Nov. 64-67, Chair. 67-; mem. House of Reps. 67-.
Leisure interests: movies, fishing.
17 Minami-Motomachi, Shinjuku-ku, Tokyo 160, Japan.
Telephone: 353-0111.

Takeuchi, Shunichi; Japanese oil executive; b. 17 Jan. 1896, Osaka; *s.* of Taketaro and Shin Takeuchi; *m.* Shizuko Yanase 1919; one *s.*; ed. Tokyo Higher Commercial School.
Mitsubishi Holding Co. 17; Mitsubishi Trading Co. Ltd. 18-40, Manager, Produce Dept., London Branch 21-29, Asst. Gen. Manager, New York Branch 34-35, Gen. Manager, San Francisco and Seattle Branches 35-40; Gen. Manager, Mitsubishi Oil Co. Ltd. 41, Dir. and Pres. 46-61, Chair. of Board 61-66, Senior Adviser 66-; Dir. Japan Productivity Centre 58-; Pres. Japan Management School 58-; Chair. of Board of Dirs. The English Language Educ. Council Inc. 63-; Vice-Pres. The Japan-British Soc., Tokyo 64-; Blue Ribbon Award 59, Order of the Rising Sun (Third Class) 66.
Leisure interests: travelling, reading, theatre-going.
5-31, 2-chome Matsugaoka, Kugenuma, Fujisawa City, Japan.
Telephone: 0466-22-3405.

Takla, Philippe; Lebanese politician and banker; b. 3 Feb. 1915; ed. Univ. Law School, Beirut.
Law practice, Beirut 35-45; M.P. 45, 47-; Minister of Nat. Economy and Communications 45-46; Minister of Foreign Affairs 49, 61-63, 64-65, 66; Gov. Bank of Lebanon 63-66, 66-67; Perm. Rep. to UN 67-68; Amb. to France 68-71; Minister of Foreign Affairs 74-.
c/o Ministry of Foreign Affairs, Beirut, Lebanon.

Takriti, Saddam Hussein; Iraqi politician; b. 1937, Tikrit, nr. Baghdad; *m.* Sajida Khairalla 1963; two *s.* two *d.*; ed. al-Karkh Secondary School, Baghdad, al-Qasr al-Aini Secondary School, Cairo, Cairo and Baghdad Univs.
Joined Arab Baath Socialist Party while at Secondary School in Baghdad 57; sentenced to death for attempted execution of Abdul Karim Qassim 59; joined leadership of Cairo branch of Baath Party 62; returned to Iraq following revolution Feb. 63; mem. 4th Regional Congress and 6th National Congress of Baath Party 63; mem. Regional Leadership of Baath Party in Iraq following overthrow of Party rule Nov. 63; mem. 7th National Congress, Syria 64; arrested for plotting overthrow of Abdul Salam Aref Oct. 64; elected mem. leadership by 8th National Congress while still in prison 65; Deputy Sec. Regional Leadership of Baath Party 66; played prominent role in July 68 revolution; Acting Deputy Chair. Revolutionary Command Council 68-69; Deputy Chair. Revolutionary Command Council Nov. 69-; Deputy Sec. Regional Leadership in 7th Regional Congress July 68; mem. Nat. Leadership of Party in 10th National Congress April 70.
Baath Party Headquarters, Baghdad, Iraq.

Tal, Josef; Israeli composer; b. 1910, Poland; ed. Berlin State Acad. of Music.
Went to Israel 34; taught piano and composition at Jerusalem Acad. of Music 37. Dir. 48-52; now Head, Dept. of Musicology. Hebrew Univ., Jerusalem; Dir. Israel Centre for Electronic Music 61-; has appeared

with Israel Philharmonic Orchestra and others as pianist and conductor; concert tours of Europe, U.S.A., Far East; UNESCO Scholarship for research in electronic music; mem. Acad. of Arts, West Berlin; Israel State Prize 70.
Works include: *Saul at Ein Dor* 57, *Amnon and Tamar* 61, *Ashmedai* 69 (operas), Symphony No. 1 53, No. 2 60, *Concerto for Harpsichord and Electronics* 64, *Double Concerto* (for violin and violoncello) 70, *Masada 1967* 73, other cantatas, quintets, music for ballet and several books on the theory of music.
Department of Musicology, Hebrew University Jerusalem; Home: 3 Dvora Haneviyah Street, Jerusalem, Israel.
Telephone: 30211 (Office); 228736 (Home).

Talbot, Frederick Hilborn; Guyanese diplomatist; b. 13 Oct. 1927, Georgetown; *m.*; ed. Allen Univ., South Carolina, Yale and Columbia Univs. and Univ. of Calif. (Berkeley).
Pastor, St. Peter's A.M.E. Church, Georgetown; Caribbean Consultant of Church World Service; Chair. Guyana Council of Churches; mem. World Methodist Org., Board of Poor Law Commrs. of Guyana, Govt. Hospitals Cttee., etc.; Perm. Rep. to UN 71-72; Amb. to U.S.A. 73-75.
c/o Ministry of Foreign Affairs, Georgetown, Guyana.

Talbot, Phillips; American organization executive; b. 7 June 1915, Pittsburgh, Pa.; *s.* of Kenneth Talbot and Gertrude Talbot; *m.* Mildred Fisher 1943; one *s.* two *d.*; ed. Univs. of Illinois, Chicago, London Univ., and Aligarh Muslim Univ., India.
Newspaper reporter 36-38; Fellow London Univ. 38-39; U.S. Naval service 41-46; Foreign Corresp. 46-48, 49-50; Visiting Asst. Prof. of Political Science, Chicago Univ. 48; Exec. Dir. American Univs. Field Staff Inc. 51-61; Asst. Sec. of State for Near Eastern and South Asian Affairs, Dept. of State 61-65; Amb. to Greece 65-69; Pres. Asia Soc.; Ph.D. (Univ. of Chicago) 54, Hon. LL.D. (Mills Coll.) 63.
The Asia Society, 112 East 64th Street, New York, N.Y. 10021, U.S.A.

Talboys, Brian Edward, M.P.; New Zealand farmer and politician; b. 7 June 1921, Wanganui; *s.* of F. P. Talboys; *m.* P. F. Adamson 1950; two *s.*; ed. Wanganui Collegiate School, and Victoria Univ., Wellington.
Served R.N.Z.A.F in Second World War; joined *New Zealand Dairy Exporter* 50, later Asst. Ed.; has 500-acre farm, Heddon Bush, Southland; M.P. 57-. Parl. Under-Sec. 60-62; Minister of Agriculture 62-69, of Educ. 69-72, of Science 64-72; Minister of Industries and Commerce and Minister of Overseas Trade Feb.-Dec. 72; Deputy Prime Minister, Minister of Foreign Affairs, Overseas Trade and Nat. Devt. Dec. 75-; National Party.
Parliament House, Wellington; and 134 Park Street, Winton, Southland, New Zealand.
Telephone: 44-595 (Home).

Taleghani, Khalil, B.SC.; Iranian civil engineer and politician; b. 13 Sept. 1913, Teheran; *s.* of Ali Asghar and Sareh Taleghani; *m.* Jamileh Mohseni 1947; three *s.*; ed. American Coll. of Teheran, and Univ. of Birmingham, England.
Junior engineer, England 37-39; Engineer, Persian Army 39-41; Chief Engineer, Technical Dir., Dir. of Ebtekar and other construction companies and Golpayegan Water Co. 41-51; Minister of Agriculture Dec. 51-June 52, July 52-March 53 and 55-56; Minister of State 56-59; Dir. Taleghani-Tashakori Co. (consulting engineers); Manager Karaj Dam Authority 54-59; Chair. Industrial and Mining Development Bank of Iran 60-63; Dir. Taleghani-Daftari (consulting engineers); Chair. B. F. Goodrich Tyre Manufacturing Co., Iran; Chair. Pars Paper Manuf. Co.; Chair. Manem Con-

sulting Engineers Asscn.; Fellow, A.S.C.E.; Homayoun Medal (1st Order), Taj Medal.
Leisure interests: fishing, water-skiing, music.
Home: Baghe-Bank Street, Golhak, Teheran; Office: 42 Khoshbin Street, Fisher Abad, Teheran, Iran.
Telephone: 861984 (Home); 831026 (Office).

Talhouni, Bahjat Khadr al-; Jordanian lawyer and politician; b. 1913, Ma'an; *m.*; three *c.*; ed. Damascus Univ.
Former Pres. Court of Appeal; Minister of Interior, Minister of Justice and Chief of Royal Court 53-60; mem. of Senate 60-63, 64-74, Pres. 74-; Prime Minister 60-62, 64-65, Oct. 67-March 69, Aug. 69-June 70; Minister for Foreign Affairs 67-68, of Defence 68-69, of Interior April-Sept. 68; Chief of Royal Cabinet 63-64, 69, 73-74; mem. Consultative Council 67-; Arab and foreign decorations.
The Senate, Amman, Jordan.
Telephone: 22110.

Tali, Alhaji Yakubu Tolon Na; Ghanaian Chief and diplomatist; b. Tolon; *s.* of Al-Hassan Sulemana and Ayishetu Dindow; *m.* Amina Abudulai 1938; two *s.* six *d.*; ed. Achimota.
Teacher, Northern Territories 38-47; Tali Na (Chief of Tali) 47-53; Tolon Na (Chief of Tolon) 53-; Chair. Dagomba Native Authority Council 49, later Dagomba District Council; mem. Gold Coast Legislative Assembly, later Ghana Legislative Assembly 51-, fmr. Deputy Speaker; Pres. Northern Territories Council 53-; High Commr. of Ghana in Nigeria 65-67; Ghana Mission to UN 60, 61, 69; Ghana Amb. to Yugoslavia, Bulgaria and Romania 70-72; High Commr. to Sierra Leone and concurrently Amb. to Guinea 72-75; mem. Coussey Constitutional Cttee. 49, Commonwealth Parliamentary Confs. Kuala Lumpur 63, Jamaica 64; Northern People's Party.
Leisure interests: riding, polo, pets, travel, golf.
c/o Ministry of Foreign Affairs, Accra, Ghana.

Tallchief, Marjorie; American ballerina; b. 1927; *m.* George Skibine (*q.v.*) 1947; two *s.*; ed. Beverly Hills High School, Calif.
Daughter of the Chief of the Osages Indians; studied with Bronislava Nijinska; joined American Ballet Theatre; created role of Medusa in *Undertow*; Prima Ballerina, Ballet de Monte Carlo 48, American Ballet Theater 60; created leading roles in *Somnambula*, *Concerto Barrocco*, *Les Biches*, *Boléro*, *Idylle*, *Prisoner of the Caucasus* and *Annabel Lee*; Première Danseuse Étoile, Paris Opera 57-, leading roles in *The Firebird*, *Les Noces Fantastiques*, *Giselle*, *Conte Cruel*, *Concerto* and numerous other ballets; Prima Ballerina, Hamburg State Opera 65-; Chevalier du Nicham-Iftikar.
c/o Harkness Foundation, 15 East 69 Street, New York, N.Y., U.S.A.

Talmadge, Herman Eugene; American politician; b. 9 Aug. 1913, Telfair County, Georgia; *s.* of Eugene and Mattie Thurmond Talmadge; *m.* Elizabeth Shingler 1941; two *s.*; ed. Univ. of Georgia.
Practised law in Atlanta 36-41; served with U.S. navy leaving with rank of Lieut-Commdr. 41-45; Gov. of Georgia 48-55; U.S. Senator from Georgia 57-; mem. American Bar Asscn., Farm Bureau Fed.; Chair. Richard B. Russell Library Foundation 71-74; Democrat.
109 Senate Office Building, Washington, D.C., U.S.A.
Telephone: 202/224-3643.

Talû, Naim; Turkish banker and politician; b. 22 July 1919, Istanbul; *s.* of Havva Mirat and Mehmet Nizamettin; *m.* Gevher Erdoğan 1946; two *d.*; ed. Faculty of Economics, Istanbul Univ.
Joined Türkiye Cumhuriyet Merkez Bankasi (Central Bank of Repub. of Turkey) 46, Chief 52, Asst. Dir. of

Ankara Branch 55-58, Dir. of Exchange Dept. 58-62, Asst. Gen. Dir. 62-66, Acting Pres. and Gen. Dir. 66-67, Pres. and Gen. Dir. 67-70, Chair. Board and Gov. 70-71; Chair. Foreign Investment Encouragement Cttee. 67-68; Chair. Banks Asscn. of Turkey 67-71; Sec.-Gen. Cttee. for Regulation of Bank Credits 67-70; Minister of Commerce Dec. 71-April 73; Prime Minister April-Oct. 73; mem. Ankara Educ. Foundation, Soc. for Protection of Children in Turkey.
Leisure interests: playing bridge, sailing, swimming, tennis.
Başbakan, Ankara, Turkey.
Telephone: 12-73-59.

Talvela, Martti Olavi; Finnish opera and concert singer; b. 4 Feb. 1935, Hiitola; *s.* of Toivo and Nelly Talvela; *m.* Anna Kääriäinen 1957; one *s.* two *d.*
Teacher Lahti Music High School 58; Royal Opera House, Stockholm 61-62; performances at Deutsche Oper, Berlin, Staatsoper, Hamburg, Vienna, Munich, Royal Opera, Covent Garden, Metropolitan Opera, N.Y., La Scala, Milan, also in Rome, San Francisco, Tokyo, Bayreuth, Salzburg 62-; Artistic Dir. Savonlinna Opera Festival, Finland 72-; has made numerous recordings, television appearances; Pro Finlandia 73; Finnish State Prize 73.
Leisure interests: music, books, fishing.
c/o John Coast Management, 1 Park Close, London, S.W.1, England.

Talwar, Raj Kumar, M.A., C.A.I.I.B.; Indian banker; b. 3 June 1922, Gujrat, West Punjab.
Joined State Bank of India 43, Sec. and Treas. Hyderabad Circle 65-66, Bombay Circle 66-68, Man.-Dir. 68-69, Chair. 69-; *ex-officio* Chair. seven subsidiary banks; Vice-Pres. Indian Inst. of Bankers 69-; mem. Small Scale Industries Board, Gov. Board of Nat. Inst. of Bank Management, Indian Inst. of Management, Ahmedabad; Dir. Industrial Reconstruction Corpn. of India Ltd., Calcutta; Regional Sec. Aurobindo Soc. for W. India.
State Bank of India, Central Office, New Administrative Building, Madam Cama Road, Bombay 400 021; and Dunedin, 5 J. M. Mehta Road, Bombay 400 006, India.

Tambo, Oliver; South African politician; b. 1917; ed. Anglican mission schools and Univ. Coll. of Fort Hare, Cape Province.
Teacher, Secondary School; Solicitor, Johannesburg, 51-60; banned from attending meetings 54-56 and for five years 59-; arrested on treason charges 56, charges withdrawn 57; Dep.-Pres. African Nat. Congress 58-67, Pres. 67-; escaped to London 60; mem. del. of exiled reps. of S. African parties to Third Conf. of Independent African States, Addis Ababa 60; attended UN Gen. Assembly (15th Session) 60; Head, External Mission of African Nat. Congress of South Africa.
African National Congress of South Africa, P.O. Box 2239, Dar es Salaam, Tanzania; and Africa Unity House, 3 Collingham Gardens, London, S.W.5, England.

Tamboura, Amadou, L. en D.; Upper Voltan international civil servant; b. 31 Dec. 1933; ed. primary schools in Djibo and Ouahigouya, Bamako Lycée in Mali, and Univs. of Dakar and Paris.
Customs Inspector 62; envoy to GATT 63; Div. Inspector of Customs and First Counsellor to Embassy of Upper Volta in Brussels 64; Chief, Third Div. Ouagadougou Customs; Sec.-Gen. Customs Union of States of West Africa until 72, of Communauté Economique de l'Afrique de l'Ouest 72-73; Counsellor to Prime Minister for Financial and Econ. Affairs and Int. Co-operation Jan. 74; Technical Counsellor to Minister of Finance April 74; Minister of Finance 75-.
Ministry of Finance, Ouagadougou, Upper Volta.

Tamiya, Hiroshi, D.SC.; Japanese biologist; b. 5 Jan. 1903, Osaka; s. of Koreharu and Masayo Tamiya; m. Nobuko Seida 1928; one d.; ed. Imperial Univ. of Tokyo.

Professor of Botany, Univ. of Tokyo 39-55; Dir. of Inst. of Applied Microbiology, Univ. of Tokyo 55-63; Dir. The Tokugawa Inst. for Biological Research 46-70; mem. Special Cttee. of Int. Biological Programme 64-74, Vice-Pres. 67-74; Chair. Japanese Nat. Cttee. for Int. Biological Programme 64-74; Editor *Archiv für Mikrobiologie, Journal of Biochemistry, Plant and Cell Physiology, Journal of General and Applied Microbiology*; mem. Japan Acad., Deutsche Akademie der Naturforscher; Foreign Assoc. U.S. Nat. Acad. of Sciences; Prize and Medal from Fujiwara Foundation; Acad. Prize from Acad. of Japan.

Publs. scientific works on metabolism of fungi, action mechanisms of respiratory enzymes, kinetics of enzyme action, mass-cultures of algae, mechanism of photosynthesis, growth physiology of micro-algae.

Leisure interest: music.

Shinjuku-ku, Shimotochiai 1-363, Tokyo, Japan.

Telephone: 03-951-3172.

Tammes, Arnold J. P., LL.D.; Netherlands international lawyer; b. 10 July 1907, Groningen; ed. Univ. of Groningen.

Foreign Editor, *Nieuwe Rotterdamsche Courant*, Rotterdam; Prof. of Public Int. Law and Int. Relations, Univ. of Amsterdam 47-72; mem. Perm. Court of Arbitration; Pres. Netherlands Press Council 59-69; mem. UN Int. Law Comm. 67-; Rep. at several Confs. of IAEA and mem. del. to most sessions of UN Gen. Assembly 53-; mem. Royal Netherlands Acad. of Sciences.

Publs. *Internationaal Publiekrecht* and various reports and articles.

c/o Faculty of Political and Social Sciences, University of Amsterdam, Spui 21, Amsterdam, Netherlands.

T'an Chen-lin; Chinese politician; b. 1902, Yu-hsien, Hunan; ed. Juichen Red Army Univ. and Moscow Red Army Univ.

Joined CCP 26; participated in Autumn Harvest Uprising 27; Political Commissar in Red Army during Civil and Sino-Japanese Wars; mem. 7th Cen. Cttee. of CCP 45; Gov. of Chekiang 49-50; Sec. CCP Chekiang 49-52; Gov. of Kiangsu 52-55; mem., Sec. of Secr., Deputy Sec.-Gen. 8th Cen. Cttee. of CCP 56; mem. Politburo, CCP 58-67; Vice-Premier, State Council 59-; Dir. Office of Agriculture and Forestry, State Council 62-67; Vice-Chair. State Planning Comm. 62-67; criticized and removed from office during Cultural Revolution 68; mem. 10th Cen. Cttee. of CCP 73.

People's Republic of China.

T'an Ch'i-lung; Chinese party official; b. 1912, Kiangsi.

Director Political Dept., Hunan-Hunpeh-Kiangsi Border Region 37; Political Commissar Guerilla Force 43, People's Liberation Army 44-49; Deputy Sec. CCP Chekiang 49-52, Sec. 52-55; Political Commissar Chekiang Mil. District, PLA 52-55; Gov. of Chekiang 52-55; Acting Gov. of Shantung 54; Alt. mem. 8th Cen. Cttee. of CCP 56; Sec. CCP Shantung 55-56, Second Sec. 56-61, First Sec. 61-67; Gov. of Shantung 58-63; First Political Commissar Tsinan Mil. Region, PLA 63; Sec. E. China Bureau, CCP 65-67; criticized and removed from office during Cultural Revolution 67; Alt. mem. 9th Cen. Cttee. of CCP 69; Vice-Chair. Fukien Revolutionary Cttee. 70; Sec. CCP Fukien 71; Sec. CCP Chekiang 72, First Sec. 73-; Vice-Chair. Chekiang Revolutionary Cttee. 73; mem. 10th Cen. Cttee. of CCP 73.

People's Republic of China.

Tan Chin Tuan, Tan Sri, B.S.M., C.B.E., J.P.; Singapore banker and company director; b. 21 Nov. 1908, Singapore; ed. Anglo-Chinese School, Singapore.

Member Singapore Municipal Comm. 39-41; Deputy Pres. Singapore Legislative Council 51-55; mem. Singapore Exec. Council 48-55; Chair. Kinta Ellas Tin Dredging Ltd. 69-74, Oversea-Chinese Banking Corpn. Ltd. 66-, Fraser & Neave Ltd. 57-, Great Eastern Life Assurance Co. Ltd. 69-, Int. Bank of Singapore 74-, Malayan Breweries Ltd. 57-, Wearne Bros. Ltd. 74-, Overseas Assurance Corpn. Ltd. 69-, Robinson & Co. Ltd. 57-, Sime Darby Holdings Ltd. 73-, The Straits Trading Co. Ltd. 65-; Dir. Gopeng Consolidated Ltd. 67-, Petaling Tin Berhad 67-, Tronoh Mines Ltd. 67-, United Malacca Rubber Estates Berhad 69-; Dir. Tanjong Tin Dredging Ltd. 69-75; Pres. Raffles Hotel Ltd. 69-; Fellow, Inst. of Bankers (London) 65, Australian Inst. of Man. 62.

Oversea-Chinese Banking Corporation Ltd., Upper Pickering Street, Singapore 3 (from mid-1976: OCBC Centre, Chulia Street, Singapore 1); Home: 42 Cairnhill Road, Singapore 9.

Tan Siew Sin, Hon. Tun, S.S.M., J.P.; Malayan businessman and politician; b. 21 May 1916, Malacca; s. of late Tun Tan Cheng Lock and Toh Puan Yeo Yeok Neo; m. Lim Cheng Neo 1947; three d.; ed. High School Malacca and Raffles Coll., Singapore.

Malacca Municipal Commr. 46-49; mem. Fed. Legislative Council 48-, mem. Standing Cttee. on Finance 49-55; mem. Rubber Producers' Council 51-57, Vice-Chair. 57; mem. Rubber Industry Replanting Board 52-57, Vice-Chair. 57; Pres. Malayan Estate Owners' Asscn. 56, 57; mem. Malacca Chinese Advisory Board 50-55; Hon. Sec. Malacca Branch, Malayan Chinese Asscn. 49-57, Chair. Malacca Branch 57-61, Vice-Pres. Malayan Chinese Asscn. 57-61, Pres. 61-74; Fed. Minister of Commerce and Industry 57-59, Minister of Finance, Malaya 59-63, Malaysia 63-69; Minister with Special Functions May 69-Sept. 70; Minister of Finance 70-74; Assoc. mem. IMF Cttee. of Twenty 73-; Treas.-Gen. Alliance Party 59-69, Vice-Chair. 61-; Chair. Commonwealth Parl. Asscn.; Pro-Chancellor Malaysia Nat. Univ. 71-; Dir. Unitac Ltd. 51-57, Malaka Pinda Rubber Estates Ltd., United Malacca Rubber Estate Ltd., Leong Hin San Ltd. 41-57, Sime Darby Holdings Ltd. 74, Siemens Components Sdn. Bhd. 74, Highlands and Lowland Para Rubber Co. Ltd. 74; Hon. LL.D. (Univ. of Malaya) 65; Grand Cross Order of Leopold II (Belgium) 67, Seri Setia Mahkota 67, Order of Sikatuna (Class Data) of the Philippines 68, Bintang Mahaputera Kelas Dua of Indonesia 70.

Leisure interests: shooting, reading.

Universiti Kebangsaan Malaysia, P.O. Box 1124, Jalan Paritai Baru, Kuala Lumpur 22-12, Malaya, Malaysia.

Telephone: 27171.

Tanaka, Isaji; Japanese politician; b. 1906, Hyogo Prefecture.

Lawyer 32; mem. Kyoto Municipal Assembly 33; Democratic Party mem. of the Diet 46, joined Liberal Party 48, subsequently elected twelve times to House of Reps. from Kyoto Prefecture; fmr. Minister of Justice, re-appointed 72-73; Liberal Democratic Party.

c/o House of Representatives, Tokyo, Japan.

Tanaka, Kakuei; Japanese politician; b. 4 May 1918, Niigata Prefecture; s. of Kazuki Tanaka and Fume Tanaka; m. Hanako Sakamoto 1942; one d.; ed. Chuo Technical High School, Tokyo.

Established own construction business 37; building contractor in Tokyo 40-47; mem. Lower House of Parl. 47-; Parl. Vice-Minister of Justice Oct.-Nov. 48; Minister of Posts and Telecommunications (Kishi Cabinet) 57-58; Chair. Policy Research Council of Liberal Dem. Party 61-62; Sec.-Gen. Liberal Democratic Party 65-66, Dec. 68-July 71; Minister of Finance 62-65; Chair. Research Comm. on Municipal Policy, Liberal Dem. Party 67-68; Minister of Int. Trade and Industry 71-72; Pres. Liberal Dem. Party and Prime

Minister 72-74; Chair. Board of Dirs., Echigo Traffic Co. Ltd. 60-.
Leisure interest: golf.
Publ. *A Proposal for Remodelling the Japanese Archipelago.*
12-19-12, Mezirodai, Bunkyo-ku, Tokyo, Japan.
Telephone: 03-943-0111.

Tanaka, Kyubei, B.ECON.; Japanese banker; b. 8 March 1903, Wakayama Pref.; s. of Roichi and Maki Tanaka; m. Kyoko Etoh 1935; one s. one d.; ed. Econ. Dept., Tokyo Imperial Univ.
Managing Director, The Mitsui Bank Ltd. 55-58, Senior Man. Dir. 58-61, Deputy Pres. 61-65, Pres. 65-68, Chair. 68-74, Dir., Counsellor 74-; Blue Ribbon Medal.
Leisure interests: "Go", reading.
The Mitsui Bank Ltd., 1-2, Yurakucho 1-chome, Chiyoda-ku, Tokyo 100; Home: 35-20, Sanno 1-chome, Ota-ku, Tokyo 143, Japan.
Telephone: 501-1111 (Office); 774-2777 (Home).

Tanaka, Masami; Japanese politician; ed. Tokyo Univ.
Member House of Reps. (seven times); Chair. Social Cttee. of Liberal Democratic Party Policy Affairs Research Council; Parl. Vice-Minister of Health and Welfare; Minister of Health and Welfare Dec. 74-.
Ministry of Health and Welfare, Tokyo, Japan.

Tananayev, Ivan Vladimirovich; Soviet inorganic and analytical chemist; b. 4 June 1904, Serpovoe, Tambov Region; S. of Vladimir Alexandrovich and Maria Ivanovna Tananayev; m. Galina Semionovna 1929; two d.; ed. Dept. of Chemistry, Polytechnical Inst., Kiev.
Assistant in Analytical Chemistry, Kiev Polytechnical Inst. 25-30, Docent 30-34; Chief of Analytical Chemistry Laboratory, Acad. of Sciences of Georgian S.S.R., Tbilisi 34-35; Science worker, Inst. of Gen. and Inorganic Chemistry of Acad. of Sciences of U.S.S.R., Moscow 35-39, Doctor and Prof. 39-, Head, Analytical Laboratory and Rare Elements Laboratory 39-48, Deputy Dir. 48-54; mem. C.P.S.U. 42; Corresp. mem. U.S.S.R. Acad. of Sciences 46-58, mem. 58-; mem. Inorganic Chemistry Section of IUPAC 59-63; Lecturer, Inst. of Chemical Technology 62-; Editor-in-Chief *Inorganic Materials* 64-; State Prizes 49, 51, 71; Mendeleev Gold Medal 73.
Leisure interests: playing and composing music.
Publs. *The Physico-Chemical Analysis Method in Analytical Chemistry* 50, 56, 59, 61, *The Chemistry of Metal Fluorides* (13 edns. 38-62), *Ferrocyanides of Metals* (9 edns. 38-58), *Rare Elements Chemistry* 54, 55, 57, 59, 62, *Phosphates of Metals* 62, *The Chemistry of Fluorine Compounds of Actinides* 63, *The Chemistry of Germanium* 67, *The Chemistry of Ferrocyanides of four valent metals* 72; more than 300 articles.
Institute of General and Inorganic Chemistry of U.S.S.R. Academy of Sciences, 31 Leninsky Prospekt, 117071 Moscow, U.S.S.R.

Tanassi, Mario; Italian politician; b. 17 March 1916, Ururi, Campobasso; s. of Vicenzo Tanassi and Lucia Carrozza; m. Enrica Pappalardo 1943; three d.; ed. Italian public schools.
Vice-Sec. Italian Socialist Democratic Party (P.S.D.I.) 50, Sec. 56-66 and Feb.-June 72, Pres. 69-75, Sec. 75-76; Co-Sec Unified Italian Socialist Party (P.S.I.) 66-69; mem Chamber of Deputies 63-; Minister of Industry and Commerce 68-69; Minister of Defence 70-72, 72-73, 73-74, of Finance March-Oct. 74.
Leisure interest: country life.
c/o Ministry of Finance, Rome; and Largo Messico 7, Rome, Italy.

Tanco, Arturo R., Jr., M.I.L.R.; Philippine government executive; b. 22 Aug. 1933, Manila; s. of Arturo V. Tanco, Sr., and Felicia Roxas; m. Patricia Pickett

1962; one s. two d.; ed. De la Salle Coll., Manila, Ateneo de Manila Univ., Union Coll. of New York, Cornell and Harvard Univs.
General Man. and mem. Board, Philippine Investment Management Inc. (PHINMA) 56; Pres. and Gen. Man. Management and Investment Devt. Associates Inc. (MIDA) 64; Under-Sec. for Agriculture, Dept. of Agriculture and Natural Resources 70-71; fmr. Sec. of Agriculture and Natural Resources.
Leisure interest: football (soccer).
Publs. articles in magazines and newspapers including *The Financial Times* (London) and *The Sunday Times Magazine* (London).
Department of Agriculture, Diliman, Quezon City; Home: No. 3 Second Street, Villamar Court, Parañaque, Rizal, Philippines.
Telephone: 99-89-46, 99-87-41 (Office).

Tanford, Charles, PH.D.; American professor of biochemistry; b. 29 Dec. 1921, Halle, Germany; s. of Max and Charlotte Tanford; m. Lucia Brown 1948 (divorced 1968); three c.; ed. New York and Princeton Univs.
Lalor Fellow, Harvard Univ. 47-49; Asst. Prof., Univ. of Iowa 49-54, Assoc. Prof. 54-59, Prof. 59-60; Prof. Duke Univ. 60-70, James B. Duke Prof. of Physical Biochemistry 70-; Guggenheim Fellow 56-57; mem. Nat. Acad. of Sciences.
Leisure interests: photography, hiking, travel.
Publs. *Physical Chemistry of Macromolecules* 61, *The Hydrophobic Effect* 73; 175 scientific articles in various journals.
Department of Biochemistry, Duke University, Durham, N.C. 27710; Home: 1430 Mangum Street, Durham, N.C. 27701, U.S.A.
Telephone: 684-5805 (Office); 688-8912 (Home).

Tang Ming-chao; Chinese United Nations official; b. 1910, Kwangtung Province; ed. Tsinghua Univ. and Univ. of California, U.S.A.
Former mem. Council, Chinese People's Inst. on Foreign Affairs, Chinese People's Asscn. for Friendship with Foreign Countries; Deputy to Nat. Congress, People's Repub. of China; mem. del. to UN Gen. Assembly 71; Under-Sec.-Gen. Dept. of Political Affairs, Trusteeship and Decolonization, UN April 72-.
United Nations, First Avenue, New York, N.Y. 10017, U.S.A.

Tange, Sir Arthur Harold, Kt., C.B.E., B.A.; Australian diplomatist; b. 18 Aug. 1914, Sydney; s. of Charles Tange and Maud Kingsmill; m. Marjorie Shann 1940; one s. one d.; ed. Univ. of W. Australia.
Economist; Econ. Dept. Bank of N.S.W. 38-40; various Australian Govt. Depts., Canberra 42-45; First Sec., Dept of External Affairs 45; First Sec., Australian Mission to UN, N.Y. 46-48; Counsellor, UN Div., Canberra 48-50; Asst. Sec. Dept. of External Affairs 51-53; Minister, Australian Embassy, Washington, D.C. 53-54; Sec. External Affairs 54-65; High Commr. to India and Amb. to Nepal 65-70; Sec. Dept. of Defence 70-; mem. Australian del. Bretton Woods Monetary Conf., UN Preparatory Conf. UN Gen. Assembly 46, 47, 50, 51, and Econ. and Social Council, Reparations Conf., Paris; ILO, Paris, Montreal and San Francisco; Commonwealth Confs., London, Colombo, Sydney 49-63, etc.
Leisure interests: music, tennis, stream fishing.
32 La Perouse Street, Canberra, A.C.T. 2603, Australia.
Telephone: 958879.

Tange, Kenzo, DR.ENG.; Japanese architect; b. 4 Sept. 1913, Osaka; m. Toshiko Kato 1949; one d.; ed. Tokyo Univ.
Member Japanese Architects Asscn., Hon. mem. American Acad. of Arts and Letters, Akad. der Künste, Germany; Hon. Fellow American Inst. of Architects;

Prof. Univ. of Tokyo; Royal Gold Medal, Royal Inst. of British Architects 65; AIA Gold Medal, American Inst. of Architects 66; Medal of Honour, Danish Royal Acad. of Fine Arts, and several other awards; Hon. Dr. Arts, Harvard Univ.; Hon. doctorate Sheffield Univ.; Hon. Dr. Fine Arts, Univ. of Buffalo, N.Y.; Hon. Dr.-Ing., Technische Hochschule, Stuttgart; Hon. Dr. Arch., Politecnico di Milano, Italy; Grande Médaille d'Or, Acad. Française 73.

Buildings include: Peace Memorial Park and Buildings, Hiroshima, Tokyo City Hall, Tokyo, Kurashiki City Hall, Kurashiki, Kagawa Prefectural Govt. Office, Takamatsu, Roman Catholic Cathedral, Tokyo, Nat. Gymnasiums for 1964 Olympic Games, Tokyo, Skopje City Centre Reconstruction Project, Skopje, Yugoslavia, Yamanashi Press and Broadcasting Centre, Yamahashi, Master Plan for Expo 70, Osaka, Fiera District Centre, Bologna, Italy.

Publs. *Katsura* 60 (English edn. 60), *A Plan for Tokyo, 1960* 61 (English edn. 61), *Ise* 62 (English edn. 65), *Japan in the Future* 66, *Kenzo Tange, 1946-1958* 66, *Kenzo Tange, 1958-1964* 66, *Kenzo Tange 1964-1969* 70 (English, French and German edns. 70).

1702 Mita Tsunamachi Park Mansion, 34-3, 2-chome, Mita, Minatoku, Tokyo, Japan.

Tangney, Dame Dorothy Margaret, D.B.E., B.A.; Australian politician; b. 1911; ed. Univ. of W. Australia.

Teaching staff Education Dept. Western Australia; Hon. Life Assoc. Univ. of W. Australia; mem. Standing Cttee. of Convocation Univ. of W. Australia; mem. Federal Exec. Australian Labour Party; Senator for W. Australia 43-68 (first woman to be elected to Commonwealth Senate).

12 Mary Street, Claremont, W.A. 6010, Australia.

Tanida, Toshio; Japanese shipping executive; b. 1897; ed. Tokyo Higher Commercial School.

Joined Mitsubishi Goshi Kaisha 18, Mitsubishi Trading Co. 18, Man. Steamship Dept. (Kobe branch) 40, Man. Kobe branch 42, Taipeh (Formosa) branch 42, Dir. Mitsubishi Steamship Co. Ltd. 46, Man. Dir. 46; Man. Dir. Kyokuto Shipping Co. Ltd. 49; Man. Dir. Mitsubishi Shipping Co. Ltd. 49, Senior Man. Dir. 49, Vice-Pres. 57, later Pres.; Chair. Japan Tanker Owners' Asscn. 54-; Dir. Japanese Shipowners' Asscn. 59-.

2-20 Marunouchi, Chiyoda-ku, Tokyo, Japan.

Taniguchi, Toyosaburo; Japanese textile executive; b. 29 July 1901, Osaka, Japan; s. of Fusazo and Etsu Taniguchi; m. Kinu Yashiro 1928; two s. two d.; ed. Tokyo Univ.

Director Osaka Godo Spinning Co. Ltd. 29-31; Dir. Toyobo Co. Ltd. 31-42, Exec. Vice-Pres. 51-59, Pres. 59-66, Chair. of Board 66-72, Gen. Adviser 72-; Auditor, Japan Exlan Co. Ltd. 56-66; Rep. Dir. Kansai Cttee. for Econ. Devt. 59-60; Pres. Toyobo-Howa Textile Eng. Co. Ltd. 61-; Junior Vice-Pres. IFCATI 64-66, Senior Vice-Pres. 66-68, Pres. 68-70; Chair. Japan Spinners Asscns. 66-68; Vice-Pres. Japan Tax Asscn. 67-; Pres. Expo Textile Asscn. 67-71, Japan Textile Color Design Center 68-72, Japan Textile Fed. 70-71; Supreme Adviser, Japan Textile Fed. 71-; Blue Ribbon Medal (Ranju Hosho) 65; Osaka Governor's award as man of merit for industry 68; First Class Order of Sacred Treasure (from Japanese Emperor) 73.

Leisure interests: golf, Haiku (17 syllables version).

Toyobo Co. Ltd., 8 Dojma Hamadori 2-chome, Kita-ku, Osaka, 530 Japan; Home: 283 Gunge Kakiuchi, Mikage-cho, Higashinada-ku, Kobe, 658 Japan.

Telephone: 06-344-1331 (Office); 078-851-2327 (Home).

Taniguchi, Yoshiro, D.ENG.; Japanese architect; b. 24 June 1904, Kanazawa; s. of Yoshiro and Nao-e Taniguchi; m. Kinu Mitsui 1931; one s. two d.; ed. Tokyo Imperial Univ.

Assistant Prof., Tokyo Univ. of Engineering 31-43,

Prof. 43-45, Prof. Emer. 65-; Dir. Museum Meiji-mura, Inuyama 65-; mem. Cultural Properties Specialists Council of Japan 52-; mem. Japan Acad. of Arts; Prizes of Japan Inst. of Architecture 42, 49, 56; Award of Japan Acad. of Arts 61.

Works include: Nat. monument for the unknown war-dead, Tokyo 59, Palace for Crown Prince of Japan 60, Hotel Okura, Tokyo 62, Imperial Theatre 66, Gallery of Eastern Antiquities at Tokyo Nat. Museum 68, Tokyo Nat. Museum of Modern Art 69, Hotel Okura Amsterdam, Amsterdam (in collaboration) 71.

7-11-7, Koyama, Shinagawa-ku, Tokyo, Japan.

Telephone: 03-781-1990.

Tannery, Jean-Paul; French business executive; b. 11 May 1911, Colmar; s. of Jacques and Suzanne (née Molk) Tannery; m. Yvonne Pilliard 1933; three s. one d.; ed. Lycées Montaigne and Louis-le-Grand, and Ecole Nat. Supérieure des Mines, Paris.

Engineer, Société des Aciéries de Longwy 34-53, Dir. Longwy works 45; Asst. Dir.-Gen. Société Lorraine-Escaut (merger of Aciéries de Longwy, Senelle-Maubeuge and Escaut-et-Meuse) 53-62, Dir.-Gen. 62-66; Dir.-Gen. Société Usinor (merger of Usinor and Lorraine-Escaut) 66; Dir.-Gen. Vallourec 67-, Dir. 68-, Pres.-Dir.-Gen. 73; Dir. of several companies; Officier Légion d'Honneur; Chevalier des Palmes académiques; Croix de Guerre.

Vallourec S.A., 7 Place du Chancelier Adenauer, 75016 Paris; Home: 48 rue du Docteur-Blanche, 75016 Paris, France.

Telephone: 288-56-27 (Home).

Tannous, Afif'I, B.A., M.A., PH.D.; American government official; b. 25 Sept. 1905, Bishmizzeen, Koura, Lebanon; s. of Ishak and Theodora Tannous; m. Josephine Milkey 1941; two s.; ed. American Univ. of Beirut, St. Lawrence Univ., Canton, N.Y., and Cornell Univ.

Admin. position with British Govt. in Sudan 29-31; with Education Dept., Govt. of Palestine and Rural Improvement Programme 31-33; taught Social Science at American Univ. of Beirut and directed rural improvement work 33-37; taught Social Science at Univ. of Minn., U.S.A. 40-43; joined U.S. Dept. of Agriculture, as Middle East specialist, later Head of Middle East Div.; Advisory Editor, *Middle East Journal* 47-; Lecturer on Middle East, School of Advanced Int. Studies, Washington, D.C. 48-51; Deputy Dir. U.S. Technical Co-operation Service for Lebanon 51-54; Co-ordinator, Dept. of Agriculture Services to Technical Co-operation Admin. 54-61; mem. U.S. Agricultural Mission to Middle East 46; FAO Agricultural Mission, Greece 46, UN Economic Survey Mission Middle East 49; Chief Africa and Middle East Branch, Foreign Agric. Service 56-61; Area Officer, Near East and Africa 61-71; Retd. Jan. 71; mem. Board of Int. Centre for Dynamics of Devt., Washington, D.C. 72-; Researcher and writer on Middle East Devt.; Deputy Dir. U.S. Exhibit, Cairo Int. Agricultural Exhbn. 61; Founder mem. Soc. for Int. Devt.; mem. U.S. Dept. of Agriculture Team for Appraisal of Agricultural Devt. in Egypt Oct.-Nov. 75; mem. American Acad. of Political and Social Science, American Asscn. for Advancement of Science, American Sociological Asscn., American Agricultural Econ. Asscn.

Leisure interests: hunting, hiking, gardening, reading.

6912 Oak Court, Annandale, Va. 22003, U.S.A.

Telephone: 256-0767.

Tanoé, Appagny; Ivory Coast diplomatist; b. 1 Oct. 1929; ed. Univ. de Bordeaux.

Former Head Doctor, Centre Hospitalier, Abidjan; Vice-Pres. Econ. and Social Council of the Ivory Coast 61-64; Amb. to France 65-.

Embassy of the Ivory Coast, 102 avenue Raymond-Poincaré, 75016 Paris, France.

Tans, Jean Guillaume Hubert; Netherlands politician; b. 19 Jan. 1912; s. of J. W. Tans and C. Tans-Schrijnemaekers; m. J. B. M. van Hardenburg 1943; five s.; ed. Univ.
Teacher in Secondary schools; mem. Second Chamber of Parl. 54-70; mem. Municipal Council of Maastricht 55-66; mem. Provincial States of Limburg 58-66; mem. Party Cttee. Netherlands Labour Party 61-, Chair. 65-70; Chair. Prep. Cttee., Medical Faculty, Univ. of Maastricht 70-; Chair. Governing Body, State Univ. of Limburg 75-; Freeman of Town of Maastricht 75; Knight of Order of the Lion (Netherlands).
Leisure interests: reading, gardening, walking.
Schweibergerweg 41, Mechelen-Wittem, Netherlands.
Telephone: 04455-1273; 043-88889.

Taofinu'u, H.E. Cardinal Pio; Samoan ecclesiastic; b. 9 Dec. 1923, Falealupo, Savaii; s. of Solomona Taofinu'u and Mau Solia.
Ordained priest 54; Bishop of Samoa and Tokelau 68-; cr. Cardinal by Pope Paul VI March 73.
Leisure interests: gardening, music, art.
Publ. The Kava Ceremony is a Prophecy 73.
Cardinal's Office, P.O. Box 532, Apia, Western Samoa, Telephone: Apia 95.

Tape, Gerald Frederick, M.S., PH.D.; American physicist and scientific administrator; b. 29 May 1915, Ann Arbor, Mich.; s. of Henry A. Tape and Flora Simmons Tape; m. Josephine Waffen 1939; three s.; ed. Eastern Michigan Univ., and Michigan Univ.
Assistant in Physics, Eastern Mich. Univ. 33-35, Univ. of Mich. 36-39; Instructor in Physics, Cornell Univ. 39-42; Staff mem. Radiation Laboratory, Mass. Inst. of Technology 42-46; Asst., later Assoc. Prof. of Physics Univ. of Ill. 46-50; Asst. to Dir. 50-51, Deputy Dir., Brookhaven Nat. Laboratory 51-62; Vice-Pres. Associated Univs. Inc. 62, Pres. 62-63, 69-; U.S. Atomic Energy Commr. 63-69; U.S. Rep. to IAEA with rank of Amb. 73-; mem. President's Science Advisory Cttee. 69-73; mem. Defense Science Board 70-74, Chair. 70-73; mem. AEC High Energy Physics Advisory Panel 69-74; mem. IAEA Scientific Advisory Panel 72-74; mem. Energy Research and Devt. Agency Gen. Advisory Cttee. 75; mem. Nat. Science Foundation Advisory Group on Science Programs 75-; Dir. Atomic Industrial Forum Inc. 70-73; Dir. Science Service Inc. 71-; Fellow, American Physical Soc., American Nuclear Soc., American Asscn. for Advancement of Science; mem. American Astronomical Soc.; Hon. D.Sc. (E. Michigan Univ. 64); Army-Navy Certificate of Appreciation 47; Dept. of State Tribute of Appreciation 69; Sec. of Defense Meritorious Civilian Service Medal 69; Dept. of Defense Distinguished Public Service Medal 73.
Publs. co-author with L. J. Haworth Relay Radar Chapter of Massachusetts Institute of Technology Radiation Laboratory Technical Series; co-author with Dr. F. K. Pittman and M. F. Searl Future Energy Needs and the Role of Nuclear Power 64, Proceedings of Third International Conference on Peaceful Uses of Atomic Energy 64, Proceedings of the Thermionic Electrical Power Generation Symposium, Stresa 68, Why We Test 68, National Policy on Peaceful Uses of Nuclear Explosives 69.
6717 Tulip Hill Terrace, Washington, D.C., U.S.A.
Telephone: 301-229-6264.

Tàpies, Antoni; Spanish painter; b. 13 Dec. 1923; self-taught.
First one-man exhbn., Barcelona 48, later in Paris, New York, London, Zürich, Rome, Milan, Munich, Stockholm, Hanover, Washington, Pasadena, Buenos Aires, Caracas, Düsseldorf, Bilbao, Madrid and Barcelona; French Govt. Scholarship 50; UNESCO Prize, Venice Biennale and Pittsburgh International Prize 58, Guggenheim Prize 64, Rubens Prize 72.
C. Zatagoza 57, Barcelona, Spain.

Taranczewski, Wacław; Polish painter; b. 4 March 1903, Czarnków Wielkopolski; s. of Sylwester and Waleria Taranczewski; m. Wanda Hryniewiecka; ed. Acad. of Fine Arts, Cracow and Warsaw.
Organized Poznań Higher School of Art 45; Prof. of Monumental Painting, Cracow Acad. of Arts 47-72, Prof. Emeritus 72-; works exhibited Brussels Int. Exhbn. 35, Paris Exhbn. of Modern Art 45, XXIX Venice Biennale 58, etc.; Guggenheim Foundation Nat. Prize 58, Prize of Minister of Culture and Art (1st Class) 69, State Prize 72 and numerous other awards; easel and mural paintings, also cycles: Mała Malarka (The Little Painter), Koncert w atelier (Concert in the Studio), Martwa natura ze świątkiem (Still Life with Seated Christ), Martwa natura z wiolonczelą (Still Life with 'Cello), Krakowska Wenus z Willenford (Cracow Venus from Willenford), Okno (Window); also numerous decorative works for churches, including polychromes in Poznań, Radom, Warsaw, stained-glass windows in Warsaw Cathedral, polychromes for the Philharmonic Hall, Poznań, and decorated ceilings in the State Council.
Ul. Siemaszki 13 m. 6, 31-201 Cracow, Poland.

Tarasov, Nikolai Nikiforovich; Soviet politician; b. 1911; ed. Moscow Textile Inst.
Foreman, Shop Superintendent, Dir. of Spinning Mill, Deputy Head of Cotton Mill, Orethovo-Zuevo 35-42; Soviet Army 42-45; Factory Head Engineer, Head Engineer, Cotton Industry Central Admin. of Moscow Region, Head, Cotton Industry Central Admin. of Ivanovo Region 45-52; Dep. Minister of Light Industry of U.S.S.R. 52-53; Head, Consumer Goods Dept., U.S.S.R. Council of Ministers 53-55; Dep. Chair., U.S.S.R. State Planning Cttee. 55-57; Dep. Chair. Vladimir Econ. Council 58-60; Dep. Chair. All Russian Econ. Council 60-62; Chair. State Cttee. for Light Industry of U.S.S.R. State Planning Cttee. 62-65; Minister of Light Industry 65-; mem. C.P.S.U. 42-; Alt. mem. Central Cttee. C.P.S.U. 66-; Deputy to U.S.S.R. Supreme Soviet 66-.
Ministry of Light Industry, 15 Verkhnyaya Krasnoselskaya, Moscow, U.S.S.R.

Tarazi, Salah El Dine, L. en D., D. en D.; Syrian diplomatist; b. 1919; ed. Coll. des Frères, Damascus and Faculté Française de Droit, Beirut.
Lawyer 40-47; Lecturer and Asst. Prof. of Law, Damascus Univ. 46-48; Ministry of Foreign Affairs 49-50; Chargé d'Affaires, Brussels 51-53; Alt. Perm. Rep. to UN 53-56; Sec.-Gen., Ministry of Foreign Affairs 56-57; Ambassador to U.S.S.R. 57-58; Ambassador of U.A.R. to Czechoslovakia 58-59, to People's Repub. of China 59-61; Perm. Rep. of Syria to UN 62-64; Amb. to U.S.S.R., concurrently accred. to Finland 64; fmr. Amb. to Turkey; Judge, Int. Court of Justice Feb. 76-; Syrian, Belgian and Czech awards.
Publ. Les Services Publics Libano-Syriens 46.
International Court of Justice, Peace Palace, The Hague 2012, Netherlands.

Tarbell, Dean Stanley, A.B., A.M., PH.D.; American professor of chemistry; b. 19 Oct. 1913, Hancock, N.H.; s. of Sanford M. Tarbell and Ethel L. Millikan; m. Ann Tracy 1942; two s. one d.; ed. Thayer High School, Winchester, N.H., and Harvard Univ.
Postdoctoral Fellow, Ill. 37-38; Instructor, rising to Houghton Prof. of Chem. and Chair. of Dept., Univ. of Rochester 38-67; Distinguished Prof. of Chem., Vanderbilt Univ. 67-; R. C. Fuson Lecturer, Nevada 72; mem. Nat. Acad. of Sciences, American Acad. of Arts and Sciences; Herty Medallist 73.
Leisure interests: reading, travel.
Publs. About 185 research papers in organic chemistry 36-.
Department of Chemistry, Vanderbilt University, Nashville, Tenn. 37235, U.S.A.
Telephone: 322-2714.

Tardieu, Jean; French writer; b. 1 Nov. 1903; *m.* Marie-Laure Tardieu-Blot; one *d.*; ed. Lycée Condorcet and Univ. de Paris.

With Radiodiffusion Télévision Française (O.R.T.F.), Head Drama Section 44-46, Dir. Club d'essai-centre d'Etudes 46-60, Dir. France musique O.R.T.F. 54-64, Admin. Counsellor 64-74; Chevalier Légion d'Honneur; Chevalier Arts et Lettres; Grand Prix de Poésie (Acad. Française) 72.

Publs. *Accents, Le Témoin invisible, Figures, Monsieur Monsieur, Un Mot pour un autre, La Première Personne du singulier, Une voix sans personne, Théâtre de chambre, L'espace et la Flûte, Poèmes à jouer, De la peinture abstraite, Choix de poèmes, Histoires obscures, Il était une fois, deux fois, trois fois* (children's book), *Pages d'écriture, Le fleuve caché, Les Portes de toile, La part de l'ombre, Scripts, Formeries, Obscurité du jour*; translations of German poems and plays (Goethe, Hölderlin). 72 boulevard Arago, 75013 Paris, France.

Tariki, Abdallah; Saudi Arabian oil executive; b. 19 March 1919; *s.* of Houmoud and Lolwa Tariki; *m.* 1st Eleanore Nicholas 1948, 2nd Maha Jumblatt 1969; two *c.*; ed. Univs. of Cairo and Texas.

Studied at Univ. of Texas and worked as trainee with Texaco Inc. in W. Texas and Calif. 45-49; Dir. Oil Supervision Office, Eastern Province, Saudi Arabia (under Ministry of Finance) 49-55; Dir.-Gen. of Oil and Mineral Affairs (Saudi Arabia) 55-60; Minister of Oil and Mineral Resources 60; Dir. Arabian American Oil Co. 59-62; Leader Saudi Arabian Del. at Arab Oil Congresses 59, 60; Independent Petroleum Consultant 62-; Chair. Arab Petroleum Consultants; co-founder of OPEC; publisher of monthly petroleum magazine *Naft El-Arab*; adviser to Iraqi, Algerian and Kuwait govts. on oil matters.

Leisure interest: breeding Arab horses.

KAC Building, Floor 10, Apt. 3, Sharie Hilali, Kuwait; Home: P.O. Box 22699, Kuwait City, Kuwait.

Telephone: 415860, 412561 (Office); 443466 (Home).

Tarjanne, Päivö Kaukomieli; Finnish diplomatist; b. 4 May 1903, Hämeenlinna; *s.* of A. J. Tarjanne and Hellin Makkonen; *m.* Annu Ritavuori 1932; three *s.*; ed. Univs. of Helsinki and Paris, and Inst. Int. des Hautes Etudes, Paris.

Attaché, Ministry of Foreign Affairs 28; Attaché, Stockholm 29-30; Sec. Ministry of Foreign Affairs 30-32; First Sec. Berne and Geneva (mem. of perm. del. to League of Nations) 32-34; Counsellor, Stockholm 34-38; Dir. of the Admin. Section of the Ministry of Foreign Affairs 39-45 (rank of Minister 42); Minister to Norway 45-50, to Iceland 47-50; Sec.-Gen. of Ministry of Foreign Affairs 50-53; Minister to Denmark 53-55, Amb. 55-56; Amb. to Sweden 56-61, to Denmark 61-70; mem. Chapter of the Order of the White Rose of Finland and of the Order of the Lion of Finland 70-.

Kuhatie 21A, SF-02170 Espoo 17, Finland.

Telephone: 90-426256.

Tarjanne, Toivo, M.A., LL.M.; Finnish jurist; b. 8 Feb. 1893, Helsinki; *s.* of Onni Tarjanne and Josefina Veijola; *m.* Eeva Lundelin 1929; two *d.*; ed. Helsinki Univ.

Sec. Ministry of Commerce and Industry 31-32, to Chancellor of Justice 32-42; Judge, Supreme Administrative Court 43; Governor of Province of Vasa 43-44; Chancellor of Justice 44-50; Pres. Supreme Court and Chair. High Court of Impeachment 50-63; Chancellor, Order of Finnish White Rose and Order of Finnish Lion 63-73.

Pohjoiskaari 40, 00200 Helsinki 20, Finland.

Telephone: Helsinki 67-5160.

Tarka, Joseph Sarwuan; Nigerian politician; b. 10 July 1932, Igbor, Tiv Division; *s.* of Chief Tarka Nachi; *m.*; six *c.*; ed. Gboko Primary School, Katsina-Ala Middle Secondary School and Bauchi Teachers' Training Coll.

Teacher, Provincial Secondary School, Tiv Native Admin.; mem. House of Reps. 54; Fed. Commr. for Transport 67-71, for Communications 71-74; del. to Nigerian Constitutional Conf. 57-58, Pan African Conf. 59; Pres. Intergovernmental Maritime Consultative Org. (IMCO) 71-73.

Leisure interests: tennis, photography, reading detective novels, listening to jazz records, Tiv folk-songs.

c/o Ministry of Communications, Lagos, Nigeria.

Tarski, Alfred, PH.D.; American (b. Polish) professor of mathematics; b. 14 Jan. 1902, Warsaw; *m.* Maria Josephine Witkowski 1929; one *s.* one *d.*; ed. Univ. of Warsaw.

Instructor, Polish Pedagogical Inst., Warsaw 22-25; Prof. Żeromski's Lycée, Warsaw 25-39; Docent and Adjoint Prof. Univ. of Warsaw 25-39; Research Assoc. Harvard Univ. 39-41; Visiting Prof. Coll. of City of New York 40-41; mem. Inst. for Advanced Study, Princeton 41-42; Lecturer, Univ. of Calif., Berkeley 42-45, Assoc. Prof. 45-46, Prof. of Mathematics 46-68, Emer. 68-; Visiting Prof. Nat. Univ. of Mexico 57; Research Prof. Miller Inst. for Basic Research in Science 58-60; Visiting Flint Prof. of Philosophy, Univ. of Calif., Los Angeles 67; Shearman Memorial Lecturer, Univ. Coll., London 50, 66; Visiting Prof. Catholic Univ. of Chile 74-75; mem. U.S. Nat. Acad. of Sciences; Corresp. Fellow, British Acad.; Foreign mem. Royal Netherlands Acad. of Sciences and Letters; fmr. corresp. mem. Polish Acad. of Arts and Sciences; Hon. mem. Dutch Mathematical Soc.; Past Pres. Asscn. for Symbolic Logic, Int. Union for History and Philosophy of Science; Past Chair. U.S. Nat. Cttee. Int. Union for History and Philosophy of Science; Hon. D.Sc., Catholic Univ. of Chile 75.

Publs. *The Concept of Truth in Languages of Deductive Sciences* 33, *Geometry* (with Z. Chwiałkowski and W. Schayer) 35, *Introduction to Logic and the Methodology of Deductive Sciences* 36, *Direct Decompositions of Finite Algebraic Systems* (with B. Jónsson) 47, *A Decision Method for Elementary Algebra and Geometry* 48, *Cardinal Algebras* 49, *Undecidable Theories* (with A. Mostowski and R. M. Robinson) 53, *Logic, Semantics, Metamathematics* 56, *Ordinal Algebras* 56, *The Completeness of Elementary Algebra and Geometry* 67, *Cylindric Algebras, Part I* (with L. Henkin and J. D. Monk) 71.

Home: 462 Michigan Avenue, Berkeley, Calif. 94707; Office: Department of Mathematics, University of California, Berkeley, Calif. 94720, U.S.A.

Telephone: 415-524-2094 (Home); 415-642-2721 (Office).

Tartakower, Arie, DR. IUR., D.RER.POL.; Israeli (b. Polish) university professor; b. 24 Sept. 1897, Brody; *s.* of Nathan Tartakower and Sophia Fichman; *m.* Malvina Schickler; one *s.* (died 1944); ed. Univ. of Vienna.

Co-founder Zionist Labour Movement and Chair. Zionist Labour Party, Poland 22-29; Lecturer, Inst. of Jewish Sciences, Warsaw 32-39; Dir. Dept. of Relief and Rehabilitation of World Jewish Congress (U.S.A.) 39-46; fmr. Professor, Lecturer and Head, Dept. of Sociology of the Jews, Hebrew Univ., Jerusalem; fmr. Chair. Israel Exec., World Jewish Congress; mem. General Council World Zionist Org.; mem. World Secr., Zionist Labour Movement; Chair. World Asscn. for Hebrew Language and Culture; Co-founder and fmr. Pres. Israel Asscn. for UN.

Publs. include: *History of the Jewish Labour Movement, Jewish Emigration and Jewish Policy of Migration, The Jewish Refugee, Jewish Wanderings in the World, The Wandering Man, The Jewish Society, The Israeli Society, History of Colonization, Jewish Colonization in the Diaspora, History of Jewish Nationalism, The Tribes of Israel* (3 vols.).

1 Ben Yehuda Road, Jerusalem, Israel.

Telephone: Jerusalem 222889.

Tasca, Henry J., M.B.A., PH.D., LL.D.; retd. American diplomatist; b. 23 Aug. 1912, Providence, R.I.; *m.* Lina M. Federici; four *c.*; ed. Temple Univ., Univ. of Pennsylvania and London School of Economics and Political Science.
Economic Analyst, Div. of Trade Agreements, Dept. of State 37-38; Asst. Dir. of Trade Regulation and Commercial Policy Project 39-40; Econ. Adviser to Nat. Defense Comm. 40; U.S. Treasury Dept. Rep. at Embassy in Rome 45-48; Alt. U.S. Exec. Dir. Int. Monetary Fund; concerned with Marshall Plan operations as U.S. mem. in Europe, Deputy to Amb. W. Harriman to "Three Wise Men" NATO group, later apptd. Deputy U.S. Special Rep. in Europe; apptd. by Pres. Eisenhower as Special Rep. for Korean Econ. Affairs 53; Dir. of U.S. Operations Mission in Italy; Econ. Counsellor U.S. Embassy at Bonn 56-60; Deputy Asst. Sec. of State for African Affairs 60-65; Amb. to Morocco 65-69, to Greece 69-74; war service in U.S. Navy as Lieut.-Commdr. 40-45; Hon. LL.D. Temple Univ., Medal of Freedom 46; Distinguished Service Award (Korea); Grand Cordon of Ouissam Alaouite (Morocco); Order of Merit, Cavaliere di Grand Croce.
c/o Dept. of State, 2201 C Street, N.W., Washington, D.C., U.S.A.

Tashiro, Kikuo; Japanese newspaper executive; b. 22 April 1917; ed. Waseda Univ.
Joined *Asahi Shimbun* 40; City Editor 59; Managing Editor 66; Exec. Dir. in charge of Editorial Affairs 69-.
Asahi Shimbun, 6-1, 2-chome, Yuraku-cho, Chiyoda-ku, Tokyo, Japan.

Tassara González, Gen. Luis; Chilean army officer; b. 26 Feb. 1908; *m.* Blanca Jimenez; two *s.* three *d.*
Infantry and Staff Officer; a UN Mil. Observer in Kashmir 51-52, 56-57; fmr. Instructor, Nat. Defence Acad., Chile; later Chief of Joint Operations, Armed Forces Staff; later Dir. of Army War Acad. 61; Sec. Nat. Security Council; Chief Intelligence Services, Armed Forces Gen. Staff; C.-in-C. Southern Reg. 61-64; Chief Mil. Observer, UN Mil. Observer Group in India and Pakistan (UNMOGIP) 66-.
c/o UNMOGIP, United Nations, New York City, N.Y. 10017, U.S.A.

Taswell, Harold Langmead Taylor, M.COM.; South African diplomatist, b. 14 Feb. 1910, Cape Town; *s.* of Stephen Taswell and Helen Simkins; *m.* Vera Blytt 1940; three *d.*; ed. Christian Brothers Coll., Pretoria, and Univ. of Cape Town.
Department of External Affairs 37-, Berlin 37-39, London 39, The Hague 40, New York 40-46; Consul, Elisabethville 46-49; Int. Trade and Econ. Section, Dept. of External Affairs, Pretoria 49-51; First Sec., Wash. 51-56; Consul-Gen., Luanda, Angola 56-59; High Commr. of S. Africa in Fed. of Rhodesia and Nyasaland 59-61, Accredited Diplomatic Rep. 61-63, Accredited Diplomatic Rep. in S. Rhodesia 63-64; Head, Africa Div., Dept. of Foreign Affairs, Pretoria 64; Amb. to U.S.A. 65-71, to UN, Geneva 71-Feb. 75.
Leisure interest: walking.
c/o Ministry of Foreign Affairs, Pretoria, South Africa.

Tata, Jehangir Ratanji Dadabhoy; Indian industrialist; b. 29 July 1904.
Joined Tata Sons Ltd. 26; Chair. Tata Sons Private Ltd., Tata Industries Private Ltd., The Tata Iron and Steel Co. Ltd., The Tata Oil Mills Co. Ltd., Tata Chemicals Ltd., Tata Ltd., London, Tata Inc., New York, Tata Inst. of Fundamental Research, Indian Hotels Co. Ltd., Sir Dorabji Tata Trust, Lady Tata Memorial Trust, J. N. Tata Endowment, Nat. Centre for the Performing Arts, Homi Bhabha Fellowships Council, Air-India, Gov. Board Family Planning Foundation; Pres. Court of Indian Inst. of Science, Bangalore; Dir. Tata Engineering and Locomotive Co. Ltd., Investment

Corpn. of India Ltd.; mem. Indian Airlines, Atomic Energy Comm.; Trustee, Gandhi Smarak Nidhi, Kasturba Gandhi Nat. Memorial Trust; Trustee, Jawaharlal Nehru Memorial Fund; first pilot to qualify in India holding a private licence from 29-; solo flight India-England 30; founded Tata Airlines 32; Hon. Air Vice-Marshal Indian Air Force; Officier Légion d'Honneur 54, Padma Bhushan 55; Hon. D.Sc. (Allahabad) 47.
Office: Bombay House, Bruce Street, Bombay 1; Home: The Cairn, Altamount Road, Bombay 26, India.

Tatad, Franciso, LITT.B.; Philippine writer and politician; b. 4 Oct. 1939; ed. Univ. of Santo Tomas, Manila.
Former Corresp. Agence France-Presse; fmr. Columnist *Manila Daily Bulletin*; Press Sec. and Presidential Spokesman 69-; Sec. of Public Information 72-.
Department of Public Information, Malacanang, Manila; Home: 2 Arfel Homes, Diliman, Quezon City, Philippines.

Tatarkiewicz, Władysław, PH.D.; Polish philosopher; b. 3 April 1886, Warsaw; *s.* of Ksawery Tatarkiewicz and Maria Brzezinska; *m.* Teresa Potworowska 1919; one *s.*; ed. Warsaw, Zürich, Paris, Berlin and Marburg Univs.
Professor of Philosophy, Warsaw Univ. 15-62, Emer. Prof. 62-; mem. fmr. Polish Acad. of Learning; mem. Polish Acad. of Sciences, Int. Inst. of Philosophy; Hon. mem. Int. Cttee. of History of Art; mem. Serbian Acad. of Sciences 72; mem. several other Polish and foreign scientific and learned socs.; Commdr. Cross, Order of Polonia Restituta 38, with Star 58, State Prize 66, Légion d'Honneur (France), and other decorations.
Publs. *Historia filozofii* (History of Philosophy) 31, (7th edn. 70), English edn.: *Nineteenth Century Philosophy* 73, and *Twentieth Century Philosophy* 73; *Les trois morales d'Aristote* 32, *Skupienie i marzenie* (Concentration and Dreaming) 35, *O szczęściu* (On Happiness) 48 (5th edn. 70), English edn.: *Analysis of Happiness* 75; *Dominik Merlini*, (Italian edn. 69), *Historia Estetyki* (History of Aesthetics) 60, English edn. Vol. I-III 70-74, *Droga do filozofii i inne rozprawy filozoficzne* (Way to Philosophy and other philosophical papers) 71.
Ul. Chocimska 35, m. 10, 00-791 Warsaw, Poland.
Telephone: 45-20-80.

Tatay, Sándor; Hungarian writer; b. 6 May 1910, Bakonytamási; *s.* of Lajos Tatay and Teréz Varga, *m.* Maria Takacs 1944; one *d.*; ed. Sopron, Pécs; Journalist *Kelet Népe* 37-.
Leisure interest: vineyard.
Publs. *Thunderstorm* 41, *The Simeon Family* (5 vols.) 55-59, *White Carriage* 60; *The House under the Rocks* (film) 58; children's books and short stories.
Gyöngyösi, u. 53, H-1131 Budapest XIII, Hungary.
Telephone: 409-523.

Tate, Allen, LITT.D.; American writer and university professor; b. 19 Nov. 1899, Winchester, Ky.; *s.* of John Tate and Eleanor Varnell; *m.* Helen Heinz 1966; one *s.* one *d.*; ed. Georgetown Preparatory School, and Vanderbilt Univ.
Guggenheim Foundation Fellow 28-30; Prof. of English, Univ. of North Carolina 38-39; Resident Fellow in Poetry, Princeton Univ. 39-42; Ed. of *The Sewanee Review* 44-47; Visiting Prof., Univ. of Chicago 49; Prof. of English, Univ. of Minnesota 51-67; Visiting Prof., Univ. of Rome 53-54; American Acad. of Arts and Letters Award 48; Bollingen Prize for Poetry 56, Acad. of American Poets Award 63; Gold Medal Società Dante Alighieri 62; mem. Univ. of Oxford 58-59, Nat. Inst. of Arts and Letters, American Acad. of Arts and Letters 64.
Publs. *The Fathers* 38, *Poems 1922-1947* 48, *On the*

Limits of Poetry 48, *The Hovering Fly* 48, *The Forlorn Demon* 53, *Collected Essays* 59, *Poems* 60, *Essays of Four Decades* 68, *The Swimmers and other selected poems* 70, *Memories and Opinions: Miscellaneous Essays* 75.
Running Knob Hollow Road, Sewanee, Tenn. 37375, U.S.A.
Telephone: 598-5849.

Tate, James Hugh Joseph, LL.D.; American politician; b. 1910; ed. Northeast Evening High School, Strayer's Business Coll., Tucker Inst., St. Joseph's Coll. and Temple Univ. Law School.
Member Pennsylvania Legislature 40-46; Vice-Chair. Democratic City Cttee., Philadelphia 52-; mem. Philadelphia City Council 51-55, Pres. 55-62, Acting Mayor of Philadelphia 62-63, Mayor 64-70; Chair. Delaware River Port Authority 62-63; Pres. U.S. Conf. of Mayors 70-71; mem. Exec. Cttee. Nat. Urban Coalition 67-.
4029 N. 7th Street, Philadelphia 40, Pa., U.S.A.

Tati, Jacques (Jacques Tatischeff); French actor and film director; b. 9 Oct. 1908, Le Pecq; *m.* Micheline Winter 1944; one *s.* one *d.*
Formerly music-hall artist; films directed include *Gai Dimanche, Soigne ton Gauche, L'Ecole des Facteurs, Jour de Fête, Les Vacances de Monsieur Hulot, Mon Oncle, Tati No. 4* (later called *Playtime*), *Yes Monsieur Hulot* (later called *Traffic*), *Parade* 74; Scenario Prize, Venice Film Festival 49 and Grand Prix du Cinéma Français 50 for *Jour de Fête*, Int. Critics' Prize, Cannes Film Festival and Prix Louis Delluc for *Les Vacances de Monsieur Hulot* 53; Special Prize, Cannes Film Festival for *Mon Oncle* 58; "Oscar" and New York Critics' Award for best foreign film; French Cinema Acad. Grand Prix for *Playtime* 68.
Specta Films, 12 rue du Château, 92250 La Garenne-Colombes; Home: 9 rue Voltaire, 78100 Saint-Germain-en-Laye, France.
Telephone: 782-19-97 (Office).

Taton, (André) René, D. és L.; French historian; b. 4 April 1915, L'Echelle (Ardennes); *m.* Juliette Battesti 1945; two *c.*; ed. Faculté des Sciences, Nancy and Paris, Ecole Normale Supérieure de St. Cloud.
Research Asst., Nat. Centre of Scientific Research 46, rising to Research Dir. 64-; Prof. Ecole pratique des Hautes Etudes 64-, Dir. Centre for Research into History of Science, Ecole des Hautes Etudes 64-; mem. Acad. Int. d'Histoire des Sciences; Lauréat Académie des Sciences; Sec.-Gen. of Int. Union of the History and Philosophy of Sciences 55-72, Vice-Pres. 72-.
Publs. *L'oeuvre scientifique de Gaspard Monge* 51, *L'oeuvre mathématique de G. Desargues* 51, *Causalités et Accidents de la Découverte Scientifique* 58 (translated into English, Spanish, Japanese), ed. *Histoire Générale des Sciences* (4 vols.), (translated into English, Italian, Spanish, Portuguese), numerous articles on the history of mathematics and the history of sciences in general.
12 rue Colbert, 75002 Paris; Home: 64 rue Gay-Lussac, 75005 Paris, France.
Telephone: 742-76-59 (Office).

Tátrai, Vilmos; Hungarian violinist; b. 7 Oct. 1912, Kispest; *s.* of Vilmos Tátrai and Maria Obernauer; *m.* Zsuzsa Kreismann 1938; one *s.* one *d.*; ed. National Conservatoire, Budapest.
Teacher 46-53; First Violinist, Budapest Symphony Orchestra 33; mem. Radio Orchestra 38; Leading Violinist Metropolitan State Concert Orchestra 40-; Founder-Leader Tátrai String Quartet 46, and led it on tours throughout Europe 52-; Founder-Leader Hungarian Chamber Orchestra 57-; Prof. of Music, Budapest Acad. of Music 65-; First prize, Béla Bartók Competition 48, Liszt Prize 52, 72, Kossuth Prize 58, Eminent

Artist of Hungarian People's Republic, Labour Order of Merit golden degree.
Leisure interests: walking, photography.
Raoul Wallenberg u. 4; and Zenemüvészeti Föiskola, Liszt Ferenc tér. 2, H-1136 Budapest XIII, Hungary.
Telephone: 110-529.

Taube, Henry, B.S., M.S., PH.D.; American professor of chemistry; b. 30 Nov. 1915, Saskatchewan, Canada; *s.* of Samuel Taube and Albertina Tiledetzki Taube; *m.* Mary Alice (née Wesche) 1952; two *s.* two *d.*; ed. Univs. of Saskatchewan and Calif. (Berkeley).
Instructor Univ. of Calif. at Berkeley 40-41; Instructor-Asst. Prof. Cornell Univ. 41-46; Asst. Prof., Prof. Univ. of Chicago 46-61; Prof. of Chem., Stanford Univ., Calif. 62-; Guggenheim Fellow 49-55; mem. Nat. Acad. of Sciences; American Chem. Soc. Awards 55, 60, Chandler Medal of Columbia Univ., Kirkwood Award, Harrison Howe Award, Rochester Section, ACS, 60; Nichols Medal, New York Section, ACS 71; Willard Gibbs Medal, Chicago Section, ACS 71; F. P. Dwyer Medal, Univ. of N.S.W. 73.
Leisure interests: record-collecting, gardening.
Publs. Approx. 190 research papers in chemical re-activity.
Department of Chemistry, Stanford University, Stanford, Calif. 94305; 441 Gerona Road, Stanford, Calif. 94305, U.S.A.
Telephone: 415-328-2759.

Taubman, (Hyman) Howard, A.B.; American journalist, author and critic; b. 4 July 1907; ed. Cornell Univ. Journalist 29-; with *New York Times* 30-, Drama Critic 60-65, Critic-at-Large 65-72; Hon. Mus.D. (Cornell Univ. and Oberlin Coll.); mem. Philadelphia Music Acad. 59-.
Publs. *Opera Front and Back* 38, *Music as a Profession* 39, *Music on My Beat* 43, *The Maestro, The Life of Arturo Toscanini* 51, *How to Build a Record Library* 53, *How to Bring up Your Child to Enjoy Music* 58, *The Making of the American Theatre* 65.
New York Times, Times Square, New York City, N.Y.; Home: 41 W. 83rd Street, New York, N.Y. 10024, U.S.A.

Taufa'ahau Tupou IV, G.C.V.O., K.C.M.G., K.B.E., B.A., LL.B.; H.M. the King of Tonga; b. 4 July 1918; eldest son of the late Queen Salote Tupou III of Tonga and the late Hon. Uiliame Tungi, C.B.E., Premier of Tonga; ed. Newington Coll. and Sydney Univ., N.S.W.; married H.R.H. Princess Mata'aho 47; four children, of whom the eldest, Crown Prince Tupoutoa, is heir to the throne.
Premier of Tonga 49-65; King of Tonga 65-; Chancellor of the University of the South Pacific 70-73; Hon. LL.D. The Palace, Nuku'alofa, Tonga.

Taus, Josef, LL.D.; Austrian banker and politician; b. 8 Feb. 1933, Vienna; *s.* of Josef Taus and G. Schinko; *m.* Martha Loibl 1960; ed. Univ. of Vienna.
Journalist; law practice; with Austrian Inst. of Econ. Research; Sec. and Head of Econ. Div., Girozentrale und Bank der Österreichischen Sparkassen AG 58, mem. Man. Board 67-68, Chair. and Man. Dir. 68-75; fmr. Man. Sparinvest-Kapitalanlage G.m.b.H.; mem. Parl.; State Sec. Fed. Ministry of Communications and Nationalized Enterprises 66-67; Fed. Chair. Austrian People's Party (ÖVP) Aug. 75-.
Österreichische Volkspartei, Kärntnerstrasse 51, 1010 Vienna; Home: Kahlenberger Strasse 44/2/2, A-1190 Vienna, Austria.
Telephone: (0222) 52-26-21 (Office); (0222) 36-16-05 (Home).

Tautscher, Anton, DR.RER.POL., DR.JUR.; Austrian economist; b. 1906, Veitsch, Steiermark; *s.* of Alexander and Josefine Tautscher; *m.* Hedy Mosdorfer 1936; two *d.*; ed. Univ. of Graz.

Lecturer in Nat. Economy and Finance at Univ. of **Graz** 40-48, Asst. Prof. 48-55, Prof. 55-; Rector of Karl Franzens Univ. of Graz 57-58, 65-66.
Publs. *Ernst Ludwig Carl, Der Begründer der Volks-wirtschaftslehre* 39, *Bankenverstaatlichung, Zur Frage des gestuften Zinses* 46, *Staatswirtschaftslehre des Kameralis-mus* 47, *Geschichte der Volkswirtschaftslehre* 50, *Die Öffentliche Wirtschaft* 53, *Die Grenzen der Besteuerung* 54, *Einkommenspolitik und Genossenschaften* 55, *Wirtschaftsethik* 57, *Vom Arbeiter zum Mitarbeiter, Quantitative und qualitative Sozialpolitik* 61, *Hand-buch der Oesterreichischen Wirtschaftspolitik* 61, *Grund-sätze der modernen Sozialpolitik* 61, *Lebensstandard und Lebensglück* 63, *Die Wirtschaft als Schicksal und Aufgabe, Ges. Aufsätze* 65, *Die Elite aus Geist und Verantwortung, zur gegenwärtigen Wirtschaftsordnung* 65, *Schicksal oder Aufgabe des Menschen* 66, *Wesen und Aufgabe des Akademikers* 66, *Wesen und Würde des Beamtens* 66, *Die Stellung des Hochschulprofessors in der Gesellschaft von heute* 66, *Steigender Steuerdruck bei sinkendem Geldwert* 67, *Die Stellung des Lehrers in der Gesellschaft von heute* 68, *Der ökonomische Leviathan oder die wirtschaftliche Übermacht des Staates* 69, *Die Österreichische Wirtschaftsordnung* 71, *Wirtschafts-geschichte Österreich* 73.
Schröttergasse 7, Graz, Austria.

Tavares, Amandio Joaquim, M.D.; Portuguese univer-sity professor; b. 1900, Valpaços; *m.* Maria da Purifi-cação Gomes Sampayo Tavares 1928; one *s.*; ed. Univ. of Oporto.
Lecturer Univ. of Oporto 22-27; Asst. Prof. of Anatomy, Histology and Embryology 27-29; Asst. Prof. of Patho-logical Anatomy 29-32, Prof. 32-70; Vice-Pres. Inst. of High Culture 42-52; Rector of the Univ. of Oporto 46-61; Hon. Rector 61; Pres. Portuguese Asscn. for the Advancement of Sciences 50-64; Pres. Scientific Re-search Council (Inst. of Higher Culture) 52-65; Pres. Legal Medicine Council of Oporto 59-70; Dir., Dept. of Pathology, Hospital Escolar de S. João, Oporto 62-70; Pres. Portuguese Pathology Soc. 63-69; Vice-Pres. First Section, Nat. Education Junta 65-70; Dir. Research Centre for Anatomical and General Pathology, I.A.C. 41-72; mem. Lisbon Acad. of Sciences, New York Acad. of Sciences and several Portuguese and foreign scientific socs.; numerous honours and decorations.
Publs. About 200 books and articles on anatomy, anthropology, pathological anatomy and education.
Rua dos Lagos 48, Senhora da Hora, Portugal.
Telephone: 950444.

Taverne, Dick, Q.C.; British politician; b. 18 Oct. 1928, Sumatra; *s.* of Dr. N. J. M. Taverne and L. V. Taverne; *m.* Janice Hennessey 1955; two *d.*; ed. Charterhouse School and Balliol Coll., Oxford.
Called to the Bar 54; Labour M.P. for Lincoln 62-72; Q.C. 65; Parliamentary Under-Sec. of State, Home Office 66-68; Minister of State, Treasury 68-69; Finan-cial Sec. to the Treasury 69-70; resigned as Labour M.P. to fight seat as Democratic Labour candidate 72, M.P. for Lincoln 73-Oct. 74; mem. European Parl. 73-74; Dir. Inst. for Fiscal Studies 71-, Equity and Law Life Assurance Co. Ltd. 72-, BOC Int. 75-.
Leisure interests: squash, sailing.
Publ. *The Future of the Left* 74.
60 Cambridge Street, London, SW1V 4QQ, England.
Telephone: 01-826-0166.

Taverner, Sonia; Canadian ballerina; b. 18 May 1936, Byfleet, Surrey; *d.* of H. J. Taverner; ed. Elmhurst Ballet School, and Royal Ballet School, London, and ballet school in New York.
Joined Royal Ballet 55, toured U.S.A. and Canada; joined Royal Winnipeg Ballet 56, leading dancer 57, ballerina 62-66; appeared with Royal Winnipeg Ballet, Commonwealth Arts Festival, London 64; joined "Les Grands Ballets Canadiens" Spring 66, as principal

dancer; appeared as guest artist with the Boston Ballet Co., in Swan Lake 67; Guest teacher Les Grands Ballets Canadiens Summer School 70; principal artist with The Pennsylvania Ballet 71-; guest artist with Toronto, Winnipeg and Vancouver Symphony Orches-tras; has toured extensively over North America, Jamaica and U.K.
Leisure interests: cooking, books.
The Drake, 1512 Spryce Street, Philadelphia, Pa. 19102, U.S.A.
Telephone: K15-2072.

Taviani, Paolo Emilio; Italian politician; b. 6 Nov. 1912; ed. Univ. of Genoa.
Professor in History of Economic Theory at Genoa Univ.; leader Partisan War 43-45; organizer of Christian Democratic Party (in Genoa area) 43; mem. Con-stituent Assembly 46-48; mem. Parl. 48-; Deputy Sec. Christian Democratic Party 46-49, Sec. 49-50; Editor *Civitas* 50-; Italian Rep. to Schuman Plan Conf. 51 and to later E.D.C. Confs.; Under-Sec. for Foreign Affairs 51-53; Minister of Defence 53-58, of Finance 59-60, of Treasury 60-62, of Interior 62-68, for interventions in Southern Italy 68-72, for Budget, Econ. Planning and Southern Devt. 72-73, of the Interior 73-74.
Publs. include *Social Reformers of the Italian Risorgi-mento* 40, *Social Prospects* 45, *Ownership* 46, *The Schu-man Plan* 52, *Atlantic Solidarity and European Com-munity* 57, *Defence of Peace* 58, *Christian Principles and Democratic System* 65, *The Concept of Utility in Economic Theory Vol. I* 68, *Vol. II* 70, *Utility, Economics and Morals* 70, *The Problem of Development and the "Cassa del Mezzogiorno" Experience*.
Via di Fontanegli 33, Bavari, Genoa, Italy.

Tavolaro, Silvio, D.IUR.; Italian jurist; b. 28 Oct. 1900; ed. Univ. degli Studi, Rome.
Judge 22; Justice of Court of Appeals 41-47; Justice of Supreme Court of Italy 47-55, Presiding Judge 55-58; Chief Justice of Court of Appeals, Rome 58-62; Chief Justice of Supreme Court 62-70; fmr. Perm. mem. Supreme Council of Judiciary; mem. Cttee. on Conten-zioso Diplomatico, Ministry of Foreign Affairs; mem. Acad. of Biological and Moral Sciences; Hon. mem. Roman Soc. of Legal Medicine; mem. Exec. Cttee. World Asscn. of Judges; Chair. Asscn. for Cultural Exchange of Italian and German Jurists; Knight Grand Cross Order of Malta; Medal for Social Redemp-tion; First Class of Sacred Treasure of Japan; Grosses Bundesverdienstkreuz.
Publs. Essays and articles on constitutional law, family law and the judiciary.
38 Via Casperia, Rome, Italy.

Távora, Virgilio de Moraes Fernandes; Brazilian politician; b. 29 Sept. 1919, Fortaleza; *s.* of Manuel do Nascimento Fernandes Távora and Carlota Augusta de Moraes; *m.* Luiza Moraes Correia 1953; one *s.* one *d.*; ed. Colégio Militar of Fortaleza, and Rio de Janeiro.
Military career: 2nd Lt. 39, Lt. 41, Capt. 44, Major 50, Lt.-Col. 55, Col. 60; Head União Democrática Nacional 53, 59, 61; mem. Chamber of Deputies 50-58, 66-70, Senate 71-; Candidate for Gov. of Ceará 58; Minister of Transport, Communications and Public Works Sept. 61-June 62; Gov. of Ceará 63-66; mem. NOVACAP (org. which built Brasília 58); Dr. h.c. Universidade Federal Ceará, Escola de Administração Ceará.
Leisure interests: classical music, historical research.
SQS111-B1. H- Apto. 302, Brasília; Rua José Lourenço, 435 Fortaleza, Ceará, Brazil.
Telephone: 43-8352 (Brasília); 24-2511 (Fortaleza).

Tavoulareas, William Peter; American oil executive; b. 9 Nov. 1919, Brooklyn; *s.* of Peter W. and Mary (née Palise) Tavoulareas; *m.* Adele Maciejewska 1941; two *s.* one *d.*; ed. St. John's Univ., Jamaica.
Joined Mobil Oil Corpn. 47, Man. Middle East Account-

ing Dept. 57, Man. Corporate Planning and Analysis Dept. 59; Vice-Pres. for Plans and Programmes, Mobil International Oil Co. 61; Vice-Pres. Mobil 63; Dir., mem. Exec. Cttee. and Senior Vice-Pres. 65; Pres. North American Div. 67; Pres. Mobil Oil Corpn. Sept. 69-; Hon. D.C.S. and Young Business Man of the Year Award, St. John's Univ.

Leisure interests: swimming, boating, reading.

150E 42nd Street, New York, N.Y. 10017; Home: Harbor Road, Sands Point, N.Y., U.S.A.

Telephone: 212-883-3616 (Office); 516-883-7255 (Home).

Tawes, J. Millard; American banker and politician; b. 8 April 1894; ed. Wilmington Conf. Acad., and Sadler's, Bryant and Stratton Business Coll.

Clerk of Court, Somerset County, Md. State 30-38; Comptroller 38-47; State Bank Commr. 47-50, Comptroller 50-58; Gov. of Maryland 59-66; Sec. Dept. Nat. Resources, Md. 69-71; fmr. Sec.-Treas. Crisfield Shipbuilding Co.; fmr. Pres. Nat. Asscn. of State Auditors, Comptrollers and Treasurers, Maryland State Firemen's Asscn.; mem. Board of Visitors and Govs., Washington Coll., Board of Trustees, Wesley Junior Coll., Dickinson Coll., Board of Dirs., McCready Memorial Hospital; Democrat.

Hall Hwy, Crisfield, Md. 21817, U.S.A.

Tax, Sol, PH.D., PH.B.; American university professor; b. 30 Oct. 1907, Chicago, Ill.; s. of Morris Paul Tax and Kate (Hanowitz) Tax; m. Gertrude Jospe Katz 1933; two d.; ed. Univs. of Wisconsin and Chicago.

Member Logan Museum North African Expedition 30; field research, Apache Indians 31, Fox Indians 32-34; Investigator, and later Ethnologist, Carnegie Inst. 34-48; field research in Guatemala and Chiapas (Mexico) 34-43; Research Assoc. in Anthropology, Univ. of Chicago 40-44, Assoc. Prof. 44-48, Prof. of Anthropology 48-; Assoc. Dean Social Sciences Div. 48-53, Chair. Anthropology Dept. 55-58; Dean Univ. Extension 63-68; Assoc. Editor *American Anthropologist* 48-52, Editor 53-56; Editor *Current Anthropology* 57-74, Viking Fund Publications in Anthropology 59-68; Gen. Editor *World Anthropology*, Proceedings IX Int. Congress of Anthropological and Ethnological Sciences; Fellow American Anthropological Asscn. (Pres. 58-59), Center for Advanced Study in the Behavioral Sciences 69-70; Man-Nature Project in Chiapas, Mexico 56-59; Chair. Cttee. on Darwin Centenary (1859-1959) 56-59; U.S. Nat. Comm. for UNESCO 59-65, Exec. Cttee. 63-65; Consultant, U.S. Office of Educ. 65-70; Special Adviser, Smithsonian Inst. 65-, and Dir. of its Center for Study of Man 69-; mem. Board of Advisers, Council on Int. Communication 66-; Pres. Int. Union of Anthropological and Ethnological Sciences; Viking Medallist 61; Medal of Govt. of Czechoslovakia 69; D. Hum. Litt. (Wis. Univ.) 69; Hon. LL.D., Wilmington College 74; Hon. D.Sc., Univ. del Valle de Guatemala 74; Hon. Fellow Royal Anthropological Inst., Slovakian Anthropological Soc. of Slovak Acad. of Sciences, Chilean Anthropological Soc., Ethnological Soc. of Hungary.

Publs. *Heritage of Conquest: The Ethnology of Middle America* 52, *Penny Capitalism, A Guatemalan Indian Economy* 53, 63; Editor for 29th Int. Congress of Americanists Proceedings 49-52, *Civilizations of Ancient America* 51, *Acculturation in the Americas* 52, *Indian Tribes of Aboriginal America* 52, *Evolution After Darwin* (3 vols.) 60, *Anthropology Today—Selections* 62, *Horizons of Anthropology* 63, *The Draft: A Handbook of Facts and Alternatives* 67, *The People Versus the System* (ed.) 68.

1700 E. 56th Street, Chicago, Ill. 60637, U.S.A.

Telephone: DO3-0990.

Taylor, Alan John Percivale, M.A.; British historian; b. 25 March 1906, Southport; s. of Percy Lees Taylor and Constance Thompson; four s. two d.; ed. Oriel Coll., Oxford.

Rockefeller Fellow in Social Sciences 29-30; Lecturer in History, Univ. of Manchester 30-38; Fellow of Magdalen Coll., Oxford; fmr. Univ. Lecturer in Int. History. Leisure interests: fell walking, W. C. Fields.

Publs. *The Italian Problem in European Diplomacy 1847-49* 34, *Germany's First Bid for Colonies* 38, *The Course of German History* 45, *The Habsburg Monarchy 1809-1918* 48, *From Napoleon to Stalin* 50, *Rumours of Wars* 52, *The Struggle for Mastery in Europe 1848-1914* 54, *Bismarck* 55, *Englishmen and Others* 56, *The Trouble-Makers* 57, *The Russian Revolution of 1917* (TV lectures) 58, *The Origins of the Second World War* 61, *The First World War* 63, *Politics in Wartime* 64, *English History 1914-1945* 65, *From Sarajevo to Potsdam* 66, *Europe: Grandeur and Decline* 67, *War by Timetable* 69, *Churchill: Four Faces and the Man* (with others) 69, *Beaverbrook* 72, *The Second World War* 75, *Essays in English History* 75.

13 St. Mark's Crescent, London, NW1 7TS, England. Telephone: 01-485-1507.

Taylor, Arthur Robert, M.A.; American business executive; b. 6 July 1935, Elizabeth, N.J.; s. of Arthur Earl Taylor and Marion Hilda Scott; m. Marion McFarland 1959; ed. Brown Univ.

Assitant Dir. of Admissions, Brown Univ. 57-60; Asst. Vice-Pres. The First Boston Corporation 64-66, Vice-Pres. 66-70, Dir. 69-70; Vice-Pres. (Finance), Int. Paper Co. 70-71, Exec. Vice-Pres. 71-72, Dir. 71-72; Pres. and Dir. CBS Inc. 72-; mem. Council on Foreign Relations; Trustee, Bucknell Univ., Brown Univ., Asia Soc. and Japan Soc.

Publs. Article in *Harvard Review of Business History* 71, chapter in *The Other Side of Profit* 75.

Columbia Broadcasting System Inc., 51 West 52nd Street, New York, N.Y. 10019, U.S.A.

Taylor, Edward Plunket, C.M.G., B.SC.; Canadian industrialist; b. 29 Jan. 1901, Ottawa; s. of Lt.-Col. P. B. Taylor and Florence Magee; m. Winifred Thornton Duguid 1927; one s. two d.; ed. Ashbury Coll., Ottawa Collegiate Inst., and McGill Univ., Montreal.

President, Lyford Cay Co. Ltd., Windfields Farm Ltd.; Chair. New Providence Devt. Co., The Royal Bank of Canada Int. Ltd., Int. Housing (Cayman) Ltd., Int. Housing Ltd.; Dir. Argus Corpn. Ltd., Massey-Ferguson Ltd., The Royal Bank of Canada, Trust Corpn. Ltd., London, Trust Corpn. of Bahamas Ltd., etc.; Joint Dir.-Gen. Munitions Production 40; Exec. Asst. to Ministry of Munitions and Supply 41; Pres. War Supplies Ltd., Washington, D.C. 41; Pres. and Vice-Chair. British Supply Council in North America Sept. 41; Dir.-Gen. British Ministry of Supply Mission Feb. 42; Canadian Deputy mem. on Combined Production and Resources Board Nov. 42; Canadian Chair. Joint War Aid Cttee. U.S.-Canada Sept. 43; Chair. and Chief Steward Jockey Club of Canada; Hon. Chair. Ontario Jockey Club.

Lyford Cay, Nassau, Bahamas.

Taylor, Elizabeth; British film actress; b. 27 Feb. 1932; m. 1st Conrad Nicholas Hilton, Jr. 1950 (div.); m. 2nd Michael Wilding (div.), two s.; m. 3rd Mike Todd 1957 (died 1958), one d.; m. 4th Eddie Fisher 1959 (div.); m. 5th Richard Burton (q.v.) 1964 (div. 1974, remarried 1975), one adopted d.; ed. Byron House, Hawthorne School, and Metro-Goldwyn-Mayer School.

Films include *Lassie Come Home, National Velvet, Little Women, A Place in the Sun, Ivanhoe, Elephant Walk, Rhapsody, Beau Brummel, The Last Time I Saw Paris, Giant, Raintree County, Cat on a Hot Tin Roof, Butterfield 8, Cleopatra, The V.I.P.s, The Sandpiper, Who's Afraid of Virginia Woolf, The Taming of the Shrew, Dr. Faustus, Reflections in a Golden Eye, The Comedians, Boom, Secret Ceremony, The Only Game in Town, Hammersmith is Out, Under Milk Wood, Zee &*

Co., *Night Watch* 73, *Ash Wednesday* 74, *Identikit* 74, *The Bluebird* 75; Acad. Award (Oscar) for Best Actress for *Butterfield 8* 60, for *Who's Afraid of Virginia Woolf* 67; Silver Bear Award for *Hammersmith is Out*, Berlin 72.

c/o Major D. Neville-Willing, 85 Kinnerton Street, London, S.W.1, England.
Telephone: 01-235-4640.

Taylor, Harold McCarter, C.B.E., T.D., M.SC.(NZ), M.A., PH.D.; British university official; b. 13 May 1907, Dunedin, New Zealand; s. of James and Louisa (née McCarter) Taylor; m. 1st Joan Sills 1933 (died 1965), 2nd Judith Samuel 1966; two s. two d.; ed. Otago Boys' High School, Dunedin, New Zealand, Univ. of Otago and Clare Coll., Cambridge.
University Lecturer in Mathematics, Univ. of Cambridge 33-45; Treasurer, Univ. of Cambridge 45-53, Sec.-Gen. of the Faculties 53-61; Vice-Chancellor Univ. of Keele Oct. 61-67, retd.; Rede Lecturer, Univ. of Cambridge 66; Fellow, Soc. of Antiquaries 61, Vice-Pres. 74-; mem. Royal Comm. on Historical Monuments 72; Lt.-Col. Royal Artillery 39-45; Smith's Prize, Univ. of Cambridge 32, John Henry Lefroy Medal, Royal Artillery 46, Alice Davis Hitchcock Medallion, Soc. of Architectural Historians 65.
Leisure interests: ski-mountaineering, history of architecture.
Publs. *Anglo-Saxon Architecture* (with Joan Taylor) 65, *Why Should We Study The Anglo-Saxons?* 66, numerous archaeological articles in nat. journals.
192 Huntingdon Road, Cambridge, CB3 0LB, England.
Telephone: Cambridge 76324.

Taylor, Henry J., D.LITT.; American diplomatist, author, journalist, economist; b. 2 Sept. 1902; ed. Lawrenceville School, N.J., and Univ. of Virginia.
Entered newspaper profession 18; war correspondent in Second World War, accredited to all theatres of war; Amb. to Switzerland 57-61; columnist United Features Syndicate 61-; Chair. of Board, Silicone Paper Company of New York, Inc., Waldorf Astoria Hotel, Advisory Board Chemical Bank, etc.
Publs. *Germany's Economy of Coercion, Time Runs Out, Men in Motion, Men and Power, An American Speaks His Mind, The Big Man* (novel), *Men and Moments,* etc.
45 Rockefeller Plaza, New York, N.Y. 10020, U.S.A.

Taylor, Hobart, Jr.; American lawyer and government official; b. 17 Dec. 1920, Texarkana, Texas; s. of Hobart Taylor, Sr. and Charlotte Wallace; m. Lynette Dobbins 1951; two s.; ed. Prairie View State Coll., Texas, Howard Univ., and Univ. of Michigan.
Admitted to Michigan Bar 44; Research Asst. Michigan Supreme Court 44-45; Private Law Practice, Detroit 45-48; Asst. Prosecuting Attorney, Wayne County 49-50, Corpn. Counsel 51-61; Senior Partner Taylor, Patrick, Bailer, Wexler and Brookins (law firm) 58-61; Special Counsel, Pres. of U.S.'s Cttee. on Equal Employment Opportunity 61-62, Exec. Vice-Chair. 62-65; Special Asst. to Vice-Pres. Lyndon B. Johnson 61-63; Assoc. Counsel to Pres. Johnson 64-65; Dir. Export-Import Bank 65-68, Great Atlantic and Pacific Tea Co. 71-, Standard Oil Co. of Ohio 71-, Westinghouse Electric Corpn. 71-, Aetna Life & Casualty Co. 73-; mem. Board of Govs., Amer. Nat. Red Cross; Partner Dawson, Riddell, Taylor and Davis 68-; many hon. degrees and awards, including Commdr., Légion d'Honneur of Repub. of Ivory Coast.
Office: 723 Washington Building, Washington, D.C. 20005, U.S.A.

Taylor, Sir James, Kt., M.B.E., D.SC., PH.D., F.R.I.C., H.F.I.MIN.E., F.R.S.A.; British industrial consultant; b. 16 Aug. 1902, Sunderland; s. of James and Alice Taylor; m. Margaret Lennox Stewart; two s. one d.; ed. Bede Coll., Sunderland, Rutherford Coll., Newcastle-upon-Tyne, Univs. of Durham, Utrecht, Cambridge and the Sorbonne.
Joined Nobel Div., I.C.I. Ltd. 28, Research Dir. 46, Joint Man. Dir. 51, Dir. 52-64; Chair. Yorkshire Imperial Metals Ltd. 58-64, Imperial Aluminium Co. Ltd. 59-64, Imperial Metal Industries Ltd. 62-64; Pres. Inst. of Physics and Physical Soc. 66-68; Deputy Chair. Royal Ordnance Factories Board 59-72 (mem. 52-72); Dir. Fulmer Research Inst. Ltd., Oldham International Ltd. 65-71; Chair. Chloride Silent Power Ltd. 74-; Hon. mem. Newcomen Soc. (U.S.A.) 70; mem. Council of R.S.A. 64-, Chair. 69-71, Vice-Pres. 69-; mem. Court of Brunel Univ. 67-; Pres. Research and Devt. Soc. 70-; Medal of the Soc. of the Chemical Industry 65, Silver Medal, Royal Soc. of Arts 69, Silver Medal for Service to the Chemical Soc. 72; Hon. F.Inst.P. 72; Hon. D.Sc. (Bradford), Hon. D.C.L. (Newcastle.)
Leisure interests: gardening, writing.
Publs. include *On the Sparking Potentials of Electric Discharge Tubes* 27, *Detonation in Condensed Explosives* 52, *British Coal Mining Explosives* 58, *Solid Propellent and Exothermic Compositions* 59, *The Modern Chemical Industry in Great Britain* 61, *Arts, Crafts and Technology* 69, *New Horizons in Research and Development* 71, *The Scientific Community* 73, lectures and numerous articles in learned journals.
Culvers, Seale, Nr. Farnham, Surrey, GU10 1JN, England.
Telephone: Runfold 2210.

Taylor, John Wilkinson, A.B., A.M., PH.D.; American educationist; b. 26 Sept. 1906, Covington, Ky.; s. of John Wesley and Ethel (née Wilkinson) Taylor; m. 1st Katherine Wright 1939 (dissolved 1951), one s.; m. 2nd Helen Green 1952 (died 1966); m. 3rd June Fairbank 1966; seven stepchildren; ed. Columbia Coll., Columbia Univ., Vanderbilt Univ., Univs. of Berlin, Paris, London and Vienna.
Teacher 29-30; Asst. Teachers Coll., Columbia Univ. 27-30, Instructor in Education 30-36; Teacher, Kaiser Friedrich Realgymnasium, Berlin 30-31; Broughton High School, Raleigh, N.C. 31-32; Educational Adviser to Pres. John Day Publ. Co 32-33; Asst. in Education and Dir. Foreign Study, Columbia Univ. 34-35; Asst. to Chair. New Coll., Columbia Univ. 35-37, Chair. of Admissions, Scholarships, Loans, Curriculum and Personnel Guidance Cttees. 37-38; Assoc. Prof. of Comparative Education and Admin. Asst. to Pres. Louisiana State Univ. 38-40, Dir. Bureau of Educational Research 41-43; served as Capt. to Lieut.-Col. U.S. Army 43-46; Dir. of Studies, Mil. Govt. School and Holding Centre, Natousa, N. Africa 42-43; Chief Education and Religious Affairs Branch, U.S. Mil. Govt. for Germany 44-47 and U.S. Rep. Quadripartite Education Cttee. for Germany 45-47; Pres. Univ. of Louisville, Ky. 47-50; Deputy Dir.-Gen. of UNESCO 51-54, Acting Dir.-Gen. 52-53; Exec. Dir. Chicago Educational Television Asscn. 54-71; Chicago Council on Foreign Relations 54, mem. Board of Dirs. 70-72; Pres. and mem. Board of Dirs., Learning Resources Inst. 63-70, Midwest Educational T.V. Network, Inc. 64-68; mem. Round Table Meeting on Contribution to Peace of UNESCO 66; mem. Film Industry Advisory Board, Chicago Int. Film Festival 65-; Chair. Board Chicago City Colls. 66-; mem. numerous commissions and advisory cttees.; U.S. Legion of Merit, Légion d'Honneur, and numerous American and foreign decorations.
Leisure interests: golf, bridge.
Publ. *Youth Welfare in Germany* 36.
Office: 180 North Michigan Avenue, Chicago, Ill. 60601; Home: 1244 North State Street, Chicago, Ill. 60610, U.S.A.
Telephone: 312-269-8000 (Office); 312-787-3347 (Home).

Taylor, Lauriston Sale, A.B., D.SC.; American physicist; b. 1 June 1902, Brooklyn, N.Y.; s. of Charles Taylor and Nancy Sale; m. Azulah Walker 1925 (deceased 1972), two s.; m. 2nd Robena Harper Taylor 1973; ed. Stevens Inst. of Technology, Cornell, Columbia Univs.

Bell Telephone Labs., New York City 22-; Nat. Bureau of Standards (N.B.S.) 27-64, Chair. Nat. Comm. Radiation, Protection and Measurements 29-64, Pres. Nat. Council 64-; mem. Int. Comm. on Radiological Protection 28-69, mem. Emer. 70; Eighth Fighter Command, Ninth Air Force, Europe 43-45; Chief Biophysics Branch A.E.C. 47-48; Chief Atomic and Radiation Physics Div. 50-62, Assoc. Dir. N.B.S. 62-64; mem. Int. Comm. on Radiation Units and Measurements 28-34, Sec. 34-50, Chair. 53-69, Hon. Chair. and mem. Emer. 69-; Special Asst. to Pres., Nat. Acad. of Sciences 65-70; Exec. Dir. Advisory Comm. to Office of Emergency Preparedness 65-71; Pres. of Nat. Council on Radiation Protection and Measurements 64-; Hon. D.Sc. (Univ. of Pennsylvania and St. Procopius Coll.).

Leisure interests: cabinet making, plumbing, electrical work.

Publs. 16 books and about 140 papers principally on X-radiation measurement and protection.

7407 Denton Road, Bethesda, Md. 20014, U.S.A.
Telephone: 301-652-5096.

Taylor, Gen. Maxwell Davenport; American army officer (retd.); b. 26 Aug. 1901; ed. U.S. Military Acad., West Point.

Commissioned Second Lieut. Corps of Engineers 22; various assignments in U.S. and abroad; Instructor in French and later Asst. Prof. of Spanish, U.S. Mil. Acad., West Point 27-32; attended Field Artillery School and Commd. and Gen. Staff School 32-35; with American Embassy, Tokyo 35-37 and 37-39; Asst. Mil. Attaché, Peking 37; at Army War Coll., Washington, D.C. 39-40; special mission to Latin American countries 40; commd. 12th Field Artillery Battn. 40-41; duty at Office of Sec. of Gen. Staff 41-42; Chief of Staff and Artillery Commdr. 82nd Infantry Div. 42; served overseas in Sicilian and Italian campaigns 43-44; commd. 101st Airborne Div. invasions of Normandy and Holland, Ardennes and Central European campaigns 44-45; Supt. U.S. Mil. Acad., West Point 45-49; Chief of Staff, European Commd. H.Q., Heidelberg 49; U.S. Commdr. Berlin 49-51; Asst. Chief of Staff for Operations, Dept. of the Army 51, Deputy Chief of Staff for Operations and Admin. of Army 51-53; Commdr. 8th Army Feb. 53-55, General June 53 and U.S. Army Forces, Far East Nov. 54-April 55; C.-in-C. UN Command and Far East Command April 55; Chief of Staff U.S. Army 55-59; Pres. Lincoln Center for the Performing Arts 61; Mil. Rep. of Pres. 61-62; Chair. Joint Chiefs of Staff 62-64; Amb. to Repub. of Viet-Nam 64-65; mem. Foreign Intelligence Advisory Board 65-68, Chair. 68; Consultant to the Pres.; Pres. Inst. of Defense Analyses; decorations include D.S.C., D.S.M. (four times), Silver Star; D.S.O. (U.K.), Hon. C.B. (U.K.); Commdr. de la Légion d'Honneur (France); French and Belgian Croix de Guerre, etc.; Hon. D.Eng. (N.Y. Univ.); Hon. LL.D. (Bowdoin Coll., Williams Coll., Univ. of Mo., Pa. Mil. Coll., Trinity Coll., Yale Univ., Lafayette Coll., Seoul Nat. Univ., Philips Univ.).

Publs. The Uncertain Trumpet 60, Responsibility and Response 67, Swords and Plowshares 72.

2500 Massachusetts Avenue, N.W., Washington, D.C. 20008, U.S.A.

Taylor, Paul B.; American modern dancer and choreographer; b. Allegheny County, Pa.; s. of Paul B. Taylor and Elizabeth P. Rust; ed. Virginia Episcopal School, Syracuse Univ., Juilliard School of Music, Metropolitan School of Ballet and Martha Graham School of Contemporary Dance.

Former dancer with the companies of Martha Graham, George Balanchine, Charles Weidman, Anna Sokolow, Merce Cunningham, Katherine Litz, James Waring and Pearl Lang; now dancer-choreographer-director, The Paul Taylor Dance Co.; since 56 has undertaken 18 foreign tours, 28 tours throughout U.S.A. and 10 seasons on Broadway; Guggenheim Fellowship 61, 65; Chevalier, Ordre des Arts et des Lettres; Centennial Achievement Award (Ohio State Univ.) 70; several int. awards for choreography.

Choreography includes: Three Epitaphs 56, Rebus 58, Tablet 60, Junction 61, Fibers 61, Insects and Heroes 61, Tracer 62, Piece Period 62, Aureole 62, Party Mix 63, Scudorama 63, Duet 64, From Sea to Shining Sea 65, Post Meridan 65, Orbs 66, Agathes' Tale 67, Lento 67, Public Domain 68, Private Domain 69, Churchyard 69, Foreign Exchange 70, Big Bertha 70, Fetes 71, Book of Beasts 71, Guests of May 72, So Long Eden 72, Noah's Minstrels 73, American Genesis 73, Untitled Quartet 74, Sports and Follies 74.

The Paul Taylor Dance Foundation, 550 Broadway, New York, N.Y. 10012, U.S.A.
Telephone: 212-431-5562.

Taylor, Paul Schuster, M.A., PH.D., LL.D.; American economist; b. 9 June 1895, Sioux City, Iowa; s. of Henry Taylor and Rose Schuster; m. 1st Katharine Whiteside 1920, 2nd Dorothea Lange 1935; one s. two d.; ed. Wisconsin and California Univs.

Member staff Calif. Univ. 22-62 and Prof. of Economics 39-62, Chair. of Dept. 52-56, Emer. 62-; Chair. Inst. Int. Studies 56-62; Chief Investigator of Mexican Labour in U.S. for Social Science Research Council 27-29; Consultant Nat. Comm. on Law Observance and Enforcement 30-31; Latin-American Fellow of Guggenheim Foundation 31; Regional Labour Adviser Resettlement Administration 35-36; Pres. California Rural Rehabilitation Corpn. 36-43; Consultant Social Security Board 36-40, U.S. Dept. of Interior 43-52, Export-Import Bank 52, Int. Co-operation Admin. (now U.S. Agency for Int. Development) 55, 58, 59, 61, 62, 63, 66, 67, 68, UN 60, 63; Visiting Prof. Inst. of Land Reclamation, Univ. of Alexandria 62-63; Research Dir. California Labor Fed. 70, Consultant 71.

Publs. Sailors' Union of the Pacific 23, Mexican Labour in the U.S. 28-32, A Spanish-Mexican Peasant Community 33, An American-Mexican Frontier 34, An American Exodus (with Dorothea Lange) 39, 69, Slave to Freedman 70, Communist strategy and tactics of employing peasant dissatisfaction over conditions of land tenure for revolutionary ends in Vietnam 70, Georgia Plan 1732-1752 72.

1163 Euclid Avenue, Berkeley, Calif. 94708, U.S.A.
Telephone: 415-524-3880.

Taylor, Most Rev. Robert Selby, M.A.; British ecclesiastic; b. 1 March 1909, Cumberland; s. of late Robert Taylor; unmarried; ed. Harrow School, St. Catharine's Coll., Cambridge and Cuddesdon Coll.

Ordained Deacon 32, Priest 33; Mission Priest, Diocese of Northern Rhodesia 35, Principal Diocesan Theological Coll. 39; Bishop of Northern Rhodesia 41-51, of Pretoria 51-59, of Grahamstown 59-64; Archbishop of Cape Town 64-74; Hon. D.D.

Seaspray, Main Road, Kalk Bay, Cape Province, South Africa.
Telephone: 8-5588.

Taylor-Smith, Ralph Emeric Kasope, B.SC., PH.D., A.R.I.C., F.R.I.C.; Sierra Leonean organic chemist and diplomatist; b. 24 Sept. 1924; m.; four c.; ed. Univ. of London.

Demonstrator, Woolwich Polytechnic, London 56-59; Lecturer Fourah Bay Coll., Univ. of Sierra Leone 59-62, 63, Senior Lecturer 65, Dean Faculty of Pure and Applied Science 67, Assoc. Prof. 68, 69; Solomon B. Caulkner Post-Doctoral Fellow, Weizmann Inst. of

Science, Israel 62-63; Research Assoc. Princeton Univ., N.J. 65-69; Visiting Prof. Kalamazoo Coll., Mich. 69-70; Amb. to People's Repub. of China 71-74; High Commr. in the U.K. (also accred. to Denmark, Norway and Sweden) 74-; Chair. Board of Dirs., Sierra Leone Petroleum Refinery Co. 70; mem. Board of Educ. of Sierra Leone 70; served on numerous acad. and public cttees.

Publs. conf. papers and articles in scientific journals including a series of studies, *Investigations on Plants of West Africa* (I-XII).

Sierra Leone High Commission, 33 Portland Place, London, W1N 3AG, England.

Tchaikowsky, André; British concert pianist and composer; b. 1 Nov. 1935, Warsaw, Poland; ed. Paris Conservatoire, Warsaw Conservatory, private tuition under Stefan Askenase, composition studies with Nadia Boulanger.

Compositions: *Sonata for Clarinet and Piano* 59, *Inventions for Piano* 60-61, *Love's End* (Song Cycle) 64-67, *String Quartet* 66-68, *Ariel* (Song Cycle) 69, *Concerto for Piano and Orchestra* 66-71.

Leisure interests: reading, classical literature and drama, solitary walking, chess.

c/o Harrison & Parrott, 22 Hillgate Street, London, W.8, England.

Telephone: 01-229-9166.

Tchanqué, Pierre; Cameroonian civil servant; b. 16 Dec. 1925, Douala; s. of Noutchang and Najeukam Tchanqué; m. Odette Tchanqué 1967; two s. two d.; ed. Univ. de Paris.

Former Dir. of Public Accounts; Sec.-Gen. Ministry of Finance; Dir. Société Nationale d'Investissement du Cameroun; Pres. of Council, CIMENCAM; Dir. of various companies; Sec.-Gen. Union Douanière et Economique de l'Afrique Centrale (UDEAC) July 70-; Officier et Chevalier de l'Ordre National (Cameroon) and decorations from Tunisia and Fed. Germany.

Leisure interests: games and sport, especially football.

Union Douanière et Economique de l'Afrique Centrale (UDEAC), B.P. 969, Bangui, Central African Republic.

Telephone: 28-08.

Tcherepnin, Alexander; American (b. Russian) composer, pianist and conductor; b. 21 Jan. 1899, St. Petersburg; s. of Nicolai and Marie (née Benois) Tcherepnin; m. Lee Hsien-ming 1937; three s.; ed. St. Petersburg Conservatory and Paris.

Western debut, recital in London 22; concert tours in France and Western Europe 22-, U.S.A. 26-, China, Japan 34, 35, 36, 37, U.K., Scandinavia 46, Egypt 48; Prof. San Francisco Music and Art Inst. 48; Prof. Piano and Composition De Paul Univ., Chicago 49-64; Prof. Acad. Int. d'été, Nice 59-62; Prof. Mozarteum, Salzburg 62; mem. Nat. Inst. of Arts and Letters, U.S.A. 74; Schotts' Int. Prize for *Concerto da Camera*, Glinka Prize (France) 59, David Bispham Award for *The Farmer and the Nymph* 60, Achievement Award, Immigrants Service League 60; Knight, Arts and Letters (France) 68; Hon. D.Mus. (Chicago Musical Coll., Roosevelt Univ.) 51, (Cleveland Inst. of Music) 74.

Compositions include four symphonies, four operas including *Ol-Ol, Die Hochzeit der Sobeide*, ten ballets including *Ajanta's Frescoes, La Femme et son Ombre, Trepak*, six piano concerti, numerous pieces for piano, for orchestra, chamber music, songs, choral music, film and theatre music.

Publ. *An Anthology of Russian Music*.

Boosey & Hawkes, 295 Regent Street, London, W1A 1BR, England.

Tcherina, Ludmila; French actress and dancer; b. 10 Oct. 1924, Paris; d. of Avenir Tchemerzine and Stéphane Finette; m. 1st Edmond Audran (deceased), 2nd Raymond Roi 1953; ed. privately and studied under Yvan Clustine.

First dancer and choreographer, Ballets de Monte Carlo 40-44, Ballets de Paris 51-58; founded Compagnie de Ballet Ludmila Tcherina 58.

Chief appearances include: Ballets: *Romeo and Juliet* (with Serge Lifar) Paris 42, *Giselle* La Scala Milan 54, Bolshoi Theatre Moscow 59, *Le Martyre de Saint Sébastien* Paris Opéra 57, *Les Amants de Teruel* Théâtre Sarah Bernhardt Paris 59, *Gala* (by Salvador Dali and Maurice Béjart) Venice 61, Brussels and Paris 62, etc.

Films: *The Red Shoes, The Tales of Hoffmann, Clara de Montargis, La Légende de Parsifal, La Nuit s'achève, Oh! Rosalinda, A la Mémoire d'un Héros, La Fille de Mata-Hari, Honeymoon, Les Amants de Teruel* (Cannes Film Festival, French Entry 62), *Jeanne au Bûcher*, etc.; French TV appearances include: *Salomé, Bonaparte, La Possédée, La Dame aux Camélias*.

Exhibited drawings and gouaches in Paris 62 and New York 62, gouaches and sculptures in Paris 66, gouaches, lithographs and sculptures in Zurich 67, paintings in Geneva 72 and Paris 73; Prize for Best Feminine Performance, Vichy Film Festival for *La Nuit s'achève* 50, First Prize Dance Film Festival, Buenos Aires for *A la Mémoire d'un Héros* 52, "Oscar" for Best Feminine Performance by a Foreign Actress in *Tales of Hoffmann* 52, Paris Gold Medal 59, Chevalier de l'Ordre des Arts et des Lettres 62, Oscar Italien de la Popularité, Chevalier, Légion d'Honneur 70.

42 cours Albert 1er, 75008 Paris, France.

Telephone: 359-18-33.

Tchoungi, Simon Pierre; Cameroonian doctor and politician; b. 28 Oct. 1916; ed. Ecole Primaire Supérieure, Centre Médicale, Ayos, Ecole de Médecine, Dakar, and Univ. de Paris à la Sorbonne.

Former Dir. of Office, Ministry of Public Health and Population, then of Ministry of Public Works; Dir. Int. Relations, Ministry of Public Health and Population 59-60; Dir. of Public Health for Cameroon 61-; Minister of Public Health and Population 61-64; Minister of Nat. Economy 64-65; Sec. of State to the Presidency 65; Prime Minister of East Cameroon 65-72; numerous decorations.

B.P. 1057, Yaoundé, Cameroon.

Tebaldi, Renata; Italian soprano opera singer; b. 1 Feb. 1922; ed. Arrigo Boito Conservatory, Parma, Gioacchino Rossini Conservatory, Pesaro, then pupil of Carmen Melis and Guiseppe Pais.

Début Rovigo 44; has sung the principal soprano operatic roles in America and Europe.

1 Piazza Guastella, Milan, Italy.

Tebbit, Sir Donald Claude, K.C.M.G., M.A.; British diplomatist; b. 4 May 1920, Cambridge; m. Barbara Margaret Olson Matheson 1947; one s. three d.; ed. Perse School, Cambridge, Trinity Hall, Cambridge Univ.

Royal Naval Voluntary Reserve 41-46; Foreign Office 46-48; Second Sec., British Embassy, Washington, D.C. 48-51; Foreign Office 51-54; First Sec. (Commercial), Bonn 54-58; Private Sec. to Minister of State, Foreign Office 58-61, Counsellor 62, Sec. Cttee. on Representational Services Overseas 62-64; Counsellor and Head of Chancery, Copenhagen 64-67; Head of W. and Gen. Africa Dept., Commonwealth Office 67; Asst. Under-Sec. of State, FCO 68; Commercial Minister, Washington, D.C. 70-71, Minister 71-72; Deputy Under-Sec. of State, FCO 73-76; High Commr. to Australia 76-.

British High Commission, Commonwealth Avenue, Canberra, A.C.T., Australia; Home: Hill Cottage, Hill Close, Harrow on the Hill, Middx., England.

Tebbutt, Arthur Rothwell, M.A., PH.D.; American statistician; b. 10 Nov. 1906, New Bedford, Mass.; s. of James and Rosetta Tebbutt; m. Frances Benson 1932; two s.; ed. Brown and Harvard Univs.

Harvard Econ. Soc. 27-28; Asst. Editor *Review of Economic Statistics* 29-30; Instr. in Statistics, Harvard Graduate School of Business Admin. 30-35; Asst. Prof. of Econs., Brown Univ., and Dir. Bureau of Business Research 35-40; Prof. of Statistics, Northwestern Univ. 40-74, Emer. 74-, Dean of the Graduate School 45-51; Vice-Pres. American Asscn. of Graduate Schools 49, Pres. 50; Educational Consultant to French Ministry of Economic Affairs 56-57; Consultant to business firms; Republican.

Leisure interests: golf occasionally.

Publs. *Behavior of Consumption in Business Depression* 33, *Introduction to Economic Statistics* (with W. L. Crum and A. C. Patton) 38, *Government Regulation of Sugar in World War II* 44.

1862 Sherman Place, Evanston, Illinois, U.S.A. Telephone: 312-869-3822.

Tedder, 2nd Baron, cr. 46, of Glenguin; **John Michael Tedder,** Bt., M.A., SC.D., D.SC., F.R.S.E.; British professor of chemistry; b. 4 July 1926, London; s. of the late Marshall of the R.A.F. the 1st Lord Tedder, G.C.B., and of Rosalinde Wilhelmina Tedder (née Maclardy); m. Peggy Eileen Growcott 1952; two s. one d.; ed. Dauntsey's School, Wilts., Magdalene Coll., Cambridge, Univ. of Birmingham.

Lecturer in Chem., Sheffield Univ. 54-62, Reader in Organic Chem. 62-64; Roscoe Prof. of Chem., Queens Coll., Dundee 64-69; Purdie Prof. of Chem., St. Salvator's Coll., St. Andrews Univ. 69-; mem. Court of St. Andrews Univ. 71-.

Publs. *Basic Organic Chemistry* (Parts I-V) 66-73, *Valence Theory* 66; original papers in *Journal of the Chemical Society, Transactions of the Faraday Society* and other learned journals.

Department of Chemistry, University of St. Andrews, St. Andrews, Fife, KY16 9ST; Home: Little Rathmore, Kennedy Gardens, St. Andrews, Fife, Scotland.

Teelock, Sir Leckraz, Kt., C.B.E., M.B., CH.B., D.T.M., L.M.; Mauritian diplomatist; b. 4 March 1909, Mauritius; m. Vinaya Kumari Prasad 1948; one s. one d.; ed. Royal Coll. of Mauritius and Univ. of Edinburgh.

Member Legislative Council of Mauritius 59-63; Commr. for Mauritius in U.K. 64-March 68; High Commr. in U.K. March 68-; Amb. to the Holy See, Belgium, Norway, Luxembourg, Denmark, Sweden, Finland, the Netherlands and to the EEC.

Leisure interests: reading, philately.

Mauritius High Commission, Grand Buildings, Northumberland Avenue, London, W.C.2, England. Telephone: 01-930-2895.

Teets, William I.; American business executive; b. 16 Oct. 1917, Lake Hopatcong, N.J.; s. of William Teets and Grace Barrett; m. Jane Deming 1940; three s.; ed. Northern Univ., Ada, Ohio.

Joined Electrolux 42, Treas. 53, Vice-Pres. (Finance) 61, Dir. 64, Pres. 67, Chair. 69; Chair. Fuller Brush 69; Pres. Consolidated Foods Corpn. 70-75.

Leisure interests: boating, swimming, golf.

63 Indian Hill Road, Winnetka, Ill. 60093, U.S.A. Telephone: 251-5060 (Home).

Teir, Grels, BARR.-AT-LAW; Finnish lawyer and politician; b. 26 Feb. 1916, Lappfjärd; s. of Frans and Hilja (née Hannelius) Teir; m. Doris Häggblom 1950; one s. two d.

Member of Parl. 51-; Chair. of youth org. of Swedish People's Party 53-56, Vice-Chair. of S.F.P. 56-70; Chair. Swedish Group in Parl. 63-64, 66-68, 71-72, Standing Cttee. on law-procedure in Parl. 58, 66-68, 70, 72-; Vice-Chair. of Finnish Property Union 67-73; Dir. Gamlakarleby Helsingfors Aktiebank 59-71; Minister of Transport and Communications 64-66, of Trade and Industry 68-70, 72; Dir. Gen. of the State Treasury 73-.

Parliament Building, Helsinki; Home: Parksvängen 13 D 44, 00200 Helsinki 20, Finland. Telephone: 6923551 (Home).

Teixeira Pinto, Luis Maria, PH.D.; Portuguese economist and politician; b.1927; ed. Instituto Superior de Ciências Econômicas e Financeiras, Technical Univ. of Lisbon, and Univ. of Paris.

Assistant Prof. Instituto Superior de Ciências Econômicas e Financeiras 48-62; Sec. Econ. Studies Dept. Portuguese Industrial Asscn. 50-52; mem. Centre for Econ. Studies, Nat. Statistical Inst. 52-55; Adviser, Commercial Dept., Export Development Fund, Paris 55-56; Prof. Instituto de Altos Estudos Militares 57-62; Dir. Dept. of Econ. Studies and Projects, Nat. Development Bank 60-62, Vice-Gov. Nat. Development Bank 62-70; Minister of Econ. 62-March 65.

Publs. *Algumas notas sobre o Equilíbrio Keynesiano* 57, *L'évolution de la théorie de la croissance économique* 57, *Alguns Aspectos da Teoria do Crescimento Econômico* 57, *Portugal e a Integração Económica Europeia* 60, *The Economic Growth of Small Nations: the Portuguese Case* 60, *A Unidade Económica Nacional* 60, *Políticas de Desenvolvimento Econômico* 62, *O Comércio Internacional e os preços dos factores produtivos, L'Economie Portugaise, Problemas do Desenvolvimento Econômico Africano.*

Avenida Infante Santo, 66-7 C. Esq., Lisbon, Portugal.

Tejada, Marquis de (*see* Coronel de Palma, Luis).

Tejan-Sie, Sir Banja, G.C.M.G.; Sierra Leonean public official; b. 7 Aug. 1917, Moyamba, S. Province; s. of the late Alpha Ahmed Tejan-Sie; m. Admira Stapleton 1946; three s. one d.; ed. Bo School, Prince of Wales School, Freetown, and London School of Econs.

Station clerk, Sierra Leone Railway 38-39; Nurse, Medical Dept. 40-46; Council of Legal Educ. 47-51, called to Bar, Lincoln's Inn 51; Nat. Vice-Pres., Sierra Leone People's Party 53-56; mem. Keith Lucas Comm. on Electoral Reform 54; Police Magistrate, E. Province 55, N. Province 58; Hon. Sec. Sierra Leone Bar Asscn. 57-58; Senior Police Magistrate, Provinces 61; Speaker of House of Reps. 62-67; numerous official visits to other countries; Chief Justice 67-70; Acting Gov.-Gen. April 68-70, Gov.-Gen. Sept. 70-April 71; numerous decorations.

Leisure interests: music, books.

3 Tracy Avenue, London, N.W.2, England. Telephone: 01-452-2324.

Tejchma, Józef; Polish politician; b. 14 July 1927, Markowa; ed. Acad. of Political Sciences, Higher School of Social Sciences.

Active leader of Rural Youth Union (Wici Z.M.W.) 45-48; instructor for school youth problems, Cen. Board of Polish Youth Union (Z.M.P.) 48; plenipotentiary, Cen. Board of Z.M.P. at Nowa Huta 51-54; Deputy Head of the Organizational Dept. Cen. Board of Z.M.P. 54-55; Co-organizer Z.M.W., Chair. Organizational Cttee., Provisional Board and later Central Board 56-63; Head of Agricultural Dept. Polish United Workers' Party (P.Z.P.R.) Central Cttee. 63-64; mem. P.Z.P.R. 52-; Deputy mem. Central Cttee. 59-64, mem. 64-, Sec. Central Cttee. 64-72; mem. Politburo Nov. 68-; mem. Seym 52-; Vice-Chair. of Presidium of All-Polish Cttee. of Nat. Unity Front June 71-, Vice-Premier March 72-; Minister of Culture and Art Feb. 74-; Order of the Banner of Labour 1st Class 64, Medal of 30th Anniversary of People's Poland, and others.

Ministerstwo Kultury i Sztuki, Krakowskie Przedmieście 15/17, 00-071 Warsaw, Poland.

Tekoah, Yosef; Israeli diplomatist; b. 4 March 1925; s. of Saul and Dvora Tekoah; m. Ruth Weidenfeld 1952; two s. one d.; ed. Université L'Aurore, China, and Harvard Univ.

Instructor in Int. Relations, Harvard Univ. 47-48; Dep. Legal Adviser, Ministry of Foreign Affairs 49-53; Dir. Armistice Affairs, and Head Israeli Dels. to Armistice Comms. with Egypt, Jordan, Syria and Lebanon 53-58; Dep. Perm. Rep. to UN 58, Acting Perm. Rep. 59-60; Amb. to Brazil 60-62, to U.S.S.R. 62-65; Asst. Dir.-Gen. Ministry of Foreign Affairs 66-68; Perm. Rep. to UN 68-75; Pres. Ben-Gurion Univ. of the Negev 75-.
Ben Gurion University of the Negev, P.O. Box 2053, Beersheba, Israel.

Telegdi, Valentine L., M.SC., PH.D.; American physicist; b. 11 Jan. 1922, Budapest; s. of late George Telegdi and of Elea Telegdi (née Csillag); m. Lidia Leonardi 1950; ed. Lausanne Univ. and Swiss Fed. Inst. of Technology.
Assistant, Swiss Fed. Inst. of Technology 47-50; Instructor, Univ. of Chicago 51-53, Asst. Prof. 53-56, Assoc. Prof. 56-58, 58-71, Enrico Fermi Distinguished Service Prof. 71-; Nat. Science Foundation Senior Postdoctoral Fellow, CERN, Geneva 59, Guest Prof. 70; mem. Nat. Acad. of Sciences, American Acad. of Arts and Sciences; American Physical Soc.; Loeb Lecturer, Harvard Univ. 66.
Leisure interests: travel, gastronomy, jazz.
Publs. numerous articles in professional journals.
The Enrico Fermi Institute, University of Chicago, 5630 Ellis Avenue, Chicago, Ill. 60637, U.S.A.
Telephone: 753-8641.

Teles, José Manuel Galvão, LL.M.; Portuguese diplomatist; b. 1938, Lisbon.
President, Catholic Univ. of Youth; practised law in Lisbon, opposition defence in judicial trials; founder, active mem. and dir. of several political and cultural orgs. opposing Govts. of Salazar and Caetano, including *Pragma, O Tempo e O Modo, Centro Nacional de Cultura*; Opposition Candidate in election to Nat. Assembly 69; worked with Council of the Revolution and with Provisional Govts. April 74-; mem. Comm. drafting Electoral Law for Constituent Assembly, Comm. guiding negotiations between Portuguese Govt. and liberation movements in Mozambique (FRELIMO) and Angola 74-75; Perm. Rep. to UN Nov. 75-.
Permanent Mission of Portugal to the United Nations, 777 Third Avenue, 27th Floor, New York, N.Y. 10017, U.S.A.

Tellenbach, Gerd, PH.D.; German university professor; b. 17 Sept. 1903, Berlin-Lichterfelde; s. of Leo Tellenbach and Margarete Eberty; m. Marie-Elisabeth Gerken; two s. one d.; ed. Univs. of Freiburg and Munich.
Asst., Prussian Historical Inst. in Rome 28-33; Lecturer, Heidelberg, Giessen, and Würzburg Univs. 33-38; Prof., Giessen 38-42, Münster 42-44; Prof. of Medieval and Modern History, Univ. of Freiburg, and Dir. Historical School 44-63; Dir. German Historical Inst., Rome 62-72; Prof. Univ. of Freiburg 72-; D. h.c. Ph. et Litt. (Louvain), Hon. D.Litt. (Glasgow).
Publs. include: *Die bischöflich passauischen Eigenklöster und ihre Vogteien* 28, *Römischer und christlicher Reichsgedanke in der Liturgie des früheren Mittelalters* 34, *Libertas, Kirche und Weltordnung im Zeitalter des Investiturstreites* 36, *Königtum und Stämme in der Werdezeit des deutschen Reiches* 39, *Church, State and Christian Society* 40, *Die Entstehung des deutschen Reiches* 40, *Goethes geschichtlicher Sinn* 49, *Europa im Zeitalter der Karolinger, Historia Mundi V* 56, *Studien und Vorarbeiten zur Geschichte des grossfränkischen und frühdeutschen Adels* 57, *Zur Bedeutung der Personenforschung für die Erkenntnis des früheren Mittelalters* 57, *Kaisertum, Papstum und Europa im hohen Mittelalter, Historia Mundi VI* 58, *Neue Forschung über Cluny und die Cluniacenser* 59, *Repertorium Germanicum II* 33-61, *Der Sybyllinische Preis, Schriften und Reden zur Hochschulpolitik 1946-1963* 63, *Empfehlungen zur Neuordnung des Studiums in den Philosophischen Fakultäten* 66, *Saeculum Weltgeschichte III and IV* 67, *V* 70, *Monumenta Germanica historica: Liber memorialis Romaricensis* (with E. Hlawitschka and K. Schmid) 70.
Faculty of Philosophy, Albert-Ludwigs-Universität Freiburg, Belfortstrasse 13, Freiburg; Home: Hintere Steige 4, 78 Freiburg/Br., Federal Republic of Germany.
Telephone: 56497.

Teller, Edward, PH.D.; Hungarian-born American scientist; b. 15 Jan. 1908, Budapest, Hungary; s. of Ilona and Max Teller; m. Augusta Mary Harkanyi 1934; one s. one d.; ed. Karlsruhe Technical Inst., and Univs. of Munich and Leipzig.
Research Assoc., Leipzig 29-31, Göttingen 31-33; Rockefeller Fellow, Copenhagen 34; Lecturer, Univ. of London 34-35; Prof. of Physics, George Washington Univ. 35-41, Columbia Univ. 41-42; Physicist, Manhattan Engineer District 42-46; Prof. of Physics, Univ. of Chicago 46-52; Physicist, and Asst. Dir. Los Alamos Scientific Laboratory 49-52; Consultant, Univ. of Calif. Radiation Laboratory, Livermore 52-53, Assoc. Dir. Lawrence Radiation Laboratory 54-, Dir. 58-60; Prof. of Physics Univ. of Calif. 53-60, Prof. of Physics-at-Large 60-70, Univ. Prof. 70-, Prof. Emer. 75-; Chair. Dept. of Applied Science, Univ. of Calif. 63-66; Assoc. Dir. Emer. Lawrence Livermore Laboratory 75-; mem. Nat. Acad. of Sciences, American Acad. of Arts and Sciences, U.S.A.F. Scientific Advisory Board, etc.; Fellow, American Nuclear Soc.; Sr. Research Fellow, Hoover Inst. for War, Revolution and Peace 75-; Joseph Priestley Memorial Award 57, Albert Einstein Award 59, Midwest Research Inst. Award, Living History Award 60; Enrico Fermi Award 62, Robins Award of America 63; Harvey Prize 75; Hon. D.Sc. (Yale, Alaska, Fordham, George Washington, S. Calif., St. Louis, Clarkson Coll., Clemson Univ.); Hon. LL.D. (Mount Mary).
Leisure interests: chess, hiking, piano.
Publs. *The Structure of Matter* (with F. O. Rice) 49, *Magneto-Hydrodynamic Shocks* (with F. de Hoffmann) 50, *Theory of Origin of Cosmic Rays* 54, *Our Nuclear Future* (with A. Latter) 58, *Legacy of Hiroshima* (with Allen Brown) 62, *The Reluctant Revolutionary* 64, *Constructive Uses of Nuclear Explosives* (with Talley, Higgins & Johnson) 68, *Great Men of Physics* (with others) 69, *General Remarks on Electronic Structure* 70, *The Hydrogen Molecular Ion* 70, *General Theory of Electron Structure* 70.
University of California, Lawrence Livermore Laboratory, P.O. Box 808, Livermore, Calif. 94550; 1573 Hawthorne Terrace, Berkeley, Calif., 94708 U.S.A.
Telephone: 415-447-1100 Ext. 3444.

Telli Boubacar, H.E. Diallo; Guinean lawyer and diplomatist; b. 1925, Poredaka, Mamou district; m. Kadiatou Diallo; two s. one d.; ed. Lycée de Dakar, Lycée Louis Le Grand, Paris, Faculté de droit, Sorbonne, L'Ecole Nationale de la France d'Outre-Mer.
Called to the bar 51; Asst. Public Prosecutor, Senegal 54, later with Court of Cotonou, Dahomey and Court of Appeal, Dakar; served on staff of French High Commissioner, Dakar; Sec.-Gen. Grand Council, French West Africa 57-58; Amb. to U.S.A. 58-61 and Perm. Rep. to the UN 58-64; Vice-Pres. 17th Session of UN Gen. Assembly 61-62; Chair. special Cttee. on Apartheid of UN Gen. Assembly 63-64; Sec.-Gen. Org. of African Unity 64-72; Minister of Justice Aug. 72-.
Ministry of Justice, Conakry, Guinea.

Tembo, John Zenas Ungapake; Malawi politician; b. Sept. 1932; ed. senior primary school, Kongwe, Mlanda School, Ncheu, Blantyre Secondary School and Roma Univ. Coll., Basutoland.
Worked for Colonial Audit Dept., Zomba 49-March 55; studied at Roma Univ. Coll. 55-58; fmr. mem. African

Students' Rep. Council; attended course for educational diploma, Salisbury, Rhodesia Dec. 58-Nov. 59; teacher, Kongwe Secondary School 59-61; mem. Legislative Council for Dedza 61-62; Parl. Sec. for Finance 62-64; M.P. for Dedza North 64, resigned May 70; Minister of Finance 64-68, concurrently Minister of Trade, Industry, Devt. and Planning 64-68; Minister of Trade and Finance Dec. 68-Aug. 70; Gov. Reserve Bank of Malawi Aug. 70-.

Reserve Bank of Malawi, P.O. Box 565, Blantyre, Malawi.

Temin, Howard M., PH.D.; American professor and virologist; b. 10 Dec. 1934, Philadelphia, Pa.; s. of Henry and Annette (née Lehman) Temin; m. Rayla G. Greenberg 1962; two d.; ed. Swarthmore Coll., California Inst. of Tech.

Postdoctoral Fellow, Calif. Inst. of Tech. 59-60; Asst. Prof. of Oncology, Univ. of Wis., Madison 60-64, Assoc. Prof. 64-69, Prof. 69-; Prof. of Cancer Research at Wis. Alumni Research Foundation 71-; American Cancer Soc. Prof. of Viral Oncology and Cell Biology 74-; mem. Nat. Acad. of Sciences 74; U.S. Steel Foundation Award in Molecular Biology, Nat. Acad. of Science 72, Griffuel Prize, Asscn. for Research against Cancer, Villejuif 72, American Chem. Soc. Award in Enzyme Chem. 73, G. H. A. Clowes Award and Lectureship, American Asscn. for Cancer Research 74, Gairdner Foundation Int. Award (shared) 74, Albert Lasker Award in Basic Medical Science 74, Nobel Prize in Physiology or Medicine (shared) 75.

Publs. author and co-author of over 100 articles and contributions to books.

McArdle Laboratory for Cancer Research, University of Wisconsin, 450 North Randall Avenue, Madison, Wis. 53706, U.S.A.

Telephone: (608) 262-1209.

Temple, George, C.B.E., F.R.S., D.SC., M.A.; British mathematician; b. 2 Sept. 1901, London; s. of James Temple and Frances Compton; m. Dorothy Carson 1930; ed. Birkbeck Coll., and Trinity Coll., Cambridge. Assistant at Birkbeck Coll. 22-24; Asst. Lecturer in Mathematics City and Guilds Coll. 24-28; Asst. Prof. Royal Coll. of Science 30-32; Prof. of Mathematics King's Coll. London 32-53; Chief Scientific Adviser to Minister of Civil Aviation July 47-49; Sedleian Prof. of Natural Philosophy, Oxford Univ. 53-68, now Prof. Emer.; Emer. Fellow, Queen's Coll., Oxford; Chair. Aeronautical Research Council 61-64; Hon. D.Sc (Dublin, Louvain Univs.); Hon. D.Lit. (Western Ontario) 69.

Publs. *Introduction to Quantum Theory,* 31, *Rayleigh's Principle* 33, *General Principles of Quantum Theory* 34, *An Introduction to Fluid Dynamics* 58, *Cartesian Tensors* 60, *The Structure of Lebesgue Integration Theory* 71.

341 Woodstock Road, Oxford, England.

Temple, Shirley (*see* Black, Shirley Temple).

Templer, Field Marshal Sir Gerald Walter Robert, K.G., G.C.B., G.C.M.G., K.B.E., D.S.O.; British army officer; b. 11 Sept. 1898, Colchester; s. of late Lieut.-Col. Walter Francis Templer, C.B.E., D.L.; m. Ethel Margery Davie 1926; one s. one d.; ed. Wellington Coll., and Royal Military Coll., Sandhurst.

Joined Royal Irish Fusiliers 16; served in First World War, operations in North-West Persia and Mesopotamia 19-21, operations in Palestine 36; Brevet Major 35, Brevet Lieut.-Col. 38; commd. 2nd Corps, 47th (London) Div., 1st Div., 56th (London) Div. and 6th Armoured Div. between 42 and 44; Dir. Mil. Govt. 21st Army Group 45-46; Dir. Mil. Intelligence, War Office 46-48; Vice-Chief Imperial Gen. Staff 48-50; G.O.C.-in-C. Eastern Commd. 50-52; High Commr. and Dir. of Operations, Fed. of Malaya 52-54; Chief Imperial Gen.

Staff 55-58; Col. Royal Horse Guards (now Blues and Royals) and Gold Stick to H.M. the Queen 63-; H.M. Lieut. for Greater London 66-73; Trustee Nat. Portrait Gallery 58-72, Imperial War Museum 59-66, Historic Churches Preservation Trust 63-; mem. Nat. Army Museum Council 60-; mem. Council, Outward Bound Trust 54-; Constable of Tower of London 65-70; mem. Cttee. of Inquiry into Security Procedures and Practices 61; Hon. D.C.L. (Oxford), Hon. LL.D. (St. Andrews).

Flat 7, 31 Sloane Court West, London, SW3 4TE, England.

Templeton, John M., M.A., LL.D., L.H.D.; British investment counsellor; b. 29 Nov. 1912, Winchester, Tenn., U.S.A.; s. of Harvey M. and Vella Handly Templeton; m. Irene Reynolds Butler 1958; two s. one d.; ed. Yale Univ., Balliol Coll., Oxford Univ.

President of Templeton, Dobbrow and Vance Inc., Investment Counsellors, N.Y. 40-60, Templeton Growth Fund Ltd., Toronto 54-, Lexington Research Investing Corpn. 55-65, Corporate Leaders of America 59-62, First Trust Bank Ltd., Nassau 64-, Chief Execs. Forum 67-68, Board of Trustees, Princeton Theological Seminary 67-73, Templeton Investment Counsel Ltd., Nassau 73-, Lyford Cay Property Owners Asscn. Ltd. 73-75; f. Templeton Foundation Prize for Religion 73-; Treas. Young Presidents' Foundation 52-56; Gov. Investment Counsel Asscn. of America 60-61; Chair. Finance Cttee., United Presbyterian Comm. on Ecumenical Mission 60-69; Dir. Magic Chef Inc., U.S.A. 67-, Chase Manhattan Trust Co. Ltd., Nassau 68-, Caribbean Utilities Co. Ltd., Cayman Islands 70-; Trustee Wilson Coll., U.S.A. 51-62; mem. United Presbyterian Council of Theological Seminaries 64-, Chartered Financial Analysts, Phi Beta Kappa, Zeta Psi.

c/o Lyford Cay Club, Box N7776, Nassau, Bahamas.

Telephone: 809-327-4295.

Templeton, Malcolm J. C.; New Zealand diplomatist; b. 12 May 1924, Dunedin; m. Barbara Elaine Gill 1956; two s. two d.; ed. Otago Univ.

Joined Ministry of Foreign Affairs 46; held diplomatic posts in U.S.A. 51-57; Head UN Div., later Defence Div., Ministry of Foreign Affairs 57; Counsellor, London 62, Minister 64-67; Imperial Defence Coll., London 63-64; Asst. Sec. of Foreign Affairs 67-72; seconded to Prime Minister's Dept. as Deputy Perm. Head 72; Acting Deputy Sec. of Foreign Affairs Jan.-May 73; Perm. Rep. to UN Aug. 73-; rep. to several int. confs., including meetings of Colombo Plan, SEATO Council, Commonwealth Prime Ministers, S. Pacific Forum, UN Law of the Sea Conf.

Permanent Mission of New Zealand to United Nations, 733 Third Avenue, 22nd Floor, New York, N.Y. 10017, U.S.A.

Tendryakov, Vladimir Fedorovich; Soviet writer; b. 5 Dec. 1923, Makarovskaya, Vologda Region; ed. Gorki Literary Inst., Moscow.

Army service 41-43; Corresp. *Ogonyok* 51-54; admitted to Union of Soviet Writers 54; mem. Communist Party of the U.S.S.R. 48-; Order of Red Banner of Labour.

Publs. short stories: *Sredi Lesov* (In the Fields), *Ne ko Dvoru* (Ill Suited) 54, *Tugoi Uzel* (The Tight Knot) 56; novels: *Padenie Ivana Chuprova* (The Fall of Ivan Chuprov) 53, *Uchabyi* (Pits and Bumps) 57, *Chudotvornaya* (The Wonder-Worker) 58, *Za Beguschim dnem* (For Running Day) 60, *Hahodka* (The Find) 64, *Svidanie s Nefertiti* (Meeting with Nefertiti) 64, *Wonder-Working* 67, *Apostol* (Finish) 69, *One Day Butterfly-Short Life* 70, *Three Bags Litter Wheat* 72, *Spring Madonna* 73, *Night After Co-Graduates* 74, etc.; scenarios: *Alien In-Laws* 55, *Miracle Worker* 60, *Short Circuit* 61, *The Trial* 62; film; *Spring Madonna* 75.

Union of Writers of the U.S.S.R., 52 Ulitsa Vorovskogo, Moscow, U.S.S.R.

Tenenbaum, Michael, M.S., PH.D.; American business executive; b. 23 July 1914, St. Paul, Minn.; *m.* Helen Zlatovski 1941; two *d.*; ed. Harvard Univ. and Univ. of Minnesota.

Joined Inland Steel Co. 36; Gen. Man. Research and Quality Control 61-66, Vice-Pres., Research 66-68, Vice-Pres., Steel Manufacturing 68-71, Pres. and Dir. 71-; Chair. Caland Ore Co., Jackson City Iron Co.; Dir. Inland Steel Coal Co., Inland Steel Mining Co., Inland Lime and Stone Co., INRYCO, Inland Steel Container Co., Inland-Ryerson and Son Inc., Jos. T. Ryerson and Son. Inc., Continental Illinois Corpn., Continental Illinois Nat. Bank and Trust Co. of Chicago; mem. American Inst. of Mining, Metallurgical and Petroleum Engineers, Metallurgical Soc. (Pres. 68, Fellow 71), Iron and Steel Inst. (American and Int.), The Metals Soc. (U.K.), Nat. Acad. of Eng.; Fellow American Soc. for Metals; Hon. D.Sc. (Northwestern Univ.); recipient of several achievement awards.

Leisure interests: gardening, golf, music.

Publs. articles in prof. journals.

Inland Steel Company, 30 West Monroe Street, Chicago, Ill. 60603, U.S.A.

Teng Hsiao-p'ing; Chinese politician; b. 1904, Kuang-an, Szechuan; ed. French School, Chungking, in France and Far Eastern Univ., Moscow.

Dean of Educ., Chungshan Mil. Acad., Shensi 26; Chief of Staff Red Army 30; Dir. Propaganda Dept., Gen. Political Dept., Red Army 32; on Long March 34-36; Political Commissar during Sino-Japanese War; mem. 7th Cen. Cttee. of CCP 45; Political Commissar 2nd Field Army, People's Liberation Army 48-54; First Sec. E. China Bureau, CCP 49; Sec.-Gen. Cen. Cttee. of CCP 53-56; Minister of Finance 53; Vice-Chair. Nat. Defence Council 54-67; Vice-Premier, State Council 54; mem. Politburo, CCP 55-67; Sec., Secr. of Cen. Cttee., CCP 56-67; Gen.-Sec. 8th Cen. Cttee. of CCP 56; criticized and removed from office during Cultural Revolution 67; mem. 10th Cen. Cttee. of CCP 73; mem. Politburo, CCP 74-76; Vice-Chair. Mil. Affairs Cttee. of CCP Central Cttee. 75-76; Chief of Gen. Staff, PLA 75-76; Vice-Premier, State Council 75-76.

People's Republic of China.

Teng Ying-ch'ao; Chinese party official; b. 1903, Hsinyang, Honan; *m.* Chou En-lai 1925 (died 1976); ed. Tientsin No. 1 Girls' Nat. School.

Arrested for involvement in May 4th Movt. 19; studied in France 20; participated in Long March 34-36; Dir. Women's Work Dept., Cen. Cttee. of CCP 37; Alt. mem. 7th Cen. Cttee. of CCP 45; Vice-Chair. Nat. Women's Federation of China 53-; mem. 8th Cen. Cttee. of CCP 56, 9th Cen. Cttee. 69, 10th Cen. Cttee. 73.

People's Republic of China.

ten Holt, Friso; Netherlands painter and etcher; b. 6 April 1921, Argeles-Gazost, France; *m.* A. Taselaar 1946; two *s.* one *d.*; ed. Rijksakademie van Beeldende Kunsten, Amsterdam.

Paintings mainly of swimmers, landscapes and nudes, portraits and figures; Prof. of painting, Rijksakademie van Beeldende Kunsten, Amsterdam 69-; one-man exhibitions in Netherlands since 52, London 59, 62, 63, 65, 69; Group exhbns. at Beaverbrook Art Gallery, Canada, and Tate Gallery, London 63, Biennale Salzburg 64, Carnegie Inst., Pittsburgh 64, Netherlands travelling exhbn. 57-58; works in collections in Netherlands, Sweden, U.K., France and America.

Major works: stained-glass windows for churches in Amsterdam and The Hague.

Leisure interest: horse riding.

Keizersgracht 614, Amsterdam, Netherlands.

Telephone: 230736.

Tennant, Sir Peter Frank Dalrymple, Kt., C.M.G., O.B.E., M.A.; British company director and industrial adviser; b. 29 Nov. 1910, Hoddesdon; *s.* of George F. D.

and Barbara (née Beck) Tennant; *m.* 1st Hellis Fellenius 1934, 2nd Galina Bosley 1953; one *s.* two *d.* and one step *s.*; ed. Marlborough Coll. and Trinity Coll., Cambridge.

Fellow, Queens' Coll., Cambridge 33-47, Lecturer in Scandinavian languages 33-39; diplomatic service 39-52, served in Stockholm, Paris and Berlin; Overseas Dir., later Deputy Dir.-Gen. Fed. of British Industries 52-65; Dir. Gen. British Nat. Export Council 65-71; Industrial Adviser, Barclays Bank International 72-; Dir. Barclays Bank S.A., Paris, C. Tennant Sons & Co. Ltd., London, Prudential Assurance, Company Ltd., Anglo-Rumanian Bank; Chair. Gabbitas Thring Educ. Trust; Deputy Chair. London Chamber of Commerce; mem. Academic Council Wilton Park, Gov. Body Int. Briefing Centre, Farnham Castle, Quality Assurance Council; fmr. mem. Design Council, BBC Advisory Council.

Leisure interests: country pursuits, painting, travel, languages.

Publs. *Ibsen's Dramatic Technique, The Scandinavian Book.*

Anchor House, Linchmere Road, Haslemere, Surrey, GU27 3QF, England.

Telephone: Haslemere 3124.

Tennekoon, Herbert Ernest, M.B.E., B.A., F.R.S.A., F.I.B.A.; Ceylonese administrator; b. 30 Sept. 1911, Kandy; *s.* of L. B. Tennekoon and Nanda Rambukwella; *m.* Norma Wickremasinghe 1940; one *s.* two *d.*; ed. St. Anthony's Coll., Kandy and Univs. of Colombo, London, and Oxford.

Entered Ceylon Civil Service 35, held various judicial and admin. appointments 36-52; Commr. of Lands 53; Commr. for Registration of Indian and Pakistani Residents 54; Controller of Immigration and Emigration 57; Acting Perm. Sec. to Ministry of Defence and External Affairs 58, Perm. Sec. 60; Acting Perm. Sec. to Ministry of Commerce, Trade, Food and Shipping 61; Perm. Sec. to Ministry of Agriculture, Lands, Irrigation and Power 63; Sec. to Treasury and Perm. Sec. to Ministry of Finance 63; Special Adviser to GATT, Geneva 65; Amb. to Japan 66; Dir. Asian Productivity Org. 68-; Gov. Cen. Bank of Ceylon 71-.

Leisure interests: golf, music.

Central Bank of Ceylon, Colombo; Home: Bank House, 206 Bauddhaloka Mawatha, Colombo 7, Sri Lanka.

Telephone: 27486 (Office); 81506 (Home).

Tennekoon, William; Ceylonese banker; b. 1 June 1912, Peradeniya; *s.* of Punchi Banda Tennekoon and Bandara Menike Ratnayake; *m.* Daisy Dingiri Menike Wadugodaputiya 1941; one *s.* two *d.*; ed. St. Anthony's Coll. Kandy, Trinity Coll., Kandy, and Univ. Coll. of Ceylon.

First Agent (Kandy Branch), Bank of Ceylon 41-43, Deputy Accountant 43-47, Accountant 47-49, Head Office Man. 49-50; Chief Accountant, Cen. Bank of Ceylon 50-55, Dir. of Bank Supervision 51-57, Dep. Gov. 57-67, Gov. 67-71; Alt. Exec. Dir. Int. Monetary Fund 53-54, 62-64, Int. Bank for Reconstruction and Devt. 54-55; Dir. Devt. Finance Corpn. of Ceylon 59-62, 65-67; Exec. Dir. Asian Devt. Bank 71-.

Leisure interests: gardening, reading, sports.

Asian Development Bank, Metropolitan Building, Commercial Centre, Ayala Avenue, Makati, Rizal; Home: 14 Real Street, Urdaneta Village, Makati, Rizal, Philippines.

Telephone: Manila 88-51-48.

Tennyson, Sir Charles Bruce Locker, Kt., C.M.G., M.A., F.R.S.L.; b. 8 Nov. 1879, London; *s.* of Hon. Lionel and Mrs. Eleanor Bertha Mary (née Locker) Tennyson; *m.* Ivy Gladys Pretious 1929; one *s.*; ed. Eton Coll., and King's Coll., Cambridge.

Called to Bar 06; Asst. Legal Adviser Colonial Office 11; Deputy Dir. Federation of British Industries 19;

Sec. Dunlop Rubber Co. Ltd. 28-48; Vice-Pres. Fed. of British Industries; Hon. Fellow King's Coll., Cambridge, Royal Coll. of Art, Bedford Coll., Hon. LL.D. (Cambridge), Hon. D.Litt. (Leicester).

Publs. *Cambridge from Within* 12, *Alfred Tennyson* 49; (Editor) *Shorter Poems of Frederick Tennyson* 13, *The Devil and the Lady* (by Alfred Lord Tennyson) 30, *Unpublished Poems of Alfred Tennyson* 31, *Life's All a Fragment* 53, *Six Tennyson Essays* 53, *Stars and Markets* 57, *Dear and Honoured Lady* (with Hope Dyson) 70, *The Tennysons* (with Hope Dyson) 74.

23 The Park, London, N.W.11, England.

Tenzing Norgay, G.M.; Nepalese mountaineer; b. about 1914 in eastern Nepal, migrated to Bengal 32.

Took part (as porter) in expeditions under Shipton 35, Ruttledge 36 and Tilman 38; joined small expedition to Karakoram 50, and French expedition to Nanda Devi 51, when he and one Frenchman climbed the east peak; Sirdar to both Swiss expeditions 52, joining assault parties and reaching about 28,000 feet; Sirdar to British Everest expedition 53, when he and Hillary reached the summit on May 29th; Dir. of Field Training, Himalayan Mountaineering Inst., Darjeeling 54-.

1 Tonga Road, Ghang-La, Darjeeling, West Bengal, India.

Tepavač, Mirko; Yugoslav politician; b. 1923.

Joined Tito's partisans 41, served throughout war; later served as Amb. to Hungary; Deputy Foreign Sec. 59-65; First Sec. C.P. in Vojvodina, Serbia until 69; Federal Sec. for Foreign Affairs 69-72.

Department of Foreign Affairs, Belgrade, Yugoslavia.

Terao, Takeo; Japanese banker; b. 5 April 1905; ed. Tokyo Univ.

Nomura (now Daiwa) Bank 29-, Dir. 47-, later Managing Dir., Pres. 50-73, Chair. 73-; Vice-Pres. Fed. of Bankers' Asscn. of Japan and Osaka Bankers' Asscn.

Daiwa Bank Ltd., 21 Bingomachi, 2-chome, Higashi-ku, Osaka 541, Japan.

Terebilov, Vladimir Ivanovich; Soviet lawyer; b. 18 March 1916, Leningrad; ed. Leningrad Inst. of Law.

Regional Public Procurator 39-49; Senior Scientific Worker and Scientific Sec., Inst. of Criminology 49-57; Deputy Head of Board of Public Procurators, U.S.S.R. 57-61; mem. U.S.S.R. Coll. of Public Procurators 61-62; Vice-Chair. of U.S.S.R. Supreme Court 62-70; Minister of Justice 70-; Deputy to U.S.S.R. Supreme Soviet 70-; Order of Red Banner of Labour.

U.S.S.R. Ministry of Justice, 15 Ulitsa Vorovskogo, Moscow, U.S.S.R.

Terenzio, Pio-Carlo, LL.D.; Italian international civil servant; b. 4 Sept. 1921, Lausanne, Switzerland; s. of Rodolfo Arnoldo Terenzio and Katherine Agopian; m. Luisa de Notaristefani 1950; two s.; ed. Univs. of Rome and Geneva.

Joined Int. Labour Office (ILO) 48; Officer in charge of Relations with Int. Orgs, UNESCO 48-60, Dir. in charge of Congo Operations 60-63, Dir. Bureau of Relations with Member States 63-69, Dir. Bureau of Personnel 69-70; Sec.-Gen. Inter-Parl. Union (IPU) Aug. 70-.

Publ. *La rivalité anglo-russe en Perse et en Afghanistan* 47.

Inter-Parliamentary Union, Place du Petit-Saconnex, 1211 Geneva 28; 10 chemin Colladon, Petit-Saconnex, Geneva, Switzerland.

Telephone: 34-41-50 (Office); 98-22-94 (Home).

Teresa, Mother (Agnes Gonxha Bojaxhiu); Albanianborn Roman Catholic missionary; b. 27 Aug. 1910, Skopje, now Yugoslavia.

Joined Sisters of Loretto 28; worked at Loretto insts. in Ireland and India; Principal St. Mary's High School, Calcutta; founded the Missionaries of Charity 50; through the Missionaries of Charity has set up over

fifty schools, orphanages and houses for the poor in India and other countries; opened Nirmal Hriday (Pure Heart) Home for Dying Destitutes 52; started a leper colony in West Bengal 64; Pope John XXIII Peace Prize 71, Templeton Foundation Prize 73.

Missionaries of Charity, Nirmal Hriday Home for Dying Destitutes, 5A Lower Circular Road, Calcutta, India.

Tereshkova, Valentina Vladimirovna Nikolayeva-; Soviet cosmonaut; b. 6 March 1937; m. Andriyan Nikolayev (q.v.); ed. Yaroslavl Textile Coll. and Zhukovsky Air Force Engineering Acad.

Former textile worker, Krasny Perekop textile mill, Yaroslavl, and textile mill Sec., Young Communist League; mem. C.P. of the Soviet Union March 62-; cosmonaut training March 62-; made 48 orbital flights of the earth in spaceship *Vostok VI* 16th June to 19th June 63; first woman in world to enter space; Deputy to U.S.S.R. Supreme Soviet 62-70; Chair. Soviet Women's Cttee. 68-; mem. Supreme Soviet Presidium 74-; Pilot-Cosmonaut of U.S.S.R., Hero of Soviet Union, Order of Lenin (twice), Gold Star Medal, Joliot-Curie Gold Medal, World Peace Council 66; Order of the Nile (Egypt) 71.

Zvezdny Gorodok, Moscow, U.S.S.R.

Terkelsen, Terkel M.; Danish journalist; b. 8 Nov. 1904, Tjaereborg; m. Ella Schmidt 1929; three d.

London Ed. of *Berlingske Tidende* 37-40 and 45-46; Political Intelligence Dept. of the Foreign Office, and Commentator B.B.C. Danish Service 41-45; mem. of the Danish Council, London (Free Danes) 40-45; Chief Ed. *Berlingske Tidende* and *Berlingske Aftenavis* 46-72; Chair. Board of *Berlingske Tidende* and subsidiary cos. 73-75, Editorial Adviser 75-; Chair. Fed. of Danish Newspapers 69-72, Danish Nat. Cttee. of the Int. Press Inst. 69-72; mem. Exec. Cttee. Training Coll. for Journalists, Aarhus 69-72; Hon. C.B.E.

Leisure interests: fishing, shooting.

Holck Winterfeldts Alle 6, 2900 Hellerup; Office: *Berlingske Tidende*, Pilestraede 34, 1147 Copenhagen K, Denmark.

Telephone: Copenhagen 157575 (Office), HE 7227 (Home).

Terman, Frederick Emmons, A.B., SC.D.; American electrical and radio engineer; b. 6 June 1900, English, Ind.; s. of Lewis and Anna (née Minton) Terman; m. Sibyl Walcutt 1928; three s.; ed. Stanford Univ., Mass. Inst. of Technology.

Instructor Electrical Eng., Stanford Univ. 25-27, Asst. Prof. 27-30, Assoc. Prof. 30-37, Prof. and Exec. Head Dept. 37-45; Dir. Harvard Univ. Radio Research Laboratory 42-45; mem. Vacuum Tube Development Cttee. NDRC and JCB 43-46; mem. Divs. 14 and 15 of Nat. Defence Research Cttee. 42-45, Naval Research Advisory Cttee. 56-64, Chair. 57-58; Dean of School of Engineering, Stanford Univ. 45-58, Provost 55-65, Vice-Pres. 59-65, Emeritus 65-; Pres. SMU Foundation for Science and Engineering 65-74; mem. Nat. Acad. of Sciences, Chair. Engineering Section 53-56, Council 56-59; Founder mem. Nat. Acad. of Engineering; mem. American Philosophical Soc.; Vice-Pres. Inst. Radio Engineers 40, Pres. 41, Dir. 40-43, 48-49, Medal of Honor 50, Founders Award 62; Vice-Pres. American Soc. of Eng. Educ. 49-51; AIEE Educ. Medal 56, Lamme Medal 64; mem. Board of Foreign Scholarships 60-66, Medal for Merit 48; Herbert Hoover Medal, Stanford Alumni Asscn. 69; Hon. Sc.D. (Harvard, B.C. and Syracuse Univs.).

Publs. *Transmission-Line Theory* (with W. S. Franklin) 27, *Radio Engineering* 32, 37, 47, *Measurements in Radio Engineering* 35, *Fundamentals of Radio* 38, *Radio and Vacuum Tube Theory* (in collaboration with U.S. Mil. Acad. staff) 40, *Radio Engineers' Handbook* 43,

Electronic Measurements (with J. M. Pettit) 52, *Electronic and Radio Engineering* 55.
445 El Escarpado, Stanford, Calif., U.S.A.
Telephone: 415-321-1646.

Terracini, Umberto Elia, LL.D.; Italian journalist; b. 27 July 1895, Genoa; *m.* Marialaura Gagno 1948; one *s.*; ed. law school.
Convicted many times in early twenties for activity in the workers' movement; sentenced by special Fascist Tribunal to 23 years' imprisonment June 25; released after the overthrow of Mussolini Aug. 43; Pres. of Constituent Assembly until April 48; Senator May 48-; mem. of Italian Communist Party; collaborator on *Ordine Nuovo* (founded 1919); Pres. of Communist Group of Senate.
Leisure interests: music (piano), pictures.
Via Dogana Vecchia 29, Rome, Italy.

Terray, Jean Pierre; French banker; b. 28 July 1906
President Banque de l'Union Européenne 68; Pres., Compagnie Financière de l'Union Européenne 68-71, now Hon. Pres. and Dir.; Pres. and Dir.-Gen. Banque Franco-Arabe d'Investissements Internationaux 71; Pres. Crédit Chimique 72, Anjou Devts. Property Ltd. (Australia); Dir. Lille-Bonnières-Colombes, Roussel Uclaf, Chrysler France, Centrale Roussel Nobel, Le Continent, Moet Hennessy.
29 avenue Georges Mandel, 75016 Paris, France.

Terrenoire, Louis; French journalist and politician; b. 10 Nov. 1908.
Former trade union Sec.; Editor *La Voix Sociale*, *Nouveau Journal de Lyon* 30-31, Editorial Sec. *L'Aube* 32-39, later Editor; Sec. Conseil Nat. de la Résistance 44; captured and deported; Deputy to Nat. Ass. from Orne 45-51; Sec.-Gen. Rassemblement du Peuple Français (R.P.F.) 51-54; Dir. News and Information, Radiodiffusion-Télévision Française July-Nov. 58; Dep. from Orne 58, 62-73; Minister of Information Feb. 60-Aug. 61; Minister attached to Office of Prime Minister Aug. 61-Apr. 62; Sec.-Gen. Union pour la Nouvelle République 62; mem. European Parl. 63-73, Vice-Pres. 67-73; mem. Union pour la Nouvelle République (U.N.R.), Pres. Ass. Group 59-60; Officier Légion d'Honneur, Croix de Guerre, Rosette de la Résistance.
6 rue de Rémusat, 75016 Paris, France.

Terry, Luther Leonidas; American physician and public health administrator; b. 15 Sept. 1911, Red Level, Ala.; *s.* of James and Lula (née Durham) Terry; *m.* Beryl Reynolds 1940; two *s.* one *d.*; ed. Birmingham-Southern Coll., and Tulane Univ.
Chief, Medical Services, Public Health Service Hospital Baltimore 43-53, Chief Cardiovascular Clinic 50-53, Chief. Gen. Medicine and Experimental Therapeutics at P.H.S. Nat. Heart Inst. 50-58, Asst. Dir. 58-61; Dir. Residency Training Program, Nat. Heart Inst. 53-61; Chair. Cardiovascular Research Training Cttee. 57-61; Surgeon-Gen. U.S. Public Health Service 61-65; Visiting Prof. for Medical Affairs, Univ. of Pennsylvania 65-71, Prof. of Medicine and Prof. of Community Medicine, Oct. 65-75, Adjunct Prof. Community Medicine 75-; Chief U.S. Del., WHO 61-65; mem. Expert Comm. on Cardiovascular Disease, Smoking and Disease, WHO 75-; Asst. Prof. Johns Hopkins Univ. School of Medicine 53-61; Fellow, American Coll. of Physicians 43, Gov. 61-65, Master 73-; mem. Board of Overseers, Harvard Univ. School of Public Health; Fellow, American Coll. of Cardiology; Cttee. mem. American Heart Assen.; mem. Nat. Board of Medical Examiners; mem. Board of Dirs. Nat. Soc. for Medical Research; Diplomat, American Board of Internal Medicine; mem. Nat. Acad. of Sciences; Chair. Cttee. on Veterinary Medicine, Research and Educ.; mem. and officer numerous professional orgs.; Hon. D.Sc.

(Birmingham-Southern Coll., Jefferson Medical Coll., Tulane Univ., Univ. of Rhode Island and Rose Polytechnic Inst.), Hon. LL.D. (Calif. Coll. of Medicine and Univ. of Alaska), Hon. M.D. (Woman's Medical Coll. of Pennsylvania), Hon. LL.D. (Union Coll. New York) 64, Hon. D.Sc. (McGill Univ. Montreal) 66, Hon. D.Sc. (Alabama Univ.), Hon. D.Sc. (St. Joseph's Coll. Pa.), Hon. LL.D. (Marquette Univ.) 68, (Philadelphia Coll. of Pharmacy and Science) 70; numerous Hon. Fellowships and awards.
Leisure interests: fishing, hunting, tennis.
College Hall, University of Pennsylvania, Philadelphia, Pa. 19104, U.S.A.
Telephone: 215-594-7231.

Terzakis, Anghelos; Greek novelist and dramatist; b. 16 Feb. 1907, Nauplia; *m.* Luisa Vogasari 1936; one *s.*; ed. Univ. of Athens.
Sec. Nat. Theatre 37, and later apptd. Dir. of Repertory, Artistic Dir. and Gen. Dir.; Theatre Critic and Literary Contributor to Athens daily newspaper *Vima*; editor *Epoches* magazine 63-67; mem. of Athens Acad., Commdr. Order of King George; First Prize of Athens Acad.
Leisure interest: film.
Publs. include: (novels) *The Violet City* 37, *Princess Izabo* 45, *Without a God* 51, *Secret Life* 57; (plays) *Emperor Michael* 36, *The Cross and the Sword* 39, *Theophano* 56, *The Mediterranean Night* 58, *The Lady in White Gloves* 62, *Thomas the Apostle* 62, *The Ancestor* 70; (history) *Greek Epic* 64; (essays) *To the Tragic Muse* 70.
23 Odos Strat., Syndesmou (136), Greece.
Telephone: 618-223.

Tesauro, Giuseppe, M.D.; Italian gynaecologist; b. 21 June 1898, Avellino; *s.* of Beniamino Tesauro and Antonietta Ranucci; *m.* Maria Grazia Benedetti; two *s.*; ed. Univ. of Naples.
Titular Prof. of Obstetrics and Gynaecology, Univ. of Sassari 35-36, Univ. of Messina 36-43, Dean Faculty of Medicine, Messina 39-43; Titular Prof. of Clinical Obstetrics and Gynaecology and Dir. of Clinical Obstetrics and Gynaecology, Univ. of Naples 43-; Rector, Univ. of Naples 59-; Pres. Società Italiana di Ostetricia e Ginecologia 59-61; Pres. Int. Fertility Assen. 62-66, Pres. Int. Fed. of Gynaecology and Obstetrics 64-67; official of numerous medical and govt. orgs.
Publs. *Cancer du col de l'utérus sur moignon d'hystérectomie subtotale* 28, *Sur le développement de tumeurs dans les ovaires soumis à l'action des rayons X* 28, *Über Erzeugung von Ehrlich-Adeno-Carcinomen-Tieren* 32, *Die Bewertung des eklamptischen Anfalls* 32, *La sterilità femminile* 39, *Conceptions actuelles sur le diagnostic et le traitement du cancer de l'utérus* 53, *Le dépistage du cancer de l'utérus par la méthode cytologique* 54, *Les isotopes radioactifs dans l'étude de la circulation amniotique* 58, *L'influence de l'isoimmunisation Rh sur la mortalité du nouveau-né* 59, *Déséquilibres métaboliques hormonaux gravidiques et anomalies congénitales* 60, *Thalassemia and Fertility* 62, *Arteriografia pelvica dopo isterectomia radicale* 63, *Trattato Italiano di Ginecologia* 64.
51 Via S. Brigida, Naples, Italy.
Telephone: 320421.

Tesch, Emmanuel Camille Georges Victor; Luxembourg business executive; b. 9 Dec. 1920, Hespérange; *s.* of Georges Tesch and Marie-Laure Weckbecker; *m.* Thérèse Laval 1949; one *s.*; ed. Technische Hochschule, Aachen and Eidgenössische Technische Hochschule, Zürich.
Engineer, Manufacture de Tabacs Heintz van Landewyck; Man. Dir. Société Générale pour le Commerce de Produits Industriels (SOGECO); joined ARBED as auditor 58, Dir. 68, Chair. Gen. Man. 72, Chair. Board 72; Pres. Columeta S.A. 72, ARBED Finance S.A. 72,

SALEM S.A. 74, Groupement des Industries Sidérurgiques Luxembourgeoises 73, Chambre de Commerce du Grand-Duché de Luxembourg 74; Deputy Chair. Stahlwerke Röchling-Burbach GmbH 73; Dir. SIDMAR S.A., Cie. Maritime Belge, Cie. Financière de l'Union Européenne, Eschweiler Bergwerks-Verein, F. & G. Carlswerk AG., F. & G. Fabrik Elektrischer Kabel, Companhia Siderurgica Belgo-Mineira S.A., Talleres Metalúrgicos San Martin "TAMET", SOGECO S.A.; Conseiller Société Générale de Belgique; Médaille de la Résistance (France); Chevalier, Ordre de la Couronne de Chêne (Luxembourg); Ordre de la Couronne (Belgium); Commdr. Order of Orange-Nassau (Netherlands); Cavaliere di Gran Croce (Italy); Order of Tudor Vladimirescu (Romania).
Leisure interests: shooting, fishing, gardening, literature.
Administration Centrale de l'ARBED, avenue de la Liberté, Luxembourg; Home: La Cléchère, Kockelscheuer, Luxembourg.
Telephone: 47-921 (Office); 36-81-68 (Home).

Teshigahara, Sofu (Koichi); Japanese artist in flower arrangement (Ikebana), sculptor and calligrapher; b. 1900, Tokyo; s. of Hisatsugu Teshigahara; m. Hama Teshigahara 1925; one s. one d.
Founded Sogetsu Ikebana School 27; numerous int. awards.
Publs. many books on Ikebana in English and other languages.
Sogetsu School, 1-1-4, Shibuya, Shibuya-ku, Tokyo 150, Japan.
Telephone: (03) 407-6181.

Tetley, Glen; American ballet director and choreographer; b. 3 Feb. 1926, Cleveland, O.; s. of Glenford Andrew Tetley and Mary Eleanor Byrne; ed. Franklin and Marshall, Lancaster, Pa. and New York Univ.
Performed with Hanya Helm, José Lunion, Pearl Lang, John Butler modern dance cos.; principal dancer, New York City Opera; leading soloist, Robert Joffrey Ballet, Martha Graham Dance Co., American Ballet Theater, Jerome Robbins' Ballet U.S.A.; formed own company 62-69; dancer and choreographer, Nederlands Dans Theater, Co-Artistic Dir. 69-; with Ballet Rambert; guest choreographer Royal Danish, Swedish, Norwegian Ballets; Dir. Stuttgart Ballet.
Performances: *Kiss me Kate, Out of this World, Amahl and the Night Visitors*; choreography: *Pierrot Lunaire 62, Sargasso, The Anatomy Lesson, Circles, Imaginary Film, Arena, Small Parades, Mutations, Embrace Tiger and Return to Mountain, Ziggurat, Rag Dances, Ricercare, Field Figures, Laborintus, Mythical Hunters, Gemini, Chronocromie, Threshold, Moveable Garden, Voluntaries, Le Sacre du Printemps*.
c/o Stuttgart Ballet, Württembergisches Stadttheater, 7 Stuttgart, Obereschlossgarten 6, Federal Republic of Germany.

Tett, Sir Hugh Charles, Kt., A.R.C.S., B.SC., D.I.C.; b. 28 Oct. 1906, Exeter, Devon; s. of late James Charles Tett and of Florence Tett (née Lihou); m. 1st Katie Sargent 1931 (died 1948), 2nd Joyce Lilian (née Mansell) 1949; two d.; ed. Univ. Coll., Exeter, and Royal Coll. of Science, London.
Esso Petroleum Co. 28-67, Chair. 59-67; Chair. Addis Ltd. 73, Bristol Composite Material Ltd. 74; Dir. Esso-Europe 66-68, Pirelli Gen. Cable Works Ltd. 70, Black and Decker Ltd. 70, Bristol Composite Materials Ltd. 72; Pro-Chancellor Univ. of Southampton 67-; Fellow Imperial Coll., London 64; Hon. D.Sc. (Southampton 65, Exeter 70).
Leisure interest: golf.
Flat 115, Portsea Hall, Portsea Place, London W2 2BZ, England.
Telephone: 01-262 6220.

Teuber, Hans-Lukas, PH.D.; American physiologist; b. 7 Aug. 1916, Berlin, Germany; s. of Eugen and Rose (Knopf) Teuber; m. Marianne Liepe 1941; two s.; ed. Coll. Français, Berlin, Univ. of Basle and Harvard Univ.
Assistant in psychology, Harvard Univ. 41-42; Research Assoc. later Prof. of Psychiatry and Neurology, New York Univ. Coll. of Medicine, 47-61; Prof. and Chair. Dept. of Psychology, Mass. Inst. of Technology 61-; mem. Council, Int. Brain Research Org. UNESCO; Eastman Prof., Oxford Univ. (U.K.) 71-72; mem. various public scientific panels, etc.; mem. Nat. Acad. of Sciences, American Acad. of Arts and Sciences, A.A.A.S., American Neurological Asscn., American Psychological Asscn., etc.; Dr. h.c. Univ. Claude Bernard (Lyons) 75, Univ. of Geneva 75; K. S. Lashley Award 66, Apollo Achievement Award (NASA) 69, Kenneth Craik Award (St. John's Coll., Cambridge) 71.
Publs. *Visual Field Defects after Penetrating Missile Wounds of the Brain* (co-author) 60, *Somatosensory Changes after Penetrating Brain Wounds in Man* 60, chapters in books and articles in journals.
Department of Psychology, Building E10-012, Massachusetts Institute of Technology, Cambridge, Mass. 02139, U.S.A.

Tévoédjré, Albert, D. ès SC. ECON. et SOC., L. ès L.; Dahomeyan politician and international civil servant; b. 1929, Porto Novo; m. Isabelle Ekué 1953; three s.; ed. Toulouse Univ., Fribourg Univ., Institut Universitaire des Hautes Etudes Internationales, Geneva, Sloan School of Management and M.I.T. (Advanced Programme for Senior Executives).
Teaching assignments include: Lycée Delafosse, Dakar, Senegal 52-54, Cahors, France 57-58, Lycée Victor Ballot, Porto Novo 59-61, Geneva Africa Inst. 63-64, Georgetown Univ., Washington D.C. 64; Sec. of State for Information 61-62; Sec.-Gen. Union Africaine et Malgache (U.A.M.) 62-63; Research Assoc. Harvard Univ., Centre for Int. Affairs 64-65; Int. Labour Office 65-, Regional Dir. for Africa March 66, Asst. Dir.-Gen. 69-75, Deputy Dir.-Gen. 75; Dir. Int. Inst. for Labour Studies 75-; fmr. Chief Editor *L'Etudiant d'Afrique Noire*; founder mem. Promotion Africaine (society to combat poverty in Africa); founder-mem. Nat. Liberation Movt. and mem. Cttee. 58-60; Deputy Sec.-Gen. of Nat. Syndicate of Teachers, Dahomey 59-60.
Publs. *L'Afrique Revoltée 58, La Formation des cadres africains en vue de la croissance économique 65, Pan-Africanism in Action 65, L'Afrique face aux problèmes du socialisme et de l'aide étrangère 66, Une Stratégie du Progrès social en Afrique et la Contribution de l'OIT 69*, etc.
International Labour Office, Geneva; Home: Le Manoir des Amadies, 1245 Collonge-Bellerive, Switzerland.
Telephone: (022) 98-52-11 (Office); 022-52-33-86 (Home).

Tewson, Sir Vincent, C.B.E., M.C.; British trade union official; b. 4 Feb. 1898; ed. Bradford.
Served First World War; Sec. Org. Dept. of TUC 25-31; Asst. Gen. Sec. 31-46; Gen. Sec. 46-Sept. 60; mem. Econ. Planning Board July 47-60; Vice-Chair. *Daily Herald* 46-60; Pres. Int. Confed. of Free Trade Unions (ICFTU) 51-53; Part-time mem. London Electricity Board 60-68; mem. Independent Television Authority 64-69.
7 Campana Court, Blenheim Road, Barnet, Hertfordshire, England.

Tézenas du Montcel, Robert; French civil servant; b. 22 Sept. 1902; ed. St. Etienne, Univs. of Lyons and Paris.
Auditor, Cour des Comptes 30; Colonial Inspector 34; Overseas Inspector-Gen. 48; Dir.-Gen. Ministry for Relations with Associated States 50; Pres. Admin.

Council, Institut d'émission de l'A.O.F. et de Togo 55; Pres. Overseas Tourist Office 55; Pres. Central Bank of West African States 59-64; Dir. of Gen. Inspection of Overseas Affairs 64; Pres. Cie. Financière France-Afrique 65, Union de Participations de France et d'Outre-mer 65-; Dir. Caisse Centrale de réescompte 66-72, Soc. industrielle et forestière des allumettes 67-, Int. Bank of W. Africa 69-73; Grand Officier de la Légion d'Honneur, Croix de Guerre, Conseiller Référendaire Hon. à la Cour des Comptes, foreign honours.
Leisure interest: Fmr. Pres. "Groupe de Haute Montagne".
Publ. *Ce Monde qui n'est pas le nôtre.*
77 boulevard Général-Koenig, 92200 Neuilly-sur-Seine, France.

Thacher, Nicholas Gilman; American diplomatist; b. 20 Aug. 1915, Kansas City, Mo.; s. of John H. and Edith (née Gilman) Thacher; m. Jean Louise Naffziger 1947; two s. one d.; ed. Princeton and Fordham Univs. and Univ. of Pennsylvania.
Banker, New York City 37-42; entered foreign service 47; Third Sec., Karachi 47-49; Vice-Consul, Calcutta 50-51, Consul 52; Indian Affairs Officer, Dept. of State 53-54; Officer in charge of Afghanistan-Pakistan Affairs 54-56; First Sec., Baghdad 56-58; Nat. War Coll. 58-59; Deputy Dir. Office of Near Eastern Affairs, Dept. of State 59-62; Counsellor, Jeddah 62-65; Minister-Counsellor, Teheran 65-70; Amb. to Saudi Arabia 70-73; Vice-Pres. Wells Fargo Bank, San Francisco, Calif. 74-.
3919 Washington Street, San Francisco, Calif. 94118, U.S.A.

Thacker, Maneklal Sankalchand; Indian engineer; b. 3 Dec. 1904; ed. Univ. of Bristol, England.
Worked for Bristol Corpn. Electricity Dept. 27-31; worked with Calcutta Electric Supply Corpn. 31-47; Prof. of Electrical Technology and Power Engineering, Indian Inst. of Science 47-49; Dir. Indian Inst. of Science 49-55; Dir. Scientific and Industrial Research and Additional Sec. to the Ministry of Natural Resources and Scientific Research 55-57; Sec. to Govt. of India in Ministry of Scientific Research and Cultural Affairs and Dir.-Gen. Council of Scientific and Industrial Research 57-62, mem. Planning Comm. 62-; fmr. Chair. Commonwealth Scientific Cttee.; Pres. UN Conf. on the Application of Science and Technology 63, 65; Hon. D.Sc., D.Eng., D.Litt.; numerous gold medals; Padma Bhushan 55.
44 Kushak Road, New Delhi, India.

Thailand, King of (*see* Bhumibol Adulyadej).

Thajeb, Sjarif, M.D.; Indonesian diplomatist; b. 7 Aug. 1920, Peureula, Atjeh; s. of Tueku Tjhi Hadji Mohamad Thajeb, Ulubalang of Peureula and Raden Aju Nurhamidah Thajeb; m. Nunijati Hidajat Prawirodiprodjo; one s. three d.; ed. Jakarta Medical Coll., Harvard Medical School, Temple Univ. School of Medicine, Philadelphia, Pa. and Army Staff and Command School, Jakarta.
Former army doctor; Lecturer, Children's Div., Dept. of Medicine, Univ. of Indonesia; Pres. Univ. of Indonesia; Minister of Higher Educ. and Sciences; Vice-Chair. of Parl.; Amb. to U.S.A. 71-74; Minister of Educ. and Culture 74-; participant in several int. paediatric confs.; Hon. doctorate, Univ. of Mindanao (Philippines); several medals and decorations.
Leisure interests: music, theatre, golf, bowling.
Publs. papers and articles on various subjects published in numerous paediatric magazines and journals.
Ministry of Education and Culture, Jakarta, Indonesia.

Thalmann, Ernesto A., DR. IUR.; Swiss diplomatist; b. 14 Jan. 1914, Bellinzona; s. of Friedrich Thalmann and Clara Good; m. Paula Degen 1943; two s. one d.; ed. Univ. of Zürich.

Lawyer, District Court of Zürich 40; Fed. Dept. of Public Economy 41; Attaché, Swiss Fed. Political Dept. 45; Sec. Extraordinary Powers Cttee. and the Cttee. of Foreign Affairs of the Nat. Council 46; Second Sec. of Legation 47; Dep. Chief, Press and Information Service, Swiss Fed. Political Dept. 47; Sec. Swiss del. UN Conf. for Freedom of Press and Information, Geneva 48; Swiss Legation, Paris 49, First Sec. 51; Swiss Legation, Prague 52; Dep. Chief, Division of Organization and Admin. Affairs, Swiss Political Dept. 54-57; Counsellor and Dep. Chief of Mission, Swiss Embassy in U.S.A. 57-60, Minister-Counsellor 60-61; Perm. Observer to UN with rank of Amb. 61-66; Chief, Div. for Int. Orgs., Fed. Political Dept. 66-71; Special Mission in Jerusalem after Six-Day War, as Personal Rep. of UN Sec.-Gen. 67; Sec.-Gen. of Fed. Political Dept. and Dir. of Political Affairs 71-75; Amb. to U.K. 76-.
Leisure interest: gardening.
Embassy of Switzerland, 16-18 Montagu Place, London, W1H 2BQ; Residence: 21 Bryanston Square, London, W1H 7FG, England.
Telephone: 01-723 0701 (Office and Residence).

Thammasak, Sanya; Thai lawyer and politician; b. 1907, Bangkok; ed. Bangkok and London.
Former Chief Justice, Supreme Court; fmr. Rector, Thammasat Univ.; Pres. Privy Council 69-73; Prime Minister 73-75; Vice-Pres. World Buddhist Fed., Buddhist Assen. of Thailand.
c/o Buddhist Association of Thailand, 41 Phra Aditya Street, Bangkok, Thailand.

Thapa, Surya Bahadur; Nepalese politician; b. 20 March 1928, Muga, East Nepal; s. of Bahadur Thapa; m. 1953; one s. two d.; ed. Allahabad Univ., India.
House Speaker, Advisory Assembly to King of Nepal 58; mem. Upper House of Parl. 59; Minister of Forest, Agriculture, Commerce and Industry 60; Minister of Finance and Econ. Affairs 62; Vice-Chair. Council of Ministers, Minister of Finance, Econ. Planning, Law and Justice 63; Vice-Chair. Council of Ministers, Minister of Finance, Law and Gen. Admin. 64-65; Chair. Council of Ministers, Minister of Palace Affairs, 65-69; mem. Royal Advisory Cttee. 69-72; arrested Aug. 72; Tri-Shakti-Patta 63, Gorkha Dakshinbahu I 65; several Nepalese and foreign awards.
Naxal, Katmandu, Nepal.

Thatcher, Rt. Hon. Margaret Hilda, P.C., M.P., M.A., B.SC.; British barrister and politician; b. 13 Oct. 1925; d. of the late Alfred Roberts; m. Denis Thatcher 1951; one s. one d. (twins); ed. Grantham High School and Somerville Coll., Oxford.
Research chemist 47-51; called to the Bar, Lincoln's Inn 53; M.P. for Finchley 59-; Parl. Sec. Ministry of Pensions and Nat. Insurance 61-64; Chief Opposition Spokesman on Educ. 69-70; Sec. of State for Educ. and Science 70-74; Leader of Conservative Party Feb. 75-; Hon. Bencher, Lincoln's Inn 75; Conservative.
House of Commons, London, S.W.1, England.

Thayer, William Paul; American business executive; b. 23 Nov. 1919, Henryetta, Okla.; s. of Paul E. Thayer and Opal Marie Ashenhurst; m. Margery Schwartz 1947; one d.; ed. Wichita High School North, Univs. of Wichita and Kansas.
Served in U.S. Navy 41-45; Pilot, TWA 45-47; Chief Experimental Test Pilot, Chance Vought Corpn. 48-50; Chief Flight Test, Northrop Aircraft Co. 50-51; Sales Man. Chance Vought Corpn. 51, Sales and Service Man. 52, Vice-Pres. Sales and Service 54, Vice-Pres. Washington, D.C. Operations 58, Vice-Pres. and Gen. Man. Vought Aeronautics Div. 59; Pres. Chance Vought 63, subsequently Senior Vice-Pres. Ling-Temco-Vought Inc. 63; Exec. Vice-Pres. Ling-Temco-Vought Inc. 64; Pres. LTV Aerospace Corpn. 65; Chair. of Board and Chief Exec. Officer, Ling-Temco-Vought Inc. (name changed to LTV Corpn. 72) 70-; Distinguished Flying

Cross, Air Medal with Nine Clusters, Distinguished Service Award, etc.
Leisure interests: flying, hunting and golf.
P.O. Box 5003, Dallas, Texas 75222; Home: 10200 Hollow Way, Dallas Texas 75229, U.S.A.
Telephone: 742-9555 (Office).

Thé, Guy Blaudin de, M.D., PH.D.; French cancer research specialist; b. 5 May 1930, Marseilles; ed. Faculty of Medicine, Marseilles, Sorbonne, Paris.
Research Asst., Duke Univ. Medical Centre, U.S.A. 61-63; Visiting Scientist, Laboratory of Viral Oncology, Nat. Cancer Inst., U.S.A. 63-65; Head of Unit of Electro-microscopy, Centre Nat. de Recherche Scientifique 65-67; Chief, Unit of Biological Carcinogenesis, WHO Int. Agency for Cancer Research, Lyons 67-; Consultant to Inst. de cancérologie et d'immunogénétique 70-; mem. Scientific Council, Ligue nat. française contre le cancer 72-; mem. Soc. française de Microscopie électronique, Soc. française de Microbiologie, Royal Microscopic Soc. of England, American Soc. for Cell Biology, American Asscn. for Cancer Research, A.A.A.S., American Soc. of Electron Microscopy, European Asscn. for Cancer Research, European Asscn. for Cell Biology.
Publs. many publs. on the cell virus relationship on avian and murine leukemia viruses.
International Agency for Research on Cancer, 16 avenue Maréchal Foch, 69 Lyons, France.
Telephone: 52-33-26, 52-32-40.

Theocharis, Reghinos D., PH.D.; Cypriot economist and banker; b. 10 Feb. 1929, Larnaca; s. of Demetrios and Florentia Theocharis; m. Madeleine Loumbou 1954; one s. one d.; ed. Graduate School of Economics, Athens, Univ. of Aberdeen, and London School of Economics.
Inspector of Commercial Education, Cyprus 53-56; at London School of Economics 56-58; Chief, Economic Development Unit, Bank of Greece, Athens 58-59; Minister of Finance in Cyprus Provisional Govt. March 59-Aug. 60; Minister of Finance Aug. 60-62; Gov. of Bank of Cyprus 62-75; Prof. Highest School of Econs. and Commercial Sciences, Athens 75-; Hon. Fellow, London School of Econs 71.
Leisure interests: chess, gardening.
Publ. *Early Developments in Mathematical Economics* 61.
c/o Bank of Cyprus Ltd., P.O.B. 1472, Nicosia, Cyprus.
Telephone: 64064.

Theodorakis, Mikis; Greek composer; b. 29 July 1925, Chios (Greek Island); s. of Georges Michel Theodorakis and Aspasia Poulaki; m. Myrto Altinoglou 1953; one s. one d.; ed. secondary and high school, Greece, Athens Conservatoire and Paris Conservatoire.
Joined resistance against German occupation of Greece 43; arrested and deported during civil war 47-52; moved to Paris 53 and studied under Olivier Messiaen (q.v.); first public concert *Sonatina* (for pianoforte), Paris 54; set to bouzouki music the poem *Epitaphios* by Iannis Ritsos 58-59 and subsequently wrote numerous other successful songs; Ballet music for *Antigone* (first performed in London by Dame Margot Fonteyn) and *Les Amants de Teruel*; returned to Greece 61; leader Lambrakis youth movement; mem. of Parl. 63; arrested for political activities 67, released April 70; resigned from Communist Party March 72; United Left candidate, parliamentary election Nov. 74; Gold Medal, Moscow Shostakovitch Festival 57; Corbey Prize, U.S.A. 57; First Prize Athens Popular Song Festival 61; Sibelius Award, London 63.
Works include: *Sinfonia* (oratorio) 44, *Love and Death* (voice, strings) 45-48, *Assi-Gonia* (orchestra) 45-50, *Sextet for Flute* 46, *Oedipus Tyrannus* (strings) 46, *Greek Carnaval* (ballet suite) 47, *First Symphony* (orchestra) 48-50, *Five Cretan Songs* (chorus, orchestra) 50, *Orpheus and Eurydice* (ballet) 52, *Barefoot Battalion*

(film) 53, *Suite No. 1* (four movements, piano and orchestra) 54, *Poèmes d'Eluard* (*Cycle* 1 and *Cycle* 2) 55, *Suite No. 2* (chorus, orchestra) 56, *Suite No. 3* (five movements, soprano, chorus, orchestra) 56, *Illmet by Moonlight* (film) 57, *Sonatina No. 1* (violin, piano) 57, *Les Amants de Teruel* (ballet) 58, *Sonatina No. 2* (violin, piano) 58, *Antigone* (ballet) 58, *Epitaphios* (song cycle) 59, *Deserters* (song cycle) 58, *Epiphania* (song cycle) 59, *Honeymoon* (film) 60, *Phoenician Women—Euripides* (theatre music) 60, *Axion Esti* (pop oratorio) 60, *Electra-Euripides* (film), *Phaedra* (film) 62, *The Hostage* (song cycle) 62, *The Ballad of the Dead Brother* (musical tragedy) 62, *Zorba the Greek* (film), *The Ballad of Mathausen* (song cycle) 65, *Romiossini* (song cycle) 65, *Lusistrata—Aristophanes* (theatre music) 66, *Romancero Gitano* (Lorca) (song cycle) 67, *Sun and Time* (song cycle) 67, *Arcadias* Nos. 1-10 (song cycles) 68-69, *Canto General* (Pablo Neruda) (pop oratorio) 72, *Z* (film), *Etat de Siège* (film) 73, *Ballads* (song cycle) 75.
Publs. *Journals of Resistance* 72, *Culture et Dimensions Politiques* 73.
111 rue Notre-Dame-des-Champs, 75006 Paris, France.
Telephone: 326-1466.

Theodorakopoulos, Ioannis, PH.D.; Greek philosopher; b. 28 Jan. 1900, Sparta; s. of Nikolaos and Panagiota Theodorakopoulos; m. Penelope Kakridis 1935; two d.; ed. Univs. of Athens, Vienna and Heidelberg.
Prof. of Philosophy Univ. of Salonika 25-33, Univ. of Athens 39-67, Panteios School of Political Science 50-; Minister of Educ. 45 and 66; Chair. Greek Nat. Theatre Cttee.; mem. Acad. of Athens, Pres. 63, now Sec.-Gen.; cttee. mem. Int. Inst. of Philosophy, Fed. Int. Soc. of Philosophy, Union Acad. Int., Brussels; hon. mem. Goethehaus (Frankfurt); Editor *Archives of Philosophy Theory of Science* 29-41 and *Philosophia* 71-; Hon. LL.D. (Univ. of Athens, Ohio).
Publs. *Platons Dialektik des Seins* 27, *Theory of Knowledge* 28, *Plotins Metaphysik des Seins* 29, *Philosophy and Psychology* 29, *The Philosophy of Kant* 30, *The Philosophy of Heraclitus* 30, *Philosophy of Art* 31, *Philosophy of Education* 32, *The Problem of the Philosophy of History* 32, *History and Life* 36, *An Introduction to Plato* 40, *Plato's Phaedrus* 48, *System of Ethics* 48, *Studies of Christian and Philosophical Thought* 52, *A Philosophical Interpretation of Goethe's Faust* 56, *Plato, Plotinus, Origenis* 59, *Plato's Theory of Ideas* 60, *Dialogue, Dialectic and our Times* 61, *The Place of Hellenism in the Contemporary World* 61, *Philosophie und Religion* 61, *Greece and Europe* 63, *Philosophy and Life* 67, *Die Hauptprobleme der Platonischen Philosophie* 72, *Contemporary Philosophical Currents* 72, *Introduction to Philosophy*, 4 Vols. 74-75.
Akadimia Athinon, Odos Panepistimiou, Athens, Greece.
Telephone: 611-560.

Theorell, Hugo, M.D.; Swedish biochemist; b. 6 July 1903, Linköping; s. of Ture Theorell and Armida Bill; m. Margit Alenius 1931; three s.; ed. Royal Caroline Medico-Surgical Inst., Stockholm.
Asst. Prof. of Chemistry Uppsala Univ. 32; Head Biochemistry Dept., Nobel Inst. Stockholm 37-70; Sec.-Gen. Swedish Society of Physicians and Surgeons 40-45, Chair. 46-47, 57-58, Hon. mem. 56-; mem. State Research Council for Natural Sciences 50-54, for Medical Sciences 58-64; Chair. Swedish Chemical Soc. 47-48, Pres. Int. Union of Biochemistry 67-73; mem. Royal Swedish Acads. of Science, Engineering Sciences and of Music, Royal Danish Acad. of Sciences and Letters, Norwegian Acad. of Science and Letters, Accad. dei XL, Rome, American Acad. of Arts and Letters, Nat. Acad. of Sciences, American Philosophical Soc.; hon. mem. New York Acad. of Sciences; foreign mem. Royal Society, Polish Acad. of Sciences, Indian Acad. of Sciences, Acad. Royale de Médicine, Belgium, Akad.

Leopoldina, Halle, Bayerische Akad. der Wissenschaften, Munich, American Coll. of Physicians; Nobel Prize in Physiology or Medicine 55; Commdr. 1st Class Royal Order of the Northern Star; Commdr. Royal Norwegian Order of St. Olaf; Officer, Brazilian Order of Southern Cross; Commdr. Légion d'Honneur; Commdr. 1st Class Order of Finnish Lion; principal research in field of enzymes; Dr. h.c. (Paris, Philadelphia, Louvain, Brussels, Rio de Janeiro, Kentucky and Michigan).
Leisure interest: violin-playing.
Nobel Institute of Medicine, Stockholm 60, Sweden.

Thesiger, Wilfred, C.B.E., D.S.O., M.A.; British traveller; b. 3 Jan. 1910, Addis Ababa, Ethiopia; s. of the Hon. Wilfred Thesiger, D.S.O., and Kathleen Mary Vigors; ed. Eton and Magdalen Coll., Oxford.
Explored Danakil country of Abyssinia 33-34; Sudan Political Service, Darfur and Upper Nile Provinces 35-39; served in Ethiopia, Syria and Western Desert with Sudan Defence Force and Special Air Service, Second World War; explored the Empty Quarter of Arabia 45-50; lived with the Madan in the Marshes of Southern Iraq 50-58; awarded Back Grant, Royal Geographical Soc. 36, Founders Medal 48; Lawrence of Arabia Medal, Royal Central Asian Soc. 55; David Livingstone Medal, Royal Scottish Geographical Soc. 61; W. H. Heinemann Bequest, Royal Soc. of Literature 64; Burton Medal, Royal Asiatic Soc. 66; Hon. D.Litt. (Leicester).
Leisure interests: photography, travel in remote places.
Publs. *Arabian Sands* 58, *The Marsh Arabs* 64.
15 Shelley Court, Tite Street, London, S.W.3, England. Telephone: 01-372-7213.

Thestrup, Knud, CAND.JUR.; Danish judge; b. 27 Aug. 1900, Proestø; s. of Dyrlage P. Thestrup and Ingeborg Madsen; m. Jenny Marie Birgitte Knudsen 1925; one s. two d.; ed. Københavns Universitet.
Assistant Judge, Øster and Vester Han 24, Herning and Hammerum 29-45; in Frøslev Concentration Camp 44-45; Act. Judge Western Div. of High Court 45-47; Judge, Viborg Criminal Court 47-53, Court at Herning 53-; Minister of Justice 68-72; mem. Folketing (Parl.) 47- (2nd Vice-Chair. 64-), Parl. Finance Cttee. 50-, Conservative Party Parl. Group 56- (Vice-Chair. 58-); Conservative Party Gen. Council 57- (Chair. 65-); mem. Nordic Council 52-, Chair. of the Council's Cttee. of Nine 59-60, of the Council's Legal Cttee. 60-; Knight Order of Dannebrog (1st Class), Commdr., Swedish Order of Vasa.
Leisure interest: reading.
Rosenvaemget Allee 10, 2100 Copenhagen, Denmark.

Thiam, Doudou; Senegalese fmr. Minister of Finance, Economic Affairs and Planning; see *The International Who's Who 1975-76*.

Thiel, Frans Joseph Frits Marie Van; Netherlands politician; b. 1906; ed. Univ. of Nijmegen.
Former lawyer; M.P. 48-52, 56-; Minister of Social Works 52-56; Speaker Second Chamber of Parl. 63-72; Catholic.
Warandelaan 11A, Helmond, Netherlands.
Telephone: 22010.

Thiele, Ilse; German politician; b. 4 Nov. 1920; ed. secondary school.
Shorthand typist; mem. Communist Party 45, SED 46; founder mem. Democratic Women's League (DFD), first Pres. 53-; mem. Central Cttee. SED; mem. Volkskammer; mem. Council of State.
Demokratischer Frauenbund Deutschlands (DFD), 108 Berlin, Clara-Zetkin-Strasse 16, German Democratic Republic.

Thielicke, Helmut, D.THEOL., DR. THEOL., D.PHIL, D.D.; German theologian; b. 4 Dec. 1908, Wüppertal-

Barmen; s. of Reinhard and Lore Thielicke; m. Marie-Luise Herrmann 1937; three s. one d.; ed. Univs. of Greifswald, Marburg, Erlangen and Bonn.
Prof. at Heidelberg 36-40; Parish Priest Ravensburg 41-42; head of Theological Office of Württemberg Church 43-45; Prof. of Systematic Theology at Univ. of Tübingen 45-54; Rector Univ. of Tübingen and Pres. Conf. of Rectors, German Fed. Republic 51; Prof. of Systematic Theology, Univ. of Hamburg 54-, Rector 60; Hon. Dr.Theol. (Heidelberg Univ.), Hon. D.D. (Glasgow Univ.), Hon. LL.D. (Waterloo Univ., Canada). Hon. Litt.D. (Hickory, N.C.).
Leisure interest: photography.
Publs. *Das Verhältnis zwischen dem Ethischen und dem Aesthetischen* 32, *Geschichte und Existenz* 35, 64, *Fragen des Christentums an die moderne Welt* 47, *Tod und Leben* 46, *Theologie der Anfechtung* 49, *Der Nihilismus* 50 (Japanese, English trans.), *Der Glaube der Christenheit* 47, *Zwischen Gott und Satan* 46 (English trans.), *Theologische Ethik* (English trans.), 4 vols., 51, 55, 58, 64, *Das Gebet, das die Welt umspannt* 45, 11th edn. 63 (English, Dutch, Swedish, Japanese, Norwegian, Finnish, Danish, Afrikaans trans.), *Das Leben kann noch einmal beginnen* 56, *Das Bilderbuch Gottes* 57, 4th edn. 63 (U.S., Norwegian, Danish, Swedish, Dutch, Brazilian, Italian, Portuguese and Japanese trans.), *Wie die Welt begann* 60 (English, Dutch, Danish, Swedish trans.), *Gespräche über Himmel und Erde: Begegnungen in U.S.A.* 64 (U.S., Finnish trans.), *Leiden an der Kirche* 65 (U.S., Dutch, Japanese trans.) 65, *Der evangelische Glaube: Grundzüge der Dogmatik* Vol. I, *Prolegomena* 68, Vol. II, *Gotteslehre und Christologie* 73, *Und wenn Gott wäre* 70.
2 Hamburg 13, Sedanstrasse 19, Federal Republic of Germany.
Telephone: 0411-4123-3806.

Thier, Jacques de, LL.D.; Belgian lawyer and diplomatist; b. 15 Sept. 1900, Heusy; m. Mariette Negroponte 1946 (died 1973); three step-s.; ed. Univ. of Liège.
Mem. of the Bar, Liège and Verviers 23; attached to the Prime Minister's Cabinet, Brussels 29-32; Diplomatic Service 30-65; Attaché, Berlin 32; Chargé d'Affaires, Athens 35, Teheran 36; First Sec., Berlin 37-38; First Sec., then Counsellor, Washington 38-44; Chargé d'Affaires, Madrid 44-46; Political Dept., Ministry of Foreign Affairs 47; Asst. Head of Belgian Mission in Berlin 47-; Consul-Gen., New York 48-55; Pres. Soc. of Foreign Consuls in N.Y. 54; mem. Belgian Dels. to UN Gen. Assemblies 56-60; Ambassador to Mexico 55-58, to Canada 58-61, to United Kingdom 61-65; Perm. Rep. to Western European Union (W.E.U.) 61-65, retd; Counsellor COMETRA Oil Co.; Chair. Belgian Nat. Cttee. of United World Colls.; Hon. G.C.V.O., Grand Officier Ordre Léopold II (Belgium), and numerous other decorations.
Leisure interests: golf, travelling, reading.
38 avenue des Klauwaerts, 1050 Brussels, Belgium.
Telephone: 649-07-58.

Thiess, Frank, DR.PHIL.; German author; b. 13 March 1890; ed. Univs. of Berlin and Tübingen.
War service 15; on editorial staff of *Berliner Tageblatt* 15-18; theatrical producer in Stuttgart 20-21; dramatic critic in Hanover 21-23; Mem. Akademie der Wissenschaften und der Literatur, Mainz, Kuratorium: Ostdeutscher Kulturrat, DOG, Mainz, PEN Club of Austria; Hon. mem. VDS; Knight of Mark Twain Soc., U.S.A.; Hon. mem. Bruckner Soc., U.S.A.
Publs. *Der Tod von Falern, Angelika ten Swaart, Die Verdammten, Das Gesicht des Jahrhunderts, Abschied vom Paradies, Das Tor zur Welt, Der Leibhaftige, Der Zentaur, Der Kampf mit dem Engel, Narren, Geschichte eines unruhigen Sommers, Erziehung zur Freiheit, Die Zeit ist reif, Der Weg zu Isabelle, Stürmischer Frühling, Der ewige Taugenichts, Wir werden es nie wissen,*

Tsushima, Das Reich der Dämonen, Caruso, Puccini, Ideen zur Natur-und Leidensgeschichte der Völker, Katharina Winter, Die Blüten welken, aber der Baum wächst, Der heilige Dämon, Die Strassen des Labyrinths, Tödlicher Karneval, Don Juans letzte Tage, Die Herzogin von Langeais, Die Wirklichkeit des Unwirklichen, In Memoriam Wilhelm Furtwängler, Das Menschenbild bei Knut Hamsun, Das Werther-Thema in Hamsuns "Mysterien", Der unbequeme Mitmensch, Hamsuns "Auf überwachsenen Pfaden", Theater ohne Rampe, Geister werfen keinen Schatten, Gäa, Ursprung und Sinn des Ost-West Gegensatzes, Die griechischen Kaiser, Sturz nach oben, Das Gesicht unseres Jahrhunderts-heute, Theater ohne Vorhang, Verbrannte Erde, Freiheit bis Mitternacht, Plädoyer für Peking, Der Schwarze Engel, Zauber und Schrecken (Die Welt der Kinder), Reich der Dämonen (new version), *Dostoyewski-Realismus am Rande der Transzendenz, Jahre des Unheils, Der Zauberlehrling.*
Park Rosenhöhe, Darmstadt, Federal Republic of Germany.

Thiessen, Peter Adolf, DR. PHIL. HABIL.; German chemist; b. 6 April 1899; ed. Univs. of Breslau, Freiburg and Göttingen.
Dozent, Univ. of Göttingen 26, Head of its Inst. of Inorganic Chemistry; Extraordinary Prof. 32; Univ. of Frankfurt 34, Münster 35, Berlin 35; Dir. Kaiser-Wilhelm-Inst. of Physical Chemistry 35; scientific work in U.S.S.R. 45-56; Prof. of Physical Chemistry, Humboldt Univ., Berlin 56-64, Prof. Emeritus 64-; mem. Deutsche Akad. der Wissenchaften zu Berlin, Dir. of its Inst. of Physical Chemistry, Emer. 64-; Hon. Chair. Research Council of D.D.R.; mem. Exec. Council Deutscher Kulturbund; Hon. mem. Chamber of Technology; non-resident mem. of Acad. of Sciences, U.S.S.R. 66; Hon. Dr. rer. nat. 59; U.S.S.R. State Prize (1st Class) 51, Order of Lenin 51, Order of Red Labour Banner 56, Nat. Prize 1st class 58, Order of Banner of Labour 59, Fatherland Gold Order of Merit 59, Distinguished People's Scientist 64.
Akademie der Wissenschaften der D.D.R., 108 Berlin, Otto-Nuschke-Strasse 221-2; Rudower Chausse 5, 1199 Berlin-Adlershof, German Democratic Republic.
Telephone: 67-701-05.

Thieu, Lt.-Gen. Nguyen Van (*see* Nguyen Van Thieu).

Thieulin, Gustave Léon Pierre; French dairy research scientist; b. 20 July 1903, Emanville; s. of Amand Gustave Thieulin and Leonie Blactot; m. Germaine Pfeiffer 1929; two s.; ed. Ecole Nat. Vétérinaire d'Alfort, Inst. Pasteur, Inst. Nat. Agronomique.
On staff of Paris and Seine Veterinary Service 28-, in charge of Milk Research and Control Laboratory 41-, Deputy Dir. 46; Deputy Prof. of Production, Hygiene and Control of Milk, Ecole Nat. Vétérinaire d'Alfort 32, Inst. Nat. Agronomique 38; Director of Service Vétérinaire Sanitaire (Paris and Seine Dept.) 61-; Contrôleur-Gén. Services Vétérinaires, Ministry of Agriculture 65-; Dir. and Editor-in-Chief of *Le Lait;* Consultant FAO; Consultant, mem., Sec.-Gen. (and fmr. Pres.) Acad. Vétérinaire; mem. Acad. Nat. de Médecine; Higher Council of Public Hygiene; Laureate of the Acad. des Sciences, Acad. Nat. de Médecine, Acad. d'Agriculture and Acad. Vétérinaire; Officier de la Légion d'Honneur, Chevalier du Mérite Social, Officier du Mérite Agricole; Officier des Palmes Académiques; Officier de la Santé Publique, Officier du Mérite Militaire.
Leisure interests: bridge, equitation, tennis.
Publs. *Manuel d'Analyse du Lait, des Oeufs et des Produits Laitiers, La Viande* (*nature, preparation, distribution*), and 181 scientific and technical papers.
113 avenue Victor Hugo, 75116 Paris; 48 avenue Président Wilson, 75116 Paris; and Tourny (Eure 27), France.
Telephone: 727-7924 and 727-5398.

Thimann, Kenneth Vivian, B.SC., A.R.C.S., D.I.C., PH.D.; American biologist and educationist; b. 5 Aug. 1904, Ashford, Kent, England; s. of Phoebus and Muriel (Harding) Thimann; m. Ann Mary Bateman 1929; three d.; ed. Caterham School, and Imperial Coll., London.
Instructor in Biochemistry, California Inst. of Technology 30-35; Lecturer, Harvard Univ. 35-36, Asst. Prof. 36-39, Assoc. Prof. 39-46, Prof. of Biology 46-62, Higgins Prof. of Biology 62-65; Prof. of Biology and Provost Crown Coll., Univ. of Calif. at Santa Cruz 65-72, Prof. Emer. 72-, Chair. Board of Studies in Biology 73-; Acting Dean of Natural Sciences 65-66; Visiting Prof. Univ. of Paris 54-55, Univ. of Mass. 74; Pres. Soc. of Gen. Physiologists 49-50, American Soc. of Plant Physiologists 50, American Soc. of Naturalists 55, Botanical Soc. of America 60, American Inst. of Biological Sciences 65; Pres. XI Int. Botanical Congress, Seattle Aug. 69, Pres. VIII Int. Congress on Plant Growth Substances, Tokyo 73; Frank Hatton Prize for Chemistry 24, Stephen Hales Prize, American Soc. of Plant Physiologists 36 and Barnes hon. life membership; mem. Nat. Acad. of Sciences (Councillor 68-71), Philosophical Soc. (Councillor 72-75), American Acad. of Arts and Sciences; Foreign mem. Royal Soc. (London) 69, Accad. Nazionale dei Lincei (Rome), Acad. Nat. Roumaine des Arts et Sciences, Akad. Leopoldina, Botanical Socs. of Japan and the Netherlands; Dr. h.c. (Univs. of Basle and Clermont-Ferrand).
Leisure interests: music, garden.
Publs. *Phytohormones* (with F. W. Went) 37, *Les Auxines* 55, *The Action of Hormones in Plant and Invertebrates* (with B. Scharrer and F. Brown) 48, *The Life of Bacteria* 55, 63 (German trans. 64), *The Natural Plant Hormones* 72, *Hormones in the Life of Plants* 76, and about 250 papers in scientific journals; Editor *Vitamins and Hormones* vols. 1-20, 43-62, *The Hormones* vols. 1-5, 48-63.
Thimann Laboratories, Division of Natural Sciences, University of California, Santa Cruz, Calif. 95064, U.S.A.
Telephone: 408-429-2418.

Thin, U Tun, PH.D.; Burmese economist; ed. Rangoon, Michigan and Harvard Univs.
Chairman Econ. Dept., Univ. of Rangoon; Dir. Cen. Statistics and Econs. Dept., Ministry of Planning, Burma; Alt. Exec. Dir. IMF for Burma, Ceylon, Japan and Thailand; Asst. Dir. IMF Asian Dept. 59-66, Deputy Dir. 66-72, Dir. 72-.
Asian Department, International Monetary Fund, 19th and H Streets, N.W., Washington, D.C. 20431, U.S.A.
Telephone: 202-477-2911.

Thiry, Marcel, D. en D.; Belgian writer; b. 13 March 1897; ed. Univ. of Liège.
Awarded Prix Verhaeren 26, Prix triennal de Poésie 35, Grand Prix Quinquennal de Poésie 58, Prix Bernheim 63, Grand Prix quinquennal de littérature 65; elected to Belgian Acad. royale de langue et de littérature françaises 39, Perpetual Sec. 60-.
Publs. Poetry: *Toi qui pâlis au nom de Vancouver* 24, *Plongeantes Proues* 25, *L'Enfant Prodigue* 27, *Statue de la Fatigue* 34, *La Mer de la Tranquillité* 38, *Ages* 50, *Poésie* 58, *Vie Poésie* 61, *Le Festin d'Attente* 63; Prose: *Marchands* 37, *Echec au Temps* 45, *La Belgique pendant la Guerre* 47, *Juste* 53, *Simul* 57, *Comme si* 59, *Le grand Possible* 60, *Le Tour du monde en guerre* 65, *Nondum Jam non* 66, *Le poème et la langue* 67.
Vaux-sous-Chèvremont, Belgium.
Telephone: 04-65-09-27.

Thode, Henry George, C.C., M.B.E., M.SC., PH.D., D.SC., LL.D., F.R.S., F.R.S.C., F.C.I.C.; Canadian chemist and university administrator; b. 10 Sept. 1910, Dundurn, Sask.; s. of Charles H. and Zelma Thode; m. Sadie

Alicia Patrick 1935; three s.; ed. Univs. of Saskatchewan and Chicago, and Columbia Univ.

Instructor, Pennsylvania Coll. for Women 35-36; Research Asst., Columbia Univ. 36-38; Research Chemist U.S. Rubber Co., N.J. 38-39; Asst. Prof. of Chemistry, McMaster Univ. 39-42, Assoc. Prof. 42-44, Head Dept. of Chemistry 48-52, Vice-Pres. 57-61, Dir. of Research 47-61, Pres. 61-72, Vice-Chancellor 61-72, Prof. of Chemistry 44-; Principal Hamilton Coll., McMaster Univ. 44-63; Research Chemist, Atomic Energy Project 43-46, Consultant 45-51; Consultant Atomic Energy of Canada Ltd. 51-; Visiting Prof. and Sr. Foreign Scientist, Nat. Science Foundation, Calif. Inst. of Technology 70; Dir. Hamilton Health Asscn. 48-68, Western New York Nuclear Research Centre 65-73, Atomic Energy of Canada Ltd. 66-, Fidelity Mortgage and Savings Corpn. 68-, Steel Co. of Canada Ltd. 69-; mem. Royal Society of Canada (Pres. Section III 50-51), Pres. 59-60; Pres. Chemical Inst. of Canada 51-52; mem. Nat. Research Council 55-61, Defence Research Board 55-61, Board of Govs., Ontario Research Foundation 56-, Comm. on Atomic Weights, Inorganic Chemistry Div., Int. Union of Pure and Applied Chemistry 63-; Hon. LL.D. Univ. of Saskatchewan; Hon. D.Sc. Univ. of Toronto, Univ. of British Columbia, Acadia Univ., Laval Univ., McGill Univ., Queen's Univ., Royal Military Coll., Canada, York Univ.; Chemical Inst. of Canada Medal 57; Royal Soc. of Canada Tory Medal 59.

Leisure interests: swimming, farming, golf.

Publs. numerous papers on nuclear chemistry, isotope chemistry, isotope abundances in terrestrial and extraterrestrial material, separation of isotopes, magnetic susceptibilities, electrical discharges in gases, sulphur concentrations and isotope ratios in lunar materials.

Nuclear Research Building, McMaster University, 1280 Main Street West, Hamilton, Ont., L8S 4K1, Canada.

Telephone: 416-525-9140, Ext. 4249 (Office).

Thom, Ronald James, F.R.A.I.C.; Canadian architect; b. 15 May 1923, Penticton, B.C.; ed. Vancouver School of Art.

Began career as concert pianist; studied art; taught in Vancouver School of Art and at School of Architecture, Univ. of British Columbia; Partner, Thompson, Berwick, Pratt, Vancouver 58; R. J. Thom Architects, Toronto 63-; has lectured at univs. throughout Canada; Fellow, Royal Architectural Inst. of Canada; mem. Royal Canadian Acad. of Arts, Ontario Asscn. of Architects, Architectural Inst. of B.C.; Hon. LL.D. (Trent Univ.) 71, Hon. D.Eng. (Nova Scotia Technical Coll.) 73.

Publs. many articles on architecture in arts journals.

The Thom Partnership, 47 Colborne Street, Toronto, Ontario; Home: 95 Meadowcliffe Drive, Scarborough, Ontario, Canada.

Thomas, Baron (Life Peer), cr. 71, of Remenham in the Royal County of Berkshire; **(William) Miles (Webster) Thomas,** Kt., D.F.C.; British industrialist; b. 2 March 1897, Wrexham, N. Wales; s. of William Henry Thomas and Mary Elizabeth Webster; m. Hylda Nora Church 1924; one s. one d.; ed. Bromsgrove School.

Served armoured car squadrons, R.F.C. and R.A.F., First World War; Man. Dir. Wolseley Motors Ltd. 36-40; Vice-Chair. Morris Motors Ltd. Wolseley Motors Ltd., Morris Commercial Cars Ltd., M.G. Car Co. Ltd., Riley Motor Co. Ltd., Morris Industries (Exports) Ltd., S.U. Carburettor Co. Ltd., Mechanisations and Aero Ltd. 40-47; Pres. Motor Trades Asscn. 34; Chair. Cruiser Tank Production Group; mem. Advisory Panel on Tank Production 41-45; Chair. British Tank Engine Mission to U.S. 42; Pres. Soc. Motor Manufacturers and Traders 47; Dir. Colonial Development Corpn. 47-51,

Deritend Stamping Co. 62-74; Chair. S. Rhodesian Govt. Development Comm. 47-50; Deputy Chair. BOAC 48-June 49, Chair. 49-56; Pres. IATA 51-52; Chair. Monsanto Chemicals Ltd. 56-63, Dir. Monsanto Europe Ltd. 63-65; Chair. British Productivity Council 59, Devt. Corpn. for Wales 58-67; Chair. Agricultural Central Trading Ltd. 62-67, Nat. Savings Movement 65-70, Pres. 65-72.

Leisure interests: shooting, fishing, photography.

Publ. *Out on a Wing* (autobiography) 64.

Remenham Court, Henley-on-Thames, Oxfordshire, England.

Telephone: Henley 5400.

Thomas, André Jean, D. EN MED., D. ÈS SC.; French biologist; b. 4 April 1905, Besançon; s. of Albert Thomas and Marie-Louise Sulter; m. Suzanne Anne-Marie Dautrement 1940; one s. two d.; ed. Lycée de Besançon and Faculté de Médecine, Paris.

Professor, Faculté des Sciences, Paris 46-50, Titular Prof. of Cellular Biology 51-, Dir. Centre for Cellular Physiology 55-; Deputy Dir. Ecole des Hautes Etudes 42-45, Dir. 46-; mem. Inst. Pasteur 29-68, Head of Cellular Biology Science 51-68; mem. Acad. des Sciences (Inst. de France), Acad. nationale de Médecine, and many other scientific socs.; Hon. Fellow, Int. Coll. of Surgeons; Officier, Légion d'Honneur, Ordre de Léopold (Belgium); Médaille de la Résistance.

Université de Paris VI, Centre de Physiologie cellulaire, 7 quai Saint-Bernard, 75005 Paris; Home: 8 rue Pierre et Marie Curie, 75005 Paris, France.

Telephone: 336-25-25, Ext. 34-20 (Office); 326-59-04 (Home).

Thomas, Sir Ben Bowen, Kt., B.A., M.A., LL.D.; former British civil servant; b. 1899, Ystrad Rhondda, Glam., S. Wales; s. of Jonathan and Ann Thomas; m. 1st Rhiannon Williams 1930 (died 1932), one d.; m. 2nd Gweneth Ellis Davies 1941 (died 1963); ed. Rhondda Grammar School, Univ. Coll. of Wales, Aberystwyth, and Jesus Coll., Oxford.

Lecturer in Adult Education, Univ. of Wales 22-27; Warden of Colegharlech 27-40; Dir. of Extra Mural Studies, Univ. of Wales 40-45; Chair. South Wales Manpower Board 41-45; Permanent Sec., Welsh Dept., Ministry of Education 45-63; mem. Exec. Board UNESCO 54-62, Chair. 58-60; Pres. Nat. Inst. of Adult Education 64-71, Univ. Coll. of Wales, Aberystwyth 64-, Welsh Council of UN Asscn. 64-68; Pres. Baptist Union of Wales 66-67; Pres. Hon. Soc. of Cymmrodorion 69-; Chair. North Wales Asscn. of the Arts; mem. Councils and Governing Bodies Univ. of Wales, Nat. Museum of Wales, Nat. Library of Wales, Independent Television Authority 64-70, Royal Comm. on the Constitution 69-73, etc.; Knight Bachelor 50; Hon. Fellow Jesus Coll., Oxford 63; Hon. LL.D. (Wales).

Leisure interests: strolling, travel.

Publs. *Economic History of Wales* (in Welsh), *The Old Order* (in English) 40, *The Ballads of Glamorgan* 52, *The Balladmonger's Mirror* 58 (both in Welsh), *Aber 1872-1972* 72; numerous articles in learned journals on Welsh literary and historical subjects.

Wern, Bodlondeb, Bangor, North Wales.

Telephone: Bangor 2971.

Thomas, Rt. Hon. George (see Thomas, Rt. Hon. Thomas George).

Thomas, Henri, L. ès L.; French writer and poet; b. 7 Dec. 1912; ed. Strasbourg Univ.

Teacher till 39; Forces 40-47; Programme Asst. B.B.C. French Section 47-58; Lecturer in French, Brandeis Univ. Mass., U.S.A. 56-60; in charge German Dept. Gallimard's Publishing House 60-; Prix Sainte-Beuve 56, Prix Médicis 60; Prix Fémina 61; Prix Valéry Larbaud 70; Chevalier Légion d'Honneur.

Publs. Verse: *Travaux d'Aveugle, Signe de Vie, Le Monde Absent, Nul Désordre*; Novels: *Le Seau à*

Charbon, Le Précepteur, La Vie Ensemble, Les Déserteurs, Le Porte-à-faux, La Nuit de Londres, La Dernière Année, John Perkins (Prix Médicis 6o), *Le Promontoire* (Prix Fémina 61), *La Chasse aux trésors, Le Parjure, Sous 6 Lien du Temps, La Relique, Tristan, le Dépossédé*; Short stories: *La Cible, Histoire de Pierrot.*
Editions Gallimard, 5 rue Sébastien-Bottin, 75007 Paris, France.

Thomas, Ivor Bulmer-, M.A.; British writer and politician; b. 30 Nov. 1905, Cwmbran, Mon.; s. of Alfred Ernest and Zipporah Thomas; m. 1st Dilys Llewelyn Jones 1932 (died 1938), one s.; 2nd Margaret Joan Bulmer 1940, one s. two d.; ed. St. John's and Magdalen Colls., Oxford.
Editorial staff of *The Times* 30-37; Chief Leader writer *News Chronicle* 37-39, on staff *Daily Telegraph* 52-56; served R. Fusiliers 39-42; Labour M.P. for Keighley 42-48, Independent, later Cons. 48-50; Parl. Sec. Ministry of Civil Aviation 45-46; Parl. Under-Sec. of State Colonial Office 46-47; mem. Gen. Synod of Church of England; Chair. Exec. Cttee. Historic Churches Preservation Trust 52-56; Sec. Ancient Monuments Soc. 57-; Hon. Dir. Friends of Friendless Churches 57-; Convener British Group Inst. Int. des Civilisations Différentes 59-; Joint Hon. Sec. Friends of St. John's 62-75 (Hon. Treas. 69-75); Chair. Redundant Churches Fund 69-; Fellow, Soc. of Antiquaries of London 70-.
Leisure interest: athletics.
Publs. *Coal in the New Era* 34, *Gladstone of Hawarden* 36, *Top Sawyer* 38, *Greek Mathematics* 39-42, *The Problem of Italy* 46, *The Socialist Tragedy* 49, *The Party System in Great Britain* 53, *Growth of the British Party System* 65, *Cio che è originale e cio che è derivato negli Elementi di Euclide* 73, *St. Paul: Teacher and Traveller* (editor) 75.
12 Edwardes Square, London, W8 6HG, England.
Telephone: 01-602-6267.

Thomas, Jean; French educationist; b. 10 Dec. 1900, Marseille; s. of Louis Augustin Thomas and Valentine Abric; ed. Ecole Normale Supérieure.
Répétiteur Ecole Normale Supérieure; Prof. Poitiers and Lyon Univs.; Chef de Service, Ministry of Nat. Education; Dir. Cultural Activities UNESCO 46-54; Asst. Dir. Gen. 54-60; Inspecteur-Gén. de l'Instruction Publique; Pres. Conseil du Bureau Int. d'éducation; Pres. Comm. Nat. pour l'éducation, la science et la culture; Commdr. Légion d'Honneur, Médaille de la Résistance, Commdr. des Palmes Académiques, Ordre des Arts et Lettres.
Publs. include *Le Romantisme Contemporain, L'Humanisme de Diderot, Sainte-Beuve et l'Ecole Normale, Le Vrai Système de Dom Deschamps, UNESCO, Education en Europe: Tendances Actuelles et Problèmes Communs, Des Maîtres pour l'Ecole de Demain, Les Grands Problèmes de l'Education dans le Monde.*
8 bis boulevard de Courcelles, Paris 17e, France.
Telephone: 622-34-49.

Thomas, John Frederick, M.A.; American international social welfare official; b. 24 Jan. 1907, Minneapolis, Minn.; s. of Frederick G. Thomas and Johanna M. Delene; m. 1st Harriet Larson Thomas 1943, two d.; m. 2nd Jean Meyers Sims Thomas 1972; ed. Univs. of Minnesota and Maryland.
Phyllis Wheatley Settlement House, Minn. 33-39; Nat. Youth Admin. Personnel, Minn. 39-42; served in U.S. Army 42-45; Welfare/Resettlement Officer UNNRA/IRO, U.S. Zone, Germany 45-52; Operations Officer, Intergovernmental Cttee. for European Migration (ICEM) 56-62; Dir. Cuban Refugee Programme, U.S. Govt. 62-68; Dir. Refugee Programme and Adviser to Govt. of S. Vietnam 68-69; Dir. ICEM 69-; Joseph Chamberlain Award 57, Superior Service Award (U.S. Govt.) 64, Social Service Medal (S. Vietnam Govt.) 68,

Rockefeller Service Award 69, Norwegian Refugee Council Medal 69, Nansen Ring 71, Vasco da Balboa Grand Cross (Panama) 72.
Leisure interests: bowling, ice-skating, golf.
Publ. *Planned International Migration and Multilateral Co-operation.*
16 avenue Jean Trembley, 1211 Geneva 19, Switzerland.
Telephone: 34-22-00.

Thomas, Llewellyn Hilleth, PH.D., D.SC.; American professor of theoretical physics; b. 21 Oct. 1903, London, England; s. of Charles James Thomas and Winifred May Thomas fmrly. Lewis; m. Naomi Estelle (Frech) Thomas 1933; one s. two d.; ed. Merchant Taylors School, Trinity Coll. Cambridge and Inst. of Theoretical Physics, Copenhagen.
Professor of Physics, Ohio State Univ. 29-43, 45-46; Physicist and Ballistician, Ballistic Research Lab., Aberdeen Proving Ground, Md. 43-45; mem. of Senior Staff, Watson Scientific Computing Lab., and Prof. of Physics, Columbia Univ. New York 46-68; Univ. Prof. N. Carolina State Univ., Raleigh 68-; mem. Nat. Acad. of Sciences 58; Smith Prize 25.
Leisure interests: mountain-walking, chess.
Publs. Over 100 papers in scientific journals.
Department of Physics, North Carolina State University, Raleigh, N.C. 27607; Home: 3012 Wycliff Road, Raleigh, N.C. 27607, U.S.A.
Telephone: 919-755-7515 (Office); 919-787-9050 (Home).

Thomas, Orlando Pendleton, B.S., M.B.A.; American rubber company executive; b. 14 June 1914, Forney, Tex.; s. of William Pendleton and Lottye Trail; three s.; ed. East Texas State Coll., Univ. of Texas, Wharton School of Univ. of Pennsylvania, New York Univ., and Harvard School of Business Admin.
U.S. Navy, Second World War; Sinclair Oil Corpn. 45-; Asst. Comptroller 54-57, Vice-Pres. 57-60, Dir. 60-; Exec. Vice-Pres. 60-64, Pres. 64-69, Chief Exec. Officer 68-69; on merger of Sinclair Oil Corpn. into Atlantic Richfield Co. March 69, became Chair. Exec. Cttee.; Chair. B. F. Goodrich Co. 71-; Dir. of Bristol-Myers Co., Kraftco Corpn., Rubber Mfrs. Asscn.; mem. Board of Trustees, Mutual Life Insurance Co. of N.Y.; Nat. Dir., mem. Exec. Cttee., Boy's Clubs of America; Hon. Dir. American Petroleum Inst.; mem. Newcomen Soc. in N. America, mem. Policy Cttee. Business Roundtable, Canadian Council; Trustee Eisenhower Exchange Fellowships, Conf. Board; Hon. LL.D. (East Texas State Univ.).
Leisure interest: golf.
B. F. Goodrich Co., 500 South Main Street, Akron, Ohio 44318, U.S.A.

Thomas, Rt. Hon. Peter, P.C., Q.C., M.P.; British barrister and politician; b. 1920; ed. Epworth Coll., Rhyl and Jesus Coll., Oxford.
Member of Parl. for Conway 51-66, for Hendon (South) 70-74, for Barnet, Hendon (South) 74-; Parl. Sec. Ministry of Labour 59-61; Under-Sec. Foreign Office 61-63; Minister of State for Foreign Affairs 63-64; Opposition Spokesman on Law and Foreign Affairs 64-66; Sec. of State for Wales 70-74; Chair. Conservative Party 70-72; Pres. Nat. Union of Conservative Asscns. 74-76; Master of the Bench, Middle Temple; Recorder of Crown Court; Conservative.
House of Commons, London, S.W.1, England.

Thomas, Philippe Henri André; French business executive; b. 25 Feb. 1918, Paris; m.; four c.; ed. Ecole Polytechnique.
Inspector of Finances 46; Private Sec. to Minister of Industry and Commerce 51; joined Pechiney 52, Head, Thermo-Electric Dept. 55, Dir. in charge of Dept. of Metals and Uses of Atomic Energy 62, Asst. Dir.-Gen. 65, Dir.-Gen. 68; Admin. Pechiney June 70-, also Aluminium de Grèce, Tréfimétaux; Pres. Dir.-Gen. Organico 58-63; Vice-Pres., Dir.-Gen. Aluminium

Français 64-67; Vice-Pres., Dir.-Gen. Pechiney-Ugine Kuhlmann 72-75, Pres. 75-; Chevalier, Légion d'Honneur; Croix de Guerre.

Pechiney, 23 rue Balzac, 75008 Paris, France.

Thomas, Rev. Ronald Stuart; Welsh clergyman and poet; ed. Univ. of Wales and St. Michael's Coll., Llandaff.

Ordained Deacon 36, Priest 37; Curate of Chirk 36-40, of Hanmer 40-42; Rector of Manafon 42-54; Vicar of St. Michael's, Eglwysfach 54-68, of Aberdaron 68-; Heinemann Award of Royal Soc. of Literature 56 for *Song at the Year's Turning*; Sovereign's Gold Medal for Poetry 64.

Publs. *Stones of the Field* (privately published) 47, *Song at the Year's Turning* 55, *Poetry for Supper* 58, *Tares* 61, *The Bread of Truth* 63, *Pieta* 66, *Not That He Brought Flowers* 68, *H'm* 72, *Selected Poems 1946-1968* 74.

The Vicarage, Aberdaron, Pwllheli, Gwynedd, Wales.

Thomas, Rt. Hon (Thomas) George, P.C., M.P.; British politician; b. 29 Jan. 1909; ed. Tonypandy Grammar School and Univ. Coll. of Southampton.

M.P. for Central Cardiff 45-50, W. Cardiff 50-; Parl. Under-Sec. of State, Home Office 64-66; Minister of State, Welsh Office 66-67, Commonwealth Office 67-68; Sec. of State for Wales 68-70; Deputy Speaker, House of Commons, Chair. Ways and Means Cttee. 74-76, Speaker Feb. 76-; Vice-Pres. Methodist Conf. 59-60; Labour.

Publ. *The Christian Heritage in Politics*.

Speaker's House, London, S.W.1; Home: Tilbury, 173 King George V Drive East, Heath, Cardiff, Glamorgan, Wales.

Thomas, Tracy Yerkes, A.B., M.A., PH.D.; American mathematician; b. 8 Jan. 1899, Alton, Ill.; s. of Tracy Reeve Thomas and Blanche Ailene Yerkes; m. Virginia Rowland 1928; one s.; ed. Rice Inst., and Princeton Univ.

National Research Fellow in Physics, Univ. of Chicago 23-24, in Mathematics Zürich Univ. 24-25, Harvard and Princeton Univs. 25-26; Asst. Prof. of Maths. Princeton Univ. 26-31, Assoc. Prof. 31-38; Prof. of Maths. Univ. of Calif. 38-44; Prof. of Maths. Indiana Univ. 44-69, Chair. of Dept. 44-54, Head Graduate Inst. for Applied Maths. 50-54, Dir. Graduate Inst. for Maths. and Mechanics 54-56, Distinguished Service Prof. of Maths. 56-69; Visiting Prof. Univ. of Calif., San Diego, at La Jolla 62-63, at Los Angeles 65-66, 67-68; Prof. in Residence, Univ. of Calif., Los Angeles 69-70; Fellow Indiana Acad. of Sciences, Royal Astronomical Soc.; mem. Soc. Eng. Science, American Math. Soc., Math. Asscn. of America, Nat. Acad. of Sciences.

Publs. include: *The Elementary Theory of Tensors* 31, *The Differential Invariants of Generalized Spaces* 34, *Concepts from Tensor Analysis and Differential Geometry* 61 (2nd edn. 65), *Plastic Flow and Fracture in Solids* 61, and papers on relativity theory, cosmology, plasticity, fracture, gas dynamics, shock waves, tensors, differential geometry and extended theory of conditions for discontinuities over moving surfaces.

249 N. Glenroy Avenue, Los Angeles, California 90049, U.S.A.

Telephone: 213-472-6562.

Thomaz, Admiral Américo de Deus Rodrigues; Portuguese naval officer and politician; b. 19 Nov. 1894, Lisbon; m. Gertrudes Ribeiro da Costa Rodrigues Thomaz 1922; ed. Naval Coll., Lisbon.

Midshipman 14; served on convoy duty to Great Britain and France during the First World War in the cruiser *Pedro Nunes* and the destroyers *Douro* and *Tejo*; 2nd-Lieut. 18; transferred to Hydrographic Board 19; served on board the hydrographic vessel *Cinco de Outubro* 20-36; 1st-Lieut. 22, Lieut.-Commdr. 31; Sec. Ministry of Marine 36-44, in charge of hydrographic survey of Portuguese coast; Commdr. 39; Pres. Nat. Mercantile Marine Board 40-44; Capt. 41; Minister of Marine 44-58; Rear-Admiral 51; Admiral 70; mem. Int. Council for the Exploration of the Sea, Fisheries Comm. and numerous other Portuguese and int. nautical, hydrographical and meteorological cttees.; Pres. of Portugal 58-74; in exile following coup April 74; living in Brazil.

Thompson, Sir Edward Hugh Dudley, Kt., M.B.E., T.D.; British company executive; b. 12 May 1907; ed. Uppingham and Lincoln Coll., Oxford.

Solicitor 31-36; Asst. Managing Dir. Ind. Coope and Allsopp Ltd. 36-39, Managing Dir. 39; Army Service 39-45; Managing Dir. Ind Coope Ltd. 45-55, Chair. 55-62; Chair. Brewers' Soc. 59-61; Dir. Allied Breweries Ltd. (Chair. and Chief Exec. 61-68), P-E Consulting Group, Sun Alliance and London Insurance Ltd.; High Sheriff of Derbyshire 64; Fellow, British Inst. of Management; Assoc. mem. Parl. Group for World Govt.

Culland Hall, Brailsford, Derbyshire, England.

Telephone: Brailsford 247.

Thompson, Edward K(ramer), A.B., D.HUM.LITT.; American editor; b. 17 Sept. 1907; ed. Univ. of North Dakota.

Editor Foster Co. *Independent*, Carrington, N.D. 27; City Ed. *Fargo* (N.D.) *Morning Forum* 27; Picture Ed., Asst. News Ed. *Milwaukee Journal* 27-37; Assoc. Ed. *Life* 37-42, Asst. Man. Ed. 45-49, Man. Ed., later Ed. 49-67; Ed. Smithsonian Inst. magazine 69-; served with U.S. Armed Forces 42-45; decorated Legion of Merit, Hon. O.B.E., Joseph Henry Medal, Smithsonian Inst. 73.

Home: 1601 28th Street, N.W., Washington, D.C. 20007; Office: Smithsonian Institution, Washington, D.C. 20560, U.S.A.

Thompson, Floyd LaVerne; American aeronautical engineer and research administrator (retd.); b. 25 Nov. 1898; ed. South Lyon High School, Salem, Michigan, and Univ. of Michigan.

Langley Research Center, Nat. Aeronautics and Space Admin. (NASA) 26-68, Aeronautical Engineer 26-45, Chief of Research 45-52, Assoc. Dir. 52-60, Dir. 60-68; Fellow American Inst. of Aeronautics and Astronautics; mem. American Asscn. for the Advancement of Science; NASA Award for Outstanding Leadership 63; Hon. D.Sc. Univ. of Mich., Coll. of William and Mary, Virginia.

94 Alleghany Road, Hampton, Virginia 23661, U.S.A.

Thompson, Sir Harold (Warris), Kt., C.B.E., F.R.S.; British chemist; b. 15 Feb. 1908; ed. King Edward VII School, Sheffield, Trinity Coll., Oxford, and Kaiser Wilhelm Inst. for Physical Chemistry, Berlin-Dahlem.

Fellow of St. John's Coll., Oxford 30-75; Reader in Spectroscopy, Oxford Univ. 54-64, Prof. of Physical Chemistry 64-75; mem. Council Royal Soc. 59-60, 61-64, 65-71, Vice-Pres. 63-64, 65-71, Foreign Sec. 65-71; Chair. British Nat. Cttee. for Chemistry 60-66; mem. Bureau Int. Union of Pure and Applied Chemistry (IUPAC) 63-71, Vice-Pres. 71-73, Pres. 73-75; Pres. Int. Council of Scientific Unions (ICSU) 63-66; mem. U.K. UNESCO Comm.; Chair. Great Britain/China Cttee. 72-; Vice-Chair. Football Asscn.; Editor *Spectrochimica Acta* 57-, *Advances in Spectroscopy* Vol. I 59, Vol. II 61; Chevalier Légion d'Honneur (France), Grand Service Cross (Fed. Repub. of Germany), Aztec Eagle (Mexico), and several other awards.

St. John's College, Oxford; Home: 33 Linton Road, Oxford, England.

Telephone: Oxford 58925.

Thompson, Homer Armstrong, B.A., M.A., PH.D.; Canadian-born American classical archaeologist; b. 7 Sept. 1906, Devlin, Ont.; s. of William J. and Gertrude Thompson; m. Dorothy Burr 1933; three d.; ed. Univs. of British Columbia and Michigan.

Staff mem., American School of Classical Studies excavations of the Athenian Agora 29-, Field Dir. 45-67; Prof. of Classical Archaeology, Toronto Univ. 33-47, Head of Dept. of Art and Archaeology 46-47; Prof., Princeton Inst. for Advanced Study 47-; Asst. Dir., Curator of Classical Collection, Royal Ont. Museum, Toronto 33-47; George Eastman Visiting Prof., Oxford Univ. 59-60; Geddes-Harrower Prof. of Greek Archaeology and Art, Aberdeen Univ. 64-65; Distinguished Visitor Australian-American Educ. Foundation; Corresp. Fellow British Acad.; Hon. mem. German Archaeological Inst., Soc. for Promotion of Hellenic Studies, Greek Archaeological Soc., Royal Soc. of Arts and Letters (Gothenburg), Acad. of Sciences (Heidelberg), Royal Swedish Acad., Soc. of Antiquaries (London); mem. American Philosophical Soc., American Acad. of Arts and Sciences; Commdr. Order of the Phoenix (Greece); Gold Medal Archaeological Inst. of America 72; Hon. LL.D. (Univs. of Toronto and British Columbia); Litt.D (Univ. of Michigan); L.H.D. (Dartmouth Coll., Univs. of Athens, Lyons, Freiburg, New York).
Leisure interests: gardening, mountaineering.
Publs. Studies in topography, architecture, sculpture and ceramics of ancient Athens (chiefly in *Hesperia*) 34-; *The Agora of Athens* (with R. E. Wycherley) 72.
Institute for Advanced Study, Princeton, N.J.; and 134 Mercer Street, Princeton, N.J. 08540, U.S.A.
Telephone: 609-924-4400.

Thompson, James Burleigh, Jr., PH.D.; American geologist; b. 20 Nov. 1921, Calais, Maine; s. of James B. and Edith (Peabody) Thompson; m. Eleanora Mairs 1957; one s.; ed. Dartmouth Coll. and Mass. Inst. of Technology.
Instructor in Geology, Dartmouth Coll. 42-46; Research Asst. in Geology, M.I.T. 46-47; Instructor in Petrology, Harvard Univ. 49-50, Asst. Prof. in Petrography 50-55, Assoc. Prof. of Mineralogy 55-60, Prof. 60-; mem. American Asscn. for the Advancement of Science, American Geophysical Union, American Acad. of Arts and Sciences, Nat. Acad. of Sciences, Geochemical Soc. (Pres. 68-69); Fellow, Geological Soc. of America, Mineralogical Soc. of America (Pres. 67-68); Faculty Fellowship, Fund for Advancement of Educ. (Ford Foundation) 52-53, Guggenheim Fellowship 63, Arthur L. Day Medal, Geological Soc. of America 64.
Leisure interests: skiing, mountain climbing.
Publs. articles on metamorphic petrology and geology of the Northern Appalachians in professional journals.
Department of Geological Sciences, Harvard University, Cambridge, Mass. 02138; Home: 20 Richmond Road, Belmont, Mass., U.S.A.
Telephone: 617-484-9525.

Thompson, Robert Henry Stewart, C.B.E., M.A., D.SC., D.M., B.CH., F.R.C.P., F.R.C.PATH., F.R.S.; British chemical pathologist; b. 2 Feb. 1912, Croydon; s. of Dr. Joseph H. Thompson and Mary E. Rutherford; m. Inge V. A. Gebert 1938; one s. two d.; ed. Trinity Coll., Oxford, and Guy's Hospital Medical School, London.
Adrian Stokes Travelling Fellowship to Hospital of Rockefeller Inst. for Medical Research, N.Y. 37-38, Gillson Research Scholar in Pathology, Society of Apothecaries, London 38; Fellow and Tutor, Univ. Coll., Oxford 38-47; Demonstrator in Biochemistry; Oxford Univ. 38-47; served as Major in R.A.M.C. 44-46; Dean of Medical School, Oxford 46-47; Prof. of Chemical Pathology, Guy's Hospital Medical School, Univ. of London, and Consulting Chemical Pathologist to Guy's Hospital 47-65; Courtauld Prof. of Biochemistry, Middlesex Hospital Medical School, Univ. of London 65-75; Trustee, Wellcome Trust 63-; awarded Radcliffe Prize for Medical Research, Oxford 43; mem. Biochemical Society; Fellow, Royal Society of Medicine;

Sec.-Gen. Int. Union of Biochemistry 55-65; mem. British Nat. Cttee. for Biochemistry 67-70.
Leisure interest: gardening.
Publs. *Biochemistry in Relation to Medicine* (with C. W. Carter) 53, *Biochemical Disorders in Human Disease* (with I. D. P. Wootton) 3rd edn. 70; numerous papers in medical and scientific journals.
27 Wheeler Avenue, Oxted, Surrey, England.
Telephone: Oxted 3526.

Thompson, Robert Norman, B.SC., D.C., LL.D., F.R.G.S.; Canadian politician and educator; b. 17 May 1914, Duluth, Minn.; s. of Theodore Olaf Thompson and Hannah Olafson Thompson; m. Hazel Maxine Kurth 1939; five s. three d.; ed. Provincial Normal School, Calgary, Garbutt's Business Coll., Calgary, Bob Jones Univ., Greenville, Univ. of British Columbia, Palmer Coll. of Chiropractic and Wheaton Coll.
Public school teacher, Alberta 34-36; chiropractor 39-40; service in Second World War 40-43; Officer Commanding Imperial Ethiopian Air Force Acad. 43-44; Asst. Headmaster Haile Selassie Secondary School, Ethiopia 44-46; Dir. of Educ. Kaffa Province, Ethiopia 46; Dir. of Provincial Educ. Ministry of Educ., Ethiopia 47-51; Headmaster Haile Selassie Secondary School, Addis Ababa 47-51; diplomatic missions for Ethiopian Govt. 46-58; Educ. Dir. Sudan Interior Mission 52-58; Pres. Social Credit Asscn. Canada 60-61; Nat. Leader, Social Credit Party 61-67; Conservative M.P. 68-72; Prof. of Political Science, Waterloo Lutheran Univ. 68-72; Nat. Co-ordinator of Organization, Canadian Conservative Party 68-72; Chair. of Board World Vision of Canada 66-; Pres. Gospel Recording of Canada 71-73; Pres. Evangelical Fellowship of Canada 71-; Pres. Thompson Assocs. Ltd.; Dir. Greenarctic Consortium, B.C. and Yukon Regional Chamber of Commerce; Vice-Pres. Trinity Western Coll., Vancouver; Fellow, Royal Geographical Soc., London; Knight Commdr. Order of St. Lazarus of Jerusalem; mem. Inter-Parl. Union, Commonwealth Parl. Asscn. NATO Parl. Asscn., Gideons Int., Christian Businessmen of Canada Int.; Commdr. Ethiopian Star of Honour.
Leisure interests: reading, camping, hiking, farming.
Publs. *Common Sense for Canadians, Canadians, It's Time You Knew, Canadians Face Facts*.
House of Commons, Ottawa; 8989 Hudson Bay Street, Fort Langley, B.C., Canada.
Telephone: (604) 534-5381 (Office); (604) 534-1366 (Home).

Thompson, Thomas Miller, B.A., B.S.; American transportation executive; b. 25 July 1917; one s. two d.; ed. Western Reserve Univ., Cleveland, Ohio.
General American Transportation Corpn. 39-, East Chicago 39-41, Union Refrigerator Transit Div. 41, Office Manager, Cleveland 45-52, Asst. Vice-Pres. Chicago 52-58, Dir. and Vice-Pres. 58-60, Pres. 60-61, Chair. of Board and Chief Exec. Officer 61-; U.S. Marine Corps 42-45; official of other companies and civic orgs.
Leisure interests: golf, reading.
General American Transportation Corporation, 120 South Riverside Plaza, Chicago, Illinois 60680; Home: 777 Sunset Ridge Road, Northfield, Illinois 60093, U.S.A.

Thompson, Tyler; American government official; b. 21 Sept. 1907, Elmira, N.Y.; s. of Merle D. Thompson and Louise Henry Thompson; m. Ruth Hunt 1931; one s. one d.; ed. Princeton Univ.
Vice-Consul Cherbourg, France 31-33, Marseille 33-37; Sec. of Embassy and Vice-Consul, Paris 37-41; Vice-Consul, Zürich 41; Vichy, France 41-42; interned 42-44; Consul, Oran, Algeria June-Sept. 44, Marseille Oct.-Dec. 44; Sec. of Embassy and Consul, Paris 44-46; Dept. of State 46; Chief Div. of Foreign Service Planning 46-49; Student Nat. War Coll. 49-50; Counsellor, Prague 50-51;

Exec. Dir. Bureau of European Affairs, Dept. of State 52-55; Minister to Canada 55-60; Ambassador to Iceland 60-61; Dir.-Gen. of Foreign Service 61-64; Ambassador to Finland 64-69; retd.
Leisure interests: sailing, skiing, fishing, tennis.
The Eddy, Hancock, Maine 04640, U.S.A.

Thomsen, Christian; Danish politician; b. 1909, Svostrup, Co. Viborg.
Trained as nursery-man and worked in various gardening establishments abroad; Foreman, Brostrøm Nursery 33-34; Municipal Horticulturist, Viborg 38-; mem. Viborg Town Council 40-50; mem. Folketing for Viborg 53-; Minister of Agriculture 64-68, for Fisheries 71-73; mem. Exec. Cttee. Danish Garden Workers' Trade Union; mem. numerous cttees. dealing with agriculture and related subjects; mem. Danish Del. to Council of Europe 62-64; Social Democrat.
Folketing, Copenhagen, Denmark.

Thomsen, Ib; American business executive; b. 8 Oct. 1925, Copenhagen, Denmark; s. of Niels Thomas and Magda Marie Thomsen; m. Lisa Edith Voss 1947; two s. one d.; ed. Harvard Univ. Graduate School of Business Admin.
Joined Goodyear Int. Corpn. 52; Treas. Goodyear-India 57-58; Treas. Goodyear-U.K. 58, Financial Dir. and Sec. 61, Asst. to Man. Dir. 64, Deputy Man. Dir. 64, Man. Dir. 66; Vice-Pres. Goodyear Int. Corpn. 71, Pres. Aug. 72-; Dir. and Exec. Vice-Pres. Goodyear Tire & Rubber Co. 73-.
Goodyear International Corporation, 1144 East Market Street, Akron, Ohio 44316; Home: 15 Southwood Road, Akron, Ohio 44313, U.S.A.
Telephone: 794-2026 (Office); 867-6910 (Home).

Thomsen, Knud, M.SC.; Danish industrial executive and politician; b. 1908, Aalborg.
With Int. Patent Bureau 31; on staff of Tech. Univ. 31-32; industrial and commercial training in paint and lacquer industry 33-36; Asst. Man. Kemisk Vaerk, Koge, then Man. 46-66; Chair. Asscn. of Chem. Industries 52-; mem. Cttee. of Fed. of Danish Industries 55-; mem. Cttee. of Acad. of Tech. Sciences 62-; Chair. Board of Dirs. of Research Lab. of Paint and Varnish Industry 65-; Dir. Ballin and Hertz (leather) 60-, Carlsberg Brewery Council 60-, Cold Stores Ltd. 62-, Glent and Co. 66-; mem. Folketing 60-; mem. Gen. Council of Conservative Party 65-, Chair. of Conservative Foundation 65-; Minister of Commerce 68-71.
The Folketing, Copenhagen, Denmark.

Thomsen, Roszel C.; American judge; b. 17 Aug. 1900, Baltimore, Md.; s. of William E. Thomsen and Georgie A. (Cathcart) Thomsen; m. Carol Griffing Wolf 1929; one s. two d.; ed. Boys Latin School, Baltimore, Johns Hopkins Univ., and Univ. of Maryland.
Legal practice, Soper, Bowie and Clark 22-27, partner, Clark, Thomsen and Smith 27-54; Trustee, Goucher Coll. 36-, Chair. Board of Trustees 54-67; U.S. Dist. Judge, Maryland District 54-55, Chief Judge 55-70; U.S. District Judge 70-; Instructor in Commercial Law, Johns Hopkins Univ. 33-43, Law School, Univ. of Maryland 52-55; mem. Judicial Conf. of United States 58-64; mem. Advisory Cttee. on Civil Rules 60-70, Co-ordinating Cttee. for Multiple Litigation 62-68, Cttee. to Implement the Criminal Justice Act of 1964 64-74, Interim Advisory Cttee. on Judicial Ethics 69-73, Cttee. on Admin. of the Criminal Law 71-73; Chair. Standing Cttee. on Rules of Practice and Procedure of the U.S.A. 73-.
Leisure interests: literature, drama.
506 United States Court House, 111 North Calvert Street, Baltimore, Maryland 21202, U.S.A.
Telephone: Mulberry 5-3522.

Thomson, David Spence, M.C., M.P.; New Zealand dairy farmer and politician; b. 14 Nov. 1915, Stratford;

m. June Grace 1942; one s. three d.; ed. Stratford Primary and High School.
Territorial Army 31-59, served Middle East 39-42, Prisoner of war 42-45, Brigadier (Reserve of Officers); Chair. Federated Farmers Sub-provincial Exec. 59-63; M.P. for Stratford 63-; Minister of Defence, Minister in charge of Tourism, Minister in charge of Publicity 66-Feb. 67; Minister of Defence, Minister Asst. to Prime Minister, Minister in charge of War Pensions, Minister in charge of Rehabilitation Feb.-March 67; Minister of Defence, Minister of Tourism, Minister Asst. to Prime Minister, Minister in charge of Publicity, Minister in charge of War Pensions, Minister in charge of Rehabilitation March 67-Dec. 69; Minister of Defence, of Police, in charge of War Pensions, in charge of Rehabilitation 69-72; Assoc. Minister of Labour and Immigration 71-72, Minister Feb.-Nov. 72; Minister of Justice Nov. 75-; National Party.
Leisure interests: fishing, golf, music.
Bird Road, Stratford, New Zealand.

Thomson, Rt. Hon. George Morgan, P.C.; British journalist and politician; b. 16 Jan. 1921, Stirling, Scotland; s. of James Thomson; m. Grace Jenkins 1948; two d.; ed. Grove Acad., Dundee.
Royal Air Force 40-45; Editor *Forward* 46-53; M.P. 52-72; Chair. Commonwealth Educ. Council 59-64; Chair. Parl. Group for World Govt. 62-64; Minister of State, Foreign Office 64-66, Jan.-Aug. 67; Chancellor of Duchy of Lancaster 66-67; Sec. of State for Commonwealth Affairs 67-68; Minister without Portfolio 68-69; Chancellor of Duchy of Lancaster and Deputy Foreign Sec. (with special responsibility for European Affairs and Common Market negotiations) Oct. 69-June 70; Opposition Spokesman on Defence 70-72; Chair. Standing Conf. of British Refugee Organizations 71-; Chair. David Davies Memorial Institute 71-; Chair. Labour Cttee. for Europe 72-73; mem. Comm. of European Communities, with special responsibility for Regional Policy 73-; Hon. LL.D. (Dundee Univ.) 67, D.Litt. (Heriot-Watt Univ.) 73; Labour.
Leisure interests: swimming, walking.
EEC Commission, 200 rue de la Loi, 1040 Brussels, Belgium; 7 Carver Road, London, S.E.24, England.

Thomson, James E.; American (naturalized) business executive; b. 29 June 1905, Ontario, Canada; m. Dorothy Miskimin 1927; one s. one d.
Joined Merrill Lynch as runner 24, Exec. Vice-Pres. 64-66, Pres. 66-68, Vice-Chair. April 68, Chair. and Chief Exec. Officer 68-70; Gov., American Stock Exchange 62-66; Gov., New York Stock Exchange 66-69.
Leisure interests: bridge, golf.
165 Broadway, New York, N.Y. 10006; and 1000 Minisink Way, Westfield, N.J. 07090, U.S.A.

Thomson, Sir John, K.B.E., T.D., M.A.; British banker; b. 3 April 1908, Oxfordshire; s. of Guy and Evelyn Vera (Hughes) Thomson; m. Elizabeth Brotherhood, 1953; ed. Winchester Coll. and Magdalen Coll. Oxford.
High Sheriff of Oxfordshire 57; Vice-Chair. Barclays Bank Ltd. 56-58, Deputy Chair. 58-62, Chair. 62-73, now Dir.; Chair. Nuffield Medical Trustees, Nuffield Orthopaedic Trust; Pres. British Bankers Asscn. 64-66; Dir. Union Discount Co. of London 60-74; Lord Lieut. of Oxfordshire 63-; mem. Royal Comm. on Trade Unions and Employers Asscns. 65-68; Steward and Trustee, Jockey Club; Deputy High Steward, Oxford Univ.; Curator, Oxford Univ. Chest 49-74; Hon. D.C.L. (Oxon.); Knight of the Order of St. John.
Woodperry House, Woodperry, Oxford, England.

Thomson, Hon. Kenneth (Roy), B.A., M.A.; Canadian newspaper proprietor; b. 1 Sept. 1923, Toronto; s. of Lord Thomson of Fleet (*q.v.*) and Edna Alice Irvine;

m. Nora Marilyn Lavis 1956; two *s.* one *d.*; ed. Upper Canada Coll. and Cambridge Univ.

Served with Canadian Air Force during Second World War; in Editorial Dept., *Timmins Daily Press*, Timmins, Ont. 47; Advertising Dept. *Galt Reporter* 48-50, Gen. Man. 50-53; directed U.S. and Canadian Operations of Thomson Newspapers in Toronto 53-68; Deputy Chair. Times Newspapers Ltd. 66-67, Chair. 68-70, Co-Pres. 71-; Pres. and Dir. Thomson Newspapers Ltd.; Joint Chair. Thomson Organisation Ltd. 71-; Dir. Abitibi Paper Co. Ltd., Toronto, The Toronto Dominion Bank, Imperial Life Assurance Co. of Canada, Toronto.

Leisure interests: collecting antiques and paintings.

Thomson Newspapers Limited, Thomson Building, 65 Queen Street West, Toronto 102, Ontario, Canada; and Times Newspapers Ltd., New Printing House Square, Gray's Inn Road, London, WC1X 8EZ, England; Home: 8 Castle Frank Road, Toronto 5, Ontario, Canada; and 8 Kensington Palace Gardens, London, W.8, England.

Thomson, Richard Murray, B.A.SC.(ENG.), M.B.A.; Canadian banker; b. 14 Aug. 1933, Winnipeg, Man.; *s.* of H. W. Thomson; *m.* Heather Lorimer 1959; ed. Univ. of Toronto, Harvard Business School, Queen's Univ., Kingston, Ont.

Joined Toronto-Dominion Bank, Head Office 57, Senior Asst. Man., St. James & McGill, Montreal 61, Asst. to Pres., Head Office 63, Asst. Gen. Man. 65, Deputy Chief Gen. Man. 65, Vice-Pres., Chief Gen. Man., Dir. 71, Pres. 72-; Dir. Eaton's of Canada, Canadian Gypsum Co., S. C. Johnson & Co. Ltd., Texasgulf Inc., Cadillac Fairview Corpn. Ltd., Union Carbide of Canada; Trustee, Hospital for Sick Children. Leisure interests: golf, tennis, skiing.

Toronto-Dominion Bank, King and Bay Streets, Toronto 1; and 69 Dawlish Avenue, Toronto, Ont., Canada.

Thomson, Virgil, A.B.; American composer and critic; b. 25 Nov. 1896, Kansas City, Mo.; *s.* of Quincy A. and May Gaines Thomson; ed. Harvard Univ., and studied under Nadia Boulanger and Rosario Scalero.

Assistant Instructor in Music, Harvard Univ. 21-25; Organist, King's Chapel, Boston 22-23; lived in Paris 25-40; Music Critic *N.Y. Herald Tribune* 40-54; Pulitzer Prize in Music 49; Gold Medal Nat. Inst. of Arts and Letters 66; Brandeis Award 68; mem. American Acad. of Arts and Letters, American Acad. Arts and Sciences; Officier Légion d'Honneur; Hon. D.F.A. (Syracuse Univ.), Hon. Litt.D. (Rutgers Univ.), Litt. Hum. Doc. (Park Coll., Roosevelt Univ., Fairfield Univ.), D.Mus. (N.Y. Univ., Univ of Mo.).

Publs. *The State of Music* 39, *The Musical Scene* 45, *The Art of Judging Music* 48, *Music Right and Left* 51, *Virgil Thomson* (memoirs) 66, *Music Reviewed 1940-54* 67, *American Music since 1910* 71.

Compositions include: three operas: *Four Saints in Three Acts* 28, *Filling Station* (ballet) 38, *The Mother of Us All* 47, *Lord Byron* 68, *Parson Weems and the Cherry Tree* (ballet) 75; incidental music for plays and films, including: *The Plow that Broke the Plains* 36, *The River* 37, *Louisiana Story* 48, *The Goddess* 57, *Power Among Men* 57, *Journey to America* 64; three Symphonies and many shorter works for orchestra (incl. twelve Portraits and eight Suites), a Cello Concerto, a Flute Concerto, a Concertino for Harp, two String Quartets, and other chamber music; four Piano Sonatas and many short piano pieces, songs and choruses; *Missa pro Defunctis* for men's and women's choirs and orchestra.

Leisure interest: cooking.

222 West 23rd Street, New York, N.Y. 10011, U.S.A.

Thomson of Fleet, 1st Baron (cr. 64), of Northbridge in the City of Edinburgh; **Roy Herbert Thomson,** G.B.E. (father of Kenneth Thomson, *q.v.*); British newspaperman; b. 5 June 1894; *s.* of Herbert Thomson; *m.* Edna Alice Irvine 1916 (died 1951); ed. Jarvis Collegiate, Toronto, Canada.

Chair. The Scotsman Publications Ltd., Scottish Television Ltd. until 69, Thomson Organisation of Great Britain Ltd., Thomson Newspapers Ltd. (Toronto), Northern Broadcasting Co. Ltd., Thomson Newspapers Inc. (U.S.A.) and other companies; Vice-Pres. Periodical Proprietors' Asscn. Ltd.; Trustee, Reuters; Dir. The Royal Bank of Canada Trust Corpn., Security Trust Co. of Birmingham Ltd.; fmr. Chancellor, Memorial Univ. of Newfoundland 61; Fellow Royal Soc. of Arts; Fellow British Inst. of Management; Commdr. Royal Order of Phoenix, Greece; Hon. D.Litt. (St. John's Memorial Univ., Newfoundland); Hon. D.C.L. (New Brunswick Univ.); Hon. LL.D. (Northern Mich. Univ.); Hon. H.L.D. (L.I. Univ., N.Y.).

Publ. *After I Was Sixty* 75.

Office: Thomson Organisation Limited, P.O. Box 47G, 4 Stratford Place, London, W1A 47G; Home: Alderbourne Arches, Fulmer, Bucks., England.

Thondaman, Savumiamoorthy; Ceylonese agriculturalist; b. 30 Aug. 1913; ed. St. Andrew's Coll., Gampola.

Member Ceylon Parl. 47-51, 60-; mem. ILO Asian Advisory Cttee., Substitute Deputy mem. Governing Body of ILO; Leader, Ceylon Workers' Congress; Leader of struggle for political and econ. rights by one million persons of Indian origin in Sri Lanka.

Wavendon Group, Rambod, Sri Lanka.

Thonemann, Peter Clive, M.SC., D.PHIL., F.P.S.; British physicist; b. 3 June 1917; ed. Univs. of Melbourne and Sydney and Trinity Coll., Oxford.

Commonwealth Research Scholar (Sydney Univ.) 44-46; I.C.I. Fellow, Clarendon Laboratory, Oxford, 46-49; Head of Controlled Thermonuclear Research A.E.R.E., Harwell 49-60, Deputy Dir., Culham Laboratory of the Atomic Energy Authority 65-66; Prof. of Physics and Head of Dept., Univ. Coll., Swansea 68-.

Department of Physics, University College, Swansea, Singleton Park, Swansea, Wales; 33 Cumnor Hill, Oxford, England.

Thorley, Sir Gerald Bowers, Kt., T.D.; British business executive; b. 1913, Burton-on-Trent; *m.* Beryl Preston (née Rhodes) 1947; one *s.* one *d.*; ed. Ratcliffe Coll., Leicester.

Joined Ind Coope & Allsopp 35; mil. service and prisoner-of-war 39-45; Dir. Ind Coope 47, later Chair.; Dir. Allied Breweries Ltd. 61, Vice-Chair. 67, Deputy Chair. 69, Chief Exec. and Chair. 70-Sept. 75; Govt. Dir. and Chair. British Sugar Corpn. April 68-; Chair. Metropolitan Estate and Property Corpn. (MEPC) 76-; Dir. Rockware Glass Co., British American-Tobacco Co. Ltd. 74-.

Leisure interests: gardening, golf, agriculture.

Home: Church House, Bale, Fakenham, Norfolk, England.

Telephone: Thursford 314.

Thorn, Gaston, D. EN D.; Luxembourg politician; b. 3 Sept. 1928, Luxembourg; *s.* of Edouard Thorn and Suzanne Weber; *m.* Liliane Petit 1957; one *s.*; ed. Univs. of Montpellier, Lausanne and Paris.

Admitted to Luxembourg Bar; Pres. Nat. Union of Students, Luxembourg; mem. Legislature 59-; mem. European Parl. 59-69, Vice-Pres. Liberal Group; Pres. Democratic Party, Luxembourg 61-; Minister of Foreign Affairs 69-, of Foreign Trade, Civil Service, Physical Educ. and Sport 69-74; Prime Minister 74-; Pres. Liberal Int. 70-; Pres. of 30th Session of the UN Gen. Assembly Sept. 75-(Sept. 76).

Leisure interests: lecturing, tennis, golf.

Office of the Prime Minister, Luxembourg; and 1 rue de la Forge, Luxembourg.

Telephone: 420-77.

Thorn, George Widmer, M.D.; American physician; b. 15 Jan. 1906, Buffalo, N.Y.; s. of George W. and Fanny (Widmer) Thorn; m. Doris Weston 1931; one s.; ed. Coll. of Wooster, Ohio.

House Officer, Millard Fillmore Hospital, Buffalo (N.Y.) 29-30; Asst. Univ. of Buffalo 31-34; Rockefeller Fellow in Medicine, Harvard Medical School and Mass. Gen. Hospital 34-35; Asst. Prof. Dept. of Physiology, Ohio State Univ. 35-36; Assoc. Prof. of Medicine, Johns Hopkins Medical School, Assoc. Physician Johns Hopkins Hospital 36-42; Physician-in-Chief, Peter Bent Brigham Hospital, Hersey Prof. of Theory and Practice of Physic, Harvard Univ. 42-72 (Emer. 72); Samuel A. Levine Prof. of Medicine, Harvard Medical School 67-72 (Emer. 72); Dir. of Research, Howard Hughes Medical Inst. 56-; mem. Corpn. and of Exec. Cttee. of Corpn. of Mass. Inst. of Technology 65-; First Wingate Johnson Visiting Prof., Bowman Gray School of Medicine, Wake Forest Univ. 72; Consultant U.S. Public Health Service, etc.; Fellow, Royal College of Physicians, London; mem. Nat. Advisory Cttee. on Radiation; Trustee, Diabetic Fund; numerous awards including John Philips Memorial Award (American Coll. of Physicians) 55, Modern Medicine Award 61, George Minot Award (American Medical Asscn.) 63, Robert H. Williams Award (Asscn. of Profs. of Medicine) 72; Hon. mem. Soc. Colombiana de Endocrinologia (Bogotá), Royal Soc. of Medicine (Great Britain); mem. Royal Acad. of Medicine (Belgium), Norwegian Medical Soc., Swedish Medical Soc.; First Lilly Lecturer, Royal Coll. of Physicians, London 66; Commdr. Order of Hipólito Unanue (Peru).

Leisure interests: tennis, music, arboriculture.

45 Shattuck Street, Boston, Mass. 02115; 983 Memorial Drive, Cambridge, Mass. 02138, U.S.A.

Telephone: 617-876-6410 (Home).

Thorn, Sir Jules, Kt.; British business executive. Chairman, Thorn Electrical Industries Ltd. 37-(Aug. 76), Man. Dir. 37-69; Fellow of British Inst. of Management; Hon. Master of the Bench of Middle Temple 69.

Thorn Electrical Industries Ltd., Thorn House, Upper St. Martin's Lane, London, WC2H 9ED, England.

Thornbrough, Albert A.; American business executive; b. 1912; ed. Kansas State Coll.

President, Chief Exec. Officer and Dir., Massey-Ferguson Ltd., Toronto.

200 University Avenue, Toronto, Ontario, Canada.

Thorndike, Dame Sybil, C.H., D.B.E.; British actress; b. 24 Oct. 1882, Gainsborough, Lincs.; d. of Canon A. F. W. and Agnes (née MacDonald) Thorndike; m. Lewis Casson 1908 (died 1969); two s. two d.; ed. Rochester High School.

Began theatrical career touring U.S.A. in Shakespearian repertory 03; with Miss Horniman's Co., Manchester 08-09, leading parts 11-13; management in London 22-27; South African tour 28; toured Middle East, Australia and New Zealand 32-33; several tours with Old Vic 40-42; tour of Belgium, France and Germany 45-46; recital tour of Australasia, Africa, Far East, Israel and Turkey 54-56, of Australia 62.

Recent plays include: *A Family Reunion* 56, *The Potting Shed* (London and New York) 56, *The Chalk Garden* (London and Australia) 57-58, *Eighty in the Shade* 59, *Waiting in the Wings* 60-61, *Vanity Fair* 62, *Uncle Vanya* 62, *The Reluctant Peer* 64, *Season of Goodwill* 64, *Return Ticket* 65, *Arsenic and Old Lace* 66, *The Viaduct* 67, *Night Must Fall* 68, *There Was an Old Woman* 69; Films: *Dawn, Prince and the Showgirl, Big Gamble, Hand in Hand*; Hon. D.Litt. (Oxford), Hon. LL.D. (Southampton, Surrey, Durham, Manchester and Edinburgh Univs.).

Leisure interests: piano playing, reading.

Publs. *Religion and the Stage, Lillian Baylis* (with Russell Thorndike), *Favourites* (Editor) 73.

98 Swan Court, London, S.W.3, England.

[*Died 9 June 1976.*]

Thorneycroft, Baron (Life Peer), cr. 67, of Dunston in the County of Stafford; **(George Edward) Peter Thorneycroft,** P.C.; British barrister and politician; b. 26 July 1909; ed. Eton and Royal Military Acad., Woolwich.

Commissioned service in Royal Artillery 30-33; called to Bar, Inner Temple 35; practised in Birmingham; served Royal Artillery in Second World War; Conservative M.P. for Stafford 38-45, for Monmouth 45-66; Parl. Sec., Ministry of War Transport 45; Pres. of the Board of Trade 51-57, Chancellor of the Exchequer 57-58; Minister of Aviation 60-62, of Defence 62-64; Sec. of State for Defence April-Oct. 64; Dir. Pirelli Ltd. Dec. 64-, Securicor Ltd. 69-; Chair. Pirelli Gen. Cable Works Ltd. 67-, Pye of Cambridge Ltd. 67-, Pye Holdings Ltd. 67-, SITPRO (Simplification of Int. Trade Procedures) 68-75, Pirelli Ltd. 69-, Trust Houses Forte Ltd. 71-, British Overseas Trade Board 72-75; Chair. of Conservative Party Feb. 75-.

House of Lords, London, S.W.1, England.

Telephone: 01-219-4093.

Thornton, Charles Bates, B.C.S.; American business executive; b. 22 July 1913, Knox Co., Tex.; m. Flora Laney Thornton; two s.; ed. Texas Technological Coll., George Washington Univ., and Columbia Univ.

U.S. Army Air Force, Second World War, Consultant to Commdg. Gen. A.A.F. 46, to Under-Sec. Dept. of State 47; Dir. of Planning, Ford Motor Co. 46-48; Vice-Pres., Chair., Exec. Cttee., Hughes Aircraft Co. 48, Asst. Gen. Man. 48-53; Vice-Pres. Hughes Tool Co. 48-53; Chair. and Pres. Litton Industries Inc. 53-61, now Chair. of the Board and Chief Exec. Officer; Dir. United Calif. Bank, Cyprus Mines, Inc.; Dir. and mem. Finance Cttee. Trans World Airlines Inc.; many other directorships; mem. Emergency Cttee. for American Trade, The Business Council, and of many other asscns. and cttees.; Trustee, Univ. of S. Calif.; Hon. D.C.S. (George Washington Univ.), Hon. D.Iur. (Texas Technological Coll. and Univs. of S. Calif. and Pepperdine); Distinguished Service Medal, Legion of Merit, and many civilian awards.

Office: 360 North Crescent Drive, Beverly Hills, Calif. 90213, U.S.A.

Thorp, Willard Long, A.M., PH.D.; American economist; b. 24 May 1899, Oswego, N.Y.; s. of Rev. Charles N. Thorp and Susan Long (Thorp); m. Clarice F. Brows; one s. two d.; ed. Amherst Coll., Univ. of Michigan, and Columbia Univ.

Taught Econs. at Univ. of Michigan and Amherst Coll. 26-34; Research Staff of the Nat. Bureau of Econ. Research 23-33; Chief Statistician N.Y. State Board of Housing 25-26; Dir. U.S. Bureau of Foreign and Domestic Commerce 33-34; Dir. Econ. Research, Dun & Bradstreet Inc. and Editor of *Dun's Review* 35-40; Econ. Adviser to Sec. of Commerce 39-40; Chair. of Board of Gen. Public Utilities Corpn. 40-46; Dep. to Asst. Sec. of State for Econ. Affairs 45-46; asst. Sec. of State for Econ. Affairs 46-52; U.S. rep. UN Econ. and Social Council 46-50; Prof. of Econs., Amherst Coll. and Dir. Merrill Center for Econs. 52-65; Fellow American Acad. of Arts and Sciences; Dir. Nat. Bureau Econ. Research 56-; Trustee Associated Gas and Electric Corpn. 40-46, Brandeis Univ. 56-62; American Asscn. Univ. Profs. Council 57-60; Foreign Bondholders Protective Council 58-63; Nat. Comm. on Money and Credit 58-61; Acting Pres. Amherst Coll. 57; Chief UN Econ. Survey Mission to Cyprus 60; Chief, President's Special Econ. Mission to Bolivia 61; Chair. Development Assistance Cttee. O.E.C.D. 63-67; Senior Fellow, Council on Foreign Relations, N.Y.C. 68-69; Phi Beta

Kappa Visiting Scholar 69; Consultant, Admin. Man., UN 70-72; Distinguished Visiting Prof. Univ. of Florida 71; Hon. LL.D. (Marietta, Amherst, Albright Colls., Univs. of Mass., Michigan).
Publs. *The Integration of Industrial Operation* 24, *Business Annals* 26, *Economic Institutions* 28, *The Structure of Industry* (co-author) 41, *Trade, Aid or What?* 54, *The New Inflation* (co-author) 59; contrib. to *Recent Economic Changes, Cyprus: Suggestions for a Development Program* 61; Editor: *Economic Problems in a Changing World* 39, *The United States and the Far East* (American Assembly series 56), 62, *Development Assistance Efforts and Policies* 63, 64, 65, 67, *The Reality of Foreign Aid* 71.
9 Harkness Road, Amherst, Mass. 01002, U.S.A.
Telephone: 413-256-8019.

Thorpe, Rt. Hon. (John) Jeremy, P.C., M.P.; British politician; b. 29 April 1929; m. 1st Caroline Allpass 1968 (died 1970), one s.; m. 2nd Maria (Marion) Stein, fmr. Countess of Harewood, 1973; ed. Rectory School, Conn., Eton Coll. and Trinity Coll., Oxford.
Barrister, Inner Temple 54; mem. Devon Sessions; mem. Parl. for North Devon 59-; Treas. UN Parl. Group 62-67; Hon. Treas. Liberal Party 65-67, Leader 67-76.
Publs. *To All Who Are Interested in Democracy* 51, *Europe: The Case for Going In* 71.
House of Commons, London, S.W.1, England.

Thorpe, William Homan, M.A., SC.D., F.R.S.; British zoologist specializing in animal behaviour; b. 1 April 1902, Hastings, Sussex; s. of Francis Homan Thorpe and Mary Amelia Thorpe (née Slade); m. Winifred Mary Vincent 1936; one d.; ed. Mill Hill School and Jesus Coll., Cambridge.
Research Fellow of Int. Educ. Board (Rockefeller Foundation), Univ. of Calif. 27-29; Research Entomologist, Farnham Royal Parasite Lab. of Imperial Bureau of Entomology 29-32; Tutor, Jesus Coll., Cambridge 32-45, Senior Tutor 45-47; Lecturer in Entomology, Univ. of Cambridge 32-59; Leverhulme Research Fellow in E. Africa 39; Dir. Sub-Dept. of Animal Behaviour, Univ. of Cambridge 59-69; Prof. of Animal Ethology, Univ. of Cambridge 66-69; Pres. Asscn. for Study of Animal Behaviour 48-52, Soc. of British Entomology 51-53, British Ornithologists' Union 55-60, Section D (Zoology), British Asscn. (Sheffield) 56; Prather Lecturer in Biology, Harvard Univ. 51-52; Visiting Prof. Univ. of Calif. 58; Eddington Lecturer 60; Riddell Lecturer, Durham Univ. 61; Fremantle Lecturer, Balliol Coll., Oxford 62-63; Gifford Lecturer, St. Andrews Univ. 69-71; Pres. Jesus Coll., Cambridge 69-72.
Leisure interests: music, swimming.
Publs. *Learning and Instinct in Animals* 56, *Current Problems in Animal Behaviour* (edited with O. L. Zangwill) 61, *Bird Song: The Biology of Vocal Communication and Expression in Birds* 61, *Biology and the Nature of Man* 62, *Science, Man and Morals* 65, *Duetting and Antiphonal Song in Birds: its Extent and Significance* 72, *Animal Nature and Human Nature* 74; numerous papers on entomology, ornithology, comparative physiology and animal behaviour in scientific journals.
Sub-Department of Animal Behaviour, University of Cambridge, Madingley, Cambridge; Home: 9 Wilberforce Road, Cambridge, England.
Telephone: Madingley 301 (Office); Cambridge 50943 (Home).

Thorson, Hon. Joseph Thorarinn, P.C., B.A., LL.B., J.D., LL.D.; Canadian judge; b. 15 March 1889; ed. Winnipeg Collegiate Inst., Manitoba Coll., and New Coll., Oxford.
Barrister (Middle Temple) 13, Manitoba 13; served with B.E.F. France First World War, Capt. 16-19; Dean, Manitoba Law School 21-26; law practice 27-41; K.C.

30; Canadian del. to L.N. Assembly 38; mem. House of Commons for Winnipeg South Centre 26-30, for Selkirk 35 and 40; Liberal; Chair. War Expenditures Cttee. 41; mem. Privy Council for Canada and Ministry for Nat. War Services 41-42; Pres. Exchequer Court of Canada 42-; Pres. Int. Congress of Jurists, Berlin 52, Athens 55; Hon. Pres. Int. Comm. of Jurists.
20 Crescent Road, Rockcliffe, Ottawa, Canada.

Thorsteinsson, Eggert G.; Icelandic politician; b. 6 July 1925; ed. technical school and private studies.
Mason, Reykjavík 47-53; mem. Central Cttee. Labour Party 48-; mem. Althing 53-; Asst. Man. State Housing Inst. 61-65; Minister of Social Affairs and Fisheries 65-71.
Althing, Reykjavík, Iceland.

Thorsteinsson, Pétur; Icelandic diplomatist; b. 1917, Reykjavík; m. Oddny Stefansson 1948; three s.; ed. Univ. of Iceland.
Entered Ministry of Foreign Affairs 44; served Moscow 44, Ministry of Foreign Affairs 47; Del. to F.A.O. Assembly, Washington 49; Sec. Icelandic F.A.O. Cttee. 48-51; Chief of Div., Ministry of Foreign Affairs 51, Head, Commercial Division 50-53; Chair. Inter-Bank Cttee. on Foreign Exchange 52-53; Minister to U.S.S.R. 53-56, Ambassador 56-61 (concurrently Minister to Hungary 55-61 and to Romania 56-61); Ambassador to German Fed. Republic (concurrently Ambassador to Greece and Minister to Switzerland and Yugoslavia) 61-62, to France (concurrently Perm. Rep. to NATO and OECD) 62-65, concurrently Amb. to Belgium 62-65, to Luxembourg 62-65, to EEC 63-65; Amb. to U.S.A. 65-69, concurrently accred. to Argentina, Brazil, Canada and Mexico and Minister to Cuba; Sec.-Gen. Ministry for Foreign Affairs 69-; Commdr. with Star Order of the Icelandic Falcon; Belgian, French, Luxembourg, Norwegian, Danish, Swedish and Finnish decorations.
Ministry of Foreign Affairs, Reykjavík, Iceland.
Telephone: 25-000.

Thrane, Hans Erik, M.ECON.; Danish diplomatist; b. 14 April 1918, Copenhagen; s. of Julius Peter Thrane and Frieda Jensen; m. Gerda Boye 1941; two s.; ed. Københavns Universitet.
Danish Foreign Service 45-; Econ. Attaché, Paris 48-52; Ministry of Foreign Affairs, Copenhagen 52-56; Econ. Counsellor, Washington 56-59; Alt. Exec. Dir., Int. Bank for Reconstruction and Devt. 58-59; Ministry of Foreign Affairs, Copenhagen 59-66, Minister 62, Asst. Undersec. of State for Econ. Affairs 64; Amb. and Perm. Rep. to European Free Trade Asscn. (EFTA), and Perm. Rep. to UN Office and other int. orgs. in Geneva 66-74; Chair. of Council, Gen. Agreement on Tariffs and Trade (GATT) 68-71; Amb. to Norway 74-.
Leisure interests: sailing, skiing, mountaineering.
Kgl. Dansk Ambassade, Olav Kyrresgt. 7, Oslo 2 (Mail Address: Postuttak, Oslo 1); Private: Villaveien 31, Oslo, Norway.
Telephone: 44-18-46 (Office); 60-77-31 (Private).

Thulin, Ingrid; Swedish actress; b. 27 Jan. 1929, Sollefteå; d. of Adam Thulin and Nanna Larsson; m. 1st Claes Sylwander 1951, 2nd Harry Schein 1956; ed. Royal Dramatic Theatre School, Stockholm.
Has appeared in many modern and classical plays for Royal Dramatic Theatre, Stockholm, and for municipal theatres of Malmo and Stockholm until 62; has also appeared on Broadway, the Italian stage and U.S. T.V.; many national and int. awards.
Films include: *When Love Comes to the Village* 50, *Wild Strawberries* 57, *So Close to Life* 58, *The Face* 58, *The Judge* 60, *The Four Horsemen of the Apocalypse* 61, *Winter Light* 62, *The Silence* 63, *La Guerre est finie* 68, *The Damned* 70, *Cries and Whispers* 73, *A Handful of Love* 74, *La Cage* 75.

Kevingestrand 7B, Danderyd, Sweden; San Felice Circeo and Sacrofano, Italy.
Telephone: 08-755-68-98 (Sweden).

Thunholm, Lars Erik, C.B.E.; Swedish business executive; b. 2 Nov. 1914, Stockholm; ed. Stockholm School of Economics, Univ. of Stockholm.
Joined Svenska Handelsbanken 38, Econ. Adviser and Man. of Econ. Dept. 48-55; Head of Fed. of Swedish Industries 55-57; Man. Dir. Skandinaviska Banken, Stockholm (now Skandinaviska Enskilda Banken) 57-65, Chief Man. Dir. 65-; Chair. of Board, Banque Scandinave en Suisse, Scandinavian Bank Ltd., Kockums Mekaniska Verkstads AB; Vice-Chair. Svaenska Dagbladet; mem. of Board ADELA Investment Co. AS, Ship Mortgage Int. (Sweden) N.V., Billeruds AB, Bofors AB, Försäkrings AB Skandia, AB Iföerken, Cementa AB, Svenska Tändsticks Aktiebolaget, Svenska Unilever AB, Gränges; Chair. Stockholm Chamber of Commerce 71-, Swedish British Soc. and mem. of other insts.; Kt. Commdr. of the Royal Order of Vasa.
Publs. *Svenskt Kreditvasen* 10th edition 69, *Bank-vasendet i utlandet* 4th edn. 69, *Bankerna och penning-politiken* 64.
c/o Skandinaviska Enskilda Banken, 106 40 Stockholm, Sweden.

Thurlow, 8th Baron, cr. 1792; **Francis Edward Hovell-Thurlow-Cumming-Bruce,** K.C.M.G.; British diplomatist; b. 9 March 1912, London; s. of 6th Baron Thurlow and Grace Catherine Trotter; m. Yvonne Diana Wilson 1949; two s. two d.; ed. Shrewsbury School and Trinity Coll., Cambridge.
Assistant Principal, Dept. of Agriculture for Scotland 35-37, Dominions Office 37; Asst. Sec. Office of U.K. High Commr. in New Zealand 39-44, in Canada 44-46; Principal Private Sec. to Sec. of State 46-48; Asst. Sec. Commonwealth Relations Office (C.R.O.) 48; Head of Political Div., Office of U.K. High Commr. in India 49-52; Establishment Officer, C.R.O. 52-54, Head of Commodities Dept. 54-55; Adviser on External Affairs to Gov. of Gold Coast 55-57, Deputy High Commr. for U.K. in Ghana 57-58; Asst. Under-Sec. of State, C.R.O. 58; Deputy High Commr. for U.K. in Canada 58-59, High Commr. in New Zealand 59-63, High Commr. in Nigeria 64-66; Gov. and C.-in-C. Bahamas 68-72.
Leisure interests: golf, fishing.
The Old Vicarage, Mapledurham, Reading, Berks.; 16 Warwick Avenue, London, W.2, England.
Telephone: Kidmore End 3339 (Country); 01-723-7525.

Thurmond, Strom; American lawyer, farmer and politician; b. 5 Dec. 1902, Edgefield, S.C.; s. of J. William and Eleanor Gertrude Thurmond (née Strom); m. 1st Jean Crouch 1947 (died 1960), 2nd Nancy Moore 1968; one s. two d.; ed. Clemson Coll.
Teacher, South Carolina Schools 23-29, Superintendent 29-33; admitted to the Bar 30, served as City and County Attorney; State Senator 33-38; Circuit Judge 38-46; Gov. of South Carolina 47-51; Trustee, Bob Jones Univ.; Chair. South Carolina Democratic Del. and mem. Nat. Exec. Cttee. 48; mem. American Bar Assen., Clemson Alumni Assen.; decorations include Legion of Merit with Oak Leaf Cluster, Bronze Star with "V", Purple Heart, Croix de Guerre, Croix de la Couronne, Army Commendation Ribbon, Congressional Medal, Honor Soc. Nat. Patriot's Award 74, American Legion Distinguished Public Service Award 75; Hon. LL.D., Hon. D.M.S., Hon. L.H.D., Hon. D.C.L., Hon. Litt.D.; U.S. Senator from South Carolina 54-; active service in Europe and Pacific 42-46; fmr. Maj.-Gen. in U.S. Army Reserve (now retd.); Republican.
Senate Office Building, Washington, D.C. 20510; Home: Box 981, Aiken, South Carolina, U.S.A.
Telephone: 202-224-5972.

Thurston, Raymond LeRoy, PH.D., M.A.; American diplomatist; b. 4 Feb. 1913, St. Louis, Mo.; m. 1st Elizabeth Sherman 1934 (divorced), 2nd Gabriella Mariani 1970; one d.; ed. Washington Univ., and Univs. of Texas and Wisconsin.
Diplomatic Service, Toronto, Naples, Bombay 37-45; Asst. Chief, S. Asian Affairs, Dept. of State 45-49; First Sec./Counsellor Moscow 49-51; Dir. E. European Affairs, Dept. of State 52-55; Counsellor, Athens 55-57, Paris 57-61; Minister to NATO 61; Dep. Dir. Operations Center, Dept. of State 61; Amb. to Haiti 61-63; State Dept. Adviser to Commdr., Air Univ. 63-65; Amb. to Somalia 65-69; Visiting Prof. of Political Science, Univ. of Nevada 69-71; Visiting Prof. of Government Chapman Coll., Calif. 71-; Assoc. Prof. Center for Int. Studies, Chapman Coll., World Campus Afloat, then Dean and Dir. of Program Devt., now Off-Campus Rep. (Chapman Coll.) 75-.
Leisure interests: golf, chess, swimming.
5400 Ocean Boulevard, 3-7 Sarasata, Fla. 33581, U.S.A.; "Il Piccolo Campo", La Gina, 06069 Tuoro sul Trasimeno, Perugia, Italy.
Telephone: (813) 349-4338 (U.S.A.).

Thygesen, Jacob Christoffer, M.A.; Danish industrialist; b. 11 April 1901, Kolding, Jutland; s. of S. Thygesen; m. Rigmor Thygesen 1932; one s.; ed. Copenhagen Univ.
Worked in Danish Foreign Service 26-30; joined The Danish Distilleries Ltd. 30, Man. Dir. 53-71; Barrister, High Court 39; Chair. Fed. of Danish Industries 61-66; Pres. Nat. Cttee. Int. Chamber of Commerce 59-66; mem. Acad. of Technical Science 56-, Atomic Energy Comm. 64-68; Vice-Pres. Business and Industry Advisory Comm. to OECD (BIAC), Paris 66-68; Chair. Danish Section, European League for Econ. Co-operation; Chair. The National Bank of Denmark, Superfos Ltd., The Royal Chartered Fire Insurance Co. Ltd.; Dir. Scandinavian Tobacco Co. Ltd., Synthetic Ltd., and other industrial cos. and foundations; Commdr. 1st Grade Order of Dannebrog; Knight, Order of Orange-Nassau (Netherlands), Grand Officer, Order of the Crown (Belgium).
Leisure interest: golf.
Amaliegade 22, 1256 Copenhagen K, Denmark.

Thyssen-Bornemisza de Kaszon, Baron Hans Heinrich; Swiss industrialist and administrator; b. 13 April 1921; ed. Real Gymnasium, The Hague, Fribourg Univ.
Positions held: Pres. Supervisory Board Thyssen-Bornemisza Group NV; Pres. Bremer Vulkan Schiffbau und Maschinenfabrik, Bremen, Thyssengas GmbH, Duisburg; Dir. Heineken NV, Heineken Holding NV, Nederlandse Crediet bank NV, Amsterdam; picture collection housed and exhibited in Villa Favorita, exhibited in Nat. Gallery, London 61.
Villa Favorita, 6976 Castagnola di Lugano, Switzerland.

Tibandebage, Andrew Kajungu; Tanzanian diplomatist; b. circa 1921, Kasheshe; s. of Kajungu and Isabella; m. Catherine Mahuruzi 1946; two s. six d.; ed. Makerere Coll. and London Univ. Inst. of Education.
Schoolteacher Tabora 45-54, Headmaster Bugene Middle School, Karagwe 55, Head of Mathematics Section, St. Thomas More Secondary School, Ihungo, Bukoba 56-61; Ministry of External Affairs 62-; Counsellor in London 62; Head Tanganyika Embassy to Fed. Germany 62-63, Ambassador 63-64; Ambassador of Tanzania to the Congo (Kinshasa) 64-67; Principal Sec. at Ministry of Information and Tourism 67; Tanzanian Amb. to France 68-70; Personal Asst. to Pres. 70-72; Amb. to Zaire (also accred. to Burundi and Rwanda) 72-.
Leisure interest: reading Dickens.
B.P. 1612, Kinshasa, Zaire.

Tidemand, Otto Grieg; Norwegian shipping executive and politician; b. 18 June 1921, Oslo; ed. Commercial High School, Oslo.

Royal Norwegian Air Force, Canada, England 41-45; shipping business 45-65, mem. Stove Shipping, and Christian Smith Shipping Co., Oslo; Minister of Defence 65-70; Minister of Commerce and Shipping June 70-March 71; Chair. Finance Cttee., Conservative Party 52-; Oslo Conservative Party 70-.

The Storting, Oslo, Norway.

Tiekso, Anna-Lisa, M.A.; Finnish politician; b. 14 March 1929, Kemi; m.

Member of Parl. 51; active in youth and women's orgs. of Finnish People's Democratic League; later, Councillor of rural commune of Kemi; mem. of Cen. Cttee. of C.P. 66-, also of its Exec. Cttee.; First Min. for Social Affairs 68-70; Minister for Health and Social Welfare Feb.-March 71.

Communist and Socialist Union Party, Simonkatu 8B, Helsinki, Finland.

Tiemann, Norbert Theodore; American governor and businessman; b. 18 July 1924, Minden, Neb.; s. of Martin William Tiemann and Alvina T. Rathert; m. Lorna Lou Bornholdt 1950; one s. three d.; ed. Univ. of Neb., Midland Lutheran Coll., Neb.

Assistant County Agent, Lexington 49-50; Asst. Man. Neb. Hereford Asscn. 50; army service 43-46, 50-52; Exec. Sec. Nat. Livestock Feeders Asscn., Omaha 52; Dir. of Industry Relations Nat. Livestock and Meat Board, Chicago 52-54; Mayor of Wausa 56-62; Pres. Commercial State Bank, Wausa 57-; Republican Gov. of Neb. 67-71; Fed. Highway Admin. 73-; mem. board of dirs. Lutheran Church of America, mem. American Legion.

8440 Brook Road, McLean, Virginia 22101, U.S.A.

Tien Wei-hsin; Chinese army officer.

Deputy Dir., Gen. Political Dept., People's Liberation Army.

People's Republic of China.

Tietjens, Norman Orwig, PH.B., M.A., J.D.; American judge; b. 8 July 1903; s. of Otto P. and Corinne H. (née Orwig) Tietjens; m. Lucretia Larkin 1936; two d.; ed. Brown Univ. and Univ. of Michigan.

Admitted to Ohio Bar; Assoc., Williams, Eversman and Morgan, Toledo 30-32, private legal practice 32-33; Special Counsel, Fed. Emergency Admin. of Public Works 33-37; Counsel, U.S. Maritime Comm. 37-38; Attorney, Office of Gen. Counsel, U.S. Treasury Dept. 38-39, Asst. Gen. Counsel 39-50; Judge, Tax Court of the U.S. 50-61, Chief Judge 61-67; Achievement Award of Tax Soc. of N.Y. Univ. 64, and other awards.

Office: U.S. Tax Court, Washington, D.C.; Home: 3509 Overlook Lane, Washington, D.C., U.S.A.

Tikhonov, Andrei Nikolayevich; Soviet mathematician and geophysicist; b. 30 Oct. 1906, Gagarin, Smolensk Region; ed. Moscow State Univ.

Postgraduate, Junior Scientific Worker, Moscow State Univ. 27-35; Senior Scientific Worker, Dept. of U.S.S.R. Acad. of Sciences Inst. of Theoretical Physics 35-58; Deputy Dir. U.S.S.R. Acad. of Sciences Inst. of Applied Mathematics 53-; Prof. Moscow State Univ. 36; Corresp. mem. U.S.S.R. Acad. of Sciences 39-66, mem. 66-; Lenin Prize 66.

Publs. Works on theoretical pluralistic topology, on mathematical physics and on geophysics.

U.S.S.R. Academy of Sciences, 14 Leninsky prospekt, Moscow, U.S.S.R.

Tikhonov, Nikolai Alexandrovich; Soviet engineer and politician; b. 1905; ed. Dniepropetrovsk Metallurgical Inst.

Assistant locomotive driver, technician and student 27-30; engineer, later Chief Engineer and Dir. Metallurgical plant, Dniepropetrovsk; Chief, main board of

U.S.S.R. Ministry of Ferrous Metallurgy 30-55; Deputy Minister of Ferrous Metallurgy 55-57; Chair. Council of Dniepropetrovsk Econ. Region 57-60; Vice-Chair. U.S.S.R. Scientific Econ. Council 60-65; Vice-Chair. U.S.S.R. Council of Ministers 65-; Alt. mem. C.P.S.U. Cen. Cttee. 61-66, mem. 66-; Deputy to U.S.S.R. Supreme Soviet 58-.

Council of Ministers, the Kremlin, Moscow, U.S.S.R.

Tikhonov, Nikolai Semyonovich; Soviet writer and poet; b. 4 Dec. 1896, Leningrad.

First work published 18; del. Paris Conf. for Defence of Culture 35; Chair. Soviet Peace Cttee. 49-; Chair. Cttee. for Literature and the Arts, Lenin Prize Cttee.; Deputy to U.S.S.R. Supreme Soviet 50-, Vice-Chair. Soviet of Nationalities; Sec. of Board, U.S.S.R. Union of Writers; State Prizes 41, 48, 51, 53, Lenin Prize Winner 70, Int. Lenin Peace Prize 58, T. Shevchenko Ukrainian S.S.R. State Prize, Shota Rustaveli Georgian S.S.R. State Prize, K. Khetagurov North Ossetian A.S.S.R., Gold Medal Hammer and Sickle; Order of Lenin (three times); Order of the Red Banner of Labour; Hero of Socialist Labour 66; Order of Patriotic War (twice); J. Nehru Prize 67.

Publs. Poetry: *The Horde, Mead* 22, *Poems of Kakhetia* 35, *Friend's Shadow* 35-36, *Kirov is with us* 41, *Year of Fire* 42, *Poems of Yugoslavia* 47, *Georgian Spring, Two Streams* 51, *At the Second World Congress of Supporters of Peace* 61, *May Morning* 61, *Poems* 61, *The Morning of Peace* 62; also *Leningrad Stories* 42, *Novels and Stories* 48, *Stories of Pakistan* 50, *White Miracle* (travels) 56, *Collected Works* (6 vols.) 59, *Selected Lyrics* 64, *Stories* 64, *Double Rainbow* 64, *From the View of Friends* 67, *The Green Darkness* 67, *Novels* 67.

U.S.S.R. Union of Writers, 52 Vorovskogo Ulitsa Moscow, U.S.S.R.

Tikriti, Saddam Hussain (*see* Takriti, Saddam Hussain).

Tillinghast, Charles C., Jr., PH.B., J.D.; American lawyer and corporation executive; b. 30 Jan. 1911, Saxton's River, Vt.; s. of Charles C. and Adelaide Barrows (Shaw) Tillinghast; m. Lisette Micoleau 1935; one s. three d.; ed. Brown and Columbia Univs.

Admitted N.Y. Bar 35; Deputy Asst. District Attorney N.Y. County 38-40; partner, Hughes, Hubbard & Ewing and successor firm of Hughes, Hubbard, Blair & Reed 42-57; Vice-Pres. and Dir. Bendix Corpn. 57-61; Dir. of several cos.; Pres., Chief Exec. Officer and Dir. Trans World Airlines Inc. 61-69, Chair. and Chief Exec. Officer 69-; mem. Conference Board 65-; Hon. L.H.D. (S. Dakota School of Mines and Technology 59); Hon. LL.D. (Franklin Coll. 63, Redlands Univ. 64, Brown Univ. 67, Drury Coll. 67).

Leisure interests: golfing, shooting, gardening, woodworking.

Office: 605 3rd Avenue, New York, N.Y. 10016; Home: 56 Oakledge Road, Bronxville, New York, N.Y. 10708, U.S.A.

Timakov, Vladimir Dmitriyevich; Soviet microbiologist; b. 22 July 1905, Pustotino, Ryazan Region; m. Maria Timakova 1927; one d.; ed. Tomsk Univ.

Postgraduate Tomsk Univ. 29-31; Research Assoc. Tomsk Medical Inst. 31-34; Research Assoc., Asst. Prof., Head of Chair, Medical Inst., Inst. of Epidemiology and Microbiology, Ashkhabad 34-41; People's Commissar of Public Health, Turkmen S.S.R.; Scientific Dir. Inst. of Microbiology and Epidemiology 41-45; Dir. Gamaleya Inst. of Epidemiology and Microbiology 45-53, Head of Dept. 63-66; Head of Chair, Second Moscow Medical Inst. 49-; Corresp. mem. U.S.S.R. Acad. of Medical Sciences 48, now mem., Vice-Pres. 57-63, Pres. 66-; Academician, U.S.S.R. Acad. of Sciences 68-; Chair. Board U.S.S.R. Soc. of Epidemiologists, Microbiologists and Infectionists; Deputy Editor *Big Medical*

Encyclopaedia; mem. Exec. Int. Asscn. of Micro-biologists, Turkish Med. Soc., Purkinyě Soc., Czecho-slovakia; numerous decorations.
Leisure interests: walking in the forest, picking up mushrooms.
U.S.S.R. Academy of Medical Sciences, 14 Solyanka Ulitsa, Moscow; Home: Serafimovicha 2, Flat 200, Moscow, U.S.S.R.
Telephone: 237-23-69 (Home).

Timár, Dr. Mátyás; Hungarian politician; b. 1923, Mòhacs; ed. Univ. of Laio.
Former leather worker; Hungarian Communist Party 43-; fmr. teacher Faculty of State and Legal Sciences, Loránd Eötvös Univ. of Sciences; afterwards Head Finance Faculty, Karl Marx Univ. of Econs., Budapest; Ministry of Finance 49-, Deputy Minister of Finance 55-57, 60-62, Minister of Finance 62-67; Deputy Chair. Council of Ministers 67-75; mem. Central Cttee. Hungarian Socialist Workers' Party 66-, mem. Political Econ. Board attached to HSWP Cen. Cttee. 75-; mem. State Planning Cttee. 73-; Pres. Nat. Bank of Hungary 75-.
Publs. *Economic Development and Directive Systems in Hungary* 68, *Economic Policy in Hungary 1967-1973* 73.
Office of the President of the National Bank of Hungary, H-1850, Budapest, Hungary.
Telephone: 112-600.

Timm, Bernhard, DR. PHIL. NAT.; German business executive; b. 1909, Pinneberg (Holstein); ed. Reform-realgymnasium Altona and Univ. of Heidelberg.
Worked in private laboratory of Prof. Dr. Carl Bosch, Heidelberg 34-36; joined Badische Anilin- & Soda-Fabrik A.G. (BASF) (chemicals) 36, Dir. 50-, Deputy Chair. of Management Board 52-65, Chair. 65-74, Chair. Supervisory Board 74-; Deputy Chair. Supervisory Board Mannheimer Versicherungsgesellschaft, Mann-heim, Deutsche Shell A.G., Hamburg; mem. Supervisory Board Allgemeine Elektricitäts-Gesell-schaft AEG-Telefunken, Berlin/Frankfurt, Con-tinental Gummi-Werke A.G., Hanover, Preussag A.G., Hanover, Hugo Stinnes AG, Mülheim, Rhenus AG, Mannheim; Chair. Verein zur Förderung der Krebsfor-schung in Deutschland e.V., Heidelberg; mem. Pre-sidium of Asscn. of German Chemical Industry, Frankfurt/Main; mem. Vorstandsrat des Deutschen Museums, Munich, Wissenschaftrats, Köln-Marienburg; mem. Kuratorium "Deutsche Sporthilfe", Frankfurt/Main; Hon. Prof. 66, Hon. Dr. Ing. 69, Hon. Senator 69, Univ. of Heidelberg; Castner Medal, Soc. of Chemical Industry, London 70; Dr. rer.Nat. h.c. (Univ. of Mainz) 69; Grosses Bundesverdienstkreuz mit Stern 69.
69 Heidelberg, Am Rosenbusch 1, Federal Republic of Germany.

Timmis, Denis William; Canadian pulp and paper company executive; b. 3 Dec. 1919, Bickley, England; ed. Wellington Coll., England.
Trainee accountant Peat, Marwick, Mitchel & Co. 38-47; army service in India, Burma 39-46; Corporate Sec. Bowaters Newfoundland Pulp and Paper Mills Ltd. 50; Corporate Sec. Bowater Southern Paper Corpn. 52, Exec. Vice-Pres. 57; Man. Dir. Tasman Pulp and Paper Co. Ltd., New Zealand 60; Deputy Chair. Gen. Man. Bowaters U.K. Pulp and Paper Mills 63; Consultant, Sandwell and Co. Ltd., Vancouver 64; Man. Special Projects, MacMillan Bloedel Ltd. 64, Group Vice-Pres. Pulp and Paper 68, Exec. Vice-Pres. Operations 70-73, Dir. 70-, Pres. and Chief Exec. Officer April 73-; Dir. Canadian Imperial Bank of Commerce 73-, Canadian Pacific Ltd. 74-, Canadian Gen. Electric.
MacMillan Bloedel Ltd., 1075 West Georgia Street, Vancouver, B.C. V6E 3R9, Canada.

Timmons, Benson E. L., III; American diplomatist; b. 2 March 1916, Sapulpa, Okla.; s. of Benson E. L. Timmons, Jr., and Mary Frances Jones; m. 1st Ruth

Hunt, two s.; m. 2nd Sanya Bezencenet 1964; ed. Univ. of Georgia, and Balliol Coll., Oxford (Rhodes Scholar). Instructor in Economics, Univ. of Georgia 37-38; Asst. to Dir., Foreign Funds Control, U.S. Treasury 40-42; Lt.-Col. U.S. Army 42-46; Exec. Asst. to Asst. Sec. of Treasury 46-48; Deputy Dir., then Dir. of U.S. Eco-nomic Cooperation Mission to France 48-55; Minister for Economic Affairs, U.S. Embassy, Paris 54-55; Dir., Office of European Regional Affairs, Dept. of State 55-59; Counsellor and Consul-Gen., American Embassy, Stockholm 59-61; Minister and Dep. Chief. of Mission, American Embassy, New Delhi 61-63; Amb. to Haiti 63-67; Deputy Sec.-Gen., OECD 67-73; U.S. Legion of Merit; M.B.E.; Officier Légion d'Honneur; Chevalier Order of Saints Maurice and Lazarus (Italy); Officer Order of the Crown of Italy; Bronze Star (U.S.); Commdr. Nat. Order of Merit, Italy; Grand Cross, Order of Honour and Merit, Republic of Haiti.
Leisure interests: boating, riding, reading, art.
c/o Department of State, Washington, D.C. 20520, U.S.A.

Timofeyev, Nikolai Vladimirovich; Soviet politician; b. 1913; ed. Urals Forestry Engineering Inst.
Former stevedore, Siberia; later Chief Engineer and Dir. timber enterprise 35-50; Chief Engineer East Siberian Timber Trust 50-55; Deputy Minister of Paper and Woodworking Industry 55-56, Minister 56-57; Chair. Econ. Council, Kostroma 57-62, North West 62-65; Minister of Timber, Paper, Pulp and Wood-working Industry, U.S.S.R. 65-68, of Timber and Woodworking Industry 68-; mem. C.P.S.U. 43-; mem. Central Auditing Comm. 66-; Deputy to U.S.S.R. Supreme Soviet 66-; awarded Orders of Red Star, Badge of Honour and other decorations.
U.S.S.R. Ministry of Timber and Woodworking Indus-try, 2/16 Ul. Gritsevets, Moscow, U.S.S.R.

Timofeyeva, Nina Vladimirovna; Soviet ballet dancer; b. 11 June 1935; ed. Leningrad Ballet School.
With Ballet Company of the Leningrad Kirov State Academic Theatre of Opera and Ballet 53-56; Deputy to Supreme Soviet of the U.S.S.R.; mem. Bolshoi Theatre 56-; has toured with Bolshoi Ballet in U.S.A., Fed. German Repub. and other countries; People's Artist of the R.S.F.S.R. 63; People's Artist of U.S.S.R. 69; prizewinner at three int. classic dance competitions. Principal roles: Odette-Odile (*Swan Lake*), Marta (*Giselle*), Laurensia (*Laurensia*), Yegina (*Spartacus*), Kitri (*Don Quixote*), Mistress of the Copper Mountain (*Stone Flower*), Diane Mireille (*Flames of Paris*), Gayane (*Gayane*), Raymonda (*Raymonda*); Princess Aurora (*Sleeping Beauty*), Leili (*Leili and Medjnun*), Mekhmene Banu (*Legend of Love*), Giselle (*Giselle*), Asel (*Asel*), Bacchante (*Faust*), Masha (*Nutcracker*), Shopeniana.
State Academic Bolshoi Theatre of the U.S.S.R., ploshchad Sverdlova 1, Moscow, U.S.S.R.

Tinbergen, Jan; Netherlands economist; b. 12 April 1903, The Hague; s. of Dr. D. C. Tinbergen and Jeannette van Eek; m. Tine Johanna De Wit 1929; four d.; ed. Leiden Univ. (Doctor of Physics).
Staff of Central Bureau of Statistics, The Hague 29-36, 38-45; Business cycle research expert, League of Nations, Geneva 36-38; Dir. Central Planning Bureau, The Hague 45-55; Prof. of Development Planning, Univ. of Rotterdam 33-; mem. Netherlands Acad. of Sciences; Erasmus Prize 67; Nobel Prize for Econs. 69.
Leisure interests: grandchildren, languages, drawing.
Publs. *Business Cycles in the U.S.A. 1919-1939* 39, *On The Theory of Economic Policy* 52, *Economic Policy: Principles and Design* 56, *Selected Papers* 59, *Shaping the World Economy* 62, *Development Planning* 68, *Income Distribution* 75.
Haviklaan 31, The Hague, Netherlands.
Telephone: 070-394884.

Tinbergen, Nikolaas, PH.D., F.R.S.; British zoologist; b. 15 April 1907, The Hague, Netherlands; s. of Dirk C. Tinbergen and Jeannette van Eek; m. Elisabeth A. Rutten 1932; two s. three d.; ed. High School, The Hague, Univ. of Leiden, Netherlands, and Vienna and Yale, U.S.A.
Professor Experimental Zoology, Leiden 47; Lecturer in Animal Behaviour, Oxford Univ. 49, Reader 60, Prof. 66-74; naturalized British citizen 55; Hon. mem. many learned socs.; Hon. D.Sc. (Univs. of Edinburgh, Leicester); Bölsche Medal; Italia Prize TV documentaries 69; Godman-Salvin Medal, Jan Swammerdam Medal; Nobel Prize for Physiology or Medicine 73.
Leisure interests: drawing, photography, observing animals and people.
Publs. *The Study of Instinct* 51, *The Herring Gull's World* 53, *Curious Naturalists* 58, *Animal Behaviour* 65, *Signals for Survival* (filmed with Hugh Falkus) 70, *The Animal in its World, Vol. I* 72, *Vol. II* 73.
88 Lonsdale Road, Oxford, OX2 7ER, England.
Telephone: Oxford 58662.

Tindemans, Leo; Belgian politician; b. 16 April 1922, Zwijndrecht; m. Rosa Naesens 1960; two s. two d.; ed. State Univ. of Ghent, Catholic Univ. of Louvain.
Member, Chamber of Deputies 61-; Mayor of Edegem 65-; Minister of Community Affairs (Dutch speaking) 68-71; Minister of Agriculture and Middle Class Affairs 72-73; Deputy Prime Minister and Minister for the Budget and Institutional Problems 73-74; Prime Minister April 74-; Vice-Pres. European Union of Christian Democrats; Charlemagne Prize 76; Christian Socialist.
Leisure interests: reading, writing, walking.
Publs. several books on constitutional and int. problems.
Wetstraat 16, Brussels; Home: Jan Verbertlei 24, 2520 Edegem, Belgium.
Telephone: 02/513-80-20 (Office).

Tiné, Jacques Wilfrid Jean Francis, L.E.N.D.; French diplomatist; b. 24 May 1914, Algiers; s. of Edouard Tiné and René Pittaluga; m. Helena Terry 1948; one s. one d.; ed. Lycée d'Alger, Faculté de Droit and Ecole Libre des Sciences Politiques, Paris.
Entered diplomatic service 38; Counsellor French Embassy, Copenhagen 49-50, UN 50-55, London 55-61; Minister Plenipotentiary, Rabat, Morocco 61; Deputy Perm. Rep. to UN 63-67; Dir. for Europe, Ministry for Foreign Affairs 67-69; Amb. to Portugal 69-73; Diplomatic Counsellor to the Govt. Dec. 73-75; Perm. Rep. to NATO 75-; Pres. Office Nat. de Diffusion Artistique; Officier, Légion d'Honneur, Croix de Guerre, Commdr. de l'Ordre Nationale du Merite, Commdr. des Arts et Lettres.
120 rue du Bac, Paris 7e; and 5 rue de l'Arbre Sec, Fontainebleau, France.
Telephone: 548-0876; 422-2777.

Ting Sheng; Chinese army officer; b. 1912, Kiangsi; ed. Red Army School and Mil. Coll.
Participated in Long March 34-35; Battalion Commdr. 37; Div. Commdr. 4th Field Army 49; Commdr. 54th Army, People's Liberation Army, Tibet 54-55; Deputy Commdr. Sinkiang Mil. Region, PLA 63-68, Canton Mil. Region, PLA 68; mem. 9th Cen. Cttee. of CCP 69; Sec. CCP Kwangtung 71; Commdr. Canton Mil. Region, PLA 72-73; Chair. Kwangtung Revolutionary Cttee. 72; First Sec. CCP Kwangtung 72-73; mem. 10th Cen. Cttee. of CCP 73; Commdr. Nanking Mil. Region, PLA 74-.
People's Republic of China.

Tinkham, Michael, M.S., PH.D.; American professor of physics; b. 23 Feb. 1928, near Ripon, Wis.; s. of Clayton H. and Laverna Krause Tinkham; m. Mary S. Merin 1961; two s.; ed. Ripon Coll., Ripon, Wis., Mass. Inst. of Technology (M.I.T.) and Univ. of Oxford.
Research Asst., Univ. of Calif. (Berkeley) 55-57, Asst.

Prof. of Physics 57-59, Assoc. Prof. of Physics 59-61, Prof. of Physics 61-66; Gordon McKay Prof. of Applied Physics and Prof. of Physics, Harvard Univ. 66-; mem. Nat. Acad. of Sciences; Fellow, American Acad. of Arts and Sciences; Guggenheim Fellow 63-64; Buckley Prize 74.
Publs. *Group Theory and Quantum Mechanics* 64, *Superconductivity* 65, *Introduction to Superconductivity*; numerous articles in journals.
Department of Physics, Harvard University, Cambridge, Mass. 02138; Home: 98 Rutledge Road, Belmont, Mass. 02178, U.S.A.
Telephone: 617-495-3735 (Office).

Tinoco, Pedro Rafael; Venezuelan lawyer and politician; 4 Oct. 1927, Caracas; s. of Dr. Pedro R. Tinoco Smith; m. Carmen Montilla de Tinoco 1965; one d.; ed. Bois Gentil, Vaud, Switzerland, Peekshill Mil. Acad., N.J., and Central Univ. of Venezuela.
Former Prof. of Public Finances and Econs., Central Univ. of Venezuela; Pres., Nat. Banking Asscn. 62-65; Founder and Pres., Inst. de Capacitación Bancaria; mem. Nat. Energy Council, Fed. Chambers of Commerce (Pres. Petroleum Cttee.); fmr. Vice-Pres. and Pres., Board of Dirs., Banco Mercantil y Agrícola; Elected rep., Fed. District in Nat. Congress; Minister of Finance 69-72; Luis Sanojo Prize 55-56.
Leisure interests: horse-riding, yachting, chess.
Publs. *Comments on the Venezuelan Income Tax Law* 50, *Petróleo-Factor de Desarrollo* 68.
Escritorio Tinoco, P.O. Box 221, Caracas, Venezuela.
Telephone: 81-02-81/2.

Tiomkin, Dimitri; American (naturalized) composer; b. 1899, near St. Petersburg, Russia; m. 1st Albertina Rasch 1927 (died 1967), 2nd Olivia Cynthia Patch 1972; ed. St. Petersburg Conservatory.
Studied under Glazunov in St. Petersburg and under Busoni in Berlin; commenced musical career as a pianist making frequent appearances as soloist with the Berlin Philharmonic Orchestra during 1920's; gave two-piano recitals in Paris with his colleague Raskov; debut at Carnegie Hall, New York 26; composed film score for *Alice in Wonderland* 33, followed by *Lost Horizon* 37; co-producer (with Carl Foreman q.v.), *McKenna's Gold*; exec. producer and general music dir. of the Soviet-American film on the life of Tchaikovsky; Chevalier, Légion d'Honneur; Chevalier, Ordre des Arts et des Lettres; Cruz de Caballero de la Orden de Isabel la Católica; Hon. life mem. of Amer. Inst. of Fine Arts; four Academy Awards (Oscars) for film scores and numerous other awards; has composed scores for over 160 films including: *The Moon and Sixpence, I Confess, Shadow of a Doubt, Friendly Persuasion, Giant, The Court Martial of Billy Mitchell, 55 Days at Peking, The Alamo, The Fall of the Roman Empire, High Noon, The High and the Mighty, The Old Man and the Sea, The Guns of Navarone, The Sundowners, The Long Night.*
Publ. *Please Don't Hate Me.*
Suite 2270, 1900 Avenue of the Stars, Los Angeles, Calif. 90065, U.S.A.

Tioulong, Gen. Nhiek; Cambodian fmr. Deputy Prime Minister; see *The International Who's Who 1975-76.*

Tippett, Sir Michael Kemp, Kt., C.B.E.; British composer; b. 2 Jan. 1905, London; ed. Royal Coll. of Music.
Taught at Hazelwood School until 31; Dir. of Music, Morley Coll. 40-52; Dir. Bath Festival 70-73; Hon. D.Mus. (Cantab.) 64, (Leeds) 64, (Dublin) 65, (Oxford) 67, (Bristol) 70; Hon. Dr. Univ. (York) 66; Hon. mem. Amer. Acad. of Arts and Letters 73.
Works include: *String Quartet No. 1* 35, *Piano Sonata No. 1* 37, *Concerto for Double String Orchestra* 39, *A Child of Our Time* 41, *Fantasia on a Theme of Handel, for Piano and Orchestra* 42, *String Quartet No. 2* 43, *Symphony No. 1* 45, *String Quartet No. 3* 46, *Little Music for*

Strings 46, *Suite for the Birthday of Prince Charles* (*Suite in D*) 48, *The Heart's Assurance* 51, *The Midsummer Marriage* 52, *Fantasia Concertante on a Theme of Corelli for String Orchestra* 53, *Divertimento on "Sellinger's Round", for Chamber Orchestra* 53-54, *Concerto for Piano and Orchestra* 55, *Sonata for Four Horns* 55, *Symphony No. 2* 57, *Crown of the Year* 58, *King Priam* (opera) 61, *Magnificat and Nunc Dimittis* 62, *Piano Sonata No. 2* 62, *Incidental Music to The Tempest* 62, *Praeludium for Brass, Bells and Percussion* 62, *Concerto for Orchestra* 63, *The Vision of St. Augustine* 66, *The Knot Garden* (opera) 69, *The Shires Suite* 65-70, *Songs for Dov* 70, *Symphony No. 3* 72, *Piano Sonata No. 3* 73.
Publ. *Moving into Aquarius* 59.
Promotion Department, Schott & Co., 48 Great Marlborough Street, London, W.1, England.
Telephone: 437-1246.

Tirikatene-Sullivan, The Hon. Tini Whetu Marama, B.A.; New Zealand social worker and politician; b. 9 Jan. 1932, Ratana Pa, Via Wanganui; d. of the late Hon. Sir Eruera Tirikatene and of Lady Tirikatene; m. Dr. Denis Sullivan; one s. one d.; ed. Rangiora High School, Victoria Univ. of Wellington, Nat. Univ. of Australia.
Secretary, Royal Tour Staff for visit of H.M. Queen Elizabeth II and H.R.H. The Duke of Edinburgh 53-54; fmr. Social Worker, Depts. of Maori Affairs, Social Security and Child Welfare; mem. for Southern Maori, House of Reps. 67-; Minister of Tourism 72-; Assoc. Minister of Social Welfare 72-74; Minister for the Environment 74-75.
Leisure interests: dress designing, fabric printing, ethnic handicrafts, contemporaneous home . interior design, Ikebana floral arrangements.
Parliament Buildings, Wellington; Home: 260A Tinakori Road, Wellington, New Zealand.

Tishler, Max, M.S., PH.D.; American organic and medicinal chemist and university professor; b. 30 Oct. 1906, Boston, Mass.; s. of Samuel and Anna Gray Tishler; m. Elizabeth M. Verveer, 1934; two s.; ed. Tufts Coll. and Harvard Univ.
Research Assoc. Harvard Univ. 34-36, Instructor in Chem. 36-37; Research Chemist Merck & Co., Inc. 37-41, Section Head in charge of Process Devt. 41-44, Dir. of Devt. Research 44-53, Vice-Pres. for Scientific Activities 54-56; Vice-Pres. and Exec. Dir. Merck Sharp & Dohme Research Labs. Div. 56-57, Pres. 57-69; mem. Board of Dirs. Merck & Co., Inc., 62-, Senior Vice-Pres. Research and Devt. 69-70; Univ. Prof. of Sciences, Chair. Dept. of Chemistry, Wesleyan Univ. Middleton, Conn. 70-; Co-editor *Chemistry and the Economy*, American Chemical Soc.; mem. Editorial Board *Separation Science*; mem. Science Board of Govs. Weizmann Inst.; Trustee Tufts Univ., Union Coll.; mem. numerous advisory councils and cttees. of various educational orgs.; fmr. mem. Board of Dirs. and Awards Cttee. Industrial Research Inst., Asscn. Harvard Chemists (Pres. 46); mem. Research and Devt. Section Pharmaceutical Manufacturers Asscn., etc.; mem. Nat. Acad. of Sciences, American Acad. of Arts and Sciences, American Asscn. for Advancement of Science, American Chem. Soc. (Chair. Organic Chem. Div. 51, Pres. 72), Soc. of Chemical Industry (Chair. American Section 66-67, Hon. Vice-Pres. 68), American Inst. of Chemists, N.Y. Acad. of Sciences, Chem. Soc. (London), Chem. Soc. of Japan, Swiss Chem. Soc., Conn. Acad. of Arts and Sciences; hon. mem. Société Chimique de France; Dir. Royal Soc. of Medicine Foundation; numerous honours and awards including Industrial Research Inst. Award 61, Chem. Industry Medal of Soc. of Chem. Industry 63, Chem. Pioneer Award of American Inst. of Chemists 68, Priestley Medal of American Chem. Soc. 70; Hon. D.Sc. (Tufts, Bucknell, Philadelphia Coll. of Pharmacy and Science, Upsala

Coll., Univ. of Strathclyde, Rider Coll., Fairfield Univ.), Hon. D.Eng. (Stevens Inst. of Tech.).
Leisure interest: horticulture.
Publs. Co-author: *Chemistry of Organic Compounds* 37, *Streptomycin* 49; Editor-in-Chief, *Organic Syntheses* Vol. 39; over 100 scientific publs. in the fields of vitamins, steroids, antibiotics, sulfonamides.
Department of Chemistry, Wesleyan University Middletown, Conn. 06457, U.S.A.

Tito, Marshal (**Josip Broz**); Yugoslav politician; b. 25 May 1892.
Mechanic; served in Austro-Hungarian Army 14-15; imprisoned in Russian concentration camps 15-17; participated in the Russian revolution; returned to Yugoslavia and worked as machinist and mechanic until 27; Dist. Sec. of trade union of metal workers 27-28; took active part in illegal Yugoslav Communist Party; sentenced to six years' imprisonment for conspiracy 28; after release left the country, helped recruit Yugoslavs for the Int. Brigade in Spanish Civil War 36-38; returned to Yugoslavia before Second World War; after the German invasion organized Partisan Forces; elected Marshal of Yugoslavia and Pres. Nat. Liberation Cttee. 43; Prime Minister and Minister of Nat. Defence 45-53; Pres. of the Republic 53-, Life Pres. 74; Gen. Sec. C.P. Secr. 53-66, Chair. League of Communists 66-, and Supreme Commdr. of the Armed Forces 53-; Nat. Hero decoration (twice), Order of Lenin (U.S.S.R.), Jawaharlal Nehru Award for Int. Understanding 74.
Offices of the President of the Republic, Belgrade, Yugoslavia.

Titov, Col. Herman Stepanovich; Soviet air force officer and cosmonaut; b. 11 Sept. 1935; ed. secondary school, Volgograd Pilots' School and Zhukovsky Air Force Eng. Acad.
Training for space flight 60-61; in space-ship *Vostok II* circled earth 17 times during a journey of 25 hours Aug. 6-7, 61; mem. Young Communists' League; Candidate mem. Communist Party until 61, Full mem. 61-; student, Zhukovsky Air Force Engineering Acad. 68; Deputy, Supreme Soviet of U.S.S.R.; Pres. Viet-Nam-Soviet Friendship Soc.; Hero Soviet Union 61, Order of Lenin, Gold Star Medal, and other awards.
Zvezdny Gorodok, Moscow, U.S.S.R.

Titov, Vitali Nikolayevich; Soviet politician; b. 1907; ed. Kharkov Building and Engineering Inst.
Worker, later Dir. State Farm 23-35; Teacher, Kharkov Building and Eng. Inst. 36-41; mem. C.P.S.U. 38-; teacher, later party organiser, Kazakhstan 41-44; party work, Ukraine 44-62; Sec. Dist. Cttee., then Sec. Second Sec. Kharkov Regional Cttee., Ukraine C.P. 44-50; Sec., Second Sec. Kharkov Regional Cttee. 50-53, First Sec. 53-61; mem. Central Cttee. of C.P.S.U. 56-, mem. Secr. of Presidium of Central Cttee. of C.P.S.U. 61-65; Chair. C.P.S.U. Comm. on Ideological Questions 62-65, Second Sec. Communist Party of Kazakhstan 65-70; First Vice-Del. of U.S.S.R. to Council for Mutual Econ. Assistance 70-; Deputy to U.S.S.R. Supreme Soviet 54-, Chair. Credentials Comm., Soviet of Union; mem. Planning and Budgetary Comm. 74.
U.S.S.R. Delegation to Council for Mutual Economic Assistance, Moscow, U.S.S.R.

Tixier, Claude, L. ès L., D. ès D.; French economist; b. 22 Nov. 1913, Paris; m. Simone Lamy 1939; two s. three d.; ed. Arts and Law Faculties and Ecole des Sciences Politiques, Univ. of Paris.
Deputy Inspector of Finances 39, Inspector of Finances 42; Deputy Dir. to Ministry of Nat. Economy 45; Chief, Service of Economic Survey 46; Dir. Cabinet of Sec. of State for the budget 47; Deputy Dir. Cabinet of Minister of Finances 48; Dir. Cabinet of Prime Minister (Finances) 48; Dir. Cabinet of Minister of

Finances 49; Dir.-Gen. of Finances to the Algerian Ministry, Algiers 49-58; Vice-Pres. European Investment Bank July 58-62; Pres. and Dir.-Gen. Banque Industrielle de Financement et Crédit 62-67; Vice-Pres. Banque Worms 67; Pres. Unibail 74; Chevalier de la Légion d'Honneur.
Leisure interests: theory of numbers, cosmology.
15 boulevard Haussmann, Paris 9e; and 5 square des Ecrivains Combattants, Paris 16e, France.
Telephone: 260-3520 (Office); 224-62-55 (Home).

Tizard, Robert James, M.A.; New Zealand teacher; b. 7 June 1924, Auckland; s. of Henry James and Jessie Mae Tizard (née Philips); m. Catherine Anne Maclean 1951; one s. three d.; ed. Auckland Grammar School, Auckland Univ.
Served in R.N.Z.A.F., Canada, U.K. 42-46; Junior Lecturer in History, Auckland Univ. 49-53, teaching posts 55-57, 61-62; mem. Parl. 57-60, 63-; Minister of Health and State Services 72-74; in charge of State Advances Corpn. 72-73; Deputy Prime Minister, Minister of Finance 74-75; Deputy Leader of Opposition Dec. 75-.
Leisure interests: golf, squash.
Parliament Buildings, Wellington; Home: 27 Aragon Avenue, Auckland 5, New Zealand.

Tlass, Gen. Mustapha; Syrian army officer and politician; b. 2 May 1932, Rastan (Homs); s. of Abdul Kader; m. Lamyaa al-Jabri 1958; two s. one d.; ed. Mil. and Law Colls.
President of Damascus Mil. Tribunal 66; Deputy Minister of Defence 68; Chief of Staff of the Army and Armed Forces 68; mem. Regional Command, Arab Baath Party, mem. Politburo; mem. People's Council 71; Deputy Commdr.-in-Chief of the Army 72; Minister of Defence 72-; took part in war against Israel 73; many Syrian, Arab and foreign decorations.
Leisure interests: reading and writing books, sport.
Ministry of Defence, Damascus, Syria.

Tobey, Mark; American artist; b. 11 Dec. 1890; ed public schools.
Fashion artist, Chicago 17-22; teacher Seattle 22; travelled in Europe and Near East 25-27; taught at Dartington Hall, England 31-37; studied art in China and Japan 34; worked on Fed. Art Project; Exhibitions in Paris (Musée des Arts Decoratifs 61), London (Whitechapel Gallery 61), Berne, then Amsterdam 66, Düsseldorf 66, London (Hanover Gallery) 68; works in Kunstmuseum, Basle, Tate Gallery, London and in several American galleries. and museums, including Museum of Modern Art, N.Y., U.S.A.
[*Died 24 April* 1976.]

Tobias, Phillip Vallentine, PH.D., D.SC., M.B.B.CH., F.R.S.(S.A.), F.L.S., F.R.A.I.; South African professor of anatomy; b. 14 Oct. 1925, Durban; s. of the late Joseph Newman Tobias and Fanny Norden (née Rosendorff); ed. St. Andrew's School, Bloemfontein, Durban High School, Univ. of the Witwatersrand and Emmanuel Coll., Cambridge.
Lecturer in Anatomy, Univ. of Witwatersrand 51-52, Senior Lecturer 53, Prof. and Head of Anatomy Dept. 58-; Visiting Prof. Cambridge Univ.; founder Pres. Inst. for the Study of Man in Africa, Anatomical Soc. of Southern Africa, South African Soc. for Quaternary Research; mem. numerous int. asscns.; Fellow, Royal Anthropological Inst. of Great Britain and Ireland, Royal Soc. of South Africa, Linnean Soc. of London; sometime Vice-Pres. and acting Exec. Pres. South African Asscn. for the Advancement of Science; Pres. Royal Soc. of South Africa 70-72; Trustee Leakey Foundation, Pasadena, Calif.; British Asscn. Medal 52; Simon Biesheuvel Medal 66; South Africa Medal 67; Senior Captain Scott Medal 73.

Leisure interests: archaeology, philately, music, books, people.
Publs. *Chromosomes, Sex-cells and Evolution* 56, *Olduvai Gorge* Vol. II 67, *Man's Anatomy* (with M. Arnold) 68, *The Brain in Hominid Evolution* 71, *The Meaning of Race* 72; many articles in scientific journals.
Department of Anatomy, University of the Witwatersrand Medical School, Hospital Street, Johannesburg; 602 Marble Arch, 36 Goldreich Street, Hillbrow, Johannesburg, South Africa.
Telephone: 724-1561 (Office); 642-9176 (Home).

Tobin, Austin J(oseph), A.B., LL.B.; American lawyer and ports executive; b. 25 May 1903, Brooklyn, New York; s. of Clarence J. and Katharine (Moran) Tobin; m. 1st Geraldine Farley 1925 (died 1966), 2nd Rosaleen C. Skehan 1967; one s. one d.; ed. Holy Cross Coll., Mass., and Fordham Univ.
Admitted to New York Bar 28; Asst. Gen. Counsel, Port of New York Authority 35-42, Exec. Dir. 42; Pres. Port Authority, Trans Hudson 62-; Port Consultant, Thailand Govt. and World Bank, on organization of Israel Ports Authority; mem. Board of Trustees Stevens Inst. of Technology, N.J. and U.S. Council, Int. Chamber of Commerce; mem. Board of Dirs. Tri-Continental Corpn. Acad. of Political Sciences, and legal asscns.; Chair. Conf. on State Defense; mem. Municipal Forum of N.Y., Soc. Friendly Sons of St. Patrick; Hon. D. of Civil Law (Pace Coll.); awards include Chevalier Légion d'Honneur and Cavaliere Ordine al Merito; Hon. LL.D. (Adelphi Coll. and Tuskegee Inst.); Hon. D.Eng. (Stevens Inst. of Technology).
Homes: 200 East 66th Street, New York, N.Y. 10021, and Bay Road, Quogue, N.Y. 11959, U.S.A.

Tobin, James, M.A., PH.D.; American economist; b. 5 March 1918, Champaign, Ill.; s. of late Louis Michael and of Margaret Edgerton; m. Elizabeth Ringo 1946; three s. one d.; ed. Harvard Univ.
U.S. Navy 42-46; Teaching Fellow in Economics, Harvard Univ. 46-47, Junior Fellow 47-50; Assoc. Prof. of Economics, Yale Univ. 50-55, Prof. 55-57; Dir. Cowles Foundation for Research in Economics, Yale Univ. 55-61; Sterling Prof. of Economics, Yale Univ. 57- (on leave 61-62), Chair. Dept. of Econs. 74-(76); Visiting Prof. Univ. of Nairobi, Kenya 72-73; mem. President's Council of Economic Advisers 61-62; mem. Nat. Acad. of Sciences 72-.
Leisure interests: skiing, sailing, tennis.
117 Alden Avenue, New Haven 15, Conn.; and Yale University, New Haven, Conn., U.S.A.
Telephone: 203-436-2330.

Tobriner, Walter N.; American lawyer; b. 2 July 1902, Washington, D.C.; s. of Leon Tobriner and Blanche Barth Tobriner; m. Marienne E. Smith 1933; one s. one d.; ed. Friends School, Washington, Princeton Univ., and Harvard Univ. Law School.
Legal practice, Washington 26-61; Prof. of Law, Nat. Univ. Law School 30-50; Army Service 43-46; mem. Board of Education 52-57, Pres. 57-61; Pres., Board of Commissioners, District of Columbia 61-67; Amb. to Jamaica 67-69; Consultant, Agency for Int. Devt. 69; Chair. Nat. Capital Housing Authority; mem. D.C. Armory Board 61-67.
Leisure interest: woodworking.
6100 Thirty-third Street, N.W., Washington, D.C., U.S.A.

Todd, Baron (Life Peer), cr. 62, of Trumpington in the County of Cambridge; **Alexander Robertus Todd,** D.SC., D.PHIL., F.R.S.; British chemist; b. 2 Oct. 1907, Glasgow; s. of Alexander Todd, J.P.; m. Alison Sarah Dale 1937; one s. two d.; ed. Glasgow, Frankfurt a.M. and Oxford Univs.
Assistant in Medical Chemistry 34-35, Beit Memorial Research Fellow 35-36, Edinburgh Univ.; mem. staff

Lister Inst. Preventive Medicine, London 36-38; Sir Samuel Hall Prof. of Chemistry and Dir. Chemical Laboratories Manchester Univ. 38-44; Prof. Organic Chemistry Cambridge Univ. 44-71, Master, Christ's Coll. 63-; Managing Trustee, Nuffield Foundation 50-73, Chair. 73-; Chair. Advisory Council on Scientific Policy 52-64; Pres. Chemical Soc. 60-62; Master, Salters' Co. 61-62; Chancellor, Univ. of Strathclyde 65-; Chair. Royal Comm. on Medical Educ. 65-68; Chair. Govs. United Cambs. Hospitals 69-74; Pres. Royal Soc. 75-; Trustee, Ciba Foundation; awarded Meldola Medal 36, Lavoisier Medal, French Chemical Soc. 48, Davy Medal of Royal Soc. 49, Royal Medal 55; Cannizarro Medal, Italian Chemical Soc. 58; Longstaff Medal, Chemical Soc. of London 63, Copley Medal, Royal Soc. 70; foreign mem. Indian Nat. Acad. of Science, Polish Acad. of Sciences, Nat. Acad. of Sciences, U.S.A., Österreichische Akad. der Wissenschaften, Ghana Acad. of Sciences, Akad. Naturf. Halle, American Acad. of Arts and Sciences, American Phil. Soc., Australian Acad. Sciences, Royal Soc., Edinburgh; Hon. mem. Royal Australian Chemical Inst., Nobel Prize for Chemistry 57; Hon. LL.D. (Glasgow, Calif., Edinburgh and Manchester); Hon. D.Litt. (Sydney); Hon. Dr.rer.nat. (Kiel); Hon. D.Sc. (Durham, London, Madrid, Exeter, Leicester, Melbourne, Aligarh, Wales, Yale, Sheffield, Harvard, Adelaide, Australian Nat. Univ., Liverpool, Oxford, Warwick, Paris, Michigan, Strasbourg, Strathclyde). The Master's Lodge, Christ's College, Cambridge, England.

Todd, (Reginald Stephen) Garfield, D.D.; Rhodesian rancher and politician; b. 13 July 1908, Invercargill, New Zealand; s. of Thomas and the late Edith Todd; m. Jean Grace Wilson; three d.; ed. Otago Univ., Univ. of Witwatersrand, and Glen Leith Theological Coll. Worked with Thomas Todd & Sons Ltd., Invercargill, N.Z.; Superintendent Dadaya Mission, Southern Rhodesia 34-53; M.P. 46-58; Pres. United Rhodesia Party 53-58; Prime Minister 53-58; Minister of Ladour 54-58; Minister of Native Education 55-57; Minister of Labour and Social Welfare 58; founded (with Sir John Moffat) Central Africa Party 59, Pres. 59-60; founded New African Party, July 61; Dir. Hokonui Ranching Co. Ltd.; restricted to his ranch for 12 months Oct. 65; imprisoned Jan. 72, under house arrest Feb. 72-; Hon. LL.D. Leisure interest: Chair., Governing Board of Dadaya Mission (religious and educational). P.O. Dadaya, Rhodesia. Telephone: 01222 Shabami.

Todorov, Stanko; Bulgarian politician; b. 10 Dec. 1920, Pernik Region; m. Sonya Todorova 1947; two s. Active in Resistance Movement 41-44; mem. Nat. Assembly; Minister of Agriculture 52-58; Sec. Central Cttee. Bulgarian C.P. 58-59, 66-71; Full mem. Politburo 61-; Deputy Prime Minister 59-66; Perm. Bulgarian Representative to Council for Mutual Econ. Assistance (COMECON) 62-66; Chair. Council of Ministers July 71-. Ministerski Suvet, Sofia, Bulgaria.

Todorović, Mijalko; Yugoslav politician; b. 25 Sept. 1913, Knić, Kragujevac; m. Milica 1940; two s. one d.; ed. Belgrade Univ. In Nat. Liberation Movement 41-45; first as Political Commissar of Brigade, then of Division, and Corps, and finally of First Yugoslav Army; Asst. Minister of Nat. Defence and Head of Provisional Administration for Supplies 45-48; Minister of Agriculture and Forestry 48-53; Pres. of Econ. Cttee., Fed. Exec. Council 53-58; Vice-Pres. Fed. Exec. Council 58-63; Vice-Pres. Fed. Assembly and Pres. of Fed. Chamber 63-66; mem Exec. Cttee. Yugoslav League of Communists, Sec. 66-69; mem. Exec. Bureau of the Presidency 69-71; Pres. Fed. Assembly 71-74; Orders of Nat. Hero, Nat. Liberation, Partisan Star, etc.

Leisure interests: tennis, hunting. Publs. *Disalienation of Labour, Socio-Political Foundations of the Equality of the Republics and Peoples of Yugoslavia, Reorganization of the League of Communists —an Objective Need of the Working Class, Some Questions of Our Economic System, Self-government—Historical Strive of the Working Class.* Užička ul. 23, Belgrade, Yugoslavia.

Toennies, Jan Peter, PH.D.; American physicist; b. 3 May 1930, Philadelphia, Pa.; s. of Dr. Gerrit Toennies and Dita Jebeus; m. Monika Zelesnick 1966; two d.; ed. Amherst Coll., Brown Univ. Assistant, Bonn Univ., Fed. Repub. of Germany 62-65, Privat Dozent 65-67, Dozent 67-69; Scientific mem. Max-Planck-Inst. für Strömungsforschung (Fluid Dynamics) 69-; Extraordinary Prof. Göttingen Univ. 71-; Hon. Prof. Bonn Univ. 71-; Physics Prize, Göttingen Acad. of Sciences 64. Leisure interest: sailing. Publs. *Chemical Reactions in Shock Waves* (with E. F. Greene) 64, *A Study of Intermolecular Potentials with Molecular Beams at Thermal Energies* (with H. Pauly) in *Advances in Atomic and Molecular Physics* 65, *Molecular Beam Scattering Experiments*, contribution in *Physical Chemistry, an Advanced Treatise* 74, *Rotationally and Vibrationally Inelastic Scattering of Molecules* 74. Max-Planck-Institut für Strömungsforschung, Bottingerstrasse 6-8, 3400 Göttingen; Home: Dahlmannstrasse 19, 3400 Göttingen, Federal Republic of Germany. Telephone: 0551-44051 (Office); 0551-42645 (Home).

Toepfer, Alfred Gustav Carl Kurt; German businessman, philanthropist and conservationist; b. 13 July 1894, Hamburg-Altona; s. of Carl J. and Engel Maria (née Volkmer) Toepfer; m. Emma J. Klima 1922; three s. two d.; ed. Höhere Handelsschule. Founded own export-import firm trading in corn, animal foodstuffs and rape-seeds, Hamburg 19; founder and Chair. Stiftung F.V.S., Hamburg; hon. mem. Austrian Acad. of Sciences; Dr. h.c. (Kiel); Hon. Senator, Univs. of Hamburg and Innsbruck. Leisure interests: walking, conservation. Publs. numerous publications on agrarian policies, conservation, etc. 2000 Hamburg 1, Ballindamm 2/3, Federal Republic of Germany.

Toeplitz, Heinrich, LL.D., DR. IUR.; German judge; b. 5 June 1914, Berlin; s. of Georg Toeplitz (died 1918) and Margarete Toeplitz (died 1964); m. Ruth Toeplitz 1946; one s. two d.; ed. König-Wilhelm Gymnasium, Breslau, Univs. of Breslau and Leipzig. Military service 40; enforced labour, France and Netherlands 44-45; Junior Barrister, Berlin 45-47; Dept. of Justice, Town Council, Gross-Berlin 47-50; Sec. of State in D.D.R. Ministry of Justice 50-60; Pres. of Supreme Court of D.D.R. 60-; mem. Volkskammer 51-; mem. Presidium of Governing Body of Christlich-Demokratische Union Deutschlands (CDU) 52-; Vaterländischer Verdienstorden in Silber, Ehrenspange zum Vaterländischen Verdienstorden in Gold. Oberstes Gericht der Deutschen Demokratischen Republik, Littenstrasse 13, 102 Berlin, German Democratic Republic.

Toeplitz, Jerzy, LL.B., PH.D.; Polish film critic and historian; b. 24 Nov. 1909, Kharkov, U.S.S.R.; m. Izabella Stanisława Górnicka 1943; three d.; ed. Warsaw. Co-founder "Start" (film asscn.) 29, Sec. and Vice-Pres. 30-34; film work in England and Italy 35-37; mem. Cen. Council for Film Industry 38; Rector and Prof. State Theatrical and Film Higher School, Łódź 48-68; Pres. Int. Fed. of Film Archives (FIAF) 48-; Vice-Pres. Int.

Film and Television Council; mem. Int. Bureau of Historical Research 52-; mem. Jury, Int. Film Festival, Karlovy Vary 51, 52 and 56, Venice Documentary Film Festival 57, 62, Cannes 58, 65, Venice 60, 64, Mar del Plata 61, Moscow 59, 61, Bergamo 63, 64, Florence 65, Cracow 64, 65, San Sebastian 66, New Delhi 69; Dir. Inst. of Art, Polish Academy of Science 61-68; Visiting Prof. Univ. of Calif. 67; Head of Cinema Dept., Inst. of Art 68-72; Dir. Film and Television School, Australia.

Publs. *Historia Sztuki Filmowej (History of Cinematographic Art)* Vol. I 55, Vol. II 56, Vol. III 59, Vol. IV 69, Vol. V 71, *Film i telewizja w U.S.A. (Film and T.V. in U.S.A.)* 64, *Hollywood and After* 74.

The Film and Television School, 11-15 Lyonpark Road, North Ryde, N.S.W. 2113; Home: 19/30 Archer Street, Chatswood, N.S.W. 2067, Australia.

Telephone: 888-3066 (Office); 41-4825 (Home).

Toft, H. C.; Danish politician; b. 1914, Thisted, Jutland; *s.* of L. Toft and Anna Johansen; *m.* Nina Jørgenson 1943; two *s.*
Forest Ranger 36; fought in Russo-Finnish War of 39-40; Farmer Bjørndalgård 43; mem. Folketing 57-; Auditor of Nat. Accounts 68-69; Minister of the Interior July 69-Oct. 71; Chair. Conservative Cttee. of Youth Movement of Thisted 37-38, Bldg. and Eng. Cttee. of Agronomic Soc. of Thy District 46-62, Conservative Parl. Group 68-69; mem. Parl. Foreign Affairs Cttee., Board of Dirs. of Danmarks Nationalbank 68, Nordic Council.
Bjørndalgård, 7790, Hvidbjerg, Thy, Denmark.

Togbe, Jacques Dabra; Togolese diplomatist; b. 3 May 1930, Akloa; *m.*; three *c.*; ed. primary and secondary schools in Togo and Dahomey, Univs. of Montpellier and Paris and Inst. des Hautes Etudes d'Outre-Mer, Paris.
Inspector of Labour and Head of the Labour Inspection Service 65-68; Dir.-Gen. of Labour and Social Security 68-72; Deputy Sec.-Gen. Rassemblement du Peuple Togolaise, also mem. Political Bureau 69-71; Prof. of Labour Law and Social Security, Ecole Nat. d'Admin. Togolaise 65-72; Amb. and Perm. Rep. to UN April 72-; Officer, Order of the Leopard (Zaire).
Permanent Mission of Togo to United Nations, 112 East 40th Street, New York, N.Y. 10017, U.S.A.

Togni, Giuseppe; Italian politician; b. 5 Dec. 1903; *m.* Bianca Corbin 1930; four *c.*; ed. Spoleto Technical Inst., Univs. of Pisa and Rome.
Dir. of "Gruppo Marmi" of Soc. Montecatini; mem. Consultative Council 45; Deputy to Constituent Ass. 46-48; mem. Chamber of Deputies 48-68; Under-Sec. of State, Ministry of Labour and Social Security 47, Minister of Industry and Commerce 47, for Economic Co-ordination 48, of Industry and Commerce 50-51, of Transport 53, of State Participation 57, of Public Works 57-60, of Industry and Commerce 63, of Posts and Telecommunications 73-74; mem. Senate 68-; Prof. Univ. of Rome; Pres. Italian Confed. of Management, Higher Inst. of Management, Italian Asscn. of Public Relations; Pres. Nat. Inst. of Foreign Trade 49; Grand Cross of Sovereign Military Order of Malta, Vatican Order of St. Gregory the Great, Order of Merit Fed. Repub. of Germany, Grand Commdr. Légion d'Honneur, and many others; Christian Democrat.
Via Giovanni Paisiella 53, Rome, Italy.

Toh Chin Chye, PH.D.; Singapore physiologist and politician; b. 10 Dec. 1921; ed. Raffles Coll., Singapore, Univ. Coll., London Univ., and National Inst. for Medical Research, London.
Founder, People's Action Party, Chair. 54-; Reader in Physiology, Univ. of Singapore 58-64; Research Assoc., Univ. of Singapore 64; Deputy Prime Minister of Singapore 59-68; Minister for Science and Technology 68-75;

Minister for Health 75-; mem. Parl. Singapore 59-; Chair. Board of Govs., Singapore Polytechnic 59-75; Vice-Chancellor, Univ. of Singapore 68-75; Chair. of Board of Govs. Regional Inst. for Higher Educ. and Devt. 70-75.
Ministry of Health, Palmer Road, Singapore 2; and 23 Greenview Crescent, Singapore 11, Singapore.

Tokaryev, Aleksandr Maksimovich; Soviet politician; b. 1921; ed. Kuibyshev Inst. of Construction Engineers. Member C.P.S.U. 42-; Soviet Army service 40-45; Komsomol Leader 49-51; Sec. Stavropol, later First Sec. Novo Kuibyshev City Cttees. of C.P. 51-55; Sec. Kuibyshev Regional Cttee. of C.P. 58-59; Chair. Exec. Cttee. Kuibyshev Regional Soviet of Working People's Deputies 59-63; First Sec. Kuibyshev Regional Cttee. of C.P. 63-67; Minister of Industrial Construction, U.S.S.R. 67-; mem. Central Cttee. C.P.S.U. 66-; Deputy to U.S.S.R. Supreme Soviet 62-.
U.S.S.R. Ministry of Industrial Construction, Moscow, U.S.S.R.

Tokunaga, Masatoshi; Japanese politician; b. 25 Aug. 1913.
Director Japan Bereaved Asscn.; mem. House of Councillors 59-; Deputy Minister of Health and Welfare; Standing Chair., Ministry of Finance; Minister of Transport 73-74.
12-17, Sasuke, 2-chome, Kamakura City, Kanagawa Prefecture 248, Japan.

Tolbert, William Richard, Jr., B.A.; Liberian politician; b. 13 May 1913, Bensonville; *s.* of William and Charlott Tolbert; *m.* Victoria David 1936; two *s.* six *d.* (one deceased); ed. Liberia Coll. (now Univ.).
Liberian Treasury 35, Disbursing Officer 36-53; mem. House of Reps. 43-51; Vice-Pres. of Liberia 51-71, Pres. July 71-; Pres. Baptist World Alliance for Africa 65-70; fmr. Chair. Board of Directors, Bank of Liberia; Hon. D.C.L., Hon. D.D. (Liberia Univ.); numerous Liberian and foreign decorations.
The Executive Mansion, Monrovia, Liberia.

Toledo Piza, Arthur Luiz de; Brazilian painter and print-maker; b. 1928.
Painter and exhibitor 43-; moved to Paris 52; regular exhibitor at Bienal of São Paulo and of Ljubljana since 51; Triennali of Grenchen since 58; One-man exhibitions in Brazil, Germany, Yugoslavia, U.S.A. and Paris; works in many important museums and private collections; Purchase Prize 53, and Nat. Prize for Prints São Paulo Biennale 59, Prizes at biennales at Ljubljana 61, Santiago 66, Venice 66, and Grenchen Triennale 61.
16 rue Dauphine, Paris 6e, France.

Tolkunov, Lev Nikolayevich; Soviet journalist; b. 22 Jan. 1919, Bukreevka, Kursk Region; ed. Gorky Inst. of Literature, Moscow and Higher Party School of C.P.S.U.
Sub-Editor and Military Correspondent *Pravda* 38-44; Deputy Exec. Sec. and Head of Dept. *For a Lasting Peace, For a People's Democracy* 47-51; Deputy Editor, later Editor, People's Democracies Dept. *Pravda* 51-57; Deputy Chief of Central Cttee. of C.P.S.U. Dept. for Liaison with Communist and Workers' Parties in other Communist Countries 61-65; Editor-in-Chief *Izvestia* 65-76; Chair. of Board of Novosti Press Agency 76-; Alt. mem. C.P.S.U. Central Cttee. 66-; Deputy to U.S.S.R. Supreme Soviet 66-, mem. Foreign Affairs Comm., Soviet of Nationalities, Vice-Chair. U.S.S.R. Parliamentary Group; Orders of Lenin, Red Banner of Labour, Red Star and medals.
Novosti, Pushkinskaya pl. 2, Moscow, U.S.S.R.

Tolloy, Giusto; Italian politician; b. 3 Nov. 1907; ed. Accad. Militare, Modena and Scuola di Guerra.
Major in Second World War, then founded anti-fascist

Partito Italiano del Lavoro, later merged with Partito Socialistà Italiano (P.S.I.); mem. Cttee. P.S.I. 47-, Organising Chief 50-54; mem. Chamber of Deputies 48-58; Senator 58-; Pres. of P.S.I. Group in the Senate; Vice-Pres. Foreign Comm. and Italian section Inter-Parliamentary Union; Minister of Foreign Trade 66-68. The Senate, Rome, Italy.

Tolstikov, Vasili Sergeyevich; Soviet politician and diplomatist; b. 1917; ed. Leningrad Inst. of Railway Engineering.
Soviet Army 41-46; construction orgs., Leningrad 46-52; mem. C.P.S.U. 48-; party and Soviet work 52-57; First Deputy Chair. Exec. Cttee. Leningrad Soviet of Workers' Deputies 57-60; Sec., later Second Sec. Leningrad Regional Cttee., C.P.S.U. 60-62, First Sec. 62-70; Amb. to People's Republic of China 70-; mem. Presidium of U.S.S.R. Supreme Soviet 62-71; mem. Central Cttee. of C.P.S.U. 61-; Deputy to U.S.S.R. Supreme Soviet 62-.
Soviet Embassy, Peking, People's Republic of China.

Tolstikov, Yevgeniy Ivanovich, D.SC.; Soviet polar explorer; b. 9 Feb. 1913, Tula; m. Nina Nikolayevna 1937; one s. one d.; ed. Moscow Hydrometeorological Inst.
Head of the Soviet drifting station SP-4 in the Arctic 54-55; head of the Soviet Int. Geophysical Year Aroarctic Expedition to Mirny 58-59; Deputy Chief, Main Dept. of Northern Sea Route of Ministry of Merchant Marine 55-63; Deputy Head Main Board for Hydro-meteorological Services for U.S.S.R. Council of Ministers 63-; mem. C.P.S.U.; Hero of U.S.S.R.; State Prize Laureate.
Leisure interests: literature, sport.
Main Board for Hydrometeorological Services for U.S.S.R. Council of Ministers, Pereulok Pavlika Morzova 12, Moscow, U.S.S.R.

Tolubko, Gen. Vladimir Fedorovich; Soviet army officer; b. 1914; ed. Military Acad. of Tank and Mechanized Forces and Acad. of Gen. Staff.
Teacher in secondary school 31; Soviet Army 32-; soldier, officer cadet, tank, platoon, company Commdr. 32-38; at Military Acad. of Tank and Mechanized Forces 38-41; Squadron Commdr., Chief of Staff of Tank Div., Commdr. of Tank Brigade, Chief Staff Officer of Tank Corps 41-46; on staff of U.S.S.R. Ministry of Defence, then First Deputy Commdr. Rocket Forces, later Commdr. Siberian Mil. District 46-69; Commdr. Far Eastern Mil. District 69-; Deputy to U.S.S.R. Supreme Soviet 70-.
Ministry of Defence, 34 Naberezhnaya M. Thoreza, Moscow, U.S.S.R.

Tomal, Zdzisław; Polish politician; b. 19 March 1921, Rogów, Kazimierza Wielka; ed. Higher School of Agriculture, Wrocław.
Active in ZMW (Rural Youth Union—"Wici") 38; during Second World War, fought with Peasant Battns. in Pińczów; after war worked for Wici and Peasant Movement; worked in Presidium of Voivodship Nat. Council, Wrocław 47-56; Vice-Pres. Voivodship Cttee. of ZSL (United Peasant Party), Wrocław 57; Chair. Presidium of Voivodship People's Council, Koszalin 57-66; mem. ZSL Cen. Cttee. 59-, mem. Presidium of ZSL Cen. Cttee. 64-, Vice-Pres. Cen. Cttee. 73-; Deputy to Seym 64-; Vice-Pres. Council of Ministers 69-76; Chair. Polish Cttee. for Preservation of the Environment Oct. 70-; decorations include Order of Banner of Labour 1st and 2nd Class, Officer's Cross of Order of Polonia Restituta.
c/o Urząd Rady Ministrów, Aleje Ujazdowskie 1/3, 00-583 Warsaw, Poland.

Tomasini, René François; French civil servant and politician; b. 14 April 1919; ed. Univ. de Strasbourg.
Early service in Provincial Prefectures; Technical Counsellor to French Resident-Gen. Morocco 54, Dir. of Work and Social Questions 55-57; Dir. Centre for

re-orientation of French repatriated from Morocco and Tunisia 57; Deputy 58-; Sec.-Gen. Nat. Council of Union pour la Nouvelle République (U.N.R.) 61-67, Asst. Sec.-Gen. of U.N.R. 61-67; mem. Nat. Secretariat of U.N.R. 67; Sec. of Nat. Council of U.D.R. 68; mem. European Parl. Assembly 62-71; Vice-Pres. U.N.R.-U.D.T. in Nat. Assembly 62, U.D.R. 68-72; Sec.-Gen. U.D.R. 71-72; Pres. Higher Council of Electricity and Gas 66; Mayor of Corny 61-67, Mayor of Les Andelys 65-72; Conseiller Gén. of Eure region 68-; Sec. of State attached to Prime Minister, responsible for Relations with Parl. 74-; Chevalier Légion d'Honneur, Croix de Guerre, Médaille de la Résistance.
Assemblée nationale, Paris 7e; and Le Clan, Noyers-les-Andelys, Eure, France.

Tómasson, Tómas Ármann, M.A.; Icelandic diplomatist; b. 1 Jan. 1929, Reykjavík; s. of Tómas Tómasson and Gudrun Thorgrimsdottir; m. Heba Jónsdóttir 1957 (divorced); two s. one d.; ed. Reykjavík Grammar School, Univ. of Illinois, Fletcher School of Law and Diplomacy and Columbia Univ.
Entered Icelandic foreign service 54; Sec., Moscow 54-58; Ministry for Foreign Affairs 58-60; Deputy Perm. Rep. to NATO and OECD 60-66; Chief of Div., Ministry for Foreign Affairs 66-69, Deputy Sec.-Gen. of Ministry 70-71; Amb. to Belgium and EEC and Perm. Rep. on North Atlantic Council Aug. 71-; Order of the Falcon (Iceland) and decorations from France and Sweden.
Avenue des Lauriers 19, 1150 Brussels, Belgium; c/o utanríkisráduneytid, Reykjavík, Iceland.
Telephone: 2151035 and 7311187 (Belgium); 25000 (Iceland).

Tomaszewski, Henryk; Polish graphic artist and designer; b. 10 June 1914, Warsaw; m.; one s.; ed. Warsaw Acad. of Fine Arts.
Worked with Film Polski 47-52; Scenographer, Syrena Theatre 50-52; Prof. Warsaw Acad. of Fine Arts 52-; mem. Asscn. of Polish Plastic Artists, Alliance Graphique Internationale; five 1st Prizes, Int. Exhbn. of Posters, Vienna 48, State Prize, 2nd Class 53, Premier's Prize for Illustrations in Children's Books 58, 1st Prize, VII Biennale of Arts, São Paulo 63, Silver Medal, Int. Biennale of Posters, Warsaw 66, Gold Medal 70, Knight's Cross, Order of Polonia Restituta 54, Commdr.'s Cross 59; one-man exhbns.: Bienne, Switzerland 69, Museum of Posters, Warsaw 72; works exhibited: Nat. Gallery, Warsaw, Museum of Modern Art, New York, Museum of Modern Art, São Paulo, Fagersta Library, Stockholm, Kunstgewerbe Museum, Zurich, Museum Villa Hugel, Essen.
Publ. *Książka zażaleń* (Book of Complaints).
Ul. Szpitalna 8 m. 17, 00-031 Warsaw, Poland.

Tomaszewski, Henryk; Polish choreographer, ballet master and mime; b. 11 Nov. 1919, Poznań; ed. Ballet School, Ivo Gall's Studio.
Member of F. Parnell Ballet Ensemble, then of Wrocław Opera Ballet 49-56; organized Mime Studio 55 (name changed to Mime Theatre 56); now Artistic Man. Wrocław Mime Theatre; won 1st Prize, World Festival of Youth, Moscow with his first programme; Medal of French Critics, Festival of Nations 62, Gold Medal, Swedish Soc. of Dance 63, Gold Star, VIII Int. Festival of Dance 71, Knight's Cross, Order of Polonia Restituta, Press Prize, Wrocław, Minister of Culture and Arts Prize, 2nd Class 62; performances in Europe, America and Africa; ballets: *Process* (from Kafka) 66, *Gilgamesh* 68, *Klątwa* (by Wyspiański) 69, *Odejście Fausta* 70, *Menażeria Cesarowej Filissy* (with F. Wedekinda), *Peer Gynt* 74, *Księżniczka Turandot* (by C. Gozzi) 74.
Al. Dębowa 16, 53-121 Wrocław, Poland.

Tombaugh, Clyde William, M.A.; American astronomer; b. 4 Feb. 1906, Streator, Ill.; s. of Muron and Adella Tombaugh (née Chritton); m. Patricia Edson 1934; one s. one d.; ed. Univ. of Kansas.

Assistant Astronomer, Lowell Observatory, Flagstaff, Arizona 29-43; Science Instructor, Arizona State Coll. 43-45; Optical Physicist and Astronomer, White Sands Missile Range 46-55; Astronomer, New Mexico State Univ. 55-59; Assoc. Prof. Dept. of Earth Sciences and Astronomy, New Mexico State Univ. 61-65, Prof. 65-, Emer. 73-; mem. Amer. Astronomical Soc. 31-, Meteoritical Soc. 32-; mem. Int. Astronomical Union Comm. on Planets and Satellites; planetary searches and observations, including the Moon, Mars, Venus, Jupiter and Saturn; discovered ninth planet, Pluto 30, and five new galactic star clusters and one globular star cluster; Hon. D.Sc. (Univ. of Arizona); Fellow, American Inst. of Aeronautics and Astronautics; numerous awards.
Leisure interest: grinding, polishing and figuring telescope mirrors.
Publs. *The Search for Small Natural Earth Satellites* 59 (co-author), *Lectures in Aerospace Medicine* 60, 61, *The Trans-Neptunian Planet Search* 61, *Geology of Mars*, and over 30 other papers.
P.O. Box 306, Mesilla Park, New Mexico 88047; and Dept. of Astronomy, Box 4500, New Mexico State University, University Park, New Mexico, U.S.A.
Telephone: 505-526-9274 (Home); 646-2107 (Office).

Tombazos, George; Cypriot politician; b. 2 Feb. 1919, Morphou; s. of Christos and Maria Tombazos; m. Diana Tombazos 1960; two s.; ed. Pancyprian Gymnasium, Cyprus College, Dentists' School of Athens.
Worked as dentist at Morphou 50-66; M.P. for Nicosia 60-66; Minister of Agricultural and Natural Resources 66-70; Head Central Information Service 70-75; Minister of Communications and Works 75-.
Ministry of Communications and Works, Nicosia, Cyprus.

Tomeh, Georges J., M.A., PH.D.; Syrian university professor and diplomatist; b. 1 March 1921; ed. American Univ. of Beirut and Georgetown Univ.
Attaché, London, and Alt. Del. to UNESCO 45-46; Syrian Embassy, Washington 47-52; Alt. Gov. Int. Monetary Fund 50; Dir. UN and Treaties Dept., Ministry of Foreign Affairs, Damascus 53-54; Asst. Prof of Philosophy and Asst. to Dean of Arts and Sciences, American Univ. of Beirut 54-56; Dir. Research Dept., Ministry of Foreign Affairs, Damascus 56-57; Consul-Gen., New York 57-58, Consul-Gen. of United Arab Republic in New York 58, Minister, New York 61; Consul-Gen. and Deputy Perm. Rep. of Syria to UN 61-63; Minister of Economy, Syrian Arab Republic 63; Prof. of Philosophy, Syrian Univ. 64-65; Perm. Rep. to UN 65-72.
Publs. *The Climax of Philosophical Conflict in Islam* 53, *Islam* 57, *The Constitution and Electoral Laws of Syria, Where Islam and Christianity Meet* 60, *The Dynamics of Neutralism in the Arab World* 64, *Challenge and Response: A Judgement of History* 69.
Ministry of Foreign Affairs, Damascus, Syria.

Tomic, Romero Radomiro; Chilean lawyer, politician and diplomatist; b. 7 May 1914; ed. Universidad Católica de Chile.
Newspaper Editor 37-41; mem. Chamber of Deputies 41-45, 45-49, Senate 50-53, 61-65; founded Christian Democratic Party (PDC) 35, Chair. of Youth Movement 35-37, Nat. Chair. of Party 46-47, 52-53; Ambassador to U.S.A. 65-68; Leader of PDC 69-; Presidential candidate 70.
Publs. numerous political essays and *The Inter-American System and the Regional Market* 58.
Partido Demócrata Cristiano, Santiago, Chile.

Tomkins, Sir Edward Emile, G.C.M.G., C.V.O.; British diplomatist; b. 16 Nov. 1915, Jubbulpore, India; s. of late Lt. Col. E. L. Tomkins and Marie Louise de

Marigny; m. Gillian Benson 1955; one s. two d.; ed. Ampleforth Coll., and Trinity Coll., Cambridge.
Entered diplomatic service 39; mil. service 40-44; has served at British Embassies in Moscow, Paris, Bonn and Washington; Amb. to the Netherlands 70-72, to France Nov. 72-75.
Leisure interests: travel, music, gardening, skiing, golf.
Winslow Hall, Winslow, Buckingham, MK18 3HL; and 17 Thurloe Place Mews, London, S.W.7, England.
Telephone: Winslow 2323; 01-589 9623.

Tomkins, Rt. Rev. Oliver Stratford, M.A., D.D.; British theologian; b. 9 June 1908, Hankow, China; s. of Rev. Leopold Charles Fellows Tomkins and Mary Katie Stratford; m. Ursula Mary Dunn 1939; one s. three d.; ed. Trent Coll., Christ's Coll., and Westcott House, Cambridge.
Asst. Gen. Sec. Student Christian Movement 33-36; editor *Student Movement* Magazine 36-40; Vicar Holy Trinity Church, Millhouses, Sheffield 40-45; Assoc. Gen. Sec. World Council of Churches and Sec. of its Comm. on Faith and Order 45-52; Warden of Theological Coll., Lincoln 53-59; Bishop of Bristol 59-Oct. 75; World Council of Churches Cen. Cttee. 68-74.
Leisure interests: family life and frivolous reading.
Publs. *The Wholeness of the Church* 49, *The Church in the Purpose of God* 50, *Lund 1952: The Report of the Third World Conference on Faith and Order* (ed.), *The Life of Edward Woods* 57, *A Time for Unity* 64, *Guarded by Faith* 71.
14 St. George's Square, Worcester, WR1 1HX, England.
Telephone: Worcester 25330.

Tomlinson, Sir Frank Stanley, K.C.M.G.; British diplomatist; b. 21 March 1912, Batley, Yorkshire; s. of late John Derrick Tomlinson and Mary (née Laycock) Tomlinson; m. Nancy Gleeson-White 1959; ed. High Pavement School, Nottingham and Univ. College, Nottingham.
Consular Service in Japan 35-41, Saigon 41-42; served in U.S.A. 43-45, Consul, Washington 45; Acting Consul-Gen., Manila 45-46, Chargé d'Affaires 46-47; First Sec., Foreign Office 47-51; Counsellor, Washington 51-54; Head of S.E. Asia Dept., Foreign Office 54-59; served Berlin 59-61; Deputy Perm. U.K. Rep. to North Atlantic Treaty Org. (NATO) 61-64; Consul-Gen., New York 64-66; High Commr. in Ceylon 66-69; Deputy Under-Sec. of State, Foreign Office 69-72; mem. Gov. Body School of Oriental and African Studies 72-; Chair. Council of Int. Social Service 73-, Royal Soc. for Asian Affairs 74-; Hon. LL.D. Nottingham Univ.
Leisure interests: reading, trout fishing, wine.
6/24 Buckland Crescent, London, N.W.3, England.
Telephone: 01-722-6445.

Tomonaga, Sin-itiro, D.SC.; Japanese physicist; b. 31 March 1906, Tokyo; s. of Sanjuro and Hide Tomonaga; m. Ryo Tomonaga 1940; two s. one d.; ed. Third High School, Kyoto, and Kyoto Imperial Univ.
Research student, Inst. of Physical and Chemical Research 32-39; studies, Univ. of Leipzig 37-39; Asst., Inst. of Physical and Chemical Research 39-40; Lecturer, Tokyo Bunrika Univ. (absorbed into Tokyo Univ. of Educ. 49) 40, Prof. of Physics 41-69; Dir. of Inst. of Optical Research, Kyoiku Univ. (Tokyo Univ. of Educ.) 63-69; Pres. Tokyo Univ. of Educ. 56-62; Pres. Science Council of Japan 63-69; Japan Academy Prize 48, Order of Culture 52, Lomonosov Medal (U.S.S.R.) 64; Nobel Prize for Physics 65.
Publs. *On the photo-electric production of positive and negative electrons* 34, *Innere Reibung und Wärmeleitfähigkeit der Kernmaterie* 38, *On a Relativistically Invariant Formulation of the Quantum Theory of Wave Fields* 46, *On the Effect of the Field Reactions on the Interaction of Mesotrons and Nuclear Particles I, II, III, IV* 46-47, *A Self-Consistent Subtraction Method in*

Quantum Field Theory I, II 48, *Remarks on Bloch's Method of Sound Waves to Many-Fermion Problems* 50.
3-17-12, Kyonan-cho, Musashino City, Tokyo, Japan.
Telephone: 0422-32-2410.

Tomorowicz, Bohdan; Polish diplomatist; b. 1 April 1923, Warsaw; ed. Main School of Planning and Statistics, Warsaw.
In Polish Air Force in U.K. in Second World War; Editor, Polish radio 46-47; party posts, staff of Polish Workers' Party, later the Polish United Workers' Party 45-57; Counsellor, Polish Embassy, London 57-63; Deputy Dir. Dept. of Int. Orgs. Ministry of Foreign Affairs, Warsaw 63-66; Amb. and Perm. Rep. to UN, New York 66-69; Ministerial Counsellor, Ministry of Foreign Affairs, Warsaw 70; at Polish Inst. of Int. Affairs June 71-; Gold Cross of Merit, Knight Cross of Order of Polonia Restituta.
Polski Instytut Spraw Międzynarodowych, ul. Warecka 1, Warsaw, Poland.

Tömpe, István; Hungarian politician; b. 2 Jan. 1909, Budapest; *s.* of Benö Tömpe and Jolán Sugár; *m.* Jolán Kovács 1948; one *s.* one *d.*
Upholsterer by original trade; joined workers' movement 28, C.P. 29; lived in France 29-34; fought in Spain during Civil War; returned to Hungary 41, arrested 42; held different party functions after 45; held leading posts in Ministries for Home Affairs, and Agriculture 46-48; Deputy Minister of Armed Forces 56, of Home Affairs and of Agriculture 58-62; Chair. Hungarian Radio and Television 62-74; Chair. State Cttee. for Radio and TV 74-; Sec. of State 74-; Vice-Pres. Int. Radio and TV Org. 73-75; mem. Hungarian Socialist Workers' Party Cen. Cttee., mem. Agitation and Propaganda Board attached to HSWP Cen. Cttee. 75-
Leisure interest: wild-game shooting.
Office: Magyar Rádió és Televizió Bisottság, H-1800 Budapest VIII, Bródy Sándor-utca 5/7, Hungary.
Telephone: 338-330.

Tomsky, Nikolay Vasiliyevich; Soviet sculptor; b. 12 Dec. 1900, Ramushevo, Novgorod Region; ed. Leningrad Technical School of Fine Arts.
Represented at exhibitions in the U.S.S.R., India, China, Indonesia, Finland, German Democratic Repub., Bulgaria, Hungary, Egypt, Paris Universal Exhibition 37, New York World's Fair 39, 28th and 29th Venice Biennale 56, 58; mem. of U.S.S.R. Acad. of Fine Arts 49-, Pres. 68-; mem. Lenin Peace Prize Cttee. 73; State Prizewinner 41, 47, 49, 50, 52, Lenin Prizewinner 72; People's Artist of the U.S.S.R.; Hero of Socialist Labour; several awards.
Works include: Monuments to Kirov (Leningrad) 38, Lenin (Voronezh, Saransk, Orel, Murmansk, Tashkent, Berlin and Kuibyshev) 40, 58, 63, Apanasenko (Belgorod) 49, Chernyakovsky (Vilnius) 50, Gogol (Moscow) 52, Nakhimov (Sebastopol) 59, Lomonosov (Moscow) 53, Kutuzov (Moscow) 73, and many sculptural portraits; Hero of the Soviet Union, Young Partisan, Lenya Golikov (Novgorod) 64.
U.S.S.R. Academy of Arts, 21 Kropotkinskaya Ulitsa, Moscow, U.S.S.R.

Ton Duc Thang; North Vietnamese politician; b. 20 Aug. 1888, Long Xuyen Province, South Viet-Nam.
Went to France and joined French Navy 12; returned to Saigon 20; joined Viet-Nam Revolutionary Youth Soc. 25; imprisoned by French on Pulo Condore Island 29-45; mem. Communist Party of Indo-China 30; held exec. Party and Govt. posts 45-, including Deputy Chair., then Chair. of Standing Cttee. of Democratic Republic of Viet-Nam (D.R.V.) Nat. Assembly; Chair. of Central Cttee. Presidium of Viet-Nam Fatherland Front; mem. Central Cttee. of Working People's Party of Viet-Nam; Vice-Pres. D.R.V. 60-69, Pres. Sept. 69-;

Chair. Central Board of Vietnamese-Soviet Friendship Soc.; at Congress of Working People's Party of Viet-Nam 51, 60; Leader Nat. Assembly Del. to U.S.S.R. 56; Lenin Int. Prize for Promotion of Peace Among Nations, Order of Lenin of U.S.S.R. 67.
Office of the President, Hanoi, Democratic Republic of Viet-Nam.

Tončić-Sorinj, Lujo, LL.D.; Austrian landowner and politician; b. 12 April 1915, Vienna; *s.* of Dušan and Mabel von Tončić-Sorinj; *m.* Renate Trenker 1956; one *s.* four *d.*; ed. Grammar School, Salzburg, and Univs. of Vienna and Zagreb.
Assistant to Chair. S.E. Europe Dept., Berlin Univ. 40-44; Military Service 41-44; Head of Political Dept., Austrian Research Inst. for Econs. and Politics 46-49, Editor *Berichte und Informationen* 46-49; mem. Parl. for Land Salzburg 49-66; Chair. Legal Cttee. of Austrian Parl. 53-56, Foreign Affairs Cttee. 56-59; in charge of Foreign Affairs questions, Austrian People's Party 59-; Austrian mem. Consultative Assembly of Council of Europe 53-66, Vice-Pres. Political Comm.; Vice-Pres. Council of Europe 61-62; Minister of Foreign Affairs 66-68; Sec.-Gen. Council of Europe 69-74; Grosses Goldenes Ehrenzeichen am Bande (Austria) and other decorations.
Leisure interests: history, geography, swimming, diving.
5020 Salzburg, Schloss Fürberg, Pausingerstrasse 11, Austria.
Telephone: 06222-73437.

Tonga, King of (*see* Taufa'ahau Tupou IV).

Tonkin, Hon. John Trezise, M.L.A.; Australian politician; b. 2 Feb. 1902, Boulder; *s.* of John Trezise Tonkin and Julia Carrigan; *m.* 1st Rosalie Cleghorn 1929 (died 1969), one *s.* two *d.*; *m.* 2nd Joan West 1971.
Member W. Australia Legislative Assembly 33-; Minister of Educ. and Social Services 43; Deputy Leader of Opposition 47; Minister for Educ., Works and Water Supplies 53; Deputy Premier 55-59; Deputy Leader of Opposition 59-67, Leader 67-71; Premier of W. Australia, Treas. and Minister of Cultural Affairs 71-74; Leader of Opposition 74-; Fellow, Australian Soc. of Accountants; Labor Party.
Leisure interest: gardening.
Parliament House, Perth, Western Australia.
Telephone: 218993.

Tooley, John, M.A.; British administrator; b. 1 June 1924, Rochester, Kent; *s.* of late H. R. Tooley; *m.* 1st Judith Craig Morris (dissolved 1965), three *d.*; *m.* 2nd Patricia J. N. Bagshawe 1968, one *s.*; ed. Repton School and Magdalene Coll., Cambridge.
Secretary, Guildhall School of Music and Drama 52-55; Asst. to Gen. Admin., Royal Opera House, Covent Garden 55-60, Asst. Gen. Admin. 60-70, Gen. Admin. 70-.
Leisure interests: sailing, theatre.
12, Earl's Court Gardens, London, S.W.5, England.
Telephone: 01-370-2956.

Toom, Lieut.-Gen. Willem den; Netherlands air force officer and politician; b. 11 July 1911, Rotterdam; *m.* Jeannette Niessink; three *c.*; ed. Royal Military Acad., Breda, Netherlands, and General Staff Coll.
Cadet, Netherlands Royal Mil. Acad. 30-33; Air training 36-37; Prisoner of war 40-45; Maj. 48; Head, Operations Section of the Air Force Staff, Lt.-Col 50; Head Air Force Section European Defence Comm., Paris 52-53; Col. 53; Asst. Chief of Staff, Air Force 53-55; C.O. Airbase Ypenburg 55-56; Air Commodore, C.O. Air Force Training Centre, Arnhem 56-58; Netherlands Mil. Rep., SHAPE, and Mil. Adviser of Netherlands Perm. Rep., NATO, Paris 58-60; Maj.-Gen. Deputy Chief of Staff, Air Force 60-63; Dir. Air Force Procurement 63; State Sec. of Defence (Air Force) 63-65; Chair.

NATO Air Defence Ground Environment System Policy Board, Paris 65-67; Minister of Defence 67-72; Commdr. Order of Orange-Nassau, War Commemoration Cross, Medal for Freedom and Peace, Commdr. Order of Black Star (France), Grand Cross of the Order of the Right Hand of the Gurkha of Nepal, Grand Cross of the Order of Merit of the Fed. Repub. of Germany, Knight of Order of Netherlands Lion.
Laan van Clingendael 133, The Hague, Netherlands.

Toon, Malcolm, M.A.; American diplomatist; b. 4 July 1916, Troy, N.Y.; s. of George Toon and Margaret Broadfoot; m. Elizabeth J. Taylor 1943; one s. two d.; ed. Tufts Univ., Fletcher School of Law and Diplomacy, and Harvard Univ.
Research Technician, Nat. Resources Planning Board 39-41; Ensign, Lt.-Commdr., U.S. Naval Reserve 42-46; in U.S. Foreign Service 46-; Amb. to Czechoslovakia 69-71, to Yugoslavia 71-75; Amb. to Israel 75-; Superior Honor Award, Dept. of State 65.
Leisure interests: golf, tennis, hunting, fishing.
71 Hayarkon Street, Tel-Aviv, Israel.

Toothill, Sir John Norman, Kt., C.B.E.; British engineering executive; b. 11 Nov. 1908, Leicester; s. of John Harold Toothill and late Helena Toothill; m. Ethel Amelia Stannard 1935; ed. Beaminster Grammar School, Dorset.
Engineering apprentice, Tilling Stevens, Maidstone 30; Chief Cost Accountant Ferranti Ltd., Hollinwood, Lancs. 34-43, Gen. Man. (Scotland) 43-68, Dir. Ferranti Co. 58-75 (retd.); Chair. Cttee. of Inquiry into Scottish Economy 61; Dir. A.I. Welders Ltd., Inverness, Edinburgh Investment Trust, Edinburgh, W. A. Baxter & Sons Ltd., Fochabers, R. W. Toothill Ltd., Darlington; Vice-Pres. Scottish Council, Devt. and Industry Council; Gov. Coll. Aeronautics, Cranfield; Hon. LL.D., Hon. D.Sc.
Leisure interests: fishing, shooting.
St. Germain's, Longniddry, East Lothian, Scotland.
Telephone: Longniddry 52106.

Tope, Trimbak Krishna, M.A., LL.B.; Indian lawyer and teacher; b. 28 Feb. 1914, Yeola, Nasik District; one s. three d.; ed. Bombay Univ.
Professor of Sanskrit, Ramnarain Ruia Coll. 39-47; Advocate, Bombay High Court 46; Prof. of Law, Govt. Law Coll. 47, Principal and Perry Prof. of Jurisprudence 58-; Vice-Chancellor, Univ. of Bombay 71-; Pres. Maharashtra Samajik Parishad.
Leisure interest: gardening.
Publs. *Why Hindu Code?*, *Indian Constitution*, *A Modern Sage*.
University of Bombay, Bombay 32, India.
Telephone: 255726 (Office); 259887 (Office-Personal); 291750 (Home).

Töplitz, Heinrich (see Toeplitz, Heinrich).

Topolski, Feliks; British painter; b. 14 Aug. 1907, Warsaw, Poland; s. of Edward Topolski and Stanisława Drutowska; m. 1st Marion Everall 1944 (divorced 1975), one s. one d.; m. 2nd Caryl Stanley 1975; ed. Acad. of Art, Warsaw, Paris and Italy.
Came to England 35; official war artist from 40 to 45; works in British Museum, Victoria and Albert Museum, Tate Gallery, Imperial War Museum, Glasgow, Nottingham, Edinburgh, Toronto, Brooklyn, Texas Univ., Melbourne, Tel Aviv, Delhi, Warsaw, Singapore and in Buckingham Palace, London; exhibitions in Europe, Canada, U.S., India and Australia.
Publs. *The London Spectacle* 35; illustrated Bernard Shaw's *Geneva* 39, *In Good King Charles's Golden Days* 39, *Pygmalion* 41; *Penguin Prints* 41, *Britain in Peace and War* 41, *Russia in War* 42, *Three Continents* 44-45, *Portrait of G. B. S.* 46, *Confessions of a Congress Delegate* 49, *88 Pictures* 51, *Topolski's Chronicle* 53-, *Sketches of Gandhi* 54, *The Blue Conventions* 56, *Topolski's Chronicle for Students of World Events* 58, *Topolski's Legal London* 61, *Face to Face* 64, *The United Nations: Sacred Drama* (with Conor Cruise O'Brien) 68, *Holy China* 68, *Shem Ham Japeth Inc. U.S.A.* 69, *Paris Lost* 73.
Bridge Arch 158, opposite Artists' Entrance, Royal Festival Hall, London, S.E.1, England.

Topolski, Jerzy; Polish historian; b. 20 Sept. 1928, Poznań; ed. Univ. of Poznań.
Doctor 51-56, Docent 56-61, Assoc. Prof. 61-68, Prof. 68-; with Inst. of Social Sciences of Cen. Cttee., Polish United Workers' Party (PZPR) 51-54; with Inst. of History, Polish Acad. of Sciences (PAN) -54, now mem. Cttee. of Historical Sciences, Corresp. mem. PAN 71-; with Inst. of History, Poznań Univ. 54-, Head of Dept. of Methodology of History 73-; mem. Editorial Staff *Studia Filozoficzne*; mem. Cen. Board, Int. Asscn. of Econ. History; State Prize, 2nd Class 70, Knight's Cross, Order of Polonia Restituta, Award of Pomeranian Griffin.
Publs. *Methodology of History* 68, *Narodziny kapitalizmu w Europie XIV-XVIII wieku*, *Świat bez historii* 72, *Wielkopolska poprzez wieki* 73, *Zarys dziejów Poznania* 73, co-author *Dzieje Wielkopolski* 69.
Ul. Pamiątkowa 26 m. 2, 61-505 Poznań, Poland.

Toraldo di Francia, Giuliano; Italian physicist; b. 17 Sept. 1916, Florence.
Professor of Physics, Univ. of Florence 58-; Pres. Int. Comm. of Optics 66-69, Soc. Italiana di Fisica 67-73; Thomas Young Medal, Inst. of Physics and Physical Soc.; C. E. K. Mees Medal, Optical Soc. of America.
Publs. *Electromagnetic Waves* 56, *La Diffrazione della Luce* 58, *L'indagine del mondo Fisico* 76.
Via Panciatichi 56-27, Florence, Italy.

Torbert, Horace Gates, Jr.; American diplomatist; b. 7 Oct. 1911, Washington, D.C.; s. of Horace Gates Torbert and Alice K. Coyle; m. Anne C. Holloway 1942; two s.; ed. Yale and Harvard Univs., and U.S.A. National War Coll.
Industrial firm 34-46; army service 42-46; U.S. Foreign Service Officer 47-, Second Sec., Spain 47-50, Second Sec., Austria 50-51, First Sec. 51, Asst. Dep. Commr. 52; Consul, Salzburg 54; Officer-in-Charge Italian-Austrian Affairs, Dept. of State 56; Dir. Office of Western European Affairs, Dept. of State 57-58; Counsellor of American Embassy, Italy 58-61, Chargé d'Affaires, Hungary 61-62, Ambassador to Repub. of Somalia 62-65; Deputy Asst. Sec. of State (Congressional Relations) 65-70; Amb. to Bulgaria 70-72; Legion of Merit, M.B.E. (mil.), Superior Honor Medal.
3041 Sedgwick Street, N.W., Washington, D.C. 20008, U.S.A.

Torbov, Zeko Nicolchov, DR.JUR., DR.PHIL.; Bulgarian university professor; b. 15 April 1899, Orechovo; s. of Nicolcho Mihailov Torbov and Raina Ivancheva Popova; m. Valentina Ilieva Topusova 1962; ed. Univs. of Berlin, Göttingen, Paris and Rome.
Advocate in Orechovo 25; Teacher in Philosophy and German, Sofia 31-42; Priv. Doz. in Philosophy of Law, Sofia State Univ. 42; Prof. 45; Assoc. Prof. in German Language and Law, Mil. Acad. Sofia 39-48; Assoc. Prof. in Law Univ. for Financial and Administrative Sciences, Sofia 44-46; Dean, Faculty of Law, State Univ. Sofia 47-48; mem. and Sec. of Bulgarian Philosophical Club Sofia 35-44, Bulgarian Sociological Soc. 31-45; mem. Int. Vereinigung für Rechts und Sozialphilosophie, Union of the Scientific Workers in Bulgaria, Kant-Gesellschaft, Mainz; Herder-Prize for Science of Univ. of Vienna 70.
Leisure interest: gardening.
Publs. *Die Sozialgesetzgebung in Bulgarien* 23, *Über die Friessche Lehre vom Wahrheitsgefühl* 29, *Rationalismus und Empirismus in der Rechtswissenschaft* 43,

Naturrecht und Rechtsphilosophie 47, Bulgarian translation of Kant's *Kritik der reinen Vernunft* 67, *Kritik der praktischen Vernunft* 74; and several books in Bulgarian on philosophy and law.
Ul. Giovanni Gorini 7, Sofia V, Bulgaria.
Telephone: 44-29-78.

Törnqvist, Erik Olof; Finnish international finance official; b. 20 July 1915; *m*.; two *s*.; ed. Abo Acad.
Registrar, Board of Customs Statistical Bureau 39-40; Price Control Cttee. 40-41; Research Fellow, Bank of Finland 40-42; Sec. Price Council 42-45, Price and Wage Council 46; Sec.-Gen. Econ. Council 46-47; Dir. War Reparation Board 47-49; Dir.in-Chief Econ. Dept. Ministry of Finance 49; Chair. Finance Comm. 49-61; Sec.-Gen. Econ. Planning Council 51-53; Principal Sec. to Prime Minister 53-54; Chair. Finnish Group, Nordic Econ. Co-operation Cttee. 56-57; Chief of Section, UN Econ. Comm. for Europe (ECE) 57-59, Econ. Comm. for Latin America (ECLA) 59-61; Expert, UNTAB 62-63; Chair. ECE Conf. of Senior Econ. Advisers 64; Chair. Finnish Delegation to Nordic Council 68-70; Exec. Dir. IBRD, IFC and IDA Nov. 70-72; Amb. to Mexico Nov. 72-; del. to UN Gen. Assembly 65, 67 and other int. confs.; Chair. and mem. several govt. cttees.; Cmmdr. Finnish Lion Order.
Leisure interest: golf.
Embajada de Finlandia, Homero 136 (Polanco), México 5, D.F., Mexico.

Torre, Xavier; French diplomatist and government official; b. 11 Sept. 1910, Paris; *s*. of Jean-Paul Torre and Marie-Dominique Mary; *m*. Alberte Richard 1936; ed. Lycée de Bastia, Lycées Saint-Louis and Louis-le-Grand, Paris, and Faculty of Law, Univ. of Paris.
Department of Economic Affairs, Central Admin Ministry of French Overseas Territories 36, successively Deputy Head, Head Office of Production and Trade; Deputy Dir. in Charge of Overseas Plan 48, Joint Dir. 52; Sec.-Gen. of Government Gen., French West Africa 54; High Commr. to Cameroun 58-60; Head European Economic Community Fact Finding Mission in Congo 62-63; Admin. Optorg. 64, Vice-Pres. 65, Pres. 69; Officier, Légion d'Honneur and other decorations.
2 rue Victor-Daix, 92 Neuilly-sur-Seine, France.
Telephone: 637-42-30.

Torre Nilsson, Leopoldo; Argentine film director; b. 1924.
Films include: Co-Director with Leopoldo Torres Ríos: *El Crimen de Oribe* 50, *El Hijo del Crack* 53; Director: *El Muro* 47, *Días de Odio la Tigra* 54, *Para Vestir Santos* 55, *Graciela el Protegido* 56, *La Casa del Angel* 57, *Precursores de la Pintura Argentina* 57, *El Secuestrador* 58, *Fin de Fiesta* 60, *Un Guapo del 900* 60, *La Mano en la Trampa* (Grand Prix of Int. Film Press Federation, Cannes) 61, *Piel de Verano* 61, *70 veces 7* 62, *Homenaje a la hora de la Siesta* 62, *La Terraza* 63, *El ojo de la cerradura* 66, *Cavar un foso, Monday's Child* 67, *Martin Fierro* 68, *El santo de la Espada* 71, *Güemes, Boquitas Pintadas* 74.
Av. Santa Fé 836, 12°, Buenos Aires, Argentina.

Torres, José Garrido, M.A. (Econ.); Brazilian economist; b. 13 Jan. 1915, Rio de Janeiro; *s*. of late José Garrido Torres and of Olga Coelho Costa; *m*. Lucilia Vieira Garrido Torres; one *s*. one *d*.; ed. New York Univ. Head Brazilian Trade Bureau, New York 47-52; Commercial Attaché, Washington 47-52; Chair. Nat. Econ. Council 57-58; Exec.-Dir. Superintendency of Currency and Credit (S.U.M.O.C.) 58-59; mem. Nat. Econ. Council 54-58, and 59-64; Pres. Banco Nacional do Desenvolvimento Econômico 64-67; Pres. Embraplan S.A., A.S.P.E. (Exec.'s Pension Asscn.), Leasing & Serviços S.A.; mem. Advisory Council Siemens do Brasil, Banco Aymoré, Vidraria Santa Marina; mem. numerous national dels. to international conferences; writer of several papers on Brazilian economic problems

and foreign trade; mem. Technical Council of Nat. Trade Confederation and Econ. Council of Nat. Confederation of Industry; Fellow Royal Econ. Soc.; mem. American Econ. Asscn.; Charter-mem. Catholic Econ. Asscn. U.S.A.; Commdr. Order of Leopold (Belgium); Great Officer of Military Order of Christ of Portugal; Tamandarés Medal.
Leisure interests: reading, collecting rare books, music, birds.
Rua Humberto de Campos 1003, Rio de Janeiro, Brazil.

Torres Gonzales, Gen. Juan José; Bolivian army officer and politician; b. 5 March 1919, Cochabamba; *m*. Emma Obleas de Torres; three *s*. one *d*.; ed. Military Artillery Coll. of Argentina.
Chief of Staff and Instructor of Artillery Regiments, Mil. Coll. of Bolivia; Commdr. Second Artillery Div.; Mil. Attaché, Brazil; Amb. to Uruguay; Minister of Labour and Social Security; Chief of Staff, Armed Forces 67-68, organized campaign against Che Guevara; Sec.-Gen. Supreme Council of Nat. Defence 69; C.-in-C. Armed Forces 69-July 70; Pres. of Bolivia Oct. 70-Aug. 71; Condor de los Andes (Bolivia), Guerrilleros Lanza, Merito Aeronáutico, Constancia Militar por la Orden Brasileña del Pacificador (Brazil).
c/o Peruvian Embassy, La Paz, Bolivia.

Torres Manzo, Carlos; Mexican economist, banker and politician; b. 25 April 1923; ed. Universidad Nacional Autónoma de México, post-graduate Univs. of London, Tokyo.
Special inspector of C.E.I.M.S.A., Head of Dept. de Política Comercial de la Secretaría de Industria y Comercio; Admin. Man., Compañía Nacional de Subsistencias Populares, Pres. of Colegio de Economistas and Sec. Gen. of Liga de Economistas Revolucionarios; Chair. of Asociación de Comerciantes del Banco del Pequeño Comercio; Sec. of Industry 70.
c/o Secretaría de Industria y Comercio, Mexico, D.F., Mexico.

Torresi, François; French public servant; b. 23 Oct. 1898; ed. Ecole Centrale des Arts et Manufactures, Ecole Supérieure d'Electricité, and Univ. de Paris à la Sorbonne.
Former Asst. Head Central Technical Service, Compagnie Parisienne de Distribution d'Electricité; fmr. Asst.-Dir. of Production and Transport, Electricité de France, later Head of Thermic Production, now Hon. Dir.; Del.-Gen. Association Technique pour l'Energie Nucléaire 63-73; Officier Légion d'Honneur.
5 rue André-Colledebœuf, 75016 Paris, France.

Torrijos Herrera, Brig.-Gen. Omar; Panamanian army officer; b. 13 Feb. 1929, Santiago, Panama; *m*.; three *c*.; ed. Mil. School, El Salvador, U.S.A., Venezuela.
Commissioned Second Lieut., Panama Nat. Guard 52; Lieut. Col. 66; with Cen. American Defence Board, El Salvador; led coup d'etat Oct. 68; Commdr. Panama Nat. Guard 68-; Col. 68; Brig.- Gen. 69; Chief of Govt. 72-.
National Guard Headquarters, Panama City, Panama.

Torroja, José María, DR.SC.; Spanish professor of astronomy and geodesy; b. 29 Aug. 1916, Madrid; *s*. of José María and Isabel Torroja; *m*. Aurora Torroja 1962; two *s*.; ed. Univ. of Madrid.
Geographical Engineer, Instituto Geografico, Madrid 42-52; Astronomer, Observatory of Madrid 52-67; Prof. of Astronomy and Geodesy, Univ. of Madrid 45-75; Vice-Rector, Univ. of Madrid 67-75; mem. Real Academia de Ciencias Exactas, Físicas y Naturales.
Publs. several publications on astronomy and geodesy.
Islas Filipinas 50, Madrid 3, Spain.
Telephone: 2544721.

Tortelier, Paul; French cellist and composer; b. 21 March 1914; ed. Conservatoire Nat. de Musique de Paris.

First Cellist Monte Carlo 35-37; 3rd Cellist Boston Symphony Orchestra 37-40; 1st Cellist Soc. des Concerts du Conservatoire de Paris 46-47; solo cellist with leading orchestras (Europe, U.S.A., Israel, etc.) 47-56; Prof. Conservatoire Nat. Supérieur de Musique de Paris 56-, Folkwang Musikhochschule, Essen; mem. Soc. des Auteurs compositeurs et éditeurs de musique; Hon. mem. Royal Acad. of Music, London; Dr. h.c. Leicester Univ. 72.
Works: Two Cello Concertos, Concerto for Two Cellos, *Symphonie Israélienne*, Cello Sonata, Suite for Unaccompanied Cello, *Trois Petits Tours* (cello and piano), *Spirales* (cello and piano), *Elegie*, *Toccata* (cello and piano), duos for two cellos; Cadenzas for Haydn, Schumann, Boccherini and K. P. E. Bach concertos; edition of Sammartini Sonata; Six Studies for Cello and Piano; Concerto for Violin and Orchestra; Concerto for Piano and Orchestra; Offrande.
Publ. *How I Play, How I Teach* 73.
Scheppener Weg 4b, 4300 Essen 16, Federal Republic of Germany.

Tosar, Hector A.; Uruguayan composer and pianist; b. 1923; ed. Montevideo, and Conservatoire Nationale de Musique, Paris, and Ecole Normale de Musique, Paris (under D. Milhaud, J. Rivier and A. Honegger).
Professor of History of Music and Musical Analysis, Conservatorio de Música, Montevideo 51-60; Prof. of Harmony, Composition and Analysis, and Chief of Theory Dept., Conservatorio de Música de Puerto Rico 61; Guggenheim Fellowships, U.S.A. 46-47, 60-61.
Principal works: *Symphony for Strings* 59, *Te Deum* for bass, chorus and orchestra 59, *Sinfonia Concertante* for piano and orchestra 61.

Toshima, Kenkichi, B.S.; Japanese metallurgical engineer and business executive; b. 30 June 1902, Osaka; s. of Yasukichi and Haru Toshima; m. Michiko Tamiya 1933; three d.; ed. Kyoto Univ.
Kobe Steel Ltd., Kobe 32-, Dir. 49-53, Man. Dir. 53-56, Senior Man. Dir. 56-58, Pres. 58, Chair. 72-74, Adviser 74-; First Class Order of the Sacred Treasure, Chevalier Légion d'Honneur.
Leisure interests: golf, Utazawa.
Office: Kobe Steel Ltd., 36-1, 1-Chome, Wakinohama-cho, Fukiai-ku, Kobe; Home: 15-16 Rokurokuso-cho, Ashiya City, Hyogo Prefecture, Japan.
Telephone: Kobe 251-1551 (Office); Ashiya 22-4561 (Home).

Tötterman, Richard Evert Björnson, LL.M., D.PHIL.; Finnish diplomatist; b. 10 Oct. 1926, Helsinki; s. of B. Björn Tötterman and Katharine Clare Wimpenny; m. Camilla S. Veronica Huber 1953; one s. one d.; ed. Univ. of Helsinki and Brasenose Coll., Oxford.
Entered Ministry for Foreign Affairs 52; several diplomatic posts in Stockholm 54-56, Moscow 56-58, at Ministry of Foreign Affairs 58-62, Berne 62-63, Paris 63-66; Deputy Dir. Ministry of Foreign Affairs 66; Sec.-Gen. Office of Pres. of Finland 66-70; Sec.-Gen. Ministry of Foreign Affairs 70-75; Amb. to U.K. 75-; Knight Commdr. Order of the White Rose (Finland); Grand Cross, Order of Dannebrog (Denmark), Order of Merit (Austria), Order of Homayoun (Iran), Order of Orange-Nassau (Netherlands), Order of the Pole Star (Sweden), Order of the Falcon (Iceland); Grand Officer Ordre de la Couronne (Belgium), Order of St. Olav (Norway); Hon. K.C.V.O., Hon. O.B.E.
14 Kensington Palace Gardens, London, W.8, England.
Telephone: 01-730-0771/5.

Touffait, Adolphe Auguste; French lawyer; b. 29 March 1907; ed. Faculty of Law, Rennes.
Director Research into War Crimes, Ministry of Justice 45-46; Civil Dir. Ministry of Armed Forces 47-48; Minister of State for Information 49-50; Dir. of Cabt. of Vice-Pres. of Council 53-54; Minister of French

Overseas Territories 55-56; Dir. of Cabt. Ministry of Justice 57-58; First Deputy Attorney for the Repub., later Attorney 58; Counsellor, Court of Cassation 61; Dir. of Personnel and Gen. Admin., Insp. Gen. of Judicial Services, Ministry of Justice April-Nov. 62; First Pres. Court of Appeal of Paris 62-67, now Solicitor-Gen., Court of Cassation 68-; Commandeur, Légion d'Honneur.
8 boulevard Julien-Potin, 92 Neuilly-sur-Seine (Seine), France.

Toukan, Baha Ud-Din; Jordanian diplomatist; b. Salt, East Bank; m.; two s. one d. (Queen Alia of Jordan); ed. American Univ., Beirut.
After graduation entered civil service; served in court of late King Abdullah of Jordan; Gov. of Balqaa District; transferred to Ministry of Foreign Affairs 47; Consul-Gen., Jerusalem 47; Minister Plenipotentiary to Cairo and Ankara 48; Under-Sec. Ministry of Foreign Affairs; Rep. of Arab League in Rome 66-70; Perm. Rep. to UN 71-72; Amb. to Italy 72-73; mem. of Senate 73; Amb. to Yugoslavia 75-.
Jordanian Embassy, Uzun Mirkova 2/11, Belgrade, Yugoslavia.

Toulemon, Robert, L.en D.; French civil servant; b. 2 July 1927, Montagnac-le-Crempse (Dordogne); s. of Henri Toulemon and Henriette Chaussade; m. Madeleine Fargeot 1951; three s.; ed. Univs. of Toulouse and Paris, Institut d'Etudes Politiques de Paris and Ecole Nationale d'Administration.
Inspector of Finance 54-57; Special Mission, Ministry of Finance 58; Head of Lectures, Institut d'Etudes Politiques de Paris 58-60; Technical Adviser, Office of Sec. of State for Econ. Affairs and Foreign Trade 58-60; Special Mission, Foreign Econ. Affairs Nov. 58; Head, Export Credit Section, Ministry of Finance and Econ. Affairs 60-62; Chef de Cabinet to Vice-Pres. of Comm. of EEC 62-63; Dir. of Section in Foreign Dept. of EEC 63-67; Gen. Dir. of Industrial Affairs 68-71, of Industrial, Technological and Scientific Affairs 71-73; Inspector of Finance 73-; Dir. of Cabinet of Minister of Co-operation July 74-.
Leisure interests: tennis, chess.
Rue Monsieur 20, 75007 Paris; Home: Rue d'Assas 41, 75006 Paris, France.
Telephone: 783-46-71 (Office); 222-16-59 (Home).

Toumbas, Vice-Admiral John N., D.S.O.; Greek naval officer and politician; b. 24 Feb. 1901; m. Yvonne-Agnes Bondi 1944; ed. naval and military schools.
Distinguished Naval service, Second World War; Commdr. Salamis Dockyard 45; Naval Attaché Washington 46; Commdr., Naval Cadet School 46-47; Dir. of Personnel, Admiralty 47-49; Supreme Commdr. Coastal Defence Forces 49-51; C.-in-C. Coastal Defences 50-52; Nat. Military Rep., NATO Command HQ, Paris 52; C.-in-C. of the Fleet 52-53; Liberal M.P. 56, Centre Union 58-64; Minister of State Nov.-Dec. 63; Minister of the Interior Feb. 64-Jan. 65; Minister of the Interior and Public Order (Security) July-Aug. 65, of Industry Sept. 65-May 66, of Foreign Affairs May-Dec. 66; Gold Medal for Outstanding Bravery; Grand Commdr. of Phoenix; War Cross (four awards), U.S.A. Legion of Merit, Romanian Grand Cross of August 23rd Order, Yugoslavian Grand Cross of the Star Order, Grand Cross of the Holy Tomb Order, Grand Commdr. of Danish Order.
Leisure interests: athletics, motoring, swimming.
Publ. *Enemy in Sight* (memories of World War II) 54 (Academy Award).
10 Alopekis Street, Athens 139, Greece.
Telephone: 714-048.

Touré, Ahmed Sekou; Guinean trade unionist and politician; b. 9 Jan. 1922; ed. Ecole Coranique, French Guinea Primary Schools, Ecole Professionnelle Georges Poiret, Conakry.

Entered Post and Telecommunications Service, French Guinea 41; Sec.-Gen. Syndicat du Personnel des P.T.T., mem. Comm. Consultative Fédérale du Travail, mem. Guinea Comm. Consultative Territoriale, Comms. Mixtes Paritaires et Administratives 45; Comptable, Trésoreries (Cadre Supérieur), Sec.-Gen. Syndicat des Employés du Trésor 46; founder-mem. Rassemblement Démocratique Africain (RDA) 46; Sec.-Gen. Union Territoriale, Confédération Générale du Travail (CGT) 48; Sec.-Gen. CGT Co-ordination Cttee., French West Africa and Togoland 50; Sec.-Gen. Guinea Democratic Party 52-; Territorial Counsellor 53; Pres. Confédération Générale des Travailleurs d'Afrique Noire (CGTA) 56, Mayor of Conakry, Deputy from Guinea to French Nat. Assembly 56; mem. Comité Directeur Fédéral, Union Générale des Travailleurs de l'Afrique Noire (UGTAN) Jan. 57-; Territorial Counsellor, Conakry, Grand Counsellor, French West Africa, Vice-Président du Conseil, Govt. of Guinea May 57; Vice-Prés. RDA Oct. 57; Président du Gouvernement (Head of State), Republic of Guinea (upon declaration of independence following referendum) Oct. 58- (re-elected 61, 63, 68, 74), Prime Minister 58-72; Lenin Peace Prize 60.
Présidence de la République, Conakry, Guinea.

Touré, Ismaël; Guinean politician; b. 1925; ed. in France.
Head, Kankan Meteorological station; mem. Kankan Municipal Council 56; mem. Faranah Territorial Assembly; Minister of Works 57-59, of Posts, Telegraphs and Transport 59-61; Minister of Public Works and Transport 61-62; Minister of Econ. Development 63-68; Minister of Finance 68-72, of the Economy and Finance Domain 72-; led Guinea del. to All-African People's Conf. 60; del. to UN 60, 61; mem. Political Bureau Parti Démocratique de Guinée.
Ministry of the Economy and Finance Domain, Conakry, Guinea.

Touré, Mamoudou, L. EN D., PH.D.; Mauritanian diplomatist and administrator; b. 1928; ed. Univs. of Dakar and Paris and Ecole Nationale de la France d'Outre-Mer.
Served in Admin. of French Overseas Territories, Paris 57-58; Counsellor and Head of Service de Pays et Territoires d'Outre-Mer associés, Secr. of EEC Council of Ministers, Brussels 58-61; Amb. to France, U.K., Fed. Germany, Belgium, Spain and EEC 61-62; Sec.-Gen. Comm. for Technical Co-operation in Africa, Lagos 62-63; Consultant for co-ordination of bi-lateral programmes, UNICEF 63-65; Dir. UN African Inst. for Econ. Devt. and Planning, Dakar 65-66; Dir. African Dept. IMF 67-.
International Monetary Fund, 700 19th Street, N.W., Washington, D.C. 20431, U.S.A.

Tournier, Gilbert Edouard; French business executive and writer; b. 18 July 1901; ed. Lycée Janson de Sailly, and Ecole Polytechnique, Paris.
With Compagnie nationale du Rhône since its foundation in 33, fmr. Sec.-Gen., Dir., retd. 66; Founder Soc. d'Etudes Mer du Nord-Méditerranée; with Compagnie nat. d'aménagement du Bas Rhin-Languedoc and Soc. du développement du Sud-Est; Founder Vallée Impériale and Editorial Cttee. *Delta;* Officier Légion d'Honneur, Commdr. des Palmes académiques et du Mérite National, Officier de l'Economie nationale et du Mérite commercial.
Publs. *Rhône, dieu conquis, Le Rhône, fleuve-dieu, vous parle, Babel ou le vertige technique, Je n'ai pas de métier, Le Coeur des Hommes;* writer of film scripts: *Fleuve-dieu, Sont morts les bâtisseurs, Confluent sans âge, Suite magique, Quatuor élémentaire, Les Deux Parts.*
95 rue Pierre-Brunier, Caluire, Rhône, France.

Tournier, Michel, L. ès L., L en D., D.PHIL.; French author; b. 19 Dec. 1924, Paris; s. of Alphonse and Marie-Madeleine (née Fournier) Tournier; ed. Saint-

Germain en Laye, and Univs. of Paris (Sorbonne) and Tübingen.
Grand Prix du Roman, Acad. Française 67, Prix Goncourt 70; mem. Académie Goncourt 72.
Leisure interest: photography.
Publs. *Vendredi ou les Limbes du Pacifique* 67, *Le Roi des Aulnes* 70, *Les Météores* 75.
Le presbytère, Choisel, 78460 Chevreuse, France.
Telephone: 052-05-29.

Tousey, Richard, A.B., A.M., PH.D.; American physicist; b. 18 May 1908, Somerville, Mass.; s. of Coleman Tousey and Adella R. H. (Hill) Tousey; m. Ruth Lowe 1928; one d.; ed. Tufts and Harvard Univs.
Instructor Harvard Univ. 33-36; Research Instructor Tufts Univ. 36-41; Physicist in Optics Div., Naval Research Laboratory 41-58, Head of Rocket Spectroscopy Branch, Space Science Div. (fmrly. Atmosphere and Astrophysics Div.) 58-; Henry Norris Russell Lecturer, American Astronomical Soc. 66; Whiting Fellow, Harvard Univ. 29-31, Bayard Cutting Fellow 35-36; mem. Nat. Acad. of Sciences of U.S.A.; Fellow American Academy of Arts and Sciences, American Physical Society, Optical Society of America, American Geophysical Union; member American Astronomical Soc. (Vice-Pres. 64-66), A.A.A.S., and numerous other U.S. and int. socs.; Hon. D.Sc. (Tufts Univ.); several awards, including Prix Ançel Award of Soc. Française de Photographie 62, Henry Draper Medal of Nat. Acad. of Sciences 65, Navy Award for Distinguished Achievement in Science 63, Eddington Medal of Royal Astronomical Soc. 64, NASA Exceptional Scientific Achievement Medal 74.
Leisure interests: music, ornithology.
Publs. Numerous articles in various technical journals.
Code 7140, U.S. Naval Research Laboratory, Washington, D.C. 20375; Home: 7725 Oxon Hill Road, S.E., Washington, D.C. 20021, U.S.A.
Telephone: 202-767-3441 (Office).

Toussaint, Michel; D. EN DROIT; Belgian politician; b. 26 Nov. 1922, Namur; ed. Univ. of Liège.
Lawyer, Barreau de Namur 54; mem. Council, Order of Lawyers of Barreau de Namur 70; Local Councillor, Namur; First Alderman of Namur 65; mem. Senate 63, Vice-Pres. 71; Minister, Sec. of State for Nat. Educ. 66-68; Minister of Nat. Educ. 73-74, of Foreign Trade 74-.
Ministère du Commerce Extérieur, Brussels, Belgium.

Tovar Llorente, Antonio, DR. EN FIL. Y LET.; Spanish university professor; b. 17 May 1911, Valladolid; s. of Antonio Tovar and Anselma Llorente; m. Consuelo Larrucea 1942; three s. two d.; ed. Univs. of Valladolid and Madrid, Sorbonne and Univ. of Berlin.
Under-Secretary for Press Affairs 40; Prof. of Latin, Univ. of Salamanca 42-63, Rector of Univ. 51-56; Visiting Prof. Univ. of Buenos Aires 48-49; Univ. Nac. Tucumán 58-59; Visiting Prof. Univ. of Illinois 60-61, Prof. of Classics 63-67; Prof. Univ. of Tübingen 67-; Hon. D.Phil. (Munich, Buenos Aires); Hon. mem. Acad. Vasca, Bilbao 74, Akad. der Wissenschaften, Heidelberg 75; mem. Royal Acad. of Spain 68.
Leisure interest: music.
Publs. *En el Primer Giro: Estudios sobre la antigüedad* 41, *Lengua gótica* 46, *Gramática histórica latina: Sintaxis* 46, *Vida de Sócrates* 47, *Estudios sobre las primitivas lenguas hispánicas* 49, *Aristóteles Retórica* (text and trans.) 53, *Socrate, sa vie et son temps* 54, *Eurípedes, Alcestis y Andromaca* (text and trans.) 55, *Un Libro sobre Platón* 56, *The Basque Language* 57, *El Euskera y sus Parientes* 59, *Platón, el Sofista* (text and trans.) 59, *Euripides, Bacantes y Hécuba* (text and trans.) 60, *Ensayos y peregrinaciones* 60, *The Ancient Languages of Spain and Portugal* 61, *Catálogo de las Lenguas de América del Sur* 61, *Propercio* (text and trans.) 63, *Tendido de Sol* 68, *An Introduction to Plato* 69, *El telar*

de Penélope 71, *Novela Española e Hispanoamericana* 72, *Sprachen und Inschriften, Studien zum Mykenischen, Lateinischen und Hispanokeltischen* 73, *Iberische Landeskunde: Baetica* 74.
Seminar Vergl. Sprachwiss., Universität Tübingen, Mohlstr. 54, 74 Tübingen, Federal Republic of Germany.
Telephone: 29-2413.

Tovstonogov, Georgi Aleksandrovich; Soviet producer; b. 28 Sept. 1915, Tbilisi; s. of Aleksandr Andreyevich Tovstonogov and Tamara Grigorievna Papitashvili; *m.*; two *s.*; ed. Lunacharsky Inst. of Theatrical Art.
Actor and Asst. Dir. Tbilisi 31; studied at Lunacharsky Inst. 33-38; Dir. Griboyedov Russian Drama Theatre, Tbilisi 38-46; produced in Central Theatre for Children, Moscow 46-49; Producer Leningrad Komsomol Theatre 49-56; Chief Dir. Leningrad State Bolshoi Drama Theatre 56-; State and Lenin prizewinner, People's Artist of the U.S.S.R.
Productions include *Even a Wise Man Stumbles*, *The Storm* (Ostrovsky), *An Optimistic Tragedy* (Vishnievsky), *On the Road to Immortality*, *The Sixth Floor* (from the French of A. Jeri), *Fox and Grapes*, *The Idiot* (Dostoievsky), *Sorrow from the Mind* (Griboyedov), *Virgin Soil Upturned* (Sholokhov), *Three Sisters* (Chekhov), *Barbarians* (Gorky), *Inspector General* (Gogol), *Philistines* (Gorky), *Last Summer in Chulimsk* (Vampilov), *Three Sacks of Weedy Wheat* (Tendrjakov), *The Story of a Horse* (Tolstoy).
Leisure interest: collecting masks.
Leningrad State Academic Bolshoi Drama Theatre, 65 Fontanka, Leningrad, U.S.S.R.

Towe, Peter Milburn, M.A.; Canadian diplomatist; b. 1 Nov. 1922, London, Ont.; s. of Allen M. and Clare Durdle Towe; *m.* Carol Krumm 1953; one *s.* two *d.*; ed. Univ. of W. Ontario and Queen's Univ.
Joined Dept. of External Affairs 48, served in Washington, Bonn, Beirut, Paris; Deputy Dir. Gen., External Aid Office 62-67; Minister, Canadian Emb., Washington 67-72; Amb. and Perm. Rep. to OECD 72-75.
Leisure interests: golf, fishing.
c/o Department of External Affairs, Ottawa, Canada.

Toweett, Taaitta, B.A., HONS., B.A. (philosophy); Kenyan politician; b. 1925; ed. Alliance High School and Makerere Coll., Uganda, and Univ. of South Africa.
Member Legislative Council 58-; Minister of Labour and Housing 61-62, of Lands, Survey and Town Planning 62-63, of Educ. 69-74, of Housing and Social Services 74-.
Publ. *Tears over a Dead Cow* (short stories).
P.O. Box 45958, Nairobi, Kenya.
Telephone: 31650 (Office); 89535 (Home).

Tower, John; American politician; b. 29 Sept. 1925; ed. Southwestern Univ., Texas, Southern Methodist Univ., and London School of Economics and Political Science, England.
Radio Announcer, Beaumont, Texas 48, Taylor, Texas 48-49; Insurance Agent, Dallas 50-51; Assistant Professor of Political Science, Midwestern University Texas 51-61; U.S. Senator from Texas (elected to fill vacancy caused by election of Lyndon Johnson as Vice-President of U.S.A.; re-elected 66, 72) May 61-; Republican.
Senate Office Building, Washington, D.C., U.S.A.

Towers, Graham Ford, C.C., C.M.G., B.A.; Canadian banker; b. 29 Sept. 1897, Montreal; s. of William C. and Caroline Auldjo Towers; *m.* Mary Godfrey 1924; ed. Montreal High School, St. Andrews Coll., and McGill Univ.
Lieutenant Canadian Army 15-19; joined Royal Bank of Canada Montreal 20, Accountant Havana Branch 22, Inspector Foreign Dept. 24, Chief Inspector 29, Asst. Gen. Man. 33; Gov. Bank of Canada 34-54; Chair. Foreign Exchange Control Board 39-51; Chair. Nat. War Finance Cttee. 43-45; Pres. Industrial Devt. Bank

D.C. 46-54; Hon. LL.D. (McGill 44, Queen's 54); Hon. D.C.L. (Bishops Univ.) 61.
Leisure interest: golf.
Publ. *Financing Foreign Trade* 21.
260 Park Road, Rockcliffe, Ont., Canada.

Townes, Charles Hard, M.A., PH.D.; American physicist; b. 28 July 1915, Greenville, S. Carolina; s. of Henry Keith and Ellen Sumter Hard; *m.* Frances H. Brown 1941; four *d.*; ed. Furman and Duke Univs., California Inst. of Technology.
Assistant Calif. Inst. of Technology 37-39; mem. Technical staff, Bell Telephone Laboratories 39-47; Assoc. Prof. of Physics, Columbia Univ. 48-50, Prof. 50-61; Exec. Dir. Radiation Laboratory 50-52, Chair. Dept. of Physics 52-55; Vice-Pres. and Dir. of Research, Inst. for Defense Analyses 59-61; Provost and Prof. of Physics, Mass. Inst. of Technology 61-66, Inst. Prof. 66-67; Univ. Prof., Univ. of Calif. 67-; Trustee Carnegie Inst. of Washington 65-, Board of Dirs. Perkin-Elmer Corpn. 66-, Rand Corpn. 65-70, Gen. Motors 73-, Bulletin of the Atomic Scientists 64-69; Chair. Science and Technology Advisory Comm. for Manned Space Flight, Nat. Aeronautics and Space Administration 64-69; Chair. Space Science Board, Nat. Acad. of Sciences 70-73; Trustee, Woods Hole Oceanographic Inst. 71-74, Science Advisory Cttee., Gen. Motors 71-73; Guggenheim Fellow 55-56; Fulbright Lecturer, Paris 55-56, Tokyo 56; Scott Lecturer, Cambridge 63; mem. Scientific Advisory Board, U.S.A.F. 58-61; President's Science Advisory Cttee. 66-70, Vice-Chair. 67-69; Centennial Lecturer, Univ. of Toronto 67; mem. Editorial Board *Review of Scientific Instruments* 50-52, *Physical Review* 51-53, *Journal of Molecular Spectroscopy* 57-60, etc.; Fellow American Physical Soc. (Council mem. 59-62, 65-, Pres. 67), Inst. of Electrical and Electronics Engineers; mem. Soc. Française de Physique (Council mem. 56-58), Physical Soc. of Japan, American Acad. of Arts and Sciences, American Philosophical Soc., American Astronomical Soc., American Assen. of Physics Teachers Space Program Advisory Council, NASA, National Acad. of Sciences; Hon. mem. Optical Soc. of America; numerous awards include Comstock Award (Nat. Acad. of Sciences) 59, Stuart Ballantine Medal (Franklin Inst.) 59, 62, Exceptional Service Award (U.S.A.F.) 59, Rumford Premium (American Acad. of Arts and Sciences) 61, David Sarnoff Award in Electronics (American Inst. of Electrical Engineers) 61, John A. Carty Medal (Nat. Acad. of Sciences) 62, Thomas Young Medal and Prize (Inst. of Physics and Physical Soc., England) 63, Nobel Prize for Physics 64, Joseph Priestley Award (Dickinson Coll.) 66; Distinguished Service Award, Calif. Inst. of Technology 66; Churchman of the Year Award 67, Golden Plate Award, American Acad. of Achievement 69, Distinguished Public Service Medal (NASA) 69; Medal of Honor, Inst. of Electrical and Electronics Engineers 67; Michelson-Morley Award 70; Wilhelm Exner Award 70; recipient of numerous hon. degrees, including D.Litt., Sc.D., Dott.Ing., LL.D., L.H.D.; holder of patents in electronics, including fundamental patents on masers and lasers, etc.
Leisure interest: natural history.
Publs. *Microwave Spectroscopy* 55, *Quantum Electronics* (editor) 60, *Quantum Electronics and Coherent Light* (editor) 65; other scientific papers on microwave spectroscopy, molecular and nuclear structures, radio astronomy, masers and lasers, etc.
University of California, Department of Physics, Berkeley, Calif. 94720, U.S.A.

Townsend, Lynn A.; American motor car executive; b. 12 May 1919, Flint, Mich.; s. of Lynn A. Townsend and Georgia E. Crandall; *m.* Ruth Mildred Laing 1940; three *s.*; ed. Univ. of Michigan.
Accountants, Briggs and Icerman 39-41, Ernst and

Ernst 41-44, 46-47; Supervisory Accountant and Partner, Touche, Niven, Bailey and Smart 47-57; Comptroller, Chrysler Corpn. 57-58, Group Vice-Pres. (Int. Operations) 58-60, Dir. 59, Admin. Vice-Pres. 60-61, Pres. 61-66, Chief Exec. Officer 66-75, Chair. of the Board 67-75.

c/o Chrysler Corporation, P.O. Box 1919, Detroit, Mich. 48231; and Bloomfield Hills, Michigan 48013, U.S.A. Telephone: 956-3251.

Toyoda, Eiji; Japanese motor executive; b. 12 Sept. 1913, Kinjo, Nishi Kasugai-gun, Aichi-ken; s. of Heikichi and Nao Toyoda; m. Kazuko Toyoda; three s. one d.; ed. Tokyo Univ.

President, Toyota Motor Co. Ltd. 67-; Dir. Aishin Seiki Co. Ltd. 65-, Toyota Automatic Loom Works Ltd. 69, Aichi Steel Works Ltd. 61-, Toyota Machine Works Co. Ltd. 64-, Toyota Central Research and Devt. Laboratories Inc. 60, Toyota Motor Sales Co. Ltd. 71-, Towa Real Estate Co. Ltd. 53-, Toyota Motor Sales U.S.A. Inc. 57-, Chiyoda Fire and Marine Insurance Co. Ltd. 73-; Chair. Japan Automobile Mfrs. Asscn. 72-, Japan Motor Industrial Fed. 72-; Exec. Dir. Japan Fed. of Employers' Assccns. 67, Fed. of Economic Orgs. 67; Blue Ribbon Medal 71.

Leisure interests: reading, music.

Office: 1 Toyota-cho, Toyota-shi, Aichi-ken; Home: 12 Yagen, Takemachi, Toyota-shi, Aichi-ken, Japan. Telephone: 0565-28-2121 (Office); 0565-52-7535 (Home).

Trabucchi, Alberto, LL.D.; Italian lawyer; b. 26 July 1907, Verona; m. Nanda Nanni Sparavieri 1945; five c.; ed. Liceo Maffei, Verona, Univ. of Padua.

Assistant, Istituto di Filosofia del Diritto, Padua 29-35; Lecturer in Civil Law, Univ. of Ferrara 36-40; Prof. of Private Law, Univ. of Venice 38-52; Prof. of Civil Law, Univ. of Padua 42-, of Roman Law 43-45, of Private Comparative Law 49-60; Mayor of Illási (Verona) 50-; Judge, Court of Justice of European Communities 62-; Advocate-Gen., Court of Justice of European Communities 72-; Dir. of *Giurisprudenza Italiana* and *Rivista diritto civile*.

Publs. *Il Matrimonio putativo* 36, *Il Dolo nella teoria dei vizi del volere* 37, *Codice delle Comunità Europee* 62, *Commentario Trattato C.E.E.* 65, *Istituzioni di Diritto civile* 75.

Via Rudena 39, Padua, Italy; and 3 rue Lavandier, Luxembourg.

Telephone: 20-615 (Padua); 20-851 (Luxembourg).

Tracy, Honor Lilbush Wingfield; British authoress; b. 19 Oct. 1913, Bury St. Edmunds, Suffolk; d. of Humphrey Tracy and Christabel May Clare Miller; ed. Grove School, Highgate, London.

Foreign Corresp. *The Observer* 47-50.

Leisure interests: travelling, gardening, botany and wild life.

Publs. Travel: *Kakemono: A Sketchbook of Postwar Japan* 50, *Mind You, I've Said Nothing* 53, *Silk Hats and No Breakfast* 57, *Spanish Leaves* 64, *Winter in Castille* 73; Fiction: *The Deserters* 54, *The Straight and Narrow Path* 56, *The Prospects are Pleasing* 58, *A Number of Things* 59, *A Season of Mists* 61, *The First Day of Friday* 63, *Men at Work* 66, *The Beauty of the World* 67, *Settled in Chambers* 68, *The Butterflies of the Province* 70, *The Quiet End of Evening* 72, *In a Year of Grace* 75.

Four Chimneys, Achill Sound, Co. Mayo, Ireland. Telephone: Achill Sound 45.

Traglia, H.E. Cardinal Luigi; Italian ecclesiastic; b. 3 April 1895, Albano Laziale.

Ordained priest 17; Titular Bishop of Caesarea in Palestine 37; fmr. Dep. Vicar-Gen. of Rome and Consultor to the Supreme Sacred Congregation of the Holy Office; Chair. Preparatory Cttee. Roman Diocesan Synod 59-60; created Cardinal by Pope John XXIII 60; Pro-Vicar General of The Pope for Rome and district

until 65, Vicar-Gen. 65-68, Chancellor 68-73; Dean Sacred Coll. of Cardinals 74-; Chair. Episcopal Comm. directing Activities of Italian Catholic Action Movement 61-; mem. Sacred Congregations of the Holy Office, of Eastern Church, of the Sacraments and of the Evangelization of Peoples (de Propaganda Fide).

Palazzo della Cancelleria, Piazza della Cancelleria 1, 00186 Rome, Italy.

Train, Russell Errol, LL.B.; American conservationist; b. 4 June 1920, Washington, D.C.; s. of Rear Admiral Charles R. Train and Errol C. (Brown) Train; m. Aileen Bowdoin 1954; one s. three d.; ed. St. Albans School, Washington, D.C., Princeton and Columbia Univs.

Attorney, Congressional Joint Cttee. on Internal Revenue Taxation 48; Clerk (Chief Counsel), House Cttee. on Ways and Means 53, Minority Adviser 55; Treasury Dept. 56; Judge, Tax Court of U.S.A. 57-65; Pres. Conservation Foundation 65-69; mem. Nat. Water Comm. 68-69; Under-Sec. of the Interior 69-70; Chair. Council on Environmental Quality 70-73; Dir. Environmental Protection Agency 73-; fmr. Pres. and fmr. Vice-Pres. and Dir. World Wildlife Fund; fmr. Dir. American Cttee. for Int. Wildlife Protection; mem. Exec. Cttee., Int. Union for Conservation of Nature and Natural Resources; several hon. degrees.

Environmental Protection Agency, Washington, D.C. 20460, U.S.A.

Trąmpczyński, Witold; Polish economist; b. 22 Oct. 1909, Podlesie; m. Róża Trąmpczyński 1945; one s. one d.; ed. European and American Univs.

Rockefeller Fellow, Univ. of Vienna 34-35; Asst. at Univ. of Poznań 35-38; Rockefeller Fellow, Harvard Univ., Univ. of Chicago, Berkeley Univ., and London School of Econs. 38-39; Lecturer and Asst. Prof., Univ. of Poznań 39; working in Bank Emisyjny (Issue Bank) in Cracow 39-45; Prof., Univ. of Cracow 45-46; Deputy Gen. Man. Nat. Bank of Poland 45-47, Gen. Man. 47-53, Pres. 54-56; Vice-Minister of Finance 50-56; Minister of Foreign Trade Dec. 56-68; Prof. High School of Planning and Statistics, Warsaw 60-; First Deputy Pres. Planning Comm. attached to Council of Ministers 68-71, Acting Chair. March-Oct. 71; Deputy to Seym 69-72; Amb. to U.S.A. 72-; mem. Polish Workers' Party 47-48, Polish United Workers' Party 48-, Deputy mem. Cen. Cttee. 64-71; decorations include Order of Banner of Labour 1st Class 59, 64.

Leisure interests: motoring, horse riding.

Publs. *Notion of Capital* 36, *Capitalism* 39.

Polish Embassy, 2640 16th Street, N.W., Washington, D.C., U.S.A.; Home: 14 Wiejska, 00-490 Warsaw, Poland.

Tran Buu Kiem; Vietnamese politician; b. 1921, Can Tho; ed. Faculty of Law, Hanoi Univ.

Member of Indo-Chinese Student Org.; organized a popular uprising in Saigon 45; Sec.-Gen. Admin. and Resistance Cttee. for Southern Region of Viet-Nam, Indo-Chinese Student Org., Deputy Dir. for Econ. Services in Southern Region 50; Deputy Sec.-Gen. Cen. Cttee. of Democratic Party 60; mem. Cen. Cttee. NLF; Pres. Student Union of South Viet-Nam; head of NLF Del. to Paris Conf. on Viet-Nam; Minister to Presidency May 75-.

Provisional Revolutionary Government of South Viet-Nam, Saigon, South Viet-Nam.

Trân Thien Khiem, Gen.; Vietnamese army officer and politician; b. 15 Dec. 1925.

Army Service 47; held off attempted coup against Pres. Diem 60, took part in coup against him 63; with Gen. Nguyen Khan led coup removing Gen. Duong Van Minh 64; Defence Minister and C.-in-C. 64; Amb. to U.S.A. Oct. 64-Oct. 65, to Rep. of China Oct. 65-May

68; Minister of the Interior 68-73, Deputy Prime Minister March-Aug. 69, Prime Minister 69-75, Minister of Defence 72-75; flew to Taiwan April 75.

Tran Van Chuong, S.J.D.; Vietnamese lawyer and diplomatist; b. 1898, Phu-Ly; *s.* of Tran Van Thong and Bui Thi Lan; *m.* Than Thi Nam Tran 1922; one *s.* two *d.*; ed. Univ. of Paris.
Lawyer, South and North Viet-Nam 26-47; Vice-Pres. Grand Council for Econ. and Financial Interests of Indo-China 38; mem. Fed. Council of Indo-China 40; Minister of Foreign Affairs and Vice-Premier 45; Judge, Franco-Vietnamese Court of Cassation and Council of State 53-54; Minister of State, Repub. of Viet-Nam 54; Amb. to United States 54-63, to Brazil 59-63, to Mexico 62-63; Minister to Argentina 60-63.
Leisure interest: lecturing.
Publ. *Essai sur l'Esprit du Droit Sino-Annamite* 22.
5601 Western Avenue, N.W., Washington, D.C. 20015, U.S.A.
Telephone: 244-5249.

Tran Van Huong; Vietnamese politician; b. 1 Dec. 1903.
Former schoolteacher; participated in Viet-Minh resistance against French; Prefect of Saigon 54 and 64; Prime Minister Repub. of Viet-Nam 64-65, 68-69; Vice-Pres. of Repub. of Viet-Nam 71-75, Pres. 21-28 April 75; Hon. Corporal Repub. of Viet-Nam Armed Forces 74.

Tran Van Lam; Vietnamese politician and pharmacist; b. 30 July 1913, Cho Lon; ed. Hanoi Univ.
Charter Sec.-Gen. Viet-Nam Pharmacists Asscn. 51-52; elected Saigon City Council 52; mem. Cttee. for Protection of Econ. Interests of the South Vietnamese People 52-54; Speaker, Constituent Assembly; First Legis. Assembly 56-57; Majority Leader in Assembly 57-61; Amb. to Australia and New Zealand 61-64; Chair., Board Viet-Nam Commercial and Ind. Bank 64-67; Chair., Cong Thuong Dia Oc Cong Ty 66-67; Man. Dir., Saigon Duoc Cuoc 64-67; Minister of Foreign Affairs 69-73; Speaker of Senate 73-75.

Tran Van Tra, Gen.; Vietnamese army officer and politician (also known by other names Tu Chi and Tran Nam Trung); b. 1918, Quang Ngai Province, S. Viet-Nam.
Alternate mem. Cen. Cttee. Lao Dong Party; Deputy Chief of Staff, North Vietnamese Army; Chair. Mil. Affairs Cttee., Cen. Office of South Viet-Nam (COSVN) 64-; rose to rank of three-star general May 75; head of mil. cttee. controlling Saigon and District May 75-Jan. 76.
Central Office of South Viet-Nam, Saigon, South Viet-Nam.

Traore, Col. Moussa; Mali army officer and politician; b. 25 Sept. 1936, Kayes; ed. Training Coll., Fréjus, Cadets Coll., Kati.
Became N.C.O. in French Army; returned to Mali 60; promoted Lieut. 64, Col. 71; at Armed Forces Coll., Kati until 68; led coup to depose Pres. Modibo Keita Nov. 68; Pres. Mil. Cttee. for Nat. Liberation (Head of State) Nov. 68-, also Prime Minister Sept. 69-; Pres. Conf. of Heads of State, Union Douanière des Etats de l'Afrique de l'Ouest 70.
Office of the President, Comité militaire de libération nationale, Bamako, Mali.

Traore, Seydou; Mali diplomatist; b. 3 Feb. 1927, Sofara; *s.* of Adama Traore and Mpegue Toure; *m.* Arlette Eugenie Traore 1963; one *s.* two *d.*; ed. Ecole Nationale de France d'Outre-Mer and Orientation à la Fonction Internationale, Paris.
Technical Adviser, Ministry of Commerce 60; Dir. of Econ. Affairs 61; Technical Adviser, Ministry of Foreign Affairs 62, Chief Legal Div. 63, Head Econ. Div. 64; Dir. of Cabinet of Ministry for Co-operation and

Technical Assistance 64; Amb. to Belgium, Sweden, Fed. Germany and EEC 68-69; Amb. to U.S.A. 69-75; Perm. Rep. to UN 70-75; del. to UN Gen. Assembly 62, 63, ECOSOC meetings 62, UNCTAD meetings 64, 68 and sessions of the Council of Ministers of OAU.
c/o Ministry of Foreign Affairs, Bamako, Mali.

Trapeznikov, Vadim Aleksandrovich; Soviet power engineer; b. 28 Nov. 1905, Moscow; ed. Moscow Higher Technical School.
Power Engineer, All-Union Electrotechnical Inst. 28-33; Instructor, Moscow Power Eng. Inst. 30-39, Prof. of Automation and Electrical Machine Building 39-41; Inst. of Automation and Telemechanics, U.S.S.R. Acad. of Sciences 41-, Dir. 51-; Corresp. mem. U.S.S.R. Acad. of Sciences 53-60, mem. 60-; mem. C.P. 51-; Chief Editor *Automation and Telemechanics*, U.S.S.R. Acad. of Sciences; Deputy Chair., State Cttee. for Science and Technology; mem. Exec. Cttee., Int. Fed. of Automatic Control; Hero of Socialist Labour 65; Order of Red Banner of Labour State Prize 51.
Publs. *Design Principles for a Series of Asynchronous Machines* 37, *Automatic Checking of Linear Dimensions in Manufactured Articles* 47, *Generalized Conditions of Proportionality and Optimum Geometry of Transformers* 48, *Cybernetics and Automatic Control* 62, *Problems of Technical Cybernetics in Institute of Automation and Telemechanics* 64.
Institute of Automation and Telemechanics, 81 Profsoyuznaya ulitsa, Moscow, U.S.S.R.

Trautman, Gerald Hough, LL.B.; American business executive; b. 27 Aug. 1912; *s.* of Newton E. and Madelaine (Hough) Trautman; ed. Stanford and Harvard Univs.
Admitted to Calif. Bar 37; partner, McCutchen, Doyle, Brown, Trautman and Enersen 37-65; Pres. Greyhound Corpn. 66-70, Dir. 66-, Chair. of Board and Chair. Exec. Cttee. 68-; Chair. of Board and Chair. Exec. Cttee. Armour and Co. 69-; Chair. Greyhound Computer Corpn., Gen. Fire and Casualty Co., Greyhound Leasing and Financial Corpn., Greyhound Finance and Leasing Corpn. A.G.; Dir. numerous other Greyhound subsidiaries and industrial concerns; mem. American Bar Asscn.
Office: Greyhound Tower, Phoenix, Ariz. 85077; Home: 6246 Bret Hill Drive, Scottsdale, Ariz. 85253, U.S.A.

Trautmann, Rezsö; Hungarian politician; b. 1907.
Structural engineer; Chair. Nat. Office of Building Construction 53; Deputy Minister of Building Industry 51-53, Minister 57-68; mem. Pres. Council; Pres. Scientific Soc. of Bldg.
Presidential Council, Kossuth Lajos tér 1/3, H-1357 Budapest V, Hungary.

Travell, Janet, M.D.; American physician; b. 17 Dec. 1901, New York, N.Y.; *d.* of J. Willard Travell and Janet E. Davidson; *m.* John William Gordon Powell 1929; two *d.*; ed. Wellesley Coll. and Cornell Univ. Medical Coll.
Former medical practice in New York; Assoc. Prof. of Clinical Pharmacology, Cornell Univ. Medical Coll. 51-61; Official Physician to the White House 61-65; Assoc. Clinical Prof. of Medicine, George Washington Univ. School of Medicine 61-70, Prof. Emer. 70-; Special Consultant to Surgeon-Gen., U.S.A.F. 62-64; Chair. Inaugural Medical Care and Public Health Cttee., Washington, D.C. 65; Fellow, N.Y. Acad. of Medicine, Royal Soc. of Medicine, etc.; Pres. North American Acad. of Manipulative Medicine 68-69; Hon. Dr. of Medical Sciences (Woman's Medical Coll. of Pa.) 61; Hon. D.Sc. (Wilson Coll.) 62; mem. many professional insts.
Leisure interests: home, gardening, tennis, horseback riding, reading.

Publs. Scientific papers and autobiography *Office Hours: Day and Night* 69.
4525 Cathedral Avenue, N.W., Washington, D.C. 20016, U.S.A.
Telephone: 202-363-9090.

Treadwell, (Charles) James, C.M.G.; British diplomatist; b. 10 Feb. 1920; s. of the late C. A. L. Treadwell; m. Philippa Perkins 1946; three s.; ed. Wellington Coll., N.Z., Univ. of N.Z.
Military service 39-45; Sudan Political Service and Judiciary 45-55; at Foreign Office 55-57; with High Comm., Lahore 57-60, Embassy, Jeddah 60-62; Deputy High Commr. for Eastern Nigeria 65-66; Head of Joint Inf. Services Dept., FCO 66-68; Political Agent, Abu Dhabi 68-71; Amb. to United Arab Emirates 71-73; High Commr. in Bahamas 73-75; Amb. to Oman 75-.
British Embassy, P.O. Box 300, Muscat, Oman.

Tréca, Albert, D. EN D.; French diplomatist; b. 5 Nov. 1917, Mouriez; s. of Albert Tréca and Gabrielle Froissart; m. Jacqueline Cuvelier 1946; two s. four d.; ed. Collège de Passoy à Froyennes and Faculté de Droit, Paris.
With Résidence Générale de France, Morocco 46-56; Ministry of Foreign Affairs, Paris 56-59; Counsellor, Tripoli 60-62; Amb. to Niger 64-68; Dir. du Cabinet, Sec. of State for Foreign Affairs 68-71; Amb. to Ethiopia Sept. 71-; Chevalier, Légion d'Honneur, Officier de l'ordre national du mérite, Croix de Guerre.
Leisure interests: hunting, golf.
Ambassade de France, Omedla Road, P.O. Box 1464, Addis Ababa, Ethiopia.

Tredgold, Rt. Hon. Sir Robert Clarkson, P.C., K.C.M.G., Q.C.; Rhodesian lawyer and politician; b. 1899; ed. Hertford Coll., Oxford.
Served First World War; called to Bar, Inner Temple 23; practised Southern and Northern Rhodesia; M.P. for Insiza District 34-43; Minister of Justice and Defence S. Rhodesia 35-43, Minister of Native Affairs 41-43; High Court Judge 43-50; Chief Justice 50-55; Chief Justice Fed. of Rhodesia and Nyasaland 55-60; mem. Commonwealth Judicial Cttee. Privy Council.
Publs. *The Rhodesia that was My Life* 68, *Xhosa: Tales from the African Veld* 73.
43 Jelliman Avenue, Marandellas, Rhodesia.

Tréfouël, Jacques; French scientist; b. 9 Nov. 1897, Le Raincy, Seine-et-Oise; m. Thérèse Boyer 1921; ed. Univ. of Paris.
Worked at the Institut Pasteur 20-40, Dir. 40-64, Hon. Dir. 64-; mem. Acad. des Sciences, Vice-Pres. 64, Pres. 65, Acad. Nat. de Médecine, Vice-Pres. 66, Pres. 67, Acad. de Chirurgie, Acad. de Pharmacie, etc.; Dr. h.c. (Oxford, Cambridge, Laval, Rio de Janeiro, Rutgers, Athens, Uppsala, Liège, Oslo, Brussels Univs.); Grand Officier de la Légion d'Honneur, Grand Croix de l'Ordre National du Mérite, and numerous other decorations; author of many scientific studies, particularly on Sulfamides and Sulfones, some jointly with Madame Thérèse Tréfouël.
Leisure interests: woodwork and iron-work.
207 rue de Vaugirard, Paris 15e; and Institut Pasteur, 28 rue du Dr. Roux, Paris 15e, France.
Telephone: 734-53-40.

Treholt, Thorstein; Norwegian farmer and politician; b. 13 April 1911, Skoger, Vestfold; ed. Vestfold School of Agriculture and State Farmers Training School.
Assistant to Oppland County Agric. Officer 38; District Agric. Officer, Brandbu 39-47; Travelling Inspector, Agric. Loan Fund 48-49; Lecturer, Valdres Agric. School 49, Dir. of School 51-60; Asst. Sec., Ministry of Agric. 54-57; mem. Storting 58-, Chair. Parl. Agric. Cttee. 61-65, Vice-Chair. 65-69; Minister of Agric. March 71-Oct. 72, Oct. 73-; Labour Party.
Ministry of Agriculture, Oslo; 2760 Brandbu, Norway.
Telephone: Brandbu 1450.

Treichl, Dr. Heinrich; Austrian banker; b. 31 July 1913, Vienna; s. of Dr. Alfred and Dorothea Treichl (née Baroness Ferstel); m. Helga Ross 1946; two s.; ed. Univs. of Frankfurt, Germany and Vienna.
Dir. Banque des Pays de l'Europe Centrale, Paris, Mercur Bank AG and Länderbank Wien AG, Vienna 36-39; Partner, Ullstein and Co., Vienna 46-55; Dir. Österreichische Industrie- und Bergbauverwaltungs GmbH, Vienna 56-58; Dir. Creditanstalt-Bankverein, Vienna 56-, Chair. of Man. Board 70-; mem. Board of Govs. Österreichische Nationalbank; Pres. Austrian Bankers Asscn.; Head Banking Section, Fed. Chamber of Commerce; Vice-Pres. Vienna Stock Exchange; Grosses Goldenes Ehrenzeichen Republik Österreich; Commdr. Order Homayoun; Commdr. Légion d'Honneur.
Leisure interests: literature, hunting, skiing.
A-1030 Vienna, Salmgasse 2, Austria.
Telephone: 73-31-50.

Treiman, Sam Bard, S.M., PH.D.; American professor of physics; b. 27 May 1925, Chicago, Ill.; s. of Abraham Treiman and Sarah (Bard) Treiman; m. Joan Little 1952; one s. two d.; ed. Northwestern Univ. and Univ. of Chicago.
Joined Princeton Univ. 52, Professor 63-; Sloan Fellow; Guggenheim Fellow; mem. Nat. Acad. of Sciences, American Acad. of Arts and Sciences.
Leisure interests: tennis, reading.
Publs. *Formal Scattering Theory* (with M. Grossjean), *Lectures on Current Algebra* (with R. Jackiw and D. Gross) 72; and numerous papers in professional journals.
60 McCosh Circle, Princeton, N.J. 08540 (Home); Physics Dept., Princeton University, Princeton, N.J. 08540, U.S.A. (Office).
Telephone: 924-0592 (Home); 452-4350 (Office).

Trejos Fernández, José Joaquín; Costa Rican university professor and politician; b. 18 April 1916, San José; s. of Juan Trejos and Emilia F. de Trejos; m. Clara F. de Trejos 1936; five s.; ed. Univ. of Chicago.
Former Prof. of Statistical Theory and Dean, Faculty of Econ., Univ. of Costa Rica; Pres. of Costa Rica 66-70; Partido Unión Popular (PUP).
Leisure interests: music, history.
Publs. *Reflexiones sobre la Educación*, 2nd edn. 68, *Ocho Años en la Política Nacional—Ideales Políticos y Realidad Nacional*, Vol. I 73, Vol. III 73, Vol. IV 73, Vol. II 74.
Apartado 1313, San José, Costa Rica.
Telephone: 24-24-11.

Trelford, Donald Gilchrist, M.A.; British journalist; b. 9 Nov. 1937, Coventry; s. of Mr. and Mrs. T. S. Trelford; m. Janice Ingram 1963; two s. one d.; ed. Bablake School, Coventry, Selwyn Coll., Cambridge.
Pilot Officer, R.A.F. 56-58; Cambridge Univ. (Open Exhibitioner in English) 58-61; worked on newspapers in Coventry and Sheffield 61-63; Editor *Times of Malawi* and Corresp. in Africa, *The Times, Observer,* BBC 63-66; joined *Observer* as Deputy News Editor 66, Asst. Man. Editor 68, Deputy Editor 69-75, Dir. and Editor Jan. 76-.
Leisure interests: golf, cricket, squash.
The Observer, 8 St. Andrew's Hill, London, EC4V 5JA, England.
Telephone: 01-236 0202.

Trelles Montes, Dr. Oscar; Peruvian physician and politician.
Psychiatric practice, Lima; fmr. Minister of Public Health; Prime Minister and Minister of Interior July 63-Jan. 64; Ambassador to France 64-65; Sec.-Gen. Partido Acción Popular 65-68.
Partido Acción Popular, Nicolás de Piérola 677, Lima, Peru.

Tremblay, Paul, B.A., LL.B., L.SC.SOC.; Canadian diplomatist; b. 6 July 1914, Chicoutimi, Quebec; s. of François and Eugénie Tremblay; m. Gertrude Nadeau; one s. two d.; ed. Univ. of Montreal, McGill and George Washington Univs.

Department of External Affairs 40-; Second Sec. Washington 43-46, Santiago 46-49; Dept. of External Affairs, Ottawa 49-51; Second Sec. The Hague 51-54; Del. to NATO and OEEC, Paris 54-57; Dept. of External Affairs, Ottawa 57-59; Amb. to Chile 59-62; Perm. Rep. to UN, New York 62-66; Amb. to Belgium and Luxembourg and EEC 66-70; Assoc. Under-Sec. of State for External Affairs 70-73; Amb. to the Holy See Oct. 73-.

Embassy of Canada, Via della Conciliazione 4/D, 00193 Rome, Italy.

Tremelloni, Roberto; Italian political economist and politician; b. 30 Oct. 1900, Milan; m. Emma Nascimbene 1928; one d.; ed. Univs. of Turin and Geneva.

Under-Secretary Ministry for Industry 46, Minister 47; Deputy to Parl. 48-; Minister for European Economic Co-operation 48 and Del. to O.E.E.C. 49; Pres. Parl. Comm. on Unemployment and Milan Electricity Authority 52; Minister of Finance 54-55; Pres. Parl. Cttee. on Free Competition Limits 61; Treasury Minister 62-63; Minister of Finance 64-65, of Defence 66-68; Pres. of Budget Comm. of Chamber of Deputies 69-70; Social Democrat.

Leisure interest: economic literature.

Publs. include: *La Storia dell'Industria Italiana Contemporanea, L'Industria Tessile Italiana, L'Italia in un' Economia Aperta* and *Il Danaro Pubblico.*

Chamber of Deputies, Rome; and Via Pellegrini 18, Milan, Italy.

Trench, Sir David, G.C.M.G., M.C.; British colonial administrator; b. 2 June 1915, Quetta, Pakistan; s. of W. L. C. and Margaret (née Huddleston) Trench; m. Margaret Gould 1944; one d.; ed. Tonbridge and Jesus Coll., Cambridge.

Colonial Admin. Service, British Solomon Islands 38, mil. service there 42-46, later held several posts in Pacific; Hong Kong 50, Deputy Colonial Sec. 59-61; High Commr. for Western Pacific 61-64; Gov. and C.-in-C. Hong Kong April 64-Oct. 71; Vice-Chair. Advisory Cttee. on Distinction Awards, Dept. of Health and Social Security 72-; Hon. LL.D. Univ. of Hong Kong and Chinese Univ. of Hong Kong.

Leisure interests: golf, photography.

Barwood, The Milldown, Blandford Forum, Dorset, England.

Trend, Baron (Life Peer), cr. 74, of Greenwich in Greater London; **Burke St. John Trend,** P.C., G.C.B., C.V.O.; British civil servant; b. 2 Jan. 1914; s. of late Walter St. John Trend; m. Patricia Charlotte Shaw 1949; two s. one d.; ed. Whitgift School, and Merton Coll., Oxford.

Entered Civil Service (Ministry of Education) 36, Treasury 37, Asst. Private Sec. to Chancellor of the Exchequer 39-41, Principal Private Sec. 45-49, Under-Sec. to Treasury 49-55, Office of Lord Privy Seal 55-56, Deputy Sec. of the Cabinet 56-59, Third Sec. Treasury 59-60, Second Sec. Treasury 60-62, Sec. to Cabinet 63-73; Rector Lincoln College, Oxford 73-; Trustee Nuffield Foundation 73-, British Museum 73-; Dir. Hudson Bay Co. 73-, Provident Life Insurance Asscn. 74-.

Lincoln College, Oxford, England.

Trendota, Józef; Polish politician; b. 14 Jan. 1921, Tarnów; ed. Higher School of Economics, Katowice.

Bank Clerk, Communal Savings Bank, Tarnów 39-43; worked at Tar Paper Factory, Tarnów 43-45; at Wholesale Chemical Enterprise, Katowice 45-47; managerial posts in Central Board of Chemical Industry, Gliwice; teaching and research at Faculty of Econs. of Chemical Industry, Higher School of Econs., Katowice 48-51; Dir. of Dept. Ministry of Finance 51-53; Deputy Minister of Finance 53-69, Minister June 69-Dec. 71; Chair. State Board of Prices March 72-; mem. Polish United Workers' Party (PZPR); Order Polonia Restituta, Order of Banner of Labour 1st Class, etc.

Państwowa Komisja Centralna, ul. Świętokrzyska 12, 00-044 Warsaw, Poland.

Trengganu, H.R.H. The Sultan of; Tunku Ismail Nasiruddin Shah Ibni Almarhum Sultan Zainal Abidin, D.K., D.K.M., D.M.N., S.P.M.T., K.C.M.G.; Ruler of Trengganu State; b. 24 Jan. 1907.

Joined Trengganu Civil Service 29, later served as High Court Registrar and Chief Magistrate; acceded to throne of Trengganu 45, installed 49; Timbalan Yang di-Pertuan Agung (Deputy Head of State) of Malaya, later Malaysia 60-66, Yang di-Pertuan Agung (Head of State) 66-70.

Istana Badariah, Kuala Trengganu, Trengganu, Malaysia.

Trepczynski, Stanisław; Polish politician; b. 7 April 1924, Łódź; m.; two s.; ed. Łódź Univ.

Member Łódź Cttee., Polish Workers' Party, later Polish United Workers' Party 46; Sec. Polish Peace Cttee. 51; Sec. Organizational Cttee., Conf. of IPU 59, Assembly of World Fed. of UN Asscns. 60; Head, Office of Secretariat, Cen. Cttee., Polish United Workers' Party (PZPR) 61-70; Deputy Minister of Foreign Affairs March 71-; mem. Cen. Cttee. PZPR Dec. 71-; Pres. UN Gen. Assembly 73; several Polish decorations, including Order of Banner of Labour 2nd Class, Officer's Cross Order of Polonia Restituta, Silver Medal (IPU).

Publs. *Socialism and National Development* (co-author) 71 and articles on international affairs.

Ministerstwo Spraw Zagranicznych, Aleja I Armii Wojska Polskiego 23, Warsaw, Poland.

Trethowan, (James) Ian (Raley); British broadcasting executive; b. 20 Oct. 1922, High Wycombe; s. of Major J. J. R. Trethowan, M.B.E. and late Mrs. Roy Trethowan; m. Carolyn Reynolds 1963; three d.

Newspaper Reporter, Norwich and York; Observer, Fleet Air Arm during Second World War; Political Corresp. *Yorkshire Post* 47; Political Corresp. *News Chronicle* 55; Newscaster and Diplomatic Corresp., Independent Television News (ITN), then Deputy Editor 58, and later Political Editor; Commentator on politics and current affairs, British Broadcasting Corpn. (BBC) 63-70, Man. Dir. Radio 70-75, Man. Dir. BBC TV 76-; Political Contributor, *Economist* 50-58, 65-67, *The Times* 67-69; mem. Cttee. on Official Secrets Acts 71-72; Univ. of Calif. Award for programme about U.S.A. 61.

BBC, Broadcasting House, Portland Place, London, W.1; 15 Pembroke Square, London, W.8, England. Telephone: 01-937-4489.

Treurnicht, Andries Petrus, M.A., PH.D., M.P.; South African politician; b. 19 Feb. 1921, Piketberg; s. of Andries Petrus Treurnicht and Hester Johanna E. Albertyn; m. Engela Dreyer 1949; four d.; ed. Piketberg High School, Univ. of Stellenbosch, Theological Seminary, Stellenbosch and Univ. of Cape Town.

Minister, Dutch Reformed Church 46-60; Editor *Die Kerkbode* 60-67, *Hoofstad* 67-71; mem. Parl. for Waterberg 71-; Deputy Minister of Bantu Admin. and Educ. Jan. 76-.

Publs. thirteen publications on various religious subjects.

383 Bergkaree Avenue, Lynnwood, Pretoria, South Africa. Telephone: 788205.

Trevaskis, Sir (Gerald) Kennedy (Nicholas), K.C.M.G., O.B.E.; British diplomatist; b. 1 Jan. 1915, Hove, Sussex; s. of Rev. Hugh Kennedy Trevaskis and

Gwendolen Eva Constance Myfanwy Tizard; *m.* Sheila Harrington 1945; two *s.* one *d.*; ed. Marlborough and King's Coll., Cambridge.

Colonial Admin. Service 38, Cadet, N. Rhodesia; British Mil. Admin., Eritrea 41-48, British Admin. 48-50; Dist. Officer, N. Rhodesia 50-51; Political Officer, Western Aden Protectorate 51-52, Deputy British Agent 52-54, Adviser and British Agent 54-Jan. 63; Deputy High Commr. for Aden and the Protectorate of South Arabia Jan.-June 63, High Commr. June 63-Dec. 64; Dir. Sunningdale Oils.

Leisure interests: gardening, beagling.

Publs. *A Colony in Transition: the British Occupation of Eritrea* 60, *Shades of Amber* 68.

The Old Vicarage, Chaddleworth, Berks., England.

Trevelyan, Baron (Life Peer), cr. 68; **Humphrey Trevelyan,** K.G., G.C.M.G., C.I.E., O.B.E.; retired British diplomatist; b. 27 Nov. 1905, Hindhead, Surrey; *s.* of Rev. George Philip Trevelyan; *m.* Violet Margaret (*d.* of Gen. Sir William Bartholomew, G.C.B., C.M.G., D.S.O.); two *d.*; ed. Lancing Coll., and Jesus Coll., Cambridge.

Joined Indian Civil Service 29; Indian Political Service 32-47; Political Agent in Indian States; Sec. to Agent-Gen. for India in Washington, D.C. 44-46; Joint Sec., Ministry of External Affairs, New Delhi 46-47; entered H.M. Foreign Service 47; Counsellor, Baghdad Embassy 48; Economic and Financial Adviser to U.K. High Commr. in Germany 51-53; Chargé d'Affaires, Peking, 53-55; Amb. to Egypt 55-56; Under-Sec. UN 58; Amb. to Iraq 58-61; Deputy Under-Sec. Foreign Office 62; Amb. to U.S.S.R. 62-65; High Commr. in Aden 67; Pres. Council of Foreign Bondholders 65-; Dir. British Petroleum Co. Ltd. 65-75, Gen. Electric Co. Ltd., British Bank of the Middle East; Chair. of Trustees, British Museum; Chair. Royal Inst. of Int. Affairs; Hon. Fellow, Jesus Coll., Cambridge; Hon. LL.D. (Cambridge) 70; Hon. D.C.L. (Durham) 73; Hon. D.Litt. (Leeds) 75.

Publs. *The Middle East in Revolution* 70, *Worlds Apart* 71, *The India We Left* 72, *Diplomatic Channels* 73.

13 Wilton Street, London, S.W.1, England.

Telephone: 01-235-4503.

Trevor-Roper, Hugh Redwald; British historian; b. 15 Jan. 1914, Glanton, Northumb.; *s.* of Dr. B. W. E. and Mrs. Trevor-Roper; *m.* The Lady Alexandra Haig 1954; ed. Charterhouse and Christ Church, Oxford.

Research Fellow, Merton Coll., Oxford 37-39; Student of Christ Church, Oxford 45-57; Regius Prof. of Modern History in the Univ. of Oxford 57-; Dir. Times Newspapers Ltd. 74-.

Publs. *Archbishop Laud* 40, *The Last Days of Hitler* 47, *Hitler's Table Talk* (Editor) 53, *The Gentry 1540-1640* 54, *The Poems of Richard Corbett* (Editor, with J. A. W. Bennett) 55, *Historical Essays* 57 (American title, *Men and Events* 58), *Hitler's War Directives* (Editor) 64, *The Rise of Christian Europe* 63, *Religion, the Reformation and Social Change* 67 (American title *The Crisis of the 17th Century* 68), *The Philby Affair* 68, *Queen Elizabeth's First Historian* 71.

Oriel College, Oxford; and 8 St. Aldate's, Oxford, England.

Telephone: 43388.

Trezise, Philip H.; American analyst and diplomatist; b. 27 May 1912, Calumet, Michigan; *s.* of Norman R. and Emma A. Trezise; *m.* Ruth E. Dorsey 1938; two *s.*; ed. Univ. of Michigan.

Research Assoc. Univ. of Michigan until 41; Analyst, Office of Defense Transportation 42; Office of Strategic Services, U.S. Navy 43-46; Chief Research Analyst, then Chief of Div. of Research for Far East, State Dept. 46, Chief of Div. of Research for Near East and Africa, later Deputy Dir. Office of Intelligence and Research, mem. Policy Planning Staff; Nat. War Coll. 49-50; Minister for Econ. Affairs, U.S. Embassy, and Dir. of Agency for Int. Devt. (AID) Mission, Tokyo

57-61; Deputy Asst. Sec. of State for Econ. **Affairs** 61-65; Head of U.S. Del. to Org. for Econ. Co-operation and Devt. (OECD) Jan. 66-69; Asst. Sec. of State for Econ. Affairs 69-72; Senior Fellow, Brooking Inst. 71-; mem. Nat. Comm. on Supplies and Shortages 75-; President's Award for Distinguished Fed. Civilian Service 65.

c/o Department of State, Washington, D.C.; Home: 6900 Broxburn Drive, Bethesda, Md., U.S.A.

Telephone: 229-3443 (Home).

Triboulet, Raymond, L. en DROIT, L. ès L.; French politician; b. 3 Oct. 1906, Paris; *s.* of Maurice Triboulet and Josèphe Wagner; *m.* Luce Chauveau 1928; three *s.* three *d.*; ed. Univ. of Paris.

Active in French Resistance 41-44; Sous-Préfet for Bayeux region 44-46; Regional Inspector for Rhine-Palatinate 46; Mem. Parl. 46-; founder of Federalist group in French Parl.; Pres. of Gaullist Parl. Group (Social Republicans) 54-58; Minister of War Veterans Jan.-Oct. 55; mem. ECSC Common Assembly 57; Pres. Union of New Republic (U.N.R.) 58; Minister of War Veterans 59-63, of Co-operation 63-66; re-elected Deputy 58, 62, 67 and 68; mem. European Parl. 67; Pres. U.D.E. group 68; Pres. D-Day Commemoration Cttee.; Chevalier Légion d'Honneur; Croix de Guerre; Resistance Medal; O.B.E., and other decorations.

Publs. *Les Billets du Négus* 39, *Sens dessus dessous* 51, *Des Vessies pour des Lanternes* 58, *Halte au Massacre* 66.

119 rue Brancas, 92310 Sèvres, France.

Tricart, Jean Léon François; French university professor; b. 16 Sept. 1920, Montmorency; *s.* of François Tricart and Lea Cordonnier; *m.* Denise Casimir 1944; four *s.*; ed. Lycée Rollin, Paris, and Univ. de Paris à la Sorbonne.

Assistant Lecturer, Univ. de Paris 45-48; Lecturer Univ. of Strasbourg 48-49, Asst. Prof. 49-55, Prof. 55-; Vice-Dean, mem. of Univ. Senate 67-70; Principal Asst., Geological Map of France 60; Founder-Dir. Centre of Applied Geography, Strasbourg 56-; Pres. Applied Geomorphology Comm. of Int. Geographical Union 60-68; Head of numerous technical co-operation missions in Senegal, Mauritania, Ivory Coast, Guinea, Togo, Mali, Brazil, Chile, Venezuela, Peru, Panama, El Salvador, Colombia, Uruguay and IICA, FAO, UNDP and UNESCO Senior Consultant 68-; scientific assessor of IRAT.

Leisure interest: philately.

Publs. include numerous scientific articles and *Principes et Méthodes de la Géomorphologie* 65, *Traité de Géomorphologie* (with A. Cailleux), 6 vols. to date.

Centre de Géographie Appliquée, Université Louis-Pasteur, Strasbourg, 43 rue Goethe, 67000 Strasbourg; and 85 route de la Meinau, 67100 Strasbourg-Meinau, France.

Telephone: 35-43-00, ext. 279 (Office); 39-09-86 (Home).

Tricornot de Rose, Comte François de; French diplomatist; b. 3 Nov. 1910; *m.* Yvonne Daday 1933; two *d.*; ed. Ecole Libre des Sciences Politiques, Paris.

Secretary Embassy to U.K. 37-40, Italy 45-46; mem. French del. to UN 46-50; Minister to Spain 52-56; Ministry of Foreign Affairs, Paris 56-60; mem. Atomic Energy Comm. (Paris) 50-64; Pres. European Nuclear Research Org. (CERN) 58-60; Deputy Chief of Staff, Nat. Defence 61-62; mem. Board Institut Français d'Etudes Stratégiques 62-64; Ambassador to Portugal 64-69; Amb. and Perm. Rep. to North Atlantic Council 70-75; Amb. de France; Officier Légion d'Honneur, Croix de Guerre.

Leisure interests: golf, skiing, shooting.

Home: 5 rue du Faubourg Saint-Honoré, 75018 Paris, France.

Triffin, Robert, LL.D., PH.D.ECON.; American economist; b. 5 Oct. 1911, Flobecq, Belgium; *s.* of François Triffin and Céline van Hooland; *m.* Lois Brandt 1940;

three *s*.; ed. Kain-lez Tournai, Louvain Univ., Harvard Univ.

Instructor, Harvard 39-42; Chief Latin American Div., Bd. of Govs. Fed. Reserve System 42-46; Int. Monetary Fund, Chief Exchange Control Div. 46-48, Chief Rep. in Europe 48-49; Special Policy Adviser, Econ. Co-operation Admin. and Alternate U.S. Rep. European Payments Union 49-51; Frederick William Beinecke Prof. of Economics and Master of Berkeley Coll., Yale Univ. 51-; headed numerous monetary and banking reorganization missions to Latin American countries, Iran, etc.; Consultant to UN 52; Council of Econ. Advisers (U.S.) 53-54, 61; Consultant OEEC 57-58, EEC 58-; Vice-Pres. American Economic Asscn. 66-67; mem. Council of Economic Advisers, Société d'Econ. Pol. (Paris); mem. American Acad. of Arts and Sciences, World Acad. of Art and Science, Assoc. Acad. Royale de Belgique; Commdr. Ordre de la Couronne (Belgium) 73; Wells Prize, Harvard 39.

Leisure interests: reading, bridge, hiking, horseback riding.

Publs. *Monopolistic Competition and General Equilibrium Theory* 40, *Monetary and Banking Reform in Paraguay* 46, *Europe and the Money Muddle* 57, *Gold and the Dollar Crisis* 60, *The Evolution of the International Monetary System: Historical Reappraisal and Future Perspectives* 64, *The World Money Maze: National Currencies in International Payments* 66, *Our International Monetary System: Yesterday, Today and To-morrow* 68, *The Future of the Pound* 69.

Office: 403A Yale Station, Yale University, New Haven, Conn. 06520; Home: 125 High Street, New Haven, Conn. 06520, U.S.A.

Telephone: 436-8580 (Office); 777-4380 (Home).

Trillo Pays, Dionisio Martin Enrique; Uruguayan author and librarian; b. 1909; ed. Univ. of the Republic, Montevideo.

Dir. Nat. Library of Uruguay 47-; mem. Nat. Comm. for Archives of Artigas 47; mem. Council on Legal Rights of Authors 47; Editor *Asir*, literary review 49-.

Publs. *Mediodía* (play) 40, *Pompeyo Amargo* 42, *Zarzas* (stories) 44, *Estas hojas no caen en otoño* 46, *El patio de los naranjos* (play) 50.

Biblioteca Nacional, Guayabo 1793, Montevideo, Uruguay.

Trintignant, Jean Louis Xavier; French actor; b. 11 Dec. 1930; ed. Faculté de Droit, Aix-en-Provence.

Films include: *Et Dieu créa la femme, Club de Femmes, Les Liaisons dangereuses, L'Eté violent, Austerlitz, La Millième Fenêtre, Pleins Feux sur l'assassin, Coeur battant, L'Atlantide, Le Jeu de la vérité, Horace 62, Les Sept Péchés capitaux, Le Combat dans l'île, Il Sorpasso, Il Successo, Château en Suède, La Bonne Occase, Mata Hari agent H 21, Angélique marquise des anges, Meurtre à l'italienne, La Longue Marche, Le 17e ciel, Paris brûle-t-il?, Un homme et une femme, Safari diamants, Un homme à abattre, L'homme qui ment, Les Biches, Le Voleur de crimes, Z, Ma nuit chez Maud, Disons un soir à diner, L'Américain, La Mort a pondu un oeuf, L'Amour à cheval, Le Conformiste, Si douces, si perverses, Le Train, Le Mouton Enragé 74, Les Violons du Bal 74, Le Jeu avec le Feu 74.*

c/o Art Media, 37 rue Marbeuf, 75008 Paris, France.

Trip, Fokele Hendrik Pieter; Netherlands politician; b. 10 Oct. 1921, Amersfoort; *m*.; three *s*. three *d*.; ed. Univ. of Amsterdam.

Officer in Army Information Service, Indonesia 46-49; Sec. Management Board, Polak and Schwarz Scents and Flavours Industries, Zaandam; Chair. Management Board of Dutch branch Int. Flavors and Fragrances, Chair. Exec. Board controlling European branches -72; Chair. Exec. Board State Univ., Utrecht 72-; Nat. Pres. Catholic Industrial Pastoral Work

Asscn.; Minister of Science Policy and Univ. Educ. 73-; mem. Radical Political Party.

Second Chamber of States General, Het Binnenhof, The Hague, Netherlands.

Tripathi, Kamalapati; Indian politician.

Member, Legislative Assembly of Uttar Pradesh 36-; Minister for Irrigation and Information and later for Home Affairs, Educ. and Information, U.P.; Deputy Chief Minister of Uttar Pradesh 69-71, Chief Minister 71-73; Minister of Shipping and Transport 73-75, of Railways Feb. 75-; mem. Rajya Sabha 73-.

Ministry of Railways, New Delhi, India.

Tripp, (John) Peter, C.M.G.; British diplomatist; b. 27 March 1921; ed. Sutton Valence School, Institut de Touraine.

Royal Marines 41-46; Sudan Political Service 46-54; H.M. Foreign Service (later Diplomatic Service) 54-, Amb. to Libya 70-74; High Commr. in Singapore 74-.

British High Commission, Tanglin Circus, Singapore 10, Singapore.

Trivedi, Sir Chandulal Madhavlal, K.C.S.I., C.I.E., O.B.E., B.A.; Indian civil servant; b. 2 July 1893; *s*. of Madhavlal and Ujamben Trivedi; *m*. Kusum Trivedi 1906; one *s*.; ed. Bombay Univ., Elphinstone Coll., Bombay, and St. John's Coll., Oxford.

Entered I.C.S. 17; served as Asst. Commr., Central Provinces 17-21; after serving in various capacities, posted as Dep. Sec. to Govt. of India Home Dept. 32-35 (Act. Joint Sec. April-Sept. 34); Sec. to Govt. of India Secretariat Organization C tee. 35-36; Commr. Berar 36, Chattisgarh Div. 36-37; Chief Sec. to Govt. C.P and Berar 37-Mar. 42; Sec. to Govt. of India War Dept. July 42-Jan. 46; Gov. of Orissa April 46-Aug. 47; Gov. of Punjab from Aug. 15th 47-53; Gov. of Andhra 53-56; Gov. of Andhra Pradesh 56-57; mem. Planning Comm. Govt. of India 57-63; Chair. Madhya Pradesh Police Comm. 64-65; Hon. LL.D. (Punjab Univ.); Hon. D.Litt. (Andhra Univ.); Padma Vibhushan award 56; Chancellor Gujarat Ayurveda Univ. Nov. 66-; Pres. Bharat Scouts and Guides 67-73.

Leisure interests: walking, gardening, reading.

Chandra-Bhuvan, Kapadwanj, Gujarat, India.

Troadec, René; French fmr. overseas governor; b. 6 July 1908, Finistère; *s*. of François Troadec and Victorine Morin; *m*. Suzanne Bellec 1934; two *s*. four *d*.; ed. Paris Univ. Law Faculty, and Ecole Nat. de la France d'Outre-Mer, Paris.

Admin., Middle Congo 34-39; officer in War 39-45; Dir. of Recruitment, Ecole Nat. de la France d'Outre-Mer 45-48; Sec.-Gen. French West African Ex-Servicemen's Office 48-53; Commdr., Cercle Dimbroko, Ivory Coast 54; Sec.-Gen. French Somaliland Govt. 54-56; Sec.-Gen. Ivory Coast 56; Gov. and High Comm., Chad 56-59; Sec.-Gen. French Equatorial Africa Govt. 59-60; First Councillor of Gen. High Comm. in Brazzaville 59-60; adviser to Sec. of State for Overseas Territories 61-66; Man. attached to the Gen. Management of Thomson-C.S.F. 66-73; Commdr. Légion d'Honneur, Compagnon de la Libération, Rosette de la Résistance, Croix de Guerre.

Leisure interest: sea fishing.

10 rue Voltaire, 29200 Brest, France.

Troclet, Léon-Eli; Belgian barrister and politician; b. June 1902, Liège; *m*. Mlle. Jakob 1935; one *d*.; ed. Univ. of Liège.

Leader of Socialist youth movement 18; Provincial Councillor, Liège 28-32; Prof. and Dir. Ecole de Droit Admin. et de Police 32-45; Belgian Del. to L. of N. 31, 61; Senator 44; Minister of Labour and Social Insurance 45-49; Vice-Pres. of Bourse du Travail (Labour Exchange) and of Unemployment Claims Comm. 34; juridical assessor to Arbitration Tribunal of Liège 27-45; mem. of clandestine Walloon Economic Council and

Cttee. of Walloon Congress 43-44; Prof. of Law and Social Legislation, Univ. of Brussels; mem. European Parliament and Pres. of its Social Affairs Cttee.; Del. to ILO 45-69; Chair. ILO 50-51; Minister of Labour and Social Welfare 54-58; Minister of State 68; Govt. del. to ILO 45-66; mem. Coll. d'Impulsion de Benelux 69; Vice-Pres. Cttee. of Independent Experts, Council of Europe 72-; Socialist.

Leisure interests: law, sociology.

Publs. *La réglementation de l'assurance chômage* 38, *La Wallonie et les Allocations familiales* 39, *L'influence de la guerre sur les contrats de travail et d'emploi* (2 vols.) 41, *Guide pratique de législation sociale* 42, *Problèmes belges de la sécurité sociale* 49, 62, *Signification sociale du déficit de l'Assurance-maladie* 50, 63, *Législation Sociale Internationale* (3 vols.) 52-62, *Droit Social Européen* 64, *Statut Juridique des représentants de Commerce* 64, *La loi sur la protection des rénumérations* 65.

2 Avenue des Prisonniers Politiques, 1150 Woluwé-St. Pierre, Brussels, Belgium.

Telephone: 02/622046.

Trofimuk, Andrei Alexeevich; Soviet petroleum geologist; b. 16 Aug. 1911, Khvetkovichi, Byelorussia; ed. State Univ. of Kazan.

Head Geologist and Scientific Leader of Central Research Laboratory of the "Vostokneft" Trust 34-40; Chief Geologist "Ishimbaineft" Trust 40-42, "Bashneft" Soc. 42-50; Chief Geologist, Main Oil and Gas Exploration Dept., Ministry of Oil Industry of U.S.S.R. 50-53; Dep. Dir. All-Union Oil and Gas Scientific Research Inst. 53-55, Dir. 55-58; Dir. Inst. of Geology and Geophysics, Siberian Branch, U.S.S.R. Acad. of Sciences 58-; mem. U.S.S.R. Acad. of Sciences 58-; mem. U.S.S.R. Acad. of Sciences Presidium, First Vice-Chair. Siberian Branch; Editor *Geology and Geophysics*; Hero of Socialist Labour 44, State Prizes 46, 50, Hon. Scientist of R.S.F.S.R. 57, Order of Lenin 50, Order of Red Banner of Labour 59, 61.

Publs. *On the Nature of Ishimbaevo Oil-Bearing Massifs* 36, *An Outline of Tectonics and Oil Content of Volga-Ural Region* 39, *Oil Content of Paleozoic Beds of Bashkiria* 50, *Conditions of Formation of Oil Deposits of Ural-Volga Oil-Bearing Region* 55, *Gas Resources of the U.S.S.R.* 59, *Oil and Gas Content of Siberian Platform* 60, *Gas-Bearing Prospects of the U.S.S.R.* 63, *Geology and Oil and Gas Content of West Siberian Lowland, a New Oil-Bearing Province of the U.S.S.R.* 63, *Oil- and Gas-Bearing Basins of the U.S.S.R.* 64, *Tectonics and Oil and Gas-Bearing prospects of Platform Regions of Siberia* (with Yu. A. Kosygin) 65, *Some Questions on the Theory of Organic Origin of Oil and the problem of Diagnostics of Oil-Source Beds* (with A. E. Kontorovich) 65, *On the Methods of Calculation of Prognostic Reserves of Oil* 66.

Akademgorodok, Novosibirsk 90, U.S.S.R.

Trofin, Virgil, E.ECON.; Romanian politician; b. 23 July 1926, Lipovăţ, Vaslui County; ed. Bucharest Acad. of Economics.

Member Cen. Cttee. revolutionary youth org. 45-47, First Sec. of its Cen. Cttee. 56-64; mem. Romanian Communist Party (R.C.P.) 45-; Alt. mem. Cen. Cttee., R.C.P. 55-60, mem. Cen. Cttee. 60-, Sec. Cen. Cttee. 65-71, mem. Exec. Cttee. of Cen. Cttee. 68-, Standing Presidium of Cen. Cttee. 68-74; Chair. Nat. Union of Agricultural Production Co-operatives 69-71; Deputy Grand Nat. Assembly 57; mem. Defence Council of Romania 69-74; Chair. Gen. Trade Union Confederation 71-72; Vice-Chair. Council of Ministers and Minister of Home Trade 72-74; Hero of Socialist Labour 71.

c/o Council of Ministers, Bucharest, Romania.

Troll, Carl, PH.D.; German professor of geography; b. 24 Dec. 1899, Gabersee, Upper Bavaria; s. of Dr. med. Theodor Troll; m. Elisabeth Kuerschner 1930; five s. four d.; ed. Univ. of Munich.

Assistant in Geographical Inst., Univ. of Munich 22; Lecturer in Geography 25; Prof. of Geography, Univ. of Berlin 30; Prof. of Econ. Geography 36; Prof. of Geography and Dir. of Geographical Inst., Univ. of Bonn 38-, now Emer. Prof.; Rector Bonn Univ. 60-61; scientific expeditions to S. America 26-29; expedition to E. Africa 33-34; scientific leader of the German Himalaya expedition to Nanga Parbat 37; expedition to Abyssinia 37, to Mexico 54; mem. Acads. of Berlin, Munich, Halle, Bucharest, Mainz, Vienna, Helsinki, Rome, Venice, Buenos Aires, Copenhagen, La Paz, Barcelona; Hon. mem. 17 scientific socs. in 9 countries; Pres. Int. Geographical Union 60-64; Carus Medal 38, Vega Medal 51, Ritter Medal 59, Victoria Medal 62, Martin Behaim Medal 59, Penck Medal 64, Madan Mohan Malviya Medal 71; Dr.Sc. h.c., Dr.Phil. h.c., and other awards.

Leisure interests: theatre and concerts.

Publs. *Diluvial Geology* 24, *Bolivian Andes* 29, *Geography of South America* 30, *Vegetation of N.W. Himalaya* 39, *Colonial Land Planning of Africa* 41, *Glaciology* 42, *Geomorphology* 44, *Periglacial Geomorphology* 47-48, *Geography in Germany 1933-1945* 47, *Tropical Mountains* 59, *Physiognomy of Tropical Plants* 59, *Gr. Herder Atlas* 58, *Seasonal Climates of the Earth* 64, *Landscape Ecology and High Mountain Research* 66, *Air Photo Interpretation* 66, *Plural Societies of Developing Countries* 66, *Geo-Ecology of the Tropical Americas* 68, *Problems of Geomorphological Research* 69, *Mapping of Land Use in the Rhinelands, Geo-ecology of the High Mountain Regions of Eurasia* 72, *Water Supply by Qanats and Universal History* 72; Editor of *Erdkunde* 47-71; Editor of *Bonner Geogr. Abhandl.* 47-, of *Colloquium Geographicum* 50-, of *Arbeiten zur Rheinischen Landeskunde* 52-, of *Erdwissenschaftliche Forschung* 68.

Rheinbacherstrasse 55, 53 Bonn/Rhein-1, Federal Republic of Germany.

Telephone: 636036.

Troll, Wilhelm, DR.PHIL.; German university professor; b. 3 Nov. 1897, Munich; s. of Dr. Theodor and Elisabeth (née Hufnagel) Troll; m. Margareta Weissenberg 1925; ed. Humanistisches Gymnasium and Univ. of Munich.

Privatdozent Univ. of Munich 25; Prof. of Botany, Univ. of Halle/Saale 32; Prof. of Botany and General Biology, Univ. of Mainz 46, now Prof. Emer.; Dr. rer. nat. h.c. (Univ. of Heidelberg) 67; Corresp. mem. American Botanical Soc. 69.

Leisure interests: natural philosophy, Goethe-research.

Publs. *Vergleichende Morphologie* 36-42 (reprinted 67-68), *Allgemeine Botanik* (4th edn.) 73, *Praktische Einführung in die Pflanzenmorphologie* 54-57 (reprinted 73-75), *Die Infloreszensen* Vol. I 64, Vol. II/1 69.

Institut für Spezielle Botanik, 6500 Mainz, Postfach 3980; Home: 6500 Mainz, Oberer Laubenheimer Weg 19, Federal Republic of Germany.

Telephone: 392626.

Trowbridge, Alexander B.; American organization executive; b. 12 Dec. 1929, N.J.; s. of A. Buel and Julie Chamberlain Trowbridge; m. Nancey Horst 1955; two s. one d.; ed. Phillips Acad., Andover, Mass., and Princeton Univ.

U.S. Marine Corps during Korean War; with overseas operations of several petroleum companies in Cuba, El Salvador, Panama and Philippines; Pres. and Div. Man. Esso Standard Oil Co. of Puerto Rico until 65; Asst. Sec. of Commerce for Domestic and Int. Business 65-67; Acting Sec. of Commerce Feb. 67-May 67, Sec. of Commerce May 67-68; Pres. American Management Asscn. 68-70, Conf. Board Inc. 70-76, U.S.-Korea Econ. Council; Vice-Chair. Atlantic Council (U.S.); Dir. Allied Chemical Corpn., then Vice-Chair. of Board 76-.

Leisure interests: tennis, skiing.

2 Colonial Road, White Plains, N.Y. 10605, U.S.A.

Troyanovsky, Oleg Aleksandrovich; Soviet diplomatist; b. 24 Nov. 1919, Moscow; ed. Moscow Foreign Languages Inst., Moscow Inst. of Philosophy, Literature and History.

Diplomatic service 44; took part in many important confs.; Amb. to Japan 68-76.

c/o Ministry of Foreign Affairs, 32-34 Smolenskaya-Sennaya ploshchad, Moscow, U.S.S.R.

Troyat, Henri (*pseudonym* of Tarasoff); French writer; b. 1 Nov. 1911, Moscow, U.S.S.R.; *m.* Marguerite Saintagne 1948; one *s.* one *d.*; ed. Lycée Pasteur, and Law Faculty, Univ. of Paris.

Member Acad. Française 59-; Légion d'Honneur.

Publs. *Faux-Jour* (Prix Populiste) 35, *L'Araigne* (Prix Goncourt) 38, *La Neige en Deuil* (Grand prix littéraire de Monaco) 52, *Tant que la terre durera* (three vols.) 47-50, *Les semailles et les moissons* (five vols.) 53-58, *La Lumière des Justes* (five vols.) 60-, *Les Eyglétière* (three vols.) 65-67, *Les Héritiers de l'avenir* 68, *Anne Predaille* 73, *Le Moscovite* 74, etc.; biographies: *Dostoïevsky, Pouchkine, Tolstoi, Gogol.*

Académie Française, quai de Conti, Paris 6e, France.

Trudeau, Rt. Hon. Pierre Elliott, P.C., M.P.; Canadian lawyer and politician; b. 18 Oct. 1919, Montreal, Quebec; *s.* of Charles-Emile Trudeau and Grace Elliott; *m.* Margaret Sinclair 1971; three *s.*; ed. Collège Jean-de-Brébeuf, Montreal, Univ. of Montreal, Harvard Univ., Univ. of Paris, and London School of Economics.

Called to Bar, Province of Quebec 43, then studied at Harvard, Paris and London; subsequently employed with Cabinet Secr., Ottawa; later practised law, Province of Quebec; one of founders of *Cité Libre* (Quebec review); Assoc. Prof. of Law, Univ. of Montreal 61; mem. House of Commons 65-; Parl. Sec. to Prime Minister Jan. 66-April 67; Minister of Justice and Attorney-Gen. April 67-July 68; Leader of Liberal Party and Prime Minister of Canada April 68-; Dr. h.c. Duke Univ. 74; Freedom of City of London 75.

Publs. *La Grève de l'Amiante* 56, *Canadian Dualism/La Dualité Canadienne* 60, *Deux Innocents en Chine Rouge* 61, *Federalism and the French Canadians* 68, *Résponses* 68; and numerous articles in Canadian and foreign journals.

Prime Minister's Residence, 24 Sussex Drive, Ottawa, Canada.

Telephone: 613-992-4211.

Trueheart, William Clyde, B.S., M.A.; American diplomatist; b. 18 Dec. 1918, Chester, Va.; *s.* of William Cheatham Trueheart and Sallie Leftwich Shepherd; *m.* Phoebe Anna Everett 1948; two *s.*; ed. Phillips Exeter Acad. and Univ. of Virginia.

Navy Dept. 42; U.S. Army 43-46; Atomic Energy Comm. 47-49; Dept. of State 49-54; Deputy Dir. Political Affairs, U.S. Del. to NATO, Paris 54-58; Exec. Asst. to Sec.-Gen., Baghdad Pact Org., Ankara 58-59; First Sec., London 59-61; Counsellor, with rank of Minister, Saigon 61-64; Dir. Office of S.E. Asian Affairs, Dept. of State 64-66; Senior Foreign Policy Seminar, Dept. of State 66-67; Deputy Dir. for Co-ordination, Bureau of Intelligence and Research, Dept. of State 67-69; Amb. to Nigeria 69-71; Adviser to Commdt., Maxwell Air Force Base 71-73; Adviser to Office of Environmental Affairs, Dept. of State 73-74; Consultant, U.S. Senate Select Cttee. on Intelligence 75-76.

5012 Hawthorne Place, N.W., Washington, D.C. 20016, U.S.A.

Trueta, Joseph, M.A., M.D., F.R.C.S.; b. 27 Oct. 1897; Spanish-born British surgeon; ed. Barcelona Inst. and Univ.

House Surgeon, Santa Creu Hospital, Barcelona 21, Asst. Surgeon 28; Auxiliary Prof. Barcelona Univ. 32; Dir. of Surgery, Gen. Hospital of Catalonia, Barcelona Univ. 35; Acting Surgeon-in-Charge Accident Service, Radcliffe Infirmary Oxford 42-44; Nuffield Prof. of Orthopaedic Surgery, Oxford 49-66, Prof. Emer. 66-; Hon. mem. British Orthopaedic Asscn. 40; Hon. F.R.C.S. (Canada); Hon. Fellow American Coll. of Surgeons; Hon. mem. Italian, French, German and S. American socs. of Orthopaedics and Traumatology, Portuguese Orthopaedic Soc., Scandinavian Orthopaedic Soc., Foreign Assoc., French Acad. of Surgery; Hon. Pres. Int. Soc. Surgery and Traumatology; Dr. h.c. (Oxford, Buenos Aires, Rio de Janeiro, Bogotá, Gothenburg Univs.); Commdr. Southern Cross, Officier, Légion d'Honneur.

Publs. *Els tumors Malignes Primitius dels Ossos* 35, *La Hidatidosi Ossia* 36, *Tractament de les Fractures de Guerra* 38, *Treatment of War Wounds and Fractures* 39, *Principles and Practice of War Surgery* 43, *The Spirit of Catalonia* 46, *Studies of the Renal Circulation* (in collaboration) 47, *Atlas of Traumatic Surgery* 49, *Handbook on Poliomyelitis* (in collaboration) 56, *Studies of the Development and Decay of the Human Frame* 68, *Gathorne Robert Girdlestone* 71.

Rambla de Catuluña 74, Barcelona, Spain.

Truffaut, François; French film director; b. 6 Feb. 1932; ed. secondary school.

Former journalist, cinema critic, publisher of *Cahiers du Cinéma* and *Arts*; Film Dir. 57-; First Prize Cannes Festival for *Les 400 Coups* 59; U.S. Nat. Soc. of Film Critics' Award for Outstanding Director of the Year for *Baisers Volés* 69; Prix Méliès for *L'Enfant Sauvage* 70; Acad. Award for Best Foreign Film (*La Nuit Américaine*) 74.

Films: *Les Mistons, Les 400 Coups, Tirez sur le Pianiste, Jules et Jim, L'Amour à Vingt Ans, La Peau Douce, Fahrenheit 451, La Mariée était en Noir* 67, *Baisers Volés* 68, *La Sirène du Mississippi* 69, *L'Enfant Sauvage* 70, *Domicile Conjugal* 70, *Les Deux Anglaises et le Continent* 71, *Une Belle Fille Comme Moi* 72, *La Nuit Américaine* 73, *L'Histoire de Adèle H.* 75, *L'Argent de Poche* 76.

Publs. (with Helen G. Scott) *Hitchcock* 67, *Les Aventures d'Antoine Doinel* 70, *Les Filmes de ma Vie* 75.

5 rue Robert-Estienne, Paris 8e, France.

Truhaut, René Charles, D. ès sc.; French toxicologist; b. 23 May 1909, Pouzauges (Vendée); *s.* of Jules Truhaut and Sidonie Lucas; ed. Lycée de La Roche-sur-Yon, Facultés de pharmacie et des sciences de Paris.

Chief Pharmacist psychiatric hospitals (Seine) 37-; Head of Lab., Inst. of Cancer 30-41, Head of Chemical Research 41-48; Head of Research Inst. Gustave Roussy 49-; Prof. of Toxicology and Industrial Hygiene, Faculté de Pharmacie, Paris 49-60, Titular Prof. 60-; Head of teaching of industrial toxicology, Inst. of Industrial Medicine, Paris 55-; Sec.-Gen. European Cttee. for the Study of the Protection of Populations against the long-term effects of Toxicity (EUROTOX); Adviser to numerous int. orgs. including WHO, FAO, ILO, Perm. Int. Comm. of Occupational Medicine, Int. Union Against Cancer, Council of Europe, EEC Int., Union of Pure and Applied Chemistry; mem. Conseil supérieur d'Hygiène publique de France and of numerous nat. comms. on public health; mem. Acad. des Sciences (Inst. de France), Acad. Nat. de Médecine.

Leisure interests: history, old paintings, Rugby football.

Publs. *Les Facteurs chimiques de cancérisations* 48, *Les Fluoroses* 48, *Les Dérivés organiques halogénés doués d'activité insecticide* 48, *Toxicologie des produits phytopharmaceutiques* 52, *Traitement d'urgence des intoxications* 57, *Précis de Toxicologie* 60, *Compentido de Toxicologia* 62, *Potential Carcinogenic Hazards from Drugs* 67.

Centre de recherches toxicologiques de la Faculté des Sciences Pharmaceutiques et Biologiques de l'Université René Descartes, 4 avenue de l'Observatoire, Paris 6e, France.

Telephone: 326-26-80, ext. 206.

Trujillo Molina, General Hector Bienvenido; Dominican army officer and politician; b. 1908; ed. Univ. of Santo Domingo.

Entered Army 26; Chief of Staff of Army 36; Supervisor-Gen. of National Police 38-43; Secretary of War, C.-in-C. of Army and Navy 44; succeeded his brother as Pres. of the Dominican Republic 52-60; Prof. American Int. Acad., Washington; corresp. mem. Nat. Athenaeum Arts and Sciences, Mexico; holds numerous military and other decorations of his own and foreign countries.
Living abroad.

Truong Nhu Tang; Vietnamese lawyer and politician; b. 1923, Cholon; ed. Univ. of Paris.

Controller-General, Viet-Nam Bank for Industry and Commerce; Dir.-Gen. Viet-Nam Sugar Co., Saigon; Sec.-Gen. People's Movement for Self-Determination 64-65; mem. Saigon Cttee. for Restoration of Peace; Pres. Viet-Nam Youth Union 66-67; imprisoned 67-68; joined Nat. Liberation Front 68; Minister of Justice, Provisional Revolutionary Govt. of S. Viet-Nam 69- (in Saigon 75-).
Ministry of Justice, Saigon, South Viet-Nam.

Tryoshnikov, Alexey Fyodorovich, D.SC.; Soviet polar explorer; b. 14 April 1914, Pavlovka village, Ulyanovsk Region; ed. Leningrad Univ.

Head of the Soviet drifting station SP-3 in the Arctic 54-55; Head Soviet Int. Geophysical Year Antarctic Expedition to Mirny 56-58; Dir. Arctic and Antarctic Scientific Research Inst., Leningrad 60-; mem. C.P.S.U. 44-; Hero of Socialist Labour 49; State Prize 71.
Ul. Kuibysheva 1/5, kv. 121, Leningrad; and The Arctic and Antarctic Research Institute, Leningrad, U.S.S.R.

Trypanis, Constantine Athanasius, M.A., D.PHIL., LITT.D.; Greek university professor; b. 22 Jan. 1909, Chios; s. of Athanasius G. Trypanis and Maria Zolota; m. Aliki Macris 1942; one d.; ed. Univs. of Athens, Berlin and Munich.

Lecturer in Classical Literature Athens Univ. 39; Bywater and Sotheby Prof. of Byzantine and Modern Greek, Univ. of Oxford 47-68; Univ. Prof. of Classics, Univ. of Chicago 68-74; Minister of Culture and Science 74-; Emer. Fellow, Exeter Coll., Oxford; Fellow, Royal Soc. of Literature, Int. Inst. of Arts and Letters; Archon Hieromnemon of the Oecumenical Patriarchate, Megas Archon Hieromnemon 72; Visiting Prof., U.S. univs. 63, 64, 65, 66; Visiting mem. Inst. for Advanced Study, Princeton 59-60; Corresp. mem. of Inst. for Balkan Studies, Salonica, Center for Neo-Hellenic Studies, Austin, Texas, Acad. of Athens 72.
Leisure interests: tennis, painting, walking.
Publs. *The Influence of Hesiod upon the Homeric Hymn to Hermes* 39, *Alexandrian Poetry* 43, *Tartessos, Phanagorea, Alexandria eschate* 45, *Medieval and Modern Greek Poetry* 51, *Pedasus* 55, *The Stones of Troy* 57, *Callimachus* 58, *The Cocks of Hades* 58, *Sancti Romani Melodi Cantica* 63, *Pompeian Dog* 64, *Fourteen Early Byzantine Cantica* 68, *Sancti Romani Melodi Cantica II* 70, *The Penguin Book of Greek Verse* 72, *The Glass Adonis* 73, *The Homeric Epics* 75.
Ministry of Culture and Science, Athens, Greece.

Trzebiatowski, Włodzimierz, D.SC.; Polish chemist; b. 25 Feb. 1906, Grodzisk; s. of Dr. Casimir Trzebiatowski and Wanda Grossman; m. B. Jeżowska 1935; ed. Inst. of Technology, Lwów.

Assistant, Chemistry Dept., Inst. of Technology, Lwow 29-37; Prof. of Inorganic Chemistry Univ. of Lwow 38-45, Univ. and Inst. of Technology, Wrocław 46-68; Dir. Inst. for Low Temperature and Structure of Polish Acad. of Sciences Wrocław 67-74; Dir. Int. Laboratory of High Magnetic Fields and Low Temperatures, Wrocław 68-; Vice-Pres. Polish Acad. of Sciences 69-71, Pres. 71-; mem. Polish United Workers'
Party, Cen. Cttee. 71-; mem. Presidium of All-Polish Cttee. of Nat. Unity Front 72-; Doctor h.c. Univ. of Wrocław; Corresp. mem. Polish Acad. of Sciences 52-56, mem. 56-; mem. Chem. Soc., London; American Chem. Soc., Asscn. F. et J. Joliot-Curie, Int. Union of Pure and Applied Chem., Int. Union of Crystallography; foreign mem. Acad. of Sciences, Czechoslovakia 73, G.D.R. 74, Bulgaria 74; State Prize in Chem. 55, 74; Commdr. Cross Polonia Restituta, Order of Banner of Labour 64, 70; Gold Medal, Slovakian Acad. of Sciences 73; Order of Builders of People's Poland 74; Gold Medal, Polish Teachers' Asscn. 74; Medal of 30th Anniversary of People's Poland 74.
Publs. *The Structure of Metals* 53, *X-Ray Structural Analysis* (with K. Lukaszewicz) 60, *Inorganic Chemistry* (4 vols. in Polish and German) 60-68; over 100 papers on the structure and magnetic properties of rare metal compounds and alloys.
ul. Gierymskich 20, 51-636 Wrocław, Poland.
Telephone: 4836-99.

Ts'ao Li-huai; Chinese army officer; b. Fukien.
Chief of Staff Garrison Command H.Q., Yenan 42; Commdr. 49th Army, 4th Field Army 49; Commdr. 4th Field Army 53; Commdr. of Air Force, People's Liberation Army 56, Lieut.-Gen. 56, Deputy Commdr. 56-; mem. 9th Cen. Cttee. of CCP 69, 10th Cen. Cttee. 73.
People's Republic of China.

Ts'ao Ssu-ming; Chinese army officer.
Secretary CCP Sinkiang 71; Commdr. Sinkiang Mil. Region, People's Liberation Army 73-.
People's Republic of China.

Tsarapkin, Semyon Konstantinovich; Soviet diplomatist; b. 4 June 1906, Nikolaev, Ukraine; ed. Moscow Oriental Inst.

Worker in smelting plant; transferred for advanced political training; Deputy Head, Head, Second Eastern Dept., later Far Eastern Dept., Ministry of Foreign Affairs 37-44; Head, U.S.A. Dept. 44-47; Minister, Soviet Embassy, Washington 47-49; Deputy Perm. Rep. to UN Security Council 49-54; Head of Div. for Int. Orgs., Moscow 54-66; Head Soviet del. to Geneva Disarmament Talks 61-66; Amb. to Fed. Repub. of Germany 66-71; Amb. at large 71-; Orders of Red Banner of Labour, Badge of Honour, Great Patriotic War (1st Class), etc.
Ministry of Foreign Affairs, 32-34 Smolenskaya-Sennaya ploshchad, Moscow, U.S.S.R.

Tsatsos, Konstantinos; Greek philosopher, lawyer and politician; b. 1 July 1899; s. of Demetrius Tsatsos and Theodora Eustratiadi; m. Jeanne Seferiades 1930; two d.; ed. School of Law, Athens Univ. and Univ. of Heidelberg.

Practised law 21; Assoc. Prof. of Law, Athens Univ. 30-32, Prof. of Law 32; Minister of the Interior and of Press and Air 45; mem. Parl. for Athens 46-50, 63-67; Minister of Education 49; Under-Sec. of State for Economic Co-ordination 50-51; Minister attached to Prime Minister 56-61; Minister of Justice 3-21 April 67; Minister of Cultural Affairs and Science July-Oct. 74; Pres. of Greece June 75-; fmr. Pres. Acad. of Athens, mem. 61-.
Publs. *Der Begriff des Positiven Rechts* 28; in Greek: *The Problem of Interpreting the Law* 32, *The Problem of the Sources of the Law* 41, *Social Philosophy of the Ancient Greeks* 38, *Palamas* 35, *Dialogues on Poetry* 39, *Greece on the March* 53, *At the Roots of American Democracy* 55, *The Social Philosophy of the Ancient Greeks, Politics, Aphorisms and Thoughts* (4 vols.), *Demosthenes-Cicero, Aesthetics* (2 vols.), *Essays on Legal Philosophy*.
Office of the President, Athens, Greece.

Tsatsos, Vice-Admiral Konstantinos; Greek naval officer; b. 1901; ed. Naval Cadet College.
Sub-Lieutenant 23; served in destroyers as Exec. Officer and Commanding Officer; Commdr. 40; Commanding

Officer H.H.M.S. *Aspis*; served with SHAEF, Frankfurt, and as Naval Attaché, Paris, before returning to Greece; A.D.C. to the King 46; Capt. 47; held various naval appointments, including Chief of Naval Personnel, Ministry of the Navy; Rear-Admiral 52; Chief Naval Training, C.-in-C. Royal Arsenal 53; C.-in-C. Fleet 53-57; Deputy Chief of Naval Operations 57-58; Chief and NATO Commdr. Eastern Mediterranean 58; C.-in-C. Naval Operations 58-59.
Vassileos Constantinou 61, Kifissia, Athens, Greece.

Tschudi, Hans-Peter, LL.D.; Swiss politician; b. 22 Oct. 1913; ed. Basle Univ.
Professor of Labour Law, Basle Univ. 52-59; Head of Home Dept. Govt. of Basle 53-59; mem. Council of States, Fed. Assembly 56-59; mem. Fed. Council 60-73, Vice-Pres. Jan.-Dec. 64, Jan.-Dec. 69, Pres. Jan.-Dec. 65, Jan.-Dec. 70; Head of Dept. of the Interior 60-73; mem. Assembly, Int. Red Cross; Socialist.
Publs. *Die Ferien im schweizerischen Arbeitsrecht* 48, *Koalitionsfreiheit und Koalitionszwang* 48, *Die Sicherung des Arbeitsfriedens durch das schweizerische Recht* 52, *Gesamtarbeitsvertrag und Aussenseiter* 53.
c/o Comité International de la Croix-Rouge, Avenue de la Paix 17, 1211 Geneva, Switzerland.

Tsedenbal, Yumzhagiyin; Mongolian politician; b. 17 Sept. 1916; ed. in Mongolia and U.S.S.R.
Teacher then Deputy Minister later Minister of Finance 39-40; Sec.-Gen. Central Cttee. Mongolian People's Revolutionary Party 40-54, First Sec. 58-; Deputy C.-in-C. Mongolian Army 41-45; Chair. State Planning Comm. 45-48; Deputy Chair. Council of Ministers 48-52, Chair. 52-74; Chair. Presidium, the People's Great Hural 74-; Order of Lenin 44, Order of Kutuzov (1st Class) 45, Hero of the Soviet Union, Order of Sukhbator 66; Hon. mem. Acad. of Sciences.
Government Palace, Ulan Bator, Mongolian People's Republic.

Tselikov, Alexander Ivanovich; Soviet metallurgist; b. 20 April 1904, Moscow; ed. Bauman Higher Technical School, Moscow.
Designer, Engineer, metallurgical plants 25-35; Lecturer, Higher Schools 35-45; Research Work, U.S.S.R. Research and Designing Inst. for Metallurgical Eng. 45-. Dir. 59-; mem. C.P.S.U. 45-; mem. U.S.S.R. Acad. of Sciences 64-; State Prize (thrice); Lenin Prize 64; Hero of Socialist Labour 64.
Publs. Basic works on designing and developing of new metallurgical and foundry equipment.
U.S.S.R. Academy of Sciences, 14 Leninsky Prospekt, Moscow, U.S.S.R.

Tseng Shao-shan; Chinese party official; b. 1910, Hunan.
On Long March 34-35; Regimental Commdr. 38; Brigade Commdr. 41; Deputy Commdr. E. Szechuan Mil. District, People's Liberation Army 50-52; Lieut.-Gen. PLA 57; Commdr. Tsinan Mil. Region, PLA 57; Political Commissar Shenyang Mil. Region, PLA 60; mem. 9th Cen. Cttee. of CCP 69; Second Sec. CCP Liaoning 71, First Sec. 75-; Vice-Chair. Liaoning Revolutionary Cttee. 73, Chair. 75-; mem. 10th Cen. Cttee. of CCP 73.
People's Republic of China.

Tseng Ssu-yu; Chinese army officer; b. 1907.
Staff Officer Red 1st Front Army 35; Commdr. 4th Column, N. China PLA 48; Lieut.-Gen. Shenyang Mil. Region, PLA 60, Deputy Commdr. 65-67; Commdr. Wuhan Mil. Region, PLA 67-73; mem. 9th Cen. Cttee. of CCP 69; First Sec. CCP Hupeh 71-73; mem. 10th Cen. Cttee. of CCP 73; Commdr. Tsinan Mil. Region, PLA 74-.
People's Republic of China.

Tsevegmid, Dondogiin; Mongolian biologist and diplomatist; b. 26 March 1915; ed. Moscow Univ.
Teacher 30-45; Chancellor Ulan Bator Univ., and Chair. Cttee. of Sciences 59-60; Deputy Minister of Foreign Affairs 60-62; Ambassador to People's Republic of China 62-67; Del. to UN 61; Chancellor Ulan-Bator Univ. 67-72; Chair. People's Great Hural of Mongolia 69-73; Deputy Prime Minister 72-; Corresp. mem. Mongolian Acad. of Sciences; Dr. h.c. Moscow Lomonosov and Berlin Humboldt Univs.
Publs. *The Ecological and Morphological Analyses of the Duplicidentate* 50, *Fauna of the Transaltai* 63, *Selected Works* 46, 56, 74.
Government Palace, Ulan Bator, Mongolia.

Tsiranana, Philibert; Malagasy politician; b. 18 Oct. 1912; ed. Univ. of Montpellier.
Teaching until 55; mem. Majunga Provincial Assembly, Pres. 56; mem. fmr. Malagasy Representative Assembly 52-58; Deputy from Madagascar to French Nat. Assembly 56-59; Prime Minister, Malagasy Republic 58-59, Pres. of the Cabinet 59-May 72; Pres. (Head of State) 60-Oct. 72.
Tananarive, Madagascar.

Tsitsin, Nikolay Vasiliyevich; Soviet botanist and geneticist; b. 18 Dec. 1898, Moscow; ed. State Agricultural Inst., Saratov.
Worked on selection and genetics of Spring and Winter wheat, Scientific-Research Inst. of Drought, Saratov 27-32, Head, Selection Dept. 32; later Dir. Scientific Research Inst. of Grain Econ., Omsk; Dir. All-Union Agricultural Exhibition, Moscow 37-57; mem. and fmr. Vice-Pres. Lenin All Union Acad. of Agricultural Science 57-; mem. C.P.S.U. 38-; mem. U.S.S.R. Acad. of Sciences 39-, Yugoslav Acad. of Science and Arts; Dir. Cen. Botanical Garden, U.S.S.R. Acad. of Sciences 45-; Dr. h.c. Jena Univ.; Hon. mem. Romanian Acad. of Sciences; Corresp. mem. German Acad. of Agricultural Sciences; Chair. U.S.S.R.-India Friendship Soc.; State Prize 43, Hero of Socialist Labour 68, Order of Lenin and other decorations.
Publs. *Problem of Winter and Perennial Wheats* 35, *Advancement of Winter Crops to East* 40, *Pyrethrum* 41, *Transformation of Cultivated Plants* 43, *Investigations in the Field of Vegative-Reproductive Hybridization* 46, *Problem of Grains: Leading Link in Agriculture* 46, *Remote Hybridization of Plants* 53, *Darwin and Problems of Modern Biology* 57, *Activated Creoline* 57, *Representatives of the New Species of Wheat, Triticum Agropyrotriticum Perenne (Cicin)* 58, *New Species and Varieties of Wheat Obtained Experimentally* 59, *New Varieties of Branchy Wheats* 60, *Remote Hybridization and the Origination of New Species* 60, *New Varieties of Winter Rye* 61, *Hybrids Triticum × Elymus (gig. and arenarius)* 61, *Wheat-elymus Amphidiploids* 63, *Hybridization of Rye with Couch-Grass* 63.
Central Botanical Garden of U.S.S.R., Academy of Sciences, Botanicheskaya ulitsa 4, Moscow U-276, U.S.S.R.

Tsolov, Tano; Bulgarian politician; b. 27 June 1918; ed. High Commercial School, Commercial Acad. and Higher School for Finance and Admin.
Young Communist League 34-40; mem. Communist Party 40-; student, political prisoner and partisan, Young Communist League and Party functionary 40-44; First Sec. of the Regional Cttee. of the C.P. and Chair. Regional Cttee. of the Fatherland Front, Byala Slatina 44-50; Industry, Building and Transport Dept., Cen. Cttee. of the C.P. 50-52; mem. Cen. Cttee. of the C.P. 57; Minister Heavy Industry 52-59; Chair. Cttee. for Industry and Technical Progress 59; Sec. Cen. Cttee. of the C.P. 59-62; Cand. mem. of Political Bureau 62; mem. of Political Bureau 66; Deputy Chair. Council of Ministers 62-71; Chair. Council for Industry and Con-

struction at Council of Ministers 62-66; Chair. State Planning Cttee. 68-71; Permanent Rep. of the People's Republic of Bulgaria in the Council for Mutual Econ. Assistance (SIV) 66-74, Chair. Exec. Cttee. 73-74; Chair. Comm. for Econ., Scientific and Technical Co-operation at Council of Ministers 66; First Deputy Chair. Council of Ministers 71-.
Council of Ministers, Sofia, Bulgaria.

Tsoumbas, Gen. Vassilios; Greek army officer (retd.) and politician; b. 1914; ed. Athens Mil. Acad.
Commissioned 53; Brig. Gen. 63; Maj. Gen. 65, Lt.-Gen. 67; Chief of Army 68-72; Minister of Public Order 72-73, of the Interior Dec. 73-July 74; arrested Oct. 74.

Tsukasa, Tadashi; Japanese publisher and book executive; b. 5 Oct. 1893, Aichi Prefecture; s. of Moritsune Tsukasa and Nobu Hiramatsu; m. Yoshiko Miyawaki 1922; two s. three d.
With Maruzen Co. 06-, Dir. 40-, Pres. 47-71, Chair. 71-; Vice-Pres. Tokyo Chamber of Commerce and Industry; Chair. Tokyo Stationery Industrial Asscn., Japan Book Importers Asscn.; mem. Board of Trustees and Dir., Japanese Nat. Cttee. of Int. Chamber of Commerce; Pres. Tokyo Distribution Center Co.; Vice-Pres. Tokyo Trade Fair Asscn.; Dir. Tokyo Foreign Trade Asscn.; Rotarian; 2nd Class Order Rising Sun 64, Ordre des Arts et Lettres (France) 63, First Class Order of the Sacred Treasure 71.
Leisure interests: gardening, earthenware.
No. 3-10, Nihombashi 2-chome, Chuo-ku, Tokyo; and 15-5, 1-chome, Kitazawa, Setagaya-ku, Tokyo, Japan. Telephone: (03) 272-7211 (Office); (03) 467-1755 (Home).

Tsur, Yaakov; Israeli diplomatist; b. 18 Oct. 1906, Vilno; s. of Samuel and Bella Tsur; m. Vera Gotlib 1928; one s. one d.; ed. Hebrew Coll., Jerusalem, Univ. of Florence and Sorbonne.
Member staff daily newspaper *Haaretz*, Tel-Aviv 29; Dir. French Dept. and later Co-Dir. Propaganda Dept. Jewish Nat. Fund, Jerusalem 30; special Zionist missions, Belgium, Greece, France 34-35, Bulgaria and Greece 40; Liaison officer with G.H.Q. British Troops in Egypt 43-45; Head del. to Greece 45; Pres. Israeli Army Recruiting Cttee. Jerusalem 48; Minister to Argentina 49-53, Uruguay 49-53, Chile 50-53, and Paraguay 50-53; Ambassador to France 53-59; Chair. Jewish National Fund 59-; Chair. Zionist Gen. Council 61-68; Pres. Central Inst. for Relations with Ibero-America, Bialik Inst. Publication Soc.; Grand Officier Légion d'Honneur.
Publs. *Juifs en Guerre* 47, *The Birth of Israel* 49, *Shacharit Shel Etmol* (Autobiography) 65 (French trans.—*Prière du Matin* 67, English trans.—*Sunrise in Zion* 68), *Ambassador's Diary* (Hebrew) 67 (French trans. *Prélude à Suez* 69), *La Révolte Juive* 70 (also Spanish and Italian trans.), *Portrait of the Diaspora* 75.
P.O. Box 283, Jerusalem; and c/o Jewish National Fund, Jerusalem, Israel.
Telephone: 39013 (Office); 33811 (Home).

Tubby, Roger W.; American diplomatist (retd.); b. 30 Dec. 1910, Greenwich, Conn.; s. of George Prentiss Tubby and Frances Kidder; m. Anne Walton Williams 1936; one s. three d.; ed. Choate School, Yale Univ., and London School of Economics.
Newspaperman 38-42, Board of Econ. Warfare 42-44; Asst. to Administrator, Foreign Economic Admin. 44-45; Dir. Information Office Int. Trade, Dept. of Commerce 45-46, Press Officer, Dept. of State 45-50; Asst. Press Sec. The White House 50-52, Acting Press Sec. Oct.-Dec. 52, Press Sec. Dec. 52; Personal Asst. Democratic Pres. Candidate 56; Editor and Publisher, *Adirondack Daily Enterprise*, Saranac Lake 53-61; Dir. Public Relations, Democratic Nat. Cttee. 60; Asst. Sec. for Public Affairs, Dept. of State 61-62; Amb. and Perm. Rep. to UN, etc., Geneva 62-69; Dean, Foreign Service Inst., Dept. of State 69-72; Dir. Devt. Paul Smith's Coll., N.Y. 72-; Trustee, Trudeau Foundation, Coll. of the Atlantic; mem. Acad. of Political Sciences; Candidate U.S. Congress 74; Democrat.
Trudeau Road, Saranac Lake, N.Y. 12983, U.S.A.

Tucci, Giuseppe, PH.D.; Italian orientalist; b. 5 June 1894, Macerata; ed. Rome Univ.
Lieutenant 15-19; leader scientific expeditions to Tibet and Nepal; Prof. of Religions and Philosophy of India and the Far East, Rome Univ. 33-65; mem. Royal Italian Acad.; Hon. mem. Soc. Asiatique (Paris), Asiatic Soc. (Calcutta); leader archaeological missions in Pakistan, Afghanistan and Iran 56-; Pres. Middle and Far East Inst.; Hon. Prof. Univ. of Kolosvar, Delhi, Louvain, Teheran, Visva-Bharati (Shantiniketan).
Publs. *Storia della filosofia cinese antica* 22, *Il Buddhismo* 26, *Doctrines of Maitreyanatha, Secrets of Tibet, Predinnaga Buddhist Logic, Indo-Tibetica* (7 vols.), *Tibetan Painted Scrolls* 49, *Asia Religiosa* 46, *Tibetan Folksongs* 49, *The Tombs of the Tibetan Kings* 50, *A Lhasa e Oltre* 50, *Tra Giungle e Pagode* 54, *Preliminary Report of two Scientific Expeditions in Nepal* 56, *Minor Buddhist Texts*, Part I 56, Part II 58, Part III 71, *Storia della Filosofia Indiana* 58, *Nepal* 60, *Theory and Practice of the Mandala* 61, *Il Trono di Diamante* 67, *Tibet, Land of Snows* 68, *Die Religionen Tibets* 70, *Archaeologia Mundi: Tibet* 73.
Via della Crocetta 8, s. Polo dei Cavalieri, Rome, Italy.

Tuchkevich, Vladimir Maximovich, D.SC.; Soviet physicist; b. 29 Dec. 1904, Yanoutsi Village, Chernovitsk Region; ed. Kiev State Univ.
Head of Laboratory, All-Ukrainian Radiological Inst. 31-35; Head of Lab., Leningrad Radiological Inst. 35-36, Ioffe physico-technological Inst., U.S.S.R. Acad. of Sciences 36-, Dir. 68-; mem. C.P.S.U. 52-; corresp. mem. U.S.S.R. Acad. of Sciences 68-70, mem. 70-; Honoured Scientist of R.S.F.S.R. 66; Lenin Prize 66; State Prize 42.
Ioffe Physico-Technological Institute, U.S.S.R. Academy of Sciences, Politekhnicheskaya ulitsa 2, Leningrad, U.S.S.R.

Tuchman, Barbara W., B.A.; American writer; b. 30 Jan. 1912; ed. Radcliffe Coll., Cambridge, Mass.
Research Asst., Inst. of Pacific Relations, New York City 34, Tokyo 35; Editorial Asst. *The Nation*, New York City 36, Spain 37; Staff writer *War in Spain*, London 37-38; American Corresp. *New Statesman*, London 39; with Far East News Desk, Office of War Information, New York City 34-45; Trustee, Radcliffe Coll. 60-72; mem. Nat. Portrait Gallery Comm. 71-; mem. Nat. Inst. of Arts and Letters; Authors' Guild, Authors' League; Fellow, American Acad. of Arts and Letters; Pres. Soc. of American Historians; Pulitzer Prize 63, 72; numerous hon. degrees.
Publs. *The Lost British Policy* 38, *Bible and Sword* 56, *The Zimmermann Telegram* 58, *The Guns of August* 62, *The Proud Tower* 66, *Stilwell and the American Experience in China 1911-45* 71, *Notes from China* 72; contributions to major magazines.
c/o Russell & Volkening, 551 Fifth Avenue, New York, N.Y. 10017, U.S.A.

Tuck, James Leslie, M.SC., M.A., O.B.E.; British-born American physicist; b. 9 Jan. 1910, Manchester, England; s. of James H. Tuck and Selina Jane Reece; m. Elsie Mary Harper 1937; one s. one d.; ed. Manchester Cen. Grammar School, Manchester and Oxford Univs.
Dalton Scholar and Demonstrator, Manchester Univ. 32-37; Salter Research Fellow, Oxford Univ. 37-39; Adviser to Lord Cherwell on Prime Minister's Staff 39-42; Principal Scientific Adviser, Ministry of Defence 42-44; Principal Scientific Officer, British Mission to

Manhattan Project (Atom Bomb), Los Alamos, New Mexico 44-46; Supervisor, Dept. of Advanced Studies, Clarendon Laboratory, Oxford 46-49; Research Assoc., Chicago Univ. Inst. for Nuclear Studies 49-50; Assoc. Division Leader, Physics Div., Los Alamos Scientific Laboratory, Univ. of California 50-72, Dir. of Controlled Fusion Research 52-73, Consultant 73-; Walker-Ames Visiting Prof., Univ. of Washington 74; Visiting Prof., Univ. of Waikato, N.Z. 74; Regents Lecturer, Univ. of Calif., San Diego April 75; Fellow, American Physical Soc., Guggenheim Fellow, Fellow, American Asscn. Advancement of Science (AAAS).

Leisure interests: skiing, chess, tennis.

Publs. Numerous papers on Accelerators, Physics of Explosives (Munroe Effect), Nuclear Cross Sections and Thermonuclear Research.

Los Alamos Scientific Laboratory, Los Alamos, New Mexico 87544; 2502 35th Street, Los Alamos, New Mexico 87544, U.S.A.

Telephone: (505) 667-5111 (Lab.); (505) 662-6323 (Home).

Tucker, Gardiner Luttrell, PH.D.; American physicist; b. 6 Sept. 1925, New York; s. of Dr. Ernest Eckford Tucker, D.O., and Katherine May Luttrell; m. Helen Harwell 1954; two s. one d.; ed. Columbia Coll., and Columbia Univ., New York.

With IBM Corpn. 52-67; Research Physicist Watson Laboratories, N.Y. 52-53; Man. Semiconductor and Transistor Research, Poughkeepsie, N.Y. 54-56; Man. Corporate Research Analysis and Planning 57-59; Man. Research Laboratory, San José 59-60; Dir. Devt. Engineering World Trade Corpn. 61-62; Dir. of Research 63-67; with U.S. Dept. of Defense 67-73; Deputy Dir. Defense Research and Engineering for Electronics and Information Systems 67-68; Principal Deputy Dir. Defense Research and Engineering 69; Asst. Sec. of Defense for Systems Analysis 70-73; with U.S. Dept. of State 73-; Asst. Sec.-Gen. for Defence Support, NATO 73-; Phi Beta Kappa 47, Sigma Xi 51, Dept. of Defense Distinguished Public Service Award 72.

Leisure interest: piano.

Publs. *The Magnetic Moment of the Helium Atoms is the Metastable Triplet State* (with Vernon Hughes) 52, *Nuclear Spin-Echo Storage* (with Anderson, Hahn, Walker et al) 54, *A Twenty-Five Year Look at the Future of Research in the Nation* 64.

Room J. 322, North Atlantic Treaty Organization, Brussels; Home: 219 avenue de Tervuren, 1150 Brussels, Belgium.

Telephone: Brussels 41-44-00, Ext. 2249 (Office).

Tucker, Sir Henry James, K.B.E.; Bermudan politician; b. 1903, Bermuda; m. Catherine Newbold Barstow 1925; two s. one d.; ed. Saltus Grammar School, Bermuda and Sherborne School, U.K.

Worked in New York with various stock exchange houses and a bank 24-34; joined Bank of Bermuda 34, Gen. Man. 38-70; mem. House of Assembly 38-48, 53-; mem. Exec. Council 42-48; formed United Bermuda Party 64, Leader 64-71; Leader, Exec. Council 68-71.

Leisure interests: golf, philately.

The Lagoon, Paget, Bermuda.

Tudor, James Cameron, M.A.; Barbadian politician and diplomatist; b. 18 Oct. 1919, St. Michael; ed. Keble Coll., Oxford.

President, Oxford Union 42; Broadcaster, BBC 42-44; Lecturer, Reading Univ. 44-45; taught History at Combermere School, Barbados 46-48, Civics and History at Queens Coll., British Guiana 48-51; Sixth Form Master, Modern High School, Barbados 52-61; freelance journalist, lecturer and broadcaster 52-61; mem. Legislature 54-72; Gen. Sec. Democratic Labour Party 55-63, Third Vice-Chair. 64-66; Minister of Educ. 61-67; Minister of State for Caribbean and Latin American Affairs 67-71; Leader of House of Reps.

65-71; Minister of External Affairs 71-72; Leader of Senate 71-72; High Commr. in U.K. 72-76; Perm. Rep. to UN Jan. 76-; mem. Council, Univ. of the West Indies 62-65.

Permanent Mission of Barbados to the United Nations, 866 United Nations Plaza, Suite 527, New York, N.Y. 10017, U.S.A.

Tueni, Ghassan, M.A.; Lebanese newspaper editor; b. 5 Jan. 1926; m. Nadia Hamadeh; two s.; ed. Amer. Univ. of Beirut and Harvard Univ.

Lecturer in Political Science, Amer. Univ. of Beirut 47-48; Editor-in-Chief, *An-Nahar* (daily newspaper) 48-; Man.-Dir. of An-Nahar Publishing Co. 63-; Co-founder of Lebanese Acad. of Law and Political Science 51, Lecturer 51-54; M.P. for Beirut 53-57; mem. Lebanese del. to UN Gen. Ass. 57; founded Middle East Business Services and Research Corpn. 58, Chair. 58-70; founder, Chair. and Man.-Dir. of Press Cooperative, S.A.L. 60-; Deputy Prime Minister and Minister of Information and Nat. Educ. 70-71; arrested Dec. 73, appeared before mil. tribunal and then released in accordance with press laws; Minister for Social Affairs and Labour, Tourism, Industry and Oil July 75-.

An-Nahar, P.O. Box 11-226, Beirut (Office); Ras Kafra, Beit Mery, Lebanon.

Tugwell, Rexford Guy, B.S., M.A., PH.D., LITT.D., LL.D.; American political scientist; b. 10 July 1891; ed. Univ. of Pennsylvania.

Instructor and Asst. Prof. of Economics, Columbia Univ. 20-31, Prof. 31-37; Asst. Sec. Dept. of Agriculture 33, Under-Sec. and Admin. Resettlement Admin. 34-37; Chair. New York City Planning Comm. 38-41; Chancellor Univ. of Puerto Rico 41-42; Gov. of Puerto Rico 41-46; Dir. Inst. of Planning, Univ. of Chicago 46-52; Prof. of Political Science 46-57, Prof. Emeritus 57-; Development Consultant, Univ. of Puerto Rico 61-64; Research Prof. Political Science, Univ. of S. Illinois, Carbondale 65-66; Visiting Prof. London School of Econs. 49-50; Woodrow Wilson Award, Amer. Political Science Asscn.

Publs. *The Economic Basis of Public Interest* 22, *American Economic Life* 25, *Industry's Coming of Age* 27, *The Industrial Discipline* 33, *The Battle for Democracy* 35, *Redirecting Education* 35, *The Fourth Power* 39, *Changing the Colonial Climate* 42, *The Stricken Land* 46, *The Place of Planning in Society, with Special Reference to Puerto Rico* 54, *A Chronicle of Jeopardy* 55, *Great Cities of the World* (co-author) 55, *The Democratic Roosevelt* (Woodrow Wilson Award) 57, *The Art of Politics* 58, *Early American Contributors* (co-author) 60, *The Enlargement of the Presidency* 60, *The Light of Other Days* 62.

Box 4068, Santa Barbara, Calif. 92705, U.S.A.

Tu'ipelahake, H.R.H. Prince Fatafehi, C.B.E.; Tongan politician; b. 7 Jan. 1922, second son of the late Queen Salote Tupou III and the late Hon. Uiliame Tungi, C.B.E.; Premier of Tonga; married H.R.H. Princess Melenaite 47; six children; ed. Newington Coll., Sydney, N.S.W., and Gatton Agricultural Coll., Queensland.

Governor of Vava'u 52-65; Prime Minister of Tonga 65-, also Minister for Foreign Affairs, Agriculture, Tourism and Telegraphs and Telephones; Chair. Tonga Copra Board and Tonga Produce Board.

Office of the Prime Minister, Nuku'alofa, Tonga.

Tuke, Anthony Favill; British banker; b. 22 Aug. 1920, Berkhamsted, Herts.; s. of late Anthony William Tuke and Agnes Edna Tuke (née Gannaway); m. Emilia Mila Antic 1946; one s. one d.; ed. Winchester Coll., Magdalene Coll., Cambridge.

Scots Guards 40-46; joined Barclays Bank Ltd. 46; various appts. in Barclays Bank Ltd. including Chair. Birmingham Board 64-68; Vice-Chair. Barclays Bank Int. Ltd. (fmrly. Barclays Bank D.C.O.) 68-72, Chair. 72-; Vice-Chair. Barclays Bank Ltd. 72-73, Chair. Oct.

73-; Dir. Merchants Trust Ltd., Mercantile and Gen. Reinsurance Co. Ltd.; mem. Board various subsidiary cos. in Barclays Group; Deputy Chair. Cttee. of London Clearing Bankers 74.
Leisure interests: lawn tennis, gardening.
Barclays Bank Ltd., 54 Lombard Street, London, E.C.3; Home: 68 Frognal, London, NW3 6XD, England. Telephone: 01-435-8895 (Home).

Tukey, Harold Bradford, B.S., PH.D.; American horticulturist; b. 30 Sept. 1896, Berwyn, Ill.; s. of James Bradford Tukey and Armenia Mehrhof; m. 1st Margaret Davenport 1918 (died 1930), 2nd Ruth Schweigert 1932; three s. two d.; ed. Illinois Univ., and Univ. of Chicago. Horticulturist in charge of Hudson Valley Fruit Investigations 23-27; Chief in Research New York State Agricultural Experimental Station and Prof. of Pomology Cornell Univ. 27-45; Head Dept. of Hort. Mich. State Coll. 45-63, Prof. Emeritus 63; awarded Jackson Dawson Memorial Medal 48; Fellow American Asscn. for the Advancement of Science, American Soc. Hort. Science, Royal Horticultural Soc., London, Vice-Pres. 65-; hon. mem. Société Nat. d'Horticulture de France; Sec. American Soc. for Horticultural Science 27-47, Pres. 47; Ed. *Proceedings* 27-49; Pres. American Pomological Soc. 51-53, Int. Soc. for Horticultural Science 62-66; Pres. XVII Int. Hort. Congress 66; mem. Exec. and Editorial Staff *Rural New Yorker* 20-64; Assoc. Editor *American Fruit Grower*; Editorial Board *Review of Plant Physiology*; Marshall P. Wilder Medal 46, Norman Jay Coleman Award 56; American Horticultural Council Citation 57; Gold Medal Award 67; Liberty Hyde Bailey Medal 67; Hon. D.Hort.Sc. (Hanover Inst. of Technology).
Publs. *The Pears of New York* 21, *The Pear and its Culture* 29, *Plant Regulators in Agriculture* 54, *Dwarfed Fruit Trees* 64.
The Maples, Woodland, Mich. 48897, U.S.A.

Tukey, John W(ilder), PH.D., SC.D.; American statistician; b. 16 June 1915, New Bedford, Mass.; s. of Ralph H. Tukey and Adah M. Tasker; m. Elizabeth Louise Rapp 1950; ed. Brown Univ. and Princeton Univ. Fine Instructor, Mathematics, Princeton Univ. 39-41, Asst. Prof. 41-48, Assoc. Prof. 48-50, Prof. 50-66, Prof. of Statistics 65-, Donner Chair of Science 76-; mem. Tech. Staff, Bell Telephone Labs. 45-58, Asst. Dir. of Research 58-61, Assoc. Exec. Dir. Research 61-; mem. President's Science Advisory Cttee. 60-63; Nat. Advisory Cttee. for Oceans and Atmosphere 75-; mem. Nat. Acad. of Sciences 67, American Acad. of Arts and Sciences, American Philosophical Soc.; Hon. mem. Royal Statistical Soc.; Guggenheim Fellow 49-50; Fellow, Inst. of Mathematical Statistics (Pres. 60), American Statistical Asscn. (Vice-Pres. 55-57), American Soc. of Quality Control, American Asscn. for the Advancement of Science (Chair. 72, 74); Samuel Wilks Medal, American Statistical Asscn. 65; Nat. Medal of Science 73; Hon. Sc.D. (Brown Univ., Yale Univ., Case Inst. of Technology, Univ. of Chicago).
Leisure interest: table tennis.
Publs. *Convergence and Uniformity in Topology, Statistical Problems of the Kinsey Report* (with W. G. Cochran and F. Mosteller), *The Measurement of Power Spectra from the Point of View of Communications Engineering* (with R. B. Blackman) 59, *Exploratory Data Analysis*, Vols. I-III 70-71, *Robust Estimates of Location: Survey and Advances* (with others) 72, *The Statistics CumIndex*, Vol. I (with J. L. Dolby) 73, *Index to Statistics and Probability*, Vols. II-V (with others) 73-75; more than 150 technical papers.
Office: Fine Hall, P.O. Box 708, Princeton, N.J. 08540; 1A-219 Bell Telephone Laboratories, Murray Hill, N.J. 07974; Home: 115 Arreton Road, Princeton, N.J. 08540; Summer: P.O. Box 304, Westport Point, Mass. 02791, U.S.A.

Telephone: 609-452-4219 (Fine Hall); 201-582-4507 (Bell Telephone); 609-924-5095 (Home); 617-636-2612 (Summer).

Tuna, Ahmet Nusret; Turkish politician; b. 1916, Mucur, Kireşehir.
Has worked as a teacher, lawyer and journalist; Senator for Kastamonu 61; Deputy Chair. of Justice Party in Senate until 73; Minister of Agriculture 73-74; Justice Party.
c/o Ministry of Agriculture, Ankara, Turkey.

Tunney, James Joseph (Gene); American former boxer and businessman; b. 25 May 1897, New York, s. of John Joseph Tunney and Mary Lydon Tunney; m. Mary Josephine Lauder 1928; three s. one d.; ed. La Salle Acad.
With Ocean Steamship Co., New York 12-17; served with U.S. Marine Corps 18-19; won light heavyweight championship of American Expeditionary Forces, Paris 19; professional boxer 19-28, won World Heavyweight Championship 26, retired undefeated 28; Dir. Industrial Bank of Commerce, New York City, Pittston Co., New York City; Commdr. U.S.N.R. to direct athletic and physical fitness programme for the U.S. Navy 41; Capt. 45; LL.D. h.c. (Ithaca Coll.).
Publs. *A Man Must Fight, Arms For Living.*
Stamford, Connecticut, U.S.A.; Office: 200 Park Avenue, New York, N.Y. 10017, U.S.A.

Tunney, John V., B.A., LL.B.; American politician; b. 26 June 1934, New York City; s. of Gene Tunney (*q.v.*) and Mary Lauder Tunney; two s. one d.; ed. Westminster School, Simsbury, Conn., Yale Univ., Univ. of Virginia School of Law and Acad. of Int. Law, The Hague.
Practised law, New York City 59-60; Judge Advocate, U.S. Air Force 60-63; taught Business Law at Univ. of Calif., Riverside; mem. U.S. House of Representatives 64-70; Senator from California 71-; Democrat.
Leisure interests: tennis, sailing, skiing, handball.
United States Senate, Washington, D.C. 20510, U.S.A. Telephone: 202-224-3841.

Tuominen, Leo Olavi, M.A.; Finnish diplomatist; b. 19 Jan. 1911, Turku; s. of Johan Tuominen and Johanna Johansson; m. Helene Habert 1938; one s. three d.; ed. Univ. of Turku.
Joined Foreign Service 34; served Paris 34-38, Riga 38-39, and Warsaw 39, Ministry of Foreign Affairs 40; Sec. of Section, Ministry of Foreign Affairs 41-43, Chief of Section 43-46; served Antwerp 46-47; First Sec. Legation, Brussels 47-48; Asst. Dir. of Commercial Division, Ministry of Foreign Affairs 48-50; Permanent Del. to Int. Organisations, Geneva 50-52; Minister to Argentina, Chile and Uruguay 52-55; Dir. Commercial Division, Ministry of Foreign Affairs 55-56; Sec. of State, Ministry of Foreign Affairs 56-57; Amb. to U.K. 57-68, to Italy, Cyprus and Malta 68-69, to Sweden 69-72, to U.S.A. 72-; Grand Cross Icelandic Order of the Falcon, Order of the Lion of Finland, Order of the North Star of Sweden; Grand Officer, Orders White Rose (Finland), of Merit (Argentina), K.B.E.; Commdr., Léopold II (Belgium), the Crown (Italy), the Oak Crown (Luxembourg), Orange-Nassau (Netherlands), Officier Légion d'Honneur; Hon. Dr. Humane Letters (North Mich. Univ.) 74.
Leisure interests: athletics and slalom.
Finnish Embassy, 3001 Woodland Drive, N.W., Washington, D.C., U.S.A.

Tupini, Giorgio; Italian industrial executive; b. 26 June 1922, Rome; ed. Rome Univ.
Member of Parl. 48-53; fmr. Under-Sec. Prime Minister's Office; with Istituto per la Ricostruzione Industriale (I.R.I.) 53-; fmr. Pres. and Managing Dir. Navalmeccanica of Naples; fmr. Dir. and mem. Exec. Cttee. Finmeccanica; Chair. Società Finanziaria Cantieri

Navali (FINCANTIERI) 59-67; Chair. and Man. Dir. Società Finanziaria Meccanica (FINMECCANICA) 68-74; Chair. Alitalia June 74-.
Alitalia, Palazzo Alitalia, Piazzale Giulio Pastore, 00144 Rome, Italy.

Tupua Tamasese Lealofi IV; Samoan politician and doctor; b. 8 May 1922, Apia; *m.* Lita 1953; five *c.*; ed. Fiji School of Medicine and postgraduate studies at Suva.
Medical practitioner 45-69; succeeded to Paramount Chief (Tama-a-Aiga) of Tupua Tamasese 65; mem. Council of Deputies 68-69; M.P. Feb. 70-; Prime Minister of Western Samoa 70-73, 75-.
Leisure interests: reading, golf.
Office of the Prime Minister, Apia, Western Samoa.
Telephone: 323.

Tureck, Rosalyn; American concert artist, conductor and professor; b. 14 Dec. 1914, Chicago; *d.* of Samuel Tureck and Monya Lipson; ed. Juilliard School of Music, New York.
Debut in Chicago 23; first New York appearance 31; concert tours U.S.A. and Canada 37-, Europe 47-, South Africa 59, South America 63, Israel 63, World Tour (Far East and India) 71; repeated appearances at major int. festivals; specializes in the keyboard works of J. S. Bach, played on the piano, harpsichord, clavichord, antique and electronic instruments; conductor 56-; Lecturer, Philadelphia Conservatory of Music 35-42, Mannes School of Music 40-44, Juilliard School of Music 43-55, Columbia Univ. 53-55; Visiting Prof. of Music, Washington Univ., St. Louis 63-64; Prof. of Music, Univ. of Calif., San Diego 66-72, Regents Lecturer 66; Lecturer, Univ. of Cincinnati 63, 74, Univ. of Chicago 66, Univ. of Connecticut 67, Roosevelt Univ., Chicago 69, Georgia Southern Univ. 70, Peabody Coll. 72, Inst. for Special Studies Juilliard School of Music 72, Mt. Holyoke Coll. 74, Royal Coll. of Music, Royal Acad. of Music, Trinity Coll. of Music, Guildhall School of Music and Drama, Barber Inst. Oxford Univ. 74; Visiting Fellow, St. Hilda's Coll., Oxford 74, Hon. Life Fellow 74-; Visiting Fellow, Wolfson Coll., Oxford 75; Founder-director of Composers of Today 51-55, Tureck Bach Players 57, Int. Bach Soc. 66, Int. Bach Soc. Orchestra 67, Inst. for Bach Studies 68; mem. many musical socs.; First Prize, Greater Chicago Piano Playing Tournament 28; Hon. D.Mus., Colby Coll. 64, Roosevelt Univ. 68, Wilson Coll. 68.
Recordings: *The Well-tempered Clavier* (Books I and II), *Goldberg Variations, Six Partitas, Italian Concerto, French Overture, Introduction to Bach, A Bach Recital, A Harpsichord Recital.*
Publs. *An Introduction to the Performance of Bach* (3 vols.) 59-60 (trans. into Japanese 66, Spanish 72), *A Critical and Performance Edition of J. S. Bach's Chromatic Fantasia and Fugue*; numerous articles in various periodicals; Editor: *Paganini, Niccolo—Perpetuum Mobile 50, J. S. Bach—Sarabande, C Minor 60, Scarlatti, Alessandro—Sarabande and Gavotte.*
c/o Columbia Artists Management Inc., 165 West 57th Street, New York, N.Y. 10019, U.S.A.

Turkevich, Anthony Leonid, PH.D.; American professor of chemistry; b. 23 July 1916, N.Y.C.; *s.* of Rev. L. J. Turkevich and Anna (Chervinsky) Turkevich; *m.* Ireene T. Podlesak 1948; one *s.* one *d.*; ed. Columbia Grammar School, Curtis High School, Dartmouth Coll., Hanover N.H., Princeton Univ.
Research Assoc. Physics Dept. Univ. of Chicago 40-41; Research Assoc. Manhattan Project, Columbia Univ., Univ. of Chicago, Los Alamos Scientific Lab. 42-46; Asst. Prof. Enrico Fermi Inst. and Chemistry Dept. Univ. of Chicago 46-48, Assoc. Prof. 48-54, Prof. 54-, James Franck Prof. of Chemistry 65-70, Distinguished Service Prof. 70-; Consultant to U.S. Atomic Energy Comm. Labs. 46-; mem. Nat. Acad. of Sciences, Amer.

Chem. Soc., Amer. Phys. Soc., Royal Soc. of Arts (London), Amer. Soc. for the Advancement of Science; E. O. Lawrence Award of U.S. Atomic Energy Comm. 62, Nat. Acad. of Sciences Award 67, Atoms for Peace Prize 69, American Asscn. of Arts and Sciences 69.
Leisure interests: hiking, reading.
Publs. articles on intra-nuclear cascades, on chemical analysis of the moon and on high energy nuclear reactions.
Enrico Fermi Institute, University of Chicago, 5640 South Ellis Avenue, Chicago, Ill. 60637, U.S.A.
Telephone: 312-753-8626.

Turki, Brahim, LIC. EN DROIT; Tunisian diplomatist; b. 13 Nov. 1930; *m.* 1961; one *s.* two *d.*
Teacher of Arabic until 56; Admin., Secr. of State for Foreign Affairs 56-59, Head Dept. of Econ. Affairs 59; econs. course UN Gen. Secr. 59-60; Counsellor Ministry of Foreign Affairs 60-61; Principal Private Sec. to Sec of State for Foreign Affairs 61-62; rank of Minister Plenipotentiary 62; Consul-Gen., Paris 62-65; Minister, Tunisian Embassy, Algeria 65-67; Dir. Political Affairs, Ministry of Foreign Affairs 67-70; Amb. to The Netherlands 70-73, to U.K. March 74-; participated in many sessions of UN Gen. Assembly and OAU; Commdr. Order of Repub. of Tunisia; many foreign decorations.
Tunisian Embassy, 29 Prince's Gate, London, SW7 1QG, England.

Türkmen, İlter; Turkish diplomatist; b. 1927, Istanbul; *s.* of Behçet Türkmen and Nuriye Türkmen; *m.* Mina Türkmen 1953; one *s.* one *d.*; ed. Galatasaray Lycée, Istanbul, Faculty of Political Sciences, Ankara. Director-General of Policy Planning Dept., Ministry of Foreign Affairs 64; Asst. Sec.-Gen. for Political Affairs 67; Amb. to Greece 68, to U.S.S.R. 72; Perm. Rep. to UN 75-.
Permanent Mission of Turkey to the United Nations, 866 Second Avenue, 15th Floor, New York, N.Y. 10017, U.S.A.
Telephone: (212) 421-5630.

Turnbull, David, PH.D.; American professor of applied physics; b. 18 Feb. 1915, Elmira, Ill.; *s.* of David Turnbull and Luzetta A. Murray; *m.* Carol M. Cornell 1946; two *s.* one *d.*; ed. Monmouth Coll., Ill., and Univ. of Illinois.
Faculty, Case School of Applied Science, Cleveland, Ohio 39-46; Scientist, Research Lab., Gen. Electric Co., Schenectady, N.Y. 46-62; Man. Chemical Metallurgy Section, Gen. Electric Research Lab., Schenectady 50-58; Gordan McKay Prof. of Applied Physics, Harvard Univ. 62-; mem. Nat. Acad. of Sciences; Fellow, American Acad. of Arts and Sciences; Inst. of Metals Lecturer, American Inst. of Mech. Engineers 61; Hon. Sc.D. (Monmouth (Ill.) Coll.).
Leisure interests: history, hiking.
Publs. Co-editor (with Seitz and Ehrenreich) *Solid State Physics Series*; Co-Editor (with Dorem and Roberts) *Growth and Perfection of Crystals* 58; scientific publs. and reviews on nucleation, crystal growth, diffusion, liquids, glass state.
Pierce Hall, Harvard University, Cambridge, Mass 02138; Home: 77 Summer Street, Mass. 02193, U.S.A.
Telephone: 495-2838 (Univ.).

Turnbull, George Henry, B.SC., F.I.MECH.E., F.I.P.E., F.I.M.I., F.I.M.; British business executive; b. 17 Oct. 1926, London; *s.* of Batholomew and Pauline A. Turnbull; *m.* Marion Wing 1950; one *s.* two *d.*; ed. Bablake and Henry VIII schools, Coventry Technical Coll., and Birmingham Univ.
Personal Asst. to Technical Dir. Standard Motor Co. 50-51; Liaison Officer between Standard Motor Co. and Rolls-Royce 51-53; Exec. in charge Experimental Div., Standard Motor Co. 54-55; Works Man. Petters Ltd.

55-56; Div. Man. Car Production, Standard Motor Co. 56-59, Gen. Man. 59-62; Dir. and Gen. Man. Standard Triumph Int. Ltd. 62-68; Man. Dir. British Leyland Austin Morris 68; Deputy Man. Dir. British Leyland Motor Corpn. 68-73, Man. Dir. May-Sept. 73; Man. Dir. Austin Morris British Leyland U.K. 68-73; Vice-Pres., Dir. Hyundai Corpn., Seoul 74-; mem. Man. Board, Engineering Employers' Fed.; mem. Birmingham Chamber of Commerce and Industry; Fellow, Inst. of Dirs.
Leisure interests: golf, tennis.
902/1002 Namsan Motors, Namsan, Seoul, Republic of Korea.

Turnbull, Sir Richard Gordon, G.C.M.G.; British overseas administrator; b. 7 July 1909, St. Albans, Herts.; s. of Richard Francis Turnbull and Livia Causley; m. Beatrice Wilson 1939; two s. one d.; ed. Univ. Coll., London, and Magdalene Coll., Cambridge.
With Colonial Admin. Service Kenya, District Officer 31-48, Provincial Commr. 48-53, Minister for Internal Security and Defence 54; Chief. Sec. of Kenya 55-58; Gov., Tanganyika 58-61; Gov.-Gen. 61-62; Chair. Cen. Land Board, Kenya 63-64; High Commr. for Aden and the Protectorate of South Arabia 65-67; Fellow, Univ. Coll., London, Hon. Fellow, Magdalene Coll., Cambridge.
Wharfe House, Henley-on-Thames, Oxon., England.
Telephone: Henley 2170.

Turner, Francis John, D.SC.; American professor of geology; b. 10 April 1904, Auckland, New Zealand; s. of Joseph H. Turner and Gertrude K. Turner (née Reid); m. Esmé R. Bentham 1930; one d.; ed. Auckland Grammar and Auckland Univ., New Zealand.
Lecturer in Geology, Univ. of Otago, New Zealand 26-46; Prof. of Geology, Univ. of Calif., Berkeley, U.S.A. 46-72; Sterling Fellow, Yale 38-39; Guggenheim Fellow 51, 60; Fulbright Fellow (Australia) 56; O.A.S. Mission to Univ. of São Paulo, Brazil 62; Pres. Mineralogical Soc. of America 69; mem. Nat. Acad. of Sciences (U.S.A.) 56-; Hector Medal, Royal Soc. N.Z. 51; Lyell Medal, Geol. Soc., London 69; Hon. D.Sc. (Auckland Univ.) 63.
Leisure interests: travel, paintings of classical schools, wine.
Publs. *Evolution of Metamorphic Rocks* 48, *Igneous and Metamorphic Petrology* (with J. Verhoogen) 51, 66, *Petrography* (with J. Williams and C. M. Gilbert) 53, *Structural Analysis of Metamorphic Tectonites* (with L. E. Weiss) 63, *Metamorphic Petrology* 68, *The Earth* (with J. Verhoogen et al.) 70, *Igneous Petrology* (with I. S. E. Carmichael and J. Verhoogen) 74.
2525 Hill Court, Berkeley, Calif. 94708, U.S.A.
Telephone: 415-845-6764 (Home).

Turner, Hon. John Napier, P.C., Q.C.; Canadian politician and lawyer; b. 7 June 1929, Richmond, Surrey, England; s. of Leonard and Phyllis (née Gregory) Turner; m. Geills McCrae Kilgour 1963; three s. one d.; ed. schools in Ottawa, and Univs. of British Columbia, Oxford and Paris.
·Member of Parl. 62-; Minister without Portfolio 65; Registrar-Gen. 67; Minister of Consumer and Corporate Affairs Jan. 68; Solicitor-Gen. April 68; Minister of Justice and Attorney-Gen. July 68-71; Minister of Finance 72-75; Liberal.
Leisure interests: tennis, squash, canoeing, skiing.
House of Commons, Ottawa; Home: 555 Prospect Avenue, Rockcliffe Park, Ottaway, Ont. K1M 0X6, Canada.

Turner, Sir Mark (*see* Turner, Sir Ronald Mark Cunliffe).

Turner, Sir Michael William, Kt., C.B.E., M.A., F.Z.S.; British banker; b. 25 April 1905, Winchester; s. of late Sir Skinner Turner and late Lady Turner; m. Wendy Spencer (née Stranack) 1938; three s.; ed. Marlborough Coll., and Univ. Coll., Oxford.

Joined Hongkong and Shanghai Banking Corpn. 26, Chair. and Chief Man. 53-62; interned in Singapore 42-45; Regional Dir. Nat. Westminster Bank; mem. London Advisory Cttee. The Hongkong Bank Group, and various cos.; Colonial Police Medal 56; Commdr. Order of Prince Henry the Navigator (Portugal) 63; Hon. LL.D. (Hong Kong).
Leisure interests: fishing and shooting.
Kirawin, Cliveden Mead, Maidenhead, Berkshire, England.
Telephone: Maidenhead 24718.

Turner, Sir Ralph Lilley, M.C., M.A., LITT.D., F.B.A.; British oriental scholar; b. 5 Oct. 1888, Charlton; s. of George Turner, O.B.E.; m. Dorothy Rivers Goulty 1920 (died 1972); one s. three d.; ed. Perse School, and Christ's Coll., Cambridge.
Fellow of Christ's Coll., Cambridge 12, Hon. Fellow 50; Lecturer in English and Sanskrit, Queen's Coll., Benares 13; attached 2/3rd Gurkha Rifles, Indian Army Reserve of Officers 15-19; Prof. of Indian Linguistics, Hindu Univ. of Benares 20; Prof. of Sanskrit, London Univ. 22-54, Emeritus 54-; Dir. School of Oriental and African Studies Sept. 37-57; mem. Advisory Cttee. on Education of the Colonies and other cttees.; Hon. Fellow School of Oriental and African Studies (London) 57, Deccan Coll. (Poona) 58; hon. mem. Soc. Asiatique (Paris), Deutsche Morgenländische Gesellschaft, American Oriental Soc., Linguistic Soc. of America, Linguistic Soc. of India, etc.; corresp. mem. Norske Videnskaps-Akademi; foreign corresp. Institut de France (Acad. des Inscriptions et Belles Lettres); Hon. Fellow Ceylon Acad. of Letters; Hon. D.Litt. (Banaras), Hon. D.Lit. (Ceylon, London, Visva-Bharati); Gorkha Dakshina Bahu (First Class) of Nepal.
Leisure interest: comparative philology.
Publs. *Gujarati Phonology* 21, *The Position of Romani in Indo-Aryan* 27, *A Comparative and Etymological Dictionary of the Nepali Language* 31, *The Gavimath Inscription of Asoka* 32, *Report to the Nuffield Foundation on a Visit to Nigeria* (with J. T. Saunders and D. Veale) 46, *Some Problems of Sound Change in Indo-Aryan* 60, *A Comparative Dictionary of the Indo-Aryan Languages* 66, *Indexes volume* (with Dorothy R. Turner) 69, *Phonetic Analysis Volume* 70, *Collected Papers 1912-1973*.
Haverbrack, Barrels Down Road, Bishop's Stortford, Herts., England.
Telephone: Bishop's Stortford 54135.

Turner, Sir (Ronald) Mark (Cunliffe), Kt.; British banker; b. 29 March 1906, London; s. of Christopher R. Turner and Jill H. P. Cunliffe; m. Margaret Wake 1939; three s. two d.; ed. Wellington Coll., Berks.
With M. Samuel and Co. Ltd., Merchant Bankers 24; Robert Benson and Co. Ltd., Merchant Bankers 34; Ministry of Econ. Warfare 39-44, Foreign Office 44-45; Under-Sec. Control Office for Germany and Austria 45-47; Chair. Mercantile Credit Co. Ltd. 57-73; Deputy Chair. Kleinwort, Benson Ltd. 66-71, Rio Tinto Zinc Corpn. 66-75, Chair. 75-; Chair. British Home Stores 68-, Bank of America Int. Ltd. 71-.
Leisure interests: shooting, golf.
3 The Grove, Highgate Village, London, N.6, England.

Turner, William Cochrane, B.S.; American diplomatist and business executive; b. 27 May 1929, Red Oak, Iowa; s. of James Lyman Turner and Josephine Cochrane Turner; m. Cynthia Dunbar 1955; three s.; ed. Northwestern Univ.
Vice-President and Dir., Western Management Consultants Inc. 52-60, Pres. and Dir. 60-74, Pres. and Dir. Western Management Consultants Europe S.A. 68-74; Dir. Ryan-Evans Drug Stores Inc. 68-72, First Nat. Bank of Arizona 71-74; Amb. and U.S. Rep. to OECD 74-; mem. U.S. Advisory Comm. on Int. Educ. and Cultural Affairs 69-74, Nat. Review Board 70-74,

Center for Cultural Interchange between East and West, Panel on Int. Information, Educ. and Cultural Relations, Center for Strategic and Int. Studies 73-75, Western Int. Trade Group 70-74, Brookings Inst. Urban Policy Conf.; Pres. and Dir. Phoenix Symphony Asscn.; Dir. American Graduate School for Int. Management 71; Nat. Trustee, Nat. Symphony Orchestra Asscn. 73; mem. Inst. of Management Consultants 72-74, Board of Govs. American Hosp. of Paris 74, Board of Trustees, American School of Paris, Saint-Cloud 75.
Leisure interests: tennis, symphony, opera, international political and economic relations.
19 rue de Franqueville, 75016 Paris, France; Home: 4201 North 63rd Place, Scottsdale, Ariz. 85251, U.S.A. Telephone: 524-9737 (Office).

Turpin, Raymond Alexandre; French professor of medicine; b. Nov. 1895, Pontoise (Val d'Oise); *m.* Simone Gaillochet 1931; six *c.*; ed. Faculty of Medicine, Paris.
Served in First World War as Auxiliary Doctor in 9th Infantry Regt., Verdun 16; Hosp. Intern as part of medical training 21; Prof., Faculty of Medicine, Paris 47; created Inst. of Progenesis, attached to the Faculty of Medicine 59; made first BCG vaccinations against tuberculosis with Weill-Hallé 21; discovered the electromyographic anomalies of tetany 42; initiated the study of human genetics in France and discovered chromosome irregularities; mem. Acad. de Médecine, Acad. des Sciences and numerous other learned socs. in France and abroad; Médaille Militaire, Commdr. de la Légion d'Honneur; many awards.
Publs. include *Tétanie de l'enfant, Hérédité des prédispositions morbides, La Progenèse, Les Chromosomes Humains, Caryotypes normaux et variations pathologiques* (with J. Lejeune).
94 avenue Victor Hugo, 75116 Paris, France.

Turrettini, Bernard, LIC.JUR., M.B.A.; Swiss diplomatist; b. 1911, Paris, France; ed. Univ. of Geneva, Switzerland, and Harvard Business School, Mass., U.S.A.
Bank employee, New York 39-40; entered Fed. Political Dept., Berne 40, diplomatic posts in Rio de Janeiro, Algiers, Paris and Washington 40-51; Dir. Communications Section of Div. of Int. Orgs., Fed. Political Dept. 51-54, Deputy Chief of Div. of Int. Orgs. 59-61; Swiss Del. to Cen. Comm. for Navigation of the Rhine, Strasbourg 51-59; Amb. to Venezuela and Minister in Panama 61-63, Amb. to Trinidad and Tobago 63-64, to Panama 64-66; Perm. Observer of Switzerland at UN 66-74; Amb. to Sweden April 74-.
Skeppsbron 20, Box 1237, 111 82 Stockholm 1, Sweden. Telephone: 23-15-50.

Turski, Stanisław, PH.D., D.SC.; Polish mathematician; b. 15 May 1906, Sosnowiec; *s.* of Władysław Turski and Maria Michalska; *m.* Olga Ameisen 1934; two *s.*; ed. Jagiellonian Univ., Cracow.
Professor and Rector, Gdańsk Polytechnic School 45-49; mem. of Parl. 47-52; Prof., Warsaw Polytechnic School 49-51; Dir. of Dept., Ministry of Educ. for Higher Learning 49-51; Prof., Warsaw Univ. 51-, Rector 52-69; Dir. Computer Science Inst. of Warsaw Univ. 69-; Pres. Polish Cybernetical Soc. 66-70; decorated Order of Builders of People's Poland, Commdr. of Polonia Restituta (with Star), Officier Légion d'Honneur, Lion de Finlande (avec l'Etoile), Oder-Neisse-Baltic Medal and others.
Leisure interest: hunting.
Instytut Maszyn Matematycznych UW, Pałac Kultury i Nauki, Warsaw; Home: ul. Konopczyńskiego 5/7, Warsaw, Poland.
Telephone: 268258 (Office).

Turski, Zbigniew; Polish composer and conductor; b. 16 Oct. 1908, Warsaw; *m.* Halina Turska; three *d.*; ed. in Warsaw.

Musical Dir. of Warsaw Radio 37-39; Dir. of Baltic Philharmonic Orchestra 45-46; Lecturer, State Superior Theatrical School 48-49; Consultant, Teatr Współczesny (Modern Theatre), Warsaw 57-; Pres. Polish Union of Composers 59-60; Gold Medal Olympic Arts Contest, London 48, Prize at 2nd Festival of Polish Music 55, Award of Union of Composers, Minister of Culture and Art Prize 57, State Prize 68; holder of numerous decorations.
Works include three Symphonies, Sinfonia de Camera, Violin Concerto, two String Quartets, cantatas *The Airs* and *The Vistula* on poems by Broniewski and Fiszer, theatre and film music.
c/o Union of Polish Composers, Rynek Starego Miasta 27, Warsaw, Poland.
Telephone: 174058.

Turyn, Alexander, PH.D.; Polish-American philologist; b. 26 Dec. 1900, Warsaw; *s.* of Arnold Turyn and Ernestyna Glazer; *m.* Felicia L. Sachs 1926; one *s.*; ed. Warsaw and Berlin Univs.
Instructor Warsaw Univ. 25, Docent 29, Prof. Extra. of Classical Philology 35-39; Lecturer, Univ. of Michigan 41; Assoc. Prof. New School for Social Research, New York 42-45; Prof. Univ. of Illinois 45-69; mem. Center for Advanced Study 62-69, Prof. Emeritus 69-; corresp. mem. Polish Acad. Cracow, Acad. of Athens; research collaborator, Vatican Library 60-66; Foreign mem. Istituto Lombardo (Milan); Hon. mem. Epistemonike Hetaireia, Athens; Fellow, Guggenheim Foundation 59; Award of Merit, American Philological Asscn. 60; Hon. Ph.D. (Athens Univ.) 65.
Publs. *Observationes metricae* 23, *Studia Sapphica* 29, *De Aelii Aristidis codice Varsoviensi atque de Andrea Taranowski et Theodosio Zygomala* 29, *De codicibus Pindaricis* 32, *The Manuscript Tradition of the Tragedies of Aeschylus* 43, *Pindari Epinicia* 44, *The Manuscripts of Sophocles* 44, *Pindari Carmina cum fragmentis* 48, *The Sophocles Recension of Manuel Moschopulus* 49, *Studies in the Manuscript Tradition of the Tragedies of Sophocles* 52, *The Byzantine Manuscript Tradition of the Tragedies of Euripides* 57, *Codices graeci Vaticani saeculis XIII et XIV scripti annorumque notis instructi* 64, *Dated Greek Manuscripts of the Thirteenth and Fourteenth Centuries in the Libraries of Italy* 72, *Demetrius Triclinius and the Planudean Anthology* 73, *Michael Lulludes, a Scribe of the Palaeologan Era* 74.
801 South Maple Street, Urbana, Ill. 61801, U.S.A. Telephone: 217-367-3911.

Turzún-Zadé, Mirzo; Soviet writer and poet; b. 5 Sept. 1911, Kishlak Karatak, Tadzhik S.S.R.; *s.* of Tursun and Holbibi Turzún-Zadé; *m.* Saodat Turzún-Zadé; two *s.* one *d.*; ed. Tadzhik Education Inst.
Literary work 31-; mem. Acad. of Sciences, Tadzhik S.S.R. 51-; People's Poet of Tadzhik S.S.R.; Deputy Supreme Soviet 46-; Chair. Soviet Afro-Asian Solidarity Cttee. 56-; First Sec. Union of Writers of Tadzhik S.S.R. 46-; mem. Central Cttee. C.P. of Tadzhikistan; Sec. U.S.S.R. Union of Writers 66; mem. Cttee. on Lenin Prizes under U.S.S.R. Council of Ministers; mem. U.S.S.R. Cttee. in Defence of Peace and World Peace Council; mem. Comm. for Foreign Affairs, Union of Soviets; U.S.S.R. State Prize, Lenin Prize, Rudaki Tadzhik S.S.R. State Prize in Literature, J. Nehru Prize, Hero of Socialist Labour, Hammer and Sickle Gold Medal, Order of Lenin (four times), Red Banner of Labour (three times), Badge of Honour (twice), Order of Kirill and Metodii (first degree).
Publs. Play: *The Sentence* 34; poems: *Spring and Autumn* 37, *Indian Songs* 48, *Hissar Valley, Child of his Fatherland, Tahir and Zukhra, I am from the Free East* 51, *Hasan Arobakesh* 54, *Voice of Asia* 57, *Eternal Light* 57, *My Dear* 60, *Selected Works* (3 vols.) 60, *Path of a Sun Ray* 64, *Epoch, Life and Creative Work* 65, *The Globe* 66,

From Gang to Kreml 70, *Selected Works* (2 vols.) 71, *My Century* 73, *Complete Works* (6 vols.) 73-76.
734025 Dushaube, Ordzomikidzet 2, U.S.S.R.
Telephone: 2-25-93.

Tuthill, John Wills; American diplomatist; b. 10 Nov. 1910, Montclair, N.J.; *s.* of Oliver B. Tuthill and Louise Jerolem Wills; *m.* Erna Margaret Lüders 1937; one *s.* one *d.*; ed. Coll. of William and Mary, New York Univ., and Harvard Univ.
Private banking 32-36; Investment Counsel 36-37; Instructor and Asst. Prof. Northeastern Univ. 37-40; Foreign Service Officer 40-, Canada, Mexico, SHAEF, U.S. Military Govt., Berlin, Dept. of State, Stockholm, London, Bonn, Paris, Dept. of State 59-60; American Ambassador to Organisation for Economic Co-operation and Development (OECD) 61-62, to the European Communities 62-66, to Brazil 66-69; Prof. of Int. Politics, Johns Hopkins Univ., School of Advanced Int. Studies, Bologna, Italy 69; Dir.-Gen. and Gov., Atlantic Inst. for Int. Affairs, Paris 69-.
Leisure interests: reading, skiing, tennis, riding, swimming.
Atlantic Institute, 120 rue de Longchamp, Paris 16e; Home: 5 rue de Lota, Paris 16e, France.
Telephone: 727-24-36.

Tutin, Dorothy, C.B.E.; British actress; b. 8 April 1930, London; *d.* of Dr. John Tutin and A. E. Fryers; *m.* Derek Waring 1963; one *s.* one *d.*; ed. St. Catherine's, Bramley, Surrey, and Royal Acad. of Dramatic Art, London.
Appeared at Stratford Festival 58, 60; took part in Shakespeare Memorial Theatre tour of Russia 58; Shakespeare recital before Pope, Vatican 64; *Evening Standard* Award as Best Actress 60, Variety Club of Great Britain Award for Best Film Actress 72.
Leisure interest: music.
Principal roles: Rose (*The Living Room*), Katherine (*Henry V*), Sally Bowles (*I am a Camera*), St. Joan (*The Lark*), Catherine (*The Gates of Summer*), Hedwig (*The Wild Duck*), Viola (*Twelfth Night*), Juliet (*Romeo and Juliet*), Ophelia (*Hamlet*), Dolly (*Once More, With Feeling*), Portia (*The Merchant of Venice*), Cressida (*Troilus and Cressida*), Sister Jeanne (*The Devils*) 61, 62, Juliet (*Romeo and Juliet*) and Desdemona (*Othello*), Stratford-on-Avon 61, Varya (*The Cherry Orchard*) 61, Prioress (*The Devils*), Edinburgh 62, Polly Peachum (*The Beggar's Opera*) 63, Hollow Crown, New York 63, Queen Victoria (*Portrait of a Queen*) 65, Rosalind (*As You Like It*), Stratford on Avon 67, Los Angeles 68, Queen Victoria (*Portrait of a Queen*), New York 68, *Old Times* 71, Peter Pan 71, 72, *What Every Woman Knows* 73, 75, *A Month in the Country* 74.
Films include: *The Beggar's Opera, The Importance of Being Earnest, A Tale of Two Cities, Cromwell, Savage Messiah.*
c/o Peter Browne Management, 13 St. Martin's Road, London, S.W.9, England.

Tuttle, O. Frank; American professor of geochemistry; b. 25 June 1916, Olean, N.Y.; *s.* of Orvel Delano Tuttle and Lucy Holmes; *m.* Dawn Hardes 1941; two *d.*; ed. Pennsylvania State Coll. and Mass. Inst. of Technology.
Physical chemist, Geophysical Lab., Washington 42-45, U.S. Naval Research Lab., Washington 45-47; Petrologist, Geophysical Lab. 47-53; Prof. of Geochemistry and Chair. Div. of Earth Sciences, Pa. State Univ. 53-59; Dean, Coll. of Mineral Industries 59-60; Prof. of Geochemistry, Penn. State Univ. 60-65; Prof. of Geochemistry, Stanford Univ. 65-67; now retd. Mineralogical Soc. of America Award (first recipient) 51 and Roebling Medal 75; Day Medal, Geological Soc. of America 67; mem. Nat. Acad. of Sciences 68.
Leisure interests: studying securities, cabinet making, hiking.

Publs. 78 scientific papers, two books.
4850 West Lazy C Drive, Tucson, Ariz. 85705; Box 16, Greer, Ariz. 85927, U.S.A.
Telephone: 602-624-3168.

Tutuola, Amos; Nigerian writer; b. 1920, Abeokuta, W. Nigeria; *s.* of Charles and Esther Tutuola; *m.* Victoria Tutuola 1947; four *s.* four *d.*; ed. Mission Schools.
Worked on father's farm; trained as coppersmith; served with R.A.F. Second World War; Nigerian Broadcasting Corpn., Ibadan 45-.
Leisure interests: farming, writing.
Publs. *The Palm-Wine Drinkard* 52, *My Life in the Bush of Ghosts* 54, *Simbi and the Satyr of the Jungle* 55, *The Brave African Huntress* 58, *The Feather Woman of the Jungle* 62, *Ajaiyi and His Inherited Poverty* 67.
c/o Nigerian Broadcasting Corporation, Broadcasting House, Ibadan, Nigeria.
Telephone: 61660/26.

Tuve, Merle Antony, B.S., M.A., PH.D.; American research physicist; b. 27 June 1901; ed. Univ. of Minnesota, Princeton Univ., and Johns Hopkins Univ. Instructor in Physics Princeton Univ. 23-24, Johns Hopkins Univ. 24-26; Physicist and Staff mem. Carnegie Inst. of Washington 26-46, Dir. Dept. of Terrestrial Magnetism 46-66; Chair. Section T, Nat. Defence Research Cttee. and Office of Scientific Research and Devt. 40-45; Chair. Advisory Panel on Radio Astronomy, Nat. Science Foundation 53-; U.S. Comm. for the Int. Geophysical Year; Editor *Journal of Geophysical Research* 49-58; Trustee Johns Hopkins Univ.; Fellow American Physical Soc., Inst. of Radio Engineers, American Asscn. for the Advancement of Science; mem. Nat. Acad. of Sciences, Home Sec. 66-, American Acad. of Arts and Sciences and American Philosophical Soc.; Presidential Medal for Merit 46, C.B.E. 48, Bowie Medal 63, and many other awards; Hon. Sc.D. (Case, Kenyon, Williams, Johns Hopkins, Univ. of Alaska), Hon. LL.D. (Augustana and Carleton).
Publs. *Exploration of the Upper Atmosphere (Ionosphere) by Radio Pulse Methods* 25-29, *High Voltage Techniques for Nuclear Physics* 30-35, *Resonance Levels in the Atomic Nucleus* 35-37, etc.
Home: 135 Hesketh Street, Chevy Chase, Md.; Office. Carnegie Institution of Washington, 5241 Broad Branch Road, N.W. Washington, D.C. 20015, U.S.A.

Tuzo, Gen. Sir Harry Craufurd, G.C.B., O.B.E., M.C., A.D.C. GEN., M.A.; British army officer; b. 26 Aug. 1917, Bangalore, India; *s.* of John A. Tuzo and Annie K. Craufurd; *m.* Monica P. Salter 1943; one *d.*; ed. Wellington Coll. and Oriel Coll., Oxford.
Regimental Service, Royal Artillery 39-45; staff appts. Far East 46-49; Royal Horse Artillery 50-51, 54-58; mem. Staff, School of Infantry 51-53; Gen. Staff Officer, War Office 58-60; Commdg. Officer, 3rd Regt. Royal Horse Artillery 60-62; Asst. Commdt., Sandhurst 62-63; Commdr. 51 Gurkha Infantry Brigade 63-65; Imperial Defence Coll. 66; Chief of Staff, British Army of the Rhine 67-69; Dir. Royal Artillery 69-71; Gen. Officer Commanding, Northern Ireland 71-72; C.-in-C. BAOR and Commdr., Northern Army Group, NATO 72-76; Deputy Supreme Allied Commdr. Europe Feb. 76-.
Leisure interests: music, sailing, shooting.
Publs. articles in professional publications.
c/o Army & Navy Club, Pall Mall, London, S.W.1, England.

Tweter, Clifford; American banker; b. 6 Oct. 1907; ed. Northwestern School of Commerce.
With Continental-Ill. Nat. Bank & Trust Co., Chicago 25-41; with California Bank, Los Angeles 41-, Asst. Vice-Pres. 43-45, Vice-Pres. 45-54, Exec. Vice-Pres., Dir. 54-, Pres. 59-69; Pres. and Dir. United California

Bank; Chair. Western Bancorporation (fmrly. First-America Corpn.) until 74, now Chair. Exec. Cttee., Dir. Office: 707 Wilshire Boulevard, Los Angeles, Calif. 90017, U.S.A.

Twigt, Bernard Tielsman, DR. ECON.; Netherlands transport economist; b. 3 Dec. 1912, Rotterdam; s. of Vincent Twigt and Petronella Anna Breedveld; m. Alice Klapwijk 1946; one s.; ed. Rotterdam Univ. of Economics.
Deputy Chief of Administration and Finance, International Civil Aviation Org. (ICAO), Montreal 49-56; Asst. Dir. of Admin. and Gen. Services, United Nations Relief and Works Agency for Palestine, Beirut 56-59; Sec. UN Joint Staff Pension Fund, New York 59-60; Chief Admin. Officer, UN Emergency Force, Gaza 60-62; Chief Admin. Officer, UN Operation in the Congo, Léopoldville 62-63; Assoc. Dir., Joint Admin. Div., Technical Asst. Board, UN, New York 63-64; Sec.-Gen. Int. Civil Aviation Org. (ICAO), Montreal Aug. 64-70; Dir. European Office, UN Children's Fund (UNICEF) Aug. 70-.
Leisure interests: sport, tennis, swimming.
22 chemin du Pommier, 9 Saconnex (Geneva), Switzerland.
Telephone: 33-20-73.

Twining, Gen. Nathan F.; American air force officer; b. 11 Oct. 1897; ed. U.S. Military Acad., Infantry School, Air Corps Tactical School, Commd. and Gen. Staff School.
Commissioned Second Lieut. Infantry 18; transferred to Air Corps 24; advanced through grades to Lieut.-Gen. 45, Gen. 50; Chief of Staff to Commdg. Gen. S. Pacific 42-43; Commdg. Gen. 13th Air Force, Solomon Islands 43, 15th Air Force, Italy 44-45, 20th Air Force, Pacific 45, Alaska 47-50; Vice-Chief of Staff U.S.A.F. 50-53, Chief of Staff 53-57; Chair. Joint Chiefs of Staff 57-60 (retd.); Vice-Chair. Holt, Rinehart and Winston 61-67; awarded D.S.M. (Army and Navy), Legion of Merit with oak leaf cluster, D.F.C., Air Medal, etc.; Hon. K.B.E. (U.K.).
25 North Live Oak Road, Hilton Head Island, S.C. 29928, U.S.A.

Twisleton-Wykeham-Fiennes, Sir Maurice Alberic, Kt., C.ENG., F.I.MECH.E.; British company director; b. 1 March 1907, London; s. of Alberic Arthur Twisleton-Wykeham-Fiennes and Gertrude Theodosia Pomeroy-Colley; m. 1st Sylvia Mabel Joan Finlay 1932, 2nd Erika Hueller von Huellenried 1967; two s. three d. (by 1st marriage); ed. Repton School, Derbyshire, and Armstrong Coll., Newcastle.
Manager, Pneumatic Tool Dept., Sir. W. G. Armstrong Whitworth and Co. 30-37; Commercial Asst. to Man. Dir. United Steel Companies Ltd.; Gen. Works Dir. Brush Electrical Engineering Co. Ltd. 42-45; Managing Dir. Davy and United Engineering Co. Ltd., Sheffield 45-60; Man. Dir. Davy-Ashmore Group 60-69, Chair. 61-69; Dir. Continuous Casting Co. Ltd. 57-69; Clyde Crane and Booth Ltd. 61-68, Simon Engineering Ltd. 62-69, North Sea Marine Engineering Construction Co. Ltd. 64-69, Metallurgical Equipment Export Co. Ltd. 64-67; Pres. Iron and Steel Inst. 62-63; Steel Industry Adviser (UN) to Govt. of Peru 74-; Hon. Vice-Pres. Indian Inst. of Metals; Hon. mem. American Iron and Steel Inst., Hon. mem. Verein Deutscher Eisenhütten-leute; Chair. CBI Overseas Scholarships Board; Gov. Yehudi Menuhin School.
Leisure interest: music.
Gowers Close, Sibford Gower, Banbury, Oxon., England.
Telephone: (029-578) 292.

Tyerman, Donald; British journalist; b. 1 March 1908, Middlesbrough, Yorks.; s. of Joseph Tyerman and Catherine Tamar Day; m. Margaret Charteris Gray

1934; two s. three d.; ed. Gateshead-on-Tyne Secondary School and Brasenose Coll., Oxford.
Lecturer Univ. Coll. Southampton 30-36; Asst. and later Deputy Editor *The Economist* 37-44; Deputy Editor *The Observer* 43-44; Asst. Editor *The Times* 44-55; Editor *The Economist* 56-65; Chair. Exec. Board Int. Press Inst. 61-62; mem. Exec. Cttee. Overseas Devt. Inst.; Dir. Economist Newspaper Ltd. 59-69, United City Merchants Ltd.; Editor of Twentieth Century Studies for Hodder and Stoughton; mem. of Council, Univ. of Sussex 66-75; Gov. London School of Econs. 57-75; mem. Press Council 64-69; Hon. Treas. The Save the Children Fund 67-75.
Leisure interests: reading, watching games and television, the countryside.
41 Buckingham Mansions, West End Lane, London, N.W.6; and Holly Cottage, Westleton, Saxmundham, Suffolk, England.
Telephone: 01-435-1030 (London); 0728-73-261 (Suffolk).

Tyler, William Royall; American government official; b. 17 Oct. 1910, Paris, France; s. of Royall Tyler and Elisina de Castelvecchio; m. Bettine Mary Fisher-Rowe 1934; one s. one d.; ed. Oxford and Harvard Univs.
Guaranty Trust Co., New York City 34-38; Programme Manager Short Wave Radio Station Boston 40-42; Office of War Information, New York 42, North Africa 43-44, France 44-45; Dept. of State 45-, Counsellor, Paris 48-54; Deputy Dir. Office of Western European Affairs, Washington 54-57, Dir. 57-58; Political Counsellor, Bonn 58-61; Deputy Asst. Sec. of State for European Affairs, Dept. of State 61-62, Asst. Sec. of State 62-65; Amb. to Netherlands 65-69; Dir. Dumbarton Oaks Research Library and Collection (Harvard Univ.) Washington, D.C. 69-; Corresp. mem. Mass. Historical Soc., Acad. de Dijon; Assoc. mem. Centre Européen d'Etudes Burgondo Médianes; Fellow, American Acad. of Arts and Sciences; Chevalier, Légion d'Honneur.
Leisure interests: history of art, history, music.
Publs. *A Moment of Silence* (trans. from Dutch), *Dijon and the Valois Dukes of Burgundy* 71.
1735 32nd Street N.W., Washington, D.C. 20007, U.S.A.
Telephone: 232-3101.

Tynan, Kenneth, B.A., F.R.S.L.; British writer; b. 2 April 1927, Birmingham; s. of Sir Peter Peacock and Letitia Tynan; m. 1st Elaine Dundy 1951, 2nd Kathleen Halton 1967; one s. two d.; ed. Magdalen Coll., Oxford.
Director of Repertory Theatre, Lichfield 49; directed plays in and around London and on television 50-51; Drama Critic *The Spectator* 51; Drama Critic *Evening Standard* 52-53; Drama Critic *Daily Sketch* 53-54; Drama Critic of *The Observer* 54-63; Script Editor of Ealing Films 56-58; Drama Critic of *The New Yorker* 58-60; TV. producer 61-62; Literary Manager Nat. Theatre 63-73; Film Critic *The Observer* 64-66, Arts Columnist 68-69; co-author (with Roman Polanski) of screen adaptation of *Macbeth* 70.
Leisure interests: food, wine.
Publs. *He that Plays the King* 50, *Persona Grata* (with Cecil Beaton) 53, *Alec Guinness* 53, *Bull Fever* 55, *Curtains* 61, *Tynan Right and Left* 67, *A View of the English Stage 1944-63* 75, *The Sound of Two Hands Clapping* 75; plays: *The Quest for Corbett* (with Harold Lang) 56, *Oh Calcutta* 69.
20 Thurloe Square, London, S.W.7, England.

Typolt, Jiři, c.sc.; Czechoslovak economist and politician; b. 20 June 1930, Prague; m. Nina Močlavá 1954; two s.; ed. Moscow State Inst. of Economics.
State Planning Office 54-59; State Planning Comm. 59-68, Dept. Head until 63, Head of Prices Dept. 63-68; Head of Income Policy Dept., Ministry of Econ. Planning 68-69; Minister-Chair. Fed. Cttee. for Prices

69; mem. Econ. Council of Govt. of C.S.S.R. 69-70; Vice-Dir. Research Inst. of Econ. Plannng 70, ICA Cybernetic Agency 70-.

Leisure interests: photography, cars.

Publs. *Price Formation in the New Economic Management* (with Janza) 58, co-author *Planning of Prices of Industrial Products* 59, co-operated on *The Role of Finance in Czechoslovakia's Present Economy* 59, *New Regulations of Price Formation of Products and Services* 60, *Price Formation in Various Economics* (*New York*) 67.

ICA Cybernetic Agency, Na Perštyně 1, Prague, Czechoslovakia.

Telephone: (Home) 34-27-60.

Tzounis, Ioannis Alexander; Greek diplomatist; b. 13 Oct. 1920, Bucharest, Romania; *s.* of Alexander and Mathilde (née Politis) Tzounis; *m.* Helen Besi 1962; one *s.*; ed. Univ. of Athens and French Inst., Athens.

Joined diplomatic service 47; posts at Ministry of Foreign Affairs, Athens, 47-50, 59-62, 67-69; Vice-Consul, San Francisco 51, Acting Consul-Gen. 54; Chief Information Officer, Greek Embassy, Washington, D.C. 55; Counsellor, Moscow 62, Chargé d'Affaires 63-65; Counsellor, London 65-67; Amb. to Turkey 69-73; Dir.-Gen. for Political Affairs, Ministry of Foreign Affairs Dec. 73-; mem. del. to UN Gen. Assembly 51, 54, del. to Geneva Tripartite Conf. on Cyprus July-Aug. 74; Knight Commdr., Royal Order of Phoenix, Order of Golden Star (Yugoslavia), Tudor Vladimiresco (Romania), Maple (Luxembourg); Commdr. Royal Order of George I, Légion d'Honneur.

Leisure interests: photography, sailing.

c/o Ministry of Foreign Affairs, Athens, Greece.

U

Ubac, Raoul; Belgian painter; b. 1910; ed. Sorbonne and Ateliers de la Grande Chaumière.
Settled in Paris 32; work in surrealist photography 32-39; abandoned photography for pen-drawing, gouache, painting and sculpture of slates; exhbns. Paris 43, London and Brussels 46, Galerie Maeght (Paris) 50, 55, 58, 64, 66, Basel Kunsthalle 54, Zürich and São Paulo 57, Carnegie Inst. (Pittsburgh) 58, Dokumenta (Kassel and Geneva) 59, Dunn Int. Exhbn., London 63; Musée d'Art moderne, retrospective exhbn. Paris 68; works in New York Museum of Modern Art, Kunstmuseum, Basle, Carnegie Foundation, Pittsburgh, Musée d'Art Moderne, Paris and Brussels, and in numerous private collections.
Publs. Illustrations for poems of André Frénaud and for *Pierre Ecrite* by Yves Bonnefoy, *Proximité du Murmure* by Jacques Dupin, etc.
11 rue d'Orchampt, 75018 Paris, France.

Ubbelohde, Alfred R. J. P., C.B.E., F.R.S., M.A., D.SC., F.R.I.C., F.INST.P., M.I.CHEM.E.; British professor of thermodynamics; b. 14 Dec. 1907, Antwerp, Belgium; s. of F. C. Ubbelohde and Angele Verspreeuwen; ed. St. Paul's School, London, and Christ Church, Oxford.
Dewar Fellow, Royal Inst. 35-40; with Ministry of Supply 40-45; Prof. of Chem., Queen's Univ., Belfast 45-54, Dean of Faculty of Science 47-51; Prof. of Thermodynamics, Imperial Coll. of Science and Technology, London Univ. 54-75, Head of Dept. of Chemical Engineering and Chemical Technology 61-75, Prof. Emer. and Sr. Research Fellow 75-; Chair. Fire Research Board 56-61, Science and Engineering Panel of British Council 64-74; Pres. Council of Institut Solvay 57-64, 65-, Faraday Soc. 63-65; Dir. Salters' Inst. of Industrial Chemistry 59-75; mem. Agric. Research Council 66-; Van't Hoff Memorial Lecturer, Royal Netherlands Acad.; mem. Pontifical Acad., Göttingen Acad.; Hon. Laureate (Padua Univ.); Dr. h.c. (Univ. Libre, Brussels); Hon. D.Sc. (Belfast); Alfred Egerton Medal, Combustion Inst. 71; Messel Medal, Soc. of Chemical Industry 72; George Shakel Award, American Carbon Soc. 75, Paul Lebeau Gold Medal, Société des Hautes Températures et Réfractaires 75.
Leisure interest: farming.
Publs. *Modern Thermodynamical Principles* 37, 2nd edn. 52, *Time and Thermodynamics* 47, *Man and Energy* 54, (2nd edn.) 63, *Graphite and its Crystal Compounds* 60, *Melting and Crystal Structure* 65; papers in proceedings and journals of scientific socs.
48 Cottesmore Court, Stanford Road, London, W.8; Platt's Farm, Burwash, Sussex, England.

Uchida, Tsuneo; Japanese politician; b. 1907; ed. Tokyo Univ.
Member, House of Reps.; Dir. Property Custodian Bureau of Ministry of Finance; Parl. Vice-Minister for Int. Trade and Industry, subsequently for Science and Technology; Chair. House of Reps. Commerce and Industry Cttee.; Chair. Liberal-Democratic Party Tax System Research Council; Minister of Health and Welfare 70-71; Dir. Econ. Planning Agency 73-Dec. 74.
House of Representatives, Tokyo, Japan.

Udall, Stewart Lee; American politician; b. 31 Jan. 1920; ed. Univ. of Arizona.
Served U.S. Air Force, Second World War; admitted to Arizona Bar 48, practised law, Tucson 48-54; mem. House of Reps. 55-61, mem. Interior and Insular Affairs Cttee., Labor and Education Cttee.; Sec. of the Interior 61-69; Chair. of Board, Overview Group (int. consulting firm working to create a better environment for mankind); Visiting Prof. in Environmental Humanism, Yale School of Forestry; Democrat.
Publ. *The Quiet Crisis.*
1700 Pennsylvania Avenue, Washington, D.C. 20006, U.S.A.

Udaltsov, Ivan Ivanovich, CAND. SC.; Soviet historian; b. 12 March 1918, Moscow State Univ. and Postgraduate Courses of Inst. of History of U.S.S.R. Acad. of Sciences.
Took part in Second World War 40-45; postgraduate student, scientific assoc., Inst. of Slavonic Studies, U.S.S.R. Acad. of Sciences; Head of Dept., mem. Editorial Board *Voprosy istorii* (Problems of History), *Slavyane* (Slavs), *Novaya i noveishaya istoriya* (Modern and Recent History) 45-50; mem. staff C.P.S.U. Central Cttee. 50-59, 62-65; Dir., Inst. of Slavonic Studies, U.S.S.R. Acad. of Sciences 59-62; diplomatic service 65-70; Chair. of Board, Novosti Press Agency 70-76; Alt. mem. C.P.S.U. Cen. Cttee. 71-; Deputy to Supreme Soviet 74-; mem. Foreign Affairs Comm., Soviet of Nationalities; Order of Red Banner of Labour (twice), Badge of Honour, White Lion, Mil. Cross (Czechoslovakia) and medals.

Udink, Berend Jan; Netherlands politician; b. 12 Feb. 1926, Deventer; m. Anneke van Drumpt 1949; one s. two d.; ed. School of Economics, Rotterdam, and Ecole des Hautes Etudes Commerciales, Univ. of Lausanne.
Deputy Sec. Rotterdam Chamber of Commerce 53-58, Sec. 58-63; Lecturer, School of Econs., Rotterdam, and Dir. Central Inst. for Traffic Engineering 50-63; Dir. of Central Chamber of Netherlands for Export Promotion 62-67; mem. Nat. Advisory Council for Aid to Developing Countries 65-; Chair. Protestant Group in the Rijnmond Council 65-; Exec. mem. of Board, OGEM Rotterdam; Minister without Portfolio, responsible for Aid to Developing Countries 67-71, of Housing and Physical Planning 71-73, also Minister of Transport 72-73.
Burg, Lefèvre de Montignylaan 109, Rotterdam, Netherlands.
Telephone: 010-222328.

Udoma, Sir (Egbert) Udo, LL.B., M.A., PH.D.; Nigerian lawyer; b. 21 June 1917, Ibekwe Ntanaran Akama Opobo, S.E. State; s. of Chief Udoma Inam and Adiaha Edem; m. Grace Bassey 1950; six s. one d.; ed. Methodist Coll., Uzuakoli, Trinity Coll., Dublin, Ireland, St. Catherine's Coll., Oxford.
Called to the Bar, Gray's Inn, London 45; practised as barrister and solicitor, Supreme Court, Nigeria 46-61; mem. House of Reps. 52-59; Judge, Lagos High Court 61-63; Chief Justice of Uganda 63-69; Justice Supreme Court of Nigeria 69-; Chancellor Ahmadu Bello Univ. 72-; Nat. Pres. Ibibio State Union 47-63; mem. Nigeria Marketing Co. 52-54; Man. Cttee. West Africa Inst. for Oil Palm Research 53-63; Vice-Pres. Nigeria Bar Asscn. 57-61; mem. Int. Comm. of Jurists, World Asscn. of Judges; Chair. Board of Trustees King George V Memorial Fund 64-69; Patron Nigeria Soc. of Int. Law 68-; awarded title of Obong Ikpa Isong Ibibio 61; Hon. LL.D. Ibadan Univ. 67, Ahmadu Bello Univ. 72, Trinity Coll., Dublin 73.
Leisure interests: billiards, gardening, walking.
Supreme Court, Lagos, Nigeria.
Telephone: 21651.

Udovichenko, Petr Platonovich; Soviet (Ukrainian) diplomatist and educationist; b. 1914; ed. Novomoskovsky Pedagogical Inst.
Professor of History, Teachers Inst., Dneprodzerhiński

34-39; Asst. to Minister, Head of Dept. of Political Affairs, Ministry of Foreign Affairs, Ukraine 44-52; Pro-Rector, Kiev State Univ. 52-58; Ukrainian Perm. Rep. to UN 58-61; teacher, Kiev State Univ. 61-67; Minister of Educ. of Ukrainian S.S.R. 67-.
Ministry of Education, Kiev, U.S.S.R.

Ueki, Shigeaki; Brazilian politician; b. 1935, São Paulo; ed. Catholic Univ. of São Paulo.
With private cos. until 67; Adviser to Minister of Trade and Industry 67-68; later Commercial Dir. PETROBAS, and mem. Council of Nat. Bank for Econ. Devt. (BNDE); Minister of Mines and Energy April 74-.
Ministério das Minas e Energia, Brasília, Brazil.

Uffen, Robert James, PH.D., D.SC., P.ENG., F.R.S.C., F.G.S.A.; Canadian geophysicist; b. 21 Sept. 1923, Toronto, Ont.; s. of James Frederick Uffen and Elsie May (Harris) Uffen; m. Mary Ruth Paterson 1949; one s. one d.; ed. Univs. of Toronto, Western Ontario and Calif. at Los Angeles.
Lecturer, Univ. of Western Ontario 51-53, Asst. Prof. of Physics and Geology 53-57, Assoc. Prof. of Geophysics 57-58, Prof. and Head of Dept. of Geophysics 58-61, Acting Head Dept. Physics 60-61; Principal Univ. Coll. of Arts and Science, London, Ont. 61-65; Dean Coll. of Science, Univ. of Western Ontario 65-66; Vice-Chair. Defence Research Board, Ottawa 66-67, Chair. 67-69; Chief Science Adviser to the Cabinet 69-71; Dean, Faculty of Applied Science, Queen's Univ., Kingston, Ont. 71-; Research Fellowship, Inst. of Geophysics, U.C.L.A. 53; mem. Council of Regents Colls. of Applied Arts and Technology 66-69, 73-, Nat. Research Council of Canada 63-66, Science Council of Canada 67-71, Defence Council 67-69; Dir. Canadian Patents and Devt. Ltd. 65-70; mem. Club of Rome 69-; Chair. Canadian Engineering Manpower Council 73-74; Dir. Centre for Resource Studies 74-, Ont. Hydro 74-. (Vice-Chair. 75); Councillor, Asscn. of Professional Engineers of Ont. 75-; Hon. D.Sc. (Queen's Univ., Univ. W. Ontario).
Leisure interests: painting, skiing, boating, old bottles.
Publs. papers on geophysics, operations research, evolution and science policy.
167 Fairway Hill Crescent, Kingston, Ont., Canada. Telephone: 613-546-4981.

Ugueto, Luis; Venezuelan international finance official; b. 24 Aug. 1936, Caracas; s. of Angel Ugueto and Maria Cristina Arismendi; m. Maria Otánez 1959; two s. one d.; ed. Universidad Católica "Andrés Bello", Caracas and London School of Economics.
Resident Inspection Engineer, Ministry of Public Works 58-62; Adviser, Central Bank of Venezuela and Ministry of Finance, Caracas 62-63; Exec. Aerovías Venezolanas, S.A., Caracas 62-67; Exec. Dir. Banco de Comercio, Caracas 66-69; mem. Board Public Admin. Comm., Caracas 69-70; Dir.-Gen. Ministry of Finance 69-70; Exec. Dir. IMF 70-72; Sec. Caucus of Latin American and Philippines Govs. to the IMF and IBRD 70-72; Minister Counsellor for Econ. Affairs, Venezuelan Embassy in Wash. D.C. 71-74, Deputy Chief of Mission 72-74; Exec. Dir. IBRD 72-74, Deputy Cttee. of Twenty 72-73; Pres. Banco Hipotecario de Aragua 74-; Adviser and mem. Board Banco de Venezuela 74-.
Banco Hipotecario de Aragua, Centro comercial Casa, Calle Carabobo, cruce calle Páez, Apdo. 286, Maracay, Aragua, Venezuela.

Uhlenbeck, George Eugene, PH.D.; American (naturalized 1952) professor of theoretical physics; b. 6 Dec. 1900, Jakarta, Indonesia; s. of Eugene Marius Uhlenbeck and Anna Beeger; m. Else Renee Ophorst 1927; one s.; ed. Univ. of Leiden.
Associate Professor, Univ. of Michigan 27-35; Prof. Univ. of Utrecht 35-39, Univ. of Mich. 39-61, Rockefeller Univ., New York 61-71; mem. Radiation Lab., Cambridge, Mass. 42-45; Lorentz Prof., Leiden 54-55;

Van der Waals Prof., Amsterdam 63-64; mem. Nat. Acad. of Sciences, Accad. dei Lincei; Max Planck Medal 64, Lorentz Medal 70; Hon. Ph.D. Notre Dame Univ., Case Inst., Univ. of Colorado, Yeshiva Univ.
Leisure interest: reading, especially history.
Publs. *Threshold Signals* (with J. L. Lawson) 50, *Lectures in Statistical Mechanics* (with G. W. Ford) 63; contributions to professional journals.
130 East 63rd Street, New York, N.Y. 10021; and The Rockefeller University, New York, N.Y. 10021, U.S.A.
Telephone: PL2-4887; 360-1767.

Uhlmann, Hans; German engineer and sculptor; b. 27 Nov. 1900; ed. Berlin Technical Inst.
First exhibition of metallic sculptures 45; Prof. Berlin Acad. of Fine Arts 50-; rep. at many int. exhbns. including Brussels Int. Exhbn. 58, *Expo 67*, Montreal 68; one-man exhbn. at Berlin Akad. der Künste 68; mem. Akad. der Künste (Berlin); Kunstpreis (Berlin) 50; German Prize, Unknown Political Prisoner Monument Competition 53; Deutscher Kritiker Preis 54; Grafik Preis (Lugano) 60; Cornelius Preis (Düsseldorf) 61.
Schorlemer Allee 21, Berlin 33, Federal Republic of Germany.

Ujfalussy, József, PH.D.; Hungarian musicologist; b. 13 Feb. 1920, Debrecen; s. of Dr. Géza Ujfalussy and Margit Mándy; ed. Debrecen Univ., Music Academy, Budapest.
Secondary school teacher 43-46; education organizer, Budapest 46-48; Section Head, then Chief Dept. Leader Ministry of Culture 49-55; Prof. of Aesthetics of Music and Theory of Music, Budapest Acad. of Music 55-; Fellow Inst. of Musicology 69; Fellow Hungarian Acad. of Sciences Bartók Archives 61, Dir. 73-; Corresp. mem. Hungarian Acad. of Sciences 73-; mem. Hungarian UNESCO Cttee.; mem. Board Fed. of Hungarian Musical Artists; Erkel Prize 61, Kossuth Prize 66.
Publs. *Bartók breviárium* (with Vera Lampert) 58, (2nd edn. 74), *Debussy* 59, *A valóság zenei képe* (The Musical Image of Reality) 62, *Béla Bartók* Vols. I and II 65, 70.
Csévi-utca 19b, H-1025 Budapest II, Hungary.
Telephone: 364-884.

Ulam, Stanisław Marcin, D.SC.; American scientist; b. 13 April 1909, Lwów, Poland; s. of Joseph Ulam and Anna Auerbach; m. Françoise Aron 1941; one d.
Came to U.S. on invitation of Inst. for Advanced Study, Princeton, N.J. 36; mem. Soc. of Fellows and Lecturer, Harvard Univ. 36-40; Asst. Prof. Univ. of Wis. 41-43; Staff mem. and later Research Adviser, Los Alamos Scientific Laboratory, N.M. 44-67, now Consultant; also Prof. and Chair., Dept. of Mathematics, Univ. of Colo.; Visiting Prof., Harvard Univ., Mass. Inst. of Technology and Univs. of Colo. and Calif. at La Jolla; Board .of Govs. Weizmann Inst. of Science; Chair. Mathematics Section, American Asscn. for the Advancement of Science; mem. American Acad. of Arts and Sciences, Nat. Acad. of Sciences, American Philosophical Soc.; Polish Millenium Prize.
Leisure interests: chess, tennis.
Publs. *A Collection of Mathematical Problems* 60, *Mathematics and Logic* (with M. Kac) 68, *Sets, Points, Universes* 74, *Adventures of a Mathematician* 76; over 100 research papers in mathematics and physics.
c/o Mathematics Department, University of Colorado, Boulder, Colo., and Mathematics Department, University of Florida, Gainesville, Fla. 32608; Home: 1122 Old Santa Fé Trail, Santa Fé, New Mexico 87501, U.S.A.
Telephone: 492-7148 (Office); 983-1710 (Home).

Ulanfu; Chinese (Mongolian) party official; b. 1906, Suiyuan; ed. Mongolian-Tibetan School, Peking, Far Eastern Univ., Moscow.
Joined CCP 25; Alt. mem. 7th Cen. Cttee. of CCP 45; Chair. Inner Mongolia People's Govt. 47-67; Commdr., Political Commissar Inner Mongolia Mil. Region,

People's Liberation Army 47-67; Vice-Premier, State Council 54-; Chair. Nationalities Comm. 54-67; First Sec. CCP Inner Mongolia 54-67; Gen. 55; Alt. mem. Politburo, CCP 56-67; criticized and removed from office during Cultural Revolution 67; mem. 10th Cen. Cttee. of CCP 73.
People's Republic of China.

Ulanova, Galina Sergeyevna; Soviet ballerina; b. 10 Jan. 1910; ed. Leningrad Choreographic School.
Debut in Kirov Theatre 28, dancing the Chopin Suite (produced as *Les Sylphides* by Diaghilev Ballet); became star at the Kirov Theatre and then of the Bolshoi Ballet and danced many leading parts; has also made musical films including *Etoiles du Ballet Russe* shown at Int. Film Festival, Cannes 54; now teaches ballet at Bolshoi Choreographic School; People's Artist of the U.S.S.R; four State Prizes, Lenin Prize 57.
Principal roles: Odette-Odile (*Swan Lake*), Aurora (*Sleeping Beauty*), Masha (*The Nutcracker*), Giselle (*Giselle*), Maria (*Bakhchisarai Fountain*), Cinderella (*Cinderella*), Juliet (*Romeo and Juliet*), Parasha (*The Copper Horseman*), Tao Khoa (*The Red Flower*).
Publ. *Ballets Soviétiques* (The making of a ballerina).
State Academic Bolshoi Theatre, 1 Ploshchad Sverdlova, Moscow, U.S.S.R.

Ullastres Calvo, Alberto, LL.D.; Spanish economic historian and politician; b. 1914, Madrid; s. of Emilio and Jesusa Ullastres Calvo; ed. Madrid Univ.
Captain in Engineers (in reserve) of army; Prof. of Political Economy and Finance, Madrid Univ., Prof. of Econ. History, Leo XIII Ints.; Minister of Commerce 57-65; Amb. to the European Communities 65-; mem. Acad. of Moral and Political Sciences; Great Crosses Carlos III, Isabel la Católica (Spain) and of Germany, Austria, Colombia, Paraguay, Argentina, Egypt, Mauritania.
Leisure interests: metaphysics, gardening.
Spanish Delegation to the European Communities, 23-27 rue de la Loi, 1040 Brussels, Belgium.
Telephone: 13-88-50.

Ullendorff, Edward, M.A., D.PHIL.; British university professor; b. 25 Jan. 1920; s. of Frederic and Cilli Ullendorff; m. Dina Noack 1943; ed. Univs. of Jerusalem and Oxford.
War service in Eritrea and Ethiopia 41-46; Asst. Sec., Govt. of Palestine 46-47; Research Officer, Oxford Univ. Inst. of Colonial Studies 48-49; Lecturer, later Reader, in Semitic Languages, St. Andrews Univ. 50-59; Prof. of Semitic Languages, Manchester Univ. 59-64; Prof. of Ethiopian Studies, London Univ. 64-, Head of Africa Dept., School of Oriental and African Studies (SOAS); Chair. Asscn. of British Orientalists 63-64, Anglo-Ethiopian Soc. 65-68, Editorial Board of *Bulletin of SOAS* 68-; Schweich Lecturer, British Acad. 67; Pres. Soc. for Old Testament Study 71; Vice-Pres. Royal Asiatic Soc. 75-; Fellow, British Acad.; Haile Sellassie Prize for Ethiopian Studies 72, Hon. D. Litt. (St. Andrews Univ.).
Leisure interests: music, motoring in Scotland.
Publs. *Exploration and Study of Abyssinia* 45, Catalogues of Ethiopic MSS in the Bodleian Library 51, the Royal Library, Windsor Castle 53, Cambridge Univ. Library 61; *The Semitic Languages of Ethiopia* 55, *The Ethiopians* 60, 3rd edn. 73, *Comparative Grammar of the Semitic Languages* 64, *An Amharic Chrestomathy* 65, *Ethiopia and the Bible* 68, *Solomon and Sheba* 74, translated and annotated Emperor Haile Sellassie's autobiography 76 and others; articles and reviews in journals of learned socs.
School of Oriental and African Studies, London University, London, W.C.1; The Athenaeum, Pall Mall, London, England.
Telephone: 01-637 2388 (Office).

Ullmann, Liv Johanne; Norwegian actress; b. 16 Dec. 1938, Tokyo, Japan; d. of late Viggo Ullmann and of Janna (Lund) Ullmann; m. Dr. Gappe Stang 1960 (dissolved 1965); one d.
Worked in repertory company, Stavanger 56-59; has appeared at Nat. Theatre and Norwegian State Theatre, Oslo; Best Actress of the Year, Nat. Soc. of Critics in America 69, 70, 74; N.Y. Film Critics Award 73, 74; Hollywood Foreign Press Asscn.'s Golden Globe 73; Best Actress of the Year, Swedish T.V. 73, 74; Donatello Award (Italy) 75; Bambi Award (Fed. Repub. of Germany) 75; nominated for Tony Award as Best Stage Actress, debut on Broadway in *The Doll's House* 75.
Films include: *Pan* 65, *Persona* 66, *The Hour of the Wolf* 68, *Shame* 68, *The Passion of Anna* 69, *The Night Visitor* 71, *The Emigrants* 72, *Cries and Whispers* 72, *Pope Joan* 72, *Lost Horizon* 73, *40 Carats* 73, *The New Land* 73, *Zandy's Bride* 73, *Scenes from a Marriage* 74, *The Abdication* 74.
Plays include: *Brand* 73, *The Doll's House* 75; *The Six Faces of Women* (TV).
Svingen 3, Strommen, Norway.

Ulrich, Franz Heinrich; German business executive; b. 6 July 1910; ed. German Univs.
Member of Board of Man. Dirs. Deutsche Bank AG; Chief Exec. 76-, mem. Board of Management 76-; Chair. Supervisory Board Daimler Banz AG, Stuttgart, Deutsche Texaco AG, Hamburg, Deutsche Ueberseeische Bank, Berlin/Hamburg, Enka Glanzstoff AG, Wuppertal, Klöckner-Humboldt-Deutz AG, Cologne, Mannesmann AG, Düsseldorf, Otto Wolff AG, Cologne, Bergmann-Elektricitäts-Werke AG, Berlin; Deputy Chair. Supervisory Board Allianz-Versicherungs AG, Munich/Berlin, Bayer AG, Leverkusen, Berliner Disconto Bank AG, Berlin, Siemens AG, Munich; mem. Supervisory Board Münchener Rückversicherungs-Gesellschaft, Munich, Zentralgesellschaft VFW-Fokker mbH, Düsseldorf.
Deutsche Bank AG, Königsalle 45, Düsseldorf, Federal Republic of Germany.

Ulveseth, Ingvald Johan; Norwegian politician; b. 25 Aug. 1924, Fjell, Hordaland; ed. Norwegian Inst. of Technology.
Consultant Construction Engineer, Bergen 49-52; Municipal Engineer, Fjell 52-61; mem. Fjell Municipal Council and Exec. Cttee. 56-67, Mayor 58-65; with Brodrene Ulveseth, Bergen 61-65; Under-Sec. of State, Ministry of Local Govt. and Labour 64-65; mem. Storting (Parl.) 65-; Chair. Man. Board *Bergens Arbeiderblad* 68-; Deputy Chair. Standing Cttee. on Industry 69-73; mem. Board Norsk Hydro 70-; Gov. Sogn and Fjordane 71-73; Minister of Industry 73-; Labour.
Ministry of Industry, Oslo Dep., Norway.

Umba Kyamitala, M.SC.; Zairian mining executive; b. 20 Feb. 1937, Elisabethville (now Lubumbashi); s. of Ngoie Mbuluku and Mwamba Kima; m. Ngoie Ya Kachina 1961; two s. one d.; ed. Nat. Univ. of Zaire and U.S.A.
Employed in mine at Kipushi, La Générale des Carrières et Mines du Zaïre (Gécamines) 67, Planning and Admin. of Mines and Quarries 69, Dir. of Mines and Quarries 72, Gen. Man. Nov. 73-; mem. American Asscn. of Mining Engineers and Metallurgists; major projects: sub-level excavation in Northwest Massif 67; application of machinery to opencast mining.
Leisure interest: swimming.
Gécamines, B.P. 45, Lubumbashi, Zaire.
Telephone: 91-105.

Umri, Gen. Hassan; Yemen Republican politician.
Took part in revolution against Imamate 62, Minister of Transport Sept.-Oct. 62, of Communications Oct. 62-April 63; mem. Council of Revolutionary Command 62-

63; Vice-Pres. of Yemen 63-66; mem. Political Bureau 63-66; Prime Minister Jan.-April 65, July 65-Sept. 66, Dec. 67-Sept. 68; Mil. Gov.-Gen. of Yemen Sept. 68-July 69; also C.-in-C. of Army; Prime Minister Aug.-Sept. 71; in exile in Lebanon until Jan. 75; returned to Yemen A. R. Jan. 75.

Underwood, Benton J., M.A., PH.D.; American psychologist; b. 28 Feb. 1915, Center Point, Iowa; s. of Willie B. and Blanche C. Underwood; m. Hazel Louise Olson 1939; two d.; ed. Cornell Coll., Univ. of Missouri and State Univ. of Iowa.
Public School Teacher 36-39; U.S. Navy 42-46; Asst. Prof. Northwestern Univ. 46-48, Assoc. Prof. 48-52, Prof. 52-, Chair. Dept. of Psychology 67-70; mem. Nat. Acad. of Sciences; Warren Medal (Soc. of Experimental Psychologists) 64; Hon. D.Sc. (Cornell Coll.).
Publs. *Experimental Psychology* 49 (revised edn. 66), *Psychological Research* 57, *Meaningfulness and Verbal Learning* 60.
Department of Psychology, Northwestern University, Evanston, Ill. 60201; Home: 1745 Stevens Drive, Glenview, Ill. 60025, U.S.A.
Telephone: 492-7359 (Office); PA-4-3063 (Home).

Underwood, Cecil H., M.A., LL.D.; American politician and businessman; b. 5 Nov. 1922; ed. Salem Coll., West Virginia Univ.
U.S. Army Reserve Corps. 42-43; high-school teacher 43-46; mem. staff Marietta Coll. 46-50; Vice-Pres. Salem Coll. 50-56; Vice-Pres. Island Creek Coal Co. 61-64; Public Relations Counsellor 64-; mem. West Virginia House of Delegates 44-56 and Minority Floor Leader 49-54; Gov. of West Virginia 57-61; Temp. Chair. Republican Nat. Convention 60; Dir. Civic Affairs, Northeastern Region, Monsanto Co. 65-66; Vice-Pres. Govt. and Civic Affairs, Monsanto Co., Washington, D.C. 67-; Pres. Fanswood Inc., Huntington 68-; mem. Governing Council, Nat. Municipal League 66-; Pres. Cecil H. Underwood Asscns. 65-; Pres. Bethany Coll. 72-; eight hon. degrees.
Pendleton Heights, Bethany, W. Va. 26032, U.S.A.

Underwood, Eric John, C.B.E., PH.D., F.R.S.; Australian professor of agriculture; b. 7 Sept. 1905, London, England; s. of James Underwood and Elizabeth (née Lowe) Underwood; m. Erica Reid Chandler 1934; two s. two d.; ed. Univs. of Western Australia, Cambridge and Wisconsin Univs.
Research Officer in Animal Nutrition, Dept. of Agriculture, Western Australia 32-45; Hackett Prof. of Agriculture and Dir. Inst. of Agriculture, Univ. of W. Australia 46-70; mem. of Exec. Commonwealth Scientific and Industrial Org. 66-75; Centennial Prof. of Nutrition Univ. of Calif. 68; Pres. Australian and New Zealand Asscn. for the Advancement of Science 73; Harkness Fellow, Commonwealth Fund of New York 36; F.A.A., F.A.I.A.S., F.A.S.A.P.; Hon. mem. American Inst. of Nutrition; Hon. D.Rur.Sci. (Univ. of New England); Hon. D.Sc.Agric. (Univ. of W. Australia); Hon. D.Agric. Sci. (Univ. of Melbourne); Gold Medal of Australian Inst. of Agricultural Science 51, Kelvin Medal of Royal Soc. of W. Australia 59, Farrer Memorial Medal 67; Burnett Medal, Australian Acad. of Science 73.
Leisure interests: reading, gardening.
Publs. *Principles of Animal Production* 46, *Trace Elements in Human and Animal Nutrition* 56, 3rd edn.) 71, *The Mineral Nutrition of Livestock* (F.A.O./C.A.B.) 66; and approx. 100 research papers and reviews.
Commonwealth Scientific and Industrial Research Organization, Private Bag, P.O., Wembley, W.A.6014; Home: 3 Cooper Street, Nedlands, W. Australia.
Telephone: 87-4233 (Office); 86-2620 (Home).

Unger, Leonard, A.B.; American diplomatist; b. 17 Dec. 1917, San Diego, Calif.; s. of Louis Allen and Rachel Seidman Unger; m. Anne Axon Unger 1944; three s. two d.; ed. Harvard Univ.
National Resources Planning Board 39-41; Dept. of State 41-, served Trieste, Naples; Officer in Charge of Politico-Military Affairs, European Regional Affairs Div., State Dept. 53-57; Dep. Chief of Mission, American Embassy, Bangkok, Thailand 58-62; Ambassador to Laos 62-64; Deputy Asst. Sec. of State for Far Eastern Affairs 65-67; Amb. to Thailand 67-74, to Taiwan 74-.
Leisure interests: music, gardening, reading, tennis.
American Embassy, 2 Chung Hsiao Road, Sec. 2, Taipei, Taiwan; Home: 12701 Circle Drive, Rockville Md. 20850, U.S.A.

Ungerer, Paul; German merchant and company executive; b. 12 March 1912, Frankfurt am Main; s. of Friedrich Ungerer and Katharina Brenner; m. Leyda Pezzini 1941; one s.; ed. mercantile apprenticeship.
Joined DEGUSSA as apprentice in Precious Metals Dept. 30, specialist training in all depts. and subsidiaries 34, del. to DEGUSSA Agent in Shanghai 35, Man. of DEGUSSA Office in Shanghai 40, of Branch Office in Hamburg 49, Head of Carbon Black and Pigments Div., Frankfurt 54, Deputy Vice-Pres. of Exec. Board 61, Pres. 73-.
Leisure interests: music, fine arts in general, travelling.
DEGUSSA, Weissfrauenstrasse 9, 6000 Frankfurt 1, Federal Republic of Germany.
Telephone: 0611 2182290.

Unsöld, Albrecht Otto Johannes, DR.PHIL.; German physicist; b. 20 April 1905, Bolheim, Württemberg; s. of Johannes Unsöld and Clara Müller; m. Dr. Liselotte Kühnert 1934; three s. one d.; ed. Univs. of Tübingen and Munich.
Assistant, Inst. of Theoretical Physics, Univ. of Munich 27; Fellow, Int. Educ. Board 28; Lecturer, Univ. of Munich 29, Univ. of Hamburg 30; Prof. of Theoretical Physics, Dir. Inst. of Theoretical Physics and Observatory, Univ. of Kiel 32-73; corresp. mem. Bavarian Acad. of Sciences, Göttingen Acad. of Sciences; Assoc. Royal Astronomical Soc., London; Hon. mem. Royal Astronomical Soc. of Canada; Copernicus Prize 43, Catherine Wolfe Bruce Gold Medal Astronomical Soc. of the Pacific 56; Gold Medal of Royal Astronomical Soc. 57; Dr.rer.Nat. h.c. Utrecht State Univ. 61, Univ. of Munich 72; Univ. Medal Liège 69; Hon. D.Sc. (Edinburgh) 70; foreign mem. Provinciaal Utrechts Genootschap van Kunsten en Wetenschappen, Utrecht 61; mem. Int. Acad. of Astronautics, Paris 61, Deutsche Akademie der Naturforscher Leopoldina, Halle, 62, Kungliga Fysiografiska Sällskapet i Lund 65; Fellow American Asscn. for Advancement of Science 68; Cothenius Gold Medal of Deutsche Akad. der Naturforscher Leopoldina, Halle 73.
Leisure interests: painting, music.
Publs. *Physik der Sternatmosphären* 38 (2nd edn. 55). *Der neue Kosmos* 67 (2nd edn. 74); translations into English, Italian, Japanese 68, *Sterne und Menschen* (essays and lectures) 72.
Sternwartenweg 17, Kiel 23, Federal Republic of Germany.
Telephone: 84205.

Untermeyer, Louis; American author; b. 1 Oct. 1885, New York City; s. of Emanuel and Julia (Michael) Untermeyer; m. Bryna Ivens; three s.
Contrib. Editor *The Liberator* and *The Seven Arts;* Lecturer Amherst, Knox, Michigan and other univs.
Leisure interests: playing with a household of cats and pottering in the garden.
Publs. include: *Roast Leviathan* 23, *Food and Drink* 32, *Chip—My Life and Times* 33, *Poetry—Its Appreciation and Enjoyment, The Donkey of God* 33, *Selected Poems and Parodies* 35, *Rainbow in the Sky* 35, *Play in Poetry* 37, *Heinrich Heine: Paradox and Poet* (2 vols.) 37, *From Another World* (autobiography) 39, *Stars to*

Steer By 40, *Modern American and British Poetry* (revised) 42, *A Treasury of Great Poems* 42, *A Treasury of Laughter* 46, *The Book of Noble Thoughts* 46, *The Love Poems of Robert and Elizabeth Browning* 47, *An Anthology of the New England Poets* 48, *The Inner Sanctum*, *Walt Whitman* 49, *The New Modern American and British Poetry* 50, *The Best Humor Annual* 50, 51, 52, *The Magic Circle* 52, *Makers of the Modern World* 55, *A Treasury of Ribaldry* 56, *Lives of the Poets* 59, *Britannica Library of Great American Writing* 60, *Long Feud: Selected Poems* 62, *The Letters of Robert Frost to Louis Untermeyer* 63, *The World's Great Stories* 64, *Labyrinth of Love* 65, *Bygones: An Autobiography* 65, *The Paths of Poetry* 66, *The Firebringer and Other Stories* 68, *The Pursuit of Poetry* 69, *Men and Women: The Poetry of Love* 70, *Cat O'Nine Tales* 71, *Great Humor* 72, *Fifty Modern American and British Poets: 1920-1970* 73.
Great Hill Road, Newtown, Conn., U.S.A.
Telephone: 203-426-2383.

Upadhyay, Shailendra Kumar; Nepalese diplomatist; b. 13 Sept. 1929, India; *s.* of Gopal Prasad Upadhyay and Uma Devi Upadhyay; *m.* 1st Sharmistha Upadhyay, 2nd Beena Sharma; three *s.*; ed. Benares Hindu Univ. Founder member Communist Party of Nepal 50, mem. Cen. Cttee. and Political Bureau 50-56; Founder Communist Party of Nepal 58; Asst. Minister for Forests, Food and Agriculture 62-64; Minister in charge of Panchayat 65; mem. Nat. Panchayat 63-71; Vice-Chair. Nat. Planning Comm. 69; Minister for Home and Panchayat and Minister for Land Reforms and Information 70-71; Perm. Rep. to UN June 72-.
Leisure interests: reading, riding, trekking, painting, golf.
Permanent Mission of Nepal to United Nations, 711 Third Avenue, Room 1806, New York, N.Y. 10017; 430 500 East 77th Street, New York, N.Y. 10021, U.S.A.; 5/108 Jawala Khel, Lalitpur, Kathmandu, Nepal.
Telephone: YU6-1989 (Office); 737-2633 (Home); 21587 (Nepal).

Updike, John Hoyer, A.B.; American writer; b. 18 March 1932; ed. Shillington High School, Pennsylvania, and Harvard Coll.
Reporter on the magazine *New Yorker* 55-57.
Publs. *The Carpentered Hen* (poems) 58, *The Poorhouse Fair* (novel) 59, *The Same Door* (short stories) 59, *Rabbit, Run* (novel) 60, *Pigeon Feathers and Other Stories* 62, *The Centaur* (novel) 63, *Telephone Poles and Other Poems* 63, *Assorted Prose* 65, *Of the Farm* (novel) 65, *The Music School* (short stories) 66, *Couples* (novel), *Midpoint and other poems* 69, *Bech: A Book* 70, *Rabbit Redux* 72, *Museums and Women and Other Stories* 72, *Buchanan Dying* (novel) 74, *A Month of Sundays* (novel) 75, *Picked-up Pieces* 76.
Labor-in-Vain Road, Ipswich, Mass. 01938, U.S.A.

Upmark, Erik Gustaf Johan; Swedish administrator; b. 1904, Uppsala; *s.* of Col. Johan Upmark and Jenny Dahlberg; *m.* Maja Erhardt 1928; two *s.* two *d.*; ed. Uppsala Hoegre Allmaenna Laeroverk, and Technical Univ., Stockholm.
With Vattenbyggnadsbyraan A.B. 27; with Messrs. Rendel, Palmer and Tritton 28; Sec. Swedish Water Power Asscn. 35; Chair. State Fuel and Power Comm. 47; Gen. Man. Swedish State Rlys. 49-69; Chair. State Geotechnical Inst. 71-76; mem. Royal Swedish Acad. of Engineering Sciences, Chair. Transport Research Comm. 69-74; Pres. Int. Union of Railways 67-68.
Leisure interest: botany.
Home: Storgatan 44, S-11455 Stockholm, Sweden.
Telephone: 08-603247.

Uquaili, Nabi Baksh Mohammed Sidiq, F.C.A.; Pakistani chartered accountant and banker; b. 11 Aug. 1913, Karachi; *m.* 1947; one *s.* one *d.*
Experience of agricultural banking, commercial banking, central banking, exchange control and industrial and investment banking for over thirty years; Controller of Foreign Exchange, State Bank of Pakistan 51-58; Rep. of Pakistan, Econ. and Social Council of UN, 57 and 58; Man. Dir. Pakistan Industrial Credit and Investment Corpn. 58-66; Minister of Finance 66-69; Consultant to World Bank; mem. Board several financial and industrial enterprises in Pakistan; Vice-Chair. Board of Dirs. Habib Bank (Overseas) Ltd.; Grösses Bundesverdienstkreuz; awarded Sitara-i-Quaid-i-Azam 61; Sitara-i-Pakistan 64.
Leisure interests: reading, gardening.
22 F Dawood Colony, Stadium Road, Karachi-5, Pakistan.
Telephone: 225432 (Office); 411013 (Home).

Urabe, Shizutaro; Japanese architect; b. 31 March 1909; ed. Kyoto Univ.
Kurashiki Rayon Co. Ltd. 34-64; Lecturer (part-time) in Architecture, Osaka Univ. Technical Course 54-55; Lecturer (part-time) in Architecture, Kyoto Univ. Technical Course 62-66; Pres. K.K., S. Urabe & Assoc. Architects 62-; Prize of *Mainichi Shuppan Bunka Sho* (publication) 61; Osaka Prefecture Architectural Contest Prize 62; *Annual of Architecture* Prize 63; Architectural Inst. of Japan Prize 64; Osaka Prefecture Order of Merit 65.
Buildings include: Ohara Museum (Annex) 61, Suita Service Area 63 and other offices of Japan Road Corpn. 65, Kurashiki Int. Hotel 63, Aizenbashi Hospital and Nursery School, etc. 65, Asahi Broadcasting Co. Ltd. (consultant) 66, Tokyo Zokei Univ. 66, Tokyo Women's Christian Coll., Research Inst. 67.
Offices: S. Urabe and Assoc. Architects, 7th Floor, New Hankyu Building, 8, Umeda, Kita-ku, Osaka; Shin-Nihonbashi Building, 3-1, Nihonbashi-dori, Chuo-ku, Tokyo; Home: 1-181, Kotoen, Nishinomiya Hyogo, Japan.

Urbanik, Kazimierz, D.SC.; Polish mathematician; b. 5 Feb. 1930, Krzemieniec; ed. Wrocław Univ.
Docent 57-60, Assoc. Prof. 60-64, Prof. 64-; Corresp. mem. Polish Acad. of Sciences (PAN) 65-73, mem. 73-, now mem. Presidium of PAN and Vice Dir. and mem. Scientific Council of Mathematical Inst.; Dir. Mathematical Inst. of Wrocław Univ. 67-; mem. Editorial Staff, *Studia Mathematica, Zeitschrift für Wahrscheinlichkeitstheorie und verwandte Gebiete, Journal of Multivariant Analysis*; mem. many Polish and foreign socs.; Knight's and Officer's Crosses, Order of Polonia Restituta, Prize of Polish Mathematical Soc., State Prize, 2nd Class 64, City of Wrocław Prize 70, Order of Banner of Labour, 2nd Class 74, Medal of 30th Anniversary of People's Poland 74.
Leisure interests: tourism, motoring, cooking secrets of various nations.
Publs. over 100, mainly concerned with the theory of probability, achievements in prediction theory, generalized processes and universal algebras.
Ul. Stefczyka 8, 51-662 Wrocław, Poland.

Urbański, Tadeusz; Polish university professor; b. 26 Oct. 1901, Krasnodar; *s.* of Rajmund Urbański and Jadwiga Pogorzelska; *m.* Jadwiga Maciejowska 1926; two *d.*; ed. Warsaw Technical Univ.
Chemical industry Poland and France 24-32; Asst. Prof. of Organic Technology, Warsaw Technical Univ. 33-36, Prof. 36-39, 46-72, Prof. Emer. 72-; Dean, Faculty of Chemistry 38-39, 46-50; Chemist C.N.R.S., Paris 40; Principal Exp. Officer Ministry of Supply, London 40-46; Dir. Inst. Organic Chemistry, Polish Acad. Sciences 58-68; Sen. Foreign Fellow N.S.F., U.S.A. and Visiting Prof. Univs. Tien-Tsin (China) 58, Illinois and Maryland 65-66, London 70,Queen's Kingston, Ont. 74; Visiting Scientist Nat. Chemical Laboratory, Poona 73; Pres. Polish Chemical Soc. 50, 68-70; mem. Polish Acad. of Sciences; foreign mem. German Acad. Leopoldina; mem. IUPAC Bureau 57-61; Sec.

Div. Cttee. of Organic Chemistry IUPAC 61-65; Nat. Rep. Comm. on Molecular Structure and Spectroscopy IUPAC 61-; mem. Editorial Advisory Boards of several int. journals; State Prizes 49 and 52; van't Hoff Award 61, Sniadecki Medal, Polish Chemical Soc. 65; Copernicus Medal of Polish Acad. of Sciences 73; Jurzykowski Foundation Award, New York 73; Commdr. Cross with Star, Order Polonia Restituta.
Leisure interest: lawn tennis.
Publs. *Theory of Nitration* (in Polish) 54, *Chemie und Technologie der Explosivstoffe*, 3 vols. 61-64 (English 64-67), *Nitro Compounds* (Editor) 64.
Office: Koszykowa 75, 00-662 Warsaw; Home: Nowo-wiejska 22/27, 00-665 Warsaw, Poland.
Telephone: 28-13-28.

Uren, Thomas; Australian politician; b. 28 May 1921, Balmain, Sydney.
Served with Royal Australian Artillery 39, 2nd Australian Imperial Force 41, in Changi prisoner-of-war camp 42-45; mem. Parl. for Reid 58-; mem. Fed. Parl. Labor Party Exec. 69-; First Minister of Urban and Regional Devt. 72-75; del. to Australasian Area Conf. of Commonwealth Parl. Asscn., Darwin 68, to Australian Parl. Mission to Europe 68, to Commonwealth Parl. Asscn. Conf., Canberra 70; Labor Party.
Parliament House, Canberra, A.C.T., Australia.

Urey, Harold Clayton, B.S., PH.D., D.SC.; American chemist; b. 29 April 1893, Walkerton, Ind.; s. of Samuel Clayton Urey and Cora Rebecca Reinoehl; m. Frieda Daum Urey 1926; one s. three d.; ed. Univs. of Montana and California.
Research chemist, Barrett Chemical Co. 18-19; Instructor, Univ. of Montana 19-21; American-Scandinavian Foundation Fellow, Copenhagen 23-24; Assoc. in Chem., Johns Hopkins Univ. 24-29; Assoc. Prof. Columbia Univ. 29-34, Prof. 34-45; Dir. of War Research, SAM Laboratories 40-45; Distinguished Service Prof. of Chem., The Enrico Fermi Inst. for Nuclear Studies, Univ. of Chicago 45-52, Martin A. Ryerson Prof. 52-58; Visiting Prof., Oxford 56-57; Prof. at large, Calif. 58-70; Visiting Prof., U.K. 71; mem. Nat. Acad. of Sciences, etc.; foreign mem. Royal Soc. (London), and Swedish, Belgian, Irish, Indian and American Scientific Socs.; Hon. D.Sc. (Princeton, Montana, Newark, Columbia, Oxford, Washington and Lee, Michigan, Athens, Yale, MacMaster, Indiana, Durham, Birmingham, Saskatchewan, Pittsburgh, Chicago, Manchester, Israel Inst. of Technology Franklin & Marshall Coll. and Gustavus Adolphus Coll.); Hon. LL.D. (Calif., Wayne, Notre Dame Univs.); D.Hum. (Hebrew Union Coll.); many awards and prizes including Nobel Prize for Chem. 34, Willard Gibbs Medal (American Chemical Soc.) 34, Davy Medal (Royal Soc., London) 40, Franklin Medal 43, Medal for Merit 46, Cordoza Award 54, Nat. Medal for Sciences 64, American Acad. Achievement Award 66, Linus Pauling Award 70, NASA Scientific Achievement Award 73, V. M. Goldschmidt Medal, Geochemical Soc. (Utah) 75.
Leisure interests: gardening, raising of orchids.
Publs. *Atoms, Molecules and Quanta* (with A. E. Ruark) 30, *The Planets* 52.
Revelle College, University of California, San Diego, La Jolla, Calif.; Home: 7890 Torrey Lane, La Jolla, Calif. 92037, U.S.A.
Telephone: 453-2000-1451 (Office); 714-454-1640 (Home).

Ürgüplü, Ali Suat Hayri; Turkish politician; b. 1903, Damascus, Syria; m.; one s.; ed. Lycée Galatasaray, Istanbul, and Univ. of Istanbul.
Turkish Sec. Mixed Courts of Arbitration 26-29; Magistrate Supreme Commercial Court, Istanbul 29-32; in private legal practice 32-39; mem. Turkish Nat. Assembly 39-46; Minister of Customs and Monopolies 43-46; resigned and left People's Party 46; re-elected to Grand Nat. Assembly 50 and joined Democratic Party;

mem. and Vice-Chair. Council of Europe 50-52; Amb. to Fed. Repub. of Germany 52-55, to U.K. 55-57, to U.S.A. 57-60, to Spain 60; Senator (Independent) 61-63 (Presidential Appointee) 66-; Speaker of Senate 61-63; Prime-Minister Feb.-Oct. 65; Prime Minister designate April-May 72.
Sahil Cad 19, Yesilyurt, Istanbul, Turkey.

Uri, Pierre Emmanuel; French professor and economic consultant; b. 20 Nov. 1911, Paris; s. of Isaac Uri and Hélène Kahn; m. Monique Blanchetière 1939; two s. two d.; ed. Lycée Henri IV, Ecole Normale Supérieure and Princeton Univ.
Professor of Philosophy 36-40; Research Economist 44-47; Econ. and Financial Adviser to French Planning Comm. 47-52; Prof. Nat. School of Public Admin. 47-51; Econ. Dir. European Coal and Steel Community (ECSC) 52-59, Econ. Adviser, Common Market 58-59; European Rep., Lehman Brothers 59-61; Econ. Consultant, particularly Counsellor for Studies, Atlantic Inst. 62-; Chair. Experts' Group on Long Term Development in European Economic Community 60-64; Chair. Experts' Group on Competitive Capacity of the European Community 68-70; Prof., Univ. Paris IX 69-; Vice-Chair. UN Group on Multinational Corpns. 73-74; mem. French Econ. and Social Council 74-; Chevalier de la Légion d'Honneur, Croix de Guerre, etc.
Leisure interests: theatre-going, travelling.
Publs. *La réforme de l'enseignement* 37, *Le fonds monétaire international* 45, *French National Economic Budgets* 47-48, *Report of French Delegation on Treaty of Paris Instituting the Coal and Steel Community* 51, *Report of the Inter-Governmental Committee on the Common Market and Euratom* 56, *Report on the Economic Situation of the European Community Countries* 58, *Dialogue des Continents* 63, *Une Politique Monétaire pour L'Amérique Latine* 65, *Pour gouverner* 67, *From Commonwealth to Common Market* 68, *Un Avenir pour L'Europe Agricole* 71, *Trade and Investment Policies for the '70's* 71, *Plan quinquennal pour une Révolution* 73, *L'Europe se gaspille* 73, *Développement sans dépendance* 74, *Report on the Introduction of a Capital Gains Tax in France* 75.
1 avenue du Président Wilson, 75116 Paris, France.
Telephone: 723-97-42.

Uris, Leon Marcus; American writer; b. 3 Aug. 1924; ed. High School.
Served with the United States Marine Corps 42-45.
Publs. *Battle Cry* 53 (novel and screenplay), *The Angry Hills* 55, *Exodus* 57, *Mila 18* 60, *Gunfight at the OK Corral* (screenplay), *Armageddon* 64, *Topaz* 67, *QB VII* 70; with others *Exodus Revisited* (Photo essay) 59.
c/o Doubleday Publishing Co., Inc., Garden City, N.Y. 11530, U.S.A.

Urquhart, Alastair Hugh, C.B.E.; Australian stockbroker; b. 3 Nov. 1919, Manly, N.S.W.; s. of late G. R. Urquhart; m. Joyce Muriel Oswald 1947; two d.; ed. Sydney Church of England Grammar School.
Senior Partner, Australian stockbroking firm; mem. Sydney Stock Exchange 49-, Chair. 59-66; Vice-Pres. Australian Associated Stock Exchanges 60-63, Pres. 59, 64-66; Army Service 40-45; official of commercial and civic orgs.
Leisure interests: golf, surfing, yachting.
Office: 15 O'Connell Street, Sydney 2000, N.S.W.; Home: 4 Wentworth Place, Point Piper, Sydney 2027, N.S.W., Australia.

Urquhart, Brian E.; British United Nations official; b. 19 Feb. 1919, Bridport, Dorset; s. of Murray Urquhart and Bertha (née Rendall); m. 1st Alfreda Huntington 1944, two s. one d.; m. 2nd Sidney Howard 1963, one s. one d.; ed. Westminster School and Christ Church, Oxford.
Army service 39-45; Personal Asst. to Exec. Sec. of Preparatory Comm. of UN, London 45-46; Personal

Asst. to Trygve Lie, First Sec.-Gen. of UN 46-49; has served in Office of UN Sec.-Gen. since 49; served in various capacities relating to peace-keeping operations in Office of UN Under-Sec.-Gen. for Special Political Affairs 54-71; Exec. Sec. 1st and 2nd UN Int. Confs. on Peaceful Uses of Atomic Energy 55, 58; Deputy Exec. Sec. Preparatory Comm. of IAEA 57; Asst. to Sec.-Gen.'s Special Rep. in the Congo July-Oct. 60; UN Rep. in Katanga, Congo, Nov. 61-Feb. 62; Asst. Sec.-Gen. UN July 72-Jan. 74; Under Sec.-Gen. for Special Political Affairs UN Feb. 74-.
Publ. *Hammarskjöld* 73.
131 East 66th Street, New York, N.Y. 10021, U.S.A.

Urrutia Aparicio, Carlos, PH.D.; Guatemalan internationalist; b. 6 Jan. 1927, Guatemala; m. María Graciela Angel de Urrutia 1957; three s. one d.; ed. Colegio de Infantes Guatemala, Univ. of Dayton, Ohio, George Washington Univ., Washington, D.C., and American Univ., Washington, D.C.
Pan American Union 55-58; Alt. Perm. Rep. of Guatemala to UN 58; Consul-Gen. of Guatemala in New York 58-60; Ambassador of Guatemala to Organization of American States (OAS) and Perm. Rep. to Council of OAS 60-63; special OAS envoy to Uruguay and Paraguay 63; Chief, OAS Div. of Gen. Information 63-65, Technical Dir. of the OAS Chronicle, and Special Asst. to Dept. of Information and Public Affairs 65-68; Adviser to OAS Asst. Sec.-Gen. 68-75; Adviser to Special Cttee. of XIII Meeting of Consultation of Ministers of Foreign Affairs 69; Dir. of OAS Office in Panama 75-; Order of Rubén Dario (Nicaragua) and Order of El Quetzal (Guatemala).
Leisure interests: horseback riding, reading, playing pool.
Publs. *Juridical Aspects of the Anglo-Guatemalan Controversy: in Re Belize* 51, *Opúsculo sobre el Derecho de Asilo Diplomático* 52, *Puerto Rico, América y las Naciones Unidas* 54, *Diplomatic Asylum in Latin America* 60, *Páginas internacionales de la vida democrática de Guatemala* 61.
Office of the General Secretariat, Organization of American States, Calle Uruguay 2-49, Panama, Panama.
Telephone: 64-1349, 64-3367; 69-0910 (Home).

Ursi, H.E. Cardinal Corrado; Italian ecclesiastic; b. 26 July 1908; s. of Riccardo Ursi and Apollonia Sterlicchio.
Ordained Priest 31; Bishop of Nardo 51, Archbishop of Acorensa 61, Archbishop of Naples 66-; created Cardinal by Pope Paul VI 67.
Largo Donnaregina 23-80134, Naples, Italy.
Telephone: 449118.

Ursu, Ioan, PH.D.; Romanian physicist; b. 5 April 1928, Mânăstireni, Cluj; s. of Ioan Ursu and Ana Abrudan; m. Lucia Flămându 1930; two s. one d.; ed. Univ. of Cluj and Univ. of Princeton, U.S.A.
Assistant Prof., Univ. of Cluj 49, Prof. and Head of Dept. 60, Vice-Rector 61; Prof. and Head of Dept., Univ. of Bucharest 68-; Dir.-Gen., Inst. for Atomic Physics 68-; Pres. State Cttee. for Nuclear Energy 69-, Nat. Council for Science and Tech. 72-; Corresp. mem. Romanian Acad. 63, mem. 74-; mem. Board of Govs. IAEA 71, Vice-Pres. 72; mem. Exec. Council, European Physical Soc. 68, Vice-Pres. 75-; mem. Romanian Soc. of Physics and Chem., Physical Socs. of U.S.A., Belgium, France; mem. Board of Int. Soc. of Magnetic Resonance, Cttee. of Assen. of Mechanical and Physical Energy Research Establishments (AMPERE); mem. Grand Nat. Assembly; Order of Labour, Order of Star of the Socialist Republic of Romania, Order of Tudor Vladimirescu, Order of 23rd August, Grosses Verdienstkreuz mit Stern und Schulterband (Fed. Repub. of Germany) and others.
Publs. *Rezonanţa Electronică de Spin* 65, *La Résonance Paramagnétique Electronique* 68, *Magnetic Resonance and Related Phenomena* (Ed.) 71, *Energia atomică* 73

and about 100 papers on atomic and nuclear physics, nuclear materials, nuclear technologies, solid state physics, interaction of radiation with matter.
National Council for Science and Technology, str. Roma 32-34, Bucharest 1; Institutul de Fizica Atomica, P.O. Box 35, Bucharest; Home: Str. Grigore Mora 24, Bucharest 1, Romania.
Telephone: 33-43-01 (Council); 80-47-90 (Institute).

Urwick, Lt.-Col. Lyndall, O.B.E., M.C., M.A., F.B.I.M., M.I.P.E., C.I.MECH.E.; British industrial management consultant; b. 3 March 1891, Malvern, Worcs.; s. of late Sir Henry Urwick; m. 1st Joan Wilhelmina Bedford 1923, one s. one d.; 2nd Betty Warrand 1941, one s. one d.; ed. New Coll., Oxford.
Member staff Rowntree and Co. Ltd. 22-28; Dir. Int. Management Inst. Geneva 28-33; Chair. Urwick, Orr and Partners Ltd. (management consultants) 34-63; Consultant H.M. Treasury 40-42; G.S.O.1, Petroleum Warfare Dept. 42-44; Chair. Cttee. on Education for Management 47; Vice-Chair. British Inst. of Management 47; Gold Medal Int. Cttee. for Scientific Management 51; Wallace Clark Int. Management Award 55; Henry Laurence Gantt Gold Medal 61; The Taylor Key 63; Bowie Medal 68; Knight of St. Olaf (Norway) 48; Hon. D.Sc. (Univ. of Aston) 69; Hon. LL.D. (Univ. of York, Toronto) 72.
Publs. *The Meaning of Rationalisation* 29, *Distribution in Europe and the U.S.A.* 31, *Management of To-morrow* 33, *Organising a Sales Office* 37, *Committees in Organization* 37, *The Development of Scientific Management in Great Britain* 38, *Dynamic Administration* 41, *The Elements of Administration* 44, *The Making of Scientific Management*, Vol. I, *Thirteen Pioneers* 45, Vol. II, *British Industry* 45, Vol. III, *The Hawthorne Experiments* 48, *Freedom and Co-ordination* 49, *Management Education in American Business* 54, *The Pattern of Management* 56, *Leadership in the XX Century* 57, *Organisation* 66.
Urwick Orr & Partners Ltd., 50 Doughty Street, London, WC1N 2LS, England; and 83 Kenneth Street, Longueville, N.S.W. 2066, Australia.
Telephone: 01-405 4683; and Sydney 422102.

Usami, Makoto; Japanese banker; b. 5 Feb. 1901, Tokyo; s. of Katsuo Usami; m. Hiroko Nakamura 1937; ed. Keio Univ.
Entered Mitsubishi Bank Ltd. 24, Man. Econ. Research Dept. 47, Man. Gen. Affairs Dept. 49, Dir. 50, Dir. and Man. Head Office 51-54, Man. Dir. 54-59, Deputy Pres. 59-61, Pres. 61-64; Gov. Bank of Japan 64-Dec. 69. Chair. Board of Counsellors, Keio Univ. 66-; Chair. Fed. of the Bankers' Asscn. of Japan 62-63.
Leisure interests: Japanese chess, reading.
Room 524, Marunouchi Yaesu Building 6-2, 2 Marunouchi, Chiyoda-ku, Tokyo 100; Home: 24-15, 2 Minami-Aoyama, Minato-ku, Tokyo, Japan.
Telephone: 211-2670 (Office); 401-8675 (Home).

Usery, William J.; American industrial relations executive; b. 21 Dec. 1923, Hardwick, Ga.; ed. Georgia Mil. Coll., Mercer Univ.
Served U.S. Navy 43-46; Maintenance Machinist, Armstrong Cork Co. 49-55; Grand Lodge Rep., Int. Asscn. of Machinists and Aerospace Workers (IAM), AFL-CIO 56, IAM Special Rep., Cape Canaveral Air Force Test Facilities 56, IAM Rep. to President's Missile Sites Labor Cttee. 61-67; Co-ordinator for Union Activities, Manned Spacecraft Center, Houston, Tex.; Co-founder, Cape Kennedy Labor-Management Relations Council 67, Chair. 68; Asst. Sec. of Labor for Labor-Management Relations 69-73, Sec. of Labor Feb. 76-; Dir. of Fed. Mediation and Conciliation Service 73-76; Special Asst. to the Pres. 74-75, for Labor-Management Negotiations 75-76; Democrat.
Department of Labor, 14th Street and Constitution Avenue, N.W., Washington, D.C. 20210, U.S.A.

Ushakov, Konstantin Alekseyevich; Soviet stage designer and theatre director; b. 1908; ed. Central Inst. of Theatrical Art and State Inst. of Theatrical Art.

Apprentice Painter Korsh Theatre 20-22; Asst. Chief Painter Moscow Bolshoi Drama Theatre (now Stanislavsky and Nemirovich-Danchenko Theatre of Opera and Ballet) 22-27; Head of Design Section, Deputy Art Dir., Dir., Moscow Theatre of Operetta 27-47; Chief. of Dept of Art Affairs, Moscow City Soviet of Working Peoples' Deputies 41-53; Chief of Board of Culture Dept., Moscow Soviet 53-65; Senior Teacher, Dir. of Faculty, State Inst. of Theatrical Art 64; Dir. Moscow Arts Theatre 65-, toured France, Bulgaria, Hungary, Austria, Japan; Order of Red Banner of Labour; Honoured Cultural Worker, R.S.F.S.R. and several decorations.

Publs. On problems of history, theory and practice of theatre and culture.

Moscow Arts Theatre, 3 Proyezd Khudozhestvennogo teatra, Moscow, U.S.S.R.

Ushakov, Nikolai Alexandrovich, D.SC.; Soviet international lawyer; b. 19 Nov. 1918, Moscow.

Research Prof., Inst. of State and Law, U.S.S.R. Acad. of Sciences 48-; Chief of Editorial Board, *International Law* (annual); mem. Perm. Court of Arbitration, The Hague; mem. UN Int. Law Comm. 67-; Exec. Sec. UN Assen. in U.S.S.R.; mem. Int. Law Assen.; Vice-Pres. Soviet Int. Law Assen.; lectures in int. public law at Moscow, Kiev and Leningrad Univs.; has participated in various confs. on questions of int. law.

Publs. over 40 learned publications in the field of int. law.

Institute of State and Law of U.S.S.R. Academy of Sciences, ul. Frunze 10, Moscow, U.S.S.R.

Usher Arsène, Assouan, M.A.; Ivory Coast lawyer and politician; b. 1930; ed. Bordeaux and Poitiers Univ.

Lawyer, Court of Appeals, Poitiers 55-56; Cabinet attaché of M. Houphouet-Boigny 56; Asst. Dir. Caisse des Allocations Familiales 57-59; Conseiller Général 57-59; Deputy Vice-Pres. Nat. Assembly 59-60; Lawyer, Court of Appeals, Abidjan 59; Head, Ivory Coast Perm. Mission to UN 61-67; Minister of Foreign Affairs 67-; mem. UN Security Council 64-67.

Ministry of Foreign Affairs, Abidjan; and Cocody-Abidjan, Ivory Coast.

Usherwood, Kenneth Ascough, C.B.E., M.A., F.I.A.; British insurance executive; b. 19 Aug. 1904, London; s. of late H. T. Usherwood and Lettie Ascough; m. 1st Molly Tidbeck 1933 (dissolved 1945), 2nd Mary Reepmaker d'Orville 1946; one s. one d.; ed. City of London School and St. John's Coll., Cambridge.

Joined Prudential Assurance Co., Ltd. 25, Deputy Gen. Man. 47-60, Gen. Man. 61-67, Dir. 68-, Deputy Chair. 69-70, Chair. 70-75; Dir. of Statistics, Ministry of Supply 41-45; Chair Industrial Life Offices Assen. 66-67; Pres Inst. of Actuaries 62-64.

Prudential Assurance Co., Ltd., Holborn Bars, London, E.C.1; Home: 24 Litchfield Way, London, N.W.11, England.

Telephone: 01-405-9222 (Office); 01-455-7915 (Home).

Uslar-Pietri, Arturo; Venezuelan writer and politician; b. 16 May 1906, Caracas; s. of Arturo Uslar and Helena Pietri de Uslar; m. Isabel Braun 1939; two s.; ed. Univ. Central de Venezuela.

Professor of Political Economy, Univ. Cen. de Venezuela 37-41; Sec. to Pres. of Venezuela 41-43; Minister of Nat. Educ. 39-41, of Finance 43, of Foreign Affairs 45; Prof. of Latin American Literature, Columbia Univ., New York 47, of Venezuelan Literature, Univ. Cen., Caracas; mem. Acad. Venezolana de la Lengua, Acad. of Social and Political Sciences, Acad. of History, Venezuela; Senator, Nat. Congress 58; Ind. Candidate for Pres. Dec. 63; holds numerous int. awards.

Publs. novels: *Las lanzas coloradas* 31, *El camino de El Dorado* 47, *El laberinto de fortuna* 2 vols.; stories: *Barrabás y otros relatos* 26, *Red* 36, *Treinta hombres y sus sombras* 49, *Pasos y Pasajeros* 65; essays: *Las Nubes* 51, *Del hacer y deshacer de Venezuela* 63, *La ciudad de nadie* 60, *Oraciones para despertar*; poems: *Manoa* 72; plays: *Teatro* 58, *Chúo Gil y las tejedoras* 60, and several monographs.

Avenida Los Pinos 49, La Florida, Caracas, Venezuela., Telephone: 74-05-65.

Usman, Brig. Musa; Nigerian air force officer; b. 1940 Enugu; s. of Alhaji Usman Kakagida (Nigerian Army) and Hadiza Abdalla (Royal Family of Igala); m. 1965; one s. three d.; ed. Ibadan Goodbye School, Kaduna, St. Michael School, Zaria Mil. Training School, Zaria, Ghana Accra Regular Officers' Special Training School, Officer Cadet School, Aldershot, England, Royal Mil. Acad. Sandhurst, and Army Infantry School, Georgia, U.S.A.

Served in Congo in UN Peace Keeping Force; later C.O. of Nigerian Air Force, Kaduna; Mil. Gov. of N.E. State of Nigeria 67-75; Acting Brig.-Gen. Oct. 72.

Leisure interest: tennis.

Office of the Governor of N.E. State, Maiduguri, Nigeria.

Usmani, Ishrat Husain, PH.D.; Pakistani scientist and administrator; b. 15 April 1917; ed. Aligarh Univ., Bombay Univ. and Imperial Coll. of Science and Technology, London.

Joined Madras Cadre of Indian Civil Service 42; fmr. Chief Controller of Imports and Exports, Pakistan; fmr. Chair. W. Pakistan Mineral Development Corpn.; Chair. Pakistan Atomic Energy Comm. 60-72; Sec. Ministry of Educ. 69-, of Science and Technology 72-; Chair. Pakistan Power Comm. 61-62; Chair. Board of Govs., IAEA Vienna 62-63; mem.-Sec. Scientific Comm., Pakistan 59-61; fmr. Chair. Nat. Science Council, Pakistan; Hon. Consultant to UN Sec.-Gen. on Nuclear Non-proliferation Treaty; Hon. Vice-Pres. U.K. Inst. of Nuclear Engineers.

Ministry of Science and Technology, Islamabad, Pakistan.

Usmanov, Gumer Ismagilovich; Soviet politician; b. 1932; ed. Kazan Agricultural Inst.

Member C.P.S.U. 53-; Teacher, First Sec. District Cttee. of Young Communist League 50-56; Sec., later, Second, and then First Sec. Chistopolsk City Cttee. of C.P., then Chief, Production Collective State Farm Dept. 62-65; First Sec. Buinsky District Cttee. of C.P. 65-66; Chair. Council of Ministers, Tatar A.S.S.R. 66-; Deputy to U.S.S.R. Supreme Soviet 66; mem. Comm. for Construction and Building Material Industry.

Council of Ministers of Tatar A.S.S.R., Kazan, U.S.S.R.

Ussoskin, Moshe; Israeli social worker; b. 8 March 1899, Moghilev-Podolsk, Russia; s. of Elijahu-Eli and Dvora Ussoskin; m. Miriam Griner 1934; one d.

Zionist work in Bessarabia 17; Controller Bank Moldova Bucharest and Co-Dir. Branche Reni 18-28; Dir. American Joint Distribution Cttee. and Foundation for Hungary, Turkey and Balkan countries 28-41; Dir. Cen. Bank for Jewish Co-operatives in Romania 33-41; in Israel 41-; Senior Officer Migdal Ins. Co. Jerusalem 41-48; exec. comm. Union Credit Co-operatives in Palestine 42-47; Dir.-Gen. and Treas. *Keren Hayessod* United Israel Appeal 49-68; mem. Board Israel Land Devt. Co., Jerusalem Econ. Corpn., Binjaneh Haumah Ltd., and others; mem. Presidium of World Fed. of Bessarabian Jews; Board of Govs. Hebrew Univ. Jerusalem; has organized much relief work for refugees.

Publs. Co-Editor of co-operative monthly *Die Genossenschaft Czernowitz-Bukovina*; *Social Welfare among Jews in Bessarabia*, *Social Welfare among Jews in Saloniki (Greece)*, *Struggle For Survival* 75, and many articles on

co-operative, economic, zionist, and Jewish matters in many languages.
16 Arlosorof Street, Jerusalem 92181, Israel.
Telephone: (02)-31854.

Ustinov, Gen. Dmitri Fedorovich; Soviet politician and administrator; b. 1908; ed. Military Inst. of Mechanics. Worked in Research Inst. 34-37; Construction Engineer later Deputy Head of Construction Bolshevik plant 35-40, Dir. 41; People's Commissar for Armaments 41-46; Minister of Armaments 46-53; Minister of Defence Industries 53-57; Deputy Chair. Council of Ministers, U.S.S.R. 57-63, First Deputy Chair. 63-65; Minister of Defence April 76-; Chair. Supreme Council of Nat. Economy 63-65; Sec. Cen. Cttee. of Communist Party of Soviet Union 65-, Alt. mem. Political Bureau 66-76, mem. 76-; Deputy to U.S.S.R. Supreme Soviet 46-50, 57-; Hero of Socialist Labour, Order of Lenin, Hammer and Sickle Gold Medal (twice).
Ministry of Defence, 34 Naberezhnaya M. Thoreza, Moscow, U.S.S.R.

Ustinov, Peter Alexander, C.B.E., F.R.S.A.; British dramatist and actor; b. 16 April 1921; s. of late Jona Ustinov and Nadia Benois; ed. Westminster School and London Theatre Studio.
Entered theatre as actor 39; first appearance in revue writing own material, Ambassador's Theatre, London 40; first appearance in films 40; served in army 42-46; wrote and directed films: *School for Secrets* 47, *Vice-Versa* 48, *Private Angelo* 49, *Billy Budd* 62, *Lady L* 65; collaborated on screenplay *The Way Ahead* 44; appeared in plays: *Crime and Punishment* 46, *Frenzy* 48, *Love in Albania* 49, *The Love of Four Colonels* 51; appeared in films: *The Way Ahead* 44, *Odette* 50, *Hôtel Sahara* 51, *Quo Vadis* 51, *Beau Brummel* 54, *The Egyptian* 54, *We're no Angels* 55, *Lola Montes*, *Spartacus*, *Billy Budd* 62, *Topkapi* 63, *John Goldfarb* 64, *Lady L* 65, *Blackbeard's Ghost* 66, *The Comedians* 67, *Viva Max!* 70, part-author and star *Hot Millions* 68, *Hammersmith Is Out* (also dir.) 71, *One of Our Dinosaurs Is Missing* 75; directed opera, *The Magic Flute*, Hamburg 68, appeared in play *The Unknown Soldier and his Wife* 73, directed, designed and appeared in opera *Don Quichote*, Paris 74; mem. British Film Acad.; Rector, Univ. of Dundee 68-74; three Emmy Awards for best TV actor of year.
Plays: *House of Regrets* 42, *Blow Your Own Trumpet* 43, *The Banbury Nose* 44, *The Tragedy of Good Intentions* 45, *The Indifferent Shepherd* 48, *The Man in the Raincoat* 49, *The Love of Four Colonels* 51, *The Moment of Truth* 51, *No Sign of the Dove* 53, *Romanoff and Juliet* 56, *Photo Finish* 62, *The Life in My Hands* 63, *Half Way up the Tree* 67, *The Unknown Soldier and his Wife* 67, *Who's Who in Hell* 74; short stories: *Add a Dash of Pity* 59, *The Frontiers of the Sea* 66; novels: *The Loser* 60, *Krumnagel* 71.
c/o Christopher Mann Ltd., 140 Park Lane, London, W.1, England; and La Datcha, Les Diablerets, Vaud, Switzerland.

Ustor, Dr. Endre; Hungarian lawyer; b. 1 Sept. 1909, Budapest; m. Lili Havas; no c.
Head, Int. Law Dept., Ministry of Foreign Affairs 57-75; hon. Prof. Karl Marx Univ. of Econs., Budapest 68-; mem. Perm. Court of Arbitration, The Hague 61-; mem. UN Int. Law Comm. 67-, Chair. 74-75, UN Admin. Tribunal 76-; Assoc. mem. Inst. of Int. Law, Belgium 67-.
73 Fodor-U, 1124 Budapest, Hungary.
Telephone: (00361) 457-611.

Utchenko, Sergei Lvovich; Soviet historian; b. 1 Dec. 1908; ed. Leningrad State Univ.
Assistant Prof. Leningrad State Univ. 39-41; served in Soviet Army 41-46; Prof. of Ancient History, Moscow State Univ. 50-54, Moscow Inst. of Historical Archives 54-; Head Ancient History Section, Inst. of History, U.S.S.R. Acad. of Sciences 50-; mem. C.P.S.U. 31-; Order of the Red Star and military medals.
Publs. More than 70 works including *The Law of Licinius Sextus 'De Modo Agrorum'* 47, *Sallust's Letter to Caesar* 50, *The Ideological and Political Struggle at Rome on the Eve of the Fall of the Republic* 52, *The Crisis of the Polis and the Political Views of the Roman Stoics* 55, several chapters in *World History*, Vol. II 56, *The Crisis of the Roman Comitiae* 59, *The Concept of Popular Sovereignty in Republican Rome* 60, *From the Caesar's Consulate to the Tribunate of Claudius* 61, *The Roman Army in the First Century B.C.* 62, *The Crisis and the Fall of the Roman Republic* 65, *As One Historian Sees It* 66, *Ancient Rome: Events, People, Ideas* 69, *Cicero and his Time* 73.
Institute of History, 19 ul. Dm. Ulyanova, Moscow, U.S.S.R.

Utzerath, Hansjörg; German theatre director; b. 20 March 1926; ed. Kepler Oberschule, Tübingen.
Began as actor, later in theatre management in Düsseldorf, and then in production; Chief Stage Man., Düsseldorfer Kammerspiele 55-59, Dir. 59-66; Intendant, Freie Volksbühne, Berlin Jan. 67-; Guest Producer at Staatstheater Stuttgart, Münchener Kammerspiele and Schiller-Theater, Berlin 59-.
c/o Freie Volksbühne, Berlin 15, Schaperstrasse 24, Germany.

Utzon, Jørn; Danish architect; b. 9 April 1918, Copenhagen; ed. Royal Acad. of Fine Arts, Copenhagen. Joined Helsinki Office of Alvar Aalto (q.v.) after Second World War; won travelling scholarships to Morocco and U.S.A.; designer of furniture and glassware; won competition for design of Sydney Opera House 57, worked on project in Denmark 57-63, in Sydney 63-66 (resigned as architect); won competition for design of Zürich Schauspielhaus 66; architect of a housing scheme near Fredensborg, his own house, Bank Melli Iran, Teheran etc.; Fellow, Royal Australian Inst. of Architects 65; Ehrenpreis, Bund Deutscher Architekten 66, Gold Medal, Royal Australian Inst. of Architects 73, and other awards.
3150 Hellebaek, Denmark.

Uzan, Aharon; Israeli agriculturist; b. Tunisia. Emigrated to Israel 49; co-founder, settler, Moshav Ghilat, in Negev 49, Sec., later Head of supply network; mem. Knesset (Parl.) 65-69; Deputy Minister of Agriculture 66-69; Gen. Sec. Tnuat Hamoshavim 70-74; Minister of Communications March-June 74, of Agriculture June 74-, of Communications March 75-; Labour Party.
Ministry of Agriculture, Jerusalem, Israel.

Uzuner, Ali Riza; Turkish politician and forest engineer; b. 1 April 1926; s. of Esat and Hanife Uzuner; m. Aysel Uzuner 1968; one d.; ed. School of Forestry. Director, Research Inst. of Forestry 56-61; mem. Nat. Assembly 61-72; Minister of Labour 71-73; mem. Nat. Security Council; Expert, Ministry of Forestry.
Leisure interests: sport, theatre, social politics, opera. Publs. research articles published in various newspapers and periodicals.
Republican People's Party, Uludag sok. 13/6, Maltepe, Ankara, Turkey.

V

Vader, Arthur Pavlovich; Soviet politician; b. 1920; ed. C.P.S.U. Higher Party School.
School director 42-48; party work 48-52; Sec. Tallinn City C.P. Cttee. 52-59, Cen. Cttee. C.P.S.U. 59-63; Chair. Party Control Cttee. of Estonia C.P. 63-64; Deputy Chair. Estonian Council of Ministers 63-64; Second Sec., Cen. Cttee., C.P. of Estonia 64-70; Chair. Presidium, Supreme Soviet of Estonian S.S.R. 70-; Vice-Chair. Presidium, U.S.S.R. Supreme Soviet 70-; Alt. mem. Cen. Cttee. of C.P.S.U. 66-71, mem. 71-; Deputy to U.S.S.R. Supreme Soviet 62-.
Presidium of Supreme Soviet of Estonian S.S.R., Tallinn, U.S.S.R.

Vadim, Roger (Plemiannikov); French film director; b. 26 Jan. 1928; *m.* 1st Brigitte Bardot (*q.v.*) 1952 (divorced), 2nd Annette Stroyberg 1958 (divorced), 3rd Jane Fonda (*q.v.*) 1967 (divorced), 4th Catherine Schneider 1975.
Actor; script-writer and Asst. Dir. with Marc Allegret; reporter *Paris-Match* 52-54; independent film dir. 55-; writer and dialogue for *Futures Vedettes, Cette Sacrée Gamine, En Effeuillant la Marguerite*; dir. and dialogue *Et Dieu Créa la Femme, Sait-on Jamais, Les Bijoutiers du Clair de Lune, Les Liaisons Dangereuses, Et Mourir de Plaisir, Le Repos du Guerrier, Le Vice et la Vertu, La Ronde, La Curée, Histoires Extraordinaires, Barbarella, Metzengerstein* 69, *Pretty Maids in a Row, Hellé, Don Juan* 73, *La Jeune Fille Assassinée* 74.
6 avenue Frédéric-Leplay, 75007 Paris; Home: La Fontaine Richard, Saint-Ouen-Marchefroy, 28 Berchères-sur-Vesgres, France.

Vagnozzi, H.E. Cardinal Egidio, PH.D., S.T.D., J.C.D.; Vatican diplomatist; b. 2 Feb. 1906; ed. Lateran Pontifical Seminary and Lateran Pontifical Univ.
Papal Secretariat of State, Vatican City 30-32; Sec., then Auditor and Counsellor, Apostolic Delegation, Washington, D.C. 32-42; Counsellor, Lisbon 42, Vatican 42-46, Paris 46-48; Chargé d'Affaires, Counsellor, Papal Internunciature, India 48-49; Apostolic Del., then Papal Nuncio to Philippines 49-58; Apostolic Del., Washington, D.C. 58-67; mem. Council Public Ecclesiastical Affairs, Congregations for the Bishops 67, for the Eastern Churches 69, for Evangelization of Peoples 75; mem. Supreme Tribunal of Apostolic Signature 72; cr. Cardinal 67; Pres. Comm. of Cardinals for the Prefecture of Econ. Affairs of the Holy See 68-; Commandeur Légion d'Honneur, Order of Sikatunan, Grand Cross of Order of Holy Sepulchre.
Prefettura degli Affari Economici della Santa Sede, Vatican City, Rome, Italy.

Vago, Constantin, PH.D., D.SC.; French university professor and research director; b. 2 May 1921; *s.* of Vincent Vago; *m.* Catherine Sary 1944; one *s.* one *d.*; ed. Univs. of Debrecen and Marseilles.
Director, Lab. of Cytopathology, Nat. Inst. for Agron. Research, Saint-Christol 58-; Research Dir. Nat. Inst. of Agron. Research of France 62; Prof. of Pathology and Microbiology, Univ. of Science, Montpellier 64-; Dir. Lab. of Comparative Pathology, Univ. of Montpellier 64-; mem. Acad. of Sciences of France, Acad. of Agric. of France, N.Y. Acad. of Science; Past Pres. Int. Soc. for Invertebrate Pathology; mem. numerous scientific socs.; Ordre de la Légion d'Honneur, Ordre du Mérite, and other decorations.
Leisure interests, sculpture, swimming.
Publs. *Invertebrate Tissue Culture* 72, and about 300 publs. on comparative pathology, invertebrate tissue culture, invertebrate virology, chlamydial diseases, comparative oncology.
University of Sciences, Place Eugéne Bataillon, 34060 Montpellier, France.
Telephone: 639144; 522017.

Vago, Pierre; French architect and town planner; b. 30 Aug. 1910, Budapest, Hungary; *s.* of Joseph and Ghita (Lenart) Vago; (re)*m.* Nicole Cormier 1968; two *s.* two *d.*; ed. Ecole spéciale d'Architecture, Paris.
Editor-in-Chief *Architecture d'Aujourd'hui* 32-48, Pres. of Cttee. 48-75, Dir. 76-; Founder and Sec.-Gen. Int. Reunions of Architects 32-48 and Int. Union of Architects 48-69, Hon. Pres. 69-; Head Architect for Reconstruction 48-56; Pres. Int. Council, Soc. of Industrial Design 63-65; fmr. Vice-Pres. Confed. of French Architects; mem. Jury of many Int. Competitions; architect and town planner in Belgium, Austria, France, Germany, Tunisia, Luxembourg, Israel and Italy; Prof. and Dir. of Studies Ecole Supérieure d'Architecture St. Luc de Belgique; honours include hon. mem. of R.I.B.A. and membership of numerous architectural socs.; Doc. h.c. (Univ. of Stuttgart), Prof. h.c. (Tech. Univ., Budapest); Chevalier Légion d'Honneur, Commdr. Grégoire le Grand.
Major works include: Basilica St. Pius X, Lourdes and other churches, Central Bank of Tunis, Library of Univ. of Bonn, Univ. of Lille, several buildings in France, Fed. Rep. of Germany, North Africa and Israel.
Leisure interest: history.
17 quai Voltaire, Paris 7e, France.
Telephone: 261-20-96 and 97.

Vahidi, Iraj, M.SC., PH.D.; Iranian politician; b. 1927, Khorramshahr; ed. Univs. of Teheran and Durham.
Formerly engineer, Ministry of Roads; fmr. mem. Board of Dirs. Independent Irrigation Inst., subsequently Man. Dir.; Technical Asst. to Ministry of Water and Power; Man. Dir. Khouzestan Water and Power Authority; Minister of Agriculture 71, of Water and Power 71-74, of Energy 74-.
Ministry of Energy, Teheran, Iran.

Vaizey, John, M.A., D.TECH., D.LITT.; British economist and writer; b. 1 Oct. 1929, London; *s.* of Ernest and Lucy (Butler) Vaizey; *m.* Marina Stansky 1961; two *s.* one *d.*; ed. Cambridge Univ.
United Nations, Geneva 52-53; Fellow, St. Catharine's Coll., Cambridge 53-56; Lecturer in Econ. History, Oxford Univ. 56-60; Dir. Research Unit in Econs. of Educ., Univ. of London 60-61; Fellow and Tutor, Worcester Coll., Oxford 62-66; Prof. of Econs. and Head of School of Social Sciences, Brunel Univ., London 66-75; Vice-Chancellor Monash Univ. 76-; Visiting Prof. Univ. of Calif. 66-67; Consultant to OECD, UN, ILO; Dir. Acton Soc. Trust 61-; mem. Public Schools Comm. 66-68, Nat. Council for Educational Technology 67-73, U.K. Comm. for UNESCO 65-71, Inner London Educ. Authority 70-72, Gov. Board, Int. Inst. for Educational Planning; Gladstone Prizeman, Univ. of Cambridge 54; Eleanor Rathbone Lecturer, Univ. of Liverpool 66; Trustee King George VI and Queen Elizabeth Foundation; Gov. Ditchley Foundation; Centenary Visiting Prof., Univ. of Adelaide.
Leisure interests: writing, travel, arts.
Publs. *The Costs of Education* 58, *Scenes from Institutional Life* 59, *The Brewing Industry 1886-1951* 60, *Some Economic Aspects of Educational Development in Europe* (with Michel Debeauvais) 60, *Guinness's*

Brewery in the Irish Economy 1759-1876 (with Patrick Lynch) 61, *The Economics of Education* 62, *Education for Tomorrow* 62, revised 66, *The Control of Education* 63, *The Residual Factor and Economic Growth* (Editor) 65, *Economics of Education* (Editor, with E. A. G Robinson) 66, *Barometer Man* 67, *Resources for Education* (with John Sheehan) 68, *The Sleepless Lunch* 68, *Capitalism* 71, *The Type to Succeed* 70, *Social Democracy* 71, *The Political Economy of Education* (with Keith Norris and John Sheehan) 72, *The Economics of Research and Technology* (with Keith Norris) 73, *History of British Steel* 74, numerous pamphlets and articles.

Monash University, Wellington Road, Clayton, Victoria 3168, Australia.

Vajda, Georges; French Hebraist; b. 18 Nov. 1908; ed. Séminaire Rabbinique, Budapest, and Paris, and Ecole des Langues Orientales, Sorbonne.

Professor, Séminaire Israélite de France 36-; Lecturer, Ecole Pratique des Hautes Etudes 37, Dir. 54-; Head of Oriental Section, Institut de Recherche et d'Histoire des Textes 40-; Prof. Univ. de Paris 70-.

Publs. *Introduction à la Pensée Juive du Moyen Age* 47, *La Théologie ascétique de Bahya ibn Paquda* 47, *Répertoire des Catalogues et Inventaires de Manuscrits Arabes* 49, *Un Recueil de Textes Historiques Judéo-Marocains* 51, *Index Général des Manuscrits Arabes Musulmans de la Bibliotheque Nationale* 53, *Juda ben Nissim Ibn Malka, Philosophe juif marocain* 54, *Les certificats de lecture dans les manuscrits arabes de la B.N. de Paris, L'amour de Dieu dans la Théologie juive du moyen age* 57, *Album de Paléographie Arabe* 58, *Isaac Albalag, averroïste juif* 60, *Recherches sur la Philosophie et la Kabbale* 62, *Le Dictionnaire des Autorités d'Ad-Dimyati* 62, *Ya'aqov ben Sheshet, Sefer Meshiv Devarim Nekhohim* 68, *Le Commentaire d'Ezra de Gerone Sur le Cantique des cantiques* 69, *Deux Commentaires Karaites sur l'Ecclesiaste* 71, *Isaac Albalag, Sefer Tiqqun Ha-De'ot* (A Hebrew Abridgement of Ibn Malka's Commentary) 73, *Revue des Etudes Juives* (Editor).

Institut de Recherche et d'Histoire des Textes, 40 avenue d'Iéna, Paris 16e; and 51 rue Saint-Placide, Paris 6e, France.

Vajpayee, Atal Bihari, M.A.; Indian politician; b. 25 Dec. 1926; ed. Victoria Coll. Gwalior, D.A.V. Coll., Kanpur.

Member, Indian Nat. Congress 42-46; mem. Lok Sabha 57-62, 67-, Rajya Sabha 62; mem. Rashtriya Swayam-sewak Sangh 41; founder mem. Bharatiya Jana Sangh, Pres. 68-; Chair. Public Accounts Cttee. 69-70.

Publs. *Amar Balidan, Mrityuya Hatya, Jana Sangh our Musalman.*

1 Ferozeshah Road, New Delhi 1, India.
Telephone: 387-446.

Valcárcel Vizcarra, Luis Eduardo, D.PHIL., LL.D.; Peruvian ethnologist; b. 1891; ed. Univ. del Cuzco and Col. Peruano del Cuzco.

Professor of Peruvian History, Univ. del Cuzco 17-30, Dir. Univ. Archaeological Museum 23-30; Dir. Peruvian Archaeological Museum, Lima 30-44; Dir. Bolívar Museum, Lima 30; Dir. National History Museum, Lima 44-65, Dir. Emer. 65-; Prof. Univ. of Lima 31-63; fmr. Dir. Ethnological Inst., Lima 46; Minister of Educ. 45-47; Prof. Emeritus Univ. of San Marcos; Order of Aztec Eagle (Mexico); Order of the Sun (Peru).

Publs. *Historia Incaica* 25, *Tempestad en los Andes* 27, *Mirador Indio* (essays) 37, *Cuentos y Leyendas Incas* 38, *Historia de la Cultura Antigua del Perú* 43, *Ruta Cultural del Perú* 45, *Historia del Perú Antiguo* 3 vols. 64, etc.

Lord Cochrane 456, Miraflores, Lima, Peru.
Telephone: 22764.

Valdés González-Roldán, Antonio; Spanish politician and transport administrator; b. 1927; m.; four c.

Chief Exec., Traffic and Planning Service, Dirección Gen. de Carreteras 60-66; responsible for traffic circulation and transport in municipality of Madrid 66-73; Adviser to RENFE (State Railway Org.) Sept.-Dec. 73; Lecturer on Transport, Inst. of Local Admin. Studies; Minister of Public Works Dec. 73-.

Ministerio de Obras Públicas, Madrid, Spain.

Valencia-Ibañez, Gen. Edmundo; Bolivian army officer and diplomatist; b. 8 March 1928, La Paz; s. of Juan de Dios Valencia and Sara Ibañez de Valencia; m. Violeta Collazos de Valencia 1950; three s. one d.; ed. various military colls.

Former Mil. Attaché, Paris; Minister of Nat. Economy, of Industry and Commerce and of Finance (a.i.); fmr. Gov. IDB; Amb. to U.S.A. 71-75, also accred. to Canada 72; Perm. Rep. of Bolivia to OAS 72; Pres. Sugar-Cane and Sugar Board (CNECA), Fábrica Nacional de Fósforos (Nat Match Co.), Inst. for Promotion of Investment in Bolivia (INPIBOL), Nat. Council for Electricity; decorations from Bolivia, Argentina, China and the Vatican.

Leisure interest: reading.
c/o Ministerio de Relaciones Exteriores, La Paz, Bolivia.

Valenti, Jack; American film executive and government official; b. 1922; m. Mary Margaret Wiley; one s. two d.; ed. High School, Houston, Univ. of Houston and Harvard Business School.

Former office boy, oil company; U.S. Air Force, Second World War; Special Asst. to President Johnson 63-66; Pres. Motion Picture Asscn. of America 66-, Asscn. of Motion Picture and Television Producers Inc. 66; Dir. American Film Inst. 67.

1600 I Street, N.W., Washington, D.C. 20006, U.S.A.

Valentine, Alan, M.A.; American historian and former administrator; b. 23 Feb. 1901, Glen Cove, N.Y.; s. of Charles Post Valentine and Annie Laurie Valentine; m. Lucia Norton 1928; one s. two d.; ed. Swarthmore Coll., Univ. of Pennsylvania, and Oxford Univ. (Balliol Coll.).

Instructor, Univ. of Pennsylvania 21-22; with Oxford Univ. Press in U.K. and U.S. 25-28; Asst. Prof. of English and Dean of Men, Swarthmore Coll. 28-32; Prof. in History, Arts and Letters Dept., Yale Univ., and Chair. of Board of Admissions and Master of Pierson Coll. 32-35; Pres. Univ. of Rochester 35-50; Chief of Mission to Netherlands for Econ. Co-operation Admin. 48-49; Econ. Stabilisation Dir. 50-51; Pres. Cttee. for Free Asia 51-52; Grand Officer Order of Orange-Nassau (Neths.); several hon. degrees.

Publs. *The English Novel* 27, *Biography* 27, *Dusty Answers* 41, *The Age of Conformity* 53, *Vigilante Justice* 55, *Trial Balance* 56, *Education of an American* 58, *Lord George Germain* 62, *1913: Year of Transition* 62, *Fathers to Sons* 63, *Lord North* (2 vols.) 67, *Lord Stirling* 69, *The British Establishment 1760-1784* (2 vols.) 70, *The American Academy in Rome* (with Lucia Valentine) 73.

7 Lafayette Road, Princeton, N.J. 08540, U.S.A.
Telephone: 609-924-6625.

Valerio, Giorgio; Italian engineer and industrialist; b. 20 March 1904, Milan; m. Viviana Talan Lubovitch 1935; two s. one d.; ed. Milan Engineering Univ.

With Società Edison Milan (now Montecatini Edison S.p.A.) 27, Man. Dir. 52-65, Vice-Chair., Man. Dir. 61-65, Chair. and Chief Exec. Officer 65-70; Vice-Chair. Sincat, Palermo, Chatillon, Milan; Dir. Soc. Italiana per le Strade Ferrate Meridionali, Florence, Riunione Adriatica di Sicurtà, Trieste; La Fondiaria, Florence.

Foro Bonaparte 31, Milan, Italy.

Valéry, François; French diplomatist; b. 17 July 1916; ed. Univ. of Paris.
Auditor, Cour des Comptes 44; Technical Counsellor at the Peace Conf. 46; mem. French del. to Council of Ministers for Foreign Affairs on the Marshall Plan and to Tripartite Confs. on Germany 46-50; Head of Section of Econ. Co-operation and Integration, Ministry of Foreign Affairs 48; Conseiller Référendaire, Cour des Comptes 50; Perm. Del. of France to OEEC 56-61, to OECD 61-; Vice-Pres. Exec. Cttee of OECD 67-; Chevalier de la Légion d'Honneur.
Organisation for Economic Co-operation and Development, 2 rue André-Pascal, Paris 16e; Home: 3 rue Léon-Mignotte, 91-Bièvres, France.

Valle, Inger Louise; Norwegian politician; b. 28 Nov. 1921, Oslo; ed. Commercial Coll., and law studies.
Appointed to Price Directorate 51, transferred to Consumer Council 58, Head of Legal and Econ. Section 58-71; mem. Baerum Municipal Council 67-71; mem. Arbeiderpartiet (Labour Party); Chair. Nordic Cttee. for Consumer Problems; mem. Labour Party Environment Conservation Cttee. and Democracy Cttee.; Minister of Family and Consumer Affairs 71-72, of Consumer Affairs and Govt. Admin. 72, of Justice and Police Oct. 73-.
Ministry of Justice and Police, Oslo, Norway.

Vallejo Arbeláez, Joaquin; Colombian civil engineer, politician and diplomatist; b. 4 Oct. 1912; s. of Nestor Vallejo and Maria Arbeláez; m. Nelly Mejia 1937; four s. five d.; ed. Escuela Nacional de Minas.
Director of Public Educ., Antioquia 36-38; Prof. of Mathematics, Physical Sciences and Philosophy, Univ. of Antioquia and Nat. School of Mines 35-39; Deputy to Provincial Assembly, Antioquia 37-39; mem. Nat. Assembly 39-; Pres. of Aliadas McKesson Laboratories 44-64; Minister of Devt. 57; Minister of Finance and Public Credit 65-66; Perm. Rep. to UN 69-70; Minister of the Interior 70; mem. Board of Dirs. of Public Works Dept., and several private corpns.
Leisure interests: philosophy, sciences, agriculture, economics.
Publs. Articles on development, economics, philosophy, politics, regional integration, education.
Apartado aereo 253, Palmira, Colombia.
Telephone: 631-8665.

Vallenthin, Wilhelm, DR.JUR.; German business executive; b. 24 July 1909.
Chairman Supervisory Board, Berliner Disconto Bank A.G., Berlin, Hemmoor Zement A.G., Karstadt A.G., Essen, Hutschenreuther A.G., Selb, Polyphon Film und Fernsehgesellschaft G.m.b.H., Hamburg, Schmalbach-Lubeca G.m.b.H., Braunschweig, Zeiss-Ikon A.G.; Deputy Chair. Supervisory Board, Schiffshypothekanbank zu Lübeck A.G.; mem. Supervisory Board, Deutsche Shell A.G., Hamburg, Europemballage Corpn., Brussels, Norddeutsche Affinerie, Hamburg, Phoenix Gummiwerke A.G., Hamburg-Harburg, Salzgitter A.G., Berlin/Salzgitter-Brütte; mem. Advisory Board, Deutsche Beteiligungsgesellschaft G.m.b.H., Frankfurt (Main), Hako-Werke Hans Koch & Sohn, Bad Oldesloe; mem. Board Deutsche Bank A.G., Frankfurt (Main), Stiftung Estel, Arnheim.
2 Hamburg 55, Elbchaussee 474, Federal Republic of Germany.

Vallentin, Maxim, Prof.; German theatrical producer and director; b. 9 Oct. 1904, Berlin; s. of Richard Vallentin and Elise Zachow-Vallentin; m. Edith Wolff 1924; one s.
Debut Schlossparktheater and Max Reinhardt Theatre, Berlin; founder and producer, Das Rote Sprachrohr (revolutionary workers' theatre), Berlin until 33; in Czechoslovakia and U.S.S.R. until 45, German announcer and radio-drama producer, Moscow Radio; returned to Weimar (D.D.R.) 45; founded German Theatre Inst.;

Chief Producer, Das Junge Ensemble, Weimar; Chief Producer and Dir. Maxim Gorki Theatre, Berlin 52-68; productions include works of Cervantes, Kleist, J. R. Becher, Fr. Wolf, Gorki, etc.; Assoc. German Acad. of Arts; two Nat. Prizes, two Nat. Orders of Merit, Order of Banner of Labour; Medal of Merit of D.D.R., J. R. Becher Gold Medal, Fritz Heckert Medal, Silver Medal (Czechoslovakia), Deed of Honour (U.S.S.R.), etc.
Publs. on German Stanislavski reception and German Gorki reception.
Leisure interests: improvisation, sculpture.
Akademie der Künste der Deutschen Demokratischen Republik, 104 Berlin, Robert-Koch-Platz 7, German Democratic Republic.

Valli, Romolo; Italian director and actor; b. 7 Feb. 1925, Reggio Emilia; ed. Univ. of Parma.
Joined Il Carrozzone group of actors producing their own plays 49; at Piccolo Teatro di Milano under direction of Giorgio Strehler 52-54; founded and managed Compagnia dei Giovani with Giorgio De Lullo, Rosella Falk, (q.v.), and Elsa Albani; directed Pirandello's *Six Characters in Search of an Author* and *Rules of the Game* at the World Theatre Season, London 65, 66; Artistic Dir. Festival of Two Worlds, Spoleto 72-; Principal actor and director of own company with Giorgio De Lullo 74-75; participated in the films: *The Leopard, Death in Venice, The Garden of the Finzi Continis, Boom, 1900*, etc.; Nastri d'argento, La Grolla d'oro, l'Olimpo d'oro, Nettuno d'oro, Premio Anna Magnani etc.
Compagnia di Prosa Romolo Valli, Via Luigi Settembrini 17-a, Rome, Italy.

Vallindas, Petros G., LL.D., POL. SC.M.; Greek university professor; b. 1912; ed. Univs. of Athens and Berlin.
Attorney-at-Law 34-; Asst. Prof. Univ. of Athens 38-44; Prof. School of Pol. Science 38-46; Dir. of Legislative Studies, Ministry of Justice 38-41; Prof. of Private Int. and Comparative Law Univ. of Thessalonica 44-61; Dir. Hellenic Inst. of Int. and Foreign Law 39-60; Hon. Legal Adviser to Ministry of Foreign Affairs 47-, mem. Hague Permanent Court of Arbitration; mem. Council Int. Association of Legal Science; mem. Governing Council, Rome Int. Inst. for Unification of Private Law; Assoc. mem. Inst. of Int. Law; Legis. Counsellor in charge gen. codification of Greek laws; mem. Int. Acad. of Comparative Law, Council Int. Faculty of Comparative Law at Luxembourg.
Publs. *Studies on Private Law*, Editor: *Uniformity of Interpretation of Conventions on Private International Law* 32, *Greek Private International Law During the First Half of the 19th Century* 35, *Public Policy in Private International Law* 37, *Private International Law* (two Vols. with G. Streit) 37, *Theoretical Principles of Private International Law of the Greek Civil Code* 42, *Introduction to Private International Law* 43, *Nationality Law* 43, *Contributions to the Law of Leases in Ancient Greek Law* (with N. Pantazopoulos) 48, *Introduction to Comparative Law* 51, *Introduction to English Private Law* 51, *Vocabulary of the Charter of the United Nations and of the Statute of the International Court of Justice* 53, *Cases on the General Principles of Civil Law* 56, *Nationality Code of 1955* 57, *Introduction to the Science of Law* (5th edn.) 58.
4 Sekeri, Athens, Greece.

Vallois, Henri Victor, D.M., D.SC.; French anthropologist; b. 11 April 1889, Nancy; m. A. d'Autheville 1918.
Prosector, Faculty of Medicine, Univ. of Montpellier 14; Prof. of Anatomy Univ. of Toulouse 22; Dir. Institut de Paléontologie humaine 43; Prof. Natural History Museum 41; Hon. Dir. Musée de l'Homme 61-; mem. Acad. Nat. de Médicine, France, Akad. der Wissenschaften, Vienna, Akad. der Wissenschaften und der Litteratur, Fed. Germany, etc.; Huxley Medal

Royal Anthrop. Inst., England, Viking Medal Wenner-Gren Inst., U.S.A.; Officier Légion d'Honneur; many hon. degrees.

Publs. *Traité d'Anthropologie* 26, *Anthropologie de France* 42, *Les Races Humaines* 44, *Les Hommes Fossiles* 46, *Les Primates* 55, *Les Pygmées du Cameroun: Anthropologie et Ethnologie* (with P. Marquer), *Les Mésolithiques de France* (with S. de Félice); editor *L'Anthropologie, Archives de l'Institut de Paléontologie humaine, Bulletins de la Société d'Anthropologie de Paris.*

57 rue Cuvier, Paris 5e, France.
Telephone: 535-42-12.

Valsecchi, Athos; Italian politician; b. 26 Nov. 1919, Gravedona (Como); s. of Eufrasio Valsecchi and Giuditta Oldrini; m. Marisa Gallegioni 1948; three c.
Deputy for Como Constituency, Sondrio-Varese 48-63; mem. Parl. Comm. on Finance and Treasury 48-, Vice-Pres. 53-58, Pres. 60-63; mem. Comm. on Industry and Commerce 57-58; mem. Exec. Cttee. Christian Democrat Parl. Group 54-58; mem. European Parl. Assembly and Vice-Pres. Comm. for Budget and Admin. 57-60; Under-Sec. of State for Budget (Italy) 58-59, Under-Sec. of State for Finance 59-60, 63-68; Senator 63-; Minister of Agriculture and Forestry 68-69, of Posts and Telecommunication 69-70, of Health Feb.-June 72, of Finance 72-73; Pres. Italo-German and Italo-French Cttees. for Econ. Co-operation 58-; Pres. Inst. for European Economy 67-; Mayor of Chiavenna 51-.
Senato della Repubblica, Rome; and Via Giancarlo Bitossi 21, Rome, Italy.
Telephone: 344990.

Van Aal, Henri-François; Belgian journalist and politician; b. 4 Jan. 1933, Alicante, Spain; ed. Paris and Harvard Univs.
Journalist with Radio-Télévision Belge 58-, sub-editor of *Journal Parlé* and *Journal Télévisé* and TV *Enquêtes et Reportages*; organized seminar on information problems at Dept. of Social Communications of Catholic Univ. of Louvain; Deputy for Brussels 71-; fmr. Sec. of State at Ministry of Foreign Affairs; Minister of French Culture, Deputy Minister for Brussels Affairs and Sec. of State for Housing June 74-; fmr. Political Sec., Parti Social Chrétien.
Ministry of French Culture, Brussels, Belgium.

Van Allen, James Alfred, B.S., M.S., PH.D.; American physicist; b. 7 Sept. 1914, Mount Pleasant, Iowa; s. of Alfred Morris and Alma Olney van Allen; m. Abigail Fithian Halsey II 1945; two s. three d.; ed. Iowa Wesleyan Coll. and State Univ. of Iowa.
Research Fellow, Carnegie Inst., Washington 39-41, Physicist 41-42; Physics Laboratory, Johns Hopkins Univ. 42, 46-50; Lieut.-Commdr. in U.S. Navy 42-46; Head of Dept. and Prof. of Physics and Astronomy, Univ. of Iowa 51-; Guggenheim Research Fellow at Brookhaven Nat. Laboratory 51; Research Associate Princeton Univ. Project Matterhorn 53-54; Dir. expeditions to study cosmic radiation Central Pacific 49, Alaska 50, Arctic 52, 57; mem. Rocket and Satellite Research Panel 46, Chair. 47-58, Exec. Cttee. 58-; mem. Advisory Cttee. on Nuclear Physics, Office of Naval Research 57-60; mem. Space Science Board, Nat. Acad. of Sciences 58-70; Consultant, President's Science Advisory Cttee.; mem. Cosmic Radiation, Rocket Research and Earth Satellite Panel, Int. Geophysical Year; Fellow, American Physical Soc., American Geophysical Union, American Rocket Soc., Inst. of Electrical and Electronics Engineers, American Astronautical Soc., American Acad. of Arts and Sciences; mem. Royal Astronomical Soc. (U.K.); founder mem. Int. Acad. of Astronautics; Assoc. Editor *Physics of Fluids* 58-62, *Journal of Geophysical Research* 59-67; mem. Editorial Board *Space Science Reviews* 62-;

several awards and medals and numerous Hon. D.Scs.; discoverer of the "Van Allen Belt" of radiation around the earth and a pioneer of high-altitude rocket research.
Publs. *Physics and Medicine of the Upper Atmosphere, Rocket Exploration of the Upper Atmosphere,* and 200 scientific papers; Editor *Scientific Use of Earth Satellites.*
Department of Physics and Astronomy, University of Iowa, Iowa City, Iowa 52242, and 5 Woodland Mounds Road, R.F.D. 5, Iowa City, Iowa 52240, U.S.A.

Van Atta, C(hester) M(urray), PH.D.; American physicist; b. 25 May 1906, Portland, Ore.; s. of Lester Claire and Martha Amelia (Murray) Vanetta; m. Rosalind Isenstein 1930; two s. three d.; ed. Reed Coll., and New York Univ.
Nat. Research Fellow, Mass. Inst. of Technology 33-35, Research Associate 35-38, Asst. Prof. 38-40; Physicist Naval Ordinance Laboratory 40-43; Physicist Lawrence Radiation Laboratory Univ. of California 43-46; Prof. of Physics and Chair. Division Physical Sciences and Mathematics, Southern California 46-50; Physicist Lawrence Radiation Laboratory, Univ. of California 50-; Consultant on Vacuum Technology to the Kinney Vacuum Division of the New York Air Brake Co. 37-65; Head Project for controlled thermonuclear research programme at the Berkeley and Livermore sites of the Lawrence Radiation Laboratory; Assoc. Dir. Univ. of Californian Lawrence Radiation Laboratory, Livermore 55-70, Asst. to the Dir. 70-73; mem. of Board Berkeley Science Capital Corpn., San Francisco 61-; Head, del. of American scientists to research insts. in U.S.S.R. working on controlled fusion research; Fellow, American Physical Soc. and American Asscn. for the Advancement of Science; mem. American Vacuum Soc., Smithsonian Nat. Assocs.
Publs. *The Design of High Vacuum Systems, Vacuum Science and Engineering* 65, and research papers in the fields of nuclear physics and particle accelerators.
University of California, Lawrence Radiation Laboratory, Berkeley, Calif. 94720, and Livermore, Calif. 94550; Home: 166 Caldecott Lane, Apt. 401 Oakland, Calif. 94618, U.S.A.
Telephone: 415-549-0566.

van den Bergh, Lieut.-Gen. Hendrik; South African security officer.
Former Head of Security Branch and Adviser to Prime Minister on Security; Head of Bureau of State Security May 69-; accompanied Prime Minister Vorster on his visit to Liberia and to the Victoria Falls Conf. on Rhodesia.
c/o Bureau of State Security, Pretoria, South Africa.

van den Hoven, Helmert Frans; Netherlands business executive; b. 25 April 1923, IJsselmonde; m. Dorothy Ida Bevan 1950; one s.
Joined Unilever NV, Rotterdam 38, at London Office 48-50, at Unilever Office, Turkey 51-62, Chair. 58-62; Chair. Van den Bergh en Jurgens BV 62; Dir. Unilever 70; Vice-Chair. Unilever Ltd., Chair. Unilever NV 75.
Unilever NV, Burg-s' Jacobplein 1, Rotterdam, Netherlands.

van der Byl, Pieter Kenyon Fleming-Voltelyn; Rhodesian politician; b. 11 Nov. 1923, S. Africa; ed. Cape Town, Cambridge and Harvard Univs.
Tobacco farmer in Rhodesia 46-; mem. of Parl. 62-; Deputy Minister of Information 64-68; Minister of Information, Immigration and Tourism 68-74, of Foreign Affairs and Defence Aug. 74-.
Ministry of Foreign Affairs, Salisbury, Rhodesia.

van der Kemp, Gerald, M.V.O.; French museum curator; b. 5 May 1912; m. Florence Harris; two s. two d.; ed. Institut d'Art et d'Archéologie, Sorbonne.
With Musée du Louvre 36-41; Asst. Musée National d'Art Moderne 41-45; Curator of the Museums of Versailles, Trianons and Jeu de Paume 45-53, Chief

Curator 53-, Insp. Gen. Nat. Museums 72-; mem. Institut de France; Officier de la Légion d'Honneur. Château de Versailles, Seine-et-Oise, France.
Telephone: 950-5832.

van der Merwe, Schalk Willem, M.B., CH.B.; South African medical practitioner and politician; b. 18 Sept. 1922, Citrusdal, Cape Prov.; ed. Paarl Hoër Jongenskool, Univs. of Cape Town and South Africa.
Practised as Gen. Practitioner, District Surgeon at Keimoes, Cape Prov. 47-66; mem. Parl. 66-; Deputy Minister of the Interior, Social Welfare, Pensions and Coloured Affairs 70-72; Minister of Health, Coloured, Rehoboth and Nama Affairs 72-76, of Health, Planning, Environment and Statistics Jan. 76-.
Ministry of Health, Private Bag X399, Pretoria, South Africa.

van der Meulen, Jozef Vital Marie, B.POL.SC.; Belgian diplomatist; b. 1 March 1914, Melsele-Waas.
Inspector of Finances; Dir.-Gen. Ministry of Econ. Affairs; mem. Exec. Cttee. European Agency for Nuclear Energy; now Amb., Perm. Rep. to European Communities; Hon. Sec. Council of Ministers; Hon. Chef de Cabinet, Prime Minister, Minister of Econ. Affairs; mem. Board Francqui Foundation.
62 rue Belliard, Brussels, Belgium.

van der Pol, Cornelis, B.SC., PH.D.; South African chemical engineer; b. 26 July 1925, Jutphaas, Netherlands; s. of Paul van der Pol and Neeltje Bosman; m. Fleur Edith de Lange 1951; one s. one d.; ed. Univ. of the Witwatersrand, Univ. of Queensland, Australia.
With Sugar Milling Research Inst., Durban 52-57; Asst. Gen. Man., Doornkop Sugar Co., and later Gen. Man. Ubombo Ranches Ltd., Swaziland 57-64; Man. Dir. responsible for cane growing, sugar milling and refining operations in S.A., Huletts Group 64-68; Dir., Huletts Corpn. Ltd. 68-70, Chief Exec. Officer 70-72, Group Man. Dir. July 72-; mem. of the board of many subsidiary cos. in Huletts Group; mem. Prime Minister's Scientific Advisory Council.
Leisure interests: music, gardening.
Huletts Corporation Ltd., 213 West Street, Durban; and P.O.Box 248, Durban 4000, South Africa.

Van der Post, Laurens Jan, C.B.E.; British writer and explorer; b. 13 Dec. 1906.
War service in Syria, Africa and the Far East 39-45; prisoner of war 43-45; Asst. to British Minister, Batavia 45-47; leader of several expeditions in Africa for British Govt. and on his own account; produced the film *The Lost World of the Kalahari* 56.
Publs. *In a Province* 34, *Venture to the Interior, A Bar of Shadow* 52, *The Face Beside the Fire* 53, *Flamingo Feather, The Dark Eye in Africa* 55, *The Lost World of the Kalahari* 58, *The Heart of the Hunter* 61, *The Seed and the Sower* 62, *Journey into Russia* 64, *A Portrait of All the Russias* 67, *The Hunter and the Whale* 67, *A Portrait of Japan* 68, *The Night of the New Moon* 70, *A Story like the Wind* 72, *A Far Off Place* 74, *A Mantis Carol* 75, *Jung and the Story of our Time* 76.
27 Chelsea Towers, Chelsea Manor Gardens, London, S.W.3. England.

Van der Spuy, Johannes Petrus; South African politician and diplomatist; b. 24 Nov. 1912; ed. Univ. of Stellenbosch and Univ. Coll. of Orange Free State.
Member of Parl. 61-67; Amb. to Austria 69; Minister of Educ. and Culture 69-76, of Posts and Telecommunications, Social Welfare and Pensions 76-.
Ministry of Posts and Telecommunications, Pretoria, South Africa.

van der Stee, Alphons Petrus Johannes Mathildus Maria; Netherlands politician; b. 30 July 1928, Terheyden, North Brabant; ed. Catholic Univ., Nijmegen.
Joined Begeijn, van Arkel and Co. 56, Partner 60; Chair. Arnhem section, Catholic People's Party 59-63,

mem. Exec. Cttee. and Treasurer, Catholic People's Party 65, Chair 68; Sec. of State for Finance 71-73; Minister of Agriculture and Fisheries 73-.
Ministry of Agriculture and Fisheries, Bezuidenhoutseweg 73, The Hague, Netherlands.

van der Stoel, Max, LL.M., M.A.; Netherlands politician; b. 3 Aug. 1924, Voorschoten; m. Maria Johanna Aritia de Kanter; one s. four d.; ed. Univ. of Leyden.
International Sec. Labour Party (Partij van de Arbeid) 58-65; mem. Exec. Board Socialist Int. 58-65; mem. First Chamber of Parl. 60-63, Second Chamber 63-65, 67-73; State Sec. of Foreign Affairs 65-66; mem. Assembly Council of Europe 67-72; North Atlantic Assembly, European Parl. 72-73; Minister of Foreign Affairs 73-; Pres. Exec. Board, Netherlands Inst. for Peace Research; mem. Koos Vorrink Inst. 63; Grand Cross Order of Merit (Italy), Order of Republic (Tunisia), Order of the White Rose (Finland) and other decorations.
Ministry of Foreign Affairs, Plein 23, The Hague, Netherlands.

van Doorn, Henri Willem; Netherlands politician; b. 6 Oct. 1915, The Hague; ed. Leiden State Univ.
Public Prosecutions Dept., Rotterdam 42, Head Political Investigation Dept. 45; Advocate-Fiscal, Special Tribunal, The Hague 47-51; Deputy Public Prosecutor, Rotterdam 51-56; Chair. Roman Catholic People's Party 54-62; mem. Parl. 56-68; joined Radical Political Party 68; Chair. Roman Catholic Broadcasting Corpn. 61; mem. Board Netherlands Radio Union, Netherlands Television Foundation; Minister for Culture, Recreation and Social Welfare 73-.
Ministry of Cultural Affairs, Recreation and Social Welfare, Steenvoordelaan 370, Rijswijk, Netherlands.
Telephone: (070) 94-92-33.

van Kemenade, Josephus Antonius, PH.D.; Netherlands sociologist; b. 6 March 1937, Amsterdam; m. Anna Maria Nijman 1961; two s. one d.; ed. Catholic Univ., Nijmegen.
Part-time Research Adviser, Catholic Inst. for Socio-ecclesiastical Research 60-65; Dir. Inst. of Applied Sociology 65; Part-time Lecturer in Sociology of Educ., Catholic Univ., Nijmegen 65, Senior Lecturer 69, Prof. 70, mem. Exec. Board 72; Minister of Educ. and Science May 73-; Chair. Educ. Cttee. of Dr. Wiardi Beckman Inst., Board of Govs., School of Journalism, Working Party on Sociology of Educ., Univs. Inst. for Socio-scientific Research (SISWO), Educ. Cttee. of Netherlands Univs. Council; mem. many other educ. cttees. and editorial boards of several publs.
Ministerie van Onderwijs en Wetenschappen, 1 Nieuwe Uitleg, The Hague, Netherlands.

van Laethem, Gabriel; French international official; b. 4 Jan. 1918, Paris; m.; three c.; ed. Ecole Supérieure de Commerce et d'Industrie de Lille, Ecole des Sciences Politiques, Paris.
Fought with French Forces in N. Africa and Italy during World War II; joined diplomatic service; Asst Consul, Shanghai 45-48; First Sec., Washington, D.C. 49-54; First Counsellor to Gen. Commr. for Indo-China 54; Head of Bilateral Technical Assistance, Paris; Dir.-Gen. of Office of High Commr. of France in Morocco; Sec.-Gen. French Co. of the Sahara 58; Gen. Man., Dir. of Office of Industrial Co-operation in Algiers 66-70; Amb. to Australia 71-74; Under-Sec.-Gen. for Econ. and Social Affairs, UN 74-.
United Nations Secretariat, New York, N.Y. 10017, U.S.A.

van Lynden, Baron Diederic Wolter; Netherlands diplomatist; b. 22 April 1917, Amsterdam; m. Anne Heathcote 1945; two s. one d.; ed. Royal Netherlands Naval Coll., Den Helder.
Royal Netherlands Navy 37-48; Foreign Service 49-,

serving in New York (UN), London, Vienna and three times at Ministry of Foreign Affairs 49-70; Dir.-Gen. for Political Affairs, Ministry of Foreign Affairs 70-74; Amb. to Fed. Repub. of Germany Nov. 74-.

Leisure interests: drawing, reading, swimming, walking, shooting.

Publs. articles in Netherlands periodicals on political affairs and on int. law.

Royal Netherlands Embassy, 53 Bonn, Strässchensweg 2, Federal Republic of Germany.

Telephone: (02221)-238091.

Van Praagh, Dame Margaret (Peggy), D.B.E.; British ballet director and teacher; b. 1 Sept. 1910; ed. King Alfred School, London.

Dancer with Dame Marie Rambert 33; examiner for Cechetti Soc. 35; dancer, Sadler's Wells Ballet 41-46; Ballet Mistress Sadler's Wells Theatre Ballet 46-51; Asst. Dir. to Dame Ninette de Valois 51-56; Artistic Dir., Borovansky Ballet, Australia 60-61; Artistic Dir., The Australian Ballet 62-74; mem. Victorian Council of the Arts; Hon. D.Litt., Univ. of New England, N.S.W. 74.

Publs. *How I became a Ballet Dancer*, *The Choreographic Art* (with Peter Brisnon).

Flat 24, 248 The Avenue, Parkville, Victoria 3052, Australia.

Telephone: 38-5773.

van Tamelen, Eugene Earl, PH.D.; American professor of chemistry; b. 20 July 1925, Zeeland, Mich.; s. of Gerrit van Tamelen and Henrietta (Vanden Bosch) van Tamelen; m. Mary Ruth Houtman 1951; one s. two d.; ed. Hope Coll. and Harvard Univ.

Instructor, Univ. of Wisconsin 50-52, Asst. Prof. 52-56, Assoc. Prof. 56-59, Prof. 59-61, Homer Adkins Prof. 61-62; Prof. of Chem. Stanford Univ. 62-, Chair. Dept. of Chem. 74-; Prof.-Extraordinarius Univ. of Groningen, Netherlands 67-74; G. Haight Travelling Fellow 57, Guggenheim Fellow 65, 73; Research Stereochem., Biochem., Photochem. and Organic and Inorganic Chem. 53-; mem. Nat. Acad. of Sciences, American Acad. of Arts and Sciences, American Chemical Soc., Chemical Soc., London; Editor *Bioorganic Chemistry*; Hon. D.Sc. (Bucknell Univ., Hope Coll.); Pure Chemistry Award, American Chemical Soc. 61, Leo Hendrick Baekeland Award 65, A.C.S. Award for Creative Work in Synthetic Organic Chem. 70.

Leisure interests: architecture and building, theatre, travel, gardening.

Stanford University, Stanford, Calif. 94035; Home: 23570 Camino Hermoso, Los Altos Hills, Calif.; 127 Cormorant Way, Pajaro Dunes, Calif., U.S.A.; 1 Smugglers' Cove, Cap Estate, Castries, St. Lucia, West Indies.

Telephone: 415-321-2300 (Office); 415-941-2356 (Home, Calif.); 415-497-3507 (St. Lucia).

Van Veelen, Evert; Netherlands business executive; b. 13 Nov. 1911, IJmuiden; m. M. Habermehl; six s. three d.

With Admin. Dept. Hoogovens 27-31, Commercial Dept. 31-49, Man. 49-53; Man. Dir. Wm. H. Müller en Co. NV 53-65; mem. Man. Board Estel NV Hoesch Hoogovens 72-75, Chair. Board of Man. 75-; mem. Man. Board Hoogovens IJmuiden BV 72-75, Chair. Board of Man. 75-; Chair. Board of Man. Estel NV Hoesch Hoogovens and Koninklijke Nederlandsche Hoogovens en Staalfabriken NV 75-; mem. Man. Board Hoesch Werke AG; Knight, Order of Netherlands Lion.

ESTEL NV Hoesch-Hoogovens, Barbarossastraat 35, Nijmegen; Home: Wilhelminaplein 7, Wassenaar, Netherlands.

Telephone: 080-269111 (Office).

Van Vleck, John Hasbrouck, A.M., PH.D.; American professor; b. 13 March 1899, Middletown, Conn.; s. of Edward Burr Van Vleck and Hester Raymond Van

Vleck; m. Abigail Pearson 1927; no c.; ed. Univ. of Wisconsin and Harvard Univ.

Instructor in Physics, Harvard Univ. 22-23; Asst. Prof. Minnesota 23-26, Assoc. Prof. 26-27, Prof. 27-28; Prof. Wisconsin Univ. 28-34; Prof. Harvard Univ. 34-, Hollis Prof. of Mathematics and Natural Philosophy 51-69, Emer. Prof. 69-; Dean of Engineering and Applied Physics 51-57; Guggenheim Foundation Fellow 30; Lorentz Prof., Leiden Univ. 60; Eastman Prof., Oxford Univ. 61-62; Pres. American Physical Soc. 52; mem. Nat. Acad. of Sciences, American Philosophical Soc. American Acad. of Arts and Sciences; foreign assoc. of several acads., many hon. degrees; Albert A. Michelson Award, Case Inst. 63; Irving Langmuir Prize 65; Nat. Medal of Science 66; Chevalier Légion d'Honneur.

Leisure interests: Japanese prints, travel.

Publs. *Quantum Principles and Line Spectra* 26, *Theory of Electric and Magnetic Susceptibilities* 32.

Lyman Laboratory of Physics, Harvard University, Cambridge, Mass. 02138, U.S.A.

Van Zandt, John Parker, B.S., PH.D.; American economist; b. 16 Jan. 1894, Chicago, Ill.; s. of George Van Zandt and Grace Goodspeed; m. Lydia Van Hagan 1937; no c.; ed. Univs. of Chicago, Washington and Calif.

Captain U.S. Air Service 18-26; Pres. Scenic Airways 27-29; European Aviation Rep., Ford Motor Co. 29-31; Pacific Rep., Pan-American Airways 35-38; Consultant, Civil Aeronautics Board 39-42; Senior Staff member, The Brookings Inst. 42-47; Pres. Aviation Research Inst. 47-50; Deputy to Asst. Sec. of the Air Force 50-53; Aviation mem. U.N. Transport Survey Mission to Central America 52-53; Aircraft Section NATO 53-59; Pres. European Technical Services 59-.

Leisure interests: travel, golf.

Publs. *European Air Transport on the Eve of War* 40, *Geography of World Air Transport* 44, *Civil Aviation and Peace* 44, *World Aviation Annual* (Editor-in-Chief) 48. 3900 Cathedral Ave., N.W., Washington, D.C. 20016, U.S.A.

Vanamo, Jorma Jaakko, L. en D.; Finnish diplomatist; b. 30 Oct. 1913, Mouhijärvi; s. of Eino Jaakko Vanamo and Sigrid Emilia Vanamo; m. Hanna Hongisto 1938; two s. one d.; ed. Univ. of Helsinki.

Diplomatic Service 39-, Moscow 40-41, Ministry of Foreign Affairs 41-45, Moscow 45-48, Ministry of Foreign Affairs 49-51; Counsellor, Stockholm 51-53, Washington 54-56; Dir. of Admin. Div., Ministry of Foreign Affairs 56-58; Ambassador to Poland 58-62, Minister to Romania 58-60, to Bulgaria 58-62; Ambassador to U.S.S.R., also accred. to Afghanistan and Mongolia 63-67; Sec. of State, Ministry of Foreign Affairs 67-70; Amb. to Italy, also accred. to Cyprus and Malta 70-75; Amb. to Sweden 75-.

Leisure interests: music, photography.

Office: Regeringsgatan 67, 103 82 Stockholm; Home: V. Trädgårdsgatan 13, 111 53 Stockholm, Sweden.

Telephone: 24 02 70 (Office).

Vance, Cyrus Roberts, B.A., LL.B.; American lawyer and fmr. government official; b. 27 March 1917, Clarksburg, W. Va.; s. of John Carl and Amy Roberts Vance; m. Gracie Elsie Sloane 1947; one s. four d.; ed. Kent School and Yale Univ.

Lieutenant, U.S. Navy 42-46; Asst. to Pres. The Mead Corpn. 46-47; Simpson, Thacher and Bartlett, N.Y. (law firm) 47-61, Partner 56-61, 69-; Special Counsel, Preparedness Investigating Subcttee., Cttee. on Armed Services of the U.S. Senate 57-60; Consulting Counsel to Special Cttee. on Space and Astronautics, U.S. Senate 58; Gen. Counsel, Dept. of Defense 61-62; Chair. Cttee. Adjudication of Claims of the Admin. Conf. of the U.S. 61-62; Sec. of the Army 62-64; Dep. Sec. of Defense 64-67; Pres. Johnson's Special Envoy on Cyprus Situation 67, on Korean Situation 68; negotiator at Paris talks on Viet-Nam 68-69; Dir. Pan American World Airways

69-; Chair. Board of Rockefeller Foundation; Pres. Bar Asscn. of City of N.Y. 74-; mem. Board of IBM (Int. Business Machines Corpn.), New York Times Co.; mem. U.S. Supreme Court, American Bar Asscn., N.Y., State Bar Asscn.; Fellow, American Coll. Trial Lawyers; Medal of Freedom 69.
One Battery Park Plaza, New York, U.S.A.
Telephone: 212-483-9000.

Vandeputte, Robert M. A. C., D. en D., D. en SC. POL. ET SOC.; Belgian banker and university professor; b. 1908, Antwerp; m. Marie-Louise Cauwe 1938; three c.; ed. Univs. of Louvain, Nijmegen, Paris, Berlin and Berne.
Called to Antwerp Bar 30; Prof. Univ. of Louvain 36-; Cabinet Chief, Ministry of Econ. Affairs 39-40; Sec.-Gen. Asscn. Belge des Banques 40-42 ; Dir. Banque Nat. de Belgique 43-44, Gov. 71; Man. Dir. Société Nat. de Crédit à l'Industrie 44-48, Pres. 48-71; Regent Banque Nat. de Belgique 54-71; mem. Caisse Générale d'Epargne et de Retraite 58-; Dir. and mem. Directing Cttee. Société Nat. d'Investissement 62-71; Pres. Inst. de Réescompte et de Garantie 73-; Administrateur, Palais des Beaux-Arts de Belgique 66-; mem. Conseil Supérieur des Finances 69-71; Pres. Hoger Inst. voor Bestuurs- en Handelswetenschappen 59-; Commdr. Order of the Crown and Knight Order of Léopold, (Belgium); Officer Order of Merit (Italian Repub.); Commdr. Order of St. Gregory the Great (Holy See); Gr. Officer, Order of Leopold II (Belgium), and other awards.
Publs. in Dutch: *Beginselen van Nijverheidsrecht, Handboek voor Verzekeringen en Verzekeringsrecht;* in French: *Quelques aspects de l'Activité de la Société Nationale de Crédit à l'Industrie, Le Statut de l'Entreprise.*
Boulevard de Berlaimont 5, 1000 Brussels; Home: Avenue de Tervueren 282, 1150 Brussels, Belgium.
Telephone: 217-63-00 (Office).

Vanderpoorten, Herman, LL.D.; Belgian politician; b. 25 Aug. 1922; ed. Atheneum Berchem-Antwerp and Rijksuniversiteit te Gent.
Attorney 45; County Councillor, Antwerp 49-58; Town Councillor and Deputy Justice of the Peace, Lier 59; mem. Chamber of Representatives 61-65; Senator 65; Minister of Interior 66-68, of Justice 73-; Pres. Liberal Flemish Asscn. 57-66.
Ministry of Justice, Brussels; and Antwerpsesteenweg 2, Lier, Belgium.

Vanistendael, August Albert Joseph; Belgian trade unionist and social worker; b. 1917; ed. Secondary School of the Fathers of Don Bosco.
Factory Worker, Belgium 34-36; Bank Employee, Brussels 36-37; Local Branch Trade Union Sec. 38; Sec.-Gen. Nat. Federation of Christian Trade Unions in Hotel Trade, Brussels 38-40; Public Admin. 40-44; Nat. Sec. Hotel Trade Section, Nat. Fed. of Christian T.U.s of Food Industry 44-45; Sec. Nat. Fed. of Clerical Employees, Brussels 45-47; Asst. Sec.-Gen., Int. Fed. of Christian Trade Unions (IFCTU), Utrecht 47-52; Sec.-Gen. Brussels 52, Pres. Co-operation and Solidarity; Lecturer, Univ. of Louvain 63; Lay auditor at Ecumenical Council Vatican II 66; mem. Pontifical Comm. Justice and Peace 67; mem. Joint Exploratory Cttee. of Roman Catholic Church and World Council of Churches on Justice, Devt. and Peace 67; Sec.-Gen. of Int. Co-operation for Socio-Econ. Devt. (CIDSE).
Publs. poetry: *Schakel Der Ziel* 45, *Pool en Tegenpool* 51; novel: *Barbara.*
CIDSE, 6 rue de la Limite, Brussels 3; Co-operation and Solidarity, 158 rue Joseph II, Brussels 4; Home: Prinses Lydialaan 16, Heverlee, Belgium.
Telephone: 17-53-59 and 18-05-87 (CIDSE); 34-42-60 (Co-operation and Solidarity).

Vanprapar, Kamol; Thai lawyer; b. 7 Dec. 1908; ed. Ministry of Justice Law School, Nat. Defence Coll.

Public Prosecutor 30-68; Dir.-Gen. Public Prosecutor's Dept. 68-72; Minister of Justice 72-73, of the Interior 73-74; Knight Grand Cordon, Order of the Crown of Thailand; Knight Grand Cross, Order of the White Elephant.
644/3 Samsen Road, Bangkok 3, Thailand.
Telephone: 815601 (Home).

Varda, Agnès; French film writer and director; b. 30 May 1928; m. Jacques Demy (q.v.); one s. one d.; ed. Séte, Herault, and Univ. de Paris à la Sorbonne.
Official Photographer, Théâtre National Populaire 51-61; Reporter and Photographer for *Réalités, Plaisir de France, Marie-France* and other magazines; Prix Méliès 62 (*Cleo de 5 à 7*), Prix Louis Delluc 65 (*Le Bonheur*), Bronze Lion, Venice Festival 64 (*Salut les Cubains*), Silver Bear, Berlin Festival 65 (*Le Bonheur*); 1st Prize, Oberhausen (*Black Panthers*), Popular Univs. jury (*Lions Love*) 70.
Full-length films: *La Pointe-Courte* 54, *Cleo de 5 à 7* 61, *Le Bonheur* 64. *Les Créatures* 65, *Loin du Vietnam* 67, *Lions Love* 69, *Nausicaa* 70, *Daguerreo Types* 74; Short-length films: *O Saisons, O Châteaux* 57, *L'Opéra-Mouffe* 58, *Du côté de la Côte* 58, *Salut les Cubains* 63, *Uncle Yanco* 67, *Black Panthers* 68, *Réponse de Femmes* 75.
86 rue Daguerre, Paris 14e, France.
Telephone: 734-57-17.

Vargas, Lt.-Gen. Jesús Miranda; Philippine army officer and international official; b. 22 March 1905; ed. Manila North High School and Philippine Constabulary Acad.
Philippine Constabulary 30-36; Philippine Army 37-51; Chief of Staff 54-56; Mil. Adviser to SEATO 54-56; retired from armed forces 56; Sec. of Nat. Defence 57-59; Chair. Board of Dirs. Nat. Waterworks and Sewerage Authority 57-59; Vice-Pres. Philippine-American Life Assurance Co. 59-; Pres. Philippine-American Management and Financing Co. 60-; Chair. Board of Trustees Ramon Magsaysay Award Foundation 62-65; Sec.-Gen. South East Asia Treaty Org. (SEATO) 65-72; many decorations.
Philippine-American Life Assurance Co., Philamlife Building, UN Avenue, Ermita, Manila, Philippines.

Vargas Llosa, Mario; Peruvian writer; b. 28 March 1936; ed. Cochabamba (Bolivia), Universidad de San Marcos, Lima, and Universidad de Madrid.
Former journalist *La Crónica* Lima, *La Industria,* Piura, and La Radio Panamericana, Lima, Agence-France Presse, Paris; broadcaster on Latin American services of Radiodiffusion Télévision Française; Lecturer in Latin American Literature, Queen Mary Coll., London Univ.; Prix Leopoldo Alas 58, Prix Biblioteca Breve 62, *Crítica Española* Prize 63, Rómulo Gallegos Prize 67.
Publs. include: *Los Jefes* 58, *La Ciudad y los perros* 62, *La Casa Verde* 65, *Los Cachorros* 66, *Conversación en la Catedral* 70.
c/o Embassy of Peru, London, S.W.1, England.

Varley, Rt. Hon. Eric Graham, M.P.; British politician; b. 11 Aug. 1932, Poolsbrook, Derbys.; m. Marjorie Turner 1955; one s.; ed. Secondary Modern and Technical Schools, and Ruskin Coll. Oxford.
Apprentice Engineer's Turner 47-52; Engineer's Turner 52-55; Mining Industry Craftsman 55-64; Nat. Union of Miners' Branch Sec. 55-64; mem. Area Exec. Cttee., Derbys. 56-64; mem. Parl. for Chesterfield 64-; Asst. Govt. Whip 67-68; Parl. Private Sec. to Prime Minister 68-69; Minister of State, Ministry of Technology 69-70; Sec. of State for Energy 74-75, for Industry June 75-.
Leisure interests: gardening, reading, sport.
House of Commons, London, SW1A OAA, England.

Várnai, Zseni; Hungarian poetess; b. 25 May 1890, Nagyvázsony; m. Andor Peterdi 1910; one s. one d.
Awarded Silver Degree of Order of Liberty for work in

movement of nat. resistance during German occupation, and First Degree of the József Attila Prize 54; awarded Munka erdemrend (Degree of Works) 58, 60, Golden Degree of Order of Works 65, 68, Literary Prize of Hungarian Trade Union 69; Literary Prize of the Native Place District Council 69.
Leisure interests: reading, classical music.
Publs. *Katonafiamnak* (*To My Soldier Son*), *Vörös tavasz* (*Red Spring*), *Anyasziv* (*Mother Heart*), *A fájdalom könyve* (*Book of Grief*), *Gracchusok anyja* (*Mother of the Gracchi*), *Furulyaszó, Örömök kertje* (*Garden of Joys*), *A mesélő erdö* (*The Forest of Tales*), *Im itt az irás* (*Lo, Here is the Writing*), *Kórus szopránban* (*Soprano Choir*), *Fekete bárány* (*Black Lamb*), *Én mondom és te add tovább, Legyen meg a Te akaratod!, Ég és föld között* (*Between Earth and Heaven*), *Mint viharban a falevél* (*Like a Leaf in the Tempest*), *Egy asszony a milliók közül* (*A Woman of the Millions*), Vols. I and II, *Aldot asszonyok* (*Blessed Women*), *Száz vers a szabadságért* (*Hundred Poems for Liberty*), *Várnai Zseni válogatott versei* 55, *Fényben, viharban* (*In Light and Lightning*) (novel), *Igy égtem, énekeltem* (*In Flames I Sang*) 58, *Feltámadás* (*Resurrection*) (Dramatic poem) 59, *Peace!* (poems), *Légy boldog te Világ* (*O World, Be Happy*) (poems) 61, *Élők, vigyázzatok!* (*People, be on your guard!*) (poems) 62, *Nem volt hidba . . .* (*It was not in vain*) 62, *A Woman of the Millions* (autobiography) 63, 74, *Nyugtalan madár* (*Restless Bird*) (poems) 66, *Ének az anyáról* (*Songs upon the Mother*) 68, *Tündérkert* (*Fairyland*) (poems for children) 68, *Borostyán* (*Amber*) 69, *Idő Heroldja* (*Time's Herald*) 71, *Vers és virág* (*Song and Flower*) 73.
Keleti Károly u. 27, H-1024 Budapest 11, Hungary.
Telephone: 361-346.

Vårvik, Dagfinn; Norwegian politician; b. 8 June 1924, Leinstrand; s. of Kristian and Helga Vårvik; m. Bjørg Presttrø 1951; one s. two d.; ed. Univ. of Oslo.
Secretary to Parl. Group, Centre Party 52-61; mem. editorial staff, *Nationen* 61-63, Chief Editor 63-; Minister of Finance 67-71, of Prices and Wages 65-71, of Foreign Affairs 72-73; Chair. Centre Party 73-.
Senterpartiet, Arbeidergatan 4, Oslo; Home: Theodor Løvstads vei 38, Oslo 2, Norway.
Telephone: 33.50.90 (Office); 55.76.11 (Home).

Vas, István; Hungarian poet; b. 24 Sept. 1910, Budapest; s. of Pál Vas and Erzsebet Augenstein; m. 1st Etel Nagy 1936, 2nd Maria Kutni 1945, 3rd Piroska Szántó 1951.
Publisher's Reader 46, wrote poems and essays for the Press; noted as translator of plays by Shakespeare, Racine, Schiller, Molière, O'Neill, poems by Apollinaire and Eliot, and novels from French, German and English; Kossuth Prize 62, Order of Labour 70, Pro Arte Medal 73, Chevalier Palmes Académiques 73.
Publs. Collected Essays: *Az Ismeretlen Isten* (The Unknown God); poems: *Mit akar ez az egy ember?* (Collected Poems), *Önarckép a Hetvenes Evekböl* (Self-portrait in the Seventies); autobiographical novel: *Nehéz szerelem* (Hard Love).
Home: H-1013 Budapest, Groza Péter rakpart 17, Hungary.

Vasarely, Victor; French (b. Hungarian) artist; b. 1908; ed. Budapest Bauhaus.
Studied medicine; settled in Paris 30; one-man exhbns. Budapest 29-33, Europe 45-56, Rose Fried Gallery, New York City 58, World House Gallery, N.Y.C. 61, 62, Montevideo 58, Hanover Gallery, London 62, Pace Gallery, Boston 62; group exhbns. in Paris, Stedelijk Museum, Amsterdam, Documenta III, Kassel, Gallery Chalette, N.Y.C., Sidney Janis Gallery, N.Y.C., Solomon R. Guggenheim Museum, New York, and in São Paulo, Rio de Janeiro and Montevideo, Tate Gallerv, London 64; permanently represented in Museum of Modern Art,

New York, Musée St. Etienne, Paris, Albright Knox Gallery, Harvard, Tate Gallery, London, Stedelijk Museum, Amsterdam, and in Buenos Aires, Montevideo, Brussels, Reykjavík, São Paulo, Helsinki, etc.; Musée Vasarely at Château de Gordes, Vaucluse, opened 71; Prix de Critique (Brussels) 55, Guggenheim Int. Award for Merit 64, Guggenheim Prize (New York) 64, Ljubljana Award 65, São Paulo Biennale Award 65, Grand Prix de la VIIIeme Biennale de São Paulo 65, Carnegie Award 67, Ministry of Foreign Affairs Prize Tokyo Biennale 67, Painting Prize of Carnegie Inst. 67, First Prize of Premier Biennale de la Gravure Cracovie (Poland) 68, Première Palette d'Or Festivale Internationale de Peinture Cagnes-sur-Mer (France) 69; Hon. citizen of New Orleans 66, Hon. Prof. in Applied Arts, Budapest 69, Chevalier, Légion d'Honneur 70.
83 rue aux Reliques, 77410 Annet-sur-Marne, France.

Vásáry, Tamás; Hungarian concert pianist; b. 11 Aug. 1933; m. Ildiko Kovacs 1967; ed. Franz Liszt Univ. of Music, Budapest under Lajos Hernadi, Jozsef Gat and Zoltan Kodàly.
First solo performance at age of eight; studied at Franz Liszt Acad. until 54; remained at Franz Liszt Acad. to teach theory; recitals in Leningrad, Moscow and Warsaw; settled in Switzerland 58; London debut 61, New York 62; debut as conductor in Menton Festival of Music 71; has since appeared in Europe, S. Africa, S. America, U.S.A., Canada, India, Thailand, Hong Kong, Australia, Japan and Mexico; records for Deutsche Grammophon; Liszt Prizes: Queen Elizabeth (Belgium), Marguerite Longue (Paris); Chopin Prizes: Int. Competition, Warsaw, Int. Competition, Brazil; Bach and Paderewski Medals (London).
Principal recordings: three records of works of F. Liszt; nine records of works of Chopin.
Leisure interest: writing fiction.
9 Village Road, London, N.3, England.

Vasconcellos Motta, H.E. Cardinal Carlos Carmelo de; Brazilian ecclesiastic; b. 1890.
Ordained priest 18; Titular Bishop of Algiza 32; Bishop of São Luis do Maranhão 35-44; Archbishop of São Paulo 44-64, of Aparecida 64-; created Cardinal by Pope Pius XII 46; mem. Sacred Congregations of Religious, of Ceremonies and of Seminaries and Univs.
Praça N. Sra. Aparecida 273, Aparecida, São Paulo, Brazil.

Vasey, Sir Ernest Albert, K.B.E., C.M.G.; Kenyan financial consultant; b. 27 Aug. 1901; m. 1st Norah Mary Mitchell 1923, 2nd Hannah Strauss 1944; two s.
Nairobi Town Council 39-50; mem. Kenya Legislative Council 45, mem. for Health and Local Govt. 50-51, for Education, Health and Local Govt. 51-52; Minister for Finance and Development 52-59; Minister for Finance, Tanganyika 60-62, Financial and Econ. Adviser, World Bank Development Service 62-66, Resident Rep., IBRD in Pakistan 62-66; 2nd Class Brilliant Star of Zanzibar, Hilal-i-Quaid-i-Azam of Pakistan 66.
Leisure interests: drama, bridge.
Publs. *Report on African Housing* 50, *Economic and Political Trends in Kenya* 56.
P.O. Box 14235, Nairobi, Kenya.
Telephone: 25208 (Office); 43461 (Home).

Vashchenko, Grigory Ivanovich; Soviet politician; b. 1920; ed. Kharkov Engineering Coll. and U.S.S.R. Polytechnic Inst.
Factory worker in Kharkov and Nizhny Tagil 38-58; Party Official 58-63; First Sec. Kharkov Regional Cttee. C.P. of Ukraine July 63-72; Vice-Chair. Ukrainian S.S.R. Council of Ministers 72-; Alt. mem. Political Bureau, Central Cttee. C.P. Ukraine; mem. C.P.S.U. Central Cttee. 66; Deputy to U.S.S.R. Supreme Soviet

66-; Chair. Planning and Budget Comm., Soviet of Union 74-; mem. C.P.S.U. 43-.
Ukrainian Council of Ministers, Kiev, U.S.S.R.

Vasilevsky, Marshal Alexander Mikhailovich; Soviet army officer and politician; b. 30 Sept. 1895, Novopokrovskoe, Ivanovo Region; ed. Military Acad. of General Staff.
Served 14-18 war and Civil War; various posts in People's Commissariat of Defence and Volga Mil. Area 31-36; Deputy Chief of Staff, U.S.S.R. Armed Forces 41-42, Chief of Staff 42-45, 46-49; Deputy Commissar for Defence 42-44; C.-in-C. Byelorussian Front and Far East 45; Minister of Defence 49-53, Dep. Minister of Defence 53-57, Insp.-Gen., Ministry of Defence 59-; Hero of Soviet Union (twice), Order of Lenin (seven times), Victory (twice), Order of Red Banner (twice), Suvorov 1st Class Red Star and numerous other decorations.
c/o Ministry of Defence, Naberezhnaya M. Thoreza 34, Moscow, U.S.S.R.

Vasiliev, Vladimir Viktorovich; Soviet ballet dancer; b. 1940; ed. Bolshoi Theatre Ballet School.
With Bolshoi Theatre Ballet 58-; Honoured Artist of the R.S.F.S.R.; Lenin Prize 70.
Principal roles: The Prince (*Nutcracker*), Pan (*Valpurgis Night*), The Poet (*Chopiniana*), Danila (*Stone Flower*), Prince Charming (*Cinderella*), Batyr (*Shurale*), Andrei (*A Page of Life*), Basil (*Don Quixote*), Albert (*Giselle*), Frondoso (*Laurencia*), Medjnun (*Leili and Medjnun*); also appeared in *The Humpbacked Horse* and *Spartacus*.
State Academic Bolshoi Theatre of the U.S.S.R., 1 Ploshchad Sverdlova, Moscow, U.S.S.R.

Vass, Mrs. István; Hungarian politician; b. 1915, Budafok; d. of János Metzker; m. István Vass 1931; one s. two d.
Worker in Rubber Factory, later welder; mem. Communist Party 39; mem. Presidium Hungarian Peace Council; M.P. 53-; Deputy Speaker 55-63, Speaker 63-67, Deputy Speaker 67-May 71; Sec. Patriotic People's Front 56-60; Gen. Sec. Democratic Fed. of Hungarian Women 50-56, Pres. 56-57; mem. Pres. Council of Hungary.
Leisure interests: angling, cooking.
c/o Presidential Council, Kossuth Lajos tér 1/3, H- 1357 Budapest V, Hungary.

Vaucelles, Count Pierre Louis Joseph de; French diplomatist; b. 13 Feb. 1907; ed. Ecole Fénelon, Lycée Condorcet and Institut catholique de Paris.
Foreign Service 32-; Attaché Bucharest 32-37; Sec. Berlin 37-40, Budapest 40-43; Sec. Brussels 44-46, Counsellor 46-48; at Ministry of Foreign Affairs 48-50; Counsellor Brussels 50-52, Minister 52-54; Ambassador to Iraq 54-56; Asst. Perm. Rep. to UN 57-60; Dir. diplomatic section Institut des hautes études de défense nationale 60-63: Ambassador to Venezuela 63-68, to Norway 68-71; Commdr. Légion d'Honneur, Commdr. Etoile noire, Grand Officier Ordre de la Couronne (Belgium); Commdr. Ordre de Léopold, Grand Cross, Orders of Francisco de Miranda and Libertador (Venezuela), Grand Cross, Order of Saint Olav (Norway).
5 rue Marietta Matrin, Paris 16e; and Chateau Filhot, 33118 Sauternes, France.
Telephone: 647-9936 (Paris).

Vaughan, Sir (George) Edgar, K.B.E.; British professor and former diplomatist; b. 24 Feb. 1907, Cardiff; s. of William John and Emma Kate (Caudle) Vaughan; m. Elsie Winifred Deubert; one s. two d.; ed. Cheltenham Grammar School and Jesus Coll., Oxford.
Vice-Consul, Hamburg 31; Second Sec. and Vice-Consul, La Paz 32-35; Vice-Consul, Barcelona 35-38, Buenos Aires 38-44; Chargé d'Affaires and Consul-Gen.,

Monrovia 45-46; Consul, Seattle 46-49; Consul-Gen., Lourenço Marques 49-53, Amsterdam 53-56; Minister and Consul-Gen., Buenos Aires 56-60; Ambassador to Panama 60-63, to Colombia 64-66; Special Lecturer in History, Univ. of Saskatchewan (Regina Campus) 66-67, Prof. of History 67-74, Dean of Arts and Science 69-73; Fellow, Royal Historical Soc. 65-; Hon. Fellow, Jesus Coll., Oxford 66-.
Leisure interests: golf, swimming.
27 Birch Grove, London, W3 9SP, England.

Vaughan, Dame Janet Maria, D.B.E., D.M., F.R.C.P., M.A.; British doctor and university official; b. 18 Oct. 1899, Clifton, Bristol; d. of William Wyana Vaughan and Margaret (née Symonds) Vaughan; m. David Gourlay 1930; two d.; ed. Univ. Coll. Hospital and Somerville Coll., Oxford.
Assistant Clinical Pathologist, Univ. Coll. Hospital 27-29; Rockefeller Travelling Fellow 29-30; Beit Memorial Fellow 31-34; Leverhulme Fellow, Royal Coll. of Physicians 34-35; Clinical Pathologist British Post-Graduate Medical School 35-39; Dir. N.W. London Blood Supply Depot 39-45; Principal Somerville Coll. 45-67, Hon. Fellow 67-; Chair. Oxford Regional Hospital Board 50-51; Dir. Medical Research Unit for Research on Bone-Seeking Isotopes 50-; mem. Royal Comm. for Equal Pay 44-45, Phillips Cttee. on Econs. and Problems of the Provision for Old Age 53, Commonwealth Scholarship Comm. 64-, Cttee. on Libraries of Univ. Grants Cttee. 65-67; Trustee Nuffield Foundation.
Leisure interests: gardening, travel.
Publs. *The Anaemias* 34, *The Physiology of Bone* 70, 2nd edn. 75, *The Effects of Irradiation on the Skeleton* 73, and numerous scientific papers.
1 Fairlawn End, First Turn, Wolvercote, Oxford, England.
Telephone: Oxford 54111.

Vaughan, (John) Keith, C.B.E.; British painter, designer and illustrator; b. 23 Aug. 1912, Selsey, Sussex; s. of E. G. S. Vaughan and G. R. M. Macingtosh; ed. Christ's Hospital.
Lecturer in Painting Central School of Art, London 52-56, Slade School 57-; Resident Painter State Univ. of Iowa 60; first one-man exhbn. London 46, others in New York, London, Buenos Aires, São Paulo, retrospective exhbn. Whitechapel Art Gallery, London 62; represented in public galleries: Tate Gallery, Victoria and Albert Museum, etc., London, Fitzwilliam Museum, Cambridge and provincial museums in U.K.; Nat. Gallery of Scotland; Nat. Gallery of New South Wales; Toronto Museum; Albright-Knox Museum, Buffalo, Wadsworth Atheneum, Conn., Art Inst. of Chicago, Yale Univ., Iowa Univ.; Hon. A.R.C.A.; Design of the Year Award, Council of Industrial Design 58.
Major works: Central Mural for Dome of Discovery, Festival of Britain 51, Ceramic Mural Corby New Town 54, Mural for L.C.C. Aboyne Estate 63; Illustrated Books: *Une Saison en Enfer*, Rimbaud 49, *Tom Sawyer*, Twain 51.
Publ. *Journal and Drawings* 66.
9 Belsize Park, London, N.W.3; and Harrow Hill, Toppesfield, Halstead, Essex, England.
Telephone: 01-794-4966.

Vaughan, Ralph Thomas, B.A., Q.C., LL.D.; Canadian airline executive; b. 12 July 1919, Halifax; s. of Francis William Vaughan and Lillian Clare Hemsworth; m. Elinore Gavin 1950; three s. one d.; ed. St. Mary's and Dalhousie Univs.
News Editor, *Halifax Herald* 46-48; called to Bar of Nova Scotia 48; Partner, Fielding, O'Hearn & Vaughan 48-51; Exec. Asst. to Premier of Nova Scotia 51-54; Asst. to Pres. Canadian Nat. Railways 55-66, Vice-Pres. CNR, Sec. CNR and Air Canada 66-72, Vice-Pres., Asst. to Chair., Sec. Air Canada 71-73, Pres. 73-, Vice-Pres., Asst. to Chair., Sec. CNR 72; mem. Board of

Govs., St. Mary's Univ. 70, Cttee. on Property and Devt., St. Mary's Univ. 72; Hon. LL.D. (St. Mary's Univ.) 69.
Leisure interest: golf.
Air Canada, 1 Place Ville Marie, Montreal, Quebec H3B 3P7; Home: 393 Devon Avenue, Town of Mount Royal, Quebec, Canada.
Telephone: 874-4931 (Office).

Vaughan, Sarah; American jazz singer; b. 27 March 1924, Newark, N.J.; *d.* of Ada Vaughan; *m.* 3rd Marshall Fisher; one *d.*
Began singing career 42; has sung with bands of Earl Hines, Billy Eckstine and John Kirby Como; Vocalist Award, *Downbeat* 46-52.
Leisure interests: sewing, golf.
Recordings include *I'll Wait and Pray, It's Magic, Tenderly, Misty, Broken Hearted Melody.*
c/o James Harper & Assocs., 13063 Ventura Boulevard, Studio City, Calif. 91604, U.S.A.

Vaughn, Jack Hood, M.A.; American diplomatist; b. 18 Aug. 1920; ed. Univs. of Michigan, Pennsylvania and Mexico.
U.S. Marine Corps 43-46; Univ. Instr. 46-49; U.S. Information Service, Costa Rica and Bolivia 49-51; Agency for Int. Development, Panama, Bolivia, Washington, Senegal 52-61; Regional Dir. for Latin America, Peace Corps 61-64; Ambassador to Panama 64-65; Asst. Sec. for Latin American Affairs 65-66; Dir. The Peace Corps 66-69; Amb. to Colombia 69-70; Pres. Nat. Urban Coalition 70-72; Dean Int. Affairs, Florida Int. Univ. 72.
806 Connecticut Avenue, Washington, D.C. 20006, U.S.A.

Vaughn, William Scott; American business executive; b. 8 Dec. 1902, Kansas City, Mo.; *s.* of Dr. Harry Scott Vaughn and Florence Sloan Vaughn; *m.* Elizabeth Harper 1928; two *d.*; ed. Vanderbilt Univ., Rice Inst., Oxford Univ., England, and Rochester Inst. of Technology.
Eastman Kodak Co. 28-, Asst. to Gen. Manager, Kodak European Companies, Kodak Ltd., London 34-35, Asst. to Gen. Manager, Eastman Kodak Co., Rochester 46, Asst. Vice-Pres. 49, Vice-Pres. and Asst. Gen. Manager 50, First Vice-Pres. Tennessee Eastman Co. and Texas Eastman Co. 52, First Vice-Pres. Eastman Chemical Products Inc. 53, Pres. and Dir. 56, Vice-Pres. and Gen. Man. Eastman Kodak Co. 58, Dir. 59-73, Pres. 60-66, Chair. Board of Dirs. 67-70, Chair. Exec. Cttee. 66-70; Dir. Kodak Ltd., London 62-70, Kodak-Pathé, Paris 62-70, Canadian Kodak Co. Ltd. 60-70, Kodak A.G., Stuttgart 66-70; Dir. Lincoln First Bank of Rochester (mem. Advisory Comm.), Rochester Gas and Electric Corpn.; Chair. Finance Comm., mem. Board of Trustees, Colgate Rochester Divinity School; Pres. Board of Trust Vanderbilt Univ.; Trustee of several educational orgs.; Hon. LL.D. (Rochester Inst. of Technology).
Eastman Kodak Co., 343 State Street, Rochester, New York, 14650, U.S.A.
Telephone: 716-325-2000.

Vázquez Carrizosa, Alfredo, LL.D.; Colombian lawyer and diplomatist; b. 9 Feb. 1909, Bogotá; *s.* of Dr. Alfredo Vázquez-Cobo and Ana Carrizosa-Tanco; *m.* Lucía Holguín 1961; ed. Université Catholique de Louvain, Belgium.
Former lecturer in Public International Law and Constitutional Law, Bogotá; fmr. Secretary-Gen., Ministry of Foreign Affairs; fmr. Acting Head, Ministry of Foreign Affairs; fmr. Asst. Publisher *La República* (daily); mem. House of Reps. 60-62; fmr. Sec.-Gen. of Presidency; fmr. Amb. to Belgium; Rep. to Org. of American States 64-70; Minister of Foreign Affairs 70-74; Amb. to U.K. 75-; mem. Perm. Court of Arbitration, The Hague 75.
Leisure interests: music, art, automobiles.

Publs. *Lectures on Public International Law* (2 vols.) 59-60, *Colombia y la Política del Mar* 72, *El Concordato* 73, *Roncador Quita Sueño y Serrana* 74, *Los Derechos Humanos y la Tragedia de Chile* 75, *El Nuevo Derecho del Mar* 76.
Embassy of Colombia, Flat 3a Hans Crescent, London, SW1X 0LR, England.

Veasey, Josephine, C.B.E.; British (mezzo-soprano) opera singer; b. 10 July 1930, London; *m.* Ande Anderson 1951 (divorced 1969); one *s.* one *d.*
Member of chorus Covent Garden Opera Company 48-50, returned as soloist 55; now principal mezzo-soprano, Royal Opera House, Covent Garden; has sung every major mezzo-soprano role in repertory; many recent foreign engagements have included Salzburg Festival, La Scala, Milan, Metropolitan Opera House, N.Y., and Paris opera; has made recordings with Karajan, Solti and Colin Davis; Hon. R.A.M.
13 Ballard's Farm Road, South Croydon, Surrey, CR2 7JB, England.
Telephone: 01-657-8158.

Večeřa, Bohuslav; Czechoslovak politician; b. 14 May 1925, Pavlínov; ed. Party Coll., Cen. Cttee. of C.P.S.U., Moscow.
Has worked in agricultural sphere for Communist Party 50-; Sec. Regional Cttee. C.P. of Czechoslovakia, Liberec 56-67; Minister-Chair. Fed. Cttee. for Agriculture and Food 70; Minister of Agriculture and Food of C.S.S.R. 71-; Deputy to House of the People, Fed. Assembly 71-; Award for Merit in Construction, Order of Labour 75.
Ministry of Agriculture and Food, Těšnov 65, Prague 1, Czechoslovakia.

Vedel, Vice-Admiral A. H.; Danish naval officer; b. 1 Sept. 1894, Copenhagen; *s.* of Helge and Charlotte (Braëm) Vedel; *m.* Kirsten Lützen 1921; two *s.* two *d.*
Lieutenant 16, Lieut.-Commander 23, Commander 32, Captain 39, Vice-Admiral 41; Chair. Danish Del. to Scandinavian Defence Cttee. 48-49; C.-in-C. Danish Navy 41-58; fmr. Lecturer in Strategy, Danish Naval Acad.; fmr. Chair. Danish Naval Scientific Society; Vice-Pres. Danish Royal Geographical Society 46-73; Chair. Danish Pearyland Expedition to Greenland, Cttee. for navigation in Greenland Waters 59; Pres. UNESCO Intergovt. Conf. on Oceanographic Research, Copenhagen 60; mem. of Cttee. Danish Galathea Expedition round the World; fmr. Board mem. East Asiatic Co. Ltd.; Dr. h.c. (Univ. of Copenhagen).
Rypevej 13, Hellerup, Copenhagen, Denmark.
Telephone: Hellerup 4302.

Veen, Christian van, DR.JUR.SC.; Netherlands politician; b. 19 Dec. 1922, Barneveld; *m.* Petronilla G. de Korte; one *s.* one *d.*
Official, Office of the Town Clerk, Rijswijk 50-60; Town Clerk, Hoogeveen 60-64, Groningen 64-67; Parliamentary Under Sec. for the Interior 67-71; Minister of Educ. and Science 71-73; Pres. Fed. of Netherlands Industry 74-.
Prinses Beatrixlaan 5, The Hague, Netherlands.
Telephone: 814171.

Végh Villegas, Alejandro; Uruguayan industrial engineer and politician; b. 22 Sept. 1928; ed. Escuela de Ingeniería de Montevideo, Univ. of Harvard.
Professor, Escuela de Ingeniería, Montevideo; Prof. Universidad Nacional de Buenos Aires; consultant in power economy in Venezuela; Planning Adviser, Hidronor, S.A., Argentina; Adviser, Planning Ministry of Brazil; Consultant of IDB, OAS, ECLA and IBRD; Under-Sec. of State, Ministry of Industry and Trade 67; Dir., Planning and Budget Office 68; Minister of Finance July 74-.
Ministerio de Economía y Finanzas, Montevideo, Uruguay.

Veibel, Stig, DR. PHIL.; Danish university professor; b. 19 April 1898, Korsør; *s.* of Bertel Christian Veibel and Vilhelmine Petersen; *m.* Ellen Kirk 1940; two *d.*; ed. Royal Technical Coll., Copenhagen.

Assistant, Dept. of Organic Chemistry, Univ. of Copenhagen 20-31; Lecturer in Organic Chemistry, Royal Technical Coll., Copenhagen 32-44, Prof. 44-68; mem. of Acad. of Technical Sciences 43, of Danish Royal Acad. of Sciences 55; Pres. Danske Kemiske Foreningers Faellesraad for Internationalt Samarbejde (Danish Nat. Council of Chem.) 46; Chair. Danish Chemical Soc. 47-50; mem. of Bureau of Int. Union of Chem. 47-51; Hon. mem. French Chemical Soc. 57, Polish Chemical Soc. 59, Finnish Chemical Soc. 69, Danish Chemical Soc. 75; Hon. Dr. Univ. of Bordeaux 61; Corresp. mem. Acad. of Sciences, Paris 61.

Leisure interest: literature.

Publs. *Vejledning i organiske stoffers identification* 26, 37, 47, *Studier over nitreringsprocessen* 29, *Kemiens Historie i Danmark* 39, *Dansk kemisk bibliografi 1800-1935* 43, *Organisk Kemi I-II* 51, 58-59, *The Identification of Organic Compounds* 54, 61, 66, 71, *Identification des substances organiques* 57, Russian edn. 57, German edn. 60, Czechoslovak edn. 64, *Determination of hydroxyl groups* 72.

4 Enighedsvej, DK 2920 Charlottenlund, Denmark. Telephone: (01) OR 5776.

Veil, Simone, L.EN.D.; French lawyer and politician; b. 13 July 1927, Nice; *d.* of André Jacob and Yvonne Steinmetz; *m.* Antoine Veil 1946; three *s.*; ed. Paris Univ.

Lawyer; Attaché, Ministry of Justice 57-59, Asst. 59-65; Technical Adviser to Office of René Pleven, Keeper of the Seals; Sec.-Gen. Conseil Supérieure de la Magistrature 70-74; mem. ORTF Admin. Council 72-74; Minister of Health May 74-; Chevalier Ordre Nat. du Mérite; Médailles de l'Educ. surveillée et de l'admin. pénitentiaire.

Publ. *L'Adoption, données médicales, psychologiques et sociales* (with Prof. Launay and Dr. Soule) 69.

8 avenue de Ségur, 75007 Paris; Home: 11 Place Vauban, 75007 Paris, France.

Vekua, Ilya Nestorovich; Soviet mathematician; b. 23 April 1907, Sheshelety, Georgia; ed. Georgian State Univ., Tbilisi.

Research work in U.S.S.R. Acad. of Sciences and Georgian Acad. of Sciences 30-52; mem. C.P.S.U. 43-; Prof. Moscow Univ. 52-57; corresp. mem. U.S.S.R. Acad. of Sciences 46-58, mem. 58-; mem. Presidium Siberian Dept. of U.S.S.R. Acad. of Sciences 58-; Rector, Novosibirsk Univ. 59-65; Vice-Pres. Acad. of Sciences of Georgian S.S.R. 65-66; Rector Tbilisi Univ. 66-; mem. Editorial Board U.S.S.R. Acad. of Sciences 59-; Deputy U.S.S.R. Supreme Soviet 66-; mem. Comm. for Public Educ., Science and Culture, Soviet of Union; State Prize 50, Lenin Prize 63, Hero of Socialist Labour, Order of Lenin (three times), "Hammer and Sickle" Gold Medal and other decorations.

Publs. *New Methods of Solving Elliptical Equations* 48, *Systems of First Order Differential Equations of the Elliptical Type and Boundary Problems with an Application to the Theory of Shells* 52, *Generalised Analytic Functions* 59, *Fixed Special Points of Generalised Analytical Functions* 62, *New Methods in Mathematical Shell Theory* 65.

Georgian University, Prospekt Tchavtchavadze 1, Tbilisi, U.S.S.R.

Velasco Alvarado, Maj.-Gen. Juan; Peruvian army officer; b. 16 June 1910, Piura; *m.* Consuelo Gonzales de Velasco; two *s.* four *d.*; ed. Escuela de Cadetes.

Captain 40, Major 45, Lieut.-Col. 49, Col. 55, Brig.-Gen. 59, Gen. of Div. 65; taught at mil. schools; Head of 29th Infantry Battn.; Head of Chorrillos Mil. School and School of Infantry; Chief of Staff CIMP; Gen.

Commdr. 2nd Light Div.; Mil. Attaché in France; Chief of Staff, 1st Mil. Region; Gen. Insp. of Army; Army Del. at Interamerican Defense Cttee.; Gen. Chief of Staff of Army; Head of Joint Chiefs of Staff; led coup to depose Pres. Belaúnde Oct. 68; Pres. of Peru 68-75; numerous awards from Peru and France.

c/o Oficina del Presidente, Lima, Peru.

Velasco Ibarra, José María, DR.JUR.; Ecuadorean politician; b. 19 March 1893; ed. San Gabriel Coll., Central Univ. of Quito and Univ. de Paris à la Sorbonne.

Secretary of the Council of State; Attorney-Gen. of Quito; Deputy to Nat. Congress; Pres. of Republic 34-35, 44-47; newly elected Constitutional Pres. of Republic for term 52-56, 60-64 (deposed Nov. 61) elected for fifth term June 68. deposed Feb. 72; now in exile; Leader of Federación Nacional Velasquista (FNV); mem. Academia Ecuatoriana; decorated by Venezuela, Colombia, Bolivia, Chile, Argentina, El Salvador, France, Spain, Austria, etc.

Publs. *Conciencia o Barbarie, Tragedia Humana y Cristanismo, Experiencias Jurídicas Hispano-americanas, Derecho Internacional del Futuro, Caos Político en el Mundo Contemporáneo, Servidumbre y Liberación,* etc.

Veldkamp, Dr. G. M. J.; Netherlands politician; b. 27 June 1921, Breda; *s.* of J. J. Veldkamp and J. Siebel; *m.* 1948; one *s.* four *d.*; ed. Tilburg Catholic Economic Univ.

Board of Labour, Breda 41-50; Scientific Adviser, Social Insurance Section, Ministry of Social Affairs and Public Health 50-52; Lecturer, Coll. for Social Service Work, and at Technical Coll. 47-52; Chair. for Diocese and mem. Nat. Social Charitable Centre 47-52; Chair. Roman Catholic Party, Municipal Council of Breda 50-52; Sec. of State for Econ. Affairs 52-61; Minister of Social Affairs and Public Health 61-67; Chair. of Royal Cttee. for Unification and Codification of Social Law; Chair. of European Inst. for Social Security, Int. Inst. for Temporary Work; mem. of Board, Int. Soc. for Gerontology; Catholic Party.

Leisure interests: organ playing, cooking, gardening. Neuhuyskade 4, The Hague, Netherlands. Telephone: 244785.

Velloso, João Paulo dos Reis, PH.D.; Brazilian economist and politician; b. 1931, Parnaiba; *s.* of Francisco Augusto de Castro Velloso; *m.* D. Gelza Armond da Trinidade Velloso; two *s.*; ed. Universidade do Estado da Guanabara, Conselho Nacional de Economia, Fundação Getúlio Vargas and Yale Univ.

Worked at Chamber of Deputies; various posts with *IAPI* 53-54; joined Banco do Brasil 55; Assessor to Pres. 57-61; Ministry of Finance 61-62; founder and Sec.-Gen. Inst. of Applied Econ. Research (*IPEA*), Ministry of Planning; Minister of Planning and General Co-ordination Oct. 69-.

Ministério de Planejamento, Brasília, Brazil.

Veltchev, Boris Lazarov; Bulgarian politician; b. 1914; ed. secondary-technical education.

Sofia Municipality 33-41; mem. Central District Cttee., Bulgarian Communist Party, Sofia 40, Sec. 41; political imprisonment 41-44; successively mem. Sofia Council of Syndicalists, Sec. Municipal Employees Trade Union, Instructor at Regional Cttee. of C.P., Sofia 44-48, Sec. 48; Deputy Editor *Party Activist* magazine 48-49; Sec. Sofia City Cttee. of C.P. 49-52; Deputy Head, Trade Union and Youth Dept., Cen. Cttee. of Bulgarian Communist Party 52-54, Head 54-59; First Sec. Regional Cttee. of C.P., Sofia 59; Sec. Cen. Cttee. of Bulgarian Communist Party 59-, mem. Politburo 62-; Chair. of Party and State Control Cttee. of the Party and Council of Ministers 62-63; Deputy National Assembly; mem. State Council; Chair. Parl. Group of C.P. at Nat. Assembly.

Central Committee of Bulgarian Communist Party, Sofia, Bulgaria.

Venkataraman, Krishnasami, PH.D., D.SC., F.N.A.; Indian university professor; b. 7 June 1901, Madras; s. of P. S. Krishnaswami; m. Shakuntala Subramaniam; one d.; ed. Univs. of Madras and Manchester.
Professor of Organic Chem., Forman Christian Coll., Lahore 29-34; Reader, Dept. of Chemical Technology, Univ. of Bombay 35-38, Prof. and Dir. Chemical Tech. Dept. 38-57; Dir. Nat. Chemical Lab., Poona 57-66; Pres. Indian Chemical Soc. 59, 60; mem. Deutsche Akademie der Naturforscher Leopoldina 60; Padma Bhushan 61; Hon. Dr. of D. E. Mendeleev Inst. of Chemical Technology, Moscow 62; Visiting Prof. Purdue Univ. Feb.-June 62; Reilly Lecturer, Univ. of Notre Dame March 62; Hon. mem. Polish Chemical Soc.
Leisure interests: fiction, bridge.
Publs. *The Chemistry of Synthetic Dyes*, Vols. I and II 52, Editor, Vols. III-VII 71-74; articles on pure and applied organic chemistry in *Review of Textile Progress*, Kirk-Othmer's *Encyclopaedia of Chemical Technology*, Zechmeister's *Progress in the Chemistry of Organic Natural Products, Pointers and Pathways in Research* 63, *Chemistry of Flavonoid Compounds, The Flavonoids*, and over 250 papers, etc.
National Chemical Laboratory, Poona 8, India.
Telephone: Poona 54818, 58399.

Vennamo, Veikko Emil Aleksander, LL.L.; Finnish politician; b. 11 June 1913, Jaakkima; s. of Emil Fennander and Sivi Haikala; m. Sirkka Tuominen 1944; one s. two d.
Barrister-at-Law 39; Sec.-Gen. Emergency Resettlement Board 40-41; Chief, Bureau for Reconstruction of the Rural Districts of Ceded Karelia 42-43; Acting Chief Resettlement Dept., Ministry of Agriculture 43, Chief 44-59; M.P. 45-62, 66-; accounting and econ. dept. Board of Customs 60-; mem. Board of Dirs. Treasury Office, and of Programme Council of Finnish Broadcasting Corpn. 46-47; Chair. Finnish Small Farmers Party (later Rural Party) 59-; Presidential candidate 68; mem. Helsinki Town Council.
Leisure interests: foreign policy, historical interests, travelling.
c/o Finnish Small Farmers (Rural) Party, Pohhjois—Rautatienkatu 15 B Helsinki; Ritokalliontie 1, 00330 Helsinki 33, Finland.
Telephone: 48-2915, 86-8076 (summer).

Ventura, Raúl Jorge Rodrigues, DR.HIST., DR.JUR.SC.; Portuguese university professor and politician; b. 1919; ed. Univ. of Lisbon.
Former Public Prosecutor, Setúbal and later Chief of Dept. Inst. Nacional de Trabalho e Providência and Sec. to Under-Sec. of Corporations and Social Assistance; Under-Sec. of State for Overseas Territories 53-55, Minister for Overseas Territories 55-58; Prof. of Law, Lisbon Univ.; corresp. mem. Inst. of Law, Nat. Univ. of Argentina, Inst. of Labour, Univ. of São Paulo and Inst. of Social Law, Lisbon.
Rua Fernão Mendes Pinto 34, Lisbon, Portugal.

Venturi, Robert, M.F.A.; American architect; b. 25 June 1925, Philadelphia, Pa.; s. of Robert C. Venturi and Vanna Lanzetta; m. Denise Scott Brown 1967; one s.; ed. Princeton Univ.
Fellow, American Acad. in Rome 54-56; Assoc. Prof., School of Fine Arts, Univ. of Pennsylvania 59-65; Charlotte Shepherd Davenport Prof., Yale Univ. 65-70; Partner, Venturi and Rauch (architects and planners) 64-; Rome Prize, American Acad. in Rome.
Leisure interest: travel.
Publs. *Complexity and Contradiction in Architecture* 66, *Learning from Las Vegas* (with Denise Scott Brown and Steven Renour) 72; numerous articles in professional journals.
Venturi and Rauch, 333 South 16th Street, Phila-

delphia, Pa. 19102; Home: 6904 Wissahickon Avenue, Philadelphia, Pa. 19119, U.S.A.
Telephone: (215) 735-7400 (Office); (215) 849-1150 (Home).

Venzo, Mario, S.J.; Italian painter; b. 14 Feb. 1900; ed. Accademia di Belle Arti, Venice.
Painter in Paris 26-39; entered Society of Jesus 40; exhibitions in Milan 51-53, Rio de Janeiro 55, Turin 58, Trieste 61, Zürich 64, Munich and Berne 65, Monte Carlo and Padua 66, Turin and Milan 67, Zurich 68, Rome 70; First Prize Ucai, Vicenza 50, Monte Carlo 66, Nat. Exhbn. Prize, Milan, Turin 72.
Major works: *Via Crucis* (Lonigo) 60, *Crocefissione* (Coll. Pio-Latino-Americano, Rome) 62, *Via Crucis* (Villa Cavalletti, Frascati) 64, *Crocefissione* (Alte, Vicenza) 65, *Via Crucis* (Prospiano) 67, paintings in Galleria d'Arte di Venezia, Museo Civico di Vicenza, Museo di Brescia, Galleria d'arte Moderna di Milano.
Aloysianum, Gallarate, Varese, Italy.
Telephone: 796167.

Vercors (*pseudonym* of Jean Bruller); French writer, graphic artist and engraver; b. 26 Feb. 1902, Paris; s. of Louis Bruller and Ernestine (née Bourbon) Bruller; m. 1st Jeanne Barusseau (divorced), 2nd Rita Barisse; three s.; ed. Ecole alsacienne, Paris.
Early career as graphic artist and engraver; Founder *Editions de Minuit* with Pierre de Lescure 41; many lecturing tours throughout the world since 45; mem. PEN Club; Hon. Pres. National Cttee. of Writers.
Major works (graphic art and engraving): *21 recettes de mort violente* 26, *Hypothèses sur les amateurs de peinture* 27, *Un homme coupé en tranches* 29, *Nouvelle clé des songes* 34, *L'Enfer* 35, *Images rassurantes de la guerre* 36, *Silence* 37, *La Danse des vivants* (160 prints) 38, *Hamlet* (French adaptation, with aqua-forte illustrations) 65.
Publications: *Le Silence de la Mer* 41, *La Marche à l'Etoile* 43, *Le Sable du Temps* 45, *Les Armes de la Nuit* 46, *Les Yeux et la Lumière* 48, *Plus ou moins homme* 50, *La Puissance du jour* 51, *Les Animaux dénaturés* 52, *Les pas dans le sable, Portrait d'une amitié* 54, *Divagations d'un Français en Chine* 56, *Colères* 56, *P.P.C.* 57, *Sur ce rivage* vol. 1 58, vol. 2 58, vol. 3 60, *Sylva* 61, *Zoo ou l'Assassin philanthrope* (play) 63, *Les Chemins de l'Etre* (with P. Misraki) 65, *Quota ou les Pléthoriens* (with P. Coronel) 66, *La Bataille du Silence* 67, *Le Radeau de la Méduse* 69, *Le Fer et le Velours* (play) 69, *Oedipe* (play) 70, *Hamlet et Oedipe* 70, *Sillages* (novel) 72, *Sept Sentiers du Désert* (short stories) 72, *Questions sur la Vie* 73, *Comme un Frère* (novel) 73, *Tendre Naufrage* (novel) 74, *Ce que je crois* (essay) 75.
Moulin des Iles, Faremoutiers, Seine-et-Marne, France.

Verdeţ, Ilie; Romanian politician; b. 10 May 1925, Comăneşti, Bacău County; ed. Acad. of Econ. Studies, Bucharest.
Member Romanian C.P. 45-; worked in the Party local organs of Banat Region 48-54; Head of Section in Central Cttee. Romanian C.P., First Sec. Hunedoara Regional Party Cttee. 54-65; mem. Central Cttee. Romanian C.P. 60-; Deputy to Grand Nat. Assembly 61-; Alt. mem. Exec. Cttee. of Central Cttee. of R.C.P. 65-66, mem. 66-; mem. Perm. Presidium of Central Cttee. 66-74, Sec. Cen. Cttee. 74-; Deputy Chair. Council of Ministers of Socialist Repub. of Romania 65-66, First Deputy Chair. 66-74; Chair. Cen. Council of Workers' Control over Econ. and Social Activity 74-; Hero of Socialist Labour 71.
Council of Ministers of Socialist Republic of Romania, Bucharest, Romania.

Verdier, Abel; French diplomatist; b. 15 March 1901, Lille; m. Suzanne Maertens 1935; two s. two d.; ed. Lycées Lakanal et Janson de Sailly and Université de Paris à la Sorbonne.

Assistant Consul, London 30-35; Consul, Saarbrücken 35-39; mem. French Mission for Economic Warfare, England 39-40; Ministry of Foreign Affairs 41-50; Ambassador to Colombia 50-55, to UNRWA, Beirut 55-57, to Finland 60-64; Ministry of Foreign Affairs 64-67, retd.; Officier Légion d'Honneur, Médaille de la Résistance, Croix de Guerre (39-45) and foreign decorations.
Leisure interests: history, literature, gardening.
Publs. *La Constitution fédérale de la République d'Autriche* 24, *Manuel Pratique des Consulats* 33, 47, 57, 63, 74, *Formulaire à l'Usage des Consulats* 47, 57, 63, 74, *Les Amours italiennes de Lamartine—Graziella et Lena* 63, *La vie sentimentale de Lamartine* 70, 72.
8 rue du Général Camou, 75007 Paris, France.
Telephone: 705-56-63.

Verdon-Smith, Sir (William) Reginald, Kt.; British business executive; b. 5 Nov. 1912, London; s. of late Sir William George Verdon-Smith, C.B.E., and late Florence Jane (Anders) Verdon-Smith; m. Jane Margaret Hobbs 1946; one s. one d.; ed. Repton School and Brasenose Coll., Oxford.
President, Soc. of British Aircraft Constructors 46-48; Chair. British Aircraft Corpn. (Holdings) Ltd. 68-72; Deputy Chair. Lloyds Bank Ltd., Lloyds and Scottish Ltd.; Chair., Dir. Lloyds Bank Int. Ltd. 73-; Dir. Lloyds Bank California 75-.
Leisure interests: golf, sailing.
Lloyds Bank Ltd., 71 Lombard Street, London EC3P 3BS; and 13 Redcliffe Parade West, Bristol BS1 6SP, England.
Telephone: 01-626-1500.

Verdoorn, Frans, PH.D.; Netherlands scientist and editor; b. 1906; ed. Univs. of Utrecht, Vienna and Geneva.
Assistant, Botanic Gardens, Buitenzorg 30; Founder and Man. Editor The Chronica Botanica Co. 33-37; Botany Sec., Int. Union of Biological Science 35-53; Research Assoc., Harvard Univ. 40-; Tech. Adviser, Neth. Indies Govt. 43-49; Organizing Dir. Los Angeles Arboretum 48-49; Dir. Biohistorical Inst., Utrecht Univ. 57-; Gen. Sec., Int. Biohistorical Comm. 48-; mem. Zeeuwsch Genootschap; hon. foreign mem. of many acads. and socs.; First Mary Soper Pope Medal 46; Centenary Medal, French Botanical Soc. 54; Netherlands Soc. for History of Science Medal 63; Editor *Annales Bryologici* 28-39, *Annales Cryptogamici et Phytopathologici* 42-, *Biologia* 46-, *Bryopgyta Arduennae Exsiccata* 27-29, *Chronica Botanica* 35-, *Hepaticae Selectae et Criticae* 30-39, *Lotsya* 48-, *Musci Selecti et Critici* 38-40, "*A New Series of Plant Science Books*" 38-, *Pallas* 48-.
Publs. *De Frullaniaceis 1-18*, *Manual of Bryology* 32, *Manual of Pteridology* 38, *Aims and Methods of Biological History* 44, *Plants and Plant Science in Latin America* 45, *Science and Scientists in Neth. Indies* (with P. Honig) 45, *The Modern Arboretum* 48.
Biohistorical Institute, University of Utrecht, 187 Nieuwe Gracht, Utrecht, Netherlands.

Verdross, Alfred, DR.IUR.; Austrian jurist; b. 1890, Innsbruck; s. of Ignaz and Edda Verdross Edler von Drossberg; m. 1st Elisabeth Maurocordato 1917 (died 1952), 2nd Trude Kren 1953 (died 1968); three d.; ed. Vienna, Munich and Lausanne Univs.
Prof. Vienna Consular Acad. 22-38; Prof. of Int. Law and Philosophy of Law Vienna Univ. 24-, Dean of Law Faculty 31-32, 47-48 and 58-59, Rector of the Univ. 51-52; mem. UN Int. Law Comm. 57-66; Hague Perm. Court of Arbitration 58-; Judge, European Court of Human Rights 59-; mem. Austrian Acad. of Sciences; mem. Inst. of Int. Law, Vice-Pres. 52, Pres. 59-61; Pres. Int. Conf. in Vienna for the codification of the law of diplomatic relations 61; Dr. h.c. Univs. of Salamanca, Paris, Frankfurt, Vienna, Salzburg, Innsbruck, Louvain

and Salonika; Austrian Hon. Medal for Arts and Sciences, Grand Cross of St. Sylvester and Order of Malta.
Leisure interest: walking.
Publs. *Die Einheit des rechtlichen Weltbildes* 23, *Die Verfassung der Völkerrechtsgemeinschaft* 26, *Grundlinien der antiken Rechts- und Staatsphilosophie* (2nd edn.) 48, *Abendländische Rechtsphilosophie* 58 (2nd edn. 63), *Völkerrecht* (5th edn.) 64; important papers in the *Recueil des Cours de l'Académie de droit international* include *Le Fondement du Droit International* 27, *Les Règles Générales du Droit International de la Paix* 29, *Idées Directrices de l'Organisation des Nations Unies* 53. *Statisches und dynamisches Naturrecht* 71, *Die Quellen des universellen Völkerrechts* 73.
Pokornygasse 23, 1190 Vienna, Austria.
Telephone: 36-32-96.

Veres, József; Hungarian engineer and politician; b. 1906.
Resistance Movement, Second World War; party, state and econ. official 45-; Mayor of Budapest 58; mem. Central Cttee. of Hungarian Socialist Workers' Party 59-; Minister of Labour 63-70; Red Banner Order of Merit.
Ministry of Labour, H-1370 Budapest V, Szabadság ter 15, Hungary.

Vereschagin, Leonid Fedorovich; Soviet physicist; b. 29 April 1909, Kherson, Ukraine; s. of F. V. Vereschagin and M. P. Vereschagina; m. E. N. Andreeva 1944; one s. one d.; ed. Odessa Inst. of People's Education.
Postgraduate 30-33; Chief Engineer Research Bureau, Kharkov Turbogenerator Factory 33-34; Chief Engineer Ukrainian Physical-Technical Inst., Kharkov 34-39; Dir. Lab. Inst. of Organic Chemistry, U.S.S.R. Acad. of Sciences 39-54; Dir. Lab. of Physics of Superhigh Pressures, U.S.S.R. Acad. of Sciences 54-58; Dir. Inst. for High Pressure Physics, U.S.S.R. Acad. of Sciences 58-; Prof. Moscow State Univ. 53-; Corresp. mem. U.S.S.R. Acad. of Sciences 60-66, mem. 66-; mem. Royal Swedish Acad. of Engineering Sciences 73; U.S.S.R. State Prize 52; Lenin Prize 61; Hero of Socialist Labour 63, Order of Lenin (three times), "Hammer and Sickle" Gold Medal and other awards.
Leisure interest: photography.
Institute for High Pressure Physics, U.S.S.R. Academy of Sciences, Moscow Region, Podolsk District, Akademgorodok, U.S.S.R.

Verey, Michael John, T.D., M.A.; British merchant banker; b. 12 Oct. 1912, London; s. of late Henry Edward Verey and late Lucy Alice Verey; m. Sylvia Mary Wilson 1947; two s. one d.; ed. Eton Coll., Trinity Coll., Cambridge.
Joined Helbert Wagg and Co. Ltd. 34; served in Warwickshire Yeomanry, Middle East and Italy becoming Lieut.-Col. 39-45; Chair. Brixton Estate Ltd. 71, Schroders Ltd. 73, Accepting Houses Cttee. 74, Broadstone Investment Trust Ltd., Charities Official Investment Fund; Vice-Chair. Commercial Union Assurance Co. Ltd.; Dir. Boots Co. Ltd., Darling Holdings Ltd., British Petroleum Co. Ltd., Invest (Italy), Negit S.A. (Luxembourg); mem. Covent Garden Authority 61-66, Inst. of Directors; mem. and Vice-Pres. British Bankers' Asscn.; High Sheriff of Berkshire 68.
Leisure interests: gardening, and travel.
Flat 16, No. 1 Sloane Court East, London, S.W.3; Little Bowden, Pangbourne, Berkshire, England.
Telephone: 730-6946 (London); Pangbourne 2210.

Verghese, Boobli George; Indian journalist; b. 21 June 1927, Maymyo; s. of Lt.-Col. G. and Anna Verghese; m. Jamila Barakatullah; two s.; ed. The Doon School, Dehra Dun, St. Stephen's Coll., Delhi and Trinity Coll., Cambridge.

Assistant editor, *The Times of India* Bombay 49, transferred to New Delhi Bureau 51; Chief, New Delhi News Bureau, *Times of India* 56-62; Asst. Editor, *Times of India*, Bombay 62-66; Information Adviser to Prime Minister of India 66-68; Editor, *Hindustan Times* 69-.
Leisure interest: music.
Publs. *Himalayan Endeavour* 62, *Our Neighbour Pakistan* 64, *Design for Tomorrow* 65, *Beyond the Famine* 67, *An End to Confrontation* 72.
The Hindustan Times, Post Box 40, New Delhi 1, India.
Telephone: 387707.

Verghese, Rev. Thadikkal Paul (*see* Gregorios, Bishop Paul).

Verhoogen, John, PH.D.; American professor of geophysics; b. 1 Feb. 1912, Brussels, Belgium; s. of Dr. René Verhoogen and Lucy Vinçotte; m. Ilse Goldschmidt 1939; two s. two d.; ed. Univs. of Brussels and Liège and Stanford Univ.
Assistant, Univ. of Brussels 36-39, Fonds National de la Recherche 39-40; with Mines d'Or de Kilo-Moto 40-43; Gov.-Gen. Belgian Congo 43-46; Prof. of Geophysics, Univ. of Calif. at Berkeley 47-; mem. Nat. Acad. of Sciences; Day Medal, Geological Soc. of America.
Leisure interest: doing nothing.
Publs. *Igneous and Metamorphic Petrology* (with F. J. Turner) 51, *Metamorphic Reactions* (with F. J. Turner and W. S. Fyfe) 58, *The Earth* 70.
Department of Geology and Geophysics, University of California, Berkeley, Calif. 94720; Home: 2100 Marin Avenue, Berkeley, Calif. 94707, U.S.A.
Telephone: 415-642-2575 (Office); 415-526-8061 (Home).

Verity, Calvin William, Jr., B.A.; American steel executive; b. 26 Jan. 1917, Middletown, Ohio; s. of C. William Verity, Sr. and Elizabeth O'Brien Verity; m. Margaret Burnley Wymond 1941; two s. one d.; ed. Phillips Exeter Acad. and Yale Univ.
With Armco Steel Corpn., Middletown, Ohio 40-, Dir. Org. Planning and Devt. 57-61, Dir. of Public Relations 61-62, Asst. to Pres. 62-63, Vice-Pres. and Gen. Man. 63-65, Exec. Vice-Pres. 65-66, Pres. 65-71, Chair., Chief Exec. Officer 71-, Pres. 74; Dir. U.S. Chamber of Commerce, First Nat. Bank, Middletown, Mead Corpn., Dayton, Ohio, Business Int., New York, Boston Co., Bonston, Mass., Taft Broadcasting Co., Cincinnati, Thunderbird Graduate School of Int. Management, Glendale, Ariz.; mem. Pres. Export Council; Vice-Chair. Board of Trustees Ford's Theatre Soc., Wash. D.C.; Hon. D.H., Univ. of Dayton.
Leisure interests: golf, hunting, tennis.
Armco Steel Corporation, Middletown, Ohio; Home: 600 Thorn Hill Lane, Middletown, Ohio, U.S.A.
Telephone: 513-423-8689.

Verne, Claude Marie Jean, D.MED., D.SC.; French physiologist; b. 4 Oct. 1890, Saint-Julien; m. Louise Douin 1912; three c. (one died 1958); ed. Paris Univ.
Professeur sans chaire, Univ. de Paris 32, of Biology 46, of Histology 55-62, Hon. Prof. 62-; Dir. Institut d'Histochimie; Gen. Sec. Asscn. Française pour l'Avancement des Sciences 26-; Pres. de l'Académie de Médecine 68; Vice-Dean Paris Faculty of Medicine 46-62; mem. the European Tissue Culture Club; Founder-Pres. Soc. française d'Histochimie.
Publs. *Les pigments dans l'organisme animal* 19-29, *Recherches histophysiologiques sur poumon et graisses* 23-26, *Recherches sur les cultures des tissus* 30, 46, *Histochimie des graisses* 28-36, 38-42, *Précis d'histologie* 60, *La vie cellulaire hors de l'organisme* 37, *Recherches histochimiques sur les enzymes* 46-61, *sur les glandes surrénales et le pancréas* 50-57, *sur l'auto-historadiographie avec S.35* 56-58, *Etudes sur les Cellules hépatiques cultivées in*

vitro 60-66, *L'Histologie* 66, *La Culture de Tissus* (with Hébert) 67.
38 rue de Varenne, Paris 7e, France.

Vernejoul, Robert de; French professor of clinical surgery; b. 28 March 1890, Montcaret, Dordogne; s. of E. de Vernejoul and Lucie Laurens; m. Madeleine Hotz 1926; two s. one d.; ed. Lycée Blaise Pascal, Clermont Ferrand and Facultés de Médecine, Paris and Marseilles.
Former Professor of Clinical and Experimental Surgery, Faculté de Médecine, Marseilles, Hon. Prof. 63-; mem. Institut Français (Acad. des Sciences), Acad. Nationale de Médecine; Grand Officier, Légion d'Honneur; Croix de Guerre; Médaille de la Résistance.
Leisure interest: golf.
96 rue Sylvabelle, 13 Marseilles 6e, France.
Telephone: 37-56-47.

Verner, Paul; German politician; b. 26 April 1911.
Former metal worker; mem. Kommunistische Partei Deutschlands 29-39; Editor-in-Chief *Junge Garde* 33; in Spanish Civil War 36-39; prison in Sweden 39-43, fitter in Sweden 43-45; Co-founder Freie Deutsche Jugend (F.D.J.); mem. Secretariat Central Council of F.D.J. 46-49; mem. Central Cttee. Sozialistische Einheitspartei Deutschlands (S.E.D.) 50-, mem. Secretariat 50-53, 58-; mem. Volkskammer 58-; Sec. Greater Berlin District S.E.D. 59-; mem. Politburo, S.E.D. 63-; mem. Council of State 71-; Vaterländischer Verdienstorden in Silber.
Sozialistische Einheitspartei Deutschlands, 102 Berlin, Am Marx-Engels Platz 2, German Democratic Republic.

Vernier-Palliez, Bernard Maurice Alexandre, L. ÈS D.; French business executive; b. 2 March 1918; m. Denise Silet-Pathe 1952; one s. three d.; ed. Ecole Libre des Sciences Politiques, Ecole des Hautes Etudes Commerciales.
Head of Welfare, Régie Nationale des Usines Renault 45-47, Sec. to Sec.-Gen. 47-48, Sec.-Gen. 48-67, Deputy Man. Dir. 67-71, Pres. Dir.-Gen. 76-; Pres. Dir.-Gen. SAVIEM 67-74; Del.-Gen. for commercial vehicles, coaches and buses, Régie Renault 75-76; Pres. Berliet 75-76; Vice-Pres. Supervisory Board of SAVIEM 75-76; Officier de la Légion d'Honneur, Croix de Guerre, Médaille de la Résistance.
R.N.U.R., 34 quai du Point du Jour, 92109 Boulogne-Billancourt, France.
Telephone: 609-64-14.

Vernon, Sir James, C.B.E., PH.D.; Australian business executive; b. 13 June 1910, Tamworth; s. of Donald Vernon; m. Mavis Lonsdale-Smith; two d.; ed. Sydney Univ., Univ. Coll. London.
Chief Chemist, Colonial Sugar Refining Co. Ltd. (C.S.R.) 38-51, Senior Exec. Officer 51-56, Asst. Gen. Man. 56-57, Gen. Man. 58-72; Dir. C.S.R. Ltd., Commercial Banking Co. of Sydney Ltd., M.L.C. Ltd., United Telecasters Sydney Ltd.; Chair. Martin Corpn. Ltd., Commonwealth Cttee. of Econ. Inquiry 63-65, Australian Post Office Comm. of Inquiry 73-74, Mfg. Industries Advisory Cttee.; Pres. Australia/Japan Business Co-operation Cttee.; Vice-Pres. Australian Industries Devt. Asscn.; mem. Chase Manhattan Advisory Cttee.; Fellow Royal Australian Chemical Inst.; Hon. D.Sc. (Sydney and Newcastle); Leighton Memorial Medal, Royal Australian Chemical Inst. 65; John Storey Medal, Australian Inst. of Management 71.
Leisure interests: fishing, theatre, music.
27 Manning Road, Double Bay, N.S.W. 2028, Australia.

Vernon, William Michael; British business executive; b. 17 April 1926, Cheshire; s. of late Sir Wilfred Vernon; m. Rosheen O'Meara 1952; one s.; ed. Marlborough Coll. and Trinity Coll., Cambridge.
Joined Spillers (millers and animal food manufacturers) as trainee 48, Dir. 60-, Joint Man. Dir. 62-67,

Deputy Chair. 67-68, Chair. Aug. 68-; Dir. Electrical and Musical Industries Ltd. 73-.
Leisure interests: sailing, shooting, skiing.
Spillers Ltd., Old Change House, Cannon Street, London, E.C.4; Home: Ropley House, nr. Alresford, Hants., England.

Vernov, Sergey Nikolayevich; Soviet physicist; b. 10 July 1910, Sestroretsk, Leningrad Region; ed. Leningrad Polytechnic Inst.
Corresponding mem. U.S.S.R. Acad. of Sciences 53-68. Academician 68-; mem. I.G.Y. Cttee. of the U.S.S.R. 57; in Radium Inst., U.S.S.R. Acad. of Sciences 31-36; P. N. Lebedev Inst. of Physics, Acad. of Sciences 36-; Prof. Moscow Univ. 44-; State prizewinner 49; Lenin Prize 60; Order of Lenin and other awards.
Publs. *Latitudinal Effect of Cosmic Rays in the Stratosphere and Verification of Cascade Theory* 45, *Study of Interaction of Primary Components of Cosmic Rays with Matter in the Stratosphere* 49, *Study of Cosmic Rays* 58, *Discovery of Research on Radiation Belt of the Earth* 60, *Investigation of the Earth's Radiation Belts at Altitude of 0-400 kilometres* 64, *On the Assymmetry of Intensity of Fast Electrons in Conjugated Points at Certain Heights* 64, *A Study of Cosmic Rays at Altitudes of 200-400 km.* 65.
Moscow State University, Leninskie Gory, Moscow, U.S.S.R.

Veronese, Vittorino, D.IUR.; Italian administrator; b. 1 March 1910.
Formerly Editor *Studium*; fmr. Gen. Sec. Catholic Movement of Univ. Graduates, Prof. Inst. of Social Sciences, Athenaeum Angelicum, Rome, Pres. Catholic Action, Pius XII Foundation, Cen. Inst. of Credit, Consorzio di Credito per le Opere Publiche; Sec. Perm. Int. Congress of Lay Apostolate, Rome; mem. Italian Del to UNESCO 48-58; mem. Italian Nat. UNESCO Comm.; mem. UNESCO Exec. Board 52-56, Pres. 56-58; Dir.-Gen. UNESCO 58-61; resigned Nov. 61; Chair. Board of Dirs. of Banco di Roma 61, Vice-Chair. Banco di Roma (France) Paris, Banco di Roma (Belgium) Brussels; Vice-Chair. Banco di Roma (Ethiopia), Addis Ababa; Dir. and mem. Exec. Cttee. of Fondazione Cini, Venice; Dir. Società Italiana per l'Organizzazione Internazionale; Chair. Italian Cttee. for Human Rights; mem. Pontifical Comm. for Justice and Peace, Vatican City 67; Vice-Pres. Int. Consultative Liaison Cttee. for Literacy, UNESCO.
Banco di Roma, 307 Via del Corso, Rome, Italy.

Verosta, Stephan Eduard, LL.D.; Austrian lawyer and diplomatist; b. 16 Oct. 1909, Vienna; s. of Rudolf Verosta and Elisabeth (née Szalay) Verosta; m. Maria Stuehler 1942; two s. one d.; ed. Gymnasium, Vienna, Univ. of Vienna and studied in Paris, Geneva and Acad. of International Law, The Hague.
Legal practice 32-35, Judge 36-; Legal Dept., Austrian Foreign Office 35-38, Deputy Legal Adviser 45-48, 49-51; Counsellor, Austrian Legation, Rome, Minister, Budapest 51-52; Head of Legal Dept., Foreign Office 53-56; Ambassador to Poland 56-61; Austrian Del. to various int. confs. and UN; mem. Perm. Court of Arbitration, The Hague 57-; Consultant to Foreign Office 62-; Dozent in Int. Law, Univ. of Vienna 46-, Prof. of Int. Law, Jurisprudence and Int. Relations 62; Chair. U.S.-Finnish Comm. of Conciliation 64-; mem. Dutch-Fed. German Comm. of Conciliation, Inst. de Droit Int. 61; mem. Appeals Board, Council of Europe 74; mem. Austrian Acad. of Science 64; mem. Founding Cttee. UN Univ. 72; numerous decorations.
Leisure interests: collecting old books, stamps.
Publs. *Les Avis consultatifs de la Cour Permanente de Justice Internationale*, etc. 32, *Jean Dumont und seine Bedeutung für das Völkerrecht* 34, *Liberale und planwirtschaftliche Handelspolitik* (with Gottfried Haberler) 34, *Richterliches Gewohnheitsrecht in Österreich* 42, *Die*

Satzung der Vereinten Nationen 46, *Die internationale Stellung Österreichs von 1938-1947* 47, *Die geschichtliche Kontinuität des österreichischen Staates und seine europäische Funktion* 54, *Johannes Chrysostomus, Staatsphilosoph* 60, *Geschichte des Völkerrechts* 64, *International Law in Europe and Western Asia between 100-650 A.D.* 66, *Dauernde Neutralität* 67, *Theorie und Realität von Bündnissen Heinrich Lammasch, Karl Renner und der Zweibund 1897-1914* 71, *L'histoire de l'Académie de Droit International de la Haye* 73.
1180 Vienna, Hockegasse 15, Austria.
Telephone: 47-13-48.

Verret, (Louis Joseph) Alexandre, B.A., B.S., LL.M.; Haitian journalist, teacher and diplomatist; b. 5 June 1914, Port-au-Prince; s. of Ciceron L. Verret and Virginia Vallès-Verret; m. Denise Gabriel 1946; three d.; ed. Inst. St. Louis de Gonzague, Port-au-Prince, and Faculté de Droit, Port-au-Prince.
Assistant Dir. of *La Tribune* (newspaper) 42; Prof. of Social Sciences, Univ. of Haiti 46-58; Attaché 58-59, Second Sec. 59-60, First Sec. 60, Consul-Gen. of Haiti 60, Minister-Counsellor 71; Alt. Rep. to UN Gen. Assembly 60-61, Rep. for Haiti on several UN cttees. 61-; Rep. to UN Gen. Assembly 63-; Amb., Deputy Perm. Rep. of Haiti to UN 73; Vice-Pres. UN Gen. Assembly 74-; mem. "Le Cercle d'Or" 65, Inter-American Bar Asscn. 67, American Soc. of Int. Law 68.
Leisure interests: theatre, classical music, playing and composing piano music.
Publs. Poetry and literary and scientific articles in newspapers and periodicals.
Permanent Mission of Haiti to the United Nations, 801 Second Avenue, New York, N.Y. 10017, U.S.A.; 20 Rue de la Révolution, Port au Prince, Haiti.
Telephone: MU62368 (New York).

Verrett, Shirley; American mezzo-soprano singer; b. 31 May 1931, New Orleans; d. of Elvira and Leon Verrett; m. Louis Lomonaco 1963; one d.; ed. Juilliard School of Music, N.Y.
Appeared in title role of *Carmen*, Spoleto Festival 62, Bolshoi Opera, Moscow 63, N.Y. City Opera 66, Florence 68; debut as Carmen at Metropolitan Opera, N.Y. 68; appeared as Amneris (*Aida*) and Eboli (*Don Carlos*) at Covent Garden 67-68; appeared in *Maria Stuarda* with American Opera Soc. 68; appeared as Lady Macbeth (*Macbeth*), opening night La Scala 75; other roles include Dido (*Les Troyens*) and leading roles in *Samson et Dalila*, *Il Trovatore*, *Norma*, *Orfeo* (Gluck), *La Favorita* (Donizetti), *Macbeth* (Verdi); appears frequently at the leading opera houses of U.S.A. and Europe including La Scala, Milan, Rome, Paris and Vienna; numerous concert and recital tours include performances of oratorio, etc., expecially Verdi's *Requiem*.
Leisure interests: cooking, musical biographies, collecting English and American antiques, collecting engravings of famous singers.
c/o Basil Horsfield, Artists International Management, 5 Regent's Park Road, London, N.W.1, England.

Verykios, Dr. Panaghiotis Andrew; Greek diplomatist; b. 24 July 1910, Athens; m. Mary Dracoulis 1939; three s.; ed. Univ. de Paris, Ecole Libre des Sciences Politiques, and Acad. of Int. Law, The Hague.
Greek Diplomatic Service 35-; Army Service 39-40; Vice-Consul, Bourgas, Bulgaria 40-41; Sec. and Acting Consul-Gen., Lisbon 42-45; First Sec. Ministry of Foreign Affairs, Athens 45-47; First Sec., London 47-50; Counsellor, Athens 50-52; Deputy Perm. Rep. at NATO, Paris 52-54; Counsellor, Paris 54-56; Head of NATO Dept., Athens 56-60; Amb. to Netherlands 60-64, to Denmark, also accred. to Norway and Iceland 64-67; Amb. to U.K. 67-69; Amb. to Spain 69-70; retd. 71; Greek Mil. Cross; Knight Commdr. Royal Orders of

George I and Phoenix (Greece) and several foreign decorations.
Leisure interests: music, philately.
Publ. *La Prescription en Droit International* 34.
Iras 6, Ekali, nr. Athens, Greece.
Telephone: Athens 8031216.

Verzili, Danilo, DR.POL.SC.; Italian banker; b. 5 Oct. 1909, Monteantico (Grosseto); s. of Angelo and Anito Burroni; m. Teresa Dodet 1950; one s. one d.; ed. Univs. of Siena and Florence.
Secretary-General, Confederazione Italiana dei Dirigenti di Azienda (CIDA) 45-71; Pres. Banca Toscana, Florence 66-69; Pres. Monte dei Paschi di Siena 59-; Pres. Fondazione Accademia Musicale Chigiana Siena 66-, Società Autostrada Tirrenica 68-; Dir. Istituto di Credito per le Imprese di Pubblica 60-, United Bank for Africa 67-, AICI 71-, Società Finanziaria Internazionale 71-; Cavaliere di Gran Croce al Merito della Repubblica Italiana and several other decorations.
Viale Rinaldo Franci n. 12, Siena; Via Aurelia Antica n. 286, Rome, Italy.
Telephone: 20.202 (Siena); 622.0033 (Rome).

Veselsky, Dr. Ernst Eugen; Austrian politician; b. 2 Dec. 1932, Vienna; s. of Maria and Rudolf Veselsky; m. Franziska Raser 1956; one s. one d.
Joined Econ. Section, Vienna Chamber of Labour 56; Head, Econ. Section, Vorarlberg Chamber of Labour 59; Sec. Vienna Chamber of Labour 63; Exec. Sec., Econ. and Social Advisory Board (subsidiary body of Joint Council for Wages and Prices) 65; mem. Board of Dirs., Austrian Nat. Bank 69-70; mem. Nationalrat 70-; State Sec. in Fed. Chancellery 70-.
Leisure interests: modern arts, books, music, sport.
Aslangasse 51, A-1190 Vienna, Austria.
Telephone: 32-42-61.

Vesey-FitzGerald, Brian Seymour; British naturalist; b. 1900, Wrexham, Wales; s. of Percy Seymour Vesey-Fitzgerald, C.S.I., and Mary Brigid Jones; m. 1st Catherine Nash 1930 (died 1960), 2nd Mary Julius Hunt 1961; ed. Dover Coll. and Keble Coll., Oxford.
Editor *The Field* 38-46; mem. Honourable Soc. of Cymmrodorion; Vice-Pres. Gamekeepers' Assocn.; Editor County Books 46-; Pres. British Fairground Soc. 55-63.
Leisure interests: bird watching, gardening, chess.
Publs. *A Book of British Waders* 38, *Hampshire Scene* 40, *Farming in Britain* 42, *Field Fare* 42, *A County Chronicle* 42, *Hedgerow and Field* 43, *Gypsies of Britain* 44, *British Game* 46, *The Book of the Horse*, *It's My Delight* 47, *The Book of the Dog*, *A Child's Biology*, *Hampshire*, *British Bats* 48, *Bird Biology for Beginners* 49, *Background to Birds* 49, *Rivermouth* 49, *The River Avon* 51, *Borrow in Britain* 53, *Winchester* 53, *Cats* 55, *Nature Recognition* 55, *The Domestic Dog* 57, *The Beauty of Cats* 58, *The Beauty of Dogs* 60, *Your Book of Dogs* 62, *Cat Owner's Encyclopaedia* 63, *Foxes in Britain* 64, *Dog Owner's Encyclopaedia* 65, *Animal Anthology* 65, *Portrait of the New Forest* 66, *Enquire Within About Animals* 67, *Garden Alive* 67, *The World of Fishes* 68, *The World of Reptiles* 68, *The Domestic Cat* 69, *The Vanishing Wildlife of Britain* 69.
c/o Laurence, Pollinger Ltd., 18 Maddox Street, London, W.1, England.

Vetter, Heinz-Oskar; German trade unionist; b. 21 Oct. 1917, Bochum; s. of Oskar and Martha (née Berge) Vetter; m. Lieselotte Bleil 1947; one d.; ed. Akad. für Wirtschaft und Politik, Hamburg.
With Harpener Bergbau AG, Dortmund 46-49, shop steward with trade union; studied at Akad. für Wirtschaft und Politik, Hamburg; Sec. IG Bergbau und Energie 52, mem. Exec. 60, Vice-Chair. 64; Chairman, Deutscher Gewerkschaftsbund May 69-; Vice-Pres. Int. Confederation of Free Trade Unions; Pres. European Confederation of Free Trade Unions,

European Trades Union Confed. 74-; Bundesverdienstkreuz.
Leisure interests: books, music, crafts.
Deutscher Gewerkschaftsbund, 4000 Düsseldorf, Hans-Böckler-Haus am Kennedydamm, Postfach 2601; Home: 4330 Mülheim/Ruhr, von-Berhing-Strasse 2, Federal Republic of Germany.
Telephone: Düsseldorf 4301/200.

Vialar, Paul; French writer; b. 18 Sept. 1898; ed. Lycée Janson-de-Sailly, Paris.
Former Pres. Société des Gens de Lettres; Hon. Pres. Syndicat des Ecrivains Français; Hon. Pres. Fed. Nat. des Sociétés d'Auteurs; Pres. Asscn. des Ecrivains Sportifs; Pres. Int. Writers' Guild; Hon. Pres. Syndicat Nat. des Auteurs et Compositeurs; mem. Council of Alliance Française; Commdr. de la Légion d'Honneur, Ordre des Arts et Lettres; Croix de Guerre; and numerous foreign awards.
Publs. 15 plays and 90 novels including *La rose de la mer* (Prix Femina) 39, *La mort est un commencement* (8 vols.) (Grand Prix de la Ville de Paris) 48, *Chronique française du XXème Siècle* (10 vols. completed), *Les Invités de la chasse* 69, *Les Députés*, *Ceux du cirque*, *Safari vérité* 70, *Mon seul amour*, *la Caille et le Butor* 72, *La Croule* 74.
34 Avenue Victor Hugo, Boulogne sur Seine, France.

Vichit-Vadakan, Vinyu; Thai economist and educationist; b. 21 July 1937; s. of Luang and Prapapan Vichit-Vadakan; m. Chantima Vichit-Vadakan 1967; two s. one d.; ed. Univ. of Fribourg.
Economist, Nat. Econ. Devt. Board 62-71; Acting Dean Faculty of Econs., Thammasat Univ. 71-72, Dean 72-73; Dir. UN Asian Inst. for Econ. Devt. and Planning Jan. 74-.
Leisure interest: reading.
United Nations Asian Institute for Economic Development and Planning, P.O. Box 2-136, Sri Ayudhya Road, Bangkok, Thailand.
Telephone: 815400.

Vick, Sir (Francis) Arthur, Kt., O.B.E., D.SC., PH.D., LL.D.; British physicist; b. 5 June 1911, Solihull, Warwicks.; s. of Wallace Devenport Vick; m. Elizabeth Dorothy Story 1943; one d.; ed. Waverley Grammar School and Birmingham Univ.
Assistant Lecturer in Physics, Univ. Coll., London 36, Lecturer 39-44; Asst. Dir. of Scientific Research, Ministry of Supply 39-44; Lecturer in Physics, Manchester Univ. 44-47, Senior Lecturer 47-50; Prof. of Physics, Univ. Coll. of North Staffordshire (now Univ. of Keele) 50-59, Vice-Principal 50-54; Dep. Dir. Atomic Energy Research Establishment, Harwell 59-60, Dir. 60-64, Dir. Research Group 61-64, mem. for Research U.K. Atomic Energy Authority 64-66; mem. Advisory Council on Research and Devt., Ministry of Power 60-63; mem. Governing body, Nat. Inst. for Research in Nuclear Science 64-65; mem. Nuclear Safety Advisory Cttee., Ministry of Power 60-66, Univ. Grants Cttee. 59-66; Pres. Asscn. of Teachers in Colls. and Depts. of Educ. 64-72, Hon. mem. 72; Pres. and Vice-Chancellor, Queen's Univ., Belfast Oct. 66-76; Hon. mem. Asscn. for Science Educ. 69; Chair. Acad. Council of Royal Defence Acad. 69; Knight Commdr. Liberian Humane Order of African Redemption 62.
Leisure interests: music, gardening, the countryside.
Vice-Chancellor's Lodge, Lennoxvale, Belfast BT9 5BY, Northern Ireland; Home: Fieldhead Cottage, Fieldhead Lane, Myton Road, Warwick, CU34 6QF, England.
Telephone: 0232-665370; 0926-41822 (Home).

Vickers, Jon, C.C.; Canadian tenor; 29 Oct. 1926, Prince Albert, Saskatchewan; s. of William Vickers and Merle Mossip; m. Henrietta Outerbridge 1953; three s. two d.
Began career as concert and opera singer in Canada; joined Royal Opera House, Covent Garden (London) 57; sang at Bayreuth Festival, Vienna State Opera, San

Francisco, **Chicago Lyric Opera, Metropolitan Opera, New York, La Scala, Milan, Paris Opera, Athens Festival, Salzburg Festival,** etc.; Hon. LL.D. Univ. of Saskatchewan; Hon. C.L.D. Bishop's Univ.
Major roles include Pollione in *Norma*, Herod in *Salome*, Alvaro in *Forza*, Laca in *Jenufa*, title role in *Otello*.
c/o Metropolitan Opera Co., New York City, N.Y., U.S.A.

Victor, Paul-Emile, LIC. ÈS SC., DIPL. D'ETHNOLOGIE; French explorer and civil engineer; b. 28 June 1907, Geneva, Switzerland; *m.* 1st Eliane Decrais 1946, 2nd Colette Faure de la Vaulx 1961; three *s.* one *d.*; ed. Lycée Rouget de Lisle (Lons-le-Saulnier), Ecole Centrale de Lyon, Faculty of Science and Letters and Inst. of Ethnology, Paris.
Greenland Expedition 34-35; crossed Greenland by dog sleigh 36; wintered on east coast of Greenland 36-37; trans-Alpine crossing by dog sleigh Nice-Chamonix 38; expedition to Lapland 39; Second Naval Attaché for France in Scandinavia 39-40; U.S. Air Force (parachutist commanding Nome flight of Alaska search and rescue squadron) 42-46; has organized and directed the Expeditions Polaires Françaises (missions Paul-Emile Victor—Arctic and Antarctic expeditions) since 47; Pres. French Antarctic Cttee. Int. Geophysical Year; Pres. Groupe Paul-Emile Victor for the Protection of Man and his Environment 73-; Head of Int. Glaciological Expedition to ·Greenland; Chair. Int. Logistics Group of Scientific Cttee. on Antarctic Research; Officier de la Légion d'Honneur, Grand Croix de l'Etoile d'Anjouan, Officer of the Orders of Vasa and Dannebrog; Gold Medal of the Royal Geographical Soc. (London), Vega Gold Medal (Sweden), Médailles spéciales de l'Administration des Monnaies.
Leisure interests: skiing, swimming, deep sea diving, painting, engraving.
Publs. *Boréal* 38, *Banquise* 39, *Apoutsiak* 47, *Aventure Esquimau* 48, *La Grande Faim* 58, *Pôle Sud* 60, *La Voie Lactée* 61, *L'Homme à la Conquête des Pôles* 62, *Pôle Nord* 63, *Poèmes Eskimo* 65, *Tahiti* 66, *Pôle Nord-Pôle Sud* 67, *Terres Polaires, Terres Tragiques* 71, *Eskimos, nomades de glaces* 72, *La prodigieuse histoire des pôles* 74, *Chiens de traîneaux compagnons du risque* 75, *Mes aventures polaires* 75, *La vie des Eskimos* 75.
Expéditions Polaires Françaises, 47 Avenue du Maréchal Fayolle, 75116 Paris, France.
Telephone: 504-17-71.

Vidal, Gore; American writer; b. 3 Oct. 1925; ed. Phillips Acad., Exeter, N.H.
Served in U.S. Army 43-46; Edgar Allen Poe award for Television 55; Drama Critic *Reporter* (magazine) 59; Democratic-Liberal Candidate for U.S. Congress from New York 60; Pres. Kennedy's Advisory Council on the Arts 61-63; Co-Chair. People's Party 70-72.
Publs. Novels: *Williwaw* 46, *In a Yellow Wood* 47, *The City and the Pillar* 48, *The Season of Comfort* 49, *A Search for the King* 50, *Dark Green, Bright Red* 50, *The Judgment of Paris* 52, *Messiah* 54, *Julian* 64, *Washington, D.C.* 67, *Myra Breckinridge* 68, *Two Sisters* 70, *Burr* 72, *Myron* 74, *1876* 76; short stories: *A Thirsty Evil* 56; plays: *Visit to a Small Planet* 56, *The Best Man* 60, *Romulus* 62, *Weekend* 68, *An Evening with Richard Nixon* 72; film scripts and adaptations: *Wedding Breakfast, I Accuse, Ben Hur, Suddenly Last Summer, The Best Man*; essays: *Rocking the Boat* 63, *Reflections upon a Sinking Ship* 69, *Homage to Daniel Shays* 72; criticism in *Partisan Review, The Nation, New York Review of Books, Esquire*, etc.
Via di Torre Argentina 21, Rome, Italy.

Videla, Lt.-Gen. Jorge Rafael; Argentine army officer and politician; b. 1925, Mercedes, Province of Buenos Aires; *m.* Alicia Hartridge; six *c.*; ed. Nat. Mil. Coll. and War School.

Commissioned in Infantry 44; Lieut. in Vigilance Co., Ministry of War 46; with Motorized Army Regt. 47-48; Nat. Mil. Coll. 48; Student, War School, with rank of Army Capt. 51-54; Staff Officer, Nat. Mil. Coll. 54-56; Adviser to Office of Mil. Attaché, Washington, D.C. 56-58; Staff Officer, Army Gen. Command 62-65, 66-68; Col. 65; engaged on course in Strategy, Army Centre of Higher Studies 65-66; Lieut.-Col., Chief of Cadet Corps 68; Second in Command and Chief of Staff, Fifth Infantry Brigade 68-70; Chief of Operations, Third Army Corps 70-71; Brig., Head of Nat. Mil. Coll. 71-73; Chief of Army Gen. Staff 73-75, of Joint High Command 75; C.-in-C. of Army Aug. 75-; led coup to depose Pres. María Perón March 76; leader of mil. junta, then Pres. of Argentina March 76-; fmr. mem. Inter-American Defence Board, Washington, D.C.
Oficina del Presidente, Casa Rosada, Buenos Aires, Argentina.

Vidor, King Wallis; American film director; b. 8 Feb. 1895; ed. Galveston High School and Peacock Military Acad. San Antonio, Texas.
Productions include: *The Big Parade, The Crowd, Hallelujah, The Citadel, Duel in the Sun, H. M. Pulham Esq., The Fountainhead, War and Peace, Solomon and Sheba*.
Publs. *A Tree is a Tree* (autobiography) 53, *King Vidor on Film Making* 73.
Suite 104, 201 Lasky Drive, Beverly Hills, Calif., U.S.A

Vieillard, Roger; French artist; b. 9 Feb. 1907, Le Mans, Sarthe; *s.* of Edmond Vieillard and Madelaine Magimel; *m.* Anita de Caro, painter, 1939; ed. Univ. of Paris.
Took part in exhbns. by Jeune Gravure Contemporaine, Société des Peintres Graveurs, Salon de Mai, Biennales of Venice, and São Paulo; works exhibited in Paris (Bibliothèque Nat., Galerie de France, la Hune, Adrien Maeght, Galerie Coard), London (Hanover Gallery), Rotterdam (Boymans Museum), Berne (Musée de Berne), Galerie d'Art Moderne, Basle, Galerie le Garrec Sagot; has specialized in line engraving; prints in French and foreign museums and private collections; works at Manufacture Nat. de Sèvres, Musée Nat. Monnaies et Médailles; Vice-Pres. Comité Nat. de la Gravure Française, Comité Nat. du Livre Illustré française, Société·des Peintres Graveurs; Chevalier de la Légion d'Honneur, Officier des Arts et des Lettres.
Leisure interests: banking, economics.
Principal works: Illustrations for: *La Fable de Phaeton d'Ovide* 39, *Hommage a Rimbaud* 44, *Poèmes de Jean Tardieu* 45, *Discours de la Méthode* 48, *L'Ecclésiaste* 51, *Le Banquet de Platon* 52, *Poèmes d'André Frenaud* 56, *Eléments* 56, *Retour du Pays d'Ombre* 72, *Voyage en Pays Circulaire* 73.
7 rue·de l'Estrapade, Paris 5e, France.
Telephone: Odéon 40-78.

Vieira da Silva, Marie-Hélene; French artist; b. 13 June 1908, Lisbon, Portugal; *m.* Arpad Szenes; ed. Acad. de la Grande Chaumière under Bourdelle and Despiau.
Sculptor 28-; influenced by Siennese school of painting; studied painting under Dufresne, Friesz, Fernand Léger and Bissière, also engraving under Hayter, *L'Atelier 17*; first one-man exhbn. 32; in Portugal 39, Brazil 40-47, settled in Paris 47; one-man exhbns. at Galerie Pierre 48, 51, 55, Galerie Jeanne Bucher (nine between 37 and 71), Galerie Knoedler, New York 61, 63, 66; Retrospective Exhbns. at Kestner-Gesellschaft 58, Musée de Grenoble, Galleria Civica d'Arte Moderna, Turin, Museum of Modern Art, Paris, Boymans van Beuningen, Rotterdam 69, Kunsternes Hus, Oslo 70, Kunsthalle, Basle, Fondation Calouste Gulbenkian, Lisbon; works in the major galleries of the world; 1st Int. Prize São Paulo Biennial

61; Prix Nat. des Arts, Paris 66; Commdr. des Arts et Lettres.
c/o Guy Weelen, 8 avenue Frochot, Paris 9e, France.

Vienne, Robert (Baron de); French industrialist; b. 23 Jan. 1904.
President, Dir.-Gen., Constructions mécaniques et électriques Capri-Codec S.A. 63-; mem. Soc. of French Civil Engineers; Chevalier, Légion d'Honneur.
32 rue Ernest-Renan, Colombes (Seine), France.

Viereck, Peter, B.S., M.A., PH.D.; American poet, historian and dramatist; b. 5 Aug. 1916, New York; s. of George S. and Margaret (Hein) Viereck; m. 1st Anya de Markov 1945 (divorced 1970); one s. one d.; m. 2nd Betty Martin Falkenberg 1972; ed. Harvard Univ. and Christ Church, Oxford.
Teaching Asst., Harvard Univ. 41-42, Instructor in German Literature and tutor 46-47; History Instructor, U.S. Army, Univ. of Florence, Italy 45; Asst. Prof. History, Smith Coll. 47-48; Assoc. Prof. Mount Holyoke Coll. 48-55, Prof. of European and Russian History 55-; U.S. State Dept. mission of cultural exchange to U.S.S.R. Sept.-Oct. 61; awarded Tietjens Prize for Poetry 48, Pulitzer Prize for Poetry 49; Guggenheim Fellow, Rome 49-50; Visiting Lecturer Univ. of Paris, American Univ., Beirut, and American Univ. Cairo 66; L.H.D. Olivet Coll. 59.
Publs. *Metapolitics—from the Romantics to Hitler* 41, *Terror and Decorum* (poems) 48, 73, *Who Killed the Universe* 48, *Conservatism Revisited—The Revolt Against Revolt—1815-1849* 49, *Strike Through the Mask: New Lyrical Poems* 50, 73, *The First Morning: New Poems* 52, 73, *Shame and Glory of the Intellectuals* 53, 65, *Dream and Responsibility: The Tension Between Poetry and Society* 53, *The Unadjusted Man: a New Hero for Americans* 56, 62, 73, *Conservatism: From John Adams to Churchill* 56, *The Persimmon Tree* (poems) 56, *The Tree Witch: A Poem and Play* 61, 73, *Metapolitics: The Roots of the Nazi Mind* 61, 65, *Conservatism Revisited and the New Conservatism: What Went Wrong?* 62, 65, *New and Selected Poems* 67.
Mount Holyoke College, South Hadley, Mass. 01075; Home: 12 Silver Street, South Hadley, Mass., 01075, U.S.A.
Telephone: 413-534-5504 (Home).

Vietoris, Leopold, PH.D.; Austrian professor of mathematics; b. 4 June 1891; s. of Dipl. Ing. Hugo Vietoris and Anna (née Diller) Vietoris; m. 1st Klara von Riccabona (died 1935), 2nd Maria von Riccabona 1936; six d.; ed. Technische Hochschule, and Univ. of Vienna.
Lecturer, Staatserziehungsanstalt, Vienna 19-20; Asst. in Maths., Technische Hochschule, Graz 20-22; Asst. in Maths., Univ. of Vienna 22-27; Rockefeller Fellowship, Amsterdam 25-26; Prof. of Maths., Univ. of Innsbruck 27-28; Technische Hochschule, Vienna 28-30, Univ. of Innsbruck 30-61, Emeritus Prof. 61-; mem. Acad. of Science, Vienna 60; Hon. mem. Austrian Mathematical Soc. 65, Österreichisches Ehrenzeichen für Wissenschaft und Kunst 73.
Leisure interests: mountaineering, skiing.
Publs. *Point Set Theory, Topology, Numerical Analysis, Foundations of Probability Theory, Glaciology.*
Kaiserjägerstr. 40, A-6020 Innsbruck, Austria.
Telephone: 0043-05222/245354.

Viglione, Gen. Andrea; Italian army officer; b. 24 Aug. 1914, Turin; m. Romana Rocco 1946; three d.; ed. Infantry and Cavalry Mil. Acad., Army War Coll.
Battalion Commdr. 52-53; Commdr. 76th Infantry Regiment 59-60; Commdt. Advanced Staff Course, War Coll. 64-65; Head First Dept. Army Gen. Staff 65-66; Commdr. Infantry Div. "Folgore" 66-67, Xth Military Command of Southern Region 71-72, VIIIth Military Command of Central Region 72-73; Head Army Gen. Staff 73-75; Head of Defence Gen. Staff 75-; Knight of Grand Cross of Order of Merit of Repub. of

Italy, Knight of Magistral Grace of the Sovereign Military Order of Malta and other military awards.
Stato Maggiore Difesa, Via XX Settembre 11, Rome, Italy.

Vignes, Alberto Juan; Argentine diplomatist; b. 5 Dec. 1896, Morón; m. Carmen Croppi 1922; ed. Univ. of Buenos Aires.
Head Int. Labour Office, Ministry of External Affairs 21; First Sec., Chargé d'Affaires Austria, Yugoslavia and Hungary 22-28, Sweden, Denmark, Norway and Finland 30-35, Czechoslovakia 36-37, Yugoslavia 38-41, Hungary 41-43; Amb. 46; Dir. of State Ceremonial 46-47; Under-Sec. of External Affairs 48-73, Minister 73-75; Vice-Pres. del to UN Assembly 48, Pres. 73; Pres. Argentine Diplomatic Circle 67-72; Pres. special del. to Fourth Conf. of Non-Aligned Countries, Algeria 73; Pres. del. to Conf. of American Chancellors, Mexico and Washington 74; Pres. del. to OAS Ordinary Assembly 74; numerous foreign decorations.
Ministerio de Relaciones Exteriores y Culto, Buenos Aires, Argentina.

Vila, George Raymond, A.B., S.M., A.M.P.; American business executive; b. 3 March 1909, Philadelphia, Pa.; s. of Joseph S. Vila; ed. Wesleyan Univ., Massachusetts Inst. of Technology, Harvard Graduate School of Business Administration.
Joined Naugatuck Chemical Div., Uniroyal Inc. 36, various sales and research posts 36-57, Vice-Pres. and Gen. Man. 57, Group Exec. Vice-Pres. Uniroyal Inc. 57-60, Pres. 60-74, Chair. 64-74; Chair. Uniroyal Ltd. (Canada, Scotland); Dir. Rubber Manufacturers' Asscn., Chemical Bank, Church and Dwight Co. Inc., Hon. D.Eng. (Clarkson Coll. of Technology).
Publs. *Critical Analysis of T-50 Test* 39, *Action of Organic Acceleration in Buna S* 42, *Plastication and Processing of GR-S* 43, *Approach of Statistical Methods to Manufacture of Synthetic Rubber* 44, *A New Era in Synthetics in Rubber to Match Plastics?* 55, *Tires: An Expanding Market for Chemicals* 56, *1960 Outlook for In-Process Materials* 59, *Economics and Trends in Rubber and the Newer Rubber-Like Materials* 59.
West Woods Road, Sharon, Conn. 06069, U.S.A.

Vilcek (Wilczek), Miroslav, L. ès L.; Yugoslav international official; b. 25 Sept. 1923, Zagreb; s. of Ivan Wilczek and Zora Bijelic; m. Andjelija Bogdanovic 1958; ed. Lausanne Univ. (economics), Bern Univ. (law and admin.) and Belgrade Univ. (English language and literature).
Interned in Italy and Switzerland during Second World War 42-45; Attaché, Yugoslav Legation, Bern, and mem. several dels. to int. confs. 45-49; Secr. of State for Foreign Affairs, Belgrade (Desk for Social and Humanitarian Int. Orgs., and Consular Dept.) 50-55; Head of Dept. for Foreign Relations and Information, Belgrade City Council 55-59; Sec. of Television Programme Cttee. of Asscn. of Yugoslav Broadcasting Stations, Belgrade 59-63; Dir. of Television Programme (Eurovision) Div., and Sec. TV Programme Cttee. of European Broadcasting Union, Geneva March 63-.
Leisure interest: philately.
Publs. Articles on human rights and int. public law in professional periodicals in Belgrade 50-55.
European Broadcasting Union, 1 rue de Varembé, Geneva, Switzerland.
Telephone: 33-24-00.

Vîlcu, Vasile; Romanian politician; b. 26 Sept. 1910, Ciamurlia de Jos, Constanţa County; m. Inda Vîlcu; one s. one d.; ed. Party High School, "Stefan Gheorghiu".
Member Romanian Communist Party (R.C.P.) 29-; imprisoned Tîrgu Jiu 41-44; Sec. Doli District Cttee. of R.C.P. 44-46, Tulcea District Cttee. of R.C.P. 46-47; First Sec. Dobrogea Region Cttee. of R.C.P.

56-65; Alt. mem. Cen. Cttee. of R.C.P. 58-60, mem. 60-; Alt. mem. Exec. Cttee. of Cen. Cttee. of R.C.P. 65, mem. 66-; Deputy, Grand Nat. Assembly 48-52, 57-; Chair. Council of Nat. Union of Agricultural Production Co-operatives 66-69; mem. Exec. Bureau of Nat. Cttee. of Socialist Unity Front 68; Vice-Pres. State Council 69-75; First Sec. Constanta County Cttee. of R.C.P. 71-; Hero of Socialist Labour 71.
Central Committee of the Romanian Communist Party, Bucharest, Romania.

Vilela, H.E. Cardinal Avelar Brandão; Brazilian ecclesiastic, b. 13 June 1912, Viçosa.
Ordained priest 35; consecrated Bishop of Petrolina 46; Archbishop of Teresina 55, of São Salvador da Bahia March 71-; cr. Cardinal by Pope Paul VI 73.
Palácio Arquiepiscopal do Campo Grande, Praça da Sé 1, Salvador, Est. da Bahia, Brazil.
Telephone: 3-2979.

Vilhjalmsson, Thor; Icelandic lawyer; b. 9 June 1930, Reykjavík; s. of Vilhjalmur Th. Gislason and Inga Arnadottir Gislason; m. Ragnhildur Helgadottir Vilhjalmsson 1950; one s. three d.; ed. Reykjavík Grammar School, St. Andrews Univ., Scotland, Univ. of Iceland, New York Univ. and Univ. of Copenhagen.
Assistant Lecturer, Univ. of Iceland 59-62, part-time Lecturer 62-67; Prof. 67-, and Dean, Faculty of Law 68-70, Dir. Inst. of Law 74-; Dep. Judge Reykjavík Civil Court 60-62, Judge 62-67; Pres. Asscn. of Icelandic Lawyers 71-74; Judge, European Court of Human Rights 71-; mem. Icelandic Del. to UN Gen. Assembly 63, UN Sea-Bed Cttee. 72, 73, to Law of the Sea Conf. 74, 75, and other int. confs.; Editor Icelandic Law Review 73-.
Publs. *Civil Procedure I-IV* and studies on human rights and legal history.
Faculty of Law, University of Iceland, Reykjavík, Iceland.
Telephone: 25088.

Viljoen, Hon. Marais; South African politician; b. 2 Dec. 1915, Robertson; m. Dorothea Maria Brink 1940; ed. Jan Van Riebeeck High School, Cape Town, and Univ. of Cape Town.
Manager, *Die Transvaler Boekhandel* 40-43; Organizer, Nat. Party 43-51, Information Officer 51-53; mem. Transvaal Provincial Council for Pretoria 49-53; mem. Parl. for Alberton, Transvaal 53-; Deputy Minister of Labour and of Mines 58-62; Deputy Minister of Interior, Educ., Arts and Science, of Labour and of Immigration 62-66; Minister of Labour and of Coloured Affairs 66-70, also Minister of Interior May-Dec. 70; Minister of Labour and Posts and Telecommunications 70-76; Pres. of Senate Jan. 76-.
The Senate, Cape Town, South Africa.

Villa, José García, A.B.; Philippine poet and critic; b. 5 Aug. 1914, Manila; s. of Dr. Simeon Villa and Maria García; two s.; ed. Univs. of the Philippines, of New Mexico and Columbia Univ.
Associate Editor New Directions Books 49; Cultural Attaché Philippine Mission to UN 53-63; Dir. N.Y. City Coll. Poetry Workshop 52-63, Prof. of Poetry, New School for Social Research 64-73; Philippines Presidential Adviser on Cultural Affairs 68-; Guggenheim Fellowship 43, Bollingen Fellowship 51, Rockefeller Grant 64; American Acad. of Arts and Letters Award 42, Shelley Memorial Award 59, Pro Patria Award 61, Philippines Cultural Heritage Award 62, Nat. Artist in Literature 73; Hon. D.Litt., (Far Eastern Univ.) 59, Hon. L.H.D. (Univ. of Philippines) 73.
Leisure interests: dogs, plants, cooking.
Publs. *Footnote to Youth* (stories) 33, *Many Voices* 39, *Poems by Doveglion* 41, *Have Come, Am Here* 42, *Volume Two* 49, *Selected Poems and New* 58, *Poems*

Fifty-five 62, *Poems in Praise of Love* 62, *Selected Stories* 62, *The Portable Villa* 63, *The Essential Villa* 65; Editor: *A Celebration for Edith Sitwell* 48, *Doveglion Book of Philippine Poetry* 75.
780 Greenwich Street, New York City 14, N.Y., U.S.A.

Villalba, Jovito; Venezuelan politician; b. 1908; ed. Liceo Caracas, Universidad Central de Venezuela and Universidad Libre, Colombia.
Former Prof. of Constitutional Rights and Political Theory, Universidad Central, Venezuela; Sec., Federation of Venezuelan Students 28; imprisoned 28-34; Sec.-Gen. Nat. Democratic Party 36; exile in Colombia 36-38; Founder, Unión Republicana Democrática 46, now leader; exiled 52-57; Leader, Junta Patriótica 58; Presidential Candidate 63, 73.
Unión Republicana Democrática, Caracas, Venezuela.

Villanueva, Carlos Raúl; Venezuelan architect; b. 30 May 1900, London, England; s. of Carlos Villanueva and Paulina Astoul; m. Margot Arismendi 1933; three s. one d.; ed. Lycée Condorcet, Paris, and School of Architecture, Ecole Nationale des Beaux Arts, Paris.
Founding Professor, Faculty of Architecture, Univ. of Venezuela, Caracas; mem. Acad. of Natural Sciences, Venezuela; Hon. mem. Soc. of Architects of Colombia, American Inst. of Architects, Royal Inst. of Architects (U.K.); Corresp. mem. UNESCO Int. Cttee. for Monuments, Arts Sites, History and Archaeological Excavations; numerous awards and architectural prizes; D.Arch. h.c. Univ. of Venezuela.
Major works: Plaza de Toros, Maracay; Los Caobos Museum, Caracas; Gran Colombia School, Caracas; urban renewal of el Silencio, Caracas; low cost settlements, Maracaibo and Caracas; Inst. for Petroleum Engineering, Universidad Nacional del Zulia, Maracaibo; Univerisity City, Caracas; office building, Fundación La Salle, Caracas; Museo "Jesús Soto", Ciudad Bolívar.
Quinta Caoma, 27 avenida de los Jabillos, La Florida, Caracas, Venezuela.
Telephone: (02) 749594.

Villar Mir, Juan Miguel; Spanish engineer and politician; b. 30 Sept. 1931; m. Silvia de Fuentes Bescos; three c.; ed. Madrid and Washington, D.C.
Assistant Dir.-Gen. of Ports; Dir.-Gen. of Labour; Deputy Prime Minister for Economic Affairs and Finance Dec. 75-.
Leisure interests: sport and reading.
Ministerio de Hacienda, Madrid, Spain.

Villas Bôas, Claudio; Brazilian anthropologist and explorer; b. 1916, Botucatu, São Paulo; s. of Agnelo and Arlinda Villas Bôas; brother of Orlando Villas Bôas (q.v.).
Has lived in the Brazilian jungle around the River Xingu and worked among the Indians since 45; founded aid posts for Indians and opened airstrips in the jungle; worked in the Indian Protection Service; Fundação Nacional do Indio 67-; Gold Medal, Royal Geographical Soc.
Leisure interests: reading, philosophy, ethnology, classical music.
Parque Nacional do Xingu, Praça Franklin Roosevelt 278, Apto 123, São Paulo, SP, Brazil.

Villas Bôas, Orlando; Brazilian anthropologist and explorer; b. 1914, Botucatu, São Paulo; s. of Agnelo and Arlinda Villas Bôas; m. Marina Lopes de Lima Villas Bôas; one s.; brother of Claudio Villas Bôas (q.v.).
Has lived in the Brazilian jungle around the River Xingu and worked among the Indians with his brother since 45; co-founder (with his brother) for the establishment of the Parque Nacional do Xingu (Brazil's most

important reservation for Indians); Dir. 61-; Gold Medal, Royal Geographical Soc.
Leisure interests: theatre, reading, travel.
Parque Nacional do Xingu, Rua Capital Federal 309 01259, São Paulo, Brazil.

Villaseñor, Eduardo, B.A.; Mexican economist; b. 1896, Angamacutiro, Michoacán; s. of J. Jesús Villaseñor and Rosario Angeles; m. 1st Margarita Ureta 1933 (marriage dissolved), 2nd Laura Wells 1949; one s. three d.; ed. Univ. Michoacana, Univ. of Mexico, London School of Economics.
Professor, Political Economy, Nat. School of Agriculture 21-25; Head, Dept. of Co-operative Socs., Nat. Bank of Agricultural Credit 26-28; Sec. Mexican-British Claims Comm. 28-29; Commercial Attaché Legation London 29-31; Head Consular Div. Dept. of Foreign Affairs 31-32; Head Div. of Publs., Dept. of Finance and Public Credit 32; mem. Nat. Banking Comm. 32-33; Prof. of Int. Trade, Faculty of Economics, Univ. Mexico; Sec. Board Nat. Mortgage Bank of Urban and Public Works; Sec. Nat. Council Economy 32-34; Consul-Gen. New York 35; Pres. Nat. Agricultural Bank 36-37; Under Sec. for Finance and Public Credit 38-40; Dir.-Gen. Banco de México, S.A. 40-46; Pres. Banco del Atlántico 49-65; Chair. of Board Banco de la Ciudad de México, S.A. 66-71; Commdr. de la Légion d'Honneur.
Leisure interests: painting, antique collecting, golf.
Publs. *Extasis, novela de aventuras* 28, *Nuestra Industria Textil de Algodón* 34, *Inter-American Trade and Financial Problems* 41, *The Inter-American Bank: Prospects and Dangers* 41, *Some Aspects of Mexico's War Economy* 43, *Ensayos Interamericanos Reflexiones de un economista* 44, *De la Curiosidad y otros papeles* 45, *Episodio* 52, *The English are they Human?* 53, *La Farce et la Mori au Mexique* 57, *Stabilité ou Développement de l'Economie Mexicaine* 57, *Los Recuerdos y los Días* 60, *Memorias-Testimonio* 74.
Reyna 73, Mexico 20, D.F., Mexico.
Telephone: 5-48-20-13.

Villella, Edward, B.S.; American ballet dancer; b. 1 Jan. 1936, New York; m. Janet Greschler 1962, divorced 1970; one s.; ed. N.Y. State Maritime Coll.
Joined N.Y. City Ballet 57, becoming soloist within a year, now Premier Dancer; originated leading roles in George Balanchine's *Bugaku*, *Tarantella*, *Stars and Stripes*, *Harlequinade*, *Jewels*, *Glinkaiana*, *A Midsummer Night's Dream*; first danced his famous role of *Prodigal Son* 60; has also danced leading roles in *Allegro Brillante*, *Jeux*, *Pas de Deux*, *Raymonda Variations*, *Scotch Symphony*, *Swan Lake*; choreographed *Narkissos*; has appeared at Bolshoi Theatre, with Royal Danish Ballet and in London, and made numerous guest appearances; choreographed and starred in revivals of *Brigadoon*, *Carousel*; *Dance* magazine award 65; mem. Nat. Council on the Arts; Golden Plate Award (American Acad. of Achievement) 71.
New York City Ballet, New York State Theatre, Lincoln Center Plaza, New York, N.Y. 10023, U.S.A.
Telephone: 212-TR7-4700.

Villeméjane, Bernard de; French business executive; b. 10 March 1930, Marseilles; s. of Pierre and Marie-Thérèse (née Getten) de Villeméjane; m. Françoise Boucheronde 1965; two s.; ed. Ecole Polytechnique and Ecole des Mides, Paris.
With Direction des Mines et de la Géologie, French West Africa 55-60; Ministry of Industry 60-61; Engineering Adviser, Banque Rothschild 61-62; Deputy Man. Dir. Société Penarroya 63, Man Dir. 67, Chair. of Board and Man. Dir. 71-; Man Dir. Société Le Nickel 71-74, Imetal 74-; Chair. of Board and Man. Dir. S.M. le Nickel S.L.N. 74-; Dir. of various other French companies.

Office: 1 boulevard de Vaugirard, 75751 Paris 15; Home: 102 rue d'Assas, 75006 Paris, France.
Telephone: 538-52-33.

Villiers, Alan John, D.S.C., F.R.G.S.; Australian author and sailor; b. 23 Sept. 1903, Melbourne; s. of Leon Joseph Villiers and Anastasia Edith (née Hayes) Villiers; m. Nancie Wills 1940; two s. one d.; ed. State schools in Melbourne.
Went to sea in sailing ships 20; mem. pioneer pelagic whaling voyage into Ross Sea, Antarctica 23-24; part-owner Finnish 4-mast barque 30-34; master-owner full-rigged ship *Joseph Conrad* 34-36; sailed Arab deep-sea dhows 38-39; Royal Navy 40-46; Master, Outward-Bound Sea Schools' training ships 49-50; voyage in Portuguese 4-mast schooner Grand Banks and Greenland 50; Commanded barque *Mayflower II* 57; Trustee Nat. Maritime Museum for twenty years; Gov. Cutty Sark Soc.; Vice-Pres. Soc. for Nautical Research, mem. Ships Cttee. Maritime Trust, Tech. Cttee., H.M.S. *Victory*; Commdr. Portuguese Order of Santiago; Camõens Prize for Literature 54.
Publs. *Falmouth for Orders* 29, *By Way of Cape Horn* 30, *Cruise of the Conrad* 37, *Sons of Sinbad* 40 and new edn. (U.S.A.) 69, *The Way of a Ship* 50, *The Quest of the Schooner Argus* 57, *The Western Ocean* 57, *Give me a Ship to Sail* 58, *Oceans of the World* 63, *Captain Cook, the Seaman's Seaman* 67, *The War with C. Horn* 71, *The Bounty Ships of France* 72, *Captain Conrad* 76.
1A Lucerne Road, Oxford, OX2 7QB, England.
Telephone: Oxford 55632.

Villiers, Georges; French commercial administrator; b. 15 June 1899; ed. Lycée de Lyon, Ecole nationale supérieure des Mines, Saint-Etienne.
Mayor of Lyon 41-42, deported to Germany 43-45; Pres. Nat. Council of French Employers 46-66; Pres. Council of Industrial Federations in Europe 64-70; Pres. French Cttee. of the Int. Chamber of Commerce; Gov. European Cultural Foundation; Pres. of Comm. for Int. Econ. Relations of the C.N.P.F.; Treas. and then Pres. Advisory Econ. and Industrial Cttee. to OECD 66-68; Commdr. Légion d'Honneur, Croix de Guerre (39-45) and other European int. awards.
62 Avenue Henri Martin, Paris, France.
Telephone: 504-05-08.

Villot, H.E. Cardinal Jean; French ecclesiastic; b. 11 Oct. 1905; ed. Séminaire de l'Institut Catholique, Paris and Collège Angélique, Rome.
Ordained priest 30; Vice-Rector Catholic faculties of Lyon 42-50; Sec.-Gen. of the French Episcopate 50; Bishop of Vinda and Auxiliary to Cardinal Feltin 53-59; Coadjutor Archbishop of Lyon 59-65; Under-Sec. Ecumenical Council 62-65; Archbishop of Lyon 65-67; Prefect of the Sacred Congregation of the Council 67-69; Sec. of State, Vatican 69-; Chamberlain Oct. 70-; cr. Cardinal 65.
Apostolic Palace, Vatican City, Rome, Italy.

Vimond, Paul Marcel; French architect; b. 20 June 1922, La Meurdraquière; s. of Ernest Vimond and Marie Lehuby; m. Jacqueline Lefèvre 1945; two s. two d.; ed. Lycée de Coutances, Ecole préparatoire des beaux-arts de Rennes and Ecole nationale supérieure des beaux-arts, Paris.
Member Jury of Nat. School of Fine Arts; mem. Diocesan Comm. on Sacred Art, Paris; Chevalier des Arts et des Lettres and of Pontifical Order of Merit; Premier Grand Prix de Rome 49.
Major architectural works include: Architect in charge of Int. Exhbn. of Sacred Art, Rome 53; responsible for films and architectural reconstructions of tomb of Saint Peter, Rome; Buildings in Paris for: Assemblée de l'Union française, Conseil économique et social, Union de l'Europe occidentale, Organisation de co-opération

et de développement économiques; planner and architect for Palais d'Iéna, Paris; town planner for Cherbourg; Atomic Power Station, The Hague; two theatres, three churches in Paris, hotels, restaurants, hospitals, and numerous lycées in France; technical insts. at Besançon, Montpellier, Paris, Orsay, Nice, Toulon, Troyes; Faculty of medicine, Nice; many telephone exchanges and ten large postal sorting offices in Paris region and provinces; sorting offices in Riyadh, Jeddah and Dammam and project for television centre in Saudi Arabia.
Leisure interests: painting, golf.
Office: 23 rue de Lubeck, 75116 Paris; and 91 avenue Niel, Paris 17e, France.
Telephone: 720-59-53, 720-59-57 and 720-59-61 (Office); 924-87-84 (Home).

Vimont, Jacques Pierre, L. en D.; French diplomatist; b. 17 July 1911, Paris; s. of Marcel and Alice (née Durantet) Vimont; m. Anne Brun 1942; one s. two d.; ed. Lycée de Nice, Faculté de Droit, Paris and Ecole Libre des Sciences Politiques.
Attaché Belgrade 38; Dir. Adjoint du Cabinet Résidence Gén., Tunis 39-42; Ministry of Foreign Affairs 44-46; Counsellor to Sherifian Govt. 46-49; Counsellor, Berne 49-50; Sec.-Gen. Tunisian Govt. 50-51; Counsellor, Rio de Janeiro 51-53; Dir. Adjoint de Cabinet Ministry of Foreign Affairs 53-54; Minister-Counsellor, Washington 54-57; Dir. of Personnel, Ministry of Foreign Affairs 58-65; Amb. to Mexico 65-69, to Czechoslovakia 70-73, to U.S.S.R. 73-; Commdr. Ordre du Mérite, Commdr. Légion d'Honneur.
French Embassy, Ulitsa Dimitrova 43, Moscow, U.S.S.R.

Vincent, Daniel, D. ès SC., M.D., PHARM.D.; French doctor and pharmacologist; b. 12 Oct. 1907, Dortan, Ain; s. of Albert Vincent and Marie-Thérèse Blanc; m. Marie-Louise Doucet-Bon 1933; one s. three d.; ed. Univ. of Lyon.
Head medical chemist, Faculty of Medicine and Pharmacy, Univ. of Lyon, and Head of Medical Clinic 38-39; Prof. Faculty of Medicine and Pharmacy, Toulouse 43 and Lyon 65; Biologist of Hospitals in Lyon 69; Regional Insp. of Pharmacy 42-45 and Principal Insp. 55; mem. Regional Council Ordre des Pharmaciens, Toulouse 50-65, New York Acad. of Sciences 61; Lauréat de l'Inst. de France, Prix Pourat 39; Lauréat de l'Acad. de Médecine, Prix Marc Sée 45, Prix Jansen 61.
Les Crètes 54 avenue Valioud, 69110 Ste. Foy-Les-Lyon, France.
Telephone: (78) 36-00-56.

Vincent, Eric R. P., C.B.E., LITT.D., D.PHIL., M.A.; British university professor (emeritus); b. 10 Dec. 1894, Hampstead, London; s. of Charles Vincent and Hannah Phillips; m. Ivy Barrow Simonds 1923, one d.; ed. Berkhamsted School and Christ Church, Oxford.
Interned in Germany as civil prisoner of war 14-18; Lecturer in Italian, King's Coll., Univ. of London 22; Univ. Lecturer in Italian Language and Literature Oxford 27-34; Prof. of Italian, Cambridge 35-62, Emeritus 62-; Life Fellow of Corpus Christi Coll., Cambridge, Pres. 54-59; served Foreign Office 39-45; Commendatore Ordine Al Merito della Repubblica Italiana; fmr. Pres. of Asscn. Int. di Studi Italiani; mem. Italian Arcadian Acad.; British Acad. Serena Medal 73.
Leisure interests: book and art collecting.
Publs. *Ardengo Soffici, Six Essays on Modern Art, Preface and Notes,* 22 *Gabriele Rossetti in England* 36, *The Commemoration of the Dead* (Foscolo's *Sepolcri*) 36, *Byron, Hobhouse and Foscolo* 49, *Ugo Foscolo, An Italian in Regency England* 53; and other works.
Sandhills Cottage, Salcombe, Devon, England.
Telephone: Salcombe 3154.

Vincent, Olatunde Olabode; Nigerian banker; b. 16 May 1925, Lagos; s. of Josiah O. and Comfort A. Vincent; m. Edith Adenike Gooding; three s. one d.; ed. C.M.S. Grammar School, Lagos, Chartered Inst. of Secs., London, Univ. of Manchester, and Admin. Staff Coll., Henley, England.
Nigerian Army 42-46; Financial Sec.'s Office 47-65; Fed. Ministry of Finance 56-61; Asst. Gen. Man. Central Bank of Nigeria 61-62, Deputy Gen. Man. 62, Gen. Man. 63-66, Adviser 73-75, Deputy Gov. 75-; Vice-Pres. African Devt. Bank, Abidjan, Ivory Coast 64-73; Part-time Lecturer in Econs., Extra-Mural Dept., Univ. Coll. of Ibadan 57-60; mem. Lagos Exec. Devt. Board 60-61; mem. Cttee. which set up Nigerian Industrial Devt. Bank; Dir. Nigerian Industrial Devt. Bank 64-66, Nigerian Security Printing and Minting Co. Ltd., Lagos, 75-; Chair. Capital Issues Comm., Lagos, 75-; mem. Cttee. of Nine which set up African Devt. Bank; mem. Soc. for Int. Devt.; Econ. and Financial Adviser, African Church Inc., Lagos; Auditor African Church Cathedral (Bethel), Lagos.
Leisure interests: reading (mainly history and magazines), walking, listening to African and light classical music, gardening.
Central Bank of Nigeria, P.O. Box 12194, Lagos; 2 Glover Road, Ikoyi, Lagos, Nigeria.
Telephone: 53700 and 25086.

Vinci, Piero; Italian diplomatist; b. 1912; ed. University of Rome.
Diplomatic Service 38-, Switzerland, Bulgaria 38-47; Head of Press Section, Ministry of Foreign Affairs, Rome 47-49; First Sec. Beirut 49-53; Consul-Gen. London 53-55; Head of Political Office for Relations with Africa and the Middle East, Ministry of Foreign Affairs, Rome 55-59; Head of UN Division 59-60; Chief of Cabinet to Deputy Prime Minister and Minister of Foreign Affairs 60-63; Perm. Rep. to UN 64-73; Presidential Cttee. (Political) of 23rd Gen. Assembly of the UN 68; Italian Rep. to UN Security Council 71; mem. of Board of UNITAR 73; Amb. to U.S.S.R. 73-75; Perm. Rep. to UN 75-.
Permanent Mission of Italy to UN, 747 Third Avenue, 35th Floor, New York, N.Y. 10017, U.S.A.

Vinde, Pierre L. V., JUR.CAND., PHIL.CAND.; Swedish civil servant; b. 15 Aug. 1931, Paris, France; s. of Victor Vinde and Rita Wilson; m. Ann-Marie Persson 1957; one s. one d.; ed. Schools in France, Sweden and U.K., Univs. of Uppsala and Stockholm.
In Prime Minister's Office 57-58; Ministry of Trade 58-60; Ministry of Finance 61-, Budget Dir. 70-74, Under-Sec. 74-; mem. Board Devt. Assistance Agency 62-65, Inst. of Defence Org. and Management 68-70, Nat. Audit Office 69-74, Agency for Admin. Devt. 74-; Deputy Group of Ten 74-; Chair. Board of Dirs. Bank of Sweden 74; mem. Police Comm. 62-64, Defence Comm. 65-68; Chair. Relocation of Gov. Administration Comm. 70-72.
Publs. *Hur Sverige styres* (The Government of Sweden) 68, *Swedish Government Administration* 71.
Finansdepartementet, Fack, S-103 10 Stockholm; Sveriges Riksbank, Box 2119, S-103 13 Stockholm, Sweden.
Telephone: 08-7631000 (Finansdepartementet); 08-228200 (Riksbank).

Vines, William Joshua, C.M.G.; Australian business executive and farmer; b. 27 May 1916, Terang; s. of Percy V. and Isabella Vines; m. Thelma J. Ogden 1939; one s. two d.; ed. Haileybury Coll., Victoria.
Army service, Middle East, New Guinea and Borneo 39-45; Sec. Alexander Fergusson Pty. Ltd. 38-47; Dir. Goodlass Wall and Co. Pty. Ltd. 47-49, Lewis Berger and Sons (Australia) Pty. Ltd. and Sherwin Williams Co. (Aust.) Pty. Ltd. 52-55; Man. Dir. Lewis Berger and Sons (Victoria) Pty. Ltd. 49-55; Managing Dir. Lewis

Berger & Sons Ltd. 55-60; Managing Dir. Berger, Jensen & Nicholson Ltd. 60-61; Man. Dir. Int. Wool Secr. 61-69, mem. Board 69-; Chair., Man. Dir. Dalgety Australia Ltd.; Chair. Carbonless Papers (Wiggins Teape) Pty. Ltd.; Dir. Commercial Union Assurance Co. of Australia Ltd., Port Phillip Mills Pty. Ltd., Tubemakers of Australia Ltd., Assoc. Pulp and Paper Mills Ltd.

Leisure interests: golf, swimming.

73 Yarranabbe Road, Darling Point, Sydney; Old Southwood, Tara, Queensland, Australia.

Telephone: 328-7970 (Sydney); 89R (Tara).

Vinicchayakul, Serm D. en D.; Thai politician and lawyer; b. 2 June 1908; m. Chomsri Poshyananda 1941; two s. two d.; ed. Assumption Coll. and Faculté de Droit, Univ. of Paris.

Appointed Sec. Gen. of Judicial Council 46; Gov. Bank of Thailand 46-47, 52-54; Prof. of Law Thammasat Univ. 54; Under-Sec. for Finance 54-65; Gov. IBRD, IFC and IDA 65; Minister of Finance 65-71; Minister of Finance 72-73; Chair. Exec. Board of Econ. and Social Devt. Council 72; Senator 74-; Knight Grand Cross (First Class), Order of Chula Chom Klao; Knight Grand Cordon (Special Class), Order of the White Elephant; Knight Grand Cordon, Order of the Crown of Thailand.

159 Asoke Road, Bangkok, Thailand.

Vinograd, Jerome, M.A., PH.D.; American professor of chemistry and biology; b. 9 Feb. 1913, Milwaukee, Wis.; s. of Oscar Vinograd and Bertha Bernstein Vinograd; m. Sherna Shalett 1937; two d.; m. 2nd Dorothy Colodny 1975; ed. Univ. of Minnesota, Univ. of Berlin, Univ. Coll. London, Univ. of Calif., Los Angeles, and Stanford Univ., Palo Alto.

Research Assoc., Stanford Univ. 39-41; Research Chemist, Shell Devt. Co., Emeryville, Calif. 41-51; Senior Research Fellow in Chem., Calif. Inst. of Technology 51-56; Research Assoc., Calif. Inst. of Technology 56-65; Prof. of Chem. and Biology, Calif. Inst. of Technology 65-; Visiting Prof. Albert Einstein Medical Coll. 67; mem. Nat. Acad. of Sciences 68; American Acad. of Arts and Sciences 69; Recipient, Kendall Award of American Chemical Soc. 70; Burroughs Wellcome Lecturer, Harvard Medical School 70; Jessie W. Beams Lecturer, Univ. of Virginia 72; Falk-Plaut Lecturer, Columbia Univ. 72; mem. Nat. Inst. of Health, Nat. Cancer Inst. Molecular Control Working Group 72-.

Publs. Approximately 100 scientific articles, including chapters in monographs.

Divisions of Chemistry and Chemical Engineering, Building 164-30, California Institute of Technology, 1201 East California Boulevard, Pasadena, Calif. 91125; Home: 635 Old Mill Road, Pasadena, Calif. 91108, U.S.A.

Telephone: 213-795-6811, Ext. 2053.

Vinogradov, Ivan Metveyevich; Soviet mathematician; b. 14 Sept. 1891, Mirolyub, Pskov Region; ed. Leningrad Univ.

Lecturer and later Prof. Perm Univ. 18-20; Prof. Leningrad Polytechnical Inst. and Leningrad Univ. 20-34 (founded Chair. of Numbers, Leningrad Univ.); mem. U.S.S.R. Acad. of Sciences 29-, Dir. Steklov Inst. of Mathematics 32-; hon. mem. London Mathematical Society, Netherlands Mathematical Society, American Philosophical Society, Royal Society, London, American Acad. of Arts and Sciences, Royal Danish Acad. of Sciences, Indian Mathematical Society, Hungarian Acad. of Sciences, Italian Acad. of Sciences; foreign mem. Serbian Acad. of Sciences 59-; mem. Royal Soc., London 60-; Corresp. mem. French Acad. of Sciences, German Acad. of Sciences; Hero of Socialist Labour 45; State Prize 41, Lenin Prize 72, four Orders of Lenin,

"Hammer and Sickle" Gold Medal, Lomonosov Gold Medal; Hon. Ph.D. (Oslo Univ.) 50.

Publ. *New Methods in Analytic Theory of Numbers.*

Steklov Mathematics Institute, U.S.S.R. Academy of Sciences, 28 Ulitsa Vavilova, Moscow, U.S.S.R.

Vinogradov, Vladimir Alexandrovich; Soviet historian and diplomatist; b. 1907; ed. Leningrad Univ.

Former Prof. of History; Diplomatic Service 39-; Counsellor, Turkey 40, Amb. 40-48; Head, Dept. of UN Affairs, Ministry of Foreign Affairs 48-50; Chair. U.S.S.R. Council of Ministers Radio Cttee. 50-53; Amb. to France 53-65; on staff of Ministry of Foreign Affairs 65-67; Amb. to Egypt (fmrly. United Arab Repub.) 67-73; Head Perm. Mission to UN, Geneva Jan. 74-; mem. Central Auditing Comm. of C.P.S.U. 62-66; Grand Croix Légion d'Honneur.

Permanent Mission of the U.S.S.R. to the United Nations Office, Geneva, Switzerland.

Violardo, H.E. Cardinal Giacomo; Vatican ecclesiastic; b. 10 May 1898, Govene, Alba.

Ordained 23; Titular Bishop of Satafi 66-; Sec. for Sacred Congregation for Following the Sacraments; cr. Cardinal 69.

Piazza del Sant' Uffizio 11, 00193 Rome, Italy.

Telephone: 698-4203.

Viollet, Paul; French engineer; b. 10 Nov. 1919, Paris; s. of Louis Viollet and Paule Mornard; m. Laetitia de Royer-Dupré 1944; one s. two d.; ed. Coll. Stanislas, Paris, Ecole Polytechnique de Paris and C.P.A. de Paris.

Manager Cie. de Saint-Gobain 56-61; Vice-Chair. and Gen. Man. Produits Chimiques Pechiney-Saint-Gobain 61-72; Dir., Gen. Man. of Rhône-Progil 72-75; Gen. Man. Rhône-Poulenc Polymères 75-; Chair. Syndicat Professionnel des Fabricants de Matières Plastiques et de Résines Synthétiques; Dir. Philagro, Distugil, Sodefine, Société des Industries Chimiques du Nord de la Grèce (Athens), Reposa (Madrid); Vice-Chair. Naphtachimie, Union des Industries Chimiques; Chevalier de la Légion d'Honneur.

22 avenue Montaigne, 75008 Paris; Home: 112 avenue de Versailles, 75016 Paris, France.

Telephone: 256-40-00.

Viot, Jacques Edmond, L. ÈS L.; French diplomatist; b. 25 Aug. 1921, Bordeaux; m. Jeanne de Martimprey de Romecourt 1950; ed. Bordeaux and Paris lycées and Ecole Normale Supérieure and Ecole Nationale d'Admin.

Lecturer in French, Univ. of Dublin 45-47, Ecole Nat. d'Admin. 48-50; Foreign Office 51-53, Second Sec., London 53-57; First Sec., Rabat 57-61; held various posts in central admin. 61-72; Amb. to Canada 72-; Officier, Légion d'Honneur, Officier, Ordre Nat. du Mérite.

French Embassy, 42 Sussex Drive, Ottawa, Ont. K1M 2C9, Canada.

Telephone: 232-1795; 233-4016.

Vira, Dharma; Indian civil servant and diplomatist; b. 20 Jan. 1906; ed. Lucknow and Allahabad Univs., and London School of Economics and Political Science.

Joined Civil Service 30; Joint Magistrate Aligarh 30-34, Almora 34-36, Bareilly 36; Joint Sec. Industries and Agricultural Exhibition, Lucknow 36-37; Officiating District Magistrate, Bareilly 37; District Magistrate, Etah 37-38, Almora 38-41; with Commerce Dept., Govt. of India 41-44, Deputy Sec. Industries and Civil Supplies Dept. 44-45, Textile Commr. 45-47, Joint Sec. to Cabinet 47-50; Principal Private Sec. to Prime Minister 50-51; Commercial Adviser, High Comm. London 51-53; Ambassador to Czechoslovakia 54-56; Sec. Ministry of Works. Housing and Rehabilitation 56-63; Chief Commr. for Delhi 63-64; Cabinet Sec. and Sec. to the Council of Ministers 64-66; Chair. Atomic

Energy Comm. and Sec. Dept. of Atomic Energy 66; Gov., Punjab and Haryana 66-67; Gov. of W. Bengal 68-69; Gov. of Mysore 69-72.
A 53 Vasant Vihar, New Delhi, India.

Virata, Cesar Enrique, B.S.BUS.ADM., B.S.MECH.ENG., M.B.A.; Philippine finance executive; b 12 Dec. 1930, Manila; s. of Enrique Virata and Leonor Aguinaldo; m. Joy Gamboa 1956; two s. one d.; ed. Univ. of Pa., U.S.A. and Univ. of the Philippines.
Dean, Coll. of Business Admin., Univ. of the Philippines 61-69; Chair. and Dir. Philippine Nat. Bank 67-69; Deputy Dir.-Gen. Presidential Econ. Staff 67-68; Under-Sec. of Industry 67-69; Chair. Board of Investments 67-70; Sec. of Finance 70-; Chair. Land Bank of the Philippines 73-; mem. Monetary Board; mem. Nat. Econ. and Devt. Authority 72-; L.H.D. h.c., D.P.A. h.c.
Leisure interests: tennis, pelota filipina, golf, reading.
c/o Department of Finance, Manila; Home: 63 East Maya Drive, Quezon City, Philippines.
Telephone: 59-52-62 and 59-71-39 (Office); 99-74-19 (Home).

Virolainen, Johannes, PH.D.; Finnish politician and farmer; b. 31 Jan. 1914, Viipuri; ed. Helsinki Univ. (Agriculture and Forestry).
Vice-Chair. Agrarian Party 46-64, Chair. 65- (name of party changed to Centre Party 65); Second Minister of Interior 50-51; Second Minister of Prime Minister's Office 51; Minister of Educ. 53-54, 68-70, of Foreign Affairs 54-56, 57, 58, of Agriculture 61-63; Deputy Prime Minister 57-58, 62-63, 68-70; Prime Minister 64-66; Speaker of Parl. 66-69; First Minister of Finance 72-75; Chair. Nat. Planning Council 56-66; Grand Crosses Orders of Merit (Argentina), Leopold (Belgium), Dannebrog (Denmark), Hawk (Iceland); Grand Officer Order of Polonia Restituta (Poland).
Kirkniemi, Lohja, Finland.

Virta, Nikolai Evgenievich; Soviet writer; b. 19 Dec. 1906, Lasovka, Tambov Region.
Journalist 23-35; State prizewinner (4 times).
Publs. plays: *Earth* 37, *Slander* 39, *Our Daily Bread* 47, *Plot of the Doomed* 48, *Endless Horizons* 57, *In Summer the Sky is High* 60, *Three Stones of Faith* 60, *Operation Czech Forest* 61, *Thirst* 61, *Golgotha* 61 , *Winds Blew and Blew* 62, *Niagara Falls* 62, *Secret of Clemance and Son* 64; novels: *Loneliness* 35, *The Adventurer* 37, *Evening Bells* 51, *Steep Hills* 55, *Soil Returned* 60, *The One We don't Know* 60, *Our Bertha* 60, *Field Marshal* 61, *Aksushka* 62, *Two Days of their Life* 62, *Fast Running Days* 65, *Novels of Last Years* 65, *Cat with a Long, Long Tail* 66, *The End of a Career* 67.
U.S.S.R. Union of Writers, 52 Vorovskogo ulitsa, Moscow, U.S.S.R.

Visentini, Bruno, D.IUR.; Italian lawyer, politician and business executive; b. 1 Aug. 1914, Treviso; ed. Univ. of Padua.
Member Consultative Assembly; Under-Sec. of Finance, Govt. of Alcide de Gasperi; Vice-Chair. Istituto per la Ricostruzione Industriale (I.R.I.) until 73; Chair. Olivetti e C., S.p.A. until 74; Vice-Chair. Confindustria until 74; Dir. Montecatini-Edison; fmr. Prof. of Commercial Law, Univ. of Urbino; Lecturer in Business Law, Univ. of Rome; Pres. Italian Venice Cttee.; mem. Parl.; Minister of Finance Nov. 74-; Radical Republican.
Ministry of Finance, Rome; Home: 14 Via Bacone, Rome, Italy.
Telephone: 689-788.

Vishnevskaya, Galina Pavlovna; Soviet singer; b. 1926, Leningrad.
Studied with Vera Garina 42-52; Leningrad Musical Theatres 44-52; joined Bolshoi Theatre 52-; numerous parts in operas, notably Leonora in *Fidelio*, and Tatiana in *Eugene Onegin* (also in the film), Aida (*Aida*), Kupava (*Snow Maiden*), Liza (*Queen of Spades*), Chio-Sio-San (*Madame Butterfly*), Margaret (*Faust*),

Natasha (*War and Peace*), Cherubino (*Marriage of Figaro*); People's Artist of R.S.F.S.R. and U.S.S.R.
State Academic Bolshoi Theatre of U.S.S.R., 1 Ploshchad Sverdlova, Moscow, U.S.S.R.

Visscher, Maurice B., M.S., PH.D., M.D.; American professor of physiology; b. 25 Aug. 1901, Holland, Mich.; s. of Johannes W. Visscher and Everdena Bolks; m. Janet Gertrude Pieters 1925; two s. two d.; ed. Hope Coll., Holland, Mich., and Univ. of Minnesota.
Professor and Head of Dept. of Physiology, Univ. of Minnesota 36-68, Regent's Prof. of Physiology 67-; Pres. American Physiological Soc. 48-49; Board of Dirs. of *Biological Abstracts* 49-53, Council of Int. Orgs. of Medical Sciences 52-55; Pres. 52-65; Nat. Soc. for Medical Research, Pres. 65-; Sec.-Gen. Int. Union of Physiological Sciences 53-59; Pres. Soc. for Experimental Biology and Medicine 67-69; Chair. U.S. Nat. Cttee. for Int. Union of Physiological Sciences 60-69; mem. U.S. Nat. Acad. of Sciences, American Philosophical Soc.; Fellow, American Acad. of Arts and Sciences; American Heart Asscn. Outstanding Achievement Award.
Publs. *Ethical Constraints and Imperatives in Medical Ethics* 75; Editor: *Chemistry and Medicine* 40, *Claude Bernard, Experimental Medicine* 67, *Humanistic Perspectives in Medical Ethics* 72; Chair. Editorial Cttee. *Handbook of Physiology* (15 vols.) 56-57; approx. 200 papers in physiology journals.
Office: Univ. of Minnesota, Stone Research Laboratory, 421 29th Avenue S.E., Minneapolis, Minn. 55414; Home: One Orlin Avenue S.E., Minneapolis, Minn. 55414, U.S.A.
Telephone: 373-5248.

Visser 't Hooft, Willem Adolph, DR. THEOL., D.D.; Netherlands ecclesiastic; b. 20 Sept. 1900, Haarlem; s. of Hendrik P. Visser 't Hooft and Jacoba Lieftinck; m. Henriette Boddaert 1924 (died 1968); two s. one d.; ed. Univ. of Leiden.
Member of the staff of World Cttee. of Y.M.C.A. 24; Gen. Sec. World Student Christian Fed. 29; Gen. Sec. World Council of Churches 38-66, Hon. Pres. 68-; Editor of *The Student World* 28-38; Editor *The Ecumenical Review* 48-66; Grand Cross of the Order of Merit, Fed. Repub. of Germany 57 Officer Legion of Honour 59; Wateler Peace Prize 62; Cross of the Great Commdr. of the Holy Sepulchre 63; Commdr. Order of St. Andrew 63; Order of St. Vladimir 64; Commdr. Order of the Netherlands Lion 65; Hon. Commdr. Order of St. John 66; Peace Prize of German Book Trade 66; Award of Family of Man 66; Grotius Medal 66; Sonning Prize, Copenhagen 67; Hon. Citizenship of Geneva 67; Hon. D.D. (Aberdeen, Princeton, Toronto, Geneva, Yale, Oberlin, Oxford, Harvard, Tokyo, Paris, Brown Univ., Berlin, Zürich, Louvain), Hon. Prof. of Theological Faculty of Budapest 47, and Theological Acad. in Moscow 64; Hon. Fellow, Hebrew Univ., Jerusalem 72, Open Univ. 74.
Publs. *The Background of the Social Gospel in America* 28, *Anglo-Catholicism and Orthodoxy* 33, *None Other Gods* 37, *The Church and its Function in Society* (with Dr. Oldham) 37, *Wretchedness and Greatness of the Church* 44, *The Struggle of the Dutch Church* 46, *Le Conseil oecuménique des Eglises, sa nature et ses limites* 46, *Rembrandt et la Bible* 47, *The Kingship of Christ* 47, *La Renovación de la Iglesia* 52, *The Meaning of Ecumenical* 53, *The Ecumenical Movement and the Racial Problem* 54, *The Renewal of the Church* 56, *Rembrandt and the Gospel* 57, *The Pressure of our Common Calling* 59, *No Other Name* 63, *Peace among Christians* 67, *Memoirs* 73, *Has the Ecumenical Movement a Future?* 74.
150 Route de Ferney, 1211 Geneva 20, Switzerland.

Visseur, Pierre, LL.D.; Swiss international administrator; b. 10 June 1920, Bré; s. of Pierre L. Visseur and Charlotte van Aken; m. Suzy Butikoffer 1947; one s.

two *d.*; ed. Univs. of Basle, Geneva and Berne, and Inst. of International Studies, Geneva.

Secretary-General, European Div., World Brotherhood 50-62; Dir. World Fed. for Mental Health 63-68; Dir. Pharmaceutical Proprietary Asscn. of Europe (AESGP) 69-; Past Pres. Fed. of Private and Semi-Official Int. Orgs. in Geneva.

Leisure interests: mountaineering, gardening, history.

Publ. *Evolution of Control of International Labour Legislation* 46.

10 Avenue des Amazones, 1224 Chêne-Bougeries, Geneva, Switzerland; 135 Avenue Wagram, Paris 17e, France.

Telephone: 022-484697 (Geneva); 227-33-39 (Paris).

Viswanathan, Kambanthodath Kunhan, B.A., B.L.; Indian administrator; b. 4 Nov. 1914, Mattancheri, Kerala; *s.* of Kunhan and Lakshmi Viswanathan; *m.* Saradamani Devi (deceased); four *s.*

Legal practice in Cochin 38; mem. Cochin Assembly, later mem. Travancore-Cochin Assembly 48-50; mem. Kerala Assembly 57, re-elected 60; Sec. Congress Legislature Party 57-59, 60-64; Gen. Sec. Kerala Pradesh Congress Cttee. 66-69, Convener ad hoc 69, Pres. 70-73; Editor *The Republic*, Malayalam weekly 67-69; Gov. of Gujarat 73-.

Raj Bhavan, Shahibag, Ahmedabad-380004, Gujarat, India.

Telephone: 66477.

Viswanathan, Venkata; Indian civil servant; b. 25 Jan. 1909; ed. Central Coll., Bangalore, Univ. Coll., London, and Balliol Coll., Oxford.

Indian Civil Service 30-; Asst. and Joint Magistrate, Agra, Azamgarth, Banaras 31-36; District Magistrate, Banaras 36; Asst. Settlement Officer and Settlement Officer, Bahraich, Kheri 36-40; Under-Sec., Govt. of India 40, Deputy Sec. 42; Sec. to Rep. of Govt. of India in Ceylon 43; Additional Deputy Sec. and Sec. to Rep. of Govt. of India with Govt. of Burma 44; Registrar of Co-operative Socs. U.P. 46; District Magistrate, Dehra Dun 47; Indian Alt. Del. on UN Comm., Palestine 47; Deputy High Commr. in Pakistan 47-48; Chief Sec. and Adviser Madhya Bharat 48-50; Chief Commr., Bhopal 50-52; Joint Sec. Ministry of States and Ministry of Home Affairs 52-58; Special Sec. Ministry of Home Affairs 58, Sec. 61-64; Chief Commr., Delhi 64-66; Lieut.-Gov. Himachal Pradesh 66-67; Gov. of Kerala 67-74.

c/o Office of the Governor, Trivandrum, Kerala, India.

Vital Brazil, Alvaro; Brazilian civil engineer and architect; b. 1909; ed School of Polytechnic and Fine Arts, Rio de Janeiro.

Former Prof. of Colégio Santo Antonio Maria Zacarias and of the French Lycée; Mem. Inst. of Brazilian Architects; two first awards in competitions for architectural design (São Paulo and Minas Gerais); mem. of the Executive Council of Inst. of Brazilian Architects.

Av. Presidente Vargas 590, Rio de Janeiro, R.J. Brazil.

Vitali, Felice Antonio; Swiss radio and television official; b. 24 March 1907, Bellano; *s.* of Battista and Leonie Vitali; *m.* Hilda Schlatter 1930; ed. St. Gall Gymnasium and Commercial Coll.

Editor *Die Presse* 28; Radio Berne 29; Editor *Schweizer Radio Zeitung* 30; Dir. Radio Svizzera Italiana 31-47; corresp. Swiss Radio in Berlin 48-57; Project-leader UNESCO Radio Advisory Mission to Libya 57-58; Head of Information Services, Swiss Television (Zürich) 58-67; Programme Liaison of Swiss Television, Lugano 67-; Prix Pisa of the Prix Italia 62 (for TV documentary).

Leisure interests: walking, gardening.

Radio plays: *I tre amici, La capanna del Bertuli, Idol und Masse, Kraftwerk Mittelmeer, Flut ohne Ebbe, Kampf um die öffentliche Meinung* 55, *Atome für die*

Politik 56, *Die sieben Kiesel* 61; Television documentaries: *Der alte Mensch, Was war der Generalstreik? Kranke Menschen, halbe Hilfe, Urteil ohne Richter, Testfall Celerina, Die Polizei des Bürgers, Frau Grossrätin, Hauptmann Grüninger, Die Barriere, Das Wagnis: Partner im Rollstuhl, Betrifft Friedrich Glanser.*

Publs. *Reporter erleben England, Confidenze del Microfono, Radiohörer das geht dich an, Der alte Mensch und das Fernsehen, Altersprogramme—Ghetto oder Treffpunkt.*

Ronco Nuovo, 6911 Comano-Lugano, Switzerland.

Telephone: (091)-51-12-50.

Vitsaxis, Vassilios, PH.D.; Greek diplomatist; b. 22 Oct. 1920, Athens; *s.* of George and Iphigenia Vitsaxis; *m.* Zoe-Ketty Ioannidou 1946; no *c.*; ed. Univ. of Athens.

Entered diplomatic service 46; Liaison Officer of Greek Govt. to Balkan Cttee. of UN 47; later Sec., Paris; mem. Del. to Council of Europe; Consul, Belgium; Counsellor and Chargé d'Affaires, Perm. Mission of Greece at UN and Consul-Gen., New York; Counsellor, Ankara 64, Minister-Counsellor and Chargé d'Affaires 65-66; Amb. and Perm. Del. to Council of Europe 66-69; Amb. to U.S.A. 69-72; Amb. to India, Nepal, Sri Lanka, Bangladesh, Burma, Malaysia, Singapore, Thailand 73-, fmrly. accredited to Indonesia and the Republic of Viet-Nam; mem. Inst. of Int. and Private Law; Grand Commdr. Royal Order of George I, Grand Commdr. of Phoenix, Commdr. of the Holy Sepulchre (Jerusalem) and Golden Cross of the Crown (Belgium).

Leisure interests: photography, poetry, ham radio.

Publs. *The Influence of Greek Philosophy in the Evolution of Roman Law, Studies in Hellenic Labour Law; Reflets* (collection of poetry).

Embassy of Greece, 188 Jor Bagh, New Delhi, India.

Telephone: 617854; 387119.

Vivian, Robert Evans, M.A., PH.D.; American university dean; b. 20 April 1893, Melvin, Ill.; *s.* of Rev. Robert L. and Blanche Weatherby Vivian; *m.* Belle Doyle 1919; two *s.*; ed. Univ. of Southern Calif. and Columbia Univ.

Engineering Dept., Home Telephone Co., Los Angeles 12-14; Teacher High School and Junior Coll. and Chief of Assay Office, Kern County, Calif. 18-28; Asst. to Prof. Columbia Univ. 29; electrochemical engineer in charge pilot plant operations Int. Agricultural Corpn. 30-31; research Chemist, later Development Engineer, Gen. Chemical Co., N.Y. 31-35; Dir. of Research, Metals Disintegrating Co., Elizabeth, N.J. 35-37; Prof. and Head of Dept. Chemical Engineering Univ. of Southern Calif. 37-42, Dean of School of Eng. 42-58, Emeritus 58-; Chair. Eng. Div., Long Beach State Coll. 58-64, Emeritus Dean 64-; mem., Sec. and Chair. several chemical asscns.; mem. Eng. Coll. Admin. Council 48-51, George Westinghouse Award Cttee. 49-51; Chemical Production Specialist, M.S.A., U.S. Govt. Mission to Italy 52, Technical Consultant M.S.A., U.S. Govt. in S.E. Asia 53; Educational Consultant Northrop Inst. of Technology, Calif. 64-73; Hearing Board of Air Pollution, Control District, Los Angeles County 70-75; Hon. Sc.D. (Northrop Inst. of Technology 68, Univ. of S. Calif. 69).

Leisure interests: church work, gardening, tennis, history.

Office: Room 502, Vivian Hall of Engineering, University of Southern California, Los Angeles 90007; Home: 862 Victoria Avenue, Los Angeles 5, Calif., U.S.A.

Vladimirov, Vasily Sergeyevich, D.SC.; Soviet mathematician; b. 9 Jan. 1923, Djaglevo, Leningrad region; *s.* of Sergei Ivanovich Vladimirov and Maria Semenovna Vladimirova; *m.* Nina Jakovlevna Ovsjannikova 1948; two *s.*; ed. Leningrad State Univ.

Junior Research Worker, Leningrad Dept., V. A.

Steklov Inst. of Mathematics, U.S.S.R. Acad. of Sciences 48-56; Senior Research Worker, Steklov Inst. of Maths., Moscow 56-69, Head, Dept. of Mathematical Physics 69-; Prof. Physico-technical Inst. 65-; mem. C.P.S.U. 44-; corresp. mem. U.S.S.R. Acad. of Sciences 68-70, mem. 70-; State Prize 53; Gold Medal of A. N. Liapounov 71; Orders of the Labour Red Banner 67, 73; Order of Lenin 75.
Leisure interests: skiing, fishing, tennis.
Publs. works in the field of numerical methods of problems solution of mathematical physics; analysis of transfer equation; theory of holomorphic functions of several complex variables and distribution theory, and their applications in mathematical physics.
Steklov Institute of Mathematics, Vavilova Street 42, B-333 Moscow, U.S.S.R.
Telephone: 135-14-49 (Office); 135-55-71 (Home).

Vladychenko, Ivan Maximovich; Soviet trade union official; b. 16 Jan. 1924, Mokrii, Donetsk Region; ed. Donetsk Industrial Inst.
Soviet Army 41-45; mem. C.P.S.U. 43-; miner, Donbuas 51-52; Second Sec. Chistiakov City Cttee., then First Sec. Sniezhnansk Dist. Cttee., Ukraine C.P. 52-59; Chair. Central Cttee. Miners' Union 59-63; Sec. All-Union Central Council of Trade Unions 63-; mem. Central Auditing Comm. of C.P.S.U. 61-66; Alt. mem. Central Cttee. of C.P.S.U. 66-.
All-Union Central Council of Trade Unions, Leninsky prospekt 42, Moscow, U.S.S.R.

Vlerick, Andreis; Belgian economist and politician; b. 11 Sept. 1919, Kortryk; s. of Alphonse Vlerick and Afra van Elstraete; m. Cécile Sap 1945; no c.; ed. Catholic Univ. of Louvain, Cambridge and Harvard Univs.
Professor of Econs. and Management, Univ. of Ghent; Minister-Sec. of State for Regional Economy (Flemish) 68-72; Minister of Finance Jan. 72-73; Senator Nov. 71-; Christian Social Party.
Leisure interests: travel, reading, swimming.
Publs. several books on Flemish regional economy; *Development Aid* 67, *Monetary Reform and European Integration* 73.
The Senate, 1000 Brussels; and Ketelpoort 23, 9000 Ghent, Belgium.

Vlielander Hein, François Emile, D.C.L., O.B.E.; Netherlands industrialist: b. 22 Jan. 1916, The Hague; m. E. G. H. Dijckmeester; ed. Univ. of Leiden.
Joined Philips Eindhoven 41-43; mil. service 44-47; head of mil. mission Germany 48-49; Dir. NIVAG (construction company) 49-50; banker 51-53; Dir. N.V. Hollandsche Draad-en Kabelfabriek 53-61; Chair. Exec. Cttee. N.K.F. Groep N.V. Jan. 71-; Commdr. Order Industry and Agriculture of Cuba.
Office: N.K.F. Groep B.V. Rijswijk (Z.H.), J. C. van Markenlaan 5, Netherlands; Home: 83 Boekenrodeweg, Aerdenhout, Netherlands.
Telephone: 070-99-31-12 (Office).

Vo Nguyen Giap, Gen.; Vietnamese army officer; b. 1912, Quangbinh Province; ed. French Lycée in Hué, and law studies at Univ. of Hanoi.
History teacher, Thang Long School, Hanoi; joined Viet-Nam C.P. in early 1930s; fled to China 39; helped organize Vietminh Front, Viet-Nam 41; Minister of Interior 45, became Commdr.-in-Chief of Vietminh Army 46; defeated French at Dien Bien Phu 54; now Deputy Prime Minister, Minister of Defence and C.-in-C., Democratic Repub. of Viet-Nam; mem. Politburo Lao-Dong Party.
Publs. *People's War, People's Army, Big Victory, Great Task* 68.
Ministry of Defence, Hanoi, Democratic Republic of Viet-Nam.

Vogel, Friedrich, DR.OEC.PUBL.; German publisher; b. 23 Feb. 1902; ed. Hindenburg-Gymnasium, Düsseldorf and Univs. of Greifswald, Cologne and Munich.
Partner Verlag Handelsblatt G.m.b.H.; Handelsblatt publications include *Handelsblatt, Chemische Industrie, Der Betrieb, Der Schrottbetrieb, Wirtschaft und Wettbewerb, Die Absatzwirtschaft, Die Atomwirtschaft, Zeitschrift für Verkehrswissenschaft*; Chair. Special Comm. for Int. Collaboration, Zentralausschuss der Werbewirtschaft; mem. Board Verein Rheinisch-Westfälischer Zeitungsverleger e.V.; mem. Board Akademie für Absatzwirtschaft, Deutsch-Französischer Kreis, Advisory Body Deutsch-Englische Gesellschaft; Hon. Pres. Union of European Econ. and Financial Press.
Elbinger Weg 3, 4 Düsseldorf 30, Federal Republic of Germany.
Telephone: 83881.

Vogel, Brig.-Gen. Herbert Davis, DR. ING., M.S., C.E., B.S.; American civil servant; b. 26 Aug. 1900, Chelsea, Mich.; s. of Lewis P. Vogel and Pearl M. Davis; m. Loreine Elliott 1925; two s.; ed. Univs. of Michigan and California, U.S. Military Acad. and Berlin Technical Univ.
Commissioned U.S. army 24, served through all ranks to Brigadier-Gen.; Builder and Dir. Waterways Experiment Station 30-34; District Engineer, Pittsburgh, Pa. 40-43; S.W. Pacific Theatre 44-45; District Engineer, Buffalo, N.Y. 45-49; Maintenance Engineer and Lieut.-Gov., Panama Canal 49-52; Engineer S.W. Division, Dallas 52-54; Chair. Tennessee Valley Authority 54-62; mem. Beach Erosion Board 46-49, Mississippi River Comm. 52-54, Board of Engineers for Rivers and Harbours 52-54; mem. Perm. Int. Council of Perm. Int. Asscn. of Navigation Congresses 57-64, Hon. mem. 67-; Engineer Adviser, Int. Bank for Reconstruction and Devt. 63-67; Consulting Engineer, Principal of Herbert D. Vogel Associates 68-; mem. U.S. Cttee. Int. Comm. on Large Dams; Licensed professional engineer, N.Y., Tex., Tenn., Dist. of Columbia; Dir. Int. Gen. Industries; Fellow A.S.C.E.; Nat. Dir. S.A.M.E.; mem. Nat. Soc. of Professional Engineers, Benjamin Franklin Fellow, R.S.A., London, Industrial Cttee., American Power Conf., American Inst. of Consulting Engineers, Nat. Water Policy Cttee., ASCE; Occupant of George W. Goethals Chair of Mil. Construction, U.S. Army Engineer School; Legion of Merit; Distinguished Service Medal; Knight Grand Cross, First Class Order of the Most Noble Order of the Cross of Thailand; Colon Alfaro Medal; Philippine Liberation and Ind. Medals; mem. Order of the Carabao.
Leisure interests: travel, gardening, reading.
Office: 601-2 Washington Building, Washington, D.C. 20005; Home: 3033 Cleveland Avenue, N.W., Washington, D.C. 20008, U.S.A.
Telephone: 202-638-0010 (Office); 202-Co5-3033 (Home).

Vogel, Rudolf, DR.ING.; German business executive; b. 10 Feb. 1918, Hamburg; s. of Paul and Meta (née Liebetrau) Vogel; m. Marianne Ahlers 1950; one s. one d.; ed. Staatslehranstalt and Univ. of Hamburg and Technische Hochschulen, Brunswick and Aachen.
Head clerk Gutehoffnungshütte Sterkrade AG 54-64; Man. Ottensener Eisenwerke G.m.b.H., Hamburg 64-68; mem. Exec. Board, Salzgitter Maschinen AG 68-75, Consultant 75-; Consultant Salzgitter AG 75-; mem. of supervisory board of co. in Iran.
Leisure interests: reading, music, hiking, travel.
332 Salzgitter 51, Jägerweg 6, Federal Republic of Germany.
Telephone: 05341-31733.

Vogelsang, Günter; German business executive; b. 20 Jan. 1920, Krefeld.
Former mem. Management Board Mannesmann AG;

Chair. Management Board Fried. Krupp G.m.b.H. 68-72, Blohm u. Voss AG, Hamburg, Dornier G.m.b.H.; Deputy Chair. Daimler-Benz AG, Stuttgart; mem. Board Dirs. Deutsche Bank AG, Frankfurt, Stahlwerke Röchling-Burbach G.m.b.H., Völklingen/Saar, Ruhrkohle AG, Essen, Rheinstahl AG, Essen, Gerling-Konzern, Köln.

4000 Düsseldorf-Oberkassel, Kaiser-Friedrich-Ring 84, Federal Republic of Germany.

Voghel, Baron Franz de; Belgian banker; b. 21 Dec. 1903, Brussels; *m.* Marie-Antoinette François; one *s.* two *d.*; ed. Univ. of Louvain.

Director of Banking Comm. 33-45; Prof. Univ. of Louvain; mem. Conseil Central de l'Economie, Banque Centrale du Congo, Fonds des Rentes, Commission Bancaire; Minister of Finance Aug. 45-July 46; fmr. Deputy Gov. Nat. Bank of Belgium; fmr. Pres. Institut de Réescompte et de Garantie; Pres. Palais des Beaux-Arts, Brussels; mem. Monetary Cttee. EEC 58-; awarded U.S. Medal of Freedom.

Publs. *Contrôle des banques, Statut légal des banques.*

Office: 78 rue du Commerce, 1040 Brussels; Home: 9 rue des Sablons, Brussels 1000, Belgium.

Telephone: 511-73-30.

Vogt, Ernst, S.T.L., S.S.D.; Swiss ecclesiastic; b. 30 Jan. 1903, Basle; *s.* of Emil and Anna Vogt; ed. Innsbruck Univ.

Professor of Sacred Scripture, Theological Faculty São Leopoldo 39-48; Prof. of Old Testament Exegesis, Pontifical Biblical Inst., Rome 49-.

Publs. *Os Salmos Traduzidos e Explicados* 51, *Lexicon Aramaicum Veteris Testamenti* 71.

Via della Pilotta 25, 00187 Rome, Italy.

Telephone: 686-453.

Vogt, Hersleb; Norwegian diplomatist; b. 20 May 1912, Oslo; *s.* of Lorentz Vogt and Ida Fabricius; *m.* Inger Hansen 1947; ed. Univ. of Oslo.

Entered Diplomatic Service and served Ministry of Foreign Affairs 36, Paris and Luxembourg 37, Rome 38; Ministry of Foreign Affairs London 44, Oslo 45, Brussels and Luxembourg 48, London and Dublin 49; Minister to Japan 53-58, Ambassador 58; Ambassador to German Fed. Repub. 58-63, to Denmark 63-67, to France 67-73, to Sweden 73-; Commdr. Order of St. Olav; Norwegian War Participation Medal (with Star); C.V.O.; Commdr. Order of Phoenix (Greece); Grand Cross Order of Rising Sun (Japan); Grand Cross (First Class), Order of Merit (Fed. Repub. of Germany); Grand Cross, Order of Dannebrog (Denmark); Grand Commdr. French Legion of Honour.

Royal Norwegian Embassy, Strandvägen 113, 115 27 Stockholm, Sweden.

Telephone: 67-06-20.

Vogt, Joseph, DR. PHIL.; German university professor; b. 23 June 1895, Schechingen; *s.* of Dionys and Josephine (née Fischer) Vogt; *m.* Gertrud Dimroth 1931; one *s.* five *d.*; ed. Lyceum Mergentheim, Gymnasium Rottweil, and Univs. of Tübingen and Berlin.

Graduated 21; became lecturer 23; Prof., Univs. of Tübingen 26, Würzburg 29, Breslau 36, Tübingen 40, 46, Freiburg 44; Prof. Emer., Univ. of Tübingen 62; mem. Akad. der Wissenschaften und der Literatur, Mainz; Corresp. mem. Heidelberger Akad.; Hon. mem. Österreichische Akad.; Foreign mem. Acad. Inscriptions et Belles Lettres; Medal, Cultori di Roma 71.

Publs. *Die alexandrinischen Münzen* 24, *Herodot in Ägypten* 29, *Römische Republik* 32 (6th edn. 73, Italian edns. 39, 68), *Ciceros Glaube an Rom* 35, *Kaiser Julian und das Judentum* 39, *Vom Reichsgedanken der Römer* 42, *Constantin der Grosse und sein Jahrhundert* 49, 60, 73 (Spanish edn. 56), *Gesetz und Handlungsfreiheit* 55, *Struktur der antiken Sklavenkriege* 57, *Wege zum historischen Universum* 61 (Japanese edn. 66, Spanish 71), *Der Niedergang Roms* 65 (Italian edn. 65, English 67,

Spanish 68), *Sklaverei and Humanität* 65, 72 (Italian edn. 69, English edn. 74, American edn. 75).

74 Tübingen, Im Rotbad 10, Federal Republic of Germany.

Telephone: 63011.

Vogüé, Comte Arnaud de; French businessman; b. 11 June 1904.

Admin. Ecole Supérieure des Sciences Economiques et Commerciales (Essec) 68; Hon. Pres. Cie. de Saint-Gobain Pont-à-Mousson 70-; Admin. Cie. Financière de Suez, La Cellulose du Pin, La Générale Sucrière; Officier, Légion d'Honneur, Croix de Guerre, Commdr. Palmes Académiques.

Home: 48 rue du Docteur-Blanche, Paris 16e; and le Peseau, 18 Boilleret; Office: 62 boulevard Victor Hugo, Neuilly-sur-Seine, France.

Voitec, Ştefan; Romanian politician; b. 19 June 1900, Corabia, Olt County; one *d.*; ed. Bucharest Polytechnic and Bucharest Univ.

Former Leader, Social-Democratic Party of Romania; Minister of Nat. Educ. 44-48; mem. Cen. Cttee. and Alt. mem. Political Bureau, Romanian Workers' Party (now Romanian Communist Party) 55-65; mem. Exec. Cttee. of Central Cttee., Romanian Communist Party 65-; Minister of Home Trade 55-56, of Consumer Goods Industry 57-59; Deputy Chair. Council of Ministers 48-49, 56-61; Pres. Grand Nat. Assembly 61-74, Vice-Pres. State Council 61-65, 74-; mem. Acad. of Social and Political Sciences 70-; Hero of Socialist Labour 64.

State Council, Bucharest, Romania.

Volcker, Paul A., M.A.; American banker and government official; b. 5 Sept. 1927, Cape May, N.J.; *s.* of Paul A. and Alma Klippel Volcker; *m.* Barbara Marie Bahnson 1954; one *s.* one *d.*; ed. Princeton Univ., Harvard Univ. Graduate School of Public Admin., and London School of Econs. and Political Science.

Special Asst. Securities Dept., Fed. Reserve Bank of N.Y. 53-57; Financial Economist, Chase Manhattan Bank, N.Y.C. 57-62, Dir. of Forward Planning 65-69; Dir. Office of Financial Analysis, U.S. Treasury Dept. 62-63, Deputy Under-Sec. for Monetary Affairs 63-65, Under-Sec. Monetary Affairs 69-74; Pres. N.Y. Fed. Reserve Bank Aug. 75-; mem. Board Fed. Nat. Mortgage Asscn., Overseas Private Investment Corpn.; mem. Board and Pres. Environmental Financing Authority; Phi Beta Kappa (Princeton), Admin. Fellowship (Harvard), Rotary Foundation Fellow (L.S.E.), Arthur S. Flemming Award (Fed. Govt.), U.S. Treasury Dept. Exceptional Service Award, Alexander Hamilton Award.

c/o Treasury for Monetary Affairs, Main Treasury Building, Washington, D.C. 20220, U.S.A.

Volfkovich, Semyon Isaakovich; Soviet inorganic chemist and technologist; b. 23 Oct. 1896, Ananyev, Ukraine; ed. Moscow Inst. of Nat. Econ.

Scientific Research Inst. of Fertilizers and Insecto-fungicides 21-; Prof. Moscow Inst. of Nat. Economy 29-; Prof. Moscow Univ. 47; Pres. All-Union Mendeleyev Soc. 63-; mem. Acad. of Sciences of the U.S.S.R. 46-; Mendeleyev prizewinner 32, State prizewinner 41; awarded three Orders of Lenin, Order of the Red Banner of Labour, Mendeleyev Gold Medal 66.

Publs. *New Cycle of Wet Processing of Phosphorites* 28, *Technology of Nitrogen Fertilizers* 35, *General Chemical Technology* 59 (2 vols), *The Role of Physical and Chemical Analysis in the Technology of Fertilizers* 61, *Chemistry in Agriculture, Hydrothermal Treatment of the Phosphates* 64.

Scientific Research Institute of Fertilizers and Insecto-fungicides, Leninsky prospekt 55, Moscow, U.S.S.R.

Volk, H.E. Cardinal Hermann, PH.D., TH.D.; German ecclesiastic; b. 27 Dec. 1903, Steinheim/Main; *s.* of Philipp Volk and Maria Kaiser; ed. Hochschule, Mainz, Univs. of Freiburg and Münster.

Ordained Priest, Mainz 27; Curate 27-35; Asst. Pastor 39-41; Pastor, Nidda 41-46; Prof. of Dogmatics, Univ. of Münster 46-62, Rector 54-55, Hon. Prof. 62; Papal House Prelate 56; Bishop of Mainz 62-; Hon. Prof., Univ. of Mainz 63; cr. Cardinal 73.
Publs. eighty-one works, including *Die Kreaturauffassung bei Karl Barth* 38, *Emil Brunners Lehre von der ursprünglichen Gottebenbildlichkeit des Menschen* 39, *Schöpfungsglaube und Entwicklung* 55, *Christus und Maria* 55, *Sonntäglicher Gottesdienst* 56, *Gesammelte Schriften I* 61, *Gesammelte Schriften II* 66, *Priestertum heute* 72.
Am Rosengarten 2, D-6500 Mainz, Federal Republic of Germany.
Telephone: 06131-82415.

Volkenshtein, Mikhail Vladimirovich; Soviet physicist; b. 23 Oct. 1912, St. Petersburg (now Leningrad); *s.* of Vladimir Mikhailovich Volkenshtein and Maria Mikhailovna Volkenshtein; *m.* Stella Iosifovna Alenikova 1947; one *s.* one *d.*; ed. Moscow Univ.
Specialist in molecular physics, polymers, biophysics and spectroscopy; Research Assoc. Karpov Physico-Chemical Inst. 33-41, Optical Inst. 42-48; Prof. Leningrad Univ. 45-53, 62-67; Prof. Inst. of High Molecular Compounds, Acad. of Sciences 48-67, Inst. of Molecular Biology 67-; Corresp. mem. U.S.S.R. Acad. of Sciences 66-; State Prize 50.
Leisure interests: painting, literature.
Publs. *Vibrations of Molecules* 49 (2nd edn. 74), *Molecular Optics* 51, *Structure of Molecules* 55, *Configurational Statistics of Polymeric Chains* 58 (English edn. 63), *Molecules and Life* 65 (English edns. 70, 74), *Enzyme Physics* 67 (English edn. 70), *Molecular Biophysics* 75 (English edn. 76).
Institute of Molecular Biology, U.S.S.R. Academy of Sciences, Ul. Vavilova 32, Moscow, U.S.S.R.

Volkov, Alexander Petrovich; Soviet government official; b. 1910; ed. Moscow Aviation Inst.
Secretary Moscow Regional Party Committee 50-52, Chair. Moscow Region Exec. Cttee. (Mayor of Moscow) 52-56; Chair. State Cttee. for Labour and Wages of U.S.S.R. Council of Ministers 56-74; mem. U.S.S.R. Council of Ministers 56-74; mem. C.P.S.U. Central Cttee. 56-71; Deputy to U.S.S.R. Supreme Soviet 54-; Order of Lenin (twice), Red Banner of Labour, Badge of Honour and other awards.
State Committee for Labour and Wages, 1 Kuibyshev Square, Moscow, U.S.S.R.

Volpe, John Anthony; American engineer and politician; b. 8 Dec. 1908, Wakefield, Mass.; *s.* of Vito and Filomena Volpe; *m.* Jennie Benedetto 1934; one *s.* one *d.*; ed. Wentworth Inst., Boston, Mass.
President, John A. Volpe Construction Co. 33-69; Comm. of Public Works, Mass. 53-56; Fed. Highway Administrator 56-57; Gov. of Mass. 60-62, 64-69; U.S. Sec. of Transportation 69-73; Amb. to Italy 73-; mem. President's Urban Affairs Council 69-; Past Chair. Nat. Governors' Conf.; Republican; Grand Officer, Order of Merit (Italy) 57, Knight of Malta 60.
Leisure interests: golf, family activities.
United States Embassy, Via Vittorio Veneto 119A, Rome, Italy; Home: Villa La Pariola, 5 Viale G. Rossini, Rome, Italy.
Telephone: 4674 (Office).

Volynov, Col. Boris Valentinovich; Soviet cosmonaut; b. 18 Dec. 1934; ed. School of Military Pilots and Zhukovsky Air Force Engineering Acad.
Air Force Fighter Pilot 56-59; with Cosmonaut Training Unit 59-; mem. C.P.S.U. 58-; Commdr. of space ship *Soyuz-5* which orbited Earth and formed first manned orbital station with *Soyuz-4*; Hero of Soviet Union, Gold Star medal, Order of Lenin, Red Star, Pilot-

Cosmonaut of the U.S.S.R., K. Tsiolkovsky Gold Medal of the U.S.S.R. Acad. of Sciences and other awards.
Zvezdny Gorodok, Moscow, U.S.S.R.

Von Beckh, Harald J., M.D.; Argentine medical scientist; b. 17 Nov. 1917, Vienna, Austria; *s.* of Johannes A. and Elisabeth von Beckh (née Flach-Hillé); ed. Theresianum High School, Vienna and Vienna Univ.
Career devoted to aviation and later to space medicine, and in particular to weightlessness and its effects on living organisms; Lecturer Aeromedical Acad. Berlin 41, Buenos Aires Nat. Inst. of Aviation Medicine 47; joined staff of U.S. Air Force Aeromedical Field Laboratory, Holloman Air Force Base, N.M. 56, Scientific Dir. Oct. 58-64; Chief Scientist 64-70; Dir. of Research, Aerospace Medical Research Dept., Naval Air Devt. Center 70-; Prof. of Human Physiology, New Mexico State Univ. 59-70; mem. Armed Forces/Nat. Research Council Cttee. on Bio-Astronautics 58-61; mem. Space Medicine Cttee. of Int. Astronautical Fed. 61-, Int. Acad. of Astronautics; hon. mem. German Rocket Soc., Medical Asscn. of Armed Forces of Argentina, Portuguese Centre of Astronautical Studies, Spanish Soc. of Aerospace Medicine, Austrian Astronautical Soc.; Fellow, British Interplanetary Soc., Aerospace Medical Asscn.; Assoc. Fellow, American Inst. of Aeronautics and Astronautics; Senior mem. American Rocket Soc. (Pres. Holloman Section 59-61); mem. Int. Acad. of Aviation Medicine; Arnold D. Tuttle Award of the Aerospace Medical Asscn. 72, Melbourne W. Boynton Award of the American Astronautical Soc. 72, Hermann Oberth Honor Ring, Hermann Oberth Soc. 75.
Leisure interests: French and Spanish literature, flying.
Publs. *Fisiología del Vuelo* 55, *Basic Principles of Aerospace Medicine* 60; numerous papers in *Journal of Aviation Medicine* and *Journal of the British Interplanetary Society* and other aeronautical and aeromedical journals in U.S.A., Great Britain, Germany, Argentina and Spain.
P.O. Box 1220, Warminster, Pa. 18974, U.S.A.
Telephone: 215-672-9000, Ext. 2189.

von Eckardt, Felix; German journalist; b. 18 June 1903.
With *Hamburger Fremdenblatt* and *Münchener neueste Nachrichten* 24-26; foreign correspondent of *Verlag Ullstein* 26-29; Press Attaché, German Embassy in Brussels 29-32; employed in film industry 33-45; f. *Weser-Kurier* in Bremen 45 and became Editor-in-Chief; Head of Press and Information Dept., German Federal Govt. 52-55; Perm. Observer to UN 55-56; Head of Press and Information Dept., German Fed. Govt. 56-62; Fed. German Representative in Berlin 62-65; mem. Bundestag 65-; Christian Democrat.
2941 Funnix bei Wilhelmshaven, Federal Republic of Germany.

von Euler, Ulf Svante, M.D.; Swedish professor; b. 7 Feb. 1905, Stockholm; *s.* of Prof. Hans von Euler and Prof. Astrid (Cleve) von Euler; *m.* 1st Jane Sodenstierna 1930, 2nd Dagmar Cronstedt 1958; two *s.* two *d.*; ed. School of Medicine, Stockholm.
Professor of Physiology, Karolinska Inst., Stockholm 39-71; mem. Medical Research Council of Sweden 55-61; Nobel Cttee. for Physiology and Medicine 53-65; Pres. Nobel Foundation 65-75; Foreign Assoc. U.S. Nat. Acad. of Sciences 72-; Foreign mem. Royal Soc. 73; Nobel Prize for Medicine 70; Dr. h.c. (Rio de Janeiro, Umeå, Dijon, Ghent, Tübingen, Buenos Aires, Edinburgh, Madrid, Manchester).
Publs. *Noradrenaline* 56, *Prostaglandins* 68, and many medical papers.
Sturegatan 14, Stockholm, 11436 Sweden.
Telephone: 08-63-65-59.

von Hirschberg, C. F. G.; South African diplomatist; b. 13 Jan. 1926, Jamestown; *m.* Mary Wadley 1949; two *s.* one *d.*; ed. Univ. of Cape Town.

Entered foreign service 48; served in London 52-57, Vienna 57-62; served in Dept. of Foreign Affairs, Pretoria 62-67, Head UN and Int. Orgs. Div. 66-67; mem. South African del. to gen. confs. of IAEA 57-61, alt. Gov. 57-62; del. to UN Gen. Assembly 67-74; Minister to Perm. Mission to UN 68-70; Amb. Extra-ordinary, Plenipotentiary and Perm. Rep. to UN 70-74; Consul-Gen., Tokyo, Japan 75-.
Leisure interests: golf, tennis, boating.
c/o Ministry of Foreign Affairs, Pretoria, South Africa.

von Koerber, Hans Nordewin, PH.D.; American educationist and orientalist; b. 23 July 1886, Treptow, Pomerania, Germany; s. of Friedrich T. Freiherr von Koerber and Helene E. von Otto; m. Hildegard E. von Boetticher 1955; ed. Berlin and Marburg Univs.
Ethnographical Expedition, Central Africa 05-07; Linguistic Research, Central Africa 07-08; Ethno-graphic and Linguistic Research, Siberia, Central Asia, West China and Tibet 09-10 and 12-14; Lecturer in Oriental Linguistics, Bonn 11-12; Linguistic Research and Instruction, British India 14-20; Lecturer Marburg Univ. 20-21; Linguistic Research, Dutch Indies 21-22; Lecturer in Comparative Religion, Stralsund, Germany 23-24; Lecturer in Comparative Religion and Prof. of Oriental Linguistics, Univ. of Amoy, China 24-25; Prof. of Oriental Linguistics and Lecturer in German and French, Univ. of the Philippines 26-28; Prof. of Asiatic Studies and Dir. Foundation of Asiatic Studies, Univ. of S. Calif. 28-52, Prof. Emeritus 52-; Guest Prof. in Asian Studies and the great religions of the world in Colls. and Univs. of S. Calif. 52-66; Founder Divine Word Founda-tion Inc. 62; ordained Minister of Covenant Church of America; Grand Prior, Order of St. John of Jerusalem, and other orders.
Leisure interests: the study of nature and railroads.
Publs. *Das Tibetische Verbalsystem* 19, *Die Morphologie des Tibetischen* 21, *Tibetan Literature—Its Contribution Through Western Explorers* 35, *Morphology of the Tibetan Language* 35, *A Word on Philology* (Hewett Memorial) 37, *Kuan Yin: The Buddhist Madonna* 41, *About Basic Concepts and Words in Languages* 46, compiler and translator of Chinese, Japanese and German sections in *Aviation Dictionary in Nine Languages* (Lanz) 44, *Reminiscences in Education* 58, *The Cosmic Mystery* 63, *A New Revelation, Why?* 65, *The Significance of Matter* 68, *The Contamination of Divine Truth* 69, *A New Light Shines out of Present Darkness* 70.
Warner Springs, Calif. 92086, U.S.A.
Telephone: 714-782-3361.

von Plehwe, Friedrich-Karl, C.V.O.; German civil servant and diplomatist; b. 25 April 1912, Langfuhr; s. of the late Gen. Gustav von Plehwe and Dorothea von Reichel; m. 1st Anneliese Nette 1936 (died 1962), 2nd Helga Dahm 1964; two s. one d.; ed. Classics School, Königsberg, Univ. of Göttingen.
Cavalry Staff Officer, Asst. Mil. Attaché, regular army 30-45; joined Ferrostaal AG, Frankfurt and Hamburg 49-51; mem. Secr. for German Del., Paris 52-55, Sec.-Gen. Status of Forces Conference, Bonn 55-57, Counsel-lor Perm. Del. to NATO, Paris 57-60, Minister-Counsel-lor 60-62, Political Dept. Ministry Foreign Affairs, Bonn 62-67, Deputy Sec.-Gen. WEU, London 67-74, Acting Sec.-Gen. 74-.
Leisure interests: riding, golf, stalking.
Publs. *Schicksalsstunden in Rom* 67 (publ. in English as *The End of an Alliance* 71), *Internationale Organisationen und die moderne Diplomatie* 72, *Reiter, Streiter und Rebell* 76.
Western European Union, 9 Grosvenor Place, London, SW1X 7HL, England.
Telephone: 01-235 5351.

von Wechmar, Rudiger Freiherr; German journalist and diplomatist; b. 1923, Berlin.

With German News Service (DPD); joined United Press 48, Head of Bonn Bureau 54-58; Press Attaché, German Consulate-Gen., N.Y. 58; Head of E. European Bureau, Zweites Deutsche Fernsehen, Vienna 63; Dir. German Information Centre N.Y. 68; Deputy Head of Govt. Press and Information Office 69, State Sec., Head of Govt. Press and Information Office, Chief Govt. Spokesman 72-74; Perm. Rep. to UN July 74-.
Permanent Mission of Federal Republic of Germany to the United Nations, 600 Third Avenue, New York, N.Y. 10016, U.S.A.

Vondeling, Dr. Anne; Netherlands politician; b. 2 March 1916, Appelscha; m. Antonia Agnes van 't Hof 1941; two s. one d.; ed. Agricultural Univ., Wageningen.
Agricultural expert with the Provincial Authorities of Friesland 40-45; Dir. of an Accountancy Bureau, adviser on taxes 45-58; mem. Parl. (Socialist) 46-58, 59-65, 67-, Chair. 69-; Minister of Agriculture Jan.-Dec. 58; Deputy Prime Minister and Minister of Finance 65-66; Chair. Parl. Lower House 72-; fmr. Prof. of Int. Econ. Orgs., Univ. of Groningen; Chair. Dutch Labour Party.
Leisure interests: poetry, sport.
Europaplein, Leeuwarden, The Netherlands.
Telephone: 05100-23496.

Vonnegut, Kurt, Jr.; American author; b. 11 Nov. 1922; ed. Cornell Univ., Carnegie Inst. of Technology and Univ. of Chicago.
Served with U.S. Army as Infantry Combat Scout, World War II; prisoner of war Dresden 45; police reporter, Chicago City News Bureau 45-47; public relations officer, G.E.C. Schenectady 47-50; contrib. *Saturday Evening Post, Collier's, Galaxy,* etc.
Publs. novels: *Player Piano* 52, *The Sirens of Titan* 59, *Mother Night* 61, *Cat's Cradle* 63, *God Bless you, Mr. Rosewater* 65, *Slaughterhouse-Five* 69, *Happy Birthday, Wanda Jane* (play) 71, *Between Time and Timbuktu* 72, *Breakfast of Champions* 73, *Wampeters, Foma and Granfalloons* 74; short stories: *Welcome to the Monkey House* 68.
Scudder's Lane, West Barnstable, Mass. 02668, U.S.A.

Vonsovsky, Sergei Vasilievich; Soviet physicist; b. 2 Sept. 1910, Tashkent; ed. Leningrad State Univ.
Engineer, Chief Engineer, Ural Physical-Technical Inst. 32-39; Junior Scientific Worker, Senior Scientific Worker, Inst. for Investigation of Metals, for Metallo-physics and Metallurgy, Urals Branch of U.S.S.R. Acad. of Sciences 39-47; Chief Dept., Deputy Dir. Inst. of Physics of Metals, Urals Branch of U.S.S.R. Acad. of Sciences 47-; Corresp. mem. U.S.S.R. Acad. of Sciences 53-66, mem. 66-; Chair. Presidium Urals Scientific Centre, U.S.S.R. Acad. of Sciences 71-; Hero of Socialist Labour, Order of Lenin, etc.
Urals Scientific Centre of the U.S.S.R. Academy of Sciences, Ulitsa Pervomaiskaya 91, Sverdlovsk-Oblastnoi, U.S.S.R.

Voronov, Avenir Arkadyevich, D.SC.; Soviet auto-mation specialist; b. 28 Nov. 1910, Lomonosov; s. of Arkady Vasilyevich Voronov and Vera Dmitrievna Bystrova; m. Nina Petrovna Alexandrova 1938; one s. one d.; ed. Leningrad Polytechnic Inst.
Engineer, Gorky electrical power plant 38-39; army service 39-46; mem. C.P.S.U. 43-; Lecturer Moscow Bauman Higher School 46-48; Research Assoc., Inst. of Automation and Telemechanics, U.S.S.R. Acad. of Sciences 48-55; Lecturer, Moscow Power Inst. 48-55; Head of Lab., Vice-Dir. Inst. of Electromechanics 55-64, Inst. of Control Problems 64-70; Lecturer, Leningrad Polytechnical Inst. 55-64, Moscow Inst. of Radioengineering, Electronics and Automation 64-70; Deputy Chair. Presidium, Far Eastern Scientific Centre, U.S.S.R. Acad. of Sciences 71-; Dir. Inst. of Automation and Control Processes 71-; Academician, U.S.S.R. Acad. of Sciences 70-.

Publs. (in Russian) *The Elements of Automatic Regulation Theory* 50, *Digital Analogues for Automatic Control Systems* 60, *Fundamentals of Automatic Control Theory* Part I 65, Part II 66, Part III 70, *Operations Research and Control* 70.
Far Eastern Scientific Centre, U.S.S.R. Academy of Sciences, 50 Leninskaya St., 2 Vladivostock, U.S.S.R. Telephone: 2-31-98.

Voronov, Gennadi Ivanovich; Soviet politician; b. 31 Aug. 1910, Rameshki, Tver Region; ed. Tomsk Industrial Inst.
First Sec. Chita Communist Party 48-55; Deputy to Supreme Soviet 50-54; mem. Cen. Cttee. of Supreme Soviet 52-54; U.S.S.R. Deputy Minister of Agriculture 55-57; First Sec. Orenburg Regional Party Cttee. 57-61; First Deputy Chair. Bureau for the R.S.F.S.R. 61-62; Chair. of Council of Ministers of R.S.F.S.R. 62-71; Chair. People's Control Cttee. 71-; Alt. mem. Presidium of Cen. Cttee. of C.P.S.U. 61, mem. Oct. 61-66, mem. Politburo 66-73; Deputy to Supreme Soviet of U.S.S.R. 50-; Order of Lenin 70.
U.S.S.R. People's Control Committee, Ulitsa Kuibysheva 21, Moscow, U.S.S.R.

Vorozhtsov, Nikolay Nikolayevich; Soviet chemist; b. 6 July 1907, Tomsk; ed. Bauman Higher Technical School, Moscow.
Member Staff U.S.S.R. Comm. for Investigation of Natural Resources 28-30; Scientific Worker State Inst. of High Pressures 30-38; mem. C.P.S.U. 42-; Chief Dept. Kazakh State Univ. 38-43; Scientific Supervisor, Research Inst. for Organic By-products and Dyestuffs 43-47; Chief Dept. Mendeleev Chemical-Technical Inst. Moscow 45-58; Dir. Novosibirsk Inst. of Organic Chem. of Siberian Dept. of U.S.S.R. Acad. of Sciences 58-; Corresp. mem. U.S.S.R. Acad. of Sciences 58-66, mem. 66-; State Prize 52, Order of Lenin and other awards.
Publs. Works on technology of organic dyestuffs and intermediate products.
Akademgorodok, Prospekt Nauki 17, Novosibirsk, U.S.S.R.

Vorrink, Irene; Netherlands lawyer and politician; b. 7 Jan. 1918, The Hague.
Member of Legal Staff, Industrial Insurance Admin. Office, Amsterdam; Clerk of Social Insurance Appeals Board, Utrecht 61-63; Clerk of Social Insurance Appeals Board, Amsterdam 65-69, Vice-Chair., and Vice-Pres. of Civil Service Appeals Board 69-73; mem. First Chamber of States Gen. 69-; Minister of Health and the Environment 73-.
Ministry of Health and the Environment, The Hague, Netherlands.

Vorster, Balthazar Johannes, B.A., LL.B.; South African lawyer and politician; b. 13 Dec. 1915, Jamestown, Cape Province; s. of W. C. and E. S. Vorster; m. Martini Malan 1941; two s. one d.; ed. Sterkstroom High School and Stellenbosch Univ.
M.P. for Nigel 53-; Deputy Minister of Educ., Arts and Science and of Social Welfare and Pensions 58-61; Minister of Justice 61-66; Minister of Justice, Police and Prisons 66; Prime Minister 66-; Leader National Party 66-; Chancellor Univ. of Stellenbosch 68-.
Union Buildings, Pretoria; Groote Schuur, Cape Town; Libertas, Bryntirion, Pretoria, Republic of South Africa. Telephone: 699-121; 743151.

Voss, August Edwardovich; Soviet politician; b. 30 Oct. 1916, Saltykovo, Omsk Region; ed. Teacher-Training Inst., C.P.S.U. Higher Party School and C.P.S.U. Acad. of Social Sciences.
Soviet Army service 40-45; Party Official in Latvia 45-49; Head of Dept. of Science and Culture, Central Cttee., Latvian C.P. 53-54; Party Official at Central Cttee., Latvian C.P. 54-60; Sec. Central Cttee., Latvian C.P.

60-66, First Sec. 66-; Deputy to U.S.S.R. Supreme Soviet 66-; Chair. Comm. for Public Educ., Science and Culture, Soviet of Union, and Latvian Supreme Soviet; mem. C.P.S.U. Central Cttee. 71-.
Central Committee, Communist Party of Latvia, Riga, U.S.S.R.

Voss, Ralph J.; American banker; b. 1910, Eagle Grove, Iowa; m. Eleanor Madsen; one s. one d.; ed. Univ. of Minnesota, Northwestern Univ.
Assistant to Pres. and Senior Vice-Pres. United California Bank 46-60; Pres., Chief Exec. Officer, First Nat. Bank of Oregon 60-73, Chair. 72-75; Dir. Western Bancorporation 65-, Pres., Chief Admin. Officer 72-73, Pres., Chief Exec. Officer Dec. 73-75, Chair., Chief Exec. Officer 75-; Outstanding Achievement Award (Univ. of Minnesota) 73.
Leisure interest: music.
Western Bancorporation, 707 Wilshire Boulevard, Los Angeles, Calif. 90017, U.S.A.
Telephone: (213) 614-3001.

Voth, Reinhold; German politician and businessman; b. 23 March 1930, Würzburg; ed. Würzburg Univ.
Member of Bavarian State Diet Nov. 58-Sept. 72, Chair. of cultural sub-cttee. 64-70; Deputy Chair. Christian Social Union (CSU) parl. group 66-70; State Sec. Ministry for Labour and Social Affairs Dec. 70-Sept. 72; mem. Radio Council, Bavarian Radio Jan. 60-Sept. 72, Chair. March 65-April 72, Man. Dir. Oct. 72-; Chair. CSU in Unterfranken until 72; Chair. Board of Trustees, Hochschule für Politik, Munich; Govt. Dir. Bavarian State Pensions Office; mem. supervisory board, St. Bruno-Werk, Würzburg; hon. mem. Man. Board, Bavarian Schools Asscn.
Bayerischer Rundfunk, Rundfunkplatz 1, Munich 2, Federal Republic of Germany.

Voyadjis, Apostolos, LL.D.; Greek lawyer; b. 1904, Karditsa; m. Elisabeth Koumli 1939; one d.; ed. Univ. of Athens, Rutgers Univ. and Centre d'Education Ouvrière, Paris.
Lawyer in Karditsa and Athens 28-67; Chair. of Popular Library in Karditsa, and Night Schools 37-39; served in war (on Albanian front) 41; mem. of Nat. Resistance Movement 41-44; organized Socialistic Fed. 46-50; legal adviser to Greek Labour Gen. Confederation 48-58; mem. (also Chair.) Social Policy Cttee. and Social Insurance Cttee. 50-67; taught labour law and labour relations in seminars of the Greek Labour Gen. Confederation of the (fmr.) European Productivity Org. 55-58, and at the Greek Productivity Centre 55-68; del. in missions to study productivity problems in Sweden, Switzerland, France and Denmark; visited Common Market to study trade union problems 66; Minister of Labour 68-70; Pres. Legislative Consultative Cttee. 71.
Leisure interests: reading, walking in woods, swimming, liberal arts.
Publs. *The Condemnation of Imperialism and Principles of Universality* 47, *Policy of Wages in Greece* 56, *Full Employment as Social Policy* 57, *Handicraft as a Factor in Modern Economy* 58, *Labour Relations*, a survey on labour union legislation in Common Market countries, Greece and Turkey 66, *Social Peace and Social Justice* 70.
Ministry of Labour, Greece, Athens.

Voznessensky, Andrey Andreyevich; Soviet poet; b. 12 May 1933, Moscow; ed. Moscow Architectural Inst. Member Union of Soviet Writers, mem. Board 67-; Hon. mem. American Acad. of Arts and Letters 72.
Publs. poems: *The Masters* 59, *Longjumeau* 64, *Anti-worlds* 64; collections: *Parabola* 60, *Mosaic* 60, *Heart of Achilles* 66, *Verses* 67.
U.S.S.R. Union of Writers, Ulitsa Vorovskogo 52, Moscow, U.S.S.R.

Vranckx, Alfons, LL.D.; Belgian university professor and politician; b. 24 Jan. 1907, Kessel-Lo, Brabant.
Formerly Prof. of Constitutional Law, Univ. of Ghent; mem. Chamber of Reps. 32-47, 65-; mem. Council of State 47-65; Minister of Interior 65-66, of Justice 68-72; Socialist.
Maria Theresia Straat 90, B-3000, Leuven, Belgium.

Vratuša, Dr. Anton; Yugoslav diplomatist and politician; b. 21 Feb. 1915, Doljnja Slaveča; ed. Univ. of Ljubljana.
Colonel in Yugoslav People's Army 41-45; various appointments in Ministry of Foreign Affairs and Fed. Exec. Council 45-; mem. Fed. Assembly 65-; mem. numerous dels. to UN; Pres. Yugoslav Nat. Comm. for UNESCO; Dir. Inst. for Social Sciences; Prof. at School of Political Sciences, Belgrade; Perm. Rep. to UN 67-69; Prof. of Political Sciences, Belgrade Univ. 69; Deputy Minister of Foreign Affairs 69-71; Vice-Pres. Fed. Exec. Council Dec. 71-; Pres. Fed. Council for Socio-Political System 73-.
Publs. numerous works on self-management system in Yugoslavia and international relations.
Federal Executive Council, Belgrade, Yugoslavia.
Telephone: 338-165.

Vredeling, Henk; Netherlands politician; b. 20 Nov. 1924; ed. Agricultural Univ., Wageningen.
Member of Second Chamber of the States Gen. 56-; mem. European Parl.; Socio-econ. Adviser to Agricultural Workers' Union; Minister of Defence 73-.
Ministry of Defence, The Hague, Netherlands.

Vredenburgh, Dorothy McElroy, B.S.; American politician; b. 8 Dec. 1916, Columbus, Miss.; m. 1st Peter Vredenburgh 1937, 2nd John Bush 1960; ed. Mississippi State Coll. for Women and George Washington Univ.
U.S. Steel Corpn., Birmingham, Alabama 37-40; Nat. Committee woman, Alabama Young Democrats 41-50; Asst. Sec. Young Democrats of America 41-43; Co-Chair. Jackson Day, Ala. 44; Vice-Pres. Young Democrats of America 43-48, Act. Pres. 44-45; Sec. Democratic Nat. Convention, Washington, D.C. (first woman to hold this position) 44, 48, 52, 56, 60, 64, 68, 72; Vice-Pres. Mississippi State Coll. for Women Alumnae Asscn. 58-60; Democrat.
Leisure interests: needlework, drama.
Democratic National Committee, 1625 Massachusetts Avenue, N.W., Washington, D.C. 20036, U.S.A.
Telephone: (202) 797-5900.

Vrethem, Åke Torulf; Swedish engineer and businessman; b. 25 March 1912, Vretakloster; s. of Simon and Antina (Johansson) Vrethem; m. Brita Maria Sjögren 1940; four s. one d.; ed. Royal Inst. of Technology.
Joined State Power Board 34, Chief Engineer 44-48; Asst. Man. Dir. ASEA 48, Man. Dir. 49-61, Chief Exec. Dir. ASEA Group 61-; Dir. Fed of Swedish Industries 53-73; Gen. Export Asscn. of Sweden 54-72; Chair. Swedish Asscn. of Electrical Industries 67-72; mem. Council Int. Chamber of Commerce 57-; mem. The Conf. Board (U.S.A.) 61-; Pres. of Swedish Council of the European Movement 61-72; Pres. Swedish Standards Asscn. 62-73; Pres. Int. Org. for Standardization (ISO), Geneva 74-76; Knight Order of the North Star, Commdr. (First Class) Order of Vasa; Hon. D.Tech. (Chalmers Inst. of Technology, Gothenburg) 60, Hon. D.Sc. (Cranfield Inst. of Technology) 74.
ASEA Group Office, P.O. Box 3281, S-10365 Stockholm; Home: Strandvägen 33, S-18262 Djursholm, Sweden.
Telephone: 7-55-42-43.

Vries, Egbert de, DR. AGR.; Netherlands economist; b. 29 Jan. 1901, Grypskerke; s. of Jan de Vries and Johanna Willemina Luuring; m. 1st Tine Berg 1924 (died 1945), 2nd Alexandrine Duvekot 1947; five s. two d.; ed. Univ. of Wageningen.

Government service in Netherlands East Indies 24-41; Head of Div. for Gen. Econ. Affairs in Dept. of Econ. Affairs 38-41; Prof. of Agricultural Econs. and Dean of Agricultural Faculty, Univ. of Batavia 41-46; returned to Netherlands 46; Prof. of Tropical Agricultural Econs., Univ. of Wageningen, and adviser to Netherlands Ministry of Overseas Affairs 47-50; Chief of Econ. Resources Div. of Econ. Dept. of Int. Bank for Reconstruction and Devt. 50-52; Chief of Econ. Div. of Technical Operations Dept. 52-53, Agricultural Div. 53-56; Chair. Working Cttee. of Dept. of Studies, Div. Church and Soc., World Council of Churches 54-61; mem. of Cttee. on Devt. Countries, World Council of Churches 62; Rector Inst. of Social Studies, The Hague 56-66; Dir. Netherlands Univs. Foundation for Int. Co-operation 56-66; Chair. Nat. Org. for Int. Aid 56-61, Vice-Chair. 61-66; Prof. of Int. Devt., Univ. of Pittsburgh 66-73; Fellow, Inst. of Social Studies 66; Vice-Chair. Board of Council for Study of Mankind 68-70, mem. 70-; partner in consultancy on econ. and public admin. 73-; Trustee Obon Foundation 71-, Chair. Board of Trustees 75-; Trustee Interfuture 71-; Knight, Order of Netherlands Lion 50; Commdr. Order of Orange-Nassau 66; Prof. Emer. Public and Int. Affairs, Univ. of Pittsburgh 73.
Leisure interests: gardening, stamps.
Deerlake Park, Chalkhill, Pa. 15421, U.S.A.
Telephone: 412-438-4776.

Vriesland, Victor Emanuel van; Netherlands writer; b. 1892; ed. Gymnasium, The Hague, and Univ. of Dijon.
Arts and Literary Editor of *Nieuwe Rotterdamsche Courant*; Dir. of *De Groene Amsterdammer*; Editor of *De Vrije Bladen, Forum, Kroniek van Kunst en Kultuur*, and at present of *De Nieuwe Stem*; Pres. C. V. De Bezige Bij GA; Hon. mem. of Society of Authors; mem. of Arts Council; Vice-Pres. Bd. of Bureau of Musical Authors' Rights; fmr. Pres. Netherlands P.E.N. Centre, Dir. of Bureau of Authors' Rights, Vice-Pres. Int. Fed. of P.E.N. Clubs, now Int. Pres.; Editor several publishing houses; Order of Leopold II (Belgium); Légion d'Honneur; Order of Orange-Nassau; Hon. D.Litt. (Leyden); Constantyn Huyghens Prize, Prize Kunstenaarsverzet.
Publs. Essays: *De Cultureele Noodtoestand van het Joodsche Volk* 15, *Herman Hana* 20, *Grondslag van Verstandhouding* 46, *Vereenvoudigingen* 52, *Onderzoek en Vertoog* (2 vols.) 58, etc.; verse: *Voorwaardelijk Uitzicht* 29, *Vooronderzoek* 46, *Le Vent se couche* 49, *Tegengif* 59, etc.; plays: *Dor verlorene Sohn* 25, *Havenstad* 33; novel: *Het Afscheid van de Wereld in drie Dagen* 26; anthologies: *Winterboek W.B., Spiegel van de Ned. Poezie door alle eeuwen* (3 vols. 39, 53, 54), *In den Hof van Eros* 40, *Werk en de Mens Nico van Suchtelen* 48, *De Vergetenen* 55, etc., also short stories and many translations.
Weesperzijde 25, Amsterdam, Netherlands.

Vrigny, Roger, L. ès L.; French writer; b. 19 May 1920; ed. Collège oratorien de Rocroy-Saint-Léon, Paris, Lycée Condorcet, Paris, and Univ. of Paris.
Professor of Literature, Collège Rocroy-Saint-Léon; Founder of *Le Miroir* Theatre Co. 50; broadcaster and radio producer; Prix Femina 63.
Publs. novels: *Arban, Lauréna, Barbegal, La Nuit de Mougins, Fin de Journée, Le Serment d'Amboise* (Prix Femina), *La Vie brève* 72, *Pourquoi cette joie?* 74; farce: *Marute*; sketches: *L'Enlèvement d'Arabelle, L'Impromptu du réverbère*; comedy: *Les Irascibles*; mystery: *La Dame d'Onfrède*.
Home: 4 rue Jean-Ferrandi, 75016 Paris, France.

Vu Van Mau, LL.B., LL.D.; Vietnamese lawyer, diplomatist and politician; b. 25 July 1914; ed. Univ. of Hanoi and Univ. of Paris.
Lawyer, Hanoi 49; Dean, Faculty of Law, Univ. of

Saigon 55-58, Prof. of Law 65; First Pres. Vietnamese Supreme Court of Appeal 55; Minister of Foreign Affairs 55; Sec. of State for Foreign Affairs 56-63 (resgnd.); Pres. Viet-Namese Nat. Asscn. of Comparative Law; Amb. to U.K., Belgium and Netherlands 64-65; Senator 70-75; Prime Minister 28-30 April 75.
Publs. Legal Works in French and Vietnamese.

Vuillequez, Jean; American mining executive; b. 7 March 1911, New York; s. of Gustave Vuillequez and Suzanne Veyrey; m. Germaine Bardet 1937; one s. one d.; ed. New York City public schools and New York Univ.
President, Dir. Ametalco Inc. 64-72, Chair. 72-; Exec. Vice-Chair. Roan Selection Trust Ltd. 68-; Vice-Chair. Ametalco Ltd., U.K. 70-; Vice-Chair. RST Int. Metals Ltd. 70-72, Chair. 72-74; Chair. Ametalco Ltd. 73-; Pres. RST Int., Inc. 73-; Chief Exec. Amax Zambia, Inc. 73-; Vice-Chair. AMAX Inc. 74-.
Leisure interests: reading, sports.
AMAX Inc., AMAX Center, Greenwich, Conn. 06830, U.S.A.
Telephone: (203) 622-3000.

Vul, Benzion; Soviet physicist; b. 22 May 1903, Belay Cerkov, Kiev; s. of Moysai Vul and Basia Vul; m. Sofia Frenkel 1927; one d.; ed. Electrotechnical Faculty of Polytechnic Inst., Kiev, Physical-Technical Inst., Leningrad.
Red Army volunteer 20-21; at Physical Inst. of U.S.S.R. Acad. of Sciences 33-, founded Laboratory of Physics of Dielectrics 33 (reorganized as Laboratory of Physics of Semiconductors 50), now Chair.; mem. Editorial Board of Soviet Encyclopaedia 51; Chair. Scientific Council of Physics and Chem. of Semiconductors 60-; Vice-Pres. IUPAP 72-; Lenin Prize, State Prize, Hero

of Socialist Labour, 5 Orders of Lenin and other orders and medals.
Leisure interests: philosophy, skiing, swimming.
Publs. *Edge Dielectric Breakdown* 31, *Progressive Breakdown in Solid Dielectrics* 32, *Electrical Breakdown in Compressed Gases* 40, *Dielectric Constant of Titanates* 45, *Capacitance of P-N Junctions* 54; papers in *Proceedings of the International Conference on Physics of Semiconductors* 58, 60, 62, 64, 66, 68, 72, 74.
P.N. Lebedev Physical Institute, Academy of Sciences of the U.S.S.R., Leninski Prospect 53, Moscow 1352320, U.S.S.R.

Vuong Van Bac; Vietnamese diplomatist; b. 1927, Bac Ninh, N. Viet-Nam; ed. Hanoi Univ., Michigan State Univ., Vanderbilt Univ., U.S.A.
Admitted to Hanoi Bar Asscn. 52, Saigon Bar Asscn. 54; Prof. of Constitutional and Political Science, Nat. Inst. of Admin. 55; Chair. Dalat Univ. 65; Sec.-Gen. Viet-Nam Lawyers' Fed. 61; mem. Council of Lawyers, Saigon High Court 62-68, Board of Dirs. Viet-Nam Council on Foreign Relations 68; Legal Adviser to Repub. of Viet-Nam Liaison and Observation Del. at Paris talks 68; Amb. to U.K. 72-73; Minister of Foreign Affairs 73-75; has attended numerous int. confs. on legal and econ. affairs.

Vutthi, Thoutch, LL.D.; Khmer diplomatist; b. 23 May 1930, Phnom Penh; m.; ed. Univ. of Aix-en-Provence, France.
Head Political Affairs Bureau, Ministry of Foreign Affairs 59-60; with Perm. Mission to UN 60-61, Deputy Perm. Rep. 64-66; Dir. Political Affairs, Ministry of Foreign Affairs 66-67; Minister-Counsellor, Peking 67-70; Amb. to Repub. of Viet-Nam 70-71, to Indonesia 71-73, concurrently accred. to Malaysia 71-72; Perm. Rep. to UN 73-74.

W

Wächter, Eberhard; Austrian opera-singer; b. 8 July 1929, Vienna; *m.* 1954; three *s.* three *d.*; studied with Elisabeth Rado, Vienna.

Début with Volksoper, Vienna; mem. State Opera, Vienna 55-; has sung in Germany, France, Holland, England, Spain, U.S.A. and Italy, Bayreuth Festival, Salzburg Festival, etc.

Vienna XIX, 46 Fel. Mottlstrasse, Austria.

Telephone: 3417-212.

Wachtmeister, Count Wilhelm Hans Frederik; Swedish diplomatist; b. 29 April 1923, Wanås; *s.* of Count Gustaf Wachtmeister and Countess Margaretha Wachtmeister (née Trolle); *m.* Countess Ulla Wachtmeister (née Leuhusen); one *s.* two *d.*; studied law.

Attaché, Foreign Office 46-47, Embassy in Vienna 47-49, in Madrid Feb.-May 49, in Lisbon 49-50, Foreign Office 50-52; Second Sec. Foreign Office 52-55; Second Sec. Embassy in Moscow 55-56, First Sec. 56-58; Special Asst. to Sec.-Gen. of UN 58-62; Head of Div. for UN Affairs, Foreign Office 62-63, Head of Div. 63-65, Head of Dept. July-Oct. 65, Asst. Under-Sec. of State 65-66; Amb. to Algeria 66-68; Deputy Under-Sec. of State and Head of Political Div. 68-74; Amb. to U.S.A. June 74-; Hon. LL.D.

Royal Swedish Embassy, 600 New Hampshire Avenue, N.W., Washington, D.C. 20037; Residence: 3900 Nebraska Avenue, N.W., Washington, D.C. 20016, U.S.A.

Telephone: (202) 362-3270 (Residence).

Wachuku, Hon. Jaja Anucha, M.A., LL.B., LL.D.; Nigerian lawyer and politician; b. 1918, Umunkpeyi; *s.* of Chief Ndubisi and Ngwanchiwa Wachuku; *m.* Rhoda Idu Onumonu 1951; two *s.* three *d.*; ed. Nigeria Govt. Coll., Umuahia, Higher Coll., Yaba, Gold Coast People's Coll., Adidome and Trinity Coll., Dublin.

Law practice in Eire 44-47; returned to Nigeria 47; mem. Ngwa Native Authority Council 49-52; mem. Eastern House of Assembly 51-53, Fed. House of Reps. 52-66 (Speaker 60); Minister of Econ. Devt. 60-61; Acting Perm. Rep. to UN 60-61; Minister of Foreign Affairs and Commonwealth Relations 61-63, of External Affairs 63-65, of Aviation 65-66; fmr. Chair. UN Conciliation Comm. in the Congo; Man. Dir. Jawach Properties and Devt. Corpn. 66-; mem. Nsulu Community Council, Ngwa Div. 70, Chair. of Council 70-; mem. N.C.N.C.

Ugo Ngwa, P.O. Box 100, Nbwasi, East-Central State, Nigeria.

Wacker, Alfred, LL.B.; Swiss lawyer and diplomatist; b. 8 Jan. 1918, Zürich; *s.* of Paul Wacker; *m.* Chantal Thormann 1950; one *s.* two *d.*; ed. Universität Bern.

Swiss Foreign Office 45-50, 58-60; at Embassy, German Fed. Repub. 50-55, Budapest 55-57; Counsellor, Mexico 61-64; Deputy Head, Swiss Mission to European Econ. Community (EEC) 64-66; Deputy Sec.-Gen. European Free Trade Asscn. (EFTA) 66-73; Amb., Perm. Rep. to Council of Europe 73-.

7 rue Schiller, 67000 Strasbourg, France.

Telephone: 35-15-17.

Wada, Tsunesuke; Japanese business executive; b. 3 Nov. 1887; ed. Kobe Univ.

Furukawa Mining Co.; later with Furukawa Trading Co.; fmr. Man. Dir. and Pres. Fujitsu Ltd., Chair. 58-; fmr. Man. Dir., Pres. Chair., Adviser Fuji Electric Co. Ltd.

Fuji Electric Co. Ltd., 1-1 Marunouchi, Chiyoda-ku, Tokyo; Kami-osaki 2-8-12, Shinagawa-ku, Tokyo, Japan.

Wadati, Kiyoo; Japanese meteorologist; b. 8 Sept. 1902, Nagoya; *s.* of Yotaro and Kin Wadati; *m.* Kuniko Wadachi 1928; three *s.* four *d.*; ed. Tokyo Univ.

Entered Meteorological Observatory; has conducted research into earthquakes, tidal waves etc.; Dir.-Gen. Japan Meteorological Agency 56-63; fmr. Pres. Science Council of Japan; Pres. Saitama Univ. 63; Pres. Japan Acad.

Publs. *Earthquakes, Kisyo No Jiten (Encyclopaedia of Meteorology), Kaiyo No Jiten (Encyclopaedia of Oceanography).*

1-8 Naitomachi, Shinjiku-ku, Tokyo, Japan.

Telephone: 03-341-3503.

Wade, Emlyn Capel Stewart, Q.C., LL.D., F.B.A., J.P.; British barrister; b. 31 Aug. 1895, Saffron Walden, Essex; *s.* of C. S. D. Wade and E. L. Wade (née Holden); *m.* Mary Esmé Cardew 1924; four *d.*; ed. St. Lawrence Coll., Ramsgate and Gonville and Caius Coll., Cambridge.

Principal, Law Society's School of Law 26-28; Fellow of St. John's Coll. Cambridge 28-31; Tutor, Gonville and Caius Coll. Cambridge 31-39, Fellow 31-; Downing Prof. of Laws of England, Univ. of Cambridge 45-62; Reader in Constitutional Law, Council of Legal Education 45-66; U.K. Del. to Cttee. on European Unity, Paris 48-49; mem. of Departmental Cttees. on Law of Defamation 39, Electoral Law 44, Law of Limitations 48, Law Reform 52-63; Pres. Soc. of Public Teachers of Law 50-51; served in Army 15-19 and 39-42; Hon. D.C.L. Durham Univ.

Leisure interest: gardening.

Publs. *Constitutional Law* (with the late G. Godfrey Phillips) 31 (8th edn. 70, with A. W. Bradley), (Editor) *Dicey, The Law of the Constitution,* 10th edn. (with new Introduction) 59.

17 Sculthorpe Road, Fakenham, Norfolk, England.

Telephone: Fakenham 2565.

Wade, Robert Hunter, M.A.; New Zealand diplomatist; b. 14 June 1916, Balclutha; *s.* of R. H. Wade; *m.* Avelda Grace Peterson 1941; two *s.* two *d.*; ed. Waitaki School, Otago Univ., Victoria Univ.

New Zealand Treasury 39; Eastern Group Supply Council, Delhi 41; N.Z. Govt. Offices, Sydney 43; N.Z. High Comm. Canberra 47; Head, Eastern Political Div., Wellington 49; N.Z. Embassy, Wash. 51; N.Z. High Comm., Ottawa 56; Dir. Colombo Plan Bureau, Colombo 57; Dir. External Aid, Wellington 59; N.Z. Commr. in Singapore and Borneo 62; High Commr. to Malaysia 63; Deputy High Commr., London 67; N.Z. Amb. to Japan and Repub. of Korea 69; Deputy Sec.-Gen. of the Commonwealth Secr., London 72, Amb. to Fed. Repub. of Germany and Switzerland 75-.

New Zealand Embassy, 53 Bonn-Bad Godesberg, Turmstrasse 4, Federal Republic of Germany.

Telephone: Bad Godesberg 37-59-39.

Wadia, Sophia; Indian editor; b. 13 Sept. 1901, Bogotá, Colombia; *m.* Bahman P. Wadia 1928; ed. Lycée Molière, Paris, Columbia Univ., New York, School of Oriental and African Studies, London.

Lecturer; founder-organizer P.E.N. All-India Centre; Pres. Indian Inst. of World Culture, Bangalore, Balkan-Ji-Bari, Asian Book Trust; Vice-Pres. Bombay City Council for Child Welfare; assoc. United Lodge of Theosophists; Editor *Aryan Path* 29- and *The Indian P.E.N.* Bombay 34-; also worker in women's social, educational and cultural movements.

Leisure interests: philosophy, literature, music.

Publs. *The Brotherhood of Religions, Preparation for Citizenship.*
Theosophy Hall, 40 New Marine Lines, Bombay 400-020, India.
Telephone: 292173.

Wadsworth, James Jeremiah, A.B., LL.D.; American politician and administrator; b. 12 June 1905, Groveland, N.Y.; s. of James W. and Alice Hay Wadsworth; m. 1st Harty G. Tilton (died 1965), 2nd Mary A. Donaldson 1967; one d.; ed. Yale Univ.
Member, New York State Assembly 31-41, Asst. Industrial Relations Man., Curtiss Wright Corpn. 41-45; Dir. Public Interest Div., War Assets Corpn. 45-46; Dir. Govt. Liaison, Air Transport Asscn. of America 46-48; Special Asst. to Administrator, ECA (Marshall Plan) 48-50; Dep. later Acting Admin. Fed. Civil Defense Admin. 50-53; Dep. U.S. Rep. to U.N. 53-60, U.S. Rep. 60-61; Pres. Peace Research Inst. 61-62; Board of Trustees, Freedom House 61-63; mem. Exec. Cttee. of Dag Hammarskjöld Foundation 62-65, Fed. Communications Comm. 65-69; U.S. del. INTELSAT Consortium Conf. 69-70; retd. 70.
Leisure interests: sports, writing, painting, ceramics, photography, music, farming.
Publs. *The Price of Peace* 62, *Power and Order* 63, *A Warless World* 63, *The Glass House* 66.
3909 Avon Road, Geneseo, N.Y. 14454, U.S.A.
Telephone: 716-243-3896.

Wadsworth, Jeffery Page Rein; Canadian banker; b. 27 July 1911, Toronto; s. of William Rein and Mildred (Jeffery) Wadsworth; m. Elizabeth C. Bunting 1940; one d.; ed. Lakefield College School and Upper Canada College.
Joined the Canadian Bank of Commerce 28, Gen. Man. 56, Dir. and Vice-Pres. 57, Vice-Pres. and Gen. Man. Canadian Imperial Bank of Commerce 61, Pres. 63, Vice-Chair. 64, Deputy Chair. 70, Pres., Deputy Chair. and Chief Exec. Officer 71, Chair. and Chief Exec. Officer 73-; Vice-Pres. Board of Dirs. Confederation Life Insurance Co.; Dir. Calif. Canadian Bank, Holt, Renfrew and Co. Ltd., Pilot Insurance Co.; Hon. Chair. Board of Govs. Lakefield Coll. School; Gov. Univ. of Waterloo.
Leisure interests: golf, skiing, sailing, fishing.
Canadian Imperial Bank of Commerce, Commerce Court, Toronto, Ont.; Home: 7 Austin Terrace, Apt. 4, Toronto, Ont., Canada.

Wagenhöfer, Carl Friedrich; German banker; b. 24 Feb. 1910, Nuremburg; s. of Karl Wagenhöfer and Johanna Bauer; m. Gretl Hofman 1937; one s. one d.; ed. Univs. of Erlangen, Vienna, Kiel and Munich.
Department of Finance, Bavaria 37-39; Army Service 39-45; Chief of Section for Interministerial and Superregional Questions, Dept. of Finance, Bavaria 47-52; Sec. of State, Senate of Free and Hanseatic City of Hamburg 52-56; Pres. of Landeszentralbank in Bavaria 56-; mem. Central Bank Council of Deutsche Bundesbank 56-.
Leisure interests: literature concerning philosophy, theology and history of art; photography.
Publs. *Der Föderalismus und die Notenbankverfassung* 57, *Währungspolitik in der Sozialen Marktwirtschaft* 61.
Landeszentralbank, Ludwigstrasse 13, 8 Munich 22; Hermine-Bland-Strasse 1, 8 Munich 90, Federal Republic of Germany.
Telephone: 23700200 (Office); 64 89 64 (Home).

Wagner, Sir Anthony Richard, K.C.V.O., D.LITT.; British Garter King of Arms; b. 6 Sept. 1908, London; s. of Orlando H. Wagner and Monica Bell; m. Gillian M. M. Graham 1953; two s. one d.; ed. Eton and Balliol Coll., Oxford.
Portcullis Pursuivant 31-43; Richmond Herald 43-61; War Office 39-43; Private Sec. to Minister of Town and Country Planning 44-45; mem. Advisory Cttee. on Historic Buildings 47-66; Registrar, Coll. of Arms 53-60; Sec. of Order of the Garter 52-61; Jt. Register of Court of Chivalry 54-; Garter Principal King of Arms 61-; Inspector of Regimental Colours of the Order of St. John 61-; Knight Principal Imperial Soc. of Knights Bachelor 62-; Genealogist of the Order of the Bath 61-72, of the Order of St. John 61-; Trustee, Nat. Portrait Gallery 73-.
Publs. *Historic Heraldry of Britain* 39, *Heralds and Heraldry in the Middle Ages* 39, *Heraldry in England* 46, *Catalogue of English Mediaeval Rolls of Arms* 50, *The Records and Collections of the College of Arms* 52, *English Genealogy* 60, *English Ancestry* 61, *Heralds of England* 67, *Pedigree and Progress* 75.
College of Arms, Queen Victoria Street, London, E.C.4; 68 Chelsea Square, London, S.W.3; Wyndham Cottage, Aldeburgh, Suffolk, England.
Telephone: 01-248-4300.

Wagner, Aubrey Joseph; American engineer; b. 12 Jan. 1912, Hillsboro, Wis.; s. of Joseph M. and Wilhelmina F. Wagner; m. Dorothea J. Huber 1933; three s. one d.; ed. Univ. of Wisconsin.
Tennessee Valley Authority 34-, successively Junior Hydraulic Engineer, Asst. Hydraulic Engineer, Assoc. Navigation Engineer, Asst. Chief, River Transportation Branch, Act. Chief. later Chief Navigation and Transportation Branch, Asst. Gen. Man. 51-54, Gen. Man. 54-61, Dir. 61-62, Chair. 62-; mem. Nat. Acad. of Eng. 73; Hon. LL.B. (Newberry Coll.), Hon. degree in Public Administration (Lenoir Rhyne Coll., N.C.); N. W. Dougherty Award (Univ. of Tenn.) 69, Lambda Chi Alpha Order of Achievement 70.
Leisure interests: fishing, woodworking.
Publs. Articles in various journals and magazines.
Tennessee Valley Authority, 403 New Sprankle Building, Knoxville, Tennessee 37902; Home: 201 Whittington Drive, Knoxville, Tennessee 37919, U.S.A.
Telephone: 615-632-3554 (Office); 615-693-4779 (Home).

Wagner, Carl, PH.D.; German physical chemist; b. 25 May 1901, Leipzig; s. of Julius Wagner; ed. Univ. of Leipzig.
Professor, Technische Hochschule, Darmstadt 34-45; Scientific Adviser, Ordnance Research and Devt. Div., Fort Bliss. U.S.A. 45-49; Visiting Prof. of Metallurgy, Mass. Inst. of Technology, U.S.A. 49-55, Prof. of Metallurgy 55-58; Head Max-Planck-Inst. für physikalische Chemie, Göttingen 58-66, Staff mem. 67-; Palladium Medal, Electrochemical Soc. 51, Willis R. Whitney Award, Nat. Asscn. of Corrosion Engineers 57, Bunsen Medal, Deutsche Bunsengesellschaft 61, Gauss Medal, Braunschweigische Wissenschaftliche Gesellschaft 64; Dr. rer. nat. h.c. (Technische Hochschule, Darmstadt), Dr. Ing. E.h. (Bergakademie Clausthal-Technische Hochschule).
Publ. *Thermodynamics of Alloys* 62.
Home: Wohnstift C-309, D 34 Göttingen-Geismar; Office: Max-Planck-Institut für biophysikalische Chemie, 34 Gottingen-Nikolausberg, Am Fassberg, Federal Republic of Germany.

Wagner, Claude; Canadian politician; b. 4 April 1925.
Former Asst. Crown Prosecutor; first elected to Quebec Assembly Oct. 64; Attorney-Gen., Quebec 64-66; resigned from Quebec Assembly after defeat in elections for Liberal Party leadership 70; Judge of Sessions Court 70-72; Leader Progressive Conservative Party Oct. 72-; Conservative Party External Affairs Spokesman Dec. 72-.
Headquarters of the Progressive Conservative Party, 178 Queen Street, Ottawa, Ont., Canada.

Wagner, Gerrit Abram, LL.M.; Netherlands oil executive; b. 21 Oct. 1916; ed. Leiden Univ.
Royal Dutch/Shell Group 46-, working in various parts of world; Vice-Pres. Compañía Shell de Venezuela 59-61, Pres. 61-64; Man. Dir. N.V. Koninklijke Nederlandsche

Petroleum Maatschappij, Shell Petroleum Co. 64-; mem. Principal Dir. of Shell Petroleum N.V. 64-; Pres. Royal Dutch Petroleum Co. 71-; Dir. Shell Oil Co. 71-, Chair. 72-; Dir. Shell Canada Ltd. 71-; Order of Francisco de Miranda, Second Class (Venezuela), Knight Order of the Netherlands Lion; Hon. C.B.E. (U.K.); Officier Légion d'Honneur.

N.V. Koninklijke Nederlandsche Petroleum Maatschappij, Carel van Bylandtlaan 30, The Hague; Home: Teylingerhorstlaan 13, Wassenaar, Netherlands.

Wagner, Hellmuth, DR. IUR.; German lawyer and industrial official; b. 17; ed. Staatliches Kaiserin-Augusta-Gymnasium, Berlin, and Münster Univ.
Compulsory labour service 36; apprenticeship in textile industry 36-38; Military Service 38-45; legal and political science studies, Münster Univ. 48-51; Legal Adviser to Gütersloh Town Council 51-52, Federation of German Industries 52-; Managing Dir., Federation of German Industries 63-75, mem. Man. Board 68-; consulting mem. Pres. Board 75-.
Publs. articles on business management.
Bundesverband der Deutschen Industrie, Oberländer Ufer 84-88, 5 Cologne 51, Federal Republic of Germany.
Telephone: 3708-1.

Wagner, Philip Marshall; American newspaper columnist and viticulturist; b. 18 Feb. 1904, New Haven, Conn.; m. 1st Helen Crocker 1925, 2nd Jocelyn McDonough 1940; two c.; ed. Kent School, and Univ. of Michigan.
With General Electric Co. 25-30; Editorial Writer, *Baltimore Evening Sun* 30-36, London Corresp. *Baltimore Sun* 36-37, Editor *Evening Sun* 38-43, Editor *Baltimore Sun* 43-64; writer of syndicated newspaper column on public affairs 64-; with wife has introduced new grape varieties into American viticulture; American del. Fédération Nat. de la Viticulture Nouvelle; Officier du Mérite Agricole, France.
Publs. *American Wines and How to Make Them* 33, *Wine Grapes and How to Grow Them* 37, *The Wine-Grower's Guide* 45, *American Wines and Wine Making* 56, *H. L. Mencken* (American Writers Series) 66; Edited (with Dr. Stanford V. Larkey) *Turner on Wines* 41.
Boordy Vineyard, Box 38, Riderwood, Md., U.S.A.
Telephone: 301-823-4624.

Wagner, Robert F., B.A., LL.B.; American lawyer and public official; b. 20 April 1910; ed. Yale Univ., Harvard School of Business Administration, School of Int. Relations, Geneva, and Yale Law School.
Mem. N.Y. State Assembly 38-41; served American Air Force 41-45; Tax Commr., N.Y. City 46; Commr. Dept. of Housing and Buildings, N.Y. City 46-47; Chair. N.Y. Planning Comm. 47-49; Borough Pres. of Manhattan 50-53; Mayor of New York 54-65; Partner, Wagner, Quillinan and Tennant 66-68, 72-; Amb. to Spain 68-69; Chair. Nationalities Div., Dem. Nat. Cttee. 62; Bronze Star, Presidential Unit Citation, Croix de Guerre and six battle stars; Hon. LL.D. (Long Island Univ., Fordham Univ. and Brooklyn Law School).
Empire State Building, 350 5th Avenue, New York, N.Y. 10001, U.S.A.

Wagner, Wolfgang Manfred Martin; German festival director; b. 30 Aug. 1919, Bayreuth; s. of Siegfried Wagner and Winifred Williams; brother of late Wieland Wagner; m. Ellen Drexel 1943; one s. one d.
Director, Bayreuth Festival.
Festspielhügel 3, 8580 Bayreuth, Federal Republic of Germany.
Telephone: 20721.

Wahi, Prem Nath, M.D., F.R.C.P.; Indian doctor; b. 10 April 1908; ed. K.G. Medical Coll., Lucknow, London Hospital Medical School, London, and New England Deaconess Hospital, Boston, U.S.A.

Professor of Pathology, S.N. Medical Coll., Agra 41-; Principal, S.N. Medical Coll., Agra 60-; Dean, Faculty of Medicine, Agra Univ. 61-64; Dir. WHO Int. Reference Centre and Cancer Registry 63-; mem. Expert Panel of WHO on Cancer, Lyon, France 65-; has attended numerous int. conferences on cancer; Lady Brahamachari Readership, Calcutta Univ. 65; Fellow, Nat. Inst. of Sciences, India; Founder Fellow, Coll. of Pathologists, London 63; Founder Fellow, Indian Acad. of Medical Sciences 64.
S.N. Medical College, Agra (U.P.), India.

Wahl, Jacques Henri; French government official; b. 18 Jan. 1932, Lille; s. of Abraham Wahl and Simone Kornbluth; m. Inna Cytrin 1969; two s. one d.; ed. Institut d'Etudes Politiques, Paris, Univs. of Lille and Paris, Ecole Nat. d'Administration.
Inspecteur des Finances 61-65; Treasury Dept. 65-68; Special Asst. to Ministers of Econ. and Finance, François Ortoli 68-69, Valéry Giscard d'Estaing 69-71; Asst. Dir. of the Treasury for Int. Affairs 71-73; Chair. Invisible Transactions Cttee., OECD 71-73; Lecturer Inst. d'Etudes Politiques and Ecole Nat. d'Administration, Paris 69-73; Financial Minister, French Embassies, U.S.A. and Canada 73-; Exec. Dir. IMF, IBRD 73-; Chevalier, Ordre Nat. du Mérite, Commdr. de l'Ordre National de Côte d'Ivoire, Officier de l'Ordre du Mérite de la République Centrafricaine, Chevalier de l'Ordre du Mérite de Haute Volta.
Residence: 5100 Van Ness Street, N.W., Washington, D.C. 20016; International Monetary Fund, Room 13-118, 700 19th Street, N.W., Washington, D.C. 20431, U.S.A.
Telephone: (202) 244-4328 (Res.); (202) 477-3861 (IMF).

Wahlen, Friedrich Traugott; Swiss agriculturalist and politician; b. 10 April 1899, Mirchel, Berne; s. of Johann Wahlen and Katharina Stucki; m. Helen Hopf 1923; ed. Swiss Fed. Inst. of Technology, Zurich.
Asst. Inst. of Agronomy, Fed. Inst. of Technology, Zürich 20-22; Supervising Analyst Dominion Seed Laboratory, Quebec, then Chief Analyst Dominion Dept. of Agriculture, Ottawa with Canadian Civil Service 22-29; Dir. Swiss Experiment Station of Agriculture, Oerlikon, Zürich 29-43; Prof. of Agronomy, Fed. Inst. of Technology, Zürich 43-49; Chief of the Section of Agricultural Production and Home Economics in the Swiss War Food Office and Commr. for Food Production 38-42 and 42-45, organizing the Wahlen Plan for assuring Switzerland's food supplies during the Second World War; mem. Swiss Council of States (Senate) 42-49; Dir. Agriculture Division, F.A.O., Washington 49-50, Rome 51-57; Chief Expanded Tech. Asst. Programme F.A.O. 50-52; Deputy Dir.-Gen. F.A.O. 57-58; Federal Councillor (Justice and Police) 59, (Public Economy) 60-June 61, (Political Dept.) July 61-65; Pres. Swiss Confederation 61; Chair. Comm. for Revision of the Swiss Constitution 67-; mem. Royal Swedish Acad.; Marcel Benoist Prize 40. etc.; Hon. Dr. of Medicine, Univ. of Zürich 46; Hon. Dr. of Agricultural Sciences, Univ. of Göttingen, and Laval Univ., Quebec; Hon. Dr. of Law, Univ. of Basle; Hon. Dr. of Tech. Sciences, Swiss Fed. Inst. of Technology.
Leisure interests: too many to mention.
39 Humboldtstrasse, Berne, Switzerland.
Telephone: 031-41-23-55.

Wahrhaftig, Zorach, DR.JUR.; Israeli lawyer and politician; b. 2 Feb. 1906, Warsaw, Poland; m.; three s. one d.; ed. Univ. of Warsaw.
Private law practice, Warsaw 32-39; Vice-Pres. Mizrachi, Poland 20-39; mem. of exec. Keren Hayesod, Hechalutz Hamizrachi, World Jewish Congress; Deputy Dir. Inst. of Jewish Affairs, New York 43-47; Vice-Leumi Law Dept. 47; mem. Provisional State Council 48; mem. of Knesset; Deputy Minister for Religious Affairs 56-61; Minister of Religious Affairs 61-74;

Chair. Knesset Constitution, Law and Justice Cttee.; mem. Jewish Law Research Inst., Ministry of Justice 48; Lecturer on Talmudic Law, Hebrew Univ.; Chair. of Exec., Bar-Ilan Univ.

Publs. *Starvation over Europe* 43, *Relief and Rehabilitation* 44, *Where Shall they Go?* 46, *Uprooted* 46, *Hazaka in Jewish Law* 64, and many publs. in Hebrew on Israeli Law and Religion.

The Knesset, Jerusalem, Israel.

Waidelich, Charles J., B.S., C.E.; American business executive; b. 2 May 1929, Columbus, O.; *s.* of Bernard H. Waidelich and Alberta L. Poth; *m.* Margaret E. Finley 1952; one *s.* one *d.*; ed. Purdue Univ.

Engineer, Cities Service Oil Co. 51-53; Asst. to Pres. Cities Service Pipeline Co. 56-59; Pipeline Co-ordinator, Cities Service Co. 59-65; Transport Co-ordinator 65-66; Staff Vice-Pres. Operations Co-ordination 66-68; Vice-Pres., Operations, Tenn. Corpn. 68-69; Exec. Vice-Pres. and Dir., Cities Service Co. 70-71, Pres. 71-.

Leisure interests: reading, sport, bridge, gardening.

Cities Service Co., 110 West 7th Street, Tulsa, Okla. 74119; Home: 2161 Forest Blvd., Tulsa, Okla. 74114, U.S.A.

Wain, John Barrington, M.A.; British writer; b. 14 March 1925, Stoke-on-Trent, Staffs.; *s.* of Arnold A. and Anne Wain; *m.* Eirian James 1960; three *s.*; ed. High School, Newcastle-under-Lyme and St. John's Coll., Oxford.

Lecturer in English Literature, Univ. of Reading 47-55; resigned 55 to become free-lance writer and literary critic; occasional academic assignments incl. Churchill Visiting Prof., Univ. of Bristol 67, Visiting Prof., Centre Universitaire Expérimental, Vincennes, France and George Elliston Lecturer on Poetry, Univ. of Cincinnati, U.S.A.; 1st holder, Fellowship in Creative Arts, Brasenose Coll., Oxford Univ. 71-72; Prof. of Poetry, Oxford Univ. 73-; Fellow Brasenose Coll. 73-; Dir. 1st "Poetry at the Mermaid" Festival, London 61; James Tait Black Memorial Prize for *Samuel Johnson* 74.

Leisure interests: walking, canoeing.

Publs. poetry: *Mixed Feelings* 51, *A Word Carved on a Sill* 56, *Weep Before God* 61, *Wildtrack* 65, *Letters to Five Artists* 69, *The Shape of Feng* 72, *Feng* 75; novels: *Hurry on Down* 53, *Living in the Present* 55, *The Contenders* 58, *A Travelling Woman* 59, *Strike the Father Dead* 62, *The Young Visitors* 65, *The Smaller Sky* 67, *A Winter in the Hills* 70; stories: *Nuncle and other Stories* 60, *Death of the Hind Legs* 66, *The Life Guard* 71; play: *Harry in the Night* 75; non-fiction: *Preliminary Essays* 57, *Sprightly Running* (autobiog.) 62, *Essays on Literature and Ideas* 63, *The Living World of Shakespeare* 64, *A House for the Truth* 72, Editor *Johnson as Critic* 74, *Samuel Johnson* 74.

c/o Macmillan and Co. Ltd., Little Essex Street, London, W.C.2, England.

Wajda, Andrzej; Polish film director; b 6 March 1926, Suwałki; *m.* 1st Beata Tyszkiewicz 1967 (divorced), one *d.*; *m.* 2nd Krystyna Zachwatowicz 75; ed. Acad. of Fine Arts, Cracow and Film Acad., Łódź.

Assistant Stage Man. 53; Film Dir. 54-; Stage Man., Teatr Stary, Kraków 73-; Polish State Prize for film *Pokolenie* (Generation), Silver Palm for *Kanał*, Cannes 57, Fipresci Prize for *Popiół i Diament*, Venice 57, *The Birch Wood*, Milan 70, and for *Landscape after Battle*, Milan 71, Silver Prize for *The Wedding*, San Sebastian 73, Grand Prix for *Krajobraz po bitwie*, Colombo, Sri Lanka 73, State Prize 74, Grand Prix Moscow Film Festival 75 and Int. Prize Chicago Festival 75 for *The Promised Land*.

Films: *Pokolenie* (Generation) 54, *Idę do słońca* (I'm Going to the Sun) 55, *Kanał* (Canal) 56, *Popiół i Diament* (Ashes and Diamonds) 57, *Lotna* 59, *Niewinni Czarodzieje* (Innocent Sorcerers) 59, *Samson* 60, *Serbian Lady Macbeth* 61, *Love at 20* 61, *Popioły* (Ashes) 65,

Bramy raju (Gates of Paradise) 67, *Wszystko na sprzedaż* (Everything for Sale) 68, *Przekładaniec* (Jigsaw Puzzle) (for TV) *Polowanie na muchy* (Hunting Flies) 69, *Macbeth* (for TV) 69, *Krajobraz po bitwie* (Landscape after Battle) 70, *The Birch Wood* 70, *Pilatus* (for TV) 71, *Mistrz i Małgorzata* (Master and Margaret) (for Fed. German TV) 72, *Wesele* (Wedding) 72, *Ziemia Obiecana* (The Promised Land) 75; directed plays: *Hatful of Rain* 59, *Hamlet* 60, *Two on the Seesaw* 60, *Wesele* 62, *The Demons* 63, *Play Strindberg* 69, *The Devils* 71, *Sticks and Bones*, Moscow 72, *Der Mittmacher* 73, *November Night* 74, *The Danton Affair* 75; scenography for *Hatful of Rain*, *The Demons*, *November Night*.

Film Polski, ul. Mazowiecka 6/8, Warsaw; Home: 14 Haukego Street, 01-540, Warsaw, Poland.

Wakeley, Sir Cecil (Pembrey Grey), Bt., K.B.E., C.B., M.CH., D.SC., F.R.S. (Edin.), F.R.C.S., K.ST.J.; British surgeon; b. 5 May 1892; *m.* Elizabeth Muriel Nicholson-Smith 1925; three *s.*; ed. Dulwich Coll., and London Univ.

Surgical Specialist Royal Navy 15-19, Surgeon Rear-Admiral 39-46; Arris and Gale Lecturer 24-25, Arnot Demonstrator 34, Hunterian Prof. 29, 34, 37, 40, 42, Hunterian Orator 55, Thomas Vickary Lecturer 57; Erasmus Wilson Lecturer 28, 30-33, 35-38, Bradshaw Lecturer 47; Hunter Prof. and Orator, Royal Coll. of Surgeons 55, Hunterian Orator Hunterian Soc. 61; Examiner in Surgery 33-43, Pres. Royal Coll. of Surgeons 49-54; at present Consulting Surgeon King's Coll. Hospital, Senior Surgeon Royal Masonic Hospital and Belgrave Hospital for Children, Consulting Surgeon West End Hospital for Nervous Diseases and to Royal Navy 30-; Lecturer in Anatomy, London Univ. 19-67; fmr. mem. and Treas. of the Gen. Medical Council; mem. Exam. Board R.N.; Vice-Pres. and Chair. Council Imperial Cancer Research Fund; Vice-Pres. British Empire Cancer Campaign; Editorial Sec. *British Journal of Surgery*; Editor *Annals of R.C.S.* 47-69; Editor *Medical Press* 33-53; Chair. Medical Sickness Finance Corpn., Int. Exhibition Co-operative Wine Soc. Ltd., Hunterian Trustees, Royal Coll. of Surgeons, Wakeley Bros.; Vice-Chair. Medical Sickness Society; Legion of Merit U.S.A.; Order of the Nile 2nd Class, Chevalier de la Légion d'Honneur, Order of Southern Cross (Brazil); Hon. F.A.C.S., Hon. F.R.A.C.S.; Hon. F.R.C.S. (Edin. and Ireland); Hon. LL.D. (Glasgow, Lahore, Leeds), Hon. D.Sc. (Delhi and Colombo).

Leisure interests: stamp collecting and gardening.

Publs. *Modern Treatment Yearbook* 35-, *A Textbook of Surgical Pathology*; Editor: Rose and Carless' *Manual of Surgery* 22-, *Surgical Diagnosis*, Treves and Wakeley's *Handbook of Surgical Operations*, *Aids to Surgery*, *The Pineal Gland*, *Synopsis of Surgery*, *Surgery for Nurses and Medical Dictionary*.

240 Maidstone Road, Chatham, Kent ME4 6JN, England.

Telephone: Medway 45946.

Walcha, Helmut; German organist and harpsichordist; b. 27 Oct. 1907, Leipzig; *s.* of Emil Walcha and Anna Ficker; *m.* Ursula Koch 1939; ed. Leipzig Inst. of Music.

Organist and Prof. of Music Frankfurt/Main 29; Prof. Music Inst., Frankfurt/Main; Organist, Dreikönigs Kirche, Frankfurt/Main.

Leisure interest: literature.

Compositions: *Choral Preludes* (3 vols.).

Recordings: incl. complete works of Bach for organ solo and for harpsichord solo.

Hasselhorstweg 27, Frankfurt/Main, Federal Republic of Germany.

Telephone: 65-35-24.

Wald, George, PH.D.; American university professor; b. 18 Nov. 1906, New York; *s.* of Isaac W. and Ernestine Rosenmann; *m.* Dr. Ruth Hubbard; one *s.* one *d.*;

ed. New York Univ. and Columbia Univ., New York. National Research Council Fellow, Kaiser Wilhelm Inst., Berlin and Heidelberg, Univ. of Zurich and Univ. of Chicago 32-34; Tutor in Biochemical Sciences, Harvard Univ. 34-35, Instructor in Biology 35-39, Faculty Instructor 39-44, Assoc. Prof. of Biology 44-48, Prof. 48-, Higgins Prof. of Biology 68-; Visiting Prof. of Biochemistry, Univ. of Calif., Berkeley 56; Nat. Sigma Xi Lecturer 52; Chair. Div. Cttee. on Biology and Medical Sciences, Nat. Science Foundation 54-56; Guggenheim Fellow 63-64; Overseas Fellow, Churchill Coll., Cambridge 63-64; mem. Nat. Acad. of Sciences; Eli Lilly Prize, American Chemical Soc. 39; Lasker Award, Public Health Asscn. 53; Proctor Award, Asscn. for Research in Ophthalmology 55; Rumford Medal, American Acad. of Arts and Sciences 59; Ives Medal, Optical Soc. of America 66; Paul Karrer Medal in Chemistry, Univ. of Zürich 67; co-recipient Nobel Prize for Medicine 67; T. Duckett Jones Memorial Award 67, Bradford Washburn Medal 68, Max Berg Award 69, Joseph Priestley Award 70.
Department of Biology, Harvard University, Cambridge, Mass. 02138, U.S.A.

Wald, Richard C.; American journalist; s. of Joseph S. and Lily (Forstate) Wald; m. Edith May Leslie 1953; two s. one d.
Reporter later Man. Editor *N.Y. Herald Tribune* 55-66; Asst. Man. Editor *Washington Post* 67; Exec. Vice-Pres. Whitney Communications Corpn. N.Y.C. 68-; Vice-Pres. News NBC, Pres. 73-; Dir. *Columbia Spectator.*
30 Rockefeller Plaza, New York, N.Y. 10020; Home: 35 Orchard Road, Larchmont, New York, N.Y. 10538, U.S.A.

Waldbrunner, Karl; Austrian engineer and politician; b. 25 Nov. 1906, Vienna; m. Friedl Sinkovc 1969; one s. one d.; ed. Vienna Technical Univ.
Engaged in construction of power stations and plants in U.S.S.R. after completion of engineering studies; returned to Austria to become chief engineer of a steel works 37; active mem. of Social Democratic Party since student days, illegal political activity during German occupation; mem. Nationalrat 45-71; State Sec. for Commerce, Business, Industry, and Transport 45; transferred to Federal Ministry of Insurance and Economic Planning; Minister to U.S.S.R. 46; participated in Austrian Treaty negotiations in London 47-49; Sec. Socialist Party of Austria 46-56; Minister of Transport and Nationalised Industries 49-56, of Communications and of Electric Power Development 56-62; Deputy Pres. of Nat. Council 62-70, Pres. 70-71; Vice-Pres. Austrian Nationalbank 72-; Deputy Chair. Socialist Party 65-74; Hon. Pres., Fed. of Socialist Univ. Graduates, Intellectuals and Artists.
Leisure interests: socialist university and cultural organizations, travel, photography.
Office: Österreichische Nationalbank, Postfach 61, A-1011 Vienna; Home: Bickellgasse 12, Vienna 1120, Austria.
Telephone: 43-60-901 (Office).

Waldenström, Erland; Swedish civil engineer and company director; b. 4 June 1911, Malmö; s. of Martin Waldenström and Hedvig Lion; m. Dorothy Ethel Boleyn 1945; one s. two d.; ed. Royal Inst. of Technology.
Engineer, Korsnäs Sågwerks AB, Gävle 34, 36-40; Expert, Tech. Research and Devt. Swedish Fed. of Industries 40-46; Official Expert and Sec. State Cttee. on Tech. Research 41-42; Chief, Tech. Office, Svenska Cellulosa AB, Sundsvall 42-46, Chief Engineer 47-49; Industrial Counsellor UN Econ. Comm. for Europe (EEC), Geneva 48; Dir. Luossavaara-Kiirunavaara AB 50-, Pres. 50-57; Pres. Gränges AB 50-71, Chair. Board 71-; Dir. Fed. of Swedish Industries 51-, Chair. 71-73;

Dir.-Gen. Export Asscn. of Sweden 51-59, 73-74, Chair. 71-73; Dir. Swedish Employers' Confed. 51-72; Dir. Liberian American-Swedish Minerals Co. (LAMCO) (Monrovia) 55-75, Chair. 75-; Dir. Ironmasters Fed. 55-62; Dir. Liberian Iron Ore Ltd. (Toronto) 58-70, Chair. and Pres. 70-; Chair. Swedish Mining Asscn. 57-59; Dir. Skandinaviska Enskilda Banken 57-, Vice-Chair. 68-; Chair. LAMCO Joint Venture 60-75; Chair. Swedish LAMCO Syndicate 63-; Dir. AB Bofors (Bofors) 60-; Chair. Thiel Art Gallery 61-; Dir. Stockholm School of Econs. 61-; Dir. S.A. Cockerill-Ougrée-Providence et Espérance-Longdoz (Seraing) 70- (Espérance-Longdoz 64-70); Chair. Gränges American Corpn. 71-; Chair. Concert Asscn. of Stockholm 73- (mem. Board 56-73); mem. Royal Swedish Acad. of Eng. Sciences 48, Centre d'Etudes Industrielles Foundation Board (Geneva) 70; Fellow, Royal Soc. of Arts, London 68-.
Publs. *On Industrial Progress in Sweden* 42, *Waste and Residual Products in Forestry* 42, *Development Trends in Forestry* 46; also several essays on technical and economic questions.
Gränges, Fack S-103 26, Stockholm 16; Home: Villa Gröndal, Manillavägen 17, Djurgården, S-115 25, Stockholm, Sweden.

Waldenström, Jan Gosta, M.D.; Swedish professor of medicine; b. 17 April 1906, Stockholm; s. of Prof. Henning Waldenström and Elsa Laurin; m. 1st Elisabet Waldenström 1932, 2nd Karin Nordsjö 1957; five s. two d.; ed. Univs. of Uppsala and Cambridge, Technische Hochschule, Munich.
Various positions at Academic Hospital, Uppsala; Prof. of theoretical medicine, Uppsala 47; Prof. of practical medicine, Univ. of Lund 50-72; Physician-in-Chief, Dept. of Gen. Medicine. Gen. Hospital, Malmö 50-72; foreign mem. Nat. Acad. of Sciences of U.S.A.; Hon. mem. Royal Soc. of Medicine, London and other foreign acads.; Jahre Scandinavian Prize in Medicine 62, Gairdner Award 66, Paul Ehrlich Prize 72; hon. degrees from Univs. of Oslo, Dublin, Mainz, Oxford, Paris, London, Innsbruck and Poitiers.
Leisure interests: history, botany, travelling, art.
Publs. *Studien über Porphyrie,* 37, *Monoclonal and polyclonal hypergammaglobulinemia* 68, *Diagnosis and Treatment of Multiple Myeloma* 70; numerous publications on metabolic, hematologic and other subjects of internal medicine; chapters in many textbooks.
Department of Medicine, Malmö General Hospital, S 214 01 Malmö; Home: Sanekullavägen 17, S 217 74 Malmö, Sweden.
Telephone: 040/91-62-02.

Waldheim, Kurt, LL.D.; Austrian diplomatist and United Nations official; b. 21 Dec. 1918; m. Elisabeth Ritschel Waldheim 1944; one s. two d.; ed. Consular Acad. of Vienna, Univ. of Vienna.
Entered foreign service 45; served Ministry of Foreign Affairs; mem. Austrian Del. to Paris, London and Moscow for negotiation on Austrian State Treaty; 1st Sec. 45-47; served Paris 48-51; Counsellor and Head of Personnel Div., Ministry of Foreign Affairs 51-55; Perm. Austrian Observer to UN 55-56; Minister to Canada 56-58, Amb. to Canada 58-60; Dir.-Gen. for Political Affairs, Ministry for Foreign Affairs 60-64; Perm. Rep. to UN 64-68; Chair. Outer Space Cttee. of UN 65-68, 70-71; Fed. Minister for Foreign Affairs 68-70; Perm. Rep. to UN 70-71; Candidate for Pres. of Austria 71; Sec.-Gen. of UN 72-; several decorations.
Publ. *Der österreichische Weg* (The Austrian Example).
United Nations, New York, N.Y. 10017, U.S.A.
Telephone: Plaza 4-1234, ext. 5012.

Walding, Joseph A.; New Zealand politician; b. 1926, Christchurch; m.; six d.; ed. Wellington and Dunedin.
Served in Merchant Navy, World War II, France, Atlantic and Pacific; City Councillor, Palmerston North; mem. Parl. for Palmerston North 67-; founder,

Man. Dir. Export Co.; Minister of Overseas Trade, the Environment, Recreation and Sport 72-75, also Assoc. Minister of Foreign Affairs 72-75, fmr. Pres., Sec. Palmerston North Workers' Educ. Asscn.

Leisure interests: music chess, fishing, golf.

c/o Ministry of Overseas Trade, Wellington, New Zealand.

Waldock, Sir (Claud) Humphrey (Meredith), Kt., C.M.G., O.B.E., Q.C., D.C.L.; British international lawyer; b. 13 Aug. 1904, Colombo, Ceylon; s. of F. W. Waldock and Lizzie K. Souter; m. Ethel B. Williams; one s one d.; ed. Uppingham School, and Brasenose Coll., Oxford.

Barrister-at-Law 28; Fellow of Brasenose Coll. 30-47; Principal Admiralty 40; Asst. Sec. 43; Principal Asst. Sec. 44-45; U.K. Commr., Italo-Yugoslav Boundary Comm. 46; attached as Under-Sec. to Foreign Office; U.K. Rep. on Comm. for Statute of Free Territory of Trieste, Paris Conf. 46; Chichele Prof. of Public Int. Law Oxford 47-72; Assoc. Inst. of Int. Law 50-61, mem. 61-; mem. European Comm. of Human Rights 54, Pres. 55-61, Judge 66-74, Vice-Pres. 69-71, Pres. 71-74; mem. Int. Law Comm. 61-73; Special Rapporteur on the Law of Treaties; mem. Perm. Court of Arbitration 65-; Chair. Cttee. of Inquiry into Oxford Univ. Press 67-70; Judge, Int. Court of Justice 73-; mem. Swedish-Finnish, Swedish-Swiss, Swedish-Turkish, German-Swiss, American-Danish, Chilean-Italian, Danish-Norwegian and Swedish-Spanish Conciliation Comms.; Fellow of All Souls Coll., Oxford 47-72; Bencher Gray's Inn (Treasurer 71); Hon. Fellow Brasenose Coll.; King Christian X of Denmark Liberty Medal 46; Commdr. Order of Isabel la Católica of Spain 61, Order of the Dannebrog (Denmark) 69; Grand Officer Order of Merit (Chile) 69.

Publs. *English Law of Mortgages* 38, *The Regulation of the Use of Force* 52, *General Course in Public International Law* 62, articles in learned journals; Editor *The British Year Book of International Law* 55-74, 6th Edn. of Brierley's *Law of Nations* 63.

International Court of Justice, Peace Palace, The Hague 2012, Netherlands; Home: 6 Lathbury Road, Oxford, England.

Telephone: 58227 (Home).

Waldron-Ramsey, Waldo Emerson, LL.B., B.SC., LL.M., PH.D.; Barbadian diplomatist; b. 1 Jan. 1930, Barbados; s. of late Wyatt Waldron-Ramsey and of Delcina Waldron-Ramsey; m.; one s. two d.; ed. Schools in Barbados, London School of Economics, Middle Temple, London, Hague Acad. of Int. Law, and Univs. in Yugoslavia.

Legal Adviser and Welfare Officer, London Transport Exec. 56-57; practising barrister, London 57-60; Marketing Economist, Shell Int. 60-62; Rep. of Tanzania at UN 62-70; High Commr. for Barbados in London (also Amb. to France, Netherlands, and Fed. Repub. of Germany) 70-71; UN Legal Expert in field of Human Rights 67-71, on Israel 68-71; Perm. Rep. to UN 71-; Teaching Fellow, Univ. of Chung-Ang, Seoul, Repub. of Korea 74-; Grand Officer, First Class (Haiti), Grand Officer (First Class) of the Fahia Mêtrei of the Khmer Repub.; Hon. Ph.D., Hebrew Univ., Jerusalem, Hon. LL.D., Univ. of Phnom Penh; decorations from several Afro-American and other socs. in U.S.A. in recognition of work for human rights at UN; mem. American Acad. Political and Social Science, American Soc. of Int. Law, American Petroleum Inst. (Marketing).

Leisure interests: cricket, table tennis, contract bridge, hiking.

Permanent Mission of Barbados to the United Nations, 866 United Nations Plaza, Suite 527, New York, N.Y. 10017, U.S.A.

Wales, Prince of, and Earl of Chester (cr. 58), H.R.H. The Prince Charles Philip Arthur George, K.G., G.C.B., Duke of Cornwall and Rothesay, Earl of Carrick, Baron of Renfrew, Lord of the Isles and Great Steward of Scotland (cr. 52); eldest son of Queen Elizabeth II and Prince Philip, Duke of Edinburgh, and heir apparent to the throne of the United Kingdom of Great Britain and N. Ireland; b. 14 Nov. 1948; ed. Cheam School, Gordonstoun School, Geelong Grammar School, Trinity Coll., Cambridge, and Univ. Coll. of Wales, Aberystwyth.

Invested as Prince of Wales 69; Flight-Lieut, R.A.F. 71; entered Royal Navy 71, Lieut. 73, assumed command of H.M.S. *Bronington* 76; Col.-in-Chief Royal Regiment of Wales 69-; Col. Welsh Guards 74-; represented H.M. the Queen at memorial service for Prime Minister of Australia 67, at Fiji independence celebrations 70, at requiem mass for Gen. Charles de Gaulle 70, at Bahamas independence celebrations 73, at funeral Prime Minister of New Zealand 74, at Fiji centenary celebrations 74, at coronation of King of Nepal 75, at Papua New Guinea independence celebrations 75; Personal A.D.C. to H.M. the Queen 73-; Pres. Welsh Environment Foundation 71-; Vice-Pres. Soc. of Friends of St. George's and Descendants of K.G.s 68-; Great Master of the Order of the Bath 75-; Chair. Admin. Council King George's Jubilee Trusts 75-; Freeman of several companies and cities; Queen Elizabeth II Coronation Medal 53, Grand Cross, White Rose of Finland 69, Grand Cordon, Supreme Order of the Chrysanthemum of Japan 71, Grand Cross Order of House of Orange 72, Grand Cross Order of Oak Crown of Luxembourg 72, Knight of the Order of the Elephant of Denmark 74, Grand Cross Order of Ojasvi Rajanya of Nepal 75, Order of the Seraphim of Sweden 75.

Buckingham Palace, London, S.W.1, England.

Walker, Ardis Manly, B.S.; American engineer, poet and writer; b. 9 April 1901, Keysville, Calif.; s. of William Brannon Walker and Etta May Bole; m. Gayle Mendelssohn 1937; ed. Univ. of California, and Univ. of Southern California.

Mem. Technical Staff Bell Telephone Laboratories, New York City 27-32; poet and writer on American-Indian lore and early Californian history; also lecturer.

Leisure interests: collecting and researching Western Americana, conservation, exploring High Sierra Nevada.

Publs. *Quatrains* (verse), *Muse, American Lyric Poetry, Sierra Prologue, Poets on Parade, Poetry Digest, The Winged Word, Mission Sonnets, Francisco Garces, Man and Missionary, Pioneer Padre, The Manly Story, Judas on the Kern, Sierra Sonnets, Last Gunmen, Freeman Junction, Walker Pass, Borax Smith: an Evaluation, Kern River Vignettes, The Rough and the Righteous, High Choice* (verse), *Vigor* (verse), *Haiku and Camera, West From Manhattan, The Prospectors* (verse), *The Pageant* (verse).

P.O. Box 37, Kernville, Calif. 93238, U.S.A.

Telephone: 376-6296.

Walker, Charles Edward, M.B.A., PH.D.; American economist; b. 24 Dec. 1923, Graham, Tex.; s. of Pinkney Clay Walker and Sammye McCombs Walker; m. Harmolyn Hart 1949; one s. one d.; ed. Univs. of Tex. and Pa.

Pilot, U.S.A.F. World War II; Instructor in Finance and later Asst. and Assoc. Prof., Univ. of Tex. 47-54; Assoc. Economist, Fed. Reserve Bank of Phila. 53-54; Economist and Special Asst. to Pres. of the Repub. Nat. Bank of Dallas 55-56; Vice-Pres. and Financial Economist, Fed. Reserve Bank of Dallas 58-61; Asst. to the Sec. of the Treas. 59-61; Exec. Vice-Pres., American Bankers' Asscn. 61-69; Under-Sec. of the Treas. 69-72; Deputy Sec. of the Treas. 72-73; Chair. President's Advisory Council on Minority Enterprise, American Council for Capital Formation; Vice-Chair. Joint Council on Econ. Educ.; Hon. LL.D., Ashland Coll. 70.

Leisure interests: small craft flying, golf, music.
Publs. *The Banker's Handbook* 66 (co-editor); numerous articles in economic and other journals.
1661 Crescent Place, N.W. Washington, D.C. 20009, U.S.A.
Telephone: 202-232-7470 (Home).

Walker, Sir (Charles) Michael, K.C.M.G.; British diplomatist; b. 22 Nov. 1916, Simla, India; s. of late Col. C. W. G. Walker and Mrs. Walker; m. Enid Dorothy McAdam 1945; one s. one d.; ed. Charterhouse, and New Coll., Oxford.
Army service 39-45; Dominions Office 47-49; First Sec. British Embassy, Washington 49-51; Office of High Commr., Calcutta and New Delhi 52-55; Establishment Officer Commonwealth Relations Office 55-58; Imperial Defence Coll. 58-59; Asst. Under-Sec. of State and Dir. of Establishments and Org., Commonwealth Relations Office 59-62; High Commr. in Ceylon 62-65, in Malaysia 66-71; Sec. to Overseas Devt. Admin., Foreign and Commonwealth Office 71-73; High Commr. in India 74-.
Leisure interests: gardening, fishing, golf.
British High Commission, Shantipath, Chanakyapuri, New Delhi, India; Home: 40 Bourne Street, London, S.W.1, England.

Walker, Daniel, J.D.; American state governor; b. 6 Aug. 1922, San Diego, Calif.; m. Roberta Dowse 1947; three s. four d.; ed. U.S. Naval Acad. of Northwestern Univ.
Administrative Aide to Gov. Adlai E. Stevenson II (Illinois) 52; with Hopkins, Sutter, Owen, Mulroy, Wentz and Davis (law firm) 53-66; Vice-Pres. and Gen. Counsel, Marcor and Vice-Pres., Gen. Counsel and Dir. Montgomery Ward & Co. 66-71; Pres. Chicago Crime Comm. 68-69; Gov. of Illinois 73-; Hon. D.Hum.Litt. (Carroll Coll.) and several awards for distinguished service.
Leisure interests: hunting, tennis.
Publs. *Spotlights on Organized Crime, Rights in Conflict, Military Law* (Textbook).
State Capitol, Springfield, Ill., U.S.A.

Walker, Sir (Edward) Ronald, C.B.E., M.A., PH.D., LITT.D., D.SC.(ECON.); Australian economist and diplomatist; b. 26 Jan. 1907, Cobar; s. of Frederick T. Walker; m. Louise Donckers 1933; one s. one d.; ed. Univ. of Sydney and Cambridge Univ.
Lecturer in Economics, Univ. of Sydney 27-38; Prof. of Economics, Univ. of Tasmania 39-46; Economic Adviser, N.S.W. Treasury 38-39, Govt. of Tasmania 39-42; Deputy Dir.-Gen. Australian Dept. of War Organisation of Industry 42-45; Economic Counsellor for Europe and Counsellor, Australian Embassy, Paris 45-50; Exec. mem. Australian Nat. Security Resources Board 50-52; Ambassador to Japan 52-55, to U.N. 56-59, and Australian Rep. on the Security Council 56-57; Chair. UNESCO Exec. Board 47-48, Pres. UNESCO Gen. Conf. 49; Chair. U.N. Experts on Full Employment 49; Australian Rep. on Disarmament Comm. 56-58, on Econ. and Social Council 62-64 (Pres. 64), Advisory Cttee. on Application of Science and Technology 64; Amb. to France 59-68, to Fed. Repub. of Germany 68-71, to OECD 71-73; Adviser to Govt. on Multinat. Corpns. 73.
Publs. *An Outline of Australian Economics* 31, *Australia in the World Depression* 33, *Money* (co-author) 35, *Unemployment Policy* 36, *War-time Economics* 39, *From Economic Theory to Policy* 42, *The Australian Economy in War and Reconstruction* 47, *National and International Measures for Full Employment* (in collab.) 50.
1 rue de Longchamp, Paris 16e, France.

Walker, Herbert John; New Zealand chartered accountant and politician; b. 2 June 1919, Rangiora; s. of Robert J. Walker and Margaret J. Johnston; m. Phyllis Tregurtha 1942; three s.

Accountant, Lincoln Agricultural Coll. 54-60; Lincoln Coll. Board of Govs. 60-70; Pres. Canterbury Trustee Savings Bank 69; mem. Parl. 60-; Minister of Tourism, Minister of Broadcasting 69-72, also Postmaster-Gen. Feb.-Dec. 72; Minister of Social Welfare Dec. 75-; Order of St. Lazarus of Jerusalem.
Leisure interest: community activities.
Ministry of Social Welfare, Wellington; 36 Jennifer Street, Christchurch, New Zealand.
Telephone: 49-090 (Wellington); 515703 (Christchurch).

Walker, Sir H(orace) Alan, Kt.; British brewing executive; m.; one s. two d.
Managing Dir., United Molasses until 56; Chief Exec. Mitchells and Butlers 56-61, Bass Mitchells and Butlers 61-64, Chair. and Chief Exec. 64-67; Chair. Bass Charrington Ltd. 67-76, Pres. 76-; Chair. Thomas Cook Feb. 76-; Dir. Eagle Star Insurance Co. Ltd., Staplegreen Insurance Holdings Ltd., Standard Broadcasting Corpn. (U.K.) Ltd., etc.; part-time mem. and Chair. Western Region, British Rail Board; fmr. Chair. Fed. of Commonwealth Chambers of Commerce.
Leisure interests: opera and ballet.
7 Grosvenor Gardens, London, SW1H 0BW, England.
Telephone: 01-834-3121.

Walker, John, B.A.; American art museum director; b. 24 Dec. 1906, Pittsburgh, Pa.; s. of Hay and Rebekah (Friend) Walker; m. Lady Margaret Gwendolen Mary Drummond 1937; one s. one d.; ed. Harvard Univ., and with Berenson in Florence.
Assoc. in charge of Fine Arts, American Acad. in Rome 35-39; Chief Curator, Nat. Gallery of Art, Washington 39-69, and Dir. 56-69; Trustee, American Fed. of Arts, Nat. Trust for Historic Preservation, A. W. Mellon Educational & Charitable Trust, Wallace Foundation; mem. Advisory Council, Inst. of Fine Arts of New York Univ.; mem. Board of Advisers of Dumbarton Oaks, Art Advisory Panel, British Nat. Trust, White House Historical Asscn.; Hon. D.F.A. (Tufts, Brown Univs., La Salle Coll.); Hon. D.Litt. (Notre Dame, Washington and Jefferson Univs.), and other hon. degrees; Officier de la Légion d'Honneur.
Leisure interests: chess, bridge.
Publs. *A Guide to the Gardens and Villas of Italy* (with Amey Aldrich) 38; edited: *Great American Paintings from Smibert to Bellows 1729-1924* (with Macgill James) 43, *Masterpieces of Painting from the National Gallery of Art* (with Huntington Cairns) 44, *Great Paintings from the National Gallery of Art* (with Huntington Cairns) 52; *Paintings from America* 51, *Bellini and Titian at Ferrara* 56, *The National Gallery of Art, Washington* 56, *Treasures from the National Gallery of Art* (with Huntington Cairns) 62, *The National Gallery of Art, Washington. D.C.* 63, *Pageant of Painting* 66, *Self-Portrait with Donors* 74.
4th Floor, 1729 H Street, N.W., Washington, D.C. 20006, U.S.A.
Telephone: 298-8064.

Walker, John Charles, M.S., PH.D.; American plant pathologist; b. 6 July 1893, Racine, Wis.; m. 1st 1920 (wife died 1966), 2nd 1966; one s.; ed. Univ. of Wisconsin.
Asst. in Plant Pathology, Univ. of Wisconsin 14-17, Instr. 19, Asst. Prof. 19-25, Assoc. Prof. 25-28, Prof. 28-64, Prof. Emer. 64-; Scientific Asst., U.S. Dept. of Agriculture 17-19, Asst. Pathologist 19-25, Agent 25-45, Collaborator 45-; mem. Nat. Acad. of Sciences, American Phytopathological Soc., Botanical Soc. of America, American Soc. of Naturalists; E.C. Stakman Award (Univ. of Minn.) 72.
Leisure interests: bowling, travel.
Publs. *Diseases of Vegetable Crops* 52, *Plant Pathology* 50 (3rd edn. 69).
14016 North Newcastle Drive, Sun City, Arizona 85351, U.S.A.
Telephone: 977-3788.

Walker, Rt. Hon. Peter Edward, P.C., M.B.E., M.P.; British businessman and politician; b. 25 March 1932; s. of Sydney and Rose Walker; m. Tessa Joan Pout 1969; two s. one d.; ed. Latymer Upper School.

Chair. Rose, Thomson, Young and Co. Ltd. (Lloyd's Brokers) 56-70; Deputy Chair. Slater Walker Securities Ltd. 64-70; Dir. Adwest Ltd. 63-70; mem. Lloyd's 69-75; Parl. candidate for Dartford 55 and 59, M.P. for Worcester 61-; mem. Nat. Exec. of Conservative Party 56-; Nat. Chair. Young Conservatives 58-60; mem. Conservative Commonwealth Council Gen. Cttee. 60; Parl. Private Sec. to Leader of House of Commons 63-64; Opposition Spokesman Finance and Economics 64-66, Transport 66-68, Housing and Local Govt. 68-70; Minister of Housing and Local Govt. June-Oct. 70; Sec. of State for the Environment 70-72, for Trade and Industry 72-74; Opposition Spokesman on Trade and Industry March-June 74, Defence June 74-Feb. 75; Conservative.

House of Commons, London, S.W.1; Home: Martin Court, Martin Husingtree, Droitwich, Worcestershire, England.

Walker, Wilbert A.; American accountant; ed. Tarentum and Irwin public schools, Univ. of Pittsburgh.

Junior Accountant, Ernst and Ernst 34-39; Sales and System Staff, Int. Business Machines Corpn. 40; joined U.S. Steel Corpn. 41, Vice-Pres. Accounting, Dir. Carnegie-Illinois Steel Corpn. 49, U.S. Steel Corpn. 51, Vice-Pres., Comptroller 56, Admin. Vice-Pres., Comptroller 59, Exec. Vice-Pres., Comptroller 67, Dir. 68-, Chair. Finance Cttee. 70, Pres. 73-; mem. Financial Execs. Inst., American Inst. of Accountants, Pa. Inst. of Certified Accountants and others.

Publ. co-author *Industrial Internal Auditing* 51.
U.S. Steel Corporation, 600 Grant Street, Pittsburgh, Pa. 15230, U.S.A.

Walkup, William Edmondson; American business executive; b. 31 May 1918, Nashville, Tenn.; s. of John Pegram and Marion (Edmondson) Walkup; m. Dorothy Elizabeth Sanborn 1939; two s. one d.; ed. Univ. of Calif. at Los Angeles and Nat. Univ. of Mexico.

Mail Clerk, Signal Oil and Gas Co. (later named The Signal Companies, Inc.) 39, at Crude Oil Dept., Huntington Beach 43-48, Admin. Asst. to Pres. 48-55, Controller 55-58, Dir. 55-, Vice-Pres. Finance 58-62, Group Vice-Pres.-Staff 62-64, Senior Exec. Vice-Pres. Jan. 64-68, Exec. Vice-Pres. and Vice-Chair. The Signal Cos., Inc. April 68-69, Exec. Vice-Pres. and Chair. of the Board April 69-; Dir. The Garrett Corpn., Mack Trucks, Inc., UOP Inc.

Leisure interests: golf, reading, gardening.
The Signal Companies, Inc., 9665 Wilshire Boulevard, Beverly Hills, Calif. 90212; Home: 1140 Brooklawn Drive, Los Angeles, Calif. 90024, U.S.A.
Telephone: 213-278-7400 (Office).

Wall, Baron (Life Peer), cr. 76, of Coombe in Greater London; **John Wall,** Kt., O.B.E., C.I.E.E., F.B.I.M., C.I.E.R.E.; British computers executive; b. 15 Feb. 1913, London; s. of Harry A. F. and Marie Wall; m. Gladys E. Wright 1939; two s. (twins) one d.; ed. Wandsworth School and London School of Econs.

With O. T. Falk & Co., merchant bankers 33; Ministry of Food 39, Under-Sec. 46; Deputy Head, Finance Dept., Unilever Ltd. 52, Head Org. Div. 56; Dir. Electric and Musical Industries 58, Man. Dir. 60; Deputy Chair. Post Office Board 66; Chair. Int. Computers (Holdings) Ltd. and Int. Computers Ltd. 68-72; Chair. Burrup Mathieson Ltd. 73-; Dir. Laporte Industries Ltd. 68-, Exchange Telegraph (Holdings) Ltd. 72-, Grundy (Teddington) Ltd. 72-; Dir. and Deputy Chair. Data Recording Instruments Ltd. 74-; Fellow

Royal Statistical Soc., Assoc. mem. Operational Research Soc.; Officer, Order of Orange-Nassau.
Leisure interest: golf.
Wychwood, Coombe End, Kingston-upon-Thames, Surrey, England.

Wall, Frederick Theodore, B.CHEM., PH.D.; American physical chemist; b. 14 Dec. 1912, Chisholm, Minn.; s. of Peter Wall and Fanny Rauhala Wall; m. Clara Vivian 1940; two d.; ed. Univ. of Minn.

Instructor to Prof. of Chem., Univ. of Ill. 37-64, Dean of Graduate Coll. 55-63; Prof. of Chem., Univ. of Calif. at Santa Barbara 64-66, Vice-Chancellor Research 65-66; Vice-Chancellor Graduate Studies and Research, and Prof. of Chem., Univ. of Calif. at San Diego 66-69; Editor *Journal of Physical Chemistry* 65-69; Exec. Dir. of American Chem. Soc. 69-72; Prof. of Chem., Rice Univ. 72-; Chair. Board of Trustees, Universities Space Research Asscn. 69-73, Vice-Chair. Council of Insts. 73-74, Chair. 74-75; Fellow American Acad. of Arts and Sciences; mem. Nat. Acad. of Sciences; Corresp. mem. Finnish Chemical Soc.; American Chemical Soc. Award in Pure Chem. 45, Univ. of Minn. Outstanding Achievement Award 59.

Publs. *Chemical Thermodynamics* 58, (3rd edn. 74); numerous scientific articles on statistics of macromolecular configurations, rates of chemical reactions, and polymeric electrolytes.
Department of Chemistry, Rice University, Houston, Texas 77001, U.S.A.
Telephone: (713) 527-8101.

Wallace, Bruce, PH.D.; American professor of genetics; b. 18 May 1920, McKean, Pa.; s. of George E. and Rose Paterson Wallace; m. Miriam Covalla 1945; one s. one d.; ed. Columbia Coll. and Columbia Univ.

Research Assoc., Dept. of Genetics, Carnegie Inst. of Washington 47-49; Geneticist, later Asst. Dir., Biological Laboratory, Cold Spring Harbour, N.Y. 49-58; Assoc. Prof., Cornell Univ. 58-61, Prof. of Genetics 61-; mem. Nat. Acad. of Sciences 70-72, American Acad. of Arts and Sciences.

Publs. *Radiation, Genes, and Man* (with Th. Dobzhansky) 59, *Adaptation* (with A. M. Srb) 61, *Chromosomes, Giant Molecules and Evolution* 66, *Topics in Population Genetics* 68, *Genetic Load* 70, *Essays in Social Biology* 72.
416 Mitchell Street, Ithaca, N.Y. 14850, U.S.A.
Telephone: 607-273-7895.

Wallace, Dan(iel Philip), B.A., M.A.; Canadian government officer; b. 27 Sept. 1910; m. Frances Godsoe 1954; one s.; ed. Dalhousie Univ., Halifax, Nova Scotia, Oxford Univ. and Harvard Univ.

Associate Prof. of English, St. Francis Xavier Univ., Nova Scotia 36-38; Sec. Nat. Film Board, Ottawa 42-47; Exec. Asst. to Minister, Dept. of Nat. Health and Welfare, Ottawa 47-54; Chief Sec. Dept. of Nat. Defence, Ottawa 54-56; Exec. Officer to Prime Minister 57; Dir. of Travel and Information, Province of Nova Scotia, Halifax 58-61; Asst. Dir. Canadian Govt. Travel Bureau, Ottawa 61-65, Dir. 65-73; Gen. Dir. Canadian Govt. Office of Tourism 73-75; retd.
1823 Beattie Avenue, Ottawa, Ont., Canada.

Wallace, DeWitt; American publisher; b. 12 Nov. 1889; m. Lila Bel Acheson 1921; ed. California Univ. With Webb publishing Co. 11-15, Brown and Bigelow 16; sergeant in U.S. Army 17-19; Founder-Editor *Reader's Digest* 21-65, Chair. and majority shareholder 21-73, now Dir.
Leisure interests: collecting paintings (particularly French impressionists).
Byram Lake Road, Mount Kisco, N.Y., U.S.A.

Wallace, Doreen (Mrs. D. E. A. Rash), M.A.; British writer; b. 18 June 1897, Lorton, Cumberland; d. of R. B. A. Wallace and Mary Elizabeth Peebles; m.

Rowland H. Rash 1922; one *s.* two *d.*; ed. Malvern Girls' Coll., and Somerville Coll., Oxford.
Fmr. teacher; anti-tithe publicist; novelist and reviewer.
Leisure interests: painting, gardening, stirring up politics.
Publs. *Esques* (with E. F. A. Geach) 18, *A Little Learning, The Gentle Heart, The Portion of the Levites, Creatures of an Hour, Even Such is Time, The Tithe War* 33, *Barnham Rectory* 34, *Latter Howe* 35, *Going to Sea* 36, *Old Father Antic* 37, *The Faithful Compass* 37, *The Time of Wild Roses* 38, *A Handful of Silver* 39, *East Anglia* 39, *English Lakeland* 40, *The Spring Returns* 40, *Green Acres* 41, *Land from the Waters* 44, *Carlotta Green* 44, *The Noble Savage* 45, *Billy Potter* 46, *Willow Farm* 48, *How Little We Know* 49, *Only One Life* 50, *In a Green Shade* 50, *Root of Evil* 52, *Sons of Gentlemen* 53, *The Younger Son* 54, *Daughters* 55, *The Interloper* 56, *The Money Field* 57, *Forty Years On* 58, *Richard and Lucy* 59, *Mayland Hall* 60, *Lindsay Langton and Wives* 61, *Woman with a Mirror* 63, *The Mill Pond* 66, *Ashbury People* 68, *The Turtle* 69, *Elegy* 70, *An Earthly Paradise* 71, *A Thinking Reed* 73, *Changes and Chances* 75.
Manor House, Wortham, Diss, Norfolk, England.
Telephone: Diss 2763.

Wallace, George Corley; American lawyer and politician; b. 25 Aug. 1919; *m.* 1st Lurleen Wallace (died 1968), 2nd Cornelia Ellis Snively 1971; ed. Univ. of Alabama.
Former state judge, Alabama; fmr. mem. Alabama State Legislature; Gov. of Alabama 63-67, 71-; candidate for Pres. American Ind. Party 68; shot and wounded in assassination attempt 15 May 72; Order of Lafayette Freedom Award 73; Democrat.
State Capitol Building, Montgomery, Ala. 36104; and 1142 S. Perry Street, Montgomery, Alabama, U.S.A.

Wallace, Walter Wilkinson, C.B.E., D.S.C.; British overseas administrator; b. 23 Sept. 1923, Edinburgh; *s.* of late Walter W. Wallace and of Helen M. Douglas; *m.* Susan Blanche Parry 1955; one *s.* one *d.*; ed. George Heriot's School, Edinburgh.
Captain, Royal Marines 42-46; Asst. District Commr., Sierra Leone 48-54; Principal, Colonial Office 55-57; District Commr., Sierra Leone 57-61; Provincial Commr. 61, Devt. Sec. 62-64; Establishment Sec., Bahamas 64-67; Sec. to the Cabinet, Bermuda 68-73; H.M. Commr., Anguilla 73; Gov. of British Virgin Islands 74-.
Leisure interest: golf.
Government House, Tortola, British Virgin Islands; Home: Becketts, Itchenor, W. Sussex, England.
Telephone: Birdham 512438 (Home).

Wallach, Eli, M.S. IN ED.; American actor; b. 7 Dec. 1915, Brooklyn, N.Y.; *m.* Anne Jackson 1948; one *s.* two *d.*; ed. Univ. of Texas, City Coll. of New York, Neighbourhood Playhouse School of Theatre.
Started theatre career 46, film career 55; Donaldson Award, Tony Award, British Film Acad. Award 56; acted in plays: *The Rose Tattoo, The Teahouse of the August Moon, Camino Real, Luv, Typists and Tiger*; films include *Baby Doll* 56, *The Line-Up* 58, *Seven Thieves* 59, *The Magnificent Seven* 60, *The Misfits* 61, *How the West Was Won* 62, *The Victors* 63, *The Moonspinners* 64, *Lord Jim* 65, *Genghis Khan* 65, *How to Steal a Million* 66, *The Good, the Bad and the Ugly* 67, *The Tiger Makes Out* 67, *Mackenna's Gold* 68, *Cinderella Liberty* 73.
Leisure interest: photography.
c/o Actors' Equity Association, 165 West 56th Street, New York, N.Y. 10036, U.S.A.

Wallenberg, Jacob; Swedish banker; b. 27 Sept. 1892, Stockholm; ed. School of Economics, Stockholm.
Asst. Man. Stockholms Enskilda Bank 18, Vice-Man. Dir. and mem. Board 20, Man. Dir. 27-46. Vice-Chair. of Board 46-50, Chair. 50-69; Chair. Förvaltnings AB

Providentia, AB Investor, Stora Kopparbergs Bergslags AB, AB Astra, Svenska Tändsticks AB; Bergvik och Ala AB; mem. Board Nobel Foundation 52-68; Chair. of Board, Knut and Alice Wallenberg Foundation 66-; Dr. h.c. (Econ.) and Dr. med. h.c.; Hon. mem. Royal Swedish Acad. of Eng. Sciences; Commdr. Grand Cross Order of Vasa, Commdr. Grand Cross Order of Polar Star, Commdr. 1st Class Order of Dannebrog (Denmark), Commdr. of White Rose of Finland, Knight Legion of Honour.
Leisure interests: yachting and shooting.
Knut och Alice Wallenbergs stiftelse, Kungsträdgårdsgatan 8, 114 47 Stockholm, Sweden.
Telephone: 22-19-00.

Wallenberg, Marcus; Swedish banker; b. 5 Oct. 1899, Stockholm; *s.* of Marcus Wallenberg and Amalia Hagdahl; *m.* 1st Dorothy Helen Mackay 1923, one *s.* one *d.*; *m.* 2nd Baroness Marianne de Geer of Leufsta 1936.
Assistant Man. Stockholms Enskilda Bank 25, Deputy Man. Dir. 27-46, Man. Dir. 46-58, Vice-Chair. 58-69, Chair. 69-71; Chair. Skandinaviska Enskilda Banken 72-; Swedish Del. trade negotiations with Great Britain 39-43, Finland 40-44, and Great Britain and U.S.A. 43-44; Chair. and Dir. of many Swedish and foreign companies; Chair. Swedish Banks Asscn. 49-51, 55-57, Industrial Inst. for Econ. and Social Research 50-75, Hon. Chair. 75-; Vice-Chair. and Chair. Fed. of Swedish Industries 59-64; Chair. Council of European Industrial Feds. 60-63, Business and Industrial Advisory Cttee. to OECD 62-64; Chair. Swedish Nat. Cttee. Int. Chamber of Commerce 51-64, Hon. Chair. 64-; Pres. Int. Chamber of Commerce 65-67; Co-Chair. ICC-UN/GATT Econ. Consultative Cttee. 69-71; mem. of Board, Knut and Alice Wallenberg Foundation and Nobel Foundation; Dr. h.c. (Royal Inst. of Technology, Stockholm and Stockholm School of Econ.).
Leisure interests: tennis, yachting, shooting.
Skandinaviska Enskilda Banken, Kungsträdgårdsgatan 8, Stockholm 16, Sweden.
Telephone: 08/22-19-00.

Waller, Ivar, PH.D.; Swedish physicist; b. 11 June 1898, Flen; *s.* of Dir. Erik Waller and Signe Frigell; *m.* Irène J. L. Glucksmann 1932; ed. Uppsala Univ.
Lecturer Uppsala Univ. 25, Prof. and Dir. Inst. for Theoretical Physics 34-64, Emeritus 64-; mem. Swedish Acad. of Sciences, Reg. Soc. Uppsala, Royal Physiographical Soc. Lund, Det Norske Videnskapsakademie, Oslo; Dr. h.c., Leiden 65.
Leisure interests: skiing, travelling.
Publ. *Theoretische Studien zur Interferenz- und Dispersionstheorie der Röntgenstrahlen* 25, various papers.
Institute for Theoretical Physics, S-75220 Uppsala; Home: Tradgardsgatan 10, S-75220 Uppsala, Sweden.
Telephone: 018-115159 (Office); 018-136075 (Home).

Waller, Sir (John) Keith, Kt., C.B.E.; Australian diplomatist; b. 19 Feb. 1914, Melbourne; *m.* Alison I. Dent 1943; two *d.*; ed. Scotch Coll., Melbourne, and Univ. of Melbourne.
Mem. Dept. of External Affairs 36-37; Personal Sec. W. M. Hughes 37-40; Second Sec. Australian Legation Chungking 41; Sec.-Gen. Australian del. San Francisco Conf. 45; First Sec. Australian Legation Rio de Janiero 45; Chargé d'Affaires 46 and First Sec. 47 Washington; Consul-Gen. Manila 48; Officer in charge Political Intelligence Division Canberra 50; External Affairs Officer, London 51; Ambassador to Thailand 57-60, to U.S.S.R. 60-62; First Asst. Sec. Dept. of External Affairs 62-64; Ambassador to U.S.A. 64-70; Head Dept. of Foreign Affairs 70-74; retd.
17 Canterbury Crescent, Deakin, A.C.T. 2600, Australia.

Waller, William; American politician; b. 21 Oct. 1926; ed. Memphis State Univ. and Univ of Mississippi.
Member law firm, Waller & Fox 52-72; Gov. of Miss.

72-76; leader of several trade missions 72-75; Chair. Tennessee-Tombigbee Waterway Devt. Authority; Co-Chair. for States of Appalachian Regional Comm.; Nat. Chair. for State Govs. in Payroll Savings Cttee. of Treasury Dept.; mem. Exec. Cttee. of Nat. Govs. Conf. 74; Democrat.

c/o State Capitol, Jackson, Miss. 39205, U.S.A.

Walling, Cheves (Thomson), PH.D.; American professor of chemistry; b. 28 Feb. 1916, Evanston, Illinois; s. of Willoughby George Walling and Frederika Christina Haskell; m. Jane Ann Wilson 1940; one s. four d.; ed. Harvard Univ. and Univ. of Chicago.

Research chemist, E. I. du Pont de Nemours and Co. 39-43, U.S. Rubber Co. 43-49; Technical Aide, Office of Scientific Research and Devt. 45; Research Supervisor, Lever Bros. Co. 49-52; Prof. of Chem., Columbia Univ. 52-70; Chair., Dept. of Chem., 63-66; Distinguished Prof. of Chem., Univ. of Utah 70; Editor *Journal of the American Soc.* 75-; mem. Nat. Acad. of Sciences, American Acad. of Arts and Sciences.

Leisure interests: skiing, sailing, photography, hiking.
Publs. numerous research publications; *Free Radicals in Solution* 57.
Department of Chemistry, Univ. of Utah, Salt Lake City, Utah, 84112; Home: 2784 Blue Spruce Drive, Salt Lake City, Utah, U.S.A.
Telephone: 801-581-8336 (Office); 801-277-7565 (Home).

Wallis, Sir Barnes (Neville), Kt., C.B.E., F.R.S., F.I.C.E.; British aeronautical engineer; b. 26 Sept. 1887, Ripley, Derbyshire; s. of Dr. and Mrs. C. Wallis; m. Mary F. Bloxam 1925; two s. two d.; ed. Christ's Hospital.

Trained as Marine Engineer with J. S. White and Co. Ltd.; Asst. Chief Designer, Vickers Ltd. 13-15; Army and R.N. A.S. 15; Chief Designer, Airship Dept., Vickers Ltd. 16-21; Chief Engineer, Airship Guarantee Co. (responsible for design and construction of R.100) 23-30; Chief Designer, Structures, Vickers Aviation Ltd. 30-37; Asst. Chief Designer, Vickers-Armstrongs Ltd. Aviation Section 37-45; Chief of Dept. of Aeronautical Research and Development, British Aircraft Corpn. Ltd., Weybridge Div. 45-71; invented geodetic construction; designed Wellington bomber; designed "skipping bomb" used to burst Moehne and Eder dams, also Grand Slam and other bombs; invented "swing-wing" aircraft, in which flight is controlled by varying the geometry of the flying surfaces; Royal Designer for Industry; R.Ae.S. Silver Medal 28, 37; Ewing Medal, I.C.E. 45; Founder's Medal, Air League 62; Albert Medal of Royal Soc. 68; Kelvin Gold Medal, Inst. of Civil Engineers 68; Royal Soc. Royal Medal 75; Hon. Fellow, Churchill Coll., Cambridge, Inst. of Science & Technology, Univ. of Manchester; Senior Fellow, Royal Coll. of Art; Hon. D.Sc. (Bristol, London, Cambridge, Loughborough, Oxford); Hon. M.I.M.E., F.S.E., F.R.Ae.S.

Leisure interests: reading, gardening, walking and many other interests.
White Hill House, Effingham, Surrey, England.
Telephone: 01-259-52027.

Walser, Martin, DR. PHIL.; German writer; b. 24 March 1927, Wasserburg/Bodensee; s. of Martin Walser and Augusta Schmid; m. Käthe Jehle 1950; four d.; ed. Theologisch-Philosophische Hochschule, Regensburg, and Univ. of Tübingen.

Writer 51-; Group 47 Prize 55, Hermann-Hesse Prize 57, Gerhart-Hauptman Prize 62, Schiller Prize 65.

Publs. short stories: *Ein Flugzeug über dem Haus* 55, *Lügengeschichten* 64; novels: *Ehen in Philippsburg* 57, *Halbzeit* 60, *Das Einhorn* 66, *Fiction* 70, *Die Gallistl'sche Krankheit* 72, *Der Sturz* 73, *Jenseits der Liebe* 76; plays: *Der Abstecher* 61, *Eiche und Angora* 62, *Überlebensgross Herr Krott* 63, *Der Schwarze Schwan* 64, *Die Zimmerschlacht* 67, *Ein Kinderspiel* 70, *Das Sauspiel* 75; essays:

Beschreibung einer Form, Versuch über Franz Kafka 61, *Erfahrungen und Leseerfahrungen* 65, *Heimatkunde* 68, *Wie und wovon handelt Literatur* 73.
7773 Nussdorf/Bodensee, Zum Hecht 32, Federal Republic of Germany.
Telephone: 4131.

Walsh, Alan, M.SC.TECH., D.SC., F.INST.P., F.A.I.P., F.A.A., F.R.S.; British research physicist; b. 19 Dec. 1916, Darwen, Lancs.; s. of Thomas Haworth Walsh and Betsy Alice Robinson; m. Audrey Dale Hutchinson 1949; two s.; ed. Darwen Grammar School and Manchester Univ.

At British Non-Ferrous Metals Research Asscn. 39-46; seconded to Ministry of Aircraft Production 43; with Commonwealth Scientific and Industrial Research Org. (C.S.I.R.O.), Australia 46-, Asst. Chief of Div. of Chemical Physics, C.S.I.R.O. 61-; Hon. mem. Soc. for Analytical Chem., Royal Soc. of New Zealand; Foreign mem. Royal Acad. of Sciences, Stockholm; Pres. Australian Inst. of Physics 68-69; Hon. D.Sc. Monash Univ.; Hon. Fellow, Chemical Soc., London 72-; Torbern Bergman Memorial Lecturer, Swedish Chem. Soc. 76; Britannica Australia Science Award 66; Royal Soc. of Victoria Medal 69; Talanta Gold Medal 69; Maurice Hasler Award, Soc. for Applied Spectroscopy (U.S.A.) 72; James Cook Medal, Royal Soc. of N.S.W. 76.

Leisure interests: gardening, golf.
Publs. numerous papers in scientific journals.
Division of Chemical Physics, Commonwealth Scientific and Industrial Research Organisation, P.O. Box 160, Clayton, Victoria 3168; Home: 11 Dendy Street, Brighton, Victoria 3186, Australia.
Telephone: 544-0633 (Office); 92-4897 (Home).

Walsh, Capt. Don, PH.D., M.S., M.A., B.S.; American naval officer; b. 1931, Berkeley, Calif.; s. of J. Don and Marta G. Walsh; m. Joan A. Betzmer 1962; one s. one d.; ed. San Diego State Coll., Texas A. & M. Univ. and U.S. Naval Acad.

Entered navy 50, submarine service 56; became Officer-in-Charge Submersible Test Group and Bathyscaph *Trieste* 59, made record dive to 35,780 ft., Jan. 60; Submarine service 62-64; at Dept. of Oceanography, Texas A. & M. Univ. 65-68; commanded submarine *Bashaw* 68-69; Scientific Liaison Officer Submarine Devt. Group One 69-70; Special Asst. to Asst. Sec. of the Navy for Research and Devt., Wash. 70-73; Research Fellow Woodrow Wilson Int. Center for Scholars 73-74; Deputy Dir. Naval Laboratories 74-; mem. American Geophysical Union, American Asscn. for Advancement of Science, U.S. Naval Inst., etc.; Dir. American Soc. for Oceanography; Legion of Merit; Gold Medals from City of Trieste and Chicago Socs. and other awards.

Leisure interests: writing, travel, sailing and flying.
Office of Naval Laboratories, Room 1062, Crystal Plaza 5, Washington, D.C. 20360; Home: 3406 Gallows Road, Annandale, Va. 22003, U.S.A.
Telephone: 3-202-692-2766 (Office); 703-573-1888 (Home).

Walston, Baron (Life Peer), cr. 61, of Newton, Cambridge; **Henry David Leonard George Walston**, J.P., M.A.; British farmer and politician; b. 6 June 1912, Cambridge; s. of Sir Charles Walston and Florence Einstein; m. Catherine Macdonald 1935; three s. two d; ed. Eton and King's Coll., Cambridge.

Research Fellow in Bacteriology, Harvard Univ. 34-35; mem. Hunts. War Agricultural Cttee. 39-45, Cambs. Agricultural Cttee. 48-50; Dir. of Agriculture, British Zone of Germany 46-47; Agricultural Adviser for Germany to Foreign Office 47-48; Counsellor of Duchy of Lancaster 48-54; Trustee Rural Industries Bureau; mem. Home Office Cttee. on Experiments on Living Animals May 63-64; Deputy Chair. Council of Royal

Commonwealth Soc. April 63-64; Parliamentary Under-Sec. of State for Foreign Affairs 64-67; Special Amb. of British Govt. at Presidential Inaugurations in Mexico 64, Colombia 66, Liberia 67; Parl. Sec., Board of Trade Jan.-Aug. 67; Crown Estate Commissioner 67-; Chair. Inst. of Race Relations 68-71; Chair. East Anglia Regional Econ. Planning Council 70-, Great Britain/East Europe Centre 74-, Centre of East Anglian Studies, Univ. of East Anglia 75-; Del. to Council of Europe 71-; mem. European Parl. 75-, Commonwealth Devt. Corpn. 75-; Labour.

Leisure interests: shooting, sailing.

Publs. *From Forces to Farming* 44, *Our Daily Bread* 52, *No More Bread* 54, *Life on the Land* (with John Mackie) 54, *Land Nationalisation, For and Against* 58, *Agriculture under Communism* 61, *The Farmer and Europe* 62, *The Farm Gate to Brussels* 70.

Town's End Spring, Thriplow, Royston, Herts.; A14 Albany, Piccadilly, London, W.1, England; Marquis Estates, St. Lucia, West Indies.
Telephone: Fowlmere (Herts.) 388.

Waltari, Mika; Finnish writer; b. 19 Sept. 1908, Helsinki; s. of Toimi Waltari and Olga Johansson; m. Marjatta Luukonen 1931; one d.; ed. Helsinki Univ.
Literary Critic *Maaseudun Tulevaisuus* 32-42, Finnish Radio 37-38; Editor *Suomen Kuvalehti* 36-38, State Information Office 39-40, 41-44; mem. Finnish Acad. 57; D.Phil. h.c. (Turku Univ.) 70; Pro Finlandia award 52, Commdr. Finnish Lion 60, etc.
Publs. *The Egyptian* 49, *Michael the Finn* 50, *The Sultan's Renegade* 51, *The Dark Angel* 53, *A Nail-Merchant at Nightfall* 55, *Moonscape* 56, *The Etruscan* 56, *The Tongue of Fire* 58, *The Secret of the Kingdom* 61, *The Tree of Dreams* 65, *The Roman* 66.
Tunturikatu 13, Helsinki 10, Finland.

Walter, William Grey, M.A., SC.D.; British neurophysiologist; b. 19 Feb. 1910, Kansas City, Mo.; s. of Karl Walter and Margaret Hardy; m. 1st Katherine Monica Ratcliffe 1933, 2nd Vivian Joan Dovey 1947, 3rd Lorraine Josephine Aldridge 1958 (divorced 1973); three s.; ed. Westminster School, and King's Coll., Cambridge.
Scientific Consultant, Burden Neurological Inst., Bristol 39-; founder and Foreign Sec. Electroencephalographical Soc. 42; co-founder Int. Fed. of Socs. for Electroencephalography and Clinical Neurophysiology (Hon. Pres.), *Electroencephalography and Clinical Neurophysiology* (co-editor) 47; mem. WHO Study Group on Psychobiological Development of the Child 53-56; co-founder and Council mem. Int. Asscn. of Cybernetics 56; mem. UNESCO Study Group for Establishment of Int. Brain Research Org. 59-60.
Leisure interests: tennis, skin diving, gliding.
Publs. *The Living Brain* 53, *Further Outlook* (*The Curve of the Snowflake*) 56; numerous papers.
20 Richmond Park Road, Flat 2, Bristol, BS8 3AP, England.
Telephone: 0272-312702.

Walters, Peter Ingram, B.COM.; British oil executive; b. 11 March 1931, Birmingham; s. of Stephen and Edna F. (née Redgate) Walters; m. Patricia Anne Tulloch 1960; two s. one d.; ed. King Edward's School, Birmingham and Univ. of Birmingham.
Served R.A.S.C. 52-54; joined BP 54, Vice-Pres. BP North America 65-67, Gen. Man. Supply and Devt. 69-70, Regional Dir. Western Hemisphere 71-72; Dir. BP Trading Ltd. 71-73, BP Chemicals Int. 72; Man. Dir. The British Petroleum Co. Ltd. Feb. 73-.
Leisure interests: golf, gardening.
10 Stormont Road, Highgate, London, N.6, England.
Telephone: 01-340-4029.

Walters, Sir Roger Talbot, K.B.E., F.R.I.B.A., F.I.-STRUCT.E.; British architect; b. 31 March 1917, Chorley

Wood, Herts.; s. of Alfred Bernard Walters; ed. Oundle School, Architectural Asscn. School of Architecture, Liverpool Univ.
Entered office of Sir E. Owen Williams 36; Directorate of Constructional Design, Ministry of Works 41-43; served in Royal Engineers 43-46; Architect, Timber Devt. Asscn. 46-49; Principal Asst. Architect, E. Region, British Railways 49-59; Chief Architect (Devt.), Directorate of Works, War Office 59-62; Deputy Dir.-Gen. Research and Devt., Ministry of Public Bldgs. and Works 62-67, Dir.-Gen. for Production 67-69, Controller Gen. 69-71; Architect and Controller of Construction Services, Greater London Council 71-.
Department of Architecture and Civic Design, Greater London Council, Room N174, The County Hall, Westminster Bridge, London, S.E.1; Home: 40 Farley Court, Allsop Place, London, N.W.1, England.
Telephone: 01-633-3515 (Office); 01-486-4128 (Home).

Walters, Maj.-Gen. Vernon Anthony; American army officer; b. 3 Jan. 1917, New York City; s. of Frederick J. and Laura (O'Connor) Walters; ed. St. Louis Gonzaga School, Paris, Stonyhurst Coll., England.
Second Lieut. U.S. Army 41, rising to rank of Lieut.-Gen., served N. Africa, Italy; mil. attaché Brazil 45-48; mil. attaché at large, Paris 48-50; Asst. to Deputy Chief of Staff SHAPE, Paris 51-56; staff asst. to Pres. Eisenhower 56-60; mem. NATO Standing group 56-60; army attaché U.S. Embassy, Rome 60-62; defence attaché U.S. Embassy, Rio de Janeiro 62-67; served Viet-Nam 67; defence attaché U.S. Embassy, Paris 67-72; Deputy Dir. CIA 72-76; interpreter to Pres. Truman, Eisenhower, Nixon; Distinguished Service Medal with oak leaf cluster, Distinguished Intelligence Medal, Legion of Merit with oak leaf cluster, Bronze Star, Air Medal (U.S.), Army Commendation, Commdr. Legion of Honour, Croix de Guerre with palms, War Cross (Brazil), Bronze Medal Valor (Italy).
2295 S. Ocean Blvd., Palm Beach, Fla. 33480, U.S.A.

Walther, Gebhardt von; German diplomatist; b. 19 Dec. 1902, Düsseldorf; m. Anneliese Gierlichs 1953; one s.; ed. Univs. of Cologne and Göttingen.
Attaché, Foreign Office, Berlin 29-32; Vice-Consul, Beirut 32-34; Consulate-Gen., Memel 34-36; Sec. Moscow 36-41; Consul Tripoli 41-43; Counsellor, Ankara 43-45; worked in German machine tool industry 45-51; Minister, Paris 51-56; Ambassador to Mexico 56-58, to Brazil 58-59; Perm. German Rep. to NATO 59-62; Amb. to Turkey 62-66, to U.S.S.R. 66-68; Exec. Vice-Pres. Deutsche Gesellschaft für Auswärtige Politik e.V. 68-.
Leisure interest: golf.
Deutsche Gesellschaft für Auswärtige Politik, 53 Bonn, Adenaueralle 133; Home: 5039 Hahnwald bei Köln, Oberbuschweg 214, Federal Republic of Germany.
Telephone: 22-00-91 (Office); Wesseling 64900 (Home).

Walton, Ernest Thomas Sinton, M.A., M.SC., PH.D.; Irish university professor; b. 6 Oct. 1903, Dungarvan, Co. Waterford; s. of Rev. John A. Walton; m. Winifred I. Wilson 1934; two s. two d.; ed. Methodist Coll., Belfast, Trinity Coll., Dublin, and Cambridge Univ.
Fellow Trinity Coll. Dublin 34-74, Fellow Emeritus 74-, Erasmus Smith's Prof. of Natural and Experimental Philosophy 46-74; awarded Hughes Medal, Royal Society (jointly with Sir John Cockcroft) 38; Nobel Prize in Physics (jointly with Sir John Cockcroft) 51, for pioneer work in the field of nuclear physics; Hon. D.Sc. (Belfast Univ. 59, Gustavus Adolphus Coll. 75).
Leisure interest: gardening.
26 St. Kevin's Park, Dartry Road, Dublin 6, Ireland.
Telephone: 971-328.

Walton, Sir William Turner, Kt., o.m.; British composer; b. 29 March 1902, Oldham; m. Susana Gil de Halton 1948; ed. Cathedral School, and Christ Church, Oxford.

Gold Medal Royal Philharmonic Soc. 47; Hon. Mus. Dr. (Oxford, Cambridge, London, Durham, Manchester, Trinity Coll., Dublin, Univ. of Ireland, Cork, Sussex); Hon. F.R.C.M., F.R.A.M.

Works include Pianoforte Quartet (Carnegie award) 18, String Quartet (unpublished) 21, *Façade* (with Edith Sitwell) 23 and 26, *Siesta* for small orchestra 26, *Portsmouth Point* 26, Sinfonia Concertante for piano and orchestra 28, Viola Concerto 29, *Belshazzar's Feast* 31, Three Songs for Soprano 32, Symphony 35, *Crown Imperial* (Coronation March) 37, *In Honour of the City of London* 37, Violin Concerto 39, *Music for Children* 40, *Scapino* (comedy overture) 41, incidental music to film *The Foreman Went to France* 42, to Gielgud production *Macbeth* 42, to Olivier's *Henry V* 44-45, *Quest* (ballet) 42, *String Quartet* 47, *Hamlet* (film) 47, Violin Sonata 49, *Orb and Sceptre* (Coronation March) 53, *Te Deum* 53, *Troilus and Cressida* 54, *Richard III* (film music) 55, *Johannesburg Overture* 56, 'Cello Concerto 56, *Partita* 57, *Anon in Love*, Second Symphony 60, *Gloria* 61, *A Song for a Lord Mayor's Table* 62, *Variations on a Theme by Hindemith* 63, *The Twelve* (anthem) 65, *Missa Brevis* 66, *The Bear* 67, *Capriccio Burlesco* 68, *Battle of Britain* (film music) 69, *Improvisations on an Impromptu of Benjamin Britten* 69, *Five Bagatelles for Guitar* 71, *Magnificat and Nunc Dimittis* 72, *Jubilate* 72, *Sonata for String Orchestra* 72, *Cantico del Sole* 74.

c/o Oxford University Press, 44 Conduit Street, London, W1R 0DE, England.

Wan Li; Chinese government official; b. Szechuan. Vice-Minister of Building Construction 52-56; Minister of Urban Construction 56-58; Sec. CCP, Peking 58-66; Vice-Mayor of Peking 58-66; criticized and removed from office during Cultural Revolution 67; Minister of Railways 75.

People's Republic of China.

Wan Waithayakon, Prince Krommun Naradhip Bongsprabandh, M.A.; Thai diplomatist and politician; b. 25 Aug. 1891, Bangkok; s. of H.R.H. Prince Naradhip Prabandhbongs and Mom Luang Tuansri Worawan; m. 1st Momchao Phibun Benchang Kitiyakara 1920, 2nd Mom Proi Suphin Bunnag 1930; one s. (deceased), one d.; ed. Marlborough Coll., Balliol Coll., Oxford, and Ecole des Sciences Politiques, Paris.

Sec. Thai Legation, Paris 17-19; Private Sec. to Minister of Foreign Affairs 19-24; Under-Sec. of State for Foreign Affairs 24-26; Minister to London 26-30; Adviser to Premier's Office and Foreign Office, Bangkok 33-46; Ambassador to U.S.A. 47-52; Permanent Del. to U.N. 47-59; Pres. U.N. Gen. Assembly 56-57, Conf. on Law of the Sea 58, 60; Minister of Foreign Affairs 52-58; Deputy Prime Minister 59-68; Rector, Thammasat Univ. 63-71; Rapporteur, Asian-African Conf., Bandung 55; Hon. D.Litt. (Chulalongkorn), Hon. D.Pol.Sc. (Thammasat), Hon. D.Law (Columbia, New York, Fairleigh Dickinson), Hon. D.C.L. (Oxford); Knight of the Most Illustrious Order of the Royal House of Chakri.

Leisure interest: word coining.

26 Soi 20, Sukhumvit Road, Bangkok, Thailand.

Telephone: 913346.

Wanamaker, Pearl Anderson, B.A.; American educator; b. 18 Jan. 1899, Wash.; d. of Nils Anderson and Johanna Hellman; m. Lemuel A. Wanamaker 1927; two s. one d.; ed. Western Washington Coll. of Education, Univ. of Washington.

Rural teacher 17-21; High School teacher 22-23, 28-41; County Supt. of Schools 23-27; mem. Wash. State House of Reps. 29, 33, 35, Wash. State Senate 37, 39; Supt. of Public Instruction. State of Wash. 41-57; Pres. Nat.

Educational Assen. 46-47; Pres. Nat. Council of Chief State School Officers 50; Gov. American Nat. Red Cross 52-55; Rep., Scholastic Magazines 59-; Chair. Task Force for Women and Girls in Educ. 73-74; Altrusa Int. Distinguished Service Award for 45-47; American Education Award 49, and Achievement Award, Women's Nat. Press Club 50, Quota Club of Seattle 51; Curator, Wash. State Historical Soc. 51-; Woman of the Year Award, Seattle B'nai B'r'ith 55; Wash. State Arts Comm. 61-67; Hon. LL.D. (Miami Univ., Ohio, Mills Coll.); Hon. L.H.D. (Columbia Univ., Smith Coll.).

Leisure interests: art, politics.

415 W. Mercer Street, Seattle, Washington 98119, U.S.A.

Telephone: AT4-7938.

Wanamaker, Sam; American actor and film and theatre director; b. 14 June 1919, Chicago, Ill.; s. of Maurice Wanamaker and Molly Bobele; m. Charlotte Holland 1940; three d.; ed. Drake Univ., Iowa, and Goodman Theatres, Chicago.

Dir. Jewish Peoples' Inst., Chicago 39-40; radio acting New York 40-41; acted in *Café Crown* 41 and *Counterattack* 42, Broadway; U.S. Army 42-45; actor and dir. 46-; Artistic Dir. New Shakespeare Theatre, Liverpool 57-59; three-picture contract with M.G.M. 68; acted in and directed *Joan of Lorraine* (Broadway) 46; acted in *My Girl Tisa* 47, *Christ in Concrete* 49, *Denning Drives North* 51; directed *Gentleman from Athens* 48, *Goodby my Fancy* 49, *Caesar and Cleopatra, Revival of Gardsman*; acted in and/or directed *Winter Journey, The Shrike, The Rainmaker, Threepenny Opera, The Big Knife, A Hatful of Rain, A View from the Bridge, Reclining Figure, Othello, The Rose Tattoo* 59, *A Far Country* 61; acted in film *Taras Bulba* 62; directed on Broadway plays *Children from Their Games* (Irwin Shaw) 62, *Case of Libel* (Louis Nizer) 63, *A Murderer Among Us* (Louis Nizer) 63; directed at Covent Garden opera *King Priam* (Tippett) 63, *Forza del Destino* (Verdi) 63; acted in film *Those Magnificent Men in their Flying Machines* 64; directed and acted in *Macbeth*, Goodman Theatre, Chicago 64; acted in film *The Spy Who Came in From the Cold* 65; directed or acted in TV films *The Defenders, For the People, Gunsmoke, The Baron* 62-66; acted in and/or directed (TV) *The Day the Fish Came Out* 66, *Warning Shot* 66, *The Eliminator* 67, and TV films *Custer, The Hawk, Lassiter, Cimmarron Strip, Court Martial, The Champions, Lancer* 66-67; director *The Chinese Visitor* 68, *The File of the Golden Goose* 68, *The Executioner* 69, *Catlow* 69-70; founder Globe Playhouse Trust and World Centre for Shakespeare Studies 70-71; producer *The Black Camels of Qashran* 72, *War and Peace* (opening production Sydney Opera House) 73, John Player Season at Bankside Globe Playhouse 72-73, Shakespeare Birthday Celebrations Southwark Cathedral 72-73; acted in films *The Law, The Spiral Staircase*, produced Dickens, Shakespeare and Bankside summer festivals 74, acted in film *The Sell Out*, directed film *Sinbad's Journey* 75, acted in film *The Voyage* 75, directed *Paradise Lost* (Penderecki), Chicago 76.

Leisure interest: art.

The Globe Playhouse, 40 Bankside, The Liberty of the Clink, Southwark, London, S.E.1, England.

Wanchoo, Kailas Nath; Indian judge; b. 25 Feb. 1903, Mandsaur (Madhya Pradesh); s. of Pandit Pirthi Nath and Bishanpati Wanchoo; m. Mohini (d. of Pandit Brijmohau Nath Zutshi) 1928; one s. two d.; ed. Pandit Pirthi Nath High School, Kanpur, Muir Central Coll., Allahabad, and Wadham Coll., Oxford.

Magistrate and Judge, United Provinces (later Uttar Pradesh) 26-51; Judge, Allahabad High Court 47-51; Chief Justice, Rajasthan High Court 51-58; Judge, Supreme Court of India 58-67; Chief Justice of India 67-68; Chair. Railway Accidents Inquiry Cttee.,

Ministry of Railways 68-69; Chair. Board of Arbitration (JCM) Ministry of Labour 68-75, Direct Taxes Inquiry Cttee., Ministry of Finance 70-71, Comm. of Inquiry into Corruption Charges, W. Bengal 74-75; Kashmiri Pandit Benefit Trust, New Delhi; Hon. LL.D. (Agra Univ.).
Leisure interests: gardening, reading.
6 Friends Colony, New Delhi 14, India.
Telephone: 630504 (Home).

Wand, Rt. Rev. and Rt. Hon. (John) William (Charles), K.C.V.O., P.C., D.D., D.LITT.; British ecclesiastic; b. 25 Jan. 1885, Grantham, Lincs.; s. of A. J. H. Wand and E. A. O. Turner; m. Amy Agnes Wiggins 1911; one s. (deceased) one d.; ed. King's School, Grantham, St. Edmund Hall, Oxford, and Bishop Jacob Hostel, Newcastle-on-Tyne.
Curate of Benwell 08-11, Lancaster 11-14; Vicar-Choral of Sarum 14-19; Lecturer Sarum Theological Coll. 14-20; Tutor 20-24; Temporary Chaplain to the Forces 15-19; Hon. Chaplain 19-22 and 25-; Chaplain to the R.A.F. 22-25; Vicar of St. Mark, Sarum 19-25; Fellow, Dean, and Tutor Oriel Coll. Oxford 25-34; Lecturer in Theology St. Edmund Hall 28-31; Univ. Lecturer in Church History 31-34; Archbishop of Brisbane and Metropolitan of Queensland 34-43; Senior Chaplain (Anglican), 1st Military District, Australian Military Forces 35-43; Bishop of Bath and Wells 43-45; Bishop of London 45-55, Canon Residentiary of St. Paul's 56-69; Dean of the Chapels Royal 45-55; Hon. Chaplain R.N.V.R. 47-; Editor *Church Quarterly Review* 56-68; Hon. Fellow St. Edmund Hall, Oxford 38, Oriel Coll. 41, King's Coll. London 56; Hon. D.D. (Oxford, London), S.T.P. (Columbia), S.T.D. (Toronto), D.Litt. (Ripon, U.S.A.), D.D. (W. Ontario).
Leisure interests: reading and writing.
Publs. *The Golden String* 26, *The Development of Sacramentalism* 28, *History of the Modern Church* 30, *The Old Faith and the New Age* 33, *History of the Early Church* 35, *New Testament Letters* 44, *God and Goodness* 47, *The Spirit of Church History* 48, *The Latin Doctors* 48, *The Authority of the Scriptures* 49, *White of Carpentaria* 49, *The Greek Doctors* 50, *The High Church Schism* 51, *What Paul Said* 52, (Editor) *The Anglican Communion* 48, (Joint Author) *Oxford and the Groups* 34, *Westminster Commentary* 34, *First-Century Christianity* 37, *European Civilisation* 37, *Union of Christendom* 38, *The Four Councils* 51, *What the Church of England Stands For* 51, *The Second Reform* 53, *The Mystery of the Kingdom* 53, *The Life of Jesus Christ* 55, *The Four Great Heresies* 55, *Seven Steps to Heaven* 56, *The Road to Happiness* 57, *True Lights* 58, *The Church Today* 60, *The Anglican Communion in History and Today* 61, *Doctors and Councils* 62, *St. Augustine's City of God* 63, *The Atonement* 63, *The Temptation of Jesus* 65, *Reflections on the Collects* 65, *Reflections on the Epistles* 66, *Transfiguration* 67, *What St. Paul Really Said* 69, *Reflections on the Gospels* 69, *Christianity: A Historical Religion?* 71, *Letters on Preaching* 74.
Homes of St. Barnabas, Lingfield, Surrey, England.
Telephone: Dormans Park 260.

Wandel, Paul, DR. h.c.; German journalist and diplomatist; b. 16 Feb. 1905.
Engineer; mem. Communist Party 23; Pres. Communist Group, Mannheim City Council; Chief Ed. Communist *Deutsche Volks-Zeitung* after 45; Minister of Education; fmr. Sec. Central Cttee. Socialist Unity Party (S.E.D.); Ambassador to People's Republic of China 58-60; Deputy Minister of Foreign Affairs 60-63; Pres. Liga für Völkerfreundschaft 64-.
108 Berlin, Thälmannplatz 8-9, German Democratic Republic.

Wang Chen; Chinese government official; b. 1909, Liuyang, Hunan.
Regimental Political Commissar 30; Alt. mem. 7th Cen.

Cttee. of CCP 45; Commdr. of 1st Army Corps, 1st Field Army, People's Liberation Army 49; Commdr. Sinkiang Mil. Region, PLA 50; Minister of State Farms and Land Reclamation 56; mem. 8th Cen. Cttee. of CCP 56, 9th Cen. Cttee. 69, 10th Cen. Cttee. 73; Vice-Premier of State Council 75.
People's Republic of China.

Wang Cheng; Chinese government official.
Vice-Minister of Posts and Telecommunications 49-54; Commdr. People's Liberation Army Signal Corps 59; Minister Fourth Ministry of Machine Building 63-.
People's Republic of China.

Wang Chia-tao; Chinese party official.
Major-General, Commdr. Heilungkiang Mil. District, People's Liberation Army 64-; Vice-Chair. Heilungkiang Revolutionary Cttee. 67, Chair. 70; Alt. mem. 9th Cen. Cttee. of CCP 69; First Sec. CCP Heilungkiang 71; Alt. mem. 10th Cen. Cttee. of CCP 73.
People's Republic of China.

Wang Chien; Chinese party official.
Deputy Sec.-Gen. Rural Work Dept., CCP Cen. Cttee. 55; visited Eastern Europe 55; Sec. CCP Shansi 57, Second Sec. 66-67, Sec. 73, First Sec. 75-; Gov. of Shansi 65-67; Alt. mem. 10th Cen. Cttee. CCP 73; Vice-Chair. Shansi Revolutionary Cttee. 73, Chair. 75-.
People's Republic of China.

Wang Huai-hsiang; Chinese party official.
Political Commissar 3rd Field Army 49; Deputy Political Commissar Kirin Mil. District, People's Liberation Army 64; Chair. Kirin Revolutionary Cttee. 68; mem. 9th Cen. Cttee. of CCP 69; First Sec. CCP Kirin 71; mem. 10th Cen. Cttee. of CCP 73.
People's Republic of China.

Wang Hung-wen; Chinese party official; b. 1937.
Worker Shanghai No. 17 Cotton Textile Mill; Founded Shanghai Workers Revolutionary Rebel Gen. H.Q. during Cultural Revolution 67; Vice-Chair. Shanghai Revolutionary Cttee. 68; Sec. CCP Shanghai 71; Political Commissar Shanghai Garrison District, People's Liberation Army 72; Vice-Chair. CCP 73-; mem. Standing Cttee. of Politburo, CCP 73.
People's Republic of China.

Wang Kuo-chan; Chinese diplomatist; b. 1911.
Former Deputy to Third Nat. People's Congress in Peking; fmr. Amb. to German Democratic Repub. and Poland; Pres. Chinese People's Asscn. for Friendship with Foreign Countries; Amb. to Australia 73-.
Embassy of the People's Republic of China, Canberra, Australia.

Wang Ling, M.A., PH.D.; Chinese historian; b. 23 Dec. 1918, Nangtung, Kiang Su Province; s. of C. C. Wang; m. Ruth Burkitt 1961; two s.; ed. National Central Univ., China, and Trinity Coll., Cambridge.
Junior Research Fellow, Inst. of History and Philology, Academia Sinica 41-44; Senior Lecturer, Nat. Fu-tan Univ. 44-45. Assoc. Prof. 45-46; Assistant to J. Needham, F.R.S., Cambridge Univ. 46-57; Visiting Lecturer, Cambridge Univ. 53; Snr. Lecturer Canberra Univ. Coll., Melbourne Univ. 57-59; Assoc. Fellow, Nat. Acad. of Science, Academia Sinica 55-57; Senior Lecturer Univ. Coll., Australian Nat. Univ., Canberra 60-61, Assoc. Prof. 61-63; Professorial Fellow, Inst. of Advanced Studies, Australian Nat. Univ. 63-; Visiting Prof. of Chinese Literature, Cornell Univ. 65; Visiting Prof. of Chinese Classics, Wisconsin Univ. 65-66; mem. Comm. for the History of the Social Relations of Science of the Int. Union for the History of Science 48-56; corresp. mem. Int. Acad. of History of Science, Paris 64-.
Publs. *Science and Civilisation in China* (asst. to Dr. J. Needham, F.R.S.) Vol. I 54, Vol. II 56, Vol. III 59, Vol. IVa 62, Vol. IVb 64, Vol. IVc 71, *Heavenly Clockwork*

(asst. to Dr. J. Needham) 60, *A Study on the Chiu Chang Suan Shu* 62.
Institute of Advanced Studies, Australian National University, Canberra, A.C.T. 2600, Australia.
Telephone: Canberra 493171.

Wang Liu-sheng; Chinese party official.
Major-General People's Liberation Army, Shanghai 64; Deputy Political Commissar Nanking Mil. Region, PLA 66; Alt. mem. 9th Cen. Cttee. of CCP 69; First Political Commissar Wuhan Mil. Region, PLA 72; Second Sec. CCP Hupeh 72; Alt. mem. 10th Cen. Cttee. of CCP 73.
People's Republic of China.

Wang Pi-ch'eng; Chinese army officer; b. 1912, Hunan.
Deputy Commdr. Chekiang Mil. District, People's Liberation Army 49, Commdr. 51; Maj.-Gen. PLA 55; Commdr. Shanghai Garrison District, PLA 55-61; Deputy Commdr. Nanking Mil. Region, PLA 61; Deputy Commdr. Kunming Mil. Region, PLA 69, Commdr. 72-; Second Sec. CCP Yunnan 71; First Vice-Chair. Yunnan Revolutionary Cttee. 72; mem. 10th Cen. Cttee. of CCP 73.
People's Republic of China.

Wang Shang-jung; Chinese army officer; b. 1906, Shansi; ed. Sun Yat-sen Univ., Moscow.
On Long March 34; Div. Commdr., Red Army 36; Commdr. Tsinghai Mil. District 49; Lt.-Gen. 55; Alt. mem. 8th Cen. Cttee. of CCP 58; Dir. Combat Dept., People's Liberation Army Gen. Staff H.Q. 59-66; criticized and removed from office during Cultural Revolution 67; Deputy Chief of Gen. Staff, PLA 74.
People's Republic of China.

Wang Shou-tao; Chinese communications specialist; b. 1907, Liu-yang, Hunan; ed. State Agriculture School, Changsha, Peasant Movt. Training Inst.
Joined CCP 25; Sec. CCP Hunan-Hopei-Kiangsu Special Cttee. 28; revolutionary work in Shanghai 30-32; Political Commissar on Long March 34; Alt. mem. 7th Cen. Cttee. of CCP 45; Gov. of Hunan 50-52; Vice-Minister of Communications 52-54; Dir. Sixth Staff Office, State Council 54-58; mem. 8th Cen. Cttee. of CCP 56; Minister of Communications 58-64; Sec. Cen.-South Bureau, CCP 64-67; Vice-Chair. Kwangtung Revolutionary Cttee. 68-; mem. 9th Cen. Cttee. of CCP 69; Sec. CCP Kwangtung 71-; mem. 10th Cen. Cttee. of CCP 73.
People's Republic of China.

Wang Tung-hsing; Chinese party official.
Bodyguard of Mao Tse-tung 47; Capt. of Guards of Cen. Cttee., CCP 47-49; Capt. of Guards, Gen. Admin. Council 49-54; Vice-Minister of Public Security 55-58, 62-; Vice-Gov. of Kiangsi 58-60; Sec. CCP Kiangsi 58-60; mem. Cen. Cultural Revolution Group 67; Dir. Admin. Office of Cen. Cttee., CCP 69; Alt. mem. Politburo, 9th Cen. Cttee. of CCP 69; mem. Politburo, 10th Cen. Cttee. of CCP 73.
People's Republic of China.

Wang Yang; Chinese government official.
Minister of Seventh Ministry of Machine Building 75.
People's Republic of China.

Wang Yi; Chinese army officer.
Major-General People's Liberation Army 64; Commdr. Tientsin Garrison District, PLA 69-; Vice-Chair. Tientsin Revolutionary Cttee. 70; Sec. CCP Tientsin 71.
People's Republic of China.

Wangchuk, Jigme Singye; King (Druk Gyalpo) of Bhutan; b. 11 Nov. 1955; s. of late Druk Gyalpo Jigme Dorji Wangchuk and of Queen Ashi Kesang; ed. North Point, Darjeeling, Ugyuen Wangchuk Acad., Paro, also in England.

Crown Prince March 72; succeeded to throne 24 July 72, Crowned 2 June 74; Chair. Planning Comm. of Bhutan March 72-; C.-in-C. of Armed Forces.
Royal Palace, Thimphu, Bhutan.

Wangensteen, Owen Harding, B.A., B.S., M.D., PH.D.; American surgeon; b. 21 Sept. 1898, Lake Park, Minn., s. of Owen Wangensteen (Norwegian) and Hannah Hanson; m. 1st Helen C. Griffin 1923; 2nd Sarah Ann Davidson 1954; two s. one d.; ed. Univ. of Minnesota.
Intern Univ. Hospital Minneapolis 22; Fellow in Medicine, Univ. of Minnesota 23; Fellow in Surgery, Mayo Clinic 24; Resident Surgeon, Univ. Hospital 25; Instructor in Surgery, Univ. of Minnesota 26, Asst. Prof. 27; Asst. Surgical Clinic and Physiological Inst., Berne 27-28; Assoc. Prof. of Surgery, Univ. of Minnesota 28, Dir. Dept. of Surgery 30-67, Prof. of Surgery 31-66, Regents' Prof. of Surgery 66-; co-Editor *Surgery* 37-70; Pres. Minn. Pathological Soc., Halsted Surgical Soc., Minn. Medical Foundation 48-54, Minn. Acad. of Medicine 53, Heart Council 54-57, American Coll. of Surgeons 59, Research Facilities Council 59, American Chapter of Int. Surgical Soc. 69-70; Consultant to U.S.P.H.S.; Hon. mem. Hellenic Surgical Soc., Athens, Norwegian Acad. of Science, Royal Coll. of Surgeons of Edinburgh, Royal College of Surgeons of Ireland, Argentine Surgical Soc.; mem. Nat. Acad. of Sciences 66-; Pres. American Surgical Asscn. 68-69; awarded Samuel D. Gross Prize Philadelphia Acad. of Surgery 35, John Scott Award 41, Alvarenga Prize Philadelphia Coll. of Medicine 49, American Cancer Soc. Award 49, Pittsburgh Surgical Soc. Award 58, Medallion and membership of French Nat. Acad. of Medicine 59, Distinguished Service Award, Univ. of Minn. 60, Passano Award 61, American Cancer Soc. Special Citation 62; corresp. mem. German Surgical Congress 60; the Outstanding Minnesotan Award 69; Quinquennial Lannelongue Prize, French Acad. of Surgery 67; Distinguished Service Award, American Medical Asscn. 68, American Surgical Asscn. 76; Hon. Fellow, Royal Coll. of Surgeons, London 62; Dr. h.c., Sorbonne 62; Hon. LL.D., Univ. of Buffalo 46; D.Sc. (Univ. of Chicago 56, St. Olav Coll. 58, Temple Univ. 61, Hamline Univ. 63).
Publs. *The Therapeutic Problem in Bowel Obstruction* 37, 42, 55, *Cancer of the Esophagus and Stomach* 51, 56, *Experimental and Clinical Journal;* publs. on therapeutic aspects of intestinal obstruction.
Office: University of Minnesota Medical School Complex, P.O. Box 610, Minneapolis, Minn. 55455; 2832 W. River Road, Minneapolis 55406, Minn., U.S.A.
Telephone: 612-373-5944 (Office); 612-729-3884.

Wankel, Felix; German research engineer; b. 13 Aug. 1902, Lahr/Schwarzwald; s. of Rudolf and Gertrud (née Heidlauff) Wankel; m. Mi Kirn; ed. Volksschule and Gymnasium.
Employed at Druckerei-Verlag, Heidelberg 21-26; partner in engineering works 27-32; worked in own research workshop in Lahr for B.M.W. (Bayrische Motorenwerke) 34-36; engaged in research and devt. work at W.V.W. (Wankel-Versuchs-Werkstätten) for R.L.M. (Air Ministry) 36-45; continued work at Technische Entwicklungsstelle, Lindau, for Goetzewerke, Borsig, N.S.U. 51-60; now Dir. TES Inst.; inventor and developer of rotary combustion engine—"Wankel-Motor"; Gold Award Verein Deutscher Ingenieure 69, Hon. Dr.Ing. Munich 69, Grosses Bundesverdienstkreuz 70, Franklin Medal, Philadelphia Inst. 71, Bavaria Order of Merit 73.
Leisure interests: reading history and poetry, architecture, protection of animals, vegetarianism, pacifism, running, rowing.
Publs. *Voraussetzungen für das Untersuchen der Kolbenringabdichtung* 41. *Kurzbericht über scheiben- und walzengesteuerte Verbrennungsmotoren* 44, *Einteilung*

der Rotationskolbenmaschinen 63 (English trans. 65); several articles in journals.

Office: Technische Forschungs- und Entwicklungsstelle der Fraunhofergesellschaft, Lindau/Bodensee, Fraunhoferstrasse 10; Home: 899 Lindau/Bodensee, Bregenzerstrasse 82, Federal Republic of Germany.

Telephone: 5277 (Office); 5953 (Home).

Wansbrough-Jones, Sir Owen Haddon, K.B.E., C.B., M.A., PH.D., F.R.I.C.; British scientist; b. 25 March 1905, Attleborough, Norfolk; s. of Arthur and Beatrice Anna Wansbrough-Jones (née Slipper); ed. Gresham's School, Holt, and Trinity Hall, Cambridge.

Chemical research Univ. of Cambridge 26-30; Berlin 31; Fellow of Trinity Hall 30-46; Asst. Tutor 32, Tutor 34, Hon. Fellow 56; Departmental Demonstrator, Dept. of Colloid Science, Cambridge 31-39; granted Emergency Comm. in Army 40; miscellaneous Gen. Staff and technical appointments 40-46; Dir. of Special Weapons and Vehicles 46; demobilized as Brig. April 46; Scientific Adviser to Army Council 46-50; Principal Dir. of Scientific Research (Defence), Ministry of Supply 51-53, Chief Scientist, Ministry of Supply 53-59; Treas. Faraday Society 49-60; Dir. Albright and Wilson Ltd. 59-65, Exec. Vice-Chair. 65-67, Chair. 67-69; Prime Warden Goldsmiths Company 67-68; mem. Council Natural Environment Research Council 68-74; Dir. British Oxygen Int. 60-76.

Leisure interests: gardening and shooting.

The Guild House, Long Stratton, Norfolk; 7 King Street, St. James's, London, S.W.1, England.

Telephone: 0508-30410 (Norfolk); 01-930-8608 (London).

Warburg, Sir Siegmund George, Kt.; British merchant banker; b. 30 Sept. 1902, Tübingen, Germany; s. of Georges Warburg and Lucie Kaulla; m. Eva Maria Philipson 1926; one s. one d.; ed. Reutlingen Gymnasium, and Urach Humanistic Seminary.

Partner, M. M. Warburg and Co., Hamburg 30-38; Dir. New Trading Co., London 38-46, Kuhn Loeb and Co., New York 56-64, S. G. Warburg and Co., London 46-69; Pres. S. G. Warburg & Co., London 70-; German Grand Cross of Merit, other decorations.

30 Gresham Street, London, E.C.2, England.

Ward, Dame Barbara, D.B.E., B.A. (Lady Jackson); British journalist and economist; b. 23 May 1914; d. of Walter and Teresa Ward; m. Commdr. (now Sir) Robert Jackson (q.v.) 1950; one s.; ed. The Convent, Felixstowe, Lycée Molière and Sorbonne Paris, Germany, and Somerville Coll., Oxford.

University Extension Lecturer 36-39; Asst. Editor of *The Economist* 40; Gov. of Sadler's Wells and Old Vic Theatres 44-53, Trustee 43-; Gov. of B.B.C. 46-50; Hon. mem. American Acad. of Arts and Sciences; mem. Pontifical Comm. for Justice and Peace; Visiting Scholar and Carnegie Fellow, Harvard Univ. 57-68, Albert Schweitzer Prof. of Int. Econ. Devt., Columbia Univ. 68-73; Pres. Int. Inst. for Environment and Devt.; hon. degrees from Fordham, Smith, Columbia, Harvard, Georgetown, Utah and Boston Univs., Canisius, Lake Forest and Kenyon Colls.; Labour.

Publs. *The International Share-Out* 38, *Turkey* 41, (part-author) *Hitler's Route to Baghdad* 39, *A Christian Basis for the Post-War World* 41, *The West at Bay* 48, *A Policy for the West* 51, *Faith and Freedom* 54, *The Interplay of East and West* 57, *Five Ideas that Change the World* 59, *India and the West* 61, *The Rich Nations and the Poor Nations* 62, *Nationalism and Ideology* 66, *Spaceship Earth* 66, *The Lopsided World* 68, *The Widening Gap* (editor) 71, *Only One Earth* 72 (with René Dubos).

c/o I. Hunter, 21 Smith Terrace, London, SW3 4DL, England.

Ward, David, C.B.E., F.R.C.M.; British (bass) opera singer; b. 3 July 1922, Dumbarton, Scotland; s. of James Ward and Catherine Bell; m. Eily V. S. Ruther-

ford 1960; ed. St. Patrick's Coll., Dumbarton and Royal Coll. of Music.

Joined Sadlers Wells Opera Company 52, Royal Opera House, Covent Garden 60; freelance singer 65-; has appeared at many of the world's major opera houses including La Scala, Milan, Vienna State Opera and Metropolitan Opera House, New York; noted for interpretation of Wagnerian roles, especially Wotan in *Der Ring der Nibelungen*; Hon. R.A.M.; Hon. LL.D. (Strathclyde Univ.).

Leisure interests: golf, swimming, theatre.

14 Clarence Terrace, Regent's Park, London, N.W.1, England.

Warde, George A.; American airline executive; m. Doris Darius; one d.; ed. Hofstra Coll. Hempstead, Univ. of Alabama.

Apprentice mechanic LaGuardia Airport 40; held various posts within American Airlines, American Overseas Airlines; joined Pan American World Airways; Man. Production Schedules and Control, American Airlines Maintenance and Engineering Center, Tulsa 60, Vice-Pres. Maintenance and Engineering; Senior Vice-Pres. Operations, American Airlines 68, Exec. Vice-Pres., Gen. Man., mem. Board 71, Pres., Chief Exec. Officer 72-74; mem. Board, Nat. Bank of Tulsa, British-American Chamber of Commerce; Flight Safety Foundation; mem. American Inst. of Aeronautics and Astronautics and many other socs.

American Airlines, Inc., 633 Third Avenue, New York, N.Y. 10017, U.S.A.

Wardhana, Ali, M.A., PH.D.; Indonesian economist and politician; b. 6 May 1928, Surakarta, Central Java; m. Renny Wardhana 53; one s. three d.; ed. Univ. of Indonesia, Jakarta and Univ. of California (Berkeley), U.S.A.

Director of Research Inst. of Economic and Social Studies 62-67; Prof. of Economics, Univ. of Indonesia 67-, Dean Faculty of Econs. 67-; Adviser to Gov. of Cen. Bank 64-68; mem. team of experts of Presidential Staff 66-68; Minister of Finance 68-; Chair. Cttee. of Board of Governors of the IMF on Reform of the Int. Monetary System and Related Issues 72-74; Grand Cross Order of Léopold II (Belgium), Grand Cross Order of Orange Nassau (Netherlands).

Leisure interests: reading, tennis, bowling, swimming.

5, Jalan Brawijaya III, Kebayoran Baru, Jakarta, Indonesia.

Warhol, Andy; American film maker and artist; b. 8 Aug. 1931; s. of James and Julia (Von) Warhol.

Exhibitions at Leo Castelli Gallery and Stable Gallery N.Y.C., Ferus Gallery, Los Angeles, Morris Gallery, Toronto, Rubbers Gallery, Buenos Aires, Sonnebend Gallery, Paris; 6th Film Culture Award 64, Los Angeles Film Festival Award 64.

Films include: *Sleep* 63, *Eat* 63, *Kiss* 63, *Empire* 64, *Harlot* 64, *My Hustler* 65, *Chelsea Girls* 66, *Bike Boy* 67, *Lonesome Cowboys* 68, *Blue Movie* 69, *Imitation of Christ* 69; dir. by Paul Morrissey: *Flesh* 69, *Trash* 71, *Women in Revolt* 72, *Heat* 72, *Blood for Dracula* 74, *Flesh for Frankenstein* 75.

Publ. *The Philosophy of Andy Warhol (From A to B and Back Again)* 75.

c/o The Castelli Gallery, 4 East 77th Street, New York City, N.Y., U.S.A.

Waring, Hon. Frank Walter, B.A., B.COM.; South African politician; b. 7 Nov. 1908, Kenilworth, Cape Prov.; s. of Frank Richard Waring; m. Joyce Barlow; three c.; ed. S. African Coll. School and Cape Town Univ.

Grain Broker; M.P. 43-72; Minister of Information 61-66, of Tourism 63-72, of Indian Affairs, Sport and Recreation 66-72; Nat. Party.

252 Ocean View Drive, Presnaye, Sea Point, Cape Town, South Africa.
Telephone: 495020/495080.

Waris, Klaus, PH.D.; Finnish economist; b. 17 March 1914, Helsinki; s. of Dr. Erkki Warén and Katri Cannelin; m. Elina Leppänen 1939; two s. one d.; ed. Turku, Helsinki Univ.
Chief, Economic Affairs Division, Ministry of Finance 46-49; Prof. Economics Finnish Inst. of Technology 49-52; mem. Man. Board Bank of Finland 52-57; Gov. Bank of Finland 57-67; Chancellor, Helsinki School of Econs. 67-; Gov. for Finland, Int. Monetary Fund 58-68. Kartanontie 12, Helsinki 33, Finland.
Telephone: 482-979.

Wark, Sir Ian William, Kt., C.M.G., C.B.E., D.SC., PH.D.; Australian physical chemist; b. 8 May 1899, Melbourne: s. of W. J. and F. E. Wark; m. Elsie Evelyn Booth 1927; one d.; ed. Scotch Coll., Melbourne, and Univs. of Melbourne, London and Calif. (Berkeley).
Exhibition of 1851 Science Research Scholarship 21-24; Lecturer in Chemistry, Univ. of Sydney 25; Research Chemist, Electrolytic Zinc Co. of Australasia Ltd. 26-39; **Commonwealth Scientific and Industrial Research Organisation, Chief, Div. of Industrial Chemistry 40-58**, Dir. Chemical Research Laboratories 58-60, mem. of Exec. 61-65; Chair. Commonwealth Advisory Cttee. on Advanced Educ. 65-71; Hon. Consultant to CSIRO Minerals Research Laboratories 71-; Gen. Pres. Royal Australian Chemical Inst. 57-58; Fellow, Australian Acad. of Science 54-, Treas. 59-63; hon. mem. Australasian Inst. Mining and Metallurgy 60-, Fellow Univ. Coll. London 65; Australia and New Zealand Asscn. for the Advancement of Science Medal 73.
Leisure interests: golf, fishing for trout.
Publs. *Principles of Flotation* (monograph) 38, (revised with K. L. Sutherland 55), *Why Research?* 68.
31 Linum Street, Blackburn, Victoria 3130, Australia.
Telephone: Melbourne 877-2878.

Warner, Sir Frederick Archibald, G.C.V.O., K.C.M.G., M.A.; British businessman, farmer and fmr. diplomatist; b. 2 May 1918, Bournemouth; s. of Frederick A. Warner and Marjorie M. Winants; m. Simone Georgina de Ferranti 1971; two s.; ed. Royal Naval Coll., Dartmouth and Magdalen Coll., Oxford.
Served Royal Navy 32-37, 39-46; joined Foreign Office 46; served in Moscow 50-51, Rangoon 56-58, Athens 58-59; Amb. to Laos 65-67; Minister, NATO 67-68; Deputy Perm. Rep. to UN 69-70; Amb. to Japan 72-75; Dir. Guinness Peat (Overseas), Mercantile and Gen. Reinsurance Co.
L6 Albany, Piccadilly, London, W.1; Laverstock, Bridport, Dorset, England.
Telephone: 01-734 2356 (London); Broadwindsor 543 (Dorset).

Warner, Harry B., M.S.; American chemical engineer and business executive; b. 7 July 1916, Columbus, Ohio; s. of Harry Albert and Marie (Flynn) Warner; m. Vesta Marie Engel 1940; two s. (twins), one d.; ed. Ohio State Univ.
With B. F. Goodrich Chemical Co. 39-64, Vice-Pres. devt. 54-58, marketing 58-60, Pres. 60-64; Group Vice-Pres. B. F. Goodrich Co. 64-67, Pres. 67-74; mem. Board of Dirs. B. F. Goodrich 66-74, Special Exec. Consultant 74-; mem. Board of Govs. and fmr. Pres. Cleveland Engineering Soc.; fmr. Dir. American Inst. of Chemical Engineers, mem. and fmr. Pres. Cleveland Section; mem. Exec. Cttee. American Section of Soc. for Chemical Industry; Dir. Rubber Mfg. Asscn.; mem. Advisory Council Nat. 4-H Foundation, Advisory Comm. Univ. of Akron Coll. of Engineering, Nat. Industrial Council of Opportunities Industrialization Center of America; Trustee Akron City Hospital.

B. F. Goodrich Company, 500 South Main, Akron, Ohio 44318, U.S.A.
Telephone: 216-379-2252.

Warner, Jack L.; American film executive; b. 1892; ed. public schools, Youngstown, Ohio.
Former singer; pioneer, with brothers, of talking films 26-28; Pres. and Dir. Warner Bros. Pictures Inc.; mem. Pres.'s Nat. Advisory Cttee. on Jobs for Veterans 71-; numerous decorations and awards including, Officier Légion d'Honneur; Commdr. Order of British Empire; Officier Ordre de la Couronne (Belgium); Cross of Merit, 1st Class (Fed. Germany); Medal for Merit (U.S.A.); First World War Peace Prize; Hollywood Foreign Corresp. Asscn. Award for production, *The Life of Emile Zola* 37, *Casablanca* 43; Acad. Award for Producer of Best Picture, *My Fair Lady* 64; David di Donatella Award for Best Picture 65.
1900 Avenue of the Stars, Century City, Calif. 90067, U.S.A.

Warner, John Christian, A.B., M.A., PH.D.; American physical chemist; b. 28 May 1897, Goshen, Ind.; s. of Elias and Addie Plank Warner; m. Louise Hamer 1925; two s.; ed. Indiana Univ. and Univ. of Mich.
Instructor in Chem., Indiana Univ. 21-24; Research Chemist, Wayne Chemicals 24-26; Instructor, Carnegie-Mellon Univ. 26-28, Asst. Prof. 28-33, Assoc. Prof. of Chem. 33-36, Assoc. Prof. of Metallurgy 36-38, Prof. of Chem. and Chair. of Dept. 38-49, Dean Graduate Studies 45-50, Vice-Pres. 49-50, Pres. 50-65, Pres. Emer. 65-; on Manhattan Project 43-45; Consultant to foundations and industries 65-; Pres. Electrochemical Soc. 52, American Chemical Soc. 56; mem. Nat. Acad. of Sciences; Hon. doctorates from 14 univs. and colls.; Pittsburgh American Chemical Soc. Award 45, Gold Medal of American Inst. of Chemists 53, Pennsylvania Award for Excellence in Educ. 66.
Leisure interests: performing arts, travel, literature, educational innovation.
Publs. include *Physical chemistry of iron and steelmaking* 51; numerous articles in journals.
1124 Oliver Building, Pittsburgh, Pa. 15222; Home: 825 Morewood Avenue, Apartment H-4, Pittsburgh, Pa. 15213, U.S.A.
Telephone: 412-281-4910 (Office); 412-621-2744 (Home).

Warner, John W., B.S., LL.B.; American government official; b. 18 Feb. 1927, Washington, D.C.; s. of late Dr. John W. Warner and of Martha (Budd) Warner; m. Catherine Conover Mellon; one s. two d.; ed. public schools in Washington, D.C., school of Naval Research Laboratory, Washington, D.C., Washington and Lee Univ. and Univ. of Virginia Law School.
In U.S. Navy attained rank of Electronic Technician 3rd Class 44-46; subsequently enlisted in U.S. Marine Corps Reserve, active duty as Communications Officer 50-52, Captain in Marine Corps Reserve 52-61; Admitted to the Bar 54; private practice 54-56; in U.S. Attorney's office as Special Asst. 56, Asst. 57, trial lawyer 60-; joined campaign staff of then Vice-Pres. Richard Nixon 60; Associated with law firm Hogan & Hartson 60, gen. partner 64; Dir. of Ocean Affairs as rep. of Dept. of Defense 71; Under-Sec. of U.S. Navy 69-72, Sec. 72-74; Dir. American Revolution Bicentennial Admin. 74-; head of U.S. Del. to Moscow on naval affairs.
American Revolution Bicentennial Admin., 736 Jackson Place, N.W., Washington, D.C. 20276, U.S.A.

Warner, Leslie Harry; American industrial executive; b. 1911; ed. Wichita State Univ. and Harvard Univ. Graduate School of Business Admin.
Automatic Electric Co. 37; Man. Dir. Automatic Electric do Brasil, S.A., São Paulo 38-42; Vice-Pres. Automatic Electric Sales Corpn., New York City 42-46; Commercial Man., Automatic Electric Co., Chicago 46-47; Pres. Automatic Electric Sales Corpn., Chicago

47-54, Leich Electric Co., Genoa, Ill., Leich Sales Corpn., Chicago 54-55, Automatic Electric Co. 55-57; Exec. Vice-Pres. (Mfg.), Gen. Telephone & Electronics Corpn., New York City 57-61, Pres. 61-, Pres. and Chief Exec. Officer 66-71, Chair. and Pres. 71-72, Chair. and Chief Exec. Officer 72-; Dir. numerous subsidiary and other cos.
General Telephone & Electronics Corporation, 730 Third Avenue, New York, N.Y. 10017, U.S.A.

Warner, Rawleigh, Jr., A.B.; American business executive; b. 13 Feb. 1921, Chicago, Ill.; s. of late Rawleigh Warner and Dorothy Haskins Warner; m. Mary Ann de Clairmont 1946; two d.; ed. Lawrenceville School and Princeton Univ.
Mobil Oil Corpn. 53-; Asst. to Financial Dir. Socony Vacuum Overseas Supply Co. 53-56; Man. Econs. Dept., Mobil Oil Corpn. 56-58, Man. Middle East Affairs Dept. 58-59, Regional Vice-Pres. for Middle East 59-60; Exec. Vice-Pres. Mobil Int. Oil Co. 60-63, Pres. 63; Dir. Exec. Vice-Pres. and mem. Exec. Cttee. Mobil Oil Corpn., with responsibility for Mobil Int. and Mobil Petroleum Corpn. Inc. 64-65, Pres. Mobil Oil Corpn. 65-69, Chair. 69-; Dir. American Petroleum Inst., Marcor Inc., American Telephone and Telegraph Co., American Express Co. and American Express Int. Banking Co., Time Inc., Caterpillar Tractor Co., Chemical New York Corpn. and Chemical Bank, Nat. Council for U.S.-China Trade; Trustee, Lawrenceville School, Woodrow Wilson Int. Center for Scholars; Chair. Princeton Univ. Council for Univ. Resources; mem. The Business Council, White House Labor-Management Cttee.
Leisure interests: golf, walking, reading (mystery and adventure).
Mobil Oil Corporation, 150 East 42nd Street, New York, N.Y. 10017, U.S.A.
Telephone: 212-883-2405.

Warner, Rex; British writer; b. 9 March 1905; ed. Wadham Coll., Oxford.
Schoolmaster in Egypt; Classics Master at Raynes Park County School; Dir. British Inst., Athens 45-47; Prof. Univ. of Connecticut 64-74; retd.
Publs. *Poems* 37, *The Wild-Goose Chase* 37, *The Professor* 38, *The Aerodrome* 41, *Why Was I Killed?* 43, *Poems and Contradictions* 45, *The Cult of Power* 46, *Men of Stones* 49, *John Milton* (biography) 50, *Men and Gods* 50, *Greeks and Trojans* 51, *Views of Attica* (travel) 51, *Escapade* 53, *Eternal Greece* 53, *The Vengeance of the Gods* 54, *The Greek Philosophers*, *The Young Caesar* 58, *Imperial Caesar* 60, *Pericles the Athenian* 63, *The Converts* (novel) 67, *Athens at War* 70, *Men of Athens* 72; translations of *Medea*, *Hippolytus* and *Helen* (Euripides), *Prometheus Bound* (Aeschylus) *Anabasis* (Xenophon, entitled *The Persian Expedition*), *The Peloponnesian War* (Thucydides), *The Fall of the Roman Republic* (Plutarch) 58, *Caesar's War Commentaries* 59, *Confessions of St. Augustine* 63, *Pericles the Athenian* 63, *Poems* and *The Greek Style* (Seferis) 63 and 66, *History of My Times* (Xenophon) 66, *Moral Essays* (Plutarch) 71, *Men of Athens* 72.
Anchor House, St. Leonard's Lane, Wallingford, Oxon., England.

Warnock, Geoffrey James, M.A.; British philosopher; b. 16 Aug. 1923, Leeds; s. of James Warnock, O.B.E., M.D., M.A.; m. Helen M. Wilson 1949; two s. three d.; ed. Winchester Coll. and New Coll., Oxford.
Fellow, Magdalen Coll., Oxford 49, 53-71, Brasenose Coll. 50-53; Principal, Hertford Coll., Oxford 72-; Visiting Lecturer, Univs. of Illinois and Wisconsin and Princeton Univ.; Hon. Fellow, New Coll., Oxford.
Leisure interests: cricket, golf.
Publs. *Berkeley* 53 (2nd edn. 69), *English Philosophy*

since 1900 58 (2nd edn. 69), *Contemporary Moral Philosophy* 67, *The Object of Morality* 71.
Hertford College, Oxford, England.
Telephone: Oxford 41434.

Warnock, Maurice John; American business executive; b. 28 Dec. 1902, Silverton, Oreg.; s. of James Clark and Mary (Spahr) Warnock; m. 1st Isabel Cherry 1930 (died 1974), two s.; m. 2nd Gertrude Baur 1975; ed. Oregon High School, Silverton and Univ. of Oregon.
With Armstrong Cork Co., Lancaster, Pennsylvania 26-, Salesman, Floor Div., Seattle 27-29, District Manager 29-30, Asst. Sales Manager, Floor Div., Lancaster 30-41, Asst. Gen. Sales Manager, Lancaster 41, Dir. of Advertising and Promotion, Lancaster 41-43, Treas. 43-59, Vice-Pres. and Treas. 50-59, Dir. 59-, Senior Vice-Pres. 59-61, First Senior Vice-Pres. 61-62, Exec. Vice-Pres. 62, Pres. 62-68, Chair. of Board 68-; Dir. Armstrong Cork Co. Ltd., England 62-; Dir., Armstrong Cork (Australia) Pty. Ltd. 61-; mem. Board of Dirs. Home Capital Funds Inc., Selas Corpn. of America and numerous other asscns.
Leisure interest: golf.
Armstrong Cork Co., Liberty and Charlotte Streets, Lancaster, Pa.; Home: 191 Eshelman Road, Lancaster, Pa., U.S.A.
Telephone: 717-393-0317.

Warnock, William, B.A., LL.D.; Irish diplomatist; b. 22 Sept. 1911, Dublin; s. of Frank Warnock and Susan Twamley; m. Dorothy Murray; two s. two d.; ed. The High School, Dublin, Trinity Coll., Dublin, and Hochschule für Politik, Berlin.
Entered Dept. of External Affairs as Cadet 35; Sec., Berlin 38, Chargé d'Affaires a.i., Berlin 39-44; Head of Section; Dept. of External Affairs, Dublin 44-47; Chargé d'Affaires, Stockholm 47-50; Minister to Switzerland Feb. 50-54, also accredited to Austria March 52-54; Asst. Sec. Dept. of External Affairs 54-56; Minister to Fed. Republic of Germany 56-59, Amb. 59-62; Amb. to Switzerland and Austria 62-64, to India 64-67, to Canada 67-70, to U.S.A. 70-73, to Switzerland 73-, concurrently accred. to Austria 73-74, concurrently accred. to Israel 75-; Gustav V Medal (Sweden), Grand Cross of Order of Merit (Fed. Repub. of Germany).
Leisure interest: touring, preferably on foot.
Embassy of Ireland, 9 Dufourstrasse, 3005 Berne, Switzerland.

Warren, Frederick Miles, C.B.E., F.N.Z.I.A., A.R.I.B.A., DIP.ARCH.; New Zealand architect; b. 10 May 1929, Christchurch; s. of M. B. and J. Warren (née Hay); ed. Christ's Coll., Auckland Univ. School of Architecture.
Worked for late C. W. Wood, F.N.Z.I.A. 46-47, for late R. C. Munroe, A.N.Z.I.A. 48; joined partnership with late G. T. Lucas 56; started firm Warren and Mahoney 58, Senior Partner; Fellow, New Zealand Inst. of Architects 65; Warren and Mahoney awarded N.Z.I.A. Gold Medal for Dental Nurses' Training School 60, for Christchurch Memorial Garden Crematorium 64, for Christchurch Coll. Halls of Residence 69, for Christchurch Town Hall and Civic Centre 73; won Architectural Competition for design of Condominium Offices, New Hebrides 66.
Leisure interests: yachting, water-colouring, sketching.
65 Cambridge Terrace, Christchurch 1, New Zealand.
Telephone: 62-684.

Warren, Jack Hamilton; Canadian diplomatist; b. 10 April 1921; m. Hilary J. Titterington; four c.; ed. Queen's Univ., Kingston, Ont.
Royal Canadian Navy 41-45; joined Dept. of External Affairs 45; served in London 48-51; transferred to Dept. of Finance and served as Financial Counsellor, Washington, D.C. and as Alt. Dir. for Canada, IMF and IBRD 54-57; Canadian Del. to OECD and NATO

57-58; Asst. Deputy Minister of Trade and Commerce 58-64; Chair. GATT Contracting Parties 62-65; Deputy Minister of Trade and Commerce 64-68, of Industry, Trade and Commerce 68-71; High Commr. to U.K. 71-74; Amb. to U.S.A. June 75-.
1746 Massachusetts Avenue, N.W., Washington, D.C. 20036, U.S.A.

Warren, Robert Penn, B.A., B.LITT.; American university professor and writer; b. 24 April 1905, Guthrie, Ky.; s. of Robert Franklin Warren and Anna Ruth Penn; m. 1st Emma Brescia 1930 (divorced 1951), 2nd Eleanor Clark 1952; one s. one d.; ed. Vanderbilt, Oxford and Yale Univs. and Univ. of California.
Asst. Prof., Southwestern Coll. 30-31, Vanderbilt Univ. 31-34; Asst. Prof. Louisiana State Univ. 34-36, Assoc. Prof. 36-42; Prof. Univ. of Minnesota 42-50; Lecturer Yale Univ. 50-51, Prof. of Playwriting 51-56, of English 61-73; Poetry, Library of Congress 44-45; a Founder and Editor *Southern Review* 35-42; mem. American Acad. of Arts and Letters, American Acad. of Arts and Sciences, American Philosophical Soc.; Hon. Fellow. Modern Language Asscn.; Rhodes Scholarship, Houghton Mifflin Literary Fellowship 36, Guggenheim Fellowship 39-40 and 47-48; Levinson Prize 36, Caroline Sinker Prize 36, 37, 38, Shelley Memorial Award 42, Pulitzer Prize for Fiction 47, Southern Prize 47, Robert Melzer Award (Screen Writer's Guild) 49, Millay Award (American Poetry Soc.), Nat. Book Award, Pulitzer Prize for Poetry 58, Sidney Hillman Award for Journalism 59, Irita Van Doren Award (*New York Herald Tribune*) 65; Bollingen Prize in Poetry 67; Nat. Medal for Literature 70; Hon. Litt.D., LL.D.; Van Wyck Brooks Poetry Award 70, Bellaman Award 70, Jefferson Lecturer, Nat. Endowment for the Humanities 74, Thoreau-Emerson Medal, American Acad. of Arts and Sciences 75.
Leisure interests: gardening, walking, swimming.
Publs. *John Brown: The Making of a Martyr* 29, *XXXVI Poems* 36, *An Approach to Literature* (with Cleanth Brooks and John Purser) 37, *Understanding Poetry* (with Cleanth Brooks) 38, *Night Rider* (novel) 39, *At Heaven's Gate* (novel) 43, *Eleven Poems on the Same Theme* 42, *Selected Poems* 44, *All the King's Men* (novel) 46, *Circus in the Attic* (stories) 48, *World Enough and Time* (novel) 50, *Brother to Dragons* (verse) 53, *Band of Angels* (novel) 55, *Segregation: The Inner Conflict of the South* 56, *Promises* (verse) 57, *Selected Essays* 58, *The Cave* (novel) 59, *You, Emperors and Others* (verse) 60, *The Legacy of the Civil War* 61, *Wilderness* (novel) 61, *Flood* (novel) 64, *Who Speaks for the Negro?* 65, *Selected Poems, New and Old* 66, *Incarnations: Poems 1966-68* 68, *Audubon: A Vision* (a poem) 69, *Meet Me in the Green Glen* 72, *American Literature: the Makers and the Making* (with Cleangh Brooks and R. W. B. Lewis), *Or Else* (poem), *Poems 1968-74* 74, *Democracy and Poetry* 75, *Selected Poems 1923-75* 76.
2495 Redding Road, Fairfield, Conn. 06430, U.S.A.

Warren, Shields, A.B., M.D.; American physician; b. 26 Feb. 1898, Cambridge, Mass.; s. of William M. and Sara B. Warren; m. Alice Springfield 1923; two d.; ed. Boston Univ., Harvard Medical School.
Professor of Pathology, Harvard Medical School (New England Deaconess Hospital) 48-65, Prof. of Pathology, Emeritus 65-; Chair. Corpn. and Trustees, Boston Univ. 61-69; U.S. Rep. UN Scientific Cttee. on the Effects of Atomic Radiation 55-63; Consultant, U.S. Atomic Energy Comm. 59-; Special Consultant, Dept. of Defense (Health and Medical) 59-62; Chair. Cttee. on Pathological Effects of Atomic Radiation 55-60, Life Sciences Cttee. NASA 71-74; mem. Nat. Acad. of Sciences 62-; Hon. D.Sc., Hon. S.D., Hon. LL.D.; many awards.
Publs. *Medical Science for Everyday Use* 27, *Pathology of Diabetes Mellitus* 30, 4th edn. 66, *A Handbook for the Diagnosis of Cancer of the Uterus* (with O. Gates) 47, 48, 49, *Introduction to Neuropathology* (with S. P. Hicks) 50, *Medical Effects of the Atomic Bomb in Japan* (with A. W. Oughterson) 56, *Pathology of Ionizing Radiation* 61.
194 Pilgrim Road, Boston, Mass. 02215, U.S.A.

Wartiovaara, Otso Uolevi; Finnish diplomatist; b. 16 Nov. 1908, Helsinki; s. of J. V. Wartiovaara and Siri Wartiovaara (née Nystén); m. Maine Alanen 1936; three s.; ed. Helsinki Univ. Law School.
Entered Foreign Service 34; Attaché, Paris 36-39; Sec. and Head of Section, Ministry for Foreign Affairs 39-42; Counsellor, Stockholm 42-44; Consul, Haaparanta (Sweden) 44-45; Head of Section, Ministry of Foreign Affairs 45-49; Counsellor, Wash. 49-52; Head of Admin. Dept. Ministry of Foreign Affairs 52-54, Head of Legal Dept. 54-56; Minister to Yugoslavia, also accred. to Greece 56-58; Amb. to Yugoslavia, also accred. to Greece 58-61; Amb. to Austria 61-68, also accred. to Vatican 66-68; Perm. Rep. to Int. Atomic Energy Org., Vienna 61-68; Amb. to U.K. 68-74; decorations from Finland, Austria, Greece, Vatican, Yugoslavia, Sweden, U.K. and Norway.
Leisure interest: shooting.
Lutherinkatu 6A, Helsinki 10, Finland.

Washburn, Sherwood L., PH.D.; American professor of anthropology; b. 26 Nov. 1911, Cambridge, Mass.; m. Henrietta Pease 1938; two s.; ed. Harvard Univ.
Anatomy Dept., Columbia Univ. Medical School 39-47; Dept. of Anthropology, Univ. of Chicago 47-58; Prof. of Anthropology, Univ. of Calif. at Berkeley 58-; mem. Nat. Acad. of Sciences; Viking Fund Medal 60, Ciba Foundation Medal 65, Huxley Medal 67.
Publs. on human evolution.
Department of Anthropology, University of California, Berkeley, Calif. 94720; Home: 2797 Shasta Road, Berkeley, Calif. 94708, U.S.A.
Telephone: 415-642-2897 (Office) 415-843-5326 (Home).

Washington, Walter E., LL.B.; American government official; b. 15 April 1915, Dawson, Georgia; m. Bennetta Bullock; one d.; ed. Howard Univ. and Howard Law School.
Executive Dir. Nat. Capital Housing Authority, Washington, D.C. until Nov. 66; Chair. New York City Housing Authority Nov. 66-67; Commr. of District of Columbia and Mayor of Washington 67-74; Mayor D.C. 75-; 13 hon. degrees.
408 T Street, N.W., Washington, D.C. 20001, U.S.A.

Wass, Sir Douglas William Gretton, K.C.B., M.A.; British civil servant; b. 15 April 1923, Wallasey, Cheshire; s. of Arthur W. and Elsie W. Wass; m. Dr. Milica Pavicic 1954; one s. one d.; ed. Nottingham High School, St. John's Coll., Cambridge.
Scientific Research with Admiralty 43-46; Asst. Principal, Treasury 46, Principal 51; Commonwealth Fund Fellow, U.S.A. 58-59; Fellow, Brookings Inst., Washington 59; Private Sec. to Chancellor 59-61; Private Sec. to Chief Sec. 61-62; Alt. Exec. Dir. to IMF and Financial Counsellor, British Embassy, Washington 65-67; Under-Sec. of Treasury 68, Deputy Sec. 70, Second Perm. Sec. 73, Perm. Sec. 74-.
Leisure interest: golf.
6 Dora Road, Wimbledon, London, S.W.19, England.
Telephone: 01-946-5556.

Wasserburg, Gerald Joseph, M.SC., PH.D.; American professor of geology and geophysics; b. 25 March 1927, New Brunswick, N.J.; s. of Charles Wasserburg and Sarah Levine Wasserburg; m.; two s.; ed. Univ. of Chicago.
Rifleman, U.S. Army Second Infantry Div. 43-46; with Resurrection Mining Co. 47; Juneau Ice Field Research Project, Alaska 50; Consultant Argonne Nat. Labora-

tory, Lamont, Ill. 52-55; Research Assoc. Enrico Fermi, Inst. for Nuclear Studies, Chicago 54-55; Asst. Prof. of Geology, Calif. Inst. of Technology 55-59, Assoc. Prof. of Geology 59-62, Prof. of Geology and Geophysics 62-; Vice-Chair. Lunar Sample Analysis Planning Team, MSC, NASA 70; mem. Lunar Sample Review Board 70-72, Science Working Panel 71-73, Physical Sciences Cttee. 71-; Editor *Earth and Planetary Science Letters* 67-75; mem. Nat Acad. of Science; Fellow American Acad. of Arts and Sciences, American Geophysical Union, Geological Soc. of America; Combat Infantryman's Badge, Purple Heart; Exceptional Scientific Achievement Medal, NASA 70; Arthur L. Day Medal, Geological Soc. of America 70; Distinguished Public Service Medal, NASA 72; James Furman Kemp Medal, Columbia Univ. 73, Leonard Medal, Meteor Soc. 75.
Publs. more than 100 research papers in scientific journals, in the field of geochemistry and geophysics and the application of the methods of chemical physics to problems in the earth and planetary sciences; major researches: determination of the time scale of the solar system, chronology of the moon, establishment of dating methods using long-lived natural radioactivities, study of geological processes using nuclear and isotopic effects as a tracer in nature and the application of thermodynamic methods to geological systems.
California Institute of Technology, Division of Geological and Planetary Sciences, 1201 East California Street, Pasadena, Calif. 91125; Home: 2100 Pinecrest Drive, Altadena, Calif. 91101, U.S.A.
Telephone: 213-795-6841 (Office); 213-798-8171 (Home).

Watanabe, Tadao; Japanese banker; b. 3 Sept. 1898, Hokkaido; s. of Teruo Watanabe and Haruko Watanabe; m. Minoru Mita 1926; two s.; ed. Tokyo Univ.
Joined Bank of Japan 24; transferred to Sanwa Bank 45, Man. Dir. 45-46, Senior Man. Dir. 46-47, Pres. 47-60, Chair. 60-; Man. Dir. Kansai Econ. Fed.; Dir. Ohbayashi Road Construction Co., Fujita Tourist Enterprise Co., Mainichi Broadcasting Co., Osaka UNESCO Asscn. and numerous other socs.; Auditor Osaka Gas Co.; Adviser Teijin Ltd., Kansai Electric Power Co., Takashimaya Co., Toyo Trust and Banking Co., Fed. of Econ. Org., Japan Fed. of Employers' Asscn.; Pres. Sandwa Midori Fund.
Leisure interests: appreciation and collection of paintings, golf.
4-10 Fushimimachi, Higashi-ku, Osaka; 1-18 Kawanishicho, Ashiyashi, Hyogo Prefecture; 5-16-35, Roppongi, Minato-ku, Tokyo, Japan.
Telephone: 0797-22-2910 (Ashiya); 03-583-2715 (Tokyo).

Watanabe, Takeshi; Japanese banker and financial consultant; b. 15 Feb. 1906, Tokyo; s. of Chifuyu Watanabe (fmr. Minister of Justice) and Yoshiko Watanabe; m. Fusako Yamakawa 1933; three s. two d.; ed. Law School of Tokyo Imperial Univ.
Ministry of Finance, Japan 30, serving as Chief Liaison Officer, Chief of the Ministers' Secr. and Financial Commr.; Minister, Japanese Embassy in Washington 52-56; Exec. Dir. for Japan, Int. Bank for Reconstruction and Devt.—IBRD (World Bank) and Int. Monetary Fund (IMF) 56-60; Int. Financial Consultant 60-65; Adviser to Minister of Finance, Japan, in charge of preparatory work for the establishment of the Asian Devt. Bank 65; Pres. Asian Devt. Bank, Manila 66-72; Chair. Trident Int. Finance Ltd., Hong Kong 72-; Adviser to Bank of Tokyo; Chair. Japanese Comm. of Trilateral Comm.
Leisure interests: photography, golf.
Publs. *Japanese Finance in Early Post-War Years* (in Japanese) 66, *Diary of the ADB President.*
35-19 Oyama-cho, Shibuya-ku, Tokyo, Japan.

Waterhouse, Sir Ellis Kirkham, Kt., C.B.E.; British professor of fine arts; b. 16 Feb. 1905, Epsom; m. Helen

Thomas 1949; two d.; ed. Marlborough Coll., New Coll., Oxford, and Princeton Univ., New Jersey.
Assistant, Nat. Gallery, London 29-33; Librarian, British School at Rome 33-36; Fellow Magdalen Coll., Oxford 38-47; Dir. Nat. Galleries of Scotland 49-52; Barber Prof. of Fine Arts and Dir. of Barber Inst., Univ. of Birmingham 52-70; Dir. of Studies Paul Mellon Centre for Studies in British Art (London) 70-73; Kress Prof. in Residence, Nat. Gallery of Art, Washington, D.C. 74-75; mem. Exec. Cttee. Nat. Art Collections Fund 72-; Officer Orange-Nassau, Ordine al Merito della Republica Italiana.
Publs. *Roman Baroque Painting* 37, *Reynolds* 41, *British Painting 1530-1790* 53, *Gainsborough* 58, *Italian Baroque Painting* 62, *Reynolds* 73.
Overshot, Hinksey Hill, Oxford, England.

Waters, Aaron Clement, B.SC., M.SC., PH.D.; American geologist; b. 6 May 1905, Waterville, Wash.; s. of Richard J. Waters and Hattie Lovina Clement Waters; m. Elizabeth P. von Hoene 1940; two d.; ed. Univ. of Wash. and Yale Univ.
Instructor in Geology, Yale Univ. 28-30, Asst. Prof., Stanford Univ. 30-33, Assoc. Prof. 33-38, Prof. 38-42, 45-51; Staff Geologist and Research geologist, U.S. Geological Survey 42-45; Prof. of Geology, Johns Hopkins Univ. 52-63, Univ. of Calif. at Santa Barbara 63-67; Prof. of Earth Sciences, Univ. of Calif. at Santa Cruz 67-72; Emeritus 72-; Guggenheim Fellow, Nat. Science Foundation Senior Postdoctoral Fellow; mem. Nat. Acad. of Sciences, American Acad. of Arts and Sciences.
Leisure interests: varied and changeable.
Publs. Textbooks (co-author) 51, 4th edn. 75; over 100 articles in professional journals.
Division of Natural Sciences, University of California, Santa Cruz, Calif. 95064; Home: 308 Moore Street, Santa Cruz, Calif. 95060, U.S.A.
Telephone: 408-429-2881 (Office); 408-426-3764 (Home).

Watkinson, 1st Viscount (cr. 64), of Woking in the County of Surrey; **Harold Arthur Watkinson,** P.C., C.H.; British politician and business executive; b. 25 Jan. 1910, Walton-on-Thames; s. of Arthur Gill Watkinson and Mary Casey; m. Vera Langmead 1939; two d.; ed. King's Coll., London.
Conservative M.P. 50-64; Parl. Sec. Ministry of Labour 52-55; Minister of Transport and Civil Aviation 55-59, Minister of Defence 59-62; Dir. Midland Bank 64-, Deputy Chair. 69, British Insulated Callender Cables Ltd. 68-(76); Group Man. Dir. Schweppes Ltd. 63-69, Exec. Chair. Cadbury Schweppes Ltd. 69-74; Chair. Cttee. for Exports to U.S.A. 64-67; Council British Inst. of Management 68-70; Pres. Inst. of Grocery Distribution 70-72; Chair. Confederation of British Industry Cttee. on company responsibility 73, Deputy Pres. CBI 75-76, Pres. May 76-.
Leisure interests: sailing, mountaineering, walking.
Dibbles, West Clandon, nr. Guildford, Surrey, England.

Watson, Cecil James, B.S., M.S., M.D., PH.D.; American physician, scientist and professor of medicine; b. 31 May 1901, Minneapolis; s. of James Alfred Watson and Lucia Louise Coghlan Watson; m. Joyce Petterson 1925; ed. Univs. of Minn., Mich., Munich and Technische Hochschule.
Pathologist and Dir. of Laboratories, Minn. Gen. Hospital 26-28, Pathologist and Dir. Northwest Clinic, Minot, N. Dakota 28-30; Nat. Research Council Fellow 31-32; Fellow and Resident in Medicine, Minn. Gen. and Univ. of Minn. Hospitals 32-34; Asst. Prof. of Medicine, Univ. of Minn. 34-36, Assoc. Prof. and Dir. Div. of Internal Medicine 36-42, Prof. and Chair. Dept. of Medicine 42-66, Distinguished Service Prof. 61-, Dir. Univ. of Minn. Unit for Teaching and Research in Internal Medicine, Northwestern Hospital, Minn. 66-72,

Regent's Prof. of Medicine 68-, Senior Consultant 72-; Pres. Cen. Soc. for Clinical Research 44, American Soc. for Clinical Investigation 47, Asscn. of American Physicians 61, American Clinical and Climatological Asscn. 66; mem. Nat. Acad. of Sciences; Hon. M.D. (Univs. of Mainz and Munich); numerous lectureships and awards including Gordon Wilson Lecture and Medal, American Clinical and Climatological Asscn. 47, Lecturer and Hon. mem. Harvey Soc., N.Y.C. 48, Modern Medicine Award 59, James F. Bell Distinguished Service Award, Minn. Medical Foundation of Univ. of Minn. 61; F. V. Müller Medal, Munich 69; Kober Medal, Asscn. of American Physicists 72; Fogarty Scholar and Medal N.I.H. Bethesda Md. 72.
Leisure interests: skiing, wilderness fishing, travel, history.
Publs. Numerous scientific articles and chapters; and some non-scientific addresses and essays.
Northwestern Hospital, Minneapolis, Minn. 55407; Home: 3318 Edmund Boulevard, Minneapolis, Minn., U.S.A.
Telephone: 874-4210 (Office); 722-7381 (Home).

Watson, Sir Francis John Bagott, K.C.V.O., F.B.A., F.S.A.; British museum director and civil servant; b. 24 Aug. 1907, Dudley, Worcs.; s. of Hugh Watson and Ellen Marian (née Bagott); m. Mary Rosalie Gray Strong 1941 (died 1969); one s. (adopted); ed. Shrewsbury School, and St. John's Coll., Cambridge.
Registrar Courtauld Inst. of Art 34-38; Asst. Keeper, later Asst. Dir. Wallace Collection 38-63, Dir. 63-74; Asst. Surveyor of the King's (later the Queen's) Works of Art 46-63, Surveyor 63-72, Adviser for The Queen's Works of Art 72-; Trustee, Whitechapel Art Gallery 49-; Chair. Furniture History Soc. 66-; Slade Prof. of Fine Art, Oxford Univ. 69-70; Chair. Walpole Soc. 70-; Hon. M.A. (Oxford).
Leisure interest: travel.
Publs. *Canaletto* 49 (2nd edn. 54), *Southill, A Regency House* (with others) 51, *Catalogue of the Furniture in the Wallace Collection* 56, *Louis XVI Furniture* 59 (revised French edn. 63), *The Choiseul Gold Box* 63, *Wrightsman Catalogue* (vols. I, II) 66 (vols. III, IV) 70 (vol. V) 74, *Eighteenth Century Gold Boxes of Europe* (with others), *The Guardi Family of Painters* 66, *Tiepolo* 66, *Fragonard* 67, *The French Bronze 1500-1800* 68, *Catalogue of Pictures and Drawings in the Wallace Collection* (16th edn.) 68.
33 Whittingstall Road, London, S.W.6, England.

Watson, James Dewey, B.S., PH.D.; American biologist; b. 6 April 1928, Chicago, Ill.; s. of James D. and Jean Mitchell Watson; m. Elizabeth Lewis 1968; two s.; ed. Univ. of Chicago, and Univ. of Indiana.
Research Fellow, U.S. Nat. Research Council, Univ. of Copenhagen 50-51; Fellow U.S. Nat. Foundation, Cavendish Laboratory, Univ. of Cambridge, England 51-53; Senior Research Fellow in Biology, Calif. Inst. of Technology 53-55; Asst. Prof. of Biology, Harvard Univ. 55-58, Assoc. Prof. 58-61, Prof. 61-; Dir. Cold Spring Harbor Laboratory 68-; mem. Nat. Acad. of Sciences, Danish Acad. of Arts and Sciences, American Acad. of Arts and Sciences, American Soc. of Biological Chemists; Senior Fellow, Soc. of Fellows, Harvard Univ. 64-70; Hon. Fellow of Clare Coll., Univ. of Cambridge 67; Lasker Award 60, Nobel Prize for Medicine (with F. H. C. Crick and M. F. H. Wilkins) 62, and other awards; Hon. D.Sc. (Chicago, Indiana), Hon. LL.D. (Notre Dame Univ.).
Leisure interests: bird-watching, walking.
Publs. *Molecular Biology of the Gene* 65 (2nd edn. 70, 3rd edn. 76), *The Double Helix* 68; papers on structure of deoxyribonucleic acid (DNA), on protein synthesis and on the induction of cancer by viruses.
Biological Laboratories, Harvard University, 16 Divinity Avenue, Cambridge, Mass. and Cold Spring

Harbor Laboratory, Cold Spring Harbor, Long Island, New York, N.Y. 11724; Home: Bungtown Road, Cold Spring Harbor, New York 11724, U.S.A.
Telephone: 617-495-2341.

Watson, John Hugh Adam, C.M.G., M.A.; British diplomatist; b. 10 Aug. 1914, Leicester; s. of J. C. Watson and Alice Tate Watson; m. Katharine Anne Campbell 1950; two s. one d.; ed. Rugby, and King's Coll., Cambridge.
Entered Diplomatic Service 37; British Legation Bucharest 39, British Embassy, Cairo 40-44, Moscow 44-47; Foreign Office 47-50; British Embassy, Washington 50-56; Head of African Dept., Foreign Office 56-59; Minister and Consul-General, Senegal 59-60, Ambassador to Mali Fed. 60, to Senegal, Togo and Mauritania 60-62, to Cuba 63-66; Asst. Under-Sec. of State, Foreign Office 66-68; Diplomatic Adviser to British Leyland Motor Corpn. 68-73; Dir.-Gen. Int. Asscn. for Cultural Freedom 74-; Fellow, Nuffield Coll., Oxford 62-63.
Leisure interests: theatre, travel, historical research.
Publs. *War of the Goldsmith's Daughter, Emergent Africa, The Nature and Politics of the Third World.*
53 Hamilton Terrace, London, N.W.8; and Sharnden Old Manor, Mayfield, Sussex, England.
Telephone: 01-286-6330.

Watson, Thomas J., Jr.; American business executive; b. 8 Jan. 1914, Dayton, Ohio; m.; six c.; ed. Brown Univ.
With International Business Machines Corpn. 37-40; with U.S. Air Force 40-45; Dir. International Business Machines Corpn. 46-, Pres. 52-61, Chief Exec. Officer 56-71, Chair. of Board 61-71, Chair. Exec. Cttee. 71-; Dir. Bankers Trust Co.; Trustee, Rockefeller Foundation, Brown Univ., Calif. Inst. of Technology, American Museum of Nat. History, Inst. for Advanced Study; Dir. Pan American World Airways; Citizen Regent Smithsonian Inst.; U.S. Air Medal, Presidential Medal of Freedom, Légion d'Honneur, other foreign awards.
Home: Meadowcroft Lane, Greenwich, Conn.; Office: Old Orchard Road, Armonk, New York, N.Y. 10504, U.S.A.

Watt, Rt. Hon. Hugh, P.C.; New Zealand politician; b. 1912; ed. Seddon Technical Coll.
Former dir. in sheetmetal and engineering company; mem. Parl. for Onehunga 53-75; Minister of Works and Electricity 57-60; Deputy Prime Minister, Minister of Labour 72-74, of Works and Devt. 74-75; mem. Cabinet to Dec. 75; High Commr. to U.K. and Amb. to Ireland 75-76.
c/o New Zealand House, London, SW1Y 4TQ, England.

Watts, Helen; British contralto; b. Haverfordwest, South Wales.
Singer in Glyndebourne and BBC choruses; toured Russia with English Opera Group 64; Concert tours in U.S.A. 67-; has sung at the Salzburg Festival, Covent Garden and the Hong Kong Festival; major appearances with many of Europe's leading orchestras and conductors; four Promenade concerts 74.
Recordings include *Handel Arias, Orfeo, B Minor Mass,* Beethoven's *Mass in C Minor, The Apostles, Götterdämmerung.*
c/o Harold Holt Ltd., 122 Wigmore Street, London, W1H oDJ, England.
Telephone: 01-935-2331.

Waugh, Alec; British novelist; b. 8 July 1898, London; s. of Arthur Waugh and Catherine Raban; brother of the late Evelyn Waugh; m. 1st Joan Chirnside 1932 (died 1969), two s. one d.; m. 2nd Virginia Sorensen 1969; ed. Sherborne and Royal Mil. Coll., Sandhurst.
Served with Dorset Regt. First World War, rejoined Regt. 39, served with B.E.F. France 40; Staff Capt.

Mines Dept. 40, M.E.F. 41-42, P.A.I.C. 43-45, retd. with rank of Major 45.
Publs. *The Loom of Youth* 17, *Kept* 25, *Nor Many Waters* 28, *Hot Countries* 30, *Most Women . . .* 31, *So Lovers Dream* 31, *Wheels Within Wheels* 33, *The Balliols* 34, *Jill Somerset* 36, *Going Their Own Ways* 38, *No Truce with Time* 41, *His Second War* 44, *Unclouded Summer* 48, *The Lipton Story* 50, *Where the Clocks Chime Twice* 52, *Guy Renton* 53, *Island in the Sun* 56, *The Sugar Islands* 58, *In Praise of Wine* 59, *Fuel for the Flame* 60, *My Place in the Bazaar* 61, *The Early Years of Alec Waugh* 62, *A Family of Islands* 64, *The Mule on the Minaret* 65, *My Brother Evelyn and Other Profiles* 67, *Wines and Spirits* 68, *A Spy in the Family* 70, *Bangkok: the Story of a City* 70, *The Fatal Gift* 73, *A Year to Remember: an autobiographical account of 1931* 75, *Brief Encounter* (novel based on play by Noel Coward) 75.
c/o Brandt-Brandt, 101 Park Avenue, New York 17, N.Y., U.S.A.

Way, Sir Richard, K.C.B., C.B.E.; British civil servant and university administrator; b. 15 Sept. 1914, London; *s.* of Frederick Way and Clara Way (née Willetts); *m.* Ursula Joan Starr 1947; one *s.* two *d.*; ed. Polytechnic Secondary School, London.
Joined Civil Service 33; Perm. Under-Sec. of State for War 60-63; Perm. Sec. Ministry of Aviation 63-66; Chair. Lansing Bagnall Ltd. 67-69; Chair. London Transport 70-74; Principal, King's Coll., London 75-; American Medal of Freedom (with bronze palm) 46; Commdr. Order of St. John of Jerusalem 74.
Manor Farm, Shalden, Alton, Hants., England.
Telephone: Alton 82383.

Wayne, John (Marion Michael Morrison); American film actor; b. 26 May 1907; ed. Univ. of S. California.
Films include: *Stagecoach* 39, *The Long Voyage Home* 40, *Reap The Wild Wind* 42, *A Lady Takes a Chance* 43, *Tall in the Saddle* 44, *They Were Expendable* 45, *Red River* 46, *Wake of the Red Witch* 48, *Sands of Iwo Jima* 49, *Operation Pacific* 50, *The Quiet Man, Jet Pilot, Big Jim McLain* 51-52, *Fort Apache, Island in the Sky, Hondo, The High and the Mighty, The Searchers, Blood Alley, The Conqueror* 55, *Wings of Eagles* 56, *Barbarian and Geisha* 58, *Horse Soldiers* 59, *North to Alaska, Hatari, McLintock* 64, *The Sons of Katie Elder* 65, *El Dorado* 67, *The Green Berets* 67, *True Grit* 69 (Acad. Award for Best Actor 70), *Chisum* 69, *Rio Lobo* 70, *The Cowboys* 72, *Cahill* 73, *McQ* 74, *Brannigan* 74, *Rooster Cogburn* 75.
c/o Batjac Productions Inc., Paramount Studios, Hollywood, Calif. 90056, U.S.A.

Ważyk, Adam; Polish poet; b. 17 Nov. 1905, Warsaw; *s.* of Beniamin and Hanna Ważyk; *m.* Maria Krawczyk 1948; two *d.*; ed. Univ. of Warsaw.
Co-editor *Kuznica* (weekly) 45-50; Editor *Tworczosc* (monthly) 50-54; Polish PEN-Club Award 50; State Prize 53; Commdr. Cross of Order Polonia Restituta 55; Medal of 30th Anniversary of People's Poland 74.
Leisure interest: mathematics.
Publs. Verse: *Wiersze zebrane* (Collected Poems),*t Poemat dla doroslych* (A Poem for Adults) 55, *Labiryn* (Labyrinth), *Wagon* (The Carriage), *Surrealism* (anthology) 73; Novels: *Mity rodzinne* (Family Myths), *Epizod* (Episode); Essays: *Mickiewicz i wersyfikacja narodowa* (Mickiewicz and National Versification), *Kwestia gustu* (Matter of Taste) 67, *Gra i doświadczenie* (The Play and the Experience) 74; numerous translations of French and Russian poets and of Horatius.
Aleja Róż 8, 00-556 Warsaw, Poland.
Telephone: 287878.

Weaver, Robert C., B.S., M.A., PH.D.; American economist and government official; b. 29 Dec. 1907, Washington, D.C.; *s.* of Mortimer G. Weaver and Florence

Freeman Weaver; *m.* Ella Haith Weaver 1935; one *s.* (deceased); ed. Harvard Univ.
Adviser on Negro Affairs (Dept. of the Interior) 33-37; Consultant (Housing Div., Public Works Admin.) 34-37; Special Asst. to Admin., U.S. Housing Authority 37-40; Chief, Negro Employment and Training (Office of Production Man. and later War Production Board) 40-44; Visiting Prof. New York Univ. 48-50; Dir. Opportunity Fellowships (J. H. Whitney Foundation) 50-55; Dep. Commr. of Housing, N.Y. State 55, Rent Admin. 55-59; Consultant, Ford Foundation 59-60; Vice-Chair. Housing and Redevelopment Board, N.Y. City 60-61; Admin. Housing and Home Finance Agency 61-66; fmr. Chair. Nat. Asscn. for the Advancement of Colored People, mem. Advisory Comm. U.S. Housing Census for 1960, Nat. Comm. for Selection (Fulbright Fellowships), Exec. Cttee. of Action; Dir. Lavenburg Foundation; Sec. Dept. of Housing and Urban Devt. 66-68; Pres. Bernard Baruch Coll., City Univ. of New York (C.U.N.Y.) 69-70; Distinguished Prof. of Urban Affairs, Hunter Coll., C.U.N.Y. 70-; Chair. of Board FNMA 61-68; LL.D. (Harvard).
Publs. *Negro Labor: A National Problem* 46, *The Negro Ghetto* 48, *The Urban Complex* 64, *Dilemmas of Urban America* 65.
Office: 790 Madison Avenue, New York, N.Y. 10021; Home: 215 East 68th Street, New York, N.Y. 10021, U.S.A.
Telephone: (212) 360-2807.

Weaver, Warren, B.S., C.B., PH.D.; American science executive; b. 17 July 1894, Reedsburg, Wis.; *s.* of Isaiah and Kittie Belle (Stupfell) Weaver; *m.* Mary Hemenway 1919; one *s.* one *d.*; ed. Univ. of Wisconsin.
Assistant Prof. of Maths., Throop Coll. 17-18, Calif. Inst. of Technology 19-20; Asst. Prof. of Maths., Univ. of Wisconsin 20-25, Assoc. Prof. 25-28, Prof. and Chair. of Dept. 28-32; Dir. Div. of Natural Sciences and Agriculture, Rockefeller Foundation 32-55, Vice-Pres. for Natural and Medical Sciences 55-59; Air Service, U.S. Army 17-19; Chair. Section D-2 40-42, and Chief of Applied Mathematics Panel, Nat. Defense Research Cttee. of Office of Scientific Research and Development 43-46; Fellow, Exec. Cttee. American Asscn. for Advancement of Science 50-52, Pres. 54, Chair. Board of Dirs. 55; mem. Board Scientific Consultants, Sloan-Kettering Inst. for Cancer Research 51-54, Chair. Scientific Policy Cttee. 55-59, Trustee 54-67, Vice-Pres. 58-59; Vice-Chair. Memorial Sloan-Kettering Cancer Center 60-67, Chair. Scientific Policy Cttee. 60-67; Chair. Basic Research Group, Research and Development Board 52-53; mem. American Philosophical Soc. 44-, Councillor 57-60; mem. Board Nat. Science Foundation 56-60; Vice-Pres. Alfred P. Sloan Foundation 59-64, Trustee 56-67, Consultant on Scientific Affairs 64-; mem. Nat. Advisory Cancer Council, U.S. Public Health Service 57-60; Vice-Chair. Health Research Council, City of New York 58-60; Pres. Public Health Research Inst. of City of New York Inc. 61-63; Chair. Board of Trustees and Fellow, Salk Inst. for Biological Studies 62-; mem. Board of Dirs. Scientists' Inst. for Public Information 63-67, Nat. Acad. of Sciences 69-; Fellow American Acad. of Arts and Sciences; mem. New York Acad. of Sciences 63-; Fellow 64-; King's Medal for Service in the Cause of Freedom; Medal for Merit (U.S.A.); Officier Légion d'Honneur (France); Public Welfare Medal, Nat. Acad. of Sciences 57; Hon. LL.D. (Wis.), Hon. D.Sc. (Drexel Inst. of Technology, São Paulo, Pittsburgh, New York Univs.), D.Eng. (Rensselaer Polytechnic Institute), D.Hum.Litt. (Univ. of Rochester); UNESCO Kalinga Prize 65, Arches of Science Award 65.
Leisure interest: Lewis Carroll and *Alice in Wonderland*.
Publs. *The Electromagnetic Field* (with Max Mason) 29, *Mathematical Theory of Communication* (with Claude

Shannon) 49, *Lady Luck—The Theory of Probability* 63, *Alice in Many Tongues* 64, *U.S. Philanthropic Foundations: Their History, Structure, Management and Record* 67, *Science and Imagination* 67, *Scene of Change* 70; Editor *The Scientist Speaks.*
Second Hill, Rural Route 3, New Milford, Connecticut 06776, U.S.A.

Webb, James Edwin, A.B.; American government official and industrialist; b. 7 Oct. 1906, Granville County, N.C.; s. of John Frederick and Sarah Gorham Webb; m. Patsy Aiken Douglas 1938; one s. one d.; ed. Univ. of N. Carolina and George Washington Univ. Law School.
Employed at R. G. Lassiter & Co., Raleigh, N.C. 24-25; Bureau of Educational Research Univ. of N.C. 28-29; Parham & Lassiter (Attorneys) Oxford, N.C. 29-30; Sec. to Congressman Edward W. Pou 32-34; Personnel Dir. and Asst. to Pres., Sperry Gyroscope Co. Inc., Brooklyn, N.Y. 36-41, Sec. and Treas. 41-43, Vice-Pres. 43-44; Gardner, Morrison & Rogers (Attorneys) Wash., C.D. 45-46; Exec. Asst. to Under-Sec. of Treas. 46; Dir. Bureau of Budget 46-49; Under-Sec. of State 49-52; Dir. Kerr-McGee Oil Industries Inc. 52-61, 69-; Admin. Nat. Aeronautics and Space Admin. (NASA) 61-68; Dir. Gannett Co. 69-, Sperry Rand Corpn. 69-, McGraw-Hill Inc. 72-; Trustee George Wash. Univ. 51-63, Cttee. for Econ. Devt. 52-, Nat. Geographic Soc. 66-; mem. and Treas. Nat Acad. of Public Admin. 69-; Regent, Smithsonian Inst. 70-; mem. Govt. Procurement Comm. 72-73; Chair. Meridian House Foundation, Wash., D.C. 62-70; mem. American Bar Asscn., Bar Assocn. of D.C., Soc. of Public Administrators (Pres. 66-67), Acad. of Political and Social Science; Collier Trophy 66, Oklahoma Hall of Fame 67; NASA Distinguished Service Medal 68; President's Medal of Freedom 68; Goddard Memorial Trophy 71; N. Carolina Public Service Award 71, Oklahoma State Univ. Henry G. Bennett Distinguished Service Award 73, Gen. Accounting Office Award for Public Service 73; Hon. Sc.D. (Notre Dame, Wash., New York and other universities), Hon. LL.D. (Syracuse Univ. and others), etc.
Publs. *Governmental Manpower for Tomorrow's Cities* 62, *Space Age Management* 68, *NASA as an Adaptive Organization* 68, *Leadership Evaluation in Large-Scale Efforts* 72, *Management Leadership and Relationships* 72.
Home: 2800 36th Street, N.W., Washington, D.C. 20007, U.S.A.

Weber, Ernst, D.SC., D.PHIL., D.ENG.; Austrian engineer; b. 6 Sept. 1901, Vienna; s. of Hermann Rudolf Weber and Josefine Pauline Swoboda; m. 1st Irma Lintner (divorced 1933), 2nd Charlotte Sonya Escherich 1936; two step d.; ed. Vienna Technical Univ.
Research Engineer Oesterreichische Siemens-Schuckert Co. Vienna 24-29; Design Engineer Siemens-Schuckert Co. Berlin 29-30; Visiting Prof. Polytechnic Inst. of Brooklyn, N.Y. 30-31, Research Prof. of Electrical Engineering 31-41, Head Research and Graduate Study in Electrical Engineering 42-45; Head Dept. of Electrical Engineering and Dir. of Microwave Research Inst. 45-57, Vice-Pres. for Research 57-63; Pres. Polytechnic Inst. of Brooklyn 57-69, Pres. Emer.; Chair. Nat. Acad. of Sciences; Consultant PRD Electronics Inc.; Founding mem. Nat. Acad. of Eng.; mem. Nat. Acad. of Sciences, Nat. Research Council Comm. on Sociotechnical Systems; Pres. Inst. Radio Engineers 59; Pres. Inst. of Electrical and Electronics Engineers 63.
Leisure interests: mountain climbing, music.
National Academy of Sciences, 2101 Constitution Avenue, N.W., Washington, D.C. 20418; Home: P.O. Box 1619, Tryon, N.C. 28782, U.S.A.
Telephone: (202) 389-6331 (Office); (704) 859-6224.

Weber, Prof. Gerhard; German architect; b. 11 June 1909, Mylau, Saxony; m. Elise Ebert; one s.; ed.

Kunstgewerbeakademie, Dresden, and Bauhaus, Dessau/Berlin.
Buildings: industrial and administrative, swimming pools, radio and television studios of the Hessischer Rundfunk; AFN Frankfurt; Deutschlandfunk Köln; Staatsoper Hamburg, Nationaltheater Mannheim; August-Thyssen-Hütte laboratories; Atomic reactor, Technische Universität Munich.
Leisure interests: objets d'art, fruit and viticulture.
8131 Allmannshausen, Zieglerweg, 14 Federal Republic of Germany.
Telephone: 08151 5816.

Wechsler, James A.; American editor; b. 1915; ed. Columbia Univ.
Editor *Columbia Spectator* 34-35; Student Advocate 36-37; Asst. Editor *Nation* magazine 38-39; Labour Editor, PM newspaper 40-41; Washington Bureau Chief, *New York Post* 42-44, Washington Correspondent 46-49, Editor, Editorial Page 49-61; Editorial Page Columnist and Editor 61-; U.S. Army 45.
Publs. *Revolt on the Campus* 35, *War Propaganda and the United States* (with Harold Levine) 40, *Labor Baron* 44, *The Age of Suspicion* 53, *Reflections of an Angry Middle-Aged Editor* 60, *In a Darkness* 72.
Home: 185 West End Avenue, New York, N.Y. 10023; Office: 210 South Street, New York, N.Y. 10002, U.S.A.

Weckmann-Muñoz, Luis, PH.D., LL.D., M.A.; Mexican diplomatist and historian; b. 7 April 1923, Ciudad Lerdo, Durango; s. of José Bernardo Weckmann and Ana Muñoz; m. Ibone de Belausteguigoitia 1972; ed. Nat. Univ. of Mexico, Univs. of Paris and Calif., Inst. des Hautes Etudes Int. and Ecole des Chartes, Paris.
Successively Sec. of Legation and Chargé d'Affaires, Czechoslovakia, Sec. of Embassy and Chargé d'Affaires, France 52-59; Dir.-Gen. for Int. Educ. Affairs and Exec. Sec.-Gen. Mexican Nat. Council for UNESCO 59-64; Minister Plenipotentiary and Chargé d'Affaires, France 65-66; Amb. to Israel 67-69, to Austria 69-72, to Fed. Repub. of Germany 73-74; Special Rep. of UN Sec.-Gen. to Iran and Iraq April-June 74; Special Rep. of UN Sec.-Gen. in Cyprus 74-75; Amb. to Iran 76-; Vice-Pres. 1st Interamerican meeting on Science and Technology, Washington; UNESCO's expert for Latin America on Cultural Exchanges.
Leisure interest: reading.
Publs. *La Sociedad Feudal* 44, *Las Bulas Alejandrinas de 1943 y la Teoría Política del Papado Medieval* 49, *El Pensamiento Político Medieval y una nueva base para el Derecho Internacional* 50, *Les origines des Missions Diplomatiques Permanentes* 53, *Panorama de la Cultura Medieval* 62, *Les Relaciones Franco-Mexicanas (1823-1885)* vol. I 61, vol. II 63, vol. III 72.
Mexican Embassy, 15 Avenue Hafez, Avenue Mohammed Reza Shah, Yousef Abad, P.O. Box 1917, Teheran, Iran.

Wedel, Cynthia C., M.A., PH.D.; American voluntary worker and church and community lecturer; b. 26 Aug. 1908, Dearborn, Mich.; d. of Arthur Pierson Clark and Elizabeth (née Haigh) Clark; m. Rev. Theodore O. Wedel 1939 (died 1970); ed. Northwestern Univ., George Washington Univ.
Paid jobs: professional Church work, Episcopal Church, New York 31-39; Teacher, Nat. Cathedral School, Washington, D.C. 39-49; Lecturer, American Univ. 57-60; Assoc. Gen. Sec. Nat Council of Churches 69-72; Assoc. Dir. Center for a Voluntary Soc. 69-73; volunteer work: Pres. Nat. Council of Churches 69-72, World Council of Churches 75-; Chair. Nat. Council of Orgs. for Children and Youth 73-75; Trustee, Virginia Theological Seminary 71-, Washington Theological Consortium 72-; Board mem. Girl Scouts of the U.S.A. 60-66; Nat. Chair. of Volunteers, American Red Cross 73-; Church Woman of the Year 57; Hon. D.Lit.

(Western Coll., Elmshurst Coll., Moravian Coll., Fordham Univ., Smith Coll.).

Leisure interests: travel, reading.

Publs. *Happy Issue* 62, *Faith or Fear and Future Shock* 74; many articles in journals and magazines.

National Headquarters, American Red Cross, Washington, D.C. 20006; Home: 4800 Fillmore Avenue, Alexandria, Va. 22311, U.S.A.

Telephone: (202) 857-3634 (Office); (703) 578-4978 (Home).

Wedgwood, Dame (Cicely) Veronica, O.M., D.B.E., M.A., F.R.HIST.S., F.R.S.L.; British author and historian; b. 20 July 1910; d. of the late Sir Ralph Wedgwood; sister of Sir John Wedgwood (*q.v.*); ed. Lady Margaret Hall, Oxford.

President English Centre Int. PEN Club 51-57; Pres. English Association 55-56; Clark Lecturer, Cambridge 57-58; Northcliffe Lecturer, University of London 59; mem. Arts Council 58-61, 66-67; mem. Royal Comm. on Historical MSS 53-, Inst. of Advanced Study, Princeton 52-68; Trustee Nat. Gallery, London 63-68, 70-; Officer, Order of Orange-Nassau, Goethe Medal 59; mem. American Acad.; Fellow, British Acad. 75; Hon. D.Litt. (Univs. of Oxford, Sheffield, Keele, Sussex, Smith Coll., Liverpool and Harvard Univ.), Hon. LL.D. (Univ. of Glasgow).

Leisure interests: poetry, painting, theatre.

Publs. *Strafford* 35, *The Thirty Years' War* 38, *Oliver Cromwell* 39, *William the Silent* 44, *Velvet Studies* 46, *Richelieu* 49, *English Literature in the Seventeenth Century* 50, *The Last of the Radicals* 51, *Montrose* 52, *The King's Peace* 55, *The King's War* 58, *Truth and Opinion* 60, *Poetry and Politics Under the Stuarts* 60, *Thomas Wentworth: A Revaluation* 61, *The Trial of Charles I* 64, *Milton and his World* 69, *The Political Career of Rubens* 75.

c/o Department of History, University College, London, W.C.1, England.

Wedgwood, Sir John Hamilton, Bt., T.D., F.R.S.A., F.R.G.S.; British master potter; b. 1907, Newcastle upon Tyne; s. of Sir Ralph L. Wedgwood and Iris Veronica (née Pawson); brother of Dame Veronica Wedgwood (*q.v.*); m. Diana Hawkshaw; four s. (one deceased) one d.; ed. Winchester Coll., Trinity Coll., Cambridge, and in France, Germany, etc.

Joined Josiah Wedgwood and Sons Ltd. 31, Dir. 35 and Deputy Chair. 55-66; Chair. Artistic Framing Ltd. 70-; mem. British Nat. Export Council 64-66; Chair. Anglo-American Relations Cttee., Lakenheath Airbase 71-; Hon. LL.D. (Birmingham).

Leisure interests: mountaineering, walking, spelaeology, travel.

Artistic Framing Limited, Dobles Lane, Holsworthy, North Devon, EX22 6HN, England.

Telephone: Holsworthy 253332.

Weedon, Basil Charles Leicester, C.B.E., F.R.S., D.SC., F.R.I.C.; British chemist, university teacher and administrator; b. 18 July 1923, London; s. of the late Charles William Weedon; m. Barbara Mary Dawe 1959; one s. one d.; ed. Wandsworth School, Imperial Coll. of Science and Tech., Univ. of London.

Research Chemist, ICI Ltd. (Dyestuffs Div.) 45-47; Lecturer in Organic Chem., Imperial Coll. of Science and Tech. 47-55, Reader 55-60; Prof. of Organic Chem., Queen Mary Coll., Univ. of London 60-75; Vice-Chancellor, Univ. of Nottingham 76-; Meldola Medal, Royal Inst. of Chem.; Tilden Lecturer of Chem. Soc.

Publs. numerous papers in scientific journals, mainly in *Journal of the Chemical Society*.

University of Nottingham, University Park, Nottingham, NG7 2RD, England.

Telephone: Nottingham 56101.

Weeks, Edward A., B.S., LITT.D.; American journalist; b. 19 Feb. 1898, Elizabeth, New Jersey; s. of Edward A. Weeks and Frederika Suydam; m. 1st Frederika Watriss 1925 (died 1970); one s. one d.; 2nd Phoebe Adams 1971; ed. Cornell, Harvard and Cambridge Univs.

MSS. reader and salesman with Horace Liveright. Inc., N.Y. City 23; Assoc. Editor *Atlantic Monthly* 24-28, Editor 38-66; Editor Atlantic Monthly Press 28-37, Senior Editor 66-; Overseer, Harvard Univ. 45-51; Trustee, Wellesley Coll. 47-65, Colonial Williamsburg 58-67, Pittsburgh and Rochester Univs. 60-68; Dir. Magazine Publishers' Asscn. 61-63; Dir. American Field Service 63-71; Vice-Chair. United Negro Coll. Fund 63-; Fellow American Acad. Arts and Sciences.

Leisure interests: conservation, fishing, golf, books.

Publs. *This Trade of Writing* 35, *Great Short Novels* (Ed.) 41, *The Pocket Atlantic* (Ed.) 46, *The Open Heart* 55, *Jubilee—One Hundred Years of the Atlantic* (Ed. with Emily Flint) 57, *In Friendly Candor* 59, *Breaking into Print* 62, *Boston: Cradle of Liberty* 65, *The Lowells and Their Institute* 66, *Fresh Waters* 68, *The Moisie Salmon Club: A Chronicle* 71, *My Green Age* 74, *Myopia, A Centennial History, 1875-1975* 75.

Home: 59 Chestnut Street, Boston, Mass.; Office: 8 Arlington Street, Boston, Mass. 02116, U.S.A.

Telephone: 617-536-9500 (Office).

Weerasinghe, Oliver, O.B.E., F.R.I.B.A., M.T.P.I.; Ceylonese city planner and diplomatist; b. 29 Sept. 1907, Colombo; s. of Joseph Victor Weerasinghe and Maria Caroline Tudugalla; m. Christobel Beatrice Kotelaweta 1942; one s. one d.; ed. Royal Coll., Colombo Ceylon, and Univ. of Liverpool, England.

Directed planning and development of new city of Anuradhapura, Ceylon 40-56; Head Town and Country Planning Dept., Ceylon 47-56; Chair. Board of Improvement Commrs., Colombo 53-56; Chief, Planning and Urbanization Section, Dept. of Econ. and Social Affairs, UN, New York 56-64; Exec. Sec. UN Seminar on Regional Planning, Tokyo 58, UN Expert Group on Metropolitan Planning, Stockholm 61, UN Symposium on New Towns, Moscow 64; Deputy Dir. Centre for Housing, Building and Planning, UN, New York 65; del. to twentieth session of UN General Assembly; Amb. of Ceylon to the U.S.A. 65-71, and Mexico 67-71; Distinction in Town Planning, Royal Inst. of British Architects 46.

Leisure interest: golf.

Publ. *Town Planning in Ceylon* 47.

Ministry of Foreign Affairs, Colombo, Sri Lanka.

Weeratunge, Conrad Edward Somadasa, M.B., B.S., F.R.C.G.P.; Ceylonese diplomatist and health specialist; b. 30 July 1924; s. of late Mr. and Mrs. William Weeratunge; m. Dayanitha Nathalie Gunaratne 1950; one s. three d.; ed. Royal Coll., Colombo and Univ. of Ceylon.

Member of Court, Univ. of Ceylon 53-59, Board of Regents 71-72; Sec., Ministry of Health 70-74; Chair. Nat. Comm. of Health Planning 71-74; Dir. State Pharmaceutical Corpn. 71-74; Chair. Advisory Comm. on Post-graduate Medical Educ. 71-72; Chair. WHO Regional Comm. 72, Tech. Discussions, 27th World Health Assembly 74; WHO Expert Adviser Panel, Public Health Admin. 72-; Founder Pres. Sri Lanka Asscn. for Population Studies 72-73; Amb. to U.S.S.R., Romania, Poland, Czechoslovakia, Hungary and German Democratic Repub. 74-.

Leisure interests: photography, music.

Embassy of Sri Lanka, 24 ulitsa Shepkina, Moscow, U.S.S.R.; 35 Bagatalle Road, Colombo 3, Sri Lanka.

Telephone: 281-92-91, 281-63-63 (Office).

Weese, Harry, American architect; b. 30 June 1915, Evanston, Ill.; s. of Harry Ernest Weese and Marjorie Mohr Weese; m. Kate Baldwin 1945; three d.; ed. Yale Univ. School of Architecture, Mass. Inst. of Technology, Cranbrook Acad. of Art.

Research Asst. Bemis Housing Foundation, Mass. Inst. Technology (prefabricated and low-cost housing) 39; Principal, Baldwin, & Weese (architects) 40-42; U.S. Navy 42-46; Senior Designer, Chicago office Skidmore, Owings & Merrill 46-47; independent practice 47-; manufacturing plant for Cummins Engine Co., Columbus, Indiana 50-64.

Principal works: U.S. Embassy, Accra, Ghana, Hyde Park Redevelopment Project, Chicago, Arena Stage, Washington D.C., Elvehjem Art Center, Univ. of Wisconsin, Milwaukee Center for the Performing Arts, Wisconsin, Metro Rapid Rail Transit System, Washington Metropolitan Area Transit Authority, Washington D.C., IBM Building, Milwaukee, Time & Life Building, Chicago, Technical Center, Cummins Engine Co., Columbus, Staff Housing Air India, Bombay, Crown Center Hotel, Kansas City, Physical Education Building, Education and Communications Building, Student Services, Building Classroom Office Building, Univ. of Illinois Chicago Circle Campus, U.S. Courthouse Annex, Chicago, Fine Arts Center, Carleton Coll., Social Sciences Campus, New York State Univ., Buffalo-Amherst Campus, Student and Fine Arts Centers, Drake Univ., Terman Eng. Center, Stanford Univ., Calif.; Loop Subway System Study, CTA Determination of System and Design Elements (with American Bechtel) for Chicago Central Transportation District; Redevt. of Station and Devt. of Air Rights, Union Station Terminal, Kansas City, Mo.

Leisure interests: sailing, skiing, tennis.

Office: 10 West Hubbard Street, Chicago, Ill. 60610; Home: 314 West Willow Street, Chicago, Ill. 60614, U.S.A.

Telephone: 467-7030 (Office); MI-2-1498 (Home).

Węgrzyn, Stefan, D.ENG.; Polish scientist; b. 20 May 1925, Cracow; s. of Jan Węgrzyn and Maria Wilgocka; ed. Silesian Technical Univ., Gliwice.

Assistant, Electrical Dept. Silesian Technical Univ. 49, Asst. Prof. 54-60, Prof. 61-; Deputy Dir. for Scientific Affairs, Inst. of Automation, Polish Acad. of Sciences 62-; corresp. mem. Polish Acad. of Sciences 64-73, mem. 73-, mem. Presidium 74-; mem. Council of Science and Technics 72-, Deputy Dir. Centre of Scientific Research, Polish Acad. of Sciences, Katowice Voivodship; Knight's Cross of Order Polonia Restituta 64; State Prize 66; Medal of 30th Anniversary of People's Poland 74; Dir. h.c. (Univ. of Lille, France) 73.

Publs. *Rachunek operatorowy* 55, *Podstawy automatyki* 63, 72, 74, *Calcul Opérationnel en électrotechnique* 67, *Introduction à l'étude de la Stabilité dans les espaces métriques* 71.

Politechnika Śląska, 44-100 Gliwice, Katowicka 16; Home: Konarskiego 11 m. 3, Gliwice, Poland.

Telephone: 91-46-73 (Office); 91-01-10 (Home).

Wehner, Herbert; German journalist and politician; b. 11 July 1906; ed. Realschule.

Mem. Saxon Provincial Parl. 30-32; resistance movement 30-; emigrated to various countries including U.S.S.R. and Sweden 35-46; later Editor, Hamburg; Chair. Hamburg Union, Sozialdemokratische Partei Deutschlands (S.P.D.), Dep. Chair. Federal S.P.D. 58-73, Parl. Leader 69-; mem. Bundestag 49-; Minister of All-German Affairs 66-69.

Beim Schlump 36, Hamburg 13, Federal Republic of Germany.

Wei Kuo-ch'ing; Chuang party official; b. 1914, Tunglan, Kwangsi.

Regimental Commdr. 33; on Long March 34-35; Deputy Political Commissar 10th Army Corps, 3rd Field Army, People's Liberation Army 49; Mayor of Foochow 49; Gov. of Kwangsi 55-58; Alt. mem. 8th Cen. Cttee. of CCP 56; Sec. CCP Kwangsi 57-61, First Sec. 61-68; Chair. Kwangsi People's Govt. 58-68; First Political

Commissar Kwangsi Mil. District, PLA 64-73; Sec. Cen.-South Bureau, CCP 66; Political Commissar Canton Mil. Region, PLA 67-; Chair. Kwangsi Revolutionary Cttee. 68; mem. 9th Cen. Cttee. of CCP 69; First Sec. CCP Kwangsi 71-75; First Sec. Kwantung CCP Cttee. 75-; mem. Politburo, 10th Cen. Cttee. of CCP 73.

People's Republic of China.

Wei Tao-ming, LL.D.; Chinese diplomatist and politician; b. 1899; ed. Univ. de Paris à la Sorbonne.

Minister of Justice 28-29; Mayor of Nanking 30-32; Sec.-Gen. Executive Yuan 37-41; Amb. to France 41-42, to U.S.A. 42-46; Vice-Pres. Legislative Yuan 46-47; Gov. Taiwan Province 47-49; Adviser to Pres. Repub. of China 49-64; Amb. to Japan 64-66; Minister of Foreign Affairs 66-71.

Publ. *Le Cheque en Chine.*

No. 10, Lane 119, Roosevelt Road, Sec. I, Taipei, Taiwan.

Weichmann, Herbert; German politician; b. 23 Feb. 1896, Landsberg; s. of Dr. Wilhelm Weichmann and Irma (née Guttentag); m. Dr. Elsbeth Greisinger 1928; one s.; ed. Univs. of Breslau, Frankfurt (Main), Heidelberg and New York.

Provincial Judge, Breslau 26-27; Prussian Govt. posts 27-33; emigrated to France 33-40, U.S.A. 41-48; Pres. Hamburg Audit Court 48-57; Senator for Finance, Hamburg 57-65; Chief Burgomaster of Hamburg 65-71; mem. Bundesrat; Pres. Bundesrat 68-69; Vice-Pres. Int. Inst. of Public Admin.; Social Democrat; Hon. Prof. Hamburg Univ. 64-; hon. citizen Hamburg and Minneapolis, U.S.A.

Am Feenteich 8, Hamburg 76, Federal Republic of Germany.

Weicker, Lowell Palmer, Jr., LL.B.; American senator; b. 16 May 1931, Paris, France; s. of Lowell Palmer Weicker and Mary (Bickford) Paulsen; m. Mary Louise Godfrey 1953; three s.; ed. Lawrenceville School, Yale Univ. and Univ. of Virginia.

State Rep. in Conn. Gen. Assembly 63-69; U.S. Rep., Fourth Congressional District, Conn. 69-71; Senator from Conn. 71-; 1st Selectman of Greenwich 64-68; mem. Select Cttee. for Investigation of the Watergate Case 73; Senate Cttee. on Govt. Operations, Commerce, Select Cttee. on Small Businesses; Republican.

Leisure interests: tennis, sailing, history.

342 Russell Building, Washington, D.C. 20510, U.S.A. Telephone: 202-225-4041.

Weidenfeld, Sir (Arthur) George, Kt.; British publisher; b. 13 Sept. 1919; s. of Max and Rose Weidenfeld; m. 1st Jane Sieff 1952, one d.; m. 2nd Barbara Skelton Connolly 1956; m. 3rd Sandra Whitney Payson 1966; ed. Piaristen Gymnasium, Vienna, Univ. of Vienna and Konsular Akademie.

B.B.C. Monitoring Service 39-42; B.B.C. News Commentator on European Affairs on B.B.C. Empire and North American service 42-46; Foreign Affairs columnist, *News Chronicle* 43-44; Political Adviser and Chief of Cabinet of President Weizmann of Israel; founder of Contact Books 45; f. Weidenfeld & Nicolson Ltd. 48; Chair. Weidenfeld & Nicolson Ltd. 48-, Arthur Barker Ltd.

Leisure interests: opera, travel.

Publ. *The Goebbels Experiment* 43.

9 Chelsea Embankment, London, S.W.3, England.

Weidlein, Edward Ray, M.A.; American scientist; b. 14 July 1887, Augusta, Kansas; s. of Edward Weidlein and Nettie (Lemon) Weidlein; m. Hazel Butts 1915 (deceased); three s.; ed. Univ. of Kansas.

Industrial Fellow, Univ. of Kansas 10-12; Senior Fellow, Mellon Inst., Pittsburgh 12-16, Asst. Dir. and later Assoc. Dir. 16, Acting Dir. 17-18, Dir. 21-51, Pres. 51-56 (retd.); Chair. Board of Trustees Mellon Inst. 51-55;

Emer. Trustee Univ. of Pittsburgh 21-; Chief of Chemicals Branch W.P.B. 40-42, and Head Technical Consultant, W.P.B. 42-46; Pres. Regional Industrial Devt. Corpn. Fund 62-71; Fellow, American Asscn. for Advancement of Science, N.Y. Acad. of Sciences, Royal Soc. of Arts; mem. American Chemical Soc. (Pres. 37, Dir. 38-47), awards include Chemical Industry Medal 35, Naval Ordnance Devt. Award 47, Priestley Medal 48, Certificate of Appreciation (Depts. of Army and Navy) 48; William Proctor Prize from Scientific Research Soc. of America 61; Richard Beatty Mellon Award 61; Founder's Award American Inst. of Chemical Engineers 66; several hon. degrees.
Leisure interests: golf, hunting and fishing.
Publs. with William A. Hamor: *Science in Action*, *Glances at Industrial Research*.
"Weidacres", P.O. Box 45, Rector, Pa. 15677, U.S.A. Telephone: 238-2202.

Weigl, Henry, B.A., LL.B.; American business executive; b. 6 July 1912, New York; s. of Otto and Lottie Weigl; m. 1st Gladys Hines 1940 (deceased), 2nd Marie Babington 1969; two d.; ed. New York Univ., and Harvard Univ.
Standard Brands Inc. 43-, Gen. Counsel 48-56, Vice-Pres. 54-56, Exec. Vice-Pres. 56-60, Dir. 56-, Pres. and mem. Exec. Cttee. 60-75, Chief Exec. Officer 64-75, Chair. 75-.
Standard Brands Inc., 625 Madison Avenue, New York City, N.Y. 10022; Home: 164 Clapboard Ridge Road, Greenwich, Conn. 06830, U.S.A.

Weihs, Dr. Oskar; Austrian politician; b. 19 April 1911, Vienna; ed. Hochschule für Bodenkultur, Vienna. Employed at Bacteriological Inst., Mödling and Wiener Molkerei 34-35; political activities 35-38; employed with the Milch- und Fettwirtschaft Südmark 38-40; army service and prisoner-of-war 40-45; Deputy Dir. Styrian Chamber for Blue and White-Collar Workers 46; mem. Nationalrat 59-; Minister for Agriculture and Forestry May 70-; Socialist Party.
Federal Ministry of Agriculture and Forestry, Vienna, Austria.

Weikop, Ove Vilhelm; Danish businessman and politician; b. 21 April 1897, Copenhagen; m. 1918; one s. one d.
Began career as retail dealer in textiles 16; Pres. Danish Textile Retailers' Asscn. (Dansk Textil Union) 38-50; Pres. Mogensen & Dessau, Odense, Ove Weikop & Son, Østerbros Messe; mem. Maritime and Commercial Court 40-50; mem. City Council, Copenhagen 33-41; Alderman 41-50; mem. Parl. 47-68; Minister of Trade 50-51; Burgomaster of Copenhagen 51-71; Commdr. Order of Dannebrog; Grand Officer Order of Orange Nassau (Netherlands), Order of the Crown; Knight Commdr. of Victorian Order; Commdr. Crown of Thailand.
Home: Borgmester Jensens Alle 22, Copenhagen.

Weil, André; French mathematician; b. 6 May 1906, Paris, France; m. Eveline Gillet 1937; two d.; ed. Ecole Normale Supérieure, Paris, and Univs. of Rome, Göttingen and Paris.
Professor, Aligarh Muslim Univ. 30-32; Faculty of Science, Univ. of Strasbourg 33-39; Faculty of Philosophy, Univ. of São Paulo 45-47; Prof., Dept. of Mathematics, Univ. of Chicago 47-58; Prof. Inst. for Advanced Study, Princeton 58-; Foreign mem. Royal Soc. (U.K.) 66.
Institute for Advanced Study, Princeton, N.J. 08540, U.S.A.

Weinberg, Alvin M., S.M., PH.D.; American physicist and scientific administrator; b. 20 April 1915, Chicago, Ill.; s. of Jacob and Emma Levinson Weinberg; m. Margaret Despres 1940 (died 1969), two s.; m. 2nd Gene Kellerman 1974; ed. Univ. of Chicago.

Biophysics research Univ. of Chicago 39-42; Hanford reactor design Univ. of Chicago Metallurgical Laboratory 42-45; Section Chief Physics Div., Oak Ridge Nat. Laboratory 45-47, Dir. Physics Div. 47-48, Research Dir. 48-55; Dir. Oak Ridge Nat. Laboratory 55-73; Dir. Office of Energy Research and Devt., Fed. Energy Office 74-, Inst. for Energy Analysis 75-; mem. Scientific Advisory Board to the Air Force 55-59; mem. President's Science Advisory Cttee. 60-63; Fellow, American Nuclear Soc. American Physical Soc.; mem. American Acad. of Arts and Sciences, Nat. Acad. of Eng.; mem. Nat. Acad. of Sciences, Cttee. on Science and Public Policy of Nat. Acad. of Sciences 63-66, Council of Nat. Acad. of Sciences 67-70; mem. Pres. Nixon's Task Force on Science Policy 69, Nat. Cancer Plan Evaluation Cttee. 72; co-recipient Atoms for Peace Award 60, Ernest O. Lawrence Memorial Award of Atomic Energy Comm. 60, Univ. of Chicago Alumni Medal 66, Heinrich Hertz Energy Prize 75; contributions to nuclear technology in reactor theory, reactor design, breeder reactor systems, implications of nuclear energy; formulation of science policy; energy supply and demand.
Leisure interests: piano, tennis, swimming.
Publs. *The Physical Theory of Neutron Chain Reactors* (with Eugene P. Wigner) 58, *Reflections on Big Science* 67.
Institute for Energy Analysis, Oak Ridge Associated Universities, P.O. Box 117, Oak Ridge, Tenn. 37830; Home: 111 Moylan Lane, Oak Ridge, Tenn. 37830, U.S.A.
Telephone: 202-456-6511 (Office); 615-483-6045 (Home).

Weinberg, Steven, PH.D.; American physicist; b. 3 May 1933, New York; s. of Fred and Eva Weinberg; m. Louise Weinberg 1954; one d.; ed. Cornell Univ., Univ. of Copenhagen and Princeton Univ.
Columbia Univ. 57-59; Lawrence Radiation Lab. 59-60; Univ. of Calif. (Berkeley) 60-69; Prof. of Physics, Mass. Inst. of Technology 69-73; Higgins Prof. of Physics, Harvard Univ. 73-; Sr. Scientist, Smithsonian Astrophysical Observatory 73-; Scott Lecturer, Cavendish Laboratory 75; mem. Nat. Acad. of Sciences, American Acad. of Arts and Sciences, Council for Foreign Relations; mem. Council, American Physical Soc.; Oppenheimer Prize 72; Richtmeyer Lecturer 74.
Leisure interest: mediaeval history.
Publs. *Gravitation and Cosmology* 72, and over 90 articles.
Department of Physics, Harvard University, Cambridge, Mass. 02138, U.S.A.

Weinberger, Caspar; American government official; b. 18 Aug. 1917, San Francisco; s. of Herman and Cerise Carpenter (Hampson) Weinberger; m. Jane Dalton 1942; one s. one d.
Served with AUS 41-45; with Heller, Ehrman, White and McAuliffe 47-69, partner 59-69; mem. Calif. State Legislature 52-58; Vice-Chair. Calif. Repub. Centennial Comm. 60-62, Chair. 62-64; Chair. Calif. Gov. Org. and Econ. 67-68; Dir. Finance Calif. 68-69; Chair. Fed. Trade Comm. 70; Deputy Dir. Office of Management and Budget 70-72, Dir. 72-73; Counsellor to Pres. 73; Sec. of Health, Educ. and Welfare and in charge of natural resources 73-75; Chair. Pres. Cttee. Mental Retardation; mem. Bd. Govs. U.S. Nat. Red Cross, Dir. Yosemite Inst., Board Trustees John F. Kennedy Center for Performing Arts, American Bar Asscn., State Bar Calif.
Department of Health Education and Welfare, Washington, D.C. 20201, U.S.A.

Weiner, Mervyn Lester, B.COM., B.PHIL.; Canadian development finance official; b. 30 Oct. 1922, Montreal; s. of Louis Weiner and Beatrice Feinstein; m. Shirley R. Hurwitz 1951; one s. one d.; ed. McGill Univ., Balliol Coll., Oxford, Univ. of Pennsylvania and Johns Hopkins Univ.

Instructor, Wharton School of Commerce and Finance, Univ. of Pennsylvania 48-49; Instructor Johns Hopkins Univ. 49-51; Econ. Affairs Officer UN 50; IBRD officer 51-, Research Economist 51-55, Country Economist 55-61, Loan Officer 61-63, Div. Chief 63-65, Economic Adviser, later Chief Economist, Western Hemisphere Dept. 65-69, Dir. Public Utilities Projects Dept. 69-72, Dir. Asia Region Projects Dept. 72-74, Regional Vice-Pres. S. Asia 74-75, Dir.-Gen. Operations Evaluation 75-.
Leisure interests: sailing, photography.
1818 H Street, N.W. Washington, D.C. 20433; Home: 3206 Cummings Lane, Chevy Chase, Md. 20015, U.S.A. Telephone: 202-393-6360 (Office).

Weinstock, Sir Arnold, Kt., B.SC.(ECON.); British business executive; b. 29 July 1924; ed. Univ. of London. Junior Admin. Officer, Admiralty 44-47; with Private Group of Companies engaged in finance and property development 47-54; Man. Dir. Radio and Allied Industries Ltd. (now Radio and Allied Holdings Ltd.) 54-63; Dir. General Electric Co. Ltd. 61-; Man. Dir. 63-; Man. Dir. Nat. Nuclear Corpn. 73-; Dir. Rolls-Royce (1971) Ltd. 71-73; Dir. numerous other companies.
7 Grosvenor Square, London, W.1, England.

Weir, Hon. Walter C.; Canadian politician; b. 7 Jan. 1929; s. of James Dixon Weir and Christina Maude Cox-Smith; m. Harriet Thompson 1951; three s. one d.; ed. elementary and secondary education, Portage la Prairie, Manitoba.
Private business (funeral director), Minnedosa, Manitoba 53-63; Minister of Municipal Affairs, Manitoba 61-63, Acting Minister of Public Works 62, full Minister of Public Works Nov. 62-66; Minister of Highways 65-67; Leader of Manitoba Progressive Conservative Party and Premier of Manitoba Nov. 67-June 69; Leader of the Opposition June 69-.
Leisure interests: curling, golf.
Home: 670 Wellington Crescent, Winnipeg 9, Manitoba, Canada.
Telephone: 284-2175 (Home).

Weisgal, Meyer Wolf; American journalist and executive; b. 10 Nov. 1894, Kikol, Poland; m. Shirley Hirschfeld 1923; two s. one d.; ed. Columbia Univ.
National Sec. Zionist Org. of America 21-30; Dir.-Gen. Palestine Pavilion, World's Fair, New York 39-40; Personal Political Rep. Dr. Weizmann in U.S.A. 40-48; Organizer, American Section Jewish Agency for Palestine, Sec.-Gen. 43-46; Organizer and Exec. Vice-Chair. American Cttee. Weizmann Inst. 46-59; Chair. Exec. Council Weizmann Inst. of Science, Israel 49-, Pres. 66-70, Chancellor 70; del. World Zionist Congress 24-; fmr. Editor *The New Palestine* (New York) 21-30, *Jewish Standard* (Toronto) 30-32; Hon. D.Phil. (Weizmann Inst. of Science) 64; Hon. D.Sc. (Brandeis Univ.), Hon. D.Phil. (Hebrew Univ. Jerusalem), 69; Rothschild Prize 69.
Publs. *Chaim Weizmann: Statesman, Scientist, Builder of the Jewish Commonwealth* 44, *Chaim Weizmann, A Biography by Several Hands* (Editor) 63, *Chaim Weizmann, Letters and Papers* (Gen.-Editor) 68, ... *So Far* (autobiography) 72, *The Letters and Papers of Chaim Weizmann* (Editor) 73, and numerous Jewish and Zionist pamphlets.
14 Neveh Weizmann, Rehovoth, Israel; and 240 Central Park South, New York 19, N.Y.. U.S.A.
Telephone: 03-951721 (Israel); CI-7-3753 (New York).

Weiss, Gerhard, DR. RER. OEC.; German economist and politician; b. 30 July 1919, Erfurt, Thuringia; ed. Deutsche Akad. für Staats- und Rechtswissenschaft, Humboldt-Univ. Berlin.
Commercial training 35-37, subsequently clerk in export firm; mem. Staff, Head of Dept. in a Thuringia Province Ministry 49-51; Head of Dept.. Ministry of Foreign and Inter-German Trade of D.D.R. 51-54;

Deputy Minister of Foreign and Inter-German Trade 54-65; Deputy Chair. of Council of Ministers (65-) and Perm. Rep. of D.D.R. to Council for Mutual Econ. Assistance (COMECON) 67-; Candidate mem., Central Cttee. of Socialist Unity Party 67-; mem. Volkskammer 67-; Vaterländischer Verdienstorden der D.D.R. (Bronze); Orden Banner der Arbeit; Order of Merit of Repub., First Class (Egypt); Grand Cordon of Order of Repub. (Egypt).
Council of Ministers of D.D.R., 102 Berlin, Klosterstrasse 47, German Democratic Republic.

Weiss, Herman L.; American business executive; b. 22 July 1916, Cleveland, Ohio; m. Pauline McCabe; one s.; ed. Case Inst. of Technology.
Joined General Electric Co. 39; Gen. Man. Lamp Div. 59; Vice-Pres. 61; Group Exec., Consumer Products Group 62; Exec. Vice-Pres. and mem. President's Office Jan. 68; Vice-Chair. and Dir. Gen. Electric Co. Dec. 68-.
General Electric Company, 3135 Easton Turnpike, Fairfield, Conn. 06431, U.S.A.

Weiss, Paul Alfred, PH.D.; American biologist; b. 21 March 1898, Vienna, Austria; s. of Carl S. and Rosalia Weiss; m. Maria Helene Blaschka 1926; ed. Univ. of Vienna.
Asst. Dir. Biology Research Inst., Acad. of Sciences, Vienna 22-29; Sterling Fellow, Yale Univ. 30-32; Prof. of Zoology, Univ. of Chicago 33-54; Prof., Rockefeller Inst., New York 54-64; Prof. and Dean Graduate School of Biomedical Sciences, Univ. of Texas 64-66; Prof. Emer. Rockefeller Univ. 66-; Visiting Prof. at many Univs.; mem. Science Advisory Cttee. of Pres. of U.S.A. 58-60; Chair. Div. Biology and Agriculture, Nat. Research Council 51-55, Biology Council, Nat. Acad. Sciences 53-58, U.S.A. Nat. Comm., Int. Union Biological Sciences 53-64; Consultant, U.S. Dept. of State; mem. U.S. Nat. Acad. Sciences, mem. Council 64-67; mem. Royal Swedish Acad. Science, Serbian Acad. Science, German Acad. of Science, Leopoldina, American Philosophical Soc., American Acad. Arts and Science; Max-Planck Soc. Pres. Growth Soc. 41, Harvey Soc. 62-63; Pres. Int. Soc. Cell Biology 65-68; Vice-Pres. American Asscn. for Advancement of Science 52-53; Hon. M.D., Hon. Dr. med., Hon. Sc.D., Hon. Dr. med. and surg., Hon. Dr. rer. nat.; U.S. Army-Navy Citation for Outstanding Merit, Leitz Award, Weinstein Award of UN Cerebral Palsy Asscn., John F. Lewis Prize and Lashley Prize of American Philosophical Soc., and other awards.
Leisure interests: art, writing, music.
Publs. *Entwicklungsphysiologie der Tiere* 30, *Aus den Werkstätten der Lebensforschung* 31, *Principles of Development* 39, *Dynamics of Development: Experiments and Inferences* 68, *Life, Order and Understanding* 70, *Biomedical Excursions* 71, *Within the Gates of Science and Beyond* 71, *Hierarchically Organized Systems* 71, *The Science of Life: The Living System—a System of Living* 73, *Knowledge in Search of Understanding* 75, over 350 scientific papers on growth, development, nerve function, theoretical biology, etc.
Rockefeller University, New York, N.Y. 10021, U.S.A.
Telephone: 360-1578.

Weiss, Peter; Swedish (b. German) writer; b. 16; ed. Art Academy, Prague.
Emigrated from Germany 34, lived in England 34-36, in Czechoslovakia 36-38, in Sweden 39-; painter, film producer and writer; Charles Veillon Prize for Literature 63; Heinrich-Mann-Preis, Akademie der Künste (E. Berlin) 66.
Publs. Prose: *Der Schatten des Körpers des Kutschers* 60, *Abschied von den Eltern* 61, *Fluchtpunkt* 62, *Das Gespräch der drei Gehenden* 63, *Rekonvaleszenz* (diary) 72; Plays: *Nacht mit Gästen* 63, *Die Verfolgung und Ermordung Jean-Paul Marats* 64 (film 67), *Die Er-*

mittlung 65, *Gesang vom Lusitanischen Popanz* 66, *Viet-Nam Dialogue* 67, *Wie dem Herrn Mockinpott das Leiden ausgetrieben wird* 68, *Trotzki im Exil* 70, *Hölderlin* 71.
c/o Suhrkamp Verlag, Lindenstrasse 29-35, 6 Frankfurt-am-Main, Federal Republic of Germany.

Weisskopf, Victor Frederick, PH.D.; American (b. Austrian) physicist; b. 1908, Vienna; *m.* Ellen Trede 1934; one *s.* one *d.*; ed. Vienna and Göttingen Univs. Research Associate, Berlin 31-32; Zürich Inst. of Technology 32-36, Rockefeller Foundation Fellow, Copenhagen and Cambridge 36-37; Instructor of Physics, Univ. of Rochester 37-40, Asst. Prof. 40-43; Group Leader, Los Alamos Scientific Laboratory 43-47; Prof. of Physics, Mass. Inst. of Technology 45-; mem. Directorate, European Org. for Nuclear Research 60-61, Dir.-Gen. 61-65; Pres. American Physical Soc. 60; corresp. mem. French, Scottish, Austrian and Bavarian Acads. of Sciences; foreign mem. Danish Soc. of Sciences; Hon. Fellow, French Soc. of Physics, Royal Soc. of Edinburgh, Weizmann Inst., Israel; Max Planck Medal 50; Bors Pregel Award (U.S.A.) 71, Cino del Duca Award (France) 72; several hon. degrees.
Publs. *Theoretical Nuclear Physics* (with J. Blatt) 52, *Knowledge and Wonder* 62, *Physics in the Twentieth Century* 72.
36 Arlington Street, Cambridge, Mass. 02140, U.S.A. Telephone: 617-868-2390.

Weissman, George; American tobacco executive; b. 12 July 1919; *m.* Mildred Stregack; two *s.* one *d.*; ed. Coll. of City of New York, New York Univ. and Univ. of Illinois.
United States Navy 42-46; Samuel Goldwyn 46-48; Account Exec., Benjamin Sonnenberg 48-52; Asst. to Pres. and Dir. of Public Relations, Philip Morris Inc. 52-53, Vice-Pres. 53-57, Vice-Pres. and Dir. of Marketing 57-59, Dir. 58-, Exec. Vice-Pres. 59-66, mem. Exec. Cttee. of Board of Dirs. 64-; Chair. of Board and Chief Exec. Officer, Philip Morris International 60-67, Pres. 64-67; Pres. and Chief Operating Officer Philip Morris Inc. 67-73, Vice-Chair. Board of Dirs. 73-; Dir. Benson and Hedges (Canada) Ltd. 58-70, Philip Morris (Australia) 60-67, Fabriques de Tabacs Réunies 63-67; Pres. and Dir. Philip Morris Int. Finance Corpn. 68-73; Dir. Miller Brewing Co. 69-, Mission Viejo Co. 70-, Harlem Savings Bank, Avnet Inc., Lincoln Center; Trustee, Lincoln Center Fund, Baruch Coll. Fund, Assoc. UM-YWHAs of Greater N.Y.; mem. Board of Dirs. Film Soc. of Lincoln Center Board of Visitors City Univ. N.Y. and City Coll. N.Y., Graduate Advisory Board of Baruch Coll. of N.Y.; Commdr. Order of Merit of Italy.
Philip Morris Incorporated, 100 Park Avenue, New York City, N.Y. 10017; Home: 81 Manursing Way, Rye, New York 10580, U.S.A.
Telephone: 212-679-1800 (Office); 914-967-5845.

Weitnauer, Albert, DR.JUR.; Swiss diplomatist; b. 30 May 1916, Blumenau, Brazil; *s.* of Albert Weitnauer and Stephanie (née Hoeschl); unmarried; ed. Basle Gymnasium and Basle Univ.
Entered Swiss Govt. Service 41; Legal Adviser to Cen. Office of War Economy 41-46; transferred to Div. of Foreign Trade 46, First Head of Section 51; Econ. Counsellor, Swiss Legation, London 53-54, Swiss Embassy, Washington 54-58; Swiss Govt. Del. for Trade Agreements and Head of Swiss Del. to GATT 59-71; also Del. for Special Missions 66-71 (apptd. Minister Plenipotentiary 61, Amb. 66); Amb. to U.K. 71-75.
Leisure interests: golf, reading, study of languages.
Publs. articles in periodicals on questions of Swiss foreign policy, European integration and world trade.
c/o Eidgenössisches Politisches Departement, 3003 Berne, Switzerland.

Weitz, Paul J.; American astronaut; b. 25 July 1932, Erie, Pa.; *m.* Suzanne M. Berry; one *s.* one *d.*; ed. Pennsylvania State Univ. and U.S. Naval Postgraduate School.
Reserve Officer Training Corps, Pennsylvania State Univ.; assigned to destroyer duty 54; completed flight training 56; tactics instructor, Naval Air Station, Jacksonville, Fla. 56-60; project officer, various air-to-ground delivery tactics projects, China Lake, Calif. 60-62; detachment officer-in-charge, Naval Air Station, Whidbey, Wash. until 66; selected by NASA as astronaut April 66; crew mem. *Skylab* mission 73.
NASA Johnson Space Center, Houston, Tex. 77058, U.S.A.

Weitz, Raanan; Israeli rural development planner; b. 27 July 1913, Rehovoth, Israel; *s.* of Joseph and Ruchama Weitz; *m.* Rivka Schechtman; one *s.* one *d.*; ed. Hebrew Gymnasia, Jerusalem, Hebrew Univ., and Univ. of Florence.
Agricultural Settlement Dept., Jewish Agency 37-, fmr. Village Instructor now Head of Dept.; Chair. Nat. and Univ. Institute of Agriculture 60-66; Head Settlement Study Centre 63-; service with Intelligence Corps, British 8th Army, Second World War; fmr. mem. Hagana; mem. Exec., Zionist Org. 63-; Prof. Rural Regional Devt., School of Social Work, Haifa Univ. 73.
Publs. *Agriculture and Rural Development in Israel: Projection and Planning* 63, *Rural Planning in Development Countries* (editor) 65, *Agricultural Development—Planning and Implementation* 68, *Rural Development in a Changing World* (editor) 71, *From Peasant to Farmer: a Revolutionary Strategy for Development* 71, *Urbanization and the Developing Countries: Report on the Sixth Rehovot Conference* (editor) 73, and papers on problems of comprehensive planning.
Zionist Organisation, Jerusalem; Home: Moshav Ora, Hare-Yehuda Mobile P.O., Israel.
Telephone: 02-39261 (Office); 02-419680 (Home).

Weiz, Herbert; German politician; b. 27 June 1924, Cumbach; ed. Univs. of Jena and Berlin and Technische Hochschule, Dresden.
Former employee, VEB Optima Büromaschinenwerk, Erfurt and VEB Carl Zeiss, Jena; mem. Sozialistische Einheitspartei Deutschlands (S.E.D.) 46-, now mem. Cen. Cttee.; State Sec. for Research and Technology 62; Deputy Chair. Council of Ministers 69-, and Minister for Science and Technology; Order of Banner of Labour, Vaterländischer Verdienstorden.
Ministerrat, Berlin, German Democratic Republic.

Weizman, Gen. Ezer; Israeli air force officer and politician; b. 1924, Tel-Aviv; nephew of Chaim Weizmann (1st Pres. of Israel); *m.*; two *c.*; ed. R.A.F. Staff Coll.
Officer, Israel Air Force 48-66 and fmr. Commanding Officer, I.A.F.; Chief General Staff Branch 66-69; Minister of Transport 69-Aug. 70; Chair. Exec. Cttee. Herut Party 71-.
28 Hageffen Street, Ramat Hasheram, Israel.

Weizsäcker, Carl-Friedrich von, DR.PHIL.; German university professor; b. 1912; ed. Univs. of Berlin, Göttingen and Leipzig.
Asst. Univ. of Leipzig 33-36, Kaiser-Wilhelm-Inst. für Physik, Berlin-Dahlem 36-41; Prof. Univ. of Strasbourg 42-45; Dir. of Dept. Max-Planck-Inst. für Physik, Göttingen 46-57; Prof. of Philosophy, Hamburg 57-69; Hon. Prof. Univ. of Munich; Dir. Max-Planck-Inst. for Research into the Preconditions of Human Life in the Modern World, Starnberg 70-.
Publs. *Zum Weltbild der Physik* 44, *Die Geschichte der Natur* 48, *Die Verantwortung der Wissenschaft im Atomzeitalter* 57, *Atomenergie und Atomzeitalter* 57, *Physik der Gegenwart* (with J. Juilfs) 58, *The Relevance of Science* 64, *Thoughts about the Future* (three speeches) 66, *The Insecure Peace* 69, *Die Einheit der Natur* 71.

Office: Max-Planck-Institut zur Erforschung der Lebensbedingungen der Wissenschaftlich-technischen Welt, D813 Starnberg, Riemerschmidstrasse 7; Home: 8135 Söcking, Alpenstrasse 15, Federal Republic of Germany.

Wejchert, Kazimierz, DR.TECH.SC.; Polish architect; b. 14 March 1912, Smoleńsk; s. of Kazimierz and Wiktoria Wejchert; m. 1st Janina Pawluc 1932, 2nd Hanna Adamczewska-Wejchert 1962; one s. two d.; ed. Warsaw Polytechnic.
Professor Warsaw Polytechnic 46-; Chief Planner, Tychy New Town 51-; (Wejchert works in permanent collaboration with Prof. Dr. H. Adamczewska-Wejchert, his wife); Dir. Town Planning Inst., Faculty of Architecture, Warsaw Polytechnic 70-, Polish Town Planning Asscn. (Chair. 52-54); numerous prizes in town planning and architectonic competitions including First Prize for Warsaw Town Center 58; Nat. Prize (First Class) with H. Adamczewska-Wejchert for planning and realization of the North part in Tychy new town 64; numerous decorations and prizes.
Leisure interests: iris growing, water colouring, photography, wandering.
Major projects include plans for many towns in Olsztyn and Szczecin districts 47-49, for towns, Garwolin 48, Olsztyn, Starachowice 50, regional plan for industrial towns in Upper Silesia, plan for Katowice town centre. Publs. *Miasteczko polskie jako zagadnienie urbanistyczne* (A Small Polish Town as an Urbanistic Problem) 47, *Tereny sportowe w osiedlach* (Sports Grounds in Housing Estates) 54, *Nowe Tychy* (Tychy New Town) 60, *Miasto na Warsztacie* (Town on the Drawing Board) 69, *Elementy Kompozycji Urbanistycznej* (Elements of Spacecomposition) 74, *Town in the Making* (in English) 74.
Ul. Norwida 57, 43-100 Tychy; and Ul. Orężna 45, 02-937, Warsaw, Poland.
Telephone: 27-42-33 (Tychy); 42-28-87 (Warsaw).

Welensky, Rt. Hon. Sir Roy (Roland), K.C.M.G.; Rhodesian politician; b. 20 Jan. 1907, Salisbury; s. of Swedish Jewish father and South African Dutch mother; m. 1st Elizabeth Henderson 1928 (died 1969), one s. one d.; m. 2nd M. Valerie Scott, one d.; ed. Primary School, Salisbury.
Worked for Rhodesia Railways (beginning as fireman and engine driver) 24-53; M.L.C. Northern Rhodesia 38-53; mem. Exec. Council 40-53; Dir. of Manpower 41-46; Leader of the Unofficial Mems. 46-53; Dep. Prime Minister Fed. Govt. of Rhodesia and Nyasaland 53-56, Min. of Transport 53-56, of Posts 53-56, Prime Minister and Minister of External Affairs 56-63, of Defence 56-59; Pres. United Federal Party 56-63; Leader New Rhodesia Party Aug.-Dec. 64.
Leisure interests: fishing, reading, light and grand opera, music.
Publ. *Welensky's 4,000 Days* 64.
82 Queen Elizabeth Road, Greendale, P.O.B. 804, Salisbury, Rhodesia.
Telephone: SBY 23338.

Wellek, René, LITT.D., PH.D., D. ÈS L.; American professor of comparative literature; b. 22 Aug. 1903, Vienna, Austria; s. of Bronislav Wellek and Gabriele von Zelewski; m. 1st Olga Brodská 1932 (deceased), 2nd Nonna Dolodarenko 1968; one s.; ed. Gymnasium and Charles Univ., Prague and Princeton Univ.
Instructor, Smith Coll. 28-29, Princeton Univ. 29-30; Docent, Charles Univ. 31-35; Lecturer of Czech Language and Literature, School of Slavonic Studies, Univ. of London 35-39; Prof. of English, Univ. of Iowa 39-46; Prof. of Slavic and Comparative Literature, Yale Univ. 46-52, Sterling Prof. of Comparative Literature 52-72, Emeritus Prof. 72-; twelve hon. degrees, three Guggenheim awards.

Publs. *Immanuel Kant in England* 31, *The Rise of English Literary History* 41, *Theory of Literature* (with Austin Warren) 48, *A History of Modern Criticism* (four vols.) 55-65, *Dostoevsky* 62, *Essays on Czech Literature* 63, *Concepts of Criticism* 63, *Confrontations* 65, *Discriminations* 70.
45 Fairgrounds Road, Woodbridge, Conn., U.S.A.

Wellenstein, Edmund P.; Netherlands civil servant; b. 20 Sept. 1919, The Hague; m.; six c.; ed. Univ. of Amsterdam.
Travelling Sec. World Student Service Fund 45-46; Official, Queen's Cabinet 46-50; Head of German Section, Deputy Dir. for European Affairs, Ministry of Foreign Affairs 50-52; Sec. of Working Group, High Authority of European Coal and Steel Community 53-67, Sec. 56, Sec.-Gen. 60-68; Dir.-Gen. for Foreign Trade, Comm. of the European Communities 68-70; Head del. for the negotiations for the enlargement of Communities 70-72; Dir.-Gen. for External Relations 73; Co-Pres. for EEC Devt. Comm. of Int. Conf. for Econ. Co-operation Feb. 76-.
c/o Commission of the European Communities, 200 rue de la Loi, 1040 Brussels, Belgium.

Weller, Thomas Huckle, A.B., M.S., M.D.; American scientist and university professor; b. 1915, Ann Arbor, Mich.; s. of Carl V. and Elsie H. Weller; m. Kathleen R. Fahey 1945; two s. two d.; ed. Harvard Univ. and Univ. of Michigan.
Teaching Fellow, Harvard Medical School 40-42; served Medical Corps, U.S. Army 42-45; Asst. Resident, Children's Hospital, Boston 46-47; Research Fellow Harvard Medical School 47-48, Instructor 48-49, Assistant Prof. Tropical Public Health, Harvard School of Public Health 49, Assoc. Prof. 50-54, Richard Pearson Strong Prof. and Head of Dept. 54-; Asst. Dir. Research Div. of Infectious Diseases, Children's Medical Center, Boston 49-55; Dir. Comm. on Parasitic Diseases, Armed Forces Epidemiological Board 53-59; Consultant on Tropical Diseases, U.S. Public Health Service; Dir. Center for Prevention of Infectious Diseases, Harvard School of Public Health 66-; mem. Nat. Acad. of Sciences; winner (jointly) of E. Mead Johnson Award 53, Kimble Methodology Award 54, Nobel Prize in Medicine and Physiology 54; Ledlie Prize 63; Hon. LL.D.
Publs. Papers on infectious diseases, tropical medicine, virus cultivation (especially poliomyelitis and mumps), the etiology of varicella, cytomegalic inclusion disease and rubella, herpes zoster, laboratory diagnosis of schistosomiasis.
Home: 56 Winding River Road, Needham, Mass.; Office: Harvard School of Public Health, 665 Huntington Avenue, Boston, Mass. 02115, U.S.A.

Welles, (George) Orson; American actor and producer; b. 6 May 1915; ed. Todd School, Woodstock, Ill.
Fmr. actor Gate Theatre, Dublin; founded Mercury Theatre 37, now Vice-Pres.; Producer, Writer and Dir. R.K.O. Radio Pictures 39-40; mem. Actors Equity Asscn., American Fed. Radio Artists; Claire Senie Award for foremost achievement in American Theatre 38; Associate Editor *Free World Magazine*; mem. American Acad. of Arts and Sciences 70-; Special Acad. Award 71; Life Achievement Award, American Film Inst. 74.
Directed plays: *Horse Eats Hat* 36, *Dr. Faustus*, *Cradle Will Rock* 37, *Julius Caesar* 37, *Shoemaker's Holiday*, *Heartbreak House*, *Danton's Death* 38; produced and acted in *Othello* (London) 51, *Moby Dick* (London) 55, *King Lear* (New York) 56; wrote and acted in *Chimes at Midnight* 60.
Films: *Citizen Kane* (wrote, produced, directed, acted) 40, *The Magnificent Ambersons* (wrote, dir., prod.) 42, *Journey into Fear* (wrote, prod., acted) 42, *Jane Eyre*

43, *Tomorrow is Forever* 45, *The Lady from Shanghai* (wrote, prod., dir., acted) 46, *Macbeth* (adapted, dir., acted) 47, *Cagliosto* 47, *The Third Man* 49, *The Black Rose* 50, *Versailles* 55, *Confidential Report* (wrote, dir., acted) 55, *Moby Dick* 55, *Othello* (adapted, dir., acted) 56, *The Long Hot Summer* 58, *Compulsion* 59, *Ferry to Hong Kong* 59, *Crack in the Mirror* 60, *David and Goliath* 61, *The Trial*, *The V.I.P.s* 63, *I'll Never Forget What's 'Is Name* 67, *A Man for All Seasons* 67, *The Kremlin Letter* 69, *The Immortal Story* (dir.) 69, *Waterloo* 70, *Ten Days' Wonder* 72, *F for Fake* (wrote, dir., acted) 74, *The Other Side of the Wind* (dir.) 74.
Publs. *Mr. Arkadin* 57; Editor with Roger Hill: *Everybody's Shakespeare* 33, *Mercury Shakespeare* 39; Play: *Chimes at Midnight* (film 64).
10464 Bellago Road, Bel Air, California, U.S.A.

Wells, Rear-Adm. David Charles, C.B.E.; Australian naval officer; b. 19 Nov. 1918, Inverell, N.S.W.; s. of Charles Valentine Tighe Wells and Dorothy Margaret Wells (née Cardale); m. Joan Moira Alice (née Pope) 1940; one s. three d. (one adopted); ed. St. Peter's Coll., Adelaide, Royal Australian Naval Coll.
Communications Officer, Royal Naval Air Station, Culdrose 50-51; attended RN Staff Course, Greenwich 52; In Command, HMAS *Queenborough* 54-55; Dir. of Plans, Navy Office 59-60; In Command, HMAS *Voyager* 61-62; Deputy Dir. RN Staff Coll. Greenwich 62-64; attended Imperial Defence Coll. 65; In Command, HMAS *Melbourne* 65-66; Commdg. Officer Royal Australian Navy Air Station, Nowra (HMAS *Albatross*) 67; Flag Officer-in-Charge, East Australia Area 68-69; Deputy Chief of Naval Staff 70-71; Commdr. Australia, New Zealand and U.K. Forces (ANZUK) in Malaysia and Singapore 72-73; Flag Officer Commdg. H.M. Australian Fleet 74.
Leisure interest: farming.
Ministry of Defence, Navy Office, Canberra, A.C.T.; Home: Morundah, Sackville North, N.S.W. 2756, Australia.

Wells, Herman B., B.S., A.M., LL.D.; American educationist; b. 7 June 1902, Jamestown, Indiana; s. of Joseph Granville and Anna Bernice (née Harting) Wells; ed. Univs. of Illinois and Wisconsin, and Indiana Univ.
Asst. Cashier, First Nat. Bank, Lebanon, Ind. 24-26; Asst., Dept. of Economics, Univ. of Wisconsin 27-28; Field Sec. Indiana Bankers' Asscn. 28-31; Sec. and Research Dir. Study Comm. for Indiana Financial Instns. 31-33; Instr. in Economics Indiana Univ. 30-33, Asst. Prof. 33-35; Supervisor Div. of Banks and Trust Cos. and Div. of Research and Statistics, Dept. of Financial Instns. State of Indiana 33-35, Sec. Comm. for Financial Instns. 33-36; Dean and Prof. School of Business Admin. Indiana Univ. 35-37, Acting Pres. of Univ. 37-38, Pres. of Univ. 38-62, Chancellor 62-; Pres. Indiana Univ. Foundation 62-69, Chair. of Board 37-62, 69-72, Vice-Pres. and Chair. Exec. Cttee.; Chair. American Council on Educ. 44-45; Trustee, Carnegie Foundation for Advancement of Teaching 41-62; adviser cultural affairs Mil. Govt., U.S. Zone, Germany 47-48; mem. UNESCO Comm. of Experts on German Questions 49-50; U.S. Nat. Comm. for UNESCO 51-55, Vice-Chair. 53-54; mem. U.S. del. to UN 57; adviser to Pakistan Ministry of Educ. 59; Vice-Pres. Int. Asscn. of Univs. 55-60; Head U.S. Del. SEATO Preparatory Comm. on Univ. Problems 60; Chair. Board Nat. Research Inst. for the Arts; Chair. Board of Trustees, Educ. and World Affairs 63-70; mem. President's Cttee. on U.S.-Soviet Trade Relations 65; mem. Review Cttee. on Haile Sellassie I Univ. 66-; mem. Nat. Cttee. on U.S.-China Relations 69-; mem. Board Lilly Endowment; Hon. degrees from twenty-four univs. and colls.; Commander's Cross of Order of Merit, Fed. Repub. of Germany and other orders.

Leisure interest: travelling.
1321 East 10th Street, Bloomington, Ind.; Indiana University, Bloomington, Ind., U.S.A.
Telephone: 812-336-6275 (Home); 812-337-6647 (Office).

Wells, John West, PH.D.; American geologist; b. 15 July 1907, Philadelphia, Pa.; s. of Raymond Wells and Maida West; m. Elizabeth Baker 1932; one d.; ed. Univ. of Pittsburgh and Cornell Univ.
Instructor in Geology Univ. of Texas 29-31; Instructor-Prof. of Geology Ohio State Univ. 38-48; Geologist U.S. Geological Survey 46-; Prof. of Geology Cornell Univ., N.Y. 48-73, Prof. Emer. 73-; Bikini Scientific Resurvey 47; Arno Atoll Expedition for Pacific Science Board 50; Fulbright Lecturer Univ. of Queensland, Australia 54; Fellow, Geological Soc. of America; mem. Paleontological Soc. (Pres. 61-62), Paleontological Research Inst. (Pres. 61-64), Soc. of Vertebrate Paleontology, Soc. of Systematic Zoology, Soc. for Study of Evolution, History of Science Soc., Nat. Acad. of Sciences.
Leisure interests: history of geology, prize books.
104 Brook Lane, Ithaca, New York 14850, U.S.A.
Telephone: 607-272-8454.

Welsh, Matthew E., B.S.ECON., DR.JUR.; American politician; b. 15 Sept. 1912, Detroit, Mich.; s. of Mathew W. Welsh and Inez Empson; m. Mary Virginia Homann 1937; two d.; ed. Wharton School of Commerce (Univ. of Pennsylvania), Indiana Univ., and Univ. of Chicago.
State Rep., Indiana Gen. Assembly 40-43; served U.S. Navy 44-46; U.S. Attorney, S. District of Indiana 50-52; private law practice 52-60; Democratic candidate for Gov. 56; State Senator 54-61; Gov. of Indiana 61-65; Chair. U.S. Section, Int. Joint Comm., U.S. and Canada 65-70; Democrat Candidate for Gov. of Indiana 72; official of numerous legal, educational and religious bodies; received six hon. degrees, Partner Bingham, Summers, Welsh and Spilman.
Leisure interests: reading and walking.
2700 Indiana Tower, Indianapolis, Indiana 46204, U.S.A.
Telephone: 317-635-8900.

Welty, Eudora, B.A.; American writer; b. 1909; ed. Mississippi State Coll. for Women, Univ. of Wisconsin and Columbia Univ.
Member American Acad. of Arts and Letters 69; Gold Medal, Nat. Inst. Arts and Letters 72; Pulitzer Prize for Fiction for *The Optimist's Daughter* 73.
Publs. *A Curtain of Green* 41, *Robber Bridegroom* 42, *The Wide Net* 43, *Delta Wedding* 46, *The Golden Apples* 49, *The Ponder Heart* 54, *The Bride of Innisfallen* 55, *The Shoe Bird* 64, *Losing Battles* 70, *One Time, One Place* 71, *The Optimist's Daughter* 72.
1119 Pinehurst Street, Jackson, Miss., U.S.A.

Wende, Jan Karol; Polish politician; b. 25 July 1910, Warsaw; s. of Stanisław and Elżbieta Wende (née Wesołogórska); m. Zofia Eisele 1945; one s.; ed. Univ. of Warsaw and Wolna Wszechnica Polska.
Former writer, critic and political journalist; Democratic Clubs and Democratic Party 37-39; educational activity in Polish emigration centres in U.S.S.R. 39-43; Mil. Service in Polish Army in U.S.S.R. 43-44; Gen. Sec. Presidium of Polish Cttee. of Nat. Liberation 44; Deputy Minister of Culture and Art 45; Amb. to Yugoslavia 45-50; Sec.-Gen. Cttee. for Cultural Co-operation with Foreign Countries 50-56; leading posts in Democractic Party 44-, mem. Presidium of Central Cttee. 45-71, Vice-Chair. Central Cttee. 58-61, 69-71, Gen. Sec. Presidium of Cen. Cttee. 61-69; Deputy to Seym 52-72, Chair. Comm. of Culture and Fine Arts 57-61, Vice-Marshal 61-71; mem. of Presidium and Sec. All-Polish Cttee. of Nat. Unity Front 58-71; mem. Exec. Cttee., Interparliamentary Union 67-72; Order

of Builders of People's Poland, Order Polonia Restituta 2nd Class, Order of Banner of Labour 1st and 2nd Class, Gold Cross of Merit, etc.
Publs. novels: *Drogi cztowiecze* (Human Roads) 37, *Pokolenie 1905 roku* (The Generation of 1905) 39, *Parliament in Poland* 66, *Poland and the Soviet Union*, *The Splendour and Shadows of the II Republic* 69.
Aleja I Armii Wojska Polskiego, 16 Warsaw, Poland.

Wendt, Frantz; Danish civil servant; b. 24 Feb. 1905, Hörby, Holbäk; s. of Hans and Nitetis (née Kjerulff) Wendt; m. Eve Conradt-Eberlin 1930; one s. one d.; ed. Univs. of Copenhagen, Harvard and the Sorbonne.
Assistant Professor of Modern History and Civics, Univ. of Copenhagen 35-43; Sec.-Gen. Inst. of Econs. and History, Copenhagen 36-43; Exec. Dir. Danish Div., Norden Asscn. 43-53; Sec.-Gen. Danish Secr. of the Nordic Council 52-75.
Leisure interests: chess, British and French biography, French poetry.
Publs. include *The Nordic Council and Co-operation in Scandinavia* 59.
Ahlmanns allé 11, 2900 Hellerup, Denmark.
Telephone: (01) 43-27-22.

Wenger, Antoine, Rév. Père; French theologian, journalist and historian; b. 2 Sept. 1919, Rohrwiller (Bas Rhin); s. of Charles and Philomène Gambel; ed. Sorbonne, Strasbourg Univ.
Director of Oriental Theology, Univ. Catholique de Lyon 48-56, Prof. 56; Chief Editor *La Croix* 57-69; Pres. Fédération Internationale des Directeurs de Journaux Catholiques 57-65; mem. Pontifical Marian Acad., Rome 59; Prof. of Ancient Christian Literature Strasbourg Univ. 69-73; Ecclesiastical Counsellor to the French Amb. to the Holy See 73-.
Publs. *L'Assomption dans la tradition orientale* 55, *Homélies Baptismales inédites de St. Jean Chrysostome* 57, *La Russie de Khrouchtchev* 59, *Vatican II, Première Session* 63, *Vatican II, Deuxième Session* 64, *Vatican II, Troisième Session* 65, *Quatrième Session* 66, *Upsal, le Défi du Siècle aux Eglises* 68.
Via Piave 23, 00187 Rome, Italy.
Telephone: 46-38-41.

Went, Frits W., PH.D., D.SC.; American professor of botany; b. 18 May 1903, Utrecht, Netherlands; s. of Prof. F. A. F. C. Went and C. J. Went-Tonckens; m. Catherine H. van de Koppel 1927; one s. one d.; ed. Univ. of Utrecht.
Botanist, later Head, Treub Lab., Botanical Gardens, Buitenzorg (now Bogor), Java 28-32; Prof. of Plant Physiology Calif. Inst. of Technology 33-58; Dir. Missouri Botanical Garden 58-63; Prof. of Botany Washington Univ. 58-65; Head of Lab. of Desert Biology, Desert Research Inst., Univ. of Nevada and Distinguished Prof. of Botany, Univ. of Nevada 65-; Visiting Prof. Univ. of Vienna March-July 76; mem. Nat. Acad. of Sciences; Foreign mem. or Corresp. mem. of Netherlands, Belgian and French Acads. of Science; Hon. Ph.D. (Univs. of Paris and Uppsala Methodist Central College, Mo.), Hon. D.Sc. (McGill Univ.); Hon. LL.D (Univ. of Alberta); Hodgkin Medal of Smithsonian Inst.
Leisure interests: gardening, hiking.
Publs. *Phytohormones* (with K. V. Thimann) 37, *The Experimental Control of Plant Growth* 57, *The Plants* 63.
Laboratory of Desert Biology, Desert Research Institute, University of Nevada, Reno, Nev. 89507; Home: Lodestar Lane 3450, Reno, Nev. 89503, U.S.A.
Telephone: 702-784-6744 (Office); 702-786-1543 (Home).

Wentworth, Hon. William Charles, M.A.; Australian politician; b. 8 Sept. 1907, Sydney; s. of Mr. and Mrs. W. C. Wentworth; m. Barbara Baird 1935; three s. one d.; ed. The Armidale School and New Coll., Oxford.
Financial Adviser, N.S.W. Treasury 33-36; mem. of Parl. for Mackellar 49-; Minister for Social Services and Minister in charge of Aboriginal Affairs 68-71; Liberal.
Leisure interests: hiking, anthropology.
1 Redman Road, Dee Why, N.S.W., Australia.
Telephone: 98-0287 (Home).

Wentzel, Gregor, PH.D.; American physicist; b. 17 Feb. 1898, Düsseldorf, Germany; m. Anna L. Wielich 1929; one s.
Professor of Physics, Univ. of Leipzig, Germany 26-28, Univ. of Zurich, Switzerland 28-48, Univ. of Chicago, U.S. 48-69; mem. Nat. Acad. of Sciences; Hon. D.Sc. (Swiss Fed. Inst. of Technology; Max Planck Medal, German Physical Soc. 75.
77 Via Collina, Ascona (Ticino), Switzerland.
Telephone: 093-355529.

Werblan, Andrzej, DR.POL.SC.; Polish politician; b. 30 Oct. 1924, Tarnopol; ed. Warsaw Univ. and Inst. of Social Sciences of Cen. Cttee. of PUWP.
Active mem. Polish Socialist Party 47-48; mem. Polish United Workers' Party (PUWP) 48-, Deputy mem. Cen. Cttee. 48-56, mem. Cen. Cttee. 56-, mem. Secr. Cen. Cttee. 71-74, Sec. Feb. 74-; Sec. PUWP Voivodship Cttee., Kielce 48-51; Head, Propaganda Dept., PUWP Cen. Cttee. 56-60, Head, Educ. Dept. 60-71; mem. Secretariat PUWP Cen. Cttee. 71-75, Sec. Cen. Cttee. Dec. 75-; Editor-in-Chief, *Nowe Drogi* 72-74, Chair. Editorial Council 74-; Deputy to Seym 52-57, 61-, Vice-Marshal of Seym 71-72; mem. Presidium, Cen. Board Union of Fighters for Freedom and Democracy; Chair. Polish Group, Inter-Parl. Union (IPU) Oct. 71-; Prof. Extraordinary, Silesian Univ. 74-; Head, Inst. of Basic Problems of Marxism-Leninism, Cen. Cttee. of PUWP 74-; Commdr. Cross of Order of Banner of Labour 1st Class, Order of Polonia Restituta, Order of Builders of People's Poland 74, etc.
Polska Zjednoczona Partia Robotnicza, Nowy Świat 6, 00-497 Warsaw, Poland.

Werner, Ernest George Germain; Netherlands oil executive; b. 23 Dec. 1920, The Hague; m. Elly Agnese Asmussen 1945; two s.; ed. Technological Univ. of Delft.
Joined Royal Dutch/Shell Group as research chemist at Amsterdam laboratory 45; subsequent appointments in chemical engineering and research at Amsterdam, London and the Pernis refinery; Head of Plastics, Resins and Elastomers Div. 61-63, of Industrial and Agricultural Chemicals Div. 63-64; Manufacturing Co-ordinator for Chemicals 64-67, Dir. for Chemicals 67-70; Man. Dir. N.V. Koninklijke Nederlandsche Petroleum Maatschappij (Royal Dutch) 70-, Shell Petroleum Co. Ltd. 70-; Principal Dir. Shell Petroleum N.V. 70-.
N.V. Koninklijke Nederlandsche Petroleum Maatschappij, 30 Carel van Bylandtlaan, The Hague; Home: 3 Doornweg, Wassenaar, Netherlands.
Telephone: 771435 (Office).

Werner, Pierre; Luxembourg lawyer and politician; b. 29 Dec. 1913, Saint André, Lille, France; m. Henriette Pescatore 1939; three s. two d.; ed. Univ. of Paris and Luxembourg.
Practising lawyer 38-39 and 44-45; with Banque Générale du Luxembourg 39-44; with Ministry of Finance 45; Commr. of Bank Control 45-53 and of Nat. Savings 48-53; Sec. to the Council of Govt. 49-53; Minister of Finance and of the Armed Forces 53-58; Prime Minister and Minister of Finance 59-64; Prime Minister, Min. of Foreign Affairs, of Treasury, and of Justice 64-66; Prime Minister, Minister of Treasury and of Civil Service 67-69; Prime Minister, Minister of Finance and Minister of Cultural Affairs 69-74; Gov. European Investment Bank 58-74; Chair. EEC Cttee. on Monetary Union 74; Chair. Parl. group Christian Socialists 74-; Christian Social Party; numerous Luxembourg and foreign decorations.

Publs. various publs. on European and monetary matters.

2, Rond-Point Robert Schuman, Luxembourg.
Telephone: 225-74.

Wertheimer, Pierre; French surgeon; b. 23 July 1892, Lyons; s. of Dr. Paul Wertheimer and Jeanne L. Grunwald; m. Germaine Kahn 1919; one s. one d.; ed. Faculté de Médecine, Lyons.
Professor, Faculté de Médecine, Lyons 26; Hospital Surgeon 30; Titular Prof. of Clinical Surgery 44-65, Hon. Prof. 65-; Hospital Administrator 50-; mem. Acad. des Sciences, Acad. de Médecine, Acad. de Chirurgie; Croix de Guerre; Commdr. Légion d'Honneur.
69 Lyon 6e, 21 avenue du Maréchal-de-Saxe, France.
Telephone: 52.27.01.

Werthén, Hans Lennart Oscar, D.TECH.; Swedish business executive; b. 15 June 1919, Ludvika; s. of Oscar F. and Mabel (née Evans) Werthén; m. Britta Ekström 1950; three d.; ed. Royal Inst. of Technology, Stockholm.
Assistant Prof., Royal Inst. of Technology, Stockholm 42-46, Chief of Television Research 47-51; Chief of Television Research Lab., AGA AB 52-56; Vice-Pres. (Engineering) Norrköpings Elektrotekniska Fabrikers AB (NEFA) (Philips) 56-59; Vice-Pres. L. M. Ericsson, Telefon AB, Stockholm 60, Senior Vice-Pres. 63-67; Pres. AB Electrolux 67-74, Exec. Chair. 74-; Royal Order of Vasa.
Leisure interests: history, music, mountain climbing.
AB Electrolux, 104 45 Stockholm; Home: Karlavägen 67VI, 114 49 Stockholm, Sweden.
Telephone: (08) 13 01 00 (Office); (08) 61 08 00, 62 24 67 (Home).

Wesker, Arnold; British playwright; b. 24 May 1932, Stepney, London; s. of Joseph Wesker and Leah Wesker (née Perlmutter); m. Doreen (Dusty) Cecile Bicker 1958; two s. one d.; ed. mixed elementary schools and Upton House Central School, Hackney, London.
Left school 48, worked as furniture maker's apprentice, carpenter's mate, bookseller's assistant; R.A.F. 50-52 (ran drama group); plumber's mate, road labourer, farm labourer, seed sorter, kitchen porter and pastry-cook; studied nine months, London School of Film Technique; Arts Council Bursary 59; Dir. Centre 42, 61-70; Encyclopaedia Britannica Competition, 1st Prize (for *Chicken Soup with Barley*), 3rd Prize 61 (for *The Kitchen*); Premio Marzotto Drama Prize (for *Their Very Own Golden City*) 64; Gold Medal, Premios el Espectador y la Crítica (for *The Kitchen*) 73; began directing his own plays: *The Four Seasons*, Cuba 68, world première of his own play *The Friends* at Stadsteatern, Stockholm 70, London 70, *The Old Ones*, Munich, *Their Very Own and Golden City*, Aarhus 74.
Leisure interest: listening to gramophone records.
Plays: *The Kitchen* 57, The trilogy—*Chicken Soup with Barley* 58, *Roots* 59, *I'm Talking about Jerusalem* 60, *Chips with Everything* 62, *Menace* 63, *Their Very Own and Golden City* 64, *The Four Seasons* 65, *The Friends* 70, *The Old Ones* 72, *The Journalists* 72, *The Wedding Feast* 73, *The Merchant* 75; Publs.: *Fears of Fragment-ation* (essays and lectures), *Six Sundays in January* (miscellaneous), *Love Letters on Blue Paper* (short stories) 74, *Say Goodbye You May Never See Them Again* (text to accompany book of paintings by John Allin) 74.
27 Bishops Road, London N.6, England.
Telephone: 01-340-5125.

Wesselmann, Tom, B.A.; American artist; b. 23 Feb. 1931, Cincinnati, Ohio; s. of Edwin W. and Grace D. Wesselmann; m. 2nd Claire Selley 1963; one s. one d.; ed. Univ. of Cincinnati, Art Acad. of Cincinnati and Cooper Union, N.Y.
Taught art New York City Junior and Senior High Schools 59-62; one-man exhbns. 61-, incl. Tanager

Gallery, New York 61, Green Gallery, New York 62, 64, 65, Museum of Contemporary Art, Chicago 68, Newport Harbor Art Museum, Calif. 70, Jack Glenn Gallery, Calif. 71, Calif. State Univ. 74, Sidney Janis Gallery 66, 68, 70, 72, 74.
Leisure interests: nature, wildlife.
231 Bowery, New York, N.Y. 10012, U.S.A.
Telephone: 228-3930.

West, Frederic W., Jr., B.SC.; American steel executive; b. 18 Feb. 1919, Philadelphia, Pa.; s. of Frederic Wultze West and Marion Etta (Nill) West; m. Ruth Virginia Landers 1947; three s. one d.; ed. Cornell Univ.
Joined Bethlehem Steel Corpn. 41; Mil. service 42-45, 50-51; Asst. Gen. Man. Sales 69-70, Vice-Pres. Manufactured Products, Sales 70-73, Dir. 73-, Exec. Vice-Pres. 73-74, Pres. Aug. 74-; mem. American Iron and Steel Inst., the Conf. Board Inc., Advertising Council Industries Advisory Cttee., Econ. Club of New York, The Newcomen Soc. in North America, Board of Trustees, St. Luke's Hospital, Bethlehem, Pa.; Bronze Star.
Bethlehem Steel Corpn., Bethlehem, Pa. 18016, U.S.A.
Telephone: 215-694-2424.

West, John C., LL.B.; American state governor; b. 27 Aug. 1922; s. of late Shelton J. West and of Mattie (Ratterree) West; m. Lois Rhame 1942; three c.; ed. Univ. of South Carolina.
Elected to S. Carolina Senate 54, re-elected 58, 62; Lieut.-Gov. of S. Carolina 66-70; Gov. of S. Carolina 70-74; fmr. Attorney with firm of West, Holland, Furman and Cooper; mem. various cttees. and civic orgs.; Democrat.
Office of the Governor, State Capitol, Columbia, S. Carolina, U.S.A.

West, Mae; American actress; b. 17 Aug. 1892, Brooklyn.
Stage appearances include *Little Nell the Marchioness* 97, *East Lynne*, *The Fatal Wedding*, *A la Broadway* 11, *A Winsome Widow* 12, *Such is Life* 13, *Sometime* 18, *Demitasse* 19, *The Mimic World* 21, *Sex* 26, *The Wicked Age* 27, *Diamond Lil* 28, *The Constant Sinner* 31, *Catherine Was Great* 44; films include, *Night after Night* 32, *She Done Him Wrong* 33, *I'm no Angel* 33, *Bell of the Nighties* 34, *Goin' to Town* 35, *Klondike Annie* 36, *Go West, Young Man* 36, *Every Day's a Holiday* 37, *My Little Chickadee* 40, *The Heat's On* 43, *Myra Breckenridge* 70.
Publs. *Goodness Had Nothing to Do With It* 59, *Diamond Lil*, *The Constant Sinner*, *On Sex, Health and ESP* 75.
514 Pacific Coast Highway, Santa Monica, Calif. 90402, U.S.A.

West, Morris (Langlo); Australian author; b. 26 April 1916, Melbourne; ed. Univ. of Melbourne.
Teacher of Modern Languages and Mathematics, New South Wales and Tasmania 33-39; Army service 39-43 Nat. Brotherhood Award, Nat. Council of Christians and Jews 60, James Tait Black Memorial Prize 60, Royal Soc. of Literature Heinemann Award 60 (All prizes for *The Devil's Advocate*); Fellow, Royal Soc. of Literature, World Acad. of Arts and Sciences; Hon. D. Litt. (Santa Clara Univ., Calif.).
Publs. *Gallows on the Sand* 55, *Kundu* 56, *Children of the Sun* 57, *The Crooked Road* (English title *The Big Story*) 57, *Backlash* (English title *Second Victory*) 58, *The Devil's Advocate* 59, *Daughter of Silence* 61, *The Shoes of the Fisherman* 63, *The Ambassador* 65, *The Tower of Babel* 68, *The Heretic* (play) 70, *Scandal in the Assembly* (with Robert Francis) 70, *Summer of the Red Wolf* 71, *The Salamander* 73, *Harlequin* 74.
c/o Paul R. Reynolds Inc., 12 East 41st Street, New York City, N.Y. 10017, U.S.A.

West, Dame Rebecca, D.B.E.; British novelist and journalist; b. 21 Dec. 1892, Edinburgh; d. of Charles and Isabella Campbell (Mackenzie) Fairfield; m. Henry

Maxwell Andrews 1930; one *s.*; ed. George Watson's Ladies Coll., Edinburgh.

Contributor to leading British and American journals *The Daily Telegraph, Sunday Times, N.Y. Herald Tribune, Harper's Magazine, Atlantic Monthly, Sunday Telegraph*; mem. American Acad. Arts and Sciences; Hon. mem. American Acad. of Arts and Letters; D.Litt. New York Univ. U.S.A.; Order of St. Sava; Chevalier Légion d'Honneur 57; A. C. Benson Silver Medal for Literature 66, Companion of Literature 67. Leisure interests: swimming, photography.

Publs. include *Henry James* 16, *The Return of the Soldier* 18, *The Judge* 22, *The Strange Necessity* 28, *Harriet Hume* 29, *D. H. Lawrence: An Elegy* 30, *St. Augustine* 33, *The Rake's Progress* (with David Low) 34, *The Harsh Voice* 35, *The Thinking Reed* 36, *Black Lamb and Grey Falcon* 42, *The Meaning of Treason* 49, *A Train of Powder* 55, *The Fountain Overflows* 57, *The Court and the Castle* 58, *The Vassall Affair* 63, *The New Meaning of Treason* 64, *The Birds Fall Down* 66.

c/o Macmillans, Little Essex Street, London, W.C.2, England.

Westerberg, Karl Arne Rickard; Swedish business executive; b. 11 June 1917, Dalarö; *s.* of Rickard and Märtha Westerberg; *m.* Siv Andersson 1946; one *d.*; ed. Royal Inst. of Technology, Stockholm.

Managing Director, Halmstads Järnverks AB 59-66; Pres. and Chief Exec. Officer, Sandvik Group 67-; Knight Commdr. of Royal Order of Vasa.

Leisure interests: tennis, reading.

Sandvik AB, S-811 01 Sandviken 1; Home: Hedåsen, S-811 00 Sandviken, Sweden.

Telephone: 26 00 00 (Office); 25 94 78 (Home).

Westerfield, Putney, B.A.; American business executive; b. 9 Feb. 1930, New Haven, Conn.; *s.* of Ray and Beatrice Westerfield; *m.* Anne Montgomery 1954; two *s.* one *d.*; ed. Choate School and Yale Univ.

Vice-Pres. and Co-founder, Careers Inc. 50-52; Man. Southeast Asia Operations, Swen Publications; service with Dept. of State in Korea, Washington, Saigon 53-59; Asst. to Publisher of *Time* 57-59, Asst. to Circulation Dir. 59-61, Circulation Dir. 61-66, Asst. Publisher 66-68; Asst. Publisher of *Life* 68-69; Publisher of *Fortune* 69-73; Pres. Chase World Information Corpn. 73-75; Assoc. Boyden Assocs. Int. 76-.

Leisure interests: reading, music, tennis, swimming.

206 Madison Avenue, New York, N.Y. 10016; Home: Dairy Road, Greenwich, Conn. 06830, U.S.A.

Telephone: 203-869-8884.

Westergaard, Mogens Christian Wanning, D.SC.; Danish geneticist; b. 12 June 1912, Copenhagen; *s.* of Henry and Mathilde (née Wanning) Westergaard; *m.* Ebba Caspersen 1936; one *s.* two *d.*; ed. High School, Horsens and Univ. of Copenhagen.

Amanuensis, Genetics Dept., Royal Veterinary Agricultural Coll. 36-49; Lecturer, Univ. of Copenhagen 46-49, Prof. and Chair. Dept. of Genetics 49-62; Research Assoc., Carlsberg Foundation 62-; Fellow, Royal Danish Acad. of Science and Letters; Foreign Assoc., Nat. Acad. of Sciences, U.S.A.; Fellow Arctic Inst., N. America; Foreign mem. Royal Physiographical Soc., Sweden; Hon. mem. British Genetical Soc., Mendelian Soc., Sweden, and Nordic Genetical Soc.; Munksgaard Prize.

Leisure interests: mystery and crime, hiking.

Publs. *Man's responsibility to his genetic heritage* 55, *The mechanism of sex determination in dioecious flowering plants* 58, Co-author: *The Flowering Plants of Greenland* 58, *The Synaptinemal complex* 72.

91 Abildgaardsvej, DK-2830, Virum, Denmark.

Telephone: (02) 857065.

Westerman, Sir (Wilfred) Alan, Kt., C.B.E., M.A.ECON., B.ED., ED.D.; Australian business executive; b. 25

March 1913, New Zealand; ed. Knox Grammar School, Univs. of Tasmania, Melbourne and Columbia.

Former Lecturer in Rural Sociology, Columbia Univ.; Trade Commr. Service 46-49; Dir. Trade Promotion and Int. Trade Relations 49-53; First Asst. Sec., Dept. of Commerce and Agriculture 53-58; Chair. Commonwealth Tariff Board 58-60; Sec. Dept. of Trade and Industry 60-71; Exec. Chair. Australian Industry Devt. Corpn. 71-.

P.O. Box 1483, Canberra, A.C.T. 2601, Australia.

Westerterp, Theodorus Engelbertus (Tjerk); Netherlands politician; b. 2 Dec. 1930, Rotterdam; *m.* 1954; ed. High School Breda, Univ. of Nijmegen.

Journalist 49-53; Civil Servant European Parl. 53-63; mem. Parl. 63-71; State Sec. for Foreign Affairs 71-73; Minister of Transport and Public Works 73-; Grand Officer Order of Bernardo O'Higgins (Chile); Grand Cross Order of the Lion (Finland); Grand Cross (Italy); Catholic People's Party.

Ministry of Transport, The Hague, Netherlands.

Westmoreland, Gen. William Childs; American retd. army officer; b. 26 March 1914, Spartanburg County, S. Carolina; *s.* of James R. and Eugenia Childs Westmoreland; *m.* Katherine S. Van Deusen 1947; one *s.* two *d.*; ed. U.S. Military Acad.

U.S. Army 36-72; Maj.Gen. 56, Lieut.-Gen. 63, Gen. 64; Battery Officer, Oklahoma and Hawaii 36-41; Commdg. Officer, 34th Field Artillery Battalion 42-44; Executive Officer 9th Infantry Div. 44, Chief of Staff 44-45, Commdr. 60th Infantry Regiment, Germany 45, 504th Parachute Infantry Regiment, Fort Bragg 46-47; Chief of Staff, 82nd Airborne Div. 47-50; Instructor, Command and Gen. Staff Coll., and Army War Coll. 50-52; Commdr. 187th Airborne Regimental Combat Team, Korea and Japan 52-53; Deputy Asst. Chief of Staff G1, for Manpower Control, Dept. of Army 53-54, Sec. Gen. Staff 55-58; Commanding Gen. 101st Airborne Div. and Fort Campbell, Kentucky 58-60; Supt. U.S. Military Acad., West Point 60-63; Commdr. 18th Airborne Corps, Fort Bragg 63-64; Deputy Commdr. U.S. Military Assistance Command Viet-Nam 64, Commdr. 64-68; Chief of Staff, U.S. Army, The Pentagon 68-72; retired from army 72.

Leisure interests: tennis, squash, golf.

Publ. *War In Vain* 76.

P.O. Box 1059, Charleston, S.C. 29402, U.S.A.

Telephone: 803-577-7793.

Weston, Garry Howard, B.A.; business executive; b. 1927, Toronto, Canada; *s.* of Willard Garfield Weston (*q.v.*); *m.* Mary Ruth Kippenberger; three *s.* three *d.*; ed. Sir William Borlase School, Marlow, New Coll., Oxford, and Harvard Univ.

Director, Allied Bakeries Ltd. (U.K.) 50-; Man. Dir. Ryvita Co. Ltd. (U.K.) 50-56, and Ryvita Co. (Australia) Pty. Ltd. 54; Dir. Fortnum and Mason 52; Chair. of Directors Weston Holdings (Australia) Pty. Ltd. 54, and Man. Dir. Weston Biscuit Co. (Australia) Pty. Ltd. 54; Vice-Chair. Assoc. British Foods Ltd. (U.K.) 60-68, Chair. 68-; Dir. George Weston Foods Ltd. (Australia) 62-.

Weston Centre, 40 Berkeley Square, London, W.1; 11 Upper Phillimore Gardens, London W.8, England.

Weston, Willard Garfield; Canadian businessman; b. Canada 1898; father of Garry Howard Weston (*q.v.*); ed. Harbord Collegiate Inst., Toronto.

Served with Canadian Engineers First World War, joined George Weston Ltd. Toronto 19-, Vice-Pres. 21; Man. 22, now Chair.; founder and Chair. George Weston Holdings Ltd., Weston Biscuits Co., Allied Bakeries Ltd.; Chair. George Weston Ltd., Toronto, and Weston Biscuit Co. New Jersey; Pres. Assoc. British Foods Ltd. 67-; Cons. M.P. for Macclesfield, England 39-45.

Weston Centre, 40 Berkeley Square, London W.1, England.

Wetmore, Alexander, M.S., PH.D., D.SC.; American biologist and ornithologist; b. 18 June 1886, North Freedom, Wis.; *s.* of Dr. Nelson Franklin Wetmore and Emma Amelia Woodworth; *m.* 1st Fay Holloway 1913, 2nd Annie Beatrice van der Biest Thielen 1953; ed. Kansas and George Washington Univs.

Asst. Biologist and Biologist, Biological Survey Dept. of Agriculture 10-24; Asst. Sec. Smithsonian Inst., Dir. U.S. Nat. Museum 25-44, Sec. 45-52, Research Assoc. 53-; Trustee Textile Museum, Washington, George Washington Univ., Research Corpn. 47-53, Pacific War Memorial, Wildlife Inst.; Dir. Gorgas Memorial Inst. for Tropical Medicine; mem. Advisory Cttee., Int. Wildlife Protection; mem. Int. Comm. Bird Protection, Joint Latin-American Study 45-47; Sec.-Gen., 8th American Science Congress 40; Vice-Chair. Nat. Advisory Cttee. for Aeronautics 45-52; Trustee Nat. Gallery of Art 45-52; Dir. Canal Zone Biological Area 40-46; Past Pres. Explorers' Club; Pres. X Int. Ornithological Congress, Sweden 50; Chair. Cttee. on Classification and Nomenclature for 5th edn. *Check-list of North American Birds* publ. 57.

Leisure interest: study of living birds.

Publs. *The Migration of Birds* 27, *Birds of Porto Rico and the Virgin Islands* 27, *Fossil Birds of North America* 31, *Birds of Haiti and the Dominican Republic* 31, *Book of Birds* 37, *Check-List of the Fossil and Prehistoric Birds of North America and the West Indies* 56, *Birds of Coiba Island Panama* 57, *Revised Classification for Birds of the World* 60, *Song and Garden Birds* 64, *Water, Game and Prey Birds* 65, *Birds of Panama*, Part I 65, part II 68, Article on Archaeopteryx for *Encyclopaedia Britannica* 71, *Birds of Panama*, Part III 72.

5901 Osceola Road, Washington, D.C. 20016; and c/o Smithsonian Institution, Washington, D.C. 20560, U.S.A.

Telephone: 320-4623 (Home); 381-5291 (Office).

Wetmore, Robert Bernard Norton, M.B.E.; Rhodesian (retired) civil servant and diplomatist; b. 31 Aug. 1911, Beira, Mozambique; *s.* of late J. N. Wetmore; *m.* 1st Phyllis Grace Jones 1940 (died 1964), 2nd Monica M.E. Fenn 1966; three *s.*; ed. Prince Edward School, Salisbury.

Government Service (Treasury) 29-37; Manager Southern Rhodesia Publicity Office, Johannesburg 37-42; Supply Office 42-46; Assistant Food Controller, Salisbury 47-50; Secretary at High Comm., Pretoria 51-55; Consul-Gen. in Mozambique 55-57; Counsellor for Rhodesia and Nyasaland Affairs, British Embassy, U.S.A. 57-62; Under-Sec. External Affairs, Salisbury 62-64; Accredited Diplomatic Representative for Rhodesia in South Africa 64-65; Sec. for External Affairs 65-67.

Leisure interests: golf, gardening, carpentry and travel.

2 Wetmore Close, Highlands, Rhodesia.

Telephone: 42656 (Home).

Wetter, Rear-Admiral (Sten) Erik P:son; Swedish naval officer and businessman; b. 4 April 1889, Stockholm; *s.* of Pres. Albert Petersson and Ada Wetter; *m.* Maja Carlander 1924; one *s.* four *d.*; ed. Swedish and Leghorn Naval Academies.

Lt. Commdr. Royal Swedish Navy 18, Commdr. 31, Rear-Admiral 43, Dep. Dir. Navy Board 43-45; mem. (Liberal) First Chamber of Riksdag 45-47; Vice-Pres. Board Swedish Ballbearing Co. (SKF) 54-62; Pres. Board A. B. Bofors 46-66; Pres. Board Home Lines Inc. 53-; Man. Dir. Swedish Orient Line 31-51; A.D.C. to H.R.H. the Crown Prince 27, Chief A.D.C. to H.M. the King 50, First Marshal of the Court to H.M. the King of Sweden 52-62; Hon. Dr. Univ. Lund 74; 3 Swedish orders and 12 foreign orders.

Leisure interest: archaeology, especially etruscology.

Fredrikshovsgatan 5, 115 22 Stockholm, Sweden.

Telephone: Stockholm 08/62-67-94.

Wey, Vice-Admiral Joseph Edet Akinwale, O.F.R.; Nigerian naval officer and marine engineer (retd.); b. 7 March 1918, Calabar; *s.* of George Akinlaja Wey and Margaret Arit-Ekpo; three *s.* three *d.*; ed. Holy Cross School, Lagos, Methodist School, Ikot Ekpene and St. Patrick's Coll., Calabar.

Engineer Cadet-in-Training, Nigerian Marine 39; Marine Engineer Second Class 50-56; Sub-Lieut. Engineer, Nigerian Navy 56-59; First class Marine Engineer 59-; Lieut. 58, Lieut.-Commdr. 60; transferred to Exec. Branch and promoted Commdr. 62; Commdg. Officer of Base and Naval Officer in Charge, Apapa 62-63; Capt. and Chief of Naval Staff 63; served in India 63-64; Commodore 64; in command, Nigerian Navy 64; Rear-Admiral 67-71; mem. Supreme Mil. Council 66-, Fed. Exec. Council 67-75; Commr. for Establishments and Service Matters 67-75, also acting Commr. for Labour 71; Vice-Admiral 71-75, Chief of Staff, Supreme HQ 73-75; Chair. Admin. Cttee. of Nigerian Defence Acad. and responsible to the C.-in-C. for Armed Forces.

Leisure interests: reading, swimming, boating.

Supreme Headquarters, Dodan Barracks, Lagos, Nigeria.

Telephone: 23315.

Weyand, Gen. Frederick Carlton; American army officer; b. 15 Sept. 1916, Calif.; *s.* of Frederick C. and Velma Semans Weyand; *m.* L. Arline Langhart 1940; one *s.* two *d.*; ed. Univ. of Calif., Berkeley, Nat. War Coll., Washington, and Infantry School, Fort Benning.

Commissioned 38; mem. Berkeley Police Dept. 39-40; active service 41; served in India, Burma, China 44-45; Intelligence duties 46-49; Battalion Commdr. and 3rd Div. Operations Officer, Korea 50-51; Exec. Officer, Sec. of Army 54-57; Brigade Commdr., Berlin 58-60; Legislative Liaison with Congress 60-64; Commdr. U.S. 25th Infantry Div. 64-67; Field Force Commdr., Vietnam 67-68; Mil. Rep. to Paris Peace Talks 69-70; Deputy Commdr. and Commdr. U.S. Mil. Assistance Command, Viet-Nam 70-73; Vice-Chief of Staff of the Army 73-74; Chief of Staff 74-; Distinguished Service Cross, Silver Star, Distinguished Service Medal, Legion of Merit.

Leisure interests: sport (golf and tennis), music (guitar and saxophone), reading (history).

Department of the Army, The Pentagon, Washington, D.C. 20310; Apt. 1236, Makaha Valley Towers, Waianae, Hawaii, U.S.A.

Weyerhaeuser, Frederick King; American timber executive; b. 16 Jan. 1895; ed. Yale Univ.

President Weyerhaeuser Sales Co., St. Paul, Minn. 29-59, Weyerhaeuser Co. 56-60, Chair. 55-56 and 60-66; Dir. First Trust Co. of St. Paul 31-, Rock Island Corpn. 46-, First Nat. Bank of St. Paul 46-, Great Northern Railway Co. 46-; Trustee, Minnesota Mutual Life Insurance Co. 39-.

Home: 294 Summit Avenue, St. Paul, Minn. 55102; Office: First National Bank Building, St. Paul, Minn. 55101, U.S.A.

Weyerhaeuser, George Hunt, B.S.; American timber executive; b. 8 July 1926, Seattle; *s.* of late J. P. Weyerhaeuser and Helen Walker Weyerhaeuser; *m.* Virginia Wagner 1948; two *s.* four *d.*; ed. Yale Univ.

Served in U.S. Navy 44-46; Weyerhaeuser Co. 47-, serving respectively as: Shift Supt. 49-51, Wood Products Man. 54, Asst. to Exec. Vice-Pres. 57-58, Man. Wood Products Group, later Vice-Pres. 58; elected to Board of Dirs. 60; Exec. Vice-Pres. for Wood Products, Timber and Lands 61-, Exec. Vice-Pres. for Operations 64-, Pres. and Chief Exec. Officer 66-; Pres. and Dir. Weyerhaeuser Int. Inc., Weyerhaeuser Int. S.A., Weyerhaeuser Real Estate Co., Weyerhaeuser American Corpn., Weyerhaeuser Co.; Dir. Boeing Co., Puget Sound Nat. Bank, Barlow Weyerhaeuser Packaging

Investments (Pty.) Ltd., R-W Paper Co., Weyerhaeuser Canada Ltd., and others; mem. Board of Trustees, Charles Wright Acad., Weyerhaeuser Co. Foundation; mem. Business Council, Japan-Calif. Asscn., Advisory Council Stanford Research Inst., Yale School of Forestry and Natural Environment, etc.
Leisure interest: tennis.
Weyerhaeuser Company, Tacoma, Washington 98401, U.S.A.
Telephone: 924-2345.

Weymann, Gert; German theatre director and playwright; b. 31 March 1919, Berlin; s. of Hans Weymann and Gertrud Israel; ed. Grammar School, Berlin, and Berlin Univ.
Assistant Dir., later Dir. Berlin theatre; worked as Dir. in several W. German cities and New York; Lecturer in Drama Dept., American universities 63, 66; Lecturer at Goethe Inst., Berlin 70-; perm. ind. mem. SFB (radio and television plays); Gerhart Hauptmann Prize for *Generationen* 54.
Plays: *Generationen, Eh' die Brücken verbrennen*; TV Plays: *Das Liebesmahl eines Wucherers, Familie*; Radio Plays: *Der Anhalter, Die Übergabe.*
1 Berlin 31, Karlsruherstrasse 7, Germany.
Telephone: 885 1861.

Weynen, Wolfgang, LL.D.; German press agency executive; b. 5 July 1913, Nilvingen, Alsace Lorraine; s. of Wilhelm Weynen and Maria Weynen (née Bremer); m. Lieselotte née Hoffmann 1964; one d.; ed. Univs. of Bonn, Paris, Königsberg and Leipzig.
Legal adviser and Deputy Gen. Man. Chamber of Industries and Commerce, Wiesbaden 46-48, Gen. Man. 48-55; Gen. Man. Deutsche Presse-Agentur 55-; Pres. of Alliance Européenne des Agences de Presse 56, Chair. Satellite Sub-Cttee. of Int. Press Telecommunications Cttee. (IPTC) 65, mem. Presidency Cultural Cttee. of German-Korean Friendship Asscn., Vice-Pres. IPTC 67-68; Chair. IPTC 68; Board of Vereinigte Wirtschaftsdienste, Frankfurt; Grosses Verdienstkreuz der Republik Österreich, Chevalier Légion d'Honneur, Grosses Silbernes Ehrenzeichen der Republik Österreich, Commdr. Cross of Italian Repub., Bundesverdienstkreuz 1st Class, Federal German Repub., Knight, Royal Order of Vasa, Sweden.
Publs. *Die Arbeitszeitregelung in kontinuierlichen Betrieben* 38, *Nachrichten im Zeitalter der Satelliten* 69.
dpa-Deutsche Presse-Agentur, 2 Hamburg 13, Mittelweg 38; Home: 2 Hamburg 20, Brabandstrasse 7, German Federal Republic.
Telephone: 4113300 (Office); 51-59-82 (Home).

Weyrauch, Wolfgang Karl Joseph; German writer; b. 15 Oct. 1907, Königsberg; m. Margot von Kurnatowski 1946; two s. two d.; ed. Humanistisches Gymnasium, Johann Wolfgang Goethe-Universität, Frankfurt, and Humboldt Universität in Berlin.
Publisher's Reader *Berliner Tageblatt* 34-38, Deutscher Verlag, Berlin 38-39; Editor *Ulenspiegel*, Berlin 46-48; Publisher's Reader, Rowohlt Verlag, Hamburg 50-58; Hörspielpreis der Kriegsblinden for *Totentanz* 62; Stereo Hörspielpreis der Rundfunkindustrie und ARD 67; Johann-Heinrich-Merck Honour of Darmstadt 72; Andreas-Gryphius Prize 73; mem. of Jury Leonce und Lena preis für neue Lyrik; mem. Deutsche Akademie für Sprache und Dichtung, PEN-Zentrum of Fed. Germany.
Leisure interest: detective stories.
Publs. *Der Main* (legend) 34, *Auf der bewegten Erde* (story) 46, *Von des Glücks Barmherzigkeit* (poems) 47, *Die Davidsbündler* (story) 48, *Tausend Gramm* (anthology) 49, *An die Wand geschrieben* (poems) 50, *Woher kennen wir uns bloss?* (radio play) 52, *Die Minute des Negers* (ballad) 53, *Bericht an die Regierung* (story) 53, *Die japanischen Fischer* (radio play) 55, *Gesang, um nicht zu sterben* (poems) 56, *Mein Schiff, das heisst*

Taifun (stories) 59, *Anabasis* (radio play) 59, *Expeditionen* (anthology) 59, *Ich lebe in der Bundesrepublik* (anthology) 60, *Totentanz* (radio play) 61, *Dialog mit dem Unsichtbaren* (radio plays) 62, *Das tapfere Schneiderlein* (radio play) 63, *Die Spur* (poems) 63, *Alle diese Strassen* (anthology) 65, *Alexanderschlacht* (radio play) 65, *Etwas geschieht* (story) 66, *Das erste Haus hiess Frieden* 66, *Ausnahmezustand* (anthology) 66, *Ich bin einer, ich bin keiner* (stereo radio play) 67, *Auf der bewegten Erde* (stories) 67, *Lyrik aus dieser Zeit* (anthology with Johannes Poethen) 67, *Federlese P.E.N. Almanach* (anthology with Benno Reifenberg) 67, *Feuer, Wasser, Luft und Erde* (radio play) 68, *Geschichten zum Weiterschreiben* (stories) 69, *Wie geht es Ihnen?* (stereo radio play) 70, *11 Autoren über 1 Jahrzehnt* (anthology) 70, *Wie geht es Ihnen?* (story) 71, *Ein Clown sagt* (story for children) 71, *Im Conjunctiv* (radio play) 72, *Mit dem Kopf durch die Wand* (stories, poems, essays and a radio play) 72, *Das Ende von Frankfurt am Main* (stories) 73, *Wer fängt an?* (radio play) 74, *Dostojevskij* (radio play) 74.
Darmstadt, Alexandraweg 23, Federal Republic of Germany.
Telephone: 46759.

Wharton, Clifton R., Jr., PH.D.; American economist and university president; b. 13 Sept. 1926, Boston, Mass.; s. of Hon. Clifton R. Wharton Sr.; m. Dolores Duncan; two s.; ed. Boston Latin School, Harvard Univ., Johns Hopkins Univ. School of Advanced Int. Studies and Univ. of Chicago.
Head of Reports and Analysis Dept., American Int. Asscn. for Econ. and Social Devt. 48-53; Exec. Assoc. in Agricultural Econs., Agricultural Devt. Council 57-58, stationed in Malaysia 58-64, Dir. of the Council's American Universities Research Program 64-66; Act. Dir. 66-67, Vice-Pres. 67-69; Pres. Michigan State Univ. Jan. 70-; Visiting Prof., Univ. of Malaysia during period 58-64, Stanford Univ. 64-65; fmr. mem., Advisory Panel on East Asian and Pacific Affairs of U.S. Dept. of State, Southeast Asian Devt. Advisory Group of Agency for Int. Devt. (AID), Presidential Task Force on Agriculture in Vietnam, etc.; Dir. or Trustee of numerous orgs. including Equitable Life Assurance Soc., Asia Soc., Overseas Devt. Council, Rockefeller Foundation, Ford Motor Co., Burroughs Corpn., Carnegie Foundation.
Michigan State University, East Lansing, Mich. 48823, U.S.A.

Wheare, Sir Kenneth Clinton, Kt., C.M.G., F.B.A., D.LITT.; British (b. Australian) former college principal; b. 26 March 1907, Warragul, Victoria; s. of Eustace Leonard and Kathleen Wheare; m. 1st Helen Mary Allan 1934, 2nd Joan Randell 1943; three s. two d.; ed. Scotch Coll., Melbourne, Univ. of Melbourne, and Oriel Coll., Oxford.
Lecturer Christ Church, Oxford 34-39; Beit Lecturer in Colonial History, Oxford 35-44; Fellow of Univ. Coll. Oxford 39-44, Dean 42-45; Gladstone Prof. of Govt. and Public Admin., Univ. of Oxford, Fellow of All Souls Coll. 44-57, Fellow of Nuffield Coll. 44-58; Rector Exeter Coll. Oxford 56-72; Pro-Vice-Chancellor Oxford Univ. 58-64, 66-72, Vice-Chancellor 64-66; Pres. British Acad. 67-71; Constitutional Adviser to Nat. Convention of Newfoundland 46-47, to Confs. on Central African Fed. 51, 52, 53; Rhodes Trustee 48-; mem. Univ. Grants Cttee. 59-63; Chancellor, Liverpool Univ. 72-; Fellow of All Souls Coll., Oxford; Hon. Fellow of Univ. of Exeter, Oriel, Nuffield and Wolfson Colls., Oxford; Hon. L.H.D. (Columbia), Hon. LL.D. (Exeter, Liverpool and Manchester), Hon. Litt.D. (Cambridge).
Leisure interest: cooking.
Publs. *The Statute of Westminster* 31, 33, *The Statute of Westminster and Dominion Status* 38 (5th edn. 53), *Federal Government* 46 (4th edn. 63), *Abraham Lincoln*

and the United States 48, *Modern Constitutions* 51, *Government by Committee* 55, *The Constitutional Structure of the Commonwealth* 60, *Legislatures* 63, *Maladministration and its Remedies* 73.
55 Park Town, Oxford, England.
Telephone: Oxford 53775.

Wheatley, Dennis Yeats, F.R.S.A., F.R.S.L.; British author; b. 8 Jan. 1897, London; *s.* of Albert David Wheatley and Florence Lady Newton; *m.* 1st Nancy M. Robinson 1924, one *s.*; *m.* 2nd Joan Gwendoline Johnstone 1931; ed. H.M.S. *Worcester*, and privately in Germany.
Served in army in First World War 14-19; entered father's Mayfair wine business becoming sole owner 26; Dir. of numerous companies; Liveryman of Vintners Company 18, Distillers Company 22; sold business 31; gave up active wine business for writing 32; re-commissioned in R.A.F.V.R. 41 and appointed to Joint Planning Staff; worked in Office of War Cabinet 41-45; Bronze Star (Mil.), U.S.A.; Pres. Old Comrades Asscn. 2/1 London Brigade 64-.
Leisure interests: collecting books, Georgian furniture and travel.
Publs. *The Forbidden Territory* 33, *A Private Life of Charles II*, *Black August* 34, *The Devil Rides Out*, *The Eunuch of Stamboul* 35, *They Found Atlantis*, *Murder off Miami* 36, *Red Eagle* 37, *The Golden Spaniard* 38, *The Scarlet Impostor*, *Faked Passports* 40, *The Black Baroness* 41, *Come into my Parlour* 46, *The Launching of Roger Brook* 47, *The Shadow of Tyburn Tree* 48, *The Rising Storm* 49, *The Second Seal* 50, *The Man Who Killed the King* 51, *To the Devil a Daughter* 54, *The Island where Time Stands Still* 55, *The Ka of Gifford Hillary* 56, *The Prisoner in the Mask* 57, *Traitor's Gate* 58, *Stranger than Fiction*, *The Rape of Venice* 59, *The Satanist* 60, *Saturdays with Bricks*, *Vendetta in Spain* 61, *Mayhem in Greece* 62, *The Sultan's Daughter* 63, *Bill for the Use of a Body* 64, *They Used Dark Forces* 64, *Dangerous Inheritance* 65, *White Witch of the South Seas* 68, *Evil in a Mask* 69, *Gateway to Hell* 70, *The Ravishing of Lady Mary Ware*, *The Devil and all his Works* 71, *The Strange Story of Linda Lee* 72, *The Irish Witch* 73, *Desperate Measures* 74, *Library of the Occult*.
60 Cadogan Square, London, S.W.1, England.
Telephone: 01-584-4881.

Wheeldon, John Murray, B.A.; Australian barrister, solicitor and politician; b. 9 August 1929, Subiaco, W. Australia; *s.* of Murray Walter and Marjorie Lillian Wheeldon; *m.* Judith Tanya Shaw; two *s.* one *d.*; ed. Perth Modern School, Univ. of Western Australia.
Member Australian Labor Party, W. Australian State Exec. 52-; Senator 65-; Chair. Australian Parl. Cttee. on Foreign Affairs and Defence 73-75; Minister for Repatriation and Compensation June 74-Nov. 75, for Social Security June-Nov. 75.
Parliament Offices, 191 St. Georges Terrace, Perth, W.A. 6000, Australia.

Wheeler, John Archibald, D.SC., PH.D.; American physicist; b. 9 July 1911, Jacksonville, Fla.; *s.* of Dr. Joseph Lewis Wheeler and Mabel Archibald; *m.* Janette Latourette Zabriskie Hegner 1935; one *s.* two *d.*; ed. Johns Hopkins Univ.
National Research Council Fellow, New York and Copenhagen 33-35; Asst Prof. of Physics, Univ. of N.C. 35-38; Asst. Prof. of Physics, Princeton Univ. 38-42, Assoc. Prof. 45-47, Prof. 47-66, Joseph Henry Prof. of Physics 66-; Physicist, Manhattan Project of U.S. Govt., Chicago, Wilmington, Hanford 42-45; Dir. Project Matterhorn, Princeton 51-53; Lorentz Prof., Univ. of Leiden 56; Fulbright Prof., Univ. of Kyoto 62; Guggenheim Fellow, Paris and Copenhagen 49-50; visiting Fellow Clare Coll. Cambridge 64; mem. Editorial Board, *Physical Review*, *Review of Modern Physics*; Chair. Joint Cttee. of American Physical Soc and

American Philosophical Soc. on History of Theoretical Physics; mem. U.S. Gen. Advisory Cttee. on Arms Control and Disarmament 69-; Fellow, American Physical Soc. (Pres. 66, mem. Council), American Philosophical Soc., A.A.A.S. (mem. Board of Dirs. 63-68); mem. American Acad. of Arts and Sciences, Nat. Acad. of Sciences; Trustee Battelle Memorial Inst.; Hon. Sc.D. (Western Reserve, Yeshiva and Yale Univs., Univs. of N.C. and Pa. and Middlebury Coll.); A. Cressy Morrison Prize, N.Y. Acad. of Sciences 47, Albert Einstein Prize, Strauss Foundation 65, Enrico Fermi Award, U.S. Atomic Energy Comm. 68, Franklin Medal of Franklin Inst. 69, Nat. Medal of Science 71.
Leisure interests: swimming, sculpture in nature.
Publs. *Geometrodynamics* 62, *Gravitation Theory and Gravitational Collapse* 65, *Spacetime Physics* 66, *Einstein's Vision* 68, *Relativity* 71.
The Joseph Henry Laboratories, Princeton University, Princeton, N.J. 08540; Home: 30 Maxwell Lane, Princeton, N.J. 08540, U.S.A.
Telephone: 609-452-4387 (Office); 609-924-4262 (Home).

Wheeler, Sir (Robert Eric) Mortimer, C.H., Kt., C.I.E., M.C., T.D., M.A., D.LIT. (London), F.R.S., F.B.A., F.S.A.; British archaeologist; b. 10 Sept. 1890, Glasgow; *m.* Tessa Verney 1914 (died 1936); one *s.*
Served France, Italy and Germany in First World War; Keeper, Archaeological Dept., Nat. Museum of Wales 20-24, Dir. Museum 24-26; Lecturer in Archaeology Univ. of Wales 20-24; Keeper and Sec. London Museum 26-44; Lecturer in British Archaeology and Hon. Dir. Inst. of Archaeology Univ. of London 34-44; Dir.-Gen. of Archaeology India 44-48; Prof. Archaeology of Roman Provinces, Univ. of London 48-55; Archaeological Adviser to Govt. of Pakistan 48-50; Prof. of Ancient History to Royal Acad. of Arts 65-; directed archaeological excavations Colchester 17 and 20, Caernarvon 21-23, Brecon 24-25, Caerleon 26-27, Lydney 28-29, St. Albans 30-33, Maiden Castle, Dorset 34-37, Brittany 38, Normandy 39, India 44-48, Pakistan 50, 58, etc.; Pres. Cambrian Archaeological Asscn. 31, South-Eastern Union of Scientific Societies 32, British Asscn. Conf. of Dels. 33, Museums Asscn. 37-38, Indian Museums Asscn. 47-48, Pakistan Museums Asscn. 49; Royal Archaeological Inst. 50; Vice-Pres. Society of Antiquaries 35-39, Sec. 39-40, Dir. 40-44, 49-54, Pres. 54-59; Trustee, British Museum 54-59 and 63-73; Sec. British Acad. 49-68; Commr. Royal Comm. on Historical Monuments (England) 39-58; Fellow, Univ. Coll., London 22; Lieut.-Col. R.A. 39-43, Brig. 43; served in Africa and Italy 41-43; Hon. D.Litt. (Oxford, Bristol, Delhi, Wales, Ireland, Liverpool); Gold Medal Soc. of Antiquaries 44; Petrie Medal, Univ. of London 51; Lucy Wharton Drexel Medal, Univ. of Pennsylvania 62.
Publs. Books on Roman London, Prehistoric and Roman Wales, London and the Saxons, the Belgic and Roman cities of Verulamium, Maiden Castle, Ancient Pakistan; *The Indus Civilisation*, *Archaeology from the Earth*, *Rome beyond the Imperial Frontiers*, *Early India and Pakistan*, *Still Digging* (autobiography), *Charsada*, *Roman Art and Architecture*, *Civilizations of the Indus Valley and Beyond*, *Alms for Oblivion* (collected papers), *Flames over Persepolis*, *The British Academy 1949-68*.
c/o British Academy, Burlington House, London, W.1, England.

Wheelock, John Hall; American poet; b. 9 Sept. 1886, Long Island, N.Y.; *s.* of William Efner Wheelock and Emily Charlotte Hall; *m.* Phyllis Edwalyn de Kay 1940; ed. Harvard, Göttingen and Berlin Univs.
Member staff Charles Scribner's Sons 11, Editor 26, Dir. 32, Sec. 32-42, Treas. 42-57, retd.; member, American Acad. of Arts and Letters; Hon. Consultant in American Letters to the Library of Congress; hon. mem. Poetry Soc. of America; Chancellor Acad. of

American Poets; Bollingen Poetry Prize (co-winner) 61; Medal for Achievement in the Arts of The Signet Soc. (Harvard Univ.) 65, Poetry Soc. of America Gold Medal for Notable Achievement in Poetry 72, and other awards.

Leisure interests: walking, swimming, reading, chess.
Publs. *Verses by Two Undergraduates* (with Van Wyck Brooks) 05, *The Human Fantasy* 11, *The Beloved Adventure* 12, *Love and Liberation* 13, *Alan Seeger, Poet of the Foreign Legion* 18, *Dust and Light* 19, *Theodore Roosevelt: a Bibliography* 20, *The Black Panther* 22, *The Bright Doom* 27, *Collected Poems* 36, *Poems Old and New* 56, *The Two Knowledges: An Essay on a Certain Resistance* 58, *The Gardener and other Poems* 61, *What is Poetry?* 63, *Dear Men and Women: New Poems* 66; *By Daylight and in Dream: New and Collected Poems, 1904-1970, In Love and Song* 71; Editor: *The Face of a Nation, Poetical Passages from the Writings of Thomas Wolfe* 39, Editor to Author, *The Letters of Maxwell E. Perkins* 50, *Poets of Today* (annually) 53-61.
350 East 57th Street, New York City, N.Y. 10022, U.S.A.
Telephone: Plaza 8-3322.

Whelan, Eugene; Canadian farmer and politician; b. 11 July 1924, Amhurstburg, Ont.; s. of Charles B. and Frances L. (Kelly) Whelan; m. Elizabeth Pollinger 1960; three d.; ed. Windsor, Ont., vocational and technical school.
Former mem. Board of Governors, Ont. Fed. of Agriculture; fmr. Dir. United Co-operatives, Ont.; fmr. Pres. Essex Co. Fed. of Agriculture; mem. House of Commons 62- (re-elected 63, 65, 68); Parl. Sec. to the Minister of Forestry 68-72; Minister of Agriculture Nov. 72-; mem. of numerous farming orgs.; Kt. of Colombus.
Ministry of Agriculture, Ottawa, Ontario; Home: 641 Front Road North, Amherstburg, Ontario N9V 2X6, Canada.
Telephone: 736-4042 (Home).

Whelan, William Joseph, B.SC., PH.D., D.SC.; British biochemist; b. 14 Nov. 1924, Salford; s. of William Joseph Whelan and Jane Antoinette Bertram; m. Margaret Miller Birnie 1951; ed. Univ. of Birmingham.
Assistant Lecturer, Univ. of Birmingham 47-48; Asst. Lecturer, Lecturer and Senior Lecturer, Univ. Coll. of N. Wales 48-55; Senior mem. Lister Inst. of Preventive Medicine 56-64; Prof. and Head of Biochemistry Dept., Royal Free Hosp. Medical School, Univ. of London 64-67; Prof. and Chair. of Biochemistry Dept., Univ. of Miami, U.S.A. 67-; Gen. Sec. Int. Union of Biochemistry 73-; Alsberg Award, American Asscn. of Cereal Chemists 67, CIBA Medal of the British Biochemical Soc. 69, Award of Merit, Japanese Soc. of Starch Science 75.
Publs. (editor) *Control of Glycogen Metabolism* 64, 68, *Carbohydrate Metabolism and its Disorders* 68, *Biochemistry of Carbohydrates* 75.
Department of Biochemistry, University of Miami, P.O. Box 520875, Miami, Fla. 33152; Home: Apt. 1003, 1420 South Bayshore Drive, Miami, Fla. 33131, U.S.A.
Telephone: (305) 547-6265 (Office); (305) 373-8039 (Home).

Wheldon, Sir Huw P., Kt., O.B.E., M.C.; British (Welsh) television executive; b. 7 May 1916, Prestatyn; s. of late Sir Wynn Wheldon and of Lady Wheldon; m. Jacqueline Mary (née Clarke) 1956; one s. two d.; ed. Friars School, Bangor and London School of Econs.
With Kent Education Cttee. 39; active service 40-45; Dir. Arts Council for Wales 46; Festival of Britain Directorate 49; B.B.C. Television 52, Producer 53-62, Head of Documentary Programmes 62, Head of Music and Documentary Programmes 63-65, Controller of Programmes 65-68, Man. Dir. Television 69-75; Special Adviser BBC 75-; Chair. and mem. Council London

School of Econs.; mem. Council, Hon. Soc. of Cymmrodorian, Nat. Film School Council, Royal Coll. of Art; Guild of Television Producers Award for Best British Documentary 58; Ford Foundation Award 59; TV Soc. Silver Medal 63; Hon. Fellow, London School of Econs., Manchester Coll. of Arts and Design; Fellow, Royal Soc. of Arts; Hon. D. Litt. (New Univ. of Ulster) 75.
Leisure interest: golf.
Publ. *Monitor: An Anthology* 62.
120 Richmond Hill, Richmond, Surrey, England.

Whinnery, John Roy, PH.D.; American professor of electrical engineering; b. 26 July 1916; s. of Ralph Vincent and Edith Bent Whinnery; m. Patricia Barry 1944; three d.; ed. Modesto Junior Coll. Calif., Univ. of Calif. Berkeley.
Student Engineer to Research Engineer, Gen. Electric Co. 37-46; Lecturer, Union Coll., Schenectady, N.Y., 45-46; Univ. of Calif., Berkeley, Lecturer, Assoc. Prof., Prof., Chair. of Dept., Dean of Coll. 46-; (on leave from Univ. of Calif.) Guggenheim Fellow E.T.H. Zurich Switzerland 59; Head of Microwave Tube Research at Hughes Aircraft Co., Culver City Calif. 52-53; visiting mem. of Tech. Staff, Bell Telephone Laboratories 63-64; Visiting Prof. Stanford Univ. 69-70; Research Professorship in Miller Inst. for Basic Research in Science 73-74; mem. of Nat. Acad. of Engineering 65; Nat. Acad. of Sciences 73; Educ. Medal Inst. Electronics and Electrical Engineers.
Leisure interests: hiking, skiing, golf, writing poetry and children's stories.
Publs. *Fields and Waves in Modern Radio* (with Simon Ramo) 44, 52; *World of Engineering* 65, *Fields and Waves in Communication Electronics* (with Simon Ramo and T. Van Duzer) 65, *Introduction to Electronic Systems Circuits and Devices* (with D. O. Pederson and J. J. Studer) 66, technical articles and patents on microwaves and lasers.
Department of Electrical Engineering and Computer Sciences, Univ. of Calif., Berkeley, Calif. 94720; Home: 1 Daphne Court, Orinda, Calif. 94563, U.S.A.
Telephone: (414) 642-1030 (Office); (415) 254-3098 (Home).

Whipple, Fred Lawrence, A.B., PH.D.; American astronomer; b. 5 Nov. 1906, Red Oak, Iowa; s. of Harry Lawrence Whipple and Celestia (MacFarland) Whipple; m. 1st Dorothy Woods 1928, 2nd Babette Samuelson 1946; one s. one d.; ed. Univ. of California.
Member Staff Harvard Coll. Observatory 31; in charge of Oak Ridge Station 32-37; Instructor 32-38, Lecturer 38-45, Associate Prof. 45-50, Prof. of Astronomy 50-; Chair. Cttee. on Concentration in the Physical Sciences 47-49; Chair. Dept. Astronomy, Harvard Univ. 49-56; Research Associate Radio Research Laboratory 42-45, in charge of Confusion Reflectors "Window" (radar countermeasure); Dir. Smithsonian Inst. Astrophysical Observatory 55-73, Senior Scientist 73-; mem. Rocket and Satellite Research Panel 46-, U.S. Nat. Advisory Cttee. on Aeronautics Sub-Cttee. 46-52, U.S. Research and Development Board Panel 47-52, U.S. Nat. Cttee. I.G.Y. 55-59, Advisory Panel on Astronomy to the Nat. Science Foundation 52-55 and Chair. 54-55; mem. Div. Cttee. for Mathematical and Physical Sciences 64-, many other scientific cttees., etc.; Project Leader Harvard Radio Meteor Project 58-; Phillips Prof. of Astronomy, Harvard Univ. 68-; mem. NASA Optical Astronomy Panel, Astronomy Missions Board 68; mem. NASA Science and Technology Advisory Cttee. 69; mem. NASA Comet and Asteroid Working Group 71-72, Chair. 72-; Voting Rep. of U.S.A. in Int. Astronomical Union 52 and 55; Associate Editor *Astrophysical Journal* 52-54, *Astronomical Journal* 54-56, 64-; Editor *Planetary and Space Science* 58-; Editor *Harvard's Announcement Cards* 52-60; Editor *Smithsonian Contributions to Astrophysics* 56-; Lowell Lecturer, Lowell Inst.

Boston 47; Vice-Pres. American Astronomical Soc. 48-50, 60-, Cttee. on Space Research (COSPAR) 60-; Ed. Board *Space Science Reviews* 61-; Ed. Cttee. *Annual Review of Astronomy and Astrophysics* 65-; Associate, Royal Astronomical Soc. 70; Donohue Medals, Pres. Certificate of Merit, J. Lawrence Smith Medal of Nat. Acad. of Sciences, Exceptional Service Award (U.S.A.F.), Liège Univ. Medal, Space Flight Award, Commr. of Order of Merit for Research and Invention; Distinguished Federal Civilian Service Award from President Kennedy and other awards; mem. R.S.A., Benjamin Franklin Fellow 68-; Leonard Medal, Meteoritical Soc. 70, Nat. Civil Service League's Career Service Award for Sustained Excellence 72, Kepler Medal, A.A.A.S.; Hon. M.A., Hon. D.Sc., Hon. D.Litt., Hon. LL.D.

Leisure interests: scuba diving, stochastic painting, cycling.

Publs. *Earth, Moon and Planets* 42, 63, 68, and many scientific papers.

Smithsonian Astrophysical Observatory, 60 Garden Street, Cambridge, Mass. 02138; and 35 Elizabeth Road, Belmont, Mass. 02178, U.S.A.

Whipple, George Hoyt, B.A., M.D.; American pathologist; b. 28 Aug. 1878, Ashland, N.H.; s. of Ashley Cooper Whipple and Frances Anna Hoyt; m. Katharine Ball Waring 1914; one s. one d.; ed. Yale Univ., and Johns Hopkins Univ.

Associate Prof. of Pathology, Johns Hopkins Univ. 09-14; Resident Pathologist, Johns Hopkins Hospital 10-14; Prof. of Research Medicine, Univ. of California 14-21; Dean, Univ. of Rochester 21-53, Prof. 21-55; joint recipient of Nobel Medicine Prize for research in the treatment of anaemia 34; Trustee Rockefeller Foundation 27-43; Trustee Gen. Education Board 36-43; mem. Board of Scientific Dir. Rockefeller Inst. 36-53; Trustee 39-60, Trustee Emeritus 60; mem. Nat. Acad. of Sciences and American Philosophical Society; hon. mem. Pathological Society of Great Britain and Ireland 45-, Int. Asscn. for Dental Research 60-; foreign corresp. mem. British Medical Asscn.; Hon. Fellow, American Acad. of Oral Pathology; many awards and medals.

Leisure interests: fishing, shooting.

Apartment 208, The Valley Manor, 1570 East Avenue, Rochester, N.Y. 14610; 260 Crittenden Boulevard, Rochester, N.Y. 14642, U.S.A.

Whistler, Laurence, C.B.E., B.A., F.R.S.L.; British writer and glass engraver; b. 21 Jan. 1912, Eltham, Kent; s. of Henry Whistler and Helen Ward; brother of the late Rex Whistler; m. 1st Jill Furse 1939 (died 1944), one s. one d.; m. 2nd Theresa Furse (younger sister of Jill Furse) 1950, one s. one d.; ed. Stowe School, Balliol Coll., Oxford.

Served World War II, commissioned 41; Hon. Fellow, Balliol Coll.; King's Gold Medal for Poetry 35, Atlantic Award for Literature 45; work on glass includes: goblets in point-engraving and drill, engraved church windows and panels at Sherborne Abbey, Moreton, Dorset, Checkendon, Oxon., Ilton, Somerset, Eastbury, Berks., Guards' Chapel, London; exhbns.: Agnews, Bond Street 69, Marble Hill, Twickenham 72, Corning Museum, U.S.A. 74.

Publs. *Sir John Vanbrugh* (biography) 38, *The English Festivals* 47, *Rex Whistler, His Life and His Drawings* 48, *The World's Room* (Collected Poems) 49, *The Engraved Glass of Laurence Whistler* 52, *Rex Whistler: the Königsmark Drawings* 52, *The Imagination of Vanbrugh and His Fellow Artists* 54, *The View From This Window* (poems) 56, *Engraved Glass* 52-58, *The Work of Rex Whistler* (co-author) 60, *Audible Silence* (poems) 61, *The Initials in the Heart: the story of a marriage* 64,

To Celebrate Her Living (poems) 67, *Pictures on Glass* 72, 75.

Little Place, Lyme Regis, Dorset, England.

Telephone: Lyme Regis (02-974) 2355.

Whitaker, Thomas Kenneth, M.SC.(ECON.); Irish banker; b. 8 Dec. 1916, Rostrevor, Co. Down; s. of Edward Whitaker and Jane O'Connor; m. Nora Fogarty 1941; five s. one d.; ed. Christian Brothers' School, Drogheda.

Entered Irish Civil Service 34; Sec. Dept. of Finance 56-69; Dir. Cen. Bank of Ireland 58-69, Gov. 69-; Pres. Econ. and Social Research Inst.; Hon. D.Econ.Sc. (Nat. Univ. of Ireland).

Leisure interests: angling, golf, music.

Publ. *Financing by Credit Creation*.

Central Bank of Ireland, Fitzwilton House, Wilton Terrace, Dublin 2; Home: 148 Stillorgan Road, Donnybrook, Dublin 4, Ireland.

Whitcomb, Hon. Edgar D.; American lawyer, businessman and politician; b. 6 Nov. 1917; s. of John W. Whitcomb and Louise Doud; m. Patricia Louise Dolfuss 1951; one s. four d.; ed. Indiana Univ.

United States Army Air Corps World War II; mem. Indiana State Senate 51-54; Asst. U.S. Attorney Southern District Ind. 55-56; Chair. Great Lakes Comm. 65-66; Sec. of State of Ind. 66-68, Gov. 69-73; Dir. World Trade Center, Indianapolis, U.S. Auto Club 73-; retd. Col. U.S.A.F. Reserve; Hon. LL.D. Indiana Univ. 74; Republican.

Leisure interests: cycling, sailing and riding.

Publ. *Escape from Corregidor*.

636 North Poplar, Seymour, Indiana 47274, U.S.A.

Telephone: 317-248-8511 (Office); 812-522-5454 (Home).

White, Baroness (Life Peer), cr. 70, of Rhymney, Mon.; **Eirene Lloyd White;** British politician; b. 9 Nov. 1909, Belfast; d. of late Dr. Thomas Jones; m. John Cameron White 1948 (died 1968); ed. St. Paul's Girls' School, and Somerville Coll., Oxford.

Ministry of Labour 41-45; Parl. journalist 45-49; Labour M.P. for E. Flintshire 50-70; Parl. Under-Sec. of State, Colonial Office 64-66; Minister of State, Foreign Office 66-67; Minister of State for Wales 67-70; mem. Nat. Exec. Cttee., Labour Party 47-53, 57-72, Chair. 68-69; Deputy Chair. Metrication Board 72-76; Chair. Land Authority for Wales 75-; mem. Royal Comm. on Environmental Pollution 74-, British Waterways Board 74-; Pres. Nat. Council of Women (Wales); Pres. Council for the Protection of Rural Wales; Vice-Pres. British Commonwealth League.

36 Westminster Gardens, Marsham Street, London, SW1P 4JD, England.

Telephone: 01-828-3320.

White, Abraham, M.A., PH.D.; American professor of biochemistry; b. 18 March 1908, Cleveland, Ohio; s. of Morris and Lena White; m. Edna Shapiro 1937; no c.; ed. Univs. of Denver and Mich.

Postdoctoral Research Fellow, Physiological Chem., Yale Univ. School of Medicine 31-33, Instructor 33-37, Asst. Prof. 37-43, Assoc. Prof. 43-48; Prof. and Chair. Dept. of Physiological Chem., Univ. of Calif. School of Medicine, Los Angeles 48-51; Vice-Pres. and Dir. of Research, Chemical Specialities Co., Inc., N.Y.C. 51-53, Visiting Lecturer in Biochem., Coll. of Physicians and Surgeons, Columbia Univ.; Prof. and Chair. Dept. of Biochem. and Assoc. Dean, Albert Einstein Coll. of Medicine 53-72; Distinguished Scientist Syntex Research Laboratories 72-; Consulting Prof. of Biochemistry, Stanford Univ. School of Medicine 72-; mem. Nat. Acad. of Sciences; Hon. L.H.D. (Yeshiva), Sc.D. (Univ. of Denver) 75; Eli Lilly Prize 38, Distinguished Alumni Award (Denver) 60, Sesquicentennial Alumni Award (Univ. of Mich.) 67, Borden Award 69.

Leisure interests: classical music, art, theatre, archaeology, anthropology.

Publs. *Principles of Biochemistry* (co-author), and approximately 200 articles in scientific journals.

580 Arastradero Apt. 507, Palo Alto, Calif. 94306, U.S.A.

Telephone: 415-493-1492.

White, Elwyn Brooks, B.A.; American writer and editor; b. 11 July 1899; ed. Cornell Univ.

Comment writer, reporter, and contributor to *The New Yorker* magazine; also contributed monthly department called "One Man's Meat" to *Harper's* 38-43; Presidential Medal of Freedom 63; Laura Ingalls Wilder Award 70; Nat. Medal for Literature 71; Hon. Litt.D. (Dartmouth Coll., Hamilton Coll., Univs. of Maine, Yale, Harvard, Bowdoin Coll., Colby Coll.).

Publs. *The Lady is Cold* 29, *Is Sex Necessary?* (with James Thurber) 29, *Every Day is Saturday* 34, *The Fox of Peapack* 38, *Quo Vadimus?* 39, *One Man's Meat* 42, enlarged 44, *Stuart Little* 45, *The Wild Flag* 46, *Here is New York* 49, *Charlotte's Web* 52, *The Second Tree from the Corner* 54, *The Points of My Compass* 62, *The Trumpet of the Swan*; editor (with Katharine S. White) *A Subtreasury of American Humor* 41.

25 West 43rd Street, New York, N.Y. 10036; and North Brooklin, Maine, U.S.A.

White, Sir Frederick William George, K.B.E., M.SC., PH.D., F.A.A., F.R.S.; Australian physicist; b. 1905, Wellington, New Zealand; s. of W. H. White; m. Elizabeth Cooper 1932; one s. one d.; ed. Victoria Univ. Coll., New Zealand, and Cambridge Univ.

Post-graduate work at Cavendish Laboratory, Cambridge 29-31; Demonstrator in Physics, Lecturer in Physics, King's Coll. London 31-37; Prof. of Physics, Canterbury Univ. Coll. New Zealand 37; seconded to Council for Scientific and Industrial Research as Chair. Radiophysics Advisory Board 41; Chief Div. of Radiophysics 42; Exec. Officer C.S.I.R. 45, mem. Exec. Cttee. 46, Chief Exec. Officer Commonwealth Scientific and Industrial Research Organisation (CSIRO) 49-56; Deputy Chair. CSIRO 57-59, Chair. 59-70; Hon. D.Sc. (Monash Univ., Melbourne, Australian Nat. Univ., Canberra, Univ. of Papua New Guinea).

Leisure interests: fishing, walking.

Publ. *Electromagnetic Waves* 34.

57 Investigator Street, Red Hill, Canberra, A.C.T., Australia.

White, George David Lloyd, M.V.O., M.A.; New Zealand diplomatist; b. 21 March 1918, Nelson; s. of G. D. and F. E. White; m. Miranda Turnbull 1946; one s.; ed. Canterbury Univ., Christchurch.

Served with New Zealand Army in Middle East 41-45; Econ. Stabilization Comm. 45-49; joined Ministry of Foreign Affairs 49; Econ. Counsellor, London 54-55; Counsellor, Wash. 56-58, Chargé d'Affaires 58-60; Deputy High Commr. to U.K. 61-64; Deputy Sec. for Foreign Affairs 64-72; Amb. to U.S.A. 72-.

Leisure interests: golf, tennis, fly fishing.

Embassy of New Zealand, 19 Observatory Circle, N.W., Washington, D.C. 20008, U.S.A.

Telephone: 202-265-1721.

White, Sir Harold Leslie, Kt., C.B.E., M.A., F.L.A.A., F.A.H.A.; Australian librarian; b. 14 June 1905; s. of James White and Beatrice Hodge; m. Elizabeth Wilson, M.B.E.; two s. two d.; ed. Wesley Coll., Melbourne, and Queen's Coll. of Melbourne Univ.

Commonwealth Parl. Library 23-67, Parl. Librarian 47-67; Nat. Librarian, Nat. Library of Australia 47-70; Chair. Standing Cttee. Australian Advisory Council on Bibliographical Services 60-70; Gov. Australian Film Inst. 58-; Chair. Advisory Cttee. Australian Encyclopaedia 70-; mem. Nat. Memorials Cttee. 75-, Australian Cttees. for UNESCO, Australian Nat. Film Board; mem. UNESCO Int. Cttee. Bibliography, Documentation and Terminology 61-65; Fellow Acad. of Social Sciences of Australia; retd. 70.

Publ. (ed.) *Canberra: A Nation's Capital.*

Home: 27 Mugga Way, Red Hill, Canberra, A.C.T. 2600, Australia.

White, Lee Calvin, B.S., LL.B.; American lawyer and government official; b. 1 Sept. 1923, Omaha, Neb.; m. Dorothy Cohn 1944; five c.; ed. Univ. of Nebraska, and Lehigh Univ.

Lawyer, Div. of Law, Tennessee Valley Authority 50-54; Legislative Asst. on staff of Senator John F. Kennedy 54, 55-57; Counsel to Senate Small Business Cttee. 57-58; Admin. Asst. to Senator Cooper of Kentucky 58-61; Asst. Special Counsel to Pres. Kennedy 61-64; Special Counsel to President Johnson March 65-66; Chair. Fed. Power Comm. 66-69; in private practice of firm White, Fine and Ambrogne; Campaign Man. for R. Sargent Shriver 72.

1156 15th Street, N.W., Washington, D.C. 20005, U.S.A.

Telephone: 202-659-2900.

White, Michael James Denham, D.SC., F.R.S., F.A.A.; Australian geneticist; b. 20 Aug. 1910, London; s. of James Kemp White and Una Theodora Chase; m. Isobel Mary Lunn 1939; two s. one d.; ed. Univ. Coll. London.

Assistant Lecturer in Zoology, Univ. Coll. London 33-36, Lecturer 36-46; Rockefeller Foundation Fellow, Columbia Univ. 37-38; Reader in Zoology, Univ. Coll. London 47; Guest Investigator, Carnegie Inst. of Washington, Dept. of Genetics 47; Prof. of Zoology, Univ. of Texas 47-53; Senior Research Fellow, Commonwealth Scientific and Industrial Research Org. (CSIRO), Canberra, Australia 53-56; Prof. of Zoology, Univ. of Missouri 57-58; Prof. of Zoology, Univ. of Melbourne 58-64, Prof. of Genetics 64-; Fellow, Australian Acad. of Science 55, Royal Soc. (U.K.) 61; Hon. Foreign mem. American Acad. of Arts and Sciences 63; Mueller Medal, Australian and N.Z. Asscn. for the Advancement of Science 65, Companion of the Order of Australia.

Leisure interest: travel.

Publs. *The Chromosomes* 37 (numerous later edns. and translations), *Animal Cytology and Evolution* 45, 54, 73, *Genetic Mechanisms of Speciation in Insects* (editor) 74; numerous papers in scientific journals.

Department of Genetics, University of Melbourne, Parkville, Victoria 3052; Home: 23 Leicester Street, North Balwyn, Victoria 3104, Australia.

Telephone: 345-1844, Ext. 6246 (Univ.); 85-79033.

White, Patrick, B.A.; Australian writer; b. 28 May 1912, London, England; s. of Victor White and Ruth Withycombe; ed. Cheltenham Coll., and King's Coll., Cambridge.

Intelligence officer, R.A.F., World War II; W. H. Smith & Son Award 59; Nobel Prize for Literature 73; Companion, Order of Australia 75.

Publs. *Happy Valley* 39, *The Living and the Dead* 41, *The Aunt's Story* 48, *The Tree of Man* 55, *Voss* 57, *Riders in the Chariot* 61, *The Burnt Ones* 64, *Four Plays* 65, *The Solid Mandala* 66, *The Vivisector* 70, *The Eye of the Storm* 73, *The Cockatoos* 74.

20 Martin Road, Centennial Park, Sydney, N.S.W., Australia.

White, Robert M., II; American journalist; b. 6 April 1915, Mexico, Mo.; s. of L. Mitchell White and Maude (née See) White; m. Barbara Spurgeon 1948; one s. three d.; ed. Missouri Military Acad., and Washington and Lee Univ.

With United Press 39; Army service 40-45; Pres.,Co-Ed. and Co-Publisher *Mexico* (Missouri) *Ledger* 45-; Ed. and Pres. *New York Herald Tribune* Aug. 59-Feb. 61; Dir.

American Newspaper Publishers' Asscn. 55-63, Treas.
62-63; Dir. New York World's Fair (64-65); fmr. Chair.
Associated Press Nominating Cttee.; fmr. Chair. and
Pres. of Board Inland Daily Press Asscn.; Dir. Ste-
phen's Coll.; Pres. See TV Co. 65-; American Cttee. Int.
Press Inst., Vice-Chair. 68-71; Dir. American Soc. of
Newspaper Editors 68-70; Dir. Missouri Mil. Acad.;
Pres. Sigma Delta Chi (Nat. Soc. of Journalists) 67-68;
Visiting Prof., Univ. of Missouri 68-69; mem. Pulitzer
Prize Jury for Journalism 64-66; Chair. American Soc.
of Newspaper Editors Freedom of Information Cttee.
70-72; Chair. Missouri Free Press-Fair Trial Cttee. 70-
74; mem. Board of Dirs. Mexico Bank of Commerce,
Associated Press, Commerce Bancshares Inc., Butler
Mfg. Co., Board of Dirs. Wash. Journalism Center 72-,
McArthur Memorial Foundation, State Historical Soc.
of Missouri, Missouri Public Expenditure Survey,
Board of Dirs. Commerce Bank of St. Louis, Washington and Lee Univ. Alumni Inc.; Pres. Mark Land Co.
56-; Distinguished Service to Journalism Award, Univ.
of Missouri 67, Nat. Newspapers Asscn. Pres. Award
of Merit 67.
Leisure interests: hunting, golfing.
Publs. *A Study of the Printing and Publishing Business
in the Soviet Union* (co-author), *China Journey*.
3 Park Circle, Mexico, Mo. 65265; Office: 300 N.
Washington St., Mexico, Mo. 65265, U.S.A.
Telephone: 314-JU-1-1111 (Office); 314-JU-1-2522
(Home).

White, Robert Mayer, SC.D.; American meteorologist;
b. 13 Feb. 1923, Boston, Mass.; *s.* of David and Mary
White; *m.* Mavis Seagle 1948; one *s.* one *d.*; ed. Harvard
Univ., and Massachusetts Inst. of Technology.
War Service with U.S. Air Force; executive at Atmos-
pheric Analysis Laboratory, Geophysics Research
Directorate, Air Force Cambridge Research Center
52-58, Chief of Meteorological Devt. Laboratory 58;
Research Assoc. Massachusetts Inst. of Technology 59;
Travelers Insurance Companies 59-60, Pres. Travelers
Research Center, Hartford 60-63; Chief of Weather
Bureau, U.S. Dept. of Commerce 63-65; Admin.
Environmental Science Services Admin., U.S. Dept. of
Commerce 65-70; mem. Exec. Cttee. American Geo-
physical Union, Marine Technological Soc., Royal
Meteorological Soc.; mem. of numerous weather re-
search cttees., Commr. Int. Whaling Comm.; Chair.
U.S. Cttee. of World Meteorological Org., Administra-
tor, Nat. Oceanic and Atmospheric Administration 71-.
Leisure interests: gardening, reading.
National Oceanic and Atmospheric Administration,
U.S. Department of Commerce, Washington, D.C.
20230; 8306 Melody Court, Bethesda, Md. 20034, U.S.A.
Telephone: 202-967-3567 (Office); 301-365-3927 (Home).

White, Theodore H., A.B.; American writer; b. 6 May
1915, Boston, Mass.; *s.* of David White and Mary
(Winkeller) White; *m.* Nancy Bean 1947 (divorced
1971); one *s.* one *d.*; ed. Boston Latin School and
Harvard Univ.
Far Eastern Correspondent, *Time* magazine 39-45; Ed.
New Republic 47; European Corresp.-in-Chief, Overseas
News Agency 48-50; Chief European Corresp. *The
Reporter* magazine 50-53, Nat. Corresp. 54-55; Nat.
Corresp. *Colliers* 55-56; Consultant to Columbia Broad-
casting System 61-64; mem. Board of Overseers,
Harvard Coll.; mem. Board of Dirs. Encyclopaedia
Britannica; Air Medal 44; Ben Franklin Award;
Overseas Press Club Award; Pulitzer Prize 62, Emmy
Award 64, 67.
Leisure interests: boating, painting, talk.
Publs. *Thunder out of China* 46, *Stilwell Papers* 48, *Fire
in the Ashes* 53, *The Mountain Road* 58, *The View from
the Fortieth Floor* 60, *The Making of the President 1960*
61, *The Making of the President 1964* 65, *Caesar at the
Rubicon* 68, *The Making of the President 1968* 69, *The

Making of the President 1972 73, *Breach of Faith: The
Fall of Richard Nixon* 75.
168 East 64th Street, New York 21, N.Y., U.S.A.

White, William Smith; American journalist; b.
20 May 1907; ed. Univ. of Texas.
Held various posts with Associated Press (News
Editor, War Editor and War Corresp.); mem. Washing-
ton staff, *The New York Times* 45-57; Chief Congres-
sional corresp. 57-58; nationally syndicated Political
Columnist 58-; Regents Prof. Univ. of Calif. (Berkeley)
57-58; Contributing Editor *Harper's* Magazine 60-62;
Pulitzer Prize in Letters, etc.
Publs. *The Taft Story* 54, *Citadel: The Story of the U.S.
Senate* 57, *Majesty and Mischief: A Mixed Tribute to
F.D.R.* 61, *The Professional: Lyndon B. Johnson* 64,
*Home Place: The Story of the U.S. House of Representa-
tives* 65, *The Responsibles* 72.
2101 Connecticut Avenue, Washington, D.C. 20008,
U.S.A.

Whitehead, George William, PH.D.; American mathe-
matician; b. 2 Aug. 1918, Bloomington, Ill.; *s.* of
George William Whitehead and Mary Gutschlag
Whitehead; *m.* Kathleen Ethelwyn Butcher 1947; ed.
Univ. of Chicago.
Instructor in mathematics Purdue Univ. 41-45,
Princeton Univ. 45-47; Asst. Prof. of Math. Brown
Univ. 47-48, Assoc. Prof. 48-49; Asst. Prof. of Math.
Mass. Inst. of Technology 49-51, Assoc. Prof. 51-57,
Prof. 57-; Fellow, American Acad. of Arts and Sciences
54; mem. Nat. Acad. of Sciences 72-.
Publs. *Homotopy Theory* 66, *Recent Advances in Homo-
topy Theory* 70, and articles in scientific journals.
Room 2-284 Massachusetts Institute of Technology,
Cambridge, Mass. 02139; Home: 25 Bellevue Road,
Arlington, Mass. 02174, U.S.A.
Telephone: 617-253-4991; 617-643-0911 (Home).

Whitehouse, Alton Winslow, Jr., LL.B.; American oil
executive; b. 1 Aug. 1927, Albany, N.Y.; *s.* of Alton
Winslow and Catherine L. Whitehouse; *m.* Helen
MacDonald 1953; two *s.* one *d.*; ed. Univ. of Virginia.
Associate Partner, McAfee, Hanning, Newcomber,
Hazlett & Wheeler 52-68; Vice-Pres. and General
Counsel, Standard Oil Co. of Ohio 68-69, Senior Vice-
Pres. and Gen. Counsel 69, Pres. and Chief Operating
Officer 70-.
Leisure interests: hunting, fishing, golf.
Office: 1750 Midland Building, Cleveland, Ohio 44115;
Home: 34700 Cedar Road, Cleveland, Ohio 44040,
U.S.A.
Telephone: 575-5482 (Office); 216-461-2370 (Home).

Whitelaw, Rt. Hon. William (Stephen Ian), C.H.,
M.C., D.L., M.P.; British politician; b. 28 June 1918,
Edinburgh; *s.* of Mr. and Mrs. W. A. Whitelaw; *m.*
Cecilia Doriel Sprot; four *d.*; ed. Winchester Coll. and
Trinity Coll., Cambridge.
Member of Parliament for Penrith and Border Div. of
Cumberland 55-; Parl. Private Sec. to Chancellor of
Exchequer 57-58; Asst. Govt. Whip 59-61; a Lord
Commr. of the Treasury 61-62; Parl. Sec. Ministry of
Labour July 62-Oct. 64; Opposition Chief Whip Nov.
64-June 70; Lord Pres. of Council and Leader of House
of Commons 70-72; Sec. of State for N. Ireland 72-73,
for Employment Dec. 73-74; Chair. Conservative Party
74-75; Deputy Leader of the Opposition 75-.
Leisure interests: golf, shooting.
House of Commons, London, S.W.1, England.

Whitlam, Edward Gough, Q.C., B.A., LL.B., M.P.;
Australian barrister and politician; b. 11 July 1916,
Melbourne; *s.* of H. F. E. Whitlam; *m.* Margaret Dovey
1942; three *s.* one *d.*; ed. Knox Grammar School,
Sydney, Canberra High School, Canberra Grammar
School and Univ. of Sydney.
Royal Australian Air Force 41-45; admitted to New
South Wales Bar 47; mem. House of Representatives

52-; mem. Parl. Cttee. on Constitutional Review 56-59; mem. Federal Parl. Exec. of Australian Labor Party 59-; Deputy Leader of Australian Labor Party in Federal Parliament 60-67, Leader 67-; Prime Minister 72-75, concurrently Minister of Foreign Affairs 72-73. Publs. *The Constitution v. Labour* 57, *Australian Foreign Policy* 63, *Socialist Policies within the Constitution* 65, *Australia—Base or Bridge* (Evatt Memorial Lecture) 66, *Beyond Vietnam—Australia's Regional Responsibilities* 68, *An Urban Nation* 69, *The New Federalism* 71, *Towards a New Australia—Australia and her Region* 72, *Labor in Power* 72.
Parliament House, Canberra, A.C.T., Australia.
Telephone: 733200.

Whitman, Marina von Neumann, M.A., PH.D.; American economist; b. 6 March 1935, New York, N.Y.; d. of John von Neumann and Mariette Kovesi (Mrs. J. B. H. Kuper); m. Robert F. Whitman 1956; one s. one d.; ed. Radcliffe Coll. and Columbia Univ.
Lecturer in Econs., Univ. of Pittsburgh 62-64, Asst. Prof. 64-66, Assoc. Prof. 66-71, Prof. of Econs. 71-; Senior Staff Economist, Council of Econ. Advisers 70-71; mem. President's Price Comm. 71-72; mem. President's Council of Econ. Advisers (with special responsibility for int. monetary and trade problems) 72-73; mem. President's Advisory Group on Contributions of Tech. to Econ. Strength 75-76; Distinguished Public Service Prof. of Econs., Univ. of Pittsburgh 73-; mem. American Econ. Asscn.; mem. Board of Overseers, Harvard Univ. 72-, Council on Foreign Relations, Trilateral Comm., Comm. on Critical Choices for Americans, Brookings Panel on Econ. Activity 74; mem. Board of Dirs. Mfrs. Hanover Trust Co., Westinghouse Electric Corpn., Marcor Inc.
Publs. various books and articles on economic topics.
Department of Economics, University of Pittsburgh, Pittsburgh, Pa. 15260; Home: 5440 Aylesboro Avenue, Pittsburgh, Pa. 15217, U.S.A.
Telephone: 412-624-5710 (Office).

Whitney, Hassler, MUS.B., PH.D.; American educator; b. 23 March 1907; ed. Yale and Harvard Univs.
National Research Fellow 31-33; Instr. in Maths., Harvard Univ. 33-35; Asst. Prof. 35-40; Assoc. Prof. 40-46; Prof. 46-52; Prof. Inst. for Advanced Study 52-; Research Mathematician, Nat. Defense Research Cttee. 43-45; mem. Nat. Acad. of Sciences, American Philosophical Society; Hon. S.D.
Institute for Advanced Study, Olden Lane, Princeton, N.J., U.S.A.

Whitney, John Hay; American diplomatist and newspaper publisher; b. 17 Aug. 1904, Ellsworth, Maine; s. of Payne and Helen (Hay) Whitney; m. 2nd Betsey Cushing Roosevelt 1942; two d.; ed. Groton School, Oxford Univ., and Yale Univ.
Senior partner, J. H. Whitney & Co., New York; Chair. Whitney Communications Corp., New York; fmr. Chair. Bd. of Freeport Sulphur Co.; Chair. John Hay Whitney Foundation; served U.S.A.F. in Second World War; fmr. special adviser on public affairs, Dept. of State; mem. Board of Govs. New York Hospital; Fellow, Yale Corpn. 55-70, Senior Fellow 70-73; Trustee, Museum of Modern Art; Amb. to U.K. 57-61; Publisher and Editor-in-Chief *New York Herald Tribune*, New York 61-67; Pres. and Publisher *New York Herald Tribune*, European Edition 61-67; Chair. *International Herald Tribune*, Paris 67-; mem. Nat. English Speaking Union of U.S.A.; Graduate mem. Business Council; Vice-Pres. and Trustee Nat. Gallery of Art; First American recipient Benjamin Franklin Award of R.S.A. 63; mem. Corpn. for Public Broadcasting 70-72; Hon. LL.D. (Columbia, Colgate Univ., Brown Univ., Exeter Univ., Colby Coll.); Hon. L.H.D. (Kenyon Coll.); Hon. M.A. (Yale Univ.).
110 West 51st Street, New York, N.Y. 10020, U.S.A.

Whitteridge, Sir Gordon (Coligny), K.C.M.G., O.B.E.; British diplomatist; b. 6 Nov. 1908, Thornton Heath, Surrey; s. of W. R. Whitteridge; m. 1st Margaret Lungley 1938 (died 1942), 2nd Jane Driscoll 1951; one s.; ed. Whitgift School, Croydon, and Univ. of Cambridge.
Joined Consular Service 32, service in Bangkok, Batavia and Medan; Foreign Office 42; 1st Sec., Moscow 48-49; Consul-Gen. Stuttgart 49-51; Counsellor and Consul-Gen. Bangkok 51-56; Consul-Gen. Seattle 56-60, Istanbul 60-62; Ambassador to Burma 62-65, to Afghanistan 65-68; Chair. Anglo-Thai Soc. 71-.
Leisure interests: tennis, music.
13 Grimwade Avenue, Croydon, Surrey CR0 5DJ, England.
Telephone: 01-654-3591.

Whittingham, Air Marshal Sir Harold Edward, K.C.B., K.B.E., M.B., CH.B., F.R.C.P. (LOND.), F.R.C.P. (EDIN.), F.R.F.P.S. (GLASGOW), D.P.H., D.T.M. AND H., K.ST.J.; British pathologist and tropical diseases and aviation medicine specialist; b. 3 Oct. 1887, Portsmouth; s. of the late Rear-Adm. William Whittingham and Elizabeth Annie Crowley; m. 1st Agnes Seright 1912 (died 1966), one s. one d.; m. 2nd Rita White 1966; ed. Christ's Hospital, Greenock Acad., and Glasgow Univ.
Pathologist and Asst. Dir. of Research, Royal Cancer Hosp. Glasgow 10-14; Scottish Nat. Red Cross 14-15; served R.A.M.C. India and Mesopotamia 16-17; Pathologist R.A.F. 18-24, Dir. of Pathology 25-30; Lecturer in Biochemistry London School of Hygiene and Tropical Medicine 26-30; Consultant in Hygiene, Pathology and Tropical Medicine R.A.F. 30-39; C.O. R.A.F. Central Medical Establishment 34-40; Dir. of Hygiene Air Ministry and Chief Exec. Officer Flying Personnel Research Cttee. 39-41; promoted Air Marshal 41; Dir.-Gen. R.A.F. Medical Services 41-46; Medical Adviser British Red Cross Society 46-48; Dir. Medical Services BOAC 48-56; Chair. Med. Cttee., Int. Air Transport Asscn. 50-57; Lecturer, Aviation Medicine, Royal Inst. Public Health and Hygiene 50-73; Medical Adviser Commonwealth Devt. Corpn. 56-66, Medical Consultant 66-; Chair. Flying Personnel Research Cttee. 49-67; Hon. Civil Consultant in aviation medicine to the R.A.F. 67-; Consultant on aviation medicine to BEA 57-; mem. WHO Expert Cttee. on Sanitation of Int. Airports, advisory panels on Int. Quarantine, Environmental Sanitation 53-74, Int. Acad. of Astronautics; Hon. Physician to the King 38-46; Hon. mem. Assocs. of Clinical Pathologists, Mil. Surgeons, U.S.A., Soc. of Med. Consultants to Armed Forces, U.S.A.; decorations include Knight Grand Cross Order of St. Olav (Norway), Commdr. U.S. Legion of Merit, North Persian Memorial Medal, Cross and Star of Order of Polonia Restituta; Chadwick Gold Medal and Prize 25; John Jeffries Award, Inst. of Aero Sciences, U.S.A. 44; Stewart Memorial Award 70; Hon. F.R.C.S. (Edinburgh) and Hon. F.R.S.M. (London); Hon. Fellow, Aero-Medical Assocn., Hon. LL.D. (Glasgow).
Leisure interests: sketching, photography, motoring.
26 Marlborough Gardens, Lovelace Road, Surbiton, Surrey, England.
Telephone: 01-399-8648.

Whittle, Air Commodore Sir Frank, K.B.E., C.B., M.A., F.R.S., C.ENG., R.A.F. (retd.); British aeronautical expert; b. 1 June 1907, Coventry; s. of M. Whittle; m. Dorothy Lee 1930; two s.; ed. Leamington Coll., Royal Air Force Coll., Cranwell, and Cambridge Univ.
Posted to 111 Fighter Squadron as Pilot Officer 28; attended Flying Instructors' Course 29; Flying Instructor at No. 2 Flying Training School, Digby 30; Test Pilot, Marine Aircraft Experimental Estab., Felixstowe 31-32; attended Officers' Course of Engineering at Henlow 32-34; Cambridge Univ. 34-37; posted to Special Duty List to continue work on Whittle

jet-propulsion gas turbine 37-46; Technical Adviser on Engine Design and Production to the Controller of Supplies (Air), Ministry of Supply 46-48; retd. R.A.F. 48; Technical Adviser to BOAC 48-52; consultant to Power Jets (Research and Devt.) Ltd 50-53; Bataafsche Petroleum Maatschappij, The Hague 53-57; Technical Adviser on Devt. of Whittle Turb-Drill by Bristol Siddeley Engines 61-66 and Rolls-Royce 66-70; mem. Livery, Guild of Air Pilots and Air Navigators; Hon. mem. Eng. Inst. of Canada; Hon. Fellow, Aeronautical Soc. of India; Hon. M.I.Mech.E.; Hon. F.R.Ae.S.; Gold Medal (Royal Aeronautical Soc.); James Alfred Ewing Medal; Daniel Guggenheim Medal 46; Kelvin Gold Medal for 47; Melchett Medal 49; Rumford Medal of Royal Soc. 50; Gold Medal of Fed. Aéronautique Internationale 51; Churchill Medal of Soc. of Engineers; Albert Medal of Royal Soc. of Arts 52; Franklin Medal, U.S.A. 56; John Scott Award, City of Philadelphia 57; U.S. Legion of Merit; first recipient Goddard Award of American Inst. of Aeronautics and Astronautics 65; Award of Merit City of Coventry 66; Christopher Columbus Medal and Prize (Genoa) 66; Hon. Fellow, Soc. of Experimental Test Pilots (U.S.A.) 66; Int. Hall of Fame, San Diego 68; Hon. Fellow, American Inst. of Aeronautics and Astronautics 68; Tony Jannus Award 69; Hon. Freeman Royal Leamington Spa; Hon. mem. Société Royale Belge des Ingénieurs; Hon. D.Sc. (Oxford, Manchester, Bath, Warwick, Leicester, Exeter), Hon. Sc.D. (Cambridge), Hon. LL.D. (Edinburgh), Hon. D.Tech. (Technical Univ. of Norway).
Leisure interests: walking, tennis, reading.
Publs. *The Early History of the Whittle Jet-Propulsion Gas Turbine* (First James Clayton Lecture) 45, *Jet: The Story of a Pioneer*.
c/o Williams and Glyn's Bank, Whitehall, London, S.W.1, England.

Whyte, William Hollingsworth; American writer; b. 1 Oct. 1917, West Chester, Pa.; s. of William Hollingsworth Whyte and Louise Price; m. Jenny Bell Bechtel 1964; one d.; ed. Princeton Univ.
Worked for Vick Chemical Co. 39-41; served with U.S. Marine Corps 41-45; joined *Fortune* Magazine 46, Asst. Man. Editor 51-58; Dir. Street Life Project 70-, Municipal Art Soc. of N.Y., N.Y. Landmarks Conservancy; Vice-Chair. Conservation Foundation; mem. American Conservation Assn., N.Y. State Environmental Board; Benjamin Franklin Award 55; LL.D. h.c., Grinnell Coll.
Leisure interests: conservation, urban planning, photography.
Publs. *Is Anybody Listening* 52, *The Organisation Man* 56, *The Exploding Metropolis* 59, *Cluster Development* 64, *The Last Landscape* 68.
175 East 94th Street, New York, N.Y. 10028, U.S.A.
Telephone: 369-0014.

Wiarda, Gérard J.; Netherlands judge; b. 4 Sept. 1906, Amsterdam; ed. in Amsterdam.
Advocate, Rotterdam; Deputy Judge and Judge, Arrondissement Court, Amsterdam; fmr. Prof. of Admin. Law, Univ. of Utrecht; Judge, Netherlands Supreme Court 50, Vice-Pres. 68-72, Pres. 72-; Judge, European Court of Human Rights 67-; mem. Royal Netherlands Acad. of Sciences; Pres. Benelux Court of Justice.
Wassenaarseweg 170, The Hague, Netherlands.

Wibaux, Fernand, DR. EN DROIT; French diplomatist; b. 21 July 1921, Paris; s. of René Wibaux and Marcelle Caudrelier; m. 1st Jaqueline Piezel (deceased); m. 2nd Jeanine Petrequin; one s. two d.; ed. Lycée de Lille and Faculté de Droit, Paris.
Civil Service admin., Algeria 44; Attaché to Sec. of State for Overseas Territories 49, to Minister of Merchant Marine 50-51, to High Commr., French W. Africa 52-56; Chief Asst. to Ministers for Overseas Territories 56-58; Dir.-Gen. Niger Office 56; Consul-Gen. Bamako 60-61;

Amb. to Mali 61-64; Dir. Office de Coopération et d'Accueil Universitaire 64-; Amb. to Chad 68-74; Dir. of Cultural and Social Affairs, Ministry of Co-operation Oct. 74-; Croix de Guerre; Officier de la Légion d'Honneur.
Ministère de la Coopération, 20 rue Monsieur, 75700 Paris, France.

Wiberg, Kenneth Berle, B.S., PH.D.; American professor of chemistry; b. 22 Sept. 1927, New York; s. of Halfdan Wiberg and Solveig Berle; m. Marguerite Louise Koch 1951; two s. one d.; ed. Mass. Inst. of Technology and Columbia Univ.
Instructor, Univ. of Washington 50-52, Asst. Prof. 52-55, Assoc. Prof. 55-57, Prof. 58-62; Prof., Yale Univ. 62-68, Chair. Dept. of Chemistry 68-71, Whitehead Prof. of Chemistry 68-; Visiting Prof., Harvard Univ. 57-58; A. P. Sloan Foundation Fellow 58-62, J. S. Guggenheim Fellow 61-62; mem. Nat. Acad. of Sciences, American Acad. of Arts and Science; California Section Award of American Chemical Soc. 62, J. F. Norris Award of American Chemical Soc. 73.
Publs. *Laboratory Technique in Organic Chemistry* 60, *Interpretation of NMR Spectra* 64, *Physical Organic Chemistry* 64, *Oxidation in Organic Chemistry* (Editor) 65, *Computer Programming for Chemists* 66, *Sigma Molecular Orbital Theory* (with Sinanoglu)70; approx. 150 articles in scientific journals.
Department of Chemistry, Yale University, 225 Prospect Street, New Haven, Conn. 06520, U.S.A.
Telephone: 203-436-2443.

Wibisono, Jusuf, LL.D.; Indonesian politician; b. 28 Feb. 1909, Magelang, Cen. Java; s. of Kunto Kismo Bahuatmodjo; m. Sumijati Sontodihardjo 1936; three s. one d.; ed. Faculty of Law, Jakarta.
Vice-Chair. Working Cttee., Cen. Nat. Cttee. 45-46; Vice-Minister of Economic Affairs 46-47; mem. of Parl. 50-56, Minister of Finance 51-52 and 56-57; mem. Exec. Council of Masjumi Party 48-59; Pres. Indonesian Islamic Trade Union S.B.I.I. (since 61 GASBIINDO) 67-72, Hon. Pres. 66-67; mem. Muhammadijah Exec. Board 56-59, Provisional People's Congress 60-68; mem. of Parl. 60-68; mem. Exec. Board Nat. Front 60-66; Pres. and Dir. Perdania Bank Ltd. 58-; Pres. Council of Advisers, Islamic Commercial Asscn. 67-; Pres. Tjokroaminoto Univ. 68-73.
Leisure interests: photography, reading books on economics, politics, Islam and history.
Publs. *Marriage, Polygamy and Divorce in Islam* 37, *Excursion behind the Iron Curtain* 52.
Jl. Proklamasi 40 (Pegangsaan Timur 40), Jakarta, Indonesia.
Telephone: 82042.

Wichterle, Otto, D.TECH., D.SC.; Czechoslovak chemist; b. 27 Oct. 1913, Prostějov; s. of Karel Wichterle and Slávka Podivínská; m. Ludmila Zahradníková 1938; two s.; ed. Czech Technical Univ., Prague, and Medical Faculty, Charles Univ., Prague.
Assistant Lecturer, Inst. of Experimental Organic Chemistry, Czech Technical Univ., Prague 35-39; Head of Polymer Dept., Bata-Zlín 40-42, 44-45; Gestapo prisoner 42-43; Asst. Prof. Faculty of Chemistry, Czech Tech. Univ., Prague 45, later Prof.; Prof. Coll. Macromolecular Chem., Technical Univ., Prague 49-69; Academician, Czechoslovak Acad. of Sciences 55-76; Head of Dept. of Macromolecular Chem., Inst. of Chem. 55-59; Inst. of Macromolecular Chem., Dir. 59-70, Scientist 70-; Chair. Comm. for Macromolecular Chem.; mem. Bureau Int. Union of Pure and Applied Chem. 62-; Deputy Chair. Scientific Collegium for Chem. and Chemical Technology, Czechoslovak Acad. of Sciences, Prague 63; mem. Exec. Cttee. Int. Union of Pure and Applied Chem. 67; Deputy to Czech Nat. Council 68-69; Deputy to House of Nations, Fed. Assembly 69; Pres. Union of Czech Scientific Workers 69-70; State Prize

54; Order of Labour 66; Klement Gottwald State Prize 67.

Leisure interests: mechanical workshop, gardening.

Publs. Numerous papers and *Foundations of Preparative Organic Chemistry* (with others) 51, *Organic Chemistry* 52, 55, *Inorganic Chemistry* (with Petrů) 53, 56, *Macromolecular Chemistry* 57.

Office: Institute of Macromolecular Chemistry, Prague 6, Na Petřinách 1888; Home: Farni B1, 162 00 Prague 6, Czechoslovakia.

Telephone: Prague 35-3351 (Office); Prague 355070 (Home).

Wickberg, Erik E.; Swedish Salvation Army officer; b. 6 July 1904; ed. Uppsala, Berlin, Stockholm, The Salvation Army Int. Training Coll., and Staff Coll.

Salvation Army 25-; appointments in Scotland, Berlin, London; Divisional Commdr. Uppsala 46-48; Chief. Sec. Switzerland 48-53, Sweden 53-57; Territorial Commdr., Germany 57-61; Chief of Staff, Int. Headquarters London 61-69; General of The Salvation Army 69-74; Commdr. Order of Vasa 70, Order of Moo Koong-Wha (Korea) 70, Grand Cross of Merit (Fed. Rep. of Germany).

Leisure interests: reading, fishing, chess.

Publs. *In Darkest England Now* 74, and articles in Salvation Army periodicals and year book.

International Headquarters of the Salvation Army, 101 Queen Victoria Street, London, E.C.4, England.

Telephone: 01-236-5222.

Wickman, Krister, LL.B., PH.D.; Swedish bank governor and former politician; b. April 1924, Stockholm; s. of Johannes Wickman.

At Nat. Swedish Inst. of Econ. Research 51; Under-Sec. of State at Ministry of Finance 59; mem. Parl. 67-73; mem. Cabinet and Minister without Portfolio for Econ. Policy 67; Minister for Industry 69-71, for Foreign Affairs 71-73; Sec. of Parl. Standing Cttee. on Banking and Currency 53-58; Vice-Chair. of Board LKAB Mining Co. 62-67; Chair. of Board Swedish Film Inst. 63-67; Chair. of Board and mem. Board of Govs. Bank of Sweden 64-67, Gov. 73-; Chair. Econ. Policy Council 68-71; Dir. BIS 73-, SAS 74-; Social Democrat.

Sveriges Riksbank, Box 2119, S-10313, Stockholm, Sweden; Home: Haga Trädgård, 17153 Solna, Sweden.

Telephone: 08/228200 (Office); 08/828818 (Home).

Widdemer, Margaret; American poet and novelist; b. 30 Sept. 1893, Doylestown, Pa.; d. of Rev. Howard T. and Alice De Witt Widdemer; m. R. H. Schauffler 1919 (deceased).

Former Vice-Pres. Board Poetry Soc. of America; Board Dirs. Pen and Brush Club; Lecturer, New York Univ. 45-48; Lecturer on fiction and co-dir. 45-65, Writers' Conf., Chautauqua, N.Y.; Hon. M.A. (Middlebury); Hon. Litt.D. (Bucknell).

Leisure interests: swimming, folk-song, research in extrasensory perception.

Publs. *Why Not?* 16, *Factories* (poems) 17, *Old Road to Paradise* 81 (Poetry Society Pulitzer Prize 19), *The Year of Delight* 21, *Graven Image* 23, *Gallant Lady* 26, *More Than Wife* 27, *Collected Poems* 27, *Road to Downderry* (poems) 32, *Golden Rain* 33, *Back to Virtue, Betty* 34, *Other Lovers* 35, *Hill Garden* (poems) 36, *Eve's Orchard* 37, *Do You Want to Write?* 37, *Hand On Her Shoulder* 38, *Ladies Go Masked* 39, *She Knew Three Brothers* 40, *Lover's Alibi* 40, *Let Me Have Wings* 41, *Angela Comes Home* 42, *Constancia Herself* 44, *Lani* 48, *Red Cloak Flying* 50, *Lady of the Mohawks* 51, *Prince in Buckskin* 52, *Basic Principles of Fiction Writing* 53, *Golden Wildcat* 54, *Great Pine's Son* 54, *Dark Cavalier: collected poems* 58, *Buckskin Baronet* 60, *Golden Friends I Had* (memoirs) 64, *The Red Castle Women* 68, *A Rope to Hang my Love* 72.

c/o Doubleday and Company Inc., 277 Park Avenue,

New York City, N.Y.; Winter: One W 67th Street, New York City, N.Y.; Summer: Barbour Road, Canada Lake, N.Y., U.S.A.

Widdrington, Peter Nigel Tinling, M.B.A.; Canadian business executive; b. 2 June 1930, Toronto; s. of Gerrard Widdrington and Margery (MacDonald) Widdrington; m. Betty Ann Lawrence 1956; two d.; ed. Pickering Coll., Newmarket, Ont., Queen's Univ. and Harvard Business School.

Assistant Regional Man. Labatt's Ontario Breweries Ltd. 57, Regional Man. 58; Gen. Man. Kiewel and Pelissiers, Winnipeg 61; Gen. Man. Labatt's Manitoba Breweries Ltd. 62, Labatt's B.C. Breweries Ltd. 65; Pres. Lucky Breweries Inc., San Francisco 68; Vice-Pres. Corporate Devt., John Labatt Ltd. 71, Senior Vice-Pres. 73, Pres. 73-; Dir. Canada Trust 74-.

John Labatt Ltd., 451 Ridout Street North, London, Ont., Canada.

Telephone: 519-673-5112.

Widerberg, Bo; Swedish film director; b. 8 June 1930. Had twelve different jobs before military service; fmr. literary critic.

Films: *Barnvagnen* (The Pram) 62, *Kvarteret Korpne* (Raven's End) 63, *Kärlek 65* (Love 65) 65, *Elvira Madigan* 67, *Adalen '31* 69 (Award for Best Foreign Film, U.S. Film Critics Guild), *Joe Hill* 71, *Fimpen* (Stubby) 74.

Publs. *Kyssas* (short story) 52, *Erotikon* (novel) 57, *En stuhl, Madame* (autobiographical short story) 61, *Den gröna draken* (novel), *Visionen i svensk film* (essays).

c/o Svenska Filminstitutet, Kungsgatan 48, Stockholm C, Sweden.

Widerström, Ulf E.; Swedish business executive; b. 8 June 1914; ed. Royal Technical Highschool, Stockholm.

Engineer, AB Vattenbyggnadsbyrån 37-40 and Bridge Section, The Nat. Swedish Road Admin. 40-42; joined AB Skånska Cementgjuteriet 42; Dir. and Head of the Malmö Regional Admin. 59-65; Sr. Vice-Pres. 63-65; Pres. 65-; board mem. of Svenska Handelsbanken, Savoy Hotel, Skånska Cementgjuteriet and of 30 cos. in the Skanska Group, including Sepco (Paris), Skanska Baugesellschaft (Hamburg), C. G. Jensen A/S (Denmark), Ohlsson & Skarne AB, SENTAB, The Federation of Swedish Contractors of Building and Public Works (Chair.), The Int. Federation of European Contractors of Building and Public Works (London), Gunnebo Bruk.

AB Skånska Cementgjuteriet, Fack S-103 40 Stockholm 40, Sweden.

Telephone: 24 75 00.

Widgery, Baron (Life Peer), cr. 71, of South Molton in the County of Devon; **John Passmore Widgery,** P.C., Kt., O.B.E., T.D.; British judge; b. 24 July 1911; s. of Samuel Widgery; m. Ann Kermode 1948; ed. Queen's Coll., Taunton.

Solicitor 33; Royal Artillery 39-45; called to Bar, Lincoln's Inn 46; practised South-Eastern Circuit; Q.C. 58; Recorder of Hastings 59-61; Judge of High Court of Justice (Queen's Bench Div.) 61-68; Lord Justice of Appeal 68-71; Lord Chief Justice 71-; Vice-Chair. Home Office Advisory Council on Penal System 66-70.

Royal Courts of Justice, Strand, London, W.C.2, England.

Wieczorek, Janusz; Polish politician; b. 15 Oct. 1910, Brzóza, near Warsaw; ed. Warsaw Univ. Dept. of Law. Head of Dept. in Ministry of Social Welfare -39; mem. resistance movement in Murnau prisoner-of-war camp 39-45; Admin. Officer, Ministry of Labour and Social Welfare 45-48; admin. posts in Office of Presidium of Council of Ministers 48-50; Vice-Chair. State Board of Regular Posts 51-56; Deputy Head of Office of Council

of Ministers, Vice-Minister 56-65, Head of Office, Minister 65-; mem. Polish Socialist Party 45-48, Polish United Workers' Party (PZPR) 48-; Chair. Council for Protection of Monuments of Struggle and Martyrdom 60-, Cttee. for Construction of Children's Health Centre 68-; mem. Cen. Board, Union of Fighters for Freedom and Democracy (ZBOWiD), Presidium of Cen. Comm. for Prosecution of Nazi War Criminals in Poland; Order of Banner of Labour, 1st Class 59, 2nd Class 64, Cross Virtuti Militari, 5th Class 64 and others.
Urząd Rady Ministrów, Al. Ujazdowskie 1/3, 00-583 Warsaw, Poland.

Wieczorowski, Robert E.; American international finance official; b. 1 July 1927; *m.*; two *c.*; ed. Yale and Loyola Univs.
Executive Sec., Chamber of Commerce, Norwich, Conn. 51-52; served in Korea 52-54; joined retail sales dept., A. G. Becker & Co., Inc., Chicago 55, Vice-Pres. 65-69; Dir. Mid-America Devt. Asscn. 66-67; Exec. Dir. for U.S.A., IBRD, IFC and IDA -73; current business activity in private investments; mem. Chicago Council on Foreign Relations 56-, Pres. 64-66; mem. Chicago Bar Asscn.; Dir. USA-UNA of Chicago 68-69.
3501 Springland Lane, N.W., Washington, D.C. 20008, U.S.A.

Wien, Lawrence A., A.B., LL.B.; American lawyer; b. 30 May 1905; *m.* Mae Levy 1929; two *d.*; ed. Columbia Univ.
Admitted to New York Bar 27; Senior Partner Wien, Lane and Malkin and predecessors 51-; Trustee Citizens Budget Comm., New York 56-, Brandeis Univ. 57-, (Chair. 66-70), Consolidated Edison Co. of New York Inc. 63-, Educational Broadcasting Corpn., Inst. of Int. Education; Dir. Borden Inc. 65-; Chair. Board of Trustees Fed. of Jewish Philanthropies (Pres. 60-63); Vice-Chair. Board of Trustees Lincoln Center for the Performing Arts Inc., New York; Creator Wien Int. Scholarship Program at Brandeis Univ. 57, Nat. Scholarship Program at Columbia Univ. School of Law 59; mem. Board of Trustees, Columbia Univ. 64-70, Bar Asscns. of New York City, New York State, American Bar Asscn., New York County Lawyers' Asscn., Nat. Panel of American Arbitration Asscn.
60 East 42nd Street, New York, N.Y. 10017, U.S.A.

Wiener, Alexander S., A.B., M.D., F.A.C.P., F.C.A.P., F.A.S.C.P., F.R.C.P.; American serologist and hematologist; b. 16 March 1907, Brooklyn, N.Y.; *s.* of George and Mollie (née Zuckerman) Wiener; *m.* Gertrude Rodman 1932; two *d.*; ed. Cornell Univ., and State Univ. N.Y. Coll. of Medicine.
Senior Bacteriologist (Serology) Office of Chief Medical Examiner of New York City; attending Immunohematologist, Jewish Hospital of Brooklyn 53-, Adelphi Hospital 53-74; Assoc. Prof. Forensic Medicine, N.Y. Univ. School of Medicine 60-, Prof. 68-; pioneer discoverer of Rh blood types, affiliate Royal Soc. of Medicine; Fellow, Royal Coll. of Physicians 73, American Medical Asscn., American Acad. of Forensic Sciences, N.Y. Acad. of Sciences, American Asscn. Advancement of Science; mem. American Asscn. Immunology, Genetic Soc., founder and first Pres. Soc. Study of Blood; corresp. mem. Acad. des Sciences, Inscriptions et Belles Lettres de Toulouse 69; Deutsche Akademie der Naturforscher Leopoldina 70; Lasker Award; Passano Foundation Award; Karl Landsteiner Award, Silver Medal American Soc. of Clinical Pathology; Joseph P. Kennedy Int. Award, etc.; Dr. h.c. Univ. of Toulouse 69.
Leisure interests: music (piano) and composing, mathematics, the arts.
Publs. *Blood Groups and Transfusion* 35 (3rd edn. 43), *An Rh-Hr Syllabus* 54 (2nd edn. 63), *The Rh-Hr Blood Types* 54, *Heredity of the Blood Groups* 58, *Advances in*

Blood Grouping (vols. I, II and III) 61, 65, 70, *A-B-O Groups and Lewis Types* 76.
Home: 90 Maple Street, Brooklyn, N.Y. 11225; Office: 64 Rutland Road, Brooklyn, N.Y. 11225, U.S.A.
Telephone:212-IN9-5259(Home);212-BU2-3434(Office).

Wieringa, Robert T.; American business executive; b. 1924.
Vice-President Gillette Co., Pres. Toni and Paper-Mate subsidiaries; Senior Vice-Pres. of Consumer Products Group, Warner-Lambert Co. 68, Dir., mem. Exec. Cttee., Exec. Vice-Pres. 72, Pres., Chief Exec. Officer Parke, Davis & Co., Pres., Chief Operating Officer Warner-Lambert Co. 73-, Vice-Chair. and Chief Admin. Officer 75-.
Warner-Lambert Co., 201 Tabor Road, Morris Plains, N.J. 07950, U.S.A.

Wierzbicki, Eugeniusz; Polish architect; b. 31 March 1909, Chanżenkowo.
Member of Polish Asscn. of Architects (SARP) 36-, Pres. Warsaw Branch 51-53, of Cen. Board 53-55, now mem. Council and Collective Judge; Senior Designer, Warsaw Design Office of Gen. Architecture; First Prizes in collaboration with W. Kłyszewski (q.v.) and J. Mokrzyński (q.v.) 40; State Prize, 3rd Class 51, 2nd Class 55, 1st Class 74, Knight's Cross, Order of Polonia Restituta 57, Gold Award of Rebuilding of Warsaw 58, Hon. Prize of SARP 68, of Katowice Branch of SARP 72, Order of Banner of Labour, 2nd Class 69, Prize of Minister of Construction, 1st Class 73.
Publs. numerous articles in newspapers.
Al. Wyzwolenia 2 m. 54, 00-570 Warsaw, Poland.

Wiese und Kaiserswaldau, Benno von, DR. PHIL.; German university professor; b. 25 Sept. 1903, Frankfurt am Main; *s.* of the late Leopold von Wiese und Kaiserswaldau; *m.* Ilse von Gavel 1931; one *s.* one *d.*; ed. Univs. of Leipzig, Vienna, Heidelberg.
Lecturer in German Literature Univ. Bonn 29; Prof. Univ. Erlangen 32-43; Prof. Univ. Münster 43-57; Visiting Prof. Univ. of Indiana (Bloomington) 54-55; Princeton Univ. 55-56; Prof. Univ. Bonn 57-71; Visiting Prof., Univ. of Minnesota and Univ. of California 67-68; mem. Düsseldorfer Akademie für Forschung des Landes Nordrhein-Westfalen; Hon. Dr. Hum.Litt. (Univ. of Chicago).
Publs. *Die deutsche Tragödie von Lessing bis Hebbel* 48, *Friedrich Schiller* 59, 63, *Die deutsche Novelle von Goethe bis Kafka* Vol. I 56, Vol. II 62; *Eduard Mörike* 50, *Zwischen Utopie und Wirklichkeit* 63, *Von Lessing bis Grabbe* 68, *Karl Immermann* 69.
53 Bonn-Ippendorf, Bergstrasse 33, Federal Republic of Germany.
Telephone: 282794.

Wiesner, Jerome Bert, M.S., PH.D.; American professor and communications engineer; b. 30 May 1915; *m.* Laya Wainger 1940; three *s.* one *d.*; ed. Univ. of Michigan.
Chief Engineer Library of Congress, Washington 40-42; mem. staff M.I.T. Radiation Laboratory, Cambridge; Mass. 42-45; mem. staff Univ. of California, Los Alamos Laboratory 45-46; Prof. of Electrical Eng., Assoc. Dir. and Dir. Research Lab. of Electronics, Chair. Dept. of Electrical Eng., M.I.T. 48-61; Dean of Science 64-66, Provost 66-71, Pres. 71-; Special Asst. to Pres. for Science and Technology, Dir. Office of Science and Technology, White House 61-64; mem. Pres.'s Science Advisory Cttee. 58-68, Inst. of Radio Engineers, Acoustical Soc. of America, Fed. of American Scientists, American Soc. for the Advancement of Science, Nat. Acad. of Sciences, Nat. Acad. of Eng., of American Acad. of Arts and Science, American Asscn. of Univ. Professors, Geophysical Union, American Soc. Eng. Educ., American Philosophical Soc.
Leisure interests: politics, writing, sailing, skiing.

Publ. *Where Science and Politics Meet* 64.

c/o Massachusetts Institute of Technology, Cambridge 39, Mass.; Home: 61 Shattuck Road, Watertown, Mass., U.S.A.

Telephone: 617-253-4665 (Office).

Wiesner, Karel František, R.N.DR., F.R.S.C., F.R.S.; Canadian chemist; b. 25 Nov. 1919, Prague, Czechoslovakia; s. of Karel František Wiesner and Eugenie Sterova; m. Blanka Pevná 1942; one s.; ed. Real-Gymnasium, Chrudim and Charles Univ., Prague, Czechoslovakia.

Assistant to Prof. J. Heyrovský, Inst. for Physical Chemistry, Charles Univ., Prague 45-46; Prof. of Organic Chemistry, Univ. of New Brunswick, Canada 48-62, Research Prof. Natural Products Research Center, Univ. of N.B. 64-; Dir. of Chemistry, Ayerst Laboratories, Montreal 62-64; Post-doctoral Fellow, Zurich, Switzerland 46-48; C.I.C. Palladium Medal 63, Officer Order of Canada 75; Hon. D.Sc. (Univs. of New Brunswick, Western Ontario, Montreal).

Leisure interests: tennis, cross-country skiing, boating.

Publs. About 163 scientific papers on electrochemistry, structure determination, synthesis, reaction mechanisms and the kinetics of fast reactions determined from rate-controlled polarographic currents.

Natural Products Research Center, University of New Brunswick, Fredericton, New Brunswick; Home: 814 Burden Street, Fredericton, New Brunswick, Canada.

Telephone: 506-453-4780 (Office); 506-454-4007 (Home).

Wigg, Baron (Life Peer), cr. 67, of the Borough of Dudley; **George Edward Cecil Wigg,** P.C.; British politician; b. 28 Nov. 1900; ed. Fairfields Council Schools and Queen Mary's School, Basingstoke, Hants. Army Service 19-37, 40-46; M.P. 45-67; fmr. Parl. Private Sec. to Rt. Hon. E. Shinwell; mem. Racecourse Betting Control Board 58-61, Totalisator Board 61-64; Paymaster-General 64-67; Chair. Horse Race Betting Levy Board 67-72; Pres. Betting Office Licensees' Asscn. 73-; Labour.

Publ. *George Wigg* 72.

117 Newcastle Road, Trent Vale, Stoke-on-Trent, Staffs., England.

Wiggins, Archibald Lee Manning, B.A.; American retired railroad executive, banker and newspaper publisher; b. 9 April 1891, Durham, N.C.; s. of the late Archie Lee Wiggins and Margaret London (Council) Wiggins; m. Pauline Lawton 1915; two s. two d.; ed. Univ. of N. Carolina.

Former banker; Lecturer Graduate School of Banking, Rutgers Univ. 44-57; Under-Sec. U.S. Treasury 47-48; Chair. of Board Bank of Hartsville 48-63, Atlantic Coast Line, Louisville and Nashville, and Clinchfield Railroad Cos. 48-61; Dir. American Telephone and Telegraph Co. 50-63; Chair. of Board Alico Land Devt. Corpn. 60-63; now Chair. of Board Pauline and Lee Wiggins Foundation Inc., Policy Advisory Cttee., Easter Seal Soc. for Crippled Children and Adults of South Carolina Inc.; Chair. Board of Dirs. Hartsville Publishing Co.; Trustee, North Greenville Coll. S.C. Foundation of Independent Colls. Inc.; Pres. S.C. Bankers' Asscn. 31-32, American Bankers' Asscn. 43-44, Trust Co. of S.C. 41-69; mem. Advisory Council Fed. Reserve Board 46; Dir. American Cancer Soc. 46-49; Treas. American Nat. Red Cross 47-48; Chair. S.C. State Reorganization Comm. 48-50; Chair. S.C. Governor's Tax Advisory Cttee. 53-54, Fiscal Survey Comm. of S.C. 55-58, Gov. of S.C. Advisory Cttee. on Higher Educ. 61-62; Hon. LL.D. (Univs. of North Carolina, South Carolina, Duke Univ. Campbell Coll.).

306 E. Home Avenue, Hartsville, S.C. 29550, U.S.A.

Telephone: 803-332-3791.

Wiggins, James Russell; American newspaperman; b. 4 Dec. 1903; ed. Luverne (Minn.) High School, and USAF Air Intelligence School.

With *Rock County Star* 22-30; Editorial Writer *St. Paul Dispatch* and *St. Paul Pioneer Press* 30-33, Washington Correspondent 33-38, Man. Editor 38-42, 45-46; U.S. Army Air Force 42-45; Asst. Publisher *New York Times* 46-47; Man. Editor *The Washington Post* 47-55, Vice-Pres. 53-60, Exec. Editor 55-60, Editor and Exec. Vice-Pres. 60-68; Perm. Rep. to UN 68-69; Editor, publisher *Ellsworth American* 69-; Eliza Lovejoy Award 54, John Zenger Award 57, Golden Key Award 60.

Publ. *Freedom or Secrecy* 56.

Water Street, Ellsworth, Maine 04605, U.S.A.

Wightman, Arthur Strong, PH.D.; American professor of mathematics and physics; b. 30 March 1922, Rochester, N.Y.; s. of Eugene Pinckney and Edith Stephenson Wightman; m. Anna-Greta Larsson 1945; one d.; ed. Yale Coll. and Princeton Univ.

Instructor in Physics, Yale Univ. 43-44; U.S. Navy 44-46; Instructor in Physics, Princeton Univ. 49, Asst. Prof., Assoc. Prof.; Prof. of Mathematical Physics, Princeton Univ. 60-; mem. Nat. Acad. of Sciences; Dannie Heinemann Prize in Mathematical Physics 69; D.Sc. h.c. (Eidgenössische Technische Hochschule, Zürich) 69.

Leisure interests: art, music, tennis.

Publ. *PCT, Spin and Statistics and All That* (with R. F. Streater) 64.

Joseph Henry Laboratories of Physics, Princeton University, Box 708, Princeton, N.J. 08540; Home: 30 The Western Way, Princeton, N.J. 08540, U.S.A.

Telephone: 609-452-4392 (Office); 609-921-7779 (Home).

Wigner, Eugene Paul, DR.ING.; American physicist; b. 17 Nov. 1902, Budapest, Hungary; s. of Antal and Elisabeth Wigner (née Einhorn); m. 1st Amelia Z. Frank 1936 (died 1937); m. 2nd Mary A. Wheeler 1941; one s. one d.; ed. Müegytem, Budapest and Technische Hochschule, Berlin.

Lecturer, Technische Hochschule, Berlin 28; Prof. of Mathematical Physics, Princeton Univ., on part-time basis 30-36; Prof. of Physics, Univ. of Wisconsin 37-38; Thomas D. Jones Prof. of Mathematical Physics, Princeton Univ. 38-71; Visiting Lecturer, Univ. of Massachusetts 71; Visiting Prof. Louisiana State Univ. 72-74, also at Technion, Haifa 73; mem. of Visiting Cttee., Nat. Bureau of Standards 47-51, Board of Dirs., Oak Ridge Inst. of Nuclear Studies 47-50; mem. Gen. Advisory Cttee. to U.S. Atomic Energy Comm. 52-57, 59-64; on leave of absence at the Metallurgical Laboratory, Univ. of Chicago (Plutonium Project) 42-45; on leave of absence as Dir. of Research and Development of the Clinton Laboratories, Oak Ridge, Tenn. 46-47, as Lorentz Lecturer, Inst. Lorentz, Leyden, Neths. 57; mem. American Physical Soc., American Mathematical Soc., American Philosophical Soc., Nat. Acad. Sciences, American Acad. of Arts and Sciences, Franklin Soc. (Franklin Medal 50), Royal Netherlands Acad., Austrian Acad. of Sciences, American Nuclear Soc. (Dir. 60-61); foreign mem. Royal Society 70; corresp. mem. Akad. der Wissenschaften, Göttingen; Vice-Pres. American Physical Society 55, Pres. 56; Dir. Int. School of Physics, Enrico Fermi Course 29, Varenna 63, Nat. Acad. Sciences Harbour Project 63; Dir. (on leave of absence) Civil Defense Project, Oak Ridge Nat. Laboratory 64-65; Medal for Merit 46; Fermi Award 58; numerous honorary degrees; Atoms for Peace Award 60, Max Planck Medal of German Physical Soc. 61, Nobel Prize for Physics 63, George Washington Award of the American Hungarian Studies Foundation, Semmelweiss Medal of American Hungarian Medical Asscn. 65, U.S. Nat. Medal of Science 69, Albert Einstein Award 72.

Leisure interest: wandering.

Publs. *Gruppentheorie und ihre Anwendungen auf die Quantenmechanik der Atomspektren* 31 (English edn. 59), *Nuclear Structure* (with L. Eisenbud) 58, *Physical*

Theory of Neutron Chain Reactors (with A. M. Weinberg) 58, *Project Harbour Summary Report* (with R. Park) 64, *Symmetries and Reflections* 67, *Who Speaks for Civil Defense* (editor) 68, *Survival and the Bomb* 69.
Jadwin Hall, Princeton Univ., P.O. Box 708, Princeton, N.J. 08540; and 8 Ober Road, Princeton, N.J., U.S.A.
Telephone: 609-452-4335.

Wigny, Pierre L. J. J.; Belgian politician; b. 18 April 1905, Liège; m. Lily Borboux 1929; three c.; ed. Liège and Harvard Univs.
Secretary-General Centre d'Etudes pour la Réforme de l'Etat 36-40; Pres. PSC Studies Centre 45-46; Minister of the Colonies 47-50; mem. (PSC) Chamber of Reps. 49-71, Vice-Pres. 68-71; Sec.-Gen. Int. Inst. of Differing Civilizations (INCIDI) 52-58; Pres. Political Econ. Soc. of Belgium 54-58; mem. European Parl. Assembly and ECSC Common Assembly 52-58, Pres. Christian Democratic Group 58; Minister of Foreign Affairs 58-61, Justice 65-66, Justice and French Culture 66-68; Prof. of Law, Louvain Univ. and Faculty of Namur; mem. Acad. Royale de Belgique, Acad. (Royale) des Sciences d'Outre-Mer, Brussels and Paris; Pres. Comm. Royale des Monuments et des Sites; Pres. Caisse Nat. de Crédit Professionnel.
Leisure interest: gardening.
94 Avenue Louise, Brussels, Belgium.
Telephone: 11-16-67.

Wijsenbeek, Louis Jacob Florus, D.D.L., D.H.A.; Netherlands museum curator; b. 21 April 1912; ed. Gymnasium Erasmianum, Rotterdam and Leiden Univ.
On staff of Ministry of Education, Arts and Sciences 39-40; Asst. Keeper Municipal Museum, The Hague 40-42; Recuperation Officer in Austria 45-47; Dir. of Delft Museums 47-51; Dir. Municipal Museum, Bredius Museum and Costume Museum, The Hague 51-; Pres. I.C.O.M. Cttee. for Museum Architecture; Vice-Pres. Royal Acad. of Arts, The Hague, Netherlands, Asscn. of Museum Dirs., Netherlands Cttee. of I.C.O.M.; Commdr. Order of Mexican Eagle, Hon. M.V.O., Officer, Royal Gurkha Order of Nepal; Officer of Swedish Order of Vasa, Royal Netherlands Order of Orange Nassau, Order of Crown of Belgium, Chevalier de la Légion d'Honneur, Knight of the Order of Pius IX, Gold Medal of Merit, 1st Class (Italy).
Publs. *Het Tijdperk van de Camera Obscura* 40, *Mij spreekt de Blomme een tale* 52, *Pablo Picasso* 54, *Vraagstukken bij het Bouwen van Musea* 58, *Piet Mondriaan* 62 (German edn. 68, English and Dutch 69), *Delfts Zilver* 69.
Gemeentemuseum, Stadhouderslaan 14, The Hague, Netherlands.

Wijting, Lt.-Gen. Alexander Johannes Wilhelm; Netherlands air force officer; b. 29 June 1925, Magelang, Indonesia; s. of D. A. Wijting and J. F. C. Müsler; m. Margaret E. Lyle-Stewart 1946; one s. one d.; ed. Netherlands Air Staff Coll., Netherlands Defence Study Centre.
Escaped occupied territory 42; R.A.F. Fighter Pilot 44-46; Royal Netherlands Air Force 46-, Deputy Dir. Personnel 69, Deputy Chief of Staff 71, Commdr. Tactical Air Command 73; Chair. Netherlands Joint Chiefs of Staff Cttee. 73-, Chief of Defence Staff 76-; Knight Order of Netherlands Lion; Officer Order of Orange-Nassau; Cross of Merit; Chevalier Légion d'Honneur.
Leisure interest: sailing.
Jozef Israëlsplein 11, The Hague, Netherlands.
Telephone: 070-24-27-81.

Wilanowski, Włodzimierz, M.ENG.; Polish engineer and airline executive; b. 12 Feb. 1915, Ros; s. of Walenty and Irena Wilanowski; m. Maria Wilanowska 1943; two d.; ed. Warsaw Polytechnic.
Worked in aircraft construction 34-39; prisoner-of-war

40-42; air technologist 42-44; Chief Technologist of aircraft plants 44-58; Technical Dir. Aviation Inst. 58-60; Dir. aircraft construction centre 60-65; Technical Dir. LOT Polish airlines 65-69; Dir.-Gen. LOT Polish Airlines 69-; Silver and Gold Cross of Merit, Knight's Cross of Polonia Restituta, Banner of Labour (2nd class) and other civil and military decorations.
Leisure interests: tourism and football.
Publs. articles in technical journals.
Polskie Linie Lotnicze, Ul. Grójecka 17, 02-021 Warsaw; Home: Ul. Złota 64-66, 00-821 Warsaw, Poland.
Telephone: 22-55-46 (Office); 20-09-14 (Home).

Wilberforce, Baron (Life Peer), cr. 64; **Richard Wilberforce,** C.M.G., O.B.E., M.A.; British judge; b. 11 March 1907, Jullundur; s. of Samuel Wilberforce and Katherine Sheepshanks; m. Yvette Lenoan 1947; one s. one d.; ed. Winchester Coll. and Oxford Univ.
Fellow, All Souls Coll., Oxford 32-; Chief, Legal Div., Control Comm., Germany 45; U.K. Rep. Legal Cttee. Int. Civil Aviation Org. (ICAO) 49-; Judge, High Court 61-64; Lord of Appeal in Ordinary 64-; mem. Perm. Court of Arbitration 64-; Chair. Exec. Council, Int. Law Asscn. 65-; High Steward, Oxford Univ. 67-; Chair. Court of Inquiry into Electricity Workers' Dispute 70-71, Mineworkers' Dispute 72; Hon. D.C.L., LL.D.
Leisure interests: music, golf, philately, the turf.
Publ. *The Law of Restrictive Practices and Monopolies* (joint author) 57.
8 Cambridge Place, London, W.8, England.
Telephone: 01-937-4895.

Wilbur, Richard (Purdy), M.A.; American poet and university professor; b. 1 March 1921, New York City; s. of Lawrence L. Wilbur and Helen Purdy Wilbur; m. Charlotte Ward 1942; three s. one d.; ed. Amherst Coll., and Harvard Univ.
Asst. Prof. of English, Harvard Univ. 50-54; Assoc. Prof. Wellesley Coll. 54-57; Prof. Wesleyan Univ. 57-; mem. Nat. Inst. of Arts and Letters, American Acad. of Arts and Sciences, Soc. of Fellows of Harvard Univ. 47-50; Guggenheim Fellow 52-53, Ford Fellow 61, Guggenheim Fellow 63; Chancellor, Acad. of American Poets, PEN; Pres. American Acad. of Arts and Letters 74-; mem. Dramatists Guild; Harriet Monroe Prize 48; Oscar Blumenthal Prize 50; Prix de Rome from American Acad. of Arts and Letters 54-55; Edna St. Vincent Millay Memorial Award 56; Nat. Book Award; Pulitzer Prize 57, co-recipient Bollingen Translation Prize 63; co-recipient Bollingen Prize in Poetry 71; Prix Henri Desfeuilles 71; Brandeis Creative Arts Award 71; Shelley Memorial Prize 73.
Leisure interests: tennis, walking, herb gardening.
Publs. *The Beautiful Changes and other poems* 47, *Ceremony and other poems* 50, *A Bestiary* (anthology, with Alexander Calder) 55, *The Misanthrope* (trans. from Molière) 55, *Things of this World* (poems) 56, *Poems 1943-1956* 57, *Candide* (comic opera, with Lillian Hellman and others) 57, *Poe* (edition of his poems with introduction and notes) 59, *Advice to a Prophet* (poems) 61, *Tartuffe* (trans. from Molière) 63, *The Poems of Richard Wilbur* 63, *Loudmouse* (for children) 63, *Poems of Shakespeare* (with Alfred Harbage) 66, *Walking to Sleep* (new poems and translations) 69, *School for Wives* (translations) 71, *Opposites* (Children's Verse, illustrated by the author) 73, *The Mind-Reader* 76.
Box KK, Wesleyan Station, Middletown, Conn. 06457; and Dodwells Road, Cummington, Mass. 01026, U.S.A.
Telephone: 203-347-0045 (Middletown); 413-634-5420 (Cummington).

Wild, Earl; American pianist and composer; b. 26 Nov. 1915, Pittsburgh, Pa.; s. of Royland and Lillian G. Wild; ed. Carnegie Technical Coll., Pittsburgh.
Studied with Selmar Jansen, Egon Petri, Helene

Barrere, Volya Cossack and Paul Doguereau; first American soloist to perform with NBC Orchestra conducted by Toscanini 42, has performed with symphony orchestras and given recitals in many countries; has appeared with Sir Malcolm Sargent, Jascha Horenstein, Sir Georg Solti, Arthur Fiedler; played first TV piano recital; has played for 7 Presidents of U.S., incl. inauguration of Pres. J. F. Kennedy; Music Dir. Palm Springs Museum; numerous recordings for RCA, EMI, Columbia and Vanguard Records.
Leisure interest: writing poetry.
Compositions incl. *The Turquoise Horse* (choral work) and ballet, oratorio, solo piano music, choral work and songs.
291 Lilliana Drive, Palm Springs, Calif. 92262, U.S.A.

Wild, Rt. Hon. Sir (Herbert) Richard (Churton), P.C., K.C.M.G.; New Zealand chief justice; b. 1912, Blenheim; s. of Dr. L. J. Wild; m. Janet Grainger 1940; two s. two d.; ed. Feilding High School and Victoria Univ. of Wellington.
Admitted to bar 34; practised as solicitor, Wellington 39-57; Queen's Counsel 57; Solicitor-Gen. 57-65; Chief Justice of New Zealand 66-; Hon. LL.D. (Victoria), Hon. Bencher, Inner Temple.
Supreme Court, Wellington; Home: 10 Homewood Avenue, Karori, Wellington, New Zealand.

Wild, John Paul, F.R.S., F.A.A., M.A., SC.D.; Australian radio astronomer; b. 1923, Sheffield, England; s. of Bessie (née Arnold), and the late Alwyn H. Wild; m. Elaine Poole Hull 1948; two s. one d.; ed. Whitgift School, Croydon, England and Peterhouse, Cambridge.
Radar Officer, Royal Navy 43-47; Researcher in Radio Astronomy, especially of the Sun, Radiophysics Div. of Commonwealth Scientific and Industrial Research Org. (C.S.I.R.O.), N.S.W., Australia 47-, Chief of Division 71-, Dir. C.S.I.R.O. Solar Radio Observatory, Culgoora, N.S.W. 66-; Pres. Radio Astronomy Comm. of Int. Astronomical Union 67-70; Foreign mem. American Philosophical Soc.; Foreign Hon. mem. American Acad. of Arts and Sciences; Corresp. mem. Royal Soc. of Sciences, Liège; Edgeworth David Medal, Hendryk Arctowski Gold Medal of Nat. Acad. of Sciences U.S., Balthasar van der Pol Gold Medal of Int. Union of Radio Science, Herschel Medal of Royal Astronomical Soc.
Publs. Various papers on radio astronomy in scientific journals.
Division of Radiophysics, Commonwealth Scientific and Industrial Research Organisation, P.O. Box 76, Epping, N.S.W. 2121, Australia.
Telephone: Sydney 869-1111.

Wilder, Billy; American film writer, producer and director; b. 22 June 1906, Austria.
Former reporter, Berlin; writer *People on Sunday, Emil and the Detectives*, Germany; went to U.S. 34; writer and dir. *Mauvaise Graine*, Paris; writer in collaboration *Bluebeard's Eighth Wife, Midnight, Ninotchka, What A Life, Arise, My Love, Hold Back The Dawn, Ball of Fire*; Dir. and collaborator *The Major and the Minor, Five Graves to Cairo, Double Indemnity, The Lost Weekend, The Emperor Waltz, A Foreign Affair, Sunset Boulevard*; Producer, dir. and writer (in collaboration): *The Big Carnival, Stalag 17, Sabrina, Love in the Afternoon, Some Like It Hot, The Apartment, One, Two, Three, Irma La Douce, Kiss Me, Stupid, The Fortune Cookie, The Private Life of Sherlock Holmes, Avanti*; co-producer, dir. and writer (in collaboration) *The Seven Year Itch*; dir., collaborator *The Spirit of St. Louis, Witness for the Prosecution, The Front Page*; six Academy Awards (for *Lost Weekend, Sunset Boulevard* and *The Apartment*).
Universal Studios, Universal City, Calif. 91608, U.S.A.

Wilder, Raymond Louis, PH.B., SC.M., PH.D., SC.D.; American professor of mathematics; b. 3 Nov. 1896,

Palmer, Mass.; s. of John Louis Wilder and Mary Jane Shanley; m. Una Maude Greene 1921; one s. three d.; ed. Brown Univ. and Univ. of Tex.
Instructor, Univ. of Tex. 21-24; Asst. Prof., Ohio State Univ. 24-26; Asst. Prof.. then Prof., Univ. of Mich. 26-47, Research Prof. 47-67; Prof. Emer. 67-; Josiah Willard Gibbs Lecturer 69; Pres. American Mathematical Soc. 55-56, Mathematical Asscn. of America 65-66; Visiting Prof. Univ. of Calif. at Santa Barbara 69-; Distinguished Service Award, Mathematical Asscn. of America 72; mem. American Nat. Acad. Sciences.
Leisure interests: piano, hiking, anthropology.
Publs. *Lectures in Topology* (Co-Editor with W. L. Ayres) 41, *Topology of Manifolds* 49, 2nd edn. 63, *Introduction to the Foundations of Mathematics* 52, 2nd edn. 65, *Evolution of Mathematical Concepts* 68.
2427 Calle Montilla, Santa Barbara, Calif. 93109, U.S.A.
Telephone: 805-965-4449.

Wilgus, A. Curtis, M.A., PH.D.; American historian, bibliographer and university professor; b. 2 April 1897, Platteville, Wis.; s. of James Wilgus and Flavia McGurer; m. 2nd Karna Steelquist 1947; one s.; ed. Univs. of Wisconsin and Calif.
Assistant Instr. in History, Univ. of Wisconsin 22-24; Assoc. Prof. of History, Univ. of South Carolina 24-30, Prof. George Washington Univ. 30-51; Dir. School of Inter-American Studies, and Prof. of History, Univ. of Florida 51-63, Dir. Caribbean Confs. 50-67; Vice-Chancellor Int. Inst. of Arts, San Juan, Puerto Rico and Miami 67-69; Visiting Prof. of Inter-American Studies, Inter-American Univ. of Puerto Rico, Spring 72, Spring 74; Consultant to Dir., North-South Center of Puerto Rico 71-72; organizer, charter mem. and Pres. Inter-American Bibliographical and Library Asscn.; charter mem. Soc. for Advancement of Educ.; Dir. Pan-Am Foundation; Dir. U.S. Branch, Eloy Alfaro Int. Foundation; mem. Nat. Council, Inst. of Int. Educ.; corresp. mem. Acad. of American Franciscan History; Foreign corresp. *Panama American*; mem. Board Americas Foundation; awards include U.S., Venezuelan, French and Swedish honours; Editor *World Affairs* 40-51, *Inter-American Bibliographical Review* 40-43, *Doors to Latin America* 50-, *Latin American Monographs* 57-63, *Grandes Figures de l'Amérique* series 57-60, *Gateway to Latin America* series 64-65, *Library of Latin American History and Culture* series 65, Editor *Source Books and Studies on Latin America* 69; Founder *Journal of Inter-American Studies* 59, Chair. Board of Editors 63.
Publs. *An Outline of Hispanic American History* 27, *A History of Hispanic America* 31, *Histories and Historians of Hispanic America* 36, 42, 65, *Outline-History of Latin America* (with Dr. Raul d'Eca) 39, *Development of Hispanic America* 41, 69, *Latin America in Maps* 43, *Readings in Latin-American Civilization* 46, Editor *Modern Hispanic America* 33, *The Caribbean Area* 34, *Argentina, Brazil and Chile since Independence* 35, 63, *Colonial Hispanic America* 36, 63, *South American Dictators* 37, 63, *Hispanic American Essays* 42, 70, *The Caribbean at Mid-Century* 51, *The Caribbean: Peoples, Problems and Prospects* 52, *The Caribbean: Contemporary Trends* 53, *The Caribbean: Its Economy* 54, *The Caribbean: Its Culture* 55, *The Caribbean: Current Political Problems* 56, *The Caribbean: Contemporary International Relations* 57, *The Caribbean: British, Dutch, French, United States* 58, *The Caribbean: Natural Resources* 59, *The Caribbean: Education* 60, *The Caribbean: The Central American Area* 61, *The Caribbean: Contemporary Colombia* 62, *The Caribbean: Venezuelan Development* 63, *Latin American History* (with Raul d'Eca) 63, 65, 66, 67, *The Caribbean: Mexico Today* 64, *The Caribbean: Its Health Problems* 65, *The Caribbean: Current U.S. Relations* 66, *The Caribbean: Hemispheric Role of The Caribbean* 67,

Historical Dictionaries of Latin America, 23 vols. (editor) 67-, *Historical Atlas of Latin America* 67, 69, *Latin America 1492-1942: A Guide to Historical and Cultural Development before World War II* 73, *Latin America in the Nineteenth Century* (a selected bibliography) 73, *Historiography of Latin America 1500-1800* 75.
Leisure interest: book reviewing.
Home: 1140 N.E. 191st Street, North Miami Beach, Fla.; 130 East 67 Street, New York City, New York, U.S.A.

Wilkes, Maurice Vincent, M.A., PH.D., F.R.S., F.I.E.E., F.B.C.S.; British university professor; b. 26 June 1913, Dudley; s. of Vincent J. Wilkes, O.B.E.; m. Nina Twyman 1947; one s. two d.; ed. King Edward VI School, Stourbridge, and St. John's Coll., Cambridge.
University Demonstrator 37; Radar and Operational Research, Second World War; Univ. Lecturer and Acting Dir. of Mathematical Lab., Cambridge 45, Dir. 46-70; Head of Computer Lab. 70-; Prof. of Computer Technology, Univ. of Cambridge 65-; mem. Measurement and Control Section Cttee., Inst. of Electrical Engineers 56-59; First Pres. British Computer Soc. 57-60; mem. Council Int. Fed. for Information Processing 60-63, Council of the Inst. of Electrical Engineers 73-; Touring Lecturer Assen. for Computing Machinery 67; Harry Goode Memorial Award, American Fed. of Information Processing Socs. 68; Distinguished Fellow, British Computer Soc. 73; Foreign hon. mem. American Acad. Arts and Sciences 74-.
Publs. *Oscillations of the Earth's Atmosphere* 49, *Preparation of Programs for an Electronic Digital Computer* 51, 58, *Automatic Digital Computers* 56, *A Short Introduction to Numerical Analysis* 66, *Time-Sharing Computer Systems* 68, 72, 75.
Computer Laboratory, Corn Exchange Street, Cambridge, England.
Telephone: 52435.

Wilkins, Graham John; British business executive; b. 22 Jan. 1924, Mudford, Somerset; s. of George W. and Ann May Wilkins (née Clarke); m. Daphne Mildred Haynes 1945; ed. Yeovil School, Univ. Coll. of South West, Exeter.
Managing Dir. Beecham Research Laboratories 61; Chair. Beecham Pharmaceutical Div., Dir. Beecham Group Ltd. 64, Man. Dir. (Pharmaceuticals) 73; Exec. Vice-Chair. Beecham Group Ltd. 74-75, Chair. 75-; Vice-Chair. Proprietary Asscn. of Great Britain 66-68, Pres. Asscn. of British Pharmaceutical Industry 69-71; Chair. Medico-Pharmaceutical Forum 72, 73.
Leisure interests: golf, motor yacht cruising, travel.
Beecham Group Ltd., Beecham House, Great West Road, Brentford, Middx.; Home: Alceda, Walton Lane, Shepperton-on-Thames, Middx., England.
Telephone: Walton 27714 (Home).

Wilkins, Maurice Hugh Frederick, C.B.E., M.A., PH.D., F.R.S.; British molecular biologist; b. 15 Dec. 1916, Pongaroa, New Zealand; s. of E. H. Wilkins and Eveline Whittaker; m. Patricia Chidgey 1959; two s. two d.; ed. St. John's Coll., Cambridge.
Research on luminescence of solids, Physics Dept. Birmingham Univ.; Ministry of Home Security and Aircraft Production 38; Manhattan Project (Ministry of Supply), Univ. of California 44; Lecturer in Physics, St. Andrews Univ. 45; Medical Research Council, Biophysics Unit, King's Coll., London 46, Deputy Dir. 55-70, Dir. 70-72, Dir. Neurobiology Unit (Cell Biophysics Unit 74-), MRC 72-; Prof. of Biophysics and Head of Dept., King's Coll. 70-, Fellow 73-; Pres. British Soc. for Social Responsibility in Science 69; Hon. mem. American Soc. of Biological Chemists 64; Foreign Hon. mem. American Acad. of Arts and Sciences 70; Albert Lasker Award, American Public

Health Asscn. 60; Joint Nobel Prize for Physiology or Medicine 62; Hon. LL.D.
Leisure interest: gardening.
Publs. Papers on luminescence and topics in biophysics e.g. molecular structure of nucleic acids and structure of nerve membranes.
Department of Biophysics, King's College, 26-29 Drury Lane, London, W.C.2; 30 St. John's Park, London, S.E.3, England.
Telephone: 01-836-8851.

Wilkins, Roger C.; American insurance executive; b. 6 June 1906, Houlton, Me.; s. of George and Amanda Wilkins (née Carson); m. Evelyn McFadden, 1933; one d.; ed. Univ. of Maine.
Joined Travelers Corpn. 29, Vice-Pres. 53, Sen. Vice-Pres. 65, Dir. and Chair. of Finance Cttee. 68, Pres. and Chief Exec. Officer 69-71, Chair. 71-74, Chair. Exec. Cttee. 74-; Chair. Broadcast Plaza Inc.; Dir. Prospect Co., Conn. Bank and Trust Co., Conn. Natural Gas Co., Chemical Express Co., United Aircraft Corpn., Allis-Chalmers Corpn.; Dir./Trustee U.S. Chamber of Commerce, American Life Insurance Asscn. of America, Nat. Telephone Co., Wells Fargo Mortgage Investors and of numerous other business and philanthropic concerns; Hon. LL.D. (Univ. of Hartford, Ricker and Trinity Colls.).
Leisure interests: golf, fishing, horticulture.
Office: Travelers Corpn., 1 Tower Square, Hartford, Conn. 06115; Home: Talcott Notch Road, Avon, Conn. 06001, U.S.A.
Telephone: 203-277-2886 (Office); 203-677-2508 (Home).

Wilkins, Roy; American administrator; b. 30 Aug. 1901, St. Louis, Miss.; s. of William and Mayfield (Edmundson) Wilkins; m. Aminda Badeau 1929; ed. Univ. of Minnesota.
Managing Editor *The Call,* Kansas City, Mo. 23-31; joined staff of Nat. Asscn. for the Advancement of Colored People (N.A.A.C.P.) as Asst. Exec. Sec. 31, Administrator 50-55, Exec. Sec. 55-64, Exec. Dir. 64-; Chair. U.S. Del. to Int. Conf. on Human Rights 68; Theodore Roosevelt Award 68; U.S. Medal of Freedom 68; Joseph Prize for Human Rights 75; Hon. degrees from Atlanta Univ., Notre Dame Univ., Boston Univ., Columbia Univ., Fordham Univ., etc.
147-15 Village Road, Jamaica, N.Y. 11435, U.S.A.

Wilkinson, Sir Denys Haigh, Kt., D.SC., M.A., PH.D., SC.D., F.R.S.; British physicist and university professor; b. 5 Sept. 1922, Leeds; s. of Charles and Hilda Wilkinson; m. 1st Christiane Clavier 1947, three d.; m. 2nd Helen Sellschop 1967; ed. Jesus Coll., Cambridge.
Worked on British Atomic Energy Project 43-46, on Canadian Atomic Energy Project 45-46; Demonstrator 47-51, Lecturer 51-56 and Reader 50-57 Cavendish Laboratory of Univ. of Cambridge; Fellow, Jesus Coll., Cambridge 44-59, Hon. Fellow 61-; Student of Christ Church, Oxford 57-; Prof. of Nuclear Physics Clarendon Laboratory of Univ. of Oxford 57-59, Prof. of Experimental Physics 59-76, Head of Dept. of Nuclear Physics 62-76; Vice-Chancellor Sussex Univ. Sept. 76-; Rutherford Memorial Lecturer of British Physical Soc. 62; mem. Governing Board Nat. Inst. for Research in Nuclear Science 58-64; Queen's Lecturer Berlin 66; mem. Science Research Council 67-70; Chair. S.R.C. Nuclear Physics Board 68-70; Chair. Physics III Cttee. CERN, Geneva 71-75; Hon. D.Sc. (Univ. of Saskatchewan, Utah State Univ.); Holweck Medallist of French and British Physical Socs. 57, Hughes Medal of the Royal Soc. 65; Bruce-Preller Prize of Royal Soc. of Edinburgh 69; Battelle Distinguished Prof., Univ. of Washington 70; Cherwell-Simon Memorial Lecturer, Oxford 70; Tom W. Bonner Prize of American Physical Soc. 74; Tizard Memorial Lecturer 75.
Leisure interests: early music and art, ornithology.

Publs. *Ionization Chambers and Counters* 50, Editor *Isospin in Nuclear Physics* 69, and many articles in learned journals.
University of Sussex, Falmer, Brighton, Sussex, BN1 9QX, England (from Sept. 1976).

Wilkinson, Geoffrey, PH.D., F.R.S.; British professor of inorganic chemistry; b. 14 July 1921, Todmorden; s. of Henry and Ruth Wilkinson; m. Lise Sølver Schou 1953; two d.; ed. Todmorden Secondary School, Imperial Coll., London.
Junior Scientific Officer, Nat. Research Council of Canada 43-46; Research Assoc., Radiation Lab., Univ. of Calif. 46-50, Mass. Inst. of Technology 50-51; Asst. Prof. Harvard Univ. 51-55; Prof. Inorganic Chem., Imperial Coll., London 56-; Foreign mem. Royal Danish Acad. of Science, American Acad. of Arts and Sciences, Nat. Acad. of Sciences; Hon. Counsellor Spanish Research Council; Hon. D.Sc. (Edinburgh); Lavoisier Medal, Nobel Prize for Chem. 73.
Leisure interest: organic chemistry.
Publs. *Advanced Inorganic Chemistry* (with F. A. Cotton) 3rd edn. 72, *Basic Inorganic Chemistry* (with F. A. Cotton) 76, and over 300 scientific papers.
Chemistry Department, Imperial College, London, SW7 2AY, England.

Wilkinson, Sir Harold, Kt., C.M.G.; British oil executive; b. 24 Feb. 1903.
Formerly: Deputy Chair. The Shell Transport and Trading Co. Ltd.; Man. Dir. The Shell Petroleum Co. Ltd., Shell Exploration Co. Ltd., Shell Int. Petroleum Co. Ltd.; Principal Dir. of Bataafse Petroleum Mij. N.V.; Chair. Canadian Shell Ltd., Shell Tankers Ltd.; Vice-Chair. Shell Caribbean Petroleum Co. (New York); Dir. Bataafse Internationale Chemie Mij. N.V., Shell Int. Chemical Co. Ltd., Shell Oil Co. (New York), retired July 64; U.S. Medal of Freedom with Bronze Palm 51, Knight Commdr. Order of Merit, Ecuador.
La Sologne en Ballègue, Epalinges 1066, nr. Lausanne, Switzerland.

Wilkinson, Kenneth Grahame, B.SC., F.C.G.I., D.I.C., C.ENG., F.R.AE.S., F.C.I.T., F.S.L.AE.T.; British business executive; b. 14 July 1917, London; ed. Shooters Hill School, London, Coll. of Aeronautical Engineering, Chelsea and Imperial Coll., London.
Aerodynamics Dept., Royal Aircraft Establishment 38-46; Supt. Performance and Analysis, British European Airways 46-52, Schedules Planning Man. 52-59, Fleet Planning Man. 60-61, Asst. to Chief Maintenance Engineer 61-62, Asst. Chief Engineer 62-64, Chief Engineer 64-70, Man. Dir. Mainline BEA 71-72, Chair. 72-; Man. Dir. Rolls-Royce (1971) Ltd. 72-74, Vice-Chair. and mem. Board 74-76; Eng. Dir., British Airways April 76-; Hon. D.Sc.
Leisure Interests: gliding, swimming.
British Airways Board, Air Terminal, Victoria, London, S.W.1, England.
Telephone: 01-828-6822.

Wilkinson, Sir Peter (Allix), K.C.M.G., D.S.O., O.B.E.; British retd. diplomatist; b. 15 April 1914, India; s. of late Capt. Osborn Cecil Wilkinson and late Esmé Barbara Cramer-Roberts; m. Mary Theresa Villiers March 1945; two d.; ed. Scaitcliffe, Englefield Green, Rugby School and Corpus Christi Coll., Cambridge.
Commissioned in Second Bn., Royal Fusiliers 35; Acting Head of British Mil. Missions to Polish and Czechoslovak Armies 40, Mil. Service in Middle East, Italy and Balkans 40-45; Chief of Political Branch, Political Div., British Comm. for Austria 45-47; First Sec., British Legation, Vienna 47-48; Foreign Office 48-52; First Sec., British Embassy, Washington, D.C. 52-55; Sec.-Gen., Summit Conf. of Heads of Govt., Geneva 55; Counsellor, British Embassy, Bonn 55-60; Head Perm. Under Sec.'s Dept. Foreign Office 60-63;

Under-Sec. Cabinet Office 63-64; Chief Civilian Instructor, Imperial Defence Coll. 64-66; Amb. to Repub. of Vietnam 66-67; Asst. Under-Sec. 67-68; Deputy Under-Sec. and Chief Clerk, Foreign and Commonwealth Office 68-70; Amb. to Austria 70-72; Cross of Valour (Poland), Order of White Lion (Czechoslovakia).
Leisure interests: fishing, reading, gardening.
Mill House, Charing, Kent, England.

Wilkinson, Sir (Robert Francis) Martin, Kt.; British stockbroker; b. 4 June 1911, Blackheath, London; s. of the late Sir Robert Pelham Wilkinson and the late Phyllis Marian Wilkinson; m. Dora Esme Arendt 1936; three d.; ed. Repton School.
Partner, de Zoete and Gorton 36-70, de Zoete and Bevan 70-; mem. London Stock Exchange (now United Stock Exchange) 33-, mem. Council 59-, Deputy Chair. 63-65, Chair. 65-73, Chair. United Stock Exchange March-June 73.
Leisure interest: gardening.
Kixes, Sharpthorne, Sussex; 25 Finsbury Circus, London E.C.2, England.
Telephone: 01-588-4141.

Wilkomirska, Wanda; Polish violinist; b. 11 Jan. 1929, Warsaw; d. of Alfred Wilkomirski and Dorota Temkin; m. Mieczysław F. Rakowski (q.v.) 1952. two s.; ed. Łódź Conservatory and in Budapest and France.
Public debut at age of 7 years; first appearance with orchestra aged 15, in Cracow; studied under Irena Dubiska (Łódź), Ede Zathureczky (Budapest) and Henryk Szeryng (Paris); Polish State Prize 52, 64; several foreign prizes, including Bach Competition award of Dem. German radio; Officer's Cross of Polonia Restituta 53; Order of Banner of Labour 2nd class 59, 1st Class 64; Minister of Culture and Arts Prize, 1st Class 75; numerous recordings; now appears frequently with most of the major orchestras throughout the world.
Leisure interests: theatre, literature, sports.
Ul. Dabrówki 13, 03-909 Warsaw, Poland.
Telephone: 175-843.

Willatt, Sir Hugh, Kt., M.A., F.R.S.A.; British fmr. solicitor and arts administrator; b. 25 April 1909, Nottingham; s. of Robert John Willatt and Marguerite Gardner; m. Evelyn Gibbs, A.R.E., A.R.C.A. 1945; ed. Repton and Pembroke Coll., Oxford.
Qualified as Solicitor 34, practised in family firm in Nottingham until 60, Partner in Lewis Silkin & Partners, Westminster 60-68; mem. Arts Council Drama Panel 55-68, Chair. 60-68; Sec.-Gen. of Arts Council of Great Britain 68-75; Fellow, Royal Soc. of Arts 74; mem. Boards of Nottingham Playhouse, Mercury Trust Ltd. (Ballet Rambert) and Nat. Theatre at various times.
Leisure interests: reading, travel and sport.
4 St. Peter's Wharf, Hammersmith Terrace, London, W.6, England.
Telephone: 01-741-2707.

Willcocks, David Valentine, C.B.E., M.C., M.A., MUS.B., F.R.C.O., F.R.C.M.; British conductor; b. 30 Dec. 1919, Newquay, Cornwall; s. of T. H. Willcocks; m. Rachel Blyth 1947; two s. two d.; ed. Clifton Coll. and King's Coll., Cambridge.
Fellow, King's Coll., Cambridge 47-51; Organist Salisbury Cathedral 47-50, Worcester Cathedral 50-57; Conductor Worcester Three Choirs Festival and City of Birmingham Choir 50-57; Organist King's College, Cambridge 57-74; Lecturer in Music, Cambridge Univ. and Cambridge Univ. Organist 57-74; Conductor Cambridge Univ. Music Soc. 58-73; Musical Dir. Bach Choir, London 60-; Pres. Royal Coll. of Organists 66-68; Dir. Royal Coll. of Music, London 74-; Hon. R.A.M., Hon. F.R.C.C.O., F.R.S.C.M.

Leisure interests: golf, swimming.
Royal College of Music, Prince Consort Road, London, SW7 2BS, England.
Telephone: 01-589-3643.

Willebrands, H.E. Cardinal Johannes Gerardus Maria, DR. PHIL.; Netherlands ecclesiastic; b. 4 Sept. 1909, Bovenkarspel; s. of Herman Willebrands and Afra Kok; ed. Warmond Seminary, Holland.
Ordained 34; Chaplain, Begijnhof Church Amsterdam 37-40; Prof. of Philosophy, Warmond 40, Dir. 45; Pres. St. Willibrord Asscn. 46: organized Catholic Conf. on Ecumenical Questions 51; Sec. Vatican Secretariat for Promoting Christian Unity 60, Pres. 69-; created Bishop 64; created Cardinal 69; appointed Archbishop of Utrecht 75.
Publs. *La Liberté religieuse et l'oecuménisme; Ecumenismo e problemi attuali, Oecuménisme et Problèmes actuels; Bibel, ekumenik och sekularisering; Christus, Zeichen und Ursprung der Einheit in einer geteilten Welt.*
Segretariato per l'unione dei cristiani, Via dell'Erba 1, Rome 1-00193, Italy.
Telephone: 698-4181.

Willers, Thomas F., B.A.; American corporation executive; b. 13 July 1919, Niagara Falls, N.Y.; s. of Frederick E. and Laura (Couture) Willers; m. Jean Campbell 1938; three s. one d.; ed. Dartmouth Coll.
With Hooker Chemical Corpn. 41-71, Pres. 63-71; Pres. Occidental Petroleum Corpn. 68-70, Vice-Chair. Board 70-71; Pres. and Dir. Champion Int. (fmrly. U.S. Plywood-Champion Papers Inc.) 72-75, Chair. of Board and Chief Exec. Officer 73-75.
P.O. Box 1407, Greenwich, Conn. 06830, U.S.A.

Willesee, Donald Robert; Australian politician; b. 14 April 1916, Derby, W. Australia; m.; four s. two d.; ed. state schools.
Member of Senate 49-, Leader of Opposition in Senate 66-67, Deputy Leader 69-72; Special Minister of State, Minister Assisting the Prime Minister 72-73; Minister for Foreign Affairs 73-75, Leader of Australian Del. to UN Gen. Assembly 73, 74; mem. Joint Cttee. on Foreign Affairs 67, Privileges Cttee. 69; mem. several Parl. dels. abroad.
The Senate, Parliament House, Canberra, A.C.T., Australia.

Willey, Rt. Hon. Frederick Thomas, P.C., M.P.; British politician; b 1910; m. Eleanor Snowdon 1939; two s. one d.; ed. Johnston School, Durham, and St. John's College, Cambridge.
Called to Bar, Middle Temple 36; M.P. 45-; Parl. Private Sec. to Rt. Hon. J. Chuter Ede 46-50; Parl. Sec. to Ministry of Food 50-51; fmr. Dir. North-Eastern Trading Estates Ltd.; fmr. River Wear Commissioner; fmr. mem. Consultative Assembly, Council of Europe and Assembly, Western European Union; Minister of Land and Natural Resources 64-67; Minister of State, Ministry of Housing and Local Govt. 67; mem. Council, Save the Children Fund; Chair. Select Cttee. on Educ. and Science 68; Chair. Select Cttee. Members' Interests, Race Relations, Parl. and Scientific Cttee.; Vice-Chair. Parl. Labour Party; Labour.
Publs. *Plan for Shipbuilding, Education: Today and Tomorrow, An Enquiry into Teacher Training, The Honourable Member.*
11 North Square, London, N.W.11, England.

Willey, Gordon Randolph, M.A., PH.D.; American archaeologist; b. 7 March 1913, Chariton, Ia.; s. of Frank Willey and Agnes Caroline Wilson; m. Katharine Winston Whaley 1938; two d.; ed. Univ. of Arizona and Columbia Univ.
Instructor in Anthropology Columbia Univ. 42-43; Anthropologist, Bureau of American Ethnology, Smithsonian Inst. 43-50; Bowditch Prof. of Mexican and Central American Archaeology, Harvard Univ.

50-; mem. Nat. Acad. of Sciences; Wenner-Gren Medal for Archaeology 53, Order of Quetzal, Republic of Guatemala 68.
Leisure interests: tennis, swimming, English literature and literary criticism.
Publs. *Archaeology of the Florida Gulf Coast 49, Prehistoric Settlement Patterns of the Viru Valley, Peru 53, Method and Theory in American Archaeology 58, Prehistoric Maya Settlements in the Belize Valley 65, An Introduction to American Archaeology Vol. I 66, Vol. II 71, Excavations at Altar de Sacrificios, Guatemala 73, A History of American Archaeology* (co-author) 73.
Peabody Museum, Harvard University, Cambridge, Mass. 02138; Home: 25 Gray Gardens E., Cambridge, Mass., U.S.A.
Telephone: UN8-7600, Ext. 2249 (Office); EL4-1287 (Home).

Williams, Albert L.; American business machine executive; b. 17 March 1911, Berwick, Pa.; s. of William F. and Mabel (née Lynn) Williams; m. 1st Ruth Bloom 1931 (died 1964), 2nd Katherine Carson 1966; one s. one d.; ed. Beckley Coll.
Student Sales Rep., Int. Business Machines Corpn. (IBM) 36, Sales Rep. 37, Controller 42-47, Treas. 47, Vice-Pres. and Treas. 48-51, mem. Board of Dirs. 51-, Exec. Vice-Pres. 54-61, Pres. 61-66, Chair. Exec. Cttee. Board of Dirs. 66-71, Chair. Finance Cttee. 71-; Dir. Mobil Oil Corpn., First Nat. City Bank (N.Y.), Gen. Foods Corpn., Eli Lilly and Co.; Trustee, Alfred P. Sloan Foundation; Chair. President's Comm. on Int. Trade and Investment Policy 70-71.
International Business Machines Corporation, Old Orchard Road, Armonk, N.Y. 10504, U.S.A.

Williams, Carroll Milton, S.B., A.M., PH.D., M.D.; American professor of biology; b. 2 Dec. 1916, Richmond, Va.; s. of George Leslie and Jessie Hendricks Williams; m. Muriel Voter Williams 1941; four s.; ed. Univ. of Richmond and Harvard Univ.
Assistant Prof., Harvard Univ. 46-48, Assoc. Prof. 48-53, Prof. 53-66, Bussey Prof. of Biology 66-; Jr. Prize Fellow of Harvard Soc. of Fellows 41-45, Guggenheim Fellow 55-56; Fellow, American Acad. of Arts and Sciences; mem. Nat. Acad. of Sciences (Chair. Zoology Section 70-72), American Philosophical Soc., Inst. of Medicine of Nat. Acad. of Sciences; Hon. D.Sc.; Annual Research Prize of A.A.A.S. 50, Boylston Prize and Gold Medal of Harvard Medical School 61, George Ledlie Prize of Harvard Univ. 67, H. T. Ricketts Award of Univ. of Chicago 69.
Leisure interests: music, entomology.
Publs. Over 170 scientific articles on biology with special reference to insects.
The Biological Laboratories, Harvard University, 16 Divinity Avenue, Cambridge, Mass. 02138; Home: 27 Eliot Road, Lexington, Mass., U.S.A.

Williams, Cecil Beaumont, O.B.E., B.A., DIP.ED.; Barbadian civil servant and diplomatist; b. 8 March 1926, Barbados; s. of George and Violet Williams; m. Dorothy Marshall 1952; two s. one d.; ed. Harrison Coll. Barbados, Durham Univ., New Coll. Oxford and Econ. Devt. Inst., IBRD.
Permanent Sec. Ministry of Educ. 58, Ministry of Trade, Industry and Labour 58-63; Dir. Econ. Planning Unit 64-65; Man. Industrial Devt. Corpn. 66-67; High Commr. to Canada 67-70; Perm. Sec. Ministry of External Affairs 71-74; Amb. to U.S.A. and Perm. Rep. to OAS June 74-.
Leisure interests: golf, tennis, music, reading.
Embassy of Barbados, 2144 Wyoming Avenue, N.W., Washington, D.C. 20008; Home: 4850 Linnean Avenue, N.W., Washington, D.C. 20008, U.S.A.

Williams, Emlyn, C.B.E., M.A.; British actor and dramatist; b. 26 Nov. 1905, Mostyn, Wales; s. of Richard and Mary Williams; m. Molly O'Shann 1935 (deceased); two *s.*; ed. County School, Holywell, and Christ Church, Oxford.

First London stage appearance in *And So To Bed*, Savoy Theatre 27; since then has appeared in most of his own plays and also in *The Winslow Boy* 47, *Montserrat* 50, *The Wild Duck* 55, *Shadow of Heroes* 58, *A Man for All Seasons* (New York) 62-63, *The Deputy* (New York) 64, *A Month in the Country* 65-66, *Forty Years On* 69, and at the Old Vic and the Memorial Theatre, Stratford-on-Avon; solo theatrical performances as Charles Dickens 51, 52, 61, 70, 75, and as Dylan Thomas (*A Boy Growing Up*) 55, 57, 58 and 64; has played in the films *The Last Days of Dolwyn, Another Man's Poison, Ivanhoe, The Deep Blue Sea, I Accuse, Beyond This Place, The Wreck of the Mary Deare, The L-Shaped Room, The Eye of the Devil, The Walking Stick, David Copperfield*; Hon. LL.D. (Bangor).

Plays: *A Murder Has Been Arranged* 31, *Glamour, Full Moon, Vessels Departing, Spring 1600, Night Must Fall* 35, *He Was Born Gay* 37, *The Corn is Green* 38, *The Light of Heart* 40, *The Morning Star* 41, *The Druids Rest* 44, *The Wind of Heaven* 45, *Trespass* 47, *Accolade* 50, *Someone Waiting* 53, *Beth* 58; adapted *The Late Christopher Bean, A Month in the Country*; *George* (autobiog. Vol I) 61, *Emlyn* (autobiog. Vol. II) 73; study of murder *Beyond Belief* 67; wrote, directed and played in the film *The Last Days of Dolwyn* 48.

Leisure interests: reading, walking.

123 Dovehouse Street, London, S.W.3, England.

Williams, Rt. Hon. Eric Eustace, P.C., C.H., B.A., D.PHIL.; Trinidadian politician; b. 25 Sept. 1911; ed. Tranquillity Intermediate School, Queen's Royal Coll., Port of Spain, and Oxford Univ.

Professor Social and Political Science Howard Univ., Washington 39; Julius Rosenwald Fellowships 40 and 42; Consultant British Section Anglo-American Caribbean Comm. 43-44; Sec. Agricultural Cttee. Caribbean Comm. 44-46; Consultant Caribbean Comm. 46-48; Deputy Chair. Caribbean Research Council, Caribbean Comm. 48-55; Chief Minister and Minister of Finance, Planning and Development, Trinidad 56-61, Premier 59; Minister of External Affairs 61-64; Prime Minister independent state of Trinidad and Tobago Sept. 62-, also Minister of Finance, Planning and Devt. 67-71, also Minister for External Affairs 73-75, also Minister for Finance 75-; Pro-Chancellor Univ. of W. Indies until 71; Hon. LL.D. (Univ. of New Brunswick) 65; Hon. D.C.L. (Oxford).

Publs. *The Negro in the Caribbean* 42, *Capitalism and Slavery* 44, *Education in the West Indies* 50; Editor *Caribbean Historical Review; Documents on British West Indian History, 1807-1833* 52, *The British West Indies at Westminster, Pt. I 1789-1823* 53, *A History of the People of Trinidad and Tobago* 62, *Documents of West Indian History* 63, *Capitalism and Slavery* 64, *British Historians and the West Indies* 65, *Inward Hunger* 69, *From Columbus to Castro* 70.

Prime Minister's Residence, La Fantasie Road, Port of Spain, Trinidad.

Williams, G. Mennen, A.B., J.D.; American lawyer and politician; b. 23 Feb. 1911, Detroit; *s.* of Henry Phillips and Elma Christina (Mennen) Williams; *m.* Nancy Lace Quirk 1937; one *s.* two *d.*; ed. Princeton Univ., and Univ. of Michigan Law School.

Attorney, Social Security Board, Washington, D.C. 36-37; Asst. Attorney Gen., State of Michigan 38-39; Exec. Asst. to U.S. Attorney Gen. 39-40, Special Asst., Criminal Division 40-41; served U.S. Navy 42-46; Deputy Dir., Office of Price Admin., Michigan 46-47; Democratic mem. Michigan Liquor Control Comm. 47-48; former mem. law firm of Griffiths, Williams & Griffiths; Gov. of Michigan 49-60; Sec. of State for African Affairs 61-66; Amb. to Philippines 68-69; Justice, Michigan Supreme Court 71-; Legion of Merit; Grand Officer Order of Orange-Nassau (Netherlands); Grand Commdr. Royal Order of Phoenix (Greece); Humane Band of African Redemption (Liberia), Polonia Restituta (Polish Govt. in Exile), Pro Merito Latvia; Hon. LL.D. (Wilberforce, Michigan, Michigan State, Western Michigan, Liberia, World, Puerto Rico and Lincoln Univs., Aquinas Coll., St. Augustine's Coll., Ferris Inst.); Dr. of Humanities (Lawrence Inst. of Technology); Democrat.

Leisure interests: golf, fishing, tennis.

Office: Michigan Supreme Court, Law Building, Lansing, Mich. 48901; and 1425 Lafayette Building, Detroit, Mich. 48226; Home: 25 Tonnancour Place, Grosse Pointe Farms, Mich. 48236, U.S.A.

Williams, Harrison Arlington, Jr., B.A., LL.D.; American lawyer and politician; b. 10 Dec. 1919; ed. Oberlin Coll., Ohio, Columbia Univ. Law School, and Georgetown Univ. Foreign Service School.

Seaman on a minesweeper and Navy pilot during Second World War; mem. U.S. House of Reps. 53-56; U.S. Senator from New Jersey 59-; Chair. U.S. Senate Cttee. on Labour and Public Welfare 71-; Democrat.

Home: Holland Road, Bedminster, N.J.; Office: 970 Broad Street, Newark, N.J.; also Senate Office Building, Washington, D.C. 20510, U.S.A.

Williams, Ian George Keith, B.SC.ECON.; British international civil servant; b. 19 Nov. 1921, Southsea, Hants.; *s.* of George James and Dorothy Gertrude (née Hollier) Williams; *m.* Florence Davies 1946; one *d.*; ed. Purbrook Park County High School and privately.

Royal Artillery (Field) 41-46; Principal, Board of Trade and Ministry of Supply 46-55; Senior Staff U.K. Atomic Energy Authority 55-66; Deputy Dir.-Gen., OECD Nuclear Energy Agency 66-.

Leisure interests: golf, opera.

38 boulevard Suchet, 75016 Paris, France.

Telephone: 524-96-60.

Williams, Jack Kenny, M.A., PH.D.; American university administrator; b. 5 April 1920, Galax, Va.; *s.* of Floyd W. and Mary J. (Vass) Williams; *m.* Margaret Pierce 1943; two *d.* and one foster *d.*; ed. Emory and Henry Coll. and Emory Univ.

High School teacher, Va. 40-42; mem. Clemson Univ. Faculty 47-66; Dean, Graduate School, Clemson Univ. 57-60, Dean of Faculties 60-63, Vice-Pres. for Academic Affairs 63-66; Commr. Co-ordinating Board, Texas Coll. and Univ. System 66-68; Vice-Pres. for Academic Affairs, The Univ. of Tennessee System 68-70; Pres. The Texas A. & M. Univ. and The Texas A. & M. System 70-; Chair. Comm. on Colls., Southern Asscn. of Colls. and Schools; mem. Board of Trustees, Nat. Coll. Entrance Examination Board; mem. Philosophical Soc.; Texas; Hon. LL.D. (Univ. of Fla. and Austin Coll.); Hon. Litt.D. (Emory and Henry Coll.).

Publ. *Vogues in Villainy* 59.

Texas A. & M. University, College Station, Texas 77843; Home: 102 Throckmorton Street, College Station, Texas 77840, U.S.A.

Telephone: 713-845-4331 (Office); 713-845-5929 (Home).

Williams, John; British guitarist; b. 24 April 1941, Melbourne; ed. Friern Barnet Grammar School, and Royal Coll. of Music, London.

Studied guitar with Segovia at Accad. Chigiana, Siena; has toured widely in Europe, America, Japan and Soviet Union; numerous transcriptions and gramophone recordings as solo guitarist and with Philadelphia Orchestra and English Chamber Orchestra; founded The Height Below (ensemble) with Brian Gascoigne.

c/o Harold Holt Ltd., 122 Wigmore Street, London, W.I, England.

Williams, John Bell, LL.B.; American lawyer and politician; b. 4 Dec. 1918; ed. Hinds Junior Coll., Raymond, Mississippi, Univ. of Mississippi and Jackson School of Law.

Admitted Miss. State Bar 40; gen. law practice, Raymond, Miss. 40-46; Prosecuting Attorney, Hinds County, Miss. 44-46; mem. U.S. House of Representatives 46-66; Gov. of Miss. 67-72; Democrat.
Raymond, Miss. 39154, U.S.A.

Williams, John Henry, M.A., PH.D., SC.D. (HON.); American economist; b. 21 June 1887, Ystrad, Wales; *s.* of John Hamer and Margaret Williams; *m.* 1st Jessie Monroe 1915 (died 1960), 2nd Katherine McKinstry 1962; two *d.*; ed. Brown and Harvard Univs.
Instructor in English, Brown Univ. 12-15; Frederick Sheldon Travelling Fellow, Harvard to Argentina 17-18; Asst. Chief Latin American Div., U.S. Dept. of Commerce 18; Asst. Prof. of Econs., Princeton 19-20; Assoc. Prof. of Banking, Northwestern Univ. 20-21; Asst. Prof. of Econs., Harvard Univ. 21-25, Assoc. Prof. 25-29, Prof. 29-33; Occasional Consultant U.S. Treasury and State Dept. 30-40; Del. Agenda Cttee. World Econ. and Monetary Conf. 32-33; Econ. Adviser, Fed. Reserve Bank of New York 33-52, Vice-Pres. 36-47, Econ. Consultant 56-64; Head, State Dept. Mission to investigate Latin American exchange problems 34; Occasional Consultant, OEEC, Paris 48-50; mem. ECA Advisory Cttee. on fiscal and monetary problems 48-51; Consultant, ECA, Paris, London, Switzerland; Dean, Graduate School of Public Admin., Harvard 37-47; Nathaniel Ropes Prof. of Political Economy, Harvard 33-57, Emer. 57-; William L. Clayton Prof. Int. Econ. Affairs, The Fletcher School of Law and Diplomacy, Tufts Univ. 57-63, Emer. 63-; mem. Randall Comm. 53-54.
Leisure interests: reading, sports.
Publs. *Argentine International Trade Under Inconvertible Paper Money* (Wells Prize) 20, *Annual Studies of Balance of Payments of U.S.* 19-23, *Post-War Monetary Plans and Other Essays* 44, (co-author) *Financing American Prosperity* 45, *Economic Stability in the Modern World* 52, *Economic Stability in a Changing World* 53.
318 Clemence Hill, Southbridge, Mass. 01550, U.S.A. Telephone: 764-7580.

Williams, John Richard; American radio broadcaster and politician; b. 29 Oct. 1909, Los Angeles, Calif.; *s.* of James Morris Williams and Laura LaCossitt; *m.* Vera May 1942; two *s.* one *d.*; ed. High School and Junior Coll.
Connected with Radio Station KOY 29-66; elected Mayor of Phoenix, Ariz. 55; Gov. of State of Ariz. 66-75.
Leisure interests: radio broadcasting, writing.
2323 North Central Avenue, Phoenix, Ariz. 85004, U.S.A.

Williams, Kenneth Rigby; British chartered accountant; b. 25 Aug. 1936, Stockport; *m.*; one *s.* one *d.*; ed. Haywood Grammar School, Manchester and Inst. of Chartered Accountants.
Articled Clerk, Rhodesian audit firm 59-62; Head Office Accountant, Rhodesian Breweries Ltd. 62-63; Branch Accountant 63-65, Chief Accountant 65-67; Financial Controller, Beer Div., S.A. Breweries 67-68, subsequently apptd. Group Financial Controller and later Group Commercial Man.; Group Gen. Man. S.A. Breweries 73-; Fellow, Inst. of Chartered Accountants of England and Wales.
Leisure interests: golf, tennis, reading.
The South African Breweries Ltd., P.O. Box 1099, 2 Jan Smuts Avenue, Johannesburg, South Africa.

Williams, Laurence Frederic Rushbrook, C.B.E., M.A., B.LITT., F.R.HIST.S., F.R.S.A., J.P.; British historian; b. 10 July 1890, London; *s.* of Laurence Williams; *m.* Freda May Chance 1923; two *s.* one *d.*; ed. Univ. Coll., Oxford.
Lecturer Trinity Coll. Oxford 13; Fellow All Souls Coll. Oxford 14-21; Lecturer in Medieval History Queen's

Univ. Canada 13-14; Prof. of Modern Indian History Allahabad Univ. 14-19; attached to Gen. Staff, Army Headquarters, India 18; Literary Asst. to Pres. Indian Cen. Publicity Board and special duty Indian Constitutional Reforms 18; Dir. Cen. Bureau of Information 20-25; Sec. to Indian Del. Imperial Conf. 23; Political Sec. to Maharaja of Patiala 25, to Chancellor of Princes 26-30; Foreign Ministry Patiala 25-31; mem. Legislative Assembly 24-25; Joint Dir. Indian Princes Special Organization 29-31; Adviser to Indian States Del., Round Table Conf. 30-31, 32; Dir. Eastern Services, B.B.C. 41-44; fmr. Dir. Min. of Information Middle East Section; Editorial Dept. of *The Times* 44-55; Vice-Pres. Indo-British Historical Soc.; Editor Murray's *Handbook to India, Pakistan, Nepal, Bangladesh and Sri Lanka*; Adviser to His Highness the Maharao of Kutch; Hon. Editorial Adviser Pakistan Soc. of London; Hon. Adviser for Contemporary Indian History, Keesings Contemporary Archives.
Leisure interests: motoring, miniature photography.
Publs. *A Primer of Indian Administration, India's Parliament* (4 vols.), *Moral and Material Progress Report on India 1918-25* (Parl. paper), *A History of India under the Company and the Crown, An Empire Builder of the Sixteenth Century: Babur, What about India?, The State of Israel, The Black Hills, Kutch in History and Legend, The State of Pakistan* (2nd edn. 66), *The East Pakistan Tragedy* 72, *Sufi Studies East and West* 74, *Pakistan Under Challenge* 75, *Murray's Handbook* 75.
Little West Hairshaw, Stewarton, by Kilmarnock, Ayrshire, Scotland; and Athenaeum Club, London, S.W.1, England.
Telephone: Stewarton 2318.

Williams, Leonard A., M.A.(ECON.); Trinidadian international banking official; b. 1930; *m.*; one *c.*; ed. Columbia and London Univs.
Lecturer in Econs. Lincoln Univ., Mo., U.S.A. 61-62; Economist, Econ. Planning Div. Prime Minister's Office, Trinidad and Tobago 62-65; Officer in Charge of Monetary Section of Finance and Econs. Div., Min. of Finance March 65-Oct. 66; Alt. Exec. Dir. Int. Monetary Fund 66-68, Exec. Dir. 68-70; Deputy Gov., Cen. Bank of Trinidad and Tobago Nov. 70-; Chair. Nat. Insurance Board.
Central Bank of Trinidad and Tobago, Independence Square, P.O. Box 1250, Port of Spain, Trinidad.
Telephone: 62-52601.

Williams, Leslie Henry, F.R.I.C.; British company director; b. 26 Jan. 1903, London; *s.* of Edward Henry and Jessie Williams; *m.* Alice Helen Harrison 1930; one *s.*; ed. Highbury County School, and London Univ.
Imperial Chemical Industries Ltd., Paints Div. 29-, Dir. 43-46, Man. Dir. 46-48, Chair. 49-56, Dir. I.C.I. Main Board 57-60, Dep. Chair. I.C.I. Ltd., 60-67; Dir. British Nylon Spinners Ltd. 57-64, Ilford Ltd. 58-67; Chair. I.C.I. Fibres Ltd. 65-66; Pres. Royal Inst. of Chemistry 67-70; part-time mem. Monopolies Comm. 67-73; Hon. D.Sc. (Salford).
Leisure interests: garden, golf, music.
Penny Green, West End Lane, Stoke Poges, Bucks., England.
Telephone: Farnham Common 3423.

Williams, Nicholas James Donald; British solicitor and business executive; b. 21 Oct. 1925, Calcutta, India; *s.* of Nicholas T. and Daisy (Hollow) Williams; *m.* 1st Dawn Hill 1947 (dissolved), 2nd Sheila M. Dalgety 1955; three *s.* two *d.*; ed. Rugby School.
Partner, Nicholas Williams and Co., London 50-61; Senior Partner, Surridge and Beecheno, Karachi, Pakistan 55-61; Legal Adviser, The Burmah Oil Co., London 61-63, Co-ordinator, Eastern Operations 63-65,

Exec. Dir. 65-67, Asst. Man. Dir. 67-69, Man. Dir. 69-Jan. 75, also Chief Exec. 71-Jan. 75.
Leisure interest: sailing.
Charlton House, Tetbury, Gloucestershire, England.

Williams, Nick B.; American newspaper editor; b. 23 Aug. 1906; s. of John F. and Anne M. Williams; m. 1st Elizabeth Ricbenbaker 1933 (died 1973), one s. three d.; m. 2nd Barbara Steele 1973; ed. Univ. of the South and Univ. of Texas.
Editorial worker, Texas, Tennessee and California 27-58; Man. Editor *Los Angeles Times* 58, Editor 59-71, Editorial Page Columnist; Editorial Consultant, Times Mirror Co. 71-; Trustee Pitzer Coll., Calif.; D.C.L. (Univ. of the South); Kt. Order of Leopold, American Freedoms Foundation Award.
Leisure interests: art, gardening, fishing.
23 Lagunita, Laguna Beach, Calif., U.S.A.

Williams, Paul Revere; American architect; b. 18 Feb. 1896; ed. Univ. of Southern California, and Beaux Arts Inst. of Design, Los Angeles.
Architect 23-; works include private houses, Los Angeles Superior Court Building, Pearl Harbour Memorial, Honolulu, Franz Hall and Botany Building, Univ. of S. Calif.; Fellow, American Inst. of Architects; Award for Creative Planning, Los Angeles Chamber of Commerce.
Publs. *Small Homes for Tomorrow, New Homes for Today.*
Office: 3440 Wilshire Boulevard, Los Angeles, Calif. 90005; Home: 1690 Victoria Avenue, Los Angeles, Calif. 90019, U.S.A.

Williams, Raymond, LITT.D., M.A.; British writer and university lecturer; b. 31 Aug. 1921, Llanfihangel, Mon.; s. of Henry Joseph and Gwendolene Williams (née Bird); m. Joyce Dalling 1942; two s. one d.; ed. Abergavenny Grammar School, and Trinity Coll., Cambridge.
Army Service 41-45; Staff Tutor, Oxford Univ. Extra-Mural Delegacy 46-61; Univ. Lecturer in English Jesus Coll., Cambridge 61-67, Fellow 61-; Univ. Reader in Drama, Cambridge 67-74, Prof. 74-.
Leisure interest: gardening.
Publs. *Drama from Ibsen to Eliot* 52, *Drama in Performance* 54 (revised 68), *Culture and Society* 58, *Border Country* 60, *The Long Revolution* 61, *Communications* 62, *Second Generation* 64, *Modern Tragedy* 66, *Public Enquiry* 67, *Drama from Ibsen to Brecht* 68, *May Day Manifesto* (Editor) 68, *The English Novel from Dickens to Lawrence* 70, *Orwell* 71, *The Country and the City* 73, *Television: Technology and Cultural Form* 74, *Keywords* 76.
Jesus College, Cambridge, England.
Telephone: Cambridge 68611.

Williams, Richard Tecwyn, PH.D., D.SC., F.R.S.; British professor of biochemistry; b. 20 Feb. 1909, Abertillery, Mon.; s. of Richard and Mary (née Jones) Williams; m. Josephine Sullivan 1937; two s. three d.; ed. Univ. Coll. of S. Wales and Mon., Cardiff.
Research Asst., Physiology Inst., Cardiff 30-34; Lecturer in Biochem., Univ. of Birmingham 34-42; Senior Lecturer in Biochem., Univ. of Liverpool 42-48; Prof. of Biochem. St. Mary's Hosp. Medical School, London 49-, Deputy Dean 70-; Visiting Scientist Nat. Heart Inst., N.I.H., Bethesda, U.S.A. 56; Visiting Prof. of Toxicology, New York Univ. School of Medicine 65-66; Visiting Prof. for short periods, Univ. of Ibadan, Nigeria 69-; mem. Food Additives and Contaminants Cttee., Ministry of Agriculture, Fisheries and Food 64-72; mem. Horserace Anti-Doping Cttee. 71; mem. Toxicity Sub-cttee. of Cttee. on Medical Aspects of Chemicals in Food and the Environment, Ministry of Health and Social Security 72-; Howard Fox Memorial Lecturer, N.Y. Univ. School of Medicine 69; Merit Award, Soc. of Toxicology (U.S.A.) 68; D. de l'Univ.

(h.c.), Univ. of Paris; M.D. (h.c.) Univ. of Tübingen, Hon. D.Sc. (Univ. Ibadan, Nigeria) 74; CIBA Medal of Biochemical Soc. 72, 1922 Medal, Univ. of Turku, Finland 75.
Leisure interests: gardening, Welsh literature, music.
Publs. *Detoxication Mechanisms* 47, 59, and about 200 articles, mainly in *Biochemical Journal.*
Department of Biochemistry, St. Mary's Hospital Medical School, London, W.2; Home: 95 Vernon Drive, Stanmore, Middx., HA7 2BW, England.
Telephone: 01-723-1252 Ext. 119 (Office); 01-427-5554 (Home).

Williams, Robert Edmond, B.SC.; American steel executive; b. 7 Feb. 1913, San Francisco; s. of George and Ynez (Smith) Williams; m. Ellen Reinecke 1936; two s.; ed. Univ. of California at Berkeley.
U.S. Steel Corpn., 35-60, Vice-Pres. Sales, Nat. Tube Div. 60-61; Vice-Pres. Sales, Youngstown Sheet and Tube Co. 61-63, Exec. Vice-Pres. 63-65, Dir. and mem. Exec. Cttee. April 64-, Pres. 65, Chief Exec. Officer 66-70; Vice-Chair., Chief Admin. Officer, Lykes-Youngstown Corp. 69-70; Pres. and Chief Exec. Officer GF Business Equipment Inc., Youngstown 73-; Dir.-Gen. Fireproofing Co., Pittsburgh Nat. Bank, Dollar Savings & Trust Co. (Youngstown), Diamond Shamrock Corpn.; Dir. and mem. Exec. Cttee. American Iron and Steel Inst.; Dir. International Iron and Steel Inst.
1359 Virginia Trail, Youngstown, Ohio 44505, U.S.A.

Williams, Robert Martin, C.B.E., PH.D.; New Zealand mathematician; b. Christchurch; s. of Canon Henry Williams; m. Mary Constance Thorpe 1944; one s. two d.; ed. Christ's College, Canterbury Univ. N.Z., St. John's Coll., Cambridge.
Mathematician, Radar Development Laboratory, D.S.I.R., N.Z. 41-44; mem. U.K. Atomic Group in U.S.A. 44-45; mem. Applied Maths. Laboratory, D.S.I.R. 49-53, Dir. 53-62; Commr. State Services Comm. N.Z. 63-66; Vice-Chancellor Univ. of Otago 67-73; Vice-Chancellor, Australian Nat. Univ. 73-75; Chair. State Services Comm. 75-; Hon. LL.D. (Otago); mem. Int. Statistical Inst.
Publs. papers on mathematical statistics.
State Services Commission, P.B. Wellington; Home: 21 Wadestown Road, Wellington, New Zealand.

Williams, Robley Cook, PH.D.; American biophysicist and educator; b. 13 Oct. 1908, Santa Rosa, Calif.; s. of William Claude Williams and Anna Mae Cook Williams; m. Margery Ufford 1931; one s. one d.; ed. Cornell Univ.
Professor, Univ. of Michigan 49-50; Prof. of Biophysics, Univ. of Calif., Berkeley 50-59; Assoc. Dir. of Virus Lab. and Research Biophysicist, Univ. of Calif., Berkeley 50-; Prof. of Virology, Univ. of Calif., Berkeley 59-64, Prof. of Molecular Biology 64-; Chair. Dept. of Molecular Biology 64-69; mem. Nat. Acad. of Sciences; Longstreth Medal of Franklin Inst. 39, John Scott Award 54.
Leisure interest: golf.
Publs. Numerous scientific publs. in fields of physics, astronomy and biophysics.
Department of Molecular Biology, University of California, Berkeley, Calif. 94720; Home: 1 Arlington Court, Berkeley, Calif. 94707, U.S.A.
Telephone: 415-526-2063 (Home).

Williams, Roger J(ohn), M.S., PH.D.; American biochemist; b. 14 Aug. 1893, Ootacumund, Ind.; s. of Robert and Alice Williams; m. 1st Elizabeth Wood 1916 (deceased), 2nd Mabel Hobson 1953; two s. one d.; ed. Univs. of Redlands and Chicago.
Research Chemist, Fleischmann Co. 19-20; Asst. Prof. Univ. of Oregon 20-21, Assoc. Prof. 21-27, Prof. 28-31; Prof. Oregon State Coll. 32-39; Prof. of Chemistry, Univ. of Texas 39-71, Prof. Emer. 71-; Dir. Clayton

Foundation Biochemical Inst. Univ. of Texas 41-63; Research Council Food and Nutrition Board 49-53; Research Scientist, Clayton Foundation Biochemical Inst., Univ. of Texas 71-; mem. Nat. Acad. of Sciences, American Chemical Society (Pres. 57), Biochemical Society of London, etc.; Fellow American Asscn. for Advancement of Science; Mead Johnson Award 41; Chandler Medal 42; Hon. D.Sc. (Univ. of Redlands, Columbia Univ., Oregon State Coll.).
Leisure interests: golf, fishing, travel.
Publs. *An Introduction to Organic Chemistry* 27, *A Laboratory Manual of Organic Chemistry* (with R. Q. Brewster) 28, *An Introduction to Bio-chemistry* 31, *Textbook of Biochemistry* 38, *What to do about Vitamins* 45, *The Human Frontier* 46, *Biochemistry of B Vitamins* (with others) 50, *Nutrition and Alcoholism* 51, *Free and Unequal* 53, *Biochemical Individuality* 56, *Alcoholism: The Nutritional Approach* 59, *Nutrition in a Nutshell* 62, *You are Extraordinary* 67, *Nutrition Against Disease* 71, *Physicians Handbook of Nutritional Science* 75.
Office: University of Texas, Austin, Texas; 1604 Gaston Avenue, Austin, Texas, U.S.A.
Telephone: 471-3591.

Williams, Rt. Rev. Ronald Ralph, M.A., D.D., F.R.S.A.; British ecclesiastic; b. 14 Oct. 1906, Orpington; s. of Ralph and Mary Williams; m. Cicely Maud Williams 1934; ed. Gonville and Caius Coll., and Ridley Hall, Cambridge.
Tutor, St. Aidans Coll., Birkenhead 28-29; Curate, Leyton Parish Church 29-31; Chaplain, Ridley Hall, Cambridge 31-34; Examining Chaplain to Bishop of Chelmsford 31; Home Education Sec., Church Missionary Society 34-40; with Religious Division, Ministry of Information 40-45, Dir. 43-45; Commissary to Bishop of Tasmania 44; Examining Chaplain to Bishop of Durham 45; Principal, St. John's Coll., Durham 45-53; Proctor in Convocation of York 50; Hon. Canon, Durham Cathedral 53-54; Bishop of Leicester 53-; Church of England rep. to Brussels Ecumenical Centre, mem. Consultative Cttee. of Churches of European Community 73-; Pres. European Christian Industrial Movement 75-; mem. House of Lords 59-; hon. Fellow St. Peter's Coll. (Oxford).
Leisure interests: golf, climbing (member of Alpine Club), music, travel.
Publs. *Religion and the English Vernacular* 40, *The Strife Goes On* 40, *The Christian Religion* 41, *Authority in the Apostolic Age* 50, *The Perfect Law of Liberty* 53, *The Acts of the Apostles* 53, *Reading Through Hebrews* 60, *The Word of Life* (Editor) 60, *Take Thou Authority* 61, *The Bible in Worship and Ministry* 62, *The Letters of John and James* 65, *What's Right with the Church of England* 66, *I believe—and why* 71, *Faith and the Faith* 73.
Bishop's Lodge, Springfield Road, Leicester LE2 3BD, England.
Telephone: Leicester 708985.

Williams, Rt. Hon. Shirley, P.C., M.P., M.A.; British politician; b. 27 July 1930, London; d. of Sir George Catlin (q.v.) and the late Vera Brittain; m. Bernard Williams 1955 (divorced 1974); one d.; ed. Summit School, Minn., U.S.A., St. Paul's School, Somerville Coll., Oxford, and Columbia Univ.
General Sec. Fabian Soc. 60-64; M.P. for Hitchin 64-; Parl. Private Sec., Minister of Health 64-66; Parl. Sec. Minister of Labour 66-67; Minister of State, Dept. of Education and Science 67-69; Minister of State, Home Office 69-70; Opposition Spokesman on Health and Social Security 70-71, on Home Affairs 71-73, on Prices and Consumer Affairs 73-74; Sec. of State for Prices and Consumer Protection 74-, Paymaster-Gen. April 76-; mem. Labour Party Nat. Exec. Cttee. 70-; Visiting Fellow, Nuffield Coll., Oxford 67-75; Hon. D.Ed., C.N.A.A.; Labour.

Leisure interests: riding, rough walking, music, singing.
Publs. pamphlets on European Community, and economics of Central Africa; articles and broadcasts.
House of Commons, Westminster, London, S.W.1, England.
Telephone: 01-219-3000.

Williams, Stephen, PH.D.; American professor of anthropology and museum director; b. 28 Aug. 1926, Minneapolis, Minn.; s. of Clyde G. and Lois M. (Simmons) Williams; m. Eunice Ford 1962; two s.; ed. Univ. of Michigan and Yale Univ.
Historical and Archaeological Research on Caddo Indians for U.S. Dept. of Justice 54-55; Research Fellow in N. American Archaeology, Peabody Museum of Archaeology and Ethnology, Harvard Univ. 55-58; Lecturer in Anthropology, Harvard Univ. 56-58, Asst. Prof. of Anthropology 58-62, Assoc. Prof. 62-67, Prof. of Anthropology 67-, Chair. Dept. of Anthropology 67-69; mem. of Board of Freshmen Advisers, Harvard Univ. 59-60, 61-65; Asst. Curator of N. American Archaeology, Peabody Museum 57-58, Curator of N. American Archaeology 62-, Exec. Dir. for Research and Devt., Peabody Museum 67; Acting Dir., Peabody Museum 67-69, Dir. 69-; Hon. M.A. (Harvard Univ.).
Publs. *The Aboriginal Location of the Kadohodacho and Related Tribes* (in *Explorations in Cultural Anthropology*) 64, *An Outline of SE US Prehistory with Particular Emphasis on the Paleo-Indian Era* (with James B. Stoltman, in *The Quaternary of the United States*) 65, *The Waring Papers: The Collected Papers of Antonio J. Waring, Jr.* (in *Papers of the Peabody Museum* Vol. 58) 68.
Peabody Museum of Archaeology and Ethnology, Harvard University, 11 Divinity Avenue, Cambridge, Mass. 02138; Home: 103 Old Colony Road, Wellesley, Mass. 02181, U.S.A.
Telephone: 617-495-2248 (Office); 617-235-7588 (Home).

Williams, Tennessee, A.B.; American writer; b. 26 March 1911; ed. Univs. of Missouri and Iowa, and Washington Univ., St. Louis.
Awarded Pulitzer Prize 47 and 54, Drama Critics' Circle Award 44, 47, 54, 61.
Publs. *Battle of Angels* 40, *The Glass Menagerie* 44, *You Touched Me* 46, *A Streetcar Named Desire* 47, *Summer and Smoke* 48, *Rose Tattoo* 50, *Roman Spring of Mrs. Stone* 52, *Camino Real* 53, *Cat on a Hot Tin Roof* 55, *Orpheus Descending* 57, *Suddenly Last Summer* 58, *Something Unspoken* 58, *Sweet Bird of Youth* 59, *Period of Adjustment* 60, *The Night of the Iguana* 61, *The Milk Train Doesn't Stop Here Any More* 62 (Revised version 63), *The Knightly Quest* (short stories) 67, *The Two Character Play* 67, *The Eccentricities of a Nightingale* 67, *The Seven Descents of Myrtle* 68, *In the Bar of a Tokyo Hotel* 69, *Small Craft Warnings* 72, *Eight Mortal Ladies Possessed* (stories) 74, *The Red Devil Battery Sign* 74, *Moise and the World of Reason* (novel) 75, *Memoirs* (autobiography) 75.
c/o Audrey Wood, International Famous Agency Inc., 1301 Avenue of the Americas, New York, N.Y. 10019, U.S.A.

Williams, Walter Charles; American aeronautical engineer; b. 30 July 1919, New Orleans; s. of Walter C. and Emilia B. Williams; m. Helen E. Manning 1939; two s. one d.; ed. Louisiana State Univ.
Langley Memorial Aeronautical Laboratory, Nat. Advisory Cttee. for Aeronautics (NACA) 39-46; NACA Project Engineer for X-1 Experimental Aircraft Program 46-47; Head, NACA Flight Research Center, Edwards Air Force Base, California 47-59; Assoc. Dir. and Dep. Dir. Nat. Aeronautics and Space Admin. (NASA) Manned Spacecraft Center, Houston, Texas 59-63; Dep. Assoc. Admin. for Manned Space Flight Operations, NASA, Washington 63-64; Vice-Pres. Aerospace Corpn., Gen. Man. Manned Systems Div.,

El Segundo, Calif. 64-; Vice-Pres., Aerospace Corpn., Gen. Man. Vehicle Systems Division; NASA Distinguished Service Medal 62, and other awards.
4240 Reyes Drive, Tarzana, Calif. 91356, U.S.A.

Williams, Sir William Emrys, C.B.E.; British art administrator; b. 5 Oct. 1896; ed. Manchester Univ.
Tutor, Univ. of London Extra Mural Dept. 28-34; Sec. British Inst. of Adult Educ. 34-40; Chief Editor, Dir. Penguin Books 35-65; Dir. Army Bureau of Current Affairs 41-45, Bureau of Current Affairs 46-51; Sec.-Gen. Arts Council of Great Britain April 51-63; Sec. Nat. Art Collection Fund 63-70; Pres. Welsh Nat. Theatre 68-.
Publ. *Allen Lane: a Personal Portrait* 73.
Grenville Paddock, Haddenham, Aylesbury, Bucks., England.

Williams-Ellis, Lady Amabel; British writer of novels and children's books; m. Sir Clough Williams-Ellis (q.v.) 1915.
Publs. *An Anatomy of Poetry, The Big Firm, Men who Found Out, Noah's Ark, How you are Made, To Tell the Truth, A History of English Life, Learn to Love First, Headlong Down the Years, Women in War Factories, The Art of Being a Woman, The Art of Being a Parent, A Food and People Geography, Changing the World, Seekers and Finders, Modern Scientists at Work, Darwin's Moon (A Life of Alfred Russel Wallace), Life in England* 6 vols., *Gypsy Folk Tales, Out of This World* 10 vols., etc.
Plâs Brondanw, Llanfrothen, Gwynedd, North Wales.
Telephone: Penrhyndeudraeth 292.

Williams-Ellis, Sir Clough, Kt., C.B.E., M.C., LL.D., F.R.I.B.A., J.P., M.T.P.I., F.L.I.A.; British architect; b. 28 May 1883, Gayton, Northants.; m. Amabel Strachey (Lady Amabel Williams-Ellis, q.v.) 1915; one s. (deceased) two d.; ed. Oundle and Trinity Coll., Cambridge.
Authority on town-planning; founder of the Portmeirion Peninsular Colony, N. Wales; Chair. Council for Preservation of Rural Wales, Glass Industry Working Party; First Chair. Stevenage New Town Corpn.; fmr. Pres. Design and Industries Asscn.; mem. Town Planning Inst., Govt. Cttee. on Art and Industry, Univ. of Wales Art Cttee., Grand Council British Travel Asscn., Welsh Advisory Reconstruction Council; Govt. Cttee. on Nat. Parks; Welsh Cttee. Festival of Britain 51; mem. Ministry of Transport Highways Advisory Cttee., Nat. Trust Welsh Cttee.; **Town Planning Consultant to various municipalities.**
Leisure interests: travelling, building.
Works include churches, schools, hotels, clubs, village schemes; private residences in China and South Africa; Portmeirion (see above); memorial to David Lloyd George.
Publs. *The Pleasures of Architecture, England and the Octopus, Architecture Here and Now, The Architect, The Face of the Land, Britain and the Beast, Plan for Living The Adventure of Building, On Trust for the Nation, An Artist in North Wales, Town and Country Planning, Roads in the Landscape, Architect Errant,* etc.
Plâs Brondanw, Llanfrothen, Gwynedd, North Wales.
Telephone: Penrhyndeudraeth 292.

Williamson, Henry; British novelist; b. 1 Dec. 1895.
Publs. include *The Beautiful Years* 21, *Dandelion Days* 22, *The Dream of Fair Women* 24, *The Pathway* 28 (forming a tetralogy called *The Flax of Dream*), *The Lone Swallows* 22, *The Peregrine's Saga* 23, *The Old Stag* 26, *Tarka the Otter* 27 (Hawthornden Prize 28), *Tales of a Devon Village* and *Life in a Devon Village* 32, *The Gold Falcon* 33, *Salar the Salmon* 35, *The Story of a Norfolk Farm* 41, *T. E. Lawrence: Genius of Friendship* 41, *Scribbling Lark* 49, *The Phasian Bird* 50, *A Chronicle of Ancient Sunlight* (fifteen vols.) 51-69: *The Dark Lantern* 51, *Donkey Boy* 52, *Young Phillip Maddison*

53, *How Dear is Life* 54, *A Fox under my Cloak* 55, *The Golden Virgin* 57, *Love and the Loveless: A Soldier's Tale of Passchendaele 1917* 58, *A Test to Destruction* 60, *The Innocent Moon* 61, *It was the Nightingale* 62, *The Power of the Dead* 63, *The Phoenix Generation* 65, *A Solitary War* 66, *Lucifer before Sunrise* 67, *The Gale of the World* 69, *The Great War of 1914-18, Tales of Moorland and Estuary* 53, *A Clear Water Stream* 58, *The Henry Williamson Animal Saga* 60, *Collected Nature Stories* 70, *The Scandaroon* 72, *The Vanishing Hedgerow* 72 (a film treatment with David Cobham shown on BBC television and chosen for 1973 Monaco winter film show).
c/o National Liberal Club, Whitehall Place, London, S.W.1; 4 Capstone Place, Ilfracombe, Devon, England.

Williamson, Malcolm Benjamin Graham; British composer, pianist and organist; b. 21 Nov. 1931, Sydney, N.S.W., Australia; s. of George and Bessie Williamson; m. Dolores Daniel 1960; one s. two d.; ed. Barker Coll., Hornsby, N.S.W., and Sydney Conservatorium of Music.
Assistant organist, Farm Street, London 55-58; Organist, St. Peter's, Limehouse 58-60; Lecturer in Music, Cen. School of Speech and Drama, London 61-62; Exec. Cttee., Composers Guild of Great Britain 64; Composer-in-Residence Westminster Choir Coll., Princeton, N.J. 70-71; Master of the Queen's Music 75-; Sir Arnold Bax Memorial Prize 63; Hon. Dr.Mus. (Westminster Choir Coll.) 71.
Leisure interest: literature.
Compositions include: Operas: *Our Man in Havana* 63, *English Eccentrics* 64, *The Happy Prince* 64, *Julius Caesar Jones* 65, *The Violins of St. Jacques* 66, *Dunstan and the Devil* 67, *The Growing Castle* 68, *Lucky-Peter's Journey* 69, *Genesis, The Stone Wall* 71, *The Red Sea* 72, *The Winter Star* 73; Ballets: *The Display* 64, *Sun into Darkness* 66; Orchestral: Piano Concertos 58, 60, 61, Organ Concerto 61, Violin Concerto 65, *Elevamini* (Symphony) 56, *Santiago de Espada* (Overture) 56, *Sinfonia Concertante* 61, *Sinfonietta* 65, *Symphonic Variations* 65, Concerto Grosso 65, *Symphony No. 2* 69; Chamber: *Variations for Cello and Piano* 64, *Concerto for Wind Quintet and Two Pianos, Eight Hands* 65, *Pas de Quatre* (Piano and woodwind) 67; Organ: *Fons Amoris* 57, *Symphony* 60, *Vision of Christ Phoenix* 61, *Elegy JFK* 64, *Peace Pieces* 71; *The Brilliant and the Dark* (operatic sequence) 66, Two piano sonatas 67, *From a Child's Garden* (tenor and piano) 68, *Little Carols of the Saints, Hammarskjöld Portrait* 74, also choral and piano music.
32 Hertford Avenue, London, S.W.14, England.

Willingham, Ben Hill; American business executive; b. 1 June 1914; ed. Hume Fogg High School, Nashville, Vanderbilt Univ.
Joined Genesco, Inc. 33, various admin. and exec. positions, Dir. 53-, Vice-Pres. 56-58, Pres. 58-69; Vice-Pres. Burlington Industries Inc. 69-, Pres. Burlington International 70-; Dir. Third Nat. Bank of Nashville; mem. American Soc. of Corporate Execs. 60-, Newcomen Soc. of N. America, Advisory Council of the Fashion Inst. of Technology; Trustee, Foundation for Research on Human Behavior.
32 Beethovenstrasse, Zurich, Switzerland.

Willis, Baron (Life Peer), cr. 63, of Chislehurst; **Edward (Ted) Willis;** British author; b. 13 Jan. 1918, London; s. of Alfred John and Maria Harriet Willis; m. Audrey Hale 1944; one s. one d.; ed. Downhills Central School.
Royal Fusiliers 40-44; professional writer 45-; Chair. Screenwriters' Guild 58-68, Dir. World Wide Pictures 67-, Capital Radio Ltd.; Labour.
Leisure interests: tennis, badminton, watching football.
Publs. Plays: *Woman in a Dressing Gown* 56, *Hot*

Summer Night 59, *Doctor in the House* 60, *Mother* 61, *Slow Roll of Drums* 64, *Knock on any Door* 64, *Queenie* 67, *Dead on Saturday* 70; *Whatever Happened to Tom Mix* (autobiog.) 70; Novels: *Death May Surprise Us* 74, *The Left-Handed Sleeper* 75, *Man-Eater* 76; Films incl.: *Blue Lamp, Bitter Harvest, No Trees in the Street, Hunter's Walk* 73; TV Series incl.: *Dixon of Dock Green, Sergeant Cork, Crime of Passion, Hunter's Walk.*
5 Shepherds Green, Chislehurst, Kent, England.

Willis, Sir Eric Archibald, K.B.E., C.M.G.; Australian politician; b. 15 Jan. 1922, Murwillumbah, N.S.W.; *s.* of the late Archibald Clarence Willis and of Via Mabel Willis (née Buttenshaw); *m.* Norma Dorothy Knight 1951; two *s.* one *d.*; ed. Murwillumbah High School, Univ. of Sydney.
Member N.S.W. Legis. Assembly 50-, Deputy Leader of Opposition 59-65; Minister for Labour and Industry 65-71, Chief Sec. 65-72, Minister for Tourism 65-72, for Sport 71-72, for Educ. 72-76, Premier and Treas. Jan. 76-.
Leisure interest: politics.
Premier's Department, State Office Block, Sydney, N.S.W. 2000; Home: 16 Crewe Street, Bardwell Park, N.S.W. 2207, Australia.
Telephone: 20576 (Office).

Willoch, Kaare Isaachsen, CAND. OECON.; Norwegian politician; b. 3 Oct. 1928, Oslo; *s.* of Haakon Willoch and Agnes Saure; *m.* Anne Marie Jørgensen 1954; one *s.* two *d.*; ed. Ullern Gymnasium and Univ. of Oslo.
Secretary, Fed. of Norwegian Shipowners 51-53, Counsellor, Fed. of Norwegian Industries 54-63; mem. Nat. Cttee. Conservative Party 61-; Sec.-Gen. Conservative Party 63-65; Asst. Dir. Fed. of Industries 65-; Minister of Trade and Shipping 63, 65-70; mem. Storting 58-; Chair. World Bank Group 67; Chair. Conservative Party Parliamentary Group 70-74; mem. Nordic Council 70-, Pres. 73.
Leisure interests: skiing, touring.
Publs. *Personal Savings* 55, *Price Policy in Norway* (with L. B. Bachke) 58.
Blokkaveien 6B, Oslo 2, Norway.

Wills, Sir John Spencer, Kt., F.C.I.T.; British business executive; b. 10 Aug. 1904, London; *s.* of Cedric Wills and Cécile Charlotte; *m.* Elizabeth Garcke 1936; two *s.*; ed. Cleobury Mortimer Coll., Shropshire, and Merchant Taylors' School.
Chairman East Yorkshire Motor Services Ltd. 39-68, Chair. Birmingham & Midland Motor Omnibus Co. Ltd. 46-68; Chair. British Electric Traction Co. Ltd. 39-; Chair. Nat. Electric Construction Co. Ltd. 45-, Rediffusion Ltd. 47-, Rediffusion Television Ltd. 54-, Wembley Stadium Ltd. 65-; Dir. Monotype Corpn. Ltd. 47-72; Dir. of numerous other companies; Gov. Royal Shakespeare Theatre, Stratford on Avon 46-74; Fellow, Chartered Inst. of Transport (Pres. 50-51), Council of Public Road Transport Asscn. (Chair. 45-46); Hon. mem. of Council, Royal Opera House Soc. 62-74; Vice-Patron, Theatre Royal Windsor Trust 65-.
Leisure interests: complete idleness, formerly: flying, swimming, skiing, tennis, riding, shooting.
Stratton House, Stratton Street, Piccadilly, London, WIX 6AS; Beech Farm, Battle, Sussex, England.
Telephone: 01-629-8886.

Willson, Francis Michael Glenn, M.A., D.PHIL.; British professor and university administrator; b. 29 Sept. 1924, Carlisle; *s.* of late Christopher Glenn Willson and Katherine Mattick; *m.* Jean Carlyle 1945; two *d.*; ed. Carlisle Grammar School, Univ. of Manchester, Balliol and Nuffield Colls., Oxford.
War service in Merchant Navy 41-42 and R.A.F. 43-47; seconded to BOAC 46-47; Research Officer, Royal Inst. of Public Admin. 53-60; Research Fellow, Nuffield Coll., Oxford 55-60; Lecturer in Politics, St. Edmund

Hall, Oxford 58-60; Prof. of Govt., Univ. Coll. of Rhodesia and Nyasaland 61-64, Dean of Social Studies 62-64; Prof. of Govt. and Politics, Univ. of Calif., Santa Cruz 65-74, Provost of Stevenson Coll. 67-74, Vice-Chancellor College and Student Affairs 73-74; Warden of Goldsmith's Coll. 74-75; Principal of London Univ. 75-.
Leisure interests: listening to music, reading, walking.
Publs. *Organization of British Central Government 1914-1956* (with D. N. Chester) 57, 2nd edn. *1914-1964* 68, *Administrators in Action* 61.
University of London, Senate House, Malet Street, London, WC1E 7HU, England.
Telephone: 01-636-800.

Wilson, Sir Alan Herries, F.R.S.; British industrial executive; b. 2 July 1906; *m.* Margaret Monks 1934 (died 1961); two *s.*; ed. Wallasey Grammar School, and Emmanuel Coll., Cambridge.
Fellow, Emmanuel Coll. Cambridge 29-33, Hon. Fellow 59; Fellow and Lecturer, Trinity Coll. Cambridge 33-45; Univ. Lecturer in Mathematics, Cambridge 33-45; joined Courtaulds Ltd. 45, Man. Dir. 54, Deputy Chair. 57-62; Dir. Int. Computers Holdings Ltd. 62-72; Chair. Cttee. on Coal Derivatives 59-60, on Problem of Noise 60-63; Chair. and Dir. Glaxo Group Ltd. 63-73; Deputy Chair. Electricity Council 66-; mem. Iron and Steel Board 60-67; Hon. D.Sc. (Oxford), Hon. D.Sc. (Edinburgh).
Publs. *The Theory of Metals* 36, 53, *Semi-Conductors and Metals* 39, *Thermodynamics and Statistical Mechanics* 57.
65 Oakleigh Park South, Whetstone, London, N20 9JL, England.
Telephone: 01-445-3030.

Wilson, Alexander (Sandy) Galbraith; British writer and composer; b. 19 May 1924, Sale, Cheshire; *s.* of George Wilson and Caroline Humphrey; ed. Harrow School, Oxford Univ. and Old Vic Theatre School.
Contributed to revues *Slings and Arrows, Oranges and Lemons* 48; wrote revues for Watergate Theatre, London *See You Later, See You Again* 51-52; wrote musical *The Boy Friend* for Players Club Theatre 53, transferred to Wyndhams Theatre and on Broadway 54; *The Buccaneer* 55, *Valmouth* London 58, U.S.A. 60, *Divorce me Darling* 65; Dir. London revival of *The Boy Friend* 67; Composed music for *As Dorothy Parker Once Said* London 69; songs for B.B.C. television *Charley's Aunt* 69; wrote and performed *Sandy Wilson Thanks the Ladies* (one man show) London 71; wrote *His Monkey Wife* London 71.
Leisure interests: cinema, cookery, travel.
Publs. *This is Sylvia* 54, *The Poodle from Rome* 62, *I Could Be Happy* (autobiog.) 75, *Ivor* 75.
2 Southwell Gardens, London, S.W.7, England.
Telephone: 01-373-6172.

Wilson, Angus (Frank Johnstone), C.B.E., B.A., F.R.S.L.; British writer; b. 11 Aug. 1913, Sussex; *s.* of William Johnstone-Wilson and Maud (née Caney); ed. Westminster School, and Merton Coll., Oxford.
Asst. Keeper, Dept. of Printed Books, British Museum 36-55; full-time writer 55-; Lecturer, School of English Studies, Univ. of East Anglia 63-, Prof. 66-; mem. Arts Council 67-69; Chair. Nat. Book League 71-74; Pres. Dickens Fellowship 74-75; C.Lit. 72; Chevalier de l'Ordre des Arts et des Lettres 72.
Publs. *The Wrong Set* 49, *Such Darling Dodos* 50, *Hemlock and After* 52, *For Whom the Cloche Tolls* 53, *Emile Zola* 54, *The Mulberry Bush* (a play, produced Bristol Old Vic 55, Royal Court Theatre 56, published 56), *Anglo-Saxon Attitudes* 56, *A Bit off the Map* 57, *The Middle Age of Mrs. Eliot* 58, *The Old Men at the Zoo* 61, *The Wild Garden* 63, *Late Call* 64, *No Laughing Matter* 67, *The World of Charles Dickens* 70, *As if by*

Magic 73; also several (unpublished) plays for television. Felsham Woodside, Bradfield St. George, Bury St. Edmunds. Suffolk, England.

Wilson, Sir (Archibald) Duncan, G.C.M.G.; British diplomatist; b. 12 Aug. 1911, Winchester, Hants; *s.* of Archibald Wilson and Ethel Schuster; *m.* Elizabeth Fleming 1937; one *s.* (deceased) two *d.*; ed. Winchester and Balliol Coll., Oxford.
Teacher, Westminster School 36-37; Asst. Keeper, British Museum 37-39; Ministry of Economic Warfare 39-41; Foreign Office 41-45; Control Comm., Germany 45-46; Foreign Service 47-71; Berlin 47-49, Yugoslavia 51-53; Dir. of Research and Acting Librarian, Foreign Office 55-57; Chargé d'Affaires, Peking 57-59; Fellow, Center of Int. Affairs, Harvard Univ. 59-60; Asst. Under-Sec. Foreign Office 60-64; Ambassador to Yugoslavia 64-68, to U.S.S.R. 68-71; Master, Corpus Christi Coll., Cambridge 71-.
Leisure interests: music, tennis, golf.
Publ. *Life and Times of Vuk Karadžić* 70.
Corpus Christi College, Cambridge, England.

Wilson, Carroll Louis, S.B.; American scientist; b. 21 Sept. 1910, Rochester, N.Y.; *s.* of Louis Edna Wilson; *m.* Mary Bischoff 1937; one *s.* three *d.*; ed. Rochester, N.Y., and Mass. Inst. of Technology.
Assistant to Pres., Mass. Inst. of Technology 32-37; mem. Nat. Defense Research Cttee., Mission to Great Britain 41; Man. Instnl. Div., Research Corpn. of N.Y. 37-43; Senior Liaison Officer 40-42; Exec. Asst. to the Dir., Office of Scientific Research and Development, Washington, D.C. 42-46; Sec. Board of Consultants Dept. of State on Int. Control of Atomic Energy 46; Vice-Pres. and Dir. Nat. Research Corpn. of Boston 46-47; Gen. Manager U.S. Atomic Energy Comm. 47-50; Dir. Industrial Development Dept. Climax Molybdenum Co. 51-54; Pres. Climax Uranium Co. 51-54; Dir. Millipore Filter Co., Boston; Pres. and Gen. Manager Metals & Controls Corpn., Mass. 56-58; Prof. Mass. Inst. of Technology (M.I.T.) 59-; Dir. Rhode Island Hospital Trust Co.; Trustee Rhode Island Hospital, World Peace Foundation (Boston); mem. Rockefeller Brothers Fund Panel on Int. Security 57-58, Council on Foreign Relations. Dir. 64-; Dir. M.I.T. Fellows in Africa Program 60-, A. D. Little Research Inst., Edinburgh 62-; Chair. OECD Cttee. on Scientific Research 62-; mem. Expert Advisory Cttee. on Science and Development (ECOSOC) 64-, Nat. Acad. of Sciences Int. Marine Science Affairs Panel 67-, Nat. Acad. of Sciences Board on Science and Technology for Int. Devt. 68-; N.A.S. Marine Science Affairs Panel 67-69; Chair. World Peace Foundation, Boston 70-; Chair. of Board, Int. Centre for Insect Physiology and Ecology, Nairobi 70-; Dir. Study of Critical Environmental Problems 70-; Dir. Study of Man's Impact on Climate (Stockholm) 71; Adviser to Sec.-Gen. for UN Conf. on the Human Environment 71-; OECD Cttee. on Scientific Research 62-70; mem. Cttee. for Econ. Devt. Environmental Statement 71; mem. Jury, Environmental Prize, Inst. de la Vie 72; mem. Exec. Cttee. Club of Rome 71-, Trilateral Comm. (N. America, Europe and Japan) 73, Comm. on Critical Choices for Americans 73; Mitsui Prof. in Problems of Contemporary Technology, MIT 74-; Dir. Workshop on Alt. Energy Strategies 74-; mem. Cttee. Alfried Krupp von Bohlen und Halbach Prize for Energy Research 74-(77); Trustee Int. Fed. of Insts. of Advanced Studies (Stockholm) 72, Pilgrim Soc. (U.S.A.) 72; Fellow, American Acad. of Arts and Sciences, American Soc. of Mining and Metallurgical Engineers, Royal Swedish Acad. of Engineering Sciences; Medal for Merit 48; Hon. O.B.E.; Hon. Sc.D. (Williams Coll.).
Leisure interest: Provençal history.
130 Jacob Street, Seekonk, Mass., U.S.A.
Telephone: 617-336-8615.

Wilson, Sir Charles Haynes, Kt., M.A., LL.D., D.C.L., D.LITT.; British university officer; b. 16 May 1909, Glasgow, Scotland; *s.* of George Wilson and Florence Hannay; *m.* Jessie Wilson 1935; one *s.* two *d.*; ed. Glasgow Univ. and Oxford Univ.
Fellow and Tutor in Modern History, Corpus Christi Coll., Oxford 39-52, Junior Proctor 45; Principal, Univ. Coll. of Leicester 52-57; Vice-Chancellor, Univ. of Leicester 57-61; Principal and Vice-Chancellor, Univ. of Glasgow 61-; Hon. Fellow, Corpus Christi Coll., Oxford 63.
The University, Glasgow, G12 8QQ, Scotland.
Telephone: 041-339-8855.

Wilson, Colin Henry; British writer; b. 26 June 1931, Leicester; *s.* of Arthur Wilson and Annetta Jones; *m.* 1st Dorothy Troop 1951, one *s.*; 2nd Pamela Stewart 1960, two *s.* one *d.*; ed. Gateway Secondary Technical School, Leicester.
Laboratory assistant 48-49, civil servant (taxes) 49-50; R.A.F. 50, discharged on medical grounds 50; then navvy, boot and shoe operative, dish washer, plastic moulder; lived Strasbourg 50, Paris 53; later factory hand and dish washer; writer 56-; Writer in Residence, Hollins Coll., Virginia, U.S.A. 66-67; Visiting Prof., Univ. of Washington 67-68, Dowling Coll., Majorca 69, Rutgers Univ., N.J. 74.
Leisure interests: music. mathematics, wine.
Publs. incl. philosophy: *The Outsider* 56, *Religion and the Rebel* 57, *The Age of Defeat* 58, *The Strength to Dream* 61, *Origins of the Sexual Impulse* 63, *Beyond the Outsider* 65, *Introduction to the New Existentialism* 66; other nonfiction: *Encyclopaedia of Murder* 60, *Rasputin and the Fall of the Romanovs* 64, *Brandy of the Damned* (music essays) 65, *Eagle and Earwig* (literary essays) 65, *Sex and the Intelligent Teenager* 66, *Voyage to a Beginning* (autobiography) 68, *Shaw: A Reassessment* 69, *A Casebook of Murder* 69, *Poetry and Mysticism* 70, *The Strange Genius of David Lindsay* (with E. H. Visiak) 70, *The Occult* 71, *New Pathways in Psychology* 72, *Strange Powers* 73, *The Schoolgirl Murder Case* 74, *A Book of Booze* 74, *The Craft of the Novel* 75; novels: *Ritual in the Dark* 60, *Adrift in Soho* 61, *The World of Violence* 63, *Man Without a Shadow* 63, *Necessary Doubt* 64, *The Glass Cage* 66, *The Mind Parasites* 67, *The Philosopher's Stone* 69, *The Killer* 70, *The God of the Labyrinth* 70, *The Black Room* 70, *The Space Vampires* 76; Play: *Strindberg* 70.
Tetherdown, Trewallock Lane, Gorran Haven, Cornwall, England.

Wilson, Donald M.; American journalist and publishing executive; b. 27 June 1925; *m.* Susan M. Neuberger 1957; one *s.* two *d.*; ed. Yale Univ.
Air Corps Navigator, Second World War; magazine assignments in 35 countries 51-61; fmr. Far Eastern Corresp., *Life* magazine, Chief Washington Correspondent 57-61; Dep. Dir. U.S. Information Agency 61-65; Gen. Man. Time-Life Int. 65-68; Assoc. Publisher *Life* magazine 68-69; Vice-Pres. Corporate and Public Affairs, Time Inc. 69-.
Time Inc., Time and Life Building, Rockefeller Center, New York, N.Y. 10020; 4574 Province Line Road, Princeton, N.J. 08540, U.S.A.

Wilson, E(dgar) Bright, PH.D.; American professor of chemistry; b. 18 Dec. 1908, Gallatin, Tenn.; *s.* of E. Bright Wilson and Alma Lackey; *m.* 1st Emily Buckingham 1935, 2nd Therese Bremer 1955; four *s.* two *d.*; ed. Princeton Univ. and Calif. Inst. of Technology.
Teaching Fellow in Chem., Calif. Inst. of Technology 31-33, Fellow 33-34; Jr. Fellow, Harvard Univ. 34-36, Asst. Prof. of Chem. 36-39, Assoc. Prof. 39-46, Prof. 46-47, Theodore William Richards Prof. 47-; Research Dir. Underwater Explosives Research Laboratory, Woods Hole 42-44; Chief Div. 2, Nat. Defense Research

Cttee. 44-46; mem. Weapons System Evaluation Group 52-53; mem. Corp. Oceanographic Inst., Woods Hole; Fulbright Grantee and Guggenheim Fellow, Oxford 49-50; American Chemical Soc. Award in Pure Chem., Debye Award, Norris Award in Teaching of Chem., G. N. Lewis Award, Pauling Award, Rumford Medal.

Publs. *Introduction to Quantum Mechanics, with Applications to Chemistry* (with Linus Pauling) 35, *An Introduction to Scientific Research* 52, *Molecular Vibrations: The Theory of Infra-red and Raman Vibrational Spectra* (with P. C. Cross and J. C. Decius) 55.
12 Oxford Street, Cambridge, Mass. 02138, U.S.A.

Wilson, Edward B.; American advertising executive; b. 15 Aug. 1920, Bronx, N.Y.; s. of George Lovett Wilson, Jr. and Sigrid Ducander; m. Mary Abbot Cregier 1948; one s. three d.; ed. Wesleyan Univ.
First Lieut. U.S.A.F. 42-45; Production Asst., Fibre Conduit Co. 45-46; Advertising Exec., J. Walter Thompson Co. 46-73, Pres. 73-74, Chair. 74-; Dir. Mentholatum Co. 64-, J. Walter Thompson Co. 67-; N. Westchester Speech Center 67-71, Salvation Army (Chicago) 71-73; Trustee, Wesleyan Univ. 74-.
J. Walter Thompson Co., 420 Lexington Avenue, New York, N.Y. 10017; Home: Harbor Drive, Greenwich, Conn. 06830, U.S.A.

Wilson, F. Perry; American chemical engineer; b. 19 Dec. 1914, Manson, N.C.; m. Isabel Agemian; one s. one d.; ed. North Carolina State Univ.
Joined plastics laboratory, Union Carbide, Bloomfield, N.J. 41; worked for Union Carbide Canada Ltd. 49-61, Pres. Plastics Group 54, later Vice-Pres., Exec. Pres. and Dir., Union Carbide Canada Ltd., Toronto; Vice-Pres., fmr. Union Carbide Int. Co., New York 61-63, Exec. Vice-Pres. 63, Pres. 64-66; Corporate Vice-Pres. and Chair., Board of Union Carbide Eastern Inc. 66-67; Group Vice-Pres., responsible for chemicals, plastics and olefins 67-69; Pres. and Dir. Union Carbide Corpn. 69-71, Chair. of Board and Chief Exec. Officer 71-; mem., New York Chamber of Commerce; mem. and Dir., Exec. Cttee., Mfg. Chemists' Asscn., Nat. Export Expansion Council of U.S. Dept. of Commerce and Apawamis Club.
Union Carbide Corporation, 270 Park Avenue, New York, N.Y. 10017, U.S.A.

Wilson, Sir Geoffrey Masterman, K.C.B., C.M.G.; British international civil servant; b. 7 April 1910; ed. Manchester Grammar School, Oriel Coll., Oxford, and Middle Temple.
Practised law as barrister 35-39; served in British Embassy, Moscow and Russian Dept. of Foreign Office 40-45; in H.M. Treasury 47-51, 53-58; Dir. Colombo Plan Technical Co-operation Bureau 51-53; Under-Sec. Overseas Finance Div., H.M. Treasury and mem. Managing Board of European Payments Union 56-58; Financial Attaché, British Embassy, Washington and Alt. Exec. Dir. for U.K., World Bank, Int. Finance Corpn. and Int. Development Asscn. 58-61; Consultant, World Bank Sept.-Dec. 61; Dir. of Operations for South Asia and the Middle East Dec. 61-62; Vice-Pres. World Bank 62-66; Deputy Sec. Ministry of Overseas Devt. 66-68, Perm. Sec. 68-71; Deputy Sec.-Gen., Commonwealth Secretariat 71; Chair. Race Relations Board 71-74.
Race Relations Board, 5 Lower Belgrave Street, London, S.W.1; Home: 34 Sheffield Terrace, London, W.8, England.
Telephone: 01-730-6291 (Office).

Wilson, Georges; French theatre and film director; b. 16 Oct. 1921; ed. Centre d'Art Dramatique, Paris.
Acted in two plays in Grenier-Hussenot Company 47; entered Comédie de l'Ouest 50; entered Théâtre Nat. Populaire (T.N.P.) 52, played important roles in almost all the plays; Dir. *L'Ecole des Femmes, Le Client du*

Matin (Théâtre de l'Oeuvre), *Un Otage* (Théâtre de France), *La Vie de Galilée, Lumières de Bohème, La Folle de Chaillot, Le Diable et le Bon Dieu, Chêne et lapins angora, Les Prodiges* 71, *Turandot* 71; Dir. of Théâtre Nat. Populaire 63-72; Officier de l'Ordre du Mérite Nat., Chevalier de l'Ordre des Arts et Lettres.
Films directed include: *Une aussi longue absence, La jument verte, Le Caïd, Terrain Vague, Lucky Joe, Dragées au Poivre, Chair de Poule, Max et les Ferrailleurs* 70, *Blanche* 71, *Nous sommes tous en liberté provisoire* 73.
Moulin de Vilegris, Clairefontaine-en-Yvelines, 78120 Rambouillet, France.

Wilson, Rt. Hon. Sir (James) Harold, K.G., P.C., O.B.E., M.P., F.R.S.A., F.R.S.; British politician; b. 11 March 1916; s. of James Herbert Wilson and late Ethel Wilson; m. Gladys Mary Baldwin 1940; two s.; ed. Milnsbridge Council School, Royds Hall School, Huddersfield, Wirral Grammar School, Cheshire, and Jesus Coll., Oxford.
Lecturer in Economics, New Coll., Oxford 38; Fellow of Univ. Coll., Oxford and research asst. to Sir William (later Lord) Beveridge 38-39; Economic Asst. to War Cabinet Secretariat 40-41; Mines Dept. (later a part of Ministry of Labour) 41-43; Dir. Economics and Statistics, Ministry of Fuel and Power 43-44; M.P. 45-; Parl. Sec. Ministry of Works 45-47; Sec. for Overseas Trade March-Oct. 47; Pres. of Board of Trade Oct. 47-51 (resigned); mem. Nat. Exec. of Labour Party 52-76 (Chair. 61-62), and of Parl. Cttee. 54-63; Chair. Public Accounts Cttee. of House of Commons 59-63; Leader of Parl. Labour Party 63-76; Prime Minister 64-70; Leader of the Opposition 70-74; Prime Minister 74-76; Chancellor Univ. of Bradford 66-; Pres. Royal Statistical Soc. 72; Freeman, City of London 75; Hon. D.Iur (Bridgeport, U.S.A.) 64; Hon. LL.D. (Lancaster) 64, (Liverpool) 65, (Nottingham) 66; Hon. D.C.L. (Oxford) 65; Hon. D.Tech. (Bradford) 66; D.Univ. (Essex) 67.
Publs. *New Deal for Coal* 45, *In Place of Dollars* 52, *War on Want, The War on World Poverty* 53, *Purpose in Politics* 64, *The Relevance of British Socialism* 64, *The New Britain* (speeches) 64, *Purpose in Power* 66, *The Labour Government 1964-1970* 71.
House of Commons, London, S.W.1, England.

Wilson, John Leonard; Canadian judge; b. 1 Sept. 1900, Scomberg, Ontario; m. Lois Poyntz 1929; two s. one d.; ed. Univ. of Toronto, and Osgoode Hall Law School, Toronto.
Legal Practice, Toronto 26-45; Judge of Supreme Court, Ontario 45-; Pres. High Court of Justice of Cyprus 62-64; Exec. mem. World Asscn. of Judges; Hon. mem. World Peace Through Law Center 66-; Chair. Fed. Electoral Boundaries Comm. for Province of Ontario 72-73.
Leisure interests: colour photography, summer cottage, travel, and a special continuing interest in the development and welfare of Cyprus, World Association of Judges.
Apartment 1105, 9 Deer Park Crescent, Toronto 195, Ont., Canada.
Telephone: 363-4101.

Wilson, John Tuzo, C.C., O.B.E., PH.D., SC.D., LL.D., F.R.S., F.R.S.C.; Canadian geologist; b. 24 Oct. 1908, Ottawa; s. of John Armitstead Wilson, C.B.E., and Henrietta Loetitia (née Tuzo); m. Isabel Jean Dickson 1938; two d.; ed. Ashbury Coll. School, Ottawa, Univs. of Toronto and Cambridge, and Princeton Univ.
Summer field parties 24-35; Asst. Geologist, Geological Survey of Canada 36-39; Field Service and Staff (Col.), Canadian Army 39-46; Prof. of Geophysics, Univ. of Toronto 46-74, Fellow, Massey Coll., Univ. of Toronto 62-, Principal, Erindale Coll., Univ. of Toronto 67-74; Dir.-Gen. Ontario Science Centre 74-; Pres. Int. Union of Geodesy and Geophysics 57-60; Trustee, Nat.

Museums of Canada 67-74; Foreign Assoc., U.S. Nat. Acad. of Sciences; Bucher Medal, American Geophysical Union; Logan Medal, Geological Asscn. of Canada; Penrose Medal, Geological Soc. of America; Carty Medal, U.S. Nat. Acad. of Sciences; Civic Award of Merit, City of Toronto.
Leisure interests: visits to 200 univs. and 100 countries, North Pole to Antarctica, walking, and sailing the Great Lakes in a Hong Kong junk.
Publs. *Physics and Geology* (with J. A. Jacobs and R. D. Russell) 59, 2nd edn. 73, *One Chinese Moon* 59, *IGY: Year of the New Moons* 61, *Continents Adrift* (Editor) 73, *Unglazed China* 73; more than 100 scientific papers.
27 Pricefield Road, Toronto, Ont., M4W 1Z8, Canada.

Wilson, Kendrick R., Jr.; American business executive; b. 2 Jan. 1913; ed. Phillips Exeter Acad., and Dartmouth Coll.
U.S. Trust Co. of New York 36-41; Lehman Bros. 46-50; Vice-Pres. (Finance), Dir. and mem. Exec. Cttee. Avco Mfg. Co., New York City 50-57, Pres. 57-60, Chair. Board and Chief Exec. Officer 61-69, Chair. Board 70-.
Home: Shagbark Road, Wilson Point, South Norwalk, Conn. 06854; Office: Avco Corporation, 1275 King Street, Greenwich, Conn. 06830, U.S.A.

Wilson, Sir (Leslie) Hugh, Kt., O.B.E., R.I.B.A., M.R.T.P.I.; British architect and town planner; b. 1 May 1913, London; s. of Frederick C. Wilson and Ethel A. Hughes; m. Monica Chrysavye Nomico (died 1966) 1938; one s. two d.; ed. Haberdashers' Aske's School.
Assistant Architect in private practice 33-39; Asst. Architect, Canterbury 39-45; City Architect, Planning Officer 45-56; Chief Architect, Planning Officer, Cumbernauld New Town 56-62; Partner, Hugh Wilson and Lewis Womersley 62-.
Leisure interests: travel, music.
26 Charlotte Street, London, W1P 2BQ; Home: 2 Kings Well, Heath Street, Hampstead, London, NW3 1EN, England.
Telephone: 01-580-6095 (Office); 01-435-3637 (Home).

Wilson, Gen. Louis Hugh; American marine corps officer; b. 11 Feb. 1920, Brandon, Miss.; s. of Louis and Bertha (née Buchanon) Wilson; m. Jane Clark 1944; one d.; ed. Millsaps Coll.
Enlisted in Marine Corps Reserve 41, Second Lieut. 41, 9th Marine Regt., San Diego, Guadalcanal, Efate, Bougainville; Capt. 43; participated in assault on Guam 44; Company C.O., Camp Pendleton 44; Detachment Commdr., Washington, D.C. 44-46; Dean, later Asst. Dir. Marine Corps Inst., later ADC to Commanding Gen. of Fleet Marine Force, Pacific; Recruiting Officer, N.Y.; Lieut.-Col. 51; exec. posts at Basic School, Quantico, Va.; C.O., Camp Barrett 51-54; with 1st Marine Div. as Asst. G-3 in Korea 54-55, C.O. in U.S.A. 55-56; Head of Operations Section, G-3 Div. at HQ Marine Corps 56-58; C.O., Test and Training Regt., then of Basic School, Quantico 58-61; Joint Plans Co-ordinator to Deputy Chief of Staff, HQ Marine Corps 62-65; Asst. Chief of Staff, G-3 1st Marine Div., Repub. of Viet-Nam 65; Command, 6th Marine Corps District, Atlanta, Ga. 66; Brig.-Gen. 66; Legislative Asst. to Commdt. of Marine Corps 67-68; Chief of Staff, HQ Fleet Marine Force, Pacific 68-70; Maj.-Gen. 70; Command, 1st Marine Amphibious Force, 3rd Marine Div., Okinawa 70; Deputy for Educ., Dir. of Educ. Centre, Quantico 71-72; Lieut.-Gen. 72; Command, Fleet Marine Force, Pacific 72-75; Commdt. Marine Corps July 75-; Medal of Honor 44, Legion of Merit with Combat V and 2 Gold Stars, Purple Heart with 2 Stars, Cross of Gallantry with Gold Star (Repub. of Viet-Nam) 65, Order of Nat. Security Merit (Repub. of Korea), GUK-SEON Medal, 2nd Class, Commdr., Legion of Honour (Philippines).
United States Marine Corps, Department of the Navy, Washington, D.C. 20380, U.S.A.

Wilson, Olin C., PH.D.; American astronomer; b. 13 Jan. 1909, San Francisco, Calif.; s. of Olin and Sophie Wilson; m. Katherine E. Johnson 1943; one s. one d.; ed. Univ. of Calif. (Berkeley), and Calif. Inst. of Technology.
Assistant, Mount Wilson Observatory 31-36, Asst. Astronomer 36-50, Astronomer, Mount Wilson and Palomar Observatories 50-; mem. Nat. Acad. of Sciences.
Leisure interests: reading, hiking.
Publs. Numerous research papers, chiefly in stellar and nebular spectroscopy.
Office: 813 Santa Barbara Street, Pasadena, Calif. 91101; Home: 1754 Locust Street, Pasadena, Calif. 91106, U.S.A.
Telephone: 577-1122 (Office); 796-6436 (Home).

Wilson, O(wen) Meredith, B.A., PH.D.; American educator; b. 21 Sept. 1909, Colonia Juarez, Chihuahua, Mexico; s. of Guy C. and Melissa Stevens Wilson; m. Marian Wilson 1938; three s. three d.; ed. Brigham Young Univ., and Univ. of California (Berkeley).
Assistant Prof. Brigham Young Univ. 37-42, Univ. of Utah 42-44; Asst. Prof. of History, Univ. of Chicago 44-45; Assoc. Prof. of History, Assoc. Dean of Coll., Univ. of Chicago 45-47; Prof. and Dean of School of Arts and Sciences, Univ. of Utah 47-52; Sec. and Treas., Fund for Advancement of Educ. 52-54; Pres. Univ. of Oregon 54-60, Univ. of Minnesota 60-67; Chair. American Council on Educ. 58-59, mem. Exec. Cttee. 60-61, Chair. Comm. on Plans and Objectives in Higher Educ. 62-65; mem. Exec. Cttee. Carnegie Foundation for Advancement of Teaching 61-, Chair. 65; mem. Board of Dirs. Center for Advanced Study in Behavioral Sciences 61-67, Dir. 67-75 (retd.); mem. Board of Trustees Inst. of Int. Educ. 61, Vice-Chair. 62, Chair. 63-69; mem. Council on Higher Educ. in the American Republics 59-68, Co-Chair. 64-66; Chair. Nat. Advisory Council on Educ. of Disadvantaged Children 65-68; mem. Agency for Int. Devt., Univ. Relations 63-68; mem. U.S. Nat. Comm. for UNESCO 62-64; Marshman S. Wattson Memorial Plaque 62; Assoc. mem. Royaumont Foundation 71; Acad. Fellow, Shimer Coll., Ill. 71; mem. Board of Trustees: Univ. of Notre Dame; mem. Board of Univ. Research Asscn. 67-73; Chair. of the Board and Federal Reserve Agent of the Fed. Reserve Bank of San Francisco 68-; Benjamin Franklin Fellow of the Royal Soc. of Arts 69; mem. American Acad. of Arts and Sciences 71.
Leisure interest: golf.
Publ. (collaborator) *The People Shall Judge* 49.
456 Marlowe Avenue, Palo Alto, Calif. 94301, U.S.A.
Telephone: 415-327-7449.

Wilson, Perry William, M.S., PH.D.; American professor of bacteriology; b. 25 Nov. 1902, Bonanza, Ark.; s. of Commodore Lawson Wilson and Frankie Ellen Smith; m. Helen E. Hansel 1929; one s. one d.; ed. Rose Polytechnic and Univ. of Wisconsin.
Analytical Chemist, Commercial Solvent Corpn. 20-22, Research Chemist 24-25; Asst. Prof. of Bacteriology, Univ. of Wis. 34-38, Assoc. Prof. 38-43, Prof. 43-; with Consultant Fed. Security Agency 43-44; Editor *Bacteriological Reviews* 52-57; Pres. American Soc. for Microbiology 57; Guggenheim Fellow, Cambridge Univ. and Helsinki 36; mem. Nat. Acad. of Sciences; Pasteur Award of Soc. of Illinois Bacteriologists 55.
Leisure interest: gardening.
Publs. *Biochemistry of Symbiotic N-fixation* 40, *Respiratory Enzymes* (Editor) 42, *Bacterial Physiology* (Editor and Author) 51; and review articles and scientific papers on biological nitrogen.
305 Bacteriology, The University of Wisconsin, Madison, Wis. 53706; Home: 3830 Cherokee Drive, Madison, Wis. 53711, U.S.A.
Telephone: 608-262-3052 (Office); 608-233-5516 (Home).

Wilson, Peter Cecil, C.B.E.; British art auctioneer; b. 8 March 1913; ed. Eton Coll., and New Coll., Oxford. Director Sotheby and Co. London 38-, Chair. 58-; Chair. Parke-Bernet, New York 64-.
Garden Lodge, Logan Place, London, W.8, England.
Telephone: 01-373-0373.

Wilson, Ralph Frederick, O.B.E., M.COM., A.C.A.; New Zealand political executive and economist; b. 21 Sept. 1912, Invercargill, New Zealand; s. of F. R. Wilson; m. Lillias Dever 1938; two s. one d.; ed. Otago Boys' High School and Univ. of Otago.
Assistant Sec. Bureau of Industry 38; Private Sec. Minister of Supply and Industries and Commerce 41-47; Sec. N.Z. Board of Trade 50-54; Sec. N.Z. Retailers' Fed. 54-59; Gen. Dir. N.Z. Nat. Party 59-73; economist, M.Y. Walls and Assocs. 73-.
Leisure interests: lawn bowls, golf, wood sculpture.
88 Cecil Road, Wadestown, Wellington; Bowring Burgess Building, Boulcott St., Wellington, New Zealand.
Telephone: 736-171.

Wilson, Richard Lawson; American journalist; b. 3 Sept. 1905, Galesburg, Ill.; s. of Frank and Emily Wilson; m. Katherine Young Macy 1928; two d.; ed. Iowa State Coll., and State Univ.
Reporter, *Register*, Des Moines 26-29, *St. Louis Globe-Democrat* 29-30; City Editor *Register*, Des Moines 30-33, Washington D.C. Corresp. *Des Moines Register and Tribune* 33-; Washington Corresp. *Minneapolis Star and Tribune* 38-43; Chief Washington Bureau, Cowles Publications, including *Look* Magazine 38-70; Pres. National Press Club 40; Pres. Nat. Press Building Corpn. 62-72; Pulitzer Prize (for Distinguished Reporting of Nat. Affairs) 54; Headliner Award for Magazine Reporting 54; Special Citation Raymond Clapper Award 58; Centennial Award Iowa State Coll. 58; author of commentary for *Setting the Course*, the major policy statements of Pres. Nixon's first year 70 and of second volume, *A New Road for America* 72; Golden Plate Award, American Acad. of Achievement; Hon. LL.D. (Drake Univ.) 56; Hon. D.Litt. (Iowa Wesleyan Coll.).
Home: 2918 Garfield Street, N.W., Washington, D.C. 20008; Office: 952 National Press Building, Washington, D.C. 20004, U.S.A.
Telephone: 347-9111 (Office).

Wilson, Robert Rathbun, PH.D.; American professor of physics; b. 4 March 1914, Frontier, Wyo.; m. Jane Inez Scheyer 1940; three s.; ed. Univ. of Calif. at Berkeley.
Instructor, then Asst. Prof. and Head of Isotron Devt. Project, Princeton Univ. 40-43; Leader Cyclotron Group, then Head of Experimental Research Div., Manhattan Project, Los Alamos, N.M. 43-46; Assoc. Prof. of Physics Harvard Univ. 46-47; Dir. Fermi Nat. Accelerator Laboratory, Batavia, Ill. and Prof. of Physics Univ. of Chicago 67-; mem., Fed. of American Scientists (first Chair.), Nat. Acad. of Sciences, American Physical Soc., A.A.A.S.; Elliot Cresson Medal 64, Nat. Medal of Science 73.
Fermi National Accelerator Laboratory, P.O. Box 500, Batavia, Ill. 60510, U.S.A.

Wilson, Rt. Rev. Sir Roger Plumpton, K.C.V.O., M.A., D.D.; British ecclesiastic; b. 3 Aug. 1905, Manchester; s. of Canon Clifford Plumpton and Hester Marion (Wansey) Wilson; m. Mabel Joyce Avery 1935; two s. one d.; ed. Winchester Coll., and Keble Coll., Oxford.
Classical Master Shrewsbury School 28-30 and 32-34, St. Andrew's, Grahamstown, S. Africa 30-32; ordained Deacon 35; Curate St. Paul's, Liverpool 35-38; Curate St. John's, Westminster 38-39; Vicar of South Shore, Blackpool 39-45, Radcliffe-on-Trent, Notts. 45-49; Archdeacon of Nottingham 45-49; Bishop of Wakefield 49-58; Bishop of Chichester 58-74; Clerk of the Closet 63-75; mem. of Praesidium of the Conf. of European Churches 67-74.
Kingsett, Wrington, Bristol, BS18 7NH, England.

Wilson, Sir Roland, K.B.E., D.PHIL., PH.D.; Australian economist and company director; b. 7 April 1904, Ulverstone, Tasmania; s. of Thomas and Mabel (née Inglis) Wilson; m. 1st Valeska Thompson 1930 (died 1971), 2nd Joyce Clarice Chivers 1975; ed. Univs. of Tasmania, Oxford and Chicago.
Lecturer in Economics Tasmania Univ. 30-32; Economist in Commonwealth Statistician's Office 32-35; Commonwealth Statistician and Econ. Adviser to Treasury 36-40 and 46-51; Sec. Commonwealth Dept. of Labour and Nat. Service 41-46; Chair. UN Economic and Employment Comm. 48-51; Sec. to the Treasury 51-66; Dir. Qantas-Wentworth Hotel, M.L.C. Assurance Co. Ltd.; Pres. Australia-Mexico Asscn.; Hon. Fellow, The Acad. of Social Sciences in Australia 72; Hon. LL.D. (Univ. of Tasmania).
Leisure interests: cabinet-making, engineering.
Publ. *Capital Imports and the Terms of Trade* 31.
64 Empire Circuit, Forrest, Canberra, A.C.T. 2603, Australia.
Telephone: 73-1848.

Wilson, Stanley John, F.C.I.S.; South African oil company executive; b. 23 Oct. 1921, Johannesburg; s. of Joseph Wilson and Jessie Cormack; m. Molly Ann Clarkson 1952; two step s.; ed. King Edward VII School, Johannesburg, Witwatersrand Univ.
Posts held 45-73: Chartered Accountant, Savory & Dickinson; Sec. and Sales Man., Rhodesian Timber Holdings; Chair. and Chief Exec. for S. Africa, Vacuum Oil Co.; Regional Vice-Pres. for S. and E. Africa, Mobil Petroleum; Pres. Mobil Sekiyu; Pres. Mobil Europe Inc.; Pres. Mobil East Inc. 73-75; Man. Dir. The Burmah Oil Co. Ltd. 75-; Assoc., Inst. of Cost and Works Accountants, Soc. of Incorporated Accountants and Auditors; Wallace Memorial Prize, England.
Leisure interests: golf, shooting, fishing.
Burmah House, Pipers Way, Swindon, Wilts., SN3 1RE; Home: Leigh Hill, Savernake, near Marlborough, Wilts., SN3 8BH, England.
Telephone: Swindon 30151 (Office); Burbage 230 (Home).

Wilson, T(hornton Arnold), M.SC.; American aircraft company executive; b. 8 Feb. 1921, Sikeston, Mo.; m. Grace Miller; three c.; ed. Iowa State Coll. and Calif. Inst. of Technology.
Draughtsman on military transport version of B-29, The Boeing Co. 43; worked on B-47 bomber programme, then became Project Engineer for B-52; Leader of Boeing's contribution to Int. Continental Ballistic Missile Program 60; Vice-Pres. and Head of Corporate H.Q.'s Operations and Planning 64, Exec. Vice-Pres. 66, Pres. and Chief Exec. Officer April 69-72, Chair. of Board, Chief Exec. Officer Sept. 72-; Sloan Fellow Mass. Inst. of Technology 52; mem. Corpn. of Mass. Inst. of Technology, Board of Govs. of Iowa State Univ., Board of Dirs. of Seattle-First Nat. Bank; Fellow American Inst. of Aeronautics and Astronautics.
Leisure interests: Shoot pool, bee-keeping, swimming.
The Boeing Company, P.O. Box 3707, Seattle, Wash. 98124, U.S.A.
Telephone: 206-655-6707.

Wilson, William Douglas, B.A., LL.B.; South African lawyer and business executive; b. 13 July 1915; m. Beatrice Helen Buchanan 1947; one s. two d.; ed. St. John's Coll., Johannesburg, Michaelhouse, Balgowan, Cambridge Univ.
Called to the Bar (Middle Temple), London; Advocate, Supreme Court of S. Africa 38; served World War II, Air Liaison Officer S.A. Air Force and Eighth Army, Kenya, Abyssinia, Western Desert, joined Sixth S.A.

Div. and later seconded to British Army, Yugoslavia with rank of Lieut.-Col.; practised at the S. African Bar 45-46; joined Anglo American Corpn. 46, Dir. 54-57, Man. Dir. Free State Mines 57-65; Man. Dir. Charter Consolidated 56-58; Joint Deputy Chair. Anglo American Corpn. of S.A. Ltd. 70-.
Anglo American Corporation of South Africa Ltd., 44 Main Street, Johannesburg, South Africa.

Wilson Smith, Sir Henry, K.C.B., K.B.E.; British business executive; b. 30 Dec. 1904, Newcastle upon Tyne; s. of J. Wilson Smith and Annie (née Davison); m. Molly Dyson 1931; two s.; ed. Royal Grammar School, Newcastle upon Tyne, and Cambridge Univ.
Secretary's Office, Post Office 27-30; Treasury 30; Asst. Private Sec. to Chancellor of Exchequer 32-34, Principal Private Sec. 39-42; Under Sec., Treasury 42-46; Perm. Sec., Ministry of Defence 46-48; Second Sec. Treasury 48-51; Part-time mem. Nat. Coal Board 56-61; Dir. Powell Duffryn Ltd. 51-69, Chair. 57-69; Dir. Guest Keen and Nettlefolds Ltd. 51-72, Deputy Chair. 62-72; Chair. Doxford and Sunderland Shipbuilding and Engineering Co. Ltd. 62-68; Dir. Bank of England 64-70.
Leisure interests: reading and travel.
68 Cotinas Verdes, Bensafrim, Lagos, Algarve, Portugal.

Wilton, Percy Ronald; South African mining engineer and executive; b. 10 Oct. 1917, Durban; m. Glynne Elizabeth Wilton; one s. two d.; ed. Durban High School.
Joined Johannesburg Consolidated Investment Co. Ltd. as apprentice miner, Langlaagte Estates 35, and later became Mine Man., Rustenburg Platinum Mines; Asst. Consulting Eng., Head Office, Johannesburg 57-59, Consulting Eng. 59-62; Man. of Johannesburg Consolidated Investment Co. 62-66, Exec. Dir. March 66-; Chair. of Consolidated Murchison Ltd., Antimony Products (Pty.) Ltd., Di Penta Africa Construction (Pty.) Ltd., Pentacor (Pty.) Ltd., Prospects of Rhodesia (Pty.) Ltd.; Deputy Chair. Rustenburg Platinum Mines Ltd.; Pres. Companhia Moçambicana de Minas S.A.R.L., and Companhia de Minas Angolana S.A.R.L.; Dir. Argus Printing and Publishing Co. Ltd., Rhodesian Mining Investments (Pty.) Ltd. and S. Vaal Holdings Ltd.
Johannesburg Consolidated Investment Co. Ltd., Consolidated Building, corner Fox and Harrison Streets, Johannesburg; 56 Sixth Street, Lower Houghton, Johannesburg, South Africa.

Win Maung, U, B.A.; Burmese politician; b. 1916; ed. Judson Coll., Rangoon.
Joined Burmah Oil Co. after leaving coll.; then entered govt. dept.; joined Army as 2nd Lieut. 40; during Second World War took active part in resistance movement of Anti-Fascist Organization; went to India, where he received training in tactics of military and guerila warfare at Mil. Coll., Calcutta and Mil. Camp, Colombo 44; rejoined guerilla forces in Burma 45; Vice-Pres. Karen Youth Organization and Ed. *Taing Yin Tha* 45; mem. Constituent Assembly 47; Minister for Industry and Labour 47, of Transport and Communications 49; later Minister for Port, Marine, Civil Aviation and Coastal Shipping; mem. Burmese Parl. for Maubin South (Karen) 51-55 and 56-57; Pres. of the Union of Burma, 13th Mar. 57-62; detained after *coup d'état* Mar. 62-Oct. 67.
Rangoon, Burma.

Winckler, Jean-Claude Stéphane, L. en D.; French diplomatist; b. 8 Dec. 1913, Venice, Italy; s. of Henri and Marguérite (née Luigi-Phillip) Winckler; m. Elisabeth Lascelles 1939; five s.; ed. Lycée de Longchamps and Faculté de Droit de Bordeaux.
Entered foreign service 38; posts in Barcelona 38-39, Tunis 39-42, Washington 45-49, Venice 49-50, Rome 50-59; Technical Counsellor, Office of Sec. of State in

charge of Moroccan and Tunisian Affairs 57; First Counsellor, Washington 59-62; Dir. du Cabinet of Sec. of State for Foreign Affairs 62-63; Minister, Berlin 63; Minister-Counsellor and Chargé d'Affaires, Rabat 67-70; Amb. to Denmark 70-72, to Argentina 72-; Croix de Guerre, Officier de la Légion d'Honneur.
French Embassy, 1399 Cerrito, Buenos Aires, Argentina; Home: 35 rue Halle, 75014 Paris, France.

Winckler, Karl von, DR. RER. POL.; German and Austrian businessman; b. 8 Dec. 1912, Stainach (Steiermark); s. of Carl and Johanna (née Stögmüller) von Winckler; m. 1st Gertrud Dangl 1939 (died 1967), one s. one d.; 2nd Ruth Fehling 1968; ed. Univ. of Vienna.
Scientific Asst., Zweckverband Warenhäuser und Einheitspreisgeschäfte, Berlin 37-38; Private Sec. to Graf Nikolaus von Ballestrem, Gleiwitz 38-45; Man. Dir. Österreichische Kontor-G.m.b.H. Graz, Vienna, Salzburg 45-52; Deputy Dir. Buderus'sche Eisenwerke, Wetzlar 52-58, mem. Man. Board 58-, Chair. 67; Chair. Advisory Board Burger Eisenwerke A.G., Burg/ Dillkreis, Edelstahlwerke Buderus A.G., Wetzlar, Hessische Berg- und Hüttenwerke A.G., Wetzlar, Metallhüttenwerke Lübeck G.m.b.H., Lübeck, Omniplast G.m.b.H. & Co. KG, Ehringshausen; Deputy Chair. Tiroler Röhren- und Metallwerke AG, Solbad Hall; official of several other companies; mem. Man. Board, Deutsche Handelskammer in Österreich; Pres. Admin. Board Soc. of Friends and Patrons of Univ. of Giessen; Ehrensenator of Hochschule für Welthandel, Vienna, and of Univ. of Giessen; Companion Teutonic Order; Grosses Goldenes Ehrenzeichen des Landes Steiermark 72; Grand Officer Order of Merit of Sovereign Mil. Order of Malta 72; Commdr. of German Order of Merit 73.
Leisure interests: hunting, classical music.
633 Wetzlar, Am Feldkreuz 14, Federal Republic of Germany.
Telephone: 73-451.

Windelen, Heinrich; German politician and businessman; b. 25 June 1921, Bolkenhain, Silesia (now part of Poland); s. of Engelbert and Anna (née von den Driesch) Windelen; m. Ingeborg Kreutzer 1954; one s. three d.; ed. in Striegau and Univ. of Breslau.
Served in war 41-45; mem. Christian Democratic Union (CDU) 46-; mem. Bundestag 57-; Pres. Deutsche Stiftung für europäische Friedensfragen 66-; Minister for Refugees, Expellees and War Veterans Feb. 69-Oct. 69; Deputy Chair. CDU/CSU Parl. Group 69; Chair. CDU, Westphalia 71; mem. Advisory Council, Westdeutscher Rundfunk 71-.
441 Warendorf, Hermanstrasse 1, Federal Republic of Germany.
Telephone: 02581-3522.

Windeyer, Sir Brian Wellingham, Kt., F.R.C.P., F.R.C.S., F.R.C.R.; British university administrator; b. 7 Feb. 1904, Sydney, Australia; s. of Richard Windeyer, K.C. and Mabel Fuller Windeyer; m. 1st Joyce Ziele Russell 1928, one s. one d.; m. 2nd Elspeth Anne Bowrey 1948, one s. two d.; ed. Sydney Church of England Grammar School and Univ. of Sydney.
Middlesex Hospital and Medical School 31-69; Prof. of Radiology, Univ. of London 42-69, Vice-Chancellor 69-72; Consultant Advisor in Radiotherapy, Min. of Health 48-72; mem. Clinical Research Board 54-62, Chair. 68-72; mem. Medical Research Council 58-62, 68-72; Chair. Radiological Protection Board; Dean, Middx. Hosp. Medical School 54-67; Dean, Faculty of Medicine, Univ. of London 64-68; Chair., Academic Dir. Radiotherapy Dept. Mount Vernon Hospital 45-69; Chair. Inst. of Educ., Univ. of London, Kennedy Inst. of Rheumatism; Skinner Lecturer, Knox Lecturer, Faculty of Radiologists; Pres. Faculty of Radiologists 49-52; mem. Royal Comm. on Medical Educ.; Hon.

F.R.A.C.S., F.R.A.C.R., F.A.C.R.; Hon. D.Sc. (British Columbia, Wales, Cambridge), LL.D. (Glasgow).
Leisure interests: gardening, golf.
Publs. *British Practice in Radiotherapy* (co-editor) 55; articles on cancer and radiotherapy.
Moreton Gap, Thame Park Road, Thame, Oxon., England.
Telephone: Thame 2371 (Home).

Windham, Sir Ralph, Kt., M.A., LL.B.; British judge; b. 25 March 1905, Wawne, E. Yorks.; s. of Ashe Windham and Cora Middleton; m. Kathleen Fitz-Herbert 1946; two s. two d.; ed. Wellington Coll., Berks., and Trinity Coll., Cambridge.
Called to Lincoln's Inn Bar 30; Legal Draftsman, Palestine 35, District Court Judge 42; Puisne Judge, Supreme Court, Ceylon 47, Kenya 50; Chief Justice, Zanzibar 55-59; Judge of Court of Appeal for Eastern Africa 59-60; Chief Justice, Tanganyika 60-64, of Tanzania 64-65; Commr. on Foreign Compensation Comm. 65-, Vice-Chair. 69-72, Chair. 72.
Leisure interests: music, genealogy, tennis.
Moreton House, Moreton, Ongar, Essex, England.
Telephone: Moreton 222.

Windle, William F., B.S., M.S., PH.D., SC.D.; American anatomist and neurologist; b. 10 Oct. 1898, Huntingdon, Ind.; m. Ella Howell 1923; one s. one d.; ed. Denison Univ., Northwestern Univ., Medical and Graduate Schools.
Instructor, later Asst. and Assoc. Prof. of Anatomy, Northwestern Univ. 23-35; Prof. of Microscopic Anatomy, Northwestern Univ. Medical School 35-42; Prof. of Neurology and Dir. Inst. of Neurology 42-46; Prof. of Anatomy and Chair. of Dept., Univ. of Washington (Seattle) 46-47, Univ. of Pa. 47-51; Scientific Dir. Baxter Laboratories, Morton Grove (Ill.) 51-54; Chief, Neuroanatomical Sciences Laboratory, Nat. Inst. of Neurological Diseases and Blindness (Nat. Insts. of Health) 54-60, Asst. Dir. 60-61; Chief, Laboratory of Perinatal Physiology (Nat. Insts. of Health) San Juan, Puerto Rico 61-64; Hon. Prof. Anatomy, Univ. of Puerto Rico 62-64; Research Prof. and Dir. of Research, Inst. of Physical and Medical Rehabilitation, N.Y. Univ. Medical Center 64-71; research prof. Denison Univ., Granville 71-; Hon. mem. Faculty of Medicine, Univ. of Chile; *Symposia in Neuroanatomical Sciences* 54-64; Editor-in-Chief *Experimental Neurology* 59-; mem. Harvey Soc.; War—Navy Award 44, Sesquicentennial Medal, Univ. of Louisville 48, Max Weinstein Award 57, Albert Lasker Basic Medical Science Award 68.
Publs. *An Outline and Laboratory Guide to Neurology* 39, *Physiology of the Fetus* 40, *Textbook of Histology* 1st edn. 49, 2nd 53, 3rd 60, *Asphyxia* 50.
229 Cherry Street, Granville, Ohio 43023, U.S.A.

Windlesham, 3rd Baron; **David James George Hennessy,** P.C.; b. 28 Jan. 1932; s. of 2nd Baron Windlesham and Angela Mary (Duggan); m. Prudence Glynn 1965; one s. one d.; ed. Ampleforth, Trinity Coll., Oxford.
Chairman of Bow Group 59-60, 62-63; mem. Westminster City Council 58-62; Dir. Rediffusion Television 65-67; Man. Dir. Grampian Television 67-70; Minister of State Home Office 70-72; Minister of State Northern Ireland 72-73; Lord Privy Seal, Leader House of Lords 73-74; Opposition Leader, House of Lords March-Oct. 74; Joint Man. Dir. ATV Network 74-75, Man. Dir. 75-.
Publs. *Communication and Political Power* 66, *Politics in Practice* 75.
House of Lords, London, S.W.1, England.

Wingate, Henry Smith, B.A.; American mining executive; b. 8 Oct. 1905, Talas, Turkey; s. of Henry and Jane Wingate; m. Ardis Swenson 1929; two s.; ed. Carleton Coll., and Univ. of Michigan.

Associate, Sullivan and Cromwell 29-35; Asst. Sec. The Int. Nickel Co. Inc. 35-39; Sec. The Int. Nickel Co. of Canada Ltd. 39-52, Dir. 42-; Vice-Pres. 49-52; Pres. The Int. Nickel Co. of Canada Ltd., The Int. Nickel Co. Inc. 54-60, Chair. 60-72, Dir. and Chair. Advisory Cttee. 72-; Dir. of numerous companies and orgs. including: Canadian Pacific Ltd., J. P. Morgan & Co. Inc., Morgan Guaranty Trust Co. of New York, U.S. Steel Corpn., American Standard Inc., The People's Symphony Concerts N.Y., American Friends of Canada; Trustee, Seaman's Bank for Savings, N.Y.; mem. The Canadian-American Cttee. of the Nat. Planning Asscn. Washington, the Private Planning Asscn. of Canada (now C. D. Howe Research Inst.), Canadian Inst. of Mining and Metallurgy, Mining and Metallurgical Soc. of America; mem. Council on Foreign Relations; mem. and Trustee, U.S. Steel Foundation Inc.; Senior mem. The Conference Board; several Hon. LL.D. and L.H.D.
Leisure interest: genealogy.
Office: 1 New York Plaza, New York, N.Y. 10004; Home: 520 E. 86th Street, New York, N.Y. 10028, U.S.A.

Wingfield Digby, George; British author; b. 2 March 1911, Sherborne, Dorset; s. of F. J. B. Wingfield Digby and Gwendolen Hamilton Fletcher; m. Cornelia Keitler 1935; one s. (deceased); ed. Harrow, Trinity Coll., Cambridge, and Univs. of Grenoble and Paris.
Keeper, Dept. of Textiles, Victoria and Albert Museum 47-72, Keeper Emer. 72-73 (retd.).
Leisure interests: oriental porcelain, studio pottery.
Publs. *Work of the Modern Potter in England* 52, *Meaning and Symbol in Three Modern Artists* 55, *Symbol and Image in William Blake* 57, *Elizabethan Embroidery* 63, *The Devonshire Hunting Tapestries* (with Wendy Hefford) 72, *Tapestries Medieval and Renaissance* (Victoria and Albert Museum collections); joint author *History of the West Indian Peoples* (4 vols. for schools) 51-56, *The Bayeux Tapestry* 57.
72 Palace Gardens Terrace, London, W.8, England.

Winkler, Paul; French (b. Hungarian) newspaper executive; b. 7 July 1898; ed. Lycée Luthérien, and Univ. of Budapest.
Director-General *Lectures pour tous*; Dir. Opera Mundi press agency 28, Pres., Dir.-Gen. 58-; Pres. Press Alliance 40-45; Political Columnist *Washington Post* 43-45, with 1st Army 44-45; Founder *Société Edi-Monde* with Librairie Hachette 47; Founder Union of Press Syndicates, Pres. 35-39; Chair. Advertising Cttee., Int. Fed. of the Periodical Press 67-69; Vice-Pres. Fédération des associations d'éditeurs de périodiques de la Communauté économique européenne 74-; Chevalier Légion d'Honneur.
Publs. *The Thousand Year Conspiracy* 43, *Paris-Underground* 43, *Allemagne secrète* 46, *Les Sources mystiques des concepts moraux de l'Occident* 57.
100 avenue Raymond-Poincaré, 75116 Paris; 23 avenue Foch, 75116 Paris; Domaine du Pré, 77770 Chartrettes, France.

Winkler, Wilhelm, DR. JUR.; Austrian statistician and demographer; b. 29 June 1884, Prague; s. of Anna and Julius Winkler; m. 1st Clara Deutsch 1918 (died 1956), 2nd Franziska Hacker 1958; three s. one d.; ed. German Branch of Karl Ferdinands Univ., Prague.
Lecturer in Statistics, Univ. of Vienna 23; founder and fmr. Dir. Statistical Inst. of Univ. of Vienna; Chief Population Division, Bundesamt für Statistik 25-38; Extraordinary Prof. 29; Prof. 47-55, Emeritus 55-; Dean Faculty of Law and Social Sciences 50-51; Hon. Prof. Hochschule für Welthandel 48-; was retired from his professorship by the Nazi regime 38-45; Founder, Hon. Chair. Österreichische Statistische Gesellschaft; fmr. Vice-Pres. Int. Union for the Scientific Study of Population; Editor *Statistische Vierteljahresschrift* 48-58; Co-

Founder *Metrika*; organizer of Int. Demographic Congress, Vienna 59; Hon. mem. Int. Statistical Inst. and British, German, Hungarian, Mexican Statistical Socs.; mem. Austrian Acad. of Sciences, Hon. Dr. Oec. Publ. Munich Univ. 59, Hon. Dr.rer.Pol., Vienna Univ. 66; Österreichisches Ehrenkreuz für Wissenschaft und Kunst (1st Class); Offizierskreuz des Österreichischen Verdienstordens.

Leisure interests: chamber music, chess, ping-pong, theatre and films, reading, gardening.

Publs. *Statistische Verhältniszahlen* 23, *Die Einkommensverschiebungen in Oesterreich während des Weltkrieges* 30, *Statistisches Handbuch der europäischen Nationalitäten* 31, *Grundriss der Statistik* (2 vols.) 31-33, *Der Geburtenrückgang in Oesterreich* 35, *Grundfragen der Oekonometrie* 51, *Typenlehre der Demographie* 52, *International Population Conference* 59 (Co-Editor), *Mehrsprachiges Demographisches Wörterbuch* 60, *Demometrie* 69, *Verteilung der geistigen Anlagen und Leistungen der Menschen.*

Ghelengasse 30, A-1130 Vienna, Austria.
Telephone: 82-77-542.

Winnacker, Karl, DR. ING.; German chemist; b. 21 Sept. 1903, Wuppertal; *s.* of Ernst Winnacker and Martha Wallis; *m.* Gertrud Deitenbeck 1936; two *s.* one *d.*; ed. Brunswick and Darmstadt Technical Univs. Honorary Prof. Frankfurt-am-Main Univ. 53-71; Pres. (Gen. Man.) Hoechst AG until 69, Pres. Advisory Board, Hoechst AG, Hon. Pres. Advisory Board, Wacker-Chemie GmbH, Munich; mem. Advisory Board, Münchener Rückversicherungsges., Dresdner Bank, Frankfurt-am-Main, DEMAG AG, Duisburg, Degussa, Frankfurt (M), etc.; mem. industrial and scientific orgs.; Hon. Pres. Dechema; Dr.rer.Nat. h.c. (Technische Hochschule, Brunswick and Mainz Univ.), Dr.Phil. h.c. (Marburg Univ.).

Publs. *Chemische Technologie* (Co-Editor) 69-75 (7 vols.), *Nie den Mutverlieren* 71, *Challenging Years* 72, *Das unverstandene Wunder* (with K. Wirtz) 75.

Leisure interests: music, aquatic activities.

Hoechst AG, 623 Frankfurt (Main)-80; and Oelmühlweg 31A, 624 Königstein, Federal Republic of Germany.
Telephone: Frankfurt 31-60-60 (Office).

Winneke, Sir Henry Arthur, K.C.M.G., O.B.E., K.ST.J., Q.C.; Australian state governor; b. 29 Oct. 1908, Melbourne; *s.* of Judge Henry Christian Winneke; *m.* Nancy Rae 1933; two *s.*; ed. Ballarat Grammar School, Scotch Coll., Melbourne, Melbourne Univ.
Admitted to Bar 31; war service R.A.A.F. (Group Capt.) 39-46; Solicitor-Gen., Victoria 51-64, Chief Justice of Supreme Court 64-74; Lieut.-Gov. of Victoria 72-74, Gov. 74-.
Leisure interests: golf, tennis, reading.
Government House, Melbourne 3004, Victoria, Australia.
Telephone: 63-9971.

Winner, Michael, M.A.; British film producer and director; b. 1936, London; ed. Cambridge Univ.
Editor and film critic of Cambridge Univ. paper; entered film industry as film critic and columnist for nat. newspapers and magazines 51; wrote, produced and directed many documentary, TV and feature films for the Film Producers Guild, Anglo Amalgamated, United Artists 55-61; Films: *Play It Cool* (Dir.) 62, *The Cool Mikado* (Dir., writer) 62, *West 11* (Dir.) 63, *The System* (Co-producer and Dir.) 63-64, *You Must Be Joking* (original story, Dir.) 64-65, *The Jokers* (Writer, Dir.) 66, *I'll Never Forget What's 'is Name* (Producer, Dir.) 67, *Hannibal Brooks* (Producer, Dir., original story) 68, *The Games* (Dir.) 69, *Lawman* (Producer, Dir.) 70, *The Nightcomers* (Producer, Dir.) 71, *Chato's Land* (Producer, Dir.) 71, *The Mechanic* (Dir.) 72, *Scorpio* (Dir.) 72, *The Stone Killer* (Producer, Dir.) 73,

Death Wish (Dir.) 74, *Won Ton Ton—The Dog Who Saved Hollywood* (Producer, Dir.) 75.
Leisure interest: art.
Scimitar Films Ltd., 6-8 Sackville Street, London, W1X 1DD, England.
Telephone: 01-734-8385.

Winqwist, Carl-Henrik; Swedish lawyer; b. 4 Nov. 1932, Menton, France; *s.* of Folke and Annajo Winqwist; *m.* Caroline Crafoord 1959; two *s.* three *d.*; ed. Sigtunastifelsens Humanistiska Läroverk, and Univ. of Stockholm.
Chairman Swedish Conservative Student Union 59-62; Sec.-Gen. Int. Christian Democratic and Conservative Student Union 62-65; Man. Dir. of an econ. research bureau 62-68; Int. Sec. Conservative Party 65-71; Dir.-Gen. Swedish Moderate Party 68-71; with Skandinaviska Enskilda Banken 71-72; Sec.-Gen. Int. Chamber of Commerce 73-; mem. Royal Comm. of Advertising 66-74.
Leisure interests: classical music, Richard Wagner, cooking, squash.
Publs. *Sweden and Nuclear Missiles* 59, *One Europe* 62.
International Chamber of Commerce, 38 Cours Albert 1er, 75008 Paris; Home: 1 avenue Silvestre de Sacy, 75007 Paris, France.
Telephone: 359-05-92 (Office); 551-70-96 (Home).

Winspeare Guicciardi, Vittorio, M.A.; Italian diplomatist; b. 19 Aug. 1912, Catania; *s.* of Cesare and Francesca (de Malfer) Winspeare Guicciardi; *m.* Adi von Bernd 1948; one *s.* one *d.*; ed. Bocconi Univ., Milan.
Secretary Italian Embassy, London 45-49; mem. Italian Del. Paris Peace Conf. 46-47; First Sec. Italian Embassy, Bonn 51-54; Consul-Gen., Berlin 54-58; Amb. to Ireland 61-66, Czechoslovakia 66-68; Under-Sec.-Gen. UN and Dir.-Gen. UN Office at Geneva July 68-; Personal Rep. of UN Sec.-Gen. on Good Offices Mission, Bahrain 70; Special Rep. of UN Sec.-Gen. in India and Pakistan Dec. 71, Bangladesh Jan.-Feb. 72; Gran Ufficiale Ordine Al Merito della Repubblica Italiana; Hon. C.V.O.; Officier Légion d'Honneur; Commdr. Order of George I (Greece); Verdienstkreuz der Bundesrepublik Deutschland and others.
United Nations, Palais des Nations, 1211 Geneva, Switzerland.

Wint, Arthur Stanley, M.B.E., C.D., F.R.C.S.; Jamaican medical practitioner and diplomatist; b. 25 May 1920, Jamaica; *s.* of Rev. John S. and Hilda Wint (née Smith); *m.* Norma Marsh 1949; three *d.*; ed. Excelsior Coll., Jamaica, St. Bartholomews Hosp., London.
Royal Air Force 44-47; St. Bartholomews Hosp. 47-53; Univ. Hosp. of West Indies 54-57; Altringham Gen. Hosp. 58-63; Jamaican Hospitals 63-73; High Commr. in U.K. (also accred. to Denmark, Italy and Sweden) Jan. 74-.
Leisure interests: swimming, badminton.
Jamaican High Commission, 48 Grosvenor Street, London, W1X 0BJ, England.
Telephone: 01-499-8600.

Winters, Shelley; American actress; b. 18 Aug. 1922, St. Louis, Mo.; ed. Wayne Univ.
Films include: *A Thousand and One Nights, A Place in the Sun, Playgirl, Executive Suite, The Diary of Anne Frank* 58, *Odds Against Tomorrow, Let No Man Write My Epitaph, Lolita* 62, *Wives and Lovers* 63, *The Balcony* 64, *A House is not a Home* 64, *A Patch of Blue, Time of Indifference* 65, *Alfie* 65, *The Moving Target* 65, *Cleopatra Jones* 73, *Blume in Love* 74, *Whoever Slew Auntie Roo* 74, *Heaven Save Us from Our Friends* 75; Stage appearances incl.: *A Hatful of Rain* 55, *Girls of Summer* 57, *The Night of the Iguana, Cages, Who's Afraid of Virginia Woolf?*; Acad. Award for best supporting actress in *The Diary of Anne Frank* 59, Emmy Award for Best Actress 64, Monte Carlo Golden Nymph

Award 64, Int. Television Award, Cannes Festival 65.
c/o International Creative Management, 22 Grafton
Street, London, W.1, England.

Wintour, Charles Vere, M.A., M.B.E.; British journalist; b. 18 May 1917, Wimborne, Dorset; s. of F. Wintour
and Blanche Foster; m. Eleanor Baker 1940; two s.
two d.; ed. Oundle School, and Peterhouse, Cambridge
Univ.
Royal Norfolk Regiment 40, G.S.O. Headquarters,
Chief of Staff to Supreme Allied Commdr. (designate)
and SHAEF (despatches); *Evening Standard* 46, Political Editor 52; Asst. Editor *Sunday Express* 52-54;
Deputy Editor *Evening Standard* 54-57; Man. Editor
Daily Express 57-59; Editor *Evening Standard* 59-,
Chair. Evening Standard Co. 68; Gov. London School
of Econs.; Dir. Beaverbrook Newspapers 64-; Croix de
Guerre 45; Bronze Star (U.S.) 45.
Leisure interests: theatre, travel.
Publ. *Pressures on the Press* 72.
Evening Standard, 47 Shoe Lane, London, E.C.4; 32
Cranfield House, 97 Southampton Row, London,
W.C.1, England.
Telephone: 01-636-1132.

Wirkkala, Tapio; Finnish designer; b. 2 June 1915;
m. Rut Bryk 1945; one s. one d.; ed. Industrial Art
Inst., Helsinki.
Art Director, Industrial Art Inst. 51-54; designed interior, Finnish Pavilion, Brussels World Fair 58;
Smithsonian Inst. Travelling Museum Exhibition in
U.S. 56-58; seven Grande Premios in Triennales; four
prizes for designing Olympic Games stamps 52; Italian
President's Gold Medallion, Int. Ceramic Competition,
Faenza 63, 66, 67, 69; Cultural Foundation of Finland
Hon. Prize 68 and many other awards.
Itäranta 24, Tapiola, Finland.
Telephone: 46-44-14.

Wirowski, Maciej, M.ENG.; Polish engineer and politician; b. 2 March 1929, Katowice; ed. Silesian Technical Univ., Gliwice.
Assistant and Senior Asst., Dept. of Inorganic Chemistry, Silesian Technical Univ.; worked in Factory of
Chemical Reagents, Gliwice 55-60; Technical Dir. Inst.
of Inorganic Chemistry, Gliwice 60-63; Vice-Dir., later
Dept. Dir., Ministry of Chemical Industry 63-69;
Under-Sec. of State 69-71; Vice-Chair. Planning Comm.
attached to Council of Ministers 71-Nov. 74; Minister of
Chemical Industry Nov. 74-; Chair. Asscn. of Chemical
Industry Engineers and Technicians April 72-; mem.
Polish United Workers' Party; Order of Banner of
Labour, 2nd Class and others.
Ministerstwo Przemysłu Chemicznego, ul. Wspólna 4,
00-505 Warsaw, Poland.
Telephone: 28 01-82.

Wirtz, William Willard, A.B., LL.B.; American lawyer
and government official; b. 14 March 1912; ed. Univ. of
California (Berkeley), Beloit Coll., and Harvard Law
School.
Teacher 33-39; Assistant Prof. School of Law, Northwestern Univ. 39-42; Asst. Gen. Counsel, Board of
Econ. Warfare 42-43; served War Labor Board 43-45;
Chair. Nat. Wage Stabilization Board 46; Prof. of Law,
Northwestern Univ. 46-54; law practice 55-61; Under-
Sec. of Labor 61-62, Sec. of Labor 62-69; now Partner,
Wirtz and Gentry; Trustee, Penn Cen. 70; Hon. degrees
from Michigan, Rhode Island, Northwestern, Yeshiva,
and Roosevelt Univs. and Amherst, Monmouth Colls.;
Democrat.
5009 39th Street, N.W., Washington, D.C. 20016,
U.S.A.

Wischnewski, Hans-Jürgen; German politician;
b. 24 July 1922.
Served German Forces 40-45; worked in metal industry
after war; mem. Social Democrat Party 46- (Exec. Sec.

68-72); Sec. Metal Workers' Union, Cologne 52; mem.
Bundestag 57-; Chair. Young Socialists 60; Fed.
Minister for Econ. Co-operation 66-68; Chair. Stiftung
für Entwicklungsländer (Foundation for the Developing Countries) 70-72; Minister of State in Federal
Foreign Office 74-.
Am Kappellenbusch 2, 5042 Erftstadt-Liblar, Federal
Republic of Germany.

Wise, George Schneiweis; American (b. Russian)
university professor; b. 1906; ed. Columbia Univ.
Former lecturer in Sociology at Columbia Univ. and
Univ. of Mexico; business interests in U.S.A., Mexico
and Israel; Pres. Tel Aviv Univ. 63-71, Chancellor
Oct. 71-.
Tel Aviv University, Ramat Aviv, Tel Aviv, Israel.

Wise, Robert Earl; American film producer and
director; b. 10 Sept. 1914, Winchester, Ind.; s. of Earl
W. Wise and Olive Longenecker; m. Patricia Doyle
1942; one s.; ed. Franklin Coll., Ind.
Joined RKO 33, apprentice sound effects cutter, then
Asst. Editor and later Film Editor; films edited include
Citizen Kane and *The Magnificent Ambersons*; Film
Dir. 43-, directed and produced thirty-five films; Vice-
Pres. The Filmakers Group; mem. Board of Govs.,
Acad. of Motion Picture Arts and Sciences; Pres. Dirs.
Guild of America; mem. Nat. Council on the Arts; four
Acad. Awards (Best Film and Best Dir. *West Side Story*
and *The Sound of Music*), and Irving Thalberg Award,
Acad. of Motion Picture Arts and Sciences.
Films include *Curse of the Cat People* 44, *The Body
Snatcher* 45, *The Set Up* 49, *The Day the Earth Stood
Still* 51, *The Desert Rats* 53, *Executive Suite* 54, *Helen of
Troy* 55, *Tribute to a Bad Man* 56, *Somebody Up There
Likes Me* 56, *Until They Sail* 57, *Run Silent, Run Deep*
58, *I Want to Live* 58, *Odds Against Tomorrow* 59, *West
Side Story* 61, *Two for the Seesaw* 62, *The Haunting* 63,
The Sound of Music 65, *The Sand Pebbles* 66, *Star!* 68,
The Andromeda Strain 71, *Two People* 73, *The Hindenberg* 75.
c/o The Filmakers Group, 1436 North Beachwood
Drive, Hollywood, Calif. 90028, U.S.A.

Wiseman, Gen. Clarence D.; Canadian Salvation Army
leader; b. 19 June 1907, Moreton's Harbour, Newfoundland; m. Janet Kelly 1932; one s. one d.; ed.
Salvation Army Training Coll.
In command, Salvation Army centres in Canada; served
overseas as Chaplain, Canadian Forces, in World War
II, after 3 years directed all Salvation Army Welfare
Services on various fighting fronts; admin. posts in
Salvation Army in Canada 45-60, directed operations
in Kenya, Tanzania and Uganda 60-62; Principal,
Salvation Army William Booth Memorial Training
Coll., London 62-67; Head of Salvation Army work in
Canada 67-74; Gen. (Int. Leader) of the Salvation Army
May 74-; Hon. LL.D. (Newfoundland Memorial Univ.).
Salvation Army International Headquarters, 101
Queen Victoria Street, London, EC4P 4EP, England.

Wiser, Forwood C., Jr., M.B.A.; American airline
executive; b. 24 June 1921, Chester, Pa.; m. Martha
Bergey; one s. one d.; ed. Lehigh Univ., U.S. Naval
Acad. and Harvard Business School.
Naval Officer 44-49; Asst. to Vice-Pres. Container
Corpn. of America 51; Vice-Pres. Pittsburgh Standard
Conduit Co. 54-57; Asst. Vice-Pres. of Operations,
American Airlines 57-58, Vice-Pres. of Operations
58-59, 64-66, Vice-Pres. of Technical Services 59-64;
Pres., then Pres. and Chief Exec. Officer, Northeast
Airlines 66-68; Dir. and Exec. Vice-Pres. Trans World
Airlines (TWA) Oct. 68, Pres. and Chief Operating
Officer 69-75; Pres. Pan American Airlines Jan. 76-;
Trustee, U.S. Naval Acad. Foundation; mem. Fund
Council of Harvard Business School.
The Pan Am Building, New York, N.Y. 10017, U.S.A.

Wiśniewski, Włodzimierz, DR.ECON.SC.; Polish economist; b. 19 Jan. 1926, Warsaw; *s.* of Kazimierz and Aurelia Wiśniewski; *m.* Henryka Wiśniewski 1947; one *s.* one *d.*; ed. Acad. of Marine Trade, Gdynia and Gdańsk Univ.

Worked for Marine Agency and Polish Ocean Lines; later for Polish Marine Mission, London, Chief 60-63; Dir. Gdynia-America Lines, London 62-64; Dir., Western Dept., Foreign Trade Ministry 64-68; Commercial Adviser Polish Embassy, London 68-73; Under-Sec. of State, Ministry of Foreign Trade 73-74; Pres. Polish Chamber of Foreign Trade 74-; mem. Polish United Workers' Party.

Leisure interests: gardening, fishing.

Polska Izba Handlu Zagranicznego, ul. Trębacka 4, 00-074 Warsaw 1, Poland.

Telephone: 26-01-43.

Wistrand, Karl, B.C.L.; Swedish politician; b. 9 April 1889, Karlskoga; *s.* of Knut Wistrand and Louise Strokirk; *m.* Louise Follin 1936 (died 1954); ed. Uppsala Univ.

Former Judge; mem. Stockholm County Council 31-37; mem. L.N. Sub-Cttee. for Iron and Steel Statistics 34-36; Man. Dir. Employers' Asscns. of Iron and Steel and Mining Industries 20-36; Sec. Iron Works Commercial Asscn. 20-38; Del. to many Int. Labour Confs. and L.N. Assembly 38; mem., Labour Court 29-49, 1st Chamber 37-53; Pres. Board State Hosps. in Stockholm 41-59; mem. State Cttee. on Admin. Control 42-53, Vice-Pres. 50-53; Pres. State Cttee. on Nat. Expenditure 45; mem. Cttee. for the Univs. 45-50; Pres. of the Swedish Council of the European Movement 49-61, Hon. Pres. 65-; mem. Consultative Ass. Council of Europe 49-59; Chair. Museum of Medical History 52-62; Comm. for non-represented Countries 53-59; Chair. Soc. Belgo-Suédoise 56-61; mem. W. European Advisory Cttee. 54-66, Royal Science Asscn. (Uppsala); Dr. med. h.c.; Commdr. First Class Order of Vasa, Grand Officier l'Ordre Belge Léopold II, Commdr. Légion d'Honneur and other decorations.

Leisure interest: history.

Publ. *Hört och Upplevat* (memoirs) 62.

Karlbergsvägen 40, Stockholm, Sweden.

Telephone: 08-326563.

Withers, Reginald Grieve, LL.B.; Australian politician; b. 26 Oct. 1924, Bunbury, W.A.; *s.* of late F. J. Withers; *m.* Shirley Lloyd-Jones 1953; two *s.* one *d.*; ed. Bunbury and Univ. of Western Australia.

Served in Royal Australian Navy 42-46; mem. Bunbury Municipal Council 54-56, Bunbury Diocesan Council 58-59, Treas. 61-68; State Vice-Pres., Liberal and Country League of W.A. 58-61, State Pres. 61-65; mem. Fed. Exec. of Liberal Party 61-65, Fed. Vice-Pres. 62-65; mem. Senate for W.A. Feb.-Nov. 66, Nov. 67-, Govt. Whip in Senate 69-71, Leader of Opposition in Senate 72-75; Special Minister of State, Minister for A.C.T., Minister for the Media and Minister for Tourism and Recreation Nov.-Dec. 75, Leader of Govt. in Senate and Minister for Admin. Services Dec. 75-; fmr. Chair. Joint Cttee. on A.C.T., Select Cttee. on Foreign Ownership and Control of Australian Resources, Senate Standing Cttee. on Constitutional and Legal Affairs; mem. del. to Conf. of Commonwealth Parl. Asscn., Trinidad 69.

Leisure interests: swimming, reading, painting.

Parliament House, Canberra, A.C.T. 2600; and Australian Parliament Offices, Hamersley House, 191 St. George's Terrace, Perth, W.A. 6000, Australia.

Telephone: 72-6650 (Canberra); 222-991 (Perth).

Witkon, Alfred, DR.JUR.; Israeli judge; b. 23 Feb. 1910, Berlin, Germany; *m.* Greta Philipsohn 1936; ed. Univs. of Bonn, Berlin and Freiburg, and Middle Temple, London.

Called to Middle Temple Bar 36, to Palestine Bar 37; practised law, Palestine 37-48; Pres. District Court, Jerusalem 48-54; Justice Supreme Court of Israel 54-; Lecturer, Hebrew Univ. 53-69.

Publs. *Law and Society* 55, *Law and Politics* 65, *Law of Taxation* 66.

17 Shmarjahu Levin Street, Jerusalem, Israel.

Telephone: 412687.

Witkop, Bernhard, PH.D., SC.D.; American chemist; b. 9 May 1917, Freiburg (Baden), Germany; *s.* of Prof. Philipp W. Witkop and Hedwig M. Hirschhorn; *m.* Marlene Prinz 1945; one *s.* two *d.*; ed. Univ. of Munich.

Dozent Univ. of Munich 46; Matthew T. Mellon Fellow Harvard Univ., U.S. 47; Instructor and Lecturer 48-50; Special Fellow U.S. Public Health Service 50-53; Research Fellow Nat. Heart Inst. 50; Special Fellow, Nat. Inst. of Arthritis and Metabolic Diseases, Nat. Insts. of Health 52, Chief of Section on Metabolites 55, Chief of Lab. of Chemistry, Nat. Inst. of Arthritis, Metabolic and Digestive Diseases 57-; Visiting Prof., Kyoto Univ. 61, Univ. of Freiburg 62; mem. Nat. Acad. of Sciences; mem. Acad. Leopoldina-Carolina 72; Hillebrand Award of American Chemical Soc. 59; Paul Karrer Medallist; Lecturer, Univ. of Zurich 72-.

Leisure interests: languages, etymology, literature, piano, chamber music, hiking, skating, mountaineering.

Publs. *Mushroom Poisons* 40, *Curare Arrow Poisons* 42, *Yohimbine* 43, *Kynurenine* 44, *Indole Alkaloids* 47-50, *Oxidation Mechanisms, Ozonization, Peroxides* 52, *Hydroxyaminoacids, Metabolites, Building Stones and Biosynthesis of Collagen* 55, *Mescalin and LSD Metabolism* 58, *Pharmacodynamic Amines* 60, *Nonenzymatic Cleavage and Modification of Enzymes* 61, *Gramicidin A* 64, *Rufomycin* 64, *Photo-Reductions, -Additions, -Cyclizations* 66, *Microsomal Hydroxylations, Arenoxide Metabolites, "NIH-Shift"* 67, *Amphibian Venoms, Batrachotoxin, Pumiliotoxin* 68, *Norepinephrine Release, Inactivation, False transmitters* 68, *Histrionicotoxin, a selective inhibitor of cholinergic receptors* 70-72, *Interaction of Polynucleotides Stimulators of Interferon* 73-74.

National Institute of Arthritis, Metabolic and Digestive Diseases, National Institutes of Health, Bethesda, Md. 20014; Home: 3807 Montrose Driveway, Chevy Chase, Md. 20015, U.S.A.

Telephone: (301) 496-5455.

Witkowski, Józef, PH.D., D.SC.; Polish astronomer; b. 21 Feb. 1892, Odessa, Russia; *s.* of Józef and Anna (Targoni) Witkowisk; *m.* 1st Sophia Reutt, PH.D., 1920 (died 1938), 2nd Aline Lauber 1950; one *s.* one *d.*; ed. Odessa Univ.

Assistant, Odessa Observatory 18 and Cracow Observatory 19-27; Dir. Poznań Observatory 29-39, 45-63; Prof. of Astronomy Poznań Univ. 29-67, Prof. emer. 67-; Visiting Prof. Univ. of Algiers 65-66; fmr. Dean, Faculty of Sciences; fmr. Dir. Astronomical Inst. and Latitude Recording Station, Acad. of Sciences; Hon. Editor *Acta Astronomica*; Editor *Bulletin de la Société des Sciences de Poznań*; fmr. Pres. Polish Nat. Cttee. Geodesy and Geophysics; mem. Int. Astronomical Union; mem. Astronomical and Geodetic Cttee., Polish Acad. of Sciences; F.R.A.S. (U.K.); Commdr. Cross with Star of Order Polonia Restituta 73, and other decorations.

Leisure interest: classical literature.

Publs. Over 150 on astronomy, geodetical astronomy, gravimetry, cosmology, earth tides, history of astronomy.

Ulica Słoneczna 36, Poznań, Poland.

Telephone: Poznań 660209.

Witte, Peter Cornelis, LL.M.; Netherlands diplomatist and international official; b. 19 May 1916, Texel; *s.* of Cornelis Albertus Witte and Euphemia Catherina de Haan; *m.* Adolphine de Moor 1946; one *s.* two *d.*; ed. Univ. of Leyden.

Officer in Netherlands Army in Netherlands East

Indies 45-48; with Ministry of Finance 48-53; Asst. Financial Attaché, Embassy in Washington, D.C. 53-57, Financial Attaché and First Commercial Sec., London 53-64, Counsellor, New Delhi 64-68, Minister Plenipotentiary, London 68-71; Dir. of Financial and Econ. Devt. Assistance, Ministry of Foreign Affairs 71-74; Exec. Dir., IBRD, IDA, IFC Nov. 74-; Officer, Order of Orange Nassau, Commdr., Order of Repub. of Tunisia.
Leisure interests: philosophy, history.
Publs. articles on financial matters.
6201 Goldsborough Road, Bethesda, Md. 20034, U.S.A.
Telephone: (202) 477-5286 (Office); (301) 229-2763 (Home).

Witteveen, Hendrikus Johannes; Netherlands economist, politician and international administrator; b. 12 June 1921, Zeist; m. L. De Vries Feyens; four c.; ed. Netherlands School of Economics, Rotterdam.
Netherlands Cen. Planning Office 45-46; Lecturer, Netherlands School of Econs., Rotterdam 47-48, Prof. of Business Cycles and Econs. 48-63; mem. First Chamber, States-Gen. 58-63, Second Chamber 65-67; Minister of Finance 63-65, 67-71, also First Deputy Prime Minister 67-71; mem. Advisory Board Unilever N.V. 72-73, ROBECO 72-73; Man. Dir. Int. Monetary Fund 73-; Liberal.
Leisure interests: classical music, English and French literature.
International Monetary Fund, 19th and H Streets, N.W., Washington, D.C. 20431; 10817 Admiral's Way, Potomac, Md., U.S.A.
Telephone: 299-3190 (Md.).

Wittig, Georg, DR. PHIL.; German chemist; b. 16 June 1897, Berlin; s. of Prof. Gustav Wittig and Martha (née Dombrowski); m. Waltraut Ernst 1930; two d.; ed. Wilhelms-Gymnasium, Kassel and Marburg Univ.
Dozent, Marburg Univ. 26-32; Head of Dept. Technische Hochschule, Brunswick 32-37; Special Prof. Univ. of Freiburg/Br. 37; Prof. and Inst. Dir. Tübingen Univ. 44-56; Prof. Heidelberg Univ. 56-67, Emer. Prof. 67-; Baeyer Medal 53; mem. Acad. of Sciences, Munich and Heidelberg, Sociedad Química del Perú, Leopoldina Halle; Hon. mem. Swiss Chem. Asscn., New York Acad. of Sciences, Chemical Soc. (London), Soc. Chimique de France; Dannie-Heineman-Preis 65; Otto Hahn Prize 67, Ville de Paris Medal 69; Hon. Dr. of Sorbonne; Hon. Dr.rer.Nat. (Univs. of Tübingen and Hamburg); mem. de l'Académie Française; Paul Karrer Medal, Univ. of Zurich 72; Bruylants Chair Medal, Univ. of Louvain 72; Roger Adams Award, American Chemical Soc. 73, Karl-Ziegler-Preis 75.
Leisure interests: mountaineering, music.
Publs. *Textbook on Stereochemistry* 30, *Metallorganic and Carbanion Chemistry*.
Bergstrasse 35, 69 Heidelberg, Federal Republic of Germany.
Telephone: 40945.

Woelfle, Arthur W.; American business executive; b. 8 March 1920, Dunkirk, N.Y.; m. Ruth Godden; three d.; ed. Univ. of Buffalo.
Served in U.S. Marine Corps 39-45; Sec.-Treas. Bedford Products until 55; Senior Vice-Pres. Bedford Products Division, Kraftco Corpn.; Div. Product Man. Kraft's Eastern Div. 59; later various positions with Kraft Foods Division; Chief Exec. Officer Kraft Foods, Fed. Repub. of Germany 66-69; Chair. and Man. Dir. Kraft Foods Ltd., U.K. and Scandinavia 69-73; Dir. Kraftco Corpn. 73-, Vice-Chair. 73, Pres. and Chief Operating Officer 73-.
Kraftco Corporation, Kraftco Court, Glenview, Ill. 60025, U.S.A.

Woerdeman, Martinus Willem, M.D., D.SC., PH.D.; Netherlands university professor (Emer.); b. 1892, Zaandyk; s. of Martinus Woerdeman and Antje

Huysman; m. 1st Geertruida Elizabeth Polderman (died 1958), 2nd Hanna Nyman 1959; one s.; ed. Univ. of Amsterdam.
Assistant in Anatomy and Histology, Univ. of Amsterdam 14-22, Lecturer in Histology 22-25, Prof. of Histology 25-26; Prof. of Anatomy and Embryology, Univ. of Groningen 26-31; Prof. of Anatomy and Embryology and Head of Dept. of Anatomy, Univ. of Amsterdam 31-62, Dean of Faculty of Medicine 46-50; Rector of Univ. 45-46; Pres. Royal Neths. Acad. of Sciences 54-60; Pres. Univ. of Amsterdam 53-59; Chief Editor *Excerpta Medica* and *Acta morphologica neerlando-scandinavica*; foreign mem. Royal Swedish Acad. Sciences, Royal Flemish Acad. of Medicine, Nat. Acad. of Sciences, Mexico; Swammerdam Medal 50; Commdr. Order of Orange Nassau; Knight Order of Neths. Lion; Officier de la Légion d'Honneur; Knight Order of St. Sava; Hon. D.Sc. (Oxford) 50, Hon. Ph.D. (S. Africa) 59.
Leisure interests: mathematics, history.
Publs. *Atlas of Human Anatomy* 48, *Nomina anatomica Parisiensia* 57.
10 Botticellistr., Amsterdam Nw. Z, Netherlands.
Telephone: 020-723700.

Wojna, Ryszard; Polish journalist; b. 2 July 1920, Sanok; m. Elzbieta Wojna; two c.; ed. Jagiellonian Univ., Cracow and Univ. of Grenoble.
Editor, *Echo Krakowa* 48-49; Foreign Editor, *Głos Pracy*, Warsaw 51-56, Perm. corresp. in Middle East 57-61, in Bonn 63-67; Deputy editor *Życie Warszawy* 68-71, Editor 72-73; Journalist *Trybuna Ludu* 73-; mem. Presidium, Gen. Board of Polish Journalists' Asscn., Chair. Warsaw Branch 71-; Deputy mem. Cen. Cttee. Polish United Workers' Party 71-75, mem. 75-; mem. Presidium All-Polish Peace Cttee.; Officer's Cross of Order Polonia Restituta 72, State Prize for Literature and Journalism 72.
Leisure interest: skiing.
Publs. *Szkice arabskie* 64, *Spokojnie płynie Ren* 71.
Trybuna Ludu, Pl. Starynkiewicza 7, 02-015 Warsaw, Poland.

Wojtaszek, Emil; Polish administrator and diplomatist; b. 1927, Cracow; ed. Higher School of Social Sciences, Cen. Cttee. of Polish United Workers' Party, Warsaw.
Lived in France 29-44, later working as a miner 41-44; mem. French Resistance 39-44; deported to Germany 44; returned to Poland 50; worked in Vienna for World Council for Peace; asst. to chief of dept. for foreign affairs of Cen. Cttee. of Polish United Workers' Party 68-72; Vice-Minister Foreign Affairs April-May 72; Amb. to France 72-76; Minister of Admin., Regional Economy and Protection of the Environment March 76-; mem. Polish Workers' United Party; Knight's, Officer's and Commdr's Cross, Order of Polonia Restituta, Medal of 30th Anniversary of People's Poland.
Ministry of Administration, Regional Economy and Protection of the Environment, Warsaw, Poland.

Wojtyła, H.E. Cardinal Karol; Polish ecclesiastic; b. 18 May 1920, Wadowice; ed. Jagiellonian Univ., Cracow.
Ordained Priest 46; Prof. of Moral Theology at Univs. of Cracow and Lublin 53-58; Bishop of Ombi and Vicar-General of Archdiocese 58, Scholastic of Metropolitan Chapter and Vicar of Archdiocese 60-64; Archbishop of Cracow 63-; cr. Cardinal by Pope Paul VI 67; Adviser to the Council of Laymen; mem. Congregation for the Eastern Church, Congregation for the Clergy, Congregation of Sacraments and Worship, Council of Sec.-Gen. of Bishops' Synod.
Leisure interests: skiing, rowing, sport.
Publs. (In the province of Moral Theology) *Love and Responsibility* 60, 62, *Person and Work* 69, *At the Bases*

of Renovation—study of the realization of Vaticanum II 72.
Ul. Franciszkańska 3, 31-004 Cracow, Poland.
Telephone: 502-46.

Wold, Herman O. A., D.SC.; Swedish university professor; b. 25 Dec. 1908, Skien, Norway; s. of Edward M. and Betzy Omberg Wold; m. Anna-Lisa Arrhenius 1940; one s. two d.; ed. Univ. of Stockholm.
Professor of Statistics, Univ. of Uppsala 42-70; Fellow, Inst. Mathematical Statistics 46; Vice-Pres. Int. Inst. of Statistics 57-61; Fellow, American Statistical Asscn. 51, Swedish Acad. Sciences 60, mem. Nobel Econ. Science Prize Cttee. 69-; Pres. Econometric Soc. 66; Prof. of Statistics, Univ. of Gothenburg 70-75, Emeritus 75-; Hon. Fellow, Royal Statistical Soc. (U.K.) 61; Hon. Dr. Technical Univ. of Lisbon.
Leisure interests: reading, study of individual versus social functions of the arts, cycling, skiing.
Publs. *A Study in the Analysis of Stationary Time Series* 38, *Demand Analysis* 52 (Several translations), *Bibliography on Time Series and Stochastic Processes* (Editor) 65, *Mergers of Economics and Philosophy of Science* 69, *Interdependent Systems: Structure and Estimation* (Co-Author) 70, *The University in Transition I-IV* 72-75, *Soft modelling by latent variables: the non-linear iterative partial least squares (NIPALS) approach* 75.
Office: University Institute of Statistics, Kyrkogårdsgatan 10, Uppsala 75235; Home: Kyrkogårdsgatan 19, Uppsala 75235, Sweden.
Telephone: (Office) 013-111230; (Home) 018-145004.

Wold, Knut Getz, M.ECON.; Norwegian banker and economist; b. 3 Aug. 1915, Verdal; s. of Trygve and Anna Ella (née Getz) Wold; m. Astrid M. Graver; one s. two d.; ed. Oslo and Stockholm Univs.
Research Assoc., Oslo Univ. 39-40; Adviser to Norwegian Ministry of Finance in London 41-45, in Oslo 45-46; Under-Sec., Ministry of Social Affairs, Oslo 46-48; Dir. Foreign Trade Div., Ministry of Commerce 48-58; Deputy Gov. Norges Bank (Bank of Norway) 58-70, Gov. 70-; Pres. Norwegian Econ. Asscn. 63-68; Commdr. Order of Dannebrog (Denmark), St. Olav (Norway), Order of the Falcon (Iceland).
Publs. *Kosthold og levestandard* 41, *Plan for velstand, T.V.A. og Norge* 46, *Levestandardens økonomi* 49, *Økonomisk styring i et fritt samfunn* 75.
Norges Bank, Bankplassen 4, Oslo 1; Home: 7 Fougstad Gt., Oslo 1, Norway.
Telephone: 42-9850 (Office); 46-1710 (Home).

Wolfbein, Seymour Louis, PH.D.; American government official and educator; b. 8 Nov. 1915, New York; s. of Samuel Wolfbein and Fannie Katz; m. Mae Lachterman 1941; two d.; ed. Brooklyn Coll., and Columbia Univ.
Research Assoc. U.S. Senate Comm. on Unemployment and Relief 38; Economist, Research Div., Works Project Admin. 39-42; Economist, Bureau of Labor Statistics, Dept. of Labor 42-45, Head, Occupational Outlook Div. 46-49, Head, Manpower and Productivity Div. 49-50, Manpower and Employment Div. 50-59, Dep. Asst. Sec. of Labor 59-62, Dir. Office of Manpower, Automation and Training 62-65, Economic Adviser to Sec. of Labor 65-67; Visiting Prof. Univ. of Michigan 50-; Adjunct Prof. American Univ. 51-; Dean, School of Business Admin., Temple Univ. 67-; Fellow, American Statistical Asscn., American Asscn. for Advancement of Science; Distinguished Service Award, Dept. of Labor 55 and 61; Eminent Man of Guidance Award 70.
Leisure interest: painting.
Publs. *Decline of a Cotton Textile City* 42, *The World of Work* 51, *Employment and Unemployment in the U.S.* 64, *Employment, Unemployment and Public Policy* 65, *Education and Training for Full Employment* 67,

Occupational Information 68, *Emerging Sectors of Collective Bargaining* 70, *Work in the American Society* 71, *Manpower Policy: Perspectives and Prospects* 73, *Labor Market Information for Youths* 75.
Temple University, Philadelphia, Pa. 19122, U.S.A.
Telephone: 787-7676 (Office).

Wolfenden, Baron (Life Peer), cr. 74, of Westcott in the County of Surrey; **John Frederick Wolfenden,** Kt., C.B.E.; British educationist; b. 26 June 1906; s. of late G. Wolfenden; m. Eileen Lemessurier Spilsbury 1932; one s. two d. (and one s. deceased); ed. Wakefield School, and Queen's Coll., Oxford.
Henry Davison Scholar, Princeton Univ. 28-29; Fellow, Tutor in Philosophy, Magdalen Coll., Oxford 29-34; Headmaster Uppingham School 34-44; Dir. Air Training Corps 41; Headmaster Shrewsbury School 44-50; Vice-Chancellor Reading Univ. 50-63; Chair. Departmental Cttee. on Homosexual Offences and Prostitution 54-57; Chair. Univ. Grants Cttee. 63-68; Dir. British Museum 69-73; First Pres. Chelsea Coll., London Univ. 73-.
Publs. *The Approach to Philosophy* 32, *The Public Schools Today* 49, *How to Choose Your School* 52.
The White House, Guildford Road, Westcott, near Dorking, Surrey, England.
Telephone: 0306-5475.

Wolff, Etienne Charles, PH.D.; French embryologist; b. 12 Feb. 1904; ed. Univ. de Strasbourg.
Assistant at Biological Laboratory of Wimereux, Univ. of Paris 27-28; Asst. at Medical Faculty, Univ. of Strasbourg 33-37; Assoc. Prof. of Biology, Univ. of Strasbourg 37-42, Prof. of Zoology and Embryology 42-55; Prof. Collège de France 55-, Pres. Admin., Coll. de France; Dir. Inst. of Embryology and Teratology, Centre Nat. de Recherche Scientifique; Dir. Laboratory of Embryology, Ecole Pratique des Hautes Etudes, Paris; mem. Acad. des Sciences, Acad. Nat. de Médecine; Assoc. mem. Acad. Royale de Belgique; Foreign mem. Royal Swedish Acad. of Sciences; Officier Légion d'Honneur; Commdr. de l'Ordre Nat. du Mérite; Commdr. des Palmes Académiques; Prix de l'Institut de France; Dr. h.c. (Univs. of Ghent, Louvain and Geneva).
Publs. *Les Changements de Sexe* 46, *La Science des Monstres* 48, *Les Chemins de la Vie* 64.
49 bis, avenue de la Belle-Gabrielle, 94130 Nogent-sur-Marne, France.

Wolff, Hans Julius, DR. IUR.; German professor of Roman law; b. 27 Aug. 1902, Berlin; s. of Bruno Wolff and Katharina Pinner; m. Sylvia A. Plann 1944; one d.; ed. Univ. of Berlin.
Judge in Berlin 32; staff mem. *Thesaurus ling. Lat.*, Munich 33-35; Prof. of Roman Law, Nat. Univ. of Panama 35-39; Prof. of History, Oklahoma Coll. for Women, Chickasha, Okla. 45-46; Prof. of History, Oklahoma City Univ. 46-50; Law Librarian, Lecturer in Jurisprudence, Univ. of Kansas City (Mo.) 50-52; Prof. of Roman Law, Univ. of Mainz 52-55, Univ. of Freiburg (Germany) 55-; mem. Heidelberg Acad. of Sciences; Corresp. mem. Munich, Göttingen, Athens Acads. of Sciences; D.Iur.h.c. (Athens).
Leisure interest: travel.
Publs. *Written and Unwritten Marriages in Hellenistic and Postclassical Roman Law* 39, *Roman Law, an Historical Introduction* 51, *Beiträge zur Rechtsgeschichte Altgriech. u.d. Hell.-Röm. Äg.* 61, *Das Justizwesen der Ptolemäer* 62, *Die att. Paragraphe* 66, *Demosthenes als Advokat* 68, *Opuscula Dispersa* 74.
D7815, Kirchzarten, Schulhaustrasse 35, Federal Republic of Germany.
Telephone: 07661-4124.

Wolff von Amerongen, Otto; German industrialist; b. 6 Aug. 1918.
President Otto Wolff A.G.; mem. Board of Dirs. Exxon Corpn., New York; Chair., Deputy Chair. and

mem. Supervisory Boards various nat. and int. corpns.; Pres. Asscn. of German Chambers of Commerce and Industry; Pres. Cologne Chamber of Commerce and Industry; Pres. Ostausschuss der Deutschen Wirtschaft. Zeughausstrasse 2, Cologne, Federal Republic of Germany.
Telephone: Cologne 20411.

Wolfson, Sir Isaac, Bart., F.R.S.; British businessman; b. 17 Sept. 1897; m. Edith Specterman 1926; father of Leonard Wolfson (q.v.); ed. Queen's Park School, Glasgow.
Joined The Great Universal Stores Ltd. 32, Man. Dir. 34-, Chair. 46-; mem. Worshipful Company of Pattenmakers, Grand Council British Empire Cancer Campaign; Hon. Pres. Weizmann Inst. of Science Foundation; Trustee Religious Centre, Jerusalem; Founder and Trustee the Wolfson Foundation, created 55, mainly for the advancement of health, education and youth activities in the U.K. and British Commonwealth; Einstein Award for Philanthropy 67; Lehmann Award 68; Hon. Fellow, Weizmann Inst. of Science, Israel; Hon. LL.D. (London, Glasgow, Cambridge, Manchester and Strathclyde), Hon. F.R.C.P., Hon. F.R.C.S., Hon. D.C.L. (Oxford), Hon. Fellow, St. Edmund Hall, Oxford.
74 Portland Place, London, W.1, England.
Telephone: 01-580-6441.

Wolfson, Leonard G.; British retail executive; b. 1927; s. of Sir Isaac Wolfson (q.v.); m. Ruth Sterling 1949; four d.; ed. King's School, Worcester and Malvern Coll.
Director Great Universal Stores Ltd. 52-, Man. Dir. 62-; Chair. Great Universal Stores Merchandise Corpn. Ltd. 66-; Chair. and Founder Trustee Wolfson Foundation; Trustee Wolfson Coll., Oxford, The Civic Trust; Pres. Jewish Welfare Board; Hon. Fellow, Wolfson Coll., Cambridge; Hon. D.C.L. (Oxon.), Hon. Ph.D. (Tel Aviv), Hon. LL.D. (Strathclyde); Hon. Fellow, St. Catherine's Coll., Oxford.
Leisure interests: history, economics, bridge, golf.
Office: Universal House, 251/256 Tottenham Court Road, London, W.1, England.

Wolfson, Louis Elwood; American industrialist; b. 28 Jan. 1912, St. Louis; s. of Morris David and Sarah (Goldberg) Wolfson; m. 1st Florence Ruth Monsky 1936 (died 1968), 2nd Patrice Jacobs; three s. one d.; ed. Univ. of Georgia.
With M. Wolfson and Co. 34-49; officer and Dir. Fla. Pipe and Supply Co. Inc., Jacksonville, Fla. 34-49, M L and S Corpn., real estate and investments 46-56; Pres. Southern Pipe and Supply Co., Orlando, Fla. 48-57; controlling stockholder Tampa Shipbuilding Co. Inc., Fla. 45-48; Officer, Ceco. Agency Corpn. 48-; Chair. of Board Merritt-Chapman and Scott Corpn., N.Y.C. 51-69, and Pres. 53-59; Chair. of Board N.Y. Shipbuilding Corpn., Camden, N.J. 53-61, Chair. Exec. Cttee. 61-69; Chair. of Board Capital Transit Co., Washington 51-56, Newport Steel Corpn. (Ky.) 54-56; Dir. Montgomery Ward and Co. 55-56, Revday Industries Inc. 64-68; Trustee, Ga. Student Educ. Fund Inc., Brunswick, Ga., Wolfson Family Foundation Inc., Mount Sinai Hosp., Miami Beach, Ga. Gridiron Secret Soc.; mem. Boys Estate Advisory Cttee., Board of Govs. Eleanor Roosevelt Cancer Foundation American Cancer Soc. Cttee. to Advance World Wide Fight against Cancer; mem. Nat. Conf. Christians and Jews, Acad. of Political Science, Nat. Advisory Council, Synagogue Council of America, American Iron and Steel Inst.; Hon. Alumnus, Hebrew Univ. of Jerusalem.
Leisure interest: horse racing.
Office: P.O. Box 4, Jacksonville, Fla. 32201; Home: 11 Island Avenue, Miami Beach, Fla. 33139, U.S.A.

Wolman, Abel, B.A., B.SC., D.ENG.; American emeritus professor and public health engineering consultant; s. of Morris Wolman and Rose Wachsman Wolman; m. Anne Gordon 1919; one s.; ed. Johns Hopkins Univ. Assistant Engineer to Div. Engineer, Maryland State Dept. of Health 15-22, Chief Engineer 22-39; Prof. in Sanitary Engineering and Water Resources, Johns Hopkins Univ. 37-57, Prof. Emer. 59-; Editor-in-Chief *Journal* of American Water Works Asscn. 21-37; Editor *American Journal of Public Health* 55; Consultant to numerous American cities, state and federal agencies, and 50 foreign govts.; fmrly. Adviser Atomic Energy Comm., Tennessee Valley Authority, Army, Navy and Air Force, Office of Science and Tech., U.S. Geological Survey, U.S. Public Health Service, WHO, Int. Bank for Reconstruction and Devt., Pan American Health Org.; Pres. American Public Health Asscn. 39, American Water Works Asscn. 42; mem. Nat. Water Resources Board of U.S. 34-45, Cttee. on Public Eng. Policy 75; mem. Nat. Acad. of Sciences, American Geophysical Union; Hon. mem. Nat. Acad. of Eng., American Soc. of Civil Engineers, American Water Resources Asscn., American Public Works Asscn., Int. Water Quality Research Council, Md. Public Health Asscn.; Hon. Life mem., Board of Dirs., Technion, Haifa, Israel; Hon. Life Fellow, Franklin Inst.; Fellow American Asscn. for Advancement of Science; Hon. D.Eng., LL.D. (Johns Hopkins Univ.), Hon. D.Sc. (Drexel Inst., Philadelphia), Hon. D.Hum.Litt.; Special Award, Lasker Foundation of American Public Health Asscn. 60, William Proctor Prize, Scientific Research Soc. of America 67, Lewis L. Dollinger Pure Environment Award, Franklin Inst., Philadelphia 68, American Water Works Asscn., Publ. Award 73, Milton Stover Eisenhower Medal 73, U.S. Nat. Medal of Science 74.
Leisure interests: music, literature, walking, grandchildren.
Publs. *Manual of Water Works Practice* (Editor) 25, *Solving Sewage Problems* by Fuller and McClintock (Editor, and Author of several chapters) 26, *The Significance of Waterborne Typhoid Fever Outbreaks* (with Arthur E. Gorman) 31; *Water, Health and Society,* selected papers 69, and numerous articles 19-68.
209 Ames Hall, The Johns Hopkins University, Baltimore, Md. 21218; Home: 3213 North Charles Street, Baltimore, Md. 21218, U.S.A.
Telephone: 301-235-8567 (Office); 301-235-7192 (Home).

Wołoszyn, Stefan, D.PHIL.; Polish professor; b. 19 Aug. 1911, Lwów; ed. Jagiellonian Univ., Cracow, and Nicholas Copernicus Univ., Toruń.
College Teacher, Vilnius 35-41; Dir. Pedagogical Lyceum, Białystok 45-46; Research Worker, Nicholas Copernicus Univ., Toruń 46-50; Head, Faculty of Pedagogy, Adam Mickiewicz Univ., Poznań 50-53; Lecturer, Faculty of Pedagogy, Warsaw Univ. and Acad. of Physical Education (AWF), Warsaw 53-61, Prof. AWF 61-73, Rector AWF 60-71; Prof. Warsaw Univ. 61-; mem. Cttee. of Pedagogical and Psychological Sciences, Polish Acad. of Sciences 52-, Cen. Cttee. of Physical Culture and Tourism 60-, Supreme Council of Higher Educ. 66-73.
Publs. books and articles on education.
ul. Koszykowa 75m. 16, Warsaw, Poland.

Wolters, Baron Laurent; Belgian oil executive; b. 24 July 1901, Orel, Russia; s. of Emile Wolters and Mathilde (Ryndzunsky); m. Olga Bogdanova 1925 (died 1970); two s. (one died 1972) one d.
Former Chair. and Man. Dir. Petrofina, now Hon. Chair.; Dir. several subsidiary cos.; fmr. Chair. Soc. Industrielle Belge des Pétroles, Petrocongo; Officier de l'Ordre de Léopold, Officier de l'Ordre de la Couronne, Médaille de la Résistance, Croix de Guerre.
Rue de la Loi 33, 1040 Brussels; Château "Le Bisdom", 1900 Overijse, Belgium.

Wong Lin Ken; Singapore historian and diplomatist; b. 31 July 1931, Penang; *m.* Lili Tam Boeyhian 1961; two *s.* one *d.*; ed. Univ. of Malaya and Univ. of London. Raffles Prof. of History, Univ. of Singapore; mem. Editorial Board *Journal of S.E. Asian History* 60-64; Editor *Journal of the South Seas Soc.* 59-60; Chair. Adult Educ. Board 64-67; Perm. Rep. to UN 67-69; Amb. to U.S.A. 67-69; Amb. to Brazil 68-69; Minister for Home Affairs 70-72.
Publs. *A Study of the Trade of Singapore 1819-1869* 60, *The Malayan Tin Industry to 1914* 65.
Leisure interests: golf, fishing.
Department of History, University of Singapore, Singapore.

Wontner, Sir Hugh Walter Kingwell, G.B.E., C.V.O., J.P., D.LITT.; British hotelier; b. 22 Oct. 1908; *s.* of Arthur Wontner; *m.* Catherine Irvin 1936; two *s.* one *d.*; ed. Oundle, and in France.
Member Secretarial Staff of London Chamber of Commerce 27-33; Gen. Sec. Hotels and Restaurants Asscn. of Great Britain 33-38; Sec. Coronation Accommodation Cttee. 36-37; Asst. to Sir George Reeves-Smith at the Savoy Hotel 38-41; Dir. of the Savoy, Claridge's and Berkeley Hotels, London 40, Man. Dir. 41-, Chair. 48-; Chair. Savoy Theatre Ltd. 48-, Eurocard Int., S.A., Lancaster Hotel, Paris 73-; Trustee D'Oyly Carte Opera Trust, Coll. of Arms Trust, Southwark Cathedral Devt. Trust; Chair. Exec. Cttee. British Hotels and Restaurants Asscn. 57-59, Council 69-73; Pres. Int. Hotel Asscn. 62-65; Chair. Nutrition Cttee., Univ. Coll. Hosp. 45-52; mem. Lloyds 37-; mem. of Board British Travel Asscn. 50-69; mem. Historic Buildings Council for England 68-73; Chair. Coronation Accommodation Cttee. 52-53, Historic Houses Cttee. (British Tourist Authority) 65-; Master Worshipful Co. of Feltmakers 62, 73, of Clockmakers 76; Clerk of Royal Kitchens 53; Freeman of the City of London 34-, Alderman 63-, Sheriff 70-71, Lord Mayor 73-74; Lieut. of the City and J.P. 63-.
1 Savoy Hill, London, W.C.2; and Hedsor Priory, Hedsor, Buckinghamshire, England.

Wood, Arthur M., B.L.; American business executive; b. 27 Jan. 1913, Chicago; ed. Princeton Univ., Harvard Law School.
Service in Second World War; joined Sears, Roebuck and Co. 46, Co. Sec. 52-61, Vice-Pres. 56, mem. Board of Dirs. 59, Vice-Pres. and Comptroller 60-62, Vice-Pres. in charge of Far West Territory 62-67, of Midwest Territory 67, Pres. Feb. 68-73; Chair. Board of Dirs. and Chief Exec. Sears Roebuck Foundation 73-; Chair. U.S. Industrial Payroll Savings Cttee. for Chicago 74-; Dir. Allstate Insurance Co., Continental Illinois Corpn., Simpsons-Sears Ltd., Homart Devt. Co., Quaker Oats Co., Council for Financial Aid to Educ., United Way of America, Community Fund of Chicago; trustee Tax Foundation Inc., Cttee. for Econ. Devt., Art Inst. of Chicago, Rush Presbyterian St. Luke's Medical Center; mem. President's Advisory Cttee. on Labor Man., Business Council, Nat. Industrial Energy Conservation Council.
Sears Tower, Chicago, Ill. 60684, U.S.A.

Wood, Harland, A.B., PH.D.; American university professor of biochemistry; b. 2 Sept. 1907, Delavan, Minn.; *s.* of William C. and Inez (Goff) Wood; *m.* Mildred Lenora Davis 1929; three *d.*; ed. Macalester State and Iowa State Colls.
Fellow, Nat. Research Council, Biochem. Dept., Univ. of Wis. 35-36; Asst. Prof., Bacteriology Dept., Iowa State Coll. 36-43; Assoc. Prof., Physiological Chem. Dept., Univ. of Minn. 43-46; Prof. and Dir. Dept. of Biochem., Western Reserve Univ. 46-65, Prof. of Biochem., Case Western Reserve Univ. 65-, Dean of Sciences 67-69; Pres. American Soc. of Biological Chemists 59-60; Sec.-Gen., International Union of Bio-

chemistry 70-73; mem. Presidential Science Advisory Cttee., Washington, D.C. 68-72; Senior Fulbright Research Scholar, New Zealand 55; Guggenheim Fellow 62; mem. Nat. Acad. of Sciences, American Acad. of Arts and Sciences, Bayerische Akad., Germany; Hon. Sc.D. (Macalester Coll.); Eli Lilly Award in Bacteriology 42, Glycerine Award 54, Modern Medicine Award for Distinguished Achievement 68, Lynen Lecture and Medal 72; Hon. D.Sc. (Northwestern Univ.) 72.
Leisure interests: skiing, hunting, fishing.
Publs. Over 150 scientific papers; Editorial Cttee., *Journal of Biological Chemistry* 49-54, and of *Biochemistry* 64-69.
Department of Biochemistry, Case Western Reserve University, School of Medicine, 2109 Adelbert Road, Cleveland, Ohio 44106, U.S.A.

Wood, Lee Blair, B.A.; American newspaper editor; b. 7 March 1893, Corry, Pa.; *s.* of Perrie Grant and Mary Lavinia (Laing) Wood; *m.* Mildred Louise Rody 1924; ed. Corry High School, and Amherst Coll. Reporter *Cleveland Leader* 16-17; Telegraph Ed. Cleveland Press 20-22, Night Ed. 23-24, News Ed. 24-25; Man. Ed. *Oklahoma News* 25-27; News Ed. *New York Telegram* 27-28, Man. Editor 29-30 (*New York World-Telegram and The Sun*), Exec. Editor 31-60, Editor 60-62, Pres. 62-65; Pres. Scripps-Howard Investment Co. 62-.
Home: Route 2, Ridgefield, Conn. 06877; Office: c/o Scripps-Howard Newspapers, 200 Park Avenue, New York, N.Y. 10017, U.S.A.

Wood, Rt. Rev. Maurice Arthur Ponsonby, D.S.C., M.A.; British ecclesiastic; b. 26 Aug. 1916, England; *s.* of Mr. and Mrs. Arthur S. Wood; *m.* 1st S. S. Marjorie Pennell 1947 (died 1954), 2nd M. Margaret Sandford 1955; four *s.* two *d.*; ed. Monkton Combe School, Queens' Coll., Cambridge and Ridley Hall, Cambridge. Ordained 40; Curate, St. Paul's, Portman Square, London 40-43; Royal Naval Chaplain 43-47; Rector, St. Ebbe's, Oxford 47-52; Vicar and Rural Dean of Islington 52-61; Principal, Oak Hill Theological Coll., Southgate, London 61-71; Bishop of Norwich 71-; Hon. Chaplain, Royal Naval Reserve 71-; Chaplain, Commando Asscn.; Gov. Monkton Combe School, Bath, Gresham's School, Norfolk.
Leisure interests: running, hockey, sailing.
Publs. *Like a Mighty Army* 56, *Your Suffering* 59, *Christian Stability* 68.
The Bishop's House, Norwich, NR3 1SB, England.
Telephone: Norwich 29001.

Wood, Rt. Hon. Richard Frederick, P.C., M.P., D.L.; British politician; b. 5 Oct. 1920, London; *s.* of 1st Earl of Halifax, K.G., O.M., G.C.I.E.; *m.* Diana Kellett 1947; one *s.* one *d.*; ed. Eton and New Coll., Oxford. Attaché, British Embassy, Rome 40; army 40-43, wounded; M.P. 50-; Parl. Private Sec. to Minister of Pensions 51-53, to Minister of State, Board of Trade 53-54, to Minister of Agriculture and Fisheries 54-55; Joint Parl. Sec., Ministry of Pensions and Nat. Insurance 55-58; Parl. Sec., Ministry of Labour 58-59; Minister of Power 59-63, of Pensions and Nat. Ins. 63-64; Dir. Yorks. Conservative Newspapers 47-55, Hulton Press 53-55, F. J. C. Lilley and Co. Ltd. 67-70, Hargreaves Ltd. 74; Gov. Queen Elizabeth's Foundation for the Disabled; Minister for Overseas Devt. 70-74; Deputy Lieut. County of Humberside; Hon. Col., 4th Battalion, Royal Green Jackets; Hon. LL.D. (Sheffield Univ.).
Leisure interest: travel.
Flat Top House, Bishop Wilton, York YO4 1RY; and 49 Cadogan Place, London, SW1X 9RT, England.

Wood, William B., III, PH.D.; American professor of biology; b. 19 Feb. 1938, Baltimore, Md.; *s.* of Dr. W. Barry Wood, Jr. and Mary L. Hutchins; *m.* Renate Marie-Elisabeth Hartisch 1961; two *s.*; ed. Harvard Coll., Stanford Univ. and Univ. of Geneva.

National Acad. of Sciences—Nat. Research Council Postdoctoral Fellow, Univ. of Geneva 64; Asst. Prof. of Biology, Calif. Inst. of Technology 65-68, Assoc. Prof. 68-70, Prof. 70-; mem. Nat. Acad. of Sciences.
Leisure interests: music, tennis, camping.
Publs. *Biochemistry, A Problems Approach* 74, *Molecular Design in Living Systems* 74, *The Molecular Basis of Metabolism* 74; articles in professional journals.
Division of Biology 156-29, California Institute of Technology, Pasadena, Calif. 91109; Home: 1840 San Pasqual Street, Pasadena, Calif. 91107, U.S.A.
Telephone: 213-795-6841 (Office); 213-449-0317 (Home).

Woodcock, Rt. Hon. George, P.C., C.B.E.; British trade union official; b. 20 Oct. 1904, Walton-le-Dale, Lancs.; s. of Peter Woodcock and Ann (née Baxendale); m. Laura Mary McKernan 1933; one s. one d.; ed. Ruskin Coll., and New Coll., Oxford.
Cotton weaver 16-29; Sec. T.U.C. Research and Economic Dept. 36-47; Asst. Gen. Sec. T.U.C. 47-60, Gen. Sec. 60-69; Chair. Comm. on Industrial Relations 69-71; mem. cttee. on taxation of trading profits 45-51; mem. cttee. on taxation treatment of retirement provisions 50-54; mem. Royal Comm. on taxation of profits and income 51-55; mem. British Guiana Constitutional Comm. 54; mem. cttee. on working of the monetary system 57-59; Vice-Chair. Nat. Savings Cttee. 52-74; Gov. Admin. Staff Coll. 57-67; Vice Pres. ICFTU 60-69; mem. Nat. Econ. Devt. Council (NEDC) 62-69; Royal Comm. on Trade Unions and Employers' Asscns. 65-68; numerous honorary degrees.
24 Lower Hill Road, Epsom, Surrey, England.
Telephone: Epsom 22694.

Woodcock, Leonard; American labour leader; b. 15 Feb. 1911, Providence, R.I.; s. of Ernest and Margaret (née Freel) Woodcock; m. Loula Martin 1941; one s. two d.; ed. St. Wilfred's Coll., Oakmore, Northampton Town and Country School (England) and intermittent courses at Wayne State Univ.
Regional Director, UAW 47-55; Vice-Pres. UAW 55-70; Pres. Int. Union, United Automobile, Aerospace and Agricultural Implement Workers of America (UAW) 70-.
Leisure interests: music and literature.
Office: 8000 E. Jefferson Avenue, Detroit, Mich. 48214, U.S.A.
Telephone: 313-926-5201.

Woodham-Smith, Cecil C., C.B.E., M.A.; British writer; ed. St. Hilda's Coll., Oxford.
Awarded James Tait Black Memorial Prize for *Florence Nightingale* 50; Hon. D.Litt., Nat. Univ. of Ireland, Hon. LL.D., Univ. of St. Andrews; Fellow St. Hilda's Coll., Oxford 67; A. C. Benson Medal for Contribution to Literature 69.
Publs. *Florence Nightingale* 50, *Lonely Crusader* 51, *Lady in Chief* 53, *The Reason Why* 54, *The Great Hunger* 62, *Queen Victoria: Her Life and Times*, Vol. I (1819-61) 72.
44 Mount Street, London, W.1, England.

Woodhouse, Hon. Christopher Montague, D.S.O., O.B.E., M.A.; British politician; b. 11 May 1917, London; s. of Lord and Lady Terrington; m. Lady Davina Lytton (Countess of Erne) 1945; two s. one d.; ed. Winchester Coll., and New Coll., Oxford.
Commissioned R.A. 40; commanded Allied Mil. Mission in German occupied Greece 43-44; Asst. Sec. Nuffield Foundation 47; served Foreign Office in Athens 45 and Teheran 51; Fellow of Trinity Hall, Cambridge 49; Dir.-Gen. Royal Inst. of Int. Affairs 55-59; M.P. for Oxford 59-66, 70-74; Parl. Sec. Ministry of Aviation 61-62, Home Office 62-64; Chief Editor Penguin Books 60; Dir. of Educ. and Training, Confederation of British Industry 66-70; Visiting Fellow Nuffield Coll. 56; Fellow Royal Soc. of Literature; Legion of Merit

(U.S.A.); Order of Phoenix with swords (Greece); Conservative.
Leisure interests: fishing, music.
Publs. *Apple of Discord* 48, *One Omen* 50, *Dostoievsky* 51, *The Greek War of Independence* 52, *Britain and the Middle East* 59, *British Foreign Policy since the Second World War* 61, *Rhodes* (with J. G. Lockhart) 63, *The New Concert of Nations* 64, *The Battle of Navarino* 65, *Postwar Britain* 66, *The Story of Modern Greece* 68, *The Philhellenes* 69, *Capodistria* 73, *The Struggle for Greece (1941-1949)* 76.
Willow Cottage, Latimer, Bucks., England.
Telephone: Little Chalfont 2627.

Woodring, Wendell Phillips, A.B., PH.D.; American geologist and palaeontologist; b. 13 June 1891, Reading, Pa.; s. of James Daniel and Margaret Hurst Woodring; m. 1st Josephine Jamison 1918 (deceased), 2nd Merle Crisler Foshag 1965; two d. (one deceased); ed. Albright Coll., and Johns Hopkins Univ.
Geologist, U.S. Geological Survey 19-27, 30-61; Prof. of Invertebrate Palaeontology, Calif. Inst. of Technology 27-30; Emeritus mem. Nat. Acad. of Sciences (Thompson Medal 67), American Philosophical Society; Pres. Geological Society of America 53 (Penrose Medal 49); Hon. Sc.D. (Albright Coll.); hon. Research Assoc. Smithsonian Inst. 61-.
Leisure interest: gardening.
Publs. *Geology of Republic of Haiti, Miocene Molluscs from Bowden, Jamaica, Geology of Kettleman Hills Oil Field, California, Geology and Palaeontology of Palos Verdes Hills, California, Geology and Palaeontology of Santa Maria District, California, Geology and Palaeontology of the Canal Zone and adjoining parts of Panama.*
U.S. National Museum of Natural History, Washington, D.C. 20560, U.S.A.
Telephone: 202-381-5334.

Woodroofe, Sir Ernest George, Kt., PH.D., LL.D., F.INST.P., F.I.CHEM.E.; British business executive; b. 6 Jan. 1912, Liverpool; s. of Ernest George and Ada (Dickinson) Woodroofe; m. 1st Margaret Downes 1938, 2nd Enid Grace Hutchinson Arnold 1962; one d.; ed. Leeds Univ.
Director British Oil and Cake Mills Ltd. 51-56; Dir. Unilever Ltd. and Unilever N.V., in charge of Research 56-61, Vice-Chair. Unilever Ltd. 61-70, Chair. 70-74; Vice-Chair. Unilever N.V. 70-74; Dir. Commonwealth Devt. Finance Co. Ltd. 70-75, Schroders Ltd. 74-, Burton Group 74-, British Gas Corpn. 74-, Guthrie Corpn. 75-; Chair. Review Body on Doctors' and Dentists' Remuneration 75-; Visiting Fellow, Nuffield Coll., Oxford 72-; Order of Orange-Nassau 72; Hon. LL.D., Hon. D.Sc., D.Univ.
Leisure interests: fishing, golf, cinematography.
The Crest, Berry Lane, Worplesdon, Surrey, England.
Telephone: Worplesdon 2666.

Woodruff, John Douglas, C.B.E.; British writer and businessman; b. 8 May 1897, Wimbledon; m. Hon. Marie Acton 1933; ed. New Coll., Oxford.
Served under Foreign Office in Holland 17-19; Lecturer in History, Sheffield Univ. 23-24; on editorial staff of *The Times* 26-38; in charge of Press Publicity for Empire Marketing Board 31-33; with B.B.C. 34-36; Editor *The Tablet* 36-67; Chair. Tablet Publishing Co. 37-67; Dir. Hollis and Carter 48-62; Chair. Allied Circle 47-62, Associated Catholic Newspapers 53-70, B.O.W. Holdings 59-70.
Publs. *Plato's American Republic* 26, *The British Empire* 29, *Plato's Britannia* 30, *Charlemagne* 34, contributor to *Early Victorian England* 34, *Great Tudors* 35, *European Civilisation, The Grand Tour* 35, edited *Dear Sir* 36, *The Story of the British Colonial Empire* 39, *Talking at Random* 41, *More Talking at Random* 44, *Still Talking at Random* 48, *Walrus Talk* 54, *The Tichborne Claimant*

57, *Church and State* 60, *The Life and Times of Alfred the Great* 74.

Marcham Priory, nr. Abingdon, Oxon., England.

Telephone: Frilford Heath 260.

Woodruff, Sir Michael Francis Addison, Kt., F.R.S., F.R.C.S., D.SC., M.S.; British surgeon; b. 3 April 1911, London; *s.* of the late Prof. Harold Addison Woodruff and Margaret Ada Cooper; *m.* Hazel Gwenyth Ashby 1946; two *s.* one *d.*; ed. Wesley Coll., Melbourne, Queen's Coll., Univ. of Melbourne, Australia.

Served as Captain, Australian Army Medical Corps, Malaya 40-46; Tutor in Surgery, Univ. of Sheffield 46-48; Lecturer in Surgery, Univ. of Aberdeen 48-52; Prof. of Surgery, Univ. of Otago, New Zealand 53-56; Prof. of Surgery, Univ. of Edinburgh 57-; Surgeon, Edinburgh Royal Infirmary 57-; Dir. Nuffield Transplantation Surgery Unit, Edinburgh; Foreign Assoc., Acad. de Chirurgie (France) 64; Hon. mem. American Surgical Asscn. 65; Corresp. mem. Deutsche Gesellschaft für Chirurgie 68; Hon. Fellow, American Coll. of Surgeons 75; Lister Medal 69.

Leisure interests: music, sailing.

Publs. *Deficiency Diseases in Japanese Prison Camps* (with A. Dean Smith) 51, *Surgery for Dental Students* (3rd Edn.) 74, *Transplantation of Tissues and Organs* 60; articles on surgical topics and transplantation and tumour immunology.

Department of Surgery, University of Edinburgh Medical School, Teviot Place, Edinburgh, EH8 9AG; Home: The Bield, 506 Lanark Road, Juniper Green, Midlothian, EH14 5DH, Scotland.

Telephone: (031) 667-5272 (Office); (031) 441-1253 (Home).

Woodruff, Philip (*see* Mason, Philip).

Woods, The Most Rev. Frank, K.B.E., M.A., D.D., British ecclesiastic; b. 6 April 1907, Switzerland; *m.* Jean M. Sprules 1936; two *s.* two *d.*; ed. Marlborough Coll., Trinity Coll., Cambridge, and Westcott House Theological Coll., Cambridge.

Curate of St. Mary, Portsea 31-33; Chaplain Trinity Coll., Cambridge and Examining Chaplain to Bishop of Bristol 33-36; Vice-Principal Wells Theological Coll. 36-45; Chaplain to the Forces 39-45; Vicar of Huddersfield 45-52; Rural Dean of Huddersfield 45-52; Hon. Canon of Wakefield and Proctor in Convocation Wakefield 47-52; Chaplain to H.M. the King 51-52; Bishop Suffragan of Middleton and Canon Residentiary of Manchester Cathedral 52-57; Archbishop of Melbourne 57-; Chaplain (Victoria) Order of St. John of Jerusalem 62; Primate of the Church of England in Australia 71-.

Leisure interests: tennis, music, walking.

Bishopscourt, Clarendon Street, East Melbourne 3002, Australia.

Telephone: 41-3621.

Woodward, Joanne Cignilliat; American actress; b. 27 Feb. 1930, Thomasville, Ga.; *m.* Paul Newman (*q.v.*) 1958; three *d.*; ed. La. State Univ.

Films include *The Three Faces of Eve, Count Three and Pray, Long Hot Summer, No Down Payment, The Sound and the Fury, A Kiss Before Dying, Rally Round the Flag Boys, Paris Blues* 61, *The Stripper* 63, *A New Kind of Love* 63, *A Big Hand for a Little Lady* 65, *A Fine Madness* 65, *Rachel, Rachel, The Effect of Gamma Rays on Man-in-the-Moon Marigolds* 73, *Summer Wishes, Winter Dreams* 73, *The Drowning Pool* 75; numerous awards including Foreign Press Award for best actress 57, Acad. Award 57, Nat. Board Review Award 57, Best Actress Award, Soc. of Film and TV Arts 74.

c/o Creative Management, Beverly Hills, Calif., U.S.A.

Woodward, Robert Burns, A.M., B.S., PH.D.; American organic chemist; b. 10 April 1917, Boston, Mass.; ed. Massachusetts Inst. of Technology.

Post-doctoral Fellow, Harvard Univ. 37-38, mem. Soc. of Fellows 38-40, Instructor in Chemistry 41-44, Asst. Prof. 44-46, Assoc. Prof. 46-50, Prof. 50-53, Morris Loeb Prof. of Chemistry 53-60, Donner Prof. of Science 60-; Dir. Woodward Research Inst., Basle 63-; Consultant, Polaroid Corpn. 42-; Cttee. on Medical Research 44-45, War Production Board 44-45; mem. Board of Dirs. Ciba-Geigy Ltd., Basle 70-; Centenary Lecturer of Chemical Soc., London 51, Harvard Lecturer, Yale Univ. 59, Lecturer U.S.S.R. Acad. of Sciences, Leningrad 61, Weizmann Memorial Lecturer, Israel 63, etc.; mem. of Corpn. Massachusetts Inst. of Technology 66-71; Fellow, American Acad. of Arts and Sciences; mem. Nat. Acad. of Sciences, American Philosophical Soc.; mem. various foreign Acads.; Hon. Fellow, Chemical Soc., Indian Acad. of Sciences; Hon. degrees include: D.Sc. h.c. Manchester (England), New Brunswick (Canada), Yale, Harvard, Wesleyan, Bucknell Univs., Univ. of Southern California, Univ. of Chicago, Univ. of Cambridge (England), New England Coll. of Pharmacy, Colby Coll., Brandeis Univ., Univ. of Sheffield (England), Israel Inst. of Technology, Polytechnical Inst. of Brooklyn, Univ. of Western Ontario (Canada); Hon. A.M. Harvard Univ. and hon. degrees from Columbia and Louvain Univs.; John Scott Medal 45, Baekeland Medal 55, Ledlie Prize 55, Research Corpn. Award 55, Nichols Medal 56, ACS Synthetic Organic Chemistry Award 57, Richards Medal 58, Davy Medal 59, ACS Roger Adams Award 61, Pius XI Gold Medal of the Pontifical Acad. of Sciences 61, Scientific Achievement Medal 61, Priestly Medallion 62, Stas Medal of Belgian Chemical Soc. 62, Gold Medal for Creative Research in Synthetic Organic Chemistry 62, Nat. Medal of Science (U.S.A.) 64, Kirkwood Medal of Yale Dept. of Chemistry and New Haven Section of ACS 65, Nobel Prize in Chem. 65, Willard Gibbs Medal 67, Lavoisier Medal 68 and others.

Department of Chemistry, Harvard University, Cambridge, Mass. 02138, U.S.A.

Woolcott, Richard, B.A.; Australian diplomatist; b. 11 June 1928, Sydney; ed. Frankston High School, Geelong Grammar School, Univ. of Melbourne and London Univ. School of Slavonic and East European Studies.

Joined Australian Foreign Service 51; served in Australian missions in London, Moscow (twice), S. Africa, Malaya, Singapore and Accra; attended UN Gen. Assembly 62; Acting High Commr. to Singapore 63-64; High Commr. to Ghana 67-70; accompanied Prime Ministers Menzies 65, Holt 66, McMahon 71, 72 and Whitlam 73, 74 on visits to Asia, Europe, the Americas and the Pacific; Head, South Asia Div., Dept. of Foreign Affairs 73; Deputy Sec. Dept. of Foreign Affairs 74; Amb. to Indonesia March 75-.

Australian Embassy, 15 Jalan Thamrin, Gambir, Jakarta, Indonesia.

Wooldridge, Dean E., M.S., PH.D.; American engineer; b. May 1913, Chickasha, Okla.; ed. Univ. of Okla. and Calif. Inst. of Technology.

Member of technical staff, Bell Telephone Labs. 36-46; Dir. of Electronic Research and Devt., Hughes Aircraft Co. 46, subsequently Vice-Pres. for Research and Devt.; Co-founder & Pres. Ramo-Wooldridge Corpn. 53-58, Pres. Thompson Ramo Wooldridge Inc. (TRW Inc.) 58-62, Dir. until 69; Research Assoc. in Engineering, Calif. Inst. of Technology 62-; Chair. Nat. Inst. of Health Study Cttee. 64, 65; Fellow, American Acad. of Arts and Sciences, American Physical Soc., Inst. of Electrical and Electronic Engineers, American Inst. of Aeronautics and Astronautics; mem. Nat. Acad. of Sciences; Citation of Honor, Air Force Asscn.; R. E. Hackett Award 55; Distinguished Service Citation, Univ. of Okla. 60, AAAS—Westinghouse Award for Science Writing.

Publs. *The Machinery of the Brain* 63, *The Machinery of Life* 66, *Mechanical Man: The Physical Basis of Intelligent Life* 68; several articles in journals and magazines.

4545 Via Esperanza, Santa Barbara, Calif. 93110, U.S.A.

Woolford, Harry Russell Halkerston, O.B.E.; British art gallery director; b. 23 May 1905; ed. Edinburgh Coll. of Art; studied art in London, Paris and Italy.

Consultant Restorer, Nat. Gallery of Scotland; Fellow Museums Asscn., Int. Inst. for Conservation of Historic and Artistic works.

Dean Park, Golf Course Road, Bonnyrigg, Midlothian, Scotland.

Telephone: 031-663-7949.

Woollcombe, Kenneth John, M.A., S.T.D.; British ecclesiastic; b. 2 Jan. 1924, Sutton, Surrey; *s.* of Rev. Edward P. Woollcombe O.B.E., and Elsie O. Wood; *m.* Gwendoline R. V. Hodges 1950; three *d.*; ed. Haileybury Coll., Technical Coll., Wednesbury, St. John's Coll., Oxford and Westcott House, Cambridge.

Sub-Lieutenant, R.N.V.R. 45-46; Curate, Grimsby Parish Church 51-53; Fellow, Chaplain and Tutor, St. John's Coll., Oxford 53-60; Prof. of Dogmatic Theology, Gen. Theological Seminary, New York 60-63; Principal of Episcopal Theological Coll., Edinburgh and Canon of St. Mary's Cathedral, Edinburgh 63-71; Bishop of Oxford 71-; Chair. Soc. for Promotion of Christian Knowledge (S.P.C.K.) 73; Hon. Fellow St. John's Coll., Oxford 71; Hon. D.D. (Hartford, Conn.) 75.

Leisure interests: reading, music.

Publs. *Essays on Typology* (joint author) 57, and contributions to other theological publications.

Bishop's House, Cuddesdon, Oxford OX9 9HB, England.

Telephone: Garsington 323.

Woolley, Sir Richard van der Riet, Kt., O.B.E., SC.D.; F.R.S.; British astronomer; b. 24 April 1906, Weymouth, *s.* of Paymaster Rear-Admiral C. E. A. Woolley, C.M.G., and Julia Woolley (née Van der Riet); *m.* Gwyneth Meyler 1932; ed. Univ. of Cape Town, and Gonville and Caius Coll., Cambridge.

Commonwealth Fellow, Mt. Wilson Observatory 29-31; Isaac Newton Student 31-33; Chief Asst., Royal Observatory, Greenwich 33-37; John Couch Adams Astronomer, Cambridge Univ. 37-39; Dir. Commonwealth Solar Observatory, Australia 39-55; Prof. of Astronomy, Australian Nat. Univ. 50-55; Vice-Pres. Int. Astronomical Union 52-58; Pres. Australian and New Zealand Asscn. for the Advancement of Science 55; Astronomer Royal (England) 56-71; Dir., South African Astronomical Observatory Jan. 72-; Pres. Royal Astronomical Soc. 63-65; Master, Worshipful Company of Clockmakers 69; Visiting Prof. of Astronomy, Univ. of Sussex; Hon. LL.D. (Melbourne), Hon. Dr. Phil. (Uppsala), Hon. D.Sc. (Cape Town), Hon. D.Sc. (Sussex); Gold Medal, Royal Astronomical Soc. 71.

Leisure interests: playing piano, bridge, folk dancing.

Publs. *Eclipses of the Sun and Moon* (with Sir Frank Dyson) 37, *The Outer Layers of a Star* (with D. W. N. Stibbs) 53.

South African Astronomical Observatory, P.O. Box 9, Cape Province, South Africa.

Woolsey, Clinton Nathan, M.D.; American professor of neurophysiology; b. 30 Nov. 1904, Brooklyn, N.Y.; *s.* of Joseph Woodhull Woolsey and Lillian Matilda Aichholz; *m.* Harriet Runion 1942; three *s.*; ed. public schools, N.Y. State, Union Coll., Schenectady, N.Y., and Johns Hopkins Univ.

Assistant in Physiology, subsequently Assoc. Prof. of Physiology, Johns Hopkins Univ. School of Medicine 33-48; Charles Sumner Slichter Prof. of Neurophysio-

logy, Univ. of Wis. 48-, Dir. Lab. of Neurophysiology 60-73; Biomedical Unit Co-ordinator Waisman Center on Mental Retardation and Human Devt. 73-; mem. Nat. Acad. of Sciences; Fellow, American Asscn. for the Advancement of Science, American Physiological Soc. and mem. several other professional orgs; mem. Div. of Medical Science, Nat. Research Council 52-58; consultant or mem. many nat. cttees; various awards and hon. lectureships.

Office: 627 Waisman Center, University of Wisconsin, Madison, Wis. 53706; Home: 106 Virginia Terrace, Madison, Wis. 53705, U.S.A.

Telephone: 608-263-5929 (Office); 608-233-6094 (Home).

Wooster, William Alfred, SC.D., PH.D., M.A., B.SC.; British lecturer (retd.) and company director; b. 18 Aug. 1903, London; *s.* of Ernest Alfred Wooster and Rachel Johnson; *m.* Nora Ann Martin 1928; two *s.* one *d.*; ed. Deacon's School, Peterborough, Peterhouse, Cambridge Univ.

University Demonstrator, Dept. of Mineralogy, Cambridge Univ. 28, Lecturer in Dept. of Mineralogy and Petrology 35-75 (now retd.); Dir. and Co-founder, Crystal Structures Ltd. 47-; Hon. Gen. Sec. Asscn. of Scientific Workers 35-57, Pres. 64-67; Treas. World Fed. of Scientific Workers 46-73.

Leisure interests: foreign languages, pottery.

Publs. *Crystal Physics* 38, *Diffuse X-ray Reflections from Crystals* 62, *Experimental Crystal Physics* 70, *Tensors and Group Theory* 73.

339 Cherry Hinton Road, Cambridge, England.

Telephone: Cambridge 811451 (Office); Cambridge 47838 (Home).

Wootton, Baroness (Life Peer), cr. 58, of Abinger; **Barbara Frances Wootton,** M.A., J.P.; British social scientist; b. 14 April 1897, Cambridge; *d.* of James and Adela Marion Adam; *m.* 1st J. W. Wootton 1917 (died 1917), 2nd G. P. Wright 1935 (died 1964); ed. Cambridge Univ.

Director of Studies in Econs., Girton Coll., Cambridge 20-22; Research worker, T.U.C. and Labour Party 22-26; Principal, Morley Coll. for Working Men and Women 26-27; Dir. of Studies in Adult Education, Univ. of London 27-44; Reader in Social Studies, Univ. of London 44-48; Prof. of Social Studies, Univ. of London 48-52; univ. research fellow 52-57; a Governor of the BBC 50-56; Chair. Metropolitan Juvenile Courts 46-62, Nat. Parks Comm. 66-68; Countryside Comm. 68-69; A Deputy Speaker of the House of Lords 66; Hon. LL.D., Hon. D.Litt. and Hon. D.Sc.

Leisure interest: country life.

Publs. *Twos and Threes* 33, *Plan or No Plan* 34, *London's Burning* 36, *Lament for Economics* 38, *Freedom Under Planning* 45, *Testament for Social Science* 50, *Social Foundations of Wage Policy* 55, *Social Science and Social Pathology* 59, *Crime and the Criminal Law* 63, *In a world I never made* 67 (autobiog.), *Contemporary Britain* 71, *Incomes Policy: An Inquest and a Proposal* 74.

High Barn, Abinger Common, Dorking, Surrey, England.

Telephone: Dorking 730 180.

Wootton, Charles Greenwood, M.A., N.D.C.; American diplomatist; b. 8 Aug. 1924, Elizabethtown, Ill.; *s.* of Estel C. Wootton and Sarah B. Greenwood; *m.* Elizabeth Grechko 1944; one *s.* five *d.*; ed. Columbia and Stanford Univs., Nat. Defence Coll. of Canada.

Vice-Consul, Stuttgart 49; Second Sec., American Embassy, Manila 51; Consul, Vice-Consul, Bordeaux 54; Int. Economist, Dept. of Commerce 56; First Sec., Second Sec., Mission to European Communities 59; Counsellor for Econ. and Commercial Affairs, American Embassy, Ottawa 65; Counsellor for Econ. and Commercial Affairs, American Embassy, Bonn 70, Minister 71; Deputy Sec.-Gen. Org. for Econ. Co-operation and

Devt. 74-; Superior Honor Medal, Dept. of State 64, Golden Sports Medal (Fed. Germany) 73.
Leisure interests: jogging, squash, other sports, reading.
Organisation for Economic Co-operation and Development, Château de la Muette, 2 rue André-Pascal, 75775 Paris, Cedex 16, France.
Telephone: 524-8020.

Worden, Alfred M.; American astronaut; b. 7 Feb. 1932, Jackson, Mich; *s.* of Merrill Bangs Worden and Helen Crowell; *m.* 2nd Sandra Lee Wilber 1974; two *d.*; ed. U.S. Military Acad. and Univ. of Michigan.
Commissioned in Air Force; completed flight training, Texas and Florida; pilot and armament officer, 95th Fighter Interceptor Squadron, Andrews Air Force Base, Md. 57-61; attended Instrument Pilots' Instructor School, Randolph Air Force Base, Texas 63; graduated from Empire Test Pilots' School, Farnborough, U.K. 65, and from Aerospace Research Pilots' School 65; selected by NASA as astronaut April 66; designated backup command module pilot *Apollo XII* mission; Crewman, command module pilot, *Apollo XV* July 71. Publs. *Hello Earth—Greetings from Endeavour* (poetry), *A Flight to the Moon.*
Chief, Systems Study Division, Ames Research Center, Moffett Field, Calif. 94035, U.S.A.
Telephone: 415-965-5357.

Worms, Gérard Etienne; French company director; b. 1 Aug. 1936, Paris; *s.* of André Worms and Thérèse Dreyfus; *m.* Michèle Rousseau 1960; one *s.* one *d.*; ed. Lycées Carnot, Saint-Louis, and Ecole Nat. Supérieure des Mines, Paris.
Engineer, Org. commune des régions sahariennes 60-62; Head of Dept., Délégation à l'Aménagement du Territoire et à l'Action Régionale 63-67; Tech. Adviser, Office of Olivier Guichard (Minister of Industry, later of Planning) 67-69, Office of Jacques Chaban-Delmas (Prime Minister) 69-71; Asst. Man. Dir., Librairie Hachette 72-75, Man. Dir. 75-; Prof., Ecole des Hautes Etudes Commerciales 62-69; Supervisor of complementary courses, Faculty of Letters and Human Sciences, Paris 63-69; Prof., Ecole Polytechnique 74-; Chevalier, Ordre Nat. du Mérite, Chevalier, Ordre du Mérite Maritime.
Publs. *Les Méthodes modernes de l'économie appliquée* 65; various articles on economic methods in specialized journals.
61 bis, avenue de la Motte Piquet, 75015 Paris, France.
Telephone: 783-99-43.

Wormser, Olivier Boris; French diplomatist; b. 29 May 1913; *m.* Simone Colomb 1946; two *s.*; ed. Ecole libre des sciences politiques.
French Embassy, Rome 33; with Cabt. of Ministry of French Overseas Territories 34; Cabt. of Under-Sec. of State for Foreign Affairs 36; Lecturer Faculty of Law, Dijon 38-39; Del. of French Cttee. for Nat. Liberation, London 43; Sec. to French Embassy, London 45; with Cen. Admin. 48, Dir. of Econ. and Financial Affairs, Ministry of Foreign Affairs 54-66; Amb. to the U.S.S.R. 66-68; Gov. Bank of France 69-74; Dir. Bank for Int. Settlements; Amb. to Fed. Repub. of Germany 74-; Grand Officer, Légion d'Honneur.
Embassy of France, Kapellenstrasse 1a, Bonn-Bad Godesberg, Federal Republic of Germany; and 72 rue du Cherche-Midi, Paris 6e, France.

Worth, Irene; American actress; b. 23 June 1916; ed. Univ. of Calif. at Los Angeles.
Daily Mail Nat. Television Award 53-54; British Film Acad. Award for *Orders to Kill* 58; Page One Award, Newspaper Guild of New York, for *Toys in the Attic* 60; American Theatre Wing "Tony" Award for *Tiny Alice* 65; *Evening Standard* Award for Noel Coward Trilogy 66; Whitbread Anglo-American Theatre Award 67; Variety Club of Great Britain Award 67.
First appeared as Fenella in *Escape Me Never*, New

York 42; debut on Broadway as Cecily Hardern in *The Two Mrs. Carrolls* 48; London appearances in *Love Goes to Press* 46, *The Play's the Thing* 47, *Edward My Son* 48, *Home is Tomorrow* 48, *Champagne for Delilah* 49, *The Cocktail Party* 50, *Othello* 51, *A Midsummer Night's Dream* 52, *The Other Heart* 52, *The Merchant of Venice* 53, *A Day by the Sea* 53-54, *The Queen and the Rebels* 55, *Hotel Paradiso* 56, *Maria Stuart* 58, *The Potting Shed* 58, *King Lear* 62, *The Physicists* 63, *The Ides of March* 63, *A Song at Twilight* 66, *Shadows of the Evening* 66, *Come into the Garden Maud* 66, *Heartbreak House* 67, *Oedipus* 68, *Notes on a Love Affair*, Lyric Theatre, other appearances include: *The Cocktail Party*, New York 50, Old Vic tour of S. Africa 52, Shakespeare Festival, Stratford, Ont. 53, 59, *A Life in the Sun*, Edinburgh Festival 55, *Maria Stuart*, New York 57, *Toys in the Attic*, New York 60, Royal Shakespeare Theatre, Stratford 62, World tour of *King Lear* 64, *Tiny Alice*, New York 65, worked with Peter Brook's Int. Theatre Research Centre, Paris and Iran 70, 71, Hedda in *Hedda Gabler*, Stratford, Ont. 71, *The Seagull*, Chichester Festival Theatre 73, *Ghosts*, *The Seagull*, *Hamlet*, Greenwich Theatre 74; films include: *Orders to Kill* 57, *The Scapegoat* 58, *King Lear*, *Nicholas and Alexandra* 71.
38 Ladbroke Square, London, W.11, England.

Worthington, Edgar Barton, C.B.E., M.A., PH.D., F.L.S., F.R.G.S.; British scientist; b. 13 Jan. 1905, London; *s.* of Edgar Worthington and Amy Beale; *m.* Stella Johnson 1930; three *d.*; ed. Rugby School, and Gonville and Caius Coll., Cambridge.
Frank Smart Student Gonville and Caius Coll. during Fishing Surveys of African Lakes 27-30; Balfour Student Cambridge Univ. 30-33, Leader Expedition to E. African Lakes; Demonstrator in Zoology Cambridge Univ. 33-37; Scientist for African Research Survey 34-37; Dir. Freshwater Biological Asscn. of British Empire 37-46; Scientific Adviser Middle East Supply Council 43-45; Development Adviser, Uganda 46; Scientific Sec. Colonial Research Council 46-49; Seconded as Scientific Sec. East African High Comm. 47-51; Sec.-Gen. Scientific Council for Africa South of the Sahara 51-55; Deputy Dir.-Gen. (Scientific) Nature Conservancy, London 56-65; Scientific Dir. of International Biological Programme 65-; Mungo Park Medal of Royal Scottish Geographical Soc. 38.
Leisure interests: field sports, farming.
Publs. *Fishing Survey of Lakes Albert and Kioga* 29, *Fisheries of Uganda* 32, *Inland Waters of Africa* (with Stella Worthington) 33, *Science in Africa* 38, *Middle East Science* 46, *Development Plan for Uganda* 47, *Life in Lakes and Rivers* (with T. T. Macan) 51, *Survey of Research and Scientific Services in East Africa* 52, *Science in the Development of Africa* 58, *The Evolution of IBP* 75.
Colin Godmans, Furner's Green, nr. Uckfield, Sussex, England.
Telephone: Chelwood Gate 322.

Wouk, Herman, A.B.; American writer; b. 27 May 1915, New York; *s.* of Abraham Isaac Wouk and Esther Levine; *m.* Betty Sarah Brown 1945; two *s.*; ed. Columbia Univ.
Radio script-writer for leading comedians, New York 35-41; publicity work for U.S. Treasury 41-42; served U.S.N.R. 42-46; Visiting Prof. of English, Yeshiva Univ., N.Y. 52-57; Trustee, Coll. of the Virgin Islands 62-69; mem. Authors' Guild Council, U.S.A., Author's League; Hon. L.H.D. (Yeshiva Univ.); Hon. D.Litt. (Clark Univ.); Pulitzer Prize for Fiction 52, Columbia Univ. Medal of Excellence.
Leisure interests: Hebraic studies, travel.
Publs. *Aurora Dawn* 47, *The City Boy* 48, *Slattery's Hurricane* 49, *The Traitor* (play) 49, *The Caine Mutiny* (novel) 51, *The Caine Mutiny Court-Martial* (play) 53,

Marjorie Morningstar 55, *Nature's Way* (play) 57, *This is my God* 59, revised edn. 73, *Youngblood Hawke* (novel) 62, *Don't Stop the Carnival* (novel) 65, *The Winds of War* (novel) 71.

c/o H. Matson, 22 East 40th Street, New York, N.Y. 10016, U.S.A.

Woytowicz-Rudnicka, Stefania; Polish concert singer; b. 8 Oct. 1922, Orynin; d. of Michał and Domicela Zwolakowska Woytowicz; m. 1952; ed. State Higher School of Music.
Concerts in Europe, U.S.A., China, Japan; tour of Singapore, Hong Kong, New Zealand, India with Australian Broadcasting Comm.; contract with Deutsche Grammophon; also recorded with RCA Victor, Supraphon, Polskie Nagrania and others; participates in Vienna Festival, Edinburgh Festival and others; First Prize in Prague Spring Int. Singing Competition 54, State Prize, 2nd Class 64, Officer's Cross, Order of Polonia Restituta 68, Orpheus Prize, Polish Musicians' Asscn. 67, Diploma of Ministry of Foreign Affairs 70, Medal of 30th Anniversary of People's Poland 74, Prize of Minister of Culture and Arts, 1st Class 75.
Al. Przyjaciół, 00-565 Warsaw, Poland.

Wrangham, Cuthbert Edward, C.B.E.; British former business executive; b. 16 Dec. 1907, London; s. of Walter George Wrangham and Evelyn Wilberforce; m. 1st Teresa Jane Cotton 1935, 2nd Jean Behrens 1958; three s. two d.; ed. Eton Coll., and King's Coll., Cambridge.
Air Ministry and Min. of Aircraft Production 39-45; Chair. Shelbourne Hotel Ltd. 50-60; Monopolies Commission 54-56; Chair. Power Gas Corpn. Ltd. 60-61, Short Bros. and Harland Ltd. 61-67, Marine and General Mutual Life Assurance Society 61-72, C. Tennant Sons & Co. Ltd. 67-72, Doxford and Sunderland Ltd. 69-71; Joint Treas. Anti-Slavery Soc. 68-72.
Leisure interests: gardening, books, walking.
Rosemary House, Catterick, Yorkshire, England.
Telephone: Old Catterick 375.

Wrathall, John James; Rhodesian chartered accountant and politician; b. 28 Aug. 1913, Lancaster, England; s. of late T. Wrathall; m. 1946; two s.; ed. Lancaster Royal Grammar School, England.
Worked in Income Tax Dept., Southern Rhodesia 36-46; Sec. of public co. 47-49; private practice, Bulawayo 50-63; mem. Parl. 63-75, Deputy Speaker Jan.-Oct. 63; Minister of Health and Educ. 63-64, of Finance 64-75, of Posts 64-73; Deputy Prime Minister 66-75; Senator 74-75; Pres. of Rhodesia Jan. 76-; Independence Decoration.
Leisure interests: tennis, fishing.
Box 368, Salisbury, Rhodesia.
Telephone: 26666.

Wriedt, Kenneth Shaw; Australian politician; b. 11 July 1927; ed. Univ. High School, Melbourne.
Served in the Merchant Navy 44-58; State Insurance Office, Tasmania 58-67; mem. Senate 67-; Minister of Primary Industry 72-73; Minister for Agriculture June 74-Nov. 75; Leader of Govt. in Senate Feb.-Nov. 75; Labor Party.
Parliament House, Canberra, A.C.T.; Marine Board Building, Hobart, Tasmania; Home: 25 Corinth Street, Howrah, Hobart, Tasmania 7018, Australia.

Wrigge, Friedrich Wilhelm, DR.ING.; German business executive; b. 22 Dec. 1906, Hannover; s. of Heinrich Wrigge and Frieda Neddenriep; m. Käte Harcke 1934; one s. two d.; ed. Technische Hochschule, Hannover.
Assistant, Technische Hochschule, Hannover 29; Chemist, Vereinigte Aluminiumwerke AG 37, mem. Administrative Board 57-, now Chief Spokesman.
Vereinigte Aluminiumwerke AG, 53 Bonn 1, Postfach

626; Home: Am Stadtwald 43, 532 Bad Godesberg, Federal Republic of Germany.
Telephone: 02221-353674 (Home).

Wright, Benjamin Fletcher, PH.D.; American educationist; b. 8 Feb. 1900; ed. Texas and Harvard Univs.
Teacher Univ. of Texas 22-26; Instructor to Prof. of Govt., Harvard 26-49, Chair. Dept. of Govt. 42-46, of Gen. Education 46-49; President, Smith Coll. 49-59; Fellow Center Advanced Study Behavioral Sciences 59-60; Prof. of Govt., Univ. of Texas 60-; Jefferson Lecturer, Univ. of Calif. 64; Visiting Prof. of Govt., Harvard 66-67; American Acad. of Arts and Sciences; Hon. LL.D., Litt.D.
Publs. *American Interpretations of Natural Law* 31, *Contract Clause of the Constitution* 38, *Growth of American Constitutional Law* 42, *Consensus and Continuity* 58, ed. *The Federalist, The Five Public Philosophies of Walter Lippmann* 73.
1415 Wathen Avenue, Austin, Texas 78703, U.S.A.

Wright, Sir Denis Arthur Hepworth, G.C.M.G.; British diplomatist; b. 23 March 1911, Kingston upon Thames; m. Iona Craig 1939; ed. Brentwood School, and St. Edmund Hall, Oxford.
Assistant Advertising Man., Gallaher and Co. Ltd. 35-39; Vice-Consul, Constanza 40-41, Trebizond 41-43; Acting Consul, Mersin 43-45; Commercial Sec., Belgrade 46-48; Consul Chicago 49-51; Head Econ. Relations Dept. Foreign Office 51-53; Chargé d'Affaires and Counsellor, Teheran 53-55; Asst. Under-Sec. of State, Foreign Office 55-59, 62; Amb. to Ethiopia 59-62, to Iran 63-71; retd. 71; Dir. Chartered Bank, Standard Chartered Banking Ltd., Mitchell Cotts Group, and Shell Transport and Trading Co.
Duck Bottom, Flint Street, Haddenham, Aylesbury, Bucks., England.
Telephone: Haddenham 291086.

Wright, Georg Henrik von, M.A., DR. PHIL.; Finnish philosopher; b. 14 June 1916, Helsinki; s. of Tor von Wright and Ragni Elisabeth Alfthan; m. Baroness Maria Elisabeth von Troil 1941; one s. one d.; ed. Helsinki and Cambridge Univs.
Lecturer in Philosophy Univ. of Helsinki 43-46; Prof. of Philosophy Univ. of Helsinki 46-61; Prof. of Philosophy Univ. of Cambridge 48-51; sometime Fellow Trinity Coll., Cambridge; Visiting Prof. Cornell Univ. 54, 58, Univ. of Calif. 63, Univ. of Pittsburgh 66; Gifford Lecturer Univ. of St. Andrews 59-60; Research Fellow Acad. of Finland 61-; Andrew D. White Prof.-at-Large, Cornell Univ. 65-; Chancellor of Åbo Acad. 68-; Tarner Lecturer, Trinity Coll., Cambridge 69; Woodbridge Lecturer, Columbia Univ. 72; Fellow Finnish Soc. of Sciences, Royal Swedish Acad. of Sciences, British Acad., Royal Danish Acad. of Sciences; Hon. Foreign mem. American Acad. of Arts and Sciences; Pres. Philosophical Soc. of Finland 62-73; Pres. Int. Union of History and Philosophy of Science 63-65, Inst. Int. de Philosophie, Paris 75-; Dr. h.c. Univ. of Helsinki, Univ. of Liverpool, Lund Univ., Univ. of Turku.
Publs. *The Logical Problem of Induction* 41 (2nd revised edn. 57), *A Treatise on Induction and Probability* 51, *An Essay in Modal Logic* 51, *Logical Studies* 57, *The Varieties of Goodness* 63, *Norm and Action* 63, *The Logic of Preference* 63, *An Essay in Deontic Logic* 68, *Explanation and Understanding* 71, *Causality and Determinism* 74.
4 Skepparegatan, Helsinki, Finland.
Telephone: 655-192.

Wright, H.E. Cardinal John Joseph; American ecclesiastic; b. 18 July 1909, Dorchester, Boston.
Ordained 35; Titular Bishop of Egee 47; Bishop of Worcester 50-59, of Pittsburgh 59-69; Prefect of Congregation for the Clergy 69-; cr. Cardinal 69; mem. Board Nat. Inter-religious Cttee. for Peace, American

Acad. of Arts and Sciences; Knight, Commdr. of the Holy Sepulchre, Officier Légion d'Honneur, Officer Order of Merit of the Italian Republic.
Publs. *Words in Pain, The Christian and the Law, The Church: Hope of the World, Conscience and Authority.*
Piazza della Città Leonina 9, 00193 Rome, Italy.

Wright, Sir (John) Oliver, K.C.M.G., D.S.C.; British diplomatist; b. 6 March 1921, London; *m.* Marjory Osborne 1942; three *s.*; ed. Solihull School, and Christ's Coll., Cambridge.
Royal Navy 41-45; joined Foreign Office Nov. 45; served New York 46-47, Bucharest 48-50, Singapore 50-52, Berlin 54-56, Pretoria 57-58; Imperial Defence Coll. 59; Asst. Private Sec. to Foreign Sec. 60-63, Private Sec. Jan. 63-Nov. 63; Private Sec. to Prime Minister Nov. 63-June 66; Amb. to Denmark 66-69; U.K. Rep. to Northern Ireland Govt. Aug. 69-March 70; Deputy Under-Sec. of State and Chief Clerk, Foreign and Commonwealth Office 70-72; Deputy Under-Sec. for EEC and Economic Affairs 72-75; Amb. to Fed. Repub. of Germany 75-.
Leisure interests: theatre, gardening.
British Embassy, Friedrich-Ebert-Allee 77 Bonn, Federal Republic of Germany; Home: Burstow Hall, nr. Horley, Surrey, England.
Telephone: Horley 3494.

Wright, Judith Arundell; Australian writer; b. 31 May 1915; Armidale, N.S.W.; *m.* J. P. McKinney; one *d.*; ed. New England Girls' School, Armidale, N.S.W., and Sydney Univ.
Commonwealth Literary Fund Scholarship 49, 62; Lecturer in Australian literature at various Australian univs.; Fellow, Australian Acad. of Humanities; Hon. D.Litt., Univs. of Queensland and New England; Encyclopedia Britannica Writers' Award 64.
Publs. Poetry: *The Moving Image* 46, *Woman to Man* 49, *The Gateway* 53, *The Two Fires* 55, *A Book of Birds* 62, *Five Senses* 63, *The Other Half* 66, *Collected Poems* 71, *Alive* 72; criticism: *Charles Harpur* 63, *Preoccupations in Australian Poetry* 64, *Because I was Invited* 75; anthologies: *A Book of Australian Verse* 56, *New Land, New Language* 57; biography: *The Generations of Man* 58; short stories: *The Nature of Love* 66; also books for children.
c/o Angus & Robertson Ltd., P.O. Box 177, Cremorne Junction, S.W. 2090, Australia.

Wright, Louis Booker, PH.D., F.R.S.A., F.R.S.L., F.R.HIST.S.; American librarian and historian; b. 1 March 1899, Greenwood, S.C.; *s.* of Thomas Fleming and Lena Booker Wright; *m.* Frances Marion Black 1925; one *s.*; ed. Wofford Coll., and Univ. of North Carolina.
Newspaper Corresp. and Editor 18-23; Dept. of English, Univ. of N. Carolina 26-32; Guggenheim Fellow, England and Europe 28-29, 30; Visiting Scholar, Huntington Library 31-32, mem. Perm. Research Group 32-48; Visiting Prof. of Bibliography and Research Methods, Univ. of Calif., Los Angeles 34-48; Assoc. mem. of Faculty, Calif. Inst. of Technology 32-48; Dir. Folger Shakespeare Library 48-68; Chair. Advisory Board, John Simon Guggenheim Memorial Foundation 50-71; Vice-Chair., Board of Dirs., Council on Library Resources 56-; mem. Board of Dirs., Henry Francis du Pont Winterthur Museum 55-, Harry S. Truman Library Inst. 56-; Chair. Board of Visitors, Tulane Univ. 70-; Life Trustee Shakespeare Birthplace Trust, Nat. Geographic Soc.; History Consultant, Nat. Geographic Soc. 71-; Benjamin Franklin Medal, Royal Soc. of Arts 69; Hon. O.B.E. 68; Cosmos Club Award 73; numerous hon. degrees.
Leisure interests: dry fly fishing, walking.
Publs. incl. *Middle Class Culture in Elizabethan England* 35, 59, *The First Gentlemen of Virginia* 40, *The Secret Diary of William Byrd of Westover 1709-1712* 41, *The

Atlantic Frontier 47, 59, *The History and Present State of Virginia 1705 by Robert Beverley* 47, *Culture on the Moving Frontier* 52, *The Cultural Life of the American Colonies* 57, *William Byrd of Virginia, The London Diary 1717-1721, and Other Writings* 58, *Shakespeare for Everyman* 64, *The Dream of Prosperity in Colonial America* 65, *The Prose Works of William Byrd of Westover* (editor) 66, *Folger Library General Reader's Shakespeare* (editor), *Gold, Glory and the Gospel* 70, *West and by North: North America seen through the eyes of its Seafaring Discoverers* 71, and *The Moving Frontier: North America seen through the eyes of its Pioneer Discoverers* 72 (with Elaine W. Fowler), *Barefoot in Arcadia: Memories of a More Innocent Era* 74.
National Geographic Society, 17th and M Streets, N.W., Washington, D.C. 20036; Home: 3702 Leland Street, Chevy Chase, Md. 20015, U.S.A.
Telephone: 223-3426 (Office); 652-5509 (Home).

Wright, Hon. Reginald Charles, B.A., LL.B.; Australian politician; b. 10 July 1905, Tasmania; *m.*; two *s.* four *d.*; ed. Univ. of Tasmania.
Called to the Bar 28; Lecturer in Law Univ. of Tasmania 31-41, 44-45; Pres. Tasmanian Liberal Party 45-46; mem. State House of Assembly, becoming Deputy Leader of the Opposition 46-49; mem. Senate 49-; Govt. Whip 50-51; sat on numerous Parl. Cttees.; Minister for Works and in Charge of Tourist Activities 68-72; War service in Australian Imperial Force 41-44; Liberal.
The Senate, Canberra, A.C.T., Australia.

Wright, Rowland Sydney, B.SC., C.B.E., F.R.S.A., F.R.I.C.; British business executive; b. 4 Oct. 1915, Northampton; *s.* of late Sydney H. Wright and Elsie M. Wright; ed. High Pavement School, Nottingham and Univ. Coll. Nottingham.
Joined ICI Ltd. (Dyestuffs Div.) 37; Production Dir. Imperial Chemical (Pharmaceuticals) Ltd. 55-57; Production Dir. Dyestuffs Div. 57-58; Research Dir. 58-61; Joint Man. Dir. ICI Ltd., Agricultural Div. 61-63, Chair. Agricultural Div. 64-65; Dir. ICI Ltd. 66; Personnel Dir. 66-70; Dir. AE & CI Ltd. 70, Deputy Chair. 71-75; Deputy Chair. ICI Ltd. 71-75, Chair. 75-; Chair. Reorganization Cttee. for Eggs 67-68; mem. Council, Foundation for Management Educ. 67-70, Council of Chemical Industries Asscn. 68-73, British Shippers' Council 75; Pres. Inst. of Manpower Studies 71-; Vice-Pres. Soc. of Chemical Industry 71-74; Dir. Royal Insurance Co. Ltd. 73-; Gov. London Graduate School of Business Studies 75; Fellow British Inst. of Management; Trustee Civic Trust.
Leisure interests: gardening, photography.
ICI Ltd., Millbank, London, S.W.1, England.
Telephone: 01-834-4444.

Wright, Roy W., C.B.E.; British mining executive. Former Dir. Brush Engineering Co.; joined Rio Tinto Zinc Corpn. 52; subsequently Man. Dir. Rio Tinto Mining Co. of Canada; Deputy Chair., Deputy Chief Exec. Rio Tinto Zinc Corpn. 65-75, non-exec. Dir. 75-; non-exec. Dir. Palabora Mining Co., Rio Tinto S. Africa Ltd., Rio Algom Ltd., Davy Int. Ltd.; Chair. Lornex Mining Co.
Rio Tinto Zinc Corpn., 6 St. James's Square, London, S.W.1, England.

Wright, Sewall, B.S., M.S., D.SC.; American biologist; b. 21 Dec. 1889, Melrose, Mass.; *s.* of Philip Green Wright and Elizabeth Quincy Sewall; *m.* Louise Lane Williams 1921; two *s.* one *d.*; ed. Lombard Coll., Univ. of Illinois, and Harvard Univ.
Ernest D. Burton Distinguished Service Prof. of Zoology, Univ. of Chicago 37-54; Fulbright Prof. Univ. of Edinburgh 49-50; Leon J. Cole Prof. of Genetics, Univ. of Wisconsin 55-60, Prof. Emer. 60-; Pres. Genetics Society of America 34; Pres. American Society of Zoologists 44; Pres. American Society of Naturalists

52, Society for the Study of Evolution 55; Pres. 10th Int. Genetics Con. 58; mem. U.S. Philosophical Society, Nat. Acad. of Sciences, American Acad. of Arts and Sciences; Foreign mem. Royal Soc. (England), Royal Danish Acad. of Sciences and Letters; Hon. F.R.S.E., Genetical Soc.; Nat. Medal of Science 66; many hon. degrees.

Leisure interest: travel.

Publs. on genetics of guinea pigs, inbreeding, cross-breeding, statistical consequences of Mendelian heredity, evolution, *Evolution and the Genetics of Populations* Vol. 1 68, Vol. 2 69.

3905 Council Crest, Madison, Wis. 53711, U.S.A.

Wright, Stephen Junius, M.A., PH.D.; American university president; b. 8 Sept. 1910, Dillon, S.C.; s. of Dr. and Mrs. Stephen Wright; m. Rosalind E. Person 1938; ed. Hampton Inst., Howard and New York Univs.

Teacher Kennard High School, Maryland 34-36; Principal, Douglass High School 36-38; Dir. Student Teaching, North Carolina Coll. 39-41, Chair. Dept. of Educ., Act. Dean of Men 43-44; Prof. of Educ., Dir. Educ. Div., Hampton Inst. 44-45, Dean of Faculty of Educ. 45-53; Pres. Bluefield State Coll., West Virginia 53-57; Pres. Fisk Univ. 57-66, United Negro Coll. Fund Inc. 66-69; Vice-Pres. Coll. Entrance Examination Board 69-; mem. Board of Trustees Meharry Medical Coll., Hampton Inst.; mem. Board Arms Control and Disarmament Advisory Cttee., Inst. of Int. Educ. Board, Shaw Univ. Board of Trustees; mem. Nat. Council on Humanities, Policy Comm. of Nat. Assessment of Educ. Progress of the Educ. Comm. of the States; Hon. LL.D. Colby Coll., Notre Dame, Michigan State, New York and Rhode Island Univs., Morgan State Coll., Hon. D.Litt. Coll. of St. Thomas and Manhattan Coll.

Home: 595 Ramapo Road, Teaneck, N.J. 07666; Office: College Entrance Examination Board, 888 Seventh Avenue, New York, N.Y. 10019, U.S.A.

Telephone: 212-582-6210.

Wriston, Henry Merritt, A.M., PH.D.; American educationist; b. 4 July 1889, Laramie, Wyo.; s. of Henry Lincoln and Jennie Amelia Atcheson Wriston; m. 1st Ruth Colton Bigelow 1914 (died 1946), 2nd Marguerite Woodworth 1947; one s. (q.v.) one d.; ed. Wesleyan and Harvard Univs.

Instructor and Prof. of History, Wesleyan Univ. 14-25; Pres. of Lawrence Coll. 25-37; Dir. Inst. of Paper Chemistry 29-37; Pres. Brown Univ., Providence, Rhode Is. 37-55; Vice-Pres. Council on Foreign Relations 50-51, Pres. 51-64, Hon. Pres. 64-; Exec. Dir. American Assembly 55-58, Pres. 58-62, Chair. 62-66, Emer. 66-; Chair. Sec. of State's Public Cttee. on Personnel 54, President's Comm. on Nat. Goals 61; Pres. Asscn. of American Colls. 35-36, Asscn. of American Univs. 48-50; mem. Exec. Cttee. American Council of Educ. 41-44; Hon. C.B.E., Hon. ED.D., D.C.L., L.H.D., Litt.D., LL.D.

Leisure interests: gardening, water-lilies, writing.

Publs. *War Chest Practice, Report of Connecticut State Council of Defense, Executive Agents in American Foreign Relations, The Nature of a Liberal College, Prepare for Peace, Challenge to Freedom, Strategy of Peace, Diplomacy in a Democracy, Academic Procession, Policy Perspectives.*

12 Beekman Place, New York, N.Y. 10022, U.S.A.

Telephone: 3-2238.

Wriston, Walter B., B.A., M.A.; American banker; b. 3 Aug. 1919, Middleton, Conn.; s. of Henry Merritt Wriston (q.v.) and late Ruth Bigelow; m. Kathryn A. Dineen 1968; one d.; ed. Wesleyan Univ., The Fletcher School of Law and Diplomacy, Ecole Française and American Inst. of Banking.

Junior Insp., Comptrollers Div., First Nat. City Bank

46-48, Senior Insp. 48-49, Domestic Div. 49-50, Asst. Cashier 50-52, Asst. Vice-Pres. 52-54, Vice-Pres. 54-58, European District 56-58, Senior Vice-Pres. 58-59, in charge of Overseas Div. 59-61, Exec. Vice-Pres. 60-67, Pres. and Dir. First Nat. City Bank 67-70; Chair. and Dir. First Nat. City Bank and CITICORP 70- and other cos.; Trustee The Rand Corpn.; mem. Nat. Comm. for Industrial Peace, Advisory Cttee. on Reform of Int. Monetary System, Labor-Management Advisory Cttee., Business Council; Hon. LL.D. (Lawrence Coll., Brown, Tufts and Columbia Univs.), D. C. S. (Pace and St. John's Univs.).

First National City Bank, 399 Park Avenue, New York, N.Y. 10022, U.S.A.

Wroński, Stanisław; Polish politician; b. 17 June 1916 Sielec, Jedrzejów district; ed. Warsaw Univ. and Inst. of Social Sciences, Cen. Cttee. of Polish United Workers' Party, Warsaw.

Member, Communist Union of Polish Youth 30-36, Polish Workers' Party 45-48, Polish United Workers' Party (PUWP) 48-; Dep. mem. Cen Cttee., PUWP 64-68, mem. 68-; Lecturer, Inst. of Social Sciences 50-56; Scientific Worker, Polish Acad. of Sciences and Military Historical Inst. 57-62; Pres. and Editor-in-Chief, Publishing Co-operative "Książka i Wiedza" 63-71; Deputy to Seym; Vice-Chair. Seym Comm. of Culture and Art 69-72; Minister of Culture and Art 71-74, without Portfolio Feb.-June 74; mem. Council of State 74-; Chair. ZBoWid (Union of Fighters for Freedom and Democracy) 72-; Editor-in-Chief *Nowe Drogi* 74-; mem. Polish Inst. of Foreign Affairs, Inst. of History of Polish-Soviet Friendship, Polish Acad. of Sciences; mem. Cen. Board Soc. for Polish Soviet Friendship; mem. other scientific councils, etc.; Order of Banner of Labour, Grunwald Cross.

Publs. numerous papers on modern history.

Ul. Piotra Maszyńskiego, 00-485 Warsaw, Poland.

Telephone: 28-09-61 (Office).

Wrzaszczyk, Tadeusz; M.ENG.; Polish politician; b. 1932, Stradom; ed. Technical Univ., Warsaw.

Constructor at Wireless Factory T-1, Warsaw 54-56; managerial posts at Motor-Car Factory (FSO), Warsaw 56-65, Chief Engineer 62-65; Vice-Chair. Gen. Board, Polish Mechanical Engineers and Technicians Asscn. 60-65; Dir.-Gen., Motorization Industry Union 65-70; Asst. Prof. Inst. of Motor Vehicles, Warsaw Technical Univ. 70-; Minister of Engineering Industry 70-75; mem. Cen. Cttee. Polish United Workers' Party (PZPR) 71-; Vice-Chair. State Council, Chair. Planning Cttee. of Council of Ministers 75-; Order of Banner of Labour, 2nd class and other decorations.

Ministerstwo Przemysłu Maszynowego, Ul. Krucza 36, 00-522 Warsaw, Poland.

Wu Chien-Shiung, PH.D.; American professor of physics; b. 31 May 1912, Shanghai, China; d. of Mr. and Mrs. Z. Y. Wu; m. Dr. Luke C. L. Yuan 1940; one s.; ed. Nat. Central Univ. and Univ. of Calif.

Professor of Physics, Columbia Univ. 58-; mem. of Nat. Acad. of Sciences; Hon. Fellow, Royal Soc. of Edinburgh; Dr. h.c. (Princeton, Yale and Rutger's Univs. and Smith and Goucher Colls., Chinese Univ. of Hong Kong); Research Co-operation Award, Comstock Award of Nat. Acad. of Sciences, Woman of the Year Award of American Asscn. of Women, Chia-Hsin Outstanding Achievement Award.

Publs. *Beta Decay* (with S. A. Moszkouski), *Experimental Nuclear Physics* (Co-Editor with Luke C. L. Yuan), *Weak Interaction* (with T. D. Lee).

15 Claremont Avenue, New York, N.Y. 10027, U.S.A.

Wu Kuei-hsien; Chinese party official; b. 1935. Woman worker in textile mill at N.W. State Cotton Mill No. 1, Sian; mem. Shensi Revolutionary Cttee. 68; mem. 9th Cen. Cttee. of CCP 69; Deputy Sec. CCP

Shensi 71; Alt. mem. Politburo, CCP 73-; Vice-Premier of State Council 75-.
People's Republic of China.

Wu Te; Chinese party official; b. 1914, Fengjun, Hopei; ed. China Univ., Peking.
Workers leader in Tangshan 35; Regimental Political Commissar 42; Vice-Minister of Fuel Industry 49-50; Sec. CCP Pingyuan 50-52; Deputy Sec. CCP Tientsin 52-55; Deputy Mayor of Tientsin 52-53, Mayor 53-55; Pres. Tientsin Univ. 52-57; Alt. mem. 8th Cen. Cttee. of CCP 56; First Sec. CCP Kirin 56-66; Political Commissar Kirin Mil. District, People's Liberation Army 58; Sec. N.E. Bureau, CCP 61; Second Sec. CCP Peking 66; Acting Mayor of Peking 66; Vice-Chair. Peking Revolutionary Cttee. 67-72, Chair. 72; mem. 9th Cen. Cttee. of CCP 69; Head of Cultural Group, State Council 71; Second Sec. CCP Peking 71, First Sec. 72; mem. 10th Politburo, CCP 73; Second Political Commissar Peking Mil. Region, PLA.
People's Republic of China.

Wünsche, Kurt Hermann, DR. IUR.; German lawyer and politician; b. 14 Dec. 1929, Obernigk; s. of Dr. Phil. Hermann Wünsche and Hilde (née Wagner); m. Ursula Kreutzer 1952; one s.; ed. Schillerschule, Dresden, and Deutsche Akademie für Staats- und Rechtswissenschaft "Walter Ulbricht", Potsdam-Babelsberg.
Secretary of Cen. Management Cttee. of Liberal Democratic Party 54-60; Deputy Sec.-Gen. of Liberal Democratic Party 60-65, Deputy Chair. 67-; Vice-Chair. of Council of Ministers of German Democratic Repub. (D.D.R.) 66-74, also Minister of Justice; mem. Volkskammer 54-, Presidium of League for People's Friendship 61-71, Presidium of Nat. Council of Nat. Front 70-; Vaterländischer Verdienstorden der D.D.R. in Bronze and Silver, and other medals.
Publ. *Funktion und Entwicklung der Liberal-Demokratischen Partei Deutschlands im Mehrparteiensystem der Deutschen Demokratischen Republik* 64.
108 Berlin, Klara Zetkin Str. 93, German Democratic Republic.

Wurfbain, Johan Cornelis, DRS.ECON.; Netherlands economist and banker; b. 18 Sept. 1907, Arnhem; ed. Dutch School of Econs., Rotterdam.
Manager, Van Ranzow's Bank, Arnhem 36; Man. De Twentsche Bank N.V. 52; Man. Algemene Bank Nederland N.V. 64, mem. Presidium 69, Pres. 70-72, mem. Supervisory Board 72-.
Algemene Bank Nederland N.V., Amsterdam, 32 Vijzelstraat, Netherlands.

Wurmser, René Bernard; French professor of biochemistry; b. 24 Sept. 1890, Paris; m. Sabine Filitti 1936; ed. Univ. of Paris.
Director of Biophysical Laboratory of Ecole des Hautes Etudes 27-45; Prof. Faculté des Sciences, Univ. of Paris 45-60, Hon. Prof. 60-; mem. Acad. des Sciences.
Publs. *Recherches sur l'Assimilation chlorophyllienne* 21, *Oxydations et Reductions* 30, *Thermodynamique des Réactions Immunologiques* 54.
36 rue de l'Université, 75007 Paris, France.

Wurth, Pierre, D. EN D.; Luxembourg diplomatist; b. 10 June 1926, Luxembourg; m. Jeanine Rentier 1968; ed. Lycée de Garçons, Luxembourg, and Univ. of Paris.
Lawyer 51-52; Ministry of Foreign Affairs, Luxembourg 53-54; Luxembourg Embassy, Paris 54-59; Dep. Chief, Political Section, Ministry of Foreign Affairs, Luxembourg, and Perm. Rep. to Council of Europe 59-64; Perm. Rep. of Luxembourg to UN 64-68; Amb. to U.S.S.R. and Poland 68-71; Sec.-Gen., Ministry of Foreign Affairs 71-.
Ministry of Foreign Affairs, 5 rue Notre Dame, Luxembourg.

Wüst, Georg, PH.D.; German oceanographer; b. 15 June 1890, Posen; s. of Max and Clara Wüst; m. 1st Martha Weyringer 1921, 2nd Mimy Holdorf 1943; two d.; ed. Berlin Univ.
Oceanographer of the *Meteor* Atlantic Expedition 25-27 and of *Altair* Gulf Stream Expedition 38; Prof. of Oceanography, Berlin Univ. 28-45; Prof. of Oceanography, Kiel Univ. and Dir. Inst. for Marine Research Kiel 46-59, Emer. 60-; Visiting Prof., Columbia Univ. 60-64, Walker-Ames Prof., Univ. of Washington (Seattle) 62, Guest Prof., Bonn Univ. 65-67.
Leisure interests: literature, golf, navigation, Rotary Club.
Publs. *Verdunstung auf dem Meere* 20, *Florida-und Antillenstrom* 23, *Schichtung und Zirkulation des Atlantischen Ozeans* 35-38, *Kuroshio und Golfstrom* 36, *Bodentemperatur und Bodenstrom in der Pazifischen Tiefsee* 37, *Kreisläufe des Wassers* 50-51, *Wechselbeziehungen zwischen Ozean und Atmosphäre* 54, *Stromgeschwindigkeiten im Tiefen- und Bodenwasser des Atlantischen Ozeans* 55, *Stromgeschwindigkeiten und Strommengen in der Atlantischen Tiefsee* 57, *Vertical Circulation in the Mediterranean Sea* 61, *Stratification and Circulation in the Caribbean Sea* 63, *Major Deep-Sea Expeditions and Research Vessels (1873-1960)* 64, *History of Investigations of the Longitudinal Deep-Sea Circulation 1800-1922* 68, and other scientific publications.
Wohnstift Rathsberger Strasse 63, 8520 Erlangen, Federal Republic of Germany.
Telephone: Wohnstift 82-5362.

Wüthrich, Ernst; Swiss trade unionist; b. 27 Jan. 1905. Secretary, Swiss Metalworkers' and Watchmakers' Asscn. 46, Pres. 58-; Pres. Swiss Fed. of Trade Unions (Schweizerischer Gewerkschaftsbund) 70-73.
c/o Schweizerischer Gewerkschaftsbund, Postfach 64, Berne 23, Switzerland.

Wuttke, Hans A., DR.JUR.; German banker; b. 23 Oct. 1923, Hamburg; m. Maria M. Schorsch 1957; two s. two d.; ed. Univs. of Cologne and Salamanca.
With Dresdner Bank A.G. 49-54, Daimler-Benz A.G. 54-61; Partner M.M. Warburg-Brinckmann, Wirtz and Co., Hamburg 61-75; Exec. Dir. S. G. Warburg and Co., Ltd., London; Dir. S. G. Warburg and Co. Int. Holdings Ltd., Warburg Parisbas Becker Inc., N.Y.; Chair. Board of Dirs., European Australian Associates; Exec. Chair. Effectenbank-Warburg AG; Deputy Chair. Standard Elektrik Lorenz AG, Deutsche Babcock & Wilcox AG; Chair. Claudius Peters AG; mem. Board Rolls-Royce Motors Ltd., German Devt. Co. Cologne, Landeszentralbank, Hamburg, Australian United Corpn. Ltd.; Chair. Board, Hüttenmetall GmbH, Peek and Cloppenburg; Pres. Australian-New Zealand Asscn., mem. Board East Asia Asscn., Hamburg.
M.M. Warburg-Brinckmann, Wirtz and Co., Ferdinandstrasse 75, 2000 Hamburg 1, Federal Republic of Germany.
Telephone: 32-82-1.

Wyart, Jean, D. ès s.; French university professor; b. 16 Oct. 1902, Avion; m. Madeleine Bourdon 1943; one s.; ed. Ecole Normale Supérieure.
Asst. Univ. of Paris 28, Deputy Prof. 33-46; Prof. of Mineralogy, Sorbonne and Ecole de Physique et Chimie 46-; Sec. French Society of Mineralogy 31-40, Pres. 45; Dir. of Documentation Service of Nat. Centre of Scientific Research 41-; Pres. Int. Union of Crystallography 57; mem. Acad. des Sciences 59, Deutsche Akademie der Naturforscher Leopoldina 66; Hon. mem. Royal Inst. 60.
Leisure interests: sport, travel.
Université de Paris, Tour 16, 4 Place Jussieu, 75230 Paris; Home: 18 rue Pierre-Curie, Paris 5e, France.
Telephone: DAN 94-29.

Wycech, Czesław; Polish retired politician; b. 20 July 1899, Wilczogęby, Węgrów district; ed. Teachers' Inst., Warsaw.

Active in popular movement and Union of Polish Teachers before Second World War; Dir. Dept. of Education and Culture, Polish Govt. in Exile during German occupation; Pres. Union of Polish Teachers 45; Minister of Education 45-47; mem. Polish Peasant Party 45-49; mem. United Peasant Party 49-, Deputy Chair. 56-62, Chair. of Supreme Exec. 62-71; Vice-Pres. Council of State 56-57; Deputy to Seym (Parl.) 47-72, Marshal of Seym 57-71; Order of Builders of People's Poland, and other decorations.

Publs. on the history of peasant movements, including *Powstanie chłopów w 1848 r.* (The Peasant Uprising in 1848), *Z dziejów chłopskich walk o społeczne wyzwolenie* (On the History of Peasant Struggles for Social Liberation), *Z przeszłości ruchów chłopskich 1768-1861* (On the History of Peasant Movements 1768-1861), *Ks. Piotr Ściegienny 1840-1880* (Father Piotr Sciegienny 1840-1880), *Społeczna gospodarka rolna w polskiej myśli politycznej* (Socially-Run Farming in Polish Political Thought).

Ul. Koszykowa 10, Warsaw, Poland.

Wyckoff, Ralph Walter Graystone, B.S., PH.D.; American scientist; b. 9 Aug. 1897, Geneva, N.Y.; *s.* of Abram Ralph Wyckoff and Ethel Agnes Catchpole; *m.* Laura Kissam Laidlaw 1927; one *s.* two *d.*; ed. Hobart Coll., and Cornell Univ.

Instructor, analytical chemistry, Cornell Univ. 17-19; Physical Chemist, Geophysical Laboratory, Carnegie Inst. of Washington 19-27; Research Assoc., Calif. Inst. of Technology 21-22; Assoc. mem. Rockefeller Inst. for Medical Research 27-37; with Lederle Laboratories Inc. as scientist 37-40, as Assoc. Dir. in charge of virus research 40-42; Technical Dir., Reichel Laboratories Inc. 42-43; Lecturer in epidemiology, Univ. of Michigan 43-45; Senior Scientist, U.S. Public Health Service 45; Scientist Dir. 46-52; Foreign Service Reserve Officer (Science Office), American Embassy, London 52-54; Biophysicist, P.H.S. Nat. Inst. of Health 54-59; Prof. of Physics Univ. of Arizona 59-; Dir. de Recherches, Centre Nat. de la Recherche Scientifique, France 58-62, 69; Exchange Prof., Univ. of Paris 65; mem. Nat. Acad. of Sciences, American Acad. of Arts and Sciences; foreign mem. Royal Netherlands Acad. of Sciences and Literature, Royal Society, London; assoc. mem. Acad. des Sciences, Paris; hon. mem. Société Française de Minéralogie et de Crystallographie, Société Française de Microbiologie, Royal Microscopical Society, London; Hon. Fellow Indian Acad. of Sciences; Hon. M.D. (Masaryk Univ.); Hon. Sc.D. (Strasbourg).

Publs. *An Analytical Expression of the Results of the Theory of Space Groups* 22, *The Structure of Crystals* 24, 30, 34, *Crystal Structures* 48, 51, 53, 57, 58, 59, 60, 63, 64, 65, 66, 68, 69, 71, *Electron Microscopy* 49, *The World of the Electron Microscope* 58, *The Biochemistry of Animal Fossils* 72.

Department of Physics. University of Arizona, Tucson, Ariz. 85721, U.S.A.
Telephone: 602-884-1422.

Wyeth, Andrew N.; American artist; b. 12 July 1917; ed. privately.

Artist, landscape painter 36-; first one-man exhibition William Macbeth Gallery, New York 37; exhbns., Doll and Richard, Boston 38, 40, 42, 44; Macbeth Gallery 38, 41, 43, 45; Art Inst. of Chicago 41; Museum of Modern Art, N.Y.C. 43; M. Knoedler and Co., N.Y.C. 53; Mass. Inst. of Technology, Cambridge 60; Dunn Int. Exhibition, London 63; one-man exhbn., The White House, Washington, D.C. 70, Tokyo 74; mem. Nat. Inst. of Arts and Letters, American Acad. of Arts and Sciences; U.S. Presidential Medal of Freedom 63; Einstein Award 67; Hon. D.F.A. (Univ. of Maryland).
Chadds Ford, Pa. 19317, U.S.A.

Wyler, William; American film director and producer; b. 1 July 1902, Mulhouse (Alsace); *s.* of Leopold and Melanie (Auerbach) Wyler; *m.* Margaret Tallichet 1938; one *s.* three *d.*; ed. Lausanne, and Coll. de France.

Foreign Publicity for Universal Pictures one year; went to Hollywood as Asst. Dir. 20; directed films for Universal, Twentieth-Century Fox, Samuel Goldwyn Productions, Warner Bros., M-G-M and Paramount; served U.S. Army 42-45; awarded Air Medal and Legion of Merit (U.S.) and Légion d'Honneur (France); Irving Talberg Award of American Film Acad. 66 and other awards.

Leisure interests: skiing, travel, photography.

Directed films *Hell's Heroes* 31, *A House Divided* 32, *Counsellor-at-Law* 33, *The Good Fairy* 34, *The Gay Deception* 35, *These Three* 36, *Dodsworth* 36, *Come and Get It* 37, *Dead End* 37, *Jezebel* 38, *Wuthering Heights* 39 (New York Critics' Award), *The Westerner* 39, *The Letter* 40, *The Little Foxes* 41, *Mrs. Miniver* 42 (Acad. Award for direction), *The Best Years of Our Lives* 46 (Acad. Award for direction and New York Critics' Award), *The Heiress* 49, *Detective Story* 51, *Carrie* 52, *Roman Holiday* 53, *The Desperate Hours* 54, *Friendly Persuasion* 56 (Cannes Film Festival Award), *The Big Country* 57, *Ben Hur* 58 (New York Critics' Best Film of the Year, "Oscar" for directing), *The Children's Hour* (*The Loudest Whisper*) 62, *The Collector* 65, *How to Steal a Million* 65, *Funny Girl* 67, *The Liberation of L. B. Jones* 70.

1121 Summit Drive, Beverly Hills, Calif. 90210, U.S.A.

Wylie, Sir Campbell, Kt., E.D., Q.C.; British Commonwealth judge; b. 14 May 1905, New Zealand; *s.* of William James Wylie and Edith Grace Stagg; *m.* Leita Caroline Clark 1933; ed. Auckland Grammar School and Victoria Univ. of Wellington.

Barrister and solicitor, New Zealand 28; Barrister-at-Law, Inner Temple, London 50; private legal practice, New Zealand until 40; New Zealand Expeditionary Force 40-46; legal adviser, various Malay States 45-51; Attorney-Gen. Barbados 52-55, British Guiana 55-56; Attorney-General of West Indies 56-59; Federal Justice, West Indies 59-63; Chief Justice, Unified Judiciary of Sarawak, N. Borneo and Brunei 62-63; Chief Justice, High Court in Borneo (Sarawak and Sabah) 63-66; Law Revision Commr., Tonga 66-67; Chief Justice of the Seychelles 67-69; Commissioner for Law Reform and Revision, Seychelles 70-72.
1 Tiri Road, Takapuna, Auckland 9, New Zealand.
Telephone: 498091.

Wylie, Laurence William; American university professor; b. 19 Nov. 1909, Indianapolis; *s.* of William H. and Maude Stout Wylie; *m.* Anne Stiles 1940; two *s.*; ed. Indiana Univ., Institut des Etudes Politiques, Paris, and Brown Univ.

Instructor, Simmons College 36-40, Asst. Prof. 40-43; Asst. Prof. Haverford Coll. 43-48, Assoc. Prof. 48-57, Prof. 57-58, Chair. Dept. of Romance Languages 48-59; C. Douglas Dillon Prof. of French Civilization, Harvard Univ. 59-; Cultural Attaché, American Embassy, Paris 65-67.

Leisure interests: swimming, scuba diving, running.

Publs. *Saint-Marc Girardin Bourgeois* 47, *Village in the Vaucluse* 57, *Deux Villages* 66, *Les Français* 70; co-author: *In Search of France* 62, *Youth: Change and Challenge* 63, *Chanzeaux, A Village in Anjou* 67, *France: The Events of May-June 1968: A critical bibliography* 72; film: *Répertoire des gestes-signes français* 73.

Home: 997 Memorial Drive, Cambridge, Mass. 02138; 1540 William James Hall, Harvard University, Cambridge, Mass. 02138, U.S.A.
Telephone: UNiversity 8-7600, Ext. 3834.

Wyman, Jeffries, PH.D.; American molecular biologist; b. 21 June 1901, West Newton, Mass.; *s.* of Jeffries Wyman and Helen MacKay; *m.* 1st Anne McMaster

Cabot 1928 (deceased), 2nd **Rosamund Forbes** 1945 (divorced), 3rd Olga Lodigensky 1955; one *s.* one *d.*; ed. Harvard Univ., Univ. of Cambridge and Univ. Coll., London.

Member, subsequently Dir., Harvard Univ. Biological Labs. 28-50; engaged on research for U.S. Navy during World War II; Scientific Adviser, U.S. Embassy, Paris 50-53; Dir. UNESCO Middle East Science Co-operation Office, Cairo 54-58; Sec.-Gen. European Molecular Biology Org. and mem. of Council 64-69; Guest Scientist, Inst. of Biochemistry, Univ. of Rome and Regina Elena Inst. for Cancer Research, Rome 60-; Visiting Scientist, Fogarty Int. Center, Nat. Inst. of Health 71; mem. Nat. Acad. of Sciences, American Acad. of Arts and Sciences.
Leisure interests: travelling, walking, painting.
Publs. *Biophysical Chemistry*; papers in molecular biology.
Istituto Regina Elena, Viale Regina Elena 291, 00161-Rome; Home: Piazza Farnese 51, Rome, Italy; Summer Address: Les Collons-sur-Sion, Valais, Switzerland.
Telephone: 4956741 (Office); 560401 (Home).

Wyn-Harris, Sir Percy, K.C.M.G., M.B.E., K.ST.J., M.A.; British administrative officer; b. 24 Aug. 1903, London; *s.* of Percy Martin Harris and Catherine Mary Davies; *m.* Mary Moata MacDonald 1932 (died 1976); one *s.*; ed. Gresham's School, Holt, and Caius Coll., Cambridge.
District Officer, Kenya Colony 26; Labour Commr. Kenya 45, Provincial Commr. 45, Chief Native Commr. 47-49 and mem. for African Affairs in the Kenya Govt.; Governor and C.-in-C. Colony and Protectorate of the Gambia 49-58; mem. Devlin Commission in Nyasaland 59; Administrator, Northern Cameroons Oct. 60-61; Special Rep., Duke of Edinburgh's Award Scheme Overseas 62-63; mem. Mt. Everest Expeditions 33, 36.
Leisure interest: voyaging under sail.
8 Theatre Street, Woodbridge, Suffolk, England.
Telephone: Woodbridge 2911.

Wyndham White, Sir Eric, K.C.M.G., LL.B., BAR.-AT-LAW; British lawyer and international civil servant; b. 26 Jan. 1913; ed. London School of Economics, Univ. of London, and Middle Temple, London.
Practised as mem. English bar; Lecturer in Law London School of Economics; mem. British del. Int. Chamber of Commerce Berlin 37 and Copenhagen 39; war service 39-45; special asst. to European Dir. U.N.R.R.A. 45; Sec.-Gen. Emergency Economic Cttee. for Europe 46; Exec. Sec. First Session Preparatory Cttee. for Int. Trade Organization, London 46, Second Session, Geneva 47; Exec. Sec. U.N. Conf. on Trade and Employment, Havana 47-48; Exec. Sec. GATT 48-65, Dir.-Gen. 65-68; Chair. Investors' Overseas Services May 70-71.
Case Postale 470, 1200 Geneva 3 Rive, Switzerland.

Wynne-Edwards, Vero Copner, C.B.E., M.A., D.SC., F.R.S.C., F.R.S.E., F.R.S.; British zoologist; b. 4 July 1906, Leeds, Yorks.; *s.* of Rev. Canon J. R. Wynne-Edwards and Lilian Streatfeild; *m.* Jeannie Campbell Morris 1929; one *s.* one *d.*; ed. Leeds Grammar School, Rugby School and New Coll., Oxford.
Student Probationer Marine Biological Laboratory Plymouth 27-29; Asst. Lecturer Bristol Univ. 29-30; Asst. Prof. Zoology McGill Univ. Montreal 30-44, Assoc. Prof. 44-46; Regius Prof. of Natural History Aberdeen Univ. 46-74; Visiting Prof. of Conservation Univ. of Louisville Kentucky 59; Commonwealth Interchange Fellow New Zealand 62; Editor *Journal of Applied Ecology* 64-68; Pres. British Ornithologists' Union 65-70, Scottish Marine Biological Asscn. 67-73; Chair. Nat. Environment Research Council 68-71; mem. Royal Comm. on Environmental Pollution 70-74; foreign mem. Societas Scientiarum, Finland; Hon. D.Univ. (Stirling), LL.D. (Aberdeen).

Leisure interests: skiing, hill-walking, natural history.
Publs. *Animal Dispersion in Relation to Social Behaviour* 62; and scientific articles, mainly on marine and Arctic birds and population ecology.
Zoology Department, Tillydrone Avenue, Aberdeen, AB9 2TN, Scotland; Home: Ravelston, Torphins, Aberdeenshire AB3 4JR, Scotland.
Telephone: Aberdeen 40241 (Univ.); Torphins 434 (Home).

Wynter, Hector Lincoln, M.A., J.P.; Jamaican educationist and journalist; b. 27 July 1926, Cuba; *s.* of late Percival Wynter and of Mrs. Lola Parkinson; *m.* 1st Jacqueline Antrobus 1956 (dissolved), 2nd Diana Ayee 1970; three *s.* two *d.*; ed. Havana, Oxford, and London Univs.
Teacher of Spanish 45-49; Resident Tutor, Dept. of Extra-mural Studies, Univ. of W. Indies 53-55, Deputy Registrar 55-60, Dir. Extra-mural Studies 60-63; Senator 62-72; High Commr., Trinidad and Tobago 63-64; Registrar, Univ. of W. Indies 64-65; Parl. Sec. to Prime Minister on External Affairs 65-67; Minister of State for Educ. 67-69, for Youth and Devt. 69-72; mem. Exec. Board UNESCO 70-76, Chair. 75-76, Chair. Finance Cttee. 72-74; Exec. Editor *Daily Gleaner* 74-; Dir. Projects Asscn. of Caribbean Univs. 73; Chair. and mem. several statutory boards and voluntary asscns.; Rhodes Scholarship 49, Commonwealth Scholarship 49, UN Fellow 52, Journalist of the Year 73, Commonwealth Finance Journalism Scholarship 75.
Leisure interests: cricket, horse-racing, reading law.
Publs. numerous articles on education and politics.
Daily Gleaner, P.O. Box 40, Kingston; Home: 5 Monterey Drive, Kingston 6, Jamaica.
Telephone: 93-77110 (Home).

Wyschofsky, Günther; German chemist and politician; b. 1929.
Member, Cen. Cttee. Sozialistische Einheitspartei Deutschlands (S.E.D.); Minister for the Chemical Industry.
Ministerrat, Berlin, German Democratic Republic.

Wyszyński, H.E. Cardinal Stefan, DR.JUR.; Polish ecclesiastic; b. 3 Aug. 1901, Zuzela; *s.* of Stanisław and Julianna (née Karp) Wyszyński; ed. Univ. of Lublin.
Ordained Priest 24; Prof. of Sociology and Canon Law, Higher Seminary Włocławek 30-39; Rector of the Seminary and Canon of the Cathedral Assembly of Canons in Włocławek 45; Bishop of Lublin 46; Archbishop of Gniezno and Warsaw and Primate of Poland Nov. 48-; Cardinal 53; imprisoned 53-56; Organizer of Pastoral Great Novena of Millenium of Baptism in Poland 57-66; Pres. of Second Vatican Oecumenical Council; Pastoral Protector of Polish Emigration 64-.
Publs. *Główne typy Akcji Katolickiej za granicą* 31, *Dzieło Ks. Kard. Ferrari. Ideały i prace społeczno-apostolskie* 37, *Przemiany moralno-religijne pod wpływem bezrobocia* 37, *Stanowisko i zadanie duszpasterstwa wobec współczesnych ruchów społecznych* 38, *Stolica Apostolska a świat powojenny, Duch pracy ludzkiej* 46, *Droga Krzyżowa* 59, *W światłach tysiąclecia* 61, *Wielka Nowenna Tysiąclecia* 62, *Gody w Kanie, Uświęcenie pracy zawodowej* 63, *Matka Kościoła* 66, *A Strong Man Armed* 66, *The Deeds of Faith* 66, *Per la Libertà e la pace degli Uomini* 67, *Un évêque au service du peuple de Dieu* 68, *U podstaw soborowej nauki o człowieku* 68, *List do moich Kapłanów* 69, *Miłość na Codzień* 71, *Ojcze nasz-Rozważania* 71, *A ponad wszystko większa jest miłość* 71, *Kromka chleba* 72, *Wspomnienia O Janie XXIII* 72, *W sercu Stolicy* 72, *Z gniazda Orląt* 72, *Idzie nowych ludzi plemię* 73, *Sursum Corda* 74, *Kazania Świętokrzyskie* 74; works translated into many languages.
Ulica Miodowa 17, 00-246 Warsaw, Poland.
Telephone: 31 21 57.

60

X

Xanthopoulos-Palamas, Christian; Greek diplomatist; b. 1902; ed. Athens Univ.

Entered Greek Foreign Service 29; served in Balkan countries, Rome and Paris; mem. Greek del. to Paris Peace Conf. 46; del. to Council of Europe 49-52; mem. of dels. to 3rd, 6th and 7th sessions of UN Gen. Assembly; Head of Dept. of Economic Affairs at Ministry for Foreign Affairs 52-54; Perm. Rep. to UN 54-60; Gen. Dir. Ministry of Foreign Affairs 60-62; Perm. Rep. to NATO Oct. 62-67; Amb. to U.S.A. 67-69 (also accred. to Mexico and Panama); Minister for Foreign Affairs Jan.-Feb. 64; Under-Sec. for Foreign Affairs 71-72; Alt. Minister for Foreign Affairs Jan.-Sept. 72, Minister Oct.-Nov. 73; awarded Nat. Orders by Italy, Germany, France, Belgium, Argentina, Lebanon, Egypt and Yugoslavia; Commdr. Order of Phoenix; Greek Mil. Medal.

c/o Ministry of Foreign Affairs, Athens, Greece.

Xenakis, Iannis; French (b. Greek) composer, architect and engineer; b. 29 May 1922, Braïla, Romania; s. of Charchos Xenakis and Fantins Pavlou; m. Françoise Xenakis 1953; one d.; ed. Athens Polytechnic Inst., Ecole Normale de Musique, Paris (with Honegger and Milhaud) and Paris Conservatoire (under Messiaen).

Studied engineering in Athens; fought in Greek Resistance, World War II, condemned to death; went into exile in France 47; collaborated as engineer and architect with Le Corbusier 47-60; innovator of mass concept of music, Stochastic Music and Symbolic Music through probability calculus and set theory into instrumental, electro-acoustic and computerized musical composition; designer, Philips Pavilion, Brussels World Fair 58, sonic, sculptural and light composition *Polytope* for French Pavilion, Expo '67 Montreal, music and light spectacle *Persepolis* on ruins and mountain, Persepolis, Iran, *Polytope de Cluny*, Paris 72; founder and Dir. Equipe de Mathématique et Automatique Musicales, Paris, Center for Mathematical and Automated Music, Indiana Univ.; Assoc. Prof. Indiana Univ. 67-72; Assoc. Prof. Univ. of Paris I; Gresham Prof. in Music, City Univ., London; Hon. mem. American Acad. of Arts and Letters, Nat. Inst. of Arts and Letters; mem. Centre Nat. de Recherche Scientifique, France; Maurice Ravel Gold Medal 74.

Works include: *Metastasis* (for orchestra) 54, *Pithoprakta* (for string orchestra) 56, *Achorripsis* (for 21 instruments) 57, *Symos* (for 18 string instruments) 59, *Analogiques* (for 9 string instruments and magnetic tape) 59, *ST/10-1,080262* (for 10 instruments) 57-62, *Atrées* (for 10 instruments) 62, *Amorsima-Morsima* (for 4 instruments) 62, *Stratégie* (for 84 instruments and 2 conductors) 63, *ST/4-2* (for string quartet) 62, *Eonta* (for piano and brass) 63, *Akrata* 65, *Terretcktorh* 66, *Nuits* 68, *Nomos Gamma* 68, *Persephassa* 69, *Antikhthon* 71, *Aroura* 71, *Linaia-Agon* 72, *Eridanos* 73, *Cendrées* 74, *Erikhthon* 74, *Gmeeoorh* 74, *Noomena* 74, *Empreintes* 75, *Phlegra* 75, *Psappha* 75; several works for magnetic tape.

Publs. *Musiques formelles* 63, *Formalized Music* 70, *Musique Architecture* 70, *Xenakis—les Polytopes* 75, and many articles.

17 rue Victor Massé, Paris 9e, France.

Xuan Thuy; Vietnamese politician; b. 2 Sept. 1912, Hanoi.

In numerous nat. liberation movements until 45; later Editor *Cuu Quoc* (National Salvation—organ of the Viet-Minh); Pres. Asscn. of Journalists of Democratic Repub. of Viet-Nam; Deputy, Vice-Speaker and Sec.-Gen. of Nat. Assembly, Democratic Repub. of Viet-Nam; mem. Presidium Fatherland Front Cen. Cttee.; Deputy Head, Del. Democratic Repub. of Viet-Nam to Geneva Conf. on Laos 61-62; Minister of Foreign Affairs 63-65; Minister of State to head Democratic Repub. of Viet-Nam's negotiating team, Paris 68-73; Minister without Portfolio; fmr. Deputy Premier; mem. Secr. Cen. Cttee. Lao Dong Party.

Lao Dong Party, Hanoi, Democratic Republic of Viet-Nam.

Y

Yaacobi, Gad, M.SC.; Israeli politician; b. 1935, Moshav Kfar Vitkin; *m.*; three *c.*; ed. Tel Aviv Univ., School of Law and Econs.
Member Moshavim Movt. 60-67; Asst. to Minister of Agriculture, Head of Agriculture and Settlement Planning and Devt. Centre 60-66; mem. Cen. Cttee. Histadrut, Labour Union, Rafi Faction 66-; Chair. Econ. Council Rafi Faction 66-67; mem. Cen. Cttee., Secr. Labour Party; Asst. to Sec. Labour Party 66-70; mem. Parl. (Knesset) 69-, Parl. Finance Cttee. 69-70, Parl. Defence and Foreign Affairs Cttee. 74; Deputy Minister of Transport 70-74, Minister June 74-.
Publs. *The Quality of Power* 71, *The Freedom to Choose* 75, and many articles on economics and politics.
Ministry of Transport, Jerusalem, Israel.

Yacé, Philippe; Ivory Coast politician; b. 23 Jan. 1920; ed. William Ponty School, Dakar.
French Army 40-45; mem. Democratic Party of Ivory Coast (PDCI) 46-, Sec.-Gen. 59-; mem. Territorial Assembly, Ivory Coast 52-58; Deputy to Ivory Coast Constituent Assembly 58-59; Senator of the French Community 59-61; Pres. Nat. Assembly, Ivory Coast 60-; Pres., High Court of Justice 63-; Pres. Parl. Conference of EEC and African States 69-; Grand Officier, Légion d'Honneur, Grand Officier, Ordre National de la République de Côte-d'Ivoire.
National Assembly, B.P. 1381, Abidjan, Ivory Coast.

Yadin (formerly Sukenik), **Yigael,** M.A., PH.D.; Israel soldier and archaeologist; b. 21 March 1917, Jerusalem; *m.* Carmella Ruppin 1941; two *d.*; ed. Hebrew Univ. of Jerusalem.
Chief of Gen. Staff Branch, Hagana H.Q. 47; Chief of Operations, Gen. Staff, Israel Defence Forces 48; Chief of Gen. Staff Branch 49, Chief of Staff, as Lt.-Gen. 49-52; Archaeological Research Fellow, Hebrew Univ. 53-54; Lecturer in Archaeology, Hebrew Univ. 55-59, Assoc. Prof. 59-63, Prof. 63-; Dir. Excavations at Hazor 55-58, 69, Megiddo 60, 66-67, 71, Judaean Desert Caves 60-61, Masada 63-65.
Leisure interests: underwater fishing, gardening, stamp collecting, photography.
Publs. *The Scroll of the War of the Sons of Light against the Sons of Darkness* 55, 56, *The Message of the Scrolls* 57, *A Genesis Apocryphon* (with N. Avigad) 58, *Hazor I: The First Season of Excavations* 58, *Hazor II* 59, *Hazor III-IV* 61, *The Art of Warfare in Biblical Lands* 63, *Finds in the Bar-Kochba Caves* 63, *Masada: First Season of Excavations* 65, *The Ben Sirah Scroll from Masada* 65, *Masada Herod's Fort and the Zealots Last Stand* 66, *Philacteries from Qunran* 69, *Bar-Kochba* 71, *Hazor-Schweich Lectures' Series* 72, *Hazor* 75.
47 Ramban Road, Jerusalem, Israel.

Yadlin, Aharon; Israeli politician; b. 17 April 1926; ed. Hebrew Univ.
Co-founder Kibbutz Hatzerim; fmr. mem. Presidium, Israel Scouts Movement; mem. Knesset (Parl.) 59-; Deputy Minister of Educ. and Culture 64-72; Gen. Sec. Israel Labour Party 72; Minister of Educ. and Culture June 74-.
Ministry of Education and Culture, Jerusalem, Israel.

Yafi, Abdullah Aref al; Lebanese lawyer and politician; b. 1901; ed. Collège des Pères Jésuites, Beirut, and Univ. de Paris à la Sorbonne.
Admitted to Beirut Bar 26; Prime Minister and Minister of Justice 38-39; Lebanese del. to preparatory conf. for founding League of Arab States 44, to San Francisco Conf. 45; Minister of Justice and Finance 47; Prime Minister 52, 53, 54, 56, 66, 68-Jan. 69.
rue Fouad Ier, Beirut, Lebanon.

Yagodin, Gennady Alexeyevich; Soviet physical chemist; b. 3 June 1927; ed. Mendeleyev Chemical Technology Inst., Moscow.
Deputy Dean, Mendeleyev Chemical Technology Inst., Moscow 56-59, Dean, Dept. of Physical Chemistry 59-63, Prof. of Chemical Technology 59-63, 66-; Deputy Dir.-Gen. (Head of Dept. of Training and Technical Information 63-64, Head of Dept. of Technical Operations 64-66), International Atomic Energy Agency (I.A.E.A.), Vienna Sept. 63-66, Dean Dept. of Physical Chemistry, Mendeleyev Chemical Technology Inst. 66-73, Rector Inst. 73-.
Mendeleyev Chemical Technology Institute, Miusskaya Ploshchad 9, Moscow, U.S.S.R.

Yagudin, Shamil Khairulovich; Soviet ballet dancer; b. 1932; ed. Moscow Ballet School of Bolshoi Theatre.
Joined Bolshoi Theatre Ballet 52; Honoured Art Worker of R.S.F.S.R. 62; with Bolshoi Ballet has toured U.K., Bulgaria, German Democratic Repub., Denmark, India, Canada, Norway, Egypt, France, U.S.A. and Czechoslovakia.
Main roles: The Jester (*Romeo and Juliet*, Prokofiev), Karen (*Gayane*, Khachaturyan), Nurali (*Fountain of Bakhchisarai*, Afasyev), The Wicked Witch (*Swan Lake*, Tchaikovsky), Jester (*Cinderella*, Prokofiev), Petrushka (*Petrushka*, Stravinsky), Ibn Salom (*Leili and Medjnun*, Balasanyan).
State Academic Bolshoi Theatre of the U.S.S.R., Ploshchad Sverdlova 1, Moscow, U.S.S.R.

Yaguibou, Télesphore; Upper Volton diplomatist; b. 18 Oct. 1933, Pô; ed. Faculties of Law and Econs., Dakar and Paris and Inst. des Hautes Etudes d'Outre-Mer, Paris.
Judge, Court of First Instance, Bobo-Dioulasso 66-67; Sec.-Gen., Govt. of Upper Volta and Council of Ministers 67-71; responsible for relations between Govt. and Parl. 71-72; Perm. Rep. to UN Sept. 72-; fmr. del. to confs. of OAU and OCAM.
Permanent Mission of Upper Volta to United Nations, 866 Second Avenue, 6th Floor, New York, N.Y. 10017, U.S.A.

Yahya Khan, Gen. Agha Muhammad, H.P.K., H.J.; Pakistani fmr. army officer; b. 4 Feb. 1917, Peshawar; *s.* of Khan Bahadur Agha Saadat Ali Khan; *m.* Begum Fakhira Yahya 1945; one *s.* one *d.*; ed. Punjab Univ. and Indian Military Acad.
Service on N.W. Frontier before Second World War; service in Middle East and Italy, Second World War; set up Pakistan Staff Coll. 47, later Chief of Staff, Pakistan Army; Chair. Capital Comm. 59; G.O.C. East Pakistan 62; Commdr. Infantry Div. 65; C.-in-C. Pakistan Army 66-71; in charge of Admin. of Pakistan March 69, Pres. of Pakistan March 69-Dec. 71; under house arrest Jan. 72, released July 74.
Leisure interests: golf, shooting, reading.
Rawalpindi, Pakistan.

Yakas, Orestes, M.SC., PH.D.; Greek architect and politician; b. 14 Sept. 1920, Thessaloniki; *s.* of Athanase and Helene (née Xanthopoulou) Yakas; *m.* Eugenia Kerameos 1959; two *s.*; ed. Athens Nat. Polytechnic and Melbourne Univ.
In private practice in Melbourne 55; Head, Town Planning Section, Doxiades Associates 57; Chief Rep. of Doxiades Associates, Islamabad, Pakistan 59; Vice-Pres. Doxiades Associates 63; in private practice in Athens 66, also Adviser to Sec.-Gen. for Sport; Adviser to Gov. of Investment Bank 71; Minister of Mercantile Marine, Transport and Communications Aug. 71-

July 72, May-Nov. 73; Alt. Minister of Interior 72-73; Man. Dir. Yakas Consulting Group 74-.
Leisure interest: sport.
Publs. *Town Planning Elements Influencing Urban Economics* 71; many lectures, radio talks, etc.
41 Voriou Epirou Str., Philothei, Athens, Greece.
Telephone: 6822685; 6819240.

Yakovlev, Alexander Sergeyevich; Soviet aircraft designer; b. 1 April 1906, Moscow; ed. Zhukovsky Air Force Engineering Acad.
Member C.P.S.U. 38; Deputy Minister of the Aircraft Industry of U.S.S.R. 40-56; Chief Designer to Ministry of Aircraft Industry 56-; Col.-Gen. of Air Force Engineering Service; Deputy to U.S.S.R. Supreme Soviet 46-; mem. Comm. for Legislative Proposals, Soviet of Nationalities; designed sport, training, passenger, and bomber aeroplanes; Corresp. mem. U.S.S.R. Acad. of Sciences 43-; State Prize 41, 43, 44, 46, 47, 48, Hero of Socialist Labour, Orders of Lenin, Hammer and Sickle Gold Medal (twice), and many other awards.
Ministry of the Aircraft Industry, Moscow, U.S.S.R.

Yakovlev, Mikhail Danilovich, M.SC.; Soviet diplomatist; b. 8 Nov. 1910, Petropavlovka, Ukraine; ed. Leningrad State Univ.
Diplomatic Service 59-; Minister of Foreign Affairs, R.S.F.S.R. 59-60; Amb. to Congo (Léopoldville) 60-66, to Iraq 61-65; Dir. Moscow Inst. of Int. Relations 65-71; Amb. to Sweden 71-73.
c/o Ministry of Foreign Affairs, Smolenskaya-Sennaya Ploshchad, Moscow, U.S.S.R.

Yakubovsky, Marshal Ivan Ignatievich; Soviet army officer and politician; b. 7 Jan. 1912, Zaitsevo, Byelorussia; ed. Acad. of General Staff.
Soviet Army 32-; mem. C.P.S.U. 37-; Armoured Units, Second World War; Dep. Commdr. Tank Corps 44-46; Commdr. Tank Div. 48-52; Area Military Commdr., Armoured Forces 52-53; First Dep. C.-in-C. Soviet Forces in Germany 57-60, 61-62, C.-in-C. 60-61, 62-65; Area Mil. Commdr. 65-67; Deputy Defence Minister 67; Chair. Mil. Council, Chief of Armed Forces of Warsaw Pact 67-; mem. Cen. Cttee. of C.P.S.U. 61-; Deputy to U.S.S.R. Supreme Soviet 62-; mem. Credentials Comm., Soviet of Union; mem. Political Bureau of Central Cttee. of C.P. of Ukraine; Hero of Soviet Union, Gold Star Medal (twice), Order of Lenin (three), Suvorov (twice), Order of Red Banner (four), Red Star.
c/o Ministry of Defence, 34 Naberezhnaya Maurice Thorez, Moscow, U.S.S.R.

Yamagata, Shiro, B.ENG.; Japanese business executive; b. 26 Dec. 1902, Iwakuni City; s. of Osamu Yamagata and Kinuko Moriwaki; m. Setsuko Murayama, 1929; four c.; ed. Tokyo Univ.
Osaka Refinery, Mitsubishi Metal Mining Co. Ltd. 27-, Man. Osaka Refinery 47-48, Dir. 50-, Man. Dir. 56-60, Pres. 60-67, Chair. 67-71; Pres. Mitsubishi Nuclear Fuel Co. Ltd. 71-.
Leisure interest: golf.
Ohtemachi Building No. 6-1, 1-chome, Ohtemachi, Chiyoda-ku, Tokyo, Japan.
Telephone: 03-214-0051.

Yamamoto, Yoichi, B.ECONS.; Japanese business executive; b. 19 Jan. 1909, Hokkaido; s. of Makoto and Toyo Yamamoto; m. Mitsuho Asano 1939; four s. one d.; ed. Chuo Univ. School of Econs.
Staff, Fed. of Dairy Production and Sales Co-operatives of Hokkaido (later Snow Brand Milk Products Co.); Dir., Man. Sales Dept., Snow Brand Milk Products Co. 56, Man. Dir. 63, Exec. Man. Dir. 71, Pres. 73-.
Leisure interest: reading.
4-20-17 Yagumo, Meguro-ku, Tokyo, Japan.
Telephone: (717) 1812.

Yamani, Shaikh Ahmed Zaki; Saudi Arabian politician; b. 1930; ed. Cairo Univ., New York Univ. and Harvard Univ.
Saudi Arabian Government Service; private law practice; Legal Adviser to Council of Ministers 58-60; Minister of State 60-62; mem. Council of Ministers 60-; Minister of Petroleum and Mineral Resources 62-; Dir. Arabian American Oil Company 62-; Chair. of Board of Dirs. General Petroleum and Mineral Org. (PETROMIN) 62-, Coll. of Petroleum and Minerals, Dhahran 63-, Saudi Arabian Fertilizer Co. (SAFCO) 66-; Sec.-Gen. Org. of Arab Petroleum Exporting Countries (OAPEC) 68-69, Chair. 74-75; mem. several Int. Law Assens.
Publ. *Islamic Law and Contemporary Issues.*
Ministry of Petroleum and Mineral Affairs, Riyadh, Saudi Arabia.

Yamasaki, Minoru, B.ARCH.; American architect; b. 1 Dec. 1912; ed. Univ. of Washington.
Instructor of Water Colour, New York Univ. 35-36; Designer 35-45; Instructor of Architectural Design, Columbia Univ. 43-45; Chief Architectural Designer for Smith Hirchman & Grylls, Detroit 45-49; Principal, Leinweber, Yamasaki & Hellmuth, Detroit, Mich. and St. Louis, Mo. 49-55, Yamasaki, Leinweber and Assocs. 55-59; Minoru Yamasaki and Assocs. Birmingham, Mich. 59-; mem. Nat. Council on the Arts; numerous architectural honours, including American Inst. of Architects First Honor Award for McGregor Memorial Community Conf. Center, Wayne State Univ., A.I.A. Gold Medal Award 59, American Inst. of Architects First Honor Award for Reynolds Metals Regional Building 61; Hon. D.Hum. (Wayne State Univ.), Hon. D.Arch. (Michigan Univ.), Hon. D.F.A. (Rensselaer Polytechnic Inst. and Bates Coll.).
Home: 3077 Livenois Road, Troy, Mich.; Office: 1025 East Maple Road, Birmingham, Mich., U.S.A.

Yamashita, Isamu; Japanese business executive; b. 15 Feb. 1911; ed. Tokyo Imperial Univ.
Joined shipbuilding dept., Mitsui & Co. 33; entered Tamano Shipyard Ltd. (predecessor of Mitsui Shipbuilding & Engineering Co. Ltd.) 37; Man. Dir. Mitsui Shipbuilding & Engineering Co. Ltd. 62, Senior Man. Dir. 66, Vice-Pres. 68, Pres. 70-.
Mitsui Shipbuilding & Engineering Co. Ltd., 6-4, Tsukiji 5-chome, Chuo-ku, Tokyo, Japan.
Telephone: 544-3001.

Yaméogo, Antoine W.; Upper Volta financial official; b. 17 Jan. 1928, Koudougou; m. Christine Guissou 1956; two s. one d.; ed. Univ. de Bordeaux, Ecole Nationale des Impôts, Paris, and Univ. de Paris.
Inspector of publicly controlled financial bodies, France, Senegal, Mauritania and Upper Volta 55-59; Dir. of Treasury, later Commr. for Upper Volta Devt. Plan 59-61; Minister of Nat. Economy, Upper Volta 61-62; Economist with International Monetary Fund (IMF) 63-64, Alternate Exec. Dir. 64-66, Exec. Dir. 66-.
Leisure interests: hunting, farming, classical music.
International Monetary Fund, 19th and H Streets, N.W., Washington, D.C. 20431; 1614 Tuckerman Street, N.W., Washington, D.C., U.S.A.
Telephone: 477-2867 (Office); 882-6401 (Home).

Yaméogo, Maurice; Upper Voltan politician; b. 31 Dec. 1921; ed. High School.
Member of Grand Council French W. Africa 47, Minister of Agriculture 55, of Interior 56, Premier 58-60; Pres. Council of Ministers 60-66, Minister of Defence 65-66; Pres. of the Republic 60-66; mem. Rassemblement Démocratique Africain (RDA); on trial for embezzlement April 69; sentenced to 5 years hard labour May 69, sentence reduced to 2 yrs. Aug. 69, released Aug. 70.

Yanagi, Masuo; Japanese banker; b. 22 June 1900, Shimonoseki; *m.* Otome Hosoda 1926; three *s.* one *d.*; ed. Keio Univ., Tokyo.
Mitsui Bank 21-, branches in U.S.A. and Great Britain 31-33, Branch Man., Osaka 52, Man. Dir. 57, Pres. 59-64, Adviser 65-; Auditor, Mitsui Mutual Life Insurance Co. 65-, Fuji Xerox Corpn. 71-.
Leisure interests: golf, painting.
Fuji Cable Works Ltd., Fuji Xerox Corpn., 1-2 Yurakucho 1-chome, Chiyoda-ku, Tokyo, Japan.

Yancey, Robert E., B.ENG.SC.; American petroleum company executive; b. 15 July 1921, Cleves, Ohio; *s.* of George W. Yancey; *m.* Mary Estelline Tackett 1941; one *s.* one *d.*; ed. Marshall Univ.
Process Engineer, Ashland Oil 43, Gen. Superintendent of Refineries 54, Vice-Pres. of Mfg. 56, Dir. 64-, Senior Vice-Pres. 65, Pres., Ashland Chemical Co. (Div.) 67, Chief Operating Officer, Pres. Ashland Petroleum Co. 69, Pres. Ashland Oil Inc. 72-.
Leisure interests: boating, golf.
Ashland Oil Inc., P.O. Box 391, Ashland, Ky. 41101; Home: 102 Lycan Road, Bellefonte, Ky. 41101, U.S.A. Telephone: (606) 324-9849.

Yanenko, Nikolai Nikolayevich; Soviet mechanical engineer; and mathematician; b. 22 May 1921, Kuibyshev, Novosibirsk; ed. Tomsk State Univ.
Senior Lecturer, Moscow State Univ. 49-56; Scientific Assoc., Geophysical Inst., U.S.S.R. Acad. of Sciences 48-53; Head of Lab., Computing Centre, Siberian Branch, U.S.S.R. Acad. of Sciences 63-; Prof. and Chair. of Dept., Novosibirsk State Univ. 64-; corresp. mem. U.S.S.R. Acad. of Sciences 66-70, mem. 70-; mem. C.P.S.U. 52-.
Computing Centre, Akademgorodok, Novosibirsk, U.S.S.R.

Yang Chen Ning, PH.D.; Chinese professor of physics; b. 22 Sept. 1922; ed. Nat. Southwest Associated Univ., Kunming, and Univ. of Chicago.
Instructor, Univ. of Chicago 48-49; mem. Inst. for Advanced Study, Princeton, N.J. 49-55, and Prof. 55-65; Albert E. Einstein Prof. of Science, New York State Univ. 65-; Visiting Prof. Univ. of Paris 57; Hon. D.Sc. (Princeton Univ., Brooklyn Polytechnical Inst., Univ. of Wrocław); Nobel Prize in Physics 57; A. Einstein Award 57.
Department of Physics, State University of New York, Stony Brook, N.Y. 11790, U.S.A.

Yang Ch'eng-wu; Chinese army officer; b. 1904, Changting, Fukien.
Political Commissar, Red 1st Army Corps 32; Mil. District Commdr. 38; Army Corps Commdr., People's Liberation Army N. China Mil. Region 49, Chief of Staff 52; Gen. 55; Commdr. PLA Air Defence Command 56; Alt. mem. 8th Cen. Cttee. of CCP 56; Commdr. Peking Mil. Region 57-59; Deputy Chief of Staff PLA 59-68, Acting Chief of Staff 66-68; criticized and removed from office during Cultural Revolution 67; Deputy Chief of Staff, PLA 74.
People's Republic of China.

Yang Ta-yi; Chinese army officer.
Major-General People's Liberation Army 63; Deputy Commdr. Hunan Mil. District, PLA 67, Commdr. 69-; Vice-Chair. Hunan Revolutionary Cttee. 68; Deputy Sec. CCP Hunan 70.
People's Republic of China.

Yang Te-chih; Chinese army officer; b. 1910, Li-ling, Hunan; ed. Red Army Acad. and Nanking Mil. Acad.
Joined CCP 27; on Long March 34-35; Regimental Commdr., Red Army 35; Commdr. Ninghsia Mil. Region, People's Liberation Army 49; Chief of Staff Chinese People's Volunteers in Korea 51, Deputy Commdr. Chinese People's Volunteers 53-54, Commdr. 54-55; mem. Nat. Defence Council 54; Gen. 55; Alt.

mem. 8th Cen. Cttee. of CCP 56; Commdr. Tsinan Mil. Region, PLA 58-73; First Vice-Chair. Shantung Revolutionary Cttee. 67, Chair. 71; mem. 9th Cen. Cttee. of CCP 69; First Sec. CCP Shantung 71; mem. 10th Cen. Cttee. of CCP 73; Commdr. Wuhan Mil. Region, PLA 74-.
People's Republic of China.

Yang Yung; Chinese army officer; b. 1906, Liuyang, Hunan; ed. Red Army Coll.
Joined CCP 26; Regimental Deputy Commdr., Red Army 37; Commdr. 5th Army Group, 2nd Field Army, People's Liberation Army 48; Deputy Commdr. 2nd Field Army, PLA 49; Gov. of Kweichow 49-55; Deputy Commdr. Chinese People's Volunteers, Korea 54, Commdr. Chinese People's Volunteers 55-58; Alt. mem. 8th Cen. Cttee. CCP 56; Commdr. Peking Mil. Region, PLA 60-67; criticized and removed from office during Cultural Revolution 67; Commdr. Sinkiang Mil. Region, PLA 73-; Vice-Chair. Sinkiang Revolutionary Cttee. 73; Second Sec. CCP Sinkiang 73.
People's Republic of China.

Yankov, Alexander, PH.D.; Bulgarian diplomatist; b. 22 June 1924; *m.*; two *c.*; ed. Sofia Univ. and Hague Acad. of Int. Law.
Assistant Prof. of Int. Law, Sofia Univ. 51-54; Sec. Int. Union of Students, Prague 54-57; Senior Asst. Prof. of Int. Law 57-64, Assoc. Prof. 64, Prof. 68-; Counsellor, Perm. Mission of Bulgaria at UN 65-68; Vice-Chair. UN Cttee. on Peaceful Uses of the Sea-Bed 68-; mem. Court of Arbitration, Bulgarian Chamber of Commerce 70; mem. Perm. Court of Arbitration, The Hague 71; Amb. to U.K. Feb. 72-; Pres. 8th Session, Assembly of Inter-Govt. Maritime Consultative Org. 73; Chair. 3rd Main Cttee., UN Conf. on Law of the Sea, Caracas 74, Geneva 75.
Publs. several publications on international law and international relations.
Embassy of Bulgaria, 12 Queen's Gate Gardens, London, S.W.7, England.
Telephone: 01-584-9433.

Yano, Jun'ya; Japanese politician; b. 27 April 1932, Osaka; *m.* Mitsuko Yano 1961; one *s.*; ed. Kyoto Univ.
With Ohbayashi-gumi Ltd. 56-; mem. Osaka Prefectural Assembly 63; mem. House of Reps. 67-; Sec.-Gen. Komeito (Clean Govt.) Party 67-.
Leisure interests: reading, listening to music.
Komeito, 17 Minamimotomachi, Shinjuku-ku, Tokyo; 536 Mikuriya, Higashi-Osaka-shi, Osaka, Japan.
Telephone: 06-788-0443 (Osaka).

Yanofsky, Charles, PH.D.; American professor of biology; b. 17 April 1925, New York, N.Y.; *s.* of Frank Yanofsky and Jennie Kopatz Yanofsky; *m.* Carol Cohen 1949; three *s.*; ed. City Coll. of N.Y. and Yale Univ.
Research Asst. in Microbiology, Yale Univ. 51-53; Asst. Prof. of Microbiology Western Reserve Univ. 54-58; Assoc. Prof., Dept. of Biological Sciences, Stanford Univ., Prof., Dept. of Biological Sciences 61-; Herzstein Prof. of Biology 67; Pres. Genetics Soc. of America 69; Career Investigator American Heart Asscn. 69; mem. Nat. Acad. of Sciences, American Acad. of Arts and Sciences; Eli Lilly Award in Bacteriology 59, U.S. Steel Award in Molecular Biology 64, Albert Lasker Award for Basic Medical Research 71, Nat. Acad. of Sciences Award in Microbiology 72, Townsend Harris Medal, City Coll. of N.Y. 73.
Leisure interests: tennis, sports.
Publs. Scientific articles in *Proceedings* of Nat. Acad. of Sciences, etc.
725 Mayfield Avenue, Stanford, Calif. 94305, U.S.A.
Telephone: 415-323-9934 (Home); 415-497-2413, Ext. 2413 (Office).

Yanshin, Alexander Leonidovich; Soviet geologist; b. 28 March 1911, Smolensk; *s.* of Leonid Alexandrovich and Marija Petrovna Yanshina; *m.* Fidan

Taufikovna Bikkenina; one *s.*; ed. Moscow Geological Inst.

Researcher, Institute of Fertilizers 29-36, Geological Inst., U.S.S.R. Acad. of Sciences 36-56; Man. Dept. of Regional Tectonics, Geological Inst. 56-; Vice-Dir. Inst. of Geology and Geophysics, Siberian Div., U.S.S.R. Acad. of Sciences 59-; mem. U.S.S.R. Acad. of Sciences 58-; helped compile tectonic maps of U.S.S.R. 52, 56, Europe 64, Chief Editor tectonic map of Eurasia 65-66; Foreign mem. Acad. of Sciences, Mongolia 74-; State Prize 69-, Order of Lenin (three times), Order of the Red Banner of Labour (twice), Badge of Honour.

Publs. *Tectonics of Eurasia,* many works on the geology of the U.S.S.R.

Institute of Geology and Geophysics, Akademgorodok, Novosibirsk, U.S.S.R.

Telephone: 65-65-19.

Yanshin, Mikhail Mikhailovich; Soviet actor; b. 2 Nov. 1902, Ukhnov; *s.* of Mikhaie Yamshin and Alexandra Zhieva; *m.* Nonna Yanshina; ed. Moscow Art Theatre Studio School.

Moscow Art Theatre 32-; Artistic Dir. of Gypsy Romen Theatre 37-41; Chief Stage Dir. Moscow Stanislavsky Drama Theatre 50-63; principal productions include *Blood Wedding, The Wonderful Woman Shoemaker* at the Romen Theatre, *Makar Chudra* by Gorky, *Griboyedov, The Beautiful Girls* at the Moscow Stanislavsky Drama Theatre, *Front* and *The Late Love* at the Moscow Art Theatre; People's Artist of the U.S.S.R. 55, two Orders of Lenin, Order of the Badge of Honour, State prize.

Leisure interest: sport.

Moscow Art Theatre, Proyezd Khudozhestvennogo teatra 3, Moscow, U.S.S.R.

Yanushkovskaya, Tamara Petrovna, M.SC.; Soviet trade union official; b. 10 May 1924, Rzhev, Kalinin; ed. Moscow State Univ.

Soviet Army 41-44; mem. Communist Party of Soviet Union 41-; teacher in institutions of higher learning 55-63; Chair. Central Cttee. of Educ., Univ. and Scientific Workers Union 63-; mem. All-Union Central Council of Trade Unions; mem. Central Auditing Comm. of C.P.S.U. 66-71.

Central Committee of Educational, University and Scientific Workers' Trade Union, Leninsky Prospekt 42, Moscow, U.S.S.R.

Yao Wen-yuan; Chinese journalist; b. 1924.

Journalist and youth activist before Cultural Revolution; leading pro-Maoist journalist during Cultural Revolution 55-68; Editor *Wen Hui Bao* 66, *Liberation Daily* 66; mem. Cen. Cultural Revolution Group, CCP 66; Vice-Chair. Shanghai Revolutionary Cttee. 67-; Editor *People's Daily* 67-; mem. Politbureau, CCP 69; Second Sec. CCP Shanghai 71; mem. Politbureau, 10th Cen. Cttee. of CCP 73.

People's Republic of China.

Yapp, Ronald Payne Hunter; British business executive; b. 26 June 1908, London; *s.* of Sir Frederick C. Yapp and Katie Vincent Payne; *m.* Dorothy Pearl Rowland 1932; two *s.*; ed. St. Paul's School.

Director, Vickers Ltd. 58-, Man. Dir. 68-70; Dir. British Aircraft Corpn. (Holdings) Ltd. 60-.

Leisure interest: cricket.

Vickers Ltd., Vickers House, Millbank Tower, London, S.W.1, England.

Telephone: 01-828-7777.

Yarborough, Ralph Webster, LL.B.; American lawyer and politician; b. 8 June 1903, Chandler, Texas; *s.* of Charles Richard Yarborough and Nannie Spear; *m.* 1928; one *s.*; ed. Sam Houston State Teachers Coll., Huntsville, Texas, U.S. Military Acad., West Point, N.Y., and Univ. of Texas Law School.

Practised law, El Paso, Texas 27-30; Asst. Attorney-

Gen. Texas 31-34; Dir. Lower Colorado River Authority 35-36; Lecturer, Univ. of Texas Law School 35; District Judge, Austin 36-41; served in Second World War and Lt.-Col. 46; U.S. Senator from Texas 57-71; mem. Tex. Constitutional Revision Cttee. 73-; mem. and former Pres. Travis Bar Asscn.; mem. El Paso Bar Asscn.; mem. and fmr. Dir. State Bar of Texas; mem. American Bar Asscn., American Law Inst., Texas Board of Examiners 47-51, etc.; U.S. del. Inter-Parliamentary Union Conf., Brasília, Oct. 62, Dublin 65, Canberra, Easter 66, Teheran Sept. 66, Palma de Mallorca Mar. 67, Lima Sept. 68, Vienna April 69, New Delhi Oct.-Nov. 69; Democrat.

Leisure interests: reading, book and stamp collecting.

Publs.: essays on Lincoln and Houston 64, *Frank Dobie: Man and Friend* 67, *Three Men in Texas* 67.

Home: 2527 Jarratt Avenue, Austin, Tex. 78703, U.S.A.

Yariv, Brig.-Gen. Aharon; Israeli army officer; b. 1920, Latvia; *m.*; one *s.*; ed. French Staff Coll.

Emigrated to Israel 35; Capt. British Army 41-46; Haganah 46-47; various posts with Northern Command, Israel Defence Forces 48-50, Operations Div., H.Q. 51; IDF Officers' Staff Coll. 52-56; Military Attaché, Wash. and Ottawa 57-60; joined Military Intelligence 61, Dir. until 72; Special Adviser to the Prime Minister Oct. 72-73; Minister of Transport March-June 74, of Information 74-Jan. 75.

c/o Ministry of Information, Jerusalem, Israel.

Yashiro, Yukio; Japanese art historian and museum director (retd.); b. 5 Nov. 1890, Yokohama; *m.* Fumi Kimura 1925; one *s.*; ed. Tokyo Imperial Univ.

Studied art in Tokyo, Florence, London, Paris and Berlin; Prof. Imperial School of Fine Arts, Tokyo 17-42; Dir. Inst. of Art Research, Tokyo 30-42; Lecturer Harvard Univ., U.S.A. 33; Dir. The Museum Yamato Bunkakan, Nara 60-70; Commdr. Ordine al Merito (Italy).

Publs. *Sandro Botticelli* (3 vols.) 25, *Japanische Malerei der Gegenwart* 31, *Principles of Japanese Art* 43, *Masterpieces of Far Eastern Arts in European and American Collections* (2 vols.) 42, *2000 Years of Japanese Art* 58, *Art Treasures of Japan* (2 vols.) 61, *Characteristics of Japanese Art* (revised edn., 2 vols.) 65.

1013 Kitahonmachi, Oisho-cho, Nakagun, Kanagawa-ken, Japan.

Telephone: 0463-6-0354.

Yasnov, Mikhail Alexeyevich; Soviet politician; b. 1906; ed. Moscow Univ.

Member C.P.S.U. 25-; construction work, Moscow City Council 30-38; Dep. Chair. Exec. Cttee., Moscow City Council 38-49, Chair. 50-56; Dep. Minister of Town Construction U.S.S.R. 49-50; Chair. Council of Ministers R.S.F.S.R. 56-57, First Deputy Chair. 57-67; Chair. Presidium of Supreme Soviet of R.S.F.S.R. 67-; Deputy Chair. Presidium of Supreme Soviet of U.S.S.R. 67-; mem. Central Cttee. C.P.S.U. 52-; Deputy to U.S.S.R. 50- and R.S.F.S.R. Supreme Soviets.

Presidium of R.S.F.S.R. Supreme Soviet, 3 Delegatskaya ulitsa, Moscow, U.S.S.R.

Yasseen, Mustafa Kamil, D. EN D.; Iraqi international lawyer; b. 1920, Iraq; ed. Univs. of Baghdad and Paris.

Member, Baghdad Bar 42; Lecturer in Private Int. and Penal Law 50, Asst. Prof. 54; Prof. and Head, Dept. of Int. Law, Univ. of Baghdad 59; Gen. Dir. Political Dept., Ministry of Foreign Affairs 59, Dept. of Int. Orgs. 64; Amb. and Perm. Rep. to Office of UN, Geneva 66; Gen. Dir., Int. Orgs. Dept., Ministry of Foreign Affairs 71-; mem. UN Int. Law Comm. 60-, Pres. 66; Gen. Dir. Dept. of Int. Orgs. and Confs., Baghdad 71, Assoc. Inst. of Int. Law 61, mem. 71, mem. Curatorium, Hague Acad. of Int. Law; Rep. of Iraq to Governing Body, ILO 66-69; leader, Iraqi del. to Council of UNCTAD 66-69; mem. del. to UN Gen. Assembly 58-;

del. to various UN, ILO confs., etc.; Dr. h.c. (Nice) 70; Gran Cruz Civil Merit (Spain), Grand Officier Ordre National du Mérite (France).
Publs. various books and articles on int. law.
Ministry of Foreign Affairs, Baghdad, Iraq.

Yassein, Mohamed Osman, B.SC.(ECON.); Sudanese international civil servant; b. Nov. 1915, Berber; ed. Khartoum School of Administration and London School of Economics.
Joined Sudanese Political Service 45; Liaison Officer in Ethiopia 51-52; Gov. Upper Nile Province 53-55; Perm. Under-Sec. of Foreign Affairs 56-65; mem. Sudanese Del. to U.N. 56; Del. to Ind. African States Conf., Monrovia 59, to Accra Conf. on Positive Action for Peace and Security in Africa 60, to Independent African States Conf., Léopoldville 60, to Arab League 62; Special Adviser to UN on training of diplomatists 61-62; Special Envoy to Ethiopia and Somalia on border dispute 63; mem. African Unity Org. Comm. for Conciliation and Arbitration between Algeria and Morocco 63-64; organized first African Ministers of Finance Conf., Khartoum 63; mem. and Adviser, Round Table Conf. on Southern Sudan 65; mem. Int. Political Science Conf. 65; Hon. mem. Int. Inst. of Differing Civilization 66; UN Consultant with ECA 66; UN Special Adviser to Govt. of Zambia on Civil Service Structure 66-67, of Southern Yemen on Public Admin. 68-69, of Yemen Arab Repub. on Public Admin. 69; Resident Rep. UN Devt. Programme, Amman, Jordan 69-; Fellow, Adlai Stevenson Inst. for Int. Affairs, Chicago; Kt. Great Band of Humane Order of African Redemption, Liberia, Grand Officer, Order of Menelik II, Republican Order, Egypt, Star of Yugoslavia, First Order of Independence, Jordan.
Publs. *The Sudan Civil Service* 54, *Analysis of the Economic Situation in the Sudan* 58, *Problems of Transfer of Power—the Administration Aspect* 62, *Germany and Africa* 62, *Melut Scheme—an experiment in social development in developing countries* (article) 65, *The Poet's Ballet* (in Arabic) 66, *The Social, Economic and Political Role of Urban Agglomerations in Developing Countries* (article) 67, *The Reform of the Machinery of Government in the Sudan* (in Arabic) 71, *The Diplomat in Developing Countries* 71.
United Nations Development Programme in Jordan, P.O. Box 565, Amman, Jordan; Home: P.O. Box 2201, Khartoum, Sudan.

Yassin, Aziz Ahmed, PH.D., D.I.C., B.SC.; Egyptian consulting engineer; b. 13 Aug. 1918; s. of Ahmed M. Yassin and Moonira M. El-Rashidi; m. Moonira Eleanor Hartmann 1951; one s. two d.; ed. Abbassia Secondary School, Cairo Univ., and Imperial Coll., London Univ.
Ministry of Housing and Public Utilities, rising to Under-Sec. of State 39-59; Dir.-Gen. and Vice-Chair. Building Research Centre 54-59, Chair. and Pres. Tourah Portland Cement Co., Alexandria Portland Cement Co. 59-63; mem. Board of Dirs. Helwan Portland Cement Co., Sudan Portland Cement Co. 59-63; Chair. Egyptian Cement Cos. Marketing Board 59-63; Chair. and Pres. Egyptian Gen. Org. for Housing and Public Building Contracting Cos. 63-65; Minister of Tourism and Archaeology 65-67; Minister of Housing and Construction 66-68; mem. Board Asswan High Dam Authority 66-68; External Prof. in Soil Mechanics, Cairo Univ. 51-; External Prof. of Civil Engineering, Ein Shams Univ.; mem. Council of Building Research and Technology, Egyptian Acad. of Science and Technology 72-; Sec.-Gen. Fed. of Arab Engineers (FAE) 75; mem. of Council of other scientific, civil engineering and building orgs.; Order of the Republic of Egypt First Class, Order of the Banner of The Hungarian Republic First Degree, Commander's Cross with Star, Order of Resurrection of Poland.

Leisure interests: reading, economics and law.
Publs. *Model Studies on the Bearing Capacity of Piles* 51, *Bearing Capacity of Deep Foundations in Clay Soils, Testing Sand Dry Samples with the Tri-axial Apparatus* 53, *Bearing Capacity of Piles* 53, *The Industry of Building Materials in Egypt* 57.
4 Waheeb Doas Street, Maadi, Cairo, Egypt.
Telephone: Cairo 34519.

Yasui, Kaoru, LL.D.; Japanese jurist; b. 25 April 1907, Osaka; s. of Harumoto and Harue Yasui; m. Tazuko Kuki 1936; one s. one d.; ed. Tokyo Univ.
Assistant Prof. Tokyo Univ. 32-42, Prof. 42-48; Prof. Hosei Univ. 52-, Dean Faculty of Jurisprudence 57-63, Dir. 63-66; Leader (Chair. etc.) Japan Council Against Atomic and Hydrogen Bombs 54-65; Pres. Japanese Inst. for World Peace 65-; Dir. Maruki Gallery for Hiroshima Panels 68-; mem. Lenin Peace Prize Cttee.; Lenin Peace Prize 58; Gold Medal (Czechoslovakia) 65.
Leisure interests: classical music, classical literature.
Publs. *Outline of International Law* 39, *Banning Weapons of Mass Destruction* 55, *People and Peace* 55, *Collection of Treaties* 60, *My Way* 67, *The Dialectical Method and the Science of International Law* 70.
Minami-Ogikubo 3-13-11, Suginamiku, Tokyo, Japan.
Telephone: Tokyo 03-332-3580.

Yasui, Kizo; Japanese business executive; b. 2 Dec. 1899, Shiga; s. of Kizo and Suga Yasui; m. Etsuko Miyagawa 1928; one s. one d.; ed. Tokyo Univ. of Commerce.
Joined the Mitsui Bank Ltd. 26, Dir. 51, Man.-Dir. 54, Senior Man.-Dir. 57, Deputy Pres. 59; President Mitsui Petrochemicals Co. Ltd. 61; Exec. Vice-Pres. Toray Industries Inc. 63, Chair. 71-; Order of the Rising Sun 70.
Leisure interest: golf.
Toray Industries Inc., Toray Building, 2 Nihonbashi, Muromachi, 2-chome, Chuoku, Tokyo; No 5-36, 4-chome Minamiazabu, Minato-ku, Tokyo 106, Japan.
Telephone: 03-473-0520.

Yasukawa, Takeshi, B.A.; Japanese diplomatist; b. 16 Feb. 1914, Tokyo; s. of Daigoro and Matsuko Yasukawa; m. Sueko Hitomi 1946; one s. two d.; ed. Tokyo Imperial Univ.
Entered diplomatic service 39; Counsellor, Wash., D.C. 57-61; Asst. Deputy Vice-Minister for Admin., Ministry of Foreign Affairs 61-65; Dir.-Gen. American Affairs Bureau, Ministry of Foreign Affairs 65-67; Amb. to Philippines 67-69; Deputy Vice-Minister of Foreign Affairs 70-72; Amb. to U.S.A. July 73-.
Leisure interest: golf.
Embassy of Japan, 2520 Massachusetts Avenue, N.W., Washington, D.C. 20008, U.S.A.
Telephone: 234-2266.

Yates, Frank, C.B.E., SC.D., F.R.S.; British research scientist; b. 02; ed. Clifton Coll., and St. John's Coll., Cambridge.
Research Officer and Mathematical Adviser, Gold Coast Geodetic Survey 27-31; at Rothamsted Experimental Station 31-; Head of Dept. of Statistics 33-68, Deputy Dir. 58-68; Scientific Adviser to various Ministries 39-; Hon. Wing-Commdr., R.A.F. 43-45; Head of Agricultural Research Statistical Service 47-68; mem. UN Sub-Comm. on Statistical Sampling 47-51; mem. Governing Body Grassland Research Station 48-69; mem. Int. Statistical Inst. 47-; Pres. of British Computer Soc. 61-62; Royal Medal, Royal Soc. 66; Pres. Royal Statistical Soc. 67-68; Senior Visiting Fellow, Imperial Coll., London, 74-75.
Publs. *Design and Analysis of Factorial Experiments* 37, *Statistical Tables for Biological, Medical and Agricultural Research* (with R. A. Fisher) 38-63, *Sampling*

Methods for Censuses and Surveys 49-60, *Experimental Design: Selected Papers* 70.
Rothamsted Experimental Station, Harpenden, Hertfordshire, England.
Telephone: Harpenden 62271.

Ydigoras Fuentes, Gen. Miguel; Guatemalan politician and civil engineer; b. 17 Oct. 1895; ed. Mil. Acad. of Guatemala, and Guatemala Nat. Univ.
Military Attaché in Washington, Paris; Military Adviser in Peace Confs. delegation in Versailles 19; Dean of Polytechnic School; Gov. of 4 States in Guatemala; Dir. of Public Roads 38-44; Pres. Dels. to 3rd UNRRA Congress, UNESCO Congress, UN Preparatory Comm. and UN 1st Session, London 45-46, led repatriation Mission for Guatemalan Displaced Persons in Germany 46-47; mem. Neutral Observer Corps apptd. by Int. Court of Justice to organize referendum in French possessions in India 49; Minister to U.K. 45-50; Candidate for Presidency 50; Minister to Colombia 55, Amb. 56-58; Pres. of Guatemala 58-63; mem. American Society for Geographical Research.
American Society for Geographical Research.
Publs. Map of boundary sections of Guatemala and Mexico, and Map of Roads of Guatemala and El Salvador; also books on military affairs and road construction.
Living in Nicaragua.

Yefanov, V. P., (*see* Efanov).

Yefimov, B. Y., (*see* Efimov).

Yeganeh, Mohammed, M.A.; Iranian economist; b. 5 May 1923, Zanjan; s. of Ismail and Habibeh Yeganeh; m. Johanna O. Hirsch 1957; three s.; ed. Teheran Univ. and Columbia Univ., N.Y.
With UN Secr. 49-64; UN Adviser to Tunisian Govt. on Econ. Planning 58-59; Deputy Minister of Econ. 64-69; Minister of Devt. 69-70; Special Adviser to Prime Minister 70-71; Alt. Exec. Dir. Int. Bank of Reconstruction and Devt. 71-72, Exec. Dir. Int. Monetary Fund 72-73; Gov. Central Bank of Iran 73-75; Minister of State Oct. 75-; Homayoun Medal 66, Devt. Medal 67, Homayoun Medal 74.
Leisure interests: Persian poetry, music, walking.
Publs. *Perspectives décennales des développements économiques en Tunisie* 60, *Economics of the Middle Eastern Oil* (with Charles Issawi) 62, and several articles on oil and economic affairs.
Prime Minister's Office, Kakh Avenue, Teheran, Iran.
Telephone: 6161.

Yeh Chien-ying; Chinese party leader and fmr. army officer; b. 1899, Mei-hsien, Kwangtung; ed. Yunnan Mil. Inst., Sun Yat-sen Univ., Moscow, in France and Germany.
Instructor Whampoa Mil. Acad. 24; joined CCP 24; participated in Nanchang Uprising 27, Canton Uprising 27; Principal Red Army Coll. 31; Deputy Chief of Staff on Long March 34-36; mem. 7th Cen. Cttee. of CCP 45; Mayor of Peking 49; First Political Commissar Canton Mil. District, People's Liberation Army 49; Gov. of Kwangtung 49-55; Vice-Chair. Nat. Defence Council 54-; Dir. Inspectorate of Armed Forces, PLA 54-58; Marshal PLA 55; mem. 8th Cen. Cttee. of CCP 56; Pres. PLA Mil. Acad. 58; Sec., Secr. of Cen. Cttee., CCP 66; presumed Acting Minister of Nat. Defence 71-75, Minister 75-; Vice-Chair. CCP 73; mem. Standing Cttee. of Politburo, 10th Cen. Cttee. of CCP 73.
People's Republic of China.

Yeh Fei; Chinese party official; b. 1909, Fu-an, Fukien.
Guerilla leader in Fukien 26-29; joined CCP 27; Div. Commdr. New 4th Army 41; Corps Commdr. 3rd Field Army 49; Vice-Gov. of Fukien 49-54, Gov. 55-59; Mayor of Amoy 49; First Sec. CCP Fukien 55-68; Gen. 55; Alt. mem. 8th Cen. Cttee. of CCP 56; Political Commissar Foochow Mil. Region, People's Liberation Army 57-67; Sec. E. China Bureau, CCP 63-68; criticized and removed from office during Cultural Revolution 67; Alt. mem. 10th Cen. Cttee. of CCP 73; Minister of Communications 75.
People's Republic of China.

Yeh, George Kung-Chao, B.A., M.A.; Chinese politician and diplomatist; b. 1904; ed. Amherst Coll., Mass., U.S.A., and Cambridge Univ.
Prof. of English, Nat. Peking Univ. 26-27; Asst. Prof. Nat. Chinan Univ. 27-29; Prof. Tsing Hua Univ. 29-35; Prof. and Chair. Dept. Western Languages and Literature, Nat. Peking Univ. 35-39; Research Fellowship, China Foundation 37-39; Dir. British Malaya Office, Chinese Ministry of Information 40-41, Dir. U.K. Office 42-46; Counsellor and concurrently Dir. of European Affairs Dept., Ministry of Foreign Affairs 46-47; Admin. Vice-Minister of Foreign Affairs 47-49; Ambassador Extraordinary on Special Mission to Burma 47; Vice-Minister 49, Minister of Foreign Affairs (Taiwan) 49-58; Chair. Chinese Del., Seventh, Ninth and later Sessions UN Gen. Assembly; Ambassador to U.S.A. 58-61; Minister without Portfolio 61-; Special Grand Cordon, Order of Brilliant Star, Order of Propitious Clouds, many foreign decorations; Hon. LL.D. (Seoul, Amherst).
Publs. *Social Forces in English Literature, Introducing China, The Concept of Jen, Cultural Life in Ancient China* (Royal Soc. of Arts Medal 43), *On Ancient Chinese Poetry*.
The Executive Yuan, Taipei, Taiwan.

Yemelyanov, V. S., (see Emelyanov).

Yen Chia-kan, Dr., B.SC.; Chinese politician; b. 23 Oct. 1905, Soochow, Kiangsu; s. of Yen Yang-ho and Yen Wan; m. Ann Liu 1924; five s. four d.; ed. St. John's Univ., Shanghai.
Various government posts including Commr. of Reconstruction, Fukien Provincial Govt. 38-39, Finance Commr. Fukien Province, Chair. Fukien Provincial Bank 39-45; Dir. of Procurement, War Production Board 45; Communications Commr., Taiwan Provincial Govt. 45-46, Finance Commr. 46-49; Chair. Bank of Taiwan 46-49; Min ister of Econ. Affairs, Republic of China (Taiwan) 50, of Finance 50-54, 58-63; Vice-Chair. Council for U.S. Aid 50, 63; Gov. of Taiwan 54-57; Minister without Portfolio 57-58; Chair. Council for U.S. Aid 57-58; Pres. Exec. Yuan (Prime Minister) 63-72; Chair. Council for Int. Econ. Co-operation and Devt. 63-69; Vice-Pres. of Taiwan 66-75, Pres. April 75-; Hon. LL.D. (Nat. Seoul Univ., Korea) 64, Hon. D.Pol. (Nat. Chulalongkorn Univ., Thailand) 68; numerous foreign decorations.
Leisure interests: music, photography.
Office of the President, Taipei, Taiwan; 4 Section II, Chungking Road, South, Taipei, Taiwan.

Yendo, Masayoshi, B.SC.(ARCH.); Japanese architect; b. 30 Nov. 1920, Yokohama; s. of Masanao Yendo and Ima Nakamura; m. Fumi Matsuzaki 1956; two s.; ed. Waseda Univ.
Murano Architect Office 46-49; Pres. M. Yendo Associated Architects and Engineers 52-; Dir. Board, Japan Architects Asscn. 71-; Geijutsu Sensyo (Art Commendation Award) 65; Architectural Inst. of Japan Award 65.
Buildings include: Keio Terminal and Dept. Store Building 60, Resort Hotel Kasyoen 62, Yamaguchi Bank Head Office 62, 77th Building (77th Bank, Tokyo Branch) 63, Coca-Cola (Japan) Concentrating Plant 64, Yamanouchi Pharmaceutical, Yaizu Plant 67, 69, Coca-Cola (Japan) Head Office 68, Heibon-sha Limited Publishers Head Office 70, Yakult Honsha Co. Ltd. Head Office 70, Tokyo American Club 71, Taiyo Fishery Co. Ltd. Head Office 73.
Leisure interest: golf.
M. Yendo Associated Architects and Engineers,

Nakajima Building, 5-6, 8-chome, Ginza, Chuo-ku, Tokyo 104, Japan.
Telephone: 572-8321 (Tokyo).

Yeo, Edwin H., III, B.A.; American banker and government official; b. 23 May 1934, Youngstown, Ohio; s. of Edwin H. and Virginia Blevins Yeo; m. (divorced); two s. one d.; ed. Univ. of Maryland.
Served U.S. Marine Corps 52-55; with Pittsburgh National Bank 59-75, Senior Vice-Pres. 68-72, Vice-Chair. 72-75; Under-Sec. of the Treasury for Monetary Affairs Aug. 75-; also Vice-Chair. Pittsburgh Nat. Corpn.; Dir. Diston, Inc.; mem. Task Force on Municipal Credit; Chair. Greater Pittsburgh Fund Raising U.S. Olympic Cttee. 70; mem. Investment Bankers Asscn.
Leisure interest: raising Charolais cattle.
Publ. *Business News and Trends* of Pittsburgh National Bank 60-75.
United States Treasury Department, Room 3312, 15th and Pennsylvania Avenue, N.W., Washington, D.C. 20220; Home: 1358 Windy Hill Road, McLean, Va. 22101, U.S.A.
Telephone: (202) 964-5634 (Office); (703) 790-0282 (Home).

Yerby, Frank Garvin; American novelist; b. 5 Sept. 1916, Augusta, Georgia; s. of Rufus and Wilhelmina Yerby; m. 2nd Blanca Calle Pérez 1956; two s. two d. (from previous marriage); ed. Paine Coll., Fisk Univ. and Univ. of Chicago.
Teacher, Florida Agricultural and Mechanical Coll. 39, Southern Univ. 40-41; Laboratory Technician, Ford Motor Co., Detroit 41-44, Ranger Aircraft, New York 44-45; writer 44-.
Publs. *The Foxes of Harrow* 46, *The Vixens* 47, *The Golden Hawk* 48, *Pride's Castle* 49, *Flood Tide* 50, *A Woman Called Fancy* 51, *The Saracen Blade* 52, *The Devil's Laughter* 53, *Benton's Row* 54, *The Treasure of Pleasant Valley* 55, *Captain Rebel* 56, *Fairoaks* 57, *The Serpent and the Staff* 58, *Jarrett's Jade* 59, *Gillian* 60, *The Garfield Honor* 61, *Griffin's Way* 62, *The Old Gods Laugh* 64, *An Odour of Sanctity* 66, *Goat Song* 67, *Judas, My Brother* 68, *Speak Now* 69, *The Dahomean* 71, *The Girl from Storyville* 72, *The Voyage Unplanned* 74, *Tobias and the Angel* 75, *A Rose for Ana Maria* 76.
Leisure interests: photography, electronics, painting.
c/o William Morris Agency, 1350 Avenue of the Americas, New York, N.Y. 10019, U.S.A.; Edificio Torres Blancas, Avenida de América 35, Madrid, Spain.

Yetkin, Suut Kemal; Turkish scholar; b. 13 Sept. 1903, Urfa; s. of Saffet Yetkin; m. Adalet Yetkin 1932; one d.; ed. Univs. of Paris and Rennes.
Asst. Prof. of History of Art and Aesthetics, Univ. of Istanbul 33-39; Dir.-Gen. of Fine Arts, Ministry of Education 39-41; Prof. of History of Art and Aesthetics, Ankara Univ. 41-50, of History of Turkish and Islamic Arts 50-59; Rector Ankara Univ. 59-63; Prof. of Turkish Art, Columbia Univ. 63-64; mem. Académie des Sciences Morales et Politiques, Nat. Asscn. of Art Critics; Republican Party.
Publs. (in Turkish) *Philosophie de l'Art* 34, *Cours d'Esthé-tique* 42, *Les Doctrines Littéraires* 43, *Causeries Littéraires* 44, *L'Art de Leonardo da Vinci* 45, *Questions d'Art* 45, *Sur la Littérature* 53, *Les Peintres Célèbres* 55, *A. Gide: Choix de ses Ecrits Critiques* 55, *Histoire de l'Architecture Musulmane* 59; (in French) *Architecture Turque en Turquie* 62, *L'Ancienne Peinture Turque* 70, *Essaies* 72.
Kavaklidere Sok., Güney Apartments No. 23/5. Ankara, Turkey.
Telephone: Ankara 120786.

Yevtushenko, Yevgeny Alexandrovich (see Evtush-enko).

Yoder, Hatten Schuyler, Jr., A.A., S.B., PH.D.; American petrologist; b. 20 March 1921, Cleveland, Ohio; s. of Hatten Schuyler Yoder and Elizabeth Katherine (née Knieling); m. Elizabeth Marie Bruffey 1959; one s. one d.; ed. Univs. of Chicago and Minnesota and Mass. Inst. of Technology.
Active duty, U.S. Naval Reserve 42-46, MOKO expedition to Siberia 45-46, Lieut.-Commdr., retd.; Petrologist, Geophysical Laboratory, Carnegie Inst. of Washington 48-71, Dir. 71-; mem. Editorial Board *Geochimica et Cosmochimica* 58-68; N. American Editor, *Journal of Petrology* 59-68, Hon. mem. Advisory Board 68-; Assoc. Editor *American Journal of Science* 72-; Visiting Prof. of Geochemistry, Calif. Inst. of Technology 58, Visiting Prof. of Petrology, Univ. of Tex. 64, Univ. of Colo. 66, Univ. of Cape Town 67; new mineral, Yoderite named in his honour; Fellow, Mineralogical Soc. of America (mem. Council 62-64, Vice-Pres. 70-71, Pres. 71-72), Geological Soc. of America (mem. Council 66-68), American Geophysical Union (Pres. Volcanology, Geochemistry and Petrology Section 61-64, mem. Council 65-68); Corresp. Fellow, Edinburgh Geological Soc.; mem. Nat. Acad. of Sciences 58-, Geology Section Chair. 73-; mem. U.S. Nat. Cttee. for Geology 73-, for Geochemistry 73-; Mineralogical Soc. of America Award 54, Columbia Univ. Bicentennial Medal 54, Arthur L. Day Medal of Geological Soc. of America 62, A. L. Day Prize and Lectureship of Nat. Acad. of Sciences 72, A. G. Werner Medal of German Mineralogical Soc. 72.
Leisure interests: camping, trombone, rifle and pistol marksmanship, gardening.
Publs. Principal papers: *The Jadeite problem* (*American Journal of Science* Vol. 248) 50, *High-low quartz inversion up to 10,000 bars* (*Transactions* of American Geophysical Union Vol. 31) 50, *The* $MgO—Al_2O_3—SiO_2—H_2O$ *system and related metamorphic facies* (*American Journal of Science* Bowen Volume) 52, *Role of Water in Metamorphism* (Geological Soc. of America Special Paper No. 62) 55, *Experimental and theoretical studies of the mica polymorphs* (with J. V. Smith, *Mineral Magazine* Vol. 31) 56, *Origin of Basalt Magmas: an experimental study of natural and synthetic rock systems* (with C. E. Tilley *Journal of Petrology* Vol. 3 62), *Contemporaneous Basaltic and Rhyolitic Magmas* (*American Mineralogist*, Vol. 58) 73.
Geophysical Laboratory, Carnegie Institution, Washington, D.C. 20008, U.S.A.
Telephone: 202 966 0334.

Yokota, Takashi; Japanese banker; b. 31 Jan. 1909, Tokyo; ed. Keio Univ.
Joined The Nippon Kangyo Bank Ltd. 33, Dir. 58, Deputy Pres. 66, Pres. 69; Pres. The Dai-Ichi Kangyo Bank Ltd. 71-; Dir. Fed. of Bankers' Asscns. of Japan, Tokyo Bankers' Asscn. Inc.
Leisure interests: golf, reading.
The Dai-Ichi Kangyo Bank Ltd., 6-2, Marunouchi 1-chome, Chiyoda-ku, Tokyo; 5-35 Nishi-Azabu 3-chome, Minato-ku, Tokyo, Japan.
Telephone: 03-216-1111 (Office); 03-405-0510 (Home).

Yokoyama, Soichi; Japanese banker; b. 30 Nov. 1914, Tokyo; s. of Gengoro and Yone Yokoyama; m. Sumiko Mizukami 1939; one s.; ed. Hitotsubashi Univ.
Joined Yokohama Specie Bank 38; joined Bank of Tokyo Ltd. 47, Dir., Agent of New York Agency 63, Resident Dir. for Europe, London 65, Man. Dir. 65, Senior Man. Dir. 69, Deputy Pres. 72, Pres. 73-; Chair. Bank of Tokyo (Holland) NV 73-, Bank of Tokyo (Luxembourg) SA 74-; Dir. UBAN—Arab Japanese Finance Ltd., Hong Kong 74-, Banque Européenne de Tokyo SA, Paris 73-, Western American Bank (Europe) Ltd., London 73-, Fed. of Bankers' Asscns. of Japan 73-; Exec. Dir. Japan Fed. of Employers' Asscns. 73-; Trustee Japan Cttee. for Econ. Devt. 73-; mem.

Operational Council of Japan External Trade Org. (JETRO) 73-; Chair. Cttee. on Int. Finance, Fed. of Econ. Org. 74-.
Leisure interest: reading.
Bank of Tokyo Ltd., 2-1-1, Muromachi, Nihombashi, Chuo-ku, Tokyo 103; Home 14-25, Sugamo 3-chome, Toshima-ku, Tokyo 170, Japan.
Telephone: 03-270-8111 (Office): 03-918-1894 (Home).

Yong Nyuk Lin; Singapore politician and diplomatist; b. 24 June 1918, Seremban, Malaya; s. of the late Yong Thean Yong and Chen Shak Moi; m. Kwa Geok Lan 1939; two s.; ed. Raffles Coll.
Science master, King George V School, Seremban, Malaya 38-41; Overseas Assurance Corpn., Singapore, rising to Gen. Man. 41-58, resigned; Minister for Educ. 59-63; Chair. Singapore Harbour Board 61-62; Minister for Health 63-68, for Communications 68-75, without Portfolio 75-76; High Commr. in U.K. Sept. 75-.
Leisure interests: swimming, golf, stereo music.
Singapore High Commission, 2 Wilton Crescent, London, SWIX 8RW; Residence: 2 Broadwalk House, 51 Hyde Park Gate, London, S.W.7, England.
Telephone: 01-235-8315 (Office); 01-589-8451 (Residence).

Yonge, Sir (Charles) Maurice, C.B.E., D.SC., F.R.S.; British biologist; b. 9 Dec. 1899, Wakefield, Yorks.; s. of John Arthur Yonge and Sarah Edith Carr; m. 1st Martha Jane Lennox (died 1945), one s. one d.; m. 2nd Phyllis Greenlaw Fraser 1954, one s.; ed. Univ. of Edinburgh.
Baxter Natural Science Scholar, Univ. of Edinburgh 22-24; Naturalist, Plymouth Laboratory 24-27; Balfour Student, Univ. of Cambridge 27-29; Leader, Great Barrier Reef Expedition 28-29; Physiologist, Plymouth Laboratory 30-32; Prof. of Zoology, Univ. of Bristol 33-44; Regius Prof., Univ. of Glasgow 44-64; Research Fellow in Zoology, Univ. of Glasgow 65-70; Visiting Prof., Univ. of Calif., Berkeley 49, Univ. of Washington, Seattle 59; Prather Lecturer, Harvard Univ. 57; Hon. Fellow, Univ. of Edinburgh 70-; Pres. Royal Soc., Edinburgh 70-73; mem. Danish Acad. of Arts and Science, Royal Soc. of New Zealand, Calif. Acad. of Science; Hon. D.SC. (Univ. of Bristol, Heriot-Watt Univ., Univ. of Manchester); Makdougall-Brisbane Prize, Royal Soc. of Edinburgh 56; Darwin Medal, Royal Soc., London 68; Hon. Life Fellow, Pacific Science Asscn. 71.
Leisure interests: reading of history, woodwork, travel.
Publs. *The Seas* (with F. S. Russell.), *A Year on the Great Barrier Reef*, *The Sea Shore*, *Oysters*, *Guide to the Sea Shore* (with J. Barrett), *Physiology of Mollusca* (edited with K. M. Wilbur); many papers in standard scientific journals in Great Britain and U.S.A. on marine zoology, especially Mollusca and coral reefs.
13 Cumin Place, Edinburgh EH9 2JX, Scotland.
Telephone: 031-667-3678.

York, Herbert Frank, A.B., M.S., PH.D.; American physicist; b. 24 Nov. 1921, Rochester, N.Y.; s. of Herbert and Nellie York; m. Sybil Dunford 1947; one s. two d.; ed. Rochester and California Univs.
Joined staff of California Univ. Radiation Laboratory 43; attached to Y-12 Plant, Oak Ridge, Tenn. 44-45; California Univ. Graduate School 45-49; undertook, with Dr. Hugh Bradner, design and execution of major experiment in "Operation Greenhouse" (Eniwetok) 50; Asst. Prof. of Physics, California Univ. 51; headed programme, Livermore weapon development laboratory 52-54, Dir. 54-58; Assoc. Dir. California Univ. Radiation Laboratory 54-58; Dir. of Research, Advanced Research Projects Division, Inst. for Defense Analyses, Chief Scientist, Dept. of Defense Advanced Research Projects Agency 58; Dir. Defense Research and Engineering, Dept. of Defense 58-61; Chancellor, Calif. Univ. at San Diego 61-64, 70-72, Dean of Graduate Studies 69-70,

Dir. Program on Science, Technology and World Affairs, Prof. of Physics, Calif. Univ. 61-; fmr. mem. Army and Air Force Scientific Advisory Board; Vice-Chair. President's Science Advisory Cttee. 65-67, mem. 57-58, 64-68; mem. Gen. Advisory Cttee. for Arms Control and Disarmament 62-69; mem. Board of Trustees, Aerospace Corpn. 61-, Board of Trustees, Inst. for Defense Analyses 64-; mem. Exec. Cttee. Fed. of American Scientists 70-, Int. Council, Pugwash Movement 72-, Board of Dirs. Arms Control Asscn.
Publs. *Race to Oblivion* 70, *Arms Control Readings* 73, *The Advisors* 76, and various articles on physics and arms control problems.
University of California, San Diego, P.O. Box 109, La Jolla, Calif. 92037; and 6110 Camino de la Costa, La Jolla, Calif., U.S.A.
Telephone: (714) 452-3357 (Office); (714) 459-1776.

York, Susannah; British actress; b. 9 Jan. 1942, London; m.; one s. one d.; ed. Royal Acad. of Dramatic Art.
Acted in films: *Tunes of Glory* 60, *There was a Crooked Man* 60, *The Greengage Summer* 61, *Freud* 62, *Tom Jones* 63, *The Seventh Dawn* 64, *Scene Nun — Take One* 64, *Sands of the Kalahari* 65, *Scruggs* 66, *Kaleidoscope* 66, *A Man for All Seasons* 66, *Sebastian* 67, *The Killing of Sister George* 68, *Duffy* 68, *Oh What a Lovely War* 68, *The Battle of Britain*, *Lock up Your Daughters* 69, *They Shoot Horses, Don't They?* 69, *Country Dance* 70, *Jane Eyre* 70, *Zee and Co.* 71, *Happy Birthday Wanda June* 71, *Images* 72, *The Maids, Gold* 74, *Conduct Unbecoming*, *That Lucky Touch, Hostages, Mrs. Eliza Fraser;* plays: *Wings of a Dove, A Singular Man, A Cheap Bunch of Nice Flowers, The Maids, The Great Ban;* television: *The Crucible, The Creditors, La Grande Breteche, Fallen Angels.*
Publs: children's books: *In Search of Unicorns, Lark's Castle.*
c/o International Creative Management, 22 Grafton Street, London, W.1, England.
Telephone: 01-629 8080.

Yorty, Samuel William; American lawyer and politician; b. 1 Oct. 1909, Lincoln, Neb.; s. of Frank Patrick Yorty and Johanna Egan; m. Elizabeth Hensel 1938; one s.; ed. Southwestern Univ. and Univ. of S. California Admitted to Calif. Bar 39; mem. Calif. State Ass. 36-40, 49-50; U.S. Congressman, Calif. 50-54; U.S.A.F. 42-45; Mayor of Los Angeles 61-73; Republican.
Leisure interests: swimming, reading biographies, playing paddle tennis, banjo, singing.
3435 Wilshire Boulevard, Los Angeles 90012, California, U.S.A.
Telephone: (213) 380-3131.

Yoseph, Ovadya; Israeli Rabbi; b. Baghdad, Iraq.
Member, Sephardi Rabbinical Court 45; Chief of Rabbinical Court of Appeals and Deputy Chief Rabbi of Egypt (Cairo) 47; mem. regional Rabbinical Court of Petach Tiqva 51, Jerusalem 58; mem. Grand Court of Appeals, Jerusalem 65; Pres. of Great Metivta, Jerusalem; Pres. "Yeshivat Thora Ve-horaa", Tel-Aviv; mem. Management "Yeshivat Porath" Jerusalem; Pres. Cttee. of Building Fund for "Yeshivat Porath Yoseph" in the Old City; Chief Rabbi and Chief of Rabbinical Court, Tel-Aviv 68-; Sephardi Chief Rabbi of Israel Oct. 72-; Rabbi Kook Prize, Rabbi Uziel Prize.
Publs. *Yobia Omer*, several vols. of Responsa, *Hazon Ovadia.*
Chief Rabbinate, 51 Hamelech David Boulevard, Tel-Aviv, Israel.

Yoshida, Kenzuo; Japanese diplomatist; b. 19 Sept. 1917, Toyama; ed. Tokyo Univ.
Consul-General in Honolulu, U.S.A. 61-63; Counsellor, Embassy in U.K., concurrently Consul-Gen. in London 63-65, Minister in U.K. 65; Minister in Repub. of Korea

65-67; Amb. to Tanzania 67-69, concurrently to Zambia 68-69; Dir.-Gen. Immigration Bureau, Ministry of Justice, Tokyo 69-72; Dir.-Gen. Asian Affairs Bureau, Ministry of Foreign Affairs 72-73; Amb. to Australia Oct. 73-, concurrently to Nauru Jan. 74-, and to Fiji June 74-. Embassy of Japan, 112 Empire Circuit, Yarralumla, Canberra, A.C.T., Australia.

Yoshiki, Masao, DR. ENG.; Japanese engineer; b. 20 Jan. 1908, Nagasaki; s. of Tei and Kuni Yoshiki; m. Miyoko Kuwabara 1933; two s. four d.; ed. Univ. of Tokyo.
Lecturer, School of Engineering, Univ. of Tokyo 30-32; Asst. Prof., Univ. of Tokyo 32-44, Prof. of Naval Architecture, 44-68; Pres. Soc. of Naval Architects of Japan 61-63; Dean, School of Engineering, Univ. of Tokyo 62-64; Chair. Int. Ships Structures Congress 67-70; Chief Dir., Japan Soc. for the Promotion of Science 68-; Prof. Emer. Univ. of Tokyo; Commr. Space Activities Comm. 68-74; Vice-Pres. Science Council of Japan 69-72; mem. Council Science and Technology 74; Prize of Japan Acad. 66, Purple Ribbon Decoration 68.
Leisure interests: golf, Japanese chess.
Publs. Articles in journals.
43-14, Izumi 2-chome, Suginami-ku, Tokyo, Japan. Telephone: 03-328-0210.

Yoshikuni, Ichiro; Japanese civil servant; b. 2 Sept. 1916, Yokohama; s. of the late Kenzo Yoshikuni and Matsuko Yoshikuni; m. Tomiko Arai 1946; one d. one s.; ed. Tokyo Imperial Univ.
With Ministry of Commerce and Industry 40-47; mem. Board of Trade 47-48; Attorney-Gen's. Office, Legislative Bureau 48-52; Cabinet Legislative Bureau 52-, Dir. of Third Div. 59-64, Dir. First Div. 64, Asst. Dir.-Gen. 64-72, Dir.-Gen. 72-.
Leisure interests: reading, music, cinema, go (7th dan).
Publs. (co-author) Manual on the Drafting, Application and Interpretation of Law 49, Legislative Drafting 52, Dictionary of Public Finance and Accounting 74.
5-35-17 Jingumae, Shibuya-ku, Tokyo, Japan. Telephone: 03-581-1491 (Office); 03-409-0285 (Home).

Yoshimura, Junzo; Japanese architect; b. 7 Sept. 1908, Tokyo; s. of Shinzo and Tama Yoshimura; m. Takiko Ohmura 1944; one d.; ed. Tokyo Acad. of Fine Arts.
At Architectural Office of Antonin Raymond 31-42; own architectural practice 43-; Asst. Prof. in Architecture, Tokyo Univ. of Arts 45-61, Prof. 62-70, Prof. Emer. 70-; mem. Architectural Inst. of Japan, Japan Architects' Asscn.; mem., Hon. mem. Soc. de Arquitectos Mexicános 60-; Hon. Fellow American Inst. of Architects 75-; Architectural Inst. Prize 56, Parsons Medal (New York) 56, Japanese Acad. of Arts Award 75.
Leisure interests: music, travel.
Works include: Int. House of Japan, Tokyo 55, Public Kambara Hospital 56, The Motel on the Mountain, New York 56, Hotel Kowakien, Hakone, 59, Mountain House for Yawata Iron and Steel Co., Kujyu 60, N.C.R. H.Q., Tokyo 62, Americana Building, Osaka 65, Prefectural Aichi Univ. of Arts, Aichi 65-71, Aoyama Tower Building, Tokyo 69, Hotel Fujita, Kyoto 70, Japan House, New York 71, Nara Nat. Museum 73, and many residences.
2-38 Akasaka 5-chome, Minato-ku, Tokyo (Office) and 30-24 Minamidai 5-chome Nakano-ku, Tokyo, Japan (Home).
Telephone: 583-7032 (Office) and 381-1282 (Home).

Yoshiyama, Hirokichi; Japanese business executive; b. 1 Dec. 1911; ed. Faculty of Engineering, Univ. of Tokyo.
Joined Hitachi Ltd. 35, Dir. 61, Exec. Man. Dir. 64, Senior Exec. Man. Dir. 68, Exec. Vice-Pres. 69, Pres. Nov. 71-; Chair. Tokyo Atomic Industrial Consortium.

Hitachi Ltd., New Marunouchi Building, No. 5-1, 1-chome, Marunouchi, Chiyoda-ku, Tokyo 100, Japan. Telephone: 03-212-1111.

Yosizaka, Takamasa; Japanese architect and town planner; b. 13 Feb. 1917, Tokyo; s. of Syunzô Yosizaka; m. Kôno-Hukoko 1945; two s. one d.; ed. Waseda Univ., Tokyo.
Lecturer, Japan Women's Coll. 42-50, Tokyo Agricultural School 45-48, Yamanasi Univ. 56-57, Tucumán Nat. Univ., Argentina 61-62; Asst. Prof. Waseda Univ. 50, Prof. 59, Head of Dept. of Architecture 64-65, Dean of School of Science and Engineering 69-72; Man. Waseda Univ. Expedition to Equatorial Africa 58, and Leader of its MacKinley Alaska Expedition 60; Vice-Pres. Architectural Inst. of Japan 67-68, Pres. 73-74; Japanese Asscn. of Architects; Dir. Capital Region Comprehensive Planning Inst.
Principal works: Japanese Pavilion, Venice Biennale 56, Maison Franco-Japonais 59, Athénée Français 62, Gotu City Hall 62, Univ. Seminar House 65, Ikoma Space Museum 69; Projects: Redevelopment Plans for Tokada-no Baba District and Izu, Oosima, Hirosaki, Sendai.
Leisure interests: mountaineering, skiing.
Publs. Form and Environment 55, Primitive Country to Civilized Country 61, Study on Dwelling 65, Directive Proclamations 72, Moi, j'aime pas la mer (trans. into Japanese) 73.
2-17-24 Hyakunintyô, Sinziku-ku, Tokyo 160, Japan. Telephone: 03-361-1083.

Yost, Charles Woodruff, A.B.; American diplomatist; b. 6 Nov. 1907, Watertown, N.Y.; s. of Nicholas Doxtater Yost and Gertrude Cooper; m. Irena Oldakowska 1934; two s. one d.; ed. Princeton Univ. and Ecole des Hautes Etudes Internationales, Paris.
Entered foreign service 30; served Alexandria 30-32, Warsaw 32-33; free-lance journalism 33-35; served Dept. of State 35-45; Asst. to Sec. of State, San Francisco Conf. on UN 45; Sec.-Gen. to UN Del. to Berlin Conf. 45; served Bangkok 45-46; Political Adviser to U.S. Del. to UN Gen. Assembly 46; served Prague 47, Vienna 47-49; Dir. Office of Eastern European Affairs, Dept. of State 49-50; Minister in Athens 50-53; Deputy High Commr. for Austria 53-54; Minister to Laos 54-55, Ambassador 55-56; Minister in Paris 56-58; Ambassador to Syria Jan.-Mar. 58 (terminated by creation of United Arab Republic); Ambassador to Morocco 58-61; Deputy Rep. to UN Security Council 61-65; Career Ambassador 64; Rockefeller Public Service Award 64; Deputy Perm. Rep. to UN 65-66, Perm. Rep. 69-71; Lecturer in Foreign Policy, Columbia Univ. School of Int. Affairs 71-; Counsellor to UNA for U.S.A. 71-; Senior Fellow, Council on Foreign Relations 66-69; Chair. Nat. Advertising Review Board 71-73; Pres. The Nat. Cttee. on U.S.-China Relations 73-.
Leisure interests: arts, literature, swimming, riding.
Publs. The Age of Triumph and Frustration 64, The Insecurity of Nations 68, The Conduct and Misconduct of Foreign Affairs 72.
The National Committee on U.S.-China Relations, 777 United Nations Plaza, New York, N.Y. 10017, U.S.A.
Telephone: 682-6848.

Yost, Don Merlin Lee, B.S., PH.D.; American inorganic chemist and teacher; b. 30 Oct. 1893, Tedrow, Ohio; s. of William Nicholas and Viola Lorena (Lee) Yost; m. S. Marguerite Sims, 1917; one s. one d.; ed. Univ. of Calif., Univ. of Utah, and Calif. Inst. of Technology.
Du Pont Fellow, Calif. Inst. of Technology 24; Fellow Int. Educ. Board, Univs. of Uppsala, Sweden, and Berlin 28-29; Lieut.-Commdr. U.S.N.R. 36, retd. 40; Prof. of Inorganic Chemistry, Calif. Inst. of Technology 42-; A. D. Little Visiting Prof. of Chemistry, Mass. Inst. Technology; Fellow American Physical Society;

mem. Nat. Acad. of Sciences, American Acad. of Arts and Sciences; Presidential Certificate of Merit 48. Leisure interests: reading, algebra, travel.
Publs. *Systematic Inorganic Chemistry* (with H. Russell, Jnr.) 44, *The Rare Earth Elements and their Compounds* (with H. Russell, Jnr. and C. S. Garner) 47.
California Institute of Technology, Pasadena, Calif. 91109; Home: 1270 Cordova Street, Apt. 9, Pasadena, Calif. 91106, U.S.A.
Telephone: 792-5084 (Home).

Yotsumoto, Kiyoshi; Japanese business executive; b. 29 Sept. 1908; ed. Kyoto Univ.
President, Kawasaki Heavy Industries Ltd.
Kawasaki Heavy Industries Ltd., Nissei-Kawasaki Bldg., 16-1, Nakamachi-dori, 2-chome, Ikuta-ku, Kobe; P.O. Box 1140 Kobe Central; Home: 2-22-15, Minami Senzoku, Ohtaku, Tokyo, Japan.
Telephone: 726-0585.

Youde, Edward, C.M.G., M.B.E.; British diplomatist; b. 19 June 1924, Penarth, Glam.; s. of Alfred Youde; m. Pamela Fitt 1950; two d.; ed. School of Oriental and African Studies, London Univ.
Served in various diplomatic posts in China, U.S.A. and U.K. 47-65; Counsellor, Perm. Mission to UN 65-69; Private Sec. to Prime Minister 69-70; Imperial Defence Coll. 70-71; Head Personnel Services Dept., Foreign and Commonwealth Office 71-73; Asst. Under-Sec. of State, FCO 73-74; Amb. to People's Repub. of China 74-.
Leisure interests: walking, Chinese studies.
c/o Foreign and Commonwealth Office, London, S.W.1, England.
Telephone: 01-930-8440.

Younes, Mahmoud; Egyptian engineer; b. 3 April 1912, Cairo; m. 1941; two s. one d.; ed. Royal Coll. of Engineers, Cairo Univ. and Staff Officers' Coll.
Engineer with Mechanical and Electrical Dept., Ministry of Public Works, Cairo 37; army engineer 37; with Mil. Operations Directorate 43; Lecturer, Staff Officers' Coll. 44 and 47; Dir. Technical Affairs Office, G.H.Q. 52; mem. Permanent Board for Development of Nat. Production 53; Man. Dir. and Chair. Gen. Petroleum Authority 54; Counsellor, Ministry of Commerce and Industry and Mineral Wealth; Man. Dir. and Deputy Chair. Suez Canal Authority 56, Chair. 57-65; Deputy Prime Minister for Transport and Communications 65-67; Minister of Oil and Transport 67; Pres. Engineers' Syndicate 54-65; Dir. and Chair. Cie. Orientale des Pétroles d'Egypte et Soc. Coopérative des Pétroles 58-65; mem. Nat. Assembly 64-; now in private consulting office in Beirut, Lebanon; Order of Merit (Class I), Order of the Nile (Class III), Military Star, Liberation Medal, Palestine Medal, Grand Cordon of the Order of the Yugoslav Standard, Grand Officer of the Panamanian Nat. Order of Vasco Nuñez de Balboa, Republic Medal (Class III), Military Service Medal (Class I), Order of The Republic (Class I), and other decorations.
Leisure interests: swimming, reading.
P.O. Box 7272, Beirut, Lebanon.
Telephone: 349375.

Young, Col. Sir Arthur Edwin, K.B.E., C.M.G., C.V.O., K.P.M.; British police officer; b. 15 Feb. 1907, Eastleigh, Hants.; s. of Edwin Young and Gertrude née Brown; m. Ileen Turner 1970; one s.; ed. Portsmouth Grammar School.
Served Portsmouth City Police 24; Chief Constable of Leamington 38; Senior Asst. Chief Constable of Birmingham 41; Chief Constable of Hertfordshire 45; Asst. Commr. Metropolitan Police 47; Commr. of Police, City of London 50-71; Dir. of Public Safety, Allied Control Comm., Italy 43-45; Hon. Commr. of Police, New York; mem. Board of Govs. of the Police College; adviser on re-organization Gold Coast

Police 51; Commr. of Malaya Police 52, of Kenya Police 54; Inspector-Gen. Royal Ulster Constabulary 69-70; Commr. City of London Police; Officer (Brother) Order of St. John of Jerusalem; fmr. Chair. Life Guard Fed., Chair. of Council B.-P. Scout Guild, Chair. Council Police Athletic Asscn., mem. Advisory Council Nat. Police Fund, Chair. Educ. Cttee., mem. London and Home Counties Traffic Advisory Cttee.; Vice-Pres. Police Mutual Assurance Soc.; Chair. Police Council of Great Britain 67-71.
Leisure interest: walking.
Flat 3, 52 Elm Park Road, Chelsea, London, S.W.3, England.
Telephone: 01-352-6972.

Young, Brian Walter Mark; British administrator; b. 23 Aug. 1922, Ceylon (now Sri Lanka); s. of late Sir Mark Young; m.; one s. two d.; ed. Eton Coll., and King's Coll., Cambridge.
Assistant Master, Eton Coll., 47-52; Headmaster of Charterhouse 52-64; Dir. of Nuffield Foundation Sept. 64-70; mem. Central Advisory Council for Educ. 56-59; fmr. mem. U.K. Nat. Comm. for UNESCO; Dir.-Gen. Independent Broadcasting Authority Oct. 70-.
Leisure interests: watching television, reading, music, travel, skin diving and the composition of chess problems and brain teasers.
Publs. *Via Vertendi* 52, *Intelligent Reading* 64.
Independent Broadcasting Authority, 70 Brompton Road, London SW3 1EY, England.
Telephone: 01-584-7011.

Young, (Charles) Kenneth, B.A., F.R.S.L.; British author and journalist; b 27 Nov. 1916, Wakefield, Yorks.; s. of Robert William Young and Alice Jane Young (née Ramsden); m. Phyllis Young (née Dicker) 1951; three s. two d.; ed. Queen Elizabeth's Grammar School, Wakefield, Coatham School, Redcar, and Leeds Univ.
Army Service, Second World War; Foreign Office 44; B.B.C. European Service 48; *Daily Mirror* 50; Perm. Under-Sec. Dept., Cabt. Office 50; *Daily Telegraph* 52-60; Editor *The Yorkshire Post* 60-64; Political and Literary Adviser, Beaverbrook Newspapers 65-; broadcaster, Editor Television series *The Book Man* 60; Gov. Welbeck Coll. 63-73.
Leisure interests: walking, talking, music.
Publs. *D. H. Lawrence* 52, *John Dryden* (critical biography) 54, *Ford Madox Ford* 58, *A. J. Balfour* (authorized biography) 63, *Churchill and Beaverbrook* (a study in friendship) 66, *Rhodesia and Independence* 67, 2nd edn. 69, *Compton Mackenzie* 68, *Music's Great Days at the Spas and Watering Places* 68, *The Greek Passion* 69. *Sir Alec Douglas-Home* 70, *Chapel* 72, *The Bruce Lockhart Diaries* Vol. I 73, Vol. II 75, *H. G. Wells* (essay) 74, *Life of 6th Earl of Rosebery* 74, *Baldwin: A Biography* 76, *Arnold Bennett* (essay) 75.
The Daily Express, Fleet Street, London E.C.4; and 35 Central Parade, Herne Bay, Kent, England.
Telephone: 022-73-5419; and 01-353-8000 (Office).

Young, Sir Frank George, Kt. cr. 73, M.A., D.SC., PH.D., F.R.I.C., F.R.S.; British university professor; b. 25 March 1908, London; m. Ruth Eleanor Turner 1933; three s. one d.; ed. Alleyn's School and Univ. Coll., London.
Bayliss-Starling Scholar, Sharpey Scholar, and Schafer Prizeman, Univ. Coll., London 29-32; Beit Memorial Fellow at Univ. Coll., London, Univ. of Aberdeen and Univ. of Toronto 32-36; mem. of scientific staff, Medical Research Council, Nat. Inst. for Medical Research 36-42; William Julius Mickle Fellow, Univ. of London 40; Prof. of Biochemistry, St. Thomas's Hospital Medical School, Univ. of London 42-45; at Univ. Coll., Univ. of London 45-49; Sir William Dunn Prof. of Biochemistry, Univ. of Cambridge 49-75; mem. Medical Research Council 50-54; Hon.

Fellow of Trinity Hall, Cambridge; Master of Darwin College, Cambridge 64-; Fellow, Univ. Coll., London; Chair. Editorial Board *Biochemical Journal* 42-46; Pres. European Asscn. for the Study of Diabetes 65-68; mem. Royal Comm. on Medical Educ. 65-68; Treas. Int. Union of Biochemistry 67-71; Chair. MRC Clinical Endocrinology Cttee. 67-72; Chair. Advisory Cttee. on Irradiation of Food (U.K.) 67-; Pres. Int. Diabetes Fed. 70-73; Trustee, Ciba Foundation 67-; Pres. British Nutrition Foundation 70-76; Hon. Dr. (Montpellier, Rhodesia and Aberdeen Univs. and Catholic Univ. of Chile); hon. mem. of many foreign scientific and medical bodies; many lectureships held abroad.
Darwin College, Cambridge CB3 9EU, England.

Young, John W.; American astronaut; b. 24 Sept. 1930, San Francisco, Calif.; *m.* Susy Feldman; one *s.* one *d.*; ed. Georgia Inst. of Technology.
Entered U.S. Navy 52; test pilot and program man. F4H weapons system project 59-62; set world time-to-climb records in the 3,000 metre and 25,000 metre altitudes in F4B Navy fighter; served with Fighter Squadron 143, Miramar, Calif.; selected by NASA as astronaut Sept. 62; pilot of first manned *Gemini* flight, *Gemini III* 65; backup pilot for *Gemini VI* Mission 66; command module pilot of *Apollo X* Mission May 69; Commdr. *Apollo XVI* April 72; Chief U.S. Astronaut Office 75-; Fellow, American Astronautical Soc.; NASA Exceptional Services Medal 65, 66.
Leisure interest: running.
NASA Johnson Space Center, Houston, Texas 77058, U.S.A.

Young, John Zachary, M.A., F.R.S.; British zoologist; b. 18 March 1907; ed. Marlborough Coll. and Magdalen Coll., Oxford.
Fellow, Magdalen Coll., Oxford 31-45; Univ. Demonstrator in Zoology and Comparative Anatomy, Oxford 33-45; Prof. of Anatomy, Univ. Coll., London 45-74, Emeritus 74-; Rockefeller Fellow 36; BBC Reith Lecturer 50; Chair. Zoology Section, British Asscn. for Advancement of Science 57; Foreign hon. mem. American Acad. of Arts and Sciences 57, Philosophical Soc.; Royal Medal, Royal Soc. 67; Hon. D.Sc. Bristol 56, McGill 66, Bath 74, LL.D. Glasgow 74; Hon. Fellow Acad. Lincei.
Publs. *The Life of Vertebrates* 50, *Doubt and Certainty in Science* 51, *The Life of Mammals* 57, *A Model of the Brain* 64, *The Memory System of the Brain* 66, *Introduction to the Study of Man* 71, *The Anatomy of the Nervous System of Octopus Vulgaris* 71.
166 Camden Road, London, N.W.1, England.

Young, Kenneth (*see* Young, C. K.)

Young, Michael, M.A., PH.D.; British sociologist; b. 9 Aug. 1915, Manchester; ed. Dartington Hall School, London Univ. and Gray's Inn, London.
Director of Political and Econ. Planning 41-45; Sec. Research Dept., Labour Party 45-51; Dir. Inst. of Community Studies 53-; Chair. Consumers' Asscn. 56-65, Pres. 65-; Chair. Advisory Centre for Educ. 59-; Lecturer in Sociology, Cambridge Univ. 61-63, Trustee, Dartington Hall 42-; Chair. Social Science Research Council 65-68, Chair. Nat. Suggestions Centre 68-; Chair. Int. Extension Coll. 70-; Dir. Mauritius Coll. of the Air 72; Visiting Prof. Ahmadu Bello Univ., Nigeria 74; Chair. Nat. Consumer Council 75-.
Publs. *Family and Kinship in East London* (with Peter Willmott) 57, *The Rise of the Meritocracy* 59, *Family and Class in a London Suburb* (with Peter Willmott) 61, *Innovation and Research in Education* 65, *Learning Begins at Home* 67, *Forecasting and the Social Sciences* 68, *The Symmetrical Family* (with Peter Willmott) 73, *Poverty Report* (Ed.) 74.
18 Victoria Park Square, London, E.2, England.

Young, Milton R.; American politician; b. 6 Dec. 1897, Berlin, N. Dakota; *s.* of John Young and Rachel Zimmerman Young; *m.* Patricia M. Byrne 1969; ed. La Moure High School, N. Dakota State Agric. Coll. and Graceland Coll., Lamoni, Iowa.
Actively engaged in operation of his farm near Berlin, N. Dakota until 45; first elected to public office 24; mem. House of Reps., N. Dakota State Legislature 32-34; mem. N. Dakota Senate 34-45; U.S. Senator from N. Dakota 45-; Republican.
U.S. Senate, Washington, D.C., U.S.A.

Young, Wayland (*see* Kennet, 2nd Baron).

Young, Wilford Roscoe, M.S., J.D.; American oil company executive; b. 19 July 1910, Rathdrum, Idia; *s.* of Roscoe Ellsworth Young and Henrietta Anna Reiniger; *m.* Lillie Gallagher 1935; one *s.* (deceased), one *d.*; ed. Univ. of Ida., Columbia Univ. School of Business and Fordham Univ. Law School.
Joined Legal Dept., Texaco Inc. 42, General Tax Counsel 59, Vice-Pres. and Gen. Tax Counsel 69-71, Vice-Pres. and Gen. Counsel with responsibility for Legal and Tax Depts. April-Oct. 71, Senior Vice-Pres. and Gen. Counsel 71-72, Dir., Exec. Vice-Pres. and Gen. Counsel 72-74, Vice-Chair. of Board and Gen. Counsel 74-.
Texaco Inc., 135 East 42nd Street, New York, N.Y. 10017; Home: Gray Oaks Lane, Greenwich, Conn. 06830, U.S.A.
Telephone: (212) 953-6000 (Office).

Youngdahl, Luther Wallace, B.A., LL.B.; American lawyer and politician; b. 29 May 1896, Minneapolis, Minn.; *s.* of Swedish parents; *m.* Irene Engdahl 1923; two *s.* one *d.*; ed. Gustavus Adolphus Coll., St. Peter and Minnesota Coll. of Law.
Admitted to Bar 21; Asst. Minneapolis City Attorney 21-23; Partner of Judge M. C. Tifft in Law Practice 23-30; apptd. municipal Judge 30, elected district Judge 36; elected Assoc. Justice, Minnesota Supreme Court 42; Gov. of Minnesota 46-51; Judge U.S. District Court for D.C. Oct. 51-, Senior Judge 66-; served on faculty of Minneapolis-Minnesota Coll. of Law; mem. President's Comm. on Law Enforcement and the Admin. of Justice 66; Grand Cross, Order of North Star (Sweden), Royal Order of the Lion (Finland); numerous hon. degrees.
4101 Cathedral Avenue, N.W., Washington, D.C., U.S.A.

Younger, Rt. Hon. Sir Kenneth Gilmour, P.C., K.B.E.; British politician and administrator; b. 15 Dec. 1908, Dunfermline, Scotland; *s.* of James, 2nd Viscount Younger of Leckie and Maud née Gilmour; *m.* Elizabeth Kitsteen Stewart 1934; one *s.* two *d.*; ed. Winchester Coll. and New Coll., Oxford.
Called to the Bar, Inner Temple 32; army service in Second World War; Labour M.P. for Grimsby 45-59; Parl. Under-Sec. Home Office 47-50; Minister of State for Foreign Affairs 50-51; Vice-Chair. Royal Inst. of Int. Affairs 53-59, Dir. 59-70; Chair. Board of Trustees UN Inst. for Training and Research, New York 65-; Chair. Advisory Council on Penal System 66-73; Chair. Cttee. on Privacy and the Law 70-72, Hon. LL.D. (St. John's Univ., New York) 73.
Leisure interests: sailing, guitar, music.
Publs. *Fabian International Essays* 57 (Joint Editor), *The Public Service in the New States* 59, *Changing Perspectives in British Foreign Policy* 64.
3 Clareville Grove, London, S.W.7, England.
[*Died* 19 *May* 1976.]

Yourcenar, Marguerite; American (naturalized) writer; b. 8 June 1903, Brussels, Belgium; *d.* of Michel de Crayencour and Fernande de Cartier de Marchienne. Foreign mem. Belgian Acad.; Hon. D.Litt. (Smith Coll.) 61, (Bowdoin Coll.) 68; Chevalier de la Légion

d'Honneur; Officier, Ordre de Léopold; Page One Award, New York Newspaper Guild 54, Prix Combat 63, and several other awards.
Leisure interests: conservation activities, cooking with natural foods, animal protection.
Publs. *Alexis ou le Traité du vain combat* 29, *La Nouvelle Eurydice* 31, *Pindare* 32, *La Mort conduit l'Attelage* 34, *Denier du Rêve* 34, *Feux* 36, *Les Songes et Les Sorts* 38, *Nouvelles Orientales* 38, *Le Coup de Grâce* 39, *Mémoires d'Hadrien* 51 (awarded Prix Fémina Vacaresco), *Electre ou la Chute des Masques* 54, *Les Charités d'Alcippe* 56, *Sous Bénéfice d'Inventaire* 62 (awarded Prix Combat), *Le Mystère d'Alceste* 63, *L'Oeuvre au Noir* 68 (awarded Prix Fémina), *Théâtre I, II* 71, *Entretiens Radiophoniques* 72; trans. *The Waves* (Virginia Woolf) 37, *What Maisie Knew* (Henry James) 47, *Fleuve Profond, Sombre Rivière* (Negro Spirituals) 64, *Poems* (Constantine Cavafy) 58, *Hortense Flexner* 69.
Petite Plaisance, Northeast Harbor, Maine 04662, U.S.A.

Yousuf, Lieut.-Gen. Mohammed; Pakistani soldier and diplomatist; b. 14 Oct. 1908, Quetta; s. of Khan Bahadur Sharbat Khan; m. Zubeida Jehandad Khan 1936; four s. two d.; ed. Prince of Wales's Royal Military Coll. and Royal Military Coll., Sandhurst.
Joined 7th Light Cavalry 29; Brigade Major 42; commanded 18th King Edward's Own Cavalry 47; raised 12th Div. 48; G.O.C. East Pakistan 49; led Military Mission to Iran 51; Chief of Gen. Staff 51; Commdt. Pakistan Armoured Corps 52; retd. from Army 56; High Commr. for Pakistan in Australia and New Zealand 56-59, in U.K. 59-63; Amb. to Afghanistan 63-68; High Commr. to U.K. Oct. 71-Jan. 72, Amb. Jan.-May 72; Amb. to Switzerland May 72-; Sitara-i-Pakistan, Nishani Liaqat (Iran), Légion d'Honneur (France).
Leisure interests: shooting, polo, racing.
Embassy of Pakistan, Bernastrasse 47, Berne, Switzerland.

Yu Ch'iu-li; Chinese politician; b. 1914, Szechuan.
Political Commissar of Detachment, 120th Div. 34; Deputy Political Commissar Tsinghai Mil. District, People's Liberation Army 49; Lieut.-Gen. PLA 55; Dir. Finance Dept., PLA 56-57; Political Commissar Gen. Logistics Dept., PLA 57-58; Minister of Petroleum Industry 58; Vice-Chair. State Planning Comm. 65, Chair. 72-; mem. 9th Cen. Cttee. of CCP 69, 10th Cen. Cttee. 73; Vice-Premier, State Council 75-.
People's Republic of China.

Yu Hui-yung; Chinese musician and politician.
Composer of Revolutionary Model Operas; Minister of Culture 75-.
People's Republic of China.

Yu Kuo-hua; Chinese banker; b. 1914; ed. Tsinghua Univ., Harvard Univ. Graduate School, U.S.A., London School of Econs.
Secretary to Pres. of Nat. Mil. Council 36-44; Alt. Exec. Dir. Int. Bank for Reconstruction and Devt. 47-50; Alt. Exec. Dir. IMF 51-55; Pres. Cen. Trust of China 55-61; Man. Dir. China Devt. Corpn. 59-67; Chair. Board of Dirs. Bank of China 61-67, China Insurance Co. Ltd. 61-67; Alt. Gov. IBRD 64-67, Gov. for Repub. of China 67-69; Minister of Finance 67-69; Gov. Gen. Bank of China 69-; Minister without Portfolio 69-; Gov. Int. Monetary Fund 69-, Asian Devt. Bank 69-; Dr. h.c. (St. John's Univ., Jamaica, New York Univ.).
Central Bank of China, Paoching Road, Taipei, Taiwan.

Yu Pin, H. E. Cardinal Paul; Chinese ecclesiastic; b. 13 April 1901, Lan-si Sien, Kirin.
Ordained 28; Titular Bishop of Sozusa di Palestrina 36; Archbishop of Nanking 46-, (now in Taiwan); cr. Cardinal 69.
Cardinal Archbishop of Nanking, Taipei, Taiwan.

Yu Tai-chung; Chinese party official.
Commander People's Liberation Army Unit 6410, Kiangsu 68; Alt. mem. 9th Cen. Cttee. of CCP 69; Chair. Inner Mongolia Revolutionary Cttee. 70; First Sec. CCP Inner Mongolia 71; mem. 10th Cen. Cttee. of CCP 73.
People's Republic of China.

Yuan Hua-ping; Chinese army officer.
Head of Armament Dept., Gen. Logistics Dept., People's Liberation Army.
People's Republic of China.

Yudelman, Montague, B.SC., M.SC., PH.D.; American economist; b. 8 Nov. 1922, Johannesburg, S. Africa; s. of Jack Yudelman and Ida Sahl; m. 1st 1948 (divorced 1960), 2nd Sally Ann Walters 1968; two s. two d.; ed. Durham High School and Univ. of Witwatersrand, S. Africa, and Univ. of Calif., Berkeley, U.S.A.
South African Air Force 39-45; university 46-53; Technical Assistance Officer, FAO, Rome 53-56; Asst. Dir. Social Sciences, Rockefeller Foundation, New York 56-59; Research Assoc., Center for Int. Affairs, Harvard Univ. 60-62; Econ. Adviser, Govt. of Cyprus 62-63; Prof. Univ. of Mich., Ann Arbor 63-66; Adviser to Inter-American Devt. Bank, Washington, D.C. 66-68; Vice-Pres. OECD Devt. Centre, Paris 68-; Ford Foundation Fellow 53, Rockefeller Foundation Fellow 59.
Leisure interests: walking, golf, swimming.
Publs. include: *Africans on the Land* 64, *Agricultural Development in Latin America: Current Studies and Prospects* 66, *Agricultural Development and Economic Integration in Latin America* 67, *Technological Change in Agriculture and Employment in Developing Countries* 71.
16 Rue Desbordes-Valaise, Paris 16e, France.
Telephone: 525-12-02.

Yukawa, Hideki, D.SC.; Japanese physicist; b. 23 Jan. 1907, Tokyo; s. of Takuji and Koyuki Ogawa; m. Sumi Yukawa 1932; two s.; ed. Kyoto Univ.
Lecturer, Kyoto Univ. 32, Osaka Univ. 33; Asst. Prof. Osaka Univ. 36; Prof. of Physics, Kyoto Univ. 39-70 (on leave of absence 48-52); Visiting Prof., Inst. for Advanced Study, Princeton 48-49; Prof. of Physics, Columbia Univ. 51; Imperial Prize, Japan Acad. 40; Order of Decoration of Japan 43; mem. Japan Acad. 46; Foreign Assoc., Nat. Acad. of Sciences, U.S. 49; Nobel Prize for Physics 49; Prof. Emer. (Osaka and Kyoto Univs.); Dir. Research Inst. for Fundamental Physics, Kyoto Univ. 53-70; Hon. Citizen of Kyoto; Hon. Dr. Univs. of Paris and Moscow; Hon. mem. Royal Soc. of Edinburgh, Indian Acad. of Sciences, Accademia Nazionale dei Lincei, U.S.S.R. Acad. of Sciences; mem. Pontificia Academia Scientiarum; foreign mem. Royal Soc., London.
Leisure interests: literature, history.
6 Izumikawa-cho, Shimogamo, Sakyoku, Kyoto, Japan.
Telephone: (075) 721-2468.

Yukawa, Morio, G.C.V.O.; Japanese court official and fmr. diplomatist; b. 23 Feb. 1908, Morioka City; m. Teiko Kohiyama; two s.; ed. Tokyo Univ.
Entered Foreign Service 33; served U.K., Geneva; Dir. Trade Bureau Econ. Stabilization Board, Cabinet 50-51; Dir. Gen. Econ. Affairs Bureau, Foreign Office 51-52; Minister Counsellor to France 52-54; Dir. Gen. Int. Co-operation Bureau, Foreign Office 54-55; Dir. Gen. Econ. Affairs Bureau, Foreign Office 55-57; Amb. to Philippines 57-61; Deputy Vice-Minister, Foreign Office 61-63; Amb. to Belgium, Luxembourg and European Econ. Community 63-68, to U.K. 68-72; Grand Master of the Ceremonies, Imperial Household 73-.
Leisure interests: historical or biographical works, theatre, golf.
Hilltop 5-10 Sanbancho, Chiyoda-ku, Tokyo 102, Japan

Yunich, David Lawrence; American consumer companies consultant; b. 21 May 1917, Albany, N.Y.; s. of Max A. and Bessie (Feldman) Yunich; m. Beverly F. Blickman 1941; two s.; ed. Union Coll. and Harvard Graduate School of Business Administration.
L. Bamberger and Co., Newark 47-48, Pres. and Dir. 55-62; Vice-Pres. Macy's N.Y. 41-51, Senior Vice-Pres. 51-62, Pres. 62-71; Vice-Chair. Board R. H. Macy and Co. Inc. 71-73, Dir. 58-73 (retd.); Chair. Metropolitan Transportation Authority; Dir. Prudential Insurance Co., N.Y. Telephone Co., Slater Walker Co. of America Inc., U.S. Industries Inc., East River Savings Bank, Londontown Corpn. Inc., Diners Club Inc., Bowmar Instrument Corpn. Inc.; mem. N.Y. State Banking Board; Chair. of Board N.Y. Chamber of Commerce and Industry; Chair. Mayor's Council (N.Y.C.) Econ. and Business Advisors; Dir. Educ. Broadcasting Corpn., Nat. Jewish Hospital, Denver; Trustee Carnegie Hall Corpn., Albany Med. Coll., St. Vincent's Hospital, Rutgers Univ., Union Coll., Skidmore Coll.; Pres. Retail Dry Goods Asscn.; Dir. Nat. Retail Merchants Asscn., American Management Asscn.
Office: 1700 Broadway, New York City, N.Y. 10019; Home: 26 Cooper Road, Scarsdale, N.Y. 10583, U.S.A. Telephone: 914-723-65-6.

Yussof, Dr. Mohammed; Afghan politician; b. 21 Jan. 1917, Kabul; one s. one d.
Former Minister of Mines and Industries; Prime Minister and Minister of Foreign Affairs March 63-Nov. 65; Amb. to Fed. Repub. of Germany, also accred. to Denmark, Sweden and Switzerland 66-73.
c/o Ministry of Foreign Affairs, Kabul, Afghanistan.

Yusuf bin Sheikh Abdul R'ahman, Tan Sri Datuk Chik Mohamed, P.M.N., S.P.M.P., J.P., O.B.E.; Malaysian politician; b. 3 March 1907; ed. Anderson School, Ipoh, Malaysia, Newton Coll., Newton Abbot, Exeter Coll., Oxford Univ., Inner Temple, London.
Founder mem., Perak Malay League, elected Pres. 47; founder mem., UMNO, Vice-Pres. 48-50, Vice-Pres., UMNO, Malaya 51-54; mem. Perak State Council 48-54, Fed. Legislative Council 48-54; Speaker, House of Reps., Malaysia 64-; mem. several cttees. of civil orgs. and dir. numerous cos.; Dato Bendahara Perak 59; Pemangku Mahkota Negara 71.
Parliament House, Lake Gardens, Kuala Lumpur; Home: No. 1, Jalan Clifford, Kuala Lumpur, Malaysia.

Yvon, Jacques; French physicist; b. 26 April 1903, Angoulême.
Professor, Faculty of Science, Strasbourg 38-43, 46-49 held various posts with the French Atomic Energy Commissariat 49-62, scientific adviser 62-70; Prof. of theoretical physics, Sorbonne, Paris 62-; High Commr. for Atomic Energy 70-.
Commissariat à l'Energie Atomique, 29-33 rue de la Fédération, Paris 15e, France.

Z

Zababakhin, Yevgeny Ivanovich, D.SC.; Soviet physicist; b. 16 Jan. 1908, Moscow; ed. Zhukovsky Military Air Force Engineering Acad.

Teacher, Prof., Zhukovsky Military Air Force Engineering Acad. 44; mem. C.P.S.U. 49; Corresp. mem., U.S.S.R. Acad. of Sciences 58, mem. 68-.

U.S.S.R. Academy of Sciences, 14 Lenin Prospect, Moscow, U.S.S.R.

Zacharias, Jerrold Reinach, B.A., PH.D.; American physicist; b. 23 Jan. 1905; ed. Columbia Univ.

Teacher, Hunter Coll., New York City 31-40; with Radiation Laboratory, Mass. Inst. of Technology 40-45, Prof. of Physics, Mass. Inst. of Technology 46-66, Inst. Prof. 66-70, Inst. Prof. Emeritus 70-; Dir. Nuclear Science Laboratory 46-56; Assoc. Dir. Project Lexington (nuclear-powered flight) 48; Dir. Project Hartwell (undersea warfare) 50; Assoc. Dir. Project Charles 51, Project Lincoln 51-52 (both air defence); Dir. Summer Study on Distant Early Warning Line 52; Technical Dir. Project Lamp Light (continental defence) 54; Chair. Physical Science Study Cttee. 56-; mem. Nat. Acad. of Sciences; main field of research: electric and magnetic shapes of atomic nuclei, one out-growth of which has been the invention of what is claimed to be the world's most precise atomic clock.

32 Clifton Street, Belmont, Mass. 02178, U.S.A.

Zachau, Erich, DR. RER. POL.; German chartered accountant and banking official; b. 1 Nov. 1902, Elbing, E. Prussia; ed. Humanistisches Gymnasium, Elbing, and Univs. of Jena and Berlin.

Trainee, Deutsche Bank Elbing, subsequently employee of Deutsche Uberseeische Bank, Berlin; with Deutscher Sparkassen- und Giroverband and Deutsche Girozentrale-Deutsche Kommunalbank, Berlin 27-43; mem. Board Aktiengesellschaft für Wirtschaftsprüfung-Deutsche Baurevision and partner in firm of chartered accountants, Berlin and Düsseldorf 43-48; Dir. Bank deutscher Länder 48-67; Dir. Deutsche Bundesbank 67-72.

Deutsche Bundesbank, 600 Frankfurt am Main 50, Wilhelm Epstein Strasse 14, Federal Republic of Germany.

Zachrisson, Bertil, B.A.; Swedish politician; b. 2 May 1926, Gothenburg; s. of Josef Zachrisson and Emma Gustafsson; m. Birgit Lundquist 1950; two d.

Secretary, Student Christian Movement 50-53, Youth Movement of Congregational Church of Sweden 53-55, Board of Educ. 55-57; Teacher, Folk High School 57-62; Editor Svensk Veckotidning 62-73; mem. Riksdag 69-; Minister of Educ. and Cultural Affairs Oct. 73-; Social Democrat.

Utbildningsdepartementet, Fack, S-103 10 Stockholm 2, Sweden.

Zachwatowicz, Jan, DR.TECH.SC.; Polish architect; b. 4 March 1900, Gatczyno; s. of Wincenty Zachwatowicz and Jadwiga Eggert; m. 1st Maria Chodźko 1929, 2nd Izabela Kunińska 1965; two d.; ed. Warsaw Technical Univ.

Assistant, Warsaw Tech. Univ. 26-30, Adjunct 35-39, Prof. 39-70, Prof. Emeritus 70-; Conservator-Gen. of Poland and Dir. Dept. of Conservation, Ministry of Culture and Art 45-57; mem. fmr. Polish Acad. of Learning 46, Polish Acad. of Sciences 52-; Pres. Cttee. of Architecture and Town Planning, Polish Acad. of Sciences; conservation work includes uncovering and restoring fortified walls of Warsaw Old Town and plans for reconstruction of historical monuments in Warsaw and other cities; mem. Polish Architects Asscn. 30-; Hon. mem. Royal Inst. of British Architects 63, Académie d'Architecture, Paris 67; State Prize 1st Class 50; Prize of Minister of Culture and Art 1st Class 71; Honorary Prize, Polish Architects Asscn. 71; Medal of 30th Anniversary of People's Poland 74; Commdr. Cross of Order of Polonia Restituta, Order of Banner of Labour 1st Class, and several other decorations and awards.

Leisure interest: music.

Publs. Twierdza Zamość (The Fortress of Zamość) 36, Dzieje architektury polskiej (History of Polish Architecture) 52, 54, Konserwacja zabytków (The Conservation of Monuments) 56, 65, Architektura Polska X i XI w. (Polish Architecture of X-XI Centuries) 61, Architektura gotycka w Polsce (Polish Gothic Architecture) 65, Architektura Polska (Polish Architecture) 67, Współczesna architektura polska (Contemporary Polish Architecture) 68, Katedra Gnieznieńska (Gniezno Cathedral) 70, Architektura romańska w Polsie 71

Aleja Roz 8, 00-556 Warsaw, Poland.

Telephone: 284885.

Zadok, Haim J.; Israeli politician; b. 2 Oct. 1913, Poland; m. Esther Berger; two d.; ed. Warsaw Univ.

Joined Labour Zionist Movt. 30; emigrated to Palestine 35; with Haganah and Jewish Settlement Police until 48; with Israel Defence Forces in War of Independence 48; Deputy Attorney-Gen. 49-52; private law practice 52-65, 67-74; Lecturer in Commercial Law, Tel Aviv Law School 53-61; mem. Knesset (Parl.) 59-; Minister of Commerce and Industry 65-66, of Justice 74- and Religious Affairs 74; Chair. Exec. Cttee. Hebrew Univ., Jerusalem 69-74, Knesset Foreign Affairs and Defence Cttee. 70-74; mem. Advisory Council, Bank of Israel 63-74.

Ministry of Justice, Jerusalem, Israel.

Zaefferer de Goyeneche, Ana Maria, LL.B.; Argentine professor, politician and diplomatist; b. 29 Oct. 1920, Mendoza; d. of Oscar Zaefferer Silva and Berta Toro Zelaya; m. Arturo Goyeneche 1940; two d.; ed. Univ. of Buenos Aires.

Professor of Argentine History and Constitutional Law, Superior Inst. of Modern Languages and Sta. Union Coll., Buenos Aires 44-66; Prof. of Political Economy Buenos Aires Nat. Coll. 64-66; Adviser to Presidential Sec. of Statistics 56, and to Sec. of Ministry of Educ. 62; Dir. journal Tribuna Cívica 58; mem. Partido Cívico Independiente; Founder-mem. Market Social Economy Inst. 66; Perm. Rep. of Argentina to the Int. Orgs. and European Office of UN, Geneva 66-73; Pres. ICEM Exec. Cttee. 69; First Vice-Pres. Contracting Parties GATT 68; mem. ICEM mission to Wash. 68, to Europe 70.

Leisure interests: historical research, lectures on history, Society of Argentine Bibliophiles.

Publ. Historia de la Cultura Argentina 51.

Calle Paraná 1247, 6° piso, dto. B, Buenos Aires, Argentina.

Zafrulla Khan, Sir Muhammad, K.C.S.I., B.A., LL.B., HON. LL.D. (Cantab); Pakistani politician; b. 6 Feb. 1893; ed. Govt. Coll., Lahore, and King's Coll., London.

Barrister-at-Law (Lincoln's Inn); Advocate, Sialkot, Punjab 14-16; practised Lahore High Court 16-35; mem. Punjab Legislative Council 26-35; del. Indian Round Table Confs. 30, 31, 32; del. Joint Select Cttee. of Parl. on Indian Reforms 33; Pres. All-India Muslim League 31; mem. Gov.-Gen.'s Exec. Council 35-41; Leader Indian Del. to Assembly of L. of N. 39; Agent-Gen. of Govt. of India in China 42; Judge Fed. Court of India 41-June 47; Constitutional Adviser to H.H. Ruler of Bhopal June-Dec. 47; Leader Pakistan Del. to Annual Session of UN Gen. Assembly Sept.-Nov. 47;

Minister of Foreign Affairs and Commonwealth Relations, Govt. of Pakistan Dec. 47; leader Pakistan Del. to UN Security Council on India-Pakistan dispute 48-54, and to sessions of UN Gen. Assembly 47-54; Leader Pakistan del. to San Francisco Conf. on Japanese Peace Treaty 51; Leader Pakistan Del. to SEATO Conf. Manila 54; Judge at the Int. Court of Justice, The Hague 54-61, 64-73, Vice-Pres. 58-61, Pres. 70-73; Perm. Rep. to UN 61-64; Pres. 17th session UN Gen. Assembly 62-63.
Publ. *Islam: Its Meaning for Modern Man* 62.
16 Gressenhall Road, London, S.W.18, England.
Telephone: 01-874-6298.

Zagari, Mario; Italian journalist and politician; b. 1913, Milan.
During Second World War helped reorganize Socialist Party of Proletarian Unity as mem. of admin. and exec. cttees.; elected to Constituent Assembly as rep. of Socialist Party of Proletarian Unity; mem. Chamber of Deputies rep. Socialist Democratic Party 48; Sec., Social Democratic Party 49; Man. Dir. Social Democrat newspaper *La Giustizia*; attended first European Parl. at Strasbourg; mem. Central Cttee., Socialist Party; Rome Councillor 62; elected to Chamber of Deputies 63, 68 for constituency of Rome; Under-Sec. for Foreign Affairs, 2nd and 3rd Moro govts.; Minister of Foreign Trade March 70-Feb. 71, of Justice 73-74.
c/o Ministry of Justice, Rome, Italy.

Zahedi, Ardeshir, LL.B.; Iranian diplomatist; b. 16 Oct. 1928; s. of Gen. Fazlollah and Khadijeh Zahedi; *m.* Princess Shahnaz Pahlavi 1957 (dissolved); one *d.*; ed. in Teheran, American Univ. of Beirut and Utah State Univ., U.S.A.
Civil Adjutant to His Imperial Majesty the Shah of Iran 54-; Iranian Amb. to U.S.A. 59-61, to U.K. 62-67; Minister of Foreign Affairs 67-71; Amb. to U.S.A. and Mexico 73-; LL.D. (Utah State, Chungang, East Texas State and Kent State Univs.).
Embassy of Iran, 3005 Massachusetts Avenue, N.W., Washington, D.C. 20008, U.S.A.
Telephone: (202) 483-5500.

Zahir, Abdul; Afghan politician; b. 3 May 1910, Lagham; ed. Habibia High School, Kabul and Columbia and Johns Hopkins Univs., U.S.A.
Practised medicine in U.S.A. before returning to Kabul 43; Chief Doctor, Municipal Hospital, Kabul 43-50; Deputy Minister of Health 50-55, Minister 55-58; Amb. to Pakistan 58-61; Chair. House of the People 61-64, 65-69; Deputy Prime Minister and Minister of Health 64-65; Amb. to Italy 69-71; Prime Minister 71-72.
c/o Office of the Prime Minister, Kabul, Afghanistan.

Zahir Shah (*see* Mohammed Zahir Shah).

Zahn, Joachim, DR. JUR.; German business executive; b. 24 Jan. 1914, Wuppertal; s. of Hans Zahn; ed. Tübingen, Cologne, Königsberg.
Entered Civil Service, rose to rank of Regierungsrat; management board Deutsche Treuhandgesellschaft 45-54, Aschaffenburger Zellstoffwerke 55-58; Dir. Daimler-Benz AG 58-, Spokesman, Board of Management 65-71, Chair. 71-; mem. supervisory boards of Daimler-Benz subsidiary and assoc. cos. Hanomag-Henschel Fahrzeugwerke G.m.b.H., Motoren- und Turbinen-Union, Friedrichshafen and Munich, Mercedes-Benz of North America, Argentina, Australia, Canada and assocs. in Brazil, France, Italy, Spain, South Africa, Switzerland and India; Dir. Fried. Krupp G.m.b.H., Portland Zementwerke, Heidelberg, Frankfurter Versicherung AG, Frankfurter Hypothekenbank, Hannoversche Messe AG, Obermain Schuhfabrik AG; Vice-Pres. and Treas. Bundesverband der Deutschen Industrie; mem. board Verband der Deutschen Automobilindustrie; Senator Max-Planck-Soc.; Chair. Baden-Württemberg Landeskuratorium des Stifter-verbandes für die deutsche Wissenschaft; Grand Cross of Merit, Fed. Repub. of Germany.
Daimler-Benz AG, Stuttgart-Untertürkheim, Federal Republic of Germany.

Zahradník, Jindřich, ING.; Czechoslovak politician; b. 4 July 1916, Česká Třebová; ed. Faculty of Engineering, Czech Technical Univ., Prague.
Head of Dept., Czechoslovak Heavy Engineering Works 50-51; Chief Engineer, Manager of Main Admin., Head of Dept., Ministry of Heavy Engineering 51-64; Dir., Industrial Automation Works 64-65; Gen. Dir., Instruments and Automation Works 65-70; Minister-Chair. Fed. Cttee. for Industry 70; Deputy Premier of Č.S.S.R. 71-; Deputy to House of the People, Fed. Assembly 71-; mem. State Comm. for Management and Organization 65-68; mem. State Comm. for Technology 65-69; Award of Merit in Construction 66.
Government Presidium, nábř. kapt. Jaroše, Prague 1, Czechoslovakia.

Zaid bin Sultan al-Nahayan, H.H. Sheikh; President of the United Arab Emirates and Ruler of Abu Dhabi.
Former Gov. of Eastern Province; deposed his brother, Sheikh Shakhbut, and succeeded to Sheikhdom 66; Pres. Fed. of Arab Emirates 69-71; Pres. United Arab Emirates (U.A.E.) 71-.
Royal Diwan, Abu Dhabi, United Arab Emirates.

Zajfryd, Mieczysław, M.ECON.; Polish politician; b. 12 Nov. 1922, Brześć-on-the-Bug; ed. School of Planning and Statistics, Warsaw.
Employee, Polish Railways 45-53; Deputy Dir. Dept. of Trade and Tariffs, Ministry of Railways 53-56; Asst. Dir. of Rail Transport, Cen. Transport Board 56-58, Dir. of Rail Transport 58-65; Under-Sec. of State, Ministry of Transport 65; Minister of Transport Sept. 69-; mem. Polish United Workers' Party, Deputy mem. Cen. Cttee. 71-.
Ministerstwo Komunikacji, ul. Chałubińskiego 4/6, 00-613 Warsaw, Poland.

Zakaria, Haji Mohamed Ali; Malaysian diplomatist; b. 8 Oct. 1929, Kuala Lumpur; *m.* Razimah Zakaria 1957; one *d.*; ed. Univ. of Malaya, Singapore, and London School of Econs.
Served in various capacities in Malaysian Civil Service; entered foreign service 56; Second Sec., later Information Officer, London 57-59; First Sec., later Counsellor, Perm. Mission of Malaya at UN 59-65; Deputy Sec. (Gen. Affairs), Ministry of Foreign Affairs 65-67; Deputy High Commr. to U.K. 67-70; High Commr. to Canada 70-75 and concurrently Perm. Rep. to UN 70-75.
c/o Ministry of Foreign Affairs, Kuala Lumpur, Malaysia.

Zakhava, Boris Yevgeniyevich; Soviet actor and producer; b. 1896; ed. Moscow Commercial Inst.
Joined Vakhtangov's Drama Studio 14; taught drama since 17, Dir. Vakhtangov School 25-39, directed at Shchukin Theatre School 39-; with others founded Vakhtangov State Theatre in which he has acted and produced using the Stanislavsky and Vakhtangov approach 26-; People's Artist of R.S.F.S.R. and of the U.S.S.R. 67; State Prize 52, Red Banner of Labour and other awards; Hon. D.Sc. (Art) 64.
Productions include *The Badgers* (Leonov), *The Seagull* (Chekhov), *First Joys* (Fedin), *Hamlet* (Shakespeare), *The Aristocrats* (N. Pogodin), *The Great Sovereign* (Solovyev), *The Young Guard* (Fadeyev), *Yegor Bulychev and Others* (produced with participation of the author Maxim Gorky), *The Government Inspector* (Gogol); played Field-Marshal Kutuzov in *War and Peace* (Leo Tolstoy).
Publs. *Vakhtangov and His Studio* 27, *Principles of Directing* 34, *The Creative Work of E. B. Vakhtangov* 39, *Mastership of Actor and Producer* 64.
Shchukin Theatre School of Vakhtangov Theatre, Moscow, U.S.S.R.

Zakythinos, Denis; Greek historian and university professor; b. 1905, Lixouri (Ionian Islands); one *s*., ed. Gymnasium of Lixouri, Univs. of Athens and Paris.
Secretary, Institut Néo-hellénique, Univ. of Paris 31-32; Dir. Fondation Hellénique, Cité Universitaire de Paris 32-35; Dir. State Gen. Archives 37-46; Prof. of Byzantine History, Univ. of Athens 39-70, Prof. Emer. 70-; Minister of Press and Information April-Aug. 45; Prof. of History of Civilisations, High School of Political Sciences, Athens 51-57, Prof. of Modern Greek History 57-65; Dir. of review *L'Hellénisme Contemporain* 55-; Dir. Centre of Byzantine Researches 60-; Gen. Sec. Asscn. Internationale des Etudes Byzantines 61-71, Pres. 71-; Rector High School of Political Sciences 62-63; Pres. Asscn. Int. d'Etudes du Sud-Est Européen 63-65; Minister attached to Prime Minister's Office Dec. 63-Feb. 64; Pres. Hellenic Cttee. for UNESCO 74; Deputy of State of Greek Parl. Nov. 74-; mem. Acad. of Athens 66-, Vice-Pres. 73, Pres. 74-, corresp. mem. Académie des Inscriptions et Belles Lettres, France 68; foreign mem. Accademia di Scienze, Lettere e Arti, Palermo 67-, Serbian Acad. of Sciences and Arts, Belgrade 71-; Corresp. mem. Real Academia de la Historia, Madrid 73. Leisure interests: literature, photography.
Publs. include: *Le Despotat grec de Morée*, Vol. I 32, Vol. II 53, *Le chrysobulle d'Alexis III, empereur de Trébizonde, en faveur des Vénitiens* 32, *La Grèce et les Balkans* 47, *Crise monétaire et Crise économique à Byzance du XIIIe au XVe siècle* 48 (all in French), *The Slavs in Greece: Contributions in the History of Medieval Hellenism* (in Greek) 45, *Byzantium: State and Society, Historical Survey* (in Greek) 51, *The Capture of Constantinople and the Turkish Domination* (Greek and French) 54, *Turkish Domination: an Introduction to Modern History of Hellenism* (in Greek) 57, *Byzantine Texts* (in Greek) 57, *The Political History of Modern Greece* (in Greek) 62, *Byzantine Greece 392-1204* (in Greek) 65, *The Byzantine Empire 324-1071* (in Greek) 69, *Byzantine History 324-1071* (in Greek) 72, *Byzance: Etat-Société, Economie* 73; Editor *Symmeikta* (Vols. I and II) 66, 70.
31 G. Sissini Str., Athens 612, Greece.
Telephone: 718 787.

Zaldívar Larraín, Andrés; Chilean politician; b. 18 March 1936, Santiago de Chile; *s*. of Alberto Zaldívar Errázuriz and Josefina Larraín Tejada; *m*. Inés Hurtado Ruiz-Tagle 1959; four *d*.; ed. Instituto Alonso de Ercilla de los Hermanos Maristas and Univ. de Chile.
Sec. to Ministers of Supreme Court 56-59; Lawyer-Sec. to Municipality of Colina 59-63; also practised in company law and taxation; Under-Sec. of Finance 64-Jan. 68; Minister of Economy, Devt. and Reconstruction Jan.-May 68, also Minister of Finance March 68-March 71; Gov. of Inter-American Devt. Bank for Chile 69-; Pres. Sociedad Celulosa Aranco 71-; Senator for Alorcama and Coquimbo Provs. 73-; decorated by King Olaf, Norway 67; numerous missions to other American countries.
Huérfanos 1022, Oficina 1107, Santiago, Chile.
Telephone: 63593.

Zalokostas, Christos; Greek writer, politician and industrialist; b. 1896; ed. Munich Polytechnic.
Member of Parliament 46-; Parliamentary Representative of Greece, Council of Europe 53-56; represented Greece at Olympic Games (fencing), Berlin 36; World Pistol Champion 39; Popular Party.
Publs. include *The Chronicle of Slavery* 45, *King Alexander* 46, *Poverty in the Sun* 52, *Marina* 57.
Amerikis 21, Athens, Greece.

Zalzala, Abdul Hassan, M.SC., PH.D.; Iraqi banker and diplomatist; b. 1926; ed. Coll. of Law, Univ. of Baghdad and Indiana Univ., U.S.A.

Former Deputy Gov. Cen. Bank of Iraq; Amb. to Iran; Minister of Industry June 64, of Planning Nov. 64; Acting Minister of Finance 65; Amb. to Austria 65-66, to Egypt 66; Gov. Cen. Bank of Iraq Jan. 69-73; mem. Cttee. of Twenty, IMF; Amb. to Canada 74-.
Embassy of Iraq, 377 Stewart Street, Ottawa, K1N 8J6, Canada.

Zamecnik, Paul Charles, A.B., M.D.; American physician; b. 22 Nov. 1912, Cleveland, Ohio; *s*. of John Zamecnik and Mary McCarthy; *m*. Mary Connor 1936; one *s*. two *d*.; ed. Dartmouth Coll. and Harvard Medical School.
Resident, Huntington Memorial Hospital, Boston, Mass. 36-37; Intern, Univ. Hospitals, Cleveland, Ohio 38-39; Moseley Travelling Fellow of Harvard Univ. at Carlsberg Laboratories, Copenhagen 39-40; Fellow Rockefeller Inst., New York 41-42; Instructor to Prof. of Medicine, and Physician, Harvard Univ. at Mass. Gen. Hospital 42-, Exec. Sec. of Cttee. on Research 48-50, Chair. Cttee. on Research 54-56; Chair. Exec. Cttee. of Depts. of Medicine, Harvard Medical School 56-61, 64-68; Collis P. Huntington Prof. of Oncologic Medicine, Harvard Medical School 56-; Dir. John Collins Warren Laboratories of Harvard Univ. at Mass. Gen. Hospital 56-; Pres. American Asscn. for Cancer Research 64-65; Jubilee Lecturer, Biochemical Soc., London 62; mem. Nat. Acad. of Sciences; Hon. D.Sc. (Univ. of Utrecht) 66, (Columbia Univ.) 71; John Collins Warren Triennial Prize 46, 50, James Ewing Award 63, Borden Award in Medical Sciences 65, Passano Award 70.
Leisure interests: skiing, tennis, pre-Columbian and ancient art.
Publs. *Historical and current aspects of the problem of protein synthesis (Harvey Lectures Series 54)* 60, *Unsettled questions in the field of protein synthesis (Biochemical Journal 85)* 62, *The Mechanics of protein synthesis and its possible alterations in the presence of oncogenic RNA viruses (Cancer Research 26)* 66.
Huntington Laboratories, Massachusetts General Hospital, Boston, Mass. 02114, U.S.A.
Telephone: 617-726-3671.

Zamyatin, Leonid Mitrofanovich; Soviet diplomatist and journalist; b. 9 March 1922 Nizhni Devitsk, Voronezh Region; ed. Moscow Aviation Inst. and Higher Diplomatic School.
Member C.P. of Soviet Union 44-; at Ministry of Foreign Affairs 46-50; First Sec., Secr. of Minister of Foreign Affairs 50-52; Asst. Head, Third European Dept., Ministry of Foreign Affairs 52-53; First Sec., Counsellor on Political Questions of U.S.S.R. Mission to UN 53-57; Soviet Deputy Rep. on Preparatory Cttee., and later on Board of Govs., Int. Atomic Energy Agency (IAEA) 57-59, Soviet Rep. on IAEA 59-60; Deputy Head, American Countries Dept., Ministry of Foreign Affairs 60-62, Head of Press Dept. 62-70, mem. of Collegium of Ministry 62-70; Dir.-Gen. TASS News Agency 70-, Govt. Minister 72-; Deputy to U.S.S.R. Supreme Soviet 70-; mem. Comm. for Foreign Relations, Soviet of Nationalities 74-; Orders and medals of U.S.S.R.
TASS, Tverskoy bulvar 10, Moscow, U.S.S.R.

Żandarowski, Zdzisław, M.PH.; Polish politician; b. 23 Aug. 1929, Warsaw; ed. Univs. of Łódź and Warsaw. Member of Fighting Youth Union (ZMW) -48, of Polish Workers' Party (PPR) 48, now of Polish United Workers' Party (PZPR); First Sec. of Univ. Cttee., PZPR 54-56, Deputy Head and later Head of Propaganda Dept. of Warsaw Cttee. 56-60, Sec. of Warsaw Cttee. 60-69, mem. Cen. Cttee. 68-, Deputy Head of Cen. Cttee. Org. Dept. and Editor-in-Chief *Życie Partii* 69-70, Head of Org. Dept. 70-, mem. Secr. of Cen. Cttee. 72-75, Sec. of Cen. Cttee. Dec. 75-; Order of

Banner of Labour 1st and 2nd Class, Knight's Cross, Order of Polonia Restituta.
Polska Zjednoczona Partia Robotnicza, ul. Nowy Świat 6, 00-497 Warsaw, Poland.

Zanuck, Darryl Francis; American film producer; b. 5 Sept. 1902.
Formerly with Warner Bros. Pictures Inc., writer, producer and supervisor; Pres. in charge of production Darryl F. Zanuck Productions Inc.; Pres. 20th Century Fox 62-71, Chair. Emer. 71-; Medal of French Order of Arts and Letters 68.
Films include: *Wilson, How Green Was My Valley, This Above All, Grapes of Wrath, The Razor's Edge, Gentleman's Agreement, The Snake Pit, Pinky, All About Eve, David and Bathsheba, Viva Zapata!, The Snows of Kilimanjaro, The Man in the Grey Flannel Suit, Island in the Sun, The Sun also Rises, Roots of Heaven, Crack in the Mirror, The Big Gamble, Compulsion, Sanctuary, The Longest Day.*
c/o 20th Century-Fox Film Corporation, Beverly Hills, California, U.S.A.

Zanuso, Marco; Italian architect; b. 14 May 1916; ed. Politecnico de Milano.
Architectural practice 45-; mem. C.I.A.M. 56-, Istituto Naz. Urbanistica 56-; City Councillor, Milan 56-60; mem. Building Comm., Milan Corpn. 61-63, 67-69; mem. City Devt. Comm., Milan 69; Lecturer, Faculty of Architecture, Milan Polytechnic; Pres. Asscn. for Industrial Design 66-; numerous gold medals; Int. Plastic Exhbn. Prize, London 66; Gold Medal, Ministry of Industry and Commerce 66, etc.
Buildings include: H.Q. for American Co. 48; Olivetti buildings, Buenos Aires 54; Olivetti buildings, São Paulo 65; Brinnel buildings, Casella d'Asolo 66; Int. H.Q., S.G.S. Fairchild, Agrate 67; Olivetti buildings, Scarmagno (Ivrea) 68; Arflex factory, Brion Vega factory.
Studio: Via Laveno 6, Milan; Home: Piazza Castello 20, Milan, Italy.
Telephone: 4040312, 4040322 (Studio); 866127 (Home).

Zanussi, Krzysztof; Polish film director and script-writer; b. 17 June 1939, Warsaw; s. of Jerzy and Jadwiga Zanussi; unmarried; ed. Warsaw and Cracow Univs. and Łódź Higher Film School.
Vice-Chairman, Polish Film Asscn. 71-; has directed numerous short feature films and taken prizes for *Death of Provincial* 67 at the festivals of Venice, Mannheim and Valladolid; Prize of Ministry of Culture and Art 71; Prize for *Illumination*, Locarno 73; films include: *Structure of Crystals, Family Life, Illumination* 72, *The Catamount Killing* (U.S.A.) 73; TV films: *Face to Face* 67, *Credit* 68, *Mountains at Dark* 70, *Role* (Fed. Repub. of Germany) 71, *Behind the Wall* 71, (Grand Prix, San Remo Int. Film Festival 72), *Hipotese* (Fed. Repub. of Germany) 72, *Bilans Kwartalny* 74, *Nacht Dienst* (Fed. Repub. of Germany) 75.
Aleje Jerozolimskie 53/19, 00-697 Warsaw, Poland.
Telephone: 28-07-80.

Zao Wou Ki; Chinese painter; b. 1920; ed. Nat. School of Fine Arts, Hangchow.
Prof. of Design, Nat. School of Fine Arts, Hangchow 41-47; left China to live in Paris 48; exhibited in Salon de Mai, Paris 50- and in the capitals of Europe and America; Int. Prize for modern painting, Carnegie Inst., Pittsburgh 55, Chevalier Légion d'Honneur.
Works in many collections throughout Europe.
c/o Société des Artistes Indépendants, Grand Palais des Champs-Elysées, Cour la Reine, Paris 8e, France.

Zarb, Frank Gustav, M.B.A.; American government official; b. 17 Feb. 1935, New York; m. Patricia Koster 1957; one s. one d.; ed. Hofstra Univ.
Graduate trainee, Cities Service Oil Co. 57-62; General Partner, Goodbody & Co. 62-69; Exec. Vice-Pres.,

CBWL-Hayden Stone 69-71; Asst. Sec., U.S. Dept. of Labor 71-72; Exec. Vice-Pres. Hayden Stone 72-73; Assoc. Dir. Exec. Office of the Pres., Office of Man. and Budget 73-74; Administrator, Fed. Energy Admin. 74-; Distinguished Scholar Award, Hofstra Univ.
Federal Energy Administration, Washington, D.C. 20461; Home: 7704 Falstaff Road, McLean, Va. 22101, U.S.A.

Zariski, Oscar; American mathematician; b. 24 April 1899, Kobrin, Russia; s. of Bezalel and Chana Zariski; m. Yole Cagli 1924; one s. one d.; ed. Univ. of Kiev (Ukraine), and Univ. of Rome.
Fellow Int. Educ. Board 24-26; Johnston Scholar, Johns Hopkins Univ. 27-29, Assoc. 29-32, Assoc. Prof. 32-37, Prof. of Maths. 37-45; Research Prof. of Maths., Univ. of Ill. 46-47; Prof. of Maths. and Tutor in Dept. of Maths., Harvard Univ. 47-61, Dwight Parker Robinson Prof. 61-69; Dwight Parker Robinson Prof. Emer. 69-; former Editor *Transactions of the American Mathematical Society, American Journal of Mathematics, Illinois Journal of Mathematics;* fmr. Co-operating Ed. of *Annals of Mathematics;* Pres. American Mathematical Soc. 69-70; mem. Nat. Acad. of Sciences, American Acad. Arts and Sciences, American Philosophical Society, Accad. Nazionale dei Lincei; Corresp. mem. Academia Nacional de Ciencias Exactas, Físicas y Naturales de Lima, Acad. Brasileira de Ciencias; hon. mem. of Sociedade de Matematica de São Paulo, London Mathematical Society; Cole Prize in Algebra 44, Nat. Medal of Science, Washington 66; Hon. D.Sc., Coll. of Holy Cross 59, Brandeis Univ. 65, Purdue Univ. 73.
Leisure interests: sailing, bicycling, bridge.
Publs. *Algebraic Surfaces* 35, *Some Results in the Arithmetic Theory of Algebraic Varieties* 38, *The Reduction of the Singularities of an Algebraic Surface* 39, *Local Uniformisation on Algebraic Varieties* 40, *Foundations of a General Theory of Birational Correspondences* 43, *Reduction of the Singularities of Algebraic Three-dimensional Varieties* 44, *Theory and Application of Abstract Holomorphic Functions on an Algebraic Variety* 51, *Complete Linear Systems on Normal Varieties and a Generalisation of a Lemma of Enriques-Severi* 52, *The Problem of Minimal Models in the Theory of Algebraic Surfaces* 58. *Commutative Algebra* (2 vols.) (with P. Samuel) 58, 60, *Studies in Equisingularity*, 3 papers 65, 68, *General Theory of Saturation and of Saturated Local Rings*, 3 papers 71, 74.
Department of Mathematics, Harvard University, Cambridge, Mass. 02138; and 122 Sewall Avenue, Brookline, Mass. 02146, U.S.A.

Zarkhy, Alexander Grigoryevich; Soviet film producer; b. 18 Feb. 1908, Leningrad; ed. Leningrad Technicum of Dramatic Art.
Asst. Producer 28, Producer for Lenfilm 29-49, for Byelorusfilm 50-55, for Mosfilm 57-; mem. C.P.S.U. 48-; State Prize Winner 41, 46; Honoured Art Worker of Byelorussian S.S.R., People's Artist of R.S.F.S.R. 65, of the U.S.S.R. 69.
Films include: *The Wind into the Face* 29, *Hot Days* 33, *The Deputy of the Baltic* 37, *The Member of the Government* 39, *His Name is Suhi Bator* 43, *Malahov Kurgan* 44, *In the Name of Life* 46, *Nesterko* 53, *The Height* 57, *The People on the Bridge* 59, *Hallo Life* 62, *Anna Karenina* 68.
Mosfilm Studio, 1 Mosfilmovskaya ulitsa, Moscow, U.S.S.R.

Žarković, Vidoje; Yugoslav (Montenegrin) politician; b. 10 June 1927, Nedajno; s. of Milovan Žarković and Ljubica Žarković-Dakić; m. Ljiljana Mikovilović; two d.; ed. Higher Mil. Naval Acad., Djuro Djaković Higher School of Politics, Faculty of Political Sciences.
Took part in the liberation war from the beginning 41-45, holding responsible positions; staff posts in the

Army after the war; Sec. Cen. Cttee., League of Communists of Montenegro; Pres. Exec. Council of Montenegro, Assembly of Montenegro; now mem. League of Communists of Yugoslavia, also of Presidency of Socialist Fed. Repub. of Yugoslavia 74-; 1941 Partisan Memorial Medal and other high orders of war and peacetime.

Leisure interests: hunting and fishing.

Predsedništvo SFRJ, Belgrade; Home: Strumička 88c, Belgrade, Yugoslavia.

Telephone: 331-279 (Office); 415-330 (Home).

Zarodov, Konstantin Ivanovich; Soviet journalist; b. 1 Nov. 1920, Sloboda, Vologda Region; ed. Vologda Railway Engineering Coll., C.P.S.U. Higher Party School and C.P.S.U. Acad. of Social Sciences.

Member C.P.S.U. 40; Navy Service 39-46; Young Communist League Official 46-50; mem. staff *Komsomolskaya Pravda* 50-51, *For a Lasting Peace, for People's Democracy!* 54-56; at Central Cttee. of C.P.S.U. 56-61; Editor-in-Chief, *Sovietskaya Rossiya* 61-64; First Deputy Editor-in-Chief, *Pravda* 65-68; Chief Editor, *Problems of Peace and Socialism* 68-; Alt. mem. C.P.S.U. Central Cttee. 66-; Orders of Lenin, Red Banner of Labour, Red Star.

c/o Problems of Peace and Socialism, Prague, Czechoslovakia.

Zaru, Nadim Salim; Jordanian politician; b. 17 Nov. 1931, Ramallah; *m.* Samia Taktak; ed. Ramallah High School, Univ. of Houston, Texas.

Pharmacy owner for 12 years; mem. Ramallah municipal council 60-64; Owner and Dir. Zaru Travel Agency 64-68; Mayor of Ramallah 64-69; mem. Jerusalem Electric Co. 64-69; Dir. Jerusalem Water Undertaking (Ramallah District) 64-69; resisted Israeli occupation of West Bank, imprisoned then deported to Amman, Jordan 69; Rep. of W. Bank to World Conf. of Christians for Palestine 70; Minister of Transport 72-75; Chair. Aqaba Railway Corpn., Port Authority, Maritime Establishment and Free Zone Dept., and Hedjaz Railway Admin. 72-; Hon. mem. Ramallah Fed. U.S.A.; numerous decorations from Orthodox Patriarch of Jerusalem 64-66.

Leisure interests: hunting, horse riding, reading.

Ministry of Transport, Amman, Jordan.

Zavadsky, Yuri Alexandrovich; Soviet theatrical producer; b. 12 July 1894, Moscow; ed. Moscow University. At Vakhtangov Theatre 15, Moscow Art Theatre 24-31, at Gorky Theatre, Rostov 36-40; Artistic Dir. of the Red Army Theatre 32-35; Chief Stage Dir. Mossoviet Theatre 40-; Prof. Moscow State Theatrical Inst. 47; **Pres.** theatrical section of Union of Soviet Socs. for **friendship** and cultural relations with foreign countries; mem. C.P.S.U. 44-; People's Artist of the U.S.S.R. 48, State Prize 46, 51, awarded Order of Lenin (three), Order of the Red Banner of Labour, Lenin Prize 65.

Main productions: *Death of a Squadron, On the Bank of the Neva, Enemies, The Philistines, Encounter in Darkness, The Moscow Character, The Law of Honour, The Storm, The Russian Question, Boundless Vistas, Lyubov Yarovaya, Fancy Ball, Othello,* etc.

Mossoviet Drama Theatre, Bolshaya Sadovaya ulitsa 16, Moscow, U.S.S.R.

Zavala, Silvio, D. en D.; Mexican historian; b. 1909, Mérida, Yucatán; *s.* of Arturo Zavala and Mercedes Vallado; *m.* Huguette Joris 1951; one *s.* three *d.*; ed. Univ. of the South-East, Nat. Univ. of Mexico and Central Univ. of Madrid.

Centre of Historical Studies, Madrid 33-36; Sec. Nat. Museum of Mexico 37-38; founder and dir. *Revista de Historia de América* (review of Pan-American Inst. of Geography and History) 38-65; Pres. Historical Comm. of Pan-American Inst. of Geography and History 46-65; mem. Col. de México 40; life mem. El Colegio

Nacional 47; Visiting Prof. Univ. of Puerto Rico 45, Univ. of Havana 46; Prof. of History of Social Insts. of America, Nat. Univ. of Mexico; Visiting Prof. Mexico City Coll.; Prof. Smith Coll., Mexico; Dir. Nat. Museum of History, Chapultepec 46-54; Chief, Section of Education, Science and Culture of UN 47; Visiting Lecturer Harvard 53, Visiting Prof. Washington (Seattle) and Ghent 56; Perm. Del. to UNESCO 56-62, mem. Exec. Council 60-66, Vice-Pres. 62-64; Vice-Pres. Int. Council of Human Sciences and Philosophy 59-65, Pres. 65-71; Amb. to France 66-75; Pres. Colegio de México 63-66; mem. Exec. Council, Int. Cttee. for Historical Sciences; mem. Nat. Acad. of History and Geography, Mexican Acad. of History; corresp. mem. numerous Acads. of History, etc.; hon. mem. Historical Asscn. England 56, Royal Historical Soc., London 57, American Historical Asscn., Washington, D.C. 59; Prof. h.c. Colegio de San Nicolás, Morelia, Inst. of Latin American Studies, Univ. of Texas; Hon. D.Litt., Columbia Univ. 54, Ghent Univ. 57, Toulouse Univ. 65, Montpellier Univ. 67; Nat. Literary Prize, History Div., Mexico 69, History Prize, Académie du Monde Latin, Paris 74.

Publs. Many works on the Spanish colonization of America, Latin American history, New World history.

c/o Secretaría de Relaciones Exteriores, México, D.F., Mexico.

Zavala Baquerizo, Jorge Enrique; Ecuadorean lawyer and politician; b. 13 May 1922, Guayaquil; *s.* of Oswaldo Zavala Arbaiza and Ana C. Baquerizo Germán de Zavala; *m.* Carolina Egas Núñez de Zavala; four *s.*; ed. Univ. of Guayaquil.

Public Prosecutor, 2nd Criminal Tribunal of Guayas 47; Prof. of Law, Guayaquil Univ.; Provincial Counsellor Guayas 56-58; Vice-Deputy of Guayas 58-60; Pres. Guayaquil Coll. of Lawyers (twice); Constitutional Vice-Pres. of Republic of Ecuador 68-72; Pres. Acad. de Abogados de Guayaquil 73-74, 1st National Congress of Lawyers 60, National Comm. of Human Rights; Vice-Pres. various legal confs.; mem. Int. Lawyers' Comm., Int. Lawyers' Asscn., American Bar Asscn., American Judicature Soc., Int. Asscn. of Penal Law, Exec. Cttee. of World Habeas Corpus; Premio Código Civil 40, Premio Código Penal 44; Contenta Prize for university work, Premio al Mérito Científico of Municipality of Guayaquil 66.

Publ *El Proceso Penal Ecuatoriano.*

Aguirre No. 324 y Chile, Guayaquil, Ecuador.

Telephone: 512517, 516925, 512433 (Guayaquil); 523657 (Quito).

Zavala Urriolagoitia, Julio de; Bolivian diplomatist; b. 21 June 1923, Sucre; *m.*; five *c.*; ed. univs. in Chile and U.S.A.

Joined Ministry of Foreign Affairs 47; Second Sec., Washington, D.C. 49; First Sec. Perm. Mission to UN 50; Dir. Econ. Dept., Ministry of Foreign Affairs 52; Deputy for Chuquisaca Dept. 64; Sec.-Gen. Ministry of Foreign Affairs and Religion 71; Alt. Perm. Rep. to UN 71, Perm. Rep. Aug. 73-.

Permanent Mission of Bolivia to United Nations, 211 East 43rd Street, 11th Floor, New York, N.Y. 10017, U.S.A.

Zavoisky, Yevgeny Konstantinovich; Soviet physicist; b. 28 Sept. 1907, Mogiler-Podolsky, Ukraine; ed. Kazan State Univ.

Postgraduate Asst. Prof., Prof. Kazan State Univ. 30-47; Section Chief U.S.S.R. Acad. of Sciences Kurchatov Inst. of Atomic Energy 47-; Corresp. mem. U.S.S.R. Acad. of Sciences 53-64, mem. 64-; discovered and studied the paramagnetic resonance; investigated problems of use of electron-optical converter; Lenin Prize 57, State Prize 59, Hero of Socialist Labour 69, Order of Lenin (twice), etc.

U.S.S.R. Academy of Sciences, 14 Leninsky Prospekt, Moscow, U.S.S.R.

Zayyat, Mohamed Hassan El-, M.A., D.PHIL.; Egyptian diplomatist and politician; b. 14 Feb. 1915, Damietta; s. of Hassan El-Zayyat and Badia Abboud; m. Amina Taha Hussein 1948; one s. two d.; ed. Cairo and Oxford Univs.

Lecturer and Asst. Professor Alexandria Univ. 42-50; Cultural Attaché, Egyptian Embassy, Washington, D.C. 50-54, First Sec. and Counsellor 54; Chargé d'Affaires, Egyptian Embassy, Teheran 55-57, Minister Del. of Egypt on UN Advisory Council for Somaliland 57-60; Head of Dept. of Arab Affairs and Perm. Del. of U.A.R. to Arab League 60-62; Alt. Perm. Rep. of U.A.R. to UN 62-64; Ambassador to India, concurrently accred. to Nepal 64-65; Under-Sec. of State for Foreign Affairs 65-67; Deputy Minister, Chair. U.A.R. State Information Services and Govt. Spokesman 67-69; Perm. Rep. of U.A.R. to UN 69-71; mem. Nat. Congress 69-; Minister of State for Information Jan.-Sept. 72; Minister of Foreign Affairs 72-73; Adviser to the Pres. of the Repub. 73-Feb. 75; Rep. of Egypt to UN Trusteeship Council, Security Council and Eighteen Nations Disarmament Cttee. in Geneva; decorations from Egypt, Iran, Somalia, Senegal, Poland, Mauritania, Italy, Brazil, Thailand, Chad, Belgium.
Leisure interests: farming, gardening.
1 Midan Nasr, Maadi, Egypt.
Telephone: 34130.

Zbinden, Hans, DR. PHIL.; Swiss writer, lecturer and university professor; b. 26 Aug. 1893, Berne; s. of the late Marcel Zbinden and Marie Daguet; m. 1st Marina Segantini 1936 (died 1954), 2nd Ida Bieler 1962; one d.; ed. Univs. of Berne and Zürich; studied in East and West Europe and U.S.A.

Lecture tours in U.S.A. and Europe, Guest Prof., Madison; Corresp. mem. Deutsche Akad. für Sprache und Dichtung and of Deutsche Gesellschaft für Soziologie; Prof. in Cultural Sociology, Univ. of Berne; Sec. Goethe-Stiftung für Kunst und Wissenschaft, Zürich; Pres. Swiss Authors Asscn. 53-67, Hon. Pres. 67-; Hon. Pres. Int. Union der Bürgermeister für Deutsch-Französisch Verständigung 70; Bundesverdienstkreuz (Bundesrepublik Deutschland).
Leisure interests: art, walking, travelling.
Publs. *Die politischen Ideen des Vincenzo Gioberti* 19, *Zur geistigen Lage Amerikas* 31, *Technik und Geisteskultur* 33, *Der Kampf um den Frieden* 34, *Geist und Wirtschaft* 35, *Die Moralkrise des Abendlandes* 41, *Geistige Aufgaben unseres Landes* 42, *Der Schriftsteller in unserer Zeit* 43, *Albert Anker, Mensch und Werk* 44, *Der Flüchtling und die Humanität* 45, *Um Deutschlands Zukunft* 46, *Von der inneren Freiheit* 48, *Gefahren der modernen Demokratie* 48, *Welt im Zwielicht* (essays) 51, *Giovanni Segantini* 51, *Jugend und Staat* 52, *Das Spiel um den Spoel* 52, *Vermassung und Demokratie* 53, *Schulnot und Bildungskrise* 53, *Vom Buchklima unserer Zeit* 53, *Von der Axt zum Atomwerk* (essays) 54, *Schulnoete der Gegenwart* 55, *Ueber Not und Glück des Alters* 58, *Der bedrohte Mensch* 59, *Das freie Unternehmertum und die Wandlungen der Gesellschafts-Struktur* 60, *Soziale Grundprobleme der Erholung Fünftagewoche, Ferien und schöpferische Musse* 61, *Jugend und Alter in der Gesellschaft von heute* 61, *Albert Anker in neuer Sicht* 61, "*Ich bin ein Schweizerknabe*" 62, *Ohnmacht der Eliten?* 63, *Humanismus der Wirtschaft* 63, *Im Strom der Zeit* 64, *Schweizer Literatur in europäischer Sicht* 64, *Kulturprobleme der Wirtschaft* 66, *Probleme des technischen Zeitalters in sozialer und kultureller Sicht* 67, *Freiheit und Sicherheit* 69, *Polen Einst und Jetzt, Reisebilder der Jahre 1932/3* 39, 65, 69, *Europa Wohin? Voraussetzungen einer lebensfähigen europäischen Völkergemeinschaft* 69, *Der Mensch im Spannungsfeld der modernen Technik* 70, *Die geistige Situation der Jugend Heute* 71; Editor *Iris-Bücher der Kunst* 35-59; trans. Benjamin Constant *Über die Gewalt* 42, 48, 63, A. de Tocqueville *In der nordamerikanischen Wildnis* 54 and *Über die Demokratie in Amerika* Vol. I 59, Vol. II 62. Alleeweg 13, Berne, CH 3000, Switzerland.
Telephone: 031-44-3074.

Zea Aguilar, Leopoldo, PH.D.; Mexican university professor and writer; b. 30 June 1912, Mexico; s. of Leopoldo Zea and Luz Aguilar; m. Elena Prado Vertiz 1943; two s. four d.

Editor review *Tierra Nueva* 40; Prof. Escuela Nacional Preparatoria 42-47; Prof. Escuela Normal de Maestros 44-45; Prof., Faculty of Philosophy and Letters, Nat. Univ. of Mexico 44; mem. El Colegio de México 40; Pres., Cttee. for the History of Ideas, Panamerican Inst. of Geography and History; Chief of Dept. of Univ. Studies, Secretariat of Public Education 53-54; research work, Univ. of Mexico 54-; mem. Société Européenne de Culture 53-; Dir.-Gen. of Cultural Relations Foreign Office; Vice-Pres. Historical Comm. of Pan American Inst. of Geography and History 61-; Dir. of Faculty of Philosophy and Letters, Nat. Univ. of Mexico 66-70, Prof. Emer. 71; Dir.-Gen. of Cultural Broadcasting 70-; decorations from Italy, France, Peru and Yugoslavia.
Leisure interests: music, art.
Publs. *El Positivismo en México* 43, *Apogeo y Decadencia del Positivismo en México* 44, *Ensayos sobre Filosofía en la Historia* 48, *Dos Etapas del Pensamiento en Hispanoamérica* 49, *La Filosofía como Compromiso* 52, *América como Conciencia* 52, *Conciencia y posibilidad del Mexicano* 52, *El Occidente y la Conciencia de México* 53, *La Conciencia del Hombre en la Filosofía* 52, *América en la conciencia de Europa* 55, *La Filosofía en México* 55, *Esquema para una Historia de las ideas en América* 56, *Del Liberalismo a la Revolución en la Educación Mexicana* 56, *América en la Historia* 57, *La Cultura y el Hombre de nuestros Días* 59, *Latinoamérica y el Mundo* 60, *Ensayos sobre México y Latinoamérica* 60, *Democracias y Dictaduras en Latinoamérica* 60, *Amerique Latina e la Culture Occidentalie* 61, *El Pensamiento en Latinoamérica* 63, *The Latin American Mind* 63, *L'Amérique dans l'Histoire* 63, *El Pensamiento Latinoamericano* 65, *Latinamérica en la Formación de nuestro tiempo* 65, *Antología de la Filosofía Americana Contemporánea* 68, *Latin America and the World* 69, *Dependencia y Liberación en la Cultura Latinoamericana* 74, *Cultura y Filosofía en Latino-América* 76, *Dialéctica de la Conciencia Americana* 76.
Ciudad Universitaria, Torre de Humanidades, México, D.F., and Vizcainoco 14, Chimalistac, Villa Obregón, México 20, D.F., Mexico.
Telephone: 548-14-84.

Zea Hernández, Germán; Colombian lawyer and politician; b. 15 April 1905; ed. Colegio de Araújo and Univ. Libre, Bogotá.

Member Congress and Senate of Colombia at various times; Mayor of Bogotá 38-41; Comptroller-Gen. of Colombia 41; Gov. of Cundinamarca 43-44; Minister of Justice 60-62; Pres. Dirección Nacional Liberal 60; Colombian Rep. at Int. Confs. and Chief of Perm. Colombian Del. to UN 62-65; Minister of Foreign Affairs 66-68; Prof. of Constitutional and Admin. Law, Univ. Libre, Bogotá, Pres. of Univ.; mem. Academia Colombiana de Jurisprudencia; decorations from Colombia, Venezuela, Brazil, Chile, Mexico, Panama and Bolivia.
c/o Ministerio de Relaciones Exteriores, Bogotá; and c/o Universidad Libre de Colombia, Carrera 6A, No. 8-06, Bogotá, Colombia.

Zeayen, Dr. Yusif; Syrian physician and politician; b. 1931; ed. Univ. of Damascus.
Minister of Agrarian Reform 63; mem. Presidential Council 64-65; Prime Minister Sept.-Dec. 65, Feb. 66-Oct. 68; Baath Party.
c/o Baath Party, Damascus, Syrian Arab Republic.

Zech, Walther; German publisher; b. 12 Nov. 1918;
ed. Düsseldorf Realgymnasium (Hindenburgschule).
Pupil in private bank of B. Simons & Co. (now Poensgen,
Marx & Co.) Düsseldorf 37-39; war service 40-45,
prisoner of war 45-46; Dept. Man. Essen branch, "Die
Welt" Verlags G.m.b.H. 47-49; Editor Düsseldorfer
Zeitschriftenverlag 50-52; Editor and Man. Dir. VDI-
Verlag G.m.b.H., Düsseldorf 52-62; now Editor and
Man. Dir. Mainzer Verlagsanstalt und Druckerei,
Wiesbadener Tagblatt-Verlag, G.m.b.H., Verlags-und
Verwaltungsgesellschaft m.b.H. (Mainz), Rhein-Main-
Verlagagesellschaft m.b.H., Mainz and Wiesbaden
Kurier Verlag und Druckerei G.m.b.H., Wiesbaden;
mem. Exec. of Soc. of Fed. German Newspaper Pub-
lishers, Bad Godesberg, mem. Board Technical Comm.
of German Press Agencies, Hamburg, Confed. of
German Industries and Chamber of Commerce, Mainz;
mem. Presidential Council of Zentral-ausschuss der
Werbewirtschaft (ZAW); Hon. Pres. Fédération
Internationale de la Presse Périodique (FIPP), London;
mem. of Board and Treas. Int. Gutenberg-Gesellschaft,
Mainz; Adviser, Dresdner Bank A.G., Rhineland-
Pfalz, Chair. Zigarettenfabrik Rhenania G.m.b.H.,
Andernach; mem. Stifterverbund für die Deutsche
Wissenschaft, Landeskuratorium Rheinland-Pfalz;
Kuratorium Deutsche Sporthilfe.
Grosse Bleiche 44-50, D-6500 Mainz, Federal Republic
of Germany.
Telephone: 06131-1441.

Zeckendorf, William; American real estate adminis-
trator; b. 30 June 1905; ed. New York Univ.
Entered real estate business 25; Partner L. Gans 30-;
Vice-Pres. Webb & Knapp, Inc. 37, Pres. 47-62, Chair.
62-65; Webb & Knapp (Canada) Ltd., Webb & Knapp
Nat. Corpn. Washington, D.C., Chair. of Board and Dir.
Gulf States Land & Industries Inc., Colmar Surinam
Oil Co.; Dir. American Hydrofoil Lines Inc., Webb and
Knapp (Canada) Ltd.; Real Estate Adviser to the
Rockefeller family; Trustee and Dir. of many cultural
and medical bodies; Hon. LL.D. (Long Island, Ameri-
can Univs.), Hon. D.Hum.Litt. (Wilberforce Univ.);
seven foreign Awards.
383 Madison Avenue, New York, N.Y. 10017; Home:
30 Beekman Place, New York City, U.S.A.

Zeckendorf, William, Jr.; American real estate execu-
tive; b. 31 Oct. 1929, N.Y.C.; s. of William (q.v.) and
Irma (Levy) Zeckendorf; m. 1st Guri Lie 1956 (divorced
1963), two s.; m. 2nd Nancy King 1963; ed. Lawrence-
ville School and Univ. of Arizona.
Webb and Knapp Inc. 50-, Vice-Pres. 55-58, Pres.
62-65; Chair. Board Gen. Property Corpn.; Dir. Gen.
Leisure Inc.; Chair. Board Soc. Hill Towers Inc.,
Phila., Domaine La Belle Place, Montreal; Pres.
Mayfair House, N.Y.C.; Chair. Real Estate Comm.;
mem. Exec. Board N.Y. Council, Boy Scouts of
America; mem. Board of Trustees, Long Island Univ.,
Chair. Board Building and Grounds Cttee.; U.S. Army
52-54; Army Comm. Medal; Commdr. Chevaliers du
Tastevin.
Home: Croton Lake Road, Mount Kisco, N.Y.;
Office: 383 Madison Avenue, New York City 10017,
U.S.A.

Zeffirelli, Franco; Italian theatrical producer and
designer; b. 12 Feb. 1923; ed. Liceo Artistico, Florence,
and School of Agriculture, Florence.
Designer Univ. Productions Florence; actor Morelli
Stoppa Company; collaborated with Salvador Dali in
sets for *As You Like It* 48; sets for *A Streetcar Named
Desire, Troilus and Cressida* 49; set for *Three Sisters* 51;
producer and designer La Scala, Milan 52; productions
at Covent Garden, London 59-61, 64, 66, 73; The Old
Vic, London 60, Teatro dello Cometa, Rome 60, *Much
Ado About Nothing*, London and Paris 65, Verga's *La
Lupe*, Florence 65; Dir., sets and costumes for *Antony

and Cleopatra (New York) 66, *Florence, Days of Destruc-
tion* (TV) 66, Dir. *A Delicate Balance, The Promise* 67,
Venti Zecchini d'Oro 68, *Due piu due non fa piu
quattro* 69, *Cavalleria Rusticana* and *Pagliacci* (operas)
70, Beethoven's *Missa Solemnis* (TV) 70, *Saturday,
Sunday, Monday* 73; Dir. films *The Taming of the
Shrew* 66, *Romeo and Juliet* 67, *Brother Sun, Sister
Moon* 73; Prix des Nations 64.
Via due Macelli 31, Rome, Italy.

Zehrfuss, Bernard; French architect; b. 20 Oct. 1911,
Angers; s. of Henri Zehrfuss and Jeanne Hottois; m.
Simone Samama, 1950; one d.; ed. Collège Stanislas.
Head, Architecture and Urbanism Services, Tunisia
43-48; mem. Conseil Nat. de la Construction 50-53;
Consulting Architect, Ministry of Construction, Chief
Architect of Public Buildings and Nat. Palaces 53-65;
Gen. Inspector of Public Buildings and Nat. Palaces
65-68.
Projects: buildings in Tunisia, Algeria and in France
including UNESCO Building, Paris, Palais du Centre
National des Industries et des Techniques, Paris,
Renault factory at Flins, Hôtel du Mont d'Arbois,
Megève, Danish Embassy in Paris, Super-Montpar-
nasse in Paris, Science Faculty in Tunis, Société
Siemens in Paris, Société Jeumont-Schneider in
Puteaux, Société Sandoz à Rueil-Malmaison.
Office: 9 rue Arsène Houssaye, Paris 8e; Home: 23 quai
Anatole France, Paris 7e, France.
Telephone: 924-33-89.

Zeidler, D. R., C.B.E.; Australian business executive;
b. 18 March 1918, Melbourne; s. of O. W. Zeidler; m.
June Broadhurst 1943; four d.; ed. Scotch Coll., Univ.
Melbourne.
With CSIRO 41-51; joined ICI Australia Research
Dept. 52, Research Man. 53-59, Devt. Man. 59-62,
Controller Dyes and Fabrics Group 62-63, Dir. 63-71,
Man. Dir. 71-, Deputy Chair. 72-73; Chair. ICI Australia
Ltd. May 73-; Chair. Dulux Australia Ltd., Nobel
(Australasia) Pty. Ltd., Dir. ICI N.Z. Ltd., Commercial
Bank of Australia Ltd.; mem. of the Board of various
insts.; Fellow, Royal Australian Chemical Inst.; mem.
Inst. of Chemical Engs.
Leisure interests: skiing, tennis, sailing, fishing.
ICI Australia Ltd., ICI House, 1 Nicholson Street,
Melbourne; Home: 2a Grange Avenue, Canterbury,
Victoria 3126, Australia.

Zekia, Mehmed; Cypriot judge; b. 1903; m.; five c.;
ed. Univ. of Istanbul and Middle Temple, London.
Member, Legislative Council of Cyprus 30; mem.
Advisory Council of Cyprus 33; Chair. Cttee. on Turkish
Affairs 48; Advocate 31-40; District Judge 40; Pres.
District Court 47; Judge, Supreme Court 52; Judge,
High Court of Justice 60; Judge, European Court of
Human Rights 61-; Chief Justice of Cyprus 64-66.
The Supreme Court, Nicosia, Cyprus.

Zelbstein, Uri; French (b. Lithuanian) scientist; b. 10
Jan. 1912, Vilnius; s. of Philippe Zelbstein and Fryda
Milikowski; m. Paule Pougnet 1946; one s.; ed. Univ.
of Bordeaux and of Paris.
Successively Head of Laboratory and Dir. Radio-
Electronic Laboratories, fmr. Vitus Ests. 33-39; Head,
Electronic Dept., D.F. Factories 40-46; Head of
Electronic Research Dept., Nat. Soc. for Research and
Construction of Aircraft Engines (S.N.E.C.M.A.) 46-51;
Technical Dir. and Dir.-Gen. Sexta Soc. 51-58; Head of
Physics and Electronics Laboratories, later Asst. to
Pres. of Atomic Div., S.N.E.C.M.A. 60-69; Asst. to Dir.
Hispano-Suiza Div. of S.N.E.C.M.A. 69-73, Scientific
Counsellor 74-; Fellow, Royal Soc. of Arts; mem.
Accademia Teatina for Sciences (Italy), Accademia
Tiberina (Italy); laureate Acad. Int. de Lutèce, Soc.
des Écrivains des Provinces Françaises; Officer of the
Order of Merit for Research and Invention, Chevalier

de l'Ordre National du Mérite; mem. Unione della Legion d'Oro (Italy).
Leisure interests: history and philosophy of science.
1 Villa des Iris, 92220 Bagneux, France.
Telephone: 1-2536933.

Zeldovich, Yakov Borisovich; Soviet physicist; b. 8 March 1914, Minsk; ed. Leningrad Univ.
Associate Inst. of Chemical Physics, U.S.S.R. Acad. of Sciences 31-, Inst. of Applied Maths. 64-; Corresp. mem. U.S.S.R. Acad. of Sciences 46-58, mem. 58-; Prof. Moscow Univ. 66-; mem. Deutsche Akademie Leopoldina; Hon. D.Sc. (Sussex) 76, State Prize (four), Hero of Socialist Labour (three), Lenin Prize, Order of Lenin (three).
Publs. *The Theory of Combustion and Detonation by Gas* 44, *Theory of Shock Waves and an Introduction to Gas Dynamics* 46, *Development of the Anti-Particle Theory, Elementary Particle Charges and the Properties of Heavy Neutral Mesons* 56, *Experimental Investigation of Spherical Gas Detonation* 56, *Quasi-Stable States with a Strong Isotopic Spin in Light Nuclei, Spacing by Singular Potential in Turbulence Theory and in Pulse Representation* 60, *The Existence of New Light Nuclei Isotopes and Equations for the Neutron State* 60, *Higher Mathematics for Beginners* 60, 63, 65, *Physics of Shock Waves and High Temperature Hydrodynamics* 64, *Relativistic Astrophysics* 64, 65, *Survey of Modern Cosmology* 65, *Elements of Applied Mathematics* 66, *Theory of Shock Waves and High Temperature Hydrodynamic Phenomena* 67.
Institute of Applied Mathematics, Academy of Science of U.S.S.R., Moscow 125047, U.S.S.R.

Zelenka, Jan, PH.D., C.SC.; Czechoslovak journalist and broadcasting executive; b. 5 Dec. 1923, Ústí nad Orlicí; m.; one s. two d.; ed. Charles Univ., Prague.
Director-General, Czechoslovak Television Aug. 69-; Deputy to House of the People, Fed. Assembly 71-; Chair. Admin. Council Int. Radio and TV Org. 71-73; Gold Dove First Prize of Int. Leipzig TV Festival for TV Film *Great Concert* 71; Order of Labour 73.
Publs. Articles in journals and theoretical works on journalism.
Československá televize, Prague 1, nám. Gorkého 29, Czechoslovakia.

Zellerbach, Harold Lionel, B.S.; American business executive; b. 25 March 1894, San Francisco; s. of Isadore Zellerbach and Jennie Baruh Zellerbach; m. Doris Joseph 1917; two s. one d.; ed. Univ. of Calif. and Univ. of Pennsylvania.
Joined Zellerbach Paper Co. 17, Dir. 28-59; Chair. Board Dirs. 57-59, Dir. 59-, Hon. consultant Crown Zellerbach Corpn. 59-; official of cultural and educational orgs.
1 Bush Street, San Francisco, Calif. 94119, U.S.A.

Zellerbach, William Joseph; American paper industry executive; b. 15 Sept. 1920; ed. Univ. of Pennsylvania.
Crown Zellerbach Corpn. 46-, Vice-Pres. (Marketing Service) 59-, Dir. 59-; Pres. Zellerbach Paper Co. 61-; Dir. First Western Bank and Trust Co.; mem. Gen. Advisory Cttee. on Foreign Assistance Programs of the Agency for Int. Development; official of several welfare orgs.
Home: 3540 Jackson Street, San Francisco, Calif.; and 55 Hawthorne Street, San Francisco Calif., 94120, U.S.A.

Zeman, Karel; Czechoslovak film director; b. 3 Nov. 1910, Ostroměř.
Creator of numerous puppet and trick films; State Prize 57; Grand Prix for trick film *An Invention of Destruction,* Brussels Int. Exhbn. 58; Deputy Chair. Preparatory Cttee. Union of Czech Dramatic Artists 70-; Honoured Artist of Czechoslovakia 61, State Prize 57,

59; Czechoslovak Peace Prize 59, Nat. Artist 70, and other awards.
Films include: *Inspiration, King Lávra, The Treasure of Bird Island, A Trip to Prehistoric Times* (State Prize), *Baron Münchhausen, The Jester's Tale* (prizes at San Francisco Film Festival), *On the Comet* (Venice Biennial medal) 70, *Tales of a Thousand and One Nights* 74.
Film Studio/Kudlov, Gottwaldov, Czechoslovakia.
Telephone: Gottwaldov 2301; Gottwaldov 3175 (Home).

Žemla, Miroslav, LL.D.; Czechoslovak lawyer and diplomatist; b. 28 June 1925; s. of Jindřich and Karla Žemla; m. Libuše Žemla 1954; one d.; ed. Charles Univ., Prague.
Active in the resistance movt. 44-45; entered Czechoslovak foreign service 48, has served in Warsaw, Kabul, Peking, Hanoi; Alt. Head, Czechoslovak del., Control Comm. of Neutral States in Korea 54-55; Deputy Head, Dept. of Int. Orgs., Ministry of Foreign Affairs 58-64; Adviser and mem. Czechoslovak dels. to Disarmament Confs., Geneva 58-64; Amb. to Canada 64-68; Head, Group for Analysis and Programming, Ministry of Foreign Affairs 68-69; Gen. Sec. Ministry of Foreign Affairs 69-71; Amb. to U.K. 71-74; mem. del. to UN Gen. Assembly on several occasions and to other confs.; Amb., Deputy Head Legal Dept. Ministry of Foreign Affairs.
Leisure interests: music, photography, filming.
Publs. articles on international relations.
c/o Ministry of Foreign Affairs, Prague, Czechoslovakia.

Zermatten, Maurice; Swiss writer; b. 22 Oct. 1910, Saint Martin; s. of Antoine Zermatten; m. Hélène Kaiser 1941; two s. four d.; ed. Fribourg Univ.
Teacher of French literature; fmr. Pres. Société Suisse des écrivains; awarded Prix Fondation Schiller 38, Prix Bodmer 40, Prix d'honneur Schiller 46, Grand Prix catholique de littérature, Paris 59, Grand Prix Gottfried Keller 60, French Acad. Prize 61, Prix Monceau 68.
Leisure interests: flora, fauna, mycology.
Publs. *Le Cœur Inutile, Le Chemin difficile, Contes des Hauts-Pays du Rhône, Les Années valaisannes de Rilke, Les Chapelles Valaisannes, La Colère de Dieu, Le Sang des Morts, Christine, Le Pain Noir, L'Esprit des Tempêtes, Connaissance de Ramuz, Traversée d'un Paradis, Les Mains Pures, Isabelle de Chevron, La Montagne sans Etoiles, Le Lierre et le Figuier, La Fontaine d'Aréthuse, Un Lys de Savoie, Le Bouclier d'Or, Le Cancer des Solitudes, La Rose noire de Marignan, La Louve, Pays sans Chemin, Visages, Les Sèves d'Enfance, Une Soutane aux Orties, La Porte Blanche.*
Gravelone, Sion, Valais, Switzerland.
Telephone: 027-220-84.

Zetterling, Mai Elisabeth; Swedish film director, actress and writer; b. 24 May 1925; m. David Hughes; ed. Royal Theatre School of Drama, Stockholm.
Staff of National Theatre, Stockholm 43-45; first prize Venice Film Festival (*The War Game*) 63; under contract film director to Sandrews of Sweden.
London stage appearances include: *The Wild Duck* and *The Doll's House* (Ibsen), *Point of Departure* and *Restless Heart* (Anouilh), *The Seagull* (Chekhov), *Creditors* (Strindberg); acted in films: *Frenzy* 44, *Frieda* 47, *The Bad Lord Byron* 48, *Quartet* 48, *Knock on Wood* 54, *A Prize of Gold* 55, *Seven Waves Away* 56, *Only Two Can Play* 62, *The Main Attraction* 62, *The Bay of St. Michael* 63; film dir. BBC Television documentaries; Dir. and Co-writer films: *The War Game* 63, *Loving Couples* 65, *Night Games* 66, *Dr. Glas* 68, *The Girls* 68, *Flickorna* 68, Co-Dir. *Visions of Eight* 73.
Publs. *The Cat's Tale* (with David Hughes) 65, *Night Games* (also film) 66, *In the Shadow of the Sun* 74.
c/o CMA, 22 Grafton Street, London, W.1; Berry Grove, West Liss, Hampshire, England.

Zevi, Bruno; Italian architect; b. 22 Jan. 1918, Rome; s. of Guido Zevi and Ada Bondi; m. Tullia Calabi 1940; one s. one d.; ed. Graduate School of Design, Harvard Univ. and Faculty of Architecture, Univ. of Rome.
Left Italy for political reasons 39-44; Editor *Quaderni Italiani* (anti-Fascist magazine smuggled into Italy from U.S.A.) 41-43; Dir. technical magazines of U.S. Information Service in Italy 44-46; co-founder Asscn. for an Organic Architecture in Italy 46; co-Editor *Metron*, an architectural magazine 45-55; Prof. History of Modern Architecture, Univ. of Rome 48-52, Prof. History of Architecture, Univ. of Venice 48-63; **Prof. History of Architecture, Univ. of Rome 63-;** Gen. Sec. Italian Town Planning Inst. 52-68; Vice-Pres. Italian Inst. of Architecture; Editor *L'architettura—cronache e storia* 55-; architectural critic of the weekly *L'Espresso* 55-; Academician Venice Acad. of Art 53, Accad. di San Luca, Rome 60; Hon. mem. Royal Inst. of British Architects; Hon. mem. American Inst. of Architects.
Leisure interests: tennis, swimming.
Publs. *Towards an Organic Architecture* 45 (English edn. 49), *Saper Vedere l'Architettura* 48 (English edn. *Architecture as Space* 57), *Poetica dell'Architettura Neo-plastica* 53, *Architecture* (in *International Encyclopaedia of the Arts*) 58, *Biagio Rossetti, architetto ferrarese —il primo urbanista moderno europeo* 60, *Architectura in nuce* 60, *Michelangelo architetto* 64, *Erich Mendelsohn: opera completa* 70, *Cronache d'architettura* 70-75, *Saper vedere l'Urbanistica* 71, *Spazi dell' architettura moderna* 73, *Il linguaggio moderno dell'architettura* 73, *Architettura e Storiografia* 74, *Storia dell'architettura moderna* 75.
Via Nomentana 150, 00162-Rome, Italy.
Telephone: 8380481.

Zhavoronkov, Nikolai Mikhailovich; Soviet chemist; b. 7 Aug. 1907, Streletskie Vyselki, Ryazan Region; ed. Moscow Inst. of Chemical Technology.
Instructor Moscow Inst. of Chemical Technology 30-42, Prof. 42-; Dir. Karpov Physiochemical Inst. 44-48; Dir. Mendeleev Chemical Technological Inst. 48-62; Dir. Inst. of General and Inorganic Chemistry, U.S.S.R. Academy of Sciences 62-; Corresp. mem. U.S.S.R. Acad. of Sciences 53-62, mem. 62-; mem. Presidium Acad. of Sciences of U.S.S.R., Academician Sec. Dept. of Physical Chemistry and Technology of Inorganic Compounds 63-; mem. Communist Party 39-; Hero of Socialist Labour 69, State Prize 50, Order of Lenin (twice).
Publs. *Hydraulic Principles of the Scrubber Process and Heat Transfer in Scrubbers* 44, *Nitrogen in Nature and Engineering* 51, *Sources of Industrial Bonded Nitrogen* 51, *Mass Transfer in the Pellicular Absorption Process* 51, *Determining the Separation Factor of Boron Isotopes with Equilibrium Evaporation of BCl_3* 56, *Chemical Industry and Research in the Soviet Union* 56, *K. A. Timiryazev and the Nitrogen Problem* 56, *Separating Stable Boron Isotopes* 60, *Investigation of Pellicular Absorption Process with High Speed of Gas* 61, *High Temperature Gas-Liquid Chromatography* 62, *Investigation of Hydrogen Isotopic Exchange between Water and Thiolates* 62, *Principal Directions in Development of Separation Methods of Stable Isotopes* 63, *Phase Equilibria for Mixtures Acrilonitrile—Acetonitrile* 64.
Institute of General and Inorganic Chemistry of Academy of Sciences of U.S.S.R., Leninsky prospekt 31, Moscow, U.S.S.R.

Zheludev, Ivan Stepanovich; Soviet scientist; b. 7 March 1921, Novo-Adam, Velikie Luki Region; ed. Moscow State Univ.
Senior Lecturer, Moscow State Univ. 55-62, Prof. 65; Head of Laboratory of Electrical Properties of Crystals, Inst. of Crystallography, U.S.S.R. Acad. of Sciences, Moscow 61-66, 71-; Deputy Dir. (Dept. of Technical Operations), Int. Atomic Energy Agency, Vienna 66-71; Visiting Prof., Indian Inst. of Science, Bangalore 62-63.

U.S.S.R. Academy of Sciences, 14 Leninsky Prospekt, Moscow, U.S.S.R.

Zhigalin, Vladimir Fyodorovich; Soviet engineer and politician; b. 1907; ed. Leningrad Mechanical Inst.
Leningrad and Moscow factories 31-40; Chief of Dept. People's Commissariat of Heavy Machine-Building 40-45; Dep. People's Commissar, Dep., later First Dep. Minister, of Heavy Machine-Building 45-57; Dep., later First Dep. Chair., Moscow City Econ. Council 57-61, Chair. 61-63, First Dep. Chair. U.S.S.R. Council of National Economy 63-65; Minister of Heavy Power and Transport Engineering 65-; Alt. mem. Central Cttee. of C.P.S.U. 61-64, mem. Central Cttee. of C.P.S.U. 64-; Deputy to U.S.S.R. Supreme Soviet 62-; several awards.
Ministry of Heavy Power and Transport Engineering, Moscow, U.S.S.R.

Zhiri, Kacem; Moroccan diplomatist; b. 20 March 1920, Sale; s. of Mohamed and Aicha Zhiri; m. 1947; two s. two d.; ed. Inst. of Higher Studies, Rabat.
Detained for activities in independence movement of Morocco 36, 44, exiled and detained 52; fmr. Man. daily newspapers *Al-Maghrib* and *Al Alam*; Gen. Dir. Broadcasting Station of Morocco 56-59; Amb. to Senegal 60-61, to Yugoslavia 62-64, to Algeria 64-65; Dir. of Information, Ministry of Foreign Affairs 66; Perm. Del. of League of Arab States to UN, Geneva 66-68; Minister of Secondary and Technical Educ. 68-69; Amb. to Mauritania 70-72, to People's Repub. of China 72-75; Founder, Free School in Al-Jadida; Moroccan and Yugoslav decorations.
Publs. *Biography of Mohammed V* 56, *The Gold of Sous* (novel) 55, Political commentaries 56-58, Social and historical studies.
c/o Ministry of Foreign Affairs, Rabat, Morocco.

Zhivkov, Todor; Bulgarian politician; b. 7 Sept. 1911; ed. High School of Drawing and Engraving, Sofia.
Printing worker; joined Bulgarian Young Communist League 28, Communist Party 32; mem. Resistance against Nazis 41-44; candidate mem., Central Cttee., Communist Party 45, full mem. 48; First Sec., Sofia City Cttee. 48-49, candidate mem. Political Bureau and Sec. Central Cttee. 50, mem. Political Bureau 51-, First Sec. Central Cttee. 54-, mem. Nat. Assembly 45-, of Presidium 56-, Prime Minister Nov. 62-July 71; Chair. of State Council July 71-.
Publs. *Rural Co-operation* 57, *Report to Seventh Congress* 58, *Developing the Economy* 59, *UN General Assembly* 60, *Agricultural Production* 61, *The XXII Congress of the Communist Party of the Soviet Union and its Lessons for the Bulgarian Communist Party* 61.
Durzhaven Suvet, Sofia, Bulgaria.

Zhivkov, Zhivko; Bulgarian politician; b. 1915, Toshevtsi, Vidin; ed. Sofia Univ.
Young Communist League 31-, Communist Party 35-; imprisoned 42-44; mem. Cen. Cttee., later Sec., Young Communist League; fmr. Dep. to Foreign Minister; Minister of Foreign Trade 52-57, of Educ. and Culture 58-59, Deputy Prime Minister 59-62, First Deputy Chair. Council of Ministers 62-71, Deputy Chair. 71-; Chair. Cttee. for Econ. Co-ordination 69-; mem. Cen. Cttee. of Bulgarian Communist Party 54-, mem. Political Bureau 62-76; mem. Nat. Assembly.
Council of Ministers, Sofia, Bulgaria.

Zhukov, Anatoli Borisovich; Soviet biologist and forestry specialist; b. 6 Aug. 1901, Kharkov; ed. Kharkov Institute of Agriculture and Forestry.
Forestry specialist, Trostjanets Experimental Forestry Station 23-30; Dept. Chief, Central Experimental Forestry Station of Ukrainian Research Inst. of Forestry 30-37; Asst. Dir. Mokhnatch Experimental Forestry Station 37-38; Asst. Dir., Dir. Byelorussian Scientific

Research Inst. of Forestry; Asst. Prof. Byelorussian Forestry-Technical Inst. 38-41; Asst. Dir. U.S.S.R. Scientific Research Inst. of Forestry 42-56; Dept. Chief, U.S.S.R. Acad. of Sciences Forestry Inst. 56-58; Dir. U.S.S.R. Acad. of Sciences Siberian Dept Inst. of Forestry and Wood 58-; mem. U.S.S.R. Acad. of Sciences 66; Merited Worker of Sciences and Engineering of R.S.F.S.R., Order of Lenin (twice), Red Banner of Labour.
Akademgorodok, Krasńojzsk 36, U.S.S.R.

Zhukov, Yevgeny Mikhailovich; Soviet historian; b. 23 Oct. 1907, Warsaw; ed. Leningrad Oriental Inst.
Lecturer Leningrad Oriental Inst. and Leningrad Univ. 29-32; Research Worker Inst. of History, Moscow 39-41; mem. C.P. 41-; Head of Pacific Inst., U.S.S.R. Acad. of Sciences 43-50; Head of Dept., Acad. of Social Sciences 46-; Deputy Dir. Inst. of History, Moscow 54-57; Academician, Sec. of Historical Dept., U.S.S.R. Acad. of Sciences 55-71, mem. Presidium 58-; Dir. Inst. of Universal History 68-; mem. U.S.S.R. Acad. of Sciences 58-; Vice-Pres. Int. Union of Orientalists; Order of Red Banner of Labour (twice).
Publs. *Outlines of Oriental History in the Period of Imperialism* 34, *History of Japan* 39, *Outlines of History of Japanese Liberalism* 44, *International Relations on the Far East* 56, *New History of Eastern Countries: Outlines of Modern History of Japan* 57, *On dividing World History into Periods* 60.
Chief Editor *World History*, Vols. I-IX 55-62, *Soviet Historical Encyclopaedia*, Vols. I-VI 61-65.
Department of History of Academy of Sciences of U.S.S.R., ulitsa Dmitria Ulyanova 19, Moscow, U.S.S.R.

Zhuraytis, Algis; Soviet conductor; b. 1928; ed. Vilnius and Moscow Conservatoires.
Conductor Lithuanian Opera and Ballet State Theatre 51-54; Conductor of the Bolshoi Theatre 60-; Hon. Artist of R.S.F.S.R.; radio performances 55-.
State Academic Bolshoi Theatre of U.S.S.R., 1 Ploshchad Sverdlova, Moscow, U.S.S.R.

Zhurkov, Serafim Nikolayevich, D.SC.; Soviet physicist; b. 29 May 1905, Trubitckino village, Tambov Region; ed. Voronezh State Univ.
Head of Laboratory, A. F. Ioffe Physico-Technical Inst., U.S.S.R. Acad. of Sciences 30-; Prof. Leningrad State Univ. 47-; mem. Exec. Cttee., Int. Congress on Durability of Solids; Chief Editor journal *Solid Physics*; Corresp. mem., U.S.S.R. Acad. of Sciences 58, Academician 68-.
A. F. Ioffe Physico-Technical Institute, Leningrad, U.S.S.R.

Ziaie, Abdul Hakim, PH.D.; Afghan judge; b. 15 Sept. 1915; ed. Esteqlal High School, Kabul, Tokyo Univ. and the Sorbonne.
Director higher and vocational educ. 43-45; Dean, Faculty of Law and Political Science 45-47; Pres. Dept. for Secondary educ. 47-49; Educational adviser, Ministry of Educ. 55-57, Pres. of its Planning Board 56-63; Deputy Pres. Kabul Univ. 57-58; Dean, Faculty of Econs. 57-60; Dean, Faculty of Law and Political Science 60-63; Acting Deputy Minister of Educ. 61, Deputy Minister 63-65; Minister of Planning 65-67; Chief Justice of Afghanistan 67-73; has participated in over 25 int. confs. throughout the world; Kabul Acad. Prize for Literature 35; Medal of Educ. 58; Medal of Stoor 62.
Publs. all 17 of which have been published in Afghanistan, France and Japan, include: *Educational Development in Afghanistan* 51, *Afghanistan's General Progress* 56, *The Rule of Education in securing Human Rights* 64.

Ziegler, Henri Alexandre Léonard; French aviation executive; b. 18 Nov. 1906, Limoges; s. of Charles Ziegler and Marguerite Mousnier-Buisson; m. Gillette

Rizzi 1932; three s. one d.; ed. Collège Stanislas, Paris.
Officer-pilot in air-force 28; engineer, Corps aéronautique 29; Deputy Dir. Centre d'essais en vol 38; Col.-in-Chief Forces françaises de l'Intérieur (London) 44; Dir.-Gen. Air France 46-54; Dir. of Cabinet of J. Chaban-Delmas (Min. of Public Works, Transport and Tourism) 54, and of Gen. Corniglion-Molinier (Min. of Public Works) 55-56; Admin. Dir.-Gen. Soc. des Ateliers d'Aviation Louis Bréguet 57-67; Admin. Soc. des Engins Matra, Soc. France-Couleur; fmr. Pres. and mem. of Council, Asscn. Technique pour l'Energie Nucléaire (A.T.E.N.); fmr. Pres. Forum Atomique Européen (FORATOM); Pres. Dir.-Gen. Soc. AIR-Alpes; Pres. Dir.-Gen. Sud-Aviation 68-70; Pres. Dir.-Gen. Société Nationale Industrielle Aérospatiale (co. formed following merger of Sud-Aviation with Nord Aviation and Soc. d'Etudes et Réalisations d'Engins Ballistiques-SEREB) 70-73, Hon. Pres. 74-; Admin. Gérant Airbus Industrie 74-75; Pres. Union Syndicale des Industries Aérospatiales 71-73, Hon. Pres. 74-; Grand Officier Légion d'Honneur, Croix de Guerre, Rosette de la Résistance, Legion of Merit, Hon. C.B.E., French and foreign decorations.
Leisure interest: mountaineering.
12 bis avenue Bosquet, 75007 Paris; Home: 55 boulevard Lannes, 75116 Paris, France.

Ziegler, Ronald Louis, B.S.; American government official; b. 12 May 1939, Covington, Kentucky; s. of Louis Daniel and Ruby Parsons Ziegler; m. Nancy Lee Plessinger 1960; two d.; ed. Univ. of S. Calif.
Press Dir., Republican State Central Cttee. of Calif. Oct. 61-May 62; Press Aide, Richard Nixon Gubernatorial Campaign May-Nov. 62; Account Rep., J. Walter Thompson Co. Dec. 62-June 68; Press Aide, Richard M. Nixon June 68-Jan. 69; Press Sec., President Richard Nixon 69-74, Asst. to the Pres. 73-74; Man. of Int. Services, Syska and Hennessy, Washington; Outstanding Young Man Award 71.
2008 Fort Drive, Alexandria, Va., U.S.A.

Ziętek, Gen. Jerzy; Polish politician; b. 10 June 1901, Gliwice; m. Gertruda Ziętek 1925; two s. two d.
Participated in Silesian uprisings 19-21; later worked in self-government; worked in Soviet military building, U.S.S.R.; joined Polish Army, Second-in-Command R. Traugutt Third Div. 44; after the Liberation Vice-Voivoda of Silesia-Dabrowa Region, then Vice-Chair. of Presidium of Voivodship Peoples Council in Katowice 45-63, Chair. 64-73, Voivoda of Katowice Region 73-75; mem. Polish Workers' Party (P.P.R.) 45-48, Polish United Workers' Party (P.Z.P.R.) 48-, P.Z.P.R. Central Cttee. 64-; mem. Home Nat. Council (K.R.N.) then mem. Seym 47-; mem. Seym Cttee. for Building and Public Services; mem. Council of State 63-; Vice-Chair. Supreme Council of Union of Fighters for Freedom and Democracy 49-; Brig.-Gen. on retd. list 71-; Knight, Officer and Commdr. with Star, Order of Polonia Restituta 45, 53, 54; Order of Banner of Labour 1st Class 58; Order of the Builders of People's Poland 64, and others.
Leisure interests: rose growing, lawns.
Kancelaria Rady Państwa, ulica Wiejska 41618, 00-489 Warsaw, Poland.

Zijlstra, Jelle, DR. ECON.SC.; Netherlands university professor, politician and banker; b. 27 Aug. 1918, Barradeel; s. of A. J. Zijlstra and Pietje Postuma; m. Hetty Bloksma; two s. three d.; ed. Netherlands School of Economics.
Assistant Netherlands School of Economics 45-46, Lecturer 47; Prof. of Economic Sciences, Free Univ. of Amsterdam 48-52; Minister of Economic Affairs 52-59, of Finance 59-July 63; Prof. of Economic Sciences, Free Univ. of Amsterdam 63-67; Pres. Board of Govs., European Investment Bank 62-July 63; Prime Minister 66-67; Pres. Netherlands Bank May 67-; Pres. Bank for Int. Settlements and Chair. of Board of Dirs. June 67-; Gov.

Int. Monetary Fund, Washington 67-; Anti-Revolutionary Party.

Leisure interests: skiing, sailing, golf.

Publ. *The Velocity of Circulation of Money and its Significance for the Value of Money and Monetary Equilibrium* 48.

Bavoylaan 14, The Hague; De Nederlandsche Bank N.V., Westeinde 1, Amsterdam, Netherlands.

Telephone: 63133 (Office).

Ziman, John Michael, F.R.S.; British physicist; b. 16 May 1925, New Zealand; *m.*; four *c.*; ed. Hamilton High School, Victoria Coll., Wellington, Balliol Coll., Oxford.

Junior Lecturer in Mathematics, Oxford Univ. 51-53, Pressed Steel Ltd. Research Fellow 53-54; Lecturer in Physics, Cambridge Univ. 54-64, Fellow of King's Coll. 57-64, Editor *Cambridge Review* 58-59, Tutor for Advanced Students, King's Coll. 59-63; Prof. of Theoretical Physics, Univ. of Bristol 64-, Melville Wills Prof. 69-; Editor *Science Progress*; Hon. Editor *Reports on Progress in Physics*; Gen. Editor *Cambridge Monographs on Physics*; mem. Exec. Cttee., Council for Science and Society; current research interest: review, *Models of Disorder*; Rutherford Memorial Lecturer in India and Pakistan 68.

Publs. *Electrons and Phonons* 60, *Electrons in Metals* 63, *Camford Observed* (with Jasper Rose) 64, *Principles of the Theory of Solids* 65, *Public Knowledge* 68, *Elements of Advanced Quantum Theory* 69, *The Force of Knowledge* 76; numerous articles in scientific journals.

H.H. Wills Physics Laboratory, Tyndall Avenue, Bristol, Avon, BS8 1TL, England.

Telephone: 24161.

Zimbalist, Efrem; American violinist and musical director; b. 9 April 1889; *m.* Mary Louise Curtis Zimbalist (died 1970); ed. Imperial School, St. Petersburg (pupil of Leopold Auer).

Début Berlin 07; concert performances in principal cities of Europe and America; Dir. Curtis Inst. of Music, Philadelphia 41-68; composer of works for orchestra, string quartet, violin sonata, and works for voice and piano.

866 Skyline Boulevard, Reno, Nevada 89502, U.S.A.

Zimm, Bruno Hasbrouck, PH.D.; American research chemist and professor; b. 31 Oct. 1920, Woodstock, N.Y.; *s.* of Bruno L. Zimm and Louise Hasbrouck Zimm; *m.* Georgianna Grevatt 1944; two *s.*; ed. Columbia Univ.

Teaching Asst. Columbia Univ., New York 41-44; Civilian Staff mem., Atomic Energy Comm., New York, N.Y. 42-43; with Office of Scientific Research and Devt. New York, N.Y.; Research Assoc. and Instructor Polytechnic Inst. of Brooklyn 44-46; Instructor, Univ. of Calif. at Berkeley 46-47, Asst. Prof. 47-49, Assoc. Prof. 50-52; Research Assoc., Gen. Electric Research Laboratory, Schenectady, N.Y. 51-60; Prof. of Chemistry, Univ. of Calif. at San Diego 60-; Visiting Lecturer in Chemistry Harvard Univ. 50-51; Visiting Prof. Yale Univ. 60; Leo Hendrik Baekeland Award, N. Jersey Section of American Chemical Soc. 57, Bingham Medal, Soc. of Rheology 60, High Polymer Physics Prize, American Physical Soc. 63.

Leisure interests: playing clarinet, tennis, sailing.

Publs. Over 75 articles in scientific journals.

Department of Chemistry, University of California, San Diego, Box 109, La Jolla, Calif. 92037, U.S.A.

Telephone: (714) 452-4416.

Zimmerman, Charles J., B.S., M.B.A., C.L.U.; American insurance executive; b. 9 Jan. 1902; *m.* Opal Marie Smith 1942; ed. Dartmouth Coll., The Amos Tuck School of Business Admin.

Exec. Man. New York Life Underwriters' Asscn. 24-26; Gen. Agent, The Conn. Mutual Life Insurance Co. 26-46; Man. Dir. Life Insurance Agency Management Asscn. 46-56; Pres. The Conn. Mutual Life Insurance Co. 56-67,

Chair. 67-68, Chair. of Board 68-72; Founder Univ. of Hartford 57; Trustee, Dartmouth Coll. 52-72 (Chair. 70-72), Lawrence Acad., Nat. Conf. of Christians and Jews; Chair. American Coll. of Life Underwriters 65-69, Life Trustee 69-; S. S. Huebner Foundation for Insurance and Educ., Chair. 68; Dir. Inst. of Living (Pres. 68-), Life Insurance Medical Research Fund (Chair. 63-), Nat. Asscn. for Mental Health Inc., Conn. Bank and Trust Co., Connecticut Natural Gas Co., State Dime Savings Bank, Junior Achievement of Hartford Inc.; mem. Exec. Cttee. American Life Convention, Pres. Exec. Cttee. 70-; John Newton Memorial Award 51.

140 Garden Street, Hartford, Conn.; and 70 Mohawk Drive, West Hartford, Conn. 06117, U.S.A.

Telephone: 203-549-4111 (Office); 203-232-1533 (Home).

Zimmermann, Adm. Armin; German naval officer; b. 23 Dec. 1917, Blumenau, Brazil; *m.* Anneliese Nachbar; one *d.*; ed. Reform-Humanistic Gymnasium.

In Nat. Labour Service 36; Acting Sub-Lt. 39; war service, rising to rank of Lt.-Commdr.; Flotilla Commdr., group leader and nautical specialist of German Minesweeping Admin.; joined Fed. Armed Forces as Lt.-Commdr. 56; Asst. Head of Section, Fed. Ministry of Defence; Naval Attaché, London; Troop duty as Squadron Commdr.; at Fed. Armed Forces Command and Staff Coll.; Head of Section, Fed. Ministry of Defence; Commdr., German Naval Forces North Sea; Commdr.-in-Chief, German Naval Forces 70-72; Chief of Staff, Fed. Armed Forces 72-.

Leisure interests: military policy, music, tennis, skiing.

Publs. on military policy, strategy, internal structure of modern armed forces, training and education within the armed forces.

c/o Ministerium der Verteidigung, 53 Bonn-Duisdorf, Hardthöhe, Federal Republic of Germany.

Zimyanin, Mikhail Vasilievich; Soviet journalist; b. 21 Nov. 1914, Vitebsk, Byelorussia; ed. Mogilev Pedagogical Inst.

Member C.P.S.U. 39-; First Sec. Cen. Cttee., Komsomol Byelorussia 40-46; Second Sec. Gomel Regional Cttee. C.P.S.U. 46; Minister of Educ., Byelorussia 46-47; Sec. Second Sec. Cen. Cttee. C.P. Byelorussia 47-53, First Sec. 53; Ministry of Foreign Affairs 53-56, Far Eastern Dept. 57-60, Ambassador to Dem. Repub. of Viet-Nam 56-57, to Czechoslovakia 60-65; Dep. Foreign Minister 65; Editor of *Pravda* 65-76; mem. Cen. Cttee. C.P.S.U. 52-56, 66-, Sec. 76-; mem. Cen. Auditing Comm. C.P.S.U. 56-66; Vice-Chair. Council of Nationalities of U.S.S.R. Supreme Soviet 50-54; Deputy to U.S.S.R. Supreme Soviet 46-54, 66-; Awarded Orders of Lenin (twice), Red Banner, Red Banner of Labour (twice).

Pravda, 24 Ulitsa Pravdy, Moscow, U.S.S.R.

Zinder, Norton David. PH.D.; American professor and geneticist; b. 7 Nov. 1928, New York, N.Y.; *s.* of Harry Zinder and Jean Gottesman Zinder; *m.* Marilyn Estreicher 1949; two *s.*; ed. Columbia Univ. and Univ. of Wis.

Wisconsin Alumni Fund Fellow, Univ. of Wis. 48-50, Research Asst. 50-56; Asst., Rockefeller Univ. (then Rockefeller Inst.) 52-56, Assoc. 56-58, Assoc. Prof. 58-64, Prof. 64-; Editor *RNA Phages*; mem. Nat. Acad. of Sciences, American Acad. of Arts and Sciences; Columbia Medal of Excellence, Eli Lilly Award, U.S. Steel Molecular Biology Award.

Publs. *Infective Heredity in Bacteria*, Cold Spring Harbor Symposium on Quantitative Biology XVIII 53; and scientific articles in learned journals.

Home: 450 East 63rd Street, New York City, N.Y. 10021, U.S.A.

Telephone: 421-3777.

Zingarelli, Italo, LL.D.; Italian journalist and writer; b. 9 July 1891.

Editor *Ora* 10; Zürich corresp. *Corriere della Sera* 16-18 and Vienna corresp. 21; mem. staff of *Epoca* 18-21;

Editor *Secolo* 26 and its Vienna corresp. 26-27; Vienna corresp. *Stampa* and *Agenzia Stefani* until 38; toured Middle East, Asia and Europe 38-43; Foreign Editor *Il Tempo* Feb.-Dec. 45, Editor of *Libera Stampa*, Rome Dec. 45-March 46; Foreign Editor *Il Tempo* April 46; Editor *Il Globo* June 52-62.

Publs. *La marina nella guerra attuale* 15, *La marina italiana* 15, *Il Dominio del mare nel conflitto anglo-germanico* 15, *L'invasione* 19, *L'agonia del bolscevismo* 23, *Il volto di Vienna* 25, *Der Gross Balkan* 27, *Il risveglio dell'Islam* 28, *Das Erbe von Versailles* 30, *Vienna non imperiale* 30, *Vienna* 35, *La leggenda di Ognuno* 36, *Vecchia Austria* 37, *I paesi danubiani e balcanici* 38, *Vicino e lontano Oriente* 40, *Il terzo braccio di Regina Coeli* 44, *Questo e il giornalismo* 46, *I tre imperialismi* 49, *I Padroni del Mondo* 52, *Lo stivale delle mille leghe* 62, etc.

c/o *Il Globo*, Via Due Macelli 23, Rome; and Piazza Stefano Jacini 5, Rome, Italy.

Zinnemann, Fred; American (b. Austrian) film director; b. 29 April 1907; *s.* of Dr. Oskar Zinnemann and Anna F. Zinnemann; *m.* Renée Bartlett 1936; one *s.*; ed. Universität Wien and School of Cinematography, Paris.

Studied techniques of camera, lighting and mechanics, Paris; went to U.S.A. 29; directed documentaries and short films until 41, major films 41-; initiated, with others, school of realism in American Cinema; several awards including 3 Academy Awards, 4 New York Film Critics Awards, 2 Directors' Guild of America Annual Awards; Golden Thistle Award, Edinburgh Film Festival 65; Gold Medal, City of Vienna 67; Hon. Award for *A Man for All Seasons*, Moscow Film Festival 67, D. W. Griffith Award 69; Contributor to *Encyclopedia Britannica* (Film Directing).

Leisure interests: chamber music, mountain climbing.

Films include: *The Wave* (short) 35, *Crime Does Not Pay* (series of shorts) 37-41, *The Seventh Cross* 44, *The Search* 48, *Act of Violence* 49, *The Men* 50, *Teresa* 51, *High Noon* 52, *The Member of the Wedding* 53, *From Here to Eternity* (Acad. Award) 53, *Oklahoma!* 55, *A Hatful of Rain* 57, *The Nun's Story* 58, *The Sundowners* 60, *Behold a Pale Horse* 64, *A Man for all Seasons* (Acad. Award) 66, *The Day of the Jackal* 73.

128 Mount Street, London, W.1, England.

Telephone: 01-499 8810.

Zinner, Ernst; German astronomer; b. 2 Feb. 1886; ed. Jena, Munich and Lund Univs.

Observer to Geodetic Comm. 19-26; Dir. Remeis-Observatory, Bamberg 26-53; mem. Halle Acad. of Science; mem. Int. Acad. of History of Science; mem. Int. Astronomical Union; Dr. h.c. 61.

Publs. *Verzeichnis der astronomischen Handschriften des deutschen Kulturgebietes* 25, *Veröffentlichungen der Remeis-Sternwarte*, I-IV 26-39, *Geschichte der Sternkunde* 30, *Die fränkische Sternkunde im 11 bis 16 Jahrhundert* 34, *Der deutsche Kalender des Johannes Regiomontan* 37, *Leben und Wirken des Johannes Müller von Königsberg genannt Regiomontanus* 38, *Die ältesten Räderuhren und modernen Sonnenuhren* 39, *Geschichte und Bibliographie der astronomischen Literatur in Deutschland zur Zeit der Renaissance* 41, *Entstehung und Ausbreitung der copernicanischen Lehre* 43, *Astronomie Geschichte ihrer Probleme* 51, *Sternglaube und Sternforschung* 53, *Die Erklärung des Lichtwechsels der vermissten Sterne* 52, *Aus der Frühzeit der Räderuhr* 54, *Astronomische Instrumente des 11 bis 18 Jahrhunderts* 56, *The Stars Above Us* 57, *Alte Sonnenuhren an europäischen Gebäuden* 64.

Sternwartestrasse 7, 86 Bamberg, Federal Republic of Germany.

Zipf, George G.; American business executive; b. 12 Oct. 1920, Johnstown, Pa.; *s.* of late Carl H. Zipf and

of Florence G. Zipf; *m.* Susan S. Merriman 1944; one *s.* one *d.*; ed. Lehigh Univ.

Joined Babcock & Wilcox as student engineer 42, Gen. Supt. of Steel Plants 59-63, Gen. Man. Tubular Div. 63-64, Vice-Pres. 64-66, Dir. 64-, Exec. Vice-Pres. 66-67, Pres. 67-, Chief Exec. Officer 68-, Chair. 73-; Dir. Bailey Meter Co., The Continental Corpn., Continental Insurance Co., Manufacturers Hanover Trust Co., Babcock & Wilcox Canada Ltd., Krafto Corpn.; Dir. American Iron and Steel Inst.; decorated by Italian Repub.; Distinguished Life mem., American Soc. for Metals; mem. Exec. Cttee. Machinery and Allied Products Inst.

Leisure interests: photography, golf, music, gardening.

Babcock & Wilcox Co., 161 East 42nd Street, New York, N.Y. 10017; Home: 1 Deer Trail, Armonk, N.Y. 10504, U.S.A.

Telephone: 914-273-9347 (Home).

Ziv-Av, Itzhak; Israeli administrative official and journalist; b. 4 June 1907, Russia; *s.* of Abraham and Miriam Ziv-Av; *m.* Debora Kobrinsky 1934; two *s.*; ed. Inst. of Pedagogy, Smolensk.

Farmer and Manager Local Council of Magdiel settlement, Israel 26-; Man.-Editor *Haboker* (daily) 35-48; Dir. Public Relations Div., Ministry of Defence and GHQ, Israel Defence Forces 48-52; Dir.-Gen. Israel Farmers' Fed. 52-75, Chair. Central Cttee. 75-; Chair. Exec. Cttee., Co-ordinating Bureau, Israeli Econ. Orgs. 67-; Editor *Farmers of Israel* monthly 62-; mem. Board of Dirs. Jewish Nat. Fund; Chair. Board, Land Devt. Authority; mem. Council, State Land Authority.

Leisure interests: reading, gardening, travel.

Publs. *The Unknown Land, I Seek my Brethren, The Price of Freedom, Forever Ours, From Frontier to Frontier, A World to Live in, Another World,* and poetry for children.

Israel Farmers' Federation, Kaplan Street 8, Tel-Aviv; Home: Ramat-Qan, Narkissim Avenue 20, Tel-Aviv, Israel.

Telephone: 25-22-27 (Office); 79-02-27 (Home).

Zobel de Ayala, Jaime; Philippine diplomatist; b. 18 July 1934, Manila; *s.* of Don Alfonso Zobel de Ayala and Doña Carmen Pfitz y Herrero; *m.* Beatriz Miranda 1957; two *s.* five *d.*; ed. in the Philippines and Spain, and Harvard Univ.

Chairman of Board, Ayala Corpn.; Attorney-in-Fact, Ayala Corpn. and subsidiaries; Dir. Shell Refining Co., Shell Co. of the Philippines, Central Azucarera Don Pedro, San Miguel Corpn.; Amb. to U.K. 71-74; Pres. Cultural Centre of the Philippines 69-70; Comendador de la Orden del Merito Civil (Spain).

Leisure interests: golf, horseback riding, hunting, swimming, art, music.

Publs. articles on business and art for Philippine newspapers.

c/o Ministry of Foreign Affairs, Manila, Philippines.

ZoBell, Claude E., M.S., PH.D.; American microbiologist; b. 22 Aug. 1904, Provo, Utah; *s.* of E. A. and Stella Davis ZoBell; *m.* Jean E. Switzer 1946; two *s.*; ed. Utah State Univ. and Univ. of California.

Principal, Rigby (Idaho) Elementary School 24-26; Instructor, Utah State Univ. 28-29; Research Asst., Hooper Foundation 29-30; Instructor, Scripps Inst. Oceanography, Univ. of Calif. 32-36, Asst. Prof. 38-42, Assoc. Prof. 42-48, Prof. 48-72, Emeritus Prof. 72-; Chair. Div. of Marine Biology 56-60; Research Assoc., Univ. of Wisconsin 38-39; Special Fellow, Rockefeller Foundation, Europe 48-49; Participant in Galathea Round-the-World Deep Sea Expedition; first to recover living organisms from greatest depths of the sea; Assoc. Founding mem. Surtsey (Iceland) Research Soc.; Royal Danish Navy Galathea Medal 52.

Leisure interests: handicrafts, gardening.

Publs. *Marine Microbiology* 46, 230 articles or papers dealing with researches on function of bacteria as geochemical agents and in origin of oil.
2404 Ellentown Road, La Jolla, Calif. 92037, U.S.A.

Zoitakis, Gen. George; Greek army officer; b. 1910; Nafpaktos, Aitolo-Akarnania; *m.* Sophia D. Vouranzeris 1949; one *d.*; ed. Cadet School, Higher War Coll. of Greece, School of Nat. Defence, and American School of Special Arms, Germany.
Infantry 2nd Lieut. 32; 1st Lieut. 35; Captain 38; Major 46; Lieut.-Col. 49; Col. 55; Brig. 60; Maj.-Gen. 63; Lieut.-Gen. 65; Under Sec. of State for Nat. Defence April 67; Regent of Greece Dec. 67-March 72; Gen. 70; arrested Feb. 75, charged with high treason and insurrection, sentenced to life imprisonment Aug. 75; mem. Mixed Greco-Bulgarian Cttee. for settling frontier incidents, then Pres. of corresp. Greek-Yugoslav Cttee.; numerous medals.
Leisure interests: walking, reading, theatre.

Zółkiewski, Stefan, PH.D.; Polish university professor; b. 9 Dec. 1911, Warsaw; *s.* of Jan Zółkiewski and Izabela Stopczyk; *m.* 1st Wanda Fabijanowska 1935, 2nd Barbara Bormann 1949; one *d.*; ed. Warsaw Univ.
Editor-in-Chief *Kuznica*, Łódź 46-47; Dir. Inst. of Literary Research, Warsaw 49-53; Scientific Worker 53-; Editor-in-Chief *Polityka* 57-58, *Nowa Kultura* 58-61, *Kultura i Społeczeństwo* 61-68; Deputy to Seym 47-69; Prof. of the History of Polish Literature, Warsaw Univ.; mem. Polish Acad. of Sciences, fmr. Sec. for Section I of Acad. of Sciences 61-68; mem. Polish United Workers' Party 48-; Central Cttee. 54-68; State Prizes 51, 53 and 64; Minister of Higher Education 56-59; Pres. Polish Semiotic Assen.; mem. Exec. Cttee. Int. Assen. for Semiotic Studies; Order of Banner of Labour First Class 49, Commdr. Order of Polonia Restituta with Star 54, Order of Sacred Treasure of Japan, Second Class 60.
Leisure interests: art, reading, touring.
Publs. *Stare i nowe Literaturoznawstwo* (Old and New Approaches to Literature), *Spór o Mickiewicza* (Dispute over Mickiewicz), *Kultura i Polityka* (Culture and Politics) 58, *Perspektywy Literatury XX Wieku* 60, *Przepowiednie i Wspomnienia* 63, *O Kulturze Polski* (Culture of Poland) 64, *Zagadnienia Stylu* (The Problem of Style) 65, *Semiotyka a Kultura* 69, *Essais Sur la Sémiotique et Sociologie de Littérature* 71-75, *Kultura Literacka 1918-1932* (French and English edns., *The Literary Culture 1918-1932*) 73.
Al. Róż 6 m 14, 00-556, Warsaw, Poland.
Telephone: 21-39-92.

Zollinger, Heinrich Fritz, PH.D., D.SC.; Swiss professor and university administrator; b. 29 Nov. 1919, Aarau; *s.* of Dr. Fritz Zollinger and Helene Prior; *m.* Heidi Frick 1948; three *s.*; ed. Fed. Inst. of Tech. (ETH), Univ. of Basle, Massachusetts Inst. of Tech.
Chemist, Dyestuff Research Dept., CIBA Ltd. 45-60; Lecturer in Dyestuff Chem., Univ. of Basle 52-60; Prof. of Textile Chem., Fed. Inst. of Tech. 60-, Rector 73-; Pres. Organic Chem. Div. of IUPAC 75-; Werner Prize 59, Ruzicka Award 60, Lewinstein Award 64, Conrad Prize 70.
Leisure interests: clarinet, sailing, colour studies.
Publs. *Chemie der Azofarbstoffe* 58 (Russian 60), *Diazo and Azo Chemistry* 61, *Leitfaden der Farbstoffchemie* 70, (English 72, Japanese 72); volumes on aromatic chemistry in *International Review of Science* 73, 76; 200 scientific papers.
Technisch-Chemisches Laboratorium, Eidgenössische Technische Hochschule, Universitâtstrasse 6, CH-8006, Zürich; Home: Boglerenstrasse 45, CH-8700 Küsnacht, Switzerland.
Telephone: 01-32-62-11 (Laboratory); 01-90-53-08 (Home).

Zollner, Maxime-Léopold; Dahomeyan diplomatist; b. 1934; ed. Dahomey and Univ. de Paris.
Counsellor, Dahomey Perm. Mission to UN 60-63; Counsellor, Wash. 61-63; Sec.-Gen. Malagasy Union 63-64; Deputy Perm. Rep. to UN 64-67, Perm. Rep. 67; now Sec.-Gen. Int. Secr. for Volunteer Service.
International Secretariat for Volunteer Service, 10-12 Chemin de Surville, Petit Lancy, 1213 Geneva, Switzerland.

Zolotas, Xenophon, DR.ECON.; Greek university professor; b. 26 March 1904, Athens; *s.* of the late Efthymios Zolotas; *m.* Kallirhoe Ritsos 1958; ed. Univs. of Athens, Leipzig and Paris.
Professor of Econs. Univ. of Salonica 28, of Athens 31-; Chair. Board of Dirs., Agricultural Bank of Greece 36-40; Jt. Gov. Bank of Greece (after Liberation) Oct. 44-45; mem. UNRRA Council 46; Gov. of Int. Monetary Fund for Greece 46-67, mem. Greek Del. to UN Gen. Ass. 48-53; Del. to Econ. Comm. for Europe 49; mem. Currency Cttee. 50, Vice-Chair. ECE 52; Minister of Co-ordination Oct. 52; Gov. Bank of Greece 55-Aug. 67, Nov. 74-; Minister of Econ. Co-ordination July-Nov. 74; mem. "Group of Four" for remodelling of OEEC 60; Editor *Greek Review of Economics*; mem. Acad. of Athens 52-; Grand Cross of Royal Order of the Phoenix.
Publs. *Griechenland auf dem Wege zur Industrialisierung* 26, *Etalon-or en théorie et en pratique* 34, *La question de l'or et le problème monetaire* 37, *Monetary Stability and Economic Development* 58, *Economic Development and Technical Education* 59, *The Problem of the International Monetary Liquidity* 61, *Towards a Reinforced Gold Exchange Standard* 61, *Economic Development and Private Enterprise* 62, *International Monetary Order: Problems and Policies* 62, *The Role of The Banks in a Developing Country* 63, *The Multicurrency Standard and the International Monetary Fund* 63, *Monetary Equilibrium and Economic Development* 65, *Remodelling the International Monetary System* 65, *Alternative Systems for International Monetary Reform* 65, *Monetary and Economic Developments in Greece* 66, *International Labor Migration and Economic Development* 66, *The Gold Trap and the Dollar* 68, *Speculocracy and the International Monetary System* 69, *The International Money Mess* 73, *From Anarchy to International Monetary Order* 73; in Greek *Speculation Monetary Stability* 29, *Monetary Stabilization* 29, *Liberal Socialism* 44, *Economics* 44, *Monetary Problems and the Greek Economy* 50, *Inflationary Pressures in the Greek Economy* 51, *Regional Planning and Economic Development*.
Home: 25 Dionissiou Areopagitou Street, Athens 402; Office: Bank of Greece, Panepistimon Street, Athens, Greece.
Telephone: 634-647 (Office).

Zolotukhin, Grigory Sergeyevich; Soviet politician; b. 1911; ed. Agricultural Coll. and C.P.S.U. Higher Party School.
Member C.P.S.U. 39-; Exec. posts in Tambov Region 31-38; Agronomist 38-39; Young Communist League and Party Official 39-65; First Sec. Krasnodar Territory Cttee. of C.P.S.U. 66-; Alt. mem. C.P.S.U. Central Cttee. 56-66, mem. 66-; Deputy to U.S.S.R. Supreme Soviet 58-; Chair. Comm. for Agriculture, Soviet of Union; Minister of Agricultural Products Procurement 73-.
Krasnodar Territory Committee, Communist Party of the Soviet Union, Krasnodar, U.S.S.R.

Zondek, Herman, M.D.; Israeli physician; b. 4 Sept. 1887, Wronke; *s.* of Abraham Zondek and Sara Zondek (née Hollaender); *m.* Dr. Gerda Wolfsohn 1949; one *s.* one *d.*; ed. Gymnasium, Rogasen, Prussia, and Univs. of Göttingen and Berlin.
Lecturer, Friedrich Wilhelm Univ., Berlin 18-21; Dir. Municipal Hospital am Urban, Berlin 26; Prof. of Medicine, Berlin Univ. 34; Dir. Medical Div. Bikur

Holim Hospital, 34; Visiting Prof. Hebrew Univ. Medical School, Jerusalem 40; Hon. Pres. Scientific Council of Israel Medical Asscn., Israel Soc. of Internal Medicine, Jerusalem Acad. of Medicine; mem. Israel Acad. of Sciences and Humanities; affil. Royal Soc. of Medicine, London.

Publs. *Das Hungerödem* (Hunger Oedema) 20, *The Diseases of the Endocrine Glands* (German) 23, later revised and enlarged editions in German, English, French, Polish, Russian and Italian 26-58; about 250 papers on endocrine physio-pathology (first description of endocrine disorders such as myxoedema heart 18-19, pituitary hyper- and hypothyroidism 26 and various hypothalamic-pituitary syndromes 35-36, of iodine therapy in hyperthyroidism 21; elucidation of mechanisms of hormonal action and regulation 23-68); *Auf Festem Fusse, Erinnerungen eines jüdischen Klinikers* (autobiography) 73.

8 Ben Maimon Avenue, Jerusalem, Israel.
Telephone: 39001.

Zorin, Valerian Aleksandrovich; Soviet diplomatist; b. 13 Jan. 1902, Novocherkassk, Rostov; ed. High Communist Inst. of Education.

Important position in Central Cttee. of Komsomol 22-32; post-graduate student High Communist Inst. of Education 33-35; party and pedagogical work 35-41; Asst. Gen. Sec. of People's Commissariat of Foreign Affairs 41-42, Head Fourth European Dept. 43-45; Ambassador to Czechoslovakia 45-47; Deputy Minister of Foreign Affairs 47-55, 56-57, concurrently Perm. Rep. of U.S.S.R. to UN Security Council 52-53; Ambassador to Fed. Repub. of Germany 55-60; Perm. Rep. to UN 60-62; Alt. mem. Central Cttee. C.P.S.U. 56-61, mem. 61-; Amb. to France 65-71; Rep. to Geneva Disarmament Talks 60, 64; Order of Lenin (2), Order of the Red Banner (2), Badge of Honour, and other decorations.

Ministry of Foreign Affairs, 32-34 Smolenskaya-Sennaya ploschchad, Moscow, U.S.S.R.

Zornow, Gerald Bernard; American business executive; b. 3 March 1916, Pittsford, N.Y.; s. of Theodore A. and Dora (née Sweeney) Zornow; m. 1st Gaylord Baker 1940 (deceased), m. 2nd Bette Dwyer; one d.; ed. Univ. of Rochester.

Joined Eastman Kodak Co. 37; Asst. Gen. Sales Man. Rochester, N.Y. 54-56; Dir. Sales, Apparatus and Optical Div. 56-58; Vice-Pres. 58-63; Dir. 63-; Vice-Pres. (Marketing) 63-69; Exec. Vice-Pres. 69-70; Pres. and Chair. Exec. Cttee. 70-May 72, Chair. of the Board 72; Dir. Marine Midland Bank Inc., Kodak Ltd., TRW Inc.; Dir. Gen. Signal Corpn.; Chair. Marketing Science Inst.

Leisure interest: golf.
Eastman Kodak Co., 343 State Street, Rochester, N.Y. 14650, U.S.A.

Zoungrana, H.E. Cardinal Paul; Upper Voltan ecclesiastic; b. 3 Sept. 1917, Ouagadougou; ed. l'Institut Catholique de Paris, and Université Pontificale Grégorienne.

Ordained priest 42; mem. Missionary Soc. of the White Fathers; Archbishop of Ouagadougou 60-; created Cardinal 65; Pres. Symposium of Episcopal Confs. of Africa and Madagascar (SECAM).

Archbishop's House, B.P. 90, Ouagadougou, Upper Volta.
Telephone: 27-92.

Žourek, Jaroslav, LL.D.; Czechoslovak international jurist; b. 29 March 1908, Přílepy; s. of Innocenc Žourek and Francisca Solařová; m. 2nd Marie Hrubá 1950; one s. two d. (from 1st marriage); ed. Universita Karlova, Prague.

Former Asst., Seminary of Int. Law, Charles Univ., Prague; Legal Officer, Ministry of Foreign Affairs 37; Scientific and Teaching Work, Law Faculty of Charles Univ. 45-48, Assoc. Prof. 48-69; Del. of Czechoslovakia

at Conf. of Law of the Sea, Geneva 58; mem. UN Int. Law Comm. 48-61, Pres. 57-58; leading Research Assoc. in Int. Law, Czechoslovak Acad. of Sciences 54-69; Judge *ad hoc*, Int. Court of Justice, The Hague 59-60; UN expert at Conf. on Consular Relations 63; Special Adviser to Czech del. at Conf. on Law of Treaties, Vienna 68; Univ. of Geneva 68-69; Visiting Prof. Queens Univ., Kingston, Canada 69-70; Assoc. mem. Inst. of Int. Law; mem. Presiding Council Int. Court of Arbitration for Maritime and Inland Navigation, Gdynia, Pres. 64, 67; Past Pres. and now Vice-Pres. Int. Law Asscn., London; Yugoslav award for outstanding services to the country (Zaslugy Za narod).

Publs. *Définition de l'agression* 57, *Statut et Fonctions des consuls* 62; numerous studies on questions of International Law.
Living abroad.

Zrak, Jozef, ING., C.SC.; Czechoslovak politician; b. 19 July 1929, Šumiac; ed. Coll. of Agriculture and Forestry, Košice, and Acad. of Social Sciences, Central Cttee. of C.P.S.U., Moscow.

Senior Asst., Technical Coll., Košice 52-54; Deputy Chief of Dept., Central Cttee. of C.P. of Slovakia 63-65; Asst. Prof. 63; Chief Sec., Municipal Cttee. of C.P. of Slovakia, Bratislava 65-68; Sec. Central Cttee. of C.P. of Slovakia 68-69; Deputy Premier of Slovak Socialist Repub. 69-70; mem. Cen. Union Czechoslovak Students 49-51; mem. Cen. Cttee. Slovak C.P. 66-70, Secr. 66-69; Chair. Legislative Council of Govt. of Slovak Socialist Repub 69-.

Government Presidium of Slovak Socialist Republic, Bratislava, Czechoslovakia.

Zrzavý, Jan; Czechoslovak artist; b. 5 Nov. 1890, Vadín-Okrouhlice.

Member of "The Obstinates" of early 20th Century; many study trips in Italy especially Venice; worked in Brittany 23-30; figurative paintings, landscapes, still lifes, illustrator of many books; one-man exhbns. in Paris, Venice, Berlin, Dresden, Munich, Geneva and London; Nat. Artist of Czechoslovakia 66.

Malá Strana, Nové zámecké schody 6, Prague 1, Czechoslovakia.
Telephone: 53041.

Zuckerman, Baron (Life Peer), cr. 71, of Burnham Thorpe in the County of Norfolk; **Solly Zuckerman,** O.M., K.C.B., M.A., M.D., D.SC., LL.D., M.R.C.S., F.R.C.P., F.R.S.; British anatomist; b. 1904, Cape Town; s. of late Moses Zuckerman; m. Lady Joan Rufus Isaacs; one s. one d.; ed. South African Coll. School, Cape Town Univ., and Univ. Coll. Hospital London.

Demonstrator of Anatomy Cape Town Univ. 23-25; Union Research Scholar 25; Research Anatomist to London Zoological Soc. and Demonstrator of Anatomy, Univ. Coll., London 28-32; Research Assoc. and Rockefeller Research Fellow, Yale Univ. 33-34; William Julius Mickle Fellow, London Univ. 35; Beit Memorial Research Fellow 34-37; Hunterian Prof. Royal Coll. of Surgeons 37; Univ. Demonstrator Human Anatomy Dept. Oxford 34-45; Sands Cox Prof. of Anatomy, Birmingham Univ. 43-68; Prof. Emeritus Univs. of E. Anglia, Birmingham; Scientific Adviser British Mil. Orgs. 39-46; Group Capt. (Hon.) R.A.F. 43-46; Deputy Chair. Advisory Council on Scientific Policy 48-64; Chair. Nat. Resources Technical Cttee. 51-64; mem. Agricultural Research Council 49-59; Chair. Cen. Advisory Cttee. for Science and Technology 70; Trustee, British Museum (Natural History) 67-; Pres. Fauna Preservation Soc.; Hon. Sec. Zoological Soc., London; Fellow, Univ. Coll., London; Fellow Commoner, Christ's Coll., Cambridge; Pres. Parl. and Scientific Cttee. 73-76; Pres. Asscn. Learned and Professional Society Publishers 73-; Gregynog Lecturer, Univ. of Wales 56; Mason Lecturer, Univ. of Birmingham 57, Lees Knowles Lecturer, Cambridge Univ. 65, Romanes

Lecturer, Oxford Univ. 75; Rhodes Lecturer, S. Africa 75; Chief Scientific Adviser to the Govt. 64-71; Chief Scientific Adviser to Sec. of State for Defence 60-66, Hon. Fellow, Royal Coll. of Surgeons, Pharmaceutical Soc. of Great Britain 75, Hon. mem. American Acad. of Arts and Sciences; Foreign mem. American Philosophical Soc.

Publs. *The Social Life of Monkeys and Apes* 32, *Functional Affinities of Man, Monkeys and Apes* 33, *A New System of Anatomy* 61, *Scientists and War* 66, *Beyond the Ivory Tower* 70.

The Zoological Society of London, Regent's Park, London, NW1 4RY, England.
Telephone: 01-722-3333.

Zuckmayer, Carl; German (naturalized Swiss) writer; b. 27 Dec. 1896, Nackenheim/Rhein; s. of Carl and Amalie Zuckmayer; m. Alice von Herdan 1925; one d. Playwright and poet; his first play, *Kreuzweg*, was produced at the Berlin State Theatre 20; Extraordinary mem. Akademie der Künste (Germany); Kleist prizewinner 25; Georg Büchner prizewinner 29; Goethe prizewinner 52; Ordre Pour le Mérite for Science and Art 67; Heinrich Heine Prize 72.
Leisure interests: zoology, botany, mineralogy.
Publs. Plays: *Der fröhliche Weinberg* 25, *Schinderhannes* 27, *Katharina Knie* 28, *Kakadu-Kakada* (for children) 29, *Der Hauptmann von Köpenick* (also film) 31, *Der Schelm von Bergen* 34, *The Moon in the South* 37, *Bellman* 38, *Second Wind* 41, *The Last Drop* 41, *Des Teufels General* 46, *Barbara Blomberg* 49, *Der Gesang im Feuerofen* 50, *Ulla Winblad* 53, *Das kalte Licht* 55, *Der trunkene Herkules* 58, *Die Uhr Schlägt Eins* 61, *Der Rattenfänger* 75; Novels: *Magdalena von Bozen* 36, *Herr über Leben und Tod* 38, *Das Seelenbräu* 45; Verse: *Der Baum* 26; *Collected Works* (in 4 vols.) 46, 48, 50, 52, *Henndorfer Pastorale* 72; *Die langen Wege* (essay) 52; short stories: *Das Leben des Horace A. W. Tabor* 64; *Als wär's ein Stück von mir* (memoirs) 66 (English and American edn. *A Part of Myself* 70).
CH-3906 Saas-Fée, Switzerland.
Telephone: 028-48306.

Zukerman, Pinchas; Israeli violinist; b. 16 July 1948, Israel; ed. Israel Conservatory, Acad. of Music, Tel-Aviv, Juilliard School of Music, New York.
Studied with Ivan Galamian; début in New York with New York Philharmonic 69, in U.K. at Brighton Festival 69; concert and recital performances throughout U.S.A. and Europe; directs, tours and plays with English Chamber Orchestra; has performed at Spoleto, Pablo Casals and Edinburgh Festivals; Leventritt Award 67.
c/o Harold Holt Ltd., 122 Wigmore Street, London, W1H 0DJ, England.
Telephone: 01-935-2331.

Zukor, Adolph; American film producer; b. 7 Jan. 1873, Hungary.
Fmrly. in hardware, upholstery and fur businesses New York and Chicago; founder Famous Players Film Co. 12, became Famous Players Lasky Corpn. 16, built theatres in major cities, became Publix Theatres Corpn 26, name changed to Paramount Pictures Inc. 35; Chair. Board Paramount Pictures Corpn. 35, (now Chair. Emeritus).
Paramount Pictures Corpn., 1 Gulf and Western Plaza, New York, N.Y. 10023, U.S.A.

Żukrowski, Wojciech; Polish writer; b. 14 April 1916, Cracow; s. of Zygmunt Żukrowski and Jadwiga Wojtowicz; m. Maria Woltersdorf; one d.; ed. Wrocław Univ. and Jagiellonian Univ., Cracow.
War Correspondent, North Viet-Nam 54; Counsellor, Polish Embassy, New Delhi 56-58; Deputy to Seym 72-; Co-Editor *Widnokręgi* (monthly) and *Nowe Książki*; State Prize 53, Chevalier's and Officer's Cross Polonia Restituta 53, 54, Award of Minister of Nat. Defence 61, Order of Banner of Labour 1st and 2nd Class, Prize of Minister of Culture and Art 63, 65, 69, Pietrzak Prize 67, and others; mem. Polish Union of Writers and PEN Club.
Publs. Short stories: *Z kraju milozenia* (From the Land of Silence), *Piórkiem flaminga* (With a Flamingo's Quill), *Córeczka* (Little Daughter), *Okruchy weselnego tortu* (Crumbs from the Wedding Cake); Novels: *Dni klęski* (Days of Defeat), *Bathed in Fire* (Ministry of Defence Prize 61), *Kamienne Tablice* (The Stone Tables) 66, *The Lucky Devil*, *Plaża nad Styksem* (Styx Beach) 73; Travel: *Dom bez ścian* (House without Walls), *Wanderings with my Guru: India, In the Kingdom of a Million Elephants: Laos, Nieśmiały narzeczony* (Chinese legends); Essays: *W głębi zwierciadła* (Inside Mirror) 73, *Karambole* (Collisions) 73; Films: *Bathed in Fire, Direction Berlin, The Last Days, Lotna, Potop.*
00-324 Warsaw, Karowa 14/16 m 22, Poland.
Telephone: 26 16 18.

Zulu, Alexander Grey; Zambian politician; b. 3 Sept. 1924, Chipata, Eastern Province; s. of Agrippa and Tionenji Zulu; m. 1952; four s. four d.; ed. Mafuta Lower Primary School and Munali Secondary School.
Water Devt. Asst., Northern Rhodesia 50-53; Bookkeeper/Man. Kabwe Co-operative Soc. 53-62; Parl. Sec., Northern Rhodesia 63; Minister of Commerce and Industry 64, of Transport and Works 64, of Mines and Co-operatives 65-67, of Home Affairs 67-70, of Defence 70-73; Sec.-Gen. United Nat. Independence Party (UNIP) 73-.
United National Independence Party, Freedom House, P.O. Box 302, Lusaka, Zambia.

Zulu, Rt. Rev. Alphaeus Hamilton, B.A., L.TH.; South African ecclesiastic; b. 29 June 1905, Nqutu; s. of Johannes and Miriam Zulu; m. Miriam A. Magwaza 1929; one s. six d.; ed. Univ. of South Africa.
Principal, Umlazi Mission School 24-35; Asst. (Anglican) Priest, St. Faith's Church, Durban 40-52, Rector 53-60; Bishop Suffragan, Diocese of St. John's, Transkei 60-Sept. 66; Bishop of Zululand Oct. 66-; Pres. World Council of Churches 68-; arrested March 71.
Box 147, Esham, Natal; Home: Bishops House, Gezinsila, Eshowe, Natal, South Africa.
Telephone: Esham 147 (Office); Eshowe 673 (Home).

Zumwalt, Elmo Russell, Jr., B.SC.; American naval officer; b. 29 Nov. 1920, San Francisco, Calif.; s. of Dr. Elmo Russell Zumwalt and Dr. Frances Z. Frank; m. Mouza Coutelais-du-Roche 1945; two s. two d.; ed. U.S. Naval Acad., Naval War Coll., Nat. War Coll.
Commissioned Ensign, U.S. Navy 42, advanced through ranks to Adm. 70; service on *USS Phelps* 42-43, *USS Robinson* 43-45, *USS Saufley* 45-46, *USS Zellars* 46-48; Asst. Prof. Naval Science 48-50; Commdg. Officer *USS Tills* 50-51; Navigator *USS Wisconsin* 51-52; Head Shore and Overseas Bases Section, Naval Personnel, Washington 53-55; Commdg. Officer *USS Arnold J. Isbell* 55-57; LT Detailer, Naval Personnel 57; Special Asst. for Naval Personnel, Office of Asst. Sec. of the Navy, Washington 57-58, Exec. Asst., Senior Aide 58-59; Commdg. Officer *USS Dewey* 59-61; Desk Officer for France, Spain and Portugal, Office of Asst. Sec. of Defense for Int. Security Affairs 62-63; Dir. Arms Control and Contingency Planning for Cuba 63; Exec. Asst., Senior Aide, Sec. of Navy 63-65; Commdg. Officer Cruiser-Destroyer Flotilla Seven 65-66; Dir. Chief Naval Operations Systems Analysis Group, Washington 66-68; Commdr. U.S. Naval Forces, Vietnam, Chief, Naval Advisory Group Vietnam 68-70; Chief of Naval Operations 70-74; Distinguished Service Medal with Gold Star, Legion of Merit with Gold Star, Bronze Star Medal with Combat V, Navy Commendation Medal with Combat V, and many other national and foreign decorations; Hon.